P&P	*printing & publishing*	قطاع الطباعة
Philos	*philosophy*	الفلسفة
Phot	*photography*	فن التصوير
Phys	*physics*	فيزياء
Pol	*politics*	السياسة
Psych	*psychology*	علم النفس
Radio	*radio*	الراديو
Relig	*religion*	الدين
Rhet	*rhetoric*	علم البلاغة
Sci	*science*	العلم
Sociol	*sociology*	علم الاجتماع
Sport	*sport*	الرياضة
TV	*television*	التلفزيون
Tech	*technology*	التقنية
Tel	*telecommunic-ations*	الاتصالات
Theat	*theatre*	المسرح
Transp	*transport*	النقل
Zool	*zoology*	علم الحيوان

Register labels المستويات

colloq	*colloquial*	عامية (العربية)
dialect	*dialect*	دارجة (إنكليزية)
euph	*euphemistic*	ملطف
fig	*figurative*	مجازي
fml	*formal*	رسمي
hum	*humorous*	هزلي
infml	*informal*	
liter	*literary*	
offensive	*offensive*	مهين
old use	*old usage*	استخدام قديم
pej	*pejorative*	ازدرائي
sl	*slang*	لهجة سوقية
vulg	*vulgar*	فاحش

Regional labels المناطق

Algeria		الجزائر
AmE	*American English*	الإنكليزية الأمريكية
BrE	*British English*	الإنكليزية البريطانية
Egypt		مصر
Gulf		الخليج
Iraq		العراق
Jordan		الأردن
Leb	*Lebanon*	لبنان
Levant	*The Levant*	بلاد الشام
Libya		ليبيا
ME	*Middle East*	الشرق الأوسط
Mor	*Morocco*	المغرب
NA	*North Africa*	شمال إفريقيا
SA	*Saudi Arabia*	السعودية
Scot	*Scotland*	إسكتلندا
Syria		سوريا
Tunisia		تونس

Oxford Arabic Dictionary

قاموس أكسفورد العربي

Arabic–English • English–Arabic

عربي – إنجليزي • إنجليزي – عربي

Chief Editor
Tressy Arts

رئيسة التحرير

تريسي أرتس

Great Clarendon Street, Oxford, OX2 6DP,
United Kingdom

Oxford University Press is a department of the University of Oxford. It furthers the University's objective of excellence in research, scholarship, and education by publishing worldwide. Oxford is a registered trade mark of Oxford University Press in the UK and in certain other countries

First Edition published in 2014

Impression: 5

Published in the United States of America by Oxford University Press
198 Madison Avenue, New York, NY 10016, United States of America

British Library Cataloguing in Publication Data
Data available

Library of Congress Control Number: 2014932182

ISBN 978-0-19-958033-0

Printed and bound in Malaysia by Vivar Printing

Contents

المحتويات

List of contributors

فريق العمل

Chief editor رئيسة التحرير

Tressy Arts تريسي أرتس

Revising editors: المحررون المراجعون:

Arabic–English في القاموس العربي - الإنجليزي

Karen McNeil كارن مكنيل

Sawad Hussain سفاد حسين

English–Arabic في القاموس الإنجليزي - العربي

Radia Benzehra راضية بن زهرة

Mohammed Attia محمد عبد العال عطية

Miled Faiza ميلاد فايزة

Monique IJzendoorn مونيك أيزندورن

Editors: المحررون:

Arabic–English في القاموس العربي - الإنجليزي

Nadja Arusha Schwarz نادية أروشا شوارز

Mark Demmink مارك دمنك

Assia Moutahhir Teekens أسيا مطهر تيكنس

English–Arabic في القاموس الإنجليزي - العربي

Hassan Mizori حسن مزوري

Saussan Khalil سوسن محمد خليل

Farah Aboubakr فرح أبوبكر

Bilal Maanaki بلال معنقي

Nadira Auty نادرة أوتي

Ramadan Bekheet رمضان بخيت

Editorial consultant استشاري التحرير

Jan Hoogland يان هوخلاند

Translation Consultants استشاريو الترجمة

Medicine: المصطلحات الطبية:

Amr Hawary عمرو الهواري

Law/Business: المصطلحات القانونية والتجارية:

Abdul-Raouf Garoub عبدالرؤوف قاروب

Thanks also to: ساعد في التحرير:

Michael Nevadomski مايكل نيفادومسكي

Firdaous Oueslati فردوس الوسلاتي

Shelton Henderson شلتون هندرسون

Project management إدارة المشروع

Nicholas Rollin

Julie Kleeman

Angus Stevenson

Data development تطوير البيانات

Mark Baillie

Tetyana Bogdan

Claire Day

Dan Barker

Corpus development and language technology تطوير تقنيات اللغة وذخائر النصوص

Pete Whitelock

Design التصميم

Michael Johnson

Production control مراقبة الإنتاج

Karen Bunn

Preface

Arabic and English are two of the largest and most influential languages in the world. Two of the six official UN languages, they have hundreds of millions of mother-tongue speakers and many more who learn the languages in later life. Over the past few decades Arabic has become increasingly important in the English-speaking world, and English is learned and spoken by a large proportion of people in the Arab world. Yet while there is an ever growing need for people to learn and use both languages, very few modern dictionary resources exist.

The *Oxford Arabic Dictionary* is a major new work, the largest single-volume bidirectional English–Arabic dictionary in existence. Containing more than 50,000 headwords, 85,000 senses, and many thousands of examples, collocates, and sense indicators, it covers all of the core vocabulary of modern English and Modern Standard Arabic (MSA). This is a newly compiled dictionary text that is not based on any previous edition.

The dictionary is designed to be beneficial to both experienced and less advanced users. Learners of each language should find that their efforts to understand and generate the foreign language are supported by the many grammatical and idiomatic constructions that are included and translated in the dictionary. Advanced and specialist language users will benefit from detailed content that includes many specialized terms and a wide range of up-to-the-minute vocabulary.

The dictionary has been compiled with the aid of large electronic corpora of both English and Arabic (2.5 billion and 0.9 billion words respectively), and thus includes relevant, authentic language only. It was put together over the course of five years by a team of lexicographers and native speakers of both languages who were based in many different locations across the globe, including countries in the Arab world. This was made possible through the use of a pioneering Web-based electronic dictionary compilation system that enabled native speakers from each country to see and edit each other's work.

The greatest care has been taken to supply as much information as possible to guide the user to the right translation. This takes the form of grammatical and sense disambiguators, collocates, examples, and usage labels. Relevant case endings have been provided as a means of helping the student of Arabic to understand and produce Arabic correctly, and users will find that all Arabic text on both sides is fully vowelled. The dictionary's centre matter contains information on English irregular verbs, Arabic numerals, cases, months, dates, and years, as well as fully conjugated tables of all types of Arabic verb.

The *Oxford Arabic Dictionary* provides translators, students at all levels, teachers, and business people with a reference work that is without rival in authority, currency, and accuracy.

Acknowledgements

Our thanks are due to the INL, the Institute for Dutch Lexicology, for the underlying data of their Arabic–Dutch dictionary, which was used in compiling the Arabic–English side of the *Oxford Arabic Dictionary*. Special thanks go to Jan Hoogland, the chief editor of the Arabic–Dutch dictionary, who also helped to identify many of the new Arabic words included in this work.

We would like to thank the Linguistic Data Consortium, who provided the Arabic Gigaword Corpus that formed the basis of the Oxford Arabic Corpus; Nizar Habash and his colleagues in the Center for Computational Learning Systems (CCLS) at Columbia University, who made available the MADA+TOKAN system used to analyse the Arabic text in preparation for its incorporation in the Corpus tool; Tim Buckwalter, whose SAMA Arabic analyser forms the basis of the MADA system; and Lexical Computing Limited, whose Sketch Engine software was invaluable in every aspect of dictionary compilation.

تمهيد

تشترك اللغة العربية مع اللغة الإنكليزية في الأهمية من حيث أنهما من أكثر اللغات شيوعا وتأثيرا في العالم، فهما ضمن اللغات الست الرسمية في الأمم المتحدة، وكلا اللغتين يتحدث بهما مئات الملايين من البشر كلغة أصلية، كما أن هناك ملايين آخرين من البشر يسعون إلى تعلم واحدة من اللغتين وربما كليهما. وخلال العقود الأخيرة زاد الاهتمام بدراسة اللغة العربية في الدول الناطقة بالإنكليزية، كما تضاعف الاهتمام في العالم العربي بتعلم اللغة الإنكليزية في كافة المراحل الدراسية، ولكن وبالرغم من حاجة كثير من الناس إلى تعلم كلا اللغتين، فإن القواميس الحالية المتاحة لا تفي بالغرض.

وهنا يأتي قاموس أكسفورد العربي كعمل معجمي ضخم من حيث المضمون وحديث من حيث المنهج والأسلوب، فهو أضخم قاموس ثنائي عربي-إنكليزي في مجلد واحد على الإطلاق، حيث يحتوي على أكثر من 50000 كلمة رئيسية و 85000 معنى، بالإضافة إلى آلاف الأمثلة والتعبيرات المتلازمة ودلالات المعاني. ويغطي هذا القاموس جميع المفردات الأساسية الحديثة سواء في اللغة العربية أو الإنكليزية، وقد تم جمع هذه المفردات وتصنيفها وشرحها وترجمتها في عمل فريد حديث لا يستند إلى أي إصدار سابق.

وقد صُمّم هذا القاموس ليخدم احتياجات المستخدمين سواء المبتدئين أو المتقدمين، فبالنسبة للمبتدئين فسيجدون أن هناك الكثير من التعبيرات الاصطلاحية والنحوية والأمثلة المترجمة التي تساعدهم في فهم اللغة وتعلم كيفية تركيب الجمل. أما بالنسبة للمتعلمين ذوي المستوى المتقدم والمتخصصين فسيجدون أن هناك الكثير من التفاصيل الدقيقة مصنفة ومرتبة بالشكل الذي يخدم احتياجاتهم، بالإضافة إلى المصطلحات المتخصصة وكذلك المفردات التي دخلت اللغة حديثا.

وقد تم بناء هذا القاموس باتباع النظريات والوسائل الحديثة في علم صناعة المعاجم واستنادا إلى معلومات مستنبطة من ذخائر نصوص هائلة الحجم (تبلغ 2.5 مليار كلمة من اللغة الإنجليزية و 0.9 مليار كلمة من اللغة العربية) وبهذا يتسنى لنا الجزم بأن هذا القاموس يحتوي فقط على المواد المعجمية التي ترتبط بالواقع في اللغة المعاصرة، وقد تم تجميع القاموس خلال فترة تجاوزت الخمس سنوات من قبل فريق من المختصين في صناعة المعاجم والخبراء الناطقين باللغتين الذين جاؤوا من بلدان مختلفة بما فيها عدد غير قليل من الدول العربية، وقد استخدم في بناء القاموس نظام إلكتروني حديث لبناء المعاجم يضمن الاتساق في الشكل والمحتوى وينظم دورة العمل خلال مراحله المختلفة.

وقد توخينا الحرص الشديد في أن نقدم للمستخدم المعلومات الكافية التي تسهل له الوصول إلى الترجمة الصحيحة للكلمة، وهذا يشمل سرد الأمثلة وبيان التعبيرات المتلازمة ومستويات الاستخدام بما يزيل اللبس النحوي والدلالي. وقد تم إدراج علامات الإعراب في سياقاتها كوسيلة لمساعدة المتعلم على فهم العربية وكتابتها أو التحدث بها بشكل صحيح، وقد تم تشكيل كل الكلمات العربية في شطرَي القاموس. وفي وسط القاموس تم إدراج بعض المعلومات والقوائم الأساسية التي يحتاجها متعلمو الإنكليزية والعربية مثل تصريف الأفعال الإنكليزية الشاذة وقوائم بالأرقام العربية وعلامات الإعراب وجداول بأبواب الأفعال العربية وكيفية تصريفها.

وسوف يجد المترجمون والطلبة بكافة مستوياتهم ورجال الأعمال في قاموس أكسفورد العربي مرجعا أساسيا لا يضاهيه مرجع آخر من حيث الشمولية والدقة في وصف اللغة المعاصرة.

شكر وتقدير

نتوجه بوافر الشكر لمعهد صناعة القواميس الهولندية (Institute for Dutch Lexicology) لبيانات القاموس العربي الهولندي التي استخدمناها في صناعة قاموس أكسفورد العربي. ونخص بالشكر يان هوخلاند، رئيس تحرير القاموس العربي الهولندي، على مساعدته في تدقيق العديد من الكلمات العربية الجديدة والتي تم إدراجها في هذا القاموس.

كما نشكر Linguistic Data Consortium على توفير ذخيرة النصوص الهائلة Arabic Gigaword Corpus التي استخدمت في قاموس أكسفورد وكذلك نتقدم بجزيل الشكر للدكتور نزار حبش وزملائه في مركز أنظمة التعلم الحاسوبي (CCLS) بجامعة كولومبيا الذين صرحوا لنا باستخدام برنامج MADA+TOKAN الذي يتميز بالدقة في التحليل الآلي للنصوص العربية من أجل إدماجها في أدوات تحليل ذخائر النصوص. كما نشكر تيم باكوولتر الذي طور المحلل الصرفي المستخدم في البنية الأساسية للبرنامج، كما نتقدم بالشكر والتقدير لشركة Lexical Computing Limited على توفير برنامجها Sketch Engine الذي يوظف أحدث التقنيات الإحصائية في استخراج المعلومات المعجمية والذي استفدنا منه بدرجة كبيرة في بناء هذا القاموس.

Introduction

Users of the dictionary

The *Oxford Arabic Dictionary* is intended for speakers of both English and Arabic, and grammatically relevant information is included for both languages. As such, it may be said that the dictionary is intended for:

- speakers of English who want to understand Arabic
- speakers of English who want to produce Arabic
- speakers of Arabic who want to understand English
- speakers of Arabic who want to produce English.

The dictionary will serve students, translators, interpreters, teachers of Arabic or English, and anyone who is involved with either or both languages in a professional or personal capacity. As the Arabic side of the dictionary is ordered by root, the printed dictionary is not suitable for absolute beginners in Arabic, but it will be useful for anyone who has had basic training in Arabic.

The language situation in the Arabic-speaking world

In the Arab world the language is in a state known as diglossia. This means that two varieties of Arabic are used under different conditions. The first is the 'high' variety of Arabic, close to Classical Arabic, which is known as Modern Standard Arabic (MSA). This is used in written media and in official speeches and lectures. The second is the 'low' variety of Arabic, known as Colloquial or Spoken Arabic, which is spoken and not usually written.

This situation is in flux, however: in recent years colloquial written Arabic has become prevalent on the Internet, and some literature does exist in colloquial Arabic, in Egyptian Arabic in particular.
Where Standard Arabic is largely the same throughout the Arabic world, colloquial variants vary immensely from country to country and from region to region. There is no strict separation between the 'standard' and 'colloquial' languages, but instead there is a sliding scale on which any language user constantly moves.

Which language is used in the dictionary?

This dictionary focuses on the variant of Arabic commonly known as Modern Standard Arabic. This is the language as it is currently written and spoken in the media, and in which most literature and any other 'formal' written language appear. Accordingly, this dictionary does not include Classical Arabic words that are no longer in modern use, or old senses of modern words. It includes colloquial words only where no Standard equivalent could be found. In these cases, the user will find the word marked as colloquial, and the region where it is used will also be indicated. As mentioned, the line between Modern Standard Arabic and Colloquial Arabic is not clearly marked, so in order to decide what counts as MSA, it was decided that words that occur regularly in MSA texts without quotation marks could reasonably be assumed to be acceptable in MSA. A similar policy for loanwords from other languages has been applied: if the word is used often in MSA texts, then it is included. Where an English word can be translated with both a loanword and an Arabic variant, such as *computer* (كُمْبيوتَر and حاسوب, both of which are in regular use), both are included.

Although MSA is largely the same throughout the Arabic world, some regional variation does occur. It would be impossible to list all regional variations for every word, but some have been included. Variants are marked by the name of the region.

The English used in the dictionary is British English, with US variants marked at the English headword.

The selection of Arabic headwords

The headword list on the Arabic–English side of the dictionary is based on the Arabic–Dutch translation dictionary published by Bulaaq, Amsterdam.[1] This dictionary was chosen because it is up to date and because it was created using modern evidence-based methods including a large Arabic corpus, the first time an Arabic dictionary has been able to capitalize on such a resource. This makes the Bulaaq dictionary representative of MSA as it is actually used today. The *Oxford Arabic Dictionary* took corpus use a stage further, drawing on the extensive new Oxford Arabic Corpus of 0.9 billion words for verifying word usage and discovering new words. This significantly expanded the Bulaaq vocabulary, resulting in more than 26,000 Arabic headwords.

The selection of English headwords

The English side of the text derives from Oxford's English language research programme and the Oxford English Framework, a language-neutral frame for compiling bilingual dictionaries derived from corpus-based analysis. This has been extensively edited and ensures consistency and quality across the range. It was compiled with the aid of the Oxford English Corpus, a database of 2.5 billion words of real 21st-century English from around the world. Forms and spellings are consistent with those used in the *Oxford Dictionary of English*, Oxford's flagship one-volume dictionary of current English.

1 J. Hoogland, K. Versteegh, and M. Woidich (eds), *Woordenboek Arabisch-Nederlands* (Amsterdam, 2003, rev. ed. 2009).

مقدمة

هدف القاموس

يهدف قاموس أكسفورد العربي إلى تلبية احتياجات مستخدميه سواء من المتحدثين بالإنكليزية أو العربية، وقد تم إدراج معلومات نحوية مهمة في كلتا اللغتين، وقد تم تصميم هذا القاموس ليساعد تحديدا:

متحدثي الإنكليزية الذين يرغبون في فهم اللغة العربية

متحدثي الإنكليزية الذين يرغبون في استخدام اللغة العربية سواء كتابة أو تحدثا

متحدثي العربية الذين يرغبون في فهم اللغة الإنكليزية

متحدثي العربية الذين يرغبون في استخدام اللغة الإنكليزية سواء كتابة أو تحدثا

ويخدم هذا القاموس الأغراض الأساسية للطلاب والمترجمين والمدرسين العرب والإنكليز على السواء، كما أنه مرجع ضروري لأي شخص يستخدم أيا من اللغتين في حياته اليومية سواء لغرض مهني أو شخصي. ولكن لأن الجانب العربي من هذا القاموس مرتب حسب الجذر فإنه لا يتناسب في صورته المطبوعة مع المستخدمين المبتدئين الذين ليس لديهم خلفية مناسبة عن اللغة العربية، حيث أن البحث بالجذر يحتاج إلى بعض التدريب والمعرفة الأساسية باللغة العربية وكيفية تركيب الكلمات فيها.

وضع اللغة العربية

تعيش اللغة العربية في العالم العربي وضعا خاصا أطلق عليه المختصون مصطلح «الازدواجية اللغوية»، وهذا المصطلح يعني أن هناك شكلين أو مستويين مختلفين من اللغة يستخدمان في سياقين مختلفين، فهناك اللغة 'العليا' أو الفصحى، وهي اللغة المستخدمة في الكتابة والخطب والمحاضرات الرسمية، وهناك اللغة 'الدنيا' أو العامية أو الدارجة، وهي اللغة التي تستخدم في التعاملات اليومية والأحاديث والحوارات غير الرسمية وهي عادة ما تكون منطوقة وغير مكتوبة.

ولكن وضع اللغة العربية يشهد تغيرا مستمرا، ففي الأعوام الأخيرة انتشرت الكتابة باللهجات الدارجة على الإنترنت سواء في صفحات التواصل الاجتماعي أو المدونات أو البريد الإلكتروني، بل إن هناك الكثير من الأعمال الأدبية (كالشعر والرواية) التي بدأت في الظهور بالعامية وخصوصا العامية المصرية.

وإذا كانت اللغة العربية الفصحى موحدة ومشتركة في أرجاء العالم العربي بدرجة كبيرة، إلا أن اللهجات العامية تختلف من بلد إلى بلد بل ومن مدينة إلى مدينة، وجدير بالذكر أنه لا توجد حدود ومعالم واضحة تفصل الفصحى عن العامية أو تفصل اللهجات العامية عن بعضها البعض، بل إن الاختلاف يسير بشكل تدريجي ويتسم بكثير من الدمج والخلط سواء بين الفصحى والعامية أو العامية في إقليم وآخر.

ما اللغة المستخدمة في القاموس؟

يركز القاموس الذي بين أيدينا على اللغة العربية الفصحى الحديثة وهي اللغة المستخدمة في الوقت المعاصر في وسائل الإعلام الرسمية المكتوبة والمسموعة والتي يتم تأليف معظم الأعمال الأدبية بها، كما أنها اللغة التي يتم بها إصدار الرسائل والبيانات الرسمية، وبناء على هذا المنهج فإن هذا القاموس لا يشتمل على المفردات أو المعاني العربية الكلاسيكية القديمة التي لم تعد تستخدم في العصر الحديث، ولكن قد يتم إدراج بعض الكلمات العامية عندما لا يوجد مقابل مناسب في الفصحى، وفي هذه الحالة يتم توضيح أن الكلمة عامية كما يتم بيان الدولة أو المنطقة التي تستخدم فيها هذه الكلمة. وكما ذكرنا سابقا فإنه لا توجد حدود واضحة المعالم للتفرقة الجازمة بين الفصحى والعامية، ولذلك فقد اتخذنا معيارا عمليا لتحديد ما إذا كانت كلمة ما تنتمي إلى الفصحى أم لا وهو ورود هذه الكلمة في نصوص العربية الفصحى الحديثة بشكل مطرد دون أن توضع بين قوسين أو علامات تنصيص، وقد تم تطبيق نفس هذا المعيار مع الكلمات المستعارة من اللغات الأخرى، فإذا وردت إحدى هذه الكلمات بشكل متكرر في النصوص العربية فإن الكلمة تعتبر كلمة معربة ويتم إدراجها في القاموس، وإذا وجدت ترجمتان لكلمة إنكليزية إحداهما عربية والأخرى مستعارة (مثل computer التي يقابلها كُمْبيوتر وحاسوب) فإن كلتا الكلمتين يتم إدراجهما في القاموس إذا كان استخدام كليهما شائعا في اللغة العربية.

وبالرغم من أن اللغة العربية الفصحى موحدة إلى درجة كبيرة في أرجاء العالم العربي إلا أن هناك بعض الاختلافات الإقليمية سواء فيما يتعلق باللفظ أو الدلالة، وإذا كان من المستحيل سرد جميع أوجه التباين المعجمي بين الأقاليم المختلفة، فأننا أدرجنا بعض الاختلافات وأوضحنا اسم المنطقة أو الدولة المستخدم فيها هذا اللفظ أو ذاك.

وبالنسبة للغة الإنكليزية المستخدمة في هذا القاموس فهي الإنكليزية البريطانية، وفي حالة وجود مقابل في الإنكليزية الأمريكية فإننا أدرجنا شكل الكلمة بجوار المدخل الأصلي ونعلمه برمز (AmE) بين قوسين.

اختيار المداخل في اللغة العربية

تم اختيار المداخل في الجانب العربي من القاموس بناء على القاموس العربي الهولندي الذي نشرته دار بولاك في أمستردام،[1] وقد وقع اختيارنا على هذا العمل لأنه من أحدث القواميس المنشورة للغة العربية ولأنه بني اعتمادا على ذخيرة نصوص عربية ضخمة بشكل غير مسبوق مما جعل قاموس بولاك معبرا عن اللغة العربية الفصحى الحديثة كما هي مستخدمة اليوم، ولكن قاموس أكسفورد العربي لم يتوقف عند هذا الحد ولكنه قفز باللغة العربية قفزة أخرى بأن اعتمد على تحليل ذخيرة نصوص عربية هائلة تتكون من 0.9 مليار كلمة مما سهل اكتشاف الكلمات الجديدة ومعرفة الاستخدامات والمعاني المتعددة للكلمة، وقد أدى العمل مع ذخيرة النصوص هذه إلى إضافة عدد كبير من الكلمات العربية التي لم توجد في قاموس بولاك، حتى وصل عدد المداخل في قاموس أكسفورد العربي إلى أكثر من 26000 كلمة.

اختيار المداخل في اللغة الإنجليزية

يستند الجانب الإنجليزي لهذا القاموس على إطار أكسفورد الإنجليزي (Oxford English Framework) وهو عبارة عن هيكل أو بناء نموذجي تعتمد عليه مؤسسة أكسفورد في إنشاء القواميس ثنائية اللغة الجديدة، وقد تم مراجعة هذا الإطار بشكل شامل بما يضمن الاتساق والدقة في كافة مواده. وقد تم بناء هذا الإطار اعتمادا على ذخيرة نصوص ضخمة تتكون من ٢,٥ مليار كلمة تمثل اللغة الإنجليزية كما هي مستخدمة فعليا في الدول الناطقة بالإنكليزية في القرن الحادي والعشرين. وقد تمت مطابقة هجاء الكلمات في هذا القاموس مع الكلمات المدرجة في قاموس أكسفورد الإنجليزي (Oxford Dictionary of English) الذي يعد أكبر وأشمل قاموس للغة الإنكليزية في مجلد واحد من بين إصدارات أكسفورد.

[1] J. Hoogland, K. Versteegh, M. Woidich (eds) قاموس عربي– هولندي, Bulaaq, Amsterdam, 2003, rev. ed. 2009

Using this dictionary

General

The layout of the dictionary as a whole, both the English–Arabic side and the Arabic–English side, is from left to right. If an Arabic phrase continues on to the following line, it will appear on the leftmost part of that line.

The default form for verbs and verb phrases is the infinitive in English (*to drink tea*), and the third person masculine singular past tense in Arabic (شَرِبَ الشاي).

The default for nouns and noun phrases in both languages is indefinite, but for practical or grammatical reasons they may occur in the definite form.

1. Vocalization of the Arabic

All Arabic in this dictionary is fully vocalized (i.e. the diacritic signs for the vowels are written), according to the following rules:

- A hamzat wasl is written as an alif without hamza or vowel (قاعة الاجْتِماعاتِ)
- Long vowels are indicated by the lengthening letter alif, waw, or ya without the vowel mark fatha, damma, or kasra on the preceding letter (قيل ,تقولُ ,قالَ)
- However, if the ya or waw functions as a consonant (i.e. if it is followed by another vowel), the damma or kasra is given before it (سِياسة ,صُوَر). Note that if that waw or ya is double, no damma or kasra is written (عَرَبيّة ,قوّة)
- No fatha is written before ta marbuta (مَدْرَسة)
- The article al (alif-lam) is not vocalized (ال)
- Combinations of one-letter words with the article (وال ,بال ,لل) are not vocalized
- The kasra below إ is not written (إسْلام)
- No shadda is written to indicate sun letters, nor a sukun after the article to indicate moon letters (القَمَر ,الشَمْس)
- If a word ends on sukun and the following word starts with hamzat wasl, the sukun is not written, nor any auxiliary vowel (قَرَأت الكِتاب)
- Some very frequent function words (e.g. لم ,على) are not vocalized
- Dagger-alifs are not written, but fathas or proper alifs are used instead, thus: ذَلِك and رَحْمان. The exception to this rule is the name of God الله
- No case endings are given on loanwords or names, unless they end on ta marbuta or nisba (رَقْم التِلِفون).

2. Arabic case endings

Case endings have not been provided at individual headwords or translations. In multiword phrases they have been given where they are governed by a word or rule within the word combination. In the case of an isolated genitive construction, for example, the second term takes the genitive ending. The first term does not take an ending, because that would be qualified by an element outside of the expression (مُدير شَرِكةٍ).

The default case is always the nominative. For example, if a regular plural is given, it ends on ـونَ. If a noun not governed by another word is followed by a suffix, a damma is added (زَوْجَتُهُ).

3. Abbreviated forms

Grammatical information, parts of speech, usage labels, etc. are all presented in English, in full or abbreviated forms. The Arabic translations of these can be found in the list of abbreviations in the endpapers.

4. Slashes

Slashes are used for two reasons:

(i) To provide two words that are not equivalent, but which can both occur in that place in the sentence. In such cases, both the example and its translation will contain a slash:

Phrasal verbs **back away** تَهَرَّبَ; **to ~ away from a problem/confrontation** تَهَرَّبَ من مُشْكِلةٍ \ مُواجَهةٍ

The above example can be split into two sentences: *to back away from a problem:* تَهَرَّبَ من مُشْكِلةٍ and *to back away from a confrontation:* تَهَرَّبَ من مُواجَهةٍ.

Sometimes one Arabic equivalent is masculine, while the other is feminine. In such cases, a feminine ending may be provided in brackets:

ضَرْبة a powerful explosion/blast; انْفِجار \ فَرْقعة قَويّ(ة)

(ii) To indicate two equivalents in one language, which are the same in the other language. In this case either the example or the translation will contain a slash. For example قابَلَ in the example below can be translated with either *meet* or *encounter* in English:

قابَلَ *v* 1 [لاقى] to meet, to encounter; to interview; قابَلَ شَخْصاً to meet/encounter sb; to interview sb; قابَلَ شَخْصاً

And in this Arabic expression, قاع and ذَيْل are equivalents:

فَريق قابِع على وراء القُضْبانِ languishing behind bars; فَريق قابِع على قاع \ ذَيْلِ التَّرْتيبِ a team languishing at the bottom of the rankings; نِظام قابِع على صَدْرِ الشَّعْبِ a regime

5. Brackets

Brackets are used to indicate an optional part of a translation, i.e. one that the user can choose to use or not to use:

النِساء والمُرْضِعات pregnant and nursing women; النِساء نِساء الأَعْمالِ الكاتِبات \ الأَديبات (female) writers; نِساء الأَعْمالِ

Albanian /al'beɪnɪən/ **A** *n* 1 (citizen) أَلْبان، أَلْبانِيّ 2 (language) (اللُغة) الأَلْبانِيّة

If both the example and the translation contain brackets, the words contained within these brackets correspond to one another:

راعٍ *n* |رُعاة، رُعْيان، رِعاء| 1 [فَلّاح] shepherd; راعي بَقَرٍ (أَمْريكِيّ) an (American) cowboy; راعي الغَنَمِ shepherd

6. The ≈ symbol

The symbol ≈ is used to indicate that a translation is approximate but is not suitable in all circumstances. Often this is explained further in a bracketed gloss:

abbey /'abi/ *n* (*pl* **abbeys**) 1 (community) دَيْر ≈ (كَنيسة كَبيرة مع دَيْرٍ للرُهْبانِ أو للراهِباتِ) 2 (church)

7. Commas between examples

When two examples are separated by a comma and followed by a translation, this indicates that the examples are synonymous and share the same translation:

عَبَّرَ عن قَلَقِهِ، أَبْدى قَلَقَهُ to express one's concern;

to deserve ~ اِسْتَحَقَّ الأَفْضَلَ; **so much the ~, all the ~** تَغَيَّرَ إلى الأَحْسَنِ; **to change for the ~** سَيَكونُ أَحْسَن

8. Proverbs

Both languages are rich in proverbs. Rather than giving literal translations, the translators have tried to translate proverbs and expressions in the source language with a proverb or expression in the target language that conveys the same meaning. Where that has not been possible, an explanation has been provided.

9. Gender and number

The default form for the Arabic in both sides of the dictionary is the masculine singular, so *you write* is by default translated as تَكْتُبُ. Also most examples in the Arabic–English are in the masculine form. The reason for this is that the masculine singular is the most unmarked and thus simplest form.

10. Style

In modern written English, words and phrases exist at all levels.

Because of the nature of MSA as the 'higher' variant, it is sometimes hard to find a good translation for informal or vulgar English expressions that the Arabic speaker would more naturally utter in their colloquial mother tongue. Where possible, the translators have aimed to provide a suitable translation in Standard Arabic for such words and expressions.

Regarding the spelling of words with no Standard Arabic orthography, for example إنْكْليزِيّة and إنْجليزِيّة, we have opted not to choose one over another, to reflect the variation likely to be encountered in Arabic texts.

Similarly, we use Western Arabic numerals in Arabic in the English–Arabic section, and Eastern Arabic numerals in the Arabic–English section.

Arabic–English dictionary

1. Order of entries

(i) Root order

The headwords in the Arabic–English part have been ordered by root. The first word of a new root is indicated by a single guillemet (›) to its left:

مِقْشَط *n* |مَقاشِطُ| plane, file

› قَشَعَ *v* |a; قَشْع| to drive away, to disperse; قَشَعَ الظَلامَ to dispel the darkness

اِنْقَشَعَ *v* to brighten/clear up; to disperse; يَنْقَشِعُ السَحابُ

Roots are ordered alphabetically. In roots that have identical second and third radicals (حلل، دقق) the last radical has been counted, so حلل can be found between حلك and حلم.

Sometimes it is hard to distinguish between two roots with weak consonants: فول and فيل, فعو and فعي. Where these roots are very similar, they have been merged together, and can then be found alphabetically under فولفيل or فعوفعي.

In some cases we have split roots into two or more 'homographs' for clarity's sake. These can be recognized by a superscript number before the guillemet:

¹› صَفَرَ *v* |i; صَفير| to whistle

(ii) Cross-references

If the root of a headword is unclear, a cross-reference is provided to the root at which the headword can be found:

› أَب *n* see أبو

If a word is an unpredictable form or an alternative spelling of another word, a reference to that word is provided:

› قِفْ *v* see وَقَفَ

If a word looks as if it should appear under a certain root, but is instead listed alphabetically (for example loanwords), this is indicated as *listed alphabetically*:

خُبَّيْزة *n* listed alphabetically

Such words should be searched for as if all their letters are root letters, so in the case of the example above this would be under 'root' خبيزة.

(iii) Where to find certain types of words

Combinations of words with prefixes (لاسِلْكِيّ) can be found under the root of the main word (here under سلك).

Words with complex derivation (تَمَرْكَز, خَوْصَصة) are usually included under the original root (here ركز and خصص). Referrals are included where there could be confusion.

Abbreviations are listed as if their letters are root letters, so ق.ع. can be found between roots قطن and قعد.

(iv) Order within the root

Within one root, the order is as follows:

- First, all verbs that that root has, listed from Form I up to Form X

  e.g. قَبِلَ – قَبَّلَ – قابَلَ – أَقْبَلَ – تَقَبَّلَ – تَقابَلَ – اسْتَقْبَلَ

- Second, the words that consist of the radicals of the root, with short vowels only (so no affixes)

  e.g. قَبْلَ – قَبْلُ – قُبُل – قِبَل – قِبَلَ

- Third, the words that start with the first radical, in alphabetical order

  e.g. قابِل – قابِلة – قابِليّة – قُبالة – قِبالة – قُبْلة – قِبْلة – قَبْلي – قَبْليّة – قبول – قبيل – قُبَيْل – قبيلة

- Fourth, the words that contain a prefix, in alphabetical order

  e.g. اسْتِقْبال – إقبال – تَقَبُّل – تَقابُل – مُتَقابِل – مُتَقَبِّل – مُسْتَقْبَل – مُسْتَقْبِل – مُسْتَقْبَليّ – مُقابِل – مُقابَل – مُقابَلة – مُقْبِل – مُقَبِّلات – مَقْبول – مَقْبوليّة – مُقْتَبَل

Homographs (words with the same spelling but different meaning) are indicated by Roman numerals:

قابِس I *n* |قوابِس| (Elec) (power) plug; أَدْخَلَ \ وَضَعَ القابِسَ في المِقْبَس to insert the plug into the socket

قابِس II *n* |dipt f| Gabès *(city in Tunisia)*

(v) Inclusion of entries

Combinations of function words (فيما, لِأَنَّ) are often included as separate headwords.

Not all Arabic masdars (verbal nouns) and participles have been included. Inclusion depends on whether or not there is an additional meaning that cannot be directly derived/formed from the verb, an unpredictable English translation, or meaningful examples.

2. Within headwords

(i) Headword variants

If the headword has any variant spellings, these are given in a slightly smaller font, after a comma:

› إِنْجليزيّ, إِنْكْليزيّ **A** *adj* |إِنْجليزيّون, إِنْجليز| English;

(ii) Parts of speech

Headwords can contain several different parts of speech. These are indicated by capital letters: **A**. In such cases, the adjective is placed before the noun.

(iii) Regional markers

Words that are exclusive to a specific region have that region indicated after the headword and part of speech, in brackets:

› نُوَنْبِر *n* (Mor) November

Regional markers can also be used to show that a word only has a certain meaning in one region:

قَصَبة *n* **1** [أُنبوب] pipe, tube, reed; قَصَبة هَوائيّة \ الرِئة windpipe; bronchi **2** [بَلْدة] (NA) citadel; kasbah **3** [عَظْم]

or that a certain phrase is only used in a certain region:

the investigation of/into sth; مَفْرَزة الاسْتِقْصاء (Leb) detention centre

(iv) Senses

Separate senses of headwords are indicated by numbers, and illustrated by disambiguators provided in square brackets:

› نَدَب v |u; نَدْب| ① [ناحَ] to lament, to mourn (for); نَدَبَ الْمَيِّتَ to mourn the deceased ② [أَوْفَدَ] to delegate, to depute; to authorize, to commission; to appoint, to assign;

These disambiguators can be synonyms, short descriptions, typical collocates, or a field indicator (eg *Comput* for computing, *Bot* for botany. A full list of these, and their Arabic translations, is provided in the dictionary endpapers).

(v) Translations

In terms of the order of translations, the most common translation is given first.

Several translations can be separated by commas or semicolons: commas indicate that the translations on either side are more or less synonymous; semicolons indicate a slightly different level of meaning:

نَزَع v |i| ① [قَلَعَ] |نَزْع| to remove, to take away; to tear/pull out, to extract; to take off; نَزَعَ مِسْماراً to pull out a nail;

Not all Arabic words and expressions have English equivalents. Where no translation could be found, a description of the meaning has been provided in italics instead:

(الحُروف) المُقَطَّعات n B *isolated letters of unknown significance heading 29 Quranic suras*

Information in italics in brackets is also used to further clarify a translation or to provide specific context:

مِنسَر n |مَناسِرُ| beak (*of a predatory bird*)

If translations have different spellings in British or American English, the British spelling is used. If British and American English are lexically different, each is provided with the relevant regional marker:

› ناصِية n |نَواصٍ| ① [شَعْرُ مُقَدَّمِ الرَّأس] fringe (BrE), bangs (AmE);

This approach is also used in examples. Here the user can choose either the British or American equivalent in the translation:

مَكْروهٌ an accident befell him; يَنْزِلُ المِصْعَدُ the lift (BrE) elevator (AmE) is going down; يَنْزِلُ المَطَرُ it is raining;

Where an English word is followed by *before n*, this means that this word can be used as a modifier before another noun, often as equivalent of an adjective in Arabic:

نَباتيّ A adj [مَصْنوع من النَباتِ] vegetable (*before n*),

An English word that ends in a dash means that word is usually attached to the word that follows it:

ثَلْجيّ adj icy; ice-cold; snow-; عاصِفة ثَلْجيّة blizzard, snowstorm; انْهِيار ثَلْجيّ avalanche; مِياه ثَلْجيّة ice-cold

(vi) Examples and idioms

Example sentences are given to show typical usage of the headword, grammatical constructions in which it appears, and common collocations:

مَنْسوب A adj related; attributed, assigned; مَنسوب ل \ إلى related to; التُهَم المَنْسوبة إلَيْهِ the charges against him; الكَلام المَنْسوب إلَيْهِ the words attributed to him

Sometimes a word occurs in a typical phrase that does not directly apply to any of its senses. In such cases this is included as an idiom:

بَحْر من الدَم a sea of blood; بَحْر من المَشاكِل a huge number of problems ③ [وَزْن شِعْريّ] metre

Idiom في بَحْرِ هذا الأُسْبوع in the course of this week

Where examples call for non-specific subjects or objects, شَخْص has been used for persons, and شَيْء for things. In English these are translated as *sb* (for *somebody*) and *sth* (for *something*).

3. Arabic grammatical information

Grammatical information is usually provided straight after the headword, within vertical lines.

(i) Nouns/adjectives

Broken (irregular) **plurals** of nouns and adjectives are given. Words can have more than one plural. If a word can have both a broken and a sound plural, both are provided. If only a sound plural exists, this is not given.

قُوّة n |قُوًى, قُوّات| ① [جَسَديّة] strength, power; بِقُوّةٍ strongly; ضَرَبَ شَخْصاً بِقُوّةٍ to hit sb hard; وَقَعَ بِقُوّةٍ to come down

If separate senses of a word have different plurals, those plurals are indicated at the sense:

أخ n ① [شَقيق] |إخْوة, إخْوان| brother; إخْوان brothers (*in trade/company names*); الإِخْوة والأَخَوات siblings, brothers and sisters; أَخ شَقيق full brother; أَخ غَيْر شَقيق half brother; أَخوكَ your brother; بِنْت \ ابْن أَخ niece/nephew; قَتْل أَخ fratricide; لَهُ خَمْسةُ إخْوةٍ he has five brothers ② [صَديق] |إخْوان| الأخ فُلان mister/brother so-and-so; يا أخي! excuse me, sir! ③ (Chr) |إخْوان| brother; friar ④ (Pol) |إخْوان| fellow believer; الإخْوان

If a word takes any **other irregular forms**, such as an irregular genitive or an irregular feminine plural, this is also indicated, preceded by the appropriate abbreviations:

› ذو n |ذووا, أولو; f ذات; f pl ذوات; m du ذوا; f du ذاتا; gen ذي; acc ذا| owner, possessor; embodying, comprising;

Diptotic headwords (which only have two cases in the indefinite, see *Arabic cases* in the centre pages) are followed by the indicator dipt:

أحْمَر adj |dipt; حُمْر| red; أحْمَر فاتِح light red; أحْمَر قانٍ bright/vivid red; أحْمَر دَمَوِيّ blood red, scarlet, crimson;

Diptotic plurals are indicated by a damma on the last consonant:

مَقْبَرة n |مَقابِرُ| cemetery, graveyard; مَقْبَرة عائِلِيّة family grave; مَقْبَرة جَماعِيّة mass grave; مَقْبَرة عَسْكَرِيّة military

Collective nouns are indicated by *n coll*. Singular nouns can be made by adding a ta marbuta. If a singular noun deviates from that formula, or if there is no singular noun, this is also indicated:

› شاء n coll |شواء, شياء, شياه; sing n شاة| sheep; ewe

قَوْم n coll |no singular noun; أقوام| 1 [شعْب] people; tribe; بَنو قَوْمِه one's people 2 [ناس] people; عِلْيَة القَوْم the elite, the

In general, nouns are **feminine** when they end in ta marbuta or alif, and masculine when they do not. There are a few nouns, however, that are feminine, but which don't end in ta marbuta. These are given the marker f. This same marker is provided for adjectives that do not have ta marbuta added though they can only refer to a feminine noun, e.g. حامِل.

أرْض n |f; أراضٍ| 1 [قِطْعة أرْضٍ] land; soil; property; أراضٍ land; area; أرْض فِلاحيّة \ زِراعيّة farming/

There are also some words which do end on ta marbuta, but are masculine (e.g. طاغِية). These get the marker m.

Some adjectives do not add ta marbuta when referring to a feminine word. This is indicated by mf:

› خام A adj |mf| raw, crude, unprocessed; زَيْت \ نَفْط خام crude oil; حَديد خام iron ore; مادّة خام raw material;

This mf is also used to indicate that a noun can be either masculine or feminine:

نَعْل n |mf; نِعال, أنْعُل| 1 [حِذاء] shoe, sandal; اِخْلَعْ نَعْلَيْك take off your shoes 2 [سُفْل الحِذاء] sole; نَعْل حِذائِهِ the

(ii) Verbs

In **Form I verbs** the masdar(s) and the vowel(s) used in the imperfect are indicated.

› قَحَطَ v |a; قَحْط, قُحوط| to fail to happen; to fail to appear; قَحَطَ المَطَرُ the rain held off; إذا قسا القَلْبُ قَحَطَت العَيْنُ

So the a above means that the imperfect of the verb is يَقْحَط with a fatha. An i indicates a kasra, and an u a damma.

If separate senses of a verb have different masdars, these are provided at the sense level:

قَصَّرَ v |u| 1 [عَجَزَ] |قُصور| to be remiss; قَصَّرَ عن واجِباتِهِ to be remiss in one's duties; قَصَّرَ عن تَسْديد دَيْنه to fail to repay one's debts 2 [أخَذ من طولِهِ] |قِصَر| to shorten, to curtail 3 [حَصَرَ] |قَصْر| to limit, to restrict;

In cases where it is not clear which Form a verb is, this is indicated, and its imperfect is given:

آتى v |Form III; يُؤاتي| 1 [زَوَّدَ] to give; to offer; آتى الزَّكاةَ to give zakat (alms) 2 [أحْضَرَ] to bring 3 [ناسَبَ]

If a verb has an **irregular form**, this is indicated by the form in Arabic, preceded by *perfect* or *imperfect*.

› ظَلَّ v |a; ظَلّ, ظُلول; perf ظَلِلْتُ| to stay, to remain; to continue, to keep (on); ظَلَّ سَليماً \ لَطيفاً to stay healthy/

Other information provided can include:

- imperfect only: this verb is only used in the imperfect tense, e.g. انْبَغى
- imperfect or imperative only: this verb is only used in the imperfect sense and the imperative, e.g. وَذَرَ
- no imperfect: this verb is only used in the perfect tense, e.g. عَسى
- passive only: this verb is only used in the passive, e.g. غُمي

The **prepositions** used at phrasal verbs are given in vertical lines at the sense level, usually followed by some examples indicating their use:

› بَحَثَ v |a; بَحْث| 1 [فَتَّشَ] |عن| to seek, to look/search for; بَحَثَ عن شَيْءٍ to look for sth; بَحَثَ عن مَسْكَنٍ جَديدٍ

Note that this preposition only applies to the sense at which it is given. If two senses use the same preposition, the preposition is repeated at the second sense.

English–Arabic dictionary

1. Order of entries

Alphabetical order

Entries on the English–Arabic side of the dictionary are listed in strict alphabetical order, ignoring hyphens, apostrophes, and spaces. This includes abbreviations, acronyms, compound headwords, and geographical and proper names, which are treated as normal headwords.

Variant spellings that are not alphabetically adjacent are given a separate entry in the alphabetical listing and cross-referenced to the entry where the headword is treated.

The only exception to this is phrasal verbs, which are listed after their root verb.

Headwords spelled the same but with unrelated meanings (homographs) are entered separately, with a raised number following each:

bass¹ /beɪs/ *n* 1 (voice) جَهير; (singer) مُغَنٍّ جَهير الصَوْتِ
2 (instrument: double bass) كَمان أَجْهَر; (bass guitar) جيتار بيس 3 (part) [طَبَقة صَوْتٍ خَفيضٍ وَعَميقٍ];
to sing (the) ~ [غَنّى بِطَبَقةِ صَوْتٍ خَفيضٍ وَعَميقٍ]

bass² /bas/ *n* (sea fish) قاروص; (freshwater) فَرْخ

Cross-references

American words and spellings are cross-referenced to their British variants:

checkers /ˈtʃekəz/ *n* (AmE) ▸**draughts**

Inflections and spelling variants are cross-referenced to the main entry:

could /kʊd, kəd/ ▸**can¹**

2. Within headwords

(i) Alternative spellings

If the American English spelling of the headword is different to that of the British, the American spelling is given immediately after the headword. Variants are indicated by the labels (BrE) and (AmE):

colour (BrE), **color** (AmE) /ˈkʌlə/ A *n* 1 (hue) لَوْن (أَلْوان);
what ~ is it? ما لَوْنُهُ؟; **the female is brown in ~** الأُنْثى

(ii) Pronunciation

English pronunciation can be highly unpredictable. Therefore, most headwords have their pronunciation given in the International Phonetic Alphabet (IPA) immediately after the headword (a guide to IPA can be found on page xxvi). Pronunciations are not shown at compounds for which both elements can be found elsewhere in the dictionary as headwords.

(iii) Grammatical information

If the headword has any irregular or unpredictable inflections, these are provided in brackets after the part of speech:

catchy /ˈkatʃi/ *adj* (**catchier**, **catchiest**) ‹*tune, chorus*› يَعْلَقُ في الذِهْنِ

Some English adjectives can only be used attributively. These are indicated with *before n*:

carry-on /ˈkarɪɒn/ A *n* (infml) (fuss) ضَجّة
B *adj before n* ‹*luggage*› [يُمْكِنُ حَمْلُهُ على مَتْنِ طائِرةٍ];

This indicator is also used where the form changes when used attributively:

crystal clear *adj* (*before n* **crystal-clear**) 1 ‹*water*› صافٍ

(iv) Ordering within entries

Different parts of speech are indicated with capital letters: C. A new part of speech will always start on a new line in the dictionary. Idioms are given after the final part of speech in the entry, preceded by the (Idiom) sign. Phrasal verbs are given after these. The first phrasal verb is preceded by the sign (Phrasal verbs). Any phrasal verbs that follow are preceded by a bullet point.

(v) Senses, subsenses, and collocates

Different senses are indicated by numbers: 1. Disambiguators are given in brackets to distinguish the different senses:

carousel /ˌkarəˈsɛl/ *n* 1 (merry-go-round) أُرْجوحة دَوّامة
2 (for luggage) (في المَطارِ) حِزام ناقِل للأَمْتِعةِ الخَيْلِ

Typical collocates are given in guillemets (‹ ›). Subject collocates are given between double guillemets; object and other collocates in single guillemets.

circulate /ˈsəːkjʊleɪt/ A *vt* نَشَرَ (u; نَشْر) ‹*a petition, letter*›
B *vi* 1 «rumours, documents» شاعَ (i; شَيْع, شُيوع), انْتَشَرَ
2 «blood, air» دارَ (u; دَوْر, دَوَران)

Sometimes different translations within a sense are further specified by subsenses:

band /band/ *n* 1 (group of people) عُصْبة (عُصَب), زُمْرة (زُمَر), جَماعة; (group of musicians) فِرْقة (فِرَق); **a jazz**

or by different collocates:

careless /ˈkɛːləs/ *adj* ‹*mistake*› طائِش; ‹*work*› غَيْر مُتْقَنٍ;
‹*remark, driving*› مُتَهَوِّر

If one of the senses of a word is uncountable, this is indicated by [u]:

beauty /ˈbjuːti/ *n* (*pl* **beauties**) 1 [u] (of women, voices, scenery) جَمال 2 (attractive woman) حَسْناء (حِسان)

If a word can be used in a fuller form, this is indicated by the word 'also' followed by the variant form, in brackets:

beech /biːtʃ/ *n* 1 (also **beech tree**) زان 2 [u] (wood) خَشب الزانِ

(vi) Translations

Translations are ordered from left to right, separated by commas:

commendable /kəˈmɛndəb(ə)l/ *adj* ‹*effort, performance*› جَدير بِالثَناءِ, مُسْتَحْسَن

If more translations are included, the first one should be considered to be the most important/common. In cases where regional differences are noted, the Standard Arabic translation (if there is one) is given first, followed by regional translations with their region markers:

cable car *n* تيليفريك, عَرَبة مُعَلَّقة (NA, Leb)

For one-word translations, all grammatical information for the Arabic is given in brackets to the right of the translation (see the Arabic Grammatical Information section, above):

bank² /baŋk/ A *n* 1 (Fin) بَنْك (بُنوك), مَصْرِف (مَصارِفُ); announce) أَعْلَنَ (عن) ‹*a meeting*›; دَعا (u; ل) ‹*an election*›;

Any further specification or clarification of translations is contained within brackets to the left of the translation:

babysit /ˈbeibisit/ *vi* (*present participle* **-tt-**, *past tense, past participle* **-sat**) قام بِرِعايةِ أَطْفالٍ (أثناء غِيابِ الوالِدَيْن)

Not all English words and expressions have Arabic equivalents. Where no translation is possible, a definition/explanation is provided in square brackets:

bay window *n* [نافِذة غُرْفةٍ مُمْتَدّة إلى الخارِجِ]

In some cases, an English adjective + noun construction would be translated with a genitive construction in Arabic. This is indicated by the adjective being translated with a noun (or noun phrase) in the genitive:

cardiovascular /ˌkɑːdɪəʊˈvaskjʊlə/ *adj* ‹*disease, exercise*› القَلْبِ والأَوْعِيةِ الدَمَوِيّةِ

This means that *cardiovascular disease* would be translated with مَرَض القَلْبِ والأوْعِية الدَمَوِيّة.

Some transitive verbs and phrases would be translated with the object collocate in a genitive construction with a noun in the translation, e.g. *to replace the old model*: حَلَّ مَحَلَّ الطِرازِ القَديم. Due to grammatical constraints, in translations of the headwords the article of the governing noun has been provided, thus: *to replace*: حَلَّ المَحَلَّ. The user should remember to remove the article if مَحَلّ becomes the governing word of a genitive construction. Accordingly, in the translation below:

behead /bɪˈhɛd/ *vt* قَطَعَ الرَأْسَ, ضَرَبَ العُنُقَ ‹*a prisoner,*

to behead a prisoner would be translated as ضَرَبَ عُنُقَ أَسيرٍ or قَطَعَ رَأْسَ أَسيرٍ.

(vii) Examples

Examples always appear at the end of the entry or sense and include typical usages and fixed phrases. In examples, the headword is represented by a tilde ~:

bask /bɑːsk/ *vi* 1 (to lie) «sunbathers, seals» تَنَعَّمَ; **to ~ in the sun** تَنَعَّمَ بِأَشِعّةِ الشَمْسِ 2 (to revel) **to ~ in the glory of sth** تَنَعَّمَ بِمَجْدِ شَيْءٍ

Where the italic *or* is given in an example, the words before and after it should be considered synonymous and interchangeable:

cadge /kadʒ/ *vt* (infml) **to ~ sth off** *or* **from sb** [تَحَصَّلَ على شَيْءٍ بالتَطَفُّلِ على شَخْصٍ] ‹*a cigarette, lift*›

كيفية استخدام القاموس

توضيح عام

اتجاه النص في القاموس هو من اليسار إلى اليمين ويشمل ذلك الكلمات والجمل وترجماتها وترقيم الصفحات سواء في القسم الإنكليزي أو العربي، وعلى هذا فإذا جاءت جملة عربية في سطر وبقيتها في السطر التالي فإن البقية تظهر في الجزء الأيسر من السطر التالي.

تدرج الأفعال الإنكليزية في المعجم في صيغة المصدر 'infinitive' مثال (to drink tea)، أما بالنسبة للأفعال في اللغة العربية فإنها تدرج في صيغة الماضي المفرد المذكر المسند إلى ضمير الغائب (مثال: شَرِبَ الشايَ)

أما بالنسبة للأسماء فإنها تدرج بصيغة النكرة سواء في اللغة العربية أم الإنكليزية، ولكن قد ترد الأسماء في بعض الحالات في صيغة المعرفة إذا اقتضت ذلك ضرورة تطبيقية أو نحوية.

١ - طريقة التشكيل في اللغة العربية

تم تشكيل جميع الكلمات الواردة في القاموس سواء في المداخل أو الأمثلة طبقا للقواعد التالية:

- تكتب همزة الوصل كألف مجردة من الحركات والهمزات (مثال: قاعة الاجْتِماعاتِ)
- تكتب حروف المد (وهي الألف الساكنة المفتوح ما قبلها، والواو الساكنة المضموم ما قبلها، والياء الساكنة المكسور ما قبلها) دون تشكيل الحرف الذي يسبقها (مثال: قالَ، يَقولُ، قيلَ).
- أما إذا وردت الواو أو الياء في غير وظيفة المد فإنها تأتي مشكّلة وما قبلها مشكّلا كذلك (مثال: صُوَر، سِياسة). لاحظ أنه إذا جاءت الواو أو الياء مضعفة فلا تكتب الضمة أو الكسرة قبلها (مثال: عَرَبيّة، قوّة)
- لا تكتب الفتحة قبل التاء المربوطة (مثال: مَدْرَسة)
- لا يتم تشكيل أداة التعريف (الـ)
- كذلك لا يتم تشكيل حرف الجر أو العطف الداخل عليها (مثال: والـ، بالـ، للـ)
- لا تكتب الكسرة مع الهمزة أسفل الألف (مثال: إسْلام)
- لا تكتب الشدّة بعد اللام الشمسية كما لا تكتب السكون على اللام القمرية (مثال: الشَمْس، القَمَر)
- إذا انتهت كلمة بسكون وبدأت الكلمة التالية بألف وصل، فلا يكتب السكون في آخر الكلمة الأولى ولا ما يسمى بالحركات المساعدة (مثال: قَرَأْت الكِتابَ)
- لا يتم تشكيل الكلمات الوظيفية كثيرة التداول والاستخدام (مثال: لم، على)
- لا يتم كتابة الألف الخنجرية ويكتب بدلا منها فتحة أو ألف عادية (مثال: ذَلِكَ، رَحْمان)، والاستثناء الوحيد في ذلك هو لفظ الجلالة (الله)
- لا توضع علامات الإعراب على أواخر الكلمات أو الأسماء المستعارة من لغات أخرى إلا إذا انتهت بتاء مربوطة أو ياء النسبة (مثال: رَقْم التِلِفون)

٢ - علامات الإعراب في اللغة العربية

في هذا القاموس لا يتم وضع علامات الإعراب على أواخر الكلمات المفردة سواء في المداخل أو الترجمات، ولكن إذا جاءت الكلمة داخل جملة أو مسبوقة بحرف جر مثلا بما يقتضي إعرابا معينا فيتم تشكيل آخر الكلمة حسب موقعها في الجملة أو التركيب، وإذا ورد المثال أو الترجمة مثلا في شكل مضاف ومضاف إليه فيتم وضع علامة الإعراب على المضاف إليه فقط، أما المضاف فيترك بلا علامة على آخره لأنه لم يذكر معه عامل يؤثر على شكل إعرابه (مثال: مُدير شَرِكةٍ).

تعتبر حالة الرفع هي الحالة الأصلية المفترضة مع الأسماء، وتستخدم هذه الحالة عندما يتحتم اللجوء إلى أحد أشكال الإعراب فمثلا يسرد جمع المذكر السالم مع الواو والنون ـونَ. وإذا جاء اسم بلا

عامل يسبقه وأضيف هذا الاسم إلى ضمير فتوضع ضمة على الاسم (مثال: زَوْجَتُهُ).

٣- الصيغ المختصرة

لقد تم إدراج المعلومات النحوية والصرفية وأقسام الكلام ومستويات الاستخدام وغير ذلك باللغة الإنكليزية في شكل صيغ كاملة أو مختصرة. ويمكن للمستخدم أن يجد ترجمة بالعربية لهذه الرموز في قائمة الاختصارات في آخر القاموس.

٤- الخطوط المائلة

تستخدم الخطوط المائلة لخدمة غرضين:

(أ) فصل كلمتين بديلتين عن بعضهما البعض، وفي هذه الحالة تكون الكلمتان غير مترادفتين وتردان في الأصل والترجمة على السواء، ومثال ذلك:

(Phrasal verbs) **back away** تَهَرَّبَ; **to ~ away from a problem/confrontation** تَهَرَّبَ من مُشْكِلةٍ \ مُواجَهةٍ

فهذا المثال يمكن فصله إلى جملتين إنكليزيتين تقابلهما ترجمتان عربيتان، الأولى: to back away from a problem وترجمتها: تَهَرَّبَ من مُشْكِلةٍ، والجملة الثانية: to back away from a confrontation وترجمتها: تَهَرَّبَ من مُواجَهةٍ.

وقد تكون إحدى الكلمتين العربيتين مذكرة والأخرى مؤنثة، فإذا تلاهما نعت يتم إلحاق علامة التأنيث به بين قوسين، ومثال ذلك:

a powerful explosion/blast; ضَرْبة انْفِجار \ فَرْقَعة قويّ(ة)

(ب) للفصل بين كلمتين مترادفتين في إحدى اللغتين دون الأخرى، وفي هذه الحالة يرد الخط المائل الذي يفصل بين الكلمتين المترادفتين في المثال الأصلي أو الترجمة فقط. فعلى سبيل المثال كلمة قابَلَ العربية يمكن ترجمتها إلى الإنكليزية بكلمة ’meet‘ أو ’encounter‘:

قابَلَ *v* 1 [لاقى] to meet, to encounter; to interview; قابَلَ شَخْصاً to meet/encounter sb; to interview sb; **شَخْصاً**

وفي المثال التالي تستخدم كلمتي قاع و ذَيْل كبديلين مترادفين:

languishing behind bars; وراء القُضْبانِ **فَريق قابِع على قاعِ \ ذَيْلِ التَّرْتيبِ** a team languishing at the bottom of the rankings; a regime نِظام قابِع على صَدْرِ الشَّعْبِ

٥- الأقواس

تستخدم الأقواس للدلالة على جزء اختياري داخل الترجمة، أي أن الجملة أو التعبير يعد مناسبا بذلك الجزء أو بدونه، كما في الأمثلة التالية:

pregnant and nursing women; النِساء والمُرْضِعات

(female) writers; نِساء الأَعْمالِ الكاتِبات \ الأَديبات

Albanian /al'beɪnɪən/ **A** *n* 1 (citizen) (أَلْبان) أَلْبانيّ 2 (language) **(اللُغة) الأَلْبانيّة**

إذا وردت الأقواس في كل من الأصل والترجمة فإن الكلمة بين الأقواس في الترجمة تعتبر ترجمة مقابلة للكلمة بين الأقواس في الجملة أو التعبير الأصلي، كما في المثال التالي:

راعٍ *n* |رِعاء ,رُعْيان ,رُعاة| 1 [فَلّاح] shepherd; راعي بَقَرٍ an (American) cowboy; راعي الغَنَمِ shepherd **(أَمْريكيّ)**

٦- علامة القيمة التقريبية ≈

إذا استخدمت علامة القيمة التقريبية ≈ فهذا يدل على أن الترجمة تقريبية وليست مباشرة، وعادة ما تتبع هذه الترجمة بشرح بين قوسين يبين المعنى بشكل أكثر تفصيلا، كما في هذا المثال:

abbey /'abi/ *n* (*pl* **abbeys**) 1 (community) دَيْر ≈ (كَنيسة كَبيرة مع دَيْرٍ للرُهْبانِ أو للراهِباتِ) 2 (church)

٧- الفاصلة بين الأمثلة

إذا جاء مثالان بينهما فاصلة ثم أتبع المثالان بترجمة فهذا يدل على أن المثالين مترادفان في المعنى، وأن الترجمة هي للمثالين معا، ومثال ذلك:

to express one's concern; عَبَّرَ عن قَلَقِهِ ,أَبْدى قَلَقَهُ

to deserve ~ اِسْتَحَقَّ الأَفْضَلَ; **so much the ~, all the ~** سَيَكونُ أَحْسَنَ; **to change for the ~** تَغَيَّرَ إلى الأَحْسَنِ

٨- الأمثال

تعتبر كلتا اللغتين العربية والإنكليزية من اللغات الغنية بالأمثال والأقوال المأثورة، ولذلك إذا صادف المترجم مثلا أو تعبيرا شائعا في إحدى اللغتين فإنه يحاول قدر الإمكان ترجمته إلى مثل أو تعبير يؤدي نفس المعنى والغرض في اللغة الأخرى، فإذا لم يتسن ذلك فيتم شرح المعنى.

٩- الجنس والعدد

الشكل الافتراضي المجرد للكلمة في اللغة العربية هو صيغة التذكير والإفراد، ولذلك فإن جملة you write في الإنكليزية على سبيل المثال تترجم في القاموس إلى تَكْتُبُ. والسبب في هذا هو أن صيغة المذكر المفرد هي أكثر الصيغ تجريدا وبساطة من حيث عدم احتياجها إلى علامات إضافية.

١٠ - مستويات الأسلوب

توجد في اللغة الإنجليزية الحديثة مفردات وتعبيرات من كافة المستويات سواء الرسمية أو غير الرسمية، ولكن اللغة العربية الفصحى تعتبر لغة 'عليا' أو لغة رسمية، لذا يتعذر في بعض الأحيان أن نجد ترجمة في العربية الفصحى لتعبير إنجليزية سوقي أو غير رسمي، وفي هذه الحالة يحاول المترجم قدر الإمكان إيجاد ترجمة مناسبة من الفصحى تعبر عن المعنى الإنجليزية بشكل سليم.

وبالنسبة لتهجية كلمات ليس لها قواعد إملائية ثابتة، مثل إنْجليزيّة وإنْكليزيّة ولهذ فقد قررنا أن لا نختار واحدة على حساب الأخرى لنعكس الاختلافات الإملائية الموجودة في النصوص العربية.

لقد استخدمنا أيضا الأرقام العربية المغربية في القسم الأنجليزي-العربي والأرقام العربية المشرقية في القسم العربي-الأنجليزي لنعكس هذا التنوع والاختلاف.

القاموس العربي الإنكليزي

١- ترتيب المداخل

(أ) ترتيب الجذور

تم ترتيب المداخل في الجزء الخاص بالقاموس العربي الإنكليزي على حسب الجذر، ويوجد قوس مدبب صغير (〈) بجوار أول كلمة ترتبط بجذر جديد.

مِقْشَط *n* |مَقَاشِطُ| plane, file

〈 **قَشَعَ** *v* |a; قَشْع| to drive away, to disperse; قَشَعَ الظَلَامَ to dispel the darkness

انْقَشَعَ *v* to brighten/clear up; to disperse; يَنْقَشِعُ السَحابُ

الجذور العربية في القاموس مرتبة ترتيبا أبجديا، وننوه أنه إذا جاء الحرف الثاني والثالث مكررا في مادة الجذر (مثال دقق و حلل) فإنه، أي الجذر، يأتي مرتبا ترتيبا هجائيا باعتبار تسلسل جميع الحروف، وعلى هذا فيأتي الجذر حلل بين حلك و حلم.

في بعض الأحيان يكون من الصعب التفرقة بين جذرين يتوسطهما حرف علّة مثل حوز \ حيز، فيصعب تحديد ما إذا كان الوزن فول أو فيل أو ينتهيان بحرف علّة مثل قلو \ قلي فكذلك يصعب معرفة ما إذا كان الوزن فعو أو فعي، وفي هذه الحالة يدمج الجذرين معا في جذر أبجدي واحد كما لو كان الجذر فولفيل أو فعوفعي.

وفي بعض الحالات يتم الفصل بين جذرين متماثلين (يشتملان على نفس الأحرف) بغرض التوضيح فيتم وضع رقم علوي صغير قبل القوس المدبب:

〈[1] **صَفَرَ** *v* |i; صَفير| to whistle

(ب) الإحالات المرجعية

إذا كان الجذر غير واضح لكلمة ما، فيتم إدراج الكلمة وبجوارها إشارة إلى الجذر الذي تندرج تحته الكلمة، كما في المثال التالي:

〈 **أَب** *n* see **أبو**

وقد يكون لبعض الصيغ في بعض التصريفات شكلا هجائيا غير متوقع مما يجعل من العسير على المتعلم معرفة الجذر، وفي هذه الحالة يتم إدراج الصيغة في الترتيب الهجائي للقاموس مع الإشارة إلى المدخل الذي تندرج تحته هذه الصيغة، كما في هذا المثال:

〈 **قِفْ** *v* see **وَقَفَ**

قد يبدو أن كلمة ما تنتمي إلى جذر معين ولكن في الحقيقة تكون الكلمة جامدة أو مستعارة، وفي هذه الحالة تدرج الكلمة في القاموس مرتين، مرة في موضعها الطبيعي طبقا للتسلسل الأبجدي، ومرة تحت الجذر المشابه مع عبارة (listed alphabetically)، كما في المثال التالي:

خُبَّيْزة *n* listed alphabetically

وهذا يعني أن مثل هذه الكلمات ينبغي البحث عنها في القاموس حسب الترتيب الهجائي باعتبار أن كل حروفها أصلية، ففي المثال السابق ينبغي البحث عن الكلمة تحت مادة خبيزة.

(ج) كيفية البحث عن الكلمات غير قياسية البناء

إذا كانت الكلمة مركبة من جزأين والجزء الأول عبارة عن حرف أو أداة (مثل لاسِلْكيّ) فإنها تدرج في القاموس تحت الكلمة الرئيسية أو الجزء الثاني (في هذا المثال تحت مادة سلك)

الكلمات ذات الاشتقاق المركب (مثل خَوْصَصة وتَمَرْكَز) ينبغي البحث عنها تحت الجذر الأصلي (خصص، ركز)، وللتيسير على المستخدم فقد تم إضافة مثل هذه الكلمات مع الإشارة إلى الجذر الصحيح الذي تندرج تحته الكلمة.

تم إدراج الاختصارات طبقا للترتيب الهجائي باعتبار أن كل الحروف أصلية، فمثلا ق.ع. تندرج بين الجذرين قطن و قعد.

(د) ترتيب المداخل المدرجة تحت الجذر

يتم ترتيب المداخل المدرجة تحت نفس الجذر كالتالي:

- أولا، يتم إدراج الأفعال بشكل متسلسل من الباب الأول حتى الباب العاشر (فَعَلَ، فَعَّلَ، فاعَلَ، أَفْعَلَ، تَفَعَّلَ، تَفاعَلَ، انْفَعَلَ، افْتَعَلَ، افْعَلَّ، اسْتَفْعَلَ).

  مثال: قَبِلَ – قَبَّلَ – قابَلَ – أَقْبَلَ – تَقَبَّلَ – تَقابَلَ – اسْتَقْبَلَ

- ثانيا، الكلمات التي تتكون من نفس حروف الجذر دون زيادة ولكن مع الاختلاف في التشكيل.

  مثال: قَبْلَ – قَبْلُ – قُبُل – قِبَل – قِبَلَ

- ثالثا، الكلمات التي تبدأ بنفس الحرف الأول للجذر، وتدرج حسب ترتيبها الهجائي.

  مثال: قابِل – قابِلة – قابِليّة – قُبالَةَ – قِبالة – قُبْلة – قِبْلة – قَبْليّ – قَبَليّة – قَبول – قَبيل – قُبَيْلَ – قَبيلة

- رابعا، الكلمات المشتقة من الجذر والتي تلحقها أحرف زائدة في أول الكلمة تدرج تحت الجذر طبقا للترتيب الأبجدي.

  مثال: اسْتِقْبال – إقْبال – تَقَبُّل – مُتَقابِل – مُتَقَبِّل – مُسْتَقْبَل – مُسْتَقْبِل – مُسْتَقْبَليّ – مُقابِل – مُقابَل – مُقابَلة – مُقْبِل – مُقَبِّلات – مَقْبول – مَقْبوليّة – مُقْتَبَل

تم التمييز بين الكلمات المتشابهة في الهجاء والمتباينة في المعنى (homographs) باستخدام الأرقام الرومانية، كما في المثال التالي:

قابِس **I** *n* |قَوابِسُ| (Elec) (power) plug; أَدْخَلَ \ وَضَعَ القابِسَ في المِقْبَسِ to insert the plug into the socket

قابِس **II** *n* |dipt f| Gabès (*city in Tunisia*)

(ه) ما تم إدراجه ضمن المداخل

تم إدراج الكلمات الوظيفية التي تتكون من جزأين (مثال: لِأَنَّ و فيما) كمداخل مستقلة في القاموس.

لم يتم إدراج كافة المصادر وأسماء الفاعل وأسماء المفعول، ولكن ذلك اعتمد على ما إذا كان المصدر أو اسم الفاعل واسم المفعول يحمل معنى إضافيا زائدا على المعنى المشتق من الفعل أو كان لهما ترجمة إنكليزية خاصة أو استخداما سياقيا خاصا.

٢ – تفصيل المداخل

(أ) الأشكال الهجائية المختلفة للكلمة

قد يكون لكلمة ما شكلان إملائيان مختلفان أو أكثر، وفي هذه الحالة يتم إدراج الشكل أو الأشكال المختلفة بعد المدخل الرئيسي بحجم أصغر ومفصولا عنه بفاصلة، كما في هذا المثال:

إِنْجليزيّ، إِنْكْليزيّ **A** *adj* |إِنْجليز، إِنْجليزيّونَ| English;

(ب) أقسام الكلام

قد يحتوي المدخل على مادة تنتمي إلى قسمين من أقسام الكلام، أي أن الكلمة قد تستعمل مثلا كصفة واسم، وفي هذه الحالة يتم الرمز إلى كل قسم من أقسام الكلام بتسلسل من الحروف اللاتينية الكبيرة **A**، ويتم إدراج معنى الصفة قبل الاسم.

(ج) بيان المنطقة أو الدولة

إذا كان هناك مدخل معين يتم استخدامه على وجه الخصوص في إقليم أو دولة ما، فيتم الإشارة إلى ذلك بين قوسين بعد المدخل وبعد الرمز الدال على قسم الكلام، كما في المثال التالي:

نُوَنْبِر *n* (Mor) November

وتستخدم الرموز الدالة على المنطقة كذلك للدلالة على أن كلمة ما لها معنى خاص في منطقة أو دولة معينة، كما في المثال التالي:

قَصَبة *n* 1 [أُنْبوب] pipe, tube, reed; قَصَبة هَوائيّة \ الرِئة windpipe; bronchi 2 [بَلْدة] (NA) citadel; kasbah 3 [عَظْم]

أو للدلالة على أن عبارة ما تستخدم حصريا في منطقة أو دولة معينة، كما في المثال التالي:

مَفْرَزة الاسْتِقْصاءِ (Leb) the investigation of/into sth; detention centre

(د) المعاني

إذا كان للكلمة أكثر من معنى فيتم سرد تلك المعاني الواحد تلو الآخر مسبوقة برقم مسلسل داخل مربع يليه ملخص للدلالة على المعنى بين قوسين مربعين، كما في المثال التالي:

نَدَبَ v |u; نَدْب| 1 [ناحَ] to lament, to mourn (for); نَدَبَ الميِّتَ to mourn the deceased 2 [أَوْفَدَ] to delegate, to depute; to authorize, to commission; to appoint, to assign;

وبالنسبة لهذا الملخص الدال على المعنى فقد يكون كلمة مرادفة أو شرحا موجزا أو كلمة يكثر تلازمها مع مادة المدخل أو رمز يدل على مجال أو تخصص معين (مثال Comput للدلالة على الحوسبة و Bot للدلالة على علم النبات)، وهناك قائمة بكل هذه الرموز وترجمتها إلى العربية ملحقة في آخر القاموس.

(هـ) الترجمة

يتم ترتيب الترجمات المختلفة لكلمة ما حسب شيوعها، فيتم إدراج المقابل الأكثر شيوعا أولا.

وعند ورود أكثر من مقابل في الترجمة فيتم الفصل بينها بفاصلة أو فاصلة منقوطة، مع التنويه بأن الفاصلة تعني أن المقابلات المختلفة مترادفة في المعنى إلى حد كبير، أما الفاصلة المنقوطة فتعني أن كل مقابل يحمل معنى مختلفا عن الآخر، كما في المثال التالي:

نَزَعَ v |i| نَزْع| 1 [قَلَعَ] to remove, to take away; to tear/pull out, to extract; to take off; نَزَعَ مِسْماراً to pull out a nail;

ومن الجدير بالذكر أن بعض الكلمات والتعبيرات والمصطلحات العربية لا يوجد لها مقابل في اللغة الإنكليزية، وفي هذه الحالة يتم سرد شرح للمعنى باللغة الإنكليزية مميز بحروف مائلة، كما في المثال التالي:

(الحُروف) المُقَطَّعات n B *isolated letters of unknown significance heading 29 Quranic suras*

وأحيانا أيضا يتم سرد بعض المعلومات الإضافية بجوار الترجمة بين قوسين بحروف مائلة بغرض إيضاح المعنى أو لتحديد السياق الذي تستخدم فيه الكلمة، ومثال ذلك:

مِنْسَر n |مَناسِرُ| beak *(of a predatory bird)*

إذا كان لترجمة مدخل ما هجاء مختلف في الإنكليزية البريطانية والإنكليزية الأمريكية فيتم استخدام الهجاء البريطاني، أما إذا كانت الإنكليزية الأمريكية تستخدم كلمة مختلفة عن الإنكليزية البريطانية فيتم سرد كلا الكلمتين مع التوضيح برمز بين قوسين، كما في المثال التالي:

ناصِية n |نَواصٍ| 1 [شَعْر مُقَدَّم الرَّأْس] fringe (BrE), bangs (AmE);

وتم اتباع هذا المنهج أيضا في ترجمة الأمثلة بما يتيح للمستخدم اختيار ما يناسبه للترجمة سواء من الإنكليزية الأمريكية أو البريطانية، كما في المثال التالي:

مَكْروهٌ an accident befell him; يَنْزِلُ المِصْعَدُ the lift (BrE) elevator (AmE) is going down; يَنْزِلُ المَطَرُ it is raining;

إذا جاءت كلمة في الترجمة وبعدها *before n* فهذا يعني أن الكلمة تستخدم كنعت أو صفة للاسم الذي يليها، وعادة ما يأتي هذا التركيب عندما يستخدم اسم في الإنكليزية كترجمة لصفة عربية، كما في المثال التالي:

نَباتيّ A adj [مَصْنوع من النَباتِ] vegetable *(before n)*,

إذا وردت كلمة إنكليزية في الترجمة متبوعة بشرطة فهذا يعني أن الكلمة تأتي ملتصقة بالكلمة التي تليها كما في المثال التالي:

ثَلْجيّ adj icy; ice-cold; snow-; عاصِفة ثَلْجيّة blizzard, snowstorm; مِياه ثَلْجيّة ice-cold; انْهِيار ثَلْجيّ avalanche;

(و) الأمثلة والعبارات الاصطلاحية

تم سرد الكثير من الأمثلة في هذا القاموس بغرض بيان الاستخدام الشائع للكلمة والتركيبات النحوية التي تظهر فيها وكذلك المتلازمات اللفظية (collocations) التي ترتبط بها، كما في المثال التالي:

مَنْسوب A adj related; attributed, assigned; مَنْسوب ل \ إلى related to; التُهَم المَنْسوبة إلَيْهِ the charges against him; الكَلام المَنْسوب إلَيْهِ the words attributed to him

وفي بعض الأحيان قد تقع الكلمة كوحدة في عبارة تختلف في معناها الإجمالي عن معنى مفرداتها المنفصلة وهذا ما يسمى بالتعبير الاصطلاحي (idiom)، كما في هذا المثال:

بَحْر من الدَمِ a sea of blood; بَحْر من المَشاكِلِ a huge number of problems ③ [وَزْن شِعْرِيّ] metre

Idiom في بَحْرِ هذا الأُسْبوعِ in the course of this week

عندما يتحدث المثال عن أشخاص أو أشياء غير محددة فيتم استخدام لفظ شَخْص للعاقل و شَيْء لغير العاقل، وتترجم هاتان الكلمتان في الإنكليزية إلى sb اختصارا لـ somebody و sth اختصارا لـ something.

٣- المعلومات النحوية والصرفية في اللغة العربية

يتم إعطاء المعلومات الصرفية الخاصة بمادة المدخل مباشرة بعدها بين خطين عموديين.

(أ) الأسماء والصفات

إذا كان للاسم أو الصفة صيغة أو أكثر من **صيغ جمع التكسير** فيتم وضع جميع هذه الصيغ بجوار الكلمة، وإذا كانت الكلمة تجمع جمع تكسير وجمعا سالما فيتم سرد كلا الجمعين كذلك بجوار الكلمة، كما في المثال التالي، أما إذا كانت الكلمة تجمع جمعا سالما فقط فلا يتم ذكر صيغة الجمع.

قوّة *n* |**قُوًى ,قوّات**| ① [جَسَديّة] strength, power; بِقُوّةٍ strongly; ضَرَبَ شَخْصاً بِقُوّةٍ to hit sb hard; وَقَعَ بِقُوّةٍ to come down

إذا كانت المعاني المختلفة المتفرعة من أحد المداخل لها صيغ جمع مختلفة فيتم إدراج صيغ الجمع الخاصة بكل معنى على حدة في الموقع المناسب، كما في المثال التالي:

أخ *n* ① [شَقيق] |**إخْوة ,إخْوان**| brother; إخْوان brothers (*in trade/company names*); الإخْوة والأَخَوات siblings, brothers and sisters; أخ شَقيق full brother; أخ غَيْر شَقيقٍ half brother; أخوكَ your brother; بِنْت \ ابْن أَخ niece/nephew; قَتْل أَخٍ fratricide; لَهُ خَمْسَةُ إخْوةٍ he has five brothers ② [صَديق] |**إخْوان**| الأَخ فُلان mister/brother so-and-so; يا أخي! excuse me, sir! ③ (Chr) |**إخْوان**| brother; friar ④ (Pol) |**إخْوان**| fellow believer; الإخْوان

إذا كان للكلمة **صيغ متميزة** أو غير مطردة مع القواعد معتادة، كأن يكون لها شكل خاص في الرفع أو النصب أو الجر أو يتغير شكل الكلمة عند إلحاق علامة جمع المؤنث السالم، فيتم سرد جميع هذه الصيغ مع رمز مختصر يدل على الحالة التي تستخدم فيها الصيغة، كما في المثال التالي:

ذو *n* |**ذووا ,أولو**; f **ذات**; f pl **ذَوات**; m du **ذَوا**; f du **ذاتا**; gen **ذى**; acc **ذا**| owner, possessor; embodying, comprising;

المداخل **الممنوعة من الصرف** تحمل رمز dipt كما في المثال التالي:

أَحْمَر *adj* |dipt; **حُمْر**| red; أَحْمَر فاتِح light red; أَحْمَر قانٍ bright/vivid red; أَحْمَر دَمَوِيّ blood red, scarlet, crimson;

أما **صيغ الجمع الممنوعة من الصرف** فيتم سردها في القاموس مع ضمة على آخرها كما هو متبع في المعاجم العربية، كما هو مبين في المثال التالي:

مَقْبَرة *n* |**مَقابِرُ**| cemetery, graveyard; مَقْبَرة عائِلِيّة family grave; مَقْبَرة جَماعيّة mass grave; مَقْبَرة عَسْكَرِيّة military

وبالنسبة **لاسم الجمع** فيتم الإشارة إليه برمز *n coll* وكثيرا ما يصاغ المفرد من هذه الأسماء بإضافة تاء مربوطة مثل بعوض بعوضة، وبرتقال برتقالة وتمر تمرة. فإذا جاء المفرد على غير هذه الصيغة أو لم يكن للكلمة مفرد فيتم الإشارة إلى كل ذلك، كما في المثالين التاليين:

شاء *n coll* |**شِواه ,شِياء ,شِياه**; sing n **شاة**| sheep; ewe

قَوْم *n coll* |no singular noun; **أَقْوام**| ① [شَعْب] people; tribe; بَنو قَوْمِهِ one's people ② [ناس] people; عِلْيَة القَوْم the elite, the

بصفة عامة الأسماء التي تنتهي بتاء مربوطة أو بألف تكون **مؤنثة** والأسماء التي لا تنتهي بتاء مربوطة تكون مذكرة، ولكن هناك بعض الأسماء المؤنثة ولا تنتهي بتاء مربوطة، وفي هذه الحالة يتم وضع الرمز f بجوار الكلمة كما في المثال التالي. وكذلك يتم وضع هذا الرمز بجوار الصفات التي لا تنتهي بتاء مربوطة ولا تستعمل إلا مع المؤنث مثل حامِل.

أَرْض *n* |f; **أَراضٍ**| ① [قِطْعة أَرْض] land; soil; property; أَرْض فِلاحيّة \ زِراعيّة farming/ land; area; أَراضٍ

وهناك بعض الأسماء التي تنتهي بتاء مربوطة ولكنها مذكرة (مثل طاغِية) وفي هذه الحالة يتم وضع الرمز m بجوار الكلمة.

كما أن بعض الصفات لا تضاف إليها التاء المربوطة مع المؤنث، ويتم بيان ذلك بالرمز mf كما في المثال التالي:

خام A *adj* |mf| raw, crude, unprocessed; زَيْت \ نَفْط خام crude oil; حَديد خام iron ore; مادّة خام raw material;

ويستخدم الرمز mf كذلك للإشارة إلى الأسماء التي يمكن أن تستخدم بنفس اللفظ في التذكير أو التأنيث، كما في المثال التالي:

نَعْل *n* |mf; **نعال** ,**أَنْعُل**| 1 [حِذاء] shoe, sandal; اخْلَعْ نَعْلَيْكَ take off your shoes 2 [سُفْل الحِذاء] sole; نَعْل حِذائِهِ the

(ب) الأفعال

مع **الباب الأول في تصريف الأفعال** (أي الأفعال على وزن فَعَلَ) يتم ذكر حركة العين في المضارع كما يتم ذكر صيغة أو صيغ المصدر، كما في المثال التالي:

قَحَطَ *v* |a; **قَحْط** ,**قُحوط**| to fail to happen; to fail to appear; قَحَطَ المَطَرُ the rain held off; إذا قَسا القَلْبُ قَحَطَت العَيْنُ

وعلى هذا فحرف a التالي للفعل بعد علامة | في المثال السابق يعني أن المضارعة تصاغ بفتحة على العين, أي يُقْحَطُ, وبالمثل حرف i يعنى أن عين المضارعة مكسورة, و حرف u يعنى أنها مضمومة.

أما إذا اختلفت صيغة المصدر باختلاف المعنى داخل المدخل الواحد، فيتم ذكر المصدر أو المصادر المرتبطة بكل معنى على حدة، كما في المثال التالي:

قَصَرَ *v* |u| 1 [عَجَزَ] |**قُصور**| to be remiss; قَصَرَ عن واجباتِهِ to be remiss in one's duties; قَصَرَ عن تَسْديدِ دَيْنِه to fail to repay one's debts 2 [أَخَذَ من طولِهِ] |**قِصر**|

في حالة ما إذا كان باب تصريف الفعل (أو وزن الفعل) غير واضح فيتم بيان ذلك كما يتم بيان صيغة المضارع لهذا الفعل، كما في المثال التالي:

آتى *v* |Form III; **يُؤاتي**| 1 [زَوَّدَ] to give; to offer; آتى الزَكاةَ to give zakat (*alms*) 2 [أَحْضَرَ] to bring 3 [ناسَبَ]

إذا كان للفعل **تصريف غير قياسي** في إحدى الحالات الصرفية فيتم بيان ذلك مع ذكر الحالة التي ترد فيها تلك الصيغة، ويستخدم معها الرمز perfect للدلالة على الماضي و imperfect للدلالة على المضارع، كما في المثال التالي

ظَلَّ *v* |a; ظَلّ ,ظُلول; perf **ظَلِلْتُ**| to stay, to remain; to continue, to keep (on); ظَلَّ سَليماً \ لَطيفاً to stay healthy/

كما يتم إدراج معلومات صرفية إضافية عند الضرورة وهي تشتمل على المعلومات التالية:

- imperfect only أي أن الفعل لا يستخدم إلا في حالة المضارع، مثال انْبَغى
- imperfect or imperative only أي أن الفعل لا يستخدم إلا في المضارعة أو الأمر، مثال وَذَرَ
- no imperfect أي أن الفعل لا يستخدم إلا في صيغة الماضي، مثال عَسى
- passive only أي أن الفعل لا يستخدم إلا في صيغة المبني للمجهول، مثال غُمى

إذا كان للفعل **حرف جر ملازم**، يتم سرد حرف الجر ذلك بين خطين عموديين، وغالبا مع تسرد أمثلة مع ذلك التركيب لبيان كيفية الاستخدام، كما في المثال التالي:

بَحَثَ *v* |a; **بَحْث**| 1 [فَتَّشَ] |**عن**| to seek, to look/search for; بَحَثَ عن شَيْءٍ to look for sth; بَحَثَ عن مَسْكَنٍ جَديدٍ

مع ملاحظة أنه يتم إدراج حرف الجر مع المعنى المتعلق به، وإذا ارتبط به معنيان أو أكثر فيتم تكرار حرف الجر مع كل معنى على حدة.

القاموس الإنكليزي العربي

١ – ترتيب المداخل

الترتيب الهجائي

تم ترتيب المداخل في الجانب الإنكليزي العربي ترتيبا هجائيا بحتا مع التغاضي عن الشرطة والفاصلة العليا والمسافة بين كلمتين، وينطبق هذا على الاختصارات والمداخل المركبة وأسماء الأعلام وأسماء الأماكن الجغرافية التي تم إدراجها في القاموس.

إذا كان لكلمة ما هجاء (أو شكل إملائي) مختلف فيتم سرد الهجاء البديل كمدخل مستقل إذا لم يكن ترتيبه الأبجدي يتبع الكلمة الرئيسية مباشرة، وتتم الإشارة أمامه إلى المدخل الرئيسي.

والاستثناء الوحيد لهذه القاعدة هي الأفعال المركبة، حيث تندرج تحت مادة الفعل الرئيسي.

إذا اشترك مدخلان في الشكل الهجائي ولكن كان معناهما متباينا تباينا تاما (أي ليس بينهما أي علاقة منطقية أو مجازية) وهذا ما يسمى Homographs، فيتم إدراجهما في مدخلين منفصلين، كما في المثالين التاليين:

bass¹ /beɪs/ *n* ❶ (voice) جَهير ;(singer) مُغَنٍّ جَهير الصَّوْتِ ❷ (instrument: double bass) كَمان أَجْهَر ;(bass guitar) جيتار بيس ❸ (part) [طَبَقة صَوْتٍ خَفيضٍ وَعَميقٍ]; **to sing (the) ~** [غَنّى بِطَبَقةِ صَوْتٍ خَفيضٍ وَعَميقٍ]

bass² /bas/ *n* (sea fish) قاروص ;(freshwater) فَرْخ

الإحالات المرجعية

تتم الإشارة أمام الألفاظ وأشكال الهجاء الأمريكية إلى المدخل البريطاني، كما في المثال التالي:

checkers /ˈtʃɛkəz/ *n* (AmE) ▸ **draughts**

كما تتم الإشارة أمام الصيغ الصرفية غير القياسية المدرجة في القاموس إلى المدخل الرئيسي (بدون تصريف)، كما في المثال التالي:

could /kʊd, kəd/ ▸ **can¹**

٢- تفصيل المداخل

(أ) الأشكال الهجائية المختلفة للكلمة

الهجاء المتبع في هذا القاموس هو الهجاء البريطاني، وإذا كان هناك هجاء أمريكي مغاير للهجاء البريطاني فيتم ذكره مباشرة بعد مادة المدخل، ويتم الرمز إلى الأشكال الإملائية المختلفة بالرمز المناسب، فيشار إلى الهجاء الإنكليزي البريطاني بالرمز (BrE)، أما الهجاء الأمريكي فيشار إليه بالرمز (AmE)، كما في المثال التالي:

colour (BrE), **color** (AmE) /ˈkʌlə/ **A** *n* ❶ (hue) لَوْن (أَلْوان); **what ~ is it?** ما لَوْنُهُ؟; **the female is brown in ~** الأُنْثى

(ب) النطق

النطق في اللغة الإنكليزية غير قياسي ولذلك يصعب التنبؤ بالنطق الصحيح للكلمة في كثير من الأحيان، ولهذا السبب فقد تم إدراج كيفية النطق مع معظم المداخل الإنكليزية مكتوب بالأبجدية الصوتية الدولية (International Phonetic Alphabet) ويلي المدخل مباشرة في الترتيب (يمكن للمستخدم أن يجد دليلا للأبجدية الصوتية الدولية في صفحة xxvi). وفي حال اختلاف النطق الأمريكي عن النطق البريطاني فيتم إدراج النطق الأمريكي بعد النطق البريطاني متبوعا برمز (AmE). والحالة الوحيدة التي لا يتم فيها ذكر النطق مع المداخل هي الكلمات المركبة حيث يمكن للمستخدم أن يجد النطق الخاص بكل كلمة على حدة في المدخل الخاص بها.

(ج) المعلومات النحوية والصرفية

إذا كان للكلمة صيغة صرفية خاصة فيتم سردها بين قوسين بعد رمز قسم الكلام، كما في المثال التالي:

catchy /ˈkatʃi/ *adj* (**catchier**, **catchiest**) ‹*tune, chorus*› يَعْلَقُ في الذِهْنِ

بعض الصفات الإنكليزية لا ترد في اللغة إلا كنعت لاسم يتبعها (أي لا يمكن استخدامها كخبر)، وفي هذه الحالة يشار إلى ذلك بعبارة *before n* كما في المثال التالي:

carry-on /ˈkarɪɒn/ **A** *n* (infml) (fuss) ضَجّة **B** *adj before n* ‹*luggage*› [يُمْكِنُ حَمْلُهُ على مَتْنِ طائِرةٍ];

وتستخدم هذه العبارة أيضا (*before n*) إذا تغير شكل تركيب التعبير عند الاستخدام في الحالة الوصفية، كما في المثال التالي:

crystal clear *adj* (*before n* **crystal-clear**) ❶ ‹*water*› صافٍ

(د) ترتيب المعلومات في المداخل

تتم الإشارة إلى أقسام الكلام المختلفة بحروف لاتينية كبيرة مسلسلة مثل **C**، ويبدأ كل قسم جديد للكلام على سطر جديد في القاموس، ثم يلي ذلك العبارات الاصطلاحية مشارا إليها بالرمز (Idiom)، ثم الأفعال المركبة التي تندرج تحت الرمز (Phrasal verbs) ويأتي كل فعل مركب مسبوقا برمز نقطي.

(ه) المعاني والمعاني الفرعية والمتلازمات اللفظية

تم إدراج المعاني المختلفة للكلمة مسبوقة برقم مسلسل ❶، وهناك ملخص للمعنى بين قوسين للتمييز بين المعاني، كما في المثال التالي:

carousel /ˌkarəˈsɛl/ *n* ❶ (merry-go-round) أُرْجوحة دَوّامة الخَيْل ❷ (for luggage) حِزام ناقِل للأَمْتِعةِ (في المَطارِ)

ويتم سرد المتلازمات اللفظية بين أقواس مدببة صغيرة، فإذا كان المتلازم اللفظي يقع موقع الفاعل فيدرج بين قوسين مدببين

مزدوجين، أما إذا كان يقع موقع المفعول أو غير ذلك فيدرج بين قوسين مدببين فرديين، كما هو موضح في المثال التالي:

circulate /ˈsə:kjʊleɪt/ **A** *vt* نَشَرَ (نَشْر ;u) ‹*a petition, letter*› **B** *vi* **1** «rumours, documents» شاعَ (i; شَيْع ,شُيوع). انْتَشَرَ **2** «blood, air» دارَ (u; دَوْر ,دَوَران)

وأحيانا تكون المعاني لها معان فرعية ترتبط بترجمات مختلفة، فيتم تفصيل ذلك مع كل معنى، كما في المثال التالي:

band /band/ *n* **1** (group of people) عُصْبة (عُصَب), زُمْرة (زُمَر), جَماعة; (group of musicians) فِرْقة (فِرَق); **a jazz**

أو قد تختلف الترجمة باختلاف الكلمة المتلازمة مع مادة المدخل، فيتم تفصيل ذلك أيضا، كما في المثال التالي:

careless /ˈkɛːləs/ *adj* ‹*mistake*› طائِش; ‹*work*› غَيْر مُتْقَن; ‹*remark, driving*› مُتَهَوِّر

إذا كان أحد معاني الكلمة يدل على اسم غير معدود 'uncountable'، فيتم بيان ذلك بالرمز [u] في موقعه، كما في المثال التالي:

beauty /ˈbju:ti/ *n* (*pl* **beauties**) **1** [u] (of women, voices, scenery) جَمال **2** (attractive woman) حَسْناء (حِسان)

إذا كان للكلمة صيغة أخرى أكمل فيتم إيراد الصيغة الأخرى بعد المدخل بين قوسين مسبوقة بكلمة also، كما في المثال التالي:

beech /bi:tʃ/ *n* **1** (also **beech tree**) زان **2** [u] (wood) خَشَب الزانِ

(و) الترجمة

يتم سرد الترجمات مرتبة من اليسار إلى اليمين مفصولة بفاصلة، كما في المثال التالي:

commendable /kəˈmɛndəb(ə)l/ *adj* ‹*effort, performance*› جَدير بِالثَناءِ ,مُسْتَحْسَن

إذا كان للكلمة أكثر من ترجمة في اللغة العربية يتم ترتيب الترجمات بحيث تقع الترجمة الأهم والأكثر استخداما في الصدارة، وإذا كان هناك ألفاظ في الترجمة العربية خاصة بدولة أو منطقة معينة فيتم سرد ذلك (في بعض الأحيان) بعد الفصحى إن وجدت، ومع كل لفظ خاص يتم بيان الدولة أو المنطقة التي يستخدم فيها هذا اللفظ برمز بين قوسين يتبع الكلمة، كما في المثال التالي:

cable car *n* عَرَبة مُعَلَّقة, تيليفريك (NA, Leb)

وإذا كانت الترجمة العربية لفظا غير مركب فيتم سرد المعلومات النحوية والصرفية الخاصة بهذا اللفظ بين قوسين على يمين الترجمة (راجع القسم الخاص بالمعلومات النحوية والصرفية في اللغة العربية المذكور سابقا)، كما في المثالين التاليين:

bank² /baŋk/ **A** *n* **1** (Fin) بَنْك (بُنوك), مَصْرِف (مَصارِف);

announce) أَعْلَنَ (عن) ‹*a meeting*›; دَعا (u; ل) ‹*an election*›;

وإذا احتاجت الترجمة إلى توضيح أو تحديد للسياق فيتم وضع ذلك بين قوسين على يسار الترجمة، كما في المثال التالي:

babysit /ˈbeɪbisɪt/ *vi* (*present participle* **-tt-**, *past tense, past participle* **-sat**) قامَ بِرِعايةِ أَطْفالٍ (أثناء غِيابِ الوالِدَيْنِ)

وقد لا يوجد في العربية مقابل لبعض الكلمات أو التعبيرات، وفي هذه الحالة يتم سرد تعريف أو شرح للمعنى بين قوسين مربعين كما في المثال التالي:

bay window *n* [نافِذة غُرْفةٍ مُمْتَدّة إلى الخارِجِ]

في بعض الأحيان قد تترجم الصفة والموصوف في الإنكليزية إلى تركيب إضافي (مضاف ومضاف إليه) في العربية، وفي هذه الحالة تترجم الصفة منفردة باسم عربي في حالة الجر (المضاف إليه)، كما في المثال التالي:

cardiovascular /ˌkɑ:dɪəʊˈvaskjʊlə/ *adj* ‹*disease, exercise*› القَلْبِ والأَوْعِيةِ الدَمَوِيّةِ

وهذا يعني أن عبارة *cardiovascular disease* تترجم إلى مَرَض القَلْبِ والأَوْعِيةِ الدَمَوِيّةِ.

كما أن بعض الأفعال المتعدية في الإنكليزية قد لا يوجد لها لفظ مفرد يقابلها في العربية وإنما تترجم إلى تعبير مركب يشمل الفعل واسم متلازم بحيث يضاف هذا الاسم المتلازم إلى المفعول به، فمثلا *to replace the old model* تترجم إلى حَلَّ مَحَلَّ الطِرازِ القَديمِ وفي هذه الحالة فإن الفعل replace يقابله حَلَّ مَحَلَّ ولكن القواعد النحوية تمنع وجود اسم نكرة غير منون، ولذلك فضلنا أن ندرج الترجمة في القاموس بالشكل حَلَّ المَحَلَّ. وينبغي على المستخدم أن يتذكر حذف الألف واللام عند استخدام مثل هذه التراكيب داخل الجملة. وبناء على هذا ففي المثال التالي:

behead /bɪˈhɛd/ *vt* ‹*a prisoner*,› ضَرَبَ العُنُقَ ,قَطَعَ الرَأْسَ

تترجم العبارة الإنكليزية *to behead a prisoner* إلى ضَرَبَ عُنُقَ أسيرٍ أو قَطَعَ رَأْسَ أَسيرٍ.

(ز) الأمثلة

يتم إيراد الأمثلة بعد سرد المعلومات المتعلقة بالمدخل أو المعنى، وتفيد الأمثلة في بيان الاستخدام الشائع للكلمة والعبارات الثابتة التي تشترك فيها، وفي الأمثلة يتم الاستعاضة عن لفظ المدخل بعلامة تلدة ~، كما في المثال التالي:

bask /bɑːsk/ *vi* 1▸ (to lie) «sunbathers, seals» تَنَعَّمَ; **to ~ in the sun** تَنعَّمَ بِأَشِعَّةِ الشَّمْسِ 2▸ (to revel) **to ~ in the glory of sth** تَنَعَّمَ بِمَجْدِ شَيْءٍ

إذا وردت كلمة or بأحرف مائلة بين كلمتين، فهذا يعني أن كلا الكلمتين يمكن استخدامهما في السياق المذكور وتؤديان نفس المعنى، كما في هذا المثال:

cadge /kadʒ/ *vt* (infml) **to ~ sth off** *or* **from sb** [تَحَصَّلَ على ‹*a cigarette, lift*› شَيْءٍ بالتَطَفُّلِ على شَخْصٍ]

Guide to the International Phonetic Alphabet

دليل الأبجدية الصوتية الدولية

1 Consonants

b, d, f, h, k, l, m, n, p, r, s, t, v, w, and *z* have their usual English values. Other symbols are used as follows:

Symbol	Example
g	get
tʃ	*ch*ip
dʒ	*j*ar
x	lo*ch*
ŋ	ri*ng*
θ	*th*in
ð	*th*is
ʃ	*sh*e
ʒ	deci*s*ion
j	*y*es

2 Vowels

short vowels

a	c*a*t
ɛ	b*e*d
ə	*a*go
ɪ	s*i*t
i	cos*y*
ɒ	h*o*t
ʌ	r*u*n
ʊ	p*u*t

long vowels (: indicates length)

ɑː	*ar*m
ɛː	h*air*
əː	h*er*
iː	s*ee*
ɔː	s*aw*
uː	t*oo*

diphthongs

ʌɪ	m*y*
aʊ	h*ow*
eɪ	d*ay*
əʊ	n*o*
ɪə	n*ear*
ɔɪ	b*oy*
ʊə	p*oor*

triphthongs

ʌɪə	f*ire*
aʊə	s*our*

Note on trademarks and proprietary status

This dictionary includes some words which have, or are asserted to have, proprietary status as trademarks or otherwise. Their inclusion does not imply that they have acquired for legal purposes a non-proprietary or general significance, nor any other judgement concerning their legal status. In cases where the editorial staff have some evidence that a word has proprietary status this is indicated in the entry for that word by the symbol ®, but no judgement concerning the legal status of such words is made or implied thereby.

ملاحظة بشأن العلامات التجارية ووضع الملكية

يتضمن هذا القاموس بعض الكلمات التي لها، أوتأكد أن لها، وضع ملكية خاص كعلامة تجارية أو نحو ذلك. ولا يعني إدراجها في القاموس زوال وضع الملكية من الناحية القانونية أو أنها اكتسبت صفة عامة، ولا يعني أي حكم آخر يتعلق بوضعها القانوني.

في الحالات التي تحقق لدى هيئة التحرير من بعض الأدلة أن الكلمة لها صفة ملكية فقد تم الإشارة إلى ذلك عند مدخل الكلمة برمز ®، ولكن لا يعد هذا حكما صريحا أو ضمنيا بشأن الوضع القانوني لمثل هذه الكلمات.

The structure of Arabic–English entries

بنية المداخل في القاموس العربي-الإنجليزي

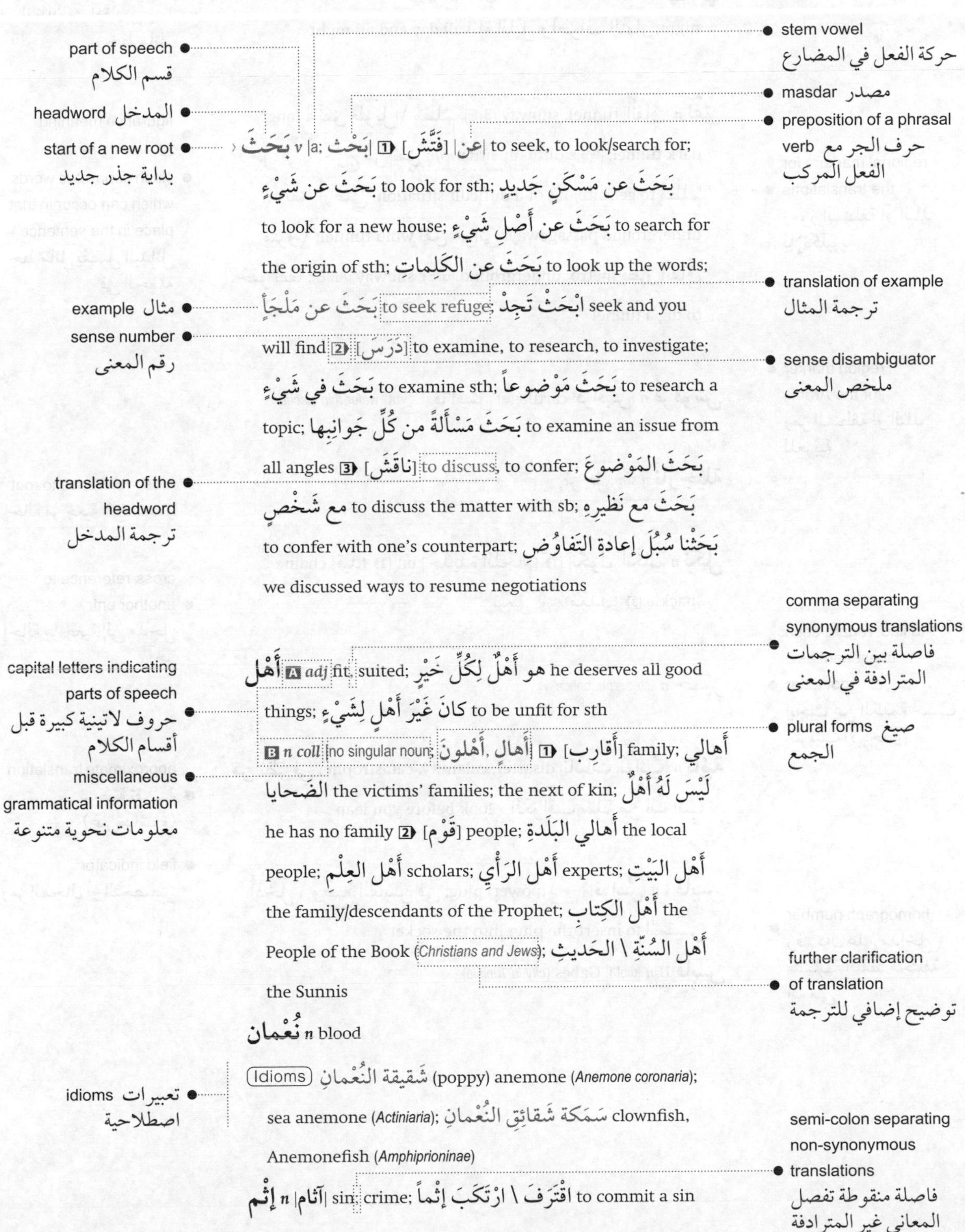

The structure of Arabic–English entries

The structure of English–Arabic entries

بنية المداخل في القاموس الإنجليزي-العربي

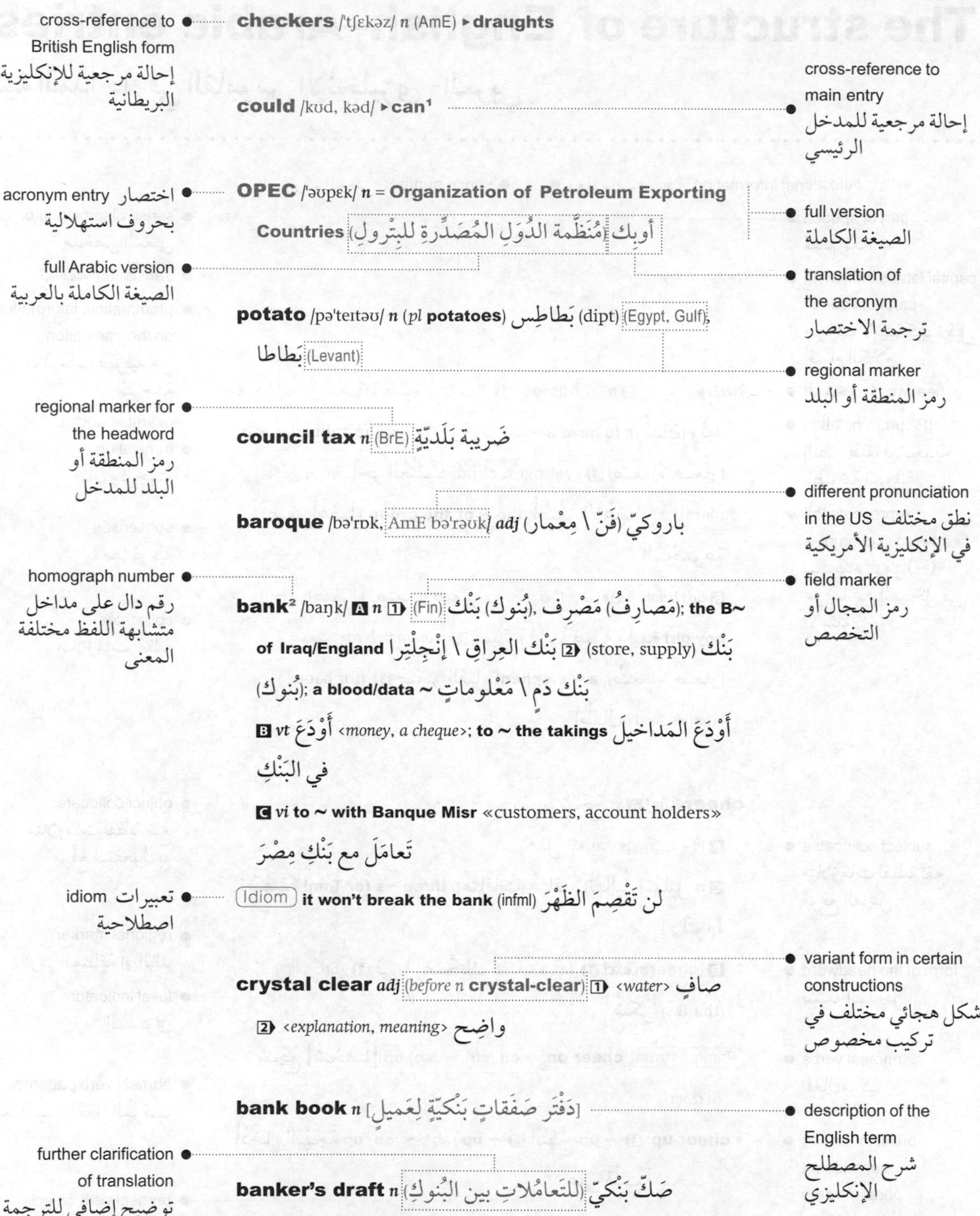
cross-reference to British English form
إحالة مرجعية للإنكليزية البريطانية
checkers /'tʃɛkəz/ n (AmE) ▸ draughts
cross-reference to main entry
إحالة مرجعية للمدخل الرئيسي
could /kʊd, kəd/ ▸ can¹
acronym entry اختصار بحروف استهلالية
OPEC /'əʊpɛk/ n = Organization of Petroleum Exporting Countries أوبك (مُنَظَّمة الدُوَلِ المُصَدِّرةِ للبِتْرولِ)
full version
الصيغة الكاملة
full Arabic version
الصيغة الكاملة بالعربية
translation of the acronym
ترجمة الاختصار
potato /pə'teɪtəʊ/ n (pl potatoes) بَطاطِس (dipt) (Egypt, Gulf), بَطاطا (Levant)
regional marker
رمز المنطقة أو البلد
regional marker for the headword
رمز المنطقة أو البلد للمدخل
council tax n (BrE) ضَريبة بَلَدِيّة
different pronunciation in the US
نطق مختلف في الإنكليزية الأمريكية
baroque /bə'rɒk, AmE bə'rəʊk/ adj باروكيّ (فَنّ \ مِعْمار)
homograph number
رقم دال على مداخل متشابهة اللفظ مختلفة المعنى
field marker
رمز المجال أو التخصص
bank² /baŋk/ A n 1 (Fin) بَنْك (بُنوك)، مَصْرِف (مَصارِفُ); the B~ of Iraq/England بَنْك العِراقِ \ إنْجِلْترا 2 (store, supply) بَنْك (بُنوك); a blood/data ~ بَنْك دَمٍ \ مَعْلوماتٍ
B vt أَوْدَعَ ‹money, a cheque›; to ~ the takings أَوْدَعَ المَداخيلَ في البَنْكِ
C vi to ~ with Banque Misr «customers, account holders» تَعامَلَ مع بَنْكِ مِصْرَ
idiom تعبيرات اصطلاحية
Idiom it won't break the bank (infml) لن تَقْصِمَ الظَهْرَ
variant form in certain constructions
شكل هجائي مختلف في تركيب مخصوص
crystal clear adj (before n crystal-clear) 1 ‹water› صافٍ 2 ‹explanation, meaning› واضِح
description of the English term
شرح المصطلح الإنكليزي
bank book n [دَفْتَر صَفَقاتٍ بَنْكِيّةٍ لِعَميلٍ]
further clarification of translation
توضيح إضافي للترجمة
banker's draft n صَكّ بَنْكِيّ (للتَعامُلاتِ بين البُنوكِ)

ا

‹ **أَ** *particle* ① [هل] **أَهُوَ مَوْجُودٌ؟** is he there?; **أَتَذْهَبُ مَعَي ؟** will you come with me? ② [أ ... أم] whether; **لا أَدْرِي أَيُحِبُّنِي أم لا** I don't know whether he loves me or not; **هو مِصْرِيٌّ سَواءٌ أَكانَ مُسْلِماً أم مَسِيحِيّاً** he is an Egyptian, whether he's a Muslim or a Christian ③ [أَلا] isn't it?; **أَلَيْسَ كَذَلِكَ؟** isn't it?; **أَما عَرَفْتَهُ؟** didn't you know him?; **أَلا تَفْهَمُنِي ؟** don't you understand me?; **أَلا يوجَدُ حَلٌّ آخَرُ؟** is there no other solution?; **وَلَكِنْ أَلا تَرَوْنَ مَعِي أَنّ ...** but don't you agree with me that ...; **أَلَمْ تَكْتُبْ كِتاباً؟** didn't you write a book? ④ [أَف، أَوَ] **أَفَتَظُنُّ أَوَتَشُكُّ في ذلك؟** do you doubt that?; **أنّ ...؟** do you think that ... ⑤ [أَلا ما \ كم \ كيف \ ...] exclamation of admiration or a wish; **أَلا كم من آلافِ السِنينِ قد مَضَت** how many thousands of years have passed ⑥ [أَلا وَهُوَ \ هي] that is (to say); being; **هَدَفُهُمْ، أَلا وَهُوَ السَلامُ** their goal, being peace

أ. *abbr* Prof. (*Professor*)

‹ **آب** *n* |dipt| (Levant, Iraq) August

‹ **أب** *n* see **أبو**

‹ **أَباجور** *n* |أباجورات| lampshade

‹ **أَبَّ** *v* |i-u; أَبًّا| ① [اشْتاقَ] to long, to yearn; **أَبَّ إلى وَطَنِهِ** to yearn for one's country, to be homesick ② [تَجَهَّزَ] to be prepared; **أَبَّ لِلسَفَرِ** to be prepared to leave

أَبابة *n* homesickness

‹ **أَبْجَدِيّ** *adj* alphabetic, alphabetical; **حَسَبَ التَرْتيبِ \ التَسَلْسُلِ الأَبْجَدِيِّ** alphabetically, in alphabetical order; **رَتَّبَ شَيْئاً تَرْتيباً أَبْجَدِيًّا** to put sth in alphabetical order, to alphabetize sth

أَبْجَدِيّة *n* alphabet; **الأَبْجَدِيّة اللاتينيّة \ العَرَبِيّة** the Roman/Arabic alphabet

‹ **أَبَدَ** *v* |i; أُبود| ① [أَقامَ | بِ] to stay (at) ② [تَوَحَّشَ] to be/become wild

أَبَّدَ *v* to make permanent, to make eternal

تَأَبَّدَ *v* ① [صارَ أَبَدِيًّا] to be/become permanent ② [تَوَحَّشَ] to become wild

أَبَد *n* |أُبود, آباد| eternity; **منذ الأَبَدِ** from time immemorial; **إلى الأَبَد, إلى أَبَدِ الآبِدينَ** forever, for all eternity; **أَبَداً** ever; never; **لا ... أَبَداً** never, by no means; not at all; certainly/absolutely not, no way; **لا شَيْءَ أَبَداً** absolutely nothing; **لن يَفْعَل ذلك أَبَداً** he will never do that; **لا أُريدُ ذلك أبداً** I don't want that at all; **هذا لَيْسَ صَحيحاً أَبَداً** that is absolutely not true; **أَملوا أَبَداً في ...** they were always hoping for ...

آبِدة *n* |أَوابِدُ| unusual thing, wonder

أَبَدِيّ *adj* everlasting, endless, eternal; **الحَياة الأَبَدِيّة** eternal life

أَبَدِيّة *n* eternity

مُؤَبَّد *adj* eternal, everlasting; **السِجْن المُؤَبَّد** life imprisonment; **حُكِمَ عَلَيْهِ بالسِجْنِ المُؤَبَّدِ** he was sentenced to life in prison

‹ **أَبَرَ** *v* |i-u; أَبْر| to sting

أَبَّرَ *v* to pollinate (*a palm tree*)

إِبْرة *n* |إِبَر, إِبْرات| ① [خِياطة] needle; **إِبْرة الخِياطةِ \ الحِياكةِ** sewing/knitting needle; **إِبْرة وَخَيْط** needle and thread; **بَحَثَ عن إِبْرةٍ في كَوْمةِ قَشٍّ** to look for a needle in a haystack; **إِبْرة العَجوز** (Zool) common brown earwig (*Labidura riparia*); **إِبْرة الراعي** (Bot) geranium (*Geranium robertianum*) ② (Med) needle; **عِلاج بالإِبَر** acupuncture ③ [الحَشَراتِ] sting; **إِبْرة النَحْلِ** bee sting ④ (Tech) needle; **إِبْرة البَوْصَلةِ** compass needle; **بَيْت الإِبْرةِ** compass

تَأْبير *n* ① (Bot) pollination ② (Med) acupuncture

‹ **أَبْراميس, أَبْرَميس** *n coll* (Zool) common bream (*Abramis brama*)

‹ **إِبْراهيم** *n* |dipt| Ibrahim, Abraham (*male given name*); سورة إِبْراهيم Ibrahim (*Sura 14*)

‹ **أَبْرَشِيّة، أَبْروشِيّة** *n* (Chr) diocese

‹ **أَبْرَميس** *n* (Zool) see أَبْراميس

‹ **إِبْريز** *n* pure gold

‹ **إِبْريق** *n* |أَباريقُ| jug, pitcher (AmE); pot, kettle; إِبْريق من القَهْوة \ الشاي a pot of coffee/tea; إِبْريق شاي teapot

‹ **أَبْريل** *n* (Mor, Egypt, Gulf) April

‹ **أَبْزَن** *n* |أَبازِنُ| washbowl

‹ **إِبْزيم** *n* |أَبازيمُ| buckle; clasp; fastening

‹ **إِبِسْتِمولوجِيا** *n* epistemology

‹ **أُبْض** *n* |آباض| hollow of the knee

إِباضِيّة *n* Ibadiyya (*Islamic sect*)

مَأْبِض *n* |مَآبِضُ| hollow of the knee

تَأَبَّطَ *v* to carry under one's arm; تَأَبَّطَ حَقيبةً to carry a bag under one's arm; تَأَبَّطَ ذِراعَ شَخْصٍ to take sb's arm; to be arm in arm with sb; تَأَبَّطَ شَرًّا to have bad intentions; Ta'abbata Sharran (*pre-Islamic Meccan poet*)

إِبْط *n* |آباط| armpit, underarm; حَلَقَ شَعْرَ إِبْطِهِ to shave one's armpits; تحت الإِبْطَيْن in the armpits

مُتَأَبِّط *adj* carrying under the arm

‹ **أَبَقَ** *v* |i-u; أَبْق، أَبَق، إِباق| to escape

إِبِل *n coll* camels

‹ **إِبْليس** *n* |dipt; أَباليسُ، أَبالِسة| (Islam) Iblis; the devil, Satan

‹ **أَبَّنَ** *v* to deliver a funeral oration; أَبَّنَ المَيِّتَ to eulogize the deceased

ابْن *n* see بنو

إِبّان *n* time; إِبّانَ، في إِبّانِ during, at the time of; إِبّانَ الحَرْبِ during the war; تُوُفِّيَ وَهُوَ في إِبّانِ شَبابِه he died in his youth

تَأْبين *n* funeral oration, eulogy; حَفْلة تَأْبينٍ memorial service; قامَ بالتَّأْبينِ to deliver a eulogy

تَأْبينيّ *adj* funerary; commemorative, memorial (*before n*); احْتِفال تَأْبينيّ memorial ceremony

مَأْبون *n* catamite, boy concubine; passive homosexual

‹ **أَبَنوس** *n* ebony (*wood*)

‹ **أَبَهَ** *v* |a; أَبْه ,ل ,ب| to pay attention (to); أَمْر لا يُؤْبَهُ لَهُ \ بِهِ an unimportant matter

أُبَّهة *n* splendour, pomp

‹ **أَب** *n* |آباء| ① [والِد] father; dad; parent; الأَبَوانِ the parents; both parents; الأَب والأُمّ father and mother; الأَب الطَبيعيّ biological/natural father; أَباً عن جَدٍّ from father to son; أَبانا (Chr) Our Father; الأَب والابْن والروح القُدُس (Chr) the Father, the Son and the Holy Spirit; أَب في العِمادِ godfather; أَب روحيّ spiritual father; كانَ أَباً روحيًّا لِشَخْصٍ to be like a father to sb; الأَب الروحيّ لِاتِّفاقيّة السَلامِ the spiritual father of the peace agreement; أَبو سَميرٍ Samir's dad; إِنَّهُ أَبٌ مِثاليٌّ لِأَوْلادِهِ a father of three (children); ثَلاثةِ أَوْلادٍ he's an ideal father to his children; من جانِبِ \ طَرَفِ الأَبِ on one's father's side; لَجْنة آباءٍ parents' committee; أَصْبَحَ أَباً to become a father ② [سَلَف] ancestor, forefather

أُبوّة *n* fatherhood; paternity; الأُبوّة الشَرْعيّة \ الطَبيعيّة legal/biological parenthood; اعْتَرَفَ بِأُبوَّتِهِ لِطِفْلٍ to acknowledge paternity of a child

أَبَويّ *adj* ① [والِديّ] fatherly, paternal; parental; السُلْطة الأَبَويّة parental/paternal authority; البَيْت الأَبَويّ the parental home; حُبّ \ حَنان أَبَويّ fatherly love; شَخْصيّة أَبَويّة a father figure ② [بَطْرِيَرْكيّ] patriarchal; نِظام أَبَويّ patriarchy; مُجْتَمَع أَبَويّ a patriarchal society

‹ **أَبو الحِنّاء** *n* (Zool) robin

‹ **أَبو الهَوْل** *n* the Great Sphinx of Giza

‹ **أَبو بَكْر** *n* ① [اِسْم شَخْصيّ] Abu Bakr (*male given name*) ② (Hist) Abu Bakr (*first Muslim caliph*)

‹ **أَبو زُرَيْق** *n* (Zool) jay

‹ **أَبو سِمْبِل** *n* Abu Simbel (*a pair of temples in Egypt*)

‹ **أَبو ظَبيّ** *n* |f| Abu Dhabi (*one of the United Arab Emirates*)

‹ **أَبو فَصادة** *n* (Zool) wagtail (*Motacilla*)

‹ **أَبو قِرْدان** *n* (Zool) cattle egret (*Bubulcus ibis*)

‹ **أَبوكاليبْس** *n* apocalypse

أَبوكاليبْسيّ *adj* apocalyptic

‹ **أَبَى** *v* |a; إِباءة، إِباء| to refuse; to reject, to turn down; يَأْبى الاعْتِرافَ بِجَرائِمِهِ he refuses to admit to his crimes; أَبى إِلّا

اللِقاءاتِ the conference took place after a series of meetings
2 |ب| to bring; to offer; لا يَأْتي الكِتابُ بِجَديدٍ the book offers nothing new; أتى بِهَديّةٍ to bring a present; من أَيْنَ أَتَيْتَ بِهَذِهِ المَعْلوماتِ؟ where did you get this information?
Idiom أتى عَلَيْهِ الدَهْرُ he lost his life

آتى v |Form III; imperf |يُؤاتي 1 [زَوَّدَ] to give; to offer; آتى الزَكاةَ to give zakat (alms) 2 [أَحْضَرَ] to bring 3 [ناسَبَ] to suit; to be suitable; آتَتْهُ الفُرصةُ he had the opportunity

آتى v |Form IV; imperf |يُؤْتي 1 [أَعْطى] to give; آتى شَخصاً شيْئاً to give sb sth; بِكُلِّ ما أوتِينا من قوّةٍ with all of our strength 2 [أَدَرَّ] to bring in, to yield; آتى ثِماراً to yield dividends, to bring benefits

تَأَتّى v 1 [تحقّق] to be/become attainable; to go well 2 [نَجَمَ] |عن ,من| to originate (from), to result (from)

آتٍ adj coming, next; following; أَجْيال آتِية future generations; الأُسْبوع الآتي next week; الأَشْخاص الآتِية أَسْماؤُهُمْ the people with the following names; كالآتي as follows

مُؤاتٍ ,مُؤاتٍ adj convenient, suitable; favourable; غَيْر مُؤاتٍ inconvenient; جاءَ في وَقْتٍ غَيْرِ مُؤاتٍ to come at an inconvenient time; فُرْصة مُواتِية a favourable opportunity; ظُروف مُواتية right circumstances; لم تكُن الظُروفُ مُؤاتِيةً لِلذَلِكَ the circumstances were not right for it

مَأْتًى n |مَآتٍ| place of origin; source; provenance

مُتَأَتٍّ adj coming, originating; مَخاطِر مُتَأَتِّية من الاسْتِثْمار risks coming from the investment

إتيمولوجيا n etymology

أَثْأَب n bayan tree

أَثَّثَ v to furnish; to equip; أَثَّثَ غُرْفَةَ جُلوسٍ to furnish a living room

أَثاث n furniture, furnishings; interior, decor; قِطْعة أَثاثٍ piece of furniture; صانِع الأَثاثِ furniture maker

تَأْثيث n furnishings, decor; furnishing, decorating; تَأْثيث حَديث \ قَديم modern/old fashioned decor

مُؤَثَّث adj furnished; شَقّة مُؤَثَّثة a furnished apartment

أَثَرَ v |i-u; |أَثْر| to pass down; أَثَرَ حَديثاً to pass down a Hadith

أَنْ يَقولَ رَأْيَهُ he insisted on speaking his mind

تَأَبّى v 1 [رَفَضَ] to refuse 2 [تَكَبَّرَ] |على| to treat high-handedly

أَبيّ adj proud; شَعْب أَبِيّ a proud people

آبٍ adj |أُباة| proud

إباء ,إباءة n 1 [رَفْض] refusal; rejection 2 [كِبْرِياء] pride

أبيب n Abib (*the eleventh month of the Coptic calendar*)

اتَّحَدَ v see وحد

اتَّخَذَ v see أخذ

اتَّزَنَ v see وزن

اتَّسَعَ v see وسع

اتَّشَحَ v see وشح

اتَّصَلَ v see وصل

اتَّضَحَ v see وضح

اتَّفَقَ v see وفق

اتَّقى ,اتِّقاء see وقي

اتَّكَأَ v see وكأ

اتَّكَلَ v see وكل

مَأْتَم n |مَآتِمُ| 1 [مَوْت] funeral 2 (Islam) *ceremonial chest-beating in Shia Islam as a display of devotion to Imam Husayn and in remembrance of his suffering*

أَتْمَتَ v |أَتْمَتة| to automate

أَتْمَتة n automation

مُؤَتْمَت adj automated, automatized

أَتان n |أُتُن ,أُتْن| female donkey

أَتون ,أَتّون n |أُتُن ,أَتاتينُ| large oven; في أَتونِ الحَرْبِ in the turmoil of war

إتْنيّ ,إِثْنِيّة see إثن

اتَّهَمَ v see وهم

إتاوة n |أتاوى| tax, duty

أُتوبيس n see أوتوبيس

أُتوماتيكيّ adj see أوتوماتيكيّ

أَتى v |i; |أَتْي ,إتْيان| 1 [جاءَ] to come; to arrive; أَتى من المَحَطّةِ to come from the station; سَآتيكُمْ غَداً I will come over tomorrow; كَما يَأْتي as follows; أَتى الاجْتِماعُ بعد سِلْسِلةٍ من

أَثِر *v* |a; أَثَر، أَثَرة |على| to consider oneself better than; أَثِر على شَخْصٍ to consider oneself better than sb else

أَثَّر *v* 1 [سَبَّبَ] to affect, to influence, to act upon; أَثَّرَ بِشِدّةٍ \ بِقوّةٍ to have a strong influence; أَثَّرَ (تأْثيراً) إيجابيّاً \ سَلْبيّاً to have a positive/negative effect; أَثَّرَ في \ على شَيْءٍ to affect sth, to influence sth; أَثَّرَ في \ على شَخْصٍ to affect sb, to influence sb; أَثَّرَ في \ على سُلوكِ شَخْصٍ to have an effect on sb's behaviour 2 [إحْساسَ الناسِ] to move, to make an impression; أَثَّرَ في الجُمْهورِ to move the audience; أَثَّرَ في شَخْصٍ تَأْثيراً عَميقاً to make a deep impression on sb, to touch sb deeply; أَثَّرَ في شَخْصٍ إلى حَدِّ البُكاءِ to move sb to tears; لا يُؤَثِّرُ ذلك في ... it doesn't matter for ..., it is of no importance regarding ...; أَثَّرَتْ حَماسَتُهُ على الآخَرينَ his enthusiasm had an effect on others

آثَر *v* |Form IV; imperf يُؤْثِرُ| to prefer, to like more; آثَرَ شَيْئاً to prefer sth; آثَرَ البَقاءَ في مَنْزِلِهِ to prefer to stay home

تَأَثَّر *v* 1 [انْفعَلَ] to be influenced; to be affected; تَأَثَّرَ (سَلْباً) بالأَحْداثِ to be (negatively) influenced by the events; تَأَثَّرَ تَأَثُّراً بالِغاً to be greatly influenced 2 [شَعَرَ] to be impressed; to be moved, to be affected, to be touched; تَأَثَّرَ بعُمْقٍ to be deeply moved; تَأَثَّرْتُ بِذَلِكَ الحادِثِ كَثيراً that accident affected me greatly; تَأَثَّرَ من كَلامِ شَخْصٍ to be hurt by sb's words; تَأَثَّرَ لِمَوْتِ صَديقِهِ to be much affected by the death of one's friend; لم يَتَأَثَّرْ بالأَمْرِ he was not affected by it

اسْتَأْثَر *v* |ب| to take exclusive possession (of), to be the sole possessor (of), to monopolize

إثْر *prep* immediately after, following; إثْرَ وُقوعِ انْفِجارَيْنِ following two explosions; واحِداً إثْرَ الآخَرِ one after the other; على \ في إثْرِهِ immediately after that; from the effects of; following on; ماتَ على إثْرِ حادِثٍ to die as the result of an accident

أَثَر *n* |آثار| 1 [عَلامة] trace, track, mark; آثار أَعْمالِ العُنْفِ traces of violence; أَثَر جُرْحٍ scar; آثار أَقْدامٍ footprints; تَرَكَ أَثَراً to leave a mark, to leave a scar; دون أَثَرٍ without a trace; اخْتَفى دون أَثَرٍ to vanish without a trace; أَخْفى آثارَهُ to cover one's tracks; اقْتَفى أَثَرَ شَخْصٍ to follow sb's tracks; لم يوجَدْ لَهُ أَيُّ أَثَرٍ there was no trace of him; في \ على أَثَرِهِ immediately after 2 [تَأْثير] effect, influence, consequence; أَثَر عَميق a strong effect; أَثَر قانونيّ a legal consequence; أَثَر حَميد \ سَيِّئ a beneficial/bad effect; أَثَر سِلْبيّ a negative effect; آثار ثانَويّة \ جانِبيّة لِدَواءٍ side effects of a medicine; سَبَّبَ آثاراً جانِبيّةً to cause side effects; كانَ لَهُ أَثَرٌ على شَخْصٍ \ شَيْءٍ to have an effect on sb/sth; كانَ لَهُ أَثَرٌ إدْمانيٌّ to be addictive; قانون ذو أَثَرٍ رَجْعيٍّ a retroactive law, an ex post facto law; عَمَل لا أَثَرَ لَهُ an ineffectual act 3 [قَديم] ancient monument, ruin; relic, artifact; آثار artifacts; ruins; عِلْم الآثارِ archaeology; عالِم الآثارِ archaeologist; آثار تَعودُ إلى القَرْنِ الثالِثَ عَشَرَ thirteenth-century artefacts; الآثار الإغْريقيّة the Greek monuments; نَقَّبَ عن الآثارِ to carry out excavations; عِلْم الآثارِ المِصْريّةِ Egyptology 4 [عَمَل فَنّيّ] work; أَثَر فَنّيّ work/piece of art; الآثار الكامِلة لِمُؤَلِّفٍ the complete works of an author 5 (Islam) *passed down tradition relating to the Prophet Muhammad and his Companions*

آثاريّ *adj* archaeological; تَنْقيب آثاريّ an archaeological dig

أَثَرة *n* egoism

أَثَريّ A *adj* antique; archaeological; أَثَريّات antiquities; بَحْث أَثَريّ archaeological research; مَتْحَف الأَثَريّاتِ museum of antiquities; بائِع أَثَريّاتٍ antique dealer

B *n* archaeologist

أَثير A *adj* favoured; كانَ أَثيراً عِنْدَها he was favoured by her

B *n* listed alphabetically

اسْتِئْثار *n* 1 [مِلْكيّة خاصّة] undivided estate 2 [احْتِكار] monopolization; exclusive power; الاسْتِئْثار بالسُّلْطةِ monopolizing power

إيثار *n* 1 [غَيْريّة] altruism 2 [تَفْضيل] preference 3 [مَوَدّة] liking, love

إيثاريّ *adj* altruistic

إيثاريّة *n* altruism

تَأَثُّر *n* |تَأَثُّرات| emotion; بِتَأَثُّرٍ moved; سَريع التَأَثُّرِ touchy, sensitive; لم يَسْتَطِعِ الكَلامَ لِشِدّةِ التَأَثُّرِ he was so moved that he was not able to speak

تَأَثُّريّة *n* (Art) Impressionism

تأثير *n* 1 [مَفْعول] effect, influence, action; affecting, influencing; result; تَأْثير إيجابيّ \ سَلْبيّ a positive/negative effect; تَأْثير نافِع a beneficial effect; تَأْثير جانِبيّ side effect; تَأْثير كَبير \ عَظيم a huge/enormous impact; تَأْثير خارِجيّ external influences; تَأْثير جَيِّد a favourable influence; تَأْثير سَيِّئ \ رَديء \ خاطِئ a bad influence; تَأْثير طَويل المَدى a long-lasting effect; كانَ لَهُ تَأْثيرٌ مُعاكِسٌ to be counterproductive; تَأْثير على شَخْصٍ \ شَيْءٍ an influence on sb/sth; التَّأْثير على هَيْئَةِ المُحَلَّفينَ manipulation of the jury; التَّأْثير على النُموِّ الاقْتِصاديِّ affecting economic growth; مارَسَ تَأْثيراً to exert influence; كانَ تحت تَأْثيرِ شَخْصٍ to be under the influence of sb; كانَ تحت تَأْثيرِ الكُحولِ to be under the influence of alcohol 2 [انْطِباع] impression; (emotional) effect; أَثَّرَ تَأْثيراً عَميقاً على شَخْصٍ to make a deep impression on sb

تَأْثيريّ *adj* inductive; المَذْهَب التَّأْثيريّ (Art) Impressionism

مُؤَثِّر **A** *adj* 1 [فَعّال] influential, effective; عَوامِل مُؤَثِّرة influential factors; لَعِبَ دَوْراً مُؤَثِّراً to play an influential role 2 [مُثير] moving, touching, emotional; impressive, imposing; exciting; قِصّة مُؤَثِّرة a moving story; حالات مُؤَثِّرة poignant cases; مَشْهَد مُؤَثِّر a moving sight; لَحْظة مُؤَثِّرة an emotional moment

B *n* (Math) operator

مَأْثَرة *n* |مَآثِرُ| feat; مَآثِر بُطوليّة \ تاريخيّة heroic/historic feats; رَوى \ عَدَّدَ مَآثِرَ شَخْصٍ to recount/enumerate sb's feats

مَأْثور **A** *adj* passed down; من المَأْثورِ أنّ … tradition has it that …; قَوْل مَأْثور tradition; saying, proverb

B *n* مَأْثورات شَعْبيّة folklore, popular tradition

مُتَأَثِّر *adj* 1 [مُصاب] affected, influenced; المَناطِق المُتَأَثِّرة the affected regions; مُتَأَثِّراً ب as a result of; تُوُفِّيَ مُتَأَثِّراً بِجراحِهِ to die as a result of one's injuries 2 [عاطِفيًّا] moved, touched, emotional; impressed; مُتَأَثِّر بِشِدّةٍ deeply touched; غَيْر مُتَأَثِّر unmoved

‹ **أَثْل**, **أَثَل** *n coll* |أُثول| tamarisk, salt cedar (*Tamarix*)

أَثيل *n* listed alphabetically

تَأْثيل *n* etymology

‹ **أَثِمَ** *v* |a; مَأْثَم ,أَثَم ,إِثْم| to sin

أَثَّمَ *v* to sin

تَأَثَّمَ *v* 1 [تابَ] to be remorseful 2 [تَجَنَّبَ الإِثْمَ] to restrain oneself

إِثْم *n* |آثام| sin; crime; اقْتَرَفَ \ ارْتَكَبَ إِثْماً to commit a sin

آثِم **A** *adj* |أَثَمة| sinful, godless; vicious, heinous; حَياة آثِمة a sinful life; جَريمة آثِمة a heinous crime

B *n* |أَثَمة| sinner; آثِم تائِب a repentant sinner

أَثيم **A** *adj* |أُثَماءُ| sinful; vicious, heinous; اعْتِداء أَثيم a vicious attack

B *n* |أُثَماءُ| sinner

‹ **إِثْمِد** *n* antimony; kohl (*traditional black eyeliner made from antimony*)

‹ **أَثْنوغرافيا** *n* ethnography

‹ **أَثْنولوجيا** *n* ethnology

‹ **إِثْنيّ**, **إِتْنيّ** *adj* ethnic; أَقَلّيّة إِثْنيّة ethnic minority

إِثْنيّة, **إِتْنيّة** *n* ethnicity

‹ **أَثير** **A** *n* 1 (Chem) ether 2 [هَواء] air; على أَمْواجِ الأَثيرِ on the air, on the radio

B *adj* see **أثر**

أَثيريّ *adj* ethereal

‹ **أَثيل** *n* ethyl

أَثيلين *n* ethylene

‹ **أَثينا**, **آثينا** *n* 1 [المَدينة] Athens (*capital of Greece*) 2 [الإلاهة] Athena (*Greek goddess*)

‹ **أَثْيوبيا** *n* Ethiopia

أَثْيوبيّ *adj*, *n* Ethiopian

‹ **أَجَّ** *v* |i-u; أَجيج| to burn, to blaze

أَجَّجَ *v* 1 [أَشْعَلَ] to light, to kindle; to inflame; أَجَّجَ النارَ to light a fire 2 [أَثارَ] to kindle, inflame; to fuel; to stir up, to stoke; أَجَّجَ ذِكْرَياتٍ to stir up memories; أَجَّجَ غَضَبَ شَخْصٍ to make sb angry; أَجَّجَ المَشاعِرَ القَوْميّةَ to stir up feelings of nationalism

تَأَجَّجَ *v* to flare, to be stirred up; to grow stronger; تَأَجَّجَت المَشاعِرُ المَذْهَبيّةُ sectarian passions flared

أُجاج *adj* salty; brackish; ماء أُجاج brackish water

مُتَأَجِّج *adj* burning, flaming; حَريق مُتَأَجِّج a fierce fire; مَشاعِر مُتَأَجِّجة بالغَضَب strong feelings of anger

[1] **أَجَرَ** *v* |u; أَجْر, إجار| ❶ [العامِلَ] to reward, to pay wages; أَجَرَ العامِلَ على عَمَلِهِ to pay the worker for his work ❷ [الدارَ] to rent (out), to let (BrE); أَجَرَ شَخْصاً داراً to rent a house to sb

أَجَّرَ *v* to rent (out), to let (BrE); to lease; أَجَّرَ لِشَخْصٍ غُرْفةً \ شَقّةً \ مَنْزِلاً to rent a room/apartment/house to sb; أَجَّرَ أَرْضاً \ حُقولاً to lease out land/fields; أَجَّرَ شِقّةً من الباطِنِ to sublet an apartment

اسْتَأْجَرَ *v* ❶ [شَيْئاً] to rent, to hire (BrE); to lease; to charter; اسْتَأْجَرَ سَيّارةً to rent a car; اسْتَأْجَرَ قِطْعةَ أَرْضٍ من شَخْصٍ to lease a piece of land from sb; اسْتَأْجَرَ طَيّارةً to charter an airplane ❷ [شَخْصاً] to hire, to take on; اسْتَأْجَرَ شَخْصاً to hire sb

إجارة *n* rent

أَجْر *n* |أُجور| ❶ [راتِب] pay; wages; salary; fee, payment; أَجْر قَليل \ كَبير a small/large fee; أُجور مُنْخَفِضة \ مُرْتَفِعة low/high wages; أَجْر الساعة hourly rate; سِياسة الأُجورِ income policy; تَخْفيض الأُجورِ lowering of wages; تَجْميد الأُجورِ wage freeze; بَيان أَجْرٍ, كَشْف الأُجورِ payslip; الحَدّ الأَدْنى للأُجورِ minimum wage; تَقاضى الحَدَّ الأَدْنى للأُجورِ to earn the minimum wage; بِدونِ أَجْرٍ unpaid, without pay; أَجْر الشَّحْنِ freight ❷ (Relig) *merit for a pious deed*; عَظَّمَ اللهُ أَجْرَكَ my sincerest condolences

أُجْرة *n* ❶ [راتِب] pay, wage, salary; دَفَعَ الأُجْرةَ to pay wages; اسْتَلَمَ الأُجْرةَ to receive wages; بَيان أُجْرةٍ payslip; أُجْرة إضافيّة extra earnings ❷ [تَكاليف] سَيّارة أُجْرةٍ taxi

أَجير *n* |أُجَراءُ| casual worker, day labourer

اسْتِئْجار *n* rent, lease; renting, leasing; عَقْد الاسْتِئْجارِ lease, rental agreement

إيجار *n* |إيجارات| ❶ [كِراء] rent; للإيجارِ for rent; بَيْت إيجارٍ a rental house; عَقْد الإيجارِ lease, rental agreement; مُدّة الإيجارِ lease term; فاتَتْ مُدّةُ الإيجارِ the lease has expired; ثَمَن \ سِعْر الإيجارِ rent; إيجار من الباطِنِ subtenancy, sublet; وَفْقاً لِعَقْدِ الإيجارِ according to the lease (agreement); وَقَّعَ عَقْدَ إيجارٍ to sign a lease; أَبْرَمَ \ أَلْغى عَقْدَ إيجارٍ to conclude/terminate a lease ❷ [سِعْر] rent; إيجار مُرْتَفِع \ قَليل a high/low rent; الإيجار الصافي base rent; إيجار مُتَرَتِّب back rent; زِيادة \ رَفْع الإيجارِ rent increase; دَفَعَ الإيجارَ to pay the rent

إيجاريّ *adj* rental; قيمة إيجاريّة rental value

تَأْجير *n* leasing, letting (BrE); شَرِكة تَأْجيرٍ leasing company; التَمَلُّك بالتَأْجير leasing

مُؤَجَّر *adj* rented, leased

مُؤَجِّر *n* ❶ [صاحِب الدارِ] landlord; العَلاقة بين المُؤَجِّرِ والمُسْتَأْجِرِ the relationship between landlord and tenant ❷ [صاحِب العَمَلِ] employer; سَرِقة أَجيرٍ لِمُؤَجِّرِه a day labourer's theft from his employer

مَأْجور **A** *adj* rented, leased; قاتِل مَأْجور hired assassin, hitman, contract killer **B** *n* worker, hired hand

مُسْتَأْجَر *adj* leased, rented

مُسْتَأْجِر *n* tenant, renter; leaseholder; مُسْتَأْجِر من الباطِنِ subtenant; العَلاقة بين المُؤَجِّرِ والمُسْتَأْجِرِ the relationship between landlord and tenant

[2] **آجُرّ** *n* brick; جِدار من الآجُرِّ a brick wall

إجّاص *n coll* pear; شَجَرة الإجّاصِ pear tree (*Pyrus*)

أَجَّلَ *v* to postpone, to delay, to adjourn, to put off, to defer, to suspend; أَجَّلَ مُحاكَمةً to adjourn a trial; أَجَّلَ مُخَطَّطاتِهِ to postpone one's plans; أَجَّلَ شَيْئاً شَهْراً to put sth off for one month; أَجَّلَ أَنْشِطَتَهُ to put off one's activities; أَجَّلَ دَعْوى to adjourn a case; أَجَّلَ شَيْئاً إلى تاريخٍ آخَرَ to postpone sth until a later date; أَجَّلَ جَلْسةً \ اجْتِماعاً إلى ما بَعْدَ الغَدِ to adjourn a session/meeting till the day after tomorrow; أُريدُ أنْ أُؤَجِّلَ هذا إلى غدٍ I'd like to leave this till tomorrow

تَأَجَّلَ *v* to be postponed; تَأَجَّلَت المُباراةُ إلى ما بعد غدٍ the game was postponed until the day after tomorrow

اسْتَأْجَلَ *v* to ask for a delay

إجْل *n* a stiff neck

آجِل *adj* ❶ [تَمَّ تَأْجيلُهُ] delayed; later, in the future; عاجِلاً أو آجِلاً sooner or later; أَسْعار العُقودِ الآجِلةِ (Fin) futures prices ❷ [مُتَعَلِّق بالآخِرةِ] *belonging to the hereafter*

أَجْل *n* من أَجْلِ, لِأَجْلِ because of, for; for the sake of; من أَجْلِهِ therefore; for his sake; فَعَلْتُ ذلك لِأَجْلِكَ \ من أَجْلِكَ I did that for you; المُفاوَضات من أَجْلِ إنْهاءِ الحَرْبِ negotiations to end the war; سافَرَ إلى الخارِجِ من أَجْلِ عَمَلِهِ he went abroad for his work; قاتَلَ من أَجْلِ الفَوْزِ to fight for victory

أَجَل *n* |آجال| **1** [وَقْت] period, (appointed) time, term; time limit; أَجَل قصير \ طَويل short/long term; قَرْض \ دَيْن قصير الأَجَلِ a short-term loan/debt; أَجَل مُدَّتُهُ ثَلاثةُ أَشْهُرٍ a three-month term; لِأَجَلٍ غَيْرِ مُسَمًّى for an indefinite period; آخِر أَجَلٍ deadline; حَدَّدَ \ ضَرَبَ أَجَلاً to fix a time; to set a deadline, to set a time limit; انْتَهى في الأَجَلِ المُحَدَّدِ to finish before the deadline; تَجاوَزَ الأَجَلَ المُحَدَّدَ to exceed the time limit, to miss the deadline; انْتَهى \ انْصَرَفَ \ انْقَضى الأَجَلُ the time limit has expired; يَبْدَأُ الأَجَلُ اعْتِباراً من يَوْمِ الغَدِ the time limit starts tomorrow **2** [مُهْلة] delay **3** [مَوْت] allotted lifespan, moment of death; حانَ أَجَلُهُ his final hour has come; إذا جاءَ أَجَلُكَ when your time is up

أَجَلْ *excl* oh yes, (yes) indeed, sure; قُلْتُ لَهُ: هل تَذْهَبُ مَعَنا؟ فَقالَ: أَجَلْ I said to him: will you come with us? and he said: oh, certainly

تَأْجيل *n* postponement, delay, adjournment, deferment, respite; تَأْجيل التَسْديد \ الدَفْع payment deferment; مَنَحَ تَأْجيل دَفْع ضَريبةٍ to grant a deferment of tax payment; تَأْجيل تَنْفيذِ عُقوبةٍ suspension of a penalty; تَأْجيل مُباراةٍ إلى أَجَلٍ غَيْرِ مُسَمًّى indefinite postponement of a match

مُؤَجَّل *adj* postponed, deferred; دَفْع مُؤَجَّل deferred payment; مُباراة مُؤَجَّلة a postponed match

‹ **أَجَم** *n coll* bushes, thicket

‹ **آجِن** *adj* brackish

‹ **أَجِنْدة** *n* **1** [مُفَكِّرة] agenda, diary; أَجِنْدة مُؤْتَمَرٍ a conference programme; أَهَمّ مَوْضوعٍ في \ على الأَجِنْدةِ the most important subject on the agenda **2** [قَصْد] agenda; أَجِنْدة سِياسيّة a political agenda; لَهُ أَجِنْدَتُهُ الخاصّةُ he has his own agenda

‹ **أَحَّ** *v* |u; أَحّ| to cough

‹ **أَحَد** *n* |f إحْدى| **1** [شَخْص] somebody, someone; anybody, anyone; لا أَحَدَ, ما من أَحَدٍ nobody, no one; ما من أَحَدٍ في المَنْزِلِ there is nobody home; لا أَحَدَ يَسْتَطيعُ أَنْ يُنْكِرَ أَنَّ ... nobody can deny that ...; لم أَرَ هُناكَ أَحَداً I didn't see anyone there; دون أَنْ يَراهُ أَحَدٌ without anybody seeing him **2** [واحِد] a, one (of); أَحَدُهُما one of (the two of) them; أَحَد المُعَلِّمينَ one of the teachers; إحْدى البَناتِ one of the girls; أَحَد أَعْضاءِ المَجْلِسِ a member of the council **3** [أَرْقام] |آحاد| آحاد ones, units **4** [يَوْم] Sunday; يَوْم الأَحَدِ Sunday; أَحَد السَعَفِ Palm Sunday; كُلَّ أَحَدٍ every Sunday **5** (Islam) الأَحَد the One (*one of the names of God*)

أُحاديّ *adj* unilateral, one-sided; عَمَل عَسْكَرِيّ أُحاديّ الجانِبِ unilateral military action; أُحاديّ اللُغةِ monolingual

أَحَدَ عَشَرَ *num* eleven

إحْدى *num* see أَحَد

حادِيَ عَشَرَ *num* eleventh

‹ **أَحِنَ** *v* |a; أَحَن| |على| to hate

‹ **أَخ** *n* see أخو

‹ **أَخَذَ** *v* |u; أَخْذ| **1** [مَسَكَ] to take; أَخَذَ شَيْئاً من الخِزانةِ to take sth out of the cupboard **2** [رَكِبَ] to take, to ride; أَخَذَ الحافِلةَ to take the bus **3** [قَبِلَ] to take, to accept; هل تَأْخُذُ 100 $ مُقابِلَ هذه الساعةِ؟ will you take $100 for this watch? **4** [سَجَّلَ] to take, to record; أَخَذَ المَقاسَ to take measurements **5** [اسْتَمْتَعَ ب] to take, to have; أَخَذَ دوشاً to take a shower **6** [دَرَسَ] to take, to study; تَأْخُذُ دُروساً في اللُغةِ العَرَبيّةِ أُسْبوعيّاً she takes Arabic classes every week **7** [بَدَأَ] to start; أَخَذَ يَتَكَلَّمُ عن شَيْءٍ to start talking about sth; أَخَذَ في الاتِّساعِ to start to expand **8** [تَناوَلَ] to take; أَخَذَ مُسَكِّناً to take a painkiller **9** [لامَ] |على| to hold against; أَخَذَ على شَخْصٍ شَيْئاً to hold sth against sb; أَخَذَ على خاطِرِهِ to feel offended **10** [تَعَهَّدَ] to take upon oneself; أَخَذَ شَيْئاً على عاتِقِهِ to shoulder sth **11** [اسْتَلَمَ] to receive, to get; أَخَذَ مُساعَدةً \ هَدِيّةً to receive help/a present; أَخَذَ قَرْضاً to take out a loan **12** [اسْتَغْرَقَ] to take; يَأْخُذُ هذا العَمَلُ ساعَتَيْنِ the work will take two hours **13** [اتَّخَذَ] to take; أَخَذَ مَجْراهُ to take its course **14** [قَبَضَ] to take by surprise; أَخَذَنا المَطَرُ

we were caught in the rain **15** [عامَلَ] to treat; أَخَذَ شَخْصاً بالحُسْنى to be kind to sb; أَخَذَ شَخْصاً بالشِدّةِ to deal severely with sb **16** [اِصْطَحَبَ] to take; أَخَذَت الأَطْفالَ إلى حَديقةِ الحَيَواناتِ she took the children to the zoo **17** [فَهِمَ] to take; نَأْخُذُ ما تَقولُهُ بِطَريقةٍ جِدّيّةٍ we take your words seriously **18** [اِسْتَحْوَذَ على] to take possession of; أَخَذَهُ الجوعُ he got hungry **19** [اِقْتَدى ب |ب|] to imitate; to adopt, to take on; أَخذ بِعاداتِ شَخْصٍ to take on sb's habits **20** [تَعَلَّمَ] to learn, to take up; أَخذ عن أَبيهِ القِراءة he learned to read from his father **21** [أَلْزَمَ] to oblige; أَخَذَ شَخْصاً بِشَيْءٍ to oblige sb to do sth

آخَذَ *v* |Form III; imperf يُؤاخِذُ| to blame, to hold against; آخَذَ شَخْصاً لا تُؤاخِذْني excuse me, pardon me, no offence; ب \ على شَيْءٍ to hold sth against sb

اِتَّخَذَ *v* **1** [أَجْرى] to take; to take on, to adopt; اِتَّخَذَ قَراراً to make a decision, to take a decision (BrE); اِتَّخَذَ إجْراءاتٍ to take measures/steps **2** [أَخَذَ] اِتَّخَذَ شَخْصاً صَديقاً to make sb one's friend; اِتَّخَذَ زَوْجةً to take a wife

أَخْذ *n* taking; أَخذ وَرَدّ discussion, debate; أَخْذ وَعَطاء give and take

اِتِّخاذ *n* taking (on)

أَخّاذ *adj* captivating, fascinating; أُسْلوب أَخّاذ a fascinating style; جَمالها الأَخّاذ her breathtaking beauty

مُؤاخَذة *n* reproach, blame; لا مُؤاخَذةَ excuse me, no offence; حُكِمَ بالمُؤاخَذةِ to be found guilty

مَأْخَذ *n* |مَآخِذُ| **1** [مَصْدَر] source; المَآخِذ bibliography, source references **2** [بَريزة] outlet, (electrical) socket **3** [إجْراء] approach, procedure; أَخَذَ الأُمورَ مَأْخَذَ الجِدِّ to take things seriously **4** [عَيْب] flaw, defect, shortcoming

مَأْخوذ *adj* **1** [مَقْبوض] taken; caught **2** |ب| taken with; fascinated by **3** |من| taken from, obtained from; derived from, adapted from

مُتَّخَذ *adj* taken; الإجْراءات المُتَّخَذة the measures taken

أَخَّرَ *v* **1** [السّاعةَ] to put/set back; أَخَّرَ ساعةً to set back a watch **2** [أَجَّلَ] to postpone, to adjourn **3** [أَبْطَأَ] to delay, to put off; to hold up, to slow down; أَخَّرَ المُفاوَضاتِ to slow down the negotiations **4** [أَوْقَفَ] to suspend, to dismiss

تَأَخَّرَ *v* to be/fall behind; to be late; to be delayed; to be slow; تَأَخَّرَ ساعةً to be one hour late, to be delayed for an hour; تَأَخَّرَ عن شَخْصٍ to be lagging behind sb; تَأَخَّرَ عن شَيْءٍ to be late for sth; تَأَخَّرَ في الجَوْدةِ not to meet the standards; تَأَخَّرَ في التَطَوُّرِ to be/lag/fall behind in development; تَأَخَّرَ عن مُنافِسِهِ (Sport) to be behind one's opponent

اِسْتَأْخَرَ *v* to be late

آخَر *adj* |dipt; f pl أُخْرَيات| other; another; مَرّةً أُخْرى once more, again, another time; الأَحْزاب الأُخْرى the other parties; من حينٍ لِآخَرَ from time to time; من عامٍ إلى آخَرَ ,من سَنةٍ إلى أُخْرى from one year to the next; بِشَكْلٍ أو بِآخَرَ one way or another; هو الآخَرُ he also; بَعْضُهُم ... وبَعْضُهُم الآخَرُ some of them ..., but others ...; هي الأُخْرى قد كَبُرَتْ she grew up too; سَأَشْتَري كِتاباً آخَرَ I will buy another book; قُتِلَ شَخْصانِ وَأُصيبَ ثَمانيةٌ آخَرونَ في الهُجومِ two people were killed and eight others were injured in the attack

آخِر **A** *adj* |أَواخِرُ, آخِرونَ| last, final; اليَوْم الآخِر Judgement Day; في آخِرِ لَحْظةٍ at the last minute; in the final moments; أَخيراً وَلَيْس آخِراً last but not least

B *n* |أَواخِرُ| **1** [طَرَف] end, top, bottom, back; إلى الآخِرِ till the end; إلى آخِرِهِ etc., et cetera, and so forth; في آخِرِهِ at the end of it; في آخِرِ الجُمْلةِ at the end of the sentence; في آخِرِ الساحةِ at the far end of the square; آخِر مَرّةٍ the last time; آخِر الأَخْبارِ \ صَيْحاتِ الموضةِ the latest news/fashion; هدَمَ شَيْئاً عن آخِرِهِ to destroy sth completely **2** [نِهاية] end; آخِر الزَمانِ end time/times, the end of days; في آخِرِ الأَمْرِ in the end, finally; في أَواخِرِ الشِتاءِ towards the end of winter; في أَواخِرِ شَهْرِ يَنايِر \ كانونِ الثاني at the end of January; في أَواخِرِ عُمْرِهِ at the end of his life; من أَوَّلِهِ إلى آخِرِهِ from beginning to end, from start to finish, from A to Z; كانَ آخِرُ ما جَرى بَيْنَهُما ... the last thing that happened between them was ... **3** (Islam) الآخِر the Last (*one of the names of God*)

أُخْرَوِيّ *adj in the hereafter*; السَعادة الأُخْرَوِيّة happiness in the hereafter

أخير **A** *adj* last, final, ultimate; recent, latest; أخيراً eventually, in the end; finally, at last; recently, lately; مُحاوَلة أخيرة a final effort; الأَيّام الأَخيرة final days (*of sth*); the last few days; Last Days (Relig); الشَهْر الأَخير last month; في المُدّةِ \ الفَتْرةِ الأَخيرة lately

B *n* last (*of a series*); end; قبل الأَخير last but one, second last; penultimate; الدَوْر قبل الأَخير the penultimate round; أخيراً وَلَيْس آخِراً last but not least; في الأَخير at the end

الآخِرة *n* the hereafter

تَأَخُّر *n* backwardness; lag, delay; كانَت البِلادُ في حالةِ تَأَخُّرٍ اقْتِصاديٍّ the country was lagging behind economically; التَأَخُّر المَدْرَسيّ educational underachievement

تَأْخير *n* delay, hold-up, slowdown; slowing down; تَأْخير لِمُدّةِ سِتِّ ساعاتٍ a six-hour delay; تَسَبَّبَ في التَأْخيرِ to cause a delay; تَأْخير دَفْعِ شَيْءٍ a delay in paying sth; تَأْخير النُموِّ stunting of growth (*physical*); slowdown in development (*mental, economic*)

مُؤَخَّر **A** *adj* delayed; back, in arrears, outstanding; مُؤَخَّراً recently, lately

B *n* **1** [جُزْء خَلْفِيّ] rear **2** [رَصيد] arrears **3** [المَهْر] *a portion of the dowry that is deferred* (*in some Muslim countries*) *as security for the wife in case of divorce*

مُؤَخِّر *n* المُؤَخِّر the Delayer (*one of the names of God*)

مُؤَخَّرة *n* **1** [قِسْم خَلْفِيّ] back, rear; مُؤَخَّرة رَأْسِهِ the back of one's head; مُؤَخَّرة سَفينةٍ stern (*of a ship*); مُؤَخَّرة طائِرةٍ the tail of an airplane; مُؤَخَّرة بُنْدُقِيّةٍ the butt of a rifle; في المُؤَخَّرةِ in back; at the back, in the rear; جَلَسَ في مُؤَخَّرةِ الصَفِّ to sit at the back of the class **2** (Anat) buttocks (fml), bum (BrE) butt (AmE) (infml)

مُتَأَخِّر **A** *adj* **1** [غَيْر مُبَكِّرٍ] late, delayed; back, outstanding; مُتَأَخِّرات outstanding payments, arrears; راتِب \ كِراء مُتَأَخِّر back pay/rent; قِطار مُتَأَخِّر a delayed train; في سِنٍّ مُتَأَخِّرةٍ at an advanced age; في ساعةٍ مُتَأَخِّرةٍ من اللَيْل late at night; مُتَأَخِّراً بِخَمْسِ دَقائِقَ five minutes late; مُتَأَخِّر عن وَقْتِهِ too late; وَصَلَتْ مُتَأَخِّرةً she arrived late; نِمْتُ مُتَأَخِّراً I overslept; **2** [مُتَخَلِّف] slow, retarded; مُتَأَخِّر عَقْلِيًّا mentally disabled

B *n* straggler; late developer; late arrival

‹ **إخْس** *excl* ugh!, yuck! (AmE)

أُخْطُبوط *n* octopus; ذِراع \ رِجْل الأُخْطُبوطِ an octopus's tentacle

‹ **أَخيل** *n* listed alphabetically

‹ **آخى** *v* **1** [بَيْنَهُما] to unite, to ally **2** [اتَّخَذَ أَخاً] to unite/ally with; آخى شَخْصاً to unite with sb

تَآخى *v* to associate as brothers

أَخ *n* **1** [شَقيق] إخْوان, إخْوة brother; إخْوان brothers (*in trade/company names*); الإخوة والأخوات siblings, brothers and sisters; أَخ شَقيق full brother; أَخ غَيْر شَقيقٍ half brother; أخوكَ your brother; بِنْت \ ابْن أَخ niece/nephew; قَتْل أَخ fratricide; لَهُ خَمْسَةُ إِخْوة he has five brothers **2** [صَديق] الأَخ إِخْوان| فلان mister/brother so-and-so; يا أَخي! excuse me, sir! **3** (Chr) إِخْوان| brother; friar **4** (Pol) إِخْوان| fellow believer; الإِخْوان المُسْلِمونَ the Muslim Brotherhood (*Islamist movement*)

إخاء *n* brotherhood, fraternity

إخائيّ *adj* brotherly (*like brothers*)

أُخْت *n* |f; أَخَوات| **1** [شَقيقة] sister; أُخْت غَيْر شَقيقةٍ half-sister; بِنْت \ ابْن أُخْتٍ niece/nephew **2** (Ling) *words that behave similarly*; كانَ وَأَخَواتُها Kana and her sisters (*verbs which shift the predicate of an equational sentence from the nominative case to the accusative case*)

أُخْت الرِمالِ *n* marram grass, beach grass (*Ammophila*)

إخْوانَجي *n* (pej) member of the Muslim brotherhood

إخْوانيّ *n* member of the Muslim brotherhood

أُخوّة *n* fraternity, brotherhood; الحُرِّيّة والمُساواة والأُخوّة liberty, equality and fraternity

أَخَويّ *adj* brotherly, fraternal; عَلاقة أَخَويّة a brotherly relationship

أَخَويّة *n* brotherhood, fraternity

تَآخ *n* brotherhood

مُؤاخاة *n* brotherhood; fraternization

‹ **أَخيل**, **آخيل** *n* Achilles; وَتَر أخيل Achilles tendon; عَقِب \ كَعْب أَخيل Achilles' heel

‹ **أَخينوس** *n* sea urchin

أَدُبَ *v* |u; أَدَب| to be well-mannered

أَدَّبَ *v* to raise well; to discipline, to punish; أَدَّبَ شَخْصاً to raise sb well; to discipline sb

تَأَدَّبَ *v* to be well-bred; to be educated; to be polite

أَدَب *n* |آداب| **1** [لِياقة] politeness, courtesy; good manners; culture, refinement; آداب اللياقة etiquette; قِلّة الأَدَب impoliteness; قليل الأَدَبِ rude, impolite; كانَ قليلَ الأَدَبِ to be rude; مُخِلّ بالآدابِ immoral, indecent; تَعَلَّمَ الأَدَبَ to learn good manners; من باب الأَدَبِ out of courtesy; بأَدَبٍ politely; تَعامَلَ مع شَخْصٍ بأَدَبٍ to be polite to someone **2** [الكِتابة] literature; الآداب literature; الأَدَب العَرَبيّ \ المُعاصِر Arabic/contemporary literature; أَدَب القُرون الوُسْطى \ النَهْضة mediaeval/Renaissance literature; كُلِّيّة الآداب ≈ the Faculty of Arts; نَظَرِيّة الآدابِ literary theory; جائزة نوبِل ل \ في الآدابِ a Nobel Prize in Literature; تاريخ الأَدَبِ the history of literature

Idiom بَيْت الأَدَبِ (old use) bathroom

أَدَبيّ **A** *adj* **1** [مُتَعَلِّق بالأَدَبِ] literary; مَجَلّة أَدَبيّة a literary journal; مُنْتَدى أَدَبيّ a literary salon; سَرِقة أَدَبيّة plagiarism **2** [أَخْلاقيّ] moral, ethical **B** *n* publication; أَدَبيّات عِلْمية \ طِبّيّة scientific/medical publications

أَديب *n* |أُدَباءُ| author, writer, novelist; أَديب كَبير a great writer

تَأَدُّب *n* good manners, civility

تَأْديب *n* discipline, punishment; مَجْلِس التَأْديبِ العَسْكَريّ military discipline board

تَأْديبيّ *adj* disciplinary; مَجْلِس تَأْديبيّ disciplinary board; إجْراء تَأْديبيّ a disciplinary action

مُؤَدَّب *adj* polite, well-mannered, well-behaved; طَلَب مُؤَدَّب a polite request; أَطْفال مُؤَدَّبون well-behaved children; غَيْر مُؤَدَّبٍ impolite, rude; جَواب غَيْر مُؤَدَّبٍ an impolite answer; كانَ مُؤَدَّباً to be well-mannered; كانَ غَيْرَ مُؤَدَّبٍ to have no manners, to be rude

مُؤَدِّب *n* educator; teacher in a Koranic school (Tunisia)

مَأْدُبة, مَأْدَبة *n* |مَآدِبُ| banquet, formal dinner; مَأْدُبة عَشاءٍ banquet, formal dinner; أَقامَ مَأْدُبةً to give a banquet; حَضَرَ مَأْدُبةً to attend a banquet

أَدَّ *v* |i-u; أَدّ| to befall, to afflict

أدارِسة *n* Idrisid dynasty (*Morocco, 788-974*)

أَدْرِياتيكيّ *n* Adriatic; البَحْر الأَدْرِياتيكيّ the Adriatic Sea

إدْريس *n* |dipt| Idris, Driss (*male given name*)

أَدْرينالين *n* adrenaline

ادَّعى *v* see دعو ادعي

1 **آدَم** *n* |dipt| **1** [اسْم شَخْصيّ] Adam (*male given name*) **2** (Relig) Adam (*the first human in the Abrahamic religions*); تُفّاحة آدَمَ Adam's apple; ابْن آدَمَ human being; بنو آدَمَ humanity; كُلُّ ابْنِ آدَمَ خَطّاءٌ to err is human

آدَميّ *n* human being

2 **إدام** *n* *anything eaten with bread*

3 **أَدَمة** *n* dermis

أَديم *n* |أُدُم| **1** [جِلْد] skin **2** [ظاهِر الشَيْءِ] surface; أَديم الأَرْضِ the surface of the earth

أَدْميرال *n* admiral

أَدّى *v* **1** [قامَ ب] to carry out, to perform, to execute; to accomplish; to fulfil, to do; أَدّى عَمَلَهُ to do one's job; أَدّى مُهِمّةً to carry out an assignment, to fulfil a task; أَدّى وَظيفةً to fulfil a function; أَدّى الخِدْمة العَسْكَريّة to perform military service; أَدّى واجِباتِهِ المَدْرَسيّة to do one's homework; أَدّى الصَلاةَ to perform prayers **2** [قادَ] |إلى| to lead, to take, to bring; أَدّى بِشَخْصٍ \ بِشَيْءٍ إلى ... to lead sb/sth to ...; يُؤَدّي هذا الدَرْبُ إلى البَحْرِ this path leads to the sea **3** [دَفَعَ] to settle; أَدّى دَيْناً to settle a debt **4** [التَحيّة أو السَلام] to convey; أَدّى السَلامَ to greet; أَدّى التَحيّةَ (العَسْكَريّةَ) to salute; أَدّى مَعْنًى to convey a meaning **5** [نَجَمَ] |إلى| to result in, to lead to; لا يُؤَدّي إلى شَيْءٍ that leads nowhere; أَدّى إلى شَيْءٍ to result in sth; يُؤَدّي إلى المَوْتِ it causes death; أَدّى إلى نَتائِجَ to lead to results

أَداء *n* |أداءات| **1** [مَسْرَحيّ] performance; أَداء مَسْرَحيّ theatrical performance; أَداء فَرْديّ solo performance; رَفَعَ \ حَسَّنَ أَداءَهُ to improve one's performance **2** [إنْجاز] performance, execution, accomplishment; تَقْييم أَداءِ الرَئيسِ evaluation of the president's performance; قَصَّرَ في الأَداءِ

to perform badly 3 [ضَرائِبَ] payment 4 [عَمَلٍ] functioning 5 (Mus) rendition

أدائيّ *n* performing; الفُنون الأدائيّة the performing arts

أدائيّة *n* (Art) performatism

أداة *n* |أدَوات| 1 [عُدّة] tool, instrument, utensil, appliance; أدَوات instruments, materials, equipment; أدَوات مَنْزِليّة housewares; أدَوات خَشَبيّة wooden utensils; أدَوات دِراسيّة educational tools; الأَدَوات السِياسيّة the political apparatus; أدَوات المائِدةِ crockery; tableware; أدَوات الطَعامِ cutlery; أدَوات الكِتابةِ writing instruments; شَريط أدَواتٍ (Comput) toolbar; صُنْدوق أدَواتٍ toolbox 2 (Ling) particle; أداة التَعْريفِ definite article; أداة التَنْكيرِ indefinite article; أداة الاسْتِفْهامِ \ النِداءِ interrogative/vocative particle

تأدية *n* payment; performance, fulfilment; تأدِيةِ الخِدْمةِ العَسْكَريّةِ the performance of military service

مُؤَدٍّ *adj* leading; الطَريق المُؤَدّي إلى الغَرْبِ the road that leads to the west

مُؤَدًّى *n* sense, meaning; substance, general purport

أديس أبابا *n* Addis Ababa (*capital of Ethiopia*)

إذْ *conj* 1 [حَيْثُ] as, since, because; إذْ أنّ now that, in view of the fact that; because, since; لا تُعاشِرْهُ إذ أنَّهُ غَيْرُ أمينٍ don't associate with him because he is not trustworthy; لم يَسْتَطِعِ السَفَرَ إذْ أُصيبَ بِمَرَضٍ مُفاجِئٍ he was not able to travel because he suddenly became sick 2 [لِلمُفاجَأةِ] then; suddenly; إذْ ذاكَ then, at that time; سَيَجِدُ نَفْسَهُ إذْ ذاكَ أمامَ خِيارَيْنِ قاطِعَيْنِ he will then find himself faced with two stark choices; بينما أنا جالِسٌ في المَطْعَمِ إذْ حَضَرَ صَديقي I was sitting in the restaurant when all of a sudden my friend showed up

إذا *conj* 1 [إنْ] when; if, whenever; إذا أَرَدْتَ التَغَيُّرَ فَلْتَبْدَأْ بِنَفْسِكَ if you want change, start with yourself; فيما إذا if, whether; فيما إذا ... أم لا if ... or not; لم يُعْرَفْ فيما إذا غادَرَ البِلادَ أم لا it is not known if he has left the country or not; إلاّ إذا except when, unless; لا يُسْجَنُ أيُّ شَخْصٍ إلاّ إذا ارْتَكَبَ جَريمةً nobody goes to prison unless he has committed a crime; هذا من المُمْكِنِ اذا ما تَوَفَّرَت الإرادةُ if the will is there it is possible; لا أدْري إذا \ ما إذا \ فيما إذا تَجادَلَ الناسُ فيما إذا كانَ الرَئيسُ مَسْؤولاً أم لا I don't know if; the people were arguing about whether the president was guilty or not 2 [إذا ب] and then, and all of a sudden; فَتَحْتُ البابَ وَإذا بِأَحْمَدَ I opened the door and there was Ahmed; وَإذا بي أَشْعُرُ بِفِقْدانِ التَوازُنِ all of a sudden I felt I lost my balance; وَإذا بِشَخْصٍ يَقِفُ إلى جانِبي suddenly there was somebody standing next to me

إذاً *adv* see إذَنْ

آذار *n* |dipt| (Levant, Iraq) March

أذَرْبَيْجان *n* |f| Azerbaijan

أذَرْبَيْجانيّ A *adj* Azerbaijani, Azeri; (اللُغة) الأذَرْبَيْجانيّة Azerbaijani/Azeri (*language*)
B *n* Azerbaijani, Azeri (*person*)

آذَرْيون *n* pot marigold (*Calendula officinalis*)

أذِنَ *v* |a; إذْن| to permit, to allow; أذِنَ بِشَيْءٍ to permit sth; أذِنَ لِنَفْسِهِ to permit oneself

أذَّنَ *v* أذَّنَ للصَلاةِ to call to prayer

آذَنَ *v* 1 [أعْلَنَ] |ب| to announce, to make known; to inform; to signal; آذَنَ بِميلادِ أُمّةٍ جَديدةٍ to herald the birth of a new nation; يُؤْذِنُ بِنِهايةِ الرَأْسْماليّةِ it signals the end of capitalism 2 [أوْشَكَ أنْ] |ب| to be on the verge; آذَنَ البَيْتُ بالسُقوطِ the house was about to collapse 3 [حَثَّ] to urge, to exhort; to call to prayer; آذَنَ المُؤَذِّنُ بالصَلاةِ the muezzin gave the call to prayer

اسْتَأْذَنَ *v* |ب، في| to ask permission; اسْتَأْذَنَ شَخْصاً ب \ في شَيْءٍ to ask sb permission to do sth

أذان *n* call to prayer

إذْن *n* permission, authorization; consent; إذْن مُسْبَق prior authorization; بِإذْنِ (من) شَخْصٍ with sb's permission; إذْن بِإذْنِ اللهِ God willing; بدونِ إذْنٍ without permission; من أجْلِ شَيْءٍ permission to do sth; كانَ عِنْدَهُ الإذْنُ he had permission; مَنَحَ (شَخْصاً) إذْنَ التَصْديرِ to give sb an export licence; طَلَبَ إذْنَ شَخْصٍ ب \ ل to ask sb permission for; حَصَلَ على إذْنِ الدُخولِ to get permission to enter; ب \ بعد \ عن إذْنِكَ with your permission, please; if that's all right with you; will you excuse me?

أُذُن *n* |f; آذان| [1] (Anat) ear; أُذُن داخِليّة \ وُسْطى \ خارِجيّة inner/middle/outer ear; طَبْلة الأُذُن eardrum; صِوان الأُذُن pinna, auricle (*outer part of the ear*); شَحْمة الأُذُن ear lobe; الْتِهاب الأُذُن ear infection; لم يُصَدِّقْ أُذُنَيْه he didn't believe his ears; ضَجيج يَصُمُّ الآذانَ a deafening noise; هَمَسَ بِشَيْءٍ في أُذُنِ شَخْصٍ to whisper sth in sb's ear [2] [مِقْبَض] handle; أُذُن فِنْجانٍ the handle of a cup

Idiom (Bot) أُذُن الدُّبِّ Aaron's rod, mullein (*Verbascum*)

إذْنيّ *adj* سَنَد إذْنيّ promissory note

أُذُنيّ *adj* auricular, ear (*before n*); القَناة الأُذُنيّة the ear canal

أُذَيْن *n* (Anat) atrium, auricle; الأُذَيْن الأَيْسَر \ الأَيْمَن the left/right atrium

أُذَيْنة *n* [1] (Anat) earlobe [2] (Hist) |m| Odaenathus (*3rd century Palmyrene king*)

اسْتِئْذان *n* permission; asking for permission; بِدونِ اسْتِئْذانٍ without permission

إيذان *n* declaration, proclamation, announcement

مُؤَذِّن *n* muezzin (*mosque official who recites the call to prayer*)

مِئْذَنة *n* |مَآذِنُ| minaret

مَأْذون [A] *adj* authorized; مَصْدَر مَأْذون an official source [B] *n* (Isl Law) *an official authorized to perform marriages*

مَأْذونيّة *n* (Syria) leave; permission

2 **إذاً, إذَنْ** *adv* so; then, therefore, in that case; واضِحٌ إذَنْ أنّ كُلَّ هذا يُمَثِّلُ تَحَدِّياً كَبيراً it is clear then that all this represents a great challenge; إنّها الحَرْبُ إذَنْ! so it is war then!

أَذِيَ *v* |a; أَذًى, أَذاة, أَذِيّة| to suffer damage, to be harmed, to be injured

أَذّى *v* to harm, to hurt, to injure; to wrong

آذى *v* |Form IV; imperf يُؤْذي| [1] [ضَرَّ] to harm, to hurt; to damage; to wrong; آذى شَخْصاً to hurt sb; to wrong sb; آذى مَشاعِرَ شَخْصٍ to hurt sb's feelings; to offend sb [2] [أَصابَ] to injure, to hurt; آذى رُكْبَتَه to hurt one's knee; لم يُؤْذِ نَمْلةً في حَياتِهِ he wouldn't hurt a fly

تَأَذّى *v* [1] [تَضَرَّرَ] to suffer damage; تَأَذَّت السَّيّارةُ the car was damaged [2] [جُرِحَ] to sustain an injury, to be injured; to be hurt; تَأَذّى ب \ من شَيْءٍ to be hurt by sth; لا أَحَدَ تَأَذّى أو قُتِلَ no one was injured or killed; مَنْ سَيَتَأَذّى مِنْها هُم النّاسُ البُسَطاءُ it's the ordinary people who will be hurt by it

أَذًى *n* [1] [ضَرَر] damage, harm; أَذًى بَدَنيّ \ نَفْسيّ bodily/emotional harm; أَذًى مادّيّ material damages; عَديم الأَذى harmless, innocuous; أَلْحَقَ أَذًى بِشَيْءٍ to damage sth, to inflict damage on sth; أَلْحَقَ أَذًى بِشَخْصٍ to harm sb; to injure sb; تَعَرَّضَ لِأَذًى to be damaged; to be harmed [2] [إهانة] offence, insult

إيذاء *n* harm, damage; abuse; إيذاء عَمْديّ deliberate harm; إيذاء بَدَنيّ \ جَسَديّ physical abuse

مُؤْذٍ *adj* harmful, hurtful

آر *n* (Meas) are (*100 square metres*)

أَراجوز *n* puppet; مَسْرَح الأَراجوز puppet show

آراميّ [A] *adj* Aramaean, Aramaic; (اللُّغة) الآراميّة Aramaic (*language*) [B] *n* Aramaean (*person*)

أَرَبَ *v* |i; أَرْب| to tighten

أَرُبَ *v* |u; إرْب, أَرابة| to be clever

أَرِبَ *v* |a; أَرَب| ب, في| to be skillful (in)

إرْب *n* |آراب| need

Idiom (مَزَّقَ شَيْئاً) إرْباً إرْباً (to tear sth) to pieces

أَرَب *n* |آراب| aim; wish

إرْبة *n* |إرَب| need

أُرْبة *n* |أُرَب| bow, knot

أُرْبِيّة *n* groin

أَريب *adj* |أُرَباءُ| clever, intelligent

مَأْرَب *n* |مَآرِبُ| goal, aim, purpose; مَأْرَب شَخْصيّ \ سِياسيّ a personal/political goal; تَحْقيق مَآرِبِهِ achieving one's goals

إرْبِد *n* |dipt f| Irbid (*city in Jordan*)

أَرْبيل *n* |dipt f| Erbil, Arbil (*capital of Iraqi Kurdistan*)

أَرْتُوازيّ *adj* artesian; بِئْر أَرْتُوازيّة an artesian well

أَرَّثَ *v* to light

إرْث *n* see ورث

أُرْثوذُكْس *adj* Orthodox; روم أُرْثوذُكْس Roman Orthodox

أُرْثوذُكْسيّ *adj* orthodox; يَهود أُرْثوذُكْسيّونَ orthodox Jews; غَيْر أُرْثوذُكْسيٍّ strictly orthodox; أُرْثوذُكْسيّ مُتَعَصِّب unorthodox

أُرْثوذُكْسيّة *n* orthodoxy

› **أَرِجَ** *v* |a; أَرَج ,أَريج| to be fragrant; to smell

أَريج *n* fragrance, pleasant smell

› **تَأَرْجَحَ** *v* to rock, to swing, to sway; to fluctuate; تَأَرْجَحَ القِطارُ بِشِدّةٍ the train swayed violently; تَأَرْجَحت الأَسْواقُ بِشِدّةٍ markets fluctuated wildly; تَأَرْجَحَ بين الحَياةِ والمَوْتِ to hover between life and death; تَأَرْجَحَ على حافةِ الحَرْبِ \ الانْهِيارِ to teeter on the brink of war/collapse

أُرْجوحة *n* |أَراجيحُ| swing; see-saw; أُرْجوحة شَبَكيّة hammock

تَأَرْجُح *n* swing; fluctuation

مُتَأَرْجِح *adj* fluctuating

› **أَرْجَنْتينيّ** *adj, n* Argentine, Argentinian

الأَرْجَنْتين *n* |f| Argentina

› **أُرْجُوان** *n* **1** [لَوْن] purple **2** (Bot) *kind of tree with red flowers*

أُرْجُوانيّ *adj* purple; لَوْن أُرْجُوانيّ purple

› **أَرَّخَ** *v* **1** [حَدَّدَ التاريخَ |ب|] to date **2** [دَوَّنَ التاريخَ] to write the history of

تاريخ *n* |تَواريخُ| **1** [أَجَل مُعَيَّن] date; dating; تاريخ الصُنْعِ date of manufacture; model year (*cars*); تاريخ البِناءِ date of construction; تاريخ الابْتِداءِ start date; تاريخ الانْتِهاءِ expiration date, final date; بِتاريخِ... dated ...; بعد التاريخِ المُحَدَّدِ بِثَلاثةِ أَسابيعَ three weeks after the specified date; يَرْجِعُ \ يَعودُ تاريخُ بناءِ المَسْجِدِ إلى... the mosque dates back to ... **2** [ما حَدَثَ في الماضي] history, past; تاريخ وَطَنيّ \ قَوْميّ national history; التاريخ الحَديث modern history; تاريخ عَريق a glorious past; عِلْم التاريخِ history; تاريخ فَنّيّ art history; عالِم التاريخِ الفَنّيِّ art historian; تَزْوير \ تَشْويه التاريخ falsification/rewriting of history; مَسار التاريخ the course of history; على مَرِّ التاريخ in the course of history; من التاريخ from the past; في التاريخِ البَعيدِ in the remote past; ما قبل التاريخ prehistory; عُصور ما قبل التاريخ prehistoric times; آثار مِمّا قبل التاريخ prehistoric artifacts; دَرَسَ التاريخَ to study history; يُعَلِّمُنا التاريخُ أنّ... history teaches us that...; اسْتَفادَ من دُروسِ التاريخِ to learn from history; لِأَوَّلِ مَرّةٍ في التاريخ for the first time in history; التاريخُ يُعيدُ نَفْسَهُ history repeats itself; كارِثة من أَفْظَعِ الكَوارِثِ في التاريخ one of the biggest disasters in history **3** [تَقْويم] calendar; التاريخ الميلاديّ \ الهِجْريّ the Christian/Islamic calendar; بِداية تاريخِنا the beginning of our calendar

تَأْريخ *n* **1** [كِتابة اليَوْمِ والشَهْرِ والسَنة] dating; التَأْريخ بالكَرْبون المُشِعّ carbon dating, radiocarbon dating **2** [تَسْجيل الأَحْداثِ التاريخيّة] historiography; the writing of history

تاريخيّ *adj* historic, historical; لَحْظة تاريخيّ(ة) \ حَدَث a historic event/moment; فُرْصة تاريخيّة a historic opportunity; المَدينة التاريخيّة historic city; the old city (*historic center of a modern city*); مَصادِر \ خَلْفِيّات تاريخيّة historical sources/backgrounds; رِواية تاريخيّة a historical novel

مُؤَرَّخ *adj* dated ...; الرِسالة المُؤَرَّخة في ٢٠ يولِيو عامَ ١٨٦٤ the letter dated July 20, 1864

مُؤَرِّخ *n* historian; مُؤَرِّخونَ مُعاصِرونَ contemporary historians

› **أَرْخَبيل** *n* archipelago

أُرْدِيّة *n* see أورد

إِرْدَبّ ,**أَرْدَبّ** *n* |أَرادِبُ| *a dry measure used in Egypt, officially equivalent to 5.62 US bushels, but varying greatly in different localities*

› **أُرْدُنيّ** *adj, n* Jordanian; المَمْلَكة الأُرْدُنيّة الهاشِميّة the Hashemite Kingdom of Jordan

الأُرْدُن *n* Jordan; نَهْر الأُرْدُن the River Jordan (BrE), the Jordan River (AmE); ما وراء الأُرْدُنِ ,شَرْق الأُرْدُنِ Transjordan

› **أَرْدُواز** *n* slate

› **أَرْز** *n* cedar (*Cedrus*)

أَرُزّ *n* rice; كيس أَرُزٍّ \ بالة a bag/sack of rice; زِراعة الأَرُزِّ rice farming

أُرْز *n* rice

أَرْزِيّة *n* (Bot) larch (*Larix*)

› **أَرِسْتُقْراطيّ ,أَرِسْتوقْراطيّ** **A** *adj* **1** [ذو عَلاقةٍ بالأَرِسْتوقْراطيّة] aristocratic; عائِلة أَرِسْتُقْراطيّة an aristocratic family **2** [أَنيق] upscale, wealthy; حَيّ أَرِسْتُقْراطيّ an upscale neighbourhood **B** *n* aristocrat

أَرِسْتُقْراطِيّة *n* aristocracy

‹ **أَرِسْطو ,أَرِسْطوطاليس** *n* Aristotle

‹ **أَرْشَفَ** *v* |i; أَرْشَفة| to archive

أَرْشيف *n* |أَراشيفُ| archives; الأَرْشيف الوَطَنيّ the National Archives

مُؤَرْشَف *adj* archived

‹ **أَرْشيدوق** *n* archduke

‹ **أَرَّضَ** *v* (Elec) to earth (BrE), to ground (AmE) (*a wire or plug*)

أَرْض *n* |f; أَراضٍ| **1** [قِطْعة أَرْض] land; soil; property; أَراضٍ land; area; أَرْض فِلاحيّة \ زِراعيّة farming/agricultural land; أَراضٍ شاسِعة huge tracts of land; أَرْض خِصْبة \ مُجْدِبة fertile/infertile land; أَراضٍ بور fallow lands; أَرْض خُصوصيّة \ مَمْلوكة للخَواصّ private property; أَراضٍ مُنْخَفِضة lowland; الأَراضي المُنْخَفِضة the Netherlands; قِطْعة أَرْض plot, tract of land; قِطْعة أَرْض فِلاحيّة \ زِراعيّة a cultivated field; 50 هِكْتاراً من الأَرْض 50 hectares of land; سِياسة الأَرْض المَحْروقة scorched-earth policy; مالِك \ صاحِب أَرْض landowner; زَرَعَ \ اسْتَصْلَحَ أَرْضاً to cultivate/develop land; اشْتَرى \ امْتَلَكَ \ باعَ أَرْضاً to buy/own/sell land **2** [كُرة أَرْضيّة] Earth; the world; كَوْكَب الأَرْض, الكُرة الأَرْضيّة the Earth; باطِن الأَرْض the Earth's core; the bowels of the Earth; على سَطْح \ وَجْهِ الأَرْض on the surface of the Earth **3** [سَطْح] ground; أَرْض مُقَدَّسة consecrated ground; فوق الأَرْض above ground, overground (BrE); تحت الأَرْض underground, subterranean; نَفَق \ سِجْن تحت الأَرْض an underground corridor/dungeon; تَجْرِبة نَوَوِيّة تحت الأَرْض an underground nuclear test; وَصَّلَ بالأَرْض (Elec) to earth (BrE), to ground (AmE) (*a wire or plug*); سَوّى شَيْئاً بالأَرْض to level sth (to the ground), to demolish sth; رَمى شَخْصاً على الأَرْض to throw sb to the floor; اضْطَجَعَ \ جَلَسَ \ سَقَطَ على الأَرْض to lie down on/sit on/fall to the ground **4** [مِنْطَقة] territory; أَراضٍ territory; أَرْض مُحايِدة neutral territory; الأَراضي المُقَدَّسة the Holy Land; الأَرْض المَوْعودة the Promised Land; أَرْض مُشْتَرَكة common ground; المُنْتَخَب صاحِب الأَرْض the home team; في \ على أَراضٍ أَجْنَبيّة on foreign soil; مُباراة على أَرْضٍ مُحايِدة a game on neutral ground; عادَ إلى أَرْضِ الوَطَنِ to return to one's native land; تَوَغَّلَ في أَراضي الأَعْداءِ to penetrate into enemy territory; غَزا أَرْضاً to invade/conquer a territory; احْتَلَّ أَراضِيَ to occupy territory

أَرَضة *n* termite

أَرْضيّ *adj* land (*before n*), ground (*before n*), earth (*before n*); terrestrial; earthly, worldly; لَغْم أَرْضيّ landmine; انْهِيار أَرْضيّ landslide; هَزّة أَرْضيّة earthquake; القِشْرة الأَرْضيّة the Earth's crust; الطابِق الأَرْضيّ the ground floor; نَفَق أَرْضيّ an underground tunnel; غَيْر أَرْضيّ extraterrestrial; مَخْلوق غَيْر أَرْضيّ an extraterrestrial, an alien; الحَياة الأَرْضيّة worldly life

أَرْضيّة *n* **1** [أَرْض] floor; ground; أَرْضيّة خَشَبيّة \ مُبَلَّطة a wooden/tiled floor **2** [أَساس] foundation, basis; هَيَّأَ الأَرْضيّةَ لِمُتابَعةِ المُفاوَضاتِ to lay the foundation for further negotiations **3** [خَلْفيّة] background

‹ **أُرْطاسِيا** *n* (Bot) hydrangea

‹ **أُرْغُن** *n* |أَراغِنُ| (Mus) organ; عَزَفَ على الأُرْغُنِ to play the organ

‹ **أَرِقَ** *v* |a; أَرَق| to be troubled; to be tormented; to be sleepless

أَرَّقَ *v* to trouble, to disturb; to torment, to torture; to keep awake; أَرَّقَهُ ضَميرُهُ to be tortured by one's conscience; شَيْء يُؤَرِّقُ مَضْجَعَهُ sth which disturbs one's sleep

أَرَق *n* sleeplessness, insomnia; عانى من الأَرَقِ to suffer from insomnia

مُؤَرَّق *adj* sleepless

‹ **أَرْقَطْيون** *n* (Bot) burdock (*Arctium*); burr

1‹ **أَراك** *n* (Bot) arak (*Salvadora persica*)

2‹ **أَريكة** *n* |أَرائِكُ| couch, sofa; جَلَسَ على الأَريكةِ to sit on the couch

‹ **أَرْكَنْساس** *n* |f| Arkansas (*US state*)

‹ **أُرومة ,أَرومة** *n* **1** [أَصْل] origin **2** [جِذْر] (tree) stump

‹ **أَرْمَنيّ ,أَرْمينيّ** **A** *adj* |أَرْمَن| Armenian; (اللُغة) الأَرْمَنيّة Armenian (*language*)

B *n* |أَرْمَن| Armenian (*person*)

أَرْمينيا *n* Armenia

‹ **أَرْنَب** *n* |أرانِبُ| rabbit; أَرْنَب بَرّيّ a wild rabbit; a hare; أَرْنَب أَليف a tame rabbit; أَرْنَب مُحَمَّر roast rabbit

أَرْنَبة *n* **1** [حَيَوان] doe (*female rabbit*) **2** [الأَنْف] tip; أَرْنَبة الأَنْفِ the tip of the nose; لا يَرى أَبْعَدَ من أَرْنَبِةِ أَنْفِهِ he can't see beyond the end of his nose

أَرْنوب *n* bunny

‹ **أُروبّا** *n* see أوروبّا

‹ **أَرى** *v* see رأي

‹ **آريّ** *adj, n* Aryan

‹ **إريتْرِيا** *n* Eritrea

إريتْرِيّ *adj, n* Eritrean

‹ **أَريحا** *n* Jericho (*city in Palestine*)

‹ **أَريزونا** *n* Arizona (*US state*)

أَريزونيّ *adj* Arizonian

‹ **أَزَرَ** *v* |u; أَزْر| to strengthen

أَزَّرَ *v* to strengthen

آزَرَ *v* to help, to support

تَآزَرَ *v* to help one another, to cooperate, to collaborate

ائْتَزَرَ *v* to put on a loincloth

أَزْر *n* strength; شَديد الأَزْرِ strong; شَدَّ من أَزْرِ شَخْصٍ to support sb

إزار *n* |f; أُزُر| *wide white cloth worn around the hips*

تَآزُر *n* mutual support, cooperation, collaboration; تَضامُن وَتَآزُر بين بَلَدَيْنِ cooperation between two countries

مُؤازَرة *n* aid, support, assistance; طَلَبَ \ لَقِيَ مُؤازَرةً to request/be given assistance; بِمُؤازَرةِ الجَيْشِ with the support of the army

مِئْزَر *n* |مَآزِرُ| apron

‹ **أَزْرو** *n* |dipt f| Azrou (*city in Morocco*)

‹ **أَزَّ** *v* |i-u; أَزيز| to buzz, to hum; يَؤُزُّ النَحْلُ the bees are buzzing; يَئِزُّ المُحَرِّكُ the engine is making a buzzing noise

أَزيز *n* buzzing, humming, zinging; أَزيز الرَصاصِ the buzzing of a bullets

‹ **أَزِفَ** *v* |a; أُزوف ,أَزَف| to come near; أَزِفَتْ ساعةُ الرَحيلِ it was nearly time to leave

‹ **مَأْزِق** *n* |مَآزِقُ| **1** [مَكان ضَيِّق] narrow passage **2** [وَرْطة] problem, critical situation; impasse; واجَهَ مَأْزِقاً to face a problem; وَقَعَ في مَأْزِقٍ to reach an impasse; خَرَجَ من مَأْزِقٍ to get out of a jam; تَخَلَّصَ من مَأْزِقٍ to resolve an impasse

‹ **أَزَل** *n* eternity; منذ (قَديمِ) الأَزَلِ from time immemorial, of old

أَزَليّ *adj* **1** [سَرْمَديّ] eternal, everlasting; الصِراع الأَزَليّ بين الخَيْرِ والشَرِّ the eternal struggle between good and evil **2** [قَديم جدًّا] ancient

أَزَليّة *n* eternity

‹ **أَزَّمَ** *v* to worsen, to aggravate; أَزَّمَ الوَضْعَ to aggravate the situation

تَأَزَّمَ *v* to be/become critical, to come to a head; to worsen, to escalate

أَزْمة *n* |أَزَمات| **1** [حالة ضيق] crisis; problem; أَزْمة إداريّة \ سِياسيّة an administrative/political crisis; أَزْمة حادّة a severe crisis; أَزْمة قَلْبيّة heart attack; أَزْمة خانِقة a suffocating crisis; أَزْمة حُكوميّة \ وِزاريّة government/cabinet crisis; أَزْمة هُويّةٍ identity crisis; أَزْمة الشَرْقِ الأَوْسَطِ the Middle East crisis; أَزْمة ثِقةٍ crisis of confidence; أَزْمة طاقةٍ energy crisis; أَزْمة مُنْتَصِفِ العُمْرِ mid-life crisis; مُواجَهة الأَزَماتِ crisis management; أَزْمة ثِقةٍ حادّة \ خَطيرة a severe/serious crisis of confidence; تَفاقُم أَزْمةِ الغِذاءِ exacerbation of the food crisis; الأَزْمة الآخِذة في خَنْقِ البِلادِ the crisis that has the country in a stranglehold; تَدارَكَ الأَزْمةَ to prevent the crisis; مَرَّ بِأَزْمةٍ to go through/undergo a crisis; سَيْطَرَ على أَزْمةٍ to be in control of a crisis; عانى من أَزْمةٍ to suffer from a crisis; حَلَّ أَزْمةً to resolve a crisis **2** (Econ) depression, crisis; أَزْمة الدولارِ dollar crisis; أَزْمة الرَهْنِ العَقاريِّ the sub-prime mortgage crisis; أَزْمة القُروضِ الائْتِمانيّةِ the credit crunch; أَزْمة الثَلاثيناتِ the crisis of the 1930s, the Great Depression

تَأَزُّم *n* escalation; complication; deterioration; تَأَزُّم وَشيك an imminent escalation; حالة تَأَزُّمٍ a crisis situation; تَأَزُّم في العَلاقاتِ a worsening of relations; تَأَزُّم الوَضْعِ deterioration of the situation

تَأْزيم *n* worsening, aggravation

مُتَأَزِّم *adj* critical, precarious; وَضْع مُتَأَزِّم a critical situation

إزْمير *n* |f| Izmir (*city in Turkey*)

إزاءَ *prep* opposite, in the face of, in front of; as compared with; جَلَسَ إزاءَ شَخْصٍ to sit opposite sb; سِعْر اليَنْ إزاءَ الدولارِ the rate of the yen to the dollar

آس[1] *n* |آسات| ace (*in playing cards*)

آس[2] *n* myrtle (*Myrtus*); الآس الشائِع common myrtle (*Myrtus communis*); الآس البَرّيّ cranberry; عَصير الآسِ البَرّيِّ cranberry juice

أُسامة *n* |dipt m| Usama, Osama (*male given name*)

أَسْباتيّ *n* see سَباتيّ

إسْبانِيا *n* Spain

إسْبانيّ **A** *adj* |إسْبان| Spanish; (اللُغة) الإسْبانيّة Spanish (*language*)

B *n* |إسْبان| Spanish person, Spaniard

إسْبِرَنْتو *n* Esperanto

أَسْبِسْتوس *n* asbestos

أَسْبِرين *n* aspirin; تَناوَلَ الأَسْبِرين to take aspirin

إسْت *n* see سته

اسْتاتيكا *n* statics (*a branch of mechanics*)

إسْتاد *n* |إسْتادات| stadium

أُسْتاذ *n* |أَساتِذة| **1**▸ [لَقَب عِلْميّ جامعيّ] professor; أُسْتاذ جامِعيّ professor, university teacher; أُسْتاذ كُرْسيٍّ professor; أُسْتاذ زائِر visiting lecturer; visiting professor; أُسْتاذ مُساعِد assistant professor **2**▸ [مُعَلِّم] teacher; أُسْتاذ الرياضيّاتِ \ الإنْجْليزيّةِ the math/English teacher; هو أُسْتاذُ اللُغة العَرَبيّة he teaches Arabic **3**▸ [في القانونِ] master; أُسْتاذ في القانونِ Master of Laws

أُسْتاذيّة *n* professorship, professorate

الإسْتانة *n* (Hist) Istanbul

إسْتَبْرَق *n* brocade

إسْتَر *n* (Chem) ester

إسْتراتيجيّ **A** *adj* strategic; مَصالِح اسْتْراتيجيّة strategic interests; شَراكة اسْتْراتيجيّة a strategic partnership; مِنْطَقة اسْتْراتيجيّة a strategic area; ذو أَهَمِّيّةٍ اسْتْراتيجيّةٍ of strategic importance

B *n* strategist

إسْتْراتيجيّة *n* strategy, tactic; إسْتْراتيجيّة خُروجٍ an exit strategy; إسْتْراتيجيّة لِشَيْءٍ a strategy for sth; إسْتْراتيجيّة لِفِعْلِ شَيْءٍ a strategy to do sth; وَضَعَ إسْتْراتيجيّةً to devise a strategy

أُسْتْرالاسِيا *n* Australasia

أوسْتُرالْيا, **أُسْتْرالِيا** *n* Australia

أوسْتُراليّ, **أُسْتُراليّ** *adj*, *n* Australian

إسْتِرْلينيّ *adj* الجُنَيْه الإسْتِرْلينيّ pound sterling

أُسْتروجين, **إسْتروجين** *n* (Med) oestrogen (BrE), estrogen (AmE)

أَسْتُغُمّاية *n* (Egypt) hide-and-seek

اسْتِمارة *n* see أمر

اسْتودِيو *n* |اسْتودِيوهات| studio; اسْتودِيو التَصْويرِ \ التِلْفِزيونِ photography/television studio

إسْتونِيا *n* Estonia

إسْتونيّ *adj*, *n* Estonian

اسْتَأْسَدَ *v* to be brave

أَسَد *n* |أُسود, آساد| **1**▸ (Zool) lion; أَسَد مُزَمْجِر a roaring lion; أَسَد البَحْرِ sea lion; أَسَد الجَبَلِ mountain lion, cougar; مُرَوِّض أُسودٍ lion tamer; رُمِيَ وَليمةً للأُسودِ to be thrown to the wolves; هذا الشِبْلُ من ذاكَ الأَسَدِ ≈ he's a chip off the old block; ≈ like father, like son; حَصَلَ على نَصيبِ الأَسَدِ من \ في شَيْءٍ to get the lion's share of sth **2**▸ (Astrol) (بُرْج) الأَسَدِ Leo

أَسَرَ *v* |i; أَسْر| to take prisoner; أَسَرَ جُنْديًّا to take a soldier prisoner

آسِر *adj* fascinating, captivating; جَمال آسِر captivating beauty

أَسْر *n* **1**▸ [حَبْس] capture; captivity; وَقَعَ في الأَسْرِ to be taken prisoner; to be put in prison **2**▸ [كُلّ] بِأَسْرِهِ completely, totally; العالَم بِأَسْرِهِ the entire world; جاؤوا بِأَسْرِهِمْ they all came

إسار *n* **1**▸ [قَيْد] strap **2**▸ (Bot) Loranthus

أُسْرة *n* |أُسَر, أُسْرات| **1**▸ [عائِلة] family; أُسْرة مالِكة \ مَلَكيّة royal family; أُسْرة مُكَوَّنة \ مُؤَلَّفة من خَمْسةِ أَفْرادٍ a family of five; رَبّ الأُسْرةِ head of the family; تَكْوين أُسْرةٍ starting a family, forming a household; تَنْظيم الأُسْرةِ family planning; رِعاية الأُسْرةِ family care, parenting; مُدَوَّنة الأُسْرةِ (Mor) the Family Code; من أُسْرةٍ مَلَكيّةٍ \ نَبيلةٍ of royal/noble blood **2** ▸ [أُسْرة حاكِمة] dynasty; الأُسْرة العاشِرة the tenth dynasty

أُسَرِيّ, أُسْرَوِيّ *adj* family (*before n*), domestic; حَياة أُسَرِيّة family life; عَلاقات أُسَرِيّة family relationships

أَسير *n* |أُسَراءُ, أَسْرى| prisoner; أَسير حَرْبٍ prisoner of war; تَبادَلَ أَسْرى حَرْبٍ to exchange prisoners of war; احْتَجَزَ أَسْرى حَرْبٍ to take prisoners of war; سَلَّمَ الأَسْرى to hand over the prisoners

إِسْرائيل *n* |dipt f| Israel

إِسْرائيليّ **A** *adj* Israeli

B *n* Israeli; Israelite

إِسْرافيل *n* |dipt| Israfel (*the angel who will blow the trumpet on Judgement Day*)

أُسْرُب *n* graphite

أَسَّسَ *v* **1** [أَنْشَأَ] to found, to establish, to set up; to base, to ground; أُسِّسَ to be based; أَسَّسَ مَدينةً to found a city; أَسَّسَ مَدْرَسةً to set up a school; أَسَّسَ جَمْعيّةً \ حِزْباً to found an association/party **2** ▸ [وَضَعَ قاعِدةً] to lay the foundation

تَأَسَّسَ *v* to be founded, to be set up; تَأَسَّسَت الشَرِكةُ عامَ ١٩٩٠ the company was founded in 1990

أُسّ *n* **1** (Math) exponent; power; اثْنانِ أُسُّ ثَلاثةٍ two to the power of three; الأُسّ الهيدْروجينيّ (Chem) pH **2** ▸ [أَساس] foundation

أَساس *n* |أُسُس, أَساسات| **1** [قاعِدة] foundation; أَساس مَتين a solid foundation; أَساس مِنَ الباطون a concrete foundation; أَساسات الكَنيسةِ the foundations of the church; حُفْرة الأَساسِ (building) excavation; حَجَر الأَساسِ cornerstone; وَضْع حَجَرِ الأَساسِ لِشَيْءٍ laying the foundation stone for sth; breaking ground on sth; وَضَعَ \ صَبَّ الأَساسَ to lay the foundations **2** ▸ [مَبْدَأ] foundation, basis, principle; أَساساً \ في الأَساسِ basically, in the main, principally; أَساس قانونيّ legal basis, legal ground; على أَساسِ ... on the basis of ..., on the strength of...; on account of...; على أَساسٍ سَنَويٍّ on a yearly basis; annualized (*interest*); على أَساسِ الاحْتِرامِ المُتَبادَلِ on the basis of mutual respect; وَضَعَ \ أَرْسى أُسُسَ شَيْءٍ to lay the foundations for sth, to lay the groundwork for sth; وَضَعَ الأُسُسَ للمُفاوَضاتِ to lay the groundwork for negotiations; اسْتَنَدَ إلى أَساسٍ راسِخٍ to be based on a firm foundation; بَنى شَيْئاً على أَساسِ شَيْءٍ to base sth on sth; لا أَساسَ لَهُ unfounded, groundless; unjustified; ادِّعاء لا أَساسَ لَهُ an unfounded allegation; لَوْم لا أَساسَ لَهُ unjustified blame; شَكاوى لَيْسَ لَها أَساسٌ unfounded complaints; تِلْكَ الاتِّهاماتُ لَيْسَ لَها أَساسٌ these accusations are baseless; لا أَساسَ لَهُ من الصِحّةِ there's no element of truth in it

أَساسيّ **A** *adj* fundamental, basic; essential, key, vital; main, principle; fundamentalist; عَمَل أَساسيّ a standard work; نِظام \ قانون أَساسيّ statute; بَحْث أَساسيّ fundamental research; جُزْء أَساسيّ a fundamental part; أَلْوان أَساسيّة primary colours; فِكْرة أَساسيّة basic thought; المَوْضوع الأَساسيّ the main theme; قَرار أَساسيّ a fundamental decision; مُخْتَلِف أَساسيّاً fundamentally different; بِصِفةٍ أَساسيّةٍ basically; chiefly, mainly; ذو أَهَمّيّةٍ أَساسيّةٍ, ذو شَأْنٍ أَساسيٍّ of vital importance, essential

B *n* fundamentalist

أُسّيّ *adj* exponential

تَأْسيس *n* foundation, founding, establishment; تَأْسيس الشَرِكةِ the founding of the company; الذِكْرى العاشِرة لِتَأْسيسِها the tenth anniversary of its establishment

تَأْسيسيّ *adj* founding, foundational; fundamental; ميثاق تَأْسيسيّ constitution; founding charter; مَرْحَلة تَأْسيسيّة foundational stage

مُؤَسَّس *adj* founded, based, set up

مُؤَسِّس *n* founder, (founding) father; مُؤَسِّس الدَوْلةِ \ حِزْبٍ the founder of the state/a party; مُؤَسِّس عِلْمِ الجَبْرِ the father of algebra

مُؤَسَّساتيّ *adj* institutional; مُسْتَثْمِرونَ مُؤَسَّساتيّونَ institutional investors

مُؤَسَّسة *n* foundation; institution, institute, organization; firm, company; مُؤَسَّسة دُوَليّة international organization; مُؤَسَّسة

خاصّة private company; مُؤَسَّسة حُكوميّة state enterprise; governmental/public institution; مُؤَسَّسة تَعْليميّة educational institute; أَسَّسَ مُؤَسَّسةً to set up a foundation

مُؤَسَّسيّ *adj* institutional; إصلاح مُؤَسَّسيّ institutional reform

‹ **إصْطَبْل, إسْطَبْل** *n* stable; إسْطَبْلات الخَيْلِ horse stables

‹ **أَسْطُرْلاب** *n* |أَسْطُرْلابات| (Hist) astrolabe

‹ **أَساطين** *n pl* |dipt| masters; authorities; celebrities; هو من أساطينِ الفَنِّ he is a master of art

‹ **إسْطَنْبول, إسْتانْبول, إسْتَنْبول** *n* |f| Istanbul

‹ **أُسْطُوانة** *n* 1 (Geom) cylinder 2 (Mech) cylinder, drum; أُسْطُوانة الغازِ gas cylinder; أُسْطُوانة التَخْميد damping cylinder; مُحَرِّك الأُسْطُواناتِ السِتِّ 6-cylinder engine 3 (Mus, Comput) record; disk; album; أَدارَ أُسْطُوانةً to play a record; إصْدار أُسْطُوانةٍ جَديدةٍ release of a new album

أُسْطُوانيّ *adj* cylindric, cylindrical

‹ **أُسْطورة** *n* |أَساطيرُ| legend, tale, myth, fable; عِلْم الأَساطيرِ mythology; أُسْطورة حَيّة a living legend

أُسْطوريّ *adj* mythical, fabulous, legendary; وَحْش أُسْطوريّ a mythical beast; شَخْصيّة أُسْطوريّة a mythical figure; صُمودُهُم الأُسْطوريّ their legendary steadfastness

‹ **أُسْطول** *n* |أَساطيلُ| fleet; squadron; (Hist) armada; أُسْطول تِجاريّ merchant fleet; أُسْطول جَوّيّ air fleet; الأُسْطول الخامِسِ (البَحْريّ) the Fifth Fleet (*portion of American Navy responsible for the Persian Gulf area*)

‹ **أَسِفَ** *v* |a; أَسَف| to regret, to feel sorry; أَسِفَ على خطأٍ \ قرارٍ to regret a mistake/decision; أَسِفَ لِسُقوطِ مَدَنيّين to regret the loss of civilian life; أَسِفَ لِإزْعاج شَخْصٍ to be sorry to disturb sb; أَسِفَ على شَيْءٍ بِشِدّةٍ to regret sth deeply, to be very sorry about sth; لم يَأْسَفْ على شَيْءٍ to not be sorry about sth, to make no apologies for sth; يُؤْسَفُ لَهُ regrettable, unfortunate; pitiful, deplorable; مِمّا يُؤْسَفُ لَهُ regrettably, unfortunately

آسَفَ *v* |Form IV; imperf يُؤْسِفُ| to make feel sorry, to make sad; يُؤْسِفُني أنْ ... I regret that ..., I am sorry that ...; يُؤْسِفُني القَوْلُ إنّ ... it pains me to say that ...

تَأَسَّفَ *v* |على| to feel sorry, to regret; تَأَسَّفَ على فَقْدانِ شَيْءٍ \ شَخْصٍ to regret the loss of sth/sb; تَأَسَّفَ على عَدَمِ حُضورِهِ to regret that one could not come

آسِف *adj* sorry; أنا آسِفٌ جِدًّا! I'm so sorry!; أنا آسِفٌ على ... I apologize for ...; أنا آسِفٌ على الإزْعاجِ pardon the disturbance; I'm sorry to bother you

أَسَف *n* regret; sorrow, grief; أَسَف عَميق deep regret; profound sorrow; مع الأَسَفِ \ ل alas, unfortunately, it's a pity that ..., it's too bad that...; مع شَديدِ الأَسَفِ ,للأَسَفِ الشَديدِ it is such a pity that...; unfortunately, (much) to my regret; يا لَلْأَسَفِ! what a shame!; أَبْدى أَسَفهُ ل ... ,أَعْرَبَ \ عَبَّرَ عن أَسَفِهِ ل ... to express one's regret at...

تَأَسُّف *n* regret

مُؤْسِف *adj* regrettable, unfortunate; pitiful, sad, depressing; أَمْر \ حادِث مُؤْسِف an unfortunate matter/event; خَبَر مُؤْسِف sad news; بِطَريقةٍ مُؤْسِفةٍ pitifully, miserably; in an unfortunate way; سوء تَفاهُم مُؤْسِف a regrettable misunderstanding; حالةُ التَعْليمِ مُؤْسِفةٌ the state of education is pitiful; كانَ مَنْظَرُهُ مُؤْسِفاً he was a sorry sight; من المُؤْسِفِ أنَّهُ لم يَنْجَحْ في الامْتِحانِ it's a pity that he didn't pass his exam; هذا مُؤْسِفٌ جِدًّا what a pity, that's too bad

مَأْسوف *adj* المَأْسوف عَلَيْهِ the departed

مُتَأَسِّف *adj* sorry, regretful; أنا مُتَأَسِّفٌ على ... I'm sorry that ...

‹ **أَسْفَلْت** *n* see سفلت

‹ **إسْفَنْج, إسْفَنْجة** *n* sponge; foam; إسْفَنْج بَحْريّ sea sponge (*animal*); natural sponge (*material*); فُرْشاة الإسْفَنْجِ foam paint brush

إسْفَنْجيّ *adj* porous, spongy; نَسيج اسْفَنْجيّ porous tissue; اعْتِلال المُخِّ إسْفَنْجيّ الشَكْلِ البَقَريّ Bovine Spongiform Encephalopathy, BSE (*mad cow disease*)

‹ **إسْفَنْدان** *n* maple; شَجَرة الإسْفَنْدانِ maple (tree); شَراب الإسْفَنْدانِ maple syrup

‹ **إسْفين** *n* |أَسافينُ| wedge

‹ **إسْقَرْبوط** *n* (Med) scurvy

‹ **أُسْقُف** *n* |أَساقِفة ,أَساقِفُ| (Chr) bishop; رَئيس أَساقِفةٍ archbishop; تاج أُسْقُفٍ mitre (*bishop's hat*); mitre saw; سامَ شَخْصاً أُسْقُفاً to ordain sb as bishop

‹ **أُسْقُفِيّ** *adj* episcopal (*of a bishop*); الكَنيسة الأُسْقُفيّة the Episcopal Church

أُسْقُفِيّة *n* diocese; episcopate, episcopacy; أُسْقُفيّة أُكْسفورْد the diocese of Oxford

‹ **إِسْقَلوب** *n* scallop

‹ **إِسْقُمْرِيّ, أُسْقُمْرِي** *n* mackerel (*Scomber scombrus*); إِسْقُمْرِيّ مُدَخَّن smoked mackerel

‹ **إِسْكِتْش, اسْكِتْش** *n* see سكيتش

‹ **اسْكُتْلَنْدا** *n* Scotland

اسْكُتْلَنْدِيّ **A** *adj* Scottish **B** *n* Scot

‹ **الإِسْكَنْدَرِيّة** *n* Alexandria (*city in Egypt*)

‹ **اسْكَنْدِينافِيّ, اسْكَنْدنافِيّ** *adj* Scandinavian

اسْكَنْدِينافِيا *n* Scandinavia

‹ **إِسْكْواش** *n* (Sport) squash; لَعِبَ الإِسْكُواش to play squash

‹ **إِسْكيمو** *n* Eskimo

‹ **أَسَل** *n* (Bot) rush (*Juncus*); أَسَل الهِنْدِ rattan

أَسِيل *adj* smooth

‹ **إِسْلام آباد** *n* |f| Islamabad (*capital of Pakistan*)

‹ **تَأَسْلَمَ, أَسْلَمة, تَأَسْلُم, مُتَأَسْلِم** see سلم

‹ **إِسْماعيل** *n* |dipt| Isma'il, Ismael (*male given name*)

إِسْماعيلِيّة *n* Ismailism (*the second largest branch of Shia Islam*)

الإِسْماعيلِيّة *n* Ismailiyya (*city in Egypt*)

‹ **إِسْمَنْت** *n* cement, mortar; concrete; إِسْمَنْت مُسَلَّح reinforced concrete

إِسْمَنْتِيّ, أَسْمَنْتِيّ *adj* concrete (*before n*), cement (*before n*); جِدار إِسْمَنْتِيّ a concrete wall

‹ **أَسِنَ** *v* |a; أَسَن| to become brackish

آسِن *adj* brackish; مياه آسنة brackish water

‹ **أَسا** *v* |u; أَسْو, أَساً| to treat; أَسا مَرِيضًا to treat a patient

أَسِيَ *v* |a; أَسًى| to be sad

أَسّى *v* to be sad

آسى *v* to comfort; آسى شَخْصاً to comfort sb

تَأَسّى *v* to be consoled

تَآسى *v* to comfort each other

أُسْوة *n* **1** [نَموذَج] example, model; أُسْوَةً بِـ ... following the model of ...; in accordance with ...; أُسْوَةً بالحُكْمِ in accordance with the verdict **2** [مِثْل] like, same as; أُسْوَةً بِبَقِيّة ... just like any other ..., same as the rest of ...; فَرْض رُخْصةٍ للمُعَلِّمينَ أُسْوةً بِبَقِيّةِ المِهَنِ imposing licenses on teachers just like any other profession; تَوْفير الخِدْماتِ البَريديّةِ السَريعةِ أُسْوةً بالدُوَلِ المُتَقَدِّمةِ offering rapid mail service, same as in developed countries

أَسًى *n* sadness, grief, sorrow, affliction, pain; أَسًى قَديم an old wound; عَلِمْنا بِبالِغِ الأَسى والحُزْنِ بِوَفاتِهِ with great sadness, we learned of his death

أَسْيان *adj* |dipt| sad; ضَحِكة أَسْيانة a sad laugh

مُؤاسٍ *adj* see وسي

مُؤاساة, مُواساة *n* consolation, comfort, sympathy; بَحَثَ عن مُؤاساةٍ في شَيْءٍ \ عند شَخْصٍ to seek comfort with sth/sb

مَأْساة *n* |مَآسٍ| **1** [مُصيبة] tragedy, drama; عاش مَأْساةً to go through a tragedy; مَأْساة إِنْسانيّة a human tragedy; مَأْساة شَخْصيّة a personal tragedy; مَآسٍ طَبيعيّة natural disasters **2** (Literat) tragedy; كَما في المَأْساةِ الإِغْريقيّة as if in a Greek tragedy

مَأْسَوِيّ, مَأْساوِيّ *adj* dramatic, tragic, painful; أَحْداث \ وَقائِع مَأْساوِيّة tragic events; خسارة مَأْساوِيّة a tragic loss; عَواقِب مَأْساوِيّة dramatic consequences

مَأْسَوِيّة *n* tragic nature

‹ **إِسْوار** *n* |أَساوِرُ, أَساوِرة| bracelet

‹ **أَسْوان** *n* |dipt f| Aswan (*city in Egypt*)

‹ **آسِيا** *n* Asia; آسِيا الوُسْطى Central Asia; آسِيا الصُغْرى Asia Minor

آسْيَوِيّ *adj*, *n* Asian

‹ **أَسِيتون** *n* (Chem) acetone

‹ **أَسْيوط** *n* |dipt f| Asyut (*city in Egypt*)

‹ **أَشَبَ** *v* |u; أَشْب| to alloy

أُشابة *n* |أَشائِبُ| permalloy

‹ **إِشْبيلِيّة** *n* Sevilla (*city in Spain*)

‹ **أَشَرَ** *v* |u; أَشْر| to saw

أَشِرَ *v* |a; أَشَر| to be haughty

أَشَّر *v* ① [أَمَّر] to mark ② [أعْطى تَأْشيرةً] to grant/provide with a visa

أَشِر *adj* haughty, arrogant

تَأْشيرة *n* visa; تَأْشيرة سِياحيّة a tourist visa; تَأْشيرة دُخولٍ \ سَفَرٍ an entry/exit visa; تَأْشيرة دُخولٍ لِدَوْلةٍ مُعَيَّنةٍ a visa for a certain country; فَرْض تَأْشيرة الدُخول requiring a visa to enter; طَلَبَ تَأْشيرةَ دُخولٍ, قَدَّمَ طَلَباً لِتَأْشيرةٍ to apply for a visa; حَصَلَ على تَأْشيرةِ دُخولٍ to get a visa; مَنَح تَأْشيرةَ دُخولٍ to provide with a visa

مُؤَشِّر *n* |مُؤَشِّرات| ① [عَلامة] indication, sign; indicator; مُؤَشِّر يَدُلُّ على أنّ ... an indication that ... ② (Mech) pointer, needle; يُشيرُ المُؤَشِّرُ إلى الشَمالِ the needle points to the north; مُؤَشِّر ساعةٍ the hand of a clock ③ (Econ) index; ارْتَفَعَ \ انْخَفَضَ المُؤَشِّرُ ٢٣ نُقْطةً the index rose/fell 23 points ④ (Comput) cursor; مُؤَشِّر الفَأْرةِ the mouse cursor; وَضْع مُؤَشِّرِ الفَأْرةِ فوق شَيْءٍ mouseover

إشْفى *n* |أشافٍ| (Tools) awl, bodkin

أُشْنة *n* lichen

أشور *n* |dipt f| Assyria

أشوريّ *adj*, *n* Assyrian

أَصَّدَ *v* to close

أَصَرَ *v* |i; أَصْر| to tighten

إصْر *n* |آصار| treaty, covenant, contract

آصِرة *n* |أَواصِرُ| bond, tie; أواصِر الصَداقةِ bonds of friendship; تَوْطيد \ تَعْميق الأواصِرِ strengthening/deepening ties

أَصيص *n* |أُصُص| flowerpot; أَصيص الزُهورِ flowerpot; أَصيص من الزُهورِ \ النَباتِ potted flowers/plants

إصْطَبْل *n* see إسْطَبْل

إصْفَهان *n* |f| Isfahan (*city in Iran*)

أَصُلَ *v* |u; أَصالة| ① [شَرُفَ] to be of noble origin ② [كانَ مُبْتَكَراً] to be original

أَصَّلَ *v* ① [إثْبات المَصْدَرِ] to establish the origin of; to etymologize; to document ② [أَسَّسَ] to found, to give a firm foundation

تَأَصَّلَ *v* to be/become rooted; to derive one's origin; تَأَصَّلَ في التَفْكيرِ الغَرْبيِّ to have its roots in Western thinking

اسْتَأْصَلَ *v* ① [اقْتَلَعَ] to uproot, to eliminate, to eradicate; اسْتَأْصَلَ شَيْئاً من جُذورِهِ to eradicate sth from its roots ② (Med) to remove, to cut (out), to excise; اسْتَأْصَلَ وَرَماً to excise a tumour; اسْتَأْصَلَ اللَوْزَتَيْنِ to remove the tonsils; اسْتَأْصَلَ بِواسِطةِ عَمَليّةٍ جِراحيّةٍ to remove surgically

اسْتِئْصال *n* ① [اقْتِلاع] removal, elimination, eradication; اسْتِئْصال الفَقْرِ eradication of poverty ② (Med) (surgical) removal, excising; اسْتِئْصال وَرَمٍ removal of a tumor; اسْتِئْصال رَحِمٍ hysterectomy; اسْتِئْصال الثَدْيِ mastectomy

أَصالة *n* authenticity; originality; أَصالة عَمَلٍ فَنّيٍّ the authenticity of a piece of art

أَصْل *n* |أُصول| ① [نَسَب] origin, source; descent, lineage, birth; أَصْل كُلِّ هذه المَشاكِلِ the source of all this trouble; بَلَد أَصْلِه one's country of origin; حِصان مَجْهول الأَصْلِ a horse of unknown breeding; هي من أَصْلٍ مِصْريٍّ, هي مِصْريّةُ الأَصْلِ she is from Egypt, she is Egyptian by birth; (مُنْحَدِر) من أَصْلٍ عَريقٍ of noble origin; في الأَصْلِ, أَصْلاً originally, primarily; essentially, basically; by definition; أَنْكَرَ أَصْلَهُ to renounce one's origins ② [أساس] fundamentals, foundation; أُصول الفِقْهِ foundations of Islamic jurisprudence; legal theory; أُصول الرِياضيّاتِ fundamentals of mathematics; أُصول المُجامَلاتِ etiquette, manners ③ (Busn) أُصول assets; أُصول شَرِكةٍ a company's assets ④ (Ling) root; أَصْل الكَلِمةِ the root of a word ⑤ [وَثيقة] original; النُسْخة الأَصْل the original text; نُسْخة طِبْقَ الأَصْلِ an accurate copy; صورة \ رَسْم طِبْقَ الأَصْلِ a true-to-life portrait

أَصْليّ *adj* ① [أساسيّ] authentic, real, true, genuine, pure; original, primary; native; لُغة أَصْليّة native language; بَلَد أَصْليّ native country; شَكْل أَصْليّ original form; ثَمَن أَصْليّ cost price; ساكِن أَصْليّ native; original inhabitant; السُكّان الأَصْليّونَ the native population; the natives; الأُسْلوب الأَصْليّ لِفَنّانٍ the authentic style of an artist; لَوْحة أَصْليّة لِرِمْبْرانْد an authentic Rembrandt painting; المَعْنى الأَصْليّ لِكَلِمةٍ the original meaning of a word; في الحالةِ الأَصْليّةِ in its original state; أَرْجَعَ \ أعادَ شَيْئاً إلى حالَتِهِ الأَصْليّةِ to restore sth to its original state ② (Ling) root (*before n*); حَرْف

أَصْليّ radical **3** (Maths) prime; عَدَد أَصْليّ prime number

أُصوليّ **A** *adj* fundamentalist; إسْلاميّون أُصوليّون fundamentalist Islamists

B *n* (religious) fundamentalist

أُصوليّة *n* fundamentalism; أُصوليّة إسْلاميّة Islamic fundamentalism

أَصيل **A** *adj* |أُصَلاءُ| original, authentic, genuine, pure; فَرَضيّة أَصيلة an original hypothesis; جَواد أَصيل thoroughbred; كَلْب أَصيل a pure-bred dog

B *n* |أَصائِلُ, آصال| late afternoon; في وَقْتِ الأَصيلِ in the late afternoon

تَأْصيليّ *adj* authentication (*before n*)

مُتَأَصِّل *adj* inherent, ingrained; deep-rooted, deep-seated; كَراهية مُتَأَصِّلة a deep-seated hatred

2 **أَصَلة** *n* (Zool) boa (*Boidae*); python (*Pythonidae*)

‹ **أَطَّرَ** *v* to frame

إطار *n* |إطارات, أُطُر| **1** [نطاق] frame, casing; إطار نافِذةٍ \ باب window/door frame; إطار مِرْآةٍ mirror frame; إطار نَظّارةٍ (eyeglass) frames; إطار لَوْحةٍ the frame of a painting **2** (Comput) window; الإطار النَشِط the active window **3** (fig) framework, scope, context; إطار تَشْريعيّ a legislative framework; في إطارِ ... within the framework of ..., as a part of ...; ضِمْنَ إطارِ النظامِ الاجْتِماعيِّ within the social framework; وَضَعَ المَوْضوعَ في إطارٍ مُعَيَّنٍ to put the matter in a particular context **4** [عَجَلة] tyre, tube; إطار خارِجيّ, إطار هَواءٍ tyre; إطار داخِليّ inner tube; إطار احْتِياطيّ spare tyre; نَفَخ إطاراً to inflate a tyre; صَلَّح إطاراً to repair a tyre **5** (P&P) box **6** [كادِر] |أُطُر| executive; الأُطُر executives, (higher) management; إطار قِياديّ staff; أُطُر مُتَوَسِّطة middle management

إطاريّ *adj* contextual; frame-like, framework (*before n*); اتِّفاقيّة إطاريّة framework agreement

تَأْطير *n* management, supervision

مُؤَطَّر *adj* framed

‹ **أَطيط** *n* **1** [صَوْت أَشْياءَ غَيْر حَيّةٍ] creaking noise; أَطيط البابِ creaking of the door **2** [جَمَلٍ] bray (*of a camel*)

‹ **أَطْلَس** **A** *n* **1** [خَرائط] atlas; أَطْلَس العالَمِ atlas of the world; بَحَثَ عن شَيْءٍ في الأَطْلَسِ to look something up in the atlas **2** [جِبال] (جِبال) الأَطْلَسِ the Atlas Mountains; الأَطْلَس الكَبير the High Atlas; الأَطْلَس المُتَوَسِّط the Middle Atlas; الأَطْلَس الصَغير the Anti-Atlas, the Lesser Atlas

B *adj* see طلس

أَطْلَسيّ *adj* Atlantic; المُحيط الأَطْلَسيّ the Atlantic Ocean; الحِلْف الأَطْلَسيّ the North Atlantic Treaty Organisation, NATO

‹ **أَطوم** *n* |أُطُم, آطِمة| (Zool) dugong, sea cow (*Dugong dugon*)

‹ **آغا, آغة** *n* agha (*official title in the Ottoman empire, now used as a personal title in some areas of the Arab world*)

‹ **إغْريقيّ** **A** *adj* |إغْريق, أَغارِقة| (ancient) Greek; الميثولوجيا الإغْريقيّة Greek mythology; (اللُغة) الإغْريقيّة ancient Greek (*language*)

B *n* |إغْريق, أَغارِقة| (ancient) Greek (*person*)

‹ **أَغُسْطُس** *n* (Egypt, Gulf) August

‹ **أَفِدَ** *v* |a; أَفَد| to approach

‹ **إفْران** *n* |dipt f| Ifrane (*city in Morocco*)

‹ **أَفْروآسِيَويّ** *adj* Afro-Asian; اللُغات الأَفْروآسِيَويّة the Afro-Asian languages

‹ **أَفَرول** *n* |أَفَرولات| jumpsuit

‹ **إفْريز** *n* |أَفاريزُ| frieze; edge; إفْريز مَنْحوت a sculptured frieze

‹ **إفْريقيّ** **A** *adj* African; شَمال إفْريقيّ Northern African; الاتِّحاد الإفْريقيّ African Union, AU

B *n* African

إفْريقيا *n* Africa; إفْريقيا السَوْداء sub-Saharan Africa; إفْريقيا الشَماليّة, شَمال إفْرِيقيا North Africa; جَنوب إفْرِيقيا South Africa

‹ **أَفْريل** *n* (Algeria, Tunisia) April

‹ **إفْشين** *n* |أَفاشينُ| (Chr) litany

‹ **أُفْشور** *n* offshore; مَصارِف الأُفْشور offshore banks

‹ **أَفْغانِسْتان** *n* |f| Afghanistan

أَفْغانيّ *adj, n* |أَفْغان| Afghan, Afghani

‹ **أَفَّ** *v* |u; أَفّ| to grumble

‹ **أَفْيون** *n* opium; إِنْتاج \ زِراعة الأَفْيونِ production/cultivation of opium; تَدْخين الأَفْيونِ opium smoking; تِجارة الأَفْيونِ the opium trade; كيلوغْرام \ طُنّ من الأَفْيونِ a kilo/ton of opium; كانَ مُدْمِناً على الأَفْيونِ to be addicted to opium

‹ **أَقّت ,مُؤَقّت** see وقت

‹ **أُقْحُوان** *n* |أَقاحيُّ| (Bot) mum (*Chrysanthemum*); أُقْحُوان المُروجِ daisy (*Leucanthemum*)

‹ **الأُقْصُر** *n* |f| Luxor (*city in Egypt*)

‹ **أُقّة** *n* |أُقَق| *a measure of weight, approx 1.25 kg*

‹ **أَقْلَمَ** *v* |i; أَقْلَمة| to acclimatize

تَأَقْلَمَ *v* to adapt oneself, to acclimatize oneself; تَأَقْلَمَ مع شَيْءٍ to adapt oneself to sth; تَأَقْلَمَ مع الظُروفِ \ الأَجْواءِ to adapt oneself to circumstances/the weather

أَقْلَمة *n* adaptation, acclimatization; adapting; أَقْلَمة مع شَيْءٍ adaptation to sth; adapting to sth

إِقْليم *n* |أَقاليمُ| **1** (Geog) district; region; province; territory; داخِلَ \ خارِجَ إِقْليمٍ inside/outside a region **2** ▶ (Meteorol) climate zone

إِقْليميّ *adj* regional; provincial; territorial; مَجْلِس إِقْليميّ provincial council; المِياه الإِقْليميّة territorial waters; على مُسْتَوًى إِقْليميٍّ at the regional level; مُسْتَشْفًى إِقْليميّ a regional hospital

إِقْليميّة *n* regionalism

تَأَقْلُم *n* adaptation, acclimatization; تَأَقْلُم مع شَيْءٍ adaptation to sth; قُدْرة على التَأَقْلُم adaptability

مُتَأَقْلِم *adj* adapted, acclimatized; كانَ مُتَأَقْلِماً مع شَيْءٍ to be adapted to sth

‹ **إِقْليد** *n* |أَقاليدُ| key

‹ **أَقَنْثة ,أَقَنْثا** *n* (Bot) acanthus (*Acanthaceae*)

‹ **أُقْنوم** *n* |أَقانيمُ| (Chr) hypostasis (*each of the three persons of the Trinity*)

‹ **أَكّاديّ** **A** *adj* Akkadian; (اللُغة) الأَكّاديّة Akkadian (*language*) **B** *n* Akkadian (*person*)

‹ **أَكادير** *n* |dipt f| Agadir (*city in Morocco*)

‹ **أَكاديميّ** *adj* academic; دِراسة أَكاديميّة academic studies

أَكاديمية *n* academy; أَكاديمية عَسْكَريّة (NA) military academy

تَأَفَّفَ *v* to grumble; to groan

أُفّ *excl* ugh!

تَأَفُّف *n* grumbling, grousing

مُتَأَفِّف **A** *adj* grumpy **B** *n* grumbler, complainer

‹ **أُفُق ,أُفْق** *n* |آفاق| **1** ▶ [خطّ السَماءِ] horizon; في الأُفُقِ on the horizon; لاحَ أَمَلٌ في الأُفُقِ there was a glimmer of hope on the horizon; وراء الأُفُقِ beyond the horizon; جَوّاب آفاقٍ globetrotter **2** ▶ [فُرْصة] perspective, prospect; فَتَحَ آفاقاً (جَديدةً) to open up new perspectives; آفاق حَسَنة a good prospect; أُفُق مُسْتَقْبَليّ future, perspective; آفاق مُسْتَقْبَليّة prospects; وَظيفة تَفْتَحُ آفاقاً مُسْتَقْبَليّةً a job with career prospects **3** ▶ [مَدى المَعْرِفةِ] horizon; وَسَّعَ أُفُقَهُ to broaden/extend one's horizons; واسِع الأُفُقِ broad-minded, open minded; ضَيِّق الأُفُقِ narrow-minded; short-sighted

أَفّاق *n* **1** ▶ [جَوّال] tramp, vagabond, vagrant **2** ▶ [من لا يَثْبُتُ على رَأْيٍ] a fickle person

أُفُقيّ *adj* horizontal; خطّ \ مُسَطَّح أُفُقيّ a horizontal line/plane

‹ **أَفَكَ** *v* |i; أَفْك| to lie

إِفْك *n* lie, untruth

أَفّاك *n* liar

‹ **أَفَلَ** *v* |u; أُفُول| to fade away; to set (*stars*); أَفَلَ نَجْمُهُ his fame has faded

آفِل *adj* |آفِلون ,أُفول ,أُفَّل| passing, transitory; declining, decreasing; vanishing, disappearing, fading

أُفول *n* disappearance, decline, fading away

‹ **أَفْلاطون** *n* |dipt| Plato (*classical Greek philosopher*)

‹ **أَفِنَ** *v* |i; أَفْن| to be stupid

أَفَن *n* stupidity

مَأْفون *adj* stupid

‹ **أَفَنْدِم** *n* (Egypt) sir; نَعَمْ يا أَفَنْدِم! yes, sir! (*often sarcastic*); أَفَنْدِم؟ sorry?, excuse me?

‹ **أَفَنْدي** *n* sir

(Idiom) يوسُف أَفَنْدي mandarin, tangerine

‹ **أَفيش** *n* |أَفيشات| placard, poster

أَكاسِيا *n* (Bot) acacia (*Acacia*)

أُكْتوبر *n* (NA, Gulf) October; في (شَهْرِ) أُكْتوبر in October; حَرْب أُكْتوبر October War (*Arab-Israeli war in 1973*)

أَكَّدَ *v* ① [ثَبَّتَ \ قَرَّرَ] to confirm, to affirm; to assure; أَكَّدَ أنّ ... to confirm that ...; أَكَّدَ ظَنًّا to confirm an assumption; أَكَّدَ لِشَخْصٍ أنّ ... to assure sb that ...; أَكَّدَ أَقْوالَ شَخْصٍ to confirm sb's story; أَكَّدَ صِحَّةَ النَبَأ to affirm a report ② [شَدَّدَ] to emphasize, to stress, to underline, to accentuate

تَأَكَّدَ *v* ① [تَثَبَّتَ] to check, to verify, to make certain; تَأَكَّدَ من شَيْءٍ to check sth, to make sure of sth; تَأَكَّدَ من أنّ ... to make sure that ...; تَأَكَّدَ من جَوابِ سُؤالٍ to check the answer to a question; تَأَكَّدَ من صِحّةِ شَيْءٍ to check the accuracy of sth ② [تَوَثَّقَ] to be affirmed, to be confirmed; تَأَكَّدَتْ هَواجِسي my foreboding was confirmed ③ [ثَبَتَ] to be certain; تَأَكَّدَ الأَمْرُ it is certain ④ [تَيَقَّنَ] to be sure, to be convinced

أَكيد *adj* certain, sure; أَكيد! certainly!, sure!; غَيْر أَكيدٍ uncertain; هذا أَمْرٌ أَكيدٌ it is an established fact, it is sure; من الأَكيد أنّ ... it is certain that ...

تَأَكُّد *n* certainty; assurance; عَدَم التَأَكُّد uncertainty; للتَأَكُّد التامّ with absolutely certainty ...; من أَجْلِ التَأَكُّد just to be sure; يُمْكِنُ التَأَكُّدُ مِنْهُ verifiable

تَأْكيد *n* |تَأْكيدات| ① [تَثْبيت] confirmation, affirmation; بالتَأْكيدِ certainly, surely; بِكُلِّ تَأْكيدٍ ,طَبْعاً بالتَأْكيدِ definitely, certainly, surely; بالتَأْكيد نَعَمْ! certainly; بالتَأْكيد لا! certainly not!; تَأْكيداً لِشَيْءٍ in confirmation of sth; هذا سَيَفْشَلُ بالتَأْكيدِ that's bound to go wrong; رَفَضَ النَفْيَ أو التَأْكيدَ to neither confirm nor deny; لم يَرِدْ تَأْكيدٌ للنَبَأ من مَصْدَرٍ مُسْتَقِلٍّ the report has not been confirmed by a reliable source ② [شَدّة] emphasis; accentuation, emphasizing; لِتَأْكيدِ شَيْءٍ to underline sth, to emphasize sth

تَأْكيديّ *adj* emphatic

مُؤَكَّد *adj* certain, sure; confirmed; من المُؤَكَّدِ أنّ ... it is certain that; من شِبْهِ المُؤَكَّدِ as good as certain; من المُؤَكَّدِ أنَّهُ لن يَرْجِعَ one thing is certain: he is not coming back; باتَ من المُؤَكَّدِ أنّ ... it has been asserted that; غَيْر مُؤَكَّدٍ uncertain; unconfirmed; مَعْلومات غَيْر مُؤَكَّدةٍ unconfirmed information

مُؤَكِّد *adj* affirming, assuring

مُتَأَكِّد *adj* certain, sure; convinced; مُتَأَكِّد تَماماً completely convinced, 100% sure; كانَ مُتَأَكِّداً من شَيْءٍ to be certain of the sth; أنا مُتَأَكِّدٌ من هذا الأَمْرِ I am certain of this matter; كانَ مُتَأَكِّداً (من) أنّ ... to be sure that ...; أنا مُتَأَكِّدٌ أَنَّهُ يَعْرِفُ ذلك I'm sure (that) he knows that

1 **أَكَرَ** *v* |i; أَكْر| to plough

أَكّار *n* ploughman

2 **أُكْرة** *n* |أُكَر| ball; sphere, globe; knob; أُكْرة بابٍ doorknob

أَكْريليك *n* acrylic

أَكْزيما ,إِكْزيما *n* eczema

أوكْسِجين ,أُكْسِجين *n* oxygen

أَكْسَدَ *v* |i; أَكْسَدة| to oxidize

تَأَكْسَدَ *v* to oxidize; to rust; يَتَأَكْسَدُ الحَديدُ iron rusts

أَكْسَدة *n* oxidation; مُضادّ الأَكْسَدةِ antioxidant

أُكْسيد ,أوكْسيد *n* |أَكاسيدُ| oxide; ثاني أُكْسيد الكَرْبون carbon dioxide, CO_2; انْبِعاثات ثاني أُكْسيد الكَرْبون CO_2 emissions; أَوَّل أُكْسيد الكَرْبون carbon monoxide; تَسَمُّم أَوَّل أُكْسيد الكَرْبون carbon monoxide poisoning

تَأَكْسُد *n* oxidation; مُضادّ التَأَكْسُدِ antioxidant

أَكْسِسْوار *n* |أَكْسِسْوارات| accessory

إِكْسير *n* elixir; potion; إِكْسير الحَياةِ elixir of life; إِكْسير الحُبِّ love potion

أَكَلَ *v* |u; أَكْل| ① [تَناوَلَ الطَعامَ] to eat; to eat up; أَكَلَ الخُضْرةَ to eat vegetables; شَخْص لا يَأْكُلُ اللَحْمةَ a person who does not eat meat; a vegetarian; لا يُؤْكَلُ inedible; هذا اللَحْمُ لا يُؤْكَلُ this meat is inedible; أَكَلَ من صَحْنٍ to eat from a plate ② [نَخَرَ] to eat away, to corrode, to erode; يَأْكُلُ الصَدأُ الحَديدَ the rust is eating away the iron ③ [حَكَّ] to itch ④ [أَخَذَ] أَكَلَ الرِبا to take usurious interest

Idioms أَكَلَ عَلَيْه الدَهْرُ وَشَرِبَ to be very old, to be obsolete; أُكِلْتُ يَوْمَ أُكِلَ الثَوْرُ الأَبْيَضُ *to seal one's fate by not preventing harm to an ally*

أَكَّلَ *v* to feed; أَكَّلَ شَخْصاً شَيْئاً to feed sb sth, to give sb sth to eat; أَكَّلَ أَطْفالَهُ to feed one's children

آكَلَ *v* |Form IV; imperf يُؤْكِلُ| to feed, to give to eat

تَأَكَّلَ *v* to be eaten; to be eaten away, to corrode; to be old/worn

تآكَلَ *v* to be eaten away, to corrode; to be old/worn; تآكَلَ تَدْريجيًّا to be gradually eaten away, to be whittled away; تآكَلَ من الداخِلِ to be eaten away from the inside, to corrode from within; تآكَلَتْ رَواتِبُهُمْ بِسَبَبِ الضرائِبِ their earnings were being eaten away by taxes

آكِل *n* |أَكَلة ,آكِلونَ| eater; آكِل لُحومٍ carnivore; آكِل لُحومِ البَشَرِ cannibal

أَكْل *n* **1** [تَناوُل] eating; جاهِز للأَكْلِ ready-to-eat; صالِح للأَكْلِ edible; غَيْر صالِحٍ للأَكْلِ inedible; فُطْرِيّات غَيْر صالِحةٍ للأَكْلِ inedible mushrooms; غُرْفة \ حُجْرة الأَكْلِ dining room; قبل \ أَثْناء \ بعد الأَكْلِ before/during/after eating; اشْتَهى الأَكْلَ to feel like eating; أَكْل لُحومِ البَشَرِ cannibalism **2** [طَعام] food, fare, nourishment; الأَكْل السَريع fast food; الأَكْل الصِحّيّ healthy food

أَكّال *n* glutton

أُكال *n* itch

أَكْلة *n* |أَكَلات| dish, meal; أَكْلة خَفيفة a small meal, a snack; أَكْلة دَسِمة a heavy meal, a rich dish

أَكول *n* glutton

تآكُل *n* **1** (Geol) erosion, weathering; تآكُل الصُخورِ rock erosion **2** [مَعادِنَ] corrosion **3** [تَحاتّ] decay

تَأَكُّل *n* erosion; corrosion

مَأْكَل *n* |مَآكِلُ| food; مَآكِل شَهِيّة delicious food; تَأْمين المَأْكَلِ والمَشْرَبِ securing food and water

مَأْكول **A** *adj* edible; فِطْر مَأْكول edible mushroom
B *n* |مَأْكولات| food, snacks; مَأْكولات سَريعة fast food; مَأْكولات hot/cold snacks; مَأْكولات ساخِنة \ بارِدة seafood; مَأْكولات خَفيفة light snacks; مَأْكولات دَسِمة fatty foods; rich foods بَحْرِيّة

مُتآكِل *adj* rusty, corroded; eroded; degraded; decayed, rotten; صُخور مُتآكِلة eroded rocks; غَضاريف مُتآكِلة eroded cartilage; جُثّة مُتآكِلة a decaying corpse

مُتَأَكِّل *adj* corroded, eroded

‹ **أَكْليروس** *n* (Chr) clergy

إكْليروسيّ *adj* (Chr) clerical

‹ **إكْليشيه** *n* |إكْليشيهات| cliché

‹ **إكْلينيكيّ** *adj* clinical

‹ **أَكَمة** *n* |أَكَمات, آكام| hill; heap of stones

‹ **إكْوادور** *n* |f| Ecuador

إكْوادوريّ *adj*, *n* Ecuadorian

‹ **أَكورْدِيون** *n* accordion

‹ **الْ** *article* the; الكِتاب the book; كِتاب الطالِبِ the student's book; الحُرِّيّة والمُساواة والأُخوّة liberty, equality, fraternity; ذَهَب للبَيْتِ to go to the house; الْتَزَم بالقَرارِ to abide by the resolution

‹ **إلاّ** *conj* **1** [ما عَدا] except, save, with the exception of, apart from, but; لا ... إلاّ ... only, merely, but, just; not ... until; لم يَأْتِ أَحَدٌ إلاّ أَحْمَدُ only Ahmed came; بيعَت البَضائِعُ إلاّ قِطْعةٌ واحِدةٌ all the goods but one have been sold; لا يُمْكِنُ أنْ تَهْبُط على هذا المَطارِ إلاّ طائِراتٌ صَغيرةٌ only small plains can land at this airport; لا إلَهَ إلاّ اللهُ there is no god but God; لم نَرَ إلاّ الأَشْجارَ we didn't see anything but trees; هذه الخُطْوةُ لَيْسَتْ إلاّ مُناوِرةً لِكَسْبِ الوَقْتِ this step is just a stalling tactic; لم تَصِلْنا الدَفْعةُ الأولى إلاّ في شَهْرِ يَنايِر we didn't receive the first payment until January; لم يَبْعَثْ لي الخَبَرَ إلاّ بالأَمْسِ he just sent me the message yesterday; لَمْ يَبْقَ لي إلاّ ثَلاثُ سَجائِرَ I have only three cigarettes left; لم تَسْتَغرِق المَعْرَكةُ إلاّ دَقيقَتَيْنِ فَحَسْب the battle lasted only two minutes **2** [إنْ لا] see إنْ 2 **3** [إلاّ أنّ] but, however; إلاّ أنّ but, however, only; كانَ يَعْتَزِمُ الإعْلانَ عَنْها إلاّ أنّ الظُروف لم تَسْمَح بِذَلِكَ he was determined to make an announcement but the circumstances didn't allow it; غابَ لَحَظاتٍ إلاّ أنّهُ ما لَبِثَ أنْ عادَ he was gone for awhile but soon returned **4** [إلاّ وَ] but, without; ما من شَهْرٍ يَمُرُّ إلاّ وَتَنْكَشِفُ فَضيحةٌ not a month passes without a scandal being discovered; ما من أَحَدٍ في الشارِعِ إلاّ وَيَعْرِفُني there is no one in the street that doesn't know me; لم يَشْعُرْ إلاّ و ... before he noticed ... **5** [إلاّ إذا] إلاّ إذا unless, except when; لا يُسْجَنُ أَيُّ شَخْصٍ إلاّ إذا ارْتَكَبَ جَريمةً nobody was imprisoned unless they had committed a crime **6** [مُنْقَطِع] لم نَرَ فَرَساً إلاّ حِماراً we didn't see any horses, just a donkey **7** [ساعة] في الساعةِ الثالِثةِ إلاّ رُبْعاً at a quarter to three; الثالِثةِ إلاّ الثُلُث twenty to three

ألا *conj* see أ

أَلاّ *conj* see لا I 2

‹ **ألاباما** *n* Alabama (*US state*)

‹ **ألاسْكا** *n* Alaska (*US state*)

[1]‹ **أَلَبَ** *v* |i-u; أَلْب| to gather

أَلَّبَ *v* |على| to incite, to agitate, to stir up; أَلَّبَ شَخْصاً (ضِدَّ \ على شَيْءٍ) to stir up sb (against sth)

تَأَلَّبَ *v* **1** [تآمَرَ] to plot, to conspire **2** [تَجَمَّعَ] to rally, to gather

تَأْليب *n* incitement; inciting, agitating, stirring up; تَأْليب شَخْصٍ على شَيْءٍ inciting sb against sth; تَأْليب الرَأْيِ العامِّ على إدارَتِهِ stirring up public opinion against his administration

[2]‹ **الألْب** *n* the Alps; (جِبال) الألْب the Alps

‹ **أَلْبانيا** *n* Albania

أَلْبانيّ **A** *adj* |أَلْبان| Albanian; (اللُغة) الأَلْبانيّة Albanian (*language*) **B** *n* |أَلْبان| Albanian (*person*)

‹ **أَلْبوم** *n* |أَلْبومات| **1** [صُوَر] album; أَلْبوم صُوَر a photo album **2** [أغانٍ] album; record; CD; أَلْبوم نانْسي عَجْرَم الجَديد Nancy Ajram's new album

‹ **إلخ** *abbr* etc., et cetera (*abbreviation of* إلى آخِرِهِ)

‹ **إلْسَلْفادور** *n* see سلفادور

‹ **آلْطو** *n* (Mus) alto

[1]‹ **أَلْف** *n* |mf; آلاف, أُلوف| **1** [عِدّة] thousand; أَلْف شُكْرٍ many thanks; أَلْف لَيْلَةٍ ولَيْلة One Thousand and One Nights, the Arabian Nights; عَشَرة آلاف ten thousand; ما يَقْرُبُ أَلْفاً around a thousand; واحِد في الأَلْفِ من السُكّانِ 0.1 percent of the population **2** [فَتْرة ١٠٠٠ سَنةٍ] millennium; الأَلْف الثاني the second millennium

أَلْفيّة *n* millennium; الأَلْفيّة الثالِثة ق م the third millennium BC; جيل الأَلْفيّة the millenials

[2]‹ **أَلِف** *n* |f| *name of the letter* أ; من أَلِفِهِ إلى يائِهِ from A to Z; أَلِف مَقْصورة alif maqsura (*long alif at the end of a word, written as a ya without dots:* ى); الأَلِف واللام alif-lam, the definite article

[3]‹ **أَلِفَ** *v* |a; أَلْف| **1** [تَعَوَّدَ] to be/become familiar with; to be/become attached to **2** [صارَ أَليفاً] to be/become tame

أَلَّفَ *v* **1** [شَكَّلَ] to form, to set up, to put together; أَلَّفَ وِزارةً \ حُكومةً to form a government **2** [تَأَلَّفَ] to compose (of), to make up; كُلُّهُمْ يُؤَلِّفونَ عائِلةً واحِدةً they are all one big family; المُهَرِّبونَ يُؤَلِّفونَ شَبَكةً دَوْليّةً للتَهْريبِ the smugglers make up an international smuggling ring **3** [كِتاباً] to write; أَلَّفَ رِوايةً \ مَقالاً to write a novel/article; أَلَّفَ قَصيدةً to write a poem **4** (Mus) to compose, to write; أَلَّفَ أُغْنيةً to compose a song (*music*); to write a song (*music with lyrics*) **5** [حَيَواناً] to domesticate, to tame; أَلَّفَ حَيَواناً to tame an animal **6** [وَفَّقَ] to reconcile; أَلَّفَ بين المُتَخاصِمَيْنِ to reconcile two contending parties

آلَفَ *v* to become familiar with

تَأَلَّفَ *v* |من| to be composed of, to consist of; يَتَأَلَّفُ المَنْزِلُ من طابِقَيْنِ the house is made up of two stories; تَتَأَلَّفُ اللَجْنةُ من خَمْسةِ قُضاةٍ the committee is composed of five judges

تآلَفَ *v* to harmonize, to be in harmony

ائْتَلَفَ *v* **1** (Pol) to form a coalition **2** [انْسَجَمَ] to go together, to harmonize; to be united; ائْتَلَفَ مع شَيْءٍ to harmonize with sth

ائْتِلاف *n* **1** [وِفاق] coalition; union; ائْتِلاف حُكوميّ (government) coalition; ائْتِلاف حاكِم ruling coalition; ائْتِلاف يَساريّ \ يَمينيّ a left/right coalition; ائْتِلاف مع حِزْبٍ آخَرَ a coalition with another party; شَريك في الائْتِلافِ coalition partner **2** (Mus) chord

ائْتِلافيّ *adj* coalition (*before n*); حُكومة ائْتِلافيّة a coalition government

إلْف *n* |آلاف| companion, close friend, intimate, confidant

أُلْفة *n* **1** [أُنْس] intimacy, familiarity; friendship; جَوّ الأُلْفةِ an intimate atmosphere **2** [اسْم شَخْصيّ] |dipt| Oulfa, Ulfa (*female given name*)

أَلِيف **A** *adj* |أُلَفاءُ| **1** [حَميم] friendly; familiar; intimate; مَكان أَلِيف an intimate place; a familiar place; وَجْه أَلِيف a familiar face **2** [داجِن] tame, domesticated, domestic; حِصان أَلِيف a tame horse; قِطّ \ كَلْب أَلِيف domestic cat/dog; حَيَوانات أَلِيفة pets

B *n* |أُلَفاءُ| close friend

تَأْلِيف *n* |تَآلِيفُ| **1** [تَشْكيل] formation; composition; تَأْلِيف الحُكومةِ الجَديدةِ the formation of the new government **2** [عَمَلٌ فَنِّيٌّ] writing; composition; تَأْلِيف موسيقيّ (musical) composition; رِواية من تَأْلِيفِ ... written by ...; رِواية من تَأْلِيفِ نَجيب مَحْفوظ a novel written by Naguib Mahfouz

مُؤَلَّف **A** *adj* composed, consisting; فَرِيق مُؤَلَّف من ٨ أَشْخاصٍ a team composed of eight people; طاقِم مُؤَلَّف من سِتّةِ أَفْرادٍ a crew of six

B *n* |مُؤَلَّفات| book, writing; مُؤَلَّفات literature, works; مُؤَلَّفات عِلْميّة \ أَدَبيّة scientific/literary works; مُؤَلَّفات حول الحَرْب العالَميّة الثانِية literature on the Second World War

مُؤَلِّف *n* author, writer, novelist; compiler, composer; مُؤَلِّف كِتابٍ the author of a book; مُؤَلِّف قاموس the compiler of a dictionary; مُؤَلِّف مَوْهوب a talented writer; مَجْهول المُؤَلِّفِ author unknown

مَأْلوف *adj* **1** [مَعْروف] familiar; مُحيط مَأْلوف familiar surroundings; شَخْص مَأْلوف a familiar person; وَجْهُكَ مَأْلوفٌ لَدَيَّ you look familiar **2** [عاديّ] conventional, customary; usual, ordinary; غَيْر مَأْلوفٍ unconventional, unusual; unfamiliar; من المَأْلوفِ (أَنّ) usually, normally

مُتَآلِف *adj* harmonious; loving

‹ **أَلْفا** *n* alpha (*Greek letter*)

‹ **أَلِفْباء** *n* |f| alphabet, ABCs; principles, fundamentals; أَلِفْباء الطَّبْخ العَرَبيّ the fundamentals of Arab cooking

أَلِفْبائيّ *adj* alphabetical; سِجِلّ \ فِهْرِس أَلِفْبائيّ an alphabetical register/index; تَرْتيب أَلِفْبائيّ alphabetical order; بِتَسَلْسُلٍ أَلِفْبائيٍّ, حَسَب التَّرْتيبِ الأَلِفْبائيِّ in alphabetical order

‹ **أَلَقَ** *v* |i; أَلْق| to sparkle, to glitter, to twinkle; أَلَقَ البَرْقُ lightning flashed

تَأَلَّقَ *v* to sparkle, to glitter, to twinkle; to shine; تَأَلَّقَ في إنْتاجٍ مَسْرَحيٍّ to shine in a theatrical production; قد تَأَلَّقَ نَجْمُها she was performing outstandingly

ائْتَلَقَ *v* to sparkle, to glitter, to twinkle

أَلْق *n* glow, brilliance

تَأَلُّق *n* glow, brilliance; sparkling, twinkling; تَأَلُّق النُّجومِ the twinkling of the stars; تَأَلُّق وَبَهاء glitter and glamour

مُتَأَلِّق *adj* **1** [مُشْرِق] shining, bright, radiant **2** [بارِز] brilliant; طالِب مُتَأَلِّق a brilliant student

‹ **إِلْكة** *n* elk (BrE), moose (AmE) (*Alces alces*)

‹ **إِلِكْترود** *n* electrode

‹ **إِلِكْترون** *n* |إِلِكْترونات| electron; إِلِكْترون حُرّ a free electron; الإِلِكْترونات في المَدار الخارِجيّ للذَّرّةِ the electrons in an atom's outer orbit

إِلِكْترونيّ *adj* electronic; e-, Web (*before n*); رِسالة إِلِكْترونيّة an email; عَبْر البَريدِ الإِلِكْترونيّ by email; كِتاب إِلِكْترونيّ e-book; قارِئ كُتُبٍ إِلِكْترونيّةٍ e-book reader; دائِرة إِلِكْترونيّة an electronic circuit; مَوْقِع إِلِكْترونيّ website; شَرِكة إِلِكْترونيّة online company; تِجارة إِلِكْترونيّة e-commerce; تَعْليم إِلِكْترونيّ e-learning; خِدْمات إِلِكْترونيّة e-services; أَجْهِزة إِلِكْترونيّة electronic devices, electronics; سَدَّدَ \ دَفَعَ بِطَريقةٍ إِلِكْترونيّةٍ to make an electronic payment

إِلِكْترونيّات *n pl* electronics; إِلِكْترونيّات اسْتِهْلاكيّة consumer electronics; صِناعة الإِلِكْترونيّاتِ the electronics industry

‹ **مُؤَلَّل** *adj* motorized

‹ **أَلِمَ** *v* |a; أَلَم| to feel pain

أَلَّمَ *v* to hurt, to cause pain; أَلَّمَ شَخْصاً to hurt sb

آلَمَ *v* |Form IV; imperf يُؤْلِمُ| to hurt, to ache, to cause pain; آلَمَ شَخْصاً to hurt sb; آلَمَ نَفْسَهُ to hurt oneself, to get hurt; آلَمَهُ بَطْنُهُ his stomach hurt; هذا يُؤْلِمُ this hurts; يُؤْلِمُهُ أَنْ ... it hurts him that ...; ماذا يُؤْلِمُكَ؟ where does it hurt?; آلَمَهُ في الصَّميمِ to be cut to the core

تَأَلَّمَ *v* to feel pain, to be in pain

أَلَم *n* |آلام| **1** [وَجَع] pain, ache; agony, suffering; أَلَم مِعَويّ intestinal pain; أَلَم نَفْسيّ emotional pain; آلام شَديدة \ حادّة severe/sharp pains; آلام مُبَرِّحة agonizing pains; أَلَم غَيْر

الله أكْبَر God is great; الله مَعَكَ God be with you, ≈ good luck; الحَمْدُ لله thank God; إكْراماً لله for God's sake; بِسْمِ الله in the name of God (*said for luck or in piety, when beginning something*); بِسْمِ الله الرَحْمنِ الرحيم in the name of God, the Compassionate, the Merciful (*formal invocation*); والله أعْلَمُ! God only knows!; الله يَرْحَمُهُ God have mercy on his soul, ≈ may he rest in peace; هذه صورةُ زَوْجي المَرْحومِ، رَحِمَهُ الله this is a picture of my late husband, may he rest in peace; بارَكَ الله, الله يُخَلّيك God bless you, ≈ thank you; الله يَرْضى عَلَيْك may God be satisfied with you (*wishing well for sb's actions*); إنْ شاءَ الله God willing, ≈ hopefully (*said when planning future activities*); إذَنْ نَراكُمْ غداً إنْ شاءَ الله! ≈ so we'll see you tomorrow then!; بِمَشيئةِ الله, بِإذْنِ الله God willing; ما شاءَ الله (*expressing appreciation, joy, praise or thankfulness for an event or person that was just mentioned*); "هذه بِنْتي صابْرينا." "ما شاءَ الله عَلَيْها!" 'This is my daughter, Sabrina.' 'Oh, isn't she beautiful!'; أُقْسِمُ باللهِ! I swear to God!; بالله عَلَيْكَ God be with you; by God; باللهِ لا تَفْعَل please don't; بِعَوْنِ الله وَتَوْفيقِه with the help of God; آمَنَ بِالله to believe in God; طَوَّلَ الله عُمْرَكَ may God give you long life; قَضاء الله \ أمْر \ حُكْم God willed/ordained it; الإنْسانُ في التَفْكيرِ والله في التَدْبيرِ man proposes, God disposes; لا إلَهَ إلاّ الله there is no god but God (*formal expression of faith in Islam*); لا حَوْلَ وَلا قوّةَ إلاّ بالله there is no power and no strength save in God (*expression of great enthusiasm, surprise or exasperation*); إنّا للهِ وَإنّا إلَيْهِ راجِعونَ to God we belong and to Him we return (*expression of exasperation or resignation*); يَلاّ see يا الله!

اللّهُمَّ *excl* **1** [هُتاف] O God!; اللّهُمَّ احْفَظْني God spare me; اللّهُمَّ ساعِدْني God help me; اللّهُمَّ اجْعَلْهُ خَيْراً please God, make it come out all right (*said when about to receive news that one fears may be bad*) **2** [إلاّ إذا] اللّهُمَّ إلاّ unless; اللّهُمَّ إلاّ إذا اتَّبَعَت الحُكومةُ سِياسةً جَديدةً unless the government will take on a new policy

إلَهيّ *adj* divine; الذَبيحة الإلَهيّة Mass; Eucharist; العِنايةُ الإلَهيّة divine providence

إلَهيّة *n* divinity, divine nature

بِلا ألَم painless; أَلَم في الرَأْسِ headache; مُحْتَمَلٍ unbearable pain; حَقْن بِلا ألَمٍ a painless injection; مُسَكِّنات الألَمِ painkillers; خَفَّفَ من آلامِ شَخْصٍ to ease sb's pain; أُصيبَ بِألَمٍ في البَطْنِ to get a stomach ache; تَلَوّى \ صَرَخَ من شِدّةِ الألَمِ to writhe/scream with pain; يَزْدادُ \ يَخِفُّ الألَمُ the pain is getting worse/better; شَعَرَ بِآلامٍ to feel pain; عانى من آلامٍ to suffer from the pain **2** (Chr) Passion (*theological term used for the suffering of Jesus in the hours before and during his crucifixion*); آلام المَسيحِ the Passion of Christ; أُسْبوع الآلامِ Holy Week

(Idiom) زَهْرة الآلام passion flower (*Passiflora*)

أليم *adj* painful; واقِع أليم a painful reality

إيلام *n* |إيلامات| pain; wound

مُؤْلِم *adj* painful, aching; غَيْر مُؤْلِم painless; تَنازُلات مُؤْلِمة painful concessions; عَمَليّة جِراحيّة مُؤْلِمة a painful operation; حادِث مُؤْلِم a painful incident

مُتَألِّم *adj* hurt; كانَ مُتَألِّماً to be hurt, to be in pain

‹ **أَلْماس** *n* diamond; أَلْماس خام \ مَصْقول a raw/polished diamond; مَنْجَم أَلْماسٍ a diamond mine; خاتَم من أَلْماسٍ a diamond ring

‹ **أَلْمانيا** *n* Germany; جُمْهوريّة أَلْمانيا الديموقْراطيّة the German Democratic Republic, GDR (*the former East Germany*)

أَلْمانيّ **A** *adj* |أَلْمان| German; (اللُغة) الأَلْمانيّة German (*language*)

B *n* |أَلْمان| German (*person*)

‹ **أَلْمِنيوم** *n* see ألومنيوم

‹ **أَلَّهَ** *v* to deify; to idolize

تَأَلَّهَ *v* to deify oneself

إلَه, **إلاه** *n* |آلِهة| god, deity; تَعَدُّد الآلِهةِ polytheism; أَقْسَمَ بِكُلِّ الآلِهةِ to swear by all the gods; عَبَدَ الآلِهةَ to worship the gods; لا إلَهَ إلاّ الله there is no god but God; يا إلَهي!, يا لَلآلِهةِ oh, my God!, good Lord!, good heavens!

الإلَهيّات *n pl* theology, divinity

إلاهة, **إلَهة** *n* goddess; أثينا إلاهةُ الحَرْبِ عند الإغْريقِ Athena is the Greek goddess of war

الله *n* God, Allah; تَاللهِ by God; واللهِ! really!, I swear!; لا واللهِ! honestly, no!; الله عَزَّ وَجَلَّ God, mighty and majestic is he;

ألوهة *n* divinity

أُلوهيّة *n* divine power; divinity; أُلوهيّة عيسى the divinity of Christ

تأْليه *n* deification, apotheosis

لاهوت *n* divinity; عِلْم اللاهوتِ theology; دَرَس عِلْمَ اللاهوتِ to study theology

ألو, **آلو** *excl* hello (*on the phone*)

ألومِنيوم, **ألَمِنْيوم** *n* aluminium (BrE), aluminum (AmE); وَرَق ألومِنيوم aluminium (BrE), aluminum foil (AmE)

إلى *prep* **1** [مَكان] to, toward; من تونس إلى الجَزائِرِ from Tunisia to Algeria; وَصَلَ إلى القاهِرةِ he arrived in Cairo **2** [زمان] until, till; إلى اللِقاءِ good-bye!, see you!; إلى مَتى ؟ for how long?; من الساعة العاشِرة إلى الخامِسةِ from ten to five; إلى غَدٍ \ الغَد until tomorrow; إلى أَجَلٍ غَيْرِ مُسَمًّى indefinitely; منذ أن يولَدَ إلى أنْ يَموتَ from birth till death **3** [تابع ل] إلَيْكَ ... here you have ..., here is ...; إلَيْكَ اقْتِراحاً here is a proposition; الأَمْرُ (عائِدٌ) إلَيْكَ it's up to you; وَما إلَيْهِ et cetera, and so on **4** [مَجازيّ] إلى غَيْرِ ذلك and the like; إلى الآخِرِ till the end; تُرْجِمَ إلى العَرَبيّةِ translated into Arabic; إلى حَدٍّ ما to a certain extent; somewhat; more or less; احْتِياجات الدَوْلةِ إلى الغِذاءِ the need of the country for food **5** [إلى أنْ] until; in such a way that

أَلْية *n* |أَلَيات| **1** [رِدْف] buttock, rump; أَلْيانِ \ أَلْيَتانِ rump, hindquarters **2** [ذَيْل] tail; fatty sheep tail (*used in cooking*)

إلْياس *n* |dipt| Ilyas, Elias (*male given name*)

الآليكْسو *n* |f| ALESCO (*Arab League Educational Cultural and Scientific Organization*)

إلينوي *n* |f| Illinois (*US state*)

أَمْ *conj* or; هل يَنْتَمي إلى الجَماعةِ أَمْ لا؟ is he part of the group or not?; هل هذا هو الحَلُّ الوَحيدُ أَمْ أنّ هُناكَ إمْكانيّةٌ أُخْرى؟ is this the only solution or is there another possibility?; شِئْنا أَمْ أَبَيْنا whether we want it or not; سَواءً كانَ أَعْمى أَمْ بَصيراً whether he is blind or sighted

إمّا *conj* either; يَجِبُ إمّا وَقْفُ المُحادَثاتِ وَإمّا تَعْليقُها the talks must either be ended or adjourned; يُؤَدّي إمّا إلى السَلامِ أو إلى الحَرْبِ it will either lead to peace or to war

أَمّا *conj* أَمّا ... فَ ... as to ..., as far as ... is concerned ...; however, on the other hand; أَمّا السُكّانُ فَهُمْ على ما يُرامُ as to the residents, they are well; أَمّا بَعْدُ so then, now to the topic (*after the preliminary greetings in a letter*)

أمارِلِّس *n* (Bot) amaryllis (*Hippeastrum or Amaryllis*)

الأَمازون, **الآمازون** *n* Amazon; غابات الأَمازون the Amazon rainforest; نَهْر الأَمازون the Amazon river

أمازيغي, **أَمازِغيّ** **A** |أمازيغ| *adj* Berber, Amazigh; (اللُغة) الأمازيغيّة Tamazight, Berber (*language*)

B *n* |أمازيغ| Berber, Amazigh (*person*)

إمْبَراطور *n* |أَباطِرة| emperor; عَصْر الأَباطِرةِ the age of empires

إمْبَراطوريّ *adj* imperial; العائِلة الإمْبَراطوريّة the imperial family

إمْبَراطوريّة *n* empire; الإمْبَراطوريّة الرومانيّة the Roman Empire; انْهيار \ سُقوط إمْبَراطوريّةٍ the collapse/fall of an empire; أَسَّسَ إمْبَراطوريّةً to found an empire

إمْبِرياليّ **A** *adj* imperialist, imperialistic; سِياسة إمْبِرياليّة imperialist policy

B *n* an imperialist

إمْبِرياليّة *n* imperialism

أُمْبولة *n* ampoule; أُمْبولة الدَواءِ an ampoule of medicine

أَمْبير *n* |أَمابيرُ| ampere, amp (*measure of electrical charge*); مِقْياس الأَمْبيرِ ammeter

أَمَد *n* |آماد| reach, range; period, span of time; قَصير الأَمَدِ of short duration, short-termed; طَويل الأَمَدِ long, long-term; خُطّة طَويلة الأَمَدِ a long-term plan; مُنْذُ أَمَدٍ طَويلٍ \ بَعيدٍ for a long time; مُنْذُ أَمَدٍ قَريبٍ for a little while now; في أَمَدٍ قَريبٍ shortly, soon, before long

أَمَرَ *v* |u; أَمْر| |ب| to order, to command, to prescribe, to instruct, to charge; أَمَرَ شَخْصاً بِأَنْ ... to order sb to ...; أَمَرَ شَخْصاً بِأَنْ يَخْرُجَ to order sb to get out; أَمَرَ شَخْصاً بِشَيْءٍ to order sb to do sth; أَمَرَ شَخْصاً بالخُروجِ \ بالسُكوتِ to order sb to get out/keep quiet; أَمَرَ بالانْسِحابِ to give orders to retreat

أَمَّرَ *v* **1** [وَلّى] to invest with authority **2** [رَسَمَ] to mark borders

آمَرَ *v* |Form III; imperf **يُؤامِرُ** ◀1▶ [شاوَرَ] to consult, to confer; آمَرَ شَخْصاً to consult sb, to confer with sb ◀2▶ [أقْنَعَ] to talk into

تَأمَّرَ *v* ◀1▶ [تَوَلّى السُلْطَةَ] to come to power ◀2▶ [تَسَلَّطَ] |على| to boss around, to bully; تَأمَّرَ على شَخْصٍ to boss sb around

تآمَرَ *v* |على| to plot, to conspire; تآمَرَ على شَخْصٍ to conspire against sb; تآمَرَ على الحُكومةِ to plot against the government

ائْتَمَرَ *v* ◀1▶ [تَشاوَرَ] to deliberate, to confer ◀2▶ [تآمَرَ] |بِ| to plot, to conspire ◀3▶ [أطاعَ] |بِ| to obey; ائْتَمَرَ بِأَمْرِ شَخْصٍ to obey sb

آمِر **A** *adj* imperious, peremptory, domineering; commanding; imperative; بِلَهْجةٍ آمِرةٍ in a peremptory tone

B *n* superior, commander, master; كانَ الآمِرَ الناهِيَ to be absolute master; آمِر الحَرَسِ الوَطَنِيِّ (Tunisia) Commander of the National Guard

أَمْر *n* ◀1▶ [طَلَب] |أوامِرُ| order, command, instruction; ordinance, decree; injunction; أَمْر قَضائِيّ a court order; أَمْر مَلَكِيّ a royal decree; أَمْر بِإلْقاءِ القَبْضِ arrest warrant; بِأَمْرِ شَخْصٍ by order of sb, at sb's command; بِأَمْرٍ من الشُرْطةِ by order of the police; (أنا) تحت أَمْرِكَ at your orders, I am at your disposal; عَدَم إطاعةِ الأوامِرِ insubordination; أَمْر بِفِعْلِ شَيْءٍ an order to do sth; الأَمْر بالهُجومِ the command to attack; أَعْطى \ أَصْدَرَ أَمْراً to give/issue an order; أطاعَ \ نَفَّذَ أَمْراً to obey/carry out an order; الْتَزَمَ \ اتَّبَعَ أَمْراً to follow orders; تَلَقّى أَمْراً to take orders; فَعَلَ شَيْئاً بِأَمْرٍ من شَخْصٍ to do sth on sb's orders; هو صاحِبُ الأَمْرِ والنَهْيِ his word is law ◀2▶ (Comput) |أوامِرُ| command; واجِهة سَطْرِ الأوامِرِ command-line interface ◀3▶ (Gram) صيغة الأَمْرِ imperative (mood)

◀4▶ [شَأْن] |أُمور| matter, affair; concern, business; thing; case; أَمْر ثانَوِيّ a secondary issue; أَمْر واقِع (an accomplished) fact, a fait accompli, status quo; خَضَعَ للأَمْرِ الواقِعِ to reconcile oneself to the facts; وَضَعَ شَخْصاً أمامَ الأَمْرِ الواقِعِ to present someone with a fait accompli; أَمْر مَفْروغ مِنْهُ a foregone conclusion; واقِع الأَمْرِ reality; أَمْرُكَ! it's up to you; في آخِرِ الأَمْرِ ultimately; في أَوَّلِ الأَمْرِ initially, at first; هو بين أَمْرَيْنِ he has two options; هو مُتَمَكِّنٌ من أَمْرِهِ he is firmly in charge; اهْتَمَّ بِأُمورِهِ الذاتيّةِ \ الشَخْصيّةِ to mind one's own business; رَتَّبَ \ نَظَّمَ الأُمورَ to arrange things; أنْهى الأَمْرَ to finish the case; أرادَ أنْ يَعْرِفَ تَفاصيلَ الأَمْرِ to want to know the details of the matter; الأُمورُ لَيْسَتْ كَذَلِكَ على الإطْلاقِ that is not the case at all; أحالَ الأَمْرَ للقَضاءِ \ إلى القَضاءِ to take a matter to court; تَدَخَّلَ في أَمْرِ شَخْصٍ to interfere in sb's business; مَهْما كانَ من أَمْرٍ whatever the case may be; لَيْسَ من أَمْرِكَ that is none of your business; هذا كُلُّ ما في الأَمْرِ that is all there is about it; الأَمْرُ الّذي أدّى إلى ... which led to ...; غادَرَ بِدونِ سابِقِ إنذارٍ، الأَمْرُ الذي أدْهَشَني he left without notice, which surprised me; وَقَّعَ الرَئيسُ الاتِّفاقيّةَ، الأَمْرُ الذي لم تُؤَيِّدْهُ المُعارَضةُ the president signed the agreement, which was not supported by the opposition

اسْتِمارة, **اسْتِمارة** *n* form; اسْتِمارة أَسْئِلةٍ questionnaire; اسْتِمارة اشْتِراكٍ registration form; مَلَأَ اسْتِمارةً to fill out a form

أَمّار *adj* inciting, instigating; النَفْس الأَمّارة بالسوءِ *the baser self that incites one to sin*

إماراتيّ **A** *adj* Emirate (*before n*) (*of the United Arab Emirates*)

B *n* Emirati

إمارة *n* ◀1▶ [بَلَد] emirate; principality; الإمارات العَرَبيّة المُتَّحِدة the United Arab Emirates ◀2▶ [مَنْصِب أمير] emirate (*the position or rank of prince*)

أمارة *n* |أمارات, أمائِرُ| indication, sign

أمير *n* |أُمَراءُ| ◀1▶ [عُضْو عائِلةٍ مَلَكيّةٍ] emir; prince; أمير الكُوَيْتِ the Emir of Kuwait; الأمير عَبْدُ اللهِ Prince Abdullah; أمير البَحْرِ admiral; صاحِب السُموِّ المَلَكيّ الأمير His Royal Highness the Prince ◀2▶ [قائِد] commander; أُمَراء الحَرْبِ warlords; أمير المُؤْمِنينَ the Commander of the Faithful (*title of the caliph and the Moroccan king*) ◀3▶ [اسْم شَخْصيّ] Amir (*male given name*)

أميريّ *adj* ◀1▶ [مَنْسوب إلى الأميرِ] royal; prince (*before n*); قَرار أميريّ a decree of the emir ◀2▶ [مَنْسوب إلى الدَوْلةِ] state (*before n*); أمْلاك أميريّة crown property

تآمُر *n* conspiracy, plot; التآمُر لِارْتِكابِ جَريمةٍ conspiracy to commit a crime; تُهْمة التآمُرِ conspiracy charges

مُؤامَرة *n* conspiracy, plot; مُؤامَرات سِياسيّة political conspiracies; مُؤامَرة أَجْنَبيّة a foreign plot; نَظَريّة المُؤامَرةِ

a conspiracy theory; مُؤامَرة ضدّ الحُكومةِ a conspiracy against the government; دَبَّرَ \ حاكَ مُؤامَرةً to hatch a plot, to plot, to conspire

مُؤْتَمَر *n* |مُؤْتَمَرات| conference, congress, meeting; مُؤْتَمَر دَوْليّ an international congress; مُؤْتَمَر صُحُفيّ \ صِحافيّ press conference; عَقَدَ مُؤْتَمَراً صُحُفيًّا to hold a press conference; مُؤْتَمَر الفيدِيو video conferencing; مُؤْتَمَر قِمّةٍ summit; مُؤْتَمَر الدُوَلِ السَبْعِ الكُبْرى the G7 meeting; مُؤْتَمَر حول السَلامِ في الشَرْقِ الأَوْسَطِ a conference on peace in the Middle East; مَرْكَز المُؤْتَمَراتِ conference centre; مائِدة المُؤْتَمَرِ conference table; عَقَدَ \ حَضَرَ مُؤْتَمَراً to hold/attend a conference; شارَكَ في مُؤْتَمَرٍ to participate in a conference; بَدَأَتْ أَعْمالُ المُؤْتَمَرِ the conference has started

مُؤْتَمِر *n* attendee (*of a conference/convention*)

مَأمور *n* commissioner; رَئِيس \ مُفَوَّض \ مَأمور \ عَميد شُرْطةٍ Chief Constable (BrE), Chief of Police (AmE); police commissioner

مَأْمورِيّة *n* [1] [مُهِمّة] order; task, assignment, mission, job; قامَ بِمَأْموريّةٍ في الخارِجِ to fulfil an assignment abroad [2] [وِحْدة إداريّة] commissioner's office

مُتَآمِر *n* conspirator

‹ **أَمْرَكَ** *v* |i; أَمْرَكة| to Americanize

تَأَمْرَكَ *v* to become Americanized

أَمْرَكة *n* Americanization

أَمْريكا, أَميرِكة *n* [1] [القارّة] America; أَمْريكا الشَماليّة North America; أَمْريكا الجَنوبيّة \ اللاتينيّة South/Latin America [2] [الوِلايات المُتَّحِدة] America, the United States

أَمْريكانيّ *adj, n* |أَمْريكان| American

أَمْريكيّ, أَميركيّ *adj, n* American

تَأَمْرُك *n* Americanization

مُتَأَمْرِك *adj* Americanized

‹ **أَمْسِ** *adv* yesterday; the recent past; ب \ في الأَمْسِ yesterday; صَباحَ أَمْسِ yesterday morning; أَمْسِ الأَوَّلَ \ أَوَّلَ أَمْسِ the day before yesterday; مَساءَ أَوَّلِ أَمْسِ the night before last

‹ **أَمْسْتِرْدام** *n* |f| Amsterdam (*capital of the Netherlands*)

‹ **أَمْشير** *n* Amshir (*the sixth month of the Coptic calendar*)

‹ **إِمَّع** *n* opportunist; sycophant

‹ **أَمْفيتامين** *n* amphetamine

‹ **أَمَلَ** *v* |u; أَمَل| to hope (for); أَمَلَ ب \ في شَيْءٍ, أَمَلَ شَيْئاً to hope for sth; أَمَلَ خَيْراً to hope for the best; أَمَلَ في التَوَصُّلِ إلى اتِّفاقٍ to hope to reach an agreement

أَمَّلَ *v* to raise hopes, to give reason to hope or expect; أَمَّلَ شَخْصاً خَيْراً to raise sb's hopes, to give sb hope

تَأَمَّلَ *v* [1] [تَفَكَّرَ] to contemplate, to think over, to reflect on, to meditate on, to consider; تَأَمَّلَ في الحَياةِ والمَوْتِ to meditate on life and death; تَأَمَّلَ مَوْضوعاً \ في مَوْضوعٍ to contemplate a matter [2] [اعْتَبَرَ] to look (intently) at, to examine; تَأَمَّلَ شَيْئاً عن بُعْدٍ to look at sth from a distance; تَأَمَّلَ شَيْئاً مَلِيًّا to take a good look at sth, to examine sth closely [3] [أَمَلَ] to hope; تَأَمَّلَ خَيْراً من شَيْءٍ to hope the best of it; تَأَمَّلَ مِنْهُ الخَيْرَ to have high hopes for sth

آمِل *adj* hopeful

أَمَل *n* |آمال| hope; أَمَل كاذِب false hope; أَعْطى شَخْصاً آمالاً كاذِبةً to give sb false hopes; آمال كَبيرة high hopes; كانَتْ لَدَيْهِ آمالٌ كَبيرةٌ حول المُسْتَقْبَلِ to have high hopes for the future; كانَ عِنْدَهُ أَمَلٌ to cherish a hope; بَصيص من الأَمَلِ a glimmer of hope; خَيْبة أَمَلٍ disappointment, letdown, disenchantment; disillusion; anticlimax; خَيْبة أَمَلٍ كَبيرة \ شَديدة a bitter disappointment; خَيْبة أَمَلٍ من \ في شَيْءٍ disappointment about sth; أَخْفى خَيْبةَ أَمَلِهِ to hide one's disappointment; خابَ أَمَلُهُ في شَيْءٍ \ شَخْصٍ to be disappointed in sth/sb; لم يُخَيِّب الآمالَ to not disappoint; على أَمَلِ أَنْ … in the hope that …; لا أَمَلَ فيهِ hopeless; وَضْع لا أَمَلَ فيهِ a hopeless situation; تَبَخَّرَ الأَمَلُ all hope has vanished; فَقَدَ \ قَطَعَ الأَمَلَ to lose hope; أَعْرَبَ عن أَمَلِهِ في … to express one's hope that …; عَلَّقَ \ عَقَدَ آمالَهُ على شَيْءٍ \ شَخْصٍ to place one's hope in sth/sb; كانَ مَحطَّ الآمالِ all hopes were riding on him; قَضى على الآمالِ to shatter all hope; تَلاشى أَمَلُنا our hopes were shattered; إنَّهُ كُلُّهُ أَمَلٌ to be full of hope; الأَمَل في غَدٍ أَفْضَلَ the hope for a better tomorrow; يَظَلُّ الأَمَلُ مَعْقوداً \ مُعَلَّقاً على … hope remains for …; خَيَّبَ اللاعِبونَ الآمالَ المَعْقودةَ عَلَيْهِم the players were straight ahead; لم يَعُدْ أمامَهُ خِيارٌ سِوى ... he had no other choice than ...

إمامة *n* imamate (*function or office of the imam*)

إماميّ *adj* مَذْهَب الشيعةِ الإماميّةِ the Imami Shiite school of jurisprudence

أَماميّ *adj* front (*before n*); foremost, forward; باب أماميّ front door; خُطوط أماميّة front lines; مَوْقِع أماميّ outpost; forward position; الصَفّ الأَماميّ the front row; مِصْباحانِ أماميّانِ headlights; دَفْع أَماميّ front-wheel drive

أُمّة *n* |أُمَم| ❶ [دَوْلة] nation; الأُمَم المُتَّحِدة the United Nations, the UN; مَجْلِس الأُمّةِ parliament ❷ [المُؤْمِنينَ] community; أُمّة مُحَمَّدٍ, أُمّة الإسْلامِ the Muslim world; أُمّة المُؤْمِنينَ the community of believers

أُمَميّ *adj* international; UN (*before n*); قوّات أُمَميّة UN troops

أُمومة *n* motherhood, maternity; رِعاية الأُمومةِ (والطُفولةِ) maternity care; إجازة \ عُطْلة الأُمومةِ maternity leave; نِظام الأُمومةِ matriarchy

أُموميّ *adj* motherly; رِعاية \ حُبّ أُموميّ(ة) motherly care/love

أُمّيّ *adj, n* illiterate

أُمّيّة *n* illiteracy; مَحْو الأُمّيّةِ the eradication of illiteracy; مُحارَبة الأُمّيّةِ the battle against illiteracy

تَأْميم *n* ❶ [مَصْدَر] nationalization; تأميم جُزْئيّ partial nationalization; تَأْميم صِناعةِ النَفْطِ nationalization of the oil industry ❷ (Geog) Tamim (*governorate in Iraq, now known as Kirkuk*)

أُمّ دُرْمان *n* |f| Omdurman (*city in Sudan*)

أَمُنَ *v* |u; أَمانة| to be reliable

أَمِنَ *v* |a; أَمْن| to be safe, to be secure; أَمِنَ من شَخْصٍ \ شَيْءٍ to be safe from sb/sth; لم يَأْمَنْ على حَياتِهِ to feel one's life is at risk

أَمَّنَ *v* ❶ [على شَيْءٍ] to insure; أَمَّنَ على شَيْءٍ ضِدّ السَرِقةِ \ الضَرَرِ \ الحَريقِ to insure sth against theft/damage/fire; أَمَّنَ على شَيْءٍ بِمِلْيونِ دولار to insure sth for one million dollars ❷ [شَخْصاً] to bring to safety ❸ [ضَمِنَ وَحَمى] to secure, to ensure; أَمَّنَ البَيْتَ ضِدّ الحَريقِ \ السَرِقةِ to secure the house against fire/burglary; أَمَّنَ مُسْتَقْبَلَهُ to secure one's future

disappointing; يَبْعَثُ على الأَمَلِ encouraging

تَأَمُّل *n* contemplation, pondering, reflection; consideration; meditation; musing; لَحْظة تَأَمُّلٍ a moment of reflection; بعد تَأَمُّلٍ all things considered; بعد تَأَمُّلٍ عَميقٍ after serious consideration; دون تَأَمُّلٍ without thought; تَأَمُّلات حول شَيْءٍ \ شَخْصٍ consideration of sth/sb

تَأَمُّليّ *adj* contemplative; نَظْرة تَأَمُّليّة a contemplative look

مُؤَمِّل *adj* hopeful, promising

مأْمول *adj* hoped for, desired; من المَأْمولِ أنْ ... it's hoped that ..., let's hope that ...; المُسْتَوى المَأْمول the desired level; حَصَلَ على المُسْتَوى المَأْمولِ من الشَفّافيّةِ to reach the desired level of transparency

أَمَّ *v* |u| ❶ (Islam) |إمامة| to lead in prayer; أَمَّ الصَلاةَ to lead in prayer; أَمَّ الناسَ في الصَلاةِ to lead people in prayer ❷ [قَصَدَ] |أَمّ| to go

أَمَّمَ *v* to nationalize; أَمَّمَ شَرِكاتٍ to nationalize companies

تَأَمَّمَ *v* to follow the example (*of sb*)

ائْتَمَّ *v* to follow the example (*of sb*)

أُمّ *n* |f; أُمَّهات| ❶ [والِدة] mother; أُمّ بَديلة surrogate mother; عيد الأُمِّ Mother's Day; حَنان الأُمِّ motherly love; لَبَن الأُمِّ mother's milk; أُمّ في العِمادِ godmother; أَصْبَحَتْ \ صارَتْ أُمًّا to become a mother ❷ [أَصْل] origin, source; أُمّ القُرى Mecca; أُمّ الدُنْيا Egypt; أُمّ الكِتابِ the Koran; the Fatiha (*the opening verse of the Koran*); أُمَّهات الكُتُبِ fundamental sources (*books*) mother tongue, native language; لُغة أُمّ native country; وَطَن أُمّ ❸ [صاحِب] owner of ..., possessor of ...; أُمّ الحِبْرِ (Zool) cephalopod; أُمّ أَرْبَعٍ وَأَرْبَعينَ centipede

Idioms بِأُمِّ عَيْنِهِ with one's own eyes, first-hand; أُمّ عَليٍّ Umm Ali (*Egyptian dessert, similar to bread pudding*); أُمُّك حورِيّة *Tunisian carrot salad with cumin, coriander and caraway*

إمام *n* |أَئِمّة| imam (*Muslim religious leader*)

أَمامَ *prep* in front of, before; opposite; أَمامَهُمْ in front of them, before their eyes; أَمامَ عَيْنَيَّ before my eyes, in front of me; إلى الأَمامِ to the front; forward, ahead, onward; قَفْزة كَبيرة إلى الأَمامِ a great leap forward; نَظَرَ إلى الأَمامِ to look

آمَنَ *v* |Form IV; imperf **يُؤْمِنُ**| to believe; آمَنَ بِشَيْءٍ to believe in sth; آمَنَ بالله to believe in God; آمَنَ بالحُرِّيّة to believe in freedom; آمَنَ بأنَّ ... to believe that ...; آمَنَ إيماناً عَميقاً بِشَيْءٍ to believe deeply in sth

تَأَمَّنَ *v* to be secured

ائْتَمَنَ *v* to entrust; ائْتَمَنَ شَخْصاً على شَيْءٍ to entrust sb with sth; to entrust sth to sb; ائْتَمَنَ شَخْصاً على سِرٍّ to entrust a secret to sb

اسْتَأْمَنَ *v* 1 [أَوْدَعَ] to entrust; اسْتَأْمَنَ شَخْصاً على مالِهِ to entrust sb with one's money 2 [طَلَبَ الأَمانَ] to ask for protection; اسْتَأْمَنَ شَخْصاً to ask sb for protection

آمِن *adj* safe, secure, peaceful; مَأْوًى آمِن a safe haven; مَلاذ آمِن a sanctuary; غَيْر آمِنٍ unsafe; كانَ آمِناً في مَكانٍ to be safe somewhere; عَلِمَ بأَنَّهُ آمِنٌ to know that one is safe

أَمْن *n* security, safety; الأَمْن العامّ public safety; أَمْن غِذائيّ food security; أَمْن قانونيّ legal certainty; أَمْن الدَوْلة, أَمْن قَوْميّ state/national security; الأَمْن الداخِليّ domestic security, internal intelligence; مَجْلِس الأَمْن (الدُوَليّ) the (UN) Security Council; جِهاز الأَمْن security, security apparatus; رِجال الأَمْن the police; إخْلال بالأَمْنِ disturbing public order; انْعِدام الأَمْنِ a lack of security; تَهْديد للأَمْنِ a security threat; ضابِط أَمْنٍ security officer; نِظام أَمْنٍ security system; قوّات الأَمْنِ security forces; حِفْظِ الأَمْنِ a مُؤْتَمَر حول السَلام والأَمْن conference on peace and security; الأَمْن في المِنْطَقة safety in the region; شَعَرَ بالأَمْن to feel safe

ائْتِمان *n* credit; بِطاقة ائْتِمانٍ a credit card; أَزْمة ائْتِمانٍ عالَميّة a global credit crisis

ائْتِمانيّ *adj* fiduciary, credit (*before n*); تَقْرير ائْتِمانيّ credit report

أَمان *n* 1 [سَلامة] safety; security; عَدَم الأَمانِ insecurity; lack of safety; حِزام أَمانٍ seat belt; بَرّ الأَمانِ safe haven/harbor, safety; في أَمانِ الله goodbye; شَعَرَ بالأَمانِ to feel safe; شُعور بالأَمانِ a sense of security; كانَ في أَمانٍ to be safe, to be out of danger 2 [حِماية] defence, protection; safeguard 3 (Hist) quarter

أَمانة *n* 1 [نَزاهة] reliability; faithfulness, fidelity, loyalty; الأَمانة الزَوْجيّة (marital) fidelity; عَدَم أَمانةٍ unreliability, disloyalty 2 [وَديعة] deposit (*sth deposited in trust*) 3 [إدارة] secretariat, secretarial department

آمِنة *n* |dipt| Amina (*female given name*)

أَمْنيّ *adj* security (*before n*), safety (*before n*); أَجْهِزة أَمْنيّة security services; شَرْط أَمْنيّ security requirement; إجْراءات أَمْنيّة safety measures; لِأَسْبابٍ أَمْنيّة for security reasons

آمين *excl* amen

أَمين A *adj* |أُمَناءُ| faithful, loyal; reliable; safe, secure; إنَّهُ في أَيادٍ أَمينةٍ he is in safe hands

B *n* |أُمَناءُ| 1 [وَظيفة] trustee, guardian; manager, chief; secretary; أَمين عامّ Secretary-General; أَمين مَكْتَبةٍ librarian; أَمين صُنْدوقٍ treasurer; cashier; مَجْلِس الأُمَناءِ board of trustees 2 [نَديم] confidant 3 [اسْم شَخْصيّ] Amin, Ameen (*male given name*)

أَمينة *n* |dipt| Amina, Amena (*female given name*)

إيمان *n* 1 [اعْتِقاد] faith, belief; أَرْكان الإيمانِ the Pillars of Faith; الإيمان بالله faith in God; إيمان راسِخ \ لا يَتَزَعْزَعُ firm/unshakeable faith; جاهَرَ بإيمانِهِ to declare one's faith 2 [اسْم شَخْصيّ] |f dipt| Eman, Iman (*female given name*)

إيمانيّ *adj* religious, belief (*before n*), faith (*before n*); عَقيدة إيمانيّة religious doctrine

تَأْمين *n* |تَأْمينات| 1 [ضَمان] assurance, safeguard, guarantee; تَمَكَّنَت القوّاتُ من تَأْمينِ وُصولِها the troops were able to assure its arrival 2 (Busn) insurance, assurance; تَأْمين صِحّيّ health insurance; تَأْمين على أَثاثِ \ عَفْشِ البَيْتِ fire and theft insurance; تَأْمين ضِدّ السَرِقة \ الحَريق insurance against burglary/fire; تَأْمين على الحَياةِ life insurance; شَرِكة تَأْمينٍ insurance company; وَكيل تَأْميناتٍ insurance agent; بوليصة \ وَثيقة تَأْمينٍ insurance policy; قِسْط تَأْمينٍ insurance premium; نِظام التَأْمينِ الاجْتِماعيّ the National Insurance system (BrE), Social Security (AmE); عَقَدَ تَأْميناً to take out an insurance policy; يُغَطّي التَأْمينُ الخَسارةَ \ الضَرَرَ the insurance covers the damage

تَأْمينيّ *adj* insurance (*before n*); غِطاء \ تَغْطِية تَأْمينيّ(ة) insurance coverage

مَأْمَن *n* refuge, safe haven; asylum; كانَ في مَأْمَنٍ من ... to be safe from ...; to be free of ...; to be immune from ...

مُؤْمِن **A** *adj* faithful

B *n* **1▸** [شَخْص يَلْتَزِمُ في العَقْد] a believer; هو مُؤْمِنٌ he is a believer; يا أَيُّها المُؤْمِنونَ O ye believers; أَمير المُؤْمِنينَ Commander of the Faithful (*historic title of the caliph and current title of the Moroccan king*); أُمّ المُؤْمِنين *wife of the Prophet Muhammad*; سورة المُؤْمِنونَ The Believers (*Sura 23*) **2▸** [إِنْسان] person, human; لا يُلْدَغُ المُؤْمِنُ من جُحْرٍ مَرَّتَيْنِ once bitten, twice shy **3▸** (Islam) المُؤْمِن the Guardian of Faith, the Giver of Security (*one of the names of God*)

مُؤَمَّن **A** *adj* safe, secured; insured, covered; مُؤَمَّن عَلَيْهِ insured; مُؤَمَّن ضدّ شَيْءٍ insured against sth; كانَ مُؤَمَّناً ضدّ الأَضْرارِ \ السَرِقةِ to be covered against damage/theft; غَيْر مُؤَمَّنٍ عَلَيْهِ uninsured, uncovered; اتِّصالات مُؤَمَّنة secure communications

B *n* insured person, policyholder; مُؤَمَّن عَلَيْهِ insured person, policyholder

مُؤَمِّن *n* insurer

مَأْمون *adj* reliable, trustworthy; safe; رَجُل مَأْمون a reliable man; مِياه الشُرْبِ المَأْمونة safe drinking water

مُسْتَأْمِن *n* insured person

‹ **أَمْهَري** *adj* Amharic; اللُغة الأَمْهَرِيّة Amharic (*language*)

[1]‹ **أَمَة** *n* |إِماء| (female) slave

[2]‹ **أُمَوِيّ** *adj* Umayyad; الدَوْلة الأُمَوِيّة the Umayyads, the Umayyad caliphate

أُمَيّة *n* |m| Umayya; بَنو أُمَيّةٍ the Umayyads, the Umayyad caliphate

‹ **أَمونِيا** *n* ammonia

‹ **أَمونِيوم** *n* ammonium; سَماد نِترات الأَمونيوم ammonium nitrate fertilizer

‹ **أَميبا, أَميبة** *n* amoeba

‹ **أَميرال** *n* admiral

‹ **أَميرِكة** *n* see أمرك

أَميرِكيّ *adj* see أمرك

‹ **أَمينيّ** *adj* amino (*before n*); حَمْض أَمينيّ amino acid

‹ **إِنْ** *conj* **1▸** [إذا] if, in case; إِنْ وُجِدَ if present; إِنْ ضَرَبْتَني ضَرَبْتُكَ, إِنْ تَضْرِبْني أَضْرِبْكَ if you hit me I will hit you; إِنْ أَرادَ الاسْتِمْرارَ عَلَيْهِ أَنْ ... if he wants to continue he will have to...; إِنْ أَرَدْنا السَلامَ فَيَجِبُ أَنْ ... if we want peace we will have to ...; الإِصْلاح صارَ صَعْباً إِنْ لم يَكُنْ مُسْتَحيلاً reform has become difficult if not impossible **2▸** [إلاّ] إِلاّ (*contraction of* **إِنْ** *and* **لا**) if not, otherwise; unless; خُطَّتُهُ مَدْروسةٌ وَإِلاّ لَما حَقَّقَ هذا النَجاحَ his plan was carefully studied, otherwise he would not have been this successful **3▸** [بعد] whether, if; سَأَلَكَ إِنْ كانَتْ مَعَكَ سَجائِرُ he asked if you have any cigarettes with you **4▸** [وَإِنْ] وَإِنْ although, though, even though, even if, albeit; القَرارُ قانونِيٌّ وَإِنْ لم يَحْضُر الجَميعُ the decision is legal even though not everybody was present; لَدَيْهِ الوَقْتُ وَإِنْ لم يَكُنْ كافِياً he has time, though not enough; اتَّسعت المُسْتَوْطَناتُ وَإِنْ لم يَتِمَّ بِناءُ مُسْتَوْطَناتٍ جَديدةٍ the settlements have been expanded but no new ones were built; هذه أَوَّل جَلْسةٍ وَإِنْ كانَت غَيْرَ رَسْمِيّةٍ this was the first meeting, albeit unofficial **5▸** [ما إِنْ] ما إِنْ يَدْخُل المُدَرِّسُ الفَصْلَ حتّى يَفْتَحَ الطُلاّبُ كُتُبَهُمْ as soon as the teacher enters the classroom the students open their books; ما إِنْ خَرَجَ من البَيْتِ وَإذا بِجَرَسِ الهاتِفِ يَرِنُّ no sooner had he left the house when the telephone rang

أَنْ *conj* that; على أَنْ on the condition (that), provided (that); قبل أَنْ before; بعد أَنْ after; يُريدُ أَنْ يَذْهَبَ إلى البَيْتِ he wants to go home; أُريدُهُ أَنْ يَقومَ بِواجِبِه I want him to do his duty; طَلَبْتُ مِنْهُ أَنْ يَقومَ بِواجِبِه I asked him to do his duty; يَجِبُ أَنْ يَقومَ بِواجِبِه he has to do his duty; يَجِبُ أَنْ أُفَكِّرَ I need to think

‹ **أَنا** **A** *pron* I, me; أَنا طالِبةٌ I am a student; كِتابي أَنا *my* book; فَقُلْتُ أَنا and then I said; هل أَنا الرابِحُ؟ am I the winner?; ها أَنا ذا here I am!; أَنا وَهُوَ he and I

B *n* ego; self

أَنانِيّ **A** *adj* selfish, egotistical

B *n* egotist

أَنانِيّة *n* selfishness, egotism

الأَناضول *n* |f| Anatolia

أَناناس *n* pineapple

أَنَّبَ *v* to reprimand, to reprove; أَنَّبَهُ ضَميرُهُ he was conscience-stricken

تَأْنيب *n* reprimand, reproof, rebuke; admonition; تَأْنيب قاسٍ a sharp reprimand; تَأْنيب شَديد اللَهْجَةِ a severe rebuke; تَأْنيب الضَمير remorse, pangs of conscience

أَنْبَج *n* mango tree

أَنْبار *n* |أَنابيرُ, أَنابِرُ| ❶ [مَخْزَن] warehouse, storehouse ❷ [مُحافَظَة] الأَنْبار al-Anbar (*province in Iraq*)

أُنْبوب, أُنْبوبة *n* see نبب

أَنْتَ *pron* you (*m sing*); أَنْتَ صَديقي you are my friend

أَنْتِ *pron* you (*f sing*)

أَنْتُمْ *pron* you (*m pl*)

أَنْتُما *pron* you (*dual*)

أَنْتُنَّ *pron* you (*f pl*)

أَنْتَرْكْتِكا *n* Antarctica

إِنْتْرانِت *n* intranet

إِنْتَرْنِت *n* Internet, the Web; صَفْحة الإِنْتَرْنِت web page; مُتَصَفِّح الإِنْتَرْنِت (web) browser; مُوَفِّر خِدْماتِ إِنْتَرْنِت Internet service provider, ISP; خِدْمة الإِنْتَرْنِت Internet cafe; مَقْهى الإِنْتَرْنِت; العَريضة النِطاقِ broadband Internet; عَبْرَ الإِنْتَرْنِت online; التَسَوُّق عَبْرَ الإِنْتَرْنِت online shopping

أَنَّثَ *v* to feminize; (Gram) to put into the feminine form

تَأَنَّثَ *v* to be effeminate, to become feminine

أُنْثَوِيّ *adj* feminine, female; womanly, woman's; خَطّ أُنْثَوِيّ feminine handwriting; مَلامِح أُنْثَوِيّة feminine features; womanly features; وَجه أُنْثَوِيّ a feminine face

أُنْثى *n* |f; أُناثى, إِناث| ❶ female; girl, woman; مَدْرَسة للإِناثِ a girls' school; كُرة الطائِرةِ للإِناثِ women's volleyball ❷ (Zool) female; أُنْثى الحِمارِ a female donkey

أُنوثة *n* femininity; ضَحِكَ \ تَكَلَّمَ بِأُنوثةٍ to speak/laugh in a feminine way; مُمْتَلِئ بالأُنوثة brimming with femininity

تَأْنيث *n* ❶ [جَعْل الشَيْءِ أُنْثَوِيًّا] feminization ❷ (Gram) *putting into the feminine form*

مُؤَنَّث *adj* ❶ [عَكْس مُذَكَّر] feminine; effeminate ❷ (Gram) feminine; "مُعَلِّمة" كَلِمةٌ مُؤَنَّثةٌ 'mu'allima' is a feminine word

أَنْثراكْس *n* anthrax

أَنْثروبولوجِيّ *adj* anthropological

أَنْثروبولوجِيا *n* anthropology

إِجّاص, إِنْجاص *n* pear

إِنْكِلْترا, إِنْجِلْترا *n* England

أَنْجلوساكْسونِيّ *adj*, *n* Anglo-Saxon

إِنْكْليزِيّ, إِنْجْليزِيّ A *adj* |إِنْجْليز, إِنْجْليزِيّونَ| English; (اللُغة) الإِنْجْليزِيّة English (*language*)
B *n* |إِنْجْليز, إِنْجْليزِيّونَ| English man/person; الإِنْجْليزِيّونَ, الإِنْجْليز the English, English people

أَنْجْليكانِيّ *adj* Anglican; الكَنيسة الأَنْجْليكانِيّة the Anglican church

إِنْجيل *n* |أَناجيلُ| gospel; بَشَّرَ \ كَرَزَ بالإِنْجيلِ to preach/spread the gospel; الأَناجيل (الأَرْبَعة) the (four) Gospels; أَهْل الإِنْجيلِ Christians

إِنْجيلِيّ A *adj* evangelical; كَنائِس إِنْجيلِيّة evangelical churches
B *n* evangelical (*person*)

أَنْدْرويْد *n* Android®

الأَنْدَلُس *n* |f| al-Andalus (*the portion of the Iberian Peninsula ruled by Muslims between 711 and 1492*)

أَنْدَلُسِيّ *adj* Andalusian

أَنْدَلُسِيا *n* Andalusia (*region in Spain*)

أَنْدورا *n* Andorra (*small principality in south-west Europe*)

إِنْدونيسِيا *n* Indonesia

إِنْدونيسِيّ A *adj* Indonesian; (اللُغة) الإِنْدونيسِيّة Indonesian, Bahasa Indonesia (*language*)
B *n* Indonesian (*person*)

إِنْدِيانا *n* Indiana (*US state*)

أَنْزيم *n* |أَنْزيمات| enzyme; أَنْزيم يَعْمَلُ على تَسْريعِ تَخَثُّر الدَم an enzyme that speeds up coagulation

أَنِسَ *v* |i; أُنْس| to be glad, to be happy; أَنِسَ بِلِقاءِ صَديقِهِ he was glad to meet his friend

أَنِسَ, أَنَسَ *v* |a; إِنْس, أَنَس 1 [تَعَوَّدَ] to be used to, to be habituated to, to get accustomed; أَنِسَ شَيْئاً to get accustomed to sth; to be habituated to sth 2 [كانَ لَطيفاً] to be friendly 3 [لاحَظَ] to notice, to perceive

أَنَّسَ *v* 1 [لاطَفَ] to put at ease 2 [حَيَواناً] to tame

آنَسَ *v* 1 [سَلّى] to entertain, to amuse; to keep company; آنَسَ وِحْدَةَ \ وَحْشَةَ شَخْصٍ to ease sb's loneliness 2 [لاحَظَ] to sense, to find

تَآنَسَ *v* to keep each other company

اسْتَأْنَسَ *v* |ب ,إلى| to feel at ease, to grow accustomed; اسْتَأْنَسَ ب \ إلى شَيْءٍ to adjust to sth; اسْتَأْنَسَ ب \ إلى شَخْصٍ to feel at ease with sb

إِنْس *n* |آناس| mankind, humankind; الإِنْس والجِنّ mankind and jinn

أُنْس *n* sociability, cordiality; familiarity

أُناس *n* people; أُناس عاديّونَ ordinary people

إِنْسان *n* man; human being; إِنْسان آليّ robot; إِنْسان بِدائيّ primitive man; عِلْم الإِنْسانِ anthropology; حُقوق الإِنْسانِ human rights; انْتِهاك حُقوقِ الإِنْسانِ a violation of human rights; سورة الإِنْسانِ Man, The Human (*Sura 76*); من صُنْعِ الإِنْسانِ man-made; الإِنْسانُ حَيَوانٌ اجْتِماعيٌّ man is a social animal; إِنْسان من لَحْمٍ وَدَمٍ a man of flesh and blood; ما أنا إلاّ إِنْسانٌ I'm only human; يُعْجِزُ الإِنْسانُ عن تَصَوُّرِ حَجْمَ المَأْساةِ one cannot imagine the size of the tragedy; الإِنْسانُ في التَّفْكيرِ واللهُ في التَّدْبيرِ man proposes, God disposes

إِنْسانَوِيّ A *adj* humanist, humanistic; النَّزْعة الإِنْسانَوِيّة humanism
B *n* humanist

إِنْسانيّ *adj* 1 [بَشَرِيّ] human; humane, humanitarian; تَصَرُّف إِنْسانيّ human behaviour; مُعامَلة إِنْسانيّة humane treatment; مُساعَدات إِنْسانيّة humanitarian aid; غَيْر إِنْسانيٍّ inhumane, inhuman, cruel, barbaric; أَعْمال غَيْر إِنْسانيّةٍ inhumane acts; عَلاقات إِنْسانيّة human relations 2 [عُلوم إِنْسانيّة] الدِراسات الإِنْسانيّة the humanities, liberal arts; كُلّيّة الآدابِ والعُلومِ الإِنْسانيّةِ Faculty of Literature and Humanities 3 [مَذْهَب] humanistic; المَذْهَب الإِنْسانيّ humanism

إِنْسانيّة *n* humanity; mankind, humankind; الإِنْسانيّة جَمْعاءَ all of humanity; جَرائِم ضِدّ الإِنْسانيّةِ crimes against humanity

آنِسة *n* |أَوانِسُ, آنِسات| Miss, young lady

إِنْسيّ *n* |أَناسيُّ| human being

أَنيس A *adj* nice, sociable, amiable
B *n* 1 [صَديق] close friend 2 [اسْم شَخْصيّ] Anis (*male given name*)

إيناس *n* 1 [لُطْف] friendliness; cordiality 2 [اسْم شَخْصيّ] |f dipt| Inass, Enas (*female given name*)

تَأَنُّس *n* (Chr) incarnation

تَأْنيس *n* domestication, taming

لاإِنْسانيّ *adj* inhuman; inhumane; تَصَرُّف لاإِنْسانيّ inhuman behaviour; لَقَدْ عومِلوا بِطَريقةٍ لاإِنْسانيّةٍ they were treated inhumanely

لاإِنْسانيّة *n* inhumanity

مُؤَانَسة *n* friendliness; sociability

مُؤْنِس A *adj* friendly, entertaining
B *n* companion, close friend

ناس *n* people; عامّة الناسِ people, the public; سورة الناس Mankind (*Sura 114*); اخْتَلَطَ بالناسِ to associate with people, to see people; هذا النَوْع من الناسِ those kind of people, people like that; ثَمّةَ أُناسٌ يَنْظُرونَ إِلَيْكَ people are watching you; من الناسِ مَنْ ... there are people who...

أَنْسولين *n* insulin; حَقَنَ بالأَنْسولين to inject insulin

إِنْش *n* (Meas) inch

أَنْطاكِية *n* Antakya (*city in Turkey*); (Hist) Antioch

أَنْغولا *n* Angola

أَنِفَ *v* |a; أَنَفة |من| to disdain, to scorn, to reject; أَنِفَ من شَخْصٍ \ شَيْءٍ to disdain sb/sth, to look down on sb/sth; أَنِفَ الكَذِبَ \ من الكَذِبِ to not like lying

اسْتَأْنَفَ *v* 1 [تابَعَ] to resume, to recommence; اسْتَأْنَفَ شَيْئاً to resume sth; سَيَسْتَأْنِفُ الجانِبانِ المُفاوَضاتِ the two sides will resume talks 2 (Law) to appeal; to lodge an appeal (against); اسْتَأْنَفَ حُكْماً \ قَراراً to appeal a verdict/decision

آنِف *adj* preceding, above; آنِف الذِكْرِ above-mentioned; آنِفاً previously, above; recently, earlier; كَما وَرَدَ آنِفاً as mentioned above, as indicated earlier

أَنْف *n* |أُنوف| nose; أَنْف مَسْدود \ مُغْلَق a blocked nose (BrE), a stuffed-up nose (AmE); أَنْف مَعْقوف \ واقِف a hooked nose; أَرْنَبة الأَنْف the tip of the nose; قَطَرات الأَنْف nose drops; فُتْحَتا الأَنْفِ nostrils; جانِب الأَنْفِ nostril; رغم \ رَغْماً عن أَنْفِه, على الرَغْم من أَنْفِه against his will, reluctantly; in defiance of him; سَدَّ أَنْفَهُ to hold one's nose; شَمَخَ بِأَنْفِه to be haughty; دَسَّ \ حَشَرَ أَنْفَهُ في شُؤونِ الغَيْر to put one's nose into other people's business; لا يَرى أَبْعَدَ من أَرْنَبةِ أَنْفِه he sees no further than his nose

(Idiom) أَنْف العِجْل snapdragon (*Antirrhinum*)

اسْتِئْناف *n* |اسْتِئْنافات| **1** [مُتابَعة] resumption, resuming; اسْتِئْناف المُفاوَضاتِ a resumption of the negotiations, resuming talks **2** (Law) appeal; عَريضة اسْتِئْنافٍ an appeal; اسْتِئْناف لِنَقْضِ الحُكْم an appeal to overturn a ruling; إجْراءات اسْتِئْنافٍ appeal procedures; فَتْرة اسْتِئْنافٍ appeal period; دَعْوى اسْتِئْنافٍ an appeal; رَبح \ خسر قَضِيّةَ اسْتِئْنافٍ to win/lose an appeal; رَفَعَ دَعْوى اسْتِئْنافٍ to lodge an appeal; قَدَّمَ اسْتِئْنافاً \ عَريضةَ اسْتِئْنافٍ to file an appeal

اسْتِئْنافيّ *adj* appeal (*before n*), appeals (*before n*); مَحْكَمة اسْتِئْنافيّة appeals court, court of appeal

أَنَفة *n* pride, honour

أَنْفيّ *adj* nasal; صَوْت أَنْفيّ a nasal sound; جُيوب أَنْفيّة nasal cavities, sinuses

أَنوف *adj* |أُنُف| proud, haughty

مُسْتَأْنِف *n* appellant

‹ **إنْفِلْوَنْزا** *n* influenza, flu; أُصيبَ بالإِنْفِلْوَنْزا to get the flu, to come down with the flu; كانَ مُصاباً, عانى من الإِنْفِلْوَنْزا بالإِنْفِلْوَنْزا to have the flu

‹ **أَنِقَ** *v* |a; أَنَق, أَناقة| to look good; to be elegant; to have style, to be stylish

أَنَّقَ *v* to make elegant

تَأَنَّقَ *v* to be elegant; تَأَنَّقَ في مَلابِسِه to dress elegantly; تَأَنَّقَ بِطَرْبوشِه وَرَبْطة عُنُقِه he cut an elegant figure in his fez and necktie

أَناقة *n* elegance, grace; chic; بِأَناقةٍ elegantly, with style

أَنوق *n* vulture; أَعَزُّ من بَيْضِ الأَنوقِ *very difficult to obtain*

أَنيق *adj* elegant, graceful; stylish, chic, fashionable, smart (BrE); سَيِّدة أَنيقة an elegant lady; قُبَّعة أَنيقة a smart hat; ثِياب أَنيقة fashionable clothing; تَصْميم داخِليّ أَنيق a stylish interior; elegant decor

مُتَأَنِّق **A** *adj* elegant; stylish, chic, fashionable

B *n* dandy (old use)

‹ **أَنْقَرة** *n* **1** (Geog) Ankara (*capital of Turkey*) **2** [صوف] angora

‹ **أَنْكَليس, أَنْقَليس** *n* eel

‹ **إنْكِلْتِرا** *n* see إنجلترا

‹ **إنْكْليزيّ** *adj* see إنجليز

‹ **أَنام, آنام** *n* mankind, humankind; all living creatures

‹ **أُنْموذَج** *n* see نموذج

‹ **أَنَمون** *n* (sea) anemone

‹¹ **إنَّ** *conj* **1** [حَرْف التَأْكيد] *particle introducing a nominal clause, in most cases not translated in English*; verily (old use); إنَّهُ رَجُلٌ لَطيفٌ he is a nice man; إنَّهُ يَعْمَلُ كَثيراً he works hard **2** [بعد فِعْلِ القَوْلِ] that; قالَ الوَزيرُ إنَّ السِياسةَ لن تَتَغَيَّرَ the minister said that the policy would not change; قالَ إنَّهُ لا مَعْلوماتِ لَدَيْه he said he had no information; قيلَ إنَّهُ أُصيبَ بِسَرَطانٍ it was said that he had cancer **3** [فَإِنَّ] ... لِذَلِكَ فَإِنَّهُ من الواضِحِ أنّ therefore it is clear that ...; في الواقِعِ فَإِنَّ العَكْسَ هو الصَحيحُ actually the opposite is true

أَنَّ *conj* **1** [حَرْف نَصْبٍ] that; خَبَر مُفادُهُ أنَّهُ لا يَسْتَطيعُ الحُضورَ a message that he cannot come; سَمِعْنا أَنَّ الوَزيرَ قد اسْتَقالَ we heard that the minister has resigned; أَخْبَرَنا بِأَنَّهُ لا يَسْتَطيعُ الحُضورَ he let us know that he could not come **2** [عَلى أَنَّ] على أَنَّ in such a sense that; as if; but, however; عامَلَهُمْ على أَنَّهُمْ أَطْفالٌ he treated them as if they were children; هُناكَ مُؤَشِّراتٌ على أَنَّهُ بِإِمْكانِ الحُكومةِ أنْ... there are indications that the government is able to...; فَقَدَ البَصَرَ وَهُوَ طِفْلٌ على أَنَّ ذلك لم يَمْنَعْهُ من مُواصَلةِ الدِراسةِ he lost his sight as a child but that didn't prevent him from pursuing his education ③ [غَيْرَ أَنَّ] غيرَ أنَّ except that, but, however

إنَّما *adv* ① [إنّ] only, merely; إنَّما فعَلَ ذلك لِجَهْلِهِ بالعَواقِبِ he only did it because he didn't know the consequences ② [لَكِنَّ] but, however; الرَجُلُ والمَرْأةُ مُتَساوِيانِ إنَّما مُخْتَلِفانِ men and women are equal but different; لَيْسَ في أوروبّا فَحَسْبُ، وَإنَّما في إفْرِيقِيا أيْضاً not only in Europe but also in Africa

كَأَنَّ *conj* as if, like; وكَأَنَّ as if; بَدا وكَأَنَّهُ مَرِيضٌ he looked as if he was ill, he seemed ill; تَصَرَّفَتْ وكَأَنَّ شَيْئاً لم يَحْدُثْ she acted as if nothing had happened

لِأَنَّ *conj* because, as, since; لم تَدْخُلِ الشُرْطةُ لأنَّ القانونَ يَمْنَعُها من ذلك the police did not enter because it is prohibited by law; لِأَنَّهُ من المُفِيدِ أنْ ... because it is useful to ...; لن تَذْهَبَ إلى المَدْرَسةِ لِأَنَّها مَرِيضةٌ she will not go to school because she is ill

2 **أَنَّ** *v* |i; أنين| to moan, to groan; أنَّ من الألَمِ to groan with pain

أَنَّة *n* moan, groan

أَنين *n* moaning, groan; أَنين الجَرْحى the moan of the wounded; أَنين الريح the moaning of the wind

أَنود *n* (Elec) anode

أَنوق *n* see أَنق

1 **أَنى** *v* |i; أَناة, أَنْي| ① [تَمَهَّلَ] to take it easy ② [حانَ] to approach, to come

تَأَنّى *v* to take it easy, to take one's time; مَنْ تَأَنّى نالَ ما تَمَنّى ≈ patience is a virtue

اسْتَأْنى *v* to wait (for); اسْتَأْنى شَيْئاً to wait for sth

إناء *n* |أوانٍ, آنِية| container, vessel; pot; إناء فاكِهةٍ fruit bowl; أوانٍ dishes; pots and pans; أوانٍ فِضِّيّة silver, silverware; أوانٍ مُسْتَطْرِقة (Phys) communicating vessels; أواني المَطْبَخِ kitchen utensils; غَسَلَ الأَوانِيَ to wash the dishes; لِكُلِّ إناءٍ غِطاءٌ ≈ there's someone for everyone

إنائيّة *n* chanterelle (*Cantharellus cibarius*); (فُطْر) الإنائِيّة chanterelle (mushrooms)

أَناة *n* deliberation; patience; طول أَناةٍ patience; ب \ في أَناةٍ, بِطولِ أَناةٍ carefully, cautiously; patiently; اسْتَمَعَ بِطولِ أَناةٍ إلى شَيْءٍ to listen patiently to sth

أَنْي, إنْي *n* |آناء| time, period; آناءَ \ في آناءِ اللَيْلِ throughout the night; آناءَ اللَيْلِ وَأَطْرافَ النَهارِ all day and all night

تَأَنٍّ *n* calmness; في التَأَنّي السَلامةُ وَفي العَجَلةِ النَدامةُ ≈ act in haste, repent at leisure

مُتَأَنٍّ *adj* slow, unhurried, calm; deliberate, thorough; دِراسة مُتَأَنِّية a thorough investigation; كانَ مُتَأَنِّياً في مُعالَجةِ المُشْكِلةِ he treated the problem with deliberation

2 **أَنّى** *pron* ① [من أَيْنَ] from where?; أَنّى لكَ هذا؟ what gave you that idea? ② [أَيْنَما] wherever ③ [كَيْف] how

أَنيميا, أَنيمِية *n* anaemia

آه *excl* oh!, ah!

أَها *excl* aha!, ha!

أَهَّبَ *v* to prepare

تَأَهَّبَ *v* to prepare oneself, to get ready; تَأَهَّبَ لِشَيْءٍ to be prepared for sth

إهاب *n* |أُهُب| (animal) skin

أُهْبة *n* |أُهَب| preparedness; على أُهْبةِ ready (to), about (to); على أُهْبةِ الاسْتِعْدادِ ready to go, about to leave; على أُهْبةِ الرَحيلِ at the ready, on standby

تَأَهُّب *n* preparedness, readiness; preparation; في حالةِ تَأَهُّبٍ at the ready; رَفَعَ دَرَجةَ التَأَهُّبِ to raise the alert level; وَضَعَ في حالةِ تَأَهُّبٍ to put at the ready

مُتَأَهِّب *adj* ready, prepared; غَيْر مُتَأَهِّبٍ unprepared; كانَ مُتَأَهِّباً لِشَيْءٍ to be ready for sth

أَهَلَ *v* |i-u; أُهول| ① [تَزَوَّجَ] to get married ② [المَكانُ] to be inhabited

أَهِلَ *v* |a; أَهَل| ب| to become familiar (with)

أَهَّلَ *v* ① [عَلَّمَ] to prepare; to educate, to train; أَهَّلَ شَخْصاً لِشَيْءٍ to train sb for sth; أَهَّلَ نَفْسَهُ كَحِرَفِيٍّ to train oneself as a professional; أَهَّلَ نَفْسَهُ لِمُواجَهةِ شَيْءٍ to prepare oneself to face sth; تَعْليم يُؤَهِّلُهُمْ لِدُخولِ الجامِعةِ an education that prepares them for university ② [رَحَّبَ] |ب| to welcome

تَأَهَّلَ *v* ① [صارَ صالِحاً (ل)] to train oneself; to qualify; to be ready; تَأَهَّلَ للدَوْرِ النِهائِيِّ (Sport) to qualify for the finals ② [تَزَوَّجَ] to get married

اسْتَأْهَل *v* to deserve, to be worthy of; تَسْتَأْهِل ذلك! serves you right!, that's just what you deserve!; كَلامُهُ لا يَسْتَأْهِلُ الرَدَّ what he said is not even worthy of a response

آهِل *adj* inhabited, populated; مَدينة آهِلة بالسُكّانِ an inhabited city; أماكِن آهِلة populated places, populated areas

أَهْل **A** *adj* fit, suited; هو أَهْلٌ لِكُلِّ خَيْرٍ he deserves all good things; كانَ غَيْرَ أَهْلٍ لِشَيْءٍ to be unfit for sth

B *n coll* |no singular noun; أهالٍ, أَهْلونَ| **1** [أقارب] family; أَهالي الضَحايا the victims' families; the next of kin; لَيْسَ لَهُ أَهْلٌ he has no family **2** [قَوْم] people; أَهالي البَلْدةِ the local people; أَهْل العِلْمِ scholars; أَهْل الرَأْيِ experts; أَهْل البَيْتِ the family/descendants of the Prophet; أَهْل الكِتابِ the People of the Book (*Christians and Jews*); أَهْل السُنَّةِ \ الحَديثِ the Sunnis

اسْتِئْهال *n* worthiness

أَهْلاً *excl* hello; أَهْلاً وَسَهْلاً! hello!, welcome!; أَهْلاً بِكَ *response to the greeting* أَهْلاً وَسَهْلاً

أَهْليّ *adj* **1** [خاصّ] private; family (*before n*); رَوابِط أَهْليّة family ties; مَدْرَسة أَهْليّة private school **2** [وَطَنيّ] civil; internal, domestic; حَرْب أَهْليّة civil war **3** [حَيَوان] tame

أَهْليّة *n* fitness; competence; qualification; أَهْليّة مَطْلوبة a required qualification; أَهْليّة قانونيّة legal capacity; أَهْليّة الزَواجِ \ النِكاحِ eligibility for marriage; أَهْليّة للعَمَلِ job qualification; عَدَم الأَهْليّةِ incompetence; عَديم الأَهْليّةِ legally incompetent; وِصاية على ناقِصِ الأَهْليّةِ guardianship over a legally incompetent person; زادَ في أَهْليّتِهِ to increase one's qualifications

تَأَهُّل *n* qualification; (ل) بِطاقة التَأَهُّلِ (Sport) qualification (for), a place (in); خَطَفَ بِطاقة التَأَهُّلِ لِنِصْفِ النِهائيّ (Sport) to snatch a place in the semi-finals

تَأْهيل *n* making fit; training, making qualified; تَأْهيل اجْتِماعيّ socialization; تَأْهيل مِهْنيّ vocational training; إعادة تَأْهيلٍ rehabilitation; إعادة تَأْهيلِ المُصابينَ rehabilitation of the injured; إعادة تَأْهيلِ المِنْطَقةِ التاريخيّةِ rehabilitation of the historic district; إعادة التَأْهيلِ الاجْتِماعيِّ social reintegration, social rehabilitation

مُؤَهَّل *adj* qualified; competent, capable; كُوادِر مُؤَهَّلة qualified staff; كانَ مُؤَهَّلاً لِشَيْءٍ to be qualified for sth

مُؤَهِّل *n* |مُؤَهِّلات| مُؤَهِّلات qualifications, abilities

مَأْهول *adj* inhabited, populated; manned; طائِرة مَأْهولة a manned aircraft; جَزيرة غَيْر مَأْهولةٍ a desert island; مَرْكَبة فَضائيّة غَيْر مَأْهولةٍ an unmanned spacecraft

مُتَأَهِّل *adj* **1** [مُتَزَوِّج] married **2** [جَدير ب] qualified

‹ **إهْليلَج** *n* **1** (Math) ellipse **2** (Bot) *Terminalia*; حَمْض الإهْليلَجِ chebulagic acid (*a product of the nut of T. chebula, considered a cure for many ailments*)

إهْليلَجيّ *adj* elliptic, elliptical; مَدار إهْليلَجيّ an elliptical orbit

‹ **أَوْ** *conj* or; هل سافرَ بالقِطارِ أو بالسَيّارة؟ did he go by train or by car?; ثَمَنُ هذا البَيْتِ ٤٠٠.٠٠٠ دينارٍ أَوْ أَكْثَرُ the price of this house is 400,000 dinars or more

‹ **آبَ** *v* |u; أَوْبة, أَوْب, إياب| to return; آبَ إلى المَنْزِلِ to return home

أَوَّبَ *v* to return

أَوْب *n* direction; من كُلِّ أَوْبٍ وَصَوْبٍ from all directions

أَوّاب **A** *adj* repentant, remorseful, regretful

B *n* **1** [نادِم] penitent **2** [اسْم شَخْصيّ] Awwab (*male given name*)

إياب *n* return (trip); مُباراة الإيابِ return match; أَقْدَمَ على رِحْلةِ الإيابِ to set out on the journey back; إياباً on the journey back; return; ذَهاباً وَإياباً back and forth; round trip

مَآب *n* return

‹ **أوبال** *n* opal

‹ **أوبِرا** *n* opera; دار أوبِرا opera house; دار أوبِرا القاهِرة the Cairo Opera House; فِرْقة أوبِرا opera company; قَدَّمَ \ عَرَضَ أوبِرا to perform an opera

‹ **أوبِريت** *n* operetta

‹ **أوبِك, أوبيك** *n* |f| OPEC (*Organization of Petroleum Exporting Countries*)

‹ **أوت** *n* (Algeria, Tunisia) August

‹ **أوتوبيس, أُتوبيس** *n* bus; أوتوبيس صَغير \ مَدْرَسيّ minibus/school bus

‹ **أوتوقْراطيّ** *adj* autocratic, dictatorial

‹ أُتوماتيكيّ, أوتوماتيكيّ *adj* automatic; أبواب أوتوماتيكيّة automatic doors; بُنْدُقيّة أوتوماتيكيّة an automatic rifle

‹ أوتيل *n* |أوتيلات| hotel

‹ أَوْج *n* highest point, peak, zenith; climax; أَوْج الشُهْرة \ السَعادة the height of fame/happiness; الحَضارة الإسلاميّة في أَوْج ازْدِهارِها Islamic civilization at its height; بَلَغَ أَوْجَهُ to reach its climax

‹ آدَ *v* |u; أَوْد, إياد| **1** [اعْوَجَّ] to be bent **2** [عَطَفَ على] to sympathize (with) **3** [أَتْعَب] to overload

أَوِدَ *v* |a; أَوَد| to bend, to curve

أَوَّدَ *v* to bend, to curve

إياد *n* **1** [حَنان] tenderness **2** [اسْم شَخْصيّ] |dipt| Iyad, Ayad (*male given name*)

‹ أُوار *n* heat, flame; thirst; أُوار الحُبّ the fiery ardor of love; اشْتَدَّ أُوارَ to heat sth up; to intensify sth; اشْتَدَّ أُوار شَيْءٍ الحَرْبِ the war intensified

الأورال *n* the Urals (*mountains in Russia*)

‹ أورانوس *n* (Astron) Uranus

‹ أورانْيوم *n* see يورانِيوم

‹ أوروبّا, أوروبّيّ *adj* أوروبا

‹ أورْج *n* (electronic) keyboard; organ

‹ أُرْدُويّة, أُرْديّة, أورْديّة *n* Urdu; (اللُغة) الأورْديّة Urdu

‹ أورُشَليم *n* |f| Jerusalem

‹ أَوُرْطة, أُورْطى *n* aorta

أَوُرْطيّ *adj* aortic; شِرْيان أَوُرْطيّ aorta; صِمام أَوُرْطيّ aortic valve

‹ أورْغ *abbr* org (*in URL*)

‹ أورْكِسْتْرا *n* orchestra; عُضْو في أورْكِسْتْرا member of an orchestra; أورْكِسْترا سِمْفونيّة a symphony/philharmonic orchestra

أورْكِسْترالِيّ *adj* orchestral

‹ أورْكيد *n* orchid

‹ أورو *n* see يورو

‹ أوروبّا, أورُبّا, أوروبّا, أُروبّا *n* Europe; أوروبّا الغَرْبيّة Western Europe

أوروبّيّ **A** *adj* European; الدُوَل الأوروبّيّة European countries; أوروبّيّ غَرْبيّ Western European

B *n* a European (*person*)

‹ أوروغُواي *n* |f| Uruguay

أوروغُوانيّ *adj*, *n* Uruguayan

‹ أورومُتَوَسِّطيّ *adj* Euro-Mediterranean

‹ أوريجانو *n* oregano

‹ أوريغون *n* |f| Oregon (*US state*)

‹ إِوَزّ *n coll* goose; إِوَزّ بَرّيّ wild goose; إِوَزّ مِصْريّ Egyptian goose (*Alopochen aegyptiacus*); إِوَزّ عِراقيّ swan

‹ أوزْبِكِسْتان *n* |f| Uzbekistan

أوزْبَكيّ **A** *adj* Uzbek; (اللُغة) الأوزْبَكيّة Uzbek (*language*)

B *n* Uzbek (*person*)

‹ أوزون *n* ozone; طَبَقة الأوزون ozone layer; الثُقْبة في طَبَقة الأوزونِ the hole in the ozone layer

‹ أوسْتُراليا *n* see أستراليا

‹ أوغَنْدا *n* Uganda

أوغَنْديّ *adj* Ugandan

‹ آفة *n* **1** [نَكْبة] plague; scourge; blight; آفة زِراعيّة a blight; آفة حَشَريّة a plague of insects; آفة المُخَدِّراتِ the scourge of drugs; كافَحَ آفةً to fight a plague **2** (Med) lesion; epidemic; آفة جِلْديّة a skin lesion **3** [عَيْب] fault, defect, failure

‹ أوقيّة *n* (Meas) ounce; uqiyya (*approx 37 grams* (*Egypt*) *or 320 grams* (*Syria*))

‹ أوكالِبْتوس, يوكالِبْتُس *n* eucalyptus (tree)

‹ أوكْرانيّ **A** *adj* Ukrainian; (اللُغة) الأوكْرانيّة Ukrainian (*language*)

B *n* Ukrainian (*person*)

أوكْرانيا *n* Ukraine

‹ أوكْسيد *n* see أكسد

‹ أوكْلاهوما *n* Oklahoma (*US state*)

‹ آلَ *v* |u; مَآل| **1** [أَدّى إلى] to lead to, to result in; آلَ الأَمْرُ إلى أنّ... eventually it resulted in ...; آلَ إلى الفَشَلِ to lead to nothing **2** [عادَ] to return to **3** [انْتَقَلَ إلى] to fall into the hands of; آلَت الشَرِكةُ بعد وَفاةِ مُؤَسِّسها إلى ابْنِهِ after the death of its founder the company fell into the hands of his son

أَوَّلَ *v* to explain, to interpret; أَوَّلَ الإنْجيلَ \ القُرْآنَ to interpret the Gospel/the Koran; أَوَّلَ شَيْئاً تَأْويلاً خاطِئاً to misinterpret sth

تَأَوَّلَ *v* to be interpreted

أَوَّل **A** *num* |dipt; أَوَّلون, أَوائِلُ; f أُولى; f pl أُولَيات| first; أَوَّلاً firstly, in the first place; at first; أَوَّلاً بِأَوَّلٍ one by one; أَوَّلاً وَقَبْلَ كُلِّ شَيْءٍ first of all; أَوَّلَ \ في all in all; أَوَّلاً وَأَخيراً at first; لِأَوَّلِ مَرَّةٍ ,لِلمَرَّةِ الأُولى for the first time; أَوَّلَ الأَمْرِ as soon as, the moment when; أَوَّلَ يَنايِر the first of January; أَوائِلُ الطَّلَبَةِ the best students; الطَّلَبَةُ الثَلاثَةُ الأَوائِلُ the first three students; في الصَّفْحَةِ الأُولى on the front page; أَحْرَزَ المَرْتَبَةَ الأُولى to become first; هَرَبَتِ المَرْأَةُ أَوَّلَ ما رَأَتِ الجُنْديَّ the woman fled as soon as she saw the soldier

B *n* |dipt| **1** [بِداية |أَوائِلُ] beginning, first part; أَوائِلُ principles; في أَوائِلِ شَهْرِ يَنايِر early in January; مِن أَوَّلِهِ from the beginning; مِن أَوَّلِهِ إلى آخِرِهِ from the beginning to the end, from A to Z **2** [سَلَف |أَوَّلونَ ,أَوائِلُ] الأَوَّلونَ ,الأَوائِلُ the forefathers; the ancients **3** (Islam) الأَوَّلُ the First (*one of the names of God*)

آل *n* **1** [أَهْل] family; house; آل مُحَمَّدٍ the family of the Prophet Muhammad; سورة آل عِمْران The Family of Imran (*Sura 3*) **2** [أَنْصار] followers

آلاتي *adj* |الآتيّة| instrumental

آلة *n* machine, device; instrument, utensil, tool; آلة حاسِبة calculator; آلة بُخاريّة steam engine; آلة رافِعة crane; آلة خِياطةٍ sewing machine; آلة تَصْوير camera; آلة موسيقيّة musical instrument; آلة وَتَريّة stringed instrument; آلة نَقْر \ إيقاع percussion instrument; عَزَفَ على آلةٍ موسيقيّةٍ to play an instrument; شَغَّلَ آلةً to switch on/operate a machine

آليّ *adj* mechanical, mechanized; automatic; إنْسان آليّ robot; ساعة آليّة watch, clock; حاسِب آليّ computer; أَسْلِحة آليّة automatic weapons; دَرّاجة آليّة motorcycle, motorbike (BrE); بِصورةٍ آليّةٍ automatically; mechanically

آليّة *n* **1** [ميكانيكيّة] mechanism; الآليّة العَرْضِ والطَلَبِ the mechanism of supply and demand **2** [عَرَبة] vehicle; machine; آليّة مُدَرَّعة armoured vehicle

أَوَّليّ *adj* primary; initial, preliminary; essential, elemental, principal; نَتائِج أَوَّليّة preliminary results; التَحْقيق الأَوَّليّ the preliminary investigation; مَصاريف أَوَّليّة initial costs; عَدَد أَوَّليّ prime (number); مَدْرَسة أَوَّليّة primary school (BrE), elementary school (AmE); اِنْتِخابات أَوَّليّة primary elections; مادّة أَوَّليّة raw material; المَوادّ الغِذائيّة الأَوَّليّة staples, staple foods

أَوَّليّة *n* **1** [أَوْلَويّة] priority; pre-eminence; أَعْطى الأَوَّليّةَ لِشَيْءٍ to give priority to sth **2** [مَبْدَأ] principle, axiom

إيالة *n* province

آيِل *adj* |إلى ,لِ| on the verge of; susceptible to, doomed to; leading to; آيِل لِلسُّقوطِ ramshackle, rickety; كُلُّ شَيْءٍ آيِلٌ لِلزَوالِ nothing lasts forever; اِتَّخَذَ كافةَ الإجْراءاتِ الآيِلةِ إلى شَيْءٍ to take all measures to accomplish sth; سُبُل آيِلة (إلى فِعْل شَيْءٍ) means (of doing sth)

أَيْلولة *n* **1** [رُجوع] returning; withdrawing, retreating **2** (Law) assignment, legal transfer; reversion; رَسْم أَيْلولةٍ probate duty (BrE), estate tax (AmE)

تَأْويل *n* |تَأْويلات| **1** [تَفْسير] interpretation, explanation; عِبارة قابِلة لِتَأْويلاتٍ مُتَعَدِّدةٍ a phrase that is open to more than one interpretation, an ambiguous phrase; عِلْم التَأْويل hermeneutics **2** (Relig) exegesis (*interpretation of the Koran*)

تَأْويليّ *adj* explanatory, interpretative; قِراءة تَأْويليّة interpretative reading

‹ **أولَئِكَ** *pron* see ذَلِكَ

‹ **أولِمْبيّ** ,**أولُمْبيّ** *adj* Olympic; الأَلْعاب الأولِمْبية the Olympic Games, the Olympics; الشُّعْلة الأولِمْبيّة the Olympic flame; لَقَب أولِمْبيّ an Olympic title; اللَجْنة الأولِمْبيّة الدُوَليّة the International Olympic Committee, the IOC

‹ **أولو** *n* see ذو

‹ **أوليغارْشيّة** ,**أوليغارْشيّا** *n* oligarchy

‹ **أوليمْبياد** *n* Olympiad

‹ **أومْليت** *n* omelette

‹ **الآنَ** *adv* now; تُشيرُ الساعةُ الآنَ إلى العاشِرةِ it is now ten o'clock; لَقَدْ فَهِمْتُكَ الآنَ now I understand you; قبل الآنَ before; بعد الآنَ, من الآنَ فَصاعِداً from now on, in the future, henceforth;

لِحَدٍّ \ إلى \ حتّى الآنَ up to now, yet; لم يَتَقَرَّرْ لِحَدٍّ \ إلى \ حتّى الآنَ it has not been decided yet

آن *n* time; آناً ... آوِنةً ... at times ... at times ...; في آنٍ (واحِدٍ) at the same time; من آنٍ إلى آخَرَ from time to time

آنَئِذٍ *adv* then, at the time, at that time

آنَذاكَ *adv* at the time, at that time, then; رَئِيس الوُزَراءِ آنَذاكَ the prime minister at the time

آنِيّ *adj* present, current

أَوان *n* |آوِنة| time; كُلّ شَيْءٍ في أَوانِهِ all in due course; آنَ الأَوانُ it's time; سابِق لِأَوانِهِ ,قبل أَوانِهِ prematurely, too soon; اسْتِنْتاج \ قَرار سابِق لِأَوانِهِ a premature conclusion/decision; تُوُفِّيَ قبل الأَوانِ to die prematurely, to die young; أَنْهى شَيْئاً قبل الأَوانِ to end sth prematurely, to abort sth; بين الآوِنةِ والأُخْرى from time to time, now and then; ... آوِنةً ... وأُخْرى... ,آناً ... آوِنةً at times ... at times ...; في الآوِنةِ الأخيرةِ lately, recently; في أَوانِهِ at the right time, timely; في غَيْرِ أَوانِهِ at the wrong time, untimely; فاتَ الأَوانُ time's up; it's too late; بعد فَواتِ الأَوانِ as time went by

إيوان *n* listed alphabetically

مَؤُونة *n* see مأن

› **أونْصة** *n* ounce

› **أَوَّهَ** *v* to moan, to groan

تَأَوَّهَ *v* to moan, to groan; تَأَوَّهَ أَلَماً to moan with pain

آهة *n* moan; sigh; آهة الأَلَمِ moan of pain; أَطْلَقَ آهةً to let out a moan

أَوّاه *excl* oh, ah; أَوّاه ماذا فَعَلْتِ؟ oh, what have you done?

تَأَوُّه *n* |تَأَوُّهات| moan

› **أوهايو** *n* |f| Ohio (*US state*)

› **أَوى** *v* |i; أُوِيّ| to accommodate, to lodge; to shelter, to harbour; أَوى شَخْصاً to accommodate sb; أَوى مُجْرِماً to harbour a criminal

آوى *v* to accommodate, to lodge; to shelter, to harbour; آوى شَخْصاً to accommodate sb; آوى لاجِئين to shelter refugees; آوى شَخْصاً عند أُسْرةٍ مُضِيفةٍ to arrange accommodation of sb with a host family

ابْن آوى *n* |بَنو آوى; f بِنْت آوى; f pl بَنات آوى| jackal

آية *n* |آيات, آي| 1▸ [مُعْجِزة] miracle, marvel, wonder; آية من آياتِ الإبْداعِ \ الجَمالِ a wonder of ingenuity/beauty 2▸ [عَلامة] token, mark; آية اللهِ ayatollah (*a sign of God*); آية الله الخُمَيْني Ayatollah Khomeiny 3▸ [قُرْآنيّة] Koranic verse; آية الكُرْسِيِّ The Verse of the Throne

إيواء *n* accommodation, lodging; sheltering, harbouring; مَرْكَز الإيواءِ relief centre; تَمَّ إيواءُ اللاجِئينَ في مُخَيَّماتٍ the refugees were housed in camps; اتِّهام بِإيواءِ الإرْهابِيّينَ a charge of harbouring terrorists

إيوائيّ *adj* housing (*before n*); سَعة \ طاقة إيوائيّة housing capacity

مَأْوًى *n* |مآوٍ| 1▸ [مَسْكَن] accommodation, lodging; وَجَدَ مَأْوًى عند أُسْرةٍ مُضِيفةٍ to find lodging with a host family; لَيْسَ لَهُ مَأْوًى to be homeless; مَأْوى سَيّاراتٍ parking; مَأْوى العُجَز retirement home 2▸ [مَلْجَأ] shelter, refuge; مَأْوًى للمُسَلَّحينَ a refuge for militants

[1]› **آيْ** *excl* ow!, ouch!

[2]› **أَيْ** *particle* that is to say, i.e.; أَلْف رِيالٍ أَيْ ما يُعادِلُ ٢٦٧ دولار one thousand riyals, or about $267

[3]› **آي النار** *n* January (*Libya under Gaddafi*)

› **إيّا** *particle* 1▸ (Gram) *a particle to which a direct or indirect object attaches when unable to attach directly to the verb*; أَعْطيني إيّاه give it to me; زِيارَتُهُ إيّاها his visit to her 2▸ [انْتَبَهْ] take care not to ...; watch out for ...; إيّاكَ والأَسَدَ ,إيّاكَ من الأَسَدِ watch out for the lion; إيّاكَ أنْ تَسْقُطَ take care not to fall

› **أَيّار** *n* |dipt| (Levant, Iraq) May

› **إيبيريّ** *adj*, *n* Iberian

› **إيثانول** *n* ethanol

› **إيحاء** *n* see وحي

› **أَيَّدَ** *v* to support, to back, to help; أَيَّدَ شَخْصاً to support sb; أَيَّدَ حِزْباً \ اقْتِراحاً to support a party/proposal; أَيَّدَ مُلاحَظةً to endorse a remark; أَيَّدَ الفِكْرةَ الّتي ... to support the thought that ...; نُؤَيِّدُ قَرارَ الوَزيرِ تَأْييداً مُطْلَقاً we totally support the minister's decision

تَأَيَّدَ *v* to be supported

تأْييد *n* |تأْييدات| support, backing, confirmation; تأْييد واسِع broad support; تأْييد أعْمى unconditional support; تأْييد حُكْمٍ upholding a verdict; تأْييد للاقْتِراح الجَديد adherence to the new proposal; تأْييداً لِشَخْصٍ \ لِشَيْءٍ in support of sb/sth; أعْلَنَ \ أعْرَبَ عن تأْييدِهِ \ لِشَخْصٍ to express one's support for sb

مُؤَيِّد *n* supporter, follower; مُؤَيِّد وَفيّ \ مُخْلِص a loyal supporter; مُؤَيِّد مُتَعَصِّب \ شَديد a fanatic/strong supporter; مُؤَيِّد الحِزْب \ الرَّئيس a supporter of the party/president

‹ **أيْداهو** *n* |f| Idaho (*US state*)

‹ **أيْدز, إيدْز** *n* AIDS; مُصاب \ مَريض بالإيدْز AIDS patient; وِقاية \ عِلاج من الإيدْز AIDS prevention/treatment

‹ **إيدْيو** *abbr* edu (*in URL*)

‹ **إدْيولوجيّ, إيدْيولوجيّ** *adj* ideological; صِراع إيدْيولوجيّ an ideological struggle

أيْدِيولوجِية *n* ideology

‹ **أيْر** *n* |أُيور| (vulg) penis

‹ **إيران** *n* |f| Iran

إيرانيّ *adj*, *n* Iranian

‹ **إيرْل** *n* earl

‹ **إيرْلَنْدا** *n* Ireland

إيرْلَنْديّ **A** *adj* Irish; (اللُغة) الإيرْلَنْديّة Irish (Gaelic) (*language*) **B** *n* Irishman; الإيرْلَنْديّون the Irish, Irish people

‹ **إيروتيكيّ** *adj* erotic

‹ **أيِسَ** *v* |a; إياس| to despair

‹ **أيْسْكريم, آيْس كْريم** *n* ice cream

‹ **أيْسْلَنْدا** *n* Iceland

إيسْلَنْديّ **A** *adj* Icelandic; (اللُغة) الإيسْلَنْديّة Icelandic (*language*) **B** *n* Icelander

‹ **إيسيسْكو** *n* |f| ISESCO (*Islamic Educational Scientific and Cultural Organization*)

‹ **آضَ** *v* |i; أيْض| **1** [عادَ] to return, to go/come back **2** [صارَ] to become

أيْض *n* metabolism; تَحْويلة أيْضٍ metabolism

أيْضاً *adv* also, too, as well; من الغَريبِ أيْضاً أنّ ... it is also strange that ...; أنا عَرَفْتُكَ أيْضاً في الحينِ I recognized you right away too; إنَّهُما أيْضاً لا يَتَكَلَّمانِ they don't talk either; لا ... فَقَطْ إنَّما ... أيْضاً ,لا ... فَحَسْبُ بَلْ أيْضاً ... not only ... but also ...; لا لِلكِبارِ فَحَسْبُ بَلْ أيْضاً للصِغارِ not just for adults but also for children

أيْضيّ *adj* metabolic; تَنْظيم أيْضيّ metabolic system; مَرَض أيْضيّ metabolic disorder

‹ **إيطاليا** *n* Italy

إيطاليّ **A** *adj* |طَلْيان| Italian; (اللُغة) الإيطاليّة Italian (*language*) **B** *n* |طَلْيان| Italian (*person*)

‹ **أيْقونة** *n* **1** (Relig) icon **2** (Comput) icon

‹ **أيْك** *n coll* bushes; أيْكة ساحِليّة mangrove

‹ **إيكولوجيّ** *adj* ecological; النِظام الإيكولوجيّ the ecosystem

إيكولوجيا *n* ecology

‹ **آيِل** *adj* see أول

أَيِّل, أَيَل, أُيَّل *n* |أيائِل| deer (*Cervidae*); سِرْب الأيائِل a herd of deer

‹ **أيْلول** *n* |dipt| (Levant, Iraq) September

أيْلولة *n* see أول

‹ **آمَ** *v* |i; أَيْمة ,أُيوم ,أَيْم| |من| to lose (*one's spouse*); آمَ من زَوْجَتِهِ he lost his wife, he became a widower; آمَتْ من زَوْجِها she lost her husband, she became a widow

أَيِّم *n* |أَيامى ,أَيِّمونَ| widower

‹ **إيميل** *n* |إيميلات| email; حِساب إيميل email account; عُنْوان إيميل email address; رِسالة إيميل email

1‹ **آنَ** *v* |i; أَيْن| to be time (for); آنَ لَكَ أنْ تَفْعَلَ ذلك it's time for you to do that; آنَ الأوانُ it's time

أيّانَ *adv* when

أيْنَ *adv* **1** [في أيِّ مَكانٍ] where; أيْنَ تَسْكُنُ؟ where do you live?; أيْنَ وَضَعْتَ قَلَمي؟ where did you put my pen?; من أيْنَ from where, whence (fml); من أيْنَ اشْتَرَيْتَ هذا؟ where did you buy this?; إلى أيْنَ where (to); إلى أيْنَ أنْتَ ذاهِبٌ؟ where are you going? **2** [على أيِّ أساسٍ] أيْنَ أنْتَ من هَذا؟ what do you think?; من أيْنَ لَكَ هذا؟ where did you get that idea?

أيْنَما *adv* wherever; نَشَرَ السَعادةَ أيْنَما ذَهَبَ to spread happiness wherever one goes

2‹ **أيَّنَ** *v* to ionize

تأيَّنَ *v* to be/become ionized

أَيُون *n* ion; أَيُون موجَب \ سالِب a positive/negative ion; بَطّارِيّة الليثِيوم أَيُون a lithium-ion battery

〈 **آيُوا** *n* Iowa *(US state)*

〈 **إيوان** *n a rectangular hall or space, usually vaulted, with one side open to the outdoors*

〈 **أَيّوب** *n* |dipt| Job, Ayub *(male given name)*

أَيّوبيّ **A** *adj* Ayyubid; السَلْطَنَة الأَيوبيّة the Ayyubid sultanate *(Muslim dynasty founded by Saladin which ruled much of the Middle East from 1171–1341 AD)*

B *n* Ayyubid; الأَيّوبيّونَ the Ayyubid dynasty

〈 **أَيّ** *adv* 1 [اِسْتِفْهام] which, what; أَيُّهُمْ أَفْضَلُ؟ which one (of them) is the best?; في أَيِّ مَكانٍ؟ where?; أَيُّ كِتابٍ هذا؟ what kind of a book is this?; أَيَّ كِتابٍ قَرَأْتَ؟ which book did you read?; لِأَيِّ سَبَبٍ؟ for what reason?; أَيُّكُما؟ which one of you (two)? 2 [أَيّ شَيْءٍ] any; أَيّ شَيْءٍ anything; بِأَيِّ ثَمَنٍ at any price; على أَيِّ حالٍ in any case, anyway; يُمْكِنُكَ الحُضورُ في أَيِّ وَقْتٍ you can come whenever you like; لم يُبْدِ أَيَّ \ أَيَّةَ مُقاوَمةٍ he didn't offer any resistance 3 [أَيّما] whatever; أَيّ من الاخْتِيارَيْنِ either of the two options; أَيًّا كانَ whichever, whatever, whoever; كُلُّ إِنْسانٍ أَيًّا كانَ everybody, no matter who; أَيًّا كانَتْ جِنْسيَّتُهُ whatever his nationality

أَيَّما *adv* 1 [أَيّ] whatever; أَيّما كانَ whatever the case 2 [لِحَدٍّ كَبير] very; انْقَسَموا على بَعْضِهِمْ أَيّما انْقِسامٍ they where very divided; رَحَّبَ بِها أَيّما تَرْحيبٍ he gave her a big welcome

أَيُّها *particle* |f أَيَّتُها| O *(old use), vocative particle;* من أَيْنَ أَنْت قادِمٌ أَيُّها الشَيْخُ؟ from where did you come, Sir?; يا أَيُّها المُؤْمِنونَ O you believers; يا أَيَّتُها المَلِكةُ O, my queen

بِ *prep* 1 [مَكان] in, at; بالقاهِرةِ in Cairo; هو مُدَرِّسٌ بالأَزْهَر he is a teacher at al-Azhar University 2 [حال] with; أنا بِخَيْر I am well; نِساء بالمَلابِسِ التَّقْليدِيَّة women in traditional clothing; أتى بِهَدِيَّةٍ to come bearing a gift 3 [زَمان] at; in; on; باللَّيْلِ at night, in the evening/night; بالنَّهار by day, in the daytime; بالأَمْسِ yesterday; بِمُناسَبَةِ شَيْءٍ on the occasion of sth 4 [بواسطة] by, by means of, with, through; بِسِكّينٍ \ بِقَلَمٍ with a knife/pen; بالقِطارِ \ بالسَّيّارةِ by train/car; باللُّغةِ العَرَبِيَّةِ in Arabic 5 [مادّة] with; filled with; accompanied by; مَليئة بالأَشْواكِ thorny; شاي بالنَّعْناعِ tea with mint; تَكَلَّلَ بالنَجاحِ to be crowned with success 6 [ثَمَن] for; at; بِثَلاثةِ دَراهِمَ for three dirhams; بِكَمْ how much? 7 [فَرْق] *specifying amount of difference*; بعد \ قبل وُصولِهِ بِيَوْمَيْن two days after/before his arrival; أَحْسَن بِكَثيرٍ much better 8 [طَريقة] with; بِشِدَّةٍ strongly, forcefully; fiercely; بِسُرْعةٍ quickly; بِصورةٍ مُسْتَمِرَّةٍ continuously; بِشَكْلٍ عامٍّ generally; بِطُرُقٍ غَيْرِ قانونيَّةٍ in illegal ways; بِشَكْلٍ أو بآخَرَ one way or another 9 [لِكُلِّ شَيْءٍ] per; مِئة بالمِئة 100 per cent; سَبْعة أَيّامٍ بالأُسْبوعِ seven days a week 10 [مع النَّفْيِ] *prefix for predicate of negative copula*; لَيْسَ الأَمْرُ بِهَذا السوءِ it's not that bad

بِمَ *pron* see بِما under **ما**

باء *n* |f| *name of the letter* ب; أَلِف باء alphabet; fundamentals; أَلِف باء الطَّبْخ the fundamentals of cooking

بُؤْبُؤ *n* (Anat) pupil; في بُؤْبُؤِ عَيْنِهِ in his pupils; (fig) his favourite; وَضَعَ شَخْصاً في بُؤْبُؤِ العَيْنِ to put sb in a favoured position; تَوَسَّعَ بُؤْبُؤُ عَيْنَيْهِ his pupils dilated

بابا *n* |m; بابَوات| 1 [أَب] dad, daddy; بابا وَماما mum (BrE) mom (AmE) and dad, mummy (BrE) mommy (AmE) and daddy 2 (Chr) pope; البابا يوحَنّا بولُس الثاني Pope John Paul II; قَداسة البابا the Holy Father; بابا الإسْكَنْدَرِيّة \ الأَقْباط Pope of the Coptic Orthodox Church of Alexandria

Idiom بابا غَنّوج baba ganoush (*aubergine dip popular in the Levant and Egypt*)

بابَوِيّ *adj* papal; السُّدّة \ الكُرْسيّ البابَوِيّ(ة) the Holy See

بابَوِيّة *n* papacy; popedom

بابايا *n* papaya

بابة *n* |m| Baba (*the second month of the Coptic calendar*)

بابْريكا *n* paprika

بابِل *n* |f| Babel, Babylon; بُرْج بابِلَ the Tower of Babel; حَدائِق بابِلَ المُعَلَّقة the Hanging Gardens of Babylon

بابِه *n* second month of the Coptic calendar

بابوج *n* |بَوابيجُ| slippers, flip-flops; من البابوجِ إلى الطَّرْبوشِ from head to toe

بابونَج *n* camomile (*Matricaria chamomilla*); شاي البابونَجِ camomile tea

باثولوجيّ A *adj* pathological; فَحْص باثولوجيّ a pathological examination

B *n* pathologist

باثولوجيا *n* pathology; الباثولوجيا الاجْتِماعيّة \ الإكْلينيكيّة social/clinical pathology

باديكير *n* pedicure

باذِنْجان *n coll* aubergine (BrE), eggplant (AmE) (*Solanum melongena*)

بَأَرَ *v* |a; بَأْر| to dig a well

بِئْر *n* |f; آبار| well; بِئْر جَوْفيّة \ أَرْتُوازيّة groundwater/artesian well; بِئْر اسْتِكْشافيّة exploratory well; آبار النِفْطِ والغازِ oil and gas wells; فوهة البِئْر well head; حَفَرَ بِئْراً to dig a well

بُؤْرة *n* |بُؤَر| spot, lesion; pool; centre; بُؤَر اسْتيطانيّة clusters of settlements; بُؤْرة شَقاءٍ a pool of misery; بُؤْرة للفَسادِ a cesspool of corruption; بُؤَر تَوَتُّرٍ في المِنْطَقةِ a hotbed of tension in the region

بار *n* |بارات| ❶ [حانة] bar; كانَ في البارِ to be in/at the bar ❷ (Phys) bar (*standard unit of pressure*)

باراغْواي *n* |f| Paraguay

بارانويا *n* paranoia

بارْبادوس *n* |f| Barbados

بارْبيتورات *n* barbiturate

بارود *n* gun powder; دُخان البارودِ gun smoke; رائحة البارودِ the smell of gunpowder; بَرْميل البارود powder keg; المِنْطَقةُ بَرْميلُ بارودٍ the region is a powder keg

باروك *n* baroque; فَنّ الباروك baroque art; عَصْر الباروك the Baroque period

باروكة *n* wig

بارومِتْر *n* barometer; البارومِتْر الزِئْبَقيّ mercury barometer; بارومِتْر الديموقْراطيّةِ العَرَبيّةِ a barometer of Arab democracy

بارون *n* baron; لَقَب بارون the title of baron; بارون المُخَدِّراتِ drug lord

باريس *n* |f| Paris

باريوم *n* barium

باز *n* |بيزان| hawk; falcon

بازار *n* |بازارات| bazaar

بازَلْت, بَزَلْت *n* basalt

بَئِسَ *v* |a; بُؤْس| to be/feel miserable; to be/become poor

ابْتَأَسَ *v* to be/become sad

بَأْس *n* ❶ [حال] لا بَأْسَ it's all right; it doesn't matter; لا بَأْسَ عَلَيْكَ! don't worry!; لا بَأْسَ في ذلك there's no problem with that, that's perfectly fine; لا بَأْسَ عَلَيْهِ he is fine ❷ [كَمّيّة أو نَوْعيّة] لا بَأْسَ بِهِ \ فيه considerable, significant; acceptable, decent; عَدَد لا بَأْسَ بِهِ a significant number; مَبْلَغ لا بَأْسَ بِهِ a considerable sum; كاتِب لا بَأْسَ بِهِ a decent writer; رَأْي لا بَأْسَ بِهِ a reasonable opinion; نُفوذُهُ لا بَأْسَ بِهِ he has significant influence ❸ [شِدّة] strength; بَأْس شَديد great power ❹ [عَذاب] misery

بُؤْس *n* misery, distress, trouble; poverty; بُؤْس مُدْقِع abject poverty; حِزام البُؤْسِ *ring of depressed suburbs around a major city*; ٨٠٪ من السُكّانِ يَعيشونَ في البُؤْسِ 80% of the residents live in poverty

بِئْسَ *excl* how dreadful; بِئْسَ المَصيرُ what a miserable fate; بِئْسَ الرَجُلُ أَنْتَ! you're such a terrible person!

بائِس **A** *adj* |بُؤَساءُ, بائِسونَ| miserable, wretched; poor; desperate; حالة \ حَياة بائِسة a miserable situation/life; طُفولة بائِسة a wretched childhood; مُحاوَلة بائِسة a desperate attempt **B** *n* |بُؤَساءُ| poor person; البُؤَساء the poor; دُموع البُؤَساءِ the suffering of the poor

بَئيس *adj* miserable, wretched

ابْتِئاس *n* sadness; depression

باسْتا *n* pasta

باسْتيل *n* pastel; أَقْلام الباسْتيل pastels

باسيفيكيّ *adj* Pacific

باشا *n* |m; باشَوات| pasha; (Egypt) Sir

باشَويّ *adj* القَصْر الباشَويّ the pasha's palace

باشَق, باشِق *n* |بَواشِقُ| sparrowhawk (*Accipiter nisus*)

باص *n* |باصات| bus, coach; باص سِياحيّ tour bus; شَرِكة باصاتٍ bus company; حادِث باصٍ bus accident; رِحْلة بالباص bus ride; مَحَطّة باصٍ \ باصاتٍ رَئيسيّة bus station; اسْتَقَلَّ الباصَ to take the bus

باطون *n* (ME) concrete; باطون مُسَلَّح reinforced concrete

باغة *n* celluloid

باكِسْتان *n* |f| Pakistan

باكِسْتانيّ *adj, n* Pakistani

باكَليت, باكيليت *n* (Chem) Bakelite®

باكو *n* |f| Baku (*capital of Azerbaijan*)

بالة *n* ❶ bale, stack, bundle; بالة تِبْنٍ \ قُطْنٍ a bale of hay/cotton ❷ second-hand goods; تاجِر البالةِ dealer in second-hand goods; مَحَلّ البالةِ charity shop (BrE), thrift store (AmE)

إبالة *n* stack, bundle

بالِسْتيّ *adj* ballistic; صاروخ بالِسْتيّ ballistic missile

بالون *n* |بالونات| balloon; بالون اخْتِباريّ trial balloon; نَفَخَ بالوناً to blow up a balloon; أَطْلَقَ بالوناً to release a balloon

بالي *n* |f| Bali

باليه *n* ballet; باليه كْلاسيكيّ \ حَديث classical/contemporary ballet; فِرْقة الباليه ballet (company); فِرْقة الباليه الوَطَنيّة \ القَوْميّة the national ballet; راقِصة الباليه ballerina

بامِية, **باميا** *n* okra (*Abelmoschus esculentus*)

بان *n coll* Egyptian willow (*Salix safsaf*)

بانْثِيون *n* pantheon

بانْجو *n* ① (Mus) banjo; عَزَفَ على البانْجو to play the banjo ② [حَشيش] (Egypt) marijuana, weed (infml), pot (infml AmE)

بانْكوك *n* |f| Bangkok

بانوراما *n* panorama

بانوراميّ *adj* panoramic

بانْيو *n* |بانْيوهات| bath, bathtub; اسْتَحَمَّ في البانْيو to take a bath

بَؤُونة *n* |m| Baona (*the tenth month of the Coptic calendar*)

بايْت *n* |بايْتات| byte; عَلامة تَرْتيبِ البايْتات byte order mark, BOM; تَشْفير الرَمْزِ مُتَعَدِّد البايْتات multi-byte character encoding

بايْنْت *n* pint

بَبْر *n* |بُبور| tiger

بَبَّغاء, **بَبْغاء** *n* |dipt; بَبَّغاوات| parrot; يُرَدِّدُ كالبَبَّغاءِ ما يَسْمَعُ he parrots whatever he hears

بَبَّغائيّة *n* ① [مَرَض] psittacosis ② [تَكْرار الكَلام] parrotism

بِت *n* (Comput) bit; صيغة تَحْويلِ نِظامِ الحُروفِ الدُوَليِّ المُوَحَّد بقوّة ٨ بِت 8-bit Unicode Transformation Format, UTF-8

بَتَّ *v* |i-u; بَتّ| ① [قَرَّرَ] to decide, to determine; بَتَّ في أَمْرٍ to decide on sth; بَتَّ في طَعْنٍ \ مَسْأَلةٍ to resolve an appeal/issue; بَتَّ في شَيْءٍ سَلْباً أو إيجاباً to decide sth one way or the other, to rule for or against sth ② [قَطَعَ] to cut off ③ [أَنْهى] to finish

انْبَتَّ *v* to be cut off; to be alienated

باتّ *adj* absolute, definite; categorical; مَنْع \ رَفْض باتّ an absolute prohibition/refusal; مَمْنوع مَنْعاً باتّاً strictly forbidden

بَتاتاً *adv* definite, absolute; مَمْنوع بَتاتاً strictly forbidden

بَتّة *n* البَتّةَ absolutely, definitely, positively; لا ... بَتّةً absolutely not; لن أَفْعَلَ ذلك البَتّةَ \ بَتّةً I will definitely not do that; هذا لا يَعْني البَتّةَ (أنّ) ... this does not at all mean that ..., this is not at all to say that ...

مُنْبَتّ *n* cut off, severed; alienated; مُنْبَتّ الصِلةِ ب \ عن شَيْءٍ disconnected from sth; (wholly) unrelated to sth

بَتَرَ *v* |u; بَتْر| to cut off, to sever; to amputate; بَتَرَ ساقاً to amputate a leg; بُتِرَتْ يَدُهُ في الحادِثِ his hand was cut off in the accident

بَتْر *n* |بُتور| cutting off, severing; amputating, amputation; حادِث بَتْرِ اليَدِ a hand-severing incident; جُرْح أَدّى إلى بَتْرِ ساقِهِ an injury resulting in the amputation of his leg; بَتْر المِنْطَقةِ الشَرْقيّةِ من خَريطةِ البَلَدِ amputating the eastern region from the country's map

أَبْتَر *adj* |dipt| ① [ناقِص] incomplete ② [بِدونِ أَطْفالٍ] childless ③ [بِدونِ ذَيْلٍ] docked, clipped (*tail*)

مَبْتور *adj* ① [مَقْطوع] amputated; كانَتْ ساقُهُ مَبْتورةً his leg has been amputated, to be missing a leg ② [غَيْر تامٍّ] incomplete, unfinished; نَصّ مَبْتور an unfinished text; جُمْلة مَبْتورة sentence fragment

البَتْراء, **البَطْراء** *n* |f| Petra (*historic site in Jordan*)

بِتْروكيماويّ, **بِتْروكيميائيّ** *adj* petrochemical; الصِناعة البِتْروكيماويّة petrochemical industry; بِتْروكيماويّات petrochemicals; مُنْتَجات بِتْروكيماويّة petrochemical products; مُجَمَّع بِتْروكيماويّ petrochemical complex

بِتْروكيماويّات *n pl* ① [صِناعة] petrochemistry ② [مَوادّ] petrochemicals

بِتْروكيمِيا *n* petrochemistry

بِتْرول, **بِتْرول** *n* petroleum, oil; بِتْرول خام \ مُكَرَّر crude/refined petroleum; تَكْرير البِتْرولِ petroleum refining; شَرِكة بِتْرولٍ oil company; تَنْقيب عن البِتْرولِ oil drilling; مُنَظَّمة الدُوَلِ المُصَدِّرةِ للبِتْرولِ \ للنَفْطِ Organization of the Petroleum Exporting Countries (*OPEC*)

بِتْروليّ *adj* petroleum (*before n*), oil (*before n*); ثَرْوة بِتْروليّة oil wealth; مُنْتَجات \ مُشْتَقّات بِتْروليّة petroleum products/ derivatives; الصِناعات البِتْروليّة the petroleum industry

1 **تَبَتَّلَ** *v* to live in chastity; *to devote one's life to God*

بَتول *n* |f| virgin; مَرْيَم البَتول (Chr) the Virgin Mary

بَتوليّة *n* virginity, chastity; celibacy; اِلْتَزَمَ البَتوليّةَ to observe celibacy

تَبَتُّل *n* celibacy

مُتَبَتِّل **A** *adj* **1** [عازِب] unmarried **2** [تَقيّ] pious, virtuous **B** *n* ascetic

2 **بَتْلة** *n* |بَتَلات, بَتْلات, بَتائِلُ| petal

بِتِلّو *n* (Egypt) veal

بَتولا *n* birch (*Betula*)

بَتونيا *n* petunia

بَثَّ *v* |i-u; بَثّ| **1** [أذاعَ] to broadcast, to transmit; بَثَّ بَرْنامَجاً to broadcast a program; بَثَّ مُباشَرةً to broadcast live **2** [نَشَرَ] to spread; بَثَّ الرُعْبَ \ الشِقاقَ to spread terror/discord; بَثَّ أَلْغاماً to lay mines

اِنْبَثَّ *v* to be spread

بَثّ *n* **1** [إذاعة] broadcast, broadcasting; بَثّ إذاعيّ \ تِلِفِزْيونيّ \ فضائيّ radio/television/satellite broadcast; بَثّ مُباشِر a live broadcast; رُخْصة البَثّ broadcasting licence; مَحَطّة \ قناة بَثّ (broadcast) station/channel; مَحَطّة بَثّ غَيْر شَرْعيّة a pirate broadcaster; اِنْقَطَعَ بَثُّهُ to go off the air; اِلْتَقَطَ بَثّاً to pick up a broadcast; تَمَّ بَثُّهُ to be broadcast **2** [نَشْر] spreading, sowing; بَثّ (بُذورِ) الفُرْقة sowing (seeds of) disunity; بَثّ الرُعْبِ spreading terror; بَثّ أَلْغامٍ sowing landmines (*in the sea or from the air*)

اِنْبِثاث *n* metastasis, spread; اِنْبِثاث السَرَطانِ إلى الأَعْضاءِ الأُخْرى metastasis of the cancer to other organs

اِنْبِثاثيّ *adj* metastatic; سَرَطان الثَدْيِ الاِنْبِثاثيّ metastatic breast cancer

مَبْثوث *adj* **1** broadcasted; بَرْنامَج مَبْثوث عَبْرَ \ على القَنَواتِ الفَضائيّة satellite TV shows; مَبْثوث على الهَواءِ مُباشِرةً aired live **2** scattered, spread; خَواطِر مَبْثوثة scattered thoughts

بَثَرَ, بَثِرَ *v* |a-i; بَثْر| to get spots (BrE) pimples (AmE)

بَثْر *n coll* |بُثور| pimples; bumps; ulcers (BrE), cankers (AmE); بَثْرة سَوْداء blackhead; بَثْر الفَمِ mouth ulcer; cold sore; بُثور الوَجْهِ facial acne

بَثِر *adj* pustulate

بَثَقَ *v* |i-u; بَثْق, بُثوق| **1** [اِنْدَفَعَ] to gush out **2** [أَخْرَجَ] to let overflow

اِنْبَثَقَ *v* **1** [طَلَعَ] to emanate; to proceed; اِنْبَثَقَ عن \ من شَيْءٍ to emanate from sth; اِنْبَثَقَتْ فِكْرةُ (شَيْءٍ) من ... the idea (of sth) emerged from ... **2** [السَيْلُ] to break forth, to gush out; اِنْبَثَقَ النورُ فَجْأةً light suddenly burst forth

اِنْبِثاق *n* emergence; emanation; outburst; اِنْبِثاق الوَعْيِ القَوْميِّ the emergence of national consciousness

مُنْبَثِق *adj* **1** [ناتِج] emanating, emerging, arising, stemming; مُنْبَثِق عن \ من ... stemming from ...; الحُكومة المُنْبَثِقة من الاِنْقِلابِ \ الاِنْتِخاباتِ the government that emerged from the coup/elections **2** (Comput) pop-up; قائِمة مُنْبَثِقة pop-up menu; إطار \ نافِذة مُنْبَثِق(ة) pop-up window; مانِع النَوافِذِ المُنْبَثِقةِ pop-up blocker

بِجاية *n* Béjaïa, Bejaya (*city in Algeria*)

بَجَحَ *v* |a; بَجْح| |ب| to rejoice at; to be proud of

تَبَجَّحَ *v* to boast, to brag; تَبَجَّحَ بِشَيْءٍ to boast about sth; تَبَجَّحَ بِأَنَّهُ فَعَلَ شَيْئاً to brag about having done sth

تَبَجُّح *n* boast; boasting, bragging; تَبَجُّح فارِغ an empty boast

مُتَبَجِّح **A** *adj* boasting **B** *n* braggart

اِنْبَجَسَ *v* **1** [سالَ] to spout; to flow; اِنْبَجَسَت الدُموعُ من عَيْنَيْهِ tears flowed from his eyes **2** [اِنْبَثَقَ] to emerge; اِنْبَجَسَ عن \ من شَيْءٍ to emerge from sth; اِنْبَجَسَت الأَسْئِلةُ من الاِجْتِماعِ questions emerged from the meeting

بَجَع *n coll* swan (*Cygnus*); pelican (*Pelecanus*)

بَجَّلَ *v* to venerate, to revere, to respect; بَجَّلَ شَخْصاً to venerate sb

تَبْجيل *n* veneration, reverence, respect; شَيْء يَسْتَحِقُّ التَبْجيلَ sth deserving of veneration

‹ **بُحْبوحة** *n* 1 [يُسْر] prosperity; بُحْبوحة مادّيّة \ ماليّة material/financial prosperity; عاشَ في بُحْبوحةٍ to live comfortably 2 [وَسَط] middle

‹ **بَحْت** *adj* pure, absolute; عَرَبيّ بَحْت a pure Arab; pure Arabic; مُصادَفة بَحْتة a total coincidence; لِأَسْبابٍ شَخْصيةٍ بَحْتةٍ for purely personal reasons

‹ **بَحَثَ** *v* |a; بَحْث| 1 [فَتَّشَ] |عن| to seek, to look/search for; بَحَثَ عن شَيْءٍ to look for sth; بَحَثَ عن مَسْكَنٍ جَديدٍ to look for a new house; بَحَثَ عن أَصْلِ شَيْءٍ to search for the origin of sth; بَحَثَ عن الكَلِماتِ to look up the words; بَحَثَ عن مَلْجَأٍ to seek refuge; اِبْحَثْ تَجِدْ seek and you will find 2 [دَرَسَ] to examine, to research, to investigate; بَحَثَ في شَيْءٍ to examine sth; بَحَثَ مَوْضوعاً to research a topic; بَحَثَ مَسْأَلةً من كُلِّ جَوانِبِها to examine an issue from all angles 3 [ناقَشَ] to discuss, to confer; بَحَثَ المَوْضوعَ مع شَخْصٍ to discuss the matter with sb; بَحَثَ مع نَظيرِه to confer with one's counterpart; بَحَثْنا سُبُلَ إعادةِ التَفاوُضِ we discussed ways to resume negotiations

باحَثَ *v* to discuss, to talk about

تَباحَثَ *v* to confer, to discuss, to have a discussion; تَباحَثَ مع شَخْصٍ في \ حول شَيْءٍ to discuss sth with sb; تَباحَثَ حول المَشاكِلِ \ النَتائِجِ to discuss the problems/results

بَحْث *n* |أَبْحاث ,بُحوثات ,بُحوث| 1 [تَفْتيش] search, quest; البَحْث عن شَيْءٍ the search for sth; مُحَرِّك بَحْثٍ search engine; 2 [دِراسة] research, study, investigation; inquiry; بَحْث شامِل an in-depth investigation; a thorough examination; بَحْث عِلْميّ scientific research; بَحْث مَيْدانيّ fieldwork; بَحْث تَجْريبيّ empirical research; بَحْث مُكَثَّف intensive research; بَحْث نَظَريّ \ تَطْبيقيّ theoretical/applied research; مَجال \ مَوْضوع البَحْثِ area/subject of research; مَرْكَز بُحوثٍ think tank; البَحْث في شَيْءٍ the study of sth; الأَمْرُ قَيْدَ \ تحت البَحْثِ the matter is under investigation; أَجْرى بَحْثاً to investigate; to hold an inquiry; قامَ بِبَحْثٍ to investigate; حَصَلَ على نَتائِجِ البَحْثِ to obtain research results; أَثْبَتَت البُحوثُ أَنّ ... research has shown that ...; المَوْضوع مَحَلّ البَحْثِ the topic in question; لا مَجالَ لِبَحْثِه هُنا we won't go into that here; تَعَمَّقَ في بَحْثِ شَيْءٍ to research sth thoroughly 3 [نِقاش] discussion; كانَ تحت \ قَيْدَ البَحْثِ to be under discussion; كانَ على بِساطِ البَحْثِ to be on the table 4 (Educ) thesis; research paper; بَحْث دِراسيّ thesis; بَحْث ماجِسْتير master thesis; كَتَبَ بَحْثاً to write a thesis 5 (Law) hearing; investigation

باحِث *n* |باحِثونَ ,بُحّاث| researcher; باحِث عَظيم a great researcher; باحِث أَكاديميّ \ جامِعيّ academic/university researcher; باحِث مُتَخَصِّص في ... a researcher specializing in ...

بَحّاثة *n* |m| scholar, researcher

بَحْثيّ *adj* research (*before n*); مُؤَسَّسة \ جامِعة بَحْثيّة research institute/university; مَشاريع بَحْثيّة research projects

مُباحَثة *n* talk, discussion; negotiation; مُباحَثات السَلامِ peace talks; مُباحَثات ثُنائيّة \ سُداسيّة bilateral/six-party talks; أَجْرى مُباحَثاتٍ مع شَخْصٍ to hold talks with sb, to conduct negotiations with sb; أَجْرى مُباحَثاتٍ تَمْهيديّةً to hold preliminary talks

مَبْحَث *n* |مَباحِثُ| investigation; study, research; (قِسْم) المَباحِثِ الجِنائيّةِ criminal investigation department (BrE), detective department (AmE)

‹ **بَحْثَرَ** *v* |i; بَحْثَرة| to disperse

‹ **بَحَّ** *v* |a; بُحاح ,بَحاح ,بَحّ| to be/become hoarse (*voice*); (قد) بَحَّ صَوْتُهُ to become hoarse; (fig) to shout oneself hoarse, to protest (in vain); بَحَّ صَوْتُنا وَنَحْنُ نُطالِبُ بِإِبْعادِهِ we called for his removal until we were blue in the face

بُحّة *n* hoarseness, croak

أَبَحّ *adj* |dipt| hoarse

مَبْحوح *adj* hoarse; صَوْت مَبْحوح a hoarse voice

‹ **أَبْحَرَ** *v* 1 [سافَرَ بَحْراً] to sail, to set sail; to travel by sea; أَبْحَرَ في سَفينةٍ to sail in a ship 2 [المَرْكَبُ] to sail, to set sail; أَبْحَرَت السَفينةُ the ship set sail; أَبْحَرَ من \ إلى مَكانٍ to sail from/to a place; أَبْحَرَ تحت الرايةِ البَريطانيّةِ to sail under the British flag

تَبَحَّرَ *v* |في| to study thoroughly, to delve into, to immerse oneself in; تَبَحَّرَ في عُلومِ الدينِ to immerse oneself in theology

مُتَبَحِّر *adj* |في| educated in, well versed in; مُتَبَحِّر في العِلْمِ well versed in science

بُخارى *n* |f| Bukhara (*city in Uzbekistan*)

بَخْت *n* |بُخوت| fortune, luck; قِراءة البَخْتِ fortune telling; سوء البَخْتِ bad luck; سَيِّءُ \ قَليل البَخْتِ unfortunate; يا بَخْتَكَ! you're in luck!

تَبَخْتَر *v* to boast; to show off; to act arrogantly; تَبَخْتَرَ ب \ في ثِيابِهِ الجَديدةِ to show off one's new clothes

بَخَّ *v* |u; بَخّ| to spray, to squirt; to vaporize; بَخَّ السُمَّ to spray poison; (fig) to poison (*relations, the political climate, etc.*)

بَخّ *n* spraying, squirting; vaporization; بَخّ الوَقودِ fuel injection

بَخّاخ *n* spray can/bottle; atomizer, vaporizer; بَخّاخ للأَنْفِ nasal spray; عَبْوة بَخّاخٍ spray bottle; جِهاز بَخّاخٍ fuel injector

بَخِرَ *v* |a; بَخْر| **1** [تَبَخَّرَ] to steam **2** [الفَمُ] to smell bad; بَخِرَ فَمُهُ he had bad breath

بَخَّرَ *v* **1** [الماءَ] to make evaporate; to make disappear; بَخَّرَ آمالَ \ أَحْلامَ شَخْصٍ to destroy sb's hopes/dreams **2** [للتَنْظيفِ] to fumigate **3** [مَكاناً] to fill with incense

تَبَخَّرَ *v* to steam; to evaporate; to go up in smoke; تَبَخَّرَ الماءُ the water evaporated; تَبَخَّرَتْ آمالُهُ \ أَحْلامُهُ his hopes/dreams have gone up in smoke

بَخَر *n* **1** [الفَمِ] bad breath, halitosis; بَخَر الفَمِ bad breath, halitosis **2** [تَبَخُّر] evaporation

باخِرة *n* |بَواخِرُ| ferry; ship, vessel; باخِرة سِياحيّة cruise ship; باخِرة مُحَمَّلة بالوَقودِ \ بالأَسْلحةِ a ship carrying oil/weapons; باخِرة شَحْنٍ \ صَيْدٍ shipping/fishing vessel; على مَتْنِ الباخِرة on board the ferry/ship

بُخار *n* |أَبْخِرة| steam; vapour, fume, emanation; أَبْخِرة سامّة toxic fumes; بُخار ماءٍ water vapour; مِكْواة بُخارٍ steam iron; steamer; حَمّام بُخارٍ sauna, steam bath

بُخاريّ *adj* steam (*before n*); steam-powered, powered; حَمّام بُخاريّ sauna; دَرّاجة بُخاريّة motorcycle; مِرْجَل \ توربين بُخاريّ steam boiler/turbine

بَخور *n* incense; بَخور مَرْيَم (Bot) cyclamen; أَحْرَقَ بَخوراً to burn incense

بَحْر *n* |بِحار، أَبْحار، بُحور، أَبْحُر| **1** [عَكْس بَرّ] sea; بَحْراً by sea; بَحْر القُلْزُمِ، البَحْر الأَحْمَر the Red Sea; البَحْر الأَسْوَد the Black Sea; البَحْر الأَبْيَض المُتَوَسِّط the Mediterranean Sea; مِنْطَقة \ حَوْض البَحْرِ الأَبْيَضِ المُتَوَسِّطِ the Mediterranean (*area*); البَحْر المَيِّت the Dead Sea; بَحْر هادِئ a calm sea; بَحْر هائِج a turbulent sea; بَحْر داخِليّ an inland sea; نَجْم البَحْرِ starfish; مُسْتَوى سَطْحِ البَحْرِ sea level; ارْتِفاع \ انْخِفاض مُسْتَوى سَطْحِ البَحْرِ the rise/fall of sea level; ٢٠ متراً فوق \ تحت مُسْتَوى سَطْحِ البَحْرِ 20 metres above/below sea level; ما وراء البِحارِ overseas; أَقاليم ما وراء البِحارِ overseas territories; في أَعالي البِحارِ، في عُرْضِ البَحْرِ on the high seas; في البَرِّ والبَحْرِ on land and at sea; نَقَّبَ عن النَفْطِ في البَحْرِ to drill for oil in the sea; رَكِبَ البَحْرَ to travel by sea; خاضَ البَحْرَ to sail the sea **2** [كَمّيّة كَبيرة] abundance; بَحْر من الدَمِ a sea of blood; بَحْر من المَشاكِلِ a huge number of problems **3** [في مَدارِ] course; في بَحْرِ in/over the course of; في بَحْرِ هذا الأُسْبوعِ in the course of this week **4** [وَزْن شِعْريّ] metre

بَحّار **A** *adj* |بَحّارون، بَحّارة| maritime **B** *n* |بَحّارون، بَحّارة| sailor, seaman

بَحْراويّ *adj* Lower Egyptian (*from the Nile Delta*)

بَحْريّ *adj* maritime, nautical, naval; sea (*before n*); نَقْل بَحْريّ shipping by sea; مَدّ بَحْريّ tsunami; قوّة بَحْريّة a naval power; القوّات البَحْريّة the navy; ميل بَحْريّ nautical mile; رِحْلة بَحْريّة sea voyage; رِياح بَحْريّة sea breeze; الوَجْه البَحْريّ the Delta Region (*in Egypt*)

بَحْريّة *n* navy; جُنْديّ البَحْريّة marine; مُشاة البَحْريّة the marines; البَحْريّة البَريطانيّة the British navy; في البَحْريّة in the navy

بَحْرَيْنيّ *adj, n* |بَحْرَيْنيّون، بَحارِنة| Bahraini

بُحَيْرة *n* |بُحَيْرات| lake; بُحَيْرة صِناعيّة artificial lake; ضِفاف البُحَيْرةِ the lake shore

إِبْحار *n* sailing; سُرْعة الإِبْحارِ sailing speed

البَحْرَيْن *n* |f| Bahrain; مَمْلَكة البَحْرَيْنِ the Kingdom of Bahrain

تَبَحُّر *n* delving (into), thorough study (of); تَبَحُّر في عُلومِ اللُغةِ a thorough study of linguistics

تَبَخُّر *n* evaporation; مُعَدَّل التَبَخُّرِ evaporation rate; حَرارة التَبَخُّرِ (Sci) heat/enthalpy of vaporization

تَبْخير *n* **1** [ماءٍ] evaporation; تَبْخير الماءِ water evaporation **2** [مَأْكَلٍ] steaming **3** [حَشَراتٍ] fumigation

مُبَخِّر *n* (Tech) evaporator

مِبْخَرة *n* |مَباخِرُ| censer, incense burner

بَخَسَ *v* |a; بَخْس| to undervalue; to disregard; to wrong; بَخَسَ شَخْصاً حَقَّهُ to wrong sb; to not give sb his due; بَخَسَ قيمةَ شَيْءٍ to undervalue sth

تَباخَسَ *v* to wrong one another

بَخْس *adj* low, insignificant; مَبْلَغ بَخْس a small amount; ثَمَن \ سِعْر بَخْس a low price

تَبْخيس *n* debasing, belittling

بَخْشيش *n* |بَخاشيشُ| see بَقْشيش

بَخِلَ *v* |a; بُخْل| to be stingy; بَخِلَ بِشَيْءٍ to be stingy with sth; بَخِلَ بِمالِهِ to be stingy with one's money; بَخِلَ على \ عن شَخْصٍ بِشَيْءٍ to withhold sth from sb

بُخْل *n* stinginess, miserliness

بَخيل **A** *adj* |بُخَلاءُ| stingy, miserly; يا لَهُ من بَخيلٍ he is so stingy

B *n* |بُخَلاءُ| miser

بُخْنُق *n* |بَخانِقُ| veil, scarf

بَدَأَ *v* |a; بَدْء| **1** [شَيْئاً] to begin, to start; بَدَأَ شَيْئاً \ بِشَيْءٍ to begin something; بَدَأَ العَمَلَ to begin work; بَدَأَ التَحَدُّثَ \ اللَعِبَ \ العامَ الدِراسيَّ to start the conversation/the game/the school year; بَدَأَ بِدراسةِ شَيْءٍ to begin researching sth; بَدَأَ يَتَكَلَّمُ عن شَيْءٍ to bring sth up; بَدَأَ يَعْمَلُ لِحِسابِهِ الخاصِّ to start one's own business; بَدَأَ يَقْرَأُ الكِتابَ he started to read the book; لَيْتَني لم أَبْدَأْ بِذَلِكَ! I wish I had never started it! **2** [شَيْءٌ] to begin, to start; يَبْدَأُ اليَوْمُ \ الفيلمُ the day/film is starting; تَبْدَأُ المُباراةُ (في تَمامِ الساعةِ التاسِعةِ) the game is starting (at nine o'clock sharp); لَقَدْ بَدَأَ العامُ الدِراسيُّ الجَديدُ the new school year has started; سَيَبْدَأُ العَرْضُ the show is starting

ابْتَدَأَ *v* to begin, to start; ابْتَدَأَ شَيْئاً \ بِشَيْءٍ to begin something

بَدْء *n* |بُدوء ,أَبْداء| beginning, start; مَوْعِد البَدْءِ starting time; بَدْء المُفاوَضاتِ \ المُحادَثاتِ the start of negotiations/talks; قبل بَدْءِ شَيْءٍ before the start of sth; عَوْداً وَبَدْءاً ,عَوْداً على بَدْءٍ starting over, going back to the beginning; اعْتَزَمَ بَدْءَ الانْسِحابِ \ المُفاوَضاتِ to be committed to begin withdrawal/negotiations

بادِئ *n* **1** [بِداية] beginning; في بادِئِ الأَمْرِ at first, initially; بادِئَ ذي بَدْءٍ first of all **2** [الَّذي بَدَأَ] the first one; the person starting; البادِئُ أَظْلَمُ the one who started the trouble is most to blame; كانَ البادِئَ بالتَسْجيلِ to be the first to score

بادِئة *n* prefix

بُداءة *n* beginning; مَحْكَمة البُداءةِ (Iraq) court of first instance (BrE), trial court (AmE)

بُدائيّ ,بِدائيّ **A** *adj* primitive; أَقْوام بُدائيّة primitive peoples; غَرائِز بُدائية primitive instincts

B *n* savage

بِداية *n* beginning, start; بِداية بَطيئة \ مُتَواضِعة a slow/modest start; بِداية مُشَجِّعة an encouraging beginning; بِداية الكِتابِ \ الشَهْرِ \ الشارِعِ the beginning of the book/the month/the street; بِداية في مَجالِ الأَدَبِ a literary debut; نُقْطة البِدايةِ starting point; بِدايةً من أَوَّلِ \ غُرَّةِ يناير as of January 1st; قبل \ بعد بِدايةِ شَيْءٍ before/after the start of sth; في البِدايةِ in the beginning, at first; في بِدايةِ التِسْعيناتِ \ القَرْنِ العِشْرينَ at the beginning of the '90s/the 20th century; من \ منذ البِدايةِ from the beginning; من البِدايةِ إلى النِهايةِ from start to finish; شَكَّلَ \ مَثَّلَ بِدايةً جَديدةً (لِشَيْءٍ) to represent a new beginning (for sth)

ابْتِداء *n* beginning, start; ابْتِداءً من from, starting, as of; ابْتِداءً من ٢٠ أَغُسْطُس from August 20th; ابْتِداءً من اليَوْمِ from today, starting today

ابْتِدائيّ *adj* primary, elementary; التَعْليم الابْتِدائيّ elementary education; مَدْرَسة ابْتِدائيّة primary school; مَحْكَمة ابْتِدائيّة court of first instance (BrE), trial court (AmE)

مُبْتَدَأ *n* **1** [مَطْلَع] beginning, start **2** (Gram) *subject of a nominal clause*

مُبْتَدِئ *n* **1** [حَديث العَهْدِ] beginner **2** (Chr) novice

مَبْدَأ *n* |مَبادِئ| **1** [أَساس] principle; basis, foundation; مَبْدَأ أَساسيّ basic principle; مَبادِئ المُساواةِ \ الديمُقْراطيّةِ the principles of equality/democracy; مَبادِئ الاقْتِصادِ \ فَنِّ الرَسْمِ the basics of economics/painting; إعْلان مَبادِئَ declaration of principles; على مَبْدَأِ المُساواةِ on the basis of equality; اتِّفاق إعْلانِ المَبادِئِ agreement in principle; من حَيْثُ المَبْدَأِ in principle **2** [عَقيدة] principle; مَبادِئ أَخْلاقيّة moral principles; شَخْص ذو \ صاحِب مَبادِئَ a principled person; مُنافٍ لِمَبادِئِه against his principles; الْتَزَمَ \ تَمَسَّكَ بالمَبادِئِ to live up to/stick to one's principles; امْتَثَل لِمَبادِئَ مُعَيَّنةٍ to follow certain principles; تَمَسَّكَ بِمَبْدَأِ ... to live by the principle of ...; حادَ عن مَبادِئِه to go/act against one's principles

مَبْدَئيّ *adj* in principle; principled; initial, preliminary; مَبْدَئيًّا in principle; مُوافَقة مَبْدَئيّة an agreement in principle; مَوْقِف مَبْدَئيّ a principled stance; تَصَوُّر مَبْدَئيّ a rough idea; تَقْدير مَبْدَئيّ an initial appraisal; رَأْسمال مَبْدَئيّ starting capital

بَدَّدَ *v* **1** [بَذَّرَ] to waste, to squander; بَدَّدَ مالَهُ to waste one's money **2** [أَزالَ] to remove, to eliminate; to dispel, to dissipate; بَدَّدَ الظُلُماتِ to dispel the darkness; بَدَّدَ الشُكوكَ \ الأَمالَ to banish all doubt/hope; بَدَّدَ مَخاوِفَ شَخْصٍ to address sb's concerns

تَبَدَّدَ *v* to be spread; to disperse; to evaporate; تَبَدَّدَت السُحُبُ the clouds have disappeared; تَبَدَّدَتْ أَحْلامُهُ his dreams have evaporated into thin air

اسْتَبَدَّ *v* **1** [طَغى] to rule despotically **2** [تَفَرَّدَ] to proceed independently; اسْتَبَدَّ بِرَأْيِه to be headstrong **3** [اسْتَحْوَذَ] to take possession, to overwhelm; اسْتَبَدَّتْ بِهِ شَهَواتُهُ he was overwhelmed by his desires; اسْتَبَدَّ بِهِ حَنينٌ he was overcome with longing

بُدّ *n* لا بُدَّ مِنْ (أَنْ \ أَنّ) ... it's necessary (that) ...; it should ...; لا بُدَّ أَنْ \ أَنّ ... it's necessary that ...; هذه الخُطْوةُ لا بُدَّ مِنْها this is a necessary step; لا بُدَّ من الإشارةِ إلى \ التَذْكير بِأَنَّ ... it should be pointed out/mentioned that ...; لا بُدَّ من وُجودِ حَلٍّ there must be a solution; لا بُدَّ من العَوْدةِ إلى السُؤالِ الأَساسيِّ we must go back to the fundamental question; لا بُدَّ لَها أَنْ تَفْعَلَ هذا she must do that

اسْتِبْداد *n* tyranny, despotism, dictatorship; absolutism; اسْتِبْداد سِياسيّ political tyranny

اسْتِبْداديّ *adj* tyrannical, dictatorial, despotic; نِظام \ حُكْم اسْتِبْداديّ a tyrannical regime/government; سُلْطة اسْتِبْداديّة tyrannical rule

اسْتِبْداديّة *n* autocracy; absolutism

تَبْديد *n* **1** [تَبْذير] waste, dissipation; تَبْديد الجُهودِ \ الطاقةِ \ المالِ a waste of strength/energy/money; تَبْديد كَبير \ فَظيع a big/enormous waste **2** [تَفْريق] dispersal; تَبْديد مَخاوِفِ شَخْصٍ addressing sb's concerns; تَبْديد الغَيْمةِ dispelling the gloom

مُبَدِّد **A** *adj* **1** [مُبَذِّر] wasteful **2** [مُفَرِّق] dispersed, scattered **B** *n* squanderer

مُسْتَبِدّ **A** *adj* tyrannical, despotic; domineering; مُسْتَبِدّ بِرَأْيِه headstrong; مَلِك مُسْتَبِدّ an absolute monarch; a tyrannical king **B** *n* despot, tyrant, dictator, autocrat; مُسْتَبِدّ عادِل a benevolent dictator

بَدَرَ *v* |u|; |بُدور| **1** to take by surprise, to come suddenly/unexpectedly **2** |من، عن| to be presented by; to come from; لم يَبْدُرْ عن السَيّارةِ أَيُّ أَعْطالٍ the car didn't give us any problems at all; بَدَرَت عن طَهْرانَ إشاراتٌ غامِضةٌ some ambiguous signals came from Tehran

بادَرَ *v* to take the initiative; to start, to set out; بادَرَ ب \ إلى (فِعْلِ) شَيْءٍ to take the initiative on sth; to start (doing) sth; بادَرَ بِإطْلاقِ النارِ to start shooting; بادَرَ شَخْصاً التَحيّةَ to be the first one to say hello to sb

تَبادَرَ *v* to occur (to one's mind); لَقَدْ تَبادَرَ إلى ذِهْني شَيْءٌ sth occurred to me

ابْتَدَرَ *v* **1** [أَسْرَعَ] to hurry to **2** [اسْتَبَقَ] to forestall, to pre-empt; to anticipate; ابْتَدَرَ حَديثَ شَخْصٍ بِسُؤالٍ to interrupt sb with a question; ابْتَدَرَها قائِلاً ... before she could say sth he said ...

بَدْر *n* |بُدور| **1** [قَمَر] full moon; بَدْر التَمامِ full moon **2** [مَدينة] |f| Badr (*town near Mecca*); مَدينة بَدْرٍ Badr City (*in Egypt*)

بادِرة *n* |بَوادِرُ| **1** [عَلامة] sign, indication; gesture; بادِرة طَيِّبة \ جَيِّدة, بادِرة خَيْرٍ a good sign; بادِرة حُسْنِ النِيَّة a token of goodwill **2** [مُبادَرة] initiative; بادِرة مَحْمودة a commendable initiative **3** [نَبات] seedling

مُبادِر **A** *adj* proactive
B *n* initiator

مُبادَرة *n* initiative; تَفْعيل مُبادَرةٍ initiative; مُبادَرة سَلامٍ peace initiative; مُبادَرة بِشَيْءٍ the initiative for sth; بِمُبادَرةٍ من شَخْصٍ on the initiative of sb; أَطْلَقَ مُبادَرةً to launch an initiative; اتَّخَذَ المُبادَرةَ \ زِمامَ المُبادَرةِ to take the initiative

بَدَعَ *v* |a; بَدْع| to introduce; to invent; to create

بَدُعَ *v* |u; بَداعة| to be marvellous

بَدَّعَ *v* **1** [تَميَّزَ] to stand out, to excel **2** (Relig) to accuse of heresy

أَبْدَعَ *v* **1** [خَلَقَ] to create **2** [أَجادَ] to stand out, to excel

ابْتَدَعَ *v* to invent, to contrive; to innovate; to create

بِدْعة *n* |بِدَع ,بِدَعات| **1** [شَيْء جَديد] novelty; innovation **2** (Relig) heresy

بَديع **A** *adj* wonderful, marvelous, fantastic
B *n* **1** [مُعْجِزة] |بَدائِع| marvel, wonder **2** [بَلاغة] عِلْم البَديع rhetoric; literary technique **3** (Islam) البَديع the Incomparable (*one of the names of God*) **4** [اسْم شَخْصِيّ] Badi' (*male given name*)

ابْتِداع *n* invention, creation; ابْتِداع نِظامٍ جَديدٍ the invention of a new system; ابْتِداع صيغةِ شَيْءٍ devising a formula for sth

ابْتِداعيّة *n* (Art) romanticism

إِبْداع *n* |إِبْداعات| creativity, inventiveness; originality; innovation; إِبْداع تَكْنولوجيّ \ فِكْريّ technological/intellectual innovation; إِبْداع فَنِّيّ artistic creativity; قِلّة \ عَدَم الإِبْداعِ a lack of creativity; حُبّ الإِبْداعِ a creative urge; قوّة الإِبْداع inventiveness; روح الإِبْداعِ creative spirit; قُدْرة على الإِبْداع a creative ability; originality

إِبْداعيّ *adj* inventive; creative; كِتابة إِبْداعيّة creative writing; قُدْرات إِبْداعيّة creative abilities

مُبْتَدِع *n* heretic

مُبْدِع **A** *adj* creative; inventive; فَنّان مُبْدِع a creative artist
B *n* **1** [خالِق] creator; inventor **2** (Islam) المُبْدِع the Originator (*one of the names of God*)

بَدَّلَ *v* **1** [غَيَّرَ] to change, to alter; بَدَّلَ مَوْقِفَهُ \ رَأْيَهُ to change one's position/opinion; لم يُبَدِّلْ شَيْئاً to not change one bit; بَدَّلَ أَماكِنَ الكَراسي to change the position of the chairs **2** [اسْتَبْدَلَ] to replace, to substitute; to exchange; بَدَّلَ عُمْلةً أَجْنَبِيّةً to exchange a foreign currency; بَدَّلَ القُماشَ الجَديدَ بالقُماشِ القَديمِ to replace the old fabric for a new one; بَدَّلَ جِلْدَهُ to shed its skin (*snake*); (fig) to completely change one's character, to go from one extreme to another

بادَلَ *v* to exchange; to reciprocate; بادَلَ شَيْئاً بِمِثْلِهِ to reciprocate sth in kind; كانَ يُبادِلُهُم التَحيّةَ بِمِثْلِها he was exchanging greetings with them; بادَلَ شَخْصاً حُبّاً بِحُبٍّ to love sb back

أَبْدَلَ *v* to replace, to substitute; أَبْدَلَ ثِيابَهُ to change one's clothes; أَبْدَلَ شَيْئاً بِغَيْرِهِ to replace sth with sth else

تَبَدَّلَ *v* to change; تَبَدَّلَ سُلوكُهُ his behaviour has changed; تَبَدَّلَ إِلى شَيْءٍ to change into sth

تَبادَلَ *v* **1** [بادَلَ] to exchange; to reciprocate; تَبادَلَ الآراءَ \ وُجْهاتِ النَظَرِ to exchange opinions/points of view; تَبادَلَ الاتِّهاماتِ to trade accusations; تَبادَلَ النَظَراتِ \ القُبُلاتِ to exchange glances/kisses; تَبادَلَ التَجارِبَ to share experiences/expertise; تَبادَلَ (أَطْرافَ) الحَديثِ to converse **2** [تَقايَضَ] to barter, to trade; تَبادَلَ الأَسْرى to exchange prisoners of war

اسْتَبْدَلَ *v* to change, to exchange; to replace, to substitute; اسْتَبْدَلَ شَيْئاً بِشَيْءٍ to change sth for sth; to replace sth with sth; اسْتَبْدَلَ أَوْراقاً مالِيّةً to exchange bank notes; اسْتَبْدَلَ قِطَعاً نَقْدِيّةً بِوَرَقةٍ مالِيّةٍ to exchange a bank note for coins; اسْتَبْدَلَ المَلابِسَ to change (one's clothes); اسْتَبْدَلَ حاسوباً جَديداً بِحاسوبٍ قَديمٍ to replace an old computer with a new one; قد اسْتَبْدَلَ التَعَصُّبَ بالتَسامُحِ to trade tolerance for extremism

بَدَل *n* |أَبْدال ,بَدَلات| **1** [عِوَض] بَدَلَ in place of, instead of; بَدَلاً من in place of, instead of; in exchange for; حَقَّقَ بَدَلاً مُجْدِياً to make a good exchange **2** [مَبْلَغ] allowance,

تَبَدُّل *n* |تَبَدُّلات| change, alteration, turn; تَبَدُّل في مَوْقِفِهِ a change in one's position

تَبْديل *n* **1** [تَصْريف] change, alteration; replacement; تَبْديل الحَرَسِ the changing of the guard; قابِل للتَبْديلِ replaceable, exchangeable; غُرْفة تَبْديلِ المَلابِسِ changing room (BrE), dressing/fitting room (AmE) **2** (Comput, Elec) switching; تَبْديل الداراتِ circuit switching; تَبْديل الرزَمِ packet switching

مُبادَلة *n* exchange; مُبادَلة تِجارِيّة trade; بَرْنامَج المُبادَلَةِ exchange programme

مُبَدِّل *n* changer; transducer; converter; مُبَدِّل سُرْعةٍ gear lever (BrE), gear shift (AmE)

مُتَبادَل *adj* mutual, reciprocal; تَفاهُم مُتَبادَل mutual understanding; مَنْفَعة مُتَبادَلَة mutual advantage; العَلاقات المُتَبادَلة بين بَلَدَيْنِ mutual relations between two countries; مَشاعِرُ الحُبِّ \ الكَراهِيَةِ (بَيْنَهُما) مُتَبادَلَةٌ their love/hate is mutual

مُتَبادِل *adj* alternating

بَدُنَ, بَدَنَ *v* |u; بَدانة| to be/become overweight

بَدَن *n* |أَبْدُن, أَبْدان| **1** [جِسْم] body; اقْشَعَرَّ بَدَنُهُ to shiver **2** [سَفينة، طَيّارة] body; hull

بادِن *adj* |بُدْن| corpulent, obese

بَدانة *n* obesity, corpulence; بَدانة مُفْرِطة obesity; مُعَدَّل البَدانةِ the obesity rate

بَدَنيّ *adj* physical, bodily; لِياقة بَدَنِيّة (physical) fitness; أذًى بَدَنِيّ bodily harm; تَرْبية بَدَنِيّة physical education; نَفْسيّ بَدَنيّ psychosomatic

بَدين *adj* |بُدْن, بُدُن, بُدَناءُ| fat, corpulent; overweight; obese; رَجُل بَدين a fat man

بَدَهَ *v* |a; بَداهة, بَدْه| to befall, to come suddenly upon; to surprise; بَدَهَ شَخْصاً to surprise sb

بَداهة *n* spontaneity; naturalness; بَداهةً a priori

بَديهة *n* impulse; intuition; سُرْعة \ حاضِر البَديهةِ agile; quick-witted; على البَديهة on an impulse; أَجابَ على البَديهةِ to answer without thinking

بَديهيّ *adj* **1** [واضِح] obvious, self-evident; natural; سُؤال بَديهيّ an obvious question; ... مِن البَديهيّ أنّ \ أنْ it's a

reimbursement; compensation; بَدَل سَكَنٍ \ سَفَرٍ housing/travelling allowance; بَدَل الإيجاراتِ (the cost of) rent; housing allowance; بَدَل الأَتْعابِ compensation for services **3** (Ling) apposition

بَدّالة *n* telephone exchange; بَدّالة هاتِفيّة \ الهاتِفِ switchboard

بَدْلة *n* |بَدَلات| suit; costume; بَدْلة رَسْمِيّة formal wear; (formal) suit; tuxedo; ceremonial dress, official robes; بَدْلة عَسْكَرِيّة military dress; لَبِسَ \ خَلَعَ بَدْلةً to put on/take off a suit; ارْتَدى بَدْلةً to wear a suit

بَديل **A** *adj* |بَدائِلُ| alternative; acting; الوَزير البَديل the acting minister; طاقة بَديلة alternative energy; طِبّ بَديل alternative medicine; حَلّ \ اقْتِراح بَديل an alternative solution/proposition; مادّة بَديلة (لِشَيْءٍ) a substitute (for sth)
B *n* |بُدَلاءُ| **1** [خِيار] alternative; option; بَديل مُناسِب \ مَقْبول a suitable/acceptable alternative; لا بَديل عن هذا there is no other choice **2** [شَخْص] replacement, substitute; stand-in, understudy; بَديل جاهِز \ مُتاح a ready/available replacement; بَديل عن حارِسِ المَرْمى substitute goalkeeper **3** [بَدَل] substitute, surrogate; بَديل سُكَّرٍ \ قَهْوةٍ a sugar/coffee substitute

إبْدال *n* |إبْدالات| **1** [تَبْديل] replacement, substitution; إبْدال نِظامٍ سِياسيٍّ بِآخَرَ replacing one political system with another **2** (Ling) phonetic change

اسْتِبْدال *n* |اسْتِبْدالات| exchange; replacement, substitution; اسْتِبْدال سَيّارةٍ قَديمةٍ trading in an old car; اسْتِبْدال العُمْلةِ currency exchange

تَبادُل *n* |تَبادُلات| exchange; trade; تَبادُل تِجاريّ trade; تَبادُل ثَقافيّ cultural exchange; تَبادُل الأَسْرى prisoner swap; تَبادُل المَعْلوماتِ \ وِجْهاتِ النَظَرِ \ الأَفْكارِ sharing information/points of view/thoughts; تَبادُل المَلِفّاتِ file sharing; بَرْنامَج تَبادُلٍ exchange programme; اتِّفاقيّة التَبادُلِ الحُرِّ free trade agreement

تَبادُليّ *adj* mutual, reciprocal, exchange (*before n*); التَدْريس \ التَعْميم التَبادُليّ reciprocal teaching; بَرْنامَج تَبادُليّ exchange programme

تَبادُلِيّة *n* reciprocity; mutual exchange

matter of course that ...; هذا من البَديهيّ that is obvious **2** [تِلْقائيّ] intuitive

بَديهيّة *n* axiom, given; common knowledge; بَديهيّات عِلْم axioms of marketing; أَصْبَحَ من البَديهيّاتِ أنّ ... التَسْويقِ it has become common knowledge that ...

‹ **بَدا** *v* |u; بَداء ,بُدُوّ| to seem, to appear, to look; to turn out, to prove; يَبْدو البَيْتُ كَبيراً \ صَغيراً the house looks big/small; يَبْدو (لي) أنّ ... apparently, evidently; على ما \ كَما يَبْدو it seems (to me) that ...; يَبْدو للوَهْلةِ الأولى (أنّ) ... to appear at first glance (that) ...; بَدا وَكَأنّهُ ... يَبْدو وَكَأنّ ... it looks like ...; بَدا أَصْغَرَ من سِنِّهِ نَجْمٌ سينَمائيٌّ to look like a movie star; to look young for one's age

أَبْدى *v* to express, to utter; to show, to display, to manifest; أَبْدى أَسَفَهُ أَبْدى الشُكْرَ \ شُكْرَهُ to show one's thanks; أَبْدى (الشَديدَ) to express one's (deepest) regrets; اسْتِعْدادَهُ \ ارْتياحَهُ to express one's willingness/satisfaction; أَبْدى اهْتِماماً (خاصًّا) بِشَيْءٍ to express a (special) interest in sth; أَبْدى رَأْيَهُ to give one's opinion

تَبَدّى *v* to manifest oneself, to appear

بَدْو *n* Bedouins, nomads; قَبائِل البَدْوِ Bedouin tribes

بادٍ *adj* clear, evident; visible; الآثارُ لا تَزالُ بادِيَةً the effects are still visible; كانَ بادِياً في الأُفُقِ to be visible on the horizon; كانَ بادِياً على وَجْهِهِ to be visible on one's face (*worry, fear, etc.*)

بادِيَة *n* |بادِيات ,بَوادٍ| desert; البادِية السوريّة \ الأُرْدُنيّة the Syrian/Jordanian desert; أَهْل البادِيَةِ nomads, Bedouins

بَداوة *n* nomadism, bedouinism; حَياة البَداوةِ nomadic life; الانْتِقال من البَداوةِ إلى الحَضارةِ the transition from nomadism to civilization

بَدَويّ **A** *adj* |بَدْو| nomadic, Bedouin (*before n*); شَعْب بَدَويّ a nomadic people; لَهْجة بَدَويّة a Bedouin dialect/accent; شِعْر \ تُراث بَدَويّ Bedouin poetry/traditions
B *n* |بَدْو| Bedouin; nomad

إبْداء *n* showing; expression; إبْداء رَأْيِهِ expressing one's opinion; حُرّيّة إبْداءِ الرَأْيِ freedom of expression

‹ **بِدونِ** *prep* see دونَ

‹ **بَذَأَ** *v* |a; بَذاء| **1** [فَحُشَ قَوْلُهُ] to use foul language **2** [أَهانَ] to abuse, to curse

بَذاءة *n* obscenity, profanity; بَذاءة اللِسانِ obscene language

بَذيء *adj* obscene, vulgar, dirty; rude; أَلْفاظ بَذيئة ,كَلام بَذيء vulgar language; نُكْتة بَذيئة a dirty joke; كَلِمة \ إشارة بَذيئة an obscene word/gesture; اسْتَخْدَمَ كَلِماتٍ بَذيئةً to use foul language

‹ **بَذَخَ** *v* |a; بَذْخ| **1** [تَكَبَّرَ] to be proud; to show off **2** [صَرَفَ] to be lavish, to be a spendthrift; بَذَخَ في الإنْفاقِ to spend lavishly

بَذَخ *n* extravagance, opulence; lavish spending; عاشَ حَياةَ بَذَخٍ to live extravagantly; أَنْفَقَ بِبَذَخٍ to spend lavishly

باذِخ *adj* luxuriant, extravagant, lavish; impressive; عُرْس باذِخ an extravagant wedding

‹ **بَذَرَ** *v* |u; بَذْر| to sow; بَذَرَ بُذورَ القَمْحِ to plant wheat; بَذَرَ بُذورَ التَوَتُّرِ to plant seeds of anxiety

بَذَّرَ *v* to waste, to squander; بَذَّرَ المالَ to waste money

بَذْر *n* |بُذور ,بِذار| seed; بُذور القُطْنِ cotton seed; بُذور الشَكِّ seeds of doubt; زَرَعَ بُذورَ to plant seeds; زَرَعَ \ بَذَرَ بُذوراً حَمَلَ بَذْراً الفِتْنةِ والشِقاقِ to sow the seeds of conflict; to bear seed

بَذْرة *n* |بَذْرات| seed; grain; germ; بَذْرة نَبْتة the seed of a plant; بَذْرة فِكْرةٍ (fig) the germ of an idea

بُذَيْرة *n* seed

تَبْذير *n* waste; wasting, squandering; تَبْذير الماءِ wasting water; تَبْذير الأَمْوالِ (العامّةِ) a waste of (public) money

مُبَذِّر **A** *adj* wasteful, profligate; شَخْص مُبَذِّر a profligate person; إنْفاق \ عَيْش مُبَذِّر extravagant spending/lifestyle
B *n* spendthrift, squanderer, waster

‹ **بَذَلَ** *v* |i; بَذْل| to give, to offer; to expend; بَذَلَ الجُهودَ to exert oneself, to make an effort; بَذَلَ الغالِيَ والنَفيسَ to take great pains, to go to great lengths; بَذَلَ تَضْحِياتٍ to make sacrifices; بَذَلَ المُسْتَحيلَ to do the impossible; بَذَلَ كُلَّ ما في وُسْعِهِ to do everything in one's power; بَذَلَ أَقْصى جُهْدِهِ لِتَحْقيقِ شَيْءٍ to take great pains to realize sth; بَذَلَ قُصارى جُهْدِهِ من أَجْلِ شَيْءٍ to go out of one's way for sth

اِبْتَذَلَ *v* **1** [تَبَذَّلَ] to be vulgar, to be indecent; to display vulgar manners, to behave indecorously **2** [امْتَهَنَ] to wear out, to make commonplace, to make trite; يَبْتَذِلُ القانونُ مَفْهومَ الإِرْهابِ the law cheapens the term 'terrorism' **3** [حَطَّ من] [قَدْرِ] to degrade, to demean; to stoop; اِبْتَذَلَ الرَئيسُ الحَياةَ السِياسيّةَ the president has degraded political life

بَذْل *n* exerting; دون بَذْلِ المَزيدِ من الجُهْدِ without any more effort; يَنْبَغي بَذْلُ الجُهودِ ل ... efforts should be made to ...; بَذْل كُلِّ الجُهودِ المُمْكِنة (لِفِعْلِ شَيْءٍ) exerting all possible efforts (to do sth)

بِذْلة *n* |بِذَل| suit; outfit; costume; uniform; بِذْلة عَمَلٍ work clothes; بِذْلة الفَضاءِ space suit; بِذْلة عَسْكَرِيّة military uniform; بِذْلة السِباحةِ swimsuit

اِبْتِذال *n* banality; vulgarity

مُبْتَذَل *adj* **1** [تافِه] trite, banal; corny, cheesy; worn out, overused; نُكْتة مُبْتَذَلة a corny joke; مَوْضوع مُبْتَذَل a banal subject; كَلام مُبْتَذَل cliché **2** (Levant) [ماء] used; مِياه مُبْتَذَلة waste water

مِبْذَلة ,مِبْذَل *n* |مَباذِلُ| nightgown; robe, dressing gown

1 ‹ **بَرِيّة** *n* |بَرايا| creature

البارِئ *n* the Evolver, the Fashioner (*one of the names of God*)

2 ‹ **بَرِئَ** *v* |a; بَراءة| **1** [خَلَصَ] |من| to be free from; to be cleared of; بَرِئَ من الدَيْنِ to be free from debt; بَرِئَ من التُهْمةِ to be cleared of the charge **2** [شُفِيَ] to be cured

بَرَّأَ *v* to acquit, to clear; بَرَّأَ شَخْصاً to acquit sb; بَرَّأَ ساحةَ شَخْصٍ بَرَّأَ شَخْصاً من تُهْمةٍ to acquit sb of a charge; بَرَّأَ شَخْصاً من جَريمةِ قَتْلٍ to acquit sb of murder; بَرَّأَ شَخْصاً من مَسْؤوليّةٍ to absolve sb of responsibility; بَرَّأَت المَحْكَمةُ ساحَتَهُ the court has acquitted him

أَبْرَأَ *v* to acquit, to clear, to discharge; أَبْرَأَ شَخْصاً من دَيْنِهِ to release sb from his debts; أُبْرِأَتْ ذِمَّتُهُ (من جَريمةٍ) he has been cleared (of a crime)

تَبَرَّأَ *v* **1** [من التُهْمةِ] |من| to be acquitted of, to be cleared of; تَبَرَّأَ من شَيْءٍ to be acquitted of sth **2** [تَخَلّى] |من| to distance oneself from, to dissociate oneself from; تَبَرَّأَ من أَصْحابِهِ to distance oneself from one's friends

اِسْتَبْرَأَ *v* to seek acquittal

بُرْء *n* cure, recovery; بُرْء من مَرَضٍ recovery from an illness

بَراءة *n* **1** [عَدَم الذَنْبِ] innocence; حُكْم بالبَراءةِ acquittal; أَثْبَتَ بَراءَتَهُ to prove one's innocence; أَقْنَعَ شَخْصاً بِبَراءَتِهِ to convince sb of one's innocence; طَلَبَ الحُكْمَ بالبَراءةِ to demand acquittal; حَكَمَ بالبَراءةِ to acquit, to discharge **2** [سَذاجة] innocence; بَراءة الأَطْفالِ the innocence of children **3** [شَهادة] license; بَراءة اخْتِراعٍ patent **4** [تَبْرِئة] dispensation

بَريء *adj* |أَبْرِياءُ ,بُراء ,إِبراء| **1** [غَيْر مُتَّهَم] innocent; بَريء كانَ بَريئاً; ضَحايا أَبْرِياء innocent victims; الساحةِ innocent; من شَيْءٍ to be innocent of sth; المُتَّهَمُ بَريءٌ حتّى تُثْبَتَ إِدانَتُهُ a suspect is innocent until proven guilty; هو بَريءٌ بَراءةَ الذِئْبِ من دَمِ يوسُفَ he is completely innocent **2** [ساذَج] innocent; طِفْلة بَريئة an innocent little girl **3** [خالٍ] |من| free from, without; بَريء من الشَوائِبِ flawless

إِبْراء *n* discharge; إِبْراء ذِمّةِ شَخْصٍ (من الدُيونِ) discharge of sb's debt

تَبْرِئة *n* acquittal; discharge; تَبْرِئة ساحةِ شَخْصٍ sb's acquittal; تَبْرِئة ذِمّةِ شَخْصٍ (من دُيونٍ) discharge of sb's debts

مُبارَأة *n* divorce by mutual consent

‹ **بْراتيسْلافا** *n* Bratislava

‹ **بَراغ** *n* |f| Prague

‹ **بَراريّ** *n* prairie

‹ **بَرازيلِيّ** *adj, n* Brazilian

البَرازيل *n* |f| Brazil

‹ **بْراغْماتِيّ** **A** *adj* pragmatic **B** *n* pragmatist

‹ **بَرافان** *n* room divider

‹ **بْرافو** *excl* bravo!

‹ **بَرافين** *n* paraffin (wax)

‹ **بَرامِسْيوم ,بَراميسْيوم** *n* (Bio) paramecium

‹ **بَراميس** *n* (Zool) see أَبْراميس

‹ **بَرْبَرَ** *v* |i; بَرْبَرة| to babble; to jabber

بَرْبَرِيّ **A** *adj* **1** [مَنْسوب إلى البَرْبَر] |بَرْبَر| Berber; (اللُغة) البَرْبَرِيّة Berber (*language*); قَبائِل بَرْبَرِيّة Berber tribes **2** [هَمَجِيّ] |بَرابِرة| barbaric; جَرِيمة بَرْبَرِيّة a barbaric crime

B *n* **1** [شَخْص من البَرْبَر] |بَرْبَر| Berber **2** [شَخْص هَمَجِيّ] |بَرابِرة| barbarian

بَرْبَرِيّة *n* barbarity, barbarism

‹ **بَرْبون, بَرْبوني** *n* (Zool) tub gurnard

‹ **بَرْبِيس** *n* (Zool) barbel

‹ **بُرْتُغالِيّ** **A** *adj* Portuguese; (اللُغة) البُرْتُغالِيّة Portuguese (*language*)

B *n* Portuguese (*person*)

البُرْتُغال *n* |f| Portugal

‹ **بُرْتُقال** *n coll* orange; عَصير بُرْتُقالٍ orange juice; شَجَرة بُرْتُقالٍ orange tree; قَشَّرَ بُرْتُقالةً to peel an orange

بُرْتُقالِيّ *adj* **1** [لَوْن] orange; قَمِيص بُرْتُقالِيّ an orange shirt **2** [مَنْسوب إلى البُرْتُقالِ] orange (*before n*); أَزْهار بُرْتُقالِيّة orange blossoms

‹ **بُرْثُن** *n* |بَراثِنُ| claw; بَراثِنِ الأَسَدِ a lion's claws; في بَراثِنِ الحَرْبِ in the grip of war; أَنْقَذَ شَخْصاً من بَراثِنِ العَدُوِّ to rescue sb from the clutches of the enemy; اِجْتَذَبَ شَيْئاً من بَراثِنِ النِسْيانِ to snatch sth from the jaws of oblivion

1 ‹ **تَبَرَّجَ** *v* to primp (infml), to get dolled up (infml)

مُتَبَرِّج *adj* made up (*face*); dressed up; unveiled

2 ‹ **بُرْج** *n* |أَبْراج, بُروج| **1** (Archit) tower; castle; بُرْج حَمامٍ dovecot; بُرْج إِرْسالٍ (broadcasting) tower; بُرْج إِرْسالٍ تِلِفِزْيونِيٍّ TV tower; بُرْج كَنِيسةٍ church tower; بُرْج قَصْرٍ \ حِصْنٍ the tower of a castle/fortress; بُرْج المُراقَبةِ control tower; watchtower; بُرْج بابِل the tower of Babel; قِمّة البُرْجِ spire, top of a tower; كانَ \ عاشَ في بُرْجٍ عاجِيٍّ to live in an ivory tower **2** (Astrol) sign (*of the zodiac*); البُروج the signs of the zodiac; دائِرة الأَبْراجِ zodiac; سورة البُروج The Constellations (*Sura 85*)

3 ‹ **بارِجة** *n* |بَوارِجُ| warship, battleship; بارِجة حَرْبِيّة warship

‹ **بَرْجَل** *n* |بَراجِلُ| compass, (pair of) compasses (BrE)

‹ **بُرْجُمة** *n* |بَراجِمُ| knuckle

‹ **بورْجُوازِيّ, بُرْجُوازِيّ** *n* bourgeois; wealthy; الطَبَقة البُرْجُوازِيّة the upper class

بورْجُوازِيّة, بُرْجُوازِيّة *n* bourgeoisie

‹ **البِرْجِيس** *n* Jupiter; لُعْبة البِرْجِيس *a home-made board game similar to pachisi*

‹ **بَرِحَ** *v* |a; بَراح| **1** [المَكانَ] to leave, to depart from; لن يَبْرَحَ مَكانَهُ he will not move from his place; (fig) he will not budge from his position; لن يَبْرَحَ الذاكِرةَ it will not be forgotten **2** [زالَ] to pass; هو ما بَرِحَ حَيًّا he is still alive

بَرَّحَ *v* |ب| to torment, to harass

بارَحَ *v* to leave, to depart from; لا تُبارِحُ الذاكِرةَ it has not been forgotten

بَراح *n* **1** [أَراضٍ] vast plain **2** [مَصْدَر] going away

البارِحة *adv* yesterday; last night; أَوَّل البارِحةِ the day before yesterday; لَيْلة البارِحةِ, اللَيْلة البارِحة last night

مُبَرِّح *adj* violent; severe; آلام مُبَرِّحة agonizing pains; ضَرَبَ شَخْصاً ضَرْباً مُبَرِّحاً to beat sb half to death

يَبْروح, يَبْروج *n* listed alphabetically

1 ‹ **بَرَدَ** *v* |u; بَرْد| to be/become cold, to cool off

بَرُدَ *v* |u; بُرود| to be/become cold

بَرَّدَ *v* to cool, to chill; بَرَّدَ الشَرابَ to chill drinks

أَبْرَدَ *v* to cool, to chill

تَبَرَّدَ *v* to cool off; to refresh oneself

بارِد *adj* **1** [عَكْس حارٍّ] cold; cool; fresh; غُرْفة بارِدة a cold/cool room; ماء \ حَليب بارِد cold water/milk; شَراب بارِد a cool drink; الحَرْب البارِدة the Cold War; الجَوُّ \ الطَقْسُ بارِدٌ اليَوْمَ it is chilly today; هَبَّتْ رِيحٌ بارِدةٌ there was a cold wind blowing **2** [فاتِر] cold, cold-hearted; cold-blooded; رَجُل بارِد a cold-hearted man; اسْتِقْبال بارِد a cool reception; نَظْرة بارِدة a cold stare; بِدَمٍ بارِدٍ in cold blood; بارِد الأَعْصابِ cool-headed; بارِد جِنْسِيًّا suffering from lack of libido; frigid **3** [سَخِيف] corny; weak; نُكْتة بارِدة a corny joke; غَنِيمة بارِدة easy prey

بَرّاد *n* **1** [ثَلّاجة] refrigerator **2** [إِبْريق شايٍ] teapot

بَرْد *n* **1** [عَكْس حَرٍّ] cold; coldness; بَرْد قارِس a bitter cold; الحَرّ والبَرْد the heat and the cold; شَعَرَ \ أَحَسَّ بالبَرْدِ to be cold; وَقَفَ \ مَشى \ اِنْتَظَرَ في البَرْدِ to stand/walk/wait in the cold 2 (Med) cold; أُصيبَ بِنَزْلَةِ بَرْدٍ to catch a cold

بَرَد *n coll* hail; حَبّات البَرَدِ hailstones; سَقَطَ البَرَدُ it was hailing

بُرَداء *n* |dipt f| malaria; feverish chill

بَرْدان *adj* |dipt| cold

بَرَدة *n* hailstone

بُرود *n* coldness; بِبُرودٍ coldly; calmly; بُرود جِنْسيّ lack of libido; frigidity; بُرود عاطِفيّ coldness, emotional distance; بُرود في العَلاقاتِ a chill in relations; بُرود الأَعْصابِ cool-headedness

بُرودة *n* 1 [بَرْد] coldness, chill; على رَغْمِ بُرودةِ الطَّقْسِ in spite of the cold; بُرودة المَساءِ the cool of the evening 2 [فُتور] coldness; بِبُرودةٍ coldly, unaffectedly; رَدَّ بِبُرودةٍ to react coldly; بُرودة الأَعْصابِ \ الدَمِ cool-headedness/cold-bloodedness

تَبَرُّد *n* cooling (off/down)

تَبْريد *n* cooling; دَوْرة تَبْريدٍ cooling system; مَحْلول تَبْريدٍ coolant; ماء تَبْريدٍ coolant water; التَبْريد بالهَواءِ air cooling; مُسْتَوْدَع تَبْريدٍ cold store; بُرْج التَبْريدِ cooling tower; جِهاز التَبْريدِ air conditioner

مُبَرَّد *adj* cooled, chilled; air-conditioned

مُبَرِّد A *adj* cooling; شاحِنة مُبَرِّدة refrigerator truck B *n* cooler; radiator; cold store

مُبَرِّدة *n* coolant; cooler; مُبَرِّدة الهَواءِ air conditioner

2 **بَرَدَ** *v* |a; بَرْد| to file

بُرادة *n* filing

مِبْرَد *n* |مَبارِدُ| file; مِبْرَد أَظافِرَ nail file

3 **بُرْداية** *n* curtain, drape; blinds

بُرْدة *n* cloak, mantle

4 **بَريد** *n* mail, post (BrE); بالبَريدِ through the post, by mail; بَريد جَوّيّ air mail; بالبَريدِ الجَوّيّ by air mail; البَريد السَريع express mail; بَريد مُسَجَّل registered post (BrE) mail (AmE); أَخَذَ شَيْئاً إِلى البَريدِ to take sth to the post; مَكْتَب بَريدٍ post office; رِسالة بالبَريدِ المَضْمونِ a registered (BrE) certified (AmE) letter; بَريد إِلِكْترونيّ email; أَرْسَلَ بالبَريدِ الإِلِكْترونيِّ to send by email; قائِمة بَريدٍ mailing list; بَريد صَوْتيّ voicemail; بَريد القُرّاءِ letters from readers; ساعي \ مُوَزِّع بَريدٍ postman (BrE), mailman (AmE); صُنْدوق بَريدٍ postbox (BrE), mailbox (AmE); letter box (BrE); post office box, PO box; صُنْدوق بَريدٍ رَقْم ٣٤٥ (ص.ب. ٣٤٥) post office box 345 (PO Box 345); وَضَعَ شَيْئاً في صُنْدوقِ البَريدِ to put sth in the letter box; اِطَّلَعَ على البَريدِ to check the mail; وَزَّعَ البَريدَ to deliver the mail; بِرُجوعِ البَريدِ by return of post (BrE), by return mail (AmE); دَفَعَ تَكاليفَ البَريدِ to pay postage

بَريديّ *adj* postal; طابَع بَريديّ stamp; حَوالة بَريديّة money order; بِطاقة بَريديّة postcard; رَمْز بَريديّ postal code; طَرْد بَريديّ parcel, package

5 **بَرْديّ** *n* papyrus sedge (*Cyperus papyrus*); وَرَق البَرْديِّ papyrus

6 **بُرَيْدة** *n* |dipt| Buraydah (*city in Saudi Arabia*)

بَرْدَعة, بَرْذَعة *n* |بَرادِعُ| saddle, packsaddle (*for a donkey*)

بَرْدَقوش *n* marjoram

بَرْذَعة *n* see بَرْدَعة

بِرْذَوْن *n* |بَراذينُ| workhorse

1 **بَرَّ** *v* |a-i; بِرّ| 1 [وَفى] to keep, to fulfil; بَرَّ بِوَعْدِهِ to keep one's promise 2 [صَدَقَ] to be honest/truthful; بَرَّ في قَوْلِهِ to speak truthfully 3 [أَدّى الطاعة] to obey; بَرَّ والِدَيْهِ to obey one's parents 4 [أَحْسَنَ] to be devoted/respectful/pious 5 [قُبِلَ] to be blessed

بَرَّرَ *v* to justify, to warrant, to account for; to excuse; الغايةُ تُبَرِّرُ الوَسيلةَ the end justifies the means; بَرَّرَ قَراراً to justify a decision; بَرَّرَ مَوْقِفَهُ to justify one's point of view; بَرَّرَ تَصَرُّفاتِهِ \ أَفْعالَهُ to justify one's behaviour/actions; بَرَّرَ المَصاريفَ الباهِظةَ to account for the high expenses

أَبَرَّ *v* to fulfil, to carry out; أَبَرَّ وَعْدَهُ to fulfil one's promise

بارّ *adj* pious; virtuous

بَرّ *n* البَرّ the Source of all Goodness (*one of the names of God*)

بِرّ *n* piety, devoutness; charity, philanthropy; خَيْرُ البِرِّ عاجِلُهُ the sooner the better

تَبْرير *n* |تَبْريرات| justification, vindication; خَطَأٌ يَتَعَذَّرُ تَبْريرُهُ an unjustifiable mistake

تَبْريريّ *adj* justifying; مَنْطِق تَبْريريّ rationalization

مَبَرّة *n* charity

مُبَرَّر *adj* justified; justifiable; غَيْر مُبَرَّر unjustified; إجْراءات \ قَرارات غَيْر مُبَرَّرة unjust measures/decisions

مُبَرِّر *n* |مُبَرِّرات| justification; grounds, reason; لا مُبَرِّرَ لَهُ unjustifiable; قَدَّمَ لِشَخْصٍ مُبَرِّراً لِشَيْءٍ to give sb a reason for sth

مَبْرور *adj* blessed; حَجّ مَبْرور a blessed pilgrimage

2 ‹ **بَرّ** *n* |بُرور| land; mainland; رَسا على البَرِّ to moor; (fig) to come to a decision; رَسا على بَرِّ الأَمانِ to be safe; بَرًّا وَبَحْراً by land and sea; on land and sea; في البَرِّ on land, on shore

بَرّانيّ *adj* outer

بَرِّيّ *adj* 1▸ [مَنْسوب إلى البَرِّ] land (*before n*), ground (*before n*); حَرْب \ مَعْرَكة بَرِّيّة ground war; قوّات بَرِّيّة land forces 2▸ [وَحْشيّ] wild, undomesticated, untamed; uncultivated; حَيَوانات بَرِّيّة wild animals; نَباتات بَرِّيّة wild plants, weeds; الحَياة البَرِّيّة wildlife

بَرِّيّة *n* |بَراريّ| wilderness; desert

3 ‹ **بُرّ** *n coll* wheat

4 ‹ **بَراريّ** *n* listed alphabetically

‹ **بَرَزَ** *v* |u; بُروز| 1▸ [نَتَأَ] to protrude; to stick out 2▸ [ظَهَرَ] to appear, to emerge, to become visible; بَرَزَتْ تَطَوُّراتٌ جَديدةٌ new developments emerged 3▸ [حَدَثَ] to come up, to arise; بَرَزَ خِلافٌ بين الدَوْلَتَيْن a conflict arose between the two countries 4▸ [تَفَوَّقَ] to stand out, to be prominent; بَرَزَ في صَفِّهِ to be near the top of one's class; to be distinguished among one's peers

بَرَّزَ *v* to excel, to be outstanding, to be excellent; بَرَّزَ في شَيْءٍ to excel in sth

بارَزَ *v* to duel; to fence

أَبْرَزَ *v* 1▸ [أَظْهَرَ] to show, to highlight; to bring out, to produce; أَبْرَزَ أَهَمِّيّةَ شَيْءٍ to highlight the importance of sth; أَبْرَزَ جَوازَ سَفَرِهِ to show one's passport; أَبْرَزَ أَدِلّةً to produce evidence 2▸ [نَشَرَ] to publish

تَبَرَّزَ *v* to defecate

تَبارَزَ *v* to duel, to fight a duel

بارِز *adj* prominent, important; outstanding, excellent; قِياديّ بارِز a prominent leader; شَخْصيّة بارِزة a prominent personality; مَرْجِع بارِز an important reference; عَلامة \ مَعْلَم بارِز(ة) a milestone; من أَبْرَزِ المُشْكِلاتِ أنّ ... one of the main problems is that ...; كانَ لَهُ دَوْرٌ بارِزٌ he played an important role; أَخَذَ مَكاناً بارِزاً to occupy a prominent position; خَصَّصَ مَكاناً بارِزاً لِشَيْءٍ to put sth in a prominent position

بِراز *n* faeces, excrement; عَيِّنة البِرازِ stool sample

بُروز *n* 1▸ [نُتوء] protrusion; relief; بُروز صَخْريّ a rocky outcrop 2▸ [تَفَوُّق] prominence; على أَساسِ بُروزِ شَخْصيَّتِهِ based on one's prominence 3▸ [ظُهور] appearance, emergence; بُروز ظاهِرةٍ the appearance of a phenomena; بُروز خِلافٍ the emergence of a conflict

بَريزة *n* listed alphabetically

إبْراز *n* showing, displaying, highlighting; إبْراز تَناقُضٍ highlighting a contradiction; طَلَبَ إبْرازَ أَدِلّةٍ demanding the presentation of evidence

تَبَرُّز *n* bowel movement, defecation; تَبَرُّز مُنْتَظِم \ غَيْر مُنْتَظِمٍ regularity/irregularity

مُبارَزة *n* duel, fight; مُبارَزة بالشيشِ fencing; المُبارَزة حول كَأْسِ العالَمِ the fight for the world title; دَعا شَخْصاً إلى المُبارَزةِ to challenge sb to a duel; دَخَلَ في مُبارَزةٍ to enter into a duel

‹ **بَرْزَخ** *n* |بَرازِخ| 1▸ (Geog) isthmus 2▸ (Islam) *the interval between death and the Day of Resurrection*

‹ **بِرْسيم** *n* clover; البِرْسيم الحِجازيّ alfalfa

1 ‹ **بُرْش** *n* |أَبْراش| mat

2 ‹ **أَبْرَش** *adj* |dipt| spotted

‹ **بَرْشِلونة** *n* Barcelona

‹ **بَرْشَمَ** *v* |i; بَرْشَمة| to rivet

بِرْشام *n coll* 1▸ (Med) capsule 2▸ (Tools) rivet 3▸ (Chr) host

بُرْشَمة *n* rivet

‹ **بَرِصَ** *v* |a; بَرَص| to have vitiligo

بَرْص *n* gecko

بَرَص *n* leprosy; vitiligo

أَبْرَص A *adj* |dipt| having vitiligo B *n person with vitiligo*

‹ **بُرْطُل** *n* |بَراطِل| mitre

بِرْطيل *n* |بَراطيل| bribe

‹ **بَرْطَمَ** *v* |i; بَرْطَمة| to pout, to purse (up) (*one's lips*)

‹ **بَرْطَمان** *n* |بَرْطَمانات| jar

‹ **بَرَعَ ,بَرُعَ** *v* |a-u; بَراعة| |في| to excel in, to be skilled in; بَرَعَ في مَجالِهِ to excel in one's field

تَبَرَّعَ *v* **1** [أَعْطى] to give, to donate, to contribute; تَبَرَّعَ بِمَبْلَغٍ كَبيرٍ لِ... to donate a large sum to ...; تَبَرَّعَ بالدَمِ to donate blood **2** [تَطَوَّعَ] to volunteer; تَبَرَّعَ بِشَيْءٍ to do sth voluntarily

بارِع *adj* skilled, skilful, competent; brilliant; مُمَثِّل بارِع a brilliant actor; تِقْنيّة بارِعة a skilful technique; كانَ بارِعاً في شَيْءٍ to be skilled in/at sth

بَراعة *n* skill, competence, proficiency

تَبَرُّع *n* |تَبَرُّعات| donation, gift; تَبَرُّع سَخيّ a generous donation; تَبَرُّع بالدَمِ blood donation; تَبَرُّع لِعَمَلٍ خَيْريٍّ a charity donation; حَمْلة تَبَرُّعاتٍ a fundraising campaign; جَمَعَ تَبَرُّعاتٍ to make a collection; جَمَعَ تَبَرُّعاتٍ لِعَمَلٍ خَيْريٍّ to collect for a good cause

مُتَبَرِّع *n* donor, contributor, supporter; مُتَبَرِّع بدَمٍ blood donor

‹ **بَرْعان** *n* (*Zool*) rock bass

‹ **بَرْعَمَ** *v* |i; بَرْعَمة| to bud; to germinate, to sprout; تُبَرْعِمُ الأَشْجارُ the trees are budding

تَبَرْعَمَ *v* to bud; to sprout; تَبَرْعَمَت البَذْرةُ the seed sprouted

بُرْعُم *n* |بَراعِمُ| bud; shoot

‹ **بُرْغيّ** *n* |بَراغيُّ| screw; bolt; شَدَّ بُرْغيًّا to tighten a screw

‹ **بَرْغَشة** *n* mosquito; midge

‹ **بُرْغُل** *n* bulgur

‹ **بُرْغوث** *n* |بَراغيثُ| flea

¹‹ **بَرَقَ** *v* |u; بَرْق| **1** [لَمَعَ] to shine, to sparkle, to glitter; to flash, to spark; بَرَقَتْ عَيْناها her eyes sparkled **2** (*Meteorol*) تَبْرُقُ السَماءُ there is lightning

أَبْرَقَ *v* **1** [أَرْسَلَ بَرْقيّةً] to telegraph, to wire **2** [السَماءُ] تَرْعَدُ السَماءُ وَتُبْرِقُ there is thunder and lightning

بارِقة *n* |بَوارِقُ| thundercloud; ما كُلُّ بارِقةٍ تَجودُ بِمائِها all that glitters is not gold

بَرّاق *adj* shining, sparkling; bright, brilliant; عَيْنانِ بَرّاقَتانِ sparkling eyes; أَلْوان بَرّاقة bright colours; الوُعود البَرّاقة والشِعارات الزائفة bright slogans and false promises

بَرْق *n* |بُروق| **1** [ضَوْء] (flash of) lightning; ضَرْبة البَرْقِ bolt of lightning; البَرْق والرَعْد thunder and lightning; بِسُرْعةِ البَرْقِ, سَريع كالبَرْقِ at lightning speed **2** [جِهاز] telegraph

بَرْقيّ *adj* telegraphic, cable (*before n*)

بَرْقيّة *n* telegram, wire; تَلَقّى بَرْقيّةً to receive a telegram; بَعَثَ \ أَرْسَلَ بَرْقيّةً to send a telegram, to telegraph

بَريق *n* |بَرائِقُ| glow, gloss, lustre; glittering; فَقَدَ بَريقَهُ to lose its lustre; بَريق الأَحْجارِ الكَريمةِ the glitter of gemstones; بَريق عَيْنَيْها a twinkle in her eyes; بَريق أَمَلٍ a spark of hope

البُراق *n* al-Buraq (*mythical steed that carried the prophet Muhammad from Mecca to Jerusalem and back*); حائط البُراقِ the Western Wall, the Wailing Wall (*in Jerusalem*)

²‹ **بَرْقة** *n* |dipt| Cyrenaica (*region in Libya*)

³‹ **إِبْريق** *n listed alphabetically*

‹ **بَرْقَشَ** *v* |i; بَرْقَشة| to paint with many colours

بِرْقِش *n* |بَراقيشُ| finch

بَرْقَشة *n being multicoloured*

مُبَرْقَش *adj* multicoloured, colourful; variegated

‹ **بُرْقُع** *n* |بَراقِعُ| veil; burka

‹ **بَرْقوق** *n coll* plum; مُرَبّى البَرْقوقِ plum jam

‹ **بَرَكَ** *v* |u; بَرْك| to kneel

بَرَّكَ *v* to make kneel down (*a camel*)

بارَكَ *v* to bless; بارَكَ شَخْصاً \ لِشَخْصٍ to bless sb, to give sb one's blessing; بارَكَ اللهُ فيكَ (may) God bless you; اللهُ يُبارِكُ فيكَ *response to* مَبْروك

أَبْرَكَ *v* to make kneel down (*a camel*)

تَبَرَّكَ *v* to be blessed

تَبارَكَ *v* to be blessed; تَبارَكَ اللهُ! praise be to God!; تَبارَكَ بِشَيْءٍ to consider sth a good sign

اسْتَبْرَكَ *v* to consider as a good sign

بَرَكة *n* blessing, benediction; بَرَكات اللهِ God's blessings; على بَرَكةِ اللهِ with God's blessing; حَبّة البَرَكةِ fennel flower, black seed (*Nigella sativa*); البَرَكةُ في البُكور ≈ the early bird catches the worm; في الحَرَكةِ بَرَكةٌ ≈ God helps those who help themselves

بِرْكة *n* |بِرَك| pond; lake; pool

تَبْريك *n* 1 [بَرَكة] blessing; benediction 2 [تَمَنِّيات طَيِّبة] good wishes

مُبارَك *adj* blessed; رَمَضانُ مُبارَكٌ! a blessed Ramadan!; عيدٌ مُبارَكٌ happy Eid!; بُقْعة مُبارَكة a blessed place

مُبارَكة *n* 1 [بَرَكة] blessing; congratulations 2 [مُوافَقة] blessing, sanction, approval; بِمُبارَكةٍ دُوَليّةٍ with international approval; أَعْطى مُبارَكَتَهُ لِشَيْءٍ to give sth one's blessing

مَبْروك A *excl* congratulations!; أَلْف مَبْروكٍ congratulations! B *adj* blessed

‹ **بِرْكار** *n* compass

‹ **بُرْكان** *n* |بَراكينُ| volcano; بُرْكان خامِد dormant volcano; بُرْكان ثائِر \ هائِج \ نَشيط active volcano; فوهة البُرْكانِ crater; ثَوران بُرْكانٍ volcanic eruption

بُرْكانيّ *adj* volcanic; صُخور بُرْكانيّة volcanic rocks; انْفِجارات بُرْكانيّة volcanic eruptions

‹ **بَرْلَمان** *n* parliament; البَرْلَمان الأوروبّيّ the European Parliament; عُضْو في البَرْلَمانِ الأوروبّيِّ a member of the European Parliament; جَلْسة البَرْلَمانِ parliamentary session; انْتَخَبَ أَعْضاءَ البَرْلَمانِ to elect the members of parliament; فازَ ب \ خَسِرَ مَقاعِدَ في البَرْلَمانِ to win/lose seats in parliament; حَصَلَ على ٢٠ مَقْعَداً في البَرْلَمانِ to win 20 seats in parliament

بَرْلَمانيّ A *adj* parliamentary; ديموقْراطيّة بَرْلَمانيّة a parliamentary democracy; لَجْنة بَرْلَمانيّة a parliamentary committee; مُناقَشة بَرْلَمانيّة parliamentary debate; دَوْرة بَرْلَمانيّة parliamentary term B *n* parliamentarian, member of parliament, MP, representative

‹ **بِرْلَنْت** *n* diamond

‹ **بَرْلين** *n* |f| Berlin

1 **بَرِمَ** *v* |a; بَرَم| |ب| to be fed up with, to be/become tired of; بَرِمَ بِشَيْءٍ to be fed up with sth

تَبَرَّمَ *v* |ب| to be fed up with, to be displeased with; to express one's displeasure with, to complain about; تَبَرَّمَ بِشَيْءٍ to express one's displeasure with sth

بَرَم *n* displeasure, dissatisfaction

بَرِم *adj* tired; discontented

تَبَرُّم *n* displeasure, dissatisfaction; تَبَرُّم من شَيْءٍ displeasure with sth; أَبْدى \ أَخْفى تَبَرُّمَهُ to show/hide one's displeasure

مُتَبَرِّم *adj* fed up, annoyed

2 **بَرَمَ** *v* |u; بَرْم| to twist; بَرَمَ الحَبْلَ to twist rope

أَبْرَمَ *v* 1 [عَقَدَ] to conclude; أَبْرَمَ مُعاهَدةً to conclude a treaty; أَبْرَمَ عَقْداً مع شَخْصٍ to enter into/make a contract with sb 2 [صادَقَ] to ratify

بَرّامة *n* 1 [لِلثُّقْبِ] drill 2 [لِنَزْعِ السَّدّادةِ] corkscrew

بَرّيمة *n* 1 [لِلثُّقْبِ] drill; auger 2 [لِنَزْعِ السَّدّادةِ] corkscrew

إِبْرام *n* conclusion (*of a pact*); إِبْرام مُعاهَدةٍ \ صَفْقةٍ conclusion of a treaty/deal; مَحْكَمة النَّقْضِ والإِبْرامِ (*Egypt*) court of cassation, ≈ supreme court

مُبْرَم *adj* 1 [مَعْقود] concluded, made, entered into; عَقْد \ اتِّفاق مُبْرَم a contract/agreement 2 [نِهائيّ] final, irreversible, irrevocable; قَدَر مُبْرَم an inescapable fate; قَرار مُبْرَم an irrevocable decision; قَضاء مُبْرَم final verdict; irreversible fate

3 **بُرْمة** *n* |بُرَم, بِرام| (earthenware) pot

‹ **بَرْمائيّ** A *adj* amphibious, amphibian; عَرَبة بَرْمائيّة amphibious vehicle; حَيَوان بَرْمائيّ amphibian B *n* |بَرْمائيّات| amphibian

‹ **بَرْمَجَ** *v* |i; بَرْمَجة| 1 [خَطَّطَ] to plan 2 (*Comput*) to program

بَرْمَجة *n* 1 [إِذاعة] programming 2 (*Comput*) programming; شَرِكة بَرْمَجةٍ software company; لُغة بَرْمَجةٍ programming language

بَرْمَجيّ *n* software (*before n*); خَطأ بَرْمَجيّ software bug

بَرْمَجيّة *n* software; بَرْمَجيّات مَفْتوحة المَصْدَرِ open-source software; بَرْمَجيّات مَجّانيّة freeware

بَرْنامَج *n* |بَرامِجُ| 1 [جَدْوَل] programme; schedule; plan; بَرْنامَج يَوْم plan for the day; بَرْنامَج طَموح an ambitious plan; بَرْنامَج دِراسيّ course of study, curriculum; بَرْنامَج

الأُمَمِ المُتَّحِدةِ الإنْمائيّ United Nations Development Programme (*UNDP*) **2** [إذاعة] programme, show; **بَرْنامَج إذاعيّ** radio programme; **قَدَّمَ بَرْنامَجاً إذاعيّاً** to present a radio programme; **بَرْنامَج تِلِفِزْيونيّ** television programme, TV show; **أَخْرَجَ \ أَنْتَجَ بَرامِجَ تِلِفِزْيونيّةً** to make/produce television programmes; **بَرْنامَج خاصّ** special; **بَرْنامَج للأَطْفالِ** children's programme; **تَفَرَّجَ على \ اسْتَمَعَ إلى بَرْنامَجٍ** to watch/listen to a programme **3** (Pol) programme, platform; **بَرْنامَج الحُكومةِ** government programme; **بَرْنامَج انْتِخابيّ** platform; **بَرْنامَج حِزْبٍ سِياسيٍّ** a political party's programme **4** (Comput) program; **بَرامِج** software; **بَرْنامَج مُساعِد \ مُلْحَق** add-on; **ثَبَّتَ بَرْنامَجاً** to install a program; **أَعَدَّ بَرْنامَجاً** to write/make a program

مُبَرْمَج *adj* programmed; **تَعْليم مُبَرْمَج** computer assisted education

مُبَرْمِج *n* programmer

‹ **بَرْمَق** *n* |بَرامِقُ| spoke; spindle, baluster

‹ **بَرْمَهات** *n* |m| Baramhat (*the seventh month of the Coptic calendar*)

‹ **بَرْموده** *n* Barmouda (*the eighth month of the Coptic calendar*)

‹ **بَرْميل ,بِرْميل** *n* |بَراميلُ| barrel; cask; **بِرْميل خشبيّ** a wooden barrel; **بِرْميل حَديديّ** an iron drum; **بِرْميل نَفْطٍ** oil barrel; a barrel of oil; **بِرْميل من الخَمْرِ** a cask of wine; **بَراميل النُفاياتِ النَوَوِيّة** nuclear waste drums

‹ **بَرْنِيّة** *n* |بَرانيُّ| clay vessel, pot

‹ **بَرْنامَج** *n* |بَرامِجُ| see برمج

‹ **بَرْنَتِيّة** *n* brent goose

‹ **بُرُنْز ,بُرُنْزِيّ** *adj* see برونز

‹ **بُرْنوس ,بُرْنُس** *n* |بَرانِسُ| burnous (*long hooded cloak*); **بُرْنُس حَمّامٍ** bathrobe

‹ **بَرْنَقَ** *v* |i; بَرْنَقة| to varnish

بَرْنيق *n* varnish

‹ **بُرْنَيْطة ,بُرْنيطة** *n* |بَرانيطُ| hat

‹ **بُرْهة** *n* |بُرَه| while, short time; moment; **بُرْهةً** a little while; **سَكَتَ بُرْهةً ثُمَّ قالَ ...** he was silent for a moment, then said ...

‹ **بَرْهَمِيّ** *n* |بَراهِمةُ| Brahman

‹ **بَرْهَنَ** *v* |i; بَرْهَنة| to prove, to demonstrate; **بَرْهَنَ (على) أنّ ...** to prove that ...; **بَرْهَنَ على صِحّةِ شَيْءٍ** to prove that sth is correct

بُرْهان *n* |بَراهينُ| proof, evidence; **بُرْهان ساطِع \ قاطِع** clear/convincing proof; **أَقامَ \ قَدَّمَ بُرْهاناً** to furnish proof; **تَقْديم البَراهينَ ضدّ مُجْرِمي الحَرْبِ** supplying evidence against war criminals

بَرْهَنة *n* proving; demonstration, attestation; **بَرْهَنة على صِحّة شَيْءٍ** proving the veracity of sth

مُبَرْهَنة *n* theorem; **مُبَرْهَنة فيثاغورَس** the Pythagorean theorem

‹ **بْروباغَنْدا** *n* propaganda

‹ **بْروبان** *n* propane

‹ **بْروتِسْتانْتيّ** *adj, n* Protestant

بْروتِسْتانْتيّة *n* Protestantism

‹ **بْروتوبْلازْما** *n* protoplasm

‹ **بُروتوكول** *n* protocol; **وَفْقاً للبُروتوكولِ** according to protocol; **بُروتوكول الإنْتَرْنِت** Internet Protocol, IP; **بُروتوكول الصَوْتِ عَبْرَ الإنْتَرْنِت** Voice over Internet Protocol, VoIP; **بُروتوكول نَقْلِ النَصّ الفائِق** hypertext transfer protocol, HTTP; **بُروتوكول التَحَكُّمِ بالنَقْلِ** transmission control protocol, TCP; **بُروتوكول نَقْلِ المِلَفّاتِ** file transfer protocol, FTP

‹ **بْروتون** *n* |بْروتونات| proton

‹ **بْروتين** *n* |بْروتينات| protein

‹ **بَرْوَزَ** *v* |i; بَرْوَزة| to frame

بْرواز ,بَرْواز *n* |بَراويزُ| frame

‹ **بُروسْتات ,بُروسْتاتا** *n* prostate; **سَرَطان البُروسْتاتا** prostate cancer

‹ **بْروش** *n* brooch

‹ **بُروفة** *n* **1** (Theat) dress rehearsal **2** (P&P) proof

‹ **بْروفِسور ,بْروفيسور** *n* professor; **بْروفِسور في الجُغْرافِيا** a professor of geography

‹ **بُروفيل** *n* profile

‹ **بْروكار** *n* brocade

‹ **بْروكْسِل** *n* |f| Brussels (*capital of Belgium*)

‹ **بْروكْلي** *n* broccoli

‹ **بْروليتاريّ** *adj, n* proletarian

بْروليتارِيا *n* proletariat

‹ **بْروناي** *n* |f| Brunei

‹ **بُرُنْز, بْرونْز** *n* bronze

بُرُنْزيّ, بْرونْزيّ *adj* bronze (*before n*); تِمْثال بْرونْزيّ a bronze statue; فازَ ب \ حَصَلَ على, أَحْرَزَ (الميدالِية) البْرونْزيّة الميدالِيةِ البرونْزيّة to win the bronze (medal)

‹ **بَرَوْنَق** *n* (*Zool*) winkle, periwinkle

1‹ **بَرى** *v* |i; بَرْي| ◀1▶ [قَلَم] to sharpen; بَرى قَلَماً to sharpen a pencil ◀2▶ [أَوْهَنَ] to weaken; to exhaust; بَراهُ المَرَضُ the disease had weakened him

بارى *v* to compete with, to play against; بارى شَخْصاً to compete with sb; to play against sb

تَبارى *v* to compete with each other; to be rivals; to meet in a contest, to play; تَبارى على كَأْسِ العالَم to compete for the World Cup; تَبارى مع شَخْصٍ to play against sb

انْبَرى *v* to undertake; انْبَرى لِفِعْلِ شَيْءٍ to set out to do sth

بَرّاية *n* (pencil) sharpener

بَرِيّة *n* |بَرايا| see برأ

تَبارٍ *n* competing; تَبارٍ في شَيْءٍ competing in sth

مُباراة *n* |مُبارَيات| match, game; competition, contest; مُباراة نِهائيّة finals; المُباراة قبل \ مُباراة رُبْع نِهائيّةٍ quarter-finals; نِصْف النِهائيّ semi-finals; مُباراة دُوَلِيّة an international (match); مُباراة وِدّيّة a friendly (match); مُباراة فَرْدِيّة singles; لَعِبَ \ خاضَ مُباراةً فَرْدِيّةً to play singles; مُباراة الذَهابِ away match; مُباراة على أَرْضِهِ home match; مُباراة الإِيابِ return game; مُباراة لِكُرةِ القَدَمِ football (BrE) soccer (AmE) match; مُباراة لِرَفْعِ الأَثْقالِ a weightlifting competition; رَبِحَ \ خَسِرَ مُباراةً to win/lose a match; لَعِبَ مُباراةً to play a match; مُباراة بين فَريقَيْنِ a match between two teams; مُباراة حول اللَقَبِ a title fight between ...; مُباراة كُرةِ القَدَمِ ضِدّ ... ,... بين a football (BrE) soccer (AmE) match against ...

مِبْراة *n* |مَبارٍ| (pencil) sharpener

مُتَبارٍ *adj* competitor

2‹ **البَريبَري, البِري بِري** *n* (*Med*) beriberi

‹ **بْرِدْج, بْريدْج** *n* bridge; لَعِبَ بْريدْج to play bridge

‹ **بَريز, بَريزة** *n* |بَرائِزُ| socket, (electrical) outlet

‹ **بَريطانيّ** *adj* British

بْريطانيا, بَريطانيا *n* بَريطانيا العُظْمى Great Britain

‹ **بَزَرَ** *v* |i; بَزْر| to sow

بَزْر *n* |بُزور| seed

بِزْر *n* |بُزور| ◀1▶ [حَبّ] seed; kernel ◀2▶ [تابل] spice

بِزْرة *n* seed

بُزَيْرة *n* (*Bot*) spur

1‹ **بَزَّ** *v* |u; بَزّ| ◀1▶ [غَلَبَ] to beat, to defeat ◀2▶ [سَلَبَ] to steal, to take away; بَزَّ شَخْصاً شَيْئاً to steal sth from sb

ابْتَزَّ *v* to blackmail; to rob; ابْتَزَّ بالتَهْديدِ to blackmail; ابْتَزَّ مالَ شَخْصٍ to extort money from sb

ابْتِزاز *n* extortion, blackmail; ضَحايا عَمَلِيّاتِ الابْتِزاز victims of extortion; ابْتِزاز الأَمْوالِ extortion of money

ابْتِزازيّ *adj* extortionate

مُبْتَزّ *n* blackmailer

2‹ **بَزّازة** *n* comforter/dummy (BrE), pacifier (AmE)

3‹ **بَزّ** *n* |بُزوز| cloth; textile; clothing

بَزّاز *n* cloth merchant

بِزّة *n* suit; بِزّة نِظامِيّة \ رَسْمِيّة uniform

‹ **بَزَغَ** *v* |u; بُزوغ| to break forth, to come out; to rise (*the sun*); to dawn (*the day*); تَبْزُغُ الشَمْسُ the sun is rising

بُزوغ *n* sunrise

‹ **بَزَقَ** *v* |u; بَزْق| to spit

بُزاق *n* spit, saliva

‹ **بَزَلَ** *v* |u; بَزْل| ◀1▶ [ثَقَبَ] to pierce ◀2▶ [الشَرابَ] to tap

بَزْل *n* (*Med*) puncture; بَزْل قَطَنيّ lumbar puncture, spinal tap

بازِلّاء *n* see بِسِلّة

بِزال *n* corkscrew

‹ **بَزَلْت** *n* see بازَلْت

‹ **بَسْباس ,بَسْباسة** *n* (Bot) fennel

‹ **بَسْبوسة** *n* basbousa (*a sweet cake soaked in syrup*)

‹ **بَسْتَرَ** *v* |i; بَسْتَرة| to pasteurize; بَسْتَرَ اللَبَنَ to pasteurize milk

بَسْتَرة *n* pasteurization

مُبَسْتَر *adj* pasteurized; حَليب مُبَسْتَر pasteurized milk

‹ **بُسْتان** *n* |بَساتينُ| garden; orchard; بُسْتان الزَيْتونِ olive orchard

بُسْتانيّ **A** *adj* garden (*before n*); horticultural **B** *n* gardener

بَسْتَنة *n* horticulture, gardening

‹ **بَسْتونيّ** *n* spades (*in playing cards*); آس البَسْتونيِّ ace of spades

‹ **بَسَرَ** *v* |u; بُسور ,بَسْر| to frown

اِبْتَسَرَ *v* to rush, to hurry; to begin prematurely

بُسْر *n coll* |بِسار| unripe date

باسور *n* |بَواسيرُ| haemorrhoid

مُبْتَسِر *adj* premature; طِفْل مُبْتَسِر a premature baby

‹ **بَسّ** *n* |بِساس| cat

‹ **بَسَطَ** *v* |u; بَسْط| **1** [نَشَرَ] to spread, to stretch out; to unfold, to unroll; بَسَطَ نُفوذَهُ على شَيْءٍ to extend one's influence over sth; بَسَطَ العَجينَ to roll out pastry; بَسَطَ ذِراعَيْهِ \ ساقَيْهِ to stretch one's arms/legs; بَسَطَ جَناحَهُ to spread one's wings **2** [سَرَّ] to make happy

بَسُطَ *v* |u; بَساطة| to be simple

بَسَّطَ *v* **1** [مَدَّ] to unfold, to open; بَسَّطَ ثَوْباً to unfold a garment **2** [يَسَّرَ] to simplify, to make simple; بَسَّطَ الأُمورَ to make things easier; بَسَّطَ الصيغةَ to simplify an equation; بَسَّطَ كَسْراً to reduce a fraction; بَسَّطَ القانونَ to simplify the law

باسَطَ *v* **1** [كانَ صادِقاً] to be sincere **2** [لَطَفَ] to be sincere

تَبَسَّطَ *v* **1** [فَصَّلَ] to speak at great length; تَبَسَّطَ في الحَديثِ to talk freely **2** [كانَ مُسْتَريحاً] to be at ease

اِنْبَسَطَ *v* **1** [اِمْتَدَّ] to stretch, to extend **2** [سُرَّ] to be happy

اِسْتَبْسَطَ *v* to consider simple

بَسْط *n* **1** [نَشْر] spreading **2** (Math) numerator; البَسْط والمَقام the numerator and the denominator

باسِط *n* الباسِط the Expander (*one of the names of God*)

بِساط *n* |أَبْسِطة ,بُسُط ,بِساطات| carpet, rug; بِساط الريحِ a flying carpet; طَرَحَ قَضِيَّةً على بِساطِ البَحْثِ to put something on the table (for discussion); سَحَبَ البِساطَ من تَحْتِ أَقْدامِ شَخْصٍ to pull the rug out from under sb

بَساطة *n* simplicity, ease; في مُنْتَهى البَساطةِ extremely simple; بِبَساطةٍ simply, easily; just like that; بِبَساطةٍ شَديدةٍ very easily; بِكُلِّ بَساطةٍ in all simplicity; plain and simple; لَيْسَ الأَمْرُ بِهَذِهِ البَساطةِ it's not that simple

بَسْطة *n* **1** [مَدًى] range, reach; بَسْطة السُلَّمِ landing (*between flights of stairs*) **2** [زِيادة] abundance

بَسيط *adj* |بُسَطاءُ| **1** [سَهْل] simple, easy; مَسْأَلة بَسيطة an easy matter; كَسْر بَسيط a simple fracture; عَمَلِيّة \ صيغة \ حَياة \ وَجْبة بَسيطة a simple operation/equation/life/meal; سُؤال بَسيط a simple question; بَسيط اليَدَيْنِ generous; لِسَبَبٍ بَسيطٍ وَهُوَ أَنّ ... for the simple reason that ... **2** [ساذَج] ناس بُسَطاءُ ordinary people **3** [طَفيف] little, small, insignificant; مَبْلَغ \ اخْتِلاف بَسيط a small amount/difference

اِنْبِساط *n* **1** [اِمْتِداد] extensiveness; extension; اِنْقِباض و اِنْبِساط العَضَلاتِ contraction and extension of muscles **2** [سُرور] joy, delight **3** (Psych) extroversion

اِنْبِساطيّ **A** *adj* extroverted, outgoing; شَخْصِيّة اِنْبِساطيّة an outgoing nature **B** *n* extrovert

اِنْبِساطيّة *n* extroversion

تَبْسيط *n* simplification; تَبْسيط الإِجْراءاتِ simplification of procedures; الإِفْراط في التَبْسيطِ oversimplification

مُبَسَّط *adj* simplified

مَبْسوط *adj* **1** [مَنْشور] spread out, extended **2** [مَسْرور] happy, cheerful

مُنْبَسَط *n* plain; مُنْبَسَط واسِع a broad plain

مُنْبَسِط *adj* **1** [مُمْتَدّ] flat; أَرْض مُنْبَسِطة plain **2** (Psych) extroverted, outgoing

‹ **بَسْطُرْمة** *n* pastrami

‹ **البُسْفور** *n* the Bosporus (*strait in Turkey separating Europe and Asia*)

‹ **بَسَقَ** *v* |u; بُسوق| to be high; to be tall

باسِق *adj* |بَواسِقُ| high; tall; نَخْل باسِق a towering palm tree

بَسْكَوِيت ,بَسْكوت *n* biscuit (BrE), cookie (AmE)

1 **بَسُلَ** *v* |u; بَسالة| to be brave

اسْتَبْسَلَ *v* to be brave, to be bold, to defy death; اسْتَبْسَلَ في الدِفاعِ عن شَيْءٍ to bravely defend sth

باسِل A *adj* |بُسَلاءُ, بَواسِلُ| brave, fearless
B *n* Basil (*male given name*)

بَسالة *n* courage, bravery

2 **بِسِلّة ,بازِلّاء** *n* peas; شورْبة بِسِلّةٍ pea soup

بَسَمَ *v* |i; بَسْم| to smile

تَبَسَّمَ *v* to smile

اِبْتَسَمَ *v* to smile; اِبْتَسَمَ لِشَخْصٍ to smile at sb; اِبْتَسَمَ لَهُ الحَظُّ fortune smiled on him; اِبْتَسَمَ اِبْتِسامةً صَفْراءَ to put on a fake smile

بَسّام A *adj* smiling
B *n* Bassam (*male given name*)

بَسْمة *n* |بَسَمات| smile

اِبْتِسام *n* |اِبْتِسامات| 1 [ضَحْك خفيف] smile 2 [اِسْم شَخْصيّ] |f dipt| Ibtisam (*female given name*)

اِبْتِسامة *n* smile; اِبْتِسامة عَريضة a broad smile; اِبْتِسامة بارِدة \ فاتِرة a cold smile; اِبْتِسامة ساحِرة \ غامِضة a charming/mysterious smile; اِبْتِسامة سَعادةٍ a smile of happiness; داعَبَتْ شَفَتَيْه اِبْتِسامةٌ, ارْتَسَمَتْ على فَمِهِ اِبْتِسامةٌ to have a smile on one's face; اِبْتَسَمَ اِبْتِسامةً ضَحْلةً to give a faint smile

مُبْتَسِم *adj* smiling; وَجْه مُبْتَسِم a smiling face

مَبْسِم *n* |مَباسِمُ| mouthpiece; nozzle

بَسْمَلَ *v* |i; بَسْمَلة| *to say* بِسْمِ اللهِ الرَحْمانِ الرَحيمِ

بَشاروش *n* see بشروش

بِشْت *n* |بُشوت| (ME) cloak

1 **بَشِرَ ,بَشَرَ** *v* |u; بُشْر, بِشْر| to rejoice, to be happy

بَشَّرَ *v* 1 [أَزْجى خبراً سارًّا] to bring news; بَشَّرَ شَخْصاً بِخَبَرٍ to bring sb good news 2 [بِدينٍ] to preach; بَشَّرَ بالدينِ الإِسْلاميِّ to preach Islam 3 [وَعَدَ] to promise; هذا يُبَشِّرُ بِخَيْرٍ that's promising!; هذا لا يُبَشِّرُ بِخَيْرٍ that does not bode well; إِنَّهُ يُبَشِّرُ بالنَجاحِ it promises to be a success

أَبْشَرَ *v* to rejoice; أَبْشَرَ بِشَيْءٍ to rejoice at sth

اسْتَبْشَرَ *v* |بِ| to rejoice (at), to be happy; اسْتَبْشَرَ بِشَيْءٍ خَيْراً to expect good things from sth; to be encouraged by sth

بَشّار *n* Bashar (*male given name*)

بِشارة *n* |بَشائِرُ| 1 [إِنْجيل] the Gospel 2 [بُشْرى] glad tidings; عيد البِشارةِ Annunciation Day

بِشْر *n* joy, delight

بُشْرى *n* good news

بَشير *n* |بُشَراءُ| 1 [نَذير] bearer of good news 2 [اِسْم شَخْصيّ] Bashir (*male given name*)

تَبْشير *n* |تَباشيرُ| evangelization, preaching (*of the Gospel*); missionary work; التَبْشير بالإِنْجيلِ preaching of the Gospel; تَباشير الفَجْرِ \ الصُبْحِ daybreak

تَبْشيريّ *adj* evangelical

مُبَشِّر *n* missionary; evangelist

مُسْتَبْشِر *adj* 1 [مَسْرور] happy, cheerful 2 [مُتَفائِل] optimistic

2 **بَشَرَ** *v* |u; بَشْر| to grate; بَشَرَ الجُبْنَ \ الجَزَرَ to grate cheese/carrots

باشَرَ *v* 1 [أَنْجَزَ] to mount, to launch; to do, to carry out; to practice; باشَرَ عَمَلَهُ to do one's job; باشَرَ مُناقَشةً to have a discussion; باشَرَ حَمْلةً to launch a campaign 2 [جامَعَ] to have sex with; باشَرَ امْرَأةً to have sex with a woman

بَشَر *n coll* |no singular noun| man; mankind, humanity; أبو البَشَرِ Adam; لا يَليقُ بالبَشَرِ unworthy of human habitation

بَشَرة *n* skin; epidermis; لَوْن البَشَرةِ (skin) colour, complexion; بَشَرة سَمْراء \ سَوْداء \ بَيْضاء olive/black/white skin, a medium/dark/light skin tone; بَشَرة ناعِمة smooth skin

بَشَريّ *adj* 1 [إِنْسانيّ] human; الدِماغ البَشَريّ the human brain; خَطَأ بَشَريّ human error; تَنْمِية المَوارِدِ البَشَرِيّة human resources development 2 [جِلْديّ] skin (*before n*), epidermal

بَشَريّة *n* mankind, humanity; البَشَرِيّة كُلُّها all mankind

مُباشِر *adj* direct; immediate; غَيْر مُباشِرٍ indirect; بِطَريقةٍ غَيْرِ مُباشِرةٍ indirectly; اِنْتِخابات مُباشِرة direct elections; تَهْديد مُباشِر an immediate threat; خَطّ \ اِتِّصال مُباشِر a direct connection; المُحيط \ الوَسَط المُباشِر the immediate vicinity;

سُؤال \ جَواب مُباشِر a direct question/answer; بَثّ مُباشِر a live broadcast

مُباشَرة *n* pursuit, practice; مُباشَرةً directly, immediately; straight, straight ahead; أمامَ البَيْتِ مُباشَرةً right in front of the house

مِبْشَرة *n* |مَباشِرُ| grater; مِبْشَرة الجُبْن cheese grater; بَشَرَ شَيْئاً بالمِبْشَرةِ to grate sth with a grater

مَبْشور *adj* grated; زَنْجَبيل مَبْشور grated ginger

3‹ **تُبُشِّر** *n* listed alphabetically

‹ **بَشْرَف** *n* (Mus) *an instrumental form in Turkish classical music*

‹ **بَشْروش, بَشَروش** *n* |بَشاروش| flamingo; طائِر البَشْروش flamingo

‹ **بَشَّ** *v* |a; بَشّ, بَشاشة| to smile

باشّ *adj* smiling

بَشاشة *n* friendliness; happiness; smile; اسْتَقْبَلَ \ قابَلَ شَخْصاً بِبَشاشةٍ to greet sb with a smile; to welcome sb warmly

بَشوش *adj* smiling; happy; بِوَجْهٍ بَشوشٍ with a smile on one's face

‹ **بَشِعَ** *v* |a; بَشَع, بَشاعة| to be/become ugly

اسْتَبْشَعَ *v* to find ugly

بَشِع *adj* ugly, hideous; repulsive; غول بَشِع a hideous ghoul; مَنْظَر بَشِع a revolting scene; جَريمة بَشِعة a monstrous crime

بَشاعة *n* ugliness

1‹ **بَشْكور** *n* |بَشاكيرُ| poker (*rod for stirring a fire*)

2‹ **بَشْكير** *n* |بَشاكيرُ| bath towel; bathrobe

‹ **بَشِمَ** *v* |a; بَشَم| |من| to be fed up (with)

أَبْشَمَ *v* to make sick; to nauseate

‹ **بَشْمَرْكة** *n* peshmerga (*Kurdish nationalist fighters*)

‹ **بَشْمَلة** *n* (Bot) loquat (*Eriobotrya japonica*)

‹ **بَشَنْس** *n* Bashans (*the ninth month of the Coptic calendar*)

‹ **بَصْبَصَ** *v* |i; بَصْبَصة| ① [الكَلْبُ] to wag; بَصْبَصَ الكَلْبُ بِذَنَبِه the dog wagged its tail ② [للمَرْأةِ] to ogle

1‹ **بَصُرَ, بَصِرَ** *v* |a-u; بَصَر| ① [رَأى] to see; to look ② [عَلِمَ] to know ③ [فَهِمَ] to understand

بَصَّرَ *v* ① [عَرَّفَ] to tell, to inform; to tell fortunes; بَصَّرَ شَخْصًا شَيْئًا \ بِشَيْءٍ to inform sb about sth ② [عَلَّمَ] to make understand

أَبْصَرَ *v* to see, to perceive, to observe; أَبْصَرَ شَيْئاً بالعَيْنِ المُجَرَّدة to see sth with the naked eye; أَبْصَرَ النورَ to be born; to come into being

تَبَصَّرَ *v* to reflect, to ponder; to realize; تَبَصَّرَ شَيْئاً \ في شَيْءٍ to reflect on sth

اسْتَبْصَرَ *v* ① [أَبْصَرَ] to see; اسْتَبْصَرَ شَيْئاً to see sth ② [كانَ ذا بَصيرةٍ] to understand ③ [تَأَمَّلَ] to reflect, to ponder; اسْتَبْصَرَ في شَيْءٍ to reflect on sth

باصِرة *n* |بَواصِرُ| eye

بَصارة *n* perception, discernment

بَصَر *n* |أَبْصار| sight, eyesight; ضَعيف البَصَرِ visually impaired; كانَ ضَعيفَ البَصَرِ to have weak eyesight; خِداع البَصَرِ illusion; مَدى \ مَجال البَصَرِ sight; range of vision; على مَدى \ مَرْمى \ امْتِدادِ البَصَرِ as far as the eye can see; في مَجالِ البَصَرِ within sight; ب \ في لَمْحِ البَصَرِ in the twinkling of an eye; فَقَدَ بَصَرَهُ to lose one's sight; رَفَعَ بَصَرَهُ to lift one's gaze; عَمِيَ \ كَفَّ بَصَرُهُ to become blind; زاغَ البَصَرُ his eyes were wandering

بَصَرِيّ *adj* optical; visual; مُعاق بَصَرِيًّا visually impaired; خِداع بَصَرِيّ optical illusion; آلات بَصَرِيّة optical instruments; وَسائِل سَمْعِيّة بَصَرِيّة audio-visual aids; عَصَب بَصَرِيّ optic nerve; كابِل الأَلْيافِ البَصَرِيّةِ optical fibre cable; ذاكِرة بَصَرِيّة visual memory; تَقْريب بَصَرِيّ optical zoom

بَصير **A** *adj* |بُصَراءُ| ① [ذو بَصَرٍ] sighted, seeing ② [فَطِن] discerning; العَيْنُ بَصيرةٌ واليَدُ قَصيرةٌ *people desire what is out of their reach*

B *n* البَصير the All-seeing (*one of the names of God*)

بَصيرة *n* |بَصائِرُ| opinion; judgement; vision, insight; discernment; أَعْمى بَصيرَتَهُ to blind one's judgement; كانَ نافِذَ البَصيرةِ to have sound judgement; كانَ ذا بَصيرةٍ to have good insight; عن بَصيرةٍ consciously

تَبَصُّر *n* ① [اعْتِبار] consideration ② [فِطْنة] discernment

تَبْصير *n* fortune-telling; informing

مُبَصِّرة *n* fortune-teller

مُتَبَصِّر *adj* perceptive

مُسْتَبْصِر *adj* ① [ذَكِيّ] bright, clever ② [عَرّاف] clairvoyant, psychic

2 **البَصْرة** *n* Basra (*city in Iraq*); بعد خَراب البَصْرة when all hope was gone; كَحامِلِ التَمْرِ إلى البَصْرةِ ≈ like carrying coals to Newcastle

3 **بِصارة** *n Egyptian dish of mashed beans and vegetables*

‹ **بَصَّ** *v* |i; بَصّ ,بَصيص| ① [نَظَرَ] to look ② [تَلأْلأَ] to shine, to sparkle

بَصّاص *n* spy, detective

بَصيص *n* ① [بَريق] glow, shine ② [قَليل] glimpse; بَصيص من الأَمَلِ a glimmer of hope

‹ **بَصَقَ** *v* |u; بَصْق| to spit (out); بَصَقَ شَيْئاً to spit sth out; بَصَقَ البَلْغَمَ to spit phlegm; بَصَقَ على شَخْصٍ \ شَيْءٍ to spit on sb/sth; بَصَقَ في وَجْهِ شَخْصٍ to spit in sb's face

بُصاق *n* saliva

بَصْقة *n* spit

‹ **بَصَل** *n coll* ① [نَوْع من الخُضَر] onions; زَرَعَ بَصَلاً to grow onions; قِشْر البَصَلِ onion skin; حَمَّرَ \ قَلى بَصَلةً to fry an onion; بَصَلة مَفْرومة a chopped onion ② [نَبات] bulb; بَصَلة التوليبِ tulip bulb; زَرَعَ أَبْصالاً to grow/plant bulbs

بُصَيْلة *n* ① [بَصَلة صَغيرة] small onion ② [المِصْباح] light bulb ③ [شَعْر] follicle; بُصَيْلة الشَعْرِ hair follicle

‹ **بَصَمَ** *v* |u; بَصْم| ① [خَتَمَ] to stamp ② [تَرَكَ بَصَماتٍ] to leave a fingerprint

بَصْم *n* stamp; imprint

بَصْمة *n* |بَصَمات| imprint; بَصْمة إِصْبَعٍ fingerprint; تَرَكَ بَصَماتٍ to leave fingerprints; تَرَكَ بَصْمةً على عالَمِ الأَدَبِ to leave one's mark on the world of literature

‹ **بَصْوة** *n* embers

‹ **بَضّ** *adj* soft

‹ **بَضَعَ** *v* |a; بَضْع| ① [قَطَعَ] to cut ② (Med) to amputate

تَبَضَّعَ *v* to buy; to shop

اسْتَبْضَعَ *v* to trade

بَضْع *n* ① [شَقّ] cut, incision ② (Med) amputation

بِضْع *n* some, a few; several; بِضْع نِساءٍ some women; بِضْعة رِجالٍ some men; بِضْع مَرّاتٍ a few times; بِضْعة أَيّامٍ a few days; بِضْعةَ عَشَرَ رَجُلاً ten-and-something men (*between 13 and 19*); بعد بِضْعِ مِئاتِ السِنينَ after a few hundred years

باضِع *n* invasive; إِجْراءات باضِعة invasive procedures

بِضاعة *n* |بَضائِعُ| goods, merchandise; بَضائِع commodities, goods; بِضاعة مُهَرَّبة contraband, smuggled goods; بَضائِع عابِرة goods in transit; حَرَكة \ نَقْل البَضائِعِ the movement of goods; قِطار البَضائِع freight train; عَرَضَ بِضاعةً to offer/display merchandise; حَمَّلَ \ أَفْرَغَ البَضائِعَ to load/unload goods

بِضْعة *n* ① piece ② see بِضْع

مِبْضَع *n* |مَباضِعُ| scalpel; lancet

‹ **بَطُؤَ** *v* |u; بُطْء| to be slow; to slow down

بَطَّأَ *v* to slow down, to hold up; بَطَّأَ السُرْعةَ to slow down, to reduce one's speed

أَبْطَأَ *v* to slow down; أَبْطَأَ في سُرْعَتِهِ to slow down, to reduce one's speed

تَباطَأَ *v* to be slow; to linger, to tarry; يَتَباطَأُ النُموُّ growth is slowing

اسْتَبْطَأَ *v* to find slow

بُطْء *n* slowness; بِبُطْءٍ slowly; سارَ بِبُطْءٍ to walk/drive slowly

بَطيء *adj* |بِطاء ,بَطيئونَ| slow; بَطيء الفَهْمِ slow on the uptake; كانَ بَطيئاً في حَرَكَتِهِ \ كَلامِهِ to move/speak slowly

إِبْطاء *n* slowing; slowdown; delay; إِبْطاء النُموِّ الاقْتِصاديِّ slowing of economic growth

تَباطُؤ *n* slowing; slowdown; delay; تَباطُؤ اقْتِصاديّ an economic slowdown; شَيْء لا يَقْبَلُ التَباطُؤَ sth which cannot be delayed

تَبْطيء *n* slowing; slowdown; delay

مُتَباطِئ *adj* sluggish; اقْتِصاد \ نُموّ مُتَباطِئ a sluggish economy/growth

‹ **بَطّاريّة** *n* ① (Elec) battery; شاحِن بَطّاريّاتٍ battery charger; عَمَلَ بالبَطّاريّاتِ to run on batteries ② (Mil) battery; نَشَرَ بَطّاريّةَ صَواريخَ to deploy a battery of rockets

‹ **بَطاطا ,بَطاطة** *n* potato

‹ **بَطّ** *n coll* duck; ذَكَر البَطِّ male duck, drake; يُبَطْبِطُ البَطُّ ducks quack; فَرْخُ البَطِّ عوّامٌ ≈ like father, like son

بَطّة *n* بَطّة الساقِ calf (*of the leg*)

‹ **بِطاقة** *n* |بَطائِقُ ,بِطاقات| ⟦1⟧ [هُويّة] card; بِطاقة تَعْريفٍ \ هُويّةٍ \ شَخْصيّة identity card, ID card; بِطاقة مَصْرَفيّة \ بَنْكيّة \ صَرْفٍ bank card, debit card; بِطاقة ائْتِمانٍ credit card; بِطاقة صُحُفيّة \ الطالِبِ press/student card; بِطاقة هاتِفيّة phonecard; بِطاقة التَعْريف الوَطَنيّة (Mor) national identity card; بِطاقة شَخْصيّة صالِحة \ نافِذة a valid identity card; بِطاقة شَخْصيّة مُزَوَّرة a forged/false identity card; بِطاقة تَعْريفٍ باسْمِ ... an identity card in the name of ...; أَبْرَزَ \ قَدَّمَ بِطاقةً شَخْصيّةً to show ID; طَلَبَ من شَخْصٍ بِطاقةَ تَعْريفِهِ to ask sb for his ID ⟦2⟧ [بَريديّة] card; بِطاقة بَريديّة postcard; بِطاقة تَهْنِئةٍ \ مُعايَدةٍ greeting card ⟦3⟧ [تَذْكِرة] ticket; بِطاقة الباصِ \ الطائِرة bus/plane ticket; حَجَزَ بِطاقةً to reserve (*a seat, etc.*); (Sport) to qualify (*for a round, tournament, etc.*) ⟦4⟧ (Sport) card; بِطاقة صَفْراء \ حَمْراء a yellow/red card; أَعْطى (لاعِبًا) البِطاقةَ الحَمْراء to give (a player) the red card; أَخَذَ بِطاقةً صَفْراء to be shown the yellow card

¹‹ **بَطَلَ** *v* |u; بُطْلان ,بُطْل| ⟦1⟧ [فَسَدَ] to be/become invalid; to be/become worthless; بَطَلَ البَيْعُ the transaction was not valid; بَطَلَ العَجَبُ to cease to be a wonder ⟦2⟧ [العامِلُ] to be unemployed

بَطَّلَ *v* to make ineffective; to put out of order

أَبْطَلَ *v* to annul, to cancel; to undo; to invalidate; أَبْطَلَ شَيْئًا to annul sth; أَبْطَلَ القاضي الحُكْمَ the judge annulled the verdict; أَبْطَلَ مَفْعولَ شَيْءٍ to render sth ineffective; أَبْطَلَ مَفْعولَ قُنْبُلةٍ to defuse a bomb

تَبَطَّلَ *v* to be idle/inactive

باطِل **A** *adj* |بُطُل ,بَواطِلُ| ⟦1⟧ [زائِف] unjust; تُهْمة باطِلة an unjust accusation; ادِّعاء باطِل an unjust allegation; باطِلاً falsely ⟦2⟧ [لاغٍ] invalid; null; حُكْم \ قَرار باطِل an invalid verdict/decision ⟦3⟧ [تافِه] futile, worthless; كَلام باطِل idle talk

B *n* |أَباطيلُ ,بُطُل ,بَواطِلُ| ⟦1⟧ [ظُلْم] injustice; صِراع الحَقِّ ضدّ الباطِلِ the struggle of truth against injustice; سَيَتَغَلَّبُ

‹ **بَطاطِس** *n pl* |dipt| potatoes; بَطاطِس مَسْلوقة boiled potatoes; بَطاطِس مَقْليّة \ مُحَمَّرة fried potatoes; chips (BrE) (French) fries (AmE); بَطاطِس مَهْروسة mashed potatoes; نَشا \ نَشاء البَطاطِسِ potato flour; قَشَّرَ البَطاطِسَ to peel potatoes; قَلى \ حَمَّرَ بَطاطِسَ to fry potatoes

‹ **بَطْبَطَ** *v* |i; بَطْبَطة| to quack

‹ **بَطَحَ** *v* |a; بَطْح| to knock down

تَبَطَّحَ *v* to lie on the floor

انْبَطَحَ *v* to lie on the floor

بَطْحاء *n* |dipt f; بِطاح| broad valley

مُنْبَطِح *adj* prone, prostrate

‹ **بِطّيخ ,بَطّيخ** *n coll* melon; بِطّيخ أَخْضَر \ شاميّ \ هِنْديّ watermelon; بِطّيخ أَصْفَر honeydew melon

‹ **بَطِرَ** *v* |a; بَطَر| ⟦1⟧ [جاوَزَ الحَدَّ كِبْرًا] to be haughty ⟦2⟧ [اسْتَخَفَّ] to be discontented; to disregard

أَبْطَرَ *v* to spoil, to make ungrateful

بَطَر *n* ⟦1⟧ [طَيْش] recklessness ⟦2⟧ [غُرور] vanity; pride; arrogance

‹ **البَطْراء** *n* see البَتْراء

‹ **بَطْرَخ** *n* |بَطارِخُ| spawn; roe

‹ **بُطْرُس** *n* Butrus, Peter (*Christian male given name*)

‹ **بَطْرَشيل** *n* (Chr) chasuble (*ornate vestment worn by Catholic or High Anglican priests*)

‹ **بِطْريق** *n* |بَطاريقُ ,بَطارِقة| ⟦1⟧ (Zool) penguin ⟦2⟧ (Hist) patrician

‹ **بَطْرَك ,بَطْريك ,بَطْرِيَرْك** *n* |بَطارِكة| patriarch; بَطْرَك مارونيّ a Maronite patriarch

بَطْرَكيّة *n* patriarchate

بَطْرِيَرْكيّ *adj* patriarchal

بَطْرِيَرْكيّة *n* patriarchate; patriarchal system

‹ **بَطَشَ** *v* |i-u; بَطْش| to attack; بَطَشَ بالعَدُوِّ to attack the enemy; بَطَشَ على لِصٍّ to overpower a thief

بَطْش *n* violence, force

باطِش *adj* strong, powerful, destructive; قوّة باطِشة a destructive power

الحَقُّ على الباطِلِ justice will prevail ② [كَلام فارِغ] أَباطيل trivialities, prattle

بَطّال *adj* unemployed

بَطالة, بِطالة *n* unemployment; بِطالة مُتَفَشِّية \ عامّة mass unemployment; البِطالة عند النِساءِ female unemployment; نِسْبة بِطالةِ \ مُعَدَّل البِطالةِ the unemployment rate; مُرْتَفِعة high unemployment; ارْتَفَعَتْ \ انْخَفَضَتْ نِسْبةُ البِطالةِ unemployment has risen/decreased; خَفَّضَ \ كافَحَ البِطالة to lower/fight unemployment

بُطْلان *n* invalidity, nullity; annulment; falsity; بُطْلان زَواج annulment of a marriage; أَثْبَتَ بُطْلانَ النَظَرِيّةِ to disprove a theory

إِبْطال *n* cancellation; nullification; إِبْطال مَفْعولِ الدَواءِ counteracting a medicine; إِبْطال مَفْعولِ قُنْبُلةٍ defusing a bomb

2 **بَطُلَ** *v* |u; بُطولة ,بَطالة| to be a hero

بَطَل *n* |أَبْطال| ① [شَخْص شُجاع] hero; بَطَل قَوْميّ national hero; بَطَل شَعْبيّ popular hero; مُكْرَهٌ أَخاكَ لا بَطَل *forced by circumstances, rather than led by courage* ② [مُدافِع] champion; بَطَل السَلام a champion of peace ③ (Cin, Literat) protagonist, main character; hero; بَطَل الفيلْمِ the star of the film; بَطَل المُلاكَمةِ \ anti-hero ④ (Sport) champion; بَطَل مُزَيَّف السِباحةِ boxing/swimming champion; بَطَل الدَوْريّ national champion; بَطَل أوروبّا \ بَطَل أولِمْبيّ European/Olympic champion; بَطَل العالَمِ world champion; بَطَل العالَمِ السابِق \ الحاليّ the former/current world champion

بُطولة *n* ① [بَسالة] heroism ② (Sport) championship, tournament; بُطولة دَوْريّة \ وَطَنيّة national championship; بُطولة كَأْسِ أوروبّا the European Cup, the European championship; بُطولة الأَلْعابِ الأولِمْبيّةِ Olympic championship; بُطولة كَأْسِ العالَمِ world championship, World Cup; بُطولة العالَمِ في كُرةِ القَدَمِ \ الشِطْرَنْجِ \ السِباحةِ the football/chess/swimming world championship; رَبِحَ \ خَسِرَ بُطولةً to win/lose a tournament; لَعِبَ في بُطولةٍ to play in a tournament; نالَ \ أَحْرَزَ لَقَبَ بُطولةِ العالَمِ to win the world title; ... جَرَت البُطولةُ في the championship was held in ... ③ (Cin, Theat) lead; دَوْر البُطولةِ the lead role; لَعِبَ دَوْرَ البُطولةِ في فيلْمٍ to star in a film; فيلْم من بُطولةِ عُمَرَ الشَريفِ a film starring Omar Sharif

بُطوليّ *adj* heroic; أَعْمال \ أَفْعال بُطوليّة heroic deeds, acts of heroism

بَطْلينوس *n* clam; limpet

بُطْم *n* (Bot) Pistacia; بُطْم عَدَسيّ mastic (*Pistacia lentiscus*)

بَطَنَ *v* |u; بُطون| to be hidden

بَطَّنَ *v* to line; to pad; بَطَّنَ تَنّورةً \ مِعْطَفاً to line a skirt/coat

أَبْطَنَ *v* ① [أَخْفى] to hide, to conceal; to keep quiet ② [ثَوْباً] to line

تَبَطَّنَ *v* ① [الوادي] to penetrate into, to become absorbed in ② [خَبَرَ] to know by experience

اسْتَبْطَنَ *v* to know thoroughly; to delve into; اسْتَبْطَنَ نِيّةَ شَخْصٍ to know what sb is up to

بَطْن *n* |أَبْطُن ,بُطون| ① (Anat) abdomen; stomach; belly; أَسْفَل البَطْنِ abdomen; تَجْويف البَطْنِ abdominal cavity; أَلَم في البَطْنِ stomach ache; أُصيبَ بِآلامٍ في البَطْنِ to have/get a stomach ache; يُقَرْقِرُ بَطْني my tummy is rumbling; سَبَّبَ لِشَخْصٍ آلاماً في البَطْنِ to give sb a stomach ache ② [حَشَرة] abdomen (*of insect*) ③ [داخِل] inside, interior; في بَطْنِ الوادي inside the valley ④ [فَرْع من العَشيرةِ] clan

باطِن *n* |بَواطِنُ| ① [داخِل] inside, interior; باطِن اليَدِ palm of the hand; باطِن القَدَمِ sole of the foot; من باطِنِ الأَرْضِ from underground; الظاهِر والباطِن the apparent and the hidden; مُقاوَلة من الباطِنِ subcontracting; أَجَّرَ \ اسْتَأْجَرَ من الباطِنِ to sublease, to sublet; عَرَفَ بَواطِنَ الأُمورِ to see through things; شَخْص مُطَّلِع على بَواطِنِ الأُمورِ insider ② (Islam) *the hidden meaning of the Koran*; الباطِن the Hidden (*one of the names of God*)

باطِنيّ *adj* ① [داخِليّ] internal; طِبّ باطِنيّ internal medicine; تَأَمُّل باطِنيّ introspection ② [سِرّيّ] esoteric, hidden

بِطانة *n* |بِطانات ,بَطائِنُ| [غِلاف] lining; بِطانة من الحَريرِ \ القَطيفةِ a silk/velvet lining; بِطانة الرَحِمِ (Anat) endometrium

بَطّانيّة *n* |بَطّانيّات ,بَطاطينُ| blanket

بطْنة *n* gluttony; البِطْنةُ تُذْهِبُ الفِطنةَ gluttony dulls the mind

بَطْنِيّ *adj* abdominal; تَجْويف بَطْنِيّ abdominal cavity

بَطين *adj* |بِطان| 1 [ضَخْم البَطْنِ] corpulent (*with a big belly*) 2 [شَرِه] gluttonous

بُطَيْن *n* ventricle (*of the heart*); البُطَيْن الأَيْسَر \ الأَيْمَن the left/ right ventricle

اسْتِبْطان *n* delving into; اسْتِبْطان الذاتِ introspection

اسْتِبْطاني *adj* introspective

الباطِنِيّة *n* Batiniyya (*pejorative term referring to those Islamic sects that believe in an inner, as well as surface, level of meaning in the Koran*)

مُبْطَن *adj* 1 [خَفِيّ] hidden, secret; veiled, disguised; إشارة مُبْطَنة a veiled reference 2 [لَهُ بِطانةٌ] lined

باطِية *n* |بَواطٍ| jug

بَظْر *n* |بُظور| clitoris

بَعْبَعَ *v* |i; بَعْبَعة| to rattle

بُعْبُع *n* |بَعابِعُ| bogeyman; goblin

بَعَثَ *v* |a; بَعْث| 1 [أَرْسَلَ] to send, to dispatch; بَعَثَ رِسالةً \ بِرِسالةٍ إلى شَخْصٍ to send sb a letter 2 [أَوْفَدَ] to delegate, to send; بَعَثَ بِوَفْدٍ رَسْميٍّ to send an official delegation; بَعَثَ شَخْصاً إلى الخارِجِ to send sb abroad 3 [أثارَ|على] to cause, to bring on; to arouse, to awaken; بَعَثَ على الشُّعورِ بـ ... to arouse feelings of ...; بَعَثَ على التَفاؤُلِ to engender optimism; بَعَثَ على الاطْمِئْنانِ \ القَلَقِ to be reassuring/ worrying; نُكْتة تَبْعَثُ على الضَحْكِ a funny joke 4 [أَخْرَجَ] to discharge, to emit, to release; بَعَثَ الدُخانَ to emit smoke 5 [أَحيا] to revive, to resurrect; بَعَثَ شَيْئاً \ شَخْصاً من المَوْتِ to raise sth/sb from the dead; بَعَثَ الحَياةَ في الاقْتِصادِ to breathe life into the economy

انْبَعَثَ *v* to be emitted; to be released; يَنْبَعِثُ الغازُ \ إشْعاعٌ gas/radiation is being emitted; انْبَعَثَتْ من فَمِهِ رائحةٌ كَريهةٌ an unpleasant odour was coming from his mouth

ابْتَعَثَ *v* to send; ابْتَعَثَت الحُكومةُ ثَلاثينَ طالِباً إلى فِرَنْسا the government sent thirty students to France

بَعْث *n* |بُعُث ,بُعوث ,بَعَثات| 1 [إرْسال] sending, dispatch; expedition; بَعْث خُبَراءَ sending experts; البُعوث الدينيّة missionary work; missionaries 2 (Relig) resurrection; البَعْث من المَوْتِ raising from the dead; يَوْم البَعْثِ the Day of Resurrection 3 (Pol) حِزْب البَعْثِ the Baath Party; اجْتِثاثِ البَعْثِ de-Baathification

باعِث *n* |بَواعِثُ| 1 [دافِع] motive; reason, cause; الباعِث على الجَريمةِ a motive for the crime; باعِث على القَلَقِ a cause for concern; بَواعث القَلَق concerns 2 (Islam) الباعِث the Resurrecter (*one of the names of God*)

بَعْثة ,بِعْثة *n* |بَعَثات| 1 [وَفْد] deputation, delegation; mission, representation; بَعْثة من الطَلَبةِ a delegation of students; البَعْثة الدِبْلوماسيّة الأَمْريكيّة US diplomatic mission; رَئيس البَعْثةِ the head of a delegation; أَرْسَلَ بَعْثةً إلى ... to send a delegation to ... 2 [رِحْلة] expedition; mission; بَعْثة عِلْمِيّة \ أَثَرِيّة a scientific/archeological expedition; بَعْثة تِجارِيّة trade mission; بَعْثة إنْجيليّة evangelical mission; اشْتَرَكَ في بَعْثةٍ اسْتِكْشافِيّةٍ to take part in an expedition

انْبِعاث *n* |انْبِعاثات| 1 [غازات] emission; انْبِعاث الغازاتِ emission of gasses; انْبِعاث ثاني أوكْسيد الكَرْبون carbon dioxide emissions 2 [نَهْضة] resurrection; renaissance; عَصْر الانْبِعاثِ the Renaissance

مَبْعَث *n* |مَباعِثُ| 1 [سَبَب] motive; cause, reason; مَبْعَث الفَخْرِ والاعْتِزازِ a source of pride; مَبْعَث قَلَقٍ \ ارْتِياحٍ a concern/ relief; التَضَخُّمُ لا يَزالُ مَبْعَثَ قَلَقٍ inflation remains a concern; مَباعِث causes, factors 2 [بَعْث] vocation, call

مَبْعوث A *adj* sent, delegated B *n* envoy, delegate, representative; مَبْعوث خاصّ للأُمَمِ المُتَّحِدةِ a special envoy of the United Nations; أَرْسَلَ \ أَوْفَدَ مَبْعوثينَ to send delegates

بَعْثَرَ *v* |i; بَعْثَرة| 1 [فَرَّقَ] to scatter, to mess up; بَعْثَرَ مُحْتَوَياتِ شَيْءٍ to ransack sth; بَعْثَرَ الأَوْراقَ to shuffle the cards; (fig) to change the game, to throw a spanner (BrE) wrench (AmE) into the works 2 [بَدَّدَ] to waste, to squander

تَبَعْثَرَ *v* 1 [تَفرَّقَ] to be disordered; to be scattered; تَبَعْثَرَتْ أَوْراقُهُ his cards were shuffled; (fig) he was knocked sideways (BrE), he was thrown for a loop (AmE) 2 [تَبَدَّدَ] to fall apart; to be wasted; تَبَعْثَرَت الجُهودُ the efforts were wasted

مُبَعْثَر *adj* scattered; messy; أَوْراق مُبَعْثَرة scattered papers; أَجْزاء مُبَعْثَرة scattered parts; شَعْر مُبَعْثَر tangled hair

بَعَجَ *v* |a; بَعْج| to slit open; to dent

انْبَعَجَ *v* to be slit open; to be dented

بَعْج *n* dent

بَعُدَ, بَعِدَ *v* |u; بُعْد| 1 [كانَ بَعيداً] to be far away, to be distant; ابْعُدْ عَنّي! go away!, get away from me!; بَعُدَت المَسافةُ the distance was great; تَبْعُدُ القَرْيةُ عن بَغْدادَ بِخَمْسةِ كيلومِتْراتٍ the village is five kilometres from Baghdad 2 [كانَ بَعيدَ الاحْتِمالِ] to be unlikely 3 [جَعَلَ بَعيداً] to keep away from; بَعُدَ بِشَخْصٍ عن هَدَفِهِ to keep sb away from his goal

بَعَّدَ *v* to remove; to exile

باعَدَ *v* |بَيْنَ| to create a distance (between), to drive apart; باعَدَ بين شَخْصٍ وَبَيْنَ تَحْقيقِ هَدَفِهِ to keep sb from his goal

أَبْعَدَ *v* to remove, to drive out; to banish, to exile; أَبْعَدَ شَيْئاً عن نَفْسِهِ to avoid sth; أَبْعَدَ عن نَفْسِهِ الشُّبْهَةَ to throw off suspicion

تَباعَدَ *v* to move away, to keep at a distance; to diverge; تَباعَدَت المَسافةُ بَيْنَهُمْ the distance between them increased

ابْتَعَدَ *v* to keep away, to avoid; to withdraw; ابْتَعَدَ عن شَيْءٍ to withdraw from sth; to distance oneself from sth

اسْتَبْعَدَ *v* 1 [اعْتَبَرَ بَعيداً] to consider (too) far; to regard as unlikely; to rule out; اسْتَبْعَدَ شَيْئاً to consider sth unlikely; لا يُسْتَبْعَدُ أنْ ... it is not inconceivable that ...; اسْتَبْعَدَ احْتِمالَ شَيْءٍ to rule out the possibility of sth 2 [اعْتَبَرَهُ غَيْرَ شائِعٍ] to exclude; to disqualify

بَعْدَ *prep* after; بَعْدَ أُسْبوعٍ after a week; بَعْدَ ذلك after that, then, next; afterwards; besides; بَعْدَ وُصولِهِ after his arrival; بَعْدَ وُصولِهِ بِيَوْمَيْنِ two days after he arrived; بَعْدَ أنْ after; بَعْدَ أنْ وَصَلَ after he (had) arrived

بَعْدُ *adv* 1 [ما زالَ] still; any more; after; فيما بَعْدُ afterwards; later (on); المَبْنى الّذي أَصْبَحَ مَدْرَسةً فيما بَعْدُ the building that later became a school; أَمّا بَعْدُ now then, now to the point; تَحيّةً طَيِّبةً وَبَعْدُ dear Sir/Sirs; هو بَعْدُ صَغيرٌ he is still young 2 [لم ... بَعْدُ] yet; لم يَصِلْ بَعْدُ he has not arrived yet; إنّنا لم نُقَرِّرْ بَعْدُ إذا كُنّا سَنُشارِكُ أم لا we have not yet decided whether to participate or not

بُعْد *n* |أَبْعاد| 1 [مَسافة] remoteness; distance; من \ عن بُعْدٍ from a distance; نَسْكُنُ على بُعْدِ ميلٍ من المَدْرَسةِ we live a mile from the school; البُعْدُ جَفاءٌ ≈ out of sight, out of mind 2 [قِياس] dimension; size; بُعْد سِياسيّ a political dimension; كانَ ذا أَبْعادٍ اقْتِصاديّةٍ to have economic dimensions; ثُلاثيّ الأَبْعادِ three-dimensional, 3D; رَسْم ثُلاثيّ الأَبْعادِ a 3D drawing; مُتَعَدِّد الأَبْعاد multidimensional

بَعْدَئِذٍ *adv* after that; لَيْسَ لَهُمْ بَعْدَئِذٍ سِوى أنْ يَقْبَلوا after that they can only accept it

بَعْدَما *conj* see ما

بَعيد *adj* |بُعَداءُ| 1 [عَكْس قَريبٍ] far (away), distant, remote; بَعيد المَنالِ unattainable, out of reach; بَعيد الأَثَرِ far-reaching; بَعيد المَدى long-term; far-reaching, long-range; extensive; صَواريخ بَعيدة المَدى long-range missiles; أَمَد بَعيد a long time ago; من بَعيدٍ from a distance; from afar; إلى حَدٍّ بَعيدٍ, إلى دَرَجةٍ بَعيدةٍ to a large extent; في الماضي البَعيد in the remote past; منذ عَهْدٍ بَعيدٍ from time immemorial; ذَهَبَ بَعيداً to go far away; كانَ بَعيداً كُلَّ البُعْدِ عَن الديمُقْراطيّةِ to be miles away from democracy; الصينُ بَعيدةٌ من هُنا China is far from here 2 [عَن الاحْتِمالِ] far-fetched, unlikely; لَيْسَ بِبَعيدٍ أنْ ... it is not unlikely that ...

بُعَيْدَ *prep* just after, shortly after

ابْتِعاد *n* |ابْتِعادات| avoidance

إبْعاد *n* removal; banishment, expatriation; deportation; إبْعاد الأَجانِبِ the deportation of foreigners

أَبْعَد *adj* |dipt; أَبْعَدونَ, أَباعِدُ| further; furthest; إلى أَبْعَدِ حَدٍّ extremely; ذَهَبَ أَبْعَدَ \ إلى أَبْعَدَ to go (even) further; أنا أَذْهَبُ إلى أَبْعَدَ من ذلك فَأَقولُ إنّ ... I would like to go beyond that and say ...

اسْتِبْعاد *n* 1 [بُعْد] unlikeliness; ruling out; اسْتِبْعاد خِيارِ / احْتِمالِ شَيْءٍ ruling out the option/possibility of sth 2 (Sport) exclusion, disqualification; اسْتِبْعاد لاعِبٍ disqualifying a player

تَباعُد *n* |تَباعُدات| 1 [بُعْد] a (great) distance; تَباعُد مَواقِفِ الطَرَفَيْنِ the distance between the two sides 2 (Comput, P&P) space; تَباعُد الأَسْطُرِ line spacing

مُبْعَد A *adj* banished; deported
B *n* exile; deportee

مُتَباعِد *adj* separate; different; divergent; على فَتَراتٍ مُتَباعِدةٍ at long intervals, now and then

مُسْتَبْعَد *adj* unlikely, improbable; ruled out; excluded; أَمْر من (غَيْر) المُسْتَبْعَد حُدوثُهُ an unlikely thing to happen; المُسْتَبْعَدِ أنْ ... it is (not) unlikely that ...; شَعَرَ بأَنَّهُ مُسْتَبْعَدٌ to feel excluded

1 **بَعْر** *n pl* droppings

2 **بَعير** *n* |أَبْعِرة, بُعْران| camel; القَشّة التي قَصَمَتْ ظَهْرَ البَعيرِ the straw that broke the camel's back

بَعْزَقَ *v* |i; بَعْزَقة| to waste, to squander

بَعْزَقة *n* waste

مُبَعْزِق *n* squanderer

بَعْض *n* 1 [بَعْض الأَشْياءِ] some, a few; بَعْض العُلَماءِ some scientists; يَقولُ بَعْضُ الناسِ ... some people say ...; يَظُنُّ بَعْضُهُمْ ... some of them think ...; في بَعْضِ المُدُنِ العَرَبِيّةِ in some Arabic cities; بَعْضَ الأَيّامِ (for) a few days; مَنْع بَعْضِ الكُتُبِ the banning of some books 2 [بَعْض الشَيْءِ] a little, a bit; بَعْضَ الشَيْءِ a little, somewhat, slightly; مُبالَغ فيهِ بَعْضَ الشَيْءِ a bit exaggerated; بَعْضَ الوَقْتِ (for) a while; اسْتَحْيى بَعْضَ الاسْتِحْياءِ to feel somewhat ashamed 3 [تَبادُل] each other, one another; ساعَدوا بَعْضُهُمْ بَعْضاً \ البَعْض to help each other; أَطْلَقوا النارَ على بَعْضِهِمْ بَعْضاً they where shooting at each other; فَصَلَهُما عن بَعْضِهما بَعْضاً he separated them from each other; الحَيَوانات الّتي تَعيشُ مع بَعْضِها البَعْض animals that live together; يَتَّصِلونَ بَعْضُهُمْ مع البَعْضِ they get in touch with one another 4 [واحِد] one, some; كانَ في بَعْضِ المُدُنِ رَجُلٌ ... in a/some/this town there was a man ...

بَعوض *n coll* mosquito

بَعْل *n* |بُعول| husband

بَعْلِيّ *n* unirrigated, rain-fed; زِراعات بَعْلِيّة rain-fed crops

بَعْلَبَك *n* |dipt f| Baalbek (*city in Lebanon*)

بَعام *n* chimpanzee

باغَتَ *v* to surprise, to take by surprise; باغَتَ العَدُوَّ to take the enemy by surprise; باغَتَ شَخْصاً بِاقْتِراحٍ to spring a proposal on sb

بَغْتة *n* surprise; بَغْتَةً suddenly, all of a sudden; by surprise; حَضَرَ بَغْتَةً to come suddenly

مُباغِت *adj* sudden; surprise; abrupt; نِهاية \ خاتِمة مُباغِتة an abrupt ending; هُجوم مُباغِت a sudden attack; عَمَلِيّة تَفْتيشٍ مُباغِتة a surprise inspection

مُباغَتة *n* sudden surprise; taking by surprise

بُغاث *n* |بِغْثان| turkey vulture

بَغْداد *n* |dipt f| Baghdad

بَغَرَ *v* |u; بُغور| to pour down

بَغْر, بَغْرة *n* downpour

بَغَضَ *v* |u; بُغْض| to hate, to loathe, to detest

بَغُضَ, بَغِضَ *v* |a-u; بُغْض, بَغاضة| to be/become hateful, to be/become despicable

بَغَّضَ *v* to make hateful

باغَضَ *v* to hate, to loathe, to detest

أَبْغَضَ *v* 1 [ضَغِنَ على] to hate, to loathe, to detest; أَبْغَضَ شَخْصاً to hate sb 2 [بَغَّضَ] to be/become hateful

تَباغَضَ *v* to hate one another

بُغْض *n* hatred, resentment, loathing; حَمَلَ في قَلْبِهِ البُغْضَ to bear hatred

بَغْضاء *n* |dipt f| hatred, hate; dislike, disgust

بَغيض *adj* hateful, odious, abhorrent; طائِفِيّة بَغيضة abhorrent sectarianism; هذا الاحْتِلال البَغيض this odious occupation

إِبْغاض *n* hatred

مُبْغِض *adj full of loathing*; مُبْغِض البَشَرِ misanthropic

مَبْغوض *adj* hateful, odious

بَغْل *n* |بِغال, أَبْغال| mule

بَغونْيا *n* begonia

بَغى *v* |i| 1 [طَمَحَ] |بُغْية| to wish, to want, to desire; to strive for, to aim at; بَغى هَدَفاً to aim at a goal; مُنَظَّمة لا تَبْغي الرِبْحَ a non-profit organization; ماذا تَبْغي أنْ تَفْعَلَ ؟ what do you want to do? **2** ◂ [ظَلَمَ] |على| بَغي; to wrong, to treat unjustly **3** ◂ [زَنا] |بِغاء| to fornicate

انْبَغى *v* |imperfect only| to be necessary; to be proper; كَما يَنْبَغي as it should be; ...: يَنْبَغي عَلَيْنا ... we should يَنْبَغي إيجادُ حَلٍّ a solution must be found; لا يَفْعَلُ أَكْثَرَ مِمّا يَنْبَغي he does no more than necessary

ابْتَغى *v* to wish, to want, to desire; to aspire, to strive for; ابْتَغى شَيْئاً to want sth; مُنَظَّمة لا تَبْتَغي الربْحَ a non-profit organization

بَغيّ *n* |f; بَغايا| prostitute; fornicator (*female*)

بَغْي *n* injustice; oppression; tyranny; يَد البَغْيِ the hand of tyranny

باغٍ **A** *adj* |بُغاة, باغونَ| **1** ◂ [ظالِم] oppressive; unjust **2** ◂ [راغب] wanting, desiring

B *n* |بُغاة, باغونَ| tyrant

بِغاء *n* prostitution; بَيْت البِغاءِ brothel; مُمارَسة البِغاءِ prostitution; مارَسَ \ تعاطى البِغاءَ to prostitute oneself; to work as a prostitute

بُغْية *n* wish, desire; purpose, aim; بُغْيَةَ with the aim of, in order to; بُغْيَةَ التَوَصُّلِ إلى حَلٍّ in order to arrive at a solution

ابْتِغاء *n* wish

مُبْتَغًى *n* endeavor; aspiration

بِفْتيك, **بِفْتاك** *n* steak

بَقّان *n* جوْز البَقّان pecan

بَقْبَقَ *v* |i; بَقْبَقة| to bubble, to gurgle, to sputter (*of water*)

بُقْجة *n* bindle (*a bundle of belongings, tied with a cloth and carried over the shoulder*)

بَقْدونِس *n* see مَقْدونس

بَقَر *n coll* cattle, cows; بَقَر الوَحْشِ antelope; بَقَرة حَلوب dairy cow; (*fig*) cash cow, golden goose; حَليب البَقَرِ (cow's) milk; لَحْم البَقَرِ beef; راعي البَقَرِ cowboy; (مَرَض) جُنونِ البَقَرِ mad cow disease, BSE; حَلَبَ \ ذَبَحَ بَقَرةً to milk/slaughter a cow; سورة البَقَرة The Cow (*Sura 2*)

بَقّار *n* herdsman, cattle hand

بَقَريّ *adj* bovine, cow (*before n*); لَحْم بَقَريّ beef; مَرَض الجُنونِ البَقَريِّ mad cow disease

بَقْس *n* (*Bot*) box, boxwood (tree)

بُقْسُماط, **بُقْسُمات**, **بُقْصُمات** *n* breadcrumbs; rusk

بَقْشيش, **بَخْشيش** *n* |بَقاشيشُ| tip, gratuity, baksheesh; أَعْطى بَقْشيشاً to tip

بَقَعَ *v* |a; بَقْع| to be spotted, to be speckled

بَقَّعَ *v* to spot, to stain; to smudge

تَبَقَّعَ *v* to be spotted; to be/become stained

بُقْعة *n* **1** ◂ [مِنْطَقة] |بِقاع| place, spot; البِقاع المُقَدَّسة the Holy Land **2** ◂ [لَطْخة] |بُقَع| spot, stain; بُقْعة دُهْنٍ grease spot; بُقْعة زَيْتٍ \ نَفْطٍ oil slick; امْتَدَّ \ انْتَشَرَ كَبُقْعَةِ زَيْتٍ to spread wildly; في \ على قَميصِها بُقْعةٌ she has a stain on her shirt **3** ◂ [نُقْطة] |بُقَع| spot; بُقَع شَمْسيّة sunspots; بُقَع حَمْراء في الجِلْدِ red spots on the skin

أَبْقَع *adj* |dipt| spotted; variegated, pied; صَيّاد السَمَكِ الأَبْقَع pied kingfisher

البِقاع *n* وادي البِقاع Bekaa Valley (*valley in Lebanon*)

مُبقَّع *adj* spotted, speckled; stained; قَنْطَريون مُبَقَّع spotted knapweed

بَقّ *n coll* **1** ◂ [حَشَرة] Argus (*genus of tick*); بَقّ الفِراشِ bed bug; شَجَرة البَقِّ elm **2** ◂ (*Comput*) bug

بَقَلَ *v* |u; بَقْل| to shoot, to sprout

بَقْل *n coll* |أَبْقال, بُقول| **1** ◂ [عُشْب] herbs; greens, vegetables; بَقْلة حَمْقاء purslane (*Portulaca oleracea*) **2** ◂ [قَطانيّ] legume

باقِلّي, **باقِلاء** *n* |dipt f| broad bean

بَقّال *n* |بَقّالة, بَقّالون| grocer

بِقالة *n* grocery store; مَحَلّ البِقالةِ grocery store

بَقْلاوة *n* baklava

بَقّان *n* listed alphabetically

بَقْويقة *n* (*Zool*) godwit; بَقْويقة مُخَطَّطة \ سَوْداء الذيلِ bar-tailed/black-tailed godwit

بَقِيَ *v* |a; بَقاء| **1** ◂ [دامَ] to stay, to remain; to continue to exist; to keep on; بَقِيَ على حالِهِ to remain unchanged; بَقِيَ حَيّاً to stay alive; بَقِيَ حِبْراً على وَرَقٍ to remain merely words on paper; to be unimplemented/unenforced; بَقِيَ الحالُ على ما هو عَلَيْهِ the situation remained as it was; بَقيتُ في بَيْروتَ ثَلاثةَ

أَبْقى *adj* longer/longest lasting; أَيُّهما الأَبْقى ؟ which of the two lasts longest?

مُتَبَقٍّ A *adj* remaining

B *n* rest, remainder

› **بِك** *n* |بَكَوات| bey (*title*)

› **بَكالوريا** *n* 1 [شَهادة] baccalaureate (*degree*) 2 [امْتِحان] baccalaureate (*annual national exam which confers the baccalaureate degree*)

› **بَكالوريوس** *n* baccalaureate, bachelor's degree

› **بَكَّتَ** *v* to censure, to rebuke

تَبْكيت *n* reprimand, rebuke; تَبْكيت الضَميرِ qualms; self-reproach

› **بَكْتيرِيّ** *adj* bacterial

بَكْتيريا ,بَكْتِريا *n* |بَكْتيريات| bacteria; عِلْم البَكْتيريا bacteriology

› **بَكَر** *v* |a; بُكور| to arrive/depart early in the morning

بَكَّر *v* to get up or rise early; to be early (at); بَكَّر المُنْتَخَبُ الوَطَنيّ ب \ في التَسْجيل the national team was first to score

باكَر *v* to be/get ahead of

أَبْكَر *v* 1 [خَرَجَ أَوَّلَ النَهارِ] to go/leave early 2 [عَجَّلَ] to hurry, to rush

ابْتَكَر *v* to invent; to think up; ابْتَكَر طَريقةً \ أُسْلوباً \ فِكْرةً to come up with a way/method/idea

بَكْر *n* |أَبْكُر ,بُكْران| young camel

بِكْر *n* |أَبْكار| 1 [شَيْء جَديد] *sth new; sth novel*; أَرْض بِكْرٍ virgin land; مُحاوَلة بِكْرٍ a first attempt 2 [مَوْلود أَوَّلاً] first born 3 [عَذْراء] virgin

باكِر *adj* early; premature; الصَباح الباكِر the early morning; في الصَباحِ الباكِرِ early in the morning, in the early hours; اسْتَيْقَظ باكِراً to rise early; سَجَّلَ هَدَفاً باكِراً to score an early goal

باكِرة *n* |بَواكِرُ| 1 [فَواكِه] first fruits; early vegetables 2 [طَليعة] forerunner, herald

باكورة *n* |بَواكيرُ| first (*before n*); هو باكورةُ زَواجِهِما he is their first child; هذه الرِوايةُ باكورةُ أَعْمالِ الكاتِبِ this is the author's debut novel

أَيّامٍ I stayed three days in Beirut; تَبْقى الذِكْرى the memory remains 2 [فَضَلَ] to be left, to remain; بَقِيَ مِنْهُ مَبْلَغٌ ضَئيلٌ a small amount of it is left; لم يَبْقَ لي إلاّ أنْ \ سِوى ... there was nothing left for me but to ...

أَبْقى *v* 1 [حافَظَ] to make stay, to ask to stay; to keep, to retain; to maintain; to save, to preserve; أَبْقى شَخْصاً على قَيْدِ الحَياةِ, أَبْقى على حَياةِ شَخْصٍ to keep sb alive 2 [تَرَكَ] to leave behind

تَبَقّى *v* to remain, to be left; ما تَبَقّى من شَيْءٍ what remains of sth; تَبَقّى ١٠٠٠ دولار $1,000 was left; لا يَتَبَقّى الكَثيرُ there is not much left; لا يَتَبَقّى إلاّ شَهْرانِ only two months remain; لا يَتَبَقّى لي إلاّ أنْ ... there is nothing left for me but to ...

اسْتَبْقى *v* to make stay, to ask to stay; to preserve; to leave behind; اسْتَبْقى شَخْصًا إلى مائِدةِ الغَداءِ to ask sb to stay for lunch

باقٍ A *adj* staying; remaining, left; البَقيّة الباقية (من شَيْءٍ) the little that remains (of sth); الأَيّام الباقِية the remaining days; المَبْلَغ الباقي the remaining sum; الحَياة الباقِية the hereafter

B *n* 1 [سائِر] |بَواقٍ| rest, remainder; باقي المَبْلَغِ the rest of the money; باقي أَنْحاءِ العالَمِ the rest of the world; بَواقي صوفٍ \ دِهانٍ leftover wool/paint 2 (*Math*) remainder 3 (*Islam*) الباقي the Everlasting (*one of the names of God*)

باقِية *n* |باقِيات ,بَواقٍ| rest; باقِيات صالِحات good deeds

بَقاء *n* staying, survival; immortality; بَقاء على قَيْدِ الحَياةِ survival; بَقاء الأَصْلَحِ survival of the fittest; بَقاء الروح بعد المَوْتِ the life of the soul after death; دار البَقاءِ the hereafter

بَقيّة *n* |بَقايا| 1 [ما بَقِيَ] rest, remainder; بَقايا جُثّةٍ remains (*of a human body*); بَقايا وَجْبةٍ leftovers; البَقيّة الباقِية (من شَيْءٍ) the little that remains (of sth); البَقيّة الباقِية من الأَمَلِ the last ounce of hope; بَقيّة المالِ the rest of the money; بَقيّةَ عُمْرِهِ for the rest of his life; بَقيّة أَنْحاءِ العالَمِ the rest of the world 2 [تَتِمّة] continuation; للكَلامِ بَقيّةٌ \ للحَديثِ to be continued

إبْقاء *n* continuation, maintenance; إبْقاء الحالِ على ما هو عَلَيْهِ maintenance of the status quo

بَكارة *n* virginity (*female*); غِشاء البَكارةِ hymen; فَضَّ بَكارةَ فَتاةٍ to take a young woman's virginity; حافَظَتْ على بَكارَتِها to keep one's virginity; فَقَدَتْ بَكارَتَها to lose one's virginity

بَكّارة *n* reel, spool

بَكْرة, بَكَرة *n* |بَكَرات, بَكَر| reel, spool; coil; pulley; بَكَرة خَيْطٍ a reel of cotton (BrE), a spool of thread (AmE)

بِكْريّ *adj* virgin (*before n*), virginal; غِشاء بِكْريّ hymen

بُكور *n* early morning; البَرَكةُ في البُكورِ ≈ the early bird catches the worm

ابْتِكار *n* |ابْتِكارات| **1** ◀ [خَلْق] creativity, ingenuity, originality; القُدْرة على الابْتِكارِ the ability to innovate **2** ◀ [اخْتِراع] invention; creation; innovation, novelty; ابْتِكارات تِكْنولوجيّة technical innovations

ابْتِكاريّ *adj* innovative, inventive; تَفْكير ابْتِكاريّ innovative thinking; الشَرِكات الأَكْثَر ابْتِكاريّةً the most innovative companies

مُبْتَكَر **A** *adj* original, new; inventive, creative; تَصْميم مُبْتَكَر an original design; حَلّ مُبْتَكَر a creative solution
B *n* |مُبْتَكَرات| invention; innovation; creation; مُبْتَكَرات تِكْنولوجيّة technological innovations; مُبْتَكَرات مُصَمِّمِ الأَزْياءِ a fashion designer's creations

مُبْتَكِر *n* inventor; creator

مُبْكِر *adj* early; premature

مُبَكِّر *adj* early; premature; إِنْذار مُبَكِّر early warning; وِلادة مُبَكِّرة a premature birth; في ساعةٍ مُبَكِّرةٍ من الصَباحِ early in the morning; في مَرْحَلةٍ مُبَكِّرةٍ in an early stage; تُوُفِّيَ في سِنٍّ مُبَكِّرةٍ to die young; نامَ \ رَحَلَ مُبَكِّراً to go to bed/leave early; أَجْرى انْتِخاباتٍ مُبَكِّرةً to hold early elections

بَكَّلَ *v* to buckle (up), to clasp, to button up

بُكْلة *n* |بُكَل| clip, barrette; buckle, clasp

بَكِمَ *v* |a; بَكَم| to be/become mute

أَبْكَمَ *v* to silence, to gag

بَكَم *n* muteness; mutism

أَبْكَم **A** *adj* |dipt; f بَكْماءُ; بُكْم| mute; أَصَمّ أَبْكَم profoundly deaf
B *n* |dipt; f بَكْماءُ; بُكْم| mute; لُغة الصُمِّ والبُكْمِ sign language

بَكى *v* |i; بُكاء| to cry, to weep; بَكى على شَيْءٍ to cry over/about sth; بَكى على الأَطْلالِ to cry over the past; to mourn what has been lost; بَكى الفَقيدَ to weep for the deceased; بَكى على كَتِفِ شَخْصٍ to cry on sb's shoulder; بَكى بُكاءً مَريراً to cry bitter tears

بَكّى *v* to make cry, to drive to tears

أَبْكى *v* to make cry, to drive to tears

تَباكى *v* to pretend to cry; تَباكى على شَيْءٍ to pretend to cry over sth

اسْتَبْكى *v* to make cry, to drive to tears; اسْتَبْكى شَخْصاً to make sb cry

باكٍ *adj* |بُكاة| crying; tearful; بِصَوْتٍ باكٍ in a tearful voice; انْفَجَرَ باكِياً to burst into tears

باكِية *n* |بَواكٍ| wailing woman

بَكّاء **A** *adj* weepy; tearful
B *n* crybaby

بُكاء *n* crying, weeping; tears, sobs; بُكاء مَكْتوم stifled sobs; بُكاء شَديد heavy crying; بَكى بُكاءً شَديداً to sob uncontrollably; نَوْبة من البُكاءِ crying fit; انْفَجَرَ \ أَجْهَشَ بالبُكاءِ to burst into tears

مَبْكى *n* حائِط المَبْكى the Wailing Wall

بَلْ *conj* as a matter of fact, in fact, actually; but; even; rather; لم تَبْدَأْ سَنةَ ١٩٧٥ بَلْ سَنةَ ١٩٧٨ she didn't start in 1975 but in 1978; هذه لَيْسَتْ كَلِماتي بَلْ هي كَلِماتُ المُؤَلِّفِ this are not my words but the words of the author; هو أَشْهَرُ الأُدَباءِ العَرَبِ، بَلْ والعَرَبيُّ الوَحيدُ الذي حَصَلَ على جائِزةِ نوبِل he is the most famous Arabic author; in fact he is the only Arab to have won a Nobel Prize; هذا لَيْسَ غالِياً بَلْ بالعَكْسِ هو رَخيصٌ this is not expensive; as a matter of fact it is cheap; أنا لا أَكْذِبُ بَلْ أَقولُ الحَقَّ I am not lying; I am telling the truth

بِلا *prep* without; بِلا شَكٍّ without a doubt, undoubtably; بِلا اسْتِثْناءٍ with no exception; أَطِبّاء بِلا حُدودٍ Médecins sans Frontières, Doctors Without Borders; شَخْص بِلا أَوْراقٍ an undocumented person

بِلاتين *n* platinum

‹ **بِلّادونا** *n* belladonna, deadly nightshade

‹ **بَلاذِر** *n* cashew (*tree and nut*)

‹ **بِلازْما** *n* ❶ (Bio) plasma; بِلازْما الدَمِ (blood) plasma ❷ (Phys) plasma; شاشة بِلازْما plasma display

‹ **بْلاسْتيك** *n* plastic; من البْلاسْتيكِ plastic; أَكْياس البْلاسْتيكِ plastic bags

بْلاسْتيكيّ *adj* plastic

1‹ **بَلْبَلَ** *v* |i; بَلْبَلة| to disturb, to trouble; to confuse, to confound; بَلْبَلَ شَخْصاً to throw sb into confusion

تَبَلْبَلَ *v* to feel uneasy; to be/become confused, to get mixed up; تَبَلْبَلَتْ أَلْسِنةُ الناسِ the language of the people was confused

بَلْبَلة *n* |بَلابِلُ| disorder, chaos, confusion; أَثارَ \ خلق بَلْبَلةً to cause confusion

تَبَلْبُل *n* confusion, confounding; تَبَلْبُل الأَلْسِنةِ a confusion of tongues

2‹ **بُلْبُل** *n* |بَلابِلُ| ❶ (Zool) bulbul; nightingale ❷ [من الإبْريق] spout

‹ **أَبْلَجَ** *v* ❶ [أَضاءَ] to dawn; أَبْلَجَ الفَجْرُ day has dawned ❷ [ظَهَرَ] to become obvious

انْبَلَجَ *v* to dawn; انْبَلَجَ الفَجْرُ day has dawned

أَبْلَج *adj* |dipt| obvious, clear; الحَقُّ أَبْلَجُ والباطِلُ لَجْلَجٌ ≈ honesty is the best policy

انْبِلاج *n* dawn; انْبِلاج الفَجْرِ daybreak

‹ **بِلْجيكا** *n* Belgium

بِلْجيكيّ *adj*, *n* Belgian

‹ **بَلَح** *n coll* dates; بَلَح البَحْرِ mussel

بُلَيْحاء *n* |dipt f| (Bot) mignonette (*Reseda*)

‹ **بَلُدَ** *v* |u; بَلادة| ❶ [قَلَّ ذَكاؤُهُ] to be ignorant ❷ [قَلَّ نَشاطُهُ] to do nothing

بَلَّدَ *v* to acclimatize, to habituate

تَبَلَّدَ *v* ❶ [أَصْبَحَ بَليداً] to become stupid ❷ [تَأَقْلَمَ] to acclimatize

بَلَد *n* |بُلْدان, بِلاد| country; بِلاد country; countries; بَلَد مُجاوِر a neighbouring country; بُلْدان بَعيدة faraway countries; بَلَد أَصْليّ country of origin; بَلَد صِناعيّ an industrial country; البُلْدان العَرَبيّة Arab countries; بِلاد الهِنْدِ \ الصينِ India/China; بَلَد من بُلْدانِ \ بَلَد من البُلْدانِ النامِيةِ a developing country; بَلَد من العالَمِ الثالِثِ a Third World country; مَصْلَحة البَلَدِ national interest; لِمَصْلَحةِ \ من أَجْلِ مَصْلَحةِ البَلَدِ for the good of the country; في جَميعِ أَنْحاءِ البِلادِ throughout the country; إِنَّهُ مَعْروفٌ في البَلَدِ كُلِّهِ he is known country-wide; بِلُغةِ البَلَدِ in the national language; مَثَّلَ بَلَدَهُ to represent one's country; غادَرَ البِلادَ to leave the country; جابَ \ طافَ البِلادَ to travel through the country; دافَعَ عن بِلادِهِ to defend one's country; سورة البَلَدِ The Country (*Sura 90*)

بَلادة *n* ❶ [غَباء] stupidity, foolishness ❷ [كَسَل] inertness

بَلْدة *n* village, town; place, spot; في خارِجِ البَلْدةِ on the outskirts of town; in the outlying areas; أَهْل \ أَبْناء البَلْدةِ locals

بَلَديّ *adj* home (*before n*), domestic, native; municipal; رَقْص بَلَديّ folk dance; قَصْر بَلَديّ town hall; المَجْلِس البَلَديّ local/city council; اجْتِماع المَجْلِس البَلَديِّ council meeting

بَلَديّة *n* municipality; رَئيس بَلَديّةٍ mayor; دار البَلَديّةِ town hall

بَليد **A** *adj* ❶ [غَبيّ] stupid, foolish; وَلَد بَليد a stupid boy ❷ [كَسْلان] lazy, inert, lethargic

B *n* fool, idiot; هو بَليدٌ he's an idiot

تِبِلْديّ *n* listed alphabetically

مُتَبَلِّد *adj* ❶ [بَليد] stupid, foolish; مُتَبَلِّد العَقْلِ slow-witted ❷ [فاتِر] apathetic, lazy

‹ **بُلْدوزِر** *n* |بُلْدوزِرات| bulldozer

‹ **بَلْسَمَ** *v* |i; بَلْسَمة| to soothe; to treat, to tend to; بَلْسَمَ جُرْحاً to soothe a wound; (fig) to repair damage; بَلْسَمَ الجِراحَ التي تَسَبَّبَتْ فيها الحَرْبُ to heal the wounds caused by the war

بَلْسَم *n* |بَلاسِمُ| ❶ [مَرْهَم] balm, balsam; liniment; بَلْسَم للشِفاهِ lip balm; بَلْسَم للشَعْرِ conditioner; كانَ بَلْسَماً لِجُروحِهِ to be balm to one's wounds ❷ (Bot) balm, balsam

‹ **بُلْشِفيّ** **A** *adj* |بَلاشِفة| Bolshevik; الثَوْرة البُلْشِفيّة the October Revolution

B *n* |بَلاشِفة| Bolshevik

بُلْشِفيّة *n* Bolshevism

‹ **بَلَشون** *n* heron

1 **بَلَّط** *v* [1] ▶ [أَرْض الدارِ] to tile; بَلَّطَ البَحْرَ to attempt the impossible [2] ▶ [الشارِعَ] to pave

بَلاط *n* [1] ▶ [أَرْض مُبَلَّطة] pavement; tiles, tiled floor [2] ▶ [مَلِكٍ] court; البَلاط المَلَكيّ \ القَيْصَريّ the royal/imperial court; ناطِق باسْمِ البَلاطِ a spokesman of the court; في البَلاطِ at court

بَلاطة *n* |بَلاطات, أَبْلِطة| tile; بَلاطة الأَرْضِيّة floor tile

تَبْليط *n* tiling; paving

مُبَلَّط *adj* paved; tiled; شارِع مُبَلَّط a paved street

مُبَلِّط *n* tiler

2 **بَلّوط** *n coll* [1] ▶ [شَجَرة] oak; شَجَرة البَلّوطِ an oak tree; طاوِلة مَصْنوعة من خَشَبِ البَلّوطِ an oak table [2] ▶ [ثَمَرة] acorn

3 **بَلْطة** *n* |بَلْطات, بُلَط| axe

بَلْطَجيّ *n* |بَلاطِجة, بَلْطَجيّة, بَلْطَجيّون| thug

4 **بُلْطيّ** *n* (Zool) tilapia

بَلْطيق *n* Baltic; بَحْر البَلْطيق the Baltic Sea; دُوَل البَلْطيق the Baltic states

بَلَعَ *v* |a; بَلْع| to swallow; بَلَعَ شَيْئاً to swallow sth; بَلَع حَبّةَ دَواءٍ to swallow a pill; بَلَعَ ريقَهُ to gulp; بَلَعَ الطُعْمَ to take the bait

أَبْلَعَ *v* to make swallow

ابْتَلَعَ *v* to swallow; to devour; ابْتَلَعَ شَيْئاً to swallow sth; ابْتَلَعَ فَريسَتَهُ to devour its prey; ابْتَلَعَتْهُ الظُلْمةُ he was swallowed by darkness; ابْتَلَعَ ثَرَواتٍ to swallow large sums of money

بالوعة *n* |بالوعات, بَواليعُ| drain; sink; culvert; sewer

بَلّاعة, بَلّوعة *n* |بَلاليعُ| drain; sink; culvert; sewer

بُلْعوم, بُلْعُم *n* |بَلاعيم| pharynx

1 **بَلَغَ** *v* |u; بُلوغ| [1] ▶ [وَصَلَ] to reach, to arrive at; بَلَغَ المَدينةَ to reach the city; بَلَغ ذَرْوَتَهُ to reach its climax; بَلَغَ التَوَتُّرُ أَشَدَّهُ tensions came to a head; بَلَغَهُ أنّ ... to learn/hear that ...; بَلَغَ من العُمْرِ الثالِثةَ he became/was three years old [2] ▶ [الكَمّيّةُ] to amount to; بَلَغ عَدَدُ القَتْلى ٦٨٢ قَتيلاً there were 682 casualties; تَبْلُغُ قيمَتُهُ مِلْيار دولار it's valued at a billion dollars; يَبْلُغ طولُهُ \ عَرْضُهُ \ ارْتِفاعُهُ ٥ أَمْتارٍ the length/width/height measures five metres [3] ▶ [نَضِجَ] to ripen; to come of age; بَلَغَ الغُلامُ the boy has come of age

بَلُغَ *v* |u; بَلاغة| to be eloquent

بَلَّغَ *v* [1] ▶ [أَوْصَلَ] to make reach; to take, to bring; to transmit, to convey; بَلَّغَ شَخْصاً \ لِشَخْصٍ تَحِيّاتِهِ to convey one's greetings to sb [2] ▶ [أَخْبَرَ] to let know, to inform; to announce, to notify; to report; بَلَّغَ شَخْصاً بِوُقوعِ حادِثٍ to inform sb that sth has happened; بَلَّغَ عن شَخْصٍ to report sb; بَلَّغَ عن جَريمةٍ to report a crime

بالَغَ *v* |في| to exaggerate, to overdo; بالَغَ في شَيْءٍ to exaggerate sth; بالَغَ في التَقْديرِ to overestimate, to overrate; لا يُبالِغُ في القَوْلِ إنّ ... he is not exaggerating when he says that ...; it is no exaggeration to say that ...

أَبْلَغَ *v* to let know, to inform, to tell; to announce; to report; أَبْلَغَ شَخْصاً شَيْئاً \ بِأَنّ ... to tell sb that ...; أَبْلَغَ شَخْصًا أنّ \ بِشَيْءٍ \ عن شَيْءٍ to inform sb of sth; أَبْلَغَ الشُرْطةَ ب \ عن شَخْصٍ to report sth/sb to the police

تَبَلَّغَ *v* to be informed (of); تَبَلَّغَ من شَخْصٍ شَيْئاً to be informed of sth by sb; لم تَتَبَلَّغ الخارِجيّةُ شَيْئاً the foreign ministry was not informed of anything

بالِغ [A] *adj* [1] ▶ [شَديد] considerable, significant; highest, greatest; serious; بِاهْتِمام بالِغٍ with great interest; أَمْر بالِغُ الأَهَمّيّةِ a matter of the highest importance; أَعْرَبَ عن بالِغِ سَعادَتِهِ to express one's utmost joy [2] ▶ [العَدَد] amounting to, numbering; نِصْف سُكّانِها البالِغِ عَدَدُهُمْ ٩ مَلايينَ نَسَمةٍ half of its population of 9 million [3] ▶ [راشِد] mature, of (legal) age, adult; sexually mature, marriageable; شَخْص بالِغ an adult; بالِغ سِنَّ الرُشْدِ of age

[B] *n* adult

بَلاغ *n* |بَلاغات| announcement, statement; notice, report, tip; reporting, declaration; بَلاغ كاذِب a hoax; أَصْدَرَ بَلاغاً to issue a communiqué; تَلَقّى بَلاغاً to receive a tip

بَلاغة *n* rhetoric; eloquence; عِلْم البَلاغةِ rhetoric; بَلاغة الكَلامِ eloquence

بَلاغيّ *adj* rhetorical

بُلْغة *n* sufficiency, adequacy

بُلوغ *n* [1] ▶ [سِنّ] maturity, adulthood; سِنّ البُلوغِ (legal) majority; وَلَد دون سِنِّ البُلوغِ a minor; في مَرْحَلةِ البُلوغِ

in adulthood [2] [وُصول] reaching, attainment, arrival; بُلوغ هَدَفٍ reaching a goal/target; بعد بُلوغِ النِهائيّاتِ after reaching the finals

بَليغ *adj* |بُلَغاءُ| [1] [فَصيح] eloquent [2] [عَميق] deep, profound; serious; أَثَر بَليغ a large effect; مُصاب بِجُروحٍ بَليغةٍ seriously wounded

إبْلاغ *n* |إبْلاغات| announcement, notification; reporting, declaration; إبْلاغ شَخْصٍ بِشَيْءٍ notifying sb of sth

تَبْليغ *n* |تَبْليغات| [1] [إعْلام] notification; reporting [2] [كِتاب] report; تَبْليغ عن الحَوادِثِ a report of the events

مُبالَغ *adj* exaggerated; كَلام \ قَوْل مُبالَغ فيهِ exaggeration

مُبالِغ *adj* exaggerating; مُبالِغ في الحَذَرِ overly careful

مُبالَغة *n* exaggeration; excess; مُبالَغة كَبيرة \ شَديدة \ خَفيفة a gross/extreme/slight exaggeration; بِلا مُبالَغةٍ without exaggerating; مُبالَغة في التَقْديرِ overestimation; مُبالَغة في الكَلامِ \ القَوْلِ \ التَصْويرِ an exaggeration

مَبْلَغ *n* |مَبالِغُ| [1] [مال] amount, sum; مَبْلَغ ضَئيل \ زَهيد a small amount; مَبْلَغ طائِل \ باهِظ a huge/exorbitant amount; مَبْلَغ مُحَدَّد a fixed sum; مَبْلَغ صافٍ net amount; مَبْلَغ مُحْتَرَم a considerable sum; مَبْلَغ لا يُسْتَهانُ بِهِ a not inconsiderable sum; المَبْلَغ بِأَكْمَلِهِ the entire amount; صَرَّفَ مَبْلَغاً من المالِ to spend a sum of money; دَفَعَ مَبْلَغاً to pay an amount; تَسَلَّمَ مَبْلَغاً قَدْرُهُ ٣٠٠٠ دينارٍ to receive a sum of 3,000 dinar; يُكَلِّفُ مَبالِغَ طائِلةً it costs a fortune [2] [نِطاق] extent, scope, range; limit; هذا مَبْلَغُ عِلْمي as far as I know; بَلَغَ مِنّي التَعَبُ مَبْلَغَهُ I am overtired

مُبَلِّغ *n* messenger; informant

بَلْغة *n* |بَلاغ| slippers

بُلْغارِيا *n* Bulgaria

بُلْغاريّ **A** *adj* |بُلْغار| Bulgarian; (اللُغة) البُلْغاريّة Bulgarian (*language*)

B *n* |بُلْغار| Bulgarian (*person*)

بِلْغْراد *n* |f| Belgrade (*capital of Serbia*)

بَلْغَم *n* |بَلاغِمُ| phlegm; mucus; طارِد للبَلْغَمِ expectorant

بَلْغَميّ *adj* phlegmy; العُقَد \ الغُدَد البَلْغَميّة lymph nodes

بَلَق *n* [1] [حَجَر] mica [2] (Egypt) حَمام البَلَقِ pigeon

أَبْلَق **A** *adj* |dipt| [مُبَقَّع] pied, spotted, speckled

B *n* |dipt| (Zool) wheatear (*Oenanthe*)

بَلْقَشة *n* (Zool) goosander (*Mergus*)

بَلْقَع *n* |بَلاقِعُ| wasteland

البَلْقان *n* |f| the Balkans

مُبَلْقَن *adj* balkanised

بَلْكونة *n* balcony

بَلَّ *v* |u; بَلّ| to wet, to moisten

بَلَّلَ *v* to moisten; بَلَّلَ شَيْئاً to moisten sth

أَبَلَّ *v* to recover

تَبَلَّلَ *v* to be/become wet

ابْتَلَّ *v* to be/become wet

بَلَل *n* moistness; humidity

بِلّة *n* moisture; humidity

(Idiom) زادَ الطينَ بِلّةً to further exacerbate the situation

بَليلة *n* balila (*Lebanese chickpea and cumin dish*)

مُبْتَلّ *adj* wet, damp, moist; شَعْر مُبْتَلّ wet hair; مَنْديل مُبْتَلّ a damp cloth

مُبَلَّل *adj* wet, damp, moist; فوطة مُبَلَّلة a damp cloth; كانَ مُبَلَّلاً بالعَرَقِ to be soaked in sweat; كانَ مُبَلَّلاً بالدُموعِ to be wet with tears

مَبْلول *adj* wet, damp, moist; خِرْقة مَبْلولة a wet rag; كانَ مَبْلولاً بالمَطَرِ to be wet with rain

بَلَم *n* anchovy

بَلِهَ *v* |a; بَلاهة, بَلَه| to be stupid, to be simple-minded

تَبالَهَ *v* to feign stupidity

بَلْهَ *excl* to say nothing of ..., let alone ...

بَلَه *n* stupidity

بَلاهة *n* stupidity, foolishness; بِبَلاهةٍ stupidly; نَظَرَ \ تَساءَلَ بِبَلاهةٍ to gaze/ask stupidly

أَبْلَه **A** *adj* |dipt| stupid, foolish, idiotic; سُؤال أَبْلَه a stupid question

B *n* fool, idiot

‹ **بِلْهارْسِيا** *n* (Med) blood fluke, bilharzia (*Schistosomiasis*)

‹ **بَلا** *v* |u; بَلْو ,بَلاء| to try, to put to the test; بَلاهُ الزَمانُ time has put him to the test

بَلِيَ *v* |a; بِلًى ,بَلاء| ① [الثَوْبُ وَنَحْوُهُ] to be/become worn out; to fray ② [الفِكْرَةُ] to be obsolete, to be worn out

بالى *v* to worry, to bother; to pay attention; to care, to be concerned; لم يُبالِ بالأَمْرِ to be unconcerned about the matter

أَبْلى *v* ① [اجْتَهَدَ] أَبْلى بَلاءً حَسَناً to prove oneself brave, to distinguish oneself in battle; to strive earnestly ② [بَلِيَ] to wear out

ابْتَلى *v* ① [جَرَّبَ] to try, to put to the test; ابْتُلِيَ بِمِحْنةٍ to meet with adversity; ابْتَلاهُ اللهُ بِشِدّةٍ God has tried him severely ② [أَصابَ] to afflict

بالٍ *adj* ① [قُماش] worn, worn-out, threadbare; ثِياب بالية worn-out clothes; ارْتَدى أَسْمالاً باليةً to be dressed in rags ② [أَفْكار] obsolete, archaic, outdated; فِكْرة بالية an outdated notion; تَقْليد بالٍ an archaic tradition

بَلاء *n* affliction, trial, tribulation; adversity; أَبْلى بَلاءً حَسَناً to prove oneself brave, to distinguish oneself in battle; to strive earnestly

بَلْوى *n* disaster, calamity

بِلًى *n* wear

بَلِيّة *n* |بَلايا| trial; misfortune, calamity; بَلِيّة من اللهِ a trial from God; أَصابَتْهُ البَلايا to suffer misfortune; شَرُّ البَلِيّةِ ما يُضْحِكُ the worst misfortune is the one that makes you laugh

ابْتِلاء *n* |ابْتِلاءات| trial, tribulation, affliction

لامُبالٍ *adj* indifferent, apathetic; careless, irresponsible; شَخْص لامُبالٍ a careless person

لامُبالاة *n* indifference, apathy; neglect

مُبالٍ *adj* attentive; mindful; careful; غَيْر مُبالٍ thoughtless, negligent; careless; unconcerned; كانَ غَيْرَ مُبالٍ بالخَطَرِ to not give a thought to the danger

مُبالاة *n* interest, attention; concern; دون مُبالاةٍ بالعَواقِبِ without thought to the consequences

مُبْتَلًى *adj* tried, tested

‹ **بْلوتو** *n* Pluto

‹ **بْلوتونيوم** *n* plutonium

‹ **بَلْوَرَ** *v* |i; بَلْوَرة| ① [جَعَلَ شَيْئاً بِلَّوْراً] to (let) crystallize ② [بَيَّنَ] to develop, to form, to formulate; to solidify; بَلْوَرَ مَوْقِفاً \ مَفْهوماً to develop a position/concept; بَلْوَرَ تَصَوُّراً واضِحاً to form a clear image

تَبَلْوَرَ *v* to crystallize; to be formed, to be developed; تَبَلْوَرَت الفِكْرةُ the idea was formed

بِلَّوْر ,بَلّور *n* |بِلَّوْرات| crystal; glass; بِلَّوْر نَقِيّ \ صَخْرِيّ pure/rock crystal; بِلَّوْر النافِذةِ window glass, windowpane; شَظِيّة بِلَّوْرٍ a glass fragment, a sliver of glass

بَلْوَرة *n* ① [بَلَّوْر] crystallization ② [تَكْوين] formation, formulation; developing; بَلْوَرة خُطّةٍ formulating a plan; بَلْوَرة تَصَوُّرٍ واضِحٍ developing a clear image

بِلَّوْرة ,بَلّورة *n* crystal; بِلَّوْرة سِحْرِيّة a crystal ball

بِلَّوْرِيّ ,بَلّوريّ *adj* crystal (*before noun*); شاشة بِلَّوْرِيّة (سائلة) liquid crystal display, LCD

تَبَلْوُر *n* ① [بلَّوْر] crystallization ② [تَكَوُّن] development; أَخَذَ في التَبَلْوُرِ to take shape

مُتَبَلْوِر *adj* crystallized; solidified; final; الاتِّفاق المُتَبَلْوِر the terms agreed upon

‹¹ **بْلوزة** *n* blouse, shirt; لَبِسَ \ ارْتَدى بْلوزةً to wear a blouse

‹² **بْلوز** *n* ① [موسيقى] blues ② [مَلابِس] blouse

‹ **بُلوفر** *n* (Egypt) sweater, pullover

‹¹ **بلى** *excl* (oh) yes; sure; indeed; أَلَيْسَ كَذَلِكَ؟ بَلى، كَذَلِكَ! isn't that right? sure it is!

‹² **بِلْية** *n* marble (*children's toy*)

‹ **بِلْيارْدو ,بِلْيارْد** *n* pool, billiards; لُعْبة البِلْيارْد a pool game, a game of billiards

‹ **بِلْيون** *num* |بَلايينُ| billion; بِبِلْيونَيْ دولار for two billion dollars; تَجاوَزَ ثَلاثةَ بَلايينِ دولار to exceed three billion dollars

‹ **بِمَ** *pron* see بِما under ما

‹ **بِما** *pron* see ما

‹ **بِنْت** *n* see بنو

‹ **البِنْتاغون** *n* the Pentagon

‹ **بَنَّج** *v* anaesthetize; بَنَّج شَخصاً to anaesthetize sb

بَنْج *n* **1** (Med) anaesthesia; طَبيب البَنْج anaesthesiologist **2** (Bot) henbanes (*Hyoscyamus*)

تَبْنيج *n* anaesthesia; طَبيب التَبْنيج anaesthesiologist

‹ **البُنْجاب** *n* |f| Punjab (*region in India*)

‹ **بَنْجَر** *n* beet; بَنْجَر السُكَّرِ sugar beet; سُكَّر البَنْجَرِ beet sugar

‹ **بَنْد** *n* |بُنود| **1** [فقرة] item; paragraph; section; بَنْد في الميزانيَةِ budget item; بَنْد مَصاريفَ (debit) item, (debit) entry; بُنود الاتِّفاقِ the terms of the agreement; وَقَعَ تحت \ في بَنْدٍ مُعَيَّنٍ to come under a certain head **2** [قانونٍ] article; item; البَنْد الرابع من المادّة ٢٣ في القانونِ الجِنائيِّ the fourth item of article 23 of the criminal code

‹ **بَنْدا** *n* panda

‹ **بَنْدَر** *n* |بَنادِر| **1** [ميناء] seaport **2** [اسْم شَخْصيّ] Bandar (*male given name*) **3** [مَرْكَز المُحافَظَةِ] (Egypt) *district capital* **4** (Zool) rhesus monkey; عامِل البَنْدَرِ Rhesus factor, Rh factor

‹ **بُنْدُق** *n coll* **1** [نَوْع من المُكَسَّراتِ] hazelnuts **2** [شَجَرة] hazel **3** (Tunisia) pine nuts

بُنْدُقيّ *adj* hazel

بُنْدُقيّة *n* |بَنادِق| rifle, gun; بُنْدُقيّة رَشّاشة \ آليّة machine gun; بُنْدُقيّة أوتوماتيكيّة automatic rifle; بُنْدُقيّة هُجوميّة assault rifle; بُنْدُقيّة ضَغْطِ الهَواءِ air rifle/airgun; صَوَّبَ \ سَدَّدَ بُنْدُقيّةً to aim a rifle; عَمَّرَ بُنْدُقيّةً to load a rifle

البُنْدُقيّة *n* Venice

‹ **بَنادورة ,بَنَدورة** *n* (Levant) tomato

‹ **بَنْدول** *n* pendulum

‹ **بِنْزان** *n* benzene

‹ **بِنْزَرْت** *n* |dipt f| Bizerte (*city in Tunisia*)

‹ **بَنْزين** *n* petrol (BrE), gas/gasoline (AmE); بَنْزين مُمْتاز \ سوبِر premium petrol, super (BrE), high octane gas (AmE); بَنْزين عاديّ normal petrol (BrE), regular gasoline (AmE); بَنْزين خالٍ من الرَصاصِ unleaded petrol; صَفيحة البَنْزينِ a tank of petrol; خَزّان بَنْزينٍ petrol tank; مِضَخّة بَنْزينٍ petrol pump; مَحَطّة بَنْزينٍ petrol/filling station (BrE), gas station (AmE); مُحَرِّك بالبَنْزينِ petrol engine; دَوّاسة البَنْزينِ accelerator (pedal), gas pedal (AmE)

‹ **بِنْس** *n* |بِنسات| penny

‹ **بِنِسلين** *n* penicillin; جُرْعة البِنْسِلين a dose of penicillin

‹ **بِنْسيلْفانيا** *n* Pennsylvania (*US state*)

‹ **بِنْصِر** *n* |بَناصِر| ring finger

‹ **بَنْطَلون** ,**بَنْطال** *n* |بَنْطَلونات| trousers (BrE), pants (AmE); بَنْطَلون الجينز jeans; رِجْل البَنْطَلونِ trouser leg (BrE), pant leg (AmE)

‹ **بَنْغازي** *n* |f| Benghazi (*city in Libya*)

بَنْغْلاديش ,بَنْجْلاديش *n* |f| Bangladesh

بَنْغْلاديشيّ ,بَنْجْلاديشيّ *adj* Bangladeshi

‹ **بَنَفْسَج** *n coll* (Bot) violet (*Violaceae*)

بَنَفْسَجيّ *adj* purple, violet; فوق بَنَفْسَجيٍّ ultraviolet

‹ **بَنْك** *n* |بُنوك| **1** [مَصْرَف] bank; البَنْك المَرْكَزيّ the Central Bank; البَنْك الدُوَليّ the World Bank; بَنْك تَوْفيرٍ \ ادِّخارٍ savings bank; مُوَظَّف في بَنْكٍ bank clerk/employee; مُدير \ صاحِب بَنْكٍ banker; قِطاع البُنوكِ banking, the banking industry; سَطْو على بَنْكٍ bank robbery; وَضَعَ المالَ في البَنْكِ to put money in the bank **2** [مَخْزَن] bank, store, repository; بَنْك المَعْلوماتِ database, databank; بَنْك الدَمِ blood bank **3** [مَقْعَد] seat; bench; كانَ قاعِداً على البَنْكِ (Sport) to be on the bench

بَنْكيّ *adj* bank (*before n*), banking (*before n*); قَرْض \ حِساب بَنْكيّ bank loan/account

اسْتِبْناك *n* (Morocco) *making use of the bank system*

‹ **بَنْكِرياس** *n* pancreas; سَرَطان البَنْكِرياسِ pancreatic cancer

‹ **بِنْكام** *n* hourglass

‹ **بَنَما** *n* Panama

1‹ **بُنّ** *n* coffee (beans); حَمَّصَ البُنَّ to roast coffee

بُنّيّ **A** *adj* brown; شَعْر بُنّيّ brown hair; عَيْنانِ بُنّيّتانِ brown eyes **B** *n* (Zool) common barbel (*Barbus barbus*)

بُنّين *n* caffeine

2‹ **بَنان** *n coll* fingertip; أَشارَ بالبَنانِ إلى to point to, to indicate; to point fingers at, to blame; عَضَّ بَنانَ النَدَمِ to sorely regret; يُشارُ إلَيْه بالبَنانِ to be famous to build a reputation; بَنى شَيْئاً بِعَرَقِهِ \ بِعَرَقِ جَبينِهِ to build sth with one's sweat and tears **2** [أَسَّسَ] to base; بَنى رَأْيَهُ على التَجارِبِ to base one's opinion on experience; بُنِيَ (على) to be based (on); بُنِيَ هذا القَوْلُ على ... this theory is based on ...; بُنِيَ على أَساسِ شَيْءٍ to be founded on sth **3** (Gram) to make indeclinable; بُنِيَ to be indeclinable; بُنِيَ على الفَتْحِ to have an invariable ending of fatha

انْبَنى *v* to be built/based

ابْتَنى *v* to build

بانٍ *n* |بُناة| builder

بَنّاء **A** *adj* constructive, positive; نَقْد بَنّاء constructive criticism; مُناقَشة إسْهام \ حَلّ بَنّاء a constructive contribution/solution; بَنّاءة a constructive discussion

B *n* builder, construction worker

بِناء *n* |أَبْنِية| **1** [تَشْييد] building, construction; (صِناعة) البِناءِ the construction industry; شَرِكة بِناءٍ construction company; عامِل بِناءٍ construction worker; رُخْصة \ تَصْريح البِناءِ building permit; حَجَر البِناءِ building block; قِطاع البِناءِ building sector; إعادة البِناءِ reconstruction, rebuilding; تَكاليف البِناءِ building costs; كانَ قَيْدَ البِناءِ to be under construction; بِناءً على... on the basis of ...; by virtue of ...; بِناءً على هذا based on that, accordingly, therefore **2** [مَبْنًى] building, edifice; هَدَمَ بِناءً to demolish a building **3** [تَرْكيب] structure; البِناء الاجْتِماعيّ the social structure/system **4** (Islam) consummation; بعد البِناءِ بِها after consummation of the marriage with her **5** (Gram) indeclinability

بِنائيّ *adj* building (*before n*), construction (*before n*); مَوادّ بِنائيّة building materials

بِناية *n* building, edifice; premises; بِناية سَكَنيّة a residential building; سَطْح \ مَدْخَل البِنايةِ the roof/entrance of a building

بُنْيان *n* structure; foundation; بُنْيان اقْتِصاديّ economic infrastructure; تَقْويض بُنْيانِ الدَوْلةِ undermining the country; كالبُنْيانِ المَرْصوصِ in solidarity

بِنْية، **بُنْية** *n* |بِنًى، بُنًى| **1** [هَيْئة] structure; infrastructure; frame, framework; بِنْية تَحْتيّة \ أَساسيّة infrastructure; بِنْية خَلَويّة

تَبَنّى *v* **1** [طِفْلاً] to adopt; تَبَنّى وَلَداً to adopt a child **2** [قَرارًا] to accept, to adopt, to embrace; تَبَنّى مَشْروعَ قانونٍ to pass a bill; تَبَنّى أَفْكاراً جَديدةً to embrace new ideas; تَبَنّى قَراراً to adopt a resolution

بَناتيّ *adj* girlish, girly; for girls, for young women

بِنْت *n* |f; بَنات| **1** [ابْنة] daughter; بِنْت عَمٍّ (female) cousin (*paternal*) **2** [فَتاة] girl, young woman; بَنات جِنْسِها all-female company, other girls; بِنْت الهَوى prostitute; مَدْرَسة للبَناتِ a girls' school **3** [عَذْراء] virgin **4** [لُعْبة الوَرَقِ] queen (*suit in playing cards*)

(Idioms) بِنْت شَفةٍ word; بَنات الصَدْرِ worries

بُنُوّة *n* paternity; إثْبات البُنُوّةِ establishing paternity

بَنَويّ *adj* filial; مَحَبّة بَنَويّة filial love

بُنَيّ *n* my little son; يا بُنَيَّ (O) my little son

بَني سُوَيْف *n* |f| Beni Suef (*city in Egypt*)

بَني مَلّال *n* |f| Beni Mellal (*city in Morocco*)

ابْن *n* |أَبْناء، بَنون| **1** [خَلَف] son; الابْن الأَكْبَر \ الوَحيد the eldest/only son; بَنو العَبّاسِ the Abbasids; ابْن آدَمَ human being; ابْن زِنا \ الحَرامِ illegitimate son, bastard; زَوْجة الابْنِ daughter-in-law; إنَّهُ ابْنُ أَبيهِ he's (definitely) his father's son **2** [إنْسان] person; ابْن البَلَدِ native, citizen; أَبْناء اليَوْمِ young people nowadays; ابْن ثَلاثينَ سَنةً a thirty-year old man; ابْن سَبيلٍ traveller; vagabond; هو من أَبْناءِ المِنْطَقةِ he is from this region

ابْنة *n* |بَنات| daughter; زَوْج الابْنةِ son-in-law

تَبَنٍّ *n* adoption; تَبَنّي أَطْفالٍ أَجانِبَ the adoption of foreign children; أَب بالتَبَنّي adoptive father

مُتَبَنٍّ *adj* **1** [مَن يَتَبَنّى] adoptive; الأَب المُتَبَنّي the adoptive father **2** [قَرار] adopting, passing; الدُوَل المُتَبَنِّية للقَرارِ the countries adopting the resolution

مُتَبَنًّى *adj* **1** [طِفْل] adopted; وَلَد مُتَبَنًّى an adopted child **2** [قَرار] adopted, passed; القَرار المُتَبَنّى في البَرْلَمانِ the resolution adopted by parliament

بَنى *v* |i; بُنْيان، بِناء| **1** [أَنْشَأَ] to build, to construct, to set up; بَنى بَيْتاً \ حائِطاً to build a house/a wall; بَنى وَطَناً to build a nation; بَنى لِنَفْسِهِ سُمْعةً to build one's future; بَنى مُسْتَقْبَلَهُ

بُهْتان *n* 1 [كَذْب] lie 2 [غَيْبة] slander

مَبْهوت *adj* amazed, perplexed

‹ **بَهَجَ** *v* |a; بَهْج| to make happy/glad

بَهِجَ *v* |a; بَهْجة, بَهَج| to be happy; بَهِجَ بِشَيْءٍ to be happy about sth

أَبْهَجَ *v* to make happy, to delight; ما يَسُرُّ العَيْنَ ويُبْهِجُ القَلْبَ that which pleases the eye and gladdens the heart

ابْتَهَجَ *v* to be happy; ابْتَهَجَ بِشَيْءٍ \ لِشَيْءٍ to be happy about sth

بَهْجة *n* happiness, joy; بَعَثَ البَهْجة to give rise to joy

بَهيج *adj* happy, cheerful; جَوّ بَهيج a cheerful atmosphere

ابْتِهاج *n* |ابْتِهاجات| joy, happiness, delight; ابْتِهاج شَديد great joy

مُبْتَهِج *adj* happy, cheerful

مُبْهِج *adj* pleasant, exhilarating

مَبْهَجة *n* |مَباهِجُ| مَباهِج الحَياةِ the pleasures of life

‹ **بَهْدَلَ** *v* |i; بَهْدَلة| to treat with contempt, to ridicule

‹ **بَهَرَ** *v* |a; بَهْر| to dazzle, to astonish; بَهَرَتْهُمْ بِجَمالِها she stunned them with her beauty

أَبْهَرَ *v* to dazzle; to astonish; أَبْهَرَ شَخْصاً to astonish sb; أَبْهَرَني بِذَكائِهِ I was astonished by his cleverness

انْبَهَرَ *v* to be dazzled; to be fascinated; انْبَهَرَ بِشَيْءٍ to be dazzled by sth

باهِر *adj* dazzling, brilliant; splendid; spectacular; نَتائِج باهِرة brilliant results; نَجاح باهِر a tremendous success; مُسْتَقْبَل باهِر a bright future; جَمال باهِر dazzling beauty

بَهار *n* |بَهارات| spice; بَهارات spices; جُزُر البَهار Maluku Islands, the Spice Islands

أَبْهَر *n* |dipt| (Anat) aorta

مُبْهِر *adj* dazzling, blinding; ضَوْء مُبْهِر a dazzling light

مُبَهَّر *adj* seasoned, spiced

مَبْهور *adj* out of breath, panting

‹ **بَهْرَجَ** *v* |i; بَهْرَجة| 1 [زَيَّنَ] to adorn; to make up 2 [زَوَّرَ] to forge, to fake

تَبَهْرَجَ *v* to dress up; to overdo one's make-up

بَهْرَج *adj* false, forged; overly made-up, showy

cell structure; البِنْية الاقْتِصاديّة economic structure, economic infrastructure; بِنْية تَحْتيّة للطاقةِ \ للاتِّصالاتِ \ للمَعْلوماتِ energy/communications/IT infrastructure; تَطْوير البِنْيةِ التَحْتيّةِ infrastructure development 2 (Literat) structure; format; بِنْية قِصّةٍ \ رِوايةٍ narrative structure; البِنْية السَرْديّة the structure of a story/novel; بِنْية القَصيدة الجاهليّةِ the format of pre-Islamic poems 3 [جَسَديّة] build; constitution, physique; بِنْية قَويّة \ نَحيفة a muscular/slim build; رَجُل مَتين البِنْيةِ a sturdy fellow; كانَ قَويَّ البِنْيةِ to have a strong constitution; كانَ ضَعيفَ البِنْيةِ to have a weak constitution, to be in bad health; كانَ سَليمَ البِنْيةِ to be in good health 4 (Ling) form, morphology

بِنْيَويّ *adj* 1 [هَيْكَليّ] structural; constitutional; systemic; خَلَل \ إصْلاح بِنْيَويّ structural defect/reform 2 (Lit) structuralist; نَقْد بِنْيَويّ structuralist literary criticism

بِنْيَويّة *n* structuralism

ابْتِناء *n* (Bio) anabolism

ابْتِنائيّ *adj* anabolic; سْتيرويْد ابْتِنائيّ anabolic steroid

مَبْنًى *n* |مَبانٍ| 1 [بِناء] building, construction, edifice; مَبْنًى خالٍ an empty building; هَدَمَ مَبْنًى to demolish a building 2 [شَكْل] form; المَبْنى والمَعْنى form and content

مَبْنيّ *adj* 1 [مُبْتَنًى] built; based 2 (Gram) indeclinable; اسْم مَبْنيّ على فَتْحةٍ a noun with an invariable fatha ending

‹ **بَنْيو** *n* see بانْيو

‹ **بَهاما** *n* جُزُر البَهاما the Bahamas

‹ **بَهَتَ** *v* |a; بُهْتان| to slander; بَهتَ شَخْصاً to slander sb

بَهِتَ *v* |a; بَهْت| 1 [اللَوْنُ] to be/become pale, to fade; to be/become bleached; بَهِتَ لَوْنُ السَتائِرِ the curtains have faded; بَهِتَ رَوْنَقُهُ its lustre has faded 2 [الصورةُ الذِهْنيّةُ] to fade; بَهِتَ في ذاكِرَتِهِ to fade from one's memory 3 [أَدْهَشَ] to amaze, to bewilder, to stagger 4 [سَكَتَ مُتَحَيِّراً] to be/become speechless; بُهِتَ to be speechless

باهِت *adj* faded; pale; lacklustre; ضَوْء باهِت a pale light, a dim light; ابْتِسامة باهِتة a wan smile; أَلْوان \ جينْز باهِت faded colours/jeans; أَزْرَق باهِت pale blue, light blue; عَرْض باهِت a lacklustre performance

بَهْرَجة *n* fanfare, hollow pomp, gaudiness

مُبَهْرَج *adj* showy

‹ **بَهْشيّة** *n* holly (*Ilex*)

‹ **أَبْهَظَ** *v* to weigh heavily on, to oppress

باهِظ *adj* exorbitant, excessive; ضَرائِب \ أَسْعار باهِظة exorbitant taxes/prices; باهِظ التَكاليفِ \ الثَمَنِ costly, excessively expensive

‹ **بَهَق** *n* (Med) vitiligo

‹ **ابْتَهَلَ** *v* to supplicate; ابْتَهَلَ إلى اللهِ أنْ ... to supplicate to God for ...

ابْتِهال *n* |ابْتِهالات| supplication; ابْتِهال إلى اللهِ supplication to God

‹ **بَهْلَوان** *n* |بَهْلَوانات| clown; acrobat; circus performer

بَهْلَوانيّ *adj* acrobatic; clown (*before n*); أَلْعاب بَهْلَوانيّة acrobatics

بَهْلَوانيّة *n* acrobatics

‹ **بُهْلول** *n* |بَهاليلُ| clown; acrobat; circus performer

‹ **أَبْهَمَ** *v* **1** [عَكْس أَوْضَحَ] to obscure, to make unintelligible **2** [الْتَبَسَ] to be obscure/unintelligible

بَهيم *adj* |بُهُم، بُهْم| pitch-black; لَيْل بَهيم a pitch-black night

بَهيمة *n* |بَهائِمُ| animal, beast; بَهائِم livestock

بَهيميّ *adj* animal (*before n*), bestial, brute; الغَرائِز البَهيميّة animal instincts

إبْهام *n* |أَباهيمُ| **1** (Anat) thumb; big toe; إبْهام الرِجْلِ the big toe **2** [غُموض] obscurity, darkness, vagueness

مُبْهَم *adj* unclear; vague, obscure; mysterious; سُؤال \ نَصّ مُبْهَم a vague question/text; شُعور مُبْهَم a vague feeling; كَلامُهُ مُبْهَمٌ his words are not clear; أَصْوات مُبْهَمة indistinct sounds; مَوْقِف مُبْهَم an unclear point of view; اسْم مُبْهَم indefinite pronoun

‹ **باهى** *v* |ب| to be proud of, to boast of

تَباهى *v* |ب| to brag about, to boast of; to show off; to pride oneself on; تَباهى بِشَيْءٍ to brag about sth; to show sth off; تَباهى بِعائِلَتِهِ to brag about one's family; تَباهى بِأنَّهُ ... to pride oneself on ...; تَباهى بِقُدْرَتِهِ على التَنْظيمِ to pride oneself on one's talent for organising; تَباهى بِسَيّارَتِهِ الجَديدةِ to show off one's new car

بَهْو *n* |أَبْهاء| foyer, parlor

بَهاء *n* beauty, splendor, magnificence; بَهاء الطَبيعةِ the beauty of nature

بَهائيّ **A** *adj* Baha'i (*before n*) **B** *n* Baha'i

بَهيّ *adj* beautiful, splendid

البَهائيّة *n* Bahai

تَباهٍ *n* boasting; self-importance, conceit

مُباهٍ **A** *adj* boasting, bragging **B** *n* braggart

مُباهاة *n* bragging

مُتَباهٍ **A** *adj* |مُتَباهونَ| boasting, bragging **B** *n* |مُتَباهونَ| braggart

‹ **باءَ** *v* |u; بَوْء| to return; to retreat; باءَ بالفَشَلِ to fail

بَوَّأَ *v* to appoint, to assign

تَبَوَّأَ *v* to hold, to occupy; تَبَوَّأَ مَنْصِباً to hold a post/position; تَبَوَّأَ العَرْشَ to take the throne; تَبَوَّأَ الحُكْمَ to come to power

بيئة، بيئة *n* **1** (Bio) environment; عِلْم البيئةِ ecology; عالِم البيئةِ ecologist; تَلَوُّث البيئةِ environmental pollution; ضَريبة البيئةِ environmental/pollution tax; حِماية البيئةِ environmental protection; سِياسة البيئةِ conservation/environmental policy; العِناية بالبيئةِ environmental care; المُحافَظة على البيئةِ saving the environment; خَطَر على البيئةِ a threat to the environment **2** (Sociol) environment; social climate; background; البيئة الاقْتِصاديّة \ الاجْتِماعيّة the economic/social climate

بيئَويّ *adj* ecological

بيئيّ *adj* ecological, environmental; عَوامِل بيئيّة ecological factors; تَلَوُّث بيئيّ environmental pollution; كارِثة بيئيّة environmental disaster; ناشِط بيئيّ environmental activist; نِظام بيئيّ ecosystem

‹ **بُواء** *n* boa (constrictor); (feather) boa

‹ **بَوَّبَ** *v* to group; to classify; to divide into chapters

المَحْظوراتِ necessity makes the forbidden permissible ❷ [باحَ] to reveal, to disclose; أَباحَ السِرَّ to tell the secret

اسْتَباحَ *v* to consider permissible; اسْتَباحَ الحُرْمَةَ to dishonour; to violate; اسْتَباحَ دَمَ شَخصٍ to allow sb to be killed

بَوْح *n* disclosure; بَوْح بِشَيْءٍ disclosure of sth

باحة *n* square; courtyard; باحة المَسْجِدِ mosque courtyard; باحة الاسْتِراحةِ rest area

إباحة *n* ❶ [إجازة] permission, allowance, authorization; permissiveness; إباحة الإجْهاضِ permitting abortion; الإباحة الجِنْسيّة sexual permissiveness ❷ [إفْشاء] disclosure

إباحيّ *adj* licentious, immoral; pornographic; مَوادّ \ صُوَر \ أَدَب أَفْلام إباحيّة pornographic material/pictures/films, porn; إباحيّ pornographic literature

إباحيّة *n* licentiousness, permissiveness; pornography

مُباح *adj* permitted, permissible, allowed; (Isl Law) permitted; طَريقة مُباحة a permissible method; وَسيلة مُباحة fair means

‹ **باخَ** *v* |u; بَوْخ, بَوَخان| to fade

بائِخ *adj* dull; banal

‹ **بوخارِسْت** *n* |f| Bucharest

‹ **بودابِسْت** *n* |f| Budapest

‹ **بودْرة** *n* powder; حَليب البودْرةِ powdered milk

‹ **بودْكاسْت** *n* |بودْكاسْتات| podcast

‹ **بودِنْج** *n* pudding

‹ **بوذا** *n* Buddha

بوذيّ *adj, n* Buddhist

البوذيّة *n* Buddhism

‹ **بارَ** *v* |u; بَوْر, بَوار| ❶ [الأَرْض] to lie fallow ❷ [السِلْعةُ] to be unsaleable ❸ [هَلَكَ] to perish, to be ruined

أَبارَ *v* to destroy, to ruin

بور *adj* |mf| fallow, undeveloped; أَرْض بور wasteland

بائِر *adj* |بور| fallow; أَرْض بائِرة wasteland

بَوار *n* ❶ [أَرْض] |بور| wasteland ❷ [هَلاك] perdition, ruin ❸ [كَساد] stagnation

(Idiom) دار البَوارِ hell

باب *n* |mf; أَبْواب, أَبْوِبة, بيبان| ❶ [مَدْخَل] door; entrance; gate; باب أَماميّ \ خَلْفيّ front/back door; باب رَئيسيّ main entrance, front door; باب خارِجيّ outside door; من البابِ الأَماميِّ through the front door; باب السَيّارةِ car door; باب المَسْرَحِ \ قاعةِ الحَفْلِ the entrance of the theatre/party hall; ثُقْب البابِ keyhole; الانْتِخاباتُ على الأَبْوابِ the elections are on their way; عَبَرَ البابَ to walk through the door; أَغْلَقَ أَبْوابَهُ to close its gates, to close down; تَرَكَ البابَ مَفْتوحاً أمام \ ل to leave the door open to; أَغْلَقَ بابَ المُناقَشةِ to cut off discussion; صَفَقَ البابَ to slam the door; لم يَتْرُكْ باباً إلا وَطَرَقَهُ ≈ to leave no stone unturned ❷ [جُزْء] chapter; section; column; في البابِ الثالِثِ in the third chapter; باب الأَخْبارِ العالَميّةِ the world news section ❸ [نَوْع] هذا لَيْسَ من بابِ المُسْتَحيلِ impossible; من بابِ أَوْلى better; من بابِ الصُدْفةِ this cannot be a coincidence

(Idiom) البابُ العالي Topkapi Palace

بَوّاب *n* doorman, doorkeeper; porter

بَوّابة *n* ❶ [باب] gate; بَوّابة تَحَكُّمٍ lock, sluice ❷ (Comput) بَوّابة إِلِكْتْرونيّة portal; بَوّابة ويب Web portal

تَبْويب *n* classification, categorization; عَلامة تَبْويب tab

مُبَوَّب *adj* classified; إعْلانات مُبَوَّبة classified ads

‹ **بوتاجاز, بوتاغاز** *n* ❶ [غاز] propane tank/cylinder; LPG tank/cylinder ❷ [فُرْن] stove

‹ **بوتاس** *n* potash

‹ **بوتاسِيوم** *n* potassium; نِتْرات البوتاسِيوم potassium nitrate, saltpetre

1‹ **بوتان** *n* |f| Bhutan (*country in South Asia*)

2‹ **بوتان** *n* butane; غاز البوتان butane

‹ **بوتْسوانا** *n* Botswana

‹ **بوتَقة** *n* crucible

‹ **بوتوكْس, بوتاكْس** *n* Botox®

‹ **بوتيك** *n* |بوتيكات| boutique

باحَ *v* |u; بَوْح, بِ| to reveal, to disclose; باحَ بِسِرٍّ to tell a secret; باحَ بِحُبِّهِ to confess one's love

أَباحَ *v* ❶ [أَجازَ] to permit, to allow; أَباحَ شَيْئاً to permit sth; أَباحَ دَمَ شَخْصٍ to allow sb to be killed; الضَروراتُ تُبيحُ

بيّارة *n* (Levant) grove, orchard

بورْجُوازيّ, بورْجُوازيّة see برجوازي

بورْسِلين *n* china, porcelain; من البورْسِلين china (*before n*), porcelain (*before n*); دُمْية من البورْسِلين porcelain doll

بورْصة *n* stock exchange/market; انْهِيار البورْصةِ stock market crash; إقْفال البورْصةِ the market's close; مُؤَشِّر أَسْعارِ البورْصةِ stock market price index, share price index; في البورْصةِ on the stock exchange

بورْكينا فاسو *n* |f| Burkina Faso

بورْما *n* Burma

بورْميّ *adj, n* Burmese

بوروندي *n* |f| Burundi

بوريه *n* purée

بوريّ *n* (Zool) mullet (*Mugil*)

بَوَّز *v* to pout; to sulk

بوز *n* |أَبْواز| snout

باسَ *v* |u; بَوْس| to kiss

بَوْس *n* kissing

بَوْسة *n* kiss

البوسْنة *n* Bosnia; البوسْنة والهَرْسَك Bosnia-Herzegovina

بوص *n coll* reed; قَلَم البوصِ reed pen

بوصة *n* inch; البوصة المُرَبَّعة square inch

بوصَلة, بَوْصَلة, بوصْلة, بوصُلة *n* compass

بوظة *n* ice cream

باع *n* |أَبْواع| fathom (old use) (*span of outstretched arms from palm to palm*); reach, capability; experience, history, tradition; باع الجَناح wingspan; قَصير الباع powerless, incapable; stingy; قُصور الباع impotence, incapacity; stinginess; طَويل الباع powerful, mighty; influential; knowledgeable; generous; كانَ لَهُ باعٌ طَويلٌ في شَيْءٍ to be experienced in sth; to have a a long tradition of sth; هو مَعْروفٌ بِطولِ باعِهِ he is known for his broad knowledge; بالباعِ والذِراعِ with all one's strength

بَوْغ *n* spore

بوغاز *n* |بَواغيزُ| (Geog) strait

بوفيه *n* [1] [خِزانة] buffet, sideboard [2] [أَطْعِمة] buffet; بوفيه مَفْتوح open buffet

بَوَّق *v* to blow

بوق *n* |أَبْواق, بوقات| [1] (Mus) horn; trumpet, clarion; bugle; نَفَخ في البوقِ to blow the horn; نَفَخَ أَبْواقَ الحَرْبِ to beat the drums of war [2] [للسَيّارة] (car) horn, hooter (BrE) [3] [ناطِق] spokesman; كانَ بوقاً للحُكومةِ to be a spokesman for the government [4] (Anat) fallopian tube; بوق فالوب fallopian tube

باقة *n* bouquet; bunch; باقة زُهورٍ \ من الزُهورِ a bouquet of flowers; باقة بَقْدونِسٍ a bunch of parsley

بَوّاق *n* trumpeter, horn player; bugler

بوكَر *n* poker (*card game*); لَعِبَ البوكَرَ to play poker

بوكْسيت *n* (Geol) bauxite

[1] **بالَ** *v* |u; بَوْل| to urinate (fml), to pee (infml), to piss (vulg)

تَبَوَّلَ *v* to urinate (fml), to pee (infml), to piss (vulg)

اسْتَبالَ *v* to make/let urinate

بَوْل *n* |أَبْوال| urine; تَحْليل البَوْلِ urinalysis; مُدِرّ للبَوْلِ diuretic; سَلَس البَوْلِ urinary incontinence

بَوْليّ *adj* urine (*before n*), urinary; مَسالِك بَوْليّة urinary passages; تَحْليل بَوْليّ urinalysis; حَصاة بَوْليّة bladder stone

تَبَوُّل *n* urination; التَبَوُّل اللاإراديّ involuntary urination

مَبْوَلة, مِبْوَلة *n* |مَباوِلُ| urinal

[2] **بال** *n* mind; heart; مَشْغول البالِ concerned, worried; طَويل البالِ patient; خالي \ مُرْتاح البالِ carefree; calm; راحة البالِ peace of mind; لم يَهْدَأْ لَهُ بالٌ he was not calm; فما بالُك ب ... let alone ...; شَغَلَ بالَهُ to worry; شَغَلَ بالَهُ بِمُشْكِل to worry about/over a problem; وَضَعَ شَيْئاً في بالِهِ to put sth in one's mind; غابَ عن البالِ to be forgotten; to be overlooked; خُذْ بالَكَ من ... mind ...!, look out for ...!; خَطَرَ على \ في بالِهِ to come to one's mind; لا يَخْطُرُ بِبالٍ unthinkable; لا على البالِ وَلا على الخاطِرِ unexpected, out of the blue

بولاق *n* |dipt mf| Bulaq (*district in Cairo*)

بولْفار *n* boulevard

‹ **تبَوْلُن** *n* تبَوْلُن الدَمِ uraemia

‹ **بولَنْدا** *n* Poland

بولَنْديّ **A** *adj* Polish; (اللُغة) البولَنْديّة Polish (*language*)

B *n* Pole, Polish person

‹ **بولو** *n* polo

‹ **بولونيا** *n* Poland

بولونيّ **A** *adj* Polish

B *n* Pole, Polish person

‹ **بوليثَر** *n* polyether

‹ **بوليس** *n* police, cop (infml)

بوليسيّ *adj* police (*before n*), cop(*before n*) (infml); كَلْب بوليسيّ police dog; دَوْلة بوليسيّة police state; رِواية بوليسيّة detective/crime novel; فيلْم بوليسيّ cop film

‹ **بوليسْتَر** *n* polyester

‹ **بوليسْتِرين** *n* polystyrene, styrofoam (AmE)

‹ **بوليصة** *n* |بَوالِصُ| policy; certificate; bill; بوليصة التَأْمِينِ insurance policy; بوليصة الشَحْنِ bill of lading

‹ **بوليفيا** *n* Bolivia

‹ **بوليمَر** *n* polymer

‹ **بولينيزيا** *n* Polynesia

‹ **بوم** *n coll* owl

‹ **بون, بَوْن** *n* (large) distance

‹ **بوهيميّ** *n* Bohemian

‹ **بوية** *n* paint

‹ **بِيانو** *n* |بِيانات, بِيانوهات| piano; بِيانو كَهْرَبائيّ an electric piano; عازِف البِيانو pianist; عَزَفَ على البِيانو to play the piano

‹ **بيبة** *n* pipe

‹ **باتَ** *v* |i; مَبيت| **1** [أَقامَ لَيْلاً] to spend the night; باتَ في مَكانٍ to spend the night in a place; باتَ عند شَخصٍ to stay at sb's place **2** [أَصْبَحَ] to become; باتَ مَعْروفاً \ واضِحاً to become famous/clear **3** [بَدَأَ] to begin, to get to the point where; باتَ يُدرِكُ he began to realize **4** [ظَلَّ] to continue to; باتَ يُواصِلُ الدِراسةَ to continue one's studies

بَيَّتَ *v* to put up for the night

أَباتَ *v* to put up for the night

بَيْت *n* **1** [البِناية] |بُيوت, بُيوتات| house; بَيْت تِجاريّ place of business; بَيْت الإِبْرةِ compass; بَيْت زُجاجيّ hothouse, greenhouse; بَيْت الراحةِ toilet (BrE), bathroom (AmE); بَيْت المالِ the treasury, the Exchequer (BrE); بَيْت الحَرامِ the Kaaba; بَيْت اللهِ the Kaaba; a mosque; بَيْت المَقْدِسِ Jerusalem; رَبّ البَيْتِ head of the household, man of the house; رَبّة البَيْتِ housewife; صاحِب بَيْتٍ homeowner, landlord; امْتَلَكَ بَيْتاً to own a house **2** [مَنْزِل العائِلةِ] home; بَيْت الزَوْجيّة \ الأَهْلِ the marital/parental home; ذَهَبَ \ رَجَعَ إلى البَيْتِ to go home; لازَمَ البَيْتَ to stay at home; وَصَلَ إلى بَيْتِه to come home; أَوْصَلَ شَخْصاً إلى بَيْتِه to take sb home; تَصَرَّفْ وَكَأَنَّكَ في بَيْتِكَ make yourself at home **3** [أُسْرة] |بُيوتات| family; البُيوتات the respectable families; أَهْل البَيْتِ the family/descendants of the Prophet **4** (Literat) |أَبْيات| verse; بَيْت شِعْرٍ a verse of poetry

بائِت *adj* old, stale; خُبْز بائِت stale bread

بَيات *n* sleep; بَيات شَتَويّ hibernation

بَيْت لَحْم *n* |f| Bethlehem

بَيْتيّ *adj* home (*before n*), house (*before n*); private; domesticated; أَدوات بَيْتيّة household goods

مَبيت *n* **1** [الإقامة لَيْلاً] overnight stay **2** [مَكان الإقامةِ] shelter for the night

‹ **بيتا** *n* beta; مَرْحَلة بيتا beta stage/phase

‹ **بيتْزا** *n* pizza

‹ **بيج** *adj* beige

‹ **بجامة, بيجامة** *n* pyjamas; يَلْبِسُ بيجامةً he is wearing pyjamas

‹ **بادَ** *v* |i; بُيود, بَيْد| to perish, to be ruined

أَبادَ *v* to destroy, to exterminate; to slaughter, to massacre; أَبادَ الحَشَراتِ to exterminate insects; أَبادَ عائِلةً كامِلةً to slaughter an entire family

بَيْدَ *conj* بَيْدَ أنّ but, however; although, nevertheless; هُوَ كَثيرُ المالِ، بَيْدَ أَنَّهُ بَخيلٌ he is rich but nevertheless stingy

بائِد *adj* past, former; النِظام البائِد the former regime; العَهْد البائِد the pre-revolutionary period

بَيْداء *n* |dipt f; بيد| desert, wilderness

إبادة *n* extermination; annihilation; إبادة جَماعيّة \ عِرْقيّة genocide

مُبيد *n* |مُبيدات| pesticide; herbicide; مُبيد حَشَريّ \ الحَشَراتِ pesticide, insecticide; مُبيد زِراعيّ agricultural pesticide; مُبيد الأَعْشابِ herbicide; اسْتِعْمال المُبيداتِ the use of pesticides

‹ **بيداغوجيّ** *adj* pedagogic

‹ **بَيْدَرَ** *v* |i; بَيْدَرة| to thresh

بَيْدَر *n* |بَيادِرُ| threshing floor

‹ **بَيْدَق** *n* |بَيادِقُ| pawn; كانَ مُجَرَّدَ بَيْدَقٍ (بِيَدِ شَخْصٍ) to be merely a pawn (for sb)

‹ **بيرة** *n* beer, lager; كَأْس \ كوب من البيرة glass of beer; مَصْنَع بيرةٍ brewery; صَنَعَ البيرةَ to brew beer

‹ **بَيْرَق** *n* flag; banner; standard

‹ **بيرو** *n* |f| Peru

‹ **بَيْروت** *n* |dipt f| Beirut

‹ **بيروفيّ** *adj*, *n* Peruvian

‹ **بيروقْراطيّ** *adj* bureaucratic; مُنَظَّمة بيروقْراطيّة a bureaucratic organization; جِهاز بيروقْراطيّ bureaucracy; مُوَظَّف بيروقْراطيّ a bureaucrat

بيروقْراطيّة *n* bureaucracy, officialdom

‹ **بيريسْكوب** *n* periscope

‹ **بَيْزار** *n* |بَيازِرة| falconer

بَيْزَرة *n* falconry

‹ **بيزَنْطيّ** **A** *adj* **1** [الإمْبراطوريّةُ] Byzantine (*before n*) **2** [مُناقَشاتٌ] futile; circular, unending; مُناقَشة بيزَنْطيّة a futile discussion; جَدَل بيزَنْطيّ an unending controversy **B** *n* Byzantine

بيزَنْطِية, بيزَنْطيا, بيزَنْطة *n* Byzantium

‹ **بيزو**, بيسو *n* peso

‹ **بيسْبول** *n* baseball; لَعِبَ البيسْبول to play baseball

‹ **بيسيتا**, بيزيتا *n* (Hist) peseta

‹ **باضَ** *v* |i; بَيْض| to lay eggs, to lay an egg; عِنْدَما يَبيضُ الديكُ ≈ when pigs fly; الدَجاجة التي تَبيضُ ذَهَباً ≈ the goose that lays the golden eggs; a cash cow

بَيَّضَ *v* **1** [لَوَّنَ بالأَبْيَضِ] to whiten; to whitewash; to bleach; بَيَّض بَيْتاً to whitewash a house; بَيَّض بَشَرَتَهُ \ أَسْنانَهُ to bleach one's skin/teeth **2** [أَبْرَأَ] to clear, to clean; بَيَّض وَجْهَهُ \ صَفْحَتَهُ to repair one's image; بَيَّض وَجْهَ شَخْصٍ to make sb appear in a favourable light; بَيَّض اللهُ وَجْهَهُ may God make him happy! **3** [نُقوداً] to launder; بَيَّض أَمْوالاً to launder money

أَباضَ *v* to ovulate

ابْيَضَّ *v* to turn white, to whiten; ابْيَضَّ وَجْهُهُ his face lit up

بَيْض *n coll* |بُيوض| **1** [حَيَواناتٍ] eggs; بَيْض طازَج fresh eggs; بَيْضة نيِّئة raw egg; بَيْضة مَسْلوقة \ مَقْلِيّة poached/fried egg; بَيْضة مَخْفوقة beaten egg; بَيْضة فاسِدة rotten egg; بَياض \ مُحّ بَيْضٍ egg white/yolk; قَشَّرَ بَيْضةً to peel an egg; حَضَنَ بَيْضةً to hatch an egg; وَضَعَ بَيْضاً to lay eggs; بَيْضة الديكِ ≈ hens' teeth (*a rare or impossible thing*); بَيْضةُ اليَوْمِ خَيْرٌ من دَجاجةِ الغَدِ ≈ better an egg today than a hen tomorrow **2** [خَليّة التَناسُلِ الأُنْثَوِيّة] ovum **3** [الذَكَرِ] testicle **4** [أَصْل] essence; بَيْضة الصَيْفِ the hottest part of the summer

بُوَيْضة *n* see بُيَيْضة

بَياض *n* **1** [عَكْس سَواد] white, whiteness; البَياضات linen, white goods; بَياض بَيْضٍ egg white; ناصِع البَياضِ immaculate white, snow-white, pearly white **2** [فَراغ] gap, lacuna; blank space; على بَياضٍ blank; شيك \ صَكّ على بَياضٍ a blank cheque; أَعْطى \ مَنَحَ شَخْصاً شيكاً على بَياضٍ to give sb a blank cheque; (fig) to give sb unlimited power **3** (Zool) *a kind of Nile fish*

بَيّاض *n* **1** [دَجاج] laying eggs; دَجاج بَيّاض laying hen **2** [مَنْ يُبَيِّضُ] house painter

بَياضات *n pl* bedding

بَيْضاء *n* |dipt f; بَيْضاوات| (Mus) minim (BrE), half note (AmE)

بَيْضاويّ *n* **1** [من دارِ البَيْضاءِ] *person from Casablanca* **2** [في البَيْتِ الأَبْيَضِ] البَيْضاويّ the Oval Office

بَيْضَويّ, بَيْضيّ *adj* oval, elliptical; ovate; egg (*before n*); شَكْل بَيْضَويّ ellipse, oval; طاوِلة بَيْضَويّة an oval table; المَكْتَب البَيْضَويّ the Oval Office

باعَ *v* |i; مَبيع ,بَيْع| to sell; باعَ شَيْئاً to sell for $100; باعَ بِمائةِ دولار to sell sth second-hand; باعَ كَمِّيّةً من السِلَعِ مُسْتَعْمَلاً to sell an amount of goods; باعَ لِشَخْصٍ مَحَلَّهُ to sell one's shop to sb; باعَ شَيْئاً في السوق العالَمِيّة \ السَوْداء to sell sth on the world/black market; باعَ نَفْسَهُ \ ضَميرَهُ (للشَيْطان) to sell one's soul (to the devil)

بايَعَ *v* **1** [حالَفَ] to acknowledge as leader; to pledge allegiance; بايَعَ شَخْصاً مَلِكاً to acknowledge sb as king **2** (Busn) to conclude a sale

أباعَ *v* to offer for sale

تبايَعَ *v* to conclude a sale/transaction

انْباعَ *v* to be sold

ابْتاعَ *v* to buy, to purchase

بَيْع *n* |بُيوعات ,بُيوع| sale; selling; بَيْع عَلَنيّ a public sale, auction; بَيْع تَأْجيريّ leasing; بَيْع بالتَجْزِئة \ بالمُفَرَّقِ retail; بَيْع بالجُمْلةِ wholesale; بَيْع بالمَزادِ sale by auction; بَيْع البُنِّ selling coffee; مَحَلّ (ل)بَيْع الكُتُبِ \ الأَثاث bookstore/furniture store; عَقْد بَيْع sale contract, deed of sale; تاريخ البَيْع date of sale; بَيْع وَشِراء negotiation, negotiating; للبَيْع for sale; كانَ عُرِضَ للبَيْع to offer sth for sale; عَرَضَ \ طَرَحَ شَيْئاً للبَيْع to be for sale; مَعْروضاً للبَيْع to cancel a sale أَلْغى البَيْعَ

بائِع *n* |باعة ,بائعونَ| seller, salesman, vendor; dealer; trader; بائِع بالتَجْزِئة \ بالمُفَرَّقِ retailer; بائِع مُتَجَوِّل street vendor; بائِع تَذاكِرَ ticket seller

بَيّاع *n* **1** [بائِع] salesman, merchant **2** [مَنْطَقة] |f| البَيّاع Bayaa' (*district in Baghdad*)

ابْتِياع *n* purchase

مُبايَعة *n* oath of allegiance; acknowledgement (*as leader*)

مَبيع *n* مَبيعات sales; مَبيعاتُ السِلاحِ \ السَيّاراتِ arms/car sales; ضَريبة المَبيعاتِ sales tax; value added tax, VAT; قِسْم \ إدارة المَبيعاتِ sales department; رَقْم المَبيعاتِ sales figures; رَقْم مَبيعاتٍ عالٍ \ مُنْخَفِض high/low sales figures; حَجْم المَبيعاتِ sales volume; ارْتَفَعَت \ انْخَفَضت المَبيعاتُ بِنِسْبةِ ٤٪ sales are up/down 4%

بيقة ,بيقيّة *n* (Bot) vetch (*Vicia*)

بَيْضيّ *adj* oval; ovate

بُوَيْضة ,بُيَيْضة *n* egg cell, ovum; بُيَيْضة مُلَقَّحة a fertilized egg cell

إباضة *n* ovulation

أَبْيَض **A** *adj* |dipt; بيض| **1** [اللَوْن] white; شَعْر أَبْيَض white/grey hair; رَجُل أَبْيَض a white man, a Caucasian man (fml); بَشْرة بَيْضاء fair skin; ذَهَب أَبْيَض white gold; الماء الأَبْيَض (Med) cataracts; الدار البَيْضاء Casablanca; البَحْر الأَبْيَض المُتَوَسِّط the Mediterranean Sea **2** [إيجابيّ] good; نهارُكَ أَبْيَض have a good day; قَلْبُهُ أَبْيَض he's a good person **3** [أَقَلّ ضَرَراً] *less harmful*; انْقِلاب أَبْيَض a bloodless coup; سِلاح أَبْيَض cutting and stabbing weapons; كِذْبة بَيْضاء a white lie **4** [فارِغ] blank; وَرَقة بَيْضاء a blank piece of paper; وَضَعَ وَرَقةً بَيْضاءَ to cast a blank ballot; فَتَحَ صَفْحةً بَيْضاءَ to start afresh, to turn over a new leaf
B *n* |dipt; بيض| a white person; البيض والسود blacks and whites

ابْيِضاض *n* whitening; ابْيِضاض الدَمِ leukaemia; أُصيبَ بِابْيِضاضِ الدَمِ to have leukaemia

البَيْضاء *n* |f| al-Bayda' (*province and city in Yemen and city in Libya*)

تَبْويض *n* ovulation

تَبْييض *n* whitening; laundering; تَبْييض أَمْوالِ المُخَدِّراتِ the laundering of drug money

تَبْييضة *n* final copy, print (*of a book*)

مَبيض ,مِبْيَض *n* |مَبايِضُ| **1** (Anat) ovary; سَرَطان المَبيضِ ovarian cancer; اسْتَأْصَلَ المَبيضَيْنِ to remove the ovaries **2** (Bot) ovary

مُبَيِّض *n* bleach; مُبَيِّض الأَسْنانِ teeth whitener

مُبَيِّضة *n* yeast; المُبَيِّضة البَيْضاء candida (*Candida albicans*); داء المُبَيِّضاتِ candidiasis, yeast infection

بَيْطار *n* |بَياطِرة| **1** [طَبيب بَيْطَريّ] veterinary surgeon (BrE), veterinarian (AmE), vet **2** [مَنْ يُرَكِّبُ نَعْلَ الحِصانِ] farrier

بَيْطَرة *n* veterinary medicine

بَيْطَريّ *adj* |بَياطِرة| veterinary; طَبيب بَيْطَريّ veterinary surgeon (BrE), veterinarian (AmE), vet; طِبّ بَيْطَريّ veterinary medicine

بيكْسِل *n* pixel

بيكُلو, بيكولو *n* piccolo

بيكين *n* |f| Beijing

بيكيني *n* bikini

بيلاروس, بيلاروسيا *n* |f| Belarus

بيمارِسْتان *n* (Hist) *medieval Islamic hospital/asylum*

بانَ *v* |i; بَيان| to be/become clear; to come to light, to come out; to show; to be exposed; بانت الحَقيقةُ the truth came out; بانَتْ عَوْرَتُهُ to be laid bare (for all to see); بانَتْ مَوْهِبَتُها her talent was clear

بَيَّنَ *v* to clarify, to make clear; to show, to demonstrate; بَيَّنَ لِشَخْصٍ شَيْئاً to show sb sth; بَيَّنَ السَّبَبَ to demonstrate the cause; بَيَّنَت الدِراساتُ أنّ … studies show that ...

بايَنَ *v* 1◀ [خالَفَ] to be contradictory to; to conflict with; to differ from; بايَنَ شَيْئاً to conflict with sth 2◀ [فارَقَ] to part with, to leave; بايَنَ شَخْصاً to leave sb

أبانَ *v* 1◀ [اِتَّضَحَ] to be/become clear 2◀ [أَوْضَحَ] to make clear, to explain

تَبَيَّنَ *v* 1◀ [ظَهَرَ] to be/become clear; to turn out, to prove, to appear; to come out; تَبَيَّنَ أَنَّهُ في صِحَّةٍ جَيِّدةٍ he turned out to be healthy; تَبَيَّنَتْ حَقيقةُ الأَمْرِ the truth came out 2◀ [أَدْرَكَ] to try to ascertain; to examine critically; تَبَيَّنَ الأَسْباب to try to find the cause

تَبايَنَ *v* 1◀ [اِخْتَلَفَ] to differ, to vary; to be contrary; تَبايَنت الآراءُ opinions differed 2◀ [تَفارَقَ] to become separated

اِسْتَبانَ *v* to be/become clear

بَيْنَ *prep* 1◀ [مَكان] between; among; بَيْنَ الجِدارِ والطاوِلةِ between the wall and the table; بَيْنَ ذِراعَيْها in her arms; مِن بَيْنِها among other things; including, among which; كانَتْ مِنْ بَيْنِها مَطْبَعةٌ among other things there was a printer; مِنْ بَيْنِهِمْ among them, among whom 2◀ [زَمان] بَيْنَ حينٍ وَآخَرَ from time to time; بَيْنَ يَوْمٍ وَلَيْلةٍ from one day to the next 3◀ [عَلاقة] العَلاقاتُ بَيْنَ الصينِ و(بَيْنَ) الوِلاياتِ المُتَّحِدةِ relations between China and the United States; بَيْني وَبَيْنَكَ between you and me; بَيْنَهُ وَبَيْنَ نَفْسِهِ inside; to himself; ليس اللَوْنُ أَخْضَرَ وَلا أَصْفَرَ وَلَكِنَّهُ بَيْنَ بَيْنَ the colour is somewhere between green and yellow; اِخْتارَ بَيْنَ شَيْئَيْنِ to choose between two things; الشُعورُ الوَطَنيُّ يَجْمَعُ بَيْنَ الناسِ national sentiment unites the people 4◀ [وَسَط] الفَتْرة ما بَيْنَ الحَرْبَيْنِ العالَمِيَّتَيْنِ the period between the two World Wars; ما بَيْنَ الساعةِ الثامنة والساعةِ العاشِرةِ between eight and ten o'clock; المِنْطَقة ما بَيْنَ الجِبالِ والبَحْرِ the area between the mountains and the sea; فيما بَيْنَ ذلك in between, meanwhile

بَيِّن *adj* clear, plain, evident, obvious; ظُلْم بَيِّن blatant injustice

بائِن *n* clear, plain, evident; طَلاق بائِن irrevocable divorce

بَيان *n* |بَيانات| 1◀ [وُضوح] clarity, obviousness; هذا غَنيٌّ عن البَيانِ that needs no explanation 2◀ [بَلاغ] declaration, statement, announcement; report; communiqué; بَيان واضِح a clear report; بَيان إداريّ administrative/official statement; بَيان رَسْميّ an official announcement; manifesto; بَيان سِياسيّ a political manifesto; بَيان وِزاريّ government policy statement; بَيانات كاذِبة false statements; بَيان حِساب bank statement; أَصْدَرَ بَياناً to issue a statement; to publish a report 3◀ [مَعْلومة] fact; بَيانات facts, details; data, information; بَيانات ناقِصة missing details; بَيانات شَخْصيّة personal data; قاعِدة بَياناتٍ database; إدارة البَياناتِ data management; جَمَعَ بَياناتٍ to collect data; خَزَّنَ \ أَدْخَلَ \ اسْتَرْجَعَ بَياناتٍ to store/enter/retrieve data 4◀ [تَفْصيل] specification 5◀ [لائِحة] register, list 6◀ [بَلاغة] eloquence; عِلْم البَيانِ rhetoric 7◀ (Ling) عَطْف البَيانِ an explanatory apposition

بَيانيّ *adj* graphic; illustrative; رَسْم بَيانيّ diagram; graph, chart

بَيِّنة *n* proof, evidence; بَيِّنة ظَرْفيّة circumstantial evidence; سورة البَيِّنة The Clear Proof (*Sura 98*); كانَ على بَيِّنةٍ من شَيْءٍ to be aware of sth; هو على بَيِّنةٍ من الأَمْرِ he knows all about it

بَيْنَما *conj* see ما

بَيْنيّ *adj* mutual, among themselves; تِجارة بَيْنِيّة bilateral trade, inter-regional trade

اِسْتِبْيان *n* |اِسْتِبْيانات| survey, poll, questionnaire; الاِسْتِبْيان العَشْوائيّ randomized survey; عَيِّنة الاِسْتِبْيانِ interviewee; sample, sampling

تَبايُن *n* |تَبايُنات| contrast; divergence, difference; تَبايُن حادّ a glaring contrast; تَبايُن في وُجْهاتِ النَظَرِ differing points of view

تِبْيان *n* explanation, clarification; uncovering, revealing; تِبْيان الحَقيقةِ establishing the truth

مُبين *adj* clear, plain, evident; الكِتاب المُبين the Koran

مُتَبايِن *adj* differing, mixed; contrasting, contradictory; divergent; أحاسيس مُتَبايِنة mixed feelings; مَواقِف مُتَبايِنة divergent positions; رُدود فِعْلٍ مُتَبايِنة mixed reactions

‹ **بَيْنا** *conj* see بَيْنَما under **ما**

‹ **بِيوتَكْنولوجِيا** *n* biotechnology

‹ **بِيوجاز** *n* biogas

‹ **بِيولوجِيا** *n* biology

بِيولوجيّ *adj* biological

1› **ت** ***abbr*** tel., telephone (*abbreviation of* **تِليفون**)

2› **تَ** ***particle*** by; **تَاللهِ** by God

› **تاء** ***n*** |f| *name of the letter* **ت**; **تاء مَرْبوطة** ta' marbuta (*feminine ending*)

› **تابو** ***n*** |**تابوهات**| taboo

› **تابوت** ***n*** |**تَوابيتُ**| coffin; sarcophagus; **تابوت العَهْدِ** the Ark of the Covenant

› **تابير** ***n*** (Zool) tapir

› **تَبْيوكة, تابْيوكا** ***n*** tapioca

› **تَأْتَأَ** ***v*** |i; **تَأْتاء, تَأْتَأة**| to stutter, to stammer

تَأْتاء ***n*** 1 [**مَصْدَر**] stammer 2 [**لَجْلاج**] stutterer, stammerer

› **تازة** ***n*** |dipt| Taza (*city in Morocco*)

› **تاكْسي** ***n*** |**تاكْسِيات**| taxi; **سائِق تاكْسي** taxi driver

› **تَوْأَم** ***n*** |**تَوائِمُ**| twin; **تَوْأمانِ** twins; **ثَلاثة تَوائِمَ** triplets; **هي حامِلٌ بِتَوْأَمٍ** she is expecting twins; **أَنْجَبَتْ تَوْأَماً** to have twins; **أخ \ أُخت تَوْأَم** twin brother/sister; **تَوْأمانِ سِياميّانِ** conjoined twins; **تَوْأَم الروحِ** kindred spirit, soulmate; **سَلا، المَدينة التَوْأَم للرباطِ** Salé, Rabat's twin city

تَوْأَمة ***n*** (town) twinning; **تَوْأَمة بين مَدينةِ أَمْسْتِرْدام وَمَدينةِ وارْسو** twinning between Amsterdam and Warsaw

مُتاءَمة ***n*** (town) twinning

› **تاميليّ** A ***adj*** Tamil; **(اللُغة) التاميليّة** Tamil (*language*) B ***n*** Tamil (*person*)

› **تانْغو, تانْجو** ***n*** tango

› **تايْلَنْد, تايْلَنْدا** ***n*** |f| Thailand

تايْلَنْديّ A ***adj*** Thai; **(اللُغة) التايْلَنْديّة** Thai (*language*) B ***n*** Thai (*person*)

› **تايْوان** ***n*** |f| Taiwan

تايْوانيّ ***adj, n*** Taiwanese

› **تايور, تايير** ***n*** |**تايورات**| outfit, (woman's) suit

› **تَبَّ** ***v*** |i; **تَبّ**| to die, to perish

اسْتَتَبَّ ***v*** to stabilize, to be/become stable; to be restored; to be established; **عِنْدَما يَسْتَتِبُّ الأَمْنُ** when security is restored

تَبّ ***n*** ! **تَبًّا!** ugh!; damn!; **تَبًّا لَكَ** damn you!, go to hell!

اسْتِتْباب ***n*** stability; stabilizing; restoration; establishment; **اسْتِتْباب الأَمْنِ** establishing security; **اسْتِتْباب الوَضْعِ الأَمْنيِّ** stabilizing the security situation; **من أَجْلِ اسْتِتْبابِ السَلامِ** in order to establish peace

مُسْتَتِبّ ***adj*** stable; **الأَمْنُ مُسْتَتِبٌّ** security is stable

› **تابوت** ***n*** *listed alphabetically*

تِبِتيّ ***adj, n*** Tibetan

التِبِت ***n*** |f| Tibet

› **تِبْر** ***n*** gold dust; gold nuggets

› **تَبْريز** ***n*** |f| Tabriz (*city in Iran*)

› **تَبِعَ** ***v*** |a; **تَبَع, تَباعة**| 1 [**تَلا**] to follow; to come after; to trail; **يَتْبَعُ** to be continued; **تَبِعَ الأَسْهُمَ** to follow the arrows; **تَبِعَ آخِرَ صَيْحاتِ الموضةِ** to keep up with the latest fashion; **تَبِعَ نَصيحةً** to take advice 2 [**الْتَزَمَ**] to follow, to obey 3 [**خَضَعَ**] to be subordinate to, to fall under, to belong to; **يَتْبَعُ الجَيْشُ وِزارةَ الدِفاعِ** the army falls under the Ministry of Defence

تابَعَ ***v*** 1 [**اسْتَمَرَّ**] to continue, to go on, to pursue; **تابَعَ أنّ ...** he went on to say that ...; **تابَعَ عَمَلَ (شَخْصٍ)** to continue (sb's) work; **تابَعَ دِراسَتَهُ** to continue one's studies 2 [**الْتَحَقَ**] to follow; **تابَعَ سَيْرَ شَيْءٍ** to follow the progress of sth; **تابَعَ دِراسةً** to study; to take a course; **تابَعَ التَطَوُّراتِ** to keep an eye on the developments 3 (Law) to prosecute; to sue, to take legal action against; **تابَعَ شَخْصاً بِتُهْمةِ السَرِقةِ** to prosecute sb for theft

أَتْبَعَ *v* to follow (up); أَتْبَعَ القَوْلَ بالعَمَلِ to suit the action to the word; أَتْبَعَ شَيْئاً بِشَيْءٍ to follow sth with sth

تتبَّعَ *v* to follow; to pursue; تتبَّعَ شَخْصاً بِنَظَراتِهِ to follow sb with one's eyes

تَتابَعَ *v* to follow in succession, to come one after the other; تَتابَعَت الأَحْداثُ بِسُرْعةٍ events came in quick succession

اتَّبَعَ *v* 1 [مَشى وراء] to follow, to pursue; اتَّبَعَ طَرِيقاً to follow a road 2 [الْتَزَمَ] to follow, to observe; to use; اتَّبَعَ أُسْلوبَ العُنْفِ to use violent means; اتَّبَعَ سِياسةً to pursue a policy; اتَّبَعَ طَرِيقةً to use a method; اتَّبَعَ الإجْراءاتِ to follow the procedures

اسْتَتْبَعَ *v* to engender; to entail, include; اسْتَتْبَعَ رَدًّا to engender a response

تَبَع *n* |أَتْباع| 1 [عُضْو] follower, adherent; أَتْباع المَذاهِبِ المُخْتَلِفةِ adherents of the different schools (of Islamic jurisprudence) 2 [اتِّباع] following; تَبَعاً ل according to, by; تَبَعاً للظَرْفِ depending on the situation

تابِع A *adj* |تابِعونَ, تُبّاع, تَبَعة| 1 [تالٍ] following 2 [خاضِع] belonging; دَوْلة تابِعة satellite (state); شَرِكة تابِعة subsidiary (company); تابِع ل belonging to, falling under, affiliated with; تابِع للحِزْبِ الحاكِمِ affiliated with the ruling party; هذا المَبْنى تابِعٌ لِوِزارة الخارِجيّة this building belongs to the foreign ministry

B *n* 1 [مُلْحَق] |تَوابِعُ| accessory; تَوابِع accessories, attachments 2 [نَصير] |تابِعونَ, أَتْباع| follower, adherent; أَتْباع followers; retinue; التابِعونَ (Islam) the Followers (*the generation of Muslims who were born after the death of the Prophet Muhammad*) 3 [مَرْؤوس] |أَتْباع| subordinate

تابِعيّة *n* citizenship; belonging, falling

تِباع *n* تِباعاً one after the other, in succession; غادَرَ الشَبابُ تِباعاً the young people left one after the other; ناقَشَ المَوْضوعاتِ الثَلاثَةَ تِباعاً he discussed the three subjects in succession

تَبِعة *n* 1 [عَقِبة] consequence; تَبِعات consequences, aftermath; تَبِعات الحَرْبِ the aftermath of the war 2 [مَسْؤوليّة] responsibility, accountability, liability; تَبِعات قانونيّة (legal) liability; تَتحَمَّلُ الحُكومةُ تَبِعاتِ النِزاعِ the government bears responsibility for the conflict

تَبَعيّة *n* dependency; subordination; submission; تَبَعيّة لِسُلْطةٍ أَعْلى submission to a higher authority; تَبَعيّة مُطْلَقة absolute dependency

تَتابُع *n* 1 [تَسَلْسُل] succession; order, sequence; وَفْقَ التَتابُعِ التاريخيِّ \ الزَمَنيِّ in chronological order; بالتَتابُعِ successively, in succession 2 (Sport) relay (race); فَريق التَتابُعِ relay team

تَتَبُّع *n* |تَتَبُّعات| tracking; سِجِلّ التَتَبُّعِ (Comput) cookies

إتْباع *n* 1 [مَصْدَر] causing to follow; subordination 2 (Mus) canon, round 3 (Ling) tautology

اتِّباع *n* following; اتِّباعاً ل in accordance with, according to; اتِّباع سِياسةٍ اقْتِصاديّةٍ following economic policy; اتِّباع خُطّةٍ following a plan

اتِّباعيّ *adj* classical

اتِّباعيّة *n* classicism

مُتابَعة *n* 1 [اسْتِئْناف] continuation; resumption 2 (Law) prosecution; legal proceedings; مُتابَعة قَضائيّة \ قانونيّة judicial/legal proceedings 3 [مُراقَبة] غُرْفة المُتابَعةِ control room

مُتَّبَع *adj* 1 [مُسْتَعْمَل] followed, used, applied; السِياسة المُتَّبَعة the policy used; الإجْراءات المُتَّبَعة لِشَيْءٍ the measures applied to sth 2 [عاديّ] current; observed; common; العادات والتَقاليد المُتَّبَعة the observed customs and traditions

مَتْبوع A *adj* followed; دَوْلة مَتْبوعة a sovereign state (*as opposed to* دَوْلة تابِعة (*a satellite state*))

B *n* superior, leader

مُتَتابِع *adj* successive, consecutive; continuous, sustained, uninterrupted, non-stop; سِلْسِلة مُتَتابِعة an uninterrupted series; مُتَتابِعاً one after the other, in succession

مُتَتَبِّع A *adj* successive, consecutive

B *n* observer, follower; مُتَتَبِّع للتَطَوُّراتِ an observer of events

تَبْغ, تِبْغ *n* |تُبوغ| tobacco; زِراعة التِبْغِ tobacco farming; دَخَّنَ التِبْغَ to smoke (tobacco)

تِبْغيّة *n* (Bot) petunia (*Petunia*)

تَبَلَ *v* |u; تَبْل| (Culin) to season; تَبَلَ بالمِلْحِ والفِلْفِلِ to season with salt and pepper

تَبَّلَ *v* to spice, to season; تَبَّلَ اللَحْمَ to season meat

تابَل ,تابِل *n* |تَوابِلُ| spice, seasoning, herb; تَوابِل حارّة hot spices

تَبّولة *n* tabbouleh (*a Levantine salad of cracked wheat mixed with finely chopped ingredients such as tomatoes, onions, and parsley*)

تَتْبيل *n* seasoning

مُتَبَّل *adj* spiced, seasoned

مَتْبول *adj* (Literat) lovesick, ravaged; قَلْبي مَتْبولٌ I'm lovesick

تِبِلْدِيّ *n* (Bot) baobab, monkey bread (tree) (*Adansonia*)

تِبْن *n* hay; straw; حُزْمة تِبْنٍ \ من التِبْنِ bale of hay; كَوْمة تِبْنٍ \ من التِبْنِ haystack; كالبَحْثِ عن إبْرةٍ في كَوْمةٍ من التِبْنِ like looking for a needle in a haystack

تُبّان *n* swimsuit, bathing/swimming costume (BrE), bathing suit (AmE)

تَبّانة *n* دَرْب التَبّانةِ the Milky Way

تاجَرَ *v* |ب ,في| to trade; to do business in, to deal in; تاجَرَ ب \ في شَيْءٍ to trade sth, to deal sth; to traffic in sth; تاجَرَ ب \ في المُخَدِّراتِ to deal drugs; to traffic in drugs; تاجَرَ شَخْصًا \ مع شَخْصٍ to do business with sb

اتَّجَرَ *v* to trade, to deal in

تاجِر *n* |تُجّار| trader, merchant, dealer; تاجِر التَجْزِئةِ \ المُفَرَّقِ \ بالتَفْرِقةِ retailer; تاجِر سَيّاراتٍ car dealer; تاجِر العَبيدِ \ الرَقيقِ slave trader; تاجِر الجُمْلةِ wholesaler; جَمْعيّة تُجّارٍ trade association (BrE), industry trade group (AmE); كِبار التُجّارِ the biggest traders

تِجارة *n* trade, commerce, business; traffic, trafficking; تِجارة دُوَليّة international trade; مُنَظَّمة التِجارةِ العالَميّةِ the World Trade Organization, the WTO; تِجارة داخِليّة domestic trade; تِجارة خارِجيّة foreign trade; تِجارة غَيْر مَشْروعةٍ \ قانونيّةٍ illegal trade, traffic, trafficking; تِجارة حُرّة free trade; مِنْطَقة تِجارةٍ حُرّةٍ free trade zone; تِجارة رابِحة \ مُرْبِحة profitable trade, lucrative business; عَمِلَ ب \ في تِجارةِ التَجْزِئةِ to be in retail; تِجارة العُمْلةِ foreign exchange business; تِجارة آجِلة \ عُقودٍ futures (trading); التِجارة بالنِساءِ trafficking of women; قِطاع تِجارة الجُمْلةِ the wholesale sector; حُرّيّة التِجارةِ freedom of commerce; غُرْفة التِجارةِ the Chamber of Commerce; مَنْع تِجارةِ العاجِ a ban on ivory trade; تِجارة مع شَخْصٍ business with sb; مارَسَ \ تَعاطى التِجارةَ to be in business, to be a trader; أدارَ تِجارةً مُرْبِحةً to do good business

تِجاريّ *adj* commercial, trading; trade (*before n*), business (*before n*); نَجاح تِجاريّ a commercial success; مُدير تِجاريّ a commercial manager; قَناة تِلِفِزْيونيّة تِجاريّة a commercial channel; عُرْف تِجاريّ trade custom; حَرَكة تِجاريّة trade, business; اتِّفاق تِجاريّ a commercial treaty; الغُرْفة التِجاريّة the Chamber of Commerce; رِياح تِجاريّة trade wind

اتِّجار *n* trade, trading, sale; إنْتاج المُخَدِّراتِ والاتِّجار بِها the production and sale of drugs; الاتِّجار بالأَسْلِحةِ \ بالبَشَرِ arms/human trafficking; الاتِّجار غَيْر المَشْروعِ smuggling

مُتاجِر *n* ⓵ [تاجِر] trader, dealer ⓶ [اسْتِغْلاليّ] profiteer

مُتاجَرة *n* trade, sale

مَتْجَر *n* |مَتاجِرُ| shop, store, business; صاحِب مَتْجَرٍ shopkeeper; tradesman; بائِع في مَتْجَرٍ sales clerk; سَرِقَ من مَتْجَرٍ to shoplift; عَمِلَ في مَتْجَرٍ to work in a shop; مَتْجَر سِلْسِليّ chain store

تُجاهَ *prep* see وجه

تَحْتَ *prep* ⓵ [مَكان] under, below, underneath, beneath; from the bottom; تَحْتَ الشَجَرةِ under the tree; من تَحْتِ ... from under ...; من تَحْتِ الأَرْضِ from underground ⓶ [مَجازيّ] تَحْتَ هذه الظُروفِ under these conditions; تَحْتَ أَعْيُنِ الناسِ under the eyes of the people; تَحْتَ قِيادةِ \ رِعايةِ ... under the guidance/protection of ...; تَحْتَ شِعارِ ... under the banner of, under the motto

تَحْتُ *adv* down, downstairs, below

تَحْتانيّ *adj* lower, under, undermost, bottom (*before n*); طابَق تَحْتانيّ basement

تَحْتيّ *adj* lower, under-; بِنْية تَحْتيّة infrastructure; مَلابِس تَحْتيّة underwear

تَحْتيّة *n* slip

أَتْحَفَ *v* |ب| to present

تُحْفة *n* |تُحَف| ⓵ [فَنّيّة] work of art, artefact, objet d'art; تُحْفة ثَمينة a valuable work of art, masterpiece ⓶ [شَيْء نادِر]

rarity; museum piece; جَمَعَ التُحَف to collect rare works

مَتْحَف *n* |مَتاحِف| museum; مَتْحَف الفُنونِ التَشْكيليّة \ الآثارِ museum of visual arts/antiquities; المَتْحَف القَوْميّ the national museum

‹ **تَحْمائيّ** *n* undersea, underwater

‹ **تَخْت** *n* |تُخوت| ➊ [جَوْقة موسيقيّة] orchestra ➋ [خِزانة] wardrobe; chest, box ➌ [مَقْعَد] couch, sofa; bed ➍ [عَرْش] throne; تَخْت المَلِك royal residence

تَخْتة *n* (Egypt) school desk

‹ **تَخَّ** *v* |u; تُخوخة| to become sour, to ferment

‹ **تُخَس** *n* porpoise

[1] ‹ **أَتْخَمَ** *v* to stuff (*with food*); أَتْخَمَ شِباكَ فَريقٍ (Sport) to score a goal against a team

مُتْخَم *adj* stuffed, filled, crammed; full, having eaten one's fill; السوقُ مُتْخَمةٌ the market is packed

[2] ‹ **تَخَمَ** *v* |i; تَخْم| to circumscribe, to set boundaries for

تاخَمَ *v* to border, to be adjacent to; تاخَمَ مِنْطَقةً \ بَلَداً to border a region/country; تاخَمَ الطَريقَ to lie adjacent to the road

مُتاخِم *adj* adjacent; near; المِنْطَقة الصَحْراويّة المُتاخِمة لِمَدينة أَسْوانَ the desert area adjacent to Aswan; المَناطِق المُتاخِمة لِلحُدودِ the borderlands

مُتاخَمة *n* proximity, contiguity

[3] ‹ **تُخَمة** *n* see وخم

‹ **تُدْرُج** *n* |تَدارِجُ| pheasant (*Phasianus colchicus*)

‹ **تَدْمُر** *n* |f| Palmyra (*ancient city in Syria*)

‹ **تُراث** *n* see ورث

‹ **تْراجيديّ** *adj* tragic

تْراجيدِيا *n* tragedy; تْراجيدِيا كْلاسيكيّة a classical tragedy; تْراجيدِيا إغْريقيّة a Greek tragedy

‹ **تْراكْتور** *n* |تْراكْتورات| tractor

‹ **تِراكوتا** *n* see تيراكوتا

‹ **تْرام, تْرام** *n* |تْرامات| tram/trolley (BrE), streetcar/cable car (AmE); سِكّة تَرامٍ tram rail; خَطّ تَرامٍ tram line; تَرام خطّ ٩ tram line 9; بالتَرامِ by tram; رَكِبَ التَرامَ to take the tram

‹ **تْرامْبولين** *n* trampoline

‹ **تْرانْزيت** *n* transit

‹ **تَرِبَ** *v* |a; تَرَب| to be/become dusty

أَتْرَبَ *v* ➊ [تَغَطّى بالتُراب] to cover with dust/earth ➋ [اِغْتَنى] to be/become rich

تَرِب *adj* dusty

تُرْب *n* soil, earth; dust

تِرْب **A** *adj* |أَتْراب| contemporary **B** *n* |أَتْراب| person of the same age, peer; contemporary

تُراب *n* |أَتْرِبة, تِرْبان| ➊ [ثَرى] ground; soil, dirt; dust; حَفْنة من التُرابِ a handful of dust; تحت التُرابِ beneath the earth; دَفَنَ رَأْسَهُ تحت التُرابِ to bury one's head in the sand ➋ [دَوْلة] territory, domain, soil; التُراب الوَطَنيّ national territory; على التُرابِ السودانيِّ on Sudanese soil

تُرابيّ *adj* ➊ [إقْليميّ] territorial; الوَحْدة التُرابيّة territorial unity ➋ [طينيّ] clay (*before n*); على المَلاعِبِ التُرابيّةِ on clay courts (*tennis*)

تُرْبة *n* |تُرَب| ground, soil; تُرْبة خَصْبة fertile ground, rich soil; تَلَوُّث التُرْبةِ soil pollution; بِنْية التُرْبةِ soil structure; تَطْهير التُرْبةِ soil sanitation; طَبيعة التُرْبةِ soil conditions; تَحْليل التُرْبةِ soil analysis

مُتْرِب *adj* dusty

‹ **تَرْبَسَ** *v* to bolt, to latch

تِرْباس *n* |تَرابيسُ, تَرابِسُ| bolt, bar, latch; deadbolt

‹ **تَرْبَنْتين** *n* turpentine

‹ **تِرْتِر** *n* sequins, spangles

‹ **تَرْجَمَ** *v* |i; تَرْجَمة| ➊ [من لُغةٍ إلى أُخرى] to translate, to render; to interpret; تَرْجَمَ كَلِمةً ب ... to translate a word as ...; تَرْجَمَ شَيْئاً من \ عن لُغةٍ إلى لُغةٍ أُخْرى to translate sth from one language into another ➋ [حَوَّلَ] to convert, to turn; تَرْجَمَ الكَلامَ إلى عَمَلٍ to turn words into action ➌ (Comput) to compile

تَرْجُمان, تُرْجُمان *n* |تَراجِمة, تَراجيمُ| interpreter, translator; اِسْتَعانَ بِتَرْجُمانٍ to call in an interpreter

تَرْجَمة *n* |تَراجِمُ| ➊ [عَمَليّة التَرْجَمةِ] translation; interpretation; تَرْجَمة فَوْريّة simultaneous translation; وِكالة \ مَكْتَب تَرْجَمةٍ

translation agency/service; أعمال التَرْجَمة translation (job/work); غَيْر قابِلٍ للتَرْجَمة untranslatable **2** [نَصّ مُتَرْجَم] translation; تَرْجَمة حَرْفيّة a literal/word-for-word translation; تَرْجَمة oral/written translation; تَرْجَمة شَفَويّة \ تَحْريريّة a free translation; تَرْجَمة مُحَلَّفة a certified/ حُرّة \ بِتَصَرُّفٍ sworn translation; تَرْجَمة على الشاشةِ subtitles; تَرْجَمة من \ عن اللُغةِ العَرَبيّةِ إلى اللُغةِ الإنْجليزيّةِ a translation from Arabic to English; قامَ بتَرْجَمةٍ to make a translation **3** [سيرة] biography; تَرْجَمة ذاتيّة autobiography

مُتَرْجِم *n* translator; interpreter; مُتَرْجِم تَحْريريّ translator; مُتَرْجِم فَوْريّ interpreter; مُتَرْجِم ل ... a translator of ...; مُتَرْجِم مُحَلَّف a sworn translator; كانَ مُتَرْجِماً في المَحْكَمةِ to be a court interpreter

‹ **تَرِحَ** *v* |a; تَرَح| to be/become sad

تَرَح *n* |أتْراح| grief, sorrow

‹ **تاريخ** *n* see أرخ

‹ **تَرْزيّ** *n* tailor

‹ **تَرَّسَ** *v* to cover/protect oneself with a shield

تَمَتْرَسَ *v* to entrench oneself

تُرْس, تِرْس *n* |أتْراس, تُروس| **1** [دِرْع] shield, buckler; سَمَك التُرْسِ (Zool) turbot (*Scophthalmidae*) **2** (Mech) gear; cog; تُروس ساعةٍ the gears of a watch; صُنْدوق التُروسِ gearbox; عُلْبة التُروسِ transmission, gearbox; جِهاز تَعْشيقِ التُروسِ clutch; غَيَّرَ التُروسَ to change gear

تِرْسة *n* |تِرَس, تِرْسات| turtle

مِتْراس *n* |مَتاريسُ| barricade, blockade; أقامَ مَتاريسَ to raise/put up barricades, to barricade; أقامَ مَتاريسَ في الشَوارعِ to barricade the streets

‹ **تَرْسانة** *n* تَرَسانة, تِرْسانة **1** [أسْلِحة] arsenal **2** [سُفُن] shipyard, dockyard

‹ **أتْرَعَ** *v* to fill (*a vessel*)

تُرْعة *n* |تُرَع, تُرْعات| canal, channel

مُتْرَع *adj* full, filled to the brim

‹ **تَرِفَ** *v* |a; تَرَف| to live in opulence

أتْرَفَ *v* to surround with luxury; to spoil

تَرَف *n* luxury; opulence, sumptuousness; عاشَ في تَرَفٍ to live luxuriously

مُتْرَف *adj* luxurious; lavish; affluent; أسْلوب حَياةٍ مُتْرَف affluent lifestyle

‹ **تِرْفاس** *n* (Bot) desert truffle (*Terfezia*)

‹ **تَرْقُوة** *n* |تَراقٍ| collarbone, clavicle

‹ **تَرَكَ** *v* |u; تَرْك| **1** [خَلا] to leave (behind), to abandon, to quit; تَرَكَ شَخْصاً (وَحيداً) to leave sb (alone); تَرَكَ أمْتِعةً to leave luggage (behind); تَرَكَ زَوْجَتَهُ to leave one's wife; تَرَكَ مالاً على الطاوِلةِ to leave money on the table; تَرَكَ دَرّاجَتَهُ في الشارعِ to leave one's bike on the street; تَرَكَ بَعْضَ الأكْلِ لِشَخْصٍ to leave some food for sb; تَرَكَ شَرِكةً to leave a company; تَرَكَ آثاراً to leave behind tracks; تَرَكَ الدِراسةَ to end one's studies, to drop out of school; تَرَكَ الخِدْمةَ العَسْكَريّةَ to leave the service; تَرَكَ شَخْصاً وَشَأْنَهُ to leave sb in peace; تَرَكَ البابَ مَفْتوحاً to leave the door open; لم يَتْرُكْ مِنْهُ شَيْئاً to completely consume sth **2** [سَمَحَ] to let, to allow; تَرَكَ شَخْصاً يَفْعَلُ شَيْئاً to let sb do sth; تَرَكَ لِشَخْصٍ شَرَفَ افْتِتاحِ المَعْرَضِ to let sb have the honour of opening the exhibition **3** [تَنازَلَ] to leave, to drop, to omit; تَرَكَ القَراراتِ لِشَخْصٍ to leave the decisions to sb; تَرَكَ كُلَّ الأسْئِلةِ الصَعْبةِ to skip all the difficult questions; تَرَكَ العاداتِ السَيِّئةَ to drop the bad habits; ما لا يُدْرَكُ كُلُّهُ لا يُتْرَكُ جُلُّهُ every little bit helps **4** [وَصيّةً] to leave (behind), to bequeath; تَرَكَ لِشَخْصٍ ثَرْوةً to leave sb a fortune; تَرَكَ أرْمَلةً مع سِتّةِ أطْفالٍ to leave a widow with six children **5** [حافَظَ على] to leave, to preserve; تَرَكَ الأُمورَ على ما هي عَلَيْهِ to leave everything as it was; to let things take their (natural) course

تَرْك *n* leaving (behind); omission; عَدَم تَرْكِ أيّةِ فُرْصةٍ not missing any opportunity; تَرْك المَنْصِبِ resignation

تَرِكة *n* legacy, inheritance, estate; قِسْمة \ تَقْسيم \ تَوْزيع التَرِكةِ division/partition/distribution of the estate; ضَريبة التَرِكةِ inheritance tax; تَرِكَتُهُ العِلْميّةُ \ الموسيقيّةُ his scientific/musical legacy

تَريكة *n* |تَرائِكُ| spinster, old maid

مَتْروك *adj* left; الأمْرُ مَتْروكٌ ل ... ≈ it's up to ...

تُرْكمانِسْتان n |f| Turkmenistan

تُرْكمانيّ A adj Turkmen; (اللُغة) التُرْكمانيّة Turkmen (language)
B n Turkmen (person)

تُرْكِيا n Turkey

تُرْكيّ A adj |أتْراك| Turkish; (اللُغة) التُرْكيّة Turkish (language)
B n |أتْراك| Turk

1 تُرْمُس n coll lupin (bean)

2 تُرْمُس n |تَرامِس| Thermos®, vacuum flask (BrE)

تِرْمومِتْر n |تِرْمومِتْرات| thermometer

تُرُنْجان n lemon balm (Melissa officinalis)

تَرانْزِسْتُر, تَرَنْزِسْتُر n 1 (Elec) transistor 2 [جِهاز رادِيو] transistor radio

تُرُنْشاه n cornflower (Centaurea cyanus)

تَرِهَ v |a; تَرَه| to concern oneself with trifles

تُرَّهة n nonsense, drivel; مُجَرَّد تُرَّهاتٍ بِلا مَعْنَى meaningless nonsense

تْروبوسْفير n troposphere

تَروتة n trout

تْروفِل n truffle (chocolate)

تْرولي n |تْروليات| trolley

تْرومْبون n trombone

تْرومْبيت n trumpet

تَتْرى adv see وتر

تِرْياق n antidote

تَريفيت n see ريف

تْريكو n (NA) tricot, jersey

تْريلْيون n trillion

تِريلْيون n |تِريلْيونات| trillion

تْرينيداد وَتوباغو n |f| Trinidad and Tobago

اتَّزَرَ v see وزر

تُسْع n (one) ninth

تاسِع num ninth (ordinal)

تاسِعَ عَشَرَ num nineteenth (ordinal)

تِسْعة num nine; تِسْعة أَطْفالٍ nine children; تِسْع فَتَياتٍ nine girls

تِسْعةَ عَشَرَ num nineteen

تِسْعونَ num ninety

التِسْعينات n pl the nineties

تْسونامي n tsunami

تْشاد n |f| Chad

تْشادِيّ adj, n Chadian

تْشارْتِر n charter flight

تِشْرين n |dipt| تِشْرين الأَوَّل (Levant, Iraq) October; تِشْرين الثاني (Levant, Iraq) November

تْشيكيّ A adj Czech; (اللُغة) التْشيكيّة Czech (language)
B n Czech (person)

تْشيكِيا, التْشيك n |f| the Czech Republic

تْشيكوسْلوفاكِيا n Czechoslovakia

تْشيللو n cello, violoncello

تْشيلي n |f| Chile

تَطْوان n |dipt f| Tetouan (city in Morocco)

تَعِبَ v |a; تَعَب| to be/become tired; تَعِبْتُ من العَمَلِ I am tired of work

أَتْعَبَ v 1 [أَرْهَقَ] to tire, to wear down/out, to fatigue; أَتْعَبَ نَفْسَهُ to tire oneself, to wear oneself out 2 [أَزْعَجَ] to bother, to annoy; أَتْعَبَ شَخْصاً بالأَسْئِلةِ to bother sb with questions

تَعَب n |أَتْعاب| 1 [عَياء] tiredness, weariness, fatigue; تَعَب جَسَديّ \ نَفْسيّ physical/mental fatigue; أَحَسَّ بالتَعَبِ to feel tired 2 [أُجْرة] fee; أَتْعاب الأَخِصّائيِّ \ الفَنّانِ \ المِعْماريِّ the fee for the specialist/artist/architect; تَلَقَّى أَتْعاباً عن شَيْءٍ to receive a fee for sth

تَعِب adj tired

تَعْبان adj |dipt| tired, weary, fatigued

مَتاعِب n pl |dipt| fatigue; discomfort; trouble, difficulty; مَتاعِب جِسْمانيّة \ جَسَديّة physical inconvenience; مَتاعِب السَفَرِ travel problems; يَوْم حافِل بالمَتاعِبِ a day full of trouble; جَلَبَ \ جَرَّ على نَفْسِهِ المَتاعِبَ to let oneself in for trouble

مُتْعَب adj tired; مُتْعَب من الحَياةِ tired of life

مُتْعِب adj tiring, strenuous; annoying, bothersome; طِفْل مُتْعِب an annoying child; عَمَل مُتْعِب strenuous work

‹ **تعتع** *v* |i; تَعْتَعة| to stammer

‹ **تَعِز** *n* |dipt f| Ta'izz (*city in Yemen*)

‹ **تَعَس، تَعِس** *v* |a; تَعْس| **1** [كانَ تَعيساً] to feel miserable **2** [هَلَكَ] to perish **3** [أَهْلَكَ] to ruin; to make miserable

أَتْعَس *v* to make miserable/unhappy

تَعْس *n* misery

تَعِس *adj* miserable, unhappy, wretched; حَياة تَعِسة a miserable life; وَضْعيّة \ حالة تَعِسة a dreadful situation

تَعاسة *n* misery; شَعَرَ بالتَعاسةِ to feel miserable

تَعيس *adj* |تُعَساءُ| miserable, unhappy; طُفولة تَعيسة a wretched childhood; حَظّ تَعيس bad luck; نَتيجة تَعيسة unfortunate results; (كانَ) في حالةٍ تَعيسةٍ (to be) in misery; مَنْظَر تَعيس a sorry sight

‹ **تَفْتة** *n* taffeta

‹ **تُفّاح** *n coll* apple; تُفّاحة آدَمَ Adam's apple; شَجَرة تُفّاحٍ apple tree; لُبّ تُفّاحةٍ an apple core

‹ **تُفْرة** *n* |تُفَر| dimple

‹ **تَفّ** *v* |u; تَفّ| to spit

تُفّ *n* |تِفَفة| dirt (*under the fingernails*); تُفّاً لَكَ pooh!

‹ **تَفَل** *v* |i-u; تَفْل| to spit

مِتْفَلة *n* |مَتافِلُ| spittoon; cuspidor (*dentistry*)

‹ **تَفْلِق** *n* (Zool) rail (*Rallidae*)

‹ **تَفْلون** *n* Teflon®

‹ **تَفِهَ** *v* |a; تَفَه، تَفاهة| to be little/insignificant

تافِه *adj* |تَوافِهُ| **1** [زَهيد] little, insignificant, trivial, petty; مَسْأَلة \ أَمْر تافِه(ة) a trivial matter; حادِث تافِه an insignificant event; مَبْلَغ تافِه a petty sum **2** [سَخيف] tasteless, insipid; فيلْم تافِه tasteless film

تَفاهة *n* futility, triviality; banality

‹ **مُتَّقِد** *adj* see وقد

‹ **أَتْقَنَ** *v* **1** [أَجادَ] to know well, to be skillful in; أَتْقَنَ شَيْئاً to know sth well, to be skillful in sth; أَتْقَنَ لُغةً to be proficient in a language; أَتْقَنَ التَعامُلَ مع شَيْءٍ to be good with sth; أَتْقَنَ شَيْئاً إِتْقاناً جَيِّداً to master sth **2** [حَسَّنَ] to perfect

تَقانة، تِقانة *n* **1** [دِقّة] perfection, precision; perfectionism **2** [تِكْنولوجيا] technology; التَقانة الحَيَويّة biotechnology; تِقانة المَعْلوماتِ information technology

تِقْنيّ **A** *adj* technical; التَفاصيل التِقْنيّة the technical details; عَبْرَ الوَسائِلِ التِقْنيّةِ المُخْتَلِفةِ through various technical means; كُلّيّة تِقْنيّة technical college (BrE), vocational school (AmE)
B *n* technician

تِقْنيّة، تَقْنيّة *n* technology; technique; تِقْنيّة عالِية high-tech; تِقْنيّة مُتَقَدِّمة \ بارِعة an advanced/outstanding technique; آخِر التِقْنيّاتِ الحَديثةِ the latest technical features; اسْتَعْمَلَ \ تَعَلَّمَ تِقْنيّةً to apply/acquire a technique

إِتْقان *n* mastery, command, thorough skill; perfection; إِتْقان لُغةٍ command of a language; في غاية \ بِمُنْتَهى الإِتْقانِ to perfection; بِكُلِّ إِتْقانِهِ with all his skill

مُتْقَن *adj* perfect, well-done; accurate, exact; تَقْليد مُتْقَن an exact imitation; فيلْم مُتْقَن a well-done film; عَمَل غَيْر مُتْقَنٍ a bungled job

‹ **تَقْوى، تَقيّة** *n* see وقي

‹ **تَكْتَكَ** *v* |i; تَكْتَكة| **1** [السَاعةُ] to tick **2** [مِن البَرْدِ] to shiver; تَكْتَكَ من البَرْدِ to shiver from the cold

‹ **تَكْتيك** *n* tactic; تَكْتيك فاشِل \ ناجِح a failing/successful tactic; تَكْتيك هُجوميّ \ دِفاعيّ an offensive/defensive tactic; اتَّبَعَ تَكْتيكاً to use a tactic

تَكْتيكيّ **A** *adj* tactical; خَطْوة تَكْتيكيّة a tactical step
B *n* tactician

‹ **تَكْريت** *n* |dipt f| Tikrit (*city in Iraq*)

‹ **تِكْساس** *n* |f| Texas (*US state*)

1‹ **تَكَّ** *v* |u; تَكّ| to trample on

2‹ **تَكَّ** *v* |u; تَكّ| to tick

تِكّة *n* ticking

3‹ **تِكّة** *n* |تِكَك| waistband; تِكّة تَنّورةٍ skirt waistband

‹ **تِكْنوقْراط** *n* technocrat

تِكْنوقْراطيّ **A** *adj* technocratic
B *n* technocrat

تِكْنوقْراطيّة *n* technocracy

تِكْنولوجيّ *adj* technological

تِكْنولوجيا, تِكْنولوجيّة *n* technology; طَوَّرَ تِكْنولوجِيا to develop a technology; تِكْنولوجِيا طِبِّيّة medical technology; تِكْنولوجيا بيولوجيّة biotechnology; تِكْنولوجِيا المَعْلوماتِ والاتِّصالاتِ information and communications technology, ICT

تِكْوانْدو, تايْكْوَنْدو *n* tae kwon do

تَكِيّة *n* |تكايا| home (*for the needy*); shrine (*of a Muslim order*)

تِلْباثيّ *adj* telepathic

تِلْباثيّة *n* telepathy

تَليد *adj* inherited; time-honoured; eternal, everlasting, endless

تِلْدة *n* tilde

تِلّيس *n* |تلاليسُ| sack

تِلِسْكوب *n* see تيليسْكوب

أَتْلَعَ *v* to stretch one's neck

تَلْعة *n* |تِلاع| hill

تِلِغْراف *n* |تِلِغْرافات| ❶ [آلة] telegraph ❷ [بَرْقيّة] telegram

تِلِغْرافيّ *adj* telegraphic

تَلِفَ *v* |a; تَلَف| to rot, to decay; to perish; يَتْلَفُ الخَشَبُ wood rots

أَتْلَفَ *v* to destroy, to damage, to ruin; أَتْلَفَ المَحْصولَ to destroy the crops

تَلَف *n* |أَتْلاف| decay, deterioration; damage, harm; قابِل لِلتَلَفِ perishable; مَوادّ غِذائيّة قابِلة لِلتَلَفِ perishables; تَلَف الأَعْصابِ nerve damage

تالِف *adj* rotten; corrupted; bad; damaged, ruined; مَوادّ غِذائيّة تالِفة rotten foodstuffs

تَلْفَزَ *v* |i; تَلْفَزة| to televise

تِلْفاز *n* |تِلْفازات| television

تَلْفَزة *n* ❶ [جِهاز] television, TV; جِهاز التَلْفَزةِ television, TV set ❷ [مُؤَسَّسة] television (*industry*)

تِلِفِزْيون, تِليفِزْيون *n* |تِلِفِزْيونات| ❶ [جِهاز] television, TV; في \ على التِلِفِزْيون on television; جَلَسَ أمامَ التِلِفِزْيون to sit in front of the television; دَليل التِلِفِزْيون TV guide; شاشة التِلِفِزْيون TV screen; فَتَحَ التِلِفِزْيون to turn on the TV ❷ [مُؤَسَّسة] television; يَشْتَغِلُ في التِلِفِزْيون he works in television; قَناة \ مَحَطّة التِلِفِزْيون television channel/station

تِلِفِزْيونيّ *adj* television/TV (*before n*)

مُتَلْفَز *adj* televised; خِطاب مُتَلْفَز a televised/TV speech

تَلْفَنَ *v* |i; تَلْفَنة| to phone, to call; تَلْفَنَ ل \ إلى شَخْصٍ to call sb

تَلْفَنة *n* telephony, telephone service; تَلْفَنة لاسِلْكيّة wireless telephony

تِلِفون, تِليفون *n* |تِلِفونات| telephone

تِلِفونيّ, تِليفونيّ *adj* telephonic, telephone (*before n*)

تِلْقاء *n* see لقي

تِلْكَ *pron* see ذٰلِكَ

تِلِكْس *n* ❶ [جِهاز] telex (*device*) ❷ [رِسالة] telex (*message*)

[1] **تَلّ** *n* |تُلول, أَتْلال, تِلال| hill, knoll, mound; dune

تَلّة *n* hill

[2] **تُلّ** *n* tulle

تَلّ أَبيب *n* |f| Tel Aviv (*city in Israel*)

تَلَم *n* |أَتْلام| furrow, rut, groove

تِلْم *n* |تِلام| burner

تَلْمَذَ *v* |i; تَلْمَذة| to take on as a pupil

تَتَلْمَذَ *v* to be/become a pupil; تَتَلْمَذَ على (يَد) شَخْصٍ to receive one's schooling/training from sb

تِلْميذ *n* |تَلامِذة, تَلاميذُ| ❶ [طالِب] pupil, student; apprentice; disciple ❷ (Chr) disciple

تِلِمْسان *n* |dipt f| Tlemcen (*city in Algeria*)

تَلْموديّ **A** *adj* Talmudic, Talmudical **B** *n* Talmudist

التَلْمود *n* the Talmud

تَلِهَ *v* |a; تَلَه| to be astonished, to be at a loss for words

تَلا *v* |u| ❶ [تَبِعَ] |تُلُوّ| to follow, to succeed ❷ [قَرَأَ] |تِلاوة| to recite, to read aloud; تَلا قَصيدةً to recite a poem; تَلا نَصًّا to read a text out loud

تالى *v* to follow

تَتالى *v* to follow one after another, to be in succession

تِلْوَ *prep* after; المَرّة تِلْوَ المَرّة time after time; الواحِدَ تِلْوَ الآخَرِ one after the other

تالٍ *adj* |تَوالٍ| following, next; اليَوْم \ السُؤال \ الصَفْحة التالي (ة) the next day/question/page; بالتالي then,

تامّ *adj* |توامٌّ| complete; finished; entire; total, utter; غَيْر تامٍّ unfinished; incomplete; هُدوء تامّ complete silence; بِمَعْزِلٍ تامٍّ in complete isolation; سِرّيّة تامّة strictest confidence; تَعاوُن \ اسْتِعْداد \ اتِّفاق تامّ total cooperation/preparedness/agreement; طاعة تامّة absolute obedience; بِشَكْلٍ تامٍّ completely, fully, entirely

تَتِمّة *n* supplement, complement; completion; continuation; sequel; تَتِمّة ل the continuation of; the sequel to; تَتمّة لِقصّةٍ the continuation of a story

تَتْميم *n* completion

تَمّ *n* swan

تَمام *n* completeness, wholeness; perfection; بَدْر التَمام full moon; بِتَمامِهِ وَكَمالِهِ to perfection; totally, entirely; كُلُّ شَيْءٍ بالتَمامِ والكَمالِ everything is perfect; تَماماً completely, totally, entirely, absolutely; exactly, precisely; مُسْتَحيل تَماماً absolutely impossible; نسيتُ تَماماً أنْ ... I completely forgot to ...; في الوَقْتِ تَماما exactly on time; في الساعةِ الخامِسةِ تَماماً ,في تَمامِ الساعةِ الخامسة at five o'clock sharp; شَخْصيّ \ سِرّيّ تَماماً strictly personal/confidential; وافَقَ شَخْصاً تَماماً to agree totally with sb; كانَ واضِحاً تَمامَ الوُضوحِ it was completely clear; تَماماً كَ ... exactly like ...

تَميمة *n* |تَمائِمُ| amulet, talisman

إتْمام *n* completion; termination, conclusion; effectuation; إتْماماً ل ... in conclusion of ...; لم يَسْتَطِعْ إتْمامَ ذلك he couldn't finish it; إتْمام مُهِمّةٍ the completion of a task

مُتَمِّم *adj* supplementary; complementary; مُتَمِّم زاوِيةٍ (Math) complementary angle; مُتَمِّم ل ... supplementary to ...; مُتَمِّم لِلجُزْءِ الأَوَّلِ supplementary to the first part

‹ **تَمّوز** *n* |dipt| (Levant, Iraq) July

‹ **تُنْباك** *n* tobacco (*for the water pipe*)

‹ **تَنْبَك** *n* tobacco (*for the water pipe*)

‹ **تَنْبَل** *n* |تَنابِلُ ,تَنابِلة| (Zool) sloth

‹ **تَنْزانيا** *n* Tanzania

تَنْزانيّ *adj*, *n* Tanzanian

‹ **تِنِس** *n* tennis; مِضْرَب تِنِس tennis racket

‹ **تَنَك** *n* tin, tinplate

subsequently; therefore, consequently; النَصُّ التالي هو نَصٌّ مُقْتَبَسٌ the following text is a quotation; لِليَوْمِ الثاني على التَوالي for the second day in a row; هو بالتالي مَسْؤولٌ therefore he is responsible; وَبالتالي دَخَلَت المِياهُ المُلَوَّثةُ البَحْرَ and consequently the polluted water flowed out to sea

تَتالٍ *n* succession

تِلاوة *n* reading, recitation; تِلاوة القُرْآنِ a reading/recitation of the Koran

مُتَتالٍ *adj* consecutive, successive, sequential; أَرْقام مُتَتالِية consecutive numbers; مُتَتالِياً in succession

مُتَتالية *n* **1** [سِلْسِلة] series, sequence **2** (Math) progression; series

‹ **تُمْبُكْتو** *n* |f| Timbuktu (*city in Mali*)

‹ **تَمْتَمَ** *v* |i; تَمْتَمة| to mumble, to mutter, to stammer; تَمْتَمَ في كَلامِهِ to mumble, to speak inarticulately; تَمْتَمَ في سِرِّهِ to mumble to himself; تَمْتَمَ بِكَلِماتٍ غَيْرِ مَفْهومةٍ to mutter incomprehensibly

تَمْتام *n* mumbler

تَمْتَمة *n* murmur, mumbling

‹ **تَمْر** *n coll* |تُمور| date; تَمْر هِنْديّ tamarind; حَمَلَ التَمْرَ إلى البَصْرةِ ,صَدَّرَ تَمْراً إلى العِراقِ to carry coals to Newcastle; شَهْر التُمور (Hist) October (*Libya under Gaddafi*)

تُمَّرة *n* warbler

‹ **تَمْرَهِنْد** *n* tamarind

‹ **تِمْساح** *n* |تَماسيحُ| crocodile; caiman; alligator

‹ **تَمَّ** *v* |i; تَمّ ,تَمام| **1** [كَمَلَ] to be finished; تَمَّ المَوْضوعُ the matter is fixed; تَمَّ إعْدادُ الكِتابِ the book is finished **2** [حَدَثَ] to happen, to take place; to become a fact; تَمَّ لَهُ ما أَرادَ he got what he wanted; تَمَّ تَوْزيعُ الأَراضي على الفَلّاحينَ the land was divided among the peasants; تَمَّ الاتِّفاقُ على هذا المَوْضوعِ an agreement was reached on the subject; تَمَّ تَسْليمُ البَياناتِ the reports were presented; تَمَّ اكْتِشافُ دَواءٍ جَديدٍ a new medicine has been discovered

تَمَّمَ *v* to complete, to finish; to carry out, to fulfil; تَمَّمَ واجِباتِهِ to perform one's duties; تَمَّمَ دِراسَتَهُ to finish one's studies

أَتَمَّ *v* to complete, to finish; to carry out; أَتَمَّ عَمَلَهُ to finish one's work; أَتَمَّ الجُمَلَ to complete the sentences

تَنَكة *n* container, tin, can; تَنَكة زَيْتِ زَيْتونٍ a tin of olive oil; تَنَكة زُبالةٍ garbage can

تَنَكيّ *adj* tin (*before n*); pewter (*before n*)

‹ **تُنّ** *n* tuna

‹ **تَنّوب** *n* spruce (*Picea*)

‹ **تَنّور** *n* |تَنانيرُ| oven (*for baking bread*); kiln; furnace

تَنّورة *n* |تَنانيرُ| skirt; تَنّورة واسِعة \ ضَيِّقة a wide/tight skirt; تَنّورة طَويلة \ قَصيرة a long/short skirt; ارْتَدَتْ تَنّورةً she put on/was wearing a skirt

‹ **تِنّين** *n* |تَنانينُ| dragon

‹ **تِهامة** *n* |dipt| Tihama (*coastal region on the Red Sea in Saudi Arabia*)

‹ **تَهْتَهَ** *v* |i; تَهْتَهة| to stammer

‹ **تُهْمة** *n* see **وهم**

‹ **تابَ** *v* |u; تَوْب| to repent; to be penitent; تابَ إلى اللهِ to turn to God in penitence

اسْتَتابَ *v* to call on sb to repent

تَوْب *n* repentance, penitence

تائِب **A** *adj* repentant
B *n* penitent

تَوّاب **A** *adj* **1** [غفور] forgiving; merciful **2** [تائِب] repentant, penitent
B *n* التَوّاب the Acceptor of Repentance (*one of the names of God*)

تَوْبة *n* repentance, penitence; سورة التَوْبة The Repentance (*Sura 9*)

‹ **توباز** *n* topaz

[1] ‹ **توت** *n* berry; mulberry; شَجَر التوتِ mulberry tree; توت الأَرْضِ strawberry

توتة *n* thymus (gland)

[2] ‹ **توت** *n* Tout (*the first month of the Coptic calendar*)

‹ **توتاليتاريّ** *adj* totalitarian

‹ **تَوَّجَ** *v* to crown; تَوَّجَ شَخْصاً مَلِكاً \ بَطَلاً to crown sb king/champion

تَتَوَّجَ *v* **1** [شَخْص] to be crowned **2** [شَيْء] to be rewarded; تَتَوَّجَت المُفاوَضاتُ بالنَجاحِ the negotiations culminated in success

تاج *n* |تيجان| **1** [إكْليل] crown; tiara **2** [للطائِرِ] crest; رَفَعَ تاجَهُ to hold up its crest **3** (Anat) crown, top (*of the head*) **4** [على سِنّ] crown (*on a tooth*) **5** (Archit) تاج عَمودٍ capital

تاجيّ *adj* شِرْيان تاجيّ coronary artery

تَتْويج *n* crowning; coronation; مِنَصّة التَتْويجِ (awards) pedestal; podium

تُوَيْج *n* corolla (*the circlet of petals on a flower*)

تُوَيْجة, تُوَيْجيّة *n* petal

مُتَوَّج *adj* crowned; غَيْر مُتَوَّجٍ uncrowned

‹ **تارة** *n* بين تارةٍ وأُخْرى at times تارةً بعد تارةٍ time after time;

‹ **تَوْراة** *n* Torah (*in Judaism*); Pentateuch (*in Christianity*)

‹ **تُرْبين, تورْبين** *n* |تورْبينات| turbine

‹ **تورْتة** *n* cake

‹ **توسْت** *n* toast

‹ **توغو** *n* Togo (*country in West Africa*)

‹ **تاقَ** *v* |u; تَوْق, تَوَقان| إلى| to long for, to yearn for; to crave; to desire; تاقَ إلى الحُرِّيّة to crave freedom; تاقَ إلى شَخْصٍ to long for sb, to desire sb; تاقَ إلى شَيْءٍ بِشدّةٍ to ache for sth, to hunger for sth

تَتَوَّقَ *v* |ل, إلى| to long for, to miss; to yearn for; to desire

تَوْق *n* yearning, longing; craving; تَوْق إلى الحُرّيّةِ yearning for freedom

تَوّاق *adj* longing, yearning; eager; craving; تَوّاق إلى السَلامِ eager for peace

تَوَقان *n* lust, desire, longing

‹ **توكة** *n* توكة الشَعْرِ hair clip

‹ **تول** *n* tulle (*a net-like cloth used for making veils or dresses*)

‹ **توليب** *n* tulip

‹ **تونة** *n* tuna

‹ **تونْجا, تونْغا** *n* Tonga

‹ **تونِس** *n* |dipt f| **1** [البَلَد] Tunisia **2** [المَدينة] Tunis (*capital of Tunisia*); تونِس العاصِمة Tunis

تونِسيّ, تونْسيّ *adj, n* Tunisian

‹ **تونيك** *n* **1** [للشَعْرِ، الجِلْدِ] tonic **2** [قَميص] tunic

تاهَ *v* |u; تَوْه| to get/be lost; to stray; to wander; تاهَ في الشَوارِعِ to wander the streets; تاهَ في الصَحْراءِ to get lost in the desert

تَوَّهَ *v* 1 [أَضَلَّ] to mislead; to lead astray 2 [حَيَّرَ] to confuse

تَوَهان *n* disorientation, confusion

تَوّ *n* |تَوًّا ,لِتَوِّه| في \ على التَوِّ immediately, right away, straightaway, at once; just, just now; في التَوِّ واللَحْظَةِ immediately; اخْتَتَمَ لِتَوِّهِ الاجْتِماعَ he just ended the meeting; اتَّصَلَتْ لِتَوِّها she just called

تْويتِر *n* Twitter®

تيتان *n* 1 (Chem) titanium 2 (Mythol) Titan

تيتانوس *n* tetanus

تيتانيوم *n* titanium

أَتاحَ *v* to permit; to grant; to make possible; أَتاحَ لِشَخْصٍ أنْ ... to allow/enable sb to ...; أُتيحَتْ لَهُ الفُرْصَةُ he got the opportunity

إتاحة *n* availability; في حالةِ إتاحةِ الفُرْصةِ لَهُ when he gets the chance

مُتاح *adj* available; المِساحة المُتاحة the available space; المَوارِد \ الوَسائِل المُتاحة the available resources/means

تايور *n* listed alphabetically

تَيّار *n* |تَيّارات| 1 [مَجْرًى] flow, stream, current; التَيّارات البَحْرِيّة ocean currents; تَيّار هَوائيّ draught (BrE), draft (AmE); air current; تَيّار بارِد \ حارّ \ قَويّ a cold/warm/strong current; تَيّار هَوائيّ صاعِد (Meteorol) thermal; تَيّار تَحْتيّ undercurrent, undertow; سُرْعة التَيّارِ rate of flow; قوّة التَيّارِ force of the current; مع \ ضدّ التَيّارِ down/upstream, with/against the current; سَبَحَ ضدّ التَيّارِ to swim against the tide; سارَ مع التَيّارِ to go with the flow; to go with the crowd 2 (Elec) current; تَيّار مُسْتَمِرّ direct current, DC; تَيّار مُتَرَدِّد alternating current, AC; تَيّار الشَبَكةِ الكَهْرَبائيّة mains current; قوّة التَيّار (الكَهْرَبائيّ) current intensity; انْقِطاع التَيّار الكَهْرَبائيّ power failure/outage, blackout 3 [مَذْهَب] trend, movement; تَيّار أدَبيّ \ سِياسيّ \ دينيّ a literary/political/religious movement; التَيّار المُعْتَدِل \ المُتَطَرِّف the moderate/extremist movement

تيرابايْت *n* |تيرابايْتات| terabyte

تيراكوتا ,**تِراكوتا** *n* terracotta

تَيْس *n* |تُيوس ,أَتْياس| (billy) goat

تَيْفود ,**تيفوئيد** *n* typhoid (fever)

تيفوس *n* typhus

تيليتِكْسْت *n* teletext

تِلِسْكوب ,**تيلِسْكوب** *n* telescope

تَيَّمَ *v* to drive mad; to spellbind, to mesmerize; تَيَّمَهُ الحُبُّ love drove him crazy

تَيْمة *n* amulet

مُتَيَّم *adj* infatuated; adoring; كانَ مُتَيَّماً بِحُبِّ شَخْصٍ to be madly in love with sb

تيْمور *n* |f| Timor (*island in South East Asia*)

تيموس *n* (Anat) thymus

تين *n* 1 [ثَمَر] fig 2 [شَجَر] fig (tree), ficus; تين شَوْكيّ prickly pear (*Opuntia*); سورة التين The Fig (*Sura 95*)

تينور *n* tenor

تينيسي *n* |f| Tennessee (*US state*)

تاهَ *v* |i; تَيْه ,تيه ,تَيَهان| to get/be lost; to stray; to wander; تاهَ في الصَحْراءِ to get lost in the desert; تاهَ في الشَوارِعِ to wander the streets

تَيَّهَ *v* 1 [أَضَلَّ] to mislead; to lead astray 2 [حَيَّرَ] to confuse

تيه *n* |أَتْياه| 1 [قَفْر] desert; wilderness; wasteland 2 [مَتاهة] labyrinth

تائِه *adj* lost; straying, wandering; تائِه في الغابةِ lost in the woods

مَتاهة *n* maze, labyrinth; مَتاهة سِياسيّة وَقانونيّة political and legal maze

تيوصوفيّة *n* see ثِيوصوفيّة

تيوقْراطيّة *n* see ثِيوقْراطيّة

‹ **ثاء** *n* |f| *name of the letter* ث

‹ **تَثاءَبَ** *v* to yawn

ثُؤَباء *n* |dipt f| yawn

تَثاؤُب *n* yawn; حَبَسَ تَثاؤُباً to suppress a yawn

‹ **ثَأَرَ** *v* |a; ثَأْر| to take revenge; ثَأَرَ لِقَتْل شَخْصٍ to avenge sb's death; ثَأَرَ من شَخْصٍ to get even with sb

أَثْأَرَ *v* to have/get one's revenge

اثَّأَرَ *v* to be avenged; to get one's revenge

ثَأْر *n* |آثار, أَثْآر, ثَأْرات| revenge, vengeance; blood revenge; retaliation; أَخَذَ ثَأْرَهُ من شَخْصٍ to take revenge on sb; to get even with sb

ثائِر *n* 1 ▸ [مُنْتَقِم] avenger 2 ▸ [ثَوْرِيّ] see **ثور**

ثَأْرِيّ *adj* vengeful, retaliatory; مُباراة ثَأْرِيّة return match

‹ **ثُؤْلول** *n* |ثَآليل| wart

‹ **ثَبَتَ** *v* |u; ثُبوت, ثَبات| 1 ▸ [اِسْتَقَرَّ] to be fixed; to stand firm; ثَبَتَ على شَيْءٍ to continue with sth; to sink one's teeth into sth; to insist on sth; to hold (on) to sth; ثَبَتَ على اتِّفاقٍ to stand by an agreement; ثَبَتَ بِذٰلِكَ المَكانِ he remained in that place 2 ▸ [صَحَّ] to be sure; to be proven; ثَبَتَ لي أنَّهُ غَيْرُ صَريحٍ I'm sure that he isn't being sincere

ثَبَّتَ *v* 1 ▸ [جَعَلَهُ راسِخاً] to strengthen; to consolidate; ثَبَّتَ الطاوِلَةَ to strengthen the table; ثَبَّتَ الاسْتِقْرار to increase stability; ثَبَّتَ مَوْقِفَهُ to stick to one's point of view; to consolidate one's position; ثَبَّتَ شَخْصاً في وَظيفَتِهِ to appoint sb permanently 2 ▸ (Phot) to fix 3 ▸ (Comput) to install 4 ▸ [عَلَّقَ] to fasten; to secure; to fix; ثَبَّتَ زِرًّا على مِعْطَفٍ to sew a button on a coat 5 ▸ [صَدَّقَ] to find; to determine

أَثْبَتَ *v* to show; to prove; to establish; to confirm; أَثْبَتَ تُهْمَةً to substantiate an accusation; أَثْبَتَ نَفْسَهُ to prove oneself; أَثْبَتَ أنّ ... to establish that ...; أَثْبَتَ وُجودَ حَمْلٍ to confirm a pregnancy; أَثْبَتَ أنَّهُ يَسْتَطيعُ التَّمْثيلَ he proved himself as an actor; أَثْبَتَ بَراءة \ إدانة شَخْصٍ to prove sb's innocence/guilt; أَثْبَتَ هُوِيَّتَهُ to prove one's identity; أَثْبَتَ شَيْئاً بِمُسْتَنَداتٍ to prove something by evidence

تَثَبَّتَ *v* to verify; to check; to ascertain; تَثَبَّتَ من شَيْءٍ to ascertain sth

اسْتَثْبَتَ *v* to verify; to check; to ascertain; اسْتَثْبَتَ من شَيْءٍ to ascertain sth

ثَبْت A *adj* |أَثْبات| firm; steadfast
B *n* |ثُبوت| index

ثَبَت A *adj* |أَثْبات| trustworthy
B *n* |أَثْبات| index; ثَبَت الكُتُب bibliography

ثابِت A *adj* |ثُبوت| 1 ▸ [دائِم] fixed; certain; constant; دَخْل ثابِت a fixed income; وَظيفة ثابِتة a steady job 2 ▸ [راسِخ] fixed; firm; stable; constant; immovable; عُمْلة \ عَلاقة ثابِتة a stable currency/relationship; دَرَجة حَرارةٍ ثابِتة a constant temperature; سُرْعة ثابِتة a constant speed; التاريخ ثابِتٌ the date is fixed; أَمْوال \ أَمْلاك \ مُمْتَلَكات ثابِتة real estate, immovable property; قَوانين الطَّبيعةِ الثابِتة the immutable laws of nature; ثابِت! at ease!; غَيْر ثابِتٍ unstable; طاوِلة غَيْر ثابِتةٍ a wobbly table; أَساس غَيْرِ ثابِتٍ an unstable basis; تَوازُن غَيْر ثابِتٍ a precarious balance 3 ▸ [مُقَرَّر] confirmed; established; حُقوق ثابِتة guaranteed rights
B *n* |ثَوابِتُ| 1 ▸ (Phys, Math) constant; الثابِت في مُعادَلةٍ رِياضيّةٍ the constant in a mathematical equation 2 ▸ [مَبْدَأ] principle; ثَوابِت سِياسيّة political principles

ثَبات *n* 1 ▸ [دَوام] durability; stability; عَدَم ثَباتٍ transience 2 ▸ [صِحّة] reliability; soundness 3 ▸ [تَمَسُّك بالرَأْي]

perseverance, persistence; ثَبات العَزيمةِ determination

4 [صَرامة] rigour

ثُبوت *n* **1** [صِحّة] certainty; ثُبوت رُؤْيةِ هِلالِ العيدِ *sighting of the new moon (start of the feast after Ramadan)*; ثُبوت الشَهْرِ *sighting of the new moon (start of the new month)* **2** [مَتانة] permanence; durability; immutability

ثُبوتيّ *adj* evidential; قوّة ثُبوتيّة evidential value

إثْبات *n* |إثْباتات| affirmation; proof; confirmation; وَسيلة إثْباتٍ evidence; وَسيلة إثْباتٍ قانونيّة legal evidence; قوّة الإثْباتِ evidential value; عِبْء الإثْباتِ burden of proof; يَقَعُ عِبْءُ الإثْباتِ على المُدَّعي the burden of proof rests with the plaintiff; شاهِد إثْباتٍ a witness for the prosecution; اسْتَطاعَ إثْباتَ هُويّتِهِ to be able to prove one's identity; وَثائِق إثْباتٍ هُويّةٍ identity papers; يُمْكِنُ إثْباتُهُ provable; demonstrable

تَثْبيت *n* |تَثْبيتات| **1** [تَأْكيد] fixing, setting; confirmation, corroboration; attachment; stabilization; strengthening, consolidation; تَثْبيت على الجِدارِ attachment or fixing to the wall **2** (Comput) installation **3** (Chr) confirmation

مُثَبَّت *adj* **1** [مُوَطَّد] fixed **2** [مُؤَكَّد] proven, established

مُثَبِّت **A** *adj* affirmative

B *n* (Chem) |مُثَبِّتات| stabilizer

ثَبَجَ *v* |u; ثُبوج| to scrawl, to scribble

ثَبَرَ *v* |u; ثُبور, ثَبْر| **1** [هَلَكَ] to perish; to die **2** [أَهْلَكَ] to ruin; to destroy

ثابَرَ *v* to persevere; to persist; ثابَرَ على المُفاوَضاتِ to persevere with the negotiations; ثابَرَ على بَذْلِ جُهودِهِ to keep making the effort; ثابَرَ في مُحاوَلاتِهِ to keep trying

ثُبور *n* decline; destruction; الوَيْل والثُبور ruin and downfall

مُثابِر **A** *adj* persevering; العَمَل المُثابِر hard work

B *n* persistent person; fighter; hard worker; النَجاحُ حَليفُ كُلِّ مُثابِرٍ slow and steady wins the race

مُثابَرة *n* persistence; perseverance; بِمُثابَرةٍ diligently

ثَبَطَ *v* |u; ثَبْط| to thwart; to obstruct, to impede; to stop; ثَبَطَ شَخْصاً عن عَمَلِهِ to prevent sb from doing his work

ثَبَّطَ *v* to thwart; to undermine; to discourage; to sap; to frustrate; ثَبَّطَ عن النَجاحِ to stand in the way of success; ثَبَّطَ عَزْمَ \ هِمّةَ شَخْصٍ to demoralize/frustrate sb

تَثْبيط *n* **1** [إحْباط] demoralization; discouragement; frustration; تَثْبيط العَزيمةِ discouragement **2** [إضْعاف] undermining, weakening

مُثَبِّط *adj* demoralizing; كانَ لَهُ مَفْعولٌ مُثَبِّطٌ للعُمّالِ it had a demoralizing effect on the workers

ثَجَّ *v* |u; ثَجّ| to flow

ثَجّاج *adj* free-flowing (*liquids*); pouring (*rain*)

ثَجيج *n* |ثُجوج| torrent

ثَخُنَ *v* |u; ثَخانة, ثُخونة| to be thick; to thicken

ثَخَّنَ *v* to thicken

أَثْخَنَ *v* to weaken; to exhaust; أَثْخَنَ في الأَرْضِ to subdue the land (*Koran 8:67*)

ثَخانة *n* thickness

ثَخين **A** *adj* |ثُخَناءُ| thick

B *n* |ثُخَناءُ| an overweight person

تَثْخين *n* binding, thickening; مادّة تَثْخينٍ binding agent, thickener

مُثَخِّن **A** *adj* thickening, binding

B *n* binding agent, thickener

ثَدْي, **ثَدًى** *n* |أَثْداء| breast; ثَدْيانِ breasts; رَضاعة الثَدْيِ breast-feeding; اسْتِئْصال الثَدْيِ mastectomy; كانَتْ مُصابةً بِسَرَطانِ الثَدْيِ to have breast cancer; ظَهَرَ ثَدْياها من فُسْتانِها her breasts showed through her dress

ثَدْييّ *n* |ثَدْييّات| mammal; الكَلْبُ من الثَدْييّاتِ dogs are mammals

ثَرَبَ *v* |i; ثَرْب| to reproach, to blame

ثَرَّبَ *v* to reproach, to blame

ثَرْثَرَ *v* |i; ثَرْثَرة| to chat; ثَرْثَرَ في مَوْضوعٍ to chat about sth

ثَرْثار **A** *adj* talkative

B *n* chatterbox

ثَرْثَرة *n* chatter, nonsense, prattle; ثَرْثَرة مُزْعِجة annoying chatter

ثَريد *n a dish of bread soaked in broth with meat*

ثَرّ *adj* abounding in water

‹ **ثَرَمَ** *v* |i; ثَرْم| to knock sb's tooth out

أَثْرَم *adj* |dipt| toothless

‹ **ثِرْموسْتات** *n* thermostat; رَفَعَ \ خفَضَ من دَرَجةِ الثِرْموستاتِ to turn the thermostat up/down

‹ **ثَرِيَ** *v* |a; ثَراء| to be/become rich

أَثْرى *v* [1] ‹ [أَغْنى] to make rich, to enrich [2] ‹ [كَثُرَ مالُهُ] to be/become rich

ثَرِيّ [A] *adj* |أَثْرِياءُ| rich; wealthy; well-to-do

[B] *n* |أَثْرِياءُ| rich/wealthy man; أَثْرِياء rich people; هو ابْنُ أَكْبَرِ الأَثْرِياءِ he is a rich man's son

ثَراء *n* |ثَرَوات| wealth, riches; بالِغ الثَراءِ immensely rich; رَجُل أَعْمالٍ بالِغ الثَراءِ an immensely rich businessman

ثَرْوة *n* wealth; riches; fortune; profusion; property; وَرِثَ ثَرْوةً to inherit a fortune; جَمَعَ ثَرْوةً to make a fortune; ثَرْوة ثَقافيّة cultural heritage; الثَرْوة الثَقافيّة القَوْميّة the national cultural heritage; ثَرْوة حَيَوانيّة livestock; ثَرْوة سَمَكيّة fish stock; ثَرَوات طَبيعيّة natural resources; ثَرَوات مَعْدِنيّة mineral resources

ثَرًى *n* ground; soil; moist earth; طَيَّبَ اللّهُ ثَراهُ ≈ (may) God rest his soul

ثُرَيّا *n* |ثُرَيّات| [1] ‹ [نَجَفة] chandelier [2] (Astron) الثُرَيّا the Pleiades, the Seven Sisters; هو منّي مَناطُ الثُرَيّا he is beyond my reach

‹ **مَثْعَب** *n* |مَثاعِبُ| trap (*of a drain*)

‹ **ثُعْبان** *n* |ثَعابينُ| (Zool) snake; ثُعْبان السَمَكِ (Egypt) eel

‹ **ثَعْلَب** *n* |ثَعالِبُ| [1] ‹ (Zool) fox; صَيْد الثَعالِبِ fox-hunt; كانَ ماكِرًا كالثَعْلَبِ to be as cunning as a fox; ثَعْلَب الماءِ otter [2] ‹ [شَخْص ماكِر] a cunning (old) fox

‹ **ثَغَرَ** *v* |a; ثَغْر| to drill through; to pierce; to perforate

أَثْغَرَ *v* to teethe

ثَغْر *n* |ثُغور| [1] ‹ [فَم] mouth; ظَهَرَتْ اِبْتِسامةٌ على ثَغْرِها a smile appeared on her lips [2] ‹ [ميناء] port

ثُغْرة *n* |ثُغْرات, ثُغَر| [1] ‹ [فَجْوة] hole; crack; breach; ثُغْرة عَميقة a yawning gap; ثُغْرة أَمْنيّة safety breach; سَدَّ \ أَغْلَقَ ثُغْرةً to fill a hole; فَتَحَ ثُغْرةً في الدِفاعِ to breach the defence [2] ‹ (fig) gap; blank; سَدَّ ثُغْرةً to fill a gap; ثُغْرة في مَعْرِفَتي a gap in my knowledge; ثُغْرة في القانونِ a loophole in the legislation

‹ **ثَغا** *v* |u; ثُغاء| to bleat

ثاغٍ *adj* bleating; ما لَهُ ثاغِيةٌ وَلا راغِيةٌ he hasn't got a penny to his name

‹ **ثُفّاء** *n* garden cress, garden peppergrass

‹ **ثُفْل** *n* |أَثْفال| sediment; deposits; pulp; sludge; lees; ثُفْل قَهْوةٍ coffee grounds; ثُفْل النَبيذِ the dregs of the wine

‹ **ثَفِنة** *n* callus

‹ **ثِقة** *n* see وثق

‹ **ثَقَبَ** *v* |u; ثَقْب| to drill through; to perforate; to punch (*a hole through*); to pierce; ثَقَبَ المَعْدِنَ to perforate the metal

ثَقَّبَ *v* [1] ‹ [خَرَقَ] to drill a hole in; to pierce, to puncture; to riddle with holes; ثَقَّبَ شَيْئًا to pierce sth [2] ‹ [أَوْقَدَ] to kindle

أَثْقَبَ *v* to light, to kindle

تَثَقَّبَ *v* to leak; to be punctured

اِنْثَقَبَ *v* to be pierced, to be punctured

ثَقْب, ثُقْب *n* |أَثْقاب, ثُقوب| hole; opening; perforation; leak; ثُقْب أَسْوَد a black hole; ثُقْب البابِ keyhole; ثُقْب في العَجَلةِ a puncture in the tyre; هُناكَ ثُقْبٌ في خَزّانِ الوَقودِ there's a leak in the fuel tank

ثاقِب *adj* penetrating, piercing; probing; sharp; نَظْرة ثاقِبة a penetrating look; عَقْل ثاقِب a keen mind; ثاقِب الفِكْرِ sharp-witted

ثِقاب *n* |ثُقُب| matchstick; عود ثِقابٍ matchstick; عُلْبة ثِقابٍ a box of matches; عود ثِقابٍ مَحْروق a burnt match; أَشْعَلَ عودَ ثِقابٍ to light/strike a match

ثَقّابة *n* drill

ثُقْبة *n* hole; ثُقْبة في ضِرْسٍ a cavity in a molar

تَثْقيب *n* piercing, perforating; آلة تَثْقيبٍ hole punch

مِثْقاب *n* |مَثاقيبُ| hole punch; drill

مُثَقَّب *adj* pierced, perforated

مِثْقَب *n* |مَثاقِبُ| drill; مِثْقَب مِرْفَقيّ hand drill; brace and bit; مِثْقَب كَهْرَبائيّ an electric drill

مَثْقوب *adj* leaking; pierced, punctured; إطار مَثْقوب a punctured tyre

اِسْتَثْقَلَ *v* to find heavy; to find annoying; to find burdensome; اِسْتَثْقَلَ المُديرُ المَهامَّ الكَثيرةَ الّتي أوكِلَتْ إلَيْهِ the manager found the many tasks that were assigned to him burdensome; اِسْتَثْقَلَ الانْتِقادَ الّذي وُجِّهَ إلَيْهِ he was annoyed by the criticism that was directed at him

ثِقْل, ثِقَل *n* |أَثْقال| ⓵ [وَزْن] weight; gravity; heaviness; ثِقْل نَوْعيّ specific gravity; يُساوي ثِقْلَهُ ذَهَباً he is worth his weight in gold; رافِع \ حامِل أَثْقالٍ weightlifter; شُعور بالثِقْلِ heavy feeling ⓶ [حِمْل] load, burden; شَكَّلَ ثِقْلاً كَبيراً to be a heavy burden ⓷ (fig) seriousness; significance; ثِقْل مَسْأَلَةٍ the seriousness of a matter

ثَقالة *n* paperweight

ثَقّالة *n* weight

ثَقيل *adj* |ثِقال, ثُقَلاءُ| ⓵ [صَعْب الحَمْل] heavy; حَقيبة ثَقيلة a heavy suitcase; صِناعة ثَقيلة heavy industry; أَسْلِحة ثَقيلة heavy weapons; ثَقيل السَمْعِ hard of hearing ⓶ [مُزْعِج] unpleasant, disagreeable; ثَقيل الظِلِّ \ الدَمِ \ الروحِ tiresome, dull; unpleasant; unbearable; كانَ ثَقيلاً على المَعِدةِ to be heavy on the stomach; هَزيمة ثَقيلة a heavy defeat ⓷ [صَعْب] hard; ثَقيل الفَهْمِ slow-witted; ثَقيل الحَرَكةِ slow; cumbersome ⓸ [عَميق] نَوْم ثَقيل a deep sleep

تَثاقُل *n* ⓵ [فُتور] laziness ⓶ [بُطْء] slowness, sluggishness

تَثْقيل *n* weighting (*adding weight to*); burdening

مُتَثاقِل *adj* slow, sluggish; lazy; laborious; dull

مِثْقال *n* |مَثاقيلُ| weight (*of approx 4.89 grams*); مِثْقال من الذَهَبِ a mithqal of gold; مِثْقال ذَرّةٍ a little bit, a tiny amount

مُثْقَل *adj* overloaded; overburdened; جِسْر مُثْقَل a bridge supporting a heavy load; بَرْنامَج مُثْقَل an overcrowded programme; مُثْقَل بالأَحْمالِ \ الأَعْباءِ heavily laden

مُثَقِّلة *n* paperweight; weight

‹ **ثَكِلَ** *v* |a; ثُكْل, ثَكَل| *to lose a child or loved one*; ثَكِلَتْ وَلَدَها she has lost her child/son

ثَكْلى *n* |f; ثَكالى| *woman who has lost her child*

‹ **ثُكْنة** *n* |ثُكَن, ثُكْنات| barracks

‹ **ثَلَبَ** *v* |i; ثَلْب| ⓵ [اِنْتَقَدَ] to criticize ⓶ [قَدَحَ] to slander

‹ **ثَقِفَ, ثَقُفَ** *v* |a; ثَقْف| to be clever, to be skilful

ثَقَّفَ *v* ⓵ [عَلَّمَ] to teach; to form; to educate; to civilize ⓶ [سَوّى وقَوَّمَ] to straighten out

ثاقَفَ *v* to fence; ثاقَفَ شَخْصاً to fence with sb

تَثَقَّفَ *v* to be trained; to be educated; تَثَقَّفَ على يَدِ... to be taught by ...

ثَقافة *n* ⓵ [حَضارة] culture; civilization; الثَقافات الشَرْقيّة the Eastern cultures; مُتَعَدِّد الثَقافاتِ multicultural; مُجْتَمَع مُتَعَدِّد الثَقافاتِ a multicultural society ⓶ [العُلوم والفُنون] civilization; culture; الفَنّ والثَقافة art and culture; ثَقافة عامّة common knowledge; ثَقافة مُضادّة counterculture

ثَقافيّ *adj* cultural; intellectual; المُسْتَوى الثَقافيّ لِشَخْصٍ the intellectual level of a person; مَرْكَز ثَقافيّ a cultural centre; اخْتِلافات ثَقافيّة cultural differences; أَنْشِطة \ أَحْداث ثَقافيّة cultural activities/events

ثَقيف *adj* |ثِقاف| skilled, proficient; clever

تَثْقيف *n* education; cultivation of the mind; edification; التَثْقيف الذاتيّ self-education

تَثْقيفيّ *adj* educational; informative; instructive

مُثَقَّف 🅐 *adj* literate; cultured; learned; educated; intellectual; رَجُل \ امْرَأة مُثَقَّف(ة) a man/woman of learning; شَخْص غَيْر مُثَقَّفٍ uneducated person; ≈ boorish/ignorant person 🅑 *n* intellectual; لُغة المُثَقَّفينَ the language of intellectuals

‹ **ثَقُلَ** *v* |u; ثِقْل| to be/become heavy; ثَقُلَ على شَخْصٍ to be a heavy burden for sb; to be too difficult for sb; ثَقُلَ عن شَيْءٍ to be too sluggish for sth; not to bother about sth

ثَقَّلَ *v* ⓵ [أَزْعَجَ] to bother; to inconvenience; ثَقَّلَ على شَخْصٍ بالأَسْئِلَةِ to bother sb with questions ⓶ [جَعَلَ ثَقيلاً] to make heavy; to weigh down; ثَقَّلَ كاهِلَ شَخْصٍ to burden sb

أَثْقَلَ *v* to burden; to weigh down with; to oppress; to overload; to swamp; أَثْقَلَ ذلك الكيسَ بالحِجارةِ he weighed the bag down with stones; أَثْقَلَ شَخْصاً بالعَمَلِ to overload sb with work; أَثْقَلَ الهَمُّ رَأْسَهُ he is weighed down by worry

تَثاقَلَ *v* to be/become slow; تَثاقَلَتْ مَشْيَتُهُ he started walking slowly

مَثْلَبة *n* |مَثالِب| shortcoming; defect

ثَلَّثَ *v* to divide into three, to trisect; to triple

ثُلْث *n* |أَثْلاث| ❶ [جُزْء] (one) third; ثُلْثانِ two thirds ❷ [عِشْرون دَقيقةً] التاسِعة إلاّ الثُلْثَ twenty to nine; ثُلُث ساعةٍ twenty minutes

ثالِث *num* third; الثالِثةُ ثابِتةٌ third time lucky (BrE), third time is the charm (AmE); الأُسْبوع الثالِث the third week; من الدَرَجةِ الثالِثةِ third-rate; طَرَف ثالِث a third party; حَلَّ في المَرْكَزِ الثالِثِ to come in third/in third place; ثالِثاً thirdly

ثالِثة *n* |ثَوالِثُ| (Mus) third; ثالِثة كَبيرة \ صَغيرة major/minor third

ثالِثَ عَشَرَ *num* thirteenth

ثالِثيّ *adj* بَلَد عالَم ثالِثيٍّ Third World country

ثالوث *n* ❶ [ثُلاثيّ] trio; *sth consisting of three parts/persons/things;* ثالوث غِنائيّ a trio of singers ❷ (Chr) Trinity ❸ (Bot) زَهْرة الثالوثِ (wild) pansy, heartsease

ثُلاثاء, ثلاثاء *n* |ثُلاثاوات, ثُلاثاءات| Tuesday; يَوْم الثُلاثاءِ Tuesday; في (يَوْم) الثُلاثاءِ on Tuesday

ثَلاثة *num* three; ثَلاثة أَطْفالٍ three children; ثَلاث فَتَياتٍ three girls; ثَلاث مَرّاتٍ في اليَوْمِ three times a day

ثَلاثةَ عَشَرَ *num* thirteen

ثَلاثون *num* thirty; ثَلاثون دَقيقةً thirty minutes

ثُلاثيّ **A** *adj* ❶ [ثَلاث مَرّاتٍ] triple; trilateral; *consisting of three parts/persons/things;* ثُلاثيّ الأَجْزاءِ tripartite; ثُلاثيّ الأَطْرافِ trilateral; ثُلاثيّ الأَبْعادِ three-dimensional; اِسْم ثُلاثيّ *full name (first name followed by father's and grandfather's name);* عَلاقة ثُلاثيّة love triangle; مُعاهَدة ثُلاثيّة a trilateral treaty; مُشاوَرات ثُلاثيّة trilateral talks; حِزام ثُلاثيّ التَثْبيتِ three-point seat belt; كَسْر ثُلاثيّ في العَظْمِ a triple bone fracture ❷ (Gram) triliteral; فِعْل ثُلاثيّ a triliteral verb

B *n* ❶ [ثَلاثة أَشْخاصٍ] trio, threesome; triad ❷ (Mus) trio

ثُلاثيّة *n* ❶ [من ثَلاثةِ أَجْزاءٍ] triptych; trilogy ❷ (Mus) triole, triplet

الثَلاثينات *n pl* the thirties

تَثْليث *n* ❶ [قِسْمة] trinity; tripling ❷ (Chr) Trinity

مُثَلَّث **A** *adj* triangular; عَلاقات مُثَلَّثة triliteral relations

B *n* |مُثَلَّثات| ❶ (Geom) triangle; مُثَلَّث مُتَساوي الأَضْلاعِ an equilateral triangle; مُثَلَّث مُتَساوي الساقَيْنِ an isosceles triangle; مُثَلَّث العَطَبِ trigonometry; حِساب المُثَلَّثاتِ warning triangle ❷ (Mus) triangle ❸ [حَرْف] *letter with three diacritical dots*

ثَلَجَ, ثَلِجَ *v* |u; ثُلوج| ❶ [السَماءُ] to snow; تَثْلُجُ السَماءُ it's snowing ❷ [بَرُدَ] to be cold ❸ [صَدْرُهُ] to be glad, to be delighted; ثَلَجَ صَدْرُهُ he was pleased

ثَلَّجَ *v* to freeze; to cool (*with ice*)

أَثْلَجَ *v* ❶ [السَماءُ] to snow; تُثْلِجُ السَماءُ it's snowing ❷ [سَرَّ] to please, to delight, to gladden; أَثْلَجَ هذا الكَلامُ قَلْبَهُ these words delighted him; أَثْلَج قرارُ الرَئيس صَدْري the president's decision made me happy

تَثَلَّجَ *v* to freeze; to become icy

ثَلْج *n* |ثُلوج| ❶ [يَسْقُطُ من السَماءِ] snow; ice; نُدْفة الثَلْجِ snowflake; كُرة ثَلْج snowball; خطّ الثَلْجِ snow line; ثُلوج أَزَلِيّة perpetual snow; رَجُل ثَلْج (لِلَّعِبِ) snowman; رَجُل الثَلْجِ (وَحْش) the Abominable Snowman; هُطول الثُلوجِ snow shower; مِياه الثُلوجِ meltwater; تَساقط \ سَقْط \ هَطْل الثَلْجِ to snow; يَتَساقطُ الثَلْجُ بِخِفّةٍ \ بِقوّةٍ it's snowing lightly/heavily; تَساقُط الثَلْجِ snowfall; أَزالَ \ جَرَف الثَلْجَ to clear/shovel the snow; يَذوبُ الثَلْجُ it's thawing; أَبْيَض كَ \ مِثْل الثَلْجِ as white as snow; مَكْسوّ \ مُكَلَّل بالثَلْجِ covered with snow; تحت الثَلْجِ under the snow ❷ [ماء مُتَجَمِّد] ice; مُكَعَّب ثَلْجٍ ice cube

ثَلاّجة *n* refrigerator, fridge; cold-storage plant; خَزَنَ شَيْئاً في الثَلاّجةِ to keep sth in the refrigerator

ثَلْجيّ *adj* icy; ice-cold; snow-; عاصِفة ثَلْجيّة blizzard, snowstorm; اِنْهِيار ثَلْجيّ avalanche; مِياه ثَلْجيّة ice-cold water; جَبَل ثَلْجيّ iceberg; بَيْت ثَلْجيّ igloo

مُثَلَّج *adj* icy, ice-cold; iced, frozen

مَثْلَجة *n* |مَثالِجُ| ❶ [لِحِفْظِ الطَعامِ] freezer compartment (BrE), freezer (AmE); icebox; cold-storage plant ❷ [نَهْر جَليديّ] glacier

مُثَلِّجة *n* freezer compartment (BrE), freezer (AmE)

ثَلَّ *v* |u; ثَلل| to ruin; to destroy; to overthrow, to topple

ثُلّة *n* |ثُلَل| group; clique; band; ثُلّة من المُشاغِبينَ a group of rioters

ثَلَمَ *v* |i; ثَلْم| **1** [فَلَّ] to blunt; to make jagged **2** [أَحْدَثَ شَقًّا] to make a crack/opening

ثَلِمَ *v* |a; ثَلَم| to be/become blunt; to be/become jagged

ثَلَّمَ *v* to blunt, to dull (AmE)

انْثَلَمَ *v* to be discredited; to be tarnished

ثَلْم *n* |ثُلوم| notch, nick; groove; serration; crack; opening, breach; ثَلْم عَميق a deep groove; أَحْدَثَ ثَلْماً to cut a notch or groove; to create a rift

ثُلْمة *n* |ثُلَم| notch; gap; score; ثُلْمة لا تُسَدُّ a void that cannot be filled; an irreparable loss

ثَمود *n* Thamud (*a people mentioned in the Koran*)

إِثْمِد *n* listed alphabetically

ثَمَرَ *v* |u; ثُمور| to bear fruit

أَثْمَرَ *v* **1** [الشَجَرُ] to bear fruit **2** [العَمَلُ أو الجُهْدُ] to yield; to be productive; المالُ الحَرامُ لا يُثْمِرُ crime doesn't pay; أَثْمَرَ زَواجُهُما عن بِنْتَيْنِ جَميلَتَيْنِ their marriage has been blessed with two beautiful daughters

اسْتَثْمَرَ *v* **1** [مالاً] to invest; اسْتَثْمَرَ في مَشْروعٍ to invest in a project; اسْتَثْمَرَ جُهْداً \ وَقْتاً في شَيْءٍ to invest energy/time in sth; اسْتَثْمَرَ مالاً في أَسْهُمٍ \ سَنَداتٍ to invest money in shares/stocks **2** [اسْتَغَلَّ] to exploit, to utilize, to put to use; to benefit (from), to profit (from); اسْتَثْمَرَ قِطْعَةَ أَرْضٍ to develop a plot of land

ثَمَر *n coll* |أَثْمار, ثِمار| fruit; ثَمَرة كاذِبة false fruit; ثِمار طازَجة fresh fruit; ثَمَرة جُهودِهِ the fruit of his efforts; جَنَى ثِمارَ شَيْءٍ to reap the fruits of sth; بَدَأَ التَشاوُرُ يُعْطي ثِمارَهُ the consultation is beginning to yield results

اسْتِثْمار *n* |اسْتِثْمارات| investing; investment; اسْتِثْمار في العَقارِ investment in real estate; اسْتِثْمار في المُسْتَقْبَلِ \ في شَرِكةٍ an investment in the future/in a company; يَتَطَلَّبُ اسْتِثْماراً it requires investment

اسْتِثْماريّ *adj* investment (*before n*)

مُثْمِر *adj* profitable, lucrative; fruitful, productive; بَحْث مُثْمِر productive research; مَشْروع مُثْمِر a lucrative project; غَيْر مُثْمِرٍ unproductive

مُسْتَثْمِر *n* investor; مُسْتَثْمِرونَ كِبار \ صِغار large/small investors; مُسْتَثْمِر أَجْنَبِيّ a foreign investor; جَذَبَ المُسْتَثْمِرينَ to attract investors

ثَمِلَ *v* |a; ثَمَل| to be/become drunk; شَرِبَ حتّى ثَمِلَ to get drunk

أَثْمَلَ *v* to make drunk

ثَمَل *n* drunkenness; intoxication

ثَمِل *adj* drunk, drunken; intoxicated

ثُمالة *n* |ثُمالات, ثُمال| dregs

ثَمْلة *n* drunkenness

ثَمَّ *adv* **1** [هُناكَ] there; there is/are; ثَمَّ حَليبٌ في الثَلاجةِ there is milk in the fridge **2** [من ثَمَّ] من ثَمَّ therefore, hence; consequently; جاءَ البَيانُ موجَزاً وَمِنْ ثَمَّ فَهُوَ لا يُلْقي الضَوْءَ على التَفاصيلِ the statement was concise and therefore sheds no light on the details

ثُمَّ *adv* then; next; subsequently; thereupon; afterwards; moreover, furthermore; ثُمَّ ماذا حَدَثَ؟ what happened next?; أَطْلَقَ الرَجُلُ الرَصاصَ على زَوْجَتِهِ ثُمَّ انْتَحَرَ the man shot his wife and then committed suicide

ثُمام *n a variety of grass*; على طَرَفِ الثُمامِ within reach

ثَمّةَ *adv* there is/are; لَيْسَ ثَمّةَ ما هو مُهِمٌّ there is nothing important; كانَتْ ثَمّةَ حاجةٌ لِ ... there was a need for ...; هل ثَمّةَ مَعْلوماتٌ؟ is there any information?

ثَمَّنَ *v* **1** [قَدَّرَ الثَمَنَ] to appraise; to evaluate; to assess; to price; ثَمَّنَ القيمةَ بِمَبْلَغٍ... to assess the value at ... **2** [قَدَّرَ] to appreciate; ثَمَّنَ قيمةَ شَيْءٍ to appreciate sth; لا يُثَمَّنُ invaluable, priceless; سَعادة لا تُثَمَّنُ inestimable happiness

ثَمَن *n* |أَثْمان, أَثْمِنة| price, cost; value; ثَمَن تَقْديرِيّ estimated value; ثَمَن باهِظ an exorbitant price; بِثَمَنٍ بَخْسٍ \ زَهيدٍ for a low/small price; بِأَيِّ ثَمَنٍ at any price; لا يُقَدَّرُ بِثَمَنٍ invaluable, inestimable; هذا مَكْسَبٌ لا يُقَدَّرُ بِثَمَنٍ this is an enormous benefit; دَفَعَ ثَمَنَ شَيْءٍ to pay the price for sth; قَبَضَ ثَمَنَ خِيانَتِهِ he got what he deserved for his treason

ثَمين *adj* valuable; expensive, costly; precious; أَشْياء ثَمينة valuables; مِلْك ثَمين a valuable possession; ضَيَّعَ وَقْتاً ثَميناً to waste precious time

تَثْمين *n* assessment; valuation, appraisal

مُثَمِّن *n* appraiser, assessor; estimator; مُثَمِّن عَقاريّ (property/land) valuer (BrE), (real estate) appraiser (AmE)

ثامِن *num* eighth

ثامِنَ عَشَرَ *num* eighteenth

ثَمانونَ *num* eighty; ثَمانونَ تِلْميذاً eighty students

ثَمانية *num* eight; ثَمانية أَشْهُرٍ eight months; ثَماني سَنَواتٍ eight years; السَنَوات الثَماني the eight years

ثَمانِيَةَ عَشَرَ *num* eighteen

ثُمْن *n* |أَثْمان| (one) eighth

الثَمانينات *n pl* the eighties

مُثَمَّن *n* octagon; مُثَمَّن مُنْتَظِم a regular octagon

ثُنَّة *n* fetlock (*joint above a horse's hoof*)

ثَنى *v* |i; ثَنْي| ❶ [طَوى] to fold (up); to pleat; to bend ❷ [صَرَفَ] to turn away, to divert; to hold back; to prevent; ثَنى [عن] شَخْصاً عن فِعْلِ شَيْءٍ to prevent sb from doing sth

ثَنَّى *v* ❶ [ضَعَّفَ] to double ❷ (Gram) to form the dual (*of a word*); to provide with two diacritical dots

أَثْنى *v* |على| to praise; to commend; to compliment; أَثْنى على شَخْصٍ to praise sb; أَثْنى على شَيْءٍ to speak highly of sth

تَثَنَّى *v* ❶ [تَضاعَفَ] to be doubled; to double ❷ [انْثَنى] to bend, to fold; to be/become bent; تَثَنَّت الأَغْصانُ the branches bent ❸ [في المَشْيِ] *to walk with a swinging gait*

انْثَنى *v* ❶ [تَثَنَّى] to bend; to be/become bent; انْثَنى ظَهْرُهُ his back became bent; لا يَنْثَني unbendable; إرادة \ عَزيمة لا تَنْثَني an iron will ❷ [انْصَرَفَ] to go away

اسْتَثْنى *v* to except; to exclude; اسْتَثْنى شَخْصاً \ شَيْئاً to make an exception for sb/sth; to exclude sb/sth

ثِنْي *n* |أَثْناء| crease; fold; pleat; plait

ثانٍ *num* second; ثانياً secondly, second; (once) again; (مَرّةً) ثانيةً a second time, again; المَلِك عَبْد اللهِ الثاني King Abdullah II; ثاني أَفْضَل \ أَجْمَل ... the second best/second most beautiful ...; الدَوْلة الثانِية سُكّاناً the second most populous country; ذَهَبَ إلى المَغْرِبِ للمَرّة الثانِية he went to Morocco for the second time

ثانَويّ *adj* secondary; minor; تَعْليم ثانَويّ secondary education; مَدْرَسة ثانَويّة secondary school, high school (AmE); ذو أَهَمّيّةٍ ثانَويّةٍ of minor importance; دَوْر ثانَويّ a minor part

ثانَويّة *n* secondary school, high school (AmE); هو مُدَرِّسُ الثانَويّةِ he is a teacher in a secondary school, he is a high school teacher (AmE); حَصَلَ على الثانَويّةِ العامّةِ he finished his secondary school education, he graduated from high school (AmE)

ثانِية *n* |ثَوانٍ| second (*unit of time*); مُؤَشِّر ثَوانٍ second hand (*of a clock*); في ثَوانٍ قَليلةٍ in a few seconds; في الثانِيةِ per second; سُرْعة الضَوْءِ هي ٣٠٠ مِلْيون مِتْرٍ في الثانِيةِ the speed of light is 300 million metres per second

ثانِيَ عَشَرَ *num* twelfth

ثَناء *n* |أَثْنِيَة| praise; commendation; compliment; eulogy; كَلِمة ثَناءٍ لِشَخْصٍ \ شَيْءٍ a word of praise for sb/sth; a eulogy for sb/sth; اسْتَحَقَّ كَثيراً من الثَناءِ \ كُلَّ الثَناءِ to deserve much/all of the praise

ثُنائيّ **A** *adj* ❶ [مُزْدَوِج] bilateral, two-sided, mutual; double, dual, bi-; مُحادَثات ثُنائيّة bilateral talks; مُشاوَرات ثُنائيّة bilateral consultations; اتِّفاقيّة ثُنائيّة a bilateral agreement; عَلاقات ثُنائيّة bilateral relations; تَبادُل ثُنائيّ mutual exchange; عالَم الاسْتِقْطابِ الثُنائيِّ a bipolar world; ثُنائيّ اللُغة bilingual ❷ (Gram) biradical ❸ (Elec) bi-, di-; صِمام ثُنائيّ diode ❹ (Math, Comput) binary; نِظام عَدٍّ ثُنائيّ binary numeral system; مِلَفّ ثُنائيّ binary file

B *n* ❶ [شَخْصانِ] duo; pair ❷ (Sport) doubles; الثُنائيّ الرِجاليّ \ النِسائيّ men's/ladies' doubles; الثُنائيّ المُخْتَلَط mixed doubles ❸ (Mus) duet

ثُنائيّة *n* ❶ [عَكْس أَحادِيّة] dualism; duality; ثُنائيّة لُغَويّة bilingualism ❷ (Mus) duet, duo

ثَنَويّة *n* dualism

ثَنِيّة *n* |ثَنايا| ❶ [طَريق] road ❷ [داخِل] في ثَنايا in, inside, among; في ثَنايا الكِتابِ within/inside the book ❸ [سِنّ أَمامِيّة] incisor

ثَنْية *n* |ثَنيات| crease; pleat; cuff (*of sleeves*); turn-up (BrE), cuff (*of pants*) (AmE); hem

أَثْناءَ *prep* during; within; in the course of; at the time of; أَثْناءَ الحَمْلِ during pregnancy; أَثْناءَ الطَعامِ during the meal; المَوْت في أَثْناءِ الاعْتِقالِ death during imprisonment; في أَثْناءِ ذلك meanwhile; في هذه \ تِلْكَ الأَثْناءِ in the meantime

اثْنا عَشَر *num* twelve; الاثْنا عَشَر duodenum

اثْنانِ *num* |f اثْنَتانِ| two; رَجُلانِ اثْنانِ two men; بِنْتانِ اثْنَتانِ two girls; نَحْنُ الاثْنانِ the two of us

اثْنَيْنِ *n* Monday; يَوْم الاثْنَيْنِ Monday

اسْتِثْناء *n* |اسْتِثْناءات| ① [الخُروج من نِطاقِ القاعِدةِ] exception; exclusion; بِاسْتِثْناءِ with the exception of, except for; بدونِ \ من دونِ اسْتِثْناءٍ without exception; فيما عَدا الاسْتِثْناءاتِ apart from exceptions; لِكُلِّ قاعِدةٍ اسْتِثْناءٌ there is an exception to every rule; وَقَّعَت الاتِّفاقيّةَ كُلُّ الجَمْعيّاتِ بِاسْتِثْناءِ جَمْعيَّتَيْنِ all associations except two signed the agreement ② (Gram) exceptive sentence; حَرْف اسْتِثْناءٍ exceptive particle (*eg* إلّا)

اسْتِثْنائيّ *adj* exceptional; extraordinary; unusual; اسْتِثْنائيًّا as an exception, exceptionally; حالة اسْتِثْنائيّة an exceptional case; إجْراءات اسْتِثْنائيّة exceptional measures; (فَقَطْ) في الحالاتِ \ الظُروفِ الاسْتِثْنائيّةِ (only) in exceptional cases/circumstances

تَثْنِية *n* ① [مُضاعَفة] doubling ② (Gram) dual

مَثْنَى *adv* two by two, in twos; two at a time

مُثَنًّى Ⓐ *n* ① [حَرْف] *letter with two diacritical dots* ② (Gram) dual
Ⓑ *adj* ① [مُزْدَوِج] double, twofold ② (Gram) in the dual

‹ **ثاب** *v* |u; ثَوْب| to return, to come back

ثَوَّبَ *v* to reward

أَثابَ *v* to reward, to repay

ثَوْب *n* |ثِياب, أَثْواب| garment; robe; dress; ثِياب clothing, clothes; لَبِسَ ثِياباً to put on/wear clothes; طاهِر الثِيابِ of impeccable character

ثَواب *n* reward in the hereafter; reward (*for good deeds*); recompense

مَثابة *n* ① [مَنجاة] refuge, resort ② [عِبارة عن] بِمَثابةِ like/as, equivalent to, tantamount to; اعْتَبَرْتُكَ دائماً بِمَثابةِ أَبي I always thought of you as my father; كانَ رَفْضُهُ للاقْتِراحِ بِمَثابةِ خَيْبةِ أَمَلٍ his rejection of the proposal was seen as a disappointment

مَثوبة *n* reward/compensation in the hereafter

‹ **ثارَ** *v* |u; ثَوْرة, ثَوَران| ① [قاوَمَ] to rebel, to revolt; to rise (up); ثارَ على شَخْصٍ \ شَيْءٍ to rebel against sb/sth ② [هاجَ] to be/become agitated; to be stirred up; to rant; to burst out; to blow up; ثارَتْ ثائرَتُهُ to fly into a rage, to lose one's temper, to become furious; ثارَ في وَجْهِ شَخْصٍ to blow up at sb

ثَوَّرَ *v* to incite revolution; to revolutionize; ثَوَّرَ الشَعْبَ to incite the people to revolt

أَثارَ *v* ① [هَيَّجَ] to arouse; to agitate, to excite; to stimulate; to stir up; أَثارَ فُضولَ شَخْصٍ to arouse sb's curiosity; أَثارَ شَهيّةَ شَخْصٍ to whet sb's appetite; أَثارَ أَعْصابَ شَخْصٍ to get on sb's nerves ② [أَحْدَثَ] to cause; to create; to unleash; to awaken; to provoke; to raise; أَثارَ الشَغْبَ to cause a riot; أَثارَ ضَجّةً to cause a stir; أَثارَ مَشاعِرَ to evoke emotions; أَثارَ شِجاراً to cause an argument; أَثارَ رَدَّ فِعْلٍ to provoke a reaction; أَثارَ الضَحِكَ to cause laughter; أَثارَ شَهْوةَ شَخْصٍ to arouse sb's desire; أَثارَ الغَيْرةَ to arouse jealousy; أَثارَ الشَكَّ لدى شَخْصٍ to arouse sb's suspicion; أَثارَ الاسْتِياء لدى شَخْصٍ to incur sb's displeasure; أَثارَ الاقْتِراحُ عِدّةَ تَساؤُلاتٍ the proposal has raised several questions; أَثارَ الشُكوكَ to raise doubts; أَثارَ انْتِباهَ شَخْصٍ to attract sb's attention; أَثارَ غَضَبَ شَخْصٍ to anger sb; أَثارَ المُؤَلِّفُ عاصِفةً من الانْتِقاداتِ the writer unleashed a storm of criticism ③ [حَرَّكَ] to excite; to incite; to provoke; to stimulate; أَثارَ شَخْصاً to excite sb ④ [طَرَحَ] to raise; to touch upon; to bring up; أَثارَ مَسْأَلةً to bring up a question

اسْتَثارَ *v* to excite; to stimulate; to stir up; to evoke; اسْتَثارَ غَضَبَ شَخْصٍ to make sb angry

ثَوْر *n* |ثيران| ① (Zool) bull; ox; مُصارَعة ثيرانٍ bullfight; مُصارِع ثيرانٍ bullfighter, matador, toreador ② (Astrol) Taurus; (بُرْج) الثَوْرِ Taurus

ثائِر Ⓐ *adj* |ثائِرونَ, ثُوّار| excited; agitated; rebellious; furious
Ⓑ *n* |ثائِرونَ, ثُوّار| ① revolutionary, rebel, insurgent ② [مُنْتَقِم] see ثأر

ثَوَران *n* outbreak; eruption; agitation, excitation; ثَوَران بُرْكانٍ volcanic eruption

ثَوْرة *n* revolution; uprising, revolt; rebellion; قِيام ثَوْرةٍ the outbreak of a revolution; الثَوْرة الفَرَنْسيّة \ الروسيّة \ الإِسْلاميّة the French/Russian/Islamic Revolution; ثَوْرة الياسَمينِ the Jasmine Revolution (*Tunisia, 2010-11*); الثَوْرة الجِنْسيّة \ الصِناعيّة the sexual/industrial revolution; ثَوْرة عارِمة violent rebellion/uprising; ثَوْرة على الحُكْمِ الدِكْتاتوريِّ a revolt against the dictatorial regime; أَشْعَلَ \ سَبَّبَ ثَوْرةً to start a revolution; أَخْمَدَ ثَوْرةً to suppress/put down an uprising

ثَوْريّ **A** *adj* revolutionary; اكْتِشاف \ فِكْرة \ حَرَكة ثَوْريّ(ة) a revolutionary discovery/idea/movement
B *n* revolutionary; rebel

ثَوْريّة *n* revolutionary spirit

إثارة *n* agitation; stimulation; provocation, incitement; awakening, arousing; مَجَلّة إثارةٍ tabloid magazine, sensationalist magazine; صُحُف إثارةٍ tabloids, tabloid press, sensationalist press; إثارة عَصَبٍ irritation of a nerve; التَشْويق والإثارة thrills and excitement; أَحْدَثَ \ سَبَّبَ إثارةً to cause a stir

اسْتِثارة *n* excitement, agitation

مَثار *n* cause; grounds; reason; motive, incentive, stimulus; occasion; مَثار الجَدَلِ contentious, controversial

مُثير **A** *adj* thrilling, exciting; fascinating, compelling, gripping; provocative; stimulating; agitating, irritating; قِصّة مُثيرة a thrilling story; خَبَر مُثير sensationalist piece of news; مُثير exciting piece of news; عَرْض مُثير a thrilling show; مُثير للأَعْصابِ nerve-racking; مُثير للشَكِّ doubtful, suspicious; مُثير للعَواطِفِ moving, touching; قِصّة مُثيرة للعَواطِفِ a moving story
B *n* |مُثيرات| stimulant

‹ **انْثالَ** *v* to crowd, to swarm, to throng; to be heaped up, to fall in a heap; to pour forth; to come over; انْثالَتْ عَلَيْنا المَشاكِلُ we were beset by problems

ثَوْل *n* |أَثْوال| swarm of bees; colony of bees

ثَوّالة *n* swarm of locusts

‹ **ثوم** *n* garlic; فَصّ ثوم a glove of garlic

‹ **ثَوى** *v* |i; مَثْوًى| **1** [أَقامَ] to stay, to live; to settle (down)
2 [ماتَ] to die; ثُوِيَ to be buried

أَثْوى *v* to lodge, to accommodate

مَثْوًى *n* |مَثاوٍ| abode, habitation, dwelling; hotel, motel, inn; place of rest; مَثْواهُ الأَخير his final resting place, his grave/tomb; لِتَكُن الجَنّةُ مَثْواهُ الأَخيرَ may he rest in peace

‹ **ثَيِّب** *n* |f; ثَيِّبات| *unmarried woman who is no longer a virgin*; widow; divorcee

‹ **ثَيْتَل** *n* mountain goat; hartebeest; wild goat; ثَيْتَل إفْريقيّ gnu, wildebeest

‹ **ثيمة** *n* theme

‹ **ثِيوصوفيّ** **A** *n* theosophist
B *adj* theosophic, theosophical

ثِيوصوفيّة, تِيوصوفيّة *n* theosophy; زاوَلَ الثِيوصوفيّةَ to practise theosophy

‹ **ثِيوقْراطيّة, تِيوقْراطيّة** *n* theocracy

ج *abbr* 1 [جَواب] answer (*abbreviation of* جَواب) 2 [عُمْلة] Egyptian pound (*abbreviation of* جُنَيْه)

جَأْب *n* wild ass

جُؤْجُؤ *n* |جَآجِئ| 1 (Naut) prow, bow 2 (Zool) breast (*of a bird*)

جَأَرَ *v* |a; جَأْر, جُؤار| 1 [البَقَر] to moo; to bellow 2 [الناس] to raise one's voice; جَأَرَ إلى اللهِ to supplicate to God; جَأَرَ بالشَكْوى (من شَيْءٍ) to complain loudly (about sth)

جاز *n* jazz; موسيقى الجاز jazz music

جَأَشَ *v* |a; جَأْش| to be agitated; جَأَشَتْ نَفْسُهُ he was agitated

جَأْش *n* agitation; رابِط \ ثابِت الجَأْشِ self-possessed, calm; رَباطة جَأْشٍ calm, composure; حافَظَ على رَباطةِ جَأْشِهِ to remain calm, to keep one's head; فَقَدَ رَباطةَ جَأْشِهِ to lose one's composure

جاكْبوت *n* jackpot

جاكيت, جاكِتة *n* |جاكيتات| jacket, coat, blazer

جالون, جَلون, غالون *n* gallon

جام *n* |جامات| cup; goblet; صَبَّ جام غَضَبِهِ على شَخْصٍ to vent one's anger on sb

جامايْكا *n* Jamaica

جامْبو *n* jumbo; طائِرة جامْبو jumbo jet

جاموس *n* |جَواميسُ| buffalo; جاموس الماءِ water buffalo

جانْفي *n* (Algeria, Tunisia) January

جاه *n* status; reputation

جاوْدار *n* rye

جاوَه *n* Java

جاوِيّ A *adj* Jawi; Javanese; اللُغة الجاوِيّة Javanese (*language*); الخَطّ الجاوِيّ Jawi alphabet (*modified Arabic script used for writing several Southeast Asian languages*)

B *n* Benjamin tree, benzoin (*Styrax benzoin*); زَيْت الجاوِيّ benzoin essential oil

1 **جَبَّ** *v* |u; جَبّ| to cancel, to nullify

جُبّ *n* |أَجْباب| 1 [خَزّان] reservoir, cistern 2 [حُفْرة] hole

2 **جُبّة** *n* |جُبَب, جِباب, جَبائِبُ| jubba (*a kaftan-like garment*)

جَبَرَ *v* |u; جَبْر| 1 (Med) to set; to splint; جَبَرَ عَظاماً to set bones 2 [أَرْغَمَ] to force 3 [ساعَدَ] to help

Idiom جَبَرَ خاطِرَ شَخْصٍ to comfort sb, to console sb

جَبَّرَ *v* to set; to splint; جَبَّرَ كَسْرَ رِجْلٍ \ ذِراعٍ to set a broken arm/leg

أَجْبَرَ *v* |على| to force, to compel, to make; أَجْبَرَ شَخْصاً على فِعْلِ شَيْءٍ to force sb to do sth; أَجْبَرَ العَدوَّ على الاسْتِسْلامِ to force the enemy to surrender; أُجْبِرَت الطائِرةُ على الهُبوطِ the plane was forced to land; أَجْبَرَني أَبي على الزَواجِ مِنْهُ my father made me marry him; أَجْبَرْتُ نَفْسي على الصَبْرِ I forced myself to be patient

تَجَبَّرَ *v* to be arrogant, to be haughty; to be tyrannical

جَبْر *n* 1 (Math) algebra; مَبادِئ عِلْمِ الجَبْرِ the fundamentals of algebra; الجَبْر والهَنْدَسة algebra and geometry 2 (Isl Law) *necessity, circumstances beyond one's control* 3 [إِلْزام] coercion, compulsion; جَبْراً by force; قامَ بالعَمَلِ جَبْراً لا طَوْعاً he did the work by force, not by choice

جابِر *n* 1 (Med) bonesetter 2 [اِسْم شَخْصيّ] Jaber (*male given name*)

جَبّار A *adj* |جَبّارونَ, جَبابِرُ, جَبابِرة| huge; great, powerful; جُهود جَبّارة a tremendous effort; مَلِك جَبّار a powerful king; قَفْزة \ خَطْوة جَبّارة a giant leap/step (forward)

B *n* |جَبّارونَ, جَبابِرُ, جَبابِرة| 1 [عِمْلاق] giant 2 (Islam) الجَبّار the Almighty (*one of the names of God*)

جَبَروت *n* tyranny; جَبَروت الاحْتِلالِ the tyranny of occupation

جَبْرِيّ **A** *adj* **1** [إِلْزاميّ] forced; compulsory; إقامة جَبْرِيّة house arrest **2** (Math) algebraic; مُعادَلة جَبْرِيّة an algebraic equation; حَلّ المُعادَلةَ جَبْرِيًّا to solve the equation algebraically **B** *n* fatalist

جَبْرِيّة *n* **1** (Philos) fatalism **2** (Islam) *Islamic school of thought emphasizing the omnipotence of God*

جَبِير *adj* arrogant

جَبيرة *n* |جَبائِرُ| cast, splint; جَبيرة على الذِراعِ a cast on the arm

إجْبار *n* forcing; coercion, compulsion; إجْبار شَخْصٍ لِفِعْلِ شَيْءٍ forcing sb to do sth; الإجْبار في الأَدْنى (Mor) (*the legal expenses) must be paid/settled*

إجْباريّ *adj* compulsory, involuntary, obligatory; مادّة إجْبارِيّة a required course; تَجْنيد إجْباريّ compulsory military service, military conscription; اسْتِقالة إجْبارِيّة forced resignation; مُساهَمة إجْبارِيّة mandatory contribution; إجْراءات إجْبارِيّة coercive measures; تَعْليم إجْباريّ compulsory school attendance; في سِنّ التَعْليمِ الإجْباريّ *of school age*

تَجْبير *n* orthopaedics

مُتَجَبِّر *adj* tyrannical, despotic

مُجْبَر *adj* forced, compelled

مُجَبِّر *n* orthopaedist

جِبْريل *n* |dipt| Gabriel; المَلاك جِبْريل the angel Gabriel

[1] **جَبَّسَ** *v* **1** [حائِطاً] to plaster; جَبَّسَ حائِطاً to plaster a wall **2** [عَظْماً] to put in a cast

جَبّاس *n* |جَبّاسونَ, جَبّاسة| plasterer

جِبْس *n* |أَجْباس| gypsum; plaster; plaster of Paris; plasterwork; مَنْجَم جِبس decorative plasterwork; ديكورات جِبْسٍ a gypsum mine

جِبْسِيّ *adj* plaster (*before n*); تِمْثال \ شَكْل جِبْسِيّ a plaster figure/piece

[2] **جَبَس** *n coll* watermelon

[1] **جَبَلَ** *v* |i-u; جَبْل| **1** [خَلَقَ] to shape; to create; جُبِلَ على to be born/made for; جُبِلَ الإنْسانُ على فِعْلِ الخَيْرِ man is naturally disposed to do good **2** [عَجَنَ] to knead

جَبّالة *n* cement mixer

جِبْلة *n* (Bio) protoplasm; جِبْلة مُجَرَّدة protoplast

جِبِلّة, جِبْلة *n* temperament, nature

مَجْبول *adj* **1** [مَخْلوط] mixed, blended; مَخْلوط بِشَيْءٍ blended with sth **2** [مائِل] disposed; كانَ مَجْبولاً على شَيْءٍ to be predisposed towards sth

[2] **جَبَل** *n* |أَجْبال, جِبال| mountain; جِبال عالِية high mountains; رَأْس \ قِمّة الجَبَلِ mountaintop, summit, peak; مُنْحَدَر الجَبَلِ mountain slope; سَفْح الجَبَلِ mountainside; تَسَلُّق الجِبالِ mountaineering, mountain climbing; هَواء الجِبالِ mountain air; جَبَل طارِق Gibraltar; الجَبَل الأَسْوَد Montenegro; جِبال الأَلْب the Alps; في الجِبالِ in the mountains; في أَعْلى الجَبَلِ on top of the mountain; في أَسْفَلِ الجَبَلِ at the foot of the mountain; في مِنْطَقةِ جِبالِ الأَطْلَسِ in the Atlas Mountains (Idiom) إكْليل الجَبَلِ rosemary

جَبَليّ *adj* mountainous, mountain (*before n*); مِنْطَقة جَبَلِيّة mountainous area; سِلْسِلة جَبَلِيّة a mountain range

جَبُنَ, جَبَنَ *v* |u; جُبْن, جَبانة| to be a coward; جَبُنَ عن شَيْءٍ to not dare to do sth

جَبَّنَ *v* **1** [صَيَّرَهُ جُبْناً] to make into cheese **2** [اتَّهَم شَخْصاً بِالجُبْنِ] to accuse of cowardice

تَجَبَّنَ *v* to curdle

جُبْن **A** *n coll* |أَجْبان| cheese; قِطْعة جُبْنٍ a piece of cheese **B** *n* cowardice; تَصَرَّفَ بِجُبْنٍ to act like a coward; بِسَبَبِ جُبْنِهِ out of cowardice; لم يَسْتَطِعْ أَنْ يَفْعَلَ ذلك بِسَبَبِ جُبْنِهِ he was unable to do that on account of his cowardice

جَبان **A** *adj* |جُبَناءُ| cowardly; عَمَل جَبان a cowardly act **B** *n* |جُبَناءُ| coward; جَبان رِعْديد a big coward

جَبّان *n* cheesemaker, cheese merchant

جَبانة *n* cowardice

جَبّانة *n* cemetery; جَبّانة الشُهَداءِ martyrs' cemetery; cemetery for the war dead

جَبين *n* |جُبُن, أَجْبِنة, أَجْبُن| forehead; مَرْفوع الجَبينِ (ME) proud; بِعَرَقِ جَبينِهِ وَصْمة عارٍ على جَبينِ (شَخْصٍ) a disgrace (to sb);

by the sweat of one's brow; قَطَّبَ الجَبِين to frown

جابَهَ *v* to face; to be faced with; جابَهَ صُعوباتٍ to be faced with difficulties

تَجابَهَ *v* to face each other

جَبْهة *n* |جِباه, جَبَهات| **1** (Anat) forehead **2** (Mil) front (line); الجَبْهة الغَرْبيّة \ الشَرْقيّة the western/eastern front; الجَبْهة الخَلْفيّة the rear; على الجَبْهةِ on the front line; (أَرْسَلَ) إلى الجَبْهةِ (to send) to the front; اخْتَرَقَ الصُفوفَ الأولى للجَبْهةِ to break through the front line; في جَبْهةٍ عَريضةٍ on a broad front **3** [مُنَظَّمة] front; جَبْهة شَعْبيّة popular front; الجَبْهة الشَعْبيّة لِتَحْرير فِلَسْطين the Popular Front for the Liberation of Palestine, the PFLP **4** (Meteorol) front; جَبْهة بارِدة cold front

جَبْهَوِيّ *adj* frontal

جَبْهِيّ *adj* frontal

مُجابَهة *n* confrontation; meeting, facing; مُجابَهة تَحَدِّيات meeting challenges; مُجابَهة مع العَدوّ a confrontation with the enemy

جَبى *v* |i; جِباية, جَبْي| to collect; to levy; جَبى الضَرائِبَ على البَضائِع to levy taxes on the goods

اجْتَبى *v* to choose, to select, to pick (out)

جابٍ *n* |جُباة| **1** [للضَرائِب] tax collector **2** [في وَسائِلِ نَقْلٍ] conductor

جَبا *n* |أَجْباء| basin, water reservoir

جِبائيّ *adj* fiscal; tax (*before n*); تَهَرُّب جِبائيّ tax evasion

تَجْبية *n* prostration

اجْتَثَّ *v* to uproot; اجْتَثَّ المُشْكِلةَ من جُذورِها to eradicate the problem from its root

جَثّ *n* beeswax

جُثّة *n* |جُثَث, أَجْثاث| body, corpse; جُثّة رَجُلٍ مَجْهولٍ the body of an unknown man; جُثّة هامِدة a lifeless body; مُسْتَوْدَع الجُثَث mortuary, morgue; نَبَشَ جُثّةً to exhume a body; إحْراق جُثّةٍ burning a corpse; cremation; جُثّة مُتَحَلِّلة a decomposed body; تَشْريح جُثّةٍ autopsy, post-mortem (examination)

جَثْل *adj* thick (*hair/forest*)

جَثَمَ *v* |i-u; جُثوم, جَثْم| **1** [جَلَسَ] to sit, to perch; جَثَمَ على صَدْرِ شَخْصٍ (fig) to weigh heavily on sb; جَثَمَ الخَوْفُ على صَدْرِهِ to be weighed down with fear **2** [هَبَطَ] to land

جاثِم *adj* |جُثَّم, جَواثِمُ| squatting; prone

جاثوم *n* |جَواثيمُ| nightmare

جُثْمان *n* |جَثامينُ| mortal remains, body, corpse; تَشْييع جُثْمانٍ funeral

جُثْمانيّ *adj* bodily

مَجْثَم *n* |مَجاثِم| perch

جَثا *v* |u; جُثُوّ| to kneel

جُثُوّ *n* genuflection; kneeling

جاثٍ *adj* kneeling; سورة الجاثِية The Kneeling (*Sura 45*)

جُحا *n* |m| Juha (*a witty, often foolish, character in many traditional folk tales*)

جَحَدَ *v* |a; جُحود, جَحْد| to deny, to renounce; جَحَدَ شَيْئاً \ بِشَيْءٍ to deny sth; جَحَدَ دينَهُ to renounce one's faith

جَحْد *n* **1** [كُفْر] absence of faith **2** [إنْكار] denial

جاحِد **A** *adj* denying; جاحِد للجَميل \ للمَعْروف ungrateful **B** *n* unbeliever

جَحود *adj* unbelieving; ungrateful

جُحود *n* denial; ingratitude, ungratefulness

جَحَرَ *v* |a; جَحْر| to be/become hollow (*eyes*)

جُحْر *n* |جُحور| hole, den, burrow; حَفَرَ جُحْراً to dig a hole, to burrow

جَحْش *n* |جِحاش, جِحْشان, أَجْحاش| foal, young donkey

جَحَظَ *v* |a; جُحوظ| to bulge, to protrude; جَحَظَتْ عَيْناهُ his eyes bulged out

جاحِظ *adj* |جُحَّظ| goggle-eyed, bug-eyed

أَجْحَفَ *v* |ب| to wrong; to harm; أَجْحَفَ بِشَخْصٍ to wrong sb

إجْحاف *n* injustice, wrong

مُجْحِف *adj* prejudiced, biased

جَحْفَل *n* |جَحافِلُ| legion, multitude, host

جَحيم *n* hell, inferno; جَحيم في الأَرْضِ hell on earth; اذْهَبْ إلى الجَحيمِ! go to hell!; قَلَبَ حياةَ شَخْصٍ جَحيماً to make

جادّة *n* main street

جَدّ *n* |أَجْداد ,جُدود| ① [أبو الأَب أو الأُمّ] grandfather, grandpa (infml); ancestor; أَجْداد ancestry; الوَطَن المَوْروث عن أَجْدادِنا the land we inherited from our ancestors; جَدّ أَعلى ancestor, forefather; جَدّ ثانٍ great-grandfather ② [جِدّيّة] seriousness; إذا جَدَّ الجَدُّ to reach a crucial point; جَدَّ الجَدُّ when push comes to shove; عَمِلَ بِجَدٍّ من أَجْلِ شَيْءٍ to labour at/over sth

جِدّ *n* seriousness; diligence; بِجِدٍّ seriously; diligently; أَقولُها بِجِدٍّ! I mean it!; جِدًّا very; كَبير جِدًّا very big; جَيِّد جِدًّا very good; تَعْبان \ جَميل جِدًّا very tired/beautiful; حارّ جِدًّا terribly hot; مُزْعِج \ صَعْب جِدًّا pretty annoying/difficult; كانَ جوعانَ جِدًّا he was awfully hungry; اخْتَلَفَ جِدَّ الاخْتِلافِ to seriously differ; أَخَذَ شَيْئاً على مَحْمَلِ الجِدِّ ,أَخَذَ شَيْئاً مَأْخَذَ الجِدِّ to take sth seriously

جَدّة *n* grandmother, grandma (infml)

جِدّة *n* ① [شَيْء جَديد] novelty, newness, recency ② [مَدينة] |dipt| Jeddah (*city in Saudi Arabia*)

جِدّي *adj* serious, earnest; مَسْأَلة جِدّيّة a serious matter; تَهْديد جِدّي a serious threat; حِوار جِدّيّ a serious discussion; جِدِّيًّا, بِشَكْلٍ جِدّيٍّ seriously, in earnest; فَكَّرَ جِدِّيًّا في شَيْءٍ to consider sth seriously

جِدّيّة *n* seriousness; بِجِدّيّةٍ seriously, in all seriousness; بِجِدّيّةٍ تامّةٍ \ بالِغةٍ extremely seriously; أَخَذَ شَيْئاً بِجِدّيّةٍ to take sth seriously; مَدى جِدّيّة شَخْصٍ في شَيْءٍ how serious sb is about sth; لم يُظْهِرْ جِدّيّةً في عَمَلِهِ he did not seem serious about his work

جَديد *adj* |جُدُد ,جُدَد| new; modern; قانون جَديد a new law; وَظيفة جَديدة a new job; مَلابِس جَديدة new clothes; تَطَوُّرات جَديدة new developments; نازيّ جَديد neo-Nazi; الموضة الجَديدة the latest fashion; السَنة الدِراسيّة الجَديدة the new school year; هذا الشَيْءُ جَديدٌ بالنِسبةِ لي that is new to me; لَيْسَ ذلك أَمْراً جَديداً that is nothing new; بَدَأَ حَياةً جَديدةً to start a new life; يُعْطيني هذا أَمَلاً جَديداً this gives me new hope; لم يَأْتِ بِجَديدٍ it has brought nothing new; من جَديدٍ again, once again, once more, anew, a second time; هل من جَديدٍ؟ is there any news?

sb's life hell; تَحَوَّلَ (المَكانُ) إلى جَحيمٍ لا يُطاقُ all hell broke loose; فَلْيَذْهَبْ إلى الجَحيمِ he can go to hell

جَحيميّ *adj* hellish

جَخَفَ *v* |i-u; جَخيف| ① [تَباهى] to brag; to take pride in ② [شَخَرَ] to snore

جَخّاف *n* boaster, braggart, swank

جَدِبَ ,جَدَبَ *v* |i; جَدْب| to be/become arid

جَدُبَ *v* |u; جُدوبة| to be/become arid

أَجْدَبَ *v* ① [المَكانُ] to be/become arid ② [القَوْمُ] to be/become poor; to be/become barren

جَدْب *n* aridness, infertility; famine; زَمَن جَدْبٍ lean times

أَجْدَب *adj* |dipt; جُدْب| barren; أَرْض جَدْباء barren land

مُجْدِب *adj* unfruitful

جَدَث *n* |أَجْداث| grave, tomb

جُدْجُد *n* |جَداجِدُ| (Zool) cricket (*Gryllidae*)

جَدَّ *v* |i; جَدّ| ① [صارَ جَديداً] to be new ② [كانَ جادًّا] to be serious, to be in earnest ③ [اجْتَهَدَ] to make every effort, to do one's best; to labour; مَنْ جَدَّ وَجَدَ ≈ seek and ye shall find; جَدَّ في طَلَبِ العِلْمِ to make every effort to acquire knowledge ④ [حَصَلَ] to have happened recently; جَدَّتْ أُمورٌ لم تَكُنْ في الحِسْبانِ things happened that were not taken into account ⑤ [اهْتَمَّ] to take seriously

جَدَّدَ *v* to renew; to renovate; to modernize; يُجَدِّدُ مَحَلَّهُ \ بَيْتَهُ he is renovating his shop/house; جَدَّدَت الجَمْعيّةُ إدارَتَها the association appointed a new board; جَدَّدوا عَقْدَهُ \ جواز سَفرِهِ they have renewed his contract/passport

أَجَدَّ *v* ① [أَحْدَثَ] to renovate; to renew ② [صارَ جادًّا] to be serious; to exert oneself

تَجَدَّدَ *v* to renew, to be revived; to happen again; تَجَدَّدَت الإضْراباتُ renewed strikes took place; تَتَجَدَّدُ الخِلافاتُ بين الدَوْلَتَيْنِ the disagreements between the two countries are resurfacing

اسْتَجَدَّ *v* ① [جَدَّدَ] to renovate; to renew ② [صارَ جَديداً] to be new; ما اسْتَجَدَّ من تَطَوُّراتٍ new developments

جادّ *adj* serious; earnest; سَعْي جادّ a serious endeavor

الجَدِيدة *n* El Jadida (*city in Morocco*)

تَجَدُّد *n* renewal; restoration; regeneration; تَجَدُّدُ القِتالِ the resumption of fighting

تَجْدِيد *n* |تَجْدِيدات| renewal; modernization; renovation, restoration; أَدْخَلَ تَجْدِيداتٍ to bring in innovations; تَجْدِيد آثارٍ إسْلامِيّةٍ renovation of Islamic monuments; تَجْدِيد مُدّةِ صَلاحِيّةِ جَوازٍ renewal of a passport; اِنْتِخابات التَجْدِيدِ النِّصْفِيِّ midterm elections

تَجْدِيدِيّ *adj* innovative

مُتَجَدِّد *adj* renewed; طاقة مُتَجَدِّدة renewable energy; مَشاكِل مُتَجَدِّدة recurring problems; مُتَجَدِّدة يَوْمِيًّا daily; updated daily

مُجِدّ *adj* diligent, assiduous

مُجَدَّد *adj* renewed; مُجَدَّداً again, anew

مُجَدِّد *n* reformer; renewer

مُسْتَجَدّ *adj* new

مُسْتَجِدّ **A** *adj* new; recent; أَحْداث مُسْتَجِدّة recent events; ظُرُوف مُسْتَجِدّة new circumstances **B** *n* |مُسْتَجِدّات| update; recent event/development; على \ في ضَوْءِ المُسْتَجِدّاتِ in light of recent events; اِسْتَعْرَضَ مُسْتَجِدّاتٍ to review recent developments

¹⟨ **جَدُرَ** *v* |u; جَدارة| to be worthy; تَجْدُرُ الإشارةُ إلى أنّ ... it is worth pointing out that ...; يَجْدُرُ بالذِكْرِ أنّ ... it is worth mentioning that ...

جِدار *n* |جُدْران, جُدُر| wall; جِدار حِمايةٍ \ نارِيّ firewall; جِدار عازِل \ فاصِل barrier; separation wall; جِدار بَطْنِيّ abdominal wall; جِدار شِرْيانٍ artery wall; جِدار الصِّينِ (العَظِيم) the Great Wall of China; جِدار الصَّوْتِ the sound barrier; بَنى جِداراً to build a wall

جَدارة *n* competence; merit; qualification; عن جَدارةٍ appropriately; بِجَدارةٍ really, truly; تَسْتَحِقُّ ذلك بِجَدارةٍ she truly deserves that; اِمْتِحان جَدارةٍ competency exam; اِمْتِحان الجَدارة اللُغَوِيّةِ language proficiency exam; أَثْبَتَ جَدارَتَهُ to prove one's worth

جِدارِيّة *n* mural

جُدْرانِيّ *adj* wall (*before n*); رُسوم \ لَوْحات جُدْرانِيّة murals, wall paintings

جَدِير *adj* |جُدَراءُ, جَدِيرونَ| worthy; worth; جَدِير بالذِكْرِ worth mentioning; جَدِير بالمُلاحَظةِ remarkable; غَيْر جَدِيرٍ unworthy; غَيْر جَدِيرٍ بالثِقةِ untrustworthy; هذا جَدِيرٌ بالمُحاوَلةِ this is worth trying

أَجْدَر *adj* |dipt| ما أَجْدَرَهُ أنْ يَفْعَلَ ذلك he was fully entitled to do that; كانَ الأَجْدَرُ بي أنْ أَسْتَمِرَّ في صَمْتي it was better for me to remain silent

²⟨ **جَدَرَ** *v* |a; جَدْر| to have smallpox; جُدِرَ to have smallpox

جَدَرة *n* scar tissue

جُدَرِيّ *n* smallpox; جُدَرِيّ الماءِ chickenpox; كانَ مُصاباً بالجُدَرِيِّ to be infected with smallpox

⟨ **جَدَعَ** *v* |a; جَدْع| to amputate, to cut off; جَدَعَ أَنْفَهُ (نِكايةً في شَخْصٍ) *to try to harm sb but really just harming oneself*

جَدْع *n* amputation

⟨ **جَدَفَ** *v* |i; جُدوف, جَدْف| to row, to paddle

جَدَّفَ *v* **1** [لَعَنَ] to curse, to rage **2** [زَوْرَقاً] to row; جَدَّفَ في بُحَيْرةٍ to row on a lake

تَجْدِيف *n* **1** [سَبّ] blasphemy, profanity, swearing; curse; اُعْتُبِرَ تَجْدِيفاً على الإسْلامِ to be considered blasphemy against Islam **2** (Sport) rowing, crew (AmE); التَجْدِيف بِمِجْدافَيْنِ kayaking

تَجْدِيفِيّ *adj* blasphemous; كَلام تَجْدِيفِيّ blasphemous language

مِجْداف *n* |مَجادِيفُ| oar; paddle

مُجَدِّف *n* **1** [على اللهِ] blasphemer **2** [بالمِجْدافِ] rower

⟨ **جَدَلَ** *v* |i-u; جَدْل| to braid; جَدَلَتْ شَعْرَها to braid one's hair

جَدَّلَ *v* to braid

جادَلَ *v* to debate, to dispute; to discuss; جادَلَ شَخْصاً to argue with sb; جادَلَ في مَسْأَلةٍ to discuss an issue; جادَلَ في صِحّةِ ادِّعاءٍ to dispute the correctness of a claim

تَجادَلَ *v* to argue, to dispute; تَجادَلَ في مَسْأَلةٍ to dispute an issue; تَجادَلَ مع شَخْصٍ to argue with sb

جَدَل *n* discussion, debate; argument; controversy; جَدَل حادّ intense debate; جَدَل دائِر (ongoing) debate; الجَدَل الدائِر

one's time in vain; دِراسة الجَدْوى feasibility study

مُجْدٍ *adj* useful; beneficial; اسْتِثْمار مُجْدٍ a worthwhile investment; غَيْر مُجْدٍ useless, pointless; كانَ تَعَبُهُ غَيْرَ مُجْدٍ his efforts were in vain; مُحاوَلة غَيْر مُجْدِيةٍ a futile attempt; من غَيْرِ المُجْدي it is useless

جَدْوَلَ *v* |i; جَدْوَلة| to arrange (*in tabular form*) ›

جَدْوَل *n* |جَداوِلُ| ◀1 [قائِمة] table; schedule; spreadsheet; جَدْوَل; chart; جَدْوَل بَيانيّ school timetable; جَدْوَل دِراسيّ schedule; جَدْوَل زَمَنيّ electronic spreadsheet; جَدْوَل حِسابيّ الجَدْوَل الدَوْريّ للعَناصِر الكيمْيائيّة agenda; جَدْوَل أَعْمالٍ periodic table of the elements; وَضَعَ جَدْوَلاً to make/create a schedule; الْتَزَمَ بِجَدْوَلٍ زَمَنيٍّ to keep to a schedule; دَوَّنَ \ قَيَّدَ شَيْئاً في الجَدْوَلِ (Law) to enter sth in the cause list; كانَ (مُدَوَّناً) في الجَدْوَل (Law) to be down for a hearing; حَسَبَ الجَدْوَل on schedule; جَدْوَل يَتَكَوَّنُ من ٣ عَواميدَ a table with three columns ◀2 [يَنْبوع] brook, stream

جَدْوَلة *n* ◀1 [جَدْوَل بَيانيّ] tabulation; حَرْف الجَدْوَلةِ tab (*indentation at the beginning of a paragraph*); tab key; tab character ◀2 [جَدْوَل زَمَنيّ] schedule, timeline; جَدْوَلة الانْسِحابِ withdrawal timeline; إعادة جَدْوَلةِ الدُيونِ debt restructuring

جَدْي *n* |جِدْيان, جِداء| kid, young goat; (بُرْج) الجَدْي Capricorn; مَدار الجَدْي tropic of Capricorn ›

جَذَبَ *v* |i; جَذْب| to pull, to draw; to attract, to allure, to entice; جَذَبَ شَيْئاً \ شَخْصاً to attract sth/sb; جَذَبَ الانْتِباهَ to attract attention; تَجْذِبُ هذه المَدينةُ الكَثيرَ من السُيّاحِ this city draws lots of tourists ›

جاذَبَ *v* to vie; to contend; جاذَبَ شَخْصاً أَطْرافَ الحَديثِ to engage sb in conversation

تَجاذَبَ *v* to attract one another; to pull back and forth; to contend; تَجاذَبَ أَطْرافَ الحَديثِ مع شَخْصٍ to chat with sb, to engage sb in conversation; تَجاذَبَهُ تَيّارانِ to be pulled in two different directions

انْجَذَبَ *v* to be attracted; انْجَذَبَ إلى شَخْصٍ \ شَيْءٍ to be attracted to sb/sth

اجْتَذَبَ *v* ◀1 [اسْتَمالَ] to lure; to attract; اجْتَذَبَ الزَبائِنَ من المُنافِسِ to lure customers away from the competition;

حول الإعْدامِ the ongoing debate about capital punishment; مُحِبّ للجَدَلِ quarrelsome; مُثير للجَدَلِ controversial; قانون \ شَخْص \ كتاب \ مَوْضوع مُثير للجَدَلِ a controversial law/figure/book/subject; عِلْم الجَدَلِ (Philos) dialectic; كانَ مَوْضِعَ جَدَلٍ to be under discussion; أَثارَ الجَدَلَ to cause controversy; حَسَمَ جَدَلاً to settle a dispute; لا جَدَلَ فيهِ indisputable; لِنَفْتَرِضْ جَدَلاً أَنّ ... let's assume for the sake of argument that ...; هذا لا يَتْرُكُ مَجالاً للجَدَلِ حول ... this leaves no room for discussion of ...

جِدال *n* |جِدالات| discussion; argument, debate, dispute; جِدال حادّ \ واسِع intense/widespread debate; لا يَقْبَلُ, لا جِدالَ فيهِ indisputable; بِلا جِدالٍ indisputably, unquestionably; هذا لا يَزالُ مَوْضوعَ الجِدالِ بَيْنَهُما that is still a subject of discussion between them

جِداليّ *adj* argumentative; controversial, debatable

جِداليّة *n* dialectic

جَدَليّ *adj* disputable, controversial, polemical; dialectical; افْتِراض جَدَليّ a disputable claim

جَدَليّة *n* dialectic

جَديلة *n* |جَدائِلُ| tress, lock (*of hair*)

تَجادُل *n* dispute, discussion

مُجادِل *adj* argumentative

مُجادَلة *n* discussion; مُجادَلة حادّة بين طَرَفَيْنِ a heated discussion between two parties; سورة المُجادَلة The Pleading (*Sura 58*)

أَجْدى *v* to be useful, to help, to benefit; لم يُجْدِ to not be useful; لا يُجْدي نَفْعاً it is no good, it does not work; هذه أَساليبُ لن تُجْدي نَفْعاً these methods will not work ›

اسْتَجْدى *v* to beg; اسْتَجْدى مالاً to beg for money; اسْتَجْدى العَواطِفَ to try to arouse compassion; اسْتَجْدى لُقْمَةَ العَيْشِ to beg for one's living/daily bread

جَدْوى *n* |f| benefit, advantage; عَدَم الجَدْوى uselessness; عَدَم جَدْوى اسْتِمْرارِ المُفاوَضاتِ the futility of further negotiations; بِدونِ \ بِلا \ بِغَيْر جَدْوى useless, pointless, futile; in vain, to no avail, to no purpose; مُحاوَلات بِدونِ جَدْوى futile attempts; ضاعَ وَقْتُهُ بِلا جَدْوى to waste

اجْتَذَبَ الجُمْهور to draw an audience; اجْتَذَبَ اسْتِثماراً \ رَأْسمالاً to attract investment/capital [2] (Phys) to attract

جَذْب *n* attraction; gravitation; bringing over; جَذْب سِياحيّ a tourist attraction; جَذْب مُسْتَخْدَمين جُدُدٍ the recruitment of new personnel

جاذِب *adj* attractive; enticing; gravitational

جاذِبيّة *n* [1] [فِتْنة] attractiveness; attraction; charm, appeal; جاذِبيّة شَديدة a great attraction; جاذِبيّة جِنْسيّة sex appeal; مَلَكَ جاذِبيّةً to have charm [2] (Phys) gravitation, gravitational force, (force of) attraction; جاذِبيّة مَغْنَطيسيّة magnetism; جاذِبيّة الأَرْضِ \ الشَّمْسِ the gravitational force of the earth/sun; مَرْكَز الجاذِبيّة centre of gravity; انْعِدام الجاذِبيّة zero gravity; قوّة الجاذِبيّة gravitation

جَذّاب *adj* attractive, sexy; captivating, charming, appealing, engaging; غَيْر جَذّابٍ unattractive; ضَحْكة جَذّابة an engaging smile; رَجُل \ امرأة جَذّاب(ة) an attractive man/woman; بَرْنامَج جَذّاب an attractive programme; قُطْب جَذّاب (fig) a magnet; a Mecca; قُطْب جَذّاب للاسْتِثْمارات الأَجْنَبيّة a magnet for foreign investment; قُطْب جَذّاب للسَّيّاح a tourist Mecca

اجْتِذاب *n* attraction; اجْتِذاب رُؤوسِ أَمْوالٍ attraction of capital; اجْتِذاب مُسْتَثْمِرينَ \ أَعْضاءٍ attraction of investors/members

انْجِذاب *n* attraction; أَحَسَّ بانْجِذابٍ نحو \ إلى شَخْصٍ to feel attracted to sb

تَجاذُب *n* attraction; gravitational force; تَجاذُب مَغْنَطيسيّ magnetism

‹ **جَذَّ** *v* |u; جَذّ| to cut off

جُذاذة *n* slip of paper; snippet

‹ **جَذَرَ** *v* |u; جَذْر| to uproot; to tear out

جَذَّرَ *v* to extract the root; جَذَّرَ (عَدَداً) to find the root (of a number)

جِذْر, جَذْر *n* |جُذور| [1] (Bot) root; من جُذورِهِ from its roots; بَحَثَ عن جُذورِهِ to search for one's roots; عالَجَ مُشْكِلةً من الجِذْرِ to treat the root of a problem; العَوْدة إلى جُذورِهِ a return to one's roots [2] (Math) root; جِذْر ٩ the root of 9; جِذْر تَرْبيعيّ \ مُرَبَّع square root; جِذْر مُكَعَّب \ تَكْعيبيّ cube root; عَلامة الجِذْرِ root sign [3] (Gram) root, stem

جِذْريّ, جَذْريّ *adj* [1] [أَساسيّ] radical; structural; تَغَيُّر جِذْريّ a radical change; غَيَّرَ شَيْئاً جِذْريًّا to change sth radically; حَلّ جِذْريّ a radical solution [2] (Math) rational; أَعْداد جِذْريّة rational numbers

مُتَجَذِّر *adj* rooted, ingrained

‹ **جَذَع** *n* |جُذْعان| young man

جِذْع *n* |أَجْذاع, جُذوع| [1] [شَجَرة] trunk, stem; stump; stalk [2] (Anat) upper part of the body; trunk, torso

‹ **جَذَفَ** *v* |i; جَذْف| to row, to oar

جَذَّفَ *v* to row, to oar; جَذَّفَ مَرْكَباً إلى الساحِلِ to row a boat to the shore; جَذَّفَ عَكْسَ التَّيّارِ to swim/row against the current

جَذْف *n* rowing

تَجْذيف *n* rowing; crew

مِجْذاف *n* |مَجاذيفُ| oar, paddle

‹ **جَذِلَ** *v* |a; جَذَل| to be happy, to rejoice

أَجْذَلَ *v* to make happy

جَذَل *n* happiness, joy

جَذِل *adj* elated, delighted, overjoyed

جِذْل *n* |أَجْذال, جُذول| stump

جَذْلان *adj* |dipt; جُذْلان, جَذالى| delighted; جَذْلان ب ... delighted with ...

‹ **جَذَمَ** *v* |i; جَذْم| to cut off; to amputate; جُذِمَ to have leprosy

جَذِمَ *v* |a; جَذَم| to be cut off

جِذْم *n* |أَجْذام, جُذوم| root

جُذام *n* leprosy; أُصيبَ بالجُذامِ to be afflicted with leprosy

جُذْمة *n* stump

أَجْذَم *adj* |dipt; جَذْمى| leprous, afflicted with leprosy; mutilated

مَجْذوم [A] *adj* leprous

[B] *n* leper; leprosy patient

‹ **جُذْمور** *n* stump

‹ **جَذْوة, جِذْوة, جُذْوة** *n* firewood; انْطَفَأَتْ جَذْوَتُهُ (fig) it died out

‹ **جَرُؤَ** *v* |u; جُرْأة ,جَراءة| |على| to dare, to risk, to venture; جَرُؤَ على فِعْلِ شَيْءٍ to dare to do sth; جَرُؤَ على قَوْلِ شَيْءٍ to dare to say sth

جَرَّأَ *v* to encourage; جَرَّأَ شَخْصاً على شَيْءٍ to encourage sb to do sth

تَجَرَّأَ *v* |على| to dare, to risk, to venture, to hazard; تَجَرَّأَ على قَوْلِ شَيْءٍ to dare to say sth

اِجْتَرَأَ *v* |على| to dare, to venture

جَراءة *n* courage, nerve

جُرْأة *n* courage, nerve, audacity

جَريء *adj* |أَجْرِياءُ ,جُرَآءُ| bold, daring, fearless; hazardous; كانَ جَريئاً to be bold; خُطّة جَريئة a bold plan; قَرار جَريء a brave decision; مُحاوَلات جَريئة valiant attempts

‹ **جَراج** *n* |جَراجات| garage

‹ **جِرافيت** *n* graphite

‹ **جِرافيتي** *n* graffiti

‹ **جِرام** *n* |جِرامات| (Egypt) see غرام

‹ **جَرانيت** *n* granite; مِن الجَرانيتِ granite; صَخْرة مِن الجَرانيت a block of granite

‹ **جَرَّبَ** *v* to try, to try out; to test, to examine; to experiment; to experience; جَرَّبَ شَخْصاً to put sb to the test; جَرَّبَ حَظَّهُ to try one's luck; جَرَّبَ حِذاءً to try on shoes; جَرَّبَ نِظاماً to test a system; جَرَّبَ سَيّارةً \ دَرّاجةً جَديدةً to try out a new car/bicycle; جَرَّبَ لَقاحاً to test a vaccine; جَرَّبَ شَيْئاً بِنَفْسِهِ to experience sth personally; سَيُجَرَّبُ على الإِنْسانِ it will be tested on humans

جَرَب *n* scabies

جِراب *n* |أَجْرِبة ,جُرُب| [1] [كيس] bag, sack; knapsack; case (for phone) [2] (Zool) marsupium, pouch; الحَيَوانات ذات الجِرابِ marsupials [3] (Anat) scrotum

جِرابيّ *n* marsupial; حَيَوان جِرابيّ marsupial

جَرْبان *adj* |جِراب ,جُرُب| mangy; scabby; كَلْب جَرْبان a mangy dog

جِرْبة *n* Djerba (*city in Tunisia*)

أَجْرَب *adj* |dipt; جُرْب ,جَرْبان| mangy; scabby

تَجْرِبة, تَجْرُبة *n* |تَجارِبُ| [1] [خِبْرة] experience; practice; تَجْرِبة رائِعة an unbelievable experience; عاشَ تَجْرِبةً to experience sth; عاشَ تَجْرِبةً عَنيفةً to go through a violent experience; اِسْتَعانَ بِتَجْرِبَتِهِ to exchange experiences; تَبادَلَ التَجارِبَ to fall back on one's experience; اِفْتَقَرَ إلى التَجْرِبةِ to have no experience; عَلَّمَتْنا التَجْرِبةُ أنّ ... experience shows us that ...; كانَتْ عِنْدَهُ تَجْرِبةٌ قَليلةٌ \ كَبيرةٌ to have little/extensive experience; بعد \ عن تَجْرِبة from experience, by experience; عَرَفَ شَيْئاً من خِلال \ بِحُكْمِ تَجْرِبَتِهِ to know sth from (personal) experience; التَجْرِبةُ أُمُّ المَدارِسِ practice makes perfect [2] [اِخْتِبار] experiment; test; تَجْرِبة نَوَويّة \ ذَرّيّة nuclear test; حَيَوان تَجارِبَ laboratory animal; فَأْر تَجارِبَ a guinea pig; مُعْطَيات مِنَ التَجْرِبة empirical data; أَجْرى تَجْرِبةً \ قامَ بِتَجْرِبةٍ to carry out an experiment; أَجْرى التَجارِبَ على الحَيَوانات to experiment on animals; بَرْهَنَت التَجْرِبةُ على أنّ ... the experiment showed that ...; عَمِلَ في مَكانٍ تحت التَجْرِبة to work somewhere for a trial period; على سَبيلِ التَجْرِبة by experiment; هذا ما زالَ تحت التَجْرِبة \ في طَوْرِ التَجْرِبةِ this is still in an experimental stage; التَجْرِبة خَيْرُ بُرْهانٍ ≈ the proof is in the pudding [3] [مُحاوَلة] try-out

تَجْريب *n* |تَجاريبُ| trial

تَجْريبيّ *adj* empirical; experimental; by experience; لَقاح تَجْريبيّ an experimental vaccine; مَسْرَح تَجْريبيّ experimental theatre; بَحْث تَجْريبيّ empirical research; فَتْرة \ مُدّة تَجْريبيّة trial period; مُباراة تَجْريبيّة training match

تَجْريبيّة *n* experimentalism; empiricism

مُجَرَّب *adj* tested; tried and tested, proven; experienced; وَسيلة مُجَرَّبة a tried and tested method; دَواء مُجَرَّب a proven remedy; رَجُل مُجَرَّب an experienced man

‹ **جَرْبوع** *n* |جَرابيعُ| (Zool) jerboa (*Dipodidae*)

‹ **جُرْثوم, جُرْثومة** *n* |جَراثيمُ| microbe, bacterium; germ; جَراثيم bacteria; عِلْم الجَراثيمِ bacteriology; مُبيد الجَراثيمِ disinfectant, antiseptic; خالٍ من الجَراثيمِ aseptic

جُرْثوميّ *adj* bacterial; bacteriological; اِلْتِهاب جُرْثوميّ a bacterial infection; أَسْلِحة جُرْثوميّة biological weapons

جَرْجَرَ *v* |i; جَرْجَرة| to drag; جَرْجَرَ خُطاهُ to shuffle along

جِرْجير *n* salad rocket (BrE), arugula (AmE) (*Eruca sativa*)

جِرْجِس *n* |dipt| Jirjis, George (*Christian male given name*)

جَرَحَ *v* |a; جَرْح| 1 [بالجُروحِ] to injure; to wound; جُرِحَ to be/get injured; جَرَحَ شَخْصاً to injure sb; جُرِحَ أَثْناءَ تَدْريبٍ to be injured during training 2 [مَشاعِرَ] to hurt; to offend; جَرَحَ شَخْصاً \ شُعورَ \ عَواطِفَ شَخْصٍ to hurt sb's feelings; جَرَحَ شَخْصاً جُرْحاً عَميقاً to offend sb deeply; جَرَحَ شَخْصاً بِكَلامِهِ to offend sb with one's remarks; جَرَحَ, جَرَحَ شَخْصاً في كَرامَتِهِ كَرامَةَ شَخْصٍ to hurt sb's pride

جَرَّحَ *v* 1 [أَلَّمَ] to injure 2 (Law) to challenge

انْجَرَحَ *v* to get wounded

اجْتَرَحَ *v* to accomplish, to perform; اجْتَرَحَ مُعْجِزةً to perform a miracle

جُرْح *n* |جُروح, جِراح| wound, injury, cut; جُرْح عَميق a deep wound; جُرْح مَفْتوح an open wound; جُروح طَفيفة slight/minor injuries; جُروح خطيرة \ بالِغة major injuries; جُروح في اليَدَيْنِ \ الرِجْلَيْنِ injuries to the hands/feet; أُصيبَ بِجِراح \ بِجُروح to suffer injuries, to be injured; خَيَّطَ \ خاطَ جُرْحاً to stitch a wound; ضَمَّدَ جُرْحاً to dress a wound; وَضَعَ إِصْبَعَهُ \ يَدَهُ على الجُرْحِ to put one's finger on it (BrE), to hit it (right) on the nose (AmE); نَكَأَ \ لَمَسَ الجُروحَ to open old wounds

جارِح *adj* 1 [الحَيَوان] predatory; طائِر \ طَيْر جارِح predatory bird 2 [الكَلام] injuring; مُلاحَظة جارِحة a nasty remark; كَلِمات جارِحة hurtful words

جارِحة *n* |جَوارِحُ| 1 [عُضْو] organ; بِكُلِّ جَوارِحِهِ with all one's heart; اسْتَمْتَعَ بِكُلِّ جَوارِحِهِ to enjoy sth to the full 2 [حَيَوان] predatory bird

جَرّاح *n* surgeon; جَرّاح القَلْبِ heart surgeon; جَرّاح الدماغِ brain surgeon; جَرّاح الأَسْنانِ dental surgeon; جَرّاح تَجْميليّ \ تَقْويميّ plastic surgeon, cosmetic surgeon; جَرّاح الأَوْعِيةِ الدَمَوِيّةِ vascular surgeon

جِراحة *n* surgery; الجِراحة الدَقيقة microsurgery; جِراحة الدِماغِ brain surgery; جِراحة في الرُكْبةِ knee surgery; جِراحة الأَعْصابِ neurosurgery; جِراحة القَلْبِ المَفْتوحِ open-heart surgery; جِراحة تَجْميلٍ cosmetic surgery; جِراحة المَناظيرِ endoscopic surgery; طاوِلة جِراحةٍ operating table; قِسْم الجِراحةِ surgical department

جِراحيّ *adj* surgical, operative; ;عَمَليّة جِراحيّة operation, surgery; عَمَليّة جِراحيّة للقَلْبِ heart surgery

جُرْحيّ *adj* traumatic

جَريح A *adj* |جَرْحى| wounded
B *n* |جَرْحى| wounded person; أَرْبَعة قَتْلى وَخَمْسة عَشَرَ جَريحاً four dead and fifteen wounded

تَجْريح *n* defamation, slander; insult; تَجْريح شَخْصيّ personal attacks

مَجْروح *adj* |مَجاريحُ| wounded, injured, hurt; إِصْبَع مَجْروح an injured finger; مَشاعِر \ كَرامة مَجْروحة wounded feelings/pride

جَرَدَ *v* |u; جَرْد| 1 [مَوْجوداتٍ] to take inventory; جَرَدَ الخَزينةَ to balance the books 2 [قَشَرَ] to peel; to bare

جَرَّدَ *v* |من| to take away, to strip, to dispossess; جَرَّدَ من الرُتْبةِ to demote; جَرَّدَ من السِلاحِ to demilitarize; جَرَّدَ الجَماعاتِ المُقاتِلة من السِلاحِ to disarm the warring parties; جَرَّدَ شَخْصاً من شَيْءٍ to deprive sb of sth; جَرَّدَ الشَعْبَ من حُقوقِهِ to deny the people their rights; جَرَّدَ شَخْصاً من مَلابِسِهِ to strip sb of their clothes

تَجَرَّدَ *v* to withdraw; to strip; تَجَرَّدَ من مَسْؤوليَّتِهِ to duck one's responsibility

جَرْد, جَرْدة *n* |جُرود| inventory; stocktaking; الجَرْد الشَهْريّ \ السَنويّ the monthly/annual stocktaking; قامَ بِجَرْدٍ to take inventory

جَراد *n coll* locust; سِرْب من الجَرادِ a cloud of locusts; جَراد البَحْرِ lobster; crayfish

جَريد *n coll* palm branches stripped of their leaves

جَريدة *n* |جَرائِدُ| 1 [صَحيفة] newspaper, paper; جَريدة يَوْميّة daily newspaper; جَريدة وَطَنيّة national newspaper; جَريدة إِقْليميّة regional newspaper; جَريدة صَباحيّة morning paper; جَريدة مَسائيّة evening paper; جَريدة رَسْميّة \ حُكوميّة official press, government newspaper; قَرَأَ الجَريدةَ to read the newspaper; قَرَأَ في الجَريدةِ to read in the newspaper; جاءَ

Idiom وَهَلُمَّ جَرًّا and so on

جَرّاء *n* من جَرّاءِ because of, due to, on account of; من جَرّاءِ شَخْصٍ because of sb; الآلام التي عانَتْها من جَرّاءِ الحَرْبِ the pain she suffered because of the war

جَرّار *n* |جَرّارات| tractor; lorry (BrE), truck (AmE)

جَرّة *n* |جِرار، جَرّات| ❶ [إناء] jar, jug, pitcher; urn; جَرّة ماءٍ a jug of water ❷ [خَطّ] stroke; بِجَرّةِ قَلَمٍ with one stroke of the pen

جَريرة *n* |جَرائِرُ| offence, crime

اجْتِرار *n* rumination

اجْتِراريّة *n* autism

مُجْتَرّ *n* ruminant

مَجَرّة *n* galaxy

مَجْرور *adj* genitive; اسْم مَجْرور a genitive noun

جَرَزَ *v* |u; جَرْز| to gorge; to gobble; to swallow

جَرَسَ *v* |i; جَرْس| to ring, to sound

جَرْس، جِرْس *n* |جُروس| timbre, tone

جَرَس *n* |أَجْراس| bell, gong, chime; جَرَس البابِ doorbell; جَرَس الإِنْذارِ warning bell/siren; جَرَس الكَنيسةِ church bell; دَقَّ \ قَرَعَ الجَرَسَ to ring the bell; يَدُقُّ \ يَرِنُّ الجَرَسُ there is someone at the door; دَقَّ جَرَسَ شَخْصٍ to ring at sb's door; الحَيّة ذات الأَجْراسِ rattlesnake

جَرْسون *n* waiter

جَرَشَ *v* |u; جَرْش| to crush, to grind; to grate

جَرَش *n* |dipt f| Jerash (*city in Jordan*)

جَريش *n* crushed grain, grits

مَجْروش *adj* ground

جَرَضَ *v* |u; جَرْض| to choke, to suffocate

جَرِضَ *v* |a; جَرَض| to suffocate

جارِض *adj* suffocating

جَرَعَ *v* |a; جَرْع| to swallow

جَرَّعَ *v* to make swallow

تَجَرَّعَ *v* to swallow; to sip

جُرْعة *n* |جُرَعات، جُرَع| ❶ [شَرْبة] swallow; gulp; drink; جُرْعة ماءٍ a drink of water; أَفْرَغَ كَأْسَهُ جُرْعةً واحِدةً to empty one's glass in one gulp; أَخَذَ \ شَرِبَ جُرْعةً (من شَيْءٍ) to take a sip

في كُلِّ الجَرائِدِ it's in all the papers; جاءَ في الجَريدةِ أَنّ ... it was in the newspaper that ...; صَدَرَ في الجَريدةِ الرَسْميّةِ to appear in the official press ❷ [نَخْلٍ] *palm branch stripped of its leaves*

أَجْرَد *adj* |dipt; جُرْد| bare; waste; desolate; أَشْجار جَرْداء bare trees; مِنْطَقة جَرْداء a desolate area; أَرْض جَرْداء barren land

تَجَرُّد *n* ❶ [عَكْس تَحَيُّز] impartiality, independence, detachment; بِكُلِّ تَجَرُّدٍ impartially ❷ [مَصْدَر] disposal

تَجْريد *n* ❶ [نَزْع] divestment, dispossession, deprivation; تَجْريد من رُتْبَتِهِ demotion تَجْريد من السِلاحِ demilitarization; ❷ (Philos) abstraction

تَجْريديّ *adj* abstract; فَنّ تَجْريديّ abstract art

مُتَجَرِّد *adj* ❶ [غَيْر مُتَحَيِّز] impartial ❷ [مُتَحَرِّر] free; مُتَجَرِّد من أَيِّ مَصْلَحةٍ without any interest, unbiased

مُجَرَّد *adj* ❶ [مَحْض] mere, sheer, sole, pure; just, merely, only; مُجَرَّد صُدْفةٍ pure chance; هذا مُجَرَّدُ كَلامٍ these are mere words; هذا لَيْسَ مُجَرَّدَ حُلْمٍ this is not just a dream; بِمُجَرَّدِ وُصولِهِ ... \ ما وَصَلَ ... بِمُجَرَّدِ ... as soon as ...; as soon as he arrived ... ❷ [عارٍ] bare, naked; free; الحَقيقة المُجَرَّدة the plain truth; فِعْل مُجَرَّد Form I verb; مِنْطَقة مُجَرَّدة من السلاحِ demilitarized zone; أَبْصَرَ \ رَأَى شَيْئاً بالعَيْنِ المُجَرَّدةِ to see sth with the naked eye ❸ [نَظَريّ] abstract; مَفاهيم مُجَرَّدة abstractions

جَرْدَل *n* |جَرادِلُ| bucket

جُرَذ *n* |جُرْذان، جِرْذان| rat

جَرَّ *v* |u; جَرّ| ❶ [سَحَبَ] to pull, to draw, to drag; جَرَّ أَصْدِقاءَهُ مَعَهُ في قَضيّةٍ to involve one's friends in a matter; جَرَّت العَرَبةَ أَرْبَعةٌ من الخُيولِ the wagon was pulled by four horses ❷ [جَلَبَ على] جَرَّ شَيْئاً على نَفْسِهِ to bring sth upon oneself

انْجَرَّ *v* to be pulled, to be drawn; انْجَرَّ على الأَرْضِ to trail along on the ground

اجْتَرَّ *v* to ruminate; to dwell on; يَجْتَرُّ ذِكْرَياتِ الماضي he lives in the past

جارور *n* |جَواريرُ| drawer

جَرّ *n* ❶ (Gram) genitive; حَرْف جَرٍّ preposition; *particle that governs the genitive* ❷ [جَذْب] pulling, traction (of sth) ② [مِقْدار] dose, dosage; dash; جُرْعة زائِدة overdose; جُرْعة من اللَقاح a dose of vaccine

جُرَيْعة *n* sip

جَرَفَ *v* |u; جَرْف| ① [كَسَحَ] to sweep away; to tear away; to wash away; جَرَفَهُ التَيّارُ he was swept away by the current; جَرَفَ البَحْرُ كُثْباناً كَبيرةً the sea washed away large tracts of dune ② [أَزالَ الوَحْلَ] to dredge

انْجَرَفَ *v* to drift; to be washed away; (fig) to get carried away; انْجَرَفَ مع \ في التَيّارِ to drift with/on the current

جُرُف, جُرْف *n* |جُروف, أَجْراف| cliff, precipice, bluff

جارِف *adj* overwhelming; violent; حُزْن جارِف overwhelming grief; عِشْق جارِف an all-consuming passion; تَيّار \ فَيَضان جارِف a violent current/flood

جارِفة *n* panzootic (*fast-spreading disease among animals*)

جاروف *n* |جَواريفُ| shovel, spade; scoop; dustpan; فُرْشاة وَجاروف dustpan and brush

جَرّاف *n* dredger

جَرّافة *n* ① [في المِياهِ] dredge, dredging machine ② [للتُرابِ] bulldozer; backhoe; excavator, dragline

انْجِراف *n* |انْجِرافات| erosion, washing away; انْجِراف التُرْبةِ erosion

تَجْريف *n* ① (Med) curettage ② [مَصْدَر] levelling; destroying; تَجْريف الأَرْضِ \ المَنازِلِ levelling land/houses

مِجْرَفة *n* |مَجارِفُ| shovel, spade; scoop; فُرْشاة وَمِجْرَفة dustpan and brush

جَرْكَسيّ *adj, n* |جَرْكَس, جَراكِسة| Circassian

جَرَمَ *v* |i; جَرْم| to commit an offence

جَرَّمَ *v* ① [اتَّهَمَ] to incriminate, to charge with a crime; جَرَّمَ شَخْصاً بِجِنايةِ السَرِقةِ to charge sb with theft ② [حَرَّمَ] to prohibit, to criminalize; قانون يُجَرِّمُ خِتانَ الإناثِ a law prohibiting female circumcision

أَجْرَمَ *v* to commit a crime; أَجْرَمَ ب \ في حَقِّ شَخْصٍ to wrong sb

جَرَم *n* لا جَرَمَ certainly, surely; لا جَرَمَ أَنَّهُ الخاسِرُ he will certainly lose

جُرْم *n* |أَجْرام, جُروم| offence, crime; بالجُرْمِ المَشْهودِ red-handed, in the act; بِجُرْمِ القَدْحِ والذَمِّ on charges of libel and slander

جِرْم *n* |أَجْرام, جُرُم| ① [جِسْم] body; أَجْرام فَلَكيّة \ سَماويّة heavenly bodies ② (P&P) format; جِرْم كَبير large format

جُرْميّ *adj* criminal; نيّة جُرْميّة criminal intent

جَريمة *n* |جَرائِمُ| crime, (criminal) offence, criminal act; جَريمة خَطيرة \ كَبيرة a serious offence; جَريمة بَشِعة \ نَكْراء a hideous crime; جَريمة سِياسيّة a political offence; جَريمة آدابٍ an act of indecency; الجَريمة المُنَظَّمة organized crime; جَريمة إِلِكْترونيّة \ الإنْتَرْنِت e-crime, cybercrime; جَريمة مَعْلوماتيّة \ حاسوبٍ computer crime; جَريمة رَقْميّة digital crime; الجَريمة الكامِلة the perfect crime; جَريمة تَعْزيريّة \ القِصاصِ \ الحُدودِ *crime in the category for which the punishment is laid down in the Koran*; جَريمة قَتْلٍ murder; جَرائِم النازيّينَ the atrocities of the Nazis; عالَم الجَريمةِ the underworld; خُطورة \ حَجْم جَريمةٍ gravity of a crime; مَكان وُقوع الجَريمةِ \ مَسْرَح الجَريمةِ the scene of the crime; عِلْم الجَريمةِ criminology; ارْتَكَبَ \ اقْتَرَفَ جَريمةً to commit a crime; ارْتَكَبَ جَريمةً أَخْلاقيّةً to commit an act of indecency; كافَحَ الجَريمةَ to fight crime

إِجْرام *n* criminality; crime; الإِجْرام المُنَظَّم organized crime; عالَم الإِجْرامِ the underworld; عِلْم الإِجْرامِ criminology; مُكافَحة الإِجْرامِ fighting crime

إِجْراميّ *adj* criminal; مُنَظَّمة إِجْراميّة a criminal organization; أَعْمال إِجْراميّة criminal acts

تَجْريم *n* incrimination; prosecution, criminal proceedings; prohibition, criminalization

تَجْريميّ *adj* incriminating

مُجْرِم *n* criminal, offender, delinquent; مُجْرِم هارِب a fugitive; مُجْرِم خَطير a dangerous criminal; مُجْرِم حَرْبٍ a war criminal; حاكَمَ مُجْرِماً to try an offender

جُرْموز *n* |جَراميزُ| (wolf) cub; cub scout

جُرْن *n* |أَجْران| ① [إناء مَنْقور] basin, trough; well; جُرْن المَعْموديّةِ baptismal font ② [بَيْدَر] threshing floor

جَرْو, جِرْو, جُرْو *n* |جِراء| puppy; cub

retaliatory action; إجْراء انْتِقاليّ transitional measure; إجْراء تَأديبيّ formality; إجْراء رَسْميّ \ شَكْليّ a disciplinary action; إجْراءات حاسِمة sweeping measures; إجْراءات صارِمة strong measures; إجْراءات قانونيّة legal proceedings; إجْراءات قَضائيّة court procedure; إجْراءات مُؤَقَّتة provisional measures; اتَّخَذَ إجْراءاتٍ to take measures; اتَّخَذَ إجْراءاتٍ مُضادّةً to take countermeasures; اتَّبَعَ الإجْراءاتِ to follow procedure; احْتَرَمَ الإجْراءاتِ الرَسْميّةَ to observe formalities; أنْهى الإجْراءاتِ الجُمْرُكيّةَ to conclude customs formalities; التَنْفيذ السَريع \ السَليم للإجْراءاتِ القانونيّةِ rapid/proper judicial process

إجْرائيّ *adj* operational, procedural; executive; سُلْطة إجْرائيّة executive power; خَطَوات إجْرائيّة procedural steps

مُجاراة *n* ❶ [مُنافَسة] match, competition; مُجاراة المَوضة keeping up with fashion; لم يَسْتَطِعْ مُجاراةَ شَخْصٍ to be unable to compete with sb ❷ [وَفْقاً] accordance, agreement; مُجاراةً ل in accordance with

مَجْرًى *n* |مَجارٍ, مَجْرَيات| ❶ [سَيْر] progress; course; channel; مَجْرًى مائيّ watercourse; مَجْرى الأَحْداثِ the course of events; جَرى مَجْرى شَخْصٍ to follow in sb's tracks; سَيْطَرَ على مَجْرَياتِ اللَعْبِ to take control of the game; عادَت المِياهُ إلى مَجاريها everything is back to normal; أَخَذَ مَجْراهُ to run its course; يَجِبُ أنْ يَأْخُذَ الحَقُّ مَجْراهُ justice must run its course ❷ [سِياق] context ❸ [خَطّ أنابيبَ] drainpipe; مَجاري التَصْريفِ sewer; شَبَكة المَجاري ,المَجاري الصِحّيّة sewage system; مِياه المَجاري sewage ❹ (Anat) tract; المَجاري التَنَفُّسيّة \ البَوْليّة respiratory/urinary tract; الْتِهاب المَجاري البَوْليّةِ urinary tract infection, UTI

‹ **جْرينادا** *n* Grenada

‹ **جْرينْلانْد** *n* |f| Greenland

‹ **جَزَّأَ** *v* to divide, to subdivide, to split up, to segment

تَجَزَّأَ *v* to divide, to be divided; to disintegrate; كانَ جُزْءاً لا يَتَجَزَّأُ من شَيْءٍ to be an indivisible/integral part of sth, to be inalienable from sth

اجْتَزَأَ *v* |ب| to content oneself with; اجْتَزَأَ بِشَيْءٍ to settle for sth

‹ **جَرى** *v* |i| جَرْي ,جَرَيان| ❶ [حَدَثَ] to happen, to take place, to occur, to come to pass; ماذا جَرى لَكَ؟ what happened to you?; تَجْري أَحْداثُ المَسْرَحيّةِ في القَرْنِ ١٧ the play is set in the seventeenth century; جَرى لَهُ حادِثٌ أَخَّرَهُ عن الحُضورِ في المَوْعِدِ something happened to him to make him late for his appointment ❷ [سالَ] to flow, to stream, to run (away); يَجْري الماءُ the water flows; جَرى سَريعاً to run fast; جَرى إلى البَحْرِ to flow to the sea; يَجْري النَهْرُ بين الجِبالِ the river flows between the mountains ❸ [رَكَضَ] to run; to rush; جَرى وراء شَيْءٍ \ شَخْصٍ to run after sth/sb

جارى *v* to follow; جارى شَخْصاً \ شَيْئاً to keep up with sb/sth; جارى شَخْصاً في الحَديثِ to go along with sb

أَجْرى *v* to carry out, to implement, to do; أَجْرى دِراسةً \ بَحْثاً to conduct a study; أَجْرى عَمَليّةً (جِراحيّةً) to perform an operation; أَجْرى مُحاوَلاتٍ to make attempts; أَجْرى انْتِخاباتٍ to hold elections; أَجْرى لِشَخْصٍ امْتِحاناً to subject sb to an examination; أَجْرى مُفاوَضاتٍ مع شَخْصٍ to carry out negotiations with sb

جَرْي *n* run; course; مُسابَقة الجَرْي (foot) race; جَرْياً على based on, following; فَعَلَ شَيْئاً جَرْياً على عادَتِهِ to do sth out of habit

جِرّيّ *n* catfish (*Siluriformes*)

جارٍ *adj* ❶ [حاليّ] current, present; ongoing; بَحْث جارٍ ongoing research; حِساب جارٍ an open account; مارِس الجاري March of this year; السَنة الجارِية the current year; الأَوْضاع الجارِية في السودانِ the current situation in Sudan ❷ [سَيّال] flowing ❸ [راكِض] running

جارِية *n* |جَوارٍ| slave girl, maidservant

جِراية ,**جَراية** *n* ration, allowance, allotment; portion; جِراية التَقاعُدِ retirement allowance, pension; بِطاقات الجِراياتِ (distribution) coupons

جَرَيان *n* course; جَرَيان نَهْرٍ \ جُرْمٍ سَماويٍّ the course of a river/heavenly body

إجْراء *n* |إجْراءات| measure, action; proceeding; إجْراء باطِل a futile measure; إجْراء إجْباريّ \ قَسْريّ a coercive measure; إجْراء احْتِياطيّ precaution; إجْراءات أَمْنيّة security measures;

جُزْء n |أَجْزاء| 1 [قِطْعة] part, portion, fraction; component, constituent; أَجْزاء احْتِياطيّة spare parts; الجُزْء الداخِليّ للبِلادِ the inland; جُزْءاً جُزْءاً little by little; في أَجْزاءٍ in parts; في جُزْءٍ من الثانِيةِ in a fraction of a second; الجُزْءِ التالي in the next part; جُزْء من الوَقْتِ part-time; عَمَل لِجُزْءٍ من الوَقْتِ part-time work; عامِل يَشْتَغِلُ جُزْءاً من الوَقْتِ a part-timer; كانَ جُزْءاً لا يَتَجَزَّأُ من شَيْءٍ to be an indivisible/integral part of sth, to be inalienable from sth 2 (Islam) *1/30 part of the Koran*

جُزْئيّ adj partial; part-time; جُزْئيًّا partly, in part, partially; وَقْت جُزْئيّ part-time; عَمَل جُزْئيّ part-time work; كُسوف جُزْئيّ للشَمْسِ a partial eclipse of the sun; مَحْكَمة جُزْئيّة (Egypt) lower court (*for minor offences*)

جُزْئيّة n جُزْئيّات details

جُزَيْء n |جُزَيْئات| particle; molecule; جُزَيْئات الغُبارِ dust particles; جُزَيْئات الحَمْضِ النَوويّ DNA molecules

جُزَيْئيّ adj molecular; البيولوجِيا الجُزَيْئيّة molecular biology; الوَزْن الجُزَيْئيّ molecular mass

تَجْزِئة n division, partition, subdivision, segmentation; قابِل للتَجْزِئةِ divisible; غَيْر قابِلٍ للتَجْزِئةِ indivisible; تِجارة التَجْزِئةِ retail; مَبيعات التَجْزِئةِ retail sales

تَجَزُّئيّة n divisibility

تَجْزيء n division

تَجْزيئيّ adj 1 [تَقْسيميّ] fractional; تَقْطير \ تَبَلْوُر تَجْزيئيّ fractional distillation/crystallization 2 [تَدْريجيّ] piecemeal; مَنْهَج تَجْزيئيّ في السِياسةِ والدينِ a piecemeal approach to politics and religion

لاتَجَزُّئيّة n indivisibility

‹ **جِزْدان, جُزْدان** n |جِزْدانات| wallet

[1]‹ **جَزَرَ** v |u; جَزْر| 1 [الماءُ] to ebb (away) 2 [نَحَرَ] to slaughter

جَزّار n |جَزّارونَ, جَزّارة| butcher; سِكّين الجَزّارِ butcher knife

جِزارة n butcher's trade; مَحَلّ الجِزارة butcher's shop

جَزْر n ebb, low tide, low water; المَدّ والجَزْر the tide; وَقْتَ الجَزْرِ at low tide

جَزَريّ A adj insular; دَوْلة جَزَريّة island state
B n islander

جَزيرة n |جُزُر, جَزائِرُ| island; جَزيرة مَهْجورة \ غَيْر مَأْهولةٍ a desert island; جَزيرة مَرْجانيّة atoll; شِبْه جَزيرةٍ peninsula; (شِبْه) الجَزيرة العَرَبيّة \ جَزيرة العَرَبِ Arabian peninsula; جُزُر القَمَرِ Comoros (*island nation in the Indian Ocean*); الجَزيرة الخَضْراء Algeciras (*city in Spain*); الجُزُر الكَناريّة Canary Islands; جُزُر الأَنْتيل Antilles; مُجْموعة جُزُرٍ archipelago; في الجَزيرة on the island; الجَزيرة Gezira (*island in the Nile in Cairo*)

الجَزائِر n |f| 1 [البَلَد] Algeria 2 [المَدينة] Algiers; الجَزائِر العاصِمة Algiers

جَزائِريّ A adj Algerian; الجُمْهوريّة الجَزائِريّة الدّيموقْراطيّة الشَّعْبيّة the People's Democratic Republic of Algeria
B n Algerian

مَجْزَرة n |مَجازِرُ| 1 [مَحَلّ الجَزّارِ] butcher's shop; slaughterhouse; مَجْزَرة إسْلاميّة Muslim butcher 2 [مَذْبَحة] slaughter, massacre, bloodbath, butchery; مَجْزَرة كَبيرة a great massacre; مَجْزَرة جَماعيّة a mass slaughter

[2]‹ **جَزَر** n coll carrot; بَشَرَ جَزَراً to scrape/peel carrots; رِزْمة جَزَرٍ a bunch of carrots; سِياسة العَصا والجَزَرةِ the carrot and the stick approach

‹ **جَزَّ** v |u; جَزّ| to mow; to clip; to shear (off); جَزَّ الصوفَ to shear wool; جَزَّ العُشْبَ to cut grass, to mow the lawn

اجْتَزَّ v to cut; to mow; to shear

جَزّازة n mower; جَزّازة عُشْبٍ lawnmower

جِزّة n |جِزَز, جَزائِزُ| wool; الجِزّة الذَهَبيّة the Golden Fleece (*Greek mythology*)

مِجَزّ n (pair of) shears

‹ **جَزِعَ** v |a; جَزَع| to be/become anxious

جَزَّعَ v to cut (up), to tear (up)

جَزْع n onyx

جَزَع n concern, anxiety; restlessness; شَعَرَ بالجَزَعِ to feel anxious; أُصيبَ بالجَزَعِ to suffer from anxiety

جُزْع n (Mech) axle

جازِع n restless, anxious

مِجْزاعة n (Bot) impatiens; busy Lizzie (BrE) (*Impatiens walleriana*)

‹ **جازَفَ** v to risk, to hazard, to venture; جازَفَ في شَيْءٍ to take a risk on sth; جازَفَ بِنَفْسِهِ \ بِحَياتِهِ to risk one's life

جُزاف *n* bulk; bulk buying; جُزافاً haphazardly; لم يَكُنْ هذا جُزافاً this is/was no accident

جُزافيّ *adj* adventurous; risky; مَشْروع جُزافيّ a venture

مُجازِف **A** *adj* reckless, rash; adventurous; رَأْسمال مُجازِف venture capital

B *n* stuntman

مُجازَفة *n* **1** ▸ [حادث مُثير] adventure; من دونِ كَبير مُجازَفةٍ without too much exaggeration **2** ▸ [مُخاطَرة] risk, hazard; بِلا مُجازَفةٍ without risk

مِجْزَفة *n* net; trawl (net)

‹ **أَجْزَلَ** *v* to give generously

جَزْل *adj* |جِزال| abundant

جَزالة *n* abundance

جَزيل *adj* |جِزال| profuse; شُكْراً جَزيلاً many thanks

1‹ **جَزَمَ** *v* |i; جَزْم| **1** ▸ [كانَ مُتأَكِّداً] to be absolutely certain; جَزَمَ شَيْئاً \ بِشَيْءٍ to be positive of sth; أَكادُ أَجْزِمُ أَنّ I am almost certain that **2** ▸ (Gram) *to put (a verb) in the jussive/apocopate*

جازِم *adj* |جَوازِمُ| distinct; positive; absolute; رَأْي جازِم strong views; قَرار جازِم an irrevocable decision; اعْتِقاد جازِم a firm belief

جَزْم *n* **1** ▸ [تأْكيد] positiveness; (dogmatic) assertion; لا يُمْكِنُ الجَزْمُ بِهِ it cannot be stated for certain **2** ▸ (Gram) jussive; apocopate; صيغة الجَزْم jussive

جَزْميّة *n* certainty; positiveness

مَجْزوم *adj* المُضارع المَجْزوم jussive; apocopate

2‹ **جَزْمة** *n* |جِزَم, جَزْمات| boot, (pair of) boots; shoe, (pair of) shoes; لَبِسَ \ نَزَعَ جَزْمةً to put on/take off boots

‹ **جَزى** *v* |i; جَزاء| **1** ▸ [كافَأَ] to reward; جَزاهُ اللّٰهُ خَيْراً may God reward him **2** ▸ [عاقَبَ] to punish, to chastise

جازى *v* **1** ▸ [كافَأَ] to reward; جازاكَ اللّٰهُ خَيْراً may God reward you **2** ▸ [عاقَبَ] to punish, to chastise

أَجْزى *v* **1** ▸ [أَثْمَرَ] to be profitable, to profit; to benefit, to be useful/beneficial; أَجْزى بِشَيْءٍ to benefit from sth **2** ▸ [قامَ مَقامَهُ] to take the place

جَزاء *n* |جَزاءات| punishment, penalty; repayment; جَزاء قاسٍ a heavy/severe punishment; جَزاء نَقْديّ fine; نُقْطة جَزاءٍ penalty point; رَكْلة \ ضَرْبة جَزاءٍ penalty (kick); مِنْطَقة جَزاءٍ penalty area; نالَ \ أَخَذَ جَزاءَهُ to get one's just deserts; هذا جَزاؤُهُ it serves him right

جَزائيّ *adj* criminal, penal; القانون الجَزائيّ criminal law

جِزْية *n* (Hist) *tax paid by Christians and Jews living under Muslim rule*

مُجازاة *n* requital, repayment

مُجْزٍ *adj* paying, profitable; sufficient; أَرْباح \ عوائِد مُجْزِية sufficient profit/proceeds; بِسِعْرٍ مُجْزٍ at a profitable price

‹ **جاسِئ** *adj* hard, stiff; جِسْم جاسِئ (Phys) a rigid body

جُسْأة *n* callus

‹ **جَسَّدَ** *v* to give concrete form; to embody; to personify; جَسَّدَ فِكْرةً to embody an idea; جَسَّدَ طُموحاتِ شَخْصٍ to reflect sb's aspirations; جَسَّدَ شَيْئاً في كَلِماتٍ to depict sth in words; جَسَّدَ الشَّرَّ to personify evil

تَجَسَّدَ *v* to materialize; to be personified, to be embodied, to be enshrined; تَجَسَّدَ ب \ في شَيْءٍ to be embodied in sth; تَجَسَّدَت الديمُقْراطيّةُ في الدُسْتورِ democracy was enshrined in the constitution

جَسَد *n* |أَجْساد| body; ارْتَعَشَ جَسَدُهُ كُلُّهُ he trembled all over his body; فَعَلَ شَيْئاً بالروح والجَسَدِ to do sth wholeheartedly; الجَسَد والروح body and mind; جَسَداً وَروحاً passionately

جَسَديّ *adj* physical, bodily, corporal; تَفْتيش جَسَديّ body search; التَصْفية الجَسَديّة assassination; killing; التَعْذيب الجَسَديّ والنَفْسيّ physical and psychological torture

تَجَسُّد *n* embodiment, personification, incarnation; تَجَسُّد الشَرِّ the embodiment of evil

تَجْسيد *n* embodiment

مُتَجَسِّد *adj* embodied; incarnate (Christ)

مُجَسَّد *adj* embodied; incarnate; الشَرّ المُجَسَّد evil incarnate

‹ **جَسَرَ** *v* |u; جُسور, جَسارة| **1** ▸ [بَنى جِسْراً] to bridge, to close; جَسَرَ هُوّةً to bridge a gap **2** ▸ [جَرُؤَ] |على| to dare, to venture; جَسَرَ على شَيْءٍ to dare to do sth

جَسَّرَ *v* to bridge; جَسَّرَ الهوّةَ بين ... to bridge the gap between ...

تَجاسَرَ *v* to dare, to venture; تَجاسَرَ على شَيْءٍ to have the courage to do sth

جِسْر *n* |جُسور| ◆1 [كوبْري] bridge; viaduct; جِسْر دَوّار swing bridge; جِسْر مُتَحَرِّك drawbridge; جِسْر مُعَلَّق suspension bridge; جِسْر عائِم pontoon bridge; جِسْر جَوِّيّ airlift; جِسْر جَوِّيّ للإِمْدادات an airlift of relief supplies; جِسْر على نَهْر a bridge across a river; على \ تحت \ عن طَريقِ الجِسْر on/under/across the bridge ◆2 (Med) جِسْر أَسْنانٍ bridge

جَسارة *n* daring; بِجَسارةٍ bravely, courageously

جَسور *adj* |جُسُر| daring; fearless

تَجْسيرِيّ *adj* bridging; قَرْض تَجْسيرِيّ bridging loan

مُتَجاسِر **A** *n* daredevil

B *adj* daring, bold

جَسَّ *v* |u; جَسّ| to touch, to feel, to finger; جَسَّ نَبْضَ شَخْصٍ to take sb's pulse, to feel sb's pulse; (fig) to feel out, to get sb's opinion

تَجَسَّسَ *v* to spy, to pry; تَجَسَّسَ لِصالِحِ العَدُوِّ to spy for the enemy; تَجَسَّسَ على العَدُوِّ to spy on the enemy

اِجْتَسَّ *v* to feel

جاسوس *n* |جَواسيس| spy; جاسوس مُزْدَوِج double agent; جاسوس أَمْريكِيّ an American spy; جاسوس لِصالِحِ أَلْمانيا a spy for Germany

جاسوسِيّة *n* espionage; spy; مُكافَحة الجاسوسِيّة counter-espionage; رِواية الجاسوسِيّة a spy novel

جَسّ *n* touch

تَجَسُّس *n* espionage, spy; spying; التَجَسُّس الصِناعِيّ industrial espionage; التَجَسُّس لِصالِحِ العَدُوِّ spying for the enemy; تُهْمة تَجَسُّسٍ a charge of espionage; طائِرة التَجَسُّسِ spy plane; مُكافَحة التَجَسُّس counter-espionage; شَبَكة التَجَسُّسِ espionage ring; بَرامِج التَجَسُّسِ (Comput) spyware

تَجَسُّسِيّ *adj* relating to espionage; espionage (before *n*); أَنْشِطة تَجَسُّسِيّة espionage activities

مَجَسّ *n* a spot that one touches; هذا خَشِنُ المَجَسِّ this feels coarse to the touch

مِجَسّ, مِجَسّة *n* |مَجاسّ, مِجَسّات| ◆1 (Mech) sensor; probe; مِجَسّ فَضائِيّ space probe ◆2 (Bio) feeler, antenna; tentacle

مَجَسّة *n* |مَجاسّ| key

جَسُمَ *v* |u; جَسامة| to be/become great, to be/become big

جَسَّمَ *v* ◆1 [بالَغَ] to exaggerate, to blow up; جَسَّمَ قَضِيّةً to exaggerate a matter ◆2 [كَبَّرَ] to magnify ◆3 [جَسَّدَ] to materialize; to embody; to give shape/form

تَجَسَّمَ *v* to take shape

جِسْم *n* |أَجْسام, جُسوم| ◆1 [جَسَد] body; جِسْم سَليم \ قَوِيّ a sound/strong body; جِسْم الإِنْسانِ the human body; وَزْن الجِسْمِ body weight; بِناء الأَجْسامِ bodybuilding; دَرَجة حَرارة الجِسْمِ body temperature; العَقْل السَليم في الجِسْمِ السَليمِ a sound mind in a sound body ◆2 [مادّة] body, object; جِسْم غَريب foreign object; جِسْم مُكَوَّر \ مُكَعَّب a spherical/cubic body ◆3 [سَفينةٍ, طائِرةٍ ...] body ◆4 (Bio) جِسْم حَيّ organism; جِسْم مُضادّ antibody; أَجْسام مُضادّة لِلحَصْبة الأَلْمانِيّة antibodies against German measles

جَسامة *n* ◆1 [خُطورة] gravity, magnitude, seriousness; جَسامة الجَريمةِ the gravity of the offence ◆2 [ضَخامة] fatness; enormity; size

جُسْمان *n* body

جُسْمانِيّ, جِسْمانِيّ *adj* physical, bodily; مَجْهود جُسْمانِيّ physical effort; بِنْية \ تَكْوين جُسْمانِيّ(ة) build; نَشاط جُسْمانِيّ physical activity

جِسْمِيّ *adj* physical, bodily, corporal; جِسْمِيًّا وَعَقْلِيًّا physically and mentally

جَسيم *adj* |جِسام| enormous, huge, immense, massive; خَطَأ جَسيم a massive error; مَسْؤولِيّة جَسيمة immense responsibility; عَواقِب جَسيمة serious consequences; ضَرَر \ أَضْرار جَسيم(ة) extensive damage

جُسَيْم *n* |جُسَيْمات| particle; فيزِياء الجُسَيْماتِ particle physics; مُسارِع الجُسَيْماتِ النَوَوِيّةِ particle accelerator

تَجْسيم *n* materialization

مُجَسَّم *adj* relief (before *n*); 3D, three-dimensional; خَريطة مُجَسَّمة relief map

مُجَسَّمة *n* replica

جَشَأَ *v* |a; جُشوء, جُشاء| to belch, to burp

جَشَّأَ *v* to belch, to burp

تَجَشَّأَ *v* to belch, to burp

جُشْأة *n* belch, burp

تَجَشُّؤ *n* belch, burp

‹ **جَشَّ** *v* |u; جَشّ| to grind, to mill

جُشّة *n* hoarseness, huskiness

أَجَشّ *adj* |dipt| hoarse, husky; بِصَوْتٍ أَجَشّ in a hoarse voice; أَصْبَح أَجَشّ الصَوْتِ to have a broken voice

‹ **جَشِعَ** *v* |a; جَشَع| to be/become greedy, to be/become covetous

جَشَع *n* greed

جَشِع *adj* greedy, covetous, avaricious, grasping

‹ **جَشِمَ** *v* |a; جَشْم, جَشامة| to undergo, to endure; جَشِمَ شَيْئاً to go through sth

تَجَشَّمَ *v* to undergo, to endure; تَجَشَّمَ شَيْئاً to undergo sth; تَجَشَّمَ عَناءَ \ مَشَقّةَ السَفرِ to endure the fatigue/discomfort of travel

‹ **جَصَّصَ** *v* to plaster, to whitewash; to stucco

جِصّ *n* plaster, plaster of Paris; gypsum; plasterwork

جَصّاص *n* plasterer

جِصّيّ *adj* plaster (*before n*)

جِصّيّة *n* (Bot) baby's breath (*Gypsophila*)

‹ **جَعْبة** *n* |جِعاب| quiver; rucksack; أَفْرَغَ ما في جَعْبَتِهِ to be spent, to use up all of one's ammunition; حَمَلَ في جَعْبَتِهِ شَيْئاً to have sth in one's arsenal; to have sth in store; حَمَلَ في جَعْبَتِهِ مُفاجَأةً to have a surprise up one's sleeve

‹ **جَعْجَعَ** *v* |i; جَعْجَعة| to rant

جَعْجَعة *n* clamour, fanfare, tumult, noise; أَسْمَعُ جَعْجَعةً وَلا أرى طَحيناً much ado about nothing

‹ **جَعَّدَ** *v* **1** [شَعْراً] to curl, to frizz; جَعَّدَت شَعْرَها to curl one's hair **2** [وَرَقاً \ مَلابِسَ] to crease, to crinkle, to crumple, to rumple; جَعَّدَ وَرَقةً \ قِطْعة وَرَقٍ to crumple a piece of paper; جَعَّدَ مَلابِسَهُ to wrinkle one's clothes

تَجَعَّدَ *v* **1** [الشَعْرُ] to curl, to frizz; يَتَجَعَّدُ شَعْرُهُ to have curly hair **2** [الوَجْهُ] to be/become wrinkled; كَبِرَتْ وَتَجَعَّدَ وَجْهُها she grew old and her face became wrinkled **3** [تَكَمَّشَ] to crease, to crinkle, to crumple; يَتَجَعَّدُ القَميصُ the shirt is wrinkled

جَعْدة *n* |جَعَدات| **1** [شَعْر] curl **2** (Bot) bugleweed, bugle (*Ajuga*); felty germander (*Teucrium polium*)

جَعْديّ *adj* curly

تَجَعُّد *n* |تَجَعُّدات| crease; creasing, crumpling

تَجْعيد *n* |تَجاعيدُ| creasing, crumpling; wrinkling; تَجاعيد في الوَجْهِ facial wrinkles; تَجْعيد الشَعْرِ curly hair, waves

مُتَجَعِّد *adj* wrinkled; curly

مُجَعَّد *adj* curled, frizzed; creased, wrinkled, wrinkly; شَعْر مُجَعَّد curly hair; وَرَقة مُجَعَّدة a crumpled piece of paper; وَجْه مُجَعَّد a wrinkled face

مِجْعَد *n* curler

مُجَعِّدة *n* curling iron

‹ **جَعْر** *n* droppings; manure

جِعْران *n* scarab, dung beetle; أَبو جِعْران scarab

‹ **جُعْضيض** *n* sow thistle (*Sonchus*)

‹ **جَعْفَر** *n* Ja'far (*male given name*)

جَعْفَريّ *adj* Ja'fari; المَذْهَب الجَعْفَريّ the Ja'fari school (*the major school of jurisprudence in Shia Islam*)

‹ **جَعَلَ** *v* |a; جَعْل| **1** [سَبَّبَ] to make, to create, to cause, to bring about; جَعَلَ شَخْصاً يَبْتَسِمُ to make sb smile; جَعَلَ شَخْصاً مُديراً to make/appoint sb manager; جَعَلَ شَخْصاً يُغَيِّرُ رَأْيَهُ to make sb change his mind; جَعَلَ شَيْئاً في مُتَناوَلِ يَدِهِ to bring sth within one's reach **2** [بَدَأَ] to begin; جَعَلَ يَفْعَلُ شَيْئاً to start doing sth; جَعَلَ الاتِّحادُ يَنْمو the union began to grow **3** [خَلَقَ] to create; جَعَلَ اللهُ السَمَواتِ والأَرْض God created the heavens and the earth

جاعَلَ *v* to bribe, to buy off

جُعَل *n* |جِعْلان| scarab, dung beetle

جِعال *n* |جُعُل| bribe; wages

‹ **جِعة** *n* beer

‹ **جُغْرافيّ** **A** *adj* geographic, geographical; أَسْماء جُغْرافيّة geographical names

B *n* geographer

جَفْنة *n* |جِفان, جَفَنات| bowl; mug

جَفا *v* |u; جَفاء| ◼1 [عَكْس آنَسَ] to avoid ◼2 [غَلُظَ] to be coarse, to be crude

جافى *v* to disagree with, to contradict, to conflict with; to offend; جافى الحَقيقةَ to be contrary to fact

تَجافى *v* to turn away

جافٍ *adj* |جُفاة| coarse, crude; blunt, harsh, unkind; كَلام جافٍ harsh words

جَفاء *n* unfriendliness; البُعْدُ جَفاءٌ out of sight, out of mind

جُفاء *n* uselessness; ذَهَبَ جُفاءً to be in vain

جَفْوة *n* alienation, estrangement

جِلاتين *n* gelatin, jello (AmE); وَرَقة جِلاتينٍ a packet of gelatin; ظَرْف جِلاتينٍ a gelatin mould (BrE), a jello mold (AmE)

جَلَبَ *v* |i-u; جَلْب| ◼1 [أَحْضَرَ] to bring, to get, to fetch; to bring along; to collect; جَلَبَ حُلولاً to come up with solutions; جَلَبَ شَيْئاً لِشَخْصٍ to bring sth for sb; ما الذي سَيَجْلِبُهُ لَنا المُسْتَقْبَلُ؟ what will the future bring us? ◼2 [سَبَّبَ] to bring about, to cause, to bring; جَلَبَ مَشاكِلَ to cause problems; جَلَبَ الإزْعاجَ \ المَتاعِبَ to bring inconvenience ◼3 [جَذَبَ] to attract, to bring in; جَلَبَ أَصْواتاً to bring in votes ◼4 [أَحْدَثَ جَلَبةً] to be noisy

جَلَّبَ *v* to rage, to rave

أَجْلَبَ *v* ◼1 [اِجْتَمَعَ] to meet, to assemble ◼2 [كَسَبَ] to earn

اِسْتَجْلَبَ *v* ◼1 [اِسْتَمالَ] to attract; to seek to attract ◼2 [اِسْتَوْرَدَ] to import; اِسْتَجْلَبَ شَيْئاً من الخارِجِ to import sth from abroad

جَلَب *n* |أَجْلاب| noise, tumult, clamour

جَلّاب *n* slave trader; (Tunisia) animal trader

جَلّابة *n* djellaba (*a long, loose garment with a pointed hood worn by both men and women in North Africa*)

جَلّابيّة *n* |جَلاليبُ, جَلّابيّات| jellabiya (*a long, loose garment native to Egypt and the Sudan Nile Valley*)

جِلْباب *n* |جَلابيبُ| jilbab (*a long, loose garment worn by some Muslim women*)

جَلَبة *n* |جَلَب| noise, tumult, clamour, racket

جُغْرافِيا, جُغْرافيّة *n* geography; الجُغْرافِيا الطَبيعيّة physical geography; الجُغْرافِيا الاجْتِماعيّة human geography; عالِم بالجُغْرافِيا geographer

جِفْت *n* forceps (*for childbirth*)

مُجَفَّد *adj* freeze-dried

جَفْر *n* fortune telling, divination; cipher, code; عِلْم الجَفْرِ numerology

جُفْرة *n* |جُفَر, جِفار| pit, hole

جَفَّ *v* |i; جَفاف| to dry (out/up); to have run dry; جَفَّت البُحَيْرةُ the lake has run dry; جَفَّ كَلامُهُ to speak coldly

جَفَّفَ *v* to dry; to wipe dry; to drain; جَفَّفَ شَعْرَهُ to dry one's hair; جَفَّفَ دُموعَهُ to dry one's tears

تَجَفَّفَ *v* to dry out/up

جافّ *adj* ◼1 [يابِس] dry, arid, barren; البُحَيْرةُ جافّةٌ the lake has dried up; عُشْب \ أَوْراق جافّ(ة) withered grass/leaves; شِفاه \ شَعْر جافّ(ة) dry lips/hair ◼2 [مُمِلّ] dry, boring; كِتاب جافّ a dry book ◼3 [فَظّ] unfriendly; discourteous, blunt; كَلام جافّ unkind words

جَفاف *n* drought; dryness; فَتْرة جَفافٍ drought; يُعاني البَلَدُ من الجَفافِ the country is suffering from drought

تَجْفاف *n* dehydration

تَجَفُّف *n* desiccation

تَجْفيف *n* drainage; drying; تَجْفيف مُسْتَنْقَعٍ marsh drainage; آلة تَجْفيفِ المَلابِسِ dryer

مُجَفَّف *adj* dried; فاكِهة مُجَفَّفة dried fruit; حَليب مُجَفَّف powdered milk

مُجَفِّف ◼A *adj* dehydrating
◼B *n* |مُجَفِّفات| dryer; مُجَفِّف الشَعْرِ hairdryer

جَفَلَ *v* |i-u; جَفْل, جُفول| to be startled; to be frightened; جَفَلَ من شَيْءٍ to be frightened by sth

جَفَّلَ *v* to frighten, to scare

أَجْفَلَ *v* to startle

جافِل *adj* |جُفّال| nervous, shy, timid

جَفْن *n* |جُفون, أَجْفان| eyelid; لم يَغْمُضْ لَهُ جَفْنٌ he did not sleep a wink; نامَ مِلْءَ جَفْنَيْهِ to sleep like a baby

اسْتِجْلاب *n* acquisition, procuring

مَجْلَبة *n* |مَجالِبُ| reason, cause; مَجْلَبة لِأَضْرارٍ cause of injury

مَجْلوب *adj* imported; شَيْء مَجْلوب من الخارِجِ sth imported from abroad

جُلْبان, **جُلُّبان** *n* peas, sweet peas

تَجَلْبَبَ *v* |ب| to wear; تَجَلْبَبَ بِجِلْبابٍ to wear a jilbab

[1] **جَلْجَلَ** *v* |i; جَلْجَلة| to rattle, to clank; to jingle; to rumble, to thunder; جَلْجَلَ الرَّعْدُ to thunder

جُلْجُل *n* |جَلاجِلُ| (little) bell; cowbell; فَضيحة بِجَلاجِلَ (Egypt) a huge scandal

جُلْجُلِيّة *n* rattlesnake; rattle

مُجَلْجِل *adj* resounding; ضَحِكَ ضَحْكةً مُجَلْجِلةً to laugh out loud

[2] **جُلْجُلان** *n* (NA) sesame

جَلِحَ *v* |a; جَلَح| to be/become bold

جَلَّخَ *v* to sharpen

جَلْخ *n* grindstone; grinder

مُجَلِّخ *n* grinder; sharpener

جَلَدَ *v* |i; جَلْد| to whip, to flog; جَلَدَ شَخْصاً بالسَّوْطِ to lash sb with a whip

جَلُدَ *v* |u; جَلْد| to persevere

جَلِدَ *v* |a; جَلَد| to freeze; جَلِدَت الأَرْضُ the ground was frozen

جَلَّدَ *v* **1** [الكِتابَ] to bind; جَلَّدَ كِتاباً to bind a book **2** [جَمَّدَ] to freeze

جالَدَ *v* to fight (with a sword); to duel; جالَدَ شَخْصاً to fight sb (with a sword)

أَجْلَدَ *v* to be frozen

تَجَلَّدَ *v* **1** [تَحَمَّلَ] |على| to endure, to suffer, to bear; to persevere; تَجَلَّدَ على شَيْءٍ to endure sth **2** [تَجَمَّدَ] to freeze; to solidify

جَلْد *n* |أَجْلاد| whipping, flogging; lash; جُلِدَ ١٠٠ جَلْدةٍ he was given 100 lashes

جَلَد *n* **1** [سَماء] sky; firmament **2** [بَرْد] freeze **3** [تَحَمُّل] endurance; sufferance, forbearance

جِلْد *n* |جُلود, أَجْلاد| **1** [مَدْبوغ] leather; من الجِلْدِ leather; جِلْد مُتَرَهِّل a leather chair **2** [بَشَرة] skin; مَقْعَد من الجِلْدِ loose skin; flabby skin; جَفاف الجِلْدِ dry skin; كانَ جِلْداً على عَظْمٍ to be skin and bones

جَلّاد *n* **1** [مُنَفِّذ] executioner **2** [بائِع] leather merchant

جَلْدة *n* lash

جِلْدِيّ *adj* leather; skin (*before n*); سِلَع \ بَضائِع جِلْدِيّة leather goods; قُفّازات جِلْدِيّة leather gloves; مَرَض جِلْدِيّ skin disease

جَليد *n* ice; جَبَل جَليدٍ iceberg; قِطْعة جَليدٍ lump of ice; كاسِحة جَليدٍ icebreaker; طَبَقة جَليدٍ سَميكة \ رَقيقة a thick/thin layer of ice; تَزَحْلُق على الجَليدِ ice skating; skiing; يَذوبُ الجَليدُ the ice is melting; إذابة الجَليد détente

جَليديّ *adj* ice (*before n*); glacial; جَبَل جَليديّ iceberg; نَهْر جَليديّ glacier; انْهِيار جَليديّ avalanche; طَبَقة جَليديّة layer of ice; الغِطاء الجَليديّ (polar) ice cap; العَصْر الجَليديّ the Ice Age

تَجْليد *n* **1** [الكُتُبِ] bookbinding; تَجْليد الكُتُبِ bookbinding **2** [غِطاء] cover, covering

مُجالِد *n* gladiator

مِجْلاد *n* |مَجاليدُ| whip

مُجَلَّد **A** *adj* bound
B *n* |مُجَلَّدات| **1** [جُزْء من مَجْموعةِ كُتُبٍ] volume **2** [غِلاف] binding, cover; في مُجَلَّد in a cover **3** (Comput) folder; directory; مُجَلَّد فَرْعيّ subfolder

مُجَلِّد *n* bookbinder

جَلَسَ *v* |i; جُلوس| to sit (down), to take a seat; جَلَسَ في مَكانٍ to sit down somewhere; جَلَسَ على كُرْسيٍّ to sit on a chair; جَلَسَ على العَرْشِ to sit on the throne; جَلَسَ إلى \ على مائِدةِ الطَّعامِ to sit at the table

جالَسَ *v* to sit with; جالَسَ شَخْصاً to sit with sb

أَجْلَسَ *v* to seat, to ask to sit down

تَجالَسَ *v* to sit with one another; to assemble, to hold a meeting

جالِس **A** *adj* |جالِسونَ, جُلوس| sitting; كانَ أَبي جالِساً على الأَرْضِ my father was sitting on the floor; رَأَيْتُهُمْ وَهُمْ

جُلوسٌ على المائِدةِ I saw them while they were sitting at the table

B *n* participant (*in a gathering*)

جَلْسة *n* meeting, session, gathering; sitting; جَلْسة مُغْلَقة a closed session; جَلْسة سِرّيّة a secret meeting; الجَلْسة الافْتِتاحيّة the opening session; جَلْسة كامِلة a plenary meeting; جَلْسة طارِئة \ اسْتِثْنائيّة an emergency meeting; جَلْسة عامّة \ مَفْتوحة \ عَلَنيّة an open meeting; جَلْسة المَحْكَمةِ court hearing; عَقَدَ جَلْسةً to convene a session; افْتَتَحَ الجَلْسةَ to open the meeting; أَجَّلَ \ رَفَعَ الجَلْسةَ to postpone/adjourn the session; أَلْغى الجَلْسةَ to cancel the meeting; حَضَرَ جَلْسةَ مُؤْتَمَرٍ to attend a conference session; جَلْسة مُنْعَقِدة في الأُسْبوعِ الماضي a session that was held last week

جِلْسة *n* manner of sitting; posture, stance

جُلوس *n* sitting, sitting down; غُرْفة \ حُجْرة الجُلوسِ living room, sitting room (BrE); تَفَضَّلْ بالجُلوسِ please have a seat

جَليس *n* |جُلَساءُ| companion; sitter, minder; جَليس الأَطْفالِ babysitter; خَيْرُ جَليسٍ في الزَمانِ كِتابٌ books are the best companions

مُجالَسة *n* association

مَجْلِس *n* |مَجالِسُ| **1** [لَجْنة] board; council; مَجْلِس تَأْديبيّ disciplinary committee; مَجْلِس قَوْميّ national assembly; مَجْلِس الحِزْبِ party council; مَجْلِس الأَعْيانِ (الأُرْدُنيّ) the (Jordanian) Senate; مَجْلِس الشَعْبِ \ النوّابِ \ الأُمّةِ parliament; عُضْو مَجْلِسِ الشَعْبِ representative of the people, Member of Parliament; مَجْلِس الوُزَراءِ cabinet; مَجْلِس الشُيوخِ \ النوّابِ (الأَمْريكيّ) (US) Senate / House of Representatives; عُضْو مَجْلِسِ الشُيوخِ \ النوّابِ senator/ representative; congressman; مَجْلِس المَجْلِس البَلَديّ \ مَجْلِس البَلَديّةِ town council; اجْتِماع المَجْلِسِ البَلَديِّ council meeting; عُضْو المَجْلِسِ البَلَديِّ (municipal) councillor (BrE) councilman (AmE); مَجْلِس الإدارةِ board (of directors); اجْتِماع مَجْلِسِ الإدارةِ board meeting; مَجْلِس الأَمْنِ (التابع للأُمَمِ المُتَّحِدةِ) the (UN) Security Council **2** (Hist) *a teacher-student gathering*

‹ **جِلِسْرين** *n* glycerine

‹ **جَلَطَ** *v* |i; جَلْط| to scrape

جَلْطة, جُلْطة *n* clot; thrombosis; جُلْطة دَمَويّة blood clot; جُلْطة دِماغيّة stroke; أُصيبَ بالجُلْطةِ to have a clot; to have a stroke; جُلْطة دَمَويّة في الدِماغ a blood clot in the brain

تَجَلُّط *n* coagulation, thrombogenesis; تَجَلُّط وَريديّ عَميق deep-vein thrombosis

‹ **جَلَفَ** *v* |u; جَلْف| to scrape

جَلُفَ *v* |a; جَلافة| to be rude; to be rough

جِلْف **A** *adj* |أَجْلاف| blunt; rough, coarse; impolite, boorish **B** *n* |أَجْلاف| lout

جَلافة *n* rudeness; coarseness

‹ **جَلَكي** *n* (Zool) lamprey

‹[1] **جَلَّ** *v* |i; جَلال| to be great; جَلَّ عن شَيْءٍ to be far above sth; جَلَّ عن الوَصْفِ to be indescribable; اللهُ عَزَّ وَجَلَّ God, the Great and Almighty

جَلَّلَ *v* **1** [عَظَّمَ] to glorify, to praise **2** [غَطّى] to cover; to envelop; جَلَّلَ شَيْئاً ب ... to envelop sth in ...

أَجَلَّ *v* to glorify; to honour; أَجَلَّ اللهَ to glorify God; أَجَلَّ وَاحْتَرَمَ شَخْصاً to honour and respect sb

تَجَلَّلَ *v* to be covered; to be enveloped

جُلّ *n* bulk, majority, major portion; جُلُّهُ most of it; جُلّ حَظِّهِ all his luck; جُلّ الأُمّةِ the majority of people; في جُلِّ الحالاتِ mostly; جُلّ ما في الغُرْفةِ everything in the room

جَلال *n* greatness, sublimity, majesty; ذو الجَلالِ والإِكْرامِ full of Majesty and Generosity (*one of the names of God*)

جَلالة *n* majesty, highness; جَلالَتُهُ His Highness; جَلالَتُكُمْ Your Highness; جَلالة المَلِك(ة) His/Her Royal Highness; صاحِب \ صاحِبة الجَلالةِ His/Her Majesty; لَفْظ الجَلالةِ *the word* الله (*God*)

جُلّة, جِلّة *n* cannonball; shot (*heavy round ball used in shot-put*); رَمْي \ دَفْع الجُلّةِ shot-put

جِلّة *n* جِلّة العُلَماءِ top scientists; top experts

جَلَل *adj* important, weighty

جَليل **A** *adj* |أَجِلّة, جَلائِلُ, أَجِلّاءُ| [عَظيم] splendid, glorious **B** *n* الجَليل the Exalted (*one of the names of God*)

إِجْلال *n* respect, reverence; إِجْلالاً لِشَخْصٍ out of respect for sb; إِجْلالاً لِذِكْرى شَخْصٍ in honour of sb's memory

مَجَلّة *n* magazine, periodical, journal; مَجَلّة أُسْبوعيّة \ شَهْرِيّة \ فَصْلِيّة a weekly/monthly/quarterly (magazine); مَجَلّة دَوْرِيّة a periodical; مَجَلّة نِسْوِيّة a women's magazine; مَجَلّة طِبِّيّة a medical journal; مَجَلّة إِلِكْتْرونِيّة e-zine; مَجَلّة حائطِيّة \ الحائطِ a poster; a bulletin board; مَجَلّة الإذاعة والتِلِفِزْيون radio and television guide; أَصْدَرَ مَجَلّةً to publish a magazine; اشْتَرَكَ في مَجَلّةٍ to subscribe to a journal

مُجَلَّل *adj* covered, enveloped; مُجَلَّل بالعار filled with shame

‹ [2] **جِلّ, جَلّ** *n* gel; جِلّ الاسْتِحْمام shower gel; جِلّ تَثْبيتِ الشَعْرِ hair gel

‹ **جُلَّنار** *n* pomegranate blossom

‹ **جَلَمَ** *v* |i; جَلْم| to shear off; to clip, to snip

‹ **جَلْمَدَ** *v* |i; جَلْمَدة| to petrify

جُلْمود *n* |جَلاميدُ| boulder

‹ **جَلا** *v* |u; جَلاء| 1 [لَمَّعَ] to polish, to burnish; جَلا الفِضّةَ to polish the silver 2 [أَوْضَحَ] to clarify; to show, to uncover; جَلا الحَقيقةَ to uncover the truth 3 [خَرَجَ] to go away, to withdraw; جَلَت القوّاتُ عن \ من المِنْطَقةِ the troops withdrew from the area 4 [أَخْرَجَ] to oust

جَلى *v* |i; جَلْي| to polish, to burnish

جَلّى *v* to show

أَجْلى *v* to evacuate, to remove; to drive away, to oust; أَجْلَوْا السُكّانَ من مَنازِلِهِمْ they evacuated the people from their homes

تَجَلّى *v* to be/become clear/evident; to show itself, to be manifest; تَجَلَّتْ إِرادَتُهُ it became clear what he wanted; تَجَلَّتْ مَوْهِبَتُها her talent was manifest; تَجَلّى في أَبْهى صُوَرِهِ it was crystal clear

انْجَلى *v* 1 [ظَهَرَ] to be/become clear; to be/become visible; انْجَلَت الحَقيقةُ the truth became clear 2 [تَبَدَّدَ] to clear up, to disperse; سَيَنْجَلي اللَيْلُ the night will end; بعد أَنْ يَنْجَلِيَ الغُبارُ after the smoke clears

اجْتَلى *v* to regard, to look

اسْتَجْلى *v* to seek to clarify; اسْتَجْلى الحَقائِقَ to try to ascertain the facts

جَلِيّ *adj* clear, plain, obvious, evident; من بِصورةٍ جَلِيّةٍ evident; من الجَلِيِّ أَنّ ... it is clear that ...

جالِية *n* |جالِيات| (immigrant) community, diaspora; الجالِية اللُبْنانِيّة في أَمْريكا the Lebanese community in the United States; أَبْناء الجالِيةِ المُسْلِمةِ members of the Muslim immigrant community

جَلاء *n* 1 [خُروج] departure, withdrawal; جَلاء الفَرَنْسِيّينَ عن الجَزائِرِ the withdrawal of the French from Algeria; عيد الجَلاء liberation day 2 [إِظْهار] clarification; uncovering, disclosure 3 [تَبَدُّد] dispelling, clearing up; dispersal 4 [وُضوح] clarity

جُلْوة *n* beauty; لَيْلة الجُلْوةِ wedding night

جَلِيّة *n* |جَلايا| fact; جَلِيّة الأَمْرِ the fact of the matter

إِجْلاء *n* 1 [إِخْلاء] evacuation; expulsion, driving away; إِجْلاء المَدَنِيّينَ من مَناطِقِ القِتالِ the evacuation of civilians from the conflict zone; إِجْلاء قُوّاتِ الاحْتِلالِ عن أَراضيهِمْ the expulsion of occupation forces from their lands 2 [سَحْب] withdrawal

اسْتِجْلاء *n* clarification, elucidation; uncovering; اسْتِجْلاء الحَقيقةِ uncovering the truth

مَجْلًى *n* |مَجالٍ| kitchen sink

‹ **جْلوكوما** *n* glaucoma

‹ **الجَليل** *n* Galilee

‹ **جُمادى** *n* |mf| جُمادى الأولى \ الأَوَّل Jumada l-Ula/l-Awwal (*the fifth month of the Islamic calendar*); جُمادى الثاني(ة) \ الآخِر(ة) Jumada l-Thaniy(a)/l-Akhir(a) (*the sixth month of the Islamic calendar*)

‹ **جُمْباز** *n* gymnastics; مارَسَ رِياضةَ الجُمْباز to do gymnastics

جُمْبازِيّ A *adj* gymnastic

B *n* gymnast

‹ **جَمْبَرِيّ** *n* (Egypt) shrimp; قَشَّرَ الجَمْبَرِيَّ to peel shrimps

‹ **جُمْجُمة** *n* |جَماجِمُ| skull, cranium; كَسْر الجُمْجُمةِ skull fracture

جُمْجُمِيّ *n* cranial

جَمَحَ *v* |a; **جُموح, جِماح, جَمْح**| to run away, to bolt; جَمَحَ الحِصانُ the horse bolted; جَمَحَ بِهِ خَيالُهُ his imagination had run away with him

جامِح *adj* 1 [طَليق من كُلِّ قَيْدٍ] extreme; unrestrained, wild; نُموّ جامِح unrestrained growth; غَضَب جامِح unrestrained anger; رَغْبة جامِحة unbridled desire 2 [هائِج] unruly, recalcitrant, refractory; حِصان جامِح an unbroken horse

جِماح *n* recalcitrance, defiance; كَبَحَ جِماحَ شَيْءٍ \ شَخْصٍ to rein sth/sb in, to put a check on sth/sb; كَبَحَ جِماحَ التَضَخُّمِ to rein in inflation

جَموح *adj* unmanageable

جُموح *n* recalcitrance, obstreperousness; uninhibitedness

جَمَدَ, جَمُدَ *v* |u; **جُمود**| 1 [صَلُبَ] to freeze; to solidify, to congeal; جَمَدَ الشَمْعِ the wax solidified 2 [تَوَقَّفَ] to be/become fixed/rigid; جَمَدَ نَظَرُهُ his look grew fixed; جَمَدَتْ أفْكارُهُ he is rigid in his ideas

جَمَّدَ *v* 1 [بالبُرودةِ] to freeze; to congeal; جَمَّدَ شَيْئاً to freeze sth; جَمَّدَ الخُضَرَ \ اللَحْمَ to freeze vegetables/meat; جَمَّدَتِ البُرودةُ أَطْرافي the cold stiffened my limbs 2 [أَبْقاهُ في وَضْعِهِ] to freeze, to block; to immobilize; جَمَّدَ شَيْئاً to put sth on ice; جَمَّدَ العَلاقاتِ (الدِبْلوماسيّة) to freeze (diplomatic) relations; جَمَّدَ أَرْصِدةَ \ حِسابَ شَخْصٍ to freeze sb's assets/account; جَمَّدَ الحَدَّ الأدْنى للأُجورِ to freeze the minimum wage

تَجَمَّدَ *v* 1 [بالبُرودةِ] to freeze; تَجَمَّدَتِ البِرْكةُ the pond has frozen up; تَجَمَّدَتِ النَوافِذُ the windows have frosted over; تَجَمَّدَتْ يداي my hands are freezing; تَجَمَّدَ بالبَرْدِ to grow numb with cold 2 [في مَكانِهِ] to freeze, to be immobilized; to be/get stuck; تَجَمَّدَ البَرْنامَجُ the program has frozen; تَجَمَّدَ في مَكانِهِ to stop dead in one's tracks 3 [صَلُبَ] to solidify

جَمَد *n* ice; frost

جامِد *adj* |**جَوامِدُ**| 1 [صُلْب] solid, hard; stiff; rigid; قالِب جامد a stereotype; مَوْقِف جامِد a rigid stand; نَظْرة جامِدة a glassy look; بِوَجْهٍ جامِدٍ stone-faced; بالمَعْنى الجامِدِ للكَلِمةِ in the narrowest sense of the word 2 [مُبَرَّد] frozen

جَماد *n* |**جَمادات**| inanimate body/being; بَقِيَ كَجَمادٍ to stand stock-still

جُمود *n* 1 [رُكود] solidity, solidness; stiffness, rigidity; deadlock, standstill; جُمود العَقْلِ the rigidity of the mind; جُمود العَلاقاتِ freezing relations; اسْتِمْرار حالةِ الجُمودِ the continuing impasse; كَسَرَ الجُمودَ to break the deadlock; تَمُرُّ المُفاوَضاتُ بِمَرْحَلةِ جُمودٍ the talks have reached total deadlock 2 [تَجَمُّد] freezing 3 [خُمول] inertia, inactivity

انْجِماد *n* freezing up/over

تَجَمُّد *n* freezing; coagulation; solidification; دَرَجة \ نُقْطة التَجَمُّدِ freezing point

تَجْميد *n* 1 [بالبُرودةِ] freezing, freeze 2 [البَقاء في وَضْعِهِ] freezing; freeze, block; immobilization, suspension; تَجْميد الأُجورِ \ الرَواتِبِ wage freeze; تَجْميد عُضْوِيّةِ شَخْصٍ suspension of sb's membership

مُتَجَمِّد *adj* frozen; بَحْر مُتَجَمِّد frozen sea; كانَ مُتَجَمِّداً من البَرْدِ to be frozen stiff with cold

مُجَمَّد *adj* frozen; immobile, stalled; لَحْم مُجَمَّد frozen meat; أَجِنّة مُجَمَّدة frozen embryos; مُفاوَضات مُجَمَّدة stalled negotiations; أَرْصِدة \ حِساب مُجَمَّد(ة) frozen assets/account

مُجَمِّد *n* freezer; freezer compartment

مُجَمِّدة *n* deep freeze, freezer

جَمَّرَ *v* to roast

جَمْر *n* 1 [بَصْوة] ember, firebrand, live coal; كانَ على أَحَرَّ من الجَمْرِ to be on tenterhooks 2 [حَصاة] small stone, pebble; رَمْي الجَمْراتِ Stoning of the Devil (*part of the Hajj ritual*)

Idiom الجَمْرة الخَبيثة anthrax

جُمّار *n* palm pith

مُجَمَّر *adj* roasted, grilled

مِجْمَرة *n* brazier; censer

جُمْرُك *n* |**جَمارِكُ**| customs; مَكْتَب جَمارِكَ customs office; مُوَظَّف جَمارِكَ customs officer; مَرَّ بالجَمارِكِ to go through customs

جُمْرُكي *adj* customs (*before n*); إجْراءات جُمْرُكيّة customs procedures; رُسوم جُمْرُكيّة tariff; تَعْرِفة \ تَعْريفة جُمْرُكيّة customs duties

جُمَّيْز *n* sycamore (fig) (*Ficus sycomorus*)

جُمَّيْز *n* listed alphabetically

جَمَشْت *n* amethyst

جَمَعَ *v* |a; جَمْع| **1** [لَمَّ] to gather, to collect; to raise; جَمَعَ مالاً to raise money; جَمَعَ ثَروةً to accumulate a fortune; جَمَعَ تَبَرُّعاتٍ to collect donations; جَمَعَ تَبَرُّعاتٍ لِعَمَلٍ صالِحٍ to raise money for a good cause; جَمَعَ مُعْطَياتٍ \ مَعْلوماتٍ to gather data/intelligence; جَمَعَ طَوابِعَ البَريدِ to collect stamps; جَمَعَ النُفاياتِ المَنْزِليّةَ to collect refuse (BrE), to pick up the garbage (AmE) **2** [أَلْحَقَ] to unite, to bring together, to join; to assemble; جَمَعَ بين شَيْئَيْنِ to join two things together; جَمَعَ بين شَخْصَيْنِ to pair off two people; جَمَعَ شَمْلَهُمْ they were reunited; جَمَعَ بَيْنَهُما الزَواجُ they were united in matrimony **3** (Math) to add (up); جَمَعَ أَعْداداً \ مَبالِغَ to add up numbers/amounts **4** (Ling) to pluralize

جَمَّعَ *v* **1** [لَمَّ] to gather, to collect; to assemble, to bring together; to raise; جَمَّعَ النّاسَ to bring people together; جَمَّعَ صُفوفَهُ to regroup; جَمَّعَ مِياهَ الأَمْطارِ to collect rainwater **2** (Comput) to assemble

جامَعَ *v* to have intercourse with, to copulate with; جامَعَ شَخْصاً to have intercourse with sb

أَجْمَعَ *v* to agree unanimously, to be agreed; أَجْمَعَ الأَعْضاءُ على أنّ ... the members were unanimously agreed that ...

تَجَمَّعَ *v* to assemble, to meet; to gather, to congregate; تَجَمَّعَ مِئاتُ المُتَظاهِرينَ أمامَ البَرْلَمانِ hundreds of demonstrators gathered in front of parliament building; تَجَمَّعَت الغُيومُ في السَماءِ clouds gathered in the sky

اجْتَمَعَ *v* to meet, to assemble, to sit; to gather, to congregate; اجْتَمَعَ عند شَخْصٍ to gather at sb's (place); اجْتَمَعَ في ساحةٍ to congregate in a square; اجْتَمَعَ في جَلْسةٍ عاجِلةٍ to meet in an emergency session; اجْتَمَعَ كُلَّ يَوْمِ اثْنَيْنِ to meet every Monday

اسْتَجْمَعَ *v* to gather, to collect; اسْتَجْمَعَ شَجاعَتَهُ to muster up one's courage; اسْتَجْمَعَ أَفْكارَهُ to gather one's thoughts

جامِع **A** *adj* comprehensive; مَشْروع جامِع a comprehensive plan; دِراسة جامِعة an exhaustive study **B** *n* **1** [مَسْجِد] |جَوامِعُ| mosque; جامِع الأَزْهَر al-Azhar mosque **2** [شَخْص] |جامِعونَ| collector; جامِع طَوابِعَ stamp collector **3** [من أَسْماءِ اللهِ] الجامِع the Gatherer (*one of the names of God*)

جامِعة *n* **1** [مُؤَسَّسة للتَعْليم العالي] university, college (AmE); خِرّيج جامِعةٍ university graduate; حَرَم الجامِعةِ campus; رَئيس مَجْلِسِ الجامِعةِ university rector (BrE), university president (AmE); عَمِلَ في الجامِعةِ to work at the university; دَرَسَ في الجامِعةِ to study at university (BrE), to be in college (AmE) **2** [اتِّحاد] union, league; جامِعة الأُمَمِ League of Nations; الجامِعة العَرَبيّة the Arab League; جامِعة الدُوَلِ العَرَبيّةِ the League of Arab States

جامِعيّ *adj* academic, university (*after n*), college (*after n*) (AmE); مُسْتَشْفى جامِعيّ a teaching hospital; مُسْتَوى جامِعيّ university-level; a university-level education; أُسْتاذ جامِعيّ university teacher, college professor (AmE); تَعْليم جامِعيّ higher education; دِراسة جامِعيّة university study; تَكْوين \ مُؤَسَّسة جامِعيّ(ة) a university education/institution

جِماع *n* (sexual) intercourse, copulation, coitus

جَماعة *n* group; community; community of faith; company, collective; صَلاة الجَماعة the congregational prayer; جَماعة من الفَنّانينَ a collective of artists; (عاش) ضِمْنَ جَماعةٍ (to live) in a community; انْضَمَّ إلى الجَماعةِ to join the group; يَدُ اللهِ مع الجَماعةِ ≈ union is strength

جَماعيّ *adj* collective; mass; communal; جَماعيًّا en masse, (all) together; تَناوُل الوَجْباتِ جَماعيًّا eating meals together; عَمَل جَماعيّ teamwork; إبادة جَماعيّة genocide; مَقْبَرة جَماعيّة a mass grave; اغْتِصاب جَماعيّ gang rape; اتِّفاق جَماعيّ a collective agreement; تَمْويل جَماعيّ crowdfunding; حُضور جَماعيّ a massive turnout; إقالة جَماعيّة mass lay-offs; رِياضة جَماعيّة a team sport; انْتِخابات جَماعيّة municipal elections; المَصْلَحة الجَماعيّة the common good

جَمْع *n* |**جُموع**| ⓵ [تَجْميع] gathering; collection; compilation; جَمْع المُعْطَياتِ data collection; جَمْع تَبَرُّعاتٍ fund raising; جَمْع الطَوابِعِ stamp collecting; جَمْع الشَمْلِ ,لَمّ الجَمْعِ reunification ⓶ (Gram) plural; جَمْع مُكَسَّر \ التَكْسيرِ broken plural; اسْم جَمْعٍ a collective noun; في (صيغةِ) الجَمْعِ (in the) plural ⓷ (Math) addition; sum

جُمْعة ,جُمُعة *n* |**جُمْعات ,جُمَع**| Friday; يَوْم الجُمْعةِ Friday; الجُمْعة الحَزينة \ العَظيمة Good Friday; صَلاة الجُمْعةِ Friday prayers; خُطْبة الجُمْعةِ Friday sermon; سورة الجُمُعة The Congregation (*Sura 62*)

جَمْعَويّ *adj* associative; إطار جَمْعَويّ associative executive

جَمْعيّ *adj* collective; وَعْي جَمْعيّ collective consciousness

جَمْعيّة *n* society, association, club; corporation, organization; جَمْعيّة سِرّيّة a secret society; الجَمْعيّة العامّة the General Assembly; الجَمْعيّة التَشْريعيّة the legislation assembly; جَمْعيّة تَعاوُنيّة a cooperative (society), a co-op; أَسَّسَ جَمْعيّةً تَعاوُنيّةً to establish a cooperative; جَمْعيّة غَيْر حُكوميّةٍ non-governmental organization, NGO; جَمْعيّة حُقوقِ الإنْسانِ Human Rights League; إدارة الجَمْعيّةِ the association board

جَميع *n* all; الجَميع all people; جَميعاً all, everybody, one and all; في جَميعِ أَنْحاءِ العالَمِ in all parts of the world; في مُتَناوَلِ (يَدِ) الجَميعِ available to everyone; هذا جَميعُهُ ضدّ القانونِ this is entirely against the law; فَشِلَتْ مُبادَراتُ الأُمَمِ المُتَّحِدةِ جَميعُها all the UN initiatives have failed

اجْتِماع *n* |**اجْتِماعات**| ⓵ [جَلْسة] meeting, gathering, assembly; اجْتِماع طارِئ emergency meeting; اجْتِماع مُطَوَّل a prolonged meeting; اجْتِماع مُصَغَّر a small meeting; اجْتِماع عاديّ \ غَيْر عاديٍّ an ordinary/extraordinary meeting; اجْتِماع سِرّيّ \ مُغْلَق a secret/closed meeting; اجْتِماع الأَعْضاءِ \ عامّ a general meeting; مَحْضَر الاجْتِماعِ the minutes of the meeting; جَدْوَل أَعْمالِ اجْتِماعٍ meeting agenda; قاعة \ غُرْفة الاجْتِماعِ meeting room; رَأَسَ اجْتِماعاً to chair a meeting; عَقَدَ اجْتِماعاً to convene a meeting; افْتَتَحَ \ حَضَرَ اجْتِماعاً to open/attend a meeting; أَنْهى الاجْتِماعَ to call the meeting to a close; كانَ في اجْتِماعٍ to be in session ⓶ [مُجْتَمَع] society; عِلْم الاجْتِماعِ sociology; social studies; أُسْتاذ عِلْمِ الاجْتِماعِ professor of sociology; عالِم اجْتِماعٍ sociologist ⓷ [تَجَمُّع] meeting, assembly; حَقّ الاجْتِماعِ freedom of assembly

اجْتِماعيّ *adj* social; societal; sociological, socio-; community (*before n*); نَشاط اجْتِماعيّ community work; بَحْث اجْتِماعيّ sociological research; حَيَوان اجْتِماعيّ a social animal; حَياة اجْتِماعيّة social life; عُزْلة اجْتِماعيّة social isolation; ظُروف \ عَلاقات اجْتِماعيّة social conditions/relationships; شَبَكة اجْتِماعيّة social network; إعْلام اجْتِماعيّ social media; خِدْمة \ مُساعَدة اجْتِماعيّة social service; المَشاكِل الاجْتِماعيّة الكَبيرة major social problems; اجْتِماعيّ ثَقافيّ sociocultural; اجْتِماعيّ اقْتِصاديّ socio-economic; عَدَم المُساواةِ الاجْتِماعيّةِ social inequality

إجْماع *n* unanimity, consensus, (general) agreement, concurrence; بالإجْماع with one accord; إجْماع في الرَّأْيِ agreement; الإجْماع على هذا المَوْضوعِ the consensus on this topic; قَرَّرَ بالإجْماعِ to decide by unanimous consensus; اتَّفَقَ (على شَيْءٍ) بالإجْماعِ to agree unanimously (on sth); قَبِلَ \ رَفَضَ اقْتِراحاً بالإجْماعِ to adopt/reject a proposal unanimously

إجْماعيّ *adj* unanimous, by common assent; قَرار \ حُكْم إجْماعيّ a unanimous decision/judgement

أَجْمَع *adj* |dipt; **أَجْمَعون**; f **جَمْعاءُ**; f pl **جُمَعُ**| whole, entire; entirely, totally, wholly; all; بِأَجْمَعِهِ entirely; العالَم أَجْمَعُهُ \ أَجْمَع \ بِأَجْمَعِهِ the whole world; العالَم الإسْلاميّ أَجْمَع the entire Islamic world; جاءَ القَوْمُ أَجْمَعُهُمْ \ بِأَجْمَعِهِمْ all the people came

تَجَمُّع *n* ⓵ [اجْتِماع] meeting, gathering; group; clustering; تَجَمُّع سِياسيّ a political grouping; a political rally; تَجَمُّع عائِليّ a family gathering; تَجَمُّع ناسٍ gathering; نُقْطة تَجَمُّعٍ gathering/rallying point; تَجَمُّع شَرِكاتٍ a conglomerate, a consortium ⓶ [مَبانٍ] complex; تَجَمُّع صِناعيّ an industrial complex; تَجَمُّع سُكّانيّ \ سَكَنيّ a housing block; an apartment complex; تَجَمُّع تِجاريّ a shopping centre, a mall (AmE)

تَجَمُّعيّ *adj* *relating to meeting/gathering*; collective

تَجْميع *n* ⓵ [جَمْع] collection, gathering; assembly; مَصْنَع تَجْميعِ سَيّاراتٍ auto assembly plant ⓶ (Math) grouping, proof; مَجْموعة شَرِكاتٍ \ مَصارِفَ consortium/bank group; كَوَّنَ مَجْموعةً to في مَجْموعاتٍ صَغيرةٍ in small groups; form a cluster/group/faction; شَكَّلَ مَجْموعةً to build up a collection **2** (Pol) union; community; المَجْموعة الأوروبّيّة European Community, EC; الدُوَل الأَعْضاء للمَجْموعة member states of the EC; انْضَمَّ إلى مَجْموعةٍ الأوروبّيّةِ to join a union **3** (Sport) set; group; المَجْموعة الأولى \ الأخيرة the first/last set; رَبِحَ \ خَسِرَ مَجْموعةً to win/lose a set

مُسْتَجْمَع *n* basin; مُسْتَجْمَع مائيّ watershed

[2] **ج.م.ع.** *abbr* Arab Republic of Egypt (*abbreviation of* جُمْهوريّة مِصْرَ العَرَبيّة)

[1] **جَمَلَ** *v* |u; جَمْل| to summarize

جَمُلَ *v* |u; جَمال| to be/become beautiful

جَمَّلَ *v* to adorn, to embellish, to beautify; to make up, to put on make-up; جَمَّلَ الوَجْهَ to beautify; (fig) to whitewash, to present a false face

جامَلَ *v* to compliment; to flatter; جامَلَ شَخْصاً to flatter sb

أَجْمَلَ *v* **1** [جَمَعَ] to sum up; to add **2** [أَوْجَزَ] to summarize; to outline

تَجَمَّلَ *v* to make oneself up, to adorn oneself

جَمال *n* **1** [حُسْن] beauty; جَمال باهِر \ رائِع a ravishing beauty; مَلِكة جَمالٍ beauty queen; عِلْم الجَمالِ aesthetics; اخْتِصاصيّ في عِلْمِ الجَمالِ aesthetician, beautician; جَمال المَنْظَرِ الطَبيعيّ the beauty of the landscape **2** [اسْم شَخْصيّ] Jamal (*male given name*)

جَماليّ *adj* aesthetic; من الناحِيةِ الجَماليّةِ aesthetically

جَماليّة *n* aesthetics

جُمْلة *n* |جُمَل| **1** (Ling) sentence; clause; جُمْلة رَئيسيّة main clause; جُمْلة مُرَكَّبة a compound sentence; جُمْلة اعْتِراضيّة \ مُعْتَرِضة parenthetical clause; جُمْلة فِعْليّة \ اسْميّة verbal/nominal sentence; جُمْلة موسيقيّة a musical phrase; شِبْه جُمْلةٍ phrase; بِناء الجُمْلةِ syntax **2** [كُلّ] whole, entire, total; جُمْلةً altogether, wholly, completely; جُمْلةً وَتَفْصيلاً entirely, completely, fully; في جُمْلَتِه in its entirety; في الجُمْلةِ \ بِ on the whole, at large; من جُمْلةِ الأُمورِ نَذْكُرُ ... of all these things we mention ... **3** [كَمّيّة كَبيرة] bulk; بالجُمْلةِ in bulk;

association; قانون التَجْميعِ associative property

تَجْميعيّ *adj* associative; assembly (*before n*); عَمَليّة تَجْميعيّة (Math) associative property; خَطّ إنْتاجٍ تَجْميعيٍّ assembly line

لااجْتِماعيّ *adj* anti-social

مُجامَعة *n* coitus, sexual intercourse

مُجْتَمَع *n* society; community, collective; مُجْتَمَع اسْتِهْلاكيّ consumer society; مُجْتَمَع مُتَكافِل \ مُتَرابِط a caring/close-knit society; المُجْتَمَع المُعاصِر \ الغَرْبيّ modern/western society; المُجْتَمَع الدُوَليّ the international community; شَرائِح المُجْتَمَع segments of society

مُجْتَمِع *adv* **1** [معاً] together, all together; هذه كُلُّها مُجْتَمِعةً all in all **2** [مُشارِك في اجْتِماعٍ] *participant in a meeting*

مُجْتَمَعيّ *adj* social; مَشاكِل مُجْتَمَعيّة social problems

مَجْمَع *n* |مَجامِعُ| academy; مَجْمَع فَنّيّ art academy; مَجْمَع اللُغة language institute

مُجَمَّع *n* complex; مُجَمَّع صِحّيّ clinic; مُجَمَّع سَكَنيّ housing block; apartment complex; مُجَمَّع تِجاريّ shopping centre, mall (AmE)

مُجَمِّع *n* (Elec) collector

مَجْموع *n* |مَجاميعُ| **1** (Busn) total, sum; total amount; يَبْلُغُ المَجْموعُ عِشْرينَ دولار the total comes to twenty dollars; مَجْموع كُلّيّ sum total **2** [جُمْلة] totality; system; مَجْموع مَجْموع من المُشارِكينَ the total number of participants; مَجْموع من القَوانينِ والأَحْكامِ a body of rules and regulations **3** (Math) sum; مَجْموع ٣ و ٤ the sum of 3 and 4

مَجْموعة *n* |مَجاميعُ, مَجْموعات| **1** [فِئة] group; collection; cluster; selection; faction; المَجْموعة الشَمْسيّة the solar system; مَجْموعة قِصَصيّة a collection of short stories; مَجْموعة كامِلة \ فَريدة \ واسِعة a complete/unique/extensive collection; مَجْموعة كَبيرة من الناسِ a large group of people; مَجْموعة من الأَصْدِقاءِ a group of friends; مَجْموعة من الجُزُرِ archipelago; مَجْموعة من الكُتُبِ \ الأُسْطُواناتِ a collection of books/records; مَجْموعة من التَجْهيزاتِ \ الاقْتِراحاتِ \ الأَنْشِطةِ a set of provisions/proposals/activities; مَجْموعة من العَوامِلِ \ المُقْتَرَحاتِ \ التَصْريحاتِ a series of factors/recommendations/statements; مَجْموعة من الأَدِلّةِ a chain of

اتَّخَذَت الحُكومةُ جُمْلَةً من الإجْراءاتِ بَيْع بالجُمْلَةِ wholesale; the government has taken a number of measures ❹ [نِظام] system; الجُمْلة العَصَبيّة the nervous system

جَميل 🅰 *adj* beautiful, pretty; handsome; lovely, graceful; nice, pleasant; فَتاة جَميلة a pretty girl; a beautiful young woman; رَجُل جَميل a handsome man; جَوّ جَميل fine weather; a good atmosphere; لَوْحة جَميلة a beautiful painting; موسيقى جَميلة lovely music; الفُنون الجَميلة the fine arts

🅱 *n* |جَمائِل| ❶ [خِدْمة] favour, service; اعْتِراف بالجَميلِ gratitude; مُعْتَرِف بالجَميلِ grateful; نُكْران الجَميلِ ingratitude ❷ [اسْم شَخْصيّ] Jamil (*male given name*)

جَميلة *n* |dipt| Jamila (*female given name*)

إجْمال *n* whole; generalization; total; على (وَجْهِ) الإجْمالِ in general; إجْمالاً in sum, in total; يَبْلُغُ عَدَدُهُمْ إجْمالاً حَوالَيْ مِائةٍ they number about one hundred in total

إجْماليّ 🅰 *adj* total, comprehensive, overall, gross; رِبْح إجْماليّ gross profit; الوَزْن الإجْماليّ gross weight; الكُلْفة \ القيمة الإجْماليّة the total cost/value; المَبْلَغ \ الدخْل الإجْماليّ the gross amount/income; تَقْدير إجْماليّ للميزانيّة an overall budget; إجْماليّ الحَصيلةِ the total yield

🅱 *n* total

أَجْمَل *adj* |dipt| more beautiful; the most beautiful; أَجْمَل فَتاةٍ the most beautiful girl

تَجْميل *n* beautification; تَجْميل وَجْهِ \ صورة شَيْءٍ making sth look better, whitewashing sth; تَجْميل وَجْهِ النِظامِ whitewashing the regime's image; جِراحة التَجْميل plastic/cosmetic surgery; اخْتِصاصيّ \ أَخِصّائيّة التَجْميلِ make-up artist, cosmetician; مُسْتَحْضَرات \ مَساحيق \ مَوادّ التَجْميل cosmetics, make-up

تَجْميليّ *adj* cosmetic, beautifying; جِراحة تَجْميليّة plastic/cosmetic surgery

مُجامِل *adj* complimentary

مُجامَلة *n* courtesy; compliment, flattery; من بابِ المُجامَلةِ out of courtesy, as a courtesy; زِيارة مُجامَلةٍ courtesy call; تَلَقّى مُجامَلةً to receive a compliment; المُجامَلات والكِذْب flattery and lies; مُجَرَّد مُجامَلاتٍ nothing but flattery; لم أَقُلْ هذا مُجامَلةً I do not say this to flatter

مُجْمَل *n* ❶ [كُلّ] whole, total, overall; كانَ الأَمْرُ بِمُجْمَلِهِ مُثيراً the issue was exciting as a whole; يُشَكِّلُ الأَجانِبُ ١٠٪ من مُجْمَلِ السُكّانِ foreigners make up 10% of the population ❷ [خُلاصة] summary

جَمّال *n* camel driver

جَمَل *n* |جِمال| camel; dromedary; جَمَل عَرَبيّ Arabian camel; الجَمَل لا يَرى حَدَبَتَهُ one never see one's own faults; لا ناقةَ لَهُ في الأَمْرِ ولا جَمَلَ he doesn't have anything to do with it; it's none of his business

جَمَلون *n* gable

جَمَّ *v* |u; جَمّ| to rest

جَمَّمَ *v* to thrive, to flourish

اسْتَجَمَّ *v* to rest, to relax; to take a break, to take a holiday (BrE) vacation (AmE); to spend time; تَسْتَجِمُّ في تُرْكِيا she is holidaying (BrE) vacationing (AmE) in Turkey

جَمّ *adj* major part

جُمّة *n* |جُمَم| wig

جَموم *adj* inexhaustible; filled with water (*of a well*)

اسْتِجْمام *n* relaxation, recreation, leisure; مَكان اسْتِجْمامٍ recreation area; رِحْلة اسْتِجْمامٍ holiday (BrE), vacation (AmE)

جُمان *n coll* pearls

جُمانة *n* |dipt| Jumana (*female given name*)

جِمْنازيوم *n* gymnasium

تَجَمْهَرَ *v* to gather, to flock (together)

جَماهيريّ *adj relating to a crowd*; حُضور جَماهيريّ a massive turnout; إقْبال جَماهيريّ a tremendous reception

جَماهيريّة *n* (Hist) People's Republic (*Libya under Gaddafi*)

جَمْهَرة *n* ❶ [جُمْهور] multitude, crowd, throng; جَمْهَرة كَبيرة من الناسِ a large crowd of people ❷ [مَصْدَر] crowding

جُمْهور *n coll* |no singular noun; جَماهيرُ| ❶ [حَشْد] crowd, multitude, mass; الجَماهير the masses; خاطَبَ الجُمْهورَ to address the crowd; جُمْهور من المُتَفَرِّجينَ a crowd of spectators ❷ [حُضور] audience; جُمْهور عَريض \ واسِع a wide audience; جُمْهور المَسْرَحِ theatre audience; جَذَبَ

الجُمْهورَ to attract an audience

جُمْهوريّ A *adj* Republican; الحِزْب الجُمْهوريّ the Republican party

B *n* Republican

جُمْهوريّة *n* republic; جُمْهوريّة مِصْرَ العَرَبيّة the Arab Republic of Egypt; جُمْهوريّة الصين الشَعْبيّة the People's Republic of China; الجُمْهوريّة العَرَبيّة المُتَّحدة United Arab Republic; جُمْهوريّة أَلْمانيا الاتِّحاديّة the Federal Republic of Germany; أَعْلَنَ الجُمْهوريّةَ to proclaim the republic

تَجَمْهُر *n* gathering; تَجَمْهُر الناسِ crowd; حَظْر التَجَمْهُر gathering ban; التَجَمْهُر غَيْر المَشْروعِ unlawful assembly

جَنَبَ *v* |u; جَنْب, جَنابة| to avoid; جَنَبَ شَيْئاً to avoid sth

جَنَّبَ *v* to spare; to keep off; جَنَّبَ شَخْصاً شَيْئاً to spare sb sth

جانَبَ *v* to avoid; to skirt; جانَبَهُ الصَوابُ to not be in the right

تَجَنَّبَ *v* to avoid, to shun, to keep away, to steer clear; تَجَنَّبَ شَخْصاً to avoid sb; تَجَنَّبَ شَيْئاً to keep away from sth; تَجَنَّبَ سُؤالاً to parry a question; تَجَنَّبَ الخَوْضَ \ الدُخولَ في شَيْءٍ to avoid getting into sth, to avoid delving into sth

اجْتَنَبَ *v* to avoid

جَنْب *n* |أَجْناب, جُنوب| 1 [جِهة] side; جَنْبَ near; beside; جَنْبَ المَكْتَبِ beside the office; جَنْباً إلى جَنْبٍ side by side; يوجَدُ المَقْهى جَنْبَ الصَيْدَليّةِ the cafe is next to the pharmacy

2 (Anat) side, flank; الجَنْبُ الأَيْسَر \ الأَيْمَن the left/right side; أَحَسَّ في جَنْبِهِ أَلَماً to have a pain in one's side; ذات الجَنْبِ (Med) pleurisy

جُنُب *adj* in a state of major ritual impurity (Islamic Law)

جانِب *n* |جَوانِبُ| 1 [جِهة] side; part; جانِباً aside; من جانِبِ by; إلى جانِبِ \ ب near, next to, beside; على الجانِبَيْنِ on both sides; جانِب أَيْمَن \ أَيْسَر right/left side; الجانِب الخَلْفيّ the back; الجانِب الغَرْبيّ the western side; الجانِب المُقابِل the opposite side; جانِب جَبَلٍ a mountainside; وَضَعَ شَيْئاً جانِباً to put sth aside; تَرَكَ مَوْضوعاً \ قَضيّةً جانِباً to let a subject/matter drop; وَقَفَ إلى جانِبِ شَخْصٍ to stand by sb; انْحازَ إلى جانِبِ شَخْصٍ to side with sb; كانَ واقِفاً جانِباً to stand aside; لِنَدَعْ هذا جانِباً ... putting that aside, ...; من جانِبٍ واحِدٍ one-sided; من كُلِّ الجَوانِبِ from all sides; إلى جانِبِ ذلك besides; من جانِبٍ ... وَمِنْ جانِبٍ آخَرَ ... on the one hand ... on the other hand ...; في الجانِبِ المُقابِلِ للشارعِ across the street; على جانِبٍ كَبيرٍ من الأَهَمّيّة of vital importance 2 [الجِسْم] side, flank, waist; أَلَم في الجانِبِ الأَيْسَرِ \ الأَيْمَنِ a pain in one's left/right side; هَجَمَ على العَدوِّ من الجانِبِ to attack the flanks of the enemy 3 [مَجْموعة] side, party; مُتَعَدِّد الجَوانِب multilateral; مُحادَثات مُتَعَدِّدة الجَوانِبِ multilateral talks; اتَّفَقَ الجانِبانِ على ... the two sides agreed to ... 4 [مَسْأَلة] aspect, facet, perspective; جَوانِب مُضيئة illuminating aspects; جَوانِب مُظْلِمة drawbacks; تَعَدُّد الجَوانِبِ multifaceted; دَرَسَ المَوْضوعَ من جَوانِبِهِ المُخْتَلِفةِ he studied the issue from different perspectives

جانِبيّ *adj* lateral, sideward, side, by-; تَأْثير جانِبيّ side effect; by-product; مَسْأَلة جانِبيّة a side issue; أَضْرار جانِبيّة collateral damage; unintended consequences; قَفْزة \ حَرَكة \ ضَغْط جانِبيّ(ة) a lateral leap/movement/pressure

جانِبيّة *n* profile

جَناب *n* جَنابُكُمْ Your Honour

جَنْبة *n* |جَنَبات| 1 [مِنْطَقة] في جَنَباتِ inside; كَظَمَ في جَنَباتِهِ ما أَحَسَّ بِهِ من أَلَمٍ he kept the pain he felt hidden deep down inside 2 (Bot) shrub

جَنوب *n* south; جَنوباً southward; جَنوبَ باريس to the south of Paris; في جَنوبِ المَغْرِب the south of Morocco

جَنوبيّ *adj* southern, south; إفْريقيا الجَنوبيّة South Africa; أَمْريكا الجَنوبيّة South America; في جِهةٍ جَنوبيّةٍ in a southerly direction

اجْتِناب *n* avoidance; abstinence

أَجْنَبيّ A *adj* |أَجانِبُ, أَجْنَبيّونَ| foreign, alien; exotic; strange; عُمّال أَجانِب foreign workers; لُغات أَجْنَبيّة foreign languages; السُكّان الأَجانِب the foreign population; نَباتات \ حَيَوانات أَجْنَبيّة exotic plants/animals; من أَصْلٍ أَجْنَبيٍّ of foreign descent

B *n* |أَجانِبُ, أَجْنَبيّونَ| foreigner, alien; immigrant; stranger; قانون الأَجانِبِ immigration law; العَداء ضدّ الأَجانِبِ aggression against foreigners

تَجَنُّب *n* avoidance; prevention; حاوَلَ تَجَنُّبَ شَيْءٍ to try and avoid sth; لِتَجَنُّبِ كُلِّ سوءِ تَفاهُمٍ to prevent any misunderstandings

تَجْنيب *n* keeping off

جُنْباز *n* see جُمْباز

جُنْجُل *n* (common) hop (*Humulus lupulus*); hops

جَنَحَ *v* |a; جُنوح| **1** [مالَ] to incline, to be inclined; جَنَحَ إلى \ ل to incline to **2** [السَفينةُ] to get stranded; to run aground; جَنَحَت السَفينةُ the ship ran aground; جَنَحَت الحيتانُ على الشاطِئِ the whales were beached

جَنَّحَ *v* to equip with wings

أَجْنَحَ *v* to make incline

جَنْح *n* side; في جَنْحِ الظَلامِ \ اللَيْلِ under cover of darkness/the night

جانِح **A** *adj* **1** [مُنْتَهِك للقانون] delinquent; الشُبّان الجانِحونَ juvenile offenders **2** [السُفُن] stranded; run aground; باخِرة جانِحة a ship run aground; حوت جانِح a beached whale
B *n* delinquent

جانِحة *n* |جَوانِحُ| rib

جَناح *n* |أَجْنِحة, أَجْنُح| **1** [طَيْرٍ أو طائرةٍ] wing; جَناح أَيْمَن \ أَيْسَر right /left wing; جَناح خَلْفيّ rear spoiler; مَقْصوص الجَناح powerless; نَشَرَ \ بَسَطَ جَناحَيْهِ to spread one's wings; على جَناحِ السُرْعة at breakneck speed; جَناح طولُهُ ٣٢ مِتْراً a wingspan of 32 metres; تحت جَناح اللَيْلِ \ الظَلامِ (fig) under the cover of darkness **2** (Mil) flank; الهُجوم على الجَناح الأَيْمَنِ an attack on the right flank **3** [مَبْنًى] wing; suite; pavilion; الجَناح الغَرْبيّ للبَيْتِ الأَبْيَضِ the West Wing of the White House; الجَناح الجَديد للمُسْتَشْفى the hospital's new wing **4** (Pol) wing; جَناح يَمينيّ \ أَيْمَن right (wing); الجَناح العَسْكَريّ the armed wing; الجَناح الأَيْسَر \ الأَيْمَن لِحِزْبٍ the left/right wing of a party; الجَناح السِياسيّ لِمُنَظَّمةٍ the political wing of an organization **5** (Sport) wing; flank; winger; جَناح أَيْمَن \ أَيْسَر right-winger/left-winger; لاعِب جَناح winger; لَعِبَ في الجَناح الأَيْمَنِ \ الأَيْسَرِ to play on the right/left wing

جُنْحة *n* |جُنَح| offence, crime; misdemeanor; مَحْكَمة الجُنَحِ misdemeanor court

جُنوح *n* **1** [السُفُن] stranding, running aground **2** [مَيْل إلى الإِجْرام] delinquency

جُنَيْح *n* aileron (*on a plane's wing*)

مُجَنَّح *adj* winged; حَشَرات مُجَنَّحة winged insects; صَمولة مُجَنَّحة wing nut

جَنَّدَ *v* **1** [صَيَّرَ جُنْديًّا] to recruit, to enlist; جَنَّدَ شَخْصاً to enlist sb into the army; جَنَّدَ شَخْصاً للتَجَسُّسِ to recruit sb as a spy **2** [الجُنودَ] to mobilize, to bring into action

تَجَنَّدَ *v* to be enlisted

جُنْد *n* |جُنود, أَجْناد| soldiers; army; ناقِلة الجُنْد المُدَرَّعة an armoured personnel carrier

جُنْديّ *n* |جُنود| soldier, serviceman; جُنْديّ مُتَطَوِّع volunteer soldier; جُنْديّ مُسْتَجِدّ recruit; جُنْديّ سابِق ex-serviceman; الجُنْديّ المَجْهول the Unknown Soldier; جُنْديّ في البَحْرِيّةِ \ مُشاةِ البَحْرِيّةِ \ القوّةِ الجَوِّيّةِ sailor/marine/airman

جُنْدِيّة *n* **1** [خِدْمة عَسْكَريّة] military service **2** [جَيْش] army

تَجَنُّد *n* military service; enlisting

تَجْنيد *n* recruitment; enlistment; mobilization; تَجْنيد إِلْزاميّ \ إِجْباريّ compulsory military service, conscription

مُجَنَّد **A** *adj* recruited
B *n* conscript

جُنْدُب *n* |جَنادِبُ| grasshopper

جَنْدَرْمة *n* gendarme; gendarmerie

جَنْدَل *n* |جَنادِلُ| **1** [صَخْر] rock, stone **2** [مَكان في النَهْر] cascade, waterfall

جُنْدول *n* |جَناديل| gondola

جِنِرال *n* general

جَنَّزَ *v* to say the burial prayers for the deceased

جَنّاز *n* funeral service, requiem mass; حَضَرَ \ أَقامَ جَنّازاً to attend/hold a funeral

جَنازة, جِنازة *n* |جَنائِزُ, جَنازات| **1** [احْتِفال] funeral, burial, interment; جَنازة رَسْمِيّة state funeral; تَشْييع الجَنازة funeral; صَلاة الجَنازةِ funeral prayer; حَضَرَ \ شَيَّعَ جَنازةً to attend a

مُتَعَدِّد الجِنْسيّاتِ multinational; عَديم الجِنْسيّةِ stateless; قوّة شَرِكة مُتَعَدِّدة الجِنْسيّاتِ a multinational (company); مُتَعَدِّدة الجِنْسيّاتِ an international force

تَجانُس *n* homogeneity; similarity, likeness; تَجانُس ثَقافيّ cultural homogeneity; عَدَم التَجانُسِ heterogeneity

تَجانُسيّ *adj* homeopathic

تَجَنُّس *n* naturalization

تَجْنيس *n* naturalization

مُتَجانِس *adj* homogeneous, having the same nature; خَليط مُتَجانِس a homogeneous mixture; مَجْموعة مُتَجانِسة a homogeneous group; غَيْر مُتَجانِسٍ heterogeneous

مُجانِس *adj* similar; related

جُنْط *n* |جُنوط| rim *(of a wheel)*

جَنَّ *v* |u; جَنّ| to cover; جَنَّ اللَيْلُ to become dark

جُنَّ *passive v* |جَنّ ,جُنون ,جِنّة| to be/become insane; هل جُنِنْتَ؟ have you gone out of your mind?; جُنَّ جُنونُهُ he went crazy

جَنَّنَ *v* to drive crazy, to drive mad (BrE); جَنَّنَ شَخْصاً to drive sb crazy

تَجَنَّنَ *v* to be/become insane

جِنّ *n coll* |sing n جِنّيّ| jinn *(intelligent, sometimes malevolent, unseen spirits)*; spirits; demons; genies; سورة الجِنّ The Jinn *(Sura 72)*

جَنائِنيّ *n* gardener

جَنان *n* |أَجْنان| heart, soul; ثابت الجَنانِ steadfast

جَنّة *n* |جَنّات ,جِنان| ❶ [فِرْدَوْس] paradise, heaven; جَنّة على الأَرْضِ heaven on earth; عُصْفور الجَنّة bird of paradise; دَخَلَ الجَنّة to enter paradise ❷ [حَديقة] garden; جَنّة عَدْنٍ the Garden of Eden ❸ [سِتْر] haven; جَنّة ضَريبيّة tax haven

جُنون *n* madness, insanity, lunacy; هذا جُنونٌ! that's insane!; جُنون العَظَمة megalomania; مَرَض جُنونِ البَقَرِ mad cow disease; في نَوْبة جُنونٍ in a fit of insanity; لا حَدَّ لِجُنونِه there is no limit to his madness; جُنَّ جُنونُهُ he went crazy; كانَ بِهِ مَسٌّ من جُنونٍ to be crazy

جُنونيّ *adj* insane; فِكْرة جُنونيّة a crazy idea; ارْتِفاع جُنونيّ في الأَسْعارِ skyrocketing prices; أَحْذِية غالِية بِشَكْلٍ جُنونيّ insanely expensive shoes

funeral service; أَقامَ جَنازةً لِشَخْصٍ to hold a funeral service for sb ❷ [مَوْكِب المُشَيِّعينَ] funeral procession

جَنْزير ,جِنْزير *n* |جَنازيرُ| ❶ [دَرّاجةٍ] (bicycle) chain ❷ [عَرَبةٍ] continuous/caterpillar tracks; جَنْزير الدَبّابةِ tank tracks/treads

جَنَّسَ *v* to grant citizenship to

جانَسَ *v* to be similar

تَجَنَّسَ *v* to be naturalized, to acquire citizenship; تَجَنَّسَ بالجِنْسيّةِ الأَمْريكيّةِ to become a (naturalized) American citizen

تَجانَسَ *v* to be alike, to be similar; تَجانَسَ مع شَيْءٍ to be of the same nature as sth

جِنْس *n* |أَجْناس| ❶ [ذَكَر أو أُنْثى] sex; gender; الجِنْس الآخَر the opposite sex; الجِنْس الخَشِن the stronger sex; الجِنْس اللَطيف \ الرَقيق \ الناعِم the fairer sex; جِنْس الإناثِ \ الذُكور the female/male sex; من كِلا الجِنْسَيْنِ of either sex; المُساواة \ التَمْييز بين الجِنْسَيْنِ gender equality/ discrimination; مِثْليّ الجِنْسِ homosexual; same-sex ❷ [جِماع] sex, (sexual) intercourse, copulation; الجِنْس الفَمَويّ oral sex; مارَسَ الجِنْسَ to have sex; مارَسَ الجِنْسَ مع شَخْصٍ to have sex with sb ❸ [نَوْع] genus; species; race, ethnic group; الجِنْس البَشَريّ the human race; اسْم جِنْسٍ genus name; إبادة الجِنْسِ genocide ❹ [صِنْف] category, type; genre; جِنْس أَدَبيّ literary genre ❺ (Gram) gender

جِناس *n* play on words; جِناس اسْتِهْلاليّ alliteration; جِناس تَصْحيفيّ anagram

جِنْسانيّة *n* sexuality

جِنْسيّ *adj* sexual, sex *(before n)*; مَرَض جِنْسيّ venereal disease; عُنْف \ اعْتِداء جِنْسيّ sexual violence/assault; تَحَرُّش جِنْسيّ sexual harassment; فَضيحة جِنْسيّة a sex scandal; شُذوذ جِنْسيّ perversion; homosexuality; اتِّصال جِنْسيّ sexual intercourse; رَغْبة جِنْسيّة libido; تَوْعِية جِنْسيّة sex education; رَجُل عاجِز جِنْسيًّا an impotent man

جِنْسيّة *n* nationality, citizenship; جِنْسيّة مُزْدَوِجة dual nationality; الجِنْسيّة البَريطانيّة British citizenship; حَمَلَ الجِنْسيّةَ البَريطانيّةَ to have British citizenship; حَصَلَ على الجِنْسيّةِ الكَنَدِيّةِ to obtain Canadian citizenship; أَعْطى شَخْصاً الجِنْسيّةَ الأَمْريكيّةَ to naturalize sb as an American citizen;

جِنّي *n* |جِنّ| see **جِنّ**

جِنِّيّة *n* (female) jinn; fairy

جَنين *n* |أَجِنّة, أَجْنُن| embryo; fetus; إِسْقاط الجَنينِ abortion; miscarriage; عِلْم الأَجِنّة embryology; اخْتِصاصيّ في عِلْمِ الأَجِنّةِ embryologist; زَرَعَ جَنيناً to implant an embryo

جُنَيْنة *n* |جَنائِنُ| garden

جَنينيّ *adj* embryonic; خَلايا جِذْعيّة جَنينيّة embryonic stem cells

أَجَنَّ *v* **1** ◀ [صَيَّرَهُ مَجْنوناً] to drive mad/insane **2** ◀ [سَتَرَ] to conceal, to hide; to veil

مِجَنّ *n* |مَجانُّ| shield

مَجْنون **A** *adj* |مَجانينُ| insane, disturbed; crazy, mad (BrE); امْرَأة مَجْنونة an insane woman; مُغامَرة مَجْنونة a crazy adventure

B *n* |مَجانينُ| madman, lunatic, maniac; fool; مُسْتَشْفى المَجانينِ insane asylum, madhouse

² ‹ **جِنّ** *n* gin

‹ **جَنى** *v* |i; جَنْي| **1** ◀ [قَطَفَ] to harvest, to pick, to gather; جَنى البَطاطِسَ to harvest potatoes; جَنى ثِمارَ الزَّيْتونِ to harvest the olives **2** ◀ [كَسَبَ] to earn; جَنى أَرْباحاً to make a profit; جَنى ثِمارَ جُهودِهِ to reap the fruits of one's labour **3** ◀ [ارْتَكَبَ] |على| to commit; to cause; to harm; جَنى على شَخْصٍ to cause sb harm

تَجَنّى *v* |على| to incriminate; to accuse falsely; تَجَنّى على شَخْصٍ to blame sb unfairly

اجْتَنى *v* to harvest, to pick

جانٍ *n* |جُناة| perpetrator, criminal, offender

جِنائيّ *adj* criminal, penal; مِسْطَرة \ إِجْراءات جِنائيّة criminal proceedings; تَحْقيق \ مُلاحَقة جِنائيّ(ة) criminal investigation/prosecution; المَباحِث الجِنائيّة detective department; تابَعَ شَخْصاً جِنائيًّا to prosecute sb; قَضيّة جِنائيّة ضِدّ شَخْصٍ a criminal case against sb

جِناية *n* offence, crime, felony; غُرْفة الجِناياتِ criminal division (*of a court*); قاضي الجِناياتِ criminal judge

مَجْنيّ **A** *adj* harvested; gained, earned; مال مَجْنيّ من عَمَليّاتِ بَيْعِ المُخَدِّراتِ money obtained from drug trafficking

B *n* المَجْنيّ عَلَيْهِ victim

‹ **جِنيف** *n* |f| Geneva; اتِّفاقيّة جِنيف the Geneva Convention

‹ **جِنيفر** *n* gin

‹ **جُنَيْه** *n* |جُنَيْهات| pound; الجُنَيْه المِصْريّ the Egyptian pound; الجُنَيْه الإِنْجليزيّ the pound sterling; الجُنَيْه الاسْتِرْلينيّ the English pound

‹ **جَهْبَذ, جِهْبِذ** *n* |جَهابِذة| great scholar; master, expert; جَهابِذة القانونِ jurists

جِهة *n* see **وجه**

‹ **جَهَدَ** *v* |a; جَهْد| to endeavour, to strive, to labour, to take pains; جَهَدَ نَفْسَهُ to exert oneself

جاهَدَ *v* to strive; to fight; جاهَدَ من أَجْلِ حُقوقِهِ to fight for one's rights; جاهَدَ في سَبيلِ اللهِ to dedicate oneself to the cause of God

أَجْهَدَ *v* to tire, to wear out; أَجْهَدَ نَفْسَهُ to overexert oneself

اجْتَهَدَ *v* to strive, to make every effort; اجْتَهَدَ في فِعْلِ شَيْءٍ to endeavour to do sth

جُهْد, جَهْد *n* |جُهود| **1** ◀ [طاقة] effort, endeavour; strain; diligence; جُهْد شَخْصيّ personal effort; جُهْد جَماعيّ a collaborative effort; جُهْد عَقْليّ \ جِسْميّ mental/physical exertion; جُهْد كَبير \ عَظيم a great/enormous effort; جُهْدَ طاقَتِهِ as much as he can; جُهْدَهُ one's every effort; بَذَلَ جُهْدَهُ to do one's best; بَذَلَ كُلَّ جُهْدِهِ to work one's fingers to the bone; بَذَلَ جُهْدَهُ من أَجْلِ شَيْءٍ \ شَخْصٍ to put oneself out for sth/sb; بَذَلَ قُصارى جُهْدِهِ لِيَتَوَصَّلَ إلى هَدَفِهِ to make every effort to reach one's goal; بِجُهْدٍ diligently; بِجُهْدٍ كَبيرٍ with much effort; عَمِلَ \ دَرَسَ بِجُهْدٍ to apply oneself to one's work/studies; فَعَلَ شَيْئاً بِكُلِّ جُهْدِهِ to do sth with all one's might; كَرَّسَ جُهْدَهُ من أَجْلِ شَيْءٍ to do one's best for sth; كافَأَ شَخْصاً على جُهْدِهِ to reward sb for their effort; بعد جُهْدٍ جَهيدٍ with strenuous and sustained effort **2** ◀ (Elec) voltage, tension; جُهْد مُنْخَفِض \ عالٍ low/high tension; فَرْق الجُهْدِ potential difference

جاهِد *adj* diligent; جاهِداً earnestly, diligently; حاوَلَ شَيْئاً جاهِداً to attempt sth in earnest; سَعى جاهِداً ل \ إلى شَيْءٍ to strive diligently for sth; عَمِلَ جاهِداً على شَيْءٍ to work hard for sth

جِهاد *n* jihad; effort, struggle; war; الجِهاد الأَكْبَر the greater jihad (*the spiritual struggle against one's ego and against temptation*); الجِهاد الأَصْغَر the lesser jihad (*the struggle to protect Islam from attack or oppression*); الجِهاد في سَبيلِ اللهِ the struggle for the cause of God

جِهاديّ **A** *adj* fighting; jihad (*before n*)
B *n* fighter; jihadi

جَهيد *adj* بعد جُهْدٍ جَهيدٍ with a strenuous and sustained effort

اجْتِهاد *n* **1** [جِدّ] diligence, application **2** (Islam) *independent judgement on a legal or theological question; individual judgement of a legal scholar*

إجْهاد *n* exhaustion; exertion; إجْهاد عَصَبيّ stress; إجْهاد جِسْمانيّ \ بَدَنيّ physical exhaustion; حالة إجْهادٍ fatigue

مُجاهِد *n* struggler; (guerrilla) fighter, resistance fighter; حَرَكة المُجاهِدينَ mujahideen movement (*Islamic guerrilla fighters*)

مُجْتَهِد **A** *adj* diligent, industrious, hard-working; طالِبٌ مُجْتَهِد a diligent student; لِكُلِّ مُجْتَهِدٍ نَصيبٌ hard work is the key to success
B *n an Islamic scholar formulating independent interpretations on legal or theological matters*

مُجْهَد *adj* exhausted, stressed

مُجْهِد *adj* strenuous, tiring

مَجْهود *n* |مَجْهودات| effort, exertion; مَجْهود فِكْريّ an intellectual effort; بَذَلَ مَجْهوداً to make an effort; مَجْهوداً جَبّاراً (لِتَحْقيقِ شَيْءٍ) to make a supreme effort (to realize sth)

جَهَرَ *v* |a; جَهْر| |ب| to reveal; to announce; to raise (*the voice*); جَهَرَ بِشَيْءٍ to announce sth; جَهَرَ بِسِرٍّ to disclose a secret

جَهُرَ *v* |u; جَهارة| to be/become loud/clearly audible (*voice*)

جاهَرَ *v* |ب| to proclaim, to say/declare openly; جاهَرَ بِشَيْءٍ to proclaim sth

أَجْهَرَ *v* to proclaim

جَهْر *n* openness; publicity; جَهْراً publicly, in public, openly; جَهْر بِشَيْءٍ publicly announcing sth

جِهار *n* openness; جِهاراً openly; جِهاراً نَهاراً in broad daylight; سَرَقَ جِهاراً نَهاراً to commit theft in broad daylight; أَبْدى رَأْيَهُ جِهاراً نَهاراً he openly gave his opinion

جَهْرة *n* جَهْرةً publicly, in public, openly; دَعا جَهْرةً إلى شَيْءٍ to openly call for sth

جَهْوَريّ *adj* loud; بِصَوْتٍ جَهْوَريٍّ in a strong voice

جَهير **A** *adj* loud; bass (*before n*); بِصَوْتٍ جَهيرٍ in a strong voice; كَمان جَهير cello
B *n* bass; جيتار الجَهير bass (guitar)

أَجْهَر *adj* |dipt| dazzled (*by bright light*)

مِجْهار *n* |مَجاهير| speaker, loudspeaker

مِجْهَر *n* |مَجاهِرُ| microscope; مِجْهَر إلِكْترونيّ electron microscope; وَضَعَ شَيْئاً تحت المِجْهَر to put sth under the microscope

مِجْهَريّ *adj* microscopic; minuscule; فَحْص مِجْهَريّ microscopic examination; جُزَيْئات مِجْهَرِيّة microscopic particles

مَجْهور *adj* (Ling) voiced; حَرْف مَجْهور a voiced consonant

جَهَّزَ *v* **1** [أَعَدَّ] to prepare, to make ready; جَهَّزَ تَرْجَمةً to prepare a translation; جَهَّزَ نَفْسَهُ لِشَيْءٍ to prepare oneself for sth; جَهِّزْ جَوازَ سَفَرِكَ have your passport ready **2** [زَوَّدَ] to provide, to supply; to equip, to fit out, to furnish; جَهَّزَ جَيْشاً to equip an army; جَهَّزَ نَفْسَهُ لِلسَّفَرِ to prepare oneself for a journey **3** (Comput) to install

أَجْهَزَ *v* |على| to kill, to finish off; أَجْهَزَ على شَخْصٍ to finish sb off

تَجَهَّزَ *v* to be equipped; to be ready/prepared; تَجَهَّزَ لِشَيْءٍ to be ready for sth

جاهِز *adj* ready, prepared; ready-made, pre-fabricated; حَلّ جاهِز a cut and dried solution; سِلْعة \ مُنْتَج جاهِز(ة) final product; وَجْبة جاهِزة a ready-made meal; مَلابِس جاهِزة ready-to-wear clothes; التَّقْريرُ جاهِزٌ the report is finished; الطَّعامُ جاهِزٌ dinner's ready; كانَ جاهِزاً لِشَيْءٍ to be ready for sth; جاهِز لِلاسْتِعْمالِ ready for use; جاهِز لِلتَّنْفيذ operational; جاهِز لِلبِناء ready for building; جاهِز لِلطَّبْع ready for press; جاهِز لِلمُغادَرة ready to leave

جاهِزِيّة *n* readiness; جاهِزِيّة لِشَيْءٍ readiness for sth

الإجْهاضِ abortion; عارَضَ الإجْهاضَ to oppose abortion

جَهِلَ v |a; جَهْل, جَهالة| to not know; to be unfamiliar with; to be ignorant; جَهِل شَيْئاً \ بِشَيْءٍ not to know sth; كانَ يَجْهَلُ القِراءةَ he didn't know how to read; يَجْهَلُ مَصيرَ شَخْصٍ to not know what happened to sb

تجاهَلَ v to ignore; to disregard; تَجاهَلَ شَخْصاً to ignore sb; تَجاهَلَ حَظْراً to disregard a ban

جَهْل n ignorance, lack of knowledge; unfamiliarity (with); جَهْلاً in ignorance; جَهْل فاحِش abysmal ignorance; نَمَّ عن جَهْلٍ to show a lack of knowledge; جَهْل بِشَيْءٍ unfamiliarity with sth; بِسَبَبِ جَهْلِهِ out of ignorance; الجَهْلُ أُمُّ الرَذائِلِ ignorance begets evil

جاهِل adj |جَهَلة, جُهَّل, جُهّال, جُهَلاءُ| 1 [غَيْر عالِمٍ] ignorant, uninformed; جاهِل بِشَيْءٍ unaware of sth; كانَ جاهِلاً to be ignorant 2 (Relig) not initiated (*Druze*)

جاهِلِيّ adj pre-Islamic; العَصْر الجاهِلِيّ the pre-Islamic period

جاهِلِيّة n pre-Islamic period; state of ignorance

جَهالة n ignorance; الفَحْص النافي للجَهالةِ due diligence

تَجاهُل n ignoring, disregard; ما لا يُمْكِنُ تَجاهُلُهُ هو أنّ ... one cannot disregard the fact that...

تَجْهيل n *keeping ignorant/misinformed/in the dark*; تَجْهيل الطَلَبة keeping the students ignorant

مَجْهَل |مَجاهِلُ| unknown/unexplored land/region/territory

مَجْهول A adj anonymous, unknown, unnamed; مَجْهولات unknown things; من أَصْلٍ مَجْهولٍ of obscure origins; عَدَد مَجْهول an unspecified number; مِنْطَقة مَجْهولة unknown territory; مَجْهول كُلِّيًّا \ بالمَرّة completely unknown; مَجْهول الهُوِيّة unidentified; قَبْر الجُنْديّ المَجْهولِ the grave of the Unknown Soldier

B n 1 [شَخْص غَيْر مَعْروفٍ] unknown; على يَدِ مَجْهولينَ at the hands of unknown persons 2 (Gram) passive; صيغة المَجْهولِ passive; مَبْني للمَجْهولِ passive; بُنِيَ على صيغةِ المَجْهولِ to be in the passive 3 (Math) unknown (*quantity or variable*)

مَجْهولِيّة n obscurity, being unknown

جُهْلول n (Zool) snipe (*Scolopacidae*)

جِهاز, جَهاز n |أَجْهِزة| 1 (Tech) machine; appliance; gadget, device; mobile phone, handset; أَجْهِزة إلِكْترونيّة \ مَنْقولة \ لاسِلْكيّة electronic/portable/wireless devices; جِهاز أَلْعابٍ (مَحْمول) (portable) game console; أَجْهِزة مَنْزِلِيّة household appliances; أَجْهِزة خارِجيّة peripheral equipment 2 [سِلْك] system, apparatus; جِهاز حُكوميّ government agency/body; الجِهاز الإداريّ \ القَضائيّ \ العَسْكَريّ the administrative/judicial/military system; جِهاز أَمْنٍ security service; جِهاز تَنْفيذيّ executive body 3 (Anat) system; جِهاز هَضْميّ digestive system; جِهاز وِعائيّ vascular system; جِهاز عَصَبيّ nervous system

تَجْهيز n equipment; تَجْهيزات equipment, gear; materials, supplies; تَجْهيزات عَسْكَرِيّة (military) ordnance; تَجْهيزات صِحّيّة sanitary fittings; تَجْهيزات أساسيّة standard equipment; تَجْهيزات إضافيّة accessories; مَطْبَخ مُجَهَّز بِكُلِّ التَجْهيزاتِ a well-equipped kitchen

تَجْهيزيّ adj preparatory, equipping; السِلَع التَجْهيزيّة durable goods; الصِناعات التَجْهيزيّة durable goods manufacturing

مُجَهَّز adj equipped, provided; prepared; مُجَهَّز بِشَيْءٍ equipped with sth

جَهَشَ v |a; جُهوش, جَهْش, جَهَشان| جَهَش بالبُكاءِ to be on the verge of tears

أَجْهَشَ v أَجْهَشَ بالبُكاءِ to be on the verge of tears

أَجْهَضَ v 1 [أَسْقَطَ الجَنينَ] to abort, to terminate; to have an abortion; أَجْهَضَتْ جَنينَها she terminated her pregnancy; she lost her baby 2 [سَقَطَ الجَنينُ] to miscarry, to have a miscarriage; أَجْهَضَتْ مَرَّتَيْنِ she has miscarried twice; أَجْهَضَتْ جَنينَها she terminated her pregnancy; she lost her baby 3 [أَفْشَلَ] to abort; to crush, to destroy; أَجْهَضَ مَسيرةَ السَلامِ to abort the peace process; أَجْهَضَ أَمَلَ \ أَحْلامَ شَخْصٍ to crush sb's hopes/dreams

جَهيض n miscarried fetus; abortion

إجْهاض n |إجْهاضات| 1 [سُقوط الجَنينِ] miscarriage; الأَدْوِيةُ المُسَكِّنةُ قد تُسَبِّبُ الإجْهاضَ painkillers could cause miscarriage 2 [إسْقاط الجَنينِ] abortion, termination of pregnancy; إجْهاض غَيْر شَرْعيٍّ illegal abortion; عَمَلِيّة

جَهُمَ *v* |u; جَهْم, جَهامة| to frown, to scowl

تَجَهَّمَ *v* to frown, to scowl; to look grim

جَهامة *n* frowning, sullenness

تَجَهُّم *n* scowl, frown; مالَ إلى التَجَهُّمِ to tend to scowl

مُتَجَهِّم *adj* grumpy, surly, sullen, grim

جَهَنَّم *n* |dipt| hell; ذَهَبَ إلى جَهَنَّمَ to go to hell; تَحَوَّلَ إلى جَهَنَّمَ to become a living hell

جَهَنَّمِيّ *adj* hellish, infernal; مُخَطَّط جَهَنَّمِيّ a fiendish plan

جَوافة *n* common guava (*Psidium guajava*); guava

جُوان *n* (Algeria, Tunisia) June

جابَ *v* |u; جَوْب| to travel, to explore; to cross, to traverse; جابَ بِلاداً to travel about a country; جابَ أوروبّا to tour Europe; جابَ الشَوارِعَ to roam the streets

جاوَبَ *v* to answer, to reply; جاوَبَ شَخْصاً to answer sb; جاوَبَ على سُؤالٍ to answer a question

أَجابَ *v* ❶ [سُؤال] to answer, to reply, to respond, to retort; أَجابَ بِأَنَّ ... to reply that...; أَجابَ شَخْصاً to answer sb; أَجابَ على \ عن شَيْءٍ to respond to sth; أَجابَ على سُؤالٍ to answer a question; أَجابَ على سُؤالٍ بالنَفْيِ to answer in the negative; أَجابَ بالإيجابِ to answer in the affirmative ❷ [إلى] to grant, to fulfil; أَجابَ شَخْصاً إلى حاجَتِهِ to answer sb's need

تَجاوَبَ *v* to harmonize, to be in accord; to respond, to comply; تَجاوَبَ مع رَغَباتِ الشَعْبِ to be in accordance with the people's wishes

انْجابَ *v* to fade, to disappear

اسْتَجابَ *v* to grant, to fulfil, to answer; to react, to respond; اسْتَجابَ لِشَيْءٍ \ اسْتَجابَ ل \ إلى شَيْءٍ to respond to sth; اسْتَجابَ لِطَلَبٍ بِإيجابيّةٍ to respond favourably to sth; اسْتَجابَ لِطَلَبٍ to comply with a request; اسْتَجابَ لِطَلَباتِ شَخْصٍ to meet sb's demands; اسْتَجابَ لِدَعْوةٍ to hear a prayer; اسْتَجابَ لِأَدْوِيةٍ \ عِلاجٍ to respond to medicine/treatment; يَجِبُ أَنْ أَسْتَجِيبَ لِنِداءِ الواجِبِ duty calls me

اسْتَجْوَبَ *v* ❶ [طَلَبَ الجَوابَ] to question, to examine, to interview; اسْتَجْوَبَ التَلاميذَ to test the students; اسْتَجْوَبَ شَخْصاً حول شَيْءٍ to question sb about sth ❷ [اسْتَنْطَقَ] to interrogate, to cross-examine; اسْتَجْوَبَ المُحامي الشاهِدَ the lawyer cross-examined the witness; اسْتَجْوَبَت الشُرْطةُ المُشْتَبَهَ بِهِ the police interrogated the suspect

جَوْب *n* travelling, touring

جَواب *n* |أَجْوِبة| ❶ [رَدّ] answer; جَواب مُلْتَبِس an ambiguous answer; كانَ حاضِرَ الجَوابِ to be ready with an answer; جَواب على سُؤالٍ an answer to a question; جَواباً على رِسالَتِكُمْ \ خِطابِكُمْ in reply to your letter ❷ (Mus) octave

جَوّاب *n* traveller, explorer, globetrotter

إجابة *n* answer, reply, response; إجابة إيجابيّة \ سَلْبيّة an affirmative/negative answer; إجابةً ل \ على شَيْءٍ in response to sth; إجابةً لِطَلَبِ شَخْصٍ at sb's request; إجابة على سُؤالٍ an answer to a question

اسْتِجابة *n* ❶ [إجابة] answering; اسْتِجابةً لِرِسالَتِكُمْ \ خِطابِكُمْ in reply to your letter ❷ (Phys) echo, resonance

اسْتِجْواب *n* |اسْتِجْوابات| interrogation, questioning, examination, cross-examination

مُجِيب **A** *adj* answering
B *n* ❶ [مُلَبٍّ] respondent; المُجيب الصَوْتيّ voicemail ❷ (Islam) المُجيب the Answerer (*one of the names of God*)

مُسْتَجْوَب *n* examinee

مُسْتَجْوِب *n* interrogator

جوبا *n* Juba (*capital of South Sudan*)

جوت *n* jute

جوجَل *n* Google®

اجْتاحَ *v* to invade; to trespass; to overwhelm; to infest; to plague; اجْتاحَت العاصِفةُ الساحِلَ the storm ravaged the coast; اجْتاحَ الغَضَبُ البِلادَ the country was filled with anger; اجْتاحَت الأَعْشابُ الضارّةُ حَديقَتَهُمْ their garden became overgrown with weeds; اجْتاحَ الجَيْشُ الأَجْنَبِيُّ شَمالَ البِلادِ the foreign army invaded the north of the country

جائِحة *n* |جَوائِحُ| disaster; epidemic; جَوائِح طَبيعيّة natural disasters

إجاحة *n* invasion; destruction

اجْتِياح *n* invasion; destruction; اجْتِياح العِراقِ the invasion of Iraq

‹ **جارَ** *v* |u; جَوْر| على| to wrong; جارَ على شَخْصٍ to treat sb unjustly

جاوَرَ *v* to border; to neighbour; to live near; إنّها تُجاوِرُ مُحافَظةَ صَلاحِ الدينِ it borders the Saladin province

أَجارَ *v* to protect; to help; أَجارَكَ اللهُ may God protect you

تَجاوَرَ *v* to be adjacent, to be neighbours; to intermix; كِتاب تَتَجاوَرُ فيهِ الأَجْناسُ الأَدَبيّةُ a book encompassing different genres; يَتَجاوَرُ المُسْلِمُ مع غَيْرِه Muslims live side by side with non-Muslims; يَتَجاوَرُ الجَبَلُ مع البَحْرِ في المِنْطَقةِ mountains border the sea in the region

اِسْتَجارَ *v* to seek protection; to shelter; اِسْتَجارَ من الرَمْضاءِ بالنارِ to jump out of the frying pan into the fire; اِسْتَجارَ بِشَيْءٍ \ شَخْصٍ to take refuge with sth/sb

جَوْر *n* |جَوْرة| tyranny; injustice; جَوْراً unjustly

جائِر *adj* unjust, unfair; oppressive; حُكْم جائِر an unjust judgement; شَرْط جائِر an unreasonable demand; عُقوبة جائِرة an unjust punishment; نَقْد جائِر unjustified criticism

جار **A** *adj* |جيران| neighbouring, adjacent; بَلَد جار a neighbouring country

B *n* |جيران| neighbour; الجارُ قبل الدارِ *good neighbours are more important than a nice house*

جِوار *n* proximity, nearness; بِجِوارِ in the neighbourhood of; في جِوارِ شَيْءٍ close by/to sth; في جِوارِ البَيْتِ in the vicinity of the house; دُوَل الجِوارِ neighbouring countries; دُوَل جِوارِ العِراقِ, الجِوارِ العِراقيِّ the countries neighbouring Iraq; عَلاقات حُسْنِ الجِوارِ good neighbourly relations; ذَهَبَ \ اِنْتَقَلَ إلى جِوارِ رَبِّهِ to meet one's Maker; جَلَسَ على الكُرْسيِّ بِجِوارِ المِدْفَأةِ he sat on the chair near the heater

تَجاوُر *n* juxtaposition

مُتَجاوِر *adj* neighbouring, adjoining, adjacent; الدُوَل المُتَجاوِرة neighbouring countries; الأَبْنِية المُتَجاوِرة adjoining properties

مُجاوِر *adj* adjoining, adjacent, neighbouring; قَرْية مُجاوِرة a neighbouring village; أُنْظُرْ إلى الشَكْلِ المُجاوِرِ see the attached diagram; مُجاوِر لـ ... adjacent to...

مُجير *n* protector, helper; يا مُجير God help us

‹ **جوخ** *n* |أَجْواخ| cloth; مَسَحَ الجوخَ to lick sb's boots

‹ **جادَ** *v* |u; جودة| ❶ [حَسُنَ] to be good ❷ [سَخا] |ب| to be generous/open-handed; to give generously; جادَ بِمالِهِ to give away one's money; ما جادَ بِهِ القَلَمُ what flowed naturally from the pen

جَوَّدَ *v* ❶ [القارِئُ] to recite ❷ [حَسَّنَ] to improve

أَجادَ *v* to master, to know well; to be skilled; أَجادَ شَيْئاً to be good at sth; أَجادَ تِقْنيّةً to master a technique; أَجادَ مِهْنَتَهُ to know one's trade; أَجادَ اللُغةَ الفَرَنْسيّةَ to be proficient in French; أَجادَ عَمَلَ شَيْءٍ to be well versed in sth; أَجادَ لُغةً إجادةً تامّةً to have an excellent command of a language

اِسْتَجادَ *v* to consider good

جَواد **A** *adj* |جود, أَجاويدُ, أَجاوِدُ, أَجْواد| generous

B *n* |جِياد, أَجْياد, أَجاويدُ| horse; racehorse; جواد أَصيل thoroughbred; راهَنَ على الجَوادِ الخاسِرِ to bet on the losing horse

جَوْدة, جودة *n* quality; class; جَوْدة عالِيَة high quality; جَوْدة فائِقة top quality; فائِق الجَوْدةِ high-quality; عَمَل فائِق الجَوْدةِ high-quality work; عَلامة الجَوْدةِ quality mark; مَعايير الجَوْدةِ quality standards; أَرْضى مَعاييرَ الجَوْدةِ to meet the quality standards; مُراقَبة \ فَحْص الجَوْدةِ quality control; اِرْتِفاع مُسْتَوى الجَوْدةِ improvement in quality

جَيِّد *adj* |جِياد| good, fine, well; جَوّ جَيِّد fine weather; مادّة جَيِّدة sound material; راتِب جَيِّد a good salary; رَجُل \ اِمْرَأة جَيِّد(ة) a good man/woman; نَصيحة \ ذَوْق جَيِّد(ة) good advice/taste; كِتاب جَيِّد a good book; كانَ في صِحّةٍ جَيِّدةٍ to be in good health; جَيِّداً well; اِسْتَمَعَ جَيِّداً to listen well; نامَ جَيِّداً to sleep well; بِ \ في شَكْلٍ جَيِّدٍ well, in the right way; جَيِّد جِدًّا very good (*examination grade*)

إجادة *n* command, mastery; proficiency; إجادة لِلُغةٍ proficiency in a language

أَجْوَد *adj* |dipt| better

تَجْويد *n* ❶ [قِراءة] recitation; Koran recitation ❷ [تَحْسين] improvement

مُجيد *adj* adept

‹ **جودو, جيدو** *n* judo; مارَسَ رِياضةَ الجودو to practise judo

مُسْتَجير *n* asylum seeker, refugee

جَوْرَب *n* |جَوارِب| sock; stocking; جَوارِب صوفيّة woollen socks; جَوارِب الحَرير silk stockings; زَوْج (من) جَوارِبَ a pair of socks; رِباط جَوْرَبٍ garters; garter belt; لَبِسَ \ خَلَعَ جَوارِبَهُ to put on/take off one's socks

جورْجِيا *n* 1 ◀ [في القَفْقاز] Georgia (*country*) 2 ◀ [في الوِلاياتِ المُتَّحِدةِ] Georgia (*US state*)

جازَ *v* |u; مَجاز, جَواز| 1 ◀ [عَبَرَ] to cross, to traverse; جازَ امْتِحاناً to pass an exam 2 ◀ [كانَ غَيْر مَمْنوع] to be/become permissible; لا يَجوزُ لَكَ أنْ ... you shouldn't ...; إنْ جازَ التَّعْبيرُ so to speak; جازَ للمَريضِ أنْ يُفْطِرَ a sick person should break the fast; لا يَجوزُ أنْ تَقومَ بِهَذا العَمَلِ she is not allowed to do this work

جَوَّزَ *v* to permit, to allow; جَوَّزَ شَيْئاً to allow sth

جاوَزَ *v* to pass; to exceed, to surpass; to overstep, to go beyond; بِتَكْلُفةٍ جاوَزَتْ ١٣٣ مِلْيون رِيالٍ at a cost exceeding 133 million riyals

أَجازَ *v* to permit, to allow; to approve; أُجيزَ to be permitted to; أجازَ (لِشَخْصٍ) شَيْئاً to allow (sb) sth; لا تُجيزُ لِنَفْسِها التَدَخُّلَ في شُؤونِ الآخَرينَ she doesn't allow herself to get involved in other people's business

تَجَوَّزَ *v* |في| to tolerate; تَجَوَّزَ في شَيْءٍ to put up with sth

تَجاوَزَ *v* 1 ◀ [تَقَدَّمَ على] to exceed, to overstep, to go beyond; to pass, to walk past; تَجاوَزَ من الجِهةِ اليُسْرى \ اليُمْنى to overtake (BrE) pass (AmE) on the left/right; تَجاوَزَ المُعَدَّلَ to surpass the average; تَجاوَزَ حُدوداً to overstep a bound; تَجاوَزَ سُلْطَتَهُ to overstep one's authority; تَجاوَزَ السُرْعةَ القُصْوى to exceed the speed limit; تَجاوَزَ عَدَدُهُم المِائَةَ they number more than one hundred 2 ◀ [أَهْمَلَ] to pass over, to ignore; تَجاوَزَ عن سَيِّئاتِ شَخْصٍ to overlook sb's shortcomings

اجْتازَ *v* to pass; to pass/go by; to go beyond; to cross; اجْتازَ الحُدودَ to overstep the limit; اجْتازَ الامْتِحانَ to pass the test; اجْتازَ مَرْحَلةً صَعْبةً to get through a hard time

اسْتَجازَ *v* 1 ◀ [طَلَبَ إجازةً] to request permission 2 ◀ [أَجازَ] to consider permissible

جائِز *adj* permissible, permitted; conceivable, possible; كانَ جائِزاً لَهُ he was allowed; من الجائِزِ أنْ ... it is possible that ...; من غَيْرِ الجائِزِ اسْتِمْرارُ الوَضْعِ على ما هو things can't continue as they are; كُلُّ شَيْءٍ جائِزٌ في هذا الزَمَنِ these days, anything's possible

جائِزة *n* |جَوائِزُ| prize, award; جائِزة تَشْجيعيّة incentive payment; الجائِزة الأولى \ الثانية \ الثالثة first/second/third prize; جائِزة نوبِل Nobel prize; تَوْزيع الجَوائِزِ handing out prizes; حَفْل تَوْزيعِ الجَوائِزِ awards ceremony; فازَ بِجائِزةٍ \ كَسَبَ جائِزةً to win a prize; حَصَدَ جَوائِزَ to win awards; أَعْطى \ مَنَحَ جائِزةً to award a prize; سَلَّمَ \ تَسَلَّمَ جائِزةً to award/receive a prize; نالَ الجائِزةَ الأولى to win first prize; مَنَحَ جائِزةً لِكِتابٍ to award a prize to a book

جَواز *n* |جَوازات| 1 ◀ [إمْكانيّة] permissibility, admissibility; permission; عَدَم جَوازِ شَيْءٍ the impermissibility of sth 2 ◀ [سَفَر] جَواز سَفَرٍ passport; جَواز سَفَرٍ صالِح a valid passport; جَواز سَفَرٍ مُنْتَهي الصَلاحيّة an expired passport; جَواز سَفَرٍ مُزَوَّر a forged passport; مُراقَبة الجَوازاتِ passport control; طَلَبَ جَوازَ سَفَرٍ to apply for a passport; أَبْرَزَ \ أَظْهَرَ جَوازَ سَفَرِهِ to show one's passport; مَلَكَ \ حَمَلَ جَوازَ سَفَرٍ أَمْريكيٍّ to have an American passport; مَدَّدَ صَلاحيّةَ جَوازِ سَفَرِهِ to renew one's passport

إجازة *n* 1 ◀ [عُطْلة] leave; holiday (BrE), vacation (AmE); إجازة مَرَضيّة sick leave; إجازة مَدْرَسيّة school holidays; أَخَذَ إجازةً to take a holiday; عِنْدَهُ إجازةٌ to have a holiday; انْتَهَتْ إجازَتي my leave has run out; كانَ في إجازةٍ to be on leave; أَخَذَ يَوْمَ إجازةٍ to take a day off; في (مَوْسِمِ) الإجازاتِ in the holiday season; قَضى إجازةً to spend a holiday; أَعْطى شَخْصاً إجازةً to give sb some time off 2 ◀ [سَماح] licence, permit; حامِل إجازةٍ licence holder 3 ◀ [شَهادة جامِعيّة] licence (*academic degree*); حامِل إجازةٍ licentiate

اجْتِياز *n* passage; لا يُمْكِنُ اجْتِيازُهُ impenetrable

تَجاوُز *n* |تَجاوُزات| excess, overstepping; violation, abuse; تَجاوُز السُرْعةِ القُصْوى exceeding the speed limit; يُمْكِنُ تَجاوُزُهُ bridgeable; مُتَّهَم بِارْتِكابِ تَجاوُزاتٍ accused of committing abuses

مُتَجاوِز A *adj* exceeding; مُتَجاوِز للحُدودِ cross-border

B *n* trespasser, transgressor

مَجاز *n* 1 [مَمَرّ] passage, passageway, corridor 2 (Literat) imagery; metaphor; figurative expression

مُجاز A *adj* authorized; كانَ مُجازاً لِفِعْلِ شَيْءٍ to be authorized to do sth; خَبير المُحاسَبةِ المُجاز chartered accountant (BrE), Certified Public Accountant/CPA (AmE)

B *n* licentiate

مَجازِيّ *adj* figurative; metaphorical; المَعْنى المَجازِيّ لِكَلِمةٍ the figurative meaning of a word; بالمَعْنى المَجازِيِّ figuratively

2 **جَوْز** *n coll* |أَجْواز| 1 [ثَمَر] walnut; nut; جَوْز هِنْدِيّ \ جَوْز الهِنْدِ coconut; لَبَن جَوْزِ الهِنْدِ coconut milk; جَوْز الطيبِ nutmeg 2 [شَجَر] walnut (tree); خَشَب الجَوْزِ walnut (*wood*); جَوْز الهِنْدِ coconut palm 3 [وَسَط] heart; centre; في أَجْوازِ in the middle; في أَجْوازِ الفَضاءِ in space

3 **الجَوْزاء** *n* (بُرْج) الجَوْزاءِ Gemini

جَوْزَل *n* |جَوازِلُ| young pigeon, squab

جاسَ *v* |u; جَوْسان, جَوْس| to investigate, to explore; to look around

جَوْسَق *n* |جَواسِقُ, جَواسيقُ| palace, villa

جَوْشَن *n* |جَواشِنُ| chest, breast

جاعَ *v* |u; جَوْع, مَجاعة| to be/feel hungry; to starve; جاعَ الأَطْفالُ the children went hungry

جَوَّعَ *v* to starve (out); جَوَّعَ مَدينةً to starve out a city; جَوِّعْ كَلْبَكَ يَتْبَعْكَ starve your dog and he will follow you (*hungry people are obedient*)

أَجاعَ *v* to starve out; أَجِعْ كَلْبَكَ يَتْبَعْكَ starve your dog and he will follow you (*hungry people are obedient*)

جوع *n* hunger; starvation; المَوْت جوعاً death by starvation; ماتَ جوعاً to starve to death; تَضَوَّرَ جوعاً to be faint from hunger; قَرَصَهُ الجوعُ to feel the pangs of hunger; قَتَلَهُ الجوعُ to die of hunger; عانى من الجوعِ to starve; أَسْكَتَ جوعَهُ to satisfy one's appetite; الجوعُ أَمْهَرُ الطَّبّاخينَ hunger is the best sauce; الجوعُ كافِرٌ a hungry man has no conscience

جائِع *adj* |جِياع, جَوَّع| hungry; starving; مَعِدة جائِعة an empty stomach; الشَّعْب الجائِع the starving population; بِنَظْرةٍ جائِعةٍ with a hungry look; كانَ جائِعاً to be hungry/starving

جَوْعان *adj* |dipt| hungry; starving

تَجْويع *n* starving (out), starvation

مَجاعة *n* famine, starvation; تَعُمُّ المَجاعةُ famine broke out; عانى من المَجاعةِ to be afflicted with famine

جَوَّفَ *v* to hollow out, to excavate

جَوْف *n* |أَجْواف| hollow, cavity; interior, inside, heart; abdomen, belly; جَوْف سَفينةٍ the hold (of a ship); في جَوْفِ الأَرْضِ in the bowels of the earth; في جَوْفِ اللَّيْلِ in the dead of night

جافِية *n* (Anat) dura; الأُمّ الجافية dura mater

جَوْفِيّ *adj* underground, subterranean; مِياه جَوْفِيّة groundwater

أَجْوَف *adj* |dipt; f جَوْفاءُ; جوف| 1 [فارِغ] hollow; empty; كَلِمات \ عِبارات جَوْفاء empty words 2 (Gram) hollow; الفِعْل الأَجْوَف hollow verb

تَجْويف *n* |تَجاويفُ| 1 [نُقْرة] hollow, excavation 2 (Anat) socket; sinus; تَجْويف أَنْفِيّ nasal cavity; تَجْويف فَمَوِيّ oral cavity; تَجْويف بَطْنِيّ abdomen

مُجَوَّف *adj* hollow, hollowed out

جَوْق, جَوْقة *n* |أَجْواق| group; band, orchestra; جَوْقة موسيقيّة music group

مُجَوْقَل *adj* airborne; قوّات مُجَوْقَلة airborne troops

جوكَر *n* joker

1 **جالَ** *v* |u; جَوْل| 1 [طافَ] to walk around, to wander (about), to roam; جالَ في (أَرْجاء) المَدينة to wander (all) around the town; جالَ على \ في مِنْطَقةٍ to tour an area; جالَ بِخاطِرِهِ to run through one's mind 2 (Comput) to surf (*the internet*)

أَجالَ *v* to circulate, to pass round; أَجالَ نَظَرَهُ to look around

تَجَوَّلَ *v* to walk around, to wander (about), to roam, to rove; to patrol; تَجَوَّلَ في مِنْطَقةٍ to tour an area; تَجَوَّلَ في المَدينة to wander round the town

جَوّال A *adj* mobile; wandering, ambulant; الإِنْتَرْنِت الجَوّال mobile internet

B n 1 [مُسافِر] traveller 2 [مَحْمول] جَوّال (هاتِف) mobile phone, mobile (BrE), cell (phone) (AmE)

جَوْلة n 1 [نُزْهة] tour, (round) trip, journey; جَوْلة تَفَقُّدِيّة an inspection tour; جَوْلة في المَصْنَعِ a tour of the factory; جَوْلة في تونِسَ a trip around Tunisia; جَوْلة على الأَقْدامِ a walking tour; قامَ بِجَوْلةٍ (قَصيرةٍ) to go on a (short) trip 2 [دَوْر] round; جَرَس الجَوْلةِ الأَخيرةِ the bell for the last round; أَجْرى جَوْلةً جَديدةً من المُباحَثاتِ to have a new round of negotiations

تَجْوال n travelling, wandering; migration; مَنْع \ حَظْر التَجْوالِ curfew; باعَ بالتَجْوالِ to sell door to door; بائِع بالتَجْوالِ door-to-door salesman; البَيْع بالتَجْوالِ door-to-door selling

تَجَوُّل n |تَجَوُّلات| wandering, roaming; مَنْع \ حَظْر التَجَوُّلِ curfew; أَعْلَنَ \ فَرَضَ حَظْرَ تَجَوُّلٍ to impose a curfew; باعَ بالتَجَوُّلِ to sell door to door

مُتَجَوِّل *adj* walking around; roaming, roving; تِجارة مُتَجَوِّلة street trading; مَكْتَبة مُتَجَوِّلة travelling library, ≈ bookmobile; سَفير مُتَجَوِّل roving ambassador; تاجِر مُتَجَوِّل itinerant trader; بائِع مُتَجَوِّل pedlar

مَجال n |مَجالات| 1 [نِطاق] space, room; مَجال جَوّيّ airspace; المَجال الجَوّيّ فوق المُحيطِ الأَطْلَسيّ the airspace over the Atlantic; خَرَقَ \ اخْتَرَقَ \ اقْتَحَمَ \ انْتَهَكَ المَجالَ الجَوّيَّ الروسيَّ to violate Russian airspace; فَسَحَ \ أَفْسَحَ المَجالَ لِشَخْصٍ to make way for sb; لا مَجالَ للشَكِّ there is no place for doubt; هذا لا يَتْرُكُ مَجالاً للجَدَلِ حول ... this leaves no room for discussion about ... 2 [مَيْدان] domain, area, field, sphere, scope; مَجال العَمَلِ sphere of activity; مَجال الفُنونِ \ العُلومِ the field of art/science; في مَجالاتٍ عِدّةٍ in many fields; خَبير في مَجالِ عِلْمِ اللُغةِ an expert in the field of linguistics; كانَ مُلِمًّا بِمَجالِ ... to be well versed in the area of ... 3 (Phys) field; مَجال مَغْنَطيسيّ \ كَهْرَبائيّ a magnetic/electric field 4 (Comput) domain; اسْم مَجالٍ domain name

[2] **جول** n joule

الجَوْلان n |f| Golan Heights; هَضْبة الجَوْلان Golan Heights

جولْف, غولْف n golf; نادي الجولْف golf club; لاعِب الجولْف golfer; مِضْمار \ مَلْعَب الجولْف golf course

جَوْلَق n (Bot) gorse, furze (*Ulex*)

جون n |أَجْوان| inlet, cove, bay

جَوْهَر A n |جَواهِرُ| essence; core; substance; جَوْهَر الديموقراطيّةِ the essence of democracy; جَوْهَر البَحْثِ the focus of the study; جَوْهَرُ المَوْضوعِ هو ... the heart of the matter is ...; في الجَوْهَرِ \ من حَيْثُ الجَوْهَرِ in essence; basically
B n coll |جَواهِرُ| jewel, gem; (fig) diamond, pearl; جَواهِر ثمينة \ نَفيسة precious stones; خاتَم مُرَصَّع بالجَواهِرِ a bejewelled ring; هذا المَبْنى هو جَوْهَرةٌ في مَرْكَزِ المَدينةِ this building is the pearl of the city centre; جَوْهَرة في الوَحْلِ a rough diamond (BrE), a diamond in the rough (AmE)

جَواهِرْجيّ n jeweller

جَوْهَريّ A *adj* essential; fundamental; substantial; جَوْهَرِيًّا in substance; مُشْكِلة جَوْهَرِيّة a key issue; اخْتِلاف جَوْهَرِيّ a fundamental difference; صِفات جَوْهَرِيّة intrinsic properties; النُّقْطة الجَوْهَرِيّة the main point
B n jeweller

مُجَوْهَر n jewel; مُجَوْهَراتٍ jewellery; المُجَوْهَراتِ الذَهَبيّة gold jewellery; بائِع المُجَوْهَراتِ jeweller

جَوّ n |أَجْواء, جِواء| 1 [طَقْس] weather; جَوّ قارِس severe weather; جَوّ خَريفيّ autumn weather; جَوّ رَبيعيّ جَميل \ مُشْمِس pleasant/sunny spring weather; الجَوُّ مُتَغَيِّر \ مُتَقَلِّبٌ the weather is changeable; حالة الجَوِّ weather conditions; تَوَقُّعات أَحْوالِ الجَوِّ weather forecast; أَحْوال الجَوِّ المُنْتَظَرة the (weather) outlook 2 [مُحيط] atmosphere, ambience, mood, feeling; جَوّ مُتَوَتِّر \ مُضْطرب a tense atmosphere; جَوّ من التَعَصُّبِ a spirit of intolerance; عَكَّرَ \ أَفْسَدَ الجَوَّ to ruin the atmosphere; نَقَّى الأَجْواءَ to clear the air; يَسودُ جَوٌّ مَرِحٌ \ كَئيبٌ a cheerful/gloomy atmosphere prevails; في أَجْواءٍ مُريحةٍ in high spirits 3 [الغِلاف الجَوّيّ] atmosphere, air, airspace; في الجَوِّ in the air; خَرَقَ أَجْواءَ بَلَدٍ to violate a country's airspace; سِلاح الجَوِّ air force; نَقَلَ شَيْئاً جَوًّا \ عن طَريقِ الجَوِّ to airlift sth

جَوّيّ *adj* 1 [مَنْسوب للجَوِّ] meteorological, weather (*before n*); atmospheric; ظُروف جَوّيّة weather conditions; ضَغْط جَوّيّ

atmospheric pressure; اضْطِرابات جَوّيّة turbulence; نَشْرة جَوّيّة weather report **2** [في الغِلافِ الجَوّيِّ] air (*before n*); بَريد جَوّيّ airmail; دِفاع جَوّيّ anti-aircraft defence; القُوّات الجَوّيّة the air force; خُطوط جَوّيّة airlines; هُجوم جَوّيّ an air attack; حَرَكة المُرورِ الجَوّيِّ air traffic; نَقْل جَوّيّ air transport, airlift

جَوِيَ *v* |a; جَوًى| *to be intensely moved* (*by love or grief*)

جُويلِية *n* (Algeria, Tunisia) July

جاءَ *v* |i; مَجيء| **1** [أتى] to come; to arrive; جاءَتْ رَسائِلُ \ أَخْبارٌ letters/news arrived; جاءَتْني رِسالةٌ من الرَئيسِ I received a letter from the president; جاءَهُ مَرَضٌ to get a disease; جاءَ من المَحَطّةِ to come from the station; جاءَ إلى الحُكْمِ to come into power; جاءَ إلى الوُجودِ to first see the light of day; جاءَ في المَرْكَزِ الأَوّلِ to take first place; ذَهَبَ وَجاءَ to pace up and down **2** [أَحْضَرَ] to bring (along); جاءَ بِشَيْءٍ \ شَخْصٍ to bring sth/sb along **3** [وَرَدَ في] to be reported, to be said; جاءَ في الجَرائِدِ أَنّ ... it says in the newspapers that...

جَيْئة, جيئة *n* coming; جيئةً وَذَهاباً to and fro; back and forth; coming and going

مَجيء *n* coming, arrival, advent; قبل مَجيءِ الإسْلامِ before the advent of Islam

[1] **جَيْب** *n* |جُيوب| **1** [في مَلابِسَ] pocket; جَيْب داخِليّ inside pocket; جَيْب مِعْطَفِهِ one's coat pocket; قاموس جَيْبٍ a pocket dictionary; دَفَعَ شَيْئاً من جَيْبِهِ الخاصِّ to pay for sth out of one's own pocket **2** [مِنْطَقة مَعْزولة] enclave, pocket; جُيوب المُقاوَمةِ pockets of resistance **3** (Math) sine; جَيْب التَمام cosine **4** (Anat) sinus; جَيْب صُدْغيّ sinus cavity; جَيْب أَنْفيّ nasal sinus; الْتِهاب الجُيوبِ (الأَنْفيّةِ) sinusitis

[2] **جيب** *n* jeep; سَيّارة جيب jeep

جيبوتي *n* |f| Djibouti; جُمْهوريّة جيبوتي Republic of Djibouti

جيتار *n* |جيتارات| guitar

جيجابايْت *n* |جيجابايْتات| gigabyte

جيد *n* |جُيود, أَجْياد| neck

جَيَّرَ *v* to whitewash; to plaster

جير *n* **1** [للبِناءِ] lime; جير حَيّ quicklime; جير مُطْفَأ slaked lime **2** (Geol) limestone; حَجَر الجيرِ limestone

جَيّار *n* quicklime

جيريّ *adj* calcareous; حَجَر جيريّ limestone

جيرْنزي *n* |f| Guernsey

الجيزة *n* Giza (*city and governorate in Egypt*)

جاشَ *v* |i; جَيْش, جَيَشان| to be excited/agitated; to rage, to thunder, to storm; to boil, to simmer; ما يَجيشُ في صَدْرِهِ من مَشاعِرِ the feelings burning in his heart

جَيَّشَ *v* to recruit, to enlist

جَيْش *n* |جُيوش| **1** (Mil) army, armed force; قائِد الجَيْشِ commander-in-chief; كانَ في الجَيْشِ to be in the army; تَطَوَّعَ للخِدْمةِ في الجَيْشِ to volunteer for military service **2** [عَدَد كَبير] army, host; جَيْش من الجَرادِ a plague of locusts; جَيْش من العاطِلينَ an army of the unemployed

جائِش *adj* surging, turbulent

جَيّاش *adj* impassioned, inflamed; agitated, excited; enraged; مَشاعِر جَيّاشة intense emotions; عَواطِف جَيّاشة passionate feelings

جافَ *v* |i; جَيْف| to stink, to be putrid (*of meat*)

جَيَّفَ *v* to be/become rotten; to stink

جيفة *n* |أَجْياف, جِيَف| carrion; (dead) body; corpse

جيفيّ *adj* الصَمْل الجيفيّ rigor mortis

جيل *n* |أَجْيال| generation; age, era; nation, people; الجيل الجَديد \ الصاعِد the new generation; الجيل الشابّ \ الناشِئ the younger generation; الجيل الأَوّل \ الثاني the first/second generation; الجيل الأَوّل من المُهاجِرينَ first-generation immigrants; الجيل الثالِث \ الرابِع (Tel) 3G/4G; الجيل المُعاصِر من الشَبابِ the young generation today; صِراع الأَجْيالِ generational conflict; ابْن جيلِهِ peer; انْتَمى إلى جيلٍ آخَرَ to belong to another generation; جيلاً بعد جيلٍ from generation to generation; تَوارَثَ شَيْئاً جيلاً عن جيلٍ to hand down sth from generation to generation

جيلاتي *n* (Egypt) ice cream

جيلاتين *n* gelatin, Jello®

جيم *n* |f| *name of the letter* ج

جين *n coll* |جينات| gene; جين سائِد \ مُتَنَحٍّ dominant/recessive gene; جينات بَشَريّة \ حَيَوانيّة human/animal genes;

عند الإنْسانِ ما يَقْرُبُ من ٣٠.٠٠٠ جينةٍ humans have approximately 30,000 genes

جينيّ *adj* genetic, gene (*before n*); هَنْدَسة جينيّة genetic engineering; عِلاج جينيّ gene therapy

‹ **جينْز** *n* jeans

‹ **جينْسِنْغ** *n* ginseng (*Panax ginseng*)

‹ **جينوم** *n* genome; خَريطة للجينوم genome map

‹ **جيهان** *n* |dipt f| Jihan (*female given name*)

‹ **جِيوسِياسيّ** *adj* geopolitical

‹ **جِيوفيزِياء** *n* |f| geophysics

جِيوفيزِيائيّ **A** *adj* geophysical

B *n* geophysicist

‹ **جِيولوجِيا** *n* geology

جِيولوجيّ *adj* geological

ح

‹ **حاء** *n* |f| *name of the letter* ح

‹ **حاخام** *n* |حاخامات| rabbi

‹ **حاشا** *particle* see حشو

‹ **حالوء** *n* house dust mite

‹ **حانوكا**, **هانوكا** *n* Hanukkah

‹ 1 **حَبَّ** *v* |i; حُبّ| to love, to like

حَبَّبَ *v* [1] [جَعَلَهُ مَحْبوباً] to make lovable/dear/attractive, to endear; حَبَّبَ نَفْسَهُ إلى شَخْصٍ to endear oneself to sb, to make oneself loved by/popular with sb [2] [أَوْصى] to recommend, to urge, to suggest [3] see also 2حبب

أَحَبَّ *v* [1] [أُغْرِمَ] to love; أَحَبَّ شَخْصاً to love sb, to care about sb; أَحَبَّ أُسْرَتَهُ \ حُرِّيَّتَهُ أَكْثَر من كُلِّ شَيْءٍ to love one's family/freedom more than anything [2] [أُعْجِبَ ب] to like; لا يُحِبُّ القَهْوة he doesn't like coffee [3] [وَلِعَ] to be fond of, to like; أَحَبَّ الأَطْفالَ \ الحَيَواناتِ to be fond of children/animals; أَحَبَّ الموسيقى to like music

تَحَبَّبَ *v* to show love, to reveal one's affections

تَحابَّ *v* to love each other

اسْتَحَبَّ *v* to prefer, to like better/more

حُبّ *n* love, affection; حُبّ حَقيقِيّ real/true love; حُبّ عُذْرِيّ courtly/platonic love; حُبّ صامِت \ غَيْر مُتَبادَلٍ an unspoken/unrequited love; حُبّ الذاتِ egoism, egotism; egocentrism; self-love; حُبّ أَبَوِيّ fatherly/paternal love; حُبّ الأُمِّ لِطِفْلِها the love of a mother for her child; حُبّ اللهِ the love of God; حُبّ الفَنِّ \ الموسيقى the love of art/music; حُبّ الوَطَنِ love for one's country, patriotism; الحُبّ بين الرَّجُلِ والمَرْأةِ the love between a man and woman; الحُبّ من أَوَّلِ نَظْرةٍ love at first sight; حُبُّهُ الأَوَّل his first love; كانَتْ حُبَّهُ الكَبيرَ she was his great love; لُغة الحُبِّ the language of love; رِسالة \ أُغْنِيّة حُبٍّ love letter/song; إِحْساس بالحُبِّ a feeling of love; لَيْسَ مَحْظوظاً في الحُبِّ he is not lucky in love; الحُبُّ أَعْمى love is blind; ما الحُبُّ إلاّ للحَبيبِ الأَوَّلِ first love is never forgotten; حُبًّا لَهُ \ بِهِ \ فيهِ for the love of him, out of love for him; عن حُبٍّ out of love; عيد الحُبِّ Valentine's day

حُبِّيّ *adj* hearty, amicable, friendly, cordial; amorous, loving, affectionate; حُبِّيًّا amicably; تَسْوِية حُبِّيّة an amicable settlement

حَبيب [A] *adj* |أَحِبّة, أَحْباب, أَحِبّاءُ| beloved, dear, loved; زَوْجي الحَبيب my beloved husband

[B] *n* |أَحِبّة, أَحْباب, أَحِبّاءُ| love, darling, sweetheart; يا حَبيبي my darling

أَحَبّ *adj* |dipt| dearer, more desirable, preferable; هذا أَحَبُّ إلَيَّ من ذلك this is dearer to me than that

مُحِبّ [A] *adj* loving, fond of; مُحِبّ للمَعْرِفة inquisitive; مُحِبّ للحَياةِ life-loving

[B] *n* lover, admirer, fan; supporter; مُحِبّ الموسيقى الكْلاسيكيّةِ a lover of classical music; مُحِبّ للطَبْخِ a cooking enthusiast; مُحِبّو السَلامِ lovers of peace

مُحَبَّب *adj* dear; pleasant; desirable; كُتُبها المُحَبَّبة her favourite books

مَحَبّة *n* love, affection; attachment; مَحَبّة البَشَرِ love of humanity/one's fellow human beings; سِمات المَحَبّةِ signs of love; characteristics of love

مَحْبوب [A] *adj* loved, dear; popular; lovable, desirable

[B] *n* darling

مُسْتَحَبّ *adj* desirable, recommendable; غَيْر مُسْتَحَبٍّ displeasing

‹ 2 **حَبَّبَ** *v* [1] (Bot) to bear/produce seed; to go to seed [2] [بَرْغَلَ] to be/become granular, to granulate [3] see also 1حبب

حَبّ *n coll* |حُبوب| **1** [قَمْح] grain, cereals; كيس حُبوبٍ a sack of grain; حَبّ الهانِ \ الهالِ cardamom (seed); مَحْصول الحُبوبِ grain crop; حَصَدَ مَحْصولَ الحُبوبِ to harvest the grain; زَرَعَ الحَبَّ to sow/grow grain; دَرَسَ الحَبَّ to thresh grain; طَحَنَ الحُبوبَ to grind/mill the grain **2** [بَذْر] seed **3** [ما يُشْبِهُ الحَبَّ] kernels, grains; حَبّ الغَمامِ hail **4** [كَرَز] حَبّ المُلوكِ cherries **5** [بُثور] pimples; حَبّ الشَّبابِ acne

حَبَب *n* (soap) bubble

حَبّة *n* **1** [قَمْح] |حُبوب| grain; granule; seed; pip; كامِل الحَبّةِ wholemeal (BrE), whole-grain (AmE); خُبْز كامِل الحَبّةِ wholemeal bread (BrE), whole-grain bread (AmE) **2** [أُرْز] |حَبّات| grain, granule; حَبّة رَمْلٍ a grain of sand; جَعَلَ من الحَبّةِ قُبّةً to make a mountain out of a molehill **3** [فاكِهة] |حَبّات| berry; حَبّة عِنَبٍ grape **4** (Med) |حُبوب| tablet, pill; حَبّة فاليوم a Valium tablet/pill; حَبّة مُنَوِّمة sleeping tablet/pill; حُبوب مُهَدِّئة analgesic tablets, painkillers; حَبّة للصُداعِ \ ضِدّ الصُداعِ headache tablet/pill, a pill against headaches; أَخَذَ \ تَناوَلَ حَبّةً to take a tablet/pill; اسْتَعْمَلَتْ حُبوبَ مَنْعِ الحَمْلِ she was on the pill **5** [بَثْر] |حُبوب| pimple, spot; blackhead **6** [مِقْياس المِساحةِ] |حَبّات| *a square measure, approx 58 square metres* **7** [مِقْياس الطولِ] |حَبّات| *a linear measure, approx 0.2 cm*

حُبَيْبة *n* little grain; small kernel

حُبَيْبيّ *adj* granular, granulated; بِنْية \ تَرْكيبة حُبَيْبيّة a granular structure

‹ **حُباحِب** *n coll* |dipt| glow-worm, firefly (*Lampyridae*)

‹ **حَبَّذَ** *v* to choose; to prefer; to approve of, to think favourably of; حَبَّذَ شَيْئاً to give preference to sth; to approve of sth; أُحَبِّذُ أَنْ يَكونَ الاجْتِماعُ هُنا I prefer the meeting to be here

حَبَّذا *excl* حَبَّذا لو ... how nice/good/great it would be if ...; it would be nice/good/great if ...; حَبَّذا الحالُ! That's great!, That's fantastic!

تَحْبيذ *n* **1** [اسْتِحْسان] approval; acclaim **2** [تَفْضيل] preference

مُحَبِّذ *n* supporter

‹ **حَبَرَ** *v* |u; حَبْر| to be glad

حَبَّرَ *v* to embellish, to refine; to write, to compose

حَبْر, حِبْر *n* |أَحْبار| prelate; *non-Muslim religious authority*; الحَبْر الأَعْظَم the Pope

حِبْر *n* ink; حِبْر صينيّ Indian ink (BrE), India ink (AmE); حِبْر سِرّيّ invisible ink; حِبْر الطِباعةِ printer's ink; عُبْوة حِبْرٍ ink cartridge; أُمّ الحِبْرِ squid; cuttlefish; مُجَرَّد حِبْرٍ على وَرَقٍ just ink on paper (*futile/meaningless*)

حَبّار *n* squid, cuttlefish

حُبارى *n* |f; حُبارَيات| (Zool) bustard (*Otididae*); أَبْلَه من الحُبارى ≈ dumb as an ox

حَبْريّ *adj* pontifical; رِسالة حَبْريّة encyclical

مِحْبَرة *n* |مَحابِرُ| inkwell

‹ **حَبَسَ** *v* |i; حَبْس| **1** [أَوْقَفَ] to stop; to obstruct, to block; حَبَسَ الكُرةَ to stop the ball; حَبَسَ أَنْفاسَهُ to hold one's breath; حَبَسَ دُموعَهُ to hold back one's tears **2** [سَجَنَ] to imprison, to detain, to lock up; حَبَسَ حَيَواناً في قَفَصٍ to lock up an animal in a cage **3** [وَقَفَ] to donate; حَبَسَ نَفْسَهُ على شَيْءٍ to devote oneself to sth

انْحَبَسَ *v* **1** [سُجِنَ] to be locked up **2** [حُصِرَ] to be held back, to be held up, to get stuck; انْحَبَسَ صَوْتُهُ his voice faltered; انْحَبَسَ المَطَرُ the rain held off

احْتَبَسَ *v* **1** [حَبَسَ] to retain; يَحْتَبِسُ الغِلافُ الجَوّيُّ الحَرارةَ the atmosphere retains heat **2** [انْحَبَسَ] to be held back; احْتَبَسَ المَطَرُ the rain stayed away **3** [سَجَنَ] to detain, to confine

حَبْس *n* |حُبوس| **1** [عُقوبة] imprisonment, custody, detention; حَبْس انْفِراديّ solitary confinement; وَضَعَ شَخْصاً في الحَبْسِ الانْفِراديّ to put sb in solitary confinement; حَبْس احْتِياطيّ preventive custody, preventive detention; حَبْس احْتِياطيّ لِمُدّةِ أُسْبوعَيْنِ two weeks in preventive custody; حَبْس على ذِمّةِ التَحْقيقِ preventive custody; عُقوبة حَبْسٍ قاسِية \ خَفيفة a harsh/light prison sentence; عُقوبة الحَبْسِ لِمُدّةِ سِتّةِ أَشْهُرٍ imprisonment; prison sentence; حَبْس لِمُدّةِ سِتّةِ أَشْهُرٍ a six-month prison sentence; حَكَمَ على شَخْصٍ بالحَبْسِ لِمُدّةِ سَنَتَيْنِ to sentence sb to two years in prison **2** [مُؤَسّسة] prison

حَبْس, حُبُس *n* |أَحْباس| *bequest for religious purposes*

حُبْسة *n* aphasia

حَبيس **A** *adj* |حُبَساءُ| confined, locked up

B *n* |حُبَساءُ| hermit

احْتِباس *n* **1** [حَبْس] retention; ظاهِرة الاحْتِباسِ الحَراريِّ the greenhouse effect; غازات الاحْتِباسِ الحَراريِّ greenhouse gases **2** [اعْتِقال] detention, arrest

انْحِباس *n* **1** [احْتِباس] barring, blocking, obstruction **2** [عَدَم الوُقوعِ] absence; انْحِباس الأَمْطارِ the absence of rain

مَحْبِس *n* |مَحابِسُ| prison, jail

مَحْبوس **A** *adj* |مَحابيسُ| imprisoned; كانَ مَحْبوساً to be in prison/custody

B *n* |مَحابيسُ| prisoner, convict

[1] **حَبَش** *n* turkey

[2] **حَبَشيّ** *adj, n* |أَحْباش| Abyssinian

الحَبَشة, الحَبَش *n* |f| Abyssinia

حَبَضَ *v* |i; حَبْض| to resonate, to reverberate

حَبَطَ, حَبِطَ *v* |a-i; حُبوط| to fail, to go wrong; to be futile

أَحْبَطَ *v* to thwart, to frustrate, to foil; أَحْبَطَ خِطَط شَخْصٍ to thwart sb's plans; أَحْبَطَ مُحاوَلةَ اغْتِيالٍ to foil an attempt on sb's life; أَحْبَطَ جُهودَ شَخْصٍ to frustrate sb's efforts

حُبوط *n* failure; futility

إِحْباط *n* frustration; إِحْباط بِسَبَبِ شَيْءٍ frustration because of sth; أَدّى إلى الإِحْباطِ to lead to frustration; العَديدُ من العامِلينَ يَشْعُرونَ بالإِحْباطِ many employees are frustrated

مُحْبَط *adj* frustrated

مُحْبِط *adj* discouraging, grim

حَبَق *n* basil

حَبَكَ *v* |i-u; حَبْك| **1** [نَسَجَ] to weave, to knit **2** [أَحْكَمَ] to tighten **3** [أَحْسَنَ تَدْبيرَهُ] to plan carefully, to devise

حِباك *n* fence; palisade

حَبْكة *n* plot, story line; حَبْكة رِوايةٍ the plot of a novel

مَحْبوك *adj* woven, knitted; tightened

[1] **حابِل** *n* snare setter, hunter; اخْتَلَطَ الحابِلُ بالنابِلِ everything became confused

حِبالة *n* |حَبائِلُ| snare

حَبْل *n* |حِبال, أَحْبال, أَحْبُل, حُبول| **1** [رِباط] rope, cord; string; cable; حَبْل غَليظ \ سَميك heavy/thick rope; قِطْعة حَبْلٍ طَويلة \ قَصيرة a long/short piece of rope; حَبْل الأَفْكارِ \ التَفْكيرِ train of thought; حَبْل المِشْنَقةِ hangman's rope; حَبْل المَساكينِ ivy; نَطّ الحَبْلِ rope-skipping, jumping rope; شَدَّ حَبْلاً to stretch a rope, to tighten a rope; شَدّ الحَبْلِ tug-of-war; أَرْخى الحَبْلَ to let out the rope, to give the rope some slack; مَشى على الحَبْلِ to walk a tightrope; لَعِبَ على الحَبْلَيْنِ to have one's cake and eat it (too); to play a double game; to double-cross; حَبْلُ الكِذْبِ قَصيرٌ lies are soon exposed; أَوْقَعَ الفَتَياتِ في حِبالِهِ to catch/get girls **2** (Anat) tendon; حَبْل شَوْكيّ spine, spinal cord; حَبْل سُرِّيّ umbilical cord; حَبْل الوَريدِ jugular vein; الحِبال الصَوْتيّة the vocal cords

أُحْبولة *n* |أَحابيلُ| **1** [مَصْيَدة] snare **2** [حيلة] trap; ruse, stratagem

[2] **حَبِلَ** *v* |a; حَبَل| to be/become pregnant, to conceive; حَبِلَتْ بِطِفْلٍ she got pregnant; she was pregnant

حَبَّلَ *v* to make pregnant

أَحْبَلَ *v* to make pregnant

حَبَل *n* pregnancy; conception; حَبَل وَهْميّ phantom pregnancy, false pregnancy; مَنْع الحَبَلِ, مانِع للحَبَلِ contraceptive; حُبوب مَنْع الحَبَلِ contraceptive pill, the pill

حُبْلى *adj* |حَبالى| pregnant; امْرَأة حُبْلى a pregnant woman

حَبْن *n* oleander

حَبَّهان *n* cardamom

حَبا *v* |u; حَبو| **1** [طِفْلٌ] to crawl **2** [وَهَبَ] to give, to present

حابى *v* to favour, to side with; حابى أَصْدِقاءَهُ to favour one's friends

حَبْوة *n* **1** [زَحْف] crawling **2** [إِعْطاء] giving

حُبْوة, حِبْوة *n* |حُبًى, حِبًى| giving

مُحاباة *n* partiality, favouritism; مُحاباة الأَقارِبِ \ الأَصْدِقاءِ nepotism

حَتَّ *v* |u; حَتّ| to scratch/scrape/rub off; حَتَّ الشَجَرَ to strip the bark off a tree

تَحاتَّ *v* **1** (Geol) to erode **2** (Phys) to corrode

حُتاتة *n* |حُتات| scraps, morsels; crumbs; debris

تَحات *n* 1 (Geol) erosion 2 (Phys) corrosion

‹ **حَتَدَ, حَتِدَ** *v* |a-u; حَتْد| to come from a good background

‹ **حِتار** *n* |حُتُر| edge, border; حِتار الظُفْر cuticle

حُتْرة *n* mouthful; drop; bit

‹ **حَتْف** *n* |حُتوف| death; لَقِيَ حَتْفَهُ to die, to meet one's end; مات حَتْفَ أَنْفِهِ to die, to meet one's end; ذَهَبَ إلى حَتْفِهِ he died a natural death

‹ **حَتَكَ** *v* |u; حَتْك| to scratch

‹ **حَتَمَ** *v* |i; حَتْم| |على| to impose on; to prescribe for

حَتَّمَ *v* to impose, to enforce; to oblige; to make necessary; حَتَّمَ شَيْئاً على شَخْصٍ to impose sth on sb

تَحَتَّمَ *v* to be obliged; سَيَتَحَتَّمُ عَلَيْهِ أَنْ ... he will have to...

حَتْم *n* |حُتوم| حَتْماً absolutely, definitely, certainly; irrevocably; inevitably; سَيُؤَدّي هذا حَتْماً إلى كارِثَةٍ this will inevitably lead to a disaster; يَجِبُ أَنْ تَرى ذلك الفيلْمَ حَتْماً you should definitely see that film

حاتِم *n* judge

حَتّامَ *conj* see حتى

حَتْمِيّ *adj* definite; inevitable, inescapable, unavoidable; كانَ الاصْطِدامُ حَتْمِيّاً the collision was inevitable; عاقِبة حَتْمِيّة an inevitable consequence

حَتْمِيّة *n* inevitability; necessity; determinism

مُحَتَّم *adj* inevitable, unavoidable

مَحْتوم *adj* inevitable, unavoidable; destined, predestined; شَرّ مَحْتوم a necessary evil; كانَ فَشَلاً مَحْتوماً it was destined to fail; لاقى مَصيرَهُ المَحْتومَ to meet one's destiny; كارِثة مَحْتومة an inevitable disaster; نِهاية مَحْتومة an inevitable end

‹ **حَتّى** A *prep* 1 [إلى وَقْتٍ] until; till, up to; حَتّى نِهايةِ المُؤْتَمَرِ until the end of the conference; حَتّى اليَوْمِ up to the present day, even now; حَتّى المَساءِ till the evening; حَتّى مَتى؟ for how long? 2 [إلى مَكانٍ] as far as, to, until; سِرْنا حَتّى المَدينةِ we walked as far as the city

B *conj* 1 [إلى أنّ] until, till; حَتّى يُحَقِّقَ أَهْدافَهُ until he has achieved his goals; حَتّى أَصْبَحَ من المُمْكِنِ أَنْ ... until it became possible to ... 2 [لِكَيْ] in order that, so that; to; سافَرَ حَتّى يَطَّلِعَ على أَحْدَثِ التَطَوُّراتِ he travelled to be informed of the latest developments; حَفِظَ المَعْلوماتِ في الكُمْبْيوتَر حَتّى لا تَضيعَ he saved the data on the computer so it wouldn't be lost 3 [حَتّى أنّ] حَتّى أنّ until; in such a way that; شاطَرَ رَأْيَهُ زُمَلاءُ كَثيرونَ حَتّى أنّ العُلَماءَ أَعْرَبوا عن قَلَقِهِمْ so many colleagues shared his opinion that the scientists started to express their concern 4 [ما ... حَتّى] ما خَرَجَ ...; he had hardly left when ...; ما كادَ يَخْرُجُ حَتّى السُكّانُ حَتّى هَدَمَ الجُنودُ بُيوتَهُمْ the residents had only just left when the soldiers destroyed their houses; ما إنْ يَدْخُلَ المُدَرِّسُ الفَصْلَ حَتّى يَفْتَحَ الطُلّابُ كُتُبَهُمْ as soon as the teacher enters the classroom the students open their books

C *adv* 1 [أَيْضاً] even, also; حَتّى الرِجالُ الطَيِّبونَ يُخْطِئونَ even good men make mistakes; لم أَشْتَرِ حَتّى كِتاباً واحِداً I didn't buy even one book; يَدْفَعُ دون حَتّى أَنْ يَنْظُرَ إلى ما يَشْتَريهِ he pays without even looking at what he's buying; لا تَثِقوا بِأَحَدٍ ولا حَتّى بي don't trust anyone, not even me 2 [وَلَوْ] حَتّى وَلَوْ even though; even if; إنّها مُسْتَعِدّةٌ للدفاعِ عَنْهُ حَتّى وَلَوْ كَلَّفَها الأَمْرُ حَياتَها she is prepared to defend him even if it costs her her life; حَتّى وَلَوْ كانَ السُمَّ الزُعافَ even though it is pure poison

حَتّامَ *conj* until when?, for how long?

‹ **حَثَّ** *v* |u; حَثّ| to urge, to incite, to spur on, to induce; to stimulate, to motivate; حَثَّ شَخْصاً على شَيْءٍ to urge sb to do sth; حَثَّ شَخْصاً على السَرِقةِ to incite sb to steal; حَثَّ شَخْصاً على الإسْراعِ \ العَجَلةِ to urge sb to hurry; حَثَّ شَخْصاً على التَفْكيرِ to set sb thinking; حَثَّ خُطاهُ to walk faster; حَثَّ خُطاهُ إلى البَيْتِ he hurried home; حَثَّتْها رَغْبَتُها في النَجاحِ she was driven by her desire to succeed

أَحَثَّ *v* to urge, to encourage; to stimulate

اسْتَحَثَّ *v* to urge; to incite; to encourage

حَثّ *n* urging; incitement; encouragement; stimulation; حَثُّهُ على اتِّخاذِ إجْراءاتٍ his insistence on taking steps

حَثيث *adj* quick, fast, rapid; جُهود حَثيثة speedy efforts; خُطَوات حَثيثة quick steps

‹ **حَثَرَ** *v* |a; حَثَر| to thicken; to solidify

احتجّ *v* ① [اِعْتَرَضَ] |على| to protest; to object; احتجّ على شيْءٍ to raise objections to sth; to protest against sth; احْتَجَّ لدى شَخْصٍ على شيْءٍ to lodge an objection with sb to sth, to protest to sb against sth; ... احْتَجَّ بأنَّ to object that ... ② [أتى بِحُجَج] |ب| to put forward as an argument; to plead ③ [تذرَّع] to give/use as an excuse ④ [شَرَح عَقْليًّا] to reason out

حاجّ *n* |حُجّاج, حَجيج| haji (*title for sb who has performed the pilgrimage to Mecca*)

حَجّ *n* |حَجّات, حِجَج| pilgrimage, hajj (*Muslim pilgrimage to Mecca*); الحَجّ إلى مَكّة the pilgrimage to Mecca; سورة الحَجّ The Pilgrimage (*Sura 22*); أدّى مَناسِكَ الحَجِّ to perform the rites of the hajj

حِجاج *n* |أَحِجّة| eye socket, orbit

حُجّة *n* |حُجَج| ① [عُذْر] excuse, pretext; بِحُجّةِ أنَّ ... under the pretence that ..., on the pretext of/that ...; اخْتلَق حُجّةً to make up an excuse ② [عِلّة] argument, reason; حُجّة قويّة \ دامغة \ مَتينة a strong/cogent/solid argument; حُجّة باهِتة \ بالِية a weak argument; حُجّة سَليمة \ داحِضة a sound/untenable argument; حُجّة مع \ ضدّ شَيْءٍ an argument for/against sth; أتى بِحُجَجٍ to present arguments; قارَعَ الحُجّةَ بالحُجّةِ to attack an argument with a counterargument; دَحَض حُجّةً to refute/invalidate/undermine an argument ③ [إثْبات] proof, evidence; إقامة الحُجّة furnishing of proof, averment

حِجّة *n* pilgrimage; حِجّة الوَداع the Farewell Pilgrimage (*the last pilgrimage of the Prophet Muhammad to Mecca*); ذو الحِجّة Dhu al-Hijja (*the twelfth month of the Islamic calendar*)

حُجّيّة *n* evidence

احْتِجاج *n* |احْتِجاجات| ① [اعْتِراض] objection, protest; احْتِجاج شَكْليّ a formal objection; احْتِجاج صامِت silent protest; عاصِفة من الاحْتِجاجاتِ a storm of protest; حَرَكة احْتِجاج protest movement; حَرَكة الاحْتِجاجِ ضدّ عَمَليّاتِ الإجْهاضِ a protest movement against abortion; حَمْلة احْتِجاجٍ protest campaign; قامَ بِحَمْلةِ احْتِجاجٍ to launch a protest campaign; مَسيرة احْتِجاجٍ protest march; مُظاهَرة

حُثالة *n* ① [راسِب] sediment, deposit, dregs; sludge ② [رَذالة] scum, trash; حُثالة الناسِ \ المُجْتَمَع riff-raff, scum, rabble

حَثا *v* |u; حَثْو| to cover

حَثاة *n* skin (*of a fruit*)

حَجَبَ *v* |u; حَجْب| ① [أَخْفى] to veil, to cover; to hide; حَجَبَ شَيْئاً عن الأَنْظارِ to hide sth from view; حَجَبَ شَيْئاً عن شَيْءٍ to screen sth off from sth; حَجَبَ الحَقيقةَ to conceal the truth; حَجَبَ زُجاجاً to cover a window; حَجَبَ مَعْلوماتٍ to withhold information ② [وَضَعَ حِجاباً] to veil; حَجَبَ وَجْهَهُ to cover one's face with a veil

حَجَّبَ *v* to veil; to screen off

تَحَجَّبَ *v* to wear a veil/headscarf

انْحَجَبَ *v* to shelter oneself, to cover oneself

احْتَجَبَ *v* ① [اخْتَفى] to hide; to disappear; احْتَجَبَت الجَريدةُ عن الصُدور the newspaper ceased publication ② [وَضَعَ حِجاباً] to be veiled, to wear a hijab; تَحْتَجِبُ النساءُ هناكَ women there wear the hijab

حاجِب *n* ① (Anat) |حَواجِبُ| eyebrow; حاجِبانِ خَشِنانِ bushy eyebrows; حاجِبانِ كَثيفانِ thick eyebrows; قَطَّبَ الحاجِبَيْنِ to knit one's brows, to frown; نَتَفَ الحاجِبَيْنِ to pluck one's eyebrows ② [بَوّاب] |حَجَبة, حُجاب| doorkeeper, doorman; chamberlain

حِجاب *n* |حُجُب, أَحْجِبة| ① [غِطاء الرَأْسِ] hijab, veil, headscarf ② [فاصِل] screen; partition; حِجاب حاجِز diaphragm ③ [تَميمة] amulet, talisman

تَحْجيب *n* veiling; concealing

مُتَحَجِّب *adj* veiled, wearing a hijab; غَيْر مُتَحَجِّبٍ unveiled, without a hijab

مُحَجَّبة *n* veiled woman, woman wearing a hijab

مَحْجوب *adj* hidden; veiled; مَحْجوب عن الأَنْظارِ hidden from sight

حَجَّ *v* |u; حَجّ| to make the pilgrimage (to Mecca), to perform the hajj

حاجَّ *v* to debate; حاجَّ شَخْصاً to debate with sb

تَحاجَّ *v* to debate, to hold a debate; to argue

احْتِجاجِ protest demonstration; قامَ بِمُظاهَرة احْتِجاجٍ to hold a protest demonstration; نَظَّمَ مُظاهَرةَ احْتِجاجٍ to organize/stage a protest demonstration; مُذَكِّرة \ عَريضة احْتِجاج (notice of) objection; أَرْسَلَ مُذَكِّرةَ احْتِجاج to lodge/file an objection (in writing); أَثارَ احْتِجاجاً to provoke protest; قَدَّمَ احْتِجاجاً (ضدّ) to lodge/file an objection (against); أَضْرَبَ احْتِجاجاً على شَيْءٍ to strike in protest of sth; احْتِجاجاً على in protest against (2) [ادِّعاء] argumentation

احْتِجاجِيّ *adj* protest (*before n*); تَظاهُرة احْتِجاجيّة protest demonstration

مُحاجّة *n* |مُحاجّ| (1) [جِدال] argumentation (2) [تَقْديم حُجَج] dispute

مُحْتَجّ A *adj* protesting
B *n* protestor

مَحَجّ *n* place of pilgrimage; destination (*of a journey*)

مِحْجاج A *adj* argumentative
B *n* (1) (*Med*) catheter; أَدْخَلَ مِحْجاجاً to insert a catheter (2) [مُجادِل] *person who loves to argue*

مَحَجّة *n* |مَحاجّ| destination (*of a journey*); أَصْبَحَت القاهِرةُ مَحَجّةَ الرُّؤَساءِ العَرَب Cairo has become the destination of the Arab presidents

1 **حَجَرَ** *v* |u; حَجْر| (1) (*Law*) to declare legally incompetent; طَلَبَت الزَّوْجةُ من القاضي أنْ يَحْجُرَ على زَوْجِها the wife requested the judge to declare her husband legally incompetent (2) [مَنَعَ] to deny access; حَجَرَ شَخْصاً \ على شَخْصٍ to deny access to sb

حَجْر *n* (1) [شَرْط] restriction, curbing; suppression; ban; حَجْر صِحّيّ quarantine (2) (*Law*) revocation/limitation of legal competence; تَمَّ الحَجْرُ على أَمْلاكِهِ his property was placed under legal guardianship

حِجْر *n* (1) [حِضْن] lap; جَلَسَ في حِجْرِ شَخْصٍ to sit on sb's lap; أَخَذَ شَخْصاً في حِجْرِهِ to take sb on one's lap (2) [مُحَرَّم] being forbidden (3) [حِصان] mare (4) (*Islam*) see 2 حجر

حُجْرة *n* |حُجَر, حُجُرات, حُجَرات| (1) [غُرْفة] room; حُجْرة تَغْيير المَلابِسِ changing room (BrE), fitting/dressing room (AmE); حُجْرة البَوّابِ porters' lodge; doorman's quarters; سورة الحُجُرات The Chambers (*Sura 49*) (2) [في السَفينةِ \ القِطارِ] cabin (*on a ship*); compartment (*on a train*)

حُجَيْرة *n* (1) [غُرْفة صَغيرة] booth, cell (2) [عُلْبة] magazine

مَحْجَر *n* |مَحاجِرُ| (1) [صِحّيّ] quarantine; مَحْجَر صِحّيّ quarantine (2) [حَبْس] prison (3) [مَقْلَع حِجارةٍ] see 2 حجر

مِحْجَر, مَحْجِر *n* |مَحاجِرُ| مِحْجَر العَيْنِ eye socket

مَحْجور A *adj* placed under guardianship
B *n* minor placed under guardianship, ward

2 **حَجَّرَ** *v* to petrify; قد حَجَّرَ الثَراءُ قَلْبَهُ wealth had turned his heart into stone

تَحَجَّرَ *v* to turn to stone, to become petrified

اسْتَحْجَرَ *v* to become petrified, to turn to stone

حَجّار *n* |حَجّارونَ| stonemason; stonecutter

حَجَر *n* |أَحْجار, حِجار, حِجارة| stone, rock; حَجَر كَريم precious stone, gem; حَجَر نَيْزَكيّ meteorite; حَجَر حَريريّ asbestos; حَجَر رَمْليّ sandstone; حَجَر القَدّاحة flint; حَجَر تَذْكاريّ memorial stone; الحَجَر الأَسْوَد the Black Stone (*in the Kaaba in Mecca*); حَجَر الزاوية cornerstone; حَجَر الفَلاسِفة the philosopher's stone; زَهْر الحَجَر lichen; على مَرْمى حَجَرٍ within a stone's throw; وَضَعَ حَجَرَ الأَساس to lay the foundation/first stone; كانَ \ شَكَّلَ حَجَرَ عَثْرة to be a stumbling block; احْذَرْ تَساقُطَ الأَحْجار! danger! falling rocks!; ضَرَبَ عُصْفورَيْن بِحَجَر واحِد to kill two birds with one stone

حِجْر *n* (1) (*Islam*) سورة الحِجْر The Rocky Tract (*Sura 15*) (2) see also 1 حجر

حَجَريّ *adj* stone (*before n*); بَيْت \ حائط حَجَريّ a stone house/wall; العَصْر الحَجَريّ the Stone Age; فَحْم حَجَريّ coal

مُتَحَجِّر A *adj* petrified; fossilized; خَشَب مُتَحَجِّر petrified wood
B *n* fossil

مَحْجَر *n* |مَحاجِرُ| (1) quarry (2) see also 1 حجر

مَحْجَريّ *adj* stone (*before n*); خامات مَحْجَريّة stone raw materials

حَجَزَ *v* |i-u; حَجْز| (1) [فَصَلَ] to separate; حَجَزَ بين الفَريقَيْنِ المُتَقاتِلَيْنِ to separate the warring parties (2) [مَنَعَ] to hold back; to restrain; حَجَزَ شَخْصاً عن شَيْءٍ to hold sb back from sth **3** [مَقْعَداً، غُرْفَةً] to reserve, to book, to make reservations for; حَجَزَ مَقْعَداً في المَسْرَحِ to reserve a seat at the theatre; حَجَزَ مائِدةً في مَطْعَمٍ to book a table in a restaurant; حَجَزَ غُرْفَةً في فُنْدُقٍ to book a room at a hotel; حَجَزَ تَذْكِرةً to book a ticket; حَجَزَ رِحْلَةً \ للسَفَرِ to book a trip **4** [صادَرَ] to impound, to confiscate, to seize; حَجَزَ على شَيْءٍ to impound sth; حَجَزَ على مُمْتَلَكاتِ شَخْصٍ to confiscate sb's property **5** [اعْتَقَلَ] to arrest, to detain

احْتَجَزَ *v* to arrest; to detain; to take/hold hostage; احْتَجَزَ شَخْصاً to take sb into custody; to hold sb hostage; احْتَجَزَ سَفينةً to place an embargo on a ship; احْتَجَزَ رِسالةً to intercept a letter

حَجْز *n* |حُجوز| **1** [مَقْعَدٍ أو غُرْفةٍ] booking, reservation; حَجْز مَقاعِدَ \ أماكِنَ reservation of seats/places **2** (Law) seizure, confiscation; attachment; embargo; حَجْز ضَريبيّ seizure of assets to pay off tax arrears

حاجِز **A** *n* |حَواجِزُ| **1** [سور] blockade, barrier, barricade; enclosure, fence; حاجِز بَشَريّ a human shield; حاجِز أَنْفيّ intranasal septum; حاجِز ناريّ firewall; حاجِز تَفْتيشٍ checkpoint; حاجِز مُرورٍ barrier; حاجِز للماءِ dike; dam; حاجِز في الطَّريقِ roadblock; سِباق ۱۱۰ م حَواجِزَ the 110-metre hurdles; حاجِز صَوْتيّ sound barrier; اخْتَرَقَ \ اجْتازَ الحاجِزَ الصَوْتيَّ to break the sound barrier; أَقامَ \ بَنى حاجِزاً to set up/build a barricade **2** [عَرْقَلة] barrier, obstacle; حاجِز نَفْسيّ a psychological barrier; حَواجِز تِجاريّة trade barriers; كَسَرَ حاجِزاً to break a barrier; تَخَطّى حَواجِزَ اللُغةِ to cross language barriers; لا يُشَكِّلُ هذا حاجِزاً مانِعاً this is not an insurmountable barrier

B *adj* دَوْلة حاجِزة buffer state; حِجاب حاجِز diaphragm

حِجاز *n* belt; rope

احْتِجاز *n* taking hostage; seizure; detention, taking into custody; احْتِجاز أَسْرى the detention of prisoners; the taking of prisoners; تَمَّ احْتِجازُهُ he was taken into custody

الحِجاز *n* |f| Hejaz (*region of Saudi Arabia in which Mecca is located*)

مُحْتَجَز **A** *adj* **1** [شَخْص] detained; held captive; taken hostage **2** [شَأْن] confiscated

B *n* prisoner; detainee

مُحْتَجِز *n* |مُحْتَجِزونَ| occupier; مُحْتَجِزو السِفارةِ the people who have taken over the embassy

مَحْجوز *adj* **1** [مَحْصور] occupied; booked, reserved; هذا المَكانُ مَحْجوزٌ this seat is taken; كُلُّ الغُرَفِ مَحْجوزةٌ all the rooms are reserved; no vacancy **2** [مَحْبوس] مَحْجوز عَلَيْهِ confiscated

‹ **احْتَجَفَ** *v* |من| to take possession of

‹ **حَجَلَ** *v* |i-u; حَجْل, حَجَلان| to hop, to frolic

حَجْل, حِجْل *n* |حُجول, أَحْجال| anklet

حَجَل *n coll* |حِجْلى, حِجْلان| partridge

حَجْلة *n* hopping; hopscotch

‹ **حَجَمَ** *v* |u; حَجْم| **1** [حَيَواناً] to muzzle **2** (Med) to cup (*a form of traditional or alternative medicine*)

حَجَّمَ *v* to restrict, to limit, to curtail; حَجَّمَ حُرّيّةَ شَخْصٍ to restrict sb's freedom; حَجَّمَ دَوْرَ شَخْصٍ to marginalize/sideline sb

أَحْجَمَ *v* |عن| to refrain from; to renounce; أَحْجَمَ عن شَيْءٍ to not do sth, to refrain from sth

حَجْم *n* |حُجوم, أَحْجام| size, dimensions, proportions; content, volume

حَجّام *n* cupper (*a person who carries out cupping*)

حِجامة *n* bloodletting

إِحْجام *n* abstention, refraining, refrainment; restraint

تَحْجيم *n* restriction, limiting, curtailment

‹ **حَجَنَ** *v* |i; حَجْن| to bend

حَجْنة *n* reed

مِحْجَن *n* |مَحاجِنُ| drag

‹ **حَجا** *v* |u; حَجْو| |ب| to assert

حاجى *v* to speak in riddles

أُحْجِيّة *n* |أَحاجِيّ, أَحاجٍ| riddle, puzzle

‹ **حِدَأة, حَدَأة, حِدْأة** *n* |حِدَأ, حِداء, حِدْآن| (Zool) kite (*Accipitridae*)

‹ **حَدِبَ** *v* |a; حَدَب| **1** [عَطَفَ] to be nice/friendly/caring; حَدِبَ على شَخْصٍ to be nice to sb; to take care of sb **2** [الظَهْرُ] to be hunchbacked

تَحَدَّثَ *v* to speak, to talk, to converse; تَحَدَّثَ مع \ إلى شَخْصٍ to speak with/talk to sb; to have a chat/conversation with sb; تَحَدَّثَ عن شَيْءٍ \ شَخْصٍ to talk about sth/sb; تَحَدَّثَ بالسوءِ عن شَخْصٍ \ شَيْءٍ to talk badly about sb/sth

تَحادَثَ *v* to speak, to talk (with each other); تَحادَثَ مع شَخْصٍ to have a conversation with sb

اِسْتَحْدَثَ *v* 1 [أَحْدَثَ] to start, to introduce; to create, to set up; اسْتَحْدَثَ مَنْصِباً to create a position/post 2 [جَدَّدَ] to renew 3 [اعْتَبَرَ حَديثاً] to consider young/new

حَدَث *n* |أَحْداث| 1 [واقِعة] event, incident, occurrence, happening; حَدَث هامّ \ خاصّ a major/special event; حَدَث كَبير \ عَظيم a big event; حَدَث سَعيد a happy event; حَدَث بارِز a striking event; حَدَث خَطير \ جِدّيّ a serious incident; حَدَث فَريد من نَوْعِهِ a one-time event; حَدَث سَنَوِيّ an annual event; حَدَث رِياضيّ sports event; أَحْداث غَيْر مُتَوَقَّعة unforeseen events; أَحْداث مُعاصِرة current events; أَحْداث الساعةِ news of the moment; صيغة الحَدَثِ infinitive; مَسْرَح الأَحْداثِ scene of the events; battlefield; crime scene; scene of the accident; pitch, field (*sports*); stage (*politics*); تَوَجَّهَت الشُرْطةُ إلى مَسْرَحِ الأَحْداثِ the police headed to the scene of the crime/incident; بَرَزَت الحَرَكةُ على مَسْرَحِ الأَحْداثِ السِياسيّة the movement emerged on the political scene; مَسْرَحُ أَحْداثِ الرِوايةِ إفْريقيا the novel is set in Africa; يَقَعُ حَدَثٌ an incident is taking place 2 [صَغير السِنِّ] minor; young man; أَحْداث juveniles, young people; سِجْن الأَحْداثِ juvenile detention centre; قاضي الأَحْداثِ magistrate in a juvenile court

حادِث *n* |حادِثات, حَوادِثُ| 1 [واقِعة] incident, event, happening, occurrence; حادِث غَريب \ مُريع a strange/terrible event; حادِث اخْتِطافٍ kidnapping, abduction; حادِث اغْتِيالٍ \ مَقْتَلٍ assassination, murder; حادِث انْفِجارٍ explosion; 2 [نَكْبة] accident; حادِث طائِرةٍ plane crash; حادِث عَمَلٍ work accident; حادِث سَيْرٍ \ مُروريّ traffic accident; حادِث مُروريّ خَطير a serious traffic accident; جُرِحَتْ في حادِثٍ مُروريٍّ she was injured in a traffic accident; مَكانَ الحادِثِ the scene of the accident; the scene of the crime; ماتَ في حادِثٍ to be killed in an accident

حَدَّبَ *v* to bend, to arch; to make convex

تَحَدَّبَ *v* to be hunchbacked; to be crooked; to be convex

حَدَب *n* |أَحْداب, حِداب| love, affection; care, solicitude

(Idiom) من كُلِّ حَدَبٍ وَصَوْبٍ from all sides/directions, from everywhere

حَدَبة *n* 1 [نُتوء] hump, lump, bump, swelling 2 [في الظَهْرِ] hunchback 3 (Mech) ridge; جِذْع \ مِحْوَر الحَدَباتِ camshaft

أَحْدَب A *adj* |dipt; حُدْب| hunchbacked; كانَ أَحْدَبَ to be hunchbacked

B *n* |dipt; حُدْب| hunchback

مُحَدَّب *adj* convex; arched; bumpy; تِلال مُحَدَّبة undulating hills

مُحْدَوْدِب *adj* convex; gibbous; hunchbacked

حِدة *n* see وحد

حَدَثَ *v* |u; حُدوث| to happen, to occur, to take place, to come about, to arise; حَدَثَ شَيْءٌ something happened, something has occurred; حَدَثَتْ مُشْكِلةٌ a difficulty arose; حَدَثَتْ خِلافاتٌ حادّةٌ داخِلَ الحِزْبِ الحاكِمِ sharp disagreements arose within the ruling party; كيف حَدَثَ هذا؟ how did that/it happen?; ماذا حَدَثَ لَكَ؟ what happened to you?; إنّ شَيْئاً من ذلك لم يَحْدُثْ nothing of the sort happened, nothing of the kind took place

حَدُثَ *v* |u; حَداثة| to be new/modern/recent; to be young

حَدَّثَ *v* 1 [رَوى] to speak, to talk; to tell; حَدَّثَ شَخْصاً عن \ في شَيْءٍ to speak with/talk to sb about sth; to tell sb about sth; حَدِّثْ وَلا حَرَجْ speak your mind, speak freely; حَدَّثَتْهُ نَفْسُهُ ب \ أنّ... his heart/inner voice told him that... 2 [جَدَّدَ] to modernize, to update, to upgrade; حَدَّثَ مَبْنًى \ أثاثاً to modernize a building/the furnishings; حَدَّثَ أَرْقاماً to update the figures; حَدَّثَ نِظاماً to update a system

حادَثَ *v* to speak to, to talk to, to converse with; to discuss with; حادَثَ شَخْصاً to talk/speak to sb; to have a conversation with sb

أَحْدَثَ *v* to cause, to make; to create, to produce; أَحْدَثَ ضَجّةً to be noisy; to cause a commotion; أَحْدَثَ قَلَقاً to cause concern; أَحْدَثَ أَصْواتاً to produce/make sounds

حادِثة *n* |حَوادِثُ| ❶ [واقِعة] occurrence, event; incident; حادِثة مَقْتَلِ السادات the murder of Sadat; حادِثة إطْلاقِ نارٍ shoot-out; مَكان الحادِثةِ the scene of the disaster/accident ❷ [نَكْبة] accident; حادِثة خَطيرة \ كَبيرة a serious/major accident; حادِثة نَوَويّة nuclear disaster; حَوادِث في المُرورِ traffic accidents; حادِثة عَمَلٍ a workplace accident; تَعَرَّض لِحادِثةِ عَمَلٍ to have a workplace accident; لَقَدْ وَقَعَتْ حادِثةٌ an accident occurred; وَقَعَتْ لَهُ حادِثةٌ he was in/had an accident

حَداثة *n* ❶ [جِدّة] modernity; newness, novelty ❷ (Art, Liter) modernism; ما بعد الحَداثةِ post-modernism

حَداثيّ *n* modernist

حُدوث *n* occurrence, incidence; كَثير الحُدوثِ common, widespread, frequent

حَديث **A** *adj* |حِداث ,حُدَثاءُ| new, modern, recent, contemporary; حَديثاً recently, lately, the other day; كِتاب ظَهَرَ حَديثاً a recently published book; حَديث الوِلادةِ newborn; حَديث الزَواجِ newlywed; العَصْر الحَديث the modern age; الفَنّ \ الموسيقى الحَديث(ة) modern art/music; عادات \ مَفاهيم حَديثة modern customs/notions; مَقال \ تَقْرير حَديث a recent article/report; اللُغات الحَديثة modern languages

B *n* |أَحاديثُ| ❶ [كَلام] conversation, talk; حَديث عن \ حَوْلَ شَيْءٍ a conversation about sth; حَديث على انْفِرادٍ private conversation, tête-à-tête; كانَ حَديثَ الجَميعِ to be the talk of the town; كانَ مِحْوَرَ حَديثِ اليَوْمِ to be on everyone's lips; جاذَبَ شَخْصاً أَطْرافَ الحَديثِ to strike up a conversation with sb; دَخَلَ مع شَخْصٍ في حَديثٍ to get into conversation with sb; بادَلَ شَخْصاً الحَديثَ to have a conversation with sb; أَشْرَكَ شَخْصاً في الحَديثِ to draw sb into the conversation; قَطَعَ \ قاطَعَ حَديثَ شَخْصٍ to interrupt sb; غَيَّرَ مَوْضوعَ الحَديثِ to change the subject; أَطالَ الحَديثَ to speak at great length; ... دارَ الحَديثُ حول the conversation was about ... ❷ [مُقابَلة] interview ❸ [شائِعة] gossip; rumour ❹ (Islam) Hadith, prophetic tradition; *narration of the words and deeds of the Prophet Muhammad*; حَديث قُدْسيّ sacred Hadith; *hadith containing the words of God repeated by the Prophet Muhammad*; عِلْم الحَديثِ science of Hadith; رَوى حَديثاً عن شَخْصٍ to narrate a Hadith from sb

إحْداث *n* ❶ [تَسْبيب] causation, causing ❷ [إبْداع] production, creation

إحْداثيّات *n pl* coordinates

أُحْدوثة *n* |أَحاديثُ| story; speech, talk; topic, subject (*of a conversation*); صارَ أُحْدوثةً it became a much discussed topic

تَحادُث *n* conversation; talk, talking, speaking

تَحَدُّث *n* talking, speaking

تَحْديث *n* modernization; update, upgrade; تَحْديث نِظامٍ system update

تَحْديثيّ *adj* innovative

مُتَحَدِّث **A** *adj* speaking

B *n* speaker; spokesman; مُتَحَدِّث رَسْميّ an official spokesman; مُتَحَدِّث حُكوميّ a government spokesman; ... مُتَحَدِّث بِاسْمِ spokesperson of ...

مُحادَثة *n* conversation, discussion; talk; مُحادَثة شَفَويّة vocal communication; مُحادَثات سِرّيّة secret talks; مُحادَثة تِليفونيّة \ هاتِفيّة telephone conversation, phone call; مُحادَثة جَماعيّة group conversation; مُحادَثة شَخْصيّة a personal conversation; مَهارة المُحادَثة conversational skills; كانَ في طَرَف في المُحادَثةِ a party to the conversation; أَجْرى مُحادَثةً مع شَخْصٍ to carry on a conversation with sb; مُحادَثاتٍ مع شَخْصٍ to have/hold talks with sb

مُحْدَث *adj* new, novel; recent; modern; المُحْدَثونَ *name for poets of the Abbasid era, vis-à-vis poets of the pre-Islamic, early Islamic, and Umayyad periods*; the moderns

مُحْدِث **A** *adj* causing, producing

B *n* creator, maker; cause

مُحَدِّث *n* ❶ [مُتَحَدِّث] speaker, talker ❷ [مُجَدِّد] modernizer; renewer ❸ (Islam) transmitter of Hadith; Hadith scholar

مُسْتَحْدَث *adj* novel

‹ **حَدَجَ** *v* |i; حَدْج| to stare at, to gaze at; to look sharply at

حَدَّجَ *v* to stare at, to gaze at; to look sharply at

‹ **حَدَّ** **I** *v* |u; حَدّ| ❶ [السِكّينَ] to sharpen, to hone ❷ [عَيَّنَ حُدوداً] |من| to restrict, to curtail, to restrain, to limit; حَدَّ من حُرِّيّةِ

حَدَّ من سُلْطَةِ شَخْصٍ to restrict/curtail sb's freedom; شَخْصٍ to restrain/check sb's power/authority ③ [جاوَرَ] to border on, to be bounded by; يَحُدُّ سوريّةَ من الشَرْقِ العِراقُ Syria borders Iraq to the east

حَدَّ II v |i| ① [السِكّينُ] [حِدّة|] to be/become sharp ② [على] to mourn (for); to wear mourning for; [شَخْصٍ |حِداد| على] حَدَّ على مَوْتِ شَخْصٍ; to mourn (for) sb حَدَّ على شَخْصٍ to mourn sb's death

حَدَّدَ v ① [عَيَّنَ] to determine, to set, to fix, to define; to mark off; حَدَّدَ المَعاييرَ to establish the criteria; حَدَّدَ القَواعِدَ \ القَوانينَ to determine the rules; حَدَّدَ الاتِّجاهَ to determine the direction, to set out the course; حَدَّدَ اتِّجاهَ الريحِ to determine the direction of the wind; حَدَّدَ السِعْرَ to set the price; حَدَّدَ مَهامَّ \ مَسْؤوليّاتٍ to define the tasks/ responsibilities; حَدَّدَ مِنْطَقةً to mark off an area; حَدَّدَ تاريخَ شَيْءٍ to date sth; حَدَّدَ مَوْعِداً to make an appointment; to set/ fix a date ② [شَحَذَ] to grind, to sharpen

أَحَدَّ v to sharpen; أَحَدَّ بَصَرَهُ في شَيْءٍ to look at sth closely, to scrutinize sth

تَحَدَّدَ v to be determined/defined; to be established, to be fixed

احْتَدَّ v to become sharper; to intensify; to be/become furious; احْتَدَّ النِقاشُ the discussion became heated

حادّ adj ① [ثاقِب] sharp, keen; pointed; سِكّين \ مِقَصّ حادّ a sharp knife/pair of scissors; أَسْنان حادّة sharp teeth; حادّ مِثْلَ الشَفْرةِ sharp as a razor; أَنْف حادّ a pointed nose; خَطّ حادّ a sharp line; نَظْرة حادّة a sharp eye ② [شَديد] vehement, violent; fierce; fiery; strong; احْتِجاج حادّ a strong protest; an angry protest; آلام حادّة sharp/stabbing pains; حادّ الطَبْعِ hot-tempered, irascible; رَدّ حادّ a sharp/fierce reaction; الْتِهاب حادّ an acute inflammation; الْتِهاب حادّ في الزائِدةِ acute appendicitis; نَقْص \ عَجْز حادّ an acute shortage; نِزاع حادّ a fierce struggle ③ [صَوْت] shrill; صَوْت حادّ a shrill voice; a high-pitched noise

حَدّ n |حُدود| ① [تَعْيين الحُدودِ] limitation, prevention; halt, stop; restriction; مُعاهَدة الحَدِّ من انْتِشارِ الأَسْلِحةِ النَوَويّةِ nuclear non-proliferation treaty; الحَدّ من الهِجْرةِ a halt to immigration; من أَجْلِ الحَدِّ من الفَسادِ in order to put a stop to corruption; حُدود اللهِ *divine restrictive ordinances or statutes, regarding things lawful and unlawful* ② [مُنْتَهًى] limit, utmost, bound; end; حَدّ زَمَنيّ time limit, deadline; الحُدود المَقْبولة \ المُباحة the accepted/permitted limits; حَدّ أَدْنى minimum, lower limit; حَدّ أَقْصى maximum, upper limit; إلى أَقْصى حَدٍّ to the limit/extreme; الحَدّ الأَقْصى لِعَدَدِ المُشارِكينَ the maximum number of participants; تحت \ فوق الحَدِّ under/ above the limit; ل \ إلى حَدِّ until, till, up to; إلى حَدٍّ ما to a certain extent, up to a point, rather; إلى هذا الحَدِّ as far as this; so far; إلى حَدٍّ كَبيرٍ to a considerable extent/degree, considerably; إلى حَدٍّ بَعيدٍ far-reaching; excessive, extreme; كانَ مُتَفائِلاً إلى أَبْعَدِ الحُدودِ to be extremely optimistic; إلى حَدِّ الآنِ up to now, so far; إلى حَدِّ النَظَرِ \ البَصَرِ as far as the eye can see/reach; في حُدودِ ... within; about; في حُدودِ القانونِ within the law; في حُدودِ الساعةِ الخامِسةِ around five (o'clock); هي في حُدودِ الثَلاثينَ she is about thirty years old; داخِلَ \ خارِجَ الحُدودِ within/without the limits; لا حَدَّ \ حُدودَ لَهُ unlimited, boundless; وَضَعَ حَدًّا لِشَيْءٍ to set a limit on sth, to put a check on something; to put a stop to something; وَصَلَ \ تَجاوَزَ الحَدَّ to reach/exceed the limit; لِكُلِّ شَيْءٍ حُدودٌ there is a limit to everything; لم يَعْرِفْ حُدوداً to know no bounds; أَوْقَفَ شَخْصاً عند حَدِّهِ to stop sb; فاقَ كُلَّ الحُدودِ to exceed all limits ③ [حاجِز] border, frontier; الحُدود الأَلْمانيّة the German border; حُدود طَبيعيّة a natural border; حُدود داخِليّة internal border; حُدود لُغَويّة language border; الحُدود المُعْتَرَف بها دُوَليًّا the internationally recognized borders; حَرَس حُدودٍ border patrol; الحُدود بين بَلَدَيْنِ the border between two countries; داخِلَ \ خارِجَ حُدودِ البَلَدِ within/ outside the borders; أَخْرَجَ شَخْصاً خارِجَ الحُدودِ to deport sb; اجْتازَ الحُدودَ to cross the border; أَغْلَقَ الحُدودَ to close the border ④ [سِكّين، سَيْف] edge; حَدّ سَيْفٍ the edge of a sword; سِلاح ذو حَدَّيْنِ a double-edged sword ⑤ (Isl Law) punishment; *penal laws of Islam*

حَدّاد n blacksmith

حِداد *n* ⓵ [حُزْن] mourning; حِداد وَطَنيّ national mourning; غَمَرَ الحِدادُ البَلَدَ the country was plunged into mourning; أَعْلَنَ يَوْمَ \ أُسْبوعَ حِدادٍ to announce a day/week of mourning ⓶ [ثِياب الحِدادِ] mourning (clothes); لَبِسَ ثَوْبَ الحِدادِ الحِدادَ to wear mourning, to be in mourning; ثَوْب الحِدادِ mourning clothes

حِدادة *n* smithery, smithing

حِدّة *n* ⓵ [شِدّة] intensity, fierceness, vehemence; sharpness, keenness; حِدّة الحَريقِ the intensity of the fire; حِدّة النَقْدِ the sharpness of the criticism; ازْدادَ حِدّةً to increase in intensity; زادَ من حِدّةِ شَيْءٍ to intensify sth; to make sth worse; رَدَّ \ احْتَجَّ بِحِدّةٍ to react/protest vehemently; وَتَزيدُ حِدّةُ السُؤالِ the question becomes (even) more urgent ⓶ [غَضَب] fury, rage

حُدوديّ *adj* border (*before n*); مِنْطَقة حُدوديّة border area, border region; نُقْطة تَفْتيشٍ حُدوديّة border checkpoint; مَرْكَز حُدوديّ border crossing (point)

حَديد *n coll* |حَدائِدُ| iron; ironware; سورة الحَديد Iron (*Sura 57*); الحَديد الخام iron ore; حَديد مُطاوِع wrought iron; حَديد مَسْبوك cast iron; من الحَديدِ المَسْبوكِ cast iron (*before n*); طَرَقَ \ عالَجَ الحَديدَ to mine for iron; اسْتَخْرَجَ حَديداً to forge iron; ضَرَبَ على حَديدٍ بارِدٍ to hammer cold iron; إنّ الحَديدَ أُطْرُق الحَديدَ وَهُوَ حامٍ strike while the iron is hot; بالحَديدِ يَفْلَحُ you have to fight fire with fire

حَديدة *n* piece of iron; object or tool made of iron

حَديديّ *adj* iron (*before n*); سِياج حَديديّ an iron fence; أدَوات حَديديّة ironware; سِكّة حَديديّة railway (BrE), railroad (AmE); track; انْضِباط حَديديّ iron discipline

الحُدَيْدة *n* al-Hudaydah, Hodeidah (*city in Yemen*)

تَحْديد *n* |تَحْديدات| ⓵ [تَعْريف] determination, fixation; arrangement; definition; عَدَم التَحْديدِ indefiniteness; على وَجْهِ التَحْديدِ precisely, exactly; to be exact; تَمَّ تَحْديدُ الوَرَمِ the tumour was localized ⓶ [حَصْر] limitation, restriction, curtailment; تَحْديد الحُرّيّةِ restriction of freedom; تَحْديد السُرْعةِ speed limit

لامَحْدود *adj* unlimited; دَعْم لامَحْدود unlimited support

لامَحْدوديّة *n* infinity, infinitude; لامَحْدوديّة الفَضاءِ the infinity of space, boundlessness of space

مُحَدَّد *adj* ⓵ [مَحْصور] limited; عَدَد مُحَدَّد a limited number; الخيرة \ المَخْزون مُحَدَّد(ة) the choice/stock is limited ⓶ [مُعَرَّف] defined, fixed; مُحَدَّد بِدِقّةٍ \ بِشَكْلٍ دَقيقٍ clearly defined; خُطّة مُحَدَّدة a well-defined plan; في إطارٍ مُحَدَّدٍ in a fixed frame; المَوْعِد المُحَدَّد the arranged date; غَيْر مُحَدَّدٍ indefinite; شُعور غَيْر مُحَدَّدٍ an indefinable feeling ⓷ [مَشْحوذ] sharp

مُحَدِّد *adj* restrictive

مَحْدود *adj* restricted, limited; كَمِّيّة مَحْدودة a limited amount; غَيْر مَحْدودٍ unlimited, unrestricted, boundless; indefinite

مَحْدوديّة *n* limitations; مَحْدوديّة مَعْرِفةِ الإنْسانِ the limitations of human knowledge

حَدَرَ *v* |i-u; حَدْر| to lower

حَدَّرَ *v* to lower; to drop

تَحَدَّرَ *v* ⓵ [نَزَلَ] to descend, to come down; تَحَدَّرَ إلى وادٍ to descend into a valley ⓶ [تَفَرَّعَ] |من| to stem from, to derive from, to descend from; تَحَدَّرَ من أَصْلٍ لُبْنانيٍّ to be of Lebanese origin

انْحَدَرَ *v* ⓵ [نَزَلَ] to descend, to come/go down, to drop; to slope (down); يَنْحَدِرُ الطَريقُ the road slopes down; تَنْحَدِرُ المِياهُ من الجِبالِ the water runs down the mountains; انْحَدَرَتْ صَخْرةٌ كَبيرةٌ من الجَبَلِ a big rock fell down from the mountain ⓶ [تَفَرَّعَ] to descend, to come, to stem; تَنْحَدِرُ من عائِلةٍ غَنيّةٍ she comes/is from a wealthy family; انْحَدَرَ من الرَسولِ to descend from the Prophet; انْحَدَرَ من الطَبَقةِ الوُسْطى للمُجْتَمَعِ to come from the middle class; انْحَدَرَ من سُلالةِ... to be descended from the House/family of...

انْحِدار *n* |انْحِدارات| ⓵ [تَراجُع] decay, decline, downfall, fall; degeneration; انْحِدار الثَقافةِ the decline of culture/civilization ⓶ [نُزول] descent; slope; gradient; انْحِدار خَفيف a gentle slope; شَديد الانْحِدارِ; انْحِدار شَديد \ قَويّ a steep slope; steep; مُنْحَدَر \ جَبَل شَديد الانْحِدار a steep slope/mountain; انْحِدار نَهْرٍ the fall of a river ⓷ [نَسَب] descent, lineage

مُتَحَدِّر *adj* descended, coming (*from*); descending, sloping downward

مُنْحَدَر *n* |مُنْحَدَرات| 1 [التَّل] slope, sloping ground; talus; مُنْحَدَر صَخْرِيّ cliff, precipice; rock face; في المُنْحَدَرِ on the slope 2 (Geog) fall

مُنْحَدِر *adj* 1 [نازِل] sloping; downhill 2 [مُتَفَرِّع] descending, originating, coming (*from*)

‹ **حَدَسَ** *v* |i-u; حَدْس| to sense, to intuit; to surmise, to guess, to conjecture

حَدْس *n* intuition, feeling; premonition; حَدْس مُخيف an anxious foreboding; تَصَرَّفَ بالحَدْسِ to act on one's intuition; تابَعَ حَدْسَهُ to follow one's intuition

حَدْسِيّ *adj* intuitive

‹ **حَدّافة** *n* see حَذّافة

‹ **حَدَقَ** *v* |i; حَدْق| 1 [بِعَيْنِهِ] to stare; to look 2 [أَحاطَ] to surround, to encircle

حَدَّقَ *v* 1 [نَظَرَ] |إلى, في| to stare at, to gaze at, to look at; حَدَّقَ إلى \ في شَيْءٍ \ شَخصٍ to stare at sth/sb 2 [أَحاطَ] to surround; حَدَّقَتْ بِهِ الأَخْطارُ he was surrounded by danger

أَحْدَقَ *v* 1 [نَظَرَ] |في| to stare at 2 [أَحاطَ] |ب| to surround, to encircle, to enclose

حَدَقة *n* |حَدَقات, حَدَق, حِداق, أَحْداق| pupil (*of the eye*)

حَدوق *n* listed alphabetically

حَديقة *n* |حَدائِقُ| garden; park; حَديقة عامّة \ عُموميّة a public park; حَديقة نَباتاتٍ a botanical garden; حَديقة الحَيَوانات zoo; في الحَديقةِ in the garden; اعْتَنى بِحَديقةٍ to tend/maintain a garden

تَحْديق *n* staring, gazing

مُحْدِق *adj* surrounding; خَطَر مُحْدِق imminent danger

‹ **حَدَلَ** *v* |i; حَدْل, حُدول| 1 [سَطَحَ] to flatten, to level 2 [ظَلَمَ] |على| to treat unjustly

مِحْدَلة *n* |مَحادِلُ| steamroller, road roller

‹ **احْتَدَمَ** *v* 1 [النارُ] to glow; to blaze, to burn (up) 2 [القِتالُ] to flare up; to break out; احْتَدَمَ القِتالُ the fight broke out; احْتَدَمَ النِقاشُ the discussion was/became heated

احْتِدام *n* |احْتِدامات| vehemence, fierceness; breaking out; heating up; paroxysm

مُحْتَدِم *adj* burning, aflame; heated; fierce; furious, enraged; مَشاكِل مُحْتَدِمة serious problems

‹ **حَدا** *v* |u; حَدْو| |على| يَحْدوهُ الأَمَلُ he is driven by hope; حَدا شَخْصاً على شَيْءٍ to urge sb to do sth

حَدِيَ *v* |a; حَدًى| |ب| to stay at, to remain at

تَحَدّى *v* to provoke, to challenge; to defy; to urge; تَحَدّى شَخْصاً أَنْ ... to provoke/challenge sb to ...; تَحَدّى القَوانينَ to defy the laws; تَحَدّى المَوْتَ to defy death

حَدْوة *n* horseshoe

تَحَدٍّ *n* |تَحَدِّيات| 1 [مُجابَهة] challenge; provocation; قَبِلَ التَحَدِّيَ to accept/take up the challenge 2 [أَمْر مُتَحَدٍّ] challenge, difficult task

مُتَحَدٍّ *n* |مُتَحَدِّونَ| challenger

‹ **حَدوق** *n* سَمك الحَدوق haddock

‹ **حادِيَ عَشَرَ** *num* see أحد

‹ **حَذِرَ** *v* |a; حَذَر, حِذْر| |من| to be cautious about, to beware, to be careful of; إحْذَرْ look out, beware; حَذِرَ من شَيْءٍ to be careful about sth

حَذَّرَ *v* to warn, to caution; حَذَّرَ من أنّ ... to warn that ...; حَذَّرَ شَخْصاً للمَرّة الأَخيرة to warn sb for the last time; حُذِّرَ to get a warning; أُحَذِّرُكَ! I'm warning you!

حاذَرَ *v* to be careful (of), to watch out (for); to be on one's guard (against), to be wary (of); حاذَرَ شَيْئًا to be on one's guard against sth

حَذَر *n* caution, cautiousness, carefulness; wariness; الحَذَرُ واجِبٌ caution is necessary; أَخَذَ حَذَرَهُ to be cautious/on the alert, to be on one's guard; أَخَذَ حَذَرَهُ من شَخْصٍ to watch out for sb; عَمِلَ \ تَصَرَّفَ بِحَذَرٍ to proceed with caution/care; عامَلَ شَيْئاً بِحَذَرٍ to treat sth with care; عامَلَ شَخْصاً بِحَذَرٍ to handle sb with kid gloves; سَأَلَ شَيْئاً بِحَذَرٍ to ask sth carefully; بِحَذَرٍ شَديدٍ with extreme caution

حَذِر *adj* cautious, careful; prudent; wary; تَعْبير حَذِر careful phrasing; حَرَكة حَذِرة a cautious move; غَيْر حَذِرٍ careless

حِذْر, حَذَر *n* caution, watchfulness; أَخَذَ حِذْرَهُ to be on one's guard; كُنْ على حِذْرٍ be cautious

حَذارِ *excl* look out, watch out; حَذارِ من ذلك! watch out for that!; be careful of that!

تَحْذير *n* |تَحْذيرات| warning, cautioning; تَحْذير صارِم a strong/stern warning; وَجَّهَ تَحْذيراً to give a warning; لم يُبالِ بالتَحْذيراتِ he didn't pay attention to the warnings

تَحْذيريّ *adj* warning (*before n*); cautionary

مُحاذَرة *n* precaution, precautionary measure, caution

مَحْذور *n* |مَحْذورات| danger; difficulty; وَقَعَ المَحْذورُ what was feared happened

‹ **حَذَفَ** *v* |i; حَذْف| **1** [شَطَبَ] to cross out, to cancel, to delete; to leave out, to omit; حَذَفَ كَلِمةً to cross out a word; to omit a word; حَذَفَ حِسابَهُ to delete one's account **2** [رَمى] |ب| to throw, to pelt; to throw away, to discard; حَذَفَ شَخْصاً بِشَيْءٍ to throw sth at sb **3** (Ling) to elide; to apocopate; to lose by apheresis

انْحَذَفَ *v* to be left out, to be omitted/deleted

حَذْف *n* **1** [شَطْب] deletion; omission **2** (Ling) elision, ellipsis; apocopation

حَذّافة, حَدّافة *n* flywheel

‹ **حِذْفار** *n* |حَذافيرُ| بِحَذافيرِهِ in its entirety, entirely, without exception; طَبَّقَ القَوانينَ بِحَذافيرِها to apply the rules/law strictly

‹ **حَذَقَ, حَذِقَ** *v* |a-i; حِذْق, حَذاقة| to be skilful/skilled, to be proficient; to master; حَذَقَ عَمَلَهُ to be good at one's job

حِذْق *n* skill, proficiency, dexterity; cleverness, intelligence; عَمِلَ شَيْئاً بِحِذْقٍ to do sth with skill; حِذْق فَنّيّ technical skill

حاذِق *adj* |حُذّاق| skilful, skilled, proficient; حِرَفيّ حاذِق a skilled craftsman

حَذاقة *n* skill, proficiency, dexterity; cleverness, intelligence

‹ **تَحَذْلَقَ** *v* to be pedantic; *to display or pretend knowledge or skill*

حَذْلَقة *n* pedantry; *exaggerated erudition, affected or forced style*

مُتَحَذْلِق **A** *adj* pedantic

B *n* pedant; يا لَهُ من مُتَحَذْلِقٍ! he is such a pedant!

‹ **حَذا** *v* |u; حَذْو| to imitate, to emulate; حَذا حَذْوَ شَخْصٍ to follow sb's example

حاذى *v* to be opposite, to face; to be/stand in front of; to run parallel to

تَحاذى *v* to be opposite to each other, to face each other

احْتَذى *v* **1** [اقْتَدى] to imitate, to copy **2** [لَبِسَ الحِذاءَ] to wear as footwear

حَذْو *n* example, model; حَذا حَذْوَ شَخْصٍ to follow sb's example

حَذْوَ *prep* opposite, face to face with, across from; parallel to

حَذّاء *n* shoemaker, cobbler

حِذاء *n* |أَحْذِية| (a pair of) shoes or boots; حِذاء عَسْكَريّ military boots; حِذاء رِياضةٍ sports shoes, trainers, pumps, sneakers; حِذاء كُرةِ القَدَمِ football (BrE) soccer (AmE) cleats; فَرْدة حِذاءٍ shoe; زَوْجا أَحْذِيةٍ \ زَوْجانِ من الأَحْذِية two pairs of shoes; قِياس حِذاءٍ shoe size; بدونِ حِذاءٍ without shoes; لَبِسَ \ خَلَعَ حِذاءً to put on/take off one's shoes; مَسَحَ حِذاءً to shine shoes; رَبَطَ \ فَكَّ شَريطَ الحِذاءِ to tie/untie a shoelace; مَسَحَ حِذاءَ شَخْصٍ to lick sb's boots

حِذاءَ *prep* opposite, face to face with, across from; جَلَسَ حِذاءَ شَخْصٍ \ بِحِذاءِ to sit opposite/facing sb; جَلَسَ حِذاءَ المُعَلِّمِ he sat down opposite the teacher; داري حِذاءَ دارِهِ my house faces his house

حَذْوة *n* |حَذَوات| horseshoe; حَذْوة الحِصانِ horseshoe

احْتِذاء *n* imitation, copying

مُحاذٍ *adj* opposite; facing; parallel; مُحاذٍ لِشَيْءٍ opposite sth, facing sth; parallel to/with sth

مُحاذاة *n* في \ بِمُحاذاةِ along, alongside; parallel to/with; نَمْشي بِمُحاذاةِ البُيوتِ we walk alongside the houses; بِمُحاذاةِ الشارِعِ along the road

‹ **حَرِبَ** *v* |a; حَرَب| to be/get angry/furious

حارَبَ *v* to fight, to battle, to combat, to wage war (*against*); حارَبَ شَخْصاً to fight with/against sb; to wage war against sb; حارَبَ العَدُوَّ to fight the enemy; حارَبَ اعْتِقاداً \ رَأْياً to oppose a view/an opinion; حارَبَ شَيْئاً بِشِدّةٍ to fight sth fiercely/with force; to oppose sth staunchly

تَحارَبَ *v* to fight; to be at war

اِحْتَرَبَ *v* to war, to fight one another

حَرْب *n* |f; حُروب| war, warfare; حَرْب أَهْلِيّة civil war; حَرْب نَوَوِيّة nuclear war; حَرْب كيمْيائيّة \ بِيولوجِيّة chemical/biological warfare; حَرْب تِجارِيّة trade war; حَرْب دينِيّة religious war; حَرْب طائِفِيّة sectarian war; حَرْب إِعْلامِيّة media war; الحَرْب البارِدة the Cold War; الحُروب الصَلِيبِيّة the Crusades; حَرْب عالَمِيّة world war; الحَرْب العالَمِيّة الأولى \ الثانِية, الحَرْب الكُبْرى \ العُظْمى World War I/II, the First/Second World War; حَرْب شَعْواء a devastating/large-scale war; حَرْب الأَسْعارِ price war, tariff war; حَرْب عِصاباتٍ guerrilla warfare; حَرْب اسْتِنْزافٍ war of attrition; الحَرْب على الإِرْهابِ \ المُخَدِّراتِ the war on terror/drugs; عِلْم الحَرْبِ war studies; فَظائِع الحَرْبِ the horrors of war, atrocities; جَرِيمة حَرْبٍ war crime; مِنْطَقة حَرْبٍ war zone; إِعْلان حَرْبٍ declaration of war; إِعْلان حَرْبٍ على بَلَدٍ a declaration of war against/on a country; مُحِبّ للحَرْبِ warlike, bellicose; الحَرْب بين فَرَنْسا وَأَلْمانيا the war between France and Germany; في سَنَواتِ \ أَيّامِ الحَرْبِ during the war years; في حالة حَرْبٍ in case of war; ما بعد الحَرْبِ post-war; دار الحَرْبِ (Hist) the Abode of War (*the war zone outside the Islamic empire*); خاضَ حَرْباً ضدّ شَخْصٍ to wage war against sb; أَشْهَرَ الحَرْبَ to declare war on sb; أَعْلَنَ الحَرْبَ على شَخْصٍ to declare war; شَنَّ حَرْباً to launch a war; to wage war; كَسَبَ حَرْباً to win a war; انْدَلَعَت الحَرْبُ war broke out

حِرْباء *n* |f; حَرابِيّ| chameleon

حَرْبة *n* |حِراب| lance, spear; spearhead; bayonet; harpoon

حَرْبِيّ *adj* war (*before n*); military (*before n*); bellicose, martial, belligerent, warlike; رَأْس حَرْبِيّ warhead; سَفِينة حَرْبِيّة warship, battleship; صِناعات حَرْبِيّة war industry, military industries

حَرْبِيّة *n* warfare; military affairs; وِزارة الحَرْبِيّةِ ministry of defence

اِحْتِراب *n* struggle; اِحْتِراب داخِلِيّ internal strife

لاحَرْب *n* non-belligerence; حالة اللاسِلْمِ واللاحَرْبِ a state of neither peace nor war

مُتَحارِب *adj* warring, belligerent; الأَطْراف المُتَحارِبة the warring parties

مُحارِب *n* warrior, combatant; مُحارِب قَدِيم war veteran, ex-serviceman

مُحارَبة *n* battle, fight, struggle; warfare; مُحارَبة الفَسادِ \ الأُمِّيّة the war on corruption/illiteracy, the fight against corruption/illiteracy

مِحْراب *n* |مَحارِيبُ| mihrab, prayer niche (*a semicircular recess in the wall of a mosque that indicates the direction of Mecca*)

‹ **حَرَثَ** *v* |i-u; حَرْث| to plough (BrE), to plow (AmE); to till, to cultivate; حَرَثَ قِطْعةَ أَرْضٍ to plough a piece of land; حَرَثَ الفَلّاحُ الحَقْلَ the farmer ploughed the field; حَرَثَ في الماءِ *to waste time and effort*

حَرْث *n* ploughing (BrE), plowing (AmE); tilling, cultivation of the soil, tillage; شَهْر الحَرْث November (*Libya under Gaddafi*)

حارِث *n* [1] [مَنْ يَحْرُثُ] |حَرّاث| ploughman (BrE); plowman (AmE) [2] [اِسْم شَخْصِيّ] Harith (*male given name*)

حِراثة *n* ploughing (BrE), plowing (AmE); cultivation of the soil, tilling (*of soil*)

حَرْثة *n* arable land

مِحْراث *n* |مَحارِيثُ| plough (BrE), plow (AmE)

‹ **حَرِجَ** *v* |a; حَرَج| [1] [ضاقَ] to be narrow/tight/close; حَرِجَ صَدْرُهُ he felt a tightness in his chest [2] [كانَ حَرِجاً] to be/become awkward/troublesome

حَرَّجَ *v* to forbid; حَرَّجَ شَيْئاً على شَخْصٍ to forbid sth to sb

أَحْرَجَ *v* [1] [أَوْقَعَ في الحَرَجِ] to embarrass; أَحْرَجَ شَخْصاً to embarrass sb [2] [حَرَّمَ] to forbid; أَحْرَجَ شَيْئاً على شَخْصٍ to forbid sth to sb

تَحَرَّجَ *v* to hold back, to hesitate; to refrain from, to avoid; to be embarrassed; لم يَتَحَرَّجْ من فِعْلِ ذلك he didn't hesitate to do it

حَرَج *n* [1] [ضيق] painful/awkward situation; distress, crisis; difficulty; أَحَسَّ بالحَرَجِ to feel awkward/uncomfortable; لا حَرَجَ go on, do not hesitate; there is no objection; لا حَرَجَ عَلَيْكَ you are at liberty; بِلا حَرَجٍ without hesitation/restraint; دَفَعَ الحَرَجَ عن نَفْسِهِ to get oneself out of an awkward situation; شَكَّلَ حَرَجاً to be awkward/annoying/painful; يا لَلْحَرَجِ! what an awkward situation! 2 [غابة] |إحراج, أَحْراج| dense forest; thicket

حَرِج *adj* awkward, uncomfortable, embarrassing; precarious, difficult, distressing, critical; مَوْقِف حَرِج an awkward position; لَحْظة حَرِجة a critical/an embarrassing moment; حالة حَرِجة a precarious/critical situation; كانَتْ حالَتُهُ حَرِجةً his condition was critical

حَراج *n* auction

حِراجة *n* forestry

حَرَجي *adj* forest (*before n*), woodland (*before n*), wooded; مِنْطَقة حَرَجيّة woodland; حَرائِق حَرَجيّة a forest fire

إحْراج *n* embarrassment, discomfiture

تَحَرُّج *n* restraint

تَحْريج *n* forestation, afforestation

مُحْرَج *adj* embarrassed

مُحْرِج *adj* embarrassing, disconcerting, awkward; precarious, difficult; أَسْئِلة مُحْرِجة awkward questions; وَضْع \ مَوْقِف مُحْرِج an awkward situation; قَضيّة مُحْرِجة a delicate matter

حَرِدَ *v* |a; حَرَد| to be/get angry, to be/get annoyed

حَرْدان *adj* angry, annoyed

حَرَّرَ *v* 1 [خَلَّصَ] to liberate; to free, to release; to relieve; حَرَّرَ شَخْصاً من شَيْءٍ to free sb from sth; حَرَّرَ غِيارَ السَّيّارةِ to put a car into neutral; حَرَّرَ مَدينةً to liberate a city 2 [كَتَبَ] to compose, to write; to edit; to draw up, to draft; حَرَّرَ مَجَلّةً \ جَريدةً to edit a magazine/newspaper; حَرَّرَ مَقالاً \ كِتاباً to edit/redact an article/a book; حَرَّرَ تَقْريراً to produce/write a report; حَرَّرَ رِسالةً to compose a letter; حَرَّرَ مَحْضَراً ضدّ شَخْصٍ to give sb a ticket; to book sb

أَحَرَّ *v* to heat, to warm

تَحَرَّرَ *v* to be freed; to get rid; تَحَرَّرَ من القُيودِ to throw off the chains

حارّ *adj* 1 [ساخِن] hot, warm; صَيْف حارّ a hot summer; يَوْم \ بَلَد حارّ a hot day/country 2 [وِدّي] hearty, warm; cordial; مُصافَحة حارّة a warm handshake; تَرْحيب \ اسْتِقْبال حارّ a warm welcome/reception; تَهانِئ حارّة warm congratulations; تَحيّة \ سَلام حارّ(ة) a warm/enthusiastic greeting; تَعازٍ حارّة heartfelt condolences; عَواطِف حارّة warm feelings 3 [مُتَّقِد] passionate, ardent; قُبُلات حارّة ardent kisses; شَوْق \ عِناق حارّ a passionate longing/embrace 4 [لاذِع] hot; تَوابِل حارّة hot spices

حَرّ *n* |حُرور| heat; حَرّ لافِح scorching heat; حَرّ لا يُطاقُ \ غَيْر مُحْتَمَل unbearable heat; مَوْجة حَرٍّ heatwave; تَجْتاحُ مَوْجةُ حَرٍّ مَناطِقَ الهِنْدِ India is experiencing a heatwave; الحَرّ والبَرْد heat and cold; بِسَبَبِ الحَرِّ because of the heat; هَرَبَ من الحَرِّ to escape from the heat

حُرّ *adj* |أَحْرار|; f pl |حَرائِرُ| 1 [غَيْر مُقَيَّدٍ] free; شَخْص حُرّ a free person; تِجارة حُرّة free trade; مِنْطَقة حُرّة free trade zone/area, duty-free zone; مِهْنة حُرّة a liberal profession; زاوَلَ عَمَلاً حُرًّا to practice a liberal profession; غَيْر حُرٍّ unfree 2 (Pol) liberal; حِزْب الأَحْرارِ the liberal party 3 [خالِص] pure, unadulterated; ذَهَب حُرّ pure gold

حَرارة *n* 1 [عَكْس بُرودةٍ] heat, warmth; حَرارة الشَّمْسِ the heat of the sun; ناقِل للحَرارةِ heat/thermal conductor; مُنَظِّم \ مُثَبِّت الحَرارةِ thermostat; الحَرارة والبُرودة heat and cold; أَعْطى حَرارةً to give off/emit heat; شَعَرَ بالحَرارةِ to feel hot 2 (Phys) temperature; دَرَجة الحَرارةِ temperature; دَرَجة حَرارةٍ قُصْوى maximum temperature; دَرَجة حَرارةٍ دُنْيا \ صُغْرى minimum temperature; دَرَجة حَرارةِ الجَوِّ ambient/air temperature; دَرَجة حَرارة الجِسْمِ body temperature; دَرَجة حَرارة الغُرْفةِ room temperature; دَرَجة حَرارةٍ عالِية \ مُنْخَفِضة a high/low temperature; حَرارة دُنْيا تَبْلُغُ ٤ دَرَجاتٍ a minimum temperature of 4 degrees; مُتَغَيِّر الحَرارةِ cold-blooded, poikilothermic (fml); ثابِت الحَرارةِ warm-blooded, homeothermic (fml); حَيَوانات ثابِتة الحَرارةِ warm-blooded animals; تَبْلُغُ الحَرارةُ ... the temperature is ...; يُشيرُ مِقْياسُ الحَرارةِ إلى ثَلاثينَ دَرَجةً the thermometer reads/indicates 30 degrees; تَنْخَفِضُ \ تَرْتَفِعُ الحَرارةُ إلى ثَماني دَرَجاتٍ the temperature drops/rises to 8 degrees 3 [حُمّى] temperature, fever; مِقْياس \ ميزان الحَرارةِ thermometer; نَظَرَ إلى مِقْياسِ الحَرارةِ to read the thermometer; قاسَ حَرارةَ شَخْصٍ to take sb's temperature; ارْتِفاع في دَرَجةِ حَرارةِ الجِسْمِ rise in body temperature (*fever*) 4 [حَماس] ardour, passion, fervour; عانَقَ اشْتاقَ إلى شَيْءٍ بِحَرارةٍ to have a burning desire for sth; وَصّى بِشَيْءٍ بِحَرارةٍ شَخْصاً بِحَرارةٍ to embrace sb warmly; to recommend sth wholeheartedly

حَراريّ ***adj*** thermal, thermo-; heat (*before n*); شُعاع حَراريّ thermal radiation; عَزْل حَراريّ thermal insulation; وَحْدة حَراريّة calorie; القيمة الحَراريّة calorific (BrE) caloric (AmE) value; مُنْخَفِض السُعْراتِ الحَراريّةِ low-calorie; غَنيّ بالسُعْراتِ الحَراريّةِ high-calorie

حَرّان ***adj*** |dipt; حَرّى f |حَرارى ,حِرار hot

حَرّة ***n*** volcanic desert ground, lava field; stony area

حُرّيّة ***n*** freedom; حُرّيّة تامّة complete freedom; الحُرّيّات العامّة basic rights; حُرّيّة التِجارةِ freedom of trade; حُرّيّة العِبادةِ freedom of worship/religion; حُرّيّة الكَلامِ freedom of speech; حُرّيّة النَشْرِ \ الصِحافة freedom of press; كَبَحَ حُرّيّةَ الصِحافةِ to restrict the freedom of press; الحِرْمان من الحُرّيّة deprivation of liberty/freedom; تَرَكَ لِشَخْصٍ الحُرّيّةَ في فِعْلِ شَيْءٍ to give/leave sb the freedom to do sth; تَرَكَ لِشَخْصٍ حُرّيّةَ التَصَرُّفِ \ الاخْتيارِ to give sb the freedom of action/choice; مِلْء الحُرّيّة a free hand; total freedom; الحُرّيّة والمُساواة والأُخوّة liberty, equality and fraternity

حَرير ***n*** |حَرائِرُ| silk; حَرير خامّ raw silk; حَرير صِناعيّ artificial silk; rayon; حَرير طَبيعيّ natural silk; حَرير صَخْريّ asbestos; ناعِم كالحَريرِ قَميص \ شال من الحَريرِ a silk shirt/shawl; as soft as silk; نَسَجَ حَريراً to weave/spin silk

حَريرة ***n*** 1 [طَحين نَباتِ الشُوفان] porridge (BrE), oatmeal (AmE); طَبَق من الحَريرةِ a plate of porridge 2 [حساء] *a light vegetarian soup traditionally eaten in North Africa*

حُرَيْرة ***n*** calorie

حَريريّ ***adj*** silk (*before n*), silken; حَجَر حَريريّ asbestos

أَحَرّ ***adj*** |dipt| hotter, warmer; أَحَرّ التَشَكُّراتِ many thanks

تَحَرُّر ***n*** liberation, emancipation, liberalization; تَحَرُّر اقْتِصاديّ \ ماديّ economic/financial liberation; التَحَرُّر من الديكْتاتوريّةِ liberation from dictatorship; تَحَرُّر من الأَسْرِ release from prison; تَحَرُّر المَرْأةِ women's liberation, the feminist movement

تَحَرُّريّ ***adj*** emancipatory

تَحْرير ***n*** 1 [تَخْليص] liberation, emancipation, liberalization; حَرَكة تَحْريرٍ liberation movement; جَبْهة تَحْريرٍ liberation front; جَيْش تَحْريرٍ liberation army; النِضال من أَجْلِ تَحْريرِ المَرْأةِ the struggle for women's liberation; مُنَظَّمة التَحْريرِ الفِلَسْطينيّة Palestinian Liberation Organization, PLO; تَحْرير التِجارةِ الدُوَليّةِ the liberalization of international trade; عيد التَحْريرِ Liberation Day 2 [كِتابة] editing; رَئيس التَحْريرِ editor-in-chief; هَيْئة \ إدارة \ مَجْلِس التَحْريرِ editorial staff; من هَيْئةِ التَحْريرِ editorial; من تَحْرير ... edited by ...

تَحْريريّ ***adj*** 1 [مَكْتوب] in writing, written; editorial; تَحْريريّ أم شَفَهيّ written or oral; امْتِحان تَحْريريّ a written exam; تَرْجَمة تَحْريريّة a written translation 2 [خاصّ بالتَحَرُّرِ] liberation (*before n*); حَرْب تَحْريريّة war of liberation

مُتَحَرِّر ***adj*** liberal; emancipated, liberated; امْرَأة \ رَجُل مُتَحَرِّر(ة) an emancipated woman/man; اتَّخَذَ مَوْقِفاً مُتَحَرِّراً to take a liberal stance

مِحَرّ ***n*** |مَحارٌ| thermometer

مِحْرار ***n*** thermometer

مُحَرِّر ***n*** 1 [مُعْتِق] liberator 2 [كِتابة] editor; مُحَرِّر سِياسيّ political editor; مُحَرِّر نُصوصٍ (Comput) text editor

حَرَزَ ***v*** |u; حَرْز| to keep, to guard, to protect; to take care of

حَرُزَ ***v*** |a-u; حَرازة| to be strongly fortified, to be impregnable; to be on one's guard

أَحْرَزَ ***v*** to obtain, to gain, to win; أَحْرَزَ تَقَدُّماً to make progress, to move forward; أَحْرَزَ لَقَباً to gain a title; أَحْرَزَ مَكانةً في ... to obtain a position in the field of ...; أَحْرَزَ المَرْتَبةَ الثالِثةَ to be/finish third; أَحْرَزَ الكَأْسَ to win the cup; أَحْرَزَ النَصْرَ to win victory; أَحْرَزَ قَصَبَ السَبْقِ ≈ to beat everyone to the punch; to score a great success

تَحَرَّزَ ***v*** to be on one's guard, to be wary

احْتَرَزَ ***v*** |من| to be cautious of, to be on one's guard against, to be wary of, to be careful of; احْتَرَزَ من شَيْءٍ to be on one's guard against sth; to take precautions against sth

حِرْز ***n*** |حُروز ,أَحْراز| 1 [تَميمة] amulet 2 [مَلْجَأ] refuge, sanctuary

اِحْتِراس *n* |اِحْتِراسات| caution, prudence, wariness; بِاحْتِراسٍ with caution, carefully

مُحْتَرِس *adj* careful, cautious; غَيْر مُحْتَرِسٍ careless

مَحْرَس *n* |مَحارِس| sentry box; guardhouse

‹ **حَرَش** *v* |i; حَرْش| to scratch

حَرَّش *v* to incite, to provoke; to sow discord; حَرَّش بين الناسِ to set people against one another

تَحَرَّش *v* ◆1 [اِسْتَفَزَّ] |ب| to provoke; to pick a quarrel with; تَحَرَّش بِرِجالِ الشُّرْطةِ to provoke the police ◆2 [تَطَفَّل] |ب| to intrude upon, to impose on; to force oneself upon; تَحَرَّش بِشَخْصٍ to force oneself/impose upon sb ◆3 [جِنْسِيًّا] |ب| to (sexually) harrass; تَحَرَّش بِامْرَأةٍ to harrass a woman

حَرْش, **حِرْش** *n* |أَحْراش, حُرُوش| wood, forest

حَرِيش *n* |حُرُش| centipede

تَحَرُّش *n* |تَحَرُّشات| provocation; obtrusion, meddling; intimidation; تَحَرُّش جِنْسِيّ sexual harassment

مُتَحَرِّش **A** *adj* harassing; provocative, defiant **B** *n* harasser

‹ **حَرْشَف** *n* |حَراشِفُ| scales

حَرْشَفِيّ *adj* scaly, scaled

‹ **حَرَص** *v* |i; حِرْص| ◆1 [اِشْتَدَّتْ رَغْبَتُهُ] |على| to desire, to want; to strive for, to aspire to; to be intent on; حَرَص على شَيْءٍ to desire/want sth; to strive for sth; to be intent on sth ◆2 [اِعْتَنى] |على| to be dedicated to; to be devoted to; حَرَص على شَخْصٍ to be dedicated to sb ◆3 [جَشِعَ] to be miserly/frugal

حِرْص *n* ◆1 [رَغْبة] desire; aspiration, wish; تابَعَ شَيْئاً بِحِرْصٍ to follow sth closely; حِرْصاً على in the desire for, in the endeavor to ◆2 [جَشَع] avarice

حَرِيص *adj* |حُرَصاءُ, حِرْصان| ◆1 [راغِب] |على| eager for, keen on; desirous of; كانَ حَرِيصاً على شَيْءٍ to be eager for sth ◆2 [بَخيل] miserly; greedy

‹ **حَرَّض** *v* to incite, to rouse, to provoke; to instigate, to stir up; حَرَّض شَخْصاً على شَيْءٍ to provoke sb to do sth; حَرَّض شَخْصاً على شَخْصٍ to set sb against sb; حَرَّض شَخْصاً على العُنْفِ to incite sb to …; شَخْصاً على …

اِحْتِراز *n* caution, prudence, circumspection; reservation, reserve

اِحْتِرازِيّ *adj* preventive, preventative, precautionary; تَدابير اِحْتِرازِيّة precautionary measures

إِحْراز *n* obtaining, acquisition, gaining

‹ **حَرَس** *v* |u; حَرْس, حِراسة| to guard; حَرَس مَبْنًى to watch a building; حَرَس مَساجِينَ to guard prisoners; حَرَس حِراسةً مُشَدَّدةً to keep/put under close surveillance; حَرَسَ المَرْمى (Sport) to keep/tend goal

اِحْتَرَس *v* to be on one's guard, to look/watch out, to beware, to be careful; اِحْتَرِسْ ! look out!; اِحْتَرَس من شَيْءٍ \ شَخْصٍ to be on one's guard against sth/sb

حَرَس *n coll* |sing n حارِس| guard, watch; escort; حَرَس عَسْكَرِيّ a military escort; الحَرَس البابَوِيّ the Papal Guard, the Swiss Guard; الحَرَس الجُمْهورِيّ the Republican/Presidential Guard; حَرَس لَيْلِيّ night watchman; حَرَس خاصّ bodyguard; الحَرَس الوَطَنِيّ (volunteer) reserve; the Territorial Army; the National Guard; حَرَس حُدودٍ border patrol; حَرَس شَرَفٍ guard of honour, honour guard; تَفَقَّدَ حَرَسَ الشَرَفِ to inspect the guard of honour; بَدَّلَ الحَرَسَ to change the guard

حارِس **A** *adj* |حُرّاس, حَرَس| vigilant, watchful; مَلاك \ مَلَك حارِس (Chr) guardian angel **B** *n* |حُرّاس, حَرَس| [خَفير] guard; watchman; sentry; attendant; حارِس سِجْنٍ jailer, prison guard; حارِس قَضائِيّ (Fin) receiver; حارِس خاصّ \ شَخْصِيّ bodyguard; عَيَّنَ شَخْصاً حارِساً خاصًّا لَهُ to hire sb as one's bodyguard; حارِس مَلاكِيّ \ مَلائِكِيّ guardian angel; حارِس المَرْمى (Sport) goalkeeper

حِراسة *n* ◆1 [مُراقَبة] guard, watch; surveillance; security; حِراسة الحُدودِ border control/security; كَلْب حِراسةٍ watchdog; وَضَعَ شَخْصاً تحت الحِراسةِ to put sb under surveillance/guard; to put someone under guard; تحت حِراسةٍ مُشَدَّدةٍ under close surveillance; under tight security; قامَ بالحِراسةِ to stand guard, to keep watch ◆2 [مُواكَبة] escort; تحت \ وَسْطَ حِراسةٍ مُسَلَّحةٍ (مُشَدَّدةٍ) under (heavily) armed escort particle; حَرْف جَرٍّ preposition; *particle that governs the genitive case* **4** [حافة] edge

حُرْف *n* (Bot) garden (pepper) cress

حِرْفة *n* |حِرَف| profession, occupation, trade; مارَس حِرْفةً to have an occupation

حَرْفيّ *adj* literal; تَرْجمة حَرْفيّة a literal translation; حَرْفيًّا literally; word for word

حِرْفيّ, **حِرَفيّ** **A** *adj* professional; craft (*before n*); artisanal (*before n*); عَمَل حِرَفيّ craft
B *n* craftsman; artisan; professional; حِرَفيّ ماهِر \ حاذِق a skilled craftsman

حَرْفيّة *n* literalism

حِرْفيّة *n* professionalism

حِرّيف *adj* spicy, piquant, hot; pungent, acrid; حِرّيفات spicy food

احْتِراف *n* professionalism; professional; كُرة القَدَم للاحْتِرافِ professional football (BrE) soccer (AmE); عَقْد احْتِرافٍ a professional contract

احْتِرافيّة *n* productivity

انْحِراف *n* |انْحِرافات| deviation, divergence, aberration; انْحِراف مِعْيارِيّ standard deviation; انْحِراف جِنْسيّ sexual perversion; انْحِراف في السُلوكِ behavioural disorder; انْحِراف سُلوكيّ abnormal behaviour; انْحِراف قِطارٍ عن سِكَّتِه train derailment

تَحْريف *n* |تَحْريفات| **1** [تَشْويه] twisting; distortion; corruption; alteration; تَحْريف الحَقائِقِ \ الحَقيقةِ distortion of the facts/truth **2** (Islam) *corruption (of God's revelation)*; تَحْريف القُرْآنِ distortion of the Koran

تَحْريفيّة *n* distortion, false interpretation; revisionism

مُحْتَرَف *n* |مُحْتَرَفات| workshop; studio, atelier

مُحْتَرِف **A** *adj* professional; مُمَثِّل مُحْتَرِف a professional actor; لاعِب مُحْتَرِف professional sports player (BrE), professional athlete (AmE); نادٍ مُحْتَرِف professional club (BrE) team (AmE)
B *n* pro, professional; فَريق مُحْتَرِفينَ professional team

مُحَرَّف *adj* twisted; corrupted; apocryphal; تَصْريحاتُه مُحَرَّفةٌ his statements/words were twisted; الأَناجيل المُحَرَّفة the apocryphal gospels

حَرَّض أَشْخاصاً على بَعْضِهِمْ بَعْضاً to provoke sb to violence; to pit people against each other

تَحْريض *n* **1** [على الشَرِّ] instigation, incitement; provocation; جَريمة; بِتَحْريضٍ من شَخْصٍ at the instigation of sb; التَحْريضِ على القَتْلِ incitement to commit murder **2** [كَهْرَبائيّ] induction

تَحْريضيّ *adj* inciting; inflammatory, provocative; تَصْريحات تَحْريضيّة inflammatory statements

مُحَرِّض **A** *adj* inciting; instigating
B *n* instigator; agitator; agent provocateur; مُحَرِّض على الإِضْرابِ instigator of a strike; الجِهة المُحَرِّضة the instigating party

حَرَّفَ *v* to distort; to corrupt; to falsify; حَرَّفَ الحَقائِقَ to distort the facts; حَرَّفَ وَثائِقَ to falsify documents; حَرَّفَ الكَلامَ عن مَواضِعِهِ to twist sb's words; حَرَّفَ كَلامَ شَخْصٍ to distort the meaning of the words

تَحَرَّفَ *v* |عن| to deviate from, to turn away from

انْحَرَفَ *v* **1** [ضَلَّ] to deviate; to stray; انْحَرَفَ عن الطَرِيقِ المُسْتَقيمِ to stray from the right path **2** [كانَ مائِلاً] to slope down, to slant

احْتَرَفَ *v* to be active in; to practise (*as a profession*); احْتَرَفَ صَيْدَ الأَسْماكِ to be a fisherman; احْتَرَفَ السِياسةَ to be a politician, to be in politics

حَرْف *n* |أَحْرُف, حُروف| **1** [أَبْجَديّ] letter, character; حُروف يونانيّة \ عَرَبيّة Greek/Arabic letters; حَرْف صَوْتيّ vowel; حَرْف هيروغْليفيّ hieroglyph; حُروف حَرْف مَطْبَعيّ type; حُروف مائِلة italics; حُروف عَريضة bold type; الحُروف الأَبْجَديّة the letters of the alphabet; حُروف كَبيرة capitals; حَرْفاً بِحَرْفٍ literally; verbatim, word for word; حَرْف الباءِ the letter ba'; انْتَهى الحَرْفُ unquote; كَلِمة من خَمْسةِ حُروفٍ a word of five letters; وَقَّع بالأَحْرُفِ الأولى to initial **2** (Gram) consonant; حَرْف ساكِن consonant; حَرْف صَحيح \ مُعْتَلّ a strong/weak letter; حُروف شَمْسيّة sun letters (*consonants that assimilate with the article*); حُروف قَمَريّة moon letters (*consonants that do not assimilate with the article*); حَرْف أَصْلِ radical; حَرْف مُتَحَرِّك *a consonant followed by a vowel*; حَرْف مَهْموس a voiceless consonant **3** [جَرّ]

مُنْحَرِف **A** *adj* **1** [شاذّ] deviating; distorted; corrupted; strange, odd; مُنْحَرِف الأَخْلاقِ immoral; آراء مُنْحَرِفة divergent opinions; dissidence **2** [مائِل] oblique; slanted, slanting; crooked
B *n* (Geom) trapezoid (BrE), trapezium (AmE); شِبْه مُنْحَرِفٍ trapezium (BrE), trapezoid (AmE)

‹ **حَرَق** *v* |i; حَرْق| to burn, to scorch; حَرَقَ نَفْسَهُ to burn oneself; حَرَقَ نَفْسَهُ بالفُرْنِ to burn oneself on the oven; حَرَقَ يَدَيْهِ to burn one's hands; حَرَقَ مَنْزِلاً to burn down a house; to set a house on fire; كانَتِ الغَيْرةُ تَحرِقُ قَلْبَهُ he was eaten up with jealousy

حَرَّقَ *v* to burn, to scorch

أَحْرَقَ *v* to burn; to scorch; to set on fire; أَحْرَقَ الخَشَبَ \ النُفاياتِ to burn wood/rubbish; أَحْرَقَ أَصابِعَهُ to burn one's fingers; أَحْرَقَ الأَخْضَرَ واليابِسَ مَعاً *to destroy indiscriminately*

تَحَرَّقَ *v* **1** [اشْتَعَلَ] to burn (up) **2** [شَوْقاً] to be consumed (*by an emotion*); to yearn for; تَحَرَّقَ عَطَشاً to be dying of thirst; تَحَرَّقَ شَوْقاً إلى شَيْءٍ to be consumed with longing for sth

احْتَرَقَ *v* to burn (up), to be burned, to be on fire; to catch fire; احْتَرَقَ عن آخِرِهِ to burn to the ground; يَحْتَرِقُ المَبْنى the building is on fire; تَحْتَرِقُ الشَمْعةُ the candle is burning; احْتَرَقَت الكَنيسةُ كُلِّيًّا the church was completely consumed by fire; قد احْتَرَقَ الطَعامُ the food got burned; احْتَرَقَتْ يَدُهُ his hand was burned

حَرْق *n* |حُروق| **1** [احْتِراق] burning, combustion; setting afire, igniting; حَرْق الأَزْبالِ \ الفَضَلاتِ garbage/waste incineration; المَوْت حَرْقاً death by fire; أَعْمال الحَرْقِ arson; حادِثة حَرْقٍ fire **2** (Med) burn; حَرْق خَطير serious burns; حَرْق من الدَرَجةِ الأولى \ الثانيةِ first/second-degree burns; أُصيبَ بِحَرْقٍ من الدَرَجةِ الثالِثةِ to suffer third-degree burns; أُصيبَ ب \ تَعَرَّضَ لِحُروقٍ to sustain burns

حارِق **A** *adj* burning; combustible, incendiary; قُنْبُلة \ زُجاجة \ عُبوّة حارِقة firebomb, incendiary bomb, Molotov cocktail; عُبوّة حارِقة an incendiary device
B *n* arsonist

حَرّاقة *n* torpedo boat; frigate

حُرْقة, حَرْقة *n* **1** [حَرْق] burning (sensation) **2** [عَذاب] agony, torment; بَكى بِحُرْقةٍ to weep in agony

حَريق *n* |حَرائِقُ| fire; حادِث \ وُقوع حَريقٍ fire (*accident*); حَريق مُتَعَمَّد arson; مُشْعِل الحَرائِقِ arsonist, firebug; أَشْعَلَ حَرائِقَ to start a fire; مُكافَحة الحَريقِ firefighting; إِنْذار الحَريقِ fire alarm; خَطَر نُشوبِ \ اشْتِعالِ الحَريقِ fire hazard; يَشِبُّ حَريقٌ a fire breaks out; a fire rages; لَقَدْ شَبَّ \ وَقَعَ حَريقٌ في بَيْتِنا we had a fire at our house; أَطْفَأَ الحَريقَ to extinguish the fire

احْتِراق *n* |احْتِراقات| burning; combustion; احْتِراق البَنْزينِ the burning of petrol (BrE) gasoline (AmE); احْتِراق الدُهونِ في الجِسْمِ the burning of fats in the body; قابِل للاحْتِراقِ combustible, flammable, inflammable; غَيْر قابِلٍ للاحْتِراقِ incombustible, non-flammable; غازات قابِلة للاحْتِراقِ flammable gases

إِحْراق *n* burning, combustion; incineration; إِحْراق جُثّةٍ cremation

تَحَرُّق *n* **1** [اشْتِعال] burning **2** [شَوْق] yearning, burning desire; التَحَرُّق إلى الحُبِّ the yearning for love

مُحْتَرِق *adj* burning, on fire; burned, scorched, charred; جُثّة مُحْتَرِقة a charred corpse; فَحْم مُحْتَرِق burning/smouldering charcoal; شَوْق مُحْتَرِق a burning desire

مِحْراق *n* burner (*of a stove*)

مُحْرَق *adj* burned

مُحْرِق *adj* burning; irritant; stinging; الشَمْس المُحْرِقة the blazing/burning sun; قُنْبُلة مُحْرِقة incendiary bomb, firebomb

مِحْرَق *n* focus, focal point

مَحْرَقة *n* **1** [فُرْن] crematorium **2** [إبادة] holocaust; المَحْرَقة (اليَهوديّة) the Holocaust **3** [كَوْمة حَطَبٍ] funeral pyre/pile **4** [للإِعْدامِ] stake

مَحْروق *adj* burned, scorched, charred; مَحْروقات fuel; *combustible materials or substances*; سِياسة الأَرْضِ المَحْروقةِ scorched earth policy

‹ **حَرْقَدة** *n* |حَراقِدُ| (Anat) Adam's apple

‹ **حَرَّكَ** *v* **1** [جَعَلَ يَتَحَرَّكُ] to move; to set in motion; to drive; حَرَّكَ قَدَمَهُ to move one's foot; لم يُحَرِّكْ ساكِناً to fail to respond; to be apathetic; حَرَّكَ عَواطِفَ شَخْصٍ to move sb; حَرَّكَ الفيلْمُ أَحاسيسي I was moved by the film **2** [زَعْزَعَ]

لاحَرَكيّة *n* 1 apathy; lethargy 2 (Med) akinesia (*the inability to initiate movement*)

مُتَحَرِّك *adj* 1 [عَكْس ثابت] movable, moving; جِسْر مُتَحَرِّك drawbridge; سَقْف مُتَحَرِّك folding/retractable roof; حِزام مُتَحَرِّك conveyor belt, (band) conveyor; رُسوم مُتَحَرِّكة (animated) cartoon; animation 2 (Gram) vowelled, vocalized; حَرْف مُتَحَرِّك a vocalized consonant

مُحَرَّك *adj* vowelled, vocalized

مُحَرِّك A *adj* *setting in motion*; قوّة مُحَرِّكة driving force; motive, motivation

B *n* 1 [جهاز] |مُحَرِّكات| engine, motor; مُحَرِّك نَفّاث \ بُخاريّ \ انْفِجاريّ jet/steam/internal combustion engine; مُحَرِّك عَنَفيّ turbojet; مُحَرِّك خارِجيّ outboard motor; مُحَرِّك رُباعيّ الأَشْواطِ four-stroke engine; كُتْلة مُحَرِّكٍ engine block; مُزَوَّد ب \ ذو مُحَرِّكٍ motorized; غُرْفة المُحَرِّكاتِ engine room; أَدارَ \ أَوْقَفَ المُحَرِّكَ to start/turn off the engine; يَدورُ المُحَرِّكُ the engine is running 2 (Comp) مُحَرِّك بَحْثٍ |مُحَرِّكات| search engine 3 (fig) |مُحَرِّكونَ| initiator, instigator; cause

حَرَمَ *v* |u; حِرْمان| to deny; to deprive; to withdraw; to exclude; حَرَمَ شَخْصاً من شَيْءٍ to forbid sb sth; حُرِمَ من شَيْءٍ to be deprived of sth; حَرَمَ شَخْصاً من حَقٍّ to deny sb a right; حَرَمَ شَخْصاً من المُشارَكةِ to exclude sb from participation; حَرَمَ شَخْصاً من الإرْثِ to disinherit sb; حَرَمَ لاعِباً من اللَعِبِ لِثَلاثِ مُبارَياتٍ to suspend a player for three games

حَرُمَ, حَرِمَ *v* |a-u; حُرْمة, حَرام| to be forbidden/taboo

حَرَّمَ *v* 1 [مَنَعَ] to forbid, to declare taboo/unlawful; to deny; حَرَّمَ شَيْئاً على شَخْصٍ to forbid sth to sb; to deny sb sth 2 [جَعَلَ مُقَدَّساً] to declare sacred; حَرَّمَ اللهُ مَكّةَ God declared Mecca a holy place

أَحْرَمَ *v* (Islam) *to enter into/be in the state of ritual consecration* (*during the pilgrimage to Mecca*)

تَحَرَّمَ *v* 1 [حُظِّرَ] to be forbidden 2 [صارَ مُقَدَّساً] to be/become sacred/sacrosanct

احْتَرَمَ *v* 1 [اعْتَبَرَ] to respect, to honor, to esteem; احْتَرَمَ شَيْئاً \ شَخْصاً to respect sth/sb; احْتَرَمَ رَأْيَ شَخْصٍ to respect sb's

to shake; to stir 3 [أَثارَ] to arouse, to excite; حَرَّكَ الشَهْوةَ to arouse desire 4 [شَكَّلَ] to vowel, to vocalize

تَحَرَّكَ *v* 1 [عَكْس سَكَنَ] to move, to be in motion, to stir; to get moving; لا تَتَحَرَّكْ! don't move!; لم يَسْتَطِعْ أَنْ يَتَحَرَّكَ he was unable to move; تَحَرَّكَ القِطارُ في مَوْعِدِه the train left on time 2 [تَوَجَّهَ |إلى|] to go

حَراك *n* 1 [نَشاط] movement, motion; بِدونِ حَراكٍ motionless 2 [تَمَلْمُل] unrest; حَراك شَعْبيّ popular unrest

حَرَكة *n* 1 [عَكْس سُكونٍ] movement; حَرَكة رِياضيّة (practice of) sports; حَرَكة لا إرادِيّة \ لا شُعورِيّة involuntary reflex; حَرَكات تَسْخينيّة warm-up; خَفيف \ ثَقيل الحَرَكةِ quick/sluggish; كَثير الحَرَكةِ active, energetic; طِفْل كَثير الحَرَكةِ an active child; عِلْم الحَرَكةِ kinetics; kinesiology; قَيَّدَ حَرَكةَ شَخْصٍ to restrict sb's movements; قامَ بِحَرَكةٍ to make a movement; في الحَرَكةِ بَرَكةٌ ≈ God helps those who help themselves 2 [فِعْل] move; manoeuvre; حَرَكة مُضادّة countermove; أَقْدَمَ على الحَرَكةِ to undertake action 3 [تَيّار] movement; حَرَكة أَدَبيّة \ سِياسيّة a literary/political movement; حَرَكة عُمّاليّة \ اسْتِقْلاليّة labour/independence movement; حَرَكة إصْلاحيّة reformism; حَرَكة تَحْريرٍ liberation movement; الحَرَكة النِسائيّة \ النِسْويّة the women's (rights) movement, feminist movement 4 (Gram) vowel; حَرَكة طَويلة \ قَصيرة a long/short vowel 5 (Transp) traffic, transportation; الحَرَكة التِجاريّة الدُوَليّة international trade; حَرَكة المُرورِ traffic; حَرَكة نَقْلِ البَضائِعِ transportation of cargo; حَرَكة الطَيَرانِ air traffic

حَرَكيّ *adj* dynamic; kinetic; in motion; *regarding movement*; motor (*before n*); تَطَوُّر حَرَكيّ motor development (*in children*); a dynamic development; نَشاط حَرَكيّ physical movement/activity; اسْم حَرَكيّ alias, nom de guerre, code name; nickname

حَرَكيّة *n* mobility; dynamics; kinetics

تَحَرُّك *n* |تَحَرُّكات| 1 [مُبادَرة] move, action, initiative; تَحَرُّك دِبْلوماسيّ diplomatic action 2 [عَكْس سُكون] movement; تَحَرُّكات الجَيْشِ troop movements; عَدَم التَحَرُّكِ immobility

تَحْريك *n* 1 [مَصْدَر] setting in motion, moving; mobilization 2 (Mech) drive opinion 2▸ [راعى] to observe, to obey; اِحْتَرَمَ القَوانِينَ to obey the law; اِحْتَرَمَ قَواعِدَ المُرورِ to obey the traffic rules; اِحْتَرَمَ كَلِمَتَهُ to keep one's word/promise

حَرَم *n* |أَحْرام| 1▸ [مَكان مُقَدَّس] sanctuary, holy place; الحَرَم الشَّرِيف the Noble Sanctuary (*the Grand Mosque in Mecca*); الحَرَم (القُدْسِيّ) الشَّرِيف the Temple Mount (*in Jerusalem*); الحَرَمانِ the two Holy Places (*Mecca and Medina*); خادِم الحَرَمَيْنِ الشَّرِيفَيْنِ Custodian of the Two Holy Mosques (*currently the king of Saudi Arabia*) 2▸ [زَوْجة] wife; حَرَم الرَّئِيس the first lady; إلى فُلانٍ وَحَرَمِهِ to Mr and Mrs So-and-So 3▸ [الجامِعةِ] campus, university grounds; في حَرَمِ الجامِعةِ on the university campus 4▸ (Sport) حَرَم المَرْمى goal area

حِرْم *n* |حُرُم| excommunication; anathema; ban

حَرام A *adj* |mf; حُرُم| 1▸ [مَمْنوع] haram; forbidden, taboo; unlawful; ابْن حَرامٍ bastard, illegitimate son; يا حَرام! poor thing!; what a shame!; حَرامٌ عَلَيْكَ! you shouldn't do that!; shame on you!; مِنْطَقة حَرام no-man's-land; prohibited area 2▸ [مُقَدَّس] sacred, holy; البَلَد الحَرام the Holy City (*Mecca*); المَسْجِد الحَرام the Holy Mosque (*surrounding the Kaaba in Mecca*); البَيْت الحَرام the Kaaba

B *n* |حُرُم| sin; transgression; عاشَ في الحَرامِ to live in sin

حَرامِيّ *n* |حَرامِيّة| thief, bandit

حِرْمان *n* 1▸ [إبْعاد] deprivation, denial; exclusion; prohibition; حِرْمان المُتَّهَم من حَقِّهِ في الدِفاعِ عن نَفْسِهِ denying the accused the right to defend himself; الحِرْمان من الإرْثِ disinheritance 2▸ [عَوَز] hardship, destitution, poverty 3▸ (Chr) excommunication

حُرْمة *n* |حُرَم, حُرُمات, حُرْمات| 1▸ [قَداسة] inviolability, sacrosanctity, holiness; حُرْمة الجَسَدِ inviolability of the body, physical integrity; انْتَهَكَ حُرْمَةَ المَنْزِلِ to trespass; انْتِهاك حُرْمَةِ المَقابِرِ desecration of graves 2▸ [مَهابة] esteem, reverence; لَهُ حُرْمَةٌ بين قَوْمِهِ to be held in high regard by one's people

حُروم *n* (Chr) excommunication

حَرِيم *n* |حُرُم, أَحْرُم, أَحارِيم| harem; *the women of a household*; women's quarters (*private part of the house where the women live*)

اِحْتِرام *n* |اِحْتِرامات| 1▸ [اِعْتِبار] respect, regard, esteem, deference; اِحْتِراماً لِ out of respect for; بِاحْتِرامٍ respectfully; deferentially; عَدَم \ قِلّة الاحْتِرامِ disrespect; عَدِيم الاحْتِرامِ disrespectful; صِيغة الاحْتِرامِ (Gram) polite form; مع كُلِّ الاحْتِرامِ with all due respect; مع فائِقِ الاحْتِرامِ, تَقَبَّلوا فائِقَ الاحْتِرامِ ≈ respectfully yours, ≈ sincerely, ≈ respectfully; فَرَضَ احْتِراماً to demand respect; أَبْدى احْتِراماً to show respect; عامَلَ شَخْصاً مُعامَلةَ احْتِرام to treat sb with respect 2▸ [اِلْتِزام] observance, honoring; adherence; اِحْتِرام هُدْنةٍ the observance of a truce; اِحْتِرام المَواعِيدِ adhering to terms; اِحْتِرام إشاراتِ المُرورِ obeying traffic signals

إحْرام *n* 1▸ [حالة المُحْرِمِ] *state of ritual consecration of the pilgrim to Mecca* 2▸ [ثَوْب المُحْرِمِ] *garments of the Mecca pilgrim*

تَحْرِيم *n* interdict, ban; prohibition, forbidding; سورة التَحْرِيم The Prohibition (*Sura 66*)

مُحْتَرَم *adj* respected, esteemed; respectable, virtuous; worthy; decent; رَجُل مُحْتَرَم a respected man; مِهْنة مُحْتَرَمة a respectable profession; دَخْل مُحْتَرَم a decent income; سِنّ مُحْتَرَمة a venerable age; سَيِّداتي وَسادَتي المُحْتَرَمونَ ladies and gentlemen

مَحْرَم *n* |مَحارِمُ| *an unmarriageable relative* (*being in a degree of consanguinity precluding marriage*); زِنى المَحارِمِ incest; زَنى بِمَحْرَمٍ to commit incest

مُحَرَّم A *adj* 1▸ [مَمْنوع] forbidden, taboo 2▸ [مَعْصوم] inviolable

B *n* 1▸ [تابو] taboo; انْتَهَكَ مُحَرَّماً to break/violate a taboo 2▸ (Islam) Muharram (*the first month of the Islamic calendar*)

مَحْرَمة *n* |مَحارِمُ| handkerchief, scarf

مَحْروم *adj* deprived, denied, bereft; أَطْفال مَحْرومونَ deprived children; مَناطِق مَحْرومة deprived areas; كانَ مَحْروماً من شَيْءٍ to be deprived of sth

‹ **حَرْمَل** *n* (Bot) African rue (*Peganum harmala*)

‹ **حَرَنَ, حَرُنَ** *v* |u; حِران, حُران| to be stubborn, to be headstrong

حَرون *adj* |حُرُن| stubborn, obstinate, refractory

‹ **تَحَرّى** *v* |عن| to investigate, to examine, to research; to inquire into, to make inquiries about; تَحَرّى عن الوَقائِعِ to examine the facts; تَحَرّى عن صِحّةِ شَيْءٍ to verify the accuracy of sth

حَزِيْران ,حُزَيْران *n* listed alphabetically

‹ **حَزَّ** *v* |u; حَزّ| 1 [آذى] to hurt; حَزَّ الأَمْرُ في نَفْسِهِ \ صَدْرِهِ \ قَلْبِهِ it hurt him/his chest/his heart 2 [قَطَعَ] to cut, to make an incision

حَزَّزَ *v* to incise, to cut

حَزّ *n* |حُزوز| notch, nick, groove; incision

حَزاز *n* 1 [أَلَم في القَلْبِ] pain in the heart 2 (Bot) moss (*Bryophyta*) 3 (Med) dandruff

حَزّة *n* notch, nick; incision

مَحَزّ *n* أَصابَ المَحَزَّ ≈ to hit the nail on the head

مُحَزَّز *adj* grooved, scored; serrated; ribbed; notched

‹ **حازوقة** *n* hiccups

حَزْقة *n* (Tech) nut (*of a bolt*)

‹ **حَزَمَ** *v* |i; حَزْم| 1 [شَدَّ بالحِزام] to pack (up); to bundle (up), to tie up; حَزَمَ حَقائِبَهُ to pack one's bags 2 [الأَمْرَ] حَزَمَ أَمْرَهُ to take/have matters firmly in hand

حَزُمَ *v* |u; حَزْم ,حَزامة ,حُزومة| to be resolute/determined

حَزَّمَ *v* to put a belt or cincture on

تَحَزَّمَ *v* to put on a belt or cincture; تَحَزَّمَ لِشَيْءٍ to prepare/ready oneself for sth

حَزْم *n* 1 [رَزْم] packing, packaging 2 [تَصَرُّف بِعَزْمٍ وَجَرْأةٍ] determination, decisiveness; بِحَزْمٍ with determination, resolutely, firmly; تَدَخَّل بِحَزْمٍ to intervene decisively; تَصَرَّفَ بِحَزْمٍ to act decisively

حازِم *adj* |حَزَمة| determined, resolute, decisive; firm, unshakeable; vigorous, energetic; bold; مَجْلِس إدارةٍ حازِم a resolute board of directors; إجْراءات حازِمة decisive actions; تَصَرُّف حازِم a determined response; مَوْقِف حازِم resolute position

حِزام *n* |حُزُم ,أَحْزِمة ,حِزامات| 1 [شَريط] belt; band; girdle, cincture; waistband; strap; حِزام جِلْدِيّ a leather belt; حِزام مُتَحَرِّك conveyor belt; حِزام النَجاةِ lifebelt, lifesaver (AmE), life preserver (AmE); حِزام الساعةِ watch band/strap; حِزام أمانٍ \ سَلامةٍ safety belt, seat belt; شَدَّ حِزامَهُ to buckle one's belt; شَدَّ الأَحْزِمةَ على البُطونِ to tighten one's belt (*to take austerity measures*); ضَرْبة تحت الحِزامِ a blow/hit below the belt

حَرِيّ *adj* worthy, suitable, appropriate; حَرِيّ بالتَقْدِيرِ estimable, honourable, worthy of appreciation; حَرِيّ بالذِكْرِ worth mentioning, considerable; حَرِيّ بالتَصْدِيقِ credible, believable

أَحْرى *adj* more appropriate; more exactly; من الأَحْرى أنْ ... it would be best to ...; أو \ بَلْ بالأَحْرى or to put it more exactly, but to put it more precisely; فَكَيْفَ بالأَحْرى ... what about ...

تَحَرٍّ *n* |تَحَرِّيات| (Law) investigation, inquiry; التَحَرِّي مع مَقْبوضٍ عَلَيْهِ the interrogation of a detainee

‹ **حَزَبَ** *v* |u; حَزْب| 1 [أَصابَ] to happen (to), to befall 2 [اِشْتَدَّ] to become serious, to intensify; to come to a crisis

حَزَّبَ *v* to form/found a party

تَحَزَّبَ *v* to form/join a party; to join forces, to make common cause; to take sides

حِزْب *n* |أَحْزاب| 1 [سِياسِيّ] party; حِزْب سِياسِيّ political party; حِزْب مُعارِض opposition (party); الحِزْب الليبيراليّ \ الاشْتِراكِيّ \ الشُيوعِيّ the liberal/socialist/communist party; الحِزْب الحاكِم the ruling party; حِزْبُ اللهِ Hezbollah (*Shiite paramilitary group and political party based in Lebanon*); نِظام الحِزْبِ الوَحِيدِ one-party system; مَكْتَب الحِزْبِ party office; زَعِيم \ رَئِيس الحِزْبِ party leader/chairman; عُضْو حِزْبٍ party member; بَرْنامَج الحِزْبِ party manifesto (BrE) platform (AmE); وَضَعَ بَرْنامَجَ الحِزْبِ to draw up the party platform; صَوَّتَ على حِزْبٍ to vote for a party; اِنْضَمَّ إلى حِزْبٍ \ اِنْتَمى to belong to/join a party; سورة الأَحْزاب The Clans (*Sura 33*) 2 [من القُرْآنِ] *a sixtieth part of the Koran*

حِزْبِيّ *adj* party (*before n*); زَعِيم حِزْبِيّ party leader, party chief

حِزْبِيّة *n* partiality, bias, favouritism; partisanship; factionalism

تَحَزُّب *n* 1 [تَحَيُّز] partiality, partisanship; factionalism 2 [تَشْكِيل حِزْبٍ] forming of a party

لاحِزْبِيّ *adj* independent, non-partisan

مُتَحَزِّب *adj* partisan; partial, biased

مُحازِب *n* partisan

‹ **حَزَرَ** *v* |i-u; حَزْر ,مَحْزَرة| to guess; to estimate; to appraise

حَزْر *n* guess, conjecture; estimation; appraisal

❷ [مِنْطَقة] zone, belt; حِزام أَمْنِيّ buffer zone; safety zone, security belt

حُزْمة *n* |حُزْمات, حُزَم| ❶ [رَبْطة] bundle; package; bunch; حُزْمة تَرَدُّدِيّة frequency band; حُزْمة ضَوْئِيّة a beam of light; حُزْمة رَسائِلَ a bundle of letters; حُزْمة سَنابِلِ القَمْحِ a sheaf of wheat; حُزْمة أَشِعّةٍ a beam of rays; حُزْمة إجْراءاتٍ a series of measures; حُزْمة من التِبْنِ a bale of straw ❷ [شَريط] zone; حُزْمة ساعيّة time zone ❸ (Comput) الحُزْمة العَرِيضة broadband; عَبْرَ الحُزْمةِ العَرِيضةِ through/via broadband

حَزِنَ *v* |a; حُزْن| to be/become sad; to grieve, to mourn; حَزِنَ على مَوْتِ شَخْصٍ to grieve for the death of sb; حَزِنَ على شَيْءٍ to be sad about sth

حَزَّنَ *v* sadden, grieve

أَحْزَنَ *v* to sadden, to make sad; أَحْزَنَ شَخْصاً to make sb sad

حُزْن *n* |أَحْزان| sadness, grief, sorrow; anguish; الشُعور بالحُزْنِ feeling of sadness; دُموع الحُزْنِ tears of sorrow; الفَرَح والحُزْن joy and sadness; حُزْناً على ... out of sadness/grief for...; كانَ مَبْعَثَ حُزْنٍ to be a cause of grief; أَعْرَب عن حُزْنِهِ على شَيْءٍ to express one's grief over sth; غَمَرَهُ الحُزْنُ he was overwhelmed by grief; غَرِقَ في أَحْزانِهِ to drown in one's sorrow

حَزِين *adj* |حَزانَى, حِزان, حُزَناءُ| sad; mournful, melancholy; كانَ حَزيناً على شَيْءٍ to be sad about sth; to grieve for sth; وَجْه حَزين a sad face; نَظْرة حَزينة a sad look; اِبْتِسامة حَزينة a sad smile; موسيقى حَزينة melancholy music

(Idiom) مالِكُ الحَزينِ egret; heron

مُحْزِن *adj* sad, miserable; saddening, depressing; tragic; حادِث مُحْزِن a sad event; a tragedy; مَشْهَد مُحْزِن a sorry sight, a mournful spectacle; أَفْكار مُحْزِنة depressing/gloomy thoughts; أَخْبار مُحْزِنة sad news; من المُحْزِنِ أَنْ نَرى it is sad to see

مَحْزون *adj* sad, sorrowful; grief-stricken

حُزَيْران, حَزيران *n* |dipt| (Levant, Iraq) June

حَسَبَ *v* |u; حَسْب, حِساب, حِسْبان, حُسْبان| to calculate, to compute; to work out; to count; حَسَبَ شَيْئاً بِدِقّةٍ to calculate sth exactly; حَسَبَ الرِبْحَ to calculate profit/interest

حَسُبَ *v* |u; حَسَب, حَسابة| to be of noble origin

حَسِبَ *v* |a-i; حِسْبان| to regard, to consider; to assume; حَسِبْتُهُ والِدَكَ I thought he was your father; I mistook him for your father; حَسِبَ الشَيْءَ سَهْلاً to consider sth to be easy; حَسِبَ حِسابَ شَيْءٍ to take something into account/consideration; حَسِبَ لِكُلِّ شَيْءٍ حِسابَهُ to take everything into account

حَوْسَبَ *v* |i; حَوْسَبة| to computerize

حاسَبَ *v* ❶ [سَوّى] to settle up; to settle an account; حاسَبَ شَخْصاً to settle up with sb, to settle accounts with sb ❷ [اِعْتَبَرَ مَسْؤولاً] to hold responsible; to call to account; حاسَبَ شَخْصاً to get even with sb; to call sb to account, to hold sb responsible; حاسَبَ شَخْصاً على تَصَرُّفاتِهِ to call sb to account for his behaviour; لا تُحاسِبْهُ على ذلك you can't count that against him; حاسِبْ نَفْسَكَ قبل أنْ تُحاسِبَ غَيْرَكَ ≈ physician, heal thyself

تَحَسَّبَ *v* ❶ [اِحْتَرَسَ] to watch out, to be careful, to be on one's guard; تَحَسَّبَ لِشَيْءٍ to watch out for sth ❷ [تَحَرّى] to try to find out; to inquire into, to look into; to investigate

تَحاسَبَ *v* to settle up; تَحاسَبَ مع شَخْصٍ to settle up (matters) with sb

اِحْتَسَبَ *v* ❶ [أَحْصى] to calculate; to do the accounts; اِحْتَسَبَ لِمَصْلَحةِ شَيْءٍ to calculate the benefit of sth; اِحْتَسَبَ بِدِقّةٍ to calculate accurately ❷ [اِعْتَدَّ] to count; to take into account; اِحْتَسَبَ شَيْئاً بِهِ to take sth into account; رَأْيُهُ لا يُحْتَسَبُ his opinion doesn't count; من حَيْثُ لا يُحْتَسَبُ out of nowhere, from an unexpected corner ❸ [اِكْتَفى |ب|] to be content ❹ [اِعْتَبَرَ] to consider ❺ [اِعْتَبَرَ مَسْؤولاً |على|] to hold responsible ❻ [تَوَقَّعَ] *to anticipate a reward in the hereafter*

حَسْب *n* sufficiency; حَسْبُنا اللهُ God suffices us; حَسْبُكَ أنْ ... you only have to ...; حَسْبي ما سَمِعْتُ I have heard enough; وَحَسْبُ \ فَحَسْبُ only, just; إنّها مَسْأَلةُ وَقْتٍ فَحَسْبُ it's only a matter of time; كانَ هذا البِدايةَ وَحَسْبُ that was just the beginning; لَيْسَ بِسَبَبِ ضَخامَتِهِ فَحَسْبُ بَلْ أَيْضاً ... not only because of its size but also ...; فَحَسْبُهُ جَهَنَّمُ Hell will settle his account

حَسَب *n* |أحْساب| ❶ [نَسَب] noble descent; ذو حَسَبٍ of noble descent ❷ [مِقْياس] measure; amount, quantity; على \ بِحَسَبِ according to, in accordance with; depending on; بِحَسَبِ القَوانِينِ الجَدِيدةِ in accordance with the new laws; بِحَسَبِ مَعْلوماتي according to my information; بِحَسَبِ قَوْلِهِ according to him; بِحَسَبِ ما إذا depending on if

حَسَبَ *prep* according to, in accordance with, as; depending on; حَسَبَ الظُروفِ depending on the circumstances; حَسَبَ ما أَعْرِفُ as far as I know; حَسَبَ ما يُقالُ according to what they say; حَسَبَ اسْتِحْقاقي as I deserve

حاسِب *n* |حاسِبات, حَواسِبُ| calculator; computer; الحاسِب الآليّ \ الإلِكْتْرونيّ computer

حاسِبة *n* calculator

حاسوب *n* |حَواسيبُ| computer; حاسوب شَخْصيّ personal computer, PC; حاسوب مَحْمول laptop; حاسوب مَكْتَبيّ desktop (computer); حاسوب دَفْتَريّ notebook; حاسوب لَوْحيّ tablet (computer); حاسوب فائِق supercomputer; أَجْهِزة \ عَتاد الحاسوبِ computer hardware/equipment

حاسوبيّ *adj* computer (*before n*), computational; بَرْنامَج حاسوبيّ computer program; رُسومات حاسوبيّة computer graphics; رُسوميّات حاسوبيّة مُتَحَرِّكة computer animation; لِسانيّات حاسوبيّة computational linguistics

حِساب *n* |حِسابات| ❶ [إحْصاء] calculation; computation; خَطَأ في الحِسابِ miscalculation; أَخْطَأَ في الحِسابِ to miscalculate, to make a miscalculation; عِلْم الحِسابِ arithmetic; أَدْخَلَ في الحِسابِ to discount; to calculate ❷ [في البَنْكِ] account; حِساب شَخْصيّ private account, personal account; حِساب جارٍ current (BrE) checking (AmE) account; حِساب بَنْكيّ \ مَصْرِفيّ \ في البَنْكِ bank account; فَتَحَ \ أَغْلَقَ حِساباً في البَنْكِ to open/close an account with a bank; أَوْدَعَ مالاً في حِسابٍ to deposit into an account; سَحَبَ مالاً من حِسابِهِ to withdraw money from one's account; حِساب ادِّخارٍ \ تَوْفيرٍ savings account; صاحِب الحِسابِ account holder; رَقْم الحِسابِ account number; كَشْف \ بَيان حِسابٍ debit notice/statement; على حِسابِ ... in the account of ❸ (Comput) account; حِساب المُسْتَخْدِمِ user account; أَنْشَأَ حِساباً to create an account ❹ [فاتورة] bill; حِساب الكَهْرَباءِ the electricity bill; على حِسابِ ... on the account of ...; at the expense of; ذلك سَيَكونُ على حِسابِ صِحَّتِهِ that will come at the expense of his health; عَمِلَ لِحِسابِ شَخْصٍ to work for sb; دَفَعَ \ سَدَّدَ حِساباً to pay a bill; دَفَعَ حِسابَ القَهْوةِ to pay for the coffee; أَدْرَجَ ٥ دولار زِيادةً في الحِسابِ to charge someone 5 dollars too much; أَدْرَجَ \ أَدْخَلَ (مَصْروفاً) في حِسابٍ to charge (sth); بِلا حِسابٍ without limit; الحِسابُ لو سَمَحْتَ bill please! ❺ [سِجِلّ الإنْفاقِ والإيراداتِ] bookkeeping, accounting; قِسْم الحِساباتِ bookkeeping section; تَفْتيش على الحِساباتِ audit of the books; حِساب رُبْع سَنَويّ quarterly accounts; حِسابات سَنَويّة annual accounts; مَسَكَ الحِساباتِ to keep the books ❻ [اعْتِبار] consideration; حَسِبَ لِكُلِّ شَيْءٍ حِسابَهُ to take everything into consideration; أَخَذَ \ أَدْخَلَ شَيْئاً في الحِسابِ to reckon with sth, to take sth into consideration ❼ (Relig) Judgement; يَوْم الحِسابِ Day of Judgement ❽ (Maths) arithmetic; أَجادَ الحِسابَ to be good at arithmetic

حِسابيّ *adj* arithmetical, mathematical; computational; عَمَليّة حِسابيّة arithmetical operation, sum; قامَ بِعَمَليّاتٍ حِسابيّةٍ to perform arithmetic

حُسْبان *n* calculation, computation; consideration, account; كانَ في الحُسْبانِ to be taken into consideration; to be expected/anticipated; ما لم يَكُنْ في الحُسْبانِ sth unexpected; sth unconsidered; على غَيْرِ حُسْبانٍ against all expectations; أَخَذَ في الحُسْبانِ to take into account; في حُسْباني I expect that...; in my opinion...; لم يَكُنْ في حُسْباني it never crossed my mind

حِسْبة *n* calculation, computation

حَسْبَما *conj* as; according to; حَسْبَما أَكَّدَ البَيانُ as was confirmed in the statement; حَسْبَما قَرَّرَ المَجْلِسُ as determined by the council; حَسْبَما أَعْلَمُ to the best of my knowledge, as far as I know

حَسيب Ⓐ *adj* |حُسَباءُ| [ذو حَسَبٍ] noble; of noble birth; respected, esteemed; من غَيْرِ رَقيبٍ وَلا حَسيبٍ unsupervised

B *n* الحَسيب the Bringer of Judgement, the Accounter (*one of the names of God*)

حَوْسَبة *n* computing; computerization; الحَوْسَبة السَحابيّة cloud computing; الحَوْسَبة الفائِقة supercomputing; الحَوْسَبة المَحْمولة \ المُتَنَقِّلة mobile computing; قِطاع الحَوْسَبة the computer industry

اِحْتِساب *n* |اِحْتِسابات| calculation

تَحَسُّب *n* precaution; تَحَسُّباً لِ in anticipation of, in case of

مُحاسِب *n* |مُحاسِبونَ| accountant; مُحاسِب قانونيّ chartered accountant (*CA*) (BrE); Certified Public Accountant (*CPA*) (AmE)

مُحاسَبة *n* bookkeeping; accountancy, accounting; ديوان المُحاسَبةِ Audit Bureau; قِسْم المُحاسَبةِ accounting department/section; comptroller's office

مُحاسَبيّ *adj* accounting (*before n*); نِظام مُحاسَبيّ accounting system; مِعْيار مُحاسَبيّ accounting standard

مُحْتَسَب *n* that for which one can expect reward in the hereafter

مَحْسوب **A** *adj* calculated; المَبْلَغ المَحْسوب the calculated amount; the result (of a calculation)
B *n* |مَحاسيبُ ,مَحْسوبونَ| protégé, favourite, pet

مَحْسوبيّة *n* nepotism; favouritism; patronage

‹ **حَسَدَ** *v* |u; حَسَد| to envy, to covet; to be jealous of; حَسَدَ شَخْصاً to envy sb, to be jealous of sb; يُحْسَدُ عَلَيْهِ enviable; وَضْعيّة \ مُهِمّة لا يُحْسَدُ عَلَيْها an unenviable position/task

تَحاسَدَ *v* to envy one another

حَسَد *n* |حُسود| envy, covetousness; jealousy; أَكَلَهُ الحَسَدُ he was consumed with jealousy; أَثارَ حَسَدَ شَخْصٍ to arouse sb's jealousy, to provoke sb's envy; بِدافِعِ الحَسَدِ out of envy

حاسِد *adj* |حُسّاد| envious, jealous

حَسود *adj* |حُسود| envious, covetous; jealous; الحَسودُ لا يَسودُ the covetous shall not prevail

‹ **حَسَرَ** *v* |i-u; حَسْر| **1** [أَزالَ] to take off, to remove **2** [كَشَفَ] to uncover, to bare; to unveil; حَسَرَ عن شَيْءٍ to uncover sth

حَسِرَ *v* |a; حَسَر ,حَسْرة| |على| to grieve; حَسِرَ على شَيْءٍ to grieve over sth; to regret sth

تَحَسَّرَ *v* |على| to moan (about), to wail (about), to lament; to be sad (over); تَحَسَّرَ على غِيابِ شَيْءٍ to lament the absence of sth

اِنْحَسَرَ *v* **1** [تَراجَعَ] to decrease; to diminish, to wane; to recede; اِنْحَسَرَ النَشاطُ الإرْهابيُّ terrorist activity has declined **2** [اِنْكَشَفَ] to be removed; اِنْحَسَرَ الماءُ عن الشاطِئِ the water retreated from the shore

حَسَر *n* weakness; حَسَر البَصَرِ myopia

حاسِر *adj* |حَواسِرُ| **1** [مَكْشوف] bare, uncovered; bareheaded; unveiled **2** [البَصَر] حاسِر البَصَرِ visually impaired; short-sighted (BrE), nearsighted (AmE)

حَسْرة *n* |حَسَرات| lamentation; grief, sorrow; يا حَسْرةً ,يا لَلْحَسْرةِ ,وا حَسْرَتي ,يا حَسْرَتاهُ alas!, what a pity!

حُسور *n* myopia, short-sightedness (BrE), nearsightedness (AmE)

حَسير *adj* |حَسْرى| fatigued, tired, exhausted; حَسير البَصَرِ myopic, short-sighted (BrE), nearsighted (AmE)

أَحْسَر *adj* |dipt| myopic, short-sighted (BrE), nearsighted (AmE)

اِنْحِسار *n* |اِنْحِسارات| decrease; recession; waning; اِنْحِسار اقْتِصاديّ economic recession; اِنْحِسار الطَلَبِ على شَيْءٍ decrease in demand for sth

تَحَسُّر *n* |تَحَسُّرات| grief; regret; heartbreak; تَحَسُّر على شَيْءٍ \ شَخْصٍ regret over sth/sb

تَحْسير *n* (Bio) moult

‹ **حَسَّ** I *v* |u; حَسّ| to sense, to feel; حَسَّ شَيْئاً \ بِشَيْءٍ to sense sth

حَسَّ II *v* |i; حِسّ ,حَسّ| to feel sorry; حَسَّ لِشَخْصٍ to feel sorry for sb

حَسَّسَ *v* to make aware, to raise awareness; الإضْرابُ حَسَّسَ الحُكومةَ بِخَطَأِ سِياسَتِها the strike made the government realize the folly of their policies

أَحَسَّ *v* to feel; to experience; to notice; أَحَسَّ بِشَيْءٍ to feel sth; أَحَسَّ بالقَلَقِ to worry, to be concerned; أَحَسَّ بِرَغْبةٍ في to feel like (having); أَحَسَّ بالفِقْدانِ to feel the loss; أَحَسَّ بِحاجةٍ إلى شَيْءٍ to feel the need for sth; أَحَسَّ أنّ ... to sense/perceive that ...

تَحَسَّسَ *v* **1** [تَلَمَّسَ] to feel (*with one's hands*); تَحَسَّسَ طَريقَهُ في الظَلامِ to grope one's way through the dark **2** [تَحَرّى] |عن| to seek information about

حاسّة *n* |حَواسُّ| sense; sensation; الحَواسّ الخَمْس the five senses; حاسّة سادِسة a sixth sense; حاسّة الشَمِّ \ اللَمْسِ

حَسَك *n coll* 1 (Bot) caltrop, thorn bush (*Tribulus terrestris*) 2 (Fishg) bones

حَسَكة *n* |حَسَك, حَسَكات| 1 [من السَمَكِ] fish bone 2 [مَدينة] الحَسَكة al-Hasakah (*city in Syria*)

حَسَكيّ *adj* thorny, prickly

حَسَمَ *v* |i; حَسْم| 1 [المَوْضوعَ] to decide, to determine; to settle, to resolve; حَسَمَ شَيْئاً مع شَخْصٍ to settle sth with sb; حَسَمَ خِلافاً \ نِزاعاً to settle a dispute; حَسَمَ نَتيجة الانْتِخاباتِ to determine the outcome of the elections 2 [خَفَّضَ] حَسَمَ ١٠ بالمِائةِ من السِعْرِ to deduct, to discount; to take 10% off the price

انْحَسَمَ *v* to be finished/completed

حَسْم *n* 1 [اتِّخاذ القَرارِ] decision, determination; عَدَم حَسْمٍ indecision; حَسْم مَصيرِ شَخْصٍ sealing sb's fate 2 [اقْتِطاع] discount, deduction; حَسْم ضَريبيّ tax reduction; حَسْم تِجاريّ dealer's discount 3 [إنْهاء] finishing; قُرْب حَسْمِ المَعْرَكةِ near/toward the end of the battle 4 [تَسْوية] settlement, settling; حَسْم المَوْقِفِ resolution of the situation

حاسِم *adj* decisive, deciding; conclusive, definitive; crucial; drastic; تَقَدُّم حاسِم a decisive lead; عُنْصُر حاسِم a decisive factor; لَحْظة حاسِمة a crucial moment; إجابة حاسِمة a definite answer; المَرْحَلة الحاسِمة the crucial phase; إجْراءات حاسِمة drastic measures; رَدَّ بِلَهْجةٍ حاسِمةٍ to reply firmly

حُسام *n* 1 [سَيْف] sword; sword edge 2 [اسْم شَخْصيّ] Hussam (*male given name*)

الحُسَيْمة *n listed alphabetically*

مَحْسوم *adj* 1 [مُقَرَّر] decided; settled, resolved; أَمْر مَحْسوم a fait accompli; an undeniable fact; نِزاع مَحْسوم النَتيجةِ a battle that has already been decided; غَيْر مَحْسومٍ undecided 2 [مُخَفَّض] cut off, severed

حَسُنَ *v* |u; حُسْن| to improve, to become good; to be/become beautiful; to be/become suitable; to be/become advisable; حَسُنَتْ أَخْلاقُ الطالِبِ the student was well-mannered; the student was moral; يَحْسُنُ بِكَ أنْ تَذْهَبَ you'd better go; حَسُنَت الأَوْضاعُ الاقْتِصاديّةُ economic conditions improved

(sense of) smell/touch; خِداع الحَواسِّ illusion; حَفَّزَ \ أَثارَ الحَواسَّ to stimulate the senses

حَسّ *n* sensation, feeling; perception

حِسّ *n* 1 [شُعور] feeling; حِسّ فَنّيّ artistry; حِسّ مُرْهَف sensitivity; حِسّ الدُعابةِ sense of humor; حِسّ باطِنيّ hunch 2 [صَوْت] faint sound; لم يَسْمَعْ حِسًّا he didn't hear a thing

حَسّاس *adj* sensitive, touchy; susceptible; allergic; ميزان حَسّاس sensitive scales; نُقْطة حَسّاسة a sore point; وَظيفة حَسّاسة a delicate position; مَوْضوع حَسّاس a delicate subject; مَعْلومات ذات طَبيعةٍ حَسّاسةٍ information of a sensitive nature; كانَ حَسّاساً لِشَيْءٍ to be sensitive/allergic to sth; ضَرَبَ على الوَتَرِ الحَسّاسِ to strike a chord; to touch a nerve

حَسّاسيّة *n* 1 [قوّة الإحْساسِ] sensitivity; حَسّاسيّة ميزانِ الحَرارة the sensitivity of a thermometer; حَسّاسيّة مُفْرِطة, الإفْراط في الحَسّاسيّةِ oversensitivity; مُفْرِط الحَسّاسيّةِ oversensitive; حَسّاسيّة للنَقْد sensitivity to criticism; قَضيّة في غايةِ الحَسّاسيّةِ an extremely delicate matter 2 (Med) irritation; allergy; حَسّاسيّة جِلْديّة irritation of the skin; حَسّاسيّة ضدّ شَيْءٍ an allergy to sth; حَسّاسيّة الطَلَعِ, حَسّاسيّة الأَنْفِ hay fever; حَسّاسيّة لِدَواءٍ an allergy to a medicine; أَعْراض حَسّاسيّةٍ allergic reactions; سَبَّبَ حَسّاسيّةً to cause irritation

حِسّيّ *adj* 1 [يُدْرَكُ بالحَسِّ] sensory; مُلاحَظات حِسّيّة sensory perceptions 2 [شَهْوانيّ] sensual; sensuous

إحْساس *n* |إحْساسات, أَحاسيسُ| feeling, sensation, perception; sentiment; إحْساس طَيِّب \ مُمْتِع a nice/pleasant feeling; قِلّة الإحْساسِ insensitivity; جهاز إحْساسٍ sensor; عَديم \ فاقِد الإحْساسِ insensitive; insensible; جَرَحَ إحْساسَ شَخْصٍ to hurt sb's feelings; فَقَدَ الإحْساسَ في جُزْءِ جَسَدِهِ to lose sensation in a part of one's body

مِحَسّة *n* |مَحاسُّ| curry comb (*a metal device with serrated ridges used for removing dirt from a body brush with which a horse is groomed*)

مَحْسوس *adj* |مَحْسوسات| sensed, felt; tangible; perceptible; دَليل مَحْسوس tangible/concrete evidence; المَحْسوسات *things perceptible to the senses*

حَسَنة *n* 1 [صَدَقة] alms (old use); money (*given to a beggar*); charity; أعْطى حَسَنةً to give alms 2 [فِعْل حَسَن] good deed; حَسَنات good works; advantages, merits

حُسْنى *n* 1 [لُطْف] kindness; بالحُسْنى amicably, with kindness; أخَذَ \ عامَلَ شَخْصاً بالحُسْنى to treat sb with kindness 2 [عاقِبة حَسَنة] happy ending, good outcome 3 see أحْسَن

حَسّون *n* |حَساسينُ| (Zool) (European) goldfinch

حُسَيْن *n* 1 [اِسْم شَخْصيّ] Hussein (*male given name*) 2 (Islam) Husayn (*ibn Ali ibn Abi Talib, grandson of the prophet Muhammed and an important figure in Shia Islam*)

إحْسان *n* 1 [تَصَدُّق] charity, almsgiving, philanthropy; performance of good works, beneficence 2 (Islam) *the interiorizing of the love of God* (*in Sufism*)

أحْسَن *adj* |dipt; أحاسِنُ| better; best; الأسْماء الحُسْنى the most beautiful names (*the 99 names of God*); بالّتي هي أحْسَنُ in a friendly way; as good as possible; in the best manner possible; على أحْسَنِ وَجْهٍ in the best way possible

اسْتِحْسان *n* 1 [تَقْدير] approval; appreciation, recognition, acclaim; لَقِيَ القَرارُ اسْتِحْساناً من المَجْلِسِ the decision was approved by the council 2 (Isl Law) *the use of one's own judgement/discretion to settle a legal or religious problem that cannot be resolved by citing sacred texts*

تَحَسُّن *n* improvement; كانَ في تَحَسُّنٍ مُسْتَمِرٍّ to continue to improve; كانَ في سَبيلِ التَحَسُّنِ to be getting better, to be on the path to improvement; هذا تَحَسُّنٌ كَبيرٌ this is a big improvement

تَحْسين *n* 1 |تَحْسينات| [تَجْويد] improvement, refinement; تَحْسينات تِقْنيّة technical refinements; أدْخَلَ تَحْسيناتٍ to make improvements 2 |تَحاسين| [تَزْيين] beautification, embellishment; ornament, decoration

مَحاسِن *n pl* |dipt| good points; merits, good qualities; amenities; مَحاسِن الأخْلاقِ high moral standards; مَحاسِن وَمَساوِئ pros and cons

مُحْسِن A *adj* charitable, beneficent; humanitarian, philanthropic

حَسَّنَ *v* to ameliorate; to improve; to beautify; to decorate; حَسَّنَ لِياقَتَهُ to improve one's condition; حَسَّنَ النَتائِجَ to upgrade the results; حَسَّنَ خِطّةً to refine a plan; حَسَّنَ مُسْتَوى المَعيشةِ to improve the standard of living

أحْسَنَ *v* 1 [أنْعَمَ] to do good (deeds); أحْسَنَ ل \ إلى شَخْصٍ to do good to sb; أحْسَنَ إلى الفُقَراءِ to be charitable to the poor 2 [أجادَ] to be good at, to know how to; to master; أحْسَنْتَ well done!, bravo!; أحْسَنَ الاخْتِيارَ to make a good choice; أحْسَنَ التَصَرُّفَ to behave well, to act properly; أحْسَنَ مُعامَلة شَخْصٍ to treat sb well; أحْسَنَ الظَنَّ بِشَخْصٍ to think highly of sb; to have faith in sb; أحْسَنَ الفَهْمَ to understand clearly

تَحَسَّنَ *v* 1 [صارَ أحْسَنَ] to improve, to get better; لَقَدْ تَحَسَّنَتْ صِحَّتُهُ his health has improved; يَتَحَسَّنُ الجَوُّ the weather is getting better 2 [تَجَمَّلَ] to put on make-up; to become more beautiful

اسْتَحْسَنَ *v* to approve of; to appreciate; to have a good opinion of; اسْتَحْسَنَ شَيْئاً \ شَخْصاً to deem sth/sb good; to have a good opinion of sth/sb; اسْتَحْسَنَ فِكْرةً to appreciate an idea; يُسْتَحْسَنُ أنْ ... it would be good/advisable if ...; يُسْتَحْسَنُ أنْ نَبْقى هُنا it would be better if we stayed; يُسْتَحْسَنُ عَدَمُ ذِكْرِهِ it's best not to mention it

حَسَن *adj* |حِسان| 1 [جَيِّد] good; حَسَناً! great!; okay!; right!; كانَ قَصْدُهُ حَسَناً he meant well; النِيّات الحَسَنة goodwill; good intentions; أبْلى بَلاءً حَسَناً (في شَيْءٍ) to show great courage (in sth); to fare well (in sth) 2 [جَميل] beautiful, handsome; حَسَن المَخْبَرِ \ المَظْهَرِ beautiful on the inside/outside 3 [اِسْم شَخْصيّ] Hassan (*male given name*)

حُسْن *n* beauty; being good; حُسْن الحَظِّ (good) luck; لِحُسْنِ الحَظِّ fortunately; حُسْن النِيّة best of intentions; حُسْن السُلوكِ good behaviour; حُسْن التَعْبيرِ euphemism; حُسْن السيرةِ good conduct

Idiom سِتّ الحُسْنِ (Bot) belladonna, deadly nightshade (*Atropa belladonna*)

حَسْناء *n* |dipt f; حِسان| beautiful woman, beauty; حَسْناء شَقْراء a beautiful blonde

B *n* **1** [وَليّ النِعْمةِ] benefactor; donor; philanthropist **2** [اسْم شَخْصيّ] Mohsen (*male given name*)

مُحَسِّن *n* improvement; beautification; مُحَسِّنات cosmetics; مُحَسِّن بَديعيّ figure of speech

مُسْتَحْسَن *adj* advisable, recommended; proper; من المُسْتَحْسَنِ أنْ ... it would be advisable/recommended to...

‹ **حَسا** *v* |u; حَسْو| to sip; to slurp

تَحَسّى *v* to drink; to sip

احْتَسى *v* to drink; to sip; احْتَسى فِنْجانَ القَهْوةِ to drink/sip a cup of coffee

حَسْو *n* soup; broth

حَساء *n* |أحْساء, أحْسِية| soup; broth; تَناوَلَ حَساءً to have soup

حُسْوة *n* |حُسْوات, حُسَوات, أحْسِية| sip, gulp; gulp

‹ **الحُسَيْمة** *n* al-Hoceima (*city in Morocco*)

‹ **حَشَدَ** *v* |i-u; حَشْد| **1** [جَمَعَ] to gather; to contract; to concentrate; حَشَدَ تَأْييداً to rally support; حَشَدَ المَوارِدَ to mobilize resources; حَشَدَ المَواهِبَ to recruit talent **2** [تَجَمَّعَ] to gather together, to assemble; حَشَدَ القوّاتِ to gather/assemble the troops

حَشَّدَ *v* to rally; حَشَّدَ القوّاتِ to rally the troops

تَحَشَّدَ *v* to gather together, to assemble

احْتَشَدَ *v* to assemble, to gather together, to congregate; احْتَشَدَ بالناسِ to be crowded with people

حَشْد *n* |حُشود| gathering, crowd, throng; حَشْد كَبير a big crowd; حُشود عَسْكَريّة amassed troops, host; حُشود من الناسِ throngs of people

حاشِد *adj* crowded; numerous

حاشِدة *n* |حَواشِدُ| (Elec) battery

مُحْتَشِد *adj* crowded, packed, full; teeming, swarming; جُمْهور مُحْتَشِد mob, crowd

‹ **حَشَرَ** *v* |i-u; حَشْر| **1** [جَمَعَ] to gather, to assemble; حُشِرَ to be gathered for the Day of Resurrection **2** [أقْحَمَ] to squeeze, to press, to shove, to stuff; حَشَرَ شَخْصاً في زاوِيةٍ to force sb into a corner; حَشَرَ نَفْسَهُ to force oneself (on); to meddle; حَشَرَ أنْفَهُ في شَيْءٍ to stick one's nose into sth

حَشْر *n* gathering, assembling; سورة الحَشْر The Gathering (*Sura 59*); يَوْم الحَشْرِ the Day of Gathering (*Judgement Day*)

حَشَرة *n* (Zool) insect; حَشَرة نافِعة \ ضارّة a beneficial/harmful insect; مُبيد الحَشَراتِ pesticide; insecticide; قَرْصة حَشَرةٍ insect bite; رَشَّ مُبيداتِ الحَشَراتِ to spray insecticides; عِلْم الحَشَراتِ entomology

حَشَريّ *adj* مَبيدات حَشَريّة insecticides

حَشَريّة *n* nosiness

مَحْشور *adj* jammed, crammed, stuck

‹ **حَشْرَجَ** *v* |i; حَشْرَجة| to hawk (up) (*to bring phlegm up from the throat*); to rattle in the throat

تَحَشْرَجَ *v* to rattle in the throat

حَشْرَجة *n* death rattle; (noisy) throat-clearing

‹ **حَشَّ** *v* |u; حَشّ| to mow, to cut; حَشَّ الحَشيشَ to cut the grass

حَشَّشَ *v* to smoke hashish

احْتَشَّ *v* to mow, to cut; to weed

حَشّاش **A** *adj* using hashish; high (*from the effects of cannabis*) **B** *n* **1** [مُحَشِّش] heavy marijuana smoker **2** (Hist) الحَشّاشونَ the Assassins (*11th-13th century Nizari Ismaili order*)

حَشيش *n* |حَشائِشُ| **1** [عُشْب] grass **2** [نَبات مُخَدِّر] hashish, hash; cannabis; زَرَعَ \ أنْبَتَ الحَشيشَ to grow cannabis; دَخَّنَ الحَشيشَ to smoke hashish; سيجارة حَشيشٍ joint; لَفَّ سيجارة حَشيش to roll a joint; عِشْرونَ جَراماً من الحَشيش twenty grams of hash

حَشيشة *n* herb; حَشيشة السُعال (Bot) coltsfoot (*Tussilago farfara*); حَشيشة الدَيْنارِ (Bot) hops (*Humulus lupulus*); حَشيشة البَحْرِ algae

مِحَشّ *n* |مَحاشُّ| **1** [مِنْجَل] sickle; scythe; billhook **2** [ما يُحَرَّكُ بِهِ النارُ] poker (*fire iron*)

مِحَشّة *n* |مَحاشّ| **1** [آلة] sickle; scythe **2** [حَصّادة] mower; (grass) trimmer (BrE), weed-whacker (AmE)

‹ **حَشْفة** *n* |حِشاف| (old use) cliff

حَشَفة *n* |حِشاف, حَشَفات| (Anat) glans (*of the penis*)

‹ **حَشَمَ** *v* |i; حَشْم| to shame, to fill with shame; حَشَمَ شَخْصاً to shame sb

حَشِمَ *v* |a; حَشَم| to be ashamed

حَشَّمَ *v* to make shy; to embarrass; حَشَّمْتَني بِتَصَرُّفاتِكَ اليَوْم you embarrassed me by your behavior today

تَحَشَّمَ *v* to be shy

اِحْتَشَمَ *v* (1) [اِسْتَحْيا] to be modest (*in dress and behavior*) (2) [خَجِلَ] to be shy

حَشَم *n* entourage, retinue

حِشْمة *n* (1) [أَدَب] decency, decorum; مُنافٍ لِلحِشْمةِ indecent (2) [اِسْتِحْياء] shyness; modesty; shame

اِحْتِشام *n* reserve; decency, propriety; تَكَلَّمَ بِاحْتِشامٍ to speak modestly

تَحَشُّم *n* modesty; shyness; reserve

مُتَحَشِّم *adj* modest; decent, demure; chaste

مُحْتَشِم *adj* modest; decent; timid; مَلابس \ لِباس مُحْتَشِم(ة) modest dress; غَيْر مُحْتَشِمٍ immodest, risqué; indiscreet

حَشا *v* |u; حَشْو| (1) [مَلَأَ] to stuff, to fill; حَشا الفُلْفُلَ بِلَحْمٍ مَفْروم to stuff peppers with minced meat; حَشا وِسادةً بالريش to stuff a pillow with feathers (2) (Med) to fill; حَشا ضِرْساً to fill a molar (3) [سِلاحاً] to load

حَشّى *v* (1) [عَلَّقَ] to annotate; to gloss (2) (Clothg) to hem

حاشى *v* to exclude

تحاشى *v* to avoid, to keep away from; لم يَتحاشَ المَخاطِرَ not to shrink from danger

حَشْو *n* |مَحاشٍ| (1) [ما يُمْلَأُ بِهِ] stuffing; filling; padding (2) (Med) filling (3) [مِنَ الكَلام] redundancy; tautology

حاشا *particle* حاشا أنْ أَفْعَلَ ذلك I would not think about doing it, far be it that I do that; حاشا لِلهِ God forbid!; حاشا لَكَ أنْ ... don't lower yourself by...

حاشِية *n* |حَواشٍ| (1) [جانِب] border (2) [هامِش] margin (3) [تَعْليق] comment; marginal note; footnote (4) [في نِهاية رِسالةٍ] epilogue, afterword; postscript (5) [مَلِكٍ] court; entourage; المَلِكة وَحاشِيَتُها the queen and her entourage

(Idioms) رَقيق الحَواشي friendly, kind-hearted; زَهْرة الحَواشي speedwell

حَشاً, حَشًى *n* |أَحْشاء| أَحْشاء intestines; في أَحْشاءِ ... inside...

حَشْوة *n* filling; stuffing; charge (*of an explosive*); حَشْوة الضِرْسِ filling (*of a tooth*); حَشْوة الشوكولاتةِ the filling of piece of chocolate

حَشِيّة *n* |حَشايا, حَشِيّات| (1) [سَرير] mattress; bedding, bedclothes; pillow, cushion (2) (Mech) gasket; حَشِيّة دائِرِيّة O-ring

اِحْتِشاء *n* (Med) infarction

تَحاشٍ *n* avoiding; refraining; abstaining, abstention

مَحْشُوّ (A) *adj* (1) [مَمْلوء] filled, stuffed; jammed; مَحْشُوّ بِأُرُزٍّ stuffed with rice; مَحْشُوّ بالأَخْطاءِ (Comput) full of bugs (2) [مُلَقَّم] loaded
(B) *n stuffed vegetable (e.g. pepper)*

مَحْشِيّ (A) *adj* stuffed, filled
(B) *n stuffed vegetable (e.g. pepper)*

حَصَبَ *v* |i-u; حَصْب| to cover with pebbles/gravel; to pave

حَصِبَ *v* |a; حَصَب| to have the measles

حَصَّبَ *v* to cover with pebbles/gravel; to pave; to supply with ballast

حَصَب *n* pebble; gravel; ballast

حَصْباء *n coll* |dipt f| pebbles; gravel; ballast

حَصْبة *n* (1) (Med) measles; كانَ مُصاباً بالحَصْبةِ to have measles; الحَصْبة الأَلْمانيّة German measles, rubella; تَطْعيم ضِدّ الحَصْبةِ الأَلْمانيّةِ German measles vaccination (2) [عاصِفة] cyclone; violent windstorm

حَصْحَصَ *v* |i; حَصْحَصة| to be/become clear; to come to light; to manifest

حَصَدَ *v* |i-u; حَصْد, حَصاد, حِصاد| to harvest, to reap; حَصَدَ الزَرْعَ to bring in the harvest; مَنْ زَرَعَ حَصَدَ you reap what you sow; مَنْ زَرَعَ الشَرَّ حَصَدَ النَدامة ≈ he who sows the wind will reap the whirlwind

أَحْصَدَ *v* to be/become ripe

اِسْتَحْصَدَ *v* to ripen, to be/become ripe; to mature

حَصْد *n* harvest, harvesting; حَصْد انْتِصاراتٍ string of victories; لِحَصْدِ ثِمارِ شَيْءٍ in order to reap the fruits of sth

حاصِدة *n* |حاصِدات, حَواصِدُ| mower; harvester, reaper; آلة حاصِدة harvester, mower (*machine*)

to lift the siege on a city **2** (Pol) embargo; حِصار تِجاريّ trade embargo; حِصار اقْتِصاديّ economic blockade; حِصار على النَفْطِ sanctions on oil; رَفَعَ حِصاراً; to lift an embargo

حَصْريّ *adj* exclusive, sole; وَكيل تِجاريّ حَصْريّ an exclusive representative; هو صاحِبُ الحَقِّ الحَصْريِّ ب ... he has the exclusive rights to ...

حَصير, حَصيرة *n* | حُصُر, أَحْصِرة | straw/reed mat

انْحِصار *n* limitation, restriction

مُحاصَر *adj* blockaded; under siege, besieged; trapped; مَقَرّ مُحاصَر headquarters under siege; مُحاصَر داخِل شَيْءٍ trapped inside sth

مُحاصِر *n* | مُحاصِرون | besieger

مُحاصَرة *n* siege, blockade; block; مُحاصَرة مَدينةٍ the siege of a city

مَحْصور *adj* **1** [مَحْدود] restricted; بَقِيَ مَحْصوراً في \ ب ... to be limited/confined/restricted to ... **2** [مُحاصَر] blocked; under siege

حِصْرِم 〈 *n* unripe grapes; sour grapes; مَنْ يَأْكُلِ الحِصْرِمَ تَضْرِسْ أَسْنانُهُ as you make your bed, so you must lie in it

حَصَّصَ 〈 *v* **1** [قَسَّمَ] to segment, to divide up (into portions) **2** [وَزَّعَ] to allot; to ration

حاصَّ *v* to share

حِصّة *n* | حِصَص | **1** [جُزْء] share, portion; quota, allotment; حِصّة (في) الرِبْحِ a share of/in the profits; حِصّة الأَسَد the lion's share; لِكُلٍّ واحِدٍ حِصَّتُهُ to each his due; نِظام الحِصَصِ quota system; تَخْصيص الحِصَص assignment of quotas **2** [دَرْس] period, lesson, class; الحِصّة الأولى \ الثانية في المَدْرَسةِ the first/second period at school; ٢٩ حِصّةً في الأُسْبوعِ 29 periods per week

تَحْصيص *n* assignment, allocation; ration

حَصُفَ 〈 *v* \|u; حَصافة\| to have insight; to have good judgment, to be wise

حُصاف *n* (Med) pellagra

حَصافة *n* wisdom, insight, sagacity; discretion; حَصافة سِياسيّة political know-how

حَصاد, حِصاد *n* harvest; حَصاد كَبير a rich harvest, an abundant harvest; حَصاد جُهودِهِ the fruits of his efforts; حَصاد مائيّ water harvesting; حَصاد الحُبوبِ grain crop; مَوْسِم الحَصادِ harvest time

حَصّاد *n* harvester

حَصّادة *n* mowing machine; grass cutter; lawnmower; حَصّادة دَرّاسة combine (harvester)

حَصيد, حَصيدة *n* | حَصائِدُ | harvest, crop

حَصَرَ 〈 *v* \|i-u; حَصْر\| **1** [حَدَّدَ] to restrict, to limit; to circumscribe; حَصَرَ الإِمْكانيّاتِ to limit the possibilities; حَصَرَ المَسْؤوليّةَ to limit liability, to mitigate responsibility **2** [أَحْصى] to enumerate, to list; to inventory **3** [أَحاطَ] to surround, to enclose

حاصَرَ *v* to besiege, to lay siege; to blockade; to encircle, to surround; حاصَرَ مَدينةً \ مَبْنًى to besiege a city/building; to surround a city/building; حاصَرَت الشُرْطةُ المَنْزِلَ the police surrounded the house; الجَيْشُ حاصَرَ القَصْرَ بِدَبّاباتٍ the army lay siege to the palace with tanks

انْحَصَرَ *v* **1** [تَحَدَّدَ] to limit oneself; to be/become restricted; انْحَصَرَ على مَكانٍ to be limited to a location **2** [تَرَكَّزَ] في \| ب to be concentrated in/at; انْحَصَرَ اللَعِبُ في وَسَطِ المَلْعَبِ gameplay was concentrated at midfield

حَصْر *n* **1** [تَحْديد] restriction, limitation; لا حَصْرَ لَهُ, يَفوقُ الحَصْرَ unlimited; innumerable, countless; إِمْكانيّات لا حَصْرَ لَها limitless possibilities; على سَبيلِ المِثالِ لا الحَصْرِ ... such as, but not limited to ...; حَصْر الإِرْثِ certification of succession **2** [حِصار] siege **3** [تَعْداد] inventory; حَصْر السِلاحِ بِيَدِ شَخْصٍ inventory of weapons in sb's possession **4** [احْتِكار] monopoly; حَصْر التَبْغِ tobacco monopoly

حَصَر *n* (Med) aphasia; *inability to speak or understand spoken language*

حُصْر, حُصُر *n* water retention; constipation; حُصْر البَوْلِ urine retention, anuria

حاصِر *n* | حاصِرات | حاصِرات بيتا beta blockers

حِصار *n* | حُصُر | **1** (Mil) siege; blockade; حِصار سَرايِيفو the siege of Sarajevo; فَكَّ \ اخْتَرَقَ حِصاراً to break a blockade, to run a blockade; to penetrate a siege; رَفَعَ الحِصارَ عن مَدينةٍ

حَصيف *adj* |حُصَفاءُ| sensible, wise; judicious; رَجُل حَصيف a wise man; رَأْي حَصيف balanced opinion

حَصَلَ *v* |u; حُصول| **1** [نالَ] |على| to obtain, to gain, to get, to receive, to achieve; حَصَلَ على شَهادةٍ to obtain a certificate; to receive a diploma; حَصَلَ على دَرَجةٍ عِلْمِيّةٍ to earn a degree; حَصَلَ على نَتيجةٍ to achieve a result; حَصَلَ على رُخْصةٍ to get a permit/licence; حَصَلَ على جائِزةٍ to win an award; حَصَلَ على حَقٍّ to acquire a right; حَصَلَ على اللُجوءِ (السِياسيِّ) to receive (political) asylum **2** [حَدَثَ] to happen, to take place; حَصَلَتْ مُضاعَفاتٌ complications arose; لَقَدْ حَصَلَ لَهُ حادِثٌ he had an accident; ماذا حَصَلَ لَكَ؟ what happened to you?

حَصَّلَ *v* **1** [جَبى] to cash, to collect; حَصَّلَ رِبْحاً to realize a profit; حَصَّلَ مَبْلَغاً to receive an amount; حَصَّلَ ضَرائِبَ to collect taxes **2** [نالَ] to obtain, to achieve, to gain; to collect; حَصَّلَ العِلْمَ to obtain knowledge **3** [اسْتَنْتَجَ] to figure out

تَحَصَّلَ *v* **1** [حُصِلَ] to be obtained **2** [حَصَلَ] to obtain

اسْتَحْصَلَ *v* |على| to obtain, to get; to procure; اسْتَحْصَلَ على شَيْءٍ to obtain sth

حاصِل *n* **1** [غَلّة] |حاصِلات| result; product; حاصِلات زِراعيّة agricultural products **2** (Math) |حَواصِلُ| outcome, total; حاصِل حِسْبةٍ \ قِسْمةٍ the outcome of a sum/division; حاصِل الضَرْبِ product **3** [المالِ] |حَواصِلُ| change; income; returns, proceeds **4** [خُلاصة] |حَواصِلُ| الحاصِلُ in short; anyway; حاصِلُ القَوْلِ in short

حَصّالة *n* cash box, kitty; piggy bank; poor box, alms box

حُصول *n* **1** [نَيْل] achievement; يُمْكِنُ الحُصولُ عَلَيْهِ في كافّةِ مَكاتِبِ البَريدِ it is available at any post office; للحُصولِ على الجِنْسيّةِ الأَمْريكيّةِ in order to obtain American citizenship **2** [حُدوث] happening, occurrence, instance; نَفى حُصولَ شَيْءٍ to deny that something happened

حَصيلة *n* |حَصائِلُ| **1** [نَتيجة] result, outcome; الحَصيلة النِهائيّة the final outcome; حَصيلة المُشاوَراتِ the results of the negotiations; حَصيلة الضَحايا death toll, *total number of victims in a disaster* **2** (Busn) proceeds, revenue; حَصيلة بَيْعٍ the proceeds from a sale; حَصيلة الأَرْباحِ profit; حَصيلة الضَرائِبِ tax revenue; تَهْبِطُ \ تَزْدادُ الحَصيلةُ the profits are decreasing/increasing **3** (Sport) score

تَحْصيل *n* |تَحْصيلات| **1** [نَيْل] obtaining; تَحْصيل حاصِلٍ a settled matter; a foregone conclusion; tautology **2** [جِباية] collection; تَحْصيل الضَرائِبِ the collection of taxes; مَكْتَب تَحْصيلٍ debt-collection agency; دَيْن تحت التَحْصيلِ outstanding debt

مُتَحَصِّل **A** *adj* obtained **B** *n* yield; intake

مُحَصِّل *n* **1** (Busn) collector; مُحَصِّل دُيونٍ \ ضَرائِبَ debt/tax collector **2** [القِطارِ] ticket collector (BrE), conductor (AmE)

مُحَصِّلة *n* outcome

مَحْصول *n* |مَحْصولات، مَحاصيلُ| yield; proceeds; product; production; مَحْصول زِراعيّ agricultural production; مَحاصيل الحُقولِ crops; مَحْصول القَهْوةِ \ القُطْنِ coffee/cotton production; يَتَراجَعُ المَحْصولُ production is declining

حَصَّنَ *v* **1** [قَوّى] to strengthen, to fortify; حَصَّنَ المَدينةَ to fortify the city; حَصَّنَ مَوْقِعَهُ to strengthen one's position **2** [طَعَّمَ] to immunize; حَصَّنَ شَخْصاً من مَرَضٍ to immunize sb against a disease

أَحْصَنَ *v* **1** [قَوّى] to fortify **2** [عَفَّ] to be chaste **3** [تَزَوَّجَ] to get married

تَحَصَّنَ *v* **1** [عَفَّ] to be chaste **2** [احْتَمى] to feel safe

حِصْن *n* |حُصون| **1** [مَعْقِل] castle, citadel; fortress, stronghold, bastion **2** [عِفّة] chastity; abstinence

حِصان *n* |حُصُن، أَحْصِنة| **1** (Zool) horse; حِصان هَزّاز rocking horse; حِصان سِباقٍ racehorse; حِصان البَحْرِ sea horse; قوّة حِصانٍ، حِصان بُخاريّ horsepower; على ظَهْرِ \ صَهْوةِ حِصانٍ on horseback; on a horse; لِكُلِّ حِصانٍ كَبْوةٌ وَلِكُلِّ عالِمٍ هَفْوةٌ ≈ to err is human; قَوِيّ كالحِصانِ as strong as an ox; حِصان هَجين a non-thoroughbred horse **2** (Sport) حِصان القَفْزِ \ الحَلَقِ vaulting horse; pommel horse, side horse **3** [في الشِطْرَنْجِ] knight (*in chess*)

حَصانة *n* **1** [فَضيلة] chastity; virtuousness **2** [مَناعة] resistance; immunity **3** [في السِياسةِ] immunity; حَصانة بَرْلَمانيّة \ دِبْلوماسيّة parliamentary/diplomatic immunity;

إحْصائيّة *n* statistics; إحْصائيّات statistics; statistical data; تُظْهِرُ \ تُثْبِتُ \ تُفيدُ الإحْصائيّاتُ أنّ ... the statistics demonstrate/prove/point out that ...

مُحْصٍ *n* المُحْصي the One to whom the number of all things is known (*one of the names of God*)

حَضَرَ *v* |u; حُضور| 1 [شَهِدَ] to attend; to be present; حَضَرَ اجْتِماعاً \ جَنازةً to attend a meeting/funeral; لم تَحْضُر الاجْتِماعَ she was not there at the meeting; حَضَرَ المَجْلِسَ to participate in the meeting; قالَ ما يَحْضُرُهُ he said whatever came into his head; حَضَرَني قَوْلُهُ his words came to mind 2 [حانَ] to come; قد حَضَرَت الصَّلاةُ the time for prayer has come; حَضَرَ العيدُ the feast has arrived 3 (Law) to appear in court; يَجِبُ أنْ يَحْضُرَ السارِقُ اليَوْمَ the thief must appear in court today

حَضَّرَ *v* 1 [أَعَدَّ] to prepare; to make ready; حَضَّرَ الغَداءَ \ اللَّحْمَ \ الحَساءَ to prepare lunch/meat/soup; حَضَّرَ الدَّرْسَ to prepare the lesson; حَضَّرَ القَهْوَةَ \ الشايَ to make coffee/tea 2 [مَدَّنَ] to civilize; to make sedentary; to urbanize

حاضَرَ *v* to lecture, to give a course of lectures; حاضَرَ في الجامِعةِ to be a university lecturer (BrE), to be a university professor (AmE)

أَحْضَرَ *v* 1 [جَلَبَ] to bring; to take; to bring along; أَحْضَرَ شَيْئاً \ شَخْصاً إلى مَكانٍ to bring/take sth/sb to a place; أَحْضَرَ جَريدةً to bring a newspaper; أَحْضَرْتُهُ مَعي I brought it with me 2 [أَعَدَّ] to prepare; أَحْضَرَ الطَّعامَ to prepare the meal 3 [أمامَ المَحْكَمةِ] to bring before; أَحْضَرَ مُتَّهَماً to bring a suspect before the court 4 [رافَقَ] to bring along; أَحْضَرْتُهُ إلى الحَفْلَةَ I brought him to the party

تَحَضَّرَ *v* to become urbanized; to be/become civilized

احْتَضَرَ *v* 1 [ماتَ] اُحْتُضِرَ to die; عَمَليّةُ السَلامِ تُحْتَضَرُ the peace process is dying 2 [حَضَرَ] to be present; to attend; to exist; احْتَضَرَ المَكانَ he was present, he was there

اسْتَحْضَرَ *v* 1 [أَحْضَرَ] to bring; to fetch; to call/fetch back 2 [طَلَبَ حُضورَهُ] to summon, to call for/up; to invoke, to conjure; اسْتَحْضَرَ الأَرْواحَ to conjure spirits 3 [تَذَكَّرَ] to recall, to call to mind; اسْتَحْضَرَ الماضِيَ to remember

تَمَتَّعَ سَحَبَ الحَصانةَ عن شَخْصٍ to remove sb's immunity; بِحَصانةٍ من شَيْءٍ to enjoy immunity from sth

حِصانيّ *adj* horse (*before n*); قُدْرة حِصانيّة horsepower

حَصين *adj* 1 [مَنيع] inaccessible; inviolable; protected, fortified; حِصْن حَصين an impregnable fortress 2 (Med) immune, resistant

إحْصان *n* chastity

تَحْصين *n* |تَحْصينات| 1 [مَصْدَر] strengthening; reinforcement 2 [تَلْقيح] immunization; resistance; تَحْصين ضِدّ مَرَضٍ immunization against a disease; حَمْلة تَحْصينٍ immunization/vaccination campaign; vaccine drive 3 [ما يُحَصَّنُ بِهِ] fortification; تَحْصينات حِصْنٍ \ مَدينةٍ \ قَلْعةٍ the fortifications of a castle/city/citadel

مُتَحَصِّن *n* holed up, dug in

مُحْصَن A *adj* married
B *n* (Isl Law) *an married person who has not committed adultery*

مُحَصَّن *adj* 1 [مُقَوّى] fortified, strengthened 2 (Med) immune; immunized, inoculated

أَحْصى *v* to count; to calculate, to compute; to add up; أَحْصى الخَسائِرَ to calculate the losses; أَحْصى على شَخْصٍ أَنْفاسَهُ to keep an eye on sb; لا يُحْصى countless, innumerable

حَصاة, **حَصْوة** *n* |حُصيّ, حَصَيات| 1 [جَمْرة] pebble 2 (Med) stone, calculus; حَصاة صَفْراويّة \ المَرارةِ gallstone; حَصاة كُلْويّة \ المَثانةِ kidney stone; عانى من حُصيٍّ كُلْوِيّةٍ to suffer from kidney stones

حَصًى *n coll* pebbles; gravel

حَصى البانِ *n* (Levant) rosemary

إحْصاء *n* |إحْصاءات| calculation; count; statistics; arithmetic; عِلْم الإحْصاءِ statistics; إحْصاء سُكّانيّ \ السُكّانِ census; مَعْهَد \ مَرْكَز \ مَصْلَحة الإحْصاءاتِ office of statistics; حَسَبَ الإحْصاءاتِ according to the statistics; قامَ بِإحْصاءٍ to compile statistics, to run the numbers

إحْصائيّ A *adj* statistical; مَعْلومات إحْصائيّة the statistical data; دِراسة إحْصائيّة statistical study/profile
B *n* statistician

the past 4 [أَعَدَّ] to prepare; اسْتَحْضَرَ دَواءً to prepare a medicine

حَضَر *n* الحَضَر civilization; the settled population

حاضِر A *adj* |حُضُور, حُضَّر| present; current; الوَقْت الحاضِر the present (time); حاضِر! at your service!; immediately!

B *n* 1 [شَخْص] |حاضِرونَ| person present; عَدَد الحاضِرينَ the number of those present 2 [الآن] the present (*time*); الماضي والحاضِر والمُسْتَقْبَل the past, present, and future; في الحاضِرِ nowadays, at present, today 3 (Gram) present tense

حَضارة *n* civilization; culture; الحَضارة الغَرْبيّة \ العَرَبيّة Western/Arab civilization; الحَضارات العَريقة ancient civilizations; الحَضارة الإغْريقيّة Greek civilization; الحَضارة البَشَريّة human civilization; تاريخ الحَضارة the history of civilization; cultural history; مَهْد الحَضارة the cradle of civilization

حَضاريّ *adj* cultural; civilized; مُجْتَمَع حَضاريّ a civilized society; تَبادُل حَضاريّ cultural exchange; بِطَريقةٍ \ أُسْلوبٍ حَضاريّ(ة) in a civilized manner

حَضْرة *n* |حَضَرات| 1 [وُجود] presence; في حَضْرةِ المَلِكِ in the king's presence 2 [لَقَب] حَضْرَتُكَ \ حَضْرَتُكُمْ you (*polite form of address*); your excellency; حَضْرة الأُسْتاذِ Professor 3 (Islam) *a collective supererogatory ritual performed by Sufi orders*

حَضَريّ A *adj* urban; sedentary

B *n* urbanite, city dweller

حُضور *n* presence, attendance; participation; حُضور كَبير a large attendance; حُضور البَديهةِ presence of mind; shrewdness, resourcefulness; بِحُضورِ \ في حُضورِ شَخْصٍ in sb's presence; في حُضورٍ عَرَبيٍّ وَدُوَليٍّ كَبيرٍ with a strong Arab and international presence; شَهِدَ الحَفْلُ حُضوراً كَبيراً there were a lot of people at the party; أَعْلَنَ عن حُضورِ شَخْصٍ to announce that sb is coming; الحُضور الحَقيقيّ (Chr) the Real Presence (*the doctrine affirming the actual presence of Jesus Christ in the Eucharist*)

حُضوريّ *adj referring to presence*; حُكْم حُضوريّ a judgement in a defended action; عَلَنيًّا وَنهائيًّا وَحُضوريًّا public, final and in the presence of the accused

حَضيرة *n* |حَضائِرُ| (Mil) squad, section; patrol; *a unit of 6 to 12 persons*

إحْضار *n* bringing

اسْتِحْضار *n* summoning; اسْتِحْضار الأَرْواحِ conjuring of spirits, communing with the dead; جَلْسة اسْتِحْضارِ الأَرْواحِ séance

تَحَضُّر *n* civilization; urbanization

تَحْضير *n* |تَحْضيرات| 1 [إعْداد] preparation; قامَ بالتَحْضيراتِ لِشَيْءٍ to make preparations for sth 2 [تَمْدين] urbanization

تَحْضيريّ *adj* preparatory; preliminary; اجْتِماع تَحْضيريّ preliminary meeting; قِسْم تَحْضيريّ (Mor) ≈ kindergarten

مُتَحَضِّر *adj* civilized; العالَم المُتَحَضِّر the civilized world; بَلَد \ شَخْص مُتَحَضِّر a civilized country/person; غَيْر مُتَحَضِّرٍ uncivilized; backwoods

مُحاضِر A *n* 1 [جامِعة] lecturer (BrE), professor (AmE) 2 (Chr) lector, reader (*sb who reads from the Bible in a church service*)

B *adj* lecturing; speaking; أُسْتاذ مُحاضِر lecturing professor

مُحاضَرة *n* lecture; (university) class; paper; حَضَرَ \ تابَعَ مُحاضَرةً attend a lecture; attend a class; أَلْقى مُحاضَرةً حول \ عن شَيْءٍ to give a lecture about sth; قاعة المُحاضَراتِ lecture hall; سِلْسِلة من المُحاضَراتِ (حول \ عن شَيْءٍ) a series of lectures (on/about sth)

مُحْتَضِر *adj* dying

مَحْضَر *n* 1 [تَقْرير] |مَحاضِرُ| minutes; report; مَحْضَر رَسْميّ official report; كاتِب المَحْضَرِ minutes secretary; حَرَّرَ مَحْضَراً, سَجَّلَ المَحْضَرَ to take/record the minutes (*of a meeting*); حَرَّرَ مَحْضَراً رَسْميًّا to take down sb's details; مُحَرِّر المَحْضَرِ officer taking sb's name 2 [حُضور] presence; في مَحْضَرِ المَلِكةِ in the queen's presence

مُحْضِر *n* (Law) مُحْضِر قانونيّ process server; bailiff

مُحَضَّر *adj* prepared; ready-made

مُسْتَحْضَر *n* |مُسْتَحْضَرات| preparation; lotion; formula, mixture; مُسْتَحْضَرات تَجْميلٍ cosmetics, cosmetic products, make-up; مُسْتَحْضَر صَيْدَلانيّ pharmaceutical preparation; حَضَّرَ مُسْتَحْضَراً (Chem) to make a preparation

حَضْرَمَوْت *n* |dipt f| Hadhramaut (*Yemeni governorate*)

‹ **حَضَّ** *v* |u; حَضّ| to urge, to exhort; to spur on; to incite; حَضَّ شَخْصاً على شَيْءٍ to urge sb to do sth

حَضِيض *n* |أَحِضّة, حُضُض| bottom; low point; وَصَلَ إلى الحَضِيضِ to hit rock bottom; هَوَتْ شَعْبِيَّتُهُ إلى الحَضِيضِ his popularity plummeted

‹ **حَضَنَ** *v* |u; حَضانة, حَضْن| ❶ [الطائِرُ] to sit (on an egg); حَضَنَ بَيْضاً to incubate an egg ❷ [عانَقَ] to embrace, to hug; حَضَنَ شَخْصاً to put one's arms around sb, to embrace sb ❸ [رَبّى] to foster, to bring up, to raise; حَضَنَ يَتِيماً to bring up an orphan

احْتَضَنَ *v* ❶ [عانَقَ] to embrace, to hold in one's arms, to hug; احْتَضَنَ شَخْصاً to embrace sb ❷ [ضَمَّ] to comprise, to contain, to make up; احْتَضَنَ رُبْعَ احْتِياطاتِ النَفْطِ to comprise a quarter of the oil reserves ❸ [رَعى] to foster, to bring up; احْتَضَنَ مُؤْتَمَراً to organize a congress; احْتَضَنَ مَشْروعاً to sponsor a project ❹ [آوى] to accommodate, to lodge

حَضْن *n* embrace, hug

حِضْن *n* |أَحْضان| breast, bosom; arms; embrace; في \ بين أَحْضان الصَحْراءِ in the middle of the desert; أَخَذَت الطِفْلَ في \ بين أَحْضانِها she took the child in her arms, she embraced the child

حاضِن **A** *adj* fostering; أُسْرة حاضِنة foster family **B** *n* ❶ [طَيْر] brood hen ❷ [راحِم] incubator (*for chickens*); hatchery

حاضِنة *n* |حَواضِنُ| ❶ (Med) incubator; ظَلَّ المولودُ أُسْبوعَيْنِ في الحاضِنةِ the baby spent two weeks in an incubator ❷ [شَخْص] child care worker; (baby)sitter ❸ [بَيْض] incubator, brooder; hatchery

حَضانة, حِضانة *n* ❶ [رِعاية الأَطْفالِ] child care; دار الحَضانةِ الأَوَّلِيّةِ day nursery (BrE), day care center (AmE); وَصَّلَ أَطْفالَهُ إلى دارِ الحَضانةِ to take one's children to the day nursery; مَدْرَسة الحَضانةِ kindergarten ❷ [تَرْبِية] (Mor) upbringing; care ❸ (Isl Law) custody (*of a mother after divorce*) ❹ (Med) incubation; فَتْرة الحَضانةِ incubation period

حُضْنة *n* brood

حَضون *adj* broody; دَجاجة حَضونة a broody hen

احْتِضان *n* embrace, hug

مَحْضَن *n* |مَحاضِنُ| incubator, nursery

مَحْضون *n person in custodial care*

‹ **حَطَبَ** *v* |i; حَطْب| to gather wood

احْتَطَبَ *v* to gather wood; to engage in logging

حَطَب *n* |أَحْطاب| firewood, brushwood; حُزْمة حَطَبٍ bundle of firewood; جمع حَطَباً to gather firewood; زادَ النارَ حَطَباً to add fuel/wood to the fire

حاطِب *n* |حُطّاب| woodcutter; lumberjack

حَطّاب *n* |حَطّابة| woodcutter; lumberjack

حِطابة *n* logging

تَحْطيب *n Egyptian martial art involving stick fighting*

‹ **حَطَّ** *v* |u| ❶ [وَضَعَ] |حَطّ| to put, to place; to unload ❷ [جَثَمَ] [الطائِرُ] |حُطوط| to land; حَطَّ على الشاطِئِ to land on the beach; حَطَّت الطائِرةُ the aircraft landed ❸ [أَنْزَلَ] |حَطّ| to reduce; to lower ❹ [من قَدْرِهِ] |حَطّ| عن to reduce; to underrate, to undervalue; حَطَّ من دَرَجةِ شَخْصٍ to reduce sb in rank, to demote

انْحَطَّ *v* ❶ [نَزَلَ] to descend, to go down; to be relegated; انْحَطَّ قَدْرُهُ \ انْحَطَّتْ سُمْعَتُهُ he has lost his reputation ❷ [تَدَهْوَرَ] to get worse, to deteriorate, to degenerate; انْحَطَّ المُسْتَوى standards have fallen, the level has dropped

انْحِطاط *n* decline; decay; deterioration; انْحِطاط الدَوْلةِ العُثْمانيّةِ the decline of the Ottoman state; انْحِطاط اللُغةِ deterioration of the language; انْحِطاط الأَخْلاقِ moral decay; عَصْر الانْحِطاطِ the Period of Decadence (*in Arabic literature*)

مَحَطّ *n* |مَحاطُّ| ❶ point; object; كانَ مَحَطَّ الأَنْظارِ all eyes were on him; كانَ مَحَطَّ الآمالِ (all) hopes were pinned on him; كانَ مَحَطَّ الكَلام people were talking about him ❷ (Mus) fermata, hold

مَحَطّة *n* ❶ [مَوْقِف] station; stop; مَحَطّة قِطارٍ railway (BrE) railroad (AmE) station ❷ [إذاعة] station, channel; مَحَطّة إذاعيّة \ إرْسالٍ تِلِفِزْيونيّة television channel/station; مَحَطّة إذاعيّة broadcasting/transmitting station; مَحَطّة الجَزيرة العَرَبيّة the al-Jazeera TV channel; بَحَثَ عن مَحَطّةٍ (أُخْرى) to search for (another) channel; اسْتَقْبَلَ مَحَطَّةً to get a station (*on television or radio*) **3** [مَصْنَع \ مُؤَسَّسة] plant, station; مَحَطّة تَكْرير refinery; مَحَطّة كَهْرَمائيّة hydro-electric power station; مَحَطّة حَراريّة coal-fired power station; مَحَطّة فَضائيّة space station; مَحَطّة بَنْزين \ وَقود petrol (BrE) gas (AmE) station; مَحَطّة أَرْصادٍ جَوّيّةٍ weather station; مَحَطّة كَهْرَبائيّة power plant; وَقَّفَ مَحَطّةً كَهْرَبائيّةً to shut down a power station; مَحَطّة نَوَوِيّة nuclear power station; فَكَّكَ مَحَطّةً نَوَوِيّةً to dismantle a nuclear power station; تُوَلِّدُ \ تُوَزِّعُ المَحَطّةُ الكَهْرَباءَ the station generates/supplies electricity

مُنْحَطّ *adj* low, base, mean; decadent; مُنْحَطّ التَّفْكير low-minded

حَطَمَ *v* |i; حَطْم| to break

حَطَّمَ *v* to break, to smash, to wreck, to demolish, to destroy; حَطَّمَ نافِذةً to smash a window; حَطَّمَ جِداراً to tear down a wall; حَطَّمَ العَدوَّ to destroy the enemy; حَطَّمَ رَقْماً قِياسيًّا to break a record; حَطَّمَ آمالَ شَخْصٍ to dash sb's hopes; حَطَّمَ القُيودَ to break one's chains; حَطَّمَ مُسْتَقْبَلَهُ to destroy one's future

تَحَطَّمَ *v* **1** [تَكَسَّرَ] to crash; to be broken; تَحَطَّمَت الطّائِرةُ في حادِثٍ the aircraft crashed; تَحَطَّمَتْ حَياتُها her life is in pieces **2** (Comput) to crash; تَحَطَّمَ المُتَصَفِّحُ the browser crashed

حُطام *n* rubble; debris; wreckage; حُطام طائِرةٍ the wreckage of a plane; أَخْرَجَ \ حَرَّرَ ناجينَ من الحُطامِ to free survivors from the wreckage; حُطام الدُّنْيا worldly goods, vanities; حُطام سَفينةٍ shipwreck, wreck

تَحَطُّم *n* destruction, devastation; (حادِث) تَحَطُّم طائِرةٍ plane crash; تَحَطُّم سَفينةٍ shipwreck, wreck

تَحْطيم *n* breaking; demolition; destruction; سَفينة تَحْطيمِ الجَليدِ icebreaker (*a ship designed for breaking through ice*); مُحاولة تَحْطيمِ الرَّقْمِ القِياسيِّ attempt to break a record; تَحْطيم الأَيْقوناتِ (Relig) iconoclasm

مُحَطَّم *adj* broken; demolished, crushed; سَقَطَ مُحَطَّماً it fell to pieces

حَظَرَ *v* |u; حَظْر| **1** [حَبَسَ الماشِيةَ في حَظيرةٍ] to stable, to house; to fence in **2** [مَنَعَ] to forbid, to prohibit, to ban; حَظَرَ شَيْئاً على شَخْصٍ to forbid sb sth; حَظَرَت السُّلْطاتُ الحِزْبَ the party was banned by the authorities

حَظْر *n* embargo, boycott; prohibition, ban; restriction; حَظْر الكَلامِ ban on public speaking; حَظْر التَجَوُّلِ curfew; حَظْر جَوّيّ air embargo; حَظْر تِجاريّ على بِلادٍ a trade embargo on a country; فَرَضَ حَظْراً تِجاريًّا to impose a trade embargo; إلْغاء حَظْرٍ the embargo was lifted; رُفِعَ الحَظْرُ التِجاريُّ the raising/lifting of an embargo; حَظْر تَوْزيعِ الأَسْلِحةِ ban on the supply of arms; حَظْر التَجارِبِ النَوَوِيّةِ a nuclear test ban; حَظْر انْتِشارِ الأَسْلِحةِ النَوَوِيّة ,حَظْر الانْتِشارِ النَوَويِّ nuclear non-proliferation; الحَظْر على المَشْروباتِ الكُحوليّةِ prohibition of the sale of alcohol; انْتَهَكَ حَظْراً to violate an embargo

حِظار *n* fence; screen; guard rail

حَظيرة *n* |حَظائِرُ| **1** [بِناية] pen, corral; stable; barn; حَظيرة الغَنَمِ sheep fold/pen; حَظيرة الطائِراتِ hangar **2** (Islam) حَظيرة الإِسْلامِ the Realm of Islam

مَحْظور **A** *adj* forbidden; illegal, outlawed; banned; تِجارة مَحْظورة illegal trade; جَماعة مَحْظورة a banned group; مَوْقِع مَحْظور a blocked website

B *n* |مَحْظورات| forbidden things; contraband; الضَروراتُ تُبيحُ المَحْظوراتِ necessity knows no law

حَظَّ *v* |a; حَظّ| to be lucky/fortunate

حَظّ *n* |حُظوظ| **1** [بَخْت] luck, fortune; fate, destiny; حَظّ عاثِر \ سَيِّئ bad luck; لُعْبة حَظٍّ game of chance; دولاب الحَظِّ the wheel of fortune; ضَرْبة حَظٍّ a stroke of luck; (شَخْص) مَنْكود الحَظِّ an unlucky person; لِحُسْنِ الحَظِّ luckily, fortunately; لِحُسْنِ حَظِّهِ أنّ he was lucky enough to; يا لَحُسْنِ حَظِّكَ you are so lucky!; lucky you!; سوء الحَظِّ misfortune; لِسوءِ حَظِّهِ أنّ … unfortunately for him …; حَظًّا سَعيداً! good luck!; تَمَنّى لِشَخْصٍ حَظًّا سَعيداً to wish sb luck; جالِب للحَظِّ mascot; جَرَّبَ حَظَّهُ to try one's luck; to take a chance; حالَفَهُ \ أَسْعَفَهُ الحَظُّ luck was on his side, fate was kind to him; واتاني الحَظُّ I was lucky **2** [حِصّة] share, part, portion; نالَ حَظَّهُ من الدِراسةِ he has done his share of studying; لا حَظَّ لَهُ من العِلْمِ his knowledge is not great

حَفْرِيّ *adj* fossil; fossilized; وَقود حَفْرِيّ fossil fuels; أَعْمال حَفْرِيّة excavation

حَفْرِيّة *n* حَفْرِيّات excavation; عِلْم الحَفْرِيّاتِ palaeontology

حَفير *n* |أَحْفار| grave; مَن حَفَرَ حَفيراً لأَخيهِ كانَ حَتْفُهُ فيهِ ≈ what goes around, comes around

حَفيرة *n* |حَفائِرُ| excavation

أُحْفورة *n* |أَحافيرُ| fossil; عِلْم الأَحافير palaeontology; عالِم الأَحافير palaeontologist

أُحْفوريّ *adj* fossil (*before n*); وَقود أُحْفوريّ fossil fuel

مِحْفَر *n* |مَحافِرُ| digger, excavator; spade; drill

‹ **حَفْر الباطِنِ** *n* |f| Hafr al-Batin (*city in Saudi Arabia*)

‹ **حَفَزَ** *v* |i; حَفْز| to spur; to stimulate, to catalyze; to encourage; حَفَزَ شَخْصاً على \ إلى شَيْءٍ to encourage sb to do sth; حَفَزَ تَطَوُّراً \ عَمَلِيّةً to stimulate a development/process

حَفَّزَ *v* to stimulate; to motivate

تَحَفَّزَ *v* to prepare/ready oneself; تَحَفَّزَ لِشَيْءٍ to prepare oneself for sth/to do sth

احْتَفَزَ *v* to be ready, to be about to

حَفْز *n* stimulation; motivation

حافِز *n* |حَوافِزُ| stimulus, incentive, impulse, motive; حافِز ل \ إلى \ على شَيْءٍ a stimulus to sth; حافِز مادّيّ \ ماليّ a financial motive, material incentive; حَوافِز بَصَرِيّة visual stimuli

حَفّاز *n* **1** (Chem) catalyst, accelerant; عامِل حَفّاز catalyst **2** (Mech) سَيّارة مُزَوَّدة بِحَفّازٍ a car equipped with a catalytic converter

تَحْفيز *n* stimulus

تَحْفيزيّ *adj* motivational, stimulating, incentive (*before n*); إِجْراء تَحْفيزيّ motivational measure

مُتَحَفِّز *adj* ready, prepared; alert

مُحَفِّز **A** *adj* stimulating
B *n* stimulant

‹ **حَفْش** *n* (Zool) sturgeon (*Acipenser sturio*)

‹ **حَفَّضَ** *v* to put a nappy (BrE) diaper (AmE) on

مَحْظوظ **A** *adj* lucky, fortunate; شَخْص مَحْظوظ lucky person; إِنَّهُ مَحْظوظٌ he is lucky; غَيْر مَحْظوظٍ unfortunate, unlucky
B *n* lucky one

‹ **حَظِيَ** *v* |a; حُظْوة| to get, to obtain; to receive; حَظِيَ ب (رُؤْيةِ شَخْصٍ) to be so lucky to (see sb); حَظِيَ بِتَأْييدٍ \ تَقْديرٍ \ مُوافَقةٍ \ اهْتِمامٍ to gain support/esteem/approval/interest; حَظِيَ بِتَأْييدِ الشَّعْبِ to enjoy/have the people's support; حَظِيَ بِتَعْديلاتٍ to have adjustments made; حَظِيَ بالتَّرْحيبِ to be welcomed; حَظِيَ بِرِعايةِ شَخْصٍ to be sponsored by sb

أَحْظى *v* to privilege, to favour

حُظْوة, **حِظْوة** *n* |حُظًا| favour, grace; privilege; نالَ حُظْوةً عند شَخْصٍ to come into favour with sb; كانَ ذا حُظْوةٍ عند شَخْصٍ to be in sb's good graces; فَقَدَ الحُظْوةَ to go/fall out of favour; to fall into disgrace

حَظِيّة *n* |حَظايا| mistress, kept woman; concubine; favourite

مَحْظِيّة *n* mistress, kept woman; concubine; favourite

‹ **حَفْحَفة** *n* rustling

‹ **حَفيد** *n* |حَفَدة, أَحْفاد| **1** [اِبْن اِبْنِهِ \ بِنْتِهِ] grandchild, grandson; اِبْن الحَفيدِ great-grandchild **2** [خَلَف] descendant

‹ **حَفَرَ** *v* |i; حَفْر| **1** [أَحْدَثَ حُفْرةً] to dig; to excavate; to drill, to bore; حَفَرَ نَفَقاً to bore a tunnel; حَفَرَ قَناةً to dig a canal; حَفَرَ بِئْراً to dig a well **2** [نَحَتَ] to engrave; to etch; to gouge; to scratch; حَفَرَ الخَشَبَ to carve/work wood, to whittle

حَفْر *n* **1** [نَقْر] digging; drilling **2** [نَحْت] inscription; engraving **3** [آثار] excavation

حافِر *n* |حَوافِرُ| hoof

حَفّار *n* **1** [نَقّار] |حَفّارات| drilling rig, derrick; excavator, digger, backhoe **2** [نَقّاش] |حَفّارات| engraver **3** [القُبور] |حَفّارونَ| digger; حَفّار قُبور gravedigger

حَفّارة *n* **1** [نَقّار] digger, excavator, backhoe **2** (Mech) drill; حَفّارة طَبيبِ الأَسْنانِ the dentist's drill

حُفْرة *n* |حُفَر| hole; pit; crater; حُفْرة عَميقة a deep hole; سَدَّ حُفْرةً to fill/stop a hole; حَفَرَ حُفْرةً to dig a hole/pit; مَنْ حَفَرَ حُفْرةً لِأَخيهِ وَقَعَ فيها ≈ what goes around comes around; أَحْدَثَ حُفْرةً to make a hole

حِفاض ,حِفاضة *n* |حِفاضات| see حِفاظة

حَفِظَ *v* |a; حِفْظ| ◀1▶ [حافَظَ] to keep, to maintain; to save; حَفِظَ السَلامَ to keep the peace; حَفِظَ الأَمْنَ to maintain security; حَفِظَ لِسانَهُ to keep quiet; حَفِظَ سِرًّا to keep a secret ◀2▶ [ذَكَرَ] to remember; to memorize; حَفِظَ اسْماً to remember a name; حَفِظَ القُرْآنَ to memorize the Koran; حَفِظَ شَيْئاً عن ظَهْرِ قَلْبٍ \ غَيْبٍ to learn sth by heart ◀3▶ [وَقى] to preserve, to guard, to protect, to shield; حَفِظَ شَخْصاً من الشَرِّ to preserve sb from evil; حَفِظَكَ اللهُ may God protect you; اللّهُمَّ احْفَظْني! God forbid! ◀4▶ (Comput) to save; حَفِظَ مِلَفًّا (بِاسْمِ \ كَ ...) to save a file (as ...); حَفِظَ التَغَيُّراتِ to save changes ◀5▶ [الْتَزَمَ] to keep; حَفِظَ كَلِمَتَهُ to keep one's word ◀6▶ [مَأْكولاتٍ] to preserve; to tin (BrE), to can (AmE)

حَفَّظَ *v* حَفَّظَ شَخْصاً شَيْئاً to make sb memorize sth; to drill sb in sth

حافَظَ *v* ◀1▶ [وَقى] |على| to maintain, to keep up; to preserve; حافَظَ على النَوْعِ to preserve the species ◀2▶ [الْتَزَمَ] |على| to maintain; to keep; حافَظَ على سُرْعَتِهِ to maintain one's speed ◀3▶ [صانَ] |على| to maintain; حافَظَ على صَداقةٍ to maintain a friendship; حافَظَ على صِحَّتِهِ to watch one's health; حافَظَ على الحَديقةِ to take care of the garden; حافَظَ على النُظُمِ \ التَقاليدِ to preserve order/traditions; تُحافِظُ الشُرْطةُ على الأَمْنِ العامِّ the police maintain order

أَحْفَظَ *v* to make memorize

تَحَفَّظَ *v* ◀1▶ [صانَ] |على| to maintain, to keep; تَحَفَّظَ على شَيْءٍ to maintain sth, to stick to sth ◀2▶ [احْتَرَزَ] |عن| to be reserved (in), to exercise restraint (in); to be careful (of); تَحَفَّظَ عن شَيْءٍ to have reservations about sth; to distance oneself from sth

احْتَفَظَ *v* |بِ| to keep, to preserve; to maintain, to uphold; احْتَفَظَ بِقيمَتِهِ to keep its value; احْتَفَظ بِشَيْءٍ لِنَفْسِهِ to keep sth for oneself; احْتَفَظ بِطَعام في الثَلاّجةِ to store food in the refrigerator; احْتَفَظَ لِنَفْسِهِ بِحَقٍّ to reserve a right; احْتَفَظَ بِهُدوئِهِ to keep one's composure

حِفْظ *n* preservation, maintenance, conservation; custody; حِفْظ الذاتِ self-preservation; حِفْظ المَفْقوداتِ lost and found; مع حِفْظِ كافّةِ الحُقوقِ all rights reserved

حافِظ *n* |حَفَظة ,حُفّاظ| ◀1▶ [مَنْ يَحْفَظُ] keeper ◀2▶ (Islam) *sb who has memorized the Koran*

حافِظة *n* |حَوافِظُ| case; حافِظة (نُقودٍ) wallet

حِفاظ *n* |حِفاظات| ◀1▶ [حِفْظ \ حِماية] preservation, maintenance, conservation; الحِفاظ على الآثارِ التاريخيّةِ the conservation of antiquities; الحِفاظ على شَيْءٍ the preservation of sth; الحِفاظ على الطَبيعةِ nature conservation ◀2▶ [لِلمَوْلودِ] see حِفاظة

حِفاض ,حِفاضة ,حِفاظ ,حِفاظة *n* nappy (BrE), diaper (AmE); حِفاظةٌ قُطْنيّة a cotton nappy; غَيَّرَ حِفاظةً to change a nappy

حَفيظ *n* |حُفَظاءُ| ◀1▶ [حارِس] keeper, preserver ◀2▶ (Islam) الحَفيظ the Preserver (*one of the names of God*); يا حَفيظُ Lord save us!

حَفيظة *n* |حَفائِظُ| grudge; resentment; rancor; أَثارَ حَفيظةً to cause resentment

احْتِفاظ *n* preserving, maintaining; مع احْتِفاظِهِ بالجِنْسيّةِ المَغْرِبيّةِ while keeping Moroccan nationality

تَحَفُّظ *n* |تَحَفُّظات| reserve, restraint, reservation; conservatism; objection; شَيْء من التَحَفُّظِ a bit of reserve; مع التَحَفُّظِ with reservation, reservedly; بِلا تَحَفُّظٍ without reservation, unreservedly; قَبِلَ شَيْئاً بِدونِ أَيّ تَحَفُّظٍ to accept sth without reservation; أَبْدى تَحَفُّظاً to exercise restraint

تَحَفُّظيّ *adj* precautionary; اعْتِقال تَحَفُّظيّ custody; إجْراءات تَحَفُّظيّة precautionary measures

تَحْفيظ *n* memorization; inculcation; (Mil) drill

مُتَحَفِّظ *adj* restrained, reserved, reticent; distant; رَدّ فِعْلٍ مُتَحَفِّظ a restrained reaction; غَيْر مُتَحَفِّظٍ indiscrete

مُحافِظ ◼A▶ *adj* conservative ◼B▶ *n* ◀1▶ (Admin) governor/governorate (*before n*) ◀2▶ (Pol) conservative; سِياسة مُحافِظة conservative politics; حِزْب مُحافِظ a conservative party; حِزْبُ المُحافِظينَ the Conservative Party; مُحافِظ جَديد neoconservative ◀3▶ [في مَتْحَفٍ] curator ◀4▶ [حارِس] keeper; guardian

مُحافَظة *n* ◀1▶ [حِفْظ] preservation, maintenance, conservation; المُحافَظة على ... ; مُحافَظةً على ... (in order) to preserve ...;

الطَبيعةِ nature conservation; المُحافَظة على النِظامِ والأَمْنِ العامِّ maintaining public order ② [مُقاوَمة التَجْديدِ] conservatism ③ (Admin) (metropolitan) province, governorate ④ [مَنْصِب] governorship

مَحْفَظة, **مِحْفَظة** *n* |مَحْفَظات, مَحافِظُ| ① [للنُقودِ] wallet; مَحْفَظة أَوْراقٍ file, portfolio; مَحْفَظة (نُقودٍ) wallet ② [حَقيبة] school bag ③ (Med) capsule

مَحْفوظ *adj* preserved, kept, reserved; جَميعُ الحُقوقِ مَحْفوظةٌ all rights reserved; أَطْعِمة مَحْفوظة preserved food; tinned food; مَحْفوظ في الذاكِرةِ committed to memory

مَحْفوظات *n pl* ① [وَثائِق] archives; أَمين المَحْفوظاتِ archivist; دار المَحْفوظاتِ المِصْرِيّة the National Archives of Egypt ② [مَأْكولات] canned food

حَفَّ *v* |i; حَفيف| ① [صَوْت] to rustle; to swish ② [أَحاطَ |ب|] to surround, to enclose; حَفَّ شَيْئاً \ بِشَيْءٍ \ حول شَيْءٍ to surround sth ③ [قَشَرَ] to scrape, to make smooth; to shave; حَفَّ الساقَيْنِ \ الوَجْهَ to remove the hair off one's legs/face

حافّ *adj* خُبْز حافّ dry bread

حافّة *n* edge, side, margin, border; bank, shore; حافّة الطَريقِ shoulder, verge; حافّة النَهْرِ riverbank; حافّة النافِذةِ windowsill; حافّة القَطْعِ cutting edge (*of a blade*); عند حافّةِ الماءِ (down) by the water; كانَ على حافّةِ القَبْرِ to stand with one foot in the grave; وَقَفَ على حافّةِ الهاوِيةِ to be/stand on the brink; جَلَسَ على حافّةِ السَريرِ to sit on the side of the bed; على حافّةِ الأَرْضِ on the edge of the world; على حافّةِ الانْهِيارِ on the verge of breakdown

حَفّاف *n* (Anat) velum; soft palate

حَفيف *n* rustling, rustle; whishing; حَفيف أَوْراقِ الأَشْجارِ the rustling of leaves; حَفيف الريحِ بين الأَشْجارِ the rustling of the wind in the trees

مِحَفّة *n* |مِحَفّات, مَحافُّ| ① [للجَرْحى] stretcher ② [للمَرْأَةِ] sedan chair; litter, palanquin

مَحْفوف *adj* surrounded; مَحْفوف بالأَخْطارِ surrounded by danger; fraught with danger

حَفَلَ *v* |i; حَفْل| ① [اجْتَمَعَ] to gather, to assemble ② [امْتَلأَ] to swarm, to crowd; حَفَلَ بِشَيْءٍ to teem with sth; to be replete/abundant with sth ③ [اهْتَمَّ |ب|] to pay attention (to)

احْتَفَلَ *v* ① [بِعيدٍ] to celebrate; to party; نَحْتَفِلُ اليَوْمَ بِعيدِ ميلادِهِ today we are celebrating his birthday; احْتَفَلَ بِعيدِ زَواجِهِ to celebrate one's wedding; احْتَفَلَ بالقُدّاسِ to celebrate Mass, to sing the Mass ② [اهْتَمَّ |ب|] to pay attention (to)

حَفْل *n* celebration, party; gathering; ceremony; حَفْل موسيقيّ concert, recital; حَفْل رِياضيّ sports event; حَفْل وَداعٍ farewell party; حَفْل نِهائيّ \ خِتاميّ closing ceremony; حَفْل اسْتِقْبالٍ رَسْميّ official/formal reception; حَفْل على شَرَفِ المَلِكةِ a gala in honour of the queen; حَفْل افْتِتاحِ المُؤْتَمَرِ the opening ceremony of the congress; أَقامَ حَفْلاً to throw a party

حافِل *adj* |حَوافِلُ, حُفَّل| |ب| full, replete, packed; بَرْنامَج حافِل a full programme; قاعة حافِلة (بالناسِ) a packed hall; يَوْم حافِل بالأَحْداثِ a day filled with events; تاريخ حافِل بالأَحْداثِ a rich history

حافِلة *n* |حافِلات, حَوافِلُ| bus; coach; حافِلة كَهْرَبائيّة trolley bus; سائِق \ مَوْقِف حافِلةٍ bus driver/stop; حافِلة رَقْم ٤٥ bus 45; رِحْلة بالحافِلةِ bus journey/trip; اسْتَقَلَّ \ رَكِبَ الحافِلةَ to take the bus; ذَهَبَ بالحافِلةِ to go by bus; فاتَتْهُ الحافِلةُ he missed the bus

حَفْلة *n* |حَفَلات| party; celebration; gathering; حَفْلة كَبيرة \ رائِعة a big/terrific party; حَفْلة خَيْرِيّة benefit/charity concert; حَفْلة تَنَكُّرِيّة a masked ball, masquerade ball; حَفْلة موسيقيّة concert, performance; recital; حَفْلة راقِصة ball; dance (party); حَفْلة غِنائيّة لِفَيْروز a performance by Fairuz; قَدَّمَ حَفْلةً to give a performance; حَفْلة زَواجٍ wedding party; حَفْلة تَأْبينٍ memorial service; حَفْلة اسْتِقْبالٍ reception; حَفْلة على شَرَفِ العَروسَيْنِ \ الزَوْجَيْنِ a party in honour of the bridal couple; في حَفْلةٍ at a party; أَحْيا \ أَقامَ حَفْلةً to give/throw a party

احْتِفال *n* |احْتِفالات| party; celebration; ceremony; feast, festival; احْتِفال سَنَويّ an annual feast; احْتِفال شَعْبيّ a popular festival; احْتِفال عارِم \ بَسيط a big/small celebration; قاعة الاحْتِفالاتِ reception room; ballroom; مَلابِس الاحْتِفالِ party clothes; full dress, evening dress;

احْتِفال بيوبيلٍ \ بِعيدٍ \ بِعيد ميلادٍ the celebration of a jubilee/feast/an anniversary; احْتِفالات بِمُناسَبةِ شَيْءٍ festivities marking the occasion of sth

احْتِفاليّ *adj* festive; حَدَث احْتِفاليّ a festive occasion; يَوْم احْتِفاليّ feast day

مُحْتَفِل **A** *adj* celebrating
B *n* **1** [مَنْ يَحْتَفِلُ] partygoer, reveler (*one who is celebrating*)
2 [قائِد الاحْتِفالِ] celebrant; officiant

مَحْفِل *n* |مَحافِل| council; gathering, meeting; المَحْفِل الاقْتِصاديّ the economic forum; مَحافِل سِياسيّة political circles; مَحْفِل ماسونيّ freemasons' lodge

‹ **حَفَنَ** *v* |u; حَفْن| to scoop up with one's hands

حَفْنة *n* |حَفَنات| handful; حَفْنة من التُرابِ a handful of dust; حَفْنة من المُشاغِبينَ a bunch of troublemakers

‹ **حَفا** *v* |u; حَفْوة| حَفا شَخْصًا \ بِشَخْصٍ to receive sb hospitably

حَفِيَ *v* |a| **1** [مَشى حافِياً] |حَفاء| to walk barefoot; to be discalced, to have bare feet **2** [رَحَّبَ] |حَفاوة; ب| to welcome; to receive

احْتَفى *v* |ب| to celebrate; احْتَفى بِعيدٍ to celebrate a feast; احْتَفى بِشَخْصٍ to fete sb

حافٍ *adj* |حُفاة| barefoot; حافي القَدَمَيْنِ barefoot; مَشى حافِياً \ حافِيَ القَدَمَيْنِ to walk/go barefoot

حَفاوة *n* welcome; بِحَفاوةٍ hospitably; اسْتَقْبَلَ شَخْصاً بِحَفاوةٍ to give sb a warm welcome

احْتِفاء *n* **1** [تَرْحيب] welcoming **2** [احْتِفال] celebration **3** [حَفاء] walking barefoot

احْتِفائيّ *adj* festive

‹ **حَقَبَ** *v* |u; حَقْب| to carry

حُقُب *n* |أَحْقاب, حِقاب| era, period; age

حِقْبة *n* |حِقَب| period, era, age; حِقْبة جَديدة a new age; الحِقْبة الاسْتِعْمارِيّة the colonial period; حِقْبة التِسْعيناتِ \ التِسْعينيّاتِ the nineties; حِقْبة من الزَمَنِ a portion of history; في تِلْكَ الحِقْبةِ من الزَمَنِ at that time; in those days

حَقيبة *n* |حَقائِبُ| **1** [شَنْطة] suitcase; bag; briefcase; حَقيبة يَدَويّة \ يَدٍ handbag; satchel; حَقيبة مَدْرَسيّة school bag; حَقيبة الظَهْرِ rucksack, backpack, knapsack; حَمَلَ حَقيبةً to carry a case/bag; وَضَعَ شَيْئاً في حَقيبةٍ to put sth into a case; حَزَمَ \ شَدَّ حَقائِبَهُ to pack one's bags **2** (Pol) portfolio, position; حَقيبة وِزارِيّة ministerial/cabinet portfolio; عَهِدَ بِحَقيبةِ الخارِجيّةِ to appoint as foreign minister; تَوْزيع الحَقائِبِ الوِزارِيّةِ allocation of ministerial portfolios, allocating cabinet seats; تَوَلّى حَقيبةَ المالِيّةِ to take on the finance portfolio

‹ **حَقَدَ, حَقِدَ** *v* |a-i; حِقْد, حَقْد| حَقَدَ على شَخْصٍ to hate sb; to have a grudge against sb; to feel malice toward sb

أَحْقَدَ *v* to embitter, to incite to hatred/resentment; أَحْقَدَ شَخْصًا على صَديقِهِ to incite sb to hate his friend

حِقْد *n* |أَحْقاد, حُقود| resentment, grudge, malice; hatred; جَريمة حِقْدٍ hate crime; أَضْمَرَ \ كَنَّ الحِقْدَ لِشَخْصٍ to have a grudge against sb; زَرَعَ الحِقْدَ في الناسِ to spread hatred among the people

حاقِد *adj* |حَقَدة| full of hatred, hateful; malevolent

حَقود *adj* |حُقُد| resentful, spiteful, rancorous; venomous; لم يَكُنْ حَقوداً to bear no ill will

‹ **حَقَرَ** *v* |i; حَقْر| to despise, to scorn, to regard with contempt; to loathe

حَقُرَ *v* |u; حَقارة| to be despicable; to be despised

حَقَّرَ *v* **1** [اسْتَهانَ] |من| to despise; حَقَّرَ من شَيْءٍ to despise sth **2** [أَذَلَّ] to humble sb; to humiliate sb

احْتَقَرَ *v* to despise, to scorn, to look down on; احْتَقَرَ شَخْصاً to despise sb; احْتَقَرَ شَخْصاً \ شَيْئاً to despise sb/sth; to look down on sb/sth

اسْتَحْقَرَ *v* to despise, to scorn, to look down on

حَقارة *n* **1** [تَفاهة] insignificance; worthlessness **2** [دَناءة] meanness, abjectness; contemptibility

حَقير *adj* |حُقَراءُ| **1** [ذَليل] poor, miserable, wretched; كوخ حَقير a poor little hut; مَسْكَن حَقير a miserable house **2** [دَنيء] low, base, despicable; حيلة حَقيرة a mean trick; شَخْص حَقير a vile/despicable person

احْتِقار *n* contempt, disdain, scorn; نَظْرة احْتِقارٍ a disdainful look; احْتِقاراً ل in contempt of; (عامَلَ) بِاحْتِقارٍ (to treat) with contempt

احْتِقاريّ *adj* disdainful, belittling; مُلاحَظة \ مَوْقِف احْتِقاريّ(ة) a disdainful remark/attitude

تَحْقير *n* contempt, disdain

تَحْقيريّ *adj* pejorative

مُحْتَقِر *adj* disdainful, contemptuous, condescending; hateful

حِقْف *n* sand dune; سورة الأَحْقاف Winding Sand Tracts (*Sura 46*)

حَقَّ *v* |i-u; حَقّ| **1** [صَدَقَ] to be true; to be correct; to be right **2** [جازَ |لِ|] to be allowed; حَقَّ لَهُ to have the right, to be entitled; حَقَّ لَهُ أَنْ ... he had the right to ...; يَحِقُّ للمَظْلوم أَنْ يُجاهِدَ في وَجْهِ الظُّلْمِ he who is wronged has the right to fight the wrong

حَقَّقَ *v* **1** [نَفَّذَ] to make come true, to carry out; to realize; to achieve, to accomplish; حَقَّقَ خِطَّةً to carry out a plan, to put a plan into effect; حَقَّقَ رَغْبَةً to fulfil a wish; حَقَّقَ هَدَفَهُ to achieve one's goal; حَقَّقَ تَقَدُّماً to make progress; حَقَّقَ نَصْراً to be victorious **2** [بَحَثَ] to investigate, to make an inquiry; حَقَّقَ في عَمَلِيَّة قَتْل to make an inquiry into a murder **3** [أَثْبَتَ] to verify; to prove to be true **4** [راجَعَ] to review, to edit; حَقَّقَ نُسْخَةً to edit a manuscript **5** [أَكَّدَ] to confirm; to assert **6** [أَثْبَتَ الهُوِيَّةَ] to identify

أَحَقَّ *v* to tell the truth; to be right

تَحَقَّقَ *v* **1** [حَدَثَ] to be realized, to be effected, to become a fact, to be fulfilled; to prove to be true, to come true; تَحَقَّقَ الحُلْمُ the dream came true **2** [تَيَقَّنَ |مِن|] to verify, to check, to make sure; تَحَقَّقَ من شَيْءٍ to check sth; تَحَقَّقَ من المُعْطَياتِ to verify data; تَحَقَّقَ من المَعْلوماتِ to verify information; تَحَقَّقَ من صِحَّة شَيْءٍ to make sure that sth is true

اِسْتَحَقَّ *v* **1** [كانَ جَديراً بِ] to deserve; to be entitled to; اِسْتَحَقَّ شَيْئاً to be entitled to sth; اِسْتَحَقَّ التَّقْديرَ \ الثناءَ \ عُقوبةً to deserve appreciation/praise/punishment; اِسْتَحَقَّ التَعَبَ to be worth the trouble; هذا ما يَسْتَحِقُّهُ it serves him right; إِنَّهُ لا يَسْتَحِقُّ ذلك he/it is not worth it; تَسْتَحِقُّ ذلك you deserve it, that's what you get! **2** [دَيْن] to be due; يَسْتَحِقُّ الدَّيْنُ the debt becomes payable

حاقّة *n* realization; الحاقّة (Islam) *the day on which the Last Judgement takes place*; سورة الحاقّة The Inevitable (*Sura 69*)

حَقّ *n* **1** [حُقوق| ذِمام] right, claim; حَقّ أَساسيّ basic right; حَقّ دُسْتوريّ basic law; حُقوق شَرْعيّة \ مَدَنيّة legitimate/civil rights; حُقوق الإِنْسانِ human rights; الإِعْلان العالَميّ لِحُقوقِ الإِنْسانِ the Universal Declaration of Human Rights; حُقوق المَرْأة women's rights; حَقّ الانْتِخابِ للنِساءِ women's right to vote; حُقوق المُؤَلِّفِ royalties; حُقوق التَّأْليفِ والطَّبْعِ والنَشْرِ copyright; جَميعُ الحُقوق مَحْفوظةٌ all rights reserved; عِلْم الحُقوقِ jurisprudence, (the study of) law; كُلِّيّة الحُقوقِ Faculty of Law (BrE), Law School (AmE); بِحَقٍّ rightly, justly; بِدونِ \ بِغَيْرِ حَقٍّ wrongfully; بِلا حُقوقٍ without rights; بِغَيْرِ وَجْهِ حَقٍّ wrongful, wrongfully; كانَ لَهُ حَقٌّ في شَيْءٍ to have the right to sth; دافَعَ عن حَقِّهِ to defend one's right; طالَبَ بِحَقِّهِ to claim one's rights; قَصَّرَ في حَقِّ شَخْصٍ to wrong sb; إِنَّهُ من حَقِّهِ it's his right; أَخَذَ حَقَّهُ بِيَدِهِ to take justice into one's own hands; المُساواة في الحُقوقِ equal rights; صِراع بين الحَقِّ والباطِلِ a struggle between good and evil; اِرْتَكَبَ جَرائِمَ بِحَقِّ شَعْبِهِ to commit crimes against one's people; سَيَتَغَلَّبُ الحَقُّ على الباطِلِ right will prevail; والحَقُّ يُقالُ in (all) fairness; لَيْسَ لَكَ هذا الحَقُّ you don't have the right to it **2** [صَواب] truth; rightness; حَقًّا really, truly, genuinely; indeed; الحَقُّ مَعَكَ you are right; كانَ على حَقٍّ to be right; كانَ الحَقُّ مَعَهُ he had right on his side; والحَقُّ أَنَّ ... it is true that ..., as a matter of fact ...; قالَ قَوْلَ الحَقِّ to tell the truth; عَلِمَ حَقَّ العِلْمِ to know perfectly well; فَهِمَ حَقَّ الفَهْمِ to understand perfectly; إِنَّهُ حَقًّا جَذّابٌ he is very attractive; هذا صَحيحٌ بِحَقٍّ it really is true; ما تَقولُهُ حَقٌّ what you say is true; الحَقّ يُقالُ the truth is spoken/said **3** (Islam) الحَقّ the Truth (*one of the names of God*)

حُقّة *n* |حُقَق، حِقاق، أَحْقاق| small pot, small box

حُقوقيّ **A** *adj* legal; juridical; تَأْييد حُقوقيّ legal support **B** *n* jurist

حُقّيّ *adj* bowl-shaped; مَفْصِل كُرَويّ حُقّيّ ball-and-socket joint

حَقيق *adj* |أَحِقّاءُ| |بِ| worthy; بِحَقٍّ وَحَقيقٍ rightly

هَدَفٍ the realization of a plan/goal; **تَحْقيق الذاتِ** self-realization; self-actualization; **قابِل للتَحْقيقِ** realistic; **يُمْكِنُ تَحْقيقُهُ** attainable; **صَعْب التَحْقيقِ** hard to attain; **هذا الهَدَفُ يَصْعُبُ تَحْقيقُهُ** that goal is hard to attain; **تَحْقيق اقْتِراحٍ \ مُقْتَرَحٍ** the implementation of a proposal; **قابِليّة التَحْقيقِ** feasibility ② [بَحْث] |**تَحْقيقات**| investigation, inquiry; **تَقْرير \ مَحْضَر التَحْقيقِ** inquiry report; **أَجْرى تَحْقيقاً** to make an inquiry, to conduct an investigation ③ (Law) |**تَحْقيقات**| interrogation, questioning; investigation, inquiry; **تَحْقيق إعْداديّ** preliminary investigation; **تَحْقيق ابْتِدائيّ** hearing, inquest; **لَجْنة تَحْقيقٍ** committee/board of inquiry; **قاضي التَحْقيقِ** examining judge/magistrate; **مَوْقوف على ذِمّةِ التَحْقيقِ** kept in preventive detention; taken into custody

تَحْقيقيّ *adj* investigative; **لَجْنة \ هَيْئة تَحْقيقيّة** an investigative committee/body

مُتَحَقِّق *adj* certain, sure, convinced

مُحِقّ *adj* legitimate, valid, justified; **هو مُحِقٌّ في حِذْرِهِ** he is right to be careful

مُحَقَّق *adj* ① [مُؤَكَّد] sure; **من المُحَقَّقِ أنّ ...** it is a fact that ..., it is sure that ... ② [مُنْجَز] realized; carried out; **رِبْح غَيْر مُحَقَّقٍ** unrealized gain/profit; **غَيْر مُحَقَّقٍ** unfulfilled

مُحَقِّق *n* ① [باحِث] inspector; detective; investigator; **مُحَقِّق صُحُفيّ** investigative reporter; **مُحَقِّق خاصّ \ سِرّيّ** private investigator ② (P&P) publisher of a text edition

مُسْتَحَقّ **A** *adj* payable, due; entitlement; **دُيون مُسْتَحَقّة لَهُ** debts owed to him

B *n* **مُسْتَحَقّ غَيْر مَدْفوعٍ** an outstanding bill; **سَدَّ مُسْتَحَقّاتٍ** to settle due payments

مُسْتَحِقّ **A** *adj* deserving, entitled; **مُسْتَحِقّ ل ...** eligible for ...

B *n* rightful claimant; beneficiary (*of a religious endowment, a waqf*)

مُسْتَحَقّات *n pl* assets, balance; **طالَبَ بالمُسْتَحَقّاتِ** to demand payment of the outstanding balance

حَقْل *n* |**حُقول**| ① [قِطْعة أَرْضٍ] field; **حَقْل خَصِب** a fertile field; **حَقْل قَمْحٍ** wheat field, cornfield (BrE); **حَقْل تَجارِبَ** proving ground; **عَمِلَ في الحُقولِ** to work in the fields; **حَقْل**

حَقيقة *n* |**حَقائِقُ**| ① [واقِع] fact; reality, truth; **الحَقيقة المُرّة** harsh reality; **حَقيقة ثابِتة \ أَكيدة** an established/confirmed fact; **حَقيقة الوَضْعِ** the actual situation; **حَقائِق واقِعيّة** real facts; **الحَقيقة والخَيال** fact and fiction; **تَقْرير مُطابِق للحَقائِقِ** a truthful report; **حَقيقةً** really, truly; **في الحَقيقةِ** in fact, as a matter of fact, actually; **أَظْهَرَ الحَقائِقَ** to bring out the facts; **كَشَفَ النِقابَ عن الحَقائِقِ** to reveal the facts; **أَلَمَّ بِمَعْرِفةِ الحَقائِقِ** to acquire factual knowledge ② [صِحّة] truth, genuineness; **الحَقيقة المُجَرَّدة** the naked truth; **حَقيقة واضِحة** a truism; **لَحْظة الحَقيقةِ** the moment of truth; **مُنافٍ للحَقيقةِ** contrary to the truth; **حَجَبَ الحَقيقةَ** to conceal the truth; **حَرَّفَ الحَقائِقَ, شَوَّهَ وَجْهَ الحَقيقةِ** to distort the truth; **اعْتَرَفَ بالحَقائِقِ** to acknowledge the truth; **هذا بَعيدٌ كُلَّ البُعْدِ عن الحَقيقةِ, هذا أَبْعَدُ ما يَكونُ عن الحَقيقةِ** that is far removed from the truth; **الرِواية الأَقْرَبُ إلى الحَقيقةِ** the story that is closest to the truth ③ [جَوْهَر] essence, core; **عَبَّرَ عن حَقيقةِ رَأْيِهِ** to give one's real opinion; **ظَهَرَ على حَقيقَتِهِ** to show one's true self/face/colors

حَقيقيّ *adj* real, true, actual; authentic; **صَديق حَقيقيّ** a true friend; **ذَهَب \ فِضّة حَقيقيّ(ة)** real gold/silver; **السَبَب الحَقيقيّ** the real/actual reason; **المَعْنى الحَقيقيّ لِكَلِمةٍ** the proper sense/meaning of a word

أَحَقّ *adj* |dipt| |ب| more deserving, more entitled; **كانَ الأَحَقَّ بالفَوْزِ** he deserved to win more

إحْقاق *n* performance, carrying out; realization

أَحَقّيّة *n* priority, precedence

اسْتِحْقاق *n* ① [الدَيْن] **تاريخ الاسْتِحْقاقِ** maturity/due date (*of a loan*); **اسْتِحْقاق الانْتِخاباتِ** the time for elections ② [اسْتِئْهال] merit; **عن اسْتِحْقاقٍ** deservedly; **بِدونِ \ بِغَيْرِ اسْتِحْقاقٍ** undeservedly; **حَسْبَ اسْتِحْقاقي** as I deserve ③ [حَقّ في شَيْءٍ] claim

اسْتِحْقاقيّة *n* entitlement

تَحَقُّق *n* ① [تَحْقيق] realization ② [إثْبات] check, verification

تَحْقيق *n* ① [تَنْفيذ] realization, actualization; fulfilment; implementation, execution; **تَحْقيق مِثالٍ \ حُلْمٍ \ أُمْنِيةٍ** the fulfilment of an ideal/a dream/wish; **تَحْقيق مَشْروعٍ **

أَلْغامٍ minefield; حَقْل نَفْطٍ oil field ❷ (Fig) field, domain, area; حَقْل عِلْميّ a scientific field; في حَقْلِ الاقْتِصادِ in the economic field ❸ (Comput) field

حَقَنَ *v* |i-u; حَقْن| ❶ [أَعْطى حُقْنةً] to inject; to give an injection; حَقَنَ شَخْصاً to give sb an injection; حَقَنَ مَريضاً بِمَصْلٍ to inject a patient with a serum ❷ [سائِلاً] to retain, to hold; حَقَنَ دَمَ شَخْصٍ to spare sb's life; حَقَنَ البَوْلَ (في مَثانَتِهِ) to hold one's urine

احْتَقَنَ *v* to accumulate, to mount up; احْتَقَنَ وَجْهُهُ his face turned red; احْتَقَنَ دَمُهُ to suffer from congestion

حَقْن *n* |حُقون| ❶ vaccination, inoculation; injection, shot; حَقْن تحت الجِلْدِ hypodermic injection ❷ (Fig) injection; حَقْن الأَمْوالِ injection of money

حُقْنة *n* |حُقَن| injection, shot; حُقْنة شَرَجيّة enema; أَعْطى حُقْنةً to give an injection; حُقْنة ضِدّ ... an injection for ...; تَلَقّى حُقْنةً to get an injection

احْتِقان *n* congestion, blood clot; تَنْفيس الاحْتِقانِ the relief of congestion; easing of a difficult situation; احْتِقان الدَمِ vascular congestion

مُحْتَقِن *adj* red; engorged, flushed, inflamed; وَجْه مُحْتَقِن a red face; عَيْنانِ مُحْتَقِنَتانِ بالدِماءِ bloodshot eyes

مِحْقَنة *n* |مَحاقِنُ| (Med) hypodermic needle; مِحْقَنة وَريديّة drip, intravenous access device, an IV; تَلَقّى مِحْقَنةً وَريديّةً to be on a drip/IV

حَقْو *n* |أَحْقاء, حِقاء| (Anat) lumbar region

احْتَكَرَ *v* to obtain the exclusive right to; to monopolize; احْتَكَرَ شَيْئاً to have/hold a monopoly on sth; احْتَكَرَ اسْماً to monopolize a name

حَكْر *n* ... هذا حَكْرٌ على this is exclusive to/only for ...

احْتِكار *n* |احْتِكارات| monopoly; exclusive right; احْتِكار بَيْعِ شَيْءٍ the monopoly on the sale of sth; كَسَرَ احْتِكاراً to break a monopoly

احْتِكاريّ *adj* monopolistic; مَوْقِع احْتِكاريّ position of monopoly; احْتَلَّ مَوْقِعاً احْتِكاريًّا to achieve/have a position of monopoly

احْتِكاريّة *n* monopolization

حَكَّ *v* |u; حَكّ| ❶ [كَشَطَ] to scratch; to rub; to chafe; حَكَّ رَأْسَهُ to scratch one's head; ما حَكَّ جِلْدَكَ مِثْلُ ظُفْرِكَ ≈ blood is thicker than water; حَكَّهُ الأَمْرُ في صَدْرِهِ it touched him deep inside ❷ [الجِلْدُ] to itch

أَحَكَّ *v* to itch

احْتَكَّ *v* ❶ [حَكَّ نَفْسَهُ] to scratch ❷ [دَعا إلى الحَكِّ] to itch; احْتَكَّ ذِراعُهُ his arm itched; يَحْتَكُّ الجُرْحُ the wound is itchy ❸ [اتَّصَلَ] to be in/come into touch/contact; احْتَكَّ بِشَخْصٍ \ شَيْءٍ to come into contact with sb/sth

حاكّ *adj* abrasive

حِكّة *n* itch

احْتِكاك *n* |احْتِكاكات| ❶ (Phys) friction; rubbing; احْتِكاك سَطْحيّ surface friction; احْتِكاك في الأَسْلاكِ الكَهْرَبائيّةِ short circuit ❷ [اتِّصال] contact; احْتِكاك مُباشِر direct contact; احْتِكاك جَسَديّ bodily contact

تَحاكّ *n* to rub/push against each other, to make contact; to make contact

مِحَكّ *n* |مَحاكُّ| touchstone; test; standard, measure; مِحَكّ السياسةِ the touchstone of the policy; وَضَعَ شَيْئاً على المِحَكِّ to test/try sth

حَكَمَ *v* |u; حُكْم| ❶ [قَضى] to judge, to pass judgement; حَكَمَ على شَيْءٍ بالصِحّةِ to judge sth as correct; حَكَمَ لِشَخْصٍ to decide in favour of sb; حَكَمَ على شَخْصٍ من خِلالِ مَظْهَرِهِ to judge sb by his appearance ❷ [سَيْطَرَ] to rule, to govern, to dominate; حَكَمَ شَعْباً \ دَوْلةً \ بَلَداً to rule a people/state/country ❸ (Law) to pass judgement, to pass sentence, to sentence, to condemn; to decide; حَكَمَ في شَيْءٍ to pass judgement on sth; to express an opinion on sth; حَكَمَ على مُجْرِمٍ to sentence a criminal; حَكَمَ على شَخْصٍ بالأَشْغالِ الشاقّةِ to sentence sb to hard labor; حَكَمَ على شَخْصٍ بالسِجْنِ لِمُدّةِ ٥ سَنَواتٍ to sentence sb to five years imprisonment; حَكَمَ على شَخْصٍ بالسِجْنِ المُؤَبَّدِ \ مَدى الحَياةِ to sentence sb to life imprisonment; حَكَمَ على شَخْصٍ بالإِعْدامِ to condemn sb to death; حَكَمَ على شَخْصٍ بالإِدانةِ \ البَراءةِ to pronounce/declare sb guilty/innocent ❹ (Sport) to referee, to umpire; حَكَمَ في مُباراةٍ to referee a match

حَكُمَ *v* |u; حُكْم| to be/become wise

حَكَّمَ *v* to arbitrate; to appoint as a judge, to let rule/judge; to appoint as a referee

حاكَمَ *v* to prosecute, to bring to trial, to try; to litigate; حاكَمَ شَخْصاً to try sb (in court); to sue sb; حوكِمَ to stand trial

أَحْكَمَ *v* 1▸ [قوّى] to strengthen, to fortify; to fasten; أَحْكَمَ سَيْطَرَتَهُ على شَيْءٍ to fasten one's grip on sth; أَحْكَمَ إغْلاقَ البابِ to close the door tight; أَحْكَمَ قَبْضَتَهُ على شَخْصٍ \ شَيْءٍ to tighten one's grip on sb/sth 2▸ [أَتْقَنَ] to master; to do well, to be proficient in

تَحَكَّمَ *v* to control, to have control of, to have sway over; to dominate; تَحَكَّمَ بِشَيْءٍ to control sth, to be in control of sth; تَحَكَّمَ في شَيْءٍ to have one's own way in sth; to decide sth oneself

تَحاكَمَ *v* to take to trial; to summon (to court)

اِحْتَكَمَ *v* 1▸ [تَقاضى] to make an appeal, to be led/guided; to invoke; اِحْتَكَمَ إلى قَوْلِ اللهِ to appeal to the word of God for judgement 2▸ [تَحَكَّمَ] to control, to dominate

اِسْتَحْكَمَ *v* to be deep-rooted

حَكَم *n* |حُكّام| 1▸ (Sport) referee, umpire; حَكَم مُساعِد linesman 2▸ (Islam) الحَكَم the Judge (*one of the names of God*)

حُكْم *n* |أَحْكام| 1▸ [سُلْطة] government, administration; rule, reign; power, authority; حُكْم مُطْلَق absolutism, absolute power; حُكْم اسْتِبْداديّ tyranny, despotism; a tyrannical regime; حُكْم إرْهابيّ reign of terror; حُكْم ديمُقْراطيّ a democratic government; نِظام حُكْمٍ فاشيّ \ عَسْكَريّ a fascist/military regime; حُكْم ذاتيّ autonomy, self-government; حُكْم ذاتيّ لِلفِلَسْطينيّين self-government for the Palestinians; مِنْطَقة حُكْمٍ ذاتيّ an autonomous area; حُكْم القِلّةِ oligarchy; حُكْم رِجالِ الدينِ theocracy; حُكْم القَويّ على الضَعيفِ the law of the jungle; نِظام حُكْمٍ polity, constitution, form of government; نِظام الحُكْمِ الدُسْتوريّ a constitutional form of government; نِظام حُكْمٍ بَرْلَمانيّ a parliamentary form of government; فَتْرة \ مُدّة الحُكْمِ period of government; تحت \ خلال حُكْمِ المَلِكِ ... under/during the reign of King ...; تَوَلّى الحُكْمَ \ زِمامَ to be in power; كانَ في الحُكْمِ جاءَ إلى الحُكْمِ to come to power, to take office; اسْتَوْلى على الحُكْمِ to come to power; تَقَلَّدَ أَعْباءَ الحُكْمِ to gain/seize power; خَضَعَ لِحُكْمِ العَدوّ to assume office; to be subjected to the enemy 2▸ (Law) judgement, verdict, sentence, decree; arbitration; حُكْم قاسٍ \ خَفيف a harsh/lenient verdict; حُكْم مُلْزِم \ دُوَليّ binding/international arbitration; حُكْم بالإعْدامِ death penalty; نَطَقَ بِحُكْمٍ to pronounce judgement; أَصْدَرَ حُكْماً to pass judgement, to give a verdict; طَعَنَ في حُكْمٍ to appeal against a judgement; نَفَّذَ حُكْماً to carry out a judgement, to execute a sentence; نَقَضَ حُكْماً to reverse a judgement; تَمَلَّصَ من حُكْمٍ to escape sentence; حُكْم بالإدانةِ conviction; حُكْم بالبَراءةِ acquittal; حُكْم حُضوريّ judgement in a defended action; حُكْم غِيابيّ judgement by default; حُكْم المَحْكَمةِ العُلْيا a decree of the Supreme Court 3▸ [قاعِدة] stipulation, clause; حُكْم قانونيّ legal ruling; خالَفَ أَحْكامَ القانونِ to break the law; أَحْكام القانونِ the stipulations of the law; للضَرورةِ أَحْكامٌ necessity knows no law 4▸ [تَقْدير] judgement, valuation; حُكْم تَقْديريّ value judgement; حُكْم صارِم a harsh judgement; حُكْم مُسَبَّق prejudice, preconception, partiality; أَحْكام مُسَبَّقة عن الأجانِبِ mistaken ideas about foreigners 5▸ [أَمْر] decree, order

(Idioms) بِحُكْمِ ... on the basis of ..., on account of ..., on the strength of ..., by virtue of ...; بِحُكْمِ عَمَلِهِ \ وَظيفَتِهِ professionally; في حُكْمِ ... as good as ..., all but ...; أَصْبَحَ في حُكْمِ المُقَرَّرِ it is all but decided

حاكِم A *adj* |حاكِمونَ, حُكّام| ruling, governing; أُسْرة حاكِمة ruling family, dynasty; مَلِك حاكِم a sovereign monarch B *n* |حاكِمونَ, حُكّام| 1▸ [مُسَيْطِر] ruler, sovereign; حاكِم بِأَمْرِهِ, حاكِم مُطْلَق absolute ruler, autocrat; حاكِم مُسْتَبِدّ tyrant, dictator; حُكّام سِياسيّونَ \ عَسْكَريّونَ political/military leaders 2▸ [مُحافِظ] governor; حاكِم وِلايةِ فْلوريدا the governor of the state of Florida; حاكِم المُسْتَعْمَرةِ the governor of the colony

حِكْمة *n* |حِكَم| 1▸ [تَعَقُّل] wisdom, prudence; insight, (good) judgement; كانَ ذا حِكْمةٍ كَبيرةٍ he had great wisdom; تَناوَلَ مُشْكِلةً بِحِكْمةٍ to handle a problem with prudence; لَيْسَ من

تَحَكُّميّ *adj* autocratic, despotic

تَحْكيم *n* arbitration, refereeing; لَجْنة \ هَيْئة تَحْكيمٍ jury; arbitration commission; تَقْرير لَجْنةِ التَحْكيمِ jury's report; مَحْكَمة التَحْكيمِ court of arbitration; لَجَأَ إلى التَحْكيمِ to go to arbitration

تَحْكيميّ *adj* arbitration, referee (*before n*), arbitration (*before n*); خَطَأ تَحْكيميّ referee error; لَجْنة تَحْكيميّة committee arbitration; jury

مُحاكَمة *n* trial; قاعة المُحاكَمةِ courtroom; بِدونِ مُحاكَمةٍ without trial; مُحاكَمة مُسْتَعْجَلة summary jurisdiction/ proceedings; أَعْدَمَ بِدونِ مُحاكَمةٍ to execute without trial; to lynch; الإعْدام بِدونِ مُحاكَمةٍ lynching

مُحْكَم *adj* solid, stable; coherent; بِناء مُحْكَم a solid structure; مُحْكَم البِناءِ solidly built, coherent; مُحْكَم الإغْلاقِ tightly/ hermetically sealed; air-tight; shut tight; مُحْكَم التَقْديرِ well-considered

مُحَكَّم *n* referee, umpire; arbitrator

مَحْكَمة *n* |مَحاكِمُ| 1 [جِسْم قَضائيّ] court (of law); tribunal; مَحْكَمة عُرْفيّة \ عَسْكَريّة court martial, military tribunal; مَحْكَمة الأَحْوالِ الشَخْصيّةِ family court; مَحْكَمة ابْتِدائيّة \ مَحْكَمة البُداءةِ \ الدَرَجةِ الأولى Court of First Instance; مَحْكَمة الاسْتِئْنافِ Court of Appeal; مَحْكَمة مَرْكَزيّة (Egypt) district court; مَحْكَمة النَقْضِ \ التَمْييزِ Court of Cassation; ≈ Supreme Court; مَحْكَمة دُوَليّة international court/tribunal; مَحْكَمة العَدْلِ الدُوَليّة \ الأوروبّيّة International/European Court of Justice; المَحْكَمة العُلْيا the highest court, Supreme Court; حُكْم المَحْكَمةِ العُلْيا verdict of the Supreme Court; مَحْكَمة كَنَسيّة ecclesiastical tribunal; مَحْكَمة جُزْئيّة lowest court in Egypt for minor offences; مَحْكَمة شَرْعيّة court dealing with family matters for Muslims; ديوان المَحْكَمةِ registry; كاتِب المَحْكَمةِ clerk of the court, registrar; مَثَلَ أمام المَحْكَمةِ to appear in court; رَفَعَ شَيْئاً إلى المَحْكَمةِ to take sth to court (*a case, dispute, complaint, etc.*) 2 [مَبْنًى] courthouse

مَحْكوم A *adj* governed, ruled; determined; convicted, condemned; هذا المَشْروعُ مَحْكومٌ عَلَيْهِ بالفَشَلِ that plan is doomed to fail; مَحْكوم بِعامِلِ الوَقْتِ determined by the time

الحِكْمةِ it is not wise; رَأْسُ الحِكْمةِ مَخافةُ اللهِ the fear of God is the beginning of wisdom; بِحِكْمةٍ wisely 2 [مَثَل] saying, proverb, piece of wisdom; حِكْمة موجَزة aphorism

حُكْميّ *adj* 1 [شَرْعيّ] legal; الانْعِقاد الحُكْميّ للمَجْلِسِ the legal convening of the board 2 [إلْزاميّ] unavoidable; obligatory, mandatory, imperative

حُكومة *n* government; cabinet; حُكومة انْتِقاليّة \ مُؤَقَّتة interim/provisional government; حُكومة ائْتِلافيّة coalition government; خِدْمة الحُكومةِ government/public service; قَرار الحُكومةِ government/cabinet decision; تَدَخُّل الحُكومةِ government intervention; سَقَطَت \ اسْتَقالَت الحُكومةُ the government has fallen/resigned; أَقالَ الحُكومةَ to dismiss/ sack the cabinet

حُكوميّ *adj* government (*before n*), state (*before n*), governmental, public; مَدْرَسة حُكوميّة state school; أَمْر حُكوميّ government/executive order; هَيْئة \ مَصْلَحة \ مُؤَسَّسة حُكوميّة a government institution/service/ organization; مُوَظَّف حُكوميّ civil servant

حَكيم A *adj* |حُكَماءُ| wise, prudent; خُطّة \ سِياسة حَكيمة a wise plan/policy; نَصيحة حَكيمة sage advice
B *n* |حُكَماءُ| 1 wise man, sage; philosopher 2 (Islam) الحَكيم the Perfectly Wise (*one of the names of God*)

حَوْكَمة *n* regulation

إحْكام *n* 1 [مَصْدَر] strengthening, fortification 2 [دِقّة] accuracy, precision, perfection

تَحَكُّم *n* 1 [سَيْطَرة] control, command; determination; التَحَكُّم بالنَفْسِ self-control; فَقَدَ تَحَكُّمَهُ بِنَفْسِهِ to lose one's self-control; التَحَكُّم في الوَضْعِ command of the situation; تَحَكُّم في \ ب التَحَكُّم في مِنْطَقةٍ control over a territory; مَصيرِ شَخْصٍ mastery of sb's fate 2 [تَشْغيل] control, regulation; تَحَكُّم لاسِلْكيّ التَحَكُّم الأَرْضيّ ground control; remote control; جِهاز التَحَكُّمِ عن بُعْدٍ remote control; لَوْحة تَحَكُّمٍ control panel; عَصا تَحَكُّمٍ (أَلْعابٍ) joystick, control stick; آلِيّة التَحَكُّمِ steering mechanism; وَحْدة تَحَكُّمٍ control unit, console; التَحَكُّمُ في الضَغْطِ \ كَمِّيّةِ الرُطوبةِ the regulation of pressure/humidity

factor; مَحْكوم عَلَيْهِ بالإعْدام sentenced to death
B *n* مَحْكوم عَلَيْهِ convict; مَحْكوم (عَلَيْه) بالإعْدامِ a condemned man/woman

مَحْكوميّة *n* prison sentence; قَضى الفَتْرةَ المُتَبَقِّيَةَ من مَحْكوميَّتِهِ to serve out the rest of one's time (in prison)

مُسْتَحْكَم *adj* deep-rooted; fortified, strong; أَزْمة مُسْتَحْكَمة a deep crisis

‹ **حَكى** *v* |i; حِكاية| to tell, to relate; حَكى قِصّةً \ حِكايةً to tell a story

حاكى *v* **1** [قَلَّدَ] to imitate, to copy, to mimic; to simulate; حاكى شَخْصاً to copy sb; حاكى الواقِعَ to imitate reality; حاكى صَوْتَ شَخْصٍ to imitate sb's voice **2** [شابَهَ] to resemble, to be like

حاكٍ *n* **1** [راوٍ] |حاكونَ, حُكاة| storyteller **2** [فونوغْراف] |حَواكٍ| gramophone, record player

حَكّاء *n* storyteller

حِكاية *n* story, tale; حِكاية مُشَوِّقة \ مُثيرة a thrilling/an exciting story; حِكاية رَمْزيّة a symbolic story; parable; allegory; دائماً نَفْسُ الحِكايةِ it's the same old story; قَرَأَ لِطِفْلٍ حِكايةً to read a child a story; سَرَدَ \ حَكى \ رَوى \ قَصَّ حِكاياتٍ to tell stories; ما الحِكايةُ؟ what's the matter?

حَكَواتي *n* storyteller

مُحاكٍ *n* |مُحاكونَ| simulator; imitator, impersonator, mimic

مُحاكاة *n* **1** [تَقْليد] imitation; simulation; مُحاكاة افْتِراضيّة a virtual simulation; جِهاز مُحاكاةِ الطَيَرانِ flight simulator **2** (Comput) simulation; simulator; المُحاكاة الرَقْميّة \ بالكُمْبْيوتَر digital/computer simulation

مَحْكيّ *adj* **1** [مَرْويّ] told, related; cited; accounted **2** [عامّيّ] colloquial, vernacular

‹ **حَلَأَ** *n* (Med) herpes simplex

1‹ **حَلَبَ** *v* |i-u; حَلْب| to milk

تَحَلَّبَ *v* to seep; to ooze; to dribble, to drip; تَحَلَّبَ ريقُهُ لِرائِحةِ الطَعام the smell of the food made his mouth water

احْتَلَبَ *v* to milk

اسْتَحْلَبَ *v* **1** [اسْتَدَرَّ] to let flow **2** [امْتَصَّ] to suck **3** [حَلَبَ] to milk **4** (Chem) to emulsify

حالِب *n* |حَوالِبُ| (Anat) ureter

حَلّاب *n* |حَلّابونَ| milkman

حِلاب *n* |حِلَب| milk bowl; *bucket or large bowl for milking cows*

حُلْبان *n* listed alphabetically

حَلْبة *n* |حَلَبات| arena, ring; circuit, track; حَلْبة سيرْكٍ circus ring; حَلْبة السِباقِ race track; الحَلْبة السِياسيّة the political arena; حَلْبة رَقْصٍ dance floor

حُلْبة, **حِلْبة** *n* (Bot) fenugreek (*Trigonella foenum-graecum*)

حَلوب *adj* |mf| (*bearing milk*); بَقَرة حَلوب dairy cow

حَليب *n* milk; حَليب دَسِم, حَليب كامِل الدَسَمِ full-cream milk; حَليب نِصْف الدَسَمِ low-fat milk; حَليب مَقْشود skim milk, non-fat milk; حَليب مُعَقَّم pasteurized milk; حَليب اصْطِناعيّ (baby) formula; عُلْبة \ زُجاجة حَليبٍ a carton/bottle of milk; مُشْتَقّات الحَليبِ dairy/milk products, dairy; سُكَّر الحَليبِ lactose, milk sugar; مَسْحوق الحَليبِ powdered/dried/dehydrated milk; حَليب الغُولة ≈ hen's teeth

مُحَلَّبيّة *n rice pudding*

مُسْتَحْلَب *n* |مُسْتَحْلَبات| (Chem) emulsion

مُسْتَحْلِب *n* (Chem) emulsifier

2‹ **حَلَب** *n* |dipt f| Aleppo (*city in Syria*)

‹ **حُلْبان** *n* (Bot) sweet pea (*Lathyrus*)

‹ **حَلَجَ** *v* |i; حَلْج, حَليج| to gin, to spin; حَلَجَ القُطْنَ to gin cotton

مِحْلَجة *n* |مَحالِجُ| cotton gin

‹ **حَلْحَلَ** *v* |i; حَلْحَلة| to remove; to cause to move, to shift something from its place

تَحَلْحَلَ *v* to move, to be removed

‹ **حَلَزَنَ** *v* |i; حَلْزَنة| to form into a spiral

حَلَزون *n* |حَلَزونات| **1** (Zool) snail; حَلَزون بَحْريّ winkle, periwinkle (*Littorina littorea*) **2** [شَكْل] spiral; helix

حَلَزونة *n* spiral; helix

حَلَزونيّ *adj* spiral-shaped, spiral (*before n*); spiraling; حَرَكة حَلَزونيّة a spiral movement

‹ **حَلِسَ** *v* |a; حَلَس| to be secluded/isolated

أَحْلَسَ *v* to cover with a blanket; to make a deal with

حِلْس *n* |أَحْلاس| horse blanket

‹ **حَلَفَ** *v* |i; حَلْف, حِلْف| to swear, to take an oath; حَلَفَ بالمُصْحَفِ to swear on the Koran; حَلَفَ باللهِ أنّ ... to swear to God that ...; حَلَفَ يَميناً to swear an oath; حَلَفَ يَميناً كاذِبةً to perjure, to commit perjury; to bear false witness

حَلَّفَ *v* to put sb under oath, to swear in; to make sb swear (an oath); حَلَّفَ شَخْصاً كَمُتَرْجِمٍ to swear sb in as a translator/interpreter

حالَفَ *v* to enter into an agreement; to be an ally; حالَفَهُ الحَظُّ luck was with him; he lucked out

تَحالَفَ *v* to enter into/form an alliance; to make a treaty; تَحالَفَ مع دَوْلَةٍ to enter into an alliance with a country; تَحالَفَ مع شَخْصٍ to make a treaty/pact with sb

اسْتَحْلَفَ *v*; to make (sb) swear; اسْتَحْلَفَهُ ألاّ يَفْعَلَهُ he made him swear not to; اسْتَحْلَفَهُ أنْ يُساعِدَ he made him promise to help

حِلْف *n* ❶ [اتِّحاد] alliance, pact; treaty; confederation, axis; الحِلْف الأَطْلَسيّ ,مُنَظَّمة حِلْفِ شَمالِ الأَطْلَسيِّ the North Atlantic Treaty Organization, NATO; حِلْف وارْسو the Warsaw Pact; حِلْف بين بُلْدانِ أوروبّا an alliance among European countries; عَقَدَ حِلْفاً to conclude an alliance; to sign a treaty; حِلْف عَدَمِ الاعْتِداءِ treaty of non-aggression ❷ [يَمين] oath

حَلْفاء ,حَلْفا ,حَلْفة *n* |f| (Bot) esparto (grass) (*Macrochloa tenacissima*)

حَلّوف *n* listed alphabetically

حَليف Ⓐ *adj* |حُلَفاءُ| friendly; allied, in league; قوّة حَليفة a friendly nation/power

Ⓑ *n* |حُلَفاءُ| (Pol) ally, confederate; حارَبَ إلى جانِبِ الحُلَفاءِ to fight on the side of the Allies; حَليف سِياسيّ a political ally; كانَ النَجاحُ حَليفَهُمْ they were successful

تَحالُف *n* alliance, treaty, pact; تَحالُف انْتِخابيّ electoral pact; قوّات التَحالُفِ the allied troops; تَحالُف مع شَخْصٍ an alliance with sb; أَقامَ تَحالُفاً to form an alliance

تَحْليف *n* swearing in; تَحْليف شاهِدٍ \ مُتَرْجِمٍ the swearing in of a witness/translator; تَحْليف اليَمينِ administering the oath

مُتَحالِف Ⓐ *adj* allied; مُتَحالِف مع الشَيْطانِ allied with the Devil

Ⓑ *n* ally; مُتَحالِف مع العَدوِّ an ally of the enemy

مُحالَفة *n* alliance, pact; confederation, confederacy

مُحَلَّف Ⓐ *adj* sworn; شاهِد مُحَلَّف a sworn witness; تَصْريح \ شَهادة مُحَلَّف(ة) a sworn statement/testimony; مُتَرْجِم \ تَرْجَمة مُحَلَّف(ة) a sworn/official translator/translation

Ⓑ *n* juror; المُحَلَّفونَ ,هَيْئَة المُحَلَّفينَ jury

‹ **حَلَقَ** *v* |i; حَلْق| to shave; to cut; حَلَقَ شَعْرَ شَخْصٍ to cut sb's hair; حَلَقَ لِشَخْصٍ to cut sb's hair; to shave sb; حَلَقَ ذَقْنَهُ to shave (oneself), shave one's beard; حَلَقَ رَأْسَهُ to shave one's head

حَلَّقَ *v* ❶ [اسْتَدارَ في طَيَرانِهِ] to fly; to glide; to fly over; حَلَّقَ في الهَواءِ \ الجَوِّ to fly/glide through the air, to soar; حَلَّقَت الطائِرةُ فوق المَدينةِ the aircraft circled above the town; حَلَّقَ كالنَسْرِ to fly/soar like an eagle ❷ [جَعَلَ كالحَلْقةِ] to circle; to make/move in circles; حَلَّقَ حَوْلَ الأَرْضِ to orbit the Earth

تَحَلَّقَ *v* to make a circle; to stand/sit in a circle; تَحَلَّقَ حول النارِ to gather around the fire

حَلْق *n* |أَحْلاق ,حُلوق| throat, gullet; حَرْف الحَلْقِ (Ling) guttural

حَلَق *n* |حِلْقان| earrings; لَبِسَ حَلَقاً to wear earrings; فَرْدة حَلَقٍ one earring; جِهاز الحَلَقِ (Sport) flying rings

حالِق *n* |حَوالِقُ ,حُلَّق| ❶ [قِمّة] height ❷ (Bot) tendril

حَلّاق *n* barber; hairdresser, hairstylist; حَلّاق للنِساءِ \ نِسائيّ (ladies') hairdresser, coiffeur; يَقُصُّ الحَلّاقُ الشَعْرَ the barber cuts hair; زارَ الحَلّاقَ to visit the barber, to go to the hairdresser

حِلاقة *n* shaving; cutting; hair cutting; صالون \ مَحَلّ حِلاقةٍ hairdressing salon, hairdresser's; barber shop, barber's; ماكينة حِلاقةٍ electric shaver; أَصْداف حِلاقةٍ razor blades; أَدَوات حِلاقةٍ shaving tackle/accessories; فُرْشة حِلاقةٍ shaving brush

حَلْقة ,**حَلَقة** *n* |حَلَقات ,حَلَق| ❶ [دائِرة] ring; circle; حَلْقة غِذائيّة food chain; حَلْقَتا الجُمْبازِ rings (*in gymnastics*); حَلْقة البابِ door knocker; حَلْقة مَفاتيحَ key ring; حَلْقة مُفْرَغة a vicious cycle; سَقَطَ في \ خَرَجَ من الحَلْقةِ المُفْرَغةِ to fall into/break a vicious cycle ❷ [قُرْط] earring; حَلْقة في الأُذُنِ a ring in one's ear; لَبِسَ حَلْقةً في أُذُنِهِ to put in/wear an earring ③ [حَلْبة] ring, arena; في حَلْقةِ المُلاكَمةِ in the (boxing) ring; حَلْقة السَمَكِ fish market ④ [من الأَشْخاصِ] circle; حَلْقة دِراسيّة a course/series of lectures; حَلْقة نِقاشٍ discussion group; panel, seminar ⑤ [سِلْسِلةٍ] link; حَلْقة مُهِمّة \ ضعيفة an important/weak link; الحَلْقة المَفْقودة the missing link; حَلْقة الاتِّصالِ the connecting link ⑥ [من مُسَلْسَلٍ] episode; instalment; حَلَقات سِلْسِلةٍ episodes of a series

حَلْقِيّ *adj* guttural; صَوْت حَلْقِيّ guttural noise

حَلَقِيّ *adj* ring-shaped, circular; دودة حَلَقِيّة (Bio) annular worm (*Oligochaeta*)

حَليق *adj* |حُلَقاءُ| shaved, shaven; حَليق الذَقْنِ clean-shaven

تَحْليق *n* ① [طَيَران] |على| flying, flight ② [ارْتِفاع] height; altitude

مِحْلاق *n* |مَحاليقُ| tendril

مِحْلَق *n* |مَحالِقُ| razor, shaver

مَحْلوق *adj* shaved, shaven

‹ **حُلْقوم** *n* |حَلاقيمُ| ① (Anat) throat, gullet ② [حَلْوى] lokum, Turkish delight

‹ **حَلَكَ**, **حَلِكَ** *v* |a-u; حُلْكة, حَلَك| to be/become pitch-black; to darken intensely

احْلَوْلَكَ *v* |Form XI| to be/become pitch-black; to darken intensely

حالِك *adj* |حَوالِكُ| pitch-black, ink-black, jet black; ظَلام حالِك pitch-darkness; لَيْلة حالِكة an ink-black night

أَحْلَك *adj* |dipt| blacker, blackest; darker; هذه هي أَحْلَكُ الفَتَراتِ التي مَرَّتْ على البِلادِ this is the darkest time the country has ever passed through

‹ **حَلَّ** I *v* |u; حَلّ| ① [فَكَّ] to untie; to untwine; to disentangle; to dissolve; حَلَّ عُقْدةً to untie a knot; حَلَّ بُرْغِيًّا to loosen a screw; حَلَّ عَرَباتِ قِطارٍ to uncouple the cars of a train; حَلَّ جَمْعِيّةً \ حِزْباً to dissolve an association/a (political) party; حَلَّ البَرْلَمانَ to dissolve/dismiss parliament ② [مُشْكِلةً] to solve, to clear up; to decipher; حَلَّ مُشْكِلةً to solve a problem; حَلَّ جَريمةً \ جريمةَ قَتْلٍ to solve a crime/murder case; حَلَّ لُغْزاً to decipher a riddle; حَلَّ مَسْأَلةً حِسابِيّةً to work out a sum; حَلَّ سوءَ تَفاهُمٍ to clear up a misunderstanding; حَلَّ شِفْرةً to decipher/crack a code ③ [أَذابَ] to dissolve

حَلَّ II *v* |i-u; حَلّ, حُلول| ① [نَزَلَ] to stop, to stay, to visit; حَلَّ مَحَلَّ شَخْصٍ to stand in for sb, to take sb's place; حَلَّ رابِعاً to become fourth ② [بَدَأَ] to set in; to fall; حَلَّ الظَلامُ darkness has fallen; حَلَّ فَصْلُ الرَبيعِ spring has come; حَلَّ عيدُ الفِطْرِ اليَوْمَ today is Eid ul-Fitr (*the feast of breaking the Ramadan fast*)

حَلَّ III *v* |i; حَلال| to be permitted, to be allowed, to be lawful

حَلَّلَ *v* ① [رَدَّ إلى عَناصِرَ] to analyse; to examine, to inspect; حَلَّلَ مَشاكِلَ to analyse problems; حَلَّلَ نَصًّا to analyse a text; حَلَّلَ دَماً to analyse blood; حَلَّلَ نَفْسِيًّا to psychoanalyse ② (Math) to resolve

أَحَلَّ *v* ① [وَضَعَ] to put, to place; أَحَلَّ شَيْئاً مَحَلَّ شَيْءٍ to replace/substitute sth with sth else ② [أَباحَ] to declare lawful, to permit, to approve (of); أَحَلَّ الحَلالَ وَحَرَّمَ الحَرامَ to permit what is lawful and prohibit what is forbidden ③ [أَبْرَأَ] |من| to discharge, to release ④ [حَقَّقَ] to establish, to bring about; أَحَلَّ السَلامَ to establish peace

تَحَلَّلَ *v* ① [الجُثّةُ] to decompose; to decay ② [تَخَلَّصَ] to free oneself; to divest oneself; تَحَلَّلَ من الْتِزاماتٍ to free oneself of obligations ③ (Islam) *to remove oneself from the ritual state of purification after the pilgrimage to Mecca*

انْحَلَّ *v* ① [انْفَكَّ] to come loose; to dissolve; to disintegrate; انْحَلَّتْ عُقْدةُ لِسانِهِ his tongue was loosened (*to talk*); انْحَلَّتِ الجَماعةُ the group disintegrated ② [ارْتَخى] to slacken; to become loose; انْحَلَّتْ عَزيمَتُهُ his determination weakened; انْحَلَّتِ الأَخْلاقُ morals have decayed

احْتَلَّ *v* ① [مِنْطَقةً] to occupy, to take; to conquer; احْتَلَّ مِنْطَقةً \ مَدينةً \ بَلَداً to occupy a region/city/country ② [مَنْصِباً، مَرْكَزاً] to hold, to occupy; to take; احْتَلَّ مَكاناً بارِزاً to hold an important position; احْتَلَّ مَكانةً بارِزةً to be of special importance, to hold a prominent position; احْتَلَّ ٥٠ مَقْعَداً في البَرْلَمانِ to have 50 seats in parliament

اسْتَحَلَّ *v* to regard as permissible

حَلّ *n* |حُلول| [1] [التَغَلُّب عَلَيْهِ] solution, way out, unraveling; تَوَصَّلَ إلى حَلٍّ وَسَطٍ ,اتَّفَقَ على حَلٍّ وَسَطٍ to come to/reach a compromise; اخْتارَ حَلاًّ وَسَطاً to choose a middle course; حَلّ مُؤَقَّت a temporary solution; الحَلّ الجَيِّد \ الصَحيح the right/correct solution; حَلّ مُبْتَكَر an innovative solution; حَلّ لِلمُشْكِلَةِ a solution to the problem; حَلّ لُغْزٍ the answer to the riddle; اقْتَرَحَ \ وَجَدَ حَلاًّ لِشَيْءٍ to propose/find a solution for something [2] [إنْهاء] dissolution; حَلّ البَرْلَمانِ the dissolution of Parliament [3] [إلْغاء] annulment; حَلّ زَواجٍ the annulment of a marriage [4] (Chr) absolution; forgiveness, pardon

حِلّ *adj* being permitted; هي حِلٌّ لِلنِكاحِ she is free to get married

حَلال *adj* halal (*slaughtered or prepared according to Islamic purity laws*); permissible, lawful; طَعام \ لَحْم حَلال halal food/meat; ابْن حَلالٍ a decent person

حَلاّل *n* solver; حَلاّل مَشاكِلَ troubleshooter, problem solver

حَلّة *n* |حِلَل| pot; حَلّة ضَغْطٍ pressure cooker

حُلّة *n* |حُلَل| garb, clothing; حُلّة العيدِ festive dress

حِلّة *n* absolution; forgiveness, pardon

حُلول *n* [1] [بِداية] beginning, arrival; حُلول سَنةٍ جَديدةٍ \ فَصْلِ الرَبيعِ the beginning of a new year/spring; بِحُلولِ العامِ at the beginning of the year; by the beginning of the year; بعد حُلولِ الظَلامِ after dusk [2] [وَضْع] putting; stopping [3] (Relig) *communion with God*

حَليل *n* |أَحِلاّءُ| husband

حَليلة *n* |حَلائِلُ| wife

احْتِلال *n* occupation; احْتِلال أَراضٍ \ مِنْطَقةٍ the occupation of land/a region; الاحْتِلال العِراقيّ للكُوَيْتِ Iraqi occupation of Kuwait; جَيْش الاحْتِلالِ army of occupation; قوّات الاحْتِلالِ occupying forces; عَهْد الاحْتِلالِ period of occupation; سُلْطات الاحْتِلالِ occupation authorities

إحْلال *n* replacement, trade; establishment; إحْلال الغازِ مَحَلَّ الفَحْمِ the replacement of coal by gas

إحْليل *n* |أَحاليلُ| (Anat) urethra

انْحِلال *n* [1] [تَفَسُّخ] loosening; disintegration; decay; انْحِلال سِياسيّ political disintegration; الانْحِلال الخُلُقيّ \ الأَخْلاقيّ the deterioration of morals, moral decay; انْحِلال الآدابِ the vulgarization of manners [2] [ارْتِخاء] الانْحِلال في العَضَلاتِ weakening of the muscles; انْحِلال رَوابِطِ العائِلةِ \ الأُسْرةِ the weakening of family ties

تَحَلُّل *n* [1] [الجُثّةِ] decay, decomposition [2] [تَخَلُّص] disengagement

تَحْليل *n* |تَحاليلُ ,تَحْليلات| [1] [الرَدّ إلى عَناصِرِه] analysis, test; تَحْليل سِياسيّ \ كيماويّ \ إحْصائيّ a political/chemical/statistical analysis; تَحْليل نَفْسيّ psychoanalysis; تَحْليل شامِل \ عَميق \ دَقيق a thorough/profound/precise analysis; تَحْليل مَوْضوعيّ \ نَقْديّ an objective/a critical analysis; تَحْليل الدَمِ blood test; تَحْليل الويب web analytics [2] (Chr) absolution [3] (Math) factorization; التَحْليل إلى عَوامِلَ factorization

تَحْليليّ **A** *adj* analytical; عَقْل تَحْليليّ an analytical mind **B** *n* analyst

مُتَحَلِّل *adj* in a state of decomposition; decomposing; decaying; جُثّة مُتَحَلِّلة a decomposing corpse

مُحْتَلّ **A** *adj* occupied; الأَراضي المُحْتَلّة the occupied territories **B** *n* occupier; المُحْتَلّ الأَجْنَبيّ the foreign occupying power

مَحَلّ *n* |مَحالّ ,مَحَلاّت| [1] [مَكان] place; مَحَلّ إقامةٍ (place of) residence; address; domicile; مَحَلّ إقامةٍ دائِم a permanent residence; في مَحَلِّهِ in its place; relevant; appropriate; سُؤال في مَحَلِّهِ a relevant question; لَيْسَ في مَحَلِّهِ, في غَيْرِ مَحَلِّهِ misplaced, inappropriate; مُزاح في غَيْرِ مَحَلِّهِ an inappropriate joke; هذا التَعْليقُ لم يَكُنْ في مَحَلِّهِ that was an inappropriate remark; حَلَّ مَحَلَّ شَخْصٍ to take sb's place, to replace sb [2] [تِجاريّ] shop; business; على حِسابِ المَحَلِّ on the house; صاحِب مَحَلٍّ shop owner [3] [مَوْضوع] مَحَلّ اهْتِمامٍ \ بَحْثٍ a point of attention/investigation; مَحَلّ خِلافٍ point of difference

مُحَلّ *adj* dissolved; disbanded; هَيْئة مُحَلّة a disbanded organisation

مَحَلّة *n* quarter, district

مُحَلِّل *n* |مُحَلِّلون| ⟨1⟩ [مَنْ يُحَلِّلُ] analyst, analyzer; مُحَلِّل نَفْسِيّ psychoanalyst; مُحَلِّل سِياسِيّ a political analyst ⟨2⟩ (Islam) *man who marries a divorced wife in order to make her lawful for her former husband again*

مَحْلول **A** *adj* dissolved

B *n* |مَحاليل| solution; مَحْلول مُشْبَع a saturated solution; مَحْلول غَيْر مُشْبَع an unsaturated solution; مَحْلول مُخَفِّف dilution

مَحَلِّي *adj* local; domestic; native; أَمْطار مَحَلِّيّة local showers; نَباتات مَحَلِّيّة native plants; المَطافِئ المَحَلِّيّة the local fire brigade; إدارة مَحَلِّيّة local government; السوق المَحَلِّيّة the local market; شَبَكة مَحَلِّيّة local area network, LAN; النَاتِج القَوْمِيّ المَحَلِّيّ gross domestic product, GDP

مُنْحَلّ *adj* ⟨1⟩ [مُفَكّ] untied; disbanded; بَرْلَمان مُنْحَلّ disbanded parliament ⟨2⟩ [مُفْسَد] immoral; decadent, corrupt; licentious, promiscuous

حَلَمَ *v* |u; حُلْم| ⟨1⟩ [رَأى في المَنامِ] |ب| to dream (about); حَلَمَ بِشَيْءٍ \ شَخْصٍ to dream about sth/sb; حَلَمَ بِأَنْ ... to dream that ... ⟨2⟩ [اِشْتاقَ] |ب| to dream (about); to fantasize (about); حَلَمَ بِسَيّارةٍ جَديدةٍ to dream about a new car

حَلُمَ *v* |a; حِلْم| to be gentle/forbearing; to remain patient

اِحْتَلَمَ *v* ⟨1⟩ [حَلَمَ] to dream; to have an erotic/wet dream ⟨2⟩ [بَلَغَ] to reach puberty

حَلَم *n coll* (Anat) nipple; حَلَمة الرَضّاعةِ teat

حُلْم *n* |أَحْلام| dream; حُلْم مُزْعِج a bad dream; حُلْم اليَقْظةِ daydream, reverie; اِسْتَغْرَقَ في أَحْلامِ اليَقْظةِ to daydream, to fantasize; قَصْر أَحْلامٍ castle in the air; بَنى قُصورَ أَحْلامٍ to build castles in the air; حَقَّقَ حُلْماً to make a dream come true; جَرى وراء الأَحْلامِ to chase a dream; تَحَقَّقَ حُلْمٌ a dream has come true; تَبَخَّرَ الحُلْمُ the dream went up in smoke; الأَحْلامُ أَهْلامٌ dreams are lies

حُلُم *n* puberty

حِلْم *n* |أَحْلام، حُلوم| ⟨1⟩ [صَبْر] forbearance; tolerance; patience ⟨2⟩ [حِكْمة] insight, discernment; wisdom

حالِم **A** *adj* dreaming

B *n* dreamer

حَلوم *n* halloumi (*a mild, firm white Cypriot cheese, used especially in cooked dishes*)

حَليم **A** *adj* |حُلَماءُ| forbearing, patient

B *n* الحَليم the Forbearing (*one of the names of God*)

حُلَيْمة *n* (Anat) papilla; حُلَيْمة لِسانيّة taste bud

حَلا *v* |u; حَلاوة| to be/become sweet; to be pleasant; تَحْلو لَهُ القِراءةُ he likes to read; كَما يَحْلو لَهُ as he likes it; أَلَمْ يَحْلُ لَكَ أَنْ تَفْعَلَ ذلك didn't you enjoy doing that?

حَلّى *v* ⟨1⟩ [زَيَّنَ] to adorn, to embellish, to decorate; to deck with jewellery ⟨2⟩ [جَعَلَهُ حُلْواً] to sweeten ⟨3⟩ [مِياهَ البَحْرِ] to desalinate

تَحَلّى *v* ⟨1⟩ [تَمَيَّزَ] to be endowed; تَحَلّى بالصَبْرِ to be endowed with patience ⟨2⟩ [تَزَيَّنَ] to adorn oneself

اِسْتَحْلى *v* to like; to be delighted by; اِسْتَحْلى شَيْئاً to be delighted by sth

حُلْو **A** *adj* sweet; pretty; pleasant; عِنَب حُلْو a sweet grape; كَلام حُلْو sweet talk; حَبّة حُلْوة *aniseed, fennel or other sweet seed*

B *n sweet/pleasant things*; قاسَمَ شَخْصاً الحَياةَ بِحُلْوِها وَمُرِّها to share the good times and the bad times with sb; في الحُلْوةِ والمُرّةِ through thick and thin, for better or for worse

حَلْي *n* |حُلِيّ| piece of jewellery; اِرْتَدى حَلْياً to wear a piece of jewellery; حُلِيّ ذَهَبيّة \ ثَمينة gold/valuable jewellery

حَلاوة *n* ⟨1⟩ [كَوْن الشَيْءِ \ الشخصِ حُلْواً] sweetness; deliciousness; grace, charm ⟨2⟩ [نَوْع من حَلَوِيّاتٍ] halawa (*a type of sweet confectionery made of sesame and sugar*)

حَلْوائيّ *n* pastry chef, confectioner

حُلْوان *n* ⟨1⟩ [بَقْشيش] tip, gratuity ⟨2⟩ [مَدينة] listed alphabetically

حَلْوانيّ *n* pastry chef, confectioner

حَلْوى *n* |f; حَلاوى| sweets, candy, confectionery

حَلْوَيات، حَلَوِيّات *n pl* sweets, candy, confectionery; pastry

حُلْوين *n* glycerine

حِلْية، حُلْية *n* |حُلىً، حِلىً| piece of jewellery

تَحْلية *n* desalination, desalinization; تَحْلية المِياهِ the desalination of water

مُحَلٍّ *adj* sweetening; مادّة مُحَلِّية sweetener

مُحَلّى *adj* 1 [بِدونِ مِلْح] desalinated; مِياه مُحَلاّة desalinated water 2 [حُلْو] sweetened; مَشْروب مُحَلّى a sweet drink

مُحَلّيّات *n pl* sweets

‹ **حُلْوان** *n* |f| 1 [مَدينة] Helwan (*city in Egypt*) 2 [بَقْشيش] see حلو\حلي

‹ **حَلّوف** *n* |حَلاليفُ| wild boar

‹ **حَم** *n* see حمو

حُمة *n* see حمو\حمي

‹ **حَمَأَ** *v* |a; حَمْأ| to dredge; حَمَأَ بِئْراً to clean out a well

حَمَأ *n* mud, mire; slush; muck

حَمْأة *n* mud, mire; slush; muck

‹ **حَماة** *n* |dipt| 1 Hama (*city in Syria*) 2 see also حمو

‹ **حَمْحَمَ** *v* |i; حَمْحَمة| to whinny

‹ **حَمِدَ** *v* |a; حَمْد| to praise; to thank; ... حَمِدَ اللهَ على to praise God that ...

حَمَّدَ *v* to praise highly; to commend, to laud

حَمْد *n* praise; commendation; الحَمْدُ لله thank God, praise be to God, thank heaven; *fine* (*as an answer to* كيف حالُك); الحَمْدُ لله على السَلامةِ thank God for your safe return, ≈ welcome back (*after a journey or an illness*)

حامِد *n* 1 [شاكِر] *one who praises* 2 [اسْم شَخْصيّ] Hamid (*male given name*)

حَمّاد *n* Hamad, Hammad (*male given name*)

حَميد A *adj* 1 [مَحْمود] praiseworthy 2 (*Med*) benign, harmless; وَرَم حَميد a benign tumour

B *n* 1 (*Islam*) الحَميد the Praised One (*one of the names of God*) 2 [اسْم شَخْصيّ] Hamid (*male given name*)

أَحْمَد *n* |dipt| 1 [اسْم شَخْصيّ] Ahmad, Ahmed (*male given name*) 2 [النَبيّ] Ahmad (*another name for the prophet Muhammad*)

تَحْميد *n pronouncing of the formula* الحَمْدُ لله

مُحَمَّد *n* 1 [اسْم شَخْصيّ] Muhammad, Mohammed (*male given name*) 2 [النَبيّ] (the prophet) Muhammad; سورة مُحَمَّد Muhammad (*Sura 47*)

مُحَمَّدي *adj concerning the prophet Muhammad*; الدَعْوة \ الرِسالة المُحَمَّدِيّة the mission/message of Muhammad; الدِيانة المُحَمَّدِيّة the Muhammadan religion (*orientalist name for Islam, generally considered offensive and incorrect*)

مُحَمَّدِيّة *n* Mohammedia (*city in Morocco*)

مَحْمود A *adj* praised

B *n* Mahmud/Mahmoud (*male given name*)

‹ **حَمْدَلَ** *v* |i; حَمْدَلة| *to pronounce the formula* الحَمْدُ لله

‹ **حَمَّرَ** *v* 1 [قَلى] to fry; to roast; to cook; حَمَّرَ اللَحْمَ to brown the meat 2 [صَبَغَ] to redden; to dye red

احْمَرَّ *v* to be/turn red; to blush; بَدَأَ يَحْمَرُّ to start to blush; احْمَرَّ وَجْهُهُ من احْمَرَّ (وَجْهُهُ) خَجَلاً he blushed with shame; الغَضَبِ his face turned red with anger

حُمَر *n* bitumen; asphalt

حَمّار *n* donkey driver

حِمار *n* |أَحْمِرة, حُمُر, حَمير| 1 (*Zool*) donkey, ass; حِمار وَحْشيّ wild donkey, onager; حِمار التَحْميل pack mule; حِمار الزَرَد zebra; قَطيع من حَمير الزَرَدِ a herd of zebras; سَمّ \ وَرْد الحِمار (*Bot*) oleander (*Nerium oleander*); جاءَ بِقَرْنَيْ حِمار to return empty-handed 2 [غَبِيّ] numbskull, ass

حُمْرة *n* 1 [لَوْن] red 2 [للتَجْميل] rouge, blush

حُمَيْرة, حُمَيْراء *n* 1 (*Med*) German measles, rubella 2 (*Bio*) redstart

أَحْمَر *adj* |dipt; حُمْر| red; أَحْمَر فاتِح light red; أَحْمَر قانٍ bright/vivid red; أَحْمَر دَمَوِيّ blood red, scarlet, crimson; شَعْر أَحْمَر red hair; أَحْمَر الشَعْرِ red-headed; البَحْر الأَحْمَر the Red Sea; الصَليب \ الهِلال الأَحْمَر the Red Cross/Crescent; مَوْت أَحْمَر a violent death; لَيْلة حَمْراء a night of passion; أَشِعّة تحت الحَمْراءِ infrared radiation; كانَتْ إشارةُ المُرورِ حَمْراء the traffic light was red; الحَمْراء the Alhambra (*palace in Granada*)

احْمِرار *n* redness; blush; glow; احْمِرار الوَجْنَتَيْن a blush on the cheeks; احْمَرَّتْ وَجْنَتاهُ احْمِراراً شَديداً a deep blush spread to his cheeks

مُحْمَرّ *adj* reddish; bloodshot; عَيْنانِ مُحْمَرَّتانِ red/bloodshot eyes; امْرَأة مُحْمَرّة الشَفَتَيْنِ a woman with red lips

مُحَمَّر *adj* seared, fried, grilled, roasted; بَطاطِس مُحَمَّرة roasted potatoes

يَحْمور **A** *adj* red (*the color of fresh blood*)

B *n* 1 (Zool) roe, roebuck; wild ass 2 (Med) haemoglobin

حَمَزَ *v* |i; حَمْز| to bite or burn the tongue; to be bitter/critical

حامِز *adj* biting; acrid; sour

حَمِسَ *v* |a; حَمَس| to be/become enthusiastic

حَمَّسَ *v* to inspire (enthusiasm), to stir; to stir up; حَمَّسَ أَتْباعَهُ to inspire one's followers; حَمَّسَ الجُمْهور to excite the crowd

تَحَمَّسَ *v* to be/become enthusiastic; to be/become fanatical/zealous; تَحَمَّس لِشَيْءٍ \ شَخْصٍ to be enthusiastic about sth/sb

حَماس *n* 1 [هِمّة] enthusiasm, fervour, passion; fanaticism; zeal; حَماس شَديد \ كَبير a great deal of enthusiasm; بِحَماسٍ with enthusiasm, passionately; fanatically; بَذَلَ جُهْدَهُ لِشَيْءٍ بِكُلِّ حَماسٍ to devote oneself passionately; دافَعَ عن شَيْءٍ بِحَماسٍ to defend something with fervour; فاضَ حَماساً to bubble over with enthusiasm; فَتَرَ حَماسُهُ his enthusiasm is flagging 2 (Pol) Hamas; حَماس (حَرَكة المُقاوَمةِ الإسْلاميّة) (the Islamic resistance movement) Hamas

حَماسة *n* enthusiasm, passion, zeal

حَماسيّ **A** *adj* enthusiastic, ardent, zealous; خِطاب حَماسيّ an enthusiastic speech

B *n* member of Hamas

تَحَمُّس *n* enthusiasm, passion; fanaticism, zealotry

تَحْميس *n* stimulation, excitement; arousal

مُتَحَمِّس **A** *adj* enthusiastic, passionate, ardent; fanatic; eager; شَخْص مُتَحَمِّس enthusiast, fanatic, maniac; خَطيب مُتَحَمِّس a passionate speaker; جُمْهور مُتَحَمِّس an enthusiastic audience/crowd

B *n* enthusiast; fanatic

حَمَشَ *v* |u; حَمْش| to irritate

[1] **حَمَّصَ** *v* to roast; to grill; to toast; حَمَّصَ القَهْوةَ to roast coffee (beans); حَمَّصَ خُبْزاً to toast bread

تَحَمَّصَ *v* to be/become roasted; to be/become toasted

حُمُّص, حِمِّص, حِمَّص *n coll* chickpeas

تَحْميص *n* roasting

مُحَمَّص *adj* roasted; toasted; خُبْز مُحَمَّص toast

مُحَمِّص *n* مُحَمِّص خُبْزٍ toaster

مِحْمَصة *n* toaster

[2] **حِمْص, حُمْص** *n* |dipt f| Homs (*city in Syria*)

حَمُضَ *v* |u; حُموضة| to be/turn/go sour; قد حَمُضَ الحَليبُ the milk has gone sour

حَمَّضَ *v* 1 [حَمُضَ] to make sour, to acidify 2 (Phot) to develop; حَمَّضَ فيلْماً to develop film

تَحَمَّضَ *v* to go/turn sour

حَمْض *n* |أَحْماض| acid; حَمْض مَعِديّ gastric juices; hydrochloric acid; حُموض أَكّالة corrosive acids; حَمْض نَوَويّ DNA; حَمْض أَمينيّ amino acid; حَمْض الكَرْبونيك carbonic acid

حامِض **A** *adj* sour; acidic; مَذاق حامِض a sour taste

B *n* |حَوامِض| 1 (Chem) sourness; acid; حامِض نَوَويّ DNA; حامِض دُهْنيّ fatty acid; أَحْماض دُهْنيّة غَيْر مُشَبَّعةٍ unsaturated fatty acids; حامِض السِتْريكِ \ الكِبْريتِ \ النِتْريت citric/sulphuric/nitric acid 2 [بُرْتُقال وَليمون] citrus

حُمّاض, حُمَّيْض *n* (Bot) sorrel (*Rumex acetosa*)

حَمْضيّ *adj* sour

حَمْضيّة *n* 1 [فاكِهة] citrus (fruit) 2 (Chem) acidity

حُموضة *n* acidity; sourness; دَرَجة الحُموضةِ level of acidity, pH value

تَحَمُّض *n* acidification

تَحْميض *n* 1 (Phot) development 2 [جَعْل الشَيْءِ حامِضاً] acidification

حَمِقَ, حَمُقَ *v* |a-u; حُمْق, حَماقة| to be stupid/foolish

حَمَّقَ *v* to regard as stupid/foolish

تَحامَقَ *v* to pretend to be stupid

حُماق *n* (Med) chicken pox, varicella

حَماقة *n* 1 [غَباء] stupidity, foolishness; تَكَلَّمَ \ تَصَرَّفَ بِحَماقةٍ to talk/act foolishly; هذا نَوْعٌ من الحَماقةِ البالِغةِ this is a sign of extreme stupidity 2 [فِعْل أو قَوْل أَحْمَق] stupidity; blunder, howler; ارْتَكَبَ حَماقةً to commit a blunder

أَحْمَق A *adj* |dipt; حُمْق, حُمُق; f حَمْقى| stupid, dumb, foolish, mad, silly; كانَ أَحْمَقَ to be stupid; عادة حَمْقاء a dumb habit; سِياسة حَمْقاء a foolish policy

B *n* |dipt; حُمْق, حُمُق; f حَمْقى; حماقى| fool, imbecile, idiot

حَمَلَ *v* |i; حَمْل| 1 [رَفَعَ] to carry; حَمَلَ صُنْدوقاً \ مُسَدَّساً \ بِطاقةً شَخْصيّةً to carry a box/pistol/identity card; حَمَلَ شَيْئاً إلى شَخْصٍ to bring sth to sb; حَمَلَ المَسْؤوليّةَ to bear (the) responsibility; حَمَلَ مَخاطِرَ to involve dangers 2 [حَبِلَ] to be/become pregnant 3 [مَلَكَ] to have, to possess; to carry; حَمَلَ اسْماً حَرَكيًّا to have a nickname; حَمَلَتْ اسْمَ زَوْجِها she used her husband's name; حَمَلَ شَهادةً to have a diploma; حَمَلَ الجِنْسيّةَ الأَمْريكيّةَ to hold American nationality; حَمَلَ فَيْروساً to carry a virus 4 [أَحَسَّ] to feel; حَمَلَ لِشَخْصٍ مَشاعِرَ الامْتِنانِ to feel gratitude towards sb 5 [هاجَمَ] to attack; حَمَلَ على شَخْصٍ to campaign against sb; to attack sb 6 [أَلْحَقَ] to ascribe (to); حَمَلَ شَيْئاً على مَحْمَلِ الجِدِّ to take sth seriously; حَمَلَ شَيْئاً على شَخْصٍ to ascribe sth to sb 7 [أَقْنَعَ] to persuade; حَمَلَ العُمّالَ على تَوْقيعِ عَريضةِ احْتِجاجٍ he persuaded the workers to sign a protest letter

حَمَّلَ *v* 1 [شَحَنَ] to load; to burden; حَمَّلَ سَفينةً to load a ship; حَمَّلَ شاحِنةً بالبَضائِعِ to load a lorry with goods 2 (fig) to pass to; حَمَّلَ شَخْصاً المَسْؤوليّةَ to give sb the responsibility; to pass on the responsibility to sb; حَمَّلَ شَخْصاً الذَنْبَ to put the blame on sb; حَمَّلَ شَخْصاً عِبْءَ شَيْءٍ to burden sb with sth 3 (Comput) to upload; حَمَّلَ مِلَفًّا to upload a file

تَحَمَّلَ *v* 1 [حَمَلَ] to carry; to take upon oneself; تَحَمَّلَ أَعْباءَ الأَضْرارِ to be responsible for the damage; تَحَمَّلَ المَسْؤوليّةَ to take on/bear the responsibility 2 [أَطاقَ] to stand, to tolerate; to bear, to endure; تَحَمَّلَ شَيْئاً to sustain/bear sth; تَحَمَّلَ الضَوْضاءَ to stand the noise; تَحَمَّلَ الحُزْنَ \ الأَلَمَ to endure grief/pain; تَحَمَّلَ مَرَضاً to come through an illness; تَحَمَّلَ شَيْئاً لِمُدّةِ ساعاتٍ to bear/tolerate sth for hours; تَحَمَّلَ شَخْصاً to tolerate sb; لم أَسْتَطِعْ أَنْ أَتَحَمَّلَهُ I couldn't stand him

تَحامَلَ *v* to treat unjustly; تَحامَلَ على شَخْصٍ to treat sb unjustly; to be prejudiced against sb; تَحامَلَ على نَفْسِهِ to overexert oneself; to pull oneself together, to take heart

احْتَمَلَ *v* 1 [تَحَمَّلَ] to stand, to tolerate; to bear, to endure; لا يُحْتَمَلُ intolerable, unbearable, insufferable; لا يَحْتَمِلُ الأَمْرُ الانْتِظارَ it can't wait; لا يَحْتَمِلُ الجَدَلَ there's no arguing about it 2 [كانَ مُمْكِناً] to be possible, to be conceivable; to be probable/likely; يَحْتَمِلُ أنْ ... it is possible that …, it might be that; it is probable likely that …

حَمْل *n* |أَحْمال, حِمال| 1 [المَرْأة] pregnancy; حَمْل وَهْميّ \ كاذِب phantom pregnancy; حَمْل خارِجَ الرَحِمِ an ectopic pregnancy; مَنْع الحَمْلِ contraception; birth control; وَسيلة مَنْعِ الحَمْلِ مانِع للحَمْلِ contraceptive, prophylactic; حُبوب مَنْعِ الحَمْلِ contraceptive pills, the pill (infml); تَناوَلَتْ حُبوبَ مَنْعِ الحَمْلِ she was on the pill; إسْقاط الحَمْلِ abortion, termination of pregnancy; أَسْقَطَ \ أَجْهَضَ الحَمْلَ to terminate a pregnancy; to perform an abortion; فَقَدَ الحَمْلَ to have a miscarriage, to miscarry 2 [الحَيَوان] gestation; conception 3 [وَزْن] load, burden; حَمْل الأَثْقالِ weightlifting 4 [حَثّ |على|] stimulus; stimulant

حَمَل *n* |أَحْمال, حُمْلان| lamb; لَحْم الحَمَلِ lamb (meat), mutton; فَخْذ الحَمَلِ leg of lamb; بُرْج الحَمَلِ Aries; كانَ كالحَمَلِ الوَديعِ to be as meek as a lamb; ذِئْب في ثَوْبِ \ جِلْدِ حَمَلٍ a wolf in sheep's clothing

حِمْل *n* |أَحْمال| burden; load

حامِل A *adj* |f; حَوامِلُ| pregnant; with child; امْرَأة حامِل a pregnant woman; بَقَرة حامِل a cow in calf; كانَتْ حامِلاً to be pregnant/expecting

B *n* |حَمَلة| 1 [صاحِب] bearer; holder; حامِل جَوازِ السَفَرِ the bearer of the passport; حامِل أَسْهُمٍ shareholder; حامِل شَهادةٍ holder of a diploma, qualified; شيك لِحامِلِهِ a cheque made payable to the bearer 2 [مِكْروب] carrier; حامِل فَيْروسِ نَقْصِ المَناعةِ المُكْتَسَبةِ carrier of the HIV virus 3 [حَمّالة] حامِل بَنْطَلونٍ braces (BrE), suspenders (AmE); حامِل مَجَلّاتٍ magazine rack 4 [حَمّال] porter; bearer

حامِلة *n* **1** (Mil) carrier; حامِلة طائِراتٍ aircraft carrier **2** [الّذي يَحْمِلُ] holder; حامِلة مَفاتيح key holder **3** [للجَرْحى] stretcher

حَمّال *n* |حَمّالة، حَمّالونَ| porter

حَمّالة *n* braces (BrE), suspenders (AmE); حَمّالة الصَدْرِ bra

حِمالة *n* **1** [عِلاقة] belt **2** [مِهْنة الحَمّالِ] *work of a porter or carrier*

حَمْلة *n* |حَمَلات| **1** [عَمَلِيّة] action; campaign; operation; حَمْلة واسِعة \ عَنيفة \ حَمْلة مَحْمومة an all-out campaign; حَمْلة انْتِخابِيّة a fierce/violent /worldwide campaign; عالَمِيّة election campaign; حَمْلة صاخِبة a noisy campaign; حَمْلة إعْلانِيّة advertising campaign; حَمْلة إعْلامِيّة \ دِعائِيّة publicity campaign; حَمْلة مُطارَدةٍ round-up; حَمْلة ضِدّ العُنْصُرِيّة a campaign against racism; شَنَّ حَمْلةً to launch a campaign; to crack down; قامَ بِحَمْلةِ اعْتِقالاتٍ to carry out a raid **2** [عَسْكَرِيّة] campaign; expedition; حَمْلة تَأْديبِيّة punitive expedition; حَمَلات نابوليون Napoleon's campaigns; حَمْلة على العَدوِّ a campaign against the enemy

حَمول *n* |mf| stoical

حُمولة *n* **1** [شَحْنة] freight; cargo; load; حُمولة سَفينةٍ ship's cargo; حُمولة من الرَمْلِ \ الرُزِّ \ بَصَلِ الزُهورِ a load of sand/ rice/bulbs; حُمولة من الكُتُبِ a load of books; سِعْر نَقْلِ حُمولةٍ freight/carriage/haulage rate; أَفْرَغَ حُمولةً to unload, to discharge cargo **2** [ثِقْل] carrying/loading capacity, tonnage; bearing/supporting power; الحُمولةُ القُصْوى ٥٠ طُنًّا a maximum load capacity of 50 tons

احْتِمال *n* |احْتِمالات| **1** [إمْكان] probability, likelihood; chance; possibility; احْتِمال ... the possibility of ...; احْتِمال ضَعيف a small chance; بَعيد الاحْتِمالِ unlikely; على قَدْرِ الاحْتِمالِ within the realm of possibility; كانَ مُهَيَّأً لِأَسْوَأ الاحْتِمالاتِ to be prepared for the worst; كانَ مَفْتوحاً على كُلِّ الاحْتِمالاتِ to be open to everything; بَقِيَ أَمامَنا فَقَط احْتِمالانِ we had only two options left; قَلَّلَ احْتِمالاتِ النَجاحِ to lessen the chances of success **2** [تَحَمُّل] endurance; قُوّة الاحْتِمالِ the strength to bear

احْتِماليّ *adj* possible, potential; مَشاكِل احْتِمالِيّة potential problems

تَحامُل *n* prejudice, partiality, bias; *unjust treatment*

تَحَمُّل *n* endurance; tolerance; لم يَسْتَطِعْ تَحَمُّلَ الأَلَمِ he couldn't stand the pain; قُدْرة على التَحَمُّلِ endurance, stamina; تَحَمُّل البَرْدِ \ الحَرارةِ tolerance for cold/heat

تَحْميل *n* **1** [شَحْن] loading; freight; حِصان تَحْميلٍ pack horse; رَصيف تَحْميلٍ loading dock; loading ramp/platform; wharf; قابِل للتَحْميلِ capable of carrying a load **2** (Comput) uploading; التَنْزيل والتَحْميل downloading and uploading; سُرْعة التَحْميلِ upload speed; تَحْميل بِلا حُدودٍ unlimited uploads

تَحْميلة *n* |تَحاميل| (Med) suppository; وَضَعَ تَحْميلةً لِشَخْصٍ to give sb a suppository

مُتَحامِل *adj* prejudiced, biased; unjust; oppressive; مُتَحامِل على شَيْءٍ \ شَخْصٍ prejudiced against sth/sb; unjust toward sth/sb

مُحْتَمَل *adj* **1** [مُمْكِن] probable, likely; possible, potential; الجاني المُحْتَمَل the suspected offender; مَشاكِل مُحْتَمَلة potential problems; من المُحْتَمَلِ probably; supposedly; سُؤال من المُحْتَمَلِ طَرْحُهُ a question that could/might be asked; من المُحْتَمَلِ أنْ يَتَأَخَّرَ القِطارُ the train will probably be late; من المُحْتَمَلِ جِدًّا أنْ ... it is perfectly possible that ..., it is quite conceivable that ...; يَبْدو من غَيْرِ المُحْتَمَلِ it seems unlikely; هذه القِصّةُ غَيْرُ مُحْتَمَلةٍ that story is unlikely; سَبَب مُحْتَمَل (Law) probable cause **2** [يُطاق] bearable; غَيْر مُحْتَمَلٍ unbearable

مَحْمَل *n* **1** [مُسْتَوًى] level; أَخَذَ شَيْئاً \ شَخْصاً على مَحْمَلِ الجِدِّ to take sth/sb seriously **2** [مِحَفّة] stretcher; litter, sedan chair, palanquin

مَحْمِل *n* |مَحامِلُ| **1** [مِحَفّة] stretcher; litter, sedan chair, palanquin **2** [دِعامة] girder; framework; مَحْمِل كُرَيّاتٍ ball bearing

مُحَمَّل *adj* loaded; laden; شاحِنة مُحَمَّلة a loaded truck; مُحَمَّلاً وَمُزَمَّلاً ≈ packed up and ready

مَحْمول **A** *adj* portable, mobile; راديو مَحْمول a portable radio; هاتِف مَحْمول mobile phone, mobile (BrE), cell (phone) (AmE); حاسوب مَحْمول laptop (computer)
B *n* (Ling) predicate

‹ **حِمْلاج** *n* blowpipe; حِمْلاج قَطْعٍ acetylene torch; cutting torch

‹ **حَمْلَقَ** *v* |i; حَمْلَقة| to stare; حَمْلَقَ في شَخْصٍ to stare at sb

‹ **حَمَّ** *v* |u; حَمّ| to heat; حَمَّ الماءَ to heat water; حُمَّ to have/get a fever

حَمَّمَ *v* [1] [غَسَلَ] to bathe, to wash; حَمَّمَ طِفْلاً to bathe a child [2] [سَخَّنَ] to heat

أَحَمَّ *v* [1] [غَسَلَ] to bathe [2] [سَخَّنَ] to heat, to warm up

تَحَمَّمَ *v* to bathe (oneself), to take a bath

اِسْتَحَمَّ *v* to bathe (oneself), to take a bath; to wash up; to shower, to take a shower; اِسْتَحَمَّ في بُحَيْرةٍ to swim in a lake, to take a dip in a lake

حُمَم *n coll* [1] [ما احْتَرَق من النارِ] ashes; *charred remnants*; حُمَم البُرْكانِ \ بُرْكانيّة lava [2] [فَحْم] charcoal

حَمام *n coll* |حَمائِمُ, حَمامات| pigeon, dove; حَمام الزاجِلِ carrier/homing pigeon; حَمام السَلامِ dove of peace; بُرْج حَمامٍ dovecote; حَمام مَحْشوّ *roast pigeon stuffed with rice and spices*

حَمّام *n* |حَمّامات| [1] [مَكان] bathroom, lavatory; bathhouse [2] [اسْتِحْمام] bath; حَمّام ساخِن \ بارِد a hot/cold bath; حَمّام مُنْعِش a refreshing bath/shower; حَمّام تُرْكيّ a Turkish bath; أَخَذَ حَمّامَ بُخارٍ to take a steambath; بُرْنُس حَمّامٍ bathrobe; أَخَذَ حَمّامَ شَمْسٍ to sunbathe; حَمّام سِباحةٍ swimming pool; حَمّام دَم bloodbath, massacre

حِمام *n* death

حَمّة *n* |حِمام, حَمّ| geyser

حُمّى *n* |f; حُمَّيات| fever; أُصيبَ \ كانَ مُصاباً بالحُمّى to get/have a fever; حُمّى صَفْراء yellow fever; حُمّى قُلاعيّة foot-and-mouth disease; حُمّى قِرْمِزيّة scarlet fever, scarlatina; حُمّى مُخّيّة شَوْكيّة meningitis; حُمّى الغِبِّ tertian fever; حُمّى القَشّ hay fever, pollinosis; حُمّى مالْطِيّة \ مُتَمَوِّجة brucellosis; مَسّ حُمّى, نَوْبة حُمّى attack of fever; مُضادّ للحُمّى antipyretic; دَواء مُضادّ للحُمّى anti-fever agent, antipyretic; شَعَرَ بالحُمّى to feel feverish; زالَتْ عَنْهُ الحُمّى his fever has passed, his fever broke; خَفَّفَ الحُمّى to bring down the fever

حَميم *adj* |أَحِمّاءُ| close, intimate; hearty, warm; familiar; اِسْتِقْبال حَميم a warm reception; عَلاقة حَميمة close ties, a warm relationship; صَديق(ة) حَميم(ة) a close friend, bosom friend; صَداقة حَميمة a close friendship

حَميميّ *adj* intimate; cordial

حَميميّة *n* intimacy; closeness; familiarity

اِسْتِحْمام *n* bath; bathing; showering

مَحْموم *adj* [1] [مُصاب بالحُمّى] feverish; كانَ مَحْموماً to have a fever, to be feverish; to have a temperature [2] [مُتَهَيِّج] wild, feverish, frantic; hectic; نَشاط مَحْموم feverish/frantic activity; تَشاوُر مَحْموم hectic consultations; سِباق مَحْموم a heated contest

‹ **حَم** *n* father-in-law; حَموُهُ his father-in-law

حَماة *n* |حَمَوات| [1] (Anat) calf [2] [أُمّ الزَوْج(ة)] mother-in-law [3] [مَدينة] listed alphabetically

‹ **حُمة** *n* |حُمًى, حُمات| sting; stinger, dart

¹‹ **حَمِي** *v* |a; حَمْية| [1] [سَخُنَ] to be/become hot; to flare up, to flame up; حَمِي الوَطيسُ fighting broke out [2] [غَضِبَ] to be/become furious

حَمّى *v* to heat; to warm up

أَحْمى *v* to heat; to overheat

حَمو *n* see حَم

حَمْو *n* heat

حُمُوّ *n* heat

حامٍ A *adj* [1] [عَنيف] heated, fierce; passionate; مُناقَشة حامية a heated discussion; مُرافَعة حامِية a passionate plea [2] [حارّ] red-hot

B *n* |حُماة| see حمي 2

حَمِيّة *n* enthusiasm, keenness; eagerness; zeal; بِلا حَمِيّةٍ coldly

إِحْماء *n* heating; warm-up; تَدْريبات الإِحْماءِ والتَسْخينِ warm-up exercise; إِحْماء المُحَرِّك warming up the engine

²‹ **حَمى** *v* |i; حَمْي, حِماية| to protect, to shelter; to defend; حَمى شَخْصاً to protect sb; حَمى شَخْصاً من ارْتِكابِ خَطأٍ to keep sb from doing wrong; حَمى نَفْسَهُ من البَرْدِ to protect oneself from the cold; حَمى الجِسْمَ من شَيْءٍ to protect the body from sth

حَمِيَ *v* |a; حَمِيّة| see حمو\حمي

حامى *v* |عن| to defend; to protect; حامى عن شَخْصٍ to defend sb

تَحامى *v* to avoid, to shun

احْتَمى *v* 1 [لَجَأَ] to seek shelter/protection/refuge; احْتَمى من الشَّمْسِ to take cover from the sun; احْتَمى بِمَكانٍ to take shelter somewhere; احْتَمى وراء حائِطٍ to take cover behind a wall 2 [امْتَنَعَ] to be put on a diet; احْتَمى عن السُّكَّرِ to not be allowed sugar

حامٍ A *n* |حُماة| protector, guardian
B *adj* see حمو\حمي 1

حامِية *n* garrison

حِمائيّ *adj* protective, protectionist (*before n*); تَدْبير \ إجْراء حِمائيّ protective measure

حِمائيّة *n* protectionism

حِماية *n* 1 [صِيانة] protection, security; shelter, cover; patronage; حِماية مَدَنيّة Civil Defence (Corps); حِماية تِجاريّة protectionism; حِماية البيئة environmental protection; الحِماية من السَرِقةِ protection against theft; حِماية من الشَّمْسِ cover from the sun; وَفَّرَ الحِمايةَ من شَيْءٍ to offer protection against/from sth; قَدَّمَ إلى شَخْصٍ حِمايةً to offer sb protection; to patronize sb; وَجَدَ الحِمايةَ to find shelter; وَقَعَ تحت حِمايةِ شَخْصٍ to be under the sb's patronage/ protection; تحت حِمايةِ الأُمَمِ المُتَّحِدةِ under protection of the United Nations; لِحِمايةِ شَيْءٍ \ شَخْصٍ for the protection of sth/sb 2 (Pol) protectorate; تحت حِمايةِ فَرَنْسا under French rule; الحِماية الفَرَنْسيّة على المَغْرِبِ the French protectorate of Morocco

حِمًى *n* protection; advocacy

حِمْية *n* diet; حِمْية صارِمة a strict diet; اتَّبَعَ حِمْيةً to be on a diet; الْتَزَمَ حِمْيةً to stick to a diet

مُحامٍ *n* |مُحامونَ| lawyer; barrister, solicitor (BrE), attorney (AmE); مُحامٍ مَجّانيّ counsel for legal aid; public defender (AmE); مُحامٍ عامّ Solicitor General; مُحامي الدِفاعِ defence lawyer; مُحامي الادِّعاءِ plaintiff's lawyer; مُحامي الحُكومةِ prosecutor; هَيْئة المُحامينَ the Bar Association; مَكْتَب مُحامينَ lawyer's office, firm of solicitors (BrE), law firm (AmE); اسْتَعانَ بِمُحامٍ to take/hire a lawyer; وَكَّلَ مُحامِياً to retain a lawyer; to be assisted by a legal adviser; يُؤازِرُ المُحامي مُوَكِّلَهُ a lawyer represents his client; طَلَبَ المُحامي الحُكْمَ بالبَراءةِ the lawyer requested acquittal

مُحاماة *n* 1 [دِفاع] defence 2 [حِرْفة المُحامي] the legal profession, the practice of law; هَيْئة المُحاماةِ the Bar Association

مَحْميّ *adj* protected, sheltered; مَحْميّ ضدّ الرِياحِ \ الأَمْطارِ sheltered from the wind/rain; مِنْطَقة مَحْميّة protected area; بَيْت مَحْميّ greenhouse; قُرْص مَحْميّ ضدّ الكِتابةِ write-protected disk

مَحْميّة *n* protectorate; preserve; مَحْمِيّة عَدَنَ البَريطانِية the British protectorate of Aden; مَحْمِيّة طَبيعيّة nature preserve

حَنَّأَ *v* to dye with henna

حِنّاء, حِنّة *n coll* henna; أبو الحِنّاءِ robin; خَضَّبَتْ شَعْرَها بالحِنّاءِ she dyed her hair with henna

مُحَنَّب *adj* bent with age

حُنْبُلة *n* |حُنْبُل| pod

حَنْبَليّ A *adj* |حَنابِلة| Hanbali; المَذْهَب الحَنْبَليّ the Hanbali school (*one of the four major schools of jurisprudence in Sunni Islam*)
B *n* |حَنابِلة| Hanbali

حَنْبَليّة *n* Hanbalism

حانوت *n* |mf; حَوانيتُ| shop; رَأْس الحانوتِ (NA) ras el hanout (*a blend of a particular shop's best spices*)

حانوتيّ *n* |حانوتيّة| 1 [صاحِب حانوتٍ] shopkeeper 2 [مُتَعَهِّد المَوْتى] undertaker; gravedigger

حَنِثَ *v* |a; حِنْث| 1 [كَذَبَ في اليَمينِ] to lie; حَنِثَ في يَمينِهِ to break one's oath; to perjure; to betray one's word; حَنِثَ نَذْراً to break a (solemn) vow 2 [أَثِمَ] to sin; to transgress, to trespass

حِنْث *n* |أَحْناث| sin; trespass; transgression

حَنْجَرة *n* |حَناجِرُ| larynx, voice box; throat; أَوْتار الحَنْجَرةِ vocal chords; الْتِهاب الحَنْجَرةِ laryngitis, sore throat; نادى بِأَقْوى ما تَسْتَطيعُ حَنْجَرَتُهُ to call out as loudly as one can

حَنْدَقوق *n* (Bot) sweet clover (*Melilot*)

حَنَش *n* |أَحْناش| snake

‹ **حَنَّطَ** *v* 1 [جِسْمَ المَيِّتِ] to embalm; to mummify 2 [الحَيَوانَ] to stuff; حَنَّطَ حَيَواناً to stuff an animal

حانِط *adj* (old use) أَحْمَر حانِط very red

حِناط *n* balm

حِنْطة *n* |حِنَط| (Bot) wheat; حِنْطة سَوْداء buckwheat (*Fagopyrum esculentum*)

حِنْطيّ *adj* wheat-colored, light brown

تَحْنيط *n* embalming; mummification

مُحَنَّط *adj* mummified, embalmed; stuffed; طائِر مُحَنَّط a stuffed bird; جُثّة مُحَنَّطة mummified remains; an embalmed body

‹ **حَنْطور** *n* عَرَبة الحَنْطورِ coach, carriage

‹ **حُنْظُب** *n* |حَناظِبُ| stag beetle

‹ **حَنْظَل** *n* bitter-apple, colocynth

‹ **حَنَفيّ** A *adj* Hanafi; المَذْهَب الحَنَفيّ the Hanafi school (*one of the four major schools of jurisprudence in Sunni Islam*)
B *n* Hanafi (*adherent of the Hanafi school*)

حَنَفيّة *n* 1 [صُنْبور] tap, faucet (AmE); spigot; ماء من الحَنَفيّةِ tap water; فَتَح الحَنَفيّةَ to open the tap; أَغْلَقَ \ سَدَّ الحَنَفيّةَ to close the tap 2 (Islam) Hanafism

حَنيف *adj* |حُنَفاءُ| true believer; الدين الحَنيف the true religion (*Islam*); الحُنَفاء *pre-Islamic monotheists*

أَحْنَف *adj* |dipt| club-footed

‹ **حَنِقَ** *v* |a; حَنَق| to be/become furious; حَنِقَ من \ على شَخْصٍ to be furious at sb

أَحْنَقَ *v* to enrage, to infuriate; أَحْنَقَ شَخْصاً to enrage sb, to infuriate sb

حَنَق *n* fury, rage, anger

حانِق *adj* furious, enraged, boiling; نَظْرة حانِقة a furious look

‹ **حَنَكَ** *v* |i-u; حَنْك| to make experienced/wise; to season; حَنَكَتْهُ التَجارِبُ he has become wise through experience; Experienced has seasoned him

حَنَّكَ *v* to make sb experienced/wise; to season sb

حَنَك *n* |أَحْناك| (Anat) palate; الحَنَك الصُلْب the hard palate; الحَنَك اللَيِّن \ الرَخو the soft palate, velum; فَلْح الشَفةِ والحَنَكِ a cleft lip and palate; harelip

حُنْك *n* |أَحْناك| experience (of life); *knowledge and skill acquired through the practical experience of things*

حُنْكة *n* experience of life, worldly knowledge; experience

حَنَكيّ *adj* (Ling) palatal; حَرْف حَنَكيّ palatal consonant

مُحَنَّك *adj* experienced, seasoned, dyed-in-the-wool; worldly-wise; سِياسيّ مُحَنَّك an experienced politician

‹ **حَنْكَليس** *n* eel

‹ **حَنَّ** *v* |i| 1 [اِشْتاقَ] |حَنين; إلى| to long (for), to yearn (for), to ache (for); حَنَّ إلى وَطَنِهِ he yearned for his country 2 [عَطَفَ] |على; حَنان, حَنّة| to feel sympathy/compassion/affection (for); حَنَّ على شَخْصٍ to feel affection for sb

حَنَّنَ *v* to blossom, to bloom

تَحَنَّنَ *v* |على| to feel pity/compassion (for)

حَنّا *n* |m| Hanna, John (*Christian male given name*)

حَنان *n* 1 [مَحَبّة] affection, sympathy; tenderness; بِحَنانٍ affectionately, tenderly; حَنانَكَ have mercy! (*when making an apology*) 2 [اِسْم شَخْصيّ] |f dipt| Hanan (*female given name*)

حَنّان *adj* |dipt| loving

حَنون *adj* loving, tender, affectionate; attached

حَنين *n* longing, yearning; homesickness; nostalgia; كانَ عِنْدَهُ حَنينٌ إلى الوَطَنِ he longed for his country

تَحْنان *n* compassion, affection

‹ **حَنا** *v* |u; حُنوّ| 1 [حَنى] to bend 2 [عَطَفَ] to like, to feel for; حَنا على شَخْصٍ to feel for sb

حَنى *v* |i; حَنْي| to bend, to bow; حَنى رَأْسَهُ to bow one's head

أَحْنى *v* to nod; أَحْنى رَأْسَهُ to nod one's head

انْحَنى *v* to bow, to bend, to curve; انْحَنى أمامَ المَلِكِ to bow to the king; يَنْحَني الطَريقُ إلى اليَمينِ the road curves to the left; تَنْحَني الأَغْصانُ the branches are bending over

حُنوّ *n* affection; tenderness

حِنْو *n* |أَحْناء| bend, twist, curve; في أَحْناءِ within

حانٍ *adj* 1 [عاطِف] sympathizing 2 [مُنْحَنٍ] bended, curved

حَنيّة *n* arc

انْحِناء *n* bend; inclination; curve

انْحِناءة *n* bow; انْحِناءة طَويلة a deep bow

أَحْوَج *adj* in greater need; هو أَحْوَجُ ما يكونُ إلى الدَّواءِ he is in great need of medication; هو أَحْوَجُ إلى هذا مِنّي he needs it more than I do

مُحْتاج A *adj* in need/want; needing, wanting; كانَ مُحْتاجاً ل \ إلى شَخْصٍ \ شَيْءٍ to need sb/sth

B *n one who is destitute*

‹ **حاذَ** *v* |u; حَوْذ| to urge on (*an animal*)

اسْتَحْوَذَ *v* |على| to take possession (of), to acquire mastery (over); to occupy, to take up; اسْتَحْوَذَ على الإعْجابِ to win admiration; اسْتَحْوَذَ على القُلوبِ والعُقولِ to win hearts and minds; اسْتَحْوَذَ على اهْتِمامِ شَخصٍ to demand sb's attention; اسْتَحْوَذَ على ٤٠ في المِائةِ to take up 40%; اسْتَحْوَذَ الأَمْرُ عَلَيْهِ كُلِّيّاً he was completely obsessed with it; اسْتَحْوَذَ القَلَقُ على تَفْكيرِه his mind was full of worry

حوذيّ *n* cabby, taxi driver; coachman

اسْتِحْواذ *n* obsession; preoccupation

اسْتِحْواذيّ *adj* obsessive

مُسْتَحْوَذ *adj* preoccupied, obsessed; مُسْتَحْوَذ على السُلْطةِ obsessed with power

‹ **حَوْذان** *n* (Bot) buttercup (*Ranunculus*)

‹ **حار** *v* |u; حَوْر| 1 [رَجَعَ] to return 2 [تَرَدَّدَ] see **حير**

حَوِرَ *v* |a; حَوَر| to be black (*eyes*)

تَمَحْوَرَ *v* to revolve, to rotate

حَوَّرَ *v* to change, to alter; to misrepresent, to warp; حَوَّرَ كَلامَ شَخْصٍ to distort sb's words

حاوَرَ *v* to talk to, to converse; to discuss; to debate; حاوَرَ شَخْصاً to talk to sb; to debate sb

تَحَوَّرَ *v* 1 [تَعَدَّلَ] to be changed/altered/modified 2 [تَحَرَّفَ] to be distorted/jumbled

تَحاوَرَ *v* to have/carry on a discussion; to dialogue; تَحاوَرَ مع شَخْصٍ to have a discussion with sb

حَوْر *n* 1 (Bot) poplar; حَوْر رَجْراج aspen 2 [نَقْص] lack

حارة *n* |حارات, حَواري| 1 [حَيّ] quarter, district; neighbourhood; حارة جَميلة a beautiful district; ابْن الحارةِ *sb from the neighbourhood*; دَعَوْنا كُلَّ أَهْلِ الحارةِ we invited the whole neighbourhood; ≈ كَمَن يَبيعُ الماءَ في حارةِ السَقّائين

مَحْنًى *n* bend; bow

مَحْنيّ *adj* bowed, curved

مُنْحَنٍ *adj* bent, curved, crooked; بِظَهْرٍ مُنْحَنٍ with a bent back

مُنْحَنًى *n* |مُنْحَنَيات| 1 [مُنْعَطَف] bend, curve 2 (Geom) curve

‹ **حَوّاء** *n* |dipt f| 1 [اسْم شَخْصيّ] Hawwa, Eve (*female given name*) 2 (Rel) Eve (*the first woman in the Abrahamic religions*)

‹ **حوت** *n* |حيتان, أَحْوات| 1 (Zool) fish, whale; صَيْد الحيتانِ whale fishing; حوت أَسْوَد orca, killer whale 2 (Astrol) بُرْج الحوتِ Pisces

‹ **أَحاثَ** *v* to root

‹ **حاجَ** *v* |u; حِياجة, حَوْج| إلى| to need

أَحْوَجَ *v* 1 [اضْطَرَّ] |إلى| to make necessary, to oblige, to force; to require; أَحْوَجَتْهُ الظُروفُ إلى ذلك circumstances forced him to do it 2 [افْتَقَرَ] to impoverish

تَحَوَّجَ *v* to do some shopping

احْتاجَ *v* 1 [اقْتَضى] to need, to have a need (for), to want (for); احْتاجَ إلى شَخْصٍ \ شَيْءٍ to need sth/sb 2 [تَطَلَّبَ] to require; يَحْتاجُ تَحْقيقُ هذا المَشْروعِ إلى مالٍ كَثيرٍ a lot of money is needed to realize this project

حاجة *n* 1 [رَغْبة] |حاجات| need, necessity, want; لا حاجة إلى ذلك that is not necessary; حاجة ماليّة financial need; حاجة ماسّة \ مُلِحّة a strong/urgent need; عند الحاجةِ in case of need, if required; صَلاة الحاجةِ the prayer of need; كانَ ب \ في حاجةٍ إلى شَخْصٍ \ شَيْءٍ to need sb/sth; كانَ في حاجةٍ إلى الهُدوءِ \ الحَرَكةِ \ الاسْتِجْمامِ to need calm/exercise/relaxation; كانَ في أَمَسِّ الحاجةِ إلى شَيْءٍ to need sth badly; سَدَّ \ لَبّى حاجةً to fill/meet a need; قَضى حاجَتَهُ to relieve oneself; إذا دَعَت الحاجةُ if the need arises; الحاجةُ أُمُّ الاخْتِراعِ necessity is the mother of invention 2 [مُتَطَلَّب] requirement 3 [شَيْء] |حَوائِج| thing, object

حاجيّات *n pl* necessities; belongings; stuff; الحاجِيّات اليَوْميّة the daily necessities

احْتِياج *n* |احْتِياجات| need, necessity, requirement; احْتِياجات needs, necessities; لَبّى \ سَدَّ الاحْتِياجاتِ to cater to/fill the needs

تَحَيَّزَ *v* ❶ [حابى] to favour; to side, to take sides; تَحَيَّزَ إلى \ عن to side with/against ❷ [كانَت لَهُ آراءٌ مُسَبَّقةٌ] to be prejudiced

انْحازَ *v* to side; انْحازَ ل \ إلى شَخْصٍ to side with sb, to be on sb's side; to favour sb

احْتازَ *v* to possess; to take possession of; احْتازَ شَيْئاً to take possession of sth

حَوْز *n* ❶ [مَصْدَر] possession ❷ [أَحْواز | أَرْض بِحَواجِز] enclosure

حَيِّز *n* |أَحْياز| room, space; حَيِّز خالٍ space; في حَيِّزِ المَفْهومِ الضَيِّقِ in the narrowest sense; احْتَلَّ \ شَغَلَ حَيِّزاً كَبيراً to take up a lot of room; to occupy a major spot; دَخَلَ حَيِّزَ التَنْفيذِ to come into effect

حائِز *n* |حائِزونَ| possessor; holder

حَوْزة *n* ❶ [مِلْك] possession; كانَ \ أَصْبَحَ في حَوْزَةِ شَخْصٍ to be/come into the possession of sb; كانَ الأَمْرُ في حَوْزَتِهِ \ في حَوْزَةِ يَدِهِ he had it in his possession ❷ [إقْليم] territory; holdings

حِيازة *n* possession

انْحِياز *n* partiality, bias; دُوَل عَدَمِ الانْحِيازِ the non-aligned countries; الانْحِياز لِشَخْصٍ taking sides with sb

تَحَيُّز *n* |تَحَيُّزات| partiality; اتَّهَمَ شَخْصاً بالتَحَيُّزِ to accuse sb of partiality; تَحَيُّز جِنْسيّ \ عِرْقيّ gender/ethnic bias; تَحَيُّز عُنْصُريّ racial prejudice; بِدونِ تَحَيُّزٍ unbiased; dispassionately

مُتَحَيِّز *adj* biased, prejudiced; partial, one-sided; مَعْلومات مُتَحَيِّزة one-sided information; حُكْم \ تَقْرير مُتَحَيِّز a biased ruling/report; صورة مُتَحَيِّزة عن الحَقائِقِ a biased version of the facts

مُنْحاز *adj* partial; biased, prejudiced; مَوْقِف مُنْحاز a biased position; أَخْبار مُنْحازة biased/coloured reporting; غَيْر مُنْحازٍ impartial, non-aligned; الدُوَل غَيْر المُنْحازة the non-aligned countries; مُنْحاز ل \ إلى التِجارة الحُرة partial towards Israel, pro-Israel

〈 **حَوْسَبَ** *n* see حسب

〈 **حاشَ** *v* |u; حَوْش| to surround, to drive into a trap

like carrying coals to Newcastle ❷ (Transp) lane ❸ [زُقاق] lane; alley; حارة السَدِّ a blind alley

حِوار *n* |حِوارات| conversation, talk; dialogue, discussion; debate; حِوار بين طَرَفَيْنِ a talk/dialogue between two parties; جَرى الحِوارُ the dialogue/discussion was held; حِوار ذاتيّ monologue

حَواريّ *n* (Chr) apostle, disciple, follower; الحَوارِيّونَ the Apostles (*the twelve chief disciples of Jesus Christ*)

حورِيّة *n* |حور, حوريّات| houri (*beautiful being of paradise*); nymph; حوريّة البَحْرِ mermaid

أَحْوَر *adj* |dipt; حور| *with beautiful black eyes*; حور عَيْنٍ houris (*beautiful beings of paradise*)

تَحاوُر *n* |تَحاوُرات| discussion

تَحْوير *n* |تَحْويرات| alteration, shuffling; distortion; falsification

مُتَحَوِّر *adj, n* mutant

مُتَمَحْوِر *adj* revolving, rotating

مَحار *n coll* ❶ [صَدَف] shell ❷ (Zool) mollusc, shellfish; oyster; mussel; مَحار مِرْوَحيّ scallop; مَحار اللُؤْلُؤِ pearl oyster

مَحارِيّة *n* shellfish; مَحارِيّات shellfish

مُحاوِر *n* speaker; conversationalist

مُحاوَرة *n* conversation; discussion, dialogue

مِحْوَر *n* |مَحاوِرُ| ❶ [مَدار] axis; pivot; مِحْوَر الأَرْضِ earth's axis; مِحْوَر الشَرِّ the Axis of Evil; مِحْوَر قُطْبيّ polar axis; مِحْوَر طوليّ longitudinal axis; دارَ حولَ مِحْوَرِهِ الطوليِّ to rotate around its longitudinal axis ❷ [مَرْكَز] core, heart, central point; كانَ ذلك مِحْوَرَ المُحادَثةِ that was the focus of the discussion; مِحْوَر أَساسيّ central point ❸ (Mech) axle, spindle; مِحْوَر طاحونةٍ the spindle of a mill ❹ (Math) مِحْوَر س x-axis; مِحْوَر ص y-axis ❺ [طَرَف] side; المِحْوَر اليَمينيّ \ التَقَدُّميّ the right/progressive party; مِحْوَر المُعارَضةِ the opposition

مِحْوَريّ *adj* pivotal, key (*before n*), central; مُشْكِلة مِحْوَرِيّة key problem; شَخْصيّة مِحْوَرِيّة key figure

〈 **حازَ** *v* |u; حَوْز, حِيازة| to obtain, to get; to gain possession of; حازَ جائِزةً \ على جائِزةٍ to win a prize

تَحَوَّزَ *v* ❶ [مَكَثَ] to stay ❷ |عن| [تَنَحّى] to turn away from

حَوَّشَ *v* to save (up); to amass, to hoard; حَوَّش مالاً to save money

حَوْش *n* |حيشان ,أَحْواش| **1** [فِناء] courtyard **2** [حَظيرة] stable; pen; enclosure **3** [ساحة حول دارٍ] yard

حوشيّ *adj* unusual; rare

تَحْويشة *n* تَحْويشة العُمْرِ nest egg (*money saved for the future*)

أَحْوَص *adj* |dipt; حوص| squinting; *with one eye closed*

حَوْصَلة *n* |حَواصِلُ ,حَوْصَلات| (Zool) crop (*a pouch in an animal's gullet where food is stored or prepared for digestion*); حَوْصَلة مَراريّة gall bladder

حُوَيْصِلة *n* **1** (Anat) bladder; حُوَيْصِلة صَفراويّة gall bladder **2** [بَثْرة] blister; vesicle, cyst

حَوْض *n* |أَحْواض ,حِياض ,حيضان| **1** (Geog) basin; حَوْض نَهْرٍ river basin; حَوْض البَحْرِ الأَبْيَضِ المُتَوَسِّطِ the Mediterranean Basin **2** [إناء] basin; sink; tub; حَوْض سِباحةٍ swimming pool; حَوْض حَمّام bathtub; حَوْض غَسيلٍ washbasin, sink; حَوْض ماءٍ water tank, cistern **3** (Naut) shipyard; حَوْض جافّ dry dock; حَوْض عائِم floating dock **4** (Anat) pelvis **5** [حَديقة] (flower) bed

(Idiom) زَهْرة الحَوْضِ (Bot) columbine (*Aquilegia*)

حَوْضيّ *adj* pelvic

حاطَ *v* |u; حَوْط ,حيطة ,حِياطة| **1** [أَحاطَ] to surround, to encircle; تَحوطُهُ العِنايةُ he is the centre of attention; يَحوطُهُ الغُموضُ it is shrouded in mystery **2** [حَفِظَ] to protect, to guard; to defend

حَوَّطَ *v* to wall (in); to enclose; حَوَّطَ حَديقةً to build a wall around a garden

حاوَطَ *v* **1** [طَوَّقَ] to surround; حاوَطَ العَدوُّ المَدينةَ the enemy surrounded the city **2** [خَدَعَ] to mislead

أَحاطَ *v* **1** [حاقَ] to surround, to encircle; أَحاطَ شَيْئًا \ بِشَيْءٍ to surround sth; to come/go with sth; أَحاطَ مَدينةً بِسورٍ to surround a city with a wall; أَحاطَ خَصْرَ شَخْصٍ to put one's arm around sb's waist; المُلابَسات \ الظُروف التي تُحيطُ بِهِ the circumstances that come with it **2** [أَدْرَكَ] to comprehend, to know; أَحاطَ بِشَيْءٍ عِلْماً to know sth thoroughly, to have comprehensive knowledge of sth; أَحاطَ شَخْصاً عِلْماً بِشَيْءٍ to inform sb of sth, to fill sb in on sth

تَحَوَّطَ *v* **1** [حَفِظَ] to protect, to guard **2** [حَذِرَ] to take care, to be on one's guard, to be cautious; تَحَوَّطَ مِن التَضَخُّمِ to hedge against inflation

اِحْتاطَ *v* |ل| to be careful of, to be on one's guard against, to watch out for; اِحْتاطَ لِشَيْءٍ to be on one's guard against sth

حائِط *n* |حَوائِطُ ,حِياط ,حيطان| **1** [جِدار] wall; حائِط فاصِل partition, dividing wall; حائِط خَلْفيّ \ داخِليّ back/inner wall; حائِط المَبْكى the Wailing Wall; تَلْبيس الحائِطِ wallcovering, wallpaper; للحيطانِ آذانٌ the walls have ears; ضَرَبَ بِهِ عُرْضَ الحائِطِ he didn't take the slightest notice of it **2** (Sport) wall

حَوْطة *n* caution, care; reserve, restraint

حيطة *n* |حِيَط| cautiousness, caution; reserve, restraint; أَخَذَ حيطَتَهُ to be on one's guard; to act with restraint; مِن بابِ الحيطةِ as a precaution, to be on the safe side

إحاطة *n* **1** [تَطْويق] encirclement **2** [دِراية] comprehension; إحاطة بالمَعْلوماتِ briefing

اِحْتِياط *n* care, cautiousness, caution; precaution; اِحْتِياط وِقائيّ precautionary measure; ضابِط اِحْتِياطٍ reserve officer; مِن باب الاحْتِياطِ ,على سَبيلِ الاحْتِياطِ as a precaution; اِتَّخَذَ اِحْتِياطاتٍ وِقائيّةً to take precautionary measures; اِتَّخَذَ الاحْتِياطاتِ اللازِمةَ to take the necessary precautions

اِحْتِياطيّ **A** *adj* **1** [وِقائيّ] preventive, preventative; اِحْتِياطِيًّا as a precaution, just in case; إجْراءات اِحْتِياطيّة precautionary measures; أَجْزاء اِحْتِياطيّة spare parts; حَبَسَ شَخْصاً حَبْساً اِحْتِياطِيًّا to remand someone in custody, to keep/hold someone in preventive custody **2** [مَنْسوب إلى الاحْتِياطِ] reserve (*before n*), spare; قوّات اِحْتِياطيّة reserve troops, reserves; إطار اِحْتِياطيّ spare (tyre), spare wheel; لاعِب اِحْتِياطيّ reserve, substitute; نُسْخة اِحْتِياطيّة extra copy, backup

B *n* reserve; اِحْتِياطيّ نَقْديّ \ النَفْط financial/oil reserves; تَوَفَّرَ عِنْدَهُ الاحْتِياطيُّ (اللازِمُ) to have the necessary reserves

مُحاط *adj* surrounded; مُحاط بِأَشْجارٍ surrounded/fenced in by trees; مُحاط بالغُموضِ shrouded in mystery; مُحاط بالأَرْضِ landlocked

مُحيط **A** *adj* surrounding
B *n* |مُحيطات| **1** [بيئة] environment; المُحيط العائليّ the family situation, the domestic environment; المُحيط الاجْتِماعيّ the social climate **2** [الضَواحي] surroundings; periphery **3** [بَحْر] ocean; المُحيط الهادِئ \ الباسيفيكيّ the Pacific (Ocean); المُحيط الأَطْلَسيّ the Atlantic (Ocean); المُحيط الهِنْديّ the Indian Ocean; المُحيط القُطْبيّ الشَماليّ the Arctic Ocean; عِلْم المُحيطاتِ oceanography **4** (Geom) circumference; perimeter; مُحيط دائِرةٍ the circumference of a circle; مُحيط مُرَبَّعٍ \ مُضَلَّعٍ the perimeter of a square/polygon

مُحيطيّ *adj* **1** [خاصّ بِمُحيطِ الشَكْلِ الخارِجيِّ] peripheral; surrounding **2** [مَنْسوب إلى البَحْرِ] oceanic **3** [بيئيّ] environmental

‹ **حافة** *n* |حَوافٍ, حافات| edge; margin; border

‹ **حاقَ** *v* |i; حَيْق| ب| to happen to, to come to; حاقَتْ بِهِ كارِثةٌ he was hit by a disaster

حَوَّقَ *v* to surround, to enclose

أحاقَ *v* |ب| to bring down (on); to draw around

مُحيق *adj* surrounding

‹ **حَوْقَلَ** *v* |i; حَوْقَلة| *to pronounce the formula* لا حَوْلَ وَلا قوّةَ إلاّ باللهِ

‹ **حاكَ** *v* |u; حَوْك, حِياك, حِياكة| **1** [نَسَجَ] to weave; to knit; حاكَ قِطْعةَ قُماشٍ to weave a cloth **2** [لَفَّقَ] to contrive; حاكَ مُؤامَرةً to hatch a plot

حَوْك *n* (sweet) basil

حائِك *n* |حاكة| weaver; knitter

حِياكة *n* weaving; knitting; إبْرة حِياكةٍ knitting needle

‹ **حالَ** *v* |u| **1** [مَنَعَ] |حَيْلولة; دون| to prevent (from), to stop (from); حالَ دون تَرَدّي الأَوْضاعِ to stop the situation from deteriorating; حالَ دون قُدومِ شَخْصٍ to prevent sb from coming; حالَ بين شَخْصَيْنِ to interfere, to stand between two people **2** [تَغَيَّرَ] |حالة| to change

حَوِلَ *v* |a; حَوَل| to squint; to be cross-eyed

حَوَّلَ *v* **1** [غَيَّرَ] to change, to transform; حَوَّلَ شَيْئاً إلى شَيْءٍ آخَرَ to change sth into sth else; حَوَّلَ الخَشَبَ إلى وَرَقٍ to turn wood into paper; حَوَّلَ مَكانَ شَيْءٍ to change the location of sth; حَوَّلَ السَيْرَ to divert traffic; حَوَّلَ الأَقْوالَ إلى أَفْعالٍ to turn words into action; حَوَّلَ اتِّجاهَ شَيْءٍ to change the course/direction of sth; حَوَّلَ دَنانيرَ إلى دولاراتٍ to exchange dinars for/into dollars **2** (Busn) to transfer; حَوَّلَ مَبْلَغاً إلى حِسابٍ to transfer an amount to an account, to pay an amount into an account; حَوَّلَ مالاً to transfer money; حَوَّلَ مالاً إلى شَخْصٍ to transfer money to sb **3** (Elec) to transform **4** [رِسالةً] to forward **5** [نَقَلَ] to move; to shift; حَوَّلَ اهْتِمامَهُ إلى شَيْءٍ \ شَخْصٍ to direct one's attention to sth/sb; حَوَّلَ نَظَرَهُ إلى شَيْءٍ to turn one's eye on sth; حَوَّلَ طَريقاً \ شارِعاً to re-route a road

حاوَلَ *v* to try, to attempt; حاوَلَ أنْ يَقْرَأَ to try to read; حاوَلَ الاتِّصالَ بِشَخْصٍ to try to reach sb; حاوَلَ الكَشْفَ عن شَيْءٍ to try to discover/find out sth; حاوَلَ عَبَثاً to make a vain/fruitless attempt; حاوَلَ قَدْرَ جُهْدِهِ to try one's best

أحالَ *v* **1** [إلى شَخْصٍ] to refer (to); أحالَ شَخْصاً إلى الطَبيبِ المُخْتَصِّ to refer sb to a specialist; أحالَ القاضي القَضيّةَ إلى مَحْكَمةٍ أُخْرى the judge referred the case to another court **2** [غَيَّرَ] |إلى| to change into **3** [سَلَّمَ] to turn over, to hand over, to pass on; أحالَ العَمَلَ إلى مُساعِدِهِ to leave the work to one's assistant

تَحَوَّلَ *v* **1** [تَغَيَّرَ] |إلى| to change into, to transform into, to become; تَحَوَّلَ إلى أميرٍ to turn into a prince; تَحَوَّلَ إلى كَوْمةِ رَمادٍ to be reduced to ashes; تَحَوَّلَتْ إشارةُ المُرورِ إلى الأَخْضَرِ the light turned green; تَحَوَّلَ من الحالةِ الصُلْبةِ إلى الحالةِ السائِلةِ to turn from solid into liquid form **2** [تَنَقَّلَ] to move (house); تَحَوَّلَ إلى دارٍ أُخْرى to move house **3** [انْصَرَفَ] to turn away, to renounce; تَحَوَّلَ من \ عن النِظامِ الشُيوعيِّ to turn away from communism

تَحَيَّلَ *v* to use cunning

تَحايَلَ *v* |على| to mislead, to deceive; تَحايَلَ على القانونِ to get around the law

احْتالَ *v* |على| to deceive, to mislead; to tempt; احْتالَ على شَخْصٍ to deceive sb; احْتالَ على الضَرائِبِ to cheat on (one's) taxes; احْتالَ على القانونِ to get around the law

احْوَلَّ *v* to squint; to be cross-eyed

اسْتَحالَ *v* 1 [صارَ مُحالاً] to be/become impossible; يَسْتَحيلُ أنْ تَذْهَبَ you can't go 2 [تَغيَّرَ] |إلى| to change (into)

حوَّل *adj* إنَّهُ رَجُلٌ حوَّلٌ قُلَّبٌ he is a fickle-hearted man

حَوْل *n* |أحْوال| 1 [سَنة] year 2 [قوّة] power; لا حَوْلَ وَلا قوّةَ إلاّ باللهِ there is no power and no strength save in God; كانَ بِحَوْلِ اللهِ لا حَوْلَ لَهُ وَلا حيلة he was completely powerless; in God's good graces, all being well

حَوْلَ *prep* 1 [ما يُحيطُ بِهِ] around; حَوْلَ القَصْرِ around the palace; نظَرَ حَوْلَهُ to look around 2 [عَنْ] about, concerning, around; دِراسة حَوْلَ شَيْءٍ a study on sth; دارَ المَقالُ حَوْلَ المَغْرِبِ the article was about Morocco 3 [تَقْريباً] about

حَيْل *n* strength; شُدَّ حَيْلَكَ! take heart!, take care!

حائِل A *adj* 1 [مُتَغيِّر|حوَّل|] variable 2 [باهِت] pale
B *n* 1 [عائِق] |حَوائِلُ| obstacle, impediment, obstruction; وَقَفَ حائِلاً دون \ أمام شَيْءٍ to stand in the way of sth
2 [حاجِز] folding screen, divider, partition; divider, partition; baffle

حال *n* |mf; أحْوال| 1 [وَضْع] situation; state, condition; position; الأَحْوال الجَوّيّة the weather conditions; دائِرة \ مَصْلَحة الأَحْوالِ المَدَنيّةِ Register Office (BrE), County Clerk's Office (AmE); قانون الأَحْوالِ الشَخْصيّةِ family law, personal status law; في الحالِ, حالاً immediately, now; في حالِ ... in case of ...; في أَفْضَلِ حالٍ \ الحالاتِ in the best condition; في هذه الحالِ in this case; على أيِّ \ كُلِّ حالٍ anyhow; مَهْما كانَت الأَحْوالُ whatever the case may be; كَما هو الحالُ as is the case; كيف الحالُ \ حالُكَ؟ how are you?; عادَ إلى حالِهِ to get back to normal; بَقِيَ على حالِهِ to remain unaltered; أُريدُ أنْ أُكَلِّمَهُ حالَ وُصولِهِ I want to talk to him as soon as he arrives; يَبْقى البَيْتُ على حالِهِ the house remains as is 2 (Ling) circumstantial accusative

حالة *n* 1 [ظَرْف] situation; circumstance; state, condition; حالة بَدَنيّة \ جَسَديّة physical condition; حالة ذِهْنيّة \ عَقْليّة mental condition; حالة نَفْسيّة mood, disposition, state of mind; mental constitution; حالة مُتَأَزِّمة crisis situation; حالة مَدَنيّة marital status; حالة المَريضِ the patient's condition; حالة الطُرُق the condition of the roads; كانَ في حالةٍ جَيِّدةٍ \ سَيِّئةٍ to be in good/bad condition, to be doing well/badly; كانَ في حالةِ اسْتِعْدادٍ \ حَرْبٍ to be in a state of readiness/war 2 [قَضيّة] case; حالة اسْتِثْنائيّة exceptional case; حالة مُسْتَعْجَلة emergency case; urgency; حالة طِبّيّة عاجِلة medical urgency; في حالةِ ... if ..., in the case that/of ...; في حالةِ الضَرورةِ in case of emergency/need; نَظَرَ في كُلِّ حالةٍ على حِدةٍ to examine sth case by case 3 (Ling) case; حالة إعْرابيّة case; حالة النَصْبِ the accusative (case)

حالَما *conj* as soon as; once; أَرْجو أنْ تَتَّصِلَ بي حالَما تَعودُ إلى بَيْتِكَ I trust you will call me as soon as you get home

حاليّ *adj* present, current; العُنْوان الحاليّ the current address; السِياسة \ المُسْتَوى \ الحُكومة الحاليّ(ة) the present politics/level/government; الرَئيس الحاليّ للجَمْعيّة the incumbent president of the society; حاليًّا at present, now, today, at this moment; في السَنةِ الحاليّةِ in the current year; this year; السِعْر الحاليّ the current price

حاليّة *n* actuality

حُؤول *n* 1 [تَحوُّل] change, transformation, turning 2 [مَنْع] prevention; الحُؤول دون الأَخْطاءِ the prevention of error

حَوالة *n* check; bill (of exchange); حَوالة بَريديّة postal/money order; حَوالة دَيْنٍ promissory note

حَوالَيْ A *prep* around, about (BrE); نَحْتَشِدُ حَوالَي النارِ we gather around the fire
B *adv* about, around, approximately; حَوالَيْ أَرْبَعةِ أَشْهُرٍ about four months

حَوْليّ *adj* temporary; periodical, cyclical; perennial; annual

حَوْليّة *n* yearbook; periodical; حَوْليّات annals; حَوْليّات الجامِعةِ the annals of the university; the university yearbooks; حَوْليّات التاريخ the pages of history

حِيالَ *prep* regarding, (related) to; رَدّة الفِعْلِ السَلْبيّة حِيالَ القِمّةِ العَرَبيّةِ the negative reaction to the Arab summit; مَناعة حِيالَ شَيْءٍ immunity to sth

تَحْويل *n* |تَحْويلات| **1** [إرْسال] referral; transfer; تَحْويل إلى قِسْمٍ آخَرَ a transfer to another department **2** [تَبْديل] change; conversion; transformation; تَحْويل شَيْءٍ إلى شَيْءٍ آخَرَ the conversion of sth into sth else; تَحْويل دَيْنٍ the conversion of a loan/debt **3** (Busn) transfer, remittance; remittance; تَحْويل إلى حِسابٍ a transfer of credit to an account **4** [نَقْل] transfer; قابِل للتَحْويلِ transferable; exchangeable; أَسْهُم قابِلة للتَحْويلِ transferable shares; غَيْر قابِلٍ للتَحْويلِ non-transferable **5** (Phys) transformation **6** [صَرْف النُقودِ] exchange

تَحْويلة *n* |تَحاويل| **1** [السِكّةِ الحَديديّة] (railroad) switch **2** [طَريق بَديل] diversion

تَحْويليّ *adj* transformational; نَحْو تَحْويليّ transformational grammar

مُتَحَوِّل *adj* changeable, variable; مُتَحَوِّل الجِنْسِ transgender

مُحال *adj* impossible; absurdity; من المُحالِ أنْ ... it is impossible that...; هو أَمْرٌ مُحالٌ it is an impossibility

مَحالة *n* (مِنْهُ \ عَنْهُ) لا مَحالةَ inevitable; undeniably; absolutely

مُحاوَلة *n* attempt; مُحاوَلة جادّة a serious attempt; مُحاوَلة جَديدة \ ناجِحة \ فاشِلة a new/successful/unsuccessful attempt; مُحاوَلة أَخيرة a final attempt; مُحاوَلات مُسْتَمِرّة constant attempts; مُحاوَلة قَتْلٍ attempted murder; مُحاوَلة وَقْفِ الحَرْبِ an attempt to stop the war; قامَ بِمُحاوَلةٍ to make an attempt

مُحْتال **A** *adj* shrewd, artful; sly, cunning **B** *n* cheat, shyster, swindler; fraud, imposter; conman

مُحَوِّل *n* |مُحَوِّلات| **1** (Elec) transformer; adapter **2** [مَصْنَع] processor

مُحَوِّلة *n* (railroad) switch

مُسْتَحيل **A** *adj* impossible; شَيْء مُسْتَحيل impossibility; مُهِمّة \ خُطّة مُسْتَحيلة an impossible task/plan; شُروط مُسْتَحيلة impossible demands/conditions; هذا مُسْتَحيلٌ that is impossible/out of the question; there is no such thing; هذا عَمَلٌ مُسْتَحيلٌ this can't be done; اعْتَبَرَ شَيْئاً من المُسْتَحيلِ to consider sth impossible **B** *n* |مُسْتَحيلات| impossibility; عُدَّ من المُسْتَحيلاتِ to be beyond the bounds of the possible

حيلة *n* |حِيَل| trick, ruse; dodge, device; حيلة بارِعة an ingenious trick; حيلة طَريفة an funny trick; حِيَل تِقْنيّة technical tricks; حِيَل سينَمائيّة special effects, stunts; حيلة لاكْتِشافِ شَيْءٍ a ruse to find out sth; واسِع الحيلةِ ingenious; لَجَأَ إلى حيلةٍ to employ a ruse; ابْتَدَعَ حيلةً to invent a trick; انْطَلَتْ عَلَيْهِ الحيلةُ he was fooled (by the trick); لم يَجِدْ حيلةً he saw no deception; ما الحيلةُ؟ what's the trick to it?

حَيْلولة *n* prevention; الحَيْلولة دون حُدوثِ أَعْمالٍ إرْهابيّةٍ the prevention of terrorist activities

إحالة *n* referring, referral; إحالة مُزْدَوِجة cross-reference; إحالة مَسْأَلةٍ على شَخْصٍ referring a matter to sb; إحالة مُجْرِمٍ إلى القَضاءِ handing a criminal over to justice

احْتِيال *n* |احْتِيالات| fraud, con, swindle; fraudulence, trickery; عَمَليّة احْتِيالٍ واسِعة النِطاقِ a massive swindle; احْتِيال ضَريبيّ tax fraud

احْتِياليّ *adj* fraudulent

أَحْوَل *adj* |dipt; حول| squinting; cross-eyed; كانَ أَحْوَلَ to have a squint; to be cross-eyed

اسْتِحالة *n* **1** [تَعَذُّر] impossibility; absurdity; اسْتِحالة الخُروجِ من المِنْطَقةِ the impossibilty of leaving the area **2** [تَحَوُّل] difference **3** (Chem) transformation, conversion; metamorphosis **4** (Chr) transubstantiation (*the conversion of the bread and wine used in the sacrament of the Eucharist into the body and blood of Christ*)

تَحايُل *n* trickery, cunning, fraud; التَحايُل على القانونِ \ الضَرائِبِ legal/ tax fraud

تَحَوُّل *n* |تَحَوُّلات| **1** [تَغَيُّر] change, transformation; turn, swing; transition; تَحَوُّل إيجابيّ a positive change; تَحَوُّل جِنْسيّ transgenderism; التَحَوُّل من نِظامٍ إلى نِظامٍ بَديلٍ the transition from one system to another; نُقْطة تَحَوُّلٍ تاريخيّة، نُقْطة تَحَوُّلٍ في التاريخِ a historic turning point; نُقْطة تَحَوُّلٍ في حَياتي a turning point in my life; شَكَّلَ نُقْطةَ تَحَوُّلٍ to be a turning point **2** (Bio) metamorphosis, transformation **3** (Phys) transformation

تَحَوُّليّ *adj* transformational; نَحْو تَحْويليّ \ تَحَوُّليّ transformational grammar

حامَ *v* |u; حَوْم, حَوَمان| to circle, to go around; to hover; حامَت الشُبُهاتُ حَوْلَهُ people doubted him; الشُكوكُ حَوْلَهُ he was suspected; حامَ حول \ على to hang around; مَنْ حامَ حول الحِمى يوشِكُ أنْ يَقَعَ فيهِ if you play with fire, you'll get burned

حَوَّمَ *v* to circle, to go around; to whirl; to hover; حَوَّمَتْ بِهِ الذِكْرَياتُ memories whirled about in his mind

حَوّامة *n* **1** [طائِرة مِرْوَحيّة] helicopter **2** [مَرْكَب بَرْمائيّ] hovercraft

حَوْمة *n* **1** [وَطيس] *the heat of battle* **2** [حَيّ] quarter

حَوى *v* |i; حَواية| **1** [تَضَمَّنَ] to contain, to hold; to comprise; تَحْوي هذه المَدينةُ ٧٠٠٠٠٠ نَسَمةٍ this city has 700,000 inhabitants **2** [اسْتَوْلى] to obtain **3** [جَمَعَ] to gather

تَحَوّى *v* to curl up; to be rolled up

احْتَوى *v* to contain; to comprise; to hold; احْتَوى شَيْئاً \ على شَيْءٍ to contain/hold sth; احْتَوى أَزْمةً to manage a crisis

حاوٍ **A** *adj* containing

B *n* **1** [فاتِن الأفاعي |حُواة|] snake charmer **2** [مُشَعْوِذ] charlatan (*a person who claims to possess magical power*)

حاوِية *n* container; حاوِية القُمامةِ \ الفَضَلاتِ skip (BrE), dumpster (AmE); سَفينة حاوِياتٍ container ship; فَرَّغَ \ شَحَنَ حاوِيةً to unload/load a container

حَوِيّة *n* |حَوايا| twist, coil

احْتِواء *n* control, management; احْتِواء الأَزْمةِ management of the crisis; احْتِواء التَكْلِفةِ cost containment

مُحْتَوًى *n* |مُحْتَوَيات| content; substance; مُحْتَوَيات contents; table of contents; مُحْتَوًى مَفْتوح open content; مُحْتَوى البَرْنامِجِ programme content; الصورة والمُحْتَوى form and content; نِظام إدارة المُحْتَوى content management system; بِدونِ مُحْتَوًى without substance; مُحْتَوى الدَسَمِ fat content

حَيْثُ **A** *adv* where; إلى حَيْثُ to where; عادَ إلى \ من حَيْثُ بَدَأَ he went back to where he started; المَدينة حَيْثُ يَسْكُنُ the city where he lives; وَصَلْنا إلى الخَرْطومِ حَيْثُ مَكَثْنا خَمْسةَ أيّامٍ we arrived in Khartoum where we stayed five days

B *conj* since, because, as; حَيْثُ أنّ because, since, as; حَيْثُ تَبَيَّنَ أنّ ... since it turned out that; من حَيْثُ with respect to ..., as to ..., regarding ...; من حَيْثُ المَبْدَأ in principle; من حَيْثُ السَلامةِ because of safety concerns; بِحَيْثُ to, so (that), in order that; أنا مَريضٌ بِحَيْثُ لا أَسْتَطيعُ الصَوْمَ I am ill, so I cannot fast

حَيْثُما *conj* wherever

حَيْثيّة *n* (Law) argument; حَيْثيّات الحُكْمِ the considerations on which the judgement is based

حادَ *v* |i; حَيْد, حُيود, مَحيد| to deviate; to keep away from; حادَ عن الحَقِّ to abandon one's principles; حادَ عن مَبادِئِهِ والصَوابِ to deviate from the right path

حَيَّدَ *v* **1** [جَعَلَهُ مُحايِداً] to neutralize **2** [وَضَعَ إلى الجانِبِ] to keep/put aside

حايَدَ *v* **1** [مالَ] to deviate **2** [تَجَنَّبَ] to avoid; to keep aloof

حِياد *n* neutrality, impartiality; aloofness; وَقَفَ على الحِيادِ to be neutral; الْتَزَمَ الحِيادَ في النِقاشِ to be/stay neutral in the discussion

حِياديّ *adj* neutral, impartial; مَوْقِف حِياديّ impartial stance

حِياديّة *n* neutrality

حَيْدة *n* **1** [مَيَلان] deviation; curving, tilting **2** [عَدَم التَحَيُّز] neutrality, impartiality

حُيود *n* diffraction (*of light or rays*)

تَحْييد *n* neutralization

مُحايِد **A** *adj* neutral; independent; بَلَد \ دَوْلة مُحايِد(ة) a neutral country/state; القاضي المُحايِد the impartial judge; لَجْنة تَحْكيمٍ مُحايِدة an independent jury; لَوْن مُحايِد a neutral color; في مِنْطَقةٍ مُحايِدةٍ on neutral ground/territory; في عِباراتٍ مُحايِدةٍ in impartial terms; بَقِيَ \ ظَلَّ مُحايِداً to remain neutral

B *n* neuter

مُحايَدة *n* keeping aloof; neutrality, impartiality

مَحيد *n* avoiding; لا مَحيدَ عَنْهُ inevitably

حَيْدَر *n* **1** [أَسَد] lion **2** [اسْم شَخْصيّ] Haydar (*male given name*)

حارَ *v* |a; حَيْرة, حَيَران| **1** [تَرَدَّدَ] to become confused, to be upset; to hesitate, to be in doubt; حارَ في أَمْرِهِ to hesitate, to waver **2** [رَجَعَ] see حور

حَيَّر *v* to confuse; حَيَّرَ شَخْصاً to confuse sb; to embarrass sb

تَحَيَّر *v* to be/become confused; to waver; تَحَيَّرَ في الأمْرِ to be confused, to be at loss, to waver

احْتارَ *v* to be/become confused

حائِر *adj* confused; حائِر في أَمْرِهِ confused, upset; helpless

حَيْران *adj* |حَيارى| confused; startled, perplexed

حَيْرة ,حيرة *n* confusion, bewilderment; في حَيْرَةٍ confused, at a loss; كانَ في حَيْرَةٍ من to be/become confused; وَقَعَ في حَيْرَةٍ أَمْرِهِ to be confused; to be helpless; to waver

مُتَحَيِّر *adj* confused, bewildered, perplexed

مُحَيِّر *adj* confusing, baffling

الحيرة *n* al-Hirah (*ancient city in Iraq*)

حيز *n* see حوز\حيز

حاصَ *v* |i; حَيْصة ,حَيْص| to flee, to escape

حيص ,حَيْص *n* escape; وَقَعَ في حيصَ بيصَ to get into trouble

مَحيص *n* escape; place of refuge; ما عَنْهُ مَحيصٌ it is unavoidable

حاضَ *v* |i; مَحاض ,مَحيض ,حَيْض| to menstruate, to have one's period

حَيْض *n* menstruation, period

حائِض *adj* |f; حَوائِضُ| menstruating; فَتاة حائِض a girl that has her period

مَحيض *n* menstruation, period; سِنّ المَحيضِ sexual maturity age (*of a girl*)

حافَ *v* |i; حَيْف| |على| to treat unjustly; حافَ على شَخْصٍ to treat sb unjustly, to do sb wrong

حَيْف *n* ① [ظُلْم] wrong, injustice ② [جَوْر] absolutism, tyranny

حَيْفا *n* Haifa (*city in Israel*)

حانَ *v* |i; حَيْنونة ,حَيْن| to come, to arrive; حانَ الوَقْتُ \ المَوْعِدُ the time has come, it's time, the moment has arrived; حانَ الوَقْتُ ل ... the time has come to; لم تَحِن الساعةُ بَعْدُ the time has not yet come; حانَ أَجَلُهُ his time has come, he is not long (for this world); حانَ لَهُ أنْ ... it's time for him to ...; حانَ دَوْرُكَ it's your turn

حَيَّنَ *v* to set a time; to update

تَحَيَّنَ *v* to wait for; تَحَيَّنَ الفُرْصةَ to wait for the opportunity

حين *n* |أحايينُ ,أَحْيان| time, period; أَحْياناً sometimes, now and then, occasionally; حيناً for some time; في حينِهِ in due time; في الحينِ immediately, directly, right away; على \ في حينِ (أنّ) while, whereas; when; في بَعْضِ الأَحْيانِ sometimes; في أَحْيانٍ كَثيرةٍ often; في أَغْلَبِ الأَحْيانِ mostly, generally; من حينٍ لِآخَرَ from time to time; حينٍ إلى حينٍ now and then, from time to time; بين حينٍ وَحينٍ now and then, from time to time; بين الحينِ والآخَرِ from time to time; كُلّ شَيْءٍ في حينِهِ all in due course; حيناً ...وَحيناً آخَرَ ... sometimes ...but other times...; من \ مُنْذُ ذلك الحينِ from then on, since (then); لا \ لم ... إلاّ بعد حينٍ only after some time

حينَ *conj* (at the time) when; حينَ كُنْتُ صَغيراً when I was young

حانة *n* bar, pub

حينَئِذٍ *adv* then, at the time; كانَ حينَئِذٍ مُوَظَّفاً حُكوميًّا at the time he was a government official

حينَذاكَ *adv* then, at the time

حينَما *conj* when, as; while; حينَما عادَ إلى البَيْتِ وَجَدَ صَديقَهُ يَنْتَظِرُهُ when he went back home he found his friend waiting for him

تَحْيين *n* update

حَيَّ ,حَيِيَ *v* |a; حَياة| to live; يَحْيا الرَّئيسُ! long live the president!

حَيّا *v* ① [أَبْقى] to keep alive; حَيّاكَ اللهُ may God grant you a long life; God keep you ② [سَلَّمَ على] to greet, to say hello; حَيّا الجَماهيرَ to greet the people

أَحْيا *v* ① [جَدَّدَ] to bring back to life, to revive; to liven up; to stimulate; أَحْيا الماضِيَ to revive the past ② [أَحْيا ذِكْرى] ذِكْرى شَخْصٍ to commemorate sb's memory ③ [أَعْطى الحَياةَ ل] to lend life to sth, to call sth into being; to resurrect sth

اسْتَحْيا ,اسْتَحى *v* |من| to be ashamed; to be/become embarrassed; اسْتَحْيا من شَيْءٍ to be ashamed of sth

حَيِيّ *adj* modest; shy; easily embarrassed

حُيَي *n* |**حُيَيّات**| (Bio) حُيَيّ مَنَوِيّ sperm cell

حَيّ **A** *adj* |**أَحْياء**| **1** [عائِش] living, alive; أُحْرِقَ حَيًّا to be burnt alive **2** [حاضِر] live; present; موسيقى حَيّة live music; تَغْطِيَة حَيّة live coverage **3** [مُشْتَغِل] live; active, working; ذَخيرة \ رَصاص حَيّ(ة) live ammunition/cartridges; لُغة حَيّة a living language; حَيّ الضَمير conscientious; عَمِلَ بِضَميرٍ حَيٍّ to act conscientiously

B *n* |**أَحْياء**| **1** [كائِن] organism, living being; عِلْم الأَحْياءِ biology; اخْتِصاصيّ في عِلْم الأَحْياءِ biologist; حَيّ دَقيق microorganism **2** [مِنْطَقة] district, quarter, neighbourhood; حَيّ فَقير \ شَعْبيّ a poor/working class neighbourhood; حَيّ راقٍ \ غَنيّ a wealthy area; الأَحْياء القَديمة the old quarters; the historic district; حَيّ سَكَنيّ جَديد a new housing development; حَيّ سَكَنيّ في دِمَشْقَ a residential area in Damascus; ساكِن الحَيِّ local resident **3** (Islam) الحَيّ the Living (*one of the names of God*)

حَيَّ *excl* come on!; حَيَّ على let's get to work!; حَيَّ على العَمَلِ come to prayer!; حَيَّ بِنا! let's go! الصَلاةِ!

حَياء *n* modesty; shame; bashfulness; قَليل الحَياءِ shameless, impudent; قِلّة الحَياءِ shamelessness, impudence; كانَ قَليلَ الحَياءِ to be shameless; بدونِ \ بِغَيْرِ حَياءٍ shameless, without shame

حَياة *n* |**حَيَوات**| **1** [عَيْش] life; حَياة زَوْجيّة married life, marriage; حَياة عائِليّة \ أُسَريّة family life; حَياة عَمَليّة working life; career; حَياة خاصّة \ شَخْصيّة private/personal life; الحَياة اليَوْميّة daily life; حَياة مُريحة \ جَميلة a comfortable/beautiful life; الحَياة الأَبَديّة eternal life; حَياة إِنْسانٍ human life; لِمَدى الحَياةِ for life, lifetime (*before n*); ظُروف الحَياةِ living conditions; أُسْلوب الحَياةِ lifestyle; مَسار الحَياةِ path (of life); في مَسارِ حَياتِها on her path; سيرة الحَياةِ career; curriculum vitae; عاشَ حَياةً مُمِلّةً \ مُثيرةً to live a boring/exciting life; هكذا هي الحَياةُ that's life; وَحَياةِ رَأْسي I swear on my life; قابِل للحَياةِ (Med) viable **2** [عَكْس مَوْت] life; على قَيْدِ الحَياةِ alive; قُبْلة الحَياةِ mouth-to-mouth resuscitation; فارَقَ الحَياةَ to depart; خاطَرَ بِحَياتِهِ to risk one's life; وَهَبَ حَياتَهُ لِوَطَنِهِ to give one's life for one's country; خافَ على حَياتِهِ to fear for one's life; ما زالَ على \ بَقِيَ على قَيْدِ الحَياةِ to stay alive; to still be alive; أَنْقَذَ حَياةَ شَخْصٍ to save sb's life; لم يَأْمَنْ على حَياتِهِ he wasn't safe; كانَ مَديناً لِشَخْصٍ بِحَياتِهِ to owe one's life to sb; لا يَأْسَ مع الحَياةِ وَلا حَياةَ مع اليَأْسِ where there is life there is hope

حَياتيّ *adj* life (*before n*); مَشاكِل حَياتيّة problems of life

حَيّة *n* **1** (Zool) snake, serpent; حَيّة سامّة \ مَسْمومة a poisonous/venomous snake; فَحيح حَيّةٍ the hissing of a snake **2** (fig) bitch

حَيَوان *n* |**حَيَوانات**| animal, beast; حَيَوان أَليف pet; domesticated animal; حَيَوانات بَرّيّة \ مائيّة wild/aquatic animals; حَيَوان مُفْتَرِس predator; حَيَوانات مَنَويّة sperm; حَيَوانات سيناءَ the animal life of the Sinai; عِلْم الحَيَوانِ zoology; عالَم الحَيَوانِ fauna, animal life; مَمْلَكة الحَيَواناتِ animal kingdom; الاتِّجار بالحَيَواناتِ animal trade; حَديقة الحَيَواناتِ zoo; جَمْعيّة الرِفْقِ بالحَيَوانِ humane society

حَيَوانيّ *adj* animal (*before n*); طَعام \ دُهْن \ بروتين حَيَوانيّ animal food/fat/protein; غَرائِز حَيَوانيّة animal instincts; إِنْتاج حَيَوانيّ animal production

حَيَويّ *adj* **1** [مَنْسوب إِلى الحَياةِ] life (*before n*); lively; مَدينة حَيَويّة a lively city; شَخْصيّة حَيَويّة a lively personality; كُتْلة حَيَويّة biomass; المَصالِح الحَيَويّة viable interests (*of a country*); مُضادّ حَيَويّ antibiotic **2** [أَساسيّ] vital, essential, crucial; central; عامِل حَيَويّ a crucial factor; وَظيفة حَيَويّة a critical role; a vital function

حَيَويّة *n* activity, liveliness, vitality; إِعادة الحَيَويّة revival; مُفْعَم بالحَيَويّةِ lively, full of life, sparkling; عَديم الحَيَويّة stuffy, dull; يَفيضُ حَيَويّةً وَنَشاطاً he is brimming with vitality and activity

إِحْياء *n* revival; revivification; إِحْياء ذِكْرى commemoration; أَعادَ إِحْياءَ المُعاهَدةِ to breath new life into the agreement; إِعادة إِحْياءِ ثَقافةٍ a cultural revival

أَحْيائيّ **A** *adj* biological; عالِم أَحْيائيّ biologist

B *n* biologist

أَحْيى *adj* livelier, more alive

اسْتِحْياء *n* shame; shyness

تَحيّة *n* |تَحايا, تَحيّات| greeting, salutation; **تَحيّة شَرفيّة** salute; **مع تَحيّاتِ** with the compliments of; **مع أطْيَبِ \ أحَرِّ التَحيّاتِ** with the kindest /warmest regards; **أَوْصِلْ \ بَلِّغْ تَحيّاتي إلى ...** say hello to..., give my regards to...; **التَحيّة العَسْكَرِيّة** the (military) salute; **أدّى التَحيّةَ (العَسْكَرِيّة)** to give the salute, to salute; to present arms; **أدّى التَحيّةَ لِشَخْصٍ** to give a salute to sb, to salute sb; to present arms to sb; **رَدَّ على التَحيّةِ العَسْكَرِيّةِ** to return the salute

مُحْيٍ *n* **المُحْيي** the Giver of Life (*one of the names of God*); **مُحْيي الدينِ** Muhyi al-Din (*male given name*)

مَحْيا *n* |مَحايٍ| life

مُحَيًّا *n* face; countenance; visage

خاء *n* |f| *name of the letter* خ

خابور *n* see خبر

خارصين *n* zinc

خاقان *n* |خَواقينُ| ruler; emperor

خام A *adj* |mf| raw, crude, unprocessed; زَيْت \ نَفْط خام crude oil; حَديد خام iron ore; مادّة خام raw material; مَوادّ خام صِناعيّة industrial raw materials; نَقْص في المَوادِّ الخامِ a shortage of raw materials

B *n* |خامات| ore; raw material

خان *n* |خانات| hostel; خان الخَليليّ Khan al-Khalili (*bazaar in Cairo*)

خانة *n* 1 [عَمود] column; الخانة الأَخيرة closing entry 2 (Math) خانة الآحادِ units; خانة العَشَراتِ tens; خانة المِئاتِ hundreds; خانة الآلافِ thousands 3 (Comput) field, box; خانة بَحْثٍ search box; خانات إلْزاميّة required fields

خانْقاة *n* |خَوانِقُ| guest house; caravanserai (BrE)

خَبأَ *v* |a; خَبْء| to hide, to conceal

خَبَّأَ *v* to hide; to conceal; خَبَّأَ شَخْصاً \ شَيْئاً to hide sb/sth; ما يُخَبِّئُ لَنا المُسْتَقْبَلُ, تُخَبِّئُ لَنا الأَيّامُ what the future has in store for us; هو غافِلٌ عَمّا تُخَبِّئُ لَهُ الأَيّامُ he doesn't know what the future may bring

تَخَبَّأَ *v* to hide, to conceal oneself; to be hidden; تَخَبَّأَ وراء شَجَرةٍ \ حائِطٍ to hide behind a tree/wall

اخْتَبَأَ *v* to hide, to conceal oneself; to be hidden; to be in hiding; اخْتَبَأَ في مَبْنًى to hide in a building; اخْتَبَأَ وراء شَجَرةٍ \ حائِطٍ to hide behind a tree/wall; اخْتَبَأَ خلال الحَرْبِ to go into hiding during the war

خابِية, خابِئة *n* |خَوابٍ| (earthenware) jar; jug; pot

خِباء *n* |أَخْبِية| 1 [خَيْمة] tent 2 [قَصَل] husk

خَبيئة *n* |خَبايا| secret, hidden thing; خَبايا القَلْبِ secrets of the heart; خَبايا النَّفْسِ secrets of the soul

مَخْبَأ *n* |مَخابِئُ| hiding place, refuge; hideout; (air-raid) shelter; مَخْبَأ آمِن a safe hiding place; بَحَثَ عن مَخْبَأٍ to look for a place to hide

مُخَبَّأ *adj* hidden; مُخَبَّآت hidden things; صَفْحة مُخَبَّأة (Comput) cached page

خَبَّ *v* |u; خَبَب| to trot

خَبَب *n* trot

خَبُثَ *v* |u; خُبْث| 1 [كانَ مُؤْذِياً] to be wicked; to be malicious 2 (Med) to be/become malignant

تَخابَثَ *v* to behave viciously

خَبَث *n* |أَخْباث| 1 [المَعْدِنِ] slag 2 [نَجَس] uncleanness

خُبْث *n* 1 [شَرّ] wickedness; malice 2 (Med) malignancy

خَباثة *n* 1 [شَرّ] wickedness; malice 2 (Med) malignancy

خَبيث A *adj* |خُبُث, خُبَثاءُ, خَبَثة| 1 [شِرّير] bad, evil, wicked, malicious; snide; بَرْمَجيّات خَبيثة (Comput) malware; نَصّاب خَبيث a wicked impostor; نَوايا خَبيثة evil intentions 2 (Med) malignant; وَرَم خَبيث a malignant tumour; الجَمْرة الخَبيثة anthrax

B *n* |خُبُث, خُبَثاءُ, خَبَثة| villain; a spiteful person

خَبَرَ *v* |u; خُبْر, خِبْرة| 1 [جَرَّبَ] to know by experience 2 [عَلِمَ] to know thoroughly

خَبَّرَ *v* to inform, to notify

خابَرَ *v* to call, to telephone; to communicate with

أَخْبَرَ *v* to inform, to tell, to notify; أَخْبَرَ شَخْصاً أنّ ... to inform/tell sb that ...; أَخْبَرْتُ أَبي بِما حَصَلَ I told my father what had happened; أَخْبَرَ الشاهِدُ الشُّرْطةَ بالحادِثِ the witness reported the accident to the police (the necessary) experience; تَبادَلَ الخِبْراتِ to exchange experiences

خَبير A *adj* |خُبَراءُ| experienced, expert, skilled; well-acquainted; سائِق خَبير an experienced driver; خَبير في مَجالِ ... experienced in the field of ...

B *n* |خُبَراءُ| 1 [إخْصائيّ] expert, specialist, authority; لَجْنة خُبَراءَ committee of experts; خَبير في عِلْمِ اللُغةِ an expert in linguistics; خَبير ضَرائِبَ tax specialist, fiscal expert; خَبير في مَجالٍ مُعَيَّنٍ an expert/authority in a particular field; اسْتَعانَ بِخَبيرٍ to call in an expert; اسْتَشارَ خَبيراً to consult an expert; في رَأْيِ الخُبَراءِ according to the experts 2 (Islam) الخَبير the All-Aware (*one of the names of God*)

إخْباريّ *adj* news (*before n*); نَشْرة إخْباريّة news, newscast (AmE); news bulletin (BrE); newsletter

اخْتِبار *n* |اخْتِبارات| 1 [امْتِحان] test, paper; اخْتِبار في الرِياضيّاتِ a maths (BrE) math (AmE) test; نَتيجة اخْتِبارٍ test results; خَضَعَ لاخْتِبارٍ to be put/subject to a test; to take a test; أَخْضَعَ شَيْئاً \ شَخْصاً لاخْتِبارٍ to put/subject sth/sb to a test; أَجْرى اخْتِباراً to take a test; اجْتازَ اخْتِباراً to pass a test 2 [تَجْرِبة] test; trial; experiment, research; اخْتِبار تِقْنيّ \ عِلْميّ a technical/scientific experiment; اخْتِبار نَفْسيّ a psychological test; اخْتِبار إكْلينيكيّ \ سَريريّ a clinical test; كانَ تحت الاخْتِبارِ to be tested; قابِل للاخْتِبارِ verifiable

اخْتِباريّ *adj* empirical; experimental; test (*before n*); عَرْض اخْتِباريّ try-out

اسْتِخْبار *n* |اسْتِخْبارات| إدارة الاسْتِخْباراتِ (military) intelligence service, secret service; secret police

اسْتِخْباراتيّ *adj* intelligence (*before n*), military intelligence (*before n*); مَعْلومات اسْتِخْباراتيّة military intelligence information

اسْتِخْباريّ *adj* intelligence (*before n*); مَعْلومات اسْتِخْباريّة intelligence information

تَخابُر *n* contact; communication

مُخابَرة *n* communication; (جِهاز\ إدارة) المُخابَراتِ intelligence service, secret service (BrE); secret police; عَميل المُخابَراتِ spy,

تَخَبَّرَ *v* to inquire about, to ask about

تَخابَرَ *v* to communicate with one another; to be in contact with one another

اخْتَبَرَ *v* to test, to put to the test; to examine; to try; أُخْتُبِرَ to take a test/an exam; اخْتَبَرَ شَخْصاً في مَعْرِفَتِهِ to test sb's knowledge; اخْتَبَرَ جَوْدةَ مَنْتوجٍ to test the quality of a product

اسْتَخْبَرَ *v* to enquire, to ask

خَبَر *n* |أَخْبار| 1 [نَبَأ] news; message; information; خَبَر مُفْرِح wonderful news; خَبَر مُؤْسِف \ حَزين sad news; خَبَر جَيِّد \ سَيِّئ good/bad news; أَخْبار جَديدة news; أَخْبار داخِليّة domestic/national news; أَخْبار خارِجيّة foreign/international news; أَخْبار رِياضيّة \ الرِياضةِ sports news; آخِر أَخْبارٍ the latest news; حَسَبَ الأَخْبارِ الأَخيرةِ according to the latest news/reports; أَخْبار (عن) شَيْءٍ \ شَخْصٍ news about sth/sb; الأَخْبار the news; نَشْرة الأَخْبارِ the news, news bulletin (BrE), newscast (AmE); قَدَّمَ \ قَرَأَ نَشْرةَ الأَخْبارِ to present/read the news; مُقَدِّم \ مُذيع نَشْرةِ الأَخْبارِ newsreader (BrE), newscaster (AmE); جَماعة أَخْبارٍ newsgroup; تَلَقَّى خَبَراً to get news, to receive a message; أَذاعَ الخَبَرَ to spread the news; أَعْلَنَ خَبَراً to make an announcement; جاءَ في الأَخْبارِ to be/come on the news; كيف الأَخْبارُ؟ how are you doing?; what's up/new?; جَمْع الأَخْبارِ news gathering; تَلَمَّسَ أَخْبارَ شَخْصٍ to seek information about sb; دارَ الخَبَرُ على الأَفْواهِ the news was going round 2 (Gram) predicate; خَبَر اسْميّ predicate; خَبَر فِعْليّ verbal predicate

خابور *n* |خَوابيرُ| 1 (Mech) pin; plug; wedge 2 (Bot) elder

خِبْرة *n* experience; knowledge, expertise; خِبْرة عَمَليّة practical experience; خِبْرة طَويلة long experience; خِبْرة واسِعة extensive experience; قَليل الخِبْرةِ inexperienced; فَريق قَليل الخِبْرةِ an inexperienced team; صاحِب الخِبْرةِ an experienced person; ذو خِبْرةٍ experienced; ذو خِبْرةٍ طَويلةٍ \ واسِعةٍ highly experienced, an old hand; قِلّة الخِبْرةِ lack of experience/expertise; بِسَبَبِ قِلّةِ الخِبْرةِ due to/through lack of experience; خِبْرة في الحَياةِ life experience; اكْتَسَبَ خِبْرةً to build up expertise; اكْتَسَبَ الخِبْرةَ اللازِمةَ to gain the necessary experience; نَقَصَتْهُ الخِبْرةُ (اللازِمةُ) to lack agent; مُخابَرات عَسْكَرِيّة \ الجَيْش military/army intelligence; وِكالة المُخابَراتِ المَرْكَزِيّة the Central Intelligence Agency, the CIA; مُخابَرة هاتِفيّة phone call

مَخْبَر *n* |مَخابِرُ| laboratory

مُخْبِر *n* [1] ◀ [مُزَوِّد بالأَخْبار] informant; حَسَبَ مُخْبِرِنا according to our informant [2] ◀ [مُحَقِّق] detective; مُخْبِر خاصّ private investigator [3] ◀ [في خِدْمةِ الحُكومة] agent; مُخْبِر سِرّيّ secret agent

مَخْبَرِيّ *adj* laboratory (*before n*); تَحْليل \ فَحْص مَخْبَرِيّ laboratory analysis/test; التَجارِب المَخْبَرِيّة laboratory experiments

مُخْتَبَر *n* |مُخْتَبَرات| laboratory

مُخْتَبَرِيّ *adj* laboratory (*before n*), lab (*before n*); تَحْليل مُخْتَبَرِيّ laboratory analysis; تَجْرِبة مُخْتَبَرِيّة laboratory test

خَبَزَ *v* |i; خَبْز| to bake; خَبَزَ خُبْزةً to bake a loaf of bread

خُبْز *n* bread; خُبْز جافّ dry bread; خُبْز أَسْمَر brown bread; wholemeal bread (BrE), whole-wheat bread (AmE); خُبْز كامِل الحَبّة wholemeal bread (BrE), whole-wheat bread (AmE); خُبْز أَبْيَض white bread

خَبّاز *n* |خَبّازون, خَبّازة| baker

خُبْزة *n* bread, a loaf of bread; خَبَزَ خُبْزةً to bake a loaf of bread

خَبيز [A] *adj* baked
[B] *n* pastry

خُبَّيْزة *n* listed alphabetically

مَخْبِز, مَخْبَزة, مَخْبَز *n* |مَخابِزُ| bakery; (عَمِلَ) في المَخْبِز (to work) in the bakery

خَبَصَ *v* |i; خَبْص| to mix, to mingle

خَبيص *n a traditional sweet dish from the Gulf region*

خَبَطَ *v* |i; خَبْط| to beat, to strike, to knock on, to pound at/on; خَبَطَ شَجَرةً بِسَيّارَتِهِ to hit a tree with one's car; خَبَطَ البابَ to knock on the door

تَخَبَّطَ *v* to stumble; to flounder; to blunder; to fumble; تَخَبَّطَ في مَشاكِلَ كَبيرة to struggle with big problems; تَخَبَّطَ في قَضيّة to blunder over an issue

خَبْطة *n* blow

تَخَبُّط *n* clumsiness

مُتَخَبِّط *adj* clumsy

خَبَلَ *v* |u; خَبْل| to drive crazy/insane; to confuse; خَبَلَهُ الحُزْنُ \ الحُبُّ grief/love drove him insane

خَبِلَ *v* |a; خَبَل, خَبال| to be crazy/insane; to go crazy; to be mentally disturbed (fml); to be/become confused

خَبَّلَ *v* to drive crazy/insane; to confuse

اخْتَبَلَ *v* to be crazy/insane; to go crazy; to be/get confused

خَبَل *n* insanity, madness; أَصابَهُ خَبَلٌ he went insane

خَبال *n* insanity, mental disorder

أَخْبَل *adj* |dipt| crazy, insane

اخْتِبال *n* insanity

مَخْبول [A] *adj* |مَخْبولون, مَخابيل| crazy, mad, insane, mentally deranged; idiotic, imbecilic
[B] *n* |مَخْبولون, مَخابيل| fool, madman; idiot

خَبا *v* |u; خَبْو, خُبُوّ| to go out, to die; تَخْبو النارُ the fire is going out

أَخْبى *v* to extinguish

خُبَّيْزة *n* (Bot) mallow

خَتَرَ *v* |u; خَتْر| to betray; خَتَرَ صاحِبَهُ to betray one's friend

خَتْر *n* betrayal

خَتَلَ *v* |i-u; خَتْل| to deceive, to fool, to dupe; خَتَلَ شَخْصاً to deceive sb

خاتَلَ *v* [1] ◀ [خادَعَ] to deceive [2] ◀ [غافَلَ] to take by surprise; خاتَلَ الصَيّادُ فَريسَتَهُ the hunter took his prey by surprise

تَخاتَلَ *v* to deceive one another

خَتْل *n* deception

خَتّال *adj* cunning, artful, shrewd

مُخاتِل *adj* deceitful; crafty; كانَ مُخاتِلاً في أَفْعالِهِ وَأَقْوالِهِ to be deceitful in word and deed

خَتَمَ *v* |i; خَتْم| [1] ◀ [طَبَعَ بالخاتَم] to seal; to stamp; خَتَمَ رِسالةً to seal/stamp a letter; خَتَمَ جَوازَ سَفَرٍ to stamp a passport; خَتَمَ طابِعاً بَريدِيًّا to stamp (the date on) a postage stamp; خَتَمَ اللهُ على قُلوبِهِمْ God has sealed their hearts [2] ◀ [أَنْهى] to finish, to conclude; to complete; to close; خَتَمَ التَحْقيقَ to close the investigation

خَثَّرَ *v* to curdle; to thicken

تَخَثَّرَ *v* to solidify; to thicken; to coagulate; يَتَخَثَّرُ السائِلُ the liquid coagulates

خاثِر *adj* syrupy, viscous; sticky; clotted, coagulated

خُثار *n* thrombosis

خَثْرة *n* clot, coagulum (fml); خَثْرة الدَم blood clot, thrombus (fml)

تَخَثُّر *n* |تَخَثُّرات| clotting, coagulation

مُتَخَثِّر *adj* clotting, coagulating

مُخَثِّر *n* coagulant; thickening agent; curdling agent, rennet

‹ **خَجِلَ** *v* |a; خَجَل| to be ashamed/embarrassed; خَجِلَ من \ لِشَيْءٍ to feel embarrassed about sth; خَجِلَ من شَخْصٍ to be ashamed in front of sb; خَجِلَ من أنْ ... to be ashamed to ...

خَجَّلَ *v* to embarrass; خَجَّلَ الوَلَدُ الفَتاةَ the boy embarrassed the girl

أَخْجَلَ *v* to embarras; أَخْجَلْتَني اليَوْمَ you embarrassed me today

خَجَل *n* shame; shyness; embarrassment; خَجَلاً out of shame; احْمَرَّ خَجَلاً \ من الخَجَلِ to blush with shame; to blush with/out of embarrassment; شُعور بالخَجَلِ a sense of shame; بدونِ خجلٍ shameless, unashamed, without any shame; تَغَلَّبَ على خَجَلِهِ to overcome one's shyness

خَجِل *adj* shy, timid, bashful

خَجْلان *adj* |خَجْلى, خَجالى| shy, timid; embarrassed

خَجول *adj* shy, timid; ashamed; طِفْل \ فَتاة خجول(ة) a shy child/girl; ضَحْكة خجولة a timid laugh

مُخْجِل *adj* embarrassing, shameful, humiliating; أَمْر مُخْجِل a humiliating performance

‹ **خِداج** *n* abortion; miscarriage

خَديج *adj* |خُدُج| premature; طِفْل خَديج premature baby

خَديجة *n* |dipt| ❶ [اِسْم شَخْصيّ] Khadija (*female given name*) ❷ [زَوْجة النَبيّ] Khadija (*first wife of the prophet Muhammad and mother of his children*)

‹ **خَدَّ** *v* |u; خَدّ| to plough; to furrow; خَدَّ الفَلّاحُ الأَرْضَ the farmer ploughed the land

خَدّ *n* |خُدود| (Anat) cheek; خَدّانِ أَحْمَرانِ red/rosy/glowing cheeks; خَدّانِ مُقَعَّرانِ sunken cheeks; مُمْتَلِئ الخَدَّيْنِ

اِخْتَتَمَ *v* to finish, to conclude; to complete; to close; اِخْتَتَمَ زِيارةً رَسْميّةً بِمُؤْتَمَرٍ صَحافيٍّ to conclude an official visit with a press conference

خَتْم *n* |خُتوم, أَخْتام| ❶ [إِنْهاء] termination, completion, closing; خَتْم التَحْقيقِ the closing of the investigation ❷ [خاتَم] stamp; seal; خَتْم التاريخ date stamp ❸ [أَثَر نَقْشِ الخاتِمِ] wax seal; stamp; فَكَّ خَتْمَ رِسالةٍ to break the seal of a letter; وَضَعَ خَتْمَهُ على شَيْءٍ to put one's stamp on sth

خاتَم, خاتِم *n* |خَواتِمُ| ❶ [طابَع] seal; stamp; signet; خاتَم التاريخ date stamp ❷ [حُلِيّ] ring; signet ring; خاتَم ذَهَبٍ \ فِضّةٍ a gold/silver ring; خاتَم الزَواج wedding ring; خاتَم الخِطْبةِ engagement ring; خاتَم في الإِصْبَعِ a ring on one's finger; لَبِسَ خاتَماً to wear a ring; كانَ خاتَماً في إِصْبَعي I had him wrapped around my finger ❸ [آخِر] *the last one*; خاتَم النَبِيّينَ the Seal of the Prophets (*i.e. Muhammad, the last of the prophets*)

خاتِمة *n* |خَواتِمُ, خَواتيمُ| ❶ [نِهاية] end, conclusion; الأُمورُ بِخَواتِمِها all's well that ends well ❷ [كَلِمة نِهائيّة] epilogue, postscript, afterword; closing speech

خِتام *n* end, conclusion; خِتام السَهْرةِ the end of the evening; في خِتامٍ \ خِتاماً at the end, finally; in conclusion; في الخِتامِ الأَمْرِ in the end

خَتّامة *n* ink pad

خِتاميّ *adj* final, concluding; كَلِمة خِتاميّة epilogue; concluding speech

اِخْتِتام *n* end, conclusion

‹ **خَتَنَ** *v* |i; خَتْن| to circumcise; خَتَنَ شَخْصاً to circumcise sb; خَتَنَ ابْنَهُ to have one's son circumcised

اِخْتَتَنَ *v* to be circumcised

خَتْن *n* circumcision

خَتَن *n* |أَخْتان| son-in-law; brother-in-law

خِتان *n* circumcision; خِتان الإِناثِ female circumcision

خِتانة *n* circumcision

‹ **خُثّ** *n* peat

مَخَثّة *n* peat bog

‹ **خَثَرَ** *v* |u; خُثور, خُثورة| to solidify; to clot, to coagulate; to curdle; يَخْثُرُ الدَمُ the blood is clotting with round/chubby cheeks; قَبَّلَ خَدَّ شَخْصٍ to kiss sb on the cheek

أُخْدود *n* |أَخاديدُ| 1 ◀ [شَقّ] furrow, groove; gorge, canyon; الأُخْدود العَظيم the Grand Canyon 2 ◀ [عَلامة مُسْتَطيلة] wrinkle

مِخَدّة *n* |مَخَدّات ,مَخادُّ| pillow, cushion

مُخَدَّد *adj* furrowed

‹ **خَدِرَ** *v* |a; خَدَر| 1 ◀ [نَمِلَ] to tingle; خَدِرَتْ ذِراعي my arm was numb 2 ◀ [اسْتَرْخى] to get high

خَدَّرَ *v* 1 ◀ (Med) to anaesthetize, to sedate; خَدَّرَ شَخْصاً to anaesthetize sb; خَدَّرَ مَوْضِعيًّا to deliver local anaesthesia; خَدَّرَ كُلِّيًّا \ جُزْئيًّا to give total/partial anaesthesia 2 ◀ [أعْطى مُخَدِّراتٍ] to drug

تَخَدَّرَ *v* 1 ◀ [فَقَدَ الحِسَّ] to be anaesthetized, to be put under an anaesthetic, to be sedated 2 ◀ [تَنَمَّلَ] to be numbed

خَدَر *n* tingling

خادِرة *n* |خَوادِرُ| chrysalis; pupa

تَخَدُّر *n* tingling

تَخْدير *n* (Med) anaesthesia; تَخْدير مَوْضِعيّ \ عامّ local/general anaesthesia; بدونِ تَخْديرٍ without anaesthesia; تحت التَخْديرِ under anaesthesia; اسْتَيْقَظَ من التَخْديرِ to recover/emerge from anaesthesia

مُخَدَّر *adj* anaesthetized, sedated, under anaesthesia

مُخَدِّر *n* 1 ◀ [مادّة] |مُخَدِّرات| drug; مُخَدِّرات drugs, narcotics; مُخَدِّر قَويّ hard drug; مُخَدِّر خفيف soft drug; مُدْمِن المُخَدِّراتِ drug addict, junkie; مُسْتَهْلِك للمُخَدِّراتِ drug user; تاجِر المُخَدِّراتِ drug dealer; تِجارة المُخَدِّراتِ drug trade, drug dealing, drug traffic; مُكافَحة المُخَدِّراتِ the fight against drugs; تَهْريب المُخَدِّراتِ drug smuggling; مُهَرِّب المُخَدِّراتِ drug smuggler; مَلِك المُخَدِّراتِ drug baron; تَبْييض أَمْوالِ المُخَدِّراتِ laundering of drug money; مُتأثِّر بالمُخَدِّراتِ under the influence of drugs; قانون المُخَدِّراتِ drug law; تَعاطى المُخَدِّراتِ to take drugs, to be on drugs; ضَبَطَ مُخَدِّراتٍ to catch/intercept/confiscate drugs 2 ◀ [طَبيب] |مُخَدِّرونَ| anaesthetist 3 ◀ [دَواء] |مُخَدِّرات| anaesthetic; انْتَهى مَفْعولُ المُخَدِّرِ the anaesthetic has worn off

‹ **خَدَشَ** *v* |i; خَدْش| to scratch; to scrape; to sully, to tarnish; خَدَشَ الجِلْدَ to scrape the skin; خَدَش كَرامةَ شَخْصٍ to undermine sb's dignity

خَدْش *n* |خُدوش| scratch, scratch mark; scrape, graze; خَدْش على المائِدةِ a scratch on the table; أُصيبَ بِخَدْشٍ to get a scrape

‹ **خَدَعَ** *v* |a; خَدْع, خُدْعة, خَديعة| 1 ◀ [احْتالَ] to deceive, to mislead, to cheat; خَدَعَ الشَّعْبَ to mislead the people; خَدَعَ صاحِبَ العَمَلِ to cheat one's employer; خَدَعَ الزَبائِنَ to deceive the clients; خَدَعَ المُسْتَهْلِكَ to deceive the consumer 2 ◀ [تَوارى] to hide

خادَعَ *v* to cheat, to deceive; خادَعَ شَخْصاً to deceive sb

تَخادَعَ *v* to cheat one another

انْخَدَعَ *v* |بِ| to be misled/deceived (by)

خَدْع *n* deceit; swindle

خادِع A *adj* misleading, deceptive; سُكون \ هُدوء خادِع a deceptive calm

B *n* impostor, cheat

خَدّاع A *adj* deceptive, delusive

B *n* impostor, swindler

خِداع *n* deception, deceit; imposture, swindle; خِداع بَصَريّ \ البَصَرِ optical illusion; عن طَريقِ \ بالخِداعِ by devious means; بالمَكْرِ والخِداع through cunning and guile

خُدْعة *n* |خُدَع| trick; ruse; خُدْعة سِحْريّة magic trick

خَديعة *n* trick, deception, ruse

انْخِداع *n* illusion; delusion

مُخادِع *n* impostor, swindler, fraud

مَخْدَع, مِخْدَع *n* |مَخادِعُ| bedroom

‹ **خَدَلَ** *v* |a; خَدَل, خَدالة, خُدولة| 1 ◀ [خَدِرَ] to become numb, to stiffen; خَدِلَت ساقُهُ his leg became numb 2 ◀ [امْتَلأَ] to be fleshy

خَدْلان *n* numbness

‹ **خَدَمَ** *v* |i-u; خِدْمة| to serve; to wait on; خَدَمَ الزَبائِنَ to serve/help the customers; خَدَمَ الوَطَنَ to serve one's country; خَدَمَ في الجَيْشِ to serve in the army; خَدَمَ مَصالِحَ شَخْصٍ to look after sb's interests; خَدَمَ مَصالِحَهُ to serve one's own interests

اسْتَخْدَمَ *v* **1** [اسْتَعْمَلَ] to use, to utilize, to make use of; to apply; اسْتَخْدَمَ عَقْلَهُ to use one's common sense; اسْتَخْدَمَ الطاقةَ الشَمْسيّةَ to use solar energy; اسْتَخْدَمَ الجَيْشُ الرَصاصَ المَطاطيَّ لِتَفْريقِ المُتَظاهِرينَ the army used rubber bullets to disperse the protesters **2** [شَغَّلَ] to employ; اسْتَخْدَمَ شَخْصاً to employ sb; اسْتَخْدَمَ شَخْصاً بِأُجْرةٍ to hire sb

خَدَّمَ *v* to hire, to employ

خادِم *n* |mf| **1** [شَخْص] |خُدّام, خَدَمة| servant, manservant; domestic servant; خادِمُ الحَرَمَيْنِ الشَريفَيْنِ the Custodian of the Two Holy Mosques (*i.e. the king of Saudi Arabia, guarding the Grand Mosque in Mecca and the Prophet's Mosque in Medina*) **2** (Comput) |خَوادِمُ| server; خادِم آمِن a secure server; خادِم بَريد إلِكْتْرونيٍّ email server

خادِمة *n* servant; maid; help

خادوم *n* (Comput) server

خَدّام *n* servant

خَدّامة *n* servant; maid; help

خَدَماتيّ *adj* service (*before n*); قِطاع خَدَماتيّ service sector

خِدْمة *n* |خِدَم, خِدْمات| **1** [شُغْل] service; خِدْمة جَيِّدة \ سَيِّئة good/poor service; خِدْمة ذاتيّة self service; خِدْمة لَيْليّة night shift; خِدْمات طِبِّيّة \ صِحّيّة health services; خِدْمات اجْتِماعيّة social services; community service; خِدْمة سَريعة fast/quick service; خِدْمات بَلَدِيّة municipal services; هَيْئة الخِدْماتِ الصِحّيّةِ (public) health service; قِطاع الخِدْماتِ the service sector; خِدْمة عَسْكَرِيّة military service, national service; خِدْمة عَسْكَرِيّة إلْزاميّة \ إجْبارِيّة compulsory military service; في الخِدْمةِ العَسْكَرِيّةِ in military service; أَدّى خِدْمةً عَسْكَرِيّةً to perform military service; عَرَضَ \ قَدَّمَ خِدْمةً to offer/provide a service; زَوَّدَ بالخِدْماتِ to render services; حَسَّنَ الخِدْمةَ to improve the service; أَيُّ خِدْمةٍ؟ can I help you?, at your service; (أنا) في خِدْمَتِكَ (I am) at your service **2** [مَعْروف] service; قَدَّمَ \ أَسْدى خِدْمةً لِشَخْصٍ to do/render sb a service; الاسْتِعْداد للخِدْمةِ readiness to help

خِدْميّ *adj* service (*before n*); القِطاع الخِدْميّ the service sector

خَدوم *adj* helpful, ready/willing to help

اسْتِخْدام *n* |اسْتِخْدامات| use; employment; consumption; سَهْل الاسْتِخْدامِ user-friendly; جاهِز للاسْتِخْدامِ ready to use; سُهولة الاسْتِخْدامِ user-friendliness; طَريقة الاسْتِخْدامِ method of use; شُروط الاسْتِخْدامِ terms of use; إعادة الاسْتِخْدامِ recycling, reuse; بِاسْتِخْدامِ ... with the use of...; أَساءَ الاسْتِخْدامَ to abuse; أَساءَ اسْتِخْدامَ سُلْطَتِهِ \ نُفوذِهِ to abuse one's power/influence; أَعادَ الاسْتِخْدامَ to recycle, to reuse

مُخَدِّم *n* |مُخَدِّمات| (Comput) server; مُخَدِّم التَطْبيقات application server

مُسْتَخْدَم **A** *adj* used; سَيّارة مُسْتَخْدَمة a used car **B** *n* employee; worker, labourer; مُسْتَخْدَمونَ staff, personnel; مُسْتَخْدَم بَنْكٍ bank employee; مُسْتَخْدَمونَ غَيْر ماهِرينَ unskilled labourers; نَقْص في عَدَدِ المُسْتَخْدَمينَ a shortage of staff; عَيَّنَ مُسْتَخْدَماً to appoint an employee

مُسْتَخْدِم *n* **1** [رَبّ العَمَلِ] employer **2** [مُسْتَعْمِل] user; مُسْتَخْدِم المُخَدِّراتِ drug user; مُسْتَخْدِم الكُمْبيوتَر computer user; حِساب المُسْتَخْدِمِ user account; اسْم المُسْتَخْدِم username; تَرْخيص المُسْتَخْدِمِ النِهائيِّ End-User Licence Agreement, EULA

‹ **خِدْن** *n* |أَخْدان| **1** [صاحِب] friend **2** [حَبيب] boyfriend; lover

‹ **خُدَيْويّ**, خِديو *n* Khedive (*title of the viceroy of Egypt under Turkish rule 1867–1914*)

‹ **خُذْروف** *n* |خَذارِفُ| spinning top

‹ **مِخْذَفة** *n* catapult (BrE), slingshot (AmE)

‹ **خَذَلَ** *v* |u; خَذْل| to abandon; خَذَلَ شَخْصاً to abandon sb

خاذَلَ *v* to leave, to abandon

تَخاذَلَ *v* to grow slack/weak; تَخاذَلَ عن خَوْضِ الأُمورِ to be too lazy to look into the matter

خِذْلان *n* failure

تَخاذُل *n* weakness, feebleness

مُتَخاذِل *adj* weak, feeble

مَخْذول *adj* |مَخاذيلُ| disappointed; failed

‹ **خَذِيَ** *v* |a; خَذًى| to submit oneself; خَذِيَ أمامَ اللهِ to submit oneself to God

اسْتَخْذى *v* to submit; اسْتَخْذى العُمّالُ أمام أرْبابِ العَمَلِ the workers submitted to the employers

خَرِئَ *v* |a; خِراء| to defecate (fml), to poo/poop (infml), to shit (vulg)

خُرْء *n* excrement (fml), poo/poop (infml), shit (vulg)

خَراء *n* excrement (fml), poo (infml), shit (vulg)

خَرَبَ *v* |i; خَرْب| to ruin, to destroy; خَرَبَ آلةً to destroy a machine

خَرِبَ *v* |a; خَراب| to be/become destroyed; to break

خَرَّبَ *v* to destroy, to devastate, to ruin, to wreck; to sabotage; خَرَّبَ بَلَداً to ruin a country

أَخْرَبَ *v* to destroy, to ruin

تَخَرَّبَ *v* to be/become destroyed, to go to ruin, to fall apart

خَرِب *adj* broken; ruined

خَراب *n* |أَخْرِبة| (state of) destruction, ruin, decay; أَخْرِبة ruins; خراب مُهَوِّل \ واسِع النِطاقِ enormous/tremendous destruction; خراب يَباب total ruin; خراب اقْتِصاديّ economic downfall; نَشَرَ الخَرابَ to spread destruction; خَلَّفَ وَراءَهُ الخَرابَ والدَمارَ to leave a trail of destruction behind; كانَ على وَشْكِ الخَرابِ to be on the brink of destruction; صارَ إلى الخَرابِ to become ruined; to go to waste; بعد خَرابِ البَصْرةِ after giving up all hope

خَرابة *n* |خَرائِبُ| خَرائِب rubble

خَرْبان *adj* broken

خُرْبة *n* |خُرَب| hole; هُناكَ خُرْبةٌ في البابِ there is a hole in the door

خِرْبة *n* |خِرَب| ruins

خَرّوبة, خَرّوب *n* listed alphabetically

تَخْريب *n* |تَخْريبات| destruction, devastation; demolition; vandalism; sabotage; تَخْريب عَمَليّةِ السَلامِ the sabotage of the peace process; أَعْمال التَخْريبِ vandalism; sabotage

تَخْريبيّ *adj* destructive, devastating; قامَ بِأَعْمالٍ تَخْريبيّةٍ to commit acts of sabotage/terror

مُخَرِّب A *adj* destructive; عَناصِر مُخَرِّبة subversive elements B *n* saboteur; vandal

خَرْبَشَ *v* |i; خَرْبَشة| ❶ [القِطّةُ] to scratch ❷ [كَتَبَ] to scrawl; خَرْبَشَ شِعاراتٍ على الجُدْرانِ to scrawl slogans on the walls

خَرْبَشة *n* ❶ [خَدْش] scratch ❷ [كِتابة] scrawl

مُخَرْبَشات *n pl* inscriptions (*in stone*); graffiti

خَرْبَطَ *v* |i; خَرْبَطة| to leave in disorder

خَرْبَقَ *v* |i; خَرْبَقة| to ruin

خَرْبَق *n* (Bot) hellebore

خَرَتَ *v* |u; خَرْت| to pierce

خَرَجَ *v* |u; خُروج| ❶ [غادَرَ] to go/come out; to leave; خَرَجَ من البَيْتِ to leave the house ❷ [تَجاوَزَ] |على| to violate, to break; خَرَجَ على القانونِ to break/violate the law ❸ [انْحَرَفَ] |عن| to exceed; خَرَجَ عن المَأْلوفِ to be unusual; خَرَجَ عن شَيْءٍ to deviate from something; خَرَجَ القِطارُ عن الخَطِّ the train has been derailed ❹ [وَصَلَ إلى حَلٍّ] to get out of; خَرَجَ من مُشْكِلةٍ to get out of a problem ❺ [تَمَرَّدَ] |على| to revolt; خَرَجَ على شَيْءٍ to revolt against sth

خَرَّجَ *v* ❶ [أَخْرَجَ] to move/take/bring out; خَرَّجَ قِطاراً عن الخَطِّ to derail a train; خَرَّجَ رِجالُ الإطْفاءِ السُكّانَ من الشَقّةِ المُحْتَرِقةِ the firefighters rescued the people from the burning apartment ❷ [الطُلّابَ] to train, to educate; تُخَرِّجُ الجامِعاتُ عَدَداً كَبيراً من الخُبَراءِ the universities train a lot of experts

أَخْرَجَ *v* ❶ [عَكْس أَدْخَلَ] to move/take/bring out; أَخْرَجَ شَخْصاً to remove sb, to throw sb out; أَخْرَجَ المالِكُ الساكِنَ من البَيْتِ the owner evicted the occupant from the house; أَخْرَجَ شَيْئاً من جَيْبِهِ to take sth out of one's pocket; أَخْرَجَ فَريقاً من المُسابَقةِ to eliminate a team ❷ [فيلْماً] to direct; أَخْرَجَ فيلْماً \ مَسْرَحيّةً to direct a film/play

تَخَرَّجَ *v* to graduate; to pass; تَخَرَّجَ من الجامِعةِ \ المَدْرَسةِ الثانَويّةِ to graduate from university/secondary school

تَخارَجَ *v* to break away

اسْتَخْرَجَ *v* to get/move/take out; to mine; to win; to extract; اسْتَخْرَجَ الغازَ \ النَفْطَ to drill for gas/oil; اسْتَخْرَجَ بُذوراً من نَباتاتٍ to extract seeds from plants; اسْتَخْرَجَ بَنْزيناً من النَفْطِ to distil petrol from oil; اسْتَخْرَجَ الفَحْمَ الحَجَريَّ to mine for coal; اسْتَخْرَجَ آثاراً to excavate antiquities

خَرْج *n* ❶ [نَفَقة] expenditure; وازَنَ بين دَخْلِهِ وَخَرْجِهِ to balance one's income and expenditure ❷ (Elec) output

خُرْج *n* |خِرَجة| saddlebag

الخارجة *n* Kharga (*an oasis in Egypt*)

الخوارج *n* the Kharijites (*members of the earliest sect in Islam*)

تَخَرُّج *n* graduation; شهادة تَخَرُّجٍ من كُلِيّةِ العُلومِ a graduate degree in science; بَحْث تَخَرُّجٍ thesis

تَخْريج *n* ⟨1⟩ [الطَلَبةِ] conferment of degree; graduation; حَفْل تَخْريج commencement ceremony; يَهْدُفُ المَعْهَدُ إلى تَخْريجِ مُتَخَصِّصينَ في المُحاسَبةِ the institute's aim is to graduate accountancy specialists ⟨2⟩ [تَفْسير] explanation; interpretation

مُتَخَرِّج *n* graduate; مُتَخَرِّج من الجامعةِ university/college graduate

مَخْرَج *n* |مَخارِجُ| ⟨1⟩ [مَنْفَذ] exit; turn; slip road (BrE), ramp (AmE); مَخْرَج خَلْفيّ back/rear exit; مَخْرَج الطَوارِئِ \ النَجاةِ emergency exit; عن طَريقِ مَخْرَجِ الطَوارِئِ through the emergency exit; سَدَّ المَخْرَجَ to block the exit ⟨2⟩ [مَفَرّ] way out; escape ⟨3⟩ [نُطْق] articulation; pronunciation; location of articulation; مَخْرَج الحُروفِ the location of articulation of the consonants ⟨4⟩ (Math) denominator

مُخْرِج *n* director; film/movie director; film-maker; مُخْرِج مَشْهور a famous director; مُخْرِج ناجح a successful director; مُخْرِج سينَمائيّ film/movie director; مُخْرِج فَنّيّ technical director; مُساعِد المُخْرِجِ assistant to the director

مُسْتَخْرَج *n* |مُسْتَخْرَجات| extract, excerpt

‹ **خَرْخَر** *v* |i; خَرْخَرة| to snore

‹ **خُرْدة** *n* |خُرْدَوات| scrapheap; scrap; خُرْدَوات bric-a-brac; junk (infml)

‹ **خُرْدُق** *n* |خَرادِقُ| buckshot

‹ **خَرْدَل** *n coll* ⟨1⟩ [تابِل] mustard; غاز الخَرْدَلِ mustard gas ⟨2⟩ (Bot) mustard

‹ **خُرْدَواتي** *n* knick-knacks

‹ **خَرَّ** *v* |i-u; خَرير| ⟨1⟩ [سَقَطَ] to fall (down); to collapse; to prostrate oneself ⟨2⟩ [الماء] to murmur, to gurgle

خَرير *n* murmur

‹ **خَرَزَ** *v* |i-u; خَرْز| ⟨1⟩ [ثَقَبَ] to pierce; to perforate; to prick; خَرَزَ شَيْئاً to pierce sth ⟨2⟩ [خاطَ] to sew; خَرَزَ الجِلْدَ to suture the skin

خَرَز *n coll* bead; خَرَزة الظَهْرِ vertebra

خارِج **A** *adj* outgoing; بَريد \ رَسائِل \ مُكالَمات (هاتِفيّة) خارِج(ة) outgoing mail/letters/calls **B** *n* ⟨1⟩ [عَكْس الداخِلِ] outside, exterior; إلى خارِجِ الحُدودِ outside the borders; خارِج عن ... from outside ...; من خارِجِ إرادَتِهِ against one's will; unintentional ⟨2⟩ [البِلادِ] foreign country, abroad; أقامَ ب \ عَمِلَ في الخارِجِ to live/work abroad; رِحْلة إلى الخارِجِ a trip abroad; من الخارِجِ from abroad ⟨3⟩ (Math) quotient

خارِجَ *prep* outside; out of; خارِجَ المُسْتَشْفى outside the hospital; خارِجَ مِصْرَ outside of Egypt; خارِجَ المُسابَقةِ out of the competition; أقامَ \ عَمِلَ خارِجَ بِلادِهِ to live/work abroad

خارِجيّ *adj* outer; outside, exterior; external; foreign; فَحْص خارِجيّ an external examination; الدائِرة \ الحَلَقة الخارِجيّة the outer circle/ring; عَلاقات خارِجيّة external relations; سِياسة خارِجيّة foreign policy; عامِل خارِجيّ an external factor; للاسْتِعْمالِ الخارِجيِّ for external use

خارِجيّة *n* وَزير \ وِزارة الخارِجيّةِ Minister/Ministry of Foreign Affairs, Foreign Secretary/Office (BrE), Secretary/Department of State (AmE)

خَراج *n* (Hist) land tax

خُراج *n* |أَخْرِجة| (Med) abscess

خُرّاج *n* |خَراريجُ| (Med) abscess

خُروج *n* ⟨1⟩ [مَصْدَر] going out, egression; exodus; departure; الخُروج من مِصْرَ the exodus from Egypt; تَسْجيل الخُروجِ signing/logging out ⟨2⟩ [باب] exit; الخُروج والدُخول the exit and the entrance

خِرّيج *n* graduate; خِرّيج جامِعةٍ university/college graduate

إخْراج *n* ⟨1⟩ [عَكْس إدْخال] taking/bringing/moving out ⟨2⟩ [فَنّيّ] direction, production; من إخْراجِ ... directed by ...; إخْراج بَرْنامَجٍ تِلِفِزْيونيٍّ the production of a television programme ⟨3⟩ (P&P) publication ⟨4⟩ (Comput) output; جِهاز إخْراجٍ output device

اسْتِخْراج *n* |اسْتِخْراجات| extraction, mining; اسْتِخْراج النَفْطِ والغازِ the extraction of oil and gas

اسْتِخْراجيّ *adj* extractive; صِناعات اسْتِخْراجيّة extractive industries

مِخْراز *n* |مَخاريزُ| awl

مِخْرَز *n* |مَخارِزُ| awl

‹ **خَرِسَ** *v* |a; خَرْس| [1] [بَكِمَ] to be/become mute [2] [سَكَتَ] to keep quiet; اخْرَسْ! keep quiet!, shut up! (infml); خَرِسَ لِسانُهُ عن الحَديثِ he was at a loss for words

أَخْرَسَ *v* to silence; أَخْرَسَ شَخْصاً to silence sb, to gag sb; أَخْرَسَتْهُ تِلْكَ الكَلِماتُ those words silenced him

خَرَس *n* muteness

أَخْرَس *adj*, *n* |dipt; خُرْسان, خُرْس| f خَرْساءُ| mute

‹ **خَرَسانة** *n* concrete; خَرَسانة مُسَلَّحة reinforced concrete

خَرَسانيّ *adj* concrete

‹ **خَرَشَ** *v* |i; خَرْش| to scratch

‹ **خَرْشَنة** *n* tern (*Sterna*)

‹ **خُرْشوف** *n* |خَراشيفُ| artichoke

‹ **خَرَصَ** *v* |u; خَرْص| [1] [حَزَرَ] to guess; خَرَصَ الفَلّاحُ الثَّمَرَ the farmer estimated the proceeds of the yield from the palms [2] [كَذَبَ] to lie

خِرْص *n* |خِرْصان| earring

‹ **خَرَطَ** *v* |i-u; خَرْط| [1] [المَعْدِنَ] to turn, to lathe; خَرَطَ كُرةً خَشَبيّةً to turn a wooden ball [2] [الوَرَقَ] to pull off; خَرَطَ وَرَقَ الشَّجَرِ to strip the leaves from the tree [3] [كَذَبَ] to lie

انْخَرَطَ *v* |في| to join; to become a member of; انْخَرَطَ في صُفوفِ الجَيْشِ to join the army

خارِطة *n* map; خارِطة أوروبّا the map of Europe; عَيَّنَ شَيْئاً على الخارِطةِ to point out sth on the map

خَرائِطيّ [A] *n* cartographer

[B] *adj* cartographic

خَرّاط *n* [1] [مُشْتَغِل في المِخْرَطةِ] turner, lather [2] [كَذّاب] braggart; liar

خِراطة *n* turning (*on a lathe*)

خَريطة *n* |خَرائِطُ| map, chart; plan; خَريطة مُفَصَّلة a detailed map; خَريطة رَقْميّة a digital map; خَريطة سِياحيّة a tourist map; خَريطة العالَم world map; خَريطة الطَّقْسِ weather chart; خَريطة مَوْقِعٍ site map; خَريطة مَرْكَزِ المَدينةِ plan of the town centre; على خَريطةٍ on a map; قَرَأَ الخَريطةَ to read the map

انْخِراط *n* joining

مِخْرَطة *n* |مَخارِطُ| lathe

مَخْروط [A] *adj* conical, cone-shaped

[B] *n* |مَخاريطُ, مَخْروطات| (Geom) cone

مَخْروطيّ *adj* conical, conic

‹ **خَرْطوش** *n coll* |خَراطيشُ| [1] [حَشْو] shell; cartridge; خَرْطوشة قَلَم حِبْرٍ the cartridge of a fountain pen [2] (Archaeol) cartouche

‹ **خُرْطوم** *n* |خَراطيمُ| [1] [الفيلِ] trunk [2] [مِياهٍ...] hose; tube; خُرْطوم حَريقٍ fire-hose [3] [في المَطارِ] خُرْطوم الطائِرةِ gangway, avio bridge

‹ **الخَرْطوم** *n* Khartoum (*capital of Sudan*)

‹ **خَرِعَ, خَرُعَ** *v* |a-u; خَرَع, خَراعة| to be/become weak

اخْتَرَعَ *v* to invent, to devise; اخْتَرَعَ شَيْئاً to invent sth; اخْتَرَعَ خُطّةً to devise a plan

خَرِع *adj* weak, feeble; soft; كانَ خَرِعاً to be/feel weak

اخْتِراع *n* |اخْتِراعات| invention; اخْتِراع البارود the invention of gunpowder; بَراءة اخْتِراع patent; قانون بَراءةِ الاخْتِراعِ patent law; مَكْتَب بَراءاتِ الاخْتِراعِ patent office; طَلَبَ بَراءةَ الاخْتِراعِ to apply for a patent; سَجَّلَ اخْتِراعاً to register a patent; حَصَلَ على بَراءةِ اخْتِراعٍ to obtain a patent; أَحْدَث اخْتِراعٍ تِكْنولوجيٍّ من اليابانِ the latest technological invention from Japan; الحاجةُ أُمُّ الاخْتِراعِ necessity is the mother of invention

مُخْتَرَع *n* |مُخْتَرَعات| invention

مُخْتَرِع *n* inventor; مُخْتَرِع عَبْقَريّ a genius inventor

‹ **خَرِفَ** *v* |a; خَرَف| to be/grow senile

خَرَّفَ *v* to grow senile

أَخْرَفَ *v* [1] [سَبَّبَ الخَرَفَ] to make senile; أَخْرَفَهُ الكِبَرُ old age made him senile [2] [أَقامَ مُدّةَ الخَريفِ] to spend the autumn

خَرَف *n* senility, dementia, senile dementia (fml)

خَرِف *adj* demented, senile; مُسِنّونَ خَرِفونَ demented elderly people; شَيْخ خَرِف a senile old man

خُرافة *n* fable; fairy tale; myth; superstition; كانَ مَبْنيًّا على خُرافةٍ to be based on superstition

خُرافيّ *adj* mythical, mythological; fabulous; legendary; fairy-tale (*before n*); شَخْصيّات خُرافيّة mythological characters

خَروف *n* |خِرْفان, خِراف| (Zool) sheep; لَحْم الخَروفِ mutton; lamb

خَريف *n* autumn, fall (AmE); خَريف العُمْرِ the autumn of life; في (فَصْلِ) الخَريفِ in the autumn

خَريفيّ *adj* autumnal; جَوّ خَريفيّ autumnal weather

‹ **خَرْفَش** *v* |i; خَرْفَشة| to mix

‹ **خَرَقَ** *v* |i-u; خَرْق| ❶ [ثَقَبَ] to perforate; to pierce; to prick; to penetrate; خَرَقَ شَخْصاً بالرَصاصِ to riddle sb with bullets; خَرَقَ بالوناً to prick a balloon ❷ [نَقَضَ] to break; to violate; to infringe on; خَرَقَ القانونَ to break the law; خَرَقَ اتِّفاقاً to violate a treaty ❸ [اخْتَرَقَ] to cross; خَرَقَ جِدارَ الصَوْتِ to break the sound barrier

خَرَّقَ *v* to tear apart

تَخَرَّقَ *v* to be torn

انْخَرَقَ *v* to be torn

اخْتَرَقَ *v* ❶ [اقْتَحَمَ] to break into/through; to penetrate; to force one's way into; اخْتَرَقَ غابةً كَثيفةً to penetrate into a dense forest; اخْتَرَقَ حاجِزَ الصَوْتِ to break the sound barrier ❷ (Comput) to hack; اخْتَرَقَ (نِظامَ) كُمْبيوتر to hack into a computer

خَرْق *n* ❶ [ثُقْب] |خُروق| hole; crack; leak ❷ [مَصْدَر] breach, violation; خَرْق واضِح \ ظاهِر a clear/blatant violation; خَرْق فاضِح a flagrant breach

خُرْق *n* clumsiness, awkwardness; fumbling

خارِق *adj* |خَوارِقُ| ❶ [نافِذ] penetrating; piercing; صِياح \ صَوْت خارِق a piercing scream/voice ❷ [غَيْر عاديّ] unusual; extraordinary; unheard-of; remarkable; قُدْرة خارِقة an extraordinary ability; جَهْد خارِق a superhuman effort; خارِق للعادةِ unusual; extraordinary; خارِق للطَبيعةِ supernatural; paranormal; preternatural; خَوارِق miracles, supernatural phenomena

خِرْقة *n* |خِرَق| rag

اخْتِراق *n* |اخْتِراقات| ❶ [تَغَلْغُل] penetration; breakthrough; breach; اخْتِراق أَمْنيّ security breach; اخْتِراق عِلْميّ a scientific breakthrough; شَهِدَ اخْتِراقاً مُهِمًّا to achieve an important breakthrough ❷ (Comput) hacking; اخْتِراق كُمْبيوتر computer hacking

أَخْرَق **A** *adj* |dipt; خُرْق| clumsy, awkward, inept; كانَ أَخْرَقَ to be clumsy; to have two left feet

B *n* |dipt; خُرْق| clumsy oaf, klutz, bungler

مُخْتَرِق **A** *adj* penetrating

B *n* hacker

‹ **خَرَمَ** *v* |i; خَرْم| ❶ [ثَقَبَ] to pierce; to perforate; خَرَمَ شَيْئاً to pierce sth ❷ [شَقَّ] to tear/rip up; خَرَمَ ثَوْباً to tear a garment

خَرَّمَ *v* ❶ [ثَقَبَ] to pierce; to perforate ❷ [شَقَّ] to tear/rip up

خَرْم *n* |خُروم| perforation

خُرْم *n* |خُروم| hole; خُرْم الإبْرةِ the eye of the needle

خَرّامة *n* hole punch; perforator

أَخْرَم *adj* |dipt| هو أَخْرَمُ الرَأْيِ he has no opinion of his own

تَخْريم *n* perforation; مِنْشار تَخْريمِ jigsaw

مُخَرَّم *adj* ❶ [وَرَق] perforated ❷ [قِماش] openwork; lacework

مَخْروم *adj* defective

‹ **خِرْنِق** *n* |خَرانِقُ| (Zool) leveret, young hare; young rabbit

‹ **خَرّوب** *n* carob; شَجَرة الخَرّوبِ carob/locust tree; خَرّوب الماعِزِ buckthorn

‹ **خَرّوبة** *n a unit of measure*

‹ **خِرْوَع** *n* castor-oil plant; زَيْت الخِرْوَعِ castor oil

‹ **خَزَب** *n* oedema

‹ **خَزَرَ** *v* |u; خَزْر| to give a sidelong glance; to give a questioning look

خَزَر *n* squint

‹[1] **خَزَّ** *v* |u; خَزّ| to pierce; خَزَّ عَدوَّهُ بِسَهْمٍ to pierce one's enemy with an arrow

[2] **خَزّ** *n* |خُزوز| silk

‹ **خَزَعَ** *v* |a; خَزْع| to cut

خِزْعة *n* (Med) biopsy

‹ **خُزَعْبَلات** *n pl* (cock-and-bull) stories

‹ **خَزَف** *n* ceramics; pottery; خَزَف صينيّ porcelain, chinaware; خَزَف مَصْقول glazed pottery; صِناعة الخَزَفِ the ceramic industry

خَزّاف *n* potter

خِزافة *n* pottery

خَزَفيّ *adj* earthenware (*before n*); china (*before n*); ceramic

خَزَق *v* |i; خَزْق| to stab

خَوْزَق *v* |i; خَوْزَقة| to impale

خازوق *n* |خوازيقُ| **1** [عَمود] pole; post; stake; foundation pile **2** [حيلة] dirty trick

اخْتَزَلَ *v* **1** [اقْتَطَعَ] to deduct; to stop; اخْتَزَلَ شَيْئاً من المالِ to deduct sth from the money **2** [رَدَّ] to reduce, to cut back on; to shorten; اخْتَزَلَ المُدّةَ إلى خَمْسةِ أَيامٍ to reduce the period to five days **3** [كَتَبَ بالرُموزِ] to write in shorthand, to use stenography

اخْتِزال *n* |اخْتِزالات| **1** [طَريقة كِتابةٍ] shorthand, stenography **2** (Phys) reduction **3** [اقْتِطاع] اخْتِزال الزَمَنِ gain in time

اخْتِزاليّ *adj* reduced, limited; partial; shorthand (*before n*); انْقِسام اخْتِزاليّ (Med) reduction division

مُخْتَزِل *n* shorthand secretary, stenographer; shorthand typist, stenotypist

خُزامى *n coll* |f; sing n خُزاماة| (Bot) lavender

خَزَنَ *v* |u; خَزْن| to store; خَزَنَ شَيْئاً في الكُمْبيوتَر to save sth on/in the computer

خَزَّنَ *v* **1** [خَزَنَ] to store; خَزَّنَ بَضائعَ to stock up/store goods; خَزَّنَ الطاقة to store energy **2** (Comput) to store, to save; خَزَّنَ مَعْلوماتٍ to store data; خَزَّنَ مِلَفّاً to save a file

اخْتَزَنَ *v* to store

خازِن *n* |خُزّان, خَزَنة| treasurer

خَزّان *n* |خَزازينُ, خَزّانات| **1** [حَوْض] tank, storage tank; reservoir; خَزّان ماءٍ water tank; خَزّان نَفْطٍ oil tank; خَزّان بَنْزينٍ petrol (BrE) gasoline (AmE) tank; a tank of petrol/gasoline; خَزّان الزَيْتِ crankcase; خَزّان وَقودٍ مَليء \ فارِغ a full/empty tank; مَلأَ الخَزّانَ بالوَقود to fill up the tank **2** [سَدّ للمِياهِ] reservoir

خِزانة *n* |خَزائنُ, خِزانات| **1** [مال] safe, strongbox; locker; الخِزانة العامّة the state treasury; وِزارة الخِزانةِ the Treasury Department **2** [دولاب] cupboard; خِزانة كُتُبٍ bookcase; خِزانة مَلابِسَ wardrobe; خِزانة عَرْضٍ showcase **3** [مَكْتَبة] خِزانة الكُتُبِ (Mor) library

خَزْنة *n* |خَزْنات| **1** [للنُقودِ] safe **2** [الرَصاصِ] magazine

خَزينة *n* |خَزائنُ| **1** [للدَفْعِ في المَحَلِّ] till, cash register; جَرَدَ الخَزينة make out the balance **2** [لِحِفْظِ الأَمْوالِ] safe, strongbox; سَرَقَ خَزينةً to crack a safe; وَضَعَ شَيْئاً في الخَزينةِ to put sth in the safe; خَزينة الدَوْلَةِ state treasury; خَزينة عَرْضٍ showcase

اخْتِزان *n* storage

تَخْزين *n* |تَخْزينات| storage; وَحْدة تَخْزينٍ خارِجيٍّ \ داخليٍّ external/main memory unit; جِهاز تَخْزينٍ storage device

تَخْزينيّ *adj* storage (*before n*); سَعة تَخْزينيّة storage capacity

مُخْتَزَن *adj* stored

مَخْزَن *n* |مَخازِنُ| **1** [مُسْتَوْدَع] warehouse, storehouse; depot; repository; shed; مَخْزَن سَفينةٍ ship's hold; مَخْزَن اسْتيداع warehouse; مَخْزَن سِلاحٍ magazine; مَخْزَن أَسْلِحةٍ arms dump, weapons depot **2** [مَحَلّ] store, shop; اشْتَرى شَيْئاً من مَخْزَنٍ to buy sth in a shop **3** (Comput) memory

مَخْزون **A** *adj* stored
B *n* |مَخْزونات| stock, supplies; مَخْزون احْتِياطيّ buffer stock; مَخْزون احْتِياطيّ من الغازِ الطَبيعيِّ a buffer stock of gas; مَخْزونُنا مَحْدودٌ our stock is limited; يَنْفَدُ المَخْزونُ the supplies are being exhausted

خَزى *v* |i; خِزْي| to disgrace; to put to shame

خَزِيَ *v* |a; خَزًى, خِزْي| to be/become despicable

أَخْزى *v* to bring shame on; أَخْزاكَ اللهُ! may God humble you!

خِزْي *n* shame; disgrace, ignominy; أَلْحَقَ بِعائلَتِهِ الخِزْيَ to disgrace one's family

مُخْزٍ *adj* humiliating; shameful; infamous

مُخْزِية *n* |مُخْزِيات, مَخازٍ| disgraceful act

خَسَأَ *v* |a; خَسْأ| to chase away

خَسِئَ *v* |a; خَسْء| to be chased away

خَسِرَ *v* |a; خُسْر, خَسارة| **1** [أَضاعَ] to lose; to forfeit; خَسِرَ حَياتَهُ to lose one's life; خَسِرَ مالاً to lose money; خَسِرَ الكَثيرَ من الوَقْتِ to lose/waste a lot of time; خَسِرَ قيمَتَهُ to lose value **2** (Sport) to lose; خَسِرَ بِفارِقِ النِقاطِ to lose on points; خَسِرَ أمامَ الفَريقِ المُضيفِ to lose to the home team

خَسَّرَ *v* to cause the loss of

أَخْسَرَ *v* to make lose, to cause a loss to

اِسْتَخْسَرَ *v* |على ,في| to grudge; اِسْتَخْسَرَ شَيْئاً على شَخْصٍ to grudge sb sth

خاسِر **A** *adj* unprofitable, loss-making (*before n*); شَرِكة خاسِرة a loss-making company; مَصْنَع سَيّاراتٍ خاسِر an unprofitable car factory; قَضِيّة خاسِرة a lost cause
B *n* loser; الرابِح والخاسِر the winner and the loser

خَسارة *n* |خَسائِرُ| loss; damage; خَسائِر مادِّيّة material damage; خَسائِر مَعْنَوِيّة non-material/emotional damage; خَسارة جَسيمة a substantial loss; خَسائِر طَفيفة minor losses; خَسائِر بَشَرِيّة loss of lives, human losses; خَسارة أَمْوالٍ loss of money/assets; عَوَّضَ خَسارَتَهُ to compensate for one's losses; خَسارة لا تُعَوَّض an irreparable loss; لم يَحْتَمِلِ الخَسارةَ to be a bad loser; كَبَّدَ العَدُوَّ خَسائِرَ فادِحةً to inflict heavy/severe losses on the enemy; تَكَبَّدَ خَسائِرَ كَبيرةً to suffer heavy/severe losses; يا خَسارةً \ لَلْخَسارةِ what a pity!, what a shame!; too bad!; باعَ شَيْئاً بِخَسارةٍ to sell sth at a loss; قَدَّرَ خَسارةً to assess the damage; أَوْقَعَ خَسارةً مادِّيّةً to inflict material/financial loss; أَنْزَلَ خَسائِرَ to inflict damage, to cause losses

خُسْران *n* loss; damage

‹ **خَسَّ** *v* |a; خَساسة ,خِسّة| **1** [قَلَّ] to decrease, to diminish; خَسَّ وَزْنُهُ to lose weight **2** [حَقَرَ] to be mean

خَسَّسَ *v* to lessen, to reduce

خَسّ *n* lettuce; رَأْس خَسٍّ a head of lettuce

خَسيس *adj* |أَخِسّاءُ| mean, low

خَسيسة *n* |خَسائِسُ| a mean trick

‹ **خَسَفَ** *v* |i; خُسوف ,خَسْف| to sink; to cause to sink; كانَ يَتَمَنّى أَنْ تَخْسِفَ بِهِ الأَرْضُ he wished the ground would swallow him up

اِنْخَسَفَ *v* to subside, to sink; اِنْخَسَفَتِ الأَرْضِيّةُ the floor/ground gave way

خَسْف *n* **1** [مَصْدَر] subsidence **2** [ذُلّ] humiliation

خُسوف *n* lunar eclipse; خُسوف جُزْئِيّ \ كُلِّيّ a partial/total lunar eclipse

اِنْخِساف *n* subsidence; اِنْخِساف الطَريقِ road subsidence

‹ **خُشاف** *n* a dessert of dried fruits and almonds

‹ **خَشَّبَ** *v* to turn into wood

تَخَشَّبَ *v* to be/grow rigid; to become woody; تَخَشَّبَتْ مَشاعِرُهُ \ عَواطِفُهُ to be/become emotionally numb; تَخَشَّبَ جِسْمُهُ his body froze, his body went rigid; تَخَشَّبَتْ ذِراعُهُ عِنْدَما أَرادَ أَنْ يَضْرِبَ أُمَّهُ his arm froze as he tried to hit his mother

خَشَب *n* |أَخْشاب| wood, timber; خَشَب لَيِّن softwood; خَشَب صَلْد \ صُلْب hardwood; خَشَب مَنْقوش \ مَحْفور woodcut, engraved wood; خَشَب مَضْغوط hardboard; خَشَب اِسْتِوائِيّ tropical hardwood; خَشَب الصَنَوْبَر pine, pine wood; خَشَب الصَنْدَل sandalwood; ناقِر \ نَقّار الخَشَبِ woodpecker; لَوْح خَشَبٍ plank, board; أَلْياف الخَشَبِ wood wool; سوس الخَشَبِ woodworm; من الخَشَبِ wooden, made of wood; يَعْفَنُ الخَشَبُ wood rots

خَشّاب *n* lumberjack; lumber merchant

خَشَبة *n* |أَخْشاب ,خَشَبات| piece of wood; plank, board; خَشَبة المَيِّتِ coffin; وَقَفَ على خَشَبةِ المَسْرَح to be on stage

خَشَبِيّ *adj* wooden; timber (*before n*); بَيْت خَشَبِيّ a wooden house; طاوِلة خَشَبِيّة a wooden table; لَوْن خَشَبِيّ colouring pencil

خَشَبِيّة *n* xylophone

تَخَشُّب *n* stiffening; rigidity; تَخَشُّب الجِسْم stiffening of the body

تَخْشيبة *n* |تَخاشيبُ ,تَخْشيبات| shed; log cabin; barracks

مُتَخَشِّب *adj* rigid; turned to wood; lignified; كانَ مُتَخَشِّباً لِشِدّةِ التَوَتُّر his body was tight with tension

‹ **خَشْخاش** *n* |خَشاخيشُ| (Bot) poppy; بِذْرة الخَشْخاشِ poppy seed

‹ **خَشْخَشَ** *v* |i; خَشْخَشة| to rustle; to rattle; to murmur; تُخَشْخِشُ الأَوْراقُ the leaves are rustling

خَشْخَشة *n* rustle; rattle; noise

خُشْخيشة *n* rattle

‹ **خُشارة** *n* remainders, leftovers; refuse

‹ **خَشْرَم** *n* |خَشارِمُ| wasps' nest; bees' nest

‹ **خَشَّ** *v* |i-u; خَشّ| to enter

خَشاش *n* vermin

‹ **خَشَعَ** *v* to be submissive; خَشَعَ في صَلاتِهِ to be deep in prayer

تَخَشَّعَ *v* to show reverence, to humble oneself

خاشِع *adj* |خَشَعة| submissive; humble

خُشوع *n* humility, submissiveness; devotion; خُشوع شَديد strong devotion; great awe

‹ **خَشْف** *n* crunching (*the sound snow makes underfoot*)

خُشْف *n* |خِشَفة, خُشوف| fawn

‹ **خَشْم** *n* |خُشوم| nose

خُشام *n* (Med) anosmia (*loss of one's sense of smell*)

خَيْشوم *n* |خَياشيمُ| 1 [سَمَك] gill 2 [أَنْف] nose

‹ **خَشُنَ** *v* |u; خُشونة| to be/become rough; to be/become coarse

خَشَّنَ *v* to roughen, to coarsen

خاشَنَ *v* to be rude/uncivil

تَخَشَّنَ *v* to roughen, to coarsen

اخْشَوْشَنَ *v* |Form XII| 1 [صارَ خَشِنًا] to roughen, to coarsen 2 [عاشَ عَيْشًا خَشِنًا] to live a rough life

خَشِن *adj* |خِشان| 1 [عَكْس ناعِم] rough; coarse; hard; chapped; خَشِن الجِسْم a heavily-built body; سَطْح \ بَشَرة خَشِن(ة) a rough surface/skin; طَقْس \ جَوّ خَشِن rough weather 2 [فَظّ] rude; unrefined; harsh; rough; رَجُل خَشِن a rude man; بِصَوْتٍ خَشِنٍ with a rough voice 3 (Sport) unsporting; لاعِب خَشِن an unsporting player; مُباراة خَشِنة an unsporting game

خُشونة *n* roughness, crudeness; rudeness; تَدَخَّلَ بِخُشونةٍ to intervene harshly; عامَلَ شَخْصاً بِخُشونةٍ to treat sb roughly; تَعامَلَ مع شَخْصٍ بِخُشونةٍ to deal roughly with sb

‹ **خَشِيَ** *v* |a; خَشْية| to fear, to be afraid of; خَشِيَ أَباهُ \ من أَبيهِ he was afraid of his father; خَشِيَ على ابْنِهِ to fear for one's son; أَخْشى أَنْ تَكونَ على صَوابٍ I am afraid that you are right

خَشّى *v* to scare, to frighten

خَشْية *n* |خَشايا| fear; dread; خَشْيةَ الفَقْرِ for fear of poverty; خَشْيةَ أَنْ يُزْعِجَها for fear that he would disturb her

‹ **خَصَبَ, خَصِبَ** *v* |a-i; خِصْب| to be fertile

خَصَّبَ *v* 1 [سَمَّدَ] to fertilize; يُخَصِّبُ السَمادُ الأَرْضَ manure makes the soil fertile; خَصَّبَ الأَرْضَ to enrich the soil 2 [لَقَّحَ] to inseminate

أَخْصَبَ *v* to be fertile

خَصِب *adj* fertile; productive; امْرَأة خَصِبة a fertile woman; غَير خَصِب infertile, sterile; barren, poor

خِصْب A *adj* fertile; productive; مادّة خِصْبة (fig) fertile ground/soil
B *n* fertility

خُصوبة *n* fertility

خَصيب *adj* fertile

إِخْصاب *n* fertilization; impregnation; إِخْصاب اصْطِناعيّ artificial insemination; الإِخْصاب بالأَنابيبِ in vitro fertilization, IVF

تَخْصيب *n* 1 [بالسَمادِ] fertilization; تَخْصيب التُرْبة fertilization of the soil; تَخْصيب الأَرْضِ بالسَمادِ fertilization of the land with manure 2 [مَوادّ نَوَويّة] enrichment; تَخْصيب اليورانيوم uranium enrichment 3 [تَلْقيح] fertilization; insemination; تَخْصيب اصْطِناعيّ artificial insemination

مُخْصِب A *adj* fertile
B *n* fertilizer

مُخَصَّب *adj* enriched; يورانيوم مُخَصَّب enriched uranium

مُخَصِّب *n* |مُخَصِّبات| fertilizer

‹ **خَصْخَصَ** *v* |i; خَصْخَصة| (Econ) to privatize; خَصْخَصَ شَرِكةَ السِكَكِ الحَديديّةِ to privatize the railways

خَصْخَصة *n* (Econ) privatization; خَصْخَصة شَرِكاتٍ حُكوميّةٍ the privatization of public services

‹ **خَصَّرَ** *v* (Clothg) to take in at the waist

خاصَرَ *v* خاصَرَ شَخْصاً to put one's arm around sb's waist

تَخاصَرَ *v* to put one's hands on/arms around each other's waist

اخْتَصَرَ *v* 1 [اخْتَزَلَ] to shorten, to cut short; to abbreviate; to summarize; اخْتَصَرَ قِصّةً to abridge a story; اخْتَصَرَ الكَلامَ to be brief; اخْتَصَرَ كَلِماتٍ to abbreviate words 2 (Math) to reduce; اخْتَصَرَ كَسْراً to reduce a fraction matters **2** [كانَ ذي صَلاحيةٍ] to be competent, to be qualified; to be authorized; اخْتَصَّ بِشَيْءٍ to be authorized to do sth, to have the power to do sth; يَخْتَصُّ قاضي النَّقْضِ بالنَظَرِ في الشَكْلِ وَلَيْسَ في المَوْضوعِ the judge of the Court of Cassation is authorized to judge the form, but not the content

خاصّ *adj* special; particular, characteristic, specific; exclusive; private, own; حالة خاصّة a special case; an extraordinary situation; اهْتِمام خاصّ special attention, special consideration; شَرِكة خاصّة a private company; القِطاع الخاصّ the private sector; private enterprise; تَأْمين خاصّ private insurance; بِصِفَةٍ خاصّةٍ especially; in particular; mainly; خاصّ ب concerning; pertaining to; belonging to; for; valid/true for; set aside for; خاصّ بِشَيْءٍ \ شَخْصٍ especially/specifically for sth/sb; مُبادَرة خاصّة a private initiative; ... الخاصّ بِهِ his own ...; اللَهْجة الخاصّة بِمَدينةِ حِمْصَ the dialect of Homs; كانَتْ لِكُلٍّ مِنْهُمْ أَسْبابُهُ الخاصّةُ بِهِ each of them had his own reasons

خاصّة *n* |خَواصُّ| **1** [ميزة] property, characteristic; خَواصّ السُكَّرِ the properties of sugar; خاصّةً especially, in particular; يَشْتاقُ إلى أُسْرَتِهِ، خاصّةً إلى ابْنِهِ الصَغيرِ he misses his family, especially his youngest son **2** [طَبَقة راقية] elite

(Idioms) خاصَّتي my (own); هذا المالُ خاصَّتي this money is mine

خاصّيّة *n* |خاصّيّات، خَصائِصُ| characteristic; property, feature, trait; peculiarity; خاصّيّة لافِتة للنَظَرِ a striking feature; خاصّيّة نَموذَجيّة a typical feature; خاصّيّة جَوْهَرِيّة an essential property

خُصّ *n* |خِصاص، أَخْصاص، خُصوص| hut

خصاص *n* gap, crevice, fissure

خُصوص *n* **1** [بالنِسْبة ل] بِخُصوصِ ... about, concerning, regarding; مَعْلومات بِخُصوصِ المَشْروعِ information on the project; ب \ في هذا الخُصوصِ in this regard, concerning this; أَوَدُّ أَنْ أُشيرَ في هذا الخُصوصِ إلى أنّ ... in this respect, I would like to point out that ... **2** [بِشَكْلٍ خاصٍّ] خُصوصاً, على (وَجْهِ) الخُصوصِ in particular, particularly, especially;

خَصْر *n* |خُصور| **1** (Anat) waist, middle; خَصْر دَقيق a slender waist; حِزام حول الخَصْرِ a belt around the waist **2** [مَلابِس] waist

خَصَر *n* frostbite

خاصِرة *n* |خَواصِرُ| (Anat) waist; flank; side; أَحَسَّ أَلَماً في خاصِرَتِهِ his side hurt

خُصار *n* (Med) chilblains; chilblained hands

اخْتِصار *n* |اخْتِصارات| **1** [اخْتِزال] abbreviation; "إلخ" اخْتِصارٌ ل "إلى آخِرِهِ" 'etc.' is short for 'et cetera' **2** [مُلَخَّص] summary; بِاخْتِصارٍ in summary/short, briefly; بِاخْتِصارٍ شَديدٍ يُمْكِنُ القَوْلُ إنّ very briefly, one could say that **3** [إيجاز] succinctness, conciseness; للاخْتِصارِ for the sake of brevity **4** (Comp) اخْتِصار رَوابِطَ URL shortening; اخْتِصار لَوْحةِ المَفاتيحِ keyboard shortcut

مُخْتَصَر **A** *adj* shortened; abbreviated; short; summary; وَصْف مُخْتَصَر a short description; تَقْرير مُخْتَصَر a summary report; طَريق مُخْتَصَر shortcut; بالمُخْتَصَرِ المُفيدِ to cut a long story short; brief and to the point

B *n* excerpt

مِخْصَرة *n* |مَخاصِرُ| baton

خَصَّ *v* |u; خَصّ, خُصوص, خُصوصيّة| **1** [تَعَلَّقَ] to concern; فيما يَخُصُّ ... as for ..., with regard to ..., in respect of ..., as far as ... is concerned; هذا لا يَخُصُّني this is none of my concern, this doesn't concern me **2** [أَفْرَدَ] to allot; خَصَّ شَخْصاً بالذِكْرِ to give sb a special mention

خَوْصَصَ *v* |i; خَوْصَصة| (NA) to privatize

خَصَّصَ *v* to designate, to allocate; to reserve, to earmark, to set aside; خَصَّصَ لِشَخْصٍ تَعْويضاً عن الضَرَرِ to award damages to sb; خَصَّصَ وَقْتاً للمُناقَشةِ to set aside time for discussion; خَصَّصَ مالاً لِشَيْءٍ to earmark money for sth; المَوْقِعُ خُصِّصَ للأَطْفالِ the site is intended for children

تَخَصَّصَ *v* to specialize; تَخَصَّصَ في عِلْمِ إدارةِ الأَعْمالِ to specialize in business administration

اخْتَصَّ *v* **1** [تَخَصَّصَ] to be specialized; to concentrate; اخْتَصَّ ب \ في شَيْءٍ to be specialized in sth; to concentrate on sth; اخْتَصَّ بالأُمورِ القانونيّةِ to be specialized in legal

عارَضَتْ كُلُّ الأَحْزابِ وَعلى الخُصوصِ حِزْبُ العَمَلِ all parties, and the Labour Party in particular, objected; الشَرْق الأَوْسَط عُموماً والعِراق خُصوصاً the Middle East in general, and Iraq in particular

خُصوصي *adj* special; private; سَيّارة خُصوصيّة private car; شَبَكة خُصوصيّة extranet

خُصوصيّة *n* **1** [ميزة] particularity **2** privacy; سِياسة الخُصوصيّةِ privacy policy; حَمى خُصوصيّةَ شَخْصٍ to protect sb's privacy

خَصيصة *n* |خَصائِصُ| particularity, characteristic; من خَصائِصِ اللَوْنِ القاتِمِ امْتِصاصُهُ للضَوْءِ one characteristic of a dark colour is that it absorbs light

خَوْصَصة *n* (NA) privatization, denationalization

اخْتِصاص *n* |اخْتِصاصات| **1** [تَخَصُّص] specialization; specialism; specialty; مُتَعَدِّد الاخْتِصاصاتِ multidisciplinary; التَنْظيمُ من اخْتِصاصِ مَجْلِسِ الجَمْعيّةِ the organization is in the hands of the association's committee; لِكُلٍّ اخْتِصاصُهُ every man to his trade **2** (Law) competence; jurisdiction; كانَ في اخْتِصاصِ المَحْكَمةِ to be within the competence of the court

اخْتِصاصيّ **A** *adj* specialist; اسْتَشارَ طَبيباً اخْتِصاصيًّا to consult a specialist (*doctor*) **B** *n* [إخْصائيّ] expert, specialist; اخْتِصاصيّ في أَمْراضِ الجِلْدِ dermatologist

أَخَصّ *adj* |dipt| في \ على الأَخَصِّ especially

أَخِصّائيّ, إخْصائيّ *n* **1** [خَبير] expert, specialist; أَخِصّائيّ تَعْليميّ educationalist, education specialist **2** (Med) specialist; أَخِصّائيّ في الأَمْراضِ الجِلْديّةِ dermatologist, skin specialist; تحت عِلاجِ أَخِصّائيٍّ under specialist treatment

تَخَصُّص *n* |تَخَصُّصات| specialization; specialism; مَجال تَخَصُّصٍ field of specialization; تَخَصُّص في طِبِّ الأَسْنانِ a specialization in dentistry

تَخَصُّصيّ *adj* specialist; مَوْضوع تَخَصُّصيّ a specialist subject/item

تَخْصيص *n* **1** [تَحْديد] allocation, allotment, setting aside; designation; assignment; تَخْصيص مَبْلَغٍ allocation of a sum of money; تَخْصيص أَرْضٍ للزِراعةِ designation of land for agriculture; تَخْصيص جائِزةٍ allocation of an award/prize **2** [خَصْخَصة] privatization; تَخْصيص شَرِكاتٍ حُكوميّةٍ privatization of public enterprises

مُتَخَصِّص *n* expert, specialist; مُتَخَصِّص في مَجالِ الضَرائِبِ tax/fiscal specialist

مُخْتَصّ **A** *adj* **1** [إخْصائيّ] specialized; مُخْتَصّ في مَجالِ ... specialized in the field of...; كانَ مُخْتَصًّا في شَيْءٍ to be specialized in sth **2** [ذو صَلاحيّةٍ] competent; المُوَظَّف \ الجِهة المُخْتَصّ(ة) the competent official/authority **B** *n* expert, specialist; مُخْتَصّ بالبيئةِ environmental specialist

مُخَصَّص *adj* |لِ| designated for, earmarked for, set aside for; focussed on; مُخَصَّص لِجِهازِ التَعْليمِ designated for the educational staff, especially for education; المَعْرِضُ مُخَصَّصٌ لِ ... the exhibition is geared towards..., the exhibition is especially for...; مُخَصَّص لِهَذا الغَرَضِ especially for this purpose; مُخَصَّص للزوّارِ reserved for visitors

مُخَصِّص *adj* characteristic; specialized

مَخْصوص *adj* special; مَخْصوص لَك especially for you

〈 **خَصَفَ** *v* |i; خَصْف| to repair (*a shoe*)

〈 **خَصْلة** *n* |خِصال| natural disposition; trait; خَصْلةُ البَدَنِ لا يُغَيِّرُها إلاّ الكَفَنُ ≈ a leopard cannot change its spots

خُصْلة *n* |خُصْلات, خُصَل| lock; tuft; خُصَل الشَعْرِ locks of hair

〈 **خَصَمَ** *v* |i; خَصْم| to discount; to subtract, to deduct; خَصَمَ مَبْلَغاً من السِعْرِ to deduct an amount from the price

خاصَمَ *v* to argue, to quarrel; to dispute

تَخاصَمَ *v* to argue, to quarrel; تَخاصَمَ مع شَخْصٍ to argue with sb; to be on bad terms with sb

اخْتَصَمَ *v* to quarrel, to argue

خَصْم *n* |أَخْصام, خُصوم| **1** [نِدّ] opponent, adversary; opposite party; opposing team; خَصْم قَوِيّ a strong opponent; خَصْم دائِم nemesis, a permanent adversary; خَصْم لَدود a fierce opponent; مُحامي الخَصْمِ counsel for the other/opposite party; الفَريق الخَصْم the opposing team **2** (Busn) deduction;

خَصْم من الراتِبِ reduction; withholding; خُصوم liabilities; خَصْم ١٠٪ على جَميع البَضائِع deduction from salary; حَصَلَ على خَصْمٍ من ثَمَنِ السِلَع 10% reduction on all goods; to get a reduction on the price of the merchandise

خِصام *n* quarrel, dispute

خُصومة *n* feud; controversy; خُصومة قَديمة بين أَشْخاصٍ an old feud between people

خَصيم *n* |خُصَماءُ, خُصْمان| adversary, opponent

مُتَخاصِم **A** *adj* arguing, fighting; كانَ مُتَخاصِماً مع شَخْصٍ to have an argument with sb, to be on bad terms with sb **B** *n* adversary; المُتَخاصِمونَ (Law) the contending parties

مُخاصَمة *n* argument; conflict

خَصى *v* |i; خِصاء| to castrate; to emasculate; خَصى قِطًّا to neuter a cat

خَصيّ *n* |خِصْية, خِصْيان| eunuch

خَصْي *n* castration

خِصاء *n* castration

خُصْية *n* |خُصًى| (Anat) testicle, testis

إِخْصائيّ *n* see خصص

مَخْصيّ *n* eunuch; حِصان مَخْصيّ gelding

خَضَبَ *v* |i; خَضْب| to colour; to dye; خَضَبَ شَعْرَهُ to dye/colour one's hair

خَضَّبَ *v* to colour, to dye

تَخَضَّبَ *v* to paint one's body *(with henna)*

خَضْب *n* pigment

خِضاب *n* pigment; dye

تَخَضُّب *n* pigmentation

خَضْخَضَ *v* |i; خَضْخَضة| to shake

خَضَدَ *v* |i; خَضْد| to break off

خَضِرَ *v* |a; خُضْرة| to be green

خَضَّرَ *v* to dye green

اخْضَرَّ *v* to be/become green

اخْضَوْضَرَ *v* |Form XII| to be/become green

خَضّار *n* grocer, vegetable seller

خُضار *n* vegetables

خَضْراوات, خَضْرَوات *n pl* |sing خَضْراءُ| vegetables; خَضْراوات طازِجة fresh vegetables; زَرَعَ \ أَنْتَجَ الخَضْراواتِ to grow vegetables

خُضْرة *n* |خُضَر| **1** [نَبات] vegetable **2** [لَوْن] green colour, greenness; دائم الخُضْرة evergreen

خُضَريّ *n* greengrocer

خَضير *adj* green; مُروج خَضيرة verdant meadows

أَخْضَر *adj* |dipt; خُضْر| green; أَخْضَر فاتِح light green; شابّ أَخْضَر greenhorn; أَعْطى شَخْصاً الضَوْءَ الأَخْضَرَ to give sb the green light; يَدُها خَضْراءُ she has green fingers (BrE), she has a green thumb (AmE)

اخْضِرار *n* becoming/turning green

مَخْضَرة *n* lawn; patch of grass

يَخْضُور *n* (Bio) chlorophyll

مُخَضْرَم *adj contemporary of the Prophet who witnessed the birth and rising of Islam; old and experienced in life; living between two eras*

خَضَّ *v* |u; خَضّ| to shake, to jolt; to churn, to agitate

خَضّ *n* shaking; يَجِبُ خَضُّ الدَواءِ قبل الاسْتِعْمالِ the medicine should be shaken before use

خَضّة *n* shock; أَحْدَثَ خَضّةً سِياسيّةً to cause a political shock

خَضَعَ *v* |a; خُضوع| to submit, to surrender; to obey; to be subject; to be subjected; خَضَعَ لِشَيْءٍ to submit to sth; to belong to sth; to fall under sth; خَضَعَ لِلسُلْطةِ to submit to the authorities; خَضَعَ لِلتَعْليماتِ to follow the instructions; خَضَعَ لِطَلَباتِ شَخْصٍ to give in to sb's demands; خَضَعَ لِعَمَليّةٍ لِتَحْقيقاتٍ to be subject to an enquiry; خَضَعَ لِتَرْميمٍ جِراحيّةٍ to undergo an operation; خَضَعَ لِتَرْميمٍ to undergo renovation

أَخْضَعَ *v* to subject; to subjugate; to submit; أَخْضَعَ شَخْصاً لِشَيْءٍ to subject sb to sth; أَخْضَعَ بَلَداً to subjugate a country

خاضِع *adj* |خُضَّع, خُضْعان| **1** [طَيِّع] submissive; humble; obedient; شَعْب خاضِع a submissive people **2** [مُلازِم] subject, liable; خاضِع لِروما subject to Rome; خاضِع للمَوضةِ subject to fashion; خاضِع للضَريبةِ liable for tax, taxable

خَضوع *adj* |خُضُع| submissive; humble

كانَ على خَطَأٍ by accident; inadvertently; بِلا خَطَأٍ flawless; to be wrong/mistaken; ارْتَكَبَ \ اقْتَرَفَ \ عَمِلَ خَطَأً to make a mistake; تَعَلَّمَ من أَخْطائِهِ to learn from/through one's mistakes; غَفَرَ لِشَخْصٍ أَخْطاءَهُ to forgive sb his mistakes; تَحَمَّلَ خَطَأً to take responsibility; صَحَّحَ خَطَأَهُ to correct a mistake; صَحَّحَ أَخْطاءَهُ to make up for one's mistakes; قَوَّمَ خَطَأً to rectify a mistake; وَقَعَ في خَطَأٍ to make a mistake

2 (Sport) foul

خِطْء *n* sin

خاطِئ **A** *adj* wrong, mistaken; incorrect; erroneous; الطَريقة الخاطِئة the wrong way; جَواب خاطِئ a wrong answer; قَرار خاطِئ a wrong decision; مَعْلومات \ تَرْجَمة خاطِئة incorrect information/translation; كانَت الرَمْيةُ خاطِئةً the shot missed

B *n* (Chr) sinner

خَطّاء *n* sinner; خَطّاء تائِب a repentant sinner; كُلُّ ابْنِ آدَمَ خَطّاءٌ ≈ to err is human

خَطيئة *n* |خَطايا, خَطيئات| sin; crime; offence; خَطيئة آدَمَ the Fall of Adam, the Sin of Adam; أُعاقَبُ على خَطيئةٍ لم أَرْتَكِبْها I am being punished for a crime I didn't commit

مُخْطِئ *adj* wrong, mistaken; كانَ مُخْطِئًا to be wrong, to be at fault; قد أَكونُ مُخْطِئًا I could/might be wrong; إذا \ إنْ لم أَكُنْ مُخْطِئًا if I am not mistaken; أَنْتَ مُخْطِئٌ في ذلك you're wrong about that

‹ **خَطَبَ** *v* |u| **1** [حَدَّثَ] |خَطابة, خُطْبة| to preach; to make/deliver a speech; خَطَبَ الشَعْبَ \ في الشَعْبِ \ إلى الشَعْبِ to preach to the people; to make a speech to the people **2** [قبل الزَواج] |خِطْبة, خَطْب| to get/become engaged; خَطَبَ فَتاةً to be engaged to a girl; to ask for a girl's hand

خاطَبَ *v* to speak to, to talk to; to address; خاطَبَ شَخْصاً to speak to sb; to address sb; خاطَبَ الضُيوفَ to make a speech to the guests; خاطَبَ شَخْصاً بِلَهْجةٍ صارِمةٍ to have a serious word with sb

تَخاطَبَ *v* to talk to each other, to have a conversation

اخْتَطَبَ *v* to be/become engaged; اخْتَطَبَ شَخْصاً to be engaged to sb

خُضوع *n* submission, surrender; obedience; الخُضوع لِشَيْءٍ \ شَخْصٍ submission to sth/sb; الخُضوع لِإرادةِ شَخْصٍ submission to sb's will; خُضوع لِلقَدَرِ surrendering to fate

إخْضاع *n* subjugation

‹ **خَضِلَ** *v* |a; خَضَل| to be/get wet; خَضِلَ ثَوْبُهُ his clothes got wet; خَضِلَتْ تُرْبةُ الوَطَنِ بالدِماءِ the nation was soaked in blood

خَضَّلَ *v* to moisten, to wet

أَخْضَلَ *v* to soak; أَخْضَلَتْنا السَماءُ the rain soaked us

اخْضَلَّ *v* to become wet; اخْضَلَّتْ لِحْيَتُهُ بالدُموع his beard was soaked with tears

‹ **خَضَمَ** *v* |i; خَضْم| to chew; خَضَمَ الأَكْلَ to chew food

خِضَمّ *n* sea; ocean; في خِضَمِّ الحَمْلةِ الانْتِخابيّةِ in the middle of the election campaign

‹ **خَطِئَ** *v* |a; خَطأ| to make a mistake

خَطَّأَ *v* to accuse of an error, to belie; to fine (Tunisia)

أَخْطَأَ *v* to make a mistake, to commit an error; to be wrong, to be mistaken; to miss; أَخْطَأَ في فِعْلِ شَيْءٍ \ التَعامُلِ مع شَيْءٍ to do/deal with sth incorrectly; أَخْطَأْتُ الفَهْمَ I misunderstood; أَخْطَأَ الهَدَفَ to miss the target; أَخْطَأَت الطَلْقةُ (هَدَفَها) the shot missed (the target); أَخْطَأَ في الإجابةِ على سُؤالٍ to give a wrong answer; أَخْطَأْتَ! you are wrong!

خَطَأ **A** *adj* wrong, incorrect; جَواب خَطَأ a wrong answer

B *n* |أَخْطاء| **1** [غَلَط] mistake, error, incorrectness, fault, flaw; خَطَأ فادِح \ كَبير \ جَسيم \ فَظيع a grave/big/enormous/terrible mistake; خَطَأ تاريخيّ a historical error; خَطَأ قَضائيّ a judicial error; خَطَأ مَطْبَعيّ misprint; a typographical error; خَطَأ كِتابيّ a writing error; خَطَأ طِبّيّ a medical error; خَطَأ حِسابيّ \ في الحِسابِ miscalculation; خَطَأ لُغَويّ a language error; خَطَأ قَواعِديّ \ أُسْلوبيّ a grammatical/stylistic mistake; خَطَأ إمْلائيّ a spelling mistake; خَطَأ مُتَعَمَّد an intentional/deliberate mistake; خَطَأ غَيْر مَقْصودٍ an unintentional mistake; خَطَأ شائِع a common mistake; أَخْطاء كامِنة hidden flaws/defects; خَطَأ في التَرْكيبِ a flaw in the assembly; خَطَأ في الحِسابِ \ الاسْتِنْتاجِ an error in the calculation/conclusion; خَطَأً \ بالخَطَإ by mistake, mistakenly;

خَطْب *n* |خُطوب| ❶ [شأْن] matter; ما خَطْبُكَ؟ what's the matter? ❷ [مَكْروه] setback

خاطِب *n* |خُطّاب, خُطَباءُ| fiancé

خاطِبة *n* matchmaker

خِطاب *n* |خِطابات| ❶ [خُطْبة] speech; oration; خِطاب افْتِتاحيّ opening speech; inaugural speech/lecture; خِطاب رَسْميّ an official speech; خِطاب مُوجَّه ل \ أمام العُمّالِ a speech to the staff; أَلْقى خِطاباً to give a speech ❷ [رِسالة] letter ❸ (Ling) discourse

خَطابة *n* rhetoric; preaching; فَنّ الخَطابةِ rhetoric, oratory

خُطْبة *n* |خُطَب| speech, oration, sermon; خُطْبة الجُمْعةِ the Friday sermon; أَلْقى خُطْبةً to preach, to give/deliver a sermon; أَعَدَّ \ حَضَّر خُطْبةً to prepare a speech

خِطْبة *n* engagement; خاتِم الخِطْبةِ engagement ring

خُطوبة *n* engagement; خاتَم الخُطوبة engagement ring; فَسَخَ خُطوبَتَهُ to break off one's engagement

خَطيب *n* |خُطَباءُ| ❶ [خاطِب] fiancé ❷ [مُحاضِر] orator; preacher; خَطيب جَيِّد \ سَيِّئ \ عَظيم a good/bad/great orator

تَخاطُب *n* conversation; speaking; لُغة التَخاطُبِ spoken language

مُخاطَب *n* ❶ (Gram) second person; ضَمير المُخاطَبِ the second-person pronoun ❷ [المُتَكَلَّم إلَيْهِ] addressed

مُخاطَبة *n* ❶ [مَصْدَر] address; مُخاطَبة الجَماهير addressing the masses ❷ [مُكالَمة] talk, conversation

مَخْطوب *adj* engaged; كانَ مَخْطوباً ل \ إلى شَخْصٍ to be engaged to sb

خَطَرَ *v* |i-u; خَطَران, خُطور| to occur; خَطَرَ لَهُ \ بِبالِهِ أنْ ... it came to his mind that ...; لَقَدْ خَطَرَ على بالي شَيْءٌ I have just thought of sth, sth just occurred to me

خَطُرَ *v* |u; خُطورة| to be/become serious, to be/become dangerous

خاطَرَ *v* |ب| to risk; خاطَرَ بِشَيْءٍ to risk sth; to put sth at stake; to wager sth; خاطَرَ بِحَياتِهِ to risk one's life

أَخْطَرَ *v* to notify, to inform; أَخْطَرَ شَخْصاً بِشَيْءٍ to let sb know about sth; أَخْطَرَ الشُرْطةَ to alert the police

تَخَطَّرَ *v* to parade, to strut

تَخاطَرَ *v* to bet; تَخاطَرَ مع شَخْصٍ على شَيْءٍ to bet sb sth

خَطَر *n* |أَخْطار, خَطَرات| danger, peril, hazard; risk; menace; خَطَر عاجِل acute danger; خَطَر مُحْدِق a threatening danger; أَكْبَر خَطَرٍ the biggest danger; مَحْفوف بالأَخْطارِ surrounded by dangers; أَخْطار المِهْنةِ the risks of the job; مِنْطَقة الخَطَرِ danger/risk zone; خَطَر على الأَمْنِ العامِّ a menace to the public order; كانَ في خَطَرٍ to be in danger/in jeopardy/at risk, to be threatened; سَفينة في خَطَرٍ a ship in need; شَكَّلَ خَطَراً على الصِحّةِ to be a threat to health; عَرَّضَ شَيْئاً للخَطَرِ to expose sth to danger; تَعَرَّضَ للخَطَرِ to be exposed to danger, to be in danger; تَلاشى الخَطَرُ the danger is over; قد زالَ خَطَرُ العَدْوى the danger of contamination has passed; حَمى شَخْصاً من الأَخْطار to protect sb from danger; تَدارَكَ الخَطَرَ to avert the danger

خَطِر *adj* dangerous, hazardous, risky

خاطِر *n* |خَواطِرُ| ❶ [بال] mind; جالَ شَيْءٌ بِخاطِرِهِ he had sth on his mind; كَلَّفَ خاطِرَهُ to take pains/pains; شَغَلَ الخَواطِرَ (وَقامَ بِشَيْءٍ) to take the trouble (to do sth); هَزَّ \ to occupy the minds; هَدَّأَ الخَواطِرَ to calm the minds; أَلْهَبَ الخَواطِرَ to stir up emotions; دارَ في خاطِرِهِ it kept going through his head; طَيَّبَ خاطِرَ شَخْصٍ to ease sb's mind; عن طيبِ خاطِرٍ by one's own free will; لا على البالِ وَلا على الخاطِرِ unexpected, out of the blue ❷ [فِكْرة] idea, thought; خَطَرَ لَهُ خاطِرٌ an idea came to his mind

Idiom من أَجْلِ خاطِرِكَ for you

خَطّار *n* pendulum

خُطورة *n* seriousness, gravity; danger; خُطورة الوَضْعِ \ المَرَضِ the seriousness of the situation/illness; خالٍ من الخُطورة without risk

خَطير *adj* |خُطْر| ❶ [هامّ] serious, grave, critical; جَريمة خَطيرة a heavy/serious crime; مَرَض خَطير a dangerous/serious/critical disease; خَطَأ \ اتِّهام خَطير a serious mistake/accusation ❷ [خَطِر] dangerous, risky, perilous; تَقاطُع خَطير a dangerous crossing; خَطير على (أَمْنِ) الدَوْلةِ dangerous to the state; عَمَلِيّة \ مَوْقِف خَطير(ة) a risky action/situation

إخْطار *n* |إخْطارات| notification, notice, information; announcement; warning; إخْطار عاجِل an urgent warning

تَخاطُر *n* telepathy

تَخاطُريّ *adj* telepathic

مَخاطِر *n pl* |dipt| dangers; واجَهَ مَخاطِرَ to encounter/defy dangers

مُخاطِر *n* adventurer

مُخاطَرة *n* risk

‹ **خَطْرَفَ** *v* |i; خَطْرَفة| to be agitated; to walk fast

‹ **خَطَّ** *v* |u; خَطّ| 1 [رَسَمَ] to sketch 2 [وَضَعَ خُطّةً] to plan; to outline; خَطَّ طَرِيقاً to outline a route 3 [كَتَبَ] to write

خَطَّطَ *v* to plan

اخْتَطَّ *v* to plan; to outline

خَطّ *n* |خُطوط| 1 [سَطْر] line; خَطّ أُفُقيّ a horizontal line; خَطّ جانِبِيّ sideline; خَطّ رَئيسيّ main line; خَطّ ساحِليّ coastline; على طولِ الخَطِّ الساحِليّ along the coastline; خَطّ زَمَنيّ timeline; خَطّ الاسْتِواءِ equator; عند \ على خطِّ الاسْتِواءِ at/on the equator; خَطّ الطول meridian; خَطّ عَموديّ altitude; a vertical line; خَطّ فاصِل dividing line, boundary; وَضَعَ خَطًّا فاصِلاً to put/place/draw a dividing line; خَطّ مُسْتَقيم a straight line; خَطّ تَنازُليّ \ تَصاعُديّ a downward/an upward curve; خَطّ مُنَقَّط a dotted line; خَطّ الذُّرْوة crest; خَطّ السَّيْرِ route; حَدَّدَ \ رَسَمَ خَطَّ سَيْرٍ to map out a route; خَطّ العَرْضِ parallel; latitude; خَطّ اعْتِراضٍ interrupt line; خَطّ الحِزْبِ the party line; مُراقِب الخَطِّ linesman; line judge; على \ خارِجَ \ داخِلَ الخَطِّ on/outside/within the line; في خُطوطٍ عَريضةٍ in broad outlines; وَضَعَ خَطًّا تحت الأَخْطاءِ to underline mistakes; اجْتازَ خَطَّ الوُصولِ to cross the finish line 2 [كِتابة يَدَويّة] handwriting; script; font; خَطّ واضِح a clear handwriting; خَطّ مائِل italic; sloping handwriting; خَطّ كوفيّ Kufic writing; خَطّ اليَدِ handwriting; فَنّ الخَطِّ calligraphy; خَطِّيًّا in writing; بِخَطِّ ... handwritten by ... 3 (Mil) line; خَطّ النارِ line of fire; تَواجَدَ على خَطِّ النارِ to be in the line of fire; خَطّ العَدوِّ the enemy lines; الخَطّ الأَوَّل \ الأَماميّ front line; انْسَحَبَ وراء الخَطِّ الأَوَّلِ to withdraw behind the front line; خَطّ دِفاعٍ line of defence; وراء \ خَلْفَ خُطوطِ الدِفاعِ behind the lines of defence; اخْتَرَقَ خَطَّ الدِفاعِ to break through the line of defence 4 (Transp) line; track, section; route; خَطّ بَحْريّ ship line; خَطّ الباصِ \ الحافِلةِ bus line; خَطّ مُباشِر a direct line; خَطّ مُنْفَرِد single track; خَطّ مُزْدَوِج double track; الخَطّ ١٢ line 12; شَرِكة الخُطوطِ الجَوّيّة airline (company); على خُطوطِ مِصْرَ للطَيَرانِ with/on EgyptAir 5 [مائيّ، كَهْرَبائيّ إلخ] pipe; خَطّ كَهْرَبائيّ electrical grid; جَدَّدَ الخُطوطَ to refurbish the pipes 6 [هاتِفيّ] telephone line; خَطّ ثابِت landline 7 (Comput) على الخطِّ online

خَطّاط *n* calligrapher

خُطّة *n* |خُطَط, خِطَط| plan; design; policy; خُطّة ناجِحة a successful plan; خُطّة خَمْسيّة a five-year plan; خُطّة طَويلة الأَجَلِ a long-range plan; خِطَط شِرّيرة evil plans; خُطّة البِناءِ construction plan; خُطّة عَمَلٍ plan of action; وَضَعَ \ رَسَمَ خُطّةً to make/draw up a plan; دَبَّرَ خُطّةً to devise a plan; سارَ وَفْقاً للخُطّة to go according to plan

خَطّيّ *adj* 1 [مَكْتوب] written; طَلَب خَطّيّ a written request; تَصْريح خَطّيّ a written statement 2 [طوليّ] linear

تَخْطيط *n* |تَخْطيطات| 1 [وَضْع الخِطَط] planning; design; plan; تَخْطيط اجْتِماعيّ a social plan; تَخْطيط عُمْرانيّ urban planning; تَخْطيط عائِليّ family planning; birth control; تَخْطيط القَلْبِ electrocardiogram, ECG; تَخْطيط طَويل المَدى long-term planning; وِكالة التَخْطيطِ الاقْتِصاديّ Economic Planning Bureau 2 [المُدُنِ والريفِ] (town and country) planning, environmental planning

تَخْطيطيّ *adj* planning (*before n*); schematic; رَسْم تَخْطيطيّ first sketch; rough draft

مُخَطَّط A *adj* 1 [تَمَّ تَخْطيطُهُ] planned 2 [مُقَلَّم] striped B *n* |مُخَطَّطات| 1 [خُطّة] plan; design; مُخَطَّط لِإنْشاءِ مَتْحَفٍ a plan to start a museum 2 [تَصْميم] sketch; working drawing, blueprint; مُخَطَّط بِقَلَمِ الرَصاصِ a pencil sketch 3 [جَدْوَل] diagram

مُخَطِّط *n* designer, planner; draughtsman (BrE), draftsman (AmE)

مَخْطوط *adj* handwritten

مَخْطوطة *n* |مَخْطوطات| manuscript; hand writing

‹ **خَطَفَ** *v* |i; خَطْف| 1 [سَرَقَ] to take away, to snatch; خَطَفَ الشَنْطةَ he snatched the bag 2 [مَرْكَبة] to hijack; خَطَفَ طائِرةً

to hijack an aircraft ③ [شَخْصاً] to kidnap, to abduct

تَخَطَّفَ *v* to take away

تَخاطَفَ *v* to snatch from one another

اخْتَطَفَ *v* ① [انْتَزَعَ] to snatch ② [مَرْكَبةً] to hijack ③ [شَخْصاً] to abduct, to kidnap; اخْتَطَفَ شَخْصاً to kidnap/abduct sb

خَطْف *n* kidnapping; hijacking; عَمَلِيّة خَطْفٍ kidnapping; hijacking

خاطِف Ⓐ *adj* |خَواطِفُ| rapid; cursory; نَظْرة خاطِفة a cursory glance, a quick look; حَرْب خاطِفة blitzkrieg

Ⓑ *n* |خاطِفونَ, خُطّاف| hijacker; kidnapper; اسْتَسْلَمَ الخاطِفونَ the hijackers surrendered

خَطّاف Ⓐ *adj* rapacious

Ⓑ *n* robber

خُطّاف *n* |خَطاطيفُ| ① [كُلّاب] (fish) hook; treble hook ② (Zool) swift (*Apodidae*); خُطّاف البَحْرِ tern (*Sternidae*)

اخْتِطاف *n* |اخْتِطافات| ① [طائِرةٍ، سَفينةٍ] highjacking ② [شَخْصٍ] kidnapping, abduction; taking of hostages

مُخْتَطِف *n* kidnapper, abductor; مُخْتَطِف طائِرةٍ hijacker (*of a plane*)

مَخْطوف *adj* snatched, abducted, hijacked

خَطِلَ *v* |a; خَطَل| to talk nonsense

خَطَل *n* nonsense, idle talk

خَطْم *n* |خُطوم| snout, muzzle, nose (*of an animal*)

خِطام *n* |خُطُم| halter (*of a camel*)

خِطْمِيّ *n* (Bot) hibiscus, rose mallow (*Hibiscus*)

خَطا *v* |u; خَطْو| ① [مَشى] to step, to pace; خَطا نحو شَيْءٍ to turn one's steps towards sth ② [تَقَدَّمَ] to stride along; to proceed; خَطا خَطَواتٍ واسِعةً to proceed with rapid strides, to make great progress

خَطّى *v* to exceed, to surpass

تَخَطّى *v* to cross; to surpass, to pass by, to overtake; تَخَطّى الحُدودَ to cross the border; تَخَطّى شَخْصاً to walk past sb; تَخَطّى الصُعوباتِ to overcome difficulties

خَطْوة ,خُطْوة *n* |خَطَوات| ① [حَرَكة] step, footstep, pace; خَطْوةً خَطْوةً step by step, inch by inch; بِخَطَواتٍ سَريعةٍ with rapid strides; بِخَطَواتٍ كَبيرةٍ \ واسعةٍ with large steps/great strides; خَطْوة كَبيرة إلى الأمامِ a big step forward; خَطْوة إلى الوَراءِ \ الخَلْفِ a step backwards; ثابِت الخُطى with a firm step; مَسافة ثَلاثِ خَطَواتٍ a distance of three steps; على بُعْدِ خَطَواتٍ قَليلةٍ at a few steps' distance; في كُلِّ خَطْوةٍ with every step; خَطْوَتانِ إلى اليَمينِ فَخَطْوَتانِ إلى اليَسارِ two steps to the right, two steps to the left; حَثَّ الخُطى to quicken one's pace; سارَ على خُطى شَخْصٍ to follow in the footsteps of sb; خَطا خَطَواتٍ واسِعةٍ في مَجالِ عِلْمِ اللُغة to make great strides in the field of linguistics; كانَ على قَيْدِ خَطْوةٍ من شَيْءٍ to be just one step away from sth ② [إجْراء] step; خَطْوة كَبيرة \ مُهِمّة a big/important step; خَطْوة مُضادّة countermove; الخَطْوة الأولى نحو \ في الطَريقِ إلى شَيْءٍ the first step towards sth; خَطْوة في الطَريقِ الصَحيحِ a step in the right direction; اتَّخَذَ خَطَواتٍ \ قامَ بِخَطَواتٍ ضدّ شَيْءٍ to take steps against sth

خَفَتَ *v* |u; خُفوت| to fade away; to die down; يَخْفُتُ الصَوْتُ the sound is fading away

أَخْفَتَ *v* ① [الضَوْءَ] to dim ② [الصَوْتَ] to silence

تَخافَتَ *v* to whisper to each other

خافِت *adj* low, soft, faint; subdued; fading; hushed; صَوْت خافِت a low voice; a faint sound; موسيقى خافِتة soft music; ضَوْء خافِت subdued lighting; لَوْن خافِت a soft colour

خَفَرَ *v* |u; خَفْر, خِفارة| to guard; to patrol

خَفَر Ⓐ *n* guard; escort; خَفَر السَواحِلِ coastguard

Ⓑ *adj* attending, on call; on guard; الطَبيب الخَفَر the attending doctor

خِفارة *n* guard, guarding; sentry duty

خَفير *n* |خُفَراءُ| guard, watchman, guardian

مَخْفَر *n* |مَخافِرُ| control post; police station; أَحْضَرَ شَخْصاً إلى مَخْفَرِ الشُرْطة to take sb to the police station

خَفَسَ *v* |i; خَفْس| ① [هَدَمَ] to tear down, to demolish ② [اسْتَهْزَأَ] to ridicule

خَفَش *n* day blindness

خُفّاش *n* |خَفافيشُ| (Zool) bat

أَخْفَش *adj* |dipt| day blind

خَفَضَ *v* |i| ⟨1⟩ [أَنْزَلَ] |خَفْض| to lower, to drop ⟨2⟩ [أَنْقَصَ] |خَفْض| to lower, to reduce ⟨3⟩ [بِنْتاً] |خِفاض| to circumcise; خَفَضَ فَتاةً to have a girl circumcised

خَفُضَ *v* |u; خَفْض| to be/become easy/carefree

خَفَّضَ *v* to reduce, to lower; to diminish, to cut back; خَفَّضَ النَفَقاتِ to cut back on expenses; خَفَّضَ الضرائِبَ \ الأَسْعارَ to lower taxes/prices; خَفَّضَ سِعْرَ \ عَدَدَ شَيْءٍ to reduce the price/the number of sth; خَفَّضَ شَيْئاً بِنِسْبَةِ ٢٠٪ to discount sth by 20%; خَفَّضَ سُرْعَتَهُ to reduce one's speed; خَفَّضَ قيمةَ العُمْلَةِ to devalue the currency; خَفَّضَ عَدَدَ العامِلِينَ to cut down/back the staff; خَفَّضَ صَوْتَهُ to drop one's voice

انْخَفَضَ *v* to descend, to sink, to go down; to diminish; to decrease; to be reduced; تَنْخَفِضُ السُرْعةُ the speed is decreasing; يَنْخَفِضُ مُسْتَوى المِياهِ the water level is going down; تَنْخَفِضُ الإيراداتُ \ العائِداتُ profits/gains are dropping; انْخَفَضَتْ قيمةُ الدولارِ the value of the dollar has gone down in value; انْخَفَضَ العَجْزُ بِنِسْبَةِ ١ في المِائةِ the deficit has been reduced by 1%; قد انْخَفَضَ سِعْرُ القَهْوَةِ من جَديدٍ the price of coffee has gone down again; انْخَفَضَ من ١٤ إلى ١٢ في المِائةِ to drop from 14% to 12%

خَفْض *n* ⟨1⟩ [إِنْقاص] lowering, lessening, decrease ⟨2⟩ (Gram) genitive

خافِض ⟨A⟩ *adj* comfortable
⟨B⟩ *n* الخافِض the Abaser (*one of the names of God*)

خافِضة *n* (Mus) damper

خِفاض *n* female circumcision, clitoridectomy

خَفيض *adj* deep, low-pitched; soft; صَوْت خَفيض a deep voice

انْخِفاض *n* |انْخِفاضات| drop; decrease, reduction, decline; انْخِفاض شَديد a heavy decrease, a strong decline; انْخِفاض في عَدَدِ الوِلاداتِ the decline in the birth rate; انْخِفاض الطَلَبِ a drop in demand; انْخِفاض عَدَدِ السُكّانِ population decrease; انْخِفاض دَرَجةِ الحَرارةِ a drop in the temperature

تَخْفيض *n* |تَخْفيضات| lowering, reduction, discount; decrease; تَخْفيض في السِعْرِ lowering of the prices; تَخْفيض الأَسْعارِ price reduction; تَخْفيض السُرْعةِ speed reduction; تَخْفيض نِسْبَةِ المَوادِّ الضارّةِ the reduction of harmful substances; اشْتَرى شَيْئاً بِتَخْفيضٍ to buy sth at a discount; تَخْفيض بِنِسْبَةِ ١٠٪ a 10% discount; مَنَحَ \ أَعْطى تَخْفيضاً give a discount

مُخَفَّض *adj* reduced; discounted

مُنْخَفَض *n* |مُنْخَفَضات| (Geog) depression, hollow; مُنْخَفَض بين تَلَّيْنِ a hollow between two hills; مُنْخَفَض جَوِّيّ a low-pressure area

مُنْخَفِض *adj* low; مُسْتَوًى مُنْخَفِض a low level; دَخْل مُنْخَفِض a low income; دَرَجة حَرارةٍ مُنْخَفِضة a low temperature; الأَراضي المُنْخَفِضة the Netherlands

خَفَّ *v* |i; خَفّ| ⟨1⟩ [خَفَضَ] to decrease, to diminish, to decline; خَفَّ الأَلَمُ the pain diminished; خَفَّ المَطَرُ the rain eased up ⟨2⟩ [عَكْس ثَقُلَ] to be/become light; أَخَذَ السارِقُ ما خَفَّ وَزْنُهُ the thief took the light objects

خَفَّفَ *v* to make lighter; to reduce, to lessen; to relieve, to alleviate; to lighten, to soften; to moderate, to temper; خَفَّفَ الضَوْءَ to dim the light; خَفَّفَ من حِدّةِ الصَوْتِ to reduce the volume; خَفَّفَ الأَلَمَ \ من الأَلَم to relieve the pain; خَفَّفَ لِشَخْصٍ مُدّةَ العُقوبةِ to reduce sb's (prison) sentence; خَفَّفَ سُرْعَتَهُ to reduce one's speed; خَفَّفَ بالماءِ to thin with water; خَفَّفَ شُروطاً to weaken conditions; خَفَّفَ من أَهَمِّيّةِ شَيْءٍ to give sth less importance

تَخَفَّفَ *v* to relieve oneself; تَخَفَّفَ من حِمْلٍ to relieve oneself of a burden

اسْتَخَفَّ *v* to disdain; to underestimate; to think little of, to attach no importance to; اسْتَخَفَّ بِشَخْصٍ to have a low opinion of sb, to look down upon sb; اسْتَخَفَّ شَيْئاً to make light of sth; اسْتَخَفَّ بِنَصيحةٍ to scorn an advice; لا تَسْتَخِفَّ بِذلِكَ don't underestimate that, don't underestimate it

خُفّ *n* |أَخْفاف ,خِفاف| slipper; mule; عادَ \ خَرَجَ \ رَجَعَ بِخُفَّيْ حُنَيْنٍ to return empty-handed

خَفاف *n* حَجَر الخَفافِ pumice (stone)

خِفّة *n* lightness

خَفيف *adj* |خِفاف ,أَخْفاف ,أَخِفّاءُ| ⟨1⟩ [عَكْس ثَقيلٍ] light; أَمْتِعة خَفيفة light luggage; شاي خَفيف light tea; شَعْر خَفيف fine hair; خَفيف الحَرَكةِ agile; energetic; خَفيف الدمِ \ الظِلِّ funny; cheerful; amiable; عاقَبَ شَخْصاً عُقوبةً خَفيفةً to give sb a light sentence **2** [ضَئيل] slight; light; اصْطِدام خَفيف a minor collision **3** [غِذاء] light; low-calorie

أَخَفّ *adj* |dipt| lighter; less; least; البْلاسْتيك أَخَفُّ وَزْناً من الزُجاج plastic is lighter/weighs less than glass

اسْتِخْفاف *n* underestimation; contempt, disregard; بِاسْتِخْفافٍ contemptuously; الاسْتِخْفاف بالآخَرينَ the underestimation of other people

تَخْفيف *n* lightening; relief, alleviation; easing; تَخْفيف (من) الألَم pain relief; التَخْفيف من حِدّةِ حِصارٍ اقْتِصاديٍّ the easing of an embargo; تَخْفيف العُسْرِ \ الحاجةِ alleviation of the need

مُخَفَّف *adj* **1** [مُرَقَّق] thinned; softened; مَحْلول مُخَفَّف dilution; حُكْم \ عِقاب مُخَفَّف a light judgement/sentence **2** [حَرْف] *consonant without shadda*

مُخَفِّف **A** *adj* softening; relieving; ظُروف مُخَفِّفة extenuating circumstances

B *n* thinner

خَفَقَ *v* |i-u; خُفوق ,خَفَقان ,خَفْق| **1** [تَحَرَّكَ] to flutter, to flap; to blow; خَفَقَ الطائِرُ بِجَناحَيْهِ the bird flapped its wings **2** [بَيْضاً] to beat, to whip; خَفَقَ بَيْضةً to beat an egg; خَفَقَ القِشْطةَ to whip cream **3** [القَلْبُ] to beat; خَفَقَ قَلْبُهُ لَها his heart beat for her

أَخْفَقَ *v* to fail, to go wrong/awry, to be unsuccessful; أَخْفَقَت المُحادَثاتُ the talks broke down; أَخْفَقَ في شَيْءٍ to fail in sth; أَخْفَقَت المُؤَسَّسةُ في تَحْقيقِ أَهْدافِها the organization failed to achieve its goals

خافِق **A** *adj* beating, fluttering, pulsing; قَلْب خافِق a beating heart

B *n* |خَوافِقُ| horizon; الخَوافِق the four quarters of the world; الخافِقان East and West

خَفَقان *n* palpitation, beating

خَفْقة *n* |خَفَقات| beat; خَفْقة القَلْبِ beating of the heart

إخْفاق *n* |إخْفاقات| failure; fiasco; flop; مَحْكوم عَلَيْهِ بالإخْفاقِ doomed to fail

مِخْفَقة *n* |مَخافِقُ| whisk; egg beater; مِخْفَقة كَهْرَبائيّة mixer

مَخْفوق *adj* whipped; whisked; beaten

خَفي *v* |i; خَفْي| to hide, to conceal

خَفِيَ *v* |a; خَفاء| to disappear; to be hidden; to be unknown; لا يَخْفى (على أَحَدٍ) أنّ ... it is well known that ...; as everybody knows ...

أَخْفى *v* to hide, to conceal; أَخْفى شَيْئاً عن شَخْصٍ to hide/conceal/keep sth for sb; أَخْفى مَشاعِرَهُ \ غَضَبَهُ to hide away one's feelings/anger; أَخْفى مَعْلوماتٍ to hold back information; أَخْفى حَقائِقَ to suppress facts; أَخْفى الضَبابُ قِمّةَ الجَبَلِ the mountain peak was shrouded in mist

تَخَفّى *v* to disguise oneself; تَخَفّى في لِباسٍ شُرْطيٍّ to disguise oneself as a police officer

اخْتَفى *v* to hide, to be hidden; to disappear, to vanish; اخْتَفى بِدونِ أَثَرٍ to disappear without a trace; اخْتَفَت الشَمْسُ وراء السُحُبِ the sun was hiding behind the clouds; اخْتَفى من الوُجودِ to cease to exist; اخْتَفى عن الأَنْظارِ to disappear from sight

اسْتَخْفى *v* to disappear, to abscond; to hide oneself, to be hidden

خَفِيّ *adj* hidden, invisible; secret; mysterious; unknown; كَنْز خَفِيّ a hidden treasure; نَظْرة خَفِيّة a secret glance; ظَلَّ خَفِيّاً to remain unnoticed

خافٍ *adj* hidden, concealed; secret; لَيْس خافِياً على أَحَدٍ أنّ ... it's no secret that ...

خافِية *n* |خَوافٍ| secret; mystery; لا تَخْفى عَلَيْهِ خافِيةٌ nothing remains hidden from him

خَفاء *n* invisibility; mystery; secrecy; في الخَفاءِ secretly; in secret

خَفِيّة *n* |خَفايا| secret; خَفايا الطَبيعةِ the secrets of nature

خُفْية *n* secrecy; خُفْيةً secretly; covertly; quietly

اخْتِفاء *n* |اخْتِفاءات| disappearance; اخْتِفاء غامِض a mysterious disappearance; قَدَّمَ بَلاغاً عن اخْتِفاءِ شَخْصٍ to report a missing person

إخْفاء *n* hiding, concealment; disguise

تَخَفٍّ *n* stealth; camouflage

مُتَخَفٍّ *adj* in disguise; undercover

مُخْتَفٍ *adj* concealed, hidden; كانَ مُخْتَفِياً في مَكانٍ to be hidden somewhere

مَخْفِيّ *adj* hidden

خَلَبَ *v* |i-u; خَلْب| to attract; to fascinate, to captivate; خَلَبَ الأَنْظارَ to attract the eyes

اخْتَلَبَ *v* to enchant, to bewitch

خِلْب *n* |أَخْلاب| claw *(of a bird)*

خَلّاب *adj* bewitching, fascinating, captivating; مَنْظَر خَلّاب a fascinating view

مِخْلَب *n* |مَخالِب| claw; سَحَبَ \ أَبْرَزَ مَخالِبَهُ to retract/bare its claws

خالَجَ *v* to preoccupy, to be on sb's mind; to trouble; خالَجَ نَفْسَهُ أَمْرٌ sth was troubling him

اخْتَلَجَ *v* to tremble, to shiver, to quiver, to shake; اخْتَلَجَ الأَمَلُ في صَدْرِهِ his heart was filled with hope

خَلْجة *n* |خَلَجات| emotion, sentiment

خَليج *n* |خُلْجان| 1 [قِطْعة من البَحْر] gulf; bay; الخَليج العَرَبِيّ the Arabian Gulf; the Persian Gulf; خَليج عَدَنَ the Gulf of Aden; خَليج العَقَبةِ the Gulf of Aqaba 2 [مَنْسوب للخَليج العَرَبِيّ] Gulf *(relating to the Persian Gulf)*; مِنْطَقة الخَليج the Gulf region; دُوَل الخَليج the Gulf states; حَرْب الخَليج the Gulf War

خَليجِيّ A *adj* Gulf *(before n)* *(pertaining to the Gulf States)*; مَجْلِس التَعاوُنِ الخَليجِيّ the Gulf Cooperation Council, the GCC; القادة الخَليجِيّونَ the leaders of the Gulf States
B *n a citizen of one of the Gulf states*; يَقْضي بَعْضُ الخَليجِيّينَ العُطْلَةَ في جَنيف some Gulf people vacation in Geneva

خَلْخَلَ *v* |i; خَلْخَلة| to destabilize

تَخَلْخَلَ *v* to be/become detached

خَلْخَل *n* |خَلاخِلُ| anklet

خَلْخال *n* |خَلاخيلُ| anklet; لَبِسَتْ خَلْخالاً فِضِّيّاً she wore a silver anklet

تَخَلْخُل *n* تَخَلْخُل العِظام osteoporosis

مُتَخَلْخِل *adj* detached

مُخَلْخَل *adj* exclusive, select; rarefied

خَلَدَ *v* |u; خُلود| to last forever; to be immortal; to live, to remain; خَلَدَ في السِجْنِ to be in prison; خَلَدَ في النَعيمِ to live in luxury

Idiom خَلَدَ إلى النَوْمِ \ الراحةِ to go to sleep, to rest

خَلَّدَ *v* perpetuate; immortalize; خَلَّدَ هذا العَمَلُ اسْمَكَ this deed has immortalized your name

أَخْلَدَ *v* 1 [خَلَّدَ] to eternize, to make immortal 2 [بالمَكانِ] to remain 3 [إلى الشَيْءِ] أَخْلَدَ إلى النَوْمِ to give in to sleep

خَلَد *n* |أَخْلاد| mind; هذا ما دارَ في خَلَدي this is what went through my mind

خُلْد *n* |خُلْدان| 1 *(Zool)* mole; خُلْد الماءِ platypus 2 [دَوام] eternity; دار الخُلْد the place of eternity *(paradise)*

خالِد *adj* 1 [أَبَدِيّ] eternal, everlasting; immortal; سِرّ خالِد an everlasting secret 2 [اسْم شَخْصِيّ] Khaled *(male given name)*

خُلود *n* 1 [أَبَدِيّة] immortality; خُلود النَفْسِ immortality of the soul 2 [اسْم شَخْصِيّ] Khulud *(female given name)*

تَخْليد *n* immortalization

خَلَسَ *v* |i; خَلْس| to steal

اخْتَلَسَ *v* to steal; to embezzle, to misappropriate; اخْتَلَسَ مالاً to embezzle/steal money; اخْتَلَسَ قُبْلَةً to steal/snatch a kiss; اخْتَلَسَ النَظَرَ إلى to peep, to glance furtively; اخْتَلَسَ النَظَرَ شَخْصٍ to peep at sb

خِلاسِيّ *n* half-breed; mulatto

خُلْسة *n* |خُلَس| خُلْسةً stealthily, surreptitiously, furtively, by stealth; نَظَرَ إلى شَخْصٍ خُلْسةً to steal a glance at sb

اخْتِلاس *n* |اخْتِلاسات| embezzlement, misappropriation; fraud; اتُّهِمَ باخْتِلاسٍ to be accused of embezzlement

مُخْتَلَس *adj* furtive, stealthy, clandestine

مُخْتَلِس *n* thief, embezzler; مُخْتَلِس النَظَرِ voyeur; peeping Tom

خَلَصَ *v* |u; خَلاص| 1 [وَصَلَ] [إلى] to finish, to conclude; خَلَصَ إلى القَوْلِ ... he concluded by saying ... 2 [صَفا] to be/become pure; خَلَصَ الماءُ من الكَدَرِ the water was purified/filtered 3 [نَجا] to be rescued, to be liberated; شَقاء لا يَدْري كيف يَخْلُصُ مِنْهُ inescapable misery

خَلَّصَ *v* 1 [صَفّى] to clear 2 [حَرَّرَ] to rescue, to save; to liberate, to free; خَلَّصَ شَخْصاً من قَلَقٍ \ عِبْءٍ to rid sb of his worries/burden; خَلَّصَ شَخْصاً من مَوْقِفٍ حَرِجٍ to rescue sb from a difficult situation; خَلَّصَ شَخْصاً من السِجْنِ to liberate sb from prison 3 [بَضائِع] |على| to clear *(customs, etc.)*;

إِخْلاص (Sura 112) ⟨2⟩ [وَفاء] faithfulness, fidelity, loyalty; إِخْلاص زَوْجِيّ marital fidelity

اسْتِخْلاص *n* |اسْتِخْلاصات| deduction, derivation; summary

تَخَلُّص *n* |تَخَلُّصات| liberation; disposal, getting rid of

تَخْليص *n* ⟨1⟩ [تَحْرير] liberation, salvation ⟨2⟩ [بَضائِعَ] clearing; تَخْليص بَضائِعَ clearance of goods

مُتَخالِص *adj* even

مُخالَصة *n* receipt; clearance (*of cheques*)

مُخْلِص *adj* dedicated; faithful; sincere, pure-hearted; صَديق مُخْلِص a loyal friend; صَديقُكَ \ صَديقَتُكَ المُخْلِص(ة) yours truly (*in a letter*)

مُخَلِّص *n* liberator; المُخَلِّص the Saviour

مُسْتَخْلَص *n* |مُسْتَخْلَصات| extract, excerpt; essence

خَلَطَ *v* |i; خَلْط| to mix, to blend, to mingle; to confuse, to mix up; خَلَطَ أَوْراق to mix wine with water; خَلَطَ الخَمْرَ بالماءِ to shuffle playing cards; خَلَطَ بين الوَقائِع \ الأَحْداثِ اللَعِبِ to mix up facts/events; خَلَطَ بين الحاضِرِ والماضي to confuse the present and the past; خَلَطَ بين شَخْصٍ وَأَخيه to confuse sb with his brother

خَلَّطَ *v* to mix, to blend, to mingle

خالَطَ *v* to mix with, to associate with, to mingle with; to interfere in/with, to meddle in; خالَطَ شَخْصاً to associate with sb; خالَطَ الناسَ to mix with society, to go out and about; خالَطَ الطَبَقَةَ الراقِيَةَ to move in the best circles

تَخالَطَ *v* to intermingle

اخْتَلَطَ *v* to mix; to be mixed; اخْتَلَطَ مع شَيْءٍ to be mixed with sth; اخْتَلَطَ عَلَيَّ الأَمْرُ the matter was confusing for me

خِلْط *n* |أَخْلاط| mix, mixture; component; الأَخْلاط الأَرْبَعة the four humours; أَخْلاط الناسِ common people

خَلّاط *n* mixer; blender

خَلّاطة *n* mixer; خَلّاطة إِسْمَنْت cement mixer

خَلْطة *n* mixture, mix, blend

خَليط *n* mixture, blend; cocktail

اخْتِلاط *n* ⟨1⟩ [امْتِزاج] mixing; اخْتِلاط المَصالِحِ a mingling of interests ⟨2⟩ (*Chem*) diffusion

خَلَّصَ على بَضائِعَ to stamp a letter; خَلَّصَ على رِسالةٍ to clear goods

خالَصَ *v* ⟨1⟩ [صافى] to act with sincerity ⟨2⟩ [صَفّى حِسابَهُ مع] to get even with

أَخْلَصَ *v* to be faithful; to be sincere

تَخَلَّصَ *v* |من| to rid oneself of, to get rid of, to free oneself from; to be saved from; تَخَلَّصَ من عِبْءٍ \ شَخْصٍ to get rid of a burden/a person; تَخَلَّصَ من مُشْكِلةٍ to get ride of a problem; تَخَلَّصَ من شُهودِ عِيانٍ to eliminate eye witnesses; تَخَلَّصَ من مُلاحِقٍ to shake off a pursuer; تَخَلَّصَ من قَبْضةِ شَخْصٍ to escape from sb's grasp; تَخَلَّصَ من الإِدْمانِ to recover from an addiction, to kick the habit; تَخَلَّصَ من عادةٍ (ضارّةٍ) to break one's (bad) habit

تَخالَصَ *v* to be even; تَخالَصَ مع شَخْصٍ to be even with someone

اسْتَخْلَصَ *v* ⟨1⟩ [اسْتَنْتَجَ] |من| to derive from, to deduce from, to conclude from; اسْتَخْلَصَ دُروساً من التَجارِبِ to draw lessons from an experience; أَسْتَخْلِصُ من كَلامِهِ أَنَّهُ مُوافِقٌ I take from his words that he agrees ⟨2⟩ [اسْتَخْرَجَ] to extract; اسْتَخْلَصَ المَعادِنَ to extract minerals

خَلَص *excl* that's it, it is over; right

خالِص *adj* |خُلَّص| pure; clear; sincere, true; ذَهَب خالِص pure gold; حَرير خالِص pure silk; صَداقة خالِصة true friendship; كُحول خالِص pure alcohol; نَبيذ خالِص undiluted wine; بِنَوايا خالِصةٍ with honourable intentions; لَكَ خالِصُ الشُكْرِ I am truly grateful; أَعْرَبَ عن خالِصِ مُؤاساتِهِ to offer one's sincerest condolences

خَلاص *n* ⟨1⟩ [نَجاة] salvation, redemption, repose; جَيْش الخَلاصِ the Salvation Army ⟨2⟩ [مَشيمة] placenta, afterbirth

خُلاصة *n* ⟨1⟩ [مُسْتَحْلَب] extract, infusion ⟨2⟩ [الكَلام] summary; خُلاصة القَوْلِ in short, to be brief ⟨3⟩ (*Comput*) RSS feed

خُلوص *n* clearness, clarity; candor, frankness

إِخْلاص *n* ⟨1⟩ [صَراحة] sincerity, uprightness; devotion, sincere faith; قالَ شَيْئاً بِإِخْلاصٍ to say sth from the heart; بِكُلِّ إِخْلاصٍ with all sincerity; سورة الإِخْلاص Sincerity

تَخْليط *n* mixing; confusion

مُخالَطة *n* association; close contact

مُخْتَلَط *adj* mixed

مُخْتَلِط *adj* mixed

مُخَلَّط *adj* mixed; غَيْر مُخَلَّطٍ unmixed

مَخْلوط *adj* |مَخاليطُ| mixed, blended

خَلَعَ *v* |a; خَلْع| 1▸ [شَلَحَ] to take off; to throw off; to remove; to pull; خَلَعَ مَلابِسَ to take off clothes, to undress; خَلَعَ كَنْزةً \ حِذاءً to take off a sweater/shoes; خَلَعَ قُبَّعةً \ نَظّارةً to take off a hat/a pair of glasses; خَلَعَ القِشْرَ عن فاكِهةٍ to remove the skin of a piece of fruit, to peel a piece of fruit 2▸ [أَقالَ] to discharge; خَلَعَ عن العَرْشِ to dethrone 3▸ (Isl Law) *to divorce (one's wife) in return for a compensation (to be paid by her)*

خَلُعَ *v* |u; خَلاعة| to be/become dissolute

تَخَلَّعَ *v* to go to pieces, to fall apart; to be/become disjointed

انْخَلَعَ *v* to come loose; to be extracted; قد انْخَلَعَ كَتْفُها her arm has been dislocated; انْخَلَعَ قَلْبي I was extremely upset

اخْتَلَعَ *v* (Isl Law) *to divorce (one's wife) in return for a compensation (to be paid by her)*

خَلْع *n* taking off (*clothes*); dislocation

خُلْع *n* (Isl Law) *divorce instigated by the wife, who has to pay compensation*

خَلاعة *n* licentiousness, profligacy

خَلاعيّ *adj* depraved, licentious; porn (*before n*), pornography (*before n*); فيلْم خَلاعيّ porn (film); مَجَلّة خَلاعيّة porn magazine

خُلْعيّ *adj* (Isl Law) طَلاق خُلْعيّ *divorce instigated by the wife, who has to pay compensation*

خَليع *adj* obscene, lewd; pornographic

مُخَلَّع *adj* loose, disjointed

مِخْلَعة *n* rack (*instrument of torture*)

مَخْلوع *adj* deposed, ousted; dislocated; الرَئيس المَخْلوع the ousted president

خَلَفَ *v* |u; خَلْف| to succeed; to follow, to come after; خَلَفَ المَلِكَ نَجْلُهُ الأَكْبَرُ the king was succeeded by his eldest son

خَلَّفَ *v* 1▸ [تَرَكَ] to leave behind 2▸ [جَعَلَهُ خَليفَتَهُ] to appoint as successor 3▸ [أَنْجَبَ] to have children

خالَفَ *v* 1▸ [بايَنَ] to be contradictory to, to conflict with; خالَفَ شَخْصاً \ شَيْئاً to conflict with sb/sth 2▸ [القانونَ] to break, to transgress; خالَفَ القانونَ to break the law; خالَفَ قاعِدةً to break a rule

أَخْلَفَ *v* to break, to fail to keep (*a promise, etc.*); أَخْلَفَ وَعْداً \ مُعاهَدةً to break a promise/treaty

تَخَلَّفَ *v* 1▸ [تَأَخَّرَ] to be/stay/fall behind 2▸ [تَغَيَّبَ] to not go/come/attend; تَخَلَّفَ عن المَجيءِ he didn't come; تَخَلَّفَ عن أَداءِ الواجِبِ to forsake one's duty

تَخالَفَ *v* to disagree

اخْتَلَفَ *v* 1▸ [تَبايَنَ] to differ, to be different; اخْتَلَفَ عن شَخْصٍ في شَيْءٍ to differ from sb in sth 2▸ [ضِدّ اتَّفَقَ] to disagree; اخْتَلَفَ مع شَخْصٍ to disagree with sb; اخْتَلَفَ في الرَأْيِ to differ in opinion; يَخْتَلِفُ الخُبَراءُ في رَأْيِهِمْ the experts disagree with each other

اسْتَخْلَفَ *v* to appoint as successor

خَلْف *n* back; إلى الخَلْفِ backwards; سارَ إلى الخَلْفِ to go backwards; to go to the rear; تَراجَعَ للخَلْفِ to take a step back

خَلْفَ *prep* behind; مَنْ يَقِفُ خَلْفَهُمْ؟ who is standing behind them?; جَلَسَ شَخْصٌ خَلْفي sb sat down behind me; سَيَأْتي شَخْصٌ خَلْفي there is someone else behind me; من خَلْفِ from behind; جاءَ من الخَلْفِ to come from behind; من خَلْفِ السَتائِرِ from behind the curtains; من خَلْفِ ظَهْرِ الرَئيسِ behind the president's back

خَلَف *n* |أَخْلاف| 1▸ [خَليفة] successor; خَلَف لِزَعيمِ الحِزْبِ a successor for the party leader; خَلَف مُناسِب a suitable successor; خَيْر خَلَفٍ لِخَيْرِ سَلَفٍ a worthy successor 2▸ [وَلَد] descendant

خِلْف *n* |أَخْلاف| nipple

خِلاف *n* |خِلافات| 1▸ [فَرْق] difference 2▸ [نِزاع] disagreement, conflict, argument, dispute, fight; خِلاف حادّ a serious conflict; خِلاف حُدوديّ a border dispute; خِلاف اجْتِماعيّ \ سِياسيّ social/political friction; نُقْطة \ مَدار خِلافٍ point of conflict; مُثير للخِلافِ controversial, provocative; خِلاف بين شَخْصَيْن a disagreement between two people; خِلاف بين

أَعْضاءِ الحِزْبِ friction between the party members; خِلاف بين سُكّانِ المَدينةِ discord within the city's population; خِلاف مع شَخْصٍ a disagreement with sb; كانَ على خِلافٍ مع شَخْصٍ to be in disagreement/conflict with sb; to collide with sb; to be at odds with sb; كانَ على خِلافٍ مع شَخْصٍ حول شَيْءٍ to be in conflict with sb about sth; إنَّهُ على خِلافٍ مع الجيرانِ he has an argument with his neighbours; سَبَّبَ خِلافاً to cause a conflict; نَشِبَ خِلافٌ a conflict arose; عاشا في خِلافٍ they lived in conflict with one another **3** [مُغايرة] خِلافاً ل contrary to, in contradiction to, in conflict with; against; خِلافاً لِما أَوْرَدَتْهُ الصُحُفُ contrary to what the newspapers said; على خِلافِ ذلك on the contrary; على خِلافِ أَحْكامِ القانونِ contrary to/against the law **4** [غَيْر] وَخِلافُهُ and the like; and others; بِخِلافِ ذلك apart from that, beside that

خِلافة *n* **1** [مَصْدَر] succession; خِلافة المَلِكِ the succession of the king **2** [إمامة] caliphate; خِلافة بَني أُمَيَّةَ the Umayyad caliphate; دار الخِلافةِ the caliph's residence

خِلافيّ *adj* controversial

خِلْفة *n* disagreement

خَلْفيّ *adj* back (*before n*), rear (*before n*); مَقْعَد خَلْفيّ back seat; صُنْدوق خَلْفيّ boot (BrE), trunk (AmE); دَفْع خَلْفيّ rear-wheel drive; الصَفّ الخَلْفيّ the back row

خَلْفيّة *n* **1** (Art) background; خَلْفيّة شاشةٍ desktop background; على خَلْفيّةِ الحَرْبِ against the background of the war **2** [تاريخ] background; خَلْفيّة ثَقافيّة \ إثْنيّة \ دينيّة a cultural/ethnic/religious background; خَلْفيّة الحَرَكةِ the background of the movement **3** [سَبَب] background, backdrop; على خَلْفيّةِ شَيْءٍ against the backdrop of sth; because of sth; القَتْل على خَلْفيّةِ الشَرَفِ honour killing

خَليفة *n* |m; خَلائِفُ, خُلَفاءُ| caliph; successor; خَليفة النَبيِّ caliph (*successor of the Prophet*)

اخْتِلاف *n* |اخْتِلافات| **1** [فَرْق] difference, distinction; diversity; اخْتِلاف صَغير \ غَيْر مَلْحوظٍ a slight/unnoticeable difference; اخْتِلاف في الطولِ \ الوَزْنِ \ السِنِّ a difference in height/weight/age; الاخْتِلاف بين شَيْئَيْنِ the difference between two things; هذا اخْتِلافٌ كَاخْتِلافِ الأَرْضِ والسَماءِ \ اللَّيْلِ والنَهارِ it's as different as night and day **2** [نِزاع] controversy; discord; اخْتِلاف حول شَيْءٍ discord about sth; كانَ على اخْتِلافٍ مع شَخْصٍ to be at odds with sb

تَخَلُّف *n* default, arrears; lag, backwardness, retardation; تَخَلُّف عَقْليّ mental disability; تَخَلُّف اقْتِصاديّ economic backwardness

مُتَخَلِّف **A** *adj* underdeveloped; backward; مِنْطَقة مُتَخَلِّفة an underdeveloped area; بَلَد مُتَخَلِّف an underdeveloped country; طِفْل مُتَخَلِّف عَقْليًّا a mentally disabled child; مُتَخَلِّف عَقْليًّا mentally disabled, having learning difficulties **B** *n* one left behind; a slow developer

مُخالِف **A** *adj* different, divergent; contrary; against; مُخالِف للدُسْتورِ unconstitutional; مُخالِف للقانونِ illegal, against the law; مُخالِف لِشُروطِ العَقْدِ contrary to the stipulations of the contract; التَعامُل بالرِبا مُخالِفٌ للشَريعةِ الإسْلاميّةِ dealing in interest is against Islamic law **B** *n* offender; dissident; مُخالِف للقانونِ offender; هَدَّدَ النِظامُ بِضَرْبِ المُخالِفينَ بِقوّةٍ the regime threatened to take a hard line on the offenders

مُخالَفة *n* **1** [القانونِ] violation, infringement, infraction; offence; مُخالَفة جَسيمة \ فاضِحة \ صارِخة \ حادّة a serious/grave offence; ارْتَكَبَ مُخالَفةً to commit an offence **2** [غَرامة] fine, penalty; ticket; مُخالَفة مُروريّة traffic violation; (traffic) ticket; حَرَّرَ مُخالَفةً to write out a fine **3** (Sport) foul

مُخْتَلَف *adj* مُخْتَلَف فيه \ عَلَيْهِ controversial, disputed; هي مَسْأَلةٌ مُخْتَلَفٌ فيها \ عَلَيْها that is a subject on which opinions differ, that is a controversial topic

مُخْتَلِف *adj* **1** [مُتَعَدِّد] different; various, diverse, all sorts of; بِمُخْتَلِفِ الطُرُقِ \ المَيادينِ in different ways/areas; في مُخْتَلِفِ مَجالاتِ العُلومِ in diverse areas of science; مُخْتَلِف الناسِ different kinds of people; مُخْتَلِف الأَنْواعِ various kinds; لِأَسْبابٍ مُخْتَلِفةٍ for different reasons; من اتِّجاهاتٍ مُخْتَلِفةٍ from different directions **2** [مُتَبايِن] different; another; else; شَيْء مُخْتَلِف something else; مُخْتَلِف تَماماً

totally different; مُخْتَلِف عن شَخْصٍ \ شَيْءٍ different from sb/sth

مُخَلَّف A *adj* left over

B *n* left overs, remnants; مُخَلَّفات refuse, waste

خَلَقَ *v* |u; خَلْق| to create, to make; خَلَقَ إمْكانيّاتٍ جَديدةً to create new possibilities; خَلَقَ فُرَصَ عَمَلٍ to create job opportunities; خَلَقَ اللهُ السَماواتِ والأَرْضَ God created heaven and earth

خَلُقَ *v* |u; خَلاقة| to be of good character

خَلِقَ *v* |a; خَلَق| to be old/shabby

خَلَّقَ *v* to perfume

أَخْلَقَ *v* to wear out; أَخْلَقَ الثَوْبُ بِسُرْعةٍ the cloth wore out rapidly

تَخَلَّقَ *v* to be shaped; تَخَلَّقَ الجَنينُ في بَطْنِ أُمِّه the embryo took shape in its mother's womb

اخْتَلَقَ *v* to invent, to make up, to fabricate; اخْتَلَقَ قِصّةً to make up a story; اخْتَلَقَ أَكاذيبَ to lie

خَلْق *n* creation; createdness; خَلْق السَماءِ والأَرْضِ the creation of heaven and earth; خَلْق القُرْآنِ the createdness of the Koran

خُلُق, **خُلْق** *n* |أَخْلاق| character, nature, disposition; أَخْلاق character; morals, morality; خُلُق نَبيل \ حَسَن a noble/good character; خُلُق سَيِّئ an evil disposition; كانَ حَسَنَ \ سَيِّئَ الخُلُقِ to be of good/bad character; كانَ دَمِثَ الأَخْلاقِ to have a gentle nature; عِلْم الأَخْلاقِ ethics; تَدَهْوُر الأَخْلاقِ moral decline; ازْدِواجيّة الأَخْلاقِ a moral double standard; عارَضَ \ ناقَضَ الأَخْلاقَ الفاضِلةَ to be contrary to good morals; القِيَم والأَخْلاق moral values/standards

خالِق *n* 1 [مُبْدِع] creator 2 (Islam) الخالِق the Creator (*one of the names of God*)

خَلّاق A *adj* creative

B *n* creator

خِلْقة *n* |خِلَق| nature, disposition

خُلُقيّ *adj* ethical

خِلْقيّ *adj* natural, congenital; عَيْب \ تَشَوُّه خِلْقيّ a congenital defect

خَلوق *adj* steadfast; upright

خَليق *adj* suitable

خَليقة *n* |خَلائِق| 1 [كائِن] creature 2 [طَبْع] natural disposition; لا يَسْتَطيعُ أَحَدٌ إخْفاءَ خَليقَتِهِ no one can hide his true nature

اخْتِلاق *n* fabrication; هذا مُجَرَّدُ اخْتِلاقٍ that is nothing more than a fabrication

أَخْلاقيّ *adj* moral; moralistic; ethical; مَسْأَلة أَخْلاقيّة an ethical question; واجِب أَخْلاقيّ a moral duty; debt of honour; اعْتِراضات أَخْلاقيّة moral objections, scruples; هذا غَيْر مَقْبولٍ أَخْلاقيًّا that is morally unacceptable

أَخْلاقيّة *n* morality

تَخْليق *n* synthesis

لاأَخْلاقيّ *adj* immoral, amoral; indecent; عَمَل لاأَخْلاقيّ an immoral act; تَصَرُّف لاأَخْلاقيّ immoral behaviour

مُخْتَلَق *adj* fabricated, invented; هذا الخَبَرُ مُخْتَلَقٌ this news is fabricated

مَخْلوق A *adj* |مَخاليقُ| created

B *n* |مَخْلوقات| creature, being; creation; مَخْلوقات الأَرْضِ earth creatures; مَخْلوق جَحود \ مُزْعِج an ungrateful/annoying creature

خَلَّ *v* |u; خَلّ| to pierce; to perforate

خَلَّلَ *v* to preserve; to pickle; خَلَّلَ شَيْئاً to pickle sth

خالَّ *v* to become friends with; to treat as a friend

أَخَلَّ *v* to break, to violate; to disturb; أَخَلَّ بِعَقْدٍ to break a contract; أَخَلَّ بالمُعاهَداتِ الدُوَليّةِ to violate international treaties; أَخَلَّ بِواجِباتِهِ to neglect one's duties; أَخَلَّ بالنِظامِ العامِّ to disturb the public order; أَخَلَّ بالنُظُمِ الاقْتِصاديّةِ \ الاجْتِماعيّةِ to disturb economic/social life

تَخَلَّلَ *v* 1 [اخْتَرَقَ] to be/come between, to intervene; to come through; to interrupt; يَتَخَلَّلُ الإعْلانُ البَرامِجَ التِلِفِزْيونيّةَ TV shows are interrupted by commercials 2 [تَوَسَّطَ] to intervene; to mediate; تَخَلَّلَ بين الطَرَفَيْنِ المُتَنازِعَيْنِ to mediate between the conflicting parties

اخْتَلَّ *v* 1 [اضْطَرَبَ] to be/become disordered; to be/become disturbed/upset 2 [العَقْلُ] to be mentally disturbed

خَلَل *n* |خِلال| imperfection; defect, fault; disorder; خَلَل تِقْنيّ a technical defect; خَلَل عَقْليّ a psychological disorder

خلا *v* |u; خُلوّ| 1 [كانَ فارِغاً] to be free; to be empty; خَلا من to be free from, to be devoid of; خَلا من الأَمْراضِ المُعْدِيةِ to be free from contagious diseases; خَلا المَكانُ من أَهْلِهِ the place was deserted; لا يَخْلو كَلامُهُ من فائِدةٍ there is some point to what he said 2 [انْفَرَدَ] to be alone; خَلا ب \ مع شَخْصٍ to be alone with sb; خَلا إلى نَفْسِهِ to be alone with oneself

خَلّى *v* 1 [أَفْرَغَ] to vacate; to evacuate 2 [تَرَكَ] to leave; خَلّى عن شَيْءٍ to give up sth

أَخْلى *v* to empty; to vacate, to evacuate; to let go; to give up; أَخْلى مَكاناً لِشَخْصٍ to make room for sb; أَخْلى الطَريقَ to clear the way; أَخْلى سَبيلَ رَهينةٍ to release a hostage; أَخْلى قَرْيةً to evacuate a village; أَخْلى بِناية to vacate a building; أَخْلى من السُكّانِ to evacuate the population; to displace the residents

تَخَلّى *v* |عن| to give up, to renounce, to abandon; to cede; تَخَلّى عن شَيْءٍ to give up sth; to recede from sth; تَخَلّى عن شَخْصٍ to let sb down; تَخَلّى عن المُتابَعةِ to dismiss; تَخَلّى عن مَكانِهِ لِشَخْصٍ to step aside for sb; تَخَلّى عن فِكْرةٍ to abandon an idea; تَخَلّى عن عَقيدَتِهِ to renounce one's faith

اخْتَلى *v* |مع ,ب| to be alone with; ما اخْتَلى رَجُلٌ بامْرَأةٍ إلاّ وكانَ الشَيْطانُ ثالِثَهُما whenever man is alone with a woman, Satan is also with them

خُلوّ *n* emptiness; vacancy

خِلْو *adj* free

خالٍ *adj* 1 [فارِغ] empty; free; شارِع خالٍ an empty street; مَقْعَد خالٍ an empty chair, a vacant seat; الاسْمُ عالٍ والمَرْبَطُ خالٍ ≈ to be all hat and no cattle (*to have a high reputation but be lacking in substance*) 2 [عَديم] free; خالي البالِ carefree; خالٍ من الدُيونِ debt-free; بَيْت خالٍ من الأَثاثِ a house without furniture; خالٍ من العَجْزِ \ الشَوائِبِ flawless/impeccable; رَجُل خالٍ من الشَفَقة a man without remorse 3 [غابِر] |خَوالٍ| bygone; في الأَيّامِ الخَوالي in bygone days

خَلا *particle* ما خَلا with the exception of, except, save; لا تُعَدُّ أوروبّا قوّةً نَوَويّةً ما خَلا بَريطانِيا وفَرَنْسا Europe is not a nuclear power, with the exception of Britain and France

خَلّ *n* |خُلول| vinegar; حامِض الخَلِّ acetic acid; زُجاجة خَلٍّ a bottle of vinegar; الزَيْت والخَلّ oil and vinegar

خِلّ *n* |أَخْلال| a close friend

خِلال, خِلالة *n* |أَخِلّة| toothpick

خِلالَ *prep* 1 [أثناء] during; within; خِلالَ فَتْرةِ الحَرْبِ during the war, in wartime; في خِلالِ سَنةٍ, خِلالَ سَنةٍ within a year; in a year; خِلالَ خَمْسِ سَنَواتٍ within five years; in five years; في خِلالِ ذلك meanwhile, in the meantime, by then; تُقَدَّمُ الطَلَباتُ خِلالَ ٢٠ يَوْماً applications must be made within 20 days; يَشْتَغِلُ خِلالَ اللَيْلِ ويَنامُ خِلالَ النَهارِ he works at night and sleeps during the day 2 [عَبْرَ] مِن خِلالِ through; by, by way of; on the basis of; من خِلالِ القَنَواتِ الدِبْلوماسيّةِ through diplomatic channels; مَرَّ من خِلالِ البَوّابةِ to pass by/through the gate; نَظَرَ مِن خِلالِ الدُخانِ إلى مَوْقِعِ الحادِثةِ through the smoke he looked at the scene of the accident

خَلّة *n* |خِلال| property, characteristic

خُلّة *n* |خُلَل| friendship

خِلّة *n* (Bot) *Ammi* (*plant which was traditionally used for toothpicks*)

خَليل *n* |خُلاّن, أَخِلاّءُ| 1 [صَديق] friend 2 [عاشِق] lover 3 [اسْم شَخْصيّ] Khalil (*male given name*)

خَليلة *n* mistress; girlfriend; concubine

اخْتِلال *n* |اخْتِلالات| disruption; disorder; disturbance; failure; اخْتِلال نَفْسيّ a psychological disorder; اخْتِلال ميزانِ القُوى a disruption of the power balance

إخْلال *n* |إخْلالات| breach, violation; disturbance; الإخْلال بالنِظامِ العامِّ disturbing the peace; الإخْلال بالعَقْدِ breach of contract

الخَليل *n* |f| Hebron (*town on the West Bank*)

تَخْليل *n* preservation, pickling

مُخْتَلّ A *adj* deranged, disturbed; مُخْتَلّ العَقْلِ demented, insane; كانَ مُخْتَلّاً عَقْليّاً to be insane; مُخْتَلّ نَفْسيّاً mentally ill B *n* مُخْتَلّ عَقْليّاً a mentally ill person, lunatic

مُخِلّ *adj* disgraceful, shameful

مُخَلَّل *adj* preserved, pickled, salted; مُخَلَّلات pickled vegetables

خَلَنْج *n* (Bot) heath, heather (*Ericaceae*)

خَلاء **A** *adj* empty, vacant; deserted; قِطْعة أَرْضٍ خَلاءٍ a vacant piece of land

B *n* **1** [فَضاء خالٍ] open country **2** [فَراغ] emptiness

خَلْوة *n* privacy; solitude

خَلَويّ *adj* **1** (Bio) cellular, cell (*before n*); اِنْقِسام خَلَويّ cellular division **2** (Tech) mobile (BrE), cellular/cell (AmE); هاتِف خَلَويّ mobile (BrE) cell (AmE) phone **3** [ناءٍ] solitary

خَلِيّة *n* |خَلايا| **1** (Bio) cell; خَلِيّة بَيْضيّة \ مَنَويّة egg/sperm cell; خَلِيّة سَرَطانيّة cancer cell; تَكاثُر الخَلايا السَرَطانيّةِ the proliferation of cancer cells; مَرْكَز خَلِيّةٍ cell nucleus; اِنْقِسام الخَلايا cell division; أُحاديّ الخَلِيّةِ unicellular, single-celled; a single-celled organism **2** (Tech) cell; خَلِيّة شَمْسيّة solar cell; خَلِيّة بَطّاريّةٍ battery cell **3** [مُنَظَّمة] cell; ring; خَلِيّة شُيوعيّة a communist cell; خَلِيّة إِرْهابيّة a terrorist cell **4** [نَحْلٍ] beehive; خَلايا الشَمْعِ honeycomb

خَلْيَويّ **A** *adj* mobile (BrE), cellular/cell (AmE); اِتِّصالات خَلْيَويّة mobile (BrE) cellular (AmE) communications; هاتِف خَلْيَويّ mobile (BrE) cell (AmE) (phone); مُشَغِّل خَلْيَويّ mobile network provider

B *n* mobile (BrE) cell (AmE) (phone); شَبَكة الخَلْيَويِّ the mobile network

اِخْتِلاء *n* |بـ| privacy; being alone with; اِخْتِلاء بِشَخْصٍ being alone with sb; اِخْتِلاء بِنَفْسِهِ being alone

إِخْلاء *n* evacuation; eviction; vacating; إِخْلاء مَسْؤوليّةٍ disclaimer; إِخْلاء مِنْطَقةِ الكارِثةِ من السُكّانِ the evacuation of the disaster area; إِخْلاء الأَراضي المُحْتَلّةِ the evacuation of the occupied territories

تَخَلٍّ *n* surrender, giving up

تَخْلِية *n* vacating; abandonment

مِخْلاة *n* |مَخالٍ| nosebag, feedbag

‹ **خَلّون** *n* (Chem) acetone

‹ **خَمان** *n* (Bot) elder, elderberry (*Sambucus*); ثَمَر الخَمانِ elderberry

‹ **خَمِجَ** *v* |a; خَمَج| to rot

خَمَج *n* rot, decay; infection; خَمَج الدَم blood poisoning, septicaemia

خامِج *adj* (Med) septic

خَمَجيّ *adj* infectious

‹ **خَمَدَ** *v* |u; خُمود| to go out, to die; to subside, to calm/die down; تَخْمُدُ النارُ the fire is going out; خَمَدَ غَضَبُهُ his anger subsided

أَخْمَدَ *v* **1** [أَطْفَأَ] to extinguish, to put out; أَخْمَدَ حَريقاً to extinguish a fire **2** [أَسْكَتَ] to suppress, to put down; أَخْمَدَ تَمَرُّداً \ اِضْطِراباتٍ to put down a rebellion/riots

خامِد *adj* inactive, dormant; extinct; بُرْكان خامِد an extinct volcano

إِخْماد *n* suppression, putting out; extinction

مُخَمِّد **A** *adj* suppressing

B *n* مُخَمِّد صَدَماتٍ shock absorber, damper (BrE)

‹ **خَمَرَ** *v* |u; خَمْر| **1** [جَعَلَهُ يَخْتَمِرُ] to ferment; to brew; to add yeast to **2** [سَتَرَ] to keep secret

خَمَّرَ *v* **1** [خَمَرَ] to ferment; to brew; to add yeast to **2** [غَطّى] to cover; خَمَّرَ الرَأْسَ بِخِمارٍ to cover the head with a veil

خامَرَ *v* overcome; خامَرَهُ الشَكُّ he was stricken with doubt

أَخْمَرَ *v* to ferment, to cause to undergo fermentation

تَخَمَّرَ *v* **1** [الخُمورُ] to ferment **2** [العَجينُ] to rise

اِخْتَمَرَ *v* to ferment, to brew; to be concocted; تَخْتَمِرُ الخُطّةُ the plan is brewing

خَمْر *n* |mf; خُمور| wine; alcohol; شَرِبَ الخَمْرَ to drink wine; اليَوْمَ خَمْرٌ وَغَداً أَمْرٌ ≈ let tomorrow take care of itself

خَمّار *n* wine seller

خُمار *n* hangover

خِمار *n* |أَخْمِرة, خُمُر| veil; khimar (*a garment worn by some Muslim women that covers the hair and torso*)

خَمّارة *n* bar, tavern, pub

خَمْرة *n* |خُمور| alcohol; wine

خَمْريّ *adj* **1** [لَوْن] wine-red, burgundy **2** [كُحوليّ] alcoholic; *containing large amounts of alcohol; related to alcohol or wine*; جَلْسة خَمْريّة *a party or get-together centered around drinking (often to excess)*

خِمّير *n* alcoholic; drunk, drunkard; addict

خَميرة *n* |خَمائِرُ| yeast; leaven, leavening; enzyme; أَضافَ الخَميرةَ إِلى العَجينِ to add yeast to the dough

اِخْتِمار *n* fermentation

تَخَمُّر *n* fermentation

تَخْمير *n* fermentation; brewing; leavening; عَمَلِيّة التَخْمِيرِ fermentation process

مُخَمَّر *adj* fermented; leavened

مُخَمِّر *adj* fermenting

مَخْمَرة *n* brewery

مَخْمور *adj* drunk

‹ **خَمَسَ** *v* |u; خَمْس| to divide into five parts

خَمَّسَ *v* to make fivefold, to quintuple; to divide into five parts

خُمْس *n* (one) fifth

خامِس *num* fifth

خامِسَ عَشَرَ *num* fifteenth

خَمّاس *n* (Hist) *sharecropper receiving one fifth of the crop*

خُماسيّ **A** *adj* fivefold; penta-; خُماسيّ الزَوايا pentagonal; مُباراة خُماسيّة pentathlon; كُرة القَدَمِ الخُماسيّة five-a-side (football) **B** quintet

خَماسين *n* khamsin (*an oppressive, hot southerly or south-easterly wind blowing in Egypt in spring*)

خَمْسة **A** *num* five **B** *n* hamsa (*a palm-shaped amulet believed to protect against the evil eye*)

خَمْسةَ عَشَرَ *num* fifteen

خَمْسونَ *num* fifty; fiftieth

خَميس *n* |أَخْمِسة| يَوْم الخَميسِ Thursday; في مَساءِ يَوْمِ الخَميس, مَساءً الخَميس on Thursday evening; خَميس الفِصْحِ \ الأَسْرارِ \ العَهْدِ Holy Thursday; خَميس الصُعودِ Ascension Day

مُخَمَّس *n* |مُخَمَّسات| (Geom) pentagon

‹ **خَمَشَ** *v* |i-u; خَمْش| to scratch

خَمْش *n* |خُموش| scratch, scratch mark

خُماشة *n* scratch, scratch mark

‹ **خَمُصَ, خَمَصَ, خَمِصَ** *v* |a-u; خَمَص, خَماصة, خُموص| to be hungry; to become thin

أَخْمَص *n* |أَخامِص| the arch of the foot; مِن (قِمّة) رَأْسِهِ إلى أَخْمَصِ قَدَمَيْهِ from head to toe

أَخْمَصيّ *adj* (Anat) plantar; اللِفافة الأَخْمَصيّة plantar fascia

‹ **خَمَلَ** *v* |u; خُمول| to be languid/weak; to hang around

خامِل *adj* lazy; lethargic, inert, inactive; languid

خُمول *n* weakness; sluggishness; inactivity; lethargy; slackness; خُمول جَسَديّ \ فِكْريّ physical/mental inactivity; تَحَرَّكَ بِخُمولٍ to move sluggishly

خَميلة *n* |خَمائِل| brushwood

مُخْمَل *n* velvet; سِرْوال من المُخْمَلِ velvet trousers (BrE) pants (AmE); مُخْمَل أَسْوَد black velvet

مُخْمَليّ *adj* velvet (*before n*)

‹ **خَمَّ** *v* |i-u; خَمّ, خُموم| to rot, to putrefy, to decay

خامّ *adj* rotten, putrid

خُمّ *n* |خِمَمة| chicken coop; poultry pen

‹ **خَمَّنَ** *v* **1** [قَدَّرَ] to estimate, to assess **2** [حَزَرَ] to guess, to conjecture; to speculate; خَمَّنَ شَيْئاً to guess (at) sth, to take a guess at sth, to take a chance on sth; خَمَّنَ ثَمَنَ شَيْءٍ to guess the price of sth; خَمَّنَ عَواقِبَ شَيْءٍ to speculate about the consequences of sth

تَخْمين *n* |تَخْمينات| estimation, guess; guessing, speculation; ارْتَكَزَ على التَخْميناتِ to be based on guesses; مُجَرَّد تَخْميناتٍ mere speculation

تَخْمينيّ *adj* estimated, speculative

‹ **خَنِثَ** *v* |a; خَنَث| to be effeminate

خَنَّثَ *v* to make effeminate

تَخَنَّثَ *v* to behave in an effeminate manner

خُنْثَويّ *adj* hermaphrodite, hermaphroditic; intersexual; androgynous; حَيَوانات خُنْثَويّة hermaphroditic animals

خُنْثَويّة *n* hermaphrodism

خُنْثى *n* |خِناث, خَناثَى| hermaphrodite

خُنوثة *n* intersexuality

مُخَنَّث *adj* effeminate

‹ **خَنْجَر, خِنْجَر** *n* |خَناجِر| dagger

‹ **خَنْدَقَ** *v* |i; خَنْدَقة| to dig a trench

تَخَنْدَقَ *v* to entrench

خَنْدَق *n* |خَنادِق| trench; ditch; هُمْ في خَنْدَقٍ واحِدٍ they're in the same boat

مُتَخَنْدِق *adj* entrenched

خِنْزِير *n* |خَنازِيرُ| (Zool) pig, swine; خِنْزِير بَرِّيّ wild boar; خِنْزِير البَحْرِ porpoise; dolphin; خِنْزِير الهِنْدِ \ غينيا guinea pig, cavia; ذَبَحَ خِنْزِيراً مُرَبّي الخَنازِيرِ pig farmer; لَحم الخِنْزِيرِ pork; to slaughter a pig

أَخْنَس *adj* |dipt| with a flattened nose

خُنْشار *n* (Bot) fern

خِنْصِر, **خِنْصَر** *n* |خَناصِرُ| (Anat) little finger, pinkie

خَنَعَ *v* |a; خُنوع| to cringe; to humble oneself

خانِع *adj* submissive, servile; cringing

خَنوع *adj* submissive, servile; cringing

خُنوع *n* submissiveness, servility; حَذا حَذْوَ شَخْصٍ بِخُنوعٍ to imitate sb slavishly

خَنْفَرَ *v* |i; خَنْفَرة| to snore

خُنْفُساء *n* |dipt f; خَنافِسُ| (Zool) beetle; scarab

خَنَقَ *v* |u; خَنْق| to strangle, to choke, to throttle; to suffocate; خَنَقَ شَخْصاً to strangle sb; خَنَقَ أَصْواتَ المُعارَضةِ to silence the voice of the opposition

خانَقَ *v* to quarrel with; خانَقَ شَخْصاً to quarrel with sb

تَخانَقَ *v* to quarrel with each other

اِنْخَنَقَ *v* to be strangled; to be suffocated, to be stifled

اِخْتَنَقَ *v* to suffocate, to choke; to be strangled; اِخْتَنَقَتْ بالدُخانِ she was choked by the smoke; اِخْتَنَقَ من الحَرِّ to suffocate from the heat

خَنْق *n* strangling, strangulation; suffocation; stifling; قَتَلَ شَخْصاً خَنْقاً to strangle sb (*to death*); ماتَ خَنْقاً to die by strangulation/ suffocation; خَنْق حُرِّيّةِ التَعْبِيرِ stifling freedom of speech; أَنْقَذَ شَخْصاً من المَوْتِ خَنْقاً to rescue sb from suffocation

خانِق [A] *adj* stuffy, stifling; suffocating; جَوّ خانِق oppressive weather; a suffocating atmosphere; سُكون خانِق an eerie silence; غاز خانِق an asphyxiating gas

[B] *n* (Tech) choke, throttle

خانوق *n* |خَوانِقُ, خَوانيقُ| (Med) croup, laryngotracheobronchitis

خُناق, **خُنّاق** *n* [1] ◀ [مَرَض الجِهازِ التَنَفُّسِيِّ] |خَوانِقُ, خَوانيقُ| diphtheria [2] ◀ [ذُبْحة] angina; خُناق الصَدْرِ angina pectoris

خِناق *n* throat; neck; ضَيَّقَ على شَخْصٍ الخِناقَ to tighten the grip around sb's throat; to press sb hard

اِخْتِناق *n* |اِخْتِناقات| suffocation, asphyxia; constriction, tightness of the chest; إِحْساس بالاخْتِناقِ an oppressive feeling; اِخْتِناق مُروريّ traffic jam; سَبَّبَ اخْتِناقاً مُروريًّا to cause a traffic jam; اِخْتِناق سُكّانيّ overpopulation

مَخْنوق *adj* suffocated; strangled; stifled

خَنَّ *v* |i; خَنين| to talk through the nose

خُنّة *n* a nasal twang

خَنين *n* nasal speech

أَخَنّ *adj* |dipt; خُنّ| nasal; صَوْت أَخَنّ a nasal voice

خَنا *v* |u; خَنًى| to use obscene language

خَنِيَ *v* |a; خَنًى| to use obscene language

خِنَّوْص *n* |خَنانيصُ| piglet

خَواجا *n* |خَواجة| sir, mister (*form of address used for Christians and Westerners*); foreigner

خُوارِزْمِيّة, **خُوارِزْم** *n* (Math, Comput) algorithm

خُوان, **خِوان** *n* |أَخْوِنة, أَخاوِينُ| (dining) table; buffet

خَوْخ *n coll* [1] ◀ [دُرّاق] (Egypt, NA) peach; قَشَّرَ \ أَكَلَ خَوْخةً to peel/ eat a peach [2] ◀ [بَرْقوق] (Syria) plum; خَوْخ أَمْلَس nectarine

خوذة *n* |خُوَذ, خوذات| helmet; لَبِسَ خوذةً to wear a helmet, to have a helmet on

خارَ[1] *v* |u| [1] ◀ [صَوْت البَهائِمِ] |خُوار| to moo, to low; تَخورُ البَقَرةُ the cow is mooing [2] ◀ [ضَعُفَ] |خَور, خُؤور| to grow weak; خارَتْ عَزيمَتُهُ he grew weak, he lost heart; خارَتْ قُواهُ he grew/was feeble

خَوِرَ *v* |a; خَوَر| to weaken

خائِر *adj* weak, strengthless

خُوار *n* mooing; bellowing; خُوار البَقَرِ the mooing of cows

خوريّ[2] *n* |خَوارِنة| priest

خورُس *n* (Chr) (church) choir

خَوْزَقَ *v* see خزق

خوص *n coll* palm leaves; wicker (*woven from palm leaves*); سَلّة خوصٍ a wicker basket, a woven basket

خَوْصَصَ *v* see خصص

to be afraid of sth/sb

خَوّاف **A** *adj* faint-hearted; cowardly

B *n* coward; chicken (infml)

خيفة *n* fear, dread

تَخَوُّف *n* |تَخَوُّفات| fear, dread; apprehension; concern

تَخْويف *n* |تَخْويفات| frightening, scaring, intimidation; مُحاوَلة تَخْويفٍ attempted intimidation

مُتَخَوِّف *adj* afraid, fearful

مَخافة *n* |مَخاوِفُ| fear; dread; مَخافة اللهِ fear of God; مَخافةَ أنْ ... for fear that ...

مَخوف *adj* feared, fearsome

مُخيف *adj* frightening, frightful, dreadful, scary, terrible; فِكْرة مُخيفة a scary thought; لَحَظات مُخيفة frightening moments; فيلْم مُخيف a horror movie

خَوَّلَ *v* **1** [مَنَحَ] to grant, to give, to concede **2** [فَوَّضَ] to authorize, to empower

خال *n* |أخْوال, خُؤولة, خُؤول| **1** [أخو الأُمِّ] (maternal) uncle; ابْن \ بِنْت خالٍ (male/female) cousin; زَوْجة خالٍ aunt; الخال حَسَن Uncle Hassan **2** [شامة] |خيلان| see **خيل**

خالة *n* (maternal) aunt; ابْن \ بِنْت خالةٍ (male/female) cousin; زَوْج خالةٍ uncle; الخالة لَيْلى Aunt Layla

خَوْليّ *n* supervisor

تَخْويل *n* authorization, empowerment

مُخَوَّل *adj* authorized, empowered, entrusted

خانَ *v* |u| خَوْن, خِيانة| **1** [خَتَرَ] to betray; to fail, to let down; خانَ وَطَنَهُ to betray one's country; خانَ أمانة شَخْصٍ to violate sb's trust **2** [في الزَّواج] to cheat (on), to be unfaithful (to); خانَ زَوْجَتَهُ to cheat on one's wife

خَوَّنَ *v* to regard as a traitor; to accuse of treason/betrayal

اخْتانَ *v* to betray, to deceive

اسْتَخْوَنَ *v* to distrust; to regard as a traitor

خائِن **A** *adj* |خَوَنة, خوّان| disloyal; treacherous; unfaithful, adulterous; زَوْج خائِن an unfaithful husband

B *n* |خَوَنة, خوّان| traitor; خائِن للوَطَنِ traitor (to one's country)

خاضَ *v* |u| خَوْض| to dive into, to plunge into; to rush into; to embark on; to go into; to become absorbed in; خاضَ الماءَ \ في الماءِ to plunge into the water, to go into the water; خاضَ في مَسْألةٍ to delve into a subject, to take up a matter; خاضَ المَعْرَكةَ to rush into battle, to join the fight; خاضَ الانْتِخاباتِ to run in the elections; خاضَ البَحْرَ to sail on the sea; خاضَ حَرْباً to wage war

خَوَّضَ *v* to wade into

مَخاضة *n* |مَخاضات, مَخاوِضُ| ford; fordable place (*in a stream*)

خافَ *v* |a| خَوْف, مَخافة, خيفة| to fear, to dread; to be afraid (of), to be scared (of); خافَ على شَيْءٍ \ شَخْصٍ to fear for sth/sb; خافَ على نَفْسِهِ to fear for his life; خافَ من شَيْءٍ \ شَخْصٍ to be afraid of sth/sb, to fear sth/sb; خافَ شَيْئاً \ شَخْصاً to fear sth/sb; أخافُ من المَوْتِ I am afraid of death; خافَ الأَبُ على ابْنِهِ من الانْحِرافِ the father feared that his son might become delinquent

خَوَّفَ *v* to frighten, to scare, to scare off; خَوَّفَ شَخْصاً to scare/frighten sb

أخافَ *v* to frighten, to scare, to intimidate; أخافَ شَخْصاً to frighten sb

تَخَوَّفَ *v* to be afraid, to be scared/frightened; تَخَوَّفَ من شَيْءٍ \ شَخْصٍ to be afraid/scared of sth/sb, to be frightened by sth/sb

خَوْف *n* fear, dread; phobia; خَوْف غَيْر مُبَرَّرٍ unjustified fear; نَظْرة خَوْفٍ a fearful look; خَوْف من شَيْءٍ fear of sth; الخَوْف من الأماكِنِ المُغْلَقةِ claustrophobia; الخَوْف من الغُرَباءِ xenophobia; الخَوْف من المُرْتَفَعاتِ fear of heights; خَوْفاً من الفَقْرِ for fear of poverty; ماتَ خَوْفاً to die of fear; to be in mortal fear; كادَ يَموتُ من الخَوْفِ to be scared to death; ارْتَعَشَ من الخَوْفِ to tremble with fear; تَصَبَّبَ عَرَقاً من الخَوْفِ he broke out in a cold sweat; خَوْف على شَيْءٍ \ شَخْصٍ fear for sth/sb; worry about sth/sb; لا خَوْفَ عَلَيْهِ don't worry about him; تَغَلَّبَ على خَوْفِهِ to overcome one's fear; يَنْتابُني الخَوْفُ I am very afraid

خائِف *adj* |خُوَّف| afraid, scared, frightened, terrified; apprehensive, anxious; كانَ خائِفاً من شَيْءٍ \ شَخْصٍ

خَوّان **A** *adj* treacherous, unreliable, disloyal
B *n* cheater, adulterer; traitor

خِيانة *n* **1** [غَدْر] disloyalty, treachery; خِيانة الوَطَنِ \ عُظْمى high treason; خِيانة المَبادِئِ abandonment of principles; خِيانة للديموقراطيّةِ betrayal of democracy; ارْتَكَبَ الخِيانةَ (العُظْمى) to commit (high) treason; أَحَسَّ بالخِيانةِ to feel betrayed **2** [زَوْجيّة] adultery; خِيانة زَوْجيّة adultery; ارْتَكَبَ خِيانةً to commit adultery

خُوّة *n* protection money

خَوى *v* |i; خَوًى ,خواء| **1** [خَلا] to be/make empty **2** [جاعَ] to be hungry

خَوِيَ *v* |a; خَواء| to be empty

أَخْوى *v* to be hungry

خاوٍ *adj* empty

خَواء *n* |أَخْوِية| emptiness, vacuum; hollowness

خابَ *v* |i; خَيْبة| to fail, to go wrong; خابَ أَمَلُهُ في شَيْءٍ \ شَخْصٍ to be disappointed in sth/sb, to be disillusioned in sth/sb

خَيَّبَ *v* to cause to fail; خَيَّبَ الأَمَلَ to disappoint, to disillusion; خَيَّبَ أَمَلَ شَخْصٍ في شَيْءٍ to disappoint sb in sth

أَخابَ *v* to disappoint

خائِب *adj* **1** [الأَمَلِ] disappointed, disillusioned; خائِب الأَمَلِ disappointed, disillusioned **2** [فاشِل] futile; unsuccessful; مُحاوَلة خائِبة a failed attempt; عادَ خائِباً to return in failure

خَيْبة *n* failure, flop; خَيْبة أَمَلٍ disappointment, disillusion, blow, let-down; anticlimax; كم كانَتْ خَيْبةُ أَمَلي كَبيرةً that was most disappointing; يا لَلْخَيْبةِ! what a disappointment!

مُخَيِّب *adj* disappointing; مُخَيِّب للأَمَلِ disappointing; خَبَر مُخَيِّب للآمالِ disappointing news; إنّ النَتيجة مُخَيِّبةٌ جِدًّا للأَمَلِ the result is very disappointing

خَيَّرَ *v* to give a choice; خَيَّرَ شَخْصاً to give sb a choice

خايَرَ *v* **1** [تَرَكَ حُرّيّةَ الاخْتِيارِ] to let choose, to enable to choose **2** [فاقَ] to surpass, to outdo

تَخَيَّرَ *v* to choose, to select, to pick

اخْتارَ *v* **1** [انْتَخَبَ] to choose, to select, to pick, to elect; اخْتارَ شَيْئاً \ شَخْصاً to choose sth/sb; اخْتارَ لَوْناً to pick a colour; اخْتارَ دِراسةً to choose a subject; اخْتارَ بين \ من... to make a choice between/from... **2** [فَضَّلَ] to prefer; اخْتارَ شَيْئاً على شَيْءٍ to prefer sth to sth else

اسْتَخار *v* to ask God for proper guidance, to seek what is best

خِيار **A** *n* **1** [اخْتِيار] choice, option; alternative; الخِيار الأَوَّل \ الثاني first/second choice; خِيار لا بَديلَ لَهُ the only choice; لا خِيارَ لي I have no choice; لَيْسَ لَنا خِيارٌ آخَرُ we have no other choice; لم يَبْقَ أَمامَنا أَيُّ خِيارٍ إلاّ أَنْ ... we had no other choice than to ...; أَبْقى البابَ مَفْتوحاً أمام كُلِّ الخِياراتِ to keep all options open **2** (Fin) option; سوق الخِياراتِ options exchange/market; اشْتَرى خِياراتٍ to buy options
B *n coll* see خير 2

خِياريّ *adj* optional; voluntary

خَيْر **A** *adj* good; better; best; على خَيْرِ ما يُرامُ couldn't be better; على خَيْرِ وَجْهٍ as good as possible; الوِقايةُ خَيْرٌ من العِلاجِ prevention is better than cure (BrE), an ounce of prevention is worth a pound of cure (AmE); حالُنا خَيْرٌ من حالِ الآخَرينَ our situation is better than others; خَيْرُها بِغَيْرِها better luck next time; خَيْرُ الأُمورِ أَوْساطُها the best way is the happy medium
B *n* |خُيور| **1** [نِعْمة] good, benefit; الخَيْر والشَرّ good and bad/evil; أَعْمال الخَيْرِ charity; فِعْل الخَيْرِ benefaction, charity; فَعَلَ خَيْراً to do good; تَمَنّى لِشَخْصٍ كُلَّ خَيْرٍ to hope for the best for sb; تَوَسَّمَ الخَيْرَ في المُسْتَقْبَلِ to have high expectations for the future; خَيْراً تَعْمَلُ شَرًّا تَلْقى no good deed ever goes unpunished **2** [رَخاء] well-being, welfare; أنا بِخَيْرٍ I'm fine, I am (doing) well **3** [ثَرْوة] plenty, ease; affluence; money, fortune, wealth

خَيِّر **A** *adj* good; philanthropic, humane, benevolent; charitable; عَمَل خَيِّر a philanthropic act
B *n* philanthropist

خَيْرات *n pl* resources, treasures; خَيْرات الدُنْيا worldly blessings; خَيْرات الطَبيعةِ the bounties of nature

خيرة *n* pick, cream, elite; خيرة الطُلّابِ the best students, the cream of the students

خَيْرِيّ *adj* charitable, benevolent, philanthropic; مَقاصِد خَيْرِيّة charity; مُؤَسَّسة \ جَمْعِيّة أَعْمالٍ خَيْرِيّةٍ a charitable institution/organization

اخْتِيار *n* choice, option, selection; اخْتِيار عَشْوائِيّ a random choice; اخْتِيارات مُتَنَوِّعة different choices; حُرِّيّة الاخْتِيارِ freedom of choice; حَسَبَ الاخْتِيارِ optional; اخْتِيار بين شَيْئَيْنِ a choice between two things; كانَ لَهُ الاخْتِيارُ to have the choice; تَرَكَ لِشَخْصٍ الاخْتِيارَ to give/leave sb the choice; يَقَعُ الاخْتِيارُ عَلَيْهِ the choice falls on him

اخْتِيارِيّ *adj* optional, elective, voluntary; المُساهَمةُ اخْتِيارِيّةٌ participation is voluntary; مادّة اخْتِيارِيّة an elective (subject)

مُخْتار **A** *adj* chosen, selected; جَماعة مُخْتارة a select group **B** *n* **1** [رَئِيس] (ME) |مَخاتِيرُ| mayor; village chief **2** [مُنْتَقًى] chosen one; مُخْتارات anthology; مُخْتارات من مُؤَلَّفاتِ ... an anthology of the works of ... **3** [اسْم شَخْصِيّ] Mukhtar/ Mokhtar (*male given name*)

[2]‹ **خِيار** **A** *n coll* cucumber; خِيار مُخَلَّل pickle, gherkin (BrE); شَرِيحة خِيارٍ a slice of cucumber
B *n* see خير 1

‹ **خَيْزُران** *n* |خيازِرُ| bamboo, cane; rattan; reed; أَثاث من الخَيْزُرانِ rattan furniture

خَيْزُرانيّة *n* (Naut) junk

‹ **خَيْش** *n* |أَخْياش, خُيوش| jute, gunny; sackcloth; canvas; كِيس (من) الخَيْشِ gunny sack

خَيْشة *n* |خِيَش, خَيْشات| piece of sackcloth; straw mattress

‹ **خاطَ** *v* |i; خَيْط| to sew; to stitch; to suture; خاطَ ثَوْباً \ قَمِيصاً to sew a garment/shirt

خَيَّطَ *v* to sew; to stitch; to suture; خَيَّطَ مَلابِسَ to sew clothes

خَيْط *n* |خُيوط, أَخْياط, خيطان| thread, yarn; خَيْط قُطْنِيّ cotton thread; خَيْط الأَسْنانِ (dental) floss; بَكَرة من الخيطانِ a reel of thread; بالإِبْرة والخَيْطِ with needle and thread

خَيّاط *n* tailor

خِياط *n* needle

خَيّاطة *n* seamstress, (female) tailor, dressmaker

خِياطة *n* sewing; tailoring; suture; أَدَوات الخِياطةِ sewing supplies; آلة خِياطةٍ sewing machine

خَيْطِيّ *adj* thread-like; stringy; بِنْية خَيْطِيّة a thread-like structure

مِخْيَط *n* |مَخايِط| needle

[1]‹ **خَيَّلَ** *v* to make believe, to pretend; to suggest; خَيَّلَ إلى شَخْصٍ أنّ ... to make sb believe that ...; يُخَيَّلُ إلَيَّ أَنَّكَ صادِقٌ it seems to me that you are telling the truth

أَخالَ *v* to be dubious

تَخَيَّلَ *v* to imagine, to fancy; تَخَيَّلَ شَيْئاً to imagine sth, to form a picture of sth; تَخَيَّلَ أَنَّهُ مَلِكٌ he imagined he was king; تَخَيَّلْ! (just) imagine!

تَخايَلَ *v* to be conceited; to boast

اخْتالَ *v* to be conceited; to boast; to swagger

خال *n* **1** [شامة] |خيلان| mole **2** [أخو الأُمّ] |أَخْوال, خُؤولة, خُؤول| see خول

خَيال *n* |خَيالات, أَخْيِلة| **1** [قوّة عَقْلِيّة] imagination; imaginative powers; خَيال خَصِب \ واسِع a vivid/lively imagination; خَيال غَيْر مُتَناهٍ a limitless imagination; شَخْص واسِع الخَيالِ dreamer; خَيال الشاعِرِ poetic imagination; عالَم الخَيالِ dreamworld; في خَيالِهِ in his imagination/fantasy; اسْتَسْلَمَ لِخَيالِهِ he surrendered to his imagination; أَثارَ الخَيالَ to excite the imagination; هذا يَفوقُ الخَيالَ it's beyond imagination; لَيْسَ من بابِ الخَيالِ أنْ ... there's a real chance that ... **2** [وَهْم] vision; fantasy; illusion; fiction; الحَقِيقة والخَيال reality and fiction; خَيال عِلْمِيّ science fiction; سَبَحَ في الخَيالِ to daydream; اعْتَبَرَ شَيْئاً من نَسِيجِ الخَيالِ to dismiss sth as a myth **3** [طَيْف] shade

خَيالة *n* ghost, spirit; shade

خَيالِيّ *adj* imaginary, fictitious, made-up, invented; مُغامَرات خَيالِيّة fantastic adventures; قِصَص خَيالِيّة fictitious stories; fiction; أَرْقام خَيالِيّة (Math) imaginary numbers; مُؤَلَّفات غَيْر خَيالِيّةٍ non-fiction

خُيَلاء *n* |dipt| snobbery; self-conceit, conceitedness; vanity; مِشْية الخُيَلاءِ an arrogant gait

اخْتِيال *n* arrogance, snobbery

أَخْيَل *n* (Zool) green woodpecker

تَخايُل *n* arrogance, snobbery

تَخَيُّل *n* |تَخَيُّلات| imagination, fantasy; visualisation; fancy; conception

تَخَيُّليّ *adj* imaginary, fantastic, fanciful

مُتَخَيَّل *adj* imaginary, illusory, unreal; لم يَكُنْ من المُتَخَيَّلِ it was unimaginable

مُخْتال **A** *adj* conceited, haughty, arrogant; مَشى مُخْتالاً كالطاووسِ to strut about like a peacock **B** *n* snob

مُخَيِّلة *n* imagination; imaginative power

2 **خَيّال** *n* |خَيّالة| horseman, rider; شُرْطة الخَيّالةِ mounted police

خَيّالة *n* cavalry

خَيْل *n coll* |no singular noun; خُيول| (Zool) horses; سِباق خَيْلٍ horse races, horse racing; خَيْل سِباقٍ racehorses; رَكِبَ الخَيْلَ to ride horses; رُكوب الخَيْل horse riding

خَيَّمَ *v* **1** [عَسْكَرَ] to camp; to pitch one's tent **2** [تَرَجَّحَ] to reign, to predominate; to permeate; خَيَّمَ الصَّمْتُ على المَدينةِ silence reigned over the city; خَيَّمَ الحُزْنُ على قَلْبي, خَيَّمَ الحُزْنُ في صَدْري grief permeated my heart **3** (Mil) to camp/bivouac

خَيّام *n* tent maker

خَيْمة *n* |خَيْمات, خِيام, خِيَم| **1** [بَيْت من القُماشِ] tent; نَسيج خَيْمةٍ tent cloth; canvas; عَمود خَيْمةٍ tent pole; نَصَبَ \ ضَرَبَ خَيْمةً to pitch a tent; هَدَمَ \ نَقَضَ خَيْمةً to take down a tent; أَقامَ في خَيْمةٍ to camp in a tent **2** (Bot) umbel

تَخْييم *n* camping

مُخَيَّم *n* |مُخَيَّمات| **1** [مُعَسْكَر] camp; مُخَيَّم اعْتِقالٍ detention camp; مُخَيَّم اللاجِئينَ refugee camp **2** [للإقامةِ في الإجازاتِ] camping site/ground

مُخَيِّم *n* camper

د

د *abbr* Dr (*abbreviation of* دُكْتور)

دَأَبَ *v* |a; دَأْب| 1 [اِعْتادَ] to persist, to persevere; دَأَبَ على شَيْءٍ to do sth consistently; to do sth repeatedly; دَأَبَ على الصَلاةِ to keep praying 2 [اِجْتَهَدَ] to do one's best; to apply oneself, to devote oneself; to be diligent; دَأَبَ على شَيْءٍ; to apply oneself to sth; دَأَبَ في الدِراسةِ to study hard

دَأْب *n* |أَدْؤُب| 1 [عادة] habit; على دَأْبِهِ according to one's habit 2 [اِجْتِهاد] diligence; في دَأْبٍ with diligence

دائِب *adj* diligent, hard-working; persistent, tireless, unceasing

دَؤُوب *adj* diligent, hard-working; العَمَل الدَؤُوب hard work; قامَ بِعَمَلٍ دَؤُوبٍ من أَجْلِ شَيْءٍ to work hard for sth; رَجُل دَؤُوب على عَمَلِهِ a man dedicated to his work; جَهْد دَؤُوب relentless effort; بَحْث دَؤُوب a thorough investigation

داب *n* سَمَك الدابِ dab (*a type of fish*)

دادائيّة, داديّة *n* (Art) Dadaism

الدار البَيْضاء *n* Casablanca (*city in Morocco*)

داكا *n* Dhaka (*capital of Bangladesh*)

داكوتا الجَنوبيّة *n* South Dakota (*US state*)

داكوتا الشَماليّة *n* North Dakota (*US state*)

دال *n name of the letter* د

داليا *n* 1 (Bot) *Dahlia* 2 [اِسْم شَخْصيّ] Dalia (*female given name*)

داما *n* see ضاما

دانْتيلاّ, دانْتيل *n* lace

دانْمارْكيّ, دانْمَرْكيّ A *adj* Danish; (اللُغة) الدانْمارْكيّة Danish (*language*)

B *n* Dane

الدانْمارْك, الدانْمَرْك *n* |f| Denmark

داوُد, داؤُد, داوود *n* |dipt| Dawud, David (*male given name*)

دايْم *n* dime

دايود *n* diode

دَبَّ *v* |i; دَبّ, دَبيب| 1 [مَشى] to shuffle, to move slowly; to creep, to crawl; دَبَّ على الأَرْضِ to crawl along the ground 2 [سَرى] to steal, to creep; to stream, to flow; دَبَّت الحَياةُ بِجَسَدِهِ to be revived; دَبَّ الشَكُّ في نَفْسِهِ doubt crept into his mind

دَبَّبَ *v* to sharpen; دَبَّبَ قِطْعَةَ حَديدٍ to sharpen a piece of iron

دابّة *n* |دَوابُّ| 1 [ما يُرْكَبُ] mount; دابّة الجَرِّ draught (BrE) draft (AmE) animal; أَغْبى من الدابّةِ dumb as a post 2 [حَيَوان] animal; beast

دُبّ *n* |دِبَبة| 1 (Zool) bear; دُبّ قُطْبيّ \ أَبْيَض polar bear 2 [دُمْية] teddy bear 3 (Astron) الدُبّ الأَكْبَر \ الأَصْغَر Ursa Major/Minor

دَبّابة *n* tank; مُضادّ للدَبّابات anti-tank; دَمَّر دَبّاباتِ العَدوِّ to destroy the enemy tanks

دَبْدوب *n* |دَباديب| teddy bear

دَبيب *n* crawling; سَمِعَ دَبيبَ أَقْدامٍ to hear the sound of footsteps

دُوَيْبّة *n* tiny animal; insect

مُدَبَّب *adj* sharp; pointed, spiky

دَبَجَ *v* |u; دَبْج| to decorate

دَبَّجَ *v* 1 [أَلَّفَ] to write (down); to compose; دَبَّجَ قَصيدةً to write a poem 2 [زَيَّنَ] to embellish, to decorate, to adorn

ديباج *n* |دَبابيجُ| *a silk garment*

ديباجة *n* preamble; introduction

دَبَح *n* (Bot) salsify (*Tragopogon*)

دَبْدَبَ *v* |i; دَبْدَبة| to make a clicking/pattering/clattering noise

دَبْدوب *n* |دَباديبُ| see دبب

دَبَرَ *v* |u; دُبور| to elapse, to go by, to pass; دَبَرَ النَهارُ \ الصَيْفُ the day/summer is over

دَبَّر *v* **1** ◀ [فَعَل] to contrive, to devise, to plot; دَبَّر خُطَّةً to hatch a plot; دَبَّر كِذْبةً \ جَواباً to come up with an excuse/answer; دَبَّر مُؤامَرةً to hatch a conspiracy **2** ◀ [حَكَمَ] الإنْسانُ يُقَدِّرُ واللهُ يُدَبِّرُ man proposes, God disposes **3** ◀ [نَظَّمَ] to organize, to arrange; دَبَّر الأُمورَ to arrange matters

أَدْبَرَ *v* to go away; to be over; أَدْبَرَ النَهارُ the day is over; أَدْبَرَ عن شَخْصٍ to turn one's back on sb

تَدَبَّرَ *v* to reflect, to consider; to treat/handle with care, to manage; تَدَبَّر أَمْرَهُ to manage one's affairs; تَدَبَّر أَمْراً \ في أَمْرٍ to consider a matter

اسْتَدْبَرَ *v* to turn one's back; اسْتَدْبَرَ شَخْصاً to turn one's back on sb

دَبْر *n* the passing of time; جَعَلَ كَلامَ شَخْصٍ دَبْرَ أُذُنَيْهِ to let sb's words go in one ear and out the other

دُبُر, **دُبْر** *n* |أَدْبار| **1** ◀ [مُؤَخِّرة] backside, buttocks, behind **2** ◀ [ظَهْر] back, rear; من دُبُرٍ from behind; وَلّى دُبُرَهُ \ الأَدْبارَ to turn tail, to run away

دابِر **A** *adj* past, bygone; يَوْم دابِر a day that has passed; أَمْسِ دابِرٌ لا يَعودُ yesterday has passed and will never return; ذَهَبَ كَأَمْسِ الدابِرِ to vanish into thin air

B *n* |دَوابِرُ| ultimate, utmost; end; قَطَعَ دابِرَ شَيْءٍ to put an end to sth

دَبور *n* west wind

دَبّور *n* |دَبابيرُ| wasp, hornet

إِدْبار *n* flight, fleeing; turning around

تَدَبُّر *n* contemplation

تَدْبير *n* |تَدْبيرات, تَدابيرُ| **1** ◀ [إِجْراء] measure; regulation, management; تَدْبير انْتِقاليّ transitional measure; تَدابير أَمْنِيّة security measures; تَدْبير المَنْزِل \ مَنْزِليّ housekeeping; التَدابير اللازِمة necessary measures; سوء التَدْبير mismanagement **2** ◀ [تَخْطيط] planning, arranging; plotting, hatching

مُدَبِّر *n* manager; originator; leader, ringleader; كانَ العَقْلَ المُدَبِّرَ للعَمَلِيّةِ he masterminded the attack

دُبْرِياج *n* clutch; دَوّاسة الدُبْرِياجِ clutch (pedal)

[1] **دَبَّسَ** *v* to pin, to attach, to staple

دَبّاسة *n* stapler

دَبّوس *n* |دَبابيسُ| pin; drawing pin (BrE), pushpin (AmE), thumbtack (AmE); staple; دَبّوس أَمانٍ safety pin; دَبّوس شَعْرٍ hair pin; دَبّوس من الذَهَبِ a gold brooch; عَلَّق شَيْئاً بِدَبّوسٍ to put sth up with a drawing pin

مِدْبَسة *n* pincushion

[2] **دِبْس** *n* syrup (*made of grapes or other fruit*); molasses

دَبْش *n* stuff; furnishings, personal belongings; clutter, mess

دَبَغَ *v* |a-i-u; دَبْغ| to tan; دَبَغَ الجِلْدَ to tan leather

انْدَبَغَ *v* to be/become tanned; جِلْدُ الخِنْزيرِ لا يَنْدَبِغُ *it is good for nothing*

دَبّاغ *n* tanner

دِباغة *n* tanning

مَدْبَغة *n* tannery

دَبِقَ *v* |a; دَبَق| ب| to stick (to), to adhere (to), to cling (to)

دَبِق *adj* sticky

دِبْق *n* (Bot) mistletoe (*Viscum*)

دَبْكة *n* debka (*Levantine folk dance*)

دُبال *n* humus, compost

دُبْلة *n* ring; دُبْلة الخُطوبةِ engagement ring; دُبْلة الزَواجِ wedding ring/band

دَبْلَجَ *v* |i; دَبْلَجة| to dub (*films, etc., into a different language*); دَبْلَج فيلْماً إلى العَرَبِيّةِ to dub a movie into Arabic

دُبْلاج *n* dubbing

مُدَبْلَج *adj* dubbed; أَفْلام مُدَبْلَجة إلى العَرَبِيّةِ movies dubbed into Arabic

دِبْلوم *n* |دِبْلومات| diploma, certificate; دِبْلوم دِراساتٍ عُلْيا a postgraduate degree

دِبْلوماسيّ, **دِيبْلوماسيّ** **A** *adj* diplomatic; السِلْك الدِبْلوماسيّ the diplomatic corps; بَعْثة دِبْلوماسِيّة diplomatic representation; عَلاقات \ أَوْساط دِبْلوماسِيّة diplomatic relations/circles; عَمَل دِبْلوماسيّ a diplomatic effort; ضَغْط دِبْلوماسيّ diplomatic pressure; في خِدْمةٍ دِبْلوماسِيّةٍ in diplomatic service; عِبارة دِبْلوماسِيّة diplomatic language; جَواب دِبْلوماسيّ a diplomatic answer

B *n* diplomat

دِبْلوماسيّة، دِيبْلوماسيّة *n* ① (Pol) diplomacy; دِبْلوماسيّة مَكّوكيّة shuttle diplomacy; دِبْلوماسيّة هادِئة quiet diplomacy ② [بَراعة، التَعامُل] diplomacy, tact, discretion

‹ **دُبَيّ** *n* |f| Dubai (*city in the United Arab Emirates*)

‹ **دَثَر** *v* |u; دُثور| to be wiped out/erased; to fall into oblivion

دَثَّر *v* ① [غَطّى] to cover; to envelop ② [أَهْلَكَ] to destroy; to annihilate

تَدَثَّر *v* to cover/shroud oneself; تَدَثَّر بِمِعْطَفٍ to wrap oneself in a coat

انْدَثَر *v* to be/become extinct, to be obliterated/wiped out

ادَّثَر *v* to cover/shroud oneself

دِثار *n* |دُثُر| blanket, cover; coat, jacket

مُدَثِّر *adj* |ب| covered (with); سورة المُدَثِّر The Covered One (*Sura 74*)

مُنْدَثِر *adj* extinct, wiped out; مِهَن مُنْدَثِرة extinct occupations; لُغة مُنْدَثِرة a dead language

‹ **دَجَّج** *v* to arm heavily; دَجَّج شَخْصاً بالسِلاحِ to heavily arm sb (with weapons)

دَجاج *n coll* chicken; دَجاجة hen; chicken; دَجاج حَبَشيّ guinea fowl; دَجاج روميّ turkey; دَجاج مَشْويّ roast chicken; أَكَلَ لَحْمَ الدَجاجِ to eat chicken; الدَجاجة الّتي تَبيضُ ذَهَباً the goose that lays the golden eggs

دَجاجيّات *n pl* game birds, wildfowl (*Galliformes*)

دُجّة *n* intense darkness

مُدَجَّج *adj* covered; armed; مُدَجَّج بالأَسْلِحةِ \ السِلاحِ heavily armed

‹ **دَجِرَ** *v* |a; دَجَر| to be/become embarrassed, to be/become confused

دَيْجور *n* |دَياجيرُ| dark, darkness

1‹ **دَجَلَ** *v* |u; دَجْل| to cheat, to swindle

دَجَّلَ *v* to deceive, to cheat

دَجّال *n* |دَجّالونَ، دَجاجِلة| swindler, charlatan, impostor; المَسيح الدَجّال Antichrist

دَجْل *n* fraud, trickery, swindle, deceit, cheat

تَدْجيل *n* fraud, deceit, trickery, cheating

2‹ **دِجْلة** *n* |dipt| Tigris (*river in the Middle East*)

‹ **دُجَمْبِر** *n* (Mor) December

‹ **دَجَنَ** *v* |u; دُجون، دَجْن| ① [أَظْلَمَ] to be/become dark, to darken ② [الحَيَوانُ] to be/become tame, to be domesticated ③ [أَقامَ] to stay, to reside; دَجَن في مَكانٍ to reside somewhere

دَجَّنَ *v* to tame, to domesticate; to cow, to subdue

داجَنَ *v* to flatter, to fawn over

أَدْجَنَ *v* ① [أَظْلَمَ] to be gloomy, to be overcast; to be rainy ② [أَقامَ] to reside, to stay; أَدْجَنَ في مَكانٍ to reside somewhere; أَدْجَنَ في بَيْتِهِ to stay at home

داجِن **A** *adj* ① [أَليف] domesticated, tame; طُيور داجِنة domesticated birds; chickens, poultry ② [مُمْطِر] dark, gloomy; rainy; سَحابة داجِنة dark cloud; rain cloud
B *n* |دَواجِنُ| pet; domestic animal; دَواجِن chickens, poultry; pets; مُرَبّي الدَواجِنِ poultry farmer; قِطاع تَرْبِيةِ الدَواجِنِ poultry farming

دُجْنة *n* ① [سَواد] darkness, dark, gloom ② [غَيْم] dark cloud

أَدْجَن *adj* |dipt| black

مُدَجَّن **A** *adj* ① [مُرَوَّض] tame, domesticated; cowed, subdued; حَيَوان مُدَجَّن a domesticated animal; شَعْب مُدَجَّن a subdued people ② [في إِسْبانيا] Mudejar (*relating to the Muslims who remained in Spain after the Reconquista*); الفَنّ \ العِمارة المُدَجَّن(ة) Mudejar art/architecture
B *n* Mudejar (*a Muslim who remained in Spain after the Reconquista*)

‹ **دُجَنْبِر** *n* (Mor) December

‹ **دَجا** *v* |u; دُجوّ| ① [أَظْلَمَ] to be/become dark ② [غَطّى] to cover

داجى *v* to flatter, to fawn over

دُجًى *n* darkness, dark

دَياجٍ *n pl* darkness; دَياجي اللَيْلِ the darkness of night

مُداجٍ *adj* adulator, flatterer; hypocrite

‹ **دَحَرَ** *v* |a; دَحْر، دُحور| to expel, to drive away; to defeat

انْدَحَرَ *v* to be expelled, to be driven away; to be defeated

انْدِحار *n* |انْدِحارات| fall, ruin; decline; انْدِحار الفاشيّة the collapse of fascism; كانَ على وَشْكِ الانْدِحارِ to be at the brink of destruction

داخَل *v* to befall, to come over (sb); داخَلَهُ الشَكُّ doubt befell him

أَدْخَل *v* to bring in; to let in, to admit; to implement; أَدْخَلَ زائِراً to let in a visitor; أَدْخَلَ شَخْصاً المُسْتَشْفى to admit sb to the hospital; أَدْخَلَ شَخْصاً إلى المَطْبَخ to let sb into the kitchen; أَدْخَلَ شَخْصاً في شَيْءٍ to involve someone in sth; أَدْخَلَ شَيْئاً; أَدْخَلَ نَفْسَهُ في أَمْرٍ to involve oneself in an issue; في جَيْبِهِ to put sth in one's pocket; أَدْخَلَ الديموقْراطِيّة to democratize; أَدْخَلَ فِكْرةً \ عادةً to introduce an idea/usage; أَدْخَلَ أَساليبَ \ عاداتٍ جَديدةً to amend; أَدْخَلَ تَعْديلاتٍ to introduce new methods/practices; أَدْخَلَ قانوناً حَيِّزَ التَنْفيذ to implement a law; أَدْخَلَ بَياناتٍ في الحاسوبِ to enter data in the computer

تَدَخَّل *v* to interfere, to intervene, to meddle; تَدَخَّلَ في شَيْءٍ to interfere in sth; تَدَخَّلَ في نِزاعٍ to intervene in a dispute; تَدَخَّلَ في حَديثٍ to intrude upon a conversation; تَدَخَّلَ في أُمورِ الغَيْرِ to meddle in other people's business; مَنْ تَدَخَّلَ في ما لا يَعْنيه نالَ ما لا يُرْضيهِ keep your nose out of other people's business

تَداخَل *v* 1 ◀ [دَخَلَ في بَعْضِهِ] to overlap; to mesh, to be interwoven 2 ◀ (Phys) to interfere

دَخْل *n* 1 ◀ [إيراد] income, earnings; الدَخْل القَوْميّ gross national product, GNP; الدَخْل الإجْماليّ \ الصافي gross/net salary; الدَخْل الاسْميّ \ الفِعْليّ nominal/actual income; دَخْل مُنْخَفِض \ مَحْدود \ بَسيط a steady income; دَخْل ثابِت a low income; دَخْل شَهْريّ monthly salary; تَوْزيع الدَخْلِ distribution of income; ضَريبة الدَخْلِ income tax; وازَنَ بين دَخْلِهِ وَخَرْجِهِ to balance one's earnings and expenses 2 ◀ [شأن] concern, business; لا دَخْلَ لَهُ بالمَوْضوعِ he doesn't have anything to do with it

داخِل *n* 1 ◀ [باطِن] inside; inner part; داخِلَ inside, in, within; من الداخِلِ from within; internal, on the inside; إلى الداخِلِ to the inside; داخِلَ المَنْزِلِ inside the house; داخِلَ العاصِمةِ inside the capital 2 ◀ [البِلادِ] الداخِل interior; في الداخِلِ inland; مُعارَضة في الداخِلِ domestic opposition; سَواءً في الداخِلِ أو الخارِج whether at home or abroad

داخِلة *n* |دَواخِلُ| innermost feelings; mind; soul

مَدْحور *adj* expelled, driven away; defeated; جَيْش مَدْحور a defeated army

دَحْرَج *v* |i; دَحْرَجة| to roll, to let roll; دَحْرَجَ الكُرةَ إلى الطَرَفِ الآخَرِ to roll the ball to the other side

تَدَحْرَج *v* to roll; تَدَحْرَجَت الكُرةُ من التَلِّ the ball rolled down the hill

دُحاس *n* (Med) whitlow

دَحَض *v* |a; دَحْض, دُحوض| 1 ◀ [أَبْطَلَ] to refute, to disprove; دَحَضَ حُجّةً to invalidate an argument 2 ◀ [بَطَلَ] to be invalid/untenable

أَدْحَض *v* to refute, to disprove

دَحْض *n* refutation; دَحْض حُجّةٍ refutation of an argument; دَحْض افْتِراضٍ \ ادِّعاءٍ refutation of a hypothesis/claim; لا يُمْكِنُ دَحْضُهُ irrefutable; بَراهين لا يُمْكِنُ دَحْضُها irrefutable evidence

داحِض *adj* unfounded, baseless, weak; حُجّة داحِضة a weak argument

مِدْحَلة *n* steamroller

دَحا *v* |u; دَحْو| to flatten, to level

دَخَر *v* |a; دُخور| (old use) to be belittled

ادَّخَر, ادِّخار, مُدَّخر see ذخر

دُخَس *n* dolphin

دَخَل *v* |u; دُخول| 1 ◀ [عَكْس خَرَجَ] to enter, to go into; دَخَلَ بَيْتاً \ في بَيْتٍ to enter a house; دَخَلَ على شَخْصٍ to enter someone's room or house; دَخَلْتُ من البابِ الخَلْفيِّ I got in through the back door; دَخَلَ مَدْرَسةً to enroll in a school; دَخَلَ المَلْعَبَ to enter the playing field; دَخَلَ بَلَداً to enter a country; دَخَلَ مُسابَقةً to enter a contest; دَخَلَ الحَرْبَ to involve oneself in the war; دَخَلَ على القانونِ تَعْديلٌ the law was amended; دَخَلَ السَنةَ الجَديدةَ to enter the new year; دَخَلَ عالَماً جَديداً to enter a new world; دَخَلَ في (صُلْبِ) المَوْضوعِ to come to the point 2 ◀ [بَدَأَ] to begin, to start; دَخَلَ وَقْتُ الصَلاةِ prayer time has started 3 ◀ [نَكَحَ] to consummate; دَخَلَ بِ \ على عَروسِهِ to consummate the marriage (*with one's bride*)

دَخَّل *v* to insert; to let in; دَخَّلَ شَيْئاً مَكاناً to insert sth somewhere

دخيلة *n* |دخائِلُ| inner core, inside; في دَخيلةِ نَفْسِهِ in one's heart

إدْخال *n* 1 [إيلاج] insertion; inclusion; الإدْخال في سِجِلٍّ recording in a register 2 (Comput) input; جِهاز إدْخالٍ input device 3 [وَضْع] implementation; insertion; إدْخال تَحْسيناتٍ \ تَعْديلاتٍ inserting improvements/amendments 4 [دُخول] entrance; admission; إدْخال إلى المُسْتَشْفى admission to the hospital

الداخِلة *n* Dakhla (*oasis in central Egypt*)

تَداخُل *n* |تَداخُلات| interference; overlap; merging; تَداخُل مَوْجاتِ الضَوْءِ interference of light waves; تَداخُل الدَواءِ مع الغذاءِ the interference of medicines with food

تَدَخُّل *n* intervention, interference, meddling; تَدَخُّل جِراحيّ a medical intervention; تَدَخُّل عَسْكَريّ \ مُسَلَّح military/armed intervention; التَدَخُّل في البوسْنة intervention in Bosnia; عَدَم التَدَخُّل non-intervention; بِفَضْل تَدَخُّل شَخْصٍ thanks to sb's intervention; تَدَخُّل في الشُؤونِ الداخِليّةِ meddling in internal affairs

مُتَداخِل A *adj* overlapping
B *n* intruder

مُتَدَخِّل A *adj* intervening, interfering; meddlesome
B *n* 1 [في جَريمةٍ] accomplice 2 [سائِل] *one who interrupts or partakes in a discussion*

مُداخَلة *n* contribution (*to a discussion*); interruption (*of a discussion*)

مَدْخَل *n* |مَداخِلُ| 1 [مَبْنًى] entrance, entry; gate, gateway; vestibule, hallway; مَدْخَل رَئيسيّ main entrance; مَدْخَل خَلْفيّ back entrance; المَدْخَل إلى الحَديقةِ the entrance to the garden 2 [طَريق] access road, driveway; أَخْلى المَدْخَلَ to clear the access road 3 [مُقَدِّمة] introduction (*to a piece of writing or music*) 4 [في قاموسٍ] entry, headword; مَدْخَل "بَيْت" the entry 'house'

مُدْخَل *n* (Comput) مُدْخَلات input

مَدْخول *n* |مَداخيلُ| income; revenue; فُقْدان المَداخيلِ loss of income; مَداخيل إضافيّة extra income

دَخَنَ *v* |a-u; دُخون ,دُخان| to smoke, to fume

دَخَّنَ *v* 1 [تَبْغاً] to smoke; دَخَّنَ السَجائِرَ \ الحَشيشَ to smoke cigarettes/pot; لا يُدَخِّنُ he doesn't smoke; دَخَّنَ بِشَراهةٍ

داخِليّ *adj* internal, inner; domestic, interior; resident; داخِليًّا internally; بَريد داخِليّ internal mail; النِظام الداخِليّ rules of procedure; مَسْأَلة داخِليّة an internal matter; خَبَر \ اجْتِماع داخِليّ an internal announcement/meeting; أَمْر \ شَأْن داخِليّ an internal matter; الأُمور \ القَضايا الداخِليّة لِبَلَدٍ the internal affairs of a country; تِجارة \ سِياسة داخِليّة domestic trade/politics; المَناطِق الداخِليّة the inland regions; السوق الداخِليّة domestic market; حَرْب داخِليّة civil war; مَدْرَسة داخِليّة boarding school; تَلاميذ داخِليّونَ resident students; مَلابِس داخِليّة underwear; نَزيف داخِليّ internal bleeding; جُرْح داخِليّ internal injury; طَبيب اخْتِصاصيّ بالأَمْراضِ الداخِليّةِ internal medicine specialist

داخِليّة *n* interior; وِزارة الداخِليّةِ interior ministry, Home Office (BrE), ≈ Department of Homeland Security (AmE)

دُخْلة *n* consummation; لَيْلة الدُخْلةِ ≈ wedding night (*night in a multi-day wedding celebration when the marriage is consummated*)

دُخول *n* 1 [وُلوج] entrance, entry, access; صَعْب الدُخولِ difficult to access; مَمْنوعٌ الدُخولُ no admittance; رَفَضَ الدُخولَ to deny حَرَمَ شَخْصاً من الدُخولِ ,السَماحَ لِشَخْصٍ بالدُخولِ access to sb; سَمَحَ بالدُخولِ to grant access; دُخول مَجّانيّ free admission; ثَمَن \ رَسْم الدُخولِ admission (fee); بِطاقة \ تَذْكِرة دُخولٍ ticket; تَأْشيرة دُخولٍ (entry) visa; عند دُخولِ المَدينةِ ,عند الدُخولِ إلى المَدينةِ while entering the city; لا يُمْكِنُ دُخولُ المِنْطَقةِ إلاّ للباحِثينَ the area is accessible to researchers only 2 [بَدْء] to start; الاسْتِعْداد للدُخولِ في الحِوارِ willingness to start a dialogue; لا يُريدُ الدُخولَ في مُواجَهةٍ عَسْكَريّةٍ he doesn't want to start an armed conflict 3 [نِكاح] consummation; بعد الدُخولِ بِها after he consummated the marriage with her 4 (Comput) login; اسْم الدُخولِ username; تَسْجيل الدُخولِ signing/logging in

دَخيل A *adj* |دُخَلاءُ| strange; from outside; intruder
B *n* |دُخَلاءُ| 1 [غَريب] stranger; newcomer; دَخيل على قَوْمٍ foreigner; outsider 2 [كَلِمة دَخيلة] loanword, borrowing; دَخيل من اللُغةِ الإنْكِليزيّةِ a loanword from English 3 [داخِل] inner self 4 [صاحِب سِرٍّ] confidant

(Idiom) (ME) دَخيلَكَ! please!

to smoke like a chimney; دَخَّنَ عُلْبَتَيْ سَجائِرَ في اليَوْمِ to smoke two packs of cigarettes a day **2** ◀ [مَوادَّ غِذائِيَّةً] to smoke (*meat, fish, etc.*)

تَدَخَّنَ *v* to smoke (*food*)

دُخْن *n* pearl millet

دُخان ,دُخّان *n* |أَدْخِنة| **1** ◀ [بُخار] smoke, fume; دُخان كَثيف dense smoke; رائِحة الدُخانِ the smell of smoke; سَحابة دُخانٍ a cloud of smoke; إِشارة دُخانٍ a smoke signal; سِتار من الدُخانِ a smoke screen; سورة الدُخان The Smoke (*Sura 44*); الغُرْفةُ مُعَبَّأَةٌ بالدُخانِ the room is full of smoke; لا دُخانَ بِلا نارٍ where there's smoke there's fire; نَفَثَ دُخانَ سيجارةٍ to exhale cigarette smoke **2** ◀ [تِبْغ] tobacco; cigarettes; عُلْبة دُخانٍ a packet of cigarettes; شَرِبَ الدُخانَ to smoke cigarettes

دُخّانيّ *adj* smoky; ضَباب دُخّانيّ smog

دُخْنة *n* **1** ◀ [طيب] incense **2** ◀ [كُدرة] smoky colour

أَدْخَن *adj* |dipt| smoky, dull gray

تَدْخين *n* smoking; مَمْنوعٌ التَدْخينُ no smoking; الرَجاءُ عَدَمُ التَدْخينِ no smoking please; أَدوات التَدْخينِ smoking paraphernalia

مُدَخَّن *adj* smoked; لَحْم مُدَخَّن smoked meat

مُدَخِّن *n* smoker; غَيْر مُدَخِّنٍ a non-smoker

مِدْخَنة *n* |مَداخِنُ| chimney; smokestack; مُنَظِّف مَداخِنَ chimney sweep; نَظَّفَ المِدْخَنةَ to clean the chimney

د.د. *abbr* rpm, revolutions per minute (*abbreviation of* **دَوْرة في الدَقيقةِ**)

دَرَأَ *v* |a; دَرْء| to ward off, to avert; دَرَأَ (عن نَفْسِهِ) مَخاطِرَ to avert danger

دَريئة *n* target

دَرابَزين *n* see دَرَبْزين

دَراخْمة ,دَراخْما *n* |دَراخْمات| drachma (*former currency of Greece*)

دْراما *n* drama, theatre

دْراميّ *adj* dramatic, theatrical

دْراماتيكيّ *adj* dramatic

دَرِبَ *v* |a; دَرَب ,دُرْبة| |على| to be used to, to be accustomed to; دَرِبَ على شَيْءٍ to be used to doing sth

دَرَّبَ *v* to train, to coach; دَرَّبَ شَخْصاً ب \ في \ على شَيْءٍ to train sb in sth; دَرَّبَ العَسْكَرَ to train the army; دَرَّبَ كَلْباً على الصَيْدِ to train a dog to hunt

تَدَرَّبَ *v* to train; to rehearse; to exercise; تَدَرَّبَ على شَيْءٍ to train for/in sth; تَدَرَّبَ على قِطْعةٍ موسيقيّةٍ \ مَسْرَحيّةٍ to rehearse a piece of music/a play; تَدَرَّبَ للأَلْعابِ الأولِمْبيّةِ to train for the Olympics; تَدَرَّبَ على رَمْيِ الجُلّةِ to train for shot-put; كانَ يَتَدَرَّبُ كُلَّ يَوْمِ أَحَدٍ he used to rehearse every Sunday

دَرْب *n* |دُروب ,دِراب| path; road; سارَ على دَرْبٍ to follow a path; مَنْ سارَ على الدَرْبِ وَصَلَ where there's a will there's a way; دَرْب التَبّانةِ the Milky Way

تَدْريب *n* |تَدْريبات| training, practice; exercise, workout; تَدْريب مُكَثَّف intensive training; تَدْريبات عَسْكَريّة military training; تَلَقّى تَدْريباً to be trained; تَدْريب مَيْدانيّ field training;

تَدْريبيّ *adj* training (*before n*); دَوْرة تَدْريبيّة training; internship; مُعَسْكَر تَدْريبيّ training camp

مُتَدَرِّب **A** *adj* trained; عَدّاؤون مُتَدَرِّبونَ trained runners; كانَ مُتَدَرِّباً على شَيْءٍ to be trained in sth

B *n* trainee; intern; كانَ مُتَدَرِّباً لدى ... to be an intern at ...

مُدَرَّب *adj* skilled; trained

مُدَرِّب *n* **1** ◀ [مُمَرِّن] instructor **2** ◀ [في الرِياضة] trainer, coach; مُدَرِّب المُنْتَخَبِ الوَطَنيِّ coach of the national team **3** ◀ [حَيَوانات] trainer (*of animals*)

دَرَبْزين ,دَرابَزين ,دَرْبَزين *n* |دَرَبْزينات| railing; banisters; دَرَبْزين سُلَّم handrail

دَرْبَسَ *v* |i; دَرْبَسة| to bolt (*a door*)

دَرْبُكّة ,دَرابُكة ,دَرْبوكة *n* darbuka, goblet drum

دَرَجَ *v* |u| **1** ◀ [مَشى] |دُروج| to become widespread; to advance gradually; دَرَجَ العُرْفُ على ... it's usual practice to ...; دَرَجَتْ موضَتُهُ it became a widespread fashion **2** ◀ [لَفَّ] |دَرْج| to wrap; دَرَجَ شَيْئاً في شَيْءٍ to wrap sth up in sth

دَرِجَ *v* |a; دَرَج| to advance gradually

دَرَّجَ *v* **1** ◀ [أَخَذَ قليلاً قليلاً] to lead gradually; دَرَّجَ شَخْصاً إلى شَيْءٍ to gradually lead sb to sth; دَرَّجَ دَرَجةَ الحَرارةِ إلى صِفْرٍ to gradually reduce the temperature to zero **2** ◀ [قَسَّمَ

[إلى دَرَجاتٍ] to divide into degrees/marks/steps, to grade, to gradate; دَرَّجَ جامِعاتٍ to grade universities 3 [عايَرَ] to gauge, to regulate, to calibrate; دَرَّجَ تِرْمومِتْراً to calibrate a thermometer

أَدْرَجَ *v* to insert; to include, to incorporate; أَدْرَجَ شَيْئاً في البَرْنامَجِ to include sth in the program; أَدْرَجَ شَخْصاً في القائِمةِ السَوْداءِ to blacklist sb; أَدْرَجَ شَيْئاً على \ في جَدْوَلِ الأَعْمالِ to put sth on the agenda

تَدَرَّجَ *v* to progress/advance gradually; تَدَرَّجَ إلى الشَمالِ to move gradually to the north; تَدَرَّجَ في سُلَّمِ النَجاحِ to steadily climb the ladder of success

اِنْدَرَجَ *v* to be included; to be categorized (as), to fall (within/under); اِنْدَرَجَ في إطارِ شَيْءٍ to fall within the framework of sth; اِنْدَرَجَ في \ تحت فئة شَيْءٍ to fall into the category of sth; تَنْدَرِجُ هذه المَقالةُ تحت بابِ الدراساتِ التَحْليلِيّةِ this article falls under the heading of analytical studies

اِسْتَدْرَجَ *v* to lure, to entice, to attract; اِسْتَدْرَجَ عُروضاً to invite bids; اِسْتَدْرَجَ شَخْصاً إلى فَخٍّ to lure sb into a trap; اِسْتَدْرَجَ شَخْصاً للحَديثِ عن شَيْءٍ to get sb to talk about sth

دَرَج *n* |أَدْراج, اِدراج| 1 [سُلَّم] stairs; ladder; صَعِدَ الدَرَجَ to climb the stairs 2 [طَريق] way, route, course; في دَرَجِ الكَلامِ in the course of talking; عادَ أَدْراجَهُ to retrace one's steps

دُرْج *n* |أَدْراج, اِدْرِجة| 1 [خِزانةٍ] drawer; فَتَحَ \ أَغْلَقَ الدُرْجَ to open/close the drawer 2 [مَقْعَد] student desk

دارِج *adj* 1 [لُغة] dialectal, colloquial, vernacular; تَكَلَّمَ باللُغةِ الدارِجةِ to speak in dialect 2 [شائِع] widespread; popular

دارِجة *n* (NA) colloquial language, dialect, spoken Arabic; الدارِجة المَغْرِبيّة Moroccan Arabic

دَرّاج *n* cyclist

دُرّاج *n* (Zool) francolin

دَرّاجة *n* bicycle; دَرّاجة هَوائيّة bicycle; دَرّاجة نارِيّة \ آلِيّة motorcycle, motorbike; دَرّاجة سِباقٍ racing bicycle; دَرّاجة مائيّة jet ski; pedalo (BrE); راكِب \ سائِق دَرّاجةٍ cyclist; سائِق دَرّاجةٍ نارِيّةٍ motorcyclist; بـ \ على الدَرّاجةِ by bicycle; ذَهَبَ بالدَرّاجةِ to go by bicycle; سِباق الدَرّاجاتِ bicycle racing

دَرَجة *n* 1 [عَلامة] grade, mark (BrE); دَرَجة سَيِّئة \ ضَعيفة a bad grade; دَرَجة جَيِّدة \ عالِية a good/high grade; قائِمة \ شَهادة دَرَجاتٍ grade list; أَعْطى دَرَجةً to give a grade; حَصَلَ على دَرَجةٍ to get a grade 2 [سُلَّم] step; rung; أَعْلى \ أَدْنى دَرَجةٍ من السُلَّمِ the top/bottom rung of the ladder 3 [مَنْزِلة] rank, class; دَرَجة أولى first class; فُنْدُق الدَرَجةِ الأولى a first-class hotel; تَذْكِرة دَرَجةٍ أولى a first-class ticket; سافَرَ في الدَرَجةِ الأولى to travel first class; من الدَرَجةِ الثانِيةِ second-rate; مُمَثِّل \ كاتِب من الدَرَجةِ الثانِيةِ a second-rate actor/writer; دَرَجة اقْتِصادِيّة / سِياحِيّة economy/tourist class 4 [حَرارةٍ] degree; دَرَجة الحَرارةِ temperature; دَرَجة الانْصِهارِ melting point; (خَمْس دَرَجاتٍ) تحت الصِفْرِ (five degrees) below zero; دَرَجَتانِ تحت \ فوق الصِفْرِ two degrees below/above zero; ٢٠ دَرَجةً مِئَوِيّةً \ فَهْرِنْهايْتِيّةً \ كَلْفِنِيّةً 20 degrees Celsius/Fahrenheit/Kelvin 5 [مَرْحَلة] stage, level, degree; بَلَغَ أَعْلى دَرَجةٍ من شَيْءٍ to reach the highest level of sth; مُعادَلة من الدَرَجةِ الثانِيةِ quadratic equation; إلى \ على هذه الدَرَجةِ so much so, to such an extent; إلى دَرَجةِ أنْ ... to the extent that ...; إلى دَرَجةٍ ما fairly, to some extent; أَقْصى دَرَجاتِ الإهانةِ the utmost humiliation; على دَرَجةٍ كَبيرةٍ / عالِيةٍ من الأَهَمِّيّةِ at a high level of importance 6 (Math) degree (*of arc*); ٣٦٠ دَرَجةً 360 degrees 7 (Sport) division; الدَرَجة الأولى the first division 8 [عِلْمِيّة] degree; دَرَجة جامِعِيّة university degree; مَنَحَ \ نالَ دَرَجةَ ماجِسْتير to award/get a masters degree

إدْراج *n* inclusion; insertion; incorporation; الإدْراج في السِجِلِّ insertion in the archive; إدْراج بَلَدٍ في قائِمةِ الدُوَلِ الداعِمةِ للإرْهابِ to include a country in the list of those that support terrorism

اِسْتِدْراج *n* solicitation; elicitation; اِسْتِدْراج عُروضٍ solicitation of bids

تَدَرُّج *n* 1 [تَقَدُّم] progress, advancement; بِتَدَرُّجٍ gradually 2 [تَرَتُّب] sequence, order

تُدْرُج *n* listed alphabetically

تَدْريج *n* gradation, classification; تَدْريجاً, بالتَدْريجِ gradually, step by step

تَدْريجيّ *adj* gradual, progressive; تَدْريجيًّا gradually; تَطَوُّر تَدْريجيّ gradual development; إصْلاح تَدْريجيّ gradual reform; على نَحْوٍ تَدْريجيٍّ in a gradual manner

تَدْريجيّة *n* gradualness

مُتَدَرِّج *adj* gradual, steady

مَدْرَج *n* |مَدارِج| runway; airstrip; وَقَفَ على المَدْرَجِ to stop on the runway; مَدْرَج المَطارِ airport runway

مُدْرَج *adj* included; listed; شَرِكات مُدْرَجة في السوقِ companies listed on the market; مَواضيع مُدْرَجة على جَدْوَلِ الأَعْمالِ topics on the agenda

مُدَرَّج **A** *adj* tiered
B *n* |مُدَرَّجات| **1** [مَقاعِد مُتَدَرِّجة] amphitheatre, gallery, lecture room; على المُدَرَّجِ in the gallery; مِنَ المُدَرَّجِ from the gallery; مُدَرَّج مَليء \ خالٍ a full/empty gallery; المُدَرَّج العُموميّ public gallery; مُدَرَّج مُغْلَق \ مَسْقوف a covered amphitheatre; مُدَرَّج زِراعيّ terrace (*agriculture*) **2** (Mus) staff; مُدَرَّج موسيقيّ staff, stave

أَدْرَد *adj* |dipt| toothless

دَرْداب *n* drumroll

دَرْدار *n* (Bot) elm (*Ulmus*)

دُرْدور *n* vortex

دَرْدَشَ *v* |i; دَرْدَشة| to chat, to prattle; دَرْدَشَ على النت to chat online

دَرْدَشة *n* chatter, chatting; دَرْدَشة مَرْئيّة video chat; غُرْفة الدَرْدَشةِ chat room

دَرَّ *v* |i-u; دَرّ| **1** [سالَ] to stream, to flow; دَرَّ الدَمْعُ tears were flowing; دَرَّ اللَبَنُ the milk flowed freely **2** [أَثْمَرَ] to yield; دَرَّ أَرْباحاً to yield profit

أَدَرَّ *v* **1** [أَثْمَرَ] to yield, to generate; أَدَرَّ سِتّةَ مَلايينَ to yield sixty million; أَدَرَّ الحَقْلُ خَيْراً وَفيراً هذا العامَ the field yielded a good crop this year **2** [أَسالَ] to let flow; دَواء يُدِرُّ البَوْلَ diuretic

اسْتَدَرَّ *v* to let flow; اسْتَدَرَّ عَطْفَ \ شَفَقةَ شَخْصٍ to arouse sb's pity

دَرّ *n* **1** [مَصْدَر] flowing; دَرّ الحَليبِ lactation **2** [حَليب] milk **3** [إنْجاز] completion; accomplishment; لِلّهِ دَرُّهُ how capable he is!

دُرّة *n* |دُرَر, دُرّات| pearl

دِرّة *n* |دِرَر| whip

دُرّيّ *adj* brilliant, twinkling, splendid

مُدِرّ *adj* |مُدِرّات| مُدِرّ للبَوْلِ diuretic

مِدْرار *n* flowing, pouring; مِدْراراً copiously, fluently

1 **دَرَزَ** *v* |u; دَرْز| to sew, to stitch

دَرْز *n* |دُروز| seam; فَتَقَ دَرْزاً to unpick a seam

دَرْزة *n* stitch; seam

مَدْروز *adj* stitched

2 **دُرْزيّ, دَرْزيّ** *adj, n* |دُروز| Druze

دَرَسَ *v* |u; دَرْس| **1** [تَعْليم] to study; to learn; دَرَسَ بِاجْتِهادٍ to study hard; دَرَسَ الطِبَّ to study medicine; دَرَسَ في كُلّيّة الزِراعةِ to study at the college of agriculture; دَرَسَ العَزْفَ على البِيانو to learn the piano **2** [تَعَمَّقَ في شَيْءٍ] to examine; to study; to consider; دَرَسَ شَيْئاً to study sth; دَرَسَ وَثيقةً بِعِنايةٍ to scrutinize a document; دَرَسَ الإمْكانيّاتِ المُخْتَلِفةَ لِشَيْءٍ to consider the various possibilities of sth; دَرَسَ شَيْئاً دِراسةً عَميقةً \ دَقيقةً to study sth thoroughly **3** (Agric) to thresh; دَرَسَ القَمْحَ to thresh wheat

دَرَّسَ *v* to teach; to instruct; to educate; دَرَّسَ شَخْصاً شَيْئاً to teach sb sth; دَرَّسَ التَلاميذَ الحِسابَ to teach pupils arithmetic; دَرَّسَ الرِياضيّاتِ \ التاريخَ to teach mathematics/history; دَرَّسَ الأَطْفالَ to teach children; دَرَّسَ في جامِعةٍ to teach at a university, to lecture; دَرَّسَ في مَدْرَسةٍ ثانَويّةٍ to teach at a secondary (BrE) high (AmE) school

دارَسَ *v* to study together with; دارَسَ شَخْصاً شَيْئاً to study sth with sb

تَدارَسَ *v* to study together with

انْدَرَسَ *v* to be/become wiped out

دَرْس *n* |دُروس| **1** [تَعْليم] lesson; دُروس لَيْليّة evening courses; دُروس خُصوصيّة private lessons; دُروس إضافيّة additional lessons; دُروس في الرَسْمِ drawing lessons; قاعة دَرْسٍ classroom; أَدَوات دَرْسٍ learning material; تَكاليف الدُروسِ tuition fee; أَثْناء الدَرْسِ during class; عِنْدَهُ دَرْسٌ من الساعةِ ٩ إلى الساعةِ ١٢ he is in class from 9 to 12; أَخَذَ دَرْساً من شَيْءٍ to learn from sth; تَلَقّى دُروساً (من شَخْصٍ) to be taught

مُدَرِّس *n* teacher, instructor; مُدَرِّس اللُغةِ العَربيَّةِ an Arabic teacher

مَدْرَسة *n* |مَدارِسُ| ❶ [مَكان التَعْليم] school; مَدْرَسة ابْتِدائيّة primary school; مَدْرَسة إعْداديّة preparatory school (BrE); middle school (AmE); junior high school (AmE); مَدْرَسة ثانَويّة secondary school (BrE), high school (AmE); مَدْرَسة عُلْيا university, college; مَدْرَسة خاصّة public (BrE) private (AmE) school; مَدْرَسة عامّة state (BrE) public (AmE) school; مَدْرَسة داخِليّة boarding school; مَدْرَسة لَيْليّة evening school; مَدْرَسة رَقْصٍ dance school; مَدْرَسة تَأْديبيّة young offender institution (BrE), youth detention center (AmE); ناظِر \ مُدير المَدْرَسةِ (school) principal; زَميل مَدْرَسةٍ schoolmate, classmate; في المَدْرَسةِ at school; بعد المَدْرَسة after school; ذَهَبَ إلى المَدْرَسةِ to go to school; دَرَسَ في المَدْرَسةِ to be in school; خَرَجَ من المَدْرَسةِ (في الساعةِ الخامِسةِ) to leave school (at 5 o'clock), to get out of school (at 5 o'clock); تَرَكَ المَدْرَسةَ to drop out of school; تَغَيَّبَ عن المَدْرَسة to be absent from school; لَعِبَ في ساحة المَدْرَسة to play in the schoolyard; يَنْتَهي دَوامُ المَدْرَسة في الساعة ١٢ school finishes at twelve o'clock ❷ [مَدْرَسة الحَياة] life experience; education (*from life's experiences*); مَدْرَسة قاسِية School of Hard Knocks ❸ [مَذْهَب] school of thought; إنَّهُ صاحِبُ مَدْرَسةٍ إبْداعيّة he's the founder of an innovative school

مَدْرَسيّ *adj* school (*before n*); كُتُب مَدْرَسيّة school books

مَدْروس *adj* thoughtful, deliberate; قَرار مَدْروس a deliberate decision

دَرَّعَ *v* to armour; دَرَّعَ سَيّارةً to armour a car

تَدَرَّعَ *v* to armour, to protect oneself

دِرْع *n* |دُروع, أَدْرُع, أَدْراع| ❶ [وِقاية] shield; armour; دِرْع بَشَريّ human shield; الدِرْع المُضادّ للصَواريخ, الدِرْع الصاروخيّ missile (defence) shield; تَدَرَّعَ دِرْعاً \ بِدِرْعٍ to wear armour ❷ (Zool) shell; armour; دِرْع سُلَحْفاةٍ turtle/tortoise shell ❸ (Hist) plate armour; mail, chain mail

دارِع *adj* armoured

دَرّاعة *n loose outer garment, slit in front*

تَدْريع *n* armour; صَفيحة \ لَوح تَدْريعٍ armour plate

(by sb); لَقَّنَ شَخْصاً دَرْساً to teach sb a lesson; حَفِظَ دَرْسَهُ to learn one's lesson; كانَ دَرْساً مُفيداً لَهُ it has been a good lesson for him; تَلَقّى دُروساً to take lessons; اسْتَفادَ من دُروسِ التاريخِ to learn from history; تَعَلَّمَ دَرْساً قاسِياً to learn a hard lesson ❷ [إمْعان] examination; consideration; إنّ الأَمْرَ قَيْدَ الدَرْسِ the matter is under consideration

دارِس *n* scholar, researcher; learner

دَرّاسة *n* (Agric) threshing machine

دِراسة *n* ❶ (Educ) study; وَقْت الدِراسةِ school time; خارِجَ \ في وَقْتِ الدِراسةِ outside/during school hours; بعد \ قبل وَقْتِ الدِراسةِ after/before school; غُرْفة الدِراسةِ study; workroom; حُجْرة الدِراسةِ classroom; تابَعَ دِراسةً to continue one's studies; أَكْمَلَ دِراسَتَهُ to finish one's studies; دِراسات تَكْميليّة a complementary course; دِراسات الشَرْق الأَوْسَط Middle Eastern Studies; الدِراسات الإسْلاميّة Islamic Studies ❷ [بَحْث] study; research; دِراسة عَميقة \ مُعَمَّقة a thorough study; دِراسة مُسْتَفيضة \ شامِلة \ دَقيقة an elaborate/extensive/accurate study; دِراسات عِلْميّة scientific/scholarly research; دِراسة حول النِظامِ الإقْطاعيِّ a study on feudalism; كانَ قَيْدَ الدِراسةِ to be under scrutiny; تُشيرُ الدِراسةُ إلى أنّ ... the study shows that ...; هذا يَسْتَحِقُّ المَزيدَ من الدِراسةِ further research is needed

دِراسيّ *adj* academic, school (*before n*); سَنة دِراسيّة academic year, school year; مَنْهَج دِراسيّ curriculum; (course) syllabus; مِنْحة دِراسيّة scholarship; fellowship; فَصْل دِراسيّ semester; quarter

دُرَّسة *n* (Bio) bunting (*Emberizidae*)

دَريس *n* hay

أَدارِسة *n* see أدرس

تَدْريس *n* education; instruction, teaching; تَدْريس جامِعيّ a university (BrE) college (AmE) education; هَيْئة التَدْريسِ faculty; teaching staff; طَريقة التَدْريس teaching method; كَفاءة التَدْريسِ teaching competence; أَحْسَنَ التَدْريسَ to teach well; عَمِلَ في سِلْكِ التَدْريسِ to work in the teaching profession

تَدْريسيّ *adj* teaching (*before n*); هَيْئة تَدْريسيّة faculty; teaching staff

مُدَرَّع **A** *adj* armoured; سَيّارة \ عَرَبة \ مَرْكَبة مُدَرَّعة armoured vehicle; قوّات مُدَرَّعة armed forces
B *n* (Zool) armadillo (*Cingulata*)

مُدَرَّعة *n* armoured vehicle; armoured car; مُدَرَّعات cavalry

‹ **دَرْفة** *n* |دَرَفات| hatch, flap; leaf (*of a door/window*)

‹ **دَرْفَلَ** *v* |i; دَرْفَلة| (Tech) to roll; دَرْفَلَ الصُلْب to roll steel

دَرْفيل *n* |دَرافيل| dolphin

‹ **دُراق** *n* goitre

دُرّاق, **دُرّاقِن** *n* (Levant) peach

دَرَقة *n* shell (*of a turtle*)

دَرَقيّ *adj* thyroid (*before n*); غُدّة دَرَقيّة thyroid gland

‹ **دارَكَ** *v* to catch, to take hold of

أَدْرَكَ *v* **1** [فَهِمَ] to realize, to understand, to be aware; أَدْرَكَ أَنّ ... to realize that ...; أَدْرَكَ الخَطَرَ to be aware of the danger; أَدْرَكَ ضَرورةَ شَيْءٍ to understand the necessity of sth; أَدْرَكَ شَيْئاً تَمامَ الإدْراكِ to be (fully) aware of sth; أَدْرَكَ أَنّ هُناكَ اعْتِراضاتٍ كَثيرةً to realize that there are many objections; لم يُدْرِكْ صُعوبةَ شَيْءٍ to not realize the difficulty of sth; لم يُدْرِكْ مَعْنى كَلِماتِهِ not to understand the meaning of his words; ما لا يُدْرَكُ كُلُّهُ لا يُتْرَكُ جُلُّهُ ≈ if you can't get what you want, take what you can get **2** [الصَّبيُّ] to be pubescent **3** [نَضِجَ] to mature **4** [القِطارَ] to take, to catch; أَدْرَكَ القِطارَ to catch the train

تَدارَكَ *v* to redress, to correct, to set right; to catch up; تَدارَكَ مُشْكِلةً to redress a problem; تَدارَكَ المَوْقِفَ to rectify the situation; تَدارَكَ خَطَأً to correct a mistake; تَدارَكَ ما فاتَ to redress for the past

اسْتَدْرَكَ *v* to correct, to rectify, to amend; to redress; اسْتَدْرَكَ المَوْقِفَ to rectify the situation; اسْتَدْرَكَ تَقْصيراً to redress a shortcoming; لَكِنَّهُ اسْتَدْرَكَ بِأَنَّ ... but he corrected himself by saying ...

دَرْك *n* lowest point, nadir; the bottom; غاصَ الغَوّاصُ إلى دَرْكِ البُحَيْرةِ the diver dived to the bottom of the lake

دَرَك *n* |أَدْراك| **1** [شُرْطة] police; الدَرَك المَلَكيّ (Mor) The Royal Moroccan Gendarmerie; رِجال الدَرَكِ police **2** [لِحاق] overtaking **3** [قَعْر] nadir, lowest level; depression

دَرَكة *n* (lowest) floor/level

دَرَكيّ *n* police officer

إدْراك *n* awareness, understanding, recognition; insight, perception; إدْراك واضِح \ جَيِّد clear/excellent insight; إدْراك عَميق deep awareness; سَهْل الإدْراكِ easily understandable; إدْراك مُتَزايِد growing awareness; سِنّ الإدْراكِ a mature age; إدْراك حِسّيّ sensory observation; الإدْراك الواعي conscious awareness; إدْراك المَشاكِلِ \ العَواقِبِ understanding of the problems/consequences; مع الإدْراكِ التامِّ لِشَيْءٍ with full awareness of sth

اسْتِدْراك *n* |اسْتِدْراكات| correction, redress, reparation

تَدارُك *n* correction, redress, reparation; control

مَدارِك *n pl* |dipt| (sensory) perception; (mental) capacity; المَدارِك الخَمْس the five senses

مُدْرَك *n* |مُدْرَكات| concept, notion

مُدْرِك *adj* aware; observant; غَيْر مُدْرِكٍ unaware; كانَ مُدْرِكاً (تَمامَ الإدْراكِ) لِشَيْءٍ to be (fully) aware of sth

‹ **دَرِمَ** *v* |a; دَرَم| to fall out; دَرِمَتْ أَسْنانُهُ his teeth fell out

دَرَّمَ *v* to cut, to clip

تَدْريم *n* تَدْريم الأَظافِرِ manicure; تَدْريم القَدَمِ pedicure

مُدَرِّم *n* مُدَرِّم أَظافِرِ اليَدِ manicure; مُدَرِّم القَدَمِ pedicure

‹ **دَرِنَ** *v* |a; دَرَن| **1** [وَسِخَ] to be/become dirty **2** (Med) to have/contract tuberculosis

دَرَن *n* |أَدْران| **1** [وَسَخ] dirt; filth **2** [سُلّ] tuberculosis, TB; دَرَن رِئَويّ, مَرَض الدَرَنِ tuberculosis, TB; أُصيبَ بالدَرَنِ to have tuberculosis

دَرِن *adj* **1** [وَسِخ] dirty **2** (Med) afflicted with tuberculosis

دَرَنة *n* outgrowth; protuberance; tubercle

تَدَرُّن *n* tuberculosis; التَدَرُّن الرِئَويّ tuberculosis

‹ **دَرْنَقة** *n* (Med) drain

‹ **دِرْهَم** *n* |دَراهِمُ| **1** [قِطْعة ماليّة] dirham; عَبْد الدِرْهَمِ money-grubber; الدِرْهَمُ الأَبْيَضُ يَنْفَعُ في اليَوْمِ الأَسْوَدِ save your pennies for a rainy day **2** [وَزْن] dirham (*approx 3 grams*)

‹ **دِرْواس** *n* (Zool) mastiff

‹ **دَرْويش** *n* |دَراويشُ| dervish (*member of a mystical order*)

دَرى *v* |i; دِراية| to know; دَرى شَيْئاً \ بِشَيْءٍ to know sth; لا أَدْري I don't know; لا يَدْري كيف \ أين \ إذا \ أنّ ... he doesn't know how/where/if/that ...

دَرّى *v* to inform, to let know; دَرّى شَخْصاً بِشَيْءٍ to let sb know sth

داري *v* 1 [لايَنَ] to treat friendlily 2 [سَتَرَ] to deceive; to not tell

أَدْرى *v* to inform, to let know; ما أَدْراكَ \ مَنْ يُدْريكَ أنّ \ ما ... you know what ... means, everyone knows what ... means

دِراية *n* 1 [خِبْرة] expertise, knowledge 2 [مَعْرِفة] knowledge, awareness; بِدونِ دِرايَتي without my knowledge; لَيْسَ لَهُ دِرايةٌ بِما يَجْري he was unaware of what was going on

لاأَدْرِيّ *adj* agnostic; المَذْهَب اللاأَدْرِيّ the agnostic school of thought; شَخْص لاأَدْرِيّ an agnostic person

لاأَدْرِيّة *n* agnosticism

مُداراة *n* friendliness; politeness; عامَلَ شَخْصاً بِمُداراةٍ to treat sb in a friendly way

دَزينة *n* dozen

دَسْتان *n* |دَساتينُ| (Mus) string, chord

دَسْتة *n* (Egypt) dozen

دَسْتَرَ *v* |i; دَسْتَرة| to constitutionalize

دُسْتور *n* |دَساتيرُ| (Pol) constitution; الدُسْتور التونِسيّ the Tunisian constitution; عَدَّلَ الدُسْتورَ to amend the constitution

دُسْتوريّ *adj* constitutional; حَظْر دُسْتوريّ على شَيْءٍ a constitutional ban on sth; حُقوق \ واجِبات دُسْتوريّة constitutional rights/duties; تَعْديل دُسْتوريّ a constitutional amendment; إصْلاحات دُسْتوريّة constitutional reform

لادُسْتوريّ *adj* unconstitutional

دَسَرَ *v* |u; دَسْر| to push, to propel

دَسْر *n* (Mech) propulsion

دِسار *n* |دُسُر| dowel; pin, peg

مِدْسَرة *n* |مَداسِرُ| 1 (Tools) punch 2 (Aviat) propeller

دَسَّ *v* |u; دَسّ| to slip, to put (secretly); to insert; دَسَّ شَيْئاً في جَيْبِهِ to slip sth into one's pocket; دَسَّ لِشَخْصٍ السُمَّ to slip sb poison; دَسَّ السَمَّ في الدَسَمِ to conspire

انْدَسَّ *v* to slip, to sneak; to infiltrate; انْدَسَّ في شَيْءٍ to slip into sth; to infiltrate sth; انْدَسَّ بين شَيْءٍ to slip between/among sth

دَسّاس *n* conspirator; plotter; العِرْقُ دَسّاسٌ what's bred in the bone will come out in the flesh

دَسيس *n* infiltrator; دَسيس في... infiltrator of ...

دَسيسة *n* |دَسائِسُ| intrigue, machination; دَسيسة اسْتِعْمارِيّة imperialist conspiracy

انْدِساس *n* infiltration; انْدِساس في ... an infiltration of ...

مَدْسوس A *adj* false, bogus, concocted, fabricated; hidden B *n* infiltrator

دِسْك *n* 1 (Med) spinal disc herniation 2 (Comput) disc

دَسْكَرة *n* |دَساكِرُ| village

دَسَم *n* fat; خالي الدَسَمِ fat-free; خَفيف الدَسَمِ low-fat; وَجْبة خَفيفة الدَسَمِ a low-fat meal; حَليب كامِل الدَسَمِ whole milk; وَضَعَ \ دَسَّ السُمَّ في الدَسَمِ *to offer sth harmful in an attractive way*

دَسِم *adj* rich, heavy, fat; وَجْبة دَسِمة a rich meal; جُبْن دَسِم full-fat cheese; حَليب دَسِم whole milk; حَليب نِصْف دَسِمٍ semi-skimmed milk (BrE), 2% milk (AmE)

دَسامة *n* fatness, fattiness

دَسّى *v* to hide, to conceal

دِسيبل *n* (Meas) decibel

دِسيغْرام *n* |دِسيغْرامات| (Meas) decigram

دِسيلِتْر *n* |دِسيلِتْرات| (Meas) decilitre

دِسيمِتْر *n* |دِسيمِتْرات| (Meas) decimetre

دِشْداشة *n* *a long-sleeved ankle-length robe traditionally worn by men in the Gulf and Levant*

مَدْشَر *n* (Mor) village

دُشّ *n* |أَدْشاش| shower; أَخَذَ دُشًّا to take a shower

دَشَّنَ *v* to inaugurate, to open, to launch; to consecrate; دَشَّنَ مَبْنًى to inaugurate a building; دَشَّنَ طَريقاً \ مَدْرَسةً to inaugurate a road/school; دَشَّنَ كَنيسةً to consecrate a church; دَشَّنَ مَرْحَلةً جَديدةً لِشَيْءٍ to inaugurate a new phase in sth

تَدْشين *n* inauguration, opening ceremony, launch; consecration; تَدْشين جِسْرٍ inauguration of a bridge; تَدْشين كَنيسةٍ consecration of a church

تَدَشّى *v* to belch

دَعَبَ *v* |a; **دُعابة**| to joke, to jest

داعَبَ *v* **1** [مَزَحَ] to romp, to frolic; to play, to tease; داعَبَ أَطْفالَهُ to frolic with one's children **2** [جِنسيًّا] to caress, to fondle, to play with (*sexually*); داعَبَ زَوْجَتَهُ to play with/caress one's wife

تَداعَبَ *v* to joke with one another

دَعِب *adj* funny, playful, joking, fun

داعِب *adj* funny, playful, joking, fun

دُعابة *n* **1** [فُكاهة] joke, jest; روح الدُعابة sense of humour; إنّها مُجَرَّدُ دُعابةٍ it's just a joke **2** [مَصْدَر] being funny

مُداعِب *adj* joking, teasing; مُداعِباً playfully

مُداعَبة *n* **1** [مُزاح] joke, jest **2** [جِنْسيّة] caress; fondling, foreplay; مُداعَبة جِنْسيّة foreplay

دَعة *n* see ودع

أَدْعَج *adj* |dipt; **دَعْجاء**, **دُعْج**| **1** [أَسْوَد] black, dark **2** [العَيْن] black-eyed, with black eyes

دَعَرَ, **دَعِرَ** *v* |a; **دَعَر**| to be lewd/obscene; to be immoral

داعِر *adj* |**دُعّار**| lewd, obscene; immoral

دَعارة, **دِعارة** *n* prostitution; مُمارِسة الدَعارة prostitute, whore; بَيْت الدَعارة brothel; دَعارة الأَطْفالِ child prostitution; مارَسَ الدَعارةَ to engage in prostitution

دَعَسَ *v* |a; **دَعْس**| to trample, to stamp on; to crush; دَعَسَ الأَرْضَ to pound the ground; دَعَسَتْهُ سَيّارةٌ to be run over by a car

دُعْسوقة *n* ladybird, ladybug (*Coccinellidae*)

تَدَعَّصَ *v* to rot, to spoil (*meat*)

دَعَّ *v* |u; **دَعّ**| to reject, to rebuff

دَعَكَ *v* |a; **دَعْك**| to rub; دَعَكَ مَرْهَماً على جِلْدِهِ to rub cream into one's skin

دَعَمَ *v* |a; **دَعْم**| **1** [أَسْنَدَ] to bear, to support; to second; دَعَمَ سَقْفاً to support a roof; دَعَمَ شَخْصاً to support sb; دَعَمَ بِوَثائِقَ to corroborate with documents **2** [ماليًّا] to support, to subsidize; دَعَمَ شَخْصاً بالمالِ to support a person financially; دَعْم العَمَلَ الاجْتِماعيَّ to support social action; دَعَمَ الزِراعةَ to subsidize agriculture

دَعَّمَ *v* to support, to aid, to substantiate; دَعَّمَ شَيْئاً بِأَرْقامٍ to substantiate sth with figures

دَعْم *n* support, subsidization; دَعْم ماليّ \ مادّيّ financial support; دَعْم فَنّيّ technical/tech support; دَعْم حُكوميّ a government subsidy; بالدَعْمِ الحُكوميِّ with government support; دَعْم حُكوميّ لِشَيْءٍ government support for sth; لَقِيَ دَعْماً to find support; بَحَثَ عن دَعْم لدى شَيْءٍ \ شَخْصٍ to look for sb's/sth's support; طَلَبَ دَعْماً حُكوميًّا to ask for a government subsidy; مَنَحَ دَعْماً حُكوميًّا to grant a government subsidy; حَصَلَ على دَعْمٍ حُكوميٍّ to get a government subsidy

داعِم **A** *adj* supporting, supportive; دَوْر داعِم a supporting role **B** *n* backer, supporter, patron

دِعامة *n* |**دِعامات**, **دَعائِم**| **1** [عِماد] pillar, support; undercarriage; دَعائِم الاقْتِصادِ the pillars of the economy **2** [شَخْص] mainstay; كانَ الرَئِيسُ السابِقُ دِعامةَ الضُعَفاءِ the former president was the mainstay of the poor

تَدْعيم *n* support; strengthening, reinforcement; تَدْعيم التَعاوُنِ strengthening cooperation

مُدَعَّم *adj* **1** [مَسْنود] supported; subsidized; substantiated; خُبْز \ وَقود مُدَعَّم subsidized bread/fuel; مُدَعَّم بِوَثائِق substantiated with documents **2** [مُقَوّى] reinforced; إِسْمَنْت مُدَعَّم reinforced concrete

مَدْعوم *adj* supported, reinforced; subsidized; غير مَدْعوم (Comput) not supported; قُروض مَدْعومة subsidized loans; مَدْعوم بِوَثائِق substantiated with documents

دَعا *v* |u| **1** [نادى |**دُعاء**|] to call; دَعا إلى الصَلاةِ to call to prayer; دَعا لِلاجْتِماعِ to call a meeting; دَعا أَعْضاءَ الجَمْعيّةِ لِلاجْتِماعِ to call a meeting for the members of the association **2** (Relig) |**دُعاء**| to invoke, to supplicate, to pray; دَعا اللهَ to invoke/pray to God **3** [سَمّى |**دُعاء**; ب|] to call; to name; دُعِيَ to be called; to be named; دَعا ابْنَتَهُ فاطِمةَ \ بِفاطِمةَ he called his daughter Fatima **4** [اسْتَضافَ |**دَعْوة**|] to invite; دَعا إلى المائِدةِ to invite to the table; دَعَوْا كُلَّ العائِلةِ إلى الحَفْلةِ they invited the whole family to the party; دَعا شَخْصاً

دَعا شَخْصاً لِإلْقاءِ مُحاضَرةٍ to invite sb to give a lecture; لِإجْراءِ اسْتِجْوابٍ to call on sb to conduct an interrogation 5 [ناشَدَ|دَعْوة] to call; to proclaim; to advocate; to appeal; to cause, to arouse; دَعا إلى أنْ ... to advocate ...; دَعا إلى to advocate for Islam; دَعا إلى السَّلامِ to call for peace; دَعا إلى حَلٍّ to call for revolution; دَعا إلى الثَّوْرةِ to call for a solution; دَعا إلى الإعْجابِ \ القَلَقِ to arouse astonishment/concern; دَعا إلى المُقاوَمةِ to call for resistance; دَعا إلى تَخْفيضِ ساعاتِ العَمَلِ to advocate for a reduction in working hours; ما الذي دَعاكَ إلى هذا الأمْرِ؟ what brought you to this?

داعى *v* to sue, to litigate, to prosecute, to take legal action against

تَداعى *v* 1 [انْهارَ] to founder, to tumble; to be on the verge of collapse 2 [دَعا بَعْضُهُم البَعْضَ] to call one another; to challenge one another

ادَّعى *v* 1 [زَعَمَ] to claim; to argue; ادَّعى أنّ ... to claim that ... 2 [زَعَمَ لِنَفْسِهِ] to claim; ادَّعى بِحَقِّهِ to claim one's right 3 [تَظاهَرَ بـ] to simulate; to feign, to pretend; يَدَّعي أنَّهُ مَريضٌ he is feigning illness; ادَّعى حُدوثَ سَرِقةٍ he faked a robbery 4 [خاصَمَ عند القاضي|على] to press charges; to summon

اسْتَدْعى *v* 1 [اسْتَحْضَرَ] to subpoena; to summon, to call; اسْتَدْعى شاهِداً to call a witness; اسْتَدْعى مُتَّهَماً to summon the suspect; اسْتَدْعى شَخْصاً لِلفَحْصِ \ لِلامْتِحانِ to call sb for the examination/test; اسْتَدْعى شَخْصاً لِلمُثولِ أمامَ المَحْكَمةِ to summon sb to appear in court 2 [طَلَبَ] to involve; to summon, to invite, to call; اسْتَدْعى مُحامِياً \ خَبيراً \ قاضِياً to involve a lawyer/expert/judge; اسْتَدْعى طَبيباً \ الشُّرْطةَ to involve a doctor/the police; اسْتَدْعى شَخْصاً إلى جَلْسةٍ to summon sb to a meeting 3 [حَذَّرَ] to alarm

دَعِيّ *n* |أدْعِياءُ| 1 [مُدَّعٍ] pretender, poser; hypocrite 2 [مُتَبَنًّى] adopted child

داعٍ *n* |دُعاة، دَواعٍ| 1 [سَبَب] occasion; consideration; reason; بِداعِي شَيْءٍ because of sth, on account of sth; بِداعِي الإصابةِ on account of injury; لا داعِيَ never mind; بِلا \ دون داعٍ unnecessary; لا داعِيَ لَهُ بالمَرّةِ unnecessary; ما \ لَيْسَ من داعٍ لَهُ that is absolutely unnecessary; لا داعِيَ لِلخَوْفِ there's no need to be scared; لا داعِيَ لَدَيْها لِلشَّكْوى she has no cause to complain; لا داعِيَ إلى التَّقْديمِ \ لِلتَّقْديمِ there's no need for introduction; كانَ داعِياً لِلقِيامِ بِشَيْءٍ to be an occasion to do sth 2 [داعِية] preacher

داعِية *n* |m| preacher; activist; داعِية السَّلامِ a peace activist; داعِية إسْلاميّ an Islamic preacher

دُعاء *n* call; prayer; supplication; اسْتَجابَ لِدُعاءِ شَخْصٍ to answer sb's prayer

دِعائيّ *adj* advertisement (*before n*); propaganda (*before n*); حَمْلة دِعائيّة advertising campaign

دِعاية *n* advertisement, ad; publicity; propaganda; دِعاية لِمَسْحوقاتِ الغَسيلِ an ad for detergent; مَكْتَب الدِعاية والإعْلانِ advertising agency

دَعْوة *n* 1 [حُضور] invitation; call; تَلَقَّى دَعْوةً to receive an invitation; لَبَّى دَعْوةً to accept an invitation; رَفَضَ دَعْوةً to turn down an invitation; صاحِب الدَعْوةِ host; اسْتَجابَ لِدَعْوةٍ to RSVP; دَعْوة لِحُضورِ اجْتِماعٍ call to attend a meeting; وَجَّهَ دَعْوةً إلى شَخْصٍ to send sb an invitation; هذه دَعْوةٌ لِلمَشاكِلِ! that is asking for trouble! 2 [دُعاء] supplication; prayer; call 3 (Relig) preaching

دَعْوى *n* |f; دَعاوى، دَعاوٍ| (Law) lawsuit; litigation; court case; trial; دَعْوى قَضائيّة legal proceedings; دَعْوى مَدَنيّة \ جِنائيّة civil/criminal proceedings; مَصاريف الدَعْوى litigation costs; دَعْوى ضِدّ \ على شَخْصٍ a lawsuit against sb; رَبِحَ \ خَسِرَ دَعْوى to win/lose a lawsuit; رَفَعَ دَعْوى to file a lawsuit; أقامَ دَعْوى to file a lawsuit; to press charges; حَوَّلَ شَيْئاً إلى دَعْوى قَضائيّةٍ to turn sth into a lawsuit; رَفَعَ \ أقامَ دَعْوى على شَخْصٍ to file a lawsuit against sb

ادِّعاء *n* |ادِّعاءات| 1 [طَلَب] claim; demand; مُمَثِّل الادِّعاءِ plaintiff's attorney 2 [زَعْم] claim; assertion; ادِّعاء أنّ the assertion that; ادِّعاء جَريء a bold assertion; ادِّعاء باطِل a false allegation; ادِّعاءات كاذِبة false claims; أصَرَّ على ادِّعاءاتِهِ to be insistent in one's assertions; وَفْقَ \ حَسَبَ ادِّعاءِ الشَرِكةِ according to the company's assertions 3 [تَظاهُر] simulation

اسْتِدْعاء *n* |اسْتِدْعاءات| **1** (Law) summons; أَصْدَرَ اسْتِدْعاءً to issue a summons; تَلَقَّى اسْتِدْعاءً to receive a summons **2** [نِداء] call; convocation; appeal; اسْتِدْعاء للتَصْوِيتِ a call for a vote

تَداعٍ *n* **1** [عاقِبة] consequence, repercussion, implication; تَداعِيات الأَزْمةِ repercussions of the crisis **2** [الأَفْكارِ] association; تَداعي الأَفْكارِ free association; brainstorming; (Literat) stream of consciousness **3** [انْهِيار] imminent collapse; decrepitude

مُتَداعٍ *adj* rickety; ramshackle; dilapidated; كوخ مُتَداعٍ a ramshackle hut

مُدَّعٍ *n* plaintiff; prosecutor; المُدَّعي العامّ \ العُموميّ (public) prosecutor, district attorney (AmE)

مَدْعاة *n* cause; مَدْعاة للفَخْرِ a matter of pride; مَدْعاة للقَلَقِ cause for concern; هذا مَدْعاةٌ للتَأَمُّلِ this is food for thought

مَدْعوّ **A** *n* invitee; guest; للمَدْعوّين فَقَطْ invitees only; اسْتَقْبَلَ المَدْعوّينَ to receive the guests; كانَ ضِمْنَ المَدْعوّين to be among the guests

B *adj* pretending; alleged, so-called

مُدَّعًى *n* المُدَّعى عَلَيْهِ defendant; accused; الطَرَف المُدَّعى عَلَيْهِ the defense

دَغْدَغَ *v* |i; دَغْدَغة| **1** [شَخْصاً] to tickle; دَغْدَغَ شَخْصاً to tickle sb **2** [لُقْمةً] to bite into pieces

دَغْدَغة *n* tickle

دَغَرَ *v* |a; دَغْر, دَغْرى| [على] to attack; to rob

داغِصة *n* |دَواغِصُ| (Anat) knee cap, patella

دَغْفَل *n* (elephant) calf; (wolf) cub

دَغَل *n* |أَدْغال ,دِغال| أَدْغال jungle; brush, thicket; في الأَدْغالِ in the jungle

مُدْغِل *adj* bushy

أَدْغَمَ *v* (Gram) to make a contraction; to assimilate

ادَّغَمَ *v* (Gram) to make a contraction; to assimilate

دُغام *n* sore throat

إدْغام *n* (Gram) contraction; assimilation; dipthong

ادِّغام *n* (Gram) contraction; assimilation; dipthong

دَفُؤَ *v* |u; دَفاءة| to be warm; to feel warm; دَفُؤَ اليَوْمُ it is a warm day

دَفِئَ *v* |a; دَفَأ ,دِفْء| to be warm; to feel warm

دَفَّأَ *v* to warm, to heat; دَفَّأَ غُرْفةً to heat a room

أَدْفَأَ *v* to warm (up); to heat (up); to keep warm; أَدْفَأَ يَدَيْهِ \ رِجْلَيْهِ to warm one's hands/feet; شَيْء يُدْفِئُ القَلْبَ sth heart-warming

تَدَفَّأَ *v* to warm oneself up; تَدَفَّأَ بالمِدْفَأةِ to warm oneself up with a heater

ادَّفَأَ *v* to warm oneself

اسْتَدْفَأَ *v* to warm oneself up; to try to warm oneself up

دِفْء *n* warmth; glow; دِفْء العَواطِفِ warm feelings; دِفْء الشَمْسِ the warmth of the sun

دافِئ *adj* warm; hot; غُرْفة دافِئة a warm room; ابْتِسامة دافِئة a warm smile; حِضْن دافِئ a warm embrace; مَساء صَيْفٍ دافِئ a hot summer evening; مَلابِس دافِئة warm clothes

دَفّاءة *n* heater; stove; fireplace

دَفيئة *n* greenhouse; دَفيئة زِراعيّة greenhouse; فِعْل الدَفيئةِ greenhouse effect; غازات الدَفيئةِ greenhouse gas

تَدْفِئة *n* heating; تَدْفِئة مَرْكَزيّة central heating; زَيْت التَدْفِئةِ heating oil; جِهاز التَدْفِئةِ heating equipment

مِدْفَأة *n* |مَدافِئُ| heater; fireplace; المِدْفَأةُ مُشْعَلةٌ the heat is on; أَوْقَدَ المِدْفَأةَ to turn on the heater

دَفْتَر *n* |دَفاتِرُ| notebook, notepad, tablet; book, register; دَفْتَر مَليء \ خالٍ a full/empty notebook; دَفْتَر اليَوْميّاتِ journal, diary; الدَفْتَر الذَهَبيّ guestbook; دَفْتَر مُلاحَظاتٍ notebook; دَفْتَر شيكاتٍ chequebook; مَسَكَ الدَفاتِرَ to keep the books

دَفْتَريّ *adj* notebook (*before n*); كُمْبيوتَر دَفْتَريّ (Comput) notebook

دِفْتيريا *n* (Med) diphtheria

دَفَرَ *v* |a; دَفْر| to push

دَفِرَ *v* |a; دَفَر| to smell (bad); to reek

دَفَعَ *v* |a; دَفْع| **1** [دَفَرَ] to push; to shove; to press; دَفَعَ سَيّارةً to push a car; دَفَعَ شَخْصاً to push sb; دَفَعَ شَخْصاً من السُلَّمِ to push sb off the ladder; دَفَعَ شَخْصاً من مَكانِهِ to shove sb out of his spot; دَفَعَ الشَرَّ عن شَخْصٍ to protect sb from distress; دَفَعَ شَخْصاً إلى الأَمامِ بِقوّةٍ to shove sb forward

وَسيلة دَفْعٍ payment method; دَفْع مُسَبَّق advance payment; دَفْع بالتَقْسيطِ payment in installments ❹ (Law) defense; plea; دُفوع شَكْلِيّة formal plea

دافِع *n* |دَوافِعُ| ❶ [مَنْ يَدْفَعُ] payer; دافِع الضَرائِبِ taxpayer ❷ [حافِز] motive; incentive; impulse; دافِع مُهِمّ an important motive; دافِع قَوِيّ a powerful incentive; دَوافِع للقِيام بِشَيْءٍ \ incentives to do sth; بِدَوافِعَ عُنْصُرِيّة \ سِياسِيّة with racist/political motives; كانَ لَدَيْه دافِعٌ لِفِعْلِ ذلك he had a motive for doing that; دافِع ل \ إلى شَيْءٍ an incentive for sth; بِدافِعِ (من) ... motivated by, driven by

دِفاع *n* ❶ [حِماية] defence; دِفاع جَوِيّ air defence; دِفاع مَدَنِيّ civil protection; الدِفاع الذاتِيّ \ عن النَفْسِ self-defence; دِفاعاً عن النَفْسِ in self-defence; الدِفاع عن المَصالِحِ defending one's interests; وَزير الدِفاعِ Defence Minister, Secretary of State for Defence (BrE), Secretary of Defense (AmE); وِزارة الدِفاعِ Ministry of Defence, Department of Defense (AmE); خَطّ دِفاعٍ line of defence; قوّات الدِفاعِ military forces; جِهاز دِفاعٍ defence apparatus; لَجْنة دِفاعٍ defence council; الدِفاع ضدّ الهُجوماتِ defence against the attacks; تَصَرَّفَ دِفاعاً عن النَفْسِ to act in self-defence; مِيزانِيّة الدِفاعِ defence budget ❷ (Sport) defence; دِفاع قَوِيّ a strong defence; لاعِب دِفاعٍ defender; دِفاع رَجُلٍ لِرَجُلٍ man-to-man marking; لَعِبَ في الدِفاعِ to play in defence ❸ (Rhet) a statement of defence; apologia ❹ (Law) defence; مُحامي \ وَكيل الدِفاعِ defence lawyer; the defence; تَوَلّى دِفاعَ شَخْصٍ to take over sb's defence; يُمْكِنُ الدِفاعُ عَنْهُ tenable, defensible; لا يُمْكِنُ الدِفاعُ عَنْهُ untenable, indefensible

دِفاعِيّ *adj* defensive, defence (*before n*); apologetic; مَوْقِف دِفاعِيّ a defensive position; سِياسة دِفاعِيّة defence policy

دَفْعة *n* |دَفَعات| ❶ [قوّة دافِعة] push; move; stroke; impulse; incentive; دَفْعة قَوِيّة a hefty push; دَفْعة أولى a first step; دَفْعة قَوِيّة في الاتِّجاهِ الصَحيحِ a strong step in the right direction; أَعْطى دَفْعةً (للاقْتِصادِ) to give a boost (to the economy) ❷ [مالِيّة] payment

دُفْعة *n* |دَفَعات, دُفُعات| ❶ [مَجْموعة] batch; year group; دُفْعة جَديدة من الطُلّابِ a new batch of students ❷ [مَرّة] time; ❷ [سَدَّدَ] to pay; دَفَعَ الحِسابَ to pay the bill; دَفَعَ مَبْلَغاً to pay an amount of money; دَفَعَ نَقْداً to pay cash; دَفَعَ أَجْراً to pay wages; دَفَعَ بالساعةِ to pay by the hour; دَفَعَ مُسَبَّقاً to pay in advance; دَفَعَ تَعْويضاً عن الضَرَرِ to pay damages; دَفَعَ الثَمَنَ غالِياً to pay a high price; دَفَعَ ثَمَنَ جَريمَتِهِ to pay for one's crime; دَفَعَ حَياتَهُ ثَمَناً لِشَيْءٍ to pay for sth with one's life; دَفَعَ ثَمانِيَةَ دولاراتٍ ثَمَناً لِتَذْكِرةِ القِطارِ to pay eight dollars for a train ticket ❸ [جَعَلَهُ يَفْعَلُ شَيْئاً] to impel; to drive (to); دَفَعَ النَفَقاتِ إلى أَعْلى to drive up costs; دَفَعَهُ الطُموحُ (إلى شَيْءٍ) ambition drove him (to sth); دَفَعَ شَخْصاً إلى الجُنونِ to drive sb to madness ❹ [أثناء الوِلادةِ] to push (*during labour*)

دافَعَ *v* to defend; to support, to side with; to plead for; دافَعَ عن شَخْصٍ \ شَيْءٍ to defend sb; دافَعَ عن نَفْسِهِ ضدّ شَخْصٍ \ شَيْءٍ to defend oneself against sb/sth; دافَعَ عن نَفْسِهِ بِعَصاً \ بِحُجّةٍ to defend oneself with a stick/an argument; دافَعَ عن مَدينةٍ ضدّ هُجوماتٍ مُعادِيةٍ to defend a city against hostile attacks; دافَعَ عن المُتَّهَمِ to defend the suspect; دافَعَ عن مَصالِحِ شَخْصٍ to defend sb's interests; دافَعَ عن فِكْرةٍ \ وِجْهةِ نَظَرٍ to defend an idea/opinion; دافَعَ عن العَدْلِ \ الديموقْراطِيّة to stand for justice/democracy; دافَعَ عن نَفْسِهِ to defend oneself; to conduct one's own defense; دافَعَتْ عن نَفْسِها بِقوّةٍ she defended herself vigorously

تَدَفَّعَ *v* to stream

تَدافَعَ *v* ❶ [القَوْمُ] to crowd; to jostle, to push/trample one another; تَدافَعوا لِشِراءِ شَيْءٍ to scramble over one another to buy sth ❷ [السَيْلُ] to stream

انْدَفَعَ *v* to be driven; to be propelled; to proceed rashly/blindly, to plunge headlong; انْدَفَعَ إلى المُقَدِّمةِ to rush to the front; انْدَفَعَ إلى خارِجِ الغُرْفةِ to rush out of the room; انْدَفَعَ وراءَ شَهَواتِهِ to be driven by one's desires

دَفْع *n* |دُفوع| ❶ (Mech) propulsion; دَفْع كَهْرَبائِيّ \ آلِيّ electric/mechanical propulsion; دَفْع نَفّاث jet propulsion; دَفْع أَمامِيّ \ خَلْفِيّ front-wheel/rear-wheel drive; دَفْع رُباعِيّ four-wheel drive; سَيّارة أَمامِيّة الدَفْعِ a front-wheel drive car; قوّة الدَفْعِ momentum ❷ [تَشْجيع] push; pushing, propelling; coercion; أَعْطى دَفْعاً قَوِيًّا لِشَيْءٍ to give sth a boost ❸ [تَسْديد] payment;

دَفَقَ v |i-u; دَفْق, دُفوق| ❶ [سالَ] to stream ❷ [صَبَّ] to pour

تَدَفَّقَ v ❶ [سالَ] to stream; to flow; to pour; to gush; to squirt; يَتَدَفَّقُ الماءُ إلى السَفينةِ water gushed into the ship; تَتَدَفَّقُ الدَمُ من الجُرْحِ blood is flowing from the wound; تَتَدَفَّقُ الأَمْوالُ على المُنَظَّمةِ money is pouring into the organisation ❷ [انْدَفَعَ] to pour in; to stream; to flock; تَتَدَفَّقُ العُروضُ offers are pouring in; يَتَدَفَّقُ اللاجِئونَ عابِرينَ الحُدودَ refugees are streaming across the border; تَدَفَّقَ الناسُ من كُلِّ حَدَبٍ وَصَوْبٍ people poured in from all directions; يَتَدَفَّقُ الصُحُفيّونَ على العاصِمةِ journalists are flocking to the capital

دَفْق n stream, flow, influx; squirt

دُفْقة n |دُفُقات, دُفْقات| surge, gush; spurt, splash

تَدَفُّق n |تَدَفُّقات| flow, influx, rush, surge; invasion; تَدَفُّق ماليّ flow of money; تَدَفُّق رُؤوسِ الأَمْوالِ \ البَضائِعِ flow of capital/goods; تَدَفُّق هائِل an huge influx; تَدَفُّق اللاجِئينَ an influx of refugees

مُتَدَفِّق adj flowing, streaming; effluent, torrential

دِفْلى n |f| (Bot) oleander (*Nerium oleander*)

دَفَنَ v |i; دَفْن| ❶ [وارى] to bury; دَفَنَ مَيِّتاً \ قَريباً to bury a deceased person/a family member; دَفَنَ شَخْصاً حَيًّا to bury sb alive ❷ [أَخْفى] to bury; to hide, to conceal; دَفَنَ الماضِيَ to bury the past; دَفَنَ رَأْسَهُ في الرِمالِ to bury one's head in the sand

دَفْن n funeral, burial; مَراسِم دَفْنٍ funeral; burial; غُرْفة دَفْنٍ burial chamber

دَفين adj |دُفَناءُ| ❶ [مَدْفون] buried ❷ [مَسْتور] secret, hidden, buried; حِقْد دَفين buried resentment; كَنْز دَفين a hidden treasure; أَشْواق \ رَغَبات دَفينة secret passions/desires

دَفينة n |دَفائِنُ| ❶ [دَفين] secret ❷ [كَنْز] treasure

مَدْفَن, مَدْفِن n |مَدافِنُ| cemetery, graveyard; tomb, vault

مَدْفون adj buried; entombed

أَدْقَعَ v to become poor

مُدْقِع adj extreme, abject; miserable, wretched; فَقْر مُدْقِع abject poverty

دَقَّ v |u; دَقّ| ❶ [طَرَقَ] to beat; to tick; to strike; دَقَّ البابَ to knock on the door; دَقَّ جَرَسَ البابِ to ring the doorbell;

دُفْعةً واحِدةً all at once; in one stroke; lump sum (*payment*); دُفْعة من المَطَرِ a rain shower

انْدِفاع n |انْدِفاعات| motivation; drive, impetus; enthusiasm; انْدِفاع شَديد an enormous drive

انْدِفاعة n surge, rush; sudden outbreak/outburst

انْدِفاعيّ adj impulsive, spur-of-the-moment; عَمَل انْدِفاعيّ an impulsive action

انْدِفاعيّة n impulsiveness

تَدافُع n stampede; crowd; jostle

مُدافِع n ❶ [مُؤَيِّد] defender; advocate; مُدافِع عن حُقوقِ الإنْسانِ human rights advocate; مُدافِع عن البيئة environmental activist ❷ (Sport) defender; مُدافِع جَناحٍ wing-back; مُدافِع الوَسَطِ centre-back; defensive midfielder; المُدافِع الحُرّ sweeper, libero; مُدافِع أَيْمَن \ أَيْسَر right-back/left-back

مِدْفَع n |مَدافِعُ| cannon; artillery; gun; مِدْفَع رَشّاش machine gun; مِدْفَع هاوُن mortar; مَدافِع مُضادّة للطائِراتِ anti-aircraft guns; مَدافِع ثَقيلة \ خَفيفة heavy/light artillery; مِدْفَع الإفْطارِ *a cannon shot marking the end of fasting during Ramadan*; مِدْفَع مِياهٍ water gun; fire hose; طَلْقة مِدْفَعٍ, قَذيفة مِدْفَعٍ artillery shell; cannonball; أَطْلَقَ قَذيفة مِدْفَعٍ to fire a shell

مِدْفَعيّ Ⓐ adj artillery (*before n*); قَصْف مِدْفَعيّ artillery shelling Ⓑ n gunner

مِدْفَعيّة n artillery; مِدْفَعيّة ثَقيلة \ خَفيفة heavy/light artillery; سِلاح المِدْفَعيّةِ artillery

مَدْفوع adj paid; إجازة مَدْفوعة الأَجْرِ paid leave; ميزان المَدْفوعاتِ balance of payments

مُنْدَفِع adj ❶ [مُنْطَلِق] reckless; impulsive; عَمَل مُنْدَفِع an impulsive act ❷ [مُتَحَمِّس] driven, motivated; inspired; enthusiastic

دَفَّ v |i; دَفيف| to flap

دَفّ n |دُفوف| (Geom) face; side

دُفّ n |دُفوف| tambourine; tabor, small drum

دَفّة n ❶ (Mech) rudder; helm; ذِراع دَفّةٍ helm; قَبَضَ على دَفّةِ التَنْفيذِ to take control/action; سَيَّرَ دَفّةَ الأُمورِ to be/stand at the helm; سَلَّمَ \ تَسَلَّمَ دَفّةَ الإدارةِ to hand over the helm; تَمَسَّكَ بِدَفّةِ الإدارةِ to hold on to the helm ❷ (P&P) cover (*of a book*)

دَقَّ مِسْماراً to hit a nail; دَقَّ وَشْماً to apply a tattoo; دُقَّتْ عُنُقُهُ he broke his neck ❷ [القَلْبُ] to beat; to pulse ❸ [سَحَقَ] to pound; دَقَّ الثِمارَ إلى مَسْحوقٍ to pound fruit into purée ❹ [رَقَّ] to be small/fine ❺ [أَحْدَثَ صَوْتاً] to ring; to strike; تَدُقُّ الساعةُ the clock is striking

دَقَّقَ *v* to specify; to scrutinize, to examine carefully; to be painstakingly accurate; دَقَّقَ مَلِيًّا في قَضِيّةٍ to get to the bottom of a case; دَقَّقَ النَظَرَ \ البَصَرَ في شَيْءٍ to scrutinize sth carefully

اِنْدَقَّ *v* to be crushed

اِسْتَدَقَّ *v* to taper; to diminish; to become fine/thin/small

دُقاق *n* grit; powder; crumbs

دَقّاقة *n* knocker (*of a door*)

دَقّة *n* knock, rap, pounding; beat, beating (*of a heart*); stroke, striking (*of a clock*)

دُقّة *n* powder

دِقّة *n* ❶ [ضَبْط] precision, accuracy, exactness; punctuality; finesse; subtlety; يَتَطَلَّبُ هذا العَمَلُ دِقّةً كَبيرةً this work requires a lot of precision; عَدَمُ الدِقّةِ inaccuracy, imprecision; فَتَّشَ كُلَّ شَيْءٍ بِدِقّةٍ تامّةٍ to examine everything thoroughly; بِدِقّةٍ كَبيرةٍ with great accuracy; بِدِقّةٍ accurately, precisely; carefully, conscientiously; exactly, minutely; حَدَّدَ شَيْئاً بِدِقّةٍ to determine sth exactly; قاسَ شَيْئاً بِدِقّةٍ to measure sth accurately; عَمِلَ بِدِقّةٍ to work conscientiously; اِلْتَزَمَ بالقَوانينِ بِدِقّةٍ to live strictly by the rules; اِفْتَقَرَ إلى الدِقّةِ to lack precision ❷ [الشاشةِ] resolution; دِقّة الشاشةِ resolution of a screen

دَقيق Ⓐ *adj* |دِقاق ,أَدِقّة| ❶ [مَضْبوط] accurate, precise, exact; close; careful, meticulous; فَحْص دَقيق a close examination; ميزان دَقيق a sensitive scale; غَيْر دَقيقٍ inaccurate, incorrect; inexact, loose; مَعْلومات دَقيقة \ غَيْر دَقيقةٍ accurate/inaccurate information; تَرْجَمة دَقيقة \ غَيْر دَقيقةٍ an exact/loose translation; قاسَ شَيْئاً بِشَكْلٍ دَقيقٍ to measure sth accurately ❷ [رَقيق] subtle; thin, fine, delicate; سِلْك دَقيق a thin cord/wire; فَرْق دَقيق a subtle difference; مَرْحَلة دَقيقة a delicate stage Ⓑ *n* flour; كيس دَقيقٍ a bag of flour

دَقيقة *n* |دَقائِقُ| ❶ [٦٠ ثانِيةً] minute; moment; دَقيقة صَمْتٍ a moment of silence; يَدومُ عَشْرَ دَقائِقَ it lasts ten minutes; دَخَلَت المُباراةُ دَقائِقَها الخَمْسَ الأخيرةَ the game is in its final five minutes ❷ (Geog) minute (*of longitude/latitude*)

تَدْقيق *n* ❶ [ضَبْط] accuracy, precision; exactness ❷ [تَحْقيق] checking, check; examination, scrutiny; audit; تَدْقيق إمْلائيّ spellcheck

مِدَقّ *n* |مَداقُّ| hammer; battering ram

مِدَقّة *n* ❶ (Bot) carpel ❷ [أَداة] pestle; tamper; hammer; هاوُن وَمِدَقّة pestle and mortar

مُدَقَّق *adj* precise, exact; checked, inspected, audited; فَواتير مُدَقَّقة checked invoices; بَيانات ماليّة مُدَقَّقة audited financial statements

مُدَقِّق *n* checker; auditor; مُدَقِّق إمْلائيّ spell check; مُدَقِّق الحِساباتِ auditor

دَقَل *n* (ship's) mast

دُقْنوش, دِقْناش *n* (Zool) shrike (*Laniidae*)

دَكّا *n* Dhaka (*capital of Bangladesh*)

ديكْتاتور, دِكْتاتور *n* dictator

ديكْتاتوريّ, دِكْتاتوريّ *adj* dictatorial; حُكْم دِكْتاتوريّ dictatorial regime

ديكْتاتوريّة, دِكْتاتوريّة *n* dictatorship; دِكْتاتوريّة عَسْكَريّة a military dictatorship

دُكْتور *n* |دَكاتِرة| ❶ [طَبيب] doctor; physician ❷ [أَكاديميّ] Dr, Doctor

دُكْتوراة, دُكْتوراه *n* doctorate, PhD; حَصَلَ على دَرَجةِ الدُكْتوراه to get a PhD; دُكْتوراه فَخْريّة an honorary doctorate; دُكْتوراه فَخْريّة في الآدابِ an Honorary Doctorate in Literature; رِسالة دُكْتوراه dissertation, (doctoral) thesis

دِكْسْتروز *n* dextrose, glucose, grape sugar

دَكَّ *v* |u; دَكّ| ❶ [هَدَمَ] to tear down; to demolish; to level to the ground ❷ [الأَرْضَ] to level, to make even

اِنْدَكَّ *v* to be crushed

دَكّة *n* |دِكَك| ❶ [مَقْعَد] bench; seat ❷ (Sport) podium ❸ (Islam) *platform in a mosque for the Koran reciter*

مِدَكّ *n* |مِدَكّات| pestle; tamper; ramrod

داكِن *adj* |دَواكِنُ| dark; dark-coloured; أَخْضَر داكِن dark green; غَيْمة داكِنة a dark cloud; زُجاج داكِن tinted glass; عُيون داكِنة dark eyes; بَشْرة داكِنة dark skin; شَعْر داكِن dark hair

دُكّان *n* |mf; دَكاكينُ| shop, store; corner shop

دُلْب *n* plane tree (*Platanus*)

دَلْبوث *n* (Bot) *Gladiolus*

دِلْتا *n* (Geog) delta; دِلْتا النيلِ the Nile delta

أَدْلَجَ *v* to set out at nightfall

دُلْدُل *n* porcupine

دَلَّسَ *v* ① [زَوَّرَ] to forge; دَلَّسَ وَثائِقَ to forge documents ② [خَدَعَ] to cheat

دالَسَ *v* to forge; to cheat; هو لا يُدالِسُ وَلا يُوالِسُ he is dead honest

تَدْليس *n* fraud, scam, deceit; embezzlement

دَلَّعَ *v* to pamper, to spoil

اِنْدَلَعَ *v* to break out; to burst out; to flare up; تَنْدَلِعُ الحَرْبُ war has broken out; يَنْدَلِعُ وَباءٌ an epidemic has broken out; اِنْدَلَعَ بِكُلِّ حِدّةٍ to flare up in full force

دَلْع *n* sticking out one's tongue; اسْم دَلْعٍ term of endearment, pet name

دَلّاع *n coll* (NA) watermelon

اِنْدِلاع *n* outbreak; flare-up; اِنْدِلاع الحَرْبِ \ الثَوْرةِ an outbreak of war/revolution

دَلَفَ *v* |i; دَلَفان ,دُلوف ,دَلْف| ① [مَشى بِبُطْءٍ] to walk with short steps, to toddle; to walk slowly, to saunter, to stroll; دَلَفَ إلى الدُكّانِ to toddle to the store ② [قَطَرَ] to drip; to trickle

دُلْفين *n* ,دولْفين |دَلافينُ| dolphin

دَلَقَ *v* |u; دُلوق ,دَلْق| ① [سَيْفاً] to draw; دَلَقَ السَيْفَ to draw one's sword ② [صَبَّ] to spill; to pour

اِنْدَلَقَ *v* to be spilled; to pour, to gush out, to stream

دَلَق *n* (Zool) marten (*Martes*)

دَلَكَ *v* |u; دَلْك| to massage; to rub; to knead; دَلَكَ العَجينَ to knead dough

دَلَّكَ *v* to massage; دَلَّكَ الرِجْلَيْنِ \ الذِراعَيْنِ to massage the legs/arms; دَلَّكَ شَخْصاً to massage sb

دَلّاك *n* massager, masseur

تَدْليك *n* massage; تَدْليك طِبّيّ \ عِلاجيّ therapeutic massage; صالون التَدْليكِ a massage parlour

مُدَلِّك *n* massager, masseur; مُدَلِّكة masseuse; مُدَلِّك طِبّيّ therapeutic masseur

دَلَّ *v* |u; دَلالة| ① [أَشارَ إلى] to show, to demonstrate; to indicate, to signify, to denote; دَلَّ على شَيْءٍ to indicate sth; دَلَّ على الشَجاعةِ to indicate courage; يَدُلُّ هذا على أنّ ... this shows that ...; تَصَرُّفاتُهُ تَدُلُّ على أَنَّهُ يَتَأَلَّمُ his behaviour shows that he's suffering; دَلَّ شَخْصاً على كَيْفيّةِ فِعْلِ شَيْءٍ to show sb how to do sth; دَلَّ شَخْصاً على \ إلى طَريقِ مَكانٍ to show sb the way to somewhere ② [تَغَنَّجَ] to be coquettish

دَلَّلَ *v* ① [بَرْهَنَ] to prove; to demonstrate; دَلَّلَ على شَيْءٍ to prove sth ② [دَلَّعَ] to coddle; to caress; to pamper, to spoil; دَلَّلَ رَضيعاً to pamper a baby; دَلَّلَ أَطْفالَهُ to spoil one's children ③ [على السِلْعةِ] to auction off; دَلَّلَ على السِلْعةِ to put the merchandise up for auction

أَدَلَّ *v* to take liberties with

تَدَلَّلَ *v* to flirt; to be coquettish

اِسْتَدَلَّ *v* ① [اِسْتَنْتَجَ] to infer; to come to the conclusion, to deduce; to derive; اِسْتَدَلَّ على شَيْءٍ to infer sth; اِسْتَدَلَّ بـ \ من شَيْءٍ على أنّ ... to infer from sth that ...; اِسْتَدَلَّ بالقَرارِ على رَأْيِهِ he used the decision to support his opinion ② [اِسْتَعْلَمَ] to inquire (about)

دالّ *adj* indicating; denotative

دالّة *n* |دَوالُّ ,دالّات| ① (Math) function ② (Ling) morpheme

دَلال *n* coquettishness

دَلّال *n* |دَلّالونَ| broker; intermediary

دَلالة *n* ① [إشارة] indication; token; للدَلالةِ على شَيْءٍ to indicate sth; دَلالةً على الثِقةِ \ التَقْديرِ \ التَعاطُفِ as a token of trust/appreciation/sympathy ② [مَعْنًى] meaning; significance; ذو دَلالةٍ significant; بالِغ الدَلالةِ extremely significant; عِلْم الدَلالةِ (Ling) semantics

دَلْهَم, **دِلْهَم** *adj* dark, gloomy; deep black

‹ **دَلّى** *v* to let down; to lower

أَدْلى *v* |ب| to express; to utter; to pronounce; أَدْلى بِتَصْريحٍ to make a statement; أَدْلى بِحُجّةٍ to put forward an argument; أَدْلى إلى شَخْصٍ بِشَيْءٍ to inform sb about sth

تَدَلّى *v* to hang down, to dangle, to hang/swing loosely; تَدَلّى من حَبْلٍ \ غُصْنٍ to hang from a rope/branch; تَدَلَّتْ من عُنُقِهِ كاميرا a camera dangled around his neck

دَلْو *n* |mf; أَدْلٍ, دِلاء, أَدْلاء| ❶ [سَطْل] bucket; أَدْلى دَلْوَهُ to do one's bit ❷ (Astrol) (بُرْج) الدَلْوِ Aquarius

دالِية *n* |دَوالٍ| ❶ [دَلْو] bucket ❷ [ساقِية] water wheel ❸ (Med) varicose vein; أُصيبَ بالدَوالي to have varicose veins ❹ [اسْم شَخْصيّ] |dipt| Dalia (*female given name*)

دَلّاية *n* pendant; دَلّاية المَفاتيحِ key chain

إدْلاء *n* delivery (*of a statement*); utterance, statement

تَدْلِية *n* dangling; lowering

مُتَدَلٍّ *adj* hanging, suspended; pendulous, droopy

‹ **دَم** *n* see دمي

‹ **الدَمّام** *n* |f| Dammam (*city in Saudi Arabia*)

‹ **دَمُثَ** *v* |u; دَمَث, دَماثة| to be gentle; to be kind/friendly

دَمَّثَ *v* to soften (*by rubbing*)

دَمِث *adj* |دِماث| soft; gentle, mild, courteous, affable; كانَ دَمِثَ الأَخْلاقِ to be well-mannered

دَماثة *adj* gentleness; mildness; kindness

‹ **دَمَجَ** *v* |u; دَمْج| ❶ [ضَمَّ] to integrate; to be inserted; to be incorporated ❷ [الشَعْرَ] to braid, to plait

أَدْمَجَ *v* ❶ [ضَمَّ] to record; to combine; to integrate; أَدْمَجَ مَدْرَسَتَيْنِ to merge two schools ❷ [الشَعْرَ] to braid, to plait

انْدَمَجَ *v* to integrate (into); to assimilate (into); to merge; to fuse; يَنْدَمِجُ المُهاجِرونَ في مُجْتَمَعِنا immigrants are assimilating into our society; تَنْدَمِجُ البُوَيْضةُ والخَليّةُ المَنَوِيّةُ the ovum fuses with a sperm; انْدَمَجَ مع شَرِكةٍ to merge with a company

دَمْج *n* merger, fusion; integration; combination, amalgamation; عَمَلِيّة الدَمْجِ merger

دِلالة *n* ❶ [حِرْفة] brokerage ❷ [أُجْرة] commission ❸ [دَلالة] meaning

دَلاليّ *adj* indicative; semantic

دَليل *n* ❶ [عَلامة] |أَدِلّة, دَلائِلُ| clue; indication; pointer; sign; دَليل على ... indication of ...; دَليل على شَيْءٍ an indication of sth; دَليل واضِح a clear indication; دَليل المِنْطَقةِ area code ❷ [حُجّة] |أَدِلّة, دَلائِلُ| evidence; exhibit; testimony; دَليل قاطِع conclusive evidence; دَليل دامِغ irrefutable evidence; دَليل زائِف forged evidence; كانَ دَليلاً على indicated; دَليل ... لِصالِحِ \ ضِدّ ... evidence for/against ...; أَفْضَل \ خَيْر دَليلٍ على هذا the best proof of this is; لِعَدَمِ تَوَفُّرِ \ كِفايةِ الأَدِلّةِ for lack of evidence; عَكَسَ مَسْؤوليّةَ إقامةِ الدَليلِ to reverse the burden of proof; قَدَّمَ دَليلاً to provide evidence; تَقْديم الأَدِلّةِ ضِدّ مُجْرِمي الحَرْبِ producing evidence against war criminals ❸ [كِتاب] |أَدِلّة, دَلائِلُ| guide; manual; دَليل سِياحيّ guide book; كِتاب دَليلٍ handbook; دَليل الهاتِف telephone directory; دَليل مَواقِعَ website directory ❹ [شَخْص] |أَدِلّاءُ| tour guide; guide; عَمِلَ دَليلاً to work as a (tour) guide

دَليليّ *n* guide (*before n*), pilot (*before n*); كَلِمة دَليليّة tag, keyword

اسْتِدْلال *n* |اسْتِدْلالات| ❶ [اسْتِنْتاج] inference, deduction, conclusion; drawing a conclusion ❷ [بَرْهَنة] evidence, proof

اسْتِدْلاليّ *adj* deductive; indicative

تَدَلُّل *n* flirtation; التَدَلُّل على شَخْصٍ a flirtation with sb

تَدْليل *n* ❶ [تَدْليع] indulgence; pampering; اسْم تَدْليلٍ nickname; pet name ❷ [إثْبات] indication; demonstration; evidence, proof; تَدْليل على فَشَلِ شَيْءٍ a demonstration of sth's failure

مُدِلّ *adj* arrogant; conceited; pretentious

مُدَلَّل *adj* pampered; spoiled; طِفْل مُدَلَّل a spoiled child

مَدْلول *n* |مَدْلولات| meaning; significance

‹ **دَلَّهَ** *v* to drive sb crazy (*with love*)

تَدَلَّهَ *v* to go crazy (*with love*); تَدَلَّهَ في حُبِّها he was madly in love with her

دَلِه *adj* out of one's mind, crazy, mad (BrE)

مُدَلَّه *adj* madly in love

‹ **ادْلَهَمَّ** *v* to be/become dark, to be deep black

انْدماج *n* integration; assimilation; merger, fusion; انْدِماج المُهاجِرينَ في المُجْتَمَعِ the assimilation of immigrants in society; حَفَّزَ على الانْدِماجِ to further integration

مُدْمَج *adj* **1** [مَحْبوك] compact; قُرْص مُدْمَج compact disc; CD-ROM **2** [غَيْر مُنْفَصِلٍ] built-in; فُرْن مُدْمَج a built-in oven

مُدَمَّج *adj* compact; firm; قُرْص مُدَمَّج compact disc; CD-ROM

مُنْدَمِج *adj* integrated; incorporated

‹[1] **دَمْدَمَ** *v* |i; دَمْدَمة| to growl; to snarl; to grumble

دَمْدَمة *n* growl

مُدَمْدِم *n* grumbler

‹[2] **دَمْدَم** *n* رَصاصة دَمْدَم (Mil) expanding bullet, dumdum (bullet)

‹ **دَمَّرَ** *v* to destroy; to demolish; to devastate; to ruin; دَمَّرَ شَخْصاً \ شَيْئاً to ruin sb/sth; دَمَّرَ سَيّارةً to destroy a car; دَمَّرَ أَسْلِحةً to destroy weapons; دَمَّرَ مَنازِلَ \ مَبانِيَ to demolish houses/buildings; دَمَّرَ بَلَداً to ravage a country

تَدَمَّرَ *v* to be destroyed; to be demolished; to be ruined; to perish

دَمار *n* destruction, demolition; ruin; havoc; سِلاح الدَمارِ الشامِلِ weapon of mass destruction, WMD

تَدْمير *n* destruction; demolition, knocking down; تَدْمير مَدينةٍ \ مَبْنًى destruction of a city/building

تَدْميريّ *adj* destructive; destroying; devastating; القوّة التَدْميريّة (لِقُنْبُلةٍ نَوَوِيّةٍ) the devastating power (of a nuclear bomb)

مُدَمِّر *adj* destroying; destructive; devastating; حَريق \ تَأْثير مُدَمِّر a devastating fire/impact

مُدَمِّرة *n* warship

‹ **دَمَسَ** *v* |u; دُموس, دَمْس| to hide; to conceal

دَمَّسَ *v* to hide; to conceal

دامِس *adj* pitch-black; dark; لَيْل دامِس a dark night

مُدَمَّس *adj* hidden; concealed; فول مُدَمَّس *Egyptian dish of mashed fava beans*

‹ **دَمَسيس** *n* (Bot) ragweed

‹ **دِمَشْق** *n* |dipt f| Damascus

‹ **دَمَعَ** *v* |a; دَمْع| to tear (up), to produce tears; دَمَعَتْ عَيْناهُ his eyes filled with tears; he was crying

أَدْمَعَ *v* to make sb cry/weep; to tear (up), to produce tears (*eyes*)

دَمْع *n coll* |دُموع| tears; ذَرَفَ دُموعاً to shed tears; سَفَكَ دَمْعاً to let one's tears flow; مَسَحَ دُموعَهُ to wipe away one's tears; حَبَسَ دُموعَهُ to stifle one's crying; دُموع الفَرَحِ \ الحُزْنِ tears of joy/sorrow; بَكى دُموعَ التَماسيحِ to shed crocodile tears; قالَ والدُموعُ في عَيْنَيْهِ he said with tears in his eyes; تَسيلُ الدُموعُ على خَدَّيْهِ tears are flowing down his cheeks

دامِع *adj* tearful; watery (*of eyes*)

دَمْعيّ *adj* tear (*before n*); lacrimal; غُدّة دَمْعيّة lacrimal gland; قَناة دَمْعيّة tear duct

مَدْمَع *n* |مَدامِعُ| lacrimal duct

‹ **دَمَغَ** *v* |a; دَمْغ| **1** [خَتَمَ] to stamp; to certify; to brand, to imprint **2** [أَبْطَلَ] to disprove; to refute; to invalidate

دامِغ *adj* valid; compelling, convincing, overwhelming, irrefutable; دَليل دامِغ irrefutable evidence; حُجّة دامِغة a compelling argument

دِماغ *n* |أَدْمِغة| brain; أُمّ الدِماغِ meninges; لِحاء الدِماغِ cortex; قِشْرة الدِماغِ cerebral cortex; قاعِدة الدِماغِ base of the brain; فَصّ الدِماغِ brain lobe; نِصْف الدِماغِ (cerebral) hemisphere; نِصْف الدِماغِ الأَيْسَر \ الأَيْمَن left/right hemisphere; عَمَل الدِماغِ brain function; هِجْرة الأَدْمِغةِ brain drain; غَسْل الدِماغِ brainwashing; إِصابة الدِماغِ brain damage; إِصابة خَطيرة في الدِماغِ severe brain damage; تَعَرَّضَ لِإِصابةٍ في الدِماغِ to incur brain damage

دِماغيّ *adj* cerebral; brain (*before n*); إِصابة دِماغيّة brain damage

دَمْغة *n* stamp; imprint; hallmark

‹ **دَمْقَرَطة** *n* democratization

ديموقراطيّة, ديمُقْراطيّة *n* democracy; مُعادٍ للديمُقْراطيّةِ anti-democratic; الديمُقْراطيّة الاجْتِماعيّة social democracy

ديمُقْراطيّ, ديموقْراطيّ **A** *n* democrat **B** *adj* democratic; الحِزْب الديموقْراطيّ the democratic party; مُنْتَخَب ديموقْراطيًا elected democratically; قَرار على غَيْر ديموقْراطيٍّ a democratic decision; الطَريقة الديموقْراطيّة undemocratic; حُكْم \ دَوْلة ديموقْراطيّ(ة) a democratic rule/country

لاديموقْراطيّ *adj* undemocratic, anti-democratic

‹ **دِمَقْس** *n* damask; raw silk

بالدَمِ to give/donate blood; نُقِلَ إلَيْه دَمٌ he underwent a blood transfusion; فَصيلة \ زُمْرة \ مَجْموعة دَمٍ blood type; دَمٍ أ إيجابيّ blood type A positive; بْلازْما دَمٍ blood plasma; صُفَيْحة \ خَليّة الدَمِ الحَمْراء \ البَيْضاء red/white blood cell; تَسَمُّم الدَمِ platelet; خِضاب الدَمِ haemoglobin; لُوَيْحة دَمٍ toxaemia; تَبَوْلُن الدَمِ sepsis; خَمَج الدَمِ uraemia; نَزيف الدَمِ haemorrhage; قَرابة الدَم blood kinship; رابِطة الدَم blood ties; من لَحْمي وَدَمي my own flesh and blood; طالَبَ بِدَمِ شَخْصٍ to demand sb's life (in retaliation); سَفْك الدِماءِ bloodshed; سَفَكَ \ أراقَ الدِماءَ to shed blood; كانَ دَمُهُ أَزْرَق \ ثَقيلاً \ خَفيفاً to be a blue blood/gloomy/funny; حَقَنَ الدِماءَ to prevent bloodshed; حَمّام دَمٍ a bloodbath, carnage; بُرودة الدَمِ sangfroid; بِدَمٍ بارِدٍ in cold blood; قَتَلَ شَخْصاً بِدَمٍ بارِدٍ to kill sb in cold blood; مُلَطَّخ بالدَمِ smeared with blood; يَداهُ تَخَضَّبَتْ أيديهِمْ he has blood on his hands; مُلَطَّخَتانِ بالدَمِ they have blood on their hands; بالدِماءِ دَفَعَ في شَيْءٍ دَمَ قَلْبِهِ to pay an arm and a leg for sth; كانَ دَمُهُ يَغْلي في عُروقِهِ his blood was boiling

دَمَوِيّ *adj* bloody; gory; violent; blood (*before n*); الدَوْرة الدَمَويّة the circulatory system; حَرْب دَمَويّة a bloody war; فيلْم دَمَويّ a gory movie

دُمْية *n* |دُمًى| doll

‹ **دُمْياط** *n* |f| Damietta (*city in northern Egypt*)

‹ **دَنَأَ ,دَنُوَ** *v* |a-u; دَناءة ,دُنوءة| to be low/despicable

دَناءة *n* baseness, meanness; عامَلَ شَخْصاً بِدَناءةٍ to treat sb shoddily

دَنيء *adj* |أَدْنياءُ ,أَدْناء| despicable, vile, mean; sleazy, sordid; جَريمة دَنيئة a despicable crime

دَنيئة *n* |دَنايا| vice

‹ **دَنْدَنَ** *v* |i; دَنْدَنة| to hum, to sing softly; to buzz; to murmur

‹ **دَنِسَ** *v* |a; دَنَس| to be/become polluted; to be/become dirty; to be defiled

دَنَّسَ *v* to dirty, to sully; to dishonour, to disgrace; to violate; دَنَّسَ حُرْمةَ to desecrate; دَنَّسَ كَنيسةً to desecrate a church; مَكانٍ to violate the sanctity of a place

تَدَنَّسَ *v* to be desecrated

‹ **مِدْماك** *n* |مَداميكُ| row of stone or tiles (*in the wall of a building*)

مِدْمَك *n* |مَدامِكُ| rolling pin

‹ **دَمِلَ** *v* |a; دَمَل| to heal (up); to scar over

انْدَمَلَ *v* to heal (up); to scar over; تَنْدَمِلُ الجُروحُ the wounds are healing

دُمَّل *n* |دَماميلُ ,دَمامِلُ| (Med) abscess; boil; sore

انْدِمال *n* healing

‹ **دُمْلُج ,دُمْلوج** *n* |دَمالِجُ| bracelet

‹ **دَمَّ** *v* |u; دَمّ| **1** [قَبُحَ] to be/become ugly **2** [طَلى] to dye

دَميم *adj* |دِمام| ugly; hideous

مِدَمّة *n* |مَدامُّ| rake

‹ **دَمَنَ** *v* |u; دَمْن| to manure, to fertilize

أَدْمَنَ *v* to be/become addicted; أَدْمَنَ شَيْئاً \ على شَيْءٍ to be/become addicted to sth; أَدْمَنَ (على) المُخَدِّراتِ to be/become addicted to drugs

إدْمان *n* addiction; إدْمان (على) المُخَدِّراتِ drug addiction; أدْوية تُسَبِّبُ \ تُؤَدّي إلى الإدْمانِ an addictive medication; عِلاج الإدْمانِ addiction treatment; rehab; تَخَلَّصَ من إدْمانٍ to rid oneself of an addiction

إدْمانيّ *adj* addictive; مادّة إدْمانيّة an addictive substance

مُدْمِن **A** *n* addict; مُدْمِن (على) مُخَدِّراتٍ drug addict **B** *adj* addicted; addictive; كانَ مُدْمِناً على شَيْءٍ to be addicted to sth

‹ **دَمَنْهور** *n* |f| Damanhour (*city in northern Egypt*)

‹ **دَمِيَ** *v* |a; دَمْي ,دَمًى| to bleed

دَمّى *v* to make bleed

أَدْمى *v* to make bleed; شَيْء يُدْمي القَلْبَ sth heartbreaking

دامٍ *adj* bloody; violent; جُرْح دامٍ a bloody wound; أَيدٍ \ ثِياب دامِية bloody hands/clothes; مَعارِك دامِية bloody battles; ثَوْرة دامِية \ نِضال دامٍ bloody revolution/strife

دَم *n* |دِماء| blood; نُقْطة دَمٍ a drop of blood; خَثْرة الدَمِ blood clot; مُحْتَقِن بالدِماءِ bloodshot; تَحْليل الدَمِ blood test; فَقْر الدَمِ anemia; ضَغْط الدَمِ blood pressure; ضَغْط دَمٍ عالٍ \ مُنْخَفِض high/low blood pressure; نَقْل الدَمِ blood transfusion; بَنْك الدَمِ blood bank; واهِب دَمٍ ,مُتَبَرِّع بِدَمٍ blood donor; تَبَرَّعَ

دَنَس n |أَدْناس| pollution, sullying; uncleanliness

دَنِس adj dirty, filthy; impure; profane

تَدْنيس n desecration; soiling, contamination; تَدْنيس الحُرْمَةِ sacrilege

مُدَنَّس adj soiled, tainted; defiled

‹ دَنِفَ v |a; دَنَف| to be seriously ill

أَدْنَفَ v أَدْنَفَهُ المَرَض the illness has exhausted him

دَنَف n a serious illness

دَنِف adj |أَدْناف| seriously ill

‹ دَنَّ v |u; دَنّ, دَنين| to buzz

دَنّ n 1 [طَنين] buzz 2 [جَرّة] |دِنان| decanter; vessel

دِنان n wine jug

دَنين n buzz

‹ دَنا v |u; دُنوّ, دَناوة| to approach, to draw near; to be close; دَنا من \ إلى شَيْءٍ to approach sth

دَنّى v to bring close

دانى v to approach; to approximate; دانى شَخْصاً to approach sb

أَدْنى v to bring close; أَدْنى شَيْئاً to bring sth close

تَدَنّى v 1 [هَبَطَ] to decline; to fall; to sink; تَدَنّى المُسْتَوى the level has dropped 2 [قَرُبَ] to approach

تَدانى v to come close to each other; to approach one another

اسْتَدْنى v to ask to come near(er), to seek to bring close

دُنوّ n approach

دانٍ adj close; near; يَعْرِفُ القاصي والداني أَنّ ... everyone knows that ...

دَناية n meanness

دُنْيا n |دُنًى| earth; world; أَقامَ الدُنْيا وَلَمْ يُقْعِدْها to make a scene; الدُنْيا صَغيرةٌ it's a small world; أُمّ الدُنْيا Egypt

دُنْيَويّ, دُنْياويّ adj worldly; secular; profane; mundane; لَذّات دُنْيَويّة worldly pleasures

أَدْنى adj 1 [أَقَلّ] lower; lowest, least; minimum; حَرارة دُنْيا \ صُغْرى minimum temperature; أَدْنى جُهودٍ least effort; المُسْتَوى الأَدْنى the lowest point; الحَدّ الأَدْنى minimum; حَدّ أَدْنى من الحَدّ الأَدْنى للحاجيّاتِ the minimum needs; التَضامُنِ a minimum of solidarity; الحَدّ الأَدْنى للأُجورِ the minimum wage; من أَدْناهُ إلى أَقْصاهُ from high to low 2 [أَقْرَب] closer by; closest by; الشَرْق الأَدْنى the Near East 3 [أَسْفَل] lower; lowest; أَدْناهُ below, hereunder; المُوَقِّع أَدْناهُ the undersigned; يُذْكَرُ في الفِقْرةِ ٥ أَدْناهُ it is mentioned in paragraph 5 below

تَدَنٍّ n decline; decrease

مُتَدَنٍّ adj low

‹ دِنيم n denim

‹ دَهْر n |دُهور, أَدْهُر| era, age; eon; إلى آخِرِ \ أَبَدِ الدَهْرِ forever; لا ... أَبَدَ الدَهْرِ never ever; صُروف الدَهْرِ the vicissitudes of fate; أَتى عَلَيْهِ الدَهْرُ to pass away; أَكَلَ عَلَيْهِ الدَهْرُ وَشَرِبَ to be/become obsolete; انْتَظَرْتُ دَهْراً I waited for ages

دَهْرِيّ A adj worldly, secular, temporal
B n atheist; heretic

‹ دَهَسَ v |a; دَهْس| to run over; to trample; دَهَسَتْهُ سَيّارةٌ a car ran him over

‹ دَهِشَ v |a; دَهَش| to be amazed; to be astonished; to be surprised; دُهِشَ to be amazed

أَدْهَشَ v to amaze; to astonish; to surprise; to stun; أَدْهَشَهُ أَنّ it surprised him that; أَدْهَشَهُ الأَمْرُ the matter surprised him; لشَدّ ما أَدْهَشَها to her amazement; لا يُدْهِشُني هذا! I'm not a bit surprised!

انْدَهَشَ v to be amazed, to be astonished; to be surprised; to marvel, to wonder; انْدَهَشَ ل \ من شَيْءٍ to be amazed by sth

دَهِش adj amazed; astonished; surprised

دَهْشة n bewilderment; amazement; astonishment; أَثارَ الدَهْشةَ to cause a stir; مُثير للدَهْشةِ amazing; عَقَلَت الدَهْشةُ لِسانَهُ to be flabbergasted; عَبَّرَ عن دَهْشَتِهِ إزاءَ to express one's amazement at

انْدِهاش n amazement; astonishment; surprise; أَثارَ الانْدِهاشَ to cause astonishment; انْدِهاش من سَيْرِ الأُمورِ amazement at what has happened

مُدْهِش adj amazing; astonishing; sensational, spectacular; cool (infml); ازْدِحام مُدْهِش a spectacular crowd; اكْتِشاف مُدْهِش an amazing discovery; تَطَوُّر \ إعْلان مُدْهِش a sensational development/disclosure; قَرار مُدْهِش a startling decision;

دُهْن *n* |دُهْنات ,دِهان ,دُهون ,أَدْهان| fat; grease; دُهون سائِلة \ نَباتِيّة \ حَيَوانِيّة liquid/vegetable/animal fats; نِسْبة الدُهْنِ fat percentage; شَفْطَ الدُهونَ liposuction

دَهّان *n* house painter

دِهان *n* |أَدْهِنة ,دِهانات| 1 [طِلاء] paint; فُرْشاة دِهانٍ paint brush; مَدَّ الدِهانَ to paint; بَخّاخ الدِهانِ spray (painting); دِهان لَمّاع gloss paint 2 [مَرْهَم] cream; balm

دُهْنِيّ *adj* fatty; greasy; oily; شَعْر دُهْنِيّ greasy hair

دَهينة *n* cream

مُداهِن A *n* flatterer
B *adj* flattering; oily, slimy

مُداهَنة *n* flattery; cajolery, sweet-talk

مُدْهِن *adj* oily, fatty, greasy

مَدْهون *adj* painted; غَيْر مَدْهونٍ unpainted; خَشَب غَيْر مَدْهونٍ unpainted wood

دَهْوَرَ *v* |i| |دَهْوَرة| to take down; to tear down; دَهْوَرَ حائطاً to tear down a wall

تَدَهْوَرَ *v* 1 [انْحَدَرَ] to decline; to deteriorate; to decay; تَدَهْوَرَت الظُروف conditions deteriorated; تَتَدَهْوَرُ حالَتُهُ الصِحِّيَّةُ his health is deteriorating; تَدَهْوَرَت التِجارةُ trade has declined sharply 2 [سَقَطَ] to fall; تَدَهْوَرَت الصَخْرةُ من أَعْلى الجَبَلِ the rock fell from the top of the mountain

تَدَهْوُر *n* decline; deterioration; decay; decadence; تَدَهْوُر التِجارةِ the deterioration of trade; تَدَهْوُر الأَوْضاعِ الاقْتِصادِيّةِ an economic downturn; تَدَهْوُر المُجْتَمَعِ degeneration of society; تَدَهْوُر الأَخْلاقِ degeneration of morals; تَدَهْوُر فِكْرِيّ intellectual decay; الازْدِهار والتَدَهْوُر flourish and decay

مُتَدَهْوِر *n* decadent; deteriorated; اقْتِصاد مُتَدَهْوِر ailing economy; مُتَدَهْوِراً deteriorating

دُهوك *n* |dipt f| Dohuk (*city in northern Iraq*)

دَهى *v* |a; دَهْو ,دَهْي| to happen to; to befall; ما دَهاكَ؟ what happened to you?

دَهِيَ *v* |a; دَهاء| to be smart

داهٍ *adj* |دُهاة| smart; clever

داهِية A *adj* |mf; دَواهٍ| smart, clever; cunning, resourceful; sly, shrewd, crafty; إِنَّهُ رَجُلٌ داهِيةٌ he's a shrewd man

سُرْعة مُدْهِشة dizzying speed; بِطَريقةٍ مُدْهِشةٍ miraculously; كانَت النَتيجةُ مُدْهِشةً the result was astonishing

مَدْهوش *adj* startled; amazed; surprised; نَظَر \ رَدَّ مَدْهوشاً a surprised look/reaction

مُنْدَهِش *adj* amazed; astonished; surprised, taken aback; confused, perplexed; كانَ مُنْدَهِشاً من شَيْءٍ he was surprised by sth

دِهْقان *n* |دَهاقِنة ,دَهاقينُ| man of importance; leading personality

دَهَكَ *v* |a; دَهْك| to grind; to crush

دِهْليز *n* |دَهاليزُ| vestibule; hall; corridor; gallery; lobby

دَهَمَ ,دَهِمَ *v* |a; دَهْم| 1 [هاجَمَ] to raid; دَهَمَت الشُرْطةُ المَنْزِلَ the police raided the house 2 [فاجَأَ] to surprise; to take by surprise; دَهَمَهُ الأَمْرُ the matter surprised him

داهَمَ *v* 1 [هاجَمَ] to raid; to attack; to storm; داهَمَ المَدينة to attack the city; داهَمَت الشُرْطةُ البَيْتَ the police raided the house 2 [فاجَأَ] surprise; to take by surprise; داهَمَهُ النَوْمُ \ المَطَرُ to be overtaken by sleep/rain

ادْهَمَّ *v* to be/become black

دَهْم *n* raid

دَهْماء *n* |dipt f| plebs, rabble

أَدْهَم *adj* |dipt; دُهْم ,دَهْماء| black; pitch-black; الدَهْماء the masses, common folk

مُداهِم *n* attacker; robber

مُداهَمة *n* raid; attack

دَهَنَ *v* |u; دَهْن| 1 [طَلى] to paint; to dye; دَهَنَ من قارورةٍ فارِغةٍ to make empty promises; دَهَنَ شَعْرَهُ to dye one's hair 2 [دَلَكَ] to lubricate, to oil, to grease; to smear; دَهَنَ الخُبْزَ بالزُبْدة to butter a slice of bread; دَهَنَ الجِلْدَ بالمَرْهَمِ to apply cream to the skin

داهَنَ *v* to flatter; to cajole, to sweet-talk; داهَنَ شَخْصاً to flatter sb

أَدْهَنَ *v* to flatter; to cajole, to sweet-talk

تَدَهَّنَ *v* to be oiled, to be greased

دَهْن *n* 1 [زَيْت] spreading; قابِل للدَهْنِ spreadable 2 [طَلْي] painting

B *n* |دَواهٍ| **1** [شَخْص] a shrewd person **2** [مُصيبة] disaster; misfortune; دَواهي الدَهْرِ life's adversities; تحت السَواهي دَواهٍ still waters run deep

دَهاء *n* cunning, guile, slyness; ingenuity, astuteness; craftiness, resourcefulness; أَظْهَرَ \ تَطَلَّبَ دَهاءً كَبيراً to demonstrate/require great resourcefulness

دو *n* doh (*the first and eighth note of a major scale*)

داء *n* |أَدْواء| disorder; disease; illness; داء عَياء an incurable disease; داء وِراثيّ a hereditary disorder; داء خَبيث a nasty disease; عانى من داءٍ to suffer from a disease; لِكُلِّ داءٍ دَواءٌ *there's a solution for everything*

دُوَيْبّة *n* see دبب

دوبارة *n* |دوبار| rope; cord; thread

دوبْلير *n* stunt double, stand-in

انْداحَ *v* to spread

دَوْحة *n* lofty tree

الدَوْحة *n* Doha (*capital of Qatar*)

داخَ *v* |u; دَوْخ| **1** [أُصيبَ بدُوارٍ] to be/become dizzy; to be/become drowsy; to feel faint, to feel ill/nauseous; بَحَثَ عن شَيْءٍ حتّى داخَ رَأْسُهُ to hunt high and low for sth; داخَ سَبْعَ دَوْخاتٍ to completely lose one's mind **2** [خَضَعَ] to obey; داخَ البَعيرُ the camel obeyed

دَوَّخَ *v* to make dizzy; to make drowsy; to make ill/nauseous; دَوَّخَ الأَلَمُ رَأْسَهُ the pain made him dizzy; رائِحَتُهُ دَوَّخَتْني its smell made me nauseous

دائِخ *adj* dizzy, giddy, light-headed; drowsy; انْبَطَحَ دائِخاً على الأَرْضِ he lay on the floor dazed

دَوْخة *n* dizziness; vertigo; أُصيبَ بالدَوْخةِ to become dazed; داخَ سَبْعَ دَوْخاتٍ to completely lose one's mind

تَدْويخ *n* to transfix, to spellbound; to befuddle

مُدَوِّخ *adj* dizzying; entrancing

دود *n coll* |ديدان| worm; caterpillar; maggot; دودة الأَرْضِ earthworm; دودة شَريطيّة roundworm, ascarid; دودة القَرْعِ tapeworm; دودة العَلَق leech; دودة الفَراشةِ caterpillar; دودة القَزِّ silkworm

دارَ *v* |u; دَوَران, دَوْر| **1** [دَوَّمَ] to turn; to rotate; to spin; to revolve; to circle; دارَ رَأْسُهُ his head was spinning; دارَ حول مِحْوَرٍ to revolve around an axis; دارَ في مَدارِهِ to revolve in its orbit; دارَ حول الأَرْضِ to circle the globe; دارَ الخَبَرُ على الأَفْواهِ word was spreading; يَدورُ المُحَرِّكُ the engine is running; تَدورُ العَجَلاتُ \ عَقارِبُ الساعةِ the wheels/hands of the clock are turning; دُرْ يَميناً turn right **2** [حول مَوْضوع] concerning; يَدورُ كُلُّ شَيْءٍ حول عَمَلِهِ everything revolves around his work

دَوَّرَ *v* **1** [جَعَلَ مُدَوَّراً] to round; دَوَّرَ الزَوايا to round the corners **2** [الآلَةَ] to propel; to start, to turn on; دَوَّرَ جِهازاً to turn on a device

داوَرَ *v* to try to deceive; ناوَرَ وَداوَرَ to wriggle every which way

أَدارَ *v* **1** [قَلَبَ] to turn (around); to turn over; to twist; أَدارَ سَيّارةً to turn a car around; أَدارَ المِفْتاحَ في القُفْلِ to turn the key in the lock; أَدارَ كُرْسِيًّا to turn a chair around; أَدارَ العِمامةَ حول رَأْسِه to wrap the turban around one's head; أَدارَ نَفْسَهُ على أَدارَ ظَهْرَهُ لِشَخْصٍ to turn one's back on sb; أَدارَ بِوَجْهِه عن الجانِبِ الآخَرِ to roll to one's other side; شَخْصٍ \ شَيْءٍ to turn away from sb/sth **2** [جِهازاً] to turn on, to start (up); to operate; to steer; أَدارَ المُحَرِّكَ to start the engine; يُديرُ المُحَرِّكُ العَجَلاتِ الأَماميّةَ the engine propels the front wheels **3** [تَوَلّى الإدارةَ] to direct; to control; to manage; to lead; أَدارَ شَيْئاً to be in charge of sth; أَدارَ مَشْروعاً to manage a project; أَدارَ شَرِكةً to run a company; أَدارَ مَتْجَراً to run a business; أَدارَ جَمْعِيّةً \ نادِياً to be on the board of an association; أَدارَ الأُمورَ الماليّةَ to hold the purse strings **4** [الشَكْلَ] to round (off) (*a shape*)

تَدَوَّرَ *v* to be/become round

اسْتَدارَ *v* **1** [الْتَفَتَ] to invert; to turn around; تَسْتَديرُ الرِياحُ the winds are changing; اسْتَدارَ نحو شَخْصٍ to turn towards sb **2** [كانَ مُدَوَّراً] to be/become round; to round; اسْتَدارَ الطَريقُ the road ran in a circle

دَوْر *n* |أَدْوار| **1** (Sport) round; دَوْر رُبْع نِهائيٍّ quarter-final; الدَوْر قبل \ نِصْف النِهائيّ semi-final; دَوْر نِهائيّ final; يَصْعَدُ إلى الدَوْرِ النِهائيِّ he is through to the final **2** (Theat, Cin) role;

دَوْر في فيلْمٍ a role in a movie; دَوْر نِسائيّ a woman's role; دَوْر مُزْدَوِج a dual role; دَوْر ثانَويّ a supporting role; لَعِبَ \ مَثَّلَ دَوْراً to play a role ❸ [طابَق] floor, storey; في الدَوْرِ الخامِسِ on the fifth floor ❹ (Astron) cycle ❺ [نَوْبة] turn; بالدَوْرِ, بِدَوْرِهِ in turn; جاءَ دَوْرُهُ it's his turn; جاءَ دَوْرُهُ ل \ في it's his turn to; أَخَذَ دَوْرَهُ في الصَفِّ to take one's place in the queue; سَبَقَ دَوْرَهُ to be out of turn; تَخَطّى دَوْرَهُ to push in (BrE), to cut (AmE); فاتَكَ الدَوْرُ your turn is over ❻ [في مَشْروعٍ] role; دَوْر رَئيسيّ main role; دَوْر المَرْأةِ \ الرَجُلِ the woman's/man's role; قامَ بِدَوْرٍ to fulfil a role; لَعِبَ دَوْراً مُهِمًّا (في شَيْءٍ) to play an important role (in sth); لَعِبَ دَوْراً حاسِماً to play a decisive role

(Idiom) الدَوْر الأَوَّل *the first round of (school) exams*

دائِر *adj* ❶ [جارٍ] in process, ongoing; happening; جَدَل دائِر controversy, debate; الصِراع الدائِر the ongoing conflict ❷ [دَوّار] running, working, in operation (*machines, etc.*)

دائِرة *n* |دَوائِرُ| ❶ (Geom) circle; round; دائِرة قُطْبيّة polar circle ❷ [حَلْقة] circle; circuit; في دائِرةٍ in a circle; round; دائِرة كَهْرَبائيّة electric circuit; دائِرة مُفْرَغة a vicious cycle; دَوائِر سِياسيّة political circles; دائِرة المُنْتَصِفِ \ الوَسَطِ centre circle; دائِرة المَعارِفِ encyclopedia ❸ [مِنْطَقة] area; district; دائِرة انْتِخابيّة constituency; دائِرة عَمَلٍ; دائِرة قَضائيّة area; دائِرة الاخْتِصاصِ jurisdiction; في \ داخِلَ دائِرةِ اخْتِصاصِ المَحْكَمةِ الابْتِدائيّةِ within the jurisdiction of the district court ❹ [مَقَرّ] office, bureau; station; department; authority; دائِرة رَسْميّة an official authority; الدَوائِر العُلْيا the higher authorities; دائِرة الشُرْطةِ police headquarters

دائِريّ *adj* round; circular; دائِريًّا, بِشَكْلٍ دائِريٍّ in a circle; round; طَريق دائِريّ ring road (BrE), beltway (AmE)

دار *n* |f; دور, دِيار, دِيارات, دِيَرة| house, home; shelter; building; دار العَدالةِ court building; دار الآثارِ museum; دار الأَيْتامِ orphanage; دار لِلمُعَوَّقينَ عَقْليًّا home for the mentally disabled; دار الإسْلامِ the abode of Islam; دار الحَرْبِ the abode of war (*outside the Muslim territories*); الدِيار المُقَدَّسة the holy places; الدار الآخِرة, دار الباقِيةِ \ القَرارِ the afterlife; دار الخُلْدِ the eternal abode; دار الكُتُبِ library; Dar al-Kutub (*well known publishing house in Egypt*); دار السينَما cinema (BrE), movie theater (AmE); دور اللَهْوِ places of entertainment; عَوْدة اللاجِئينَ إلى دِيارِهِمْ the return of the refugees to their country; في عُقْرِ دارِهِ in one's own home

دارة *n* ❶ [فيلّا] villa ❷ (Elec) circuit; دارة كَهْرَبائيّة circuit; دارة مُغْلَقة \ قَصيرة a short circuit; قاطِع الدارةِ time switch ❸ (Astron) halo; aureole

دَوّار **A** *n* |دَوّارات| ❶ [مَسْكَن كَبير] mansion ❷ (Transp) roundabout ❸ [مَلْهًى] carousel; merry-go-round **B** *adj* wandering, roaming, circulating; بائِع دَوّار roaming street vendor; كُرْسيّ دَوّار swivel chair; باب دَوّار revolving door

دُوار *n* vertigo; dizziness; دُوار السَفَرِ \ التَسارُعِ motion sickness; دُوار البَحْرِ seasickness; دُوار الجَوِّ airsickness; مُصاب بِدُوارٍ giddy; dizzy; أُصيبَ بِدُوارٍ to be/become dizzy

دَوّارة *n* whirlpool; vortex; دَوّارة الهَواءِ weather vane

دَوَران *n* ❶ [اِلْتِفاف] rotation; revolution; tour; turn; turning; الدَوَران في نَفْسِ الحَلْقةِ going around in circles; قابِل لِلدَوَرانِ revolving; بِدونِ لَفٍّ وَدَوَرانٍ without much ado ❷ [الهَواءِ، الدَمِ ...] circulation; دَوَران الدَمِ blood circulation; الدَوَران الأَكْبَر \ العامّ systemic circulation; الدَوَران الأَصْغَر pulmonary circulation; دَوَران الهَواءِ atmospheric circulation ❸ (Astron) orbit ❹ (Dance) pirouette

دَوَرانيّ *adj* rotational, rotary, circular; حَفْر دَوَرانيّ rotary drilling

دَوْرة *n* ❶ [لَفّة] rotation; revolution; turning; tour; دَوْرة حول الأَرْضِ orbiting the earth; مِقْياس دَوْراتٍ tachometer; ٩٠ دَوْرةً في الدَقيقةِ 90 rpm ❷ [الفُصولِ، الحَياةِ..] cycle; دَوْرة دَمَويّة blood circulation; الدَوْرة الشَهْريّة monthly cycle; menstruation, menstrual cycle; دَوْرة مُنْتَظِمة a regular cycle; دَوْرة المِياهِ toilet (BrE), bathroom (AmE), restroom (AmE) ❸ [حَلْقة] episode ❹ [سِلْسِلة من العَمَليّاتِ أو الحَوادِثِ] cycle; round; دَوْرة دِراسيّة \ تَعْليميّة a course; دَوْرة تَدْريبيّة training; internship; أَجْرى دَوْرةً تَدْريبيّةً to do an internship; دَوْرة انْتِخابيّة election round; دَوْرة تَشْريعيّة legislative session; دَوْرة مُشاوَراتٍ a round of talks ❺ (Sport) round; الدَوْرة الأولى \ النِهائيّة the first/final round ❻ (Transp) roundabout an administrative matter; وَثائِق إدارِيّة official documents; قانون إداريّ administrative law; قَضاء إداريّ administrative justice; عَمَل إداريّ administrative work; paperwork; مَكْتَب إداريّ قِسم إداريّ department of administration; administrative office

اسْتِدارة *n* roundness

تَدْوير *n* turning; rotation; recycling; أَعادَ التَّدْوير to recycle

مَدار *n* |مَدارات| ◀1 [مِحْوَر] axis; pivot; centre; مَدار اهْتِمامٍ the centre of attention; issue; مَدار خِلافٍ dispute; مَدار النِّقاشِ the subject of debate; على مَدارِ السَنة all year round; عَمِلَ على مَدارِ الساعةِ على مَدارِ الساعةِ around the clock; to work 24 hours a day ◀2 (Geog) tropic; مَدار السَرَطانِ Tropic of Cancer; مَدار الجَدْيِ Tropic of Capricorn ◀3 (Astron) orbit; مَدار فَضائيّ an orbit in space; في مَدارٍ حول الأَرْضِ in orbit around the world

مَداريّ *adj* ◀1 (Geog) tropical; equatorial ◀2 (Aerosp) orbital; مَحَطّة مَداريّة orbital station

مُدَوَّر *adj* round; circular; نافِذة \ مائِدة مُدَوَّرة a round window/table; الأَرْضُ مُدَوَّرةٌ the earth is round

مُدير *n* director, chief; manager; boss; مُدير عامّ director general; CEO; نائِب مُديرٍ deputy director; نائِب مُديرِ شَرِكةٍ deputy director of a company; مُدير شَرِكةٍ \ مَعْهَدٍ \ مُسْتَشْفى director of a company/institute/hospital; مُدير مَدْرَسةٍ (school) principal; مُدير مَوْقِعٍ webmaster

مُديريّة *n* ◀1 [قِسم إداريّ] directorate; department; مُديريّة عامّة directorate general ◀2 [إقْليم] (Egypt) district; province ◀3 [مَنْصِب المُدير] directorate; leadership

مُسْتَدير *adj* round; circular; نافِذة \ مائِدة مُسْتَديرة a round window/table

مُسْتَديرة *n* (Mus) whole note

‹ **دَوْرَق** *n* |دَوارِقُ| (laboratory) flask; jug, decanter

‹ **دَوْزَنَ** *v* |i; |دَوْزَنة| (Mus) to tune; to set; دَوْزَنَ العودَ \ القيثارةَ to tune the oud/guitar

مُدَوْزِن *n* (Mus) tuner

‹ **داسَ** *v* |u; |دَوْس| ◀1 [وَطِئَ] to step, to tread; to trample; داسَ شَيْئاً بالأَقْدامِ to trample sth underfoot; داسَ على القانونِ

دَوْرِيّ A *adj* periodic; regular; cyclic; عَمَلِيّة دَوْرِيّة a cyclical process; إعانات دَوْرِيّة a regular payment; اجْتِماع دَوْرِيّ a regular meeting; مُراجَعة دَوْرِيّة periodic monitoring; بِشَكْلٍ \ بِصِفةٍ دَوْرِيٍّ(ة) regularly; الجَدْوَل الدَوْرِيّ للعَناصِرِ الكيمْيائيّةِ Periodic Table of the Elements; مَجَلّة دَوْرِيّة journal; periodical; magazine; نَشْرة دَوْرِيّة newsletter; periodical
B *n* (Sport) competition; شارَكَ في الدَوْرِيِّ to participate in a competition; رَبِحَ الدَوْرِيَّ to win a sports competition; بَطَل الدَوْرِيِّ national champion

دَوْرِيّة *n* ◀1 (Mil) patrol; round; security; دَوْرِيّة عَسْكَرِيّة military patrol; زَوْرَق الدَوْرِيّة patrol boat; سَيّارة الدَوْرِيّة patrol car; قامَ بِدَوْرِيّةٍ to patrol ◀2 [مَجَلّة] periodical

دَيّار *n* monk; friar

دَيْر *n* |أَدْيار, أَدْيِرة, دُيورة| (Chr) monastery; abbey; convent; دَخَلَ الدَيْرَ to enter the monastery; دَيْر للراهِباتِ convent, nunnery

دَيْر الزور *n* |f| Deir ez-Zor (*city in Syria*)

دَيْرانيّ A *n* abbot
B *adj* monastic

إدارة *n* ◀1 [رِئاسة شَرِكةٍ أو مُؤَسَّسةٍ] administration; management; control; direction; the running of; إدارة شَرِكةٍ company management; إدارة أَعْمالٍ management; إدارة البَياناتِ data management; إدارة جامِعةٍ the administration of a university; إدارة الحُقوقِ الرَقْمِيّة digital rights management, DRM; مَجْلِس إدارةِ مُسْتَشْفًى the board of a hospital; رَئيس الإدارةِ head of administration; رَئيس مَجْلِسِ الإدارة managing director; عِلْم الإدارةِ public administration (*academic discipline*); عِلْم إدارةِ الأَعْمالِ business administration; سوء الإدارةِ mismanagement; سوء إدارةِ الأَمْوالِ financial mismanagement; أَساءَ الإدارةَ to mismanage; تَوَلّى الإدارةَ to take over management ◀2 [قِسْم أو هَيْئة] service; department; administration; إدارة حُكوميّة government administration; عَمِلَ \ اشْتَغَلَ في الإدارة to work in the administration

إداريّ *adj* administrative; managerial; official; إجْراءات إداريّة administrative procedures; الجِهاز الإداريّ administrative apparatus; التَّنْظيم \ النِظام الإداريّ organisational structure; على مُسْتَوًى إداريٍّ on an administrative level; أَمْر إداريّ

to ride roughshod over the law ◀2 [دَهَسَ] to run over; داسَتْهُ سَيّارةٌ he was run over by a car ◀3 [دَرَسَ] to thresh

دَوّاسة *n* pedal; دَوّاسة البَنْزِين accelerator, gas (pedal); \ داسَ ضَغَطَ على دَوّاسةِ الوَقودِ to hit the accelerator, to step on the gas (AmE); رَفَعَ قَدَمَهُ عن دَوّاسةِ الوَقودِ to release the accelerator, to let off the gas (AmE)

ديسة *n* jungle, forest

مَداس *n* ◀1 [حِذاء] pair of shoes ◀2 [عَجَلة] (tyre) tread

‹ **دوسَنْطاريا**, **دوسانْتاريا** *n* dysentery

‹ **دوش** *n* shower

‹ **دوطة** *n* dowry

‹ **دافَ** *v* |u; دَوْف| to blend; to mix (in)

‹ **دوق** *n* duke

دوقة *n* duchess

‹ **دالَ** *v* |u; دَوْلة| to change, to turn; to take turns, to alternate; to alternate; دالَتْ لَهُ الدَوْلةُ fortune has turned in his favour; هذا دالَتْ عَلَيْهِ الدَوْلةُ \ دَوْلَتُهُ this meant the end for him

دَوَّلَ *v* to internationalize

داوَلَ *v* ◀1 [تَناوَبَ] to discuss; to deliberate ◀2 [نالَ] to alternate; to rotate

أدالَ *v* to circulate

تَداوَلَ *v* ◀1 [تَناوَبَ] to alternate; to take turns; to exchange; تَداوَلَتْهُ الأَلْسُنُ it passed from hand to hand; تَداوَلَتْهُ الأَيْدي it was the talk of the town ◀2 [تَشاوَرَ] to deliberate; to discuss; to confer; تَداوَلَ في شَيْءٍ to discuss sth ◀3 [اِنْتَشَرَ] to circulate; to go about; to spread

دَوالَيْكَ *adv* alternately, by turns; successively, one after the other; وَهكَذا دَوالَيْكَ and so on, and so forth; فَعَلْنا ذلك دَوالَيْكَ we did that time and again

دَوْلة *n* |دُوَل| ◀1 [بَلَد] state; country; power; empire; \ دَوْلة عُظْمى كُبْرى superpower; great power; دَوْلة مُوَحَّدة a unified country; دَوْلة مُضيفة host country; دَوْلة مانِحة donor country; دَوْلة نامِية developing country; دَوْلة من دُوَلِ العالَمِ الثالِثِ one of the Third World countries; دَوْلة بوليسيّة police state; دَوْلة مُحاذِية \ مُجاوِرة neighbouring country; دَوْلة تابِعة satellite state; dependency; دَوْلة المَمْلَكة المُتَّحِدة the state of the United Kingdom; دُوَل عَدَمِ الانْحِياز Non-Aligned Countries; الدُوَل الأَعْضاء في الاتِّحاد الأوروبّيّ member state; دَوْلة عُضْو member states of the EU; جامِعة الدُوَلِ العَرَبِيّة the League of Arab States; مَجْلِس الدَوْلةِ the Council of State; وَزير الدَوْلة prime minister; رَجُل دَوْلةٍ statesman; نِظام دَوْلةٍ polity, form of government; شَأْن من شُؤونِ الدَوْلةِ state affair; حُدود الدَوْلة state border; خارِجَ حُدودِ الدَوْلةِ across the state border; من قِبَلِ الدَوْلةِ state- ◀2 (Hist) dynasty; الدَوْلة الأُمَويّة the dynasty of the Umayyads ◀3 [مَصْدَر دالَ] alternating; هذا دالَتْ عَلَيْهِ الدَوْلةُ \ دَوْلَتُهُ this meant the end for him

دَوْليّ *adj* state (*before n*); international

دُوَليّ A *adj* international; القانون الدُوَليّ international law; المُجْتَمَع الدُوَليّ an international tribunal; مَحْكَمة دُوَليّة the international community; مُنَظَّمة دُوَليّة an international organisation

B *n* international (*player*)

تَداوُل *n* ◀1 [اِنْتِشار] circulation; dissemination; spreading; prevalence; عَرَضَ شَيْئاً للتَداوُلِ to bring sth into circulation; سَحَبَ شَيْئاً من التَداوُلِ to take sth out of circulation; سُرْعة التَداوُلِ velocity of circulation; تَداوُل طَرِيقةٍ the prevalence of a method ◀2 [تَشاوُر] consultation; deliberation; counsel; القَضِيّةُ قَيْدَ التَداوُلِ the matter is still under consideration ◀3 [تَناوُب] alternation; تَداوُل السُلْطةِ (democratic) handover of power

تَداوُليّ *adj* alternating

تَداوُليّة *n* (Ling) pragmatics

تَدْويل *n* internationalization

مُتَداوَل *adj* prevailing; current; قِياس مُتَداوَل common size; عُمْلة مُتَداوَلة currency; وَسيلة دَفْعٍ مُتَداوَلة legal tender

مُداوَلة *n* deliberation; consultation; discussion; قاعة المُداوَلةِ deliberation room; غُرْفة المُداوَلةِ chamber; رُفِعَت الجَلْسةُ للمُداوَلةِ the session was adjourned for consultation

‹ **دولاب** *n* |دَواليبُ| ◀1 [خِزانة] closet; cupboard ◀2 [عَجَلة] wheel; disc; دولاب الهَواءِ Ferris wheel ◀3 [آلة] gear

‹ **دولار** *n* |دولارات| dollar

‹ **دولْفين** *n* see دلفين

دامَ *v* |u; دَوْم, دَوام| **1** [اِسْتَغْرَقَ] to last, to continue; دامَ شَهْراً to last a month; ما دامَ as long as; since, because; while he is ...; ما دامَت الأَدِلّةُ القاطِعةُ غائِبَةً as long as there's no conclusive evidence; سَأَكْتُبُ ما دُمْتُ حَيًّا I will write for as long as I live **2** [اِسْتَمَرَّ] to go on, to endure, to persist; دامَ على شَيْءٍ to go on doing sth

دَوَّمَ *v* to turn, to spin, to circle; يُدَوِّمُ الماءُ the water was whirling

داوَمَ *v* to persevere, to persist, to sustain, to carry on; داوَمَ على المُراسَلةِ to maintain a regular correspondence; نُداوِمُ على تَنْفيذِ المَشْروعِ we are persistently implementing the project

أَدامَ *v* to cause to last/continue, to perpetuate, to make (sth) permanent

اسْتَدامَ *v* to sustain, to make (sth) last/continue; to continue, to go on; اسْتَدامَ اللِقاءُ ساعاتٍ the meeting went on for hours

دَوْم *n* **1** [مَصْدَر] continuance, duration; دَوْماً constantly, always **2** (Bot) doum palm (*Hyphaene thebaica*)

دائِم *adj* lasting, enduring; continuous; durable; دائِماً! may God's blessing persist (*said by a guest after a meal or drink*); دائِماً always, forever; إقامة دائِمة permanent residence; شِفاء \ حَلّ دائِم a durable recovery/solution; إطار دائِم a permanent framework; دائِماً وَأَبداً always and forever; نَقْص \ عَجْز دائِم (في شَيْءٍ) chronic lack/deficit (of sth); هو يَزورُنا دائِماً he always visits us; أَشْجار دائِمة الخُضْرةِ evergreen trees; بِصِفةٍ دائِمةٍ \ بِشَكْلٍ دائِمٍ lasting, permanent; forever

دائِميّ *adj* permanent

دَوام *n* **1** [مُدّة] duration; working hours, office hours; دوام كامِل full-time; عَمَلَ بِدَوامٍ كامِلٍ to work full-time; نِصْف دَوامٍ part-time; غَيَّرَ \ عَدَّلَ مَواعيدَ الدَوام to change/adjust working hours; مَواعيد \ أَوْقات \ ساعات الدَوامِ opening hours, working hours, business hours; دَوام مَسائيّ evening shift **2** [اِسْتِمْرار] durability, permanence, continuity; على الدَوامِ permanently, all the time, incessantly; لن يَكْتُبَ لَهُ الدَوامُ it will not last

دَوّامة, دُوّامة *n* **1** [دَوّارة] whirlpool; vortex; دَوّامة العُنْفِ a downward spiral of violence; عاشَ في دَوّامةٍ to be in turmoil **2** [لُعْبة] (spinning) top

ديمة *n* |دِيَم| constant rain

دَيْمومة *n* continuance; لن تَكونَ هُناكَ دَيْمومةٌ للعَلاقاتِ دون سَلامٍ شامِلٍ there will be no continuance of the relationships without comprehensive peace

إدامة *n* perpetuation

اسْتِدامة *n* sustainability

تَدْويم *n* whirling, spinning

مُداوِم **A** *adj* permanent, continuing **B** *n* hardy spirit

مُداوَمة *n* perseverance, endurance

مُسْتَدام *adj* sustainable; تَنْمِية مُسْتَدامة sustainable development

مُسْتَديم *adj* permanent, continuous; durable, sustainable; عاهة مُسْتَديمة permanent disability; تَنْمِية مُسْتَديمة sustainable development

جُمْهوريّة الدومِنيكان *n* the Dominican Republic

دومينو *n* dominoes; حَجَر دومينو a domino

دومينيكا *n* Dominica

دَوَّنَ *v* to record, to write down; to list; to register; (Comput) to blog; دَوَّنَ شَيْئاً to put something down in writing; دَوَّنَ قِصَصاً to write down stories; دَوَّنَ مُعْطَياتٍ في دَفْتَرٍ to jot down data in a notebook

تَدَوَّنَ *v* to be recorded, to be listed

ديوان *n* |دَواوين| **1** [مَقْعَد] divan **2** [مَكْتَب] office; bureau; الديوان المَلَكيّ the King's/Queen's Office; ديوان المُحاسَبة the audit bureau; لُغة الدَواوينِ officialese **3** [شِعْر] collection of poems, poetry book; جَمَعَ أَشْعاراً في ديوانٍ to collect poems for an anthology **4** (Mus) octave; ديوان أَعْلى \ أَدْنى an octave higher/lower

تَدْوين *n* recording, writing down; registration; تَدْوين موسيقيّ musical notation

تَدْوينة *n* (Comput) post

مُدَوِّن *n* blogger; مُدَوِّن إلِكْتْرونيّ blogger

مُدَوَّنة *n* **1** [مُلاحَظات مَكْتوبة] record, note **2** (Comput) weblog, blog; مُدَوَّنة إلِكْتْرونيّة weblog, blog **3** [مَجْموعة قَوانين] code, body of laws; مُدَوَّنة الأُسْرةِ family code; مُدَوَّنة الأَحْوالِ

دواء *n* |أَدْوِية| medicine, medication, drug; treatment; remedy; دَواء ناجِع an effective remedy; دَواء للرَبْو a treatment for asthma; آثار ثانَويّة \ جانِبيّة لِدَواءٍ side effects of a medication; أَخَذَ \ تَناوَلَ \ تَعاطى دَواءً to take medicine; عِلْم تَرْكيبِ الأَدْوِيَةِ pharmacology; وَصَفَ (لِشَخْصٍ) دَواءً \ أَدْوِيَةً to prescribe medication (for sb); دَواء ضِدّ ضَغْطِ الدَمِ المُرْتَفِعِ medication for high blood pressure; لِكُلِّ داءٍ دَواءٌ there's a solution for every problem

دَوائيّ *adj* medicinal; pharmaceutical; مُسْتَحْضَر دَوائيّ pharmaceuticals; عُلوم دَوائيّة pharmacology

دَواة *n* |دُوِيّ, دَوَيات| inkwell

تَداوٍ *n* (medical) treatment; سافَرَ إلى المَدينةِ لِغَرَضِ التَداوي to travel to the city for treatment

مُداوٍ *n* healer

مُداواة *n* treatment; therapy; medicine

مُدَوٍّ *adj* loud; thunderous; اِنْفِجار مُدَوٍّ a thunderous explosion

دِيار بَكْر *n* |f| Diyarbakir (*city in Turkey*)

دَيافْرام *n* (Tech) diaphragm

دِيالِكْتيكيّ *adj* dialectical

دِبْلوماسي see **دِبْلوماسيّ, دِبْلوماسيّة**

دِية *n* see **ودي**

دَيّوث *n* cuckold; pimp

دَيْدَن *n* custom, habit; من دَيْدَنِهِ أَنْ يَسْتَيْقِظَ مُبَكِّراً it is his habit to wake up early

ديزل *n* diesel; diesel fuel; مُحَرِّك ديزِل a diesel engine

ديسْك *n* (Comput) disk

ديسْكو *n* nightclub; disco

دَيْسَم *n* |دَياسِمُ| bear cub

ديسَمْبِر *n* (NA, Gulf) December

دي في دي *n* |دي في دِيات| DVD; جِهاز دي في دي DVD player

ديك *n* |أَدْياك, دُيوك, دِيَكة| rooster, cock; ديك روميّ \ هِنْديّ turkey; ديك سُلْطانيّ gallinule; وَزْن الديكِ (Sport) bantamweight; بَيْضة الديكِ ≈ hens' teeth (*a rare or impossible thing*); يَصيحُ الديكُ the rooster crows

ديكيّ *adj relating to roosters*; سُعال ديكيّ pertussis, whooping cough

الشَخْصيّة the Personal Status Code

دونَ *prep* ① [بِلا] without; apart from; بِدونِ without; excluding; دونَ شُروطٍ مُسَبَّقةٍ without preconditions; قَهْوة بِدونِ حَليبٍ coffee without milk; هذه خُطّةٌ بِدونِ مَبادِئَ this is a plan without principles; لا قوّةَ بِدونِ صَلاحيّاتٍ no authority without mandatory powers; يَعْمَلونَ بِدونِ تَرْخيصٍ they work without a permit; أُعْتُقِلَ من دونِ أَيّةِ إِجْراءاتٍ قانونيّةٍ he was arrested without any legal procedures; دونَ غَيْرِهِ exclusively; لِماذا اخْتارَ هذا المَجالَ دونَ غَيْرِهِ؟ why has he chosen this field over any other? ② [تَحْتَ] under, below; beyond; دونَ ١٢٠ كم \ ساعة below 120 km/h; هو دونَ العِشْرينَ he is not yet twenty; الأَطْفال دون الخامِسةِ children under five ③ [مانِع] حالَ دونَ to prevent; to hinder; حالَ دونَ قُدومِ شَخْصٍ to prevent sb from coming; أَرادَ أَنْ يَحْضُرَ الاجْتِماعَ غَيْرَ أَنّ مانِعاً شَخْصيًّا حالَ دونَ ذلك he wanted to attend the meeting, but something personal came up that prevented it ④ [دونَ أَنْ] من دونِ أَنْ, دونَ أَنْ without; من دونِ أَنْ يَعْنِيَ ذلك أَنّ ... without this meaning that ...; من دونِ أَنْ يَلْتَفِتَ without turning around; اِبْتَسَمَ المُحاضِرُ بِدونِ أَنْ يُجيبَ عن السُؤالِ the speaker smiled without answering the question

دونيّ *adj* inferior; وَضْع دونيّ inferior position; نَظْرة دونيّة dim view

دونيّة *n* inferiority; عُقْدة \ مُرَكَّب الدونيّةِ inferiority complex

دونُم *n* dunam (*square measure, roughly 900 square metres*)

دَوّى *v* ① [سُمِعَ] to sound, to ring, to chime; to resound, to reverberate, to echo; دَوّى الرَعْدُ thunder rumbled; دَوَّتِ الأَجْراسُ the bells rang; تُدَوّي هُتافاتٌ عالِيةٌ loud cheers are resounding ② [الطائِرُ] to hover

داوى *v* to treat; داوى الجَرْحى to treat injured people; داوى شَخْصاً من مَرَضٍ to treat sb for a disease

تَداوى *v* to receive treatment

دَوِيّ *n* strike, pound, thunder; sound, echo; دَوِيّ الرَعْدِ the rumbling of thunder; دَوِيّ الانْفِجارِ the blast of the explosion; دَوِيّ المَدافِعِ the rumbling of cannons; دَوِيّ الأَسْلِحةِ النارِيّةِ the rattling of machine guns

داية *n* ① [مُوَلِّدة] midwife ② [مُرْضِعة] wet nurse

ديكتاتور، ديكتاتوريّ، ديكتاتوريّة see **دكتاتور**

ديكودراما *n* docudrama

ديكور *n* |ديكورات| decor; stage setting; مُهَنْدِس \ مُصَمِّم ديكورٍ interior designer; set designer; تَغْيير ديكوراتٍ a change of decor

ديلاوير *n* |f| Delaware (*US state*)

دَيْلَزة *n* (Med) dialysis

ديماس *n* |دَياميسُ| catacomb

ديماغوجي، ديماجوجيّ، ديماغوجيّ **A** *adj* demagogic **B** *n* demagogue

ديماغوجيّة، ديماجوجْيا *n* demagoguery, demagogy

ديموغرافيّ، ديمُغْرافيّ *adj* demographical

ديموغرافيا *n* demographics

ديموقراطيّ، ديمُقْراطيّة see **دمقرط**

دانَ[1] *v* |i; دَيْن| **1** [كانَ مَديناً] to be indebted; دانَ بِشَيْءٍ لِشَخْصٍ to owe sb sth; دانَ لِشَخْصٍ بِحَياتِهِ to owe sb one's life **2** [اِعْتَقَدَ] see **دين 2**

دايَنَ *v* to lend

أَدانَ *v* **1** (Law) to condemn; to convict; أَدانَ شَخْصاً to convict sb; أَدانَ شَخْصاً بِتُهْمةِ الغِشِّ to convict sb on charges of fraud **2** [شَجَبَ] to condemn, to denounce; أَدانَ شَخْصاً \ شَيْئاً بِشِدّةٍ to strongly condemn sb/sth

تَدَيَّنَ *v* **1** [أَخَذَ دَيْناً] to get into debt, to be indebted **2** [اِعْتَقَدَ] see **دين 2**

تَدايَنَ *v* to contract a mutual loan, to borrow money from one another

اِسْتَدانَ *v* to borrow; to get into debt, to be indebted; اِسْتَدانَ مَبْلَغاً من المالِ to borrow a sum of money

دائِن **A** *n* creditor; رَصيد دائِن credit (balance); دائِن ومَدين creditor and debtor; credit and debit; حِساب الدائِن credit **B** *adj* indebted; owing

دَيْن *n* |دُيون| debt; دَيْن مُوَحَّد consolidated debt; دَيْن الدَّوْلةِ government debt; مِقْدار \ حَجْم الدُيونِ indebtedness; إعادة جَدْوَلةِ الدُيونِ debt restructuring; دُيون مَشْكوك في تَحْصيلِها bad debts; سَدَّدَ \ قَضى دَيْناً to pay/repay a debt; اشْتَرى شَيْئاً بالدَّيْنِ to buy sth on credit; لَهُ دَيْنٌ عَلَيْنا we are indebted to him; وَعْدُ المُؤْمِنِ الحُرِّ دَيْنٌ عَلَيْهِ once you make a promise, you must keep it

دَيْنونة *n* judgement; يَوْم الدَّيْنونةِ Judgement Day, Doomsday

إدانة *n* **1** (Law) conviction; حُكْم بالإدانةِ, قَرار الإدانةِ guilty verdict, conviction; المُتَّهَمُ بَريءٌ حتّى تَثْبُتَ إدانَتُهُ the accused is innocent until proven guilty **2** [شَجْب] condemnation; إدانة شَديدة اللَهْجةِ a sharp/strong condemnation

مُدان **A** *adj* condemned, convicted **B** *n* convict; أَعْدَمَ مُداناً to execute a convict; شَنَقَ مُداناً to hang a convict

مَدين **A** *adj* indebted; owing; رَصيد مَدين credit (balance); كانَ مَديناً لِشَخْصٍ بِمالٍ to be in sb's debt; كانَ مَديناً لِشَخْصٍ to owe sb money; أنا مَدينٌ لَكَ بِحَياتي I owe you my life **B** *n* debtor; دائِن ومَدين creditor and debtor; credit and debit

مَدْيون **A** *adj* indebted; owing; أَنْتَ مَدْيونٌ لي بِأَلْفِ دينارٍ you owe me one thousand dinar **B** *n* debtor

مَدْيونيّة *n* indebtedness; عِبْء المَدْيونيّةِ debt burden; مَدْيونيّة مِقْدارُها ١١ مِلْيار جُنَيْهٍ a debt burden of 11 billion pounds

دانَ[2] *v* |i; دين| **1** [اِعْتَنَقَ ديناً] to profess; دانَ بالإسْلامِ to profess Islam **2** [كانَ مَديناً] see **دين 1**

تَدَيَّنَ *v* **1** [اِعْتَقَدَ] to be a practicing believer; to believe; to profess **2** [أَخَذَ دَيْناً] see **دين 1**

دِيانة *n* religion; belief; faith; الدِيانة اليَهودِيّة \ المَسيحيّة \ الإسْلاميّة the Jewish/Christian/Islamic faith

دين *n* |أَدْيان| religion; belief; faith; الدين الإسْلاميّ \ المَسيحيّ the Islamic/Christian religion; أَدْيان سَماوِيّة monotheistic religions; رَجُل دينٍ cleric; عالِم دينٍ theologian; رِجال الدينِ the clergy; كُلِّيّة عُلوم الدينِ the theological faculty; يَوْم الدينِ the Day of Judgment; بَشَّرَ بِدينٍ to preach a religion; نَشَرَ ديناً to propagate a religion; مارَسَ شَعائِرَ الدينِ to profess a religion; تَمَسَّكَ بِدينِهِ to hold on to one's religion; تَخَلّى عن دينِهِ to renounce one's religion; اِرْتَدَّ عن دينِهِ to desert one's faith; اِعْتَنَقَ ديناً آخَرَ to adopt another religion; ناصَرَ ديناً to adhere to a religion; أَكْمَلَ نِصْفَ دينِهِ to get married

‹ دينار n |دَنانيرُ| dinar

ديناريّ n diamonds (*in playing cards*); واحِد \ اثْنان ديناريّ ace/two of diamonds

‹ دَيْناصور n |دَيْناصورات| dinosaur

‹ دينامو n dynamo

‹ ديناميّ adj dynamic; تَطَوُّر ديناميّ a dynamic development

ديناميّة n dynamics

‹ ديناميت n dynamite; إِصْبَع ديناميتٍ dynamite stick

‹ ديناميكا n dynamics; عِلْم الديناميكا الهَوائِيَّة aerodynamics

ديناميكيّ adj dynamic; إِنْسان ديناميكيّ a dynamic person

‹ دِيو كْسين n dioxin

دينيّ adj religious; spiritual; devout; denominational; أَعْياد \ أَغانٍ دينيّة religious feasts/songs; أَسْباب دينيّة religious reasons; مَوانِع \ تَقاليد دينيّة religious objections/traditions; عَقيدة \ تَيار دينيّ(ة) a religious creed/tendency; حِزْب دينيّ a religious party; طُقوس دينيّة religious rituals; ذَبَح حَسَبَ التَعاليمِ الدينيّةِ to slaughter according to religious teachings

تَدَيُّن n religiosity; devotion; piety; godliness

لادينيّ adj secular, non-religious, anti-religious

لادينيّة n secularism, non-religiousness, anti-religiousness

مُتَدَيِّن adj religious, devout, pious, practicing

‹ **ذا** *pron* ◄1 [لِذا [هذا therefore; consequently; بِذا thereby; كَذا see كَذا ◄2 [نَصْب كَلِمَةِ ذو] see ذو

ذَلِكَ *pron* |أولئِكَ; f تِلْكَ| ◄1 [نَعْت الإشارة] that; ذَلِكَ الرَجُلُ that man; ذَلِكَ البَيْتُ that house ◄2 [ضَمير الإشارة] that; مع ذَلِكَ still, yet; nevertheless, regardless, in spite of that; شيْء من ذَلِكَ sth similar, the like; على ذَلِكَ under that condition/those conditions; consequently; thus; على ذَلِكَ ف ... therefore; consequently; ذَلِكَ وَ ... furthermore; besides; فوق ذَلِكَ moreover, furthermore, besides that; عند ذَلِكَ then, at that time; وَما إلى ذَلِكَ and the like, and so on; بِذَلِكَ under that condition/those conditions; كَذَلِكَ see كَذَلِكَ; بعد ذَلِكَ subsequently, further; afterwards; furthermore; thereafter

كَذا *adv* ◄1 [هَكَذا] thus; so ◄2 [غَيْر مُحَدَّدٍ] so-and-so; such-and-such; كَذا وَكَذا \ كَيْتَ so-and-so; في الساعةِ كَذا at such-and-such a time; اشْتَرَيْتُهُ بِكَذا مِائةِ دولار I bought it for a few hundred dollars

كَذَلِكَ *adv* also, too, as well, besides; thus, so, in the same manner; likewise; exactly like, just as; equally; ditto, the same; أَلَيْسَ كَذَلِكَ؟ isn't it?, isn't that right?; أُحِبُّها وَهِيَ كَذَلِكَ I love her, and she loves me too; أَنْتَ كَذَلِكَ سَتَفْعَلُ ذلك you'll do that as well; ماذا تَفْعَلُ والحالُ كَذَلِكَ؟ what's to be done in this situation?; والأَمْرُ كَذَلِكَ that's how it is; إذا كانَت الأُمورُ كَذَلِكَ if that's the case

لِذَلِكَ *adv* therefore, so; consequently; because of this/that; hence; وَلِذَلِكَ ف ... therefore ...

لِهَذا *adv* consequently; because of this; for this reason; thus

هَذا *pron* |هَؤُلاءِ; f هَذِهِ; m du هَذانِ; f du هاتانِ| ◄1 [نَعْت الإشارة] this; هَذا الرَجُل this man ◄2 [ضَمير الإشارة] this; كيف حَدَثَ هَذا؟ how could this happen?; هَذا وَ ... furthermore, besides; بِهَذا through this; hereby; هَذا أو ذاكَ somebody or other; بِهَذا وَذاكَ consequently; يا هَذا! hey, you!

هَكَذا *adv* thus; so; in this/that way; just as; hence; وَهَكَذا كانَتْ حَياتي and so/thus was my life; هَكَذا يَخْدَعونَ الشَعْبَ so they deceive the people

‹ **ذِئْب** *n* |ذِئاب| wolf; يَعْوي الذِئْبُ the wolf is howling; ذِئْب في ثَوْبِ \ جِلْدِ حَمَلٍ a wolf in sheep's clothing; هو بَريءٌ بَراءة الذِئْبِ من دَمِ يوسُفَ he is completely innocent; عِنَب الذِئْبِ (Bot) black nightshade (*Solanum nigrum*)

ذُؤابة *n* |ذَوائِبُ| ◄1 [شَعْر] strand; tuft ◄2 [قِمّة] top

‹ **ذاكَ** *adv* إذّاكَ, إذْ ذاكَ then, at that time; مُذْ ذاكَ since then

‹ **ذال** *n name of the letter* ذ

‹ **ذَبَّ** *v* |u; ذَبّ| ◄1 [طَرَدَ] to chase away; to drive off ◄2 [دافَعَ] to defend; ذَبَّ عن شَخْصٍ to defend sb

ذُباب *n coll* |ذِبّان| (Zool) fly; ذُباب الفَواكِهِ fruit fly; وَزْن الذُبابة (Sport) flyweight

(Idiom) ذُبابة سَيْفٍ the tip of a sword

‹ **ذَبَحَ** *v* |a; ذَبْح| to slaughter, to butcher; to cut sb's/sth's throat; to massacre; ذَبَحَ بَقَرةً to slaughter a cow; ذَبَحَ شَخْصاً to slay sb

ذَبَّحَ *v* to slaughter, to butcher

تَذابَحَ *v* to slaughter one another

ذَبْح *n* slaughter; slaughtering, butchering; ذَبْح حَلال halal butchering

ذِبْح *n* sacrifice, sacrificial animal

ذُبْحة, ذِبْحة *n* (Med) angina; ذُبْحة صَدْرِيّة angina pectoris

ذَبيح *adj* |ذَبْحى| slaughtered; كَبْش ذَبيح a slaughtered sheep; *a sheep suitable for slaughter*

ذَبيحة n |ذَبائِح| sacrifice; sacrificial animal; تَقْديم الذَّبيحةِ to make a sacrifice; قَدَّمَ خروفاً ذَبيحةً لله to sacrifice a sheep to God; فَضَلات الذَّبيحةِ offal

مَذْبَح n |مَذابِح| **1** [مَسْلَخ] slaughterhouse; abattoir **2** (Chr) altar

مَذْبَحة n |مَذابِح| massacre; slaughter, butchery; carnage; نَفَذَ \ ارْتَكَبَ مَذْبَحةً to commit a massacre; مَذْبَحة جَماعيّة mass murder; سيقَ إلى المَذْبَحةِ to be led to the slaughter

مَذْبوح adj slaughtered; slain

ذَبْذَبَ v |i; ذَبْذَبة| **1** [حَرَّكَ] to set in swinging motion **2** [تَرَكَهُ مُتَرَدِّداً] to make sb hesitate

تَذَبْذَبَ v **1** [تَحَرَّكَ] to fluctuate; to go up and down; to vibrate; تَتَذَبْذَبَ الأَسْعارُ the prices fluctuate; تَذَبْذَبَ في وَلائِهِ لِشَخْصٍ to have a wavering loyalty to sb **2** [تَرَدَّدَ] to hesitate; to waver; to be in doubt

ذَبْذَبة n vibration, oscillation; frequency; ذَبْذَبة ٥٠ ميغاهيرْتْز a frequency of 50 megahertz; ذَبْذَبات فوق صَوْتيّةٍ ultrasonic frequencies; ذَبْذَبات عالية \ مُنْخَفِضة high/low frequencies

تَذَبْذُب n fluctuation; vibration

مُتَذَبْذِب adj vibrating, wobbling; vacillating, fluctuating, changing; رَجُل مُتَذَبْذِب الآراءِ \ المِزاجِ a man whose opinions/moods fluctuate

ذَبَلَ, ذَبُلَ v |u; ذُبول, ذَبْل| to wilt; to wither, to shrivel, to dry up; يَذْبُلُ النَباتُ the plants are wilting; تَذْبُلُ الفَواكِهُ the fruit is shriveling

ذابِل adj |ذُبُل| wilted; dry; withered; أَوْراق \ أَغْصان ذابِلة dry leaves/branches

ذُبالة n |ذُبال| wick; taper

ذُبول n wilting

ذَخَرَ v |a; ذُخْر| to keep; to save; to set aside

ادَّخَرَ, اذَّخَرَ v to save; ادَّخَرَ ١٠٠٠ يورو to save 1,000 euros; ادَّخَرَ مالاً to save money; لم يَدَّخِرْ جُهْداً \ طاقةٍ to spare no effort

ذُخْر n |أَذْخار| reserve; savings; asset

ذَخيرة n |ذَخائِرُ| **1** (Mil) ammunition; munition; مَخْزَن الذَخيرةِ ammunition depot **2** [مَخْزون] supply; ذَخيرة قِدّيسٍ relic; ذَخيرة لُغَويّة, ذَخيرة النُصوصِ (Ling) corpus

ادِّخار n saving; savings; دَفْتَر الادِّخارِ deposit book; حِساب الادِّخارِ savings account

ادِّخاريّ adj saving (before n); وِعاء ادِّخاريّ savings scheme

مُدَّخَر **A** adj saved **B** n |مُدَّخَرات| reserves; savings; لَجَأَ إلى ما لَدَيْهِ من مُدَّخَراتٍ to draw on one's reserves

مُدَّخِر n saver

ذَرَأَ v |a; ذَرْء| to create

ذُرّاح n (Zool) Spanish fly (*Lytta vesicatoria*)

ذَرَّ v |u; ذَرّ| to scatter; to spread; to sprinkle; ذَرَّ رَمْلاً \ مِلْحاً to scatter sand/salt; ذَرَّ شَيْئاً في \ على شَيْءٍ to spread sth across/over sth; ذَرَّ الرَمادَ في عُيونِ شَخْصٍ to pull the wool over sb's eyes

(Idioms) ذَرَّ قَرْنُهُ to begin to show, to emerge; الخِلاف الذي ذَرَّ قَرْنُهُ أَمْسِ the conflict that emerged yesterday

ذَرّ n coll dust

ذَرّة n **1** [رَمْل \ مِلْح] grain; speck; ذَرّة رَمْلٍ a grain of sand **2** (Phys) atom; نَواة ذَرّةٍ atomic nucleus; عالِم ذَرّةٍ nuclear physicist; عَصْر الذَرّةِ the nuclear age **3** (fig) tiny amount, bit; ذَرّة من العَقْلِ a bit of common sense; وَلا ذَرّةَ not in the least bit

ذَرور n |أَذِرّة| powder; flour

ذَرّيّ adj nuclear; atomic; طاقة ذَرّيّة nuclear power; العَصْر الذَرّيّ the nuclear age; الوِكالة الدَوْليّة للطاقةِ الذَرّيّة International Atomic Energy Agency; إِشْعاع ذَرّيّ radioactivity

ذُرّيّة n |ذُرّيّات, ذَراري| descendants; offspring; progeny

ذَرَعَ v |a; ذَرْع| **1** [عَبَرَ] to cross; ذَرَعَ غُرْفةً to cross a room **2** [قاسَ] to measure; ذَرَعَ رَفّاً \ حائِطاً to measure a shelf/wall

تَذَرَّعَ v to pretend, to feign; to use as a pretext; تَذَرَّعَ بِشَيْءٍ to use sth as an excuse; تَذَرَّعَ بِحُجّةِ شَيْءٍ to use sth as a pretext; to use sth as an excuse; تَذَرَّعَ بِأَنَّهُ مَريضٌ to pretend to be ill; to feign illness; تَذَرَّعَ بالصَبْرِ to exercise patience

ذَرْع n ضاقَ ذَرْعاً بِشَخْصٍ \ شَيْءٍ to be unable to stand sb/sth; to be fed up with sb/sth

ذَرائِعيّ adj pragmatic, practical; فَلْسَفة ذَرائِعيّة a practical philosophy

ذُرْوة, ذِرْوة *n* |ذُرًى| top, peak, summit; culmination; climax; في ذُرْوةِ مَجْدِهِ at the height of one's fame; ذُرْوة المَجْدِ heyday; ذُرْوة النَشْوةِ \ اللَذّةِ orgasm; وَصَلَ إلى \ بَلَغَ ذُرْوةَ النَشْوةِ to reach a climax; to have an orgasm; شَهِدَ ذُرْوةً to experience a climax; فَتْرة الذُرْوةِ الصَباحيّة morning rush-hour

مِذْراة *n* |مَذارٍ| pitchfork; hay fork

مِذْرًى *n* |مَذارٍ| pitchfork; winnow

ذَعَرَ *v* |a; ذَعْر| to scare, to frighten; to alarm; to panic; ذُعِرَ to be frightened, to be scared; to be alarmed; to panic; ذُعِرَ من شَيْءٍ to be alarmed by sth

انْذَعَرَ *v* to panic

ذَعِر *adj*; afraid

ذُعْر *n* fear, terror; alarm, panic; بِذُعْرٍ in a panic; ذُعْر قَوِيّ intense fear; أثارَ \ أَحْدَثَ حالةً من الذُعْرِ to trigger/provoke panic; بَثَّ \ أَلْقى الذُعْرَ to cause/create panic; انْتابَتْهُ حالةٌ من الذُعْرِ to panic; اسْتَوْلى عَلَيْهِ الذُعْرُ to panic; to be scared; انْتَشَرَ الذُعْرُ panic broke out

ذُعْرة *n* (Zool) wagtail

مَذْعور *adj* afraid, scared, frightened; panicky; مَذْعوراً in panic; انْتَفَضَ مَذْعوراً عند سَماعِهِ للانْفِجارِ he trembled with fear at the sound of the explosion

ذُعاف *adj* lethal; immediately deadly (*poison*); مَوْت ذُعاف sudden death; سُمّ ذُعاف a fast-acting, deadly poison

ذَعِنَ *v* |a; ذَعَن| to give in; to submit to; to concede

أَذْعَنَ *v* |ل| to give in to, to yield to; to resign oneself to; to obey; أَذْعَنَ لِضَغْطٍ to succumb to pressure; أَذْعَنَ لِمَطالِبِ شَخْصٍ to give in to sb's demands; أَذْعَنَ لِأَمْرٍ to reconcile oneself to a situation; أَذْعَنَ لِقَرارٍ to respect a decision; أَذْعَنَ لِحُكْمٍ to accept a verdict

إِذْعان *n* acquiescence, compliance; submission; obedience

مُذْعِن *n* compliant, submissive

ذَفَر *n* stench

ذَفيف *adj* quick; light, feathery

ذَقْن *n* |mf; ذُقون| **1** [لِحْية] beard; حَلَقَ ذَقْنَهُ to shave one's beard **2** [ذَقَن] chin; غَرِقَ في عَمَلِهِ إلى \ حتّى ذَقْنِهِ to be up to one's eyeballs in work

ذَراع *adj* |mf| skilful; handy

ذِراع *n* |f; ذُرْعان, أَذْرُع| **1** (Anat) arm; ذِراع مَكْسورة a broken arm; طَوَّقَ شَخْصاً to give sb one's arm; تَأَبَّطَ ذِراعَ شَخْصٍ to embrace sb; to put one's arms around sb; وَضَعَ بِذِراعَيْهِ to put one's arms around sb's ذِراعَهُ حول كَتِفِ شَخْصٍ shoulders; مَسْنَد ذِراع armrest; بَسَطَ ذِراعَيْهِ to stretch one's arms; بالباعِ والذِراعِ with might and main **2** (Mech) arm; ذِراع تَدْويرٍ handle; ذِراع تَبْديلِ تُروسٍ gear lever (BrE), gear shift (AmE); ذِراع مِضَخّةٍ pump handle **3** [قِياس] ell (*former measure of length of between 55 and 80 centimetres*) **4** [فَرْع] division; wing; branch; الذِراع العَسْكَرِيّ the armed wing

ذَريع *adj* swift; catastrophic, abject; فَشَل ذَريع a catastrophic failure; أَخْفَقَ إِخْفاقاً ذَريعاً to fail miserably

ذَريعة *n* |ذَرائِعُ| excuse; pretense, pretext; بِذَريعةِ أَنَّ ... under the pretense that ...; بَحَثَ عن ذَريعةٍ لِتَرْكِ المَدْرَسةِ to look for an excuse to quit school

تَذَرُّع *n* excuse; pretext

ذَرَفَ *v* |i; ذَرْف, ذَرَفان| to flow; ذَرَفَ دَمْعاً سَخيناً to cry bitter tears; يَذْرِفُ الدَمْعُ tears are flowing; ذَرَفَتْ عَيْنُهُ (الدَمْعَ) to cry; to weep; ذَرَفَ دُموعاً to shed tears

ذُرْفة *n* lily-of-the-valley

ذَرَقَ *v* |i-u; ذَرْق| to drop excrement (*bird*)

ذَرا *v* |u; ذَرْو, ذَرْي| to disperse, to scatter; to carry (off), to blow (away) (*dust*); to winnow (*grain*)

ذَرّى *v* to disperse, to scatter; to carry (off), to blow (away) (*dust*); to winnow (*grain*)

أَذْرى *v* to disperse, to scatter; to carry (off), to blow (away) (*dust*); to winnow (*grain*)

تَذَرّى *v* to hide oneself; to conceal oneself; تَذَرّى بالسِتارِ to hide behind the curtain

ذارٍ *n* سورة الذاريات The Winnowing Winds (*Sura 51*)

ذُرة *n* maize (BrE), corn (AmE); ذُرة شامِيّة maize (BrE), corn (AmE); ذُرة بَيْضاء millet; ذُرة عُوَيْجة Indian millet; حَبّة ذُرةٍ kernel of maize; عِرْناس \ كوز ذُرةٍ corncob; دَقيق الذُرةِ cornflour (BrE); cornstarch (AmE)

ذَقَن, ذِقَن *n* |ذُقون ,أَذْقان| chin; نُقْرة الذَقَنِ cleft chin; ضَحِكَ على ذَقَنِ شَخْصٍ to fool sb; to pull sb's leg

ذَكَرَ *v* |u; ذِكْر ,تَذْكار| **1** [قالَ] to mention, to name; to state, to tell; to indicate; to report; to give (*data, facts*); ذَكَرَ شَيْئاً to mention sth; لن نَذْكُرَها بالاسْمِ we won't mention her by name; ذَكَرَ شَخْصاً بالخَيْرِ \ بالشَرِّ to mention sb favourably/negatively; ذَكَرَ شَخْصاً في كَلِمةِ شُكْرِهِ to mention sb in one's acknowledgements; لا يُذْكَرُ not worth mentioning, negligible; يُذْكَرُ noteworthy, important; لم يَكُنْ لَهُ دَوْرٌ يُذْكَرُ he did not have a noteworthy role; ذَكَرَ أَنَّهُ يُريدُ... he indicated that he wanted to ...; ذُكِرَ أَنَّهُ كانَ مَلِكاً it is said that he was a king; ذَكَرَ القِصّةَ بِكامِلِها لِأَبيهِ he told his father the whole story; الحالُ ما ذُكِرَ as stated before; إذا كانَ الحالُ ما ذُكِرَ if the case is as stated before **2** [تَذَكَّرَ] to remember; حَسْبَما أَذْكُرُ as far as I remember; ذَكَرَ الطالِبُ القَصيدةَ the student knew the poem by heart **3** [اسْمَ اللّهِ] to praise God; ذَكَرَ اللهَ to praise God; ذَكَرَ اسْمَ اللهِ to invoke God

ذَكَّرَ *v* to remind; to call to mind; ذَكَّرَ شَخْصاً بِشَيْءٍ to remind sb of sth; يُذَكِّرُني ذلك الكِتابُ بِأَيّامِ شَبابي that book reminds me of my youth

ذاكَرَ *v* **1** [تَكَلَّمَ] to speak; ذاكَرَ شَخْصاً في شَيْءٍ to speak to sb about sth **2** [دَرَسَ] to study, to learn; to memorize; ذاكَرَ الطالِبُ الدَرْسَ the student studied his lessons

أَذْكَرَ *v* to remind; أَذْكَرَ شَخْصاً شَيْئاً to remind sb of sth

تَذَكَّرَ *v* **1** [ذَكَرَ] to remember; to recall; تَذَكَّرَ أَنَّ ... to remember that ...; تَذَكَّرَ شَيْئاً جَيِّداً to remember sth well; تَذَكَّرَ شَيْئاً بِحَسْرةٍ to recall sth with nostalgia; لا أَتَذَكَّرُ شَيْئاً I don't remember anything; لا أَتَذَكَّرُهُ \ لا أَتَذَكَّرُ ذلك I do not remember that; هل تَتَذَكَّرُ ذلك اليَوْمَ؟ do you remember that day? **2** [تَشَبَّهَ بالذُكورِ] *to behave in a masculine way*

تَذاكَرَ *v* to consult; to confer; to deliberate; تَذاكَرَ حولَ المُسْتَقْبَلِ to deliberate on the future

اذَّكَرَ *v* to be reminded; to bear in mind; اذَّكَرَ المُديرُ المَوْعِدَ the manager took the appointment into account

اسْتَذْكَرَ *v* **1** [حَفِظَ] to commit to memory; to learn by heart **2** [تَذَكَّرَ] to remember; to recall

ذَكَر *n* **1** [عَكْسُ أُنْثى] |ذُكور ,ذُكورة| male; ذَكَر نَحْلٍ drone (*bees*); شَخْص من جِنْسِ الذُكورِ person of the male gender; ذَكَر أم أُنْثى male or female **2** [قَضيب] |ذُكور| penis; رَأْسُ الذَكَرِ glans/head of the penis; قُلْفة الذَكَرِ foreskin

ذِكْر *n* |ذُكور ,أَذْكار| **1** [إشارة] mentioning; جَدير بالذِكْرِ notable; noteworthy; سالِف \ سابِق \ آنِف الذِكْرِ aforementioned; before-mentioned; أَشادَ بِذِكْرِ شَخْصٍ to praise sb; خَصَّ شَخْصاً بالذِكْرِ to mention sb explicitly; لا مَجالَ لِذِكْرِها too many to mention; رَفَضَ ذِكْرَ اسْمِهِ he refused to give his name; اشْتَرَطَ عَدَمَ ذِكْرِ اسْمِهِ on condition of anonymity; يَسْتَحِقُّ الذِكْرَ notable; الأَعْمالُ الأَدَبيّةُ الحَديثةُ الّتي تَسْتَحِقُّ الذِكْرَ noteworthy works of modern literature **2** (Islam) invocation of God; *continuous repetition of certain words or formulas in praise of God* **3** [القُرآن] الذِكْر the Koran

ذاكِرة *n* **1** [إنْسانٍ] memory; mind; recollection; ذاكِرة قَوِيّة \ ضَعيفة an excellent/weak memory; ذاكِرة بَصَرِيّة visual memory; photographic memory; ذاكِرة سَمْعِيّة aural memory; الذاكِرة الجَماعِيّة collective memory; خَلَل في الذاكِرةِ a defective memory; فَقْد \ فِقْدان الذاكِرةِ memory loss; amnesia; عاشَ في ذاكِرةِ شَخْصٍ to live on in sb's memory; طَبَعَ \ ثَبَّتَ شَيْئاً في ذاكِرَتِهِ to imprint sth on one's mind; ما زالَ حَيًّا في الذاكِرة to still be fresh in one's mind; أَعادَ شَيْئاً \ شَخْصاً إلى الذاكِرة to bring sth/sb to mind; أَنْعَشَ ذاكِرةَ شَخْصٍ to refresh sb's memory; إنْ لم تَخُنّي ذاكِرَتي if my memory doesn't fail me; ذاكِرَتُهُ كَذاكِرةِ الجَمَلِ he has the memory of an elephant; كانَ مَنْقوشاً في ذاكِرَتِهِ to be imprinted in his memory; مَحا شَيْئاً من ذاكِرَتِهِ to banish something from one's mind; يَجِبُ أَنْ نَمْحيهِ من ذاكِرَتِنا we have to erase it from our memories; سَأَحْفَظُ هذا في ذاكِرَتي I will keep that in mind; بَقِيَ في الذاكِرةِ to stick in one's mind **2** (Comput) memory; الذاكِرةُ الحَيّة, ذاكِرةُ الوُصولِ العَشْوائيِّ RAM; الذاكِرة العامِلة working memory; سَعة الذاكِرةِ storage capacity; مَخْزون في الذاكِرةِ stored in memory

ذِكْرى *n* |f; ذِكْرَيات| **1** [تَذَكُّر] memory; commemoration, anniversary; ذِكْرى باقِية a lasting memory; ذِكْرى شَبابِهِ

a memory from one's youth; ذِكْرى مِئَوِيّة centenary (BrE), centennial (AmE); الذِكْرى ال ٢٥ لِعِيد الاسْتِقْلال the 25th anniversary of independence; ذِكْرَيات memories; memoirs; ذِكْرَيات جَميلة fond memories; لَدَيَّ ذِكْرَياتٌ مع هذه الأُغْنِيةِ this song brings back memories; في ذِكْرى شَخْصٍ \ شَيْءٍ, إحْياءً لِذِكْرى شَيْءٍ \ شَخْصٍ in memory of sth/sb; in commemoration of sth/sb; إحْياء \ تَخْليد ذِكْرى remembrance; إحْياء ذِكْرى رَسْمِيّة official commemoration; أَحْيا \ خَلَّدَ الذِكْرى to remember; to commemorate; أَحْيا ذِكْرى وَفاةِ شَخْصٍ to commemorate the anniversary of sb's death; اسْتَرْجَعَ ذِكْرى شَيْءٍ to call sth to mind; كَتَبَ ذِكْرَياتِهِ to write one's memoirs; خَلَّدَ ذِكْرى الضَحايا to commemorate the victims; كَرَّمَ ذِكْرى شَخْصٍ to honour sb's memory; احْتَفَظَ بِذِكْرَياتٍ جَميلةٍ to have good memories; اسْتَعادَ ذِكْرَياتٍ to reminisce ② [تَذْكار] souvenir; memento; remembrance; لِلذِكْرى as a souvenir; ذِكْرى لِشَخْصٍ \ لِشَيْءٍ a memento of sb/sth; دَفْتَر ذِكْرَياتٍ journal, diary; guestbook

ذَكَرِيّ *adj* male, masculine; العُضْو الذَكَرِيّ the male member

ذُكورة *n* masculinity; virility

ذُكورِيّ *adj* male, masculine; macho

ذُكورِيّة *n* machismo

اسْتِذْكارِيّ *adj* memorial (*before n*); احْتِفال اسْتِذْكارِيّ a memorial ceremony

تَذْكار, تِذْكار *n* |تَذْكارات| souvenir, memento, keepsake; أُعْطِيَ تَذْكاراً to receive a souvenir

تَذْكارِيّ *adj* memorial; commemorative; نُصْب تَذْكارِيّ monument; memorial

تَذَكُّر *n* remembering

تَذْكِرة, تَذْكَرة *n* |تَذاكِر| ① [بِطاقة] ticket; pass; admission (ticket); تَذْكِرة طَيَرانٍ \ قِطارٍ plane/train ticket; تَذْكِرة ذَهابٍ a one-way ticket; تَذْكِرة ذَهابٍ وَعَوْدةٍ \ وَإيابٍ a round-trip ticket; تَذْكِرة ذَهابٍ إلى مَدينةِ أُكْسفورْد من فَضْلِكَ a one-way ticket to Oxford, please; تَذاكِر (سَفَرٍ) إلى لُنْدُن tickets to London; تَذْكِرة سَفَرٍ أَمْسْتِرْدام – باريس a ticket from Amsterdam to Paris; تَذْكِرة سَفَرٍ دَرَجة أولى a first-class ticket; تَذاكِر لِلمُباراةِ tickets for the match ② [ذِكْرى] souvenir; memento

مُذَكَّر *adj* ① (Gram) masculine; اسْم مُذَكَّر a masculine noun ② [من لَهُ صِفاتُ الذَكَرِ] masculine, manly; امْرَأة مُذَكَّرة a mannish woman

مُذَكِّرة *n* ① [رَسْمِيّة] note; memo, memorandum; مُذَكِّرة قَصيرة a short memo; مُذَكِّرة تَفْسيرِيّة \ تَوْضيحِيّة an explanatory note; مُذَكِّرة الوَزيرِ \ ديبْلوماسِيّة a ministerial/diplomatic memorandum; مُذَكِّرة رَسْمِيّة an official note; مُذَكِّرة تَفاهُم a memorandum of understanding, MOU; أَعَدَّ \ أَبْرَمَ مُذَكِّرة تَفاهُمٍ بين ... to prepare/conclude an MOU between ... ② [يَوْمِيّات] مُذَكِّرات diary; memoirs ③ [دَفْتَر] notebook

مَذْكور *adj* mentioned; مَذْكور أَعْلاهُ \ سَلَفاً \ آنِفاً aforementioned; mentioned before/above; الكاتِب المَذْكور أَعْلاهُ the aforementioned writer; الحُجَج المَذْكورة the arguments already mentioned; المَذْكور أَدْناهُ mentioned below; below-mentioned

‹ **ذَكا** *v* |u; ذَكاء| ① [اشْتَعَلَ] to blaze; to flare up; ذَكَت النارُ \ الحَرْبُ the fire/war flared up ② [فَهِمَ] to be smart; to be intelligent ③ [فاحَ] to spread (*scent*) ④ [ذَبَحَ] to butcher

ذَكِيَ *v* |a; ذَكاء| to be smart

ذَكَّى *v* to stoke, to fuel (*a fire*)

أَذْكى *v* to stoke, to fuel (*a fire*); أَذْكى ناراً to stoke a fire; to fan the flames; أَذْكى نارَ الثَوْرةِ to fan the flames of revolution

تَذاكى *v* to pretend to be smart

ذَكِيّ Ⓐ *adj* |أَذْكِياءُ| ① [عاقِل] intelligent, smart, bright, clever; هاتِف ذَكِيّ smartphone; فِكْرة ذَكِيّة a clever idea; تِلْميذ ذَكِيّ a bright pupil; كائِنات ذَكِيّة intelligent beings; حَياة ذَكِيّة intelligent life; سُؤال ذَكِيّ a smart question; خُطْوة ذَكِيّة a smart move; أَذْكى طالِبٍ في الفَصْلِ the smartest student in the class ② [طَيِّب الرائِحةِ] fragrant
Ⓑ *n* |أَذْكِياءُ| genius; smart person

ذَكاء *n* intelligence; intellect; brightness; ذَكاء حادّ a keen intellect; ذَكاء اصْطِناعِيّ artificial intelligence, AI; حاصِل \ نِسْبة ذَكاءٍ مُرْتَفِعة \ مُنْخَفِضة high/low IQ; نِسْبة الذَكاءِ IQ; لُعْبة ذَكاءٍ puzzle game, brain training game

‹ **أَذْلَف** *adj* |dipt| *having a small and delicate nose*

‹ **ذَلْق** *n* tip of the tongue

التَذَمُّر n تَذَمُّرات| grumble, complaint; whine; discontent; التَذَمُّر الشَعْبِيّ popular discontent

مُتَذَمِّر A adj whiny, complaining; grumpy
B n whiner, complainer; grouch; nag

‹ **ذَمَّ** v |u; مَذَمّة, ذَمّ| to criticize, to disparage, to disapprove; to blame; ذَمَّ شَخْصاً to disparage sb

ذامّ adj disapproving

ذَمّ n disapproval, disparagement; invective, vituperation

ذِمّة n إذِمَم| 1 [ضَمير] conscience; على ذِمَّتي on my honour; عَديم الذِمّةِ without conscience 2 (Hist) dhimma (*rights and responsibilities of non-Muslim citizens of Islamic states*) 3 [حُرْمة] protection; security 4 [ضَمان] bail; guarantee; bond; شِراء الذِمَم buying bonds; تَبَقّى لَهُ بِذِمّةِ فُلانٍ مَبْلَغُ ... sb owes him an amount of ...

ذِمّيّ n (Hist) dhimmi (*non-Muslims citizens of Islamic states, with specified rights and responsibilities distinct from those of Muslim citizens*)

ذَميم adj reprehensible; objectionable

مَذَمّة n dispraise, censure

‹ **أَذْنَبَ** v to sin; to be guilty; أَذْنَبَ في شَيْءٍ to be guilty of sth

ذَنْب n ذُنوب| sin; guilt; offence; ذَنْبُكَ على جَنْبِكَ it's your own fault; شُعور \ إحْساس بالذَنْبِ feelings of guilt; اعْتَرَفَ بِذَنْبِهِ to admit one's guilt; to plead guilty; اعْتِراف بِذَنْبِهِ confession; admission of guilt; حَسَّسَ شَخْصاً بالذَنْبِ to make sb feel guilty; غَفَرَ اللهُ لَهُ ذُنوبَهُ God forgave him his sins; God absolved him of his sins; اقْتَرَفَ \ ارْتَكَبَ ذَنْباً to commit an offence; عُقْدة الذَنْبِ guilt complex; مَسْأَلة الذَنْبِ a question of guilt; لَيْسَ الذَنْبُ ذَنْبَهُ it's not his fault; أَحَسَّ بالذَنْبِ to feel guilty

ذَنَب n أَذْناب| 1 [حَيَوانٍ] tail; كَسَعَ ذَنَبَهُ to have its tail between its legs (*dog*) 2 [مُؤَخِّرة] trail, tail; tail end

أَبو ذُنَيْبة n tadpole

مُذْنِب A adj guilty, culpable; sinful; كانَ مُذْنِباً في شَيْءٍ to be guilty of sth
B n culprit; عَثَرَ على المُذْنِبِ ,وَجَدَ المُذْنِبَ to find the culprit

مُذَنَّب n مُذَنَّبات| comet; نَجْم مُذَنَّب comet

‹ **ذَهَبَ** v |a; مَذْهَب, ذَهاب| 1 [راحَ] to go; to leave; ذَهَبَ إلى عَمَلِهِ \ بالدَرّاجةِ \ بالسَيّارة to go by bicycle/car;

ذَلِق adj glib; smooth; fluent; ذَلِق اللِسانِ talkative

ذَلْقِيّ adj (Ling) الحُروف الذَلْقيّة liquid consonants (*generally considered to include* ل, ر, *and* ن)

ذَوْلَق n tip of the tongue

‹ **ذٰلِكَ** pron see ذا

‹ **ذَلَّ** v |i; مَذَلّة, ذِلّة, ذُلّ| to be low/lowly, to be despised/contemptible

ذَلَّلَ v 1 [أَخْضَعَ] to overcome, to surmount; ذَلَّلَ صُعوبةً to overcome a problem; ذَلَّلَت الشَرِكةُ كُلَّ العَواقِبِ the company overcame all obstacles 2 [سَهَّلَ] to level, to make even; to facilitate; ذَلَّلَ الأَرْضَ to level the terrain

أَذَلَّ v to humiliate; to abase; أَذَلَّ نَفْسَهُ لِشَخْصٍ to grovel before sb; أَذَلَّ عَدُوَّهُ to humiliate one's enemy

تَذَلَّلَ v to humiliate oneself; to lower/degrade oneself; to grovel; تَذَلَّلَ لِشَخْصٍ to grovel before sb; تَذَلَّلَ لِصاحِبِ العَمَلِ to grovel to the boss

اسْتَذَلَّ v to humiliate; to disparage; اسْتَذَلَّ عَدُوَّهُ to humiliate one's enemy

ذُلّ n degradation, ignominy; lowness, humbleness; humiliation

ذِلّة n depravity; corruption

ذَلول adj ذُلُل| submissive; docile, compliant; accommodating

ذَليل adj أَذِلّة, أَذِلاّءُ| servile, humble; obsequious

إذْلال n humiliation, abasement; prostration; إذْلال يَوْميّ daily humiliation

تَذْليل n 1 [تَحْقير] humiliation, abasement, degradation 2 [تَغَلُّب على] overcoming, surmounting; removal; تَذْليل العَقَباتِ overcoming obstacles

مُتَذَلِّل adj servile, humble; obsequious, grovelling

مُذِلّ A adj humiliating, degrading; disdainful; مُعامَلة مُذِلّة humiliating treatment; خَسارة مُذِلّة a humiliating defeat
B n المُذِلّ He who humiliates (*one of the names of God*)

مَذَلّة n humiliation, affront; obsequiousness, servility

‹ **تَذَمَّرَ** v |من| to complain (about), to grumble (about); to nag (about); to criticize; تَذَمَّرَ من شَيْءٍ to complain about sth; to nag about sth; تَذَمَّرَ من شَخْصٍ to grumble at sb

ذِمار n precious possession

بَيْتِه \ الخارِج to go to his work/his home/abroad; لَقَدْ ذَهَبَ عَلَيَّ المَوْعِدُ the appointment slipped my mind; ذَهَبَ الزوّارُ the visitors left; ذَهَبَ لِلِقاءِ رَبِّهِ he passed away; اذْهَبْ عَنّي فَلا أُريدُ سَماعَكَ go away, I don't want to hear you any more; ذَهَبَ وَجاءَ to come and go ② [بَدَأَ] to begin; ذَهَبَ يَسْبَحُ to go swimming

تَمَذْهَبَ *v* to follow, to adopt, to embrace; to be a disciple/adherent; تَمَذْهَبَ بالمَذْهَبِ السُنّيِّ to be an adherent of Sunnism

ذَهَّبَ *v* to gild, to gold-plate; ذَهَّبَ المَصوغاتِ to gold-plate jewelry

أَذْهَبَ *v* to remove

ذَهَب *n* gold; ذَهَب أَبْيَض white gold; platinum; ذَهَب أَسْوَد black gold, oil; ذَهَب عيارِ ١٨ قيراطاً 18-carat gold; سوق الذَهَبِ the gold market; مَنْجَم ذَهَبٍ a gold mine; احْتِياطيّ الذَهَبِ gold stock/reserve; قِطْعة ذَهَبٍ a gold coin; سَبيكة من الذَهَبِ gold bar; gold ingot; رُقاقة ذَهَبٍ gold leaf; ذَهَب حُرّ \ خالِص pure gold; مَوَّهَ بالذَهَبِ to gild; إذا كانَ الكَلامُ من فِضّةٍ فإنَّ السُكوتَ من ذَهَبٍ speech is silver but silence is golden; لَيْسَ كُلُّ ما يَلْمَعُ ذَهَباً ,ما كُلُّ بَرّاقٍ ذَهَبٌ all that glitters is not gold; الوَقْتُ من ذَهَبٍ time is money

ذاهِب *adj* going; إلى أَيْنَ أَنْتَ ذاهِبٌ؟ where are you going?

ذَهاب *n* journey; departure; جَيْئَةً وَذَهاباً back and forth; up and down; ذَهاباً وَإياباً ,ذَهاباً وَعَوْدةً back and forth; رِحْلة ذَهاباً وَإياباً round trip; مَشى ذَهاباً وَإياباً to walk back and forth; رِحْلة ذَهابٍ outward journey

ذَهَبيّ *adj* gold (*before n*); golden; ميدالية ذَهَبيّة gold medal; عُمْلة ذَهَبيّة gold coin; عام ذَهَبيّ للشَرِكة a prosperous year for the company; (عاشَ) عُصوراً ذَهَبيّةً (to spend) one's golden years

ذَهَبيّة *n* (*Egypt*) *houseboat used on the Nile*

مَذْهَب *n* |مَذاهِبُ| movement; school; doctrine; sect; -ism; school of Islamic law; المَذْهَب التَجْريبيّ \ العَقْلانيّ empiricism; المَذْهَب الوَهّابيّ \ السُنّيّ Wahhabism/Sunnism; انْتَمى إلى المَذْهَب الحَنْبَليّ the Hanbali school of law; اتَّبَعَ مَذْهَباً ,اعْتَنَقَ مَذْهَباً ,مَذْهَبٍ to be an adherent of a school; إنَّهُ صاحِبُ مَذْهَبٍ فِقْهيًّا to follow a school of Islamic law; إنَّهُ صاحِبُ مَذْهَبٍ إبْداعيٍّ he's the founder of an innovative movement

مُذَهَّب *adj* gilded

مَذْهَبيّ *adj* sectarian; denominational; doctrinal

مَذْهَبيّة *n* sectarianism

ذَهَلَ, ذَهِلَ *v* |a; ذُهول| ① [دَهِشَ] to be perplexed; to be dismayed; to be dumbfounded; ذَهَلَ بِشَيْءٍ to be perplexed by sth ② [شَرَدَ ذِهْنُهُ] to forget; to neglect; ذَهَلَ عن شَيْءٍ to forget sth

أَذْهَلَ *v* ① [أَدْهَشَ] to amaze; to astonish; to stagger; أَذْهَلَتْني تَصَرُّفاتُهُ his behaviour amazed me ② [أَنْسى] to distract; to make (sb) forget; أَذْهَلَتْني كَلِماتُهُ عن حُزْني his words distracted me from my grief

انْذَهَلَ *v* to be perplexed; to be baffled

ذاهِل *adj* dazed; absent, distracted, faraway; نَظْرة ذاهِلة a faraway look

ذُهول *n* ① [دَهْشة] amazement, astonishment; perplexity; أُصيبَ بالذُهولِ عند سَماعِهِ للخَبَرِ he was perplexed when he heard the news ② [شُرود الفِكْرِ] distraction; absent-mindedness

مُذْهِل *adj* amazing, astonishing; surprising; perplexing, baffling; spectacular; enormous; جَمال مُذْهِل breathtaking beauty; مَنْظَر مُذْهِل a spectacular view; كَمّيّة مُذْهِلة an enormous quantity; أَسْعار مُذْهِلة unbelievable prices

مَذْهول *adj* amazed, astonished; perplexed, baffled, confused; كانَ مَذْهولاً بِشَيْءٍ to be baffled by sth

مُنْذَهِل *adj* baffled; amazed; كانَ مُنْذَهِلاً بِشَيْءٍ to be baffled by sth

ذَهِنَ, ذَهَنَ *v* |a; ذِهْن| to understand

ذِهْن *n* |أَذْهان| intellect; mind; كانَ شارِدَ الذِهْنِ to be absent-minded; حِدّة الذِهْنِ sharpness, acumen; قَدَحَ ذِهْنَهُ في الأَمْرِ to rack one's brain over sth; ما زالَ عالِقاً في الأَذْهانِ to still be fresh in one's mind; عَلِقَ في الذِهْنِ to sink in

ذُهان *n* psychosis; عانى من ذُهانٍ to suffer from psychosis

ذُهانيّ *adj* psychotic

ذِهْنيّ *adj* intellectual; mental; مُعوَّق ذِهْنيًّا mentally disabled; رِياضة ذِهْنيّة brain teasers, mental exercise; تَرْكيز ذِهْنيّ concentration

ذِهْنيّة *n* mentality

‹ **ذو** *n* |**ذوو, أولو**; f **ذات**; f pl **ذَوات**; m du **ذَوا**; f du **ذاتا**; gen **ذي**; acc **ذا**| owner, possessor; embodying, comprising; ذو بالٍ important; ذو شأنٍ significant; important; ذَوو شأنٍ influential people; أولو أمْرٍ rulers; ذو عَقْلٍ intelligent; ذو مَعْنًى significant, meaningful; غَيْر ذي مَعْنًى insignificant, meaningless; ذو القَعْدةِ Dhu al-Qaada (*the eleventh month of the Islamic calendar*); ذو الحِجّةِ Dhu al-Hijja (*the twelfth month of the Islamic calendar*); مِعْطَف ذو لَوْنٍ أخْضَرَ a green-coloured coat; سَيّارة ذات مُحَرِّكٍ كَهْرَبائيٍّ an electric car; كانَ ذا ذَوْقٍ to have (good) taste; إنَّهُ سِلاحٌ ذو حَدَّيْنِ it's a double-edged sword

ذات *n* |f; **ذَوات**| ⟨1⟩ (Psych) ego; self; مَرْكَزيّة الذاتِ egocentrism, self-centredness; دِراسة الذاتِ introspection, self-study; حُبّ الذاتِ egotism; pride, self-esteem; مُحِبّ للذاتِ egotistical; الاعْتِماد على الذاتِ independence; self-reliance; إنْكار الذاتِ selflessness, self-denial; قائم بِذاتِهِ independent; isolated ⟨2⟩ [نَفْس] the same; similar; -self; بِذاتِهِ himself; هو ذاتُهُ \ بِذاتِهِ he himself; هو بالذاتِ he of all people; بالذاتِ above all; في (حَدِّ) ذاتِهِ as such; in itself; يُعْتَبَرُ بِحَدِّ ذاتِهِ أمْراً مُمْتازاً in itself, it is considered an excellent thing; غايةٌ بِذاتِها \ في ذاتِها a goal in itself; في ذاتِ الوَقْتِ simultaneously; من ذاتِ نَفْسِهِ spontaneously ⟨3⟩ "مُؤَنَّث "ذو see ذو

(Idioms) ذاتَ يَوْمٍ one day; ذاتَ \ في ذاتِ مَرّةٍ once

ذاتيّ *adj* own; subjective; self-; auto-; رَأْي \ حُكْم ذاتيّ a subjective opinion/judgment; صورة ذاتيّة self-portrait; selfie (infml); سيرة ذاتيّة autobiography; curriculum vitae; اكْتِفاء ذاتيّ self-sufficiency; حُكْم ذاتيّ self-determination; self-government; نَقْد ذاتيّ self-criticism; subjective criticism

ذاتيّة *n* subjectivity

‹ **ذَوات** *n* see ذو

‹ **ذابَ** *v* |u; **ذَوَبان**| ⟨1⟩ [الجَليدُ] to melt; to liquefy; to thaw; يَذوبُ الثَلْجُ the snow is melting ⟨2⟩ [تَحَلَّلَ] to dissolve; to melt away; يَذوبُ السُكَّرُ the sugar is dissolving; ذابَ غَمًّا to pine with grief; ذابَ حَياءً \ خَجَلاً to die of shame

ذَوَّبَ *v* ⟨1⟩ [الجَليدَ] to melt ⟨2⟩ [السُكَّرَ إلخ] to dissolve

أذابَ *v* ⟨1⟩ [الجَليدَ] to melt; to thaw; أذابَ زُبْدةً to melt butter; أذابَ لَحْماً to thaw meat ⟨2⟩ [السُكَّرَ إلخ] to dissolve

ذائِب *adj* melted; slushy

ذَوَبان *n* melting; dissolution; ذَوَبان الثَلْجِ \ الثُلوجِ thaw; قابِل للذَوَبانِ soluble; meltable; البْلاسْتيك قابِلٌ للذَوَبانِ plastic can melt

إذابة *n* melting

تَذْويب *n* melting; dissolution

مُذاب *adj* thawed; melted; dissolved

مُذيب *n* |**مُذيبات**| solvent

‹ **ذادَ** *v* |u; **ذَوْد**| |**عن**| to defend; to protect; ذادَ عن وَطَنِهِ to defend one's country

مِذْوَد *n* |**مَذاوِد**| feeding trough; manger; الطِفْل في المِذْوَدِ the child in the manger (*Jesus*)

‹ **ذاقَ** *v* |u; **ذَوْق, مَذاق**| ⟨1⟩ [اخْتَبَرَ طَعْمَ شَيْءٍ] to taste; to savour; to try, to sample; ذاقَ الحَساءَ to taste the soup; لم يَذُقْ طَعْمَ النَوْمِ he didn't get any sleep ⟨2⟩ [اخْتَبَرَ] to experience; ذاقَ العَذابَ to be tormented

أذاقَ *v* to cause sb to taste; أذاقَ شَخْصاً الأمَرَّيْنِ to cause trouble for sb

تَذَوَّقَ *v* ⟨1⟩ [ذاقَ] to taste; to savour ⟨2⟩ [اسْتَمْتَعَ] to enjoy; to appreciate; تَذَوَّقَ الموسيقى to enjoy music

ذَوْق *n* |**أذْواق**| taste; preference; حاسّة الذَوْقِ taste; ذَوْق سَليم \ راقٍ good/refined taste; ذَوْق رَديء bad taste; عَديم الذَوْقِ tasteless; tactless; الأذْواقُ تَخْتَلِفُ tastes differ; there's no accounting for tastes, everyone to his taste; أثَّثَ شَيْئاً بِذَوْقٍ to furnish sth tastefully; بِذَوْقٍ رَفيعٍ tasteful; tastefully; كانَ ذَوْقُهُ رَفيعاً \ مُنْحَطًّا to have good/bad taste

ذائِقة *n* taste

ذَوّاق *n* gourmet; connoisseur; gastronome

مَذاق *n* taste; مَذاق لَذيذ a delicious taste

‹ **ذَوْلَق** *n* see ذلق

‹ **ذَوى** *v* |i; **ذَوِيّ**| to wilt, to wither; to shrivel, to dry up

ذاوٍ *adj* dry; withered, wizened

‹ **ذي** *n* see ذو

ذاعَ *v* |i; ذُيوع| to circulate; to spread; to be spread; ذاعَ صيتُهُ he became famous

أَذاعَ *v* to spread; to announce; to transmit; to broadcast; أَذاعَ شَيْئاً to make sth public; to divulge sth; أَذاعَ بَرْنامَجاً to broadcast a programme; أَذاعَ شَيْئاً مُباشَرةً to broadcast sth live; أَذاعَ الأَخْبارَ to broadcast the news; أَذاعَتْ أَسْماءَ الحاضِرينَ she announced the names of the people present

ذائِع *adj* widespread; rife; ذائِع الصيتِ famous, renowned; noted; ranking; كِتاب ذائِع a best-selling book

ذُيوع *n* publicity; ذُيوع الصيتِ reputation; fame

إذاعة *n* radio; broadcast, transmission; broadcast network; يَعْمَلُ بالإذاعةِ he works in radio; مَحَطّة إذاعةٍ radio station; بَرامِج الإذاعةِ لِهَذا الأُسْبوعِ programming for this week's radio; مَحَطّة إذاعةٍ مَحَلّيّةٍ \ تِجاريّةٍ local/commercial radio station; إذاعة تِلِفِزْيونيّة telecast, TV broadcast

إذاعيّ *adj* broadcast (*before n*), broadcasting (*before n*); radio (*before n*); نِظام إذاعيّ broadcasting system; مَحَطّة إذاعيّة radio station

مِذْياع *n* |مَذاييعُ| 1 [جِهاز الراديو] radio 2 [ميكْروفون] microphone

مُذيع *n* announcer; DJ; interviewer; anchor

ذَيَّلَ *v* to append

ذَيْل *n* |أَذْيال, ذُيول| 1 [حَيَوان] tail 2 [مُلْحَق] tailpiece; trail; ذُيول ذَيْل طائِرةٍ tail of an aircraft 3 [عاقِبة] aftermath; ذَيْل الحَرْبِ the aftermath of war 4 [فُسْتان] trail, train; ذَيْل فُسْتانِ العَروسِ the train of a wedding dress

تَذْييل *n* addition, affixation; attachment, supplement, appendix; footnote

رِئة *n* lung; رِئة البَحْرِ jellyfish; طَبيب الرِئة lung specialist; ذات الرِئةِ pneumonia; كانَتْ لَهُ رِئَتانِ قَوِيَّتانِ he had good lungs; تَنَفَّسَ بِمِلْءِ رِئَتَيْه to take a deep breath

رِئَوِيّ *adj* pulmonary; lung (*before n*); اِلْتِهاب رِئَوِيّ pneumonia

راء *n* |f| *name of the letter* ر

رَأَبَ *v* |a; رَأْب| to repair

مَرْآب, مِرْآب *n* |مَرائِب| **1** [لإيواءِ السَيّارة] garage; وَضَعَ سَيّارَتَهُ في المَرْآبِ to put one's car in the garage **2** [لإصْلاح السيّارة] garage, mechanic's, shop; صاحِب مَرْآب garage owner; أَخَذَ السَيّارَة إلى المَرْآبِ to take the car to the shop

راب *n* rap, hip-hop; موسيقى الراب rap music; مُغَنّي الراب rapper

راتينَج *n* **1** (Chem) resin; راتينَج صِناعيّ synthetic resin **2** (Bot) شَجَرة الراتينَج spruce (*Picea*)

راتينَجيّة *n* spruce (*Picea*)

راد *n* (Phys) rad (*a unit of absorbed radiation dose*)

رادار *n* |رادارات| radar

رادون *n* (Chem) radon

راديكاليّ *adj* radical; اليَسار الراديكاليّ the radical left; حِزْب راديكاليّ a radical party

راديكاليّة *n* radicalism, extremism

راديو *n* radio; جِهاز راديو radio (set); فَتَحَ الراديو to turn on the radio; اِسْتَمَعَ إلى الراديو to listen to the radio

رادِيُويّ *n* radio (*before n*)

رادِيوسْكوب *n* (Phys) fluoroscope

رادِيولوجيا *n* (Phys) radiology

رادِيوم *n* (Chem) radium

رَأَسَ *v* |a; رِئاسة| to lead, to direct, to manage, to run; to chair, to preside over; رَأَسَ شَيْئاً to be the head of sth; رَأَسَ اجْتِماعاً to preside over a meeting

رَؤُسَ *v* |u; رِئاسة| to lead, to be the leader of

رَأَّسَ *v* to appoint as head/chairman; to make (sb) director/president

رَوَّسَ *v* **1** [حَدَّدَ] to point, to sharpen **2** (P&P) to supply with a header

تَرَأَّسَ *v* to chair, to preside; to be/become head/leader; تَرَأَّسَ لَجْنَةً to chair a committee

رَأْس *n* |mf; رُؤُوس, أَرْؤُس| **1** (Anat) head; رَأْس أَصْلَع \ أَقْرَع a bald head; غِطاء الرَأْسِ head covering; مَسْقَط رَأْسِه one's place of birth; قَطَعَ الرَأْسَ to behead; ضَرْبة رَأْسٍ headbutt; ضَرْبة رَأْسٍ قَوِيّة a hard headbutt; ضَرَبَ الكُرة بالرَأْسِ (Sport) to head the ball; هَزَّ الرَأْسَ to shake one's head; حَطَّمَ رَأْسَ شَخْصٍ to beat sb's brains out; صَدَمَ رَأْسَهُ to bump one's head; كَأَنَّ على رُؤُوسِهِم الطَيْرَ to be awed into silence; من (قِمّة) رَأْسِهِ إلى أَخْمَصِ قَدَمَيْه from head to foot **2** [قِيادة] كانَ على رَأْسِ شَيْءٍ to be at the head of sth **3** [حَدّ] tip; upper end; top, summit; رَأْساً immediately; رَأْس نَوَوِيّ a nuclear warhead; رَأْس مالٍ capital; رَأْس الجَبَلِ the summit of the mountain; رَأْس جِسْرٍ bridgehead; رَأْس الشَجَرة the top of the tree; رَأْس زاوِيةٍ the tip of a corner; رَأْس إبْرة \ قَلَم رَصاصٍ the tip of a needle/pencil; رَأْس السَنةِ \ العام New Year; في رَأْسِ السَنةِ on New Year's Eve; جَلَسَ على رَأْسِ المائِدة to sit at the head of the table; رَأْساً على عَقِبٍ upside down; قَلَبَ شَيْئاً رَأْساً على عَقِبٍ to turn sth upside down; مُمْتَلِئ للرَأْسِ full to the brim; رَأْسٌ بِرَأْسٍ similar **4** (Geog) cape, headland, promontory; رَأْس الرَجاء الصالِح Cape of Good Hope **5** [خُضَر] head; bulb; bunch; رَأْس خَسٍّ \ هِنْدِباءٍ a head of lettuce/endive; رَأْس ثومٍ a bulb of garlic

(Idioms) قائم بِرأْسِهِ with pleasure!; على الرَأْسِ والعَيْنِ! independent

رئاسة, رِياسة *n* leadership; presidency; chairmanship; مَجْلِس الرِئاسةِ presidential council; فَتْرة الرِئاسةِ presidency; رِئاسة عَبْدِ الناصِرِ the presidency of Nasser; اسْتَلَمَ الرِئاسةَ to gain the lead; تَوَلّى الرِئاسةَ to assume the leadership; ب \ تحت رِئاسةِ شَخْصٍ under the leadership of sb

رِئاسيّ *adj* presidential; اِنْتِخابات رِئاسيّة presidential elections; القَصْر الرِئاسيّ the presidential palace

رَأْسيّ *adj* vertical; head (*before n*)

رَأْسيّة *n* title, heading

رَئيس *n* |رُؤَساءُ| 1 [زَعيم] chairman, chairperson; president; head; chief, boss; رَئيس القِسْمِ section head; رَئيس أَرْكانٍ chief of staff; رَئيس عُمّالٍ foreman; رَئيس دَوْلةٍ head of state; رَئيس الوُزَراءِ prime minister; سِيادة الرَئيسِ His/Your Excellency the president 2 (Sport) captain 3 (Pol) president; رَئيس الوِلاياتِ المُتَّحِدةِ the president of the United States

رَئيسيّ A *adj* main, principal, chief, cardinal; السَبَب الرَئيسيّ the main reason; السُؤال الرَئيسيّ the main question; صَفْحة رَئيسيّة home page; شَخْصيّة \ دَوْر رَئيسيّ(ة) a key figure/role
B *n* الرَئيسيّات primates; كانَ من الرَئيسيّاتِ to be a primate

تَرَؤُّس *n* direction; chairmanship; leadership; presiding over; هو غَيْرُ جَديرٍ بِتَرَؤُّسِ المُنَظَّمةِ he is incapable of leading the organization

تَرْويسة *n* header, heading; letterhead

مَرْؤوس A *adj* subordinate; مَرْؤوس لِشَخْصٍ subordinate to sb
B *n* subordinate, junior

‹ **رَأْس الخَيْمةِ** *n* |f| Ras al-Khaimah (*one of the member states of the United Arab Emirates*)

‹ **رَأْسْمال** *n* |رَساميل, رُؤوس أَمْوالٍ| capital

رَأْسْماليّ A *adj* capitalist; النِظام الرَأْسْماليّ capitalism
B *n* capitalist

رَأْسْماليّة *n* capitalism

‹ **رَأَفَ, رَؤُفَ** *v* |a-u; رَأْفة, رَآفة| |ب| to take pity; to show compassion; رَأَفَ بِشَخْصٍ to take pity on sb

تَرَأَّفَ *v* |على, ب| to treat with kindness, to have mercy (with)

اسْتَرْأَفَ *v* to beg for mercy

رَأْفة *n* mercy, compassion, pity; clemency; الرَأْفة بِشَخْصٍ compassion for sb

رَؤوف A *adj* merciful
B *n* 1 (Islam) الرَؤوف the Kind (*one of the names of God*) 2 [اسْم شَخْصيّ] Ra'uf (*male given name*)

‹ **راكون** *n* raccoon (*Procyon lotor*)

‹ **رالي** *n* |راليات| rally

‹ **رِئْم** *n* |أَرْآم| white antelope

رَؤوم *adj* |mf| motherly; loving, tender (*a mother to her child*)

‹ **رام** *n* (Comput) RAM

‹ **رام الله** *n* |f| Ramallah (*city in Palestine*)

‹ **راوَنْد** *n* (Bot) rhubarb (*Rheum rhaponticum*)

‹ **رَأى** *v* |a; رَأْي, رُؤْية| 1 [أَبْصَرَ] to see; رَأى شَيْئاً to see sth; رَأى شَخْصاً \ أُمَّهُ في مَنامِهِ he saw his mother in his dream; رَأى شَيْئاً بِأُمِّ عَيْنَيْهِ to see sb/sth with one's own eyes 2 [اعْتَبَرَ] to consider, to regard, to think; رَأى أنّ ... to think that ...; ألا تَرى أنّ don't you think that; يا تُرى؟ what do you think?; I wonder; أَيْنَ ذَهَبَ يا تُرى؟ I wonder where he went?

راءى *v* to pretend, to dissimulate

أرى *v* to show, to demonstrate, to display, to exhibit; أرى شَخْصاً شَيْئاً to show sth to sb; أرى شَخْصاً حيلةً to show sb a trick; أرى شَخْصاً المَدينةَ to show sb round the city

تَراءى *v* to appear, to present oneself; يَتَراءى لي أنْ ... it seems to me that ...

ارْتَأى *v* to feel, to consider; ارْتَأى رَأْياً to have an opinion

رَأْي *n* |آراء| view, opinion; notion, idea; judgement; individual judgement (*of an Islamic jurist*); رَأْي شَخْصيّ a personal opinion; رَأْي مُخْتَلِف a dissenting opinion; رَأْي مُسَبَّق prejudice; الرَأْي العامّ the public opinion; الرَأْي السائِد the prevailing view; أَصْحاب رَأْيٍ experts; أَهْل الرَأْيِ obstinate; صُلْب الرَأْيِ adherents to a point of view; حُرّيّة الرَأْيِ freedom of opinion; اخْتِلاف الرَأْيِ a difference of opinion; اخْتَلَفَ في الرَأْيِ to disagree; أَبْدى \ أَعْطى \ طَرَحَ رَأْيَهُ في شَيْءٍ to express/give/present one's opinion about sth; غَيَّرَ رَأْيَهُ to change one's mind; كَوَّنَ رَأْيَهُ to form one's opinion; جَعَلَ شَخْصاً يُغَيِّرُ

مِرْآة *n* |مرايا| mirror; مِرْآة السَّيّارةِ rear-view mirror; أمام (وَقَف) المِرْآةِ (to stand) in front of the mirror; نَظَر في \ إلى المِرْآةِ to look in the mirror

مَرْأًى *n* sight, view, prospect; appearance; viewing; حَسَن المَرْأى beautiful; على مَرْأى من شَخْصٍ in full view of sb; على مَرْأى وَمَسْمَعِ الجَميع before the ears and eyes of everybody

مَرْئِيّ *adj* observed; visible; visual; صَوْتيّ-مَرْئيّ ,مَرْئيّ وَمَسْموع audiovisual, AV; غَيْر مَرْئِيٍّ invisible

مَرْئِيّات *n pl* video, visuals

راي *n* rai (*North African music genre*)

راي *n* (Zool) ray

رَبَأَ *v* |a; |ب| رَبْء to esteem highly

رَبَّ *v* |u; رَبّ, رِبابة| **1** [أَدَّب] to raise, to bring up (*children*); رَبَّ ابْنَهُ to raise one's son **2** [سادَ] to rule; رَبَّ القَوْمَ to rule over a people **3** [خَفَق] to beat; رَبَّ بَيْضةً to beat an egg

رابّ *n* |رَبّة| stepfather

رابّة *n* |رَوابُّ| stepmother

رَبّ *n* |أَرْباب| **1** [زَعيم] owner, proprietor; chief, leader; رَبّ العَمَلِ employer; رَبّ الأُسْرةِ the head of the family; رَبّ البَيْتِ the master of the house **2** (Relig) Lord; الرَبّ the Lord God; رَبُّنا our Lord; رَبّ العالَمينَ the Lord of the worlds; يا رَبّ oh, Lord; ذَهَبَ \ انْتَقَل إلى جِوارِ رَبِّه to meet one's Maker

رُبَّ *adv* many, many a; رُبَّ مَرَّةٍ many a time; رُبَّ كَأْسٍ شَرِبْنا we have had many drinks; رُبَّ قائِلٍ يَقولُ ... many people say ...

رَباب ,**رَبابة** *n* rebab, rebaba (*a type of string instrument*)

رُبّان *n* |رَبابِنة ,رَبابينُ| captain, commander, skipper

رَبّانيّ **A** *adj* **1** [إلَهِيّ] divine, relating to God; pious **2** (Jud) rabbinical

B *n* a godly person; rabbi

رَبّانيّة *n* godliness

رَبّة *n* owner; lady; رَبّة المَنْزِلِ \ البَيْتِ \ الأُسْرةِ the lady of the house; homemaker, housewife

رُبَّما *adv* **1** [لَعَلَّ] perhaps, maybe, possibly; إنّ الرَئيسَ رُبَّما يُواجِهُ ضُغوطاً مُتَعَدِّدةً the president might face strong

رَأْيُهُ to change sb's mind; تَمَسَّكَ بِرَأْيِهِ to stick to one's view; تَوَحَّدَ بِرَأْيِهِ to be alone in one's opinion; صَرَّحَ بِرَأْيِهِ to say frankly what one thinks; عَبَّرَ عن رَأْيِهِ to voice one's opinion; كانَ \ لم يَكُنْ لَهُ رَأْيٌ في شَيْءٍ to have an/no opinion on sth; شاطَرَ شَخْصاً رَأْيَهُ احْتَرَمَ رَأْيَ شَخْصٍ to respect sb's view; to subscribe to sb's view; اسْتَطْلَعَ رَأْيَ شَخْصٍ to ask sb's opinion; اسْتِطْلاع لِلرَأْيِ poll, survey; عَمَّقَ الرَأْيَ to broaden one's view; شَغَلَ الرَأْيَ العامَّ to engage public opinion; اسْتَقَرَّ قَرَّ الرَأْيُ على ... رَأْيُهُ على فِعْلِ ذلك he decided to do that; it was decided to ...; كانَ رَأْيُهُ أنّ ... he was of the opinion that ...; ما زالَ عند رَأْيِهِ to keep to one's opinion; حَسَبَ رَأْيِهِ الخاصِّ according to one's own opinion; في رَأْيي أنّ ... in my opinion ...; ب \ في رَأْيي أنّ ... it seems to me that ...; رَأْيي في هذه القَضِيّةِ my view on this matter; ما رَأْيُكَ فيهِ؟ what do you say to that?; إجْماع في الرَأْيِ consensus

راءٍ *n* |راؤونَ| viewer, spectator, observer; visionary

رِئاء ,**رِياء** *n* hypocrisy, insincerity, duplicity

رُؤْيا *n* |رُؤًى| vision; سِفر الرُؤْيا Revelation, the Apocalypse; رَأى رُؤًى to see/have visions; رَأى شَيْئاً في رُؤْيا to see sth in a vision

راية *n* flag, banner; الراية البَيْضاء the white flag; حامِل الرايةِ flag-bearer; تحت رايةِ الأُمَمِ المُتَّحِدةِ under the colours of the United Nations

رُؤْية *n* |رُؤًى| view; sight, vision; seeing, viewing; view, way of thinking; رُؤْية مُمْتَدّة a wide view; رُؤْية مُسْتَقْبَلِيّة a vision of the future; مَجال الرُؤْيةِ field of vision; مَدى الرُؤْيةِ visibility, visual range; رُؤْية الهِلالِ viewing the crescent (*to determine the beginning and end of the lunar month, especially Ramadan*); حَجَبَ الرُؤْيةَ عن شَخْصٍ to block sb's view; تَمَتَّعَ بِوُضوحِ الرُؤْيةِ to be insightful

رُؤْيَويّ *adj*, *n* visionary

رِياء *n* see رِئاء

تَتْرى *adv* see وتر

مُراءٍ **A** *adj* |مُراؤونَ| hypocritical, insincere, two-faced

B *n* |مُراؤونَ| hypocrite, dissembler

مُراءاة *n* hypocrisy, insincerity

رَباح *n* (Zool) genet (*Genetta*); الصَباحُ رَباحٌ the early bird catches the worm

رِبْحيّ *adj* profit (*before n*); غَيْر رِبْحيٍّ non-profit; مُنَظَّمة غَيْر رِبْحيَّةٍ a non-profit organization

رِبْحيّة *n* profitability, earnings

رَبيح *adj* profitable, lucrative

مُرابَحة *n* resale with gain (*a means of Islamic banking*)

مُرْبِح *adj* profitable, gainful, lucrative; عَرْض مُرْبِح a lucrative offer; شَرِكة مُرْبِحة a profitable company

‹ **تَرَبَّدَ** *v* to become overcast/cloudy; to cloud, to become ashen (*of a face*); تَرَبَّدَت السَماءُ the sky clouded over

ارْبَدَّ *v* to look black (*the face*)

أَرْبَد *adj* |dipt| ashy

‹ **رَبَصَ** *v* |u; رُبْص| to be on the outlook (for), to wait (for)

تَرَبَّصَ *v* |ب| to lurk, to lie in wait; to wait; to ambush; تَرَبَّصَ بالأَعْداءِ to spy on the enemy

‹ **رَبَضَ** *v* |i; رُبوض ,رَبْض| to lie down (*of an animal*); to crouch, to squat

رابِض *adj* **1** [مُتَمَدِّد] lying down **2** [سَيّارة] parked

مَرْبِض *n* |مَرابِضُ| animal pen (*area for animals to rest*)

‹ **رَبَطَ** *v* |i-u; رَبْط| to link, to connect; to bind, to tie (up), to fasten; رَبَطَ جُرْحاً to bind a wound; رَبَطَ زَوْرَقاً to tie up a boat; رَبَطَ شَيْئاً بِشَيْءٍ to connect sth to sth; رَبَطَ شَيْئاً بِإحْكامٍ to tie sth tightly; رَبَطَ مَقْطورةً بِسَيّارةٍ to connect a trailer to a car; رَبَطَ عَرَباتِ القِطارِ (بِبَعْضِها البَعْضَ) to couple railway carriages (together); رَبَطَ بِشَبَكةِ الهاتِفِ to connect to the telephone network; رَبَطَ شَرْطاً بِشَيْءٍ to attach a condition to sth; رَبَطَ حَبْلاً على شَجَرةٍ to tie a rope to a tree; رَبَطَ بين أَمْرَيْنِ to link up between two things

رَبَّطَ *v* to connect; to tie together

رابَطَ *v* to be stationed

تَرابَطَ *v* to correlate, to interrelate

ارْتَبَطَ *v* to correlate; to be connected/linked; ارْتَبَطَ بِشَيْءٍ to be connected to sth; ارْتَبَطَ بِشَخْصٍ to be in a relationship with sb; ارْتَبَطَ بِعَقْدِ الزَواجِ to be joined in matrimony;

pressure; رُبَّما سَأَكونُ في حاجةٍ إلى المُساعَدةِ maybe I'll need help; البَشَريّةُ رُبَّما نَشَأَتْ عن بِضْعةِ آلافِ شَخْصٍ humankind possibly originates from a few thousand people **2** [رُبَّ مَرّةٍ] how many times; رُبَّما ناقَشْنا هذا المَوْضوعَ how often have we discussed that subject

رُبوبيّة *n* divinity

رَبيب *n* |أَرِبّاءُ| stepson, stepchild

رَبيبة *n* |رَبائِبُ| stepdaughter

‹ **رَبَّتَ** *v* to pat, to stroke, to caress, to fondle; رَبَّتَ على كَتِفِ شَخْصٍ to pat sb on the shoulder

تَرْبيتة *n* pat

‹ **رَبِحَ** *v* |a; رِبْح| **1** [كَسَبَ] to gain, to profit **2** [فازَ] to win

أَرْبَحَ *v* to yield, to bring in

رِبْح *n* |أَرْباح| profit, gain; benefit; رِبْح صافٍ, صافي الأَرْباحِ net profit; رِبْح إجْماليّ gross profit; يَبْلُغُ الرِبْحُ الإجْماليُّ مِلْيونَ دولار the gross profit is $1 million; رِبْح مَعْقول a reasonable return; رِبْح كَبير a big profit; أَرْباح طائِلة vast profits; رِبْح مادّيّ material gain; رِبْح قَدْرُهُ ١٠٠ دولار a profit of $100; انْخِفاض الأَرْباحِ a fall in profits; فَوات \ ضَياع الرِبْحِ a loss of profit; تَوْزيع الرِبْحِ \ الأَرْباحِ profit distribution, dividend; تَوْزيع الرِبْحِ بين العُمّالِ \ المُسْتَخْدَمينَ a distribution of profits to the employees; الأَرْباح المُوَزَّعة على المُساهِمينَ the dividend paid to shareholders; اقْتِسام الأَرْباحِ profit sharing; هامِش أَرْباحٍ profit margin; قَصْد الرِبْحِ profit motive; بِ \ دون قَصْدِ الرِبْحِ for-profit/non-profit; التَكاليف والأَرْباح costs and benefits; زِيادة في \ ارْتِفاع \ نُموّ الأَرْباحِ earnings growth; نَقْص في الأَرْباحِ a decrease in profits; أَدَرَّ رِبْحاً to yield a profit; حَقَّق رِبْحاً to realize a profit; أَحْرَزَ \ حَقَّقَ \ جَنى أَرْباحاً to make a profit; أَدّى إلى أَرْباحٍ to yield a profit; عادَ عَلَيْهِ بالأَرْباحِ he's made a profit; باعَ بِأَرْباحٍ to sell at a profit; لا يَسْتَهْدِفُ الرِبْحَ non-profit; مُنَظَّمة لا تَسْتَهْدِفُ الرِبْحَ a non-profit organization

رابِح **A** *adj* profitable, lucrative, gainful; شَرِكة \ مَشْروع رابِح(ة) a profitable venture **B** *n* winner; gainer; الرابِح والخاسِر the winner and the loser of parents with their children; بِدونِ ارْتِباطٍ without obligation; إِنَّهُ شَديدُ الارْتِباطِ بـ ... he has strong ties with ...

الرِباط *n* |f| Rabat (*the capital of Morocco*)

المُرابِطونَ *n* Almoravids (*a Berber dynasty in North Africa and Spain in the 11th and 12th centuries*)

تَرابُط *n* bond, connection, link; cohesion; coherence; تَرابُط قَويّ \ شَديد a strong bond; تَرابُط بَيْنيّ interconnectedness; تَرابُط اجْتِماعيّ community spirit; أَبْدى تَرابُطاً to show cohesion

مُتَرابِط *adj* connected, joined, linked; related, associated; coherent; غَيْر مُتَرابِطٍ incoherent; disconnected, discontinuous; المُدُنُ مُتَرابِطةٌ فيما بَيْنَها the cities are connected to each other

مُرابِط *n* (Islam, NA) marabout (*a Muslim religious teacher or the shrine marking his burial place*)

مَرْبَط, **مَرْبِط** *n* |مَرابِطُ| stable (*place where animals are tied up*); stall; الاسْمُ عالٍ والمَرْبَطُ خالٍ this is the essence; هذا مَرْبَطُ الفَرَسِ ≈ to be all hat and no cattle (*to have a high reputation but be lacking in substance*)

مَرْبوط *adj* connected; tied, bound; تاء مَرْبوطة *name of the letter* ة

مُرْتَبِط *adj* connected, linked, related, allied; غَيْر مُرْتَبِطٍ without obligation; مُرْتَبِط to be related to sth; كانَ مُرْتَبِطاً بِشَيْءٍ ارْتِباطاً وَثيقاً \ مُباشِراً بِشَيْءٍ to be strongly/directly connected with sth

رَبَعَ *v* |a; رَبْع| ❶ [أَخَذَ رُبْعَهُ] to quarter ❷ [أَقامَ] to sit, to squat; to stay, to live; رَبَعَ في مَكانٍ to stay somewhere

رَبَّعَ *v* ❶ [جَلَسَ] to sit cross-legged ❷ (Math) to quadruple, to multiply by four, to increase fourfold; to square ❸ [قَسَمَ] to quarter, to divide into quarters ❹ [شَكَّلَ] to square

تَرَبَّعَ *v* to sit cross-legged

رَبْع *n* |رُبوع ,رِباع ,أَرْباع ,أَرْبُع| ❶ [مَحَلّة] quarter, residence ❷ [حَيّ] district, neighbourhood ❸ [مِنْطَقة] region, area; في رُبوعِ الجُمْهوريّةِ العِراقيّةِ within the territory of the Iraqi republic

رُبْع *n* |أَرْباع| ❶ [جُزْء] quarter, (one) fourth; الرُبْع الخالي Rub' al-Khali, the Empty Quarter (*desert in the Arabian peninsula*); رُبْع تُفّاحةٍ

to be bound by a contract

رَبْط *n* connection, link; fastening, joining; رَبْط هاتِفيّ a telephone connection; الضَبْط والرَبْط discipline

رابِط **A** *adj* binding; connective; رابِط الجَأْشِ imperturbable; composed, collected, cool

B *n* |رَوابِطُ| ❶ [عَلاقة] tie, link; bond; رَوابِط عائِليّة family ties ❷ (Comput) link; رابِط تَشَعُّبيّ hyperlink; رابِط دائِم permalink; رَوابِط مُفيدة useful links; رَوابِط خارِجيّة external links; رابِط مُعَطَّل a broken link; الرابِط لا يَعْمَلُ the link is not working

(Idiom) بِغَيْرِ ضابِطٍ ولا رابِطٍ unruly

رابِطة *n* |رَوابِطُ| ❶ [اتِّحاد] connection, link; association, league, confederation; رابِطة المُعَلِّمينَ the teachers' union; رابِطة أُمَمٍ commonwealth; الرابِطة الإسْلاميّة the Muslim League; رابِطة الشَبَكَة العالَميّة the World Wide Web Consortium, W3C ❷ [عَلاقة] bond, tie, relationship; رابِطة عائِليّة family ties; رَوابِط وَطيدة strong bonds; رابِطة الدَم blood ties; رابِطة الزَوْجيّةِ the bond of marriage; رابِطة تَعاوُنٍ cooperation; أَقامَ رَوابِطَ to establish relations; عَزَّزَ رَوابِطَ الصَداقةِ to tighten the bonds of friendship ❸ (Comput) link; hyperlink ❹ (Chem) bond

رِباط *n* |رُبُط ,أَرْبِطة| ❶ [عِصابة] band, ribbon; رِباط الساعةِ watch band; رِباط العَيْنِ blindfold; رِباط العُنُقِ tie; لَبِسَ رِباطَ عُنُقٍ to wear a tie; رِباط حِذاءٍ shoelace; زَوْج من الأَرْبِطةِ a pair of laces ❷ (Anat) ligament; رِباط مَفْصِليّ ligament ❸ (Med) bandage, dressing; رِباط مُؤَقَّت first-aid dressing ❹ (Mil) fort, stronghold

رَباطة, **رِباطة** *n* composure, calm; رِباطة الجَأْشِ imperturbability; composure

رَبْطة *n* |رَبْطات ,رِباط| ❶ [حُزْمة] bundle; bunch; pack; رَبْطة جَزَرٍ a bunch of carrots ❷ [شال] scarf; tie; رَبْطة العُنُقِ tie, necktie; رَبْطة الفَراشةِ bow tie

ارْتِباط *n* |ارْتِباطات| link, connectedness, connection; engagement, commitment; relation; correlation; ارْتِباط اجْتِماعيّ \ سِياسيّ \ شَخْصيّ social/political/personal connection; ارْتِباط وَثيق a strong commitment; ارْتِباط بِشَيْءٍ the involvement in sth; ارْتِباط الآباءِ بِأَطْفالِهِمْ the involvement a quarter of an apple; رُبْع دائِرةٍ quadrant; رُبْع سَنةٍ quarter (*three-month period*); رُبْع السَنةِ الجاري the current quarter; مَجلّة رُبْع سَنَويّةٍ the first/fourth quarter; رُبْع السَنةِ الأوّل \ الرابِع a quarterly (magazine); ثَلاثة أرْباع three-quarters, three-fourths; قَسَّمَ \ قَطَّعَ إلى أرْباع to divide/cut sth in quarters; الساعةُ الثالِثةُ والرُبْعُ \ إلاّ الرُبْعَ it is quarter past/to three ② (Astron) quarter; الرُبْع الأوّل \ الأخير the first/last quarter

رابِع ***num*** fourth

رابِعة ***n*** ① [الظُهْر] واضِح وُضوحَ الشَمْسِ في رابِعةِ النَهارِ clear as day ② [اسْم شَخْصيّ] |dipt| Rabi'a (*female given name*)

رابِعَ عَشَرَ ***num*** fourteenth

رَبّاع ***n*** ① (Sport) athlete (*wrestler, weightlifter, boxer*) ② (Agric) tenant farmer on the basis of a fourth of the proceeds of a piece of land

رُباعيّ ***n*** ① [أرْبَع مَرّاتٍ] fourfold, quadruple (*consisting of four parts or elements*); quad-; شَكْل رُباعيّ quadrangle; دَفْع رُباعيّ four-wheel drive ② (Ling) quadrilateral (*consisting of four radicals*); فِعْل رُباعيّ a quadrilateral verb

رَبْعة ***adj*** |mf| medium-sized

رُبْعيّ ***adj*** quarterly, trimestral; نَتيجة رُبْعيّة quarterly result

رُبوع ***n*** house, home

رَبيع ***n*** |أرْبِعة| spring, springtime; الرَبيع العَرَبيّ the Arab Spring; رَبيع الأوّل Rabi al-Awwal (*the third month of the Islamic calendar*); رَبيع الآخِر \ الثاني Rabi al-Akhir/al-Thani (*the fourth month of the Islamic calendar*); رَبيع عُمْرِه the prime of his life; فَصْل الرَبيع spring; عُطْلة الرَبيع spring vacation; شَهْر الرَبيع (Hist) March (*Libya under Gaddafi*); زَهْرة الرَبيع primula (*Primula*); في رَبيعِ سَنةِ ١٩٨٧ in the spring of 1987; حَلَّ الرَبيعُ! spring has come!; كانَ عُمْرُها سِتّةَ عَشَرَ رَبيعاً she was sixteen years old; إنّ تَفَتُّح وَرْدةٍ واحِدةٍ لا يَعْني حُلولَ الرَبيع one swallow doesn't make a summer

رَبيعة ***n*** |dipt| Rabi'a (*female/male given name*)

رَبيعيّ ***adj*** spring (*before n*)

أرْبِعاء ***n*** |أرْبِعاوات| Wednesday; يَوْم الأرْبِعاءِ Wednesday; في يَوْمِ الأرْبِعاءِ (on) Wednesday; يَوْمَ الأرْبِعاءِ القادِمَ \ المُقْبِلَ this Wednesday, next Wednesday; يَوْمَ الأرْبِعاءِ الماضِيَ last Wednesday; أرْبِعاء الرَمادِ (Chr) Ash Wednesday (*first day of Lent*)

أرْبَعة ***num*** four

أرْبَعةَ عَشَرَ ***num*** fourteen

أرْبَعونَ ***num*** forty; fortieth

تَرَبُّع ***n*** *cross-legged position*

تَرْبيع ***n*** ① [القَمَر] (lunar) quarter ② [مُرَبَّع] |تَرابيعُ| square

تَرْبيعة ***n*** |تَرابيعُ| square, quadrangle

تَرْبيعيّ ***adj*** square, quadratic

مُتَرَبِّع ***adj*** cross-legged; جَلَسَ مُتَرَبِّعاً to sit cross-legged

مَرْبَع ***n*** |مَرابِعُ| meadow

مُرَبَّع **A** ***adj*** ① (Geom) square ② (Math) square, squared; ١٢ مِتْراً مُرَبَّعاً 12 square metres

B ***n*** |مُرَبَّعات| ① (Geom) square, quadrangle; مُرَبَّعات لَوْحةِ شِطْرَنْج the squares of a chessboard ② (Math) square; مُرَبَّع (العَدَد) ثَلاثةٍ the square of three

مَرْبوع ***adj*** medium-sized, medium-size

‹ **رِبْقة** ***n*** |أرْباق، رِباق، رِبَق| noose; yoke

‹ **رَبَكَ** ***v*** |u; رَبْك| to confuse, to confound

رَبِكَ ***v*** |a; رَبَك| to be confused; to become involved

أرْبَكَ ***v*** to confuse, to perplex, to befuddle; أرْبَكَ شَخْصاً to confuse sb

ارْتَبَكَ ***v*** to be confused/baffled

ارْتِباك ***n*** |ارْتِباكات| confusion, perplexity, bafflement; disruption, distraction; أحْدَثَ ارْتِباكاً، تَسَبَّبَ في ارْتِباكٍ to cause confusion

مُرْبَك ***adj*** confused; perplexed

مُرْبِك ***adj*** confusing; baffling; النَتائِجُ مُرْبِكةٌ the conclusions are confusing

مُرْتَبِك ***adj*** confused; perplexed; إنَّه مُرْتَبِكٌ he is confused

‹ **تَرَبَّلَ** ***v*** to put on weight, to get fat

رَبْلة ***n*** |رَبَلات| رَبْلة الساقِ calf (*of the leg*)

مُتَرَبِّل ***adj*** corpulent, fat

‹ **رَبا** ***v*** |u; رُبُوّ، رَبْو| ① [زادَ] to increase, to grow ② [نَشَأَ] to grow up ③ [انْتَفَخَ] to rise; to swell; قد رَبا العَجينُ the dough has risen ④ (Med) to have asthma

رَبِيَ ***v*** |a; رُبِيّ| to grow up

رَبّى *v* ❶ [أَطْفالاً] to raise, to bring up; رَبّى أَطْفالاً to raise children; رَبّى شَخْصاً تَرْبِيةً تَقْليديّةً \ دينيّةً to bring up sb in a traditional/religious way ❷ [الماشِيةَ] to breed, to keep, to raise; رَبّى الخُيولَ to breed horses; رَبّى الحَمامَ \ الأرانِبَ to keep pigeons/rabbits

رابى *v* to practise usury; to lend money at interest

أَرْبى *v* ❶ [زادَ] to exceed, to be more ❷ [نَمّى] to augment, to increase

تَرَبّى *v* to be raised/brought up

رَبْو *n* asthma; مَريض الرَبْوِ asthma sufferer; نَوْبة الرَبْوِ asthma attack; مُصاب بالرَبْوِ asthmatic; كان مُصاباً بالرَبْوِ to suffer from asthma; شَخص مُصاب بالرَبْو asthma patient; الرَبْو والْتِهاب الشُعَبِ asthma and bronchitis

رابِية *n* |رَوابٍ| hill

رِباً *n* (usurious) interest; أَكَلَ الرِبا to take (usurious) interest

رَبْوة *n* |رُبىً| hill

رَبْوِيّ *adj* asthmatic, asthma (*before n*); نَوْبة رَبْوِيّة asthma attack; أُصيبَ بِنَوْبةٍ رَبْوِيّةٍ to have an asthma attack

رِبَوِيّ *adj* usurious; *relating to interest*

تَرْبَوِيّ *adj* pedagogic, pedagogical, educational; بَرْنامَج \ كِتاب تَرْبَوِيّ an educational programme/book; طَريقة تَرْبَوِيّة educational method

تَرْبِية *n* ❶ [تَثْقيف] education; upbringing; تَرْبِية دينيّة religious education; تَرْبِية صارِمة \ قاسِية a strict upbringing; تَرْبِية جَيِّدة \ صالِحة a good upbringing; تَرْبِية بَدَنيّة physical education; عَديم التَرْبِيةِ bad-mannered; وِزارة التَرْبِيةِ the Ministry of Education; كُلِّيّة التَرْبِية الفَنّيّة art school; عِلْم التَرْبِيةِ pedagogy; عالم تَرْبِيةٍ educator; تَلَقّى تَرْبِيةً to receive an education ❷ [ماشِية] breeding, keeping; تَرْبِية مُكَثَّفة factory farming; تَرْبِية الماشِيةِ cattle breeding

مُراب *n* |مُرابونَ| usurer

مُرَبٍّ *n* |مُرَبّونَ| ❶ [أَطْفالٍ] educator ❷ [حَيَواناتٍ] breeder

مَرْبًى *n* |مَرابٍ| terrarium; مَرْبًى للحَيَواناتِ البَرِّيّةِ aquarium مَرْبًى للحَيَواناتِ المائيّةِ

مُرَبّى *n* |مُرَبَّيات| jam; marmalade; بَرْطَمان مُرَبّى a jam jar

مُرَبِّية *n* nanny, nursemaid

رَتَّبَ *v* to arrange, to organize; to sort, to order, to put/set in order; رَتَّبَ شَيْئاً to put sth in order; رَتَّبَ أَفْكارَهُ to collect one's thoughts; رَتَّبَ أَثاثاً to arrange furniture; رَتَّبَ غُرْفَتَهُ to tidy one's room; رَتَّبَ أُمورَهُ to order one's affairs; رَتَّبَ تَرْتيباً أَبْجَديًّا \ هِجائيًّا \ أَلِفْبائيًّا to arrange in alphabetical order

تَرَتَّبَ *v* ❶ [رُتِّبَ] to be arranged/organized; to be sorted/ordered ❷ [وَجَبَ] |على| to be necessary/obligatory; تَرَتَّبَتْ عَلَيْهِ الدُيونُ he had debts; يَتَرَتَّبُ عَلَيْكَ دَفْعُ الإيجارِ في مَوْعِدِهِ you must pay the rent on time ❸ [نَتَجَ عن] |على| to result, to follow, to be a consequence; تَرَتَّبَ على الحَرْبِ to result from the war; لم يَتَرَتَّبْ عَلَيْهِ أَيُّ أَثَرٍ it had no effect whatsoever; تَرَتَّبَ على إِهْمالِكَ أَنَّكَ رَسَبْتَ في الامْتِحانِ due to your negligence you failed the exam

تَراتَبَ *v* to be successive

راتِب *n* |رَواتِبُ| salary, pay, wage; راتِب صافٍ net wages; راتِب إِجْماليّ gross salary; راتِب شَهْرِيّ monthly salary; راتِب أُسْبوعِيّ weekly pay; راتِب عالٍ a high salary; راتِب مُتَأَخِّر back wages; الراتِب الأَخير final salary; حَجْز الراتِبِ attachment of earnings; زِيادة \ تَخْفيض الرَواتِب increase/reduction in wages; تَخْفيض \ تَجْميد الرَواتِب wage restraint/freeze; حَوَّلَ \ دَفَعَ راتِباً to remit/pay a salary; تَقاضى راتِباً to have a salary; اسْتَلَمَ \ قَبَضَ راتِبَهُ to receive one's salary; أَدّى راتِباً to pay; حَصَلَ على زِيادةٍ في الراتِبِ to get a salary increase; أَعْطى \ مَنَحَ شَخْصاً زِيادةً في الراتِبِ to give sb a pay rise; زِيادة كَبيرة \ صَغيرة في الراتِبِ a large/small pay increase; بِدونِ راتِبٍ unpaid; راتِب قَدْرُهُ ٨٠٠٠٠ أورو a salary of 80,000 euros

رَتابة *n* monotony, routine; الرَتابة اليَوْميّة the monotony of daily life; (وَقَعَ) في رَتابةٍ (to be stuck) in a rut; كَسَرَ رَتابةً to get out of a rut

رُتْبة *n* |رُتَب| ❶ [دَرَجة] rank; رُتْبة عَسْكَريّة a military rank; أَنْزَلَ \ خَفَضَ رُتْبةَ شَخْصاً جَرَّدَ to downgrade, to demote; جَرَّدَ شَخْصاً من رُتْبَتِهِ to strip sb of his rank; كانَ أَعْلى \ أَقَلَّ رُتْبةً to be of higher/lower rank; بِرُتْبَةِ الشَرَفِ with distinction ❷ (Bio) order; رُتْبة آكِلاتِ الحَشَراتِ the order of insectivores

مَرْتَع *n* |مَراتِعُ| pasture; (fig) fertile ground, hotbed (*of evil, vice, etc.*)

‹ **رَتَق** *v* |i-u; رَتْق| to repair, to mend; to darn; رَتَقَ القَميصَ to repair a shirt; رَتَقَ الشِباكَ to mend nets

‹ **رَتَّل** *v* to recite (*in a rhythmic way*); to intone; to chant; رَتَّلَ القُرْآنَ to recite the Koran

رَتَل *n* |أرْتال| 1 [صَفّ] column; الرَتَل الخامِس the fifth column; سارَ في رَتَلٍ أُحادِيٍّ to walk in single file 2 [العَرَباتِ] convoy; رَتَل من الشاحِناتِ a convoy of trucks

رُتَيْلاء *n* |dipt f| tarantula (*Theraphosidae*)

تَرْتيل *n* recitation; song; intonation; chanting; تَرْتيل القُرْآنِ الكَريم recitation of the holy Koran

تَرْتيلة *n* |تَرْتيلات, تَراتيلُ| hymn, song of praise, religious song; chant; تَرْتيلات hymns

‹ **رَتَم** *n* (Bot) broom

‹ **رَثّ** *v* |i; رُثوثة, رَثاثة| to be ragged/worn

رَثّ *adj* |رِثاث| worn, old, shabby, threadbare; حِذاء رَثّ worn-out shoes; ثِياب رَثّة threadbare clothing; رَثّ الهَيْئةِ shabby-looking

رَثاثة *n* shabbiness, raggedness

‹ **رَثا, رَثى** *v* |i-u; رَثْو, رَثْي, رِثاء, مَرْثِية, مَرْثاة| to mourn, to lament, to bemoan; to pity; رَثا المَيِّتَ to lament the deceased; رَثا المَيِّتَ بِكَلِمةٍ to deliver an elegy for the deceased; يُرْثى لَهُ lamentable, woeful, deplorable; حالة \ وَضْعيّة يُرْثى لَها a deplorable state

رَثى *v* |i; رَثْي, رِثاء, مَرْثِية| to bemoan, to lament; to elegize

رِثاء *n* elegy, elegiac poem

رِثائيّ *adj* mournful; شِعْر رِثائيّ elegiac poetry

رَثْويّ, رَثَويّ *adj* rheumatic

رَثْية *n* |رَثَيات| arthritis; rheumatism

مَرْثاة *n* |مَراثٍ| elegy, lament; elegiac poem, dirge

مَرْثِية *n* |مَراثٍ| elegy, lament; elegiac poem, dirge

‹ **أرْجأ** *v* to postpone, to put off

إرْجاء *n* postponement

‹ **رَجَب** *n* Rajab (*the seventh month of the Islamic calendar*)

رَتيب *adj* monotonous, humdrum; dull, drab; unvarying; عَمَل رَتيب monotonous work; حَياة رَتيبة a dull existence

تَراتُبيّ *adj* hierarchical; سُلَّم تَراتُبيّ hierarchical order

تَراتُبيّة *n* order; تَراتُبيّة اجْتِماعيّة social order; تَراتُبيّة قِيادِيّة leadership hierarchy

تَرْتيب *n* |تَرْتيبات| 1 [تَنْظيم] order, arrangement; sequence, succession; بالتَرْتيبِ الأَبْجَديِّ \ الهِجائيِّ in alphabetical order; تَرْتيب زَمَنيّ chronological order; يُحاوِلُ تَرْتيبَ أفْكارِهِ he's trying to collect his thoughts 2 [إجْراء] arrangement, settlement 3 (Sport) ranking; classification; التَرْتيب العامّ the overall ranking; الأوَّل \ الثاني في التَرْتيبِ first/second in the list of rankings; تَصَدَّرَ التَرْتيبَ to lead the league

تَرْتيبيّ *adj* ordinal; ordered; hierarchic; systematic; عَدَد تَرْتيبيّ ordinal number

مُتَرَتِّب *adj* resulting, consequential

مُرَتَّب A *adj* organized, arranged, orderly; tidy, neat; غَيْر مُرَتَّبٍ disorderly

B *n* |مُرَتَّبات| salary, pay, wage; مُرَتَّب ثابِت \ عالٍ a fixed/high salary; مُرَتَّب سَنَويّ annual salary; يَبْلُغُ المُرَتَّبُ السَنَويُّ ١٠٠.٠٠٠ دولار the annual salary is 100,000 dollars; سُلَّم \ جَدْوَل المُرَتَّباتِ pay scale; بِمُرَتَّبٍ with pay; بِدونِ مُرَتَّبٍ unpaid; إجازة بِدونِ مُرَتَّبٍ unpaid leave

مَرْتَبة *n* |مَراتِبُ| 1 [مَرْكَز] rank, class, degree; مَرْتَبة مُنْخَفِضة \ مُرْتَفِعة a lower/higher rank; في المَرْتَبةِ الأولى first-rate; أدْنى \ أعْلى مَرْتَبةٍ في السُلَّمِ (الاجْتِماعيِّ) the bottom/top rung of the (social) ladder; وَصَلَ إلى أعْلى مَرْتَبةٍ to reach the highest rung; نَجَحَ بِمَرْتَبةِ الشَرَفِ to pass with credit 2 (Math) مَرْتَبة الآحادِ \ العَشَراتِ \ المِئاتِ the units/tens/hundreds 3 [حَشِيّة] mattress

‹ **رَتَج** *v* |u; رَتْج| to bolt, to bar, to lock (*a door*)

أرْتَج *v* to close tightly; أُرْتِجَ عَلَيْهِ to be speechless, to be tongue-tied

مِرْتاج *n* |مَراتيجُ| bolt

مَرْتَج *n* |مَراتِجُ| (mountain) pass

‹ **رَتَع** *v* |a; رَتْع, رُتوع| 1 [تَنَعَّمَ] to indulge, to revel 2 [الماشِيةُ] to graze, to pasture

‹ **رَجّ** *v* |u; رَجّ| to shake, to convulse
ارْتَجَّ *v* to shake, to tremble; تَرْتَجُّ الأَرْض the earth shakes
رَجّة *n* jolt, shock; convulsion
ارْتِجاج *n* |ارْتِجاجات| shock; trembling; ارْتِجاج مُخِّيّ \ دِماغِيّ concussion; ارْتِجاج مُخِّيّ خفيف \ عَنيف a light/severe concussion

‹ **رَجَحَ** *v* |a-i-u; رُجْحان, رُجوح| to outweigh; to tip (*the scales*); رَجَحَتْ إحْدى كَفَّتَي الميزانِ على الأُخْرى the balance tipped to one side
رَجَّحَ *v* to think likely/probable; to prefer/favour; رَجَّح الوَزيرُ أَحَدَ الرَأْيَيْنِ على الآخَرِ the minister preferred one view to the other
أَرْجَحَ *v* to fluctuate, to swing
تَرَجَّحَ *v* to outweigh, to be weightier
راجِح *adj* probable; preferable; راجِح العَقْلِ sensible
رَجاحة *n* wisdom
رُجاحة *n* see-saw; swing
رُجْحان *n* superiority; preponderance
أَرْجَح *adj* |dipt| على الأَرْجَح most likely
أَرْجَحِيّة *n* likelihood, probability
تَرْجيح *n* weighing
تَرْجيحِيّ *adj* ضَرْبة جَزاءٍ تَرْجيحيّة penalty kick
مُرَجَّح *adj* probable, likely; preferred, preferable; كانَ المُرَجَّحَ للفَوْزِ to be the favourite for the title; من المُرَجَّح in all probability
مَرْجوحة *n* |مَراجيحُ| swing; see-saw

‹ **رَجْرَجَ** *v* |i; رَجْرَجة| to shake; to sway
تَرَجْرَجَ *v* to shake; to bump
رَجْراج *n* shaking; swaying

‹ **رَجَز** *n* a type of poetical metre
أُرْجوزة *n* poem in the rajaz metre

‹ **رَجِسَ, رَجُسَ** *v* |a-u; رَجَس, رَجاسة| to be/become dirty, to be/become filthy
رَجِس *adj* dirty, filthy
رِجْس *n* dirt, filth; squalor

‹ **رَجَعَ** *v* |i; رُجوع| ① [عادَ] to return, to go/come back; رَجَعَ إلى الوَراءِ to walk backwards; رَجَعَ إلى الوَريثِ to fall to the heir; رَجَعَ إلى مَكانٍ to go back to a place; رَجَعَ إلى البَيْتِ to return home; رَجَعَ القَهْقَرى to start back; رَجَعَ إلى مُعْجَمٍ to consult a dictionary; رَجَعَ على عَقِبَيْهِ to turn on one's heels; رَجَعَ إلى صَوابِهِ to come round; رَجَعَ بِشَيْءٍ to take sth back; رَجَعَ بِخُفَّيْ حُنَيْنٍ to return empty handed; رَجَعَتْ بِهِ الذاكِرةُ إلى ... he thought back to ...; يَرْجِعُ الفَضْلُ في ذلك إلَيْكَ that is thanks to you ② [إلى عَصْرٍ مُعَيَّنٍ] to date, to go back; يَرْجِعُ هذا إلى عَصْرِ ... this goes back to the era of ... ③ [عن الشَيْءِ] to retract, to go back; رَجَعَ عن قَرارِهِ to go back on a decision ④ [تَعَلَّقَ ب] to derive, to be attributable; رَجَعَ السَبَبُ إلى to be caused by
رَجَّعَ *v* to return, to send/give back; رَجَّعَ الصَدى to echo
راجَعَ *v* ① [حَقَّقَ] to check, to examine, to verify, to inspect; to review, to go over; راجَع الحِسابَ to check the bill ② [لَجَأَ إلى] to consult, to refer; راجَعَ الأَرْشيفَ to refer to the archives; راجَع مَراجِع to consult the literature ③ [دَرَسَ] to rehearse; راجَعَ دَرْساً to go over a lesson ④ [شاوَرَ] to consult; راجَعَ صَديقَهُ في أَمْرٍ to consult one's friend about sth
أَرْجَعَ *v* to return, to give/send back; أَرْجَعَ شَيْئاً إلى شَخْصٍ to return sth to sb; أَرْجَعَ شَيْئاً \ شَخْصاً إلى مَكانٍ to send sth/sb back to a place; أَرْجَعَ الكِتابَ إلى المَكْتَبةِ to return the book to the library
تَرَجَّعَ *v* to reverberate, to echo
تَراجَعَ *v* ① [انْسَحَبَ] to withdraw, to retreat; تَراجَعَ خَوْفاً to recoil; تَراجَعَ إلى مَكانِهِ to go back to one's place; تَراجَعَ العَدُوُّ عن مَواقِعِهِمْ the enemy retreated from their positions ② [تَنازَلَ] |عن| to go back on, to revoke, to withdraw; تَراجَعَ عن شَيْءٍ to go back on sth; تَراجَعَ عن حُكْمٍ to reverse a judgement; تَراجَعَ عن رَأْيِهِ to change one's mind; تَراجَعَ عن إجْراءاتٍ to revoke measures; تَراجَعَ عن قَرارِهِ to reconsider a decision ③ (Econ) to collapse, to slump; to decline; يَتَراجَعُ الإنْتاجُ production is declining; تَتَراجَعُ أَسْعارُ النَفْطِ \ العُمْلاتِ the oil prices/rates are dropping; تَراجَعَتْ قُدْرَتُهُ الشِرائيّةُ his purchasing power declined; تَراجَعَ من ١٤ إلى

تَراجَعَ بِنِسْبةٍ ١٢ في المِائةِ to drop from 14 to 12 per cent; كَبيرةٍ \ هائِلةٍ to deteriorate drastically

اسْتَرْجَعَ *v* **1** [اسْتَرَدَّ] to get back, to recover, to regain, to retrieve; اسْتَرْجَعَ شَيْئاً من شَخْصٍ to get back sth from sb; اسْتَرْجَعَ ثِقَتَهُ بِنَفْسِهِ to regain one's self-confidence **2** [تَذَكَّرَ] to look back, to recall; اسْتَرْجَعَ حَدَثاً to recall an incident; اسْتَرْجَعَ ذِكْرَياتٍ to reminisce

رَجْع *n* |رِجاع| return, coming back; رَجْع الصَّوْتِ echo

راجِع *adj* returning; إنّا للهِ وَإنّا إلَيْهِ راجِعونَ to God we belong and to Him we return *(said by Muslims in times of grief)*

رَجْعة *n* |رَجْعات| cancellation; return; لا رَجْعةَ فيه \ عَنْهُ irrevocable; قَرار لا رَجْعةَ عَنْهُ an irrevocable decision

رَجْعيّ **A** *adj* **1** [ارْتِجاعيّ] retroactive; بِأَثَرٍ رَجْعيٍّ retroactively; ذو مَفْعولٍ \ أَثَرٍ رَجْعيٍّ retroactive; كانَ ذا مَفْعولٍ \ بِأَثَرٍ رَجْعيٍّ to be retroactive; للقانونِ مَفْعولٌ \ أَثَرٌ رَجْعيٌّ إلى غايةِ أَوَّلِ سِبْتَمْبَر من السَنةِ الماضيةِ the law is retroactive to September 1st of last year **2** [مُتَمَسِّك بالقَديم] reactionary; سِياسيّ \ حِزْب رَجْعيّ a reactionary politician/party **3** [يُمْكِنُ الرَّجْعةُ فيه] revocable

B *n* reactionary

رَجْعيّة *n* reactionary

رُجوع *n* return, coming back; الرُجوع إلى الوَطَنِ repatriation; بِرُجوعِ البَريدِ by return of post

رُجوعيّ *adj* backwards, retrospective; نَظْرة رُجوعيّة a retrospective look

رَجيع *n* dung

ارْتِجاع *n* reflux

ارْتِجاعيّ **A** *adj* retroactive; regressive; فَيْروس ارْتِجاعيّ retrovirus

B *n* reactionary

إرْجاع *n* return, restitution

اسْتِرْجاع *n* |اسْتِرْجاعات| **1** [اسْتِعادة] recovery, retrieval; اسْتِرْجاع المَعْلوماتِ information retrieval **2** [تَذَكُّر] retrospect

اسْتِرْجاعيّ *adj* retrieval

تَراجُع *n* |تَراجُعات| **1** [تَقَهْقُر] decline, fall-off; slowdown, downturn, slump; regression, degradation; تَراجُع بَسيط a slight decline; تَراجُع اقْتِصاديّ an economic downturn; تَراجُع في الدَخْلِ a significant decline; تَراجُع كَبير \ شَديد a drop in income; في تَراجُعٍ مُسْتَمِرٍّ in a state of continuing decline **2** [انْسِحاب] retreat, withdrawal; لم يَحْمِلْهُ الخَطَرُ على التَراجُعِ he didn't shrink from the danger

تَراجُعيّ *adj* retrogressive; خُطْوة تَراجُعيّة a step backwards

تَرْجيع *n* return, giving back

مُراجِع *n* inspector; reviewer, checker

مُراجَعة *n* **1** [فَحْص] inspection, examination; مُراجَعة دَقيقة a thorough revision; قائِمة المُراجَعة checklist; على سَبيلِ المُراجَعةِ for control **2** [اسْتِدْعاء] review; مُراجَعة للامْتِحانِ reviewing for the exam **3** (Isl Law) revocation *(of a divorce)*

مُرْتَجَع *adj* returned, sent/brought back; شيك مُرْتَجَع a bounced check

مَرْجِع *n* |مَراجِعُ| **1** [مَصْدَر] source, reference; reference book/work, handbook; المَرْجِع السابِق ibid. *(in an academic book or paper)*; راجَعَ مَراجِعَ to cite sources; ذَكَرَ مَراجِعَهُ to mention one's sources; اسْتَعْمَلَ مَرْجِعاً to use a reference book; اسْتَعانَ بِمَرْجِعٍ to consult a reference book; راجَعَ شَيْئاً في مَرْجِعٍ to look up sth in a reference work; مع \ بِدونِ ذِكْرِ المَراجِعِ with/without quotation of sources **2** [خَبير] authority

مَرْجِعيّ *adj* referential; إطار مَرْجِعيّ frame of reference; عَلامة مَرْجَعيّة bookmark

مَرْجِعيّة *n* authority

رَجَفَ *v* |u; رَجْف, رَجَفان| to tremble, to quake; to shiver

أَرْجَفَ *v* |ب| to spread *(bad news, lies or false rumours)*

ارْتَجَفَ *v* to shake, to tremble, to shiver, to quake; ارْتَجَفَ بَرْداً to shiver with cold; ارْتَجَفَ من البَرْدِ \ الخَوْفِ to shiver from the cold/with fear; ارْتَجَفَتْ فَرائِصُهُ to be trembling all over; ارْتَجَفَتْ يَداهُ his hands shook; شَعَرْتُ بالأَرْضِ تَرْتَجِفُ تحت قَدَمَيَّ I felt the ground shake under my feet

رَجْفة *n* |رَجَفات| shiver, tremble, tremor; رَجْفة الصَّوْتِ a tremor in the voice

ارْتِجاف *n* tremor; trembling

إرْجاف *n* |أَراجيفُ| false rumour

تَرْجيف *n* vibrato

مُرْتَجِف *adj* trembling, tremulous; shivery

‹ **تَرَجَّلَ** *v* [1] [نَزَلَ] to dismount, to get off (*a horse or bicycle*); to disembark, to get out of (*a vehicle*); to alight; تَرَجَّلَ عن حِصانٍ to dismount (from a horse); تَرَجَّلَ من سَيّارةٍ to get out of a car [2] [تَشَبَّهَ بِالرَجُلِ] to assume masculine manners

ارْتَجَلَ *v* to improvise, to extemporize

رَجُل *n* |رِجال| man; guy (infml), chap/bloke (infml BrE); رِجالات important men; رَجُل طَيِّب \ لَطيف a nice chap; رَجُل ذَكِيّ \ نَبيه a smart guy; الرَجُل العاديّ the common man; رَجُل قَوِيّ a strong man; رَجُل الشُرْطة policeman; عِلْم الرِجال *discipline of Islamic studies in which the narrators of Hadith are evaluated*; كُنْ رَجُلاً! be a man!; رَجُلٌ لِرَجُلٍ man to man; رَجُل بِمَعْنَى الكَلِمةِ a man's man

رِجْل *n* |f| [1] [إِنْسان] |أَرْجُل| leg; foot; إِبْهام الرِجْل the big toe; على رِجْلَيْهِ on foot; زَحَفَ على يَدَيْهِ وَرِجْلَيْهِ to go on all fours; قَدَّمَ رِجْلاً وَأَخَّرَ أُخْرى to hesitate; لا يَعْرِفُ يَدَ الشَيْءِ من رِجْلِهِ ≈ he is stupid [2] [حَيَوان] |أَرْجُل| leg; foot, paw; رِجْل أَمامِيّة foreleg [3] [شَيْء] |أَرْجُل| leg; رِجْل المائِدةِ the table leg [4] [بَنْطَلون] |أَرْجُل| (trouser) leg [5] [سِرْب] |أَرْجال| swarm; رِجْل من الجَرادِ a swarm of locusts

راجِل [A] *adj* |رُجّال, رَجّالة| walking; راجِلاً on foot [B] *n* |رُجّال, رَجّالة| pedestrian

رِجاليّ *adj* masculine, virile; صَوْت رِجاليّ a masculine voice; حَلّاق رِجاليّ barber

رِجْلة *n* (Bot) purslane (*Portulaca oleracea*)

رُجولة *n* masculinity, manliness; manhood; تَصَرَّفَ بِرُجولةٍ to behave in a manly way

رُجوليّ *adj* masculine, manly

رُجوليّة *n* masculinity; potency, virility

ارْتِجال *n* improvisation

ارْتِجاليّ *adj* improvised; unprepared, extemporaneous

ارْتِجاليّة *n* unpreparedness; improvisation

مُتَرَجِّل *n* infantry, foot soldiers

مُرْتَجَل *adj* improvised, unprepared, extemporaneous; خِطاب مُرْتَجَل an extemporaneous speech

مِرْجَل *n* |مَراجِل| boiler; cauldron; مِرْجَل بُخاريّ steam boiler

مُسْتَرْجِل *adj* mannish; فَتاة مُسْتَرْجِلة boyish girl, tomboy

‹ **رَجَمَ** *v* |u; رَجْم| [1] [رَماهُ بِالحِجارةِ] to stone; رَجَمَ شَخْصاً حَتَّى المَوْتِ to stone sb to death [2] (Islam) *the throwing of pebbles at specific locations during hajj, signifying the pilgrim's defiance of the devil* [3] [شَتَمَ] to curse, to abuse; رَجَمَ شَخْصاً بِالقَوْلِ to (verbally) abuse sb

رَجْم *n* stoning; رَجْم الغَيْبِ guesswork

راجِمة *n* |رَواجِم| rocket launcher

رَجيم *adj* cursed; stoned; الشَيْطان الرَجيم the accursed Devil

‹ **رَجا** *v* |u; رَجاء, رَجاة, مَرْجاة| [1] [طَلَبَ] to ask, to request; رَجا شَيْئاً من شَخْصٍ to request sth from sb [2] [تَوَقَّعَ] to hope; to expect; لَقيتُ هَوْلاً ما رَجَوْتُهُ I went through misery, more than I had feared; هَؤُلاءِ المَرْضى لا يُرْجى شِفاؤُهُمْ these patients are not expected to recover; لا يُرْجى مِنْهُ شَيْءٌ good-for-nothing

تَرَجّى *v* to hope; to expect

ارْتَجى *v* to hope; to expect, to anticipate; to dread

راجٍ *adj* hopeful; hoping

رَجاً *n* |أَرْجاء| في أَرْجاءِ ... throughout ...; في كُلِّ أَرْجاءِ العالَمِ all over the world

رَجاء *n* hope, expectation; request; الرَجاءُ, رَجاءً please, kindly; الرَجاءُ عَدَمُ التَدْخينِ kindly refrain from smoking; الرَجاءُ عَدَمُ الإِزْعاجِ please do not disturb; الهُدوءُ رَجاءً silence please

مَرْجاة *n* hope

مَرْجُوّ *adj* expected, hoped for; requested; النَتيجة المَرْجُوّة the desired outcome; المَرْجُوّ ... we request ...; المَرْجُوّ من جَميعِ المُواطِنينَ الالْتِزامُ بِما يَلي all citizens are asked to observe the following

‹ **رِجيم, ريجيم** *n* diet

‹ **رَحُبَ, رَحِبَ** *v* |a-u; رُحْب, رَحابة| to be wide/spacious; رَحِبَ المَكانُ the place was spacious

رَحَّبَ *v* |ب| to welcome, to bid welcome, to greet; to applaud; رَحَّبَ بِشَخْصٍ to welcome sb; رَحَّبَ بِضَيْفٍ to greet a guest; رَحَّبَ بِشَخْصٍ أَحْسَنَ تَرْحيبٍ to give sb a hearty welcome; رَحَّبَ بِشَخْصٍ تَرْحيباً حارًّا to welcome sb heartily;

رَحَّبَ الوَزِيرُ بِقرارِ الحُكُومةِ رَحَّبَ بِشَيْءٍ to welcome sth; الفَرَنْسيّةِ the minister welcomed the decision of the French government

رَحْب *adj* wide, spacious

رُحْب *n* على الرُحْبِ والسِعةِ! (you are) welcome!; اسْتَقْبَلَ شَخْصاً على الرُحْبِ والسِعةِ to welcome sb warmly

رَحابة *n* wideness; spaciousness, roominess

رَحْبة, رَحَبة *n* |رِحاب, رَحْب, رُحَب, رَحَبات| 1 [رَحابة] vastness 2 [ساحة] square

رَحِيب *adj* wide, spacious, roomy, generous

تَرْحاب *n* welcome, greeting; قابَلَ شَخْصاً بِتَرْحابٍ to receive sb with open arms; تَلَقّى شَيْئاً بِتَرْحابٍ to welcome sth

تَرْحِيب *n* |تَرْحيبات| welcoming, welcome, greeting, reception; رَحَّبَ بِشَخْصٍ تَرْحيباً تَرْحِيب حارّ a warm welcome; اسْتَقْبَلَ حارًّا \ شَديداً \ كَبيراً to give sb a warm welcome; شَخْصاً بالتَرْحيبِ to bid sb welcome; حَظِيَ بالتَرْحيبِ to be welcomed; أَلْقى كَلِمةَ التَرْحيبِ to speak a word of welcome; لاقى تَرْحيباً to gain support; تَرْحيباً ب to greet

تَرْحِيبيّ *adj* welcoming; كَلِمة تَرْحِيبيّة welcoming speech

مُرَحَّب *adj* مُرَحَّب بِهِ welcome; ضَيْف غَيْر مُرَحَّبٍ بِهِ an unwelcome guest

مَرْحَباً *excl* hello, welcome; مَرْحَباً بِكَ \ بِكُمْ *answer to* مَرْحَباً

رَحْرَح *adj* 1 [واسِع] wide, broad 2 [رَغْد] carefree, unconcerned

رَحَضَ *v* |a; رَحْض| 1 [غَسَلَ] to wash, to cleanse; to rinse 2 [رَوى] to irrigate

مِرْحاض *n* |مَراحِيضُ| 1 [أَداة] toilet; وَرَق المِرْحاضِ toilet paper; بالوعة المِرْحاضِ cesspool; غُرْفة بحَمّامٍ وَمِرْحاضٍ a room with a bath and a toilet 2 [غُرْفة] toilet (BrE), lavatory (BrE), bathroom (AmE), restroom (AmE); ذَهَبَ إلى المِرْحاضِ to go to the toilet (BrE) bathroom (AmE); \ مِرْحاض للنِساءِ لِلسَيِّداتِ ladies' toilet (BrE) restroom (AmE)

رَحِيق *n* 1 [الأَزْهارِ] nectar; جَمَعَ الرَحِيقَ to collect the nectar 2 [خَمْر] exquisite wine

رَحَلَ *v* |a; رَحيل| to depart, to leave; to emigrate, to move away; رَحَلَ من مِنْطَقةٍ to move away from an area; رَحَلَ بِلا زَمْرٍ وَلا طَبْلٍ *to leave quietly*

رَحَّلَ *v* to deport, to displace, to make leave; to evacuate, to resettle; to transport

تَرَحَّلَ *v* to wander, to roam; to be evacuated

ارْتَحَلَ *v* to depart, to leave

رَحْل *n* |رِحال| luggage, baggage; أَلْقى رِحالَهُ to stop (*during/after a journey*)

راحِل *adj* 1 [مُسافِر] travelling 2 [مَيِّت] deceased

راحِلة *n* |رَواحِلُ| *riding camel*

رَحّال A *adj* |رُحّال, رُحَّل, رَحّالة| nomadic, travelling; عَرَب رُحّال nomadic Arabs
B *n* |رُحّال, رُحَّل, رَحّالة| nomad

رَحّالة *n* voyager; explorer

رِحْلة *n* trip, journey; voyage; tour; travel; رِحْلة جَوِّيّة flight; رِحْلة فَضائيّة space travel; رَقْم الرِحْلةِ flight number; اسْتِكْشافيّة \ اسْتِطْلاعيّة expedition; قامَ بِرِحْلةٍ to go on a trip; رِحْلة بَحْرِيّة; قامَ بِرِحْلةٍ اسْتِكْشافيّةٍ to set off on an expedition; cruise; قامَ بِرِحْلةٍ بَحْرِيّةٍ to make a voyage; رِحْلة مَدْرَسِيّة school trip, field trip; ذَهَبَ في رِحْلةٍ مَدْرَسِيّةٍ to go on a school trip; رِحْلة دِراسِيّة study tour; رِحْلة جَماعِيّة group trip; نَظَّمَ رِحْلةً جَماعيّةً to organize a group trip; رِحْلة عَوْدةٍ journey home, return trip; رِحْلة عَمَلٍ business trip; رِحْلة حول العالَمِ journey around the world; تَسْتَغْرِقُ الرِحْلةُ خَمْسَ ساعاتٍ the journey takes five hours; رِحْلة على النيلِ a trip on the Nile; رِحْلة على الأَقْدامِ walking tour; رِحْلة بالمَرْكَبِ a voyage by boat; رِحْلة إلى المَغْرِبِ a trip to Morocco; رِحْلة من أَمْسْتِرْدام إلى القاهِرةِ a journey from Amsterdam to Cairo; رِحْلة طولُها ٢٠٠ كيلومِتْرٍ a journey of 200 kilometres; طَيَرانٍ تَجْرِيبيّة test flight

رَحِيل *n* departure, setting out; exit; exodus; مَوْعِد الرَحيلِ departure time; هَدَّدَ بالرَحيلِ to threaten to leave; وَدَّعَ قبل الرَحيلِ to say goodbye before departure; حانَ وَقْتُ الرَحيلِ it's time to leave; رَحيلُهُ من \ إلى بْروكْسيل his departure from/to Brussels

تَرْحال *n* departure, setting out; أَلْقى عَصا التَرْحالِ to stop (*after a journey*)

ترحيل *n* |تراحيل| ❶ [إبعاد] deportation, expulsion, banishment; ترحيل مهاجرٍ غيرِ شرعيٍّ deportation of illegal immigrants; قرار ترحيلٍ deportation order; مُهَدَّد بالتَرْحيلِ threatened with expulsion ❷ [إخلاء] evacuation

مُتَرَحِّل *adj* nomadic, migratory

مُرَحَّل *n* evacuee

مُرَحِّل *n* (Elec) relay

مَرْحَلة *n* |مَراحِلُ| ❶ stage, phase; مَرْحَلة مُبَكِّرة \ مُتَأَخِّرة an early/late stage; المَرْحَلة الثانية the second stage; مَرْحَلة ابْتِدائيّة a preliminary phase; مَرْحَلة حاسِمة a decisive stage; مَرْحَلة انْتِقاليّة transitional phase; مَرْحَلة نِهائيّة final stage; كانَ في مَرْحَلةٍ مُتَقَدِّمةٍ to be in an advanced stage; مَرَّ بِمَرْحَلةٍ to go through a phase; على مَراحِلَ in stages; فَعَلَ شَيْئاً على مَراحِلَ to do sth in stages; المَرْحَلة الأولى من التَعْليمِ الثانَويِّ the first cycle of secondary education ❷ (Aerosp) stage

مَرْحَليّ *adj* temporary; interim

رَحِمَ *v* |a; مَرْحَمة, رَحْمة| to have mercy/compassion; to be merciful; رَحِمَهُ اللهُ Lord have mercy on his soul; والدي رَحِمَهُ اللهُ my late father, bless his soul; اللهُ يَرْحَمُهُ God rest his soul; فَلْيَرْحَمْنا اللهُ! God have mercy on us!

تَرَحَّمَ *v* to plead for God's mercy; تَرَحَّمَ على أبيهِ he asked God to have mercy on his father

تَراحَمَ *v* to be kind/merciful towards each other

اسْتَرْحَمَ *v* to beg/plead for mercy; اسْتَرْحَمَ شَخْصاً to ask sb for mercy

رَحِم *n* |أَرْحام| womb, uterus; عُنُق الرَحِمِ cervix; سَرَطان عُنُق الرَحِمِ cervical cancer; اتِّساع عُنُق الرَحِمِ dilation; اسْتِئْصال \ إزالة الرَحِمِ hysterectomy

رَحْمان Ⓐ *adj* merciful
Ⓑ *n* الرَحْمان the Compassionate (*one of the names of God*); سورة الرَحْمان The Most Merciful (*Sura 55*); بِسْمِ اللهِ الرَحْمانِ الرَحيمِ in the name of God, the Compassionate, the Merciful (*formula occurring at the beginning of nearly every chapter of the Koran, and which is to be recited by Muslims at the start of an activity*)

رَحْمة *n* mercy, mercifulness, clemency, grace; عَدَم \ انْعِدام الرَحْمةِ mercilessness; عَديم الرَحْمةِ heartless; كانَ تحت رَحْمةِ شَخْصٍ to be at the mercy of sb; لَيْسَتْ في قَلْبِهِ رَحْمةٌ he has no mercy; مَنَّ عَلَيْهِ اللهُ بِرَحْمَتِهِ to receive God's grace; عامَلَ شَخْصاً بِرَحْمةٍ to treat sb mercifully; تُوُفِّيَ \ انْتَقَلَ إلى رَحْمةِ اللهِ to pass away; الْتَمَسَ الرَحْمةَ to beg for mercy; بِرَحْمةِ اللهِ by the grace of God; رَحْمة اللهِ اللامُتَناهِية God's infinite goodness

رَحوم *adj* compassionate, sympathetic

رَحيم Ⓐ *adj* |رُحَماءُ, رَحوم| merciful, compassionate; عُقوبة رَحيمة a light punishment
Ⓑ *n* الرَحيم the Merciful (*one of the names of God*); بِسْمِ اللهِ الرَحْمنِ الرَحيمِ in the name of God, the Compassionate, the Merciful (*formula occurring at the beginning of nearly every chapter of the Koran, and which is to be recited by Muslims at the start of an activity*)

اسْتِرْحام *n* plea for mercy

مَرْحَمة *n* |مَراحِم| mercy, leniency

مَرْحوم Ⓐ *adj* deceased, late; المَرْحوم والِدي my late father
Ⓑ *n* the deceased

رَحًى *n* |f; أَرْحِية, رُحِيّ, أَرْحاء| mill; quern; حَجَر الرَحى millstone; دارَتْ رَحى الحَرْبِ the war broke out

رُخّ *n* ❶ [قطْعة شِطْرَنْج] |رِخَخة, رِخاخ| rook, castle ❷ [طَيْر] roc, rukh (*a gigantic mythological bird described in the Arabian Nights*)

رَخّة *n* shower; رَخّة الشُهُبِ meteor shower

رَخُصَ *v* |u; رُخْص| to be cheap

رَخَّصَ *v* ❶ [أجاز] to allow, to permit; to license ❷ [خفض سِعْراً] to discount; رَخَّصَ الأَسْعارَ to reduce the price

أَرْخَصَ *v* to reduce the price of

اسْتَرْخَصَ *v* to find cheap

رَخْص *adj* tender, supple

رُخْصة *n* |رُخَص| permit, licence; رُخْصة مُؤَقَّتة a temporary licence; حامِل \ صاحِب رُخْصةٍ licensee; رُخْصة شَيْءٍ \ لِشَيْءٍ a licence for sth; رُخْصة قِيادةٍ driving licence (BrE), driver's license (AmE); رُخْصة قِيادةِ الطائِراتِ pilot's licence; رُخْصة إقامةٍ دائِمةٍ residence permit; سَحَبَ رُخْصةً to suspend a licence; طَلَبَ رُخْصةً to apply for a licence; مَنَحَ رُخْصةً to grant a licence; حَصَلَ على رُخْصةٍ to receive a permit

رَخيص *adj* cheap, inexpensive; شَيْء رَخيص bargain

تَرْخيص *n* |تَراخيص ,تَرْخيصات| licence; permission, authorization; تَرْخيص المُسْتَخْدِمِ النِهائيِّ End-User Licence Agreement, EULA

مُرَخَّص *adj* licensed; permitted; admissible; سَيّارة غَيْر مُرَخَّصةٍ an unlicensed car

مُرَخِّص *n* licensor

‹ **رَخَمَ** *v* |u; رَخامة| [1] [الدَجاجةُ] to incubate, to brood; to hatch; رَخَمَ بَيْضةً to hatch an egg [2] [الصَوْتُ] to soften; to be/become pleasant

رَخَم *n coll* |أَرْخام| Egyptian vulture (*Neophron percnopterus*)

راخِم *n* brooder, incubator

رُخام *n* marble; من الرُخامِ marble (*before n*); تِمْثال من الرُخامِ a marble statue

رَخامة *n* رَخامة الصَوْتِ euphony; رَخامة الشِعْرِ the euphony of poetry

رُخاميّ *adj* marble (*before n*)

رَخيم *adj* soft, pleasant, melodious, musical; صَوْت رَخيم a pleasant voice

‹ **رَخا** *v* |u; رَخاوة ,رَخاء| to be/become easy, to be/become comfortable; رَخا عَيْشُهُ to have an easy life

رَخُوَ *v* |u; رَخاوة| to be/become loose

رَخِيَ *v* |a; رَخاء| to be/become loose

أَرْخى *v* to loosen; to relax; أَرْخى عَضَلاتِ بَطْنِهِ to relax one's stomach muscles

تَراخى *v* to slacken, to become slack/lax

اِرْتَخى *v* to relax; to slacken; to become loose

اِسْتَرْخى *v* to relax, to unwind; to become loose

رَخْو *adj* loose, slack, lax; soft, flaccid, flabby; خاصِرَتُهُ الرَخْوة one's weak spot

رَخاء *n* prosperity; abundance; ease; تَحْقيق الرَخاءِ promoting prosperity; عَمَّ الرَخاءُ البِلادَ there was prosperity in the country; في الرَخاءِ والشِدّةِ for better or for worse

رُخاء *n* breeze, gentle wind

رَخاوة *n* looseness, laxity; softness

رِخْويّ [A] *adj* soft, pulpy, pappy; حَيَوان رِخْويّ mollusc, mollusk [B] *n* mollusc (*Mollusca*)

رِخْويّات *n pl* (Zool) molluscs (*Mollusca*)

اِرْتِخاء *n* relaxation; loosening; laxity; اِرْتِخاء العَضَلاتِ muscle relaxation

اِسْتِرْخاء *n* relaxation

تَراخٍ *n* loosening, relaxation; limpness, weakness; inaction, complacency; فَعَلَ شَيْئاً بِدونِ تَراخٍ to do sth strictly; التَراخي في مُواجَهةِ شَيْءٍ complacency in the face of sth

مُتَراخٍ *adj* indolent, lax, languid; slack, limp

مُرْتَخٍ *adj* loose; limp; relaxed

‹ **رَدُؤَ** *v* |u; رَداءة| to be bad

رَداءة *n* badness, wickedness

رَديء *adj* |أَرْدِياءُ| bad, wicked; inferior, defective; مادّة رَديئة shoddy material; مَنْتوج من نَوْعٍ رَديءٍ a product of inferior quality

‹ **رَدْب** *n* |رُدوب| [1] [طَريق مَسْدود] cul-de-sac, blind alley [2] (Anat) recess; cavity

‹ **رَدَح** *n* a long (period of) time; رَدَحًا من الزَمَنِ for a long period of time

‹ **رَدَّ** *v* |u; رَدّ| [1] [أَجابَ] [على] to answer, to reply, to respond; رَدَّ النَظْرةَ to look back; رَدَّ كِتابةً to write back; رَدَّ رَدًّا لائِقاً to react appropriately; رَدَّ على شَيْءٍ to respond to sth; رَدَّ على نَقْدٍ to respond to criticism; رَدَّ على الهاتِفِ to answer the phone; رَدَّ على اعْتِداءٍ to retaliate; رَدَّ على رِسالةٍ to answer a letter; رَدَّ عَلَيْها التَحيّةَ to return her greeting; رَدَّ على شَخْصٍ بالمِثْلِ to give as good as one gets; رَدَّ بِبُطْءٍ \ بِسُرْعةٍ to respond slowly/quickly; رَدَّ بِامْتِعاضٍ to react indignantly [2] [أَعادَ] to give/hand back, to return; to refund; رَدَّ الرَسائِلَ to return the letters; رَدَّ المَبْلَغَ كُلَّهُ to refund the entire amount [3] [رَفَضَ] to reject; رَدَّ تُهْمةً to reject a charge [4] [عَزا] to attribute, to ascribe; رَدَّ إلى to attribute to

رَدَّدَ *v* to repeat; to do again; رَدَّدَ أَقْوالَ شَخْصٍ to repeat sb's words

تَرَدَّدَ *v* [1] [شَكَّ] to hesitate, to be reluctant; to waver, to vacillate; تَرَدَّدَ قَليلاً to hesitate for a moment; تَرَدَّدَ في فِعْلِ شَيْءٍ to hesitate to do sth; لا تَتَرَدَّدْ (في) أَنْ ... don't hesitate

تَرْداد *n* repetition; echoing

تَرَدُّد *n* 1 [حَيْرة] hesitation, hesitance, wavering, indecision, irresolution; بِدونِ \ بلا تَرَدُّدٍ unhesitatingly, with no hesitation; بعد قَليلٍ من التَرَدُّدِ after some hesitation 2 (Phys) |تَرَدُّدات| frequency; بتَرَدُّدٍ عالٍ high-frequency; أَصْوات بَطيئة التَرَدُّدِ low-frequency tones 3 [الصَوْتِ] resonance

تَرْديد *n* repetition

مُتَرَدِّد A *adj* 1 [حائِر] hesitant, irresolute, indecisive, uncertain; مَوْقف مُتَرَدِّد an indecisive attitude 2 (Elec) alternating; تَيّار مُتَرَدِّد AC, alternating current

B *n* waverer, vacillator

مُتَرَدِّدة *n* trombone; عَزَفَ على المُتَرَدِّدةِ to play the trombone

مُرْتَدّ A *adj* apostate, renegade; قَسّ مُرْتَدّ a renegade priest

B *n* apostate, heretic; أَبْدى المُرْتَدُّ نَدَمَهُ the apostate showed remorse

مَرَدّ *n* |مَرادُّ| factor; reason, cause

مَرْدود A *adj* unacceptable, inadmissible, impermissible

B *n* |مَرْدودات| yield, pay-off, output

مَرْدوديّة *n* productivity; cost-effectiveness

مُسْتَرَدّات *n pl* rebate

رَدَسَ *v* |i-u; رَدْس| to crush; to roll; رَدَسَ شَيْئاً to crush sth

مِرْداس *n* |مَراديسُ| roller

رَدَعَ *v* |a; رَدْع| to deter; رَدَعَ شَخْصاً عن فِعْلِ شَيْءٍ to deter sb from doing sth

ارْتَدَعَ *v* |عن| to be deterred from, to be prevented from

رَدْع *n* deterrence

رادِع A *adj* deterring; إجْراءات رادِعة deterrence measures

B *n* |رَوادِعُ| deterrent; بِدونِ رادِعٍ unchecked, uncurbed

رَدْعيّ *adj* deterrent, repellent; preventing; قُدْرة رَدْعيّة deterring power

رَدْغة *n* mud

رَدَفَ *v* |u; رَدْف| to follow; to succeed

رادَفَ *v* to be synonymous

أَرْدَفَ *v* to follow; to succeed; أَرْدَفَ قائِلاً ... he continued, saying ...

to ... 2 [إلى مَكانٍ] to frequent, to visit frequently; تَرَدَّدَ على مَكانٍ بِكَثْرةٍ to visit a place frequently; تَرَدَّدَ الشابُّ على المَسْجِدِ the young man frequented the mosque 3 [الصَوْتُ] to resonate 4 [على الأَلْسِنةِ] to circulate; تَتَرَدَّدُ الشائِعاتُ the rumours are going around

ارْتَدَّ *v* 1 [رَجَعَ] to go back, to revert; to move back; to cringe, to recoil, to shrink 2 [أَعْطى نَتائِجَ عَكْسيّةً] to turn on; to backfire; سِلاح يَرْتَدُّ على أَصْحابِهِ a weapon that will turn on its users (*a strategy/action that will backfire*) 3 [عَكَسَ] to reflect; ارْتَدَّ سَلْباً على شَخْصٍ \ شَيْءٍ to reflect negatively on sb/sth 4 [عن دينٍ] to apostatize; ارْتَدَّ عن دينِهِ to abandon one's religion; ارْتَدَّ الكاتِبُ عن الإسْلامِ the writer abandoned Islam 5 [كُرة] to bounce (back), to rebound; ارْتَدَّت الكُرةُ the ball rebounded 6 (Fin) to rebound (*stocks, prices, etc.*)

اسْتَرَدَّ *v* 1 [اسْتَرْجَعَ] to retrieve, to regain; اسْتَرَدَّ كِتاباً to get a book back; اسْتَرَدَّ صِحَّتَهُ to regain one's health 2 [طَلَبَ رَدَّهُ] to reclaim; اسْتَرَدَّ شَيْئاً من شَخْصٍ to reclaim sth from sb

رادّ *adj* repulsive, repellent

رادّة *n* لا رادّةَ فيهِ there's no point in that

رَدّ *n* |رُدود| 1 [إجابة] answer, reply, response; رَدّ إيجابيّ \ سَلْبيّ a positive/negative answer; رَدّ انْتِقاميّ retaliation; رَدّ لاذِع \ حادّ a caustic/sharp response; رَدّ الفِعْلِ reaction; ما كانَ رَدُّ فِعْلِهِ؟ what was his reaction?; تَلَقّى رَدًّا to receive a response; رَدًّا على in reply to; رَدّ على سُؤالٍ an answer to a question; رَدًّا على رِسالَتِكُمْ \ خِطابِكُمْ in reply to your letter; في انْتِظارِ الرَدِّ awaiting your reply; أَخْذ وَرَدّ discussion 2 [إرْجاع] return, restitution

رَدّة *n* refrain

رِدّة *n* 1 (Islam) apostasy, renunciation of belief; أَهْل الرِدّةِ apostates 2 (Hist) *rebellion of a number of Arab tribes after the death of the Prophet Muhammad*

ارْتِداد *n* |ارْتِدادات| 1 [رُجوع] withdrawal; return; regression 2 [عن الدينِ] apostasy 3 [كُرةٍ] bounce, rebound

ارْتِداديّ *adj* هَزّة ارْتِداديّة aftershock

اسْتِرْداد *n* 1 [إرْجاع] reclamation; retrieval; recovery 2 (Econ) refund

تَرادَفَ *v* **1** [تَتابَعَ] to succeed each other **2** (Ling) to be synonymous

رِدْف *n* |أَرْداف| **1** [حَيَوانٍ] rump **2** (Anat) buttock; behind, backside, bottom (BrE); الرِدْفانِ buttocks, cheeks (infml)

رَديف *n* |رُدَفاءُ| *a person sitting behind another on a a horse or bicycle*

تَرادُف *n* |تَرادُفات| synonymity

مُتَرادِف **A** *adj* synonymous; كَلِمات مُتَرادِفة synonymous words

B *n* |مُتَرادِفات| synonym

مُرادِف **A** *adj* synonymous

B *n* |مُرادِفات| synonym; مُرادِفات وَأَضْداد synonyms and antonyms; كَلِمة قِطٍّ مُرادِفٌ لِكَلِمةِ هِرٍّ 'cat' is a synonym of 'kitty'

‹ **رَدَمَ** *v* |i-u; رَدْم| to fill (up); رَدَمَ قَناةً \ بِئْراً to fill up a ditch/well; رَدَمَ هوّةً to bridge a gap

رَدْم *n* |رُدوم| rubble; filling (up), fill; رَدْم النُفاياتِ landfill

‹ **ردمك** *abbr* ISBN, international standard book number (*abbreviation of* رَقْم دُوَليّ مِعْياريّ للكِتابِ)

‹ **رَدَنَ** *v* |i; رَدْن| to spin

رُدْن *n* |أَرْدان| sleeve

‹ **رَدْهة** *n* |رَدَهات, رَدْه, رِداه| hall, lobby, lounge

‹ **رَدِيَ** *v* |a; رَدًى| to perish, to be destroyed

رَدّى *v* **1** [أَلْبَسَ] to clothe **2** [أَسْقَطَ] to fell, to bring down

أَرْدى *v* to throw down; to destroy, to ruin; to fell, to bring down

تَرَدّى *v* to fall; to deteriorate, to become worse; تَتَرَدّى النَوْعيّةُ the quality is deteriorating

ارْتَدى *v* to dress, to get dressed; to put on; to wear; ارْتَدى مِعْطَفاً to wear a coat; to put on a coat; ارْتَدى شالاً to wear a scarf; to put on a scarf; ارْتَدى مَلابِسَهُ to get dressed

رِداء *n* |أَرْدِية| robe; dress; clothing, garment

رَدًى *n* death

ارْتِداء *n* wearing; dressing, putting on; ارْتِداء المَلابِسِ wearing clothes

تَرَدٍّ *n* deterioration, decline, fall, drop

مُتَرَدٍّ *adj* declining, deteriorating, worsening; inferior; صِناعة الصُلْبِ الأَلْمانيّة المُتَرَدّية the ailing German steel industry

مُرْدٍ *n* |مُرْدِيات| antibiotic

‹ **رَذَّ** *v* |u; رَذّ| to drizzle; رَذَّت السَماءُ it was drizzling

أَرَذَّ *v* to drizzle; أَرَذَّت السَماءُ there was a drizzle

رَذاذ *n* drizzle; أَمْطَرَت السَماءُ رَذاذاً there was a drizzle; رَذاذ خَفيف a slight drizzle

مِرْذاذ *n* |مَراذيذُ| spray, sprayer; aerosol can; atomizer

‹ **رَذُلَ** *v* |u; رَذْل| to be low or vulgar

أَرْذَلَ *v* to reject

رَذْل **A** *adj* |أَرْذال| low, despicable

B *n* |أَرْذال| *low-class, despicable person*; أَرْذال riff-raff

رَذالة *n* lowness, meanness

رَذيل *adj* |رُذَلاءُ| low, mean, despicable

رَذيلة *n* |رَذائِلُ| vice; depravity; أُمّ الرَذائِلِ the worst vice; الجَهْلُ أُمُّ الرَذائِلِ ignorance is the root of all evil; غارَق في الرَذيلةِ to lead a life of depravity

أَرْذَل *adj* lower, baser, most despicable; الأَرْذَل lowest, basest; أَرْذَل العُمْرِ feeble old age

مَرْذول *adj* depraved, despicable, mean

‹ **رَزَأَ** *v* |a; رُزْء| to wrong; to cause a loss to

رُزْء *n* |أَرْزاء| disaster, calamity, catastrophe

رَزيئة, رَزيّة *n* |رَزايا| disaster, calamity, catastrophe

‹ **مِرْزَبّة** *n* |مَرازِبُ| sledgehammer

‹ **رَزَحَ** *v* |a; رَزْح, رُزوح, رُزاح, رَزاح| to succumb, to collapse, to sag; رَزَحَ تحت ضُغوطٍ to collapse under one's load; رَزَح بِحِمْلِهِ to succumb to heavy pressure; رَزَحَ تحت نيرِ الاسْتِعْمارِ to groan under the yoke of colonialism

رازِح *adj* sagging; سُكّان رازِحونَ تحت خَطِّ الفَقْرِ residents who fall below the poverty line

‹1 **رَزَّ** *v* |u; رَزّ| to insert; رَزَّ البابَ to fix a lock on the door

رَزّة *n* staple, U bolt (*part of a lock*)

‹2 **رُزّ** *n* rice; طَحين الرُزِّ rice flour

‹ **رَزَقَ** *v* |u; رِزْق| to bless; to bestow; رَزَقَهُ اللّٰهُ بِبِنْتٍ God blessed him with a daughter; رُزِق بِطِفْلٍ to have a child

ارْتَزَقَ *v* to make/earn a living, to support oneself

اسْتَرْزَقَ *v* to seek one's livelihood; to make a living

رِزْق *n* |أَرْزاق| livelihood, living, subsistence, daily bread; *God-given material blessings*; أَرْزاق احْتِياطِيّة emergency rations; كَسَبَ رِزْقَهُ to earn a living; رِزْق من اللهِ God-given sustenance

رَزّاق *n* الرَزّاق the Provider (*one of the names of God*)

اسْتِرْزاق *n* self-support

مُرْتَزِق *adj, n* |مُرْتَزِقة| mercenary

مَرْزوق *adj* blessed

‹ **رَزَمَ** *v* |a-i-u; رَزْم| to package; to pack; to bundle

رَزْم *n* packing; bundling

رِزْمة *n* |رِزَم| bundle; pack; package, parcel; رِزْمة ثِيابٍ \ صُحُفٍ a bundle of clothes/newspapers

‹ **رَزانة** *n* poise, equanimity; stoicism; sobriety; حافَظَ على رَزانَتِهِ to preserve one's stoicism

رَزين *adj* |رِزان| demure; serious, sedate, sober; balanced

‹ **رَزِيّة** *n* see رَزِيئة

‹ **رَسَبَ** *v* |u; رُسوب| **1** [في امْتِحانٍ] to fail, to not pass, to flunk; رَسَبَ في امْتِحانٍ to fail an exam **2** (Chem) to settle, to subside, to sink

رَسَّبَ *v* (Chem) to deposit, to precipitate, to let settle

تَرَسَّبَ *v* to precipitate; to settle, to subside; تَرَسَّبَ على زُجاجِ النافِذة to settle on the window glass

راسِب **A** *adj* **1** [ما تَرَسَّبَ] residual; sedimentary **2** [فاشِل] |راسِبونَ| failing; unsuccessful
B *n* |رَواسِبُ| deposit, sediment, residue; كَوَّنَ راسِباً to form a deposit; تَتَكَوَّنُ تِلْكَ الرَواسِبُ من الرَمْلِ والطَمْيِ those deposits consist of sand and silt; راسِب من الماضي a relic from the past

رُسابة *n* sediment; precipitate

رُسوب *n* failure, flunking

رُسوبِيّ *adj* sedimentary; رُسوبِيّات sediments

تَرَسُّب *n* |تَرَسُّبات| deposit, precipitate; precipitation, sedimentation, settlement

مُتَرَسِّب *n* precipitate

‹ **رَسَخَ** *v* |u; رُسوخ| to be/become firm, to be/become entrenched; to take root; تَرْسُخُ عادةٌ a custom persists; رَسَخَتْ عَقيدَتُهُ his belief has become entrenched; رَسَخَ في شَيْءٍ to be rooted in sth

رَسَّخَ *v* to strengthen, to reinforce, to consolidate, to stabilize; رَسَّخَ أَواصِرَ الصَداقةِ to strengthen the bonds of friendship

أَرْسَخَ *v* to make fast, to fix

تَرَسَّخَ *v* to be/become deep-rooted; to take root; to be/become firm, to be/become entrenched; to solidify; يَتَرَسَّخُ الاقْتِناعُ the conviction grows

راسِخ *adj* |animate pl راسِخونَ; inanimate pl رَواسِخُ| deep-rooted, entrenched; firm, solid, stable; إيمان راسِخ a firm belief; أَساس \ مَوْقِع راسِخ a solid basis/position; انْطِباع راسِخ an indelible impression

رُسوخ *n* stability, steadiness, establishment

تَرْسيخ *n* consolidation, strengthening, establishment

‹ **رَسَّ** *v* |u; رَسّ| to bury; رَسَّ بِئْراً to sink a well; رَسَّ مَيِّتاً to bury a dead person

رُسّة *n* (Bot) arum (*Araceae*)

‹ **رُسْغ** *n* |أَرْسُغ, أَرْساغ| wrist

‹ **راسَلَ** *v* to contact, to correspond, to write; راسَلَ شَخْصاً to contact sb; راسَلَ (شَخْصاً) بِصِفةٍ مُسْتَمِرّةٍ to maintain a regular correspondence with sb

أَرْسَلَ *v* **1** [بَعَثَ] to send, to mail, to dispatch; أَرْسَلَ رِسالةً to dispatch a letter; أَرْسَلَ شَيْئاً إلى شَخْصٍ to mail sth to sb; أَرْسَلَ خبَراً إلى البَيْتِ to send a message home; أَرْسَلَ بَضائِعَ إلى أَلْمانيا to send goods to Germany; أَرْسَلَ شَخْصاً إلى المُديرِ to send sb to the manager; أَرْسَلَ شَخْصًا لِشَيْءٍ to send sb for sth; أَرْسَلَ تَقْريراً لِشَخْصٍ to send a report to sb; أَرْسَلَ إشاراتِ إِنْذارٍ to send out distress signals **2** (Sport) to serve; أَرْسَلَ الكُرةَ بِقوّةٍ to serve the ball hard

تَرَسَّلَ *v* to write, to compose; to send

تَراسَلَ *v* to correspond, to write; تَراسَلَ مع شَخْصٍ to maintain a correspondence with sb

اسْتَرْسَلَ *v* **1** [الشَخْصُ] to enlarge, to elaborate; to go on, to continue (*for a long time*); اسْتَرْسَلَ في النَوْمِ to sleep a long time; اسْتَرْسَلَ في الكَلامِ \ الحَديثِ to speak at great length **2** [الشَعْرُ] to be long and straight (*hair*)

رِسالة *n* ① [خِطاب] |رَسائِلُ, رِسالات| letter; رِسالة جَوابيّة a response; رِسالة مَفْتوحة an open letter; رِسالة مُسَجَّلة a registered letter; رِسالة مَلْغومة letter bomb; تَبادُل رَسائِل correspondence; تَبادُل الرَسائِلِ بين شَخْصَيْنِ correspondence between two people; أَرْسَلَ رِسالةً ل \ إلى شَخْصٍ to send a letter to sb; كَتَبَ لِشَخْصٍ رِسالةً to write sb a letter; رِسالة بِخَطِّ اليَدِ a handwritten letter; رِسالَتُكُم المُؤَرَّخةُ في ٦ ماي your letter dated 6 May; رِسالة بالبَريدِ المُسْتَعْجَلِ \ السَريعِ express letter ② [خَبَر] |رَسائِلُ, رِسالات| message, communication; (blog) post; رِسالة كِتابيّة \ هاتِفيّة written/telephone communication; رِسالة شَفَويّة a verbal message; رِسالة إلِكْتْرونيّة email; رَسائِل أَقْدَم \ أَحْدَث older/newer posts (*of a blog*); رِسالة نَصّيّة \ قَصيرة text message; رِسالة خَطَأ error message; تَرَكَ رِسالةً to leave a message; نَقَلَ رِسالة شَخْصٍ to deliver sb's message; أَتى بِرِسالةٍ to bring a message ③ (Educ) |رَسائِلُ, رِسالات| dissertation, thesis; رِسالة ماجِسْتير \ دُكْتوراه master's/doctoral thesis; ناقَشَ رِسالةَ دُكْتوراه to defend a dissertation ④ [مُهِمّة الرَسول] |رِسالات| mission, calling; خاتَم الرِسالاتِ the seal of messages (*message of the Prophet Muhammad*); رِسالة خالِدة \ سَماوِيّة an eternal/divine mission

رَسول *n* |رُسُل| ① (Relig) prophet; الرَسول (*usually followed by the words* صَلّى اللهُ عَلَيْهِ وسَلَّمَ *or the abbreviation* صلعم) the Prophet (Muhammad); رَسول الله the messenger of God; كِتاب اللهِ وَسُنّة رَسولِهِ the Book of God and the Sunna of his Prophet; في عَهْدِ \ عَصْرِ الرَسولِ at the time of the Prophet ② [حَواريّ] apostle, disciple ③ [مُرْسَل] messenger; runner; emissary

رَسوليّ *adj* apostolic; relating to the messenger; الكُرْسيّ الرَسوليّ the Holy See

إرْسال *n* |إرْسالات| ① [إذاعة] broadcast, transmission; إرْسال مُباشِر a live broadcast; مَحَطّة إرْسالٍ broadcasting station; جِهاز إرْسالٍ radio transmitter; وَقْت الإرْسالِ broadcasting time; انْقَطَعَ إرْسالُ المَحَطّةِ the channel went off the air; حَذَفَ إرْسالَ مَحَطّةٍ to take a station off the air ② [بَعْث] sending, forwarding; إرْسال البَضائِع the dispatch of goods; إرْسال الرَسائِلِ \ الرِزَمِ sending letters/parcels; تَكاليف \ مَصاريف الإرْسالِ shipping costs; إرْسال بالبَريد sending through the mail ③ (Sport) service, serve

إرْساليّة *n* mission; consignment, shipment; إرْساليّات تَبْشيريّة missionary work; إرْساليّة مَعوناتٍ a consignment of relief supplies

اسْتِرْسال *n* ease, naturalness, nonchalance

تَراسُل *n* messaging; تَراسُل فَوْريّ instant messaging, IM

مُراسِل *n* ① [رَسائِلَ] correspondent; pen pal ② [صُحُفيّ] correspondent, reporter; مُراسِل صُحُفيّ correspondent; مُراسِل رِياضيّ sportscaster; مُراسِل حُرّ freelance correspondent; نَنْتَقِلُ إلى مُراسِلِنا في عَمّانَ we go over to our reporter in Amman; من مُراسِلِنا (المَحَلّيّ) by our reporter (on location)

مُراسَلة *n* ① [مُكاتَبة] correspondence; مُراسَلات business correspondence; مُراسَلات شَخْصيّة personal correspondence; مُراسَلات حَيّة \ مُتَواصِلة a lively correspondence; مُراسَلة كِتابيّة written communication; مُراسَلة شَخْصٍ a correspondence with sb; عُنْوان المُراسَلةِ postal address; المُراسَلة بين شَخْصَيْنِ the exchange of letters between two people; بعد تَبادُلِ المُراسَلاتِ after some correspondence back and forth ② (Comput) messaging; مُراسَلة فَوْريّة instant messaging, IM

مِرْسال *n* |مَراسيلُ| courier, messenger

مُرْسَل Ⓐ *adj* sent; بَريد مُرْسَل sent mail Ⓑ *n* messenger; delegate, deputy; مُرْسَل إلَيْه recipient; سورة المُرْسَلات The Emissaries (*Sura 77*)

مُرْسِل *n* sender; المُرْسِلُ مَجْهولٌ sender unknown; رَدَّ إلى المُرْسِلِ to return to the sender

مُرْسِلة *n* sender; transmitter

مُسْتَرْسِل *adj* straight; flowing; شَعْر مُسْتَرْسِل straight hair

رَسَمَ *v* |u; رَسْم| ① [صَوَّرَ] to draw, to sketch; to design; to paint; to portray; رَسَمَ مَناظِرَ طَبيعيّةً to paint landscapes; رَسَمَ خُطّةً to draw up a plan; رَسَمَ شَيْئاً على وَرَقٍ to draw sth on a paper ② [وَصَفَ] to describe, to depict, to portray ③ (Chr) to ordain; رَسَمَ كاهِناً to ordain a priest command; احْتَجَّ رَسْمِيًّا to enter a formal protest; شِبْه رَسْمِيٍّ unofficial; غَيْر رَسْمِيٍّ informal; اسْتِقْبال غَيْر رَسْمِيٍّ an informal reception; رَقْم قِياسيّ غَيْر رَسْمِيٍّ an unofficial record

B *n* **1** [مُوَظَّف] official **2** رَسْمِيّات [شَكْلِيّات] formalities; ceremonies

رُسومات, رُسوميّات *n pl* graphics; رُسومات حاسوبيّة computer graphics; رُسوميّات حاسوبيّة مُتَحَرِّكة computer animation

مَراسِم *n pl* |dipt| ceremony, ritual; مَراسِم الحَجِّ the hajj rituals; حَضَرَ مَراسِمَ to attend a ceremony مَراسِم دَفْن burial;

مِرْسام *n* |مَراسيمُ| stencil; طَبَعَ بالمِرْسام to stencil

مَرْسَم *n* |مَراسِمُ| studio

مَرْسوم **A** *adj* **1** [مُصَوَّر] drawn **2** [مُدَبَّر] planned **3** [مُتَعَمَّد] deliberate

B *n* |مَراسيمُ| decree, edict, ordinance, order; مَرْسوم مَلَكيّ royal decree; أَصْدَرَ مَرْسوماً to issue a decree; بِمَرْسوم by decree; بِواسِطةِ مَرْسوم تَشْريعيٍّ by legislative decree

رَسْمَلَ *v* |i; رَسْمَلة| to capitalize

رَسَن *n* |أَرْسُن, أَرْسان| halter, bridle; رَمى بِرَسَنِ شَخْصٍ على غارِبِهِ to leave sb to his own devices

رَسا *v* |u; رَسْو| **1** [أَوْقَفَ السَفينةَ على المِرْساةِ] to anchor, to moor, to make anchorage; رَسا على الضِفَّةِ to moor ashore; رَسَت السَفينةُ في الميناءِ the ship moored in the harbour **2** [حَطَّ] to land; رَسا على جانِبِ الطَريقِ to land beside the road; رَسا بِهِ المَطافُ he has settled after many wanderings

رَسّى *v* to place a bid; to win (*a contract/job after an open bid*)

أَرْسى *v* **1** [أَوْقَفَ] to anchor, to moor; أَرْسى سَفينةً to moor a ship **2** [رَسَّخَ] to establish, to anchor; أَرْسى أُسُسَ بِناءٍ to lay the foundation of a building **3** [رَسا] to anchor, to come to anchor

رُسوّ *n* anchoring, moorage, berthing; stability

راسٍ *adj* |رَواسٍ| firm, stable; anchored, moored; سَفينة راسِية (في ميناءٍ) a ship anchored (in a harbor)

إِرْساء *n* **1** [تَرْسيخ] establishment; establishing, laying; إِرْساء أَساسِ شَيْءٍ laying the foundation for sth **2** [رُسوّ] anchorage, moorage; anchoring; مَمْنوع الإِرْساءِ moorage prohibited

تَرَسَّمَ *v* to follow, to imitate

ارْتَسَمَ *v* **1** [ظَهَرَ] to show, to become visible/manifest; to be drawn; يَرْتَسِمُ الحُزْنُ على وَجْهِهِ sadness was clearly visible on his face **2** (Chr) to be ordained; to be consecrated

رَسْم *n* **1** [صورة] |رُسوم, رُسومات| drawing; painting; illustration; figure; رَسْم هَزْليّ \ كاريكاتوريّ cartoon, caricature; رَسْم مائيّ water colour; رَسْم تَوْضيحيّ illustration; رَسْم تَخْطيطيّ \ بيانيّ diagram; رَسْم تَفْصيليّ a detailed drawing; رَسْم أَوَّليّ preliminary study; رَسْم جِداريّ mural; رُسوم مُتَحَرِّكة (animated) cartoon; مُعَلِّم الرَسْمِ art teacher; دَفْتَر الرَسْمِ sketchbook; فَنّ الرَسْمِ painting; فَنّ الرَسْمِ الحَديث modern painting; خَطَّ \ أَنْجَزَ رَسْماً to make a drawing; وَضَعَ رُسوماً to illustrate; رَسْم على الحائِطِ wall painting

2 [تَصْميم] |رُسوم, رُسومات| design, pattern; آلة رَسْم plotter **3** [وَثيقة] |رُسوم, أَرْسُم| document; رَسْم عَدْليّ (Mor) a notarial deed; رَسْم مَلَكيّ a royal decree; رَسْم وِلادةٍ \ طَلاقٍ birth/divorce certificate; رَسْم الزَوْجيّة marriage certificate

4 [ضَريبة] |رُسوم, أَرْسُم| duty, fee; رُسوم fees; رُسوم جُمْرُكيّة import duties; رُسوم جامِعيّة university tuition; رُسوم بَريديّة postage; رُسوم الدِراسةِ school fees; رُسوم تَسْجيلٍ registration fee; رَسْم مُرورٍ toll; جَبى رَسْمَ مُرور (شَيْءٍ) to levy a toll (on sth); رُسوم اسْتيرادٍ import duty; رُسوم اسْتيرادِ السَيّاراتِ \ المَوْزِ import duty on cars/bananas; فَرَضَ رُسومَ اسْتيرادٍ to impose an import duty

رَسّام *n* **1** (Art) artist, painter; مِسْنَد رَسّامٍ (painter's) easel **2** [مِهْنة] graphic artist; illustrator; draughtsman (BrE), draftsman (AmE); رَسّام مِعْماريّ \ فَنّيّ architectural/technical draughtsman

رِسامة *n* ordination; consecration

رَسْمة *n* drawing

رَسْميّ **A** *adj* official; formal; ceremonial; اسْتِقْبال رَسْميّ a formal reception; بَدْلة رَسْميّة formal wear; (formal) suit; tuxedo; ceremonial dress, official robes; شَهادة رَسْميّة an official diploma; النَتيجة الرَسْميّة the official results; وَثائِق رَسْميّة official documents; عَشاء رَسْميّ a formal dinner; تَأْكيد رَسْميّ a formal confirmation; أَمْر رَسْميّ an official to come of age; فَقَدَ \ ضاعَ رُشْدَهُ to lose one's head; ثابَ \ عادَ إلى رُشْدِهِ to come to one's senses; العَوْدة إلى رُشْدِهِ repentance

راشِد **A** *adj* **1** [بالِغ] mature, adult; تَصَرُّف راشِد mature behaviour **2** [عاقِل] discerning
B *n* **1** [بالِغ] adult **2** (Islam) *a person who follows the right way;* الخُلَفاء الراشِدونَ the rightly guided caliphs (*the first four successors of the Prophet Muhammad*)

رَشاد *n* **1** [عَقْل] reason **2** (Bot) garden cress (*Lepidium sativum*)

رَشادة *n* **1** [صَخْر] stone; rock **2** [حِكْمة] wisdom, sensibility; أكْثَر رَشادةً wiser

رُشْدي, رُشْديّ *n* Rushdi (*male given name*)

رَشيد **A** *adj* |رُشَداءُ| reasonable, rational; rightly guided; قَرار رَشيد a sensible decision; غَيْر رَشيدٍ irrational
B *n* |رُشَداءُ| **1** [شَخْص بالِغ] adult **2** (Islam) الرَّشيد the Guide to the Right Path (*one of the names of God*) **3** [اسْم شَخْصيّ] Rashid (*male given name*) **4** [مَدينة] |f| Rosetta (*city in Egypt*); حَجَر رَشيد Rosetta Stone

إرْشاد *n* |إرْشادات| **1** [هِداية] guidance; إرْشاد روحيّ spiritual care **2** [تَوْجيه] direction; information; advice; إرْشادات information; إرْشادات طِبِّيّة medical instructions; إرْشادات صِحّيّة health education; أَعْطى \ قَدَّمَ إرْشاداتٍ صِحّيّةً to provide health education; إرْشاد مُتَخَصِّص expert guidance; اتَّبَعَ إرْشاداتٍ to follow directions; حَسَبَ إرْشاداتِ شَخْصٍ on instructions from sb; إرْشادات الاسْتِعْمالِ instructions (for use)

إرْشاديّ *adj* didactic, guidance (*before n*); notice (*before n*); دَليل إرْشاديّ didactic guide; تَوْجيه إرْشاديّ guidance counselling; لَوْحة إرْشاديّة noticeboard

الرَّشيديّة *n* Errachidia (*city in Morocco*)

تَرْشيد *n* rationalization; rationing, budgeting; direction, guidance

مُرْشِد *n* **1** [روحيّ] (spiritual) guide; مُرْشِد روحيّ spiritual director **2** [سِياحيّ] travel/tourist guide; كانَ مُرْشِدَ شَخْصٍ to be sb's guide; عَمِلَ مُرْشِداً سِياحيًّا to work as a travel guide **3** [يُقَدِّمُ مَعْلوماتٍ] instructor **4** (Naut) navigator, (ship's) pilot

تَرْسِية *n* award (*of a contract/job after open bidding*)

مِرْساة *n* |مَراسٍ| anchor; سِلْسِلة المِرْساةِ anchor chain; رَفَعَ المِرْساةَ to raise (the) anchor; أَلْقى المِرْساةَ to cast anchor

مَرْسًى *n* |مَراسٍ| anchorage, mooring; berth; harbour, port

رَشَحَ *v* |a; رَشْح| to seep, to leak; رَشَحَ من السَّقْفِ to seep through the ceiling

رَشَّحَ *v* **1** [للانْتِخاباتِ أو لِمَنْصِب] to nominate; رَشَّحَ نَفْسَهُ to submit oneself as a candidate; رَشَّحَ نَفْسَهُ للانْتِخاباتِ to run in the election **2** [صَفّى] to filter; رَشَّحَ الماءَ to filter water

تَرَشَّحَ *v* to be nominated, to be a candidate

رَشْح *n* **1** [مَرَض] cold; أَدْوِية الرَّشْحِ cold medicine **2** [ماء] perspiration, sweat **3** [مَصْدَر] leaking; رَشْح المِياهِ water percolation

ارْتِشاح *n* osmosis; filtration; leak, leakage

تَرَشُّح *n* nomination; candidature

تَرْشيح *n* |تَرْشيحات| **1** [لِمَنْصِبٍ، لانْتِخاباتٍ] nomination; بِطاقة تَرْشيحٍ ballot; تَرْشيح لِوَظيفةٍ a nomination for a position **2** [تَصْفِية] filter; وَرَق تَرْشيح filter

مُتَرَشِّح *n* candidate

مُرَشَّح *n* candidate, nominee; مُرَشَّح مُناسِب a suitable candidate; مُرَشَّح قَوِيّ a strong candidate; قائِمة المُرَشَّحينَ list of candidates; كانَ مُرَشَّحاً لِشَيْءٍ to be nominated for sth; وَجَدَ \ بَحَثَ عن مُرَشَّحينَ لِشَيْءٍ to find/look for candidates for sth; المُرَشَّح للفَوْزِ the favourite (to win); مُرَشَّح للدَوْر النِهائيّ finalist; مُرَشَّح أَوَّل على القائِمةِ person heading the list of candidates

مُرَشِّح *n* |مُرَشِّحات| filter; مُرَشِّح الزَّيْت oil filter; بَدَّلَ \ نَظَّفَ مُرَشِّحَ الزَّيْتِ to replace/clean the oil filter

رَشَدَ *v* |u; رُشْد| *to be on the right way/path*

رَشَّدَ *v* to guide, to lead (*the right way*)

أَرْشَدَ *v* to lead, to guide; to counsel, to advise; أَرْشَدَ شَخْصاً في المَدينةِ to take sb round the city

اسْتَرْشَدَ *v* to consult, to ask/seek advice; to be guided

رُشْد *n* reason, rationality; ripening; maturity; سِنّ الرُّشْدِ adolescence; بَلَغَ رُشْدَهُ ,بَلَغَ سِنَّ الرُّشْدِ to reach maturity,

‹ **تَرْشَرَشَ** *v* to splatter

رَشْراش *adj* tender (*meat*)

‹ **رَشَّ** *v* |u; رَشّ| to water; to sprinkle, to spray, to splash, to spatter; رَشَّ النَباتاتِ to spray the plants; رَشَّ الحَديقةَ \ النَباتاتِ to water the garden/plants; رَشَّ المُبيداتِ to spray herbicides; رَشَّ الخَلَّ على السَلَطةِ to sprinkle lettuce with vinegar

تَرَشَّشَ *v* to splatter

رَشّ *n* |رَشاش ,رِشاش| shower; رَشّ من المَطَرِ a spatter of rain

رَشاش *n* spatter, splash, spray; رَشاش من المَطَرِ a spatter of rain

رَشّاش **A** *adj* automatic (*weapon*); سِلاح رَشّاش an automatic weapon, a machine gun

B *n* |رَشّاشات| machine gun

رَشّاشة *n* **1** [سِلاح] |رَشّاشات| machine gun **2** [مِرَشّة] watering can

رَشّة *n* sprinkle

مِرَشّة *n* |مَراشّ| spray, sprayer, spray can; (spray) nozzle; sprinkler; watering can

‹ **رَشَفَ** *v* |i-u; رَشْف| to suck; to sip; to slurp

تَرَشَّفَ *v* to slurp; to sip, to drink; to drink (up), to gulp (down)

اِرْتَشَفَ *v* to slurp; to sip, to drink; to drink (up), to gulp (down); اِرْتَشَفَتْ قَهْوَتَها she gulped down her coffee

رَشْفة *n* sip, gulp

‹ **رَشَقَ** *v* |u; رَشْق |ب| to throw, to hurl, to pelt; رَشَقَ بالحِجارةِ to throw stones; رَشَقَ الشُرْطةَ بالحِجارة to throw stones at the police; رَشَقَ شَخْصاً بِعَيْنِه \ بِبَصَرِه \ بِنَظْرةٍ to cast a glance at sb

رَشُقَ *v* |u; رَشاقة| to be shapely; to be elegant/graceful

راشَقَ *v* to throw at each other

أَرْشَقَ *v* to throw; to shoot (*an arrow*)

تَراشَقَ *v* to pelt each other

رَشاقة *n* elegance, grace, gracefulness; حَرَكات مُفْعَمة بالرَشاقةِ graceful movements; بِرَشاقةٍ elegantly

رَشيق *adj* |رُشَقاءُ| elegant, graceful; slim, slender, svelte; قَوام رَشيق a slim figure; حَرَكات رَشيقة graceful movements

‹ **رَشَمَ** *v* |u; رَشْم| to mark, to designate; to seal

‹ **رَشا** *v* |u; رَشْو| to bribe; رَشا مُراقِبَ الضَرائِبِ to bribe the tax inspector

اِرْتَشى *v* to take/accept bribes, to be corrupt; اِرْتَشى من شَخْصٍ to accept a bribe from sb

رِشاء *n* |أَرْشِية| rope

رَشْوة ,رِشْوة ,رُشْوة *n* |رُشًى| **1** [فَساد] corruption, bribery; قَضيّة رَشْوةٍ a bribery scandal; فَضيحة رَشْوةٍ a corruption case; حَقَّقَ في قَضيّةِ رَشْوةٍ to investigate a case of corruption; رَفَعَ على شَخْصٍ دَعْوَى بِتُهْمةِ الرَشْوةِ to charge sb with bribery; اِتَّهَمَ شَخْصاً بالرَشْوةِ to accuse sb of corruption **2** [مَبْلَغ] bribe, inducement, pay-off; رَشْوة كَبيرة \ صَغيرة a big/small bribe; دَفَعَ رَشْوةً to pay a bribe; تَلَقّى \ قَبِلَ \ تَقاضى رَشْوةً to take a bribe

اِرْتِشاء *n* corruption, bribery

مُرْتَشٍ *adj* corrupt; سِياسيّون مُرْتَشونَ corrupt politicians

‹ **رَصَدَ** *v* |u; رَصْد| **1** [تَرَبَّصَ] to observe, to watch; رَصَدَ العَدُوَّ to spy on the enemy **2** (Busn) to set/put aside, to earmark; رَصَدَ مالاً to earmark money; رَصَدَ مَبْلَغاً لِشَيْءٍ to set aside money for sth

رَصَّدَ *v* to earmark, to set aside (*funds*)

أَرْصَدَ *v* to balance (*an account*); to set/put aside, to earmark

تَرَصَّدَ *v* to observe, to watch; تَرَصَّدَ شَخْصاً \ شَيْئاً to spy on sb/sth

رَصْد *n* |أَرْصاد| observation, watching; تَقْرير الأَرْصادِ weather report; عِلْم الأَرْصادِ الجَوّيّة meteorology; عالِم الأَرْصادِ الجَوّيّة meteorologist

راصِد *n* |رُصّاد| monitor, observer, watcher; guard

رَصيد *n* |أَرْصِدة| balance; رَصيد مُعَلَّق an outstanding balance; رَصيد دائِن \ مَدين a credit/debit balance; رَصيد فائِض deficit; أَرْصِدة مُجَمَّدة frozen assets; رَصيد هاتِفٍ phone credit; شَحَنَ رَصيدَ هاتِفٍ to top up a phone's credit; رَصيد حِسابِ الادِّخار savings balance; اِسْتَنْفَدَ رَصيدَهُ البَنْكيَّ to exhaust one's bank account; كانَ لَهُ رَصيدٌ في البَنْكِ to have a balance at the bank; كانَ لَدَيْهِ رَصيدٌ كافٍ في حِسابِهِ he had sufficient funds in his account; بِدونِ رَصيدٍ uncovered; شيك بِدونِ رَصيدٍ a bad cheque

تَرَصُّد *n* والتَرَصُّدِ مع سَبْقِ الإِصْرارِ with premeditation

مِرْصاد *n* |مَراصيدُ| lookout, observation post

مَرْصَد *n* |مَراصِدُ| observation post; مَرْصَد فَلَكِيّ observatory

‹ **رَصّ** *v* |u; رَصّ| to compress, to press together; to pile up

رَصَّص *v* to cover with lead

تَراصَّ *v* to be pressed/packed together; to be piled up; to be/become compact

ارْتَصَّ *v* to be piled up; to be pressed together

رَصاص **A** *n* [مَعْدِن] lead; خالٍ من الرَصاصِ lead-free; قَلَم رَصاصٍ pencil
B *n coll* [سِلاحٍ ناريّ] bullet; fire, gunfire; رَصاصة مَطّاطيّة a rubber bullet; رَصاصة قاتِلة \ طائِشة a deadly/stray bullet; رَصاص حَيّ live ammunition; أَثَر رَصاصةٍ bullet hole; أَطْلَقَ رَصاصةً to fire a bullet; أَطْلَقَ وابلاً من الرَصاصِ to fire a barrage of bullets; مَثْقوب بالرَصاصِ riddled with bullets; حَكَمَ على شَخْصٍ بالإِعْدامِ رَمْياً بالرَصاصِ to sentence sb to be shot; مُقاوِم للرَصاصِ bulletproof; صَدْريّة ضدّ الرَصاصِ a bulletproof vest

رَصاصِيّ *adj* **1** [مَعْدِن] lead **2** [لَوْن] leaden (grey)

تَراصّ *n* agglutination; stacking; compaction; compactness

مُتَراصّ *adj* compact; pressed together; compressed; كانَ المُشْتَرِكونَ يَنْتَظِرونَ مُتَراصّينَ the participants huddled together waiting

مَرْصوص *adj* solid; compact; compressed, packed together

‹ **رَصَّعَ** *v* to inlay, to set, to stud; رَصَّعَ خاتِماً بالماسِ to set a ring with diamonds

رَصيعة *n* |رَصائِعُ| **1** [ميدالِية] medallion **2** [مُرَصَّع] inlay

مُرَصَّع *adj* inlaid, set (with), studded; مُرَصَّع بالذَهَبِ inlaid with gold; مُرَصَّع بالأَحْجارِ الكَريمةِ jewel-studded

‹ **رَصَفَ** *v* |u; رَصْف| to pave, to surface; رَصَفَ شارِعاً (بِأَحْجارٍ) to pave a street (with cobblestones)

رَصُفَ *v* |u; رَصافة| to be/become firm, to be/become compact

رَصَّفَ *v* to pave

تَراصَفَ *v* to be aligned; to form a line

رَصْف *n* paving, surfacing; أَعادَ رَصْفَ الشارِعِ to repave the road

رَصيف *n* |أَرْصِفة| **1** [مَكان مُرْتَفِع] pier, quay, wharf; رَصيف عائِم floating dock; رَصيف ميناءٍ pier, quay, wharf; الرَصيف; رَصيف المَحَطّةِ \ القِطارِ (station/train) platform; رَقْم أَرْبَعةٍ platform four **2** [جانِب الطَريقِ] pavement (BrE), sidewalk (AmE); رَصيف مَقْهًى \ مَطْعَمٍ cafe/restaurant terrace; على الرَصيفِ on the pavement

تَراصُف *n* alignment; تَراصُف الكَواكِبِ planetary alignment

مَرْصوف *adj* paved; طَريق مَرْصوف a paved road

‹ **رَصُنَ** *v* |u; رَصانة| to be/become calm, to be/become composed

رَصانة *n* seriousness, sobriety; calm; imperturbability

رَصين *adj* |رِصان| serious, sober, sedate; calm; رَجُل رَصين a calm man

‹ **رُضاب** *n* saliva, spittle

رُضابِيّ *adj* salivary; غُدّة رُضابيّة salivary gland

‹ **رَضْح** *n* trauma

رَضْحِيّ *adj* traumatic

‹ **رَضَخَ** *v* |a-i; رُضوخ| **1** [خَضَعَ] to yield, to bow, to give in, to acquiesce; رَضَخَ لِضَغْطٍ to give in to pressure; رَضَخ للأَمْرِ الواقِعِ to reconcile oneself to reality **2** [كَسَّرَ] to break; to crack (*nuts*)

رُضوخ *n* caving, submission, acquiescence

‹ **رَضْراض** *n* ballast (*for railways, roads*)

‹ **رَضَّ** *v* |u; رَضّ| to bruise; رَضَّ كاحِلَهُ to sprain one's ankle

رَضّ *n* |رُضوض| contusion, bruise; injury, trauma; strain, sprain

رَضّة *n* contusion, bruise; injury, trauma; strain, sprain

رَضيض *adj* bruised; crushed

مَرْضوض *adj* bruised; crushed

‹ **رَضَعَ, رَضِعَ** *v* |a-i; رَضْع, رَضاع, رَضاعة| to suckle, to nurse; رَضَعَ الثَدْيَ, رَضَعَ من الثَدْيِ to nurse at the breast

رَضَّعَ *v* to breastfeed, to nurse

أَرْضَعَ *v* to breastfeed, to nurse; أَرْضَعَ مَوْلوداً to breastfeed a baby

راضِعة *n* |رَواضِعُ| milk/baby tooth

رِضاع ,رَضاع *n* breastfeeding

رِضاعة ,رَضاعة *n* suckling; رَضاعة طَبيعيّة \ الثَدْيِ breastfeeding; رَضاعة اصْطِناعيّة bottle-feeding

رَضّاعة *n* feeding bottle

رَضْعة *n* feed *(baby's meal)*

رَضيع *n* |رُضَّع ,رُضَعاءُ ,رَضائِعُ| baby, infant

إرْضاع *n* feeding; breastfeeding

مُرْضِعة *n* **1** [امْرأة تُرْضِعُ وَلَدَ غَيْرِها] wet nurse **2** [امْرأة تُرَبّي وَلَدَ غَيْرِها] foster mother

مِرْضَعة *n* |مَراضِعُ| feeding bottle

رَضْفة *n* |رَضْف| kneecap, patella

رَضِيَ *v* |a; رِضًى ,رِضْوان ,مَرْضاة| to be satisfied/content (with); to be pleased (with); to approve (of); رَضِيَ شَيْئاً to be content with sth; رَضِيَ ب \ على \ عن شَيْءٍ to be satisfied with sth; رَضِيَ اللهُ عَنْهُ may God be pleased with him *(added to the name of companions of the Prophet Muhammad)*

رَضّى *v* to satisfy, to please; رَضّى شَخْصاً to please sb

راضى *v* to try to satisfy/please

أَرْضى *v* to satisfy, to please, to gratify, to content; أَرْضى شَخْصاً to content sb; أَرْضى الناسَ to please the people

تَرَضّى *v* to try to satisfy/please

تَراضى *v* to be/become reconciled (with each other), to make up

ارْتَضى *v* to approve, to embrace; to be satisfied; ارْتَضى شَيْئاً to be satisfied with sth

اسْتَرْضى *v* to placate, to appease; to try to satisfy/please

رَضِيّ *adj* |أَرْضِياءُ| satisfied, content

راضٍ *adj* |رُضاة| **1** [مُرْتاح] satisfied, content, fulfilled; غَيْر راضٍ dissatisfied; غَيْر راضٍ عن شَيْءٍ \ شَخْصٍ displeased with sth/sb; أَلَسْتَ راضِياً عن ذلك؟ aren't you satisfied with that? **2** [مُوافِق] willing; راضِياً أو كارِهاً willingly or unwillingly, like it or not

رِضاء *n* satisfaction, contentment, pleasure

رِضْوان *n* **1** [رِضًى] pleasure; رِضْوانُ اللهِ عَلَيْهِ may the pleasure of God be with him *(added to the name of an honoured person)* **2** [اسْم شَخْصِيّ] Ridwan, Redouan *(male given name)*

رِضًى ,رِضاً *n* **1** [اغْتِباط] satisfaction, contentment, pleasure, fulfilment; نَظْرة رِضًى a contented look; نَظَرَ بِرِضًى to look with satisfaction; بَدَتْ على وَجْهِها أَماراتُ الرِضى her face showed signs of contentment; عَدَم الرِضى dissatisfaction; عَدَم الرِضى من شَيْءٍ \ عن شَخْصٍ dissatisfaction with sth/sb; رِضى اللهِ من رِضى الوالِدَيْنِ honour thy father and thy mother **2** [اسْم شَخْصيّ] Rida *(male given name)*

إرْضاء *n* |إرْضاءات| satisfaction, contentment; صَعْب الإرْضاءِ fastidious; إرْضاءً لِوَجْهِ اللهِ to please God

اسْتِرْضائيّ *adj* conciliatory

تَراضٍ *n* **1** [تَوافُق] mutual consent **2** *(Pol)* compromise, consensus, rapprochement

تَرْضِية *n* **1** [إرْضاء] satisfaction, fulfilment; compensation **2** *(Islam) pronouncing the formula* رَضِيَ اللهُ عَنْهُ

مُرْضٍ *adj* acceptable, satisfactory; مُهِمّة مُرْضِية a rewarding task; تَسْوِية مُرْضِية an acceptable compromise; غَيْر مُرْضٍ unsatisfactory; نَتيجة غَيْر مُرْضِية an unsatisfactory outcome; جَواب غَيْر مُرْضٍ a lame answer

مَرْضاة *n* satisfaction, gratification, pleasure

رَطِبَ ,رَطُبَ *v* |a-u; رُطوبة ,رَطابة| to be/become damp, to be/become humid; to be/become wet

رَطَّبَ *v* to moisten; to soften; رَطَّبَ شَفَتَيْهِ بِلِسانِهِ to moisten one's lips with one's tongue

أَرْطَبَ *v* to moisten, to wet

تَرَطَّبَ *v* to be moistened/dampened

رَطْب *adj* moist, damp, humid; غُرْفة رَطْبة a damp room; جَوّ رَطْب humid weather; مَلابِس رَطْبة wet clothes

رُطَب *n coll* |أَرْطاب| *fresh, ripe dates*

رُطوبة *n* humidity; wetness; رُطوبة نِسْبيّة relative humidity; نِسْبة رُطوبةٍ humidity; رُطوبة الجَوّ air humidity; نِسْبة رُطوبةٍ عالِية \ مُنْخَفِضة high/low humidity; تَبْلُغُ نِسْبةُ الرُطوبةِ ١٠ بالمِائة the humidity is 10 per cent

تَرْطيب *n* wetting, dampening, moistening

مُرَطِّب *n* refreshment; moisturizer; مُرَطِّبات refreshments; كَأْس \ عُلْبة \ زُجاجة من المُرَطِّباتِ a glass/can/bottle of soft drink; مُرَطِّب الجِسْمِ body lotion

‹ **رَطْل, رِطْل** *n* |أَرْطال| ❶ (Egypt, NA) *a unit of mass equal to approximately 450 grams* ❷ (Syria) *a unit of mass equal to approximately 3.2 kilograms* ❸ [في النِظامِ الغَرْبيِّ] pound (*a unit of mass equal to 454 grams*)

‹ **رَطَمَ** *v* |u; رَطْم| to bump, to crash, to thump

ارْتَطَمَ *v* ❶ [ب| اصْطَدَمَ] to bump, to thump, to crash, to knock, to strike, to hit; ارْتَطَمَ بِشَيْءٍ to run up against sth; ارْتَطَمَ بالبابِ to hammer on the door; ارْتَطَمَ بالجِدارِ to bump against the wall; ارْتَطَمَتْ رَكْبَتُهُ بِشَيْءٍ to bang one's knee on sth ❷ [وَقَعَ] to fall, to tumble

ارْتِطام *n* |ارْتِطامات| collision; hit, impact; ارْتِطام نَيْزَكٍ \ شِهابٍ the impact of a meteor

‹ **رَطَنَ** *v* |u; رَطانة, رِطانة| to jabber, to speak gibberish

رَطانة *n* gibberish

‹ **رَعَبَ** *v* |a; رُعْب| to be frightened/afraid; to be terrified; رَعَبَ من صَوْتِ الانْفِجارِ to be frightened by the sound of the explosion

رَعَّبَ *v* to frighten, to scare; رَعَّبَتْ تَصْريحاتُهُ السُكّانَ his remarks frightened the inhabitants

أَرْعَبَ *v* to frighten, to scare; to terrify; to alarm; أَرْعَبَتْ تَصْريحاتُهُ السُكّانَ his remarks alarmed the inhabitants; إنّ ما يُرْعِبُني هو وُجودُ مُعارَضةٍ what frightens me is that there is opposition

ارْتَعَبَ *v* |من| to be frightened/scared (of/by), to be terrified (of/by); to be horrified (by); ارْتَعَبَ من شَيْءٍ to be terrified by sth; ارْتَعَبَ من رُؤْية ثُعْبانٍ to take fright at the sight of a snake

رُعْب *n* horror, terror; fear, scare; alarm; قِصّة رُعْبٍ scary story; قِصّة رُعْبٍ مُثيرة an exciting thriller; يَعُمُّ الرُعْبُ fear is prevailing; فَعَلَ شَيْئاً رُعْباً لا رُغْباً *to do sth out of fear rather than by design*

مُرْعِب 🅰 *adj* terrifying, horrifying; frightening, scary; alarming, appalling; صَوْت مُرْعِب a scary sound; مَنْظَر مُرْعِب a terrifying spectacle; فيلْم مُرْعِب a horror film 🅱 *n* creep; horror

مَرْعوب *adj* terrified; frightened, scared

‹ **رَعَدَ** *v* |a-u; رَعْد| to thunder; تَرْعَدُ السَماءُ it's thundering; تَرْعَدُ السَماءُ وَتُبْرِقُ the sky thunders and flashes; رَعَدَ لِشَخْصٍ وَبَرَقَ to threaten sb

أَرْعَدَ *v* to make tremble/shudder

ارْتَعَدَ *v* to tremble, to shudder, to shiver; ارْتَعَدَتْ فَرائِصُهُ to be terrified

رَعْد *n* |رُعود| thunder; سورة الرَعْد The Thunder (*Sura 13*); قَصَفَ الرَعْدُ a thunderstorm broke out; جَلْجَلَ الرَعْدُ the thunder rolled

راعِد *adj* thundering

رَعّاد *n coll* (Zool) electric catfish (*Malapterurus electricus*)

رِعْدة *n* tremor, shudder, shiver; trembling; أَصابَتْهُ رِعْدةٌ a tremor went through him

رَعْديّ *adj* thunderous

رِعْديد *adj* cowardly; timid; جَبان رِعْديد a big coward

‹ **رَعْرَعَ** *v* |i; رَعْرَعة| to let grow

تَرَعْرَعَ *v* to grow, to flourish; to grow up, to be raised; وُلِدَ وَتَرَعْرَعَ في مَكانٍ to be born and bred somewhere

‹ **رَعَشَ** *v* |a; رَعْش| to tremble, to shake, to shiver

أَرْعَشَ *v* to make tremble

ارْتَعَشَ *v* to tremble, to shake, to quake, to shiver; ارْتَعَشَتْ أَوْصالُهُ \ أَطْرافُهُ his limbs shuddered; ارْتَعَشَ من الخَوْفِ \ اللَذّةِ to tremble with fear/pleasure; ارْتَعَشَ من الحُمّى \ البَرْدِ \ الخَوْفِ to shake with fever/cold/fear

راعِش *adj* trembling, shaking

رَعّاش *n* (Zool) electric catfish (*Malapterurus electricus*)

رُعاش *n* quake, tremor; tic

رُعاشيّ *adj* شَلَل رُعاشيّ Parkinson's disease

رَعْشة *n* |رَعَشات| trembling, shaking, quivering; tremor, jerk, shiver; انْتابَتْهُ رَعْشةٌ to have the shakes

ارْتِعاش *n* |ارْتِعاشات| trembling, shaking, quivering

مُرْتَعِش *adj* trembling, shaking, shaky

‹ **رَعاع** *n* riff-raff, rabble

‹ **رَعَفَ** *v* |a; رُعاف, رَعْف| to bleed (*the nose*); رَعَفَ أَنْفُهُ his nose was bleeding

رُعاف *n* nosebleed; أُصيبَ بِرُعافٍ to have a nosebleed

‹ **رَعْل** *n* (Zool) drone

رُعْلة *n* wreath

رَعيل *n* |أرْعال, رِعال| leading group; generation

رَعَنَ, رَعُنَ *v* |u; رَعْن, رَعونة| to be frivolous, to be stupid/silly; رَعَنَتْهُ الشَمْسُ to have a sunstroke

رُعونة *n* folly, frivolity; stupidity

أرْعَن *adj* |dipt; رُعْن| reckless, careless, thoughtless; frivolous, hare-brained; تَصَرُّف أرْعَن indiscretion; سائِق أرْعَن a reckless driver

رَعى *v* |a; رَعْي, رِعاية, مَرْعًى| ① [الماشِيةَ] to tend, to graze ② [الماشِيةُ] to graze, to feed; يَرْعى البَقَرُ في المَرْجِ the cows are grazing in the field ③ [حَفِظَ] to guard, to protect, to watch

راعى *v* to observe, to respect, to heed, to pay attention to sth; راعى شَيْئاً to observe sth; راعى القَرارَ to comply with the decision; راعى شُعورَ شَخْصٍ to respect sb's feelings; راعى \ لم يُراعِ نَصيحةً to (not) heed advice

أرْعى *v* ① [الماشِيةَ] to graze ② [اسْتَمَعَ] to listen closely; أرْعى شَخْصاً سَمْعَهُ to listen closely to sb

اسْتَرْعى *v* to attract, to draw; اسْتَرْعى الانْتِباهَ to attract attention

رَعْي *n* grazing, pasturing; رَعْياً لَكَ may God be with you; الإفراط في الرَعْي overgrazing

راعٍ *n* |رُعاة, رُعْيان, رِعاء| ① [فَلّاح] shepherd; راعي بَقَرٍ (أمْريكيّ) an (American) cowboy; راعي الغَنَم shepherd ② [داعِم] guardian, caretaker; patron, sponsor

رِعاية *n* care, protection; رِعاية مُرَكَّزة \ مُشَدَّدة intensive care; رِعاية الفُقَراءِ care for the poor; رِعاية صِحّيّة health care; هَيْئة الرِعايةِ الصِحّيّة health service; دَوْلة رِعايةٍ a welfare state; إجازة رِعايةٍ care leave; مَرْكَز رِعايةٍ nursing home; مَرْكَز رِعاية الطِفْل child health centre; تحت رِعاية ... under the auspices of ..., sponsored by ...; في رِعايةِ اللهِ in God's care (*when saying goodbye*)

رَعَوِيّ *adj* ① [ريفيّ] rural, bucolic; pasture-; مَناطِق رَعَوِيّة pastureland ② (Chr) pastoral

رَعَوِيّة *n* citizenship, nationality

رَعِيّة *n* |رَعايا| citizen; رَعايا (كَنيسةٍ) congregation

مُراعاة *n* ① [اعْتِبار] consideration, respect; مُراعاةً لِشَخْصٍ out of respect for sb; مُراعاةً لِشُعورِها in deference to her feelings; من دونِ مُراعاةِ أحَدٍ without regard to anyone ② [الْتِزام] observance, compliance; مُراعاة قَوانينَ \ قَواعِدَ \ تَوْجيهاتٍ observance of laws/rules/regulations; مع مُراعاةِ الشُروطِ in accordance with the terms

مَرْعًى *n* |مَراعٍ| pasture, pastureland, grassland

مَرْعِيّ *adj* observed, respected; كانَ مَرْعِيّاً to be observed

رَغِبَ *v* |a; رَغْبة, رَغَب| ① [أرادَ] |في| to wish, to desire, to want; رَغِبَ (في) أنْ ... to wish that ...; رَغِبَ إلى شَخْصٍ في شَيْءٍ to ask sb for sth ② [كَرِهَ] |عن| to dislike; رَغِبَ عن شَيْءٍ to have a dislike of sth

رَغَّبَ *v* to interest, to arouse/awaken interest; رَغَّبَ شَخْصاً في شَيْءٍ to interest sb in sth

أرْغَبَ *v* to interest, to arouse/awaken interest; أرْغَبَ صَديقَهُ في فِعْلِ شَيْءٍ he made his friend interested in doing sth

رُغْب *n* فَعَلَ شَيْئاً رُعْباً لا رُغْباً *to do sth out of fear rather than by design*

راغِب *adj* |في| willing; desirous; interested (in); راغِب في شَيْءٍ desirous of sth; راغِب في التَعَلُّمِ \ الشِراءِ eager to learn/buy

رَغْبة *n* |رَغَبات, رِغاب| wish, desire; lust; رَغْبة عارِمة a fervent wish; رَغْبَتُهُ الأخيرةُ his last wish; رَغْبة مُلِحّة impulse; شَعَرَ بِرَغْبةٍ مُلِحّةٍ في عَمَلِ شَيْءٍ to feel a strong urge to do sth; كانَتْ لَدَيْهِ رَغْبةٌ في شَيْءٍ to feel like sth; انْتابَتْهُ رَغْبةٌ في فِعْلِ شَيْءٍ he was tempted to do sth; أعْلَنَ \ أبْدى رَغْبَتَهُ في أنْ ... to express the wish that ...; لَبّى رَغَباتِ شَخْصٍ to comply with sb's wish; شَعَرَ بانْعِدامِ الرَغْبةِ to feel listless; رَكَّزَ رَغْبَتَهُ على شَيْءٍ to set one's heart on sth; أشْبَعَ رَغَباتٍ جِنْسيّةً to satisfy sexual desires; رَغْبة في عَمَلٍ \ فِعْلِ شَيْءٍ a wish to do sth; رَغْبة في الحَياةِ a zest for life; الرَغْبة في النَجاحِ the wish to succeed; لا رَغْبةَ لي في ذلك I don't want that; حَسَبَ الرَغْبةِ to one's liking; عند الرَغْبةِ if (so) desired; رَغْبةً أو رَهْبةً willy-nilly

رَغيبة *n* |رَغائِبُ| wish; desire; رَغائِب desires

تَرْغيب *n* arousal of interest

مَرْغوب *adj* مَرْغوب فيهِ desirable; شَيْء مَرْغوب فيه sth desirable/wanted; object of desire; غَيْر مَرْغوبٍ فيه undesirable, unwanted; شَخْص غَيْر مَرْغوبٍ فيهِ an undesirable; حالة غَيْر مَرْغوبٍ فيها an undesirable situation; كانَ مَرْغوباً \ غَيْرَ مَرْغوبٍ فيه to be sought after/unwanted;

اعْتَبَرَ شَيْئاً مَرْغوباً \ غَيْرَ مَرْغوبٍ فيهِ to consider sth desirable/undesirable

‹ **رَغْد** *adj* pleasant, comfortable, agreeable; عاشَ في رَغْدٍ to live comfortably

رَغَد *n* comfort

رَغيد *adj* pleasant, agreeable, comfortable; well-off, affluent

‹ **رَغيف** *n* |أَرْغِفة, رُغْفان, رُغْف| loaf (*of bread*); رَغيفُ الخُبْزِ a loaf of bread

‹ **أَرْغَمَ** *v* |على| to force to, to compel to; أَرْغَمَ شَخْصاً على فِعْلِ شَيْءٍ to force sb to do sth

رَغْم, رُغْم *n* رَغْماً عن أَنْفِهِ in spite of himself; على رَغْمِ شَيْءٍ, الرَغْمِ من شَيْءٍ in spite of sth; على الرَغْمِ من \ ب despite; على الرَغْمِ مِنْهُ, رَغْماً عَنْهُ in spite of that; على الرَغْمِ من ذلك against one's will; على الرَغْمِ من إهْمالِهِ فَقَدْ نَجَحَ despite his negligence, he succeeded

رَغْمَ *prep* despite, in spite of, notwithstanding, for all; رَغْمَ أنّ although; رَغْمَ ذلك in spite of that; رَغْمَ أَنْفِهِ in spite of himself

راغِم *adj* unwilling, reluctant

رُغامى *n* |f| windpipe, trachea

إرْغام *n* force, compulsion, coercion; أَمْر إرْغامٍ writ

مُرْغَم *adj* forced; مُرْغَماً out of necessity; كانَ مُرْغَماً على فِعْلِ شَيْءٍ to be forced to do sth

‹ **رَغا** *v* |u; رَغْو| to foam, to froth, to lather; رَغا الماءُ the water foamed

رَغّى *v* to foam

أَرْغى *v* to foam; to lather; أَرْغى وَأَزْبَدَ to foam with rage

رَغّاء *n* chatterbox

رُغاء *n* grumble (*of a camel*)

رَغْوة, رُغْوة *n* |رَغاوٍ| foam, froth; lather

رَغْويّ *adj* foamy, frothy; lathery

مُرْغٍ *adj* foamy

مِرْغاة *n* |مَراغٍ| skimmer

‹ **رَفَأَ** *v* |a; رَفْء| to mend, to repair; رَفَأَ ثَوْباً to mend a garment

رَفَّأَ *v* to congratulate

رِفاء *n* harmony; conjugal bliss; بالرِفاءِ والبَنينِ good luck and blessings (*to newly-weds*)

مَرْفَأ *n* |مَرافِئُ| harbour, port

‹ **رَفَتَ** *v* |u; رَفْت| **1** [كَسَرَ] to break **2** [طَرَدَ] to dismiss

رُفات *n* rubble; (mortal) remains; رُفات قِدّيسٍ relic

مِرْفَت *n* listed alphabetically

‹ **رَفَثَ** *v* |i-u; رَفْث| to behave obscenely

‹ **رَفَح** *n* |f| Rafah (*city in Palestine*)

‹ **رَفَدَ** *v* |i; رَفْد| **1** [ساعَدَ] to support; to supplement **2** (Tech) to prop

رافَدَ *v* to assist

رافِد *n* |رَوافِدُ| tributary; الرافِدانِ the Euphrates and Tigris rivers; بِلاد الرافِدَيْنِ Mesopotamia; Iraq

رافِدة *n* |رَوافِدُ| support; girder

‹ **رَفْرَفَ** *v* |i; رَفْرَفة| to flap, to flutter; تُرَفْرِفُ الرايةُ the flag is flying; يُرَفْرِفُ العَلَمُ the flag is flapping; يُرَفْرِفُ الفَراشُ butterflies flutter

رَفْرَف *n* |رَفارِفُ| **1** [السَيارة] mudguard **2** [وِسادة] cushion

رَفْراف *n* **1** (Zool) kingfisher (*Alcedinidae*) **2** [مَدينة] |f dipt| Raf Raf (*town in northern Tunisia*)

مُرَفْرِف *adj* flapping

‹ **رَفَسَ** *v* |i-u; رَفْس| to kick; رَفَسَ كَلْباً \ خَصْماً to kick a dog/opponent; رَفَسَ حَجَرةً \ كُرةً to kick a stone/ball

رَفّاس *n* propeller

رَفْسة *n* |رَفَسات| kick

‹ **رَفْش** *n* shovel, spade

‹ **رَفّاص** *n* |رَفّاصات| **1** [مِرْوَحة السَفينة] propeller **2** [سَفينة] steamboat

‹ **رَفَضَ** *v* |i-u; رَفْض| to refuse, to decline, to reject, to turn down; to dismiss; رَفَضَ شَيْئاً to turn down sth; رَفَضَ مَشْروعاً \ اقْتِراحاً to reject a plan/proposal; رَفَضَ فِكْرةً to dismiss an idea; رَفَضَ شَكْوًى to reject a complaint; رَفَضَ طَلَباً to refuse a request; رَفَضَ دُخولي he refused me access; رَفَضَ الدَفْعَ to refuse to pay; رَفَضَ قُبولَ شَيْءٍ to refuse to accept sth; رَفَضَ أَيَّ شَكْلٍ من أَشْكالِ المُساعَدةِ to refuse

تَرَفَّعَ *v* to look down; تَرَفَّعَ عن شَيْءٍ to be above sth; تَرَفَّعَ عن شَخْصٍ to look down on sb

تَرافَعَ *v* to plead; تَرافَعَ عن شَخْصٍ to plead in sb's defence

ارْتَفَعَ *v* to rise, to go up; to increase; ارْتَفَعَت المَصاريفُ the costs are increasing; ارْتَفَعَ فوق شَيْءٍ to rise above sth; ارْتَفَعَ(ت) ثَمَنُهُ \ السِعْرُ ب ١٥٪ the price is increased by 15%; تَرْتَفِعُ قيمَتُهُ to increase in price/value; تَرْتَفِعُ أَسْعارُ البَنْزين petrol (BrE) gasoline (AmE) prices are going up; تَرْتَفِعُ دَرَجةُ الحَرارةِ the temperature is rising; يَرْتَفِعُ العَجْزُ في الميزانيّةِ بِسُرْعةٍ the budget deficit is soaring

رَفْع *n* 1 [تَعْلِية] raising, lifting; قُدْرة الرَفْع lifting capacity; رَفْع النَفَقاتِ an increase in expenses; رَفْع العُقوبةِ \ التكاليف \ رَفْع الأَثْقالِ الضَغْط an increase in punishment/costs/pressure; weightlifting 2 (Ling) nominative; رَفْع الأَفْعال the indicative; صيغة رَفْع الفِعْلِ the indicative mood; كانَ في حالةِ الرَفْع to be in the nominative

رافِع *n* 1 (Mus) sharp 2 (Islam) الرافِع the Exalter (*one of the names of God*)

رافِعة *n* |رَوافِعُ| 1 (Tools) lever, crowbar; رافِعة كَهْرَبائيّة an electric lever 2 [وِنْش] crane, winch, derrick, lifting gear; ذِراع الرافِعةِ jib; بِرافِعةٍ with a crane

رَفْعة *n* lift

رِفْعة *n* exaltedness, sublimity, highness; prestige; أَكْسَبَ شَيْئاً رِفْعةً to add lustre to sth

رَفيع *adj* 1 [سامٍ] high, exalted, sublime; refined, exquisite; ذَوْق رَفيع refined taste; مَقام رَفيع a high position; مَنْصِب رَفيع a top position; رَفيع المُسْتَوى high-ranking; وَفْد رَفيع المُسْتَوى a high-ranking delegation; شَخْص رَفيع الشَأْنِ a person of consequence 2 [رَقيق] thin, slender, fine, delicate

ارْتِفاع *n* 1 [صُعود] increase; rise; ارْتِفاع شَديد \ قَويّ a sharp rise; ارْتِفاع مُسْتَوى سَطْحِ البَحْرِ a rise in sea level; ارْتِفاع بِنِسْبة \ مِقْدارِ ١٠٪ an increase of 10%; الارْتِفاع في حَرارة الأَرْضِ global warming 2 [عُلوّ] elevation; الارْتِفاع الأَقْصى maximum height; ارْتِفاعُهُ سِتّون مِتْراً it's sixty metres high; على ارْتِفاع ٣٠٠٠ مِترٍ at an altitude of 3000 metres

any kind of assistance; رَفَض أنْ يَسْتَمِرَّ في شَيْءٍ to refuse to continue with sth

ارْفَضَّ *v* 1 [تَفَرَّق] to disperse 2 [الاجْتِماعُ] to adjourn 3 [العَرَق] to drip

رَفْض *n* refusal, rejection; dismissal; رَفْض قاطِع a firm refusal; رَفْض مُطْلَق \ عَنيف \ بِعِنادٍ an outright refusal; رَفْض الاقْتِراحِ rejection of the proposal; رَفْض التَعاوُنِ refusal to cooperate; رَفْض خُطّةِ سَلامٍ rejection of a peace plan; رَفْض مَشْروعِ قانونٍ rejection of a bill; إجابة بالرَفْضِ a negative answer

رافِض *adj* |رَوافِضُ| dismissive, rejecting; rejectionist; unwilling; مَوْقِف رافِض a rejectionist stance

رافِضة *n* rejectionist; defector, deserter; Rafida (*pejorative term for Shiite sect that only recognizes the caliphate of Ali*)

مَرْفوض *adj* unacceptable; refused, rejected; inadmissible

رَفَعَ *v* |a; رَفْع| 1 [عَلّى] to increase; to lift, to raise; to hoist, to heave; رَفَعَ شَيْئاً to lift sth; رَفَعَ السُرْعةَ to increase the speed; رَفَعَ يَدَيْهِ to put one's hands up; رَفَعَ حَقيبةً to lift a suitcase; رَفَعَ صَوْتَهُ to raise one's voice; رَفَعَ العَلَمَ to hoist the flag; رَفَعَ سِرْوالَهُ to pull up one's trousers (BrE) pants (AmE); رَفَعَ رَأْسَهُ to raise one's head; رَفَعَ إِصْبَعَهُ to hold up one's finger; رَفَعَ عَيْنَيْهِ \ البَصَرَ to lift one's eyes; رَفَعَ المَعْنَويّاتِ to invigorate the spirit; رَفَعَ الشِباكَ to draw in the nets; رَفَعَ السِعْرَ to increase the price; لَقَدْ رَفَعوا سِعْرَ ذلك المَنْتوجِ they have raised the price of that product 2 [أَلْغى] to cancel, to remit; to discontinue; رَفَع دُيوناً to cancel debts; رُفِعَت الجَلْسةُ the session was adjourned; رَفَعَ حِصاراً to lift a blockade 3 (Law) to institute, to start; رَفَع دَعْوى قَضائيّةً to institute legal proceedings; رَفَعَ دَعْوى ضِدّ \ على شَخْصٍ to sue sb 4 [سَلَّمَ] to present, to submit 5 (Gram) *to pronounce the final consonant of a word with a 'u'; to put a verb in the indicative mood; to put a noun in the nominative case*

رَفَّعَ *v* to promote; رَفَّعَ المُديرُ مُساعِدَهُ the manager promoted his assistant

رافَعَ *v* to plead; رافَعَ عن المُتَّهَمِ to plead in the suspect's defence

ترافَقَ *v* to accompany (each other); to become friends/companions; ترافَق مع شَخْصٍ to become friends with sb

رِفْق *n* kindness, mildness, gentleness; بِرِفْقٍ gently, softly, lightly; سَأَلَ أُمَّهُ بِرِفْقٍ he asked his mother gently; عامَلَ المُعَلِّمُ تَلاميذَهُ بِرِفْقٍ the teacher dealt gently with his students; جَمْعِيّة الرِفْقِ بالحَيَوانِ animal protection society

رُفْقة ,رِفْقة *n* |رِفاق ,رِفَق ,رُفَق ,أَرْفاق| company, companionship

رَفيق *n* |رِفاق ,رُفَقاءُ| 1 [صَديق] friend; companion; mate; رَفيق وَفيّ a loyal friend; رَفيق العُمْرِ life partner; رَفيق السوءِ a bad friend; رَفيق الطُفولةِ a childhood friend; رَفيق المَدْرَسةِ a school friend; رَفيق سَفَرٍ a travelling companion; رِفاق associates; أَخي وَرِفاقُهُ my brother and his friends 2 [في حِزْبٍ] comrade; الرَفيق فَهْد، الأمين العامّ للحِزْبِ comrade Fahd, the secretary general of the party 3 [اسْم شَخْصيّ] Rafiq (*male given name*)

رَفيقة *n* 1 [صَديقة] (female) companion; رَفيقة حَياةٍ life companion; بَحَثَ عن رَفيقةِ حَياتِهِ to look for one's life partner 2 [اسْم شَخْصيّ] |dipt| Rafiqa (*female given name*)

ارْتِفاق *n* (Law) easement

تَرافُق *n* accompaniment; بالتَرافُقِ مع accompanied by; together with, in conjunction with

مُتَرَفِّق *adj* charitable; mild, clement

مُرافِق *n* companion

مُرافَقة *n* 1 [مُصاحَبة] accompaniment; escort; بِمُرافَقةِ accompanied by 2 (Mus) accompaniment

مُرْفَق A *adj* attached, enclosed; مِلَفّ مُرْفَق attachment, an attached file; أُنْظُر الكُتَيِّبَ \ الصورةَ المُرْفَقَ(ة) see enclosed leaflet/photograph
B *n* |مُرْفَقات| 1 [في رِسالةٍ] enclosure; appendix; supplement 2 (Comput) attachment

مِرْفَق *n* |مَرافِقُ| 1 (Anat) elbow; التِهاب المِرفَقِ (لِلاعِبي التِنِس) tennis elbow 2 [مَصْلَحة] facility; مَرافِق عامّة municipal facilities; مَرافِق ثَقافيّة \ اجْتِماعيّة cultural/social services; مِرْفَق رِياضيّ sports centre; مَرافِق صِحّيّة medical institutions

مِرْفَقيّ *adj* cubital (*relating to the forearm*); عَمود مِرْفَقيّ crankshaft

ارْتِفاعيّ *adj* upward; قوّة ارْتِفاعيّة an upward force

تَرَفُّع *n* arrogance, disdain

مُتَرَفِّع *adj* haughty, arrogant

مُرافَعة *n* (Law) plea; pleading; defence

مُرْتَفَع *n* |مُرْتَفَعات| height, altitude; highland; مُرْتَفَع جَوّيّ a high-pressure area; المُرْتَفَعات الإِسْكُتْلَنْديّة the Highlands; مُرْتَفَعات الجولانِ Golan Heights

مُرْتَفِع *adj* high, elevated; ثَمَن \ مَبْلَغ \ سُرْعة مُرْتَفِع(ة) a high price/amount/speed; حُمّى مُرْتَفِعة a high fever; ضَغْط دمٍ مُرْتَفِع high blood pressure

مِرْفاع *n* |مَرافيعُ| crane, wench, hoist

مَرْفوع *adj* 1 [رُفِع] lifted, raised; submitted; شَعْر مَرْفوع an up-do; مَشى مَرْفوعَ الرَأْسِ to walk with one's head held high; تَقْرير مَرْفوع إلى الوِزارةِ a report that was submitted to the ministry 2 (Gram) |مَرْفوعات| imperfect (*verb*); nominative (*noun*); المُضارِع المَرْفوع the imperfect tense; كانَ مَرْفوعاً to be in the nominative

‹ **رَفَّ** *v* |i-u; رَفّ ,رَفيف| to flicker; to tremble; رَفَّتْ عَيْناهُ to flutter one's eyelids

رَفّ *n* |رُفوف ,أَرْفُف ,رِفاف| shelf, rack; رُفوف مَليئة \ خاوِية full/empty shelves; مَلَأَ الرُفوفَ to restock the shelves; على الرَفِّ on the rack; وَضَعَ شَيْئاً على الرَفِّ to shelve sth

رَفّاف A *adj* glittering, sparkling, flickering
B *n* flashing light; blinker

‹ **رَفَقَ** *v* |u; رِفْق| to be kind/friendly; رَفَقَ ب \ ل \ على شَخْصٍ to be kind to sb

رافَقَ *v* to accompany, to keep company, to escort; to be a companion/friend; رافَقَ شَخْصاً to accompany sb; رافَقَ شَخْصاً في رِحْلةٍ to accompany sb on a journey; رافَقَتْكَ السَلامةُ all the best

أَرْفَقَ *v* to attach, to enclose; to accompany; أَرْفَقَ حِساباً to enclose a bill; أَرْفَقَ مِلَفًّا to attach a file; أَرْفَقَ طَلَباً بِشَيْءٍ to accompany an application with sth; أَرْفَقَ مُرْفَقاً مع رِسالةٍ to include an enclosure with a letter

تَرَفَّقَ *v* |ب| to be kind (to); تَرَفَّقَ بِشَخْصٍ to be kind to sb

الرَقابة أَخْضَعَ لِرَقابةٍ مُشَدَّدةٍ to put through strict control; على الحُدودِ border check **2** [مَطْبوعاتٍ] censorship; رَقابة ذاتيّة self-censorship; رَقابة صارِمة strict censorship; رَقابة الصِحافةِ, رَقابة المَطْبوعاتِ censorship of print media; تَفْرِضُ تِلْكَ رَقابة على الصُحُفِ censorship of the press; الدَوْلةُ رَقابةً ثَقيلةً على الإِنْتَرْنت that country censors the Internet strictly

رَقَبة *n* **1** (Anat) |رِقاب, رَقَبات| neck **2** [شَيْءٍ] |رِقاب, رَقَبات| neck; رَقَبة الكَمانِ \ القيتار the neck of a violin/guitar; رَقَبة قِنّينةٍ \ زُجاجةٍ bottleneck **3** (Clothg) |رِقاب, رَقَبات| neck, neckline; فُتْحة الرَقَبةِ neck (*of a garment*) **4** [عَبْد] |رِقاب| slave

رَقيب *n* |رُقَباءُ| **1** [الصُحُفِ، أَفْلامٍ ...] censor; من غَيْرِ رَقيبٍ وَلا حَسيبٍ without any control **2** (Mil) sergeant; رَقيب أَوَّل sergeant first class **3** (Islam) الرَقيب the Keeper (*one of the names of God*)

تَرَقُّب *n* |تَرَقُّبات| expectation, anticipation

مُراقَب *adj* controlled; observed

مُراقِب *n* **1** [الصُحُفِ، أَفْلامٍ ...] censor **2** [مُشْرِف] inspector, controller; supervisor, overseer

مُراقَبة *n* **1** [إِشْراف] control; inspection; supervision; surveillance; مُراقَبة شَيْءٍ the supervision over sth; مُراقَبة المُراقَبة على حِصارٍ supervision of an embargo; مُراقَبة الحُدودِ border control; نُقْطة مُراقَبةٍ checkpoint; observation post; بُرْج مُراقَبةٍ control tower; watchtower; مَرْكَز مُراقَبةٍ control centre; تَقْرير مُراقَبةٍ inspection report; مُراقَبة الدَفاتِرِ الحِسابيّة the examination of the books; تحت المُراقَبةِ under observation; under surveillance; تحت مُراقَبةِ الرَئيسِ \ القائِدِ under the watchful eye of the leader **2** [الصُحُفِ] censorship

مُرْتَقَب *adj* expected; prospective

مَرْقَب *n* |مَراقِبُ| lookout, observation post; observatory

رَقَدَ *v* |u; رُقود, رُقاد| **1** [نامَ] to sleep, to rest; رَقَدَ بعد الغَداءِ to take a nap after lunch **2** [اسْتَلْقى] to lie; رَقَدَ على الفِراشِ to lie in bed **3** [في القَبْرِ] to rest, to lie (*after death*); رَقَدَ رَقْدَتَهُ الأَخيرةَ to go to one's final resting place

رَقَّدَ *v* **1** [أَنامَ] to put to sleep/bed **2** [البَيْضَ] to hatch

أَرْقَدَ *v* to put to sleep/bed

رَفَلَ *v* |u; رَفْل| to strut, to swagger; رَفَلَ ب \ في مَلابِسِهِ الغالِيةِ to show off one's expensive clothes

تَرَفَّلَ *v* to show off, to brag

رِفْل *n* |أَرْفال| train; رِفْل فُسْتانِ زِفافٍ the train of a wedding dress

رَفُهَ *v* |u; رَفاه, رَفاهة, رَفاهِية| to be comfortable/pleasant, to be luxurious

رَفَّهَ *v* to make pleasant; رَفَّهَ عَيْشَ شَخْصٍ to make sb's life pleasant; رَفَّهَ نَفْسَهُ \ عن نَفْسِهِ to relax

تَرَفَّهَ *v* to live in comfort/luxury

رَفاه, رَفاهة *n* well-being, welfare; رَفاه مادّيّ material well-being; الرَفاه العامّ the common good

رَفاهِية *n* welfare, well-being; luxury, comfort; رَفاهِية اقْتِصاديّة economic welfare; مُسْتَوى الرَفاهِيةِ level of prosperity; عَمَّت الرَفاهِيةُ البِلادَ there was prosperity in the country

تَرْفيه *n* leisure, recreation, relaxation; entertainment

تَرْفيهيّ *adj* recreational; leisure (*before n*); entertaining; مِنْطَقة تَرْفيهيّة recreation area

مُرَفَّه *adj* living well/comfortably

مُرَفِّه *n* entertainer

رَفا *v* |u; رَفْو| to mend, to darn

رَقَأَ *v* |a; رَقْأ, رُقوء| to stop flowing/bleeding

رَقَبَ *v* |u; رَقابة| to control, to supervise; to observe, to watch; to guard

راقَبَ *v* to control, to supervise, to oversee; to observe, to watch; to guard; راقَبَ شَيْئاً \ شَخْصاً to keep an eye on sth/sb; راقَبَ الأَطْفالَ to watch the children; راقَبَ الطُيورَ to observe birds; راقَبَ سُلوكَ شَخْصٍ to observe sb's behaviour; كانَ رَبُّ العَمَلِ يُراقِبُهُ بِاسْتِمْرارٍ he was constantly being watched by his employer; راقَبَ إذا ... to check whether ...

تَرَقَّبَ *v* **1** [تَرَصَّدَ] to lurk **2** [تَوَقَّعَ] to expect, to anticipate; تَرَقَّبَ شَيْئاً بِقَلَقٍ \ اهْتِمامٍ to await sth with concern/interest; تَرَقَّبَ قُدومَ شَخْصٍ to anticipate sb's arrival

ارْتَقَبَ *v* to expect

رَقابة *n* **1** [إِشْراف] control, supervision, surveillance; رَقابة دَوْريّة patrol; رَقابة دَقيقة \ مُشَدَّدة strict supervision;

راقِد *adj* |رُقود ,رُقَّد| sleeping; lying down, resting

راقِدة *n* (railway) sleeper

رُقاد *n* sleep

رَقْدة *n* sleep

مَرْقَد *n* |مَراقِدُ| ❶ [سَرير] bed ❷ [قَبْر] resting place, tomb

رَقْرَقَ *v* |i; رَقْرَقة| to sprinkle; to dilute, mix; رَقْرَقَ الماءَ to sprinkle water

تَرَقْرَقَ *v* to flow, to stream

رَقْراق *adj* misty (eyes); glittering; radiant

رَقَشَ *v* |u; رَقْش| to variegate, to mottle, to make multicoloured

رَقَّشَ *v* to variegate, to mottle, to make multicoloured; to embellish, to decorate

رَقْش *n* variegation

أَرْقَش *adj* |dipt| variegated, multicoloured, colourful

مُرَقَّش *adj* variegated; speckled

رَقَصَ *v* |a-u; رَقْص| to dance; رَقَصَ رَقْصةَ التانْجو to dance the tango; رَقَصَ في مَرْقَصٍ to dance in a club; رَقَصَ على الحَبْلِ to walk a tightrope; to walk a fine line; رَقَصَ فَرَحاً to leap for joy

رَقَّصَ *v* to make dance

راقَصَ *v* to dance with; راقَصَ زَوْجَتَهُ to dance with one's wife

أَرْقَصَ *v* to make dance

تَرَقَّصَ *v* to dance

تَراقَصَ *v* to dance (with each other)

رَقْص *n coll* dance; رَقْص بَلَديّ a folkloric dance; رَقْص شَعْبيّ folk dance; رَقْص شَرْقيّ belly dancing; رَقْص جَماعيّ group dance; فَنّ الرَقْصِ dancing; مارَسَ فَنَّ الرَقْصِ to practise the art of dance; صالة رَقْصٍ dance hall; تَعَلُّم الرَقْصِ dance class; حَلْبة \ حَلْقة رَقْصٍ dance floor; على حَلْبةِ الرَقْصِ on the dance floor; صَمَّمَ رَقْصاً to choreograph

راقِص **A** *adj* dance (*before n*); موسيقى راقِصة dance music **B** *n* dancer; راقِصة (female) dancer/entertainer; belly-dancer; راقِص حَبْلٍ tightrope walker

رَقّاص *n* |رَقّاصات| ❶ [بَنْدول] pendulum ❷ [مُحْتَرِف الرَقْصِ] dancer

رَقْصة *n* |رَقَصات| dance; هل تَسْمَحينَ لي بِهَذِهِ الرَقْصةِ؟ may I have this dance, please?

مُراقِص *n* dancing partner

مَرْقَص *n* |مَراقِصُ| ❶ [مَكان للرَقْصِ] club, nightclub ❷ [حَفْلة راقِصة] ball

مُرْقُص *n* listed alphabetically

رَقَّطَ *v* to speckle

رُقْطة *n* |رُقَط| spot, speck

أَرْقَط **A** *adj* |dipt| speckled, spotted; dotted **B** *n* leopard

مُرَقَّط *adj* speckled, spotted; فَرْو \ جِلْد مُرَقَّط spotted fur/skin; سَلْمون مُرَقَّط trout

رَقَعَ *v* |a; رَقْع| to mend, to repair; رَقَعَ ثَوْباً to mend a garment

رَقَّعَ *v* to mend, to repair

رُقْعة *n* |رِقاع ,رُقَع| ❶ [أَرْض] lot; رُقْعة الشِطْرَنْج chessboard; اتِّساع رُقْعةِ عَمَلِهِ an extension of his work ❷ [ما يُرَقَّعُ بِهِ] patch; أَشْغال الرُقْعة patchwork ❸ [خَطّ] Ruq'ah (*a variety of Arabic script*); خَطّ الرُقْعة Ruq'ah script

تَرْقيع *n* patching

مُرَقَّع *adj* patched, repaired

رَقَّ *v* |i; رِقة| ❶ [لانَ] to be/become mild, to be/become tender, to grow soft; رَقَّ (قَلْبُهُ) لِشَخْصٍ to have pity on sb ❷ [أَصْبَحَ رَقيقاً] to become thin

رَقَّقَ *v* ❶ [رَفَّعَ] to thin (out); to flatten; رَقَّقَ الخَبّازُ الرَغيفَ the baker made the bread thinner ❷ [لَيَّنَ] to soften; رَقَّقَ قَلْبَ شَخْصٍ to mollify sb ❸ [عَكْس غَلَّظَ] to thin/water down; رَقَّقَ الخَمْرَ \ الطِلاءَ to thin wine/paint ❹ [الكَلامَ] to polish; رَقَّقَ كَلامَهُ to polish up one's speech; رَقَّقَ المُتَحَدِّثُ كَلامَهُ the spokesperson spoke in polished terms

تَرَقَّقَ *v* to be refined; to be atomized

اسْتَرَقَّ *v* to enslave; اسْتَرَقَّ شَخْصاً to enslave sb

رَقّ *n* |رُقوق| parchment

رِقّ *n* ❶ [عُبودِيّة] slavery ❷ [دُفّ] |رُقوق| tambourine

رَقائِقيّ *adj* multilayered; خَشَب رَقائِقيّ plywood

رُقاق *n* flatbread

رُقاقة *n* 1 [صَفيحة] رُقاقة مَعْدَنيّة aluminium foil; رُقاقة ذَهَبٍ gold leaf 2 [قِطْعة رَقيقة] sliver, flake; chip; wafer 3 (Elec) chip; رُقاقة إلِكْترونيّة chip

رُقاقيّ *adj* scaly, flaky

رِقّة *n* 1 [وَرَق] thinness 2 [نُعومة] fineness, delicateness, delicacy; gentleness; بِرِقّةٍ gently; عامَلَ شَخْصاً بِرِقّةٍ to deal gently with sb

رَقيق A *adj* |رِقاق, أَرِقّاءُ| 1 [دَقيق] thin, slim, slender, lean; طَبَقة رَقيقة a thin layer; أُنبوب \ سَيْل رَقيق a thin pipe/trickle of water; رَقيق البِنْيةِ of slender build 2 [لَطيف] sensitive, delicate, subtle, tactful, discreet; بِعِباراتٍ رَقيقةٍ in tactful words

B *n* |أَرِقّاءُ, رِقاق| [عَبْد] slave

رَقيقة *n* |رَقائِقُ| 1 (Phot) slide 2 [قِشْرة] flake

تَرَقُّق *n* atomization; تَرَقُّق العَظْمِ osteoporosis

تَرْقيق *n* dilution, thinning down; rolling thin (*dough*)

مِرْقاق *n* |مَراقيقُ| rolling pin

مَرْقوق *adj* thin (*pastry*)

رَقَمَ *v* |u; رَقْم| 1 [كَتَبَ] to write 2 [زَوَّد بالنُقَط] to point, to provide (a text) with dots

رَقْمَنَ *v* |i; رَقْمَنة| (Comput) to digitize

رَقَّمَ *v* 1 [أَعْطى أَرْقاماً] to number 2 [زَوَّدَ بالنُقَط] to point (*a text*) 3 [رَقْمَنَ] to digitize

رَقْم *n* |أَرْقام| number, figure; numeral; digit; بالأَرْقامِ in figures; رَقْم ثُنائيّ binary number; رَقْم مُسَلْسَل serial number; رَقْم (قِياسيّ) record; رَقْم قِياسيّ عالَميّ world record; رَقْم قِياسيّ شَخْصيّ a personal record; حامِل رَقْمٍ قِياسيّ record holder; حَطَّمَ \ كَسَّرَ رَقْماً قِياسيًّا to break a record; لَوْحة أَرْقامٍ numeric keyboard; رَقْم الهاتِفِ phone number; أَدارَ رَقْماً to dial a number; رَبَّعَ \ كَعَّبَ رَقْماً to raise a number to the second/third power

رَقْميّ *adj* digital; numerical; تِقْنيّة رَقْميّة digital technology; مُجْتَمَع رَقْميّ a digital society; العَصْر الرَقْميّ the digital age; الثَوْرة الرَقْميّة the digital revolution; الصِحافة الرَقْميّة the digital press; قُرْص رَقْميّ DVD; شَبَكة رَقْميّة digital network; شَبَكة رَقْميّة للخَدَماتِ المُتَكامِلةِ Integrated Services Digital Network, ISDN; إدارة الحُقوقِ الرَقْميّةِ digital rights management, DRM; مُساعِد رَقْميّ شَخْصيّ personal digital assistant, PDA; جَعَلَ الصُوَرَ رَقْميّةً to digitize pictures

رَقيم *n* tablet; writing, text; رَقيم (من) الطين clay tablet

تَرْقيم *n* 1 [إعطاء أَرْقام] numbering 2 [رَقْمَنة] digitalization 3 [اسْتِعْمال نُقَطٍ وَفَواصِلَ] punctuation; pointing; عَلامات التَرْقيم punctuation

مُرَقَّم *adj* 1 [أُعْطِيَ رَقْماً] numbered 2 [مُزَوَّد بالنُقَط والفَواصِل] punctuated

مِرْقَم *n* |مَراقِمُ| pastel; pencil; pen; stylus

رَقَّنَ *v* to hatch

تَرْقين *n* hatching

رَقَى *v* |i; رُقْي| to charm; رَقَى المَريضَ *to say an invocation to a patient in order to ask God for recovery*

رَقِيَ *v* |a; رُقِيّ, رَقْي| to advance; to be promoted

رَقَّى *v* to advance, to further, to promote; رَقَّى شَخْصاً to promote sb; رَقَّى شَخْصاً لِرِئاسةِ القِسْمِ to promote sb to head of the department; رَقَّى تِلْميذاً إلى سَنةٍ أَعْلى to move a student up to a higher class

تَرَقَّى *v* to get promotion, to be promoted; تَرَقَّى إلى مَرْكَزِ المُديرِ to be promoted to director

اِرْتَقَى *v* 1 [تَقَدَّمَ] to advance, to be promoted, to get a promotion 2 [صَعِدَ] to rise; to ascend, to climb; اِرْتَقَى مِنْبَراً to mount the pulpit; اِرْتَقَى على العَرْشِ to ascend the throne

رُقِيّ *n* rise, promotion

راقٍ A *adj* refined, sophisticated; distinguished; superior, sublime; أُسْلوب راقٍ a lofty style; مِنْطَقة راقية a fashionable quarter; حَيّ راقٍ a respectable neighbourhood; مَنْتوجات راقية high-quality products; الطَبَقة الراقية the upper class

B *n* faith healer

رُقْية *n* |رُقًى| incantation; spell, charm

رُقَيّة *n* |dipt| Ruqayya (*female given name*)

اِرْتِقاء *n* climb

تَرْقية *n* advancement, promotion; upgrade; تَرْقية نِظامٍ system upgrade; إمْكانيّة التَرْقِيةِ promotion prospects; حَصَلَ على

تَرْقِيةٍ to get a promotion; كانَ مُرَشَّحاً للتَرْقِيةِ to be eligible for promotion; تَرْقِية إلى الدَرَجةِ الأولى promotion to the first division

مِرْقاة *n* |مَراقٍ| stairs

مَرْقًى *n* |مَراقٍ| steps

رَكِبَ *v* |a; رُكوب| to ride; to get in (*car, train*); to get on (*a bus*); to board; رَكِبَ خَيْلاً \ حِصاناً to ride a horse; رَكِبَ الدَرّاجة to ride the bicycle; رَكِبَ مَرْكَباً to sail on a boat; رَكِبَ السَيّارة to go by car; رَكِبَ البَحْرَ to sail the sea; رَكِبَ مع شَخْصٍ إلى المَدْرَسةِ to ride along with sb to school

Idioms رَكِبَ الخَطَرَ to expose oneself to danger; رَكِبَ رَأْسَهُ to be headstrong; رَكِبَ هَواهُ to do as one pleases

رَكَّبَ *v* 1 [أَرْكَبَ] to mount (*on horseback*); to make ride 2 [جَهَّزَ] to install; to assemble, to fit together, to set up; to fix; رَكَّبَ خِزانةً to assemble a cupboard; رَكَّبَ الأَجْهِزة to put together the machines; رَكَّبَ جُمْلةً to construct a sentence; رَكَّبَ بَرْنامَج كُمْبيوتَر to program a computer; رَكَّبَ آلةً من أَجْزاءٍ مُسْتَقِلّةٍ to construct a machine from loose parts 3 [وَضَعَ] to put in; to set in; رَكَّبَ أَلْواحَ الزُجاج to put in a windowpane; رَكِّبْ وَشَغِّلْ Plug and Play 4 (Chem) to combine

أَرْكَبَ *v* to mount (*sb on horseback*); to make ride

تَرَكَّبَ *v* |من| to be composed (of); تَرَكَّبَ من مُكَوِّناتٍ عَديدةٍ to be composed of several ingredients

تَراكَبَ *v* to overlap

ارْتَكَبَ *v* to commit, to perpetrate; ارْتَكَبَ خَطَأً to make a mistake; ارْتَكَبَ \ اقْتَرَفَ جَريمةً to perpetrate a crime; ارْتَكَبَ فَظائِعَ \ ذَنْباً to commit atrocities/a sin; ارْتَكَبَ هَفْوةً to commit a blunder

رَكْب *n coll* |no singular noun; أَرْكُب| caravan; procession; convoy

راكِب *n* 1 [رُكْبان ,رَكْب|[دابّةٍ| rider; horseman; راكِب دَرّاجةٍ cyclist 2 [وَسيلة نَقْلٍ] |رُكّاب| passenger; occupant; راكِب سَيّارةٍ \ قِطارٍ a car/train passenger

رِكاب *n* |رُكُب| stirrup

رُكْبة *n* |رُكْبات ,رُكَب| (Anat) knee; صَكَك الرُكْبَتَيْنِ knock knees; شَكَرَ اللهَ (أو شَخْصاً) على رُكْبَتَيْهِ to thank God (or sb) on bended knees; إلى ما فوق \ تحت الرُكْبَتَيْنِ above/below the knees

رُكوب *n* riding; mounting; boarding; رُكوب الأَمْواجِ surfing

ارْتِكاب *n* perpetration, commission (*of a crime*)

تَرْكيب *n* |تَراكيبُ ,تَرْكيبات| composition; construction; assembly, assembling, mounting; installation; تَرْكيب مُعَقَّد a complicated construction; تَرْكيب جُمْلةٍ the construction of a sentence; لُعْبة تَرْكيبٍ jigsaw (puzzle); تَرْكيب تِليفونٍ telephone connection; عَمَلِيّة التَرْكيبِ الضَوْئِيِّ photosynthesis; ذو تَرْكيبٍ جَيِّدٍ well-composed; التَرْكيب والتَشْغيل Plug and Play

تَرْكيبة *n* |تَراكيبُ ,تَرْكيبات| constitution; structure, building; تَرْكيبة الغِذاءِ the composition of food

تَرْكيبيّ *adj* structural, constructional; صيغة تَرْكيبيّة structural form

مَراكِبيّ *n* |مَراكِبِيّة| boatman, ferryman; captain

مُرْتَكِب *n* perpetrator; مُرْتَكِب حادِثٍ \ جَريمةٍ the perpetrator of an incident/crime

مَرْكَب *n* |مَراكِبُ| ship, boat, vessel, craft; مَرْكَب نَهْرِيّ inland boat; مَراكِب كَبيرة \ صَغيرة large/small vessels; مَرْكَب شِراعِيّ sailboat; مَرْكَب عُبورٍ ferry

مُرَكَّب A *adj* complex, compound; جُمْلة مُرَكَّبة a compound sentence

B *n* |مُرَكَّبات| 1 (Chem) compound; مُرَكَّب كيميائِيّ a chemical compound 2 [عُقْدة] complex; مُرَكَّب النَقْصِ inferiority complex

مُرَكِّب A *adj* component, constituent

B *n* |مُرَكِّبات| ingredient; مُرَكِّبات شَيْءٍ the ingredients of sth

مَرْكَبة *n* vehicle; carriage, wagon; مَرْكَبة فَضائيّة spacecraft

مَرْكوب *n* |مَراكيبُ| riding animal; (horse-drawn) coach

رُكْح *n* |أَرْكاح| stage (*of a theatre etc*)

رَكَدَ *v* |u; رُكود| to be motionless/still; to be stagnant

راكِد *adj* |رَواكِدُ| stagnant, still; static; ماء راكِد stagnant water; اقْتِصاد راكِد a stagnant economy

رُكود *n* 1 [سُكون] standstill; رُكود الرِياحِ calm 2 (Econ) depression, recession; رُكود اقْتِصاديّ economic stagnation;

مُتَمَرْكِز *adj* centralized, centred, concentrated; الثِقْل مُتَمَرْكِزٌ في الوَسَطِ the weight is concentrated in the middle

مُرْتَكَز *n* support; pillar, post, abutment

مُرْتَكِز *adj* based, founded; مُرْتَكِز على أساسٍ well-founded; كانَ مُرْتَكِزاً على شَيْءٍ to be based on sth

مَرْكَز *n* |مَراكِزُ| 1▸ [وَسَط] centre, middle point; focus; مَرْكَز المَدِينةِ (town) centre (BrE), downtown (AmE); كانَ مَرْكَزَ الاهْتِمام to be the centre of interest 2▸ [مَقَرّ] centre; post; مَرْكَز إداريّ administrative centre; مَرْكَز رَئيسيّ head office; مَرْكَز تِجاريّ shopping centre, mall; مَرْكَز الحَضارة \ القوّة the centre of civilization/power; مَرْكَز الشَبابِ youth centre; بَقِيَ في مَرْكَزِهِ to remain at one's post 3▸ [الهاتِفِ] (telephone) exchange; أَوْصَلَ هاتِفيًّا بالمَرْكَزِ to connect with the operator 4▸ [مَكانة] status, position, standing; post; مَرْكَز كَبير في الحُكومةِ a senior position in the government; صاحِب المَرْكَزِ الثاني the holder of the second position 5▸ (Math) centre, midpoint; مُتَّحِد المَرْكَزِ concentric

مُرَكَّز A *adj* centred; concentrated; intensive; مَحْلول مُرَكَّز a concentrated solution; عِناية مُرَكَّزة intensive care

B *n* concentrate; مُرَكَّز طَماطِم tomato concentrate; مُرَكَّز كيميائيّ chemical concentrate

مَرْكَزيّ *adj* central, centralized; centralist; مَوْقِع مَرْكَزيّ a central location; إدارة مَرْكَزيّة a centralized management; جِهاز طَرْدٍ مَرْكَزيٍّ the central bank; المَصْرِف المَرْكَزيّ centrifuge; قوّة الطَرْدِ المَرْكَزيّ centrifugal force; مِضَخّة الطَرْدِ المَرْكَزيّ centrifugal pump

مَرْكَزِيّة *n* centralization; centralism; المَرْكَزِيّة الأوروبيّة Eurocentrism

ارْتَكَسَ *v* to decline

ارْتِكاس *n* decline; relapse

رَكَضَ *v* |u; رَكْض| to run, to sprint; to race; to gallop

راكَضَ *v* to race (sb)

تَراكَضَ *v* to run together; to race, to compete (in a race)

رَكْض *n* running; run, jog

رَكَعَ *v* |a; رُكوع| to kneel (down); to bow; رَكَعَ أمام خَصْمٍ \ القانونِ to bow to an opponent/the law

رُكود البورْصةِ slackness at the stock exchange

رَكَزَ *v* |i-u; رَكْز| to fix, to embed, to place

مَرْكَزَ *v* |i; مَرْكَزة| to centralize, to concentrate

تَمَرْكَزَ *v* to be centred, to be centralized, to be concentrated; تَمَرْكَزَت الحُكومةُ في العاصِمةِ the government is centralized in the capital; تَمَرْكَزَ القِتالُ في وَسَطِ المَدِينةِ the fighting is concentrated in the city centre

رَكَّزَ *v* 1▸ [انْتِباهَهُ] |على| to concentrate on, to focus on; رَكَّزَ على شَيْءٍ to concentrate on sth 2▸ (Chem) to concentrate; رَكَّزَ مَحْلولاً to concentrate a solution 3▸ [ثَبَّتَ] to fix, to place; رَكَّزَ نَظَرَهُ \ انْتِباهَهُ على شَيْءٍ to focus one's gaze/mind on sth; رَكَّزَ الاهْتِمامَ على شَيْءٍ to concentrate on sth

تَرَكَّزَ *v* to settle; to stabilize; to concentrate, to focus; تَرَكَّزَت المُناقَشةُ حَوْلَ ... the discussion focused on ...; تَرَكَّزَتْ هذه الفِكْرةُ في عُقولِ الناسِ this idea is planted in people's minds

ارْتَكَزَ *v* to lean; to be based/founded, to rest; ارْتَكَزَ على شَيْءٍ to be founded on sth; ارْتَكَزَ على افْتِراضٍ to be based on an assumption; ارْتَكَزَ على عَصاهُ to lean on one's cane

رِكاز *n* ore; رِكاز الحَديدِ iron ore

رَكيزة *n* |رَكائِزُ| support; pillar, mast, post

ارْتِكاز *n* |ارْتِكازات| support; leaning; نُقْطة ارْتِكازٍ fulcrum, focal point; نُقَط ارْتِكازِ الجِسْرِ the abutments of the bridge

ارْتِكازيّ *adj* pivotal

تَرْكيز *n* 1▸ [إلْحاح] emphasis 2▸ [انْتِباه] concentration; تَرْكيز عَميق deep concentration; قِلّة التَرْكيزِ a lack of concentration; فُقْدان التَرْكيزِ a loss of concentration; فَقَدَ تَرْكيزَهُ to lose one's focus; قُدْرة على التَرْكيزِ power of concentration; التَرْكيز على شَيْءٍ focus on sth; عَمِلَ بِتَرْكيزٍ to work with focus 3▸ (Phys) concentration; thickening; قاسَ \ حَدَّدَ التَرْكيزَ to measure the concentration

تَمَرْكُز *n* centralization, concentration

لامَرْكَزيّ *adj* decentralized; حُكْم لامَرْكَزيّ decentralized rule

لامَرْكَزيّة *n* decentralization; حَقَّقَ اللامَرْكَزيّةَ to decentralize; حَقَّقَ اللامَرْكَزيّةَ الإداريّةَ to implement administrative decentralization

أَرْكَعَ *v* to make kneel down

راكِع **A** *adj* |رُكَّع| kneeling; bowing
B *n* |رُكَّع| kneeler

رَكْعة *n* |رُكوع ,رَكَعات| bow; prostration; *unit of Muslim prayer, consisting of a bow and two prostrations*

رُكوع *n* bow, bowing; kneeling; *a bow in Muslim prayer*

تَرْكيع *n* rendering subservient

‹ **رَكَّ** *v* |i; رَكّ ,رِكّة ,رَكاكة| to be/become weak

رَكاكة *n* weakness; inadequacy

رِكّة *n* weakness, feebleness

رَكيك *adj* |رِكاك ,رَكَكة| weak; prosaic, pedestrian; أُسْلوب رَكيك a prosaic style; بِإنْجْليزِيّةٍ رَكيكةٍ in broken English

‹ **رَكَلَ** *v* |u; رَكْل| to kick (away); رَكَلَ شَخْصاً \ شَيْئاً to kick sb/sth; رَكَلَ كُرةً to kick a ball away

رَكْلة *n* kick; رَكْلة قَوِيّة a hard kick; رَكْلة حُرّة a free kick; رَكْلة جَزاءٍ penalty (kick); تَلَقّى رَكْلةً في بَطْنِهِ to get a kick in the stomach

‹ **رَكَمَ** *v* |u; رَكْم| to pile/heap up; to accumulate

راكَمَ *v* to pile up, to accumulate; راكَمَ الخَطَأَ تِلْوَ الآخَرِ to pile one mistake on top of another

تَراكَمَ *v* to pile/heap up, to accumulate, to amass; تَتَراكَمُ الجَماهيرُ the crowd gathers; يَتَراكَمُ الغازُ gas builds up; تَراكَمَت المَشاكِلُ the problems piled up

رُكام *n* **1** [كَوْمة] pile, heap, stack; rubble; drift (*of snow*); رُكام من الرَمْلِ a heap of sand **2** (Meteorol) cumulus **3** (Geol) moraine; رُكام جَليديّ moraine

تَراكُم *n* |تَراكُمات| accumulation, building up, build-up; pile, heap; drift (*of snow*); تَراكُم المَشاكِلِ \ الأَعْمالِ \ الدُيونِ the accumulation of problems/work/debts

تَراكُمِيّ *adj* accumulated, cumulative; فائِض \ عَجْز تَراكُمِيّ accumulated surplus/deficit

مُتَراكِم *adj* accumulated; cumulative; عَمَل مُتَراكِم من وَقْتِ العُطْلةِ work that accumulated since the holidays (BrE) vacation (AmE)

مِرْكَم *n* |مَراكِمُ| accumulator, storage battery/cell

مَرْكوم *adj* piled/heaped up, accumulated

‹ **رَكَنَ** *v* |u; رُكون ,رَكْن| **1** [إلى] [وَثِقَ] to trust; to lean on, to rely on; رَكَنَ إلى الراحةِ to rest, to take it easy **2** [صَفَّ] to park; رَكَنَ سَيّارةً to park a car

رَكْن *n* parking; خِدْمة رَكْنِ السَيّاراتِ valet parking service

رُكْن *n* |أَرْكان| **1** [زاوِية] corner; رُكْن المائِدةِ the corner of the table **2** [في مَجَلّةٍ] column; رُكْن المَرْأةِ the women's page **3** (Islam) pillar; أَرْكان الإسْلامِ the (five) pillars of Islam **4** (Mil) هَيْئة الأَرْكانِ العامّة general staff; رَئيس أَرْكانٍ chief of staff

رُكْنيّ *adj* corner; ضَرْبة رُكْنِيّة corner (kick)

رَكين *adj* |رُكَناءُ| firm; stable

مِرْكَن *n* |مَراكِنُ| washtub, washbowl

مَرْكون *adj* parked; سَيّارة مَرْكونة a parked car

‹ **رَكْوة** *n* |رَكَوات| (Syria) coffee pot

‹ **رَمَث** *n* |أَرْماث| raft

‹ **رَمَحَ** *v* |a; رَمْح| to spear

رُمْح *n* |أَرْماح ,رِماح| spear; javelin; lance; رَمْي الرُمْحِ (throwing) the javelin; رامي الرُمْحِ javelin thrower

رَمّاح *n* |رَمّاحة| lancer

‹ **رَمِدَ** *v* |a; رَمَد| to be inflamed (*eye*)

رَمَّدَ *v* to incinerate

ارْمَدَّ *v* **1** [أَصْبَحَ رَماديًّا] to be/become grey/ashen **2** [أَصْبَحَ مُغَيِّماً] to cloud over **3** [الْتَهَبَ] to be inflamed (*eye*)

رَمَد *n* ophthalmia; conjunctivitis; طَبيب الرَمَدِ (Egypt) ophthalmologist

رَماد *n* |أَرْمِدة| ashes; رَماد بُرْكانيّ volcanic ash; رَماد السَجائِرِ cigarette ash; أَرْبِعاء الرَمادِ Ash Wednesday (*the first day of Lent in the Western Christian Church*); تَنفُخ في الرَمادِ you're wasting your time; ذَرَّ الرَمادَ في عَيْنَيْ شَخْصٍ to deceive sb with a smokescreen

رَماديّ *adj* grey; ashen; سَماء رَمادِيّة a grey sky; مِياه رَمادِيّة grey water

أَرْمَد *adj* |dipt; رُمْد| suffering from conjunctivitis

تَرْميد *n* burning; incineration

‹ **رَمَزَ** *v* |i-u; رَمْز| إلى| to point; to signal; to symbolize; رَمَزَ إلى شَيْءٍ to point to sth

رَمْز *n* |رُموز| 1 [إشارة] symbol, emblem, image; logo; اتَّخَذَ شَيْئاً كَرَمْزٍ to take sth as a symbol; كانَ رَمْزاً لِشَيْءٍ to represent sth; رَمْز لِلسَّلام a symbol of peace; رُموز مَشاعِرَ (Comput) emoticons 2 [عَلامة] character; code; sign; رُموز (secret) code; حَلَّ \ فَكَّ رَمْزاً to crack a code; هذه الرِسالةُ كُلُّها رُموزٌ وَأَلْغازٌ this letter is nothing but hints and riddles 3 [دَليل] mark, token; رَمْز كَرَم a generous gesture; رَمْز لِلشُّكْرِ a token of gratitude; رَمْز حُسْنِ النِيَّةِ a sign of good will

رَمْزِيّ *adj* coded; symbolic; figurative; مَعْنًى \ عَمَل رَمْزِيّ a symbolic meaning/act; فَنّ رَمْزِيّ figurative art; بادِرة رَمْزِيّة a symbolic gesture; اسْم رَمْزِيّ code name

رَمْزِيّة *n* symbolism

تَرْميز *n* encoding

مَرْموز *adj* encoded; مَرْموز إلَيْهِ represented

‹ **رَمَسَ** *v* |u; رَمْس| to bury

رَمْس *n* |رُموس, أَرْماس| grave, tomb

تُرْمُس *n* listed alphabetically

‹ **رَمَشَ** *v* |i-u; رَمْش, رَمَش| to blink; to wink; to flap/flutter (*one's eyelashes*)

رِمْش *n* |رُموش| eyelash; رُموش اصْطِناعيّة false eyelashes

رَمْشة *n* بِرَمْشةِ عَيْنٍ in the blink of an eye

‹ **رَمَص** *n* sleep (*white discharge from the eye during sleep*)

‹ **رَمِضَ** *v* |a; رَمَض| to be burning/blazing

رَمْضاء *n* |dipt f| (scorching) heat; اسْتَجارَ من الرَمْضاءِ بالنارِ to jump out of the frying pan into the fire

رَمَضان *n* |dipt; رَمَضانات, رَماضينُ| 1 (Islam) Ramadan (*the ninth month of the Islamic calendar, during which fasting is observed from dawn to sunset*); شَهْر رَمَضان المُبارَكِ \ الكَريم the blessed/noble month of Ramadan; يَخْلُطُ بين شَعْبانَ وَرَمَضانَ he doesn't know whether he's coming or going 2 [اسْم شَخْصيّ] Ramadan (*male given name*)

‹ **مَرْموط** *n* listed alphabetically

‹ **رَمَقَ** *v* |u; رَمْق| to eye; to look, to glance; رَمَقَني بِبَصَرِهِ he looked at me

رَمَّقَ *v* to stare

رَمَق *n* |أَرْماق| breath (*of life*); رَمَق أَخير final breath; حتّى آخِرِ رَمَقٍ until one's dying breath

مَرْموق *adj* prestigious, eminent, notable, distinguished, prominent; شَخْصيّة مَرْموقة an eminent person; مَكانة مَرْموقة a prominent place; prestige

‹ **رَمَكة** *n* |رَمَكات, رِماك, أَرْماك| brood-mare

‹ **رَمَّلَ** *v* to sand

أَرْمَلَ *v* to be widowed

تَرَمَّلَ *v* to be widowed

رَمْل *n* |رِمال| sand; رِمال مُتَطايِرة drifting sand; رِمال مُتَحَرِّكة quicksand; الضَرْب بالرَمْلِ geomancy; دَفَنَ الرَأْسَ في الرِمالِ to bury one's head in the sand

رَمْليّ *adj* sandy; أَرْض رَمْليّة sandy soil; ساعة رَمْليّة sandglass; حَجَر رَمْليّ sandstone

أَرْمَل *n* |dipt; أَرامِلُ| widower

أَرْمَلة *n* |أَرامِلُ, أَرامِلة| widow; أَرْمَلة السَيِّد وِسامٍ the widow of Mr Wesam

مَرْمَلة *n* |مَرامِلُ| sandpit

‹ **رَمَّ** *v* |i-u; رَمّ, مَرَمّة| to fix, to repair

رَمَّمَ *v* to restore; to repair; to renovate; رَمَّمَ بِنايةً to restore a building

رُمّة *n* |رُمَم| بِرُمَّتِهِ in its entirety; يَعيشُ الوَطَنُ بِرُمَّتِهِ في ضَياعٍ the whole country is in decline; يَنْبَغي النَظَرُ إلى المَوْضوعِ بِرُمَّتِهِ one should consider the subject in its totality

رِمّة *n* |رِمَم| cadaver; رِمَم carrion

رَميم *adj* |رَمائِمُ| decayed; worn out

تَرْميم *n* |تَرْميمات| restoration; repair; renovation

تَرْميميّ *adj* restorative

مَرَمّة *n* repair

‹ **رُمّان** *n coll* pomegranate

‹ **رَمى** *v* |i; رَمْي, رِماية| 1 [أَلْقى] to throw, to cast; to hurl, to fling; to throw away; رَمى بالحِجارةِ to throw stones; رَمى شَخْصاً بِحَجَرٍ to fling a stone at sb; رَمى شَخْصاً بالكُرةِ to pass the ball to sb; رَمى الغِلافَ \ بالغِلافِ to throw away the packaging; رَمى شَخْصاً بإهانةٍ to lob an insult at sb; رَمى شَخْصاً بِتُهْمةٍ to accuse sb ② [أَطْلَقَ النارَ] to shoot, to fire; رَمى شَيْئاً \ شَخْصاً to shoot at sth/sb; رَمى الأَرانِبَ to shoot a rabbit; رَمى سَهْماً to let loose an arrow ③ [قَصَدَ] |إلى| to aim; to intend; رَمى إلى غايةٍ بَعيدةٍ to aim at a difficult target; إلامَ تَرْمي؟ what are you getting at?

ترامى *v* ① [بَلَغَ] to reach; تَرامى إلَيَّ أنّ ... it's come to my attention that ...; تَرامى إلى سَمْعِهِ أنّ ... he has heard that ... ② [رَمى] to throw/toss over; تَرامى الكُرةَ to throw the ball over

ارْتَمى *v* to throw/fling oneself; ارْتَمى على \ تحت قَدَمَيْ شَخْصٍ to throw oneself at sb's feet

رَمْي *n* fire, firing; throwing, casting

رام *n* |رُماة| ① (Sport) pitcher ② (Mil) marksman

رِماية *n* ① [قَذْف] firing, shooting; لَوْحة رِمايةٍ target; مَيْدان الرِماية shooting range ② (Sport) archery; darts

رَمِيّة *n* |رَمِيّات, رَمايا| game (animal)

رَمْية *n* throw, cast; shot; رَمْية حُرّة a free shot; رَمْية جانِبِيّة throw-in; رَمْية صائِبَة bullseye

مُترام *adj* vast, extensive, sprawling; مُترامي الأَطْرافِ vast

مَرْمًى *n* |مَرام| ① [غَرَض] target, aim; على مَرْمى حَجَرٍ within a stone's throw ② (Sport) goal; حارِس المَرْمى goalkeeper; مِنْطَقة مَرْمًى goal area; ضَرْبة المَرْمى goal kick; سَدَّدَ الكُرةَ إلى المَرْمى to kick at goal

‹ **أَرْنب** *n* see أرنب

‹ **رِنْجة** *n* سَمَك الرِنْجةِ herring

‹ **رَنَّحَ** *v* to stagger, to reel; to sway

تَرَنَّحَ *v* to reel; to stagger; يَتَرَنَّحُ النِظامُ the system is faltering; تَرَنَّحَ من النُعاسِ to be staggering with sleepiness; تَرَنَّحَ من السُكْرِ to totter from drunkenness

تَرَنُّح *n* falter; stagger

‹ **رَنْد** *n* bay (*Laurus nobilis*); bay leaf

‹ **رَنَق** *v* رَنَّقَ النَظَرَ to stare

رَوْنَق *n* splendour, luster

‹ **رَنْكة** *n* سَمَك الرَنْكةِ herring; سِرْب من سَمَكِ الرَنْكةِ a school of herring

‹ **رَنَّمَ** *v* to hum; to sing; رَنَّمَ أُغْنِيةً to hum a song

تَرَنَّمَ *v* to hum; to intone; to chant

تَرْنيم *n* intonation; chanting

تَرْنيمة *n* |تَرانيم| song; hymn, chant

‹ **رِنْمينْبي** *n* renminbi (*official currency of China, of which the yuan is the basic unit*)

‹ **رَنَّ** *v* |i; رَنين| to ring; to jingle; to clink; يَرِنُّ الجَرَسُ the bell is ringing; يَرِنُّ المُنَبِّهُ the alarm is going off; يَرِنُّ جَرَسُ الهاتِفِ, يَرِنُّ الهاتِفُ the telephone is ringing

رَنَّنَ *v* to ring, to toll

رَنّان *adj* melodious; sonorous; اسْتَعْمَلَ كَلِماتٍ رَنّانةً to use high-sounding language

رَنّانة *n* (Mus) tuning; resonance; شَوْكة رَنّانة tuning fork

رَنّة *n* ① (Zool) reindeer, caribou (AmE) ② [صَوْت] ring, clang

رَنين *n* sound; ring, ringing; tinkle; echo; resonance; رَنين الهاتِفِ the ringing of the telephone

مِرْنان **A** *adj* ringing; clanking **B** *n* resonator

‹ **رَنا** *v* |u; رُنُوّ| |إلى| to stare at, to gaze at; رَنا إلى شَخْصٍ \ شَيْءٍ to stare at sb/sth

‹ **رَنّى** *v* to delight

‹ **رَهِبَ** *v* |a; رَهْبة| to be frightened/afraid; to fear

رَهَّبَ *v* to frighten, to scare; to intimidate; to terrorize

أَرْهَبَ *v* to frighten, to scare; to intimidate; to terrorize; أَرْهَبَ الشَعْبَ to terrorize the people

تَرَهَّبَ *v* to become a monk, to enter a monastery

راهِب *n* |رُهْبان| monk

راهِبة *n* nun, sister

رُهاب *n* phobia; رُهاب الانْغِلاق claustrophobia; مُداواة من رُهاب الخَلاءِ a therapy against agoraphobia

رَهْبانِيّ *adj* monastic

رَهْبانِيّة *n* ① [التَخَلّي عن أَشْغالِ الدُنْيا] monasticism ② [مَجْموعة رُهْبانٍ] (monastic) order

رَهْبة *n* fear, terror; رَغْبةً أو رَهْبةً willing or unwilling

رَهْبَنة *n* ① monasticism ② (monastic) order

رَهيب *adj* horrible, horrifying, horrendous, dreadful, frightful, fearful, awful; مَنْظَر رَهيب a ghastly sight; صَمْت رَهيب a dead silence; كارِثة رَهيبة a horrible disaster; جَريمة قَتْلٍ رَهيبة a gruesome murder

إرْهاب *n* terror; terrorism; الإرْهاب النازيّ the terror of the Nazis; الإرْهاب الدُوَليّ international terrorism; إرْهاب حَقيقيّ true terror; فَرَّخَ الإرْهابَ to breed terrorism; تَعَرَّضَ للإرْهابِ to be subjected to terror; كافَحَ الإرْهابَ to fight terrorism; لَطَّخَ يَدَيْه بالإرْهاب to be guilty of terrorism

إرْهابيّ **A** *adj* terrorist; حَرَكة \ تَنْظيم إرْهابيّ(ة) a terrorist movement/organization; اعْتِداء إرْهابيّ a terrorist attack; حُكْم إرْهابيّ a reign of terror; نَفَّذَ أَعْمالاً إرْهابيّةً to carry out terrorist acts
B *n* terrorist

تَرْهيب *n* intimidation, frightening

مَرْهوب *adj* dreaded; ناقِد مَرْهوب a feared critic

‹ **رَهَج ,رَهْج** *n* dust

‹ **إرْهاصة** *n* sign, symptom

‹ **رَهْط** *n* |أَراهيطُ ,أَراهِطُ ,أَرْهُط ,أَرْهاط| group, band, troop; family; tribe

‹ **رَهَفَ** *v* |a; رَهْف| **1** [حَدَّدَ] to sharpen; رَهَفَ سَيْفَهُ to sharpen one's sword **2** [رَقَّ] to make/become thinner/finer

رَهُفَ *v* |u; رَهافة| to be/become thin

أَرْهَفَ *v* to sharpen; to make thin; أَرْهَفَ أُذُنَهُ to prick up one's ears

رَهافة *n* thinness, fineness

رَهيف *adj* **1** [رَقيق] thin, slender; fine, delicate; flimsy; نَباتات رَهيفة delicate plants **2** [اسْم شَخْصيّ] Rahif (*male given name*)

مُرْهَف *adj* thin, slender; fine, delicate; sensitive; أُذُن مُرْهَفة a sharp ear; حِسّ مُرْهَف sensitivity; مُرْهَف الحِسّ sensitive

‹ **راهَقَ** *v* to be/become adolescent

أَرْهَقَ *v* to exhaust, to wear out; to burden, to oppress; أَرْهَقَ شَخْصاً to exhaust sb; أَرْهَقَ نَفْسَهُ to tax oneself; أَرْهَقَ أَعْصابَهُ to strain one's nerves; أُرْهِقَ من شَيْءٍ to be worn out by sth

إرْهاق *n* |إرْهاقات| exhaustion, weariness; overwork; strain; stress; إرْهاق عَصَبيّ stress; مَرَض الإرْهاقِ المُزْمِنِ chronic fatigue syndrome

مُراهِق *n* adolescent, teenager; تَصَرُّف المُراهِقينَ adolescent behaviour

مُراهَقة *n* adolescence; مَرْحَلة \ سِنّ المُراهَقةِ puberty; adolescence; كانَ في مَرْحَلةِ المُراهَقةِ to be going through one's adolescence; في \ خلال سِنِّ المُراهَقةِ in/during adolescence

مُرْهَق *adj* exhausted, tired/worn out, weary; overworked, overstrained; مُعَلِّم مُرْهَق an overworked teacher

مُرْهِق *adj* exhausting, tiring, wearying; strenuous, hard

‹ **رَهِلَ** *v* |a; رَهَل| to be/become soft, to be/become flabby

تَرَهَّلَ *v* to be/become soft, to be/become flabby

تَرَهُّل *n* flabbiness

مُتَرَهِّل *adj* flabby

‹ **مَرْهَم** *n* |مَراهِمُ| ointment, salve; وَصَفَ لِشَخْصٍ مَرْهَماً to prescribe an ointment for sb; دَهَنَ جُرْحاً بالمَرْهَم to put salve on a wound; دَهَنَ جِسْمَهُ بالمَرْهَم to rub ointment into one's skin

‹ **رَهَنَ** *v* |a; رَهْن| to pawn; to mortgage; رَهَنَ شَيْئاً to pawn sth

راهَنَ *v* to bet, to wager; راهَنَ شَخْصاً to make a bet with sb; راهَنَ شَيْئاً to wager sth; راهَنَ على شَيْءٍ to bet on sth; راهَنَ على حِصانٍ to bet on a horse; راهَنَ على الفَوْزِ \ النَتيجةِ to bet on the victory/outcome; راهَنَ على حَياتِهِ to gamble on one's life; راهَنَ على أنّ ... to bet that ...

أَرْهَنَ *v* to deposit as security, to pawn

تَراهَنَ *v* to bet each other

ارْتَهَنَ *v* to pawn; to pledge

اسْتَرْهَنَ *v* to demand as security

رَهْن *n* |رُهون ,رُهونات ,رِهان| **1** (Busn) deposit, security; رَهْن عَقاريّ mortgage; دَفَعَ رَهْناً to pay a deposit; مُقابِلَ رَهْنٍ on security of ..., secured by ...; رَهْن قَدْرُهُ خَمْسةُ مَلايين دولار ... قَدْرُهُ secured by five million dollars **2** [ضَمان] pledge, collateral; كانَ الشَيْءُ رَهْناً عِنْدَهُ to hold sth as collateral; أنا رَهْنُ إشارَتِكَ I am at your service

راهِن **A** *adj* current, contemporary, present, present-day; الوَقْت الراهِن the present; الحالة \ الوَضْع الراهِن(ة) the present situation; الوَضْع الراهِن للأُمورِ the current state of affairs; في الحالةِ الراهِنةِ in the present case; في الظُروفِ الراهِنةِ under the circumstances

B *n* pledger; mortgagor

رِهان *n* bet; رِهان خاسِر a losing bet; كَسَبَ \ خَسِرَ رِهاناً to win/lose a bet; قَبِلَ الرِهانَ to accept the bet

رَهْنِيّ *adj* mortgage (*before n*)

رَهْنِيّة *n* collateral; رَهْنِيّة عَقارِيّة mortgage

رَهين *adj* dependent; كانَ رَهيناً بِشَيْءٍ to be dependent on sth

رَهينة *n* |رَهائِنُ| hostage; مَصير الرَهائِنِ the fate of the hostages; احْتَجَزَ الرَهائِنَ to hold people hostage; أَطْلَقَ سَراحَ الرَهائِنِ to release the hostages

ارْتِهان *n* collateral; holding as collateral

مُراهَنة *n* bet

مُرْتَهِن *n* mortgagee

مَرْهون *adj* dependent; النَجاحُ مَرْهونٌ بِدِقّةِ التَنْفيذِ success depends on a meticulous implementation

‹ **رَهْو** *n* |رِهاء| (Zool) crane (*Gruidae*)

‹ **رُوانْدا** *n* Rwanda

‹[1] **رابَ** *v* |u; رَوْب, رُؤوب| **1** [خَثَّرَ] to curdle (*milk*) **2** [شَكَّكَ] see **ريب**

رَوَّبَ *v* to curdle

أَرابَ *v* **1** [خَثَّرَ] to curdle **2** [شَكَّكَ] see **ريب**

رائِب *adj* curdled (*milk*); لَبَن رائِب yogurt

رَوْبة *n* curd

‹[2] **روب** *n* |أَرْواب| robe/bathrobe, dressing gown; dress, gown

‹ **رَوْبَصة** *n* sleepwalking, somnambulism

‹ **روبِل** *n* rouble

‹ **روبوت** *n* robot

‹ **إرْبِيان, روبيان** *n* shrimp; prawn

‹ **روبِيّة** *n* rupee

‹ **روتين** *n* rut, routine; bureaucracy; الروتين اليَوْميّ daily routine; انْعِدام الروتينِ the lack of routine; كَسَرَ الروتين to get out of a rut

روتينيّ *adj* routine; عَمَل روتينيّ routine work; فَحْص \ مُراجَعة روتينيّ(ة) a routine examination/review

‹ **راثَ** *v* |u; رَوْث| **1** [تَبَرَّزَ] to drop dung **2** [تَباطَأَ] see **ريث**

رَوْث *n* |أَرْواث| dung, droppings; manure; رَوْث الحِصانِ horse dung

‹ **راجَ** *v* |u; رَواج| to circulate/spread; to be in vogue, to be in fashionable/popular

رَوَّجَ *v* to propagate; to promote, to push; رَوَّجَ شَيْئاً to propagate sth; رَوَّجَ مُنْتَجاتٍ to promote products; رَوَّجَ خَبَراً to spread a message

رائِج *adj* popular, in style; كانَ رائِجاً to be in style; سِلْعة رائِجة a sought-after good

رَواج *n* marketability, saleability; popularity; رَواج البَضائِعِ the distribution of goods; لاقَ رَواجاً كَبيراً to be much sought-after

تَرْويج *n* promotion; distribution; حَمْلة التَرْويج promotional campaign

تَرْويجيّ *adj* promotional; حَمْلة تَرْويجيّة promotional campaign

مُرَوِّج *n* promoter

‹ **راحَ** *v* |u; رَواح| to go; to leave, to depart; راحَ ضَحِيَّتَهُ ... to claim the life/lives of ...; راحَ ضَحِيَّةَ الهُجوم مِئةُ شَخْصٍ the attack claimed the lives of 100 people

رَوَّحَ *v* to refresh; رَوَّحَ عن نَفْسِهِ to relax

راوَحَ *v* to vary, to range; راوَحَ في مَكانِهِ to stand still, to be stalled; راوَحَ بين ٢٠٠٠ و٣٠٠٠ رِيالٍ to range between 2,000 and 3,000 riyals

أَراحَ *v* to reassure, to soothe, to calm; أَرِحْني do me a favour; أَراحَ ضَميرَهُ to ease one's conscience

أَرْوَحَ *v* to smell bad, to stink

تَرَوَّحَ *v* **1** [بالمِرْوَحةِ] to fan oneself **2** [انْتَشَرَت رائِحَتُهُ] to diffuse a strong odour, to be fragrant

تَراوَحَ *v* to vary, to range; to fluctuate; تَراوَحَ بين ٢٠٠٠ و٣٠٠٠ رِيالٍ to range from 2,000 to 3,000 riyals; تَتَراوَحُ أَعْمارُهُم بين ٢٤ و٣٠ سَنةً their ages range from 24 to 30 years

ارْتاحَ *v* to rest, to relax; to be happy/contented; ارْتاحَ لِشَيْءٍ to be happy about sth

اسْتَراحَ *v* to rest, to relax; to be relieved; to take a break; اسْتَراحَ من مَجْهودٍ to rest from an exertion; اسْتَراحَ لِمُدّةِ نِصْفِ ساعةٍ to relax for half an hour

اسْتَرْوَحَ *v* to smell, to sniff

روح *n* |mf; أَرْواح| ◄1► [نَفْس] spirit, soul; الروح (Islam) *the angel Gabriel*; روح رِياضيّة sportsmanship; روح جَديدة a spirit of innovation; روح مَعْنَويّة morale; روح جَماعيّة \ الفَريقِ team spirit; روح التَعاوُن a spirit of cooperation; روح العَصْرِ zeitgeist; روح القُدُسِ the Holy Spirit; خُلود الروح the immortality of the spirit; إزْهاق روحِ شَخْصٍ taking sb's life; تَحْضير الأَرْواحِ spiritualism; اسْتِحْضار الأَرْواحِ seance; تَقَمُّص \ تَناسُخ الروحِ reincarnation; أَسْلَمَ روحَهُ he gave up the ghost; فاضَتْ \ قُبِضَتْ روحُهُ he died; حَدَثَتْ خَسائِرُ في الأَرْواحِ people were killed; تَمَتَّعَ بِشَبابِ الروحِ to be young in spirit; الروح والجَسَد body and spirit; فَعَلَ شَيْئاً بالروحِ والجَسَدِ to do sth with all one's heart; جَسَداً وَروحاً with heart and soul; بِدونِ روحٍ lifeless ◄2► [خُلاصة] extract

ريح *n* |mf; أَرْياح ,رِياح| ◄1► [هَواء مُتَحَرِّك] wind; ريح غَرْبيّة a west wind; ريح جانِبيّة a crosswind; ريح زَعْزَع whirlwind; ريح مَوْسِميّة monsoon; ريح مُعاكِسة headwind; كانَت الرِياحُ مُؤاتِيةً \ مُعاكِسةً there was a tailwind/headwind; رِياح تِجاريّة trade wind; رِياح ضَعيفة \ مُعْتَدِلة \ قَويّة \ عاصِفة a light/moderate/strong/stormy wind; رِياح بارِدة \ قارِسة a cold/biting wind; الرِياحُ شَديدةٌ \ خَفيفةٌ there's much/little wind; رِياح خَفيفة إلى مُعْتَدِلة a light to moderate wind; نَفْحة الريحِ gust (of wind); قوّة الريحِ wind force; اتِّجاه الريحِ wind direction; سُرْعة الريحِ wind speed; كُمّ ريحٍ windsock; سُكون الرِياحِ calm; أبو رِياحٍ weathervane; تَضْعُفُ الرِياحُ the wind is falling; تَهْدَأُ الرِياحُ the wind is dropping; تُصَفِّرُ \ تَعْصِفُ الرِياحُ the wind is howling/raging; (لا) تَهُبُّ ريحُهُ he's (not) flying high; تَهُبُّ رِياحٌ غَرْبيّةٌ there is a westerly wind; هَبَّت الريحُ بِشِدّةٍ there is a strong wind; احْتَمى من الرِياحِ to sit out of the wind; كانَت الرِياحُ مَعْدومةً there was no wind; كانَت الريحُ مُواتِيةً لَهُ to have the wind in one's sails; وَضَعَ شَيْئاً في مَهَبِّ الريحِ to jeopardize sth; الرِياحُ لا تَعْبَأُ بالأَعْشابِ وَلَكِنَّها تَكْسُرُ عَظيمَ الشَجَرِ a great tree attracts the wind ◄2► [فُساء] wind; fart; أَخْرَجَ ريحاً to break wind

رَيِّح *adj* windy

رائِح *adj* departing; غادٍ وَرائِح coming and going

رائِحة *n* |رَوائِحُ| ◄1► [ما يُشَمُّ] smell, odour; رائِحة غَريبة a strange odour; رائِحة كَريهة \ نَتِنة \ عَفِنة a nasty smell; نَشَرَ رائِحةً قَذِرةً \ خارِقةً to emit a bad/pungent smell; فاحَتْ مِنْهُ رائِحةٌ كَريهةٌ to stink; تَفوحُ من هذا المَكانِ رائِحةٌ كَريهةٌ it stinks in here; مُزيل لِرائِحةِ العَرَقِ deodorant; لا رائِحةَ لَهُ odourless ◄2► [عِطْر] perfume, fragrance; رائِحة زَكيّة \ طَيِّبة fragrance; رَوائِح aromatic substances

راحة *n* |راحات| ◄1► [يُسْر] rest; ease; comfort; راحة أَبَديّة eternal rest; فَتْرة الراحةِ rest period; بَيْت الراحةِ toilet (BrE), restroom (AmE); أَحَسَّ بالراحةِ to feel at ease; أَخَذَ قِسْطاً من الراحةِ to enjoy a well-deserved rest; مُزَوَّد بِجَميعِ وَسائِلِ \ تَجْهيزاتِ \ أَدَواتِ الراحةِ fitted with all conveniences; المَريضُ بِحاجةٍ إلى الراحةِ the patient needs rest; عَدَم الراحةِ restlessness ◄2► (Anat) |راح ,راحات| palm; راحة اليَدِ palm of the hand; بِراحةِ اليَدِ with the flat of the hand

روحاني [A] *adj* spiritual; animistic; مَسائِل روحانيّة spiritual matters

[B] *n* animist

روحانيّة *n* spirituality, spiritualism; animism; روحانيّات spiritual matters

روحيّ *adj* spiritual; mental; زَعيم روحيّ a spiritual leader; غَيْر روحيّ material

روحيّة *n* spirituality; spiritualism

رَيْحان *n* |رَياحين| basil (*Ocimum basilicum*)

ارْتِياح *n* satisfaction; ease; كانَ سَبَبَ ارْتِياحٍ to give cause for satisfaction; كانَ شَديدَ الارْتِياحِ to be well pleased; بَعَثَ \ حَمَلَ على الارْتِياحِ to be satisfactory; عَبَّرَ عن ارْتِياحِهِ لِ \ إلى شَيْءٍ to express one's satisfaction with sth; شَعَرَ (لم يَشْعُرْ) بالارْتِياحِ to feel (ill) at ease; شُعور بالارْتِياحِ a sense of relief; ارْتِياح حول شَيْءٍ relief about sth; عَدَم ارْتِياحٍ discomfort

أَرْيَحي *adj* generous, munificent; liberal

أَرْيَحيّة *n* generosity, munificence

اسْتِراحة *n* 1 [فَتْرة الراحةِ] rest, break; pause; اسْتِراحة قَصيرة a short break; أَخَذَ اسْتِراحةً to take a break; أَخَذَ اسْتِراحة عَشرِ دَقائِقَ to have a ten-minute break; بِدونِ اسْتِراحةٍ without a break; في \ أَثْناءَ الاسْتِراحةِ in/during the break; بعد \ قبل الاسْتِراحةِ after/before the break 2 [مَكان] waiting room; place to rest

اسْتِرْواح *n* air intake; اسْتِرْواح الصَدْرِ \ صَدْريّ pneumothorax; اسْتِرْواح الصِفاقِ pneumoperitoneum

تَرْويح *n* diversion, recreation; تَرْويح عن النَفْسِ recreation

تَرْويحيّ *adj* recreational; بَرْنامَج تَرْويحيّ a recreational programme

مُراوَحة *n* fluctuation, variation, shift

مُرْتاح *adj* relaxed, calm; comfortable; ضَمير مُرْتاح a clear conscience; مُرْتاح النَفْسِ relieved; مُرْتاح البال carefree; عاشَ مُرْتاحَ البالِ to have peace of mind; كانَ غَيْرَ مُرْتاحٍ to be uncomfortable

مِرْوَحة *n* |مَراوِحُ| 1 [لِتَحْريكِ الهَواءِ] fan; مِرْوَحة يَدَويّة (hand) fan; مِرْوَحة سَقْفيّة ceiling fan 2 [دَوّارة] propeller; airscrew

مِرْوَحيّ *adj* relating to fans/propellers; طائِرة مِرْوَحيّة helicopter

مِرْوَحيّة *n* helicopter

مُريح *adj* restful; calming; comfortable, cosy; كُرْسيّ مُريح an easy chair; مَنْزِل \ بَيْت مُريح a comfortable house; أَحْذِية مُريحة comfortable shoes; غَيْر مُريحٍ uncomfortable; هذا الحِذاءُ غَيْرُ مُريحٍ these shoes are uncomfortable; وَضْع غَيْر مُريحٍ an unpleasant position

مُسْتَراح *n* toilet (BrE), lavatory (BrE), restroom (AmE)

مُسْتَريح *adj* relaxed; بِضَميرٍ مُسْتَريحٍ with a clear conscience

رادَ *v* |u; رَوْد| to explore; to pioneer

راوَدَ *v* 1 [عاكَسَ] to proposition; to molest; راوَدَ امْرَأةً عن نَفْسِها to proposition a woman 2 [فَتَنَ] to tempt, to try to seduce; راوَدَ خَيالَ شَخْصٍ to fire sb's imagination

أَرادَ *v* to want; to wish; to mean; أَرادَ \ لم يُرِدْ شَيْئاً to (not) want sth; أَرادَ أَنْ تَفْعَلَ شَيْئاً he wanted to do sth; أَرادَ أَنْ يَفْعَلَ شَيْئاً he wanted you to do sth; لا يُريدُ أَنْ يَحْدُثَ لَهُ هذا he doesn't want this to happen to him; ماذا تُريدُ؟ what do you want?; كَما تُريدُ as you wish, whatever you want

ارْتادَ *v* to frequent, to visit often; to attend; ارْتادَ المَقاهِيَ to frequent cafes

رائِد A *adj* |رُوّاد| pioneering, leading, trendsetting; أَفْكار رائِدة pioneering ideas; مارْكة رائِدة a trendsetting brand; دَوْر رائِد a pioneering role; لَعِبَ دَوْراً رائِداً to play a leading part
B *n* |رُوّاد| 1 [صاحِب الرِيادةِ] pioneer, groundbreaker, pathfinder; رائِد الفَضاءِ astronaut 2 [مَنْ يَتَقَدَّمُ على القَوْمِ] leader; model, example; رائِد فَريقِ كُرةِ القَدَمِ the captain of a soccer team 3 (Mil) major 4 [دَليل] guideline

رُوَيْداً *adv* رُوَيْداً رُوَيْداً gradually; رُوَيْدَكَ! ,رُوَيْداً! calm down!; بَدَأَت الموسيقى تَعْلو رُوَيْداً رُوَيْداً gradually, the music grew louder; تَقَدَّمَ رُوَيْداً رُوَيْداً نحو الجَبَلِ he slowly approached the mountain

رِيادة *n* exploration; pioneering role; رِيادة الفَضاءِ space travel; لِأَمْريكا الرِيادةُ في الأَمْرِ the US is taking the lead in this matter

رِياديّ A *adj* pioneering, path-finding; أَعْمال رِياديّة pioneering work; قامَ بِأَعْمالٍ رِياديّةٍ to break new ground
B *n* pioneer

إرادة *n* will; wish; desire; إرادة حَديديّة an iron will; إرادة الحَياةِ the will to live; فاقِد الإرادةِ weak-willed; قوّة الإرادةِ willpower; أَظْهَرَ قوّةَ إرادةٍ to show willpower; نَفَّذَ \ فَرَضَ إرادَتَهُ to get one's own way; فَرَضَ إرادَتَهُ على شَخْصٍ to force one's will on sb; بِمَحْضِ إرادَتِهِ of one's own volition; بِمِلْءِ إرادَتِهِ by one's own free will; حَسَبَ الإرادةِ as one would wish; عَدَم الإرادةِ unwillingness; خارِج عن \ دون \ بِغَيْرِ إرادَتِهِ against one's will

إراديّ *adj* voluntary; intentional; حَرَكة غَيْر إراديّةٍ an involuntary movement

لاإراديّ *adj* involuntary, unintentional, unwanted; حَرَكات لاإراديّة involuntary movements

مُراد *n* 1 [غَرَض] purpose, intention; wish; بَلَغَ مُرادَهُ to attain one's goal 2 [مَعْنًى] meaning 3 [اسْم شَخْصيّ] Murad (*male given name*)

مِرْوَد *n* |مَراوِدُ| kohl stick, eyeliner pencil

مُريد *n* novice (*in a Sufi order*); disciple; aspirant

‹ **رود آيْلانْد** *n* |f| Rhode Island (*US state*)

‹ **رودودَنْدَرون** *n* rhododendron

‹ **رازَ** *v* |u; رَوْز| to examine, to analyse; رازَ شَخْصاً to examine sb

رَوْز *n* testing; analysis

‹ **روزْماري** *n* rosemary (*Rosmarinus officinalis*)

‹ **روزْنامة** *n* calendar; almanac

‹ **رَوَّسَ** *v* see رأس

‹ **روسيّ** **A** *adj* |روس| Russian; الاتّحاد الروسيّ Russian Federation; (اللُغة) الروسيّة Russian (*language*)

B *n* |روس| Russian (*person*)

روسْيا, روسِيا *n* Russia; روسْيا البَيْضاء Belarus (*formerly called White Russia*)

‹ **روشِتّة** *n* prescription

‹ **رَوْشَن** *n* |رَواشِنُ| skylight

‹ **روش هاشَناه** *n* Rosh Hashanah (*Jewish New Year*)

‹ **رَوَّضَ** *v* to break (in), to train; to discipline; رَوَّض كَلْباً \ أَسَداً to train a dog/lion; رَوَّض فَرَساً to break a horse; رَوَّض النَفْسَ على الصَبْرِ to force oneself to be patient

تَرَوَّضَ *v* to be tamed/domesticated

تَرَيَّضَ *v* to exercise

رَوْضة *n* |رِياض, رَوْضات, رَوْض| garden; meadow; رَوْضة الأَطْفالِ kindergarten

رِياضة *n* **1** (Sport) sport (BrE), sports (AmE); exercise; رِياضة بَدَنيّة gymnastics; رِياضات مائيّة water sport (BrE) sports (AmE); رِياضة أولِمْبيّة an Olympic sport; رِياضة فَرْدِيّة an individual sport; رِياضة جَماعيّة team sport (BrE) sports (AmE); صالة \ قاعة رِياضةٍ sports hall; مارَسَ رِياضةً to play a sport; to exercise, to take (BrE) get (AmE) some exercise **2** (Math) mathematics; الرِياضة البَحْتة \ التَطْبيقيّة pure/applied mathematics **3** (Chr) رِياضة روحيّة retreat

رِياضيّ **A** *adj* **1** (Sport) sports; sportsmanlike; لاعِبة رِياضيّة sportswoman; تَقَبَّلَ شَيْئاً بِروحٍ رِياضيّةٍ to take sth with grace; ذو روحٍ رِياضيّةٍ sportsmanlike; سُلوك لارِياضيّ unsporting behaviour **2** (Math) mathematical; صيغة رِياضيّة a mathematical formula

B *n* **1** (Sport) sportsperson, sportsman **2** (Math) mathematician

رِياضيّات *n pl* mathematics; arithmetic; عالِم الرِياضيّاتِ mathematician; دَرَّسَ \ عَلَّمَ الرِياضيّاتِ to teach mathematics; كانَ نابِغاً في الرِياضيّاتِ to be good at mathematics

رِياضيّة *n* sportswoman

الرِياض *n* |f| Riyadh

تَرْويض *n* training, taming

مُرَوَّض *adj* tame, domesticated

مُرَوِّض *n* animal trainer/tamer

‹ **راعَ** *v* |u; رَوْع| **1** [خَوَّفَ] to frighten, to scare; to alarm; to appall; راعَني مَنْظَرُ الضَحايا I was appalled at the sight of the victims **2** [أَعْجَبَ] to please, to delight; راعَني جَمالُها her beauty dazzled me; راعَتْني هذه القِصّةُ this story delighted me **3** [زادَ] see ريع

رَوَّعَ *v* to frighten, to scare

أَراعَ *v* to frighten, to scare

ارْتاعَ *v* to be/become frightened

روع *n* mind, heart; سَكَّنَ \ هَدَّأَ روعَ شَخْصٍ to calm sb

رَوْع *n* dread, fear; أَثارَ رَوْعَ شَخْصٍ to frighten sb

رائِع *adj* terrific, excellent, wonderful, marvellous, magnificent, superb, splendid, glorious, sublime; يَوْم \ لَيْلة رائِع(ة) a wonderful day/evening; قِطْعة فَنِّيّة رائِعة a magnificent piece of art; مَنْظَر رائِع a beautiful view; مُغَنٍّ رائِع an excellent singer; لاعِب رائِع a great player; إِحْساس رائِع a lovely feeling; مَشْهَد رائِع a marvellous sight; حَفْل رائِع a grand party; حَديقة رائِعة a delightful garden

رائِعة *n* |رَوائِعُ| masterpiece; رائِعة من رَوائِعِ شِكْسْبير one of Shakespeare's masterpieces

رَوْعة *n* **1** [جَمال] beauty, magnificence, splendour; رَوْعة وَجَلال beauty and splendour **2** [عَظَمة] grandeur, magnificence; يا لَلرَوْعةِ how wonderful **3** [خَوْف] terror, fear

أَرْوَع *adj* |dipt| most beautiful; أَرْوَع الموسيقى the most beautiful music; على أَرْوَعِ وَجْهٍ in the best way

ترويع *n* frightening; terrorizing

مُروَّع *adj* frightened; terrified

مُروِّع *adj* dreadful, frightening, terrifying; alarming; shocking; صُوَر \ أَخْبار مُروِّعة shocking pictures/messages; جَريمة مُروِّعة a dreadful crime

مُريع *adj* dreadful, terrifying, frightening, scary; فِكْرة مُريعة a frightening thought

‹ **راغَ** *v* |u; رَوْغ| to dodge, to circumvent

راوَغَ *v* to dodge, to evade; to deceive

رَوَغان *n* evasion

مُراوِغ **A** *adj* crafty, sly, cunning, deceitful

B *n* dodger

مُراوَغة *n* dodge, evasion; equivocation, prevarication, evasiveness; deceit, trickery

‹ **راقَ** *v* |u; رَوْق| **1▸** [أَعْجَبَ] to please, to delight; راقَ المَلِكةَ أنْ ... the queen was pleased to ...; يَروقُ لَهُ الحَديثُ he likes talking **2▸** [صَفا] to be clear/transparent (*liquid*)

رَوَّقَ *v* to purify, to clean; to filter

أَراقَ *v* to shed, to spill; أَراقَ دِماءً \ أَراقَ الدِماءَ to shed blood; أَراقَ دِماءَ الأَبْرِياءِ to shed innocent blood; أَراقَ ماءَ وَجْهِهِ to lose face

رَوْق *n* |أَرْواق| **1▸** [مُقَدَّم] beginning; رَوْق اللَّيْلِ first part of the night **2▸** [سَقيفة] portico

رائِق *adj* clear, pure; serene, calm; رائِق البال \ المِزاجِ good-humoured

راووق *n* filter

رِواق, رُواق *n* |أَرْوِقة, أَرْواق| gallery, colonnade; مُشاوَرات (داخِلَ) أَرْوِقةِ البَرْلَمانِ consultations in the corridors of parliament

رِواقيّ **A** *adj* Stoic; فَلْسَفة رِواقيّة Stoic philosophy

B *n* Stoic

إراقة *n* shedding, spilling; إراقة الدِماءِ bloodshed

تَرْويقة *n* breakfast

‹ **روك** *n* (Mus) rock; موسيقى الروك rock music

‹ **رَوَّلَ** *v* to slaver, to slobber

‹ **رولّة** *n* roller; رولّة دِهانٍ paint roller

‹ **روليت** *n* roulette

¹‹ **رامَ** *v* |u; رَوْم, مَرام| **1▸** [رَغِبَ] to desire, to wish; على ما يُرامُ as it should be; fine, all right, okay; هو على ما يُرامُ he's doing well; كُلُّ شَيْءٍ على ما يُرامُ everything's going well; تَسيرُ الأُمورُ على ما يُرامُ everything is going smoothly **2▸** [زالَ] see ريم

رام *n* listed alphabetically

مَرام *n* |مَرامات| wish, hope; بَلَغَ مَرامَهُ to attain one's object; وَفْقَ المَرامِ as one would wish

²‹ **روما** *n* Rome

رومانيّ **A** *adj* |رومان| **1▸** (Geog) Romanian; Roman; Romance; الرومانيّة (اللُغة) Romanian (*language*); لُغات رومانيّة Romance languages; الإِمْبَراطوريّة الرومانيّة the Roman Empire **2▸** (Archit) Romanesque

B *n* |رومان| **1▸** [مُواطِن رومانِيا] Romanian (*person*) **2▸** [مُواطِن الإِمْبِراطوريّة الرومانيّة] Roman (*person*)

رومانِيا *n* Romania

روميّ **A** *adj* |روم| Byzantine; Greek Orthodox (*Church*); ديك روميّ turkey

B *n* |روم| Byzantine (*person*)

الروم *n* the Romans; the Byzantines; الروم الأُرْثوذُكْس the Greek Orthodox Church; سورة الروم The Romans (*Sura 30*)

³‹ **روم** *n* rum

‹ **روماتِزْم** *n* rheumatism; مُصاب بالروماتِزْم rheumatic

روماتِزْميّ *adj* rheumatic; آلام روماتِزْميّة rheumatic pains

‹ **رومانْطيقيّ, رومانْتيكيّ** *adj* romantic

رومانْطيقيّة, رومانْتيكيّة, رومانْتيكيّة *n* romanticism; romance

‹ **رومانْسيّ** *adj* romantic; شَخْص رومانْسيّ a romantic person; رَسّام \ كاتِب رومانْسيّ a romantic painter/writer; قِصّة \ فيلْم رومانْسيّ(ة) a romantic story/movie

رومانْسيّة *n* romanticism; romance

‹ **مَرْوان** *n* listed alphabetically

‹ **رَوى** *v* |i| **1▸** [سَقى] |رِيّ, رَيّ| to water, to irrigate; to give drinking water (*to an animal*); رَوى الحُقولَ to irrigate the fields **2▸** [حَكى] |رِواية| to narrate, to tell, to relate; to quote;

‹ **ريال** *n* riyal (*currency of Saudi Arabia and Qatar*)

‹ **راب** *v* |i; ريبة ,رَيْب| 1 [شَكَّكَ] to arouse suspicion, to fill with doubt 2 [خثَرَ] see **روب**

أَرابَ *v* 1 [شَكَّكَ] to arouse suspicion, to fill with doubt 2 [خثَّرَ] see **روب**

ارْتابَ *v* to suspect, to distrust; to doubt; ارْتابَ ب \ في \ من شَيْءٍ \ شَخْصٍ to distrust sth/sb; ارْتابَ في الأَمْرِ to have doubts about the matter; ارْتابَ في \ من شَيْءٍ to become suspicious of sth

رَيْب *n* doubt; بِلا رَيْبٍ without doubt; لا رَيْبَ في الأَمْرِ the matter is beyond doubt

ريبة *n* |رِيَب| doubt, suspicion

ارْتِياب *n* suspicion, distrust, mistrust; doubt; نَظْرة ارْتِيابٍ a suspicious look; بِارْتِيابٍ disbelieving; نَظَرَ بِارْتِيابٍ to look doubtful

ارْتِيابيّة *n* scepticism

مُرْتاب *adj* suspicious, distrustful, mistrustful; doubtful, sceptical, incredulous; كانَ مُرْتاباً من شَيْءٍ to be sceptical about sth

مُريب *adj* suspect, suspicious, dubious, doubtful; مَظْهَر مُريب an untrustworthy appearance

‹ **ريبورْتاج** *n* report, reportage

‹ **راثَ** *v* |i; رَيْث| 1 [تَباطَأَ] to tarry, to linger, to take one's time 2 [تَبَرَّزَ] see **روث**

تَرَيَّثَ *v* to tarry, to linger, to take one's time; تَرَيَّثَ في اتِّخاذِ القَرارِ to tarry in taking (BrE) making (AmE) the decision

رَيْثَما *conj* while, as long as; pending; until; يُسْجَنُ المُتَّهَمُ رَيْثَما يَنْتَهي التَحْقيقُ the suspect will be detained until the interrogations are completed

‹ **ريجيم** *n* see **رجيم**

‹ **رِياسة** *n* see رِئاسة

‹ **راشَ** *v* |a; رَيْش| to fledge; راشَ الطائِرُ the bird fledged

رَيَّشَ *v* to fledge; to feather

تَرَيَّشَ *v* to become wealthy

ريش *n coll* |أَرْياش ,رِياش| feathers; plumage, feathering; من الريشِ feather; حَشْوة من الريشِ a feather stuffing

رَوى قِصّةً لِشَخْصٍ to tell sb a story; رَوى الحَديثَ عن شَخْصٍ to transmit Hadith on the authority of sb

رَوِيَ *v* |a; رِيّ ,رَيّ| to drink, to quench one's thirst; to be irrigated

رَوّى *v* 1 [أَسْقى] to water, to irrigate; to give (sb) water to drink 2 [تَفَكَّرَ] to think

أَرْوى *v* to water; *to give to drink*; to sate; أَرْوى عَطَشَهُ to quench one's thirst; ظَمَأ لا يُرْوى insatiable thirst

تَرَوّى *v* to reflect, to ponder; تَرَوّى في شَيْءٍ to reflect on sth

ارْتَوى *v* to quench one's thirst

رَوِيّ *adj* thirst-quenching

راوٍ *n* |رُواة| storyteller, narrator

راية ,رِياء see **رأي**

رُواء *n* beauty

رِوائيّ A *adj* fictional, fiction (*before n*)

B *n* novelist; dramatist

رِواية *n* 1 [حِكاية] novel; story; رِواية تاريخيّة a historical novel; رِواية بوليسيّة detective story 2 [مَصْدَر] version, reading; narrative, account; تَقولُ رِوايةٌ أُخْرى إنّ ... another report says that ...; رِوايات مُخْتَلِفة لِقَضِيّةٍ \ حَدَثٍ \ حادِثةٍ different versions of a matter/event/accident

رَوِيّة *n* deliberation, thought

رَيّ *n* watering, irrigation

رَيّان A *adj* |f رَيّا; رِواء| succulent, tender, fresh; quenched, sated (*with liquid*); well-watered

B *n* (Islam) الرَيّان al-Rayyan (*the name of one of Paradise's gates, through which the observers of the fast during Ramadan will enter on the Day of Resurrection*)

أُرْوِيّة *n* |mf; أَراوِيّ| (Zool) mouflon (*Ovis aries orientalis*)

تَرَوٍّ *n* deliberation

تَرْوِية *n* consideration, deliberation

مُتَرَوٍّ A *adj* careful

B *n* deliberator

مُرَوًّى *adj* مُرَوًّى فيهِ well considered/thought out, sound

‹ **ري** *n* (Mus) ray

تريفيت *n* Riffian, Riff Berber (*language*)

ريق *n* |أَرْياق| saliva, spit; بَلَعَ رِيقَهُ to catch one's breath; على الريقِ on an empty stomach ‹

رالَ *v* |i; رَيْل| to slobber, to drool ‹

رَيَّلَ *v* to slobber, to drool

رِيالة *n* saliva, slobber, spit

مَرْيَلة ,مِرْيَلة *n* |مَرايِلُ| bib; apron

مَرْيول *n* dress; skirt

رامَ *v* |i; رَيْم| [1] [زالَ] to leave, to go away; ما رامَ مَكانَهُ he didn't move; ما يَرِيمُ يَفْعَلُ ذلك he's still doing that [2] [رَغِبَ] see **روم** ‹

رِيم ,رِئْم *n* [1] (Zool) addax, white antelope (*Addax nasomaculatus*) [2] [اسْم شَخْصيّ] |f dipt| Reem (*female given name*)

رام *n* listed alphabetically

مَرْيَم ,مَرْيَميّة *n* listed alphabetically

رانَ *v* |i; رَيْن| |على| to reign; to overcome; رانَتْ عَلَيْهِ الشُكوكُ he was assailed by doubts ‹

رِياش *n* furniture

رِيشة *n* [1] [طَيْر] feather; خَفيف كالرِيشةِ as light as a feather; وَزْن الرِيشةِ (Sport) featherweight [2] [قَلَم حِبْر] quill; nib; كَتَبَ بِرِيشةٍ to write with a quill [3] [صِباغ] paintbrush, brush [4] (Sport) shuttle; الرِيشة الطائِرة badminton [5] (Tech) blade [6] (Mus) plectrum, pick

راعَ *v* |i; رَيْع| [1] [زادَ] to increase [2] [خَوَّفَ\أَعْجَبَ] see **روع** ‹

رَيَّعَ *v* to increase

رَيْع *n* |رُيوع| yield, return

رَيْعان *n* prime; choicest part; رَيْعان الشَبابِ the prime of one's life

ريف *n* |أَرْياف| [1] [عَكْس المَدينةِ] countryside, country; أَهْل \ سُكّان الريفِ the rural population; في الريفِ in the country [2] [مِنْطَقة في المَغْرِبِ] Er Rif (*region in northern Morocco*); مِنْطَقة الريفِ Er Rif region; جِبال الريفِ Rif Mountains ‹

ريفيّ [A] *adj* rural; rustic; country (*before n*); بيئة ريفيّة a rustic ambience; تَقاليد ريفيّة rural customs; مِنْطَقة ريفيّة countryside [B] *n* peasant, country-dweller, rustic

زائير, زايير *n* |f| Zaire

زائيريّ *adj*, *n* Zairean

زِئْبَر *n* pile (*of fabric*)

زِئْبَق *n* (Chem) mercury, quicksilver

زِئْبَقيّ *adj* mercurial; mercury (*before n*)

زاج *n* sulphate

زَأَر *v* |a-i; زَأْر, زَئير| to roar

زَئير *n* roar; roaring; زَئير أَسَدٍ a lion's roar

زاغ *n* |زيغان| (Zool) chough (*Pyrrhocorax*)

زُؤام *adj* مَوْت زُؤام a sudden death

زامْبيّ *adj*, *n* Zambian

زامْبيا *n* Zambia

زان *n* beech (*Fagus*); ثَمرة الزانِ beechnut

زانة *n* pole; الوَثْب \ القَفْز بالزانةِ pole-vaulting

زاي *n* |f| *name of the letter* ز

زَبَّبَ *v* to dry grapes

زُبّ *n* |أَزْباب| (vulg) cock (vulg), dick (vulg)

زَباب *n coll* shrew

زبيب *n coll* raisin, currant

زَبَدَ *v* |u; زَبْد| to churn (*butter*)

زَبَّدَ *v* to churn (*butter*)

أَزْبَدَ *v* **1** [البَحْرُ] to foam, to froth **2** [الإنْسانُ] to foam (with rage)

زَبَد *n* |أَزْباد| foam, froth; تَطايَرَ زَبَد المَوْجِ \ البَحْرِ sea foam; تَطايَرَ الزَبَدُ من فَمِهِ to froth at the mouth

زَباد *n* قِطّ الزَبادِ (Zool) civet (*Civettictis*)

زَباديّ *adj* لَبَن زَباديّ yoghurt

زُبْدة *n* |زُبَد| **1** [مادّة] butter; عُلْبة زُبْدٍ a tub of butter; طَبَق زُبْدةٍ butter dish; زُبْدة فُسْتُقٍ pistachio butter; nut butter **2** [صَفوة] gist, main point; هذه زُبْدةُ القَوْلِ this is the gist of it, it boils down to this; زُبْدة الأَخْبارِ top news

زُبْديّ *adj* buttery

زُبْديّة, زِبْديّة *n* |زُبْديّات, زَبادي| bowl

زِبْديّة *n* avocado

مُزْبِد *adj* foaming, foamy

زَبَرَ *v* |i-u; زَبْر| **1** [شَتَمَ] to abuse, to scold **2** (Relig) to stone

زُبْر *n* penis

زَبور *n* (Book of) Psalms

زَبْرَجَ *v* |i; زَبْرَجة| to decorate, to embellish

زِبْرِج *n* |زَبارِجُ| ornament, decoration

زَبَرْجَد *n* peridot; aquamarine (*gemstone*)

زَبَّطَ *v* to quack

زَبَلَ *v* |i; زَبْل| to fertilize with manure

زَبَّلَ *v* to fertilize with manure

زِبْل *n* |أَزْبال| manure, dung

زَبّال *n* refuse collector (BrE), garbage collector (AmE)

زُبالة *n* rubbish (BrE), garbage (AmE), trash (AmE); زُبالة المَنازِلِ household rubbish; صُنْدوق الزُبالةِ dustbin (BrE), garbage/trash can (AmE); skip (BrE), dumpster (AmE); أَكْوام الزُبالةِ heaps of rubbish (BrE), piles of garbage (AmE); rubbish dump (BrE), dump (AmE)

مَزْبَلة *n* |مَزابِلُ| rubbish dump (BrE), dump (AmE); في المَزْبَلةِ on the rubbish dump; في \ إلى مَزْبَلةِ التاريخِ in/into the dustbin of history

زِبانة *n* clientele, patronage

زَجْر *n* scolding, rebuke, reprimand; الزَجْر والنَهْر scolding and admonishment (*disciplinary method*)

زَجْرِيّ *adj* repressive; تَدابير زَجْرِيّة (Law) injunctive measures

‹ **زَجَل** *n* |أَزْجال| *strophic Arabic poem in colloquial language*

زاجِل *adj* حَمام زاجِل carrier pigeon, homing pigeon

زَجّال *n poet or reciter of poems (especially* **أَزْجال***)*

‹ **أَزْجى** *v* to drive, to push, to shove

‹ **زُحار** *n* dysentery; أُصيبَ بالزُحارِ to contract dysentery

مَزْحور *adj* suffering from dysentery

‹ **زَحْزَحَ** *v* |i; زَحْزَحة| to move, to shift, to displace; to push, to shove; زَحْزَحْتُ نَفْسي بِاتِّجاهِها I pushed myself in her direction; زَحْزَحَ شَخْصاً من مَكانِهِ to force sb out of their position; زَحْزَحَت العاصِفةُ البَيْتَ من أساساتِهِ the storm displaced the house from its foundations

تَزَحْزَحَ *v* to move, to stir, to budge; لم يَتَزَحْزَحْ عن رَأْيِهِ قَيْدَ لم يَتَزَحْزَحْ قَيْدَ أُنْمُلةٍ شَعْرةٍ he didn't change his opinion at all; عن مَوْقِفِهِ he didn't budge from his position one bit

‹ **زَحَفَ** *v* |a; زَحْف| **1** [حَبا] to crawl, to creep, to slither; زَحَفَ على الأَرْضِ \ على بَطْنِهِ to crawl on the ground/on one's stomach; يَزْحَفُ الثُعْبانُ snakes slither; يَزْحَفُ الاقْتِصادُ على بَطْنِهِ the economy is crawling along **2** [تَقَدَّمَ] to march, to advance; زَحَفَ الإعْصارُ صَوْبَ تايْوان the typhoon advanced towards Taiwan; زَحَفَت الجَحافِلُ إلى شَرْقِ إفْريقيا the legions marched on East Africa

أَزْحَفَ *v* to let crawl; أَزْحَفَ الطِفْلَ he let the child crawl

زَحْف *n* march, advance; زَحْف قارّيّ continental shift; زَحْف عُمْرانيّ urban encroachment (BrE), urban sprawl (AmE)

زاحِف **A** *adj* |زَواحِفُ| crawling, creeping; نَبات زاحِف creeper, climbing plant; كُرة زاحِفة low shot (*in football*)
B *n* |زَواحِفُ| **1** (Zool) reptile **2** (Comput) زاحِف الويب Web crawler

زَحّافة *n* **1** (Sport) ski; زَحّافات flip-flops; زَحّافات ثَلْجيّة luge (*name of sport*) **2** (Tools) crawler excavator

‹ **زَحَلَ** *v* |a; زَحْل, زُحول| to move, to shift, to slide

زُحَل *n* |dipt| (Astron) Saturn; حَلَقات زُحَلَ the rings of Saturn; في مَدارٍ حول زُحَلَ in orbit around Saturn

زُبانى *n* antenna, feeler; stinger

زَبون *n* |زَبائِنُ| customer, client; guest; زَبون دائِم a regular customer; الزَبونُ مَلِكٌ the customer is always right; زَبائِن clientele; اسْتَقْبَلَ زَبائِنَ to accommodate guests; اجْتَذَبَ زَبائِنَ جُدُداً to attract new customers

‹ **زُبْية** *n* |زُبًى| *elevated place above the waterline*; بَلَغَ السَيْلُ الزُبى things have come to a head; enough is enough

‹ **زَجَّ** *v* |u; زَجّ| **1** [أَقْحَمَ] (fig) to push, to shove; زُجَّ بِهِ في السِجْنِ he was thrown in prison **2** [وَرَّطَ] to involve, to draw in, to embroil; زَجَّ شَخْصاً في شَيْءٍ to involve sb in sth; زَجَّ نَفْسَهُ في قَضيّةٍ to get oneself embroiled in an issue

زَجّاج *n* glassmaker; glazier

زُجاج *n* glass (*as a substance*); لَوْح زُجاجٍ a pane (of glass); زُجاج مُلَوَّن coloured glass; زُجاج ليفيّ glass wool (BrE), fiberglass insulation (AmE); زُجاج أَماميّ windscreen (BrE), windshield (AmE); تَحَطَّمَ \ تَهَشَّمَ الزُجاجُ the glass shattered; زُجاج مُزْدَوِج double-glazed glass (BrE), double pane glass (AmE)

زُجاجة *n* bottle; زُجاجة فارِغة \ مَليئة an empty/a full bottle; زُجاجة لِتْرٍ litre bottle; زُجاجة نَبيذٍ \ من النَبيذِ a bottle of wine; زُجاجة حارِقة \ مولوتوف Molotov cocktail, petrol bomb (BrE); أَلْقى بِزُجاجةِ مولوتوف to throw a Molotov cocktail; عُنُق زُجاجةٍ bottleneck; خَرَجَ من عُنُقِ زُجاجةٍ to get out of a tight spot

زُجاجيّ *adj* glass (*before n*), glassy; عَيْن زُجاجيّة glass eye; أَلْياف زُجاجيّة fibreglass

أَزَجّ *adj* |زُجّ| أَزَجّ الحاجِبَيْنِ with long eyebrows

‹ **زَجَرَ** *v* |u; زَجْر| **1** [وَبَّخَ] to scold; زَجَرَ شَخْصاً to scold sb; زَجَرَتْني بِنَظْرةٍ خانِقةٍ she rebuked me with a withering look **2** [مَنَعَ] |عن| to restrain, to discourage; زَجَرَ شَخْصاً عن شَيْءٍ to restrain sb from (doing) sth; زَجَرَهُ القانونُ عن السَرِقةِ the law discouraged him from stealing **3** [طَرَدَ] to drive away, to chase off

ازْدَجَرَ *v* **1** [امْتَنَعَ عن] |عن| to be discouraged from; to hold oneself back from, to refrain from; ازْدَجَرَ عن المُنْكَرِ to abstain from vice **2** [وَبَّخَ] to scold, to rebuke

‹ **زَحْلَقَ** *v* |i; زَحْلَقة| to slip, to slide; زَحْلَقَ على الدَرَجِ \ البَلاطِ to slip on the stairs/the tiles

تزَحْلَقَ *v* to glide, to slide; تزَحْلَقَ على الجَليدِ to ice-skate; to ski; to snowboard; تزَحْلَقَ على الثَلْجِ to ski

زُحْلوقة *n* |زَحاليقُ| slide

زُحْلَيْقة *n* slide

تزَحْلُق *n* **1** [على الجَليدِ \ الثَلْجِ] skating; skiing; snowboarding; تَزَحْلُق فَنّيّ figure skating; حَلْبة التَزَحْلُقِ على الجَليدِ ice rink **2** [على الماءِ] surfing; waterskiing **3** [على الرِمالِ] sandboarding

مُتَزَحْلِق *n* **1** [على الثَلْجِ] skier; skater; snowboarder **2** [على الماءِ] surfer; waterskier **3** [على الرِمالِ] sandboarder

‹ **زَحَمَ** *v* |a; زَحْم| to push, to jostle; to crowd, to cram; زَحَمَهُ الجُمْهورُ the crowd jostled him; يَزْحَمُ المَشاةُ الشَوارِعَ pedestrians crowd the streets; زَحَمَتْ بَيْتَها بالحَيَواناتِ الأَليفةِ she filled her house with pets

زاحَمَ *v* **1** [نافَسَ] to compete with sb; to crowd sb out; الصينُ تُزاحِمُ أَمْريكا على الصَدارةِ China competes with America for the lead; النَشْرُ الإلِكْتْرونيُّ يُزاحِمُ بِشِدّةٍ النَشْرَ التَقْليديَّ electronic publishing is strongly crowding out traditional publishing **2** [زَحَمَ] to push, to jostle; to crowd; زاحَموهُ على دُخولِ المِصْعَدِ they pushed him into the lift (BrE) elevator (AmE)

تزاحَمَ *v* **1** [احْتَشَدَ] to crowd together, to cram together, to jostle (each other); to be closely packed in; تَزاحَمَ الأَطْفالُ على البابِ الأَماميِّ the children crowded around the front door; تَزاحَمَ الرُكّابُ في الحافِلةِ the passengers jostled each other on the bus; تَزاحَمَتِ الأَسْئِلةُ في ذِهْنِهِ his mind was jam-packed with questions **2** [تَنافَسَ] to compete (with one another); تَزاحَمَ على كُرْسيِّ الرِئاسةِ to compete for the presidency

ازْدَحَمَ *v* to throng, to jostle, to crowd; to be crowded; تَزْدَحِمُ الأَفْكارُ في الذِهْنِ thoughts crowd the mind; يَزْدَحِمُ الشارِعُ بالمارّةِ the street is crowded with pedestrians; يَزْدَحِمُ جَدْوَلُهُ بالمَواعيدِ his schedule is packed with meetings

زِحام *n* throng, crowd; traffic; الزِحام الخانِق suffocating traffic; خَفَّفَ الزِحامَ المُروريَّ to ease traffic congestion; اخْتَفَتْ في الزِحامِ she disappeared into the crowd; ضاعَتِ المَعاني في زِحامِ الكَلِماتِ the meaning got lost in the noise

زَحْمة *n* |زَحَمات| **1** [الناسِ] throng, crowd, bustle; زَحْمة زوّارٍ a crowd of visitors; زَحْمة الأَعْيادِ the hustle and bustle of the holidays; تاهَ في زَحْمةِ التَفاصيلِ to get lost in a sea of details **2** [السَيّاراتِ] traffic; زَحْمة سَيْرٍ خانِقة a heavy traffic jam

ازْدِحام *n* crowding; traffic; ازْدِحام خانِق \ شَديد heavy traffic; ازْدِحام المُرورِ \ السَيْرِ traffic congestion; هي من أَكْثَرِ المَناطِقِ ازْدِحاماً بالسُكّانِ it is one of the most densely populated areas

تزاحُم *n* **1** [احْتِشاد] overcrowding; تَزاحُم شَديد severe overcrowding **2** [تَنافُس] competition; التَزاحُم على الوَظائِفِ the scramble for jobs

مُتزاحِم *n* **1** [مُسَبِّب الازْدِحامِ] *individual member of a throng/mob* **2** [مُنافِس] competitor, rival; مُتَزاحِم على المَقْعَدِ النِيابيِّ a rival for the parliamentary seat

مُزاحِم **A** *adj* competitive, competing **B** *n* competitor, rival

مُزاحَمة *n* **1** [زِحام] crowding, jostling; مُزاحَمة القِطاعِ الخاصِّ crowding out the private sector **2** [مُنافَسة] competition; مُزاحَمة غَيْر مَشْروعةٍ unfair competition; مُزاحَمة العِمالةِ الأَجْنَبيّةِ foreign labour competition

مُزْدَحِم *adj* busy, bustling; شارِع مُزْدَحِم a busy street; مَدينة مُزْدَحِمة a bustling city; مَوْسِم الصَيْفِ المُزْدَحِم the busy summer season

‹ **زَخّة** *n* downpour, shower; زَخّة شُهُبٍ meteor shower

‹ **زَخَرَ** *v* |a; زَخْر| |بـ| to be full of, to teem with, to burst with; زَخَرَ بالمَواهِبِ to be loaded with talent; يَزْخَرُ المَكانُ بالدَكاكينِ the place is full of shops; تَزْخَرُ مَكْتَبَتُها بالكُتُبِ her library is bursting with books; تَزْخَرُ صُفوفُ الفَريقِ بالنُجومِ the team is full of stars

تزَخَّرَ *v* **1** to be full **2** to swell, to rise

زاخِر *adj* full, chock-full, teeming; copious, abundant; قاعة زاخِرة بالحُضورِ a jam-packed hall; حَياتُها زاخِرةٌ بالإِنْجازاتِ her life is is full of accomplishments; مَلَكَ سِجِلاً زاخِراً to have a track record

زَرَدَ *v* |u; زَرْد| to swallow, to gulp (down)

اِزْدَرَدَ *v* to swallow, to gulp (down); اِزْدَرَدَتْ ريقَها \ لُعابَها she gulped

زَرَد *n* |زُرود| chain mail, coat of mail; دِرْع الزَرَدِ coat of mail

(Idiom) حِمار الزَرَدِ zebra (*Equus quagga*)

زَرَدِيّة *n* pair of pliers

زَرَّ *v* |u; زَرّ| to screw up; زَرَّ عَيْنَيْهِ to screw up one's eyes

زَرَّرَ *v* to button (up); زَرَّرَ سُتْرةً to button (up) a jacket

زِرّ *n* |أَزْرار, زُرور| ❶ [مِفْتاح] button, knob, switch; ضَغَطَ \ ضَغط الزِرَّ الأَيْمَنَ للماوْس كَبَس زِرًّا to press a button; to right-click the mouse ❷ [مَلابِس] button; خَيَّطَ زِرًّا to sew on a button; فَكَّ أَزْرارَ قَميصِهِ he unbuttoned his shirt

زُرْزور *n* |زَرازير| (Zool) starling (*Sturnus vulgaris*)

زَرَعَ *v* |a; زَرْع| ❶ (Agric) to cultivate, to grow, to produce; to plant, to sow; زَرَعَ القَمْحَ to cultivate wheat; زَرَعَ الطَماطِمَ \ الزُهورَ to grow tomatoes/flowers; زَرَعَ شَجَرةً to plant a tree; زَرَعَ بُذورَ الفِتْنةِ \ الشِقاقِ to sow seeds of discord; زَرَعَ أَلْغاماً to lay mines; زَرَعَ عَبْوةً ناسِفةً to plant an IED ❷ (Med) to transplant; to implant; زَرَعَ قَلْباً to transplant a heart; زَرَعَ شَيْئاً في الرَحِمِ to implant sth into the uterus ❸ [أَحْدَثَ] to generate, to foster; زَرَعَ الرُعْبَ \ الحِقْدَ to sow fear/hatred; زَرَعَ البَسْمةَ على وَجْهِ شَخْصٍ to put a smile on sb face

اِسْتَزْرَعَ *v* to cultivate, to grow; اِسْتَزْرَعَ الأَسْماكَ to cultivate fish

زَرْع *n* |زُروع| ❶ [نَبات] planting; crop; cutting (*plant*) ❷ (Med) transplant, transplantation; زَرْع الأَعْضاءِ organ transplant; زَرْع نِقْيِ العَظْمِ bone marrow transplant; زَرْع قَلْبٍ heart transplant; أَجْرى عَمَلِيّةَ زَرْعٍ to perform a transplant

زارِع *n* |زارِعون, زُرّاع| grower, planter, sower; زارِع القَمْحِ wheat grower

زِراعة *n* ❶ [مَصْدَر] cultivation, growing; زِراعة الخَضْرَواتِ \ القُطْنِ vegetable/cotton growing; زِراعة الأَنْسِجةِ tissue culture ❷ [حِرْفة] agriculture, farming; اِمْتَهَنَ الزِراعةَ to farm; وِزارة الزِراعةِ قِطاع الزِراعةِ agriculture sector, farming sector; the Ministry of Agriculture; الزِراعة والبَسْتَنة agriculture and horticulture; الزِراعة وَتَرْبِية الماشِيةِ agriculture and animal

زَخْرَفَ *v* |i; زَخْرَفة| to decorate, to embellish; زَخْرَفَ قَوْلَهُ \ كَلامَهُ to embellish one's words

تَزَخْرَفَ *v* to be decorated, to be embellished

زُخْرُف *n* |زَخارِف| ❶ [زينة] decoration, ornament, design; زَخارِف نَباتِيّة floral motifs; زَخارِف هَنْدَسِيّة arabesque; زُخْرُف الكَلامِ florid speech; زَخارِف مَحْفورة في الحَجَرِ \ الخَشَبِ decorative stone/wood engravings; سورة زُخْرُف The Gold Adornments (*Sura 43*) ❷ [نَعْمة] زُخْرُف الدُنْيا \ الحَياةِ worldly pleasure

زَخْرَفة *n* decoration, fittings; motif, design; الزَخْرَفة الداخِلِيّة interior decoration; زَخْرَفة نَباتِيّة a floral motif; زَخْرَفة لَفْظِيّة embellishment (*in speech*)

زُخْرُفِيّ *adj* decorative, ornamental; عَناصِر زُخْرُفِيّة ornaments

مُزَخْرَف *adj* decorated, ornamented; رُخام مُزَخْرَف ornate marble

مُزَخْرِف *n* (interior) decorator

زَخَمَ *v* |a; زَخْم| to push (forward), to propel

زَخِمَ *v* |a; زَخَم| to stink, to smell

زَخْم *n* momentum, impetus; فَقَدَ الزَخْمَ to lose momentum; تَكْتَسِبُ الاحْتِجاجاتُ زَخْماً the protests are gaining momentum; أَعْطى الزَخْمَ لِعَمَلِيّةِ السَلامِ to give impetus to the peace process

زَخَمة *n* stench

أَزْخَم *adj* |dipt| smelly

زَرَبَ *v* |u; زَرْب| to confine, to stall, to stable; زَرَبَ الماشِيةَ to stable the cattle

زَرْب *n traditional Jordanian dish usually made from chicken*

زَرْبِيّة, زُرْبِيّة *n* |زَرابِيّ| carpet, rug

زِرْياب *n listed alphabetically*

زَريبة *n* |زَرائِب| enclosure; pen, corral (AmE); زَريبة غَنَمٍ \ ماشِيةٍ sheep/cattle pen

مِزْراب *n* |مَزاريب| rain gutter, drain, spout; مِزْراب الهَدْرِ money drain (BrE), money pit (AmE); من تَحْتِ الدَلْفِ لِتَحْتِ المِزْرابِ from one calamity to another husbandry; عِلْم الزِراعةِ agricultural science, agronomy; الزِراعة المُكَثَّفة intensive agriculture; الزِراعة البيئيّة ecological/alternative farming; الزِراعة العُضْويّة organic farming ③ (Med) implantation; transplantation; زِراعة الكَبِدِ \ القَلْبِ liver/heart transplantation

زِراعيّ adj agricultural, agrarian, farm (before n); مُهَنْدِس زِراعيّ agricultural engineer; مَحاصيل زِراعيّة crops; مُنْتَجات زِراعيّة agricultural products, (agricultural) produce; الإرْشاد الزِراعيّ horticulture; جَرّار زِراعيّ tractor; مِنْطَقة زِراعيّة farming area; القِطاع الزِراعيّ the agricultural sector

زَريعة n |زَريعات, زَرائِعُ| ① [أَرْض مَزْروعة] field ② [بُذور] seed

اِسْتِزْراع n ① [زِراعة] farming, culture; اِسْتِزْراع الأَسْماكِ \ الروبيانِ fish/shrimp farming ② (Med) transplantation; اِسْتِزْراع الكَبِدِ liver transplantation

مُزارِع n farmer, grower; نِقابة المُزارِعينَ Farmers Union; مُزارِع التَبْغِ tobacco farmer

مَزْرَعة n |مَزارِعُ| farm; cultivated field; في المَزْرَعةِ on the farm; مَلَك مَزْرَعةً to have a farm; صاحِب مَزْرَعةٍ farmer; planter; مَزْرَعة دَواجِنَ \ سَمَكيّة \ رِياحٍ poultry/fish/wind farm

مَزْروع **A** adj ① (Agric) cultivated, planted; مِساحة \ أَرْض مَزْروعة cultivated area/land; أَلْغام \ قَنابِل مَزْروعة planted mines/bombs ② (Med) transplanted; عُضْو مَزْروع a transplanted organ

B n مَزْروعات crops

زَرافة n giraffe (Giraffa); رَقَبة \ عُنُق زَرافةٍ giraffe neck

1 **زَرَقَ** v |i-u; زَرْق| to inject

زَرْق n jabbing; زَرْق الإِبَرِ injections

مِزْراق n |مَزاريقُ| lance, javelin, spear

2 **زَرِقَ** v |a; زَرَق| to be/become blue

زَرَّقَ v to make blue; زَرَّقَ عَيْنَ شَخْصٍ to give sb a black eye

اِزْرَقَّ v to be/become blue; اِزْرَقَّ وَجْهُهُ his face turned blue (from asphyxiation); his face was black and blue (from beatings)

زَرَق n ① [لَوْن] blue; زَرَق السَماءِ sky blue ② (Med) glaucoma

زُرْقة n ① [لَوْن] blue; زُرْقة السَماءِ \ البَحْرِ \ عَيْنَيْها the blue of the sky/the sea/her eyes; الضارِب الى الزُرْقةِ bluish ② (Med) cyanosis

أَزْرَق adj |dipt; زُرْق| blue; أَزْرَق سَماويّ sky blue; سَماء زَرْقاء a blue sky; أَزْرَق فاتِح light blue; عَيْنانِ زَرْقاوانِ blue eyes; القُبَّعات الزَرْقاء the blue helmets (UN forces)

مُزْرَقّ adj bluish

زَرْكَشَ v |i; زَرْكَشة| to decorate, to embellish; زَرْكَشَ كَلامَهُ to embellish one's speech

زَرْكَش n embroidered silk, brocade

زَرْكَشة n decoration; motif

مُزَرْكَش adj embroidered, embellished; ثِياب مُزَرْكَشة embellished garments

زِرْنيخ, زَرْنيخ n arsenic; التَسَمُّم بالزَرْنيخ arsenic poisoning; أُكْسيد الزَرْنيخ الثُلاثيّ arsenic trioxide

زرى v |i; زِرْي, زِراية| to disparage; to reprimand, to rebuke

أَزْرى v to belittle, to disparage; to ridicule

اِزْدَرى v to disdain, to slight; اِزْدَرى الخَطَرَ to defy danger

زَرِيّ adj pitiful, miserable

زِراية n contempt, disdain

اِزْدِراء n contempt, disdain, scorn; نَظْرة كُلُّها اِزْدِراءٌ \ مِلْؤُها الاِزْدِراءُ a contemptuous look; تَكَلَّمَ بازْدِراءٍ عن شَيْءٍ \ شَخْصٍ to speak disparagingly about sth/sb; ضِحْكة \ مُلاحَظة اِزْدِراءٍ a sneering laugh/remark

اِزْدِرائيّ n pejorative, disdainful

مُزْدَرٍ adj denigratory, disdainful, disparaging

مُزْرٍ adj miserable; أَوْضاع مُزْرِية miserable circumstances

زِرْياب n (Zool) jay

زَعْتَر, سَعْتَر, صَعْتَر n thyme; a condiment made from thyme, sesame seeds, dried sumac, salt and other spices; أَوْراق الزَعْتَرِ thyme leaves

زَعَجَ v |a; زَعْج| to disturb, to interrupt; to bother, to irritate, to pester; زَعَجَ شَخْصاً في نَوْمِهِ to disturb sb's sleep

أَزْعَجَ v to disturb, to interrupt; to bother, to irritate, to pester; أَزْعَجَ شَخْصاً to bother sb; أَزْعَجَ زَميلَهُ to disturb one's colleague; هل أُزْعِجُكَ؟ am I interrupting?

اِنْزَعَجَ v to be disturbed; to be/become annoyed; to feel uneasy; اِنْزَعَجَ من شَيْءٍ \ شَخْصٍ to be annoyed by sth/sb

‹ **زَعَق** *v* |a; زَعْق| to cry, to yell, to scream, to shriek

زَعْقة *n* |زَعَقات| shout, cry, scream

زَعيق *n* shouting, screaming

‹ **زَعِل** *v* |a; زَعَل| to be/become angry; to be/become fed up

زَعْلان *adj* angry, vexed, annoyed; هي زَعْلانةٌ من نَفْسِها she's angry at herself

‹ **زَعَم** *v* |u; زَعْم| to claim, to allege, to pretend; to assert, to maintain; زَعَمَ أنّ الأَرْض مُسَطَّحةٌ to claim that the earth is flat; زَعَمَ أنّ الجَوّ سَيَتَحَسَّنُ he asserted that the weather would improve; زَعَمَ أنّ الشاهِدَ كاذِبٌ he maintained that the witness was lying

زَعُم *v* |u; زَعامة| to lead, to command

تزَعَّم *v* to lead, to command

زَعْم *n* assertion, allegation, claim; زَعْم أنّ ... a claim that ...

زاعِم *n person making a claim*

زَعامة *n* leadership, guidance; زَعامة سِياسيّة \ دينيّة political/religious leadership; بِزَعامة ... under the leadership of, led by ...

زَعيم *n* |زُعَماءُ| leader, head, chief; الزَعيم الأَكْبَر the big boss, the great leader; الزُعَماء الأوروبيّونَ \ العَرَب European/Arab leaders; زَعيم سِياسيّ political leader; زَعيم نِقابيّ union leader; زَعيم الحِزْب the party leader; زُعَماء الثَوْرة the leaders of the revolution

مَزْعَم *n* |مَزاعِم| allegation; accusation

مَزْعوم *adj* alleged, supposed, so-called; تَحَسُّن مَزْعوم a so-called improvement

‹ **زَعْنِفة, زِعْنِفة** *n* |زَعانِفُ| flipper; fin; زَعْنِفة سِباحةٍ flipper; زَوْج زَعانِفَ a pair of flippers; زَعْنِفة ظَهْريّة dorsal fin; زَعْنِفة ذَيْليّة tail/caudal fin; زَعْنِفة سَمَكة القِرْش shark fin

‹ **زَغِب** *v* |a; زَغَب| to be covered in down; to grow in (*feathers, hair*)

زَغَب *n* **1** (Zool) down, fluff; الزَغَب الناعِم soft down; ريش الزَغَب down feathers **2** [شَعْر خَفيف] fine hair (*on face or body*); الزَغَب (الخَفيف) في الجِسْمِ body fuzz

زُغْبة *n* dormouse

أَزْغَب *adj* |dipt; زُغْب| downy, fluffy, fuzzy

إزْعاج *n* nuisance, annoyance, irritation; trouble, disturbance; مَصْدَر إزْعاجٍ nuisance, annoyance; تَسَبَّبَ في ,أثارَ إزْعاجاً to cause annoyance/trouble; مِمّا أدّى إلى إزْعاجِ المُشاهِدينَ to the great annoyance of the viewers; الرَجاءُ عَدَمُ الإزْعاجِ please do not disturb

انْزِعاج *n* nuisance, annoyance, discomfort; disturbance; انْزِعاج من شَيْءٍ annoyance with sth; انْزِعاج شَديد a serious disturbance; extreme discomfort

مُزْعِج *adj* annoying, irritating, unpleasant; رَجُل مُزْعِج an annoying/unpleasant man; حَدَث مُزْعِج an unpleasant event; بَريد مُزْعِج (Comput) spam; عَمَل مُزْعِج an onerous task; شُعور مُزْعِج an unpleasant feeling; مَرَض مُزْعِج a vicious disease; أَصْوات مُزْعِجة irritating sounds; سُلوك مُزْعِج irritating behaviour; عادة مُزْعِجة an annoying habit

مُنْزَعِج *adj* irritated, irritable, annoyed, upset; بَدا مُنْزَعِجاً من شَيْءٍ to seem upset by sth

‹ **زَعِر** *adj* thin-haired

زُعْرور *n* |زَعاريرُ| (Bot) hawthorn (*Crataegus*)

أَزْعَر **A** *adj* |dipt; زُعْران| balding
B *n* |dipt; زُعْران| crook, scoundrel; مَجْموعة من الزُعْرانِ a motley crew

‹ **زَعْزَع** *v* |i; زَعْزَعة| to shake, to rock; to upset, to destabilize; زَعْزَعَ ثِقةَ شَخْصٍ to betray sb's confidence; زَعْزَعَ مَعْنَويّاتِ الجَيْشِ to undermine the army's morale; زَعْزَع اسْتِقْرار المِنْطَقةِ to destabilize the region

تَزَعْزَع *v* to shake, to wobble, to waver; لا يَتَزَعْزَعُ unshakeable, unwavering; ثِقة لا تَتَزَعْزَعُ unshakeable confidence; مَوْقِف لا يَتَزَعْزَعُ a firm stand; تَتَزَعْزَعُ عَقيدَتُهُ \ ثِقَتُهُ his faith/confidence is wavering

زَعْزَعة *n* |زَعازِعُ| convulsion; shock, concussion

مُتَزَعْزِع *adj* shaky, wobbly; كُرْسيّ مُتَزَعْزِع a wobbly chair; ثِقة مُتَزَعْزِعة shaky confidence

‹ **زُعاف** *adj* deadly poisonous; سُمّ زُعاف deadly poison

‹ **زَعْفَران** *n* **1** [زَهْرة] crocus; يُزْهِرُ الزَعْفَرانُ the crocuses are blooming **2** [تابَل] saffron

زَقا v |u; زَقْو| to crow

زَكيبة n |زَكائِبُ| bag, sack

زَكَمَ v |u; زُكِمَ ,زَكْم| to catch a cold

أَزْكَمَ v to give (sb) a cold

زُكام n cold; زُكام خَفيف a slight cold; زُكام شَديد \ حادّ a bad cold; أُصيبَ بالزُكامِ to catch a cold; كانَ مُصاباً بالزُكامِ to have a cold

مَزْكوم adj *having/suffering from a cold*; أَنْف مَزْكوم a runny nose

زَكا v |u; زُكوّ ,زَكاء ,زَكاة| 1 [نَما] to grow, to increase 2 (Relig) to be/become pure; يَزْكو القَلْبُ the heart becomes pure

زَكّى v 1 [نَمّى] to make thrive; to increase, to augment 2 [طَهَّرَ] to purify; زَكّى مالَهُ to pay alms (*zakat*) 3 [أَوْصى] to recommend

أَزْكى v to cause to grow

تَزَكّى v to give alms (*zakat*)

زَكيّ adj |أَزْكِياءُ| pure, virtuous; fragrant; زَكيّ الرائِحةِ fragrant, aromatic, sweet-smelling

زَكاة ,زَكْوة ,زَكاً n |زَكَوات| alms; zakat (*religious duty of giving alms, one of the five pillars of Islam*); زَكاة الفِطْرِ *obligatory alms at the end of the month of Ramadan*; أَدّى الزَكاةَ to give alms (*zakat*)

تَزْكِية n recommendation; sponsorship; شَهادة تَزْكِيةٍ letter of recommendation; certificate of sponsorship; مَصْدَر تَزْكِيةٍ مُمْتاز excellent reference; فازَ بالتَزْكِيةِ to win by default (*in the absence of other candidates or opponents*)

زَلَجَ v |a; زُلوج| to bolt, to lock; زَلَجَ البابَ to bolt the door

تَزَلَّجَ v to sledge (BrE), to sled (AmE); to glide, to slide; تَزَلَّجَ على الثَلْجِ to ski; تَزَلَّجَ على الماءِ to waterski; to surf; تَزَلَّجَ على الجَليدِ to ice-skate

زَلّاجة n ski; زَلّاجة مائيّة waterski

زَليج adj slippery

زُلَيْج n azulejo (*painted ceramic tile work*)

تَزَلُّج n sliding; skiing; skating; sledging (BrE), sledding (AmE); ميدان التَزَلُّجِ ice rink, skating rink; التَزَلُّج بالعَجَلاتِ roller skating

مُتَزَلِّج n skater; skier

زَغْرَدَ v |i; زَغْرَدة| *to utter trilling cries (as a manifestation of joy by Arab women)*; زَغْرَدَت النِساءُ فَرَحاً the women trilled joyfully

زَغْرَدة n |زَغاريدُ| *shrill, trilling cry of joy that is made by women*

زَغْزَغَ v |i; زَغْزَغة| 1 [أَخْفى] to hide, to conceal 2 [دَغْدَغَ] (Egypt) to tickle

زُغْلول n |زَغاليلُ| 1 [فَرْخ] squab 2 (old use) [طِفْل] small child

زَفَّتَ v to pave, to asphalt, to tar; زَفَّتَ شارِعاً to pave a road

زِفْت n asphalt; pitch; زِفْت وَقُطْران crappy, horrible

مِزْفَتة n |مَزافِتُ| steamroller

زَفَرَ v |i; زَفير| 1 [أَخْرَجَ نَفَسَهُ] to breathe out, to exhale; to sigh 2 [سُمِعَ صَوْتُ الاتِّقادِ] to crackle; تَزْفُرُ النارُ the fire crackles

زَفَر n (Chr) *the eating of meat (as opposed to abstinence during Lent)*

زَفْرة n sigh

زَفير n exhalation; الشَهيق والزَفير inhalation and exhalation

زَفْزَفَ v to whistle, to moan (*the wind*); زَفْزَفَت الريحُ the wind whistled

زَفَّ I v |i; زَفّ ,زُفوف| to hurry

زَفَّ II v |u; زَفّ ,زِفاف ,زِفافاً| 1 [زِفافاً] to lead (in a procession); زَفَّ العَروسَ to lead the bride (to the home of the bridegroom) 2 [إِلَيْهِ الخَبَرَ] to convey good news; زَفَّ الخَبَرَ إلى شَخْصٍ he conveyed the good news to sb

أَزَفَّ v to hurry, to hasten

زِفاف n wedding (party), wedding ceremony; فُسْتان زِفافٍ a wedding dress, bridal gown; لَيْلة الزِفافِ wedding night; يَوْم الزِفافِ wedding day; اِحْتَفَلَ بِزِفافٍ to celebrate a wedding

زَفّة n wedding procession

زِقّورة n ziggurat

زَقْزَقَ v |i; زَقْزَقة| to chirp; تُزَقْزِقُ العَصافيرُ the birds are chirping

زَقْزاق n (Zool) plover, lapwing; زَقْزاق شاميّ northern lapwing, peewit (*Vanellus vanellus*)

الزَقازيق n |f| Zagazig (*city in northern Egypt*)

زَقَّ v |u; زَقّ| to feed (*its young; of a bird*)

زِقّ n |أَزْقاق ,زِقاق ,زُقّان| waterskin (*receptacle for liquids*)

زُقاق n |mf; أَزِقّة| alley, lane; أَزِقّة مُتَشابِكة a maze of alleys; زُقاق ضَيِّق a narrow lane

مِزْلاج *n* |مَزاليجُ| bolt; catch, latch

مِزْلَج *n* |مَزالِجُ| sledge (BrE), sled (AmE)

مِزْلَجة *n* skate; sledge (BrE), sled (AmE); bobsleigh (BrE), bobsled (AmE); مِزْلَجة الجَليد ice rink, skating rink

‹ **زَلْزَلَ** *v* |i; زَلْزَلة| to shake, to rock; زُلْزِلَت الأَرْضُ the earth convulsed

تَزَلْزَلَ *v* to shake, to tremble, to quake

زَلْزال, زِلْزال *n* |زَلازِلُ| earthquake, earth tremor; زِلْزال عَنيف a major earthquake; مَرْكَز زِلْزالٍ epicentre; عالِم زَلازِلَ seismologist; مِقْياس الزَلازِلِ seismograph; زِلْزال بَلَغَتْ قوَّتُهُ ٤ دَرَجاتٍ على مِقْياسِ ريختَر an earthquake measuring 4.0 on the Richter scale

زِلْزاليّ *adj* seismic; نَشاط زِلْزاليّ seismic activity

زَلْزَلة *n* |زَلازِلُ| earthquake; سورة الزَلْزَلة The Earthquake (*Sura 99*)

‹ **زَلَّفَ** *v* to exaggerate, to overstate

أَزْلَفَ *v* to bring near

تَزَلَّفَ *v* |إلى| to flatter, to suck up to (infml); to fawn over; تَزَلَّفَ إلى شَخْصٍ to fawn over sb

ازْدَلَفَ *v* to flatter

زَلَفة *n* bowl

مُتَزَلِّف **A** *adj* bootlicking, sycophantic **B** *n* toady, bootlicker, sycophant

‹ **زَلَقَ, زَلِقَ** *v* |u; زَلْق| to slip; to slide, to glide; زَلَقَت السَيّارةُ في الثَلْجِ the car slipped in the snow

زَلَّقَ *v* **1** [جَعَلَ يَزْلِقُ] to make slide **2** [المَكانَ] to make slippery

أَزْلَقَ *v* to cause to slip

تَزَلَّقَ *v* to glide, to slide; to skate

انْزَلَقَ *v* to glide, to slide; to slip; انْزَلَقَ على الثَلْجِ to glide on the snow; انْزَلَقَ على الطَريقِ to slip on the road

زَلِق *adj* slippery; دَرْب زَلِق a slippery path

زَلاقة *n* slipperiness

زَلّاقة *n* slide, chute; زَلّاقة مائيّة water slide

انْزِلاق *n* skid, slip, slide; slipping, sliding; خَطَر الانْزِلاقِ danger of skidding; خَطَر الانْزِلاقِ الى الرُكودِ danger of slipping into recession; انْزِلاق أَرْضيّ landslide

انْزِلاقيّ *adj* slippery

مِزْلاق *n* |مَزاليقُ| skate

مَزْلَق *n* |مَزالِقُ| danger, pitfall; وَقَعَ في المَزالِقِ to fall into pitfalls; تَجَنَّبَ المَزالِقَ to avoid pitfalls

مُزَلِّق *n* lubricant

مِزْلَق *n* |مَزالِقُ| skate

مَزْلَقان *n* level crossing (BrE), railroad crossing (AmE)

مَزْلَقة *n* |مَزالِقُ| slide; مَزْلَقة الطَوارِئِ emergency/evacuation slide

مِزْلَقة *n* |مَزالِقُ| sledge (BrE), sled (AmE)

‹ **زَلَّ** *v* |i; زُلول, زَلّ| **1** [كَبا] to stumble, to trip **2** [أَخْطَأَ] to slip up, to make a mistake; زَلَّ لِسانُهُ to make a slip of the tongue

أَزَلَّ *v* to make stumble, to make trip

زَلَل *n* mistake, error

زُلال *n* زُلال البَيْضِ egg white, albumen

زَلّة *n* error, slip, mistake, false step; زَلّة لِسانٍ slip of the tongue

زُلّة *n* (Med) dyspnoea

‹ **زَمُتَ** *v* |u; زَمانة| to be serious, to be grave

تَزَمَّتَ *v* to be strict, to be severe

زُمَّت *n* (Zool) chough (*pyrrhocorax pyrrhocorax*)

تَزَمُّت *n* strictness, severity

مُتَزَمِّت **A** *adj* puritanical; stringent, rigid; مُتَزَمِّت في آرائِهِ rigid in his views **B** *n* puritan

‹ **زُمَّج** *n* زُمَّج الماءِ gull, seagull (*Laridae*)

‹ **زَمْجَرَ** *v* |i; زَمْجَرة| to growl, to snarl; to roar

مُزَمْجِر *adj* roaring, bellowing; أَسَد مُزَمْجِر a roaring lion; صَوْت مُزَمْجِر a bellowing voice

‹ **زَمْخَر** *n* bassoon

‹ **زَمَرَ** *v* |i-u; زَمْر, زَمير| to blow, to play (*a wind instrument*)

زَمَّرَ *v* to blow, to play (*a wind instrument*); زَمَّرَ بالمِزْمارِ to play the flute

زَمْر *n* blowing, playing (*of a wind instrument*)

زَمّار *n* flautist, flute player; oboist, oboe player

زَمّارة *n* |زَماميرُ| oboe; flute

زُمْرة *n* |زُمَر| crowd, horde, gang; زُمْرة دَمَوِيّة blood group, blood type; سورة الزُّمَر The Crowds (*Sura 39*)

زُمَرِيّ *adj* group

مِزْمار *n* |مَزاميرُ| mizmar (*a single-pipe woodwind instrument that resembles the oboe*); flute, clarinet; مِزْمار القِرْبَةِ bagpipe, bagpipes; لِسان المِزْمارِ epiglottis; عازِف مِزْمارٍ mizmar player; عَزَفَ على المِزْمارِ to play (the) mizmar

مَزْمور *n* |مَزاميرُ| psalm (*sacred song or hymn*)

‹ **زُمُرُّد** *n coll* emerald

زُمُرُّديّ *adj* emerald (green)

‹ **زَمْزَرِيق** *n* Judas tree (*Cercis siliquastrum*)

‹ **زَمْزَمَ** *v* |i; زَمْزَمة| to murmur, to mumble

زَمْزَم *n* Zamzam (*well near Mecca*)

زَمْزَمِيّة *n* water bottle, flask, canteen

‹ **زَمِعَ** *v* |a; زَمَع| to be frightened, to tremble (with fear)

أَزْمَعَ *v* to decide, to determine; أَزْمَعَ على السَفَرِ he decided to travel

زَمِع *adj* startled, shocked, frightened

مُزْمَع *adj* decided, determined, planned, scheduled; من المُزْمَع عَقْدُ جَلَساتٍ meetings have been scheduled; المُؤْتَمَر المُزْمَع انْعِقادُهُ في الصَيْفِ the conference to be held in the summer

مُزْمِع *adj* determined, decisive, resolute

1‹ **زَمَّلَ** *v* to cover up

زامَلَ *v* to be/become a colleague; to accompany

تَزَمَّلَ *v* to cover oneself up

تَزامَلَ *v* to consider each other (as) colleagues; to be companions

زَمالة *n* fellowship, camaraderie; روح الزَمالةِ collegiality

زَميل *n* |زُمَلاءُ| colleague; classmate, schoolmate; زَميلي في المِهْنَةِ my colleague (at work); زَميل دِراسةٍ fellow student, peer; هو زَميلي في القِسْمِ \ المَدْرَسةِ he is my classmate/ schoolmate

مُزَمَّل *adj* مُحَمَّل وَمُزَمَّل (ب) heavily laden (with)

مُزَمِّل *n* سورة المُزَمِّل The Enfolded One (*Sura 73*)

2‹ **إزْميل** *n* |أَزاميلُ| (*Tools*) chisel

‹ **الزَمالِك** *n* Zamalek (*island in the Nile river in Cairo*)

‹ **زَمَّ** *v* |u; زَمّ| to tie up, to fasten; زَمَّ شَفَتَيْهِ he zipped his lips

زِمام *n* |أَزِمّة| rein; bridle; leash; قَبَضَ على أَزِمّةِ الأُمورِ to take (up) the reins, to take control; أَفْلَتَ زِمامَ الأُمورِ من يَدِهِ to give up the reins, to give up control; تَوَلّى زِمامَ الأَمْرِ to be pulling the strings, to be in control; سَيْطَرَ على زِمامِ الأَمْرِ to be in charge; اتَّخَذَ زِمامَ المُبادَرةِ to take the initiative/first step

‹ **زَمِنَ** *v* |a; زَمَن, زَمانة| to be chronically ill

زَمَّنَ *v* to synchronize

زامَنَ *v* [1] [عاصَرَ] to be a contemporary of; to coincide with [2] [زَمَّنَ] to synchronize; زامَنَ الصَوْتَ والصورةَ to synchronize audio and video

أَزْمَنَ *v* to last long; to stay long; أَزْمَنَ المَرَضُ the sickness lasted a long time

تَزامَنَ *v* to coincide, to occur simultaneously; تَزامَنَ الحَدَثانِ the two events coincided; تَزامَنَ مع شَيْءٍ to coincide with sth; تَزامَنَت الاضْطِراباتُ مع زِيارةِ الرَئيسِ the disturbances coincided with the president's visit

زَمَن *n* |أَزْمان| time, duration, period; آلة الزَمَنِ time machine; مع الزَمَنِ in due time, in good time; مع مُرورِ الزَمَنِ in time, as time goes by; في زَمَنِ ... in the time of ...; في زَمَنِ الحَرْبِ العالَمِيّةِ الثانِيةِ in/at the time of the second World War; عامٍ من الزَمَنِ in a year's time; الْتَزَمَ بالزَمَنِ المُحَدَّدِ to adhere to the time limit; يَبْدو أنّ الزَمَنَ تَوَقَّفَ it seems like time has stopped; في تِلْكَ الحِقْبةِ من الزَمَنِ in those days

زَمان *n* |أَزْمِنة| time; period; مع مَرِّ الزَمانِ in good time, in due course; مُنْذُ أَزْمِنةٍ غابِرةٍ from time immemorial; من \ منذ زَمانٍ for some time (past); from way back; لم أَرَهُ منذ زَمانٍ I haven't seen him for ages; اسْتِعْمال الزَمانِ (*Mor*) school timetable

زَمانيّ *adj* [1] [مُؤَقَّت] temporary; transitory [2] [طَويلاً] long-lasting

زَمَنيّ *adj* temporal, time (*before n*); فاصِل زَمَنِيّ (time) interval; قُنْبُلة زَمَنِيّة time bomb; خطّ زَمَنِيّ timeline; بِفاصِلٍ زَمَنِيٍّ with an interval; مُرَتَّب حَسَبَ التَسَلْسُلِ الزَمَنِيِّ ,بِتَرْتيبٍ زَمَنِيٍّ ,مُرَتَّب زَمَنِيًّا in chronological order

تَزامُن *n* concurrence, conjunction, synchronization

‹ **زَنَّرَ** *v* |إلى| to glare (at)

زُنّار *n* |زَنانيرُ| ◻1 [حِزام] belt ◻2 (Hist) zunnar (*belt worn by medieval Christians and Jews in Muslim lands to mark their status as dhimmi*)

‹ **زِنْزانة** *n* dungeon; (prison) cell; زِنْزانة انْفِراديّة \ أَفْراديّة isolation cell

‹ **زَنَقَ** *v* |a-i; زَنْق| ◻1 [حَشَرَ] to drive into a corner, to press hard; to tighten, to constrict ◻2 [قَتَّرَ] to economize; to be stingy

زَنَّقَ *v* ◻1 [حَشَرَ] to drive into a corner, to press hard; to tighten, to constrict ◻2 [قَتَّرَ] to economize; to be stingy

زِناق *n* |أَزْنِقة| chin strap (*of a helmet*); *part of the bridle that passes along the throat of the horse*

‹ **زِنْك** *n* zinc; صَفيحة من الزِنْكِ a sheet of zinc

زِنْكيّ *adj* zinc (*before n*)

‹ **زَنيم** **A** *adj* |زُنَماءُ| mean, wicked

B *n* ◻1 [فَظّ] |زُنَماءُ| bastard ◻2 [غَريب] |زَنْمى| stranger, outsider

‹ **زَنَّ** *v* |u; زَنّ| to buzz (*insect*)

‹ **زَنى** *v* |i; زِناء ,زِنًى| to commit adultery, to fornicate

زانٍ *n* |زُناة| adulterer, fornicator

زانية *n* adulteress; prostitute

زِناء *n* fornication, adultery; زِناء بالجَبْرِ (Isl Law) rape

زِنًى *n* fornication, adultery; ابْن زِنًى bastard, illegitimate child

‹ **زَهِدَ** *v* |a; زُهْد| to abstain, to renounce, to forsake; زَهِدَ في \ عن شَيْءٍ to renounce sth

زَهَّدَ *v* to discourage, to deter

تَزَهَّدَ *v* to be an ascetic, to lead an ascetic life

زُهْد *n* asceticism, ascesis; abstinence, abstemiousness; حَياة زُهْدٍ an ascetic lifestyle

زاهِد *adj, n* |زُهّاد| ascetic

زَهادة *n* asceticism

زُهْديّ *adj* ascetic

زَهيد *adj* small, paltry, insignificant, meagre; أَجْر زَهيد a mere pittance; تَعْمَلُ بِأَجْرٍ زَهيدٍ she works for a mere pittance; سِعْر زَهيد a cheap price

‹ **زَهَرَ** *v* |a; زُهور ,زَهْر| ◻1 [النَباتُ] to bloom, to blossom ◻2 [أَشْرَقَ] to radiate, to shine

تَزامُنيّ *adj* synchronous, simultaneous

تَزْمين *n* synchronization

مُتَزامِن **A** *adj* synchronous, simultaneous; أَحْداث مُتَزامِنة simultaneous events; غَيْر مُتَزامِنٍ asynchronous

B *n* contemporary

مُزامِن *adj* synchronous; contemporary

مُزْمِن *adj* chronic, long-lasting, lingering; مَرَض مُزْمِن a chronic illness

‹ **زَمْهَرير** *n* bitter cold

‹ **زُنْبور** *n* |زَنابيرُ| wasp; hornet (*Vespa*); عُشّ زَنابيرَ wasp's nest; لَسْعة زُنْبورٍ wasp sting

‹ **زُنْبُرُك ,زَنْبَرك ,زُنْبُرك** *n* |زَنابِكُ| spring; زُنْبُرُك ساعةٍ a watch spring

‹ **زَنْبَق** *n coll* |زَنابِقُ| lily (*Lilium*); زَنْبَق النِمْرِ \ مُخطَّط tiger lily (*Lilium columbianum*); زَنْبَق الوادي lily of the valley (*Convallaria majalis*)

‹ **زِنْبيل ,زَنْبيل** *n* |زَنابيلُ| *a large basket made of palm leaves*

‹ **زِنة** *n* see **وزن**

‹ **زِنْج** *n coll* |زُنوج| black person; black slave; بِلاد الزِنْجِ Africa

زِنْجيّ **A** *n* |زِنج| black person

B *adj* |زِنج| *relating to a black person*

‹ **زَنْجِبار** *n* |f| Zanzibar

‹ **زَنْجَبيل** *n* ginger

‹ **زِنْجار** *n* verdigris, patina (*green or brown film on the surface of bronze or similar metals*)

زِنْجير *n* |زَناجيرُ| chain

‹ **زَنِخَ** *v* |a; زَنَخ| to be/become rancid

زَنِخ *adj* rancid, off, bad

‹ **زَنْد** *n* |زُنود| forearm; upper arm; عَظْم الزَنْدِ ulna (*the longer of the two bones in the human forearm*)

زِناد *n* |أَزْنِدة| trigger; cock (BrE), hammer (AmE) (*firing lever in a gun*); زِناد المُسَدَّسِ pistol trigger; ضَغَطَ على الزِنادِ to pull the trigger; to cock the gun; حَجَر الزِنادِ flint; قَدَحَ زِنادَ فِكْرِه to rack one's brains

‹ **زَنْدَقة** *n* atheism

زِنْديق *n* |زَناديقُ| apostate; atheist

B *n* graduate or student of Al Azhar University

الأَزْهَر *n* al-Azhar (*ancient mosque and Islamic university in Cairo*); جامِع الأَزْهَر al-Azhar Mosque and University in Cairo; شَيْخ الأَزْهَر the Grand Sheikh of al-Azhar

الزُهَرة *n* (Astron) Venus; كَوْكَب الزُهَرة Venus (*the planet*)

مُزْدَهِر *adj* prosperous, flourishing, thriving; بَلَد مُزْدَهِر a prosperous country; صِناعة مُزْدَهِرة a thriving industry

مُزْهِر *adj* blooming, in bloom

مِزْهَر *n* |مَزاهِر| mizhar (*ancient Arabic variety of the lute*)

مَزْهَرِيّة *n* (flower) vase; مَزْهَرِيّة خزفيّة a porcelain vase, a china vase

زَهَق *v* |a; زُهوق, زَهْق| **1** [ذَهَبَ واضمَحَلَّ] to disappear; زَهَقَتْ نَفْسُهُ to die; to give up **2** [فَشِلَ] to come to nothing, to fail **3** [ضَجِرَ] (Egypt) to have enough, to be fed up; زَهَقَ من شَيْءٍ to have enough of sth, to be/get fed up with sth

أَزْهَقَ *v* to destroy, to wreck; أَزْهَقَ روح شَخْصٍ to take sb's life

زاهِق *adj* |زَواهِق| useless, pointless

إِزْهاق *n* destruction

زُهْم *n* stench, foul smell

زَها *v* |u; زَهْو| **1** [تَعاظَمَ] to be/become conceited **2** [أَزْهَرَ] to bloom, to flower, to blossom **3** [أَضاءَ] to shine, to radiate

أَزْهى *v* to boast

ازْدَهى *v* to be/become conceited, to be proud

زَهْو, زُهوّ *n* vanity, conceit, pride; أَرْضى زَهْوَ شَخْصٍ to flatter sb's vanity; to appease sb

زاهٍ *adj* brilliant, bright; vivid; أَلْوان زاهِية a riot of colour, vibrant colours

زَهاء *n* brightness

زُهاء *n* about, nearly, approximately; هُم زُهاءُ أَلْفٍ there's about a thousand of them; تَجَمَّعَ هُنا زُهاءَ عَشَرةِ آلافِ لاجِئٍ approximately ten thousand refugees gathered here; عاشَ في لُبْنانَ زُهاءَ ثَلاثينَ عاماً he lived in Lebanon for nearly thirty years

زَهِيّ *adj* brilliant, bright

مَزْهُوّ *adj* arrogant, haughty, conceited

أَزْهَرَ *v* to bloom, to flower, to blossom; الحُب يَنْمو وَيُزْهِرُ love grows and blossoms; تُزْهِرُ الوَرْدُ the roses are blooming; تُزْهِرُ النَباتاتُ في الرَبيعِ the plants flower in spring

ازْدَهَرَ *v* to flourish, to prosper, to thrive; يَزْدَهِرُ الأَدَبُ \ العِلْمُ literature/science flourishes; تَزْدَهِرُ التِجارةُ business is booming

زَهْر *n coll* |أَزاهير, أَزْهار, زُهور| flower; باقة زُهورٍ \ من الزُهورِ a bouquet of flowers; سَقى الزُهورَ to water the flowers; بائِع زُهورٍ florist; ماء الزَهْرِ eau de cologne, perfume; orange blossom water

(Idiom) زَهْر النَرْدِ dice

زاهِر *adj* cheerful, rosy; bright, prosperous; shining, gleaming, luminous; مُسْتَقْبَل زاهِر a bright future

زَهّار *n* florist

زَهْرة *n* **1** (Bot) flower, blossom; كَأْس الزَهْرة calyx (*the outermost whorl of a flower*); زَهْرة الحَوْضِ columbine (*Aquilegia*); زَهْرة الرَبيعِ primula, primrose; زَهْرة اللَبَنِ (الثَلْجيّة) snowdrop (*Galanthus*) **2** [مُقْتَبَل] prime; ماتَ في زَهْرةِ شَبابِهِ he died in the prime of (his) life

زُهْرة *n* brightness, whiteness; زُهْرة الغَسيلِ bluing, blueing (*blue powder used to preserve the whiteness of laundry*)

زَهْرِيّ *adj* pink, rose; flowery, flower (*before n*)

زُهْرِيّ **A** *adj* venereal; أَمْراض زُهْرِيّة venereal diseases, sexually transmitted diseases

B *n* syphilis

زَهْرِيّات *n pl* flowering plants

زَهْرِيّة *n* (flower) vase; زَهْرِيّة فيها زُهورٌ جافّةٌ a vase of dried flowers

ازْدِهار *n* |ازْدِهارات| prosperity, growth, boom; ازْدِهار اقْتِصاديّ (economic) boom; الازْدِهار والتَدَهْوُر prosperity and decline; فَتْرة ازْدِهارٍ period of prosperity

إِزْهار *n* (Bot) florescence (*process of flowering*); فَتْرة إِزْهارٍ flowering time, flowering season

أَزْهَر *adj* |dipt| radiant, brilliant

ازْهِرار *n* (Bot) inflorescence (*process of flowering*)

أَزْهَرِيّ **A** *adj* Azhar (*before n*) (*of or pertaining to Al Azhar Mosque/University*)

‹ **زَوْبَعة** *n* |زَوابِعُ| storm, tornado, hurricane; زَوْبَعة في فِنْجانٍ a storm in a teacup (BrE), a tempest in a teapot (AmE) (*great outrage or excitement about a trivial matter*); مِحْوَر \ مَرْكَز الزَوْبَعةِ the eye of the storm

‹ **زَوَّجَ** *v* ① [أَنْكَحَ] to marry off, to give in marriage ② [قَرَنَ] to pair, to couple

زاوَجَ *v* to combine; to couple, to pair; to marry, to unite in matrimony; زاوَجَ بين عَمَلَيْنِ he combined two jobs

تَزَوَّجَ *v* to marry, to get married; تَزَوَّجَ شَخْصاً \ ب \ من شَخْصٍ to marry sb, to get married to sb; تَزَوَّجَ زَواجاً كَنَسيًّا to get married in church; تَزَوَّجَها على الكِتابِ والسُنَّةِ he married her according to Koran and Sunna; تَزَوَّجَ للمَرّةِ الثانِيةِ to remarry, to marry again

تَزاوَجَ *v* ① [حَيَوانات] to mate, to pair ② [أناس] to intermarry

ازْدَوَجَ *v* to be/become double; to duplicate

زَوْج *n* |mf; أَزْواج| ① [مُتَزَوِّج] spouse, husband; زَوْجانِ married couple; bride and groom; الزَوْج الشَرْعيّ lawful husband; زَوْج الأُمِّ stepfather; زَوْج سابِق ex-husband ② [اِثْنانِ] couple, pair; زَوْج من البَقَرِ a yoke of oxen; اشْتَرَيْتُ زَوْجاً من الأَحْذِيةِ \ زَوْجَ أَحْذِيةٍ I bought a pair of shoes

زَواج *n* marriage, matrimony, marital union; زَواج شَرْعيّ \ قانونيّ a lawful marriage; زَواج مُخْتَلِط a mixed marriage; زَواجُهُ الأَوَّل \ الثاني his first/second marriage; زَواج ناجِح a successful marriage; زَواج مَدَنيّ a civil marriage; زَواج أُحاديّ monogamy; زَواج مِثْليّ same-sex marriage, gay marriage; زَواج مُتْعةٍ (Isl Law) mut'ah (*temporary marriage, contracted exclusively for the purpose of sexual pleasure*); زَواج صوريّ, زَواج المَصْلَحةِ marriage of convenience; تَزَوَّجَ زَواجاً صوريًّا to contract a marriage of convenience; الزَواج بالوِكالةِ marriage by proxy; عَقْد الزَواجِ marriage certificate; عَقَدَ عَقْدَ زَواجٍ to contract a marriage; سِنّ الزَواجِ marriageable age; ذِكْرى زَواجِنا our wedding anniversary; حَفْلة زَواجٍ wedding party; كانَ زَواجُهُ سَعيداً \ تَعيساً he was happily/unhappily married; احْتَفَلَ بِزَواجٍ to celebrate a wedding; فَسَخَ عَقْدَ زَواجٍ to dissolve a marriage, to annul a marriage; انْهارَ زَواجُهُ his marriage broke down; طَلَبَ الزَواجَ (من شَخْصٍ) to propose (to sb); فاتَهُ قِطارُ الزَواجِ he never got married

زَواجيّ *adj* marital, marriage (*before n*)

زَوْجة *n* spouse, wife; زَوْجة وَفيّة a faithful wife; زَوْجَتُهُ السابِقةُ his ex-wife; زَوْجة الأَبِ stepmother; زَوْج وَزَوْجة husband and wife; مُتَعَدِّد الزَوْجاتِ polygamous; تَعَدُّد الزَوْجاتِ polygamy

زَوْجيّ **A** *adj* ① [زيجيّ] marital, matrimonial, conjugal, nuptial; نِزاعات زَوْجيّة domestic quarrels; حَياة زَوْجيّة married life, marriage; خِيانة زَوْجيّة infidelity, unfaithfulness; عَلاقة زَوْجيّة marital bond, marital relationship ② (Math) even; أَعْداد زَوْجيّة even numbers

B *n* (Sport) doubles; الزَوْجيّ الرِجاليّ \ النِسائيّ men's/women's doubles; الزَوْجيّ المُخْتَلَط mixed doubles

زَوْجيّة *n* matrimony, marriage, wedlock; رابِطة الزَوْجيّةِ bond of marriage; مَسْكَن \ بَيْت الزَوْجيّةِ the marital home

زيجة *n* marriage; تَعَدُّد الزيجاتِ polygamy

ازْدِواج *n* dualism, duality; ازْدِواج الشَخْصيّةِ split personality; ازْدِواج لُغَويّ \ اللُغةِ diglossia

ازْدِواجيّ *adj* dualist, dualistic

ازْدِواجيّة *n* dualism; ازْدِواجيّة لُغَويّة bilingualism; diglossia

تَزاوُج *n* mating, coupling, copulation

تَزَوُّج *n* marriage

تَزْويج *n* marrying off

مُتَزَوِّج **A** *adj* married; كانَ مُتَزَوِّجاً زَواجاً سَعيداً \ تَعيساً he was happily/unhappily married; رَجُل \ امْرَأة مُتَزَوِّج(ة) a married man/woman; غَيْر مُتَزَوِّجٍ unmarried, single

B *n* a married person

مُزْدَوِج *adj* double, twofold, two (*before n*); خَطَأ مُزْدَوِج (Sport) double fault; هَدَف مُزْدَوِج dual-purpose; (Sport) brace (*two goals*); خَطّ مُزْدَوِج (للسِكَكِ الحَديديّة) double track (railway); تَعْليم مُزْدَوِج اللُغةِ bilingual education; سَرير مُزْدَوِج a double bed; طَبَّقَ مَعاييرَ مُزْدَوِجةً to apply double standards

مِزْواج *adj* |mf; مَزاويجُ| *having been married many times*; رَجُل \ امْرَأة مِزْواج *a man/woman who has been married many times*

‹ **زاحَ** *v* |i; زَوْح, زَيَحان, زُيوح| to go away, to leave, to depart

أَزاحَ *v* to remove, to move aside, to pull away; أَزاحَت اللِثامَ عن وَجْهِها she removed the veil from her face; أَزاحَ السِتارَ عن

زور *n* falsehood, falsity; شَهِدَ زوراً perjury; شهادة الزورِ to commit perjury; اتَّهَمَ شَخْصاً زوراً to accuse sb falsely

زائِر *n* |زائِرونَ ,زوّار| visitor, guest; اسْتَقْبَلَ زوّاراً to have visitors

زار *n religious trance ceremony in Egypt*

زِيارة *n* 1 [زارَ شَخْصاً] visit; زِيارة خاطِفة \ عاجِلة quick visit; زِيارة شَيْءٍ \ شَخْصٍ a visit to sth/sb; زِيارة مَنْزِليّة house call; قامَ بِزِيارة شَخْصٍ to pay sb a visit; مَوْعِد الزِيارةِ \ أَوْقات visiting hours/time; خلال أَوْقاتِ الزِيارةِ during visiting hours; أَوْقات الزِيارةِ حَسَبَ الاتِّفاقِ surgery (BrE) doctor's office (AmE) hours by appointment only; زِيارة رَسْمِيّة state visit, official visit, formal visit; زِيارة المَلِكة الرَسْمِيّة لِليابان the Queen's state visit to Japan; رَدَّ زِيارةً to pay a return visit 2 (Relig) pilgrimage

أَزْوَر *adj* |dipt| crooked; slanting

ازْوِرار *n* turning away

تَزْوِير *n* forgery; falsification; fraud; أُتُّهِمَ بِالتَزْوِيرِ to be accused of forgery; تَزْوِير الحَقائِقِ falsification of facts; تَزْوِير الوَثائِقِ \ المُسْتَنَدات falsification of documents, forgery of documents; تَزْوِير العُمْلةِ \ النُقودِ counterfeiting

مَزار *n* |مَزارات| 1 [زِيارة] visit 2 [مُقَدَّس] shrine 3 [سِياحِيّ] مَزار سِياحِيّ tourist attraction

مُزَوَّر *adj* forged, counterfeit; false, fake; جَواز سَفَرٍ مُزَوَّر a fake passport

مُزَوِّر *n* forger, counterfeiter; مُزَوِّر العُمْلةِ \ النُقودِ counterfeiter

زَوْرَق *n* |زَوارِقُ| boat; barge; زَوْرَق شِراعِيّ sailing boat (BrE), sailboat (AmE); زَوْرَق مَطّاطِيّ rubber boat; زَوْرَق حَرْبِيّ warship; زَوْرَق سَرِيع speedboat, motor boat; زَوْرَق تَجْذِيفٍ rowing boat (BrE), rowboat (AmE)

زاغَ *v* |u; زَوْغ ,زَوَغان| 1 [ضَعُفَ] to grow weak, to weaken; زاغَ بَصَرُهُ his eyesight has weakened; زاغَتْ عَيْناهُ his eyes were tired 2 [انْحَرَفَ] |عن| to wander (from), to stray (from)

زَيَّغَ *v* to make stray; زَيَّغَهُ الشَيْطانُ Satan made him stray

أَزاغَ *v* to make stray; أَزاغَ شَخْصاً to make sb stray

زَيْغ *n* deviation, aberration; abnormal behaviour

زائِغ *adj* deviant, aberrant

زَوْفا ,زَوْفاء *n* (Bot) hyssop (*Hyssopus*)

التِمْثالِ he unveiled the statue

انْزاحَ *v* to go away, to depart, to leave

زَيّاح *n* |زَيّاحات| procession

إزاحة *n* removal; displacement; إزاحة الماءِ \ الهَواءِ the displacement of water/air

انْزِياح *n* displacement, shift

زادَ *v* |u; زِيد| 1 [وَفَّرَ] [زَوْد] to supply, to provision 2 [كَثُرَ] see زيد

زَوَّدَ *v* |ب| to provide, to supply, to deliver, to provision; زَوَّدَ اللاجِئِينَ بالطَعامِ to supply refugees with food; زَوَّدَ شَخْصاً بالأَسْلِحةِ to equip sb with arms; زَوَّدَني بالمَعْلوماتِ اللازِمةِ he provided me with the necessary information; زَوَّدَ حاسوباً بالمَعْلوماتِ to feed a computer data; زَوَّدَ قِطاعَ الصِناعةِ to supply the industry

أَزادَ *v* to supply with provisions

تَزَوَّدَ *v* to be supplied; to supply oneself; تَزَوَّدَ بالوَقودِ to refuel, to fill up

زاد *n* |أَزْوِدة ,أَزْواد| provisions, supplies; الخَطَأُ زادُ العَجولِ haste makes waste

تَزْوِيد *n* |تَزْوِيدات| supply, delivery, provision; التَزْوِيد بالأَدْوِيةِ the provision of medicines; تَزْوِيد الطائِراتِ بالوَقودِ aircraft refueling; التَزْوِيد بالمَعْلوماتِ newsfeed; briefing

مُزَوَّد *adj* supplied, equipped, furnished; مُزَوَّد بِشَيْءٍ equipped with sth

مُزَوِّد *n* supplier, furnisher, contractor; مُزَوِّد خِدْمةِ الإنْتَرْنت Internet service provider

مِزْوَد *n* |مَزاوِدُ| knapsack, provision bag

زارَ *v* |u; زِيارة| to visit, to pay a visit to, to call on; زارَ شَخْصاً to visit sb; زارَ مَدْرَسةً \ جامِعةً to visit a school/university

زَوَّرَ *v* to forge, to counterfeit; to falsify; زَوَّرَ بِطاقةً شَخْصِيّةً \ تَوْقِيعاً to forge an identity card/a signature; زَوَّرَ التارِيخَ to falsify history; زَوَّرَ نُقوداً to counterfeit money

تَزَوَّرَ *v* to be forged; to be falsified

تَزاوَرَ *v* to visit one another, to exchange visits

ازْوَرَّ *v* |عن| to turn away (from), to dissociate oneself (from)

اسْتَزارَ *v to desire sb's visit*

‹ **زَوَّقَ** *v* to decorate, to adorn, to embellish

تَزْوِيق *n* |تزاويقُ| decoration, embellishment

مُزَوَّق *adj* decorated, embellished

‹ **زالَ** *v* |i; زَيْل| to remove

زالَ *v* |a; زَوال| to disappear, to vanish; ما زالَ \ لا يَزالُ still; ما زالَ \ لا يَزالُ يَفْعَلُ شَيْئاً to keep on doing sth; ما زالَ مُسْتَمِرًّا to continue unabated; ما زالَ خائِفاً he is still afraid; لا تَزالُ على قَيْدِ الحَياةِ she is still alive; لا يَزالُ التَوَتُّرُ يَسودُ العَلاقاتِ relations are still tense; لا يَزالُ قائِماً \ مَوْجوداً it still exists; ما زالَ البَحْثُ جارِياً the investigation is still being conducted; لم تَزَل القَضِيَّةُ قَيْدَ الدِراسةِ the matter is still under study; لم يَزَل السَلامُ في الشَرْقِ الأَوْسَطِ بَعيدَ المَنالِ peace in the Middle East is still a long way off

زاوَلَ *v* to practise; زاوَلَ مِهْنَتَهُ to practise one's profession; زاوَلَ عَمَلَهُ to do one's job

زايَلَ *v* to abandon, to leave (behind)

أَزالَ *v* to remove, to dispose of, to get rid of; to eliminate; أَزالَ شَيْئاً to get rid of sth; أَزالَ الغِطاءَ عن الزُجاجةِ to remove the cap from the bottle; أَزالَ الغُبارَ to dust; أَزالَ مُشْكِلةً to overcome a problem; أَزالَ عَراقيلَ to remove obstacles

زائِل *adj* transitory, passing, temporary; حُكْم زائِل a temporary measure; ثَرْوة زائِلة fleeting wealth

زَوال *n* 1▶ [ظُهْر] noon, midday; زَوالاً, بعد الزَوالِ in the afternoon 2▶ [نِهاية] disappearance; demise; كُلُّ شَيْءٍ آيِلٌ لِلزَوالِ everything comes to an end; بعد زَوالِ الأَزْمةِ after the crisis has passed

إزالة *n* removal, elimination; إزالة العَراقيلِ the removal of obstacles; إزالة التَوَتُّرِ \ الشُكوكِ \ المَخاوِفِ dispelling tension/doubts/fears

مُزاوَلة *n* practice

مِزْوَلة *n* |مَزاوِلُ| sundial

مُزِيل **A** *adj* removing, eliminating
B *n agent for the removal of sth*; مُزِيل deodorant; مُزِيل الرائِحةِ paint stripper; مُزِيل شَعْرٍ depilatory الأَصْباغِ

‹ **زامْبي**, **زومْبي** *n* zombie

‹ **زانة** *n* listed alphabetically

‹ **زَوى** *v* |i; زَيّ| to frown

تَزَوّى *v* to withdraw, to retire

انْزَوى *v* to retire, to retreat, to seclude oneself; انْزَوى في الرِيفِ to retreat to the country

زاوِيّ *adj* angular

زاوِية *n* |زَوايا| 1▶ [رُكْن] corner; حَجَر الزاوِيةِ cornerstone (Sport) ضَرْبة \ عَلَم زاوِيةٍ corner kick/flag; زاوِية النَظَرِ \ الرُؤْيةِ point of view; نَظَرَ إلى أَمْرٍ من زاوِيةٍ أُخْرى to look at an issue from a different point of view; حَشَرَ شَخْصاً في الزاوِيةِ to drive sb into a corner 2▶ (Geom) angle; زاوِية دَورانٍ rotation angle; مُتَمِّم زاوِيةٍ complement; زاوِية حادّة \ مُنْفَرِجة an acute/obtuse angle; زاوِية قائِمة a right angle; مُثَلَّث قائِم الزاوِيةِ a right-angled triangle; ظِلّ الزاوِيةِ tangent (line); زاوِية السُقوطِ the angle of incidence

مُنْزَوٍ *adj* |مُنْزَوونَ| retired; isolated, secluded; solitary

‹ **زَيَّتَ** *v* to oil, to lubricate, to grease

زَيْت *n* |زُيوت| oil; مُسْتَوى الزَيْتِ oil level; زَيْت الوَقودِ fuel oil; زَيْت خام crude oil; زُيوت عِطْرِيّة \ نَباتِيّة \ مَعْدِنِيّة aromatic/vegetable/mineral oils; زَيْت عَبّادِ الشَمْسِ sunflower oil; زَيْت غِذائِيّ cooking oil; صَبَّ الزَيْتَ في \ فوق النارِ to pour oil on the fire

زَيْتون *n coll* 1▶ [ثَمَر] olive; زَيْت زَيْتونٍ olive oil 2▶ [شَجَرة] olive tree; غُصْن زَيْتونٍ olive branch

زَيْتونِيّ *adj* olive green; olive (*before n*)

زَيْتِيّ *adj* greasy, oily; oil (*before n*); olive green; مِصْباح زَيْتِيّ oil lamp; لَوْحة زَيْتِيّة oil painting; أَلْوان زَيْتِيّة oil colours; صَخْر زَيْتِيّ oil shale

تَزْيِيت *n* lubrication

مُزَيَّت *adj* oiled

مُزَيِّت *n* lubricant

مِزْيَتة *n* oilcan, oiler

‹ **زِيج** *n* 1▶ (Meas) plumb line 2▶ (Astrol) astronomical almanac

‹ **زادَ** *v* |i; زِيادة| 1▶ [ارْتَفَعَ] to increase, to grow; to rise; زادَ عِلْماً to increase one's knowledge; زادَ شَأْنُهُ his prestige has risen; زادَ عَدَدُ الحَوادِثِ the number of accidents has risen 2▶ [أَضافَ] to add; to increase, to raise; زادَ في المَوْضوعِ to elaborate;

زِيادة المُرَتَّب \ الإيجارِ بِنِسْبة ٣٪ a 3% increase in rent; طَلَبَ زِيادةً في المُرَتَّبِ الأَسْعارِ to ask wage/price increase; زِيادةً على ذلك for a pay rise, to ask for a raise; بِلا زِيادةٍ أو نُقْصانٍ furthermore; without addition or omission; دَفَعَ ٥٠ دِرْهَماً زِيادةً على الثَمَنِ he paid 50 dirhams on top (of the price); زِيادةً على ذلك فُصِلَ عن عَمَلِهِ on top of everything, he was fired **3** [فَرْط] surplus

زَيْدِيّة *n* Zaidiya (*Shiite sect in Yemen*)

اِزْدِياد *n* |اِزْدِيادات| **1** [نُموّ] increase, growth, rise; اِزْدِياد اسْتِهْلاكِ الطاقةِ an increase in energy consumption; اِزْدِياد التَضَخُّمِ an increase in inflation; اِزْدِياد تَدْرِيجيّ gradual increase; اِزْدِياد مُطَّرِد steady increase; ظَلَّ العَدَدُ في اِزْدِيادٍ مُسْتَمِرٍّ the number kept rising steadily **2** [وِلادة] (Mor) birth; تاريخ الاِزْدِيادِ date of birth

أَزْيَد *adj* |dipt| more

اِسْتِزادة *n* increase

تَزايُد *n* |تَزايُدات| growth, increase

تَزايُديّ *adj* incremental

مُتَزايِد *adj* increasing, growing; عَدَد مُتَزايِد من الشَبابِ an increasing number of young people; بِشَكْلٍ مُتَزايِدٍ increasingly

مَزاد *n* |مَزادات| auction, public sale; رَئِيس المَزادِ auctioneer; مَزاد إِلِكْترونيّ online auction; مَوْقِع مَزاداتٍ an auction site; في مَزادٍ عَلَنِيٍّ at a public auction; باعَ شَيْئاً في المَزادِ to sell sth by auction

مُزايِد *n* bidder

مُزايَدة *n* bidding (up); auction; مُزايَدة عَلَنِيّة public auction

مَزِيد **A** *n* **1** (Gram) *derived form of the verb* **2** [إضافة] supplement, addition; المَزِيد من ... more ...; لِلمَزِيد من المَعْلوماتِ، ... for more information, ...; اِكْتَسَبَ مَزِيداً من الخِبْرةِ to gain more experience; المَزِيد من التَوْضيحِ further explanation; يَجِبُ بَذْلُ المَزِيدِ من الجُهودِ more efforts must be made **3** [فائض] a large quantity; المَزِيد من ... a large extent of ...; مَزِيد من الخِبْرةِ lots of experience
B *adj* enhanced, increased; فِعْل مَزِيد *a derived form of the verb*

يَزِيد *n* |dipt| Yazid (*male given name*)

زير *n* |أَزْيار| water barrel; cask; زير نِساءٍ playboy, womanizer

زادَ من اِرْتِيابِ شَخْصٍ to deepen sb's hatred; زادَ من كَراهِيةِ شَخْصٍ to increase sb's suspicion; زادَ السُرْعةَ to increase the speed **3** [تَجاوَزَ] to exceed, to surpass; to be more than; زادَ على الحُدودِ to exceed the limits; مُدّة تَزِيدُ عن خَمْسِ ساعاتٍ (a period of) more than five hours; زادَ عَدَدُ السُكّانِ عن ... the population has exceeded ... **4** [وَرَّدَ] see **زود**

زَيَّدَ *v* to increase, to augment; زَيَّدَ رَأْسَمالَهُ to increase one's capital

زايَدَ *v* to outbid, to raise the bid

تَزَيَّدَ *v* to increase; تَزَيَّدَ من العِلْمِ to increase one's knowledge

تَزايَدَ *v* **1** [زادَ] to increase, to rise; يَتَزايَدُ التَوَتُّرُ tension rises **2** [في الثَمَنِ] to outbid one another

اِزْدادَ *v* **1** [كَثُرَ] to increase, to rise, to grow; اِزْدادَ قَدْرُهُ his prestige rose; اِزْدادَ عُنْفاً \ سوءاً \ ضَعْفاً to become more violent/more wicked/weaker; ما زالَ عَدَدُ سُكّانِ العالَمِ يَزْدادُ the population of China is still growing; اِزْدادَتْ نِسْبةُ المُتَعَلِّمينَ إلى الضِعْفِ the number of educated people has doubled **2** [وُلِدَ] (Mor) to be born; اِزْدادَ الوَلَدُ بالمَغْرِبِ the boy was born in Morocco; اِزْدادَتْ لَهُ بِنْتٌ he just had a daughter; اِزْدادَ يَوْمَ ٢٦ مارِس he was born on 26 March

اِسْتَزادَ *v* to want more; to ask for more

زَيْد *n* Zayd (*male given name*)

زائِد *adj* **1** [إضافيّ] additional, extra, more, added; زائِد عن اللُزومِ \ الحاجةِ superfluous; تَفْسِير زائِد additional explanation **2** [مُفْرِط] excessive, overdone; سُرْعة زائِدة excessive speed **3** (Math) plus, and; عَلامة زائِدٍ plus (sign); ٤ زائِد ٥ يُساوي ٩ four plus five equals nine

زائِدة *n* |زَوائِدُ| **1** (Anat) appendix; اِلْتِهاب الزائِدةِ appendicitis; الزائِدة الدودِيّة vermiform appendix, appendix; زائِدة أَنْفِيّة adenoids; اِلْتِهاب حادّ \ مُزْمِن في الزائِدةِ acute/chronic appendicitis; أُصِيبَ بالتِهابِ الزائِدةِ to suffer from appendicitis; اِسْتَأْصَلَ الزائِدةَ to remove the appendix **2** (Ling) affix; suffix, postfix

زِيادة *n* **1** [اِزْدِياد] increase, growth, rise; زِيادة طَفِيفة \ هائِلة a slight/substantial increase; زِيادة الإِنْتاجِ an increase in production **2** [رَفْع] addition; expansion, increase; زِيادة

‹ **زيز** *n* |زيزان| cicada

‹ **زَيْزَفون** *n* lime (tree), linden; شَجَرة الزَيْزَفونِ lime tree

‹ **زافَ** *v* |i; زَيْف| to be false, to be forged

زَيَّفَ *v* to forge, to counterfeit; to falsify

زَيْف **A** *adj* [مُزَيَّف] false; forged, counterfeit
B *n* [مَصْدَر زافَ] falseness

زائِف *adj* false; forged, counterfeit; قِصّة زائِفة an untrue story; صورة زائِفة عن الوَضْعِ a misrepresentation of the situation

تَزْييف *n* forgery, counterfeiting; تَزْييف النُقودِ counterfeiting (money)

مُزَيَّف *adj* fake, false; forged, counterfeit; جَواز سَفَر مُزَيَّف a false passport

مُزَيِّف *n* forger, counterfeiter; مُزَيِّف النُقودِ counterfeiter

‹ **زَيَّقَ** *v* (Egypt) to creak

‹ **زِمْبابْوي, زيمْبابْوي** *n* Zimbabwe

زِمْبابْويّ, زيمْبابْويّ *adj, n* Zimbabwean

‹ **زانَ** *v* |i; زَيْن| to decorate, to embellish

زَيَّنَ *v* to decorate, to embellish, to garnish; زَيَّنَ بالوَرْدِ to decorate with flowers; زَيَّنَ شَيْئاً to embellish sth; زَيَّنَ الوَجْهَ to put on make-up

تَزَيَّنَ *v* to be decorated; to dress up, to spruce up

ازْدانَ *v* to be decorated

زَيْن *adj* beautiful, pretty

زِيان *n* decoration, embellishment

زينة *n* **1** [زُخْرُف] embellishment, decoration, adornment; ornament; للزينة for decoration **2** [تَبَرُّج] toilette, *washing oneself, dressing, and attending to one's appearance*

ازْديان *n* decoration

تَزْيين *n* decoration, embellishment; للتَزْيينِ for embellishment; تَزْيين وَسَطِ المَدينةِ decoration of the city centre

تَزْييني *adj* decorative, ornamental

مُزَيَّن *adj* decorated, embellished, ornamented

مُزَيِّن *n* hairdresser, barber, coiffeur

مُزَيِّنة *n* hairdresser, hair stylist, coiffeur

‹ **زَيْنَب** *n* |dipt f| Zaynab (*female given name*)

‹ **زيورِخ** *n* |f| Zurich

‹ **تَزَيّا** *v* |ب| to put on, to get dressed; to be dressed in, to wear; تَزَيّا بالزيِّ to wear a uniform

زيّ *n* |أَزْياء| clothing, clothes, dress; costume; fashion; زيّ جَميل a nice outfit; بِزيٍّ قَوميٍّ in national costume; في زيٍّ مَدَنيٍّ in civilian clothes; زيّ مُوَحَّد a uniform; ارْتَدى الزيَّ المُوَحَّدَ \ الرَسْميَّ to wear a uniform, to be in uniform; أَزْياء نِسائيّة women's fashion; مُصَمِّم أَزْياءٍ fashion designer; عَرْض أَزْياءٍ fashion show; عارِضة أَزْياءٍ model; أَزْياء الشِتاءِ winter collection

س

س *abbr* 1 [سُؤال] question (*abbreviation of* سُؤال *in official reports*)
2 [سابق] former (*abbreviation of* سابق)

سَ *particle* particle of the future tense; see سَوْفَ; سَيَأتي غَدًا he will come tomorrow

سابِياء *n* amniotic sac, caul

ساتان *n* satin

ساتانيّ *adj* satin

ساج *n* |سيجان| teak; خَشَب السّاجِ teak

سادة A *adj* see سود1
B *n* see سود2

ساديّ A *adj* sadistic
B *n* sadist

ساديّة *n* sadism

سُؤدُد *n* see سود 2

سائِر *n* rest, remainder, other; سائِرُ أَفْرادِ العائِلَةِ the rest of the family; لم تَكُنِ اللَّيْلَةُ عاديّةً كَسائِرِ اللَّيالي it was not an ordinary night like any other

سافانا *n* savannah

ساكْس *n* saxophone, sax

ساكْسوفون *n* saxophone, sax; عازِف ساكْسوفون saxophonist; عَزَفَ على الساكْسوفون to play the saxophone

سَأَلَ *v* |a; سُؤال, مَسْألة, تَسْآل| 1 [اسْتَخْبَرَ] to ask; سَأَلَ شَخْصاً شَيْئاً to ask sb sth; سَأَلَ شَخْصاً عن شَيْءٍ \ شَخْصٍ to ask sb about sth/sb; سَأَلَ شَخْصاً عن رَأْيِه في أَمْرٍ to ask sb's opinion on sth; سَأَلَ عن سَبَبِ شَيْءٍ to ask for the reason for something; سَأَلَ نَفْسَهُ ... to ask oneself ...; سَأَلَ إذا \ ماذا ... to ask if/what ...; سَأَلَ سُؤالاً to ask a question 2 [طَلَبَ] to ask, to request; سَأَلَ شَخْصاً شَيْئاً to ask sb for sth; سَأَلَ اللهَ أنْ ... to ask God to ... 3 [كانَ مَسْؤولاً] سُئِلَ عن شَيْءٍ to be responsible for sth 4 [اسْتَعْطى] to beg

ساءَلَ *v* to ask, to question

أَسْأَلَ *v* to grant, to fulfil

تَسَأَّلَ *v* to beg

تَساءَلَ *v* to ask oneself; to ask one another; to ask, to question; تَساءَلَ عن شَيْءٍ to wonder about sth; تَساءَلَ هل ... to ask oneself whether ...

سائِل A *adj* 1 questioning 2 [مائِع] see سيل
B *n* 1 questioner; beggar 2 [ما يَسيلُ] see سيل

سُؤال *n* |أَسْئِلة| question; سُؤال مَفْتوح an open question; أَسْئِلَة مُتَكَرِّرة \ شائعة frequently asked questions, FAQ; سُؤال بَحْثٍ search query; لائِحة \ قائِمة أَسْئِلَةٍ questionnaire; سُؤال مُتَعَدِّد الاخْتِياراتِ a multiple-choice question; طَرَحَ سُؤالاً to ask a question; أَثارَ أَسْئِلَةً to raise questions; رَدَّ \ أَجابَ \ جاوَبَ على أَسْئِلَةٍ to answer questions; سُؤال لا يُمْكِنُ الإجابةُ عَنْهُ an unanswerable question; هذا هو السُؤالُ الجَوْهَريُّ that is the key question; السُؤال الذي يَطْرَحُ نَفْسَهُ the question that arises

تَساؤُل *n* |تَساؤُلات| question; دَعا إلى التَساؤُلِ to raise questions

مُتَسائِل *n* questioner

مُساءَلة *n* 1 [مَسْؤوليّة] accountability; مُساءَلة قانونيّة legal accountability, liability 2 [سائِل] questioning

مَسْأَلة *n* |مَسائِلُ| question, problem, issue; matter, case, affair; مَسْأَلة مُهِمّة an important subject; مَسْأَلة مُعَقَّدة a complicated issue; مَسْأَلة حِسابيّة sum; مَسْأَلة البِطالَةِ the unemployment problem; مَسْأَلة اللاجِئينَ the issue of asylum seekers; مَسْأَلة وَقْتٍ \ صَبْرٍ \ مُثابَرةٍ a matter of time/patience/ perseverance; ناقَشَ \ أَثارَ مَسْأَلةً to discuss/raise a question; حَلَّ مَسْأَلةً to solve a problem; تَعَمَّقَ في مَسْأَلةٍ to delve into a problem; المَسْأَلةُ لَيْسَتْ على هذا النَحْوِ that is a different matter altogether; طَرَحَ مَسْأَلةً على بِساطِ البَحْثِ \ المُناقَشةِ to consider a matter

مَسْؤول **A** *adj* responsible, answerable, accountable; الوَزير المَسْؤول the minister responsible; مَسْؤول جِنائِيًّا accountable; سُلوك غَيْر مَسْؤولٍ irresponsible behaviour; كانَ مَسْؤولاً عن شَيْءٍ to be responsible for sth; كانَ مَسْؤولاً قانونِيًّا to be legally liable

B *n* official, functionary, officer, civil servant; director, executive, manager; head; مَسْؤول كَبير a high-ranking official; المَسْؤولونَ السِياسيّونَ political officials; كِبار المَسْؤولين senior officials

مَسْؤوليّة, مَسْئوليّة *n* responsibility; liability; مَسْؤوليّة مَدَنيّة civil responsibility; مَسْؤوليّة وِزاريّة ministerial responsibility; مَسْؤوليّة خاصّة personal responsibility; مَسْؤوليّة سِياسيّة political responsibility; مَسْؤوليّة قانونيّة (legal) liability; على مَسْؤوليّتِكَ at your own risk/peril; إخْلاء مَسْؤوليّةٍ disclaimer; تأْمين المَسْؤوليّة القانونيّةِ liability insurance; إحْساس \ شُعور بالمَسْؤوليّةِ sense/feeling of responsibility; مُنْعَدِم المَسْؤوليّةِ unaccountable, not responsible; (Law) non compos mentis; ناقِص المَسْؤوليّةِ in a state of diminished responsibility; كامِل المَسْؤوليّةِ fully accountable; المَسْؤوليّة عن الأطْفالِ responsibility for the children; إنَّها مَسْؤوليّةٌ كَبيرةٌ it's a great responsibility; ذو مَسْؤوليّةٍ responsible; حَمَلَ \ تَحَمَّلَ مَسْؤوليّةً كَبيرةً to bear great responsibility; تَحَمَّلَ المَسْؤوليّةَ عن شَيْءٍ to bear the responsibility for sth; اضْطَلَعَ بالمَسْؤوليّةِ to claim responsibility; رَفَضَ المَسْؤوليّةَ to deny responsibility; وَعى مَسْؤوليّاتِهِ to be aware of one's responsibilities; أَقَرَّ بِمَسْؤوليّتِهِ عن to accept responsibility for; أَلْقى المَسْؤوليّةَ على شَخْصٍ to charge sb with the responsibility; كانَ تحت مَسْؤوليّة شَخْصٍ to fall under sb's responsibility; أَخَذَ المَسْؤوليّةَ على عاتِقِهِ to assume/shoulder the responsibility; حَمَّلَ شَخْصاً مَسْؤوليّةَ شَيْءٍ to hold sb responsible for sth; حَمَّلَ شَخْصاً مَسْؤوليّةَ تَصَرُّفاتِهِ to hold sb responsible for his actions; أَعْلَنَ مَسْؤوليّتَهُ عن الاعْتِداءِ to claim responsibility for the attack; تَقَعُ مَسْؤوليّةُ التَخْطيطِ على عاتِقِها she is responsible for the planning

‹ **سَئِمَ** *v* |a; سَأْم| to be/become bored/fed up; سَئِمَ شَيْئاً to be sick of sth; سَئِمَ عَمَلَهُ to be sick of one's work; تَسْأَمُ الحَياةَ she is tired of life; سَئِمَ من الوَضْعِ to be fed up with the situation

أَسْأَمَ *v* to bore, to weary

سَأَم *n* boredom

سَئِم *adj* bored, tired

سَؤوم *adj* weary

‹ **ساميّ** **A** *adj* Semitic; اللُغات الساميّة the Semitic languages

B *n* Semite

ساميّة *n* Semitism; لاساميّة, مُعاداة الساميّةِ anti-Semitism; مُعادٍ للساميّةِ anti-Semitic

لاساميّ **A** *adj* anti-Semitic

B *n* anti-Semite

لاساميّة *n* anti-Semitism

‹ **سامِريّ** *n* |سامِريّونَ, سَمَرة| Samaritan

‹ **سامَرّاء** *n* |f| Samarra (*city in Iraq*)

‹ **ساوْنا** *n* sauna

‹ **سَباء** *n* |f| Sheba; سورة سَباء Sheba (*Sura 34*)

‹ **سَباتيّ, أَسْباتيّ** *n* club (*in playing cards*); آس سَباتيٍّ ace of clubs

سُباتيّ *adj* carotid; شِرْيان سُباتيّ carotid (artery)

‹ **سْباغيتي, اسْباغيتي** *n* spaghetti

‹ **سْبام** *n* (Comput) spam

‹ **سَبانِخ** *n* spinach

‹ **سَبَّ** *v* |u; سَبّ| to offend, to insult; to curse (at), to call names; سَبَّ اللهَ to blaspheme; سَبَّ شَخْصاً to insult sb

سَبَّبَ *v* to cause, to bring about, to effect, to produce; سَبَّبَ شَيْئاً \ في شَيْءٍ to bring about sth; سَبَّبَ خلافاً \ مُشاجَرةً to prompt a quarrel; سَبَّبَ حَيْرةً \ في حَيْرةٍ to create confusion; سَبَّبَ الكَثيرَ من المَتاعِبِ to cause a lot of trouble; ماذا سَبَّبَ هذا؟ how did that happen?

سابَّ *v* to insult each other

تَسَبَّبَ *v* to be caused; to result, follow; to be the reason/cause; تَسَبَّبَ في حُدوثِ شَيْءٍ to cause sth to happen

تَسابَّ *v* to insult/curse each other

سَبَب *n* |أَسْباب| ① [عِلّة] cause, reason, motive; بِسَبَبِ because of ...; بِسَبَبِ ذلك therefore; بِسَبَبِ شَخْصٍ through the agency of sb; بِسَبَبِ حالةِ الجَوِّ because of the weather; سَبَب قاهِر a compelling reason; أَسْباب اقْتِصادِيّة \ مالِيّة on economic/financial grounds; أَسْباب صِحِّيّة health reasons; لِأَسْبابٍ طِبِّيّة for medical reasons; لِأَيِّ سَبَبٍ؟ why?, what for?; حَدَّدَ سَبَبَ شَيْءٍ to determine the cause of sth; رَجَعَ السَّبَبُ إلى ... the reason lies in ...; ذاكَ هو السَّبَبُ that is the reason; اقْتِراح مَشْفوع بالأَسْبابِ a reasoned proposal; ثَمَّةَ أَسْبابٌ لِقَبولِ ذلك الطَّلَبِ there are reasons to accept that request; أُطْلِقَ سَراحُ المُتَّهَمِ بِسَبَبِ عَدَمِ تَوَفُّرِ الأَدِلّةِ the suspect was released for lack of evidence ② (*Law*) title

سَبّ *n* |سُباب| insulting, abuse; cursing, swearing; أَفْرَطَ في السَّبِّ to swear excessively

سِباب *n* abuse; cursing, swearing

سَبّابة *n* forefinger, index finger

سَبَبِيّ *adj* causal; عَلاقة سَبَبِيّة a causal connection

سَبَبِيّة *n* causality

تَسْبيب *n* causation

مُتَسَبِّب Ⓐ *adj* causal

Ⓑ *n* cause

مُسَبِّب *n* |مُسَبِّبات| cause; originator; مُسَبِّب هذا الحادِثِ the cause of this accident; مُسَبِّب مَرَضٍ pathogen

مَسَبّة *n* abuse; vulgarity, swear word

1 ‹ **سَبَتَ** *v* |u; سَبْت| ① [اِسْتَراحَ] to rest, to sleep ② (*Jud*) to keep/observe the Sabbath

أَسْبَتَ *v* ① [شَتا] to hibernate ② (*Jud*) to enter on the Sabbath

سُبات *n* ① [غَيْبوبة] coma ② [نَوْم] sleep; سُبات شَتْوِيّ hibernation ③ [خُمول] lethargy

سَبْت *n* |أُسْبوت| ① [نَهار] Saturday; يَوْم السَّبْتِ Saturday; سَبْت النور Holy Saturday ② (*Jud*) السَّبْت the Sabbath

إِسْبات *n* hibernation

2 ‹ **سَبَت** *n* |سَبَتات, أَسْبِتة| basket, hamper

‹ **سَبْتة** *n* |dipt| Ceuta (*exclave and autonomous city of Spain located on the north coast of Africa*)

‹ **سِبْتَمْبِر** *n* (NA, Gulf) September

‹ **سَبَج** *n* jet

‹ **سَبَحَ** *v* |a; سِباحة| to swim; سَبَحَ على ظَهْرِه to swim on one's back; سَبَحَ في البَحْرِ \ المَسْبَحِ to swim in the sea/pool; سَبَحَ كالسَّمَكِ to swim like a fish

سَبَّحَ *v* to praise, to glorify, to exalt; سَبَّحَ اللهَ \ الرَّبَّ \ للرَّبِّ to praise God

سابِح *n* |سابِحون, سُبّاح| swimmer

سَبّاح *n* swimmer

سِباحة *n* swimming; سِباحة حُرّة freestyle; سِباحة الصَّدْرِ breast stroke; سِباحة الظَّهْرِ backstroke; سِباحة الفَراشةِ butterfly stroke; دَرْس سِباحةٍ swimming lesson; ثَوْب السِباحة swimsuit; ٢٠٠ مِتْر سِباحة على الظَّهْرِ 200 metres backstroke

سُبْحان *n* سُبْحانَ اللهِ glory to God! (*exclamation of wonderment or surprise*); اللهُ سُبْحانَهُ وَتَعالى God, glorified and exalted

سُبْحة *n* |سُبُحات, سُبَح| rosary

سَوابِح *n pl* |dipt| aquatic animals (*that live in water*)

تَسْبيح *n* |تَسابيحُ| praise, glorification (*of God*)

تَسْبيحة *n* |تَسْبيحات, تَسابيحُ| hymn, song of praise

مَسْبَح *n* |مَسابِحُ| (swimming) pool; مَسْبَح داخِلِيّ an indoor swimming pool; مَسْبَح مَكْشوف an outdoor swimming pool

مِسْبَحة *n* |مَسابِحُ| rosary, prayer beads

‹ **سَبْحَلَ** *v* |i; سَبْحَلة| *to say* سُبْحانَ اللهِ (*Glory to God*)

سَبْحَلة *n the formula* سُبْحانَ اللهِ (*Glory to God*); *saying* سُبْحانَ اللهِ

‹ **سَبْخة** *n* |سِباخ| ① [بُحَيْرة مِلْحِيّة] salt lake ② [هَوْر] marsh

تَسْبيخ *n* deep sleep, coma

‹ **سَبَرَ** *v* |i-u; سَبْر| to fathom; to sound; to explore, to probe; سَبَرَ أَغْوارَ \ عُمْقَ شَيْءٍ to explore sth's depths, to delve into sth; سَبَرَ عُمْقَ البَحْرِ to sound the depths of the sea; سَبَرَ رَأْيَ شَخْصٍ to sound out sb's opinion; سَبَرَ مَوْقِفَ شَخْصٍ to feel out sb's viewpoint; لا يُسْبَرُ غَوْرُهُ unfathomable

سَبْر *n* sounding; probing; exploring; صَعْب السَّبْرِ difficult to fathom; لا يُمْكِنُ سَبْرُهُ unfathomable

سِبار *n* probe, feeler

سَبّورة *n* board, blackboard; سَبّورة بَيْضاء whiteboard, dry-erase board; سَبّورة ذَكيّة smart board (*interactive whiteboard*); مَسَحَ السَبّورة to erase the blackboard; كَتَبَ على السَبّورة to write on the blackboard

مِسْبار *n* |مَسابيرُ| probe; sounding rod; مِسْبار فَضائيّ space probe

سَبْط *adj* |سِباط| lank, straight; شَعْر سَبْط straight hair

سِبْط *n* |أَسْباط| **1** [حَفيد] grandson, grandchild **2** [قَبيلة] tribe

سابوط *n* see شَبّوط

سُباطة *n* bunch; سُباطة مَوْزٍ a bunch of bananas

سَبَطانة *n* (gun) barrel; سَبَطانة البُنْدُقيّة the barrel of a rifle

سَبُع, سَبْع *n* |سِباع, سُبوع| predator

سُبْع *n* (one) seventh, 1/7

سابِع **A** *num* seventh, 7th; القَرْن السابِع the 7th century; الساعة السابعة seven o'clock; كانَ في السَماءِ السابِعةِ to be in seventh heaven

B *n* السابِع *a celebration held seven days after a marriage or the birth of a child*

سابِعَ عَشَرَ *num* seventeenth, 17th; القَرْن السابِعَ عَشَرَ the 17th century

سُباعيّ *adj* sevenfold; seven-lettered (*consisting of seven letters*)

سَبْعة *num* seven; سَبْع سَنَواتٍ seven years; سَبْعة أيامٍ seven days; القُرى السَبْع the seven villages

سَبْعَةَ عَشَرَ *num* seventeen; سَبْعَةَ عَشَرَ شَخْصاً seventeen people

سَبْعونَ *num* seventy; خَمْسة وَسَبْعونَ مِليون دولار $75 million; كانَ في السَبْعينَ من عُمْرِهِ to be 70 years old

سُبوع *n a celebration held seven days after a marriage or the birth of a child*

أُسْبوع *n* |أَسابيعُ| week; الأُسْبوع الماضي \ المُقْبِل last/next week; بعد أُسْبوعٍ in a week; بعد أُسْبوعَيْن in two weeks; أُسْبوعاً بعدَ أُسْبوعٍ week in, week out; عُطْلة نِهايةِ الأُسْبوعِ weekend; مَطْلَع الأُسْبوعِ the beginning of the week; مَرَّتَيْنِ في الأُسْبوعِ twice a week

أُسْبوعيّ *adj* weekly; أُسْبوعيًّا weekly

أُسْبوعيّة *n* weekly (*newspaper or periodical*)

سَبَغَ *v* |a-u; سُبوغ| **1** [طالَ] to be long; سَبَغَت النِعْمةُ the blessings lasted **2** [رَغُدَ] to be comfortable; to be abundant

أَسْبَغَ *v* |على| to shower, to overload; to give, to grant, to impart; to attribute, to ascribe; أَسْبَغَ على شَخْصٍ المَديحَ to shower sb with praise; أَسْبَغَ على شَخْصٍ صِفاتٍ مُعَيَّنةً to attribute certain qualities to sb

(Idiom) أَسْبَغَ الوُضوءَ to perform the ritual ablution correctly

سابِغ *adj* **1** [تامّ] complete, full, entire, total **2** [طَويل] long, tall

سَبَقَ *v* |i-u; سَبْق| to precede; to be/go before; سَبَقَ لِسانُهُ to stumble over one's words; سَبَقَ شَيْئاً \ شَخْصاً to precede sth/sb; سَبَقَ شَخْصاً إلى قَوْلِ شَيْءٍ to take the words out of sb's mouth; سَبَقَ شَخْصاً إلى الخَيْرِ \ المَوْتِ to be the first to do good/to die; سَبَقَ لَهُ أنْ قالَ he has said before; لم يَسْبُقْ لَهُ أنْ ... he has never ...; ما سَبَقَ preceding; ما سَبَقَ ذِكْرُهُ above-mentioned; فيما سَبَقَ previously; كَما قُلْتُ فيما سَبَقَ as I've already said; كَما سَبَقَ وَذَكَرْنا \ أَنْ ذَكَرْنا as mentioned earlier; يَسْبِقُ رِجْلَيْهِ وَرَأْسُهُ in a hurry; إلى مُسْتَوًى لم يَسْبِقْ لَهُ مَثيلٌ to an unprecedented level

سَبَّقَ *v* to put forward/ahead

سابَقَ *v* to compete with, to vie with; to race against; سابَقَ شَخْصاً to compete with sb; سابَقَ الزَمَنَ to race against time

تَسابَقَ *v* to race, to run (a race); to compete/vie with one another, to try to outdo each other

اسْتَبَقَ *v* to anticipate, to be ahead; اسْتَبَقَ الأَحْداثَ to be ahead of events

سَبْق *n* lead; antecedence; مع سَبْقِ الإصْرارِ with premeditation; تَصَرَّفَ مع سَبْقِ الإصْرارِ والتَرَصُّدِ to act with premeditation; كانَ لَهُ فَضْلُ السَبْقِ فيهِ he deserves all the credit for being first

سابِق **A** *adj* |سابِقون, سُبّاق| past; previous, last, preceding; former, ex-; سابِقاً previously; في السابِقِ before; في الصَفْحةِ السابِقةِ on the previous page; في اليَوْمِ السابِقِ لِشَيْءٍ on the day prior to sth; كَما في السابِقِ as it used to be; زَوْج سابِق \ زَوْجة سابِقة ex-husband/ex-wife; خَطيبَتُهُ السابِقة his former fiancée; وَزير سابِق a former minister; يوغوسْلافيا السابِقة the former Yugoslavia; مُناسَبة \ مَرّة سابِقة a previous occasion/time; الصَفْحة \ الحَلْقة السابِقة the last page/episode; مَواعيد \ مُحاوَلات سابِقة earlier arrangements/attempts;

مَعْلومات سابِقة prior information; المُلّاك السابِقونَ the former owners; سابِق لِأَوانِه premature

B *n* precursor; لا سابِقَ لَهُ without precedent

سابِقة *n* |سابِقات, سَوابِقُ| **1** [حادِث سابِق] precedent; شَكَّلَ سابِقةً to set a precedent; هذا لا سابِقَةَ لَهُ this is unprecedented; سابِقة هي الأولى من نوعِها في التاريخ a completely unprecedented event **2** [جَريمة مُسَجَّلة] previous conviction; سَوابِقُ criminal record; صَحيفة \ صَفْحة السَوابِقِ a criminal record; صاحِب سَوابِقَ a convicted person; كانَتْ لَدَيْهِ سَوابِقُ to have a criminal record; لا سَوابِقَ لَهُ to have a clean record **3** (Ling) prefix

سَبّاق *n* leader; forerunner

سِباق *n* |سِباقات| contest, competition; race; سِباق البَدَلِ relay race; سِباق الحَواجِزِ steeplechase, hurdles; سِباق الدَرّاجاتِ bicycle racing; سِباق السُرْعةِ (running) race; سِباق السَيّاراتِ motor sport (BrE), (car) racing (AmE); سِباق التَسَلُّحِ arms race; سِباق فَرَنْسا (للدَرّاجاتِ) Tour de France; اشْتَرَكَ في سِباقٍ to enter a race; فازَ \ خَسِرَ في السِباقِ to win/lose the race; سِباق مع الوَقْتِ \ الزَمَن a race against the clock

أَسْبَق *adj* previous, last; former, ex-; الرَئيس الأَسْبَق the former president; العام الأَسْبَق last year

أَسْبَقيّة *n* precedence, priority; seniority; أَعطى الأَسْبَقيّة لِشَيْءٍ to give priority to sth; أَخَذَ الأَسْبَقيّةَ to take precedence

اسْتِباق *n* اسْتِباقاً previously

اسْتِباقيّ *adj* proactive; pre-emptive, in advance; أُسْلوب حَلّ المَشاكِلِ الاسْتِباقيّ a proactive problem-solving approach; ضَرْبة اسْتِباقيّة pre-emptive strike

تَسابُق *n* competition, race

تَسْبيق *n* advance payment

مُتَسابِق *n* competitor, contestant; racer; runner

مُسابِق *n* competitor, contestant; racer; runner

مُسابَقة *n* **1** [مُباراة] contest, competition; race; مُسابَقة عُشاريّة decathlon; مُسابَقة دُوَليّة international contest; كانَ خارِجَ المُسابَقةِ to be out of the competition; مُسابَقة أَلْعابِ القُوى athletic competition **2** [سُؤال وَجَواب] quiz; competition; أَجْرى مُسابَقةً to hold a competition

مُسْبَق *adj* مُسْبَقاً beforehand; مُسْبَق الدَفْعِ prepaid; هاتِف جَوّال مُسْبَق الدَفْعِ a prepaid mobile (BrE) cell (AmE) phone

مُسَبَّق *adj* **1** [مُقَدَّم] advance; مُسَبَّقاً in advance; شُروط مُسَبَّقة preconditions; حُكْم \ رَأْي مُسَبَّق prejudice **2** [باكِر] premature, too early

مَسْبوق *adj* having precedent; غَيْر مَسْبوقٍ unprecedented; حُكْم غَيْر مَسْبوقٍ في التاريخ a completely unprecedented judgement

‹ **سَبَكَ** *v* |i-u; سَبْك| to found, to cast

سَبَّكَ *v* to cast

سَبّاك *n* founder, caster; plumber

سِباكة *n* plumbing

سَبيكة *n* |سَبائِكُ| bar, ingot; سَبيكة ذَهَبٍ \ فِضّةٍ a gold/silver bar

مَسْبَك *n* |مَسابِكُ| forge; foundry

مَسْبوك *adj* cast, founded; تِمْثال مَسْبوك a cast image; حديد مَسْبوك cast iron

‹ **سَبِكْتْروسْكوبي** *n* spectroscopy

‹ **أَسْبَلَ** *v* to let fall, to drop

سابِلة *n* |سَوابِلُ| السابِلة passers-by, pedestrians

سَبْلة *n* manure, dung

سَبَلة *n* ear, spike (*of grain*)

سَبيل *n* |mf; أَسْبِلة, سُبُل| **1** [طَريق] way, road, path; في سَبيلِ for the sake of; في سَبيلِ اللهِ for God's sake, for God; على سَبيلِ المِثالِ by way of illustration; ابْن سَبيلٍ traveller; اعْتَرَضَ سَبيلَ شَخْصٍ to stand in sb's way; أَخْلى سَبيلَ شَخْصٍ to release sb; يَسَّرَ \ سَهَّلَ السُبُلَ لِشَخْصٍ to pave the way for sb; مَضى إلى حالِ سَبيلِهِ to go away; لا سَبيلَ إلى فِعْلِ هذا it is impossible to do that **2** [مَلْجَأ] means, expedient; ضاقَتْ بِه السُبُلُ to see no way out; لا سَبيلَ أَمامَنا سِوى الذَهابِ إلى هُناكَ we have no other choice but to go there

‹ **سْبام** *n* listed alphabetically

‹ **سَبى** *v* |i; سَبْي, سِباء| to take prisoner/captive; سَبى عَدُوَّهُ to take one's enemy prisoner

سَبيّ *n* |سَبايا| captive, prisoner (of war)

‹ **سْبيرْتو** *n* alcohol

‹ **س.ت.** *abbr* commercial register (*abbreviation of* سِجِلّ تِجاريّ)

1 **سادِس** *num* sixth, 6th; المَلِك مُحَمَّد السادِس King Muhammad VI; القَرْن السادِس the 6th century; الساعة السادِسة six o'clock

سادِسَ عَشَرَ *num* sixteenth, 16th; القَرْن السادِسَ عَشَرَ the 16th century

سِتّة *num* six; سِتّة أَعْوامٍ ,سِتّ سَنَواتٍ six years; الدُوَل السِتّ the six countries

سِتّةَ عَشَرَ *num* sixteen; الجُنود السِتّةَ عَشَرَ the sixteen soldiers; سِتّةَ عَشَرَ عاماً sixteen years

سِتّونَ *num* sixty; sixtieth; الذِكْرى السِتّونَ لِشَيْءٍ the sixtieth anniversary of sth; كانَ في السِتّينَ من العُمْرِ to be 60 years old; منذ سِتّينَ سَنةٍ for sixty years

سُداسيّ *adj* sixfold; six-part; شَكْل سُداسيّ hexagon; مُحادَثات سُداسيّة six-party talks

سُدْس *n* (one) sixth, 1/6

سُدْسيّة *n* (Tools) sextant

مُسَدَّس *n* **1** [سِلاح] |مُسَدَّسات| handgun, pistol; revolver; مُسَدَّس رَشّاش submachine gun; مُسَدَّس مَحْشوّ a loaded gun; قِراب \ غِلاف مُسَدَّسٍ holster; سَحَبَ \ شَهَرَ \ أَشْهَرَ مُسَدَّساً to pull a gun; أَطْلَقَ الرَصاصَ بِمُسَدَّسٍ to shoot with a handgun; حَشا مُسَدَّساً to load a gun; حَمَلَ مُسَدَّساً to carry a pistol; صَوَّبَ مُسَدَّسَهُ إلى \ to aim a gun at; صَوَّبَ \ وَجَّهَ مُسَدَّساً إلى \ نحو شَيْءٍ على to aim a gun at sth **2** (Geom) hexagon

2 **سِتّ** *n* (colloq) lady, woman; سِتّ الحُسْنِ belladonna, deadly nightshade (*Atropa belladonna*)

سَتَرَ *v* |i-u; سَتْر| to cover, to veil; to disguise; to conceal; سَتَرَ شَيْئاً to disguise sth; سَتَرَت المَرْأةُ وَجْهها بالنِقابِ the woman covered her face with the veil; يَجِبُ على المَرْءِ أنْ يَسْتُرَ عُيوبَ أَخيهِ one should protect his fellow man/brother

تَسَتَّرَ *v* **1** [اِخْتَبَأَ] to hide/conceal oneself; تَسَتَّرَ بِعَباءَتِهِ to be wrapped (up) in a gown **2** [أَخْفى] to hide, to conceal, to cover up; تَسَتَّرَ على شَخْصٍ \ شَيْءٍ to hide sb/sth; تَسَتَّرَ على الفَسادِ to cover up corruption; تَسَتَّرَ الرَجُلُ على عُيوبِهِ the man concealed his failings

اِسْتَتَرَ *v* to cover oneself, to hide; to be hidden/concealed; اِسْتَتَرَ خَلْفَ شَيْءٍ to hide behind sth

سِتْر *n* |سُتور| cover; protection, shelter

ساتِر *n* |سَواتِرُ| **1** [حاجِب] covering, concealing **2** [حاجِز] barrier, obstacle; سَواتِر تُرابيّة earthen barriers **3** [الله] السّاتِر *commonly used name for God*; يا ساتِرُ ! good Lord!

سِتار *n* |سُتُر| **1** [بُرْداية] curtains, drapes; curtain, screen; السِتار الحَديديّ the Iron Curtain; سَتائِر النافِذةِ window curtains, drapes; سِتار المَسْرَحِ theater curtain; وراء \ خَلْفَ السِتارِ behind the scenes **2** [غِطاء] cover; veil; رَفَعَ السِتارَ عن شَيْءٍ to disclose sth; أَسْدَلَ السِتارَ على شَيْءٍ to close the curtain on sth; رَفَعَ السِتارَ عن تِمْثالٍ \ نُصْبٍ تَذْكاريٍّ to unveil a statue/monument; تحت سِتارِ شَيْءٍ under the guise of sth

سِتارة *n* |سَتائِرُ| curtain; سَحَبَ \ أَغْلَقَ السَتائِرَ to draw the curtains

سُتْرة *n* |سُتَر| **1** [ثَوْب] coat; jacket, blazer; tunic; سُتْرة واقِية a bulletproof vest; سُتْرة المَجانينِ straitjacket; لَبِسَ \ ارْتَدى سُتْرةً to wear a jacket **2** [سِتار] curtain; veil

اِسْتِتار *n* hiding

السَتّار *n commonly used name for God*

مُتَسَتِّر *adj* hidden; disguised

مُسْتَتِر *adj* **1** [مُخْتَفٍ] latent; نِزاع مُسْتَتِر a latent conflict **2** (Ling) ضَمير مُسْتَتِر implied personal pronoun

مَسْتور *adj* hidden; مَساتيرُ secret matters

سْتراتوسْفير *n* stratosphere

سْتْريكْنين *n* strychnine

سَتَّفَ *v* to put/stow away; to arrange

تَسْتيف *n* stowing

اِسْتِنْسِل *n* stencil

إِسْت *n* |أَسْتاه| anus

سْتيارين *n* stearin, stearic acid

سْتيرويْد, إِسْتيرويْد *n* |سْتيرويْدات| steroid; سْتيرويْد اِبْتِنائيّ anabolic steroid; سْتيرويْد قِشْريّ corticosteroid

سْتيريو *adj, n* stereo

سَجَدَ *v* |u; سُجود| **1** [رَكَعَ] to kneel (*with the forehead touching the ground*); to prostrate oneself **2** [خَضَعَ] to worship

ساجِد *adj* |سُجود, سُجَّد| prostrate (*in prayer*)

سَجّاد *n* worshipper (*of God*)

سَجّادة *n* |سَجاجيدُ ,سَجّادات| carpet, rug; prayer rug; سَجّادة فارِسيّة a Persian carpet; سَجّادة سِحْرِيّة a magic carpet; سَجّادة الصَلاةِ prayer rug; نَفَّضَ السَجّاداتِ to beat the rugs; نَسَجَ سَجّادةً to weave a carpet

سَجْدة *n* prostration (*in prayer*); سورة السَجْدة The Prostration (*Sura 32*)

سُجود *n* prostration

مَسْجِد *n* |مَساجِدُ| mosque; المَسْجِد الحَرام the Holy Mosque (*in Mecca*); المَسْجِد الأَقْصى al-Aqsa Mosque (*the third holiest site in Islam, located in Jerusalem*)

ساجور *n* |سَواجيرُ| (dog) collar

سِجارة ,سيجارة *n* see سيجارة

سَجَعَ *v* |a; سَجْع| to coo; سَجَعَ الحَمامُ the pigeon cooed

سَجَّعَ *v to speak/write in rhymed prose*

سَجْع *n* |أَسْجاع| rhymed prose

سِجاف *n* |سُجُف| curtain; diaphragm (*in a camera*)

سُجُق *n* sausage

سَجَّلَ *v* 1 [كَتَبَ] to register, to record, to enter; to note, to take/make a note of; to set down; سَجَّلَ شَيْئاً to register sth; سَجَّلَ التاريخ to note the date; سَجَّلَ هَدَفاً to score (a goal); سَجَّلَ طَلَبِيّةً to take an order; سَجَّلَ وَقْتاً مُمْتازاً to record a good time; سَجَّلَ هَزّةً أَرْضِيّةً to record an earthquake; سَجَّلَ ماركةً \ عَلامةً تِجارِيّةً to register a trademark 2 [تَسَجَّلَ] to register, to enrol, to sign up; سَجَّلَ نَفْسَهُ في المَدْرَسةِ to enrol as a student; سَجَّلَ نَفْسَهُ لِشَيْءٍ to sign up for sth 3 [على شَريطٍ] to record; سَجَّلَ الصَوْتَ to record audio; سَجَّلَ شَيْئاً على شَريطٍ to tape sth 4 [السِعْرَ] to realize (*a gain, etc.*); سَجَّلَ السَهْمُ ارْتِفاعاً تَدْريجيًّا the share rose gradually 5 (Transp) to check in

ساجَلَ *v* to compete; to vie; ساجَلَ شَخْصاً في شَيْءٍ to compete with sb for sth

تَسَجَّلَ *v* to register, to enrol; to be registered/put on record

سِجِلّ *n* |سِجِلّات| register; سِجِلّات archives; سِجِلّ عقاريّ cadastre; سِجِلّ مَدَنيّ civil registry; سِجِلّ تِجاريّ commercial register; سِجِلّ عَدْليّ criminal record; سِجِلّات عامّة a public register; سِجِلّ المَواليدِ a register of births; سِجِلّ النُزَلاءِ visitors' book; سِجِلّ التَصَفُّح \ المُتَصَفِّح browsing history; أَمين السِجِلّاتِ archivist; سِجِلّات الأَحْوالِ المَدَنِيّةِ the records of births, deaths and marriages

سِجال *n* competition; struggle, fight; سِجال حادّ fierce competition; دَخَلَ في سِجالٍ مع الوَزيرِ to have a conflict with the minister

سِجّيل *n* (Geol) marl, shale

تَسْجيل *n* |تَسْجيلات| 1 [اِكْتِتاب] registration; enrolment; signing up; تَسْجيل الدُخولِ signing/logging in; تَسْجيل الخُروجِ signing/logging out; طَلَبَ \ مَلأَ اسْتِمارةَ تَسْجيلٍ to request/complete a registration form; تَسْجيل في جامِعةٍ \ مَدْرَسةٍ enrolment in a university/school; تَنْتَهي فَتْرةُ التَسْجيلِ بعد أُسْبوعَيْنِ registration closes in two weeks 2 [على شَريطٍ] tape recording; recording; تَسْجيل تِلِفِزْيونيّ television recording; تَسْجيل الصَوْتِ audio recording; تَسْجيل حَفْلٍ موسيقيٍّ recording a concert; جِهاز تَسْجيلٍ (tape) recorder; بَدَأَ \ أَنْهى التَسْجيلَ to begin/finish recording 3 [تَقْييد] registration, registry, recording; مَكْتَب التَسْجيلِ register office; رَقْم التَسْجيل registration number; تَسْجيل أَسْماءِ الناخِبينَ the registration of voters; أَوْقَفَ \ أَلْغى التَسْجيلَ to deregister 4 (Econ) تَسْجيل شَرِكةٍ في البورْصةِ listing a company on the (stock) market

تَسْجيليّ *adj* registration (*before n*); recorded; documentary; فِلْم تَسْجيليّ documentary (film)

مُسَجَّل *adj* registered; recorded; رِسالة مُسَجَّلة a registered letter; كانَ مُسَجَّلاً to be registered

مُسَجِّل *n* |مُسَجِّلات| 1 [جِهاز] tape recorder, cassette recorder; مُسَجِّل دي في دي DVD recorder 2 [مَأْمور تَسْجيلٍ] registrar

مُسَجِّلة *n* tape recorder, cassette recorder; recorder

سَجَمَ *v* |u; سُجوم ,سِجام| to flow, to stream

انْسَجَمَ *v* 1 [اِئْتَلَفَ] to harmonize, to be in agreement; انْسَجَمَ مع شَيْءٍ to be in agreement with sth 2 [انْصَبَّ] to flow

انْسِجام *n* harmony, compatibility, congruence; عاشَ في انْسِجامٍ مع شَخْصٍ to live in harmony with sb

مُنْسَجِم *adj* harmonious; compatible; corresponding; جَوّ مُنْسَجِم a harmonious atmosphere; تَعاوُن مُنْسَجِم working well together; عَلاقة مُنْسَجِمة a harmonious relationship;

سَحَبَ نُقوداً من الأَسْواقِ to withdraw sth from the market; سَحَبَ مالاً من المَصْرِفِ to withdraw money from the bank; تراجَعَ] حِسابِهِ to take money out of one's bank account 2 عن] to retract, to withdraw, to take back, to draw back; سَحَبَ تَرْشيحَهُ to retract one's words; سَحَبَ قَوْلَهُ \ كَلامَهُ to withdraw one's candidacy; سَحَبَ قوّاتٍ to withdraw troops; سَحَبَ جَيْشاً من مِنْطَقةٍ to draw back an army from a region 3 [جَرَّ] to pull, to draw, to drag, to haul; سَحَبَ قَبْضَةً to pull a handle; سَحَبَ البيرةَ to draw beer; اسْحَبْ وأَسْقِطْ (Comput) drag and drop; سَحَبَ الحَقيبةَ الثَقيلةَ (على الأَرْضِ) to drag along the heavy suitcase; سَحَبَ الغَريقَ إلى اليابِسةِ to pull the drowning person to dry land

انْسَحَبَ *v* to withdraw, to retreat, to draw back; انْسَحَبَ الجُنودُ the soldiers retreated; انْسَحَبَ من مَشْروعٍ \ سِباقٍ to withdraw from a project/contest; انْسَحَبَ في الجَوْلةِ الثالِثةِ to drop out in the third round

سَحْب *n* withdrawal; pulling, drawing; (lottery) draw; السَحْب والإسْقاط (Comput) drag and drop

ساحِبة *n* tractor

سَحاب *n coll* |سُحُب| clouds; سُحُب clouds; سُحُب مُمْطِرة rain clouds; سُحُب مُتَراكِمة cumulus; ناطِحة السَحاب skyscraper; يَنْقَشِعُ السَحابُ the clouds are dispersing

سَحّاب *n* zip, zip fastener (BrE), zipper (AmE)

سَحابةَ *prep* during, throughout; سَحابةَ أَرْبَعةِ قُرونٍ for four centuries; قضى سَحابةَ يَوْمِهِ في شَيْءٍ to spend one's day doing sth

سَحابيّ *adj* cloud (*before n*); حَوْسَبة سَحابيّة cloud computing; تَخْزين سَحابيّ cloud storage

انْسِحاب *n* |انْسِحابات| retreat, withdrawal, pull-out, evacuation; انْسِحاب من أَراضٍ the loss of ground

مَسْحوب *adj* 1 [مُلْغًى] withdrawn; cancelled; مَسْحوب عَلَيْهِ drawee 2 [مَجْرور] drawn, pulled, dragged

مُنْسَحِب *adj* retreating, outgoing, withdrawing

سُحْت *n* |أَسْحات| ill-gotten gains; *sth forbidden*

سَحَجَ *v* |a; سَحْج| to scrape, to abrade, to file; to plane; سَحَجَ العودَ to plane wood

كانَ مُنْسَجِماً مع شَيْءٍ ألْوان غَيْر مُنْسَجِمةٍ clashing colours; to be in keeping with sth

سَجَنَ *v* |u; سَجْن| to imprison, to jail, to detain, to confine, to lock up; سَجَنَ شَخْصاً to detain sb; سَجَنَ مُجْرِمينَ to lock up criminals; سَجَنَ المُعارِضينَ السِياسيّينَ to imprison political opponents; سُجِنَ لِمُدّةِ ثَلاثِ سَنَواتٍ to be in prison for three years

انْسَجَنَ *v* to be in prison

سَجْن *n* imprisonment, detention, custody, confinement; عُقوبة سَجْنٍ prison sentence; عُقوبة سَجْنٍ مع وَقْفِ التَنْفيذِ a suspended prison sentence; فَرَضَ عُقوبةَ سَجْنٍ to impose a prison sentence; حَكَمَ على شَخْصٍ بِعُقوبةِ سَجْنٍ to sentence sb to a prison term; السَجْن مَدى الحَياةِ life imprisonment; طالَبَ بالحُكْمِ بالسَجْنِ مَدى الحَياةِ to demand life imprisonment; حُكِمَ عَلَيْهِ بالسَجْنِ مَدى الحَياة he was sentenced to life (in prison); نِظام سَجْنٍ قاسٍ \ مُعْتَدِل a harsh/mild prison system

سِجْن *n* |سُجون| prison, jail, penitentiary; دَخَلَ السِجْنَ to go to prison; أَلْقى \ زَجَّ بِشَخْصٍ في السِجْنِ to put sb in prison; قَضى ١٤ يَوْماً في السِجْنِ to be in prison for 14 days; إفْلات \ هَرَب من السِجْنِ jailbreak

سَجّان *n* (prison) warder; jailer

سَجين A *adj* |سَجْنى, سُجَناءُ| imprisoned
B *n* |سَجْنى, سُجَناءُ| prisoner, detainee; كانَ سَجيناً to be in prison; أَخْرَجَ سَجيناً to get a prisoner released; أَطْلَقَ سَراحَ سَجينٍ to release a prisoner

مَسْجون A *adj* |مَساجينُ| detained; كانَ مَسْجوناً to be in prison
B *n* |مَساجينُ| prisoner

سَجّى *v* to shroud

سَجِيّة *n* |سَجايا, سَجيّات| character, nature, disposition; character trait, characteristic; temper; طَيِّب \ حَسَن السَجيّةِ of a good disposition

مُسَجًّى *adj* shrouded; جُثْمان مُسَجًّى a shrouded corpse

سَحَبَ *v* |a; سَحْب| 1 [اسْتَرَدَّ] to withdraw, to draw back, to take back, to recall; to take out; سَحَبَ رُخْصةً to rescind a licence; سَحَبَ سَفيراً to recall an ambassador; سَحَبَ شَيْئاً من

سَحْج *n* file; abrasion; erosion

مِسْحاج *n* |مَساحِيجُ| (Tools) plane

مِسْحَج *n* |مَساحِجُ| (Tools) plane

سَحَّ *v* |i-u; سَحّ, سُحُوح| to flow, to run; سَحَّ المَطَرُ to rain (hard), to pour

سَحّاحة *n* (Chem) burette

سَحَرَ *v* |a; سِحْر| **1** [مارَسَ السِحْرَ] to bewitch, to charm, to put/cast a spell on, to bedevil; سَحَرَ شَخْصاً to bewitch sb **2** [فَتَنَ] to fascinate, to enchant, to allure, to charm

تَسَحَّرَ *v* to eat **سَحور** (*before beginning one's fast at dawn during Ramadan*)

سَحَر *n* |أَسْحار| *period of time just before dawn*; في السَحَرِ before daybreak

سِحْر *n* |أَسْحار| **1** [أَنْشِطة الساحِرِ] magic, sorcery, witchcraft; spell; سِحْر أَسْوَد \ مُؤْذٍ black magic; أَبْطَلَ مَفْعولَ السِحْرِ to break the spell **2** [جاذِبِيّة] attraction, allure, magic

ساحِر **A** *adj* |سُحّار, سَحَرة, ساحِرون| charming, enchanting, bewitching; اِبْتِسامة ساحِرة a bewitching smile

B *n* |سُحّار, سَحَرة, ساحِرون| magician, sorcerer, wizard

ساحِرة *n* |سَواحِرُ, ساحِرات| witch, sorceress; ساحِرة خَبِيثة \ قَبِيحة a wicked witch

سَحّار *n* magician, sorcerer

سُحار *n* السُحار السِليكونِيّ (Med) silicosis

سِحْرِيّ *adj* magic; عَصاً سِحْرِيّة a magic wand; الوَصْفة السَحْرِيّة the magic recipe/formula; قوّة سِحْرِيّة magical powers

سَحور *n a meal eaten before beginning one's fast at dawn during Ramadan*

مَسْحور *adj* bewitched, charmed, enchanted; قَصْر مَسْحور an enchanted castle; إِنَّهُ مَسْحورٌ بِها he is charmed by her

سُحاف *n* سُحاف رِئَوِيّ tuberculosis

سَحَقَ *v* |a; سَحْق| **1** [دَقَّ] to pulverize, to grind, to crush, to pound, to powder; سَحَقَ الحَبَّ to grind grains; سَحَقَ حَشَرةً بِقَدَمِهِ to crush an insect with one's foot **2** (fig) to crush, to overwhelm, to slaughter; سَحَقَ مُحاوَلَةَ اسْتِقْلالٍ to suppress a struggle for independence

اِنْسَحَقَ *v* to be pulverized, to be crushed/pounded; اِنْسَحَقَ تحت وَطْأَةِ شَخْصٍ to be crushed under sb's foot

سُحْق *n* distance; crushing, pounding; سُحْقاً لَهُ away with him!; سُحْقاً للدِكْتاتورِيّة away with the dictatorship!

ساحِق *adj* overwhelming, overpowering, crushing, devastating; أَغْلَبِيّة ساحِقة an overwhelming majority; نَصْر \ اِنْتِصار ساحِق a crushing victory

سِحاق *n* lesbianism

سِحاقِيّ **A** *adj* lesbian; سُلوك سِحاقِيّ lesbian behaviour

B *n* سِحاقِيّة lesbian

سَحِيق *adj* bottomless, deep; distant, remote; هاوِية سَحِيقة a bottomless abyss; زَمَن سَحِيق a long time; ماضٍ سَحِيق a distant past

إِسْحاق *n* |dipt| Ishaq, Isaac (*male given name*)

اِنْسِحاق *n* **1** [نَدَم] remorse, repentance, contrition **2** [سُحْق] crushing; اِنْسِحاق شَخْصٍ crushing sb

مُساحِقة *n* lesbian

مَسْحوق *n* |مَساحِيقُ| **1** [دَقِيق] powder, powder form; مَسْحوق غَسِيلٍ washing powder; مَسْحوق الحَلِيبِ powdered milk; مَساحِيق التَجْمِيلِ powder (*make-up*); عُلْبة المَساحِيق a (powder) compact **2** [دَواء] powder; وَصَفَ مَسْحوقاً to prescribe a powder; تَناوَلَ مَساحِيقَ to take powders

سَحَلَ *v* |a; سَحْل| to drag; سَحَلَ شَيْئاً على الأَرْضِ to drag sth on the ground

ساحِل *n* |سَواحِلُ| coast, shore; الساحِل الغَرْبِيّ \ الشَمالِيّ the west/north coast; السَواحِل الغَرْبِيّة للوِلاياتِ المُتَّحِدةِ the US West Coast; خَفَر السَواحِلِ coast guard; أمام الساحِلِ offshore; على الساحِلِ on the coast; على طول \ بِمُحاذاةِ الساحِلِ along the coast; مَدِينة على الساحِل a seaside town; ذَهَبَ إلى الساحِلِ to go to the seaside

ساحِلِيّ *adj* coastal; شَرِيط ساحِلِيّ coastal strip; إِقْلِيم \ مُقاطَعة ساحِلِيّ(ة) a coastal area

سِحْلِيّة *n* |سَحالٍ| lizard

سَواحِلِيّ **A** *adj* **1** [ساحِلِيّ] coastal **2** [اللُغة] Swahili; اللُغة السَواحِلِيّة Swahili

B *n* coastal inhabitant

مِسْحَل *n* |مَساحِلُ| grater; plane, file

‹ **سَحْلَب** *n* 1 [أورْكيد] orchid (*Orchidaceae*) 2 [شَراب] salep (*starchy preparation of the dried tubers of various orchids*); *sweetened milk drink made with salep*

‹ **سَحِمَ** *v* |a; سَحَم| to blacken, to become black

أَسْحَم *adj* |dipt| black

‹ **سَحَنَ** *v* |a; سَحْن| to pulverize, to crush; سَحَنَ شَيْئاً to pulverize sth

سَحْنة, سَحَنة, سِحْنة *n* |سُحَن, سَحَنات| appearance, look, visage; facial expression

‹ **سَحْنون** *n* (Zool) moorhen (*Gallinula*)

‹ **سِحاءة** *n* |سِحاية, سَحايا| (Anat) meninx; الْتِهاب السَحايا meningitis

سِحائيّ *adj* الْتِهاب سِحائيّ meningitis

مُسْتَحٍ *adj* bashful, shy; ashamed; صَفْصاف مُسْتَحٍ weeping willow

مُسْتَحِية *n* listed alphabetically

مِسْحاة *n* |مَساحٍ| shovel, spade

‹ **سِخْتِيان** *n* tanned goatskin leather

‹ **سُخْد** *n* placenta; afterbirth

‹ **سَخِرَ** *v* |a; سُخْريّة| to ridicule, to deride, to mock; سَخِرَ من شَخْصٍ \ شَيْءٍ to make fun of sb/sth; سَخِرَ من العَدوّ to ridicule the enemy; سَخِرَ من نَفْسِهِ to mock oneself

سَخَّرَ *v* to use, to utilize, to employ, to harness; to exploit

تَسَخَّرَ *v* 1 [سَخِرَ] to scoff, to sneer 2 [كَلَّفَهُ عَمَلاً بِلا أَجْرٍ] to reduce to servitude

ساخِر *adj* sarcastic, ironic, satirical, cynical; تَعْليق ساخِر a sarcastic comment; بَرْنامَج ساخِر a satirical programme; ضِحْكة ساخِرة a sarcastic laugh; نَظْرة ساخِرة (إلى شَيْءٍ) a cynical view (of sth)

سُخْرة *n* 1 forced labour 2 laughing stock

سُخْريّ *adj* cynical, sarcastic

سُخْرِية, سُخْرِيّة *n* ridicule, sarcasm; scorn, derision; سُخْريّة لاذِعة scathing sarcasm; سُخْريّة الأَقْدارِ \ القَدَرِ the irony of fate; مُثير للسُخْرِيّةِ ridiculous; يَدْعو ذلك إلى السُخْريّةِ that is ridiculous; كانَ عُرْضةً للسُخْرِيّةِ to be the object of derision; جَعَلَ شَخْصاً مَوْضِعَ سُخْرِيّةٍ to look a fool; أَصْبَحَ مَوْضِعَ سُخْرِيّةٍ to make a fool out of sb

تَسْخير *n* exploitation, subjugation; harnessing

مَسْخَرة *n* |مَساخِرُ| laughing stock, object of ridicule

‹ **سَخِطَ** *v* |a; سَخَط| to be/become discontented, to be/become angry; سَخِطَ ل \ من شَيْءٍ to be angry about sth; سَخِطَ على شَخْصٍ to be angry with sb

أَسْخَطَ *v* to discontent; to enrage

سُخْط, سُخُط, سَخَط *n* indignation, annoyance, dissatisfaction, discontent; سُخْط على شَيْءٍ \ شَخْصٍ dissatisfaction with sth/sb; مِمّا أَثارَ سُخْطَ الوَزيرِ to the annoyance of the minister

ساخِط *adj* indignant, annoyed, irritated, disgruntled; ساخِط على الدُنْيا embittered

‹ **سَخُفَ** *v* |u; سَخافة, سُخْف| to be/become absurd, to be/become ridiculous

سُخْف *n* foolishness, absurdity, nonsense

سَخافة *n* foolishness, absurdity, nonsense

سَخيف A *adj* |سِخاف| ridiculous, absurd, ludicrous; foolish, stupid, banal; فِكْرة سَخيفة a ridiculous idea; خَطَأ \ سُؤال سَخيف a stupid mistake/question; اسْتِنْتاج سَخيف an absurd conclusion; تَفْكير سَخيف nonsensical reasoning

B *n* |سُخَفاءُ| fool

‹ **سَخْلة** *n* |سِخال| lamb

‹ **سَخَّمَ** *v* to make black

سُخام *n* soot; ذَرّات السُخامِ soot particles

‹ **سَخُنَ** *v* |u; سُخْنة, سَخانة, سُخونة| to warm up, to be/become warm/hot

سَخَّنَ *v* to heat, to warm/heat up; سَخَّنَ الماءَ to heat water

أَسْخَنَ *v* to heat, to warm (up)

ساخِن *adj* |سُخّان| hot, warm; أَكْل ساخِن hot food; وَجْبة ساخِنة a hot meal; ماء \ جَوّ ساخِن hot water/weather; حَمّام \ دُش ساخِن a hot bath/shower; لِقاء ساخِن a heated encounter; مُناقَشة ساخِنة a heated discussion

سَخّان *n* |سَخّانات| boiler, heater; سَخّان المِياهِ water heater; أَشْعَلَ السَخّانَ to light the heater

سَدّ *n* |أَسْداد ,سُدود| ◻1▸ [حاجز مِياهِ النَهْر] dam; embankment, levee; بَنى سَدًّا to build a dam; تَقْوِية السُدودِ reinforcement of the dikes; السَدّ العالي the Aswan Dam ◻2▸ [إعاقة] obstruction, blockage, stoppage; سَدّ طَرِيقٍ roadblock ◻3▸ [دَفْع] payment

سُدّ *n* cataract

سَداد *n* ◻1▸ [دَفْع] payment; repayment ◻2▸ [صَواب] correctness; سَداد الرَأْيِ common sense

سُداد *n* obstruction

سِداد *n* |أَسِدّة| cork; stopper

سِدادة ,سَدّادة *n* cork; stopper, cap; سَدَّ قِنِّينةً بِسِدادةٍ to put a cap on the bottle

سَدّة *n* سَدّة وَريديّة (Med) venous embolism

سُدّة *n* |سُدَد| position (*of authority or responsibility*); threshold, entry; سُدّة الرِئاسةِ the presidency; سُدّة الحُكْمِ power; على سُدّةِ الحُكْمِ in power; السُدّة الرَسوليّة the Holy See

سَديد *adj* well-aimed; apt; right, correct; حُكْم سَديد an accurate judgement; جَواب سَديد a witty retort; سَديد الرَأْيِ judicious

انْسِداد *n* obstruction; انْسِداد وَريديّ embolism; انْسِداد الأَمْعاءِ intestinal obstruction; انْسِداد الأَنْفِ \ المَسالِكِ الهَوائيّةِ blockage of the nose/airways; انْسِداد في البالوعةِ \ المَجاري a stoppage in the drain/sewer system; أَدّى إلى الانْسِدادِ to stop up

تَسْديد *n* payment, settlement, clearing, discharge

تَسْديدة *n* shot; تَسْديدة إلى الهَدَفِ a shot at goal

مَسَدّ *n* replacement; سَدَّ مَسَدَّ شَيْءٍ \ شَخْصٍ to take the place of sb

مُسَدَّد *adj* paid

مَسْدود *adj* ◻1▸ [مُغْلَق] blocked; closed; مَجْرًى مَسْدود a blocked drain; أَنْف مَسْدود a blocked (BrE) stuffed up (AmE) nose; حائِط مَسْدود ,طَريق مَسْدود dead end; impasse, deadlock; وَصَلَت المُفاوَضاتُ إلى طَريقٍ مَسْدودٍ the negotiations reached an impasse ◻2▸ [مُحاصَر] blockaded

سِدْر *n coll* buckthorn (*Rhamnus*); Lote Tree (*Celtis australis*); سِدْرة المُنْتَهى (Islam) Sidrat al-Muntaha (*a Lote tree that marks the end of the seventh heaven*)

سادِر *adj* reckless, heedless, careless

سَخانة *n* heat, warmth

سُخْنة *n* fever

سُخونة *n* warmth, heat; شَعَرَ بالسُخونةِ to be hot; سُخونة الأَجْواءِ السِياسيّةِ heightened political tensions

تَسْخين *n* heating; warming up; عَيْن تَسْخينٍ hotplate; تَدْريبات بالتَسْخينِ \ بِواسِطةِ التَسْخينِ warm-up; الإحْماءِ والتَسْخينِ through heating

مُسَخِّن *n* heater; boiler

سَخا ,سَخُوَ *v* |a-u; سَخاء ,سَخاوة| to be/become generous; سَخا بِمالِهِ للمُحْتاجينَ to give generously to the needy

سَخِيَ *v* |a; سَخًى| to be generous/liberal/open-handed; سَخِيَ بِمالِهِ للمُحْتاجينَ to give generously to the needy

سَخِيّ *adj* |أَسْخِياءُ| generous, liberal, open-handed, munificent; عَرْض سَخيّ a generous offer; هِبة \ مِنْحة سَخيّة a generous donation; كانَ سَخيًّا بالإطْراءاتِ to be lavish with compliments

سَخاء *n* generosity, open-handedness; بِسَخاءٍ generously; جازى شَخْصاً بِسَخاءٍ to reward sb handsomely; هذا كَرَمٌ وَسَخاءٌ مِنْكَ that is very generous of you

سَدَّ *v* |u; سَدّ| ◻1▸ [أَغْلَقَ] to block, to obstruct, to bar; to plug (up), to stop (up); to clog; سَدَّ ثُقْباً to close a gap; سَدَّ الطَريقَ to block the road; سَدَّ ماسورةً to clog a pipe; سَدَّ المَدْخَلَ \ المَعْبَرَ to block the entrance/passage; سَدَّ شارِعاً to obstruct a street; سَدَّ البابَ to bar the door; سَدَّ فَمَهُ to close one's mouth ◻2▸ (fig) to restrain, to curb; سَدَّ العَجْزَ في الميزانيّةِ to curb the budget deficit ◻3▸ [دَفَعَ] to pay, to settle; سَدَّ حِساباً to settle a bill ◻4▸ [حاجةً] to fulfil; سَدَّ الجوعَ to satisfy hunger; سَدَّ حاجاتِ شَخْصٍ to meet sb's needs

سَدَّدَ *v* ◻1▸ [دَفَعَ] to pay, to settle, to satisfy, to pay off; سَدَّدَ دُيوناً to pay off debts; سَدَّدَ المَصاريفَ to cover the costs; سَدَّدَ المَبْلَغَ دُفْعةً واحِدةً to pay in a lump sum ◻2▸ [وَجَّهَ] to aim, to point, to level; سَدَّدَ الكُرةَ to shoot the ball; سَدَّدَ لِخَصْمِهِ ضَرْبةً he dealt his enemy a heavy blow

تَسَدَّدَ *v* to be paid/settled

انْسَدَّ *v* to be/become clogged; to be/become blocked, to be/become obstructed; انْسَدَّ بالثَلْجِ to be snowed in

سادّ *n* cataract

‹ **سُدْس, سادِس, سادِسَ عَشَرَ, سُداسيّ, سُدْسيّة, مُسَدَّس** see **ستت**

‹ **سَدَلَ** *v* |i-u; سَدْل| to let down; سَدَلَ السِتْرَ to let/put a blind down

أَسْدَلَ *v* to lower, to bring down; أَسْدَلَ السِتارَ (على شَيْءٍ) to bring the curtain down (on sth); to finish (sth)

انْسَدَلَ *v* to hang down, to be down; to droop

‹ **سَديم** *n* |سُدُم| ❶ [ضَباب رَقيق] mist, haze ❷ (Astron) nebula; سَديم السَرَطانِ the Crab Nebula

‹ **سادِن** *n* |سَدَنة| ❶ (Islam) *custodian of the Kaaba in Mecca* ❷ (Chr) sexton

سِدانة *n office of the custodian of the Kaaba*

‹ **أَسْدى** *v* to render; أَسْدى إلى شَخْصٍ خِدْمةً \ مَعْروفاً to do sb a service

سَداة *n* ❶ [خَيْط] warp (*in weaving*) ❷ (Bot) |أَسْدِية| stamen; المِدَقّة والأَسْدِية pistil and stamens

سُدًى *adv* in vain, uselessly, to no avail; ذَهَبَ سُدًى to be to no avail; ذَهَبَتْ كُلُّ مُحاوَلاتي سُدًى all my attempts came to nothing; بِسَبَبِ ذلك ذَهَبَ الكَثيرُ من الجُهْد سُدًى therefore every effort was in vain; أَضاعَ الوَقْتَ سُدًى to waste time

إسْداء *n* providing, proffering; إسْداء النَصائِح advising

‹ **سَذاب** *n* (Bot) rue (*Ruta*)

‹ **ساذِج, ساذَج** **A** *adj* |سُذَّج| naive, artless; innocent, ingenuous, unaffected; مُلاحَظة ساذِجة a naive remark; طِفْل ساذِج an innocent child; سُؤال ساذِج a simplistic question **B** *n* |سُذَّج| simpleton

سَذاجة *n* naivety; innocence, ingenuousness, simplicity; ب \ في سَذاجَتِهِ in his naivety

‹ **سَرْء, سِرْء** *n* larva, grub; spawn

‹ **سُرادِق** *n* pavilion, tent; canopy

‹ **سَراية, سَراي** *n* mansion; palace

‹ **سَرَبَ** *v* |u; سُروب| to flow; سَرَبَ دَمْعُهُ his tears flowed

سَرِبَ *v* |a; سَرَب| to leak

سَرَّبَ *v* ❶ [أَسالَ] to leak; سَرَّبَ أَسْراراً to leak secrets; سَرَّبَ مَعْلوماتٍ ل \ إلى شَخْصٍ to leak information to sb ❷ [هَرَّبَ] to smuggle

تَسَرَّبَ *v* ❶ [ماءٌ] to leak; to seep, to ooze; تَسَرَّبَ عَبْرَ السَقْفِ to seep through the roof; تَسَرَّبَ من شَيْءٍ to ooze out of sth ❷ [تَسَلَّلَ] to sneak ❸ [أَخْبارٌ] to leak out; تَسَرَّبَتْ رِسالةٌ a letter was leaked; تَتَسَرَّبُ الأَخْبارُ the news filtered out

انْسَرَبَ *v* to leak, to seep

سَرَب *n* |أَسْراب| burrow, hole, den, lair

سِرْب *n* |أَسْراب| ❶ [مَجْموعة] swarm; flock, herd; سِرْب من الجَرادِ a swarm of locusts; سِرْب من النَحْلِ a swarm of bees; سِرْب من الحَجَلِ \ البَطِّ a flight of partridges/ducks; سِرْب من النَمْلِ a colony of ants; سِرْب من السَمَكِ a school (of fish) ❷ (Aviat) formation; squadron; سِرْب من الطائِراتِ an aircraft squadron

سَراب *n* mirage; بَدا أَنَّهُ سَرابٌ it seemed to be a mirage

تَسَرُّب *n* |تَسَرُّبات| leak, infiltration; تَسَرُّب في السَقْفِ a leak in the roof; تَسَرُّب في مَحطّةٍ نَوَويّةٍ a leak at a nuclear power station; أَصْلَحَ التَسَرُّبَ to repair a leak

تَسْريب *n* leak

مَسْرَب *n* |مَسارِبُ| intake; drain, sewer; duct, conduit

‹ **سَرْبَلَ** *v* |i; سَرْبَلة| to dress

تَسَرْبَلَ *v* to wear, to put on

سِرْبال *n* |سَرابيل| garment; shirt

‹ **سِرْت** *n* |f| Sirte (*city in Libya*)

‹ **سَرَجَ** *v* ❶ [حِصاناً] to saddle ❷ [ضَفَرَ] to braid, to plait

أَسْرَجَ *v* to saddle; أَسْرَجَ خَيْلاً to saddle a horse

سَرْج *n* |أَسْرِجة, سُروج| saddle

سَرّاج *n* saddler

سِراج *n* |سُرُج| lamp

مِسْرَجة *n* |مَسارِجُ| oil lamp

‹ **سِرْجين** *n* manure

‹ **سَرَحَ** *v* |u; سُروح, سَرْح| to depart, to go away; to wander; سَرَحَ ومَرَحَ to do as one likes

سَرَّحَ *v* ❶ [أَطْلَقَ] to send away; to dismiss; سَرَّحَ مُتَّهَماً to release a suspect; سَرَّحَ شَخْصاً من السِجْنِ to release sb from prison; سَرَّحَ شَخْصاً من المُسْتَشْفى to discharge sb from hospital; سَرَّحَ عَدَداً من الضُبّاطِ to demobilize a number of officers

مَسْرَحِيّة *n* play, drama; performance; مَسْرَحِيّة كوميدية comedy; مَسْرَحِيّة غِنائيّة musical; مَسْرَحِيّة إذاعيّة radio play; كَتَبَ مَسْرَحِيّةً to write a play; مَسْرَحِيّة من فَصْلَيْنِ a play in two acts; مَثَّل في مَسْرَحِيّةٍ to appear in a play

‹ **سَرْخَس** *n* fern (*Polypodium*); السَرْخَسِيّات ferns

‹ **سَرَدَ** *v* |u; سَرْد| 1 [روى] to narrate, to recount; سَرَدَ قِصّةً to narrate a story 2 [عَدَّدَ] to enumerate, to list

سَرْد *n* narration, account; enumeration; سَرْد الحَقائِق an account of the facts

سَرْدِيّ *adj* narrative

سَرْدِيّة *n* narrative

مَسْرَد *n* |مَسارِدُ| glossary

‹ **سِرْداب** *n* |سَراديبُ ,سَرادِبُ| cellar, basement; vault; tunnel

‹ **سَرْدين** *n* sardine; عُلْبة سَرْدينٍ a tin (BrE) can (AmE) of sardines

‹ **سَرَّ** *v* |u; مَسَرّة ,تَسِرّة ,سُرور| to please, to delight, to make happy; سُرَّ بِشَيْءٍ to be happy about sth; يَسُرُّني أنْ ... it pleases me to ...; سُرَّ مَنْ رَأى *epithet for the city of Samarra*

سَرَّرَ *v* to cheer up

أَسَرَّ *v* 1 [أَفْرَحَ] to make happy, to please, to delight; أَسَرَّ الناسَ to please people; يَسُرُّني أنْ أَسْمَعَ هذا I am glad to hear that 2 [ائْتَمَنَ على سِرٍّ] to confide; أَسَرَّ إلى شَخْصٍ بِشَيْءٍ to confide sth to sb 3 [كَتَمَ] to conceal

تَسارَّ *v* to whisper, to tell each other secrets

سارّ *adj* glad, cheerful; مُفاجَأة سارّة a pleasant surprise; أَخْبار سارّة happy news; غَيْر سارٍّ unpalatable; عَواقِب غَيْر سارّةٍ unpleasant consequences

سِرّ *n* |أَسْرار| 1 [خَفِيّة] secret; سِرًّا secretly; سِرًّا وَعَلانِيَةً ,في السِرِّ والجَهْرِ secretly and openly; في السِرِّ on the quiet, in secret; سِرّ شائع an open secret; سِرّ بَنْكِيّ bank secrecy; سِرّ دَوْلةٍ state secret; سِرّ المِهْنةِ a trade secret; سِرّ المُراسَلةِ confidentiality of the mail; انْتَهَكَ سِرَّ المُراسَلةِ to breach the confidentiality of the mail; كَلِمة سِرٍّ password; أَمين \ كاتِب سِرٍّ secretary; أَمانة \ كِتابة السِرِّ secretariat; أَفْشى سِرًّا to divulge a secret; تَنَصَّتَ على سِرٍّ to overhear a secret; كَشَفَ عن سِرٍّ to disclose a secret; ائْتَمَنَ شَخْصاً على سِرٍّ to confide a secret to sb; حَكى \ كَتَمَ \ حَفِظَ سِرًّا to tell/exchange confidences; تَبادَلَ أَسْراراً

2 [مُوَظَّفاً] to fire, to dismiss 3 [الشَعْرَ] to comb; سَرَّحَ شَعْرَهُ to comb one's hair 4 [المَرْأةَ] to repudiate, to divorce (*a wife*)

سارِح *adj* wandering; سارِح الفِكْرِ absent-minded

سَراح *n* release, discharge; dismissal; إطْلاق سَراحٍ release; إطْلاق سَراحٍ مُبَكِّرٍ early release; إطْلاق سَراحٍ مَشْروط (release on) parole; أَطْلَقَ سَراحَ شَخْصٍ to set sb free; أَطْلَقَ سَراحَ السُجَناءِ بعد التَحْقيقِ to release the prisoners after interrogation

تَسْريح *n* 1 release, discharge; تَسْريح الجَيْشِ demobilization 2 [مُوَظَّف] firing, lay-off, dismissal 3 [الشَعْرِ] combing 4 [زَوْجةٍ] divorce, repudiation

تَسْريحة *n* 1 [شَعْر] hairstyle, haircut, coiffure; غَيَّرَ تَسْريحةَ شَعْرِهِ to change one's hairstyle 2 [طاوِلة بِمِرْآةٍ] dressing table, vanity

مَسْرَح *n* |مَسارِحُ| 1 [مَبْنًى] theatre, playhouse; على خَشَبةِ المَسْرَحِ on the stage; مَسْرَح في الهَواءِ الطَلْقِ open-air theatre; ذَهَبَ إلى المَسْرَحِ to go to the theatre 2 [مِهْنة المَسْرَحِ] theatre, drama; فِرْقة مَسْرَحٍ drama group; فَنّ المَسْرَحِ theatre; عالَم المَسْرَحِ the world of theatre; أَحَبَّ المَسْرَحَ to love theatre; مَثَّلَ في المَسْرَحِ to act in a play 3 [مِنَصّة التَمْثيلِ] stage; خَشَبة المَسْرَحِ stage; غادَرَ المَسْرَحَ to go off-stage; بَرَزَ \ ظَهَرَ على المَسْرَحِ to appear on the stage 4 (*fig*) scene, set; مَسْرَح الجَريمةِ the scene of the crime; مَسْرَح الأَحْداثِ the scene of events; battlefield; crime scene; scene of the accident/incident; pitch, field (*sports*); stage (*politics*); تَوَجَّهَت الشُرْطةُ إلى مَسْرَحِ الأَحْداثِ the police headed to the scene of the crime/incident; بَرَزَت الحَرَكةُ على مَسْرَحِ الأَحْداثِ السِياسيّةِ the movement emerged on the political scene; مَسْرَحُ أَحْداثِ الرِوايةِ إفْريقيا the novel is set in Africa; في المَسْرَحِ السِياسيِّ on the political scene; كانَ مَسْرَحاً لِلحَرْبِ to be the theatre of war

مَسْرَحِيّ A *adj* theatrical, dramatic; إنْتاج مَسْرَحِيّ theatrical production; عَرْض مَسْرَحِيّ theatre performance; كاتِب \ مُؤَلِّف مَسْرَحِيّ playwright; أَنْجَزَ عَمَلاً مَسْرَحِيًّا to produce a play

B *n* actor

to guard a secret; لَيْسَ سِرًّا أنّ ... it's no secret that ...; في سِرِّهِ in his heart ❷ (Chr) sacrament; الأَسْرار الأَخيرة last rites; مَنَحَ شَخْصاً الأَسْرارَ المُقَدَّسةَ الأَخيرة to administer last rites to sb

سَرّاء *n* في السَّرّاءِ والضَّرّاءِ for better or (for) worse

سِرار *n* |أَسِرّة, أَساريرُ| *line of the palm*

سُرّة *n* |سُرَر, سُرّات| (Anat) navel, belly button; umbilical; حَبْلُ السُّرّةِ umbilical cord; (fig) ties; قَطَعَ حَبْلَ السُّرّةِ (مع شَخْصٍ \ بين شَخْصَيْنِ) to sever ties (with sb/between two people); فَتْق في السُّرّةِ umbilical hernia

سُرور *n* joy, happiness, gladness, delight, cheer; بِسُرورٍ gladly; بِكُلِّ سُرورٍ with pleasure

سُرّيّ *adj* umbilical; حَبْل سُرّيّ umbilical cord

سِرّيّ *adj* ❶ [مَنْسوب للسِرِّ] secret; confidential, private; مَخْبَأ سِرّيّ a secret hiding place; مَعْلومات سِرّيّة inside information; المُقاوَمة السِرّيّة the underground resistance; رَقْم هاتِفٍ سِرّيّ an unlisted number; رِسالة سِرّيّة a personal letter; هذه الرِسالةُ سِرّيّةٌ this letter is confidential ❷ (Anat) umbilical; حَبْل سِرّيّ umbilical cord

سُرّيّة *n* |سَرايا| concubine; mistress

سِرّيّة *n* ❶ [كِتْمان] secrecy, confidentiality, privacy, discretion; في سِرّيّةٍ تامّةٍ in strict secrecy; في مُنْتَهى السِرّيّةِ strictly confidential; سِرّيّة المَصارِفِ banking secrecy; حافَظَ على السِرّيّةِ to keep secret ❷ [غُموض] mystery

سَرير *n* |أَسِرّة, سُرُر, سَرائِرُ| bed; سَرير فَرْدِيّ a single bed; سَرير مُزْدَوِج \ لِشَخْصَيْنِ a double bed; السَرير الزَوْجِيّ the marital bed; سَرير الوِلادةِ birthing bed; سَرير المَرَضِ \ المَوْتِ sickbed/deathbed; كانَ على سَرير المَوْتِ to be on one's deathbed, to be dying; لَزِمَ السَريرَ to be confined to bed; اسْتَلْقى في السَريرِ to lie in bed; عَدَد الأَسِرّةِ في مُسْتَشْفًى the number of beds in a hospital

سَريرة *n* |سَرائِرُ| ❶ [سِرّ] secret; سَرائِر intimate thoughts ❷ [داخِلة] inner self; conscience; طَيِّب السَريرةِ kind-hearted; صَفاء \ طَهارة السَريرة clarity/purity of conscience

سَريريّ *adj* clinical; عِلاج \ عِناية سَريريّ(ة) clinical treatment/care; مَوْت سَريريّ clinical death; دِراسات سَريريّة clinical studies

مَسَرّة *n* joy; مَسَرّة للنَظَرِ a joy to behold

مَسْرور *adj* happy, pleased; وَجْه مَسْرور a cheerful face; كانَ مَسْروراً بِشَيْءٍ to be pleased with sth, to be happy about sth

سَرَطَ *v* |u; سَرْط| to swallow

سَرَطان *n* |سَرَطانات| ❶ (Med) cancer; سَرَطان المَعْي intestinal cancer; سَرَطان الدَمِ leukaemia; سَرَطان الجِلْدِ \ الرِئةِ \ الثَدْيِ skin/lung/breast cancer; عِلْم السَرَطانِ oncology; اخْتِصاصيّ في أَمْراضِ السَرَطانِ oncologist; مَريض السَرَطانِ, مُصاب بالسَرَطانِ (شَخْص) cancer patient; مُسَبِّب للسَرَطانِ carcinogenic; مَوادّ مُسَبِّبة للسَرَطانِ carcinogens; كانَ مُصاباً بالسَرَطانِ to have cancer; ماتَ بالسَرَطانِ to die of cancer ❷ (Zool) crab; lobster; سَرَطان البَحْرِ crab; lobster; سَرَطان النَهْرِ crayfish ❸ [أَحَد الأَبْراجِ] Cancer; (بُرْج) السَرَطانِ Cancer (*astrological sign*); كَوْكَبة السَرَطانِ Cancer (*constellation*); مَدار السَرَطانِ tropic of Cancer ❹ (Bot) basal shoot, sucker ❺ [شَهْر] Tir (*fourth month of the Solar Hijri, or Iranian calendar*)

سَرَطانة *n* carcinoma; سَرَطانة لابِدة carcinoma in situ

سَرَطانيّ *adj* cancerous, cancer (*before n*); وَرَم سَرَطانيّ (cancerous) tumor; carcinoma; خَلِيّة سَرَطانيّة a cancer cell

مُسَرْطِن *adj* carcinogenic; عامِل مُسَرْطِن carcinogen

سَرُعَ *v* |u; سُرْعة| to hurry; to be fast

سَرَّعَ *v* to speed up, to accelerate

سارَعَ *v* to hurry, to rush, to run; سارَعَ إلى مُساعَدةِ شَخْصٍ to rush to sb's help; سارَعَ إلى القَوْلِ to hasten to say

أَسْرَعَ *v* ❶ [تَعَجَّلَ] to hurry, to rush, to run; to be fast/quick; أَسْرَعَ إلى شَيْءٍ \ شَخْصٍ to rush to sth/sb; أَسْرَعَ إلى مَكانٍ to rush somewhere; أَسْرَعَ في الاعْتِذارِ to hurriedly apologize; أَسْرَعَ حتّى لا يَتَأَخَّرَ to hurry so as not to be late; أَسْرِعْ! hurry up! ❷ [زادَ سُرْعةً] to speed up, to accelerate; تُسْرِعُ السَيّارةُ the car is accelerating

تَسَرَّعَ *v* to hurry; to be in a hurry

تَسارَعَ *v* to hurry

سِراع *n* hurry; سِراعاً quickly

سَرْعانَ, سِرْعانَ, سُرْعانَ *conj* سَرْعانَ ما soon; لَكِنَّ سَرْعانَ ما تَبْدَأُ مَوْجةُ العُنْفِ but before long a wave of violence breaks out

سُرْعة *n* 1 [عَكْس بُطْء] speed, pace, tempo; سُرْعة عالية a high speed; سُرْعة نِسْبِيّة pace; سُرْعة قُصْوى \ دُنْيا maximum/minimum speed; سُرْعة جَهَنَّمِيّة breakneck speed; سُرْعة العَمَلِ working pace; عَدّاد \ مِقْياس سُرْعةٍ speedometer; جهاز مُراقَبة سُرْعةٍ speed control; فائِق السُرْعةِ ultra fast; كُمْبيوتر فائِق السُرْعةِ an ultra-fast computer; بِسُرْعةٍ fast; بِسُرْعةٍ خارِقةٍ at a tearing pace; بِسُرْعةٍ قُصْوى at top speed; بِسُرْعةِ البَرْقِ at lightning speed; بِسُرْعة ١٢٠ كم في الساعة at a speed of 120 km per hour; مَرَّ بِسُرْعةٍ to fly by; مَرَّ الوَقْتُ بِسُرْعةٍ the time flew by; أَقْصى سُرْعةٍ maximum speed; بِأَقْصى سُرْعةٍ at full speed; تجاوَزَ السُرْعةَ القُصْوى to exceed the speed limit, to speed; خَفَّضَ السُرْعةَ, خَفَّفَ السُرْعةَ to slow down; على جَناحِ السُرْعةِ at top speed 2 (Tech) gear; ناقِل السُرْعةِ الأولى first gear; سُرْعة خَلْفِيّة reverse gear; سُرْعةٍ gear; خَمْس سُرْعاتٍ five gears; تَغْيير السُرْعةِ التِلْقائيّ automatic gear change

سَريع *adj* |سِراع| fast, quick, speedy, swift; سَريعاً soon; سَيّارة سَريعة a fast car; حَرَكة سَريعة a quick movement; نُموّ \ زِيادة سَريع(ة) rapid growth/increase; عَوْدة سَريعة a speedy return; سَريع المَفْعولِ fast-acting; سُمّ سَريع المَفْعولِ a fast-acting poison; كانَ سَريعَ الفَهْمِ to be quick-witted; سَريع كالرُمْحِ \ كالسَهْمِ swift as an arrow; في أَسْرَعِ وَقْتٍ مُمْكِنٍ as soon as possible; السَريع the express

إسْراع *n* speeding-up, acceleration, quickening; إسْراع مُفاجِئ \ شَديد sudden/strong acceleration

أَسْرَع *adj* |dipt| faster; ما أَسْرَعَ مُرورُ الأَيّامِ time flies; بِأَسْرَعِ ما يُمْكِنُ as soon as possible

تَسارُع *n* hurry, rush

تَسَرُّع *n* hurry, rush

تَسْريع *n* speeding-up, acceleration

مُتَسارِع *adj* hurrying; accelerating; تَطَوُّرات مُتَسارِعة rapid developments

مُتَسَرِّع *adj* hasty, rash, hurried; قَرار مُتَسَرِّع a rash decision; مُتَسَرِّع في إطْلاقِ أَحْكامِهِ to be hasty in one's judgement

مُسْرِع *adj* hurried, hasty; سَيّارة مُسْرِعة a speeding car; مُسْرِعاً in a hurry; عادَ مُسْرِعاً to return quickly

مُسَرَّع *adj* accelerated

مُسَرِّع *n* accelerator

‹ **سُرْعوب** *n* سُرْعوب المِنْكِ mink

‹ **سُرْعوف** *n* praying mantis (*Mantodea*)

‹ **أَسْرَف** *v* 1 [بَذَّرَ] to waste, to squander; أَسْرَفَ المالَ to squander one's money 2 [تَجاوَزَ] to go to extremes; أَسْرَفَ في شُرْبِ الخَمْرِ to drink to excess

سَرَف *n* waste, extravagance

سُرْفة *n* |سُرَف| larva

إسْراف *n* waste, extravagance; الإسْراف في شَيْءٍ to use sth to excess; الإسْراف في الشُرْبِ to drink too much

مُسْرِف A *adj* excessive, immoderate, lavish; إنْفاق مُسْرِف extravagant spending

B *n* spendthrift, squanderer

‹ **سَرَق** *v* |i; سَرِقة| 1 [شَيْئاً] to steal; سَرَقَ مالاً to steal money; سَرَقَ لَوْحةً من مَتْحَفٍ to steal a painting from a museum; سَرَقَ من الفُقَراءِ to rob the poor; لا تَسْرِقْ don't steal; (Relig) thou shalt not steal 2 [شَخْصاً] to rob; سَرَقَ شَخْصاً to rob sb

تَسَرَّق *v* to steal

انْسَرَق *v* to be/get stolen

اسْتَرَق *v* to steal; اسْتَرَقَ السَمْعَ to eavesdrop; اسْتَرَقَ النَظَرَ to spy; اسْتَرَقَ الخُطا to sneak

سارِق *n* |سُرّاق, سَرَقة, سارِقونَ| thief, robber

سَرّاق *n* thief, pilferer

سَرِقة *n* theft, robbery; سَرِقة أَدَبِيّة plagiarism; سَرِقة المَحَلاّتِ shoplifting; ارْتَكَبَ سَرِقةً to commit theft; السَرِقة بِاسْتِعْمالِ العُنْفِ robbery with violence

مُسْتَرَق *adj* sneaky, stealthy, furtive; نَظْرة مُسْتَرَقة a furtive glance

مُسْتَرِق *n person who sneaks or steals*; مُسْتَرِق السَمْعِ eavesdropper

مَسْروق A *adj* stolen

B *n* مَسْروقات stolen goods; شِراء المَسْروقاتِ buying stolen goods; سَيّارة مَسْروقة a stolen car

‹ **سَرَقُسْطة** *n* Zaragoza (*city in Spain*)

‹ **سِيرْك, سِرْك** *n* circus; ذَهَبَ إلى السِرْكِ to go to the circus

‹ **سَرْكوما** *n* sarcoma (*tumour*)

‹ **سُرْم** *n* |أَسْرام| anus

‹ **سَرْمَدَ** *v* |i; سَرْمَدة| to eternalize, immortalize

سَرْمَد *n* eternity

سَرْمَديّ *adj* eternal

سَرْمَديّة *n* eternity

‹ **سُرْناي** *n* piccolo; عَزَفَ على السُرْناي to play the piccolo

‹ **سَرَنْديب** *n* |f| Ceylon (*former name for Sri Lanka*)

1‹ **سَرْو** *n coll* cypress (*Cupressus*)

2‹ **سَراة** *n* |سَرَوات| سَرَوات القَوْمِ the leaders of the people

سَرِيّ **A** *adj* |سَراة, أَسْرِياءُ; f pl سَرايا| high-ranking; noble

B *n* see **سري**

تَسْرِية *n* pastime

‹ **سِرْوال** *n* |سَراويلُ| (a pair of) trousers (BrE) pants (AmE); سِرْوال داخِليّ underpants, underwear; سِرْوال ضَيِّق tight trousers

1‹ **سَرى** *v* |i; مَسْرًى, سَرَيان, سُرًى| **1**◂ [اِنْطَبَقَ] to be valid/current; تَسْري عَلَيْهِ to be valid; سَرى على to apply to; سَرى مَفْعولُهُ أَحْكامُ القانونِ المِصْريِّ Egyptian law applies to it **2**◂ [اِنْتَشَرَ] to spread; سَرَتْ شائِعاتٌ rumors spread **3**◂ [سالَ] to flow, to stream; سَرى السُمُّ في عُروقِهِ the poison flowed through his veins **4**◂ [سارَ لَيْلاً] to travel by night

سَرّى *v* to drive/chase away

أَسْرى *v* to travel by night

سارٍ *adj* |سُراة| **1**◂ [ساري المَفْعولِ |على|] applicable; ساري المَفعولِ valid; كانَ سارِيَ المَفْعولِ to be valid; جَواز سَفَرٍ ساري المَفْعولِ a valid passport; القَوانين \ القَواعِد السارِية المَفْعولِ the laws/regulations in force; النِظام الساري على السِلَعِ الأَجْنَبِيّةِ the system that applies to foreign goods **2**◂ [مُعْدٍ] contagious; مَرَض سارٍ a contagious disease

سارِية *n* |سَوارٍ, سارِيات| mast; boom; خَفَضَ \ أَنْزَلَ السارِيةَ to lower the mast; سارِية السَفينةِ \ المَرْكَبِ the mast of the ship

سَراية, سَراي *n* listed alphabetically

سِراية *n* communicability; transmission, contagion; سِراية المَرَضِ the disease's transmission

سَرِيّ **A** *n* |سُرْيان, أَسْرِية| creek

B *adj* see **سرو**

سَرَيان *n* circulation, currency; سَرَيان المَفْعولِ validity, taking effect; بَدَأَ سَرَيانُ المَفْعولِ to take effect, to enter into force

إِسْراء *n the night journey of prophet Muhammad from Mecca to Jerusalem*; سورة الإِسْراء The Night Journey (*Sura 17*)

مَسْرى *n* listed alphabetically

2‹ **سَرِيّة** *n* |سَرايا| company; brigade; قادَ سَرِيّةً to be in command of a company; سَرِيّة مِدْفَعِيّة battery

‹ **سورْيالِيّ, سُرْيالِيّ** **A** *adj* surrealistic; لَوْحة سُرْيالِيّة a surrealistic painting

B *n* surrealist

سورْيالِيّة, سُرْيالِيّة *n* surrealism

‹ **سُرْيانِيّ** **A** *adj* |سُرْيان, سُرْيانِيّون| Syriac, Syrian (*relating to the East Syrian Church*)

B *n* |سُرْيان, سُرْيانِيّونَ| Syriac (*a member of the East Syrian Church*)

‹ **سِرِيس** *n* (Bot) chicory (*Cichorium intybus*)

‹ **سِريلانْكا** *n* Sri Lanka

‹ **سِسْموغْراف** *n* seismograph

سِسْموغْرافِيّ *adj* seismographic

‹ **سِشْوار** *n* blow-dryer

‹ **مَسْطَبة** *n* |مَساطِبُ| مِسْطَبة, مِصْطَبة, مَسْطَبة terrace, veranda; seat, bench; جَلَسَ على المَسْطَبةِ (في الحَديقةِ) to sit on the terrace (in the garden)

‹ **سَطَحَ** *v* |a; سَطْح| **1**◂ [سَوّى] to level, to smooth, to even out **2**◂ [بَسَطَ] to spread out, to unroll

سَطَّحَ *v* **1**◂ [سَوّى] to level, to smooth, to even out; سَطَّحَ الأَرْضَ to level the site **2**◂ [بَسَطَ] to spread out

تَسَطَّحَ *v* to be spread out, to be leveled

سَطْح *n* **1**◂ [سَقْف] |أَسْطِحة, سُطوح, أَسْطُح| roof; terrace; سَطْح مَنْزِلٍ roof of a house **2**◂ [وَجْه] |سُطوح| surface, face; سَطْح ناعِم \ خَشِن a smooth/rough surface; سَطْح مائِل an inclined plane; سَطْح الشَمْسِ the surface of the sun; سَطْح الباخِرةِ deck (*of a ship*); تحت السَطْحِ under the surface; على السَطْحِ on the surface; ظَهَرَ \ بَرَزَ على السَطْحِ to surface **3**◂ (Geom)

‹ **سطا** *v* |u; سَطْوة ,سَطْو| to attack, to assault; to rob; سَطا على شَيْءٍ to break into sth; سَطا (على مَكانٍ) to rob (a place); سَطا على سَيّارة to rob sb's house; سَطا على مَنْزِلِ شَخْصٍ to rob a money transport; سَطا عَلَيْهِ لِصٌّ نَقْلِ الأَمْوالِ he was attacked by a robber

سَطْو *n* attack, assault; burglary, break-in; robbery; سَطْو مُسَلَّح armed robbery; مُحاوَلة سَطْوٍ an attempted robbery; سَطْو على بَنْكٍ bank robbery

سَطْوة *n* |سَطَوات| influence; control; power, authority

‹ **سَعة** *n* see وسع

‹ **سَعْتَر** *n* see زَعْتَر

‹ **سَعِدَ** *v* |a; سَعْد| to be/become happy; سَعِدَ بِشَخْصٍ \ شَيْءٍ to be happy about sb/sth

ساعَدَ *v* to help, to assist, to aid, to give/lend a hand; ساعَدَ شَخْصاً في شَيْءٍ على \ في شَيْءٍ to help with sth; to help sb with sth; ساعَدَ الطَبيبَ في عَمَلِيّةٍ to assist the doctor with an operation; ساعَدَ شَخْصاً على تَذَكُّرِ شَيْءٍ to help sb remember sth

أَسْعَدَ *v* to make happy, to gladden, to gratify; أَسْعَدَ شَخْصاً بِشَيْءٍ to make sb happy with sth; كم يُسْعِدُني أنْ ... it makes me so happy that ...

سَعْد *n* |سُعود| ◻1 [حَظّ] (good) luck/fortune; يَوْم سَعْدٍ a lucky day ◻2 [اسْم شَخْصيّ] Saad (*male given name*)

سُعْد *n* (Bot) galingale (*Cyperus*)

ساعِد *n* |سَواعِدُ| forearm; arm; الساعِد الأَيْمَن right hand; كانَ بِمَثابةِ الساعِدِ الأَيْمَنِ للمَلِكة he was the queen's right-hand man; شَمَّرَ عن ساعِدِهِ to roll up one's sleeves

سُعاد *n* |dipt f| Suad (*female given name*)

سَعادة *n* ◻1 [فَرَح] happiness, joy, bliss; سَعادة عائِلِيّة domestic happiness; شَديد السَعادةِ very happy; دار السَعادةِ *ancient name for Constantinople* ◻2 (Title) Excellency; سَعادَتُكُمْ Your Excellency; سَعادة السَفيرِ His Excellence the ambassador

سَعْدان *n* |سَعادينُ| monkey

سَعْدانة *n* ◻1 [قِرْدة] monkey ◻2 [حَلَم] nipple, teat ◻3 [وُصْلة] coupling unit

|سُطوح| surface; plane

سَطْحِيّ *adj* superficial, shallow; مَعْرِفة سَطْحِيّة superficial knowledge; اهْتِمام سَطْحِيّ superficial interest; عَلاقات سَطْحِيّة superficial relationships

سُطَيْح *n* facet (*of a gem*)

مُسَطَّح *adj* level, flat; الأَرْضُ مُسَطَّحةٌ عند القُطْبَيْنِ the earth is flat at the poles

‹ **سَطَرَ** *v* |u; سَطْر| to write, to jot/put down; to draw lines

سَطَّرَ *v* to write, to put/jot down; سَطَّرَ (اسْمَهُ) في التاريخ to make one's mark

سَطْر *n* |أَسْطُر ,سُطور| line; row; كَتَبَ على السَطْرِ to write on the line; قَرَأَ ما بين السُطورِ to read between the lines; المَسافة بين السُطورِ line spacing

ساطور *n* |سَواطيرُ| cleaver, meat axe

مُسَطَّر *adj* ruled, lined; striped

مِسْطَرة *n* |مَساطِرُ| ◻1 [آلة للتَسْطيرِ] ruler; مِسْطَرة حاسِبة slide rule ◻2 (Law) code; المِسْطَرة الجِنائِيّة Code of Criminal Procedure

مَسْطَرين ,مُسْطَرين *n* trowel

‹ **سَطَعَ** *v* |a; سُطوع| ◻1 [لَمَعَ] to glitter, to sparkle, to glint, to shine; يَسْطَعُ النورُ the light shines; سَطَعَ تحت الشَمْسِ to gleam in the sun ◻2 [انْتَشَرَ] to spread; سَطَعَت الرائِحةُ the fragrance spread

ساطِع *adj* |سَواطِعُ| glittering, sparkling, radiant, brilliant, luminous; نور \ ضَوْء ساطِع a dazzling light; أَضْواء ساطِعة bright lights; نَجْم ساطِع a twinkling star; وَجْه \ ابْتِسامة ساطِع(ة) a radiant face/smile; شَمْس ساطِعة a brilliant sun

سُطوع *n* brightness, brilliance, glow; سُطوع نَجْمةٍ the brightness of a star

‹ **انْسَطَلَ** *v* to be/become stoned

سَطْل *n* |سُطول ,أَسْطال| bucket; سَطْل ماءٍ a bucket of water; سَطْل مَعْدِنٍ \ خَشَبٍ a metal/wooden bucket

ساطِل *n* satellite

مَسْطول *adj* intoxicated; stoned; drunk

‹ **سِطام** *n* |سُطُم| stopper, plug

سَعْدِيّ *n* Saadi (*male given name*); السَعْدِيّونَ the Saadi dynasty (*Morocco*)

سَعوديّ **A** *adj* Saudi (Arabian); المَمْلَكة العَرَبِيّة السَعوديّة Saudi Arabia

B *n* Saudi (Arabian)

سَعيد **A** *adj* |سُعَداءُ| happy; سَنة سَعيدة happy New Year; ذِكْرَيات سَعيدة happy memories; نَهارُكَ سَعيدٌ! have a good day!; سَعيد جِدًّا بِشَيْءٍ very happy with sth; (أَتَمَنّى لَكَ) عُطْلَةً سَعيدةً \ يَوْماً سَعيداً! have a nice holiday/day!; غَيْر سَعيدٍ unhappy

B *n* |سُعَداءُ| **1** [مَحْظوظ] happy one; كانَ من السُعَداءِ to be one of the happy ones **2** [اسْم شَخْصيّ] Said (*male given name*)

بور سَعيد *n* |f| Port Said (*city in Egypt*)

مُساعِد **A** *adj* assistant

B *n* **1** [مُعين] helper, aide, assistant; مُساعِد الوَزير deputy minister **2** [رُتْبة] adjutant **3** [اجْتِماعيّ \ طِبّيّ] social worker

مُساعَدة *n* help, assistance, aid, support; relief; مُساعَدة ماليّة financial assistance; مُساعَدة إنْسانيّة humanitarian aid; مُساعَدة دُوَليّة international aid; مُساعَدة عاجِلة emergency relief; مُساعَدات عاجِلة relief supplies; مُساعَدة قَضائيّة \ قانونيّة legal assistance; مُساعَدات التَنْمِية development funds; مَكْتَب المُساعَدة help desk; تَقْديم المُساعَدةِ rendering of services; قَدَّمَ \ أَعْطى مُساعَدةً to render assistance; قَدَّمَ مُساعَدةً عاجِلةً to provide emergency aid; قَدَّمَ مُساعَداتِ التَنْمِية (إلى دَوْلةٍ) to provide development assistance (to a country); مَدَّ يَدَ المُساعَدةِ to lend aid; طَلَبَ مُساعَدةً to ask for help; أَسْرَعَ إلى مُساعَدةِ شَخْصٍ to hasten to help sb; تَلَقّى مُساعَدةً من بَعْضِ المُخْتَصّينَ he was assisted by several experts; بِمُساعَدةِ with the help of

مَسْعود **A** *adj* |مَساعيدُ| happy, contented

B *n* Masud (*male given name*)

سَعَّرَ *v* to price, to set a price; سَعَّرَ شَيْئاً to price sth

أَسْعَرَ *v* to kindle, to light; to start

اسْتَعَرَ *v* to burn, to blaze; to rage; to break out

سُعْر *n* **1** [حُرَيْرة] calorie **2** [جُنون] madness

سِعْر *n* |أَسْعار| price; سِعْر فاحِش \ باهِظ an exorbitant price; سِعْر أَدْنى a minimum price; سِعْر مِعْياريّ a standard price; سِعْر ثابِت a fixed price; سِعْر مَطْلوب asking price; سِعْر الصَرْفِ exchange rate; سِعْر الدولارِ dollar (exchange) rate; بِطاقة سِعْرٍ price tag; زِيادة \ رَفْع سِعْرٍ a price increase; مُؤَشِّر الأَسْعارِ price index; نَشْرة \ قائِمة الأَسْعارِ price list; آلِيّة الأَسْعارِ price mechanism; مُسْتَوى الأَسْعارِ price level; تَجْميد الأَسْعارِ price freeze; حَرْب الأَسْعارِ price war; تَحْديد الأَسْعارِ price control; تَحَرُّكات الأَسْعارِ price movements; سِياسة الأَسْعارِ price policy; خَفْض الأَسْعارِ price reduction; ارْتِفاع السِعْرِ \ الأَسْعارِ a rise in prices; انْخِفاض السِعْرِ \ الأَسْعارِ a fall in prices; انْخَفَضَتْ \ ارْتَفَعَتْ أَسْعارُ العُمْلاتِ the rates have fallen/risen; حَسَبَ سِعْرِ السوقِ at market value

سُعار *n* rabies, hydrophobia

سُعْرة *n* |سُعُرات| calorie; سُعْرة حَراريّة calorie

سَعير *n* |سُعُر| fire; hell

تَسْعير *n* quote, estimate; pricing; سِياسة التَسْعير pricing policy

تَسْعيرة *n* quote, estimate

مِسْعَر *n* |مَساعِرُ| calorimeter

مَسْعور *adj* |مَساعيرُ, مَسْعورونَ| mad, crazy; rabid (*dogs*); كَلْب مَسْعور a mad dog

اسْتَعَطَ *v* to sniff

سَعوط *n* snuff

سَعَفَ *v* |a; سَعْف| to help, to relieve

ساعَفَ *v* to help, to support

أَسْعَفَ *v* to help, to relieve; to save; أَسْعَفَ مَريضاً to give first aid to a patient

سَعَف *n* |سَعَفات| (palm) frond; سَعَف النَخْلِ palm frond; أَحَد السَعَفِ Palm Sunday

سَعْفة *n* ringworm, tinea; أُصيبَ بِسَعْفةٍ to have ringworm

إسْعاف *n* |إسْعافات| help, assistance; إسْعافات أَوَّلِيّة first aid; إسْعاف طارِئ \ مُسْتَعْجَل emergency care; إسْعاف المُصابينَ care for the wounded; سَيّارة إسْعافٍ ambulance; مَرْكَز الإسْعافاتِ الأَوَّلِيّة first aid station; اتَّصَلَ بالإسْعافِ to call an ambulance

مُسْعِف *n* rescuer

سَعَلَ *v* |u; سُعْلة, سُعال| to cough

مُسافَدة *n* mating

سَفَرَ *v* |i| سُفور| [اِنْكَشَفَ] ◀1▶ to unveil; سَفَرَ وَجْهُها to unveil one's face ◀2▶ سَفْر| [أَشْرَقَ] to shine; سَفَرَ الصُبْحُ the morning dawned

سَفَّرَ *v* to deport; to send on a journey

سافَرَ *v* to travel; to go on/make a journey; to leave; سافَرَ بالقِطارِ \ الباخرة \ الطائرة to travel by train/boat/air; سافَرَ إلى مَكانٍ to travel to a place; سافَرَ بَعيداً to travel far; سافَرَ عائداً to return

أَسْفَرَ *v* |عن| to result in, to end in; to yield, to bring; أَسْفَرَ عن ... to result in ...; لا يُسْفِرُ عن شَيْءٍ that leads to nothing; لم يُسْفِرْ عن نَتائِجَ to bring no results; أَسْفَرَ عن خَسارةٍ \ رِبْحٍ to yield a loss/profit

سَفَر *n* |أَسْفار| travel, journey; تَأْشيرة سَفَرٍ exit visa; وَكالة سَفَرٍ \ أَسْفارٍ travel agency; جَواز سَفَرٍ passport; ميعاد السَفَرِ departure time; رَدَّ مَصاريفَ السَفَرِ to reimburse travel expenses

سِفْر *n* |أَسْفار| book of the Bible; book; أَسْفار العَهْدِ القَديم the books of the Old Testament; سِفْر التَكْوين Genesis; سِفْر الرُؤْيا Revelations

سافِر *adj* |سَوافِرُ| ◀1▶ [غَير مُحَجَّبةٍ] unveiled; امْرَأة سافِرة *a woman who does not wear the hijab* ◀2▶ [صارِخ] blatant, bald; تَدَخُّل سافِر blatant interference

سِفارة *n* embassy; مَقَرّ \ دار السِفارةِ embassy; السِفارة البَلْجيكيّة في دِمَشْقَ the Belgian embassy in Damascus; عَمِلَ في السِفارةِ to work at the embassy

سَفْرة *n* |سَفَرات| journey, trip; سَفْرة مَدْرَسيّة school trip, field trip

سُفْرة *n* |سُفَر, سُفْرات| (Egypt) dining table

سُفور *n* unveiling

سَفير *n* |سُفَراءُ| ambassador; السَفير المِصْريّ في \ لدى أَمْريكا the Egyptian ambassador to America; اعْتَمَدَ سَفيراً to accredit an ambassador; عَيَّنَ شَخْصاً سَفيراً to appoint sb ambassador; سَعادة السَفير His Excellency the ambassador

مُسافِر **A** *adj* travelling **B** *n* traveller; passenger; مُسافِر حول العالَمِ a globetrotter; المُسافِرونَ المُتَوَجِّهونَ إلى مِصْرَ travellers to Egypt

سُعال *n* cough; سُعال ديكيّ whooping cough, pertussis; نَوْبة سُعالٍ a fit of coughing

سِعْلاة *n* |سَعالٍ, سَعالى| ◀1▶ (Zool) orangutan ◀2▶ [غول] *female demon*

سُعْلة *n* cough

أَبو سُعْن *n* stork (*Leptoptilos*)

سَعى *v* |a; سَعْي| ◀1▶ [قَصَدَ] to strive, to attempt, to endeavour, to seek; سَعى ل \ إلى شَيْءٍ to strive for sth; سَعى إلى هَدَفٍ to pursue a goal; سَعى إلى السَعادةِ \ الاعْتِرافِ to seek happiness/recognition; سَعى إلى وَظيفةٍ to solicit a position; سَعى بِيَدَيْهِ ورِجْلَيْهِ to try as hard as one can; سَعى وراء رِزْقِهِ \ لُقْمةِ العَيْشِ to seek to support oneself; تَسْعى الدَوْلةُ لِأَنْ تَكونَ عُضْواً في الاتِّحادِ الأوروبيِّ the country strives to become a member of the European Union ◀2▶ [وَشى] to betray; to slander; سَعى بِشَخْصٍ to betray sb ◀3▶ [جَرى] to run; سَعى بين الصَفا والمَرْوة to walk up and down between Safa and Marwa (*during the pilgrimage in Mecca*) ◀4▶ [تابَعَ] to chase

سَعْي *n* ◀1▶ [جُهْد] effort, endeavour, attempt; تَعْزيز السَعْيِ إلى تَحْقيقِ شَيْءٍ to step up efforts to achieve sth ◀2▶ (Islam) *walking up and down between Safa and Marwa during the pilgrimage in Mecca*

ساعٍ *n* |ساعونَ, سُعاة| messenger, courier, deliveryman; ساعي بَريدٍ postman (BrE), mailman (AmE)

مَسْعًى *n* |مَساعٍ| effort, attempt; مَسْعًى نَبيل a noble ambition

سَغِبَ *v* |a; سَغَب| to be hungry

مَسْغَبة *n* famine

سَغَل *n* malnutrition; dystrophy

سَفَحَ *v* |a; سُفوح, سَفْح| to spill; سَفَحَ الدَمَ to shed blood

سَفْح *n* |سُفوح| foot (*of a mountain*); سَفْح الجَبَل mountain slope; في سَفْحِ الجَبَلِ at the foot of the mountain

سَفّاح *n* murderer, killer, butcher

سِفاح *n* fornication; ابْن سِفاحٍ illegitimate child, bastard (vulg); سِفاح القُرْبى incest

سافَدَ *v* to mate with, to mount

سِفاد *n* mating

سَفّود *n* |سَفافيدُ| spit, skewer

تَسافُد *n* mating

أَسْفَلْت *n* asphalt

مُسَفْلَت *adj* asphalted, paved; طَرِيق مُسَفْلَت a paved road

‹ **سِفْلِس** *n* syphilis; كانَ مُصاباً بالسِفْلِس to have syphilis

‹ **سَفّان** *n* shipbuilder, shipwright

سَفِينة *n* |سَفائِن, سُفُن| boat, ship, vessel; سَفِينة تِجاريّة a merchant ship; سَفِينة ساحِلِيّة coaster; سَفِينة بُخاريّة steamship; سَفِينة حَرْبِيّة warship; سَفِينة فَضائيّة \ فَضاءٍ spaceship; سَفِينة رُكّابٍ passenger ship; سَفِينة شَحْنٍ freighter; عَنْبَر \ جَوْف سَفِينةٍ ship's hold; مُقَدِّمة سَفِينةٍ prow; مُؤَخِّرة السَفِينة stern; مُرْشِد السُفُن harbour pilot; صِناعة السُفُن \ بِناء shipbuilding; في السَفِينة on the boat; على مَتْنِ السَفِينةِ on board the ship; أَبْحَرَ في سَفِينةٍ to sail on a ship; رَكِبَ السَفِينةَ to board the ship; سافَرَ بِسَفِينةٍ to travel by ship; شَحَنَ \ جَهَّزَ سَفِينةً to load/outfit a ship; تَجْرِي السَفِينةُ the ship sails; عَوَّمَ سَفِينةً to float a ship; أَنْزَلَ سَفِينةً إلى البَحْرِ to launch a ship; السَفِينة المُتَّجِهة إلى أُسْتُراليا the boat to Australia

إسْفِين *n* listed alphabetically

‹ **سَفَنْجِيّ, سَفَنْج** see أسفنج

‹ **سَفُهَ, سَفِهَ** *v* |a-u; سَفْه, سَفاهة| to be stupid/foolish

سَفاهة *n* stupidity

سَفِيه **A** *adj* |سُفَهاءُ| **1** [أَبْلَه] stupid, foolish **2** [وَقِح] impudent

B *n* |سُفَهاءُ| fool

‹ **سَقَر** *n* hell

‹ **سَقْسَقَ** *v* |i; سَقْسَقة| to peep, to chirp

‹ **سَقَطَ** *v* |u; سُقُوط, مَسْقَط| **1** [وَقَعَ] to fall down/over; to crash/dash down; سَقَطَ قَتِيلاً to fall (in battle); سَقَطَ مَيِّتاً to drop dead; سَقَطَ من الدَرَج to tumble down the stairs; سَقَطَ من عَيْنَيْ شَخْصٍ to fall out of sb's favor; سَقَطَت الطائِرةُ على بَيْتٍ the plane fell on a house **2** [اِسْتَقالَ] to fall, to collapse; سَقَطَت الحُكُومةُ the government has fallen; لِيَسْقُط الطاغِيةُ! down with the tyrant! **3** [رَسَبَ] to fail; سَقَطَ في امْتِحانٍ to fail an exam **4** (Law) سَقَطَت القَضِيّةُ the statute of limitations has passed

أَسْقَطَ *v* **1** [أَوْقَعَ] to let fall, to drop; to bring/take down; أَسْقَطَ الرَمْلَ \ الحُطامَ to dump sand/rubbish; أَسْقَطَ طائِرةً مِرْوَحِيّةً \ طائِرةً to bring down a helicopter/aircraft; أَسْقَطَ قَنابِلَ to drop bombs **2** [حُكُومةً] to overthrow; أَسْقَطَ شَخْصاً \ شَيْئاً to

‹ **سَفَرْجَل** *n coll* |سَفارِج| (Bot) quince (*Cydonia oblonga*); مَعْجُون السَفَرْجَلِ quince jam

‹ **سَفْسَطة** *n* sophism, fallacy

‹ **سَفْسَفَ** *v* |i; سَفْسَفة| to rush (through); سَفْسَفَ عَمَلَهُ to rush through one's work

سَفْساف *adj* bad; inferior

سَفْسَفة *n* |سَفاسِفُ| nonsense, rubbish; سَفاسِف الأُمورِ nonsense

‹ **سَفَط** *n* |أَسْفاط| (fish) scales

‹ **سَفَعَ** *v* |a; سَفْع| to sunburn; to scorch (*of a hot wind*)

سَفْعة *n* burn, scorch

أَسْفَع *adj* |dipt; سُفْع| weathered; وَجْه أَسْفَع a weather-beaten face

‹ **أَسَفَّ** *v* |إلى| to stoop to

اسْتَفَّ *v* to take, to swallow (*a medicine*)

إسْفاف *n* triviality; moral decline

‹ **سَفَقَ** *v* |u; سَفْق| to slam (*a door*); to slap (*in the face*)

‹ **سَفَكَ** *v* |i-u; سَفْك| to shed; سَفَكَ الدِماءَ to shed blood; سُفِكَت الدِماءُ blood was spilled; سَفَكَ دَمْعاً to weep

سَفْك *n* shedding; سَفْك الدِماءِ bloodshed

سَفّاك *n* murderer, butcher; assassin

‹ **سَفَلَ** *v* |u; سُفُول| to be low/base; to be down

سَفُلَ *v* |u; سَفالة| to be low/base; to be down

سَفِلَ *v* |a; سَفْل| to be low/base; to be down

تَسَفَّلَ *v* to lower/abase oneself

سافِل **A** *adj* |سَفَلة| low, dirty

B *n* |سَفَلة| villain, bastard

سَفالة *n* lowness, meanness

سُفْلِيّ *adj* lower, bottom; الطابَق السُفْلِيّ the bottom floor; فَكّ سُفْلِيّ lower jaw

أَسْفَل *adj* |dipt; أَسافِلُ| **1** [أَدْنى] bottom, lower; أَسْفَلَهُ below; الجُزْء الأَسْفَل the lowest part; من الأَسْفَلِ from the bottom; من الأَسْفَلِ إلى الأَعْلى from the bottom up; من الأَعْلى إلى الأَسْفَلِ from top to bottom; في أَسْفَلِهِ on the bottom; في أَسْفَلِ الجِهةِ اليُمْنى bottom right **2** [في مَكانٍ أَسْفَلَ] below; كانَ ساكِناً في الطابَقِ الأَسْفَلِ to live on the ground floor

‹ **سَفْلَتَ** *v* |i; سَفْلَتة| to asphalt, to pave

bring down sb/sth; أَسْقَطَ حُكومةً to overthrow a government ❸ [الجَنينَ] to abort; أَسْقَطَ جَنيناً to perform an abortion ❹ (Psych) to project; أَسْقَطَ شَيْئاً على شَخْصٍ to project sth on sb ❺ (Law) أَسْقَطَ دَعْوى to drop a case; أَسْقَطَ الجِنْسِيّةَ عن شَخْصٍ to denaturalize sb

تَسَقَّطَ *v* to gather, to search for; تَسَقَّطَ الأَخْبارَ to gather information

تَساقَطَ *v* to fall, to fall/come down; تَساقَطَ شَعْرُهُ his hair fell out; تَتَساقَطُ الأَمْطارُ (بِغَزارةٍ) it's raining (very hard)

سَقَط, **سَقْط** *n* |أَسْقاط| ❶ [قُمامة] rubbish (BrE), trash (AmE); سَقَط المَتاعِ waste, offal; rubbish (BrE), trash (AmE) ❷ [شَعْر] (hair) loss ❸ [غُبار نَوَوِيّ] fallout; سَقْط إِشْعاعِيّ nuclear fallout

ساقِط *adj* |ساقِطونَ, سُقّاط| ❶ [هابِط] falling, fallen; dropped; الضَوْء الساقِط من الشُبّاكِ light falling from the window ❷ [سافِل] base, low-down; falling, fallen; امرَأة ساقِطة a fallen woman ❸ [باطِل] invalid, null (and void); لِكُلِّ ساقِطةٍ لاقِطةٌ there's someone for everyone

ساقِطة *n* prostitute

سَقّاطة *n* latch

سَقْطة *n* |سَقَطات| ❶ [غَلَط] mistake, error ❷ [وَقْعة] fall; سَقْطة حُرّة a free fall

سُقوط *n* ❶ [في المَدْرَسةِ] staying back ❷ [انْهِيار] fall; downfall, decline; collapse; سُقوط المَطَرِ rainfall; سُقوط الحُكومةِ the fall of the government; سُقوط نابوليون the downfall of Napoleon; سُرْعة السُقوطِ rate of descent

سَقيط *n* hail

إِسْقاط *n* ❶ [إِيقاع] overthrow; إِسْقاط النظامِ overthrowing the regime; الشَعْبُ يُريدُ إِسْقاطَ النِظامِ! down with the regime! ❷ [حِرْمان] withholding, deprivation ❸ [جَنين] إِسْقاط الجَنينِ miscarriage; abortion ❹ (Psych) projection ❺ (Law) إِسْقاط الجِنْسِيّةِ denaturalization

تَساقُط *n* loss (*of hair*); falling down/out/away; تَساقُط المَطَرِ rainfall; تَساقُط شَعْرٍ hair loss

مَسْقَط *n* |مَساقِط| ❶ [الرَأْسِ] مَسْقَط رَأْسٍ birthplace ❷ (Tech) projection ❸ [مَدينة] |f dipt| Muscat (*the capital of Oman*)

‹ **سُقُطْرى**, **سُقُطْراء** *n* |f| Socotra (*small archipelago off the coast of Yemen*)

‹ **مُسَقَّعة** *n* listed alphabetically

‹ **سَقَفَ** *v* |u; سَقْف| to roof; سَقَفَ بَيْتاً to roof a house

سَقَّفَ *v* to roof

سَقْف *n* |أَسْقُف, سُقُف, سُقوف| ❶ [أَعْلى البَيْتِ أو الغُرْفةِ] roof; ceiling; أَعْلى السَقْفِ ridge; سَقْف الفَمِ the roof of the mouth; عاشَ مع شَخْصٍ تحت سَقْفٍ واحِدٍ to live with sb under one roof; سَقْف واقٍ (من الشَمْسِ والمَطَرِ) shelter ❷ [الحَدّ الأَقْصى] ceiling; بَلَغَ السَقْفَ to reach the ceiling

سَقيفة *n* |سَقائِفُ| roofed passage, shelter; (wood)shed

مَسْقوف *n* covered; roofed; مَلْعَب مَسْقوف a covered stadium

‹ **سِقالة** *n* |سَقائِلُ| scaffold

إِسْقالة *n* |أَساقيلُ| scaffold

‹ **سَقِمَ** *v* |a; سَقَم| to be/become ill/sick

أَسْقَمَ *v* to make sick

سَقَم *n* |أَسْقام| illness, sickness

سَقيم *adj* |سُقُم|; f pl |سَقائِمُ| sick, ill; emaciated; صِحّة سَقيمة poor health

‹ **سُقُمْرِيّ** *n* see أَسْقُمْرِيّ

‹ **سَقى** *v* |i; سَقْي| ❶ [شَرَّبَ] to give to drink; to water (*an animal*); سَقى شَخْصاً شَيْئاً to give sb sth to drink ❷ (Agric) to irrigate, to water; سَقى النَباتاتِ to water the plants; سَقى الأَرْضَ to irrigate the land

سَقّى *v* to temper (*metal*)

ساقى *v to conclude a sharecropping contract*

أَسْقى *v* to give to drink

اسْتَقى *v* to draw; to glean, to extract; اسْتَقى من البِئْرِ to draw (water) from the well; اسْتَقى مَعْلوماتٍ من كُتُبٍ to glean information from books

اسْتَسْقى *v* ❶ [طَلَبَ مَشْروباً] to ask for a drink; الدَمُ يَسْتَسْقي الدَمَ ≈ violence begets violence ❷ [صَلّى] to pray for rain

سَقْي *n* irrigation; watering

ساقٍ *n* |سُقاة| cup-bearer

ساقِية *n* |سَواقٍ| waterwheel; irrigation ditch

سَقّاء *n* water carrier; يَبيعُ الماءَ في حارةِ السَقّائينَ he's carrying coals to Newcastle

سِقاء *n* |أَسْقِية| water bag

سِقاية *n* irrigation

اسْتِسْقاء *n* [1] [طَلَب المَطَر أو الماءِ] *request for water;* صَلاة الاسْتِسْقاءِ prayer for rain [2] (Med) oedema, edema (AmE), dropsy; اسْتِسْقاء دِماغيّ \ الرَأْسِ hydrocephalus

مُساقاة *n* sharecropping contract

مُسْتَقاة *adj* derived; مُسْتَقاة من ... derived from ...

مِسْقاة *n* |مَساقٍ| watering can

‹ **سَكَبَ** *v* |u; سَكْب| to pour (out); سَكَبَ الشايَ \ القَهْوة to pour the tea/coffee; سَكَبَ الحَساءَ to ladle out soup; سَكَبَ شَراباً لِشَخْصٍ to pour sb a drink; سَكَبَ الزَيْتَ \ البِنْزينَ على النارِ to add fuel to the fire

انْسَكَبَ *v* to be poured, to spill; يَنْسَكِبُ المَطَرُ it's pouring rain

سَكْبة *n* flower bed, bed

مَسْكَبة *n* flower bed, bed; مَسْكَبة أَزْهارٍ flower bed

مِسْكَبة *n* |مَساكِبُ| tablespoon

مَسْكوب *adj* poured out, spilled; لا تَبْكِ على اللَبَنِ المَسْكوبِ there's no use crying over spilt milk

‹ **سَكَتَ** *v* |u; سُكات, سُكوت, سَكْت| to be silent, to say nothing, to keep quiet; to fall/become/grow silent; أُسْكُتْ! shut up!; سَكَتَ عن الحَديثِ to keep quiet

أَسْكَتَ *v* to silence; أَسْكَتَ شَخْصاً to silence sb

ساكِت *adj* silent; taciturn

سَكّاتة *n* dummy (BrE), pacifier (AmE)

سَكْتة *n* |سَكَتات| (Med) stroke; infarction; سَكْتة قَلْبيّة heart failure; سَكْتة دِماغيّة cerebral infarction; أُصيبَ بِسَكْتةٍ (دِماغيّةٍ) to have a stroke

سَكوت *adj* taciturn, quiet

سُكوت *n* silence, quiet, hush; taciturnity, reticence; سُكوت! quiet!; كَسَرَ طَوْقَ السُكوتِ to break the silence; اشْتَرى سُكوتَ شَخْصٍ to pay sb hush money; أَلْزَمَ شَخْصاً السُكوتَ to put silence sb; السُكوتُ عَلامةُ الرِضا silence gives consent

سُكوتيّ *adj* taciturn; رَجُل سُكوتيّ a silent man; هو سُكوتيٌّ he isn't much of a talker

سِكّيت *adj* taciturn

إسْكات *n* silencing

مَسْكوت *adj* مَسْكوت عَنْهُ taboo

[1] **سَكَرَ** *v* |u; سَكْر| to close

[2] **سَكِرَ** *v* |a; سُكْر| to be/become drunk; شَرِبَ حتّى سَكِرَ to get drunk

أَسْكَرَ *v* to make drunk, to intoxicate; أَسْكَرَ شَخْصاً to make sb drunk

سَكَر *n* intoxicant

سُكْر *n* drunkenness, intoxication

سَكْران [A] *adj* |dipt; سُكارى, سَكارى| drunk, intoxicated; سائِق سَكْران a drunk driver; سَكْران لِدَرَجةِ الثَمالةِ dead drunk

[B] *n* (Bot) listed alphabetically

سَكْرة *n* |سَكَرات| drunkenness, intoxication; راحَت السَكْرةُ وَجاءَت الفِكْرةُ *common sense returns once one has sobered up*

سِكّير *n* alcoholic, drunk

مُسْكِر *n* |مُسْكِرات| مُسْكِرات drink, alcoholic beverage

[3] **سَكَّرَ** *v* to sugar

سُكَّر *n* [1] [مادّة حُلْوة] sugar; سُكَّر خام raw sugar; سُكَّر العِنَبِ dextrose; سُكَّر البَنْجَرِ beet sugar; سُكَّر الفَواكِهِ fructose; سُكَّر الشَعيرِ maltose; سُكَّر اللَبَنِ \ الحَليبِ lactose; قِطْعة \ مُكَعَّب سُكَّر sugar cube; مَسْحوق السُكَّرِ icing sugar (BrE), powdered sugar (AmE); نِسْبة السُكَّرِ sugar content; قَهْوة ب \ بدونِ سُكَّرٍ coffee with/without sugar; وَضَعَ السُكَّرَ في القَهْوةِ \ الشايِ to sugar the coffee/tea [2] (Med) glucose; diabetes; مَرَض السُكَّر diabetes; مُعَدَّل السُكَّرِ في الدم blood glucose level

سُكَّريّ [A] *adj* [اللَوْنِ] cream (*before n*), cream-coloured

[B] *n* diabetes; diabetic; داء (البَوْل) \ مَرَض السُكَّريِّ diabetes; كانَ مُصاباً بالسُكَّريِّ \ مُصاب بداءِ \ مَريض السُكَّريِّ diabetic; to have diabetes; عانى من مَرَض \ داءِ السُكَّريِّ to suffer from diabetes

سُكَّريّة *n* sugar bowl; سُكَّريّات sweets (BrE), candy (AmE)

[4] **مَسْكَرة** *n* listed alphabetically

‹ **سَكْران** *n* (Bot) henbane (*Hyoscyamus*)

سِكِرتير, سِكْرِتير n secretary; سِكْرِتير عامّ secretary general; سِكْرِتير الجَلْسةِ clerk of the court

سِكْرِتارِية n secretariat

سَكَروز, سُكْروز n sucrose, saccharose

سُكَّرين, سَكارين n saccharin

تَسَكَّعَ v to hang around, to loiter; to stroll, to meander; تَسَكَّعَ في شَوارِعِ المَدينةِ to loiter on the streets

تَسَكُّع n hanging around, loitering; vagrancy

مُتَسَكِّع n loiterer, vagabond; شابّ مُتَسَكِّع a loitering teen

سِكافة n shoemaking

إسْكاف n |أساكِفة| shoemaker, cobbler

إسْكافيّ n shoemaker, cobbler

سَكَّ v |u; سَكّ| to mint, to coin (*money*)

سِكّة n |سِكَك| ❶ [طَريق] road; سِكّة حَديدٍ \ حَديديّة railway (BrE), railroad (AmE); خطّ سِكّةِ الحَديدِ \ السِكَكِ الحَديديّةِ railway line; شَرِكة السِكَكِ الحَديديّةِ railways (BrE), railroad company (AmE); سِكّة المَوْتِ roller coaster ❷ [نَقْد] coin

مَسْكوكة n coin

سَكَنَ v |u| ❶ [قَطَنَ] |سَكَن, سُكْنى| to live, to occupy; to inhabit; سَكَنَ مِنْطَقةً to inhabit an area; سَكَنَ بَيْتاً \ في بَيْتٍ to occupy a house; كانَ يَسْكُنُ في بَيْتٍ he used to live in a house; سَكَنَ في المَدينةِ to live in the city; يَسْكُنُ في شِقّةٍ he lives in an apartment; سَكَنَ مع شَخْصٍ to live with sb; سَكَنَ عند شَخْصٍ to live at sb's place ❷ [هَدَأَ] |سُكون| to be/become still, to be/become calm

سَكَّنَ v ❶ [آوى] to accommodate, to lodge ❷ [هَدَّأَ] to calm, to quiet, to pacify; to alleviate, to soothe; سَكَّنَ شَخْصاً to calm sb; سَكَّنَ الأَلَمَ to alleviate the pain

ساكَنَ v to live together, to cohabit; ساكَنَ شَخْصاً to live with sb

أَسْكَنَ v to house, to shelter

تَمَسْكَنَ v to become poor

تَساكَنَ v to live together

سَكَن n ❶ [بَيْت] house, home, residence; accommodations; سَكَن مُؤَقَّت temporary accommodation; سَكَن دائِم permanent home; تَكاليف \ مَصاريف السَكَنِ living expenses; تَكاليف سَكَنٍ عالِية \ مُنْخَفِضة high/low living costs; بَحَثَ عن سَكَنٍ to look for somewhere to stay; صالِح للسَكَنِ fit for habitation, habitable; غَيْر صالِحٍ للسَكَنِ uninhabitable ❷ [إقامة] residence, residency; سَكَن دائِم permanent residence; رُخْصة السَكَنِ residence permit; بيئة السَكَنِ (everyday) environment

ساكِن **A** *adj* ❶ |ساكِنونَ| [هادِئ] calm, quiet, still; motionless, still; لم يُحَرِّكْ ساكِناً he didn't lift a finger ❷ [قاطِن] |سُكّان| residing ❸ (Phys) static; كَهْرَباء ساكِنة static electricity ❹ (Gram) *vowelless, with a sukun*

B *n* |سُكّان| resident, inhabitant; سُكّان population; بين السُكّانِ among the population; ساكِن أَصْليّ native; السُكّان الأَصْلِيّونَ the indigenous people, the natives; السُكّان المَحَلِّيّونَ the local population; قَليل \ كَثيف السُكّانِ thinly/densely populated; عِلْم السُكّانِ demography; تَزايُد السُكّانِ population growth; عَدَد سُكّانٍ population; عَدَد السُكّانِ المُطْلَق \ النِسْبيّ the absolute/relative population; اكْتِظاظ \ ازْدِحام السُكّانِ overpopulation; انْخَفَضَ \ ازْدادَ عَدَدُ السُكّانِ the population declined/increased; جَميع سُكّانِ العالَمِ world population

سُكّان n rudder

سُكّانيّ *adj* demographic, population (*before n*); تَطَوُّرات سُكّانيّة demographic developments; تَزايُد سُكّانيّ population growth; اكْتِظاظ \ اخْتِناق سُكّانيّ overpopulation; انْفِجار سُكّانيّ هائل a massive population explosion

سَكْنة n عَرَفَ حَرَكاتِ شَخْصٍ وَسَكَناتِهِ to know sb's doings

سُكْنى n |f| living; مَحَلّ سُكْنى place of residence

سَكَنيّ *adj* residential; مِنْطَقة \ حَيّ سَكَنيّ(ة) residential area

سُكون n ❶ [هُدوء] calm, tranquility; silence; سُكون تامّ a dead silence; كَسَّرَ \ شَقَّ السُكونَ to disrupt the silence ❷ (Gram) absence of vowels; sukun (*a character above a vowelless consonant*)

سِكّين n |f; سَكاكينُ| knife; سِكّين حادّة \ عَمْياء a sharp/dull knife; شَحَذَ سِكّيناً to whet a knife; شَهَرَ سِكّيناً to pull a knife; أَكَلَ بالسِكّينِ والشَوْكةِ to eat with a knife and fork

سَكينة n |سَكائِنُ| calm, serenity; وَلَّت السَكينةُ it's goodbye to peace and quiet; عادَت السَكينةُ peace has returned; أَقْلَقَ السَكينةَ to disturb the peace

إسْكان *n* housing; جَمْعِيّة إسْكانٍ housing corporation; وَحْدة إسْكانٍ housing unit; أَزْمة الإسْكانِ housing shortage

مُساكَنة *n* cohabitation, living together

مَسْكَن, مَسْكِن *n* |مَساكِنُ| house, home, residence, domicile, dwelling; مَسْكَن مُتَواضِع \ صَغير a humble abode; قِلّة مَساكِنَ a housing shortage; بِناء مَساكِنَ housebuilding; سوق المَساكِنِ the housing market; حاجة إلى مَساكِنَ housing demand; وَجَدَ \ عَرَضَ \ اسْتَأْجَرَ \ أَجَّرَ مَسْكَناً to find/offer/rent (out) a house

مُسَكِّن *n* |مُسَكِّنات| painkiller, tranquillizer, sedative; تَناوَلَ \ أَخَذَ مُسَكِّناتٍ to take painkillers

مَسْكون *adj* ① [مَأْهول] populated, inhabited; غَيْر مَسْكونٍ uninhabited; جَزيرة غَيْر مَسْكونةٍ a desert island ② [بالجُنونِ] haunted; دار مَسْكونة a haunted house; إنْسان \ شَخْص مَسْكون a person who is possessed (by the devil)

مَسْكونيّ *adj* ecumenical

مِسْكين **A** *adj* |مِسْكينونَ, مَساكينُ| poor, needy; pitiful; humble; مَخْلوق مِسْكين poor soul; عَجوز مِسْكين a pitiful old man; كانَ الحَيَوانُ المِسْكينُ جَريحاً the poor animal was wounded **B** *n* |مِسْكينونَ, مَساكينُ| wretch, (poor) soul; pauper; (يا) مِسْكين! oh, poor thing!

سْكوتِر *n* |سْكوتِرات| scooter

سْكي *n* ski; جِت سْكي jet ski

سْكيتْش, اسْكِتْش, إسْكِتْش *n* sketch

سل *abbr* cl (*abbreviation of* centilitre)

سَلا **A** *n* Salé (*city in Morocco*) **B** *v* see سلو

سَلَبَ *v* |u; سَلْب| ① [سَرَقَ] to take (away), to steal, to thieve, to rob; سَلَبَ السُيّاحَ to rob tourists; سَلَبَ شَخْصاً شَيْئاً to take sth from sb; سَلَبَ لُبَّ \ قُلوبَ الجُمْهورِ to win over the audience ② [غَنِمَ] to plunder, to loot

اسْتَلَبَ *v* to steal, to take away

سَلْب *n* ① [نَهْب] theft, stealing, plundering; سَلْب وَنَهْب looting; ابْتَغى السَلْبَ والنَهْبَ to go out looting ② [نَفْي] negation, negative; أَجابَ بالسَلْبِ to answer in the negative; سَلْباً negatively, badly, poorly; انْعَكَسَ سَلْباً على شَخْصٍ to reflect poorly on sb

سَلَب *n* |أَسْلاب| loot, plunder, booty

سالِب **A** *adj* negative; أَيّون سالِب a negative ion **B** *n* |سَوالِبُ| ① (Elec) cathode, negative pole ② (Phot) negative

سَلْبيّ *adj* ① [ضِدّ إيجابيّ] negative, unfavourable, adverse; نُفوذ سَلْبيّ a bad influence; مَوْقِف سَلْبيّ a negative attitude; عَقْليّة سَلْبيّة a negative mentality; صورة سَلْبيّة a negative image; نُقْطة سَلْبيّة demerit; جانِب سَلْبيّ drawback; كانَتْ نَتيجةُ الاخْتِبارِ سَلْبيّةً the result of the test was negative ② [غَيْر فَعّال] passive; التَدْخين السَلْبيّ second-hand smoke

سَلْبيّة *n* minus, drawback, disadvantage; الإيجابيّات والسَلْبيّات pluses and minuses; إيجابيّاتُهُ أَكْثَر من سَلْبيّاتِهِ the advantages outweigh the disadvantages

سَليب *adj* stolen

أُسْلوب *n* |أَساليبُ| ① [طَريقة] method, procedure; way, style; أُسْلوب صارِم a tough approach; أُسْلوب الحَياةِ lifestyle; أَحْدَث الأَساليب the latest methods; اتَّبَعَ أُسْلوباً آخَرَ to change course; لِكُلِّ شَخْصٍ أُسْلوبُهُ everyone has their approach ② (Art) style; أُسْلوب كِتابيّ writing style; أُسْلوب كِتابيّ واضِح a clear writing style

أُسْلوبيّ *adj* stylistic

أُسْلوبيّة *n* stylistics

مَسْلوب *adj* stolen; مَسْلوب الإرادةِ weak-willed; مَسْلوب العَقْلِ mad (BrE), crazy (AmE)

انْسَلَتَ *v* to slip away

سُلْت *n* rye

سَلْجَم *n* (Bot) rapeseed (*Brassica napus*); زَيْت سَلْجَمٍ rapeseed oil

سَلَّحَ *v* to arm; سَلَّحَ بأَسْلِحةٍ ثَقيلةٍ \ خَفيفةٍ to arm with heavy/light weapons; سَلَّحَ نَفْسَهُ بالعِلْمِ to arm oneself with knowledge

تَسَلَّحَ *v* to arm oneself, to be armed; تَسَلَّحَ بِسِكّينٍ to be armed with a knife

سِلاح *n* |أَسْلِحة| weapon; أَسْلِحة arms; سِلاح نَوَويّ \ ذَرّيّ nuclear weapon; أَسْلِحة نَوَويّة اسْتْراتيجيّة strategic nuclear weapons; أَسْلِحة ثَقيلة heavy weapons; أَسْلِحة كيمْيائيّة \ بيولوجيّة \ جُرْثوميّة chemical/biological/bacteriological

مُنْسَلَخ *n end of the month*

سَلِسَ *v* |a; سَلَس، سَلاسة| to be/become obedient; to be/become mild

أَسْلَسَ *v* to make easy, to make smooth

سَلَس *n* incontinence; سَلَس البَوْلِ urinary incontinence; مُصاب بالسَلَسِ incontinent

سَلِس *adj* mild; fluent, smooth; أُسْلوب سَلِس a smooth style; انْتِقال سَلِس للسُلْطةِ a smooth transition of power

سَلاسة *n* tractability; smoothness; بِسَلاسةٍ smoothly

سَلْسَبيل *n a spring in Paradise*; شَراب سَلْسَبيل *a deliciously cool drink*

سَلْسَلَ *v* |i; سَلْسَلة| to sequence; to interlink

تَسَلْسَلَ *v* to be successive

سَلْسَل *n* cool water

سِلْسِلة *n* |سَلاسِل| **1** [تَتابُع] series, sequence, succession, chain; سِلْسِلة غِذائيّة \ الغِذاءِ food chain; سِلْسِلة جَبَليّة \ جِبالٍ mountain range; سِلْسِلة تِلْفِزيونيّة TV series; سِلْسِلة كُتُبٍ a series of books; سِلْسِلة مَفاتيحَ bunch of keys; سِلْسِلة من الأَحْداثِ a sequence of events; سِلْسِلة من الحَوادِثِ a series of accidents **2** [عِقْد] سِلْسِلة عُنُقٍ necklace; سِلْسِلة يَدٍ bracelet

تَسَلْسُل *n* series, sequence; بالتَسَلْسُلِ consecutively; تَسَلْسُل زَمَنيّ chronology, timeline; تَسَلْسُل أَحْداثٍ a train of events; رَقْم التَسَلْسُلِ serial number

تَسَلْسُليّ *adj* serial; مَنْفَذ تَسَلْسُليّ serial port

مُتَسَلْسِل *adj* serial; continuous, sequential; تَفاعُل مُتَسَلْسِل chain reaction

مُسَلْسَل **A** *adj* continuous **B** *n* |مُسَلْسَلات| serial, series, soap; تابَعَ مُسَلْسَلاً (على التِلِفِزْيونِ) to follow a series (on TV)

سَلُطَ *v* |u; سَلاطة| to be/become impudent, to be/become insolent

سَلَّطَ *v* **1** [حَكَّمَ] to give power/authority; سَلَّطَ شَخْصاً على شَخْصٍ آخَرَ to give sb authority over sb else **2** [الأَضْواءَ] to focus; سَلَّطَ الأَضْواءَ على شَيْءٍ to shed light on sth **3** [عُقوبةً] to impose

تَسَلَّطَ *v* to overwhelm; to overcome

weapons; سِلاح أَبْيَض cutting and stabbing weapons; سِلاح ناريّ firearm; سِلاح دِفاعٍ defensive weapon; سِلاح البَحْريّةِ navy; سِلاح الطَيَرانِ \ الجَوِّ air force; مُسْتَوْدَع أَسْلِحةٍ arsenal; تِجارة أَسْلِحةٍ arms traffic; تَرْخيص السِلاحِ firearms licence; حِيازة على سِلاحٍ \ أَسْلِحةٍ دون تَرْخيصٍ illegal possession of arms; نَزْع السِلاحِ disarmament; نَزْع السِلاحِ النَوَويّ nuclear disarmament; قوّة السِلاحِ fire power; قَدَّمَ السِلاحَ to present arms; حَيّا بالسِلاحِ to present arms; أَشْهَرَ سِلاحاً to pull a weapon; أَلْقى السِلاحَ to lay down arms; لَجَأَ إلى السِلاحِ to take up arms; حَظْر (على) تَصْديرِ الأَسْلِحةِ arms embargo; الحَدّ من انْتِشارِ الأَسْلِحةِ arms control; تحت تَهْديدِ السِلاحِ at gunpoint; حِيازة سِلاحٍ \ أَسْلِحةٍ weapon possession; تِجارة أَسْلِحةٍ غَيْر شَرْعيّة illegal arms trade; سِلاح مُضادّ للطائِراتِ anti-aircraft weapons; إنَّهُ سِلاحٌ ذو حَدَّيْنِ it is a double-edged sword; مُدَجَّج بالأَسْلِحةِ \ السِلاحِ armed to the teeth

تَسَلُّح *n* armament, arms *(before n)*; تَسَلُّح نَوَويّ nuclear armament; تَسَلُّح كيمْيائيّ chemical armament; سِباق التَسَلُّحِ arms race; حَظْر التَسَلُّحِ arms embargo

تَسْليح *n* |تَسْليحات| **1** (Tech) reinforcement; حَديد التَسْليحِ rebar, reinforcing steel **2** (Mil) armament; تَسْليح نَوَويّ nuclear armament

تَسْليحيّ *adj relating to armaments*

مُتَسَلِّح *adj* armed; مُتَسَلِّح بالعِلْمِ والمَعْرِفةِ armed with knowledge

مُسَلَّح *adj* **1** (Mil) armed; غَيْر مُسَلَّحٍ unarmed; مُقاوَمة غَيْر مُسَلَّحةٍ unarmed resistance **2** (Tech) reinforced; إسْمَنْت \ باطون مُسَلَّح reinforced concrete

سُلَحْفاة *n* |سَلاحِف| turtle, tortoise

سَلَخَ *v* |a-u; سَلْخ| to skin, to flay; سَلَخَ جِلْداً to skin; سَلَخَ جِلْدَ أَرْنَبٍ to skin a rabbit; سَأَسْلَخُ جِلْدَهُ! I'll tan his hide!

تَسَلَّخَ *v* to peel

انْسَلَخَ *v* **1** [انْفَصَلَ] to come loose/off; to peel (off) **2** [مَضى] to pass/go by **3** [تَسَلَّخَ] to shed; تَنْسَلِخُ الحَيّةُ من جِلْدِها the snake sheds its skin **4** [انْسَحَبَ] |عن| to withdraw

انْسِلاخ *n* separation, detachment; alienation; metamorphosis

مَسْلَخ *n* |مَسالِخ| slaughterhouse, abattoir

سَلاطة n [1] [وَقاحة] impudence, impertinence, insolence; سَلاطة اللِسانِ incivility [2] [من خُضْرَواتٍ] see سلطة

سُلْطة n |سُلَط, سُلْطات, سُلُطات| [1] [حُكْم] authority, power, control; السُّلْطة المُطْلَقة absolute power; سُلْطة روحيّة \ زَمَنيّة religious/secular authority; السُّلْطة الحاكِمة the establishment; السُّلُطات العُلْيا the highest authorities; سُلْطة مَرْكَزيّة central government; سُلْطة تَشْريعيّة \ تَنْفيذيّة legislative/executive branch; السُّلْطة الأَبَويّة parental authority; patriarchal authority; تَسْليم السُّلْطةِ the transfer of power; تَفْريق \ فَصْل السُّلُطاتِ separation of powers; اسْتِغْلال السُّلْطةِ misuse of power; صاحِب السُّلْطةِ the ruler; انْتِقال السُّلْطةِ transfer of power; قاعِدة سُلْطةٍ power base; قاعِدة سُلْطةٍ عَريضة \ ضَيِّقة a broad/narrow power base; مارَسَ السُّلْطةَ to exercise authority; تَوَلّى السُّلْطةَ to hold power; تَمَتَّعَ بالسُّلْطةِ to have power; تَمَتَّعَ \ مارَسَ السُّلْطة القَضائيّة to exercise legal authority; كانَ في السُّلْطةِ to be in power; أَمْسَكَ بِزِمام السُّلْطةِ to seize power; حَدَّ من سُلْطةِ شَخْصٍ to curtail sb's power; تَنازَعَ \ تَصارَعَ من أَجْلِ السُّلْطةِ to struggle for power; صِراع \ نِزاع من أَجْلِ السُّلْطة power struggle; الاسْتِيلاء على السُّلْطةِ coup; اسْتِيلاء الجُنودِ على السُّلْطةِ a military coup; انْفِراد بالسُّلْطةِ autocracy; السُّلْطة على شَيْءٍ the power over sth; السُّلُطات [2] [هَيْئة حاكِمة] government, regime, authorities; السُّلُطات المَحَلّيّة the local authorities; سُلُطات وَطَنيّة national government; سُلْطة قَضائيّة judiciary; سُلْطة تَشْريعيّة legislature; سُلْطة حاكِمة government; السُّلُطات العامّة the public authorities [3] [صَلاحِية] competence; authority; سُلُطات واسِعة wide powers; سُلُطات مَمْنوحة powers granted; خَوَّلَ سُلُطاتٍ to empower; تَجاوَزَ سُلْطَتَهُ to go beyond one's authority; كانَ تحت السُّلْطةِ البَريطانيّة to fall under the British Crown; الشَّطَط في اسْتِعْمالِ السُّلْطةِ the misuse of authority

سُلْطَويّ adj authoritarian; *relating to power*

سَليط adj |سُلَطاءُ| impertinent; امْرَأة سَليطة scold; سَليط اللِسانِ sharp-tongued

تَسَلُّط n authority; حُبّ التَسَلُّطِ lust for power

تَسْليط n [1] [مَنْح سُلْطةٍ] authorizing [2] [الضَوْءِ] focusing, shedding; تَسْليط الضَوْءِ على شَيْءٍ shedding light on sth

مُتَسَلِّط adj authoritarian, domineering

مِسْلاط n projector

سَلَطة, سَلاطة[2] n salad; زَيْت السَلَطةِ salad dressing; سَلَطة خَضْراء a green salad

سَلْطَعون n crab

سُلْطان n |سَلاطينُ| [1] [حاكِم] sultan; ruler [2] [صَلاحيّة] authority; هذا شَيْءٌ ما أَنْزَلَ اللهُ بِهِ من سُلْطانٍ this is pure arbitrariness

سُلْطانيّ adj royal; *relating to the sultan*; مَرْسوم سُلْطانيّ royal decree

سُلْطانيّة n [1] [وِعاء] (salad) bowl [2] [مَدينة] Soltaniyeh (*city in Iran*)

سَلْطَنة n sultanate; سَلْطَنة عُمان the sultanate of Oman

سَلِعَ v |a; سَلَع| to crack, to split

سَلَّعَ v to crack, to split

تَسَلَّعَ v to chap (*skin*)

سِلْعة n |سِلَع| product; commodity; سِلَع goods; سِلَع اسْتِهْلاكيّة consumer goods; سِلْعة رائِجة a popular product

سِلَعيّ adj commercial; commodity (*before n*); صادِر سِلَعيّ commodity export

تَسَلُّع n chapping (*of the skin*)

سَلَفَ v |a; سَلَف| to be past; هذا كَلامٌ سَلَفَ ذِكْرُهُ this has already been said

سَلَّفَ v to lend; سَلَّفَ شَخْصاً مَبْلَغاً من المالِ to lend sb money

أَسْلَفَ v to lend, to advance

تَسَلَّفَ v to borrow

اسْتَلَفَ v to borrow; اسْتَلَفَ مَبْلَغاً (من المالِ) من شَخْصٍ to borrow a sum (of money) from sb

سَلَف n |أَسْلاف| [1] [جَدّ أَعْلى] ancestor, forefather; أَسْلاف ancestry [2] [في مَنْصِبٍ] predecessor; خَيْر خَلَفٍ لِخَيْرِ سَلَفٍ *a worthy successor* [3] [مُقَدَّم] advance; سَلَفاً in advance, beforehand, ahead of time; عَرَفَ شَيْئاً سَلَفاً to know sth in advance

سِلْف n |أَسْلاف| brother-in-law (*brother of one's spouse*)

سالِف [A] adj |سَوالِفُ, سُلّاف, سَلَف| previous, former, preceding; سالِفاً formerly; سالِف الذِكْرِ aforementioned [B] n |سَوالِفُ| sideburn

سِلْك *n* |أَسْلاك| ◀1▶ [خَيط مَعْدَنيّ] thread, string; wire, cable; line; سِلْك كَهْرَبائيّ cable; سِلْك نُحاسيّ \ حَديديّ \ فولاذيّ copper/iron/steel wire; سِلْك شائِك barbed wire; سِلْك مُقاوِم resistor ◀2▶ [هَيْئة] profession; سِلْك قَضائيّ judiciary; السِلْك السِياسيّ \ الدِبْلوماسيّ the political/diplomatic corps ◀3▶ [مِهْنة] career ◀4▶ [مَرْحَلة] (Mor) grade; السِلْك التَعْليميّ سِلْك الأَوَّل من التَعْليم الثانَويّ (Mor) the first stage of secondary education

سالِك A *adj* passable; دُروب \ طُرُق سالِكة passable roads B *n a person who follows the spiritual path*

سِلْكيّ *adj* by wire; اتِّصالات سِلْكيّة telecommunications

سُلوك *n* behaviour; سُلوك مُنْحَرِف \ غَيْر طَبيعيّ deviant behaviour; سُلوك إجْراميّ \ جانِح criminal/delinquent behaviour; سَليم السُلوكِ proper behavior; عُلوم السُلوكِ behavioural sciences; نَمَط سُلوكٍ behavioural pattern; مَبْدَأ السُلوكِ the behavioural norm; سوء سُلوكٍ misbehaviour; مُدَوَّنة (قَواعِد) ,مُذَكِّرة سُلوكٍ السُلوكِ code of conduct; أَخَلَّ بِمُذَكِّرةِ السُلوكِ to violate the code of conduct; شَهادة حُسْنِ سُلوكٍ certificate of good conduct; هو ذو سُلوكٍ حَسَنٍ he is well behaved

سُلوكيّ *adj* behavioural

لاسِلْكيّ *adj* wireless; radio (*before n*); هاتِف لاسِلْكيّ a cordless phone; عامِل لاسِلْكيّ radio operator; اتِّصالات لاسِلْكيّة wireless communications

مَسْلَك *n* |مَسالِكُ| ◀1▶ [طَريق] road, way, path; course, route; conduit; ضاقَتْ بِهِ المَسالِكُ he was at his wits' end ◀2▶ (Anat) passage; مَسالِك بَوْليّة urinary tract; إخْصائيّ المَسالِكِ البَوْليّة urologist; عِلْم المَسالِك البَوْليّة urology ◀3▶ [تَصَرُّف] behaviour

مَسْلَكيّ *adj* ◀1▶ [مِهْنيّ] professional; vocational; تَدْبير مَسْلَكيّ a professional measure ◀2▶ [سُلوكيّ] behavioural; تَغْيير مَسْلَكيّ behavioural change

سَلَّ *v* |u; سَلّ| ◀1▶ [سَيفاً] to pull out; سَلَّ سَيْفَهُ to unsheathe one's sword ◀2▶ [مَرَضٌ] سُلَّ to contract tuberculosis

تَسَلَّلَ *v* ◀1▶ [انْسَلَّ] to steal/sneak/slip in; تَسَلَّلَ إلى بَلَدٍ to enter a country illegally; تَسَلَّلَ وراء فَريسَتِهِ to stalk one's prey ◀2▶ [فَلَتَ] to sneak/steal away; تَسَلَّلَ بِهُدوءٍ to steal away quietly; تَسَلَّلَ في الوَقْتِ to slip away just in time

سُلْفة *n* |سُلَف| loan; advance; سُلْفة على الراتِبِ an advance on one's salary; طَلَبَ سُلْفةً to ask for a loan

سِلْفة *n* sister-in-law (*sister of one's spouse*)

سَلَفيّ *adj, n* Salafi, Salafist

سَلَفيّة *n* Salafism

تَسْليف *n* credit; loan; بَنْك \ مَصْرِف تَسْليفٍ lending bank

مِسْلَفة *n* cultivator, rotary tiller

سُلْفات *n* sulphate

إلْسَلْفادور *n* |f| El Salvador

سَلَقَ *v* |u; سَلْق| to boil; to poach; سَلَق بَطاطِسَ \ بَيْضاً to boil potatoes/eggs

تَسَلَّقَ *v* to climb; تَسَلَّقَ شَجَرةً to climb a tree; تَسَلَّقَ الجَبَلَ إلى قِمَّتِهِ to climb to the top of the mountain

سِلْق *n* (Swiss) chard (*Beta vulgaris*)

سُلاق *n* (Med) thrush, oral candidiasis; aphtha

سُلاّق *n* Ascension (of Jesus)

سَلوقيّ *adj, n* saluki (*breed of dog*)

سَليق *adj* cooked, boiled; نِصْف سَليقٍ half-cooked

سَليقة *n* ◀1▶ [طَبيعة] nature, disposition; instinct, intuition; بالسَليقةِ instinctively, intuitively; عَرَفَ شَيْئاً بالسَليقةِ to know sth intuitively ◀2▶ [لُغَويّة] (native speaker) intuition

تَسَلُّق *n* climbing, ascent; climb; تَسَلُّق الجَبَلِ الأَبْيَضِ the ascent of Mont Blanc

مُتَسَلِّق *n* climber; مُتَسَلِّق الجِبالِ mountaineer

مَسْلوق *adj* boiled; بَيْضة مَسْلوقة a boiled egg

سَلَكَ *v* |u; سُلوك| ◀1▶ [تَصَرَّفَ] to behave; سَلَكَ سُلوكاً جَيِّداً to behave well ◀2▶ [طَريقاً] to travel, to follow, to take; سَلَكَ مَسْلَكاً to follow a course; سَلَكَ الطَريقَ to follow a path; سَلَك طَريقَ الخَيْرِ to do good; سَلَكَ طُرُقاً جَديدةً to break new ground; سَلَكَ مَسْلَكَ شَخْصٍ to follow sb's example ◀3▶ [أَدْخَلَ] to insert

سَلَّكَ *v* to unblock; to disentangle; سَلَّكَ البالوعة to unclog the drain

أَسْلَكَ *v* to insert, to put in; أَسْلَكَ الخَيْطَ في الإبْرةِ to pass a thread through the needle

Muslim; to pretend to be religious/pious; الفَرْقُ بين المُسْلِمِ وَمَنْ يَتَأَسْلَمُ the difference between Muslims and those who pretend to be

سَلَّمَ *v* 1 [أعْطى] to hand in/over; to deliver; to produce, to submit; سَلَّمَ عُلْبَةً to deliver a parcel; سَلَّمَ نَفْسَهُ to surrender; سَلَّمَ شَخْصاً وَثائِقَ \ مُسْتَنَداتٍ to submit documents to sb; سَلَّمَ شَهادةً لِشَخْصٍ to present a certificate to sb; سَلَّمَ السُلْطَةَ إلى شَخْصٍ to hand over power to sb; سَلَّمَ شَخْصاً إلى بَلَدٍ آخَرَ to extradite sb to another country 2 [حَيّا] to send one's love/greetings; سَلَّمَ على شَخْصٍ to send sb one's love; سَلِّمْ لي على الأهْلِ say hello to the family for me 3 [رَضِيَ] to consent, to accept; سَلَّمَ بِشَيْءٍ to consent to sth 4 [اِسْتَسْلَمَ] to surrender; سَلَّمَ نَفْسَهُ للشُرْطَةِ to surrender to the police; سَلَّمَ أَمْرَهُ إلى اللهِ to entrust one's case to God 5 [خلّصَ] to preserve, to protect; صَلّى اللهُ عَلَيْهِ وَسَلَّمَ peace be upon him (*said after a prophet is mentioned*); اللهُ يُسَلِّمُكَ may God protect you (*response to* مع السَلامةِ); you're welcome (*response to* سَلِمَتْ يَداكَ); thank you (*response to* سَلامَتُكَ)

سالَمَ *v* to keep peace

أَسْلَمَ *v* 1 (Islam) to become a Muslim, to embrace Islam; أَوَّلُ مَنْ أَسْلَمَ the first to embrace Islam 2 [اِسْتَسْلَمَ] to surrender; أَسْلَمَ نَفْسَهُ إلى الشُرْطَةِ to give up the ghost; أَسْلَمَ روحَهُ to surrender to the police 3 [قَدَّمَ] to entrust; أَسْلَمَ أَمْرَهُ إلى اللهِ to entrust one's case to God

تَسَلَّمَ *v* 1 [تَلَقّى] to receive; to obtain, to get; تَسَلَّمَ رِسالةً to receive a letter 2 [تَقَبَّلَ] to accept; تَسَلَّمَ مَنْصِباً to accept a position

تَسالَمَ *v* to make peace with one another

اسْتَلَمَ *v* to receive; to obtain; اسْتَلَمَ شَيْئاً to accept delivery of sth; اسْتَلَمَ رِسالةً \ طَرْداً \ جائِزةً \ إرْثاً to receive a letter/parcel/award/inheritance

اسْتَسْلَمَ *v* to surrender, to submit, to yield, to give in; to resign oneself; اسْتَسْلَمَ لِشَيْءٍ to resign oneself to sth; اسْتَسْلَمَ لِقَدَرِهِ to resign oneself to one's fate; اسْتَسْلَمَ للاكْتِئابِ to give in to depression; اسْتَسْلَمَ للضَغْطِ to succumb to the pressure; اسْتَسْلَمَ للإغْراءِ to yield to the temptation; اسْتَسْلَمَ للأَمْرِ

انْسَلَّ *v* to sneak; to steal/sneak in; to steal away; انْسَلَّ بِسُرْعةٍ to sneak away quickly

اسْتَلَّ *v* to draw; اسْتَلَّ سَيْفَهُ to unsheath one's sword; اسْتَلَّ مُسَدَّسَهُ to draw one's gun

سُلّ, **سِلّ** *n* tuberculosis, TB, consumption (old use); عَدْوى السُلِّ TB infection; أُصيبَ بالسُلِّ to have/contract tuberculosis; كانَ مُصاباً بالسُلِّ he had TB; عانى من السُلِّ to suffer from tuberculosis

سُلالة *n* descent; family; سُلالات حَيَوانيّة \ نَباتيّة animal/plant species

سَلّة *n* |سِلال| 1 [قُفّة] basket; سَلّة فَراوْلةٍ \ تينٍ a basket of strawberries/figs; سَلّة المُهْمَلاتِ waste-paper basket (BrE), wastebasket (AmE); سَلّة من القَصَبِ a wicker basket 2 (Sport) basket; كُرة السَلّةِ basketball; لَعِبَ كُرةَ السَلّةِ to play basketball

سَليل *n* descendant, scion

سَليلة *n* 1 (Med) polyp 2 [اِبْنة] |سَلائِلُ| *female descendant*

تَسَلُّل *n* 1 [تَسَرُّب] infiltration 2 (Sport) offside; مَصْيَدة تَسَلُّلٍ offside trap; صَفَّرَ \ رَفَعَ الرايةَ للتَسَلُّلِ to whistle/raise the flag for offside; كانَ في مَوْقِفِ تَسَلُّلٍ to be offside

مُتَسَلِّل *n* intruder; اقْتَرَبَ مُتَسَلِّلاً to creep closer; كانَ مُتَسَلِّلاً (Sport) to be offside; مُتَسَلِّل لِأجْهِزةِ الكُمْبيوتَر hacker

مِسَلّة *n* |مَسالُّ, مِسَلّات| obelisk

مَسْلول *adj* tubercular, tuberculous

سَلِمَ *v* |a; سَلامة| 1 [أَمِنَ] to be safe 2 [كانَ خالِياً من] to be free 3 [مِن خَطَرٍ] to escape

Idiom سَلِمَتْ يَداكَ thank you (*said when sb brings or makes sth for you*)

تَأَسْلَمَ *v* 1 [أَسْلَمَ] to become a Muslim; يا مُلْحِدون: العالَمُ يَتَأَسْلَمُ atheists, the world is becoming Muslim 2 [صارَ إسْلامِيًّا] to be an Islamist; الشَعْبُ مُسْلِمٌ وَلَنْ يَتَأَسْلَمَ the people are Muslim but will not become Islamists 3 [تَبَنّى القِيَمَ الإسْلاميّةَ] to adopt the Islamic system; التَعْليمُ المَغْرِبيُّ يَتَأَسْلَمُ Morocco adopted the Islamic educational system 4 [تَدَيَّنَ] to become religious/pious; هل يَتَأَسْلَمُ شَعْبٌ أَمْ يَتَمَدْيَنُ؟ are the people becoming religious or are they becoming secular? 5 [ادَّعى الإسْلامَ] to pretend to be

2 [كَمال] integrity **3** [أَمْن] safety; سَلامَتُكَ! get well soon!; طَريق سَلامة المُرور traffic safety; حِزام سَلامةٍ safety belt; مع سَلامة الأَغْذِيةِ food safety; السَلامة! have a safe journey!; الحَمْدُ لله على السَلامةِ goodbye; رافَقَتْكَ السَلامةُ all the best; السَلامةِ thank God for your well-being (*said after a safe return from a journey*); إنَّهُ من أَجْلِ سَلامَتِكُمْ it is for your own safety

سُلامى *n* |f; سُلامَيات| phalanx, finger/toe bone

سُلَّمة *n* step, stair

سَلْمى *n* |f| Salma (*female given name*)

سِلْميّ *adj* peaceful, peaceable, peace (*before n*); حَلّ سِلْميّ a peaceful solution; تَسْوية سِلْميّة peace settlement; طاقة نَوَويّة سِلْميّة peaceful nuclear energy; تَفاوَضَ \ تَعايَشَ سِلْميًّا to negotiate/coexist peacefully

سِلْميّة *n* pacifism

سَليم *adj* |سُلَماءُ| **1** [سالِم] healthy; intact, complete, whole, sound; سَليم البِنْيَة \ الجَسَد able-bodied; تَرَكَ شَيْئاً سَليماً to leave sth intact; ظَلَّ \ بَقِيَ سَليماً to remain unharmed; غَيْر سَليمٍ bad; غَيْر سَليمٍ عَقْليًّا mentally deficient **2** [غَيْر مُتَضَرِّر] free; undamaged; سَليم من الأَمْراضِ free from disease **3** [صَحيح] correct; مَوْقِف \ تَصَرُّف سَليم a correct attitude/way of acting

سُلَيْمان *n* |dipt| Sulayman, Solomon (*male given name*); سَمَك سُلَيْمانَ salmon

اسْتِسْلام *n* **1** [لِلعَدُوّ] surrender, capitulation; اسْتِسْلام أَلْمانيا واليابان the surrender of Germany and Japan; وَقَّعَ الاسْتِسْلامَ to sign the surrender; أَلْزَمَ شَخْصاً بالاسْتِسْلامِ to force sb to surrender; الاسْتِسْلام للمُحْتَلِّ capitulation to the occupiers **2** [خُضوع] resignation, submission

اسْتِلام *n* **1** [تَلَقٍّ] receipt, receiving; accepting, assuming; اسْتِلام مَهامِّهِ assuming one's duties, taking office **2** [تَسْليم] transfer

إسْلام *n* Islam; دار الإسْلامِ the Islamic world; دارِس \ باحِث الإسْلامِ scholar of Islam; اعْتَنَقَ الإسْلامَ ,دَخَلَ في الإسْلامِ to convert to Islam

إسْلام أَباد *n* listed alphabetically

إسْلامَويّ *adj, n* Islamist

اسْتَسْلَمَ بعد إِلْحاحٍ طَويلٍ to reconcile oneself to the situation; to give in after much insistence

سُلَّم *n* |سَلالِمُ| **1** [دَرَج] stairs, staircase; ladder; سُلَّم حَلَزونيّ \ لَوْلَبيّ spiral staircase; سُلَّم كَهْرَبائيّ \ مُتَحَرِّك escalator; صَعِدَ \ نَزَلَ السُّلَّمَ to go up/down the stairs; تَسَلَّقَ \ صَعِدَ سُلَّماً to climb a ladder **2** [مِقْياس الرَسْمِ] scale; سُلَّم الرَواتِبِ \ الأُجورِ pay scale; سُلَّم ريخْتَر the Richter scale; حَسَبَ \ على سُلَّمٍ تَدْريجيٍّ on a sliding scale **3** (Mus) سُلَّم موسيقيّ scale **4** (fig) ladder, scale; السُلَّم الاجْتِماعيّ the social ladder

سِلْم *n* peace; أَوْقات السِلْمِ times of peace

سالِم *adj* **1** [آمِن] safe; sound; وَصَلَ سالِماً to arrive safely; عادَ سالِماً غانِماً to return safe and sound **2** (Ling) sound; جَمْع سالِم sound plural **3** [اسْم شَخْصيّ] Salim (*male given name*)

سَلام *n* **1** [تَحيّة] |سَلامات| *greeting*; السَلامُ عَلَيْكُم (وَرَحْمةُ اللهِ وَبَرَكاتُهُ) peace be with you (and God's mercy and blessings) (*a Muslim greeting*); وَعَلَيْكُم السَلامُ and with you be peace (*response to the greeting* السَلامُ عَلَيْكُمْ) **2** [أَمان] peace; سَلام عالَميّ world peace; عَمَليّة سَلامٍ peace process; مُحادَثات \ مُباحَثات سَلامٍ peace talks; مُؤْتَمَر سَلامٍ peace conference; مُبادَرة سَلامٍ peace initiative; مُفاوَضات سَلامٍ peace negotiations; مُشاوَرات سَلامٍ peace council; خُطّة سَلامٍ peace plan; اتِّفاقيّة سَلامٍ peace agreement; قوّات سَلامٍ peacekeeping force; دار السَلامِ Dar es Salaam (*former capital of Tanzania*); Paradise; *ancient name for Baghdad*; مَدينة السَلامِ *ancient name for Baghdad*; أَوْقات السَلامِ the times of peace; يا سَلامُ! how wonderful!; أَحَلَّ السَلامَ \ صَنَعَ to make peace; تَوَصَّلَ إلى اتِّفاقيّةِ \ حَقَّقَ \ أَرْسى سَلاماً to bring about peace; سَلامٍ to reach a peace agreement; مُنَظَّمة السَلامِ الأَخْضَرِ Greenpeace; عَلَيْهِ السَلامُ peace be upon him (*said when a prophet is mentioned*); عيسى \ إبْراهيم عَلَيْهِ السَلامُ Jesus/Abraham, peace be upon him; سَلامُ اللهِ على الأَنْبياءِ God's peace be upon the prophets; مُحِبّ للسَلامِ peaceful **3** (Islam) السَلام the Peace (*one of the names of God*)

سَلامة *n* **1** [جَوْدة] soundness; correctness; سَلامة النيّةِ good intentions; سَلامة الأُسْلوبِ والتَعْبيرِ correctness of usage

إسْلاميّ **A** *adj* Islamic; الشَريعة الإسْلاميّة the Islamic law

B *n* Islamist; الإسْلاميّونَ the Islamists

إسْلاميّة *n* Islamism

أَسْلَمة *n* islamisation; أَسْلَمة أوروبّا the islamisation of Europe

تَأَسْلُم *n* islamisation

تَسَلُّم *n* taking over; receipt

تَسْليم *n* **1** ◀ [تَقْديم] handing over, transfer; delivery; surrender; تَسْليم الرِسالةِ the delivery of the letter; تَسْليم الشهاداتِ \ الجَوائِزِ the presentation of the diplomas/awards; تَسْليم رُخَصِ السِياقةِ \ الجَوازاتِ the issue of drivers' licences/passports; اتِّفاق \ مُعاهَدة التَسْليم extradition treaty; اتِّفاق تَسْليمِ (المُجْرِمين) بين المَمْلَكةِ المُتَّحِدةِ وفَرَنْسا extradition treaty between the UK and France; طَلَب التَسْليمِ request for extradition; مُقابِلَ تَسْليمِ... upon receipt of... **2** ◀ [تَحيّة] greeting **3** ◀ [اسْتِسْلام] resignation, submission

لاسِلْم *n absence of peace*; حالة اللاسِلْم واللاحَرْب a state of neither peace nor war

مُتَأَسْلِم *n* a Muslim by conversion

مُسالِم *adj* peaceful, peaceable, peace-loving; مَلِك \ شَعْب مُسالِم a peace-loving ruler/people

مُسالَمة *n* conciliation

مُسْتَسْلِم *adj* resigned, submissive

مُسْتَلِم *n* recipient

مُسْلِم *n* Muslim; الإخْوان المُسْلِمونَ the Muslim Brotherhood (*Islamist political movement*)

مُسَلَّم *adj* مُسَلَّم بِهِ accepted, uncontested, indisputable; هذا مُسَلَّمٌ بِهِ that's indisputable; هذا شَيْءٌ مُسَلَّمٌ بِهِ there's no arguing about that; من المُسَلَّمِ بِهِ أنّ ... it's agreed upon that ...

مُسْلِمة *adj, n* Muslimah, Muslim (woman)

مُسَلَّمة *n* axiom, principle

‹ **سَلْمون** *n* salmon; سَلْمون طازَج fresh salmon; سَلْمون مُدَخَّن smoked salmon; شَريحة سَلْمون a salmon filet; عُلْبة سَلْمون a tin of salmon

‹ **سِلْهام** *n a long cloak with a pointed hood, worn in Morocco*

‹ **سَلا** **A** *v* |u; سُلْوان| |عن| to forget; سَلا عن شَيْءٍ \ شَخصٍ to forget sth/sb

B *n* listed alphabetically

سَلِيَ *v* |a; سُلِيّ| to forget

سَلّى *v* **1** ◀ [آنَس] to entertain, to amuse; سَلّى شَخْصاً to entertain sb; سَلّى ضُيوفَهُ to entertain one's guests; سَلّى جَماعةً to liven up a party; سَلّى شَخْصاً بِشَيْءٍ to entertain sb with sth; سَلَّتْهُ هذه الموسيقى he enjoyed this music **2** ◀ [عَزّى] to comfort, to console

أَسْلى *v* to make forget, to divert; to comfort, to console; أَسْلى شَخْصًا عن شَيْءٍ to divert sb from sth

تَسَلّى *v* to amuse oneself, to entertain oneself; to enjoy, to take pleasure (in); تَسَلّى بِشَيْءٍ to enjoy sth, to take pleasure in sth; to amuse oneself with sth

سُلْوان *n* solace, comfort

سَلْوة *n* consolation, solace, comfort

سَلْوى **A** *n* **1** ◀ [مُواساة] solace, comfort; وَجَدَ سَلْواهُ في شَيْءٍ to find comfort in sth **2** ◀ [اسْم شَخْصيّ] |f| Salwa (*female given name*)

B *n coll* (Zool) |سَلاوى; sing n سَلْواة| quail

تَسْلِية *n* |تَسالٍ, تَسْليات| entertainment, amusement, diversion, distraction, fun; مَرْكَز تَسْلِية entertainment centre; قَدَّمَ التَسْلِيةَ \ بَحَثَ عن التَسْلِيةِ to offer/seek diversion

مُسَلٍّ **A** *adj* entertaining, fun, amusing, pleasant, enjoyable; فيلْم \ كِتاب مُسَلٍّ an entertaining film/book; لُعْبة مُسَلِّية a fun game

B *n* entertainer

مَسْلاة *n* |مَسالٍ| (object of) amusement, entertainment, diversion

‹ **سِلَّور** *n* catfish

‹ **سْلوفاكيا** *n* Slovakia

سْلوفاكيّ **A** *adj* Slovak, Slovakian; اللُغة السْلوفاكيّة Slovak (*language*)

B *n* Slovak

‹ **سُلوفان, سِلوفان** *n* cellophane; وَرَق سِلوفان cellophane

‹ **سْلوفينيا** *n* Slovenia

سْلوفينيّ **A** *adj* Slovene, Slovenian; (اللُغة) السْلوفينيّة Slovene (*language*)

B *n* Slovene, Slovenian

‹ **سِلولوز** *n* cellulose

‹ **سِلولوِيْد** *n* celluloid

‹ **سَلَوِيّ** **A** *adj* (Bio) amniotic; كيس سَلَوِيّ amniotic sac; سائِل سَلَوِيّ amniotic fluid; حَيَوان سَلَوِيّ (Zool) amniote (*four-limbed animals possessing an amnion, including mammals, birds, and lizards*)

B *n* السَلَوِيّات amniotes

سَلًى *n* (Bio) amnion (*membrane enclosing an embryo or fetus*); كيس السَلّى amniotic sac

‹ **سِليكيّ** *adj* siliceous

‹ **سِليكون** *n* silicone

‹ **سم** *abbr* cm; عَرْضُهُ \ ارْتِفاعُهُ ٥ سم it is 5 cm wide/high

‹ **سَمامة** *n* (Zool) swift (*Apodidae*)

‹ **سَمْبوسة** *n* samosa (*a savory fried pastry, containing spiced vegetables or meat*)

‹ **سَمْت** *n* |سُموت| way, path; سَمْت الرَأْس (Astron) zenith

‹ **سِمة** *n* see وسم

‹ **سَمُجَ** *v* |u; سَماجة| to be ugly/repulsive

سَمِج *adj* |سَماجى| ugly; repulsive

‹ **سَمَحَ** *v* |a; سَماح| **1** [أَذِنَ] |ب| to allow, to permit; to authorize; سُمِحَ to be allowed; سَمَحَ بِأَنْ ... to allow that ...; سَمَحَ بِأَنْ يَفْعَلَ شَخْصٌ شَيْئاً to allow sb to do sth; لو سَمَحْتَ please; excuse me; إذا سَمَحْتَ لي excuse me; by your leave; أَتَسْمَحُ لي بِسُؤالٍ؟ may I ask you sth?; سَمَحَ لِنَفْسِهِ بِشَيْءٍ to permit oneself to do sth; سَمَحَ لِنَفْسِهِ بِقِسْطٍ من الراحة to allow oneself a bit of peace; سَمح لِبَلَد بالانْضِمامِ إلى الاتِّحادِ الأوروبّيّ to admit a country to the European Union; سَمَحَ بالدُخولِ to admit; سَمَحَ لِتِلْميذ بِدُخولِ المَدْرَسةِ to admit a student to a school; لا يُسْمَحُ لَنا بِأَنْ نَدْخُلَ هذا المَبْنى we are not allowed to enter this building; لا يُسْمَحُ بالتَدْخين smoking is prohibited; لا سَمَحَ اللّهُ God forbid; حتّى وَإِنْ كانَ الخَبَرُ سَيِّئاً لا سَمَحَ اللّهُ... even if, God forbid, the news were bad ... **2** [مَكَّنَ] |ب| enable, allow; تَسْمَحُ هذه الفُحوصاتُ بالكَشْفِ المُبَكِّرِ these tests enable early detection

سَمُحَ *v* |u; سَماحة, سَماح, سَمْح| to be generous/magnanimous

سامَحَ *v* to forgive; سامَحَ شَخْصاً على شَيْءٍ to forgive sb for sth; سامِحْني forgive me, I'm sorry; سامَحَهُ اللّهُ may God forgive him

تَسامَحَ *v* to tolerate, to endure, to bear; تَسامَحَ مع \ في شَيْءٍ to bear sth; تَسامَحَ مع سُلوكِ شَخْصٍ to tolerate sb's behaviour; لم يَتَسامَحْ مع هذا التَصَرُّفِ he could not put up with that behaviour

اسْتَسْمَحَ *v* to ask permission; to ask forgiveness, to apologize

سَمْح *adj* |سِماح| generous, magnanimous; tolerant

سَماح *n* permission; السَماح admission; سَماح بالدُخول بِدُخولِ اللاجِئينَ (إلى فَرَنْسا) the admission of asylum seekers (to France)

سَماحة *n* **1** [تَسامُح] kindness; اسْتَغَلَّ سَماحةَ شَخْصٍ to take advantage of sb's kindness **2** [لَقَب] eminence; سَماحة المُفْتي His Eminence the mufti

سَميح *adj* |سُمَحاءُ| **1** [سَمْح] generous, magnanimous **2** [اسْم شَخْصيّ] Samih (*male given name*)

سَميحة *n* |dipt| Samiha (*female given name*)

تَسامُح *n* tolerance, forbearance; عَدَم التَسامُح intolerance; عامَلَ شَخْصاً بِتَسامُحٍ to be accommodating towards sb; سِياسة التَسامُح policy of tolerance; التَسامُح مع آراءِ الغَيْرِ tolerance for other people's views

لاتَسامُح *n* intolerance

مُتَسامِح *adj* tolerant, forbearing, lenient; مَوْقِف مُتَسامِح a tolerant position; غَيْر مُتَسامِحٍ intolerant; مُجْتَمَع غَيْر مُتَسامِحٍ an intolerant society; سُلوك غَيْر مُتَسامِحٍ intolerant behaviour; كانَ مُتَسامِحاً مع شَخْصٍ to be tolerant of/ towards sb

مَسْموح *adj* permissible, permitted, allowed; غَيْر مَسْموحٍ بِهِ forbidden; الحَدّ المَسْموح بِهِ the (allowed) limit

‹ **سَمَّدَ** *v* to fertilize; to manure; to compost; سَمَّدَ الأَرْض to fertilize the land; سَمَّدَ النُفاياتِ to compost waste

سَماد *n* |أَسْمِدة| fertilizer; dung; compost; سَماد نَباتيّ vegetable compost; سَماد طَبيعيّ natural fertilizer; سَماد سائِل liquid fertilizer; سَماد فوسْفاتيّ \ كيمِيائيّ phosphate/chemical fertilizer; أَسْمِدة حَيَوانيّة \ عُضْويّة manures/organic fertilizers

تَسْميد *n* fertilizing; composting; تَسْميد الأَرْضِ fertilizing the land; الإفْراط في التَّسْميدِ excessive use of fertilizer

2‹ **سَميد** *n* semolina

1‹ **سَمَرَ** *v* |u; سَمَر| to talk/chat (*into the evening/night*)

سَمُرَ *v* |u; سُمْرة| to be brown (*in complexion*); to tan

سَمَّرَ *v* to nail, to fasten with a nail

سامَرَ *v* to talk/chat (*into the evening/night*)

تَسَمَّرَ *v* ① [أَصْبَحَ أَسْمَرَ] to tan ② [ثَبَّتَ بِمِسْمارٍ] to be nailed down; (*fig*) to be glued/rooted/riveted; تَسَمَّرَ في مَكانِهِ to be rooted to the spot; تَسَمَّرَ أمام شاشةِ التِلْفِزيون to be glued to the TV

تَسامَرَ *v* to talk/chat (*into the evening/night*)

اسْمَرَّ *v* to be brown (*in complexion*); to tan

سَمَر *n* ① [حَديث لَيْليّ] conversation (*during the evening/at night*) ② [اسْم شَخْصيّ] |f| Samar (*female given name*)

سَمُر *n coll* |أَسْمُر| acacia tree

سُمْرة *n* brownness (*of complexion*)

سَمّور *n* see سمور

سَمير *n* ① [مُسامِر] *a companion in night-time entertainment, a conversation partner* ② [اسْم شَخْصيّ] Samir (*male given name*)

أَسْمَر *adj* |dipt; سُمْر| brown; dark, olive (*complexioned*); خُبْز أَسْمَر brown bread; رَجُل أَسْمَر a dark-skinned/olive-skinned man; القارّة السَمْراء the Dark Continent (*Africa*); أَسْمَر فاتِح light brown

اسْمِرار *n* suntan

مُسامِر *n companion in night-time entertainment*

مِسْمار *n* |مَساميرُ| ① [وَتِد] nail; tack; مِسْمار بِرْشام rivet; مِسْمار صَدِئ a rusty nail; قَلَعَ مِسْماراً to pull out a nail; مِطْرَقة وَمَسامير a hammer and nails ② [في القَدَمِ] corn; مِسْمار القَدَمِ a corn (on one's foot)

مِسْماريّ *adj* ① [حُروف \ كِتابة] cuneiform, wedge-shaped; كِتابة مِسْمارِيّة cuneiform (script) ② (*Mil*) flechette; قَذيفة مِسْمارِيّة flechette artillery

مُسْمَرّ *adj* tanned, browned

2‹ **سَمار** *n* (*Bot*) rush (*Juncus*)

‹ **سَمَرْقَنْد** *n* |f| Samarkand (*city in Uzbekistan*)

‹ **سَمْسَرَ** *v* to act as a broker/middleman

سِمْسار *n* |سَماسِرة| broker, middleman, agent; سِمْسار أَسْهُمٍ stockbroker; سِمْسار عَقارٍ estate agent (BrE), real estate agent (AmE)

سَمْسَرة *n* brokerage; سَمْسَرة عَقارِيّة estate brokerage (BrE), real estate agency (AmE); شَرِكة سَمْسَرة brokerage firm

‹ **سَمْسَق, سُمْسُق** *n* marjoram

‹ **سِمْسِم** *n* sesame; حَبّ السِمْسِمِ sesame seeds; افْتَحْ يا سِمْسِم! open, Sesame!

‹ **سِمْط** *n* |سُموط| thread (*of a necklace*)

سِماط *n* |سِماطات, سُمُط, أَسْمِطة| *cloth on which food is served*; meal; مَدَّ السِماطَ to set the table

‹ **سَمِعَ** *v* |a; سَمْع, سَماعة| ① [بالأُذُنِ] to hear; to learn, to be told; to listen, to pay attention; سَمِعَ صَوْتاً to hear a sound; سَمِعَ أَنّ ... to hear that ...; لا يُسْمَعُ inaudible; لم أَسْمَعْ عَنْهُ أَبَداً I've never heard of him ② [الدُعاءَ] to hear, to answer; سَمِعَ دُعاءً to hear a prayer ③ [اسْتَنْطَقَ] to hear; سَمِعَ شَهادةَ شاهِدٍ to hear a witness's testimony; سَمِعَ الشُرْطيُّ شَهادةَ المُتَّهَمِ the policeman took a statement from the suspect

سَمَّعَ *v* to recite; to make/let hear; سَمَّعَ شَخْصاً الموسيقى to let sb hear the music

أَسْمَعَ *v* to let hear; to let know

تَسَمَّعَ *v* to listen; to eavesdrop; تَسَمَّعَ من وَراءِ البابِ to listen at the door

تَسامَعَ *v* تَسامَعَ بِهِ الناسُ people have heard of him, word about him got around

اسْتَمَعَ *v* |ل, إلى| to listen; to hear; to eavesdrop; اسْتَمَعَ ل \ إلى شَيْءٍ \ شَخْصٍ to listen to sth/sb; اسْتَمَعَ إلى الرادِيو to listen to the radio; اسْتَمَعَ إلى رَأْيِ شَخْصٍ to listen to sb's opinion; اسْتَمَعَت المَحْكَمةُ لِشَهادَتِهِ the court heard his testimony; اسْتَمَعَ بِانْتِباهٍ \ بِاهْتِمام to listen carefully/attentively

سَمْع *n* |أَسْماع| (sense of) hearing; ear; ضَعيف السَمْعِ hearing-impaired; ثَقيل السَمْعِ hard of hearing; رَهافة السَمْعِ a fine sense of hearing; كانَ لَدَيْهِ سَمْعٌ قَوِيٌّ \ مُرْهَفٌ he had a sharp ear; كانَ مُمْتِعاً \ مُنْفِراً للأَسْماعِ to be a delight/grate on the ear; أَرْعى شَخْصاً سَمْعَهُ to listen to sb; اسْتَرَقَ السَمْعَ to eavesdrop, to listen in, to intercept; نَفَرَتْ مِنْهُ الأَسْماعُ a terrible sound; تحت سَمْعي وَبَصَري right under my very nose; سَمْعاً وَطاعةً at your service; your wish is my command

سامِع *n* listener, hearer

سَماع *n* ⓵ [اِسْتِماع] hearing; سَبَقَ لي سَماعُ ذلك that sounds familiar to me ⓶ [في اللُغةِ] *generally accepted usage*

سَمّاعة *n* speaker; السَمّاعات speakers; headphones; سَمّاعة رَأْسٍ headphones, earphones; سَمّاعة طَبيبٍ stethoscope; سَمّاعاتُ الأُذُنِ hearing aid; earphones; سَمّاعة هاتِفٍ (telephone) receiver; رَفَعَ السَمّاعةَ to pick up the receiver

سَماعِيّ *adj* auricular; acoustic; شَهادة سَماعيّة hearsay evidence

سُمْعة *n* reputation, name, standing; سُمْعة عالَمِيّة worldwide fame; رَديء السُمْعةِ notorious; تَمَتَّعَ بِسُمْعةٍ جَيِّدةٍ \ سَيِّئةٍ to have a good/bad reputation; كانَ حَسَنَ \ سَيِّئَ السُمْعةِ to be reputable/disreputable; أَضَرَّ بِسُمْعةِ شَخْصٍ to damage sb's reputation; حافَظَ على سُمْعَتِهِ to live up to one's name; أَنْقَذَ سُمْعَتَهُ to save face; لَطَّخَ \ شَوَّهَ سُمْعةَ شَخْصٍ to discredit sb; أَساءَ إلى سُمْعةِ شَخْصٍ to injure sb's good name; مُشَوِّه للسُمْعةِ slanderer

سَمْعِيّ *adj* acoustic, auditory, auditive, aural; سَمْعِيّ بَصَرِيّ audiovisual; أَجْهِزة \ وَسائِل سَمْعِيّة بَصَرِيّة audiovisual equipment/aids

سَميع *n* |سُمَعاءُ| listener, hearer; السَميع the All-Hearing (*one of the names of God*)

اِسْتِماع *n* listening; examination; مَهارة الاِسْتِماعِ listening skills; جَلْسة اسْتِماعٍ a hearing

مُسْتَمِع *n* listener, hearer; مُسْتَمِعونَ audience; أَعِزّائي المُسْتَمِعينَ dear audience

مَسْمَع *n* earshot; على مَسْمَعٍ within earshot; على مَرْأى وَمَسْمَعِ الجَميعِ audible and visible to everyone

مِسْمَع *n* |مَسامِعُ| hearing; ear; وَصَلَ إلى مَسامِعي أنّ... it has come to my attention that...

مَسْموع *adj* audible; مَسْموع الكَلِمةِ *one whose words carry weight;* غَيْر مَسْموعٍ inaudible; مَرْئِيّ وَمَسْموع audiovisual, AV; مَسْموع بِوُضوحٍ \ بالكادِ clearly/barely audible

‹ **سَمْفونيّة, سِمْفونيّة** *n* symphony

سِمْفونيّ, سيمْفونيّ *adj* symphonic, symphony (*before n*); موسيقى سِمْفونيّة symphony music

‹1 **سَمَقَ** *v* |u; سُموق| to be/become high

سامِق *adj* |سَوامِقُ| high, lofty, towering; عُلُوّ سامِق high altitude

سُموق *n* height

‹2 **سُماق** *n* sumac (*Rhus*); sumac (*a spice made from the red berries of some varieties of sumac*)

‹ **سَمَك** *n coll* |أَسْماك, سِماك| fish; سَمَك موسى sole (*Solea solea*); plaice (*Pleuronectes platessa*); سَمَك المِياهِ العَذْبةِ freshwater fish; بائِع سَمَكٍ fishmonger, fish seller; طَبَق \ صَحْن سَمَكٍ fish dish; حَوْض السَمَكِ fish tank, fishbowl; زَعانِف سَمَكةٍ fish fins; حَساء السَمَكِ fish soup; شَوْكة السَمَكِ fish bone; صَيْد السَمَكِ fishing; صَيّاد سَمَكٍ fisherman; أَدَوات صَيْدِ السَمَكِ fishing gear; شَبَكة صَيْدِ السَمَكِ fishing net; سَفينة \ قارِب صَيْدِ السَمَكِ fishing boat; اِصْطادَ أَسْماكاً \ سَمَكاً to catch fish; قَلى \ نَظَّفَ \ طَبَخَ السَمَكَ to fry/clean/cook fish; باعَ السَمَكَ في البَحْرِ to count one's chickens before they're hatched; نَوْع من السَمَكِ fish species

Idiom عَيْن سَمَكةٍ corn (*on one's foot*)

سُمْك *n* thickness; كم سُمْكُ هذه اللَوْحةِ؟ how thick is this board?

سَمّاك *n* fishmonger, fish seller

سَماكة *n* thickness; سَماكة الجِدارِ the thickness of the wall; سَماكة الثَلْجِ the depth of the snow; بَلَغَتْ سَماكَتُها مِتْراً واحِداً to be one meter thick

سَمَكِيّ *adj* fish (*before n*); مَزْرَعة سَمَكِيّة fish farm; ثَرْوة سَمَكِيّة fisheries; fishing resources

سَميك *adj* thick, heavy; كِتاب سَميك a thick book; مِعْطَف \ كَنْزة سَميك(ة) a heavy coat/sweater

مَسْمَكة *n* |مَسامِكُ| ⓵ [حَوْض] fish pond; fish hatchery ⓶ [مَكان بَيْعِ السَمَكِ] fish shop

‹ **سَمْكَرة** *n* metalwork; وَرْشة سَمْكَرةٍ body shop

سَنْكَرِيّ, سَمْكَرِيّ *n* tinsmith; plumber

سَمَلَ *v* |a; سُمول| to be/become worn/ragged

أَسْمَلَ *v* to be worn-out, to be tattered

سَمَل *n* |أَسْمال| worn-out clothing, rag, tatters; أَسْمال بالِية rags; ارْتَدى أَسْمالاً بالِيةً to be dressed in rags

سَمَّ *v* |u; سَمّ| to poison

سَمَّمَ *v* to poison; سَمَّمَ ضَحِيَّةً to poison a victim; سَمَّمَ الطَّعامَ to poison the food; سَمَّمَ الجَوَّ \ عَلاقةً to poison the atmosphere/a relationship

تَسَمَّمَ *v* to be poisoned

سامّ *adj* |سَوامُّ| poisonous, toxic; مَوادّ سامّة toxic substances; نُفاية سامّة toxic waste; هُجوم بالغازاتِ السامّةِ an attack with poison gas

سَمّ, سُمّ, سِمّ *n* [1] |سِمام, سُموم| [مادّة سامّة] poison, toxin; سُمّ قاتِل \ سَريع المَفعولِ deadly/quick-acting poison; سُمّ الأَفْعى \ الثُّعْبانِ \ الحَيّةِ snake venom; سَمّ الحِمارِ oleander (*Nerium oleander*); عِلْم السُمومِ toxicology; بَلَعَ سُمًّا to take poison; دَسَّ السَّمَّ في الدَّسَمِ to conspire; وَضَعَ السُمَّ في الدَسَمِ *to offer sth harmful in an attractive way* [2] |سِمام, سُموم| [ثُقْب] small hole; سَمّ الإِبْرةِ the eye of a needle [3] |مَسامّ, مَسامّات| [في البَشْرة] pore; مَسامّ مَسْدودة blocked pores

سَمامة *n* listed alphabetically

سَموم *n* simoom (*a hot desert wind*)

سُمِّيّة *n* toxicity

تَسَمُّم *n* |تَسَمُّمات| poisoning; تَسَمُّم حادّ acute poisoning; تَسَمُّم الدَمِ blood poisoning; تَسَمُّم الحَمْلِ eclampsia; pre-eclampsia; تَسَمُّم غِذائيّ food poisoning; أُصيبَ بِتَسَمُّمٍ غِذائيٍّ to contract food poisoning; ماتَ بالتَسَمُّمِ to die of poisoning

تَسْميم *n* poisoning

مَسامّ *n pl* |dipt| pores; مَسامّ مَسْدودة blocked pores

مَسامّيّ *adj* porous

مَسْموم *adj* poisoned; هَدِيّة مَسْمومة a poisoned gift; (fig) a dangerous development; ماتَ مَسْموماً to die of poison

سَمِنَ *v* |a; سِمَن, سَمانة| to put on weight

سَمَّنَ *v* to fatten (up), to make fat; سَمَّنَ خَروفاً to fatten a sheep; سَمَّنَ البَقَرَ to fatten up the cows; سَمِّنْ كَلْبَكَ يَأْكُلْكَ to get small thanks for one's pains

أَسْمَنَ *v* to fatten

سَمْن *n* |سُمون| clarified butter, ghee; fat; سَمْن نَباتيّ margarine; shortening; قَلى شَيْئاً في السَمْنِ to fry sth (in fat)

Idiom سَمْن على عَسَلٍ perfect, great

سَمانة *n* سَمانة الرِجْلِ calf (*of the leg*)

سُمانى *n* |f; سُمانَيات| quail; *Phasianidae*

سَمْنة *n* clarified butter, ghee

سُمْنة *n* thrush (*Turdidae*)

سِمْنة *n* fatness, obesity; سِمْنة مُفْرِطة obesity

سَمين *adj* |سِمان|; overweight, corpulent, fat; obese; بَطْن سَمين a large belly

مُسَمَّن *adj* fat

سَمَنْجونيّ *adj* sky-blue, azure

سَمَنْدَر, سَمَنْدَل *n* salamander (*Caudata*); سَمَنْدَل الماءِ newt (*Salamandridae*)

سَما *v* |u; سُموّ| [1] [ارْتَفَعَ] to rise, to go up [2] [طَمَحَ] |إلى| to strive [3] [تَرَفَّعَ] |عن| to be too high/difficult; to exceed

سامى *v to seek to surpass*

أَسْمى *v* to raise, to elevate

تَسامى *v* to tower, to rise, to reach high

سُموّ *n* highness, loftiness, exaltedness; صاحِب \ صاحِبة السُموِّ His/Her Highness; صاحِب السُموِّ المَلَكيِّ \ المَلِك \ الأَمير His Royal Highness

سامٍ A *adj* |سُماة| high, elevated, exalted; مُوَظَّف سامٍ \ وَظيفة سامِية a high-ranking official/position

B *n* |سُماة| noble

سامي *n* Sami (*male given name*)

سَماء *n* |mf; سَماوات| [1] [جَلَد] heaven, sky; firmament; سَماء غائِمة cloudy sky; سَماء صافِية \ زَرْقاء \ رَمادِيّة \ داكِنة a clear/blue/grey/dark sky; رَفَعَ يَدَيْهِ إلى السَماءِ to throw up one's hands; (كانَ) في السَماءِ (to be) in the sky; سَماء مَليئة بالنُجومِ a star-studded sky [2] [جَنّة] heaven; كانَ في السَماءِ السابِعةِ to be in seventh heaven; يا لَلْسَماءِ good heavens; بِحَقِّ السَماءِ for heaven's sake; هِبة من السَماءِ manna from heaven

تَفْضِيلٍ comparative; superlative; اسْم اسْتِفْهامٍ interrogative; اسْم الفِعْلِ verbal noun, gerund; اسْم الفاعِلِ the active participle; اسْم المَفْعولِ the passive participle; اسْم الإشارةِ the demonstrative pronoun; اسْم عَلَمٍ proper name; اسْم جِنْسٍ generic noun; اسْم جَمْعٍ collective/mass noun; اسْم مَعْنًى abstract noun; اسْم مَكانٍ toponym

اسْميّ *adj* in name only; nominal; القيمة الاسْميّة لِأَسْهُم the nominal value of shares; جُمْلَة اسْميّة (Gram) nominal sentence

تَسْمِية *n* naming; nomenclature; name, designation, title; أَطْلَقَ تَسْمِيةً على شَخْصٍ to name sb; تَسْمِيةً عَرَبيّة لِشَيْءٍ an Arabic name for sth

مُسَمًّى **A** *adj* named, called; so-called; غَيْر مُسَمًّى indefinite; المَحَلُّ مُغْلَقٌ إلى أَجَلٍ غَيْرِ مُسَمًّى the shop is closed until further notice

B *n* **1** (Ling) denotation **2** (Math) coefficient **3** [اِسْم] name

‹ **سَنَة** *n* |سَنَوات, سِنونَ, سِنينَ| year; سَنَة ... in the year ...; في سَنَة ٥٠ ميلاديّة year of the Christian era, AD; سَنَة ميلاديّة in AD 50; سَنَة هِجْرِيّة anno Hegira, AH (*in the Muslim era*); سَنَة شَمْسيّة transitional year; سَنة كبيسة leap year; سَنَة انْتِقاليّة solar year; سَنَة ضَوْئيّة light year; سَنة ماليّة, سَنَة ضَريبيّة fiscal year; السَنة الماليّة الجارِية the current fiscal year; انْتِهاء السَنَةِ الماليّةِ (بالرِبح \ الخسارةِ) closing the fiscal year (with a profit/loss); سَنة دِراسيّة school/academic year; السَنة الدِراسيّة ٢٠١٣–٢٠١٤ academic year 2013-2014; السَنة الدِراسيّة الجَديدة \ القادِمة \ الجارِية the new/next/current school year; سَنة الوَفاةِ the year of sb's death; نِصْف سَنةٍ half a year; وِزْر \ عِبْء السِنينِ the burden of the years; رَأْس السَنةِ \ العامِ New Year; احْتَفَلَ بِرَأْسِ السَنةِ to celebrate the New Year; طالِب السَنةِ الأولى a first-year student; لِمُدّةِ سَنَتَيْنِ for two years; لِمُدّةِ سَنةٍ واحِدةٍ for one year; عَقْد \ مَشْروع لِمُدّةِ سَنةٍ (واحِدةٍ) a one-year contract/project; في سِنِّ ٣٤ at the age of 34; كُلَّ سَنةٍ وَأَنْتَ طَيِّبٌ \ بِخَيْرٍ many happy returns; سَنةً بعد سَنةٍ year after year; بعد سَنَواتٍ مُتَتالِيةٍ after consecutive years; على مَدى سِنينَ for years on end; على مَدارِ السَنةِ throughout the year; بِنْت لَها ثَلاثُ سَنَواتٍ a three-year-old girl; دِراسة من ثَلاثِ سَنَواتٍ a three-year

سَمائيّ *adj* heavenly

سَماويّ *adj* **1** [مَنْسوب إلى السَماءِ] heavenly; divine **2** [لَوْن] sky-blue, azure; أَزْرَق سَماويّ sky-blue

أَسْمَى *adj* higher, above; more exalted

مُتَسامٍ *adj* maximized

‹ **سَمّور** *n* |سَماميرُ| (Zool) sable (*Martes zibellina*)

‹ **سَمّى** *v* **1** [دَعا] to name, to call; to title, to entitle; سُمِّيَ to be called; ما يُسَمّى ب so-called; ما يُسَمّى بالحَرْبِ على الإرْهابِ the so-called 'war on terror'; يُسَمّى مُحَمَّداً \ بِمُحَمَّدٍ his name is Muhammad; تُسَمّى تِلْكَ المادّةُ عَنْبَراً that substance is called ambergris; سَمَّتْ ابْنَتَها لَيْلى she named her daughter Layla; سَمّى ابْنَهُ على أَبِيهِ he named his son after his father **2** [عَيَّنَ] to nominate, to name; سَمّى شَخْصاً لِمَنْصِبٍ to nominate sb for a post **3** [ذَكَرَ اسْمَ اللهِ] *to invoke God; to say the words* بِسْمِ اللهِ (*in the name of God*)

تَسَمّى *v* to be called/named; تَسَمّى بِاسْمٍ to be called a name

سَمِيّ *n* namesake

سُمَيّة *n* |dipt| Sumayya (*female given name*)

اسْم *n* |أَسْماء, أَسامٍ| **1** [تَسْمِية] name; اسْم عائِليّ family name; اسْم مُمْتَدّ extended name; الأَسْماء الحُسْنى the most beautiful names (*the 99 names/attributes of God*); اسْم شَخْصِيّ first name; بِاسْمِهِ الشَخْصِيِّ personally; اسْم مُسْتَعار pseudonym; (نَشَرَ) بِاسْمٍ مُسْتَعارٍ (to publish) under a pseudonym; اسْم ثُلاثيّ full name (*name followed by the name of the father and grandfather*); بِاسْمِهِ الثُلاثيِّ by one's full name; اسْم التَنْصير baptismal name; بِاسْمِ ... on behalf of ...; بِاسْمِ شَخْصٍ for sb; بِاسْمِ المُديرِ on the authority of the director; بِاسْمِ القانونِ in the name of the law; بِاسْمِهِ الحَقيقيِّ under one's own name; بِسْمِ اللهِ الرَحْمنِ الرَحيمِ in the name of God, the Compassionate, the Merciful (*said at the beginning of a letter, lecture, lesson, etc.*); طَرَحَ اسْماً to put forward a name; عَرَفَ شَخْصاً بالاسْمِ to know sb by name; نادى شَخْصاً بِاسْمِهِ to call sb by their first name; طَلَبَ عَدَمَ الكَشْفِ عن اسْمِهِ he wished to remain anonymous; كانَ اسْمُهُ جورج his name was George; ما اسْمُكَ؟ what's your name?; اسْمُهُ فادي his name is Fadi **2** (Gram) noun, adjective; اسْم تَصْغيرٍ diminutive; اسْم

training; النِصْف الأوَّل \ الثاني من السَنَةِ the first/second six months

سَنَوِيّ *adj* annual, yearly; سَنَوِيًّا yearly, annually; كِتاب سَنَوِيّ yearbook; نِصْف سَنَوِيّ half-yearly

سَنا *n* (Bot) *Senna*

سَناتور, **سِيناتور** *n* senator

سُنْبوق *n* |سَنابيقُ| skiff, boat

سُنْبُك *n* |سَنابِكُ| (Tools) punch, awl, perforator

سُنْبُل *n coll* |سَنابِلُ| ear, spike (*of grain*)

سِنة *n* see وسن

سِنْت *n* cent

سِنْترال *n* (telephone) exchange

سَنْتِلِتْر, **سَنْتيلِتْر** *n* |سَنْتِلِتْرات| centilitre

سَنْتِمِتْر, **سَنْتيمِتْر** *n* |سَنْتِمِتْرات| centimetre

سَنْتيم *n* |سَنْتيمات| centime

سِناج *n* |أَسْنِجة, سُنُج| soot

سِنْجاب *n* |سَناجِبُ, سَناجيبُ| squirrel

سَنْجَق *n* sanjak (*administrative district in the Ottoman Empire*); flag, standard

سَنَحَ *v* |a; سُنْح, سُنُح, سُنوح| 1 [أُتيحَ] to present itself, to come; سَنَحَتْ لَهُ الفُرْصةُ ل \ أنْ ... he had the opportunity to ... 2 [خَطَرَ] to occur

سانِح *adj* |سَوانِحُ| favourable, auspicious; فُرْصة سانِحة a good opportunity

سانِحة *n* |سَوانِحُ| opportunity, chance

سِنْخ *n* |أَسْناخ, سُنوخ| 1 [في الرِئَتَيْن] alveolus; سِنْخ رِئَوِيّ (pulmonary) alveolus 2 [السِنّ] root, socket (*of a tooth*) 3 [أَصْل] origin, root

سَنَدَ *v* |u; سُنود| 1 [دَعَمَ] to support, to prop, to back; تَسْنُدُ الأَعْمِدةُ الجِسْرَ the pillars support the bridge 2 [اِتَّكَأَ] to lean; سَنَدَ إلى حائِطٍ to lean against a wall

سَنَّدَ *v* to support, to prop

سانَدَ *v* to support, to back, to assist, to help; سانَدَ شَخْصاً to support sb; سانَدَ الجَيْش to support the army; سانَدَ فَريقَ كُرةِ القَدَمِ to back a football (BrE) soccer (AmE) team

أَسْنَدَ *v* 1 [نَسَبَ] to attribute, to ascribe; أَسْنَدَ شَيْئاً إلى شَخْصٍ to attribute sth to sb; أَسْنَدَ الحَديثَ إلى الوَزيرِ to attribute a statement to the minister 2 [اِتَّكَأَ] to lean; أَسْنَدَ الرَجُلُ رَأْسَهُ على حافةِ الأَريكةِ the man rested his head on the edge of the sofa 3 [عَهِدَ] to entrust, to put in charge; أَسْنَدَ إلى شَخْصٍ مُهِمّةً to entrust sb with a task; أُسْنِدَ إلَيَّ عَمَلٌ I was put in charge of a job

تَسانَدَ *v* 1 [تَآزَرَ] to support/help one another 2 [اِسْتَنَدَ] to lean; تَسانَدَ إلى شَيْءٍ to lean on sth

اِسْتَنَدَ *v* |إلى| to lean, to rest, to support; to be based; اِسْتَنَدَ إلى شَيْءٍ to lean/rest on sth; to be based on sth; اِسْتَنَدَ إلى طاوِلةٍ to lean on a table; اِسْتَنَدَ إلى وَقائِعَ to be based on facts; اِسْتَنَدَ إلى الأُسِّ to rest on a foundation

سَنْد *n* support

سَنَد *n* |أَسْناد, سَنَدات| 1 [دِعامة] support, prop, stay, pillar 2 [مُساعَدة] support, help 3 [شَخْص] pillar; كانَ سَنَداً لِنادينا he was the pillar of our club 4 [وَثيقة] document; bill; سَنَد الشَحْنِ bill of lading 5 (Busn) bond; سَنَد الخَزينةِ \ الحُكومةِ treasury/government bond; سوق السَنَداتِ bond market; سَنَد لِحامِلِهِ a bond payable to bearer; قَرْض بِسَنَداتٍ bond loan; اِشْتَرى \ باعَ سَنَداتٍ to buy/sell bonds; أَصْدَرَ سَنَداتٍ to issue bonds 6 (Islam) attribution (*of a Hadith, beginning with the source and continuing in a chain back to the prophet Muhammad*)

سِناد *n* crutch

اِسْتِناد *n* |اِسْتِنادات| leaning; اِسْتِناداً إلى ... based on ...

إِسْناد *n* |أَسانيدُ| 1 [تَكْليف] assignment; إِسْناد مُهِمّةٍ \ مَنْصِبٍ (إلى شَخْصٍ) assignment of a task/position (to sb) 2 [إِشارة] reference; إِسْناد تَرافُقِيّ cross-reference 3 (Islam) attribution (*of a Hadith, beginning with the source and continuing in a chain back to the prophet Muhammad*)

مُسانِد *n* assistant, second

مُسانَدة *n* support, backing, aid; سانَدَ شَخْصاً مُسانَدةً مالِيّةً to give sb financially backing

مُسْتَنَد *n* |مُسْتَنَدات| 1 [وَرَقة] document, paper; proof; مُسْتَنَدات documents, documentation; records 2 (Comput) file

مُسْنَد A *adj* ascribed; قُروض مُسْنَدة إلى loans granted; مُسْنَد إلى شَخْصٍ ascribed to sb; التُهْمة المُسْنَدة إلَيْه the charges against him; الجُرْم المُسْنَد إلَيْهِ the crime ascribed to him
B *n* |مَسانِدُ| (Gram) predicate

مِسْنَد, مَسْنَد *n* |مَسانِدُ| support; rest, back; مِسْنَد المَقْعَد the back of a chair; مِسْنَد الرَّأْسِ \ اليَد headrest/armrest; مِسْنَد رَسّامٍ easel; دَرَج بِمَسانِدَ \ بِلا مَسانِدَ a staircase with/without a handrail; كُرْسيّ بِمَسانِدَ \ بِلا مَسانِدَ a chair with/without arms

مَسْنود *adj* supported

سَنْدان, سِنْدان *n* |سَنادِينُ| 1 (Tools) anvil; وَقَعَ بين المِطْرَقة والسِّنْدانِ to be between a rock and a hard place 2 (Anat) سِنْدان الأُذُنِ incus

السِنْدِباد *n* السِنْدِباد البَحْرِيّ Sindbad the Sailor

سُنْدُس *n* silk brocade

سَنْدَوِتْش, سَنْدْوِيتْش *n* sandwich

سِنْدِيان *n* oak (*Quercus*)

سِنّارة *n* |سَنانيرُ| fish hook

سَنْط *n* sant tree, gum arabic tree (*Acacia nilotica*)

سِنْغافورة *n* Singapore

السِنِغال *n* |f| Senegal; نَهْر السِنِغال Senegal River

سَنْفَرة *n* sanding, emery; وَرَق السَنْفَرة sandpaper, emery paper

سَنْفور *n* Smurf

سَنْكَرِيّ *n* see سَمْكَرِيّ

تَسَنَّمَ *v* to ascend, to mount

سَنام *n* |أَسْنِمة| hump; ذُرْوة سَنامٍ peak, pinnacle; وَحيد السَنام dromedary, one-hump camel

سَنَمورة *n* anchovy

سَنَّ *v* |u; سَنّ| 1 [جَعَلَ حادًّا] to sharpen, to hone; سَنَّ قَلَمَ رَصاصٍ to sharpen a pencil 2 [قانوناً] to enact, to pass; سَنَّ قانوناً to enact a law

سَنَّنَ *v* 1 [شَحَذَ] to sharpen; to indent, to notch 2 [الأَطْفال] to teethe

أَسَنَّ *v* to age; to be advanced in years

اسْتَنَّ *v* 1 [أَسْنانَهُ] to clean (*one's teeth*) 2 [قانوناً] to enact 3 [سُنَّةً] to follow; اسْتَنَّ سُنَّةَ النَبيِّ \ بِسُنَّةِ النَبيِّ to follow the example of the Prophet

سَنَن *n* customary practice; way, method

سَنّ *n* enactment; سَنّ القَوانينِ the enactment of legislation

سِنّ *n* |mf; أَسْنان| 1 (Anat) tooth; أَسْنان teeth; أَسْنان بَيْضاء \ صَفْراء white/yellow teeth; أَسْنان دائِمة permanent teeth; سِنّ أَمامِيّة front tooth; أَسْنان الحَليبِ \ اللَبَنِ milk tooth, baby tooth; أَلَم أَسْنانٍ toothache; نَخر الأَسْنانِ caries, cavities; صانِع الأَسْنانِ dentist; طِبّ الأَسْنانِ dentistry; طَبيب أَسْنانٍ dental technician; طَقْم \ طاقِم أَسْنانٍ dentures; مينا الأَسْنانِ enamel; آذى مينا الأَسْنانِ to attack the enamel; مُقَوِّم الأَسْنانِ orthodontist; تَقْويم الأَسْنانِ orthodontics; فَرَشَ أَسْنانَهُ to brush one's teeth; تَنَضَّدَتْ أَسْنانُهُ to have straight teeth; عِلْم أَمْراض الأَسْنانِ dental care; العِناية بالأَسْنانِ periodontics; العَيْنُ بالعَيْنِ والسِنُّ بالسِنِّ an eye for an eye and a tooth for a tooth 2 (Mech) tooth; أَسْنان المُشْطِ \ التِرْسِ \ المِنْشارِ the teeth of a comb/cog/saw 3 [عُمْر] age; السِنّ الدُنْيا \ القُصْوى minimum/maximum age; سِنّ دُنْيا minimum/maximum age; سِنّ الدُنْيا لِسِياقة السَيّارة the minimum age to drive a car; سِنّ صَعْبة a difficult age; سِنّ مُحَدَّدة age limit; بَلَغَ سِنَّ الخِدْمةِ العَسْكَرِيّةِ to become of military age; وَصَلَ إلى سِنِّ التِسْعينَ to live to be ninety; تُوُفِّيَ في سِنِّ ٧٨ سَنةً he died at the age of 78; تَقَدَّمَ في السِنِّ to get on in years; مُتَقَدِّم في السِنِّ advanced in years; سَيِّد(ة) مُتَقَدِّم(ة) في السِنِّ an elderly gentleman/lady; في سِنٍّ مُتَقَدِّمةٍ late in life; في سِنٍّ مُتَأَخِّرةٍ in later years; في سِنٍّ مُبَكِّرةٍ at an early age; في سِنِّ العِشْرين at the age of twenty; طاعِن في السِنِّ of advanced years; سِنّ الدِراسةِ الإِلْزامِيّةِ school age; سِنُّهُ قد تَجاوَزَ الأَرْبَعينَ بِقَليلٍ he is a bit over forty; كم سِنُّهُ؟ how old is he? 4 (Mus) نوتة بِسِنَّيْنِ a note with two flags

سُنّة *n* |سُنَن| custom, usage; Sunna (*words and acts of the prophet Muhammad*); orthodoxy; السُنّة النَبَوِيّة, سُنّة النَبِيِّ the Sunna of the Prophet; كِتاب اللهِ وَسُنّة رَسولِهِ the Book of God and the Sunna of his Prophet

سَنون *n* toothpaste

سُنِّيّ *adj, n* Sunni

سِنِّيّ *adj* dental

تَسْنين *n* ❶ [شَحْذ] notch, indentation; grinding, sharpening ❷ [الأَطْفالِ] teething

مُسِنّ 🅐 *adj* old, aged, elderly; سَيِّد(ة) مُسِنّ(ة) an elderly gentleman/lady

🅑 *n* senior, an old/elderly person; دار المُسِنِّين rest home, old people's home

مِسَنّ *n* |مِسَنّات| sharpener

مُسَنَّن *adj* toothed, serrated; أَوْراق مُسَنَّنة serrated leaves; دولاب مُسَنَّن cog

مَسْنون *adj* sharpened; pointed

‹ **سَنة** *n* see سن

‹ **سَنا** *v* |u; سَناء| to shine; سَنا البَرْقُ lightning flashed

سَنّى *v* to facilitate, to ease

سانِية *n* |سَوانٍ| water wheel

سَنا *n* listed alphabetically

‹ **سِنودُس** *n* (Chr) synod

‹ **سِنَّوْر** *n* |سَنانير| cat

سِنَّوْرِيّ *adj* feline; حَيَوانات مُفْتَرِسة من الفَصيلةِ السِنَّوْرِيّة feline predators

‹ **سْنوكَر** *n* snooker (*a game similar to pool*)

‹ **سُنونو** *n* swallow (*Hirundinidae*)

‹ **أَسْهَبَ** *v* |في| to elaborate, to dwell; أَسْهَبَ في الحَديثِ عن شَيْءٍ to speak at great length about sth; أَسْهَبَ في شَرْحِ شَيْءٍ to explain sth in detail

سَهْب، سُهْب *n* |سُهوب| flat land, steppe

إِسْهاب *n* elaboration, elaborateness; long-windedness; بِإِسْهابٍ amply, extensively, in detail; ناقَشَ بِإِسْهابٍ to discuss in depth; تَكَلَّمَ عن شَيْءٍ بِإِسْهاب to speak about sth exhaustively

مُسْهَب *adj* lengthy, detailed, elaborate; long-winded, verbose; قِصّة \ تَقْرير مُسْهَب(ة) a lengthy story/report

‹ **سَهِدَ** *v* |a; سَهَد| to be unable to sleep

سَهَّدَ *v* to keep awake

سُهْد *n* sleeplessness, insomnia

سُهاد *n* sleeplessness, insomnia

‹ **سَهِرَ** *v* |a; سَهَر| ❶ [رَعى] |على| to guard, to watch over, to look after; to ensure; سَهِرَ على احْتِرامِ شَيْءٍ to ensure respect for sth; سَهِرَتْ جَدَّتُهُ على تَرْبِيَتِهِ his grandmother took care of his upbringing ❷ [اللَيْلَ] to stay up; سَهِرَ اللَيْلَ كُلَّهُ to stay up all night

سَهَّرَ *v* to keep awake

أَسْهَرَ *v* to keep awake

سَهَر *n* ❶ [عِناية] |على| care for; vigilance; ensuring; السَهَر على أَمْنِ شَيْءٍ ensuring the security of sth ❷ [تَيَقُّظ] staying up late, hanging out (late at night); sleeplessness, insomnia; nightlife; السَهَر في المَقْهى hanging out late at the cafe

ساهِر *adj* |سُهار| awake

سَهّار *n* night owl

سَهْران *adj* awake, up; ما زِلْتَ سَهْرانَ؟ are you still up?

سَهْرة *n* |سَهَرات| evening party, soirée; لِباس \ مَلابِس \ ثِياب \ بَدْلة السَهْرةِ evening clothes

‹ **سَهُلَ** *v* |u; سُهولة| ❶ [كانَ هَيِّناً] to be easy; يَسْهُلُ القَوْلُ إنّ ... it's easy to say (that) ...; يَسْهُلُ العُثورُ على بَيْتِهِ it's easy to find his house; لم يَسْهُلْ أَنْ نَجِدَ بَيْتَهُ it wasn't easy to find his house ❷ [كانَ مُسْتَوِياً] to be level/smooth

سَهَّلَ *v* ❶ [هَوَّنَ] to facilitate, to make easy, to ease ❷ [سَوّى] to level, to smooth

ساهَلَ *v* to be indulgent, to be mild; to show one's good will

أَسْهَلَ *v* ❶ [البَطْنَ] to purge, to relieve constipation; أَسْهَلَ البَطْنَ to purge the bowels; أُسْهِلَ to have diarrhoea ❷ [وَجَدَ الأَمْرَ سَهْلاً] to find easy

تَسَهَّلَ *v* to be/become easy

تَساهَلَ *v* to be tolerant/lenient, to tolerate; تَساهَلَ في شَيْءٍ to be lenient in sth; تَساهَلَ مع الغَيْرِ to be tolerant of other people; تَساهَلَ مع الفَسادِ to tolerate corruption

اسْتَسْهَلَ *v* to deem easy

سَهْل 🅐 *adj* easy, simple; مُهِمّة سَهْلة an easy task; حَرَكات سَهْلة easy movements; جِهاز سَهْل الاسْتِعْمالِ an easy-to-use device; سَهْل المُعاشَرةِ easy to get along with; سَهْل الهَضْمِ easily digestible; كانَ هذا العَمَلُ سَهْلاً this job was easy; هذا سَهْلٌ كَشُرْبِ الماءِ this is as easy as pie

أَسْهُم رَأْسِ المالِ share capital, equity; اِمْتِلاك أَغْلَبِيَّةِ الأَسْهُمِ controlling interest; اِجْتِماع حَمَلَةِ الأَسْهُمِ shareholders' meeting; اِجْتِماع الجَمْعِيّةِ العامّةِ لِحَمَلَةِ الأَسْهُمِ the general shareholders' meeting; اِجْتِماع اسْتِثْنائِيّ لِحَمَلَةِ الأَسْهُمِ an extraordinary shareholders' meeting **2** [نَبْلَة] |أَسْهُم,

سَهْم |سِهام, سُهوم, أَسْهُم| **3** [عَلامة] arrow; dart; رَمى بِسَهْمٍ to shoot an arrow; سَريع كالسَهْمِ swift as an arrow; الجُمْلة المُؤَشَّر عَلَيْها بالسَهْمِ the sentence marked with an arrow

سِهام *n* |dipt f| Siham (*female given name*)

مُساهِم **A** *adj* participating

B *n* **1** (Econ) partner; shareholder, stockholder; المُساهِمونَ company shareholders; جَمْعِيّة عُمومِيّة للمُساهِمينَ في شَرِكةٍ general shareholders' meeting **2** [مُشْتَرِك] participant, contributor; مُساهِم في مَشْروعٍ a participant in a project **3** (Law) accomplice

مُساهَمة *n* contribution, participation, taking part; شَرِكة مُساهَمة partnership; مُساهَمة في شَيْءٍ participation in sth; كانَتْ لَهُ مُساهَمةٌ صَغيرةٌ \ كَبيرةٌ to contribute a little/a lot

سَها *v* |u; سَهْو| |عن| to forget, to overlook; سَها عن بالِهِ to slip one's mind; سَها عن شَيْءٍ to overlook sth; سَها عن مَوْعِدٍ to forget an appointment

سَهّى *v* to make forget

أَسْهى *v* to make forget

سَهْو *n* |سِهاء| inattention, inattentiveness, absent-mindedness; negligence; سَهْواً inadvertently, mistakenly; كَلِمة سَقَطَتْ سَهْواً an accidentally omitted word; في لَحْظةِ سَهْوٍ in an unguarded moment

ساهٍ *adj* |سُهاة| inattentive; تحت السَواهي دَواهٍ still waters run deep

ساءَ *v* |u; سوء| to be/become bad/evil; to get worse, to deteriorate; ساءَ ما يَفْعَلُ what he does is bad; ساءَتْ ظُروفُ العَمَلِ في تِلْكَ الشَرِكةِ the working conditions in that company have deteriorated

أَساءَ *v* **1** [القِيامَ بِشَيْءٍ] to wrong, to do badly; mis-, ill-; أَساءَ التَصَرُّفَ to misbehave; أَساءَ فَهْمَ شَيْءٍ to misunderstand sth;

B *n* |سُهولة, سُهول| plain, level land; سَهْل قاحِل a bare plain; سَهْل واسِع a vast plain

سَهول *n* laxative, purgative

سُهولة *n* ease; بِسُهولةٍ easily; مَرَّ بِسُهولةٍ to run smoothly; حَقَّقَ شَيْئاً بِكُلِّ سُهولةٍ to sail through sth; هل الأَمْرُ بِهذِهِ السُهولةِ؟ is it that simple?; الأَمْرُ في غايةِ السُهولةِ it's extremely simple

إِسْهال *n* diarrhoea; أُصيبَ بالإِسْهالِ to have diarrhoea

تَساهُل *n* |تَساهُلات| tolerance; عَدَم التَساهُلِ intolerance; أَظْهَرَ تَساهُلاً to be lenient; عامَلَ شَخْصاً بِتَساهُلٍ to show mercy towards sb; التَساهُل مَع شَخْصٍ \ شَيْءٍ leniency towards sb/sth

تَسْهيل *n* |تَسْهيلات| **1** [تَبْسيط] simplification, facilitation, making easy **2** [مُنْشَأة] facility; تَسْهيلات مَحْدودة limited facilities; اسْتَعْمَلَ تَسْهيلاتٍ to make use of facilities

تَسْهيليّ *adj relating to facilities*; خِدْمات تَسْهيلِيّة facility services

مُتَساهِل *adj* tolerant, lenient, indulgent, merciful; مَوْقِف مُتَساهِل a tolerant stance; اتَّخَذَ مَوْقِفاً مُتَساهِلاً to take a lenient stance; غَيْر مُتَساهِلٍ intolerant

مُسْهِل **A** *adj* laxative, purgative; مَفْعول مُسْهِل a laxative effect

B *n* |مُسْهِلات| laxative, purgative

سَهَمَ, سَهُمَ *v* |u; سُهوم, سُهومة| **1** [بَهِتَ] to pale **2** [عَبَسَ] to frown

ساهَمَ *v* |في| to contribute to; to participate in, to take part in, to share in, to join in on; ساهَمَ في شَيْءٍ to take part in sth; ساهَمَ في شَرِكةٍ to participate in a company; ساهَمَ في التَكاليفِ \ تَغْطِيةِ النَفَقاتِ to share in the expenses; ساهَمَ في تَطْويرِ هذه المِنْطَقةِ to contribute to the development of this region

أَسْهَمَ *v* |في| to participate; أَسْهَمَ في شَيْءٍ to participate in sth

سَهْم *n* **1** (Econ) |أَسْهُم| share, stock; حامِل \ مالِك \ صاحِب سَهْمٍ shareholder; سوق الأَسْهُمِ the stock market; سِعْر السَهْمِ share price; تاجَرَ بالأَسْهُمِ to trade in shares; اكْتَتَبَ أَسْهُماً to acquire shares; طَرَحَ أَسْهُماً في السوق to float the company; تَهْبِطُ أَسْعارُ الأَسْهُمِ the share prices are plummeting; ارْتَفَعَ \ انْخَفَضَ سِعْرُ السَهْمِ the share price rose/fell; امْتَلَكَ أَسْهُماً في شَرِكةٍ to hold shares in a company;

scenario; لَيْسَ هُناكَ ما هو أَسْوَأُ من هذا there's nothing worse than this

مَساءة *n* |مَساوِئُ| disadvantage, shortcoming; المَحاسِن والمَساوِئ the advantages and disadvantages

مُسْتاء *adj* annoyed, offended, displeased; مُسْتاء ل \ من شَيْءٍ to be annoyed/offended by sth

مُسيء *adj* offensive, insulting; إعْلان مُسيء an offensive advertisement

سْوازيلانْد *n* |f| Swaziland

سوبْرانو *n* soprano

سوبَرْمارْكِت *n* supermarket

سوتْيان *n* bra, brassiere

ساحة *n* |ساحات, ساح| 1 [فَضاء أمام البِناءِ] square, plaza; field; site; ساحة التَحْريرِ Liberation Square; ساحة دارٍ courtyard; ساحة مَدْرَسةٍ school yard; ساحة اللَعِبِ playground 2 (fig) field; area; arena; ساحة القِتالِ battlefield; في الساحةِ الدُوَلِيَّةِ \ على الساحةِ الإقْليمِيَّةِ at the international/regional level; السِياسِيَّةِ in the political arena; غادَرَ الساحةَ to leave the arena; بَرَّأَت المَحْكَمةُ ساحَتَهُ the court has declared him innocent

سَوَّدَ *v* 1 [جَعَلَهُ أَسْوَدَ] to make black, to blacken; سَوَّدَ شَعْرَهُ to dye one's hair black; سَوَّدَ وَجْهَ شَخْصٍ to blacken sb's reputation 2 [وَضَعَ مُسَوَّدةً] to draft, to make a rough draft; سَوَّدَ دُسْتوراً جَديداً to draft a new constitution

اسْوَدَّ *v* to be/become black; اسْوَدَّ وَجْهُهُ his face clouded over

سادة A *adj* قَهْوة سادة unsweetened coffee, black coffee; شاي سادة black tea

B *n* see سَيِّد

سادِيّة, سادِيّ listed alphabetically

سَواد *n* 1 [لَوْن الأَسْوَدِ] blackness; لَيْلَة شَديدة السَوادِ a pitch-black night 2 [أَكْثَرِيّة] majority; السَواد الأَعْظَم the vast majority 3 (Geog) Sawad (*rural area of Iraq*) 4 [ثَوْب الحِدادِ] mourning (clothes)

سَوْداء *n* |dipt f| 1 [من أَخْلاطِ الجَسَدِ] black bile (*one of the four bodily humours*) 2 [كَآبة] melancholy

سَوْداوِيّ *adj* melancholy, gloomy; dejected, downcast; مِزاج سَوْداوِيّ a melancholy mood

أَساءَ مُعامَلةَ شَخْصٍ to treat sb badly; أَساءَ اسْتِعْمالَ شَيْءٍ to misuse sth; أَساءَ الظَنَّ في شَخْصٍ to think badly of sb 2 |إلى| [أَضَرَّ] to harm, to hurt; to offend, to insult; أَساءَ إلى سُمْعةِ to harm sb's/sth's image; أَساءَ إلى صورةِ شَخْصٍ \ شَيْءٍ شَخْصٍ to damage sb's reputation; أَساءَ إلى الإسْلامِ to insult Islam

اسْتاءَ *v* to take offence, to be offended; to be annoyed; اسْتاءَ من شَيْءٍ to take offence at sth; اسْتاءَ بِسُرْعةٍ to be touchy

سوء *n* evil; bad; mis-, ill-, mal-; سوء الحالِ a bad condition; سوء الإدارةِ mismanagement; سوء الاسْتِعْمالِ misuse; سوء الحَظِّ bad luck; سوء الفَهْمِ misunderstanding; سوء المُعامَلةِ ill-treatment; سوء التَغْذِيةِ malnutrition; أَهْل السوءِ evil people; ازْدادَ سوءاً to worsen; تَحَدَّثَ بالسوءِ to speak ill; وَضْع اقْتِصاديّ بالِغ السوءِ a very bad economic situation

سَوْءة *n* genital area, private parts

سَيِّئ *adj* bad; evil, wicked; تَأْثير سَيِّئ a bad influence; عادة سَيِّئة an bad habit; صِحّة سَيِّئة bad health; أَخْلاق \ نُقَط سَيِّئة bad manners/marks; نِيّة سَيِّئة evil intent; سَيِّئ النِيّةِ malicious; سَيِّئ الخُلُقِ bad-mannered; سَيِّئ الحَظِّ unfortunate; عامَلَ شَخْصاً مُعامَلةً سَيِّئةً to treat sb badly; (صار) من سَيِّئٍ إلى أَسْوَأَ (to go) from bad to worse; في حالةٍ سَيِّئةٍ in bad repair

سَيِّئة *n* 1 [خَطيئة] sin, misdeed 2 [سَلْبِيّة] downside, disadvantage

إساءة *n* 1 misdeed; إساءة اسْتِعْمالِ شَيْءٍ misuse of sth; لم يَقْصِد الإساءةَ بِذَلِكَ he didn't mean any harm 2 |إلى| [إهانة] offence, affront, insult; damage, harm; إساءة إلى الإسْلامِ an affront to Islam; إساءة إلى سُمْعةِ شَخْصٍ harm to sb's reputation

اسْتِياء *n* |اسْتِياءات| dissatisfaction, discontent, displeasure, annoyance, indignation, resentment; أَبْدى اسْتِياءَهُ to show one's annoyance; أَعْرَبَ عن اسْتِيائِهِ to express one's displeasure; أَثارَ اسْتِياءَ شَخْصٍ to offend sb; to infuriate sb; شَعَرَ بالاسْتِياءِ to feel hurt; to be offended; اسْتِياء من شَيْءٍ dissatisfaction with sth; من شِدّةِ اسْتِيائِهِ out of severe dissatisfaction

أَسْوَأ *adj* worse; worst; أَصْبَحَ في أَسْوَإِ حالٍ to come to a bad situation; في أَسْوَإِ الأَحْوالِ at worst, in the worst case

سَوْداوِيّة *n* melancholy

سُوَيْداء *n* |dipt f| melancholy, sadness; في سُوَيْداءِ قَلْبِهِ in one's heart of hearts

أَسْوَد **A** *adj* |dipt; سود, سودان; f pl سَوْداوات, سود| **1** [لَوْن] black; قاتِم \ غامِق أَسْوَد فاحِم coal-black; السُكّان السود the black population; القارّة السَوْداء Africa; the Dark Continent (old use); بالأَسْوَدِ العَريضِ in bold type; فيلْم بالأَسْوَدِ والأَبْيَضِ a black-and-white movie; الأَسْوَد والأَحْمَر all mankind **2** [سَيِّئ] black, dark; bad, evil; صَفْحة سَوْداء a dark page; قائِمة سَوْداء blacklist; السوق السَوْداء the black market; يَوْم أَسْوَد a black day; قَلْبُهُ أَسْوَدُ he is a bad person

B *n* |dipt; سود, سودان; f pl سَوْداوات, سود| black person

تَسْويد *n* **1** [عَكْس تَبْييض] blackening; تَسْويد صَفْحة \ وَجْه شَخْصٍ blackening sb's reputation **2** [كِتابة \ رَسْم مُسَوَّدة] drafting, making a rough draft

مُسْوَدّ *adj* blackish

مُسَوَّدة *n* (rough) draft; sketch; outline; مُسَوَّدة طَبْع proof; مُسَوَّدة مَشْروعِ قانونٍ (Law) draft bill; على المُسَوَّدةِ in rough; كَتَبَ على المُسَوَّدةِ to write out in draft

2 **سادَ** *v* |u; سُؤْدَد, سُؤْدُد, سِيادة| to rule, to be/become master; to dominate; to prevail; تَسودُ الغُيومُ there are a lot of clouds; سادَ جَوٌّ من التَوَتُّرِ a tense atmosphere prevailed; يَسودُ الصَمْتُ المَكانَ silence reigns; يَسودُ شُعورٌ بالرِضى a feeling of satisfaction is prevalent; سادَ الاعْتِقادُ بِأَنَّ ... there was a widespread belief that ...; الحَسودُ لا يَسودُ envy will get you nowhere

سائِد *adj* |سَوائِدُ| **1** [شائِع] prevailing, prevalent, predominant, common, current; جين سائِد a dominant gene; الرَأْي السائِد the prevailing view; نَظَرِيّة سائِدة a current theory; العُرْف السائِد هُنا the common tradition here **2** [قائِد] leading; سائِد في السوقِ market leader

سُؤْدُد *n* dominion, sovereignty

سِيادة *n* **1** [سَيْطَرة] sovereignty, supremacy, dominance, rule; سِيادة قَوْمِيّة \ وَطَنِيّة national sovereignty; سِيادة إِقْليمِيّة territorial integrity; أَعْلَنَ السِيادةَ to proclaim sovereignty; دَوْلة ذات سِيادةٍ a sovereign state **2** (Title) Excellency; سِيادة الوَزِيرِ His Excellency the minister; سِيادَتُكَ Your Excellency; ≈ you (*respectful title of address for people one does not know well*)

سِيادِيّ *adj* *relating to sovereignty*; حُقوق سِيادِيّة sovereign rights

سَيِّد *n* |أَسْياد, سادة, سادات| **1** [رَجُل] gentleman; Mr; سَيِّدي sir; (مَساءَ الخَيْرِ) أَيُّها السَيِّداتُ والسادةُ (good evening) ladies and gentlemen; أَيُّها السادةُ dear sirs **2** [مَوْلى] master, lord; chieftain; السَيِّد المَسيح the Lord Jesus; الانْتِظارُ سَيِّدُ المَوْقِفِ *it's best to wait* **3** [اِسْم شَخْصِيّ] Sayyid (*male given name*)

سَيِّدة *n* lady; madam, ma'am; Mrs; سَيِّدَتي madam, ma'am; سَيِّداتي وَسادَتي ladies and gentlemen; سَيِّدة أَعْمالٍ ناجِحة a successful businesswoman; هي سَيِّدةٌ بِمَعْنى الكَلِمةِ she is every inch a lady

سودانِيّ **A** *adj* Sudanese; فول سودانِيّ peanuts

B *n* Sudanese (*person*)

السودان *n* |f| Sudan; جُمْهورِيّة السودانِ Republic of Sudan; بِلاد السودان the Sudan

بور سودان *n* |f| Port Sudan (*city in Sudan, also the country's major port*)

سَوَّرَ *v* to fence off/in, to enclose; سَوَّرَ ساحةً to fence off a square

ساوَرَ *v* to overcome, to befall; to assault; ساوَرَتْهُ الهُمومُ he was overcome by worries

تَسَوَّرَ *v* to climb, to scale; تَسَوَّرَ سوراً to scale a wall

سور *n* |أَسْوار| **1** [سِياج] enclosure, fence, railing; تَسَلَّقَ سوراً to climb over a fence; داخِلَ \ خارِجَ الأَسْوارِ inside/outside the fences; سور حول شَيْءٍ a fence around sth **2** [حائِط] wall; سور المَدينةِ city wall; خارِجَ \ داخِلَ أَسْوارِ المَدينةِ outside/inside the city walls; بَنى سوراً to put up a wall; هَدَّمَ سوراً to break down a wall

سِوار, سُوار *n* |سُوَر, أَسْوِرة, أَساوِرُ, أَساوِرة| bracelet; wristband; سِوار ذَهَبِيّ \ فِضِّيّ a gold/silver bracelet; لَبِسَ سِواراً to wear a bracelet

سورة *n* |سُوَر| sura (*a chapter or section of the Koran*)

سَوْرة *n* vehemence, violence, intensity

إِسْوار *n* listed alphabetically

مُسَوَّر *adj* walled, enclosed (*by a wall*); fenced in; مَدينة \ حَديقة مُسَوَّرة a walled city/garden

سورِيا, سورِيّة *n* Syria; سورِيا الكُبْرى Greater Syria

سوريّ **A** *adj* Syrian; الجُمْهوريّة العَرَبيّة السوريّة Syrian Arab Republic

B *n* Syrian (*person*)

‹ **سورْياليّ** *n* see سُرْياليّ

‹ **سوريناميّ** *adj*, *n* Surinamese

السورينام *n* |f| Suriname (*Dutch-speaking country in South America*)

‹ **ساسَ** *v* |u; سِياسة| to govern, to dominate, to rule (over); ساسَ النّاسَ to rule over a people

سَوِسَ *v* |a; سَوْس| to be/become worm-eaten

سَوَّسَ *v* to decay; to be/become worm-eaten

سَيَّسَ *v* to politicize

تَسَوَّسَ *v* to be/become worm-eaten

سوس **A** *n* **1** [حَلْوى] liquorice **2** (Bot) عِرْق السوسِ, العِرْقَسوس liquorice (*Glycyrrhiza glabra*) **3** (Geog) Sousse (*region in Morocco*)

B *n coll* |سيسان| (Zool) mite; moth; woodworm; سوس الخَشَبِ woodworm

سائِس *n* |سُيّاس, سوّاس, ساسة| stableman

سَواسِية *n* see سوي

سِياسة *n* **1** [خُطّة] policy, strategy; سِياسة زِراعيّة agricultural policy; سِياسة تَشْجيعيّة incentives policy; سِياسة داخِليّة \ خارِجيّة \ اقْتِصاديّة internal/foreign/economic policy; سِياسة الحُكومةِ government policy; انْتَهَجَ \ اتَّبَعَ سِياسةً to pursue a policy; اسْتَعْمَلَ مع شَخْصٍ سِياسةَ العَصا والجَزَرة to use a carrot-and-stick approach towards sb **2** [إدارة بَلَدٍ] politics; عِلْم السِياسةِ political science; رَجُل سِياسةٍ politician; عَمِلَ بالسِياسةِ to be in politics

سِياسيّ **A** *adj* political; زَعيم سِياسيّ political leader; مُحَرِّر سِياسيّ political editor; عالِم سِياسيّ political scientist; عُلوم سِياسيّة political science; حِزْب سِياسيّ a political party

B *n* politician, statesman; سِياسيّ فاسِد a corrupt politician; سِياسيّ عَظيم a great statesman

تَسَوُّس *n* caries, cavities; tooth decay; تَسَوُّس الأَسْنانِ caries, cavities; tooth decay; مَنْعَ التَسَوُّس to prevent cavities

تَسْييس *n* politicizing

لاسِياسيّ *adj* non-political; apolitical

مُسَوَّس *adj* rotten; carious (*bones or teeth*)

‹ **سوسة** *n* |dipt| Sousse (*city in Tunisia*)

‹ **سَوْسَن** *n* **1** (Bot) iris **2** [اِسْم شَخْصيّ] |f| Sausan (*female given name*)

‹ **سوسِيو اقْتِصاديّ** *adj* socio-economic

‹ **سوسِيولوجيّ** **A** *adj* sociological

B *n* sociologist

سوسيولوجيا *n* sociology

‹ **ساطَ** *v* |u; سَوْط| to whip; ساطَ شَخْصاً to whip sb

سَوْط *n* |أَسْواط, سِياط| whip, lash, scourge; ضَرَبَ حِصاناً بالسَوْطِ to beat a horse with a whip

‹ **ساعاتيّ** *n* watchmaker

ساعة *n* |ساعات| **1** [فَتْرة ٦٠ دَقيقةً] hour; ساعة رُكود free hour; ثُلْث ساعةٍ quarter of an hour, fifteen minutes; رُبْع ساعةٍ twenty minutes; نِصْف ساعةٍ half an hour, a half hour; أَرْبَع وَعِشْرونَ ساعةً twenty-four hours; تَمُرُّ الساعاتُ مُتَثاقِلةً بَطيئةً the hours drag on; احْتاجَ لِساعةٍ من الزَمَنِ it took him an hour; بعد ساعةٍ in/after an hour; بعد ساعَتَيْنِ وَنِصْفٍ in/after two and a half hours; كُلَّ ساعةٍ \ نِصْفِ ساعةٍ on the hour/ half hour, every hour/half hour; على مَدارِ الساعةِ around the clock; الساعةُ الآنَ الخامِسةُ it's five o'clock; ساعة عَمَلٍ إضافيّة an hour of overtime **2** [وَقْت] hour; time; الساعةَ now; ساعَتَها at that/the time; in those days; وَساعَتَها كُنْتُ في البَيْتِ I was at home at the time; ساعة الذُرْوةِ rush hour; ساعات العَمَلِ working hours; خارِجَ ساعاتِ العَمَلِ outside business hours; خِلالَ \ أَثْناءَ ساعاتِ العَمَلِ during office hours; حتّى الساعةِ until now, up to now; إلى الساعةِ up to now; في ساعةٍ ما من ساعَتِهِ at once; في ساعةٍ ما at a certain point in time; (أَمْس) في مِثْلِ هذه الساعةِ at this time (yesterday); في الساعةِ الخامِسةِ \ السادِسةِ \ العاشِرةِ at five/six/ten o'clock; في ساعةٍ مُبَكِّرةٍ من الصَباحِ early in the morning; في ساعةٍ مُتَأَخِّرةٍ من اللَيْلِ well into the night; في حَوالَيْ الساعةِ الخامِسةِ around five o'clock; كم الساعةُ؟ what time is it? **3** [آلة] clock, watch, timepiece; ساعة ذَهَبيّة gold watch; ساعة مُنَبِّهة alarm (clock); ساعة رَقْميّة digital watch; ساعة رَمْليّة hourglass; ساعة شَمْسيّة sundial; ساعة يَدٍ wrist watch; ضَبَطَ \

ساقَ *v* |u; سَوْق ,سِياقة ,سِواقة ,مَساق| ① [قادَ] to steer, to drive (*a car*); to ride (*a bike*); ساقَ بِتَمَهُّلٍ to drive carefully ② [اِقْتَبَسَ] to quote, to cite ③ [بَعَثَ] to send, to dispatch; ساقَ شَخْصاً إلى المَوْتِ to drive sb to an early grave

سَوَّقَ *v* سَوَّقَ شَيْئاً to market sth

ساوَقَ *v* to harmonize

تَسَوَّقَ *v* to shop, to go shopping; تَسَوَّقَ في مَتْجَرٍ to shop at a store; تَسَوَّقَ عَبْرَ الإِنْتَرْنِت to shop online

تَساوَقَ *v* to be harmonious

اِنْساقَ *v* to drift; to be carried away, to be misled/deceived; اِنْساقَ وراء الوُعودِ الكاذِبةِ he was misled by false promises

سوق *n* |mf; أَسْواق| ① [مَكان تُباعُ فيه البَضائِعُ] market, shopping centre; souk, bazaar; سوق مَرْكَزِيّة \ مُمْتازة supermarket; سوق مَسْقوف an indoor/covered market (*as opposed to an open-air souk*); سوق الإِنْتَرْنِت internet marketplace ② (Econ) market; سوق الأَوْراقِ المالِيّةِ ,سوق الأَسْهُمِ the stock market; السوق العالَمِيّة the world market; السوق السَوْداء the black market; السوق المالِيّة the financial market; اِقْتِصاد السوق (الحُرّة) (free) market economy; آلِيّة السوقِ market forces; سِعْر السوقِ market price; قيمة السوقِ market value; بُحوث \ دِراسة السوقِ market research; غَزا السوقَ to sweep the market; طَرَحَ شَيْئاً في الأَسْواقِ to put sth on the market; حِصّة في السوقِ market share; السوق الأوروبِّيّة المُشْتَرَكة European Economic Community, EEC

سَوْق *n* driving

سائِق *n* |سائِقونَ ,سُوّاق| driver; chauffeur; سائِق السَيّارةِ the driver of the car; سائِق تاكْسي taxi driver; سائِق شاحِنةٍ trucker; سائِق دَرّاجةٍ نارِيّةٍ motorcyclist

ساق *n* |f; سيقان| ① (Anat) leg; shank; بَطّة \ رَبْلة الساقِ calf; عَظْم الساقِ shin bone; أَطْلَقَ ساقَيْهِ للريحِ to take to one's heels; جَرى على قَدَمٍ وَساقٍ to be in full swing; زاحَمَ شَخْصاً بالمَنْكِبِ والساقِ to elbow sb aside ② [حَيَوانٍ] leg; طَويل الساقِ stilt ③ (Geom) side, leg; مُتَساوي الساقَيْنِ isosceles; ساقا بِرْكارٍ the legs of a compass ④ [نَباتٍ] stalk, stem

ساقة *n* rearguard

سَوّاق *n* driver; chauffeur; سَوّاق حافِلةٍ bus driver

صَحَّحَ الساعةَ to set the clock; تَوَقَّفَت الساعةُ the clock has stopped; تَقَدَّمَت \ تَأَخَّرَت الساعةُ the clock was fast/slow; تَدورُ الساعةُ the clock is running; نَظَرَ إلى ساعَتِهِ to look at one's watch; تُشيرُ الساعةُ الآنَ إلى الخامِسةِ it's five o'clock

سُوَيْعة *n* a little time

ساغَ *v* |u; مَساغ| to be/become permissible

سَوَّغَ *v* ① [بَرَّرَ] to justify, to warrant; يُسَوِّغُ القانونُ اعْتِقالَ المُتَّهَمِ the law allows the arrest of the suspect ② [أَجَّرَ] to lease

أَساغَ *v* to swallow, to take; أَساغَ الطَعامَ to swallow the food

تَسَوَّغَ *v* to lease

اِسْتَساغَ *v* to find pleasant/agreeable; to enjoy, to like; to be able to swallow (fig), to find palatable/acceptable; اِسْتَساغَ شَيْئاً to like sth; اِسْتَساغَ الطَعامَ to enjoy the food; اِسْتَساغَ الفِكْرةَ to find an idea palatable

سائِغ *adj* ① [مُباح] permissible ② [لَذيذ] tasty, palatable; لُقْمة \ فَريسة سائِغة easy prey

تَسْويغ *n* ① [تَبْرير] justification; تَسْويغ العُنْفِ justifying violence ② [تَأْجير] leasing

مُسْتَساغ *adj* tasty, palatable; غَيْر مُسْتَساغةٍ unpalatable; فِكْرة غَيْر مُسْتَساغةٍ an unpalatable idea

مُسَوِّغ *n* |مُسَوِّغات| justification, justifying factors; مُسَوِّغ قانونِيّ legal justification, (legal) grounds

سَوَّفَ *v* to postpone

سَوْفَ ,سَـ *particle* particle of the future tense; سَوْفَ يَكْتُبُ he will write; سَنَكْتُبُ لَكُمْ we will write to you; سَوْفَ يُغادِرُ الرَئيسُ موريتانِيا اليَوْمَ the president will leave Mauritania today

تَسْويف *n* |تَسْويفات| delay; stalling

تَسْويفِيّ *adj* delaying (*before n*), stalling (*before n*)

مَسافة *n* distance, way; مَسافة طَويلة \ قَصيرة a long/short distance; قَطَعَ مَسافةً to cover a distance; المَسافة بين الأَرْضِ والشَمْسِ the distance between the earth and the sun; على مَسافةِ كيلومِتْرَيْنِ من القَرْيةِ two kilometres from the village

سوفْيِتِيّ ,سوفْياتِيّ ,سوفْيِيتِيّ *adj* |سوفْيات| Soviet; الاتِّحاد السوفْياتِيّ the Soviet Union (*Union of Soviet Socialist Republics, USSR*)

سوّاقة *n* (Comput) drive; سَوّاقة أَقْراصٍ disk drive

سوقيّ *adj* **1** [عامّيّ] vulgar, common, banal, trivial; كَلام \ لُغة سوقيّة slang نُكَت سوقيّ(ة) vulgar language/jokes; **2** [مَنْسوب إلى السوقِ] market (*before n*); قيمة سوقيّة market value

سوقيّة *n* vulgarity

سَويق *n* barley porridge

سِياق *n* |سِياقات| context; succession; سِياق الحَوادِثِ the course of events; سِياق الأَفْكارِ train of thought; سِياق الكَلام context; في هذا السِياقِ in this context; عِبارات مُقْتَطَعة من سِياقِها words taken out of context; في سِياقٍ تاريخيٍّ أَوْسَع in a wider historical context; في سِياقٍ مُتَّصِلٍ ... in a related development ...

سِياقة *n* driving; رُخْصة سِياقةٍ driving licence (BrE), driver's license (AmE); مُدَرِّس سِياقةٍ driving instructor; مَنْع السِياقةِ driving ban

انْسِياق *n* drift; getting carried away, being misled/deceived; الانْسِياق وراء العَواطِفِ getting carried away by one's emotions

تَساوُق *n* coherence; harmony

تَسَوُّق *n* shopping; مَرْكَز التَسَوُّقِ shopping centre, mall; التَسَوُّق عَبْرَ الإنْتَرْنِت online shopping

تَسْويق *n* marketing; قِسْم التَسْويقِ the marketing department

تَسْويقيّ *adj* marketing (*before n*); حَمْلة تَسْويقيّة marketing campaign

مُتَساوِق *adj* harmonious

مَساق *n* trend, development

‹ **ساكَ** *v* |u; سِواك, سَوْك| to clean; ساكَ أَسْنانَهُ to clean one's teeth (*with a miswak*)

سَوَّكَ *v* to clean (*the teeth*)

سِواك *n* |أَسْوِكة, سوك| miswak (*tooth-cleaning stick*)

مِسْواك *n* |مَساويكُ| miswak (*tooth-cleaning stick*)

‹ **سَوَّلَ** *v* to talk into; to entice

تَسَوَّلَ *v* to beg; to implore; تَسَوَّلَ في الشَوارِعِ to beg in the streets

مُتَسَوِّل *n* beggar

‹ **سولار** *n* diesel (oil/fuel)

‹ **سوليتير** *n* patience (BrE), solitaire (AmE)

‹ **سامَ** *v* |u; سِيامة| **1** [فَرَضَ] to impose **2** (Chr) to consecrate, to ordain; سامَ كَنيسةً \ مَذْبَحاً to consecrate a church/altar; سامَ كاهِناً to ordain sb a priest

سَوَّمَ *v* **1** [فَرَضَ] to impose, to force; سَوَّمَ شَخْصاً شَيْئاً to impose sth on sb **2** [أَعْلَمَ بِعَلامةٍ] to mark; سَوَّمَ الماشِيةَ to brand the cattle

ساوَمَ *v* |على| to bargain, to haggle; to compromise; ساوَمَ على شَيْءٍ to haggle over sth; to compromise on sth; إِنَّنا لن نُساوِمَ على حُقوقِنا we will not compromise on our rights

تَساوَمَ *v* to bargain

سائِمة *n* |سَوائِمُ| livestock

سِيامة *n* consecration; سِيامة قِسّيسٍ the ordination of a priest

سيماء *n* |dipt f; سِيَم| **1** [الوَجْهِ] expression, look, appearance **2** [إشارة] mark, characteristic

مُساوَمة *n* bargaining, haggling; compromise; مُساوَمة على مَبادِئِهِ compromise on one's principles

‹ **سومو** *n* sumo

‹ **سوناتة** *n* sonata

‹ **سونار** *n* sonar

‹ **سوهاج** *n* |f| Sohag (*city in Egypt*)

‹ **سَوّى** *v* **1** [عَدَّلَ] to reconcile; to settle; سَوّى خِلافاً \ نِزاعاً \ خِصاماً to settle a dispute; سَوّى قَضيّةً بالمَعْروفِ to settle a matter amicably **2** [بَسَطَ] to level, to make even, to flatten; سَوّى شَيْئاً to make sth even; سَوّى شَعْرَهُ to tidy one's hair; سَوّى سَريرَهُ to make one's bed

ساوى *v* **1** [بَيْنَهُما] to equalize, to make equal/the same, to level; ساوى بين الرِجالِ والنِساءِ to give equal treatment to men and women **2** [عادَلَ] to equal, to match; ساوى شَيْئاً to match sth; ساوى شَخْصاً في النَتائِجِ to equal sb's results; ٤ زائِد ٥ يُساوي ٩ four plus five is nine

تَساوى *v* to be/become equal/similar

اسْتَوى *v* **1** [تَساوى] to be/become equal **2** [اسْتَقَرَّ] to sit; اسْتَوى على العَرْشِ he established himself on the throne

3 [طُبِخَ جَيِّداً] to be well done/cooked; اسْتَوى على نارٍ هادِئةٍ to stew

سَوِيّ *adj* **1** [سَليم] right, proper, appropriate; normal, customary; الطَريق السَوِيّ the right path, the straight and narrow; سُلوك سَوِيّ proper behavior; غَيْر سَوِيٍّ inappropriate, improper; abnormal; عَلاقة غَيْر سَوِيّةٍ an inappropriate relationship **2** [مع بَعْضٍ] سَوِيًّا together; عَلَيْنا العَمَلُ سَوِيًّا we must work together

سَواء *adj* |أَسْواء| equal; سَواءٌ alike; سَواءٌ بِسَواءٍ equally, fifty-fifty; سَواءٌ ... أم ... regardless of whether ... or ...; سَواءٌ بِحُضورِ الناسِ أم بِغَيْرِ حُضورِهِمْ whether or not in the presence of audience; سَواءٌ \ سَواءً أكانَ صَحيحاً أم خَطَأً regardless of whether it is right or wrong; على حَدٍّ سَواءٍ, على السَواءِ both; likewise, in like manner; هي مَسْؤوليّةٌ وَطَنيّةٌ وَإنْسانيّةٌ على حَدٍّ سَواءٍ it is both a national and a humanitarian responsibility

سَواسِيَة *adj* equal; هُمْ سَواسِيَةٌ أمامَ القانونِ they are equal before the law

سِوى *prep* except, apart from; only; but; لا ... سِوى ... only; لَيْسَ مَعَهُ سِوى حَقيبةٍ واحِدةٍ he has only one suitcase with him; لم يَبْقَ مَعي سِوى صَديقي مَجْدي nobody stayed with me, apart from my friend Majdi; دون سِواهُ only he

سَوِيّة *n* سَوِيّةً together, jointly

سِيّ *n* |mf; أَسْواء| equal; similar, alike; هُما سِيّانِ عِنْدي they're both the same to me; سِيّانِ إنْ كانَ ... أم \ أو ... no matter whether it's ... or ...

سِيَّما *adv* لا سِيَّما especially, in particular, mainly; البُلْدان العَرَبيّة وَلا سِيَّما مِصْر the Arab countries, and especially Egypt; لا سِيَّما أنّ ... especially as/since ...

اسْتِواء *n* خَطّ الاسْتِواءِ equator; اجْتازَ خَطَّ الاسْتِواءِ to cross the equator; خَطّ الاسْتِواءِ المَغْنَطيسيّ the magnetic equator; ٣٤ دَرَجةً جَنوبيَّ خَطِّ الاسْتِواءِ a latitude of 34 degrees South

اسْتِوائيّ *adj* tropical, equatorial; الغابة الاسْتِوائيّة the tropical rainforest; شِبْه اسْتِوائيٍّ subtropical; دَرَجات حَرارةٍ اسْتِوائيّةٍ tropical temperatures

تَساوٍ *n* equality; تَساوي الرُتَبِ equality of ranks; بالتَساوي equally; مُوَزَّعةٍ بالتَساوي divided equally

تَسْوِية *n* arrangement, settlement, compromise; تَسْوِية وِدّيّة a friendly settlement; تَسْوِية المَدْفوعاتِ settlement of payments; تَسْوِية المَشاكِلِ العالِقةِ the settlement of existing problems; أَجْرى تَسْوِيةً مع شَخْصٍ to reach an understanding with sb; تَوَصَّلَ إلى تَسْوِيةٍ to come to an agreement

مُتَساوٍ *adj* **1** [مُساوٍ] equal, similar, alike, identical; مُعامَلة مُتَساوِية equal treatment; مُثَلَّث مُتَساوي الساقَيْنِ an isosceles triangle; مُثَلَّث مُتَساوي الأَضْلاع an equilateral triangle; غَيْر مُتَساوٍ unequal; مُعامَلة غَيْر مُتَساوِيةٍ للرِجالِ والنِساءِ unequal treatment of men and women **2** [مُسَطَّح] even, level, smooth; أَرْض غَيْر مُتَساوِيةٍ uneven terrain

مُساوٍ *adj* equal, equivalent, similar; كانَ مُساوِياً لِشَيْءٍ to be equal to sth

مُساواة *n* equality, equal rights; equalization; عَدَم المُساواةِ inequality; عَدَم المُساواةِ بين المُواطِنينَ inequality between citizens; عَدَم المُساواةِ في تَقْسيمِ شَيْءٍ inequality in the division of sth; على قَدَمِ المُساواةِ on an equal footing; عامَلَ شَخْصاً على قَدَمِ المُساواةِ to treat sb on equal terms; المُساواة أمام القانونِ equality before the law; كانَ مُنافِياً لِمَبْدَأِ المُساواةِ to be contrary to the principle of equality; مُساواة في الحُقوقِ equal rights; المُساواة بين الناسِ equality between people; المُساواة بين الرَجُلِ والمَرْأةِ equality between men and women; حَرَكة المُساواةِ بين الرَجُلِ والمَرْأةِ feminist movement; الحُرّيّة والمُساواة والأُخُوّة liberty, equality and fraternity

مُسْتَوٍ *adj* level, even; أَرْض مُسْتَوِية flat land

مُسْتَوًى *n* |مُسْتَوَيات| **1** [مَنْسوب] level; مُسْتَوى (سَطْح) البَحْرِ sea level; مُسْتَوى ارْتِفاعِ المِياهِ water level; مُسْتَوى المِياهِ الجَوْفِيّةِ water table, groundwater level **2** [مِعْيار] level, standard; مُسْتَوًى دِراسيّ educational level; المُسْتَوى المَعيشيّ standard of living; رَفيع المُسْتَوى high-quality; اخْتِلاف المُسْتَوَياتِ difference in level; دون \ فوق مُسْتَواهُ beneath/above oneself; على المُسْتَوى الأُسَريّ as a family; على مُسْتَوى الجُمْهوريّةِ \ البِلادِ on the national level;

مُشاوَرة على مُسْتَوى الوُزَراءِ \ مُسْتَوًى أوروبيٍّ a consultation at ministerial/European level; ذو مُسْتَوًى عالٍ of a high standard; على مُسْتَوًى عالٍ high-level; مُحادَثة على مُسْتَوًى عالٍ a high-level discussion; كانَ على مُسْتَوًى عالٍ \ مُنْخَفِضٍ to be of a high/low standard; حَصَلَ على مُسْتَوًى عالٍ to achieve a high level; عاشَ فوق مُسْتَواهُ to live beyond one's means; يَرْتَفِعُ \ يَنْخَفِضُ المُسْتَوى the level is rising/dropping; رَفَعَ مُسْتَوى الرَفاهةِ \ التَعْليمِ to raise the standard of prosperity/education

سُويديّ **A** *adj* Swedish; السُويديّة (اللُغة) Swedish (*language*) **B** *n* Swede

السُويد *n* |f| Sweden

السُوَيْس *n* |f| Suez (*city in Egypt*); قَناة السُوَيْسِ Suez canal

سُويسْرا *n* Switzerland

سُويسْريّ *adj*, *n* Swiss

سي *n* **1** (Mus) te, si **2** [سَيِّدي] Mr, Sir (*abbreviation for* سَيِّدي (*especially in North Africa*))

سِيّانِ *n* see سيّ

سِيانيد *n* (Chem) cyanide

سيئول *n* |f| Seoul

سابَ *v* |i; سَيْب| **1** [جَرى] to flow, to run; سابَ الماءُ the water flows **2** [غادَرَ] to leave; سابَ المُوَظَّفون خلال غِياب المُديرِ the employees left during the absence of the director **3** [تَرَكَ] to leave, to abandon; سابَتْ زَوْجَها to leave one's husband

سَيَّبَ *v* to leave, to abandon, to forsake

انْسابَ *v* to flow, to run

سائِب *adj* loose (*unpackaged*); الدَقيق السائب loose flour

انْسِياب *n* flow; انْسِياب المُرورِ the flow of traffic; تَمَّ \ جَرى بِانْسِيابٍ to run smoothly

انْسِيابيّ *adj* streamline; انْسِيابيّ الشَكْلِ streamlined

انْسِيابيّة *n* streamlining

تَسَيُّب *n* neglect, carelessness

تَسْييب *n* streamlining

سيبيريا *n* Siberia

سيتار *n* sitar

سيتِسوس، سيتِسُس *n* (Bot) golden chain (*Laburnum*)

سيتْكوم *n* sitcom

سَيَّجَ *v* to fence/hedge in; سَيَّجَ حَديقةً to fence in a garden

سِياج *n* |سِياجات| **1** [سور] fence, enclosure; barrier; railing; سِياج كَهْرَبائيّ \ مُكَهْرَب an electric fence; أَقامَ سِياجاً to put up a barrier; سِياج من خَشَبٍ a wooden fence; سِياج حول شَيْءٍ a fence around sth; داخِلَ \ خارِجَ السِياجِ inside/outside the railings **2** [من النَبات] hedge

مُسَيَّج *n* enclosed

سيجار *n* |سيجارات| cigar; دَخَّنَ سيجاراً to smoke a cigar; أَشْعَلَ سيجاراً to light (up) a cigar

سيجارة *n* |سيجارات، سَجايِرُ، سَجائِرُ| cigarette; عُلْبة سَجائِرَ a pack of cigarettes; عَقِب سيجارةٍ (cigarette) butt; دُخّان السَجائِرِ cigarette smoke; لَفَّ \ بَرَمَ سيجارةً to roll a cigarette; دَخَّنَ سيجارةً to smoke a cigarette; أَشْعَلَ \ أَطْفَأَ سيجارةً to light/put out a cigarette; وَرَق لَفِّ السَجائِرِ rolling papers

ساحَ *v* |i; سِياحة| **1** [سالَ] to flow, to run; ساحَ مِنْهُ العَسَلُ honey flowed out of it **2** [سافَرَ] to travel; to wander

سَيَّحَ *v* to make flow

أَساحَ *v* to make flow

انْساحَ *v* to spread

سائِح *n* |سائِحونَ، سُيّاح، سُوّاح| tourist; traveller; سُيّاح أَجانِب foreign tourists

سِياحة *n* tourism; سِياحة عِلاجيّة medical tourism; مَكْتَب سِياحةٍ travel agency

سِياحيّ *adj* tourist (*before n*); مُنْتَجَع سِياحيّ tourist resort; القِطاع السِياحيّ the tourist sector; سافَرَ في الدَرَجةِ السِياحيّة to travel in tourist class

[1] **ساخَ** *v* |u; سَوْخ| to sink, to go down; ساخَ في الطينِ to sink into the mud

[2] **سيخ** *n* |أَسْياخ| spit, skewer; شَوى شَيْئاً على سيخٍ to cook sth on a spit

[3] **سيخيّ** *adj*, *n* Sikh

سيدا *n* AIDS (*acquired immune deficiency syndrome, abbreviated as SIDA in several languages*)

سيدَر *n* cider

سيدي *n* CD (*compact disc*)

سارَ *v* |i; سَيْر, سَيْرورة, مَسير, مَسيرة, تَسْيار| **1** ◀ [ذَهَبَ] to go, to walk; to march; to travel; to ride; سارَ على الرَّصيفِ to walk on the pavement (BrE) sidewalk (AmE); سارَ بِسُرْعةٍ تَفوقُ سُرْعةَ الضَّوْءِ to travel faster than light **2** ◀ [بِعَجَلاتٍ] to run, to operate; لن تَسيرَ الحافِلاتُ \ الباصاتُ غَداً no buses are running tomorrow; سارَ بالغازِ to run on gas **3** ◀ [تَبِعَ] to follow, to maintain (*a behavior*); to conduct oneself **4** ◀ [الطَّريقُ] to go, to run, to lead; يَسيرُ الطَّريقُ من هُنا إلى البُحَيْرةِ the path leads from here to the lake; يَسيرُ الطَّريقُ بِمُحاذاةِ النَّهْرِ the road runs parallel to the river **5** ◀ [تَقَدَّمَ] to go; سارَ سَيْرةً حَسَنةً to go well; سارَ على خُطّةٍ to go according to plan; تَسيرُ الأُمورُ على ما يُرامُ everything's going fine

سَيَّرَ *v* **1** ◀ [تَوَلّى الإدارةَ] to lead, to manage, to run **2** ◀ [شَغَّلَ] to start up, to activate; to bring into action; سَيَّرَ جُيوشاً to bring troops into action **3** ◀ [دَفَعَ] to drive, to propel, to push along

سايَرَ *v* **1** ◀ [ماشى] to keep up/pace (with); سايَرَ شَخْصاً \ شَيْئاً to keep up with sb/sth; سايَرَ التَّيّارَ to drift with the current **2** ◀ [لاطَفَ] to humour

أَسارَ *v* to set in motion

سَيْر *n* **1** ◀ [مَشْي] walk, march; movement, course; trip, tour; سَيْر الأُمورِ \ الأَحْداثِ the course of events; سَيْر التاريخ the course of history; سَيْر قَضِيّةٍ the course of a case; تابَعَ سَيْرَهُ to continue on one's way; خَفَّفَ سَيْرَهُ to check one's step; السَّيْر جيئةً وَذَهاباً walking to and fro; أَثْناءَ السَّيْرِ during the journey **2** ◀ [حَرَكة المُرورِ] traffic; قانون السَّيْرِ traffic laws; شُرْطِيّ سَيْرٍ traffic police **3** ◀ [رباط] |سُيور| belt; drive belt; سَيْر مُتَحَرِّك conveyor belt

سَيّار *adj* ambulant; mobile; هاتِف سَيّار mobile phone (BrE), cell phone (AmE); طَريق سَيّار motorway (BrE), highway (AmE)

سَيّارة *n* car, motor car (BrE), automobile (AmE); سَيّارة مَكْشوفة a convertible; سَيّارة رِياضِيّة a sports car; سَيّارة خاصّة \ خُصوصيّة personal car; سَيّارة مُسْتَعْمَلة a second-hand car; سَيّارة مُدَرَّعة \ مُصَفَّحة an armoured car; سَيّارة مُفَخَّخة \ مَلْغومة a car bomb; سَيّارة إسْعافٍ an ambulance; سَيّارة شَحْنٍ a truck; سَيّارة رُكّابٍ a (passenger) car; سَيّارة سِباقٍ a race car; سَرِقة سَيّارةٍ car theft; بِسَيّارةِ الأُجْرة by taxi; سَيّارة أُجْرةٍ taxi; صِناعة السَّيّاراتِ the auto industry; حادِث \ حادِثة سَيّارةٍ a car crash; إطار \ دولاب سَيّارةٍ (car) tyre; تاجِر سَيّاراتٍ a car dealer; مارْكة سَيّارةٍ the make of car; سائِق سَيّارةٍ driver; مُرور السَّيّاراتِ motor (BrE) vehicle (AmE) traffic; تَعَطُّل سَيّارةٍ car trouble; ساقَ \ قادَ سَيّارةً to drive a car; ذَهَبَ \ جاءَ بالسَّيّارة to go/come by car; رَكِبَ السَّيّارةَ to ride in a car; صَفَّ السَّيّارةَ to park the car; أَمَّنَ على السَّيّارةِ to take out a car insurance; تأْمين على السَّيّارة car insurance

سيرة *n* |سِيَر| **1** ◀ [حَياة] biography; CV, curriculum vitae; سيرة ذاتيّة autobiography; سيرة الحَياة biography; سيرة النَّبِيِّ \ السيرة النَّبَوِيّة the biography of the Prophet; كَتَبَ سيرةً ذاتِيَّةً to write an autobiography; كاتِب سيرةٍ biographer **2** ◀ [سُلوك] conduct, way of life; حُسْن السيرةِ good conduct

سَيْرورة *n* process

تَسْيير *n* **1** ◀ [إدارة] management, direction, running, handling; تَسْيير ذاتيّ autonomy **2** ◀ [دَفْع] moving forward **3** ◀ [إرْسال] sending, dispatching

مَسار *n* |مَسارات| path; route; course; مَسار كَوْكَبٍ the orbit of a planet; سَلَكَ مَساراً to walk a route

مُسايَرة *n* **1** ◀ [مُجاراة] keeping up; مُسايَرة النَّسَقِ keeping pace **2** ◀ [مُداراة] flattery; humouring

مِسْيار *n* زَواج \ نِكاح المِسْيارِ misyar, travellers' marriage (*marriage wherein the spouses continue to live separately*)

مَسير *n* track, circuit; route; مَسير قَذيفةٍ the trajectory of a missile; تابَعَ مَسير شَخْصٍ to follow sb

مُسَيِّر **A** *adj* propellant, propelling **B** *n* administrator

مَسيرة *n* **1** ◀ [مَوْكِب] parade, procession; مَسيرة عَسْكَرِيّة a military parade **2** ◀ [مُظاهَرة] demonstration **3** ◀ [سَيْر] march; course; مَسيرة طَويلة a long march; مَسيرة سَلامٍ peace process; صَحَّحَ مَسيرةَ الحُكومةِ to correct the government's course **4** ◀ (Mus) march

سيراليون *n* |f| Sierra Leone

سيراميك *n* ceramics

‹ **سيرْفِر** *n* (Comput) server

‹ **سيرْك** *n* see سِرْك

‹ **سيريليّ** *adj* Cyrillic; الكِتابة السيريليّة the Cyrillic alphabet

[1] **سيرين** *n* |dipt f| Sirin (*female given name*)

[2] **سيرين** *n* (Chem) serine

‹ **سيزال** *n* (Bot) sisal (*Agave sisalana*)

‹ **سيشيل** *n* |f| Seychelles (*a 115-island country spanning an archipelago in the Indian Ocean*)

‹ **سَيْطَرَ** *v* |i; سَيْطَرة| to rule, to control, to dominate, to master; سَيْطَرَ على to dominate sth/sb; سَيْطَرَ على شَيْءٍ \ شَخْصٍ to exercise control over a people/land; شَعْبٍ \ أَرْضٍ to keep oneself under control; سَيْطَرَ على نَفْسِهِ to restrain one's emotions; سَيْطَرَ على مَشاعِرِه to bring a fire under control; سَيْطَرَ على حَريقٍ to overpower the hijackers; سَيْطَرَ على المُخْتَطِفينَ to dominate the market; سَيْطَرَ على السوقِ to bring the crises/match/situation under control; سَيْطَرَ على الأَزَمات \ المُباراةِ \ المَوْقِفِ to be overcome with despair; سَيْطَرَ عَلَيْهِ اليَأْسُ

سَيْطَرة *n* **1** [سُلْطة] domination, dominion, rule, command, supremacy; كانَ تحت سَيْطَرةِ شَخْصٍ to be under the domination of sb; جَعَلَ \ أَبْقى شَيْئاً تحت السَيْطَرة to bring sth under control; السَيْطَرة على شَعْبٍ ruling over a people **2** [تَحَكُّم] command, control; فاقِد السَيْطَرةِ unrestrained; السَيْطَرة على النَفْسِ self-control; فَقَدَ السَيْطَرةَ على نَفْسِه to lose one's self-control; فَقَدَ السَيْطَرةَ على المِقْوَدِ to lose control of the steering wheel; يُمْكِنُ السَيْطَرةُ عَلَيْه controllable; لا يُمْكِنُ السَيْطَرةُ عَلَيْهِ out of control

مُسَيْطِر **A** *adj* dominant, dominating; مُسَيْطِر على نَفْسِهِ self-controlled; كانَ مُسَيْطِراً على الأَمْرِ he was in control of the matter

B *n* ruler

‹ **سايَفَ** *v* to fence

سَيْف *n* |أَسْياف، سُيوف| sword; أبو سَيْف سَيْفُ الغُرابِ *Gladiolus*; swordfish; شَهَرَ السَيْفَ to draw one's sword; تَقَلَّدَ السَيْفَ to unsheathe one's sword; اسْتَلَّ \ سَلَّ سَيْفَهُ to draw one's sword; وَضَعَ السَيْفَ في الغِمْدِ the sheathe one's sword; سَبَقَ السَيْفُ العَذَلَ the die is cast

سَيّاف *n* |سَيّافون، سَيّافة| executioner

مُسايَفة *n* fencing

‹ **سيفون** *n* |سيفونات| siphon; سيفون دَوْرةِ المِياهِ toilet tank

‹ **سيكوباتيّ** **A** *adj* psychopathic

B *n* psychopath

‹ **سيكوسوماتيّ** *adj* psychosomatic

‹ **سيكولوجيّ** *adj* psychological

سيكولوجِيا *n* psychology

‹ **سالَ** *v* |i; سَيَلان، سَيْل| to flow, to stream; to flow/run/drain way; تَرَكَ الماءَ يَسيلُ to drain the water; يَسيلُ الحِبْرُ من القَلَمِ the ink flows out of the pen; سالَت الدُموعُ على خَدَّيْهِ tears ran down his cheeks; سالَ لُعابُهُ to salivate; سالَ لُعابُهُ على شَيْءٍ (fig) to strongly desire sth, to covet sth

سَيَّلَ *v* to liquefy, to melt, to make flow, to cause to stream

أَسالَ *v* to make flow, to cause to stream

سَيْل *n* |سُيول| stream, flow, current, torrent; سَيْل من الكَلِماتِ a torrent of words; سَيْل من الأَسْئِلةِ a barrage of questions; بَلَغَ السَيْلُ الزُبى the matter has come to a head

سائِل **A** *adj* [ضِدّ جامِد] liquid; صَمْغ \ صابون سائِل liquid glue/soap; مادّة سائِلة a liquid; أُصول سائِلة (Busn) liquid assets

B *n* **1** [ضِدّ جامِد] |سَوائِل| liquid; fluid; سَوائِل كيمْيائيّة \ قابِلة للاحْتِراقِ chemical/combustible liquids; سائِل مَنَويّ semen; امْتَصَّ السَوائِلَ to absorb liquid; لِتْران من السَوائِلِ two litres of liquid **2** [طارِح سُؤالٍ] see **سأل**

سَيّال **A** *adj* fluid, liquid; streaming, pouring; copious, abundant; كانَ قَلَمُهُ سَيّالاً he wielded a facile pen

B *n* fluid, liquid; flow; سَيّال عَصَبيّ (Med) nerve impulse

سَيَلان *n* **1** [سَوائِل] flowing **2** (Med) gonorrhoea; داء السَيَلانِ gonorrhoea

سُيولة *n* **1** [سيلان] liquid state, liquidity; flow, flowing; سُيولة المُرورِ traffic flow **2** (Busn) liquidity; سُيولة نَقْدِيّة liquidity, cash flow; سُيولة بَنْكٍ a bank's liquidity

تَسْييل *n* **1** (Phys) liquefying; تَسْييل الغازِ liquefying gas **2** (Busn) liquidation; تَسْييل المَوْجوداتِ the liquidation of assets

مُسيل *adj* liquefying; غاز مُسيل للدُموعِ tear gas; قُنْبُلة مُسيلة للدُموعِ a tear-gas canister

‹ **سيلاج** *n* silage

‹ **سيليكون** *n* silicone

‹ **سيَّما** *conj* see **سوي**

‹ **سيماء** *n* see **سوم**

‹ **سيمافون** *n* pager

‹ **سين** *n* |f| *name of the letter* **س**

‹ **سينيّ** *adj* المِحْور السينيّ x-axis

‹ **سيناء** *n* |dipt f| Sinai

‹ **سينارِيو** *n* |سينارِيُوات ,سينارِيوهات| scenario, plan, strategy; script; سينارِيو فيلْمٍ film script; كَتَبَ سينارِيو to write a script

‹ **سينما ,سِينِما ,سِينِما** *n* cinema; فَنّ السينَما cinema; مَهْرَجان السينَما film festival; ذَهَبَ إلى السينَما to go to the movies

سينَمائيّ *adj* cinematographic, cinema-; فَنّ سينَمائيّ cinematography

‹ **سيوا ,سيوة** *n* Siwa (*oasis in Egypt*)

‹ **سيّ** *n* see **سوي**

› **ش** *abbr* abbreviation for **شارِع** (*street*)

› **شاء** *n coll* |شِياه, شِياء, شِواه|; sing n |شاة| sheep; ewe

› **شادور** *n* chador (*open cloak worn by many Iranian women covering head and body*)

› **شاصي**, **شاسيه** *n* chassis

› **شَأْفة** *n* |شَأَفات| origin; اسْتَأْصَلَ شَأْفةَ الإرْهابِ to root out terrorism

› **شاكوش** *n* |شَواكيشُ| hammer

› **شال** *n* |شالات| scarf; shawl; ارْتَدى شالاً to wear/put on a shawl; شال من الصوفِ a woollen scarf

› **شاليه** *n* chalet, Swiss cottage

› **شَأَمَ** *v* |a; شَأْم| (old use) to bring bad luck

تَشاءَمَ *v* to be pessimistic; to be superstitious; تَشاءَمَ ب \ من شَيْءٍ to be pessimistic about sth

شُؤْم *n* ⓵ [تَطَيُّر] a bad omen, portent; misfortune; عَلامة شُؤْمٍ an ominous sign; كانَ نَذيرَ شُؤْمٍ على البِلادِ it was a bad omen for the country ⓶ [شَرّ] evil

تَشاؤُم *n* pessimism; نَظَرَ إلى شَيْءٍ بِتَشاؤُمٍ to have a grim/gloomy outlook on sth; دائِم التَشاؤُم eternal pessimist

تَشاؤُميّ **A** *adj* pessimistic

B *n* pessimist

مُتَشائِم **A** *adj* pessimistic; كانَ مُتَشائِماً بِخُصوصِ شَخْصٍ \ شَيْءٍ he was pessimistic about sb/sth

B *n* pessimist

مَشْؤوم *adj* |مَشائيمُ| inauspicious, ominous; unlucky; حادِث مَشْؤوم a fatal accident; خِطّة مَشْؤومة a sinister plan; في يَوْمٍ مَشْؤومٍ on a fatal day

› **شاميّ** *adj, n* (Hist) Syrian

الشام *n* (Hist) Syria; بِلاد الشامِ the Levant

› **شامْبو** *n* |شامْبُوات| shampoo

› **شَأَنَ** *v* |a; شَأْن| (old use) to become important, to become significant

شَأْن *n* |شُؤون| ⓵ [مَسْأَلة] affair, matter; case; concern; الشُؤون الداخِليّة \ الخارِجيّة domestic/foreign affairs, internal/external affairs; شُؤون العامِلينَ \ المُوَظَّفينَ personnel/staff matters, human resources; صاحِب الشَأْنِ the person concerned, the person involved; stakeholder; بِشَأْنِ ... with regard to ...; أَمْر خَطير الشَأْنِ a serious/grave matter; كَما هو الشَأْنُ ... as is the case ...; تَرَكَ شَخْصاً وَشَأْنَهُ to leave sb alone, to get off sb's back; شَأْنُكَ, أَنْتَ وَشَأْنُكَ suit yourself, do as you like; دَعْني وَشَأْني leave me alone, let me be; ذلك \ هذا لَيْسَ شَأْني that/this is none of my concern; ما شَأْنُكَ وَهَذا؟ what have you got to do with this?; لَيْسَ من شَأْنِكَ, لا شَأْنَ لَكَ في ذلك that is none of your business; شَأْنُهُ في ذلك شَأْنُ الوَزيرِ the same applies to him as to the minister; في هذا الشَأْنِ \ ب in this respect/regard, on this matter; about/concerning that ⓶ [أَهَمّيّة] rank, standing, prestige; importance; ذو شَأْنٍ significant, important; ذوو الشَأْنِ influential people; شَخْص ذو شَأْنٍ an influential/important person; رَجُل ذو شَأْنٍ عَظيمٍ a man of high esteem; شَخْص قَليل الشَأْنِ a person of little significance; لَها شَأْنٌ كَبيرٌ في الدَوْلَةِ she has great influence in the country

› **شاه** *n* ⓵ [مَلِك إيران] shah; شاه إيران Shah of Iran ⓶ [في لُعْبةِ الشِطْرَنْج] king; الشاهُ ماتَ \ ماتَ الشاهُ checkmate

› **شاهين** *n* |شَواهينُ| (Zool) peregrine falcon (*Falco peregrinus*)

› **شَأْو** *n* aim, goal, objective; بَعيد الشَأْوِ ambitious; بَلَغَتْ شَأْواً عَظيماً she has been successful in life

› **شاوَرْما** *n* shawarma (*sliced meat roasted on a vertical spit*)

› **شاويش** *n* police sergeant

‹ **شاي** *n* **1** [نبات] tea; كيس شايٍ tea bag; وَرَقة شايٍ tea leaf **2** [مَشْروب] tea; شاي ثَقيل \ خَفيف strong/weak tea; كوب \ فِنْجان من الشايِ a cup of tea; إبْريق من الشايِ a pot of tea; فِنْجان \ كوب شايٍ teacup; صينيّة شايٍ tea tray; مِصْفاة شايٍ tea strainer; شَرِبَ \ تَناوَلَ الشايَ to drink tea; أَعَدَّ \ حَضَّرَ الشايَ to make tea; صَبَّ \ سَكَبَ الشايَ to pour tea

‹ **شَبَّ** *v* **1** [تَرَبّى] |شَبيبة ,شَباب| to grow up; مَنْ شَبَّ على شَيْءٍ شابَ عَلَيْهِ always has been, always will be **2** [احْتَرَقَ] |شُبوب| يَشِبُّ to burn, to blaze; شَبَّت النارُ the fire blazed; شَبَّ حَريقٌ a fire is breaking out; a fire is raging **3** [الفَرَسُ] |شَبيب ,شِباب| to rear, to prance (*horses*)

شَبَّبَ *v* |ب| to extol, to praise highly

شابّ **A** *adj* |شَباب ,شُبّان| youthful, juvenile; young; جُمْهور شابّ a young audience **B** *n* |شَباب ,شُبّان| boy; youth, young guy/man; شَباب youth; young people; شابّ وَسيم a handsome young man; الشَباب العامِل working youth; شَباب اليَوْم today's youth

شابّة *n* |شابّات ,شَوابُّ ,شَبائِبُ| girl; young lady, young woman; شابّة طَموحة an ambitious young woman

شَبّ *n* alum

شَباب *n* youth; في شَبابِهِ in his youth, as a young man; حَبّ الشَبابِ acne; pimple; حَبّ الشَبابِ في الوَجْهِ facial acne; عانى من حَبِّ الشَبابِ to have/suffer from acne; في عِزِّ \ رَيْعانِ \ عُنْفُوانِ شَبابِها in the prime of her youth

شَبّابة *n* flute; clarinet

شَبابيّ *adj* youthful, juvenile; مَلابِس شَبابيّة young men's clothing

شَبيبة *n* youth

‹ **شِبِتّ** ,**شَبَت** ,**شِبِث** *n* (Bot) dill (*Anethum graveolens*)

‹ **شَبِثَ** *v* |a; شَبَث| (old use) |ب| to cling (to), to hang on (to); شَبِثَ بِشَيْءٍ to hold on to sth; شَبِثَ بِرَأْيِهِ to stick to one's opinion

تَشَبَّثَ *v* |ب| to cling (to), to hang on (to); to persist in; تَشَبَّثَ بِشَيْءٍ to cling to sth; to persist in sth; تَشَبَّثَ بِفِكْرةٍ to cling to an idea; تَشَبَّثَتْ بِهُوِيَّتِها she clung to her identity; تَشَبَّثَ بالماضي \ بالذِكْرَياتِ to hang on to the past/memories

شَبَث *n* |شِبْثان ,أَشْباث| (Zool) tarantula (*Theraphosidae*)

شِبِث *n* see شِبِتّ

تَشَبُّث *n* tenacity, persistence; stubbornness, obstinacy

مُتَشَبِّث *adj* tenacious, persistent; stubborn, obstinate; مُتَشَبِّث بالعاداتِ holding on to customs

‹ **شَبَحَ** *v* to bully; to threaten

شَبَح *n* |شُبوح ,أَشْباح| **1** [خَيال] ghost, spirit, apparition, spectre, phantom; مَدينة أَشْباحٍ ghost town; رَأى شَبَحاً to see a ghost **2** [هَيْئة] shape, shadowy figure; لاحَ شَبَحُ شَخْصٍ a human shape emerged **3** [فِكْرة مُخيفة] spectre, phantom; شَبَح البِطالةِ the spectre of unemployment; شَبَح الحَرْبِ the phantom of war

شَبَحيّ *adj* ghostlike

‹ **شِبْر** *n* |أَشْبار| (Meas) *span of the hand*

‹ **شَبْرَق** *n* |شَبارِقُ| (Hist) shabrack, horse blanket

‹ **شِبْشِب** *n* |شَباشِبُ| (ME) slipper

1‹ **شُباط** *n* |dipt| (Levant, Iraq) February

2‹ **شَبّوط** ,**سابوط** *n* carp (*Cyprinus carpio*); الشَبّوط الشائع \ الأوروبّيّ \ العاديّ (Zool) common carp (*Cyprinus carpio*)

‹ **شَبِعَ** *v* |a; شِبَع ,شَبْع| **1** [من الطَعام] to be/become satisfied; to be full **2** [مَلَّ] شَبِعَ من شَيْءٍ to have had one's fill of sth, to be/become fed up with sth

شَبَّعَ *v* to satisfy

أَشْبَعَ *v* to satisfy, to satiate; to drench, to saturate; أَشْبَعَ فُضولَهُ to satisfy one's curiosity; أَشْبَعَ شَخْصاً (جِنْسيًّا) to satisfy sb (sexually); جوع لا يُشْبَعُ insatiable hunger; أَشْبَعَ شَخْصاً ضَرْباً to give sb a (sound) beating; أَشْبَعَ شَوْقاً to satisfy a desire; أَشْبَعَ تَعَطُّشَهُ للسُلْطة to quench one's thirst for power; مَوْضوع أُشْبِعَ بَحْثاً an extensively researched subject

تَشَبَّعَ *v* to be/become saturated; تَشَبَّعَ بِشَيْءٍ to be saturated with sth; تَشَبَّعَ بالأَفْكار العُدْوانيّة to be full of hostile thoughts

شِبَع *n* (one's) fill

شَبْعان *adj* |شِباع ,شَباعى| satisfied, full

إشْباع *n* satisfaction, gratification; saturation; إشْباع جِنْسيّ sexual satisfaction; إشْباع السوقِ market saturation

تَشَبُّع *n* saturation; نُقْطة التَشَبُّعِ saturation point

لاتَشَبُّع *n* عَديد اللاتَشَبُّعِ polyunsaturated

مُشْبِع *adj* satisfied, sated; well-fed; غَيْر مُشْبِعٍ unsatisfied; كانَ مُشْبَعاً بِ to be saturated with, to be full of; كانَ مُشْبَعاً بالثقافة to be full of culture

مُشَبَّع *adj* ① (Elec) charged ② [بِسائِلٍ] saturated

شَبَق *n* desire, lust; eroticism; libido; شَبَق جِنْسِيّ lust; ذُرْوة الشَبَقِ orgasm, climax

شَبِق *adj* ① [شَهْوانِيّ] lustful; lewd ② [امْرَأة] امْرَأة شَبِقة nymphomaniac

شَبَكَ *v* |i; شَبْك| to be intertwined; to intertwine, to interlace; شَبَكَ شَيْئاً بِشَيْءٍ to interlace sth with sth; شَبَكَ يَدَيْهِ على بَطْنِهِ he clasped his hands over his stomach; شَبَكَ ذِراعَهُ بِذِراعِ شَخْصٍ to link arms with sb

شَبَّكَ *v* to intertwine, to interlace; to tangle (up); شَبَّكَ أَصابِعَهُ to clasp one's hands; شَبَّكَ شَيْئاً بِشَيْءٍ to intertwine sth with sth

تَشَبَّكَ *v* to be/become entangled

تَشابَكَ *v* to intertwine; to be interwoven, to be intertwined

اشْتَبَكَ *v* ① [تَقاتَلَ] to clash, to come to blows; to engage; اشْتَبَكَتْ طائِراتُنا مع طائِراتِ العَدُوِّ our fighter planes have engaged with the enemy fighter planes ② [اخْتَلَطَ] to be intertwined; to get embroiled in; اشْتَبَكَ في شَيْءٍ to get mixed up in sth

شابِكة *n* Internet

شُبّاك *n* |شَبابيكُ| ① [نافِذة] window; شُبّاك من الخَشَبِ shutter ② [بَيْع التَذاكِرِ] عند شُبّاكِ التَذاكِرِ at the box office

شُبّاكيّة *n* (NA) *sweet delicacy*

شَبْكة *n* |شَبْكات| (ME) engagement gift (*usually gold jewellery*)

شَبَكة *n* |شَبَكات, شِباك, شَبَك| ① [الصَيْد] net; شَبَكة صَيْدٍ fishing net; رَتَقَ الشِباكَ to mend nets ② net, network; grid; system; شَبَكة عالَميّة \ دُوَلِيّة a global network; شَبَكة وَطَنيّة \ قَوْميّة a national network; شَبَكة اجْتِماعيّة, شَبَكة عَلاقاتٍ اجْتِماعيّةٍ a social network; شَبَكة إِجْراميّة a criminal network; شَبَكة اتِّصالاتٍ communications network; شَبَكة عَلاقاتٍ a network of contacts; شَبَكة تَوْزيعٍ distribution network; شَبَكة أَنابيبَ \ أَسْلاكٍ tubing; grid; شَبَكة كَهْرَبائيّة (electricity/power) grid; شَبَكة إِلِكْترونيّة an electronic network; شَبَكة السِكَكِ الحَديديّة the railway network; شَبَكة قَنَواتٍ a network of canals; شَبَكة طُرُقٍ a road network; مَدَّ شَبَكة طُرُقٍ to construct a road network; مُشَغِّل شَبَكةٍ network provider ③ [إِعْلام] network; شَبَكة تِلِفِزْيونيّة television network; شَبَكة إِخْباريّة news network ④ (Comput) شَبَكة اتِّصالٍ network; شَبَكة رَقْميّة digital network; شَبَكة (اتِّصالٍ) مَحَلِّيّة local area network, LAN; الشَبَكة العالَميّة, شَبَكة الإِنْتَرْنِت العالَميّة, الشَبَكة العَنْكَبوتيّة العالَميّة the World Wide Web; على الشَبَكةِ online; خارِجَ الشَبَكةِ offline; رابِطة الشَبَكةِ العالَميّةِ the World Wide Web Consortium, W3C

شَبَكيّ *adj* ① *interwoven, as in a net*; حَوْسَبة شَبَكيّة grid computing ② (Anat) retinal; الانْفِصال الشَبَكِيّ retinal detachment

شَبَكيّة *n* (Anat) retina; اعْتِلال الشَبَكيّةِ (السُكَّرِيّ) (diabetic) retinopathy

شُبَيكة *n* |شَبائِكُ| graticule, grid

اشْتِباك *n* |اشْتِباكات| confrontation, skirmish; اشْتِباك دامٍ a bloody confrontation; اشْتِباك مُسَلَّح an armed encounter

تَشابُك *n* |تَشابُكات| entanglement; overlap; تَشابُك المَصالِحِ conflict of interest

مُتَشابِك *adj* overlapping; العَلاقات المُتَشابِكة interconnections

مُشَبَّك *adj* woven; أَسْلاك مُشَبَّكة wire mesh

مِشْبَك *n* |مَشابِكُ| ① [شَعْرٍ \ وَرَقٍ] fastener, clasp; paper clip; clip; مِشْبَك وَرَقٍ paper clip; مِشْبَك شَعْرٍ hair clip; مِشْبَك الغَسيلِ clothes peg ② [دَبّوس] pin

شِبْل *n* |أَشْبال| ① (Zool) (lion) cub; هذا الشِبْلُ من ذاكَ الأَسَدِ like father, like son ② (Sport) junior; انْتَمى إلى \ لَعِبَ مع الأَشْبالِ to belong to/play in the junior league

شَبين, شِبين *n* |أَشابينُ| ① شَبين التَعْميدِ (Chr) godfather, sponsor ② [الزَواج] best man, groomsman

إِشْبين *n* |أَشابينُ| groomsman, page

إِشْبينة *n* bridesmaid

شَبَّهَ *v* to compare; شَبَّهَها بالبَدْرِ he compared her to the full moon

شابَهَ *v* to look like, to resemble; شابَهَ شَيْئاً to bear a resemblance to sth; شابَهَ شَخْصاً to look like sb; وَما شابَهَ;

ذلك and so on; مَنْ شابَهَ أَباهُ فما ظَلَم the apple doesn't fall far from the tree

أَشْبَهَ *v* to resemble, to look like; أَشْبَهَ شَيْئاً تَمامَ الشِبْهِ to bear a striking resemblance to sth; وَما أَشْبَهَ ذلك and the like

تَشَبَّهَ *v* to imitate, to mimic

تَشابَهَ *v* to resemble one another

اشْتَبَهَ *v* 1 [في الأَمْرِ] to suspect, to have suspicions; to doubt 2 [عَلَيْهِ الأَمْرُ] to be/become confused

شَبَه *n* |أَشْباه| 1 [شَبيه] double, look-alike; يَخْلُقُ اللهُ من الشَبَهِ أَرْبَعينَ ≈ like two peas in a pod 2 [تَشابُه] resemblance; وَجْه الشَبَه similarity; common ground; أَشْباه حَسَنٍ people like Hassan; كانَ فيهِ شَبَهٌ من شَخْصٍ to bear a resemblance to sb; الشَبَهُ بَيْنَهُ والنُسْخةِ الأَصْليّةِ كَبيرٌ جدًّا the resemblance to the original is striking

شِبْه *n* |أَشْباه| almost (*before n*); demi- (*before n*); semi- (*before n*); شِبْه قارّةٍ subcontinent; شِبْه جَزيرة peninsula; شِبْه رَسْميٍّ semi-official; شِبْه عَسْكَريّ paramilitary; من شِبْهِ المُؤَكَّد almost certainly; من شِبْهِ المُسْتَحيل almost impossible; مَجْموعَتانِ شِبْهُ مُتَساوِيَتانِ two nearly identical groups

شُبْهة *n* |شُبُهات, شُبْهات, شُبَهات| suspicion, doubt; vagueness; uncertainty; كانَ فوق كُلِّ الشُبُهاتِ to be above/beyond all suspicion; حامَت الشُبُهاتُ حَوْلَها there were suspicions about her

شَبيه A *adj* |أَشْباه| similar; شَبيه بِشَيْءٍ similar to sth
B *n* |أَشْباه| counterpart

أَشْبَه *adj* |dipt| هي أَشْبَهُ بِأُمِّها she resembles her mother more than anyone else

اشْتِباه *n* |اشْتِباهات| 1 [شَكّ] suspicion, mistrust; اشْتِباه في شَخْصٍ suspicion of sb 2 [تَشابُه] resemblance, similarity

تَشابُه *n* similarity, resemblance; parallel; parallelism; تَشابُه مُذْهِل \ مُدْهِش a striking resemblance; تَشابُه تاريخيّ a historical parallel; هُناكَ تَشابُهٌ واضِحٌ \ كَبيرٌ بَيْنَهُ وَبَيْنَ أَبيهِ he bears a strong/close resemblance to his father

تَشْبيه *n* |تَشْبيهات| 1 [مُقارَنة] comparison 2 (Rhet) simile; allegory 3 (Theol) anthropomorphism (*the ascription of human characteristics to God*)

مُتَشابِه *adj* similar, resembling; جَواب \ مَوْقِف مُتَشابِه a similar answer/stance

مُشابِه *adj* similar, alike; corresponding, analogous; بِطَريقةٍ مُشابِهةٍ in a similar manner; حالات \ ظُروف مُشابِهة similar situations/circumstances

مَشْبوه A *adj* doubtful, dubious; shady, suspicious; مُمارَسات \ أَعْمال \ عَمَليّات مَشْبوهة dubious practices; قَضيّة مَشْبوهة a shady affair
B *n* suspect

مُشْتَبَه A *adj* dubious; مُشْتَبَه فيهِ suspicious; قَرار مُشْتَبَه فيهِ a dubious decision
B *n* المُشْتَبَه فيهِ suspect; مُشْتَبَه فيهِ رَئيسيّ main suspect; أَلْقَت الشُرْطةُ القَبْضَ على ثَلاثةِ مُشْتَبَهٍ فيهِمْ the police have arrested three suspects

‹ **شَباة** *n* |شَبَوات| (old use) point, tip

‹ **شَتَّ** *v* |i; شَتّ, شَتات| 1 [شَيْءٌ] to be scattered/dispersed 2 [شَيْئاً] to disperse, to scatter

شَتَّتَ *v* to scatter, to disperse

تَشَتَّتَ *v* 1 [حَطَّمَ] to shatter; to be crushed 2 [تَفَرَّقَ] to disperse; to be scattered

شَتّ *n* |أَشْتات| 1 [شَظيّة] fragment, small part 2 [أَشْياء مُتَنَوِّعة] sundries

شَتات A *adj* scattered
B *n* diaspora

شَتّانَ *excl* شَتّانَ بَيْنَهُما! how different they both are!

شَتّى A *n* various; في شَتّى مَجالاتِ العُلوم in various fields of science
B *adj* see شَتيت
C *v* see شَتيت

شَتيت *adj* |شَتّى| scattered

تَشَتُّت *n* fragmentation; diaspora; تَشَتُّت فِكْريّ distraction

‹ **شَتَرَ** *v* |i; شَتْر| (old use) to cut off

‹ **شَتَلَ** *v* |i; شَتْل| to plant; to transplant

شَتْلة *n* |شَتائِل, شُتول| cutting, scion; seedling; غَرَسَ شَتْلاً to plant seedlings

شَجَّرَ *v* to forest, to plant with trees

شاجَرَ *v* to fight (against); to quarrel/argue (with)

أَشْجَرَ *v* to be covered with trees

تَشاجَرَ *v* to dispute, to argue, to fight; تَشاجَرَ مع شَخْصٍ to quarrel with sb; تَشاجَرَ بِشَأْنِ الأَعْمالِ المَنْزِلِيّةِ to argue over chores; تَشاجَرَ من أَجْلِ شَيْءٍ to fight about sth

اشْتَجَرَ *v* to quarrel, to argue

شَجَر *n coll* |أَشْجار| tree; شَجَرة الصَنَوْبَرِ pine (tree) (*Pinus*); شَجَرة نَفْضيّة deciduous tree; شَجَرة القُضْبانِ birch (*Betula*); شَجَرة نَسَبٍ family tree; pedigree; شَجَرة عيد الميلادِ Christmas tree; أَعْلى \ رَأس \ قِمّة الشَجَرة treetop; في أَعْلى الشَجَرةِ in the treetop; إزالة الأَشْجارِ deforestation

شَجِر *adj* forested, woody

شِجار *n* fight, scuffle; argument, quarrel; شِجار عَنيف a violent argument; شِجار بِسَبَبِ \ من أَجْلِ شَيْءٍ an argument over sth; شِجار مع شَخْصٍ a quarrel with sb

شَجَرِيّ *adj* tree (*before n*); سِياج شَجَرِيّ hedge maze

شُجَيْرة *n* shrub, bush; bushes

تَشْجير *n* **1** [زَرْع الشَجَرِ] afforestation; tree planting **2** [جَدْوَل] tree (diagram)

مُشاجَرة *n* quarrel, argument, fight; arguing, squabbling; مُشاجَرة قَصيرة \ عَنيفة \ شَديدة a short/violent/severe altercation; مُشاجَرة مع شَخْصٍ a quarrel with sb

شَجُعَ *v* |u; شَجاعة| to be brave, to be courageous

شَجَّعَ *v* to encourage, to motivate, to urge (on); to support; شَجَّعَ شَخْصاً على فِعْلِ شَيْءٍ to encourage sb to do sth; شَجَّعَ نادِياً to support a team; شَجَّعَ على اسْتِعْمال حِزامِ الأَمانِ to encourage the use of a seat belt

تَشَجَّعَ *v* to be encouraged, to take heart, to keep one's spirits up

شُجاع *adj* |شُجْعان, شَجَعة| brave, courageous; valiant, intrepid; قَرار \ اخْتِيار شُجاع a brave decision/choice; مُحاوَلات شُجاعة courageous attempts

شَجاعة *n* bravery, courage; fearlessness; تَصَرَّفَ بِشَجاعةٍ to behave bravely; دافَعَ عن نَفْسِهِ بِشَجاعةٍ to put up a brave fight; شَجاعة الأَسَدِ heroism, courage of a lion

مَشْتَل *n* |مَشاتِل| nursery (*garden*)

شَتَمَ *v* |i-u; شَتْم| to insult; to abuse, to curse, to swear at; شَتَمَ شَخْصاً to swear at sb

شاتَمَ *v* to abuse; to insult

تَشاتَمَ *v* to abuse one another; to swear at one another

شَتْم *n* abuse, insult; swear word, curse

شَتيمة *n* |شَتائِمُ| abuse, insult; swear word, curse; سَيْل \ وابِل من الشَتائِمِ stream/barrage of insults; تَلَقّى وابِلاً من الشَتائِمِ to endure a torrent of abuse; أَمْطَرَ شَخْصاً بالشَتائِمِ to shower sb with abuse; كالَ لِشَخْصٍ الشَتائِمَ to heap abuse on sb; قَذَفَ شَخصاً بالشَتائِمِ to hurl insults at sb

شُتَمْبِر *n* (Mor) September

شَتا *v* |u; شَتْو| to winter, to overwinter; to hibernate

شَتّى **A** *v* to winter, to overwinter; to hibernate **B** *adj, n* see شتت

شِتاء *n* |أَشْتِية, شُتِيّ| winter; شِتاءً \ في الشِتاءِ in the winter; شِتاء قارِس a harsh winter; الشِتاء الماضي \ القادِمِ last/next winter; فَصْل الشِتاءِ winter, wintertime; في عِزِّ الشِتاءِ in the dead of winter; الشِتاءُ على الأَبوابِ winter is upon us

شِتائِيّ *adj* wintry, wintery; في لَيْلٍ \ يَوْمٍ شِتائِيٍّ on a wintry night/day

شَتْوِيّ, شَتَوِيّ *adj* wintry, wintery; جَوّ \ بَرْد شَتْوِيّ wintry weather/cold; تَوْقيت شَتْوِيّ wintertime; سُبات شَتْوِيّ hibernation; الأَلْعاب الأولِمْبِيّة الشَتْوِيّة the Olympic Winter Games

مَشْتًى *n* |مَشاتٍ| winter (sports) resort; winter residence

شَجَبَ *v* |u; شَجْب| to denounce; شَجَبَ شَيْئاً to denounce sth; شَجَبَت الاعْتِداءَ she denounced the attack

شَجَّبَ *v* to condemn

مِشْجَب *n* |مَشاجِبُ| coat rack; clothes hook

شَجَّ *v* |i-u; شَجّ| to break, to fracture; to cause a head wound

شَجّة *n* |شِجاج| skull fracture; head wound (*which leaves the skull exposed*)

شَجَرَ *v* |u; شَجْر, شُجور| to heat, to fire up; شَجَرَ الأَمْرُ بَيْنَهُمْ they had an argument

شُحّ *n* 1 [قِلّة] shortage, scarcity, lack; شُحّ في مِياهِ الشُرْبِ shortage of drinking water; شُحّ المَوادِّ الغِذائيّةِ the scarcity of food; شُحّ الأَمْطارِ the lack of rain 2 [بُخْل] stinginess

شَحيح *adj* |أَشِحّاءُ, أَشِحّة, شِحاح| stingy; frugal

مُشاحّة لا مُشاحّةَ أنّ ... it goes without saying that ..., it's undisputed that ...

‹ **شَحَذَ** *v* |a; شَحْذ| 1 [السِكّينَ] to grind; to sharpen, to whet; شَحَذَ السَكّاكينَ to sharpen knives 2 [تَسَوَّلَ] to beg

شَحْذ *n* grinding, sharpening; حَجَر الشَحْذِ grindstone

شَحّاذ *n* beggar

مِشْحَذ *n* |مَشاحِذُ| grindstone

‹ **شُحّار** *n* soot

شُحْرور *n* |شَحاريرُ| (Zool) blackbird (*Turdus*)

‹ **شَحَطَ** *v* |a; شَحْط, شُحوط| to be/become far away

شَحْطة *n* dash

‹ **شَحُمَ** *v* |u; شَحامة| to be/become fat

شَحِمَ *v* |a; شَحَم| to be/become fat

شَحَّمَ *v* to lubricate; to grease, to oil; شَحَّمَ المُحَرِّكَ \ السَيّارةَ to lubricate the engine/car

شَحْم *n* |شُحوم, شُحومات| fat; grease, lubricant; lard; أزالَ الشَحْمَ to remove grease; to remove fat; ≈ بِلَحْمِهِ وَشَحْمِهِ alive and well

شَحِم *adj* mushy (*fruit*)

شَحْمة *n* piece of fat; شَحْمة الأُذُنِ earlobe

شَحْميّ *adj* fatty, fat; greasy, oily; وَرَم شَحْميّ lipoma (*benign tumour*); الحَوامِض الشَحْميّة fatty acids

شَحيم *adj* |شُحَماءُ| fat; thick

تَشْحيم *n* lubrication; زَيْت التَشْحيمِ lubricant, lubricating oil

مُشَحِّم *n* lubricant

‹ **شَحَنَ** *v* |a; شَحْن| 1 [نَقَلَ] to transport; to carry; to ship; to load; شَحَنَ بَحْراً to transport by sea; شَحَنَ الأَثاثَ to ship furniture; شَحَنَ البَضائعَ \ النَفْطَ إلى الوِلاياتِ المُتَّحِدةِ to ship goods/oil to the United States 2 [سَفينةً] to load, to freight 3 (Elec) to charge, to recharge; to boost; شَحَنَ بَطّاريّةً to charge a battery

شَجيع *adj* |شُجَعاءُ; f pl شَجيعات, شَجائعُ| brave, courageous

تَشْجيع *n* |تَشْجيعات| encouragement; support, promotion; تَشْجيعاً by way of encouragement; تَشْجيعاً للعِلْمِ for the advancement of science

تَشْجيعيّ *adj* encouraging, motivating; سِياسة تَشْجيعيّة incentive policy

مُشَجِّع A *adj* encouraging, promising; أَخْبار \ تَطَوُّرات \ نَتائِج مُشَجِّعة encouraging news/developments/results
B *n* supporter, fan; مُشَجِّع فَريق مانْشِسْتِر يونايْتِد Manchester United fan

‹ **شَجَنَ** *v* |u| 1 [الحَمامُ] |شُجون| to coo; شَجَنَ الحَمامُ the pigeon cooed 2 [أَحْزَنَ] |شَجْن| to sadden

شَجِنَ *v* |a; شَجَن| (old use) to be/become sad; to be/become distressed

أَشْجَنَ *v* to sadden; to grieve, to distress

شَجَن *n* |أَشْجان, شُجون| sorrow, grief

‹ **شَجا** *v* |u; شَجْو| to grieve; to worry, to trouble

شَجِيَ *v* |a; شَجا| to be/become sad

أَشْجى *v* to grieve, to sadden

شَجْو *n* |أَشْجاء| sadness, grief

شَجيّ *adj* moving, touching; صَوْت شَجيّ a moving voice

شَجًى *n* a lump in the throat

مَشْجاة *n* melodrama

‹ **شَحَبَ, شَحُبَ** *v* |a-u; شُحوب, شُحوبة| to turn pale, to blanch; to look pale; شَحَبَ وَجْهُهُ his face turned pale; شَحَبَ وَجْهُها من الخَوْفِ she turned white with fear

شاحِب *adj* |شَواحِبُ| pale, white; colourless; وَجْه شاحِب a pale face; ضَوْء شاحِب a dim light; شاحِب الوَجْهِ with a pale face, as white as a sheet

‹ **شَحَتَ** *v* |a; شَحْت| to beg

شَحّات *n* |شَحّاتة| beggar

‹ **شَحَّ** *v* |i-u; شُحّ| 1 [بَخُلَ] to be stingy 2 [قَلَّ] to run out; to be/become scarce; تَشِحُّ مَوارِدُ المِياهِ the water supply is dwindling

شاحَّ *v* to be stingy/niggardly

شاحَنَ *v* 1 [خاصَمَ] to quarrel 2 [بَغَضَ] to hate

أَشْحَنَ *v* to load, to charge, to fill up

تَشاحَنَ *v* to argue, to quarrel; to hate one another

شَحْن *n* transport; shipping; شَحْن بَحْرِيّ sea freight; شَحْن جَوِّيّ air freight; شَحْن مَلابِس a shipment of clothing; شَحْن النَفْطِ بالسُفُنِ إلى أَمْريكا the shipping of oil to America

شاحِن *n* charger; شاحِن بَطّارِيّة battery charger

شاحِنة *n* lorry (BrE), truck (AmE); شاحِنة رافِعة crane; حَرَكة مُرور الشاحِناتِ lorry traffic; سائِق شاحِنةٍ lorry driver; ساقَ شاحِنةً to drive a lorry

شَحْناء *n* |dipt f| enmity, hostility

شُحْنة, شِحْنة, شَحْنة *n* |شِحْنات ,شِحَن| 1 [حُمولة] cargo, freight; شَحْنة خَطيرة \ كيمِيائيّة \ ثَمينة hazardous/chemical/precious cargo 2 (Elec) charge; شَحْنة النَواةِ ,شَحْنة نَوَوِيّة nuclear charge; شَحْنة سالِبة a negative charge; شَحْنة موجَبة \ إيجابيّة a positive charge; شَحْنة بَطّارِيّةٍ battery charge

مُشاحَنة *n* quarrel; squabbling; مُشاحَنات سِياسيّة political bickering

مَشْحون *adj* charged; جَوّ مَشْحون a charged atmosphere

شَخْبَطَ *v* |i; شَخْبَطة| to scribble; to scrawl

شَخَّ *v* |u; شَخّ| to urinate, to pee (infml), to piss (vulg)

شَخَرَ *v* |i; شَخير| 1 [حِصان] to snort 2 [مُحَرِّك] to throb 3 [الإنْسانُ] to snore

شَخَّرَ *v* to snore loudly

شَخْشَخَ *v* |i; شَخْشَخة| to rattle; to jangle

شُخْشيخة *n* |شَخاشِخُ| rattle (*toy*)

شَخَصَ *v* |a; شُخوص| 1 [نَظَرَ] to stare; to peer; شَخَصَ نَظَرُها she stared 2 [ارْتَفَعَ] to tower 3 [بَدا] to appear

شَخْصَنَ *v* |i; شَخْصَنة| to personify, to embody

شَخَّصَ *v* 1 (Med) to diagnose; شَخَّصَ المَرَضَ to diagnose the disease 2 [حَدَّدَ الهُوِيّةَ] to identify 3 [مَثَّلَ] (old use) to play (a part), to act

أَشْخَصَ *v* to send back

تَشَخَّصَ *v* to be diagnosed (*illness, disorder*); تَشَخَّصَ الداءُ the disease was diagnosed

شَخْص *n* |mf; شُخوص ,أَشْخاص| 1 [إنْسان] person, individual; figure; شَخْص ما somebody, someone; شَخص بارِز a prominent person; شَخْص حُلو المَعْشَرِ an amicable person; شَخْص مَشْبوه a suspicious person; شَخْص نَحيف a slender person; شَخص غَريب الأَطْوارِ eccentric person; تَذْكِرة واحِدة لِكُلِّ شَخْصٍ one ticket per person; كانوا خَمْسةَ أَشْخاصٍ they were five strong; كُلّ شَخْصٍ everybody, everyone 2 (Law) person; شَخْص طَبيعيّ a natural person; شَخْص مَعْنَوِيّ \ قانونيّ juristic/legal person

شَخْصانيّة *n* personalism

شَخْصِيّ *adj* personal, individual; private; شَخْصِيًّا personally, in person; مَسْؤوليّة شَخْصيّة personal responsibility; شَخْصيًّا أَرى ... personally, I think ...

شَخْصيّة *n* 1 [طَبْع] personality, character; mind; identity; شَخْصيّة فَذّة an extraordinary character; شَخْصيّة قَوِيّة a strong personality; بِطاقة شَخْصِيّة identity card; كانَتْ لَهُ شَخْصيّةٌ مُمَيَّزةٌ he was quite exceptional; كانَ مُزْدَوِجَ الشَخْصيّة to have a split personality; لَهُ شَخْصِيّةٌ ضَعيفةٌ he has no/a weak personality; انْفِصام الشَخْصيّة schizophrenia 2 [فَرْد] figure; person; شَخْصيّة مَرْكَزِيّة a key figure; شَخْصيّة تاريخيّة a historical figure; شَخْصيّة بارِزة \ ذات شَأْنٍ a prominent/notable person; شَخْصيّة مُهِمّة \ مَعْروفة an important/public figure; شَخْصيّة قِياديّة a leading figure; شَخْصيّة غامِضة an obscure figure 3 (Cin, Literat) character; part, role

تَشْخيص *n* 1 (Med) diagnosis; عِلْم التَشْخيصِ diagnostics; تَشْخيص قُزَحِيّ iridology 2 [تَمْثيل] interpretation, performance

تَشْخيصيّ *adj* diagnostic; فَحْص تَشْخيصيّ diagnostic examination

مُشَخَّص *adj* diagnosed; غَيْر مُشَخَّصٍ undiagnosed

تَشَدَّخَ *v* to burst, to pop; to crack

شَدَّ *v* |i-u; شَدّ| 1 [رَبَطَ] to fasten, to tie; to tighten, to clench; شَدَّ حَبْلاً \ خَيْطاً to stretch a rope/thread; شَدَّ الأَوْتارَ to tighten the strings; شَدَّ أَوْتارَ الرُكْبَةِ to pull a hamstring; to stretch a hamstring; شَدَّ أَوْتارَ الكَمانِ to string a violin;

شَديد *adj* |شِداد ,أَشِدّاءُ| strong, powerful; loud; harsh, severe; intense, vehement; حاجة شَديدة a dire need; عِقاب \ حُكْم \ شَهيّة شَديدة a severe punishment/judgement/pain; أَلَم شَديد a strong appetite; رَجُل شَديد a strong man; ارْتِفاع \ انْخِفاض شَديد a sharp rise/decline; عَوَز \ نَقص شَديد في شَيْءٍ a severe shortage of sth; تَحْذير شَديد اللَهْجة a stern warning; شَديد الشَقاءِ \ الحُزْن deeply unhappy; كانَ شَديدَ الاقْتِناع بِشَيْءٍ to be strongly convinced of sth; كانَ عِنْدَهُ صُداعٌ شَديدٌ he had a splitting headache; أُصيبَ بِمَرَض شَديد to be seriously ill; بِلَهْجةٍ شَديدة sharply worded

شَديدة *n* |شَدائِدُ| شَدائِد distress; hardship, affliction, adversity; تَحَمَّل \ واجَهَ شَدائِدَ to bear/face hardships

أَشَدّ *adj* |dipt| stronger; harsher; worse; أَشَدّ ما يَكونُ exceedingly; أَشَدّ غَضَباً angrier

تَشَدُّد *n* severity; strictness; بِتَشَدُّدٍ strictly; مَوْقِف غاية في التَشَدُّدِ a very strict stance

تَشْديد *n* 1 [تَقْوية] intensification, strengthening; emphasis, stress; ب \ مع التَشْديدِ على ... with the emphasis on ...; تَشْديد الإجْراءاتِ tightening of measures 2 (Gram) *doubling of a consonant*

مُتَشَدِّد A *adj* strict, stringent; severe; مُتَشَدِّد في أَفْكارِهِ rigid in his ideas

B *n* bigot; zealot; مُتَشَدِّد إسْلاميّ Islamic extremist

مُشادّة *n* controversy; quarrel, argument, dispute; مُشادّة كَلاميّة argument; مُشادّة بين شَخْصَيْن argument between two people

مِشَدّ *n* |مِشَدّات| corset

مُشَدَّد *adj* 1 [شَديد] severe; rigid; emphasized; تَدابير \ قَرارات \ إجْراءات أَمْنيّة مُشَدَّدة harsh measures/ tough decisions; heightened security measures; تحت حِراسةٍ مُشَدَّدةٍ under tight security 2 (Gram) doubled (*consonant*)

مُشَدِّد *adj* aggravating; ظُروف مُشَدِّدة aggravating circumstances

مَشْدود *adj* 1 [مَرْبوط] tense, taut; fixed; tied; قَبْضة مَشْدودة tight fist; أَعْصاب مَشْدودة tense/taut nerves; عَضَلات مَشْدودة lean muscles 2 [مَحْشور] trapped, jammed; tight

شادِر *n* |شَوادِرُ| tent; warehouse, storehouse

شَدَّتْ حِزامَها she tightened her belt; شَدَّ الزِمامَ to be pulling the strings; شَدَّ المِقْوَدَ بِكِلْتَيْ يَدَيْه to clench the steering wheel with both hands; to tighten the leash with both hands; شَدَّ بُرْغياً \ صَمولةً \ سِدادةً to tighten a screw/nut/cap; شَدَّ عَزائِمَهُ to be determined; to take matters into one's own hands; شَدَّ عَضُدَ شَخْصٍ \ شَدَّ أَزْرَ شَخْصٍ to strengthen sb's resolve; شَدَّ شَخْصٍ \ شَيْئاً to support sb/sth 2 [اسْتَحْوَذَ] to engross; to overwhelm; شَدَّني الشَوْقُ I was overcome with desire; شَدَّني المَوْضوعُ the matter intrigued me

شَدَّدَ *v* 1 [زادَ] to intensify, to strengthen; to sharpen; to tighten (up); شَدَّدَ شَيْئاً to intensify sth; شَدَّدَ الحِراسةَ to intensify the surveillance; شَدَّدَ المُراقَبةَ to tighten the supervision; شَدَّدَ العُقوباتِ to impose more severe punishments; شَدَّدَت الحُكومةُ سِياسَتَها \ الإجْراءاتِ the government intensified its policy/measures 2 [أَكَّدَ] |على| to emphasize, to stress; to accentuate, to underline; شَدَّدَ على أنّ .... to emphasize that ...; شَدَّدَ على واقِعٍ to underscore a fact; شَدَّدَ على ضَرورةِ شَيْءٍ to stress the necessity of sth; شَدَّدَ على ضَرورةِ حُدوثِ شَيْءٍ to emphasize that sth needs to happen 3 (Ling) to double a consonant in pronunciation

تَشَدَّدَ *v* to intensify; to be/become difficult

تَشادَّ *v* to discuss

انْشَدَّ *v* 1 [شَدَّ] to tauten, to tense 2 [انْجَذَبَ] |إلى نَحْوَ| to be attracted to

اشْتَدَّ *v* to intensify; to aggravate; اشْتَدَّ الأَلَمُ the pain intensified; اشْتَدَّ النِزاعُ the conflict intensified

شَدّة *n* 1 (Gram) *doubling sign over a consonant* 2 [وَرَق لَعِبٍ] شَدّة وَرَق لَعِبٍ a deck of cards

شِدّة *n* 1 [حِدّة] intensity, strength; fierceness; بِشِدّةٍ strongly, fiercely, deeply; أَلَحَّ بِشِدّةٍ to insist very strongly; ازْدادَ شِدّةً to grow more intense; تَقِلُّ \ تَزْدادُ شِدّةُ شَيْءٍ the intensity of sth is decreasing/increasing; تَكَلَّمَ \ صَرَخَ \ ضَحِكَ بِشِدّةٍ to talk/cry/laugh loudly; بَكى من شِدّةِ الفَرَحِ to weep with happiness, to cry for joy 2 [عُنْف] violence 3 [ضيق] misery; trouble, misfortune; الفَرَجُ بعد الشِدّةِ calm after the storm; بعد كُلِّ شِدّةٍ فَرَجٌ the darkest hour is just before the dawn

شادور *n* listed alphabetically

‹ **شادوف** *n* (Hist) shadoof (*a pole with a bucket and counterpoise used especially in Egypt for raising water.*)

شُدْفة *n* section; fragment

‹ **تَشَدَّقَ** *v* [1] [تَبَجَّحَ] to be loud-mouthed; to boast, to brag [2] [تَظاهَرَ] to pay lip service; تَشَدَّقَ بالديمُقْراطِيّة \ الحُرّيّة to pay lip service to democracy/freedom [3] [تَحَدَّثَ بِطولٍ وَغَضَبٍ] to rant

شِدْق *n* |أَشْداق| corner of the mouth; نَفَخَ شِدْقَيْهِ to be arrogant; ابْتَسَمَ مِلْءَ شِدْقَيْهِ to smile widely; ضَحِكَ مِلْءَ شِدْقَيْهِ he guffawed

أَشْدَق *adj* |dipt; شُدْق| large-mouthed

مُتَشَدِّق **A** *adj speaking loudly*; مُتَشَدِّق بِشَيْءٍ trumpeting sth **B** *n* braggart

‹ **شَدَنَ** *v* |u; شُدون| to be on one's own feet (*a young animal*)

شادِن *n* |شَوادِنُ| (Zool) fawn

‹ **شَدَهَ** *v* |a; شَدْه| to amaze, to astonish; شُدِهَ to be amazed

أَشْدَهَ *v* to baffle; to amaze, to astonish

انْشَدَهَ *v* to be amazed

مَشْدوه *adj* bewildered, baffled; speechless; perplexed

‹ **شَدا** *v* |u; شَدْو| to sing, to warble; شَدا بالشِعْرِ to recite poems (*in a solemn voice*)

شادٍ **A** *adj* |شُداة| [1] [رَخيم] melodious, lilting [2] [طالِب] (old use) educated, trained **B** *n* |شُداة| singer

‹ **شِدْياق** *n* |شَدايِقة| (Chr) subdeacon

‹ **شَذَّبَ** *v* to trim, to prune

مِشْذَب *n* |مَشاذِبُ| trimmer; مِشْذَب الشَعْرِ hair trimmer

‹ **شَذَّ** *v* |i-u; شُذوذ, شَذّ| to deviate

شاذّ **A** *adj* |شَواذُّ, شُذّاذ| [1] [غَيْر عاديٍّ] deviant; abnormal, unusual; peculiar, strange; وَضْع شاذّ anomaly, a strange situation; عادات شاذّة peculiar habits, strange customs; شاذّ عَقْليًّا perverted; لِكُلِّ قاعدةٍ شَواذٌّ every rule has its exceptions; شاذّ عن القاعِدةِ deviating from the rule; كانَتْ شاذّةُ الأَخْلاقِ she had eccentric manners [2] [جِنْسيًّا] perverted; homosexual **B** *n* homosexual

شُذوذ *n* aberration; anomaly, abnormality; شُذوذ جِنْسيّ sexual aberration; perversion; homosexuality

‹ **شَذْر** *n* |شُذور| fragment; nugget (*gold*); bead

شَذَر *n* شَذَر مَذَر helter-skelter, disorder

‹ **شَذا** *v* |u; شَذْو| to emit a fragrance

شَذاً *n* scent, aroma; شَذا الزُهورِ fragrance of flowers

شَذيّ *adj* fragrant

‹ **اشْرَأَبَّ** *v* |اشْرِئْباب| to stretch one's neck

‹ **شَرِبَ** *v* |a; شُرْب, مَشْرَب| to drink; شَرِبَ ماءً to drink water; شَرِبَ الدُخانَ to smoke; شَرِبَ الكُحولَ to drink (alcohol); لا يَشْرَبُ الكُحولَ he doesn't drink

شَوْرَبَ *v* |i; شَوْرَبة| to have a moustache

شَرَّبَ *v* [1] [حَشَرَ] to stuff, to fill; to impregnate, to saturate; شَرَّبَ شَيْئاً بِشَيْءٍ to fill sth with sth [2] [أَرْوى] to quench; to make drink; شَرَّبَ شَخْصاً شَيْئاً to make sb drink sth [3] [مَذْهَباً \ عَقيدةً] to indoctrinate

شارَبَ *v* to have a drink (with sb)

أَشْرَبَ *v* [1] [بَلَّلَ] to drench, to saturate [2] [سَقى] to make drink

تَشَرَّبَ *v* to absorb, to soak up

شُرْب *n* صالِح للشُرْبِ potable; ماء الشُرْبِ, ماء صالِح للشُرْبِ drinking water, potable water; غَيْر صالِحٍ للشُرْبِ undrinkable; الإِفْراط في شُرْبِ الكُحولِ excessive consumption of alcohol

شارِب *n* |شَوارِبُ| moustache; whiskers; شارِبانِ moustache; شارِب كَبير a big moustache; أَطْلَقَ شارِبَهُ to grow a moustache; لَهُ شارِبٌ كَثٌّ \ كَثيفٌ he has a bushy moustache

شَراب *n* |أَشْرِبة| [1] [مَشْروب] drink, beverage; أَدْمَنَ الشَرابَ to be an alcoholic; شَراب البُرْتُقالِ fizzy orange (BrE), orange soda (AmE) [2] [دَواء] syrup, linctus; شَرِبَ شَراباً to take a syrup; وَصَفَ (لِلمَريضِ) شَراباً to prescribe a syrup (to a patient); شَراب مُنَوِّم sedative syrup; شَراب ضِدّ السُعالِ cough syrup; مِلْعَقة \ قِنّينة شَرابٍ a spoonful/bottle of syrup

شُراب *n* |شُرابات| sock, stocking

شَرّابة, شُرّابة *n* |شَراريبُ| tassel, tuft; شَراريب fringe

شَرْبة *n* |شَرَبات| dose

شُرْبة, شورْبة n |شُرَب| 1▸ [حَساء] soup 2▸ [جُرْعة] gulp
شِرّيب n drunk, drunkard
شَوْرَب n (Zool) flycatcher
مَشْرَب n |مَشارِبُ| 1▸ [شَراب] drink, beverage 2▸ [مَيْل] tendency, inclination 3▸ [حانة] bar 4▸ [مَنْهَل] watering place
مَشْروب A n |مَشْروبات| drink, beverage; مَشْروبات كُحوليّة alcoholic drinks; مَشْروبات روحيّة spirits, liquors; مَشْروب غازيّ soft drink, soda; مَشْروبات مُنْعِشة refreshing drinks
B adj غَيْر مَشْروبٍ undrinkable
مُشَوْرَب adj having a moustache
‹ **شَرَث** n (Med) chilblain
‹ **شَرَج, شَرْج** n |أشْراج| (Anat) anus; فُتحة الشَرَج anus
شَرَجيّ adj anal; حُقْنة شَرَجيّة enema
‹ **شَرَح** v |a; شَرْح| 1▸ [أَوْضَحَ] to explain, to elucidate; to interpret; شَرَحَ شَيْئاً to explain sth; شَرَحَ شَيْئاً بِوُضوح to explain sth clearly; شَرَحَ لِشَخْصٍ أنّ ... to explain to sb that ...; شَرَحَ لِشَخْصٍ وِجْهة نَظَرِه to explain one's point of view to sb; شَرَحَ مَوْقِفَهُ لِشَخْصٍ to justify one's position to sb; شَرَحَ مَسْأَلةً \ مَوْضوعاً to explain a matter/subject; شَرَحَ ما هو قَصْدُهُ بالضَبْطِ to explain one's intention precisely 2▸ [قَطَعَ] to cut up, to slice; شَرَحَت الخُبْزَ \ اللَحْمَ she sliced the bread/meat
شَرَّح v 1▸ [جُثّةً] to dissect; شَرَّحَ جُثّةً to conduct an autopsy 2▸ [قَطَعَ] to slice
اِنْشَرَح v to be relieved; اِنْشَرَحَ صَدْرُها she was relieved
شَرْح n |شُروح| explanation, elucidation; شَرْح لِشَيْءٍ an explanation of sth; أَعْطى \ قَدَّمَ شَرْحاً to give an explanation; شَرْح واضِح \ شَفَويّ \ مُسْهَب a clear/verbal/elaborate explanation; أَمْر يَطولُ شَرْحُهُ a matter that is difficult to explain
Idiom سورة الشَرْح The Relief (*Sura 94*)
شارِح n commentator (*scholar who interprets laws*); exponent
شَريحة n |شَرائِحُ| 1▸ [قِطْعة] slice; strip; filet; شَريحة رَفيعة \ سَميكة a thin/thick slice; شَريحة خُبْزٍ \ جُبْنةٍ a slice of bread/cheese; شَريحة سَلْمون a salmon filet 2▸ [طَبَقة] segment, stratum, layer; شَرائِح المُجْتَمَعِ segments of society; شَريحة من المُواطِنينَ a segment of the population 3▸ (Phot) slide; عَرْض شَرائِحَ slideshow 4▸ (Econ) bracket; شَريحة ضَريبيّة tax bracket; أَعْلى شَريحةٍ ضَريبيّةٍ the highest tax bracket; الشَريحة الأولى \ الثانية the first/second tax bracket
اِنْشِراح n relief; ease; اِنْشِراح الصَدْرِ relief; اِنْشِراح حول شَيْءٍ relief over sth
تَشْريح n anatomy, dissection; عِلْم التَشْريح anatomy; تَشْريح جُثّةٍ autopsy, post-mortem; قامَ بِتَشْريح الجُثّةِ to perform an autopsy; تَبَيَّنَ من نَتيجةِ التَشْريحِ أنَّ ...، أَثْبَتَ التَشْريحُ بِأنَّ... the autopsy showed that ...
تَشْريحيّ adj anatomical
مُشَرِّح n pathologist; anatomist
مَشْرَحة n |مَشارِحُ| mortuary, morgue
مُنْشَرِح adj glad, happy; relieved; مُنْشَرِح الصَدْرِ relieved
‹ **شَرَخ** v |u; شَرْخ| (Egypt) to cause a crack, to crack; to split
اِنْشَرَخ v to crack
شَرْخ n |شُروخ| crack, fissure
‹ **شَرَد** v |u; شُرود, شِراد| to wander; to stray, to run away; شَرَدَ ذِهْنُها \ فِكْرُها her thoughts wandered; شَرَدَ نَظَرُهُ his gaze strayed
شَرَّد v to chase away; to displace; شَرَّدَت الفَيَضاناتُ الآلافَ the floods displaced thousands
تَشَرَّد v to be/become homeless; to roam
شارِد A adj |شَوارِدُ, شُرَّد, شُرُد| stray; wandering; كِلاب شارِدة stray dogs; شارِد الذِهْنِ absent-minded, distracted; كانَ شارِدَ النَظَرِ to stare blankly
B n |شَوارِدُ, شُرَّد, شُرُد| runaway
شارِدة n |شَوارِدُ| *something gone astray; an obscure word;* لا تَفوتُهُ شارِدةٌ وَلا وارِدةٌ he doesn't miss a thing, nothing escapes him; يَنامُ مِلْءَ جُفونِهِ عن شَوارِدِها *to torment people with the obscurity of one's language, for one's own amusement*
شُرود n شُرود الفِكْرِ absent-mindedness
شَريد adj homeless
مُتَشَرِّد A adj, n homeless; الأَطْفال المُتَشَرِّدونَ homeless children
B n homeless person, bum; vagabond

مُشَرَّد [A] *adj* homeless

[B] *n* homeless person; bum, vagabond

تَشَرْدَقَ *v* to gag, to choke

شَرْذَمَ *v* to tear apart, to divide; to split, to fragment

شِرْذِمة *n* |شَرَاذِم| [1] fragmentation; الشِرْذِمة الطائِفيّة sectarian fragmentation [2] platoon

أَشَّرَ *v* to mark

شَرَر *n coll* spark; تَطايَرَ الشَرَرُ من عَيْنَيْهِ sparks flew from his eyes; مُعْظَمُ النارِ من مُسْتَصْغَرِ الشَرَرِ little sparks kindle great fires

شَرّ [A] *adj* worse, more evil; هَزَمَهُمْ شَرَّ هَزيمةٍ he dealt them a bitter defeat; وَبَّخَ شَخْصاً شَرَّ تَوْبيخٍ to scold sb sharply

[B] *n* |شُرور| [1] [عَكْس الخَيْر] evil; نَذير شَرٍّ a bad omen; أَهْوَن الشَرَّيْن the lesser of two evils; شَرّ لا بُدَّ مِنْهُ a necessary evil; مُنْذِر بالشَرِّ ominous; يُجَسِّدُ الشَرَّ بعَيْنِه he is evil incarnate; انْكَسَرَ الشَرُّ evil is dispelled; خَيْراً تَعْمَلُ شَرًّا تَلْقى *to do sth good but get sth bad in return* [2] [خُبْث] evil, malice

شَرار *n coll* spark; شَرار النارِ sparks

شِرّير [A] *adj* |أَشْرار, أَشِرّاءُ| evil, wicked; malicious; ساحِرة شِرّيرة a wicked witch; أَرْواح \ خِطَط شِرّيرة evil spirits/plans

[B] *n* |أَشْرار, أَشِرّاءُ| villain, scoundrel

شَرِس *adj* vicious, fierce; aggressive, brutal; كَلْب شَرِس a vicious dog; مُنافَسة شَرسة \ تَنافُس شَرِس fierce competition; هَجْمة شَرِسة a ferocious attack

شَراسة *n* brutality, ferocity; قاتَلَ بِشَراسةٍ to fight fiercely

أَشْرَس *adj* |dipt; شُرْس| quarrelsome; vicious, aggressive

شِرْش *n* شِرْش اللَبَنِ whey (*watery part of milk that separates from the curds*)

شَرْشَرَ *v* |i; شَرْشَرة| to serrate

شَرْشَف *n* |شَراشِفُ| sheet, bed sheet; شَراشِف نَظيفة clean sheets; شَرْشَف مائِدةٍ \ طاوِلةٍ tablecloth

شُرْشور *n* |شَراشيرُ| (Zool) brambling (*Fringilla montifringilla*)

شَرَطَ *v* |i-u; شَرْط| [1] [اشْتَرَطَ] to stipulate; شَرَطَ شَيْئاً على شَخْصٍ to stipulate sth as a condition on sb [2] [شَقَّ] to cut into, to cut open; شَرَطَ بالمِشْرَطِ to cut with a scalpel

شَرَّطَ *v* to cut open

شارَطَ *v* to stipulate as a condition; شارَطَ شَخْصاً على شَيْءٍ to stipulate sth as a condition on sb

تَشارَطَ *v* to impose conditions on each other

اشْتَرَطَ *v* to stipulate; to impose as a condition; اشْتَرَطَ تَعْويضاتٍ to stipulate compensation

شَرْط *n* |شُروط| demand, term, clause; stipulation, condition; criterion; requirement, requisite; بِشَرْطٍ conditional; بِلا شُروطٍ unconditionally; بِشَرْطٍ واحِدٍ on one condition; شَرْط أَوَّليّ \ أَساسيّ a prerequisite; شَرْط رَئيسيّ a key requirement; شَرْط أَدْنى minimum requirement; شَرْط الجَوْدةِ quality requirement; شَرْط قانونيّ a legal provision; شَرْط ضَروريّ necessary condition, (conditio) sine qua non; شُروط صارِمة stringent requirements; شُروط قاسِية harsh conditions; strict conditions; قائِمة شُروطٍ list of demands; تَوَفَّرَتْ فيه الشُروطُ \ جَميعُ الشُروطِ he met the/all requirements; لَيْسَ شَرْطاً it is not required; على شَرْطِ أَنْ \ بِ شَرْطَ أَنْ on the condition that, provided that, subject to; فَرَضَ \ وَضَعَ شُروطاً (على) to make demands (on), to stipulate conditions; احْتَرَمَ شَرْطاً to observe a clause

شَرْطة *n* |شُرَط| dash, hyphen; شَرْطة بين كَلِمَتَيْنِ dash

شُرْطة *n* police; شُرْطة عَسْكَرِيّة military police; الشُرْطة القَضائيّة judicial police; شُرْطة الآدابِ \ الأَخْلاقِ morality police; شُرْطة الحُدودِ border police; شُرْطة الأَجانِبِ immigration police; رَجُل الشُرْطةِ policeman, police officer; رِجال الشُرْطةِ police (force); رَئيس \ مُفَوَّض \ مَأْمور \ عَميد شُرْطةٍ police commissioner, superintendent; مُدير شُرْطةٍ police chief; مَرْكَز الشُرْطةِ police station; سَيّارة الشُرْطةِ police car; جِهاز الشُرْطةِ police (force); بَدْلة الشُرْطةِ police uniform; وَحْدة شُرْطةٍ police unit; مُراقَبة الشُرْطةِ police surveillance; حِماية الشُرْطةِ police protection; كُلِّيّة الشُرْطةِ police academy; دائِرة الشُرْطةِ police headquarters, central police station; أَبْلَغَ الشُرْطةَ to inform the police; وَسْطَ حِراسةٍ مُشَدَّدةٍ من الشُرْطةِ under heavy police escort

شَرْطيّ *adj* conditional; provisional; جُمْلة شَرْطيّة (Ling) conditional clause

أَشْرَعَ *v* 1 [سِلاحاً] to draw 2 [فتَحَ] to open; أَشْرَعَ النَوافِذَ to open the windows

اشْتَرَعَ *v* to make laws

شارِع *n* 1 [طَريق] |شَوارِعُ| street; شارِع رَئيسيّ main street/main road; high street (BrE); شارِع فَرْعيّ side street/road; شارِع مُوازٍ service road; اسْم الشارِع street name; رُكْن \ زاوِية الشارِع street corner; طِفْل شارِعٍ street urchin (old use), street child; رَجُل الشارِع the man in the street, the common man; في الشارِع on/in the street; في الشارِع العَرَبيّ among the Arab population; رَأْي الشارِع العَرَبيّ the opinion of the Arab man on the street; خَرَجَ إلى الشارِع to take to the streets (to demonstrate) 2 (Law) |شارِعونَ| legislator

شِراع *n* |أَشْرِعة ,شُرُع| sail; canvas cover; الشِراع الأَماميّ foresail; jib; رَفَعَ الأَشْرِعةَ to hoist the sails; أَنْزَلَ الأَشْرِعةَ to strike the sails, to lower the sails

شِراعيّ *adj* sail (before n), sailing (before n); زَوْرَق شِراعيّ sailing boat (BrE), sailboat (AmE); طائِرة شِراعيّة glider, sailplane

شَرْعيّ *adj* legal, valid, lawful; legitimate, rightful; justified; زَوْج شَرْعيّ a lawful husband; مُتَزَوِّج شَرْعيًّا lawfully wedded; مِلْك شَرْعيّ legitimate property; المالِك الشَرْعيّ the rightful owner; الوَريث الشَرْعيّ the lawful heir; السُلْطة الشَرْعيّة the legal authority; إقامة شَرْعيّة a legal residence; مَحْكَمة شَرْعيّة sharia court; عِلْم شَرْعيّ jurisprudence; غَيْر شَرْعيٍّ illegal, unlawful, illicit, illegitimate; طِفْل غَيْر شَرْعيٍّ an illegitimate child; عَلاقة غَيْر شَرْعيّة an extramarital affair

شَرْعيّة *n* legitimacy; legality, lawfulness; عَدَم الشَرْعيّة illegality; شَرْعيّة المَطالِب the legality of the claims

شُروع *n* beginning; inauguration, entrance; الشُروع في المُفاوَضاتِ starting negotiations

شَريعة *n* |شَرائِعُ| law; الشَريعة (الإسْلاميّة) Islamic law, sharia; شَرائِع اللهِ God's laws, the divine laws; شَريعة الغابِ the law of the jungle

اشْتِراعيّ *adj* legislative; انْتِخابات اشْتِراعيّة legislative elections; مَرْسوم اشْتِراعيّ legislative decree

اشْتِراعيّة *n* legality

الشَرْع *n* the Islamic legislation

شُرْطيّ *n* police officer, policeman, cop (infml); شُرْطيّ سِرّيّ undercover agent; شُرْطيّ مُرورٍ traffic policeman

شَريط *n* |أَشْرِطة ,شَرائِط| 1 [قُماشٍ إلخ] band, strip, strap; ribbon, tape; شَريط لاصِق (adhesive) tape; شَريط حَريريّ \ جِلْديّ a silk ribbon/leather strap; قَصَّ شَريطاً to cut a ribbon; شَريط حِذاءٍ lace, shoelace; رَبَطَ شَريطَ حِذائِهِ to tie one's shoelaces 2 [مُسَجَّل] (magnetic) tape; cassette; شَريط التَصْويرِ film reel; شَريط فيديو videotape, video; على شَريطٍ on tape; شَريط تَسْجيلٍ cassette; شَريط للشابِّ خالِدٍ a cassette of Cheb Khaled; أَدارَ \ شَغَّلَ شَريطاً to play a cassette; سَجَّلَ على شَريطٍ to make a tape recording, to record on tape; كانَ مُسَجَّلاً على شَريطٍ to be (recorded) on tape 3 [خَطّ] شَريط أَدواتٍ \ عَمَلٍ (Comput) toolbar; شَريط المَهامّ (Comput) taskbar; شَريط تَقَدُّمٍ (Comput) progress bar; شَريط إخْباريّ news ticker

شَريطة *n* |شَرائِطُ| 1 [رُتْبة] chevron; على كَتِفِهِ شَريطةٌ a chevron on his shoulder 2 [شَرْط] condition; شَريطةَ أَنْ on the condition that, provided (that); شَريطةَ أَنْ يَكونَ هَدَفُهُ مُواجَهةَ الحَرَكاتِ الإرْهابيّةِ provided that his goal is to combat terrorist movements

شَريطيّ *adj* (Med) دودة شَريطيّة tapeworm (*Taenia*)

اشْتِراط *n* |اشْتِراطات| condition, stipulation, requirement; اشْتِراطات قاسِية strict requirements; اسْتَوْفى الاشْتِراطاتِ الصِحّيّةَ to meet the health requirements

إشْراط *n* conditioning

مِشْرَط *n* |مَشارِطُ| scalpel; lancet; مِشْرَط الجَرّاحِ surgeon's scalpel

مَشْروط *adj* conditional; غَيْر مَشْروطٍ unconditional; سَلام مَشْروط conditional peace; اسْتِسْلام غَيْر مَشْروط unconditional surrender; مَشْروط بـ ... contingent on

شَرْطَنَ *v* |i; شَرْطَنة| (Chr) to ordain as priest

شَرَعَ *v* |a; شُروع ,شَرْع| 1 [بَدَأَ] |في| to begin, to start; to initiate; شَرَعَ في شَيْءٍ to begin sth; شَرَعَ في مَشْروعٍ to start a project; شَرَعَ يَفْعَلُ to start to do; شَرَعَ في فِعْلِ شَيْءٍ to start doing sth; شَرَعَ في الدِراسةِ \ التَدْخينِ to start studying/smoking 2 (Law) to enact

شَرَّعَ *v* 1 (Law) to make laws 2 [سِلاحاً] to draw

أَشْرَف المَريضُ على الشِفاءِ the patient was nearly cured

تَشَرَّفَ *v* to be honoured; to feel flattered; تَشَرَّفْنا ≈ pleased to meet you; تَشَرَّفْتُ بِمَعْرِفَتِكَ it was a pleasure meeting you; تَشَرَّفْتُ بِمُقابَلةِ الرَئيسِ I had the privilege of meeting the president

اسْتَشْرَفَ *v* to look towards; اسْتَشْرَفَ المُسْتَقْبَلَ to look to the future; اسْتَشْرَفَ الآفاقَ الجَديدةَ ≈ to look into new prospects

شَرَف *n* 1 [عِرْض] honour, dignity; pride; شَرَف المِهْنةِ professional ethics; مَسْألة شَرَفٍ matter of honour; حَرَس شَرَفٍ (Mil) honour guard; دَوْرة شَرَفٍ lap of honour; ميثاق شَرَفٍ gentleman's agreement; ≈ code of honour; كَلِمة شَرَفٍ word (of honour); جَرائِم الشَرَفِ honour crimes; (قَسَماً) بِشَرَفي on my (word of) honour; أُقْسِمُ بِشَرَفي I swear; بِكُلِّ شَرَفٍ with pride, proudly; لي عَظيمُ الشَرَفِ I am very honoured; على شَرَفِ شَخْصٍ in honour of sb; اُعْتُدِيَ على شَرَفِها her honour was violated; بِرُتْبةِ الشَرَفِ (Educ) ≈ with distinction, ≈ with honors (AmE); تَخَرَّجَ بِتَقْديرِ امْتِيازٍ مع مَرْتَبةِ الشَرَفِ to graduate with distinction 2 [نَسَب] nobility; peerage

شُرْفة *n* |شُرَف ,شُرُفات| 1 [بَيْت] balcony; في الشُرْفةِ on the balcony; شُرْفة الشَقّةِ \ المَنْزِلِ the balcony of the apartment/ house; الشُرْفة المُطِلّة على ... the balcony overlooking ... 2 (Theat) balcony

شَرَفيّ *adj* honorary; عُضْويّة شَرَفيّة honorary membership; تَحيّة شَرَفيّة salute

شَريف A *adj* |أَشْراف ,شُرَفاءُ| 1 [نَبيل] noble, virtuous; distinguished, reputable; طَبْع شَريف a noble character; أُسْرة شَريفة a distinguished family 2 [فاضِل] honest, honourable, respectable; عَمَل شَريف honest work

B *n* |أَشْراف ,شُرَفاءُ| sharif (*descendant of the prophet Muhammad*); الشَريف *honorary title of the guardian of the holy places in Mecca*

اسْتِشْراف *n* futurology; اسْتِشْراف المُسْتَقْبَلِ foreseeing the future

اسْتِشْرافيّ *adj* futurological; بَحْث اسْتِشْرافيّ forward-looking research

إشْراف *n* supervision, oversight; monitoring; moderation (*of internet forum*); إشْراف مُباشِر direct supervision; إشْراف

تَشْريع *n* |تَشْريعات| legislation, issuing of rules; تَشْريع ضَريبيّ tax legislation; تَشْريعات بيئيّة environmental legislation; تَشْريعات إلَهيّة divine laws

تَشْريعيّ *adj* legislative; السُلْطة التَشْريعيّة the legislative branch; هَيْئة تَشْريعيّة a legislative body; دَوْرة تَشْريعيّة legislative session; فَراغ تَشْريعيّ a legislative gap; انْتِخابات تَشْريعيّة legislative elections; مَجْلِس تَشْريعيّ legislative council

لاشَرْعيّة *n* illegitimacy; illegality, unlawfulness

مُشْتَرِع *n* legislator

مُشَرِّع *n* legislator, lawmaker

مَشْروع A *adj* legal, lawful; legitimate; justifiable; حَقّ مَشْروع a legitimate right; بالطُرُقِ المَشْروعةِ by legitimate means; غَيْر مَشْروعٍ illegal, illicit; سُؤال \ مُلاحَظة مَشْروع(ة) a legitimate question/remark; اسْتَوْلى على شَيْءٍ بِطَريقةٍ غَيْرِ مَشْروعةٍ to misappropriate sth

B *n* |مَشاريعُ ,مَشْروعات| plan, project; venture, enterprise; concept; design; مَشْروع إداريّ an administrative concept; مَشْروع خُماسيّ five-year plan; ساهَمَ في مَشْروعٍ to participate in a project; حَقَّقَ مَشْروعاً to carry out a project; مَشْروع قانونٍ (Law) bill

مَشْروعيّة *n* legitimacy; legality

شُرْغوف *n* |شَراغيفُ| (Zool) tadpole

شَرُفَ *v* |u; شَرَف| to be/become respectable; to be noble

شَرَّفَ *v* to pay homage; to honour; يُسْعِدُني ويُشَرِّفُني it is my great pleasure and honour; شَرَّفْتُمونا ≈ thanks for coming (*when guests are leaving*); شَرَّفَنا بِزيارةٍ he honoured us with a visit; شَرَّفَتْنا بِمُقابَلةٍ she graced us with an interview

شارَفَ *v* to approach, to come near; شارَفَ على الانْتِهاءِ to near completion

أَشْرَفَ *v* 1 [راقَبَ] to supervise; to guide, to counsel; أَشْرَفَ على شَيْءٍ to supervise sth; أَشْرَفَ على بَحْثِ الطالِبِ to supervise the student's research; أَشْرَفَ على تَدْريبِ الفَريقِ to oversee the team's training 2 [أَطَلَّ] to look down; أَشْرَفَ على الجُمْهورِ to look down on the crowd; أَشْرَفَ على المَدينةِ كُلِّها to overlook the entire city 3 [أَوْشَكَ] أَشْرَفَ المَريضُ على المَوْتِ the patient was on the verge of death;

اسْتِشْراق *n* orientalism

إشْراق *n* |إشْراقات| shining, luminosity; sunshine; radiation; (spiritual) illumination إشْراق الشَمْسِ sunshine

الشارقة *n* (Geog) Sharjah (*one of the United Arab Emirates*)

الشَرْقيّة *n* (Geog) Sharqiyya (*eastern delta of the Nile*)

مُسْتَشْرِق *n* orientalist

مَشْرِق *n* |مَشارِقُ| East; Mashriq (*countries in the eastern Arab world*); من المَشْرِقِ إلى المَغْرِبِ the whole world; مَشارِق الأَرْضِ وَمَغارِبُها from East to West

مُشْرِق *adj* shining, beaming, radiant; sunny; جَوّ مُشْرِق glorious weather; شَمْس مُشْرِقة a radiant sun; يَوْم جَميل مُشْرِق a beautiful sunny day

مَشْرِقيّ *n* |مَشارِقة| inhabitant of the Mashriq (*eastern Arab world*)

شَرَقْرَق *n* (Zool) green woodpecker

شَرِكَ *v* |a; شِرْك, شِرْكة, شَرِكة| to participate, to take part; to be/ become (a) partner

شَرَّكَ *v* to partner with

شارَكَ *v* to take part, to join, to participate; to share; شارَكَ في شَرِكةٍ to participate in a company; شارَكَ في مَشْروعٍ \ تَشاوُرٍ to participate in a project/consultation; شارَكَ في حَدَثٍ to take part in an event; شارَكَ في نِقاشٍ \ مُؤْتَمرٍ to take part in a discussion/conference; شارَكَ في الاجْتِماع to attend the meeting; أُشارِكُكَ الرَأْيَ I share your opinion; شارَكَ في شَيْءٍ to share in sth; شارَكَ في دَفْعِ التَكاليف to share the costs

أَشْرَكَ *v* **1** [شَرَّكَ] to make participate; to make partner with; أَشْرَكَ المُدَرِّبُ لاعِبَهُ في المُباراة the coach put his player in the game **2** (Relig) to practise polytheism; to practise idolatry; أَشْرَكَ باللهِ to attribute associates to God, to practise idolatry

تَشارَكَ *v* to participate; to become partners; تَشارَكَ في شَرِكةٍ to participate in a company; تَشارَكَ في تَحَمُّلِ المَسْؤوليّة to share responsibility

اشْتَرَكَ *v* **1** [ساهَمَ] to take part, to participate; to join; اشْتَرَكَ في شَيْءٍ to share in sth; اشْتَرَكَ في مُسابَقةٍ to enter a competition; اشْتَرَكَ في حَرْبٍ \ نَدْوةٍ to take part in a war/ symposium **2** [في مَجَلّةٍ إلخ] to subscribe; اشْتَرَكَ في جَريدةٍ to subscribe to a newspaper

الإشْراف على شَيْءٍ supervision قَضائيّ judicial supervision; over sth; تحت \ بِإشْرافِ شَخْصٍ under supervision of sb; تحت إشْرافِ الرَئيسِ \ المُدَرِّبِ under the president's/coach's supervision; كانَ تحت الإشْرافِ الطِبّيِّ to be under medical supervision; تَوَلّى الإشْرافَ to supervise

تَشْريفة *n* تَشْريفات ceremony; رَئيس التَشْريفاتِ master of ceremonies

مَشْرَف *n* |مَشارِفُ| height; highland, high ground; مَشارِف الأَلْفيّةِ the millennium; مَشارِف المَدينةِ the outskirts of the city

مُشْرِف **A** *adj* supervising

B *n* overseer, supervisor; moderator; مُشْرِف دِراسيّ advisor; مُشْرِف مُنْتَدًى master of ceremonies, MC; مُشْرِف الحَفْلِ (Comput) forum moderator

مُشَرَّف *adj* honoured; الكَعْبة المُشَرَّفة the Holy Kaaba

مُشَرِّف *adj* respectable, honourable; عَمَل مُشَرِّف respectable work

شَرَقَ *v* |u; شَرْق| to rise; شَرَقَت الشَمْسُ the sun rose

شَرِقَ *v* |a; شَرَق| to choke; شَرِقَ بِدَمْعِه to choke on one's tears

شَرَّقَ *v* to travel east; شَرَّقَ وَغَرَّبَ to travel extensively

أَشْرَقَ *v* to shine (upon), to irradiate; to rise (*sun*); أَشْرَقَت الشَمْسُ على وَجْهِهِ the sun shone on his face; أَشْرَقَ وَجْهُهُ his face beamed

اسْتَشْرَقَ *v* to study the Orient

شَرْق *n* east; الشَرْق the Orient, the East; الشَرْق الأَوْسَط the Middle East; الشَرْق الأَقْصى the Far East; الشَرْق الأَدْنى the Near East; شَرْقَ باريس east of Paris; خَطّ طولٍ شَرْقاً eastern longitude; عِشْرونَ دَرَجةً شَرْقَ خَطِّ الطولِ 20 degrees longitude east; دِراسات الشَرْقِ الأَوْسَطِ Middle Eastern studies

شَرّاقة *n* choke

شَرْقيّ **A** *adj* eastern, east; oriental; ريح شَرْقيّة east wind; سَجّادة شَرْقيّة an oriental carpet; نِصْف الكُرة الأَرْضيّة الشَرْقيّ the eastern hemisphere

B *n* Asian

شُروق *n* sunrise; شُروق الشَمْسِ sunrise; صَلاة الشُروقِ prayer at sunrise

شَرَك *n* |شِراك, أَشْراك, شُرُك| trap, snare, (trap) net; وَقَعَ في شَرَكٍ to fall into a trap; نَصَبَ شَرَكاً لِشَخْصٍ to set a trap for sb

شِرْك *n* polytheism; idolatry; أَهْل الشِرْكِ polytheists

شِراك *n* |أَشْراك, أَشْرُك, شُرُك| shoelace, lace

شَراكة *n* partnership; شَراكة مَدَنيّة civil partnership; شَراكة بَنّاءة \ مُثْمِرة a constructive/fruitful partnership; اتِّفاقيّة شَراكةٍ اسْتِراتيجيّةٍ strategic partnership agreement

شَرِكة *n* ① [مُؤَسَّسة] company, enterprise; firm, business; partnership; شَرِكة اسْتِثْمارِيّة investment company; شَرِكة سِياحيّة tour company; شَرِكة قابِضة holding company; شَرِكة مُشْتَرَكة joint venture; شَرِكة شَقيقةٍ sister company, associate company; شَرِكة أُمّ parent company; شَرِكة تَوْزيعٍ distribution company; شَرِكة تَضامُنٍ partnership, firm; طَبيب شَرِكةٍ company doctor; شَرِكة مُساهَمةٍ مُغْلَقة a private limited company; شَرِكة مُساهَمةٍ مُغْفَلة a public limited company; شَرِكة مُساهَمةٍ مَحْدودة المَسْؤوليّةِ a limited liability company; أَصْحاب الأَسْهُمِ \ المُساهِمونَ في شَرِكةٍ company shareholders; شَرِكة مُتَعَدِّدة الجِنْسيّاتِ multinational corporation; على حِسابِ الشَرِكةِ at company expense; أَسَّسَ شَرِكةً to set up a company; كَوَّنَ \ أَسَّسَ شَرِكةَ تَضامُنٍ to create/set up a partnership; أَدارَ شَرِكةً to run a business; رَأَسَ شَرِكةً to manage a company; صاحِب شَرِكةٍ entrepreneur; company owner; هو صاحِبُ شَرِكةٍ he has a company of his own; اتِّحاد شَرِكاتٍ consortium ② [بين أَشْخاصٍ] partnership

شِرْكة *n* (Chr) (Holy) Communion

شَريك *n* |شُرَكاءُ, أَشْراك| partner, companion; associate; شَريك حَياةٍ life partner, partner in life; شَريك تِجاريّ business partner; شَريك موصٍ silent partner, financial backer; شَريك في شَرِكةٍ (business) partner, member of the firm; شَريك في الجَريمةِ accomplice, accessory; الشُرَكاء في شَرِكةٍ the partners in a firm; حِصّة الشَريكِ partner's share

اشْتِراك *n* |اشْتِراكات| ① [مُشارَكة] participation; الاشْتِراك في جَريمةٍ complicity in a crime; الاشْتِراك في شَرِكةٍ participation in a company ② [في مَجَلّةٍ أو جَمْعيّةٍ] subscription; اشْتِراك سَنَويّ annual subscription; اشْتِراك في جَريدةٍ a subscription to a newspaper; اشْتِراك في الإِنْتَرْنِت Internet subscription; بِطاقة الاشْتِراكِ subscription card; رَسْم \ سِعْر اشْتِراكٍ subscription fee; أَلْغى اشْتِراكًا to cancel a subscription; to unsubscribe; دَفَعَ الاشْتِراكَ to pay the subscription fee

اشْتِراكيّ *adj, n* socialist; الحِزْب الاشْتِراكيّ socialist party; أَفْكار اشْتِراكيّة socialist views; المُعَسْكَر الاشْتِراكيّ socialist bloc

اشْتِراكيّة *n* socialism

إِشْراك *n* ① (Relig) polytheism; إِشْراك بِاللّٰه polytheism ② [المُشارَكة] engagement, involvement; إِشْراك المُجْتَمَعِ community involvement

تَشارُكيّ *adj* participatory

تَشْريك *n* socialization

مُشارِك A *adj* participatory, participating; البُلْدان \ الفِرَق المُشارِكة the participating countries/teams
B *n* ① [مُساهِم] participant; مُشارِك في مُظاهرةٍ participant in a demonstration ② [في جَريمةٍ] accomplice, accessory; مُشارِك في ارْتِكابِ شَيْءٍ accessory to sth

مُشارَكة *n* ① [اشْتِراك] participation, involvement; مُشارَكة واسِعة widespread participation; مُشارَكة في مُباراةٍ participation in a match; مُشارَكة في قوّاتِ حِفْظِ السَلامِ participation in a peacekeeping force; مُشارَكة في الجَريمةِ complicity in a crime; اتَّهَمَ شَخْصاً بالمُشارَكةِ في الجَريمةِ to accuse sb of complicity; مَنَعَ شَخْصاً من المُشارَكةِ to sideline sb; بِمُشارَكةِ ... in cooperation with ...; المُلاحَظة بالمُشارَكةِ participant observation ② [بين أَشْخاصٍ] partnership; contractual partnership (*Islamic law*) ③ [مُساهَمة] sharing; مُشارَكة المَلَفّاتِ file sharing

مُشْتَرَك *adj* collective, common, communal; joint; mutual; مِلْكيّة مُشْتَرَكة common property, joint ownership; بَيان مُشْتَرَك a joint statement; اقْتِراح مُشْتَرَك a joint proposal; العَيْش المُشْتَرَك coexistence; الاهْتِمام المُشْتَرَك mutual interest; على حِسابٍ مُشْتَرَكٍ on a joint account; كانَ لَهُ شَيْءٌ مُشْتَرَكٌ مع شَخْصٍ he had sth in common with sb

مُشْتَرِك A *adj* accessory; مُشْتَرِك في الجَريمةِ accessory to a crime; مُشْتَرِك في ارْتِكابِ شَيْءٍ accessory to sth

B *n* **1** [مُساهِم] participant; contributor; مُشْتَرِك في المِلْكِيّة joint proprietor **2** [في مَجَلّة] subscriber; رَقْم المُشْتَرِك subscriber number

شَرْكَسِيّ *adj, n* Circassian

شَرَمَ *v* |i; شَرْم| to split; to tear, to rip

اِنْشَرَمَ *v* to become ripped

شَرْم *n* |شُروم| **1** [خَليج] cove; bay, inlet; شَرْم الشَيْخ Sharm El Sheikh (*town in Egypt*) **2** [شَقّ] crack

أَشْرَم *adj* |dipt; شُرْم| كانَ أَشْرَمَ الشَفَةِ to have a cleft lip, to be harelipped

شَرْموطة *n* |شَراميط| (ME) (vulg) whore, slut, prostitute

شَرْنَقة *n* |شَرانِق| (Zool) cocoon; شَرْنَقة الحَرير silk cocoon; شَرْنَقة الفَقْرِ the cocoon of poverty

شَرِهَ *v* |a; شَرَه| to be/become greedy, to be/become rapacious

شَرَه *n* desire, urge; eagerness; شَرَه إلى الطَعامِ gluttony; الشره المَرَضيّ \ العَصَبيّ bulimia nervosa

شَرِه **A** *adj* greedy; gluttonous, voracious; keen, avid; مُدَخِّن شَرِه heavy smoker

B *n* glutton, gobbler, guzzler

شَراهة *n* gluttony, greed; أَكَلَ بِشَراهةٍ to eat ravenously, to stuff oneself; دَخَّنَ بِشَراهةٍ to smoke like a chimney

شِرْوال *n* see سِرْوال

شَرى *v* |i; شِرىً, شِراء| to buy, to purchase, to acquire

اشْتَرى *v* to buy, to purchase; to acquire; اشْتَرى شَيْئاً to buy sth; اشْتَرى سِلَعاً من شَخْصٍ to purchase goods from sb; اشْتَرى سَيّارةً \ كِتاباً من شَخْصٍ to buy a car/book from sb; اشْتَرى لاعِبينَ to buy (sports) players; اشْتَرى مَحَلّاً to buy a shop

اسْتَشْرى *v* to intensify; to become serious; اسْتَشْرَت الرَشْوةُ corruption has become rampant

شارٍ *n* |شُراة| buyer; customer, consumer; شاري العَقارِ property buyer

شِراء *n* purchase, purchasing; acquisition; عَقْد شِراءٍ deed of purchase, purchase contract; عَقْد شِراءٍ مَبْدَئيّ initial purchase contract; وَقَّعَ \ أَبْرَمَ عَقْدَ شِراءٍ to sign/conclude a deed of purchase; سِعْر \ ثَمَن الشِراءِ purchase price; حُمّى الشِراءِ shopping fever; حَقّ خِيارِ شِراءٍ option to buy; قادِر على الشِراءِ able to purchase

شِرائيّ *adj* purchasing (*before n*); قوّة \ قُدْرة شِرائيّة purchasing power; قيمة شِرائيّة value for money

شَرْوة *n* purchase; job lot

شَرْوى *n* (fml) equal; لا يَمْلِكُ شَرْوى نَقيرٍ he hasn't got a penny to his name

شَرًى *n* urticaria, hives

شِرْيان *n* |شَرايينُ| (Anat) artery; شِرْيان تاجيّ \ إكْليليّ coronary artery; الشِرْيان الكُعْبُريّ radial artery; الشِرْيان الأَوْرَطيّ aorta; الشِرْيان السُباتيّ carotid (artery); أَمْراض شَرايينِ القَلْبِ cardiovascular disease; تَصَلُّب \ تكلّس (في) الشَرايين arteriosclerosis (*hardening of the arteries*); انْسِداد في الشِرْيانِ blockage in the artery; تَضَيُّق في الشِرْيانِ التاجيِّ stenosis of the coronary artery

شِرْيانيّ *adj* arterial, venous; نَزيف شِرْيانيّ an arterial bleeding; التَمَدُّد الشِرْيانيّ arterial expansion; الضَغْط الشِرْيانيّ arterial pressure, blood pressure; التَوَتُّر الشِرْيانيّ arterial tension

اسْتِشْراء *n* intensification; aggravation; اسْتِشْراء الطائِفيّةِ rampant sectarianism

المُشْتَري *n* (Astron) Jupiter

مُسْتَشْرٍ *adj* rampant; فَساد مُسْتَشْرٍ rampant corruption

مُشْتَرٍ *n* |مُشْتَرونَ| buyer; customer; مُشْتَرٍ خاصّ a private buyer

مُشْتَرًى *n* |مُشْتَرَيات| مُشْتَرَيات purchased goods, shopping; قِسْم المُشْتَرَيات purchasing department, procurement section

شَزَرَ *v* |i; شَزْر| to look askance at

شَزْر *n* نَظَرَ إلى شَخْصٍ شَزْراً to look askance at sb

أَشْزَر *adj* |dipt| نَظْرة شَزْراء a disapproving look

شَسَعَ *v* |a; شُسوع| to be/become wide

شاسِع *adj* vast, extensive, immense; مِنْطَقة \ أَرْض شاسِعة a vast area/terrain; فَرْق شاسِع a world of difference; على بُعْدٍ شاسِعٍ faraway; بَوْن شاسِع بين شَيْءٍ وَشَيْءٍ a far cry between sth and sth

شِصّ *n* |شُصوص| fish hook

شاطِئ *n* |شُطْآن, شَواطِئُ| beach; coast; شاطِئ رَمْليّ sandy shore; على الشاطِئِ on the beach; تَمَشّى على الشاطِئِ to walk along the beach; على طولِ الشاطِئ along the coast; نَزَلَ إلى الشاطِئ to go ashore; قُبالة شَواطِئ المَدينة off the coast of the city

مُتَشاطِئ *adj on the coast;* دُوَل مُتَشاطِئة على النيل countries on the Nile

شَطَبَ *v* |u; شَطْب| ① [حَذَفَ] to strike out, to cross off; شَطَبَ أسْماءً من قائِمةٍ to cross off names on a list; اُشْطُب العِبارةَ غَيْرَ المُناسِبةِ cross the odd phrase out; شَطَبَ النَتائِجَ to write off results; شَطَبَ شَخْصاً من لائِحةٍ to drop sb from a list ② [شَرَّحَ] to cut into slices ③ (Law) to dismiss; شَطَبَ دَعْوى to dismiss a case

شَطَّبَ *v* to cross out, to strike out

شَطْب *n* deletion, crossing out, elimination; لَوائِح الشَطْبِ check lists; شَطْب الدُيونِ debt cancellation, debt relief

تَشْطيب *n* finishing touch, completion; decorating, decoration; أعْمال تَشْطيبٍ decoration work

شَطَحَ *v* |a; شَطْح| to be far away; شطحَ بِمُخَيِّلَتِه to be lost in thought, to daydream

شَطَرَ *v* |u; شَطْر| to bisect, to divide into halves; to split; شَطَرَ الذَرّاتِ to split atoms; شَطَرَ تُفّاحةً to cut an apple in half

شَطَّرَ *v* to divide into halves

شاطَرَ *v* to share, to participate; شاطَرَ شَخْصاً رَأْيَهُ \ وجهة نَظَره to share sb's opinion; شاطَرَ شَخْصاً أَحْزانَهُ to sympathize with sb's grief; شاطَرَهُ رَأْيَهُ أَشْخاصٌ كَثيرونَ many people shared his opinion

اِنْشَطَرَ *v* to split (up), to divide; اِنْشَطَرَ (إلى) نِصْفَيْنِ \ جُزْئَيْنِ \ قِطْعَتَيْنِ to split into halves/two parts

شَطْر *n* |شُطور, أَشْطُر| ① [نِصْف] half; أَعْطاهُ شَطْرَ مالِهِ he gave him half of his property; قابل للشَطْرِ fissile, fissionable ② [جُزْء] part, piece; شَطْر من كِياني a part of myself; الشَطْر الأكْبَر من حَياتِها the biggest part of her life ③ (Math) bisector

شَطْرَ *prep* toward; يَمَّمَ شَطْرَ الجَنوبِ to head east

شاطِر Ⓐ *adj* |شُطّار| clever, smart, bright; sly
Ⓑ *n* |شُطّار| clever person

شَطارة *n* cleverness; slyness, cunningness; skill

شَطيرة *n* |شَطائِر| sandwich; شَطيرة اللَحْمِ hamburger

اِنْشِطار *n* |اِنْشِطارات| splitting, division; اِنْشِطار نَوَوِيّ splitting of atoms, nuclear fission

اِنْشِطاريّ *adj* fission (*before n*), fissionable; مَوادّ اِنْشِطاريّة fissile material, nuclear fuel; قُنْبُلة اِنْشِطاريّة fission bomb; أَسْلِحة نَوَوِيّة اِنْشِطاريّة boosted fission weapons

شِطْرَنْج, شَطْرَنْج *n* chess; شِطْرَنْج سَريع blitz chess, speed chess; قِطْعة \ حَجَر شِطْرَنْجٍ chessboard; رُقْعة \ لَوْحة شِطْرَنْجٍ chess piece; لُعْبة شِطْرَنْجٍ a game of chess; مارَسَ لُعْبَةَ الشِطْرَنْجِ to practise chess; لَعِبَ الشِطْرَنْجَ \ لُعْبَةَ شِطْرَنْجٍ to play chess/a game of chess; لاعِب شِطْرَنْجٍ chess player

شَطَّ *v* |i-u; شُطوط, شَطاط, شَطَط| to be unjust; to go too far, to go to extremes

أَشَطَّ *v* ① [ظَلَمَ] to be unjust; to go too far, to go to extremes ② [بَعُدَ] to be far away

اِشْتَطَّ *v* ① [ظَلَمَ] to be unjust; to go too far, to go to extremes ② [بَعُدَ] to be far away

شَطَط *n* excess; الشَطَط في اِسْتِعْمالِ السُلْطةِ abuse of power, abuse of authority

شَطّ *n* |شُطوط| bank, shore; شَطّ النَهْرِ riverbank; شَطّ العَرَبِ Shatt al-Arab (*estuary of the Euphrates and Tigris rivers in Iraq*)

شَطّة *n* (Bot) red pepper

شَطَفَ *v* |u; شَطْف| ① [غَسَلَ] to rinse (out), to wash (out); شَطَفَ المِرْحاضَ to flush the toilet; شَطَفَ الصُحونَ to wash the plates; شَطَفَ الزُجاجةَ \ الكَأْسَ to rinse the bottle/glass ② [شَظّى] to chip, to splinter

شُطْفة *n* chip (of wood); splinter

شَيْطان *n* see شيطن

شَظُفَ *v* |u; شَظْف| to become difficult

شَظَف *n* |شِظاف| hardship, deprivation; عانى شَظَفَ العَيْشِ to suffer hardship, to have a difficult life

شَظافة *n* hardship; شَظافة العَيْشِ hardship

شَظِيَ *v* |a; شَظًى| to crack; to splinter

شَظّى *v* to splinter

تَشَظّى *v* to splinter

شَظِيّة *n* |شَظايا, شَظِيّ| ❶ [قِطْعة] fragment, piece; chip; splinter; شَظِيّة قَذيفةٍ (Mil) shell fragment ❷ [من قُنْبُلة] (piece of) shrapnel, shell fragment; شَظايا مُتَناثِرة flying shrapnel; أَصابَتْهُ شَظِيّةٌ في رَأْسِهِ he was hit in the head by shrapnel

شَعَبَ *v* |a; شَعْب| to split, to divide

شَعَّبَ *v* to split up; to form branches, to branch off

تَشَعَّبَ *v* to branch (off), to ramify; to diverge

انْشَعَبَ *v* to split (up)

شَعْب *n coll* |no singular noun; شُعوب| people; nation, race; مَجْلِس الشَعْبِ parliament; people's assembly; إبادة الشُعوبِ genocide; مَثَّلَ الشَعْبَ to represent the people; خاطَبَ الرَئِيسُ الشَعْبَ the president addressed the people; الشَعْب الهولَنْديّ \ الكُوَيْتيّ the Dutch/Kuwaiti people

شِعْب *n* |شِعاب| (mountain) pass, col; شِعْب مَرْجانيّ coral reef; في الشِعْبِ on (top of) the col

شَعْبان *n* |dipt| Shaaban (*the eighth month of the Islamic calendar*); يُدْخِلُ شَعْبانَ في رَمَضانَ he doesn't know if he's coming or going (*is very confused*)

شَعْبانيّ *adj related to the month of Sha'ban*; زِيارة شَعْبانيّة *a visit to holy places during the month of Sha'ban*

شُعْبة *n* ❶ (Sci) |شُعَب, شِعاب| discipline, subject, field ❷ (Bot) runner, stolon ❸ (Anat) |شُعَب| bronchus; شُعَب bronchi; الْتِهاب الشُعَبِ bronchitis; كانَ مُصاباً ب \ عانى من الْتِهابِ الشُعَبِ to suffer from bronchitis, to have bronchitis; شُعَب رِئَوِيّة bronchial tubes; الْتِهاب في الشُعَبِ الرِئَوِيّةِ infection of the bronchial tubes ❹ [جُزْء] branch ❺ (Bio) |شُعَب| class

شَعْبيّ *adj* popular; common; communal; populist; حَيّ شَعْبيّ working-class neighbourhood; جَيْش شَعْبيّ militia, people's army; اسْتِفْتاء شَعْبيّ referendum; تُراث شَعْبيّ folklore; حَرَكة شَعْبيّة mass movement, popular movement; حِكْمة شَعْبيّة popular wisdom

شُعَبيّ *adj* bronchial; نَزْلة شُعَبيّة viral pneumonia

شَعْبيّة *n* popularity; populism; تَمَتَّعَ بِشَعْبيّةٍ (كَبيرةٍ) to enjoy (great) popularity; شَعْبيّة واسِعة \ عَريضة enormous/immense popularity; تَزيدُ \ تَرْتَفِعُ شَعْبيَّتُهُ his popularity is growing/increasing; عَدَم الشَعْبيّةِ unpopularity; الأَكْثَر شَعْبيّةً most popular

شُعوبيّة *n movement within the early Islamic commonwealth of nations that emphasized the superiority of the Persian people*

شُعَيْبة *n* subphylum; شُعَيْبة هَوائيّة (Anat) bronchium (*bronchial tube in the lungs*)

تَشَعُّب *n* branching (off), divergence

تَشَعُّبي *adj* hyper-; وَصْلة تَشَعُّبيّة, رابِط تَشَعُّبيّ hyperlink; نَصّ تَشَعُّبيّ hypertext

مُتَشَعِّب *adj* divergent; branched

شَعْبَذَ *v* |i; شَعْبَذة| to do tricks, to conjure; to cheat

شَعِثَ *v* |a; شَعَث| to get entangled, to get rumpled; to dishevel, to ruffle

شَعَّثَ *v* to tousle; شَعَّثَ شَعْرَ شَخْصٍ to tousle sb's hair

تَشَعَّثَ *v* to become disheveled (*hair*)

شَعَث *n* getting entangled; لَمَّ شَعَثَهُ to straighten out an issue

أَشْعَث *adj* |dipt; شُعْث| windblown, tousled, unkempt; شَعْر أَشْعَث tousled/unkempt hair

شَعَرَ *v* |u; شُعور| ❶ [أَحَسَّ] to feel, to experience; to notice, to perceive; لم يَشْعُرْ بِهِ he didn't notice it; شَعَرَ بالبَرْدِ \ الحَرارةِ to be/get/feel cold/hot; شَعَرَ بالأَلَمِ \ الحُزْنِ to feel pain/sadness; شَعَرَتْ بِوَرَمٍ في ثَدْيِها she felt a lump in her breast ❷ [نَظَمَ الشِعْرَ] to write poetry ❸ [أَدْرَكَ] to realise; to be aware, to be conscious

أَشْعَرَ *v* ❶ [أَخْبَرَ] to report; to inform, to notify ❷ [نَبَتَ لَهُ شَعْرٌ] to grow hair

تَشاعَرَ *v* to claim to be a poet

اسْتَشْعَرَ *v* to feel, to sense; to perceive

شَعْر, شَعَر *n* |أَشْعار, شُعور, شِعار| hair, head of hair; شَعْر طَويل \ قَصير long/short hair; شَعْر أَشْقَر \ أَسْمَر \ أَسْوَد \ أَحْمَر \ أَشْيَب blond/brown/black/red/gray hair; شَعْر مُجَعَّد \ مُتَجَعِّد frizzy hair, curly hair; شَعْر مُبَعْثَر tangled hair; شَعْر الصَدْرِ chest hair; شَعْر مُسْتَعار hairpiece, toupee, wig; وَضَعَ شَعْراً مُسْتَعاراً to wear a wig; أَجْعَد الشَعْرِ curly (head); نُموّ شَعْرٍ hair growth; تَساقُط شَعْرٍ hair loss; فُرْشاة شَعْرٍ hairbrush; دَبّوس شَعْرٍ hairpin; تَصْفيف \ تَسْريح شَعْرٍ hair styling; شَعْرُهُ مُصَفَّفٌ \ مُشَعَّثٌ his hair is styled/tousled; مَشَّطَ شَعْرَهُ بالمُشْطِ to comb one's hair; سَرَّحَ شَعْرَهُ بالفُرْشاةِ to brush one's hair; مُثَبِّت شَعْرٍ

hairspray; مُزيل شَعْرٍ depilatory; أزالَ الشَعْرَ to depilate; انْتَصَب شَعْرُ رَأْسِهِ his hair stood up on end

شِعْر *n* |أَشْعار| ① [قَريض] (art of) poetry; poem; شِعْر مَلْحَميّ epic (poem); شِعْر غِنائيّ lyric, lyrical poetry; أَلَّفَ شِعْراً to write poems; أَلَّفَ ديوانَ شِعْرٍ to compose a volume of poetry; أَنْشَدَ \ أَلْقى شِعْراً to recite a poem ② [مَعْرِفة] knowledge; لَيْتَ شِعْري I wish I knew ...

شاعِر *n* |شُعَراءُ| poet; شاعِر كَبير a great poet; سورة الشُعَراء The Poets (*Sura 26*)

شاعِريّ *adj* romantic; poetic; idyllic; جَوّ شاعِريّ a romantic atmosphere; قِصّة \ فيلْم شاعِريّ(ة) a romantic story/movie

شاعِريّة *n* poetics; *the state or function of being a poet*; شاعِريّة كَبيرة a great poetic genius

شَعائِريّ *adj* sacred; ritualistic, ceremonial; طَقْس شَعائِريّ ritual

شِعار *n* |شُعُر, أَشْعِرة, شِعارات| ① [عَلامة] emblem, coat of arms; logo; شِعار الاتِّحادِ union logo; شِعار الكُوَيْتِ the coat of arms of Kuwait ② [عِبارة] slogan, motto; شعار فارِغ an empty slogan; شعارات جَوْفاء empty slogans; شعارات عُنْصُريّة \ قَوْميّة racist/nationalist slogans; هَتَفَ \ أَطْلَقَ شعاراتٍ to chant slogans; تحت شِعارِ... under the banner of ...; شِعار الحَرْبِ battle cry

شَعْرة *n* hair; قَيْدَ شَعْرةٍ within a hair's breadth, barely; لم يَتَزَحْزَحْ عن مَوْقِفِه قَيْدَ شَعْرةٍ he didn't budge an inch; شَقّ الشَعْرة (just) as much

شِعْرة *n* pubic hair

شَعْريّ *adj* hair (*before n*); وِعاء شَعْريّ capillary

شِعْريّ *adj* poetic, poetical; بَحْر شِعْريّ metre; مَقْطوعة شِعْريّة verse, poem; مُخْتارات \ مُنْتَخَبات شِعْرِيّة an anthology of poetry; مَجْموعة أَعْمالٍ شِعْرِيّةٍ لِ ... collected poems of ...

شَعْرِيّة *n* vermicelli

شُعور *n* feeling, sense, perception, sensation; sentiment, emotion; شُعور غَريب a strange feeling, a funny feeling; شُعور بالارْتِياحِ \ بِعَدَمِ الثِقةِ a sense of relief/distrust; شُعور بالنَدَمِ remorse; راعى شُعورَ شَخْصٍ to respect sb's feelings; تحت الشُعور subconscious; شُعور بالذاتِ self-awareness; شُعور بالمَسْؤوليّةِ feeling of responsibility; الشُعور بالواجِبِ sense of duty

شُعوريّ *adj* aware, conscious

شَعير *n* (Bot) barley (*Hordeum vulgare*); pearl barley; سُكَّر الشَعيرِ maltose

شَعيرة *n* |شَعائِرُ| (Relig) rite, ritual; اتَّبَعَ \ مارَسَ شَعائِرَ to follow/practise rites

شُعَيْرة *n* (small) hair; شُعَيْرة دَمَوِيّة capillary

اسْتِشْعار *n* feeling, sensing; قَرْن اسْتِشْعارٍ antenna, feeler; جِهاز اسْتِشْعارٍ sensor

إشْعار *n* |إشْعارات| notification, notice; announcement; إشْعار بالدَفْعِ summons; حتّى إشْعارٍ آخَرَ till further notice

أَشْعَر *adj* |dipt; شُعْر| hairy; صَدْر أَشْعَرَ a hairy chest; كانَ أَشْعَرَ الذِراعَيْنِ \ الساقَيْنِ to have hairy arms/legs

لاشُعور *n* (Psych) subconscious, unconscious; في اللاشُعورِ in one's subconscious

لاشُعوريّ *adj* subconscious, unconscious

مَشْعَر *n* |مَشاعِرُ| feeling, emotion; رُموز مَشاعِرَ (Comput) emoticons; هَزَّ المَشاعِرَ to move, to affect; حَرَّكَ المَشاعِرَ to move, to soften; بِلا مَشاعِرَ emotionless; أَظْهَرَ مَشاعِرَهُ \ عَبَّرَ عن مَشاعِرِهِ to show/express one's feelings; كَتَمَ \ كَبَتَ مَشاعِرَهُ to suppress one's feelings; شارَكَ شَخْصاً مَشاعِرَهُ to sympathize with sb; جَرَحَ مَشاعِرَ شَخْصٍ to hurt sb's feelings; جُرِحَتْ مَشاعِرُهُ to have one's feelings hurt, to be offended; يُثيرُ هذا مَشاعِرَ مُخْتَلِفةً this evokes mixed feelings

‹ **شَعْشَعَ** *v* |i; شَعْشَعة| to shine dimly

‹ **شَعَّ** *v* |i; شَعّ, إشْعاع| to radiate, to beam; to emit

شَعَّعَ *v* to irradiate

أَشَعَّ *v* to shine; to radiate, to beam; to emit; أَشَعَّ حَرارةً to radiate heat

شُعاع *n coll* |أَشِعّة| ① [خَيْط من الضَوْءِ] beam, ray; شُعاع من الضَوْءِ a beam of light; أَشِعّة سينيّة \ إكْس X-ray; أَشِعّة فوق البَنَفْسَجيّة \ تحت الحَمْراءِ ultraviolet/infrared rays; صورة بالأَشِعّةِ السينيّةِ X-ray (image); جِهاز الأَشِعّةِ (السينيّة) X-ray machine; صَوَّرَ \ فَحَصَ بالأَشِعّةِ to X-ray; فَحْص بالأَشِعّةِ X-ray (scan) ② (Math) radius; شُعاع دولابٍ spoke

مُشْتَعِل *adj* burning, flaming, on fire; شَمْعة مُشْتَعِلة a burning candle; البَيْت المُشْتَعِل the burning house

مِشْعَل *n* |مَشاعِلُ| torch; حامِل المِشْعَل torchbearer (*lit and fig*)

‹ **شَعانين** *n* عيد \ أَحَد الشَّعانين (Chr) Palm Sunday

‹ **شَعْواء** *adj* |dipt| devastating; حَرْب شَعْواء a devastating war

‹ **شَعْوَذَ** *v* |i; شَعْوَذة| to cheat, to swindle

شَعْوَذة *n* deceiving, trickery; conjuring, art of magic

مُشَعْوِذ *n* trickster, fraud; magician, illusionist

‹ **شَغَبَ** *v* |a; شَغْب, شَغَب| to cause problems, to make trouble

شاغَبَ *v* to riot, to cause disturbance; شاغَبَ شَخْصاً to rebel against sb

تَشاغَبَ *v* to cause trouble

شَغَب *n* disturbance, row; revolt, riot; أَعْمال شَغَب riots, subversive actions; شُرْطة مُكافَحةِ الشَغَبِ riot police; سَبَّبَ \ أَثارَ شَغَباً to cause/spark a riot; أَعْمال شَغَب فظيعة \ عَنيفة \ خَطيرة terrible/violent/serious riots; وَقَعَتْ أَحْداثُ شَغَبٍ عَنيفةٌ violent riots have broken out

مُشاغِب *adj, n* rioter; troublemaker, hooligan; troublesome

مُشاغَبة *n* revolt, riot; disturbance

‹ **شَغَرَ** *v* |u; شُغور| to be open; to be vacant, to be unoccupied

شاغِر *adj* |شَواغِرُ| vacant, free; unoccupied, open; وَظيفة شاغِرة a vacancy, a vacant post; لا تَزالُ الوَظيفةُ شاغِرةً the post is still vacant; مَقْعَد شاغِر an empty chair; هل هذا الكُرْسيُّ شاغِرٌ؟ is this chair free?; شَواغِر vacancies

شُغور *n* vacancy

‹ **شَغْرَبَ** *v* |i; شَغْرَبة| to trip up

‹ **شَغَفَ** *v* |a; شَغْف| to infatuate; شُغِفَ بِشَخْصٍ حُبًّا to lose one's heart to sb, to fall in love with sb

شَغَف *n* eagerness; passion, love; craving

شَغاف *n* |شُغُف| (Anat) شَغاف القَلْب endocarditis

شَغوف *adj* passionate, impassioned; obsessed

مَشْغوف *adj* |ب| passionately in love (with)

‹ **شَغَلَ** *v* |a; شُغْل, شَغْل| ⓵ [جَعَلَهُ مَشْغولاً] to occupy; to keep busy; شَغَلَ نَفْسَهُ بِشَيْءٍ to occupy oneself with sth; شَغَلَ بالَهُ بِشَيْءٍ to worry about sth; شَغَلَتْ بالَهُ مُشْكِلةٌ \ مَسْأَلةٌ

شُعاعيّ *adj* radial; radiation (*before n*); صورة شُعاعيّة radiograph

إِشْعاع *n* |إِشْعاعات| radiation, emanation; irradiation; العِلاج بالإِشْعاعِ radiotherapy; مُعالَجة وَرَم بالإِشْعاع treating a tumor with radiation; إِشْعاع نَوَويّ \ ذَرّيّ nuclear/atomic radiation; تَعَرَّض للإِشْعاعِ (النَوَويِّ) to be exposed to (nuclear) radiation

إِشْعاعيّ *adj* radioactive; نَشاط إِشْعاعيّ radioactivity; تَلَوُّث إِشْعاعيّ radioactive contamination

إِشْعاعيّة *n* (Phys) radioactivity

تَشْعيع *n* irradiation

مُشِعّ *adj* radiant, brilliant; radioactive; يَوْم مُشِعّ a brilliant day; شَمْس مُشِعّة a radiant sun; مَوادّ مُشِعّة radioactive elements; التَأْريخ بالكَرْبون المُشِعّ carbon dating, radiocarbon dating

مِشْعاع *n* |مَشاعيعُ| radiator

مُشِعّة *n* radiator

‹ **شَعْفة** *n* summit, peak

‹ **شَعَلَ** *v* |a; شَعْل| to light, to kindle

شَعَّلَ *v* to light, to kindle; to ignite

أَشْعَلَ *v* to light, to kindle; to ignite, to set on fire; to fire, to set off; أَشْعَلَ سيجارةً to light a cigarette; أَشْعَلَ فِتْنةً to stir up discord; أَشْعَلَ الأَضْواءَ الأَمامِيّةَ لِسَيّارَتِهِ to turn on the headlights of one's car; أَشْعَلَ الشُعْلةَ الأولِمْبِيّةَ to light the Olympic flame

اشْتَعَلَ *v* to catch fire; to burn, to flame; اشتعل غَضَباً to be burning with rage; اشْتَعَلَتْ فيه النارُ to catch fire; اشْتَعَلَت المَصابيحُ the lights were turned on; اشْتَعَلَت مَعْرَكةٌ a battle broke out

شُعْلة *n* |شُعَل| flame; torch; الشُعْلة الأولِمْبِيّة the Olympic torch, the Olympic flame; كَأَنَّهُ شُعْلةُ ذَكاءٍ he is very clever; شُعْلة من الحَماس a good deal of enthusiasm

شَعيلة *n* |شَعائِلُ| (Mil) trip, switch, primer; percussion cap

اشْتِعال *n* |اشْتِعالات| combustion, burning; قابِل للاشْتِعالِ combustible, flammable, inflammable; مَوادّ قابِلة للاشْتِعالِ combustible materials; سَريع الاشْتِعالِ highly combustible; غَيْر قابِلٍ للاشْتِعالِ incombustible, non-flammable

إِشْعال *n* ignition

a problem/issue weighed on his mind; شُغِلَ بِشَيْءٍ to be occupied by sth ❷ [أَلْهى عن] to distract, to divert; to interrupt; شَغَلَ شَخْصاً to distract sb; شَغَلَ شَخْصاً عن عَمَلِهِ to distract sb from his work ❸ [مَكاناً] to take up, to occupy; to fill; شَغَلَ مَقْعَداً to occupy a seat; شَغَلَ مِساحةً to take up space; شَغَلَ وَظيفةً to fill a position; شَغَلَ مَنْصِباً حَسّاساً to hold a sensitive post

شَغَّلَ *v* ❶ [جِهازاً] to switch on, to turn on; to put into action, to activate; شَغَّلَ شَيْئاً to turn sth on; شَغَّلَ آلَةً \ جِهازاً to turn on a machine/device; شَغَّلَ بَرْنامَجاً to start a program; شَغَّلَ المُحَرِّكَ to start the engine ❷ [أَعْطاهُ عَمَلاً] to employ, to appoint; to recruit; to engage, to put to work; شَغَّلَ شَخْصاً to employ sb; شَغَّلَ شَخْصاً في وَظيفةٍ to employ sb in a position; شَغَّلَ الطُّلّابَ to put the students to work

شاغَلَ *v* to distract, to divert

أَشْغَلَ *v* ❶ [أَزْعَجَ] to interrupt ❷ [جَعَلَ شَخْصاً مَشْغولاً] to occupy, to keep busy; أَشْغَلَ الأَطْفالَ to keep the children busy ❸ [أَلْهى] |عن| to distract, to divert

تَشاغَلَ *v* ❶ [بِشَيْءٍ] |ب| to be busy, to be engaged ❷ [تَظاهَرَ الانْشِغالَ] to pretend to be busy

انْشَغَلَ *v* to occupy oneself, to busy oneself

اشْتَغَلَ *v* ❶ [شَخْص] to work, to labour; ماذا يَشْتَغِلُ \ تَشْتَغِلُ؟ what does he/she do for a living?; إِنَّهُ يَشْتَغِلُ في ... he works in ...; اشْتَغَلَ في التَّعْليمِ he used to work in education ❷ [آلة إلخ] to work, to function; to run, to operate; لا يَشْتَغِلُ التِلِفِزْيون the television does not work; كيف يَشْتَغِلُ هذا الجِهازُ؟ how does this appliance work?

شُغْل *n* |شُغول ,أَشْغال| ❶ [عَمَل] work, job; labour; post, position; شُغْل يَدَويّ manual labour, handwork; أَشْغال شاقّة hard labour; الأَشْغال العامّة \ العُمومِيّة public works (*infrastructure projects*); مَصْلَحة الأَشْغالِ العامّةِ \ العُمومِيّة public works department ❷ [نَشاط] activity; أَشْغال يَوْمِيّة daily activities ❸ [هَمّ] concern; شُغْل شاغِل foremost concern, preoccupation

شاغِل Ⓐ *adj* preoccupying; شُغْل شاغِل foremost concern, preoccupation Ⓑ *n* ❶ [مَنْ يَشْغَلُ مَنْزِلاً] |شاغِلون| occupant ❷ [هَمّ] |شَواغِل| concern, worry

شَغّال *adj* |شَغّالون ,شَغّالة| ❶ [أَجْهِزة] on; working, running; الجِهازُ \ الآلَةُ شَغّالٌ(ة) the appliance/device is working ❷ [عامِل] industrious

شَغّالة *n* ❶ [خَدّامة] cleaning lady; maid, domestic help ❷ (Zool) worker bee/ant

شَغْلة *n* (colloq Syria) matter, affair

شُغْلة *n* (Egypt) job; لا شُغْلةَ وَلا مَشْغَلة nothing to do

اشْتِغال *n* operation, functioning

أُشْغولة *n* |أَشاغيل ,أُشْغولات| distraction

الشَغِّيلة *n* working population; labourers, workers

انْشِغال *n* |انْشِغالات| preoccupation

تَشْغيل *n* ❶ [جِهاز] control; operation; تَشْغيل آلَةٍ the operation of a machine; نِظام تَشْغيلٍ operating system, OS; زِرّ تَشْغيل switch, starter; التَّرْكيب والتَّشْغيل plug and play ❷ [تَوْظيف] employment; تَشْغيل الأَطْفالِ child labour

تَشْغيليّ *adj* operational, working; دَخْل \ إيراد تَشْغيليّ operating income

مُشاغَلة *n* distraction, diversion

مَشْغَل *n* |مَشاغِل| workplace, workshop

مُشَغِّل *n* ignition; مُشَغِّل شَبَكَةٍ network operator

مَشْغَلة *n* |مَشاغِل| المَشاغِل اليَوْمِيّة the day-to-day concerns

مَشْغول *adj* occupied, busy; preoccupied; مَنْصِب مَشْغول an occupied post; كانَ مَشْغولاً to be busy; كانَ مَشْغولاً بِشَيْءٍ to be busy with sth; المِرْحاضُ مَشْغولٌ the toilet is occupied; الهاتِفُ مَشْغولٌ the phone is busy; هذه المَرْأةُ مَشْغولةٌ جِدًّا this woman is very busy; كانَ مَشْغولاً كُلَّ مَساءٍ to be busy every night; مَشْغول البالِ worried

مُنْشَغِل *adj* busy, preoccupied

شَفة *n* see شفه

شَفْر *n* |أَشْفار| ❶ [حافّة] edge, rim ❷ (Anat) edge of the eyelid

شُفْر *n* |أَشْفار| (Anat) شُفْرانِ labia (*of the vulva*)

شَفْرة *n* |شِفار ,شَفَرات| ❶ [الحَلاقة] razor blade; حادّ مِثْلَ الشَّفْرة razor-sharp ❷ [السِّكّين] blade

شَفير *n* |أَشْفار| edge; hem, border; على شَفيرِ ... on the verge of...; على شَفيرِ المَوْتِ on the brink of death

مِشْفَر *n* |مَشافِرُ| lip (of a camel)

2‹ **شَفَّرَ** *v* to encode, to code, to encrypt

شِفْرة, شيفْرة *n* code, cipher; شِفْرة وِراثيّة genetic code; حَلَّ الشِفْرةَ to decipher, to decode; شِفْرة مَصْدَريّة source code

شِفْرِيّ *adj* ciphered, encoded, code (*before n*); اسْم شِفْرِيّ code name

تَشْفير *n* encoding, coding, encryption; تَشْفير البَيانات data encryption; فَكَّ التَّشْفيرَ to decode, to decrypt

‹ **شَفْشاف** *n* sleet

‹ **شَفَطَ** *v* |i; شَفْط| to suck; شَفَطَ الدُهونَ (Med) to perform liposuction

شَفّاط *n* extractor fan, cooker hood (BrE), range hood (AmE)

شَفّاطة *n* 1▸ [مَصّاصة الشُرْبِ] straw 2▸ [مِكْنَسة كَهْرَبائيّة] vacuum 3▸ (Tools) plunger

‹ **شَفَعَ** *v* |a| 1▸ [تَوَسَّطَ] |شَفاعة| to mediate, to intercede; شَفَعَ لِشَخْصٍ عند شَخْصٍ to put in a (good) word for sb with sb 2▸ [أَضافَ] |شَفْع; ب| to add; to enclose, to attach; شُفِعَ بِشَيْءٍ to be accompanied by sth

شَفَّعَ *v* (Relig) to have (sb) mediate/plead on one's behalf (*on Judgement Day*)

تَشَفَّعَ *v* (Relig) to mediate/plead on sb's behalf (*on Judgement Day*)

اسْتَشْفَعَ *v* (Relig) to ask for mediation; to ask for intercession; شَخْص يُسْتَشْفَعُ بِهِ (Relig) an influential person

شَفْع *adj* even

شافِع *n* mediator, intercessor; intermediary

شافِعِيّ A *adj* Shafi'i; المَذْهَب الشافِعِيّ the Shafi'i school (*one of the four major schools of jurisprudence in Sunni Islam*) B *n* Shafi'i

شافِعِيّة *n* Shafi'ism (*Islamic school of religious law*)

شَفاعة *n* intercession; mediation

شَفيع *n* |شُفَعاءُ| (Chr) patron saint

اسْتِشْفاع *n* mediation; intercession

مَشْفوع *adj* accompanied; تَصْريح مَشْفوع بالقَسَم sworn statement

‹ **شَفَّ** *v* |i; شُفوف, شَفيف, شَفَّ| 1▸ [كانَ شَفّافاً] to be/become transparent 2▸ [أَفْشى] |عن| to reveal, to disclose

اشْتَفَّ *v* 1▸ [اسْتَقْصى] to search through, to go through 2▸ [شَرِبَ] to empty, to drink up, to drain

اسْتَشَفَّ *v* to conclude; to realize; to observe, to look at; اسْتَشَفَّ من كَلِماتِ شَخْصٍ to infer from sb's words; اسْتُشِفَّ to be/become clear

شَفّ *n* |شُفوف| *translucent garment*

شَفّاف *adj* transparent, translucent; obvious; غَيْر شَفّافٍ opaque; من مادّةٍ شَفّافةٍ of transparent material; وَرَق شَفّاف tracing paper, transparent paper; tissue paper

شَفّافيّة *n* transparency, translucency; obviousness

شَفيف *adj* transparent; clear, obvious

‹ **شَفِقَ** *v* |a; شَفَق| 1▸ [عَطَفَ] |على| to pity, to commiserate; to feel for 2▸ [خافَ] |على| to be/become worried

أَشْفَقَ *v* 1▸ [عَطَفَ] |على| to pity; to sympathize (with), to feel for; أَشْفَقَ على شَخْصٍ to pity sb, to have compassion for sb; أَشْفَقَ على الضَحايا to sympathize with the victims; أُشْفِقُ عَلَيْهِ I feel for him 2▸ [خافَ] |من| to beware (of), to be on one's guard (for); to be afraid (of)

شَفَق *n* |أَشْفاق| dusk; twilight; الشَفَق القُطْبِيّ الشَماليّ aurora borealis

شَفَقة *n* pity, compassion; sympathy; شَفَقةً out of pity; عَديم الشَفَقَةِ heartless, remorseless; شَخْص خالٍ من الشَفَقَةِ a heartless person; مُثير للشَفَقة pitiful, pathetic; أَثارَ الشَفَقةَ to evoke pity; هَزَّ رَأْسَهُ بِشَفَقةٍ he shook his head pityingly

شَفوق *adj* sympathetic

شَفيق *adj* |شُفَقاءُ| compassionate

إِشْفاق *n* pity, compassion; commiseration; إِشْفاقاً out of pity

مُشْفِق *adj* compassionate

‹ **شِفْنين** *n* شِفْنين بَحْرِيّ (Zool) ray (*Batoidea*)

‹ **شَفة** *n* |شَفَوات, شِفاه| 1▸ (Anat) lip; شَفة عُلْيا upper lip; شَفة سُفْلى lower lip; شَفَتانِ مُتَشَقِّقَتانِ cracked lips; بِشَفَتَيْنِ مُرْتَعِشَتَيْنِ with quivering lips; لم يَنْبِسْ بِبِنْتِ شَفةٍ he did not open his mouth; عَضَّ شَفَتَيْهِ to bite one's lips; زَمَّ شَفَتَيْهِ to purse one's lips; وَضَعَ كَأْساً على شَفَتَيْهِ to put a

مُسْتَشْفَى *n* |مُسْتَشْفَيات| hospital; infirmary; مُسْتَشْفًى جامِعِيّ university hospital; مَسْتَشْفًى عَسْكَرِيّ military hospital; مُسْتَشْفى الأَمْراضِ العَقْلِيّةِ \ النَفْسِيَةِ \ العَصَبِيَةِ psychiatric clinic, mental hospital; مُسْتَشْفى الأَطْفالِ children's hospital; ذَهَبَ إلى \ كانَ \ رَقَدَ في المُسْتَشْفى to be in hospital; المُسْتَشْفى to go to hospital

‹ **شَقِرَ** *v* |a; شَقَر| to be/become blond, to be/become fair-haired

اشْقَرَّ *v* to be blond, to be fair

شُقْرة *n* blondness

أَشْقَر **A** *adj* |dipt; شُقْر| blond; شَعْر أَشْقَر blond hair, fair hair **B** *n* شَقْراء blonde, fair-haired girl

‹ **شِقْراق** *n* (Zool) roller (*Coraciidae*)

‹ **شَقْشَق** *v* |i; شَقْشَقة| to sing, to warble; to peep, to tweet, to twitter

‹ **شَقَفة** *n* fragment

‹ **شَقّ** *v* |u| **1** [فَلَعَ] |شَقّ| to split; to cut open, to tear up; to divide, to disunite; شَقَّ شَقًّا to dig a trench; شَقَّ الحَطَبَ to split firewood **2** [طَرِيقاً] |شَقّ| to build, to construct; شَقَّ طَرِيقاً to build a road; شَقَّ طَرِيقَهُ to force one's way (through), to pull through **3** [صَعُبَ] |مَشَقّة| to be hard, to be difficult; شَقَّ الصَوْمُ على المُسافِرِ the fast was hard for the traveller; شَقَّ عَلَيْهِ أنْ ... he found it difficult to ...

شَقَّقَ *v* to split; شَقَّقَ شَيْئاً to make sth crack

تَشَقَّقَ *v* to crack, to split; to burst open; تَشَقَّقَتْ شَفَتايَ من البَرْدِ my lips have chapped with the cold

انْشَقّ *v* to split; to crack, to burst

اشْتَقّ *v* to derive; اشْتَقَّ كَلِمةً من كَلِمةٍ أُخْرى to derive a word from another word

شاقّ *adj* |شَواقّ| difficult, hard; awful; عَمَل شاقّ, أَشْغال شاقّة unremitting labour, hard work

شَقّ *n* |شُقوق| incision, cut; crack, split; groove, slot; شَقّ طُرُقٍ جَدِيدةٍ laying new roads

شِقّ *n* **1** [جانِب] side; يَنامُ على شِقِّهِ الأَيْمَنِ he sleeps on his right side **2** [نِصْف] half **3** [جُهْد] انْتِصار \ فَوْز بِشِقِّ النَفْسِ a narrow victory; بِشِقِّ النَفْسِ \ الأَنْفُسِ narrowly, barely

glass to one's lips; تَرَدَّدَ اسْمُهُ على الشِفاهِ his name was on everybody's lips; أَحْمَر الشِفاهِ lipstick; قِراءة الشَفَتَيْنِ lip-reading **2** [حافة] edge

شَفَهِيّ, شَفَوِيّ *adj* verbal, oral; اتِّفاق \ مَوْعِد شَفَوِيّ a verbal agreement/arrangement; امْتِحان شَفَوِيّ an oral examination; حَرْف \ صَوْت شَفَوِيّ (Ling) labial consonant

مُشافَهة *n* مُشافَهةً orally; verbally

‹ **شَفَى** *v* |i; شِفاء| to cure; to heal; شَفَى شَخْصاً to cure sb, to restore sb to health; شَفَى شَخْصاً من شَيْءٍ to cure sb of sth; شُفِيَ to recover, to heal; شُفِيَ من مَرَضٍ to recover from an illness; شُفِيَ من الجِراحِ to recover from an injury; شُفِيَ تَماماً to recover completely; شَفَى نَفْسَهُ \ غَيْظَهُ \ غَلِيلَهُ to take revenge

شَفَّى *v* to fillet, to debone

أَشْفَى *v* |على| to be on the verge of ...; أَشْفَى على الهَلاكِ \ المَوْتِ to have one foot in the grave

تَشَفَّى *v* **1** [شَفِيَ] to recover; to recuperate, to be cured **2** [انْتَقَمَ] |من| to take revenge; to avenge oneself

اشْتَفَى *v* **1** [بَرِئَ] to seek a cure, to be cured, to be treated; اشْتَفَى من عِلّةٍ to be cured from a disease **2** [انْتَقَمَ] to revenge oneself, to avenge oneself; اشْتَفَى من عَدوِّهِ to take revenge on one's enemy

اسْتَشْفَى *v* to take/seek a cure; to undergo treatment (in a hospital)

شافٍ *adj* healing, curative

شَفاً *n* هو على شَفا الهَلاكِ he's on the verge of breaking down; he's on the verge of giving in (*to temptation*)

شِفاء *n* |أَشْفِية| **1** [إبْلال] recovery, recuperation; cure; تَمَنَّى لِشَخْصٍ الشِفاءَ to wish sb a speedy recovery; أَتَمَنَّى لَكَ الشِفاءَ العاجِلَ! get well soon!; أَدَّى إلى الشِفاءِ to lead to recovery; المَرْضى المَيْؤوس من شِفائِهِم the incurably ill; مَرَض غَيْر قابِلٍ للشِفاءِ an incurable illness **2** [عِلاج] remedy, cure; medicine

شِفائِيّ *adj* curative, remedial, healing (*before n*); medicinal; therapeutic; قوّة شِفائيّة therapeutic effect

اسْتِشْفاء *n* cure, course of treatment

شَقْلَبة *n* somersault, flip

شَقا *v* |u; شَقْو| to sadden, to grieve

شَقِيَ *v* |a; شَقاء| to be/become unhappy

أَشْقى *v* to make miserable

تَشاقى *v* to be naughty

شَقيّ A *adj* |أَشْقِياءُ| 1 [غَيْر مُطيع] naughty, mischievous; طِفْل شَقيّ a naughty child, a brat; وَلَد شَقيّ a naughty boy 2 [تعيس] unhappy; حَياة شَقيّة a miserable existence B *n* |أَشْقِياءُ| rogue, rascal

شَقاء *n* misfortune; misery

شَقاوة *n* 1 [الأطْفالِ] mischief 2 [تَعْس] misfortune; misery

شُكّ *n* (Zool) snipe (*Gallinago gallinago*)

شَكَرَ *v* |u; شُكْر, شُكْران| to thank; شَكَرَ شَخْصاً لِشَيْءٍ \ على شَيْءٍ to thank sb for sth; شَكَرَ كُلَّ الحاضِرينَ to thank all the attendees; شَكَرَ شَخْصاً على مُساعَدَتِهِ to thank sb for their help; شَكَرَ الجُمْهورَ على حُضورِهِ to thank the audience for coming; شَكَرَ شَخْصاً من كُلِّ قَلْبِهِ (على شَيْءٍ) to thank sb wholeheartedly (for sth)

تَشَكَّرَ *v* to thank; to be grateful, to be thankful; تَشَكَّرَ شَخْصاً to thank sb

شاكِر *adj* grateful, thankful; شاكِر على شَيْءٍ grateful for sth; قَبِلَ شاكِراً to accept gratefully

شُكْر *n* |شُكور| thanks; gratitude, appreciation; شُكْراً thank you, thanks; شُكْراً جَزيلاً many thanks, thanks a lot; أَلْف شُكْرٍ thanks a million; مع جَزيلِ الشُكْرِ ل ... with many thanks to ...; شُكْراً على تَعاوُنِكَ thank you for your cooperation; الشُكْرُ للهِ, لا شُكْرَ على واجِبٍ you're welcome, don't mention it; جَدير بالشُكْرِ worthy of thanks; تَعْبير \ إِعْراب عن الشُكْرِ expression of thanks; أَلْقى كَلِمةَ شُكْرٍ to speak a word of thanks; أَسْدى الشُكْرَ لِشَخْصٍ to extend a word of thanks to sb; تَلَقّى عِباراتِ شُكْرٍ to receive thanks; عَبَّرَ عن \ عَبَّرَ لِشَخْصٍ عن شُكْرِهِ to express one's thanks to sb; جَزيل شُكْرِهِ to express one's heartfelt thanks; اسْتَحَقَّ الشُكْرَ والتَقْديرَ to deserve thanks and appreciation

شُكْران *n* thanks; صَلاة الشُكْرانِ (Chr) prayer of thanksgiving

شِقاق *n* discord, dissension; schism; شِقاق مُسْتَمِرّ ongoing rift; بَذَرَ بُذورَ الشِقاقِ to sow discord, to spread dissension

شُقّة *n* 1 [مَشَقّة] effort, trouble; exertion 2 [مَسافة] distance

شَقّة, شِقّة *n* |شِقَق| 1 [مَسْكَن] apartment, flat (BrE); سَكَنَ \ مَلَكَ شِقّةً to live in/have a flat; اسْتَأْجَرَ شِقّةً to rent a flat; شِقّة بِخَمْسِ غُرَفٍ a five-room flat 2 [شَريط] strip, band

شَقيق A *n* |أَشِقّاءُ, أَشِقّة| brother; الدُوَل العَرَبيّة الشَقيقة the Arab sister states; أَخ غَيْر شَقيقٍ stepbrother, half-brother B *n coll* |شَقائِقُ| (Bot) anemone (*Anemone coronaria*); شَقائِقُ النُعْمانِ red anemone

شَقيقة *n* 1 [أُخْت] |شَقائِقُ, شَقيقات| sister 2 (Med) migraine 3 (Bot) see شَقيق

اشْتِقاق *n* |اشْتِقاقات| (Ling) derivation; عِلْم الاشْتِقاقِ etymology; اشْتِقاق كَلِمةٍ the derivation of a word

اشْتِقاقيّ *adj* (Ling) etymological; derivational

انْشِقاق *n* |انْشِقاقات| split, rift; disunity, schism; الانْشِقاق داخِلَ الحُكومةِ the rift within the government; سورة الانْشِقاق The Sundering (*Sura 84*)

انْشِقاقيّ *adj, n* separatist

انْشِقاقيّة *n* separatism; nonconformity

مُتَشَقِّق *adj* split, cleft

مُشْتَقّ *n* |مُشْتَقّات| 1 (Ling) derived word 2 (Math) derivative 3 [مادّة] product, derivative; مُشْتَقّات الحَليبِ milk products, dairy (products); مُشْتَقّات النَفْطِ oil derivatives; مُشْتَقّات الائْتِمانِ credit derivatives

مَشَقّة *n* |مَشاقّ, مَشَقّات| effort, labour; exertion; بِمَشَقّةٍ barely, with difficulty; تَحَمَّلَ مَشاقَّ to endure hardship

مُشَقَّق *adj* 1 [مُنْفَصِل] split, cleft 2 [الجِلْد] chapped

مَشْقوق *adj* split, cleft; حَنَك \ شَفة مَشْقوق(ة) cleft palate/lip

مُنْشَقّ *adj, n* non-conformist; dissident

مُنْشَقّة *n* schistosoma; داء المُنْشَقّاتِ bilharzia, schistosomiasis

شاقول *n* plumb line, plummet

شاقوليّ *adj* vertical

شَقْلَبَ *v* |i; شَقْلَبة| to overturn, to upset

تَشَقْلَبَ *v* to do a somersault; to tumble

شَكور **A** *adj* |شُكُر| grateful, thankful

B *n* الشَّكور the Grateful (*one of the names of God*)

2 **شِكارة** *n* sack, bag; شِكارة إسْمَنْتٍ a bag of cement

شَكِسَ *v* |a; شَكاسة| to be surly/sullen

شاكَسَ *v* to pester

تَشاكَسَ *v* to treat each other gruffly

شَكِس *adj* |شُكْس| sullen, stern; moody, irritable, peevish; رَجُل شَكِس an ill-tempered man, a disagreeable fellow

مُشاكِس *adj* moody, irritable; sullen; بِطَريقةٍ مُشاكِسةٍ in a contentious manner; طِفْل مُشاكِس a naughty child

شَكْشوكة *n* (NA) *a dish of scrambled eggs with vegetables*

شَكَّ *v* |u; شَكّ| **1** [اِشْتَبَهَ] to doubt, to question; to suspect; شَكَّ في شَيْءٍ \ شَخْصٍ to doubt sth/sb, to suspect sth/sb; شَكَّ في صِحّةِ الخَبَرِ to doubt the truth of the news; شَكَّ في إمْكانيّةِ نَجاحِ شَيْءٍ to doubt whether sth will succeed **2** [طَعَنَ] to stab, to pierce

شَكَّكَ *v* to arouse suspicion; to cast doubt

تَشَكَّكَ *v* to doubt, to question; تَشَكَّكَ في شَيْءٍ to doubt sth

شَكّ *n* |شُكوك| **1** [اِرْتِياب] suspicion, mistrust; شَكّ في شَخْصٍ suspicion of sb; خامَرَهُ \ ساوَرَهُ الشَكُّ he became suspicious; ساوَرَهُ الشَكُّ في شَخْصٍ he became suspicious of sb; وَضَعَ شَخْصاً مَوْضِعَ شَكٍّ to make sb subject to suspicion **2** [عَدَم التَأكُّد] doubt; شَكّ في شَيْءٍ \ شَخْصٍ doubts about sth/sb; شَكّ في مَحَلِّهِ reasonable doubt; مَوْضِع شَكٍّ a dubious case; شُكوك scepticism; شُكوك حول شَيْءٍ scepticism about sth; بِدونِ شَكٍّ without doubt, undoubtedly; لا شَكَّ (فيهِ), لا يَقْبَلُ الشَكَّ, لا سَبيلَ إلى الشَكِّ فيه, لا يَتَطَرَّقُ إلَيْهِ الشَكُّ without a doubt; لا يَدَعُ مَجالاً للشَكِّ it leaves no room for doubt; خامَرَهُ \ راوَدَهُ شَكٌّ he had doubts; دَعا إلى \ بَعَثَ على الشَكِّ to raise doubts; هذا أَمْرٌ يَدْعو للشَكِّ this is a dubious matter; أَلْقى ظِلالاً من الشَكِّ على شَيْءٍ to raise doubts about sth; وَضَعَ شَيْئاً مَوْضِعَ شَكٍّ to cast doubt on sth; أَثْبَتَ شَيْئاً بِدونِ أَيِّ شَكٍّ to prove sth beyond doubt; ما من شَكٍّ في أَنَّ ... there is no mistaking that ...; تَغَلَّبَ على شُكوكِهِ to conquer one's scepticism

شَكّاك **A** *adj* |شُكّاك, شَكّاكون| sceptical

B *n* |شُكّاك, شَكّاكون| sceptic

شَكّة *n* prick

شُكوكيّ **A** *adj* sceptical

B *n* sceptic

مُتَشَكِّك **A** *adj* sceptical, doubting; مُتَشَكِّك في شَيْءٍ doubting about sth

B *n* sceptic

مَشْكوك *adj* مَشْكوك فيهِ doubtful, dubious; (الشَخْص) المَشْكوك فيهِ suspect; الأَمْرُ مَشْكوكٌ فيهِ the matter looks suspicious; سُمْعة مَشْكوك فيها a dubious reputation; دُيون مَشْكوك في تَحْصيلها doubtful debts

شَكَلَ *v* |u; شَكْل| **1** (Ling) to vocalize **2** [اِلْتَبَسَ] to be dubious

شَكَّلَ *v* **1** [كَوَّنَ] to form, to shape; to model, to fashion; to set up; شَكَّلَ عائِقاً to form a barrier; شَكَّلَ الحُدودَ بين دَوْلَتَيْنِ to form the border between two countries; شَكَّلَ لَجْنَةً \ فَريقاً to set up a committee/team; شَكَّلَ خَطَراً to be a danger to **2** [الكِتابَ] to vocalize

شاكَلَ *v* to resemble; أَنْتَ تُشاكِلُ أَباكَ you resemble your father

أَشْكَلَ *v* to be dubious; to be vague; to be/become difficult

تَشَكَّلَ *v* to be formed; to take shape

تَشاكَلَ *v* to resemble each other

اسْتَشْكَلَ *v* to be dubious; to be ambiguous

شَكْل *n* |شُكول, أَشْكال| **1** [صورة] picture, image; figure; شَكْل بَيانيّ diagram, graph; شَكْل تَوْضيحيّ illustration; شَكْل هَنْدَسيّ a geometric figure; شَكْل دائِريّ \ مُرَبَّع \ بَيْضَويّ a round/square/oval figure; الشَكْل المُبَيَّن أَسْفَلَهُ \ أَعْلاهُ the below/above figure **2** [هَيْئة] figure; form, shape; شَكْل جَميل a good figure; تَغَيُّر الشَكْل transformation, metamorphosis; عَديم الشَكْلِ shapeless, amorphous; بِنَفْسِ الشَكْلِ identical (in form); اتَّخذ شَكْلاً to take shape; اتَّخذَ شَكْلاً واضِحاً to take on a clear shape; غَيَّرَ شَكْلَهُ to change one's appearance; الشَكْل والمَضْمون form and content; من حَيْثُ الشَكْلِ in terms of shape **3** [طَريقة] بِشَكْلٍ عامٍّ in general; بِشَكْلٍ خاصّ in particular; بِشَكْلٍ مُباشِرٍ directly; (من) بِأَيِّ شَكْلٍ (الأَشْكالِ) in any way possible; بِشَكْلٍ ما somehow or the other **4** (Ling NA) vocalization

شِكْل *n* image, likeness

شاكِلة *n* |شَواكِلُ| 1 [طَبيعة] character; nature; على شاكِلَتِها just like her 2 [خاصِرة] flank, side

شَكْليّ *adj* formal, ceremonious; شَكْليًّا formally; غَيْر شَكْليّ informal; إجْراءات شَكْليّة, شَكْليّات formalities; قامَ بالشَكْليّاتِ to go through formalities; حَفِظَ الشَكْليّاتِ to observe the formalities

شَكْليّة *n* formalism

إشْكال *n* problem; paradox; stumbling block, obstacle

إشْكاليّ *adj* problematic

إشْكاليّة *n* problems, problematic nature; إشْكاليّة التَلَوُّثِ the problems of pollution

تَشْكيل *n* |تَشْكيلات| 1 [تَكْوين] formation, creation; forming; تَشْكيل وِزاريّ cabinet formation; تَشْكيل الإدارة الجَديدة the formation of the new management 2 [عَدَد] number, group 3 (Sport) line-up; تَشْكيل فَريق كُرةِ القَدَمِ the line-up of a football team; في تَشْكيلٍ مُعَيَّنٍ in a particular line-up 4 (Ling) vocalization

تَشْكيلة *n* 1 [مَجْموعة] assortment, variety; selection, collection; تَشْكيلة واسِعة (مِن) ... a wide assortment of ...; تَشْكيلة مُتَنَوِّعة a varied assortment; تَشْكيلة كُتُب \ من الكُتُبِ a collection of books; تَشْكيلة من المَأْكولاتِ a choice of delicacies; تَشْكيلة الأزْياءِ الصَيْفيّة summer collection (fashion) 2 (Mil, Sport) formation; line-up; تَشْكيلة مُرَبَّعة (Mil) formation; تَشْكيلة أساسيّة basic line-up

تَشْكيليّ *adj* الفَنّ التَشْكيليّ the visual arts

مُشاكَلة *n* (Ling) assimilation

مِشْكال *n* kaleidoscope

مُشْكِل *adj* problematic

مُشَكَّل *adj* 1 [مُتَنَوِّع] assorted; diverse, various 2 [مُكَوَّن] formed, shaped

مُشَكِّل *adj* component, constituent

مُشْكِلة *n* |مُشْكِلات, مَشاكِلُ| problem, difficulty; bottleneck; issue, topic; مُشْكِلة أساسيّة core/basic problem; مُشْكِلة بيئيّة environmental problem; مُشْكِلة زَوْجيّة marital problem; مَشاكِل ماليّة financial problems; مَشاكِل بيئيّة كَبيرة \ عالَميّة big/global environmental problems; مَشاكِل داخليّة \ سِياسيّة internal/political problems; واجَهَ مَشاكِلَ ماليّةً \ عانى من مَشاكِلَ ماليّةٍ to face/have financial problems; تَغَلَّبَ على المَشاكِلِ الماليّةِ to overcome financial problems; حَلَّ مُشْكِلةً \ تَغَلَّبَ على مُشْكِلةٍ to solve/overcome a problem; حَلَّ مُشْكِلةً سِلْميًّا to settle a matter amicably; واجَهَ مَشاكِلَ to face difficulties; وَقَعَ في مَشاكِلَ to get into trouble; وَقَعَ في مَشاكِلَ مع شَخْصٍ to get in trouble with sb; سَبَّبَ لِشَخْصٍ مَشاكِلَ to get sb in trouble; جَلَبَ \ أثارَ \ سَبَّبَ مَشاكِلَ to cause problems; عالَجَ مُشْكِلةً to tackle a problem; طَرَحَ مُشْكِلةً to raise a problem; بِدونِ مَشاكِلَ without a problem, smoothly; مَرَّ بِدونِ مَشاكِلَ to go smoothly; مَشاكِل بين طَرَفَيْنِ problems between two sides

شَكَمَ *v* |u; شَكْم| شَكَمَ فَرَساً to bridle a horse

أشْكَمَ *v* أشْكَمَ فَرَساً to bridle a horse

شَكيمة *n* |شَكائِمُ, شُكُم, شَكيم| 1 [لِجام] bit 2 [عِزّة] obstinacy; قَويّ الشَكيمةِ strong-willed

شَكا *v* |u; شَكْوى| 1 [اشْتَكى] to complain; to moan; شَكا شَخْصاً \ من شَخْصٍ to complain about sb; شَكا من (أنّ) he complained that 2 [تَأَلَّمَ] to have health complaints; شَكا من الألَمِ to complain about pain

شاكى *v* to file a complaint

تَشَكّى *v* to complain; to make a complaint; تَشَكّى من شَيْءٍ to complain about sth

تَشاكى *v* to complain to one another

اشْتَكى *v* to complain; to make a complaint, to lodge a complaint; اشْتَكى للإدارة to lodge a complaint with the management; اشْتَكى من أنّ ... to complain that ...; اشْتَكى من شَيْءٍ to complain about sth; اشْتَكى من الألَمِ to complain about pain; اشْتَكى من رَداءةِ شَيْءٍ to complain about the poor quality of sth; اشْتَكى شَخْصاً \ من شَخْصٍ to complain about sb

شاكٍ A *adj* complaining
B *n* plaintiff, complainant (BrE)

شَكّاء A *adj* complaining
B *n* complainer

شِكاية *n* complaint; قَدَّمَ شِكايةً to file a complaint, to complain

شَكْوة *n* complaint

شَكْوى *n* |f; شَكاوى| complaint; شَكْوى رَسْمِيّة an official complaint; ... شَكْوى ضدّ a complaint about ...; شَكْوى حول a complaint against sb; حَقّ (بِتَقْديم) الشَكْوى right of appeal; قَدَّمَ شَكْوى to file a complaint; أَعْرَبَ عن شَكْواهُ to make complaints, to air one's grievances; شَكاوى جَسَدِيّة / نَفْسِيّة somatic/psychological complaints; نَظَرَ في مَوْضوعِ شَكْوى to look into a complaint; عَريضة شَكْوى plaint

مِشْكاة *n* |مَشاكٍ, مِشْكاوات| lamp; lantern

‹ **شَلْبة** *n* Wels catfish (*Silurus glanis*)

‹ **شَلْتة** *n* |شِلَت| hassock

‹ **شَلَحَ** *v* |a; شَلْح| to take off, to pull off

شَلَّحَ *v* to undress; شَلَّح شَخْصاً to undress sb

‹ **شَلْشَلَ** *v* |i; شَلْشَلة| to drip, to dribble

‹ **شِلْق** *n* (Zool) lamprey

‹ **شَلَّ** *v* **1** [أَوْقَفَ] |u; شَلّ| to paralyze; to bring to a standstill; to disrupt; شَلَّ الحَرَكةَ to immobilize; to bring to a standstill; شَلَّ حَرَكةَ شَخْصٍ to immobilize sb; شَلَّ حَرَكةَ المُرورِ \ الإِنْتاجِ to bring the traffic/production to a standstill; شَلَّ حَرَكةَ القِطاراتِ to disrupt rail traffic **2** [أُصيبَ بالشَلَلِ] |a; شَلَل| to become paralyzed; شُلَّتْ يَمينُهُ! may his right hand be paralyzed!

أَشَلَّ *v* to paralyze, to immobilize; to bring to a standstill

انْشَلَّ *v* to be/become paralyzed; to freeze, to be put out of action; انْشَلَّتْ حَرَكةُ الطَيَرانِ air traffic was paralyzed

شَلَل *n* paralysis, palsy; شَلَل نِصْفيّ \ كُلّيّ one-sided/total paralysis; شَلَل رُعاشيّ Parkinson's disease; شَلَل الأَطْفال poliomyelitis; فَيْروس شَلَلِ الأَطْفالِ polio; لَقاح شَلَلِ الأَطْفالِ polio vaccine; أُصيبَ بِشَلَلِ الأَطْفالِ to be afflicted by/to get polio; أَعْراض الشَلَل symptoms of paralysis; أُصيبَ بالشَلَلِ to be/become paralyzed; أَصابَ الاقْتِصادَ بالشَلَلِ to paralyze the economy; أُصيبَ الاقْتِصادُ بالشَلَلِ the economy has been paralyzed

شَلّال *n* |شَلّالات| waterfall

شِلّة *n* |شِلَل| **1** [صوف] شِلّة صوفٍ a ball of wool **2** [رَهْط] gang, group

أَشَلّ **A** *adj* |dipt; شُلّ| paralyzed, paralytic

B *n* |dipt; شُلّ| paralyzed person, paralytic

مُشِلّ *adj* paralyzing, crippling

مَشْلول **A** *adj* paralyzed, lame

B *n* paralyzed person

‹ **شِلِن** *n* shilling

‹ **شِلْو** *n* |أَشْلاء| **1** [لَحْم] cut **2** [جِسْم] limb

‹ **اشْمَأَزَّ** *v* to loathe, to detest; to be nauseated; اشْمَأَزَّ من شَخْصٍ to loathe sb; اشْمَأَزَّ من شَيْءٍ to abhor sth; to get the creeps from sth

اشْمِئْزاز *n* disgust, revulsion, repugnance; horror; aversion; بِاشْمِئْزازٍ with horror; أَثارَ الاشْمِئْزاز to appal, to disgust; اشْمِئْزاز من شَيْءٍ \ شَخْصٍ disgust of sth/sb

مُشْمَئِزّ *adj* averse; nauseated

‹ **شَمْبانْزي, شِمْبَنْزي** *n* |شَمْبَنْزِيات| (Zool) chimpanzee (*Pan*)

‹ **شَمْبانِيا** *n* champagne; كَأْس من الشَمْبانِيا a glass of champagne

‹ **شَمِتَ** *v* |a; شَماتة, شَمات| ب| to gloat (at); شَمِتَ بالعَدُوِّ to gloat at the enemy

‹ **شَمَخَ** *v* |a; شُموخ, شَمْخ| to tower; to be very high; شَمَخَ بِأَنْفِهِ to be arrogant

شامِخ *adj* |شَوامِخُ, شُمَّخ| high, towering; جَبَل شامِخ a high mountain; نَسَب شامِخ noble lineage

شُموخ *n* **1** [تَكَبُّر] arrogance **2** [عُلُوّ] being high up **3** [كَرامة] self-respect, dignity

‹ **شَمَرَ** *v* |u; شَمْر| to roll up, to turn up; شَمَرَ كُمَّهُ to roll up one's sleeve; شَمَرَ عن ساقِهِ \ ساعِدِهِ to prepare oneself to do sth

شَمَّرَ *v* to roll up, to turn up; شَمَّرَ عن ساعِدَيْهِ للقِيامِ بِشَيْءٍ to buckle down to sth

تَشَمَّرَ *v* to prepare, to get ready

شَمار *n* (Bot) fennel (*Foeniculum vulgare*)

شَمْرة *n* (Bot) fennel (*Foeniculum vulgare*)

‹ **شَمَسَ** *v* |u; شُموس, شِماس| to be sunny

شَمَّسَ *v* to put (out) in the sun; شَمَّسَ شَيْئاً to lay sth in the sun

أَشْمَسَ *v* to be sunny

تَشَمَّسَ *v* to sunbathe, to bask in the sun

شَمْعُدان, شَمَعْدان, شَمْعَدان ‹ *n* |شَمْعُدانات, شَماعِد| candlestick, candleholder

شَمَلَ, شَمِلَ [1]‹ *v* |a-u; شُمول, شَمْل| 1▸ [تَضَمَّنَ] to comprise, to encompass; to contain, to hold; to cover; شَمَلَ مِنْطَقةً to encompass an area; شَمَلَ مِنْطَقةً كامِلةً to encompass an entire area; شَمَلَ شَخْصاً \ شَيْئاً بِرِعايَتِهِ to take sb/sth under one's wing; يَشْمُلُ العَفْوُ جَميعَ المُعْتَقَلين the amnesty applies to all prisoners; يَشْمُلُ القَرارُ الجَميعَ the resolution concerns everyone 2▸ [اِحْتَوى] to imply, to mean 3▸ [عَمَّ] to prevail

اِشْتَمَلَ *v* to contain, to enclose, to include; to imply, to mean; to implicate; اِشْتَمَلَ على جَميعِ المَعْلوماتِ to include all data

شامِل *adj* universal, total, complete; comprehensive, exhaustive, extensive; سَلام شامِل a comprehensive peace; بَحْث \ مُلَخَّص شامِل an extensive research/summary; وَصْف \ حِوار شامِل a comprehensive description/discussion; خُطّة شامِلة a detailed plan; مَجْموعة شامِلة a complete collection; حَظْر شامِل على شَيْءٍ a total ban on sth

شِمال *n* 1▸ [يَسار] |أَشْمُل, شُمُل, شَمائِل| left 2▸ [سِمة] |شَمائِل| characteristics

شَمْل *n* uniting, gathering; اِجْتِماع \ لَمّ \ جَمْع الشَمْلِ reunion, reunification; جَمْع \ لَمّ شَمْلِ الأُسْرةِ (ME) family reunion; شُتِّتَ شَمْلُ الأُسْرةِ the family became scattered

شَمْلة *n* |شَمَلات| 1▸ [رِداء] cape, cloak; coat 2▸ [عِمامة] turban

شَمول *n* wine

شُموليّ *adj* universal; totalitarian; حُكْم شُموليّ a totalitarian regime; نَظْرة شُموليّة a holistic view; a thorough look

شُموليّة *n* 1▸ [كُلِّيّة] thoroughness; completeness 2▸ (Pol) totalitarianism

شَميلة *n* |شَمائِل| characteristic, character trait; هو كَريمُ \ حَميدُ الشَمائِلِ he is of good character

مُشْتَمِل *adj* including; مُشْتَمِلاً على المُقَدِّمةِ including the introduction

شَمال [2]‹ *n* north; شَمالاً (to the) north of; northward; في\من الشَمالِ in/from the north; الشَمال الشَرْقيّ northeast; الشَمال الغَرْبيّ northwest; بَحْر الشَمالِ the North Sea; شَمالَ دِمَشْقَ north of Damascus

شَمْس *n* |f; شُموس| sun; غُروب الشَمْسِ sunset; تَغْرُبُ الشَمْسُ the sun is going down/is setting; طُلوع الشَمْسِ sunrise; تَطْلَعُ الشَمْسُ the sun is rising; أَشِعّة الشَمْسِ sunrays; ضَوْء الشَمْسِ sunlight; حَمّام شَمْسٍ sunbath; سَفْعة شَمْسٍ sunburn; سَفَعَتْهُ أُصيبَ بِضَرْبة الشَمْسُ to get sunburnt; ضَرْبة شَمْسٍ sunstroke; الشَمْسِ to get sunstroke; عَبّاد الشَمْسِ sunflower; اِنْقِلاب الشَمْسِ solstice; سورة الشَمْس The Sun (*Sura 91*); تُشْرِقُ الشَمْسُ the sun shines; لا جَديدَ تحت الشَمْسِ nothing new under the sun; هذا واضِحٌ مِثْل عَيْنِ الشَمْسِ that is as clear as day; تَرَبَّعَت الشَمْسُ في كَبِدِ السَماءِ the sun is at its zenith; إذا أَشْرَقَت الشَمْسُ من المَغْرِبِ ≈ when pigs fly

شَمّاس *n* |شَمامِسة| (Chr) deacon; verger

شَمْسيّ *adj* sun (*before n*); ساعة شَمْسيّة sundial; طاقة شَمْسيّة solar energy; لَوح شَمْسيّ solar panel; خَليّة شَمْسيّة solar cell; نَظّارة شَمْسيّة sunglasses; نِظام شَمْسيّ solar system; عاصِفة شَمْسيّة geomagnetic storm; الحُروف الشَمْسيّة (Gram) sun letters (*that assimilate the preceding lam of the article*)

شَمْسيّة *n* umbrella, parasol; awning; تحت شَمْسيّةٍ under a sunshade

مُشْمِس *adj* sunny, sun-drenched; بَيْت مُشْمِس a sunny house; يَوْم مُشْمِس a sunny day; شاطِئ مُشْمِس a sun-drenched beach

شَمَطَ ‹ *v* |i; شَمْط| to go grey

أَشْمَط *adj* |dipt; شَمْطاءُ f; شُمْطان, شُمْط| *having salt-and-pepper hair*

شَمَّعَ ‹ *v* 1▸ [بالشَمْعِ الأَحْمَرِ] to seal 2▸ [لَمَّعَ] to wax

شَمْع, شَمَع *n* |شُموع| wax; شَمْع طَبيعيّ beeswax; صَقَلَ \ دَهَنَ بالشَمْعِ to wax, to treat with wax; شَمْع أَحْمَر sealing wax; خَتَمَ شَيْئاً بالشَمْعِ الأَحْمَرِ to seal sth with sealing wax

شَمّاعة *n* (clothes) hanger, coat hanger; hatstand, coat stand; عَلَّقَ مِعْطَفَهُ على الشَمّاعةِ to hang one's coat on the coat stand

شَمْعة *n* |شُموع| 1▸ [لِلضَوْءِ] candle; أَشْعَلَ شَمْعةً to light a candle; أَطْفَأَ شَمْعةً to blow out a candle; شَمْعة مُشْعَلة \ مُحْتَرِقة a burning candle; شَمْعة إِشْعالٍ spark plug; شَمْعات wax candles 2▸ (Phys) candela

شَمْعيّ *adj* waxy

مُشَمَّع *adj* wax; water-repellent

شَمالِيّ **A** *adj* northern, northerly; من الجِهةِ الشَمالِيّةِ from the north, from a northerly direction; الرِياحُ شَمالِيَّةٌ the winds are northerly; قُطْبِيّ شَمالِيّ Arctic; المِنْطَقة القُطْبِيّة الشَمالِيّة the Arctic region; شَمالِيَّ مَدِينةِ دِمَشْق north of Damascus **B** *n* northerner

‹ **شَمَّ** **I** *v* |a-u; شَمِيم ,شَمّ; perf شَمَمْتُ ,شَمِمْتُ| to smell, to sniff; شَمَّ رائِحةَ الطَعام to smell food

شَمَّ **II** *v* |a; شَمَم; perf شَمِمْتُ| to be proud, to be haughty

شَمَّمَ *v* to let smell, to give to smell

أَشَمَّ *v* **1** [شَمَّمَ] to let smell, to give (sb sth) to smell **2** (Ling) to pronounce a vowel

تَشَمَّمَ *v* to investigate, to explore; to smell, to sniff; تَشَمَّمَ شَيْئاً to sniff sth; تَشَمَّمَ الزُهور to smell the flowers

اشْتَمَّ *v* **1** [شَمَّ] to smell, to sniff **2** [اكْتَشَفَ] to discover; to sense, to detect; اشْتَمَّ رائِحةَ الكِذْبِ to detect a lie

شَمَم *n* pride

شَمّ *n* **1** [الحاسّة] sense of smell; scent; حاسّة الشَمّ sense of smell; scent; شَمّ النَسيمِ (Chr Egypt) *holiday (on the first Monday following Coptic Easter) celebrating the beginning of spring* **2** [مَصْدَر] smelling, sniffing

شَمّام *n coll* **1** [فاكِهة] melon **2** [من يَشُمُّ بِدِقّة] *a person with a good nose*

أَشَمّ *adj* |dipt; شُمّ; f شَمّاءُ| noble, honourable

‹ **شَمَنْدَر** *n* (white) beet (*Beta vulgaris*); شَمَنْدَر سُكَّرِيّ \ السُكَّر sugar beet

شَمَنْدورة *n* buoy

‹ **شَنَأَ** *v* |a; شَنْء| to hate; شَنَأَ شَخْصاً to hate sb

‹ **شَنَب** *n* |أَشْناب| moustache

‹ **شَنِجَ** *v* |a; شَنَج| to convulse, to cramp, to contract

تَشَنَّجَ *v* to contract, to convulse; to tense up, to stiffen; تَشَنَّجَ العَضَلاتُ the muscles cramp up

تَشَنُّج *n* |تَشَنُّجات| cramp, (muscle) spasm, convulsion; أُصِيبَ بالتَشَنُّج to get cramp

تَشَنُّجِيّ *adj* convulsive; spastic; حَرَكات تَشَنُّجِيّة convulsive movements

مُتَشَنِّج *adj* spastic; stiff, contracted; رَقَبة مُتَشَنِّجة a stiff neck; عَضَلات \ أَطْراف مُتَشَنِّجة stiff muscles/limbs

‹ **شَنَّرَ** *v* to dishonour, to disgrace

‹ **شِنْشِنة** *n* |شَناشِنُ| nature, disposition; habit

‹ **شَنْطة** *n* |شُنَط| bag; suitcase; شَنْطة يَدَوِيّة handbag

‹ **شَنَعَ** *v* |a; شَنْع| to dishonour, to disgrace

شَنُعَ *v* |u; شَناعة ,شَنَع| to be horrible, to be abominable; to be ugly

شَنَّعَ *v* **1** [لاكَ] [على] to slander, to defame, to smear; to criticize, to denounce; شَنَّعَ على شَخْصٍ to slander sb **2** [قَبَّحَ] to make ugly

اسْتَشْنَعَ *v* to loathe

شَناعة *n* ugliness, hideousness

شَنِيع *adj* |شَنائِعُ ,شُنُع| abominable, repugnant; reprehensible; monstrous, hideous; عَمَل شَنِيع heinous act; أَفْكار شَنِيعة heinous ideas; تَصَرُّفاتُهُ شَنِيعةٌ his behaviour is reprehensible

أَشْنَع *adj* |dipt; f شَنْعاءُ| horrible, abominable

‹ **شَنْف ,شَنَف** *n* |شُنوف| ear stud, earring

‹ **شَنَقَ** *v* |u; شَنْق| to hang; شَنَقَ نَفْسَهُ to hang oneself

شَنْق *n* hanging; (مَوْت) شَنْقاً (death) by hanging; قَتَلَ شَنْقاً to kill by hanging

مِشْنَقة *n* |مَشانِقُ| gallows; قادَ شَخْصاً إلى حَبْلِ المِشْنَقةِ to lead sb to the gallows

‹ **شُنْقُب** *n* (Zool) snipe

‹ **شَنَّ** *v* |u; شَنّ| to let loose, to launch; to wage; شَنَّ انْتِفاضةً to trigger a revolt; شَنَّ حَرْباً to start a war; شَنَّ هُجوماً to launch an attack

‹ **شِهاب** *n* |شُهْبان ,شُهُب| (Astron) meteor

أَشْهَب *adj* |dipt; شُهْب; f شَهْباءُ| *with grey hair*

‹ **شَهِدَ** *v* |a| **1** [أَدْلى بِشَهادةٍ] [شَهادة] to (be) witness; to testify; شَهِدَ ل \ على شَخْصٍ to give evidence for/against sb; أَشْهَدُ أنْ لا إلَهَ إلاّ اللّٰهُ I testify that there is no God but Allah; شُهِدَ بِهِ عَلَيْهِمْ (Law Mor) *as witness the hands of the parties*; شَهِدَ باللّٰهِ to swear to God **2** [رَأى] [شُهود] to see, to witness; to experience; شَهِدَ يَوْمِيًّا to experience daily **3** [حَضَرَ] [شَهادة] to attend, to be present; شَهِدَ المَجْلِسَ to attend the session

شاهَدَ *v* [1] [رَأى] to watch, to look at, to view; to look on, to observe; شاهَدَ شَيْئاً to witness sth; شاهَدَ حُدوثَ شَيْءٍ to watch sth happening [2] [عاشَ] to experience

أَشْهَدَ *v* to call as a witness

تَشَهَّدَ *v* to profess one's faith

اسْتَشْهَدَ *v* [1] [ماتَ شَهيداً] أُسْتُشْهِدَ to die as a martyr, to fall (in battle); أُسْتُشْهِدَ في سَبيلِ الوَطَنِ to die for one's country [2] [اقْتَبَسَ |ب|] to quote, to cite; اسْتَشْهَدَ بِقَوْلِ شَخْصٍ to quote sb; اسْتَشْهَدَ بآيةٍ من القُرْآنِ to quote a Koranic verse; اسْتَشْهَدَ بِقَوْلِ كاتِبٍ to quote an author [3] [أَشْهَدَ] to call as a witness

شَهْد *n* |شِهاد| honey

شاهِد *n* [1] (Law) |أَشْهاد ,شُهود| witness; شاهِد رَئيسيّ chief witness; شاهِد زور false witness; شاهِد عِيانٍ eyewitness; شاهِد زَواجٍ witness at a wedding; كانَ شاهِداً to act as a witness; اسْتَدْعى شاهِداً to call a witness; تَبَيَّنَ من أَقْوالِ الشُهودِ أنّ ... it became clear from witness statements that ...; واللهُ شاهِدٌ على ما أَقولُ as God is my witness, I am speaking the truth; اسْتَجْوَبَ شاهِداً to examine a witness; أَخَذَ أَقْوالَ الشُهودِ to take the witnesses' statements; اسْتِجْوابُ الشُهودِ questioning of witnesses; شاهِد نَفْيٍ defence witness; شاهِد إِثْباتٍ prosecution witness [2] [قَبْر] |شَواهِدُ| gravestone, tombstone [3] [دَليل] |شَواهِدُ| quotation; reference; شاهِد من القُرْآنِ a quotation from the Koran [4] [شَخْص حاضِر] |أَشْهاد ,شُهود| witness, bystander; على رُؤوسِ الأَشْهادِ in public, for everyone to see

شاهِدة *n* tombstone

شَهادة *n* [1] [إِقْرار] statement, testimony, deposition; شَهادة كاذِبة false testimony; شَهادة شَفَوِيّة \ تَحْريرِيّة oral/written statement; حَسَبَ شَهادةِ ... on the testimony of ...; أَدّى شَهادةً, أَدْلى بِشَهادةٍ to make a statement (of evidence) [2] [دِبْلوم] diploma, certificate; qualification; شَهادة جامِعِيّة a university degree; قِسْمُ الشَهادةِ (Mor) *highest class of primary school*; حامِل شَهادةٍ certified, qualified; degree holder; حَصَلَ على شَهادةٍ to graduate; to qualify; مَنَحَ \ سَلَّمَ \ أَصْدَرَ شَهادةً to grant/give/issue a certificate; اسْتَلَمَ شَهادةً to receive a certificate; تَسَلَّمَ شَهادتَهُ to be awarded one's degree [3] [وَثيقة] deed, act; document; certificate; شَهادة طِبِّيّة a medical certificate; شَهادة المَنْشَأ certificate of origin; شَهادة \ قَيْد الميلادِ birth certificate; شَهادة فَقْرِ حالٍ certificate of insufficient means; شَهادة حُسْنِ (السَيْرةِ و) السُلوكِ certificate of good conduct; سَلَّمَ \ تَسَلَّمَ شَهادةً to present/receive a certificate [4] (Islam) shahada; profession of faith; creed; نَطَقَ بالشَهادةِ to profess one's faith

شَهيد *n* |شُهَداءُ| [1] [قَتيل] martyr; person killed in battle, fallen; ماتَ شَهيداً to die as a martyr; نُصْب تِذْكاريّ لِلشُهَداءِ a memorial to the fallen; إِحْياء ذِكْرى الشُهَداءِ the commemoration of the fallen; مَقْبَرة الشُهَداءِ war cemetery [2] [شاهِد] كَفى باللهِ شَهيداً God suffices as a witness; اللهُ على ما أَقولُ شَهيدٌ (as) God is my witness [3] (Islam) الشَهيد the Witness (*one of the names of God*)

اسْتِشْهاد *n* |اسْتِشْهادات| [1] [بِقَوْلٍ أو رَأْيٍ] quotation; اسْتِشْهاد حَرْفيّ a verbal quotation [2] [مَوْت] martyrdom

اسْتِشْهاديّ *adj* suicide (*before n*) عَمَلِيّة اسْتِشْهادِيّة suicide mission

مُسْتَشْهِد *n* martyr

مُشاهِد *n* spectator, viewer; observer, watcher; جَذَبَ \ اجْتَذَبَ المُشاهِدينَ to attract viewers; مُشاهِديَّ الأَعِزّاءَ dear viewers; عَدَد المُشاهِدينَ (audience) rating

مُشاهَدة *n* visit; view; جَدير بالمُشاهَدةِ worth seeing

مَشْهَد *n* |مَشاهِدُ| [1] [مَنْظَر] view, sight; spectacle, scene; مَشْهَد مُشَوِّق \ رائِع a fascinating/great spectacle; مَشْهَد مُؤَثِّر \ مُؤْسِف a moving/sorry sight; مَشْهَد مُضْحِك a comic scene [2] [في مَسْرَحِيّةٍ] scene; المَشْهَد الأَوَّل \ الأَخير من المَسْرَحِيّةِ the first/last scene of the play [3] [رَقْص] number; song, track [4] (Relig) holy place; tomb of a saint; مَشْهَد عَلِيّ *old name for Najaf*; مَشْهَد الحُسَيْنِ *old name for Karbala* [5] [مَدينة] |f| Mashhad (*city in Iran*)

مَشْهود *adj* [1] [مَرْئيّ] seen, observed; بالجُرْمِ المَشْهودِ in the act, red-handed [2] [بارِز] memorable; يَوْم \ حَدَث مَشْهود a memorable day/event

شَهَرَ *v* |a; شَهْر| [1] [أَعْلَنَ] to announce, to make known; شُهِرَ to be/become well-known; to be/become notorious;

شُهِرَ ب ... to be known by ... ② [سِلاحاً] to draw; شَهَرَ سِلاحاً في وَجْهِ شَخْصٍ to pull a weapon on sb

شَهَّرَ *v* ① [قَدَحَ] |ب| to slander, to defame; to abuse, to malign; شَهَّرَ بِشَخْصٍ to slander sb; شَهَّرَ بِسُمْعَةِ شَخْصٍ to blacken sb's reputation ② [جَعَلَ شَخْصاً مَشْهوراً] to make famous, to make well-known

أَشْهَرَ *v* ① [أَعْلَنَ] to announce, to declare; to display; أَشْهَرَ الحَرْبَ to declare war; أَشْهَرَ خَبَراً to announce the news ② [سِلاحاً] to draw; أَشْهَرَ سِلاحاً to draw a weapon

اشْتَهَرَ *v* ① [كانَ مَعْروفاً] to be/become well-known; اشْتَهَرَ بِشَيْءٍ to be well-known for sth ② [كانَ مَشْهوراً بِصِفةٍ إيجابيّةٍ] to be/become famous; اشْتَهَرَ بِشَيْءٍ to be famous for sth ③ [كانَ مَشْهوراً بِصِفةٍ سَلْبيّةٍ] to be/become notorious/infamous

شَهْر *n* |شُهور, أَشْهُر| ① [جُزْء سَنةٍ] month; الشَهْرُ المُقْبِل \ القادِم the coming/next month; الشُهور العَرَبيّة *the months according to the Islamic calendar*; الشُهور الميلاديّة *the months according to the Christian calendar*; شَهْر مارِس \ آذارَ the month of March; لِمُدّة شَهْرٍ for a month; في خِلالِ \ ظَرْف شَهْرٍ within a month; بعد شَهْرٍ a month later, after a month; قبل \ منذ شَهْرٍ a month ago; قبل شَهْرٍ من ذلك, قبل ذلك بِشَهْرٍ a month earlier; شَهْر العَسَل honeymoon ② [تَسْجيل عَقاريّ] شَهْر عَقاريّ, مَصْلَحة الشَهْرِ العَقاريّ land registry (service)

شُهْرة *n* ① [صيت] fame, glory; reputation; شُهْرة تِجاريّة goodwill; شُهْرة عالَميّة world fame, world repute; بِلا شُهْرةٍ inglorious; اسْم الشُهْرةِ stage name; تَمَتَّعَ بِشُهْرةٍ to enjoy fame; تَمَتَّعَ بِشُهْرةٍ عالَميّةٍ to be world-famous; اكْتَسَبَ \ حَظِيَ بِشُهْرةٍ كَبيرةٍ to earn a reputation; اسْتَحَقَّ الشُهْرةَ to be widely known; بَحَثَ عن الشُهْرةِ to search for fame ② [اسْم عائِليّ] family name, last name

شَهْرِيّ *adj* monthly; اجْتِماعات شَهْرِيّة monthly meetings; الدَخْل الشَهْرِيّ monthly income; تَصْدُرُ هذه المَجَلّةُ شَهْرِيًّا this magazine is published monthly

شَهير *adj* famous, renowned, celebrated

إِشْهار *n* commercial; publication, announcement; إِشْهار تِلِفِزْيونيّ television commercial; إِشْهار زَواجٍ wedding announcement

إِشْهاريّ *adj* promotional, commercial, advertising (*before n*); مَقْطَع إِشْهاريّ promotional film; لَوْحة إِشْهاريّة billboard

أَشْهَر *adj* |dipt| more famous, more widely known; أَشْهَر من نارٍ على عَلَمٍ *widely known*

تَشْهير *n* defamation, slander, libel

مُشاهَرة *n* مُشاهَرةً monthly, per month

مَشْهور A *adj* |مَشاهيرُ| ① [صِفة إيجابيّة] famous, renowned, celebrated; كاتِب \ رَسّام مَشْهور a famous writer/painter; لَوْحة مَشْهورة a famous painting; مَشْهور عالَميًّا world-famous; كانَ مَشْهوراً بِشَيْءٍ to be famous for sth ② [صِفة سَلْبيّة] notorious; كَذّاب \ مُجْرِم مَشْهور a notorious liar/criminal B *n* |مَشاهيرُ| celebrity; مَشاهير من عالَمِ السينَما celebrities from the world of cinema; مَشاهير عالَمِيّونَ international celebrities

‹ **شَهْرَمان** *n* shelduck, sheldrake (*Tadorna*)

‹ **شَهَقَ** *v* |a| ① [كانَ عالِياً] |شُهوق| to be very high, to tower ② [الحِمارُ] |شَهيق| to bray

شَهِقَ *v* |a; شَهيق, شُهاق, تَشْهاق| to sniff; to inhale, to breath in; to gasp; شَهِقَ غازاً to breath in gas; شَهِقَ شَهيقاً عَميقاً to inhale deeply; شَهِقَتْ لَمّا رَأَتْهُ she gasped when she saw him

شاهِق *adj* |شَواهِقُ| towering, high; مَبْنًى شاهِق a towering building; عِمارة شاهِقة a high-rise block of flats; على ارْتِفاعٍ شاهِقٍ at high altitude

شَهْقة *n* exclamation, cry, whoop; gasp

شَهيق *n* ① [إدْخال النَفَسِ] inhalation; الشَهيق والزَفير inhalation and exhalation ② [الحَمير] braying, bray

‹ **أَشْهَل** *adj* |dipt| عُيون شَهْلاء *bluish-black eyes*

‹ **شَهُمَ** *v* |u; شَهامة| to be/become courteous, to be/become chivalrous

شَهْم *adj* |شِهام| courteous, chivalrous; رَجُل شَهْم a courteous man

شَهامة *n* courtesy; chivalry; magnanimity; عَفا عن شَخْصٍ بِشَهامةٍ to forgive sb magnanimously; اعْتَرَفَ بِشَيْءٍ بِشَهامةٍ to admit something frankly

‹ **شَها** *v* |a-u; شَهْوة| to have an appetite, to feel hungry; شَها شَيْئاً to feel like sth

شَهِيَ *v* |a; شَهْوة| to feel hungry, to have an appetite

شَهّى *v* to whet the appetite; to make covetous, to fill with desire

اشْتَهى *v* to wish, to want; to desire, to covet; اشْتَهى شَيْئاً to have an appetite for sth; اشْتَهى شَخْصاً to desire sb; to have a crush on sb (infml)

شَهِيّ *adj* delicious, nice, tasty

شَهْوانيّ *adj* ① [مُثير للشَهْوة] sensual, sensuous, erotic; حُبّ شَهْوانيّ sensual love; مُتْعة شَهْوانيّة sensual pleasure ② [شَديد الرَغْبة] desirous, lascivious; نَظَرات شَهْوانيّة lustful looks

شَهْوانيّة *n* sensuality; lustfulness

شَهْوة *n* |شَهَوات| desire, lust; appetite; sensuality; شهَوات pleasures of the flesh; شَهْوة جِنْسيّة sexual desire, libido; شَهْوات حِسّيّة \ جِسْميّة \ غَريزيّة sensual/physical/instinctive desires; شَهْوة كَلْبيّة bulimia; شَهْوة للطَعام appetite; مَوْضِع شَهْوةٍ sex object; مُثير للشَهْوة sensual; أَشْبَعَ شَهَواتِه to find sexual satisfaction; أَطْلَقَ العِنانَ لِشَهَواتِه to unleash one's desires; أَثارَ شَهْوةَ شَخْصٍ to rouse sb's desire, to arouse sb; كانَ يَجْري وراء شَهَواتِه to pursue one's desires

شَهِيّة *n* appetite; قِلّة الشَهِيّة lack of appetite; شَهِيّة طَيِّبة enjoy your meal, bon appetit; أَكَل بِشَهِيّةٍ to eat with relish; فَتَحَ \ أَثارَ الشَهِيّةَ to whet the appetite; لَيْسَتْ عِنْدي شَهِيّةٌ للأَكْلِ I have no appetite

اشْتِهاء *n* liking, appetite; desire, lust

مُشَهٍّ *n* |مُشَهِّيات| مُشَهِّيات appetizers, hors d'oeuvres

‹ **شابَ** *v* |u; شَوْب ,شِياب| ① [مَزَجَ] to mix, to blend; لا تَشوبُهُ شائِبةٌ (it is) flawless ② [أَفْسَدَ] to spoil, to taint; to contaminate, to infect ③ [الشَعْرُ] see **شيب**

شَوْب *n* mix, blend

شائِبة *n* |شَوائِبُ| shortcoming, fault, defect; stain, blemish; بَريء من الشَوائِبِ spotless

مَشوب *adj* mixed, blended

‹ **شَوْبَك** *n* |شَوابِكُ| rolling pin

¹‹ **شوح** *n* (Bot) fir, spruce (*Abies*)

²‹ **شوحة** *n* (Zool) kite (*Accipitridae*)

‹ **شَوَّرَ** *v* to beckon; to gesture, to signal; شَوَّرَ إلى شَخْصٍ بِيَدِهِ to beckon to sb with one's hand

شاوَرَ *v* to consult, to take counsel; شاوَرَ شَخْصاً to consult sb

أَشارَ *v* ① [دَلَّ] [إلى] to point out, to point to, to refer to; to indicate, to show, to state; أَشارَ إلى شَيْءٍ to point to sth; أَشارَ إلى أنّ ... to point out that ...; كُلّ شَيْءٍ يُشيرُ إلى أنّ ... everything indicates that ...; أَشارَ إلى المُرْفَقاتِ to refer to the attachments; أَشارَ إلى مَقولةِ شَخْصٍ to refer to sb's words; أَشارَ إلى كِتابٍ \ مَقالٍ to refer to a book/an article, to cite a book/an article; أَشارَ إلى حَدَثٍ to refer to an event; أَشارَت الساعةُ إلى الخامِسةِ the clock showed five o'clock; تُشيرُ العَلامةُ إلى أنّ ... the sign indicates that ...; يُشيرُ ميزانُ الحَرارةِ إلى ١٨ دَرَجةً the thermometer reads 18 degrees; يُشارُ إلَيْهِ بالبَنانِ he is very famous ② [نَصَحَ] to advise; to tip off ③ [لَوَّحَ] to allude, to hint; أَشارَ إلى شَخْصٍ \ شَيْءٍ to allude to sb/sth

تَشاوَرَ *v* to consult, to deliberate, to confer; تَشاوَرَ في خُطّةٍ... to deliberate about the plan to ...; تَشاوَرَ بِخُصوصِ شَيْءٍ \ شَخْصٍ to confer about sth/sb; تَشاوَرَ (مع شَخْصٍ) في قَضيّةٍ to consult (with sb) on a case

اسْتَشارَ *v* to consult, to confer with; اسْتَشارَ شَخْصاً to consult sb; اسْتَشارَ شَخْصاً في شَيْءٍ to consult sb about sth; اسْتَشارَ خَبيراً to consult an expert; اسْتَشارَ طَبيباً to consult a doctor, to see a doctor

شارة *n* badge, tag, insignia; logo, crest; token

شِوار *n* trousseau; شِوار الزَواجِ marriage trousseau

شورى *n* |f| ① [نَصيحة] advice; advisory body; مَجْلِس الشورى (Egypt Law) advisory council, shura council; سورة الشورى The Consultation (*Sura 42*) ② (Bot) mangrove (*Avicennia marina*)

اسْتِشارة *n* consultation; اسْتِشارة طِبّيّة medical consultation; اسْتِشارة قانونيّة legal consultation; مَكْتَب اسْتِشارةٍ consulting agency; اسْتِشارة جَميعِ الأَطْرافِ المَعْنيّةِ the consultation of all the parties involved

اسْتِشاريّ *adj* consultative, advisory; مَجْلِس \ هَيْئة اسْتِشاريّ(ة) advisory council/body; مَكْتَب اسْتِشاريّ consultancy (firm)

إشارة *n* ① [عَلامة] indication, sign; clue, hint; gesture, signal; wink, nod; إشارة وِدّيّة a friendly gesture; إشارة خَفيّة a subtle hint; إشارة الصَليب (Chr) sign of the cross; إشارة شَيْءٍ a signal for sth; إشارة انْطِلاقٍ a disapproving gesture; إشارة اسْتِهْجانٍ starting signal; إشارة انْطِلاقٍ لِشَيْءٍ a starting signal for sth; أَعْطى إشارةَ الانْطِلاقِ to give the starting signal; إشارة إلى شَيْءٍ a reference to sth; في إشارةٍ إلى ... with regard to ...; اسْم الإشارةِ (Gram) demonstrative pronoun; تَلَقّى إشارةً to pick up a signal; أَعْطى \ بَثَّ إشارةً to make/send a signal; كانَ رَهْنَ إشارةِ شَخْصٍ to be at sb's disposal; الّذي سَبَقَت الإشارةُ إلَيْهِ which has been mentioned before; تَجْدُرُ الإشارةُ إلى أنّ ... it is worth mentioning that ...; اللَبيب بالإشارةِ يَفْهَمُ a word is enough to the wise [2]◂ (Transp) traffic light, traffic signal; إشارة ضَوْئيّة \ المُرورِ traffic light, traffic signal; انْتَظَرَ الإشارةَ الضَوْئيّةَ to wait for a traffic light; تَجاهَلَ \ خالَفَ \ خَرَقَ إشارةَ المُرورِ to ignore/violate/go through a traffic light; إشارة مُرورٍ حَمْراء \ خَضْراء a red/green (traffic) light [3]◂ [مَصْدَر] reference; إشارة مَرْجَعيّة (Comput) bookmark

تَشاوُر *n* |تَشاوُرات| consultation, deliberation; dialogue; تَشاوُر هاتِفيّ telephone consultation; التَشاوُر بين الطَرَفَيْنِ consultation between the two parties; بعد التَشاوُرِ المُكَثَّفِ \ الكَثيفِ after close consultation; بعد التَشاوُرِ مع شَخْصٍ after consultation with sb; قَرَّرَ شَيْئاً بعد التَشاوُرِ to decide sth after consultation

تَشاوُريّ *adj* advisory, consultative; اجْتِماع تَشاوُريّ consultative meeting

مُسْتَشار *n* [1]◂ [خَبير] expert; adviser, counsellor, consultant; councillor; مُسْتَشار قانونيّ \ ماليّ \ أَمْنيّ a legal/financial/security adviser; المُسْتَشار الأَمْنيّ للرَئيسِ the security adviser to the President; مُسْتَشار صِحّيّ a medical expert; مُسْتَشار إداريّ trustee; management consultant [2]◂ [رَئيس حُكومةٍ] Federal Chancellor; chancellor; المُسْتَشار الأَلْمانيّ German Chancellor

مُسْتَشاريّة *n* (Law) chancellery, chancery

مُشار *adj* mentioned, pointed out; مُشار إلَيْهِ aforementioned; الكاتِب المُشار إلَيْهِ آنِفاً the aforementioned author

مُشاوَرة *n* consultation; deliberation; مُشاوَرات عاجِلة emergency consultations, urgent consultations; مُشاوَرات واسِعة extensive consultations; أَجْرى \ عَقَد مُشاوَراتٍ to hold/conduct consultations; المُشاوَرات العامّة the public consultations; غُرْفة المُشاوَرةِ (judge's) chambers; أَنْهى المُشاوَراتِ to end the consultations; شارَكَ في المُشاوَراتِ to take part in the consultations

مِشْوار *n* |مَشاويرُ| ride, drive; itinerary; مِشْوار طَويل quite a ride, a long way; أَكْمَلَ المِشْوارَ (fig) to ride it out, to go the whole way; بَدَأَ مِشْوارَهُ الصَحَفيَّ في الصَحيفةِ he started his career in journalism with the newspaper

مَشورة *n* recommendation, suggestion; advice; مَشورة طِبّيّة doctor's advice; بِمَشورةِ شَخْصٍ on sb's recommendation; طَلَبَ المَشورةَ من شَخْصٍ to seek sb's advice; قَدَّمَ مَشورةً to make a recommendation

مُشير *n* (Mil) field marshal

‹ **شَوْرَب**, **شَوْرَب**, **مُشَوْرَب** see **شرب**

‹ **شورْت** *n* (pair of) shorts

‹ **شوزَن** *n* shotgun; طَلْقة شوزَن shotgun shell

‹ **أَشْوَس** *adj* |dipt; شوس, أَشاوِسُ| f شَوْساءُ| brave, courageous

‹ **شَوَّش** *v* |على| to interrupt, to disturb; to foul up; شَوَّشَ على البَثِّ to interfere with the broadcast

تَشَوَّش *v* to get confused, to get muddled (up)

شاش *n* gauze, piece of gauze; شاش مُعَقَّم sterile gauze; شاش طِبّيّ medical gauze, roller bandage

شاشة *n* [1]◂ [تَلْفَزة، حاسوبٍ] screen, monitor, display; شاشة التِلِفِزْيون television screen; شاشة كَبيرة \ صَغيرة big/small screen; الشاشة الصَغيرة television, tube; دَليل الشاشةِ TV guide; حافِظة الشاشةِ screen saver; اسْم الشاشةِ screen name; على الشاشةِ on television; شاشة من الكِرِسْتال السائِلِ Liquid Crystal Display screen, LCD screen [2]◂ [سينَما] screen, projection screen; الشاشة الفِضّيّة the silver screen

شاشيّة *n* |شَواشٍ| (NA) fez

شاويش *n* listed alphabetically

شوشة *n* a tuft of hair, lock

تَشَوُّش *n* confusion, jumble; تَشَوُّش الأَفْكارِ a jumble of thoughts

تَشْويش *n* noise, garble; disturbance, interruption

شائِق *adj* interesting, intriguing; exciting; مَوْضوع شائِق an interesting topic

شَيِّق *adj* exciting, interesting; great, super; مُباراة \ فيلْم \ كِتاب شَيِّق(ة) an exciting match/movie/book

اشْتِياق *n* |اشْتِياقات| longing, yearning, desire; الاشْتِياق لِلحُرِّيَّة the longing for freedom

تَشْويق *n* excitement, thrill; suspense; التَّشْويق والإثارة thrill and excitement

مُتَشَوِّق *adj* curious; longing, yearning; كانَ مُتَشَوِّقاً لِمَعْرِفة شَيْءٍ to be curious to know sth; كانَ مُتَشَوِّقاً لِمَعْرِفةِ شَخْصٍ to look forward to meeting sb

مُشْتاق *adj* yearning, longing, desirous

مُشَوِّق *adj* exciting, fascinating

‹ **شاك** *v* |u; شَوْك| to prick

شَوَّكَ *v* to irritate; to prick

شَوْك *n* |أَشْواك| thorn, prickle, spine; شَوْك الجَمَل (Bot) milk thistle (*Silybum*)

شائِك *adj* **1** [صَعْب] delicate, thorny; مَسْأَلة شائِكة a tricky matter; قَضِيّة شائِكة a thorny issue **2** [ذو شَوْكٍ] prickly, thorny; نَبْتة شائِكة a prickly plant; سِلْك شائِك barbed wire

شَوْكة *n* **1** [أَسَلة] |أَشْواك| prickle, thorn; spine; شَوْكة السَّمَك fish bone; شَوْكة عَقْرَبٍ scorpion sting; أَبو شَوْكةٍ (Zool) stickleback (*Gasterosteidae*); شَوْكةٌ في جَنْبِهِ a thorn in his side; شَوْكةٌ في حَلْقِ الحُكومةِ a thorn in the side of the government; كسَر شَوْكةَ شَخْصٍ to humiliate sb; to subjugate sb **2** [أَداة الأَكْل] |شِوَك, شُوَك, شَوْكات| fork; أَكَلَ بالشَّوْكةِ والسِّكّين to eat with knife and fork **3** (Tools) fork; شَوْكة دَرّاجةٍ bicycle fork

شَوْكيّ *adj* **1** (Anat) spinal; نُخاع شَوْكيّ spinal cord **2** (Bot) spiny; تين شَوْكيّ cactus pear (*Opuntia ficus-indica*)

شُوَيْكة *n* (Zool) siskin

‹ **شوكولاطة, شوكولاتة** *n* chocolate; قالِب شوكولاتةٍ a bar of chocolate; عُلْبة شوكولاتةٍ a box of chocolates

‹ **شالَ** *v* |u; شَوْل| **1** [رَفَعَ] to lift, to raise; شالَ طِفْلاً to pick up a child **2** [حَمَلَ] see **شيل**

أَشالَ *v* to raise, to lift

مُشَوَّش *adj* confused; disordered, cluttered; وَضْع مُشَوَّش a complex situation; إنَّهُ مُشَوَّشُ الفِكْرِ he is confused

مُشَوِّش *adj* confusing; disturbing

‹ **شَوِصَ** *v* |a; شَوَص| to be cross-eyed; to squint

أَشْوَص *adj* |dipt| cross-eyed; squinting

‹ **شاطَ** *v* |u; شَوْط| **1** [رَكَلَ] to kick; شاطَ كُرةً to kick a ball **2** [احْتَرَقَ] see **شيط**

شَوْط *n* |أَشْواط| **1** [جُزْء] part; قَطَعَ شَوْطاً كَبيراً في التَّقَدُّمِ to make good progress; قَطَعَ أَشْواطاً مُخْتَلِفةً to go through different stages **2** (Sport) set, half; round, stage; tour, race; الشَّوْط الأَوَّل \ الأَخير the first/last round; الشَّوْط الأَوَّل \ الثاني the first/second half; شَوْط إضافيّ extra time; سِباق على أَشْواطٍ relay (race)

‹ **شُواظ** *n* flame; passion

‹[1] **تَشَوَّفَ** *v* to long, to yearn; تَشَوَّفَ إلى شَخْصٍ to long for sb

‹[2] **الشوف** *n* Chouf (*name of a region and district in Lebanon*)

‹ **شوفان** *n* (Bot) oat (*Avena sativa*); جَريش الشوفانِ oatmeal, rolled oats

‹ **شوفينيّ** *adj, n* chauvinist

شوفينيّة *n* chauvinism

‹ **شاقَ** *v* |u; شَوْق| to fill with desire; شاقَتْهُ رُؤْيَتُها he longed to see her

شَوَّقَ *v* to arouse curiosity/interest; شَوَّقَ شَخْصاً إلى \ في شَيْءٍ to make sb curious about sth

تَشَوَّقَ *v* |إلى| to long for, to look forward to, to hanker after; تَشَوَّقَ إلى شَيْءٍ to look forward to sth; تَشَوَّقَ إلى رُؤْيةِ والِدَتِهِ to long to see one's mother; تَشَوَّقَ لِمَعْرِفةِ شَيْءٍ to be curious to know sth

اشْتاقَ *v* |إلى| to long for, to yearn for, to hanker after; اشْتاقَ إلى شَيْءٍ \ شَخْصٍ to long for sth/sb; اشْتاقَ إلى رُؤْيةِ الأَصْدِقاءِ to long to see friends

شَوْق *n* |أَشْواق| longing, yearning, desire; تَحَرَّقَ شَوْقاً to be consumed with longing; تَحَرَّقَ شَوْقاً إلى شَيْءٍ to crave sth; شَوْق عارِم craving; نَظَرات شَوْقٍ longing looks; انْتَظَرَ شَيْئاً بِكُلِّ الشَّوْقِ to look forward to sth; وَقَلْبُهُ مَليءٌ بالشَّوْق ≈ he is filled with longing; كابَدَ الشَّوْقَ to feel a longing

اِنْشالَ *v* to be lifted

شَوّال *n* |شَوّالات, شَواويلُ| Shawwal (*the tenth month of the Islamic calendar*)

أَشْوَل *adj* |dipt| left-handed

شَوَّنَ *v* to store; شَوَّنَ الغَلّةَ to store the harvest

شَوْنة *n* |شُوَن, شونات| (Egypt) granary

تَشْوين *n* |تشاوين| grain storage

شَوَنْدَر *n* (Bot) beet (*Beta vulgaris*)

شاهَ *v* |u; شَوْه| to be/become ugly

شَوِهَ *v* |a; شَوَه| to be/become ugly

شَوَّهَ *v* to deform, to mutilate; to distort, to twist; شَوَّهَ سُمْعَةَ to damage a reputation; شَوَّهَ سُمْعَةَ شَخْصٍ to tarnish sb's reputation; شَوَّهَ صَوْتاً to distort a sound; شَوَّهَ جُثّةً to mutilate a body; شَوَّهَ الطَبيعةَ to mar the landscape; شَوَّهَ الحَقائِقَ to twist the facts

تَشَوَّهَ *v* to be twisted (*words*); to be deformed, to be disfigured

أَشْوَه *adj* |dipt| deformed, disfigured

تَشَوُّه *n* |تَشَوُّهات| deformation, malformation; abnormality, defect; تَشَوُّه خِلْقيّ a congenital defect

تَشْويه *n* |تَشْويهات| defect, malformation; distortion; تَشْويه الصَوْتِ audio distortion; هذا تَشْويهٌ لِلحَقائِقِ this is a distortion of the facts

مُشَوَّه *adj* distorted, twisted; deformed, misshapen, disfigured; damaged; يَد مُشَوَّهة a deformed hand; صورة مُشَوَّهة a distorted view; لَهُ صورةٌ مُشَوَّهةٌ عن شَيْءٍ \ شَخْصٍ he has a distorted view of sth/sb; أَعْطى صورةً مُشَوَّهةً عن الأَوْضاعِ to give a distorted view of events; مُشَوَّهو الحَرْبِ war invalids

شَوى *v* |i; شَيّ| ◀1 [اللَحْمَ] to grill, to roast, to barbecue; شَوى لَحْماً to grill meat; شَوى كَباباً to grill kebab ◀2 [الفَخّارَ] to fire; شَوى الفَخّارَ to fire pottery

اِنْشَوى *v* to be grilled/barbecued

شِواء *n* grilled/roasted meat

شَوّاية *n* grill; على الشَوّايةِ on the grill

مِشْواة *n* |مَشاوٍ| barbecue; على المِشْواةِ on the barbecue

مَشْويّ *adj* grilled, roasted

شاءَ *v* |a; مَشيئة| to want, to wish; إِنْ شاءَ اللهُ God willing, hopefully; ما شاءَ اللهُ whatever God intends (*used to express an indefinite quantity, number or period of time*); amazing; إلى ما شاءَ اللهُ forever and ever, for many years to come; أَجَّلَ شَيْئاً إلى ما شاءَ اللهُ to postpone sth till God knows when; إِنْ شاءَتِ الأَقْدارُ if fate would have it; هكذا شاءَ القَدَرُ it had to be/ happen; شِئْتَ أم أَبَيْتَ whether you like it or not

شَيْء *n* |أَشْياءُ| ◀1 [جَماد] thing; object; أَهَمّ شَيْءٍ the most important thing; لا شَيْءَ nothing, nil; ثَلاث مُقابِلَ لا شَيْءَ (Sport) three to nil; كُلّ شَيْءٍ everything; أَيُّ شَيْءٍ whatever; لم أَرَ شَيْئاً I haven't seen anything; لم أُفَكِّرْ في شَيْءٍ I didn't think of anything; قبل كُلِّ شَيْءٍ before anything else; نَفْس الشَيْءِ the same ◀2 [قَليل] bit, little; شَيْئاً فَشَيْئاً bit by bit; شَيْء ما some, a little; شَيْء من الأَمَلِ some hope; شَيْء من something; بَعْض الشَيْءِ somewhat, a little; قاسٍ بَعْضَ الشَيْءِ a little severe; شَيْء من ذلك something similar ◀3 [مَوْجود] something; هذا شَيْءٌ وَذَلِكَ شَيْءٌ آخَرُ these are two (entirely) different things; في الأَمْرِ شَيْءٌ something is amiss

شاء *n* see شاء

تَشَيُّؤ *n* reification

مَشيئة *n* will; بِمَشيئةِ اللهِ God willing; مَشيئة الأَقْدارِ a whim of fate

شابَ *v* |i; شَيْب, شَيْبة, مَشيب| ◀1 [الشَعْرُ] to become grey-haired; مَنْ شَبَّ على شَيْءٍ شابَ ≈ حتّى يَشيبَ الغُرابُ when pigs fly; عَلَيْهِ a leopard can't change its spots ◀2 [مَزَجَ \ أَفْسَدَ] see شوب

شَيَّبَ *v* to give grey hair, to make hair turn grey; شَيَّبَهُ الحُزْنُ he turned grey with grief

شَيْب *n* grey hair; عَلا الشَيْبُ رَأْسَهُ his hair turned grey

شائِب *adj* |شيب, شُيّاب| grey (*of hair*)

أَشْيَب *adj* |dipt; شيب| grey-haired

شِية *n* see وشي

أَشاحَ *v* to turn away, to avert; أَشاحَ بِوَجْهِهِ to turn one's face away

شيح *n* (Bot) wormwood (*Artemisia*)

‹ **شَيَّخَ** *v* to grow old, to age

شاخَ *v* to age, to grow old

شَيْخ *n* |شُيوخ, أَشْياخ, مَشْيَخة, مَشايِخُ| **1** [مُسِنّ] elderly man, old man **2** (Pol) sheikh; مَجْلِس الشُيوخ the Upper House/Chamber **3** (Islam) master, teacher, professor (*in Islamic science*); شَيْخ الإِسْلامِ (Egypt Hist) title of the Grand Mufti

شَيْخوخة *n* old age; الشَيْخوخة المُبَكِّرة premature ageing; عِلْم الشَيْخوخةِ gerontology; أَعْراض الشَيْخوخةِ signs/symptoms of old age; طِبّ أَمْراضِ الشَيْخوخةِ geriatrics; طَبيب مُخْتَصّ بِأَمْراضِ الشَيْخوخةِ geriatrician

شَيْخوخيّ *adj* geriatric

تَشَيُّخ *n* ageing; تَشَيُّخ السُكانِ ageing of the population

مَشْيَخة *n* |مَشايِخُ, مَشْيَخات| **1** [مِنْطَقة] sheikhdom (*territory governed by a sheikh*) **2** [مَدْرَسة] faculty of an Islamic college

مَشْيَخيّ *n* Presbyterian

‹ **شادَ** *v* |i; شَيْد| to construct, to set up, to build

شَيَّدَ *v* to construct, to build, to set up; شَيَّدَ بَيْتاً \ بِنايةً to build a house/building

أَشادَ *v* to praise, to commend; أَشادَ بِشَخْصٍ \ بِذِكْرِ شَخْصٍ to sing sb's praises; أَشادَ بِجُهودِ الوَزير to praise the minister's efforts

تَشَيَّدَ *v* to be built

شيد *n* plaster, plastering, stucco; whitewash

إِشادة *n* praise, eulogy; glorification

مُشَيَّد *adj* built, constructed

‹ **شيراز** *n* |f| Shiraz (*city in Iran*)

‹ **شيزوفرينيا** *n* (Med) schizophrenia

1‹ **شيش** *n* sword, foil, rapier; لُعْبة الشيشِ fencing

2‹ **شيشة** *n* water pipe, narghile, hookah

‹ **شيشانيّ** *adj*, *n* (Geog) Chechen

الشيشان *n* |f| (Geog) Chechnya, Chechenia

‹ **شاطَ** *v* |i; شَيْط| **1** [احْتَرَقَ] to burn, to scorch; شاطَ اللَحْمُ the meat is burned; شاطَ بِهِ الغَضَبُ to be furious **2** [رَكَلَ] see **شوط**

شَيَّطَ *v* to scorch, to sear, to burn

أَشاطَ *v* to scorch, to burn

اشْتاطَ *v* |على| to be angry (with); اشْتاطَ غَضَباً to burn with anger

اسْتَشاطَ *v* to boil with rage, to be seething; اسْتَشاطَ غَضَباً to be fuming with rage

‹ **شَيْطَنَ** *v* |i; شَيْطَنة| **1** [سَوَّدَ الوَجْهَ] to demonize **2** [قامَ بِشَقاوةٍ] to make mischief

تَشَيْطَنَ *v* to get into mischief

شَيْطان *n* |شَياطينُ| devil, Satan; demon; مُحامي الشَيْطانِ the devil's advocate; السَاكِتُ عن الحَقِّ شَيْطانٌ أَخْرَسُ ≈ tell the truth and shame the devil; الشَيْطان الرَجيم Satan, the Devil

شَيْطانيّ *adj* devilish, satanic, demonic, diabolical

شَيْطَنة *n* **1** [تَسْويد الوَجْهِ] demonization **2** [شَقاوة] mischief

‹ **شاعَ** *v* |i; شَيْع, شُيوع| to spread (out); to get around, to travel; شاعَ الخَبَرُ the message went round; شاعَ المَرَضُ في البِلادِ the disease spread throughout the country

شَيَّعَ *v* to escort; *to pay final respects to the dead*; شَيَّعَ شَخْصاً to see sb off; to show a visitor to the door; شَيَّعَ جَنازةً to attend a funeral; شَيَّعَ شَخْصاً إلى القَبْرِ to escort sb to their final resting place

شايَعَ *v* to side, to take sides; to be/become a follower; شايَعَ شَخْصاً to be sb's follower

أَشاعَ *v* to spread; to divulge; أَشاعَ خَبَراً to spread a message; أَشاعَ الرَعْبَ بين الناسِ to spread fear among the people

تَشَيَّعَ *v* **1** [تَحَزَّبَ] to be biased, to be partial, to take sides **2** [صارَ شيعيًّا] to become a Shiite

شائِع *adj* widespread, common; popular; universal; طَريقة شائِعة an accepted method; أَسْئِلة شائِعة frequently asked questions; سوء تَفاهُمٍ شائِع a widespread misunderstanding; كانَ \ بَقِيَ شائِعاً to be in/come into fashion

شائِعة *n* |شائِعات, شَوائِعُ| rumour; كَذَّبَ شائِعةً to squash a rumour; هُناكَ شائِعاتٌ بِأَنَّ ... rumour has it that ...; تَتَرَدَّدُ شائِعاتٌ بِأَنَّ ... rumours are going round that ...

شيعة *n* |شِيَع, أَشْياع| **1** [طائِفة] sect; faction, party; أَشْياع followers, adherents **2** (Islam) Shia (*Shiite Islam*); شيعة عَليّ Shia (*Shiite Islam*)

شيعيّ *adj*, *n* |شيعة| Shiite

شُيوع *n* commonality; circulation; على الشُيوعِ in common; مِلْكيّة على الشُيوعِ collective ownership

شُيوعيّ **A** *adj* communist; نِظام شُيوعيّ a communist regime **B** *n* communist

شُيوعيّة *n* communism; مُناصِر للشُيوعيّةِ an adherent of communism, pro-communist; انْحِطاط الشُيوعيّةِ the fall of communism; مُعادٍ للشُيوعيّةِ anti-communist

إشاعة *n* rumour; إشاعات مُتَناقِضة \ مُتَضارِبة conflicting rumours; أَشاعَ \ نَشَرَ إشاعةً to spread a rumour; حَمْلة من الإشاعاتِ a campaign of rumours; فَنَّدَ \ كَذَّبَ الإشاعاتِ to squash/refute the rumours; راجَت الإشاعاتُ بِأَنَّ ... rumours were doing the rounds that ...

تَشَيُّع *n* **1** [تَحَزُّب] partiality, bias **2** [كانَ شيعيًّا] being a Shiite

تَشْييع *n* parting, leaving, farewell; تَشْييع المَيِّتِ *escorting the deceased to their final resting place*

مُشاع *adj* public

مُشايِع **A** *adj* biased, partial, prejudiced **B** *n* partisan, adherent

‹ **شيف** *n* chef

‹ **شيفون** *n* chiffon

‹[1] **شيك** *n* |شيكات| cheque; شيك سِياحيّ travellers cheque; عن طَريقِ شيكٍ by cheque; دَفَعَ بِشيكٍ to pay by cheque; شيك لِحامِلِهِ cheque to bearer; شيك بِدونِ رَصيدٍ a bad cheque; شيك على بَياضٍ a blank cheque

‹[2] **شِياكة** *n* chic

‹ **شيكِل, شيقِل** *n* |شَواكِلُ| shekel

‹ **شيكوريا** *n* chicory (*Cichorium intybus*)

‹ **شالَ** *v* |i; شَيْل, مَشال| **1** [حَمَلَ] to carry **2** [رَفَعَ] see **شول**

شَيّال *n* |شَيّالة, شَيّالونَ| porter, carrier

‹ **شَيْلَم** *n* (Bot) rye (*Secale cereale*)

‹ **شيلي** *n* |f| (Geog) Chile

شيليّ *adj*, *n* Chilean

‹ **شامة** *n* |شام, شامات| birthmark, mole

شيمة *n* |شِيَم| character trait, characteristic; الصَبْر من شِيَمِ الرِجالِ ≈ patience is a manly trait

مَشيمة *n* placenta; afterbirth; المَشيمة النازِلة (Med) placenta previa

‹[1] **شانَ** *v* |i; شَيْن| to dishonour, to disgrace

شائِن *adj* scandalous, outrageous; disgraceful, heinous; أكاذيب شائِنة outrageous lies; عامَلَ شَخْصاً مُعامَلَةً شائِنَةً to treat sb disgracefully

مَشين *adj* scandalous; disgraceful

‹[2] **شين** *n* |f| *name of the letter* ش

‹ **شَيْهَم** *n* (Zool) porcupine (*Hystricidae*)

‹ **ص** *abbr* **1** [صَفْحة] p., page (*abbreviation of* **صَفْحة**) **2** [صَباح] a.m., in the morning (*abbreviation of* **صَباحاً**) **3** (Islam) سورة ص Sad (*Sura 38*)

‹ **صُؤاب** *n coll* |صيبان ,صِئْبان| nit, louse egg

‹ **صابوغة** *n* (Zool) sprat (*Sprattus*)

‹ **صاج** *n inverted domed pan for cooking flatbread*

‹ **صاد** *n* |f| *name of the letter* ص

صادي *adj* المِحْوَر الصاديّ y-axis

‹ **صالة** *n* hall, (large) room

‹ **صالون** *n* |صالونات| salon, parlor

‹ **صامولة** *n* |صَواميلُ| (Tools) nut

‹ **صَأى** *v* |i; صَئِيّ| to twitter, to chirp

. **ص.ب.** *abbr* PO Box, post office box (*abbreviation of* صُنْدوق بَريدٍ)

‹ **صَبأ** *v* |a; صُبوء| to renounce, to reject, to abjure

صابِئ *n* Sabian

صابِئة *n the Sabians, a monotheistic Abrahamic religious group mentioned in the Koran*; Mandaeism (*gnostic Middle Eastern religion*)

‹ **صَبَّ** I *v* |u; صَبّ| **1** [سَكَبَ] to pour (out); to spill; صَبَّ شَيْئاً على شَيْءٍ to pour sth over sth; صَبَّ جامَ غَضَبِهِ على شَخْصٍ \ شَيْءٍ to vent one's anger on sb/sth **2** [سَبَكَ] to cast, to found, to mould; صَبَّ تِمْثالاً من البرونْز to cast a statue in bronze **3** [النَهْرُ] to flow, to empty; صَبَّ في البَحْرِ to flow into sea

صَبَّ II *v* |a; صَبابة; perf صَبِبْتُ | إلى| to love passionately

تَصَبَّبَ *v* to flow; to drip; كانَ مِعْطَفي يَتَصَبَّبُ ماءً my coat was dripping wet; تَصَبَّبَ عَرَقاً to perspire; تَصَبَّبَ العَرَقُ من جَبينِهِ his forehead was dripping with sweat

انْصَبَّ *v* **1** [انْسَكَبَ] to be poured (out) **2** [اتَّجَهَ] to be directed/aimed/turned/focused; انْصَبَّ اهْتِمامُهُ على شَيْءٍ his attention was focused on sth

صَبابة *n* passion, passionate love; craving, longing, strong desire

مَصَبّ *n* |مَصابُّ, مَصَبّات| **1** [مَخْرَج] outlet, drain; مَصَبّ المَطَر gutter **2** [النَهْر] mouth, estuary; مَصَبّ نَهْرٍ river mouth

مَصْبوب **A** *adj* cast, founded, moulded; تِمْثال مَصْبوب a cast statue

B *n* |مَصْبوبات| cast, casting

‹ **صَبَحَ** *v* |a; صَبْح| *to arrive in the morning*

صَبُحَ *v* |u; صَباحة| to be beautiful; to be handsome; to be attractive

صَبَّحَ *v* **1** [أتى صَباحًا] *to arrive in the morning* **2** [حَيّا صَباحًا] *to wish a good morning to*

أَصْبَحَ *v* **1** [صارَ] to become, to grow/turn into; أَصْبَحَ واضِحاً to become clear; أَصْبَحَ طَبيباً \ سَبّاكاً to become a doctor/plumber; أَصْبَحَ في وَضْعٍ صَعْبٍ to find oneself in a difficult situation; أَصْبَحَ هُناكَ تَأْييدٌ support arrived; أَصْبَحَ من المُمْكِنِ الآنَ أنْ ... it has now become possible to ... **2** [بَدَأَ] to begin, to start; أَصْبَحَ الصَباحُ morning came; أَصْبَحَ يَفْعَلُ شَيْئاً to start doing st **3** [اسْتَيْقَظَ] to wake up, to awaken; to get up, to rise; تُصْبِحْ على خَيْرٍ! good night! **4** [ظَهَرَ] to become clear

صُبْح *n* |أَصْباح| dawn, daybreak, morning; صَلاة الصُبْحِ morning prayer

صَباح *n* morning, dawn, daybreak; صَباحاً, في الصَباحِ in the morning; في الصَباحِ الباكِرِ early in the morning; في خِلالِ الصَباحِ during the morning; صَباحَ الخَيْرِ good morning; صَباح النورِ and a good morning to you (too) (*answer to* صَباح الخَيْر); صَباحَ اليَوْمِ this morning; صَباحَ الغَدِ tomorrow morning; ذاتَ صَباحٍ one morning

صَباحيّ *adj* morning (*before n*); صَحيفة \ جَريدة صَباحيّة morning paper

صَبوح *adj* radiant, brilliant; beautiful; handsome; attractive

صَبيح *adj* |صِباح| radiant, brilliant; beautiful, handsome, attractive

صَبيحة *n* morning; صَبيحةَ اليَوْم this morning

مِصْباح *n* |مَصابيحُ| lamp, light; lantern; مِصْباح أَماميّ headlight; مِصْباح كاشف \ كَشّاف spotlight; searchlight; مِصْباح يَدويّ \ الجَيْبِ (electric/pocket) torch (BrE), flashlight (AmE); مِصْباح مُتَوَهِّج light bulb; مِصْباح كَهْرَبائيّ electric light; مِصْباح خَلْفيّ tail light, rear light (BrE); مِصْباح زَيْتيّ oil lamp; مِصْباح الشارِعِ street light; أَطْفَأَ \ أَشْعَلَ المِصْباحَ to turn the light off/on

‹ **صَبَرَ** *v* |i; صَبْر| [1] [ثابَرَ] to be/remain patient; to endure, to bear; to persevere; صَبَرَ على شَخْصٍ to be patient with sb; اِصْبِرْ قَليلاً! wait a minute! [2] [امْتَنَعَ] to persevere, to bear patiently; لا يَسْتَطيعُ أَنْ يَصْبِرَ عن اللَحْمِ وَلَوْ يَوْماً واحِداً he can't do without meat, even for one day

صَبَّرَ *v* [1] [طَعاماً] to preserve; to can; صَبَّرَ الخُضَرَ to preserve vegetables [2] [عَزّى] to comfort, to console [3] [جُثّةً] to preserve, to embalm; صَبَّرَ جُثّةً to embalm a body [4] [حَيَواناً مَيِّتاً] to stuff, to preserve; صَبَّرَ غَزالاً to stuff a gazelle [5] [تَخَلَّصَ من الصابورةِ] to discharge ballast

تَصَبَّرَ *v* to be patient; to endure; تَصَبَّرَ على أَلَمٍ to endure pain

اِصْطَبَرَ *v* to be patient; to endure

صَبْر *n* [1] [جَلَد] patience; endurance; ب \ من خِلالِ الصَبْرِ patiently; قَليل الصَبْرِ impatient; نَفاد \ فُروغ \ قِلّة الصَبْرِ impatience; اِنْتَظَرَ شَيْئاً بِفارِغِ الصَبْرِ to await sth impatiently; الصَبْرُ جَميلٌ patience is a virtue; لا صَبْرَ لَهُ he has no patience; لِصَبْري حُدودٌ my patience has limits; نَفِدَ \ فَرَغَ صَبْري my patience is exhausted; تَطَلَّبَ كَثيراً من الصَبْرِ to require a lot of patience; اِلْتَزَمَ الصَبْرَ, تَذَرَّعَ \ تَحَلّى بالصَبْرِ to remain patient; دَعا إلى الصَبْرِ to urge patience; فَقَدَ صَبْرَهُ to lose one's patience [2] (Bot) aloe vera (*Aloe*)

صابِر *adj* [1] [مُتَحَمِّل] patient; enduring [2] [اسْم شَخْصيّ] Saber (*male given name*)

صابورة *n* ballast (*on a ship*)

صَبّار, صُبّار *n* cactus (*Cactaceae*)

صَبور A *adj* |صُبُر| patient; enduring

B *n* الصَبور the Timeless, the Patient (*one of the names of God*)

صُبَّيْر *n* prickly pear cactus (*Opuntia ficus-indica*)

تَصْبير *n* taxidermy, stuffing (*animals*)

تَصْبيرة *n* snack; تَناوَلَ تَصْبيرةً to eat a snack

‹ **صَبَعَ** *v* |a; صَبْع| to point; صَبَعَ ب \ على شَيْءٍ \ شَخْصٍ to point at sth/sb

إِصْبَع *n* |mf; أَصابِعُ| [1] [يَد] finger; toe; إِصْبَع قَدَم toe; عُقْلة إِصْبَع phalanx; رَأْس \ قِمّة الإِصْبَعِ finger tip; بَصْمة إِصْبَعٍ fingerprint; كانَ لَهُ إِصْبَعٌ في الأَمْرِ to have a finger in the pie; رَفَعَ إِصْبَعاً to raise a hand; مَصَّ إِصْبَعَهُ to suck one's finger/ thumb; أَحْرَقَ أَصابِعَهُ to burn one's fingers; أَشارَ بِإِصْبَعِهِ إلى شَخْصٍ to point one's finger at sb; وَضَعَ إِصْبَعَهُ على مَوْضِعٍ to put a finger on an issue; مَشى على أَطْرافِ أَصابِعِ قَدَمَيْهِ to tiptoe; كانَ إِصْبَعُهُ على الزِنادِ to have a one's finger on the trigger; جَعَلَ شَخْصاً كالخاتَمِ في إِصْبَعِهِ to twist sb around one's little finger; يُعَدُّ على الأَصابِعِ ≈ it can be counted on the fingers of one hand; لا يَتَجاوَزُ عَدَدَ أَصابِعِ اليَدِ الواحِدةِ it's no more than five; لم يَلْمَسْهُ وَلَوْ بِإِصْبَعٍ he didn't lift a finger [2] (Meas) inch (*linear measurement*)

‹ **صَبَغَ** *v* |a-i-u; صَبْغ, صِبَغ| [1] [لَوَّنَ] to dye; to paint, to colour; to coat, to lacquer, to varnish; صَبَغَ الأَظافِرَ to paint one's nails; صَبَغَ باباً to paint a door; صَبَغَ شَيْئاً بِطابِعٍ سِياسيٍّ to give sth a political character [2] (Chr) to baptize, to christen

اِصْطَبَغَ *v* [1] to be dyed; to be painted/coloured; to be coated/ varnished; اِصْطَبَغَ باللَوْنِ الأَصْفَرِ to be painted yellow [2] (Chr) to be baptized

صِبْغ *n* |أَصْباغ| [1] [مادّة مُلَوِّنة] dye; paint; colour, pigment, tint; lacquer, varnish; طَبَقة من الصِبْغِ a coat of paint; عُلْبة الصِبْغِ a paint can; خَلَطَ الأَصْباغَ to mix paint [2] (Bio) pigment

صَبّاغ *n* painter (*of buildings, etc.*)

صِباغ *n* |أَصْبِغة| paint, dye; lacquer

صِبْغة *n* [1] [مادّة] paint, dye [2] [لَوْن] colour, tint [3] [مَيْل] nature; tendency, inclination; taste, liking; صِبْغة احْتِفائيّة

a festive touch; أَخْرَجَ مَوْضوعاً عن صِبْغَتِهِ الأَصْلِيّةِ to take sth out of context

صِبْغِيّ A *adj* chromosome (*before n*), chromosomal; اضْطِراب صِبْغِيّ a chromosome abnormality
B *n* |صِبْغِيّات| chromosome

صِبْغِيّة *n* 1 (Bio) chromatin 2 (Bot) pokeweed (*Phytolaccaceae*)

اصْطِباغ *n* pigmentation, coloration

مَصْبَغة *n* dry cleaner's, dry cleaning; laundry service

صَبَّنَ *v* to saponify; to make into soap

صابون *n* soap; صابون سائِل liquid soap; قِطْعة من الصابونِ a bar of soap; صابون الحِلاقةِ shaving soap; رَغْوة الصابونِ suds, lather; فُقّاعة صابونٍ soap bubble; غَسَلَ يَدَيْهِ بالماءِ والصابونِ to wash one's hands with soap and water

صَبّانة *n* soap dish

مَصْبَنة *n* |مَصابِنُ, مَصْبَنات| soap factory

صَبا *v* |u; صَبْو, صَبْوة| |إلى| to long for/to, to yearn for; to strive for, to aspire to; صَبا إلى شَيْءٍ to long for sth

صَبِيَ *v* |a; صَباً, صَباء| to be/act childish, to be infantile

تَصابى *v* to be/act childish, to be infantile

صَبيّ *n* 1 [وَلَد صَغير] |صِبْيان, صِبْية| young man, youth, boy 2 [تِلْميذ] |صِبْيان, صِبْية| apprentice, novice 3 [طِفْل صَغير] |صِبْيان|; f صَبِيّة; f pl صَبايا| little one, young child, baby

صِباً, صِبًى *n* youth, childhood; مُنْذُ الصِبا since childhood

صَبْوة *n* |صَبَوات| youthful zeal/passion/desire; longing, craving

صِبْيانيّ *adj* childish, immature, infantile; adolescent, juvenile; كِتاب صِبْيانيّ children's book; خَطّ صِبْيانيّ a child's handwriting; رَدّ فِعْلٍ صِبْيانيّ a childish reaction; سُلوك صِبْيانيّ immature behaviour

صَبيّة *n* |صَبايا| (young) girl

صَحِبَ *v* |a; صُحْبة, صَحابة, صِحابة| to accompany, to escort; صَحِبَ شَخْصاً إلى مَكانٍ to accompany sb somewhere

صاحَبَ *v* to accompany, to escort, to convoy; to befriend; صاحَبَ شَخْصاً \ شَيْئاً to accompany sb/sth; صاحَبَ في العَزْفِ والغِناءِ to accompany sb in music and singing; صاحَبوهُ they kept him company

أَصْحَبَ *v* 1 [اتَّخَذَ أَصْحابًا] to make friends 2 [أَرْسَلَ مع] شَخْصٍ to send along as companion or escort

تَصاحَبَ *v* 1 [تَشارَكَ] to unite; to cooperate, to work/act together 2 [تَرافَقَ] to be friendly towards each other, to be/become friends; to associate (with)

اصْطَحَبَ *v* to accompany, to escort, to take along; اصْطَحَبَ شَخْصاً (مَعَهُ) في سَيّارَتِهِ to take sb along in one's car; اصْطَحَبَ أَوْلادَهُ في الإجازةِ to take one's children on holiday (BrE) vacation (AmE)

اسْتَصْحَبَ *v* 1 [شَيْئاً] to bring (along), to take (along); دائِماً يَسْتَصْحِبُ هذه الحَقيبةَ he always brings this suitcase 2 [شَخْصاً] to accompany, to escort; to invite/ask to come along; اسْتَصْحَبَ الأَبُ ابْنَهُ the father invited his son to come along

صاحِب *n* 1 [مالِك] |أَصْحاب, صَحابة, صُحْبة| master, owner; leader, chief; king, sovereign; صاحِب البَيْتِ the master of the house; صاحِب الأَمْرِ the person concerned; صاحِب مَصْنَعٍ industrialist; صاحِب رَأْسمالٍ capitalist; صاحِب \ صاحِبة الجَلالةِ His/Her Majesty; صاحِب \ صاحِبة السُموِّ His/Her Highness; صاحِب المَعالي His Excellency 2 [صَديق] friend, companion 3 [حَبيب] boyfriend

صاحِبة *n* 1 [صَديقة] (female) friend 2 [حَبيبة] girlfriend

صَحابيّ *n* |صَحابة, أَصْحاب| companion of the Prophet; الصَحابة the companions of the Prophet

صُحْبة *n* 1 [رِفْقة] company; في صُحْبةِ ... \ ب in the company of ... 2 [صَداقة] friendship

مُصاحِب *n* 1 [مُرافِق] companion; colleague, partner 2 (Mus) accompanist

مُصاحَبة *n* 1 [مُرافَقة] escort, company; accompaniment; بِمُصاحَبةِ ... accompanied by ... 2 [مُصادَقة] friendship, companionship

مَصْحوب *adj* |ب| accompanied; كانَ مَصْحوباً بِشَيْءٍ to be accompanied by sth; سافَرَ مَصْحوباً بالسَلامةِ to travel safely

صَحَّ *v* |i; صِحّة, صِحاح| 1 [كانَ حَقيقيًّا] to be right/correct, to be true; صَحَّ الخَبَرُ the news was true; هذا لا يَصِحُّ this isn't correct; إذا صَحَّ التَعْبيرُ so to speak 2 [شُفِيَ] to be/

get well, to recuperate, to recover, to heal ③ [انْطَبَقَ] |على| to be true for, to apply to; ما يَصِحُّ على الأَفْرادِ يَصِحُّ على الشُعوبِ what's true for the individual is true for the group

صَحَّحَ *v* to correct, to rectify; to adjust; صَحَّحَ نَصًّا \ إنْشاءً to correct a text/essay; صَحَّحَ أَخْطاءً to correct mistakes; صَحَّحَ المَسارَ to check homework; صَحَّحَ واجِباتٍ مَنْزِليّةً to correct course; صَحَّحَ مَسيرةَ الحُكومةِ to correct the course of the government; صَحَّحَ خَبَراً خاطِئاً to rectify an incorrect statement

تَصَحَّحَ *v* to be corrected/rectified, to undergo rectification

صِحّة *n* ① [عافِية] health, fitness, condition, constitution; بالصِحّةِ! صِحَّتَيْنِ! على صِحَّتِكَ! \ في ب here's to your health!, cheers; في صِحّةٍ جَيِّدةٍ \ مُمْتازةٍ in good/excellent health; صِحّة عُموميّة national health, public health (AmE); مَكْتَب صِحّةٍ (Egypt) (public) health service; مُنَظَّمة الصِحّةِ العالَميّة the World Health Organization, the WHO; عِلْم الصِحّةِ hygiene; مُضِرّ \ ضارّ بالصِحّةِ unhealthy, unwholesome; إنَّهُ غَيْرُ مُفيدٍ للصِحّةِ it isn't good for one's health; هو رَهيفُ الصِحّةِ he's in poor health; كانَ في صِحّةٍ جَيِّدةٍ, كانَ في أَتَمِّ فاضَ صِحّةً to be in good condition; تَمَتَّعَ بِصِحّةٍ جَيِّدةٍ to be in the pink; صِحّةٍ to enjoy good health; اهْتَمَّ بِصِحَّتِهِ to pay attention to one's health; أَتْلَفَ صِحَّتَهُ to undermine one's constitution; اسْتَعادَ صِحَّتَهُ (تَماماً) to recover (completely) ② [دِقّة] accuracy, precision, exactness; عَدَم صِحّةٍ inaccuracy; صِحّة الأَقْوالِ the accuracy of the statements ③ [حَقيقة] correctness, truth; authenticity, genuineness; دَرَجة الصِحّةِ degree of authenticity; شَكَّ في صِحّةِ الانْتِخاباتِ to challenge the validity of the elections; لا أَساسَ لَهُ من الصِحّةِ to be completely unfounded in fact

صِحّيّ *adj* ① [مُلائِم للصِحّةِ] healthy, health (*before n*); غِذاء صِحّيّ healthy food; غَيْر صِحّيٍّ unhealthy; مِهْنة غَيْر صِحّيّة an unhealthy occupation; حالة صِحّيّة health; تَتَدَهْوَرُ حالَتُهُ الصِحّيّةُ his health is failing ② [مَنسوب إلى الصِحّةِ] hygienic, sanitary, hygiene (*before n*); ظُروف \ تَجْهيزات صِحّيّة sanitary conditions/facilities; تَعْليمات \ إرْشادات صِحّيّة hygiene regulations

صَحيح *adj* |أَصِحّة, أَصِحّاءُ, صِحاح| ① [صَواب] right, true, correct; good; غَيْر صَحيحٍ incorrect; حِساب \ حَلّ \ قَوْل جَواب صَحيح a correct calculation/solution/answer; قَوْل صَحيح a true statement; التاريخ الصَحيح the right date; من الصَحيحِ \ لَيْسَ صَحيحاً أنّ ... it is/isn't true that ...; هل هذا صَحيحٌ؟ is that true?; هذا لَيْسَ صَحيحاً البَتّةَ this is absolutely incorrect; صَحيحٌ أَنَّهُ قامَ بِعَمَلِهِ he really did his job; تَسيرُ الأُمورُ في الطَريقِ الصَحيحِ things are moving in the right direction ② [عَدَد] round; عَدَد صَحيح a round number ③ (Islam) right, correct (*said of a Hadith*) ④ (Ling) sound (*without irregularities*); جَمْع صَحيح a sound plural; فِعْل صَحيح a sound verb

أَصَحّ *adj* |dipt| better; more correct; healthier; أو على الأَصَحِّ ... or, to be more correct ..., or rather ...

إصْحاح *n* a chapter of the Bible or the Torah

تَصْحيح *n* |تَصْحيحات| correction, rectification; revision, review; تَصْحيح أَخْطاءٍ correcting mistakes; تَصْحيح الإمْلاءِ spellchecking; أَدْخَلَ تَصْحيحاتٍ to make corrections

تَصْحيحيّ *adj* corrective, correction (*before n*)

مَصَحّة *n* sanatorium, sanitarium; مَصَحّة نَفْسيّة a mental institution/hospital; رَقَدَ في مَصَحّةٍ to stay in a sanatorium; أَدْخَلَ شَخْصاً مَصَحّةً to commit sb to a sanatorium

مُصَحِّح *n* corrector, proofreader, copy editor

صَحْراء *n* |dipt f; صَحارى, صَحارٍ| desert; الصَحْراء (الكُبْرى) the Sahara; الصَحْراء الغَرْبيّة Western Sahara; في الصَحْراءِ in the desert; رَمْل \ رِمال الصَحْراءِ desert sand; سَفينة الصَحْراءِ camel

صَحْراويّ Ⓐ *adj* desert (*before n*); أَراضٍ صَحْراويّة desert land Ⓑ *n* Saharan; desert dweller

تَصَحُّر *n* desertification

تَصْحير *n* desertification

صَحْصَحَ *v* |i; صَحْصَحة| to wake up

صَحَّفَ *v* to mispronounce; to misspell; to misread

صَحافة, صِحافة *n* journalism; press; الصِحافة المَكْتوبة the printed press; الصِحافة الرَقْميّة the digital press; في الصِحافةِ in the press; وِكالة صِحافةٍ news agency; حُرِّيّة الصِحافةِ

B *n* **1** [يَقَظة] wakefulness, alertness; consciousness; sobering up **2** [السَماءِ] clarity, clearness

صاحٍ *adj* |صُحاة, صاحونَ| **1** [مُسْتَيْقِظ] awake, alert; conscious; sober **2** [السَماء] clear, cloudless; جَوّ صاحٍ clear weather

صَحْوة *n* |صَحَوات| revival, resurgence; awakening; الصَحْوة الإسْلاميّة the Islamic revival

‹ **صَخِبَ** *v* |a; صَخَب| to shout, to yell, to clamour; to be loud/noisy, to make a racket

اصْطَخَبَ *v* to be loud/noisy, to make a racket; to shout, to yell, to clamour

صَخَب *n* noise, racket, tumult; shouting, yelling, clamour; صَخَب الاحْتِفالِ the noise from the party

صَخِب *adj* loud, noisy, boisterous

صاخِب *adj* loud, noisy, tumultuous; موسيقى صاخِبة loud music; ضَجيج صاخِب a terrible racket; مُناقَشة \ مُظاهَرة صاخِبة a lively discussion/demonstration

‹ **صَخِرَ** *v* |a; صَخَر| to be rocky; to petrify

تَصَخَّرَ *v* to petrify

صَخْر *n coll* |صَخَرات, صُخور| rock, stone, boulder; قُبّة الصَخْرة the Dome of the Rock (*in Jerusalem*); صَلْب كالصَخْرِ (as) hard as stone; ثَقيل كالصَخْرِ (as) heavy as lead; قَلْب من صَخْر a heart of stone; ارْتَطَمَت السَفينةُ بالصُخورِ the ship struck the rocks

صَخْريّ *adj* rocky, rock (*before n*); أَرْض صَخْريّة rocky ground; صوف \ حَرير صَخْريّ asbestos; النَفط \ الزَيْت الصَخْريّ shale oil

‹ **صَدِئَ** *v* |a; صَداءة| to rust, to get rusty; to corrode, to oxidize

أَصْدَأَ *v* to make rusty, to corrode, to oxidize

صَدَأ *n* rust; corrosion, oxidation; طَبَقة من الصَدَأِ a layer of rust; بُقْعة صَدَأٍ a rust stain; غَيْر قابِلٍ للصَدَأ rustproof; stainless; حَديد غَيْر قابِلٍ للصَدَأِ stainless steel; أَزالَ الصَدَأَ to remove the rust; قد غَطّاهُ \ أَكَلَهُ الصَدَأُ it's covered in/with rust

صَدِئ *adj* rusty; oxidized, corroded; مِسْمار صَدِئ a rusty nail; غَيْر صَدِئ non-rusty

‹ **صَدَحَ** *v* |a; صُداح, صَدْح| to chant, to sing; warble; يَصْدَحُ البُلْبُلُ the nightingale sings

freedom of the press; حَدَّدَ حُرّيّةَ الصِحافةِ to restrict the freedom of the press

صِحافيّ, صَحافيّ **A** *adj* journalistic; newspaper (*before n*), press (*before n*)

B *n* journalist, reporter; publicist

صَحْفة *n* |صِحاف| dish, plate, platter; bowl; saucer

صُحُفيّ, صَحَفيّ **A** *adj* journalistic; newspaper (*before n*), press (*before n*); مِهْنة صُحُفيّة a career in journalism; نَدْوة \ مُؤْتَمَر صُحُفيّ(ة) a press conference; مَرْكَز صُحُفيّ press centre

B *n* journalist, reporter; publicist; صُحُفيّ رِياضيّ a sports journalist

صَحيفة *n* |صَحائِف, صُحُف| **1** [جَريدة] newspaper, paper; صَحيفة يَوْميّة daily newspaper; صَحيفة جِداريّة placard; الصُحُف المَكْتوبة the press; الصُحُف العالَميّة \ المَحَلّيّة the international/local press; جاءَ \ ظَهَرَ في الصُحُفِ to make the paper; قالَتْ صَحيفةُ الحَياةِ إنّ ... al-Hayat newspaper said that ...; نَشَرَت الصُحُفُ أَخْباراً reports appeared in the newspaper **2** [وَرَقة] page, leaf, folio; sheet

تَصْحيف *n* |تَصْحيفات| mispronunciation; misspelling; misstatement, misrepresentation

مُصْحَف *n* |مَصاحِفُ| Koran, Koranic manuscript/codex, a copy of the Koran; المُصْحَف الشَريف (a copy of) the Holy Koran

‹ **أَصْحَل** *adj* |dipt| hoarse, husky

‹ **صَحَنَ** *v* |a; صَحْن| to grind, to mill

صَحْن *n* |صُحون| **1** [طَبَق] plate, dish, platter; bowl; saucer; صَحْن طائِر UFO, flying saucer; صَحْن هَوائيّ dish antenna; صَحْن فاكِهةٍ a dish of fruit; صَحْن سَجائِرَ ashtray **2** [الدار] courtyard, yard; صَحْن الجامِعِ a mosque courtyard; صَحْن دارٍ patio

‹ **صَحا** *v* |u; صَحْو, صُحُوّ| **1** [اسْتَيْقَظَ] to wake up, to awake; to regain consciousness, to come to/round; to sober up; صَحا من تَخْديرٍ \ تَبْنيج to recover from anaesthesia **2** [السَماء] to be clear

أَصْحى *v* to wake up, to awaken, to rouse

صَحْو **A** *adj* clear, cloudless; كانَ الجَوُّ صَحْواً the weather was clear

صَدْح *n* chant, chanting, singing; warbling (*of a bird*)

صادِح *n* |صَدَحة, صُدّاح, صُدَّح| (Mus) singer, chanter

صادِحة *n* tenor; (female) singer

مِصْدَح *n* |مَصادِح| microphone

صَدَّ *v* |u; صَدّ, صُدود| **1** [عن] to turn away/aside **2** [أعاق] to hold back, to restrain; to prevent, to stop; صَدَّ شَخْصاً عن شَيْءٍ to stop sb from doing sth **3** [دَرَأ] to keep off/out, to parry, to ward off, to repel; صَدَّ الأَسْئِلة to parry a question; صَدّ الضَرَباتِ to dodge the blows; صَدَّ هُجوماً to repel an attack; صَدَّ العَدوَّ to drive the enemy back; صَدَّ قوّاتِ العَدوِّ to ward off the enemy troops

صَدَد *n* **1** [سِياق] regard, respect, context; في هذا الصَدَدِ \ ب in this respect; في أيِّ صَدَدٍ قيلَ هذا؟ in what context was this said?; الحالة الّتي نَحْنُ بِصَدَدِها the situation in which we find ourselves **2** [يَحْدُثُ الآنَ] بِصَدَدِ currently, in the process; *periphrastic construction signifying continuous or progressive aspect*; نَحْنُ بِصَدَدِ تَأسيسِ جَمْعيّةٍ ثَقافيّةٍ we are in the process of establishing a cultural association

صَدّادة *n* stop, stopper, plug

صُدود *n* avoidance; refusal, rejection; interception

صَديد *n* pus, purulence, suppuration

مَصَدّ *n* |مَصَدّات| **1** [سَيّارةٍ] bumper, fender **2** [للأَمْواج، الريح، إلخ] breaker; buffer

صَدَرَ *v* |i-u; صُدور| **1** [الكِتابُ] to appear, to come out; to be published/issued/released; صَدَرَ أَرْبَعَ مَرّاتٍ في السَنة to appear four times a year, to be issued quarterly; صَدَرَ الكِتابُ the book was published **2** [الحُكْمُ] to be passed/pronounced; صَدَرَ الحُكْمُ في القَضيّة judgement on the case has been rendered **3** [نَشَأ] |عن| to arise/emerge, to come from, to originate from/in; صَدَرَ عَنْهُ تَصْريحٌ he gave an explanation; صَدَرَتْ عن الغُرْفة أَصْواتٌ voices came from the room; البَيانات التي تَصْدُرُ عن الوِزارة the reports that are put out by the ministry

صَدَّرَ *v* **1** [باعَ السِلَعَ إلى الخارِجِ] to export; صَدَّرَ الجُبْنَ إلى الصينِ to export cheese to China **2** [كَتَبَ مُقَدِّمةً] |ب| to write a preface/foreword

صادَرَ *v* to seize, to take possession of; to confiscate, to impound; صادَرَ شَيْئاً to take possession of something; صادَرَ الحُرّيّةَ الشَخْصيّةَ to restrict personal freedom; صادَرَ البَضائِعَ المَسْروقة to confiscate stolen goods

أَصْدَرَ *v* to publish, to issue, to release; أَصْدَرَ كِتاباً to publish a book/release a film; أَصْدَرَ فيلْماً to release a film; أَصْدَرَ مَرْسوماً to issue a decree; أَصْدَرَ اسْتِدْعاءً to issue a summons; أَصْدَرَ حُكْماً to pass judgement

تَصَدَّرَ *v* to preside, to head, to command; to lead, to take the lead; تَصَدَّرَ المائِدةَ to sit at the head of the table; تَصَدَّرَ شَيْئاً to be in charge of sth; تَصَدَّرَ الدَوْريَّ (Sport) to lead the league; تَصَدَّرَ القائِمةَ \ المُحادَثاتِ to be at the top of the list/agenda; تَصَدَّرَ الخَبَرُ الصَفَحاتِ الأولى من الصُحُفِ the news was all over the front pages

اسْتَصْدَرَ *v* to obtain, to get, to acquire

صَدْر *n* |صُدور| **1** (Anat) chest, breast; شَعْر الصَدْرِ chest hair; عاري الصَدْرِ topless; أَبو صَدْرٍ robin; سِباحة الصَدْرِ breast stroke; ضَمَّ شَخْصاً إلى صَدْرِهِ to embrace someone **2** [ثَدْيا المَرْأة] breast, bosom, bust; حَمّالة الصَدْرِ brassiere; عَمَليّة تَكْبير الصَدْرِ breast augmentation surgery **3** (Clothg) bodice; صَدْر ضَيِّق a tight bodice **4** [مُقَدَّم] foreground, front; preface, foreword; beginning; في الصَدْرِ at the forefront; صَدْر الإِسْلام the beginnings of Islam **5** [داخِلة] deepest/innermost feelings; mind; soul; بَنات الصَدْرِ worries; ضَيِّق الصَدْرِ annoyed; رَحْب الصَدْرِ generous; رَحابة الصَدْرِ generosity; كَشَفَ عن مَكْنونِ صَدْرِهِ to get sth off one's chest; كانَتْ في صَدْرِهِ رَغْبةٌ حارّةٌ he had a fervent wish; أَثْلَجَ قَرارُ الرَئيسِ صَدْري I'm delighted with the president's decision **6** (Literat) *the first half of a line of classical poetry*

صادِر **A** *adj* originating, arising, coming, emanating; issued, published; outgoing (*mail*); outbound (*train*); مَعْلومات صادِرة عن الوِزارةِ information issued by the ministry **B** *n* |صادِرات| (Busn) export product; صادِرات exports; سوق \ حَجْم \ ضَريبة الصادِراتِ export market/volume/duty; سَدَّدَ ضَريبةَ الصادِراتِ to pay export duty; ارْتَفَعَت الصادِراتُ إلى الكُوَيْتِ exports to Kuwait rose

صِدار *n* waistcoat (BrE), vest (AmE)

صَدارة *n* lead, front, forefront; precedence, prominent place; تَحْتَلُّ تِلْكَ الشَرِكةُ مَكانَ الصَدارةِ في مَيْدانِ التَشْغيلِ الآلِيِّ that company has a leading position in the field of automation; يَأْخُذُ \ يَحْتَلُّ هذا مَوْقِعَ الصَدارةِ عِنْدي that comes first with me

صُدْرة *n* |صُدَر| waistcoat (BrE), vest (AmE)

صَدْرِيّ *adj* pectoral, chest (*before n*), breast (*before n*); قَفَص صَدْرِيّ thorax

صَدْرِيّة ,صُدْرِيّة *n* **1** [حَمّالة الصَدْرِ] bra, brassiere **2** [ثَوْب يُغَطّي الصَدْرَ] waistcoat (BrE), vest (AmE); top; vest, jacket; صَدْرِيّة ضِدّ الرَصاصِ a bulletproof vest; صَدْرِيّة النَجاةِ life jacket, life vest (AmE)

صُدور *n* publication, appearance, issuance; صُدور كِتابٍ the publication of a book; أَوْقَفَ صَحيفةً عن الصُدورِ to suspend publication of a newspaper

اسْتِصْدار *n* obtaining, acquiring; issuance; سَعى لِاسْتِصْدارِ قَرارٍ to try to obtain a decision

إصْدار *n* |إصْدارات| **1** [قانونٍ] issue, issuance, issuing; إصْدار قانونٍ \ قَرارٍ \ حُكْمٍ the issuance of a law/decision/judgement **2** [نَشْر] edition, issue; publication; مَنْع الإصْدارِ publication ban; إصْدار طَبْعةٍ جَديدةٍ من مَجَلّةٍ the publication of a new issue of a magazine **3** [نُقودٍ \ طَوابِعَ ...] issue, issuance; إصْدار الأَسْهُمِ issuance of shares; إصْدار جَوازٍ issuance of a passport; سِعْر الإصْدارِ the issue price

تَصَدُّرِيّة *n* priority, precedence

تَصْدير *n* export; الاسْتيراد والتَصْدير import-export; تَصْدير الأَفْكارِ المُتَطَرِّفةِ the export of extremist ideas; سِلْعة تَصْديرٍ an export product; حَظْر \ مَنْع التَصْديرِ an export ban; حَظْر تَصْديرِ المَوادِّ الضارّةِ an export ban on hazardous materials; فَرَضَ حَظْرَ التَصْديرِ to impose an export ban; إذْن تَصْديرٍ an export permit; التَصْدير إلى الشَرْقِ الأَوْسَطِ export to the Middle East

تَصْديرِي *adj* exporting, export (*before n*); سوق تَصْديرِيّة export market

مُتَصَدِّر *adj* presiding, leading, heading; مُتَصَدِّراً leading; on top; كانَ هذا الطَلَبُ مُتَصَدِّراً لِلائحةِ الطَلَباتِ this order was on top of the list

مُصادَرة *n* confiscation, seizure, impoundment, forfeiture; expropriation, dispossession; embargo; مُصادَرة أَراضٍ expropriation of land; مُصادَرة الأَمْلاكِ the confiscation of property

مَصْدَر *n* |مَصادِرُ| **1** [مَنْشَأ] source, origin, root, inception; provenance; مَصْدَر مَفْتوح open source; بَرْمَجِيّات مَفْتوحة المَصْدَرِ open-source software; مَصْدَر تَزْكِيةٍ مُمْتاز an excellent reference; مَصْدَر مَعْلوماتٍ وَثيق الاطِّلاعِ a reliable source of information; مَصْدَر كَسْبٍ \ رِزْقٍ a source of income; المَصادِر المالِيّة الإضافِيّة additional revenue streams; مَصْدَر التَسْلِيةِ \ السَعادةِ a source of amusement/joy; مَصْدَر غَزير لِلمَعْرِفةِ an inexhaustible source of knowledge; مَصْدَر مَعْلوماتٍ \ إلْهامٍ a source of information/inspiration **2** [مُبَلِّغ] source, informant; مَصادِر عالِية المُسْتَوى high-level sources; مَصْدَر واسِع الاطِّلاعِ a well-informed source; مَصْدَر أَمْنِيّ a source within the security forces; من مَصْدَرٍ مَوْثوقٍ from a reliable source; مَصادِر مُقَرَّبة من ... \ مُطَّلِع بِهِ sources close to ...; لم يَرِدْ تَأْكيدٌ لِلنَبَأِ من مَصْدَرٍ مُسْتَقِلٍّ there's no confirmation from any independent source **3** (Gram) verbal noun, gerund

مُصَدَّر *adj* exported

مُصَدِّر **A** *adj* exporting, export (*before n*); دَوْلة مُصَدِّرة exporting country; مُنَظَّمة الدُوَلِ المُصَدِّرةِ لِلنَفْطِ Organization of Petroleum Exporting Countries, OPEC

B *n* exporter

مَصْدَرِيّ *adj* source (*before n*); كود \ شِفْرة مَصْدَرِيّ(ة) source code

مَصْدور **A** *adj* tubercular, tuberculous

B *n* tubercular

صَدَعَ *v* |a; صَدْع| to crack, to split, to tear, to rend; to break in two; صَدَعَ لَوْحاً to break a board in two; صَدَعَ بالحَقِّ to disclose; صُدِعَ to get/have a headache

صَدَّعَ *v* to split; to break; صَدَّعَ شَيْئاً to split sth; صَدَّعَ رَأْسَ \ دِماغَ شَخْصٍ to give sb a headache; to be a headache for sb

تَصَدَّعَ *v* to be/become cracked/broken; to split, to crack, to cleave; مَنْظَر تَتَصَدَّعُ لَهُ القُلوبُ a heart-rending sight;

تَصَدَّعَت المِرْآةُ \ تَصَدَّعَ الجِدارُ the mirror/wall cracked; يَتَصَدَّعُ اللَّوحُ the board is splitting

اِنْصَدَعَ *v* to be cracked/broken/split

صَدْع *n* |صُدوع| [1] [اِنْكِسار] crack, break, fracture; split, crevice; صَدْع في زَهْرِيّةٍ \ الكَأْسِ a crack in the vase/glass; رَأَبَ صَدْعاً to repair a crack [2] (Geog) fault; خطّ الصَّدْعِ fault line

صُداع *n* headache; صُداع نِصْفيّ migraine; صُداع حادّ \ رَهيب a splitting headache; شَعَرَ بِصُداعٍ to have a headache; سَبَّبَ صُداعاً لِشَخْصٍ to give sb a headache

تَصَدُّع *n* split, crack, rift, break; أَحْدَثَ تَصَدُّعاً خَطيراً to cause a deep rift

صُدْغ *n* |أَصْداغ| (Anat) temple

صُدْغيّ *adj* temporal; فَصّ \ عَظْم صُدْغيّ temporal lobe/bone

صَدَفَ *v* |i; صُدوف, صَدْف| |عن| to avoid; to avert

صادَفَ *v* to encounter by chance/coincidence; to fall/be on, to concur, to coincide; صادَفَ شَيْئاً to encounter sth; صادَفَ مَشاكِلَ to meet trouble; صادَفَ صَديقاً في الطَّريقِ to happen to meet a friend on the road; صادَفَ أَنْ حَدَثَ to happen coincidentally; صادَفَ يَوْماً \ تاريخاً to fall on a day/date; اليَوْمُ العالَميُّ للمَرْأةِ يُصادِفُ يَوْمَ الثامِنِ من مارْس International Women's Day is on March eighth

تَصادَفَ *v* to coincide, to concur; to meet/find unexpectedly, to run into/across

صَدَف *n coll* |أَصْداف| shell, shellfish; mother-of-pearl, pearl, pearl oyster; صَدَف الحَلَزونِ mollusc shell; صَدَفة الأُذُنِ auricle; داء الصَّدَفِ psoriasis

صُدْفة *n* |صُدَف| coincidence, chance; مَحْض صُدْفةٍ mere coincidence; صُدْفةً, بالصُّدْفةِ, بِطَريقِ الصُّدْفةِ \ من قَبيلِ by chance, coincidentally; تَلاقَيْنا بالصُّدْفةِ we met by chance; لم يَكُنْ هذا الأَمْرُ من قَبيلِ الصُّدْفةِ, لم يَأْتِ هذا بالصُّدْفةِ this was no coincidence; هذا لَيْسَ من بابِ الصُّدْفةِ this can't be coincidence

Idiom رُبَّ صُدْفةٍ خَيْرٌ من أَلْفِ ميعادٍ a spontaneous encounter is better than any appointment

صَدَفيّة *n* psoriasis; عانى من الصَّدَفيّةِ to suffer from psoriasis

مُصادِف *n* corresponding, analogous; يَوْم السَّبْتِ المُصادِفُ للعِشْرينَ من شَهْرِ أَبْريل the Saturday that falls on April 20th

مُصادَفة *n* coincidence, chance, accident; يا لَلْمُصادَفةِ! what a coincidence!; مُصادَفة سَعيدة a lucky coincidence; لَيْسَ مُصادَفةً أنّ ... it's no coincidence that ...; كانَ مُجَرَّدَ مُصادَفةٍ it was pure chance

صَدَقَ *v* |u; صِدْق, صَدْق| to be truthful/sincere; to be correct; صَدَقَ القَوْلَ to tell the truth; صَدَقَ في وَعْدِهِ to keep one's promise; صَدَقَ اللهُ العَظيمُ God Almighty has spoken the truth (*statement at the end of a Koranic recitation*)

صَدَّقَ *v* [1] [كَلامَ شَخْصٍ] to believe; (بِشَكْلٍ) لا يُصَدَّقُ unbelievable; قِصّة لا تُصَدَّقُ an incredible story; صَدِّقْ أو لا تُصَدِّقْ believe it or not [2] [وَثَّقَ] |على| to legalize, to ratify; to attest, to certify, to authenticate; to sanction, to approve; صَدَّقَ على مُعاهَدةٍ to ratify a treaty; صَدَّقَ على قَرارٍ to approve a resolution

صادَقَ *v* [1] [وَثَّقَ] |على| to legalize, to ratify; to attest, to certify, to authenticate; to sanction, to approve; صادَقَ على وَثيقةٍ to legalize a document [2] [صاحَبَ] to befriend, to associate with; صادَقَ شَخْصاً to befriend sb

أَصْدَقَ *v* أَصْدَقَ القَوْلَ to tell the truth

تَصَدَّقَ *v* |على| to give alms/charity (to); تَصَدَّقَ بِمالِهِ على الفُقَراءِ to give alms to the poor

تَصادَقَ *v* |مع| to befriend, to associate with; تَصادَقَ مع شَخْصٍ to befriend sb

صِدْق *n* honesty, candor, sincerity; صِدْقاً, بِصِدْقٍ sincerely, honestly, genuinely; عَبَّرَ الكاتِبُ بِصِدْقٍ عن مُعْتَقَداتِهِ the writer expressed his conviction sincerely

صادِق *adj* [1] [مُخْلِص] honest, sincere, truthful; faithful, true, loyal; frank, candid, straightforward, genuine; warm, friendly, heartfelt; تَصْريح \ جَواب صادِق an honest statement/answer; نَصيحة \ شُكْر \ اعْتِذارات صادِق(ة) sincere advice/gratitude/apologies; اهْتِمام \ إعْجاب صادِق genuine interest/admiration; صورة صادِقة a true picture; رَجُل صادِق الوَعْدِ a man of his word [2] [اسْم شَخْصيّ] Sadiq (*male given name*)

صَدَمَ *v* |i| صَدْم| 1 [اِرْتَطَمَ] to bump/crash into, to run into, to hit, to collide with; to thump, to bump, to knock; صَدَمَ شَخْصاً \ شَيْئاً to bump into sb/sth; صَدَمَ كَلْباً (بِسَيّارَتِهِ) to hit a dog (with one's car) 2 [قَلْقَلَ] to shock; صَدَمَني الخَبَرُ the news shocked me

صادَمَ *v* to bump/crash, to run into, to hit, to collide with; to clash with, to attack

تَصادَمَ *v* |مع| to bump/crash/run into, to collide with; to clash with, to conflict with; تَصادَمَ المُتَظاهِرونَ مع الشُّرْطَةِ the demonstrators clashed with the police

اِصْطَدَمَ *v* |ب| to bump/crash/run into, to collide with; to knock/strike/bang against; to clash with; اِصْطَدَمَ بالطاوِلَةِ to bump into a table; اِصْطَدَمَ بِراكِبِ دَرّاجةٍ to hit a cyclist; اِصْطَدَمَ بِجِدارٍ to crash into a wall; اِصْطَدَمَ بِشَخْصٍ to clash with sb; اِصْطَدَمَ بِجِدارٍ من الاحْتِجاجِ to come up against a wall of protest; اِصْطَدَمَت السَفينَةُ بالجِسْرِ the ship rammed a bridge

صادِم *adj* shocking; صورة صادِمة a shocking picture

صِدام *n* collision, smash, crash; clash, confrontation

صَدْمة *n* |صَدَمات| shock; impact; blow, thrust, jolt; صَدْمة كَبيرة \ قَوِيّة \ عَنيفة a big/strong/violent shock; صَدْمة مُمْتَصّ \ مُخَمِّد صَدَماتٍ كَهْرَبائيّة an electric shock; مُخَفِّف الصَّدَماتِ shock absorber; صَدْمة bumper, fender; صَدْمة حَضارِيّة culture shock; صَدْمة نَفْسِيّة trauma; صَدْمة نَفْسِيّة خَطيرة a severe trauma; تَعَرَّضَ لِصَدْمةٍ نَفْسِيّةٍ من جَرّاءِ شَيْءٍ to be traumatized by sth; سَبَّبَ \ أَحْدَثَ صَدْمةً نَفْسِيّةً to traumatize; كانَ في حالةِ صَدْمةٍ to be in a state of shock; أُصيبَ بِصَدْمةٍ to be in shock; تَعَرَّضَ لِصَدْمةٍ to get a shock; تَلَقّى صَدْمةً (عَنيفةً) to suffer a (severe) shock

اِصْطِدام *n* |اِصْطِدامات| collision, impact, crash, bump; clash, confrontation; shock; حادِث اِصْطِدامٍ collision; اِصْطِدام بِشَيْءٍ a collision with sth

تَصادُم *n* |تَصادُمات| collision, crash; clash, confrontation; shock; تَصادُم أَمامِيّ a head-on collision; تَصادُمُ الآراءِ a clash of opinions; حَدَثَ تَصادُمٌ عَنيفٌ بين قِطارَيْنِ there was a violent collision between two trains

صَداق *n* |صُدُق, أَصْدِقة| dowry, bride's/marriage portion; مُعَجَّل الصَداقِ *the portion of the dowry that is paid at the time of marriage*; مُؤَخَّر \ مُؤَجَّل الصَداقِ *the portion of the dowry that is deferred (in some Muslim countries) as security for the wife in case of divorce*

صَداقة *n* friendship, fellowship, companionship; صَداقة حَميمة a close friendship; عَلاقات صَداقةٍ friendly relations; كانَ على صَداقةٍ to be friends; حَرَصَ على صَداقةِ شَخْصٍ to remain on good terms with sb; أَلْغى الصَداقةَ to unfriend

صَدَقة *n* alms, charity

صَدوق *adj* truthful, veracious

صَديق A *adj* |أَصْدِقاءُ| friendly; قوّة صَديقة a friendly power; مُنْتَجات صَديقة للبيئةِ environmentally friendly products B *n* |أَصْدِقاءُ| 1 [صاحِب] friend, companion; صَديق حَميم \ وَفِيّ a close/true friend; هو صَديقٌ جَيِّدٌ لي he's a good friend of mine; صَديق بالمُراسَلةِ pen pal, penfriend (BrE); مَجْموعة أَصْدِقاءَ a circle of friends; كانَ صَديقاً لِشَخْصٍ to be friends with sb 2 [حَبيب] boyfriend; جاءَتْ مع صَديقِها she came with her boyfriend

صِدّيق *adj* truthful, veracious; الصِدّيق the Truthful (*epithet of caliph Abu Bakr*)

صَديقة *n* 1 [صاحِبة] (female) friend 2 [حَبيبة] girlfriend

تَصْديق *n* 1 [مُصادَقة] legalization, ratification; attestation, certification, authentication; approval, sanctioning; التَصْديق على مُعاهَدةِ ماسْتْريخْت the ratification of the Maastricht Treaty 2 [كَلامِ شَخْصٍ] belief, faith, trust, credence; عَدَم التَصْديقِ disbelief; سَريع التَصْديقِ credulous, naive

مُصادَقة *n* legalization, ratification, certification; approval

مِصْداق *n* confirmation, corroboration; touchstone, criterion; مِصْداقاً illustrating, proof of

مِصْداقيّة *n* credibility; شَخْص ذو مِصْداقيّةٍ a credible person; ضَعيف \ عَديم \ فاقِد المِصْداقيّةِ not credible; فَقَدَ مِصْداقيّتَهُ to lose one's credibility; اِفْتَقَرَ \ اِفْتَقَدَ إلى المِصْداقيّةِ to lack/lose credibility

مُصَدَّق *adj* 1 [مَوْثوق بِهِ] credible, reliable 2 [مُوَثَّق] legalized, ratified; attested, certified, authenticated; sanctioned, approved; وَثيقة مُصَدَّق عَلَيْها a legalized document

مُصادَمة *n* clash, skirmish; collision, impact; وَقعَت مُصادَماتٌ عَنيفةٌ بين المُتَظاهِرينَ والجَيْشِ violent clashes took place between demonstrators and the army

صَدِيَ *v* |a; صَدًى| to be/become very thirsty

صَدّى *v* to echo, to reverberate, to resound

أَصْدى *v* to echo, to reverberate, to resound

تَصَدّى *v* |لِ| to resist, to oppose; to fight, to combat; تَصَدّى للاسْتِغْلالِ \ للإجْرامِ to fight abuse/crime; تَصَدّى للتَبْذيرِ to combat waste

صَدًى *n* echo, reverberation, resonance; أَصْداء الحَرْبِ the repercussions of the war; تَخْطيط الصَدى an ultrasound; كانَ لَهُ صَدًى to have repercussions; وَجَدَ صَدًى طَيِّباً to get positive feedback; لَقِيَ صَدًى واسِعاً في وَسائِلِ الإعْلامِ to resonate widely in the media; أَحْدَثَ صَدًى لدى الرَأْيِ العامِّ to be well received by the public opinion; أَحْدَثَ الاقْتِراحُ صَدًى the proposal was well received

تَصَدٍّ *n* |تَصَدِّيات| resistance; confrontation

صِرْبِيّ [A] *adj* |صِرْبِيّونَ| Serbian

[B] *n* |صِرْب ,صِرْبِيّونَ| Serb

صِرْبِيا *n* Serbia

صَرُحَ *v* |u; صَراحة| [1] [كانَ صادِقاً] to be frank/candid [2] [وَضَحَ] to be clear; to be explicit

صَرَّحَ *v* [1] [أَعْلَنَ] to declare, to state, to announce, to proclaim; صَرَّحَ أنّ \ بِأنَّ ... to declare that ...; صَرَّحَ بِنَواياهُ to announce one's intentions [2] [أَوْضَحَ] to make clear; to make explicit; صَرَّحَ بِدَوافِعِهِ to make one's motives clear [3] [سَمَحَ] to permit, to allow

صارَحَ *v* [1] [أَعْلَنَ] to talk/speak frankly/openly; to confess; صارَحَ بِشَيْءٍ to openly admit sth; صارَحَها بِحُبِّهِ لَها he declared his love for her [2] [وَضَحَ] to be clear; to be explicit

صَرْح *n* |صُروح| edifice, skyscraper, high-rise; بَنى صُروحاً من الوَرَقِ \ في الهَواءِ to build castles in the air

صُراح *adj* pure, clear; قَوْل صُراح a clear statement

صَراحة *n* honesty, sincerity; frankness, candour; open-heartedness; بِصَراحةٍ frankly; بِكُلِّ صَراحةٍ in all honesty; قالَ لِشَخْصٍ الحَقيقةَ بِصَراحةٍ to tell sb the whole truth اعْتَرَفَ بِشَيْءٍ بِصَراحةٍ to admit sth frankly;

صَريح *adj* |صُرَحاءُ ,صَرائِحُ| [1] [صادِق] honest, sincere; frank, candid, open, straightforward; open-hearted; جَواب صَريح an honest answer; حِوار صَريح a candid conversation [2] [واضِح] explicit, specific, distinct; downright; مُوافَقة صَريحة explicit approval; انْتِهاك صَريح a flagrant violation; مَنْع صَريح an explicit ban; بالإشارةِ الصَريحةِ إلى with specific reference to

تَصْريح *n* |تَصْريحات ,تَصاريحُ| [1] [إقْرار] declaration, statement; announcement, proclamation, notice; تَصْريح ضَريبيّ tax return; تَصْريح صُحُفيّ press release; تَصْريح وِزاريّ government policy statement; التَصْريح الدُوَليّ لِحُقوقِ الإنْسانِ the Universal Declaration of Human Rights [2] [رُخْصة] licence, permit; تَصْريح إقامةٍ residence permit; أَصْدَرَ \ سَحَبَ تَصْريحاً to issue/withdraw a permit

مُصارَحة *n* honesty, sincerity; frankness, candour; open-heartedness

مُصَرَّح *adj* permitted, allowed; licensed; مُظاهَرة غَيْر مُصَرَّحٍ بها an illegal demonstration

صَرَخَ *v* |u; صُراخ ,صَريخ| to shout, to scream, to yell, to cry out; صَرَخَ أنّ ... to shout that ...; صَرَخَ صَرْخةً to give a cry; صَرَخَ من شِدّةِ الأَلَمِ to scream with pain; صَرَخَ في وَجْهِ شَخْصٍ to shout in sb's face

اسْتَصْرَخَ *v* to call (out) for help

صارِخ *adj* loud, noisy; glaring, shrill, piercing, sharp; flagrant; أَلْوان صارِخة glaring colours; نَقْص صارِخ في شَيْءٍ a huge deficit in sth; انْتِهاك صارِخ لِحُقوقِ الإنْسانِ a flagrant violation of human rights; تَناقَضَ \ تَعارَضَ بِشَكْلٍ صارِخٍ مع شَيْءٍ to contrast/conflict sharply with sth

صاروخ *n* |صَواريخُ| [1] (Mil, Aerosp) missile, rocket; صاروخ نَوَوِيّ nuclear missile; صاروخ إطْلاقٍ launcher; صاروخ بَعيد \ قَصير المَدى short/long-range missiles; صاروخ كُروز cruise missile; صاروخ عابِر للقارّاتِ intercontinental missiles; صاروخ مُضادّ للطائِراتِ anti-aircraft missile; أَطْلَقَ صَواريخَ على مَدينةٍ

to launch rockets at a city; فَكَّكَ صَوارِيخَ نَوَوِيَّةً to dismantle nuclear weapons **2** [مُفَرْقَعة] firecracker

صاروخيّ *adj* missile (*before n*), rocket (*before n*); هُجوم صاروخيّ missile attack

صُراخ *n* scream, shout, cry, shriek; صُراخ حادّ a piercing shriek

صَرْخة *n* |صَرَخات| scream, shout, cry, yell; صَرْخة مَكْتومة a stifled scream; صَرْخة فَزَعٍ a cry of fear; صَرَخَ \ أَطْلَقَ صَرْخةً to let out a yell

صَرْد *n* intense cold

صُرّاد *n* cirrus (cloud)

صَرَّ *v* |i; صَرير, صَرّ| to chirp, to chirrup; to grind, to gnash; to creak; to whistle, to howl (*wind*); صَرَّ ب \ على أَسْنانِهِ to grind one's teeth; يَصِرُّ البابُ \ السَّرِيرُ the door/bed creaks

أَصَرَّ *v* |على| to insist (in/on), to persist (in); to assert; أَصَرَّ على سَعْيِهِ to persist in one's pursuit; أَصَرَّ على مَطالِبِهِ to hold to one's demands; أَصَرَّ على التَّدْخِين to keep smoking; أَصَرَّ على إرادَتِهِ to impose one's will; أَصَرَّ على أَنَّهُ لا يَعْرِفُ شَيْئاً to insist that one doesn't know anything; يُصِرُّ على أَنّ ... he insists that ...

صَرّار *n* cricket; صَرّار اللَّيْلِ cricket; يَصِرُّ الصَّرّارُ crickets chirp

صُرّة *n* |صُرَر| **1** [رُزْمة] bundle; money bag, pouch, purse **2** (*Hist*) pouch with money (*for the poor people in Mecca and Medina during the Hajj*)

صَرير *n* **1** (*Med*) croup **2** [حَشَرة] chirping; creaking, squeaking, screeching; صَرير خَفيف \ مُخيف a light/ominous creaking

إصْرار *n* insistence, determination, persistence; إصْرار على شَيْءٍ insistence on sth; مع سَبْقِ الإصْرار (والتَّرَصُّدِ) premeditated; زَعَمَ \ تَشَبَّثَ \ رَفَضَ بِإصْرارٍ to doggedly insist/persist/refuse

مُصَرّ *n* turban

مُصِرّ *adj* persistent, persevering, insistent, determined; كانَ مُصِرًّا على شَيْءٍ to be insistent on sth

صَرْصَرَ *v* |i; صَرْصَرة| to chirp; to screech, to squeak

صَرْصَر *adj* ريح صَرْصَر icy gale

صُرْصور, صَرْصار *n* |صَراصيرُ| cockroach

صِراط *n* |صُرُط| path, road; way, route; الصِراط المُسْتَقيم the path of righteousness, the straight and narrow

صَرَعَ *v* |a; مَصْرَع, صِرْع, صَرْع| to bring/strike down, to crush; صَرَعَ خَصْماً to bring down an opponent; صَرَعَهُ هذا الخَبَرُ he was shattered by the news; صُرِعَ to be epileptic; to have an epileptic fit

صارَعَ *v* to fight (with), to struggle (against); to wrestle; صارَعَ من أَجْلِ البَقاءِ to fight to survive; صارَعَ المَوْتَ to struggle with death

تَصارَعَ *v* to fight/wrestle each other, to struggle (with each other); تَصارَعَ على السُّلْطةِ to wrestle for power

اصْطَرَعَ *v* to struggle, to clash, to be in conflict

صَرْع *n* epilepsy; نَوْبة صَرْعٍ an epileptic fit; عِلاج \ مُعالَجة الصَّرْعِ the treatment of epilepsy; مُصاب بالصَّرْعِ epileptic; شَخْص مُصاب بالصَّرْعِ epileptic

صِراع *n* |صِراعات| struggle, fight, battle; conflict; combat; صِراع عَقائِديّ ideological conflict; صِراع طَبَقيّ \ طَبَقاتٍ class struggle; صِراع البَقاءِ the struggle for survival; صِراع (بين) الخَيْرِ والشَّرِّ the battle between good and evil; الصِراع على السُّلْطةِ power struggle; مَسْرَح صِراعٍ battle scene; كانَ في صِراعٍ نَفْسيٍّ \ مع نَفْسِهِ to have an inner conflict; اشْتَبَكوا في صِراعٍ عَنيفٍ they were engaged in violent combat

صَرْعة *n* |صَرَعات| style, fashion, look; trend, fad; صَرْعة جَديدة a new trend

صَرْعيّ *adj* epileptic; نَوْبة صَرْعيّة an epileptic fit

صَريع *adj* |صَرْعى| **1** [مَصْروع] overcome, stricken; سَقَطَ صَريعَ مَرَضٍ to be stricken with a disease **2** (*Med*) epileptic

اصْطِراع *n* struggle, clash, conflict

مُصارِع **A** *adj* fighting; رَدَّ مُصارِعاً fighting back **B** *n* **1** (*Sport*) wrestler **2** [مُقاتِل] fighter, combatant, champion; مُصارِعُ ثيرانٍ bullfighter

مُصارَعة *n* wrestling, fight; مُصارَعة حُرّة freestyle wrestling; مُصارَعة رومانيّة Graeco-Roman wrestling; مُصارَعة ثيرانٍ bullfight

مِصْراع *n* |مَصاريعُ| **1** [البابِ] blinds, shutter; door panel; فَتَحَ البابَ على مِصْراعَيْهِ to open the door wide **2** (*Literat*) hemistich

مَصْرَع *n* |مَصارِعُ| death; لَقِيَ مَصْرَعَهُ to die; أَدّى الاشْتِباكُ إلى مَصْرَعِ شَخْصَيْن the fighting led to the death of two people

مَصْروع *adj, n* epileptic

صَرَفَ *v* |i; صَرْف| ⟨1⟩ [أَنْفَقَ] to spend, to expend; صَرَفَ مالاً to spend money; صَرَفَ وَقْتاً على شَيْءٍ \ شَخْصٍ to spend time on sth/sb ⟨2⟩ [بَدَّلَ نُقوداً] to change, to exchange; صَرَفَ دَنانيرَ إلى دولارات to change dinars into dollars; صَرَفَ شيكاً to cash a cheque ⟨3⟩ [فَصَلَ] to dismiss, to discharge, to send away; صَرَفَ تِلْميذاً عن الفَصْلِ to dismiss a student from class ⟨4⟩ [أَلْهى عن] to turn away/aside, to avert; to give up, to abandon; صَرَفَ النَظَرَ عن شَيْءٍ to avert one's eyes from sth; to pay no attention to sth; صَرَفَ النَظَرَ عن بِناءِ مَنْزِلٍ جَديدٍ to decide not to build a new house; صَرَفَ شَخْصاً عن اسْتِعْمالِ العُنْفِ to prevent sb from using violence ⟨5⟩ (Ling) to conjugate; to inflect

صَرَّفَ *v* ⟨1⟩ [أَدارَ الأُمورَ] to manage, to deal with, to arrange; صَرَّفَ الأُمورَ \ الأَعْمالَ to settle the affairs ⟨2⟩ [السائِلَ] to drain; صَرَّفَ الماءَ to drain water ⟨3⟩ [بَدَّلَ] to change, to exchange; صَرَّفَ السائِحُ الدولاراتِ إلى دَراهِمَ the tourist changed dollars to dirhams ⟨4⟩ [بَضائِعَ] to market, to sell ⟨5⟩ (Ling) to conjugate; to inflect

تَصَرَّفَ *v* ⟨1⟩ [سَلَكَ] to act, to behave; to do; تَصَرَّفَ بِسُرْعةٍ to act quickly; تَصَرَّفَ بِطَريقةٍ خاطِئةٍ to behave badly; تَصَرَّفَ تَصَرُّفاً يُثيرُ الشُبْهةَ to act suspiciously; تَصَرَّفَ تَصَرُّفَ الأَبِ to act as a father; تَصَرَّفَ كَما يَحْلو لَهُ to do as one sees fit ⟨2⟩ [بِأَشْياءٍ] |في, ب| to have, to dispose of; to manage, to administer; تَصَرَّفَ في ثَرَواتِ البِلادِ to administer the country's riches

انْصَرَفَ *v* ⟨1⟩ [ذَهَبَ] to go away, to leave, to depart; انْصَرَفَ إلى شَيْءٍ to leave for sth; انْصَرَفَ إلى وَظيفةٍ أُخْرى to switch to a different job; انْصَرَفَ يَشْتَغِلُ في التِجارةِ he went into business ⟨2⟩ [تَحَوَّلَ عَنْهُ] to turn away/aside, to avert; انْصَرَفَ عن شَخْصٍ \ شَيْءٍ to turn away from sb/sth ⟨3⟩ (Gram) to be a triptote

صَرْف *n* ⟨1⟩ (Busn) money-changing, exchange; صَرْفُ العُمْلةِ changing money; سِعْرُ الصَرْفِ exchange rate; آلةُ صَرْفٍ ATM, cash dispenser/machine (BrE) ⟨2⟩ (Ling) conjugation; inflection; عِلْمُ الصَرْفِ morphology; مَمْنوع من الصَرْفِ diptote ⟨3⟩ [إنْفاق] spending; قابِل للصَرْفِ disposable ⟨4⟩ [مَجارٍ] drainage, discharge; صَرْف صِحّيّ sewer, sewage, sanitation; شَبَكةُ الصَرْفِ الصِحّيّ sewer system ⟨5⟩ [إلْهاء] averting, turning away; بِصَرْفِ النَظَرِ عن هذا regardless of that, despite that ⟨6⟩ [كارِثة] |صُروف| adversity, misfortune; صُروفُ الدَهْرِ the vicissitudes of fortune

صِرْف *adj* pure, unmixed, unadulterated; mere, absolute; شَراب صِرْف an unadulterated drink

صَرّاف *n* ⟨1⟩ [في مَصْرِفٍ] cashier, teller; money changer; صَرّاف آلِيّ ATM, cash dispenser/machine (BrE); سَحَبَ نُقوداً من الصَرّافِ الآلِيِّ to withdraw money from an ATM ⟨2⟩ [في المَسْرَحِ] ticket seller/agent; صَرّافُ التَذاكِرِ ticket seller ⟨3⟩ [أَمينُ الخِزانةِ] treasurer, bursar

صِرافة *n* changing, exchanging (*currency*)

صَرْفيّ *adj* morphological

صَريف *n* chirp; squeaking, squealing, screech

صَيْرَفة *n* banking; money-changing

صَيْرَفيّ *n* |صَيارِفة| banker; money changer, cashier

انْصِراف *n* departure

تَصَرُّف *n* |تَصَرُّفات| ⟨1⟩ [سُلوك] behaviour, conduct, action; تَصَرُّف عَدائيّ \ مَقْبول aggressive/acceptable behaviour; تَصَرُّف شاذّ \ غَريب \ غَيْر طَبيعيّ deviant/strange/abnormal behaviour; تَصَرُّف لاإراديّ \ غَيْر مَسْؤولٍ undesirable/irresponsible behaviour; حُرّيّةُ التَصَرُّفِ freedom to do as one pleases; أَساءَ التَصَرُّفَ to misbehave; بَرَّرَ تَصَرُّفَهُ to justify one's behaviour; اسْتَهْجَنَ \ اسْتَنْكَرَ تَصَرُّفاتِ شَخْصٍ to disapprove of sb's actions; يَجِبُ عَلَيْهِ أَنْ يَتَحَمَّلَ تَبِعاتِ تَصَرُّفِهِ he has to bear the consequences of his actions ⟨2⟩ [سُلْطة] disposal; control; تَرْجَمة بِتَصَرُّفٍ a free translation; كانَ الشَيْءُ تحت \ تَصَرُّفِ شَخْصٍ to be at sb's disposal; كانَ تحت وَضَعَ \ جَعَلَ شَيْئاً في تَصَرُّفِهِ to have sth at one's disposal; تحت \ في تَصَرُّفِ شَخْصٍ to place sth at sb's disposal; كانَتْ لَهُ حُرّيّةُ التَصَرُّفِ في أَمْوالِهِ he had the freedom to do what he wants with his money

صارِم *adj* |صَوارِمُ| strict, harsh, severe; stern, serious, unrelenting; إجْراءات صارِمة harsh measures; قَوانين صارِمة strict rules; نِظام صارِم an iron discipline; جَدْوَل (زَمَنيّ) صارِم a tight schedule; سِياسة صارِمة a tough policy; مُعَلِّم صارِم a strict teacher; عِقاب \ حُكْم صارِم a severe punishment/sentence; كَلَّمَ شَخْصاً بِلَهْجةٍ صارِمةٍ to have a serious talk with sb; اتَّخَذَ مَوْقِفاً صارِماً to take an uncompromising stance

صَرامة *n* strictness, harshness, severity; fierceness; بِصَرامةٍ strictly, severely, harshly; عامَلَ شَخْصاً بِصَرامةٍ to be strict with sb; تَعامَلَ مع شَخْصٍ \ شَيْءٍ بِصَرامةٍ to be hard on sb/sth

صَريمة *n* bridle; صَريمة الجَدْيِ honeysuckle

مُنْصَرِم *adj* previous, last; elapsed, gone by; الشَهْر المُنْصَرِم last month

صارٍ *n* |صَوارٍ| mast, pole; صاري العَلَم flagpole

مِصْطَبة *n* see مَسْطَبة

مَصْطول **A** *adj* foolish, silly **B** *n* fool

صَعُبَ *v* |u; صُعوبة| to be/become difficult/hard; يَصْعُبُ عَلَيَّ فَهْمُهُ it's difficult for me to understand; يَصْعُبُ القَوْلُ إنّ ... it is difficult to say (that) ...

صَعَّبَ *v* to complicate, to make difficult/hard; صَعَّبَ البَحْثَ عن شَيْءٍ to make it difficult to search for sth

أَصْعَبَ *v* to complicate, to make more complicate/difficult

تَصَعَّبَ *v* **1** [صَعُبَ] to be/become difficult/hard **2** [صَعَّبَ] to complicate, to make difficult/hard

اسْتَصْعَبَ *v* to find/consider difficult/hard; اسْتَصْعَبَ الرِياضِيّات to find mathematics difficult

صَعْب *adj* |صِعاب| **1** [عَسير] difficult, hard, tough; complicated; مُهِمّة \ قَضية صَعْبة a difficult assignment/issue; امْتِحان صَعْب a hard exam; صَعْب الإرْضاءِ choosy, picky; طَريق صَعْب المُرورِ a difficult road **2** [عُمْلة] hard; عُمْلة صَعْبة hard currency

صُعوبة *n* **1** [تَعَب] difficulty, trouble; effort; مَرَّ بِصُعوبةٍ to progress with difficulty; تَنَفَّس بِصُعوبةٍ to breathe heavily **2** [مُشْكِلة] problem, difficulty; صُعوبات التَعَلُّمِ learning

تَصْريف *n* |تَصاريفُ| **1** [تَفْريغ] drainage, discharge; dumping; تَصْريف النَفْطِ \ المَوادِّ الكيماوِيّةِ the dumping of oil/chemicals; تَصْريف المِياهِ water draining; مِياه التَصْريفِ الصِحّيِّ sewage water; أُنْبوب تَصْريفٍ discharge pipe; قَناة تَصْريفٍ drainage canal; نِظام تَصْريفٍ sewer system **2** (Gram) conjugation, inflection, declension **3** [إدارة] managing, arranging; تَصْريف الشُؤونِ managing the affairs **4** (Busn) marketing

(Idiom) تَصاريف الدَهْرِ the vicissitudes of fortune

مُتَصَرِّف *n* administrator, manager; (provincial) governor

مَصْرِف, مَصْرَف *n* |مَصارِفُ| **1** [بَنْك] bank; المَصْرِف المَرْكَزِيّ the central bank **2** [مَجارٍ] sewer, drain; sewerage; مَصْرِف مَفْتوح an open sewer

مَصْرِفيّ *adj* bank (*before n*), banking (*before n*); بِطاقة مَصْرِفيّة bank card; قَرْض مَصْرِفيّ bank loan; حِساب مَصْرِفيّ bank account; نِظام مَصْرِفيّ banking system

مَصْروف *n* |مَصاريفُ, مَصْروفات| cost; expense, expenditure, outlay; مَصاريف expenses; المَصاريف الثابِتة fixed costs; مَصْروفات الحُكومةِ public expenditure; مَصْروف الجَيْبِ pocket money (BrE), allowance (AmE); بَنْد مَصاريفَ (debit) item, (debit) entry; مُغَطٍّ للمَصاريفِ cost-effective; قائِمة المَصاريفِ expense claim; عَوَّضَ المَصاريفَ to pay expenses; وَفى المَصاريفَ to cover the costs; قَلَّصَ المَصْروفاتِ على شَيْءٍ to reduce the costs of sth; أَنْفَقَ مَصاريفَ الدَعْوى to pay legal costs; ارْتَفَعَتْ قيمةُ المَصْروفاتِ الجارِيةِ current expenditures increased

مُنْصَرِف *adj* **1** [راحِل] departing, outgoing, leaving **2** (Gram) triptotic; غَيْر مُنْصَرِفٍ diptotic **3** [مُنْكَبّ] |إلى| devoted to, dedicated to, committed to; كانَ الكاتِبُ مُنْصَرِفاً إلى تَرْجَمةِ أَعْمالِهِ the writer dedicated himself to translating his work

صَرَمَ *v* |i; صُرْم, صَرْم| to cut off, to sever

صَرُمَ *v* |u; صَرامة| to be/become sharp/keen; to be/become severe/strict

انْصَرَمَ *v* **1** [مَضى] to pass, to elapse, to go by; to expire; انْصَرَمَ العامُ a year has passed **2** [انْقَطَعَ] to be cut off/severed

صُرْم *n* see سُرْم

difficulties; إنَّها تَسْمَعُ \ تَرى بِصُعوبةٍ she has difficulty hearing/seeing; دَرَجة الصُعوبةِ level of difficulty; وَجَدَ صُعوبةً في شَيْءٍ to have difficulty with sth; عانى من الصُعوباتِ to encounter difficulties; واجَهَ صُعوباتٍ في مادّةِ الرِياضيّاتِ to have problems with mathematics; خلَقَ \ تَجاوَزَ صُعوباتٍ to create/overcome difficulties; أَمْر لا يَخْلو من صُعوبةٍ a complicated issue

مَصاعِب *n pl* |dipt| difficulties, problems, hardships, trouble; واجَهَ مَصاعِبَ to face hardships, to have problems

صَعْتَر *n* see زَعْتَر

صَعِدَ *v* |a; صُعود| 1▸ [طَلَعَ] to rise, to ascend; to climb, to mount; صَعِدَ مُنْحَدَراً \ جَبَلاً to climb a slope/mountain; صَعِدَ إلى المِنبَرِ to ascend to the pulpit; صَعِدَ إلى عُلوٍّ قَدْرُهُ عَشَرةُ آلافِ مِتْرٍ to climb to an altitude of ten thousand meters; صَعِدَ الدَرَجَ \ السُلَّمَ to climb the stairs/ladder; صَعِدَ وَهَبَطَ to go up and down; صَعِدَ الدَمُ إلى رَأْسِهِ he got angry; يَصْعَدُ البُخارُ steam is rising 2▸ [إلى وَسيلةِ نَقْلٍ] to get in/on, to board; صَعِدَ إلى طائِرةٍ to board a plane

صَعَّدَ *v* 1▸ [زادَ من الحِدّةِ] to escalate, to intensify, to aggravate; صَعَّدَ المُشْكِلةَ to let the problem escalate 2▸ (Chem) to sublime, to sublimate

أَصْعَدَ *v* to raise, to lift, to elevate

تَصَعَّدَ *v* 1▸ [تَبَخَّرَ] to evaporate, to vaporize, to volatilize 2▸ [زادَ حِدّةً] to escalate

تَصاعَدَ *v* 1▸ [عَلا] to rise, to ascend; to mount, to climb; تَصاعَدَ التَصْفيقُ في القاعةِ applause erupted in the hall; يَتَصاعَدُ الدُخانُ smoke rises 2▸ [زادَ] to increase, to rise, to go up; تَصاعَدَتْ قيمةُ البَيْتِ the value of the house has increased

صاعِد *adj* |صُعَّد, صَواعِدُ| rising, ascending; advancing, proceeding; خَطّ صاعِد an upward path; من الآنِ فَصاعِداً from now on; من القَرْنِ التاسِعِ فَصاعِداً from the ninth century onward

صاعِدة *n* |صَواعِدُ| (Geol) stalagmite

صُعَداء *n* |dipt f| (deep) sigh; تَنَفَّسَ الصُعَداءَ to heave a deep sigh

صُعود *n* climbing, rising, ascent; ascension; صُعوداً وَنُزولاً up and down; خَميس \ عيد الصُعودِ Ascension Day

صَعيد *n* |صُعُد| 1▸ [هَضْبة] highlands, plateau; صَعيد مِصْرَ, الصَعيد Upper Egypt 2▸ [مُسْتَوى] level, plane; area, domain, sphere, field; على صَعيدٍ آخَرَ on the other hand; على الصُعُدِ كافّةً in every respect; على الصَعيدِ الوَطَنيِّ \ الدُوَليِّ at the national/international level; على الصَعيدِ الثَقافيِّ \ السِياسيِّ \ الشَخْصيِّ on the cultural/political/personal level

صَعيديّ A *adj* |صَعايِدة| *relating to Upper Egypt* B *n* |صَعايِدة| *inhabitant of Upper Egypt*

تَصاعُد *n* increase, growth, rise; escalation, mounting; تَصاعُد التَوَتُّرِ escalating tension

تَصاعُديّ *adj* increasing, growing, rising; escalating, ascending; cumulative; بِتَرْتيبٍ تَصاعُديٍّ in ascending order; ضَريبة تَصاعُديّة a progressive tax; في خَطٍّ تَصاعُديٍّ on an upward trajectory

تَصاعُديّة *n* progressiveness; progression

تَصْعيد *n* escalation; تَصْعيد أَزْمةٍ \ نِزاعٍ escalation of a crisis/conflict; تَصْعيد العُنْفِ the escalation of violence

تَصْعيديّ *adj* escalatory; تَصَرُّف تَصْعيديّ escalatory behaviour

مُتَصاعِد *adj* increasing, growing, rising, mounting, escalating; دُخان مُتَصاعِد rising smoke; التَوَتُّر المُتَصاعِد mounting tension; عُنْف مُتَصاعِد ضِدّ الأَجانِبِ increasing violence against foreigners

مِصْعَد *n* |مَصاعِدُ| lift (BrE), elevator (AmE); بِئْر المِصْعَدِ lift shaft; اِسْتَقَلَّ المِصْعَدَ to take the lift; صَعِدَ بالمِصْعَدِ إلى الطابَقِ التاسِعِ to take the lift to the ninth floor

صَعِرَ *v* |a; صَعَر| *to bend the head/neck to one side due to a disease*

صَعَّرَ *v* to have/lift one's nose in the air, to be haughty; وَلا تُصَعِّرْ خَدَّكَ للناسِ swell not thy cheek (for pride) at men

صَعِقَ *v* |a; صَعْق| to stun, to shock; صُعِقَ to be stunned; صَعَقَهُ النَبَأُ the report shocked him; صَعَقَ شَخْصاً بالكَهْرَباءِ to give sb electric shocks

صاعِق *adj* abrupt, sudden, unexpected; shocking, staggering, astounding; هُجوم صاعِق a surprise attack; خَبَر صاعِق shocking news

صاعِقة *n* |صَواعِقُ| lightning, thunderbolt; مانِعة الصَواعِقِ lightning conductor (BrE), lightning rod (AmE); قوّات صاعِقة

commandos; ضَرَبَت الصاعِقةُ البَيْتَ lightning struck the house; أَصابَتْهُ \ ضَرَبَتْهُ الصاعِقةُ he was struck by lightning

صَعْقة *n* shock; أُصيبَ بِصَعْقةٍ كَهْرَبائيّة to get an electric shock

مَصْعوق *adj* thunderstruck, stunned, shocked; مَصْعوق من الصَدْمةِ stunned by the blow

‹ **صَعْلَكة** *n* vagrancy, homelessness; loitering, loafing

صُعْلوك *n* |صَعاليك| tramp, vagrant, vagabond

‹ **صَغَرَ** *v* |u; صَغْر| to be younger than; صَغَرَ أَخاهُ بِسَنةٍ to be a year younger than one's brother

صَغُرَ *v* |u; صَغار| to be/become small, to be/become little; to be younger; صَغُرَ حَجْمُهُ he/it is smaller

صَغَّرَ *v* 1 [خَفَّضَ] to diminish, to reduce; to scale down; صَغَّرَ صورةً to scale down a photograph 2 [حَقَّرَ] to belittle, to degrade, to humiliate, to scorn; صَغَّرَ شَخْصاً to belittle sb 3 (Gram) to form the diminutive (*of a noun*)

أَصْغَرَ *v* to belittle, to degrade, to humiliate, to scorn

تَصاغَرَ *v* to cringe, to lower oneself, to act in a servile manner

اسْتَصْغَرَ *v* to underestimate, to underrate, to undervalue, to depreciate; to trivialize, to downplay; to look down on; اسْتَصْغَرَ هَديّةً to undervalue a gift; اسْتَصْغَرَ آراءَ خَصْمِه to think little of one's opponents' opinions; اسْتَصْغَرَ نَفْسَهُ to feel inferior

صِغر *n* to be small/young; مُنْذُ الصِغَرِ since childhood; العِلْمُ في الصِغَرِ كالنَقْشِ في الحَجَرِ ≈ as the twig is bent so the tree inclines

صاغِر *adj* |صَغَرة, صاغِرونَ| contemptible, despicable; humble, meek, subservient

صَغير A *adj* |صِغار| 1 [الحَجْمِ] small, little, minor, petty; العيد الصَغير the minor feast (*Eid ul-Fitr*); صِغار المُوَظَّفينَ minor officials; هو صَغيرُ القامةِ he's small in stature; كَتَبَ بِخَطٍّ صَغيرٍ to write small 2 [السِنِّ] young, small, little; طِفْل صَغير a small child; هو صَغيرُ السِنِّ he's young

B *n* |صِغار| little/young one; child, young, offspring; الصِغار والكِبار the young and the old; أَنْجَبَ صِغاراً to have young; كانَ لِلقِطّةِ صِغارٌ the cat had kittens

صَغيرة *n* |صَغائِرُ| venial sin (Isl Law); minor transgression

أَصْغَر *adj* |dipt; أَصاغِرُ; f صُغْرى| younger, youngest; smaller, smallest; lesser, minor; أَصاغِرُ (Sport) juniors', youth; آسْيا الصُغْرى Asia Minor, Anatolia; اسْتَقْبَلَ حتّى أَصاغِرَ الطُلاّبِ he accepted even the youngest students

تَصْغير *n* 1 [تَقْليص] making smaller; reduction, reducing; اسْم تَصْغيرٍ (Gram) diminutive 2 (Comput)

مُصَغَّر A *adj* diminished, decreased; miniature, micro-; اسْم مُصَغَّر diminutive; فيلْم مُصَغَّر microfiche, microfilm

B *n* |مُصَغَّرات| miniature; مُصَغَّرات فيلْميّة slides; microfiche, microfilm

‹ **صَغا** *v* |u; صَغْو| to incline, to bend

صَغِيَ *v* |a; صُغيّ| to incline, to bend

أَصْغى *v* |إلى, ل| to listen attentively to; to pay attention to, to heed; أَصْغى إلى شَخْصٍ to listen attentively to sb

صاغٍ *adj* |صاغونَ| attentive; listening; وَجَدَ أُذُناً صاغِيةً to find a sympathetic ear

إصْغاء *n* attention; listening; وَجَدَ إصْغاءً to find a sympathetic ear

‹ **صِفة** *n* see **وصف**

‹ **الصَفا** *n* al-Safa (*a hill in Mecca*)

‹ **صَفاقِس** *n* |dipt f| Sfax (*city in Tunisia*)

‹ **صَفَحَ** *v* |a; صَفْح |عن| to forgive, to pardon; صَفَحَ عن شَخْصٍ to forgive sb

صَفَّحَ *v* 1 [دَرَّعَ] to plate, to overlay; to laminate 2 [عَرَّضَ, وَطَوَّلَ] to flatten, to roll; صَفَّحَ الحَديدَ to flatten iron

صافَحَ *v* 1 [باليَدِ] to shake hands with; صافَحَ شَخْصاً to shake hands with sb 2 [لَمَسَ] to stroke, to brush

تَصَفَّحَ *v* to page/leaf through, to go through/over, to thumb, to skim; to browse, to surf (*the Internet*); تَصَفَّحَ كِتاباً to leaf through a book; تَصَفَّحَ الإنْتَرْنِت to surf the Internet, to browse the Web

تَصافَحَ *v* to shake hands (with); تَصافَحَ الخَصْمانِ the two opponents shook hands

اسْتَصْفَحَ *v* to beg forgiveness/pardon, to apologize

صَفْح *n* forgiveness; pardon, amnesty

صَفْحة *n* |صَفَحات| **1** [صَحيفة] page, leaf, folio; sheet; صَفْحة رِياضيّة \ الرِياضةِ the sports page; في الصَفْحةِ ١٢٣ on page 123; الصَفْحة الرَئيسيّة home page, main page; صَفْحة البِدايةِ home page, start page; في الصَفْحةِ كُلِّها full page; الصَفْحة الأولى front page; احْتَلَّ الصَفَحاتِ الأولى للصُحُفِ to make the front pages; تَرْقيم الصَفَحاتِ pagination; فَتَحَ صَفْحةً جَديدةً, طَوى صَفْحةَ الماضي to turn over a new leaf **2** [سَطْح] front, face; exterior, outside; surface

صَفوح *adj* forgiving, merciful

صَفيح *n* tinplate, tin; عُلْبة من الصَفيحِ a tin box; حَيّ الصَفيحِ slum

صَفيحة *n* |صَفائِحُ| **1** [لِحَفْظِ السَوائِلِ] can, tin; jerrycan, tank; container; صَفيحة بَنْزينٍ a jerrycan of petrol (BrE) gas (AmE) **2** [رَقيقة] plate, sheet; صَفيحة حَديديّة a sheet of iron

صَفيحيّ *adj* tinplated, tinny, tin (*before n*)

تَصَفُّح *n* browsing; بَرْنامَج التَصَفُّحِ (Web) browser

مُتَصَفِّح *n* (Web) browser

مُصافَحة *n* handshake

مُصَفَّح *adj* armoured, ironclad, plated; laminated; عَرَبة \ سَيّارة مُصَفَّحة armoured vehicle

مُصَفَّحة *n* armoured vehicle

صَفَدَ *v* |i; صَفْد| to shackle, to chain; to bind, to tie

صَفَّدَ *v* to shackle, to chain; to bind, to tie

صَفَد *n* |أَصْفاد| handcuff, shackle, chain

صِفاد *n* |أَصْفِدة, صُفُد| handcuff, shackle, chain

¹**صَفَرَ** *v* |i; صَفير| to whistle

صَفَّرَ *v* **1** [أَحْدَثَ صَفيراً] to whistle; صَفَّرَ بِأَصابِعِهِ to whistle through one's fingers; تُصَفِّرُ العَصافيرُ the birds are whistling **2** [أَفْرَغَ] see 2 صفر **3** [صَبَغَ بِاللَوْنِ الأَصْفَرِ] see 3 صفر

صافِرة *n* whistle; صافِرة النِهايةِ (Sport) the final whistle

صَفّارة *n* **1** [أَداة] whistle; صَفّارة الحَكَمِ the referee's whistle; نَفَخَ في صَفّارةٍ to blow a whistle **2** [صَوْت] whistle; siren; صَفّارة البِداية \ النِهايةِ the starting/final whistle; صَفّارة الإِنْذارِ (warning) siren; تَنْطَلِقُ \ تُدَوّي صَفّارةُ الإِنْذارِ the siren sounds

صُفاريّة *n* (Zool) oriole

صَفير *n* **1** [صَوْت] whistling, whistle **2** (Bot) oriole **3** [حَجَر] listed alphabetically

تَصْفير *n* whistling

²**صَفِرَ** *v* |a; صُفور, صَفَر| to be/become empty, to be/become vacant

صَفَّرَ *v* **1** [أَفْرَغَ] to empty, to clear/clean out; to evacuate; صَفَّرَ البَيْتَ من المَتاعِ to remove all the furniture from the house **2** [أَحْدَثَ صَفيراً] see 1 صفر **3** [صَبَغَ بِاللَوْنِ الأَصْفَرِ] see 3 صفر

صِفْر *n* zero; تحت الصِفْرِ below zero; نُقْطة الصِفْرِ scratch, square one; (الحَرارة) حول \ فوق نُقْطةِ الصِفْرِ around/above zero; دَرَجة الصِفْرِ المُطْلَقِ absolute zero; العَوْدة لِحالةِ الصِفْرِ returning to the starting point; خَرَجَ من شَيْءٍ صِفْرَ اليَدَيْنِ to leave empty-handed; ضَغَطَ على رَقْمِ, أَدارَ رَقْمَ الصِفْرِ to dial zero; انْخَفَضَتْ \ هَبَطَتْ دَرَجةُ الحَرارةِ (إلى) الصِفْرِ تحت الصِفْرِ, تَدَنَّتْ دَرَجةُ الحَرارةِ إلى ما دون الصِفْرِ the temperature fell below zero

صِفْريّ *adj* zero; مَجْموع صِفْريّ zero-sum game

³**صَفَّرَ** *v* **1** [صَبَغَ بِاللَوْنِ الأَصْفَرِ] to colour/paint yellow **2** [أَحْدَثَ صَفيراً] see 1 صفر **3** [أَفْرَغَ] see 2 صفر

اصْفَرَّ *v* to be/become yellow; to turn yellow/pale; اصْفَرَّ وَجْهُهُ to turn pale

صُفار *n* **1** [لَوْن أَصْفَر] yellow; صُفار البَيْضِ egg yolk **2** (Med) jaundice; hepatitis

صَفَر *n* **1** (Med) jaundice; hepatitis **2** [شَهْر] see 4 صفر

صُفْر *n* brass

صَفْراء *n* |dipt f| bile, gall

صَفْراويّ *adj* bilious; حَصاة صَفْراويّة gallstone

صُفْرة *n* yellow

أَصْفَر *adj* |dipt; صُفْر| yellow; أَصْفَر فاتِح pale yellow; نُحاس أَصْفَر brass; ضَحْكة صَفْراء a mocking laugh; fake laughter

اصْفِرار *n* turning yellow

مُصْفَرّ *adj* yellowish, yellowed; pale, wan; وَثائِق مُصْفَرّة yellowed papers; وَجْه مُصْفَرّ a pale face

صَفَقَ *v* |i; صَفْق| to slap, to hit, to strike, to cuff; to beat, to bang, to pound; لا تَصْفِق البابَ! don't slam the door!

صَفُقَ *v* |u; صَفاقة| ❶ [كانَ وَقحاً] to be impolite/insolent/impertinent/cheeky ❷ [الثَوْبُ] to be thick/heavy in texture

صَفَّقَ *v* to clap, to applaud; صَفَّقَ بِيَدَيْهِ to clap one's hands; يَدٌ واحِدةٌ لا تُصَفِّقُ two heads are better than one

اصْطَفَقَ *v* to flap; تَصْطَفِقُ الأَشْرِعةُ (في الهَواءِ) the sails are flapping (in the wind)

صِفاق *n* |صُفُق| ❶ (Med) peritoneum ❷ [عَجَلة] inner tube

صَفاقة *n* impoliteness, impertinence, insolence, cheek

صَفْقة *n* |صَفَقات| (Busn) deal, transaction; صَفْقة ماليّة a financial transaction; صَفْقة رابحة \ خاسرة a good/bad deal; عَقَدَ \ أَبْرَمَ صَفْقةً to make a deal, to finalize a deal

صَفيق *adj* |صُفَقاءُ| ❶ [وَقح] impudent ❷ [كَثيف] close-woven, thick, heavy (*of fabric*)

تَصْفيق *n* applause, clapping, ovation; تَصْفيق حارّ \ حادّ a roar of applause; عاصِفة من التَصْفيقِ thunderous applause; حَصَلَ على تَصْفيقٍ to receive applause; اسْتَقْبَلَ شَخْصاً بالتَصْفيقِ to greet sb with applause

صَفَن *n* |أَصْفان| scrotum

صَفا *v* |u; صَفاء, صُفُوّ, صَفْو| to be/become pure/clear; صَفا لِشَخْصٍ to be dedicated to sb; صَفا لَها الجَوُّ she can do as she likes; يَصْفو الجَوُّ the sky's clearing

صَفّى *v* ❶ [نَقّى] to clean, to clarify, to purify ❷ [بَضائِعَ] to liquidate, to settle, to clear; صَفّى شَرِكةً to liquidate a company; صَفّى مَحَلّاً to hold a sale ❸ [خَلَّصَ] to liquidate, to kill ❹ [سَوّى] to settle, to square, to pay; صَفّى الحسابَ to pay the bill; صَفّى خِلافاً \ مَسْأَلةً to settle a dispute/question ❺ [أَزالَ الماءَ] to drain; صَفّى البَطاطِسَ to drain the potatoes ❻ [نَفْط] to refine; to distil ❼ [قَطَّرَ] to filter, to strain; صَفّى القَهْوة to filter coffee

صافى *v* to deal honestly/be sincere with

أَصْفى *v* ❶ [خَلا] to go/do without; أَصْفى من الأَدَبِ to be impolite ❷ [نَقّى] to clean, to purify

تَصافى *v* to deal honestly/be sincere with each other

صَفَر *n* ❶ [شَهْر] Safar (*the second month of the Islamic calendar*) ❷ (Med) see صفر 3

صَفْصاف *n* willow; صَفْصاف مُسْتَحٍ weeping willow

صَفَعَ *v* |a; صَفْع| to slap; to hit, to strike; صَفَعَ شَخْصاً to slap sb

صَفْعة *n* slap, smack; blow; تَلَقّى صَفعةً على الوَجْهِ to get a slap in the face

صَفَّ *v* |u; صَفّ| to arrange, to classify; صَفَّ السَيّارةَ (Levant) to park the car; صَفَّ الحُروفَ to typeset

صَفَّفَ *v* ❶ [الشَعْرَ] to comb; to do (*hair*); صَفَّفَت شَعْرَها she did her hair ❷ [في خَطٍّ] to arrange in a row/straight line

اصْطَفَّ *v* to queue, to form a queue, to stand in line; to be aligned, to be put/arranged in a straight line

صافّة *n* سورة الصافّات Those who set the Ranks (*Sura 37*)

صَفّ *n* |صُفوف| ❶ [طابور] row, line; file, queue (BrE), line (AmE); order, arrangement, array; rank; صَفّ أماميّ front line; في صُفوفٍ مُتَراصّةٍ in close ranks; في الصُفوفِ الأولى in the front ranks; جَلَسَ في الصَفِّ الأَوَّلِ \ الأَخيرِ to sit in the front/back row; في صُفوفِ الشَبابِ among young people; سورة الصَفّ The Ranks (*Sura 6*); ضَمَّ الصُفوفَ to close ranks; سارَ في الصَفِّ to march in line; عَزَّزَ الصُفوفَ to swell the ranks; انْضَمَّ إلى الصَفِّ, أَخَذَ دَوْرَهُ في الصَفِّ to join the queue (BrE), to get in line (AmE); وَقَفَ في الصَفِّ to stand in the queue; عَمِلَ على تَشْتيتِ الصَفِّ العَرَبيِّ to spread discord among the Arabs ❷ [مُسْتَوى دِراسيّ] (ME) class, group, year; الصَفّ الثالِث the third class ❸ (Bio) class

صَفّاف *n* setter, typesetter

صُفّة *n* |صُفَف| ledge

تَصْفيفة *n* haircut; hair style, hairdo, coiffure; تَصْفيفة شَعْرٍ مُنْسَدِلة a down hairdo

مُصْطَفّ *adj* lined up, queued (up); aligned; standing in line/formation

مَصَفّ *n* |مَصافّ| ❶ [مُسْتَوًى] level; category ❷ [صَفّ] rank

مَصْفوف *adj* arranged, orderly; regulated; aligned; done, styled, coiffed (*hair*)

مَصْفوفة *n* (Math) matrix

مُصَفٍّ *n* liquidator, (official) receiver (BrE)

مِصْفاة *n* |مَصافٍ| 1 [غِرْبال] sieve, strainer, screen; filter; مِصْفاة القَهْوة coffee filter; مِصْفاة هَواءٍ air filter 2 [مَصْنَع] refinery; مِصْفاة نَفْطٍ \ بِتْرولٍ an oil refinery

‹ **صَفير** *n* sapphire

‹[1] **تَصَقَّرَ** *v* to practice falconry

صَقْر *n* |صُقور, أَصْقُر| falcon; صَقْر حَوّام buzzard (BrE), hawk (AmE)

تَصَقُّر *n* falconry

‹[2] **صاقور** *n* |صَواقيرُ| axe; hoe, mattock

‹ **صَقِعَ** *v* |a; صَقَع, صَقيع| 1 [الديكُ] to crow (*a rooster*) 2 (Meteorol) صُقِعَتْ to be covered in hoarfrost

صَقَّعَ *v* to be icy/frozen; to freeze

صُقْع *n* |أَصْقاع| 1 [مِنْطَقة] region, area; في كُلِّ أَصْقاعِ العالَمِ all over the world 2 [ناحِية] side; direction; في أَصْقاعٍ مُتَنَوِّعةٍ in different directions

صَقْعة *n* frost; severe cold

صَقيع *n* (glazed) frost, hoarfrost; صَقيع لَيْليّ night frost; عَضّة الصَقيع frostbite; صَقيع على الطَريقِ glazed frost on the road

صَقيعيّ *adj* frosty

مُصَقَّع *adj* frozen (solid)

‹ **صَقَلَ** *v* |u; صَقْل, صِقال| 1 [لَمَّعَ] to polish, to burnish, to shine; صَقَلَ المَعْدِنَ to polish metal 2 (fig) to refine, to polish, to develop, to brush up (on); صَقَلَ مَعْرِفَتَهُ to brush up one's knowledge; صَقَلَ مَواهِبَهُ to develop one's talents

صِقالة *n* |صَقائِلُ| scaffold

صَقيل *adj* |صِقال| polished, burnished; smooth; shiny, glossy; وَرَق صَقيل glossy paper

مَصْقول *adj* polished, burnished; glazed; خَزَف مَصْقول glazed pottery

‹ **صَقْلَب** *n* |صَقالِبة| Slav; الصَقالِبة the Slavs, Slavic peoples

صَقْلَبيّ A *adj* |صَقالِبة| Slavic
B *n* |صَقالِبة| Slav

‹ **صِقِلّيّ** *adj, n* Sicilian

صِقِلّيّة *n* Sicily

اصْطَفى *v* to choose, to select; اصْطَفى اللهُ الأَنْبِياءَ God chose the prophets; اصْطَفى المُديرُ عَدَداً من المُوَظَّفينَ لِإرْسالِهِمْ في بَعْثةٍ the director selected a number of employees for a delegation

صَفْو *n* clarity, purity; عَكَّرَ صَفْوَ العَلاقةِ \ الهُدوءِ to disturb the relationship/peace

صافٍ *adj* 1 [خالِص] pure, clear; bright; ذَهَب صافٍ \ فِضّة صافِية pure gold/silver; أَلْوان صافِية bright colours; هَواء صافٍ clean air; سَماء صافِية a clear sky; صافي بنَوايا صافِيةٍ with sincere intentions; صافٍ مِثْلَ البَلّورِ crystal clear 2 [عَكْس إجْماليّ] net, after tax; رِبْح صافٍ, صافي الأَرْباحِ net profit; الراتِب \ الأُجْرة الصافي(ة) net wages; غَيْر صافٍ gross; وَزْنُهُ الصافي ٢ كغ it weighs two pounds net

صَفاء *n* purity, clarity; صَفاء الذِهْنِ clarity of mind; صَفاء الماءِ water purity

صَفْوة *n* elite; the best/choice part; صَفْوة المُجْتَمَع the elite; انْتَمى إلى الصَفْوةِ to belong to the elite

صَفَويّ *adj, n* Safavid

صَفيّ *adj* |أَصْفِياءُ| clear, pure; sincere; صَديق صَفيّ a true friend

اصْطِفاء *n* selection, choice; الاصْطِفاء الطَبيعيّ natural selection

تَصْفَويّ *adj* radical; definitive; مُؤامَرة تَصْفَويّة a radical conspiracy

تَصْفِية *n* 1 (Busn) payment, settlement; تَصْفِية الحِساباتِ closing accounts 2 (Busn) sale; liquidation; تَصْفِية نِهايةِ المَوْسِمِ end of season sale; بَيْع تَصْفِيةٍ distress sale; قيمة التَصْفِيةِ liquidation value; مَصاريف التَصْفِيةِ liquidation expenses 3 (Sport) elimination, selection; مُباراة تَصْفِيةٍ elimination match 4 [قَتْل] filtering, purification, cleaning, clearing; draining; elimination; تَصْفِية عِرْقيّة ethnic cleansing; تَصْفِية البَحْثِ (Comput) search filter; تَصْفِية (نَتائِجِ) البَحْثِ الآمِنِ (Comput) safe search filter

مُصْطَفى *n* Mustafa (*male given name*)

مُصْطَفًى A *adj* chosen, selected
B *n* [مُحَمَّد] المُصْطَفى the chosen one (*a title of the prophet Muhammad*)

1‹ **صَكَّ** *v* |u; صَكّ| to slap, to strike

اصْطَكَّ *v* to shiver, to tremble, to shake; اصْطَكَّتْ أَسْنانُهُ to chatter one's teeth

2‹ **صَكّ** *n* |صُكوك| document; deed; check; وَقَّعَ صَكَّ الاسْتِسْلامِ to sign the capitulation

‹ **مَصْطَكَى, مُصْطَكَى, مُصْطَكاء** *n* listed alphabetically

‹ **صِل** *v* see وَصَلَ

1‹ **صَلَبَ** *v* |i; صَلْب| to crucify

صَلَّبَ *v* **1** [رَسَمَ إشارةَ الصَليبِ] to cross oneself, to make the sign of the cross **2** [وَضَعَ عَلامةً] to mark, to tick (BrE), to check (AmE) **3** [قَسّى] see صلب 2

صَليب *n* |صُلُب, صُلْبان| **1** [شَكْل] cross; صَليب مَعْقوف swastika; الصَليب الأَحْمَر the Red Cross; عود الصَليبِ (Bot) peony (*Paeonia*); إشارة الصَليبِ the sign of the cross; رَسَمَ إشارةَ الصَليبِ to make the sign of the cross **2** [للتَعْذيب] cross, crucifix; صَليب خَشَبيّ a wooden cross

صَليبيّ **A** *adj* cruciform, cross-shaped; cross (*before n*); حَمْلة صَليبيّة crusade

B *n* crusader

مُتَصالِب *adj* crosswise

مَصْلوب **A** *adj* crucified

B *n* crucifix

2‹ **صَلُبَ, صَلِبَ** *v* |a-u; صَلابة| to be/become hard, to harden

صَلَّبَ *v* **1** [قَسّى] to harden, to stiffen, to solidify **2** [رَسَمَ إشارةَ الصَليبِ \ وَضَعَ عَلامةً] see صلب 1

تَصَلَّبَ *v* to be/become hard, to harden, to stiffen; to be stubborn/obstinate; تَصَلَّبَ في مَوْقِفِه \ رَأْيِه to be inflexible in one's stance/opinion

صالِب *n* (Naut) keel

صَلابة *n* **1** [مَتانة] firmness, soundness; hardness, toughness; stiffness, inflexibility, rigidity; يَتَمَيَّزُ الماسُ بِصَلابةٍ عاليةٍ diamonds are characterized by extreme hardness **2** [صُعوبة] difficulty, toughness, hardness; صَلابة الحَياةِ the toughness of life

صُلْب **A** *adj* |أَصْلاب, أَصْلُب| hard, solid, firm; stiff, rigid; sturdy, robust; بِناء \ إنْشاء صُلْب solid construction; إرادة صُلْبة an iron will; تَمَسُّك صُلْب a firm grip; رَجُل صُلْب a tough man; مَعْدِن صُلْب a solid substance; صُلْب الرَأْيِ stubborn

B *n* |أَصْلاب, أَصْلُب| **1** [فولاذ] steel; صِناعة الحَديدِ والصُلْبِ the iron and steel industry **2** (Anat) lumbar region; backbone, spine; أَلَم الصُلْبِ lumbar pain; الصُلْب الأَشْرَم spina bifida **3** [لُبّ] heart, core, essence; من صُلْبِ الحَياةِ true to life; دَخَلَ في صُلْبِ المَوْضوعِ to get to the heart of the matter **4** [من ذُرِّيَّتِهِ] من صُلْبِهِ of one's own, biological (*offspring, as opposed to adopted*); لَهُ خَمْسَةُ أَطْفالٍ من صُلْبِهِ he has five children of his own

تَصَلُّب *n* **1** [تَجَمُّد] hardening; تَصَلُّب المَواقِفِ hardening of positions; تَصَلُّب المُجْتَمَعِ hardening of society **2** [صَلابة] stiffness, inflexibility, rigidity **3** (Med) sclerosis; تَصَلُّب \ تَكَلُّس (في) الشَرايينِ, شِرْيانيّ arteriosclerosis; تَصَلُّب الشَرايينِ التاجيّةِ coronary atherosclerosis

تَصْليب *n* hardening, solidification; curing

مُتَصَلِّب *adj* stiff, rigid; inflexible, strict; sclerotic; مَوْقِف مُتَصَلِّب a stubborn attitude; قَوانين مُتَصَلِّبة strict rules

‹ **أَصْلَتَ** *v* to draw, to pull out

‹ **صِلة** *n* see وصل

‹ **صُلَّج** *n coll* cocoon

‹ **صَلَحَ, صَلُحَ** *v* |a-u; صَلاح, صَلاحية| **1** [زالَ عَنْهُ الفَسادُ] to be/become correct/right/good; to be/become valid; صَلُحَ الرَجُلُ the man followed the straight path; لم يَصْلُحْ لِشَيْءٍ to be no good for sth **2** [ناسَبَ] to be adequate/sufficient; to be suitable, to fit; صَلَحَ لِشَيْءٍ \ شَخْصٍ to be suitable for sth/sb

صَلَّحَ *v* to repair, to mend, to remedy; صَلَّحَ دَرّاجةً \ راديو to repair a bicycle/radio; صَلَّحَ مَجارِيَ الماءِ to repair the water pipes; صَلَّحَ عَطَباً to remedy a defect; صَلَّحَ سِرْوالاً to mend a pair of trousers

صالَحَ *v* to make peace with; to reconcile; صالَحَ شَخْصاً to make peace with sb

أَصْلَحَ *v* **1** [أَزالَ فَسادَهُ] to repair, to mend, to remedy; to reorganize, to restructure; أَصْلَحَ شَيْئاً to repair sth; أَصْلَحَ سَيّارةً مُعَطَّلةً to repair a broken-down car; أَصْلَحَ نِظامَ

الضمانِ الاجْتِماعيِّ to reform the social security system **2** [أَدْخَلَ تَغْييراتٍ عَلَيْهِ] to reform; to review, to revise; أَصْلَحَ المُجْتَمَعَ to reform society; أَصْلَحَ قانوناً to revise a law **3** [بين الناسِ] to reconcile; أَصْلَحَ بين الزَوْجَيْنِ he reconciled the two spouses

تَصالَحَ *v* to make peace, to become reconciled; to come to terms, to come to an agreement; تَصالَحَ مع شَخْصٍ to become reconciled with sb

اصْطَلَحَ *v* **1** [اِتَّفَقَ |على|] to agree on, to accept, to adopt; اصْطَلَحَ على تَسْمِيةِ شَيْءٍ بِشَيْءٍ to call sth sth; اصْطَلَحَ على تَسْمِيةِ الحَرَكَةِ "فَتْح" the movement was called 'Fatah'; العَصْر الذي أُصْطُلِحَ على تَسْمِيَتِهِ بِعَصْرِ النَهْضةِ the period that has been called the Arabic renaissance **2** [تَصالَحَ] to be reconciled; اصْطَلَحَ الأَعْداءُ the enemies were reconciled

اسْتَصْلَحَ *v* to reclaim, to make arable; to cultivate, to develop; اسْتَصْلَحَ أَراضِيَ to reclaim land

صُلْح *n* reconciliation; صُلْح بين طَرَفَيْنِ مُتَحارِبَيْنِ reconciliation between warring parties; تَوَصَّلَ إلى الصُلْحِ to become reconciled

صالِح **A** *adj* **1** [ساري المَفْعولِ] valid; غَيْر صالِحٍ invalid; false; وَثائِق غَيْر صالِحةٍ invalid documents; حُجَج غَيْر صالِحةٍ spurious arguments; جَواز سَفَرٍ صالِح a valid passport **2** [مُسْتَقيم] righteous, pious; straight, correct, good; الصالِحات good deeds; عَمَل صالِح a good deed; زَوْج صالِح a good husband **3** [مُناسِب] suitable, fit; صالِح للزِراعةِ fit for cultivation; صالِح للأَكْلِ edible; صالِح للشُرْبِ drinkable, potable **B** *n* |صَوالِحُ| **1** interest, advantage; لِ \ في صالِحِ شَيْءٍ \ شَخْصٍ on behalf of sth/sb; الصالِح العامّ the public interest **2** [اسْم شَخْصيّ] Saleh (*male given name*)

صَلاح *n* **1** [اِسْتِقامة] righteousness; correctness, goodness; صَلاح الإدارةِ good management **2** [اسْم شَخْصيّ] Salah (*male given name*)

صَلاح الدين *n* Salah ad-Din, Saladin (*sultan who retook Jerusalem from the Christian crusaders in 1187*)

صَلاحيّة *n* **1** [سُلْطة] competence; power, authority, say; ذو صَلاحيّةٍ decision-making authority; صَلاحيّة اتِّخاذِ القَرارِ authorized; صَلاحيّة مُطْلَقة carte blanche; هو مُطْلَقُ الصَلاحيّةِ he's been given carte blanche; أَعْطى \ مَنَحَ شَخْصاً صَلاحيّةً مُطْلَقةً to give sb carte blanche; مَلَكَ الصَلاحيّةَ لِفِعْلِ شَيْءٍ to be authorized to do sth; خَوَّلَ صَلاحيّاتٍ to grant powers **2** [مَفْعول] validity; legitimacy; صَلاحيّة الأَوْراقِ النَقْديّةِ the validity of bank notes; صَلاحيّة مَحْدودة limited validity; مُدّة \ فَتْرة الصَلاحيّةِ period of validity; shelf-life; مُدّة صَلاحيّةِ جَوازِ سَفَرٍ a passport's period of validity; اِنْتَهَتْ مُدّةُ صَلاحيّتِهِ to expire; جَواز سَفَرٍ مُنْتَهي الصَلاحيّةِ an expired passport; تاريخ الصَلاحيّةِ use-by date, expiration date (AmE); اِنْتَهى \ مَضى تاريخُ الصَلاحيّةِ the use-by date has passed, it's expired (AmE); مَدَّدَ صَلاحيّةَ جَوازِ سَفَرِهِ to have one's passport renewed

صُلْحيّ *adj* conciliatory; arbitration (*before n*)

اسْتِصْلاح *n* |اسْتِصْلاحات| reclamation, cultivation; اسْتِصْلاح أَراضٍ land reclamation

اصْطِلاح *n* |اصْطِلاحات| **1** [مُصْطَلَح] term, technical term; idiom **2** [عُرْف] convention; code

اصْطِلاحيّ *adj* conventional; idiomatic

إصْلاح *n* |إصْلاحات| **1** [إزالة الفَسادِ] repair, mending; restoration; إصْلاح ذاتِ البَيْنِ reconciliation; قابِل للإصْلاحِ repairable, fixable; ضَرَر قابِل للإصْلاحِ repairable damage; لا يُمْكِنُ إصْلاحُهُ irreparable; عَمِلَ على إصْلاحِ سَيّارةٍ to work on a car **2** [إدْخال تَغْييراتٍ] reform, reformation; renewal, renovation; إصْلاحات اجْتِماعيّة \ اقْتِصاديّة \ سِياسيّة social/economic/political reforms; إصْلاحات شامِلة \ راديكاليّة comprehensive/radical reforms; إصْلاح زِراعيّ land reform; إصْلاح التَعْليمِ educational reform; خُطّة إصْلاحٍ a plan for reform; باشَرَ إصْلاحاتٍ to carry out reforms

إصْلاحيّ *adj* reform (*before n*), reformative; corrective; remedial; إجْراءات إصْلاحيّة reform measures

إصْلاحيّة *n* reformatory, reform school

تَصالُح *n* reconciliation

تَصْليح *n* |تَصْليحات| repair; تَصْليحات مُهِمّة \ بَسيطة major/minor repairs; أَعْمال تَصْليحٍ repairs; أَجْرى تَصْليحاتٍ to carry out repairs; لا يُمْكِنُ تَصْليحُهُ irreparable

‹ **صَلْصة** *n* sauce; صَلْصة الصويا soy sauce

‹ **صَلْصَل** *v* |i; صَلْصَلة| to jingle, to rattle; to clink, to clank, to clatter

صَلْصال *n* clay

صَلْصاليّ *adj* clayey, clayish

‹ **صَلِع** *v* |a; صَلَع| to be/go bald; بَدَأَ يَصْلَعُ to start going bald

صَلْعة *n* |صَلَعات| a bald spot/head

أَصْلَع *adj* |dipt; صُلْعان, صُلْع| 1 [لا شَعْرَ لَهُ] bald; رَجُل أَصْلَع a bald man 2 [بَرّاق] shining, flashing

‹ **صلعم** *abbr* PBUH (*abbreviation of* صَلّى اللهُ عَلَيْهِ وَسَلَّمَ *("peace be upon him"), said after the Prophet Muhammad is mentioned)*

‹ **صَلِف** *v* |u; صَلَف| to boast, to brag

صَلِف *adj* |صَلافى; f pl صَلائِفُ| bragging, boastful, pompous

‹ **صَلَّ** *v* |i; صَليل| to rattle, to clatter; to jingle, to tingle, to clang

صِلّ *n* |أَصْلال| cobra; adder

‹ **صالون** *n* listed alphabetically

‹ **صَلّى** *v* 1 [أَقامَ الصَلاةَ] to pray; صَلّى لله to pray to God; صَلّى بالناس to lead the people in prayer; صَلّى صَلاةَ الفَجْرِ to say the morning prayer; صَلّى الجُمْعةَ في المَسْجِدِ to say Friday prayers in the mosque 2 [بارَكَ] to bless; صَلّى اللهُ عَلَيْهِ وَسَلَّمَ peace be upon him (*said after a prophet the Prophet Muhammad is mentioned*)

صَلاة *n* |صَلَوات| prayer; صَلاة الصُبْحِ morning prayer; صَلاة الفَجْرِ morning prayer; صَلاة الظُهْرِ noon prayer; صَلاة العَصْرِ afternoon prayer; صَلاة المَغْرِب sunset prayer; صَلاة العِشاءِ night prayer; صَلاة الجَماعة communal prayer; صَلاة الجُمْعةِ the Friday prayer; الصَلاة الرَبِّيّة \ الرَبّانيّة the Lord's Prayer; صَلّى الصَلاةَ الرَبّانيّةَ to say the Lord's Prayer; أَمَّ الصَلاةَ to lead in prayer; أَذَّنَ للصَلاة to call to prayer; أَدّى \ أَقامَ الصَلاةَ to perform the prayer; حَيَّ على الصَلاةِ! come to prayer!

مُصَلٍّ *n* worshipper, person praying

مُصَلّى *n* |مُصَلَّيات| prayer room

‹ **صِلَّوْر** *n* catfish

‹ **صَلى** *v* |i; صَلْي| to roast, to grill, to broil (AmE); to burn

مُصالَحة *n* conciliation, reconciliation; settlement, arrangement; مُصالَحة وِدّيّة an amicable settlement; سِياسة المُصالَحةِ reconciliation policy

مُصْطَلَح *n* |مُصْطَلَحات| terminology; technical/professional/specialist term; مُصْطَلَحات terminology, nomenclature; مُصْطَلَحات فَنّيّة \ تِقْنيّة technical terms, jargon; مُصْطَلَحات طِبّيّة \ اقْتِصاديّة \ قانونيّة medical/economic/legal terminology

مُصْطَلَحيّ *adj* idiomatic; تَعْبير مُصْطَلَحيّ an idiomatic expression

مُصْلَح *adj* reformed

مُصْلِح *n* 1 [سياسيّ] reformer; مُصْلِح راديكاليّ a radical reformer 2 [فَنّيّ] repairman; مُصْلِح الساعاتِ watchmaker

مُصَلِّح *n* repairman

مَصْلَحة *n* |مَصالِحُ| 1 [إدارة] office, department, service; agency; مَصْلَحة الأَحْوالِ المَدَنيّةِ Register Office (BrE), Country Clerk's Office (AmE); المَصالِح الحُكوميّة the government department; مَصْلَحة الآثارِ المِصْريّة (Egypt) the archaeology department 2 [صالِح] interest; advantage, benefit; مَصْلَحة شَخْصيّة self-interest; المَصْلَحة العامّة the public interest; لِ \ في \ من مَصْلَحةِ شَيْءٍ \ شَخْصٍ for the benefit of sb/sth; من أَجْلِ مَصْلَحَتِك, في مَصْلَحَتِكَ for your own benefit; مَصْلَحة الجَماعةِ the group interest; غَلَّبَ مَصْلَحةَ الجَماعةِ to let the group interest prevail; تَعارُض \ تَضارُب \ تَشابُك a conflict of interests; صاحِب مَصْلَحةٍ the person concerned; المَصالِح وَضَع مَصْلَحة الشَعْبِ فوق كُلِ اعْتِبارٍ to put the interest of the people above everything else; حَسَمَ المُباراةَ لِمَصْلَحَتِهِ to settle the match in one's favor; رَعى مَصالِح شَخْصٍ, دافَعَ عن مَصالِحِ شَخْصٍ to act in sb's interests; خَدَمَ مَصالِحَ شَخْصٍ \ شَيْءٍ to serve sb's interest; كانَتْ لَدَيْهِ مَصْلَحةٌ فيهِ it was to his advantage

مَصْلَحيّ *adj* administrative; governmental, departmental; تَناقُض مَصْلَحيّ an administrative conflict

‹ **صَلُدَ, صَلَدَ** *v* |u; صُلودة, صَلادة| to harden, to stiffen; to be solid/compact

صَلْد *adj* |أَصْلاد| 1 [صُلْب] hard, firm, solid; طَبَقة حَجَريّة صَلْدة a hard stratum 2 [يَتَحَمَّلُ الظُروفَ الشَتَويّةَ] hardy

صَلِيَ *v* |a; صِلِيّ, صَلًى| 1 [كابَدَ] to endure, to bear 2 [النارَ] to be exposed to heat/fire

أَصْلى *v* to heat, to warm; to burn

تَصَلَّى *v* to warm up

اصْطَلى *v* to warm oneself; to get burned; لا يُصْطَلى بنارِهِ extremely brave; invincible

مُصْطَلًى *n* |مُصْطَلَيات| fireplace, hearth

‹ **صَمَتَ** *v* |u; صُموت, صَمْت| to be/become silent, to keep quiet, to shut up; صَمَتَت البَنادِقُ the guns went silent; صَمَتَ دَهْراً وَنَطَقَ كُفْراً *to speak after a long silence only to say something stupid*

صَمَّتَ *v* to silence

أَصْمَتَ *v* to silence

صَمْت *n* silence; صَمْت مُعَبِّر a pregnant silence; غارِق في الصَمْتِ in deep thought; الْتَزَمَ الصَمْتَ to be silent; وَقَفَ دَقيقة صَمْتٍ to observe a minute's silence; كَسَرَ \ قَطَعَ الصَمْتَ to break the silence; يَسودُ الصَمْتُ silence prevails

صامِت A *adj* |صَوامِتُ, صُموت| 1 [ساكت] silent, mute, quiet; مَسيرة \ مُظاهَرة \ اعْتِراض صامِت(ة) a silent march/demonstration/protest; فيلم صامِت a silent film; رَغْبة صامِتة a secret desire; الأَكْثَرِيّة الصامِتة the silent majority; وَقَفَ صامِتاً to stand silent 2 (Ling) voiceless

B *n* |صَوامِتُ| (Ling) consonant

صَموت A *adj* |mf| silent, reserved, reticent, taciturn, uncommunicative; فَتاة صَموت a silent girl

B *n a quiet person*

مُصْمَت *adj* massive, solid; unmixed, pure, unadulterated; plain, unpatterned; الجَرانيت المُصْمَت solid granite

‹ **صِماخ** *n* |أَصْمِخة| auditory canal

‹ **صَمَدَ** *v* |u; صُمود, صَمْد| to resist, to oppose, to withstand; to persevere, to persist; to stand/hold firm, to stand one's ground; to bear, to endure; صَمَدَ في وَجْهِ قوّاتِ العَدوِّ to resist enemy forces; صَمَدَ للعاصِفةِ to withstand the storm; صَمَدَ في المَعْرَكةِ to persevere in battle; صَمَدَ لِامْتِحانِ الزَمَنِ to stand the test of time

صَمَد *n* 1 [دائِم] eternity 2 (Islam) الصَمَد the Eternal (*one of the names of God*)

صامِد *adj* 1 [مَنيع] -proof, resistant; صامِد للماءِ waterproof; صامِد للريحِ والشَمْسِ resistant to the wind and the sun 2 [ثابِت] steadfast

صُمود *n* perseverance, persistence; determination, endurance

‹ **صَمَّغَ** *v* to glue, to stick, to paste

صَمْغ *n* |صُموغ| gum, resin; (tree) sap; glue, adhesive; صَمْغ عَرَبيّ gum arabic, acacia gum; شَجَرة الصَمْغِ gum (tree)

صَمْغيّ *adj* gluey, gummy, sticky

‹1 **صَمَلَ** *v* |u; صَمْل| 1 [تَصَلَّبَ] to be hard/firm 2 [ثابَرَ] to persevere, to persist, to stand firm

صَمْل *n* rigidity, stiffness; صَمْل جيفيّ rigor mortis

‹2 **صَمولة, صامولة** *n* |صَواميلُ, صَوامِلُ| (Tools) nut; صَمولة مُجَنَّحة wing nut; شَدَّ \ فَكَّ صَمولةً to tighten/loosen a nut

‹ **صِمْلاخ, صُمْلوخ** *n* |صَماليخُ| earwax

‹ **صَمَّ** *v* |u; صَمّ| 1 [سَدَّ] to close off/up; to plug; صَمَّ قارورةً to cork a bottle 2 [طَرِشَ] to be/become deaf 3 [تَعَسَّرَ] to be difficult/hard

صَمَّمَ *v* 1 [خَطَّطَ] to design; صَمَّمَ بِناية \ سَفينة \ حَديقة to design a building/ship/park; صَمَّمَ خُطَطاً to draw up plans; صَمَّمَ آلةً to design a machine 2 [عَزَمَ] to be determined/resolved; صَمَّمَ على شَيْءٍ to be determined to do sth 3 [جَعَلَ أَصَمَّ] to deafen, to make deaf

أَصَمَّ *v* 1 [جَعَلَ أَصَمَّ] to deafen, to make deaf; يُصِمُّ الآذانَ deafening; ضَجّة تُصِمُّ الآذانَ a deafening noise 2 [طَرِشَ] to be deaf

تَصامَّ *v* to pretend not to hear, to play deaf, to turn a deaf ear

صَمَم *n* deafness

صَمّ *n* deafness

صِمام *n* |أَصِمّة, صِمامات| 1 [غِطاء] valve; cap, lid, cover, top; plug, stopper; صِمام قَلْبٍ heart valve; صِمام الخُروجِ outlet valve; صِمام أَمانٍ \ أَمْنٍ safety valve; صِمام دولابِ دَرّاجةٍ the valve of a bicycle tube 2 (Elec) صِمام ثُنائيّ diode

صِمامة *n* fuse

صِمّة *n* cork; plug, stopper; صِمّة وَريديّة embolism

صَميم A *adj* true, sincere, genuine

(BrE), mailbox (AmE); postbox (BrE), mailbox (AmE); post office box; صُنْدوق بيرةٍ \ بُرْتُقالٍ \ قَرْنَبيطٍ a crate of beer/oranges/cauliflowers; كَدَّسَ صَناديقَ to pile up crates; تَفْكير خارِجَ الصُنْدوقِ thinking outside the box **2** (Busn) cash box, money box (BrE); fund, treasury; cash register; صُنْدوق التَوْفير savings bank; صُنْدوق النَقْدِ الدُوَليّ the International Monetary Fund, the IMF; أمين صُنْدوقٍ treasurer; cashier; أَدارَ صُنْدوقاً to manage a fund

صِنار *n* plane tree

صِنّارة *n* |صَنانيرُ| **1** [لِصَيْدِ السَمَكِ] hook, fish hook **2** [في المِغْزَلِ] reel, spool

صَنَعَ *v* |a; صِناعة| to manufacture, to produce, to fabricate; to make, to build, to construct; صَنَعَ سَيّاراتٍ to produce cars; صَنَعَ مَلابِسَ to manufacture clothing; صَنَعَ أَسْلِحةً كيماويّةً to produce chemical weapons; صَنَعَ البيرةَ to brew beer; صُنِعَ من الخَشَبِ (to be) made of wood; صُنِعَ في مِصْرَ made in Egypt

صَنَّعَ *v* **1** [بَلَداً] to industrialize **2** [صَنَعَ] to manufacture, to produce, to fabricate; to make, to build, to construct

صانَعَ *v* **1** [تَمَلَّقَ] to flatter **2** [رَشا] to bribe

تَصَنَّعَ *v* **1** [تَكَلَّفَ] to simulate, to pretend, to feign; تَصَنَّعَ الغَضَبَ to pretend to be angry **2** [صارَ صِناعيًّا] to industrialize

اصْطَنَعَ *v* **1** [تَصَنَّعَ] to simulate, to pretend, to feign; اصْطَنَعَ الكَرَمَ to feign hospitality **2** [صَنَعَ] to manufacture, to produce, to fabricate

صُنْع ,صَنْع *n* manufacture, production, making, construction; تاريخ الصُنْعِ year of construction; صُنْعُ الآلاتِ the manufacture of appliances; من صُنْعٍ بَلْجيكيٍّ a product of Belgium; من صُنْعِ الإنْسانِ manmade; من صُنْعِ يَدِهِ of one's (own) making; هذه الزَخْرَفة من صُنْعِ يَدِهِ this decoration is handmade

صانِع **A** *n* |صُنّاع| manufacturer, producer; maker; صانِع الأَلْعابِ (Sport) playmaker; صانِع القَرارِ decision maker **B** *adj* |صُنّاع| manufacturing, producing; الشَرِكات الصانِعة للسَيّاراتِ car manufacturers

B *n* core, heart, innermost; essence, crux; من صَميمِ قَلْبي from the bottom of my heart; دَخَلَ في صَميمِ المَوْضوعِ to get to the heart of the matter

صَميمي *adj* cordial, intimate; علاقة صَميميّة an intimate relationship

أَصَمّ **A** *adj* |dipt; صُمّ ,صُمّان| deaf; أَصَمّ أَبْكَم deaf **B** *n* |dipt; صُمّ ,صُمّان| deaf person

تَصْميم *n* |تَصْميمات ,تَصاميمُ| **1** [مُخَطَّط] plan, sketch; design; تَصْميم أَوَّليّ a preliminary sketch; تَصْميم رَقْصٍ choreography; تَصْميم داخِليّ interior design; تَصْميم مِعْماريّ \ صِناعيّ architectural/industrial design; تَصْميم مَواقِعِ الإنْتَرْنِت Web design; تَصْميم مَدْرَسةٍ جَديدةٍ a design for a new school; تَصْميم الكُرْسيّ رائِعٌ the design of the chair is excellent; وَضَعَ تَصْميماً to make a design **2** [رَسْم] design, pattern, motif; تَصْميم بَسيط a simple design **3** [عَزْم] determination, resolution; persistence, perseverance

مُصَمِّم **A** *adj* determined, resolved, resolute; كانَ مُصَمِّماً على شَيْءٍ to be set on sth; كانَ مُصَمِّماً على تَنْفيذِ الخُطّةِ to be determined to carry out a plan **B** *n* designer, planner; stylist; مُصَمِّم رَقْصٍ choreographer; مُصَمِّم أَزْياءٍ fashion designer; مُصَمِّم مَواقِعِ الإنْتَرْنِت Web designer

صُنْبور *n* |صَنابيرُ| tap, spigot, faucet (AmE); ماء من الصُنْبورِ tap water; فَتَحَ \ أَغْلَقَ الصُنْبورَ to turn on/off the tap

تَصَنَّتَ *v* |على| to listen in (to)

صَنْج *n* |صُنوج| (Mus) cymbal; gong

صَنّاجات *n pl* castanets

صِنْديد **A** *adj* |صَناديدُ| brave, courageous; adventurous; fearless **B** *n* |صَناديدُ| leader; hero

صَنْدَل *n* **1** [حِذاء مَفْتوح] |صَنادِلُ| sandal; لَبِسَ صَنْدَلاً to wear sandals **2** [سَفينة] barge, flatboat **3** (Bot) sandalwood; خَشَب الصَنْدَلِ sandalwood

صُنْدوق ,صَنْدوق *n* |صَناديقُ| **1** [عُلْبة] box, case; crate; الصُنْدوق الأَسْوَد the black box; صُنْدوق ,صُنْدوق سَيّارةٍ boot (BrE), trunk (AmE); خَلْفيّ صُنْدوق الشاحِنةِ loading platform; صُنْدوق مُصَوِّت sound box; صُنْدوق بَريدٍ letterbox

صَنائِعيّ A *adj* artisanal

B *n* artisan, craftsman

صَنّاع *adj* skilled, dexterous

صِناعة *n* |صَنائِعُ, صِناعات| 1 [تَرْكيب] manufacture, production; صِناعة النَفْطِ oil production 2 [قِطاع اقْتِصاديّ] industry; trade, craft; التِجارة والصِناعة trade and industry; صِناعة ثَقيلة \ خَفيفة heavy/light industry; صِناعة مُزْدَهِرة \ رائِجة a flourishing industry; صِناعات تَقْليديّة traditional crafts; صِناعات تَحْويليّة processing industries; صِناعة سِياحيّة \ سينَما tourist/film industry; صِناعة الإعْلانِ the advertising industry; صِناعة الإلِكْترونيّاتِ the electronics industry; صِناعة السَيّاراتِ the car industry

صِناعيّ *adj* 1 [مَنْسوب إلى الصِناعةِ] industrial; القِطاع الصِناعيّ the industrial sector; مِنْطَقة \ دَوْلة صِناعيّة an industrialized zone/country; مَجْموعة الدُوَلِ الصِناعيّةِ السَبْعِ the group of seven wealthiest industrialized nations, the G-7; ما بعد الصِناعيِّ post-industrial 2 [غَيْر طَبيعيّ] artificial; synthetic; imitation, fake; قَمَر صِناعيّ satellite; زَهْرة صِناعيّة artificial flower

صَنْعاء *n* listed alphabetically

صَنْعة *n* trade, craft, workmanship; صاحِب صَنْعةٍ craftsman; سِرّ الصَنْعةِ trade secret; تَعَلَّمَ صَنْعةً to learn a trade

صَنيع A *adj* produced, manufactured, made

B *n* 1 [عَمَل] deed, act, action 2 [حَسَنة] a good deed 3 [نَتيجة] product, result, outcome; هذا صَنيعُ الاسْتِعْمارِ this is the result of colonialism

صَنيعة *n* |صَنائِعُ| 1 [أَداة (في يَدِ شَخْصٍ إلخ)] creature, (willing) tool, puppet; صَنيعة الاسْتِعْمارِ a tool of colonialism 2 [حَسَنة] a good deed

اصْطِناعيّ *adj* artificial, synthetic, man-made; تَلْقيح اصْطِناعيّ artificial insemination; ذَكاء اصْطِناعيّ artificial intelligence, AI; مَوادّ اصْطِناعيّة synthetics

تَصَنُّع *n* 1 [تَكَلُّف] show, theatrics, dramatics, affectation; artificiality, dissimulation 2 [البَلَد] industrialization

تَصْنيع *n* 1 [صِناعة] manufacture, fabrication, production; processing; تَصْنيع الأَسْلِحةِ النَوَويّة the production of nuclear weapons; إعادة تَصْنيعِ النُفاياتِ recycling waste 2 [نَشْر الصِناعةِ] industrialization

تَصْنيعيّ *adj* industrial, industrialization (*before n*); سِياسة تَصْنيعيّة industrial policy

مُتَصَنِّع *adj* affected, unnatural, artificial; غَيْر مُتَصَنِّعٍ unfeigned

مُصْطَنَع *adj* 1 [مُتَكَلَّف] forced, affected, unnatural; كَلام مُصْطَنَع affected language; ابْتِسامة \ ضَحْكة مُصْطَنَعة a forced smile/laugh 2 [غَيْر طَبيعيّ] fabricated, synthetic 3 [مُقَلَّد] imitated, copied, duplicated; مِفْتاح مُصْطَنَع duplicate key

مُصْطَنِع *adj* artificial, fake; شَخْص مُصْطَنِع an artificial person

مَصْنَع *n* |مَصانِعُ| factory, industrial plant; صاحِب مَصْنَعٍ manufacturer, factory owner; مَصْنَع السُكَّرِ sugar factory; مَصْنَع سَيّاراتٍ car factory; مَصْنَع المُسْتَحْضَراتِ الصَيْدَليّةِ a pharmaceutical factory; سِعْر خارِجَ المَصْنَعِ price ex factory; أَنْشَأَ \ بَنى مَصْنَعاً to build a factory

مُصَنَّع A *adj* processed, manufactured

B *n* raw material

مَصْنوع *adj* made, manufactured, produced; مَصْنوعات (industrial) products; مَصْنوع باليَدِ handmade; مَصْنوع من الخَشَبِ made of wood; مادّة نِصْف مَصْنوعةٍ semi-finished products

‹ **صَنْعاء** *n* |dipt f| Sana'a (*capital of Yemen*)

‹ **صَنَّفَ** *v* 1 [بَوَّبَ] to order, to sort, to arrange; to class, to classify, to categorize, to group; صَنَّفَ شَيْئاً على أَنَّهُ ... to consider sth to be ...; صَنَّفَ المَنْتوجاتِ to classify products; صَنَّفَ النَباتاتِ \ الحَيَواناتِ to identify plants/animals; صَنَّفَ شَيْئاً حَسَبَ الحَجْمِ to arrange sth in order of size; صَنَّفَ سَيّارةً في القِطاعِ المُتَوَسِّطِ to classify a car as medium-sized; صُنِّفَ في خانةِ \ عِدادِ ... to be included in ...; to be considered part of ...; تُصَنَّفُ هذه الأَنْواعُ في عِدادِ الحَيَواناتِ المُهَدَّدةِ بالانْقِراضِ these species are considered endangered 2 [أَلَّفَ] to compile, to compose, to write 3 (Comput) to compile

صِنْف, صَنْف *n* |صُنوف, أَصْناف| class, category; type, kind; species, variety; صِنْف من التِبْغ a type of tobacco; من صِنْفٍ

صُهارة *n* (Geol) magma

صِهْرة *n* sister-in-law (*one's brother's wife*)

صَهيرة *n* (Elec) fuse

انْصِهار *n* |انْصِهارات| fusion; melting; انْصِهار نوى ذَرِّيَّةٍ nuclear fusion; دَرَجة \ انْصِهار الحَضاراتِ the fusion of cultures; نُقْطة انْصِهارٍ melting point

مُصاهَرة *n* kinship/relationship through marriage; affinity, alliance

مَصْهَر *n* |مَصاهِرُ| foundry, furnace

مِصْهَر *n* |مِصْهَرات| (Elec) fuse

‹ صِهْريج *n* |صَهاريجُ| reservoir, container, tank; cistern; صِهْريج الماءِ water reservoir; شاحِنة صِهْريجٍ tanker (*vehicle*); سَفينة صِهْريجٍ tanker (*boat*)

‹ صَهَلَ *v* |a-i; صَهيل| to whinny, to neigh; يَصْهَلُ الفَرَسُ horses whinny

صَهيل *n* whinny, neigh

‹ صَهْوة *n* |صِهاء, صَهَوات| horseback

‹ صَهْيونيّ **A** *adj* |صَهْيونيّون, صَهْيون| Zionist; الدَوْلة الصَهْيونيّة the Zionist state

B *n* |صَهْيونيّون, صَهْيون| Zionist

صَهْيونيّة *n* Zionism

مُتَصَهْيِن *n* Zionist sympathizer

‹ صابَ *v* |u; صَيْبوبة, صَوْب| to be right/correct

صَوَّبَ *v* **1** [وَجَّهَ] to aim; to direct, to focus; صَوَّبَ اهْتِمامَهُ إلى شَخْصٍ to focus one's attention on sb; صَوَّبَ نحو لَوْحةِ رِمايةٍ to aim at a target; صَوَّبَ البُنْدُقيّةَ نحو شَخْصٍ \ شَيْءٍ to aim the gun at sb/sth **2** [صَحَّحَ] to correct, to rectify; صَوَّبَ أخْطاءَهُ to correct one's mistakes

أصابَ *v* **1** [هَدَفاً] to hit, to strike; أصابَ شَيْئاً \ شَخْصاً to hit sth/sb; أصابَ مُرادَهُ to achieve one's goal; أصابَ البَرْقُ الشَجَرةَ lightning struck the tree **2** [بِجَراحٍ] to injure; to afflict; أصابَ شَخْصاً to injure sb; أصابَ نَفْسَهُ to injure oneself; أُصيبَ بـ ... to be injured by; to be struck with; to be afflicted with, to suffer from; أُصيبَ بِزُكامٍ to catch a cold; أُصيبَ بِكارِثةٍ to be struck by disaster; أُصيبَ بِمَرَضٍ \ بِسَكْتةٍ to be struck by a disease/stroke; أُصيبَ بِمَرَضٍ في كَبِدِهِ

وَضَعَ شَيْئاً ضِمْنَ صِنْفٍ مُحَدَّدٍ to place sth in a specific category واحِدٍ of the same kind;

تَصْنيف *n* **1** [تَبْويب] |تَصْنيفات| classification, division; sorting, arrangement; تَصْنيف حَسَبَ ... a division into ... **2** [صَنْف] |تَصْنيفات| category; وَضَعَ في تَصْنيفاتٍ to categorize **3** (Sport) |تَصْنيفات| league table, ranking **4** [أَدَبيّ] |تَصانيفُ| work, writing

تَصْنيفيّ *adj* typological; taxonomic; مَرْتَبة تَصْنيفيّة taxonomic rank

مُصَنَّف *n* |مُصَنَّفات| **1** [مُخْتارات] corpus, compilation **2** [كِتاب] book

مُصَنِّف *n* artist; cook

‹ صَنْفَرَ *v* |i; صَنْفَرة| to sand

صَنْفَرة *n* وَرَق الصَنْفَرةِ sandpaper, emery paper

مُصَنْفَر *adj* frosted

‹ صَنَم *n* |أصْنام| idol, image

تَصْنيم *n* idolization

‹ صِنْو *n* |أصْناء, صِنْوان| image, likeness; duplicate, twin, double; الوَلَدُ صِنْوُ أبيهِ the boy is the spitting image of his father

‹ صَنَوْبَر *n* pine (tree); إبْرة صَنَوْبَرٍ pine-needle; كوز \ حَبّة صَنَوْبَرٍ pine cone/nut; خَشَب صَنَوْبَرٍ pine, pinewood

صَنَوْبَريّة *n* (Bot) conifer; من فَصيلةِ الصَنَوْبَريّاتِ coniferous

‹ صَهْ *excl* hush

‹ أصْهَب *adj* |dipt; صُهْب| reddish, ginger

‹ صَهَد *n* heat; blaze

‹ صَهَرَ *v* |a; صَهْر| to forge, to melt, to fuse; صَهَرَ الرَصاصَ to melt lead

صاهَرَ *v* to become related by marriage; to marry into; صاهَرَ شَخْصاً to become related to sb by marriage

أصْهَرَ *v* |إلى| to become related by marriage to; to marry into; أصْهَرَ إلى شَخْصٍ to become related to sb by marriage

تَصاهَرَ *v* to become related by marriage

انْصَهَرَ *v* to melt, to liquefy; to be forged/fused/be melted

صِهْر *n* |أصْهار| **1** [زَوْج الأُخْتِ] brother-in-law (*one's sister's husband*); أصْهار in-laws **2** [زَوْج الإبْنة] son-in-law

إصابة وِراثيّة a hereditary disease; إصابة عَمَلٍ a work injury; تَعَرَّض لِإصابةٍ في الرُكْبةِ اليُسْرى to sustain an injury to one's right knee

تَصْويب *n* |تَصْويبات| 1 [تَصْحيح] correction, rectification; تَصْويب بَسيط a small correction 2 [تَوْجيه] aiming, directing; أداة التَصْويبِ sights *(of a weapon)*

مُصاب A *adj* 1 [أُصيبَ] stricken, afflicted; infected, contaminated; كانَ مُصاباً بِمَرَضٍ to be afflicted with a disease 2 injured, hurt; لاعِب مُصاب an injured player B *n* 1 [مُصيبة] disaster, calamity, catastrophe; لَحِقَهُ مُصابٌ he was struck by disaster; جَبَرَ اللهُ مُصابَكَ may God ease your suffering *(an expression of sympathy, especially on the occasion of the death of a loved one)* 2 [شَخْص] injured/wounded person, casualty; عَدَد المُصابينَ the number of casualties

مُصَوَّب *adj* aimed, pointed, directed

مُصيب *adj* accurate, correct, right; طَلْقة مُصيبة an accurate shot; كانَ مُصيباً في قَوْلِهِ to be accurate in one's statement

مُصيبة *n* |مَصائِبُ, مُصيبات| accident, misfortune, misery; catastrophe, disaster; calamity; مُصيبة قَوْميّة a national disaster; مَصائِبُ قَوْمٍ عند قَوْمٍ فَوائِدُ one man's misery is another man's fortune; أَيّةُ مُصيبةٍ هذه؟ what kind of disaster is this?

صات *v* |u; صَوْت| to tinkle, to jingle; to sound, to resound; يَصوتُ الجَرَسُ the bell rings

صَوَّتَ *v* 1 [اِقْتَرَعَ] to vote, to cast a vote; صَوَّتَ لِصالِحِ شَخْصٍ \ تَأْييداً لِشَخْصٍ to vote in favour of sb; صَوَّتَ لِحِزْبٍ to vote for a party; صَوَّتَ على \ ضِدّ شَيْءٍ to vote on/against sth; صَوَّتَ على \ ضِدّ الاقْتِراحِ to vote on/against the proposal; صَوَّتَ لليَساريّين \ لِصالِحِ اليَساريّينَ to vote for the leftists 2 [صاتَ] to shout, to cry

صَوْت *n* |أَصْوات| 1 [الإنْسانِ] voice; tone of voice; صَوْت نِسائيّ a female voice; صَوْت غِنائيّ singing voice; صَوْت مَبْحوح \ خافِت \ واهٍ \ هامِس a hoarse/soft/weak voice; صَوْت مُنْخَفِض \ خَفيض a low voice; صَوْت عالٍ \ مُرْتَفِع a raised voice; بِصَوْتٍ عالٍ aloud; تَكَلَّمَ بِصَوْتٍ عالٍ \ مُرْتَفِعٍ to speak with a raised voice; بِصَوْتٍ واحِدٍ

to suffer from a liver disease; أُصيبَ بِخَسارةٍ to suffer a loss; أُصيبَ بِجُرْحٍ \ بِجَراحٍ to get injured, to be injured; أُصيبَت البِلادُ بِمَجاعةٍ عَظيمةٍ the country was afflicted with famine; ماذا أَصابَكَ؟ what's the matter with you?; ما الذي أَصابَهُ؟ what has gotten into him? 3 [أَتى بالصَوابِ] to be right/correct; أَصابَت المُعَلِّمةُ في قَوْلِها the teacher was correct in her statement

اِسْتَصابَ *v* to consider correct/right

اِسْتَصْوَبَ *v* to agree with; to approve, to sanction; to consider correct/right; اِسْتَصْوَبَ شَيْئاً to approve sth

صَوْب *n* direction; side; من كُلِّ أَوْبٍ وَصَوْبٍ from all directions; صَوْبَ in the direction of, towards; اِتَّجَهَ صَوْبَ البَحْرِ to go towards the sea; تَنْظُرُ صَوْبَ المَدينةِ she is looking towards the city

صائِب *adj* accurate, correct; sharp, striking; اخْتِيار \ حَلّ صائِب a correct choice/solution; مُلاحَظة صائِبة an astute observation; شَكاوى صائِبة legitimate complaints; ضَرَبَ ضَرْبةً صائِبةً, رَمى رَمْيةً صائِبةً to hit the target exactly; (fig) to hit the nail on the head

صَواب *n* 1 [عَقْل] consciousness; sanity; reason; فِقْدان الصَوابِ insanity; فَقَدَ صَوابَهُ to lose one's head; غابَ عن صَوابِهِ to lose consciousness; عادَ \ رَجَعَ إلى صَوابِهِ to come to one's senses; رَدَّ شَخْصاً إلى صَوابِهِ to bring sb to reason 2 [صِحّة] accuracy, correctness, rightness; truth; صَواب أم خَطأ true or false; من الصَوابِ أنْ ... it's true that ...; أَقَرَّ لِشَخْصٍ بالصَوابِ to agree with sb; كانَ على صَوابٍ to be right; لم يَكُنْ على صَوابٍ to be wrong; هذا على جانِبٍ كَبيرٍ من الصَوابِ there's a lot of truth in this; أَمْر يُجانِبُهُ الصَوابُ a righteous case

صَوابيّة *n* aptness; correctness; أَكَّدَ صَوابيّةَ السِياسةِ to confirm the aptness of the policy

صوبة *n* greenhouse

إصابة *n* 1 [هَدَف] goal; hit; إصابة مُباشِرة direct hit; الإصابة الحاسِمة في المُباراةِ the winning goal of the match; سَجَّلَ إصابةً to score a goal 2 [أَذًى] injury, wound; harm, damage; إصابة خَطيرة a serious injury; إصابة دِماغيّة brain damage;

unanimously; بِصَوْتٍ مَجْروحٍ in a hurt voice; تَعَدُّد الأَصْواتِ polyphony; مُتَعَدِّد الأَصْواتِ polyphonous; رَفْع \ تَعْلِية الصَوْتِ raising of voice; رَفَعَ صَوْتَهُ to raise one's voice; مَيَّزَ صَوْتاً to distinguish a voice ② [ما يُسْمَعُ] sound; noise; tone; صَوْت رَهيب \ غَريب \ حادّ an awful/strange/penetrating noise; قوّة الصَوْتِ volume; مُنَظِّم الصَوْتِ volume control; مُضَخِّم الصَوْتِ megaphone; خافِت الصَوْتِ muffler; سُرْعة الصَوْتِ the speed of sound; عازِل للصَوْتِ soundproof; حُجْرة عازِلة للصَوْتِ a soundproof room; مُكَبِّر الصَوْتِ loudspeaker; بِدونِ صَوْتٍ noiseless; حاجِز \ جِدار الصَوْتِ sound barrier; خَرَقَ جِدارَ الصَوْتِ to break the sound barrier; ضَبَطَ الصَوْتَ to adjust the sound; خَفَّضَ الصَوْتَ to turn down the volume; صَدَرَتْ عَنْهُ أَصْواتٌ غَريبةٌ to make a strange sound; يَرْتَفِعُ \ يَنْخَفِضُ الصَوْتُ the volume is going up/down ③ [في انْتِخاباتٍ] vote; صَوْت ل (صالِحِ) شَخْصٍ \ شَيْءٍ a vote for sb/sth; صَوْت ضِدّ \ على شَيْءٍ a vote against/on sth; بِأَغْلَبيّةِ الأَصْواتِ with a majority of votes; نِصْف الأَصْواتِ زائِدٌ واحِدٌ half of the votes plus one; أَدْلى بِصَوْتٍ to vote; اجْتَذَبَ أَصْواتاً to get votes; فَرَزَ الأَصْواتَ to count the votes; حَصَلَ على كَثيرٍ من الأَصْواتِ to receive a lot of votes ④ (Ling) sound; صَوْت حَلْقيّ a guttural sound; عِلْم الأَصْواتِ phonology; phonetics; أَصْوات صامِتة \ صائِتة voiceless/voiced sounds

صائِت *adj* ① [رَنّان] resonant, sounding; sound (*before n*) ② (Ling) voiced; حَرْف صائِت a voiced consonant

صَوْتيّ *adj* ① [سَمْعيّ] audio, acoustic; sonic, sound (*before n*); vocal, voice (*before n*); تَسْجيل صَوْتيّ recording; عَزْل صَوْتيّ sound insulation; مَساحة صَوْتيّة vocal range; فوق صَوْتيّ supersonic; طائِرة فوق صَوْتيّةٍ a supersonic aircraft; أَجْهِزة صَوْتيّة audio equipment; الحِبال \ الأَوْتار الصَوْتيّة the vocal cords ② (Ling) phonologic; phonetic; عِلْم الصَوْتيّاتِ phonology; phonetics; النِظام الصَوْتيّ phonetic system; كِتابة صَوْتيّة phonetic transcription; مُحاكاة صَوْتيّة onomatopoeia

صَوْتيّات *n pl* ① (Ling) phonetics ② [سَمْعيّات] audio

صيت *n* fame, renown; standing, repute, reputation; صيت حَسَن \ حَميد a good/excellent reputation; ذُيوع الصيتِ reputation; سِياسيّ ذائِع الصيتِ a distinguished politician; كانَ ذائِعَ الصيتِ to have a good reputation

تَصْويت *n* vote, voting, ballot; تَصْويت سِرّيّ a secret ballot; حَقّ التَصْويتِ suffrage; حَقّ المَرْأةِ في التَصْويتِ women's suffrage; مَكْتَب \ مَرْكَز \ مَقَرّ تَصْويتٍ polling station, polling place (AmE); وَرَقة \ بِطاقة تَصْويتٍ ballot paper (BrE), ballot (AmE); حُجْرة تَصْويتٍ polling booth (BrE), voting booth (AmE); امْتَنَعَ عن التَصْويتِ to abstain from voting

تَصْويتيّ *adj* voting (*before n*); نِظام \ نَمَط تَصْويتيّ voting system/pattern

مُصَوِّت **A** *adj* voiced; sonorous, resonant **B** *n* voter; constituent

‹ **صَوْتَم** *n* (Ling) phoneme

‹ **صوجا** *n* (Bot) see صويا

‹ **أَصاخَ** *v* [إلى \ ل] to listen, to lend one's ear

‹ **صودا** *n* soda; بيكَرْبونات الصودا baking soda

‹ **صوديوم** *n* sodium

‹¹ **صَوَّرَ** *v* ① [رَسَمَ] to portray, to draw; صَوَّرَ شَخْصاً to portray sb ② [وَصَفَ] to portray, to depict, to describe; صَوَّرَ شَخْصاً على أَنَّهُ \ كَغَشّاشٍ to portray sb as a swindler; وَكَأَنَّهُ مُجْرِمٌ to depict sb as a criminal ③ (Phot) to photograph; to film; صَوَّرَ شَيْئاً to photograph sth; صَوَّرَ فيلْماً to make a film ④ [نَسَخَ] to copy, to photocopy; صَوَّرَ رِسالةً to copy a letter ⑤ [مَثَّلَ] to represent, to describe; صَوَّرَ الواقِعةَ to represent reality; صَوَّرَ شَخْصيّةً to play a character; صُوِّرَ لَهُ أنّ … it seemed to him that …

تَصَوَّرَ *v* to imagine, to visualize, to envision; تَصَوَّرَ أنّ … to imagine that …; تَصَوَّرَ شَيْئاً to visualize sth; تَصَوَّرْ! imagine!; تَصَوَّرْ أَنَّكَ رَئيسُ الدَوْلةِ imagine that you're the president; لا يُتَصَوَّرُ to be inconceivable; لا يُتَصَوَّرُ أَنَّهُمْ سَيَتَوَصَّلونَ إلى اتِّفاقٍ it's inconceivable that they will reach an agreement; حاوَلْتُ أَنْ أَتَصَوَّرَ كيف يَعيشُ هَؤُلاءِ الناسُ I tried to imagine how those people live; لا يُمْكِنُ لِعاقِلٍ أَنْ يَتَصَوَّرَ هذا a sensible person cannot imagine this

صَوَر *n* poplar; aspen

صورة *n* |صُوَر| ① [رَسْم] image, picture, illustration; portrait, figure; painting, drawing; صُوَر مُتَحَرِّكة cartoon; صورة

مُنْعَكِسة a mirror image ② (Phot) photo, photograph; shot; صورة مُكَبَّرة an enlarged photo; صورة جَوِّيّة an aerial photograph; صورة شَخْصِيّة portrait; صورة غامِضة a blurry image; صورة أَشِعّةٍ \ بالأَشِعّةِ X-ray; صورة لِأُمِّها a picture of her mother; أَلْبوم صُوَرٍ a photo album; حِدّة الصورةِ image sharpness; اِلْتَقَطَ \ أَخَذَ صورةً to take a picture; بَثَّ صُوَراً to broadcast images; الصورةُ غَيْرُ واضِحةٍ the image is blurry; صورة مُلَوَّنة a colour photograph ③ [نُسْخة] duplicate; copy, photocopy; صورة مُصَدَّقة a certified copy; صورة طِبْقَ الأَصْلِ an exact copy; صورة شَهادةِ الميلادِ a copy of the birth certificate ④ [تَصَوُّر] picture, image; representation, description; صورة مُشَوَّهة a distorted picture; صورة كامِلة \ شامِلة an overall picture; صَحَّحَ صورةً to correct a picture; رَسَمَ صورةً زائِفةً عن الوَضْعِ to misrepresent the situation; أَعْطى شَخْصاً صورةً عن شَيْءٍ to give sb a picture of sth ⑤ [طَريقة] way, manner; بِصورةٍ عامّةٍ \ خاصّةٍ in general/particular; بِصورةٍ جَلِيّةٍ evidently; بِصورةٍ غَيْرِ مَشْروعةٍ illegally ⑥ [شَكْل] form; دَفَعَ مَبْلَغاً في صورةِ ذَهَبٍ to pay an amount in gold

صُورِيّ *adj* formal; pro forma; false, sham; صورِيًّا pro forma; زَواج صورِيّ a sham marriage

تَصَوُّر *n* |تَصَوُّرات| ① [تَخَيُّل] imagination, fantasy; illusion; يُمْكِنُ تَصَوُّرُهُ conceivable; لا يُمْكِنُ تَصَوُّرُهُ inconceivable ② [مَفْهوم] concept, idea; opinion, belief; image, impression; تَصَوُّر شامِل an overall picture; على خِلافِ التَصَوُّراتِ الشائِعةِ فَإِنّ ... contrary to popular belief, ...; صَحَّحَ تَصَوُّراً شائِعاً to correct a common fallacy; اِتَّفَقَ هذا مع تَصَوُّرِهِ this corresponded with his impression

تَصَوُّرِيّ *adj* imaginary, fictitious; conceptual

تَصْوير *n* |تَصاويرُ| ① (Cin) photography; shot; take (*of a film*); آلة تَصْويرٍ camera; فَنّ التَصْويرِ photography; تَصْوير خارِجِيّ outdoor shot; بَدَأَ \ أَنْهى التَصْويرَ to start/finish shooting ② (Art) illustration; portrayal, depiction ③ [تَشْكيل] imagination, illusion; representation, description, portrayal, depiction; تَصْوير الإِرْهابِ وَكَأَنَّهُ التَهْديدُ الجَديدُ representing terrorism as if it were the new threat

تَصْويرة *n* |تَصاويرُ| image, picture; illustration; photograph; shot

تَصْويرِيّ *adj* photographic; expressive, descriptive; أُسْلوب تَصْويرِيّ an expressive style

مُتَصَوَّر *adj* imagined, conceived, visualized; غَيْر مُتَصَوَّرٍ inconceivable; من غَيْرِ المُتَصَوَّرِ أَنْ ... it's inconceivable that ...

مُصَوَّر *adj* pictured, painted, drawn; illustrated; photographed; كِتاب مُصَوَّر an illustrated book

مُصَوِّر *n* ① (Phot) photographer; مُصَوِّر مُحْتَرِف a professional photographer; مُصَوِّر صُحُفِيّ a news photographer; عَمِلَ مُصَوِّراً to work as a photographer ② [سينِمائِيّ أو تِلِفِزْيونِيّ] cameraman ③ (Islam) المُصَوِّر the Fashioner, the Shaper (*one of the names of God*)

مُصَوِّرة *n* ① [آلة] camera ② [شَخْص] (female) photographer

2 **صور** *n* |dipt f| Tyre (*city in Lebanon*)

صاع *v* |u; صَوْع| to measure; to weigh

اِنْصاعَ *v* to obey, to serve; to comply, to conform; اِنْصاعَ لِقَرارِ \ لِرَغْبةِ شَخْصٍ to comply with sb's decision/wish

صاع *n* |أَصْوُع, صيعان| صاعاً بِصاعٍ tit for tat; رَدَّ لِشَخْصٍ الصاعَ صاعَيْنِ to pay sb back twofold, to bring double retaliation on sb

اِنْصِياع *n* obedience, submission; compliance, conformity; رَفَضَ الانْصِياعَ لِأَمْرِ الرَئيس to refuse to obey the president's order

مُنْصاع *adj* obedient, submissive; docile, compliant

صاغَ *v* |u; صَوْغ, صِياغة| ① [الذَهَبَ] to forge, to smith ② [شَكَّلَ] to make, to create, to form; to draft, to draw up; صاغَ وَثيقةً \ عَقْداً to draw up a document/contract ③ [عَبَّرَ عن] to formulate, to phrase; صاغَ نَصائِحَ \ أَفْكاراً to formulate recommendations/ideas

صائِغ *n* |صاغة| jeweller, goldsmith, silversmith; صائِغ الفِضّةِ silversmith

صِياغة *n* ① [حِرْفة الصائِغِ] goldsmithing (*the profession of jeweller*) ② [تَشْكيل] modelling, forming, shaping, moulding; أَعادَ الصِياغةَ to remodel ③ [طَريقة التَعْبيرِ] formulation, phrasing; صِياغة قَرارٍ the formulation of a decision; صِياغة المَسْأَلةِ

the definition of the problem, thesis, premise; إعادة الصِياغةِ rephrasing

صيغة n |صِيَغ, صيغات| [1] [هَيْئة] form, shape; نَقْد من حَيْثُ الصيغةُ لا المَضْمونِ criticism on form rather than content; أَوْجَدَ صيغةً بَديلةً للمُفاوَضاتِ \ العَلاقاتِ to find an alternative form of negotiations/relations [2] (Gram) form; mood; voice; tense; صيغة الأَمْرِ \ الاحْتِمالِ the imperative/subjunctive (mood); صيغة رَفْعِ الفِعْلِ the indicative (mood); صيغة المَبْنيِّ للمَعْلومِ \ للمَجْهولِ the active/passive voice; صيغة الفِعْلِ verbal form; صيغة الاحْتِرام the polite form; صيغة المُنادى form of address; صيغة الجَمْع the plural (form); صيغة المُتَكَلِّم the first person; كَتَبَ بِصيغةِ المُتَكَلِّمِ to write in the first person; كانَ في صيغةِ الماضي \ المُضارِعِ to be in the past/present tense; كَلِمة مُعَلِّم على صيغةِ مُفَعِّلٍ the word 'mu'allim' corresponds to the pattern 'mufa''il' [3] (Math) formula; بواسِطةِ صيغةٍ with a formula [4] [كَلِمات مُعَيَّنة] formula, formulaic expression; صيغة مُحَدَّدة a set formula [5] [نَصّ] version; الصيغة المُنَقَّحة \ المُعَدَّلة the improved/adapted version; الصيغة النهائيّة للاقْتِراحِ the definitive version of the proposal

مَصاغ n jewelry

مَصوغات n pl jewelry; مَصوغات ثَمينة \ ذَهَبيّة expensive/gold jewelry

‹ **تَصَوَّفَ** v to be/become a Sufi, to be/become a mystic

صوف n wool, fleece; كُبّة \ كُرة من الصوفِ a ball of wool; جَوارِب من الصوفِ woollen socks

صوفيّ [A] adj [1] [من الصوفِ] wool (before n); woollen; woolly, fleecy [2] (Islam) Sufi, Sufic; mystical [B] n Sufi; mystic

صوفيّة n Sufism, mysticism

تَصَوُّف n Sufism, mysticism

مُتَصَوِّف n Sufi, mystic

‹ **صوفا** n sofa

1‹ **صالَ** v |u; صَوْل, صَوَلان| to spring, to jump, to leap; to attack, to assault; صالَ على شَخْصٍ to attack sb; يَصولُ وَيَجولُ he does as he pleases

صَوَّلَ v to wash, to cleanse

صاوَلَ v to vie, to compete

صَوْلة n [1] [حَمْلة] attack, assault [2] [سَطْوة] power, authority

2‹ **صول** n sol (military rank formerly used in Egypt and Sudan)

‹ **صَوْلَجان** n |صَوْلَجانات| [1] [مَلِكٍ] scepter; staff [2] (Sport) stick (hockey, polo); club (golf)

‹ **صامَ** v |u; صَوْم| to fast; to abstain, to refrain; صامَ عن شَيْءٍ to abstain from sth; يَصومُ المُسْلِمونَ شَهْرَ رَمَضانَ Muslims fast during Ramadan

صَوْم n fast, fasting; abstinence; أَثْناءَ الصَوْمِ during the fast; صَوْم رَمَضانَ the Ramadan fast

صائِم adj |صائِمون, صِيام| fasting; abstinent

صِيام n fasting; abstinence; وَقْت الصِيام the time of fasting; صِيام الشَهْرِ الفَضيلِ fasting during the holy month

‹ **صوماليّ** adj, n Somali

الصومال n |f| Somalia

‹ **صَوْمَعة** n |صَوامِعُ| [1] [لِخَزْنِ الحُبوبِ] silo [2] [لِلمَسْجِدِ] tower; minaret [3] [مَنْسَك] monastery cell; hermitage

‹ **صانَ** v |u; صَوْن, صِيانة| [1] [حَفِظَ] to uphold, to support; to maintain, to keep, to preserve; to safeguard, to guard, to secure; صانَ حَقًّا to uphold a law; صانَ كَرامَتَهُ to preserve one's dignity; صانَ شَخْصاً من ارْتِكابِ خَطَأٍ to keep sb from doing wrong [2] [تَعَهَّدَ بالعِنايةِ] to maintain, to keep, to tend (to), to service; صانَ حَديقةً to keep a garden; صانَ سَيّارةً to service a car

تَصَوَّنَ v to keep, to preserve (one's honour/chastity); to seclude/protect oneself

صَوْن n upholding, supporting; maintenance, preservation; safeguarding, protection; صَوْن البيئةِ protection of the environment

صَوّان n granite; flint

صُوان, صِوان n |أَصْوِنة| [1] [خِزانة] cupboard, cabinet; صِوان مَلابِسَ wardrobe (BrE), closet (AmE) [2] [الأُذُنِ] auricle

صَوّانيّ adj granite (before n)

صِيانة n maintenance, preservation; safeguarding, protection; تَكاليف الصِيانةِ the costs of maintenance; صِيانة الأَمْنِ

the maintenance of security; مَلاك الصِيانةِ guardian angel; صِيانة السَيّارةِ car maintenance/servicing

مَصون *adj* maintained, preserved, conserved; safeguarded, protected; unimpaired, untouched, unaffected, chaste; مَكانة مَصونة an unassailable position

‹ **صَوى** *v* |i; صُويّ| to squeak, to chirp

صُوّة *n* |صُوًى| landmark, road sign

‹ **صويا** *n* (Bot) soy, soybean, soya (BrE); فول الصويا soybean, soya bean (BrE); زَرَعَ الصويا to grow soybeans

‹ **صاء** *n* amniotic fluid

‹ **صاح** *v* |i; صِياح, صَيْح| **1** [صَرَخَ] to scream, to yell, to cry, to call out; صاحَ صَيْحةً to give a cry; صاحَ من الأَلَمِ to scream in pain; صاحَ بأَعْلى صَوْته to scream at the top of one's lungs; صاحَ على شَخْصٍ to yell at sb; صاحَ على أُمِّهِ to call for one's mother; صاحَ على شَخْصٍ لِيُساعِدَكَ to call out for sb's help **2** [الديكُ] to crow; يَصيحُ الديكُ the rooster crows

صَيَّحَ *v* to scream, to yell, to cry, to call out

تَصايَحَ *v* to shout at each other

صَيّاح *n* noisy person, shouter, screamer

صِياح *n* screaming, yelling, shouting; مع صِياح الديكِ before cockcrow; عَلا الصِياحُ the shouting was getting louder; انْدَلَعَ الصِياحُ shouting erupted

صَيْحة *n* scream, yell, shout, cry; صَيْحة عالِية \ حادّة a loud scream; صَيْحة الحَرْبِ battle cry; صَيْحات اسْتِنْكارٍ cheers; أَطْلَقَ صَيْحةً to let out a scream; ذَهَبَتْ صَيْحَتُهُ في وادٍ his shout went unheard

‹ **صادَ** *v* |i; صَيْد| to hunt; to fish; to catch, to trap; صادَ الأَسَدَ \ الطَيْرَ to hunt lions/birds; صادَ السَمَكَ to fish

تَصَيَّدَ *v* to hunt, to chase; to fish; to trap; تَصَيَّدَ أَخْطاءَ شَخْصٍ to pick on sb's faults

اصْطادَ *v* to hunt; to fish; to trap; اصْطادَ السَمَكَ to fish; اصْطادَ القُدَّ to fish for cod; اصْطادَ الطُيورَ \ الأَيائِلَ to hunt birds/deer; اصْطادَ في الماءِ العَكِرِ to fish in troubled waters

صَيْد *n* **1** [قَنْص] hunt, hunting; fishing; trapping, catching; صَيْد السَمَكِ fishing; صَيْد بَحْرِيّ sea fishing; صَيْد مُكَثَّف intensive fishing; صَيْد الحيتانِ whale hunt; صَيْد سَمَكِ الرَّنْكةِ herring fishing; قَصَبة الصَيْدِ fishing rod, fishing pole (AmE); زَوْرَق \ قارِب الصَيْدِ fishing boat; مَرْفَأ الصَيْدِ fishing port; أُسْطول صَيْد fishing fleet; حَظْر \ مَنْع الصَيْدِ hunting ban; fishing ban; حَقّ صَيْدِ السَمَكِ fishing right; بُنْدُقيّة صَيْدٍ hunting rifle; كَلْب صَيْدٍ hound; مَوْسِم صَيْدٍ hunting season; مِنْطَقة صَيْدٍ hunting ground; مَدينة \ قَرْية صَيْدِ السَمَكِ a fishing town/village; إفْراط في صَيْدِ السَمَكِ overfishing; صَيْد النِساءِ chasing women; خَرَجَ للصَيْدِ \ ذَهَبَ إلى الصَيْدِ to go hunting; عاشَ على صَيْدِ السَمَكِ to make a living fishing **2** [حَيَوانات] game, catch

صائِد *n* hunter; fisherman

صَيّاد *n* hunter; fisherman; صَيّاد سَمَكٍ fisherman

اصْطِياد *n* hunting; fishing; trapping; اصْطِياد الحَشَراتِ hunting insects

تَصَيُّد *n* **1** (Comp) phishing; رَسائِل تَصَيُّدٍ phishing emails **2** [الحَيَواناتِ] hunting; fishing; trapping

مِصْيادة *n* catapult

مَصْيَدة *n* hunting/fishing ground; مَصْيَدة الأَسْماكِ fishing ground

مِصْيَدة *n* |مَصايِدُ| trap, snare; net; وَضَعَ مِصْيَدةً to set a trap; وَقَعَ في المِصْيَدةِ to fall into the trap; وَقَعَ كالفَأْرِ في المِصْيَدةِ to be trapped like a rat

‹ **صَيْدا** *n* Sidon (*city in Lebanon*)

‹ **صَيْدَلانيّ** **A** *adj* |صَيادِلة| pharmaceutical, pharmacy (*before n*) **B** *n* |صَيادِلة| pharmacist

صَيْدَلة *n* **1** [عِلْم العَقاقيرِ] pharmacology; عِلْمُ الصَيْدَلةِ pharmacology **2** [أَدْوِية] pharmaceuticals

صَيْدَليّ **A** *adj* |صَيادِلة| pharmaceutical, pharmacy (*before n*); صِناعة المَوادِّ \ المُسْتَحْضَراتِ الصَيْدَلِيّةِ the pharmaceutical industry **B** *n* |صَيادِلة| pharmacist

صَيْدَليّة *n* pharmacy, chemist (BrE)

‹ **صارَ** *v* |i; صَيْر, صَيْرورة, مَصير| **1** [أَصْبَحَ] to become; صارَ فَقيراً to become poor; صارَ أَكْثَرَ ديموقْراطيّةً to become more democratic; صارَ الهِلالُ بَدْراً the moon waxed full; صارَ الماءُ بُخاراً the water turned into steam **2** [بَدَأَ] to begin, to start;

صَيْف *n* أَصْياف| summer; صَيْف مُبَكِّر \ مُتَأَخِّر \ مُمْطِر an early/late/wet summer; في الصَيْفِ in the summer; أَثْناءَ \ خلال الصَيْفِ during the summer; شَهْر الصَيْفِ (Hist) June (*Libya under Gaddafi*); قَضى الصَيْفَ to spend the summer

صَيْفِيّ *adj* summer (*before n*), summery; يَوْم صَيْفِيّ a summer day

اصْطِياف *n* summering, spending the summer; قَضى أُسْبوعَ اصْطِيافٍ على الشاطِئِ to spend a week in the summer vacationing on the coast

مُصْطاف *n* ⟨1⟩ [شَخْص] summer visitor/vacationer ⟨2⟩ [مَكان] summer home/residence, summer resort

مَصيف *n* مَصايِفُ| summer home/residence, summer resort; summer camp

مُصَيِّف *n* summer visitor/vacationer

صينِيّ ‹ **A** *adj* ⟨1⟩ [من الصينِ] Chinese; الصينِيّة (اللُغة) Chinese (*language*) ⟨2⟩ [فخّار] china, porcelain; طَقْم صينِيّ a china service

B *n* Chinese (*person*)

صينِيّة *n* صَوانِيّ, صَوانٍ, صينِيّات| ⟨1⟩ [طَبَق] (serving) tray; dish, plate ⟨2⟩ [في الفُرْنِ] baking sheet/tray

الصين *n* |f| China; بِلاد الصينِ China; جُمْهوريّة الصينِ الشَعْبِيّة the People's Republic of China; جِدار الصينِ (العَظيم) the Great Wall of China

صيوان ‹ *n* صَواوينُ| pavilion, marquee, tent

صارَ يَفْعَلُ شَيْئاً to start doing sth; صارَ يَشْتُمُ to start cursing ⟨3⟩ [حَدَثَ] to happen, to occur, to take place; صارَ ما تَوَقَّعَهُ الخَبيرُ what the expert expected, happened ⟨4⟩ [انْتَهى إلى] |إلى| to end/wind up with, to land; صارَ إلى شَخْصٍ to end up with sb; صارَتْ رِئاسةُ الجَلْسةِ إلى صَديقي my friend became chairman of the meeting

صَيَّرَ *v* to make, to cause to be/become; صَيَّرَ الحَديدَ مِفْتاحاً to make a key from iron

صَيْرورة *n* outcome, result

مَصير *n* مَصائِرُ| ⟨1⟩ [قَدَر] fate, destiny, path; مَصير قاتِم a dark fate; وَحْدة المَصيرِ solidarity; تَقْرير المَصيرِ self-determination; حَقّ تَقْرِيرِ المَصيرِ the right to self-determination; قَرَّرَ مَصيرَ شَخْصٍ to decide sb's destiny; تَرَكَ شَخْصاً يُواجِهُ مَصيرَهُ to leave sb to his own devices; شارَكَ شَخْصاً مَصيرَهُ to share sb's fate; هُمْ إخْوةٌ في المَصيرِ they share the same destiny; لا أَعْلَمُ مَصيرَهُ حتّى الآنِ even now, I don't know what happened to him; يَنْتَظِرُهُ نَفْسُ المَصيرِ he'll face the same fate ⟨2⟩ [مُفْرَد المُصْرانِ] listed alphabetically

مَصيرِيّ *adj* fateful, fatal; crucial, decisive; خَطأ مَصيرِيّ a fatal mistake; سُؤال مَصيرِيّ a crucial question; المَرْحَلة المَصيرِيّة the crucial phase

صَيَّفَ ‹ *v* to summer, to spend the summer

اصْطافَ *v* to spend the summer

ضباب *n* fog, mist; haze; ضباب كَثيف dense/thick fog; يَحُلُّ ضباب it's foggy; يَنْقَشِعُ الضبابُ the fog is lifting; الضبابُ خَفيف mist, haze; في الضَباب in the mist; غُطِّيَت الشَبابيكُ بالضَباب the windows have fogged up; ضَباب دُخانيّ smog

ضَبابيّ *adj* foggy, misty; vague, hazy, blurry; الجَوُّ ضَبابيٌّ اليَوْمَ it's foggy today; صورة ضَبابيّة a blurry photo; مَفْهوم ضَبابيّ a vague concept

ضَبابيّة *n* mist, haze; fog; ضَبابيّة صوَرٍ haziness of some photos

ضَبّة *n* |ضِباب, ضَبّات| (door) bolt, latch

مُضَبَّب *adj* vague; misty, hazy; مُسْتَقْبَل مُضَبَّب an uncertain future

ضَبَحَ *v* |a; ضَبْح| to scorch, to char

ضَبْخان *n* smog

ضَبَرَ *v* |i; ضَبْر| to gather, to collect

إضْبارة *n* |أضابيرُ, إضْبارات| file, dossier

ضَبَطَ *v* |i-u; ضَبْط| ❶ [كَبَحَ] to curb, to check; to have under control; to suppress, to restrain, to hold back; ضَبَطَ أَعْصابَهُ to keep one's nerve ❷ [قَبَضَ على] to arrest, to detain; to run in, to pick up; to catch; ضَبَطَ لِصًّا to catch a thief; ضَبَطَ السارِقَ مُتَلَبِّساً to catch the thief red-handed ❸ [عَدَّلَ] to set; to adjust, to regulate, to tune; ضَبَطَ ساعَتَهُ to set one's watch; ضَبَطَ مُحَرِّكاً to tune an engine; ضَبَطَ آلَةَ تَصْويرٍ to adjust a camera

انْضَبَطَ *v* to be (kept) in order, to be disciplined

ضَبْط *n* ❶ [دِقّة] accuracy, precision; بالضَبْطِ exactly, precisely; نَفْسُهُ \ مِثْلُهُ بالضَبْطِ exactly the same; ما قَصَدْتُهُ بالضَبْطِ exactly what I meant; في الوَقْتِ \ المَوْعِدِ بالضَبْطِ exactly on time; في النِصْفِ بالضَبْطِ exactly in the middle; في الساعةِ الثانيةَ عَشْرةَ بالضَبْطِ at precisely twelve o'clock; كاتِب الضَبْطِ

ضاد *n* |f| *name of the letter* ض; لُغة الضادِ the language of 'daad', Arabic; الناطِقونَ بالضادِ the Arabic-speaking people, the Arabs

ضَؤُلَ *v* |u; ضُؤولة, ضَآلة| to be small/insignificant

ضاءَلَ *v* to shrink

تَضاءَلَ *v* ❶ [تَناقَصَ] to diminish; تَضاءَلَ عَدَدُهُمْ their numbers decreased; تَضاءَلَ حَجْمُهُ to diminish in size; تَضاءَلَ أَمَلُهُ \ شَعْبِيَّتُهُ his hope/popularity dwindled; تَتَضاءَلُ الفُروقُ the differences are narrowing; تَضاءَلَتْ حُظوظُها her luck was running out; تَضاءَلَ تَدْريجيًّا to diminish gradually; تَضاءَلَ إلى حَدٍّ كَبيرٍ to diminish significantly ❷ [صَغُرَ] to be small/insignificant

ضَآلة *n* smallness; ضَآلة عَدَدِ الزائِرينَ the small number of visitors; نِسَب شَديدة الضَآلةِ من المِياهِ very small percentages of water

ضَئيل *adj* |ضِئال, ضُؤَلاءُ| small, little; slight; فازَ بِفارِقٍ ضَئيلٍ عن خَصْمِهِ he beat his opponent by a small margin; عَدَد ضَئيل جِدًّا a very small number

تَضاؤُل *n* decrease

ضاما, ضامة *n* draughts (BrE), checkers (AmE); لَعِبَ الضاما to play draughts; لُعْبة الضاما (a game of) draughts

ضَأْن *n coll* |sing n m ضائِن; sing n f ضائِنة| sheep; لَحْم الضَأْنِ mutton

ضَبَّ *v* |i; ضَبّ, ضُبوب| ❶ [سالَ] to seep ❷ [أَمْسَكَ بِهِ بِشِدّةٍ] |على| to grasp tightly, to hold firmly; to guard carefully; ضَبَّ على يَدِ ابْنِهِ he grasped his son's hand tightly

ضَبَّبَ *v* to bolt

أَضَبَّ *v* to be foggy, to be misty; يُضِبُّ اليَوْمُ \ المَكانُ it's foggy

تَضَبَّبَ *v* to mist over

ضَبّ *n* |ضِباب, أَضُبّ, ضُبّان| lizard; أَعْقَد من ذَنَبِ الضَبِّ *very complicated*; حتّى يَرِدُ الضَبُّ when pigs fly

(Mor) clerk of the court; كِتابة الضَبْطِ (Mor) registry, court's office **2** [كَبَح] control; ضَبْط النَفْسِ self-control; لم أَقْدُرْ على ضَبْطِ نَفْسي I couldn't control myself; لا يُمْكِنُ ضَبْطُهُ uncontrollable, out of control **3** [تَنْظيم] regularization, regulation; adjustment; ضَبْط الحِساباتِ bookkeeping

ضابِط *n* **1** [رُتْبة] |ضُبّاط| officer; رُتْبة ضابِطٍ rank of officer; ضابِط في القوّاتِ البَرِّيّةِ \ الجَوِّيّةِ an officer in the army/air force; ضابِط صَفٍّ non-commissioned officer, NCO; ضابِط اتِّصالٍ \ ارْتِباطٍ liaison officer; ضابِط الشُرْطةِ police officer; الضابِط المَسْؤول the commanding officer **2** [مِعْيار] |ضَوابِطُ| criterion, measure; standard; بدونِ ضَوابطَ unrestricted; بغَيْرِ ضابِطٍ وَلا رابِطٍ lawless; أَصْبَحَ بلا ضابِطٍ وَلا رابِطٍ to lead a loose life

ضابِطة *n* |ضَوابِطُ| **1** [مِكْبَح] brake **2** [ضابِط] standard; مَجْموعة ضابِطة (Sci) control group

ضَبْطيّ *adj* disciplinary

ضَبْطيّة *n* policing; ضَبْطِيّة قَضائيّة power of arrest

أَضْبَط *adj* |ضُبْط| ambidextrous

انْضِباط *n* discipline, order; قَليل الانْضِباطِ undisciplined; انْضِباط شَديد \ صارِم strict/stern discipline; لَجْنة الانْضِباط disciplinary tribunal; انْضِباط حَديديّ iron discipline

انْضِباطيّ *adj* disciplinary; disciplined; إجْراء انْضِباطيّ a disciplinary measure; غَيْر انْضِباطيٍّ undisciplined

مَضْبوط *adj* **1** [دَقيق] exact, precise, accurate; ساعَتي مَضْبوطةٌ my watch is right; قاسَ شَيْئاً بِشَكْلٍ مَضْبوطٍ to measure sth accurately; تَنَبُّؤ مَضْبوط an accurate prediction; عَمَل مَضْبوط a precise piece of work; عَمَل غَيْر مَضْبوطٍ sloppy work **2** [مُحَقَّق] correct, right; checked; الحِسابُ مَضْبوطٌ the bill is correct **3** [مَقْبوض عَلَيْه] run in, arrested **4** [مَحْجوز] confiscated, seized

مُنْضَبِط *adj* disciplined; غَيْر مُنْضَبِطٍ undisciplined; مُنْضَبِط في تَصَرُّفاتِه disciplined in one's behaviour

‹ **ضَبُع** *n* |أَضْبُع ,ضِباع| (Zool) hyena, hyaena

‹ **ضَبان** *n* sole; ضَبان طِبّيّ orthotic shoe insert, arch support; لَبِسَ \ اسْتَعْمَلَ ضَباناً طِبِّيّاً to wear orthotic inserts

‹ **ضَجَّ** *v* |i; ضَجيج| to be noisy, to be boisterous, to make a racket; ضَجَّت القاعةُ بالتَصْفيقِ loud applause broke out in the hall; كانوا يَضِجّونَ بالضَحِكِ they were laughing loudly

ضَجّة *n* **1** [جَلَب] noise; racket, row, din; ضَجّة هائِلة \ عالِية \ صاخِبة an huge/loud/boisterous racket; ضَجّة تُصِمُّ الآذانَ a deafening noise; بِلَجّةٍ وَضَجّةٍ with a lot of noise; بِدونِ ضَجّةٍ quietly; أَحْدَثَ ضَجّةً to make a racket, to kick up a row **2** (fig) consternation, commotion; fuss, fanfare; tumult, turmoil; ب \ بِدونِ ضَجّةٍ with/without much fanfare; ضَجّة حول شَيْءٍ commotion about sth; أَثارَ \ أَحْدَثَ ضَجّةً to make a fuss; ضَجّة قَوِيّة \ كَبيرة a great commotion; ضَجّة إعْلاميّة hype

ضَجوج *adj* noisy, clamorous

ضَجيج *n* noise; din, row, racket; أَحْدَثَ ضَجيجاً to make a racket; كَثير الضَجيج noisy, clamorous

‹ **ضَجِرَ** *v* |a; ضَجَر| |من ,ب| to be/become irritated; to have had enough, to be fed up; ضَجِرَ ب \ من شَيْءٍ to be fed up with sth

أَضْجَرَ *v* to annoy, to aggravate

تَضَجَّرَ *v* |من ,ب| to be/become irritated (by), to be/become annoyed (by)

ضَجَر *n* boredom; irritation, annoyance

ضَجِر *adj* weary; bored

مُضْجِر *adj* boring, dull, tedious

‹ **ضَجَعَ** *v* |a; ضَجْع ,ضُجوع| to lie down

ضاجَعَ *v* to have sex with; ضاجَعَ شَخْصاً to have sex with sb, to sleep with sb

أَضْجَعَ *v* to make lie down, to make sleep

اضْطَجَعَ *v* to lie (down); to rest

ضَجيع *n* bedfellow

مُضاجَعة *n* sex, sexual intercourse, coitus

مَضْجَع *n* |مَضاجِعُ| bed, couch; أَقَضَّ مَضْجَعَ شَخْصٍ to give sb sleepless nights, to deprive sb of sleep

مُضْطَجِع *adj* lying (down)

‹ **ضَحْضَحَ** *v* |i; ضَحْضَحة| to vibrate, to flicker

ضَحْضاح *adj* shallow (water), shoal

ضَحِكَ *v* |a; ضَحِك, ضِحْك, ضَحْك| to laugh; ضَحِكَ على شَخْصٍ to laugh at sb, to mock sb, to make fun of sb; ضَحِكَ من شَخْصٍ to laugh about sb; ضَحِكَ لِشَيْءٍ to laugh about sth; ضَحِكَ في سِرِّهِ to laugh heartily; ضَحِكَ من قَلْبِهِ to laugh to oneself; ضَحِكَ مِلْءَ شِدْقَيْهِ \ فَمِهِ to grin from ear to ear; مَنْ يَضْحَكُ أخيراً يَضْحَكُ كَثيراً he who laughs last, laughs best

ضَحَّكَ *v* to make laugh

ضاحَكَ *v* to jest, to joke; to banter; ضاحَكَ شَخْصاً to make fun of sb

أَضْحَكَ *v* to make laugh; أَضْحَكَ شَخْصاً to make sb laugh

تَضاحَكَ *v* to laugh; to laugh affectedly

اسْتَضْحَكَ *v* to make laugh

ضَحِك, ضَحْك, ضِحْك, ضِحِك *n* laughter, laugh, laughing; ماتَ من شِدَةِ الضَحِكِ to die laughing, to be doubled over with laughter; انْفَجَرَ بالضَحِكِ to burst out laughing; أَغْرَقَ في الضَحِكِ to have the giggles; نَوْبة من الضَحِكِ a fit of laughter; (هذا) مُثيرٌ للضَحِكِ (that is) funny; شَيْء مُثير للضَحِكِ sth to laugh at

ضَحّاك **A** *adj* giggly
B *n* joker

ضَحْكة *n* laugh; grin; ضَحْكات عالية \ صاخِبة loud laughter; ضَحْكة خَبيثة \ ساخِرة a sardonic/malicious grin; ضَحْكة صَفْراء a bitter laugh; ضَحِكَ ضَحْكةً مُتَكَلِّفةً to laugh uncomfortably; ضَحْكة عَصَبيّة a nervous laugh

ضُحْكة *n* laughing stock, object of ridicule; صارَ ضُحْكةً للناسِ he became laughing stock

ضِحْكة *n* laugh; ضِحْكة الساخِرِ a satiric laugh

ضَحوك *adj frequently laughing*

أُضْحوكة *n* |أَضاحيكُ| laughing stock, object of ridicule; أُضْحوكة خافِتة a private joke; جَعَلَ شَخْصاً أُضْحوكةً to make a fool of sb; كانَ أُضْحوكةَ المَدينةِ to be the laughing stock of the city; سَتَجْعَلُ من نَفْسِكَ أُضْحوكةً you'll make a fool of yourself

مُضْحِك *adj* funny, humorous, comic, comical; laughable; مَشاهِد مُضْحِكة comic scenes; شَخْص \ مَوْقِف مُضْحِك a comic figure/situation; فيلْم مُضْحِك a funny movie, a comedy; مَلابِس مُضْحِكة ridiculous clothes; فِكْرة مُضْحِكة a laughable idea; اعْتَبَرَ شَيْئاً مُضْحِكاً to find sth funny

مُضَحِّك *n* clown

ضَحَلَ *v* |a; ضَحْل| to be shallow

ضَحْل **A** *adj* shallow; ابْتَسَمَ ابْتِسامةً ضَحْلةً to smile faintly
B *n* |ضُحول, ضِحال, أَضْحال| shallows

ضَحا *v* |u; ضُحوّ, ضَحْو| to appear

ضَحّى *v* **1** [تَبَرَّعَ] to sacrifice; ضَحّى بِأَوْقاتِ فراغِهِ to sacrifice one's free time; ضَحّى بِشَيْءٍ من أَجْلِ شَيْءٍ to sacrifice sth for sth; ضَحّى بنَفْسِهِ في سَبيلِ الحُرّيّةِ to sacrifice oneself for freedom; ضَحّى بالنَفْسِ والنفيسِ to sacrifice life and property **2** [ذَبَحَ] to slaughter, to butcher

أَضْحى *v* to become; أَضْحى الوَلاءُ للحِزْبِ أَقْوى من الوَلاءِ للعائِلةِ loyalty to the party became stronger than loyalty to the family; أَضْحى الخَبَرُ مَعْروفاً the news became known

ضاحِية *n* |ضَواحٍ| suburb; outskirts; surroundings, environment; ضَواحٍ environs, surroundings; الضَواحي القَريبة the immediate vicinity; مَدينة عَمّانَ وَضواحيها the city of Amman and environs; في ضَواحي أَمْسْتِرْدام in the vicinity of Amsterdam

ضُحًى *n* morning, forenoon; سورة الضُحى The Morning Hours (*Sura 93*); بين عَشيّةٍ وَضُحاها suddenly

ضَحيّة, ضَحية *n* |ضَحايا| **1** [ذَبيحة] (sacrificial) offering, immolation; sacrificial animal **2** [مُصاب] victim, dupe, casualty; ضَحايا أَبْرِياء \ عُزَّل innocent/defenceless victims; ضَحايا الفَيَضانِ \ الزِلْزالِ victims of the flood/earthquake; أَصْبَحَ \ ضَحيّة الاعْتِداءِ \ الحَرْبِ a victim of the attack/war; راحَ ضَحيّةً \ ذَهَبَ \ وَقَعَ ضَحيّةَ شَيْءٍ to fall victim to sth; وَقَعَ ضَحيّةً للعُنْفِ to fall victim to violence; تَقْديم المُساعَداتِ للضَحايا aid for the victims; سَقَطَ الضَحايا there were casualties; ضَحيّة حادِثِ مُرورٍ road casualty; عَدَد الضَحايا number of casualties; وَقَعَ ضَحيّةَ عَمَليّةِ نَصْبٍ to be swindled

أَضْحَى *n* |أَضاحٍ| sacrificial animal; عيد الأَضْحى Eid al-Adha, the Feast of the Sacrifice (*religious holiday observed on the 10th of Dhu l-Hijja, celebrating Abraham's willingness to sacrifice his first-born son*)

تَضْحِية *n* sacrifice; تَضْحِية في سَبيلِ شَيْءٍ \ شَخْصٍ a sacrifice to sth/sb; بَذَلَ تَضْحِياتٍ كَبيرةً to make great sacrifices, to go to great expense; قَدَّمَ \ بَذَلَ تَضْحِيةً to make a sacrifice

‹ **ضَخَّ** *v* |u; ضَخٌّ| to pump, to drain; ضَخَّ الماءَ to pump water

مِضَخّة *n* pump, pumping station; مِضَخّة ماءٍ water pump; مِضَخّة بَنْزِينٍ petrol station (BrE), gas station (AmE); مِضَخّة الطَّرْدِ المَرْكَزِيّ centrifugal pump

‹ **ضَخُمَ** *v* |u; ضَخامة| to be/become huge

ضَخَّمَ *v* **1** [كَبَّرَ] to increase, to enlarge; ضَخَّمَ أَرْباحَهُ to increase one's profits **2** [بالَغَ] to exaggerate, to blow up, to inflate; ضَخَّمَ الأُمورَ to inflate matters **3** (Med) to distend, to swell

تَضَخَّمَ *v* to expand, to swell, to increase; يَتَضَخَّمُ المَصْنَعُ the factory is expanding; يَتَضَخَّمُ الضَجيجُ the noise is increasing

ضَخْم *adj* |ضِخام| **1** [عَظيم] enormous, colossal, huge; كِتاب \ تَقْرير ضَخْم a massive book/report; بِناء ضَخْم a colossal building; مَدينة ضَخْمة a huge city; مَبْلَغ ضَخْم a huge sum (of money); أَعْداد ضَخْمة vast quantities **2** [كَبير] big, sizeable

ضَخامة *n* enormousness, immenseness, enormity

تَضَخُّم *n* |تَضَخُّمات| **1** (Econ) inflation; تَضَخُّم ماليّ \ نَقْديّ inflation, currency depreciation; تَضَخُّم مُرْتَفِع \ ضَئيل high/low inflation; يَزْدادُ \ يَنْخَفِضُ التَضَخُّمُ inflation is rising/falling **2** (Med) inflation, swelling

تَضَخُّميّ *adj* (Econ) inflationary

تَضْخيم *n* enlarging, amplification; exaggerating

تَضْخيميّ *adj* exaggerated, inflated

مُضَخِّم *n* |مُضَخِّمات| amplifier; مُضَخِّم صَوْتٍ loudspeaker, speaker

‹ **ضادَّ** *v* to be contrary, to be opposed

تَضادَّ *v* to contradict one another

ضادّة *n* antagonist

ضِدّ *n* |أَضْداد| **1** [نَقيض] opposite **2** (Ling) *word with two opposite meanings*

ضِدَّ *prep* against, anti-, contra-; ضِدَّ سِياسةِ الحِزْبِ contrary to the policy of the party; كانَ ضِدَّ شَيْءٍ (بِحِدّةٍ) to be (sharply) opposed to sth; هذه السِياسةُ مُوَجَّهةٌ ضِدَّنا this policy is aimed against us; هل هو مَعَ قَرارِ الوَزيرِ أو ضِدَّهُ؟ is he for or against the minister's decision?; مَنْ ليس مَعي فَهُوَ ضِدّي he who is not with me, is against me

ضِدّيّ *adj* anti-, counter-; اتِّهام ضِدّيّ counter-accusation

تَضادّ *n* contrast, opposite, contradiction; تَضادّ شَديد \ حادّ a sharp contrast

مُتَضادّ *adj* opposite

مُسْتَضِدّ *n* |مُسْتَضِدّات| antigen

مُضادّ **A** *adj* opposite, opposed; anti-, counter-; جِسْم مُضادّ antibody; مادّة مُضادّة antimatter; حَرَكة \ عَمَل مُضادّ(ة) counteraction; طَلَب مُضادّ counterclaim; قوّة مُضادّة counterforce, counterbalance; إجْراءات مُضادّة countermeasures; مُضادّ للفَيْروساتِ antivirus **B** *n* (Med) مُضادّ حَيَويّ antibiotic; عالَجَ شَخْصاً \ مَرَضاً بالمُضادّاتِ الحَيَويّةِ to treat a person/disease with antibiotics

مُضادّة *n* contradiction, opposite

‹ **ضَرَبَ** *v* |i; ضَرْب| **1** [خَبَطَ] to hit, to strike, to beat; ضَرَبَ شَخْصاً to hit sb; ضَرَبَ شَخْصاً ضَرْباً مُبَرِّحاً to beat sb up; ضُرِبَ ضَرْباً مُبَرِّحاً to get beaten up; ضَرَبَ الكُرةَ to strike the ball away; ضَرَبَ إبْرةً \ حَقْنةً to inject, to give an injection; ضَرَبَ على الآلةِ الكاتِبةِ to type; ضَرَبَ على آلةٍ موسيقيّةٍ to play a musical instrument; ضَرَبَ رَقْماً قِياسيًّا to break a record; ضَرَبَ في حَديدٍ بارِدٍ to take futile steps; ضَرَبَ بِشَخْصٍ عُرْضَ الحائطِ to ignore sb, to give sb the cold shoulder; ضَرَبَ مَثَلاً to give an example; ضَرَبَ عُنُقَ شَخْصٍ to behead sb, to decapitate sb; ضَرَبَ أَجَلاً \ مَوْعِداً to make an appointment, to fix a date; ضَرَبَ عُمْلةً \ نُقوداً to mint coins/money; ضَرَبَ على الوَتَرِ الحَسّاسِ to strike the right chord **2** (Math) to multiply; ضَرَبَ ٣١ في ٥ to multiply 31 by 5 **3** [دَقَّ] to beat, to throb; يَضْرِبُ القَلْبُ the heart beats

ضَرَّبَ *v* to mix, to blend

ضارَبَ *v* to speculate, to gamble; ضارَبَ في بورْصةِ الأَوْراقِ المالِيّةِ to speculate on the stock exchange; ضارَبَ في

a severe blow; ضَرْبة مُوَفَّقة bullseye; ضَرْبة شَمْسٍ sunstroke; تَلَقّى الضَرْبةَ ضَرْبة قاضِية \ قاصِمة fatal blow, coup de grâce; وَجَّهَ ضَرْبةً قاصِمةً إلى القاضِيةَ to receive the fatal blow; شَخْصٍ to deal sb the coup de grâce; تَعَرَّضَ إلى ضَرْبةٍ to take a blow; جاءَ ضَرْبةً to deal a blow

ضَريبة *n* |ضَرائِبُ| tax; levy, levying, imposition; ضَرائِب مُباشِرة \ غَيْر مُباشِرة direct/indirect taxes; ضَريبة عَقاريّة \ الأَمْلاكِ property tax; ضَريبة جُمْرُكيّة import duty, customs duty; ضَريبة الدَخْلِ income tax, wage tax; ضَريبة المُمْتَلَكاتِ wealth tax; ضَريبة على السَيّاراتِ road tax (BrE), car/vehicle tax (AmE); ضَريبة على المَحْروقاتِ tax/levy on fuels; مَصْلَحة الضَرائِبِ tax authorities, treasury; أَخْفى شَيْئاً عن مَصْلَحةِ الضَرائِبِ to conceal sth from the tax authorities; مُفَتِّش الضَرائِبِ tax inspector; نِسْبة الضَريبةِ revenue tariff, tax rate; رَفْع \ تَخْفيض الضَرائِبِ tax increase/cut; أَعْلَنَ عن رَفْعِ الضَرائِبِ to announce a tax increase; عائِد الضَرائِبِ tax proceeds; خاضِع للضَريبةِ taxable; دَخْل \ بَضائِع خاضِع(ة) للضَرائِبِ taxable income/goods; فَرْض الضَرائِبِ taxation, levying of taxes; فَرَضَ ضَريبةً to levy taxes, to tax; حَصَّلَ ضَريبةَ الدَخْلِ to levy income tax; تَهَرَّبَ من الضَرائِبِ to evade taxes; تَهَرُّب من الضَرائِبِ tax evasion; غَشَّ في الضَرائِبِ to commit tax fraud; تَقْييم الضَريبةِ tax assessment; مُسْتَشار الضَرائِبِ tax consultant; رِبْح خاضِع للضَرائِبِ taxable profits; الراتِب الخاضِع للضَريبةِ taxable wages; الدَخْل الخاضِع للضَريبةِ taxable income; الدَخْل المُعْفى من الضَرائِبِ tax-exempt income; قانون ضَريبةِ الدَخْلِ income tax law; مُلْزَم بِدَفْعِ الضَرائِبِ obligated to pay tax, taxable; دافِع الضَرائِبِ taxpayer

ضَريبيّ *adj* fiscal, tax (*before n*); إيرادات ضَريبيّة tax revenues; غِشّ ضَريبيّ tax fraud; جَنّة ضَريبيّة tax haven; عِبْء ضَريبيّ tax burden

إضْراب *n* |إضْرابات| strike, work stoppage; إضْراب شامِل \ عامّ general strike; إضْراب قَصير a short (work) stoppage; إضْراب عن الطَعامِ hunger strike; حَقّ الإضْرابِ the right to strike; أَعْلَنَ إضْراباً to call a strike; أَنْهى إضْراباً to break a strike; إضْراب في قِطاعِ البِناءِ a strike in the construction industry

الأَسْهُمِ \ العَقارِ to speculate in shares/real estate

أَضْرَبَ *v* to strike, to be/go on strike; أَضْرَبَ عن العَمَلِ to go on strike; يُضْرِبُ عُمّالُ قِطاعِ المَعادِنِ عن العَمَلِ the metal workers are on strike; أَضْرَبَ عن الطَعامِ to go/be on a hunger strike

تَضارَبَ *v* to be contradictory, to conflict; تَتَضارَبُ الآراءُ there's a conflict of opinions

اِضْطَرَبَ *v* to be shocked; to be/become unsettled, to be/become agitated, to be/become confused; to be restless; اضْطَرَبَ شُعورُهُ he felt confused; اضْطَرَبَتْ حَرَكةُ القِطاراتِ the train traffic was disrupted

ضَرْب *n* **1** [تَخَبُّط] beating, striking; كالَ ,أَوْسَعَ شَخْصاً ضَرْباً ضَرَبَ شَخْصاً ضَرْباً مُبَرِّحاً ,لِشَخْصٍ ضَرْباً مُبَرِّحاً to beat sb (up); رَدَّ الضَرْبَ to hit back **2** (Math) multiplication; عَلامة الضَرْبِ multiplication sign; جَداوِل الضَرْبِ the multiplication tables; جَدْوَل الضَرْبِ في ٤ the four-times table **3** [نَوْع] |ضُروب| sort, variety, kind; يُعْتَبَرُ المَسْرَحُ ضَرْباً من ضُروبِ الفَنِّ theatre is considered as a form of art **4** [مَثَل] |أَضْراب| similar, like; أَحْمَد وَأَضْرابُهُ Ahmed and people like him

ضارِب **A** *adj* **1** [فاعِل ضَرَبَ] hitting, beating, giving a beating; الشَخْص الضارِب والشَخْص المَضْروب the person who did the beating and the person who got beat up **2** [مائِل إلى] إلى tending to, verging on, -ish; أَخْضَر ضارِب إلى الصُفْرةِ green verging on yellow, yellowish green

B *n* hitter, person who administers a beating

ضَرائِبيّ *adj* tax (*before n*); غِشّ ضَرائِبيّ tax fraud

ضَرْبة *n* |ضَرَبات| **1** [خَبْطة] blow, strike, bang; ضَرْبة قَوِيّة \ خَفيفة a strong/soft blow; ضَرْبة خاطِئة a miss; ضَرْبة رَأْسيّة headbutt; ضَرْبة جَوِّيّة air strike; تَلَقّى ضَرْبةً to take a blow; وَجَّهَ ضَرْبةً لِشَخْصٍ to deal sb a blow; سَقَطَ بالضَرْبةِ القاضِيةِ to go down; ضَرَبَ شَخْصاً ضَرْبةً قاضِيةً to knock sb out **2** [رَكْلة] shot, kick; ضَرْبة قَوِيّة \ خَفيفة a hard/weak shot; ضَرْبة حُرّة a free kick; ضَرْبة رُكْنيّة \ زاوِيةٍ corner (kick); ضَرْبة انْطِلاقٍ kick-off; ضَرْبة طائِرة overhead kick; ضَرْبة جَزاءٍ penalty (kick) **3** (fig) blow; ضَرْبة قاسِية \ قَوِيّة \ موجِعة

اضْطِراب *n* |اضْطِرابات| 1▸ [فَوْضى] unrest, turmoil; commotion, consternation, agitation; اضْطِرابات disturbances, unrest, riots; اضْطِرابات اجْتِماعيّة \ سِياسيّة social/political turmoil; اضْطِرابات شَديدة \ خَطيرة major/serious disturbances; اضْطِراب الوَضْعِ the restless situation; سَبَّبَ اضْطِراباً to stir up trouble, to cause a stir; وَقَعَت \ تَفَجَّرَت \ انْدَلَعَت اضْطِراباتٌ disturbances broke out; شَهِدَت العاصِمةُ اضْطِراباتٍ there was unrest in the capital; (وَقَعَ \ كانَ في) حالةِ الاضْطِرابِ (to get into/to be in) a state of turmoil; تَشْهَدُ البِلادُ اضْطِراباتٍ there's turmoil in the country 2▸ [حَيْرة] derangement, confusion; اضْطِراب نَفْسيّ internal conflict; اضْطِراب التَوَتُّر ما بعد الحَوادِثِ post-traumatic stress syndrome, PTSD; اضْطِراب الوَسْواسِ القَهْريّ obsessive-compulsive disorder, OCD; سَبَّبَ الاضْطِرابَ to cause confusion, to cause a stir 3▸ [جَوّيّ] turbulence; اضْطِرابات جَوّيّة air turbulence; اضْطِرابات شَديدة severe turbulence

تَضارُب *n* discrepancy, conflict; تَضارُب المَصالِحِ conflict of interests

مُتَضارِب *adj* contradictory, contrary, conflicting; مَصالِح مُتَضارِبة conflicting interests

مُضارِب *n* speculator; gambler

مُضارَبة *n* speculation; gambling

مُضارَبيّ *adj* speculative

مِضْراب *n* |مَضاريبُ| (Sport) bat; racket; mallet

مَضْرِب *n* |مَضارِبُ| place, spot; مَضْرِب المَثَلِ model, classic example

مُضْرِب *n* striker; مُضْرِب عن الطَعامِ hunger striker; مُضْرِب عن العَمَلِ striker

مِضْرَب *n* |مَضارِبُ| (Sport) racket; bat; mallet; مِضْرَب تِنِس tennis racket; كُرة المِضْرَبِ tennis; لَعِبَ كُرَةَ المِضْرَبِ to play tennis

مَضْروب *adj* 1▸ [ضُرِبَ] struck, hit; beaten; الشَخْص المَضْروب the person who was beaten up 2▸ [مُحَدَّد] determined, appointed; المَوْعِد المَضْروب the fixed appointment 3▸ (Math) multiplied; مَضْروب في ثَلاثةٍ multiplied by three

مُضْطَرِب *adj* restless; confused, upset; tumultuous, turbulent; زَمَن \ فَتْرة مُضْطَرِب(ة) turbulent times; نَوْم مُضْطَرِب restless sleep; كانَتْ حَرَكةُ القِطاراتِ مُضْطَرِبةً the train traffic was disrupted; عَلاقة مُضْطَرِبة an uneasy relationship; كانَ مُضْطَرِباً to be confused, to be in a muddle; ظُروف مُضْطَرِبة turbulent circumstances; إقْليم مُضْطَرِب a troubled area; مُضْطَرِب نَفْسيًّا (mentally) disturbed

‹ **ضَرَجَ** *v* |u; ضَرْج| to stain, to spot

تَضَرَّجَ *v* 1▸ [الخَدُّ] to blush 2▸ [بالدَمِ] to be stained (*with blood*)

مُضَرَّج *adj* bloody

‹ **ضَريح** *n* |أَضْرِحة, ضَرائِحُ| tomb, grave; mausoleum

‹ **ضَرَّ** *v* |u; ضَرّ| to damage, to harm, to injure; to hurt; ضَرَّ شَخْصاً \ بِشَخْصٍ to cause sb harm; لا يَضُرُّ كَثيراً بِذَلِكَ البَلَدِ it doesn't cause that country much harm; لا يَضُرُّ أَنّ ... it doesn't hurt that ..., it's no harm that ...; لا يَضُرُّهُ ذلك that doesn't hurt him; ضَرَّ بِمَصالِحِ شَخْصٍ to harm sb's interests; يَضُرُّ أَكْثَرَ مِمّا يُفيدُ it does more harm than good

أَضَرَّ *v* 1▸ [ضَرَّ] to damage, to harm, to injure; to hurt; أَضَرَّ شَخْصاً \ بِشَخْصٍ to cause sb harm; أَضَرَّ بِسُمْعةٍ to damage a reputation; أَضَرَّ بِبَيْتٍ to damage a house; التَدْخينُ يُضِرُّ بالصِحّةِ smoking is harmful to one's health 2▸ [تَزَوَّجَ على ضَرّةٍ] *to marry a second (third, fourth) wife* 3▸ [أَجْبَرَ] to force, to oblige; أَضَرَّ شَخْصاً على شَيْءٍ to force sb to do sth

تَضَرَّرَ *v* to be damaged, to be harmed; to suffer (damage); تَضَرَّرَ كَثيراً من ... to suffer badly from ...

اضْطَرَّ *v* |a| to force, to oblige, to compel; اضْطَرَّ شَخْصاً إلى شَيْءٍ to force sb to do sth; اضْطَرَّ ذلك إلى اتِّخاذِ إجْراءاتٍ سَريعةٍ that called for quick action; اُضْطُرَّ إلى شَيْءٍ to be forced/compelled to do sth; اُضْطُرِرْنا للعَوْدةِ إلى البَيْتِ we were forced to return home

ضَرَر *n* |أَضْرار| 1▸ [أَذًى] damage, harm, injury; disadvantage, loss; ضَرَر خَفيف minor damage; أَضْرار جَسيمة \ بالِغة \ فادِحة severe damage; ضَرَر مَعْنَويّ moral/emotional damage; ضَرَر جَسَديّ a physical trauma; لا ضَرَرَ في أَنّ ... there's no harm in ...; لَحِقَ بِهِ ضَرَرٌ to suffer a loss; أَحْدَثَ \ أَوْقَعَ \ أَلْحَقَ ضَرَراً to cause harm, to harm; سَبَّبَ \ أَلْحَقَ ضَرَراً

إضْرار *n* damage, harm

اضْطِرار *n* ① [إكْراه] compulsion, coercion ② [حاجة مُلِحّة] necessity, (urgent) need, exigency; عند الاضْطِرارِ if need be; in case of emergency

اضْطِراريّ *adj* coercive, compulsory, forced; urgent, emergency (*before n*); في حالاتٍ اضْطِراريّةٍ in urgent cases; هُبوط اضْطِراريّ an emergency landing; لِأَسْبابٍ اضْطِراريّةٍ for compelling reasons

مُتَضَرِّر A *adj* damaged, injured, harmed; aggrieved, hurt; كانَ مُتَضَرِّراً to be harmed
B *n* victim

مُضِرّ *adj* harmful, damaging; detrimental, adverse; تَأْثير مُضِرّ a detrimental effect; (هذا) مُضِرٌّ بالصِحّةِ (that is) harmful to one's health; مُضِرّ بالبيئةِ harmful to the environment; غَيْر مُضِرٍّ بالبيئةِ harmless to the environment, environmentally friendly

مَضَرّة *n* |مَضارُّ, مَضَرّات| damage, harm; disadvantage, detriment

مَضْرور *adj* damaged

مُضْطَرّ *adj* forced, compelled, obliged; كانَ مُضْطَرًّا أنْ ... to be forced to ...; وَجَدَ نَفْسَهُ مُضْطَرًّا لِفِعْلِ شَيْءٍ to find oneself compelled to do sth

ضَرَسَ *v* |i; ضَرْس| to bite firmly

ضِرْس *n* |ضُروس, أَضْراس| molar; ضِرْس العَقْلِ wisdom tooth; تاج الضِرْسِ (molar) crown; قَلَعَ ضِرْساً to extract a molar

ضَروس *adj* destructive, fierce; حَرْب ضَروس a fierce war

تَضاريس *n pl* |dipt| relief; تَضاريس أَرْضيّة ground elevations; تَضاريس الوَجْهِ facial wrinkles

ضَرَطَ *v* |i; ضَرْط| to fart, to pass gas

ضُراط *n* fart

ضَرَعَ *v* |a; ضُروع, ضَراعة| ① [ذَلَّ] to be humble; to humble oneself ② [سَأَلَ] to implore, to beg, to beseech

ضارَعَ *v* to match; to resemble, to look like; ضارَعَ شَخْصاً to resemble sb

أَضْرَعَ *v* to subject, to subdue; أَضْرَعَتْهُ الحُمّى the fever had weakened him

بِشَخْصٍ to cause sb harm; طالَبَ بِتَعْويضٍ عن الضَرَرِ to claim damages; حَدَّدَ الأَضْرارَ to assess the damage; أَصْلَحَ الضَرَرَ to repair the damage; بِدونِ أَضْرارٍ without damage, without an accident; أَضْرار بيئيّة environmental damage; أَخَفّ الضَرَرَيْنِ the lesser of two evils; لم يَرَ ضَرَراً في ذلك he saw no harm in it ② (Isl Law) *infliction of harm by a husband on his wife (as grounds for divorce)*

ضارّ A *adj* harmful, damaging; مَوادّ \ آثار ضارّة harmful substances/consequences; خَطَأ ضارّ a harmful mistake; غَيْر ضارٍّ harmless; مَوادّ غَيْر ضارّةٍ harmless substances; مَرَض غَيْر ضارٍّ a harmless disease
B *n* الضارّ the Harmer (*one of the names of God*)

ضارّة *n that which is harmful*; رُبَّ ضارّةٍ نافعةٌ it's a blessing in disguise

ضُرّ *n* harm, damage

ضَرّاء *n* |dipt f| adversity, misfortune; في السَرّاءِ والضَرّاءِ through thick and thin, for better or for worse

ضَرّة *n* |ضَرائِرُ, ضَرّات| *the second, third or fourth wife of a man*

ضَرورة *n* necessity, need; urgency; ضَرورة مُلِحّة an urgent need; ضَرورة مُطْلَقة an absolute necessity; ضَرورة قُصْوى highest urgency; عند الضَرورةِ القُصْوى (فَقَطْ) (only) if absolutely necessary; ضَرورة شَيْءٍ the necessity of sth; بالضَرورةِ necessarily; في حالةِ الضَرورةِ if needed, in case of emergency; ضَرورات الحَياةِ الأَساسيّة the basic necessities of life; الضَرورات تُبيحُ المَحْظوراتِ, للضَرورةِ أَحْكامٌ necessity knows no law

ضَروريّ *adj* necessary, imperative, indispensable; required; المُكَوِّنات \ الأَشْياء الضَروريّة the necessary ingredients/stuff; ضَروريّ جِدًّا badly needed, urgently required; غَيْر ضَروريٍّ unnecessary; كانَ ضَروريًّا لِشَيْءٍ to be necessary for sth; من الضَروريّ أنْ ... it is necessary that ...; لَيْسَ ذلك ضَروريًّا that is not necessary

ضَروريّة *n* necessity; ضَروريّات الحَياةِ the necessities of life; ضَروريّات الحَياةِ الأَساسيّة the basic necessities of life

ضَرير A *adj* |أَضْرار, أَضِرّاءُ| blind
B *n* |أَضْرار, أَضِرّاءُ| blind person; الأَضِرّاء the blind

تَضَرَّعَ *v* ① [إلى | ابْتَهَلَ] to implore, to beg, to beseech; تَضَرَّعَ إلى اللهِ أنْ ... to beg God to ... ② [ذَلَّ] to be humble

ضَرْع *n* |ضُروع| udder

ضِرْع *n* |ضُروع| equal, peer

ضارِع *adj* humble, submissive; entreating

ضَراعة *n* supplication, invocation

تَضَرُّع *n* |تضرُّعات| plea, entreaty, supplication

مُضارِع *n* ① (Gram) present (tense); imperfect (aspect); صيغة المُضارِع present tense; فِعْل مُضارِع an imperfect verb; حُروف المُضارِع prefixes of the imperfect; المُضارِع المَرْفوع present indicative; المُضارِع المَنْصوب subjunctive; المُضارِع المَجْزوم jussive ② [مَثيل] match, equal, parallel

مُضارَعة *n* similarity, resemblance

ضُرْغوس *n* (Bot) marsh marigold, kingcup

ضَرِمَ *v* |a; ضَرَم| to burn, to be on fire

أَضْرَمَ *v* to light, to kindle; to fan; أَضْرَمَ النارَ في شَيْءٍ to set sth on fire

اضْطَرَمَ *v* to burn, to be on fire; to flare up, to blaze up

ضِرْو *n* |أَضْرٍ, ضِراء| hunting dog

ضارٍ A *adj* |ضَوارٍ| wild, ferocious, fierce; violent; مَعْرَكة ضارية a fierce battle
B *n* |ضَوارٍ| predator

ضَراوة *n* ferocity, fierceness; ruthlessness

ضَعة *n* see وضع

ضَعْضَعَ *v* |i; ضَعْضَعة| to demolish, to tear down, to destroy; to weaken, to undermine; ضَعْضَعَ مَعْنَويّاتِ شَخْصٍ to undermine sb's morale

تَضَعْضَعَ *v* to decline, to decay, to weaken; to dissolve, to fall apart

ضَعْضَعة *n* destruction, demolition; sapping, undermining

مُتَضَعْضِع *adj* dilapidated, declining; weak

1 **ضَعُفَ** *v* |u; ضَعْف, ضُعْف| to be/become weak, to weaken, to become slack; to fade, to wane, to abate; ضَعُفَ اهْتِمامُهُ his attention faded; ضَعُفَت الرياحُ the wind has abated; لَقَدْ ضَعُفَ مَوْقِفُنا بعد ذلك الحادثِ our position is weakened by this incident; ضَعُفَ جوعاً to be faint with hunger

ضَعَّفَ *v* ① [أَضْعَفَ] to weaken, to mitigate ② [ثَنّى] see ضعف 2

أَضْعَفَ *v* to weaken, to enfeeble, to mitigate; to undermine; أَضْعَفَتْهُ الحُمّى he has been weakened by the fever; أَضْعَفَهُ الجوعُ واليَأْسُ hunger and despair weakened him; أَضْعَفَ المَعْنَويّاتِ to demoralize; أَضْعَفَ مَعْنَويّاتِ شَخْصٍ to demoralize sb

اسْتَضْعَفَ *v* to deem weak

ضَعْف, ضُعْف *n* weakness, feebleness; weakening, enfeeblement; لَحْظة ضَعْفٍ a moment of weakness; نُقْطة ضَعْفٍ weakness, weak spot, Achilles heel; ضَعْف جِنْسيّ impotence (sexual); ضَعْف الجِسْمِ \ جِهازِ المَناعة the weakening of the body/immune system; شَعَرَ بِضَعْفٍ to feel weak; ضَعْف النَظَرِ \ البَصَرِ poor eyesight; دَليل على الضَعْفِ evidence of weakness

ضَعيف *adj* |ضِعاف, ضُعَفاءُ; f pl ضَعيفات, ضَعائِفُ| weak, feeble; delicate, frail, faint; حُجّة \ شَخْصيّة ضَعيفة a weak argument/character; احْتِجاج ضَعيف a feeble protest; صِحّة ضَعيفة delicate health; شَمْس ضَعيفة a pale sun; نَتيجة ضَعيفة a poor result; ضَعيف في الرِياضيّاتِ weak in mathematics; دَليل ضَعيف weak evidence; مَوْقِف ضَعيف a weak position; كانَ مَوْقِفُهُ ضَعيفاً to not have a leg to stand on

إضْعاف *n* undermining; weakening, enfeeblement

مُسْتَضْعَف *adj* weak, feeble

2 **ضَعَّفَ** *v* ① [ثَنّى] to double, to multiply ② [أَضْعَفَ] see ضعف 1

ضاعَفَ *v* to increase, to raise; to double, to multiply; ضاعَفَ ثَلاثَ مَرّاتٍ to triple; ضاعَفوا مَجْهوداتِهِمْ they doubled their efforts; ضاعَفَ الرِهانَ to double the stakes; ضاعَفَ السُرْعة to speed up; ضاعَفَ من أَهَمّيّة شَيْءٍ to make sth more important; ضاعَفَ الحيطةَ to be extra careful

تَضاعَفَ *v* to double, to be doubled; تَضاعَفَ ثَلاثَ مَرّاتٍ to triple; تَضاعَفَ الرِبحُ profits have doubled; تَضاعَفَ عَدَدُ المُتَسابِقينَ أَرْبَعةَ أَمْثالٍ the number of contenders has quadrupled

ضِعْف *n* |أَضْعاف| double; multiple, -fold; ضِعْف تِلْكَ الكَمِّيّةِ twice as much as that; أَضْعافاً مُضاعَفةً many times; بَلَغَت زادَت الإيرادات it increased fivefold; الزِيادةُ خَمْسة أَضْعافٍ revenues have increased عَشَرة أَضْعافٍ ما كانَتْ عَلَيْهِ قبل ذلك tenfold compared to before; أُعْطيكَ أَضْعافَ ما حَلَمْتَ بِهِ I will give you many times more than you ever dreamt of

مُضاعَف **A** *adj* **1** [مُضَعَّف] doubled; تُعَدُّ تِلْكَ الدَرَجاتُ مُضاعَفةً those marks (BrE) grades (AmE) count double **2** (Gram) doubled, geminate; أَفْعال مُضاعَفة geminate verbs (*verbs where the second and third radicals are the same*)

B *n* multiple; المُضاعَف المُشْتَرَك الأَصْغَر (Math) the lowest common multiple

مُضاعَفة *n* **1** [آثار] complication; مُضاعَفات خَطيرة serious complications; مُضاعَفات طِبِّيّة medical complications; مُضاعَفات جانِبِيّة side effects; أَدّى إلى مُضاعَفاتٍ to lead to complications; تَظْهَرُ مُضاعَفاتٌ complications arise **2** [تَثْنِية] doubling; مُضاعَفة حَجْمِ الأَعْمالِ a doubling of turnover; بِمُضاعَفةِ الجُهودِ with redoubled efforts; أَضْعاف مُضاعَفة many times

مُضَعَّف *adj* doubled; جَهْد مُضَعَّف a redoubled effort; فِعْل مُضَعَّف (Gram) doubled/geminate verb

‹ **ضِغْث** *n* |أَضْغاث| mixture, mishmash, jumble; أَضْغاث أَحْلامٍ pipe dream

‹ **ضَغَطَ** *v* |a; ضَغْط| **1** [على شَيْءٍ \ سَخْصٍ] to press, to push; to squeeze, to exert pressure on; ضَغَطَ على شَخْصٍ to put pressure on sb; ضَغَطَ على زِرٍّ to push a button; ضَغَطَ على الزِنادِ to pull the trigger **2** [بالماوْس] to click; ضَغَطَ بالماوْس to click with the mouse **3** [مِلَفًّا] to compress, to zip; ضَغَطَ مِلَفًّا to compress a file

اِنْضَغَطَ *v* to be compressed, to be squeezed

ضَغْط *n* |ضُغوط| **1** [عَصْر] pressure, stress, tension; ضَغْط مائيّ \ هَيْدْروليّ hydraulic pressure; ضَغْط تَصاعُديّ \ تنازُليّ upward/downward pressure; ضَغْط زائِد excessive pressure; ضَغْط خارِجيّ external pressure; ضَغْط مُضادّ counterpressure; فارِق الضَغْطِ pressure difference; ضَغْط دَمَويّ \ الدَمِ blood pressure; قاس الضَغْطَ to measure blood pressure; الضَغْط الانْبِساطيّ \ الانْقِباضيّ (للدَم) diastolic/systolic blood pressure; ضَغْط نَفْسيّ psychological pressure; وَسيلة \ وَرَقة ضَغْطٍ lever; مُنَظِّم الضَغْطِ pressure regulator; ضَغْط العَمَلِ work pressure; عَمِلَ تحت الضَغْط to work under pressure; ضَغْط الوَقْتِ time pressure; تحت ضَغْطٍ under pressure; مارَسَ ضُغوطاً على شَخْصٍ to put pressure on sb; مارَسَ تَمْرينَ الضَغْطِ to do press-ups (BrE) pushups (AmE) **2** (Meteorol) (air) pressure; ضَغْط جَوّيّ atmospheric pressure, air pressure; انْخِفاض الضَغْطِ الجَوّيّ depression, low; مُتَوَسِّط الضَغْطِ الجَوّيّ the average air pressure; مِنْطَقة ضَغْطٍ جَوّيٍّ مُرْتَفِع \ مُنْخَفِضٍ a high-pressure/low-pressure area; يَرْتَفِعُ الضَغْطُ الجَوّيُّ the air pressure is rising; مِقْياس الضَغْطِ الجَوّيّ barometer

ضاغِط **A** *adj* oppressive; pressing, compression (*before n*); رِباط ضاغِط compression garment

B *n* (Tech) compressor

ضَغْطة *n* click

مَضْغوط *adj* pressed, compressed; خَشَب مَضْغوط hardboard, pressboard; قُرْص مَضْغوط CD-ROM; مِلَفّ مَضْغوط a compressed file

‹ **ضَغِنَ** *v* |a; ضِغْن| |على| to bear a grudge; to have an aversion; ضَغِنَ على شَخْصٍ to bear a grudge against sb

ضِغْن *n* grudge, resentment

ضَغينة *n* |ضَغائِنُ| rancour, grudge, resentment; حَمَلَ ضَغينةً على شَخْصٍ to bear a grudge against sb

‹ **ضِفْدَع، ضِفْدِع** *n* |ضَفادِعُ| (Zool) frog; toad; ضِفْدَع بَشَريّ، رَجُل ضِفْدَع frogman, diver

‹ **ضَفَر** *v* |i; ضَفْر| to braid, to plait; to intertwine, to interweave

ضَفَّر *v* to braid, to plait; ضَفَّرَتْ شَعْرَها she braided her hair

ضافَرَ *v* |على| to help, to assist, to aid; ضافَرَ على شَخْصٍ to help sb

تَضافَرَ *v* to help one another, to cooperate, to work together; to come together; تَضافَرَتْ عَوامِلُ عِدّةٌ على \ في \ ل ... various factors played a role in ...

ضَفيرة *n* |ضَفائِرُ| **1** [في الشَعْرِ] braid, plait; جَدَّلَتْ شَعْرَها في ضَفائِرَ she braided her hair **2** (Anat) plexus

تضافُر *n* [1] [تَقارُب] joining, coming together; تَضافُر جُهودٍ joining of forces [2] (Phys) convergence

‹ **ضِفّة, ضَفّة** *n* |ضِفاف| bank, shore; waterfront, waterside; الضِفّة الغَرْبيّة west bank; the West Bank (*portion of Palestine west of the river Jordan*); على ضِفّةِ نَهْرِ النيل on the banks of the Nile; على (طولِ) الضِفافِ at/by the waterside, on the shore

‹ **ضَفا** *v* |u; ضَفْو| to be abundant, to be copious

أَضْفى *v* to allot generously, to give in abundance

ضافٍ *adj* [1] [مُفَصَّل] detailed, elaborate [2] [غَزير] abundant, copious

إضْفاء *n* giving, granting

‹ **ضَلَعَ** *v* |مع| to side with

ضَلُعَ *v* |u; ضَلاعة| to be strong

ضَلِعَ *v* |a; ضَلَع| to be/become bent, to be/become crooked

ضَلَّعَ *v* to bend, to crook

تَضَلَّعَ *v* to be skilled, to be proficient; to be experienced, to be knowledgeable; تَضَلَّعَ من شَيْءٍ to be proficient in sth

اضْطَلَعَ *v* |ب| اضْطَلَعَ بِشَيْءٍ to take sth upon oneself; اضْطَلَعَ بالمَسْؤوليّة to claim the responsibility

ضِلْع, ضِلَع, ضِلَع *n* |أَضْلُع, أَضْلاع, ضُلوع| [1] (Anat) rib; ضِلْع مَكْسور \ مَرْضوض a broken/bruised rib; لَحْم الضِلْعِ chop, cutlet [2] (Geom) edge, side, leg; أَضْلاع المُثَلَّثِ \ المُرَبَّع the sides of a triangle/square; مُتَساوي الأَضْلاع equilateral

ضالِع *adj* [1] [مُتَعاوِن] involved; كانَ ضالِعاً في المُؤامَرة to be involved in the plot [2] [أَعْوَج] bent, crooked

ضُلوع *n* involvement, complicity

ضَليع [A] *adj* |ضُلَع| skilful, proficient; learned, erudite; كانَ ضَليعاً في القانونِ to be well informed about the law, to be acquainted with the law

[B] *n* |ضُلَع| expert, specialist

اضْطِلاع *n* assumption, taking upon oneself; undertaking, carrying out; نَبَّهَ شَخْصاً إلى ضَرورة الاضْطِلاع بِمَسْؤوليّاتِهِ to point out to sb the need to carry out his responsibilities

مُتَضَلِّع [A] *adj* proficient, experienced, trained, well-versed; كانَ مُتَضَلِّعاً في شَيْءٍ to be well-versed in sth

[B] *n* expert, specialist

مُضَلَّع *adj* polygonal; ribbed, corded, corrugated; شَكْل مُضَلَّع polygon

‹ **ضَلَّ** *v* |i; ضَلالة, ضَلال| [1] [تاهَ] to stray, to wander; to lose one's way, to be/get lost; ضَلَّ الطَريقَ \ عن الطَريقِ to lose one's way, to get lost; ضَلَّ سَعْيُهُ his efforts were in vain [2] (Islam) *to stray from the right path*

ضَلَّلَ *v* to mislead, to misguide; to delude, to deceive; ضَلَّلَ شَخْصاً to mislead sb

أَضَلَّ *v* to mislead, to misguide; to delude, to deceive; أَضَلَّ شَخْصاً to lead sb up the garden path

ضالّ [A] *adj* |ضُوالُّ, ضالّونَ| lost, astray; straying, wandering; erroneous, false; أَفْكار ضالّة misguided ideas

[B] *n* |ضُوالُّ| rogue; *one who is lost/has strayed*; المُؤْمِنُ الوَحيدُ في بَلَدٍ من الضالّينَ a pilgrim in an unholy land

ضالّة *n* |ضَوالُّ, ضالّات| goal, objective; wish; ضالّة مَنْشودة a long-desired goal

ضَلال, ضَلالة *n* [1] [انْحِراف] deviation, error; going astray [2] (Islam) *straying from the right path*

ضَلالة *n* lapse, error; sin

أُضْلولة *n* |أَضاليلُ| error

تَضْليل *n* deception; misguidance

تَضْليليّ *adj* misleading, deceptive

مَضَلّ *n* maze

مُضَلِّل *adj* misleading; deceptive; تَقْرير مُضَلِّل a misleading report

‹ **اضْمَحَلَّ** *v* |اضْمِحْلال| to disappear, to wane, to fade; بَدَأَتْ سُلْطَتُهُ تَضْمَحِلُّ his power began to fade; اضْمَحَلَّت القِيَمُ والأَخْلاقُ values and morals have eroded

اضْمِحْلال *n* decline, fall, deterioration; اضْمِحْلال طَبَقة الأوزونِ depletion of the ozone layer

‹ **ضَمَخَ** *v* |u; ضَمْخ| to perfume; to rub, to anoint

ضَمَّخَ *v* to anoint lavishly

مُضَمَّخ *adj* |ب| soaked with

‹ **ضَمَدَ** *v* |i; ضَمْد| to bandage, to dress

ضَمَّدَ *v* to bandage, to dress; ضَمَّدَ جَرْحاً to dress a wound

ضِماد *n coll* |ضِمادات ,ضَمائِدُ ,أَضْمِدة| bandage, dressing; وَضَعَ ضِمادةً to put on a bandage; صُنْدوق الضِماداتِ first-aid kit, band-aid box

تَضْميد *n* dressing (*of a wound*)

مُضَمَّد *adj* bandaged, dressed

ضَمَرَ *v* |u; ضُمور ,ضُمْر| to waste away; to lose weight

ضَمَّرَ *v* to make thin

أَضْمَرَ *v* to hide, to keep secret, to keep quiet; to harbour, to entertain; أَضْمَرَ حِقْداً to hold a grudge; شُعوب تُضْمِرُ العَداء لِبَعْضِها البَعْض peoples that harbour hostility toward each other; أَضْمَرَ شَيْئاً في نَفْسِهِ to keep sth to oneself; أَضْمَرَ لِشَخْصٍ الشَرَّ to harbour ill will against sb; أَضْمَرَ لِشَخْصٍ الخَيْرَ to wish sb well

ضامِر *adj* |ضَوامِرُ ,ضُمَّر| emaciated, wasted (away); slim, thin, svelte

ضُمور *n* emaciation; slenderness, slimness

ضَمير *n* |ضَمائِرُ| **1** [تَكْوين نَفْسيّ] conscience; heart, inner self; تَأْنيب \ وَخْز \ تَبْكيت الضَميرِ remorse, compunction, contrition; بَكَّتَهُ \ أَنَّبَهُ ضَميرُهُ his conscience troubled him; أَحَسَّ بِتَأْنيبِ الضَميرِ ,كانَ ضَميرُهُ يُؤَنِّبُهُ to have a guilty conscience; حَيّ الضَمير conscientious; مَعْدوم الضَميرِ unscrupulous; هو شَخْصٌ لا ضَميرَ لَهُ he is an unscrupulous person; صَوْت الضَميرِ the voice of conscience; لم يَسْمَحْ لَهُ ضَميرُهُ بِأَنْ يَفْعَلَ ذلك he did not find it in his heart to do that; أَراحَ ضَميرَهُ to soothe one's conscience **2** (Gram) pronoun; ضَمير المِلْكيّةِ possessive pronoun; ضَمير مُتَّصِل pronominal suffix; ضَمير الغائِبِ third person

ضَميريّ *adj* conscientious; واجِب ضَميريّ an obligation of conscience

إِضْمار *n* **1** (Rhet) ellipsis **2** [إِخْفاء] concealment

مِضْمار *n* |مَضاميرُ| **1** (Sport) track, course; arena; مِضْمار سِباقٍ circuit, racetrack; مِضْمار الجولْفِ golf course, golf links **2** [مَيْدان] field, domain; في مِضْمارِ ... in the field of ...; ما وَرَدَ في هذا المِضْمارِ هو ... what's available in this field is ...

مُضْمَر *adj* **1** [مَخْفيّ] hidden, secret, concealed; أَمَل \ هَدَف مُضْمَر a secret hope/goal **2** (Gram) *related to personal pronouns*; اسْم مُضْمَر personal pronoun

ضَمَّ *v* |u; ضَمّ| **1** [جَمَعَ] to unite, to join, to combine; to consist, to include; to add up; ضَمَّ أَجْزاءً إلى بَعْضِها to combine parts together; يَضُمُّ الحَيُّ الجَديدُ مائَتَيْ مَسْكَنٍ the new district consists of two hundred houses **2** [أَضافَ] to add, to join; to annex, to incorporate; ضَمَّ أَرْضاً to incorporate an area; ضَمَّ بَلَداً to annex a country; ضَمَّ أَعْضاءً جُدُداً إلى الجَمْعيّةِ to admit new members to the club; ضَمَّ مُرْفَقاً إلى رِسالةٍ to add an enclosure to a letter; ضَمَّ الصُفوفَ to close (up) the ranks **3** [حَضَنَ] to embrace, to hug; ضَمَّ شَخْصاً to embrace sb; ضَمَّ شَخْصاً إلى صَدْرِهِ to hug sb **4** (Gram) *to pronounce with the vowel u*

انْضَمَّ *v* **1** [الْتَحَقَ] |إلى| to join, to enter; انْضَمَّ إلى مَجْلِسٍ \ جَماعةٍ \ كَنيسةٍ to join a committee/group/church; انْضَمَّ إلى صُفوفِ العَدوِّ to join the enemy ranks **2** [اتَّحَدَ] to unite, to join forces

ضامّ *adj* retracting; عَضَلة ضامّة (Anat) retractor (muscle)

ضَمّ *n* **1** [جَمْع] joining, junction **2** (Pol) annexation, incorporation **3** [إِضافة] addition

ضَمّة *n* damma (*the vowel sign for u*)

ضَميمة *n* |ضَمائِمُ| addendum, appendix

إِضْمامة *n* pad

انْضِمام *n* joining, entry; الانْضِمام إلى الاتّحادِ الأوروبّيِّ entry into the European Community

مَضْموم *adj* **1** [مَجْموع] included, incorporated; joined together **2** (Gram) *with the vowel u (damma)*

ضَمِنَ *v* |a; ضَمان| to guarantee, to warrant, to safeguard; to vouch, to stand surety; ضَمِنَ شَخْصاً \ شَيْئاً to vouch for sb/sth; ضَمِنَ لِشَخْصٍ نَجاحَ شَيْءٍ to guarantee sb that sth will succeed; ضَمِنَ الأَمْنَ to guarantee safety; ضَمِنَ جَوْدةَ مُنْتَجٍ to guarantee the quality of a product

ضَمَّنَ *v* **1** [أَدْرَجَ] to enclose, to incorporate, to include; ضَمَّنَ بَحْثَهُ أَحْدَثَ النَظَريّاتِ to include the latest theories in one's study **2** (Tech) to modulate

مُتَضَمَّن *adj* included; implied

مُتَضَمِّن *adj* including, containing

مِضْمان *n* modem

مُضَمَّن *adj* embedded, included

مَضْمون A *adj* registered; guaranteed; رِسالة مَضْمونة a registered letter
B *n* |مَضامينُ| 1 [مَعْنًى] content, purport, meaning 2 (Tunisia) [شَهادة] certificate; مَضْمون وِلادةٍ birth certificate

ضَنُكَ *v* |u; ضَناكة ,ضَنْك| 1 [الشَّخْصُ] to weaken, to be/become weak 2 [العَيْشُ] to be miserable, to be wretched

ضَنْك *n* 1 [شِدّة] distress, poverty, malaise; عَيْش ضَنْكٍ a hard life 2 [ضِيق] strait

ضَنَّ *v* |a; ضَنانة| to begrudge; ضَنَّ على شَخْصٍ بِشَيْءٍ to begrudge sb sth

ضَنين *adj* |أَضِنّاءُ; f pl ضَنائِنُ| 1 [بَخيل] economical, frugal; miserly, stingy 2 [حَريص |ب] devoted, dedicated

ضَنِيَ *v* |a; ضَنًى| to pine away, to languish, to wither

أَضْنَى *v* to exhaust, to fatigue

ضَنًى *n* exhaustion, fatigue

مُضْنٍ *adj* tiring, wasting, exhausting; مَرَض مُضْنٍ a wasting disease; بَذَلَ جُهوداً مُضْنِيَةً to overstrain oneself

اضْطَهَدَ *v* to oppress, to suppress; اضْطَهَدَ الأَقَلِّيّاتِ العِرْقيّةَ to oppress ethnic minorities

اضْطِهاد *n* |اضْطِهادات| oppression, repression, tyranny; اضْطِهاد عِرْقيّ وَدينيّ persecution/oppression on account of race and religion; اضْطِهاد اسْتِعْماريّ \ شَديد colonial/forceful oppression; تَعَرَّضَ للاضْطِهاد to be oppressed, to live in oppression; جُنون الاضْطِهاد persecution complex, paranoia

مُضْطَهِد *n* oppressor, tyrant, persecutor

ضَهْر *n* |ضُهور| summit, mountaintop

ضَهْوة *n* pouch

ضاهى *v* to compare to; to be similar to, to be equal to; ضاهى الفولاذَ صَلابةً to be as strong as steel; لا يُضاهى incomparable, unmatched; أَسْعار لا تُضاهى incomparable

تَضَمَّنَ *v* to contain, to include, to comprise; ماذا يَتَضَمَّنُ هذا الاقْتِراحُ ؟ what does this proposal include?

تَضامَنَ *v* to be in accord, to stick together; to have joint/mutual responsibility; تَضامَنَ مع شَخْصٍ to have joint responsibility with sb

ضِمْن *n* inside, interior; ضِمْنَ in, among; ب \ من ضِمْنِهِمْ among them; بِضِمْنِها inclusively, including; ضِمْناً implicitly, indirectly; من ضِمْنِ المَبْلَغ included in the amount; من ضِمْنِ واجِباتِه one of his duties; يُفْهَمُ من ضِمْنِ كَلامِه أَنَّهُ غَيْرُ مُوافِقٍ it can be concluded from his words that he does not agree; كانَ التَعْليمُ الإلْزاميُّ من ضِمْنِ الحُلول المُقْتَرَحةِ compulsory education was among the proposed solutions; جاءَ ضِمْنَ بُنودِ المُعاهَدةِ أَنّ ... it is stipulated in the treaty that ...

ضامِن A *adj* |ضامِنونَ ,ضُمّان ,ضَمَنة| accountable, responsible
B *n* |ضامِنونَ ,ضُمّان ,ضَمَنة| guarantor, warrantor

ضَمان *n coll* 1 [تَأْمين] insurance, assurance, security; ضَمان اجْتِماعيّ state/public pension (BrE), social security (AmE); نِظام الضَمانِ الاجْتِماعيّ the state pensions system 2 [كَفالة] guarantee, safeguard; deposit, bail, security; ضَمان (ل) الأَمْنِ safety guarantee; ضَمان شَخْصيّ a personal guarantee; ضَمان عَيْنيّ collateral; اسْتَدانَ شَيْئاً بِضَمانٍ to borrow sth with collateral; ضَمان ماليّ security (money), bail; أَعْطى ضَمانةً مادّيّةً to provide financial guarantees 3 (Busn) guarantee, warranty; شُروط الضَمانِ warranty conditions

ضِمْنيّ *adj* implicit, tacit, hidden; اتِّفاق \ وَعْد ضِمْنيّ a tacit agreement; قَبِلَ شَيْئاً ضِمْنيًّا to take sth for granted

تَضامُن *n* solidarity, joint responsibility; تَضامُناً مع شَخْصٍ in solidarity with sb; شُعور التَضامُنِ (feeling of) solidarity; شَرِكة تَضامُنٍ partnership (firm); أَعْلَنَ التَضامُنَ مع ... to declare one's solidarity with ...

تَضامُنيّ *adj* solidarity (*before n*); عَمَل تَضامُنيّ an act of solidarity; روح تَضامُنيّة solidarity

تَضَمُّن *n* implication

تَضْمين *n* 1 [إِدْراج] implication 2 (Ling) connotation 3 (Tech) modulation (*of radio waves*); تَضْمين التَرَدُّدِ FM (*frequency modulation*)

مُتَضامِن *adj* solidary, united

إضاءة *n* lighting, illumination; اسْتَعْمَلَ الشُموعَ للإضاءةِ to use candles for lighting; إضاءة غَيْر مُباشِرةٍ indirect lighting; إضاءة الشَوارِع street lighting

مُضاء *adj* lighted, lit, illuminated

مُضيء *adj* luminous, shining

‹ **تَضَوَّرَ** *v* to writhe, to be racked (*with pain*); تَضَوَّرَ جوعاً to die of hunger, to starve to death

ضُوْر *n* extreme hunger

‹ **ضَوْضاء** *n* |dipt f| noise, din, racket; ضَوْضاء شَديدة an infernal din; أَحْدَثَ الضَوْضاءَ to make a racket

ضَوْضائيّ *adj* noise (*before n*); تَلَوُّث ضَوْضائيّ noise pollution

‹ **تَضَوَّعَ** *v* to rise, to diffuse (*fumes*)

ضَوْع *n* fragrance; diffusion, emanation

‹ **ضَوى** *v* |i; ضَيّ| ❶ [انْضَمَّ إلى] to join, to resort to ❷ [جَذَبَ] to attract, to draw

ضَوِيَ *v* |a; ضَوًى| to be thin, to be lean

أَضْوى *v* to shrink, to make lean; to weaken

انْضَوى *v* to join, to follow; to rally, to flock; انْضَوى إلى شَيْءٍ to rally around sth

ضاوٍ *adj* thin, lean

‹ **ضارَ** *v* |i; ضَيْر| to harm, to damage, to injure

ضَيْر *n* damage, harm

‹ **ضاعَ** *v* |i; ضَيْع، ضَياع| to get lost, to be lost; to perish; ضاعَتْ مِنْهُ المَفاتيحُ he lost his keys

ضَيَّعَ *v* to lose, to mislay; to waste, to squander; ضَيَّعَ وَقْتَهُ to waste one's time; يُضَيِّعُ هذا الطِفْلُ كُلَّ لُعَبِهِ that child loses all his toys; ضَيَّعَ مالَهُ to forfeit one's money; ضَيَّعَ الفُرْصةَ to miss the chance

أَضاعَ *v* to lose, to mislay; to waste, to squander; أَضاعَ وَقْتَهُ في مُشاهَدةِ التِلِفِزْيونِ to waste one's time watching television; أَضاعَ مَفاتيحَهُ he lost his keys

ضائِع *adj* |ضُيَّع، ضِياع| lost, mislaid; مِفْتاح \ قُفّاز ضائِع a lost key/glove

ضَياع *n* loss; ruin, destruction; ضَياع الفُرَصِ the loss of opportunities; نَجّى \ أَنْجى شَخْصاً من الضَياعِ to save sb

prices; رَجُل لا يُضاهيهِ في الأَهَمِّيّةِ أَحَدٌ a man unmatched in importance

ضَهًى *n* menopause

مُضاهٍ *adj* similar, alike, corresponding; أَسْعار السِلَعِ الغِذائيّةِ في الأُرْدُنِ مُضاهٍ لِأَسْعارِها في مَصْرَ the prices of food in Jordan are similar to those in Egypt

مُضاهاة *n* similarity, likeness, equivalence; لم يَسْتَطِعْ مُضاهاةَ شَخْصٍ \ شَيْءٍ to not be able to match sb/sth

‹ **ضاءَ** *v* |u; ضَوْء| to shine, to gleam

أَضاءَ *v* to light, to illuminate; أَضاءَ غُرْفةً \ قاعةً to illuminate a room/hall; أَضاءَ أَمْراً to shed light on a matter

اسْتَضاءَ *v* to seek enlightenment/insight; اسْتَضاءَ بِنارِ شَخْصٍ to go to sb for information

ضَوْء *n* |أَضْواء| light; ضَوْء كاشِف \ كَشّاف floodlight, spotlight, searchlight; ضَوْء مُعاكِس backlight; ضَوْء فوق البَنَفْسَجيِّ ultraviolet light; ضَوْء مُشْرِق \ مُعْتِم \ خافِت \ شاحِب bright/dim/faint/pale light; ضَوْء النَهارِ daylight; الأَضْواء القُطْبيّة الشَماليّة the northern lights, aurora borealis; في \ على ضَوْءِ ... in the light of ..., in view of ..., according to ...; بِسُرْعةِ الضَوْءِ at the speed of light; سارَ بِسُرْعةِ الضَوْءِ to move at the speed of light; سَلَّطَ الأَضْواءَ على شَخْصٍ to spotlight sb; ظَلَّ بَعيداً عن الأَضْواءِ to keep in the background, to keep a low profile; نَزَحَتْ عَنْهُ الأَضْواءُ he disappeared into anonymity; أَلْقى ضَوْءاً على ...; أَلْقى الضَوْءَ على ... to shed light on ...; تَسْليط الضَوْءِ على شَيْءٍ to shed light on a matter; قَضِيّةٍ the illumination of sth; سَرَقَ الأَضْواءَ to steal the limelight; أَعْطى الضَوْءَ الأَخْضَرَ لِشَيْءٍ to give the green light for sth; ضَوْء مُبْهِر dazzling light; أَطْفَأَ الضَوْءَ to turn off the light; أَشْعَلَ الأَضْواءَ to turn on the light; أَضْواء احْتِفاليّة festive lighting

ضَوْئيّ *adj* light (*before n*); مُؤَشِّر ضَوْئيّ indicator light; وَمْضة ضَوْئيّة flash of light; كَوابِل ضَوْئيّة fibre optic cables; إِعْلان ضَوْئيّ illuminated advertising; سَنة ضَوْئيّة light year; كَشّاف ضَوْئيّ torch (BrE), flashlight (AmE); floodlight; عَمَليّة التَرْكيبِ الضَوْئيِّ photosynthesis

ضِياء *n* light, brightness

as well as; إضافةً \ إضافةً إلى شَيْءٍ in addition to sth; إضافة بالإضافة إلى ذلك moreover, furthermore, besides; إضافة مَوادَّ كيمْيائيّة the addition of chemical substances 2 (Gram) genitive construction, construct state

إضافيّ *adj* additional, further, supplementary; تَكاليف إضافيّة additional costs; مُشْكِلة إضافيّة an additional problem; شَرْح إضافيّ further explanation; مُعْلومات \ تَفاصيل إضافيّة further information/details; وَسائِل \ إجْراءات إضافيّة additional means/measures; خِدْمة \ مُساعَدة إضافيّة extra service/help; ثَمَن إضافيّ surcharge, premium; عَمَل إضافيّ overtime

مُسْتَضيف *n* host; مُسْتَضيف مَواقِع Web host

مُضاف A *adj* added, attached; القيمة المُضافة the added value B *n the first noun of a genitive construction*; المُضاف إلَيْه *the second noun of a genitive construction*

مِضْياف *adj* |mf| hospitable

مُضيف A *adj* accommodating, hosting; الدَوْلة المُضيفة لِبُطولة كَأْسِ العالَمِ لِكُرة القَدَمِ the host country of the World Cup football (BrE) soccer (AmE) championship B *n* host; steward, flight attendant

مُضيفة *n* hostess; stewardess, flight attendant

ضاق *v* |i; ضِيق, ضَيْق| 1 [أَصْبَحَ \ كانَ ضَيِّقاً] to be/become narrow, to narrow; ضاقَ بِهِ المَكانُ the room closed in on him; ضاقَتْ بِهِ العيشةُ life depressed him; ضاقَ الطَريقُ the road was narrow; ضاقَتْ بِهِ السُبُلُ he was at his wits' end; يَضيقُ الوَقْتُ time is pressing, time is short 2 [تَضايَقَ] to be annoyed, to be fed up; ضِقْتُ (ذَرْعاً) بِتَصَرُّفِهِ his behaviour annoyed me

ضَيَّقَ *v* 1 [جَعَلَهُ ضَيِّقاً] to narrow, to make narrow, to reduce; ضَيَّقَ الفَجْوةَ بين شَخْصَيْنِ \ شَيْئَيْنِ to bring two people/things closer together; ضَيَّقَ سِرْوالاً to take in a pair of trousers 2 [شَدَّدَ] to oppress, to weigh; ضَيَّقَ الخِناقَ على شَخْصٍ to beset sb grievously; ضَيَّقَ على شَخْصٍ to corner sb

ضايَقَ *v* to annoy, to irritate; to oppress, to weigh; ضايَقَهُ الأَمْرُ he was inconvenienced by the matter; ضايَقَ شَخْصاً to harass sb, to nettle sb; ضايَقَ شَخْصاً بِأَسْئِلةٍ to annoy sb

from downfall; هذا مُؤَمَّنٌ ضدّ الضَياعِ أو السَرِقةِ this is insured against loss or theft

ضَيْعة *n* |ضِياع| 1 [قَرْية صَغيرة] small village, hamlet 2 [عِزْبة] country estate; ضَيْعة واسِعة a vast country estate; مالِك الضَيْعةِ landowner, lord of the manor

إضاعة *n* waste, squandering; إضاعة الوَقْتِ waste of time

تَضْييع *n* waste, squandering

مُضَيِّع *adj* wasteful, squandering; مُضَيِّع للوَقْتِ time-consuming

مَضْيَعة *n* loss, ruin; waste, squandering

ضاف *v* |i; ضِيافة, ضَيْف| to stay as a guest

ضَيَّفَ *v* to entertain, to take in as a guest

أَضافَ *v* 1 [ضَمَّ] to add, to insert, to attach; أَضافَ شَيْئاً إلى البَرْنامَجِ to insert sth into the programme; أَضافَ مَبْلَغاً to add an amount; أَضافَ التَكاليفَ الإضافيّةَ إلى الثَمَنِ (النِهائيِّ) to pass on the extra cost to the customer 2 [قالَ] to say, to add; لَكِنَّهُ أَضافَ أَنَّ ... but he added that ... 3 [اِسْتَضافَ] to take in as a guest

اِنْضافَ *v* to be added, to be attached

اِسْتَضافَ *v* 1 [آوى] to accommodate, to host; اِسْتَضافَ قِمّةً \ اِجْتِماعاً to organize a summit/meeting; اِسْتَضافَ لاجِئينَ to receive refugees; اِسْتَضافَ شَخْصاً في مَنْزِلِهِ to receive sb as a guest 2 (Comp) to host; اِسْتَضافَ مَوْقِعاً to host a site

ضَيْف *n* |ضُيوف, أَضْياف, ضيفان| guest, visitor, invitee; ضَيْف شَرَفٍ guest of honour; ضَيْف شَرَفيّ \ فَخْريّ مُهِمّ an important guest; ضَيْف عَزيز a welcome guest; ضُيوف visitors, company; دَعا ضُيوفاً to invite guests; ضُيوف غَيْر مَدْعوّينَ uninvited guests; اِسْتَقْبَلَ ضُيوفاً to receive guests, to receive visitors; نَزَلَ ضَيْفاً على شَخْصٍ to be sb's guest; غُرْفة الضُيوفِ guest room

ضِيافة *n* hospitality; حُسْن الضِيافةِ hospitality; اِسْتَغَلَّ ضِيافةَ شَخْصٍ to impose upon sb's hospitality; كانَ في ضِيافةِ شَخْصٍ to be sb's guest

اِسْتِضافة *n* hosting; اِسْتِضافة مَواقِعَ website hosting

إضافة *n* 1 [زِيادة] addendum, addition, supplement; إضافةً in addition, extra; إضافةً \ بالإضافةِ إلى besides, plus,

التَفْكِير \ الأُفُق narrow-minded; المِعْطَف ضَيِّقٌ the coat is tight; تَنّورة ضَيِّقة a tight skirt; الوَقْتُ ضَيِّقٌ time is short

ضائِقة *n* |ضَوائِقُ| malaise, misery, straits; ضائِقة اقْتِصاديّة (economic) depression; ضائِقة ماليّة lack of money, financial straits; مَرَّ في \ عانى من ضائِقةٍ ماليّةٍ to be pressed for money; عاشَ في ضائِقةٍ to be in hard trouble, to be in the dumps

ضيقة *n* hardship, deprivation

تَضَيُّق *n* narrowing, constriction; تَضَيُّق في الأَوْعِية الدَمَوِيّة (Med) stricture of blood vessels

تَضْييق *n* |تَضْييقات| narrowing, constriction

مُتَضايِق *adj* irritated, annoyed; oppressed, uncomfortable

مُضايِق *adj* annoying, disturbing, troublesome; oppressive, depressing; فِكْرة مُضايِقة a depressing thought

مُضايَقة *n* annoyance, nuisance, harassment

مَضيق *n* |مَضائِقُ, مَضايِقُ| narrow, strait; مَضيق كاليه the Straits of Dover; مَضيق جَبَلِ طارِق the Straits of Gibraltar

ضامَ *v* |i; ضَيْم| to wrong, to treat unjustly; ضامَ شَخْصاً to wrong sb

ضَيْم *n* |ضُيوم| injustice, wrong, grievance

with questions; ضايَقَهُ الجَوُّ في ذلك البَيْتِ the atmosphere in that house weighed down on him

تَضايَقَ *v* to be/become irritated, to become annoyed; to be/become anxious; تَضايَقَ من شَيْءٍ \ شَخْصٍ to get annoyed about sth/sb

ضيق *n* ① [عَكْس اتِّساع] narrowness, constriction; ضيق الشَرايينِ (Med) stricture of blood vessels; ضيق الفِكْرِ \ الأُفُقِ narrow-mindedness; ضيق المَكانِ \ المِساحةِ lack of space; ضيق في التَنَفُّسِ difficulty (in) breathing, tightness of the chest; أُصيبَ بِضيقٍ في التَنَفُّسِ he got short of breath ② [مَأْزَق] depression, distress, misery, malaise; scarcity, need, destitution; ضيق اقْتِصاديّ (economic) depression; ضيق اليَدِ poverty, destitution; ضيق ماليّ lack of money, financial straits; بِسَبَبِ ضيقٍ ماليٍّ due to lack of money; كانَ في ضيقٍ to be in trouble, to be in the dumps; الصَديقُ عند الضيق a friend in need is a friend indeed; شُعور \ إِحْساس بالضيق a sinking feeling, an oppressive feeling

ضَيْق *n* displeasure, dissatisfaction, unease

ضَيِّق *adj* narrow, tight; limited, restricted, confined; مَمَرّ \ مَدْخَل \ طَريق ضَيِّق a narrow hallway/entrance/street; ضَيِّق

ط

طاء *n* |f| *name of the letter* **ط**

طابة *n* ball

طاجيكِسْتان *n* |f| Tajikistan

طاؤوس *n* see طاووس

طَأْطَأَ *v* |i; طَأْطَأَة| to bend, to incline; to bow; طَأْطَأَ رَأْسَهُ to bend one's head

مُطَأْطِئ *adj* with bowed head; مُطَأْطِئ الرَأْسِ with bowed head

طاق *n* |طيقان| arch

طاكْسي *n* taxi, cab

طامور *n* |طَواميرُ| scroll

طاووس, طاؤوس *n* |طَواويسُ| (Zool) peacock; مَشى مُخْتالاً كالطاووسِ to strut like a peacock

طاووسية *n* طاووسيّة نَهاريّة (Zool) peacock butterfly

طاويّ *adj*, *n* Taoist

طاويّة *n* Taoism

طَبَّبَ *v* to treat medically

تَطَبَّبَ *v* to receive medical treatment

طِبّ *n* medicine; medical treatment; الطِبّ الرَسْميّ \ البَديل conventional/alternative medicine; طِبّ باطِنيّ \ داخِليّ internal medicine; طِبّ شَرْعيّ forensic medicine; طِبّ وِقائيّ preventive medicine; طِبّ بَيْطَريّ veterinary medicine; طِبّ إشْعاعيّ radiology; طِبّ تجانُسيّ homeopathy; طِبّ طَبيعيّ natural medicine; طِبّ نِسائيّ obstetrics/gynaecology; طِبّ الأَمْراضِ العَصَبيّة neurology; طِبّ نَفْسانيّ \ نَفْسيّ psychiatry; طِبّ القَلْبِ (والشَرايين) cardiology; عِلْم الطِبِّ medical science; كُلِّيّة الطِبِّ the Faculty of Medicine (BrE), Medical School (AmE); دَرَسَ الطِبَّ to study medicine; مارَسَ \ زاوَلَ مِهْنَةَ الطِبِّ to practise medicine

طِبابة *n* medicine, medical profession

طِبّيّ *adj* medical; medicinal; مُساعَدة طِبّيّة medical aid/assistance; نَباتات \ مَساحيق طِبّيّة medicinal plants/powders; فَريق \ فَحْص طِبّيّ a medical team/examination; الهَيْئة الطِبّيّة the medical staff

طَبيب *n* |أَطِبّة, أَطِبّاءُ| doctor, physician, medical practitioner; طَبيب أَسْنانٍ dentist; طَبيب مُخْتَصّ \ اخْتِصاصيّ specialist; طَبيب باطِنيّ \ داخِليّ internist; طَبيب شَرْعيّ pathologist; طَبيب نَفْسيّ \ نَفْسانيّ psychiatrist; طَبيب المِثْليّة \ تَجانُسيّ homeopath; طَبيب التَخْدير anaesthetist; طَبيب الحَلْقِ والأَنْفِ والأُذُنِ ear, nose and throat doctor; طَبيب بَيْطَريّ veterinary surgeon (BrE), veterinarian (AmE); طَبيب خاصّ personal physician; طَبيب رِياضيّ sports doctor; طَبيب عَسْكَريّ army doctor; طَبيب فَريق club doctor; الطَبيب الاسْتِشاريّ the consulting physician; الطَبيب المُعالِج the attending doctor; أَطِبّاء بِلا حُدودٍ Médecins Sans Frontières; نِقابة الأَطِبّاءِ Medical Association; زِيارة طَبيبٍ a visit to the doctor; اسْتَشارَ طَبيباً to consult (with) a doctor

تَطْبيب *n* medication; medical treatment; لَدَيْنا الأَمْوالُ الكافِيَةُ لِتَطْبيبِ أَبي we have enough money for my father's treatment

مَطَبّ *n* pit; pothole, hole; bump; وَقَعَ في مَطَبٍّ to fall into a hole

طَبَخَ *v* |a-u; طَبْخ| to cook; طَبَخَ طَعاماً لَذيذاً لِضُيوفِهِ to cook a delicious meal for one's guests

طَبْخ *n* cooking; زَيْت الطَبْخِ cooking oil; مُدّة الطَبْخِ cooking time; أَجادَ الطَبْخَ to be good at cooking

طَبّاخ *n* [1] [طاهٍ] cook; chef; طَبّاخ جَيِّد \ ماهِر a good/excellent cook; الجوعُ أَمْهَرُ الطَبّاخينَ hunger is the best sauce [2] [فُرْن] cooker; شُعْلة \ عَيْن طَبّاخٍ burner

طِباخة *n* cooking; cuisine

طَبْخة *n* meal; food; الطَّبْخةُ غَيْرُ جاهِزةٍ حتّى الآنِ the food isn't ready yet

طَبيخ *n* dish; cooked food

مَطْبَخ *n* |مَطابِخُ| 1▸ [مَكان الطَّبْخِ] kitchen 2▸ [نَوْع الطَّبيخِ] cooking; cuisine; المَطْبَخ الفَرَنْسيّ French cuisine

مِطْبَخ *n* |مَطابِخُ| stove, range; hotplate; مِطْبَخ كَهْرَبائيّ an electric hot plate

[1]‹ **طَبَّرَ** *v* *to perform the Shiite ritual of wounding the head*

تَطْبير *n* *Shiite ritual of wounding the head*

[2]‹ **طابور** *n* |طَوابيرُ| line; queue; طابور سَيْرٍ column; الطابور الخامِس the fifth column; طابور من الناسِ \ السَّيّاراتِ a line of people/cars; وَقَفَ في الطابورِ to stand in line

‹ **طَبَرْزَد** *n* (sugar) candy

‹ **طَبَرِيّا**, **طَبَرِيّة** *n* Tiberias (*city in Israel*); بُحَيْرة طَبَرِيّا the Sea of Galilee, Lake Tiberias

‹ **طَباشير** *n* chalk

طُبْشورة *n* bit/piece of chalk

‹ **طَبْطَبَ** *v* |i; طَبْطَبة| 1▸ [دَلَّعَ] to stroke, to caress; طَبْطَبَ على شَخْصٍ to caress sb 2▸ [الماءُ] to ripple, to gurgle (*water*)

‹ **طَبَعَ** *v* |a; طَبْع, طِباعة| 1▸ [نَسَخَ] to print (out); to impress; to type; to stamp; طَبَعَ كِتاباً \ رَسْماً to print a book/illustration; طَبَعَ وَثيقةً \ مِلَفًّا to print out a document/file; طَبَعَ قَميصاً to screenprint/print a T-shirt; طَبَعَ على وَرَقٍ to print on paper; طَبَعَ كَلِمةً بالحُروفِ المائِلةِ to print a word in italics; طَبَعَ شَيْئاً في ذاكِرَتِهِ to impress sth on one's mind/memory; طَبَعَ في ذِهْنِ شَخْصٍ ... to impress on sb's mind that ...; طَبَعَ رِسالةً \ نَصًّا على الكُمْبْيوتَر to type a letter/text on the computer 2▸ [خَلَقَ] to raise, to bring up; to accustom; طُبِعَ على شَيْءٍ to be raised with sth; to be accustomed to sth

طَبَّعَ *v* to normalize; طَبَّعَ العَلاقاتِ بين بَلَدَيْنِ to normalize the relations between two countries

تَطَبَّعَ *v* |ب| to take on, to assume; تَطَبَّعَ بِطِباعِ أبيهِ to take after his father; to be a chip off the old block

انْطَبَعَ *v* to be stamped; to be impressed; انْطَبَعَ في ذِهْنِهِ to be etched in one's mind

طَبْع *n* |طِباع| 1▸ [خاصيّة] nature; character; disposition; بالطَّبْعِ naturally, of course; حادّ الطَّبْعِ temperamental; passionate; اتَّسَمَ بِحِدّةِ الطَّبْعِ to be temperamental/passionate; طَبْعاً naturally, of course; obviously; that goes without saying!; طَبْعاً سَيَحْصَلُ كُلُّ الأَعْضاءِ على دَعْوةٍ naturally, all members will receive an invitation 2▸ (P&P) printing; typography; إعادة الطَّبْعِ reprint; الكِتابُ تحت الطَّبْعِ the book is being printed; جاهِز للطَّبْعِ ready for press; جَهَّزَ شَيْئاً للطَّبْعِ to prepare something for the press; صَحَّحَ مُسَوَّدةَ الطَّبْعِ to check the proofs/galleys; حُقوقُ الطَّبْعِ مَحْفوظةٌ للناشِرِ copyrights reserved to the publisher 3▸ (*Comput*) printout

طابَع, **طابِع** *n* |طَوابِعُ| 1▸ [قِطْعة صَغيرة من الوَرَقِ] stamp; طابَع بَريديّ stamp; بِدونِ طَوابِعَ unstamped; جامِع طَوابِعَ stamp collector; جَمْع طَوابِعَ stamp collecting; جَمَعَ طَوابِعَ to collect stamps; لَصَقَ طابَعاً على رِسالةٍ \ طَرْدٍ to stick a stamp on a letter/parcel 2▸ [خاتِم] seal; stamp; طابَع التاريخ date stamp; طَبَعَ شَيْئاً بِطابَعِهِ to set one's stamp/seal on sth 3▸ [ميزة] character; طابَع عَسْكَريّ a military character; احْتَفَظَ بِطابَعِهِ الخاصِّ to preserve its own character; ذو طابَعٍ خاصٍّ with a special character

طابِع *n* 1▸ printer (*person*) 2▸ signature

طابِعة *n* printer (*device*); طابِعة ليزَر laser printer

طَبّاع *n* printer (*person*)

طِباعة *n* printing; typography; طِباعة حَجَرِيّة litho, lithograph; مُنَضِّد حُروفِ الطِباعةِ typesetter; دار الطِباعةِ printing company; حُرِّيّة الطِباعةِ والنَشْرِ freedom of the press

طِباعيّ *adj* typographical; *relating to printing*; خَطَأ طِباعيّ misprint; erratum

طَبْعة *n* printing; impression; edition; issue; الطَّبْعة الأولى \ الثانية a first/second printing; طَبْعة مَحْدودة النُسَخِ \ مُعَدَّلة \ خاصّة a limited/revised/special edition

طَبيعة *n* |طَبائِعُ| 1▸ [خُلُق] nature, character; disposition, inclination; بِطَبيعةِ الحالِ naturally; obviously; of course; that goes without saying!; بِطَبيعَتِهِ by nature; الإنْسانُ بِطَبيعَتِهِ يُحِبُّ الحُرّيّةَ humans love freedom by nature; طَبيعة الإنْسانِ human nature; طَبيعة شَعْبٍ national character; طَبيعة جِنْسيّة

sexual orientation [2] [عالَم الكائنات] nature; حِماية الطَبيعة nature conservation; عُذْرِيّة الطَبيعة unspoiled nature; قوّة الطَبيعةِ force of nature; عِلْم الطَبيعةِ physics; فوق الطَبيعةِ supernatural; مُحِبّ للطَبيعة nature lover; جَمال الطَبيعةِ natural/scenic beauty; مَظْهَر من مَظاهِرِ الطَبيعةِ natural phenomenon

طَبيعيّ *adj* [1] [مَنسوب إلى الطَبيعةِ] natural; normal; self-evident; غَيْر طَبيعيٍّ unnatural; abnormal; نَزْعات غَيْر طَبيعيّةٍ (sexually) deviant tendencies; وَفاة طَبيعيّة a natural death; رَدّ فِعْلٍ طَبيعيّ a normal reaction; الأب \ الأُمّ الطَبيعيّ(ة) the biological father/mother; رَسْم بالحَجْمِ الطَبيعيِّ a life-size drawing; المَذْهَب الطَبيعيّ naturalism; تحت الظُروفِ الطَبيعيّةِ under normal conditions; ordinarily; كانَ من الطَبيعيِّ to be obvious; هذا أَمْرٌ غَيْرُ طَبيعيٍّ this is an unusual matter/issue; هذه حالةٌ غَيْرُ طَبيعيّةٍ this is an unnatural situation [2] [غَيْر مَصْنوع] natural; بطَريقةٍ طَبيعيّةٍ by natural means; الطَبيعيّات physics; الجُغْرافيا الطَبيعيّة physical geography; حُدود طَبيعيّة natural borders; مِنْطَقة طَبيعيّة wildlife area; مَناظِر طَبيعيّة خَلاّبة a beautiful landscape; ظاهِرة طَبيعيّة a natural phenomenon; مَوادّ طَبيعيّة natural materials; مَوارِد \ ثَرَوات طَبيعيّة natural resources; حَجَر طَبيعيّ (natural) stone; حَرير طَبيعيّ natural silk; أَغْذية طَبيعيّة organic food; natural food

طَبيعيّة *n* naturalism

انْطِباع *n* |انْطِباعات| impression; impressive; انْطِباع أَوَّليّ first impression; انْطِباع عَميق a deep impression; انْطِباع جَيِّد \ سَيِّئ a good/bad impression; تَرَكَ \ خَلَّفَ انْطِباعاً حَسَناً to leave a good impression; أَعْطى انْطِباعاً حَسَناً to make a good impression; أَعْطى انْطِباعاً بِأَنَّ ... to give the impression that ...; كَوَّنَ انْطِباعاً عن شَيْءٍ, خَرَجَ \ ذَهَبَ بِانْطِباعٍ عن شَيْءٍ to get an impression of sth; كانَ لَدَيْهِ الانْطِباعُ بِأَنَّ ... he was under the impression that ...; يَسودُ الانْطِباعُ بِأَنَّ ... the impression prevails that ...

انْطِباعيّ *adj* Impressionistic; Impressionist; لَوْحة انْطِباعيّة an Impressionist painting

انْطِباعيّة *n* Impressionism

تَطْبيع *n* normalization; تَطْبيع العَلاقاتِ normalization of relations

لاطَبيعيّ *adj* abnormal, unnatural

لاطَبيعيّة *n* abnormality

مَطْبَعة *n* |مَطابِعُ| printing office/company

مِطْبَعة *n* |مَطابِعُ| (printing) press; مِطْبَعة دَوّارة rotary press

مَطْبَعيّ *adj* typographical; *relating to printing*; خَطأ مَطْبَعيّ misprint; erratum

مَطْبوع [A] *adj* printed; stamped [B] *n* |مَطْبوعات| publication; printed matter

مَطْبوعة *n* publication

طَبَّقَ *v* to implement; to apply; to adopt; to enforce; طَبَّقَ شَيْئاً to implement sth; طَبَّقَ تِقْنيّةً \ مَنْهَجيّةً جَديدةً to apply a new technique/method; طَبَّقَ نِظاماً to adopt a system; طَبَّقَ قانوناً \ قاعِدةً to enforce a law

طابَقَ *v* to correspond to/with; to match (with); طابَقَ شَيْئاً to correspond to/with sth; طابَقَتْ أَوْصافُهُ أَوْصافَ أَحَدِ المُتَّهَمينَ his description matched the description of one of the suspects

أَطْبَقَ *v* [1] [أَحاطَ] to surround; أَطْبَقَ على شَخْصٍ to surround sb [2] [هَجَمَ] to (take by) surprise; أَطْبَقَ على العَدوِّ to take the enemy by surprise [3] [أَغْلَقَ] to shut; to close; أَطْبَقَ فَمَهُ \ شَفَتَيْهِ to shut one's mouth; أَطْبَقَ كِتاباً to close a book

تَطابَقَ *v* to correspond; to coincide; to be consistent; to agree; تَطابَقَ مع الحَقائِقِ to be consistent with the facts; يَتَطابَقُ الفِعْلُ مع الفاعِلِ the verb agrees with the subject

انْطَبَقَ *v* [1] [ناسَبَ] to apply; انْطَبَقَ على to apply to; تَنْطَبِقُ على هذه الجَريمةِ المادّةُ ١٠ من قانونِ العُقوباتِ article 10 of the criminal code applies to this crime [2] [وافَقَ] to correspond; to be consistent; انْطَبَقَ على شَيْءٍ to be consistent with/correspond to sth

طَبَق *n* |أَطْباق| [1] [صَحْن] dish; saucer; plate; طَبَق طائِر a flying saucer; على طَبَقٍ من ذَهَبٍ \ فِضّةٍ on a golden/silver platter; طَبَق فَضائيّ satellite dish [2] [طَعام] dish; طَبَق رَئيسيّ \ جانِبيّ main dish; قَدَّمَ طَبَقاً to serve a dish

انطباق *n* agreement; conformity

تطابُق *n* |تطابُقات| agreement; similarity; correspondence; congruence; هُناكَ تَطابُقٌ مَلْموسٌ بين هَذَيْنِ الأَمْرَيْنِ there is a striking similarity between those two matters; تَطابُق مُثَلَّثَيْنِ the congruence of two triangles

تطبُّق *n* stratification

تَطْبيق *n* |تَطْبيقات| ❶ [تَوْظيف] application; practice; implementation; تَطْبيقاً ل in accordance with, pursuant to; تَطْبيقاً للقَواعِدِ المُتَبَّعة pursuant to established rules; تَطْبيق خاطِئ misapplication; تَطْبيق عَمَلِيّ practical; دَخَلَ حَيِّزَ التَطْبيقِ to be implemented; كانَت المَنْهَجيَّةُ قابِلةً للتَطْبيقِ على أَرْضِ الواقِعِ the method was applicable in actual practice ❷ (Comput) application, app; تَطْبيق ويب Web application; مَتْجَر تَطْبيقاتٍ app store

تَطْبيقِيّ *adj* applicable; applied; practical; الاقْتِصاد \ عِلْم اللُغةِ التَطْبيقِيّ applied economics/linguistics; مَعْرِفة تَطْبيقيّة working knowledge; بَرْمَجيّات تَطْبيقيّة application software

مُتَطابِق *adj* identical; corresponding; congruent; compatible; تَوْأَمانِ مُتَطابِقانِ identical twins; مَصادِر مُتَطابِقة corresponding sources; مُثَلَّثانِ مُتَطابِقانِ two congruent triangles; مُتَطابِق فِكْرِيًّا like-minded; شَهاداتُهُم غَيْرُ مُتَطابِقةٍ their statements are incompatible

مُطابِق *adj* identical; equal; consistent; مُطابِق للواقِعِ consistent with reality

مُطابَقة *n* ❶ [مُوافَقة] agreement; conformity; uniformity ❷ (Gram) concord, agreement

مُطْبِق *adj* absolute; complete; sheer; صَمْت مُطْبِق complete silence; جُنون مُطْبِق sheer madness

مُنْطَبِق *adj* |على| applicable to; غَيْر مُنْطَبِقٍ not applicable; كانَ مُنْطَبِقاً على to be applicable to

طَبَلَ *v* |u; طَبْل| to drum, to beat a drum

طَبَّلَ *v* to drum, to beat a drum; طَبَّلَ وَزَمَّرَ *to make a fuss*

طَبْل *n* |أَطْبال, طُبول| drum; tom-tom; ضَرَبَ على الطَبْلِ to beat a drum

طَبّال *n* drummer

طَبْلة *n* drum; tabla; طَبْلة الأُذُنِ eardrum

طِبْقَ *prep* نُسْخة طِبْقَ الأَصْلِ an original copy; تَرْجَمة طِبْقَ الأَصْلِ a faithful translation; طِبْقاً لِشَيْءٍ according to sth; in accordance with sth; consistent with sth; طِبْقاً للقَواعِدِ in accordance with the rules

طابَق, طابِق *n* |طَوابِقُ| floor; storey; الطابَق الأَرْضِيّ \ السُفْلِيّ the ground floor; طابَق عُلْوِيّ upper storey/floor; في الطابَقِ العُلْوِيِّ upstairs; في الطابَقِ الأَوَّلِ \ الثاني on the first/second floor (BrE), on the second/third floor (AmE); عِمارة سَكَنيّة تَتَأَلَّفُ من عِشْرينَ طابَقاً a twenty-storeyed block of flats (BrE), a twenty-storey apartment building (AmE)

طِباق *n* ❶ [مَصْدَر] طِباق شَيْءٍ equal/identical to sth ❷ (Rhet) antithesis

طَبَقة *n* ❶ [من الأَرْضِ إلخ] layer; stratum; في طَبَقاتٍ in layers; طَبَقةً طَبَقةً layer by layer; طَبَقة أَرْضيّة a layer of the earth; a layer of soil; طَبَقة طينيّة a clay layer/stratum; طَبَقة واقِية a protective layer/coating; طَبَقة عازِلة an insulating layer; طَبَقة تَحْتيّة \ سُفْليّة \ سُفْلى \ دُنْيا a lower layer; substratum; الطَبَقة السُفْلى \ الوُسْطى \ العُلْيا \ الخارِجيّة the bottom/middle/top/outer layer; طَبَقة سَميكة \ رَقيقة a thick/thin layer; طَبَقات جَوّيّة ساخِنة \ بارِدة a hot/cold layer of air; طَبَقة سُمْكُها ٢٠ سم a layer of 20 cm; طَبَقة من الطينِ \ الزَيْتِ \ الغُبارِ a layer of mud/oil/dust; ثُغْرة في طَبَقةِ الأوزونِ the hole in the ozone layer ❷ (Sociol) stratum; class; caste; بِدونِ طَبَقاتٍ classless; طَبَقة اجْتِماعيّة social class; الطَبَقة الدُنْيا \ السُفْلى the lower class; الطَبَقة الراقِية the upper class; طَبَقة مُتَوَسِّطة \ وُسْطى the middle classes; الطَبَقة الحاكِمة \ العامِلة the ruling/working class; الطَبَقات السُفْلى في المُجْتَمَع the lower strata/ranks of society; في جَميعِ طَبَقاتِ المُجْتَمَعِ in all strata/sections of society; اسْتِغْلال الطَبَقةِ العامِلةِ the exploitation of the working class; صِراع الطَبَقاتِ class struggle; نِظام الطَبَقاتِ caste system; انْتَمى إلى طَبَقةٍ to belong to a class ❸ [طابِق] floor; storey ❹ [صِنْف] category; order ❺ (Mus) pitch

طَبَقِيّ *adj* class; مُجْتَمَع طَبَقِيّ class society

طَبَقيّة *n* classism

إطْباق *n* ❶ [إغْلاق] locking ❷ [هُجوم] attack ❸ (Gram) emphatic; حُروف الإطْباق emphatic consonants

‹ **طَرَأَ** *v* |a; طُروء| to occur, to take place, to happen; to arise; طَرَأَتْ تَغَيُّراتٌ new problems arose; طَرَأَتْ مَشاكِلُ جَديدةٌ changes in the situation occurred; طَرَأَتْ عَلَيْهِ على المَوْقِف a thought came to his mind فِكْرةٌ

طَرُؤَ *v* |u; طَراءة, طَراء| to be/become soft/weak/tender

طارِئ **A** *adj* unforeseen; حالة طارِئة an emergency; an unforeseen situation; تكاليف \ ظُروف طارِئة unforeseen expenses/circumstances

B *n* emergency

طارِئة *n* |طَوارِئُ| emergency; حالة طَوارِئَ state of emergency; في حالةِ طَوارِئَ, للطَوارِئِ in case of emergency; أَعْلَنَ حالةَ الطَوارِئ to proclaim a state of emergency; تَسْري حالةُ الطَوارِئ the state of emergency is in effect; خُطّة طَوارِئَ emergency plan; بَعَثَ إشارةَ الطَوارِئِ to send out a distress signal

‹ **طَرابُلُس** *n* |dipt f| Tripoli; طَرابُلُس (الغَرْبِ) Tripoli (*capital of Libya*); طَرابُلُس (الشامِ) Tripoli (*city in Lebanon*)

‹ **طَرابيزة** *n* side table, table

‹ **طَرِبَ** *v* |a; طَرَب| to be delighted; to be thrilled; طَرِبَ ل \ من شَيْءٍ to be delighted by sth

أَطْرَبَ *v* to delight sb; to thrill sb; أَطْرَبَني صَوْتُهُ his voice delighted me

طَرَب *n* |أَطْراب| **1** delight **2** music; آلة الطَرَبِ musical instrument

طَروب *adj* merry; lively

مُطْرِب **A** *adj* delightful; wonderful; صَوْت مُطْرِب a wonderful voice

B *n* singer; vocalist; مُطْرِب الفِرْقة the band's singer

‹ **طَرْبوش** *n* |طَرابيشُ| fez (*hat*)

‹ **طُرْبيد** *n* see طورْبيد

‹ **طَرَحَ** *v* |a; طَرْح| **1** [رَمى] to throw, to cast, to toss, to fling; طَرَحَ كُتُباً على الطاوِلةِ to throw books on the table; طَرَحَ بِضاعةً في الأَسْواقِ to launch a product **2** [عَرَضَ] to present; to propose; to submit; طَرَحَ خُطّةً to present a plan; طَرَحَ قَضيّةً للمُناقَشةِ to bring a subject/matter up for discussion; طَرَحَ على شَخْصٍ سُؤالاً to put a question to sb **3** [سَحَبَ]

طَبْليّة *n* a low round table

‹ **طابون**, **طابونة** *n* |طَوابينُ| a traditional clay oven

‹ **طَبَنْجة** *n* pistol

‹ **طُبوغْرافيّ**, **طوبوغْرافيّ** *adj* topographic; خَريطة طُبوغْرافيّة a topographic map

طُبوغْرافيا *n* topography

‹ **طُبْي** *n* |أَطْباء| teat

طابِية *n* |طَوابٍ| **1** [قَلْعة] fortress **2** [بُرْج] tower **3** [في الشَطْرَنْج] rook

‹ **طاجِن** *n* |طَواجِن| **1** [إناء] frying pan; tagine (*a shallow earthenware cooking dish with a tall, conical lid*) **2** [طَعام] tagine (*a North African stew of spiced meat and vegetables, prepared in a tagine*)

‹ **طُخْرور** *n* |طَخارير| cirrus

‹ **طِحال** *n* |طِحالات, طُحُل| spleen

‹ **طُحْلُب** *n* |طَحالِبُ| **1** [نَبات بَرّيّ] moss; algae **2** [نَبات مائيّ] seaweed; duckweed

‹ **طَحَنَ** *v* |a; طَحْن| to grind; to mill; to pulverize; طَحَنَ الحَبَّ to grind grain

تَطاحَنَ *v* to be in conflict; to quarrel

طِحْن *n* flour

طاحِن *adj* grinding; heavy; أَزْمة طاحِنة a severe crisis; مَعارِك طاحِنة heavy/fierce fighting; فَقْر طاحِن grinding poverty

طاحِنة *n* |طَواحِنُ| molar

طاحونة *n* |طَواحينُ| mill; merry-go-round; طاحونة هَواءٍ windmill; تَدورُ الطاحونةُ the mill is turning

طَحّان *n* miller

طَحين *n* flour; أَسْمَعُ جَعْجَعةً وَلا أَرى طَحيناً *much ado about nothing*

طَحينة *n* tahini (*sesame paste*)

تَطاحُن *n* conflict; quarrel

مِطْحَنة *n* |مَطاحِنُ| grinder; مِطْحَنة بُنٍّ coffee grinder

مَطْحون *adj* **1** [مَرْحيّ] ground, crushed; تُفّاح مَطْحون applesauce; بَطاطِس مَطْحونة mashed potato **2** [مَهْزوم] defeated, crushed; عادَ مَطْحوناً من الحَرْبِ to return from war defeated to lose; طَرَحَ الثِّقة ب \ في الوَزير to lose confidence in the minister **4** (Math) to subtract; to deduct; طَرَحَ ٥ من ١٠ to subtract 5 from 10

طَرَّحَ *v* to cause a miscarriage

طارَحَ *v* to exchange (*words, etc.*); طارَحَ شَخْصاً الحَديثَ \ الكَلام to have a chat with sb

تَطارَحَ *v* to exchange; تَطارَحَ الغَرامَ to make love

انْطَرَحَ *v* to be thrown; to throw oneself; انْطَرَحَ أَرْضاً to throw oneself to the ground

اطَّرَحَ *v* to discard; to dump

طَرْح *n* **1** (Math) deduction; subtraction; عَلامة طَرْح minus (sign); ناتِج طَرْح difference; remainder; ناتِج \ باقي الطَرْح ٤ من ١٠ يُساوي ٦ the difference between 10 and 4 is 6 **2** [رَمْي] throwing; طَرْح النَهْر sludge

طَرْحة *n* veil; طَرْحة عَروسٍ bridal veil

طَريح *adj* |طَرْحى| lying; prostrate; طَريح الفراشِ ill in bed; bedridden; صارَ لَها أُسْبوعانِ طَريحةَ الفِراشِ she's been bedridden for two weeks

أُطْروحة *n* dissertation; (doctoral/PhD) thesis; قَدَّمَ أُطْروحةً to present a thesis; دافَعَ عن أُطْروحةٍ to defend a thesis

مَطْرَح *n* |مَطارِحُ| place; لم يَذْهَبْ إلى أيِّ مَطْرَحٍ he wasn't going anywhere

مَطْروح *adj* submitted; raised; ناقَشَ السُّؤالَ المَطْروحَ to discuss the question raised

‹ **طَرَخْشَقون** *n* dandelion

‹ **طَرْخون** *n* (Bot) tarragon

‹ **طَرَدَ** *v* |u; طَرْد **1**| [أَبْعَدَ] to chase away, to drive away; to dispel, to expel; to throw out; to deport; طَرَدَ شَخْصاً to throw sb out; طُرِدَ من المَدْرَسة to be expelled from school; طَرَدَ شَخْصاً من حِزْبٍ \ جَمْعيّةٍ to expel sb from a party/society; طَرَدَ المُتَظاهِرين to chase away protesters; طَرَدَ شَخْصاً من دارِهِ to kick sb out of their home; طَرَدَ الأَجانِبَ to deport foreigners; طَرَدَ خَوفَ شَخْصٍ to remove/dispel sb's fears **2** [من مَنْصِبٍ] to dismiss, to fire; طَرَدَ شَخْصاً من مَنْصِبِهِ \ عَمَلِهِ to relieve sb of his duty

طارَدَ *v* to chase, to pursue; to hunt; طارَدَ شَخْصاً to chase sb; طارَدَ الشُرْطيُّ السارِقَ the policeman pursued the thief; طارَدَ أَوْهاماً to pursue delusions

اطَّرَدَ *v* to be be consistent

اسْتَطْرَدَ *v* to skip from one topic to another; to continue speaking, to go on to say

طَرْد *n* **1** [إبْعاد] expulsion; exorcism; deportation; eviction; مُهَدَّد بالطَرْدِ threatened with eviction; قامَ بِطَرْدِ الأَرْواحِ الشِرّيرة من المَريضِ he exorcized the evil spirits from the patient; جِهاز طَرْدٍ مَرْكَزيٍّ centrifuge; قوّة الطَرْدِ المَرْكَزيِّ centrifugal force; مِضَخّة الطَرْدِ المَرْكَزيِّ centrifugal pump **2** [من العَمَلِ] dismissal; discharge; طَرْد من مَنْصِبٍ \ وَظيفةٍ a discharge from office/relieve of duties **3** |طُرود| [رُزْمة] parcel; package; طَرْد بَريديّ parcel; طَرْد مَلْغوم parcel bomb; أَرْسَلَ \ سَلَّمَ \ تَسَلَّمَ طَرْداً to send/deliver/receive a package **4** (Sport) a red card

طارِد *n* repellent; طارِد حَشَراتٍ insect repellent

طارِدة *n* fighter (jet/plane)

طَرّاد, **طَرّادة** *n* boat; cruiser

طَريد *adj* **1** [عن المَنْصِبِ] dismissed; fired **2** [هارِب] fleeing

طَريدة *n* |طَرائِدُ| game animal; prey

اسْتِطْراد *n* digression; changing the subject

اطِّراد *n* regularity; uniformity; بِاطِّرادٍ regularly; constantly

مُطارِد *n* **1** [قَنّاص] driver; beater **2** [مُلاحِق] pursuer; يَهْرُبُ من مُطارِديه to run before one's pursuers

مُطارَدة *n* chase; pursuit

مُطَّرِد *adj* steady; بِسُرْعةٍ مُطَّرِدةٍ at a steady pace; بِشَكْلٍ مُطَّرِدٍ steadily

مَطْرود *adj* dismissed; fired

‹ **طُرّ** *n* طُرًّا all; every; عادى الناسَ طُرًّا he antagonized everybody

‹ **طَرَّزَ** *v* to embroider

طِراز *n* |أَطْرِزة, طُرُز| model; type; pattern; fashion; غَسّالة كَهْرَبائيّة من طِرازٍ حَديثٍ \ قَديمٍ a new/old type of washing machine; من الطِرازِ الأَوَّلِ first-rate; على أَحْدَثِ طِرازٍ in/after the latest fashion

طَرْزي *n* tailor

تَطْريز *n* embroidery

مُطَرَّز *adj* embroidered

‹ **طِرْس** *n* sheet (*of paper*)

‹ **طَرِشَ** *v* |a; طَرَش| to be deaf

طَرَش *n* deafness

طُرْشي *n* (mixed) pickles

أَطْرَش A *adj* |dipt; طُرْش| deaf; أَطْرَش أُذُنٍ واحِدةٍ deaf in one ear
B *n* |dipt; طُرْش| deaf person

‹ **طُرْطور** *n* |طَراطيرُ| *a conical cap*

‹ **طَرْطَش** *v* |i; طَرْطَشة| to splash

‹ **طَرْطوس** *n* |dipt f| Tartus (*city in Syria*)

‹ **طَرْطوفة** *n* Jerusalem artichoke; potato

‹ **طَرَفَ** *v* |i; طَرْف| 1 [العَيْنُ] to blink 2 [لَوَّنَ] to stain; طَرَفَتْ أَصابِعَها she stained her nails and fingers with henna

طَرُفَ *v* |u; طَرافة| to be original; to be strange

أَطْرَفَ *v* to bring sth new; to bring sth original

تَطَرَّفَ *v* to radicalize; to be/become an extremist

طَرْف *n* look; من طَرْفٍ خفيٍّ a furtive glance; غَضَّ الطَرْف to avert one's eyes; بِغَضِّ الطَرْفِ عن leaving aside; apart from

طَرَف *n* |أَطْراف| 1 [جانِب] side; أَطْراف مُكَعَّبٍ the sides of a cube; ... بِطَرَفِ beside (*in addresses*); من طَرَفِ on the part of; by; جاذَبَ شَخْصاً أَطْرافَ الحَديثِ to have a conversation with sb; كانَ المُفَكِّرُ مُسْتَهْدَفاً من طَرَفِ السُلُطاتِ the intellectual was targeted by the authorities; كانَتْ الخُطْوةُ الأولى من طَرَفِها she took the first step 2 [آخِر] tip; (far) end, edge; أَطْراف الجِسْمِ limbs; على أَطْرافِ الغابةِ at the edge of the forest 3 (Law) party; side; طَرَف من طَرَفٍ واحِدٍ unilateral; الطَرَفانِ the two parties; طَرَف ثالِث a third party; طَرَف طالِب a claiming party; طَرَف مَعْنيّ beneficiary; interested party/person; الأَطْراف المُتَنازِعة the disputing parties; الأَطْراف المُتَناحِرة the warring parties; الأَطْراف المُتَشاوِرة consulting partners; الأَطْراف المُتَعاقِدة contractors; contracting partners; مُتَعَدِّد الأَطْرافِ multilateral; اسْتَمَعَ إلى الطَرَفَيْنِ to hear both parties; كانَ طَرَفاً في مُعاهَدةٍ to be party to a treaty

طَرافة *n* humour; novelty; originality; لَمَسَ الطَرافةَ في شَيْءٍ to see the humour in sth

طَرْفاء *n coll* |dipt f| (Bot) tamarisk

طَرْفة *n* |طَرَفات| في طَرْفةِ عَيْنٍ at a glance

طُرْفة *n* |طُرَف| 1 [تُحْفة] novelty; curiosity; masterpiece
2 [نادِرة] anecdote

طَرَفيّ *adj* extreme; peripheral, marginal; أَجْهِزة طَرَفيّة peripheral equipment

طَريف *adj* 1 [نادِر] original; unique; strange; unusual; هَديّة طَريفة an original present; حادِثة طَريفة a strange incident
2 [مُمْتِع] funny; entertaining; نُكْتة طَريفة a funny joke

تَطَرُّف *n* extremism; radicalism; fanaticism; تَطَرُّف دينيّ \ سِياسيّ religious/political extremism; تَطَرُّف يَساريّ \ يَمينيّ right-wing/left-wing extremism

مُتَطَرِّف A *adj* extremist; radical; militant; حِزْب \ جَماعة مُتَطَرِّفة an extremist party/group; وِجْهة نَظَرٍ مُتَطَرِّفة a radical view
B *n* extremist

‹ **طَرَقَ** *v* |u; طَرْق| 1 [دَقَّ] to knock, to bang, to hammer; طَرَقَ البابَ to knock at/on the door; طَرَقَ الجِدارَ to knock on the wall; طَرَقَ أُذُنَ \ مَسْمَعَ شَخْصٍ to come to sb's ears; طَرَقَ مَوْضوعاً to broach a subject; لم يَتْرُكْ باباً إلا وطَرَقَهُ ≈ to leave no stone unturned 2 [طَريقاً] to walk (on); to tread (on); طَرَقَ طَريقاً to walk (on) a road; طَرَقَ مَيْدانَ \ مَجالَ شَيْءٍ to venture into the field of sth 3 [الحَديدَ] to forge

طُرُقيّ *v* road (*before n*); سَلامة طُرُقيّة road/traffic safety

طَرَّقَ *v* to forge; to hammer

أَطْرَقَ *v* 1 [نَظَرَ] to cast down/lower one's eyes 2 [تَأَمَّلَ] to think deeply

تَطَرَّقَ *v* 1 [ابْتَغى لِنَفْسِهِ طَريقاً] to thread through; تَطَرَّقَ الشَكُّ إلى فِكْرِهِ to begin to doubt 2 [تَكَلَّمَ] to broach; to address; to bring up; تَطَرَّقَ إلى مَوْضوعٍ to broach a subject

اسْتَطْرَقَ *v* to go on, to continue; اسْتَطْرَقَ في الكَلامِ to go on saying

طَرْق *n* hammering; knocking

طارِق A *adj* |طارِقونَ, طُرّاق| knocking
B *n* |طارِقونَ, طُرّاق| 1 [مَنْ يَطْرُقُ] night visitor; *person who knocks*;

to show sb دَلَّ شَخْصاً على الطَريقِ to ask the way; عن الطَريقِ تَلَمَّسَ the way; قَطَعَ الطَريقَ على شَخْصٍ to cut off sb's path; وَجَدَ طَريقَهُ to feel one's way; عَرَفَ الطَريقَ to know the way; الطَريقَ to find the way; أَضاعَ الطَريقَ to have lost one's way; مَهَّدَ الطَريقَ أمام شَخْصٍ to prepare/pave/smooth the way for sb; وَصَلَ إلى طَريقٍ مَسْدودٍ to reach/arrive at an impasse; فَتَحَ الطَريقَ المَسْدودَ في العَمَلِيَّةِ السِلْمِيَّةِ to break the deadlock in the peace process; ضَلَّ الطَريقَ \ عن الطَريقِ to be lost; كانَ في طَريقِ النَجاحِ to be on the road to success; كانَ على الطَريقِ الصَحيحِ to be on the right track/trail; لَيْسَ على الطَريقِ that's not on the way

طَرِيقة *n* 1 [نَمَط] |طَرائِقُ ,طُرُق| way, manner; method; procedure, process; بِهَذِهِ الطَريقة in this/that way; بِطَريقةٍ مُعَيَّنةٍ \ مُخْتَلِفةٍ in a certain/different way; بِطَرِيقةٍ أُخْرى in another way; بِنَفْسِ الطَريقة in the same way; similarly, likewise; بِطَريقَتِه (الخاصّةِ) in one's (own) way; بِطَريقةٍ سِلْمِيَّةٍ \ غَيْرِ مَشْروعةٍ by peaceful/illegal means; بِأَيَّةِ طَريقةٍ in any manner; طَريقة مُتَّبَعة an accepted method; كانَتْ اسْتَخْدَمَ \ اتَّبَعَ \ طَبَّقَ طَرِيقةً to use/follow/implement a method; هُناكَ أَكْثَرُ من طَرِيقةٍ ل ... there's more than one way to ...; سَتُحَلُّ هذه المُشْكِلةُ بِطَرِيقةٍ أو بِأُخْرى this problem will be solved, one way or another 2 (Islam) |طَرِيقات ,طُرُق| a Sufi order

طَوارِق *n pl* |dipt| Tuareg; الطَوارِق the Tuareg (people); رَجُل من الطَوارِقِ a Tuareg man

طَوارِقيّ *n* Tuareg; الثَّقافة الطَوارقِيّة Tuareg culture

مُسْتَطْرِق *adj* أَوانٍ مُسْتَطْرِقة communicating vessels

مِطْرَق *n* |مَطارِقُ| hammer

مِطْرَقة *n* |مَطارِقُ| hammer; مِطْرَقة خَشَبِيّة a wooden hammer; المِطْرَقة والمِنْجَل hammer and sickle; مِطْرَقة الرَئِيسِ (chairman's) gavel; مِطْرَقة مِخْلَبِيّة claw hammer; رَمْي \ إطاحة المِطْرَقة hammer throwing; دَقّ المِطْرَقةِ hammer-blow; دَقَّ المَسامِيرَ بِمِطْرَقةٍ to hammer in a nail; وَقَعَ بين المِطْرَقةِ والسِنْدانِ to be between a rock and a hard place

مَطْروق *adj* well-trodden; دَرْب مَطْروق a well-trodden path; فِكْرة \ مَوْضوع مَطْروق(ة) cliché

Tariq [اِسْم شَخْصيّ] 2 سورة الطارِقِ The Morning Star (*Sura 86*) (*male given name*); جَبَل طارِق Gibraltar

طَرْقة *n* |طَرَقات| knock

طَرِيق *n* |mf; طُرُق ,طُرُقات| 1 [شارِع] street, road; way, path; عَبْرَ الطَرِيقِ across the road; على (طولِ) الطَرِيقِ on/along the road; الطَريق العامّ the public road; طَريق تُرابيّ a dirt road; طَريق مُعَبَّد a paved road; طَريق مُسَفْلَت \ مُزَفَّت an asphalt road; طَريق مَسْدود a dead end; طَريق خاصّ a private road; طَريق ثانَويّ a secondary road; طَريق جانِبيّ a side road; طَريق رَئِيسيّ a main road; طَريق سَريع \ سَيّار motorway (BrE), highway/freeway (AmE); طَريق دائِريّ ring road (BrE), beltway (AmE); طَريق وَعْر an inaccessible road; الطَريق المُؤَدِّية إلى السّاحةِ the road (leading) to the square; سَطْح الطَرِيقِ road, surface; يَسار \ يَمين الطَرِيقِ the left/right side of the road; خَريطة الطُرُقِ a road map; شَبَكة الطُرُقِ a road system; مُسْتَعْمِل الطَرِيقِ a road user; مَفْرِق \ مُفْتَرَق الطُرُقِ crossroads; مُفْتَرَق \ مُلْتَقى ثَلاثةِ طُرُقٍ a fork in road; قَطَعَ الطَرِيقَ to block the road, to set up a roadblock; قاطِع طَرِيقٍ *person who sets up a roadblock to rob or attack travellers*; robber; (Hist) highwayman, footpad; شَقَّ طَرِيقاً to build a road; سَلَكَ الطَرِيقَ to follow a road; لا يَزالُ الطَرِيقُ طَوِيلاً to (still) have a long way to go; يَنْعَطِفُ الطَرِيقُ إلى اليَمينِ the road curves to the right 2 [وَسيلة] way, means; عن طَرِيقِ by means/way of, through; via; عن طَرِيقِ الطاقةِ الشَمْسِيّةِ by means of solar energy; بالطَرِيقِ الرَسْميِّ through official channels; حاوَلَ العَوْدةَ إلى العِراقِ عن طَرِيقِ تُرْكيا to try to return to Iraq via Turkey; وَجَّهَ رَسائِلَ عن طَرِيقِ القُنْصُلِ to send letters through the consul 3 [خَطّ السَيْرِ] route, way, road, path; عن طَرِيقٍ آخَر via another route; الطَرِيق المُباشِر the direct road; أَقْرَب \ أَسْرَع طَرِيقٍ the shortest/fastest route; طَرِيق جَوّيّ air route; طَرِيق شاقّ a difficult road; طَرِيق العَوْدةِ return road/route; طَرِيق السَلامِ the road to peace; الطَرِيق إلى أَمْسْتِرْدام the way to Amsterdam; كانَ على الطَرِيقِ المُسْتَقيم to be on the the straight and narrow (path); لَجَأَ إلى الطَرِيقِ الأَسْهَلِ to take the path of least resistance; اتَّبَعَ طَرِيقاً to follow a road; اتَّخَذَ طَرِيقَهُ to take the road; شَقَّ طَرِيقَهُ to work one's way; سَأَلَ

أَضْرَبَ عن الطَعام فَضَلات \ بَقايا طَعامٍ leftovers, table scraps; أَعَدَّ \ حَضَّرَ الطَعامَ to go/be on a hunger strike; to prepare food; هَنِيءَ من الطَعامِ to enjoy the food; هَنِيءَ لَهُ الطَعامُ to be satisfied; الطَعامُ جاهِزٌ the food is ready; تَناوُلُ الأَطْعِمَةِ المُخْتَلِفَة مُهِمٌّ جِدًّا it's very important to have a varied diet

طُعْمة *n* |طُعَم| food; كانَ البَيْتُ طُعْمةً للنيرانِ the house was consumed by the fire

طَعْمِيّة *n* ta'amiya (*Egyptian falafel*)

إطْعام *n* feeding

تَطْعيم *n* (Med) inoculation; vaccination; تَطْعيم طِفْلٍ ضدّ مَرَض شَلَلِ الأَطْفالِ to give a child a polio vaccine

مَطْعَم *n* |مَطاعِمُ| restaurant; eating house; مَطْعَم جامِعيّ canteen (BrE), cafeteria, dining/mess hall (AmE); مَطْعَم مَشْهور \ فَخْم a famous/fancy restaurant; مَطْعَم غالٍ \ رَخيص an expensive/cheap restaurant; مَطْعَم بيتزا pizzeria; مَطْعَم الخِدْمة الذاتيّة self-service restaurant; صاحب مَطْعَمٍ restaurateur

طَعَنَ *v* |a-u; طَعْن| ❶ [وَخَز] to stab; طَعَنَ شَخْصاً في ظَهْرِه to stab sb in the back; طَعَنَ شَخْصاً بِسِكّين to stab sb with a knife ❷ [فَنَّدَ] |في| to challenge; to contest, to appeal; طَعَنَ في قرارٍ to challenge a decision; طَعَنَ في نَتائِجِ الانْتِخاباتِ to contest the election results ❸ [شَهَّرَ] |في| to challenge; to crush; طَعَنَ فيه النُقّادُ to be crushed by the critics; طَعَنَت المَحْكَمةُ في الشاهِدِ the court challenged the witness ❹ [كَبُرَ] طَعَنَ في السِنِّ to age, to be/grow old

طَعْن *n* ❶ [بالسكّين] stabbing; قتل شَخْصاً طَعْناً to stab sb to death ❷ [هُجوم] attack; طَعْن في شَرَفِ شَخْصٍ an attack on sb's honour/good name ❸ (Law) cassation; appeal; طَريقة طَعْنٍ method of appeal; قابِل للطَعْن disputable; حُكْم قابِل للطَعْنِ a verdict that can be appealed; قَرار غَيْر قابِلٍ للطَعْنِ a irrevocable decision; هذا قابِلٌ للطَعْنِ من الناحِيةِ القانونيّة this is legally contestable

طاعِن *adj* ❶ [قرار] appellant ❷ [السِنّ] aged, old, advanced (in age); طاعِن في السِنِّ advanced in age

طاعون *n* |طَواعِينُ| plague; طاعون دُمَّلِيّ bubonic plague; طاعون الخَنازيرِ swine fever; انْدَلَعَ وَباءُ الطاعونِ an epidemic of the plague broke out

طَرِيَ *v* |a; طَراوة| to be/become soft/weak/tender

طَرّى *v* to tenderize, to soften

أَطْرى *v* to praise, to compliment; to flatter; أَطْرى على شَخْصٍ to flatter sb, to butter sb up

طَرِيّ *adj* fresh; tender; غُصْن طَرِيّ a green branch; خُضَر \ فَواكِه طَرِيّة fresh vegetables/fruit; لَحْم طَرِيّ tender meat

طَراوة *n* freshness; tenderness; softness

إطْراء *n* flattery; praise; عِبارات الإطْراءِ flattering words

طازَج *adj* fresh; خُبْز طازَج fresh bread; خُضَر \ فَواكِه طازَجة fresh vegetables/fruit

طَزاجة *n* freshness

طَشْت, طِشْت, طَسْت, طِسْت *n* |طُشوت| basin, washbasin, washtub

طَشْطَشَ *v* |i; طَشْطَشة| to spit; يُطَشْطِشُ الزَيْتُ the oil is splattering

طَعِمَ *v* |a; طَعْم| to eat

طَعَّمَ *v* ❶ (Med) to inoculate; to vaccinate; طَعَّمَ شَخْصاً ضِدّ مَرَضٍ to inoculate/vaccinate sb against a disease ❷ (Bot) to graft ❸ [زَيَّنَ] to inlay; طَعَّمَ شَيْئاً بالعاجِ to inlay sth with ivory

أَطْعَمَ *v* ❶ [أَكَّل] to feed; to nourish; to fodder; أَطْعَمَ طِفْلاً to nourish a child; أَطْعَمَ الدَجاجَ to feed the chickens ❷ (Bot) to graft

تَطَعَّمَ *v* to taste

اسْتَطْعَمَ *v* ❶ [تَلَذَّذَ] to like, to enjoy ❷ [داقَ] to taste

طَعْم *n* |طُعوم| taste, flavour; طَعْم غَريب \ حامِض a strange/sour taste; إنَّهُ طَيِّبُ الطَعْم it tastes good; كانَ طَعْمُهُ يُشْبِهُ طَعْمَ السَمَكِ to taste like fish; كانَ لَهُ طَعْمٌ \ كانَ طَعْمُهُ كَريهاً to taste bad; فقدت الفاكِهةُ طَعْمَها اللَذيذَ the fruit has lost its flavour; لم يَذُقْ للحَياةِ طَعْماً to have not experienced anything in life; لم يَذُقْ طَعْمَ النَوْمِ to not get any sleep

طُعْم *n* ❶ (Bot) graft ❷ [فَخّ] bait; اسْتَعْمَلَ شَيْئاً كَطُعْمٍ to use sth as bait ❸ (Med) |طُعوم| vaccine

طَعام *n* |أَطْعِمة| food; nourishment; meal; أَطْعِمة food; الطَعام والشَراب food and drinks; طَعام عَسير \ سَهْل الهَضْم a heavy/light meal; طَعام مُغَذٍّ substantial food; وَجْبة طَعامٍ a meal; قائِمة طَعامٍ menu; غُرْفة \ قاعة الطَعامِ dining room/hall;

طَعْنة *n* |طَعَنات| stab; طَعْنة نَجْلاء a fatal stab; طَعْنة في الظَهْرِ a stab in the back; طَعْنة سِكّينٍ stab of a knife; تَعَرَّض لِطَعْنةٍ to get stabbed; طَعَنَ شَخْصاً عِدّة طَعَناتٍ to stab sb repeatedly

مَطْعَن *n* |مَطاعِنُ| abuse, invective

‹ **طاغوت** *n* |طَواغيتُ| **1** [وَثَن] idol (*object of religious worship*) **2** [طاغ] dictator

‹ **طُغْرى, طُغْراء** *n* |dipt f; طُغْراءات| *the calligraphic monogram, seal and signature of an Ottoman sultan*

‹ **طُغْمة** *n* |طُغَم, طُغْمات| group; clique

‹ **طَغى** *v* |a; طُغْيان| **1** [سَيْطَرَ] to control; to dominate; to tyrannize; طَغى على شَيْءٍ to control sth; طَغى الفِكْرُ المُتَعَصِّبُ على المِنْطَقةِ extremism was dominant in the region; في أَجْواءٍ طَغى عَلَيْها التَفاؤُلُ in an atmosphere dominated by optimism **2** [جاوَزَ الحُدودَ] to be excessive; to exceed boundaries **3** [فاضَ] to overflow **4** [على صَوْتٍ] to drown (out); طَغى على صَوْتٍ to drown (out) a noise

طاغٍ **A** *adj* |طُغاة| **1** [دِكْتاتوريّ] tyrannical; dictatorial, oppressive **2** [الماء] *related to flooding*; مَوْجة طاغِية tidal wave **B** *n* |طُغاة| tyrant; dictator, oppressor

طاغِية *n* |m| tyrant; dictator, oppressor

طُغْيان *n* **1** [تَعَسُّف] despotism; tyranny; oppression **2** [فَيَضان] flood

طُغْيانيّ *adj* tyrannical; despotic

‹ **طَفِئَ** *v* |a; طُفوء| to go out; to die out

أَطْفَأَ *v* **1** [ناراً] to put out, to extinguish; to smother; أَطْفَأَ سيجارةً to put out a cigarette; أَطْفَأَ شَمْعةً to extinguish a candle; أَطْفَأَ ظَمَأَهُ to quench one's thirst **2** [جهازاً] to turn off, to switch off; أَطْفَأَ الضَوْءَ to turn off the light; أَطْفَأَ جِهازَ الإِنْذارِ to turn off the alarm; أَطْفَأَ الراديو to turn off the radio

انْطَفَأَ *v* to go out; to die out; انْطَفَأَ الضَوْءُ \ المِصْباحُ the light/lamp went out

طَفّاية *n* ashtray

إطْفاء *n* extinguishing; firefighting; جِهاز إِطْفاءِ الحَريقِ (fire) extinguisher; رِجال الإِطْفاءِ firefighters; مَرْكَز \ دائِرة الإِطْفاءِ fire station; سَيّارة إِطْفاءٍ fire engine; إِطْفاء نارِ الثَوْرةِ extinguishing the revolutionary fire; إِطْفاء الحَريقِ fighting the fire

إِطْفائيّ *n* fireman

إِطْفائيّة *n* fire brigade (BrE) department (AmE)

مِطْفَأة *n* |مَطافِئُ| (fire) extinguisher; رِجال المَطافِئِ firefighters; سَرِيّة \ فِرْقة المَطافِئِ fire brigade (BrE) department (AmE); مِطْفَأة سَجائِر ashtray

مُنْطَفِئ *adj* extinguished; gone out; المِدْفَأةُ \ المِصْباحُ مُنْطَفِئ(ةٌ) the stove/light has gone out

‹ **طَفَح** *v* |a; طَفْح| to overflow, to flood; to brim; طَفَحَ بالحَيَويّةِ to brim with the joy of living; طَفَحَ وَجْهُهُ بالبِشْرِ \ الفَرَحِ his face beamed with joy; تَطْفَحُ الكَأْسُ the glass is overflowing; طَفَحَ الكَيْلُ that's the limit; enough is enough

طَفْح *n* **1** (Med) rash; eruption; طَفْح القُرّاصِ nettle rash; أُصيبَ بالطَفْحِ to develop/have a rash **2** [فَيْض] flood

طافِح *adj* overflowing; replete; كانَ طافِحاً to be overflowing

مِطْفَحة *n* (Zool) skimmer

‹ **طَفَر** *v* |i; طَفْر| to jump, to leap; طَفَرَ الدَمْعُ من عَيْنَيْهِ tears came to his eyes

طافِر **A** *adj* |طَوافِرُ| mutant; جين طافِر mutant gene **B** *n* |طَوافِرُ| mutant

طَفْرة *n* **1** [قَفْزة] jump, leap; طَفْرة نَوْعيّة breakthrough; طَفْرة الأَسْعارِ a jump in prices; حَقَّقَ طَفْرةً كَبيرةً to make a big leap **2** [تَحَوُّر] mutation; طَفْرة جينيّة genetic mutation

‹ **تَطْفيش** *n* dismissal

‹ **طَفّة** *n* (Geol) travertine; طَفّة بُرْكانيّة tuff

طَفيف *adj* insignificant, minor; small, slight; petty; جُروح طَفيفة minor injuries; كَمّيّة طَفيفة a petty quantity; تَغْيير طَفيف a small change; ارْتِفاع طَفيف a slight rise in prices

مُطَفِّف *n* سورة المُطَفِّفين The Dealers in Fraud (*Sura 83*)

‹ **طَفِق** *v* |a; طَفَق| to begin; to start; طَفِقَ يَفْعَلُ شَيْئاً to start with sth

‹ **تَطَفَّلَ** *v* **1** [اسْتَفادَ | على] to beg from, to scrounge/mooch off of; تَطَفَّلَ على شَخْصٍ to mooch off of sb **2** [تَدَخَّلَ | على] to force oneself on

طَقْس *n* ① [جَوّ] weather; طَقْس مُشْمِس \ عاصِف \ رَديء sunny/stormy/nasty weather; إذا كانَ الطَقْسُ جَميلاً \ سَيِّئاً whether the weather is good/bad ② (Relig) |طُقوس| ritual, rite; أدّى طُقوساً مُعَيَّنةً to perform a ritual; طُقوس ritual, rite; طُقوس دينيّة a religious ritual

طَقْسيّ *adj* ritual, ceremonial

طُقوسيّ *adj* sacred

طَقْطَقَ *v* |i; طَقْطَقة| to rattle; to click; to crack; طَقْطَقَ أصابِعَهُ to crack one's knuckles

طَقْطَقة *n* rattle; click; crack

طَقَّ *v* |u; طَقّ| to crack; to burst

طَقْم *n* |أَطْقُم, طُقومة, طُقوم| ① [مَجْموعة] set, collection; طَقْم أَسْنانٍ (set of) false teeth; طَقْم طَناجِرَ cookware set, set of pots and pans ② [بَدْلة] suit, costume ③ [الحَيَوان] harness ④ [صينيّ] set, service; طَقْم صينيّ a china service

طاقِم *n* |طَواقِمُ| crew; cast; (ship's) company; طاقِم طائِرةٍ aircrew; طاقِم تِلِفِزْيونٍ television crew; عُضْو في الطاقِمِ crew member; بدونِ طاقِمٍ unmanned

طَلَبَ *v* |u; طَلَب, مَطْلَب| ① [سَأَلَ] to ask; to request; to order; طَلَبَ مِن شَخْصٍ to ask sth from sb; طَلَبَ شَيْئاً من شَخْصٍ ... أنْ to ask sb to ...; طَلَبَ من شَخْصٍ فِعْلَ شَيْءٍ to ask sb to do sth; طَلَبَ كَأْساً من العَصيرِ to order a glass of juice; طَلَبَ من شَخْصٍ الانْتِباهَ \ الهُدوءَ \ المُساعَدةَ to request attention/silence/assistance from sb; طَلَبَ من شَخْصٍ عَدَمَ التَدْخينِ to request that sb not smoke; طَلَبَ يَدَ فَتاةٍ to ask for a girl's hand; طَلَبَ المُسْتَحيلَ to ask for/demand the impossible; طَلَبَ بِإلْحاحٍ to urge (strongly) ② [سَعى] to search for, to look for; to gather; طَلَبَ مَعْلوماتٍ to search for information/data; طَلَبَ العِلْمَ to gather knowledge; مَنْ طَلَبَ وَجَدَ seek and ye shall find ③ [قَدَّمَ مَطْلَباً] to apply for; to consult (with); طَلَبَ اللُجوءَ to apply for a scholarship; طَلَبَ مِنْحَةً دِراسيّةً to apply for asylum; طَلَبَ نَصيحةَ البَلَديّةِ to consult (with) the municipality

طالَبَ *v* to claim, to demand; to call in; طالَبَ بِتَعْويضٍ to claim travelling expenses; طالَبَ تَكاليفَ السَفَرِ

طَفْل *n* |طُفول, طِفال| clay

طِفْل *n* |أَطْفال| ① [صَغير السِنِّ] child, infant; طِفْل حَديث الوِلادةِ a newborn; طِفْل مُعْجِزة child prodigy; أَطْفال الشَوارِعِ street urchins (old use), street children; طِبّ الأَطْفالِ paediatrics; طَبيب الأَطْفالِ paediatrician; قِسْم الأَطْفالِ paediatric/children's ward; مَرَض أَطْفالٍ childhood disease; عَدَد وَفَياتِ الأَطْفالِ infant mortality; حَديقة أَطْفالٍ playground; جَليسة أَطْفالٍ babysitter; غِذاء أَطْفالٍ baby food; رَوْضة الأَطْفالِ kindergarten; day-care centre; غَنيّ بالأَطْفالِ having many children ② [خَلَف] child, descendant; طِفْل غَيْر شَرْعيٍّ an illegitimate child; وَلَدَتْ \ وَضَعَتْ \ أَنْجَبَتْ طِفْلاً to bear a child

طِفْلة *n* (baby) girl

طِفْليّ *adj* childlike, childish; ابْتِسامة طِفْليّة a childlike smile

طُفولة *n* infancy; childhood; مُنْذُ الطُفولةِ since/from childhood; خلال الطُفولةِ in childhood; في طُفولَتِهِ in one's childhood; رِعاية \ حِماية الطُفولةِ child welfare; بَراءة الطُفولةِ the innocence of youth; أيّام \ فَتْرة الطُفولةِ childhood years; اسْتَعادَ ذِكْرَياتِ الطُفولةِ to reminisce about childhood years

طُفوليّ *adj* childlike, childish; وَجْه طُفوليّ a childlike/childish face; فَرَح طُفوليّ childlike joy

طُفوليّة *n* childishness

طُفَيْليّ Ⓐ *adj* parasitic; حَشَرات طُفَيْليّة vermin
Ⓑ *n* ① [إنْسان] |طُفَيْليّونَ| parasite, sponger ② (Zool, Bot) |طُفَيْليّات| parasite

تَطَفُّل *n* interference, intrusion

مُتَطَفِّل *n* ① [مُتَدَخِّل] meddler ② [طُفَيْليّ] profiteer

طَفا *v* |u; طَفْو| to float; to surface; to buoy; طَفا فوق السَطْحِ to float on the surface; طَفا فوق البَحْرِ to float on the sea

طَفْو *n* floating; قابليّة الطَفْوِ buoyancy

طافية *n* |طَوافٍ| buoy

طَفاوة *n* foam

طُفاوة *n* ① [على الماءِ] flotsam; *anything drifting or floating*
② [الشَمْسِ] halo (*around the sun or moon*)

طَفّاية *n* see طفأ

بِتَعْوِيضِ الخَسارةِ to claim/demand compensation for damage; طالَبَ بِشَرْحٍ \ بالطاعةِ من شَخْصٍ to demand an explanation/obedience from sb; طالَبَ بِزِيادةِ الراتِبِ to demand a wage increase; طالَبَ بِدَيْنِهِ to call in one's debt

تَطَلَّبَ *v* to require; to demand; تَطَلَّبَ شَيْئاً من شَخْصٍ to demand sth from sb; تَطَلَّبَ من شَخْصٍ أنْ ... to expect sb to ...; تَطَلَّبَ كَثيراً من الوَقْتِ to take much time; تَطَلَّبَ شَهادةً to require a diploma; تَطَلَّبَ عِنايةً خاصّةً to require special care; يَتَطَلَّبُ التَحْرِيرُ الكَثِيرَ من الطاقةِ والتَرْكِيزِ والصَبْرِ editing requires a lot of energy, concentration and patience

طَلَب *n* |طَلَبات| **1** ⟨[الْتِماس] request; claim; demand; مُقَدِّم (ب) طَلَبٍ applicant; تَقْدِيم طَلَب الاشْتِراكِ \ التَسْجِيلِ registration, application; طَلَب طَرْحِ الثِقةِ a no-confidence motion/vote; عند الطَلَبِ à la carte; بِناءً على طَلَبِ شَخْصٍ at sb's request; قَدَّمَ طَلَباً to submit/file a request/claim; قَدَّمَ طَلَباً إلى شَرِكةِ التَأْمِينِ to file a claim with the insurance company; تَقَدَّمَ بِطَلَبٍ إلى شَخْصٍ to approach sb on a matter; اسْتَجابَ لِطَلَباتِ شَخْصٍ to comply with sb's demands; رَفَضَ \ قَبِلَ طَلَباً to refuse/grant a request; وافَقَ على طَلَباتٍ to grant requests; عالَجَ طَلَباً to deal with a claim; قَدَّمَ طَلَباً لِلُّجوءِ to apply for asylum **2** (Law) claim; demand; petition; طَلَب مُضادّ counterclaim **3** (Busn) order; demand, call; العَرْض والطَلَب supply and demand; الطَلَب على مَنْتوجٍ the demand/call for a product; تحت الطَلَبِ on order; اسْتِمارة طَلَبٍ order form; قَدَّمَ طَلَباً to place an order; تَلَقّى طَلَباتٍ to obtain orders

طالِب *n* |طَلَبة, طُلّاب| **1** ⟨[دارِس] student; طالِب مَدْرَسِيّ a school student; طالِب جامِعِيّ a university/college student; طالِب في جامِعةِ دِمَشْقَ a student at the University of Damascus; طالِب فَلْسَفةٍ \ في (كُلِّيّةِ) الفَلْسَفةِ a philosophy student; جَمْعِيّة \ نادي طَلَبةٍ student union; بِطاقة الطالِبِ student card, university ID card **2** ⟨[مَنْ يَطْلُبُ] claimant, plaintiff; petitioner; طالِب بِحُقوقٍ *sb who claims his rights*

طالِبان *n* Taliban

طالِبِيّ *adj* student (*before n*); حَرَكة طالِبِيّة student movement

طُلّابِيّ *adj* student (*before n*); حَرَكة طُلّابِيّة student movement

طِلْبة *n* wish, desire; question; ما طِلْبَتُكَ؟ what do you want?, how may I help you?

طَلَبِيّة *n* order; سَجَّلَ طَلَبِيّةً to take an order; حَصَلَ على طَلَبِيّاتٍ to obtain orders

مُتَطَلَّب **A** *adj* required, necessary

B *n* |مُتَطَلَّبات| requirements; requests; مُتَطَلَّبات قانونِيّة statutory/legal requirements; لَبّى مُتَطَلَّباتٍ to comply with requests; تَوَفَّرَتْ فيهِ المُتَطَلَّباتُ to meet/fulfil requirements

مُتَطَلِّب *adj* demanding; مُتَطَلِّب كَثِيراً very/overly demanding

مُطالِب *n* claimant, plaintiff

مُطالَبة *n* demand, claim; requirement; right; مُطالَبة بِمَبْلَغِ أَلْفِ دولار a claim for a thousand dollars

مَطْلَب *n* |مَطالِبُ| **1** ⟨[طَلَب] request; demand, claim; مَطالِب *things needed or requested*; تَحْقِيق المَطالِبِ the granting of a request; تَسْوِية المَطالِبِ settlement of demands **2** ⟨[هَدَف] goal, aim; wish, desire; كانَت الوَحْدةُ العَرَبِيّةُ مَطْلَباً قَوْمِيّاً عَرَبِيّاً Arab unity was an Arab national goal; الحُرِّيّةُ مَطْلَبٌ من مَطالِبِ الناسِ everybody desires freedom

مَطْلَبِيّ *adj* required, mandatory; تَحَرُّكات مَطْلَبِيّة political action movements

مَطْلوب *adj* required, mandatory; necessary; sought-after; غَيْر مَطْلوبٍ unasked (for); أَقَلّ من المَطْلوبِ insufficient; مَنْتوج مَطْلوب a sought-after product; الأَوْراق \ التَرْخِيص المَطْلوب(ة) the required papers/licences

‹ **طَلَحَ** *v* |u; طَلاح| to be wicked, to be vicious

طَلْح *n* (Bot) acacia

طالِح *adj* wicked, vicious

‹ **أَطْلَس** **A** *adj* |dipt| gray, dull

B *n* listed alphabetically

‹ **طِلَّسْم, طِلَسْم** *n* |طَلاسِمُ| talisman; amulet; charm

‹ **طَلَعَ** *v* |u; مَطْلَع, طُلوع| **1** ⟨[ارْتَفَعَ] to rise, to ascend, to go up; to appear; to come up, to sprout; طَلَعَ وَنَزَلَ to rise and fall; طَلَعَ القَمَرُ the moon rose; طَلَعَ النَباتُ the plant sprouted **2** ⟨[ظَهَرَ] to break; يَطْلَعُ النَهارُ \ الفَجْرُ dawn is breaking **3** ⟨[صَعِدَ] to climb, to mount; طَلَعَ جَبَلاً to climb a mountain

طالَعَ *v* ❶ [قَرَأ] to read; to study; طالَعَ كِتاباً to read a book ❷ [رَأى] to see; to observe

أَطْلَعَ *v* ❶ [أَخْبَرَ] to inform, to tell; to announce; أَطْلَعَ شَخْصاً على شَيْءٍ to inform sb about/of sth ❷ [نَباتٌ] to come up, to sprout

تَطَلَّعَ *v* ❶ [نَظَرَ] |إلى| to look, to observe; تَطَلَّعَ إلى الوَراءِ to look back; تَطَلَّعَ في \ إلى وَجْهِ شَخْصٍ to observe sb's face; ❷ [تاقَ] تَطَلَّعَ (إلى شَيْءٍ) to stand by idly مَكْتوفَ اليَدَيْنِ |إلى| to aspire; to long for, to look forward to; تَطَلَّعَ إلى شَيْءٍ to aspire to sth; تَطَلَّعَ إلى العُطْلَةِ to look forward to the holidays

اطَّلَعَ *v* to examine, to study; to note, to take note; اطَّلَعَ على شَيْءٍ to look at/read sth; اطَّلَعَ على (مُحْتَوى) رِسالَةٍ to examine (the contents of) a letter

اسْتَطْلَعَ *v* to explore; to inquire; اسْتَطْلَعَ رَأْيَ شَخْصٍ to explore sb's view

طَلْع *n* pollen; غُبار الطَّلْع pollen

طالِع *n* |طَوالِعُ| horoscope; ascendant; ساءَ \ حَسُنَ طالِعُهُ to be born under an unlucky/lucky star; سَيِّء \ حَسَن الطالِعِ unlucky/lucky (person)

طَلائِعي *adj* vanguard (*before n*); لَعِبَ دَوْراً طَلائِعِيًّا to play a leading role

طَلْعة *n* ❶ [اِسْم المَرّة من طَلَعَ] flight; rise, ascent ❷ [وَجْه] appearance, looks; حَسَن \ بَهيّ الطَّلْعَةِ good-looking; مُهيب الطَّلْعَةِ a dignified appearance

طُلوع *n* rise, ascent; climb; emergence; عند طُلوعِ الفَجْرِ at (the crack of) dawn; طُلوعاً ونُزولاً up and down; طُلوع جيلٍ جَديدٍ the emergence of a new generation

طَليعة *n* |طَلائِعُ| vanguard; forward line; front, lead; طَليعة جَيْشٍ the forward line of an army; لَعِبَ في الطَّليعةِ to play up front; كانَ في طَليعةِ السِباقِ to be in the lead

طَليعيّ *adj* avant-garde

اسْتِطْلاع *n* |اسْتِطْلاعات| survey, poll; investigation, exploration; حُبّ الاسْتِطْلاعِ curiosity; حُبًّا للاسْتِطْلاعِ out of curiosity; رِحْلة اسْتِطْلاعٍ جَوِّيّة reconnaissance flight; اسْتِطْلاع للرَأْيِ opinion poll; referendum; أَظْهَرَت \ أَفادَت اسْتِطْلاعاتٌ للرَأْيِ أنّ ... opinion polls show that ...

اسْتِطْلاعيّ *adj* pilot (*before n*); reconnaissance (*before n*); دِراسة اسْتِطْلاعيّة a pilot study; بِعْثة اسْتِطْلاعيّة a reconnaissance mission

إطْلاع *n* information; education

اطِّلاع *n* |اطِّلاعات| examination, inspection; perusal; knowledge, information; على سَبيلِ الاطِّلاعِ for information; بعد الاطِّلاعِ على مُحْتَوى الرِسالةِ after examination of the letter; الاطِّلاع على أَوْراقِ قَضيّةٍ inspection of the case documents; مَصْدَر سِياسيّ واسِع الاطِّلاعِ a well-informed political source; حَصَلَ على حَقِّ الاطِّلاعِ على الوَثائِقِ to obtain the right to examine the documents

تَطَلُّع *n* |تَطَلُّعات| ❶ [تَوَقُّع] prospect; expectation ❷ [طُموح] ambition

مُسْتَطْلَع *n person interviewed in opinion poll*

مُسْتَطْلِع *n* scout, explorer

مُطالَعة *n* reading, study, perusal; قاعة المُطالَعةِ reading room; أَحَبَّ مُطالَعةَ الكُتُبِ التاريخيّةِ he loved to peruse historical books

مَطْلَع *n* |مَطالِعُ| beginning, start; في مَطْلَعِ القَرْنِ العِشْرينَ at the beginning of the century; مَطْلَع الرِسالةِ salutation (*in a letter*)

مُطَّلِع *adj* well-informed; well read; أَوْساط مُطَّلِعة well-informed circles; عَلِمَ شَيْئاً من مَصْدَرٍ مُطَّلِعٍ to learn from well-informed sources; كانَ مُطَّلِعاً على شَيْءٍ to be well informed about sth

طَلَقَ *v* |u; طَلْق ,طُلوق| ❶ [من الزَوْجِ] to get a divorce; to be divorced (*said of a woman*) ❷ [في وَقْتِ الوِلادةِ] طُلِقَتْ to be in labour

طَلُقَ *v* |u; طَلاقة| to be happy; طَلُقَ وَجْهُهُ his face beamed with happiness; طَلُقَتْ يَدُهُ he was generous

طَلَّقَ *v* to divorce (*said of a man*); طَلَّقَ زَوْجَتَهُ to divorce one's wife

أَطْلَقَ *v* ❶ [قَذَفَ] to launch; to fire, to shoot; to release, to discharge; to emit; أَطْلَقَ النارَ \ الرَصاصَ على شَيْءٍ \ شَخْصٍ to fire at sb/sth; أَطْلَقَ طَلْقةً \ سَهْماً \ رَصاصةً \ مَدافِعَ to fire a shot/arrow/bullet/cannon; أَطْلَقَ صاروخاً \ قَذيفةً to launch a missile/projectile; أَطْلَقَ بَرْنامَجاً to launch a program; أَطْلَقَ وابِلاً أَطْلَقَ مَوادَّ مُضِرّةً to emit harmful substances; أَطْلَقَ الكِلابَ على من الأَسْئِلةِ to fire/shoot questions at sb; أَطْلَقَ سَراحَ \ سَبيلَ الجُمْهورِ to set dogs on the crowd; شَخْصٍ to release sb; أَطْلَقَ يَدَ شَخْصٍ في شَيْءٍ to give/allow sb a free hand in sth; أَطْلَقَ لِحْيَتَهُ to grow one's beard; أَطْلَقَ على شَخْصٍ \ شَيْءٍ اسْماً to name sb/sth; أَطْلَقَ لِسانَهُ to talk incessantly **2** [صَيْحةً، ضِحْكةً] to utter; أَطْلَقَ صَيْحاتٍ to let out screams; أَطْلَقَ أَقْوالاً to make remarks

تَطَلَّقَ *v* **1** [أَشْرَقَ] to brighten (up); تَطَلَّقَ وَجْهُهُ his face brightened **2** [أَصْبَحَ طَليقاً] to get divorced

انْطَلَقَ *v* **1** [غادَرَ] to start, to get going; to leave, to take off; انْطَلَقَ إلى البَيْتِ to leave for home; انْطَلَقَ في الساعةِ السادسةِ to take off at six o'clock **2** [بَدَأَ] to start, to begin; انْطَلَقَ إلى \ نحو فِعْلِ شَيْءٍ to start doing sth; انْطَلَقَ في كِتابةِ رِسالةٍ to start writing a letter; انْطَلَقَ من فَرْضيّةٍ to start from a hypothesis

طَلْق I *n* talc; مَسْحوق الطَلْقِ talcum powder

طَلْق II **A** *adj* open, free, unrestrained; في الهَواءِ الطَلْقِ in the open air; كانَ طَلْقَ اللِسانِ to have a ready tongue
B *n* [وِلادة] contraction; labour pain; جاءَها الطَلْقُ her contractions started

طالِق *adj* |f| divorced; repudiated; أَنْتِ طالِقٌ I divorce you (*said to a woman*)

طَلاق *n* divorce; طَلاق بائِن, الطَلاق بالثَلاثةِ irrevocable divorce; طَلاق رَجْعيّ revocable divorce; طَلاق خُلْعيّ *divorce instigated by the wife, who has to pay a compensation*; رَسْم طَلاقٍ divorce document; سورة الطَلاق The Divorce (*Sura 65*); طَلَبَتْ من زَوْجِها الطَلاقَ she asked her husband to divorce her

طَلاقة *n* fluency, ease; بِطَلاقةٍ fluently; تَكَلَّمَ العَرَبيّةَ بِطَلاقةٍ to speak Arabic fluently

طَلْقة *n* |طَلَقات| **1** [قَذيفة] shot, gunshot; طَلْقة ناريّة shot, gunshot; طَلْقة تَحْذيريّة \ إِنْذارٍ a warning shot; طَلْقة مُحاذِية a grazing shot; مَسافة الطَلْقةِ shooting distance/range; أَطْلَقَ طَلْقةً to fire a shot; أَطْلَقَ على شَخْصٍ الطَلْقةَ القاتِلةَ to shoot sb fatally; أُصيبَ بِطَلْقةٍ to get shot; دَوَّتْ طَلَقاتٌ ناريّةٌ shots rang out **2** [اسْم مَرّةٍ من الطَلاقِ] a divorce pronouncement
3 [الوِلادة] contraction

طَليق **A** *adj* |طُلَقاءُ| free; طَليق من القُيودِ unattached; كانَ طَليقَ اليَدِ to have free play
B *n* |طُلَقاءُ| **1** [مُطَلَّق] a divorced man **2** [حُرّ] a free man (*not a slave*)

طَليقة **A** *adj* free; أَصْبَحَت البِلادُ حُرّةً طَليقةً the country became free
B *n* **1** [مُطَلَّقة] divorcée (*a divorced woman*) **2** [حُرّ] a free woman (*not a slave*)

إطْلاق *n* |إطْلاقات| **1** [قَذْف] launch, launching, firing; إطْلاق سَراحٍ release, discharge; تَبادُل إطْلاقِ النارِ gunfight; مَنصّة إطْلاقٍ launching pad; رَدَّ إطْلاقَ الرَصاصِ to shoot back **2** [مُطْلَقاً] على الإطْلاق absolutely; by far; لا \ لَيْسَ ... على الإطْلاقِ by no means, in no way, anything but; لم يَفْعَلْ شَيْئاً على الإطْلاقِ to do absolutely nothing; لن أَسْمَحَ بِهَذا على الإطْلاقِ under no circumstances will I allow that

انْطِلاق *n* departure, start; انْطِلاق نابِض a flying start; انْطِلاق مُبَكِّر a false start; خَطّ انْطِلاقٍ (starting) mark; مَكان الانْطِلاقِ start, starting place; نُقْطة انْطِلاقٍ point of departure, starting point; نُقْطة انْطِلاقِ سَفَرِنا point of departure for our journey; نُقْطة انْطِلاقِ مُناقَشةٍ \ اسْتِدْلالٍ premise of an argument/ argumentation; ضَرَبَ ضَرْبةَ الانْطِلاقِ to kick off

انْطِلاقة *n* start; انْطِلاقة خاطِئة a false start

تَطْليق *n* divorce

مُطْلَق *adj* absolute, infinite, unlimited, unrestricted; total, complete; مُطْلَقاً absolutely; لا ... مُطْلَقاً absolutely not; ضَرورة \ أَوْلَويّة مُطْلَقة an absolute necessity/priority; سُلْطة مُطْلَقة absolute power; ثِقة مُطْلَقة unconditional trust; تَوْكيل مُطْلَق unlimited power of attorney; حُكْم مُطْلَق autocratic government; حُرّيّة مُطْلَقة absolute freedom; مُطْلَق السُلْطةِ almighty; هذا الافْتِراءُ لا أَساسَ لَهُ مُطْلَقاً this is completely baseless slander; لا أَفْهَمُ مُطْلَقاً لِماذا I haven't a clue why

مُطَلَّق *adj* divorced

مُطْلَقيّ **A** *adj* totalitarian, absolutist
B *n* totalitarian, absolutist

طُمَأْنينة *n* calm; safety; trust, confidence; شُعور بالارْتِياحِ والطُمَأْنينةِ a sense of safety and security; شَعَرَ بالطُمَأْنينةِ to rest assured, to feel confident

اطْمِئْنان *n* serenity; confidence; reassurance; عَدَم الاطْمِئْنانِ anxiety, restlessness

مُطْمَئِنّ *adj* calm, at ease; لم يَكُنْ مُطْمَئِنًّا على شَيْءٍ to feel anxious/uneasy about sth; كُنْ مُطْمَئِنًّا rest assured

مُطَمْئِن *adj* comforting, reassuring, soothing; فِكْرة مُطَمْئِنة a comforting thought; هذا مُطَمْئِنٌ جِدًّا that's a great comfort/relief

‹ **طَمَثَ** *v* |u; طَمْث| to menstruate

طَمْث *n* menstrual blood; menstruation, period

طامِث *adj* |f| menstruating

‹ **طَمَحَ** *v* |a; طُموح| to be ambitious, to aspire; طَمَحَ إلى مَنْصِبٍ \ الرِئاسةِ to aspire to a position/the presidency

طامِح *adj* ambitious

طَمّاح *adj* ambitious; رَجُل طَمّاح \ غَيْر طَمّاحٍ an ambitious/unambitious man; كانَ طَمّاحاً to be ambitious

طَموح *adj* ambitious; خُطّة طَموحة an ambitious plan; رَجُل طَموح \ غَيْر طَموح an ambitious/unambitious man; كانَ طَموحاً to be ambitious

طُموح *n* |طُموحات| ambition; طُموح سِياسيّ \ عِلْميّ political/academic ambition; لَبّى الطُموحاتِ to fulfil ambitions

مَطْمَح *n* |مَطامِحُ| aim, goal, objective; ambition, aspiration; كانَ ذا مَطامِحَ عالِيةٍ \ بَعيدةٍ to have high aspirations

‹ **طَمَرَ** *v* |i-u; طَمْر| to bury; to fill up/in; طَمَرَ النُفاياتِ الكيماويّةَ to bury chemical waste; طَمَرَ قَناةً \ بِئْراً to fill in a ditch/well

طَمْر *n* filling; burial

طامور, **طومار** *n* |طَواميرُ| listed alphabetically

مِطْمَر *n* (Naut, Tools) plumb line, plummet, lead line

مَطْمور *adj* buried, covered

‹ **طَمَسَ** *v* |i-u; طَمْس| to eradicate, to obliterate, to destroy; to wipe out; to cover up, to conceal; طَمَسَ حَضارةً to destroy a civilization; طَمَسَ قَضيّةً to cover sth up; طَمَسَ الحَقائِقَ to conceal the facts; طَمَسَ الآثارَ to cover the tracks

مُطْلَقيّة *n* totalitarianism, absolutism

مُنْطَلَق *n* ⟨1⟩ [نُقْطة انْطِلاقٍ] premise; starting point; من هذا المُنْطَلَقِ from this point ⟨2⟩ (Sport) start, starting place/line

‹ **أَطَلَّ** *v* to face, to overlook; to view, to look out; أَطَلَّ على شَيْءٍ to have an overview of sth, to look out over sth; تُطِلُّ النافِذةُ على الشارِعِ the window overlooks the street; أَطَلَّ بِرَأْسِهِ من النافِذةِ to pop one's head out of the window

طَلَل *n* |طُلول ,أَطْلال| أَطْلال ruins, remains

طَلّ *n* |طِلال| ⟨1⟩ [مَطَر خَفيف] drizzle ⟨2⟩ [نَدًى] dew

إطْلالة *n* view

مُطِلّ *adj* facing, overlooking; بُيوت مُطِلّة على الساحِلِ houses facing the seashore; البُلْدان المُطِلّة على البَحْرِ الأَبْيَضِ المُتَوَسِّطِ the countries located on the Mediterranean

‹ **طُلُمْبة** *n* pump

‹ **طَلَى** *v* |i; طَلْي| to paint; to lacquer, to enamel, to varnish; طَلَى جِداراً to paint a wall; طَلَى شَيْئاً to paint/varnish sth; طَلَى البابَ بِطِلاءٍ أَخْضَرَ to paint the door green; طَلَى بالكَهْرَباءِ to galvanize

انْطَلَى *v* انْطَلَتْ عَلَيْهِ الكِذْبةُ \ الحيلةُ to be hoaxed, to be fooled

طَلّاء *n* (house) painter

طِلاء *n* paint; lacquer, varnish; polish; طِلاء كِلْسيّ \ جيريّ whitewash; طِلاء الأَحْذِيةِ shoe polish; طِلاء الأَظافِرِ nail polish; طَبَقة (من) الطِلاءِ layer of paint; عُلْبة \ أُنْبوب من الطِلاءِ a can/tube of paint; يَتَقَشَّرُ الطِلاءُ the paint is flaking/peeling off

طُلاوة, **طِلاوة**, **طَلاوة** *n* beauty

مَطْليّ *adj* coated, plated; مَطْليّ بالذَهَبِ gold-plated

‹ **طَماطِم** *n coll* |dipt| tomato; صَلْصة طَماطِمَ ketchup; حَساء \ مَعْجون طَماطِمَ tomato soup/paste; زَرَعَ الطَماطِمَ to grow tomatoes

‹ **طَمْأَنَ** *v* |i; طَمْأَنة| to ease, to calm down; to reassure, to soothe; طَمْأَنَ شَخْصاً to calm sb down, to reassure sb

اطْمَأَنَّ *v* to be calmed; to be reassured; اطْمَأَنَّ على شَخْصٍ to be reassured of sb's well-being, to check on sb; اطْمَأَنَّ إلى شَيْءٍ \ شَخْصٍ to have faith in sth/sb

انْطَمَسَ *v* to be eradicated, to be obliterated; to fade, to become faint, to become blurred; قد انْطَمَسَ ذِكْرُهُ the memory of him has faded

طَمْس *n* eradication, obliteration, extermination

انْطِماس *n* fading, blurring

طَمْطَمَ *v* |i; طَمْطَمة| to babble, to speak incomprehensibly

طَماطِم *n listed alphabetically*

طَمِعَ *v* |a; طَمَع| to covet, to desire, to lust for/after; to be keen on, to be bent on, to be eager for; طَمِعَ ب \ في شَيْءٍ to to be keen on sth, to be after sth

طَمَّعَ *v* to entice, to tempt

أَطْمَعَ *v* to entice, to tempt

طَمَع *n* |أَطْماع| desire, longing; eagerness, ambition; greed

طامِع *adj* eager; greedy

طَمّاع *adj* eager; greedy

طَماعِيّة *n* greed

مَطْمَع *n* |مَطامِعُ| ambition; goal, purpose

طِماق *n* leggings

طَمَّ *v* |u; طَمّ, طُموم| to inundate, to flood; to cover; طَمَّت الرِمالُ الطَرِيقَ the road was covered in sand

طامّة *n* calamity, disaster

طَمْأَنَ *v* to pacify, to calm down

تَطْمين *n* |تَطْمينات| reassurance

طَمَا, **طَمى** *v* |i-u; طَمْي, طُمُوّ| to overflow, to flood

طَمْي *n* sludge, silt

أَطْنَبَ *v* **1** [بالَغَ] to exaggerate **2** [في الحَديثِ] to brag; to speak in great detail/at great length

طُنْب, **طُنُب** *n* |أَطْناب| guy-rope, tent rope

إِطْناب *n* elaboration, lengthiness, exaggeration; comprehensiveness; بِإِطْنابٍ comprehensive; extensive; وَصَفَ شَيْئاً بِإِطْنابٍ to describe sth at length/in great detail

مُطْنَب *adj* elaborate; lengthy; comprehensive

طُنْبور *n* |طَنابيرُ| lute

طَنْجة *n* |dipt| Tangier (*city in in Morocco*)

طَنْجَرة *n* |طَناجِرُ| cooking pan, casserole; طَنْجَرة ضَغْطٍ a pressure cooker; طَقْم طَناجِرَ a set of pans

طَنَّشَ *v* (*Levant*) to ignore, to pretend not to notice/hear

طَنْطا *n* Tanta (*city in Egypt*)

طَنْطَنَ *v* |i; طَنْطَنة| to sound, to resound, to ring (out); to tinkle, to jingle; to buzz, to hum; طَنْطَنَت الذُبابةُ the fly buzzed; طَنْطَنَ على العودِ to strum a lute

طَنْف *n* |أَطْناف, طُنوف| corbel; overhang

طُنُف, **طُنْف**, **طَنَف**, **طَنْف** *n* |أَطْناف, طُنوف| ledge, overhang; corbel

طُنْفُسة *n* |طَنافِسُ| carpet

1 **طَنَّ** *v* |i; طَنين| to sound, to ring (out); to tinkle, to jingle; to buzz, to hum; resonate; يَطِنُّ الجَرَسُ the bell rings

طَنّان **A** *adj* bombastic, pompous; resounding, resonant; buzzing, humming; كَلِمات طَنّانة bombastic language **B** *n* **1** (*Mech*) buzzer **2** (*Zool*) hummingbird

طَنّانة *n* bumblebee

طَنين *n* ring; bleep, squeak; hum, buzz; resonance; طَنين الناموسِ the buzz of mosquitoes

2 **طُنّ** *n* |أَطْنان| (metric) ton; طُنّ من الفَحْمِ الحَجَرِيِّ a ton of coal

طَهَ *n* Taha (*male given name*); سورة طَهَ Ta-Ha (*Sura 20*)

طَهُرَ *v* |u; طُهْر| **1** [كانَ نَظيفاً] to be clean, to be pure **2** (*Islam*) to be/become pure, to be/become cleansed; *to be in a period of purity from menses*

طَهَّرَ *v* **1** [نَقّى] to clean; to cleanse; to sterilize, to disinfect; to purify; طَهَّرَ جُرْحاً to clean/disinfect a wound; طَهَّرَ مَحاقِنَ to sterilize needles; طَهَّرَ الحِزْبَ to cleanse the party; طَهَّرَ الماءَ to purify water; طَهَّرَ مِنْطَقَةً من الأَلْغامِ to sweep an area for mines **2** [خَتَنَ] to circumcise; طَهَّرَ شَخْصاً to circumcise sb

تَطَهَّرَ *v* to be/become cleansed; to cleanse oneself (*for prayer*)

اطَّهَّرَ *v* to cleanse oneself

طُهْر *n* purity, chastity; virtue

طاهِر *adj* |أَطْهار| clean, pure, chaste; virtuous; الدَم الطاهِر pure blood; طاهِر الذَيْلِ sincere, honest; طاهِر الثِيابِ of impeccable character

طَهارة *n* **1** [عِفّة] purity, chastity; virtue; طَهارة الذَيْلِ sincerity, honesty **2** (Islam) ritual purity

طَهور *n* cleansing agent

تَطْهير *n* **1** [تَنْقِية] cleaning, cleansing, washing, ablution; disinfection, sterilization; sanitation, purification; تَطْهير عِرْقيّ ethnic cleansing; تَطْهير التُرْبةِ soil sanitation **2** [خِتان] circumcision

مَطْهَر *n* (Chr) purgatory

مُطَهَّر *adj* sterile, sterilized, aseptic; cleansed

مُطَهِّر *n* **1** [مُعَقِّم] disinfectant, antiseptic; detergent **2** [خاتِن] *sb who performs circumcisions*

مَطْهَرة *n* |مَطاهِرُ| bidet

‹ **طَهْران** *n* |f| Tehran (*capital of Iran*)

‹ **مُطَهَّم** *adj* **1** [جَميل] beautiful, pretty **2** [سَمين] thick, sturdy (*horses*)

‹ **طَها** *v* |a-u; طَهْو, طَهْي| to cook; to stew; طَها بالبُخارِ to steam

طَهْو *n* cooking

طَهْي *n* cooking; مَوْقد الطَهْي cooking ring, hot plate

طاهٍ *n* |طُهاة| cook

مَطْهوّ *adj* cooked, stewed

1‹ **طَوَّبَ** *v* (Chr) to beatify; طَوَّبَ شَخْصاً to beatify sb

طوبائيّ *adj* utopian

طوبيا *n* Utopia

2‹ **طَوّاب** *n* brick maker

طوب *n coll* brick

‹ **طوبَه** *n* Touba (*the fifth month of the Coptic calendar*)

‹ **طوبوغْرافيّ** *adj* see طُبوغْرافيّ

‹ **طاحَ** *v* |u; طَوْح| **1** [تاهَ] to get lost, to go astray **2** [سَقَطَ] to fall **3** [هَلَكَ] to die

طَوَّحَ *v* |بِ| to throw; طَوَّحَ بِكُرةٍ to throw a ball

أَطاحَ *v* |بِ| to overthrow, to topple, to depose; to tackle; أَطاحَ بِمُهاجِمٍ to tackle an attacker; أَطاحَ الرَئيسَ \ بالرَئيسِ the president was deposed; أَطاحَ بالنِظامِ الحاكِمِ to overthrow the regime

تَطَوَّحَ *v* to fall

إطاحة *n* overthrowing; الإطاحة بالحُكْمِ \ إطاحة الحُكومةِ overthrowing the government

‹ **انْطادَ** *v* to rise, to soar

طَوْد *n* |أَطْواد| mountain; وَقَفَ كالطَوْدِ to be as steady as a rock

مُنْطاد *n* hot air balloon; مُنْطاد اخْتِبارٍ sounding balloon; راكِب مُنْطادٍ balloonist; بِمُنْطادٍ by air balloon; في مُنْطادٍ in an air balloon; مُنْطاد ذو مُحَرِّكٍ airship; Zeppelin

1‹ **طَوَّرَ** *v* to develop; طَوَّرَ جِهازاً \ نِظاماً \ مَشْروعاً to develop an appliance/system/project

تَطَوَّرَ *v* to develop; to evolve; to grow

طِوار, **طَوار** *n* pavement (BrE), sidewalk (AmE)

طور *n* |أَطْوار| mountain; طور سيناء Mount Sinai; سورة الطور The Mountain (*Sura 52*)

طَوْر *n* |أَطْوار| **1** [مَرْحَلة] stage, phase; period; دَخَلَ طَوْراً جَديداً to enter a new phase; كانَ في طَوْرِ التَحْضيرِ to be in the preparatory phase; إنّ المَشْروعَ لا يَزالُ في طَوْرِ الدِراسةِ the project is still in the investigatory stage **2** [حَدّ] limit; خَرَجَ عن طَوْرِهِ to lose one's self-control **3** [مَرّة] occasion, time; تارةً ... طَوْراً the one time ... the other; طَوْراً بعد طَوْرٍ time after time, time and again **4** (Phys) phase

(Idiom) غَريب الأَطْوارِ eccentric, weird

تَطَوُّر *n* |تَطَوُّرات| development; progress; evolution; تَطَوُّر اقْتِصاديّ economic development; تَطَوُّرات إيجابيّة positive developments; التَطَوُّرات الأَخيرة \ الحَديثة the latest developments; تَطَوُّر مَلْموس tangible progress; التَطَوُّرات الجارِية the current developments; نَظَرِيّة التَطَوُّرِ the theory of evolution; شَهِدَ تَطَوُّراً to undergo a development; تابَعَ التَطَوُّراتِ to follow the developments; طَرَأَتْ \ حَدَثَتْ تَطَوُّراتٌ خَطيرةٌ dangerous developments have occurred; لَيْسَ هُناكَ أَيُّ تَطَوُّرٍ there's been no progress

تَطَوُّريّ *adj* evolutionary, developmental; نَظَرِيّة تَطَوُّرِيّة evolutionary theory

تَطْوير *n* development; advancement; تَطْوير ذاتيّ self-development, self-fulfilment; لا سَبيلَ إلى تَطْويرِ مُجْتَمَعٍ إلاّ بِتَطْويرِ التَعْليمِ the only way for society to develop is through education

تطْويريّ *adj* developmental

مُتطَوِّر *adj* developed; advanced; sophisticated; مُجْتَمع مُتطَوِّر an advanced society; أَسْلِحة مُتطَوِّرة advanced weaponry

مُطَوِّر *n* developer; مُطَوِّر بَرامِج software developer; مُطَوِّر تَطْبيقاتٍ application developer

2 **طارة** *n* hoop

طُرْبيد, طورْبيد *n* |طَرابيدُ| torpedo

طَوَّسَ *v* to adorn, to embellish, to decorate

طاس *n* |طاسات| finger bowl

طاسة *n* |طاسات| frying pan

طَواشِ *n* |طَواشِية| eunuch

طَوْطَم *n* |طَواطِم| totem

طاعَ *v* |u; طَوْع| to obey, to comply; طاعَ شَخْصاً \ لِشَخْصٍ to obey sb

طَوَّعَ *v* **1** [أَخْضَعَ] to subject, to subdue **2** [في الجُنْديّة] to enlist **3** [لَيَّنَ] to make flexible

طاوَعَ *v* to obey, to comply; to consent; طاوَعَ شَخْصاً to obey sb

أطاعَ *v* to obey; to listen to; to follow; أَطاعَ شَخْصاً في شَيْءٍ to obey sb in sth; أَطاعَ أَباهُ to listen to one's father

تَطَوَّعَ *v* to volunteer; تَطَوَّعَ للخِدْمةِ في الجَيْشِ to volunteer for military service; تَطَوَّعَ بِشَيْءٍ to volunteer sth

اسْتَطاعَ *v* to be able to, can *(before v)*; اسْتَطاعَ الحِسابَ \ القِراءةَ to be able to count/read; اسْتَطاعَ فِعْلَ ذلك to be able to do that; لم يَسْتَطِعْ أَنْ يَسْتَغْنِيَ عن شَيْءٍ to not be able to do without sth; لم يَسْتَطِعْ إِنْجازَ عَمَلِه he couldn't finish his work

طَوْع *n* obedience, compliance; طَوْعاً willingly, voluntarily; طَوْعاً أو كَرْهاً willingly or unwillingly; قامَ بالعَمَلِ جَبْراً لا طَوْعاً to do a job involuntarily; كانَ طَوْعَ يَدي I had him under my thumb

طائِع *adj* obedient; compliant; يَجِبُ أَنْ تَقومَ بِواجِباتِكَ المَدْرَسيّةِ طائِعاً أو كارِهاً you have to do your homework, like it or not

طاعة *n* obedience; compliance; discipline; طاعة مُطْلَقة \ عَمْياء absolute/blind obedience; سَمْعاً وَطاعةً! at your service!; شَقَّ عَصا الطاعةِ as you wish!; عَدَم الطاعةِ disobedience; خَرَجَ عن الطاعةِ to be disobedient

طَواعِية *n* voluntariness; عن طَواعِيةٍ voluntarily

طَوْعيّ *adj* voluntarily, willingly; على أَساسٍ طَوْعيٍّ voluntarily; طَوْعيًّا of one's own accord, of one's free will

طَيِّع *adj* **1** [مادّةٍ] flexible; pliable; supple; بْلاسْتيك طَيِّع flexible plastic **2** [شَخْصٍ] obedient, compliant; accommodating, flexible; willing

اسْتِطاعة *n* ability, capability; power, capacity; كانَ في اسْتِطاعَتِهِ أَنْ يَفْعَلَ ذلك to be able to do that; حَسَبَ الاسْتِطاعة to the best of one's abilities; بَذَلَ كُلَّ ما في اسْتِطاعَتِهِ to do all/everything in one's power

إطاعة *n* obedience, compliance; عَدَم إطاعةِ الأَوامِرِ not following orders

تَطَوُّع *n* voluntariness; volunteering

تَطَوُّعيّ *adj* voluntary

تَطْويع *n* subjection, submission; تَطْويع في الجَيْشِ military recruitment

مُتَطَوِّع **A** *adj* voluntary; طاقِم مُتَطَوِّع a voluntary crew; مُتَطَوِّعاً voluntarily

B *n* volunteer

مُسْتَطاع *adj* possible, feasible; على قَدْرِ, قَدْرَ المُسْتَطاعِ as much as possible; هذا في المُسْتَطاعِ this is feasible

مُطاوِع *adj* **1** [مُطيع] obedient, compliant **2** [لَيِّن] flexible; pliable; حَديد مُطاوِع wrought iron

مُطاوَعة *n* **1** [طاعة] obedience, compliance **2** [مُرونة] flexibility, pliability

مِطْواع *adj* |مَطاويعُ| obedient, compliant

مُطَوِّع *n* mutawwa (*religious police in Saudi Arabia*)

مُطيع *adj* obedient, compliant; disciplined; dutiful; willing; غَيْر مُطيع disobedient; طِفْل مُطيع an obedient child; مُطيع للقانونِ law-abiding

طافَ *v* |u; طَوْف, طَواف, طَوَفان| to wander, to roam, to ramble; to walk around; (Relig) to circumambulate; طافَ في المَدينةِ to wander around town; طافَ بِأَنْحاءِ بَلَدٍ to rove/roam a

لا مَوْقِف \ وَضع لا يُطاق an intolerable position/situation; أُطيقُ الظُلْمَ I can't stand injustice

طَوْق *n* 1 [قُدْرة] stamina, endurance; power, control; capacity; لم يَكُنْ في طَوْقِهِ to not have the power 2 [شَيْء مُسْتَدير] |أَطْواق| hoop, band; wreath, garland; طَوْق من الياسْمين a jasmine garland; طَوْق النَجاة a life buoy 3 [حول العُنُق] |أَطْواق| collar; طَوْق عُنُق collar

طاقة *n* 1 [قُدْرة] capacity, power; potential; طاقة ماليّة financial strength; طاقة إنْتاجيّة production capacity; تَبْلُغ الطاقة الإنْتاجيّةُ ١٠٠ مِلْيون طُنٍّ سَنويًّا the production capacity is 100 million tonnes annually; لَيْسَ في طاقَتِهِ to not have the capacity; لا طاقة لَهُ ب ... not to be able to ...; هذا فوق طاقَتي this is more than I can take 2 [قوّة] energy; power; طاقة كَهْرَبائيّة electricity, electrical energy; طاقة بَطّاريّة battery power; طاقة مائيّة hydropower; طاقة نَوويّة \ ذَرّيّة nuclear/atomic energy; طاقة هَوائيّة wind power; طاقة شَمْسيّة solar energy; طاقة مُسْتَديمة \ مُسْتَدامة renewable energy; مَصْدَر طاقةٍ طَبيعيّ a natural energy/power source; تَوْليد الطاقةِ energy production; سِعْر الطاقةِ energy price; سِياسة الطاقةِ energy policy; مَحَطّة تَوْليدِ الطاقةِ الكَهْرَبائيّة a power plant; تَضْييع الطاقةِ a waste of energy; نَقْص في الطاقة energy shortage; تَوْفير الطاقةِ ,إمْداد \ تَزْويد بالطاقةِ power supply; اسْتِهْلاك \ اسْتِخْدام الطاقةِ energy consumption/use; اسْتِهْلاك مُرْتَفِع \ مُنْخَفِض للطاقةِ high/low energy consumption; اسْتَخْدَمَ الطاقةَ النَوويّةَ to use nuclear energy; احْتِياج ل \ حاجة إلى الطاقةِ energy needs/requirements; سَدَّ الحاجةَ إلى الطاقةِ to supply/meet the energy need; اسْتَنْفَدَ طاقةَ شَخْصٍ to drain sb's energy 3 [باقة] bundle, bunch; bouquet; طاقة من الزَهْرِ a bouquet/bunch of flowers

طاقَويّ *adj* energy (*before n*); مَوارِد طاقَويّة energy/power sources

طاقيّة *n* (Jud) yarmulke (*scullcap worn by some Jewish men*)

مُطاق *adj* tolerable, bearable; غَيْر مُطاقٍ intolerable, unbearable; دَرَجة حَرارةٍ مُطاقة a tolerable temperature; كانَ الأَلَمُ غَيْرَ مُطاقٍ the pain was unbearable

طوقان *n* toucan

طوفي *n* toffee

طاقَ *v* |u; طَوْق| to bear, to endure; هذا لا يُطاقُ this is unbearable

طَوَّقَ *v* 1 [حاصَرَ] to surround, to enclose; to besiege; طَوَّقَ العَدوَّ to besiege the enemy 2 [سَيْطَرَ على] to control; طَوَّقَ الأَزْمةَ to control the crisis

أَطاقَ *v* to bear, to endure; to tolerate; لا يُطاقُ unbearable, insufferable, intolerable; حَرارة لا تُطاقُ unbearable heat; country; طافَ (حول) الكَعْبةِ to circumambulate the Kaaba; طافَ بِهِ الخَيالُ بَعيداً his imagination ran wild

طَوَّفَ *v* to roam around, to wander around; to circulate

أَطافَ *v* 1 [دارَ] |على ,ب| to circle, to go around 2 [أَلَمَّ] |ب| to get to know, to acquaint with

طَوْف *n* |أَطْواف| catamaran; raft

طائِفة *n* |طَوائِفُ| 1 [جماعة] sect; confession, denomination; congregation, religious community; party; طَوائِف دينيّة religious sects; الطائِفة المَسيحيّة the Christian community; من مُخْتَلِفِ \ جَميعِ الطَوائِفِ of various/all denominations 2 (Hist) مُلوك الطَوائِفِ *the small Islamic states in Andalusia*

طائِفيّ *adj* sectarian; religious; confessional; اشْتِباكات طائِفيّة sectarian clashes; حِزْب طائِفيّ a religious party

طائِفيّة *n* sectarianism; طائِفيّة سِياسيّة sectarian politics

طَوائِفيّ *adj* sectarian

طَواف *n* round, circuit, tour; procession, circumambulation; wandering, ramble; (Relig) circumambulation (*especially of the Kaaba*); طَواف فَرَنْسا Tour de France

طَوّاف *adj* ambulant; itinerant

طوفان *n* deluge; flood, inundation; أنا وَمِنْ بَعْدي الطوفانُ after me the deluge; *I don't care what happens after I get what I want*

الطائِف *n* |f| Ta'if (*city in Saudi Arabia*)

تَطْواف *n* circumambulation, procession

مَطاف *n* circulation; في نِهايةِ \ آخِرِ المَطافِ finally, in the end; انْتَهى بِهِ المَطافُ إلى مَكانٍ to end up somewhere; رَسا بِهِ المَطافُ to (finally) settle

مُطَوِّف *n a pilgrim's guide in Mecca*

طوكيو *n* |f| Tokyo

طالَ *v* |u; طول| to be/become long; to continue; to last long; طالَ الزَمَنُ أو قَصُرَ ,to take a long time طال بِهِ العَهْدُ \ الوَقْتُ; هذا سُؤالٌ تَطولُ however long it may take; مَهْما طالَ الأَمْرُ; it's a long story ≈ إجابَتُهُ; بعد فَتْرَةٍ قد تَطولُ أو تَقْصُرُ sooner or later

طَوَّلَ *v* to lengthen

أَطالَ *v* to lengthen, to stretch; to be long; أَطالَ النَظَرَ \ الحَديثَ to watch/talk for a long time; أَطالَ العُمْرَ to prolong the life of; أَطالَ مُفاوَضاتٍ to drag out the negotiations; أَطالَ على شَخْصٍ to keep sb waiting; أَطالَ لِسانَهُ to be cheeky, to be loud-mouthed; أَطالَ اللهُ في عُمْرِهِ may God grant him a long life

تَطاوَلَ *v* 1 [تَعَدّى] |على| to attack; تَطاوَلَ على شَيْءٍ \ شَخْصٍ to attack sth/sb 2 [امْتَدَّ] to lengthen

اسْتَطالَ *v* 1 [امْتَدَّ] to be long 2 [كانَ وَقِحاً] |على| to be impertinent (to), to be rude (to); اسْتَطالَ على شَخْصٍ to be rude to sb

طول *n* |أَطْوال| 1 [امْتِداد] length; height; بالطولِ, طولاً lengthwise, longitudinal; على طولِ along; (Egypt) straight ahead; على طولِ ٢٠ مِتْراً for/over a distance of 20 metres; السَيّاراتُ مُمْتَدّةٌ على طولِ الشارِعِ the cars are parked alongside the road; في طولِ البِلادِ وَعَرْضِها throughout the country; طول حَبْلٍ \ جُمْلَةٍ \ قِصَّةٍ the length of a rope/ sentence/story; خَطُّ الطولِ (degree of) longitude; على خطِ الطولِ السادِسِ والثَلاثينَ at 36 degrees longitude; طولُ الغُرْفَةِ سِتَّةُ أَمْتارٍ the room is six metres long; يَبْلُغُ الطولُ ٣٠ مِتْراً it's 30 metres long/in length 2 [دَوام] duration; length; طول قِطْعةٍ موسيقيّةٍ the length of a composition; طول فَتْرةٍ the duration of a period; طولَ حَياتي \ عُمْري my whole life; طولَ اللَيْلِ the whole night, all night (long); انْتَظَرَ طولَ اللَيْلِ he waited all night; كانَ يَسْهَرُ اللَيْلَ بِطولِهِ he stayed up all night long

طَوْل *n* power, authority

طائِل A *adj* enormous, huge; great; immense; ثَرَوات طائِلة immense riches/wealth

B *n* use, benefit; لا طائِلَ مِنْهُ \ تَحْتَهُ, من غَيْرِ طائِلٍ useless

طائِلة *n* |طَوائِلُ| force; تحت طائِلةِ فَرْضِ غَرامةٍ under penalty of a fine; وَقَعَ تحت طائِلةِ القانونِ to be punishable under penalty of law

طالَما A *conj* [ما دامَ] as/so long as; طالَما أنّ ... since ..., as ...; طالَما أَجِدُ فيهِ as long as it's needed; طالَما اسْتَلْزَمَ الأَمْرُ ذلك so long as I'm happy with it; طالَما كانَ هُناكَ احْتِمالٌ السَعادةَ لاسْتِعادة الرَهائِنِ سالِمينَ as long as there's a chance of the hostages' safe return

B *adv* [كَثيراً ما] often, frequently; طالَما دَعا للحِوارِ he often called for dialogue

طاوِلة *n* 1 [مائِدة] table; طاوِلة الروليت \ القِمار a roulette/ gaming table; جَلَسَ حول الطاوِلة to sit down around the table 2 [لُعْبة] backgammon; لَعِبَ لُعْبةَ الطاوِلةِ to play a game of backgammon

طَوالَ, طِوالَ *prep* during, throughout, all ... (long); طَوالَ اللَيْلِ \ الصَيْفِ \ السَنةِ during the night/summer/year, the whole night/summer/year, all night/summer/year (long); طَوالَ السِنينَ الماضِيةِ all these years

طولانيّ *adj* longitudinal, lengthwise; عَضَلة طولانيّة longitudinal muscle

طوليّ *adj* lengthwise; longitudinal; مَقْطَع طوليّ lengthwise/ longitudinal section; مِحْوَر طوليّ longitudinal axis

طَويل *adj* |طِوال| 1 [مُمْتَدّ] long, lengthy; وَقْت طَويل a long time; عَمَلِيّة طَويلة الأَمَدِ a lengthy process; طَويل المَدى \ الأَمَدِ long-lasting; طَويل الأَجَلِ long-term; قَرْض طَويل الأَجَلِ a long-term loan; كانَ طَويلَ اليَدِ to have sticky fingers (to be prone to theft) 2 [مُرْتَفِع] tall; كانَ طَويلَ (القامةِ) to be tall (in stature) 3 [واسِع] considerable, extensive; طَويل الباعِ mighty, powerful; influential; generous, noble; well educated, learned, capable

طيلةَ *prep* during, throughout; طيلةَ شُهورٍ for months; طيلةَ العام throughout the year; طيلةَ عُمْرِكَ all your life

اسْتِطالة *n* (Phys) linear expansion

إطالة *n* prolongation, lengthening; إطالة أَمَدِ الاحْتِلالِ prolonging the occupation

طَيّ *n* |أَطْواء| fold; crease, pleat; folding; قابل للطَيِّ collapsible; أَبْقى مَوْضوعاً طَيَّ \ بَقِيَ \ ظَلَّ طَيَّ الكِتْمانِ to remain hidden; أَصْبَحَ طَيَّ النِسْيانِ الكِتْمانِ to keep an issue concealed; to be forgotten; أَرْفَقَ طَيًّا مَنْشوراً to enclose a leaflet; في طَيِّهِ طَيَّهُ enclosed; attached; تَجِدونَ العَريضةَ طَيَّهُ you'll find the petition enclosed; يَجِبُ طَيُّ صَفْحةِ الماضي you should close the door on the past

طيّة *n* interior; بَلاغ يَحْمِلُ في طيّاتِهِ تَهْديداً a declaration with an implied threat

طَيّة *n* fold; crease, pleat; طَيّة في صَفْحةٍ a crease in a sheet of paper; لا نَعْرِفُ ما يَحْمِلُ لَنا المُسْتَقْبَلُ في طيّاتِهِ we don't know what the future has in store for us

انْطِواء *n* self-containment; الانْطِواء على النَفْسِ self-containment

انْطِوائيّ *adj* introverted; self-contained; withdrawn; شَخْصيّة انْطِوائيّة an introverted personality

مِطْواة *n* |مَطاوٍ| pocketknife, penknife

مِطْوًى *n* |مَطاوٍ| reel, spool

مُنْطَوٍ *adj* introverted; مُنْطَوٍ على نَفْسِهِ introverted

طابَ *v* |i; طيب| to be nice/pleasant, to be agreeable; to be good; to taste good; طابَتْ لَيْلَتُكُمْ! (have) a pleasant evening!; طابَ لَهُ أَنْ ... to enjoy ...; طابَ لَهُ العَيْشُ في الخارجِ to enjoy living abroad; طابَتْ نَفْسُهُ to be happy; طابَ الطَعامُ the food was tasty

طَيَّبَ *v* 1 [جَعَلَهُ طَيِّباً] to make nice/pleasant 2 [طَعاماً] to season, to flavour 3 [عَطَّرَ] to perfume; طَيَّبَ اللهُ ثَراهُ may God have mercy on him

أَطابَ *v* to make good/pleasant

تَطَيَّبَ *v* to scent, to perfume

اسْتَطابَ *v* to love; to like, to appreciate

طيب *n* |أَطْياب| perfume, scent; سُنْبُل الطيبِ matgrass

طَيِّب A *adj* good; nice, kind, pleasant; رَجُل \ امْرَأة طَيِّب(ة) a kind man/woman; فِكْرة \ نيّة \ بِداية طَيِّبة a good idea/intention/start; كُلَّ سَنةٍ وَأَنْتَ طَيِّبٌ happy birthday; happy New Year; *phrase used for any celebration*; أَطْيَبُ التَمَنّياتِ best wishes B *n* 1 [لَطيف] a kind soul, a good man/woman 2 [اسْم شَخْصيّ] Tayib (*male given name*)

أَطْوَل *adj* |dipt| longer; longest; الزَوْج الأَطْوَل عُمْراً the surviving spouse

تَطْويل *n* lengthening, prolonging

مُتَطاوِل *adj* 1 [مُطَوَّل] prolonged, lengthy; قُرون مُتَطاوِلة long centuries 2 [وَقِح] insolent, rude

مُسْتَطيل A *adj* rectangular; مائِدة مُسْتَطيلة a rectangular table B *n* rectangle

مُطَوَّل *adj* elaborate, comprehensive; long; lengthy; time-consuming; رِحْلة مُطَوَّلة في الشَرْقِ الأَوْسَطِ a long trip through the Middle East; اجْتِماع مُطَوَّل a lengthy meeting; طَريقة مُطَوَّلة a time-consuming method/procedure; تَحَدَّثَ مُطَوَّلاً عن شَيْءٍ to discuss sth at (great/some) length, to elaborate on sth

طومار *n* |طَوامير| scroll

طَوى *v* |i; طَيّ| 1 [ثَنى] to fold (in/up/down); to wrap; طَوى غِطاءَ المَقْعَدَ الخَلْفيَّ to fold down the back seat; طَوى المائِدةِ \ طَوى وَرَقةً to fold the tablecloth/a piece of paper; طَوى (صَفْحةَ) الماضي to turn over a new leaf, to start fresh 2 [لَفَّ] to roll up; طَوى البِساطَ to roll up the carpet; to close a case 3 [قَطَعَ] to traverse; to cover; طَوى البِلادَ to traverse the country; طَوى الطَريقَ to cover the road 4 [أَخْفى] to hide; طَوى سِرًّا to hide a secret 5 [اسْتَوْلى] to overpower, to capture; اسْتَشْعَرَ الأَلَمَ يَطْوي عِظامَهُ he felt overwhelming pain in his bones

أَطْوى *v* to be/feel hungry

تَطَوّى *v* to coil (up); to curl up; تَطَوَّتِ الأَفْعى the snake coiled up

انْطَوى *v* 1 [انْثَنى] to be folded; to be wrapped; انْطَوى على نَفْسِهِ to be introverted; to be isolated 2 [تَضَمَّنَ] to contain, to include; to imply; to entail; انْطَوى على كَثيرٍ من المُتَغَيِّراتِ \ المَخاطِرِ to entail many changes/risks; انْطَوى على حُمولةٍ رَمْزيّةٍ to be symbolically charged

طَوًى *n* hunger

طَوِيّة *n* |طَوايا| conscience, conviction; سَليم الطَوِيّةِ bona fide, trustworthy; غَيْر سَليمِ الطَوِيّةِ untrustworthy; طَوِيّة الثَأْرِ vengefulness

طيبة *n* goodness; طيبة القَلْب good-heartedness; عن طيبةِ خاطِرٍ gladly, with pleasure

أَطْيَب *adj* |dipt; أَطايِبُ| better; best

طارَ *v* |i; طَيَران| ❶ [حَلَّقَ] to fly; طارَ على الخُطوطِ المَلَكيّةِ المَغْرِبيّةِ to fly with Royal Air Maroc; طارَ من \ إلى نِيويورْك to fly from/to New York; طارَ بِشَخْصٍ إلى مَكانٍ to fly sb to a place; طارَ عَقْلُهُ to lose one's head; طارَ فَرَحاً to jump for joy; تَطيرُ الطائِرةُ the airplane is flying ❷ [أَسْرَعَ] to fly, to rush; طارَ من الغُرْفةِ to rush out of the room; طارَ صيتُهُ his name spread rapidly

طَيَّرَ *v* to make fly

أَطارَ *v* to make fly

تَطَيَّرَ *v* to see an evil omen

تَطايَرَ *v* ❶ [انْتَشَرَ] to fly (up/around/over); to skim; تَطايَرَ الرَّصاصُ من فَوْقِ رُؤوسِنا the bullets flew over our heads; يَتَطايَرُ شَعْرُها (في الهَواءِ) her hair is flying (in the wind); تَتَطايَرُ مِنْهُ الشراراتُ sparks are shooting from it; تَطايَرَ الرَّمْلُ the sand flew; تَطايَرَت الأَوْراقُ the papers were blown away; تَطايَرَت القُبَّعةُ من فوق رَأْسِها the hat was blown from her head ❷ (Chem) to evaporate

طَيْر *n coll* |أَطْيار, طُيور| bird; طَيْر جارِح bird of prey; طَيْر اللَّيْلِ bat; شَهْر الطَّيْر (Hist) April (*Libya under Gaddafi*); قَفَص طُيورٍ birdcage; عُشّ الطَّيْر bird's nest; عِلْم الطُيورِ ornithology; عالِم بالطُيورِ ornithologist; سِرْب من الطُيورِ a flock of birds; وَقَفَ ساكِناً كَأَنَّ على رَأْسِهِ طَيْرٌ to stand stock-still; يُغَنّي \ يُصَفِّرُ الطَيْرُ the bird is singing/warbling; إنّ الطُيورَ على أَشْكالِها تَقَعُ birds of a feather flock together

طائِر **A** *adj* flying, airborne; طَبَق طائِر a flying saucer **B** *n* |طَيْر, طائِرات| (Zool) bird; طائِر مائيّ water bird; الطائِر المُحاكي mockingbird; طائِر رَحّال migratory bird

طائِرة *n* aircraft, aeroplane (BrE), airplane (AmE), plane; طائِرة رُكّاب airliner; طائِرة شَحْنٍ \ نَقْلٍ cargo plane; طائِرة مائيّة seaplane; طائِرة مُقاتِلة \ مُطارِدة fighter jet; طائِرة حَرْبيّة warplane; طائِرة اسْتِطْلاعٍ \ اسْتِكْشافٍ reconnaissance aircraft; طائِرة أُحاديّة المُحَرِّكِ single-engined aircraft; طائِرة نَفّاثة jet; طائِرة شِراعيّة glider; طائِرة مِرْوَحيّة \ عَموديّة \ سَمْتيّة helicopter; طائِرة وَرَقيّة kite; حامِلة \ ناقِلة الطائِراتِ (aircraft) carrier; كَبينة الطائِرةِ cockpit; تَذْكِرة \ بِطاقة الطائِرةِ an airline ticket; حادِث \ اخْتِطاف طائِرةٍ a plane crash/hijacking; تَغْيير الطائِرةِ changing planes; حَظيرة الطائِراتِ hangar; حَرَكة مُرورِ الطائِراتِ الوَطَنيّةِ \ الدُوَليّةِ national/international air traffic; على مَتْنِ الطائِرةِ aboard the aircraft; سافَرَ, اسْتَقَلَّ الطائِرةَ بالطائِرةِ to fly, to go/travel by airplane; أَقْلَعَت الطائِرةُ the plane took off; تَهْبِطُ \ تَحُطُّ الطائِرةُ the plane is descending; the plane is landing

طَيّار **A** *adj* volatile; مَوادّ طَيّارة volatile substances **B** *n* pilot; طَيّار مُساعِد co-pilot; طَيّار عَسْكَريّ \ مَدَنيّ a military/civil pilot

طَيّارة *n* ❶ [مُؤَنَّثُ طَيّار] a (female) pilot ❷ [طائِرة] aircraft, aeroplane (BrE), airplane (AmE), plane

طَيَران *n* aviation; flight; طَيَران دون تَوَقُّفٍ a non-stop flight; خَوْف من الطَيَرانِ fear of flying; الطَيَران العَسْكَريّ \ المَدَنيّ military/civil aviation; قِطاع الطَيَرانِ aviation (industry); ارْتِفاع الطَيَرانِ (flying) altitude; سُرْعة الطَيَرانِ flight speed; ساعة الطَيَرانِ flying hour; حَرَكة الطَيَرانِ air traffic; شَرِكة الطَيَرانِ airline; خَطّ الطَيَرانِ an approach route; طَريق الطَيَرانِ a flight path; عَرْض طَيَرانٍ an air show; حادِث طَيَرانٍ a plane crash; شَهادة طَيَرانٍ a flying licence; حَظْر \ مَنْع الطَيَرانِ a no-fly zone; فَرَضَ \ انْتَهَكَ حَظْرَ الطَيَرانِ to impose/violate a no-fly zone

طِيَرة, طيرة *n* an evil omen

تَطايُر *n* volatility; flying (up/around/over)

تَطايُريّة *n* volatility

مُتَطايِر *adj* volatile; diffuse; مُكَوِّنات مُتَطايِرة volatile components

مُتَطَيِّر **A** *adj* pessimistic; *believing in bad luck* **B** *n* pessimist; *sb who believes in bad luck*

مُسْتَطير *adj* imminent, impending

مَطار *n* |مَطارات| airport, airfield; مَطار دُوَليّ \ وَطَنيّ \ مَحَلّيّ an international/national/regional airport; مَطار القاهِرةِ Cairo airport; وَصَلَ إلى المَطارِ to arrive at the airport

طاشَ *v* |i; طَيْش| to be reckless/foolhardy

طَيْش *n* recklessness; thoughtlessness; تَصَرَّفَ بِطَيْشٍ شَديدٍ to behave recklessly

هذا زادَ الطينَ terracotta; زادَ الطينَ بلّةً to add fuel to the fire; إنّ الحَلَّ قَدْ زادَ الطينَ بلّةً the بِلّةً this makes it all the worse; cure is worse than the disease; اخْتِم الطينَ ما دامَ رَطْباً ≈ strike while the iron is hot

طينة *n* a piece/lump of clay; من طينةٍ واحِدةٍ of one piece; من طينَتِهِ of his kind

طيني *adj* clay; loam, mud; لَوْحة طينيّة a clay tablet; أرْض طينيّة clay/loam soil; نبتَ في الأَرْضِ الطينيّةِ to grow on clay/loam soil

‹ **طَيْهوج** *n* (Zool) grouse

طائِش *adj* reckless, thoughtless; careless, rash; frivolous; رَصاصة طائِشة a stray bullet; عَمَل طائِش a rash deed; تَصَرُّف طائِش reckless behaviour

‹ **طَيْف** *n* |طُيوف ,أَطْياف| ❶ [خَيال] vision; apparition, phantom ❷ (Phys) spectrum; أَلْوان الطَّيْفِ the colours of the spectrum

طَيْفيّ *adj* spectral; مِنْظار طَيْفيّ مِجْهَريّ microspectroscope

‹ **طَيْلَسان** *n* shawl

‹ **طَيَّنَ** *v* to daub with clay/mud

طين *n* |أَطْيان| clay; loam; mud; رَقيم (من) الطينِ a clay tablet; طين نَضيج a lump of mud; أَطْيان clay soil; كُتْلة من الطينِ

ظاء *n* |f| *name of the letter* ظ

ظَبْي *n* |ظِباء| (Zool) gazelle

ظَرِبان *n* |ظَرابينُ| (Zool) polecat; ظَرِبان أَمْريكيّ skunk

ظِرّ *n* |ظِرّان| pebble

ظَرُفَ *v* |u; ظَرْف, ظَرافة| to be charming; to be amusing/witty

تَظارَفَ *v* to affect charm; to be affected

اسْتَظْرَفَ *v* to find charming; to find amusing/witty

ظَرْف *n* |ظُروف| **1** [غِلاف] envelope; cover; covering; case; container; ظَرْف مُشَمَّع a sealed envelope; في ظَرْفٍ مَفْتوحٍ \ مُغْلَقٍ in an unsealed/sealed envelope **2** [مُناسَبة] circumstance; occasion; case; ظَرْف اسْتِثْنائيّ \ خاصّ exceptional case; ظُروف مُخَفِّفة extenuating circumstances; ظُروف مُشَدِّدة aggravating circumstances; حَسَبَ الظُروفِ according to circumstances; وَفْقاً للظُروفِ as circumstances require; تحت \ في ظُروفٍ صَعْبةٍ under difficult circumstances; في الظُروفِ الراهِنةِ under the present conditions, today; في مِثْلِ \ ظِلِّ هذه الظُروفِ under these circumstances, as things are; عند تَوافُرِ الظُروفِ when the circumstances are favourable; تَوَفَّرَت الظُروفُ المُناسِبةُ لِهَذا the circumstances are favourable for this; لم تَسْمَحْ بِهِ الظُروفُ the circumstances did not permit it; مَهْما كانَت الظُروفُ whatever the circumstances; الظُروفُ المَعيشيّةُ صَعْبةٌ جِدّاً the conditions of life are very hard **3** (Gram) adverb; adverbial adjunct; ظَرْف زَمانٍ \ مَكانٍ adverb of time/place **4** [خِلالَ] في ظَرْفِ in, within; في ظَرْفِ أَيّامٍ قَلائِلَ within a few days; في ظَرْفِ أُسْبوعٍ within a week; في ظَرْفِ سَنةٍ واحِدةٍ within one year **5** [فُكاهة] kindness; amiability; فاضَ ظَرْفاً to be very kind

ظَرافة *n* elegance, grace, gracefulness; wit, esprit

ظَرْفيّ *adj* **1** (Gram) adverbial; locative **2** [لاحِق] circumstantial; دَليل ظَرْفيّ circumstantial evidence

ظَريف *adj* |ظُرَفاءُ|; f pl |ظَرائِفُ| charming; witty, amusing, funny; pretty, cute; شابّ ظَريف a cute guy; مُلاحَظة ظَريفة a witty remark

مَظْروف **A** *adj* in an envelope; رِسالة مَظْروفة a letter in an envelope

B *n* |مَظاريفُ| envelope; cover

ظَعَنَ *v* |a; ظَعْن| to leave, to go away

ظَفِرَ *v* |a; ظَفَر| **1** [غَلَبَ] |على| to beat; to win/triumph over; to take possession; ظَفِرَ على عَدوِّهِ to beat one's opponent **2** [نالَ] |بِ| to get; ظَفِرَ بِما أَرادَ to get what you want

ظَفَّرَ *v* to make triumph, to render victorious

أَظْفَرَ *v* |بِ, على| to grant victory over

ظَفَر *n* triumph

ظَفِر *adj* triumphant; victorious

ظُفْر, ظُفُر, ظِفْر *n* |أَظْفار, أَظافِرُ| **1** [إِصْبَع] nail, fingernail; أَظافِر طَويلة \ قَصيرة long/short nails; قَلَّمَ \ بَرَدَ أَظافِرَهُ to clip/file one's nails; قَضَمَ أَظافِرَهُ to bite one's nails; مِقَصّ أَظافِرَ nail clippers; حِتار الظُفْرِ cuticle; منذ نُعومةِ أَظافِرِه since one's childhood; ذابَتْ أَظْفارُهُ his efforts were in vain **2** [مِخْلَب] claw

ظافِر *adj* triumphant; victorious

أُظْفور *n* |أَظافيرُ| nail, fingernail; طِلاء الأَظافيرِ nail polish; قَضَمَ الأَظافيرِ nail-biting

مُظَفَّر *adj* triumphant; victorious

ظَلَعَ *v* |a; ظَلْع| to limp

ظالِع *adj* lame

تَظَلَّمَ *v* |إلى| to complain to, to make a complaint to; تَظَلَّمَ إلى القاضي to make a complaint to the judge; لم يَجِدْ أَحَداً يَتَظَلَّمُ إلَيْهِ he found nobody to complain to

انْظَلَمَ *v* to suffer injustice

ظُلْم *n* injustice; unfairness; tyranny; ظُلْماً wrongfully; من الظُلْمِ أنْ... it is unjust to ...; عانى ظُلْماً \ من الظُلْمِ to suffer injustice; حارَبَ \ كافَحَ الظُلْمَ to fight injustice

ظالِم **A** *adj* |ظَلَمة, ظُلّام, ظالِمونَ| unjust, unfair, wrongful; unreasonable; قرار ظالِم an unjust decision; حُكْم ظالِم a tyrannical regime
B *n* |ظَلَمة, ظُلّام, ظالِمونَ| oppressor; tyrant

ظَلام *n* dark, darkness; gloom; ظَلام حالِك \ دامِس total darkness; حَلَّ الظَلامُ twilight set in, it grew dark; تحت جُنْحِ الظَلام under the cover of night

ظَلامِيّ *adj* ≈ reactionary; أَفْكار ظَلامِيّة reactionary ideas

ظُلْمة *n* |ظُلُمات| dark, darkness; gloom; بَحْر الظُلُماتِ (old use) the Atlantic Ocean

إظْلام *n* darkness, dimness, gloom

أَظْلَم *adj* |dipt| darker; لَيْلة ظَلْماء a pitch-black night

تَظَلُّم *n* (Law) grievance

مُظْلِم *adj* dark; gloomy; dusky; مَمَرّ مُظْلِم a dark corridor; مادّة مُظْلِمة (Phys) dark matter; لَيْلة مُظْلِمة a dark night; أَيّام مُظْلِمة dark/gloomy days

مَظْلَمة *n* |مَظالِم| **1** [ظُلْم] injustice; ارْتَكَبَ مَظالِمَ to commit iniquities **2** [شَكْوة] grievance, complaint; objection

مَظْلوم *adj* |مَظاليمُ, مَظْلومونَ| oppressed, tyrannized; treated unfairly/unjustly; wronged; كانَ مَظْلوماً to be oppressed, to suffer injustice

مَظْلوميّة *n* injustice

‹ **ظَمِئَ** *v* |a; ظَمَأ, ظَماء| to be thirsty, to be parched

ظَمَأ *n* thirst; ظَمَأ لا يُرْوى unquenchable thirst; رَوى \ أَطْفَأَ ظَمَأَهُ to quench one's thirst

ظَمِئ *adj* thirsty

ظَمْآن *adj* |dipt| thirsty, parched

‹ **ظُنْبوب** *n* |ظَنابيبُ| (Anat) shin bone, tibia

‹ **ظِلْف** *n* |ظُلوف, أَظْلاف| cloven hoof; سَعى إلى حَتْفِهِ بِظِلْفِهِ to be heading for disaster

‹ **ظَلَّ** *v* |a; ظَلّ, ظُلول; perf ظَلِلْتُ| to stay, to remain; to continue, to keep (on); ظَلَّ سَليماً \ لَطيفاً to stay healthy/friendly; ظَلَّ يَتَكَلَّمُ to keep talking; ظَلَّ على حالِهِ to stay the same, to stay the way it is; ظَلَّ عند وَعْدِهِ to keep one's word; ظَلَّ عند رَأْيِهِ to stand one's ground; كانَ وَسَيَظَلُّ as it was and will remain

ظَلَّلَ *v* **1** [أَظْلَمَ] to provide shade **2** [بِخُطوطٍ] to shade; to line

أَظَلَّ *v* to provide shade; أَظَلَّ شَخْصاً to shelter sb

تَظَلَّلَ *v* |ب| to be in the shadow (of)

اسْتَظَلَّ *v* |ب| to seek shelter (with); to seek shade (under); اسْتَظَلَّ بِحِمايةِ السُلْطةِ to seek refuge with the authorities

ظِلّ *n* |ظِلال, ظُلول, أَظْلال| **1** [اسْتِتار الضَوْءِ] shadow; shade; في ظِلِّ شَجَرةٍ in the shade of a tree; في ظِلِّ الظُروف under the circumstances; في ظِلِّ الظُروفِ الحالِيّة under the present circumstances; جِهة الظِلِّ shady side; حُكومة ظِلّ shadow cabinet; كَثير الظِلّ shady; مِنْطَقة كَثيرة الظِلِّ a shady area; ظِلّ العَيْنِ eye shadow; بَقِيَ في الظِلِّ to stay anonymous; اسْتَثْقَلَ ظِلَّ شَخْصٍ to have a strong dislike of sb **2** [حِماية] protection; في ظِلِّ شَخْصٍ under sb's protection

ظُلّة *n* |ظُلَل| **1** [كُنّة] lean-to; canopy, sunshade; تحت ظُلّةٍ under a lean-to **2** [كُشْك] stand; stall

ظَليل *adj* shady; shadowy; مِنْطَقة ظَليلة a shady area

مُظِلّ *adj* shadowy; causing shadow

مِظَلّة *n* |مِظَلّات, مَظالّ| umbrella; sunshade, sun/beach umbrella; parachute; تحت مِظَلّةٍ under an umbrella; تحت مِظَلّةِ الأُمَمِ المُتَّحِدة under the umbrella of the UN; عيد المَظَلّة (Jud) Feast of Tabernacles

مُظَلَّل *adj* shady, shadowy

مُظَلِّل *adj* causing shadow

مِظَلِّيّ *n* parachutist; paratrooper

‹ **ظَلَمَ** *v* |i; ظُلْم| to treat unjustly; to wrong; to oppress, to tyrannize; ظَلَمَ شَخْصاً to treat sb unjustly

أَظْلَمَ *v* to be/become dark; to darken; أَظْلَمَ الغُرْفةَ to darken the room; أَظْلَمَت الدُنْيا في عَيْنَيْهِ he became desperate

ظَنَّ *v* |u; ظَنّ| to think; to suppose, to believe; to suspect; ظَنَّ أنّ … to think that …; ظَنَّ في شَيْءٍ to think about/of sth; على ما \ فيما أَظُنُّ as far as I know; أَظُنُّهُ يَكْذِبُ I think that he is lying; ظَنَّ بِشَخْصٍ الظُنونَ to suspect sb of bad behaviour; ظَنَّ بِشَخْصٍ خَيْراً to have a high opinion of sb; ظَنَّ الغُرْفَةَ خالِيَةً he thought the room was empty

ظَنّ *n* |ظُنون| ① [مَصْدَر] opinion; conjecture; أَغْلَب الظَنِّ most likely; أَساءَ الظَنَّ بِشَخْصٍ to have a low opinion of sb; أَحْسَنَ الظَنَّ بِشَخْصٍ to have a high opinion of sb; to trust sb; إِنْ صَحَّ ظَنِّي فَإِنّ… if I'm not mistaken, then …; كانَ عند حُسْنِ ظَنِّ شَخْصٍ to be in sb's good books; خَيَّبَ ظَنِّي بِهِ he disappointed me ② [شَكّ] suspicion; idea; doubt; انْتابَتْهُ الظُنونُ he was overcome by doubt

ظَنين A *adj* |أَظِنّاءُ| suspicious

B *n* |أَظِنّاءُ| suspect

مَظَنَّة *n* |مَظانّ| the most likely location/place, *place where sth/sb is presumably to be found*

مَظْنون *adj* suspicious; من المَظْنونِ أنّ … supposedly

ظَهَرَ *v* |a; ظُهور| ① [أَصْبَحَ ظاهِراً] to appear, to become visible; to emerge, to show up; to stand out; to manifest itself, to become manifest/apparent; to come up, to crop up; تَظْهَرُ عَلاماتُ المَرَضِ the symptoms of the disease are becoming apparent; ظَهَرَ في المَلَأِ \ العُمومِ to appear in public; ظَهَرَ في الفَصْلِ الثالِثِ to enter in act three; تَظْهَرُ الغُيومُ the clouds are gathering; ظَهَرَ المَرَضُ الشَهْرَ المُنْصَرِمَ the disease manifested itself last month; ظَهَرَ للأَعْيانِ to become (clearly) visible ② [بَدا] to seem, to appear; to prove; على ما يَظْهَرُ seemingly; apparently; outwardly; يَظْهَرُ أَنَّهُ مُتَشائِمٌ he seems pessimistic ③ [صَدَرَ] to be published; to come out ④ [غَلَبَ |على|] to conquer

تَمَظْهَرَ *v* to (become) manifest

ظَهَّرَ *v* to confirm; ظَهَّرَ صَكًّا to endorse a document

ظاهَرَ *v* to help; to assist; to support; ظاهَرَ شَخْصاً to help sb

أَظْهَرَ *v* ① [بَيَّنَ] to show, to demonstrate; to display, to expose; أَظْهَرَ أنّ … to show that …; أَظْهَرَ شَيْئاً to produce sth; أَظْهَرَ عُيوباً to expose flaws; أَظْهَرَ آثاراً to show traces; لم يُظْهِرْ شَيْئاً he did not reveal anything; أَظْهَرَ البَحْثُ أنّ … the examination showed that …; أَظْهَرَ لِشَخْصٍ أنّ … to show sb that …; أَظْهَرَ نَشاطاً مَلْموساً to display significant activity ② (Phot) to develop ③ [أَطْلَعَ] to notify; to inform; أَظْهَرَتْ صَديقَها على سِرِّها she told her friend her secret

تَظاهَرَ *v* ① [ادَّعى] to feign, to simulate, to pretend; تَظاهَرَ بِأَنّ … to make appear as if …; تَظاهَرَ بِنَزاهةِ النَفْسِ to keep up the appearance of honesty; تَظاهَرَ بالجَهْلِ \ بِعَدَمِ المَعْرِفةِ to feign ignorance; تَظاهَرَ بالصُداعِ to pretend to have a headache; تَظاهَرَ بالنُعاسِ to feign sleep; تَظاهَرَ بِأَنَّهُ لا يَعْرِفُ شَيْئاً he acted as if he knew nothing ② [احْتَجَّ] to march, to demonstrate, to protest; تَظاهَرَ من أَجْلِ شَيْءٍ \ تَأْييداً لِشَيْءٍ to demonstrate for sth; تَظاهَرَ ضِدَّ شَيْءٍ to demonstrate against sth; تَظاهَرَ احْتِجاجاً على شَيْءٍ to hold a demonstration against sth; تَظاهَرَ ضِدَّ التَجارِبِ النَوَوِيّةِ to demonstrate against nuclear tests

اسْتَظْهَرَ *v* ① [حَفِظَ وَتَلا] to memorize; to recite ② [غَلَبَ |على|] to get/gain the upper hand ③ [كَشَفَ] (Tunisia) to show (*papers/documentation*)

ظَهْر *n* |أَظْهُر, ظُهور| ① [خَلْف] back; rear; ظَهْر كُرْسِيٍّ the back of a chair; ظَهْر اليَدِ the back of the hand; عن ظَهْرِ قَلْبٍ by heart; حَفِظَتِ القُرْآنَ عن ظَهْرِ قَلْبٍ she learned the Koran by heart ② (Anat) back; rear; أَسْفَل الظَهْرِ lower back; سِلْسِلة الظَهْرِ spine; ظَهْراً إلى ظَهْرٍ back-to-back; قَوَّسَ ظَهْرَهُ to arch one's back; كانَ ظَهْرُهُ يُؤْلِمُهُ \ يوجِعُهُ his back bothered him; أُصيبَ بِأَوْجاعٍ في الظَهْرِ to have back pain; وَلّى شَخْصاً ظَهْرَهُ, أَدارَ لِشَخْصٍ ظَهْرَهُ to turn one's back on sb; من خَلْفِ ظَهْرِ الرَئيسِ behind the chairman's back; لا تَلْعَبْ من خَلْفِ ظَهْري don't do anything behind my back; قَلَبَ شَيْئاً ظَهْراً لِبَطْنٍ to flip sth upside down; عَرَفَ شَخْصاً \ شَيْئاً ظَهْراً لِبَطْنٍ to know sb/sth inside out ③ [سَفينة] deck; ظَهْر باخِرةٍ deck; على ظَهْرِ سَفينةٍ on board a ship

ظُهْر *n* |ظُهور| noon, midday; ظُهْراً at noon; عند الظُهْرِ around noon; قبل الظُهْرِ in the forenoon; بعد الظُهْرِ in the afternoon; ظُهْرَ اليَوْمِ midday today; صَلاة الظُهْرِ midday prayer (*between 12 and 2 p.m.*)

ظهيرة *n* midday; noon; midday heat; في (وَقْتِ) الظَهيرةِ at/around noon; ظَهيرةَ اليَوْمِ midday today; ساعة الظَهيرة noon, twelve o'clock

ظواهراتيّة *n* (Philos) phenomenology

إظْهار *n* 1 [سِلَع] display 2 [عَرْض] demonstration; disclosure

الظَهْران *n* |f| Dhahran (*town in Saudi Arabia*)

تَظاهُر *n* |تَظاهُرات| 1 [مُظاهَرة] demonstration; للتَظاهُرِ for show; قامَ بالتَظاهُرِ to demonstrate, to protest 2 [ادِّعاء] feigning, pretending; simulation 3 [تَكَلُّف] fussing; affectation

تَظاهُرة *n* 1 [عَرْض] event, happening; قامَ بِتَظاهُرةٍ to put on an event; تَظاهُرة موسيقيّة \ رِياضيّة a musical/sports event 2 [مَسيرة احْتِجاج] demonstration; protest; نَظَّمَ \ سَيَّرَ تَظاهُرةً to hold a protest; تَظاهُرة احْتِجاجٍ / احْتِجاجيّة protest demonstration

تَظاهُريّ *adj* 1 [اسْتِعْراضيّ] demonstrative; بِشَكْلٍ تَظاهُريٍّ in a demonstrative way 2 [مَزْعوم] simulated; انْتِحار تَظاهُريّ suicidal gesture

تَظْهير *n* (Fin) endorsement

مُتَظاهِر *n* 1 [مُحْتَجّ] demonstrator; activist; فَرَّقَ المُتَظاهِرينَ to disperse the demonstrators 2 [مُتَصَنِّع] show-off

مُسْتَظْهِر *adj* مُسْتَظْهِراً by heart

مُظاهَرة *n* demonstration; protest march; مُظاهَرة احْتِجاجيّة protest demonstration; مُظاهَرة جَماعيّة mass demonstration; مُظاهَرة احْتِجاجاً على شَيْءٍ a demonstration against sth; مُظاهَرة تَأْييداً لِشَيْءٍ a demonstration in favour of sth

مَظْهَر *n* |مَظاهِرُ| 1 [شَكْل] appearance, look, sight; exterior, form; aspect; face, expression; figure; عادَ مَظْهَرُ المَدينةِ إلى ما كانَ عَلَيْهِ the city has regained its old look; مَظْهَر أَنيق a well-kept appearance 2 [انْطِباع] appearance; pretence; مَظْهَر خَدّاع \ خادِع façade; مَظْهَر خارِجيّ outward appearances; مَظْهَر كَذّاب \ كاذِب deceptive appearances; ظَهَرَ بِمَظْهَرِ الصَديقِ to pose as a friend; رِياضيّ المَظْهَرِ sporty

مُظَهِّر *n* (Phot) developer

ظَيّان *n* (Bot) clematis

ظاهِر A *adj* visible, perceptible; clear, evident, conspicuous; الجامِعُ ظاهِرٌ من هُنا the mosque is visible from here; بِشَكْلٍ ظاهِرٍ visibly, apparently, manifestly; ostentatiously; حَمَلَ سِلاحَهُ بِشَكْلٍ ظاهِرٍ to openly carry a weapon; غَيْر ظاهِرٍ inconspicuous; covert; latent

B *n* |ظَواهِرُ| 1 [جِهة خارِجيّة] outside; surface; في ,ظاهِراً on the outside; من الظاهِرِ from the outside; ظاهِر الكَفِّ the back of the hand 2 [مَظْهَر] (outward) appearance; في ظاهِرِ الأَمْرِ ,حَسَبَ / في الظاهِرِ evidently, obviously; apparently; حَكَمَ على شَخْصٍ بِظاهِرِهِ to judge sb by their appearance 3 (Islam) *literal meaning of a text, especially the Koran*; الظاهِر the Manifest (*one of the names of God*) 4 (Ling) literal meaning; ظاهِر اللَفْظِ literal meaning

ظاهِرة *n* |ظَواهِرُ| phenomenon; ظاهِرة مُهِمّة \ غَريبة \ جَديدة an interesting/strange/new phenomenon; ظَواهِر غامِضة \ غَيْر طَبيعيّةٍ inexplicable/supernatural phenomena; ظاهِرة حَضاريّة a cultural phenomenon; ظاهِرة طَبيعيّة a natural phenomenon; هذه ظاهِرةٌ طَبيعيّةٌ جِدًّا that is a quite natural phenomenon

ظاهِريّ A *adj* outward, external; seeming, apparent; superficial; صِفات \ تَغْييرات ظاهِريّة external characteristics/changes; تَعارُض \ تَناقُض ظاهِريّ an apparent contradiction

B *n adherent of the principle of literal interpretation of the Koran*

ظاهِريّة *n* 1 (Islam) *theological school following the principle of literal interpretation of the Koran* 2 (Philos) phenomenology

ظِهار *n words of repudiation, constituting a form of pre-Islamic divorce*

ظِهارة *n* |ظَهائِرُ| 1 (Anat) epithelium 2 [الثَوْبِ] backing

ظَهْريّ *adj* back (*before n*); dorsal

ظُهور *n* appearance; emergence; ظُهور شَبَحٍ a ghostly apparition; ظُهور التَجاعيدِ the appearance of wrinkles; ظُهور تَيّارٍ أَدَبيٍّ the emergence of a literary movement; ظُهور كِتابٍ the publication of a book

ظَهير *n* |ظُهَراءُ, أَظْهار| 1 [مُساعِد] helper; assistant 2 (Law Mor) dahir (*Royal Decree*); ظَهير شَريف Royal Decree 3 (Sport) back; ظَهير أَيْسَر left back

ع

‹ **عاد** *n* Ad (*ancient South Arabian tribe*)

‹ **عَبَأَ** *v* |a; عَبْء ,ب| to ignore, to not bother about لم يَعْبَأْ بِشَيْءٍ \ ما عَبَأَ بِشَيْءٍ \ شَخْصٍ ,شَخْصٍ to not bother about sth/sb; to not take the slightest notice of sth/sb; لم يَعْبَأْ بِتَحْذِيراتٍ to shrug off warnings

عَبَّأَ *v* 1 [جَهَّزَ] to mobilize; عَبَّأَ القُوّاتِ to mobilize the troops; عَبَّأَ الرَّأْيَ العامَّ to mobilize public opinion 2 [قَيَّدَ] to fill in; to fill out; عَبَّأَ بَياناتٍ to enter data; عَبَّأَ اسْتِمارةً to fill out a form 3 [عَلَّبَ] to pack (up), to package; يُعَبَّأُ في أَكْياسٍ بْلاسْتيكيّةٍ to be packed up in plastic bags 4 [حَمَّلَ] to charge, to fill, to load 5 [في زُجاجاتٍ] to bottle; عَبَّأَ الخَمْرَ في زُجاجاتٍ to bottle wine

عِبْء *n* |أَعْباء| load, burden; عِبْء ضَريبيّ tax burden; عِبْء الإِثْباتِ the onus of proof; أَعْباء المَسْؤوليّة the burden of responsibility; تَحَمَّلَ \ حَمَلَ عِبْئاً to bear a burden; تَحَمَّلَ العِبْءَ الأَكْبَرَ من ... to bear the brunt of ...

عابِئ *adj* غَيْر عابِئٍ indifferent, unconcerned

عَباءة *n* |عَباء ,أَعْبِئة| abaya (*a long, usually black, cloak worn by some Muslim women in public*)

تَعْبِئة *n* 1 [تَعْليب] packing, packaging; bottling; مَوادّ التَعْبِئة packing material 2 [مَلْء] filling (in/out); تَعْبِئة اسْتِمارة filling out a form 3 [تَجْنيد] mobilization; أَعْلَنَ التَعْبِئةَ to announce a mobilization

مُعَبَّأ *adj* 1 [مُعَلَّب] packed, packaged; مَكَرونة مُعَبَّأة packaged pasta 2 [مَشْحون] loaded, packed, filled; شاحِنة مُعَبَّأة غازاً \ بالغازِ a lorry (BrE) truck (AmE) loaded with gas; قَذيفة مُعَبَّأة بالفوسْفورِ a phosphorus bomb 3 [المَشْروبات] bottled; مِياه مُعَبَّأة bottled water

‹ **عَبَّ** *v* |u; عَبّ| to gulp down

عُباب *n* torrent, flood, deluge

‹ **عَبِثَ** *v* |a; عَبَث| 1 [لَعِبَ |ب] to tamper with, to play/mess around with; to fiddle with, to muddle, to fumble; عَبِثَ بالبابِ to fumble at the door; عَبِثَ بِشارِبَيْهِ to fiddle with one's mustache; عَبِثَ بِأَمْوالِ الدَوْلةِ to tamper with state money 2 [أَساءَ اسْتِعْمالَ شَيْءٍ] to violate, to infringe on; to abuse 3 [سَخِرَ] to mock

عابَثَ *v* to tease

عَبَث *n* 1 [عَمَل طائِش] tampering; fiddling (about), tinkering; bungling; العَبَث بِأَمْنِ الوَطَنِ tampering with national security; من العَبَثِ أَنْ تَفْعَلَ ذلك it is useless to do that; عَبَثاً in vain, to no avail; جاءَ \ بَحَثَ \ عَمِلَ عَبَثاً to come/search/work in vain; قد حاوَلْتُ عَبَثاً أَنْ أُقْنِعَهُ I tried to convince him, but to no avail 2 [سُخْرِيّة] mockery

عابِث A *adj* frivolous, fiddling; futile, useless; mischievous, tampering; مُحاوَلات عابِثة futile attempts; أَياد عابِثة mischievous hands

B *n* fiddler; tamperer, mischief maker

عَبَثيّ *adj* absurd, ridiculous

عَبَثيّة *n* absurdity

‹ **عَبَدَ** *v* |u; عُبودِيّة ,عُبودة ,عِبادة| to worship, to adore, to venerate; to serve; عَبَدَ شَخْصاً to adore sb; عَبَدَ اللهَ to serve God; عَبَدَ الأَوْثانَ to worship idols

عَبَّدَ *v* 1 [الطَريقَ] to pave, to surface; عَبَّدَ طَريقاً to pave a street 2 [اسْتَعْبَدَ] to enslave

تَعَبَّدَ *v* to devote oneself to the service of God

اسْتَعْبَدَ *v* to enslave, to subjugate; اسْتَعْبَدَ شَخْصاً to enslave sb; اسْتَعْبَدَ الشَعْبَ to subjugate the people

عَبْد *n* |عَبيد ,عِباد| 1 [رَقيق] slave 2 (Islam) servant (*of God*); عِباد اللهِ servants of God, humanity 3 [ناس] عِباد people; العِباد

عَبَّرَ *v* 1 [أَعْرَبَ|عن|] to express, to put into words, to utter; to phrase, to formulate; عَبَّرَ عن شَيْءٍ to express sth, to put sth into words; to express oneself about sth; to make sth known; عَبَّرَ عن رَأْيِهِ to express one's opinion; عَبَّرَ عن أمانيهِ \ شُعورِهِ \ تَقْديرِهِ to express one's wishes/feelings/esteem; عَبَّرَ عن شَيْءٍ بوُضوحٍ \ بشَكْلٍ واضِحٍ to state sth clearly 2 [فَسَّرَ] to interpret (*a dream*)

اعْتَبَرَ *v* 1 [عَدَّ] to consider, to hold, to think; to regard as, to deem, to take as; اعْتَبَرَ شَخْصاً خائِناً to consider sb a traitor; اعْتَبَرَ شَيْئاً مَقْبولاً to consider sth acceptable; اعْتَبَرَ شَيْئاً بِمَثابةِ نَجاحٍ to regard sth a success; اعْتَبَرَ تَعْليقاً إهانةً to take a remark as an insult; اعْتَبَرَ شَخْصاً غَبِيًّا to think sb is stupid; أُعْتُبِرَتْ زِيارةُ الرَّئيسِ تَهْيِئةً لاتِّفاقٍ the president's visit was regarded as a preparation to an agreement 2 [اتَّعَظَ] to be warned; اعْتَبَرَ بشَيْءٍ to learn from something; هذه عِبْرةٌ لِمَنْ يَعْتَبِرُ let that be a warning!

عَبْر *n* crossing through

عَبْرَ *prep* through, across, by way of; over; عَبْرَ الحُدودِ across the border; عَبْرَ المَمَرِّ through the hallway; عَبْرَ الطابَقِ السُّفْليِّ by way of the ground floor; عَبْرَ الصِحافةِ by way of the press; عَبْرَ القارّاتِ intercontinental; الاتِّصالات عَبْرَ الأَقْمارِ الصِناعيّةِ satellite communications

عابِر A *adj* 1 [لِمَسافاتٍ طَويلةٍ] crossing, cross-; passing; قِطار عابِر a through train; عابِر للقارّاتِ intercontinental; سَفينة عابِرة للمُحيطِ ocean liner; جَريمة عابِرة للحُدودِ cross-border crime 2 [عارِض] short, fleeting, passing; quick; مَرَض عابِر a short illness; إشارة عابِرة a fleeting reference
B *n* passer-by

عَبّارة *n* ferry, ferry boat; رَكِبَ العَبّارةَ to take the ferry; العَبّارة على النيلِ the ferry boat across the Nile

عِبارة *n* 1 [لَفْظ] expression; phrase; word; saying, proverb; عِبارة مُبْتَذَلة cliché, a worn-out phrase; عِبارة شُكْرٍ expression of gratitude, words of thanks; أَرْسَلَ عِبارةَ شُكْرٍ إلى شَخْصٍ to send sb a letter of thanks; عِبارةً فَعِبارةً word by word; عِبارات الإطْراءِ والمَديحِ words of praise; عِبارات اُقْتُطِعَتْ من سِياقِها words that are taken out of context; تَقولُ \

في هذه البِلادِ the people in this country

عابِد *n* |عابِدونَ، عُبّاد، عَبَدة| worshipper

عَبّاد *n* عَبّاد الشَمْسِ sunflower; زَيْت عَبّادِ الشَمْسِ sunflower oil; وَرَق عَبّادِ الشَمْسِ litmus paper

عِبادة *n* worship, devotion; practice of religion; عِبادة الأَصْنامِ \ الأَوْثانِ the worship of idols, idolatry; عِبادة عِشْتارَ the cult of Ishtar; أَماكِن العِبادةِ \ دور places of worship; حُرِّيّة العِبادةِ freedom of religion; عِبادة شَخْصٍ \ شَيْءٍ adoration of sb/sth; العِبادات البَدَنيّة physical acts of worship (*prayer, fasting, etc.*)

عَبْد الرَحْمان *n* Abd al-Rahman, Abdurrahman (*male given name*)

عَبْد الرَحيم *n* Abd al-Rahim, Abderrahim (*male given name*)

عَبْد العَزيز *n* Abd al-Aziz, Abdulaziz (*male given name*)

عَبْد الكَريم *n* Abd al-Karim, Abdul Karim (*male given name*)

عَبْد الله *n* Abdullah (*male given name*)

عَبْد المَلِك *n* Abd al-Malik, Abdul Malik (*male given name*)

عُبودة *n* slavery, servitude

عُبوديّ *adj* slavish, servile; مَوْقِف عُبوديّ a slavish attitude

عُبوديّة *n* slavery; حَرَّرَ شَخْصاً من العُبوديّةِ to release sb from slavery, to set sb free

تَعَبُّد *n* worship, devotion; cult

تَعْبيد *n* paving; تَعْبيد الطَريقِ paving the road

مُتَعَبِّد *adj* devout

مَعْبَد *n* |مَعابِدُ| temple; مَعْبَد يَهوديّ synagogue; مَعْبَد هِنْدوسيّ \ بوذيّ a Hindu/Buddhist temple; مَعْبَد زِيوس the temple of Zeus

مُعَبَّد *adj* metalled (BrE), paved (AmE); طُرُق مُعَبَّدة paved roads; غَيْر مُعَبَّدٍ unmetalled (BrE), unpaved/dirt (AmE)

مَعْبود *n* idol, image

عَبَدان *n* |f| Abadan (*city in Iran*)

عَبَرَ *v* |u; عَبْر, عُبور| 1 [قَطَعَ] to cross, to traverse; to pass over; to travel through; عَبَرَ الحُدودَ to cross the border; عَبَرَ الجِسْرَ to go over the bridge; عَبَرَ شارِعاً \ طَريقاً to cross a street/road; عَبَرَ نَهْراً to cross a river; to wade through a river; عَبَرَ الخَطَّ النِهائيَّ to cross the finish line; عَبَرَ الصَحْراءَ to cross the desert 2 [اسْتَوْرَدَ وَصَدَّرَ] to convey in transit

اعْتِباريّ *adj* legal, corporate; nominal, titular; شَخصيّة اعْتِباريّة legal entity

تَعْبير *n* 1 [تَعْبيرات| (عن إحْساسٍ)] expression, utterance; voicing; تَعْبير الوَجْهِ facial expression; التَعْبير عن إحْساسِهِ the expression of one's feelings; حُرّيّة التَعْبير (عن الرَأْي) freedom of speech 2 [لَفْظ] |تَعابيرُ| expression, saying; phrase, term; تَعْبير شائع a common expression; تَعْبير رَنّان a hollow phrase; تَعْبير اصْطِلاحيّ an idiomatic expression, idiom; طَريقة تَعْبيرٍ form of expression; وَسيلة التَعْبير means of expression; حَسَبَ تَعْبير فُلانٍ in so-and-so's words, according to so-and-so; بِتَعْبيرٍ آخَرَ in other words; إذا إنْ جازَ التَعْبيرُ صَحَّ التَعْبيرُ so to speak, as it were 3 [الرُؤْيا أو الحُلْم] interpretation (*of a dream*)

تَعْبيريّ *adj* (Art) expressionistic; فَنّان تَعْبيريّ expressionist; شَكْل تَعْبيريّ form of expression

تَعْبيريّة *n* (Art) expressionism

مَعْبَر *n* |مَعابِرُ| 1 [عُبور] crossing, passage 2 [مَكان عُبورٍ] passage, crossing point, gate; مَعْبَر بَحْريّ shipping lane; مَعْبَر حُدوديّ border crossing 3 [السَفينةِ] gangplank

مُعَبِّر *adj* expressive, meaningful, telling; نَظْرة مُعَبِّرة a meaningful look; عُنْوان مُعَبِّر a revealing title; حَرَكات مُعَبِّرة expressive gestures

مِعْبَر *n* |مَعابِرُ| 1 [مَرْكَب] ferry (boat); المِعْبَر إلى طَنْجةَ the ferry to Tangier 2 [جِسْر] bridge

مُعْتَبَر *adj* الحالة المُعْتَبَرة (شَرْعاً) legal competence (*for divorce*); وَهُوَ بالحالةِ المُعْتَبَرةِ (شَرْعاً) he is legally competent (*to divorce*)

عَبَسَ *v* |i; عُبوس, عَبْس| to frown; سورة عَبَسَ He frowned (*Sura 80*)

عَبَّسَ *v* to frown

عابِس *adj* frowning; sullen, surly, grouchy; وَجْه عابِس a sullen countenance

عَبّاس *n* Abbas (*male given name*)

عَبّاسيّ *adj* Abbasid; الدَوْلة العَبّاسيّة the Abbasid empire/dynasty; عَصْر العَبّاسيّينَ the Abbasid period

عَبوس *adj* frowning; sullen, surly

عُبوس *n* frowning

[طَريقة التَعْبيرِ] 2 ... as the proverb says: ... تَنُصُّ العِبارةُ: ... formulation, phrasing; بِعِبارةٍ أُخْرى in other words; بِعِبارةٍ موجَزةٍ in short; بِعِباراتٍ حادّةٍ fiercely; بِعِباراتٍ واضِحةٍ in clear terms; صيغَ بِعِباراتٍ عامّةٍ جِدّاً to be formulated in very general terms; هو عِبارةٌ عن... meaning ...

عِبْرانيّ *adj* Hebrew; اللُغة العِبْرانيّة ancient/biblical Hebrew

عَبْرة *n* tear, teardrop

عِبْرة *n* |عِبَر| warning, lesson, example; اسْتَخْلَصَ \ أَخَذَ عِبْرةً من شَيْءٍ to learn a lesson from sth; هذه عِبْرةٌ لِمَنْ يَعْتَبِرُ let that be a warning!

عِبْريّ *adj* Hebrew; اللُغة العِبْريّة Hebrew

عُبور *n* 1 [مَعْبَر] crossing, traversing; gate, passage; عُبور مُشاةٍ pedestrian crossing (BrE), crosswalk (AmE); عُبور الشارِعِ crossing the street; عُبور البَحْرِ \ النَهْرِ sea/river crossing; عُبور الحُدودِ crossing the border, border crossing; مَكان \ نُقْطة العُبورِ الحُدوديّة crossing point; نُقْطة عُبورٍ border crossing point 2 (Transp) transit; ميناء عُبورٍ transit port; بَلَد عُبورٍ transit country

عَبير *n* scent, aroma

اعْتِبار *n* |اعْتِبارات| 1 [وُجْهة نَظَرٍ] consideration, regard; اعْتِبارات أَمْنيّة security considerations; بِسَبَبِ اعْتِباراتٍ أَمْنيّةٍ for reasons of security; على اعْتِبارِ أنّ ... باعْتِبارِ أنْ ... with regard to the fact that ..., considering that ...; باعْتِبارِ التَقَشُّفاتِ in view of the cutbacks; لِاعْتِباراتٍ شَخْصيّةٍ for personal reasons; أَخَذَ شَيْئاً بِعَيْنِ الاعْتِبارِ to take sth into consideration; دون أيِّ اعْتِبارٍ without any consideration; جَدير بالاعْتِبارِ worth considering; لا يَدْخُلُ في الاعْتِبارِ it is not under consideration 2 [صِفة] capacity; باعْتِبارِهِ وَزيراً in his capacity of minister; باعْتِباري مُديرَ المَعْهَدِ as director of the institute 3 [تَقْدير] respect, regard, esteem; إعادة \ رَدّ الاعْتِبارِ restitution, rehabilitation; قَلَّلَ من اعْتِبارِ شَخْصٍ to discredit sb 4 [ابْتِداء] اعْتِباراً من from, as of, starting; اعْتِباراً من الآنِ as of now, from now on; اعْتِباراً من اليَوْمِ starting today; اعْتِباراً من ذلك اليَوْمِ from that day on; القانون الجَديد الذي يَسْري اعْتِباراً من ١ يَنايِر the new law that takes effect from the 1st of January

‹ **اسْتَعْبَطَ** *v* to play the fool

عَبِيط [A] *adj* |عُبَطاء ,عُبُط| stupid, idiotic; أنا عَبِيطٌ إذا صَدَّقْتُ شَيْئاً من ذلك! I would have to be stupid to believe that!
[B] *n* |عُبَطاء ,عُبُط| idiot, fool; جيل العُبَطاءِ a generation of idiots

اعْتِباط *n* اعْتِباطاً at random, arbitrarily

اعْتِباطيّ *adj* arbitrary, at random; قَرار اعْتِباطيّ an arbitrary decision; اعْتِقال اعْتِباطيّ arbitrary detention

‹ **عَبِقَ** *v* |a; عَبَق| to smell (of); to waft out (*a scent*); عَبِقَتْ رائِحةُ القَهْوةِ the smell of coffee wafted out; عَبِقَت الغُرْفةُ بالطيبِ the room smelled of perfume

عَبِق *adj* fragrant, sweet-smelling; رائِحة عَبِقة a fragrant scent

عابِق *adj* |ب| heavily scented with, redolent with, filled/laden with; جَوّ عابق بالدُخانِ air heavy with the smell of smoke; جَوّ عابِق بالحُبِّ an atmosphere redolent of love; جَوّ عابق بالفَسادِ a corruption-laden atmosphere

مُعَبَّق *adj* |ب| filled with

‹ **عَبْقَر** *n* fairyland, wonderland

عَبْقَريّ [A] *adj* |عَباقِرة ,عَبْقَريّونَ| brilliant, bright, ingenious; باحِث \ فَنّان عَبْقَريّ a brilliant researcher/artist; خُطّة عَبْقَرِيّة an ingenious plan; اخْتِراع عَبْقَريّ a brilliant invention
[B] *n* |عَباقِرة ,عَبْقَريّون| genius

عَبْقَرِيّة *n* genius, brilliance; عَبْقَرِيّة موزارْت the genius of Mozart

‹ **عَبْل** *adj* |عِبال| fat, chubby; plump

أَعْبَل *n* granite

أَعْبَليّ *adj* granite (*before n*)

‹ **عَبايَة** *n* see عَباءة

عُبوة ,عَبْوة *n* 1 [مِقْدار] packing, packaging; bottle; عَبوّة اقْتِصاديّة economy pack 2 [قُنْبُلة] bomb; عَبوّة ناسِفة IED (*improvised explosive device*); bomb

تَعْبَويّ *adj* mobilization (*before n*), recruitment (*before n*)

‹ **عَتَبَ** *v* |i-u; عَتْب| |على| to reproach, to blame; عَتَبَ على شَخْصٍ لِأَنَّهُ يَتَأَخَّرُ دائماً to reproach sb for being always late

عاتَبَ *v* to reproach, to blame; to reprimand; عاتَبَ شَخْصاً to reproach sb

تَعاتَبَ *v* to blame each other

عِتاب *n* reproach, blame; عاتَبَ شَخْصاً عِتاباً مُرًّا to reproach sb bitterly

عَتَبة *n* |أَعْتاب ,عَتَب ,عَتَبات| threshold, doorstep; على عَتَبةِ (عَصْرٍ جَديدٍ) on the threshold of (a new era); تحت عَتَبةِ الفَقْرِ below the poverty line; على عَتَبةِ الإفْلاسِ on the verge of bankruptcy

(Idiom) العَتَبات المُقَدَّسة the Holy Sites (*in Shia Islam, usually referring to the Iraqi cities of Karbala and Najaf*)

مُعاتِب *adj* reproachful, reproving; قالَ مُعاتِباً he said in a tone of reproach

مُعاتَبة *n* reprimand, reproof, rebuke

‹ **عَتُدَ** *v* |u; عَتاد| to prepare, to make ready

أَعْتَدَ *v* to prepare, to make ready

عَتاد *n* |أَعْتِدة| equipment; ammunition; عَتاد عَسْكَريّ military equipment; عَتاد الحاسوبِ (computer) hardware

عَتيد *adj* 1 [قادِم] next, future (*before n*); coming, new; الرَئِيس العَتيد the future president 2 [مُهَيَّأ] ready, prepared; equipped 3 [قَوِيّ] strong

‹ **عِتْر** *n* origin

عِتْرة *n* 1 [ذُرِّيّة] offspring 2 (Bot) marjoram

‹ **عَتَقَ ,عَتُقَ** *v* |i-u; عِتْق| 1 [قَدُمَ] to be/grow old; عَتَقَ الخَمْرُ the wine is mature 2 [تَحَرَّرَ] to be liberated/released; عَتَقَ العَبْدُ the slave was liberated

عَتَّقَ *v* to let ripen

أَعْتَقَ *v* to release, to liberate; أَعْتَقَ شَخْصاً من العَبودِيّةِ to liberate sb from slavery

انْعَتَقَ *v* to be liberated/released; to free oneself; انْعَتَقَ من شَيْءٍ to be liberated from something

عِتْق *n* 1 [قِدَم] ripening; maturity 2 [تَحَرُّر] release; liberty; العِتْق من النارِ salvation from hell

عاتِق *n* |عَواتِقُ| shoulder; أَخَذَ شَيْئاً على عاتِقِهِ to take sth upon oneself; أَلْقى \ وَضَعَ مُهِمّةً صَعْبةً على عاتِقِ شَخْصٍ to thrust a difficult task on sb; تَقَعُ المَسْؤوليّةُ على عاتِقِهِ the responsibility is on his shoulders

عَتاقة *n* age, vintage; maturity

عَتيق *adj* 1 [قديم] old, ancient; antique; عَتيق الطِراز antiquated, old-fashioned; أفْكار عَتيقة old-fashioned ideas 2 [حُرّ] free, liberated; البَيْت العَتيق the liberated house (*the Ka'ba*)

انْعِتاق *n* liberation, release; انْعِتاق من شَيْءٍ release from sth

مُعَتَّق *adj* ripened, old; خَمْر مُعَتَّق aged wine

‹ **عَتَلَ** *v* |i-u; عَتْل| to carry; عَتَلَ شَيْئاً to carry sth

عَتّال *n* porter, carrier

عَتَلة *n* crowbar

‹ **عَتَّمَ** *v* 1 [الأَنْوارَ] to extinguish, to put out, to turn off; to dip; عَتَّمَ الأَنْوارَ to turn off the lights; عَتَّمَ على أَمْرٍ to hush sth up 2 [لَبِثَ] ما عَتَّمَ أنْ ... it didn't take long until...

عُتْم *n* wild olive tree

عَتَمة *n* dark, darkness; في عَتَمةِ اللَيْلِ in the dark of night, under the cover of darkness

إعْتام *n* cataract

تَعْتيم *n* blackout; تَعْتيم إعْلاميّ media blackout; فَرَضَ تَعْتيماً إعْلامِيًّا to impose a media blackout

مُعْتِم *adj* dark; gloomy; faint; مَمَرّ مُعْتِم a dark passageway; ضَوْء مُعْتِم a faint light

‹ **عَتِهَ** *v* |a; عَتَه| to be/become demented; to be/become mentally disabled

عَتَه *n* dementia

عَتاهة *n* idiocy, feeble-mindedness

مَعْتوه A *adj* |مَعاتيهُ| idiotic, imbecilic; mentally disabled B *n* |مَعاتيهُ| idiot, imbecile; demented person

‹ **عَتا** *v* |u; عُتو| to be arrogant; to be violent/fierce

عَتِيّ *adj* arrogant, insolent; tyrannical, despotic

عاتٍ *adj* |عُتاة| 1 [عَنيف] strong, fierce; رِياح عاتِية a strong wind; أَمْواج \ نيران عاتِية huge waves/flames 2 [ظالِم] tyrannical 3 [مُتَكَبِّر] arrogant, presumptuous

‹ **عُثّ** *n coll* |عُثَث| moth (*Lepidoptera*)

‹ **عَثَرَ** *v* |u| 1 [وَجَدَ] |عُثور; على| to find, to come across, to discover; عَثَرَ على شَيْءٍ to find sth; عَثَرَ على شَيْءٍ في الشارِعِ to find sth in the street; لا يُعْثَرُ عَلَيْه not to be found 2 [زَلّ] |عِثار, عَثير, عَثْر| to stumble, to trip

عَثَّرَ *v* to trip, to make fall/stumble; عَثَّرَ شَخْصاً to trip sb

أَعْثَرَ *v* to trip, to make fall/stumble; أَعْثَرَ شَخْصاً to trip sb

تَعَثَّرَ *v* 1 [كَبا] to stumble, to trip; تَعَثَّرَ بِشَيْءٍ to stumble over sth 2 [تَعَرْقَلَ] to get stuck; to come to a standstill; تَعَثَّرَت المُفاوَضاتُ the negotiations have come to a standstill 3 [في الكَلامِ] to stutter

عاثِر *adj* stumbling; حَظّ عاثِر bad luck

عَثْرة *n* |عَثَرات| stumbling; false step; حَجَر عَثْرةٍ stumbling block; وَقَفَ \ كانَ \ شَكَّلَ حَجَرَ عَثْرةٍ to be a stumbling block; عَثْرةً في سَبيلِ شَخْصٍ to be a stumbling block for sb

عُثور *n* finding, discovery; العُثور على الطَريقِ finding the way

مُتَعَثِّر *adj* 1 [مُتَقَطِّع] stalled, interrupted, faltering, lagging; مُفاوَضات مُتَعَثِّرة stalled negotiations; دُيون مُتَعَثِّرة bad debts; قُروض مُتَعَثِّرة non-performing loans 2 [في الكَلامِ] broken (*speech*); stuttering

‹ **عُثْكول** *n* |عَثاكيلُ| bunch

‹ **عُثْمان** *n* |dipt| Uthman (*male given name*)

عُثْمانيّ A *adj* Ottoman; الإمْبِراطورِيّة العُثْمانِيّة the Ottoman empire; العَهْد \ العَصْر العُثْمانيّ the Ottoman period B *n* Ottoman

‹ **عُثْنون** *n* |عَثانينُ| goatee

‹ **عَثا** *v* |u; عُثوّ, عُثِيّ, عِثِيّ| to act wickedly, to cause mischief

‹ **عَجِبَ** *v* |a; عَجَب| |من| to wonder, to marvel; to be astonished/amazed; عَجِبَ من شَيْءٍ to be astonished at/over sth

أَعْجَبَ *v* 1 [أَرْضى] to please, to appeal to; تُعْجِبُني الفِكْرةُ I like the idea; هذا لا يُعْجِبُني I don't like that; هل تُعْجِبُكَ وَظيفَتُكَ الجَديدةُ؟ how do you like your new job?; لم تُعْجِبْني نَبْرةُ كَلامِهِ I didn't like his tone; إنَّهُ يُعْجِبُها she likes him, she has a crush on him 2 [اِسْتَبْدَعَ] |ب| to admire, to be impressed by; أُعْجِبَ بِشَيْءٍ \ شَخْصٍ to admire sth/sb; أُعْجِبَ بِشَخْصٍ لِمُثابَرَتِهِ to admire sb for his perseverance; أُعْجِبَ بِنَفْسِهِ to be conceited 3 [أَدْهَشَ] to amaze, to astonish

تَعَجَّبَ *v* |من| to be astonished/amazed; to wonder, to marvel; تَعَجَّبَ من شَيْءٍ \ شَخْصٍ to be astonished about sth/sb

اسْتَعْجَبَ *v* to wonder, to marvel

عَجَب *n* |أَعْجاب| **1** ◂ [شَيْء غَريب] miracle, marvel, wonder; لا عَجَبَ! no wonder!, it is not surprising!; العَجَب العُجاب wonder of wonders **2** ◂ [دَهَش] amazement, astonishment; عَجَباً!, يا لَلْعَجَبِ! how strange!; دَعا للعَجَبِ to be surprising; لَيْسَ في ذلك ما يَدْعو للعَجَبِ there is nothing strange about it; إذا عُرِفَ السَّبَبُ بَطُلَ العَجَبُ it wouldn't be strange if you knew the cause

عُجْب *n* vanity, conceit

عُجاب *adj* marvelous, amazing; very strange; العَجَب العُجاب wonder of wonders, amazing thing

عَجيب *adj* amazing, surprising; strange, remarkable, odd; ظاهِرة عَجيبة a remarkable phenomenon; حَدَث عَجيب a strange event; شِفاء عَجيب a miraculous cure; عَجيبٌ هذا that is strange; لَيْسَ (أَمْراً) عَجيباً أنّ ... it is not strange that ...

عَجيبة *n* |عَجائِبُ| wonder, marvel, miracle; عَجائِب الدُنْيا السَبْع the Seven Wonders of the World

إعْجاب *n* admiration; إعْجاب شَديد profound admiration; إعْجاب بِشَيْءٍ \ بِشَخْصٍ admiration for sth/sb; إعْجاب بالنَفْسِ conceit; جَدير بالإعْجابِ admirable; نالَ \ حازَ إعْجابَ شَخْصٍ to win the admiration of sb; كَنَّ إعْجاباً لِشَيْءٍ to have admiration for sth; كانَت مَحَطَّ إعْجابِ الجَميعِ she was admired by everyone

أُعْجوبة *n* |أعاجيبُ| wonder, miracle; بِأُعْجوبةٍ miraculously; narrowly; نَجا من المَوْتِ بِأُعْجوبةٍ to narrowly escape death

تَعَجُّب *n* astonishment, amazement; عَلامة التَعَجُّبِ exclamation mark, exclamation point (AmE); بِتَعَجُّبٍ with astonishment; ظَهَرَ عَلَيْهِ التَعَجُّبُ الشَديدُ he was obviously very surprised

مُتَعَجِّب *adj* astonished, amazed, surprised

مُعْجَب **A** *adj* pleased, admiring; مُعْجَب بِنَفْسِهِ conceited; كانَ مُعْجَباً بِشَيْءٍ to be pleased with sth; غَيْر مُعْجَبٍ بِشَيْءٍ not pleased with sth; إنَّهُ مُعْجَبٌ بِها he likes her, he has a crush on her
B *n* admirer, fan; نادي مُعْجَبينَ fan club

مُعْجِب *adj* admirable, astonishing

‹ **عَجَّ** *v* |i; عَجيج| **1** ◂ [اكْتَظَّ] |ب| to teem (with), to swarm (with), to be crawling (with); to be full (of); يَعُجُّ المَكانُ بالذُبابِ \ البَعوضِ \ النَمْلِ the place is crawling with flies/mosquitoes/ants; يَعِجُّ المَكانُ بالناسِ the place is swarming with people; يَعُجُّ بالمَواهِبِ to be teeming with talent **2** ◂ [صاحَ] to cry, to yell

عَجاج *n* |أَعِجّة| **1** ◂ [غُبار] dust **2** ◂ [دُخان] smoke **3** ◂ [صَوْت] clamour; عَجاج البَحْرِ the roar of the sea

عُجّة *n* (NA) *a baked egg dish, similar to a crustless quiche*; (Tunisia) *a dish of egg, tomatoes and peppers*

عَجيج *n* screaming, yelling

‹ **عُجْرة** *n* |عُجَر| knot; protuberance

أَعْجَر *adj* |dipt| knotty

‹ **تَعَجْرَفَ** *v* to be/become pompous, to be/become conceited

عَجْرَفة *n* arrogance, haughtiness

مُتَعَجْرِف **A** *adj* arrogant, haughty, supercilious, snobby; سُلوك مُتَعَجْرِف arrogant behaviour
B *n* snob

‹ **عَجَزَ** *v* |i; عَجْز| to be/become weak; to be incapable, to be unable; عَجَزَ عن شَيْءٍ to be incapable of sth; عَجَزَ عن وَصْفِ شَيْءٍ to be unable to describe sth, to be unable to put sth into words

عَجَّزَ *v* **1** ◂ [تَقَدَّمَ في السِنِّ] to grow old **2** ◂ [عَوَّقَ] to make feel incapable, to frustrate, to baffle; عَجَّزَني بِطَلَباتِهِ الكَثيرةِ his many demands wore me out; عَجَّزَني بِالسُؤالِ the question left me at a loss

أَعْجَزَ *v* to hold back; to keep from; أَعْجَزَ شَخْصاً عن شَيْءٍ to keep sb from sth; أَعْجَزَهُ المَرَضُ عن مُتابَعةِ دِراسَتِهِ the illness made it impossible for him to continue his studies

عَجْز *n* **1** ◂ [نَقْص] deficit, deficiency; lack, shortage; عَجْز في الميزانيّة budget deficit; عَجْز نَقْديّ deficit; عَجْز في الحِسابِ الجاري current account deficit; عَجْز قَدْرُهُ ثَلاثُمِائةِ أَلْفِ أورو a deficit of 300,000 euros; غَطّى عَجْزاً to cover a deficit; سَدَّ \ أَكْمَلَ عَجْزاً to fill/make up a deficit **2** ◂ [عَدَم القُدْرةِ] weakness; incapacity; invalidity, disablement (BrE), disability (AmE); عَجْز جِنْسيّ impotence; عَجْز دائِم permanent invalidity

عَجُز *n* |أَعْجاز| backside, behind

عاجِز 🅰 *adj* |عَجَزة| incapable, unable; disabled, invalid, infirm; عاجز عن العَمَلِ unable to work; إنّها عاجزةٌ عن العَمَلِ جُزْئيًّا she is partially disabled; عاجز جِنْسيًّا impotent; الحُكومةُ عاجِزةٌ عن تَلْبِيةِ حاجاتِ المُواطِنِينَ the government is unable to meet the people's needs; هو عاجِزٌ عن الكَلامِ he can't speak

🅱 *n* |عَجَزة| disabled person, invalid; elderly person; دار العَجَزةِ care home (BrE), nursing/retirement home (AmE)

عَجوز 🅰 *adj* |mf; عَجائِزُ, عُجُز| old, elderly; رَجُل \ امْرَأة عَجوز an old man/woman

🅱 *n* |mf; عَجائِزُ, عُجُز| an old man/woman

عَجيزة *n* |عَجائِزُ| buttocks

إعْجاز *n* إعْجاز القُرْآنِ the inimitability of the Koran

إعْجازيّ *n* miraculous; unique, inimitable; الرِحْلة الإعْجازيّة للنَبيِّ the miraculous journey of the Prophet

تَعْجيزيّ *adj* impossible; unfeasible, unattainable; أَهْداف تَعْجيزيّة unattainable goals; شَرْط تَعْجيزيّ an impossible condition; مَطالِب تَعْجيزيّة impossible demands

مُعْجِز *adj* miraculous, marvellous

مُعْجِزة *n* miracle, wonder, marvel; مُعْجِزات الطَبيعة \ التِقْنيّةِ the wonders of nature/technology; مُعْجِزة القُرْآنِ the miraculous nature of the Koran; طِفْل مُعْجِزة a child prodigy; كالمُعْجِزةِ as if by a miracle; إنَّها مُعْجِزةٌ أَنَّهُ ما زالَ حَيًّا it's a miracle that he is still alive; آمَنَ بالمُعْجِزاتِ to believe in miracles; قامَ \ أَتى \ بِمُعْجِزةٍ to work miracles; لَمْ يَتَوَقَّعْ من شَيْءٍ مُعْجِزةً to not expect a miracle from sth; الدُنْيا لا تَخْلو من المُعْجِزاتِ wonders will never cease

عَجْعَجَ *v* |i; عَجْعَجة| to roar

عَجُفَ *v* |u; عَجَف| to be thin/skinny

أَعْجَف *adj* |dipt; عِجاف| thin, skinny, lean; سَنَوات عِجاف lean years; بَقَرة عَجْفاء a skinny cow

عَجَق *n* (Levant) *a state of rushing/being busy*

عَجِلَ *v* |a; عَجَلة, عَجَل| to hurry, to hasten; to accelerate

عَجَّلَ *v* 1 [أَعْجَلَ] to quicken, to speed up; to hasten; عَجَّلَ شَيْئاً \ في شَيْءٍ to speed up sth; عَجَّلَ سَيْرَ الأَحْداثِ to speed up the course of things; عَجَّلَ بَحْثاً \ قَضيّةً to expedite an investigation/matter; عَجَّلَ الإجْراءَ to speed up a procedure 2 [اسْتَحَثَّ] to rush; عَجَّلَ شَخْصاً to rush sb 3 [دَفَعَ مُقَدَّماً] to pay in advance

عاجَلَ *v* to hurry; to be ahead of; عاجَلَ خَصْمَهُ بِضَرْبةٍ he hit his opponent before he could hit him

أَعْجَلَ *v* 1 [حَثَّ] to rush, to hurry 2 [سَبَقَ] to go ahead

تَعَجَّلَ *v* 1 [أَسْرَعَ] to hurry; to do in a hurry; تَعَجَّلَ في أَمْرٍ to do sth in a hurry 2 [حَثَّ] to rush, to urge

اسْتَعْجَلَ *v* 1 [حَثَّ] to rush, to hurry up, to speed up; اسْتَعْجَلَ شَخْصاً to hurry sb up; اسْتَعْجَلَ تَنْفيذَ مَشْروعٍ to rush the implementation of a project; اسْتَعْجَلَ الرَحيلَ to be in a hurry to go; لا تَسْتَعْجِلِ الأُمورَ don't rush things 2 [أَسْرَعَ] to hurry, to hasten, to be quick to; اسْتَعْجَلَ في العَوْدةِ to return quickly; لن أَسْتَعْجِلَ في اتِّخاذِ القَرارِ I will not take (BrE) make (AmE) a rash decision

عَجَل *n* hurry, haste; على عَجَلٍ quickly, hurriedly, hastily; ارْتَدى ثِيابَهُ على عَجَلٍ he hurriedly got dressed

عِجْل *n* |عُجول| calf; عِجْل البَحْرِ sea lion, eared/fur seal, otariid (*Otariidae*); العِجْل الذَهَبيّ the Golden Calf; أَنْف العِجْلِ snapdragon (*Antirrhinum*)

عاجِل *adj* urgent, pressing; quick; حالة عاجِلة emergency, urgent situation; أَخْبار عاجِلة breaking news; شِفاء عاجِل a quick recovery; مُساعَدة عاجِلة urgent help, emergency assistance; اجْتِماع عاجِل an emergency meeting; في القَريبِ العاجِلِ in the near future; عاجِلاً أو آجِلاً sooner or later

عُجالة *n* rush job

عَجَلة *n* 1 [دولاب] wheel; عَجَلة أَماميّة \ خَلْفيّة front/back wheel; عَجَلة القِيادةِ (steering) wheel; عَجَلات سَيّارةٍ \ دَرّاجةٍ the wheels of a car/bicycle; عَجَلات الهُبوطِ landing gear; إطار العَجَلةِ tyre; طول قاعِدةِ العَجَلاتِ wheelbase 2 [تَقَدُّم] movement, progression; process; عَجَلة الاقْتِصادِ the economy; حَرَّكَ عَجَلةَ الاقْتِصادِ to get the economy moving; عَجَلة السَلامِ the peace process; دَفْع عَجَلةِ السَلامِ advancing the peace process 3 [سُرْعة] hurry, haste; كانَ على عَجَلةٍ من أَمْرِهِ to be in a hurry; لا داعِيَ للعَجَلةِ there is no need to hurry; العَجَلة من الشَيْطانِ ≈ haste makes waste; في التَأَنّي

مُعْجَمِيّ **A** *adj* lexicographic; lexical, dictionary (*before n*); تَعْرِيف مُعْجَمِيّ dictionary definition

B *n* lexicographer; مُعْجَمِيّات lexicography

مُعْجَمِيّة *n* lexicography; عِلْم المُعْجَمِيّة lexicology

عَجْمان *n* |dipt f| Ajman (*one of the United Arab Emirates*)

عَجَنَ *v* |i-u; عَجْن| to knead; عَجَنَ عَجِينةً to knead dough

مَعْجَنَ *v* |i; مَعْجَنة| to plaster

عَجْن *n* kneading; قابِل للعَجْنِ kneadable, mouldable

عَجين *n coll* |عَجائِنُ| dough; pastry; عَجِينة مُوَرَّقة puff pastry, filo dough; عَجِينة خُبْزٍ bread dough; شَخْص عَجِينةٍ a bore, a boring/tiresome person; عَجَنَ عَجِيناً to knead dough; تَرَكَ العَجِينَ يَخْمُرُ to leave the dough to rise

مِعْجَن *n* |مَعاجِنُ| kneading trough; kneading machine

مُعَجَّنات *n pl* pastry; baked goods

مَعْجُون *n* |مَعاجِينُ| paste; cream; مَعْجُون طَماطِمَ tomato purée/paste; مَعْجُون الحِلاقةِ shaving foam; مَعْجُون الأَسْنانِ toothpaste; أُنْبوب مَعْجُونِ الأَسْنانِ a tube of toothpaste

عَجْوة *n* pressed dates

عِدْ *v* see وَعَدَ

عِدة *n* see وعد

عَدَّ *v* |u; عَدّ| **1** [حَسَبَ] to count; to calculate; عَدَّ إلى مِائةٍ to count to a hundred; عَدَّ الثَّوانِيَ to count the seconds; لا يُعَدُّ countless, innumerable **2** [اعْتَبَرَ] to consider, to regard as, to take as; عَدَّ شَيْئاً إهانةً to take sth as an insult; عُدَّ to be considered as; يُعَدُّ هذا الرَّجُلُ رَئِيسَ المُعارَضةِ this man is considered to be the leader of the opposition

عَدَّدَ *v* to enumerate, to list; عَدَّدَ أَسْماءَ المُشارِكِينَ he listed the names of the participants

أَعَدَّ *v* to prepare, to make ready; أَعَدَّ المائِدةَ to set the table; أَعَدَّ وَجْبةً ساخِنةً to prepare a hot meal; أَعَدَّ اسْتِقْبالاً حارًّا لِشَخْصٍ to prepare a warm welcome for sb; أَعَدَّ نَفْسَهُ ل ... to prepare oneself for ...; أَعَدَّ عُدَّتَهُ ل ... to make one's preparations for ...; أَعَدَّ كُلَّ شَيْءٍ لِرِحْلةٍ to make everything ready for a trip; أَعَدَّ جَوازَ سَفَرِهِ to have one's passport ready; أَعَدَّ شَخْصاً كَمُعَلِّمٍ to train sb to be a teacher

السَّلامةُ وَفي العَجَلةِ النَدامةُ ≈ act in haste, repent at leisure

4 [عَرَبة] (Iraq) vehicle; عَجَلة عَسْكَرِيّة a military vehicle

5 [دَرّاجة] (Egypt) bicycle

عَجول *adj* |عُجُل| hurried, hasty; الخَطَأُ زادُ العَجُولِ ≈ haste makes waste

اسْتِعْجال *n* haste, hurry; ضَرورة الاسْتِعْجالِ urgency; بِاسْتِعْجالٍ with haste; دَفَعَ شَخْصاً إلى الاسْتِعْجالِ to rush sb

اسْتِعْجالِيّ *adj* urgent, emergency (*before n*); الطِبّ الاسْتِعْجالِيّ emergency medicine

تَعْجيل *n* |تَعْجيلات| speeding up, hastening, expediting; التَعْجيل بالزَواجِ getting married sooner; التَعْجيل في المُساعَدةِ expedited assistance

مُتَعَجِّل *adj* hasty, hurried

مُسْتَعْجَل *adj* urgent, pressing; acute; مُعالَجة مُسْتَعْجَلة emergency treatment; الحاجِيّات \ الحالات المُسْتَعْجَلة urgent needs/cases; بَريد مُسْتَعْجَل express post (BrE) mail (AmE); مَسْأَلة مُسْتَعْجَلة an urgent matter; إصْلاح مُسْتَعْجَل an urgently needed repair; الأَمْر مُسْتَعْجَلٌ the matter cannot wait

مُسْتَعْجِل *adj* hurried, in a hurry; كانَ مُسْتَعْجِلاً to be in a hurry; كانَ مُسْتَعْجِلاً جِدًّا to be in a big hurry; كانَ مُسْتَعْجِلاً ل \ على فِعْلِ شَيْءٍ to be in hurry to do sth

مُعَجَّل *adj* **1** [عاجِل] urgent **2** [مُقَدَّم] in advance; مُعَجَّل الصَداقِ *part of the dowry that is paid at the time of marriage*

عَجَمَ *v* |u; عَجْم| to vocalize (*to provide with diacritical points or vowels*)

أَعْجَمَ *v* to vocalize (*to provide with diacritical points or vowels*)

عَجْماء *n* |dipt f| animal, beast

عُجْمة *n* vagueness, confusion (*of speech*); barbarism

عَجَمي *n* |عَجَم| foreign, non-Arab; Persian

أَعْجَمِيّ *adj* foreign, non-Arab; Persian

العَجَم *n* foreigners, non-Arabs; Persians; بِلاد العَجَمِ Persia

مُعْجَم **A** *adj* [مَنْقوط] *having diacritical points*; حُروف مُعْجَمة letters with diacritical points

B *n* |مَعاجِمُ| [قاموس] dictionary; thesaurus; مُعْجَم مُفَهْرَس concordance; عِلْم \ صِناعة المَعاجِمِ lexicography; حُروف المُعْجَمِ the letters of the alphabet; رَجَعَ إلى مُعْجَمٍ to consult a dictionary

تَعَدَّدَ *v* **1** [صارَ ذا عَدَدٍ] to be numerous; تَتَعَدَّدُ المَصادِرُ there are multiple sources **2** [زادَ في العَدَدِ] to increase; to multiply; تَعَدَّدَت الحَوادِثُ the number of accidents has risen

اعْتَدَّ *v* **1** [أَدْخَلَ في الحِسابِ] to count in; to consider important; لا يُعْتَدُّ بِهِ unimportant, insignificant; هذه الحُجَّةُ لا يُعْتَدُّ بِها that argument doesn't count; اعْتَدَّ بِنَفْسِهِ to consider oneself important **2** [اعْتَبَرَ] to deem, to regard as, to consider **3** [المَرْأَةُ] *to observe the legally prescribed period of waiting before contracting a new marriage*

اسْتَعَدَّ *v* to prepare oneself, to get ready; اسْتَعَدَّ لِشَيْءٍ to prepare (oneself) for sth; اسْتَعَدَّ لِامْتِحانٍ to prepare for an exam; اسْتَعَدَّ لِلبَرْدِ to prepare for the cold; اسْتَعَدَّ لِلرَحيل to get ready to leave; اسْتَعَدَّ لِحَفْلَةٍ to get ready for a party; اسْتَعَدَّ لِفِعْلِ شَيْءٍ to prepare to do sth

عَدَد *n* |أَعْداد| **1** [كَمِّيَّة] number; quantity; عَدَد مَشْؤوم an unlucky number; عَدَد غَيْر مَعْروفٍ \ مُحَدَّدٍ an unknown/ unspecified number; العَدَد النِهائيّ the final number; بِأَعْدادٍ كَبيرةٍ in large numbers; أَعْداد مُتَزايِدة an increasing number **2** [عَدَد من] عَدَد من a number of, some, several; عَدَد من الأَطْفالِ \ الناسِ a number of children/people; عَدَد من البَناتِ والأَوْلادِ a number of girls and boys; قَرَأْتُ عَدَداً من الكُتُبِ I read several books; سَقَطَ عَدَدٌ كَبيرٌ من الجَرْحى many people were injured **3** [رَقْم] number, figure; عَدَد صَحيح a whole number; عَدَد كَسْريّ a fraction; عَدَد طَبيعيّ a natural number; عَدَد موجَب \ سالِب a positive/negative number; عَدَد زَوْجيّ \ فَرْديّ an even/odd number; عَدَد أَوَّليّ prime (number); عَدَد قابِل \ غَيْر قابِلٍ للقِسْمةِ a divisible/ prime number; عَدَد مُرَكَّب a complex number; عَدَد تَخَيُّليّ an imaginary number; عَدَد حَقيقيّ \ جِذْريّ a real/rational number; عَدَد أَصْليّ \ رَئيسيّ cardinal (number); عَدَد تَرْتيبيّ ordinal (number) **4** [مَطْبوعة] number, issue; عَدَد خاصّ special issue; عَدَد تَجْريبيّ free trial issue **5** [من إِصْحاحٍ] verse; من إِنْجيل لوقا الإِصْحاح ١٠–العَدَد ٨ St Luke, chapter 10, verse 8

عَدّ *n* count, counting; عَدّ تَنازُليّ \ عَكْسيّ countdown; قابِل للعَدِّ countable; denumerable; أَعادَ العَدَّ to recount

عَدّاد *n* |عَدّادات| meter; counter; عَدّاد الكَهْرَباءِ electricity meter; عَدّاد سُرْعةٍ speedometer; عَدّاد الكيلومِتْراتِ milometer (BrE), odometer (AmE); عَدّاد زوّارِ المَوْقِعِ Web/hit counter; على العَدّادِ on the meter; فَتَحَ سائِقُ سَيّارةِ الأُجْرةِ العَدّادَ the taxi driver switched on the meter

عِداد *n* number; quantity; كانَ في عِدادِ المَفْقودينَ to be among the dead

عُدّة *n* |عُدَد| **1** [آلات] equipment, kit; tools, instruments **2** [اسْتِعْداد] preparedness; أَعَدَّ العُدَّةَ (لِشَيْءٍ) to really prepare (for sth)

عِدّة *n* |عِدَد| **1** [عَدَد من] a few, several; عِدّة آلافٍ a few thousand; عِدّة أَيّامٍ a few days; عِدّة رِجالٍ مَشْهورينَ some famous men; عِدّةَ مَرّاتٍ several times; قبل عِدّةِ أَشْهُرٍ some months ago; كُتُب عِدّة some books; من وُجوهٍ عِدّةٍ in many respects **2** (Isl Law) *legally prescribed period of waiting before a woman can remarry*; مُنْقَضِية العِدّةِ *a woman whose waiting period has expired*; انْقَضَتْ عِدَّتُها *her waiting period has expired*

عَدَديّ *adj* numeral, numerical; in number; التَفَوُّق العَدَديّ numerical superiority

عَديد *adj* many, numerous; العَديد من الإِمْكانيّاتِ numerous possibilities; العَديد من الإِيجابيّاتِ many advantages; أَنْواع عَديدة various kinds; سَنَوات عَديدة many years

اسْتِعْداد *n* |اسْتِعْدادات| **1** [قابِليّة] readiness, preparedness; willingness; عَدَم الاسْتِعْدادِ unwillingness; الاسْتِعْداد للتَفاوُضِ preparedness to negotiate; أَبْدى اسْتِعْداداً to indicate a willingness; على اسْتِعْدادٍ ready, prepared; willing; كانَ على أُهْبةِ الاسْتِعْدادِ to be on standby; to be on high alert; نَحْنُ على اسْتِعْدادٍ أَنْ نَحْضُرَ المُؤْتَمَرَ we are prepared to attend to the conference; أنا على أَتَمِّ الاسْتِعْدادِ I'm totally prepared **2** [إِجْراء ضَروريّ] preparation; اسْتِعْداداً ل in preparation to/for; اسْتِعْدادات preparations, preliminaries; الاسْتِعْدادات للحَفْلِ preparations for the party; قامَ ب \ أَجْرى \ اتَّخَذَ اسْتِعْداداتٍ to make preparations; يَجْري الاسْتِعْدادُ the preparations are in full swing

اعْتِداد *n* esteem; significance; عَدَم الاعْتِدادِ irrelevance; كانَ عَدَمَ الاعْتِدادِ (Law) to not be invoked; الاعْتِداد بالنَفْسِ self-esteem

مَعْدود *adj* a few, some; little; في ثوانٍ مَعْدودةٍ in a few seconds; أيّام مَعْدودة a few days

عَدَس *n coll* lentil (*Lens culinaris*); شُرْبة عَدَسٍ lentil soup; عَدَس الماءِ duckweed, water lentil (*Lemnaceae*)

عَدَسة *n* 1 [قُرْص من مادّةٍ شَفّافةٍ] lens; glass; عَدَسة مُكَبِّرة magnifying glass; عَدَسة قَوِيّة a strong lens; عَدَسة مُحَدَّبة \ مُقَعَّرة a convex/concave lens; عَدَسات نَظّاراتٍ eyeglass lenses; عَدَسة كاميرا camera lens 2 [لاصِقة] (contact) lens; عَدَسة لاصِقة contact lens, contacts; عَدَسات لَيِّنة \ صَلْبة soft/hard lenses; رَكَّبَ \ خلَعَ العَدَساتِ to put in/remove lenses; اسْتَعْمَلَ العَدَساتِ اللاصِقة to wear contacts

عَدَلَ *v* 1 |عن; عُدول| [تَخلّى] to turn away from; to abandon; عَدَلَ عن مَشْروعٍ to abandon a plan; عَدَلَ عن رَأْيِهِ to change one's opinion 2 [أَنْصَفَ] |عَدالة, عَدْل| to act justly; عَدَلَ الشَخْصَ بالشَخْصِ to treat two people equally 3 [ساوى] |عَدْل| to equal, to be equivalent to; تَعْدِلُ صَلاةُ الجَماعةِ ٢٧ ضِعْفاً صَلاةَ الفَرْدِ performing prayer in congregation is 27 times better than performing it alone

عَدَّلَ *v* 1 [أَجْرى التَغْييرَ] to change, to alter, to modify; to revise; to amend; to costumize; عَدَّلَ نَصًّا to revise a text; عَدَّلَ سِياسةَ الدَعْمِ الحُكوميِّ to restructure the policy on subsidies; عَدَّلَ مَشْروعَ قانونٍ to modify a bill; عَدَّلَ القانونَ \ الدُسْتورَ to amend the law/constitution 2 [سَوّى] adjust; عَدَّلَ المِرْآةَ الخارِجيّةَ لِسَيّارَتِهِ to adjust the outside mirror of one's car; عَدَّلَ الخُطّةَ to adjust the plan; عَدَّلَ الميزانَ to adjust the scale; عَدَّلَ مَسيرةَ الحُكومةِ to adjust the course of the government

عادَلَ *v* 1 [سَوّى] to equalize; عادَلَ نَتيجةَ المُباراةِ to level the score 2 [ساوى] to be equal/equivalent to; to be level with; to counterbalance; عادَلَ أَلْفَ دولار to be equal to one thousand dollars; عادَلَ بين الغَنيِّ وَبَيْنَ الفَقيرِ to treat rich and poor equally

تَعَدَّلَ *v* to be changed/altered/modified

تَعادَلَ *v* to be/become equal; to draw with, to tie with; تَعادَلَ الفَريقانِ the two teams tied; تَعادَلَت الأَصْواتُ the votes were evenly split

إعْداد *n* 1 [تَهْيِئة] preparation; إعْداد وَجْبةٍ the preparation of a meal; مَدْرَسة إعْدادِ المُعَلِّمينَ teacher training college; كانَ بِصَدَدِ إعْدادِ شَيْءٍ to be in the process of preparing sth 2 (Comput) installation; setting; كَيْفيّة إعْدادِ ويندوز how to install Windows; إعْدادات شَخْصيّة personal settings

إعْداديّ *adj* preparatory; مَدْرَسة إعْداديّة preparatory school (BrE); middle school (AmE); junior high school (AmE); مُعَسْكَر إعْداديّ (Sport) training camp

تَعْداد *n* |تَعْدادات| enumeration; تَعْداد سُكّانيّ \ سُكّانٍ population; تَعْداد صِفاتِ شَيْءٍ \ شَخْصٍ enumeration of sb's/sth's qualities

تَعَدُّد *n* multiplicity, plurality, multi-; تَعَدُّد الزَوْجاتِ polygamy; تَعَدُّد الاسْتِعْمالِ multi-use; تَعَدُّد الخِياراتِ many options; التَعَدُّد اللُغَويّ, تَعَدُّد اللُغاتِ multilingualism

تَعَدُّديّ *adj* multiple; نِظام سِياسيّ تَعَدُّديّ multi-party system

تَعَدُّديّة *n* pluralism, multi-; نِظام التَعَدُّديّةِ الحِزْبيّةِ multiparty system; تَعَدُّديّة سِياسيّة political pluralism; تَعَدُّديّة ثَقافيّة multiculturalism

مُتَعَدِّد *adj* numerous, multiple, multi-; various; وَسائط مُتَعَدِّدة multimedia; احْتِمالات مُتَعَدِّدة various possibilities; مُتَعَدِّد الأَشْكالِ multiform, polymorphous; اخْتِيارات مُتَعَدِّدة various choices, many options; multiple-choice; مُتَعَدِّد اللُغاتِ multilingual; المَغْرِبُ بَلَدٌ مُتَعَدِّدُ اللُغاتِ Morocco is a multilingual country; مُجْتَمَع مُتَعَدِّد الثَقافاتِ a multicultural society; قُوّات مُتَعَدِّدة الجِنْسيّاتِ multinational forces; في أَماكِنَ مُتَعَدِّدةٍ in various places

مُسْتَعِدّ *adj* prepared, ready; willing, inclined; كانَ مُسْتَعِدًّا لِشَيْءٍ to be prepared for sth; كانَ مُسْتَعِدًّا لِفِعْلِ شَيْءٍ to be willing to do sth; كانَ مُسْتَعِدًّا لِتَقْديمِ تنازُلاتٍ to be ready to make concessions, to be willing to compromise; الطائِرةُ مُسْتَعِدّةٌ للانْطِلاقِ the plane is ready for take-off; غَيْر مُسْتَعِدٍّ unprepared, unwilling

مُعْتَدّ *adj* proud; arrogant

مُعَدّ *adj* prepared, made; مُعَدّ في البَيْتِ home-made

مُعَدّات *n pl* equipment; materials; مُعَدّات عَسْكَرِيّة military equipment

مِعْداد *n* |مَعاديدُ| abacus

تَعادُل الفَريقَيْنِ 0-0 tie; هَدَف التَعادُلِ equalizer; تَعادُل سَلْبيّ the teams tied 2-2; خَرَجَ بالتَعادُلِ to end in بِهَدَفَيْنِ لِكُلٍّ مِنْهُما a draw 3 (Chem) neutralization

تَعادُليّ *adj* equalizing; balanced; الهَدَف التَعادُليّ the equalizer

تَعْديل *n* |تَعْديلات| change, alteration, modification; adjustment; amendment; costumization; تَعْديل وِزاريّ cabinet reshuffle; تَعْديل القَواعِد adjustment of the rules; اقْتِراح تَعْديلِ a proposed amendment; حَقّ التَعْديلِ the right of amendment; اقْتَرَحَ \ قَدَّمَ تَعْديلاً to introduce an amendment; قَبِلَ تَعْديلاً to accept an amendment; أَدْخَلَ تَعْديلاً to make a modification

تَعْديليّ *adj* modulating; مَخْزون تَعْديليّ reserve stock; مَرْسوم تَعْديليّ amendment decree

مُتَعادِل *adj* balanced; equal; tied; وَضَعَ شَخْصاً على مُسْتَوًى مُتَعادِلٍ مع ... to put sb on the same level with ...; خَرَجَ الفَريقانِ مُتَعادِلَيْنِ the teams came out tied

مُعادِل A *adj* equal; equivalent

B *n* equivalent

مُعادَلة *n* 1 [مُساواة] equalization, leveling 2 (Math) equation; مُعادَلة بِمَجْهولَيْنِ an equation with two unknowns; مُعادَلة تَرْبيعيّة ,من الدَرَجةِ الثانِيةِ a quadratic equation

مُعْتَدِل A *adj* moderate, temperate, mild; مُناخ \ جَوّ مُعْتَدِل a temperate climate; المَناطِق المُعْتَدِلة the temperate zones; سُرْعة مُعْتَدِلة moderate speed; تَيّار مُعْتَدِل a moderate movement; مَوْقِف مُعْتَدِل a moderate point of view; مَطالِب مُعْتَدِلة moderate demands; مُعْتَدِل السَعةِ \ القامةِ medium-sized

B *n* moderate

مُعَدَّل A *adj* changed, modified; revised; غَيْر مُعَدَّلٍ unchanged

B *n* |مُعَدَّلات| 1 [مُتَوَسِّط] average, mean; المُعَدَّل القَوْميّ the national average; مُعَدَّل السُرْعةِ the average speed; فوق \ تحت المُعَدَّلِ above/below average; تَجاوَزَ \ تَعَدّى المُعَدَّلَ to rise above the average; ارْتَفَعَت دَرَجةُ الحَرارةِ عَشْرَ دَرَجاتٍ عن مُعَدَّلِها الطَبيعيّ the temperature was ten degrees above normal 2 [نِسْبة] rate; مُعَدَّل المَواليدِ birth rate; مُعَدَّل ثابت fixed rate; مُعَدَّل صَرْفٍ exchange rate; مُعَدَّل نَقْلِ البَياناتِ bandwidth

اعْتَدَلَ *v* 1 [تَوَسَّطَ] to be moderate; to be balanced; اعْتَدَلَ المِيزانُ to balance the scales; to make a balance 2 [اسْتَقامَ] to straighten up; اعْتَدَلَ في جِلْسَتِهِ to sit straight

عَدْل A *adj* |عُدول| fair, honest; لَيْسَ عَدْلاً that is unfair; شاهِد عَدْلٍ an honest witness

B *n* 1 [إنْصاف] justice; وِزارة العَدْلِ Ministry/Department of Justice; وَزير العَدْلِ the Minister of Justice; كاتِب العَدْلِ notary (public); دار \ قَصْر العَدْلِ the Palace of Justice, the law court; مَحْكَمة العَدْلِ الدُوَليّة the International Court of Justice; روح العَدْلِ والإنْصافِ sense of justice; بِعَدْلٍ وَإنْصافٍ in all fairness; أَقامَ العَدْلَ to see justice done; قَسَّمَ شَيْئاً بِعَدْلٍ to divide sth fairly 2 (Islam) العَدْل the Just (*one of the names of God*)

عَدَل *n* |عُدول| (Mor) notary witness

عِدْل *n* |عُدول, أَعْدال| saddlebag

عادِل A *adj* just, fair; غَيْر عادِلٍ unjust, unfair; تَقْسيم عادِل a fair distribution; حُكْم عادِل a just verdict; مُعامَلة عادِلة fair treatment

B *n* Adil, Adel (*male given name*)

عَدالة *n* 1 [إنْصاف] justice; العَدالة الاجْتِماعيّة social justice; سَيْف العَدالةِ the sword of justice; انْعِدام \ غِياب العَدالةِ injustice; حَقَّقَ العَدالةَ to achieve justice; تَجْري العَدالةُ مَجْراها justice taking its course 2 [سُلْطة قَضائيّة] justice; دار العَدالةِ the Palace of Justice; قَصْر العَدالةِ (NA) courthouse, the Palace of Justice

عَدْليّ *adj* judicial; forensic; notarial; وَثيقة عَدْليّة a judicial document

عُدول *n* rescinding; reversing; عُدول خِطْبَتِهِ breaking one's engagement; عُدول اسْتِقالَتِهِ rescinding one's resignation

عَديل *n* |عُدَلاءُ| 1 [مَثيل] equal; هذا اللاعِبُ لَيْسَ لَهُ عَديلٌ this player is unequalled 2 [زَوْج أُخْتِ الزَوْجةِ] brother-in-law (*husband of one's wife's sister*)

اعْتِدال *n* moderation; بِاعْتِدالٍ moderately, in moderation; أَكَلَ \ شَرِبَ بِاعْتِدالٍ to eat/drink moderately

اعْتِداليّ *adj*, *n* moderate

تَعادُل *n* |تَعادُلات| 1 [تَكافُؤ] equality; تَعادُل الأَصْواتِ an equal number of votes 2 (Sport) draw, tie; تَعادُل بِدونِ أَهْدافٍ,

‹ **عَدِمَ** *v* |a| عَدَم| to lack; to miss; عُدِمَ to be lacking; to have disappeared

أَعْدَمَ *v* to execute; أَعْدَمَ شَخْصاً رَمْياً بالرَصاصِ to bring sb before a firing squad; أَعْدَمَ شَخْصاً شَنْقاً to execute sb by hanging; أَعْدَمَ شَخْصاً بِسَبَبِ جَرِيمةِ قَتْلٍ to execute sb for murder; أُعْدِمَ دون مُحاكَمةٍ to be executed without trial

انْعَدَمَ *v* to disappear; to be absent; انْعَدَمَ الخَوْفُ من قَلْبِهِ there was no more fear in his heart

عَدَم *n* 1 [لا شَيْء] nothing; من العَدَمِ out of nothing 2 [فِقْدان] lack, want, absence; un-, in-, non-; عَدَم الاسْتِعْدادِ unwillingness; عَدَم التَسامُحِ intolerance; عَدَم الشَرْعِيّةِ unlawfulness; illegitimacy; عَدَم النَوْمِ insomnia; عَدَم الإمْكانِيّةِ impossibility; عَدَم التَنْظِيمِ disorganisation; عَدَم التَدَخُّلِ non-intervention; عَدَم اسْتِقْرارٍ instability; عَدَم الاهْتِمامِ lack of interest; عَدَم الكَفاءةِ incompetence; لِعَدَمِ كِفايةِ الأَدِلّةِ for lack of evidence; أَكَّدَ عَدَمَ وُجودِ أَيّةِ مَشاكِلَ بين البَلَدَيْنِ he assured that there was no problem at all between the two countries

عادِم A *adj* 1 [غَيْر مَوْجودٍ] non-existent 2 [الكيمْياء والصَيْدَلة] waste; مِياه عادِمة waste water

B *n* |عَوادِمُ| exhaust fumes/gas; waste; غاز العادِمِ exhaust gas; أُنْبوب عَوادِمِ \ أُنْبوب العادِمِ \ العَوادِمِ exhaust, tailpipe; أُنْبوب العادِمِ \ العَوادِمِ سَيّارةٍ the tailpipe of a car; صِمام العادِمِ exhaust valve; انْبِعاث غازاتِ العَوادِمِ the emission of exhaust fumes

عَدَمِيّ A *adj* nihilistic

B *n* nihilist

عَدَمِيّة *n* nihilism

عَديم *adj* |عُدَماءُ| 1 [فَقير] poor 2 [بِلا] lacking; deprived of; without, -less, un-; عَديم الحَرَكةِ motionless; عَديم الحَياءِ lifeless; عَديم الأَهَمِّيّةِ unimportant; عَديم الحُقوقِ without rights; عَديم الشَفَقةِ pitiless, without mercy; عَديم العاطِفة unfeeling

إعْدام *n* |إعْدامات| execution; إعْدام فَوْرِيّ a summary execution; إعْدام الجاني execution of the culprit; الإعْدام شَنْقاً death by hanging; الإعْدام رَمْياً بالرَصاصِ execution by a firing squad; عُقوبة الإعْدامِ the death penalty; حُكْم بالإعْدام a death sentence; حَكَمَ على شَخْصٍ بالإعْدامِ to sentence sb to death; نَفَّذَ حُكْماً بالإعْدامِ to execute/carry out the death sentence; يُعاقَبُ على القَتْلِ بالإعْدامِ the punishment for murder is the death penalty

انْعِدام *n* |انْعِدامات| lack, absence; un-, in-, non-, -less; انْعِدام الثِقةِ a lack of confidence; انْعِدام إمْكانِيّةٍ impossibility; انْعِدام الأَمْنِ insecurity; انْعِدام الجاذِبِيّة weightlessness, zero gravity

مُعْدِم *adj* poor

مَعْدوم *n* absent; wanting, non-existent; كانَ دَوْرُهُ مَعْدوماً he had no role; أَصْبَحَت الفُرَصُ مَعْدومةً there are no more chances

مُنْعَدِم *adj* non-existent, wanting

‹ **عَدَن** *n* |dipt f| Aden (*city in Yemen*); خَليج عَدَنَ the Gulf of Aden

عَدْن *n* Eden; جَنّة عَدْنٍ the Garden of Eden

تَعْدين *n* mining

تَعْدينيّ *adj* mining (*before n*); مَصالِح تَعْدينيّة mining interests

مَعْدِن *n* |مَعادِنُ| mineral; metal; مَعادِن خَفيفة \ ثَقيلة light/heavy metals; مَعادِن نَفيسة \ ثَمينة \ كَريمة precious metals; مَعْدِن خام ore; عِلْم المَعادِنِ mineralogy; صِناعة المَعادِنِ metal industry; صِناعة تَحْويلِ المَعادِنِ metalworking industry; اسْتِخْراج المَعادِنِ mining; كَلَل المَعادِنِ metal fatigue; من المَعْدِنِ metal (*before n*); لَبَّسَ المَعادِنَ to refine metals

مَعْدِنيّ *adj* metal (*before n*); mineral (*before n*); شَمْعَدان مَعْدِنيّ a metal candle holder; زُيوت مَعْدِنيّة mineral oils; ماء مَعْدِنيّ mineral water

‹ **عَدْنان** *n* |dipt| Adnan (*male given name*); *name of the traditional ancestor of the Adnani Arabs of northern, central and western Arabia*

‹ **عَدا** *v* |u| 1 [رَكَضَ] |عَدْو| to run; to race; to trot; يَعْدو الحِصانُ the horse trots 2 [ظَلَمَ] |عُدْوان, عَداء; على| be hostile towards sb; to treat unjustly 3 [عَدّى عن] |عَدْو| to exceed, to go beyond; لا يَعْدو أَنْ يَكونَ ... , لا يَعْدو كَوْنَهُ ... it's no more than ...; لا يَعْدو أَنْ يَكونَ كَذّاباً he is just a liar; لا يَعْدو كَوْنَهُ حِبْراً على وَرَقٍ it's nothing more than ink on paper 4 [سَرَقَ] |عَدْو; على| to steal; عَدا على شَيْءٍ to steal sth

عَدّى *v* 1 [عَبَرَ] to cross; عَدّى نَهْراً to cross a river 2 [أَغْفَلَ] |عن| to leave, to abandon

عادى *v* to be hostile to; عادى شَخْصاً to be hostile towards sb

عَدّاء *n* runner, racer; عَدّاء المَسافاتِ الطَويلةِ a long-distance runner; عَدّاء جَيِّد \ سَريع a good/fast runner

عِدائيّ, عَدائيّ *adj* hostile, inimical; war-minded; اتَّخَذَ مَوْقِفاً عَدائيًّا to be hostile; لُغة عَدائيّة hostile language; نَظَرات عَدائيّة hostile glances

عَداوة *n* hostility, animosity, enmity; عاشَ في عَداوةٍ to live in hostility; دَخَلَ في عَداوةٍ to enter into hostilities; كَشَحَ لِشَخْصٍ بالعَداوة to nurture hostile feelings

عَدْوائيّ *adj* infectious; مَرَض عَدْوائيّ an infectious disease

عُدْوان *n* aggression, hostile action; hostility; يَسْتَمِرُّ العُدْوانُ hostilities continue; العُدْوان الثُلاثيّ the Tripartite Aggression (*the Suez crisis*)

عُدْوانيّ *adj* hostile; aggressive; نَظَرات عُدْوانيّة hostile glances; مَوْقِف عُدْوانيّ hostility

عُدْوانيّة *n* aggressiveness, aggression; hostility

عَدْوى *n* |f| infection, contamination; عَدْوى فَيْروسيّة \ بَكْتيريّة a viral/bacterial infection; خطَر العَدْوى danger of infection; مَصْدَر عَدْوى a source of infection; الوِقاية من \ مُحارَبة العَدْوى prevention of infection; انْتِقال عَدْوى contamination; نَقَلَ عَدْوى to spread an infection; أُصيبَ بِعَدْوى to be infected; عَدْوى ب ... an infection with...

اعْتِداء *n* |اعْتِداءات| attack, assault; اعْتِداء جِنْسيّ sexual assault; اعْتِداء عَنيف a violent attack; اعْتِداء بَدَنيّ physical aggression; مُنَفِّذ اعْتِداءٍ attacker; اعْتِداء واغْتِصاب assault and rape; مُعاهَدة عَدَمِ الاعْتِداءِ non-aggression pact; اعْتِداء على شَخْصٍ \ شَيْءٍ an attack on sb/sth; تَسَبَّبَ الاعْتِداءُ في مَقْتَلِ شَخْصَيْنِ the attack took the lives of two people

تَعَدٍّ *n* |تَعَدِّيات| ❶ [اعْتِداء] assault ❷ [على الحُقوقِ] violation, infringement; التَعَدّي على حُقوقِ شَخْصٍ violation of sb's rights

مُتَعَدٍّ *adj* (Gram) transitive; فِعْل مُتَعَدٍّ a transitive verb; فِعْل غَيْر مُتَعَدٍّ an intransitive verb

مُعادٍ *adj* hostile; مُعادٍ لِشَيْءٍ \ شَخْصٍ hostile to sth/towards sb

مُعاداة *n* hostility, animosity; anti-; مُعاداة الساميّةِ anti-Semitism; مُعاداة الأَجانِبِ xenophobia

مُعْتَدٍ *n* aggressor, attacker

أَعْدى *v* to infect, to contaminate; أَعْدى شَخْصاً to infect sb; أَعْدى شَخْصاً بِمَرَضٍ \ بفيروسٍ to infect sb with a disease/virus

تَعَدّى *v* ❶ [جاوَزَ] to exceed; تَعَدّى السُرْعةَ to speed, to exceed the speed limit; تَعَدّى الحُدود to exceed the limits; لا يَتَعَدّى العِشْرينَ من عُمْرِهِ he is under twenty years old; لا يَتَعَدّى أَنْ يَكونَ ... ,كَوْنَهُ ... it's nothing more than ...; لا يَتَعَدّى كَوْنَهُ شائعةً it's nothing more than rumors ❷ [ظَلَمَ] |على| to attack, to assault; to violate; تَعَدّى على مُمْتَلَكاتِ الغَيْرِ to vandalize sb else's property; تَعَدّى على حُقوقِ شَخْصٍ to infringe on sb's rights ❸ (Gram) to be transitive; يَتَعَدّى هذا الفِعْلُ إلى مَفْعولٍ this verb has an object

تَعادى *v* to be hostile to one another

اعْتَدى *v* ❶ [هَجَمَ] |على| to attack, to assault; to batter, to molest; اعْتَدى على شَخْصٍ to assault sb; اعْتَدى بالضَرْبِ to lay hands upon sb, to come to blows with sb ❷ [اغْتَصَبَ] |على| to rape, to violate, to (sexually) assault; اعْتَدى على امْرَأةٍ to rape a woman

اسْتَعْدى *v* |على| to ask for help/assistance; اسْتَعْدى على شَخْصٍ to ask sb for help/assistance

عَدوّ *n* |أَعْداء, عِدًى| ❶ [خَصْم] enemy; عَدوّ لَدود \ أَلَدّ mortal enemy; عَدوّ الدَوْلةِ enemy of the state; عَدوّ في ثَوْبِ صَديقٍ ≈ a wolf in sheep's clothing; جَعَلَ شَخْصاً عَدوًّا لَهُ to make an enemy of sb; لَدَيْهِ أَعْداءٌ كَثيرونَ he has many enemies ❷ (Mil) enemy; جُنود العَدوِّ the enemy soldiers; جَيْش \ نيران العَدوِّ (the) enemy army/fire; مِنْطَقة العَدوِّ enemy territory; قاتَلَ \ دَحَرَ \ هَزَمَ العَدوَّ to fight/roll back/beat the enemy

عَدْو *n* (Sport) race; running

عادِية *n* |عادِيات, عَوادٍ| ❶ [مُصيبة] setback, adversity; misfortune ❷ (Islam) سورة العادِيات The Coursers (*Sura 100*)

عَدا *particle* ما عَدا except (from), apart from, save, but; كُلّ أَيّامِ الأُسْبوعِ ما عَدا يَوْمَ الجُمْعةِ every day except Friday; فيما عَدا ذلك apart from that

عَداء, عِداء *n* |عَداءات| hostility, animosity; anti-; العَداء للساميّةِ anti-Semitism; أَوْقَفَ \ اسْتَأْنَفَ العَداءَ to suspend/resume hostilities

عُذْر *n* |أَعْذار| excuse; عُذْر غَيْر مَقْبولٍ a bad/poor excuse; دون عُذْرٍ مَقْبولٍ without a valid excuse; اخْتَلَقَ عُذْراً to concoct an excuse; التَمَسَ \ انْتَحَلَ الأَعْذارَ to make up excuses; تَعَلَّلَ بِعُذْرٍ to use an excuse; قَدَّمَ عُذْراً to give an excuse; لا عُذْرَ لِهَذا there is no excuse for it; عُذْر أَقْبَح من ذَنْبٍ *the excuse is worse than the sin*

عَذْراء *n* |dipt f; عَذْراوات, عَذارى| ⟨1⟩ [بِكْر] virgin; (بُرْج) العَذْراءِ Virgo; مَرْيَم العَذْراء the Virgin Mary; الطَبيعة العَذْراء virgin nature ⟨2⟩ [حَشَراتٍ] pupa, cocoon

عُذْرة *n* virginity

عُذْريّ *n* ⟨1⟩ [من قَبيلة عُذْرة] Udhri; حُبّ عُذْريّ Udhri love (*genre of classical love poetry characterized by unfulfilled longing*) ⟨2⟩ [عَفيف] chaste; virginal; تَوالُد عُذْريّ (Bio) parthenogenesis; الوِلادة العُذْريّة the Virgin Birth

عُذْريّة *n* virginity; فَقَدَتْ عُذْريَّتَها to lose one's virginity

اعْتِذار *n* |اعْتِذارات| apology, excuse; اعْتِذار صادِق a sincere apology; قَبِلَ اعْتِذارَ شَخْصٍ to accept sb's apologies; مع اعْتِذارِنا على ... with our apologies for ...; قَدَمَ اعْتِذارَهُ عن عَدَمِ حَضورِ شَيْءٍ to apologize for one's inability to attend sth, to turn down the invitation to sth

تَعَذُّر *n* impossibility; في حالِ تَعَذُّرِ تَوْفيرِ شَيْءٍ in case sth is not able to be provided; بِسَبَبِ تَعَذُّرِ قُدومِ شَخْصٍ because of absence of sb

مُتَعَذِّر *adj* impossible, unfeasible, impracticable; كانَ أَمْراً مُتَعَذِّراً to be impossible; من المُتَعَذِّر أن ... it's impossible to ...

مَعْذِرة *n* |مَعاذِرُ| excuse, forgiveness; المَعْذِرة sorry, forgive me; مَعْذِرة طِبِّيّة a medical excuse, a doctor's note; رَجا المَعْذِرةَ من شَخْصٍ عن شَيْءٍ to beg sb's pardon for sth

عِذْق *n* |أَعْذاق, عُذوق| cluster, bunch

عَذَلَ *v* |u; عَذْل| to reproach, to blame; عَذَلَ شَخْصاً to blame sb

عَذْل, عَذَل *n* reproach, blame; سَبَقَ السَيْفُ العَذَلَ ≈ the die has been cast

عاذِل *n* |عُذّال| critic, censurer

عَرَّبَ *v* to Arabize; to Arabicize, to translate into Arabic

أَعْرَبَ *v* ⟨1⟩ [عَبَّرَ] |عن| to put into words; to express, to utter; أَعْرَبَ عن أَسَفِهِ to express one's regret ⟨2⟩ (Gram) to inflect, to decline; أَعْرَبَ اسْماً to decline a noun

مُعْدٍ *adj* infectious, contagious; مَرَض مُعْدٍ an infectious disease; ضَحِك مُعْدٍ contagious laughter

مَعْدى *n* escape; لا مَعْدى عَنْهُ there is no escape from it

مُعَدِّية *n* ferry, ferry boat; سافَرَ بالمُعَدِّية إلى إنْجِلْترا to go to England by ferry

عَذُبَ *v* |u; عُذوبة| to be/become sweet; to be/become fresh

عَذَّبَ *v* to torture; to abuse; to torment; عَذَّبَ سَجيناً \ مُعارِضينَ سِياسيّينَ to torture a prisoner/political opponents; عَذَّبَ طِفْلاً to abuse a child

تَعَذَّبَ *v* to be tortured/tormented

اسْتَعْذَبَ *v* to find sweet/pleasant/agreeable; اسْتَعْذَبَ شَيْئاً to like/enjoy sth; اسْتَعْذَبَ الغِناءَ to like the singing

عَذْب *adj* |عِذاب| sweet; nice, agreeable, pleasant; fresh; ماء عَذْب fresh water; طَعام عَذْب nice food; حَديث عَذْب sweet/kind words

عَذاب *n* |عَذابات, أَعْذِبة| torture, torment; agony; عَذاب طَويل long agony

عُذوبة *n* charm; sweetness

تَعْذيب *n* torture, torment; abuse; تَعْذيب نَفْسيّ psychological abuse; مُعَسْكَر للتَعْذيب prison camp; تَعَرَّضَ للتَعْذيبِ to be tortured

مُعَذِّب **A** *adj* painful, tormenting, agonizing **B** *n* tormentor

عَذَرَ *v* |i; عُذْر, مَعْذِرة| to excuse; to forgive; عَذَرَ شَخْصاً to forgive sb

أَعْذَرَ *v* ⟨1⟩ [الشَخْصُ] to have an excuse; قد أَعْذَرَ مَنْ أَنْذَرَ *one who has given fair warning is absolved of blame* ⟨2⟩ [الشَخْصَ] to forgive; to excuse; أَعْذَرَ شَخْصاً to forgive sb

تَعَذَّرَ *v* to be impossible; تَعَذَّرَ التَأَكُّد من شَيْءٍ to be impossible to verify sth; تَعَذَّرَ عَلَيْهِ الذَهابُ بِسَبَبِ ... he couldn't go because ...

اعْتَذَرَ *v* ⟨1⟩ [تَأَسَّفَ] to apologize; اعْتَذَرَ عن تَصَرُّفِهِ to apologize for one's behaviour; اعْتَذَرَ إلى \ ل شَخْصٍ to apologize to sb ⟨2⟩ [عن الحُضورِ] to decline, to beg off, to turn down, to send one's regrets; اعْتَذَرَ عن حُضورِ الحَفْلةِ to decline the invitation to the party

تَعَرَّبَ *v* to become an Arab; *to adopt the language and customs of the Arabs*

اِسْتَعْرَبَ *v* 1 [كانَ مُسْتَعْرِباً] to be an Arabist 2 [تَعَرَّبَ] *to adopt the language and customs of the Arabs*

عَرّاب *n* godfather

عَرّابة *n* godmother; العَرّاب والعَرّابة godfather and godmother, godparents

عَرَبة *n* cart; coach, carriage; wagon; car, vehicle; عَرَبة يَدَوِيّة \ عَرَبة يَدٍ wheelbarrow; عَرَبة مُدَرَّعة armoured car; عَرَبة بَرْمائيّة amphibious vehicle; عَرَبة إسْعافٍ ambulance; عَرَبة أطْفالٍ pram (BrE), stroller (AmE)

عَرَبيّ A *adj* |عَرَب| Arab, Arabian; Arabic; دُوَل عَرَبيّة Arab countries; شِبْه الجَزيرةِ العَرَبيّةِ the Arabian Peninsula; اللُغة العَرَبيّة Arabic (*language*); الأدَب العَرَبيّ Arabic literature B *n* |عَرَب| Arab; جَزيرة العَرَبِ the Arabian Peninsula; كَلام العَرَبِ Arabic (*language*)

عُروبة *n* Arabism; pan-Arabism

عُروبيّ *adj, n* pan-Arabist

اِسْتِعْراب *n European interest in Arabic language and culture*

إعْراب *n* |إعْرابات| (Gram) declension, case (endings); marking declension/case; إعْراب اسْمٍ the declension of a noun; marking a noun's case; إعْراب جُمْلةٍ declension of a sentence; marking the case endings of a sentence; مَحَلُّ هذه الكَلِمةِ من الإعْراب مَفْعولٌ بِهِ the declension of this word marks it as the object of the sentence

إعْرابيّ *adj* حالة إعْرابيّة declension, case

أعْرابيّ *adj, n* |أعْراب| Bedouin

تَعْريب *n* Arabization

مُسْتَعْرِب *n* Arabist

مُعْرَب *adj* declinable

مُعَرَّب *adj* Arabized; translated into Arabic

‹ **عَرْبَدَ** *v* |i; عَرْبَدة| to revel (drunkenly), to carouse

عَرْبَدة *n* drunken revelry; binge; orgy

عِرْبيد *n* drunken reveler, carouser

مُعَرْبِد *n* roisterous, boisterous (*associated with drinking*)

‹ **عَرْبَنَ** *v* |i; عَرْبَنة| to make a down payment

عُرْبون, عَرَبون *n* |عَرابينُ| down payment, deposit; token; عُرْبون تَقْديرٍ a token of appreciation

‹ **عَرَبيزيّ** *n* Arabizi (*Arabic written with Latin characters and numbers on the Internet and phones*)

‹ **عَرَجَ, عَرِجَ** *v* |a-u; عُروج, عَرَج, عَرَجان| to limp, to hobble

عَرَّجَ *v* 1 [تَوَقَّفَ] to stop/pass (by), to halt; عَرَّجَ ب \ على مَكانٍ (في طَريقِهِ) to stop by someplace (on one's way) 2 [انْحَرَفَ] to turn; عَرَّجَ عن الطَريق to turn off the road 3 [تَعَرَّجَ] to zigzag

أعْرَجَ *v* to cripple, to lame

تَعَرَّجَ *v* to wind, to curve, to meander; تَعَرَّجَ الطَريقُ the road was winding

اِنْعَرَجَ *v* 1 [الطَريقُ] to wind, to curve, to meander 2 [عن الطَريق] to turn; انْعَرَجَ عن الطَريقِ to turn off the road

أعْرَج A *adj* |dipt; عُرْج| lame, cripple; حِصان أعْرَج a lame horse B *n* |dipt; عُرْج| disabled person

تَعَرُّج *n* zigzag; طَريق \ نَهْر كَثير التَعَرُّجاتِ a winding road/river; سِباق التَعَرُّج (Sport) slalom

مُتَعَرِّج *adj* winding; zigzagging; طَريق \ نَهْر مُتَعَرِّج a winding road/river

مِعْراج *n* 1 [سُلَّم] |مَعاريجُ| ladder; stairs 2 (Islam) mi'raj (*the ascension of the Prophet Muhammad into heaven*); لَيْلة الإسْراءِ والمِعْراجِ *the Muslim festival celebrating the Prophet's Night Journey to the seven heavens*

مَعْرَج *n* |مَعارِجُ| stairway, staircase; كانَ في مَعارِجِ التَقَدُّم to be in the ascent; سورة المَعارِج The Ascending Stairways (*Surah 70*)

مُعَرَّج *adj* winding, zigzagging

مُنْعَرَج *n* |مُنْعَرَجات| curve, twist, zigzag

‹ **عُرْجون** *n* |عَراجينُ| 1 [عِنَب] *a dried out bunch of grapes* 2 [فُطْر] *Podaxis* (*genus of fungi*)

‹ **عَرادة** *n* catapult, ballista

‹ **عَرار** *n* (Bot) *Pulicaria*

عَرّة *n* tic

[اقْتَرَحَ] ◀3 to take a matter to court عَرَض قضيّةً أمام القضاءِ to suggest, to propose; عَرَض فِكْرةً to propose an idea; عَرَض على شَخصٍ خُطّةً \ قضيّةً to put a plan/case before sb [عالَجَ] ◀5 he got an idea عُرِضَتْ لَهُ فِكْرةٌ to occur; [ظَهَرَ] ◀4 to handle, to deal with; لم تَعْرِض الأَمْرَ كما يَجِبُ you didn't handle the matter the way you should have ◀6 (Theat) to perform; عَرَض مَسْرَحيّةً \ أوبيرا to perform a play/opera ◀7 [أعادَ النَظَرَ] |مع| to review

عَرَّض *v* ◀1 [جَعَلَهُ مُعَرَّضاً] to expose, to put through; عَرَّض نَفْسَهُ \ شَخْصاً \ شَيْئاً ل \ إلى خَطَرٍ to expose oneself/sb/sth to danger; عَرَّض سُمْعَتَهُ للخَطَرِ to endanger one's reputation; عَرَّض نَفْسَهُ لِعُقوبةٍ to risk punishment; عَرَّض مَريضاً لِفَحْصٍ to examine a patient ◀2 [أَشارَ إلى] |ب| to accuse indirectly; عَرَّض بِشَخْصٍ to accuse sb indirectly ◀3 [جَعَلَ عَريضاً] to broaden

عارَضَ *v* to resist, to offer resistance; to oppose, to contradict; عارَض الإجْراءاتِ to strongly oppose sth; عارَض شَيْئاً بِشِدّةٍ to resist the measures; عارَض شَخْصاً في شَيْءٍ to oppose sb on sth

أَعْرَضَ *v* ◀1 [أَدارَ ظَهْرَهُ لَهُ] to turn away; أَعْرَض عن شَخْصٍ \ شَيْءٍ to turn away from sb/sth ◀2 [ظَهَرَ] to appear

تَعَرَّضَ *v* to be exposed, to expose oneself; to sustain; تَعَرَّض للنَقْدِ to be exposed to criticism; تَعَرَّض للتَعْذيبِ to be tortured; تَعَرَّض لِلإشْعاعِ \ للأَشِعّة to be exposed to radiation; تَعَرَّض لِضَرَرٍ to sustain damage; تَعَرَّض لِأَلَمٍ شَديدٍ to suffer severe pains; تَعَرَّض للصُعوباتِ to encounter difficulties

تعارَضَ *v* to be contradictory, to conflict (with), to go against; تعارَض مع شَيْءٍ to conflict with sth; تَعارَضَتْ أَقوالُهُما they contradicted each other; يَتَعارَضُ رَأْيُهُمْ مع رَأْيِنا their opinion goes against ours

اعْتَرَضَ *v* ◀1 [أعاقَ] to obstruct, to impede, to hinder; to intercept; اعْتَرَض مَسيرةَ \ طَريقَ \ سَبيلَ شَيْءٍ to obstruct sth; اعْتَرَض سَبيلَ المُخَطَّطاتِ to foil plans; اعْتَرَض سَيْرَ البَرْنامَجِ to obstruct the programme; اعْتَرَض سَبيلَ شَخْصٍ to stand in sb's way; إنَّهُ يَعْتَرِضُ سَبيلي بِاسْتِمْرارٍ he's always in my way;

مَعَرّة *n* disgrace

عِرْزال *n* |عَرازيلُ| hut, shack; tree house

عُرْس *n* |أَعْراس| wedding

عِرْس *n* |أَعْراس| spouse; husband; wife

عِرْسيّات *n pl* (Zool) weasel family (*Mustelidae*)

عَروس *n* ◀1 [عَروسة] |f ; |عَرائِسُ| bride; العَروسانِ the bride and groom, the bridal couple; طَرْحة عَروسٍ bridal veil; يَلْعَبُ الأَطْفالُ لُعْبةَ العَروسِ والعَريسِ the children are playing house ◀2 [عَريس] |عُرُس| groom

(Idioms) عَروس البَحْرِ mermaid; عَرائِس النيلِ water lily

عَروسة *n* |عَرائِسُ| ◀1 [في الزِفافِ] bride; عَريس وَعَروسة bride and groom ◀2 [لُعْبة] doll; puppet; مَسْرَح العَرائِسِ puppet theatre

عَريس *n* |عِرْسان| groom; عَريس وَعَروسة bride and groom

ابْن عِرْسٍ *n* weasel (*Mustela*); *Mustelidae*

عَرَّشَ *v* (Bot) to climb

اعْتَرَشَ *v* (Bot) to climb

عَرْش *n* |عُروش, أَعْراش| ◀1 [مَقْعَد المَلِكِ] throne; قاعة العَرْشِ throne hall/room; عيد العَرْشِ *celebration of the accession to the throne*; جَلَسَ \ اسْتَوى على العَرْشِ to sit on the throne; تَبَوَّأَ \ تخلّى ,اعْتَزَلَ العَرْشَ to ascend the throne; اعْتَلى العَرْشَ to abdicate the throne; خَلَعَ شَخْصاً عن العَرْشِ to dethrone sb ◀2 [الطائِر] nest

عَريش *n* |عُرُش| ◀1 [عَرَبة] pole, shaft ◀2 [للكَرْمِ] trellis (*for grapes*)

العَريش *n* see عريش

العَريش *n* |f| El Areesh (*city in Egypt*)

تَعْريشة *n* pergola, arbour; trellis

عَرْصة *n* |عِراص, أَعْراص, عَرَصات| courtyard

عَرَضَ *v* |i; |عَرْض| ◀1 [أرى] to show, to demonstrate; to exhibit, to display, to expose; عَرَض بَضائِعَهُ to display one's wares; عَرَض مَلابِسَ to display clothing; عَرَض فيلْماً to show a film; عَرَض أَعْمالَ فَنّانٍ to exhibit the works of an artist; عَرَض طَريقة عَمَلِ شَيْءٍ to demonstrate the workings of sth ◀2 [قَدَّمَ] to offer, to present; عَرَض مَبْلَغاً كَبيراً to offer a large amount; عَرَض على شَخْصٍ المُساعَدةَ to offer to help sb;

العقبات التي تعترِضُ مسيرة السلامِ obstacles to the peace process **2** [احْتَجَّ |على] to object to, to protest against; to resist; اعْترَضَ على شَيْءٍ to lodge an objection to sth

اسْتَعْرَضَ *v* **1** [نَظَرَ في] to consider, to examine; اسْتَعْرَضَ |مع| [أَعادَ النَظَرَ] to examine the possibilities **2** الإمْكانيّاتِ to review **3** (Mil) to hold a parade

عَرْض *n* |عُروض| **1** [سَعة] width, breadth; خَطّ العَرْضِ latitude, parallel; دَرَجة العَرْضِ degree of latitude; بالعَرْضِ breadthwise; عَرْضُهُ ٥ أَمْتارٍ it is 5 metres wide **2** [تَقْديم] offer; supply; عَرْض خاصّ a special offer; عَرْض نِهائيّ final offer; عَرْض مُتَنَوِّع a wide selection; العَرْض والطَلَب supply and demand; رَفَضَ \ قَبِلَ عَرْضاً to accept an offer; قَدَّمَ عَرْضاً to make an offer; تَلَقّى عَرْضاً to receive an offer; تَقَدَّمَ بِعَرْضٍ **3** [مَعْرِض] demonstration; exhibition, display, show; قاعة \ صالة عَرْضٍ showroom; عَرْض تاريخيّ retrospective; قابِل للعَرْضِ presentable; عَرْض أَزْياءٍ fashion show; قَدَّمَ عَرْضاً لِشَيْءٍ to give a demonstration of sth **4** (Theat, Mus, Cin) performance, show; عَرْض سينَمائيّ \ فيلْمٍ a film screening, the showing of a film; عَرْض مَسْرَحيّ a theatrical performance; قَدَّمَ عَرْضاً مَسْرَحيًّا to present a theatrical performance; عَرْض أَوَّل premiere; تَمَّ عَرْضُهُ الأَوَّلُ it had its premiere; عَرْض بَطيء slow motion; جِهاز العَرْضِ projector; حَضَرَ عَرْضاً to attend a performance; قَدَّمَ عَرْضاً to give a performance **5** [بَيان] presentation, talk, lecture; account; عَرْض الوَقائِعِ an account of the facts; قَدَّمَ \ أَلْقى عَرْضاً عن \ حول المَعادِنِ to give a presentation about minerals **6** [مَوْكِب] parade

عَرَض *n* |أَعْراض| **1** (Med) symptom; عَرَض جانِبيّ side effects, adverse effects; أَعْراض انْسِحابيّة withdrawal symptoms; عَرَض من أَعْراضِ الْتِهابِ الرِئةِ one of the symptoms of pneumonia; مُحارَبة \ مُكافَحة الأَعْراضِ treatment of (the) symptoms; بَدَتْ عَلَيْهِ أَعْراضُ مَرَضٍ to show the symptoms of a disease **2** (Philos) accident

عُرْض *n* |أَعْراض| **1** [وَسَط] middle; في عُرْضِ البَحْرِ on the high/open sea; في عُرْضِ الطَريقِ in the middle of the road; رَجُل من عُرْضِ الناسِ a working-class man **2** [جانِب] side (Idiom) ضَرَبَ شَيْئاً \ بِشَيْءٍ عُرْضَ الحائِطِ to flout sth, to completely disregard sth; to neglect sth

عِرْض *n* |أَعْراض| honour, virtue; هَتَكَ عِرْضَ شَخْصٍ to disgrace sb; to violate sb, to rape sb; صانَ عِرْضَهُ to keep one's honour

عارِض *n* **1** [مَنْ يَعْرِضُ] |عارِضون| exhibitor; demonstrator; عارِضة أَزْياءٍ fashion model **2** (Law) |عارِضونَ| petitioner **3** [حَدَث] |عَوارِضُ| incident; (temporary) disturbance, obstacle

عارِضة *n* **1** [رافِدة] |عَوارِضُ| joist, beam; doorpost; عارِضة ثابِتة a fixed joist **2** (Sport) |عَوارِضُ| crossbar; رَدَّتِ العارِضةُ الكُرةَ the ball hit the crossbar; عَلَتِ الكُرةُ العارِضةَ the ball went over (the goal) **3** [اضْطِراب] |عَوارِضُ| disturbance; عَوارِض جَوّيّة atmospheric disturbances

عَراضة *n* parade

عُرْضة *n* target; object; كانَ عُرْضةً لِشَيْءٍ to be exposed to sth; كانَ عُرْضةً للسُخْرِيّة \ النَقْدِ to be exposed to mockery/criticism; كانَ عُرْضةً لِمَرَضٍ to be exposed to a disease

عَرْضيّ *adj* breadthwise; crosswise; horizontal; مَقْطَع عَرْضيّ cross section

عَرَضيّ *adj* **1** (Med) symptomatic; ظاهِرة عَرَضيّة symptom **2** [عابِر] coincidental, accidental; passing; مُلاحَظة عَرَضيّة a casual remark; انْفِجار عَرَضيّ an accidental explosion

عَروض *n* (Literat) metre; عِلْم العَروضِ metrics, prosody

عَروضيّ *adj* prosodic; وَزْن عَروضيّ metre

عَريض *adj* |عِراض| wide, broad; طَريق \ نَهْر عَريض a broad street/river; ابْتِسامة عَريضة a broad smile; كانَ عَريضَ الكَتِفَيْنِ to have broad shoulders; كانَتْ عَريضةَ الوِرْكَيْنِ she had wide hips

عَريضة *n* |عَرائِضُ| petition, appeal; عَريضة احْتِجاجٍ letter of protest; تَقْديم عَريضةٍ petitioning; قَدَّمَ عَريضةً لِشَخْصٍ to present a petition to sb; وَقَّعَ عَريضةً to sign a petition

اسْتِعْراض *n* |اسْتِعْراضات| **1** [مَوْكِب] parade; اسْتِعْراض عَسْكَريّ a military parade **2** [بَحْث] examination, survey; review; اسْتِعْراض العَلاقاتِ a review of the relations **3** [عَرْض] display; اسْتِعْراض الطُيورِ display, courtship (*of birds*); اسْتِعْراض العَضَلاتِ show of muscles; اسْتِعْراض القوّةِ display of power [4] (*Comput*) browsing; اسْتِعْراض مُبَوَّب tabbed browsing

اسْتِعْراضيّ *adj* demonstrative; مَسيرة اسْتِعْراضيّة protest march, demonstration; مَشْهَد اسْتِعْراضيّ spectacle

اعْتِراض *n* |اعْتِراضات| [1] objection, protest; اعْتِراضات أخْلاقيّة moral objections; اعْتِراض شَكْليّ a formal objection; اعْتِراض على حُكْمٍ objections to a verdict; دون أيِّ اعْتِراضٍ without any objection; كانَتْ لَدَيْهِ اعْتِراضاتٌ على شَيْءٍ \ شَخْصٍ to have objections to sth/sb; أتى ,قَدَّمَ اعْتِراضاتٍ بِاعْتِراضاتٍ to raise objections; عَبَّرَ عن اعْتِراضاتٍ to express objections; سَجَّلَ اعْتِراضاً على شَيْءٍ to enter/lodge/make a protest against sth; لم يَقْبَلْ أيَّ اعْتِراضٍ he could not bear being contradicted; لا اعْتِراضَ على حُكْمِ اللهِ *one cannot go against God's will*; واجَهَ اعْتِراضاتٍ to encounter difficulties [2] interception; اعْتِراض صاروخٍ intercepting a rocket

اعْتِراضيّ *adj* [1] [احْتِجاجيّ] protest (*before n*), remonstrative; مَسار اعْتِراضيّ protest march; قَضِيّة اعْتِراضيّة retrial [2] [بين قَوْسَيْنِ] parenthetical; جُمْلة اعْتِراضيّة a parenthetical sentence

إعْراض *n* turning away; في إعْراضٍ reluctantly

تَعارُض *n* contradiction, conflict; لا تَعارُضَ فيهِ it is not contradictory

تَعَرُّض *n* exposure; التَعَرُّض للضَوْءِ exposure to light

تَعْريض *n* [1] [جَعَلَ عُرْضةً] exposure; التَعْريض المُفْرِط لِشَيْءٍ excessive exposure to sth [2] [تَوْسيع] broadening, widening [3] [إلْماع] indirect accusation

مُتَعارِض *adj* contradictory; conflicting; inconsistent; أحاسيس مُتَعارِضة contradictory/mixed feelings; غَيْر مُتَعارِضٍ consistent

مُسْتَعْرِض *adj* crosswise, transverse

مُعارِض [A] *adj* opposite; مَوْقِف مُعارِض an opposite point of view; فَريق مُعارِض opposing team; حِزْب مُعارِض opposition party
[B] *n* adversary, opponent; كانَ مُعارِضاً لِشَيْءٍ to be an opponent of sth; أعْلَنَ نَفْسَهُ مُعارِضاً لِشَيْءٍ to declare oneself an opponent of sth

مُعارَضة *n* opposition; resistance; protest; مُعارَضة سِياسيّة political opposition; مُعارَضة قَوِيّة \ شَديدة strong opposition; مُعارَضة إجْراءٍ protest against a measure; مُعارَضة الاسْتِفْتاءِ resistance to the referendum; حِزْب المُعارَضةِ opposition party; زَعيم المُعارَضةِ opposition leader; قابَلَ \ واجَهَ مُعارَضةً to encounter resistance

مُعْتَرِض [A] *adj* [1] [مُخالِف] opposing, against; إنّها مُعْتَرِضةٌ على تَعْيينِهِ she is against his nomination; صاروخ مُعْتَرِض interceptor missile [2] [جُمْلة] جُمْلة مُعْتَرِضة subclause
[B] *n* adversary, opponent

مَعْرِض *n* |مَعارِضُ| exhibition; exposition; fair; مَعْرِض لَوْحاتٍ an exhibition of paintings; مَعْرِض صُوَرٍ a photo exhibition; مَعْرِض الكِتابِ the book fair; نَظَّمَ \ أقامَ مَعْرِضاً to organize/hold an exhibition; زارَ \ شاهَدَ مَعْرِضاً to visit/see an exhibition

مُعَرَّض *adj* exposed; كانَ مُعَرَّضاً ل ... to be exposed to ...; to be susceptible to ...

مَعْروض [A] *adj* |مَعْروضات| [1] [أُظْهِرَ] shown; offered; proposed; كانَ مَعْروضاً لِلبَيْعِ to be for sale [2] [مَرْفوع] pending
[B] *n* |مَعْروضات| (exhibited) article; قائِمة مَعْروضاتٍ catalogue

‹ **عَرْطَنيثا** *n* (*Bot*) *Cyclamen*

‹ **عَرْعَر** *n* juniper (*Juniperus*); حَبّة \ ثَمَرة العَرْعَرِ juniper berry

‹ **عَرَفَ** *v* |i; عِرْفان ,مَعْرِفة| [1] [عَلِمَ] to know; to find out; عَرَفَ شَيْئاً to know sth; to find out sth; عَرَفَ شَيْئاً حَقَّ المَعْرِفةِ to be sure about sth; كيف عَرَفْتَ ذلك؟ how do you know that?; لا أعْرِفُ I don't know; لا أعْرِفُ الطَريقَ I don't know the way; واللهِ لا أعْرِفُ هذا I really don't know; عُرِفَ ب ... to be known as/for ...; عُرِفَ باسْمِ ... to be known as ..., to be called ...; عُرِفَ اليَوْمَ أنّ ... today it came out that ... [2] [مَيَّزَ] to recognize; عَرَفَ شَخْصاً من صَوْتِهِ to recognize sb by his voice [3] [اعْتَرَفَ] to admit; to acknowledge; عَرَفَ المُتَّهَمُ بِذَنْبِهِ the suspect admitted his guilt

عَرَّفَ *v* [1] [أعْلَمَ] to inform; to announce; عَرَّفَ شَخْصاً بِشَيْءٍ to inform sb about/of sth [2] [قَدَّمَ] to introduce; عَرَّفَ شَخْصاً ب \ على شَخْصٍ آخَرَ to introduce sb to sb else [3] [حَدَّدَ] to determine; to define, to specify, to characterize; عَرَّفَ

حُكْم عُرْفيّ martial law; فَرْض الأَحْكامِ العُرْفيّةِ imposition of martial law

عَريف *n* |عُرَفاءُ| ◆1 [سَيِّد] master; عَريف الحَفْلةِ Master of Ceremonies ◆2 [خَبير] expert, authority ◆3 (Mil) corporal; وَكيل عَريفٍ vice-corporal ◆4 (Educ) teaching assistant

اعْتِراف *n* ◆1 [إقْرار] confession; اعْتِراف كامِل a full confession ◆2 |ب| [شَخْصٍ، دَوْلةٍ] recognition; الاعْتِراف بِفِلَسْطينَ the recognition of Palestine; الاعْتِراف بِحُقوقِ شَخْصٍ the recognition of sb's rights; على أساسِ اعْتِرافِ كُلٍّ مِنْهُما بالآخَرِ on the basis of mutual recognition; حَصَلَ على الاعْتِرافِ to gain recognition; سَحَبَ اعْتِرافَهُ بِشَيْءٍ to withdraw one's recognition of sth ◆3 (Chr) confession; سِرّ الاعْتِرافِ secret of the confessional; تَقَدَّمَ إلى الاعْتِرافِ to go to confession

أَعْرَف *adj* |dipt| knowing better; better acquainted; أَعْرَف بالمَوْضوعِ better acquainted with the subject

تَعارُف *n* |تَعارُفات| |على| acquaintance; التَعارُف الأَوَّل the first acquaintance; مَوْقِع تَعارُفٍ dating site; لِقاء لِلتَعارُفِ a get acquainted meeting; التَعارُف على شَخْصٍ acquaintance with sb; يَعودُ تَعارُفُنا إلى... we have known each other since ...

تَعَرُّف *n* ◆1 [لِأَوَّلِ مَرّةٍ] acquaintance ◆2 [مَعْرِفة] recognition; realization; identification

تَعْرِفة *n* tariff; تَعْرِفة جُمْرُكيّة customs tariff

تَعْريف *n* ◆1 [تَحْديد] definition; determination; identification; وَضَعَ تَعْريفاً to give a definition; بِطاقة تَعْريفٍ identity card, ID; business card ◆2 [إعْلام] announcement, notification ◆3 [مُقَدِّمة] introduction; preface, foreword; تَعْريف الناشِرِ the publisher's foreword ◆4 (Gram) definiteness; أَداة \ حَرْف التَعْريفِ the definite article; التَعْريف والتَنْكير definiteness and indefiniteness

تَعْريفة *n* tariff; charge; تَعْريفة مُوَحَّدة flat rate; تَعْريفة عالِية \ مُنْخَفِضة a high/low tariff; تَعْريفة الدُخولِ entrance charge, admission; زِيادة \ رَفْع تَعْريفةٍ a tariff increase; حَسَبَ \ حَدَّدَ تَعْريفةً to charge/determine a tariff

تَعْريفيّ *adj* بِطاقة تَعْريفيّة identity card

عَرَّفَ مَعْنَى كَلِمةٍ ,كَلِمةً to define a word; عَرَّفَ نَفْسَهُ (ب ...) to identify oneself (as ...) ◆4 (Chr) عَرَّفَ شَخْصاً to hear sb's confession ◆5 (Gram) to make definite

تَعَرَّفَ *v* ◆1 [عَرَفَ] to become acquainted, to get to know; تَعَرَّفَ على \ إلى شَخْصٍ to become acquainted with sb; تَعَرَّفَ على \ إلى شَيْءٍ to get to know sth ◆2 [مَيَّزَ] to recognize; تَعَرَّفَ على الجاني to recognize the perpetrator

تَعارَفَ *v* to become acquainted with one another

اعْتَرَفَ *v* ◆1 [أَقَرَّ] |ب| to confess to, to admit; اعْتَرَفَ المُشْتَبَهُ بِهِ the suspect confessed to it; اعْتَرَفَ بِشَيْءٍ to confess to sth; اعْتَرَفَ بِجَريمةٍ to confess to a crime; اعْتَرَفَ بِخَطَئِهِ to admit one's mistake; اعْتَرَفَ بالواقِعِ to face the truth, to be realistic; اعْتَرَفَ لِشَخْصٍ بالجَميلِ to be grateful to sb; اعْتَرَفَ أنّ \ بِأَنَّ ... to confess that ...; اعْتَرَفَ لِشَخْصٍ بِأَنَّهُ على حَقٍّ to admit that sb is right ◆2 (Chr) |ب| to confess; اعْتَرَفَ بِذُنوبِهِ to confess one's sins ◆3 |ب| [بِقانونيّةِ شَيْءٍ] to acknowledge, to recognize; اعْتَرَفَ بِدَوْلةٍ to recognize a state; لم يَعْتَرِفْ بِشَرْعيّةِ شَيْءٍ to not recognize the legitimacy of sth

عَرْف *n* fragrance, scent

عُرْف *n* |أَعْراف| ◆1 [تَقاليد] convention; custom, practice; كَما كانَ العُرْفُ السائِدُ في ذلك الوَقْتِ as was the custom in that time ◆2 (Law) customary law; عُرْف قَبَليّ tribal law; عُرْف تِجاريّ trade custom ◆3 [ديك] comb; عُرْف الديكِ cockscomb; (Bot) cockscomb (*Celosia*) ◆4 [طائِرٍ] crest ◆5 [حِصانٍ أو أَسَدٍ] mane ◆6 (Islam) سورة الأَعْراف The Heights (*Sura 7*)

عارِف ◼A *adj* knowing; conscious of; familiar with; عارِف بالظُروفِ aware of the circumstances; أنا عارِفٌ هذا I know that

◼B *n* person who knows/is familiar; العارِفونَ (بالأُمورِ) those who are in the know (about the matter)

عَرّاف *n* fortune-teller, sooth-sayer

عِرافة *n* fortune-telling

عِرْفان *n* knowing; عِرْفان الجَميلِ gratitude; recognition

عُرْفيّ *adj* conventional; customary, common; habitual; قانون عُرْفيّ customary law; زَواج عُرْفيّ *marriage without an official contract*; ≈ common law marriage; مَحْكَمة عُرْفيّة court-martial;

عن المُنْكَرِ (SA) Committee for the Promotion of Virtue and the Prevention of Vice, Saudi religious police

عَرَفات *n* 1 (Geog) جَبَل عَرَفاتٍ Mount Arafat (*hill east of Mecca*); يَوْم عَرَفاتٍ *the ninth day of the month Dhu al-Hijjah* 2 [اسْم شَخْصيّ] Arafat; ياسِر عَرَفات Yasser Arafat (*Palestinian statesman*)

عَرَق *v* |u; عَرْق| to nibble off

عَرِق *v* |a; عَرَق| to sweat, to perspire; عَرِقَ كَثيراً \ بِشِدّةٍ to sweat a lot/heavily

عَرَّق *v* to make sweat

أَعْرَق *v* 1 [الشَجَرُ] to strike/take root 2 [عَرَّقَ] to make sweat

تَعَرَّق *v* to strike/take root

عَرَق *n* 1 [الجِسْمِ] sweat, perspiration; رائِحة العَرَقِ odour of sweat, body odour; قَطْرة عَرَقٍ drop of sweat; ب \ من عَرَقِ جَبينِهِ by the sweat of one's brow; تَصَبَّبَ عَرَقاً to break into a sweat, to be wet with perspiration; سَبَحَ في عَرَقِهِ to be soaked in sweat; كانَ العَرَقُ يَقْطُرُ من جَبينِه his forehead was dripping with sweat; كَلَّفَ كَثيراً من الجَهْدِ والعَرَقِ to take/cost blood, sweat and tears 2 [شَراب] arak (*an anise-flavoured distilled alcoholic drink*)

عِرْق *n* 1 (Anat) |عُروق| vein; blood vessel; عُروق وَشَرايين veins and arteries; عِرْق النَسا sciatica; انْقِباض العُروقِ vascular constriction; جَرى في العُروقِ to run through the veins; جَعَلَ الدَمَ يَجْمُدُ في عُروقي it made my blood run cold 2 [جِذْر] |عُروق| root; عِرْق السوسِ liquorice 3 [وَرَقةٍ] |عُروق| vein, nerve; عُروق وَرَقةٍ the veins of a leaf 4 [جِنْس] |أَعْراق| race; مُتَعَدِّد الأَعْراقِ multiracial 5 [أَصْل] descent; العِرْقُ دَسّاسٌ what's bred in the bone will come out in the flesh

عِراقيّ *adj, n* Iraqi

عَرْقان *adj* |dipt| sweaty

عَرَقة *n* cross-beam

عِرْقيّ *adj* racial, ethnic; إبادة عِرْقيّة, تَطْهير عِرْقيّ ethnic cleansing; اخْتِلافات عِرْقيّة ethnic differences; صِراع \ نِزاع عِرْقيّ an ethnic conflict; عَلاقات عِرْقيّة race relations

عَرَقيّة *n* (Egypt) *white cotton skullcap*

عِرْقيّة *n* racism

مُتَعارَف *adj* مُتَعارَف عَلَيْهِ known; customary, usual; conventional; كَما هو مُتَعارَفٌ عَلَيْهِ as is well-known; بالشَكْلِ المُتَعارَفِ عَلَيْهِ in its usual form

مُعْتَرَف *adj* recognized, acknowledged; شَهادة مُعْتَرَف بِها دُوَليًّا an internationally recognized certificate

مُعَرَّف *adj* (Gram) definite; كَلِمة مُعَرَّفة a definite word; غَيْر مُعَرَّفٍ indefinite

مُعَرِّف *n* identifier; username

مَعْرِفة *n* |مَعارِف| 1 [عِلْم] knowledge; learning; acquaintance; skill; مَعْرِفة واسِعة broad knowledge; erudition; مَعْرِفة عامّة general knowledge; مَعْرِفة سَطْحيّة superficial knowledge; مَعْرِفة الذاتِ self-knowledge; مَعْرِفة بالناسِ judgement of character; قِلّة المَعْرِفةِ a lack of knowledge; ignorance; نَظَريّة المَعْرِفةِ theory of knowledge, epistemology; شَجَرة المَعْرِفةِ the tree of knowledge; مُجْتَمَع مَعْرِفةٍ knowledge society; وِزارة المَعارِفِ Ministry of Education; دائِرة المَعارِفِ encyclopaedia; جَدير بالمَعْرِفةِ worth knowing; حَسَبَ مَعْرِفَتي as far as I know, to my knowledge; عَرَفَ شَخْصاً مَعْرِفةً حَميمةً to know sb well; عَمَّقَ مَعْرِفَتَهُ to gain more knowledge 2 [شَخْص] acquaintance, friend; contact; مَعارِف ذَوو نُفوذٍ influential friends; مَعْرِفة عَمَلٍ business contact 3 (Gram) a definite noun; المَعْرِفة والنَكِرة definite and indefinite

مَعْرِفيّ *adj* cognitive; knowledge (*before n*); نَقْص مَعْرِفيّ a lack of knowledge

مَعْروف **A** *adj* known; famous; كاتِب مَعْروف a well-known writer; غَيْر مَعْروفٍ unknown; unrecognizable; شَخْص غَيْر مَعْروفٍ an unknown person; مَعْروف بِذَكائِهِ known for his cleverness; من المَعْروفِ أنّ ... it is known that ...
B *n* 1 [جَميل] favour; ناكِر المَعْروفِ ungrateful; طَلَبَ من شَخْصٍ مَعْروفاً to ask sb for a favour; أَسْدى لِشَخْصٍ مَعْروفاً to do sb a favour; صاحِبُ المَعْروفِ لا يَقَعُ فَإنْ وَقَعَ وَجَدَ مُتَّكَأً ≈ what goes around comes around 2 [فِعْل حَسَن] good; friendliness; بالمَعْروفِ in a friendly manner; الأَمْر بالمَعْروفِ (Islam) promotion of virtue (*the personal duty of all Muslims to encourage good behavior*); هَيْئة الأَمْر بالمَعْروفِ والنَهْي

عَريق *adj* |عُرُق, عِراق| **1** [قديم] old, ancient; ميراث عَريق ancient heritage **2** [كَريم] noble; عَريق النَسَبِ \ الأَصْلِ of noble descent

العِراق *n* Iraq

تَعَرُّق *n* graining (*wood*); marbling (*stone*); خَشَب صَلْد ضَيِّق التَعَرُّقِ a fine-grained hardwood

مُتَعَرِّق *adj* sweaty; وَجْه مُتَعَرِّق a sweaty face

مَعْروق *adj* **1** [مُجَزَّع] veined; يَد مَعْروقة a veined hand **2** [نَحيل] lean, slender

‹ **عُرْقوب** *n* |عَراقيبُ| **1** (Anat) Achilles tendon **2** [كاذِب] Urqub (*a notorious liar in Arabic folklore*); أَكْذَب من عُرْقوبٍ a bigger liar than Urqub; مَواعِد عُرْقوبٍ false promises

عُرْقوبيّ **A** *adj* false, deceitful; وَعْد عُرْقوبيّ a false promise **B** *n* liar

‹ **عِرْقِسوس** *n* liquorice

‹ **عَرْقَلَ** *v* |i; عَرْقَلة| to obstruct, to impede, to hinder, to cross; عَرْقَلَ السَيْرَ \ المُرورَ to obstruct traffic; عَرْقَلَ مُخَطَّطاتٍ to thwart plans; عَرْقَلَ عَمَلِيّةَ السَلامِ to undermine the peace process; عَرْقَلَ التَطَوُّرَ to obstruct development

تَعَرْقَلَ *v* to be obstructed; to get stuck

عَرْقَلة *n* **1** [إعاقة] hindering **2** [عائِق] |عَراقيلُ| obstacle, hindrance, barrier; بدونِ عَراقيلَ without hindrance, unimpeded; وَضَعَ \ أزالَ عَراقيلَ to put up/remove obstacles

مُعَرْقِل *n* obstacle; obstructionist

‹ **عَرَكَ** *v* |u; عَرْك| to rub; عَرَكَ شَيْئاً to rub sth

عارَكَ *v* to fight with

تَعارَكَ *v* to fight one another; تَعارَكَ مع شَخْصٍ to fight with sb

اعْتَرَكَ *v* to fight with

عِراك *n* fight, struggle, battle; عِراك بالأَيْدي a fist fight

عَريكة *n* |عَرائِكُ| disposition; كانَ لَيِّنَ العَريكةِ to have a gentle nature; to be docile, to be pliable

مُعْتَرَك *n* |مُعْتَرَكات| arena; battlefield, theatre (of war); المُعْتَرَك السِياسيّ the political arena

مَعْرَكة, مَعْرُكة *n* |مَعارِكُ| **1** [قِتال] battle; fight; مَعْرَكة دامِية \ عَنيفة a bloody/fierce battle; مَعْرَكة عاتِية \ مَريرة a raging/bitter fight; مَعْرَكة حامِية \ ضارِية a heated/ferocious battle; مَعْرَكة بَحْرِيّة a sea battle; مَعْرَكة غَيْر مُتَكافِئةٍ an unequal fight; مَعْرَكة كَلاميّة verbal contest; مَعْرَكة انْتِخابيّة electoral struggle; مَعْرَكة العَلَمَيْنِ the battle of El Alamein; مَعْرَكة بين جَيْشَيْنِ a battle between two armies; مَيْدان المَعْرَكةِ battlefield; تَرْتيب المَعْرَكةِ battle array; مَعْرَكة ضِدّ شَيْءٍ \ شَخْصٍ a war against sth/sb; في خِضَمِّ المَعْرَكةِ in the heat of battle; شَنَّ مَعْرَكةً to go into battle; خاضَ مَعْرَكةً to fight a battle; إنَّها مَعْرَكةٌ خاسِرةٌ it's a lost case **2** [مَيْدان قِتالٍ] battlefield; arena

‹ **عَرِم** *adj* aggressive, violent; powerful, strong

عارِم *adj* enormous, huge; intense; overwhelming; شَوْق عارِم an intense desire; تَصْفيق \ نُموّ عارِم an enormous applause/growth; سَعادة عارِمة overwhelming joy; فَوْضى عارِمة enormous chaos; ضَجّة عارِمة a tremendous noise

‹ **عَرَمْرَم** *adj* violent, vehement; strong; جَيْش عَرَمْرَم a huge army

‹ **عَرين** *n* |عُرُن| lair, den, hole

‹ **عِرْناس** *n* |عَرانيسُ| staff; distaff; عِرْناس الذُرة corncob

‹ **عِرْنين** *n* |عَرانينُ| عِرْنين الأَنْفِ the bridge of the nose

‹ **عَرا** *v* |u; عَرْو| to strike; عَراهُ التَعَبُ he was getting tired

اعْتَرى *v* to strike

عُرْوة *n* |عُرًى| **1** [مَلابِس] buttonhole **2** [الفوطةِ] (hanging) loop

(Idiom) عُرى الصَداقةِ the bonds of friendship

‹ **عَرِيَ** *v* |a; عُرْيِة, عُرْي| **1** [الشَخْصُ] to be naked **2** [الشَيْءُ] to be bare; عَرِيَت الشَجَرةُ من \ عن أَوْراقِها the tree was losing its leaves

عَرّى *v* **1** [جَرَّدَ] to undress; to bare; عَرّى شَخْصاً to undress sb **2** [حَتَّ] to lay bare, to uncover, to denude

تَعَرّى *v* **1** [خَلَعَ المَلابِسَ] to get undressed; to strip; تَعَرّى من ثِيابِهِ to take off one's clothes **2** [تَخَلَّصَ] to be bare; to be uncovered; تَعَرَّت الشَجَرةُ من أَوْراقِها the tree lost its leaves; تَعَرّى على حَقيقتِهِ أمامَ كُلِّ الناسِ the truth about him was revealed to the people

عارٍ *adj* |عُراة| **1** [بِدونِ مَلابِسَ] naked, nude, bare; ذِراعانِ \ ساقانِ عارِيَتانِ bare arms/legs; عاري القَدَمَيْنِ barefoot; عارٍ بِصَدْرٍ bare-chested **2** [خالٍ] void; عارٍ من كُلِّ عَيْبٍ without flaws; عارٍ من الصِحّةِ not true

عارِية *n* loan

عَراء *n* |أَعْراء| open air; في العَراءِ in the open air; نامَ في العَراءِ to sleep in the open

عُرْيان *adj* |عَرايا| naked, nude

عُرْيانيّ *adj* nudist, naturist

عُرْيانيّة *n* nudism, naturism

اسْتِعْراء *n* exhibitionism

تَعَرٍّ *n* nudity

تَعْرِية *n* [1] [تَجْريد] undressing; uncovering [2] (Geog) erosion; تَعْرِية التُرْبةِ erosion of the soil; تَعْرِية الشاطِئِ المُتَزايِدة increased erosion of the coastline; كانَ عُرْضةً للتَعْرِية to be subject to erosion

عَزَبَ *v* |i-u; عُزوب| to be far; عَزَبَ الأَمْرُ عن ذِهْنِهِ he stopped thinking about it

عَزُبَ *v* |u; عُزوبة| to be single/unmarried

عَزَب *adj* |dipt; عُزّاب, أَعْزاب| single

عازِب A *adj* |عُزّاب| single, unmarried; أُمّ عازِبة a single mother

B *n* |عُزّاب| bachelor

عِزْبة *n* |عِزَب| country estate, farm

عُزوبة *n* bachelorhood

عُزوبيّة *n* bachelorhood; حَفْل تَوْديعِ العُزوبيّةِ bachelor party

أَعْزَب A *adj* |dipt| single, unmarried; رَجُل أَعْزَب \ امْرَأة عَزْباء a single man/woman

B *n* bachelor

عِزَّت *n* |dipt| Izzet (*male given name*)

عَزَّرَ *v* to reprimand, to reprove

تَعْزير *n* punishment

عَزْرائيل *n* |dipt| Azrael (*the angel of death*)

عَزَّ *v* |i; عِزّ, عِزّة, عَزازة| [1] [كانَ قَوِيًّا] to be strong/powerful; اللهُ عَزَّ وَجَلَّ God, Mighty and Majestic is He [2] [كانَ صَعْباً] to be difficult; عَزَّ عَلَيْهِ أَنْ يَتْرُكَها it was hard for him to leave her [3] [كانَ عَزيزاً] to be dear [4] [نَدَرَ] to be rare

عَزَّزَ *v* to strengthen; to consolidate; عَزَّزَ مَوْقِفَهُ to strengthen one's position; عَزَّزَ وَضْعَهُ كَزَعيمٍ to strengthen one's position as leader; عَزَّزَ فَرْضيّةً بِحُجَجٍ to support a thesis with evidence; عَزَّزَ سُلوكَ طِفْلٍ to encourage a child's behaviour

أَعَزَّ *v* [1] [أَحَبَّ] to esteem; to love [2] [عَزَّزَ] to strengthen

تَعَزَّزَ *v* to be strengthened; to consolidate

اعْتَزَّ *v* to be proud; اعْتَزَّ بِشَيْءٍ \ شَخْصٍ to be proud of sth/sb

عِزّ *n* power, force; height, peak; في عِزِّ الصَيْفِ \ الشِتاءِ in the height of summer/in the dead of winter; في عِزِّ النَهارِ in broad daylight; في عِزِّ شَبابِهِ in the prime of his life

عَزّة *n* |dipt| Azza (*female given name*)

عِزّة *n* glory; power; عِزّة النَفْسِ self-respect; pride

عَزيز A *adj* |أَعِزّة, أَعِزّاء| [1] [قَوِيّ] powerful, strong [2] [مَحْبوب] dear, beloved; صَديق عَزيز a dear friend; ذِكْرَيات عَزيزة precious memories; عَزيزي أَحْمَدُ dear Ahmed; هذا عَزيزٌ عَلَيَّ that's dear to me [3] [غالٍ] costly

B *n* (Islam) العَزيز the Almighty, the Honorable (*one of the names of God*)

اعْتِزاز *n* pride; اعْتِزاز بالنَفْسِ self-respect; أَبْدى اعْتِزازَهُ بِ \ بِأَنَّ ... to express one's pride in ...

تَعْزيز *n* |تَعْزيزات| strengthening, reinforcement; consolidation; تَعْزيز العَلاقاتِ strengthening of relations; تَعْزيز السُلْطةِ consolidation of power; تَعْزيز القُوّاتِ reinforcement of the troops; تَلَقّى تَعْزيزاً to be reinforced; طَلَبَ تَعْزيزاً to call in reinforcements

مُعْتَزّ *adj* proud

مُعِزّ *n* (Islam) المُعِزّ the Giver of Honour (*one of the names of God*)

مُعَزَّز *adj* strengthened, reinforced

مُعَزِّز *n* |مُعَزِّزات| booster

عَزَفَ *v* |i; عَزْف| [1] [على آلةٍ موسيقيّةٍ] |على| to play; عَزَفَ على البيانو to play the piano [2] [صَوَّتَ] تَعْزِفُ الريحُ the wind is howling [3] [عَفَّ] |عن| to turn away; to stop; عَزَفَ عن الدراسة to quit school

عازِف *n* player; performer; عازِف مُنْفَرِد soloist; عازِف العودِ oud player; عازِف البِيانو pianist

عَزّاف *n* musician

اعْتِزال *n* seclusion; retreat; retirement; اعْتِزال المَلِكِ abdication

أَعْزَل *adj* |dipt; عُزْل, عُزَّل| unarmed; مَدَنِيونَ عُزْل unarmed civilians

المُعْتَزِلة *n* Mu'tazila (*Islamic school of theology based on reason*)

انْعِزال *n* isolation, seclusion

انْعِزاليّ **A** *adj* isolationist; secluded; عاشَ حَياةً انْعِزاليّةً to lead a secluded life

B *n* hermit

انْعِزاليّة *n* isolationism

مُعْتَزَل *n* retreat, hideaway

مَعْزِل *n* |مَعازِلُ| isolation; quarantine; ب \ في مَعْزِلٍ عن شَيْءٍ isolated from sth; عاشَ في مَعْزِلٍ عن الناسِ to live secluded from the world

مَعْزول *adj* isolated, separated; insulated; مُسْتَوْطَنة مَعْزولة an isolated settlement; مَعْزول عن الأَهْلِ separated from his family

مُنْعَزِل *adj* isolated, secluded; solitary; بَيْت مُنْعَزِل an isolated house

عَزَمَ *v* |i; عَزْم, عَزيمة| to decide; to resolve, to determine; عَزَمَ شَيْئاً \ على شَيْءٍ to decide sth; to intend to do sth

عَزَّمَ *v* to enchant, to cast a spell on

اعْتَزَمَ *v* to resolve, to intend to; to be determined; اعْتَزَمَ فِعْلَ شَيْءٍ \ أَنْ يَفْعَلَ شَيْئاً to be determined to do sth

عَزْم *n* **1** [قَصْد] decision; intention; أَعْلَنَ عَزْمَهُ to announce one's decision; أَثْبَتَ \ أَكَّدَ عَزْمَهُ to confirm one's decision; ثَنى شَخْصاً عن عَزْمِهِ to dissuade sb from his purpose; عَقَدَ العَزْمَ على شَيْءٍ to set one's mind on sth **2** [تَصْميم] purpose, determination **3** (Tech) torque

عازِم *adj* determined, resolved; firm

عَزّام *adj* determined, resolved

عَزيمة *n* |عَزائِمُ| **1** [تَصْميم] determination; resoluteness, resolve; ثَبَّطَ عَزيمةَ شَخْصٍ to discourage sb; خارَتْ عَزيمَتُهُ his resolve faltered **2** [رُقْية] spell, incantation **3** (Isl Law) provision

تَعْزيم *n* exorcism

عَزوف **A** *adj* |عن| disinclined, averse to; عَزوف عن الزَواجِ averse to marriage

B *n* |عن| aversion; أَعْلَنَ عَزوفَهُ عن ... he expressed his aversion to ...

مِعْزَف *n* |مَعازِفُ| (stringed) instrument

مَعْزوفة *n* piece of music

عَزَقَ *v* |i; عَزْق| to hoe; عَزَقَ الأَرْضَ to hoe the soil

مِعْزَق, مِعْزَقة *n* |مَعازِقُ| hoe; pickaxe

عَزَلَ *v* |i; عَزْل| **1** [انْفَرَدَ] to isolate, to separate; عَزَلَ نَفْسَهُ عن العالَمِ الخارِجيِّ to isolate oneself from the outside world; عَزَلَ المَرْضى to quarantine the sick **2** [أَقالَ] to release, to dismiss; عَزَلَ شَخْصاً عن مَنْصِبِهِ to remove sb from office **3** (Tech) to insulate; عَزَلَ غُرْفةً \ بَيْتاً \ تَمْديداً to insulate a room/house/pipe

انْعَزَلَ *v* to be/become isolated; to seclude oneself; انْعَزَلَ عن الناسِ to cut oneself off from other people

اعْتَزَلَ *v* to withdraw; to resign; اعْتَزَلَ الخِدْمةَ مُبَكِّراً to retire early; اعْتَزَلَ السِياسةَ to withdraw from politics

عَزْل *n* **1** [تَفْرِقة] separation, segregation; isolation; عَزْل عُنْصُريّ racial segregation; apartheid; سِياسة عَزْلِ بَلَدٍ a policy of isolating a country **2** [إقالة] disposing, impeachment; discharge, dismissal; عَزْل الرَئيسِ impeachment of the president **3** [تَزْويد بِعازِلٍ] insulation **4** [لِمَنْع الحَمْلِ] withdrawal, coitus interruptus

عازِل **A** *adj* |عَوازِلُ| **1** [حاجِز] isolating; separation; جِدار عازِل barrier, a separation wall; مِنْطَقة عازِلة buffer zone **2** [فاصِل] insulating; مادّة عازِلة insulation material

B *n* |عَوازِلُ| insulation; عازِل صَوْتيّ \ حَراريّ sound/thermal insulation; عازِل ذَكَريّ \ جِنْسيّ condom; وَضَعَ عازِلاً to apply insulation

عُزْلة *n* isolation, separation, seclusion; solitude; في عُزْلةٍ in seclusion; يَعيشُ في عُزْلةٍ he leads a secluded life; في عُزْلةٍ عن العالَمِ secluded from the world; خَرَجَ من عُزْلَتِهِ to come out of one's isolation; أَصْبَحَ في عُزْلةٍ to be isolated; أَخْرَجَ شَخْصاً من عُزْلَتِهِ to drag sb out of his isolation; سَكَنَ في عُزْلةٍ to live in an isolated place

عُسْرة *n* 1 [شِدّة] distress 2 [فَقْر] poverty

عَسير *adj* difficult, hard; صِراع عَسير a hard struggle

إعْسار *n* (Law) insolvency

أَعْسَر *adj* |dipt| left-handed

مُتَعَسِّر *adj* difficult, hard; وِلادة مُتَعَسِّرة obstructed labor

مُعْسِر *adj* poor

‹ عَسَّ *v* |u; عَسّ, عَسس| to patrol by night

عاسّ *n* |عُسّاس, عَسَس| night watchman

عَسّاس *n* night watchman

‹ عَسْعَسَ *v* |i; عَسْعَسة| to become dark (*the night*)

‹ عَسَفَ *v* |i; عَسْف| to oppress, to tyrannize

تَعَسَّفَ *v* 1 [ظَلَمَ] to oppress, to tyrannize 2 [تَصرَّفَ بِطُغْيانٍ] to behave tyrannically

اعْتَسَفَ *v* 1 [فَعَلَ جُزافاً] to do at random 2 [أَجْبَرَ] to force, to compel, to coerce

عَسْف *n* despotism, tyranny

عَسّاف *n* tyrant, oppressor

عَسْفيّ *adj* oppressive; حَرْب عَسْفيّة oppressive war

تَعَسُّف *n* tyranny, despotism, oppression; arbitrariness; عانى من التَعَسُّفِ to suffer from oppression

تَعَسُّفيّ *adj* 1 [اسْتِبْداديّ] repressive, despotic, oppressive; إجْراءات تَعَسُّفيّة repressive measures; حُكْم تَعَسُّفيّ despotic government 2 [اعْتِباطيّ] arbitrary; قَرار تَعَسُّفيّ an arbitrary decision; اعْتِقال تَعَسُّفيّ arbitrary detention

مُتَعَسِّف **A** *adj* despotic, oppressive; نِظام مُتَعَسِّف an oppressive regime

B *n* despot

‹ عاسوق *n* kestrel

‹ عَسْقَل *n* turnip

‹ عَسْقَلان *n* |f| Ashkelon (*city in Israel*)

‹ عَسْكَرَ *v* |i; عَسْكَرة| to camp; to encamp

عَسْكَر *n coll* |no singular noun; عَساكِرُ| military; soldiers; حُكْم العَسْكَرِ military rule

عَسْكَريّ **A** *adj* |عَسْكَريّون, عَساكِرُ| military; الخِدْمة العَسْكَرِيّة military service; عَمَلِيّة عَسْكَرِيّة a military operation; قوّات

‹ عَزا, عَزى *v* |u; عَزْو| إلى| to ascribe to, to attribute to; to blame; عَزا الفَشَلَ إلى ... to blame the failure on ...; عُزِيَ الانْفِجارُ إلى تَسَرُّبٍ غازيٍّ the explosion was due to a gas leak

عَزّى *v* to offer one's condolences; عَزّى شَخْصاً to offer one's condolences to sb; عَزّى في وَفاةِ شَخْصٍ to offer one's condolences on the death of sb

تَعَزّى *v* to find solace

اعْتَزى *v* |إلى| to trace (back) one's descent to

عَزاء *n* 1 [تَعْزِيّة] comfort, consolation 2 (Islam) *Shiite mourning ceremony*

تَعْزِية *n* |تَعازٍ| condolence; sympathy; تَعازٍ حارّة heartfelt sympathy; سِجِلّ التَعازي condolence book; بِطاقة تَعْزِية condolence card; رَفَعَ \ قَدَّمَ تَعازيه to extend/offer one's condolences; أَحَرّ التَعازي accept my sympathies

مُعَزٍّ **A** *adj* comforting

B *n* mourner

‹ يَعْسوب *n* |يَعاسيبُ| 1 [مَلِكة النَحْل] queen (bee) 2 [حَشَرة ذات أَرْبَعةِ أَجْنِحةٍ] dragonfly (*Odonata*)

‹ عَسْجَد *n* gold

‹ عَسَرَ, عَسُرَ, عَسِرَ *v* |a-i-u; عُسْر, عُسُر, عَسَر| 1 [اشْتَدَّ] to be/become difficult/hard; يَعْسُرُ عَلَيْهِ قَبولُ مِثْلَ هذا الكَلامِ it is hard for him to accept that kind of talk 2 [المَدينَ] to press

عَسَّرَ *v* to make difficult

أَعْسَرَ *v* 1 [فَقُرَ] to be/become poor 2 [المَرْأةُ] to have a difficult delivery

تَعَسَّرَ *v* to be/become difficult

اسْتَعْسَرَ *v* to find difficult, to have problems with; اسْتَعْسَرَ شَيْئاً to find sth difficult

عَسِر *adj* difficult; hard (*of water*)

عُسْر *n* 1 [ضيق] hardship; need, distress; عُسْر ماليّ financial trouble; خَفَّفَ عُسْرَ شَخْصٍ to relieve sb's distress; في اليُسْرِ والعُسْرِ in rain or shine; إنّ بعد العُسْرِ يُسْراً after hardship comes ease 2 (Med) difficulty; عُسْر البَوْلِ difficulty urinating; عُسْر القِراءةِ dyslexia; مُعانٍ من عُسْرِ القِراءةِ dyslexic

عَسّارة *n* fruit press

عَسْكَرِيّة (military) troops; التَحيّة العَسْكَرِيّة salute; شِبْه عَسْكَرِيّ paramilitary

B *n* |عَسْكَرِيّونَ, عَساكِرُ| **1** [جُنْديّ] soldier **2** [في الشِطْرَنْج] pawn

مُعَسْكَر *n* |مُعَسْكَرات| **1** [مُخَيَّم] camp; encampment; مُعَسْكَر صَيْفيّ summer camp; مُعَسْكَر إعْداديّ \ تَدْريبيّ training camp; مُعَسْكَر اعْتِقالٍ prison camp; concentration camp; مُعَسْكَر لِلاّجِئينَ refugee camp; أَقامَ مُعَسْكَراً to set up camp **2** [أَنْصار] camp; المُعَسْكَر المُؤَيِّد لِإسْرائيلَ the pro-Israel camp

‹ **عَسَّلَ** *v* to sweeten with honey

عَسَل *n* |أَعْسال, عُسول| honey; عَسَل أَسْوَد molasses; عُلْبة عَسَلٍ a jar of honey; زَهْر العَسَلِ honeysuckle; شَهْر العَسَلِ honeymoon; ما زالا في شَهْرِ العَسَلِ they are still on their honeymoon; رِحْلة شَهْر العَسَلِ honeymoon (trip)

(Idiom) سَمْن على عَسَلٍ perfect, great

عَسّال *n* bee-keeper

مَعْسول *n* sweet, sugary; كَلام مَعْسول flattery

‹ **عُسْلُج, عُسْلوج** **A** *adj* tender, fragile

B *n* |عَسالِجُ| twig

‹ **عَسى** *v* |no imperfect| to be possible; عَسى أنْ يَكونَ مَريضاً it's possible that he's sick; ما عَساني أنْ أَقولَ؟ what can I possibly say?

‹ **عَشِبَ, عَشُبَ** *v* |a-u; عَشَب, عَشاب| to be covered with grass

عَشَّبَ *v* to be covered with grass

عُشْب *n coll* |أَعْشاب| grass; herb; عُشْبة a blade of grass; عُشْبة البَواسيرِ lesser celandine, pilewort (*Ranunculus ficaria*); عُشْب طِبِّيّ a medicinal herb; أَعْشاب ضارّة weeds; أَعْشاب بَحْرِيّة seaweed; آكِل الأَعْشابِ herbivore; مُبيد الأَعْشابِ herbicide; الحُبوب والأَعْشاب grains and grasses; قَصّ الأَعْشابَ to cut/mow the grass

عاشِب *n* |عَواشِبُ| herbivore

عُشْبِيّ *adj* grass (*before n*), vegetation (*before n*), herbal; مَلْعَب عُشْبِيّ grass court (*tennis*)

مُعْشِب *adj* grass-covered, grassy

مُعْشَوْشِب *adj* grass-covered, grassy

‹ **عِشْتار** *n* |dipt f| Ishtar (*the Assyrian and Babylonian goddess of fertility, war, love, and sex*)

‹ **عاشَرَ** *v* **1** [رافَقَ] to associate with, to seek the company of; عاشَرَ شَخْصاً to associate with sb; عاشَرَ صَفْوةَ القَوْمِ to move in the best circles; عاشَرَ الناسَ to mix with other people **2** [جامَعَ] to have a sexual relationship with

تَعاشَرَ *v* to associate with each other; to live together

عُشْر *n* |أَعْشار, عُشور| **1** [جُزْء] (one) tenth **2** (Hist) tithe

عاشِر *num* tenth; المَرّة العاشِرة the tenth time; الساعة العاشِرة ten o'clock

عاشوراء *n* |dipt| Ashura (*Shi'a day of mourning for the martyrdom of Husayn*)

عَشائِرِيّ *adj* tribal

عُشارِيّ **A** *adj* **1** (Math) decagonal **2** (Sport) decathlon (*before n*)

B *n* **1** (Math) decagon **2** (Sport) decathlon

عَشْرة *num* ten; عَشْر بَقَراتٍ \ عَشَرة دَفاتِرَ ten cows/notebooks; عَشَرات الكُتُبِ dozens of books

عِشْرة *n* association; company, companionship

عِشْرونَ *num* twenty; عِشْرونَ دَقيقةً twenty minutes; لِعِشْرينَ عاماً for twenty years; القَرْن العِشْرونَ the twentieth century

عَشْرِيّ *adj* lasting ten years; خُطّة عَشْرِيّة ten-year plan

عُشْرِيّ *adj* decimal; عَدَد عُشْرِيّ decimal; النِظام العُشْرِيّ the decimal system

عَشْرِيّة *n* decade

عَشير *n* **1** [عِرْس] husband; wife **2** [مُرافِق] companion

عَشيرة *n* |عَشائِرُ| clan; عَشيرة مُعادِية \ مُنافِسة a hostile/rival clan

اثْنا عَشَرِيّة *n* Twelver Shi'a

العِشْرينات *n pl* twenties; شَخْص في العِشْريناتِ من عُمْرِهِ a person in his twenties

مُعاشَرة *n* **1** [مُخالَطة] association; companionship; هو حَسَنُ المُعاشَرةِ he is good company, he has a pleasant manner; سَهْل المُعاشَرةِ easy to get along with; آداب المُعاشَرةِ etiquette, good manners **2** [مُساكَنة] living together; مُعاشَرة جِنْسِيّة cohabitation

مَعْشَر *n* |مَعاشِرُ| community; يا مَعْشَرَ الناسِ! O people!; نَحْنُ مَعْشَرَ العَرَبِ we, the Arabs

مُسْتَوْطَنات عَشْوائيّة squatter settlements; اخْتيار \ عَيِّنة عَشْوائيّ(ة) a random choice/sample; أَطْلَقَ النارَ بِصورةٍ عَشْوائيّةٍ to shoot randomly

عَشْوة *n* darkness, dark

عَشًى *n* night-blindness; عَشًى لَيْليّ night-blindness

عَشيّة *n* |عَشايا, عَشيّات| late afternoon, early evening; eve; في العَشيّةِ in the early evening; بين عَشيّةٍ وَضُحاها overnight, from one day to the next; عَشيّةَ الانْتِخاباتِ on the eve of the elections; عَشيّةَ (انْعِقادِ) القِمّةِ \ المُؤْتَمَرِ on the eve of the summit/conference

أَعْشى *adj* night-blind

〈 **عَصَبَ** *v* |i; عَصْب| to bind, to tie; to wind, to wrap; عَصَبَ العَيْنَيْنِ to blindfold

عَصَّبَ *v* to bind, to tie; to bandage; عَصَّبَ عَيْنَيْ شَخْصٍ to blindfold sb; عُصِّبَتْ عُيونُهُ to be blindfolded

تَعَصَّبَ *v* to be/become a fanatic, to be/become a zealot

عَصَب *n* |أَعْصاب| nerve, nerves; temper; أَعْصاب ضَعيفة \ قَويّة weak/strong nerves; أَعْصاب فولاذيّة \ حَديديّة iron nerves, nerves of steel; طَبيب أَعْصابٍ neurologist; جَرّاح الأَعْصابِ neurosurgeon; غاز الأَعْصابِ nerve gas; أَلَم العَصَبِ الوَرْكيّ sciatica; مُتَوَتِّر الأَعْصابِ nervous, tense; مُثير للأَعْصابِ nerve-racking; بارِد الأَعْصابِ cool-headed; هُدوء \ بُرودة الأَعْصابِ cool-headedness; بِبُرودةِ الأَعْصابِ cool-headedly; حافَظَ على بُرودةِ أَعْصابِهِ to stay calm; فَقَدَ أَعْصابَهُ to become nervous, to be rattled; تَمالَكَ أَعْصابَهُ to control one's temper; فَقَدَ السَيْطَرةَ على أَعْصابِهِ to lose one's temper; انْهارَتْ أَعْصابُهُ to have a (nervous) breakdown; أَثارَ أَعْصابَ شَخْصٍ to get on sb's nerves; وَتَّرَ أَعْصابَ شَخْصٍ to make sb nervous

عُصاب *n* neurosis; عُصاب نَفْسيّ neurosis

عِصابة *n* |عِصابات, عَصائِبُ| 1 [زُمْرة] gang, band; عِصابة مُجْرِمينَ a gang of criminals; عِصابة لُصوصٍ a pack of thieves; عِصابة تَهْريبِ المُخَدِّراتِ gang of drug smugglers; عِصابة شَبابٍ a gang of youths; رَجُل عِصابةٍ gangster; أَعْضاء العِصابةِ gang members; رَئيس \ زَعيم عِصابةٍ gang leader;

〈 **عَشَّشَ** *v* to nest

عُشّ *n* |أَعْشاش, عِشاش, عِشَشة, عُشوش| nest; عُشّ الطَيْرِ bird's nest

مُعَشِّش *adj* nesting; هذا مَكانٌ رَئيسيٌّ للطُيورِ المُعَشِّشةِ this is a prime spot for nesting birds

〈 **عَشِقَ** *v* |a; عِشْق| to love (passionately), to adore; عَشِقَ شَخْصاً to love sb

عَشَّقَ *v* 1 [رَبَطَ] to couple; عَشَّقَ العَرَباتِ بِقِطارٍ to couple carriages to a train 2 [سَيّارةً] to engage the clutch

تَعَشَّقَ *v* to love (passionately), to adore

عِشْق *n* love; passion

عاشِق A *adj* |عاشِقون, عُشّاق| in love, loving; عاشِق للفَنِّ art-loving

B *n* |عاشِقون, عُشّاق| lover; admirer; عاشِق مُتَيَّم \ وَلْهان a passionate lover; عاشِق الرِياضةِ sports fan; عيد العُشّاقِ Valentine's Day

عِشْقيّ *adj* erotic; قِصّة عِشْقيّة an erotic story

عَشيق *n* |عُشّاق| lover; عَشيقة mistress; لَدَيْه عَشيقةٌ he has a mistress

تَعْشيق *n* 1 [رَبْط] coupling 2 [سَيّارة] transmission

مَعْشوق A *adj* beloved

B *n* beloved, sweetheart

〈 **عَشا, عَشِيَ** *v* |u; عَشْو| to be night-blind

عَشّى *v* to give dinner

تَعَشّى *v* to have dinner, to dine; تَعَشّى في مَطْعَمٍ to have dinner at a restaurant

عَشيّ *n* early evening

عَشاء *n* |أَعْشِية| dinner; عَشاء بَسيط \ وافِر a simple/ample dinner; العَشاء الرَبّانيّ \ الإلَهيّ (Holy) Communion; العَشاء الأَخير \ السِرّيّ the Last Supper; وَجْبة العَشاءِ dinner, evening meal; حَفْلة عَشاءٍ dinner party; أَقامَ وَليمةَ عَشاءٍ to give a dinner; تَناوَلَ العَشاءَ to have dinner

عِشاء *n* evening; صَلاة العِشاءِ evening prayers

عَشْواء *n* |dipt| خَبْطَ عَشْواءَ haphazardly

عَشْوائيّ *adj* arbitrary, random; عَشْوائيًّا, بِشَكْلٍ عَشْوائيٍّ, بِطَريقةٍ عَشْوائيّةٍ at random, indiscriminately; مُلاحَظات عَشْوائيّة random comments; بَريد عَشْوائيّ junk email;

حَرْب عِصاباتٍ guerrilla war ❷ [ضِماد] band; headband; عِصابة الرَّأْسِ headband

عُصابيّ *adj* neurotic

عَصَبة *n* blood relationship

عُصْبة *n* |عُصَب| union, league, federation; عُصْبة الأُمَمِ League of Nations

عَصَبون *n* |عَصابينُ| neuron

عَصَبيّ *adj* nervous; nerve (*before n*), neuro-; irritable, irritated; عَصَبيّ المِزاجِ short-tempered; رَدّ عَصَبيّ an angry reaction; خَليّة عَصَبيّة neuron; مَرْكَز عَصَبيّ nerve centre; أَلَم عَصَبيّ neuralgia; الجِهاز العَصَبيّ the nervous system; الجِهاز العَصَبيّ المَرْكَزيّ the central nervous system; طِبّ الجِهازِ العَصَبيّ neurology; حَرَكة عَصَبيّة a nervous tic; انْهِيار عَصَبيّ a nervous breakdown

عَصَبيّة *n* ❶ [تَعَصُّب] loyalty, solidarity; nationalism; عَصَبيّة قَبَليّة \ طائفيّة tribalism/sectarianism ❷ [في المِزاجِ] irritability, short-temper

عَصيب *adj* difficult, hard; أيّام عَصيبة hard times; كانَ وَقْتاً عَصيباً it was hard times

تَعَصُّب *n* fanaticism, zealotry; intolerance; تَعَصُّب أَعْمى blind fanaticism; تَعَصُّب دينيّ \ سِياسيّ religious/political intolerance; تَعَصُّب عُنْصُريّ racism; تَعَصُّب ضدّ الأجانِبِ intolerance towards foreigners

تَعَصُّبيّ *adj* fanatical; intolerant; حَرَكة تَعَصُّبيّة fanatical organization

مُتَعَصِّب **A** *adj* fanatical; militant; مَجْموعات مُتَعَصِّبة militant groups

B *n* fanatic, zealot; extremist

مَعْصوب *adj* ❶ [مَرْبوط] tied, wrapped; مَعْصوب العَيْنَيْنِ blindfolded ❷ [مُضَمَّد] bandaged

عَصيدة *n* |عَصائِدُ| hot wheat/farina cereal; *thickened farina cereal, similar to polenta*; mush

عَصَرَ *v* |i; عَصْر| to press; to squeeze, to wring out; to juice; عَصَرَ بُرْتُقالةً to juice an orange; عَصَرَ ثَوْباً to wring out a garment

عَصَّرَ *v* to modernize, to update

عاصَرَ *v* to be a contemporary; عاصَرَ شَخْصاً to be a contemporary of sb

تَعَصَّرَ *v* to be pressed, to be squeezed out

تَعاصَرَ *v* to be contemporaneous

انْعَصَرَ *v* to be pressed, to be squeezed out

اعْتَصَرَ *v* to press out

عَصْر *n* |عُصور, أَعْصُر| ❶ [دَهْر] period; age, era; العَصْر الحَجَريّ \ البرونْزيّ \ الحَديديّ the Stone/Bronze/Iron Age; العَصْر الحَجَريّ القَديم the Palaeolithic (Period); عَصْر جَليديّ an ice age; العَصْر النَوَويّ \ الذَرّيّ the atomic age; عَصْر الحاسِبِ الآليّ the computer age; العُصور القَديمة antiquity, ancient times; العَصْر العُثْمانيّ the Ottoman period; العَصْر الجاهِليّ the Jahiliyya period (*the period prior to the revelation of the Koran*); العُصور الوُسْطى the Middle Ages; عَصْر الرَسولِ the time of the Prophet; روح العَصْرِ the spirit of the age; ابْن عَصْرِهِ a child of one's time; مُتَطَلَّبات العَصْرِ modern standards; عَصْراً بعد عَصْرٍ for centuries; في عَصْرِنا الحاضِرِ nowadays; على مَرِّ العُصورِ in the course of time; منذ أَقْدَمِ العُصورِ since time immemorial; منذ عُصورٍ بَعيدةٍ since ancient times; عند مُنْطَلَقِ عَصْرٍ جَديدٍ at the beginning of a new era; واكَبَ عَصْرَهُ to keep up with the times ❷ [بعد الظُهْرِ] afternoon; صَلاة العَصْرِ afternoon prayers; سورة العَصْرِ The Time (*Sura 103*)

عاصِرة *n* (*Anat*) (anal) sphincter; constrictor

عَصّارة *n* ❶ [للحَمْضيّاتِ] press ❷ [للغَسيلِ] wringer

عُصارة *n* juice; عُصارة مَعِديّة \ هَضْميّة gastric/digestive juices

عُصاريّ *adj* succulent; نَبات عُصاريّ succulent (plant)

عَصْريّ *adj* modern, contemporary; مَلابِس عَصْريّة fashionable clothing; موسيقى عَصْريّة contemporary music

عَصْريّة *n* modernism

عَصير *n* |عَصائِرُ| juice; عَصير فَواكِهَ fruit juice; عُلْبة \ قِنّينة \ كَأْس عَصيرٍ a carton/bottle/glass of juice; شَرِبَ عَصيراً to drink juice

إِعْصار *n* |أَعاصيرُ| storm; hurricane, cyclone; tornado; إِعْصار حَلَزونيّ hurricane; إِعْصار عَنيف a severe storm; إِعْصار مَداريّ \ اسْتِوائيّ a tropical storm; مَرْكَز الإعْصارِ the eye of

‹ **عَصَمَ** *v* |i; عِصْم| ⓵ [مَنَعَ] to hold back, to restrain; to prevent; عَصَمَهُ اللهُ عن \ من الخَطَأ God made him infallible ⓶ (Med) to immunize

اعْتَصَمَ *v* ⓵ [لَجَأَ] to entrench oneself, to sit-in; to take cover, to seek refuge; اعْتَصَمَ بِبِنايةٍ \ سِفارةٍ to take cover in a building/embassy; اعْتَصَمَ احْتِجاجاً على شَيْءٍ to stage a sit-in in protest of sth ⓶ [حَفِظَ] to maintain; اعْتَصَمَ بالصَمْتِ to maintain silence

اسْتَعْصَمَ *v* ⓵ [الْتَجَأَ] ب| to seek refuge with ⓶ [امْتَنَعَ] to resist (*a temptation*)

عاصِمة *n* |عَواصِمُ| capital; تونس \ الجَزائِر العاصِمة Tunis/ Algiers (*to distinguish the cities from the eponymous countries*)

عِصام *n* Essam, Issam (*male given name*)

عِصاميّ *adj* self-taught, self-made; فَنّان عِصاميّ a self-taught artist

عِصْمة *n* ⓵ [التَنَزُّه عن الخَطَأ] infallibility; عِصْمة من الخَطَأ infallibility ⓶ [الزَواج] *a legal stipulation of a marriage contract in which the wife maintains the right to a divorce*; العِصْمةُ في يَدِها she has the right to get a divorce

اعْتِصام *n* |اعْتِصامات| ⓵ [لُجوء] taking cover ⓶ [تَمَسُّك] maintenance ⓷ [امْتِناع عن العَمَلِ] occupation, sit-in; اعْتِصام الكُلّيّة a sit-in at the college

أَعْصَم *adj* غُراب أَعْصَم (Zool) chough

مِعْصَم *n* |مَعاصِمُ| wrist; مَفْصِل المِعْصَم wrist joint

مَعْصوم *adj* infallible; inviolable; مَعْصوم من الخَطَأ infallible; البابا مَعْصومٌ من الخَطَأ the Pope is infallible; لا أَحَدَ مَعْصومٌ من الخَطَأ no one is infallible

‹ **عَصاً** *n* |f; عِصِيّ| stick, rod, wand; عَصاً سِحْرِيّة magic wand; عَصا القِيادةِ control stick; عَصا الراعي (Bot) bistort (*Polygonum Bistorta*); شَقَّ عَصا الطاعةِ to be disobedient; أَمْسَكَ العَصا من الوَسَطِ to be take a moderate position; أَلْقى عَصا التَرْحالِ to settle down; الوَثْب \ القَفْز بالعَصا pole vaulting; لا يَعْرِفُ الأَلِفَ من العَصا he doesn't know anything; اسْتَعْمَلَ سِياسةَ العَصا والجَزَرة to use the carrot-and-stick policy

عَصَويّ *adj* (Med) bacillary; فَيْروس عَصَويّ baculovirus

عُصَيّة *n* ⓵ (Med) bacillus ⓶ [عَصًا صَغيرة] rod, stick

the storm; هَبَّ إعْصارٌ \ هَبَّتْ كالإعْصارِ like a whirlwind; ضَرَبَ إعْصارٌ المَناطِقَ الغَرْبِيّةَ a storm was raging; أَعاصيرُ a hurricane hit the western areas; اكْتَسَحَ الإعْصارُ القَرْيةَ the village was devastated by a hurricane

مُعاصِر Ⓐ *adj* modern, contemporary; الفَنّ \ الموسيقى المُعاصِر (ة) modern art/music; العالَم المُعاصِر the modern world; المُجْتَمَع المُعاصِر modern society Ⓑ *n* contemporary

مِعْصَرة, مِعْصَر *n* |مَعاصِرُ| press

‹ **عَصْرَنَ** *v* |i; عَصْرَنة| modernize, to bring up to date

عَصْرَنة *n* modernization

‹ **عَصَّ** *v* |a; عَصَص, عَصّ| to become hard

‹ **عُصْعُص, عُصْعُصة** *n* |عَصاعِصُ| tail bone, coccyx

‹ **عَصَفَ** *v* |i; عَصْف, عُصوف| to storm, to rage, to blow; عَصَفَت الريحُ في البَحْرِ there was a storm at sea; عَصَفَت الريحُ في وَجْهِهِ the wind was blowing in his face; عَصَفَ بِشَيْءٍ to blow sth away; بَلَد تَعْصِفُ بِهِ الفَوْضى a country where chaos rules

عاصِف *adj* windy, stormy; turbulent; جَوّ عاصِف stormy weather; حَياة عاصِفة a turbulent life

عاصِفة *n* |عَواصِفُ| storm, gale; عاصِفة هَوْجاء a heavy storm; عاصِفة رَعْدِيّة thunderstorm; عاصِفة ثَلْجِيّة snowstorm, blizzard; عاصِفة رَمْلِيّة sandstorm; عاصِفة شَمْسِيّة geomagnetic storm; عاصِفة من الاحْتِجاجاتِ a storm of protests; قوّة العاصِفةِ storm/gale force; تَهُبُّ العاصِفةُ there is a storm, it is storming; هَدَأَت العاصِفةُ the storm has calmed

عُصافة *n* chaff

عَصْفة *n* a gust of wind

‹ **عُصْفُر** *n* safflower (*Carthamus tinctorius*)

عُصْفور *n* |عَصافيرُ| bird; عُصْفور دوريّ sparrow; عُصْفور الجَنّةِ bird of paradise; عَصافير بَطْنِهِ the rumbling of one's stomach; يَطيرُ العُصْفورُ the bird is flying; أَصابَ عُصْفورَيْنِ بِحَجَرٍ واحِدٍ to kill two birds with one stone; عُصْفورٌ في اليَدِ خَيْرٌ من أَلْفٍ على الشَجَرة a bird in the hand is worth two in the bush

‹ **عَصَلَ** *v* |u; عَصْل| to bend, to twist

‹ **عَصْلَجَ** *v* |i; عَصْلَجة| to lock; عَصْلَجَ(ت) العَجَلةُ \ المِقْوَدُ the wheel/steering wheel was locked

عَضوض *adj* biting, mordacious

أَعْضَلَ *v* to be difficult; to be a riddle

عَضَل *n coll* muscle; عَضَلة باسِطة extensor muscle; عَضَلات مَدارِيّة sphincter muscles; قوّة العَضَلاتِ muscular strength; كُتْلة عَضَلاتٍ muscle mass; آلام العَضَلاتِ aching muscles; مَفْتول العَضَلاتِ muscular; اسْتِعْراض العَضَلاتِ muscle flexing; انْسِداد (في) عَضَلةِ القَلْبِ myocardial infarction; تَقَلُّص في العَضَلاتِ muscle cramp; مَزَّقَ \ رَضَّ عَضَلةً to tear/strain a muscle; أَحْمى \ سَخَّنَ العَضَلاتِ to loosen (up) the muscles, to warm up; أَبْرَزَ عَضَلاتِهِ to show one's muscles

عُضال *adj* incurable; مَرَض عُضال an incurable disease

عَضَليّ *adj* muscle (*before n*); تَقَلُّص عَضَليّ muscle contraction; جُهْد عَضَليّ physical exertion

مُعْضِلة *n* |مُعْضِلات, مَعاضِلُ| problem, dilemma; puzzle; مُعْضِلة طِبِّيّة a medical problem

عُضْو *n* |mf; أَعْضاء| 1 [في مُنَظَّمةٍ، نادٍ...] member; عُضْو عامِل full member; عُضْو شَرَفٍ, فَخْريّ \ شَرَفيّ a member of honour; عُضْو قِياديّ a leading member; أَعْضاء مَجْلِسِ البَلَديّة \ اللَّجْنةِ the members of the council/committee; قائِمة \ لائِحة الأَعْضاءِ membership list; دَوْلة عُضْو في المَجْموعةِ الأوروبّيّةِ a member state of the European Union 2 [الجِسْم] member, organ, limb; أَعْضاء تَناسُليّة sexual/reproductive organs, genitals; عُضْو اصْطِناعيّ prosthesis; عُضْو التَّذْكيرِ the male member; التَبَرُّع بِأَعْضاءٍ organ donation

عُضْويّ *adj* 1 [بِأَعْضاءٍ] organic; كائِنات عُضْويّة organisms 2 [مَنْسوب إلى العُضْوِ] organ (*before n*); فَشَل عُضْويّ organ failure 3 [غَيْر صِناعيٍّ] organic; نُفايات عُضْويّة organic waste; كيمِياء عُضْويّة organic chemistry; أَسْمِدة عُضْويّة organic fertilizers; وَقود عُضْويّ biofuels; الزِراعة العُضْويّة organic farming; الغِذاء \ الطَعام العُضْويّ organic food

عُضْويّة *n* 1 [انْتِماء] membership; عُضْويّة حِلْفِ شَمالِ الأَطْلَسيِّ NATO membership; عُضْويّة البَرْلَمانِ membership of parliament; بِطاقة عُضْويّةٍ membership card; أَلْغى عُضْويَّتَهُ to resign one's membership; طَرَدَ شَخْصاً من العُضْويّةِ to expel sb as a member; حَرَمَ \ اسْتَثْنى \ اسْتَبْعَدَ شَخْصاً من

عَصى *v* |i; عِصْيان| to disobey, to resist; to rebel, to mutiny; عَصى شَخْصاً \ شَيْئاً to disobey sb; to rebel against sb; عَصى على فَهْمِهِ to be difficult to understand

عاصى *v* to resist, to oppose, to defy

اسْتَعْصى *v* to be impossible; اسْتَعْصى على الفَهْمِ to be incomprehensible; اسْتَعْصى على الحَلِّ to be unsolvable

عاصٍ A *adj* |عُصاة| disobedient; recalcitrant
B *n* |عُصاة| rebel, insurgent

عِصْيان *n* disobedience, resistance; rebellion, mutiny; عِصْيان مَدَنيّ civil disobedience; عِصْيان مُسَلَّح armed resistance

اسْتِعْصاء *n* conundrum

العاصي *n* Orontes River, Asi River (*river in the Levant*)

مُسْتَعْصٍ *adj* insurmountable; unsolvable; incurable; قَضيّة مُسْتَعْصِية an intractable issue; أَزْمة \ مُشْكِلة مُسْتَعْصِية على الحَلِّ an unsolvable crisis/problem; مَرَض مُسْتَعْصٍ a persistent disease

مَعْصِية *n* |مَعاصٍ| 1 [إِثْم] sin; ارْتَكَبَ مَعْصِيةً كُبْرى to commit a mortal sin 2 [عِصْيان] disobedience

عَضْب *adj* sharp, keen

عَضَدَ *v* |u; عَضْد| to help, to support

عاضَدَ *v* to support, to assist, to help

تَعاضَدَ *v* to cooperate

عَضُد *n* |أَعْضاد| 1 (Anat) upper arm; عَظْم العَضُدِ humerus; شَدَّ عَضُدَ شَخْصٍ to support/assist sb 2 [مُساعِد] support, aid, assistance; هو عَضُدي المَتينُ he is my prop and stay

عِضادة *n* post; عِضادة البابِ door post

تَعاضُد *n* cooperation

تَعاضُديّة *n* cooperation

مُعاضَدة *n* assistance, help, aid, support

عَضَّ *v* |a; عَضّ, عَضيض| to bite; عَضَّ الكَلْبُ الجارَ the dog bit the neighbour

Idiom عَضَّ إِصْبَعَهُ to regret sth, to be sorry

عَضّاض *adj* biting; كِلاب عَضّاضة biting dogs

عَضّة *n* bite; عَضّة من التُفّاحة a bite out of the apple; عَضّة كَلْبٍ a dog bite

العُضْوِيّة to exclude sb from membership; تُكَلِّفُ العُضْوِيّةُ ٤٠ لِيرةً the membership fee is 40 lira 2 [حَيّ] organism; عُضْوِيّات مُعَدَّلة وِراثيًّا genetically modified organisms

لاعُضْوِيّ *adj* inorganic, non-organic

مُتَعَضٍّ *adj* organic; غَيْر مُتَعَضٍّ inorganic, non-organic; كائِن مُتَعَضٍّ organism

عَطِبَ *v* |a; عَطَب| to be destroyed; to spoil; عَطِبَت الفاكِهةُ the fruit has spoiled

أَعْطَبَ *v* to destroy; to damage; أَعْطَبَ سَيّارةً عَطَباً خَفيفاً \ شَديداً to slightly/heavily damage a car

عَطَب *n* defect; trouble

مَعْطوب *adj* damaged

عَطَّرَ *v* to perfume, to scent

تَعَطَّرَ *v* to perfume oneself; تَعَطَّرَ بِعِطْرٍ to put on perfume/cologne

عَطِر *adj* fragrant

عِطْر *n* |عُطور, عُطورات| perfume; cologne; زُجاجة عِطْرٍ a bottle of perfume; مَحَلّ عُطورٍ perfume shop; تَفوحُ مِنْهُ رائِحةُ العِطْرِ he smells of cologne

عاطِر *adj* fragrant, sweet-smelling; aromatic

عَطّار *n* perfume seller

عِطْرِيّ *adj* fragrant

مُعَطَّر *adj* perfumed; aromatic; زُيوت مُعَطَّرة aromatic oils; صابون مُعَطَّر perfumed soap

عُطارِد *n* |dipt| (Astron) Mercury

عَطَسَ *v* |i-u; عُطاس, عَطْس| to sneeze

عُطاس *n* sneezing; نَوْبة عُطاسٍ a sneezing fit

عَطْسة *n* sneeze

عَطِشَ *v* |a; عَطَش| to be thirsty

عَطَّشَ *v* to make thirsty; هذا الطَّعامُ يُعَطِّشُ this food makes you thirsty

أَعْطَشَ *v* to make thirsty

تَعَطَّشَ *v* |ل, إلى| to thirst for, to hunger for, to yearn for; تَعَطَّشَ للدَمِ to thirst for blood; تَعَطَّشَ للسُلْطةِ \ للنَجاحِ to hunger for power/success; تَعَطَّشَ للمالِ to lust for money

عَطَش *n* thirst; أَرْوى عَطَشَهُ to quench one's thirst

عَطِش *adj* |عِطاش| thirsty

عَطْشان *adj* |dipt; عِطاش; f عَطْشى| thirsty; كانَ عَطْشانَ to be thirsty

تَعَطُّش *n* thirst, hunger; التَعَطُّش للمالِ a lust for money; التَعَطُّش للدَمِ a thirst for blood, bloodthirstiness

مُتَعَطِّش *adj* thirsty, hungry, yearning; مُتَعَطِّش للدِماءِ bloodthirsty; نِمْر مُتَعَطِّش للدِماءِ a bloodthirsty tiger; كانَ مُتَعَطِّشاً للمَعْرِفةِ to have a thirst for knowledge; كانَ مُتَعَطِّشاً للمُغامَرة \ للانْتِقام to be out for adventure/revenge

عَطَفَ *v* |i; عَطْف| 1 [أَشْفَقَ] |على| to sympathize with, to feel compassion for; to like; عَطَفَ على شَخْصٍ to sympathize with sb 2 [أَمالَ] to bend; عَطَفَ غُصْناً to bend a twig 3 [مالَ] to turn; عَطَفَ إلى ناحِيةٍ to turn into a direction; عَطَفَ عن شَخْصٍ to turn away from sb

تَعَطَّفَ *v* 1 [تَلَطَّفَ] to deign, to be so kind as to 2 [حَنَّ] |على| to feel sympathy/compassion

تَعاطَفَ *v* |مع| to sympathize with, to feel compassion for; تَعاطَفَ مع شَخْصٍ to sympathize with sb

انْعَطَفَ *v* to turn; انْعَطَفَ إلى اليَسارِ \ اليَمينِ to turn left/right

اسْتَعْطَفَ *v* to seek sympathy/compassion; to implore

عَطْف *n* 1 [رَحْمة] sympathy, liking; attachment, affection; العَطْف على الفُقَراءِ sympathy for the poor 2 (Gram) أَداة \ حَرْف عَطْفٍ conjunction; عَطْف النَسَقِ coordination

عاطِفة *n* |عَواطِفُ| 1 [شُعور] emotion, feeling, sentiment; عَواطِف جَيّاشة overwhelming emotions; انْساقَ وراء عَواطِفِهِ to be guided by one's emotions; عَواطِف الشُكْرِ feelings of gratitude; عَواطِف بُغْضٍ \ كُرْهٍ hatred; حَرَّكَ عَواطِفَ شَخْصٍ to move sb 2 [شَفَقة] sympathy, liking, compassion

عاطِفِيّ *adj* emotional, sentimental; sensitive; loving, tender; نَوْبة عاطِفِيّة a sentimental mood; مُغامَرة عاطِفِيّة a romantic escapade; أُغْنِيّة عاطِفِيّة a love song; غَيْر عاطِفِيٍّ unemotional; insensitive; مُقابَلة عاطِفِيّة an emotional encounter

عاطِفِيّة *n* sensitivity; sentimentality

عِطاف *n* |أَعْطِفة, عُطُف| coat, cloak

عَطْفة *n* twist; curve, turn

عَطوف *adj* |عُطُف| sympathetic, compassionate; affectionate

اسْتِعْطاف *n* entreaty, request, plea

انْعِطاف *n* |انْعِطافات| bending; curve

تَعاطُف *n* sympathy, compassion; تَعاطُف مع شَخْصٍ \ شَيْءٍ sympathy for sb/sth; عَبَّرَ عن تَعاطُفِهِ مع شَخْصٍ to express one's sympathy for sb

مُتَعاطِف **A** *adj* sympathetic; هو مُتَعاطِفٌ مع الأَفْكارِ الشُيوعِيَّةِ he has communist sympathies **B** *n* sympathizer

مِعْطَف *n* |مَعاطِفُ| coat, cloak; مِعْطَف دافِئ a warm coat; مِعْطَف مَطَرِيّ a raincoat; لَبِسَ \ ارْتَدى مِعْطَفاً to wear a coat; خَلَعَ مِعْطَفَهُ to take off one's coat

مَعْطوف *adj* bent; curved

مُنْعَطَف *n* |مُنْعَطَفات| **1** [طَريق] bend, curve; مُنْعَطِف حادّ a sharp bend **2** [نُقْطَةُ التَحَوُّلِ] turn, turning point; مُنْعَطِف حاسِم a crucial turning point

عَطِلَ *v* |a; عَطَل| to lack; عَطِلَ من شَيْءٍ to lack sth; عَطِلَ عن العَمَلِ to be unemployed

عَطَّلَ *v* **1** [كَسَرَ] to break, to destroy, to wreck, to put out of action; عَطَّلَ سَيّارةً to wreck a car **2** [أَوْقَفَ] to hinder, to obstruct, to hold up; to stop; to suspend, to delay; عَطَّلَ شَخْصاً عن مُمارَسةِ عَمَلِهِ to keep sb from doing their job; عَطَّلَ مَشْروعاً to delay a project; عَطَّلَ قانوناً to block a law; عَطَّلَ مَصالِحَ شَخْصٍ to harm sb's interests

تَعَطَّلَ *v* **1** [عَطِبَ] to break (down), to fail; تَعَطَّلَ المُحَرِّكُ the engine failed; تَعَطَّلَتِ السَيّارةُ the car broke down; تَعَطَّلَ التِلْفازُ the TV broke **2** [تَأَجَّلَ] to be obstructed/hindered; to be postponed/delayed; to be stopped/at a standstill; تَعَطَّلَتِ المُفاوَضاتُ the negotiations broke down **3** [عن العَمَلِ] to be unemployed; تَعَطَّلَ عن العَمَلِ to be unemployed

عُطْل *n* |أَعْطال| defect, breakdown, trouble; عُطْل تِقَنِيّ \ فَنِّيّ a technical malfunction; عُطْل في المُحَرِّكِ a defect in the engine; أَصْلَحَ عُطْلاً to repair a defect

عاطِل **A** *adj* unemployed; عاطِل عن العَمَلِ unemployed **B** *n* unemployed (person); عَدَد العاطِلينَ the number of unemployed, the unemployment rate

عَطالة *n* unemployment

عُطْلة *n* |عُطْلات, عُطَل| holidays (BrE), vacation (AmE); leave; عُطْلة مَدْرَسِيّة school holidays; عُطْلة نِهايةِ الأُسْبوعِ weekend; عُطْلة رَسْمِيّة a public holiday; عُطْلة الصَيْفِ \ العُطْلة الصَيْفِيّة summer holiday; عُطْلة لِمُدّةِ أُسْبوعٍ \ شَهْرٍ a day's/week's holiday; يَوْم عُطْلةٍ holiday, day off; في العُطْلةِ in the holidays; هو في عُطْلةٍ ,عِنْدَهُ عُطْلةٌ he is on leave, he has a holiday; قَضى العُطْلةَ على الشاطِئِ \ الساحِلِ to spend one's holiday at the beach

تَعَطُّل *n* **1** [تَوَقُّف] blocking, obstruction; تَعَطُّل حَرَكةِ المُرورِ \ السَيْرِ blocking traffic **2** [آلةٍ] failure, breakdown **3** [عن العَمَلِ] unemployment

تَعْطيل *n* **1** [تَوْقيف] obstruction; discontinuance, stopping; suspension; تَعْطيل عُبْوةٍ ناسِفةٍ defusing a bomb **2** [كَسْر] breaking, wrecking, destruction

مُتَعَطِّل *adj* unemployed; inactive, stalled; عَمَلِيّة السَلامِ المُتَعَطِّلة the stalled peace process

مُعَطَّل *adj* broken, out of order, damaged; لَوْحة مَفاتيحَ مُعَطَّلة a faulty keyboard; كومْبيوتَر مُعَطَّل a broken computer; رابِط مُعَطَّل a broken link; عَمَلِيّة السَلامِ المُعَطَّلة the broken-down peace process; التِلِفِزْيونُ مُعَطَّلٌ the television is not working

عَطَنَ *v* |i-u; عَطْن| **1** [الجِلْدَ] to soak hides (*for tanning*) **2** [الكَتّانَ] to soak

عَطِنَ *v* |a; عَطَن| to rot, to decay

عَطِن *adj* rotten; رائِحة عَطِنة a bad/foul smell

أَعْطى *v* to give, to hand over; أَعْطى شَخْصاً هَدِيّةً to give sb a present; أُعْطِيَ هَدِيّةً to get a present; أَعْطى شَخْصاً حُبَّهُ to give sb one's love; أَعْطى واجِباً to give an assignment; أَعْطى شَخْصاً دَرْساً to give sb a lesson; أَعْطى شَخْصاً الكَلِمةَ to let sb speak

تَعاطى *v* **1** [تَناوَلَ] to use, to take; تَعاطى أَدْوِيةً to take medicines; تَعاطى المُخَدِّراتِ to use drugs **2** [قامَ بِهِ] to occupy oneself; تَعاطى مع شَيْءٍ to occupy oneself with sth, to be busy with sth; to be involved with sth; to handle sth, to deal with sth; تَعاطى السِياسةَ to be engaged in politics; تَعاطى مع مَوْضوعٍ to deal with a subject

طَبيب العِظامِ osteoporosis; طِبّ \ جراحة العِظامِ orthopaedics; orthopaedist; كانَ رَفيعَ \ غَليظَ العِظامِ to have light/heavy bones; كانَ جِلْداً على عَظْمٍ to be (nothing but) skin and bone; أَحَبَّتْهُ / كَرِهَتْهُ إلى حَدِّ العَظْم she absolutely loved/hated it

عِظَم *n* greatness, magnitude

عِظاميّ *adj* 1 [من العَظْمِ] bone (*before n*), osteological 2 [مُصاب بالبارانويا] paranoid, paranoiac; هَذَيان عِظاميّ paranoid delirium 3 [شَريف] noble, aristocratic

عَظَمة *n* greatness; magnificence, grandeur; prestige; عَظَمة الله God's greatness; صاحِب العَظَمة His Highness; جُنون العَظَمةِ megalomania; كانَ مُصاباً بِجُنونِ العَظَمةِ to be a megalomaniac; أَكْسَبَ شَيْئاً عَظَمةً to give sth prestige

عَظْميّ *adj* bony, bone (*before n*); هَيْكَل عَظْميّ skeleton; أيادٍ \ أَصابِع عَظْميّة bony hands/fingers

عَظيم A *adj* |عِظام, عُظَماءُ, عَظائِمُ| 1 [ضَخْم] enormous, gigantic, immense; عَظيم الشَأْنِ very important; بِناء عَظيم a huge building; نَجاح عَظيم an enormous success 2 [رائِع] great, magnificent, formidable, splendid; mighty, powerful; إِنْجاز عَظيم a tremendous achievement; امرَأة \ زَوْجة عَظيمة a great woman/wife; فُرْصة عَظيمة an excellent opportunity B *n* (Islam) العَظيم the Magnificent (*one of the names of God*); واللهِ العَظيم by God, the Almighty; yes, really!

أَعْظَم *adj* |dipt; أَعاظِمُ| greater; more important; بَريطانيا العُظْمى Great Britain; جَريمة عُظْمى major crime; أَغْلَبيّة عُظْمى a vast majority

تَعْظيم *n* glorification, exaltation

مُعْظَم *n* majority, most of; major part; مُعْظَم الشَبابِ most of the young people; مُعْظَم حَياتِهِ most of his life; في مُعْظَم المَناطِقِ in most areas

مُعَظَّم *adj* exalted; جَلالة المَلِكِ المُعَظَّمِ His Royal Highness

‹ **عَظاية, عَظاءة, عِظاية** *n* |عَظايا| lizard

‹ **عَفَج** *n* (Anat) duodenum

‹ **عَفَر** *v* |i; عَفْر| to cover with dust

عَفَر *n* |أَعْفار| dust

أَعْفَر *adj* |dipt| dust-coloured

‹ **عَفْرَتة** *n* mischief

اسْتَعْطى *v* to beg

عَطاء *n* 1 [مَصْدَر] giving; الأَخْذ والعَطاء give and take 2 [هِبة] |أَعْطِية| gift 3 (Busn) |عَطاءات| offer, tender; قَدَّمَ عَطاءً to make/submit an offer

عَطيّة *n* |عَطايا| 1 [هَدِيّة] gift 2 [اسْم شَخْصيّ] Atia, Atiya (*male given name*)

إعْطاء *n* giving; donation

تَعاطٍ *n* 1 [مُعامَلة] use, taking; تَعاطي المُخَدِّراتِ drug use, drug abuse 2 [عَلاقة] involvement; treatment; التَعاطي مع التَطَوُّراتِ الجَديدةِ dealing with the new developments

مُتَعاطٍ *n* user; مُتَعاطي مُخَدِّراتٍ drug user

مِعْطاء *adj* |مَعاطٍ, مَعاطيُّ| generous, giving

مُعْطًى *n* |مُعْطَيات| fact; مُعْطَيات facts, data; مُعْطَيات واقِعيّة factual information; مُعْطَيات سَليمة valid facts; مُعْطَيات تاريخيّة historical facts; على أَساسِ مُعْطَياتٍ رَسْميّةٍ on the basis of official data; إنّ المُعْطَياتِ مُتَوافِرةٌ there is sufficient information

‹ **عَظاءة** *n* see عَظاية

‹ **عِظة** *n* see وعظ

‹ **عَظُمَ** *v* |u; عِظَم| 1 [كانَ عَظيماً] to be/become great, to be/become magnificent; عَظُمَ في عَيْنَيَّ he has risen in my esteem 2 [كانَ كَريهاً] to be hard/painful; عَظُمَ عَلَيْهِ الأَمْرُ it was hard for him

عَظَّمَ *v* 1 [مَجَّدَ] to glorify, to exalt 2 [كَبَّرَ] to make greater; عَظَّمَ أَهَمِّيّةَ شَيْءٍ to attach too much importance to sth; عَظَّمَ اللهُ أَجْرَكَ may God multiply your reward

أَعْظَمَ *v* to regard as enormous; to attach great importance to; to glorify

تَعَظَّمَ *v* |ب| to boast about; to be proud of; تَعَظَّمَ بِشَيْءٍ to boast about sth

تَعاظَمَ *v* 1 [كَبُرَ] to become bigger; to be huge/enormous; تَعاظَمَ الخَطَرُ the danger has grown 2 [تَكَبَّرَ] to be proud/arrogant

اسْتَعْظَمَ *v* to regard as great/tremendous

عَظْم *n* |أَعْظُم, عِظام| bone; عَظْم الزَنْدِ ulna; عَظْم نُخاعيّ marrowbone; (Sci) medullary bone (*in birds and dinosaurs*); الْتِهاب العِظامِ osteitis, inflammation of the bones; تَخَلْخُل العِظامِ

عِفْريت *n* |عَفاريتُ| **1** [جِنّ] ifrit, demon; وَضَعَ شَيْئاً على كَفِّ عِفْريتٍ to jeopardize sth; كانَ على كَفِّ عِفْريتٍ to be in jeopardy **2** [طِفْل شَقِيّ] rascal

عَفَسَ *v* |i; عَفْس| to remove

عَفْش *n* **1** [أَثاث] furniture; household effects **2** [حَقائِب] luggage

عَفْص *n* gallnuts, oak apples (*unnatural growths on oak trees caused by insects*)

عُفوصة *n* bitterness

عَفَّ *v* |i; عَفاف, عِفّة| |عن| to abstain (from); to be chaste/virtuous; عَفَّ اللِسانَ to hold one's tongue; عَفَّ عن شَيْءٍ to abstain from sth

تَعَفَّفَ *v* to be chaste/virtuous

عَفاف *n* **1** [طُهْر] virtue, chastity **2** [اِسْم شَخْصِيّ] Afaf (*female given name*)

عِفّة *n* virtue; chastity; حافَظَتْ على عِفَّتِها \ فَقَدَتْ عِفَّتَها she maintained/lost her chastity; حِزام العِفّة chastity belt

عَفيف **A** *adj* |أَعِفّة, أَعِفّاءُ| chaste, virtuous; فَتاة عَفيفة a virtuous girl; غَيْر عَفيف unchaste
B *n* Afif (*male given name*)

تَعَفُّف *n* abstinence; chastity; virtuousness

عَفِنَ *v* |a; عَفَن| to rot, to decay; to mould

عَفَّنَ *v* to cause to rot, to spoil

تَعَفَّنَ *v* to decay, to rot; to mould; تَتَعَفَّنُ الفَواكِهُ fruit rots; يَتَعَفَّنُ الخُبْزُ bread moulds; تَعَفَّن في السِجْنِ to rot in prison

عَفَن *n* |أَعْفان| mould; decay, rot

عَفِن *adj* bad, decayed, rotten; mouldy, musty; خُبْز عَفِن mouldy bread; تُفّاحة عَفِنة a rotten apple; رائِحة عَفِنة a foul smell

عُفونة *n* decay, rot; mould; رائِحة العُفونةِ a smell of mould

تَعَفُّن *n* rotting, decay, decomposition; في حالةِ تَعَفُّنٍ شَديد in an advanced state of decomposition

مُتَعَفِّن *adj* rotten, bad; decayed, decomposed; تُفّاحة مُتَعَفِّنة a rotten apple; جُثّة مُتَعَفِّنة a decomposed body

عَفا *v* |u; عَفْو| **1** [سامَحَ] to forgive, to pardon; عَفا عن شَخْصٍ to extend forgiveness to sb; عَفا اللهُ عَمّا مَضى ≈ let bygones be bygones **2** [مَحا] to efface, to wipe out; عَفا الأَثَرَ to wipe away any trace; عَفا عَلَيْهِ الزَمَنُ to be out of date **3** [اِمَّحى] to be/become effaced

عَفّى *v* to wipe out; عَفّى الآثارَ to wipe out the traces

عافى *v* to heal; عافاكَ اللهُ get well soon!

أَعْفى *v* |من| to exempt from, to grant dispensation from; to discharge from, to relieve of, to release from; to give amnesty; أَعْفى شَخْصاً من وَظيفَتِهِ to discharge sb from office; أَعْفى شَخْصاً من مُهِمَّتِهِ to relieve sb of his task; أَعْفى شَخْصاً من عُقوبةٍ to let sb off a punishment; أَعْفى شَخْصاً من المُلاحَقةِ القَضائيّةِ to acquit sb; أُعْفِيَ من الخِدْمةِ to be exempt from military service

تَعافى *v* to be cured; تَعافى من مَرَضٍ to be cured of a disease

اِسْتَعْفى *v* **1** [اِسْتَقالَ] to resign **2** [طَلَبَ العَفْوَ] to ask forgiveness

عَفُوّ *n* العَفُوّ the Pardoner (*one of the names of God*)

عَفْو *n* pardon, amnesty; mercy; عَفْو عامّ amnesty, general pardon; مُنَظَّمة العَفْوِ الدُوَليّة Amnesty International; العَفْوُ عند المَقْدِرة *a pardon in spite of one's power (to punish)*; طَلَب العَفْوِ a request for pardon; طَلَبَ \ اِلْتَمَسَ العَفْوَ to request a pardon; to beg for mercy; قَدَّمَ \ رَفَضَ طَلَبَ العَفْوِ to submit/refuse a request for pardon; مَنَحَ شَخْصاً العَفْوَ to grant sb forgiveness; to pardon sb

(Idioms) عَفْواً, العَفْوَ you're welcome; excuse me; عَفْوَ الخاطِرِ spur of the moment

عافِية *n* |عافِيات, عَوافٍ| health; اِسْتَعادَ عافِيَتَهُ (تَماماً) to (fully) recover; يُعْطيكَ العافِية May God give you health; thank you

عَفْوِيّ *adj* spontaneous; شَخْص عَفْوِيّ a spontaneous person; رَدّ فِعْلٍ عَفْوِيّ a spontaneous reaction; بِشَكْلٍ عَفْوِيٍّ spontaneously

عَفْوِيّة *n* spontaneity; بِعَفْوِيّةٍ spontaneously

اِسْتِعْفاء *n* **1** [اِسْتِقالة] resignation **2** [طَلَب العَفْوِ] request for pardon

إِعْفاء *n* |إِعْفاءات| **1** [إِبْراء] exemption, dispensation; remission; discharge, acquittal; إِعْفاء جُمْرُكِيّ duty-free;

عُقْب *n* |أَعْقاب| tip, end; outcome; عُقْب سيجارةٍ \ بُنْدُقيّةٍ cigarette/rifle butt; في أَعْقابِ (immediately) after, following, in the aftermath

عاقِبة *n* |عَواقِبُ| consequence, implication, result, effect; عَواقِب ماليّة financial consequences; عَواقِب وَخيمة \ جَسيمة severe/far-reaching consequences; سوء العاقِبة negative consequences; setback; رَبَطَ العَواقِبَ بِشَيْءٍ to attach consequences to sth; تَحَمَّلَ عَواقِبَ شَيْءٍ to bear the consequences of sth; أَدّى إلى عَواقِبَ to lead to consequences; أَنْذَرَ بالعَواقِبِ to warn about the consequences; تَنْجِمُ عَنْهُ عَواقِبُ it has consequences; بِدونِ عَواقِبَ without adverse effects; with impunity

عُقاب *n* |عِقْبان, أَعْقُب| eagle

عِقاب *n* punishment, sanction; punishing; عِقاب بَدَنيّ corporal punishment; بِغَيْرِ عِقابٍ, دون عِقابٍ unpunished, with impunity; فَعَلَ شَيْئاً دون عِقابٍ to do sth with impunity

عِقابيّ *adj* punitive, penal, punishment (*before n*); إجْراءات \ تَدابير عِقابيّة punitive measures; مُؤَسَّسة عِقابيّة a penal institution

عَقَبة *n* |عِقاب, عَقَبات| obstacle, barrier; impediment, hindrance; مَثَّلَ \ شَكَّلَ عَقَبةً لِشَيْءٍ to be an obstacle to sth; أَزالَ عَقَبةً to remove an obstacle; حَطَّمَ عَقَبةً to break a barrier

عُقْبى *n* |f| consequence, result, effect

عُقوبة *n* punishment, sanction, penalty; عُقوبة خَفيفة \ شَديدة \ صارِمة a light/severe/harsh punishment; عُقوبة تَأْديبيّة disciplinary action; عُقوبة جَسَديّة corporal punishment; عُقوبة سِجْنٍ imprisonment; عُقوبات ضدّ بِلادٍ sanctions against a country; فَرَضَ \ رَفَعَ العُقوباتِ to impose/lift sanctions; أَوْقَعَ \ فَرَضَ عُقوبةً على شَخْصٍ to inflict/impose punishment on sb

عُقَّيب *n* (Zool) harrier (*bird*)

العَقَبة *n* ❶ [مَدينة أُرْدُنيّة] Aqaba; خَليج العَقَبة Gulf of Aqaba ❷ [بالقُرْبِ من مَكّةَ المُكَرَّمةِ] Aqaba (*a hill near the city of Mecca*)

تَعاقُب *n* |تَعاقُبات| succession, sequence; alternation; تَعاقُب الأَجْيالِ succession of generations; تَعاقُب اللَّيْلِ والنَهارِ the alternation of night and day; بالتَعاقُبِ by turns, in succession, back-to-back

إعْفاء من الخِدْمةِ tax exemption; إعْفاء ضَريبيّ \ من الضَرائِبِ exemption from military service; قَدَّمَ طَلَباً للإعْفاءِ العَسْكَريّةِ to request an exemption; مَنَحَ إعْفاءً to grant an exemption ❷ [صَفْح] pardon, remission

مُعافاة *n* recovery

مُعافًى *n* healthy, fit

مُعْفًى *adj* exempted; مُعْفًى من الضَرائِبِ \ الرُسومِ tax-free, duty-free

عَقَبَ *v* |u; عَقْب| to follow; to succeed; عَقَبَ أَباهُ to succeed one's father

عَقَّبَ *v* ❶ [عَلَّقَ على] to comment (on); عَقَّبَ على شَيْءٍ to comment on sth ❷ [تَلا] to follow; to succeed

عاقَبَ *v* ❶ [قاصَّ] to punish; عاقَبَ مُجْرِماً \ تِلْميذاً to punish a criminal/student; عاقَبَ على التَصَرُّفاتِ السَيِّئةِ to punish bad behaviour; عاقَبَ شَخْصاً على سَرِقةٍ to punish sb for stealing; عاقَبَ شَخْصاً عِقاباً شَديداً \ عُقوبةً قاسِيةً, عاقَبَ شَخْصاً بِصَرامةٍ \ بِشِدّةٍ to punish sb severely; يُعاقِبُ عَلَيْهِ القانونُ to be punishable by law; مُخالَفة يُعاقِبُ عَلَيْها القانونُ an offence punishable by law ❷ [ناوَبَ] to take turns

أَعْقَبَ *v* ❶ [خَلَفَ] to follow; to succeed; الفَتْرة التي أَعْقَبَت الحَرْبَ العالَميّةَ الثانِيةَ the period following the second world war ❷ [وَلَدَ] to have offspring

تَعَقَّبَ *v* to follow, to go after; to pursue; تَعَقَّبَ شَخْصاً في الشارِعِ to follow sb on the street; تَعَقَّبَ آثارَ شَخْصٍ to track sb; تَعَقَّبَ النَجاحَ \ المُتْعةَ to pursue success/pleasure; تَعَقَّبَ خُلْسةً to shadow

تَعاقَبَ *v* ❶ [تَلا] to succeed each other; تَعاقَبَت الأَيّامُ the days came one after the other ❷ [تَناوَبَ] to take turns; تَعاقَبَ على الكَلامِ to take turns speaking

عَقِب *n* |أَعْقاب| ❶ [مُؤَخِّر القَدَمِ] heel; رَأْساً على عَقِبٍ upside down; رَجَعَ على عَقِبَيْهِ to follow sb; سارَ في أَعْقابِ شَخْصٍ to turn back; نَكَصَ عن عَقِبَيْهِ to give up ❷ [ذُرِّيّة] offspring, descendants ❸ [بُنْدُقيّة] butt; عَقِب بُنْدُقيّةٍ rifle butt; عَقِب سيجارةٍ cigarette butt

عَقِبَ *prep* (immediately) after, following on; عَقِبَ المُحاضَرةِ following the lecture

تَعاقُبِيّ *adj* successive, consecutive; alternating; تَرْتيب تَعاقُبِيّ successive order; أَلْعاب الأَدْوارِ التَعاقُبِيَّة role-playing games

تَعَقُّب *n* |تَعَقُّبات| following; pursuit

تَعْقيب *n* |تَعْقيبات| comment; تَعْقيباً \ في تَعْقيبٍ على شَيْءٍ commenting on sth

مُتَعاقِب *adj* successive; حُكومات مُتَعاقِبة successive governments

مُعاقَب *adj* punishable; punished مُعاقَب عَلَيْهِ

مُعاقَبة *n* punishment

يَعْقوب *n* listed alphabetically

عَقابيل *n* |dipt| herpes

عَقَدَ *v* |i; عَقْد| ① [رَبَطَ] to tie, to knot; عَقَدَ حَبْلاً حول طَرْدٍ to tie a string around a package; عَقَدَ لِسانَ شَخْصٍ to silence sb; عَقَدَ قَلْبَهُ على شَيْءٍ to lose one's heart to sth; عَقَدَ أَمَلاً على شَيْءٍ to place one's hope in sth; عَقَدَ العَزْمَ على شَيْءٍ to set one's mind on sth ② [أَبْرَمَ] to conclude, to make, to close; عَقَدَ زَواجاً to contract a marriage; عَقَدَ صَفْقَةً to close a deal ③ [مُؤْتَمَراً] to hold, to arrange; عَقَدَ مُؤْتَمَراً \ اجْتِماعاً to hold a conference/meeting; عَقَدَ مُباحَثاتٍ to hold talks ④ [السائِلَ] to reduce, to thicken

عَقَّدَ *v* ① [رَبَطَ] to tie, to knot ② [صَعَّبَ] to complicate; عَقَّدَ قَضِيَّةً to complicate a matter

أَعْقَدَ *v* to coagulate; to clot

تَعَقَّدَ *v* ① [عُقِدَ] to be knotted/tied; تَعَقَّدَ لِسانُهُ he was tongue-tied ② [صَعُبَ] to be complicated; تَعَقَّدَ الأَمْرُ the matter was/became complicated

تَعاقَدَ *v* to contract; to make a contract, to make an agreement/deal; تَعاقَدَ مع شَخْصٍ على شَيْءٍ to make a contract with sb on sth; تَعاقَدَ مع مُمَثِّلٍ \ لاعِبِ كُرةِ القَدَمِ to hire an actor/soccer player (on contract)

انْعَقَدَ *v* ① [عَجَزَ عن الكَلامِ] to be knotted/tied; انْعَقَدَ لِسانُهُ he was tongue-tied ② [التَأَمَ] to be held; انْعَقَدَ الاجْتِماعُ the meeting was held

اعْتَقَدَ *v* to believe, to think, to suppose; اعْتَقَدَ في الأَشْباحِ to believe in ghosts; اعْتَقَدَ أَنَّ ... to believe that ..., to be under the impression that ...; لا أَعْتَقِدُ I don't think so; على ما أَعْتَقِدُ in my opinion

عَقْد *n* |عُقود| ① [من الأَعْدادِ] decade; (a group of) ten; العَقْد المُقْبِل \ الماضي \ الأَخير the next/past/last decade; وَصَلَ إلى العَقْدِ السابِعِ من عُمْرِهِ to reach the age of seventy ② [وَثيقة] contract; deed, act; covenant; عَقْد طَويل \ قَصير الأَجَلِ a long-term/short-term contract; عَقْد غَيْر مُحَدَّدِ المُدَّةِ an open-ended contract; عُقود مُعَطَّلة suspended contracts; عَقْد عَمَلٍ employment contract; عَقْد عَمَل ثابِت \ مُؤَقَّت a permanent/temporary work contract; عَقْد زَواج a marriage contract; مُدّة العَقْدِ contract duration; مَدَّ مُدَّةَ العَقْدِ to extend a contract; فَسَخَ \ أَنْهى \ أَلْغى \ جَدَّدَ عَقْداً to break/terminate/cancel/renew a contract; أَخَلَّ بِعَقْدٍ to breach a contract; الإِخْلال بالعَقْدِ breach of contract; وَقَّعَ على عَقْدٍ, أَمْضى عَقْداً to sign/execute a contract; الْتَزَمَ بِشُروطِ العَقْدِ to keep to the conditions of a contract; أَبْرَمَ عَقْداً مع شَخْصٍ to enter into/make a contract with sb; دَوَّنَ شَيْئاً في عَقْدٍ to lay something down sth in a contract; يَنْتَهي العَقْدُ the contract is expiring ③ [مَصْدَر] holding (*of a meeting*); concluding (*of a contract*)

عِقْد *n* |عُقود| necklace, chain; عِقْد ذَهَبِيّ \ من الذَهَبِ a gold necklace; واسِطة العِقْدِ the gem in the crown, the pièce de résistance; لَبِسَ عِقْداً to wear a necklace

عَقائِدِيّ *adj* religious; dogmatic, doctrinal; ideological; حِزْب عَقائِدِيّ a religious party; صِراع \ خِلاف عَقائِدِيّ ideological differences, a doctrinal dispute; اتِّجاه عَقائِدِيّ denomination

عُقْدة *n* |عُقَد| ① [خَيْطٍ \ شَعْرٍ] knot; tie; فَكَّ عُقْدَةً to untie a knot ② (Anat) node; سَرَطان العُقْدةِ اللِمْفاوِيّة lymphoma ③ (Naut) knot; سارَ بِسُرْعةِ ١٥ عُقْدةً to travel at a speed of 15 knots ④ (Bot) knot, gnarl; leaf bud ⑤ [مُشْكِلة] problem ⑥ (Psych) complex; عُقْدة نَقْصٍ inferiority complex; عُقْدة ذَنْب guilt complex; عُقْدة أوديب Oedipus complex; لَدَيْهُ عُقْدةٌ نَفْسِيَّةٌ he has a complex

عَقيد *n* |عُقَداءُ| (Mil) colonel

عَقيدة *n* |عَقائِدُ| ① [مَبْدَأ] faith, creed, belief; conviction; ideology; حُرِّيّة العَقيدةِ freedom of religion; freedom of conscience; العَقيدة الإِسْلامِيّة the Islamic faith ② [تَعْليم] doctrine, dogma

اعْتِقاد *n* ① [فِكْر] conviction, view, opinion, belief; idea, conception; اعْتِقاد خاطِئ a misconception; اعْتِقاد راسِخ a deep-seated belief; اعْتِقاد باطِل a false belief; الاعْتِقاد أنّ ... the conviction that ...; دَعا ل \ دَفَعَ إلى \ أدّى إلى الاعْتِقادِ أنّ ... to lead to the conviction that ...; أَعْتَقِدُ كُلَّ الاعْتِقادِ أنّ ... I am absolutely convinced that ...; هُناكَ اعْتِقادٌ بِأَنَّ ... it is believed that ...; في اعْتِقادي in my view/opinion; على عَكْسِ الاعْتِقادِ السائِدِ \ الشائِع contrary to the prevailing view; يَذْهَبُ العُلَماءُ إلى الاعْتِقادِ بِأَنَّ ... scientists are of the opinion that ...; يَسودُ اعْتِقادٌ أنّ ... the opinion prevails that ..., it is believed that ...; إنّ هُناكَ ما يَدْعو إلى الاعْتِقادِ بِأَنَّ ... there is reason to believe/assume that ... ② (Relig) |اعْتِقادات| faith, creed, belief; religious conviction; doctrine; حُرِّيّة الاعْتِقادِ freedom of religion

أَعْقَد *adj* |dipt| ① (Bot) knotty, gnarled ② [أَصْعَب] more complicated; أَعْقَد من ذَنَبِ الضَبِّ very complicated

انْعِقاد *n* holding, taking place; مَوْعِد انْعِقادِ الاجْتِماع the date of the meeting

تَعاقُد *n* ① [إبْرام عَقْد] making of a contract ② [اتِّفاق] contract, agreement; تَعاقُد وَظيفيّ employment contract; فَسْخ \ تَجْديد تَعاقُدِهِ termination/renewal of one's contract

تَعاقُديّ *adj* contractual; الْتِزامات تَعاقُديّة contractual obligations

تَعَقُّد *n* |تَعَقُّدات| complicatedness, complexity; تَعَقُّد مُشْكِلةٍ \ أَمْرٍ the complexity of a problem/matter

تَعْقيد *n* |تَعْقيدات| complication; complexity; تَعْقيدات بيروقراطيّة bureaucratic complications; ازْدادَ الأَمْرُ تَعْقيداً the matter was getting more complicated; وما يَزيدُ الأَمْرَ تَعْقيداً هو أنّ ... what complicates matters even more is that ...

مُتَعاقِد *n* party (to a contract); المُتَعاقِدانِ the two parties

مُعْتَقَد *n* |مُعْتَقَدات| ① [عَقيدة] conviction, belief; مُعْتَقَد دينيّ piety, religious belief; حُرِّيّة المُعْتَقَدِ freedom of belief ② [تَعْليم] doctrine, dogma

مُعَقَّد *adj* complex, complicated, difficult; مَسْأَلة \ مُشْكِلة مُعَقَّدة a complex issue/problem; حالة \ قَضيّة مُعَقَّدة a complicated situation/case; رَقْم مُعَقَّد (Math) a complex number

مِعْقَد *n* pancreas

‹ **عَقَرَ** *v* |i; عَقْر| ① [حَيَواناً] to slaughter; to wound; عَقَرَ حَيَواناً to slaughter an animal ② [عَقُمَ] to be/become sterile, to be/become infertile

عَقُرَ *v* |u; عُقْر| to be/become sterile, to be/become infertile

عاقَرَ *v* to be addicted; عاقَرَ الخَمْرةَ to be addicted to alcohol

أَعْقَرَ *v* to stun, to stupefy

عُقْر *n* ① [عُقْم] sterility, infertility ② [وَسَط] middle; في عُقْرِ دارِهِ in one's own backyard, on one's own turf/territory

عاقِر *adj* |mf; عُقَّر; f pl عَواقِرُ| sterile, infertile; رَجُل \ امرأة عاقِر an infertile man/woman

عَقار *n* |عَقارات| real estate, property; سِمْسار في العَقاراتِ estate agent (BrE), real estate broker/agent (AmE); اسْتَثْمَرَ في العَقاراتِ to invest in real estate

عَقّار Ⓐ *adj* snappy; هذا الكَلْبُ عَقّارٌ this dog bites Ⓑ *n* |عَقاقيرُ| medicine, drug; عَقاقير مُنَشِّطة stimulants; تَناوَلَ عَقاقيرَ مُنَشِّطةً to use stimulants

عَقاريّ *adj* real estate (before n); بَنْك \ مَصْرَف عَقاريّ mortgage lender; شَهْر عَقاريّ ≈ land register; ضَرائِب عَقاريّة property taxes; مُمْتَلَكات عَقاريّة real estate, (real) property; رَهْن \ قَرْض عَقاريّ mortgage; أَزْمة الرَهْنِ العَقاريِّ the mortgage crisis

عَقاقيريّ Ⓐ *adj* pharmacological Ⓑ *n* pharmacologist

عَقيرة *n* voice; رَفَعَ عَقيرَتَهُ to raise one's voice

مُعاقِر *n* مُعاقِر (ل)الخَمْرِ alcoholic

مُعاقَرة *n* addiction; مُعاقَرة الخَمْرِ alcohol addiction

‹ **عَقْرَب** *n* |mf; عَقارِبُ| ① (Zool) scorpion; الأَقارِبُ عَقارِبُ one's relatives are one's worst enemies ② (Astrol) (بُرْج) العَقْرَب Scorpio ③ [الساعةِ] hand (of a clock); عَقْرَب الدَقائِقِ وعَقْرَب الساعاتِ the minute hand and the hour hand; في اتِّجاهِ عَقارِبِ الساعةِ clockwise

‹ **عَقَصَ** *v* |i; عَقْص| to braid, to plait; عَقَصَتْ شَعْرَها to braid one's hair

عِقْصة *n* braid

عَقيصة *n* |عَقائِص| braid

مِعْقَص *n* |مَعاقِص| curler; curling iron

عَقْعَق *n* |عَقاعِق| magpie

عَقَفَ *v* |i; عَقْف| to bend; عَقَفَ شَيْئاً to bend sth

انْعَقَفَ *v* to be bent

أَعْقَف *adj* |dipt| bent

مَعْقوف *adj* bent; قَوْسانِ مَعْقوفانِ square brackets; مِنْقار مَعْقوف a hooked beak; صَليب مَعْقوف swastika

عَقَّ *v* |u; عَقّ| to be disobedient/disrespectful; عَقَّ الوَلَدُ والِدَهُ the boy was disrespectful to his father

عاقّ *adj* disrespectful; disobedient; طِفْل عاقّ a disobedient child

عُقوق *n* disobedience; disrespect

عَقيق *n* |عَقائِق| ① [حَجَر كَريم] agate; عَقيق يَمانيّ onyx; عَقيق أَحْمَر garnet ② [وادٍ ضَيِّق] canyon, gorge

عَقيقة *n* |عَقائِق| (Mor) Aqiqah (*the slaughter of an animal to celebrate the birth of a child*)

عَقَلَ *v* |i; عَقْل| ① [كانَ عاقِلاً] to be endowed with reason ② [فَهِمَ] to understand, to grasp; لا يُعْقَلُ أنْ ... it is incredible that ...; it is unreasonable that ... ③ [البَعيرَ] to tie up; عَقَلَت الدَهْشة لِسانَهُ he was struck dumb

عَقَّلَ *v* to bring to reason; to make reasonable

تَعَقَّلَ *v* to be/become rational, to be/become sensible

اعْتَقَلَ *v* to arrest, to detain; اعْتَقَلَ الجُناةَ to arrest the perpetrators

عَقْل *n* |عُقول| sense, reason; brain, intellect; عَقْل سَليم a sound mind; ذو عَقْلٍ, راجِح العَقْلِ intelligent, smart; قِلّة العَقْلِ stupidity, brainlessness; ضِرْس \ سِنّ العَقْلِ wisdom tooth; كانَ مُخْتَلَّ العَقْلِ he was mentally disturbed, he was out of his mind; كانَ العَقْلَ المُدَبِّر للعَمَليّةِ he was the brains behind the operation; شَغَّلَ \ اسْتَخْدَمَ عَقْلَهُ to use one's brains; فَقَدَ عَقْلَهُ to lose one's mind; فاقَ عَقْلَهُ it was beyond his comprehension; العَقْلُ السَليمُ في الجِسْمِ السَليمِ a sound mind in a sound body

عاقِل **A** *adj* |عُقّال, عُقَلاءُ, عاقِلونَ| ① [حَكيم] sensible, rational; wise; intelligent; التَفْكير العاقِل rational thinking; كائِنات عاقِلة intelligent beings; غَيْر عاقِلٍ irrational; foolish, unwise; اخْتِيار غَيْر عاقِلٍ a foolish choice; سُلوك غَيْر عاقِلٍ irrational behaviour; أَيّ إنْسانٍ عاقِلٍ every right-minded person ② (Relig) *initiated into the doctrines of the Druze religion* ③ (Gram) human, animate; غَيْر عاقِلٍ non-human, inanimate; جَمْع عاقِل animate plural **B** *n* |عُقّال, عُقَلاءُ, عاقِلونَ| right-minded person; كُلّ عاقِلٍ every right-minded person

عُقّال *n* cramp

عِقال *n* |عُقُل| iqal (*headband holding the kufiya*); *cord used to tie up a camel*; أَطْلَقَ شَخْصاً من عِقالِهِ to release sb from his chains

عَقْلانيّ *adj* rational, mental; sensible; الواقِعيّة العَقْلانيّة the plain truth; عَقْلانيًا rationally, reasonably; غَيْر عَقْلانيّ unwise; irrational

عَقْلانيّة *n* rationalism; بِعَقْلانيّةٍ sensibly, rationally; تَصَرَّفَ ب \ بِعَقْلانيّةٍ to deal with sth in a sensible way تَعاطى مع شَيْءٍ بِعَقْلانيّةٍ

عُقْلة *n* |عُقَل| ① [غُصْن] sprig ② [في السِرْكِ] trapeze

عَقْليّ *adj* mental, intellectual; rational; التَطَوّر العَقْليّ intellectual development; تَوازُن عَقْليّ mental balance; نَظَر عَقْليّ a rational view; مُعاق عَقْليًا having a mental disability

عَقْليّة *n* mentality, attitude; عَقْليّة تِجاريّة a businesslike attitude; عَقْليّة سَلْبيّة a negative mentality

عَقول *n* camel thorn tree (*Acacia erioloba*)

عَقيلة *n* |عَقائِل| wife

عَقيليّ *adj* قُرْص عَقيليّ bundt cake

اعْتِقال *n* |اعْتِقالات| arrest, detention, imprisonment, internment; اعْتِقال عَسْكَريّ military detention; اعْتِقالات عَشْوائيّة arbitrary detention; اعْتِقال في مُعَسْكَراتٍ internment in camps

تَعَقُّل *n* wisdom, prudence, reason; صَوْت التَعَقُّلِ the voice of reason

لاعَقْلانيّ *adj* irrational

لاعَقْلانيّة *n* irrationality

مُتَعَقِّل *adj* sensible, right-thinking

عَكِرَ v |a; عَكَر| to become cloudy; to become murky/muddied; عَكِرَت السَماءُ the sky became cloudy; عَكِرَت العَلاقاتُ the relations are tainted

عَكَّرَ v to disturb, to spoil, to ruin; عَكَّرَ الجَوَّ to ruin the atmosphere; عَكَّرَ صَفْوَ الجَوِّ بتَصَرُّفِهِ his behaviour ruined the atmosphere; عَكَّرَ على شَخْصٍ صَفْوَ يَوْمِهِ to ruin sb's day; عَكَّرْتَ صَفْوَ يَوْمي you ruined my day; عَكَّرَ المُناخَ السِياسيَّ to poison the political climate; عَكَّرَ صَفْوَ الهُدوءِ to disturb the peace

تَعَكَّرَ v to become murky/muddy; to be disturbed; تَعَكَّرَ الماءُ the water became murky

عَكِر adj murky, muddy; ماء عَكِر murky water; (fig) troubled waters; اصْطادَ في الماءِ العَكِرِ to go fishing in troubled waters

تَعْكير n making murky; disturbance, ruining, spoiling

مُتَعَكِّر adj murky; disturbed

مُعَكَّر adj murky

عِكْرِش n (Bot) *Aeluropus*

تَعَكَّزَ v |على| to lean (on)

عُكّاز n |عَكاكيزُ| crutch; cane, walking stick; مَشى على عُكّازَيْنِ to walk with crutches; تَوَكَّأَ على عُكّازِهِ to lean on one's cane

عَكَسَ v |i; عَكْس| 1 [رَدَّ] to reflect; عَكَسَ الماءُ صورَتَهُ the water reflected his image; عَكَسَ الضَوْءَ \ الصَوْتَ to reflect light/sound; عَكَسَ رَغْبَةً to reflect a wish; عَكَسَ جُرْأةً to show courage 2 [قَلَبَ] to reverse, to invert; عَكَسَ كَلامَ شَخْصٍ to twist sb's words; عَكَسَ أَحْرُفَ كَلِمَةٍ to reverse the letters of a word

عاكَسَ v 1 [تَحَرَّشَ بـ] to hit on, to flirt with; to harass, to trouble; عاكَسَ بِنْتاً to hit on a girl, to flirt with a girl; to harass a girl 2 [ضادَّ] to be contrary to, to counteract; عاكَسَ التَيّارَ to go against the tide

تَعاكَسَ v to be reversed

انْعَكَسَ v 1 [الضَوْءُ] to be reflected, to reflect; يَنْعَكِسُ الشُعاعُ \ الضَوْءُ \ الصَوْتُ radiation/light/sound is reflected 2 [أَثَّرَ] to be reflected; to have repercussions; انْعَكَسَ على شَيْءٍ to have repercussions on sth; انْعَكَسَ إيجابيًّا \ سَلْبيًّا to have a positive/negative effects

مُعْتَقَل A adj arrested, detained, imprisoned B n 1 |مُعْتَقَلات| [سِجْن] prison camp; كانَ في مُعْتَقَلٍ to be in a prison camp; رَحَّلَ السُجَناءَ إلى مُعْتَقَلاتٍ to transport the prisoners to prison camps 2 |مُعْتَقَلون| [سَجين] detainee, prisoner; مُعْتَقَل سِياسيّ a political prisoner, a prisoner of conscience

مَعْقِل n |مَعاقِلُ| 1 [حِصْن] fortress, citadel, stronghold 2 (fig) stronghold, bulwark, bastion; مَعْقِل المُحافِظين a conservative stronghold

مَعْقول adj reasonable, rational, sensible; comprehensible; حُجّة مَعْقولة a sensible argument; مُبَرِّر مَعْقول a reasonable excuse; حَلّ مَعْقول a smart solution; سِعْر \ طَلَب مَعْقول a reasonable price/demand; بـ \ مُقابِلَ سِعْرٍ مَعْقولٍ for a reasonable price; غَيْر مَعْقولٍ unreasonable; incomprehensible; absurd, preposterous; من المَعْقولِ reasonably

مَعْقوليّة n reasonableness, rationality

عَقْلَنَ v |i; عَقْلَنة| to rationalize

عَقُمَ v |u; عُقْم| to be infertile/sterile; عَقُمَ خَيالُهُ he is unimaginative

عَقَّمَ v 1 [شَيْئاً] to disinfect; to sterilize; عَقَّمَ جُرْحاً to disinfect/clean a wound; عَقَّمَ الحَليبَ to pasteurize milk; عَقَّمَ آلاتٍ جِراحيّةً to sterilize surgical instruments 2 [شَخْصاً] to sterilize, to make infertile

تَعَقَّمَ v to be sterile

عُقْم n infertility, sterility

عَقيم adj |عِقام، عُقُم| 1 [عاقِر] infertile; sterile 2 [بِلا جَدْوى] useless, pointless; ineffective; نِقاش عَقيم a pointless discussion; حُبّ عَقيم hopeless love

تَعْقيم n 1 [إبادة الجَراثيمِ] sterilization; disinfection, cleansing; تَعْقيم المِياهِ water purification 2 [مَنْع الوِلادةِ] sterilization; تَعْقيم إجْباريّ forced sterilization

تَعْقيميّ adj sterilizing; تَأْثير تَعْقيميّ sterilizing effect

مُعَقَّم adj 1 [عَديم البَكْتيرِيا] sterile, sterilized; حَليب مُعَقَّم pasteurized milk 2 [عَقيم] sterilized

مُعَقِّم n disinfectant, antiseptic

عَكَفَ *v* |i-u; عُكوف| 1 ⟨[أَقْبَلَ] |على| to apply/devote oneself to, to focus on; عَكَفَ على قَضِيَّةٍ to apply oneself to a matter; عَكَفَ على العِبادةِ to devote oneself to worship; عَكَفَ على نَفْسِهِ to focus on oneself, to be self-centred 2 ⟨[لَزِمَ] to stick (to); عَكَفَ في البَيْتِ to stay at home 3 ⟨[أَبْعَدَ] to keep (from); عَكَفَ شَخْصًا عن الزواج to keep sb from marrying

تَعَكَّفَ *v* to isolate oneself; to retire; تَعَكَّفَ في مَكانٍ to isolate oneself in a place

اعْتَكَفَ *v* |في| to retire to, to withdraw to; اعْتَكَفَ في بَيْتِهِ to retire to one's home

عاكِف *adj* |عُكَّف, عُكوف, عاكِفونَ| devoted (to), focussed (on), engaged (in)

اعْتِكاف *n* retirement, withdrawal; *a long stay in the mosque*

عَكَّة, عَكّا *n* Acre, Akko (*city in Israel*)

عَكَمَ *v* |i; عَكْم| to bundle

عَلَّبَ *v* to can; to pack (up); عَلَّبَ خُضاراً \ فاكِهةً to can vegetables/fruit

عُلْبة *n* |عُلَب, عِلاب| 1 ⟨[صُنْدوق] box, case; tin; bin; pack, packet, carton; عُلْبة سَجائِرَ a pack of cigarettes; عُلْبة كَعْكٍ a packet of biscuits (BrE) cookies (AmE); عُلْبة حَليبٍ a carton of milk; عُلْبة سُكَّر \ دَقيق a package of sugar/flour; عُلْبة كِبْريتٍ \ شاي a box of matches/tea; عُلْبة التَّشْغيل remote control; عُلَب اللَيْلِ night clubs 2 ⟨[لحِفْظ السَّوائِل والأَطْعِمة] can, tin; عُلْبة فاصولْيا a can of beans; فَتَحَ عُلْبةً to open a can; مِفْتاح العُلَبِ can opener; عُلْبة (من) الشاي a tin of tea; عُلْبة الأَطْعِمةِ المَحْفوظة a can of preserved food; عُلْبة من المُرَطِّباتِ a can of soda 3 ⟨[في السَّيارة] gearbox; عُلْبة التُروسِ \ السُّرعاتِ gearbox; عُلْبة (تُروسٍ) أوتوماتيكيّة \ يَدَوِيّة an automatic/manual transmission

تَعْليب *n* packing, packaging; canning

مُعَلَّب A *adj* packed; canned; مَوادّ غِذائِيّة مُعَلَّبة canned foods B *n* |مُعَلَّبات| can; مُعَلَّبات canned foods

عالَجَ *v* 1 ⟨[مَرْضى] to treat; عالَجَ جُروحَ شَخْصٍ to treat sb's wounds; عالَجَ مَريضاً to treat a patient 2 ⟨[عامَلَ] to deal with, to handle, to approach; عالَجَ قَضِيّةً to deal with a matter; عالَجَ مُشْكِلةً بِطَريقةٍ أُخْرى to approach a problem

عَكْس *n* opposite, reverse, contrary; بالعَكْسِ on the contrary; the other way round; على عَكْسِ ... as opposed to ..., contrary to ...; على العَكْسِ من ذلك contrary to that, in contrast with that; on the other hand; العَكْسُ بالعَكْسِ vice versa; العَكْسُ صَحيحٌ \ هو الصَّحيحُ the opposite is true; أَثْبَتَ العَكْسَ to prove the opposite; حتّى \ إلى أنْ يَثْبُتَ العَكْسُ until the contrary is proven; لَيْسَ ... بَل العَكْسُ تَماماً it is not ... but rather quite the opposite

عاكِس A *adj* reflecting, reflective; مِفْتاح عاكِس switch B *n* |عَواكِسُ| switch

عَكْسِيّ *adj* reverse, opposite; نَتيجة \ مَفْعول \ أَثَر عَكْسِيّ(ة) counterproductive; العَدّ العَكْسِيّ counting backwards; عَكْسِيًّا in the the opposite direction, the other way round

انْعِكاس *n* |انْعِكاسات| 1 ⟨ reflection; repercussion; انْعِكاس ضَعيف a pale reflection; انْعِكاس سَلْبِيّ backlash; انْعِكاسات الواقِعِ reflections of reality; انْعِكاس الضَوْءِ في المِرْآةِ the reflection of light in the mirror; زاوِية الانْعِكاسِ the angle of reflection 2 ⟨[انْقِلاب] reversal, inversion; قابِل للانْعِكاسِ reversible

انْعِكاسِيّ *adj* reflexive; فِعْل انْعِكاسِيّ reflexive verb

مُتَعاكِس *adj* opposite; conflicting; في اتِّجاهاتٍ مُتَعاكِسةٍ in opposite directions

مُعاكِس *adj* opposite, reverse; counter-, contra-; رُؤْية مُعاكِسة an opposing opinion; مَفْعول مُعاكِس an opposite effect; هُجوم مُعاكِس a counter-attack; سَيّارة مُعاكِسة an oncoming car; سارَ في الاتِّجاهِ المُعاكِسِ to go in the opposite direction; مَصالِحُهُمْ مُعاكِسةٌ لِمَصالِحِنا their interests conflict with ours

مُعاكَسة *n* 1 ⟨ [تَحَرُّش ب] propositioning, hitting on, flirting (with); harassment; المُعاكَسات الهاتِفِيّة harassing phone calls 2 ⟨[مُضادّة] counteraction

مَعْكوس *adj* opposite, reverse; مَنْطِق مَعْكوس perverse logic; مَعْكوساً the other way round

مُنْعَكِس *adj* reflected; فِعْل مُنْعَكِس reflex; زاوِية مُنْعَكِسة an obtuse angle

عُكّاشة, عُكاشة *n* 1 ⟨ (Zool) spider 2 ⟨[بَيْت العَنْكَبوتِ] spiderweb, cobweb

عَلِقَ *v* |a; عُلوق ,عَلَق| **1** [أَلْصَقَ] to stick, to cling; to catch, to get stuck; عَلِقَ في شَبَكَةٍ to get caught up in a net; لا يَعْلَقُ بِذِهْنِهِ الكَثيرُ there is not much that sticks in his mind **2** [أَحَبَّ] to be attached; عَلِقَ بِشَيْءٍ \ شَخْصٍ to be attached to sth/sb **3** [حُشِرَ] to get trapped/jammed

عَلَّقَ *v* **1** [دَلّى] to hang, to suspend; عَلَّقَ عَلَماً to hang a flag; عَلَّقَ مِعْطَفاً على عَلّاقَةٍ to hang a coat on a hook/hanger; عَلَّقَ لَوْحَةً على الجِدارِ to hang a painting on the wall **2** [ثَبَّتَ] to fasten, to fix **3** (fig) to attach, to hang, to set; to make dependent/conditional; عَلَّقَ أَهَمِّيّةً على شَيْءٍ to attach significance/importance to sth; عَلَّقَ على شَخْصٍ الآمالَ to hang one's hopes on sb **4** [شَرَحَ] to comment; عَلَّقَ على شَيْءٍ to comment on sth **5** [أَجَّلَ] to suspend; عَلَّقَ أَعْمالَهُ to suspend one's activities

تَعَلَّقَ *v* **1** [اِسْتَمْسَكَ] to hang, to stick, to cling; تَعَلَّقَ بِخَشَبَةٍ to cling to a piece of wood **2** [تَشَبَّثَ] to be attached; تَعَلَّقَ بِشَيْءٍ \ شَخْصٍ to be attached to sb; تَعَلَّقَ بِحُبِّ شَخْصٍ to be devoted to sb **3** [خَصَّ |ب] to concern, to be connected with; to be related to; to depend on; فيما يَتَعَلَّقُ ب ... concerning ...; with regard/respect to ..., as regards ...; فيما يَتَعَلَّقُ بِذَلِكَ as for that, with respect to that; تَعَلَّقَ بِشَيْءٍ \ بِشَخْصٍ to be related to sth/sb; to concern sth/sb

عَلَق *n coll* **1** (Zool) leech; دودة العَلَقِ leech **2** [جَلْطة دَمَويّة] blood clot; خَلَقَ الإنسانَ من عَلَقٍ He created man from a clot (Koran); سورة العَلَق The Clot (Sura 96)

عالِق **A** *adj* **1** [غَير مَفْصولٍ فيهِ] outstanding, pending, unresolved; المَشاكِل العالِقة unresolved problems; قَضيّة عالِقة a pending case **2** [مَحْشور] stuck, jammed
B *n* (Bot) عَوالِق plankton

عَلائِقيّ *adj* relational

عَلاقة *n* |عَلاقات ,عَلائِقُ| **1** [بين أَشْخاصٍ] relationship, relation, affiliation, bond; contact; عَلاقة شَخْصية a personal relationship; عَلاقة جِنْسيّة sexual relations; عَلاقات دُوَلِيّة \ ثُنائيّة international/bilateral relations; عَلاقات دِبْلوماسيّة diplomatic relations; عَلاقة أَخَويّة a brotherly relationship;

in a different way **3** [تَناوَلَ] to treat; عالَجَ مَوْضوعاً to treat a subject

تَعالَجَ *v* to be treated

اِعْتَلَجَ *v* to fight, to struggle

عِلْج *n* |عُلوج| barbarian; ill-mannered person

عِلاج *n* treatment, therapy; cure; عِلاج طِبّي medical treatment; عِلاج نَفْسيّ psychotherapy; عِلاج طَبيعيّ physiotherapy; عِلاج جينيّ gene therapy; العِلاج بالإشْعاع radiotherapy; طُرُق عِلاج بَديلة \ طَبيعيّة alternative/natural medicine; طَبَّقَ عِلاجاً to apply treatment; خَضَعَ لِعِلاجٍ to undergo treatment; تَلَقّى عِلاجاً to get/receive treatment; كانَ تحت عِلاج طَبيبٍ to be under medical treatment; الوِقاية خَيْرٌ من العِلاج an ounce of prevention is worth a pound of cure

عِلاجيّ *adj* therapeutic; medical; طُرُق عِلاجيّة therapeutic methods; السِياحة العِلاجيّة medical tourism

مُعالِج **A** *adj* attending; الطَبيب المُعالِج للمَريض the attending physician
B *n* **1** (Comput) processor; مُعالِج صُغْرِيّ microprocessor; chip **2** (Med) therapist

مُعالَجة *n* **1** [مَوْضوع] treatment, handling, dealing with; approach; مُعالَجة قَضيّةٍ the handling of a case; مُعالَجة مُشْكِلةٍ dealing with a problem; الأَمْرُ قَيْدَ المُعالَجة the matter is being attended to **2** [مَرَضٍ] treatment, cure; المُعالَجة الكيميائيّة chemotherapy; مُعالَجة وِراثيّة genetic treatment; لا يُمْكِنُ مُعالَجةُ هذا المَرَضِ there is no treatment for this illness **3** [أَثْناء الصُنْعِ] processing, treatment; مُعالَجة النُفاياتِ processing of waste; مُعالَجة المُعْطَياتِ \ الأَرْقامِ data/number processing

عُلْعُل *n* lark

عَلَفَ *v* |i; عَلْف| to feed

عَلَّفَ *v* to feed

أَعْلَفَ *v* to feed

عَلَف *n* |أَعْلاف ,عِلاف ,عُلوفة| feed, fodder; عَلَف مُرَكَّز concentrated feeds

مِعْلَف *n* |مَعالِفُ| trough, feeder

عَلاقة زَوْجيّة marital relations; عَلاقة عاطِفيّة \ غَراميّة a (romantic) relationship, romance; عَلاقة حُبٍّ a love affair; عَلاقة صَداقةٍ bonds of friendship; عَلاقة لوطيّة \ سِحاقيّة a homosexual/lesbian relationship; عَلاقات اجْتِماعيّة social contacts; عَلاقات تِجاريّة مع دَوْلةٍ commercial relations with a country; العَلاقات العامّة public relations, PR; عَلاقة جَيِّدة \ سَيِّئة a good/bad relationship; عَلاقة قَويّة \ وَثيقة \ مَتينة strong ties/bonds; عَلاقة وَطيدة a strong/steady relationship; عَلاقات حَميمة close/intimate contacts; عَلاقات حُسْنِ الجِوارِ friendly relations; العَلاقة مع الجيرانِ \ الأَبَوَيْنِ the relation with the neighbours/parents; العَلاقة بين مَجْموعَتَيْنِ the relations between two groups; تَوْثيق \ تَعْزيز \ تَوْطيد العَلاقاتِ strengthening of the relations; تَطْبيع العَلاقاتِ normalization of the relations; بُرود في العَلاقاتِ a chill in relations; كانَتْ لَهُ عَلاقةٌ بِشَخْصٍ to have a relationship with sb; كانَ على عَلاقةٍ مع فَتاةٍ to be in a relationship with a girl; كانَ على عَلاقةٍ مُمْتازةٍ بِشَخْصٍ to have an outstanding relationship with sb; بَنى عَلاقةً مع شَخْصٍ to enter into relations with sb; أَقامَ عَلاقةً مع شَخْصٍ to establish relations with sb; to take up with sb; قَطَعَ العَلاقاتِ to break off relations/contact; رَبَطَ عَلاقةً مع \ ب \ بين ... to link ...; اسْتَأْنَفَ العَلاقاتِ مع بَلَدٍ to resume relations with a country; أَنْهى عَلاقةً ,وَضَعَ حَدًّا لِلعَلاقةِ to end a relationship [2] ◂ [بين أَشْياءَ] relation, connection, correlation; عَلاقة مُتَبادَلة correlation, interconnection; عَلاقة مُباشِرة \ مَنْطِقيّة an immediate/logical connection; عَلاقة سَبَبيّة a causal connection; عَلاقة بين قَضيَّتَيْنِ a connection between two things; العَلاقة بين البِطالةِ والإِجْرامِ the connection between unemployment and crime; كانَتْ لَهُ عَلاقةٌ مع \ بِشَيْءٍ to be related to sth; لم تَكُنْ لَهُ عَلاقةٌ بالمَوْضوعِ he had nothing to do with the matter; أَثْبَتَ وُجودَ عَلاقةٍ بين أَمْرَيْنِ to demonstrate a connection between two things

عَلّاقة *n* coat/clothes hanger; hat rack; على عَلّاقةٍ on a hanger

عُلَّيْق *n* blackberry; قَطَفَ \ جَنى عُلَّيْقاً to pick/harvest blackberries

تَعَلُّق *n* attachment; تَعَلُّق بِشَيْءٍ attachment to sth; تَعَلُّقُهُ بِوَطَنِه one's attachment to one's country

تَعْليق *n* [1] ◂ [مُلاحَظة] |تَعْليقات ,تَعاليقُ| commentary, comment, remarks; note; التَّعْليق المُرافِق accompanying commentary; تَعْليق على صورةٍ photo caption; تَعْليق على مُباراةِ كُرةِ القَدَمِ commentary on a football (BrE) soccer (AmE) match; لا تَعْليق no comment; بدونِ تَعْليقٍ enough said; كانَ لَدَيْه تَعْليقٌ على الأَمْرِ he had comments on the matter; امْتَنَعَ عن التَّعْليقِ to have no comment; رَفَض أَيَّ تَعْليقٍ to decline to comment [2] ◂ [تَعْطيل] suspension; postponement; تَعْليق البَرْنامَج النَّوَويّ suspension of the nuclear program [3] ◂ [تَثْبيت] attachment; hanging [4] ◂ (Tech) (wheel) suspension [5] ◂ [حُروف] ligature

تَعْليقة *n* |تَعاليقُ| note, annotation

مُتَعَلِّق [A] *adj* [1] ◂ [مُتَمَسِّك] attached; كانَ مُتَعَلِّقاً بِشَيْءٍ \ شَخْصٍ to be attached to sth/sb [2] ◂ [مُتَّصِل] connected, related, concerning; كَلامُهُ المُتَعَلِّق بالرَّئيسِ his words regarding the president; مَعْلومات مُتَعَلِّقة بِأَوْقاتِ الافْتِتاح information on opening hours; مُتَعَلِّق بالأَمْرِ concerned [3] ◂ [مُتَوَقِّف] dependent; كانَ مُتَعَلِّقاً بِشَيْءٍ to depend on sth; to be connected with sth; هذا مُتَعَلِّقٌ بِأَبيه it depends on his father [B] *n* مُتَعَلِّقات belongings

مُتَعَلِّقات *n pl* belongings; جَمَعَ مُتَعَلِّقاتِه to gather one's belongings

مِعْلاق *n* |مَعاليقُ| hanger; hook

مُعَلَّق [A] *adj* hung, hanging; pending, outstanding; جِسْر مُعَلَّق suspension bridge; الحَدائِق المُعَلَّقة the hanging gardens; امْرَأة مُعَلَّقة a separated but not divorced woman; مَسائِل مُعَلَّقة pending questions; دَيْن \ رَصيد مُعَلَّق an outstanding debt/balance; مُعَلَّق على depending on; hung/hanging on [B] *n* المُعَلَّقات a collection of seven pre-Islamic Arabic poems

مُعَلِّق *n* commentator; المُعَلِّق على مُباراةِ كُرةِ القَدَمِ the commentator on a football (BrE) soccer (AmE) match

‹ **عَلْقَم** *n* |عَلاقِمُ| (Bot) colocynth, bitter apple (*Citrullus colocynthis*); مُرّ مِثْلُ العَلْقَم as bitter as gall

‹ **عَلَكَ** *v* |i-u; عَلْك| to chew

عِلْك *n coll* |أَعْلاك ,عُلوك| chewing gum; مَضَغَ العِلْكَ to chew gum

عَلِمَ *v* |a; عِلْم| to know; to learn, to find out; عَلِمَ شَيْئاً \ بِشَيْءٍ to know/find out sth; عَلِمَ شَيْئاً عِلْمَ اليَقِينِ to know something for sure; عَلِمَ أَنَّ ... to know/find out that ...; قد عَلِمْنا أنّ ... we learned/heard that ...; عُلِمَ أَنَّ ... it's common knowledge that ...; على ما \ بِقَدْرِ ما أَعْلَمُ as far as I know; لا أَعْلَمُ شَيْئاً I know nothing about it; من أَيْنَ تَعْلَمُ ذلك ؟ how do you know that?, where did you get that?

عَلْمَنَ *v* |i; عَلْمَنة| to secularize

عَلَّمَ *v* ⓵ [دَرَّسَ] to teach, to instruct, to train; to educate; عَلَّمَ شَخْصاً شَيْئاً to teach sb sth; عَلَّمَ شَخْصاً الأَبْجَدِيّةَ to teach sb the alphabet; عَلَّمَ شَخْصاً الانْضِباطَ \ مَهاراتٍ to teach sb discipline/skills ⓶ [وَسَمَ] to mark

أَعْلَمَ *v* to let know, to inform; to tell; أَعْلَمَ شَخْصاً بِشَيْءٍ to inform sb of/about sth; أَعْلَمَ بالنَّتِيجةِ to announce the result

تَعَلَّمَ *v* to learn, to study; تَعَلَّمَ القِراءةَ to learn to read; تَعَلَّمَ مِهْنةً to learn a trade/profession; تَعَلَّمَ شَيْئاً على يَدِ شَخْصٍ to be taught sth by sb; تَعَلَّمَ كَثيراً من شَخْصٍ to learn a lot from sb; تَعَلَّمَ أَنَّ ... to learn that ...

تَعالَمَ *v* to pretend to be knowledgeable; تَعالَمَ على شَخْصٍ to pontificate to sb

اسْتَعْلَمَ *v* to inquire, to ask (for information); اسْتَعْلَمَ شَخْصاً to ask sb for information; اسْتَعْلَمَ عن شَيْءٍ to make inquiries into/about sth; اسْتَعْلَمَ عَمّا إذا ... to inquire if/whether ...

عَلَم *n* |أَعْلام| ⓵ [راية] flag, banner; حامِل العَلَمِ flag-bearer; سارِية العَلَمِ flagpole; يُرَفْرِفُ العَلَمُ the flag is waving; رَفَعَ \ نَكَّسَ العَلَمَ to raise/lower the flag; خَفَّضَ العَلَمَ to fly the flag at half-mast ⓶ [إشارة] sign, mark; أَشْهَر من نارٍ على عَلَمٍ *very well-known* ⓷ (Gram) اسْم عَلَمٍ proper noun ⓸ [إنْسان مَشْهور] celebrity, (eminent) personality; عَلَم من أَعْلامِ الفِكْرِ one of the great thinkers

عِلْم *n* ⓵ [مَعْرِفة] knowledge; awareness, notice; بِدونِ \ دون عِلْمي without my knowledge; بِعِلْمِ شَخْصٍ with the knowledge of sb; عن غَيْرِ عِلْمٍ بالمَوْضوعِ without any knowledge of the subject; على حَدِّ عِلْمي, حَسَبَ عِلْمي as far as I know; على عِلْمٍ بِأَنَّ ...، عِلْماً أَنَّ ... in the knowledge

عَلَّ *v* |i; عَلّ| ⓵ [مَرِضَ] to be/fall ill ⓶ [أَمْرَضَ] to make ill; عُلَّ to be/fall ill

عَلَّلَ *v* ⓵ [بَيَّنَ عِلَّتَهُ] to substantiate; to explain; to justify; عَلَّلَ ظاهِرةً to explain a phenomenon; عَلَّلَ وِجْهةَ نَظَرِهِ to substantiate one's point of view; عَلَّلَ قَراراً \ خِياراً to justify a decision/choice; عَلَّلَ شَيْئاً بِأَسْبابٍ شَخْصِيّةٍ to cite personal reasons ⓶ [صَبَّرَ] to occupy; to palm/fob off; عَلَّلَ نَفْسَهُ بالأَوْهامِ to delude oneself; عَلَّلَ النَّفْسَ بالآمالِ to entertain hopes; عَلَّلَ شَخْصاً بالوُعودِ to palm sb off with promises

أَعَلَّ *v* to make ill

تَعَلَّلَ *v* ⓵ [اتَّخَذَهُ حُجّةً] to use as an excuse/pretext; to pretend; تَعَلَّلَ بِشَيْءٍ to give/use sth as an excuse; تَعَلَّلَ بِصُداعٍ to pretend to have a headache; تَعَلَّلَ بالانْشِغالِ to pretend to be busy ⓶ [تَلَهّى] to occupy; تَعَلَّلَ بالأَمَلِ to cling to hope

اعْتَلَّ *v* to be/fall ill

عِلّة *n* ⓵ [داء] |عِلّات, عِلَل| illness; defect; عِلَل الشَّيْخوخةِ diseases of old age; أَخَذَ الأُمورَ على عِلّاتِها to take things as they are ⓶ [حُجّة] |عِلَل| reason, cause; excuse; عِلّة واهِية a weak excuse; ارْتِباط المَعْلول بِعِلَّتِهِ a causal connection ⓷ (Gram) defectiveness, weakness; حُروف العِلّةِ weak letters

عَليل *adj* |أَعِلّاءُ| ⓵ [مَريض] sick, ill; صِحّة عَليلة bad health ⓶ [ناعِم] mild; نَسيم عَليل a mild breeze

اعْتِلال *n* |اعْتِلالات| illness; impairment; morbidity; الاعْتِلال الدِّماغِيّ brain dysfunction

تَعِلّة *n* excuse, pretext

تَعْليل *n* |تَعْليلات| explanation; justification; substantiation; تَعْليل مَعْقول a plausible explanation

لَعَلَّ *particle* see لعل

مُعْتَلّ *adj* ⓵ [مَريض] weak, sickly ⓶ (Gram) defective, weak; أَفْعال مُعْتَلّة defective verbs

مُعَلَّل *adj* substantiated; justified; شَكّ مُعَلَّل justifiable doubt; غَيْر مُعَلَّلٍ تَعْليلاً كافِياً not sufficiently substantiated, ill-substantiated

مَعْلول Ⓐ *adj* ill, sick Ⓑ *n* effect; العِلّة والمَعْلول cause and effect; ارْتِباط المَعْلول بِعِلَّتِهِ a causal connection that ...; on the understanding that ...; كانَ على عِلْمٍ بِشَيْءٍ to know sth, to be aware of sth; أَحاطَ شَخْصاً عِلْماً بِشَيْءٍ to inform sb of sth, to let sb know about sth; أَخَذَ عِلْماً بِشَيْءٍ to take note of sth; العِلْمُ في الصِغَرِ كالنَقْشِ في الحَجَرِ ≈ what's learned in the cradle lasts to the grave **2** [دِراسة] |عُلوم| science; study, -ology; العُلوم التَجْريبيّة the empirical sciences; عِلْم الفَلَك astronomy; عُلوم الحاسِبِ الآليِّ computer science; عِلْم السُكّانِ sociology; عِلْم الاِجْتِماعِ psychology; عِلْم النَفْسِ demography; عُلوم دينيّة geology; عِلْم الطَبَقاتِ الأَرْضيّة theology; عُلوم العَرَبيّة Arabic linguistics; عِلْم الأَمْراضِ الجِلْديّة dermatology; العُلوم الإِنْسانيّة humanities; arts; الرِياضيّات والعُلوم الطَبيعيّة mathematics and natural science; كُلّيّة العُلومِ الطَبيعيّة Faculty of Natural Sciences; نَقْل \ اِنْتِقال العِلْمِ transfer of knowledge; اِلْتَمَسَ العِلْمَ to study

عالَم *n* |عالَمونَ, عَوالِمُ| **1** [دُنْيا] world, earth; عالَم أَحْسَن \ أَفْضَل a better world; العالَم السُفْليّ the underworld; العالَم كُلُّهُ the whole world; بَطَل العالَم world champion; رَبّ العالَمينَ Lord of all creation; تاريخ العالَمِ the history of the world; رِحْلة حول العالَمِ a trip around the world; في العالَمِ in the world **2** [مُجْتَمَع] world; العالَم العَرَبيّ \ الغَرْبيّ the Arab/Western world; العالَم القَديم \ الجَديد the Old/New World; العالَم الثالِث the Third World; بَلَد عالَم ثالِثيّ a Third World country; اِنْقَطَعَ عن العالَمِ الخارِجيِّ to be cut off from the outside world **3** [بيئة] world, scene; العالَم الأَدَبيّ the literary scene; العالَم العِلْميّ the scientific world; العالَم الحِسّيّ والعالَم الروحيّ the physical and spiritual worlds; عالَم كُرة القَدَمِ the football (BrE) soccer (AmE) scene; عالَم الإِجْرامِ the world of crime/criminals, the underworld; عالَم الحَيَوانِ the animal world; يَعيشُ في عالَمِهِ الخاصِّ he is/lives in his own world

عالِم *n* |عُلَماءُ| **1** [دارِس] scientist, scholar; عالِم الجيولوجيا geologist; عالِم الفيزياءِ physicist; عالِم كَبير a great scientist; عُلَماء بارِزونَ prominent scientists; لِكُلِّ عالِمٍ هَفْوةٌ *even the best make mistakes* **2** (Islam) Islamic scholar

عالَمْثالِثيّ *adj* Third World (*before n*)

عالَميّ *adj* world (*before n*), international, worldwide, global; تَطَوُّرات \ مَشاكِل عالَميّة global developments/problems; مُنَظَّمة عالَميّة a worldwide organization; حَظْر عالَميّ an international embargo; الاِقْتِصاد العالَميّ world economy; نِظام تَحْديد المَواقِعِ العالَميّ Global Positioning System, GPS; مَعْروف عالَميّاً known throughout the world

عالَميّة *n* internationalism, universality

عَلامِ *adv* see علو\علي

عَلامة *n* |عَلامات, عَلائِمُ| **1** [إشارة] sign, mark; عَلامة حَسَنة \ سوءٍ, سَيِّئة a good/bad sign; عَلامة مُمَيِّزة \ عَلامة خَيْرٍ an identifying mark; عَلامة مائيّة watermark; وَضَعَ عَلامةً to put a sign; to mark, to check, to tick; زَوَّدَ شَيْئاً بِعَلامةٍ to mark sth; عَلامات تَدُلُّ على شَيْءٍ indications of sth **2** [رَمْز] sign; symbol; عَلامة الاِسْتِفْهامِ question mark; عَلامة التَعَجُّبِ exclamation mark, exclamation point (AmE); عَلامة التَنْصيصِ quotation mark, quote, inverted comma (BrE); بين عَلامَتَي التَنْصيصِ between/in quotation marks; فَتَحَ \ أَغْلَقَ عَلامَتَي التَنْصيصِ to quote/unquote, to open/close inverted commas (BrE); عَلامات التَرْقيمِ punctuation; أَضافَ عَلاماتِ التَرْقيمِ (إلى نَصٍّ) to punctuate (a text) **3** [دَرَجة] mark, point; نالَ الطالِبُ في الاِمْتِحانِ ١٢ عَلامةً من ٢٠ the student got 12 out of 20 points on the exam **4** [تِجاريّة] brand (name); عَلامة تِجاريّة brand (name), trademark; عَلامة تِجاريّة مُسَجَّلة a registered trademark; قانون العَلاماتِ التِجاريّةِ trademark law; اِسْتَعْمَلَ عَلامةً تِجاريّةً to use a trademark **5** [في الطَريق] road/traffic sign; عَلامة الطَريقِ road sign; عَلامة قِفْ stop sign **6** (Comput) bookmark

عَلّامة *n* expert, scholar, master

عَلْمانيّ **A** *adj* secular, profane, non-religious, worldly; طَبيعة عَلْمانيّة a secular nature; دَوْلة عَلْمانيّة a secular state **B** *n* **1** [غَيْر مُتَدَيِّن] layman **2** [مُؤَيِّد العَلْمَنةِ] secularist

عَلْمانيّة *n* secularization

عُلْمة *n* cleft lip

عَلْمَنة *n* secularization

عِلْميّ *adj* scientific; بَحْث عِلْميّ scientific research; غَيْر عِلْميٍّ unscientific; خَيال عِلْميّ science fiction; فيلْم خَيالٍ عِلْميٍّ a science fiction film

تَعْليمات طِبِّيّة واضِحة \ صارِمة explicit/strict instructions; doctor's orders; حَسَبَ التَعْليماتِ as prescribed/instructed; أَعْطى \ أَصْدَرَ تَعْليماتٍ to give instructions/orders; تَلَقّى تَعْليماتٍ to be instructed; اتَّبَعَ \ نَفَّذَ التَعْليماتِ to follow instructions; الْتَزَمَ بالتَعْليماتِ to adhere to the instructions 4 [وَضْع العَلاماتِ] marking

تَعْليميّ *adj* educational, instructional; وَسيلة تَعْليميّة teaching method; مُؤَسَّسة تَعْليميّة educational institution

مُتَعالِم *n* know-it-all

مُتَعَلِّم *adj* educated; غَيْر مُتَعَلِّم uneducated

مَعْلَم *n* |مَعالِمُ| 1 [حَدّ] contour, outline; مَعالِم الوَجْهِ facial features; المَعالِم الرَئيسيّة للسِياسة outlines of the policy; واضِح المَعالِم clearly outlined; اتَّضَحَتْ مَعالِمُهُ to take shape 2 [عَلامة مُتَمَيِّزة] landmark; highlight, sight; مَعالِم سِياحيّة tourist sites; مَعْلَم من مَعالِم الفَنِّ العَرَبيِّ one of the highlights of Arab art 3 [في الطَريق] milestone

مُعْلِم A *adj* informing
B *n* informer

مُعَلِّم *n* teacher, instructor; master; مُعَلِّم قاسٍ a strict teacher; مُعَلِّم في مَدْرَسةٍ ابْتِدائيّةٍ primary school teacher; مَعْهَد تَكْوينِ \ إعْدادِ المُعَلِّمينَ teachers' training college; يُمارِسُ مِهْنةَ مُعَلِّمٍ, يَعْمَلُ مُعَلِّماً he works as a teacher

مَعْلَمة *n* encyclopedia

مُعَلْمَن *adj* secularized, secular; مُجْتَمَع مُعَلْمَن a secular society

مَعْلوم *adj* known; غَيْر مَعْلومٍ unknown; من المَعْلومِ أنّ ... it is known that ...; صارَت الحَقيقةُ مَعْلومةً the truth became known

مَعْلوماتيّ *adj* information (*before n*); computer (*before n*), digital; تِقْنيّة مَعْلوماتيّة information technology, IT; شَبَكة مَعْلوماتيّة (computer) network; أَمْن مَعْلوماتيّ information security; جَرائِم مَعْلوماتيّة computer crime; الحَرْب المَعْلوماتيّة cyberwar

مَعْلوماتيّة *n* information science, informatics

مَعْلومة *n* fact; piece of information; مَعْلومات information, data, facts, details; knowledge; مَعْلومات أَساسيّة basic information, background; مَعْلومات مَوْثوق بها reliable information; مَعْلومات لا يوثَقُ بها unreliable information;

عَليم A *adj* |عُلَماءُ| omniscient; اللهُ العَليم the Omniscient God
B *n* العَليم the Omniscient (*one of the names of God*)

عَوْلَمة *n* globalization; العَوْلَمة المُتَزايِدة advancing globalization; عَوْلَمة الاقْتِصادِ economic globalization

اسْتِعْلام *n* |اسْتِعْلامات| inquiry; information; اسْتِعْلامات information; مَكْتَب اسْتِعْلاماتٍ information office; help desk

إعْلام *n* informing, information; إعْلام اجْتِماعيّ social media; وِزارة الإعْلامِ Ministry of Information; وَسائِل الإعْلامِ the media, mass media; وَسائِل الإعْلامِ السَمْعيّة والبَصَريّة, وَسائِل الإعْلام المَرْئيّة والمَسْموعة audiovisual media; نَشَرَ عَبْرَ وَسائِلِ الإعْلامِ to spread/publish through the media

إعْلاميّ A *adj* informative; information (*before n*); media (*before n*); حِوار إعْلاميّ an informational talk; مَكْتَب إعْلاميّ information office; سَيَكونُ لِهَذا الاجْتِماعِ طابَعٌ إعْلاميٌّ it will be an informative meeting; مَصْدَر إعْلاميّ a source of information; حَمْلة إعْلاميّة a media campaign; مَرْكَز إعْلاميّ media centre; ضَجّة إعْلاميّة fanfare, hype, publicity
B *n* media personality

أَعْلَم *adj* |dipt| more learned; واللهُ أَعْلَمُ God knows; how should I know?; who knows; هي أَعْلَمُ بِذَلِكَ مِنّي she knows more about it than I do

تَعَلُّم *n* learning; تَعَلُّم اللُغاتِ الأَجْنَبيّةِ learning foreign languages; عَمَليّة التَعَلُّم the learning process; صُعوبات التَعَلُّم learning difficulties/disabilities

تَعْليم *n* |تَعاليمُ, تَعْليمات| 1 [تَدْريس] education; teaching, training; تَعْليم ابْتِدائيّ primary education; تَعْليم أَساسيّ basic education; تَعْليم ثانَويّ secondary education; تَعْليم عالٍ higher education; تَعْليم جامِعيّ a university education; تَعْليم مِهْنيّ vocational training; تَعْليم إضافيّ extra training; تَعْليم إجْباريّ \ إلْزاميّ compulsory education; التَعْليم الذاتيّ home study; فَنّ التَعْليم didactics; the art of teaching; تَجْديد التَعْليم educational reform; نِظام تَعْليمٍ educational system; وَزير (التَرْبِيةِ و)التَعْليم the Minister of Education; تَمَتَّعَ بالتَعْليمِ, تابَعَ \ تَلَقّى تَعْليماً to be educated, to get an education; عَمِلَ في قِطاعِ التَعْليمِ to be a teacher 2 [مَبادِئ] teachings 3 [تَوْجيه] instruction, direction, order; تَعْليمات

بَنْك المَعْلوماتِ data bank; عَصْر المَعْلوماتِ the information age; تِكْنولوجِيا المَعْلوماتِ والاتِّصالاتِ information and communication technology, ICT; مَعْلومات حول \ بِخُصوصِ \ عن ... information about/concerning/on ...; حَصَلَ على \ تَلَقّى \ تَوَصَّلَ إلى مَعْلوماتٍ to get information; زَوَّدَ بِمَعْلوماتٍ, أَعْطى \ قَدَّمَ \ وَفَّرَ مَعْلوماتٍ to provide information; كانَتْ لَدَيْهِ مَعْلوماتٌ to have information; اِحْتاجَ إلى مَزيد من المَعْلوماتِ to need more information

مَعْلوميّة *n* knowing, knowledge

مُعَوْلَم *adj* globalized

‹ **أَعْلَنَ** *v* to make public, to announce; to declare, to proclaim; أَعْلَنَ شَيْئاً \ عن شَيْءٍ to announce sth, to make an announcement; to make sth public; أَعْلَنَ الاسْتِقْلالَ to proclaim independence; أَعْلَنَ عن قَوانينَ to promulgate laws; أَعْلَنَ عن عَفْوٍ عامٍّ to issue a general pardon; أَعْلَنَ حالَةَ الطَّوارِئِ to proclaim a state of emergency; أَعْلَنَ الحَرْبَ على بِلادٍ to declare war upon a country; أَعْلَنَ حُبَّهُ لَها he declared his love for her; أَعْلَنَ عن رَأْيٍ to put forward an opinion; أَعْلَنَ النَّتيجَةَ to announce the results; أَعْلَنَ عن فَصْلِ شَخْصٍ to give sb notice; أَعْلَنَ تَأْييدَهُ to express one's support; أَعْلَنَ تَقْريراً to make a report public; أُعْلِنَ عن نَبَأِ وَفاتِهِ أَمْسِ his death was announced yesterday; أَعْلَنَ أنَّ ... to announce that ...

عَلَن *n* public; في العَلَنِ, عَلَناً in public, publicly; ظَهَرَ في العَلَنِ to appear in public

عَلانِيَة *n* public; عَلانِيَةً in public, publicly; openly; عَلانِيَة الجَلَساتِ the public nature of the sessions

عَلَنِيّ *adj* public, open; سُكْر عَلَنِيّ public drunkenness; دَعْم عَلَنِيّ public support; عُنْف عَلَنِيّ assault and battery; مُحاكَمة عَلَنِيّة a public trial; بِشَكْلٍ عَلَنِيٍّ, عَلَنِيًّا publicly, in public

إِعْلان *n* |إعْلانات| ① ◀[إِخْبار] announcement, notice; proclamation; declaration; publication; إعْلان رَسْمِيّ (مِن الحُكومَةِ) an official announcement (from the government); إعْلان شَيْءٍ \ الإعْلان عن شَيْءٍ the announcement of sth; إعْلان تَرْشيح نَفْسِهِ the announcement of his candidacy; الإعْلان عن حالةِ الطَوارِئِ the proclamation of a state of emergency; إعْلان مَبادِئَ a statement of principles; إعْلان حَرْبٍ a declaration of war; الإعْلان العالَمِيّ لِحُقوقِ الإنْسانِ the Universal Declaration of Human Rights ② ◀[تِجارِيّ] advertising; advertisement, ad; commercial; إعْلان تِلِفِزْيونِيّ television commercial; بَثَّ \ أَذاعَ إعْلاناتٍ تِلِفِزْيونِيّةً to broadcast television commercials; سِلْسِلة إعْلاناتٍ تِلِفِزْيونِيّةٍ series of commercials; ≈ commercial break; مَكْتَب الدِعايَةِ والإعْلانِ advertising agency; وَضَعَ إعْلاناً في صَحيفةٍ to put an advertisement in a paper; رَدَّ على إعْلانٍ to answer an advertisement ③ ◀[لافِتة] poster; bill; إعْلان مُغْرٍ an attractive poster; لَوْحة إعْلاناتٍ notice board (BrE), bulletin board (AmE)

إِعْلانِيّ *adj* advertising (*before n*); حَمْلة إعْلانِيّة advertising campaign; لَوْحة إعْلانِيّة billboard; فَقْرة إعْلانِيّة promo, commercial

مُعْلَن *adj* announced; غَيْر مُعْلَنٍ عَنْهُ unannounced

مُعْلِن *n* advertiser; جَذَبَ المُعْلِنينَ to attract advertisers

‹ **عَلا** *v* |u; عُلُوّ| ① ◀[اِرْتَفَعَ] to be high/elevated; to go up, to rise, to climb; to increase; عَلا الصَوْتُ the sound was getting louder; عَلا النَهْرُ the river was rising; عَلا التَصْفيقُ there was loud applause ② ◀[كانَ أَعْلى] to tower over; to rise above; تَعْلو المَآذِنُ المَنازِلَ the minarets are towering above the houses; يَعْلو القانونُ فوق الاتِّفاقاتِ الفَرْدِيّةِ the law comes before individual agreements ③ ◀[صَعِدَ] to climb; to mount; عَلا شَجَرةً to climb (up) a tree; عَلَتِ الكُرةُ العارِضةَ the ball went over the goal

Idiom يَعْلو وَجْهَهُ الحُزْنُ grief is written all over his face

عَلِيَ *v* |a; عَلاء| to rise

عَلّى *v* to raise, to lift; عَلّى الحَواجِزَ to raise obstacles

أَعْلى *v* to raise, to lift; أَعْلى قَدْرَهُ to raise one's prestige

تَعالى *v* to rise (above), to tower (above), to stand out (above); to look down (on); تَعالى على شَيْءٍ to rise above sth; تَعالى على شَخْصٍ to look down on sb; قَوْلُهُ تَعالى the Almighty said (*introducing a Koranic quotation*); اللهُ سُبْحانَهُ وَتَعالى, اللهُ تَعالى God, glorified and exalted is He; اِنْتَقَلَ إلى رَحْمَتِهِ تَعالى المَأْسوفُ عَلَيْهِ ≈ the dearly departed has gone to his eternal reward (*in obituaries*)

Idiom تَعالَ! come here!

اعْتَلى *v* to mount, ascend; اعْتَلى العَرْشَ \ المَسْرَح to mount the throne/podium

اسْتَعْلى *v* 1 [عَلا] to be high/higher 2 [صَعِدَ] to climb 3 [رَآهُ عالِياً] to consider high

عُلُوّ *n* 1 [ارْتِفاع] height, altitude 2 [سُمُوّ] exaltedness (Idiom) أَثْبَتَ عُلُوَّ كَعْبِهِ to prove one's mettle

عَلِيّ A *adj* high; exalted
B *n* [اسْم شَخْصِيّ] Ali (*male given name*); أُمّ عَلِيّ Umm Ali (*Egyptian dessert, similar to bread pudding*); عَلِيّ بابا Ali Baba

عالٍ A *adj* 1 [مُرْتَفِع] high, elevated; أَمْواج عالِية high waves; حَصيلة عالِية a high yield; عالي الهِمَّةِ with great ambitions; تَعْليم عالٍ higher education 2 [صَوْت، غَيْر مُنْخَفِض] high-pitched; صَوْت عالٍ a high-pitched voice 3 [صَوْت، قَوِيّ] loud; تَكَلَّمَ \ صَرَخَ \ ضَحِكَ بِصَوْتٍ عالٍ to talk/scream/laugh out loud; شَجَّعَ شَخْصاً بِصَوْتٍ عالٍ to applaud sb loudly
B *n* العالي the Sublimely Exalted (*one of the names of God*)

عَلٍ، عَلُ *n* عَلاً \ عَلٍ \ عَلُ من from above

عَلاء *n* 1 [رِفْعة] sublimity, nobility 2 [اسْم شَخْصِيّ] Alaa (*male given name*); عَلاء الدين Aladdin; Ala al-Din (*male given name*)

عَلامَ *adv* about/on what; what for

عِلاوة *n* (extra) allowance; bonus; raise; addition; تَلَقّى عِلاوةً to receive an allowance; دَفَعَ عِلاوةً to pay a surcharge; فَرَضَ عِلاوةً to impose extra charge; عِلاوةً على in addition to; عِلاوةً على ذلك in addition to that, on top of that

عَلَوِيّ *adj, n* Alawi (*prominent religious minority in Syria*)

عُلْوِيّ *adj* upper; الطابَق العُلْوِيّ the top floor, the upper storey

عَلَوِيّة *n* Alawites

عَلى *prep* 1 [مَكان] on, on top of; over; وَضَعَ شَيْئاً على الأَرْضِ to put sth on the floor/ground; عَلى حُدودِ ... at the border of ...; عَلى الحائِطِ on the wall; أَخَذَ المِخَدَّةَ من عَلى الكُرْسِيِّ he took the pillow from the chair; عَلى مَتْنِ سَفينةٍ on board a ship 2 [واجِب] obliged; عَلَيَّ أَنْ أَكونَ في البَيْتِ في الساعةِ الثامِنةِ I have to be home at eight o'clock; ما عَلَيْهِ إلاّ \ سِوى أَنْ ... he only has to ...; لي عَلَيْهِ عِشْرونَ دِرْهَماً he owes me 20 dirham; لا عَلَيْكَ never mind 3 [رَغْم] in spite of; وَعَلى ذلك كُلِّهِ نَحْنُ باقونَ in spite of that we are still there; عَلى الرَغْمِ مِنْهُ in spite of him 4 [حال] عَلى أَضْواءِ الشُموعِ by candlelight; عَلى غَيْرِ انْتِظارٍ unexpectedly; ما زالَ عَلى ما هو عَلَيْهِ his situation has not changed; الشِقّةُ سَتَبْقى عَلى حالِها the apartment will stay as it is 5 [مَجازِيّ] عَلى ذلك on that condition; عَلى امْتِدادِ ... along, over; during, throughout; عَلى حِسابِ ... at the expense of ... 6 (Math) divided by; سِتّةٌ عَلى اثْنَيْنِ تُساوي ثَلاثةً six divided by two is three 7 [عَلى أَنّ] هو كَسْلانُ عَلى أَنَّهُ سَيَنْجَحُ he's lazy but he will succeed anyway 8 [ساعةٍ] at; عَلى الساعةِ العاشِرةِ at ten o'clock

عُلًى *n* highness

عَلْياء *n* |dipt f| 1 [مُرْتَفَع] loftiness, highness; upper class 2 [اسْم شَخْصِيّ] Alia (*female given name*)

عِلِّيّة *n* attic (room)

اسْتِعْلاء *n* superiority; مُرَكَّب الاسْتِعْلاءِ superiority complex; بِاسْتِعْلاءٍ supercilious

اسْتِعْلائِيّ *adj* supercilious, superior

اعْتِلاء *n* climbing, mounting, ascending

أَعْلى *adj* |عُلًى ,أَعالٍ; f عُلْيا| higher; upper, highest; الطَبَقة العُلْيا the top layer; the upper class; في أَعالي الجِبال high in the mountains; أَعْلاهُ above; انْظُرْ أَعْلاهُ see above; انْظُرْ الشَكْلَ البَيانِيَّ أَعْلاهُ see the above diagram; من الأَعْلى إلى الأَسْفَلِ from top to bottom; سَقَطَ من أَعْلى إلى أَسْفَلَ to fall all the way down; بِأَعْلى صَوْتِهِ at the top of one's voice; سورة الأَعْلى The Most High (*Sura 87*)

تَعْلِية *n* elevation, uplift

مُتَعالٍ A *adj* high; superior; سُلوك مُتَعالٍ superior behaviour; أَفْكار مُتَعالِية thoughts of superiority
B *n* المُتَعالي the Supremely Exalted (*one of the names of God*)

مُسْتَعْلٍ *adj* 1 [مُرْتَفِع] superior 2 (Gram) حُروف مُسْتَعْلِية *consonants which are pronounced with the tongue lifted towards the throat:* خ، ص، ض، غ، ط، ظ *and* ق

مَعالٍ *n* elevation, exaltedness; مَعالي الأُمورِ noble things; صاحِب المَعالي مَعالي الوَزيرِ His Excellency the Minister; His Excellency

عِلِّيون *n pl* Illiyun (*the highest part of heaven*)

ع.م. عم *abbr* peace be upon him, PBUH (*abbreviation of* عَلَيْهِ السَّلامُ)

عَمّا *pron* see ما

عَمَدَ *v* |i; عَمْد| ① [دَعَمَ] to support, to prop (up); عَمَدَ السَّقْفَ to support the roof ② [قَصَدَ] to go; عَمَدَ إلى السوقِ to go to the market ③ [نَوى] |إلى| to intend, to mean, to be going; عَمَدَ إلى فِعْلِ شَيْءٍ to do sth intentionally; عَمَدَ إلى إطْلاقِ النارِ to shoot intentionally

عَمَّدَ *v* (Chr) to baptize

تَعَمَّدَ *v* ① [قَصَدَ] to intend, to do intentionally/on purpose, to do deliberately; to aim at; تَعَمَّدَ إلْحاقَ الضَرَرِ بالآخَرينَ to intentionally cause damage to others ② (Chr) to be baptized

اعْتَمَدَ *v* ① [اتَّكَأَ] |على| to lean on/against, to rest on/against; to be based on; اعْتَمَدَ على عَصاهُ to lean on one's cane; اعْتَمَدَ على شَخْصٍ to lean on sb; اعْتَمَدَ على افْتِراضٍ to be based on an assumption; اعْتَمَدَ على حَقائِقَ to be based on facts ② [اتَّكَلَ] |على| to rely on, to depend on, to trust in; اعْتَمَدَ على عائِلَتِهِ to depend on one's family; اعْتَمَدَ على نَفْسِهِ to rely on oneself; اعْتَمَدَ على اللهِ to trust in God; اعْتَمَدَ على كَلامِ شَخْصٍ to take sb at his word; اعْتَمَدَ على احْتِياطاتِهِ to use one's reserves; اعْتَمَدَ على شُهْرَتِهِ \ تَجْرِبَتِهِ \ نَجاحِهِ to live on one's fame/experience/success; لا يُعْتَمَدُ عَلَيْهِ unreliable ③ [وافَقَ] to approve, to ratify; to accredit; اعْتَمَدَ قَراراً to approve of a decision; اعْتَمَدَ سَفيراً to accredit an ambassador

عَمْد Ⓐ *n* intention

Ⓑ *adj* intentional; قَتْل عَمْد murder, homicide; القَتْل العَمْد مع سَبْقِ الإصْرارِ premeditated murder; عَمْداً intentionally, deliberately, on purpose; خالَفَ القَوانينَ عَمْداً to intentionally break the law

عامود *n* see عَمود

عِماد *n* |عَمَد| ① [دِعامة] pillar; الشَبابُ عِمادُ المُسْتَقْبَلِ young people are the future ② (Mil) general ③ (Chr) baptism; أَب في العِمادِ godfather ④ [اسْم شَخْصيّ] Emad, Imad (*male given name*)

عِمادة *n* deanship; تَوَلّى العِمادةَ to hold the position of dean

عُمْدة *n* |عُمَد| mayor; village chief

عَمْديّ *adj* intentional, deliberate; إضْرار عَمْديّ intentional damage

عَمود، عامود *n* ① [دعامة] |أَعْمِدة، عُمُد| pillar; post, pole; column; عَمود فِقْريّ spinal/vertebral column, backbone; كانَ العَمودَ الفِقْريَّ لِشَيْءٍ to be the backbone of sth; عَمود النورِ lamp post; عَمود الكَهْرَباءِ power pole/pylon; عَمود دُخانٍ column of smoke; عَمود خَيْمةٍ tent pole ② [كَلِماتٍ \ أَرْقام] |أَعْمِدة| column, section; كاتِب عَمودٍ columnist; في العَمودِ الثالِثِ in the third column ③ (Mech) |أَعْمِدة، عُمُد| shaft; عَمود إدارةٍ drive shaft; عَمود مِرْفَقيّ crankshaft

عَموديّ *adj* vertical, upright; حَرَكة عَموديّة a vertical movement; ارْتَفَعَ عَموديّاً to go straight up; طائِرة عَموديّة helicopter; خَطّ عَموديّ a vertical line; perpendicular

عَميد *n* |عُمَداءُ| ① [زَعيم] head, chief; captain ② [رَئيس كُلِّيّةٍ] dean; provost, chancellor ③ (Mil) brigadier-general

اعْتِماد *n* ① [اتِّكال] dependence, reliance; confidence; الاعْتِماد على نَفْسِهِ self-reliance; هذا شَخْصٌ يُمْكِنُ الاعْتِمادُ عَلَيْهِ he is sb you can rely on ② [مُصادَقة] ratification; approbation; confirmation; أَوْراق \ كُتُب اعْتِمادٍ credentials; قَدَّمَ أَوْراقَ اعْتِمادِهِ to present one's credentials ③ (Busn) |اعْتِمادات| credit, loan; اعْتِماد جارٍ \ مُحَدَّد الأَجَلِ continuous/fixed credit; كِتاب اعْتِمادٍ letter of credit; بِطاقة اعْتِمادٍ credit card

اعْتِماديّة *n* reliability

تَعَمُّد *n* intention, purpose; premeditation, forethought; تَعَمُّد فِعْلِ شَيْءٍ doing sth intentionally; تَعَمُّد الإساءةِ إلى شَخْصٍ intentionally insulting sb

تَعْميد *n* (Chr) baptism

مُتَعامِد *adj* orthogonal, rectangular, perpendicular

مُتَعَمَّد *adj* intentional; مُتَعَمَّداً intentionally; غَيْر مُتَعَمَّدٍ unintentional

مُعْتَمَد Ⓐ *adj* official, recognized; approved; مَبْعوث مُعْتَمَد an accredited envoy

Ⓑ *n* delegate, representative; agent; مُعْتَمَد سامٍ High Commissioner

مُعْتَمِد *adj* |على| dependent on, relying on

مُعْتَمَديّة *n* commission, commissioner; legation; مُعْتَمَديّة اللاجِئين commission for refugees

مَعْمَدانيّ **A** *adj* Baptist; الكَنيسة المَعْمَدانيّة the Baptist Church **B** *n* Baptist

مَعْمودِيّة *n* (Chr) baptism

عَمَرَ *v* |u; عُمْران, عَمْر| ① [سَكَنَ في] to live in, to inhabit ② [بَنى] to build ③ [عاشَ طَويلاً] to live long

عَمَّرَ *v* ① [جَعَلَهُ آهِلاً] to populate, to make inhabited; to build; عَمَّرَ بَيْتاً to build a house ② [زَرَعَ] to cultivate; عَمَّرَ الأَرْضَ to cultivate the land ③ [عاشَ طَويلاً] to give a long life; عَمَّرَهُ اللهُ God gave him a long life

أَعْمَرَ *v* to populate

اعْتَمَرَ *v* ① [زارَ] to visit; to perform the umrah (*the lesser pilgrimage*) ② [لَبِسَ] to wear (*on one's head*); اعْتَمَرَ عِمامةً \ قُبَّعةً to wear a turban/hat

اسْتَعْمَرَ *v* to colonize; اسْتَعْمَرَ مِنْطَقَةً to colonize a region

عَمْر *n* life; age; لَعَمْري \ لَعَمْرُكَ upon my/your life!

عُمْر *n* |أَعْمار| ① [حَياة] life; life span; فُرْصة العُمْرِ the chance of a lifetime; أَصْدِقاء العُمْرِ friends for life; مُتَوَسِّط عُمْرِ شَخْصٍ \ شَيْءٍ life expectancy of sb/sth; طول عُمْرِهِ all his life; في زَهْرةِ العُمْرِ in the prime of his life; حتّى نِهايةِ العُمْرِ till the end; إنْ كُتِبَ لَهُ العُمْرُ if only he lives long enough; أَطالَ \ أَمَدَّ اللهُ في عُمْرِهِ may God give him long life; عُمْري my everything (*term of endearment*) ② [أَبَداً] عُمْرُهُ لم يَذْهَبْ إلى المَدْرَسةِ he (had) never attended school ③ [سِنّ] age; لم أَرَ مِثْلَهُ! I've never seen anything like it!; عُمْر افْتِراضيّ expected lifespan (*of a product*); عُمْر جِهازٍ \ سَيّارةٍ the life of a device/car; فِئة أَعْمارٍ age group; مُتَوَسِّط العُمْرِ middle-aged; عُمْرُهُ عِشْرونَ سَنةً he is twenty years old; من نَفْسِ العُمْرِ of the same age; في الثّامِنةِ من عُمْرِهِ at the age of eight; رَجُل من عُمْرِ ٣٥ سَنةً a man at the age of 35; بِعُمْرِ نوحٍ as old as Methuselah; إنَّهُ من عُمْري he is of my age; من كُلِّ الأَعْمارِ of all ages; مُناسِب لِكُلِّ الأَعْمارِ suitable for all ages, U-rated (BrE), G-rated (AmE); كم عُمْرُكَ؟ how old are you?; بَلَغَ الرابِعةَ والسِّتّينَ من العُمْرِ to reach the age of sixty four; مَنْ يَتَجاوَزُ عُمْرُهُ ثَمانِيةَ عَشَرَ عاماً people over eighteen; تَتَراوَحُ أَعْمارُهُمْ بين ١٣ و ٢٤ عاماً their ages range from 13 to 24

عُمَر *n* |dipt| Umar, Omar (*male given name*)

عامِر **A** *adj* ① [آهِل] inhabited, populated ② [زاخِر] full; مائِدة عامِرة a full table; عامِر بالناسِ filled with people **B** *n* [اسْم شَخْصيّ] Amir, Amer (*male given name*)

(Idiom) أُمّ عامِر hyena

عِمارة *n* |عِمارات, عَمائِر| ① [مَبْنًى] building, block of flats (BrE), apartment building (AmE); عِمارة مُؤَلَّفة من اثْنَيْ عَشَرَ طابَقاً a twelve-storey building; انْهَدَمَت العِمارةُ the building collapsed; عِمارة مَكاتِبَ office building ② [تَشْييد] architecture; هَنْدَسة \ فَنّ العِمارة architecture

عُمْران *n* ① [إعْمار] building ② [ثَقافة] civilization, culture ③ [اسْم شَخْصيّ] Imran, Umran (*male given name*)

عِمْران *n* |dipt| سورة آل عِمْرانَ The Family of Imran (*Sura 3*)

عُمْرانيّ *adj* architectural, constructional; urban; تَوَسُّع عُمْرانيّ urbanization, urban expansion

عَمْرة *n* |عَمَرات| hat, headgear

عُمْرة *n* |عُمَر| umrah (*the non-mandatory lesser pilgrimage made by Muslims to Mecca, which may be performed at any time of the year*)

عَمْرو *n* Amr (*male given name*)

عُمْريّ *adj* age (*before n*); فِئة عُمْرِيّة age group; مَرْحَلة عُمْرِيّة stage of life

عَمير *adj* inhabited, populated

اسْتِعْمار *n* colonization; colonialism; الاسْتِعْمار الجَديد neocolonialism; القَضاء على الاسْتِعْمار decolonization

اسْتِعْماريّ *adj* colonial, colonialist; ماضٍ اسْتِعْماريّ a colonial history; حُكْم اسْتِعْماريّ \ هَيْمَنة اسْتِعْمارِيّة colonial rule; colonial government; قُوّات \ دُوَل اسْتِعْمارِيّة colonial powers/countries; سِياسة اسْتِعْمارِيّة colonial policy, settlement policy

اسْتِعْمارِيّة *n* colonialism

إعْمار *n* construction, building (up); إعادة الإعْمارِ reconstruction; إعادة إعْمارِ البِلادِ بعد الحَرْبِ the reconstruction of the country after the war

المَعْمورة *n* the (inhabited) world; في كُلِّ أَنْحاءِ المَعْمورةِ all over the world

تَعْمير *n* |تَعْميرات| construction, building; urbanization

مُسْتَعْمَر *adj* colonized

مُسْتَعْمِر **A** *adj* colonial; دَوْلة مُسْتَعْمِرة a colonial country **B** *n* colonist

مُسْتَعْمَرة *n* colony; settlement; مُسْتَعْمَرة سابِقة a former colony; أَسَّسَ \ أَنْشَأَ مُسْتَعْمَرةً to found/establish a colony; مُسْتَعْمَرة طُيورٍ a bird colony

مُعْتَمِر *n* someone who performs the umrah

مِعْمار *n* architect; architecture

مِعْماريّ **A** *adj* architectural; construction (*before n*); مُهَنْدِس مِعْماريّ architect; أُسْلوب \ طِراز مِعْماريّ architectural style, architecture; فَنّ مِعْماريّ architecture **B** *n* |مِعْماريّة| architect

مُعَمَّر **A** *adj* long-lived, very old; شَجَرة مُعَمَّرة an ancient tree **B** *n* Muammar (*male given name*)

مُعَمِّر **A** *adj* perennial; نَباتات مُعَمِّرة perennials **B** *n* colonist

مَعْمور *adj* inhabited, populated; بَيْت مَعْمور an occupied house

أَعْمَش *adj* |dipt; عُمْش| bleary-eyed

عَمُقَ *v* |u; عَماقة, عُمْق| to be/become deep

عَمَّقَ *v* to deepen, to make deep/deeper; to dig out, to dredge; عَمَّقَ نَهْراً \ قَناةً to deepen a river/canal; عَمَّقَ ميناءً to dredge a port; عَمَّقَ مَعْرِفَتَهُ to deepen one's knowledge

أَعْمَقَ *v* to deepen

تَعَمَّقَ *v* [1] |في| [تَبَحَّرَ] to delve into, to be/become absorbed in, to immerse oneself in; to study thoroughly; تَعَمَّقَ في مَوْضوعٍ to delve into a subject; تَعَمَّقَ في دِراسةِ شَيْءٍ to study sth thoroughly; تَعَمَّقَ في الأَدَبِ to be/become immersed in literature [2] [عَمَّقَ] to deepen; تَعَمَّقَت الانْقِسامات divisions deepened

عُمْق, عَمْق *n* |أَعْماق| depth; profundity; عُمْق البِئْرِ the depth of the well; عُمْق التَفْكيرِ profundity, thoughtfulness; على عُمْقِ أَلْفِ مِترٍ at a depth of a thousand metres; في عُمْقِ الصَحْراءِ in the middle of the desert; في أَعْماقِ اللَيْلِ in the middle of the night; من أَعْماقِ قَلْبي from the bottom of my heart; يَدُلُّ هذا على عُمْقِ حُبِّهِ this shows how deep his love is; بِعُمْقٍ deeply, thoroughly; قَرَأَ شَيْئاً بِعُمْقٍ to read sth thoroughly

عَميق *adj* |عِماق, عُمُق| deep; profound, thorough; هوّة عَميقة a deep gorge; خِزانة عَميقة a deep closet; أَثَر عَميق a deep impression; دِراسة عَميقة a thorough study; صَوْت عَميق a deep voice; حُبّ عَميق deep love

تَعَمُّق *n* [1] [عُمْق] depth; profundity, thoroughness; بِتَعَمُّقٍ deeply, thoroughly [2] [تَعْميق] delving, immersion; thorough study; التَعَمُّق في دِراسَتِهِ immersion in one's studies

تَعْميق *n* deepening; تَعْميق المَعْرِفةِ deepening of knowledge

مُعَمَّق *adj* deep, profound; thorough; بَحْث مُعَمَّق a thorough investigation

عَمِلَ *v* |a; عَمَل| [1] [اشْتَغَلَ] to work, to be employed; to act; to be active; كانَ يَعْمَلُ to be working/at work; عَمِلَ مُدَرِّساً to be a teacher; عَمِلَ على شَيْءٍ to work at/on something; عَمِلَ لدى شَرِكةٍ to work for/at a company; عَمِلَ ساعاتٍ إضافيّةً to work overtime/extra hours; عَمِلَ تحت سُلْطةِ شَخْصٍ to operate under the authority of sb [2] [تَحَرَّكَ] to run, to work; تَعْمَلُ السَيّارةُ بالبَنْزين the car runs on petrol (BrE) gas (AmE); يَعْمَلُ هذا المُوَلِّدُ بالغاز this generator runs on gas [3] [أَظْهَرَ أَثَرَهُ] to work, to be effective; عَمِلَ عَمَلَهُ! it worked!; يُعْمَلُ بِهَذا القانونِ في حالةِ الطَوارِئِ this law is in effect during the state of emergency [4] [فَعَلَ] to do; to perform; عَمِلَ العَكْسَ to do the opposite; عَمِلَ صالِحاً to do a good deed [5] (Gram) to govern; إنّ الفِعْلَ يَعْمَلُ في المَفْعولِ the verb governs the object

عامَلَ *v* to treat, to handle, to deal with; عامَلَ شَخْصاً باحْتِرام to treat sb with respect; عامَلَ شَخْصاً مُعامَلةً عَدائيّةً to treat sb with hostility; عامَلَ شَخْصاً مُعامَلةً ظالِمةً to treat sb unfairly

أَعْمَلَ *v* to make work; to use; أَعْمَلَ آلةً to use an instrument; أَعْمَلَ ذِهْنَهُ to put one's mind to work, to use one's brains

تَعامَلَ *v* to treat, to handle, to deal with; to do business; تَعامَلَ بِدونِ رَسْميّاتٍ to interact on an informal level; تَعامَلَ مع

شَخْصٍ to do business with sb; to deal with sb; تَعامَلَ مع مُشْكِلةٍ to deal with a problem; تَعامَلَ مع مَوْضوعٍ to treat a topic; تَعامَلَ مع شَكْوى to deal with a complaint; تَعامَلَ مع شَيْءٍ بِحَذَرٍ to handle sth with care

اِعْتَمَلَ *v* to be/become agitated

اِسْتَعْمَلَ *v* 1 [اِسْتَخْدَمَ] to use, to apply, to employ; to utilize; اِسْتَعْمَلَ جِهازاً to use a device; اِسْتَعْمَلَ العُنْفَ to use violence; اِسْتَعْمَلَ مُسَدَّساً to use a gun 2 [اِتَّخَذَهُ عامِلاً] to employ

عَمَل *n* |أَعْمال| 1 [وَظيفة] work, employment; job, post; عَمَل جَديد a new job; عَمَل وَظيفيّ administrative/office work; رَبّ \ صاحِب العَمَلِ employer; مُدير أَعْمالٍ manager; خِبْرة في العَمَلِ work experience; مَشاكِل في العَمَلِ problems at work; عَمَل في شَرِكةٍ a job at a company; باحِث عن عَمَلٍ looking for work; وَجَدَ عَمَلاً to find a job; أُقيلَ من عَمَلِهِ to be dismissed/fired; كانَ عِنْدَهُ عَمَلٌ to have a job; تَعَطَّلَ عن العَمَلِ to be/become unemployed; عاطِل عن العَمَلِ unemployed, jobless; بِدونِ عَمَلٍ ثابِتٍ without a permanent job 2 [شُغْل] work, labour; عَمَل شاقّ \ عَسير heavy/difficult work; عَمَل \ أَعْمال يَدَويّ(ة) manual work; handicrafts; عَمَل تَطَوُّعيّ \ طَوْعيّ voluntary/volunteer work; عَمَل جَماعيّ teamwork; عَمَل مَيْدانيّ fieldwork; أَعْمال مَنْزِليّة housework, housekeeping; أَعْمال مُوَجَّهة seminar; عَمَل بِراتِبٍ \ بِأُجْرةٍ a paid job; عَمَل غَيْر مَدْفوعِ الأَجْرِ unpaid work; عَقْد \ اتِّفاقيّة عَمَلٍ employment contract; جَوّ \ أَجْواء العَمَلِ work climate; تَوْزيع العَمَلِ division of labour, distribution of work; غُرْفة \ حُجْرة العَمَلِ study; يَوْم عَمَلٍ working day; سَنة عَمَلٍ year of service; مُدّة العَمَلِ working hours; رِحْلة عَمَلٍ business trip; طَريقة عَمَلٍ method (of working); مَكان العَمَلِ place of work; shop floor; مَحَطّة عَمَلٍ workstation; تَصْريح \ رُخْصة عَمَلٍ work permit (BrE) visa (AmE); سوق العَمَلِ job market; حُبّ العَمَلِ, رَغْبة في العَمَلِ zest for work; وِزارة العَمَلِ Ministry of Labour; شُروط عَمَلٍ terms of employment; زِيارة عَمَلٍ working visit; خُطّة عَمَلٍ plan of work/action; مَجال العَمَلِ field/sphere of action; رَقْم الأَعْمالِ returns, turnover; فُرْصة عَمَلٍ job opportunity; عَمَل قَيْدَ التَّنْفيذِ work in progress; الحَقّ في العَمَلِ the right to work; أَعْمال business; رَجُل أَعْمالٍ businessman; جَدْوَل الأَعْمالِ agenda; work scheme; بَدَأَتْ أَعْمالُ المُؤْتَمَرِ the conference has started; أَوْقات \ مَواعيد \ ساعات العَمَلِ working hours; وَفَّرَ فُرَصَ العَمَلِ to create employment; خَلَقَ فُرَصَ عَمَلٍ للآلافِ to create thousands of new jobs; عاجِز عن العَمَلِ disabled; التَّوَقُّف عن العَمَلِ walkout; أَضْرَبَ \ تَوَقَّفَ عن العَمَلِ to stop work, to go on strike; أَنْجَزَ أَعْمالاً, قامَ بِأَعْمالٍ to do work; قد انْتَهى العَمَلُ the work is done; صَرَفَ شَخْصاً عن عَمَلِهِ to keep sb from work; هَيّا للعَمَلِ! get to work! 3 [فِعْل] deed, act, action; عَمَل مُرْعِب \ مَهول \ فَظيع atrocity, gruesome deed; عَمَل غَبيّ \ ذَكيّ a stupid/clever move; عَمَل صالِح \ خَيْريّ a good deed; charity; عَمَل سَيِّئ an evil deed; أَفْضَل الأَعْمالِ very good deeds (Islam); عَمَل نِقابيّ a union action; عَمَل حَرْبيّ act of war; قامَ بِأَعْمالِ الخَيْرِ to practise charity; عَمَل وَحْشيّ cruelty; اِرْتَكَبَ أَعْمالاً وَحْشيّةً to commit cruelties; (نُريدُ) أَعْمالاً لا أَقْوالاً actions speak louder than words; العَمَل بالمُعاهَدةِ acting according to the agreement; تَعَطَّلَ العَمَلُ بالدُّسْتورِ the coming into force of the constitution has been delayed; عَمَلاً بِ ... according to; مَجْموعة عَمَلٍ action committee 4 [مَحْصَل] work, piece of art; عَمَل فَنّيّ piece of art; الأَعْمال الكامِلة لِمُؤَلِّفٍ the collected works of an author 5 [أَداء] working, functioning; عَمَل آلةٍ \ جِهازٍ the working of a device 6 (Gram) government 7 (Admin) district

عامِل A *adj* working; active; effective; شَباب عامِل young workers; الطَّبَقة العامِلة the working class; المُنَظَّمات العامِلة في مَجالِ حُقوقِ الإنْسانِ organisations active in the field of human rights; يَد عامِلة workmen; manpower

B *n* 1 [مُسْتَخْدَم] |عامِلونَ, عُمّال| worker, workman; employee; عامِل نَشيط a hard worker; عامِل أَجْنَبيّ a foreign worker; عامِل يَدَويّ \ حِرَفيّ craftsman; عامِل صِيانةٍ repairman; serviceman; عامِل بِناءٍ construction worker; عُمّال workers, personnel, staff; حِزْب العُمّالِ the Labour Party; عَدَد العامِلينَ number of workers/employees 2 [عُنْصُر] |عَوامِلُ| factor; element, constituent; عامِل هامّ \ إيجابيّ an important/positive factor; عامِل الوَقْتِ the element of time 3 (Math) |عَوامِلُ| factor; حَلَّلَ عَدَداً إلى عَوامِلَ to factor a number **4** (Gram) |عَوامِلُ| governor; عامِل الفِعْلِ the governor of the verb **5** (Admin) |عُمّال| governor; prefect

عامِلة *n* **1** [مُسْتَخْدِمة] (female) worker **2** (Zool) worker (*bee/ant*)

عَمالة *n* (Mor) province

عِمالة *n* **1** [عُمّال] manpower, workers, labour; عِمالة مُدَرَّبة skilled workers/labour; عِمالة الأَطْفالِ child labour; عِمالة رَخيصة cheap labour; عِمالة أَجْنَبِيّة foreign workers; نَقْص في العِمالةِ a manpower shortage **2** [خِيانة] treason; على تُهْمةِ العِمالةِ on charge of treason **3** [عُمولة] commission; brokerage

عُمّاليّ *adj* workers', labour (*before n*), working-class; نِقابة عُمّاليّة a workers' trade union

عَمَلانيّ *adj* practical; operational

عُمْلة *n* |عُمُلات, عُمْلات| currency, money; عُمْلة صَعْبة \ قَوِيّة a hard/strong currency; عُمْلة ضَعيفة \ سَهْلة a weak/soft currency; عُمْلات أَجْنَبِيّة foreign currencies; عُمْلة مُتَداوَلة an accepted currency; عُمْلة زائِفة \ مُزَيَّفة forged/counterfeit money; عُمْلات صَغيرة change; عُمْلة وَرَقِيّة paper money; سوق \ بورْصة العُمْلاتِ exchange market; تِجارة العُمْلةِ exchange dealings; سِعْر (صَرْفِ) العُمْلةِ exchange rate; خَفْض \ انْخِفاض سِعْرِ \ قيمةِ العُمْلةِ devaluation; انْخِفاض قيمةِ العُمْلةِ currency devaluation; ارْتِفاع سِعْرِ \ قيمةِ العُمْلةِ a rise in the exchange rate

عَمَليّ *adj* functional, handy, useful; practical; pragmatic; حَجْم \ جِهاز عَمَليّ a handy size/device; نَهْج عَمَليّ a pragmatic method; الحَياة العَمَلِيّة daily life; العُلوم العَمَلِيّة applied sciences; عَمَليّ لِلسَفَرِ handy for travelling; غَيْر عَمَليٍّ impractical, inefficient, useless; شَيْء غَيْر عَمَليٍّ a useless thing; نَظَرِيًّا وَعَمَلِيًّا in theory and in practice

عَمَليّاتيّ *adj* operational; قُدْرة عَمَليّاتِيّة operational capacity

عَمَليّة *n* **1** (Med) operation, surgery; عَمَلِيّة جِراحِيّة surgery; عَمَلِيّة قَيْصَرِيّة Caesarean section, c-section; طاوِلة عَمَلِيّاتٍ operating table; غُرْفة العَمَلِيّاتِ operating room, OR; أَجْرى عَمَلِيّةً (جِراحِيّةً) to operate, to perform an operation; أُجْرِيَتْ لَهُ عَمَلِيّةٌ he had surgery; هو بِحاجةٍ إلى عَمَلِيّةٍ he needs surgery **2** [حَمْلة] operation, undertaking; action; عَمَلِيّة عَسْكَرِيّة a military operation; عَمَلِيّات مَصْرِفِيّة banking operations; يَحْتَسِبُ المَصْرِفُ عُمولةً لِمُعْظَمِ العَمَلِيّاتِ the bank charges for most transactions; عَمَلِيّة مالِيّة a financial transaction; عَمَلِيّة خَطْفِ طائِرةٍ hijacking of a plane; أَجْرى \ نَفَّذَ عَمَلِيّةً انْتِقامِيّةً to take retaliatory action **3** [إجْراء] process; عَمَلِيّة سَلامٍ peace process

عُمولة *n* commission; brokerage; أَخَذَ عُمولةً على شَيْءٍ to earn a commission for sth; اقْتَطَعَ عُمولةً to charge a commission

عَميل *n* |عُمَلاءُ| **1** [وَكيل] agent, representative; عَميل تِجاريّ dealer **2** [زَبون] client, customer; عُمَلاء clientele **3** [سِياسيّ] agent, spy; collaborator; عَميل سِرّيّ a secret agent, spy; عَميل لِلمُخابَراتِ البَريطانِيّةِ an agent of the British secret service, a British spy

اسْتِعْمال *n* |اسْتِعْمالات| use, utilization, application; اسْتِعْمال يَوْميّ everyday use; اسْتِعْمال داخِليّ \ خارِجيّ internal/external use; اسْتِعْمال دَواءٍ the use of a medicine; طَريقة الاسْتِعْمالِ way of using/to use; رُسوم اسْتِعْمالٍ usage fees; سوء الاسْتِعْمالِ abuse, misuse; improper use; إعادة الاسْتِعْمالِ reuse; recycling; أَعادَ الاسْتِعْمالَ to recycle; سَهْل الاسْتِعْمالِ easy to use, handy, user-friendly; سُهولة الاسْتِعْمالِ user-friendliness; إرْشادات \ دَليل \ تَعْليمات الاسْتِعْمالِ instructions, users' manual, instructional guide; إرْشادات اسْتِعْمالٍ واضِحة \ غَيْر واضِحةٍ clear/unclear instructions; حَسَبَ إرْشاداتِ الاسْتِعْمالِ according to the directions/instructions; غَيْر صالِحٍ لِلاسْتِعْمالِ unusable, not fit for use; لِلاسْتِعْمالِ الشَخْصيِّ for (one's own) personal/private use; بِاسْتِعْمالِ ... with the use of ...; من كَثْرةِ الاسْتِعْمالِ because of frequent use; راجَ \ شاعَ اسْتِعْمالُ هذا المَنْهَج this method was frequently used

تَعامُل *n* dealing, handling, treatment; التَعامُل مع مُشْكِلةٍ dealing with a problem; يُجيدُ التَعامُلَ مع الأَطْفالِ he's good with children

مُتَعامِل **A** *adj* in use

B *n* **1** [تاجِر] dealer, handler; مُتَعامِل مُعْتَمَد \ مُرَخَّص authorized/licensed dealer; مُتَعامِل بِالقِطَعِ الأَجْنَبِيّةِ foreign currency dealer **2** [زَبون] customer, client

عامّ *adj* ① [عَكْس خاصّ] general; public; common; prevalent; انْتِخابات عامّة general elections; إضْراب عامّ a general strike; قانون \ قاعِدة عامّ(ة) a general rule; المُدير العامّ the general manager; بِشَكْلٍ عامٍّ in general; بِوَجْهٍ عامٍّ generally speaking; بِصِفَةٍ عامّةٍ in a general sense ② [عُموميّ] public; القِطاع العامّ the public sector; الرَأْي العامّ public opinion; الإدارة العامّة public administration; الحَياة العامّة public life; المُدَّعي العامّ, النِيابة العامّة the public prosecutor; النِظام العامّ public order

عامّة *n* |عَوامّ| ① [الناس] people; العامّة the people; العَوامّ the common people; (Chr) the laity; عامّة الناس the masses; ordinary people; هو من عامّةِ الناسِ he is an ordinary/working-class man ② [عُموم] generality; عامّةً \ بعامّةٍ in general

عامّي *adj* common, ordinary; لَهْجة عامّيّة dialect, colloquial language, spoken Arabic

عامّيّة *n* (ME) dialect, colloquial language, spoken Arabic; العامّيّة المِصْريّة Egyptian Arabic

عَمّ *n* |أَعْمام, عُمومة| uncle (*one's father's brother*); *term of respect for older male*; ابْن \ بِنْت عَمٍّ (male/female) cousin; زَوْجة عَمٍّ aunt

عَمَّ *conj* see عَمّا under **ما**

عِمامة *n* |عَمائِم| turban; اعْتَمَرَ عِمامةً to wear a turban

عَمّة *n* aunt (*one's father's sister*); ابْن \ بِنْت عَمّةٍ (male/female) cousin; زَوْج عَمّةٍ uncle

عُموم *n* generality, prevalence; whole, total; على العُمومِ anyway, in any case (*when changing topics, or returning to the main topic after a digression*); بِوَجْهِ العُمومِ generally speaking; عُموماً in general; on the whole; في عُمومِ البِلادِ throughout the country; مَجْلِس العُموم (البَريطانيّ) (the British) House of Commons; لاقَت الإجْراءاتُ تَرْحيباً عند عُمومِ المُواطِنينَ the measures were welcomed by all citizens

عُموميّ *adj* public; general; مَدْرَسة عُموميّة a public school; النَقْل العُموميّ public transport; الجَمْعيّة العُموميّة General Assembly

عُموميّة *n* generality

عَميم *adj* comprehensive, all-embracing

تَعْميم *n* |تَعْميمات| ① [جَعْل الشَيْءِ عامًّا] popularization; extrapolation; making public ② [مَنْشور] circular (letter)

مُسْتَعْمَل *adj* used, in use; second-hand; بَضائِع مُسْتَعْمَلة second-hand goods; سَيّارة مُسْتَعْمَلة a used car; غَيْر مُسْتَعْمَلٍ unused

مُسْتَعْمِل *n* user

مُعامِل *n* |مُعامِلات| (Math) coefficient; مُعامِل تَفاضُليّ derivative; مُعامِل الذكاءِ IQ; مُعامِل ارْتِباطٍ correlation coefficient

مُعامَلة *n* ① [تَعامُل] treatment; approach; مُعامَلة وَحْشيّة brutal treatment, cruelty; المُعامَلة بالمِثْلِ reciprocity; سوء المُعامَلةِ ill-treatment; سوء مُعامَلةِ الحَيَواناتِ cruelty to animals; أَساءَ المُعامَلةَ to mistreat; أَساءَ مُعامَلةَ شَخْصٍ to mistreat sb; مُعامَلة تَفْضيليّة preferential treatment; تَلَقّى مُعامَلةً تَفْضيليّةً to get preferential treatment ② (Isl Law) transaction; مُعامَلة ماليّة a financial transaction

مَعْمَل *n* |مَعامِل| ① [مَصْنَع] factory, plant, mill; workshop; مَعْمَل تَكْريرٍ refinery; مَعْمَل لِمُعالَجةِ الغازِ a gas processing plant ② [مُخْتَبَر] laboratory

مَعْمَليّ *adj* laboratory (*before n*)

مَعْمول *adj* valid; كانَ مَعْمولاً بِهِ to be valid, to be in force, to be effective; التَقاليد المَعْمول بها the prevailing traditions; قانون مَعْمول بِهِ a law in force

عِمْلاق **A** *adj* |عَمالِقة| gigantic, huge, giant; دار نَشْرٍ عِمْلاقة a giant publisher; شَجَرة عِمْلاقة a huge tree **B** *n* |عَمالِقة| giant; عِمْلاق في الأَدَبِ a great writer

عَمَّ *v* |u; عُموم| to be/become general; to be/become common, to spread, to prevail; تَعُمُّ المَجاعةُ في إثْيوبيا there is a famine in Ethiopia; يَعُمُّ السَلامُ المِنْطَقةَ peace prevails in the area; عَمَّ الرَخاءُ البِلادَ the country was prospering

عَمَّمَ *v* ① [اسْتَعانَ بالعُموميّاتِ] to make general, to generalize, to extrapolate; عَمَّمَ نَتائِجَ التَجارِبِ على الحَيَواناتِ على الجِنْسِ البَشَريِّ to extrapolate the results of animal testing to humans ② [نَشَرَ] to popularize; to make public; to make open/accessible to the public; عَمَّمَ البَحْثَ العِلْميَّ to popularize scientific research; عَمَّمَ قَراراً to make a decision public; عَمَّمَ التَعْليمَ to make education accessible for everyone ③ [أَلْبَسَهُ عِمامةً] to put on/wear a turban

تَعَمَّمَ *v* to wear a turban

اعْتَمَّ *v* to put on/wear a turban

مُعَمَّم *adj* [1] [لابِس عِمامةٍ] wearing a turban [2] [عَكْس مُخَصَّص] generalized

عَمّان *n* |dipt f| Amman (*capital of Jordan*)

عُمان *n* |dipt f| Oman; سَلْطَنة عُمان the Sultanate of Oman

عُمانيّ *adj, n* Omani

عَمِهَ *v* |a; عَمَه| to wander about

عَمِيَ *v* |a; عَمًى| to be/become blind

عَمّى *v* [1] [صَيَّرَهُ أَعْمى] to blind [2] [جَعَلَهُ غَيْرَ واضِحٍ] to obscure, to obfuscate; عَمّى الكَلامَ to speak in riddles

أَعْمى *v* to blind; أَعْماهُ الغَضَبُ \ الحُبُّ he was blinded by anger/love

تَعَمّى *v* to be/become blind

تَعامى *v* to turn a blind eye (to); تَعامى عن الحَقيقةِ to turn a blind eye to the truth; تَعامى عَمّا يَجْري to turn a blind eye to what's happening

عَمًى *n* blindness; عَمى الكَلِماتِ dyslexia, word blindness; مُصاب بِعَمى الأَلْوانِ colour-blind

أَعْمى **A** *adj* |dipt; عُمْيان, عُمْي| blind, blinded; إيمان \ غضب أَعْمى blind faith/anger; طاعة \ كَراهِية عَمْياء blind obedience/hate; أَعْمى القَلْبِ misled

B *n* |عُمْيان, عُمْي| a blind person; أَعْمى يَقودُ أَعْمى the blind leading the blind; الأَعْوَرُ بين العُمْيانِ مَلِكٌ in the country of the blind, the one-eyed man is king

تَعامٍ *n* blindness; التَعامي عن شَيْءٍ blindness about sth

تَعْمِيةٌ *n* obfuscation; encryption; دُخان \ ضَباب تَعْمِيةٍ a smoke screen

مُعَمًّى **A** *adj* blinded; obscure; كَلام مُعَمًّى veiled language

B *n* |مُعَمَّيات| riddle, puzzle

عَنْ *prep* [1] [اِبْتِعاد] from; of; out of; انْعَزَلَ عَنْ شَيْءٍ to be isolated from sth; بَعيد عَنْ far from; عَنْ يَمينِهِ on his right/right-hand side; عَنْ طيبِ خاطِرٍ willingly [2] [حَوْلَ] about, on; أَفْكارُهُ عَنِ الاشْتِراكِيّةِ his thoughts on socialism; جَعَلَ الفيلْمَ صورةً عَنْ زَمَنِهِ he made the film a picture of his time; ماذا عَنْها؟ what about her?; how is she doing?; حَدَّثَ عن شَيْءٍ to speak about sth [3] [سَبَب] out of, because of; عَنْ خَوْفٍ \ حاجةٍ out of fear/need; عَنْ أَمْرِهِ on his command; عَنْ حُبٍّ out of love; نَتَجَ \ نَجَمَ عَنْ سوءِ التَفاهُمِ to follow from a misunderstanding [4] [سِنّ] تُوُفِّيَ عَنْ ٧٨ سَنةً he died at the age of 78 [5] [رِواية] on the authority of; فيلْم عَنْ رِوايةٍ لِ ... a film based on a novel of ...; نَقَلَت الصَحيفةُ عَنْ مَسْؤولينَ في الوِزارةِ ... the paper wrote on the authority of ministry officials; حَدَّثَني فُلانٌ عَنْ فُلانٍ x told me on the authority of y [6] [عَنْ طَرِيقِ] عَنْ طَرِيقِ through, by means of; عَنْ طَرِيقِ الطاقة الشَمْسِيّةِ through solar power [7] [مُنْذُ] عَنْ \ عَمّا قليلٍ next, later عَمّا قريبٍ soon, shortly; عَنْ \ عَمّا قليلٍ next, later

عِنَب *n coll* |أَعْناب| grapes; وَرَق عِنَبٍ (stuffed) grape leaves, dolma; عِنَب الثَعْلَبِ, عِنَب الذِئْبِ black nightshade; سُكَّر العِنَبِ grape sugar, glucose, dextrose; عُنْقود عِنَبٍ a bunch of grapes

عُنّاب *n coll* (Bot) jujube (*Ziziphus jujuba*)

عَنْبَر *n* [1] (Zool) |عَنابِرُ| sperm whale [2] [عِطْر] ambergris [3] [مَخْزَن] storehouse, magazine; hangar, shed [4] [صالة] ward, section; factory floor

عَنِتَ *v* |a; عَنَت| [1] [أَثِمَ] to sin [2] [لَقِيَ الشِدّةَ] to suffer adversity

تَعَنَّتَ *v* to be stubborn; to be obstinate, to be intransigent; تَعَنَّتَ في آرائِهِ to stubbornly hold to one's opinion

عَنَت *n* adversity; misfortune, misery; distress

تَعَنُّت *n* intransigence, obstinacy

مُتَعَنِّت **A** *adj* obstinate, intransigent; stubborn, headstrong; مَوْقِف مُتَعَنِّت an obstinate stance

B *n* mule, obstinate person

عَنْتَر *n* Antar (*male given name*)

عَنْتَرة *n* |m| Antar (*pre-Islamic Arabian hero and poet*)

عَنْتَرِيّة *n cycle of stories relating the deeds of Antar*

مُتَعَنْتِر *n* braggart

عِناج *n* (Med) lumbago

عُنْجُهِيّة *n* haughtiness, arrogance

عَنَدَ *v* |i-u; عُنود, عَنَد| to be headstrong

عانَدَ *v* to be headstrong/stubborn; to offer resistance; عانَدَ شَخْصاً to offer resistance to sb

عِنْدَ *prep* **1** [ظَرْف مَكانٍ] at, on, with; عِنْدَ الحُدودِ on the border **2** [ظَرْف زَمانٍ] at; عِنْدَ الفَجْرِ at dawn; عِنْدَ غُروبِ الشَّمْسِ at sunset; عِنْدَ ذَلِكَ \ عِنْدَها at that moment **3** [مَكان] place; house; تَعالَ عِنْدَنا come over to our house; بَعْدَما خَرَجْتُ من عِنْدَه after I had left his place; تَعْمَلُ عِنْدَنا منذ شَهْرٍ she has worked with us for a month **4** [حَقّ، مِلْك] to have (*with following possessive*); عِنْدي دَرْسٌ I have class; عِنْدي خَبَرٌ مُحْزِنٌ I have some bad news; لا مالَ عِنْدَنا we have no money; ليس عِنْدَنا مالٌ we have no money on us; لَيْسَ لَهُ عِنْدي أيُّ طَلَبٍ he can't make any demands on me; لَيْسَ لَهُ عِنْدي لَهُ مِن جَوابٍ I have no answer for him; لَهُ عِنْدي ۱۰۰ دولار I owe him 100 dollars **5** [ظَنّ] عِنْدي in my opinion; عِنْدَهُ أنّ ... he thinks that ...; هذا عِنْدَهُ أَفْضَلُ this is better to him **6** [في حالةِ] if, when; عِنْدَ اللُّزومِ if necessary

عِناد *n* obstinacy, stubbornness; عِناد شَديد severe obstinacy; بِعِنادٍ stubbornly; أَصَرَّ بِعِنادٍ to persist obstinately

عِنْدَئِذٍ *adv* at that time, then; at that moment; عِنْدَئِذٍ سَيَتَبَيَّنُ then it will be clear; عِنْدَئِذٍ انْدَلَعَت النيرانُ then a fire broke out

عِنْدَما *conj* see ما

عَنود *adj* |mf; عُنُد| stubborn; عَقَبة عَنود a major obstacle

عَنيد **A** *adj* |عُنُد| stubborn, obstinate, headstrong; مُقاوَمة عَنيدة obstinate resistance; مَوْقِف عَنيد a rigid stance; رَغْبة عَنيدة an indomitable will

B *n* |عُنُد| mule, stubborn person

مُعانِد *adj* stubborn

عَنْدَلة *n* song of the nightingale

عَنْدَليب *n* |عَنادِلُ| nightingale (*Luscinia megarhynchos*)

عَنْز *n* |أَعْنُز, عُنوز, عِناز| goat

عَنَسَ *v* |u; عَنْس, عُنوس| to be/become a spinster, to be unmarried

عانِس *n* |f; عَوانِسُ| spinster, old maid

عُنوسة *n* spinsterhood

عُنْصُر *n* |عَناصِرُ| **1** [مُكَوِّن] element; component, ingredient; constituent; عُنْصُر جَوْهَرِيّ \ أَساسِيّ an essential element; العُنْصُر الرَئيسِيّ the main ingredient; (Math) the principal component; عُنْصُر مُهِمّ an important constituent; عُنْصُر مَعْنَوِيّ لِجَريمةٍ a material element of a crime; عَناصِر سامّة \ غَيْر ضارّةٍ poisonous/harmless ingredients; عَناصِر إِلِكْترونيّة electronic components; مَجْموعة رِياضيّة مُكَوَّنة من خَمْسةِ عَناصِرَ a mathematical set that has five elements **2** (Chem) element; عَناصِر مُشِعّة radioactive elements; عَناصِر ثابِتة stable elements; عَناصِر اصْطِناعيّة synthetic elements; الجَدْوَل الدَوْرِيّ لِلعَناصِرِ الكيمْيائيّة the periodic table of the elements **3** (Philos) element; العَناصِر الأَرْبَعة the four elements **4** [شَخْص] element, person; عَناصِر مَشْبوهة \ مَشْكوك فيها suspicious/shady characters; عَناصِر هَدّامة subversive elements; جَيْش من خَمْسينَ أَلْفَ عُنْصُرٍ an army of fifty thousand men **5** [جِنْس] race; species; العُنْصُر البَشَرِيّ the human species, man

عُنْصُرِيّ **A** *adj* racist; عِبارات عُنْصُرِيّة racist remarks; كَراهِية عُنْصُرِيّة racial hatred; تَمْييز \ مَيْز عُنْصُرِيّ, تَفْرِقة عُنْصُرِيّة racism, racial discrimination; racial segregation

B *n* racist

عُنْصُرِيّة *n* racism

العَنْصَرة *n* Pentecost; عيد العَنْصَرة (the Festival of) Pentecost

عُنْصُل *n* |عَناصِلُ| (Bot) sea onion (*Drimia maritima*)

عَنُفَ *v* |u; عُنْف| **1** [قَسا] |على| to treat severely/harshly; عَنُفَ على شَخْصٍ to treat sb severely; to come down on sb **2** [اشْتَدَّ] to intensify, to become more violent; عَنُفَت الاشْتِباكاتُ the fighting intensified

عَنَّفَ *v* to reprimand; عَنَّفَ شَخْصاً to reprimand sb; to come down on sb

أَعْنَفَ *v* to treat severely/harshly

عُنْف *n* **1** [شِدّة] intensity; ازْدادَ عُنْفاً to become more intense **2** [قُوّة] violence; عُنْف بَدَنِيّ physical violence; عُنْف مُضادّ (violent) retaliation; مَوْجة عُنْفٍ a wave of violence; بِعُنْفٍ by force; roughly, violently; عامَلَ شَخْصاً بِعُنْفٍ to treat sb roughly; بِدونِ عُنْفٍ non-violent; اسْتَعْمَلَ العُنْفَ to use violence/force; لَجَأَ إلى العُنْفِ to resort to violence; نَبَذَ العُنْفَ to renounce violence; أَعْمال العُنْفِ acts of violence, violence; قُتِلَ في أَعْمالِ العُنْفِ to be killed violently

عَنَفَة *n* (Mech) turbine; عَنَفة غازيّة gas turbine

عُنْفُوان *n* prime; vigor, power; في عُنْفُوانِ شَبابِهِ in the prime of his youth

عَنَفيّ *adj* turbo; مُحَرِّك عَنَفيّ turbo engine

عَنيف *adj* |عُنُف ,عَنيفونَ| ◀1 [غاشِم] harsh, cruel; violent; طاغِية عَنيف a cruel tyrant; جَريمة قَتْلٍ عَنيفة a cruel murder; حَمْلة عَنيفة a violent action ◀2 [شَديد] severe, fierce, heavy; violent; قِتال \ مُشاجَرة \ مَعارِك عَنيف(ة) heavy fighting; مُناقَشة \ شِجار عَنيف(ة) a heated discussion; قَصْف عَنيف heavy bombing; زِلْزال عَنيف a violent earthquake; اِنْفِجار عَنيف a huge explosion; اشْتِباكات عَنيفة violent clashes ◀3 [قاسٍ] rough, rude; بِلَهْجةٍ عَنيفةٍ in harsh tones

تَعْنيف *n* reprimand, reproof; assault, abuse; تَعْنيف جَسَديّ physical assault; corporal punishment

لاعُنْف *n* non-violence, peacefulness

لاعُنْفيّ *adj* non-violent, peaceful

لاعُنْفيّة *n* non-violence, peacefulness

مُعَنَّف *adj* treated harshly, abused; reprimanded; نِساء مُعَنَّفات victims of domestic violence

‹ **عانَقَ** *v* to embrace, to hug; عانَقَ شَخْصاً to embrace sb; عانَقَ شَخْصاً بِحَرارةٍ to embrace sb warmly

تَعانَقَ *v* to embrace each other; تَعانَقَ بِقوّةٍ to embrace each other fervently

اِعْتَنَقَ *v* to adhere to, to support; to be converted, to adopt, to embrace; to profess; اِعْتَنَقَ وِجْهةَ نَظَرٍ to embrace a point of view; اِعْتَنَقَ ديناً to embrace/profess a religion; اِعْتَنَقَ الإسْلامَ to embrace Islam; to convert to Islam, to be a convert to Islam; اِعْتَنَقَ مَذْهَباً سِياسيًّا to support a political movement

عُنُق *n* |f; أَعْناق| neck; عُنُق دَقيق a slender neck; عُنُق مُتَيَبِّس a stiff neck; عُنُق زُجاجةٍ bottleneck; عُنُق الرَحِمِ cervix; رَبْطة العُنُقِ tie, necktie; ضَرْب العُنُقِ decapitation, beheading; قَطَعَ \ ضَرَبَ عُنُقَ شَخْصٍ to decapitate sb; دُقَّتْ \ كُسِرَتْ عُنُقُهُ to break one's neck; حول \ في العُنُقِ around the neck

عَناق *n* |أَعْنُق ,عُنوق| young goat; عَناق الأَرْضِ desert lynx (*Caracal caracal*)

عِناق *n* embrace, hug; عِناق حارّ \ حَميم a warm/tight embrace; تَبادَلَ العِناقَ to hug one another

عَنْقاء *n* |dipt f| phoenix

اِعْتِناق *n* conversion, embrace, adoption; اِعْتِناقُهُ للإسْلامِ his conversion to Islam

أَعْنَق *adj* |dipt| long-necked; عَنْقاء phoenix; griffin

مُعانَقة *n* embrace, hug

‹ **عُنْقود** *n* |عَناقيدُ| bunch, cluster; عُنْقود عِنَبٍ a bunch of grapes; عُنْقود نَجْميّ a star cluster; آخِر العُنْقودِ the youngest of the bunch

عُنْقوديّ *adj* cluster (*before n*); قُنْبُلة عُنْقوديّة cluster bomb

‹ **عَنْكَبوت** *n* |mf; عَناكِبُ| spider; بَيْت \ نَسيج \ شَبَكة العَنْكَبوت spiderweb, cobweb; شَبَكة العَنْكَبوت العالَمِيّة the (World Wide) Web; خَيْط \ خُيوط العَنْكَبوتِ spider's silk; سورة العَنْكَبوت The Spider (*Sura 29*)

عَنْكَبوتيّ *adj* spider-like; Internet/Web (*before n*); الشَبَكة العَنْكَبوتيّة the Internet, the Web; مَوْقِع عَنْكَبوتيّ website

‹ **عَنَّ** *v* |i-u; عَنَن ,عَنّ| to arise, to take shape; عَنَّتْ لَهُ فِكْرةٌ a thought occurred to him; عَنَّ على بالِ شَخْصٍ to occur to sb

عَنان *n* clouds; وَصَلَ إلى عَنانِ السَماءِ to go sky-high, to reach the stratosphere

عِنان *n* |أَعِنّة| rein, bridle; قادَ حِصاناً من عِنانِهِ to lead a horse by the reins; أَرْخى العِنانَ to loosen/slacken the reins; أَطْلَقَ العِنانَ لِشَخْصٍ \ لِشَيْءٍ to unleash sb/sth, to give free rein to sb/sth; أَطْلَقَ العِنانَ لِشَهَواتِهِ to give (free) rein to one's desires; أَطْلَقَ العِنانَ لِأَفْكارِهِ to give one's thoughts free rein; مُطْلَق العِنانِ unbridled, unleashed

عُنّة *n* impotence

عِنّين *adj* impotent

‹ **عَنا** *v* |u; عُنوّ| to yield, to submit; عَنا للهِ to submit to God

عَنْوة *n* violence, force; عَنْوةً by force; دَخَلَ عَنْوةً to enter by force, to force one's way into

‹ **عَنْوَنَ** *v* |i; عَنْوَنة| ◀1 [رِسالةً] to address; عَنْوَنَ رَسائِلَ to address letters ◀2 [الصَحيفةُ] to run a headline; عَنْوَنَت الصَحيفةُ أَمْسِ: ... the headline in yesterday's paper was: ...

عُنْوان *n* |عَناوين| ① [مَكان الإقامة] address; عُنْوان بَريديّ mailing address; اسْم وَعُنْوان name and address; عُنْوان مَوْقِع URL, Web address; بِدونِ عُنْوانٍ ثابِتٍ of no fixed abode; سَكَنَ \ أَقامَ في عُنْوانٍ to live at an address; هل لَدَيْكَ عُنْوانُه؟ do you have his address? ② [رَأْسيّة] title; headline; عُنْوان فَرْعيّ subtitle; عُنْوان كِتابٍ \ مَقالةٍ the title of a book/article; عَناوين الصُحُفِ newspaper headlines; صَفْحة العُنْوانِ title page; يَحْمِلُ الكِتابُ عُنْوانَ ... the book is titled ...

عَنْوَنة *n* ① [رِسالةً] addressing ② [إلْصاق بِطاقاتٍ] labelling

مُعَنْوَن *adj* |ب| titled, entitled

عَنَى *v* |i| ① [دَلَّ على] |عَنْي| to mean; يَعْني meaning, i.e.; so ..., um ...; أَعْني بِذٰلِكَ ... I mean by that ...; ماذا تَعْني تِلْكَ الكَلِمةُ؟ what is the meaning of that word?; هذا يَعْني الشَيْءَ الكَثيرَ لي this means a lot to me ② [أَهَمَّ] |عِناية| to concern, to affect, to preoccupy; هذا لا يَعْنيكَ إطْلاقاً that is none of your business

عَنِيَ *v* |a; عَناء| to toil; عُنِيَ ب to take care of, to see to, to look after, to concern oneself with; to be worried about; عُنِيَ بِمَريضٍ \ طِفْلٍ to look after a patient/child; عُنِيَ بِتَرْبِيةِ الأَطْفالِ to concern oneself with the upbringing of the children

عانى *v* to suffer, to endure; عانى من شَيْءٍ to suffer from sth; عانى من مَرَضٍ to suffer from a disease; عانى من الصُداعِ to have a headache; عانى من قَلْبِهِ \ التَنَفُّسِ to have heart/breathing problems; عانى الفَقْرَ \ الجوعَ to suffer (from) hunger/poverty; عانى نَقْصاً to suffer a shortage; عانى الأَمَرَّيْنِ to go through hell and back

تَعَنّى *v* to toil

اعْتَنى *v* |ب| to take care of, to look after, to concern oneself with; اعْتَنى بِشَخْصٍ to take care of sb; to pay attention to sb; اعْتَنى بِنَفْسِهِ to take care of oneself; اعْتَنى بِحَيَوانٍ \ بِنَباتٍ to take care of an animal/plant; اعْتَنى بِمَريضٍ \ بِطِفْلٍ to look after a patient/child; اعْتَنى بِشَعْرِهِ to take care of one's hair; لا يُعْتَنى بِهِ that is of no importance

عَناء *n* pains, trouble, bother; دون عَناءٍ without any trouble; بِقَليلٍ من العَناءِ without too much trouble; عَناء السَفَرِ travel fatigue

عِناية *n* ① [اهْتِمام] care, attention, concern; العِناية الإلَهيّة divine providence; العِناية بالصِحّةِ wellness, health care; العِناية بالأُسْرةِ caring for one's family; عِنايةُ ... for the (personal) attention of ...; بِعِنايةٍ with care, carefully; فَحَصَ شَيْئاً بِعِنايةٍ to examine sth with care; تَرَكَ شَيْئاً تحت عِنايةِ شَخْصٍ to entrust sth to sb's care; أَوْلى شَيْئاً عِنايةً خاصّةً to pay special attention to sth; وَجَّهَ عِنايةً فائِقةً لِشَيْءٍ to handle sth with the utmost care ② [رِعاية] (medical) care, nursing; عِناية طِبّيّة \ نَفْسيّة medical/psychological care; حَصَلَ على عِنايةٍ to receive care; أَعْطى عِنايةً جَيِّدةً to provide good care; تَلَقّى عِنايةً جَيِّدةً to be well cared for; احْتاجَ إلى العِنايةِ to need care; رَقَدَ في غُرْفةِ العِنايةِ الفائِقةِ \ المُرَكَّزةِ to be in intensive care

اعْتِناء *n* care

مُعاناة *n* suffering; distress; مُعاناة قاسِية immense suffering; مُعاناة لا تُطاقُ \ لا تُحْتَمَلُ unbearable/intolerable suffering; خَفَّفَ من مُعاناةِ شَخْصٍ to alleviate sb's suffering; تَحَمَّلَ المُعاناةَ to endure suffering

مُعْتَنٍ *adj* careful, thoughtful

مُعْتَنًى *adj* مُعْتَنًى بِهِ well-cared-for

مَعْنَويّ *adj* ① [عَكْس مادّيّ] non-physical, spiritual; ضَرَر مَعْنَويّ non-physical harm ② [أَخْلاقيّ] moral; دَعْم مَعْنَويّ moral support; روح مَعْنَويّة morale, spirit ③ [ضِمْنيّ] implicit; عامِل مَعْنَويّ (Gram) covert governor ④ [مَنْسوب إلى المَعْنى] semantic; *relating to meaning*

Idiom شَخْص مَعْنَويّ a legal entity

مَعْنَويّات *n pl* morale; spirit; مَعْنَويّات عالية high morale; مَعْنَويّات القوّاتِ troop morale; انْهارَتْ مَعْنَويّاتُهُ his morale was destroyed, he became demoralized; رَفَعَ المَعْنَويّاتِ to boost morale, to raise spirits; رَفَعَ مَعْنَويّاتِ شَخْصٍ to boost sb's morale; حَطَّمَ \ كَسَرَ مَعْنَويّاتِ شَخْصٍ to crush sb's morale

مَعْنًى *n* |مَعانٍ| ① [مَدْلول] meaning, sense, import; مَعْنًى ضِمْنيّ implicit meaning; مَعْنًى إضافيّ connotation; additional meaning; بالمَعْنى الحَقيقيِّ \ الدَقيقِ \ الواسِعِ للكَلِمةِ in the real/strict/broad sense of the word; بِكُلِّ ما في الكَلِمةِ

بِعَهْدِهِ to keep one's promise; قَطَعَ على نَفْسِهِ عَهْداً to make a vow; نَكَثَ عَهْدَهُ to break one's promise 3 ◀ [وَقْت] period, age, era; time; عَهْد انْتِقاليّ transitional period; في عَهْدِ المَلِكِ فاروق in the time of King Faruq; حَديث العَهْدِ recent, new; منذ عَهْدٍ حَديثٍ recently; for a short time now; منذ عَهْدٍ بَعيدٍ for a long time; طالَ بِهِ العَهْدُ it took a long time 4 ◀ [عِلْم] knowledge; acquaintance; أنا قَديمُ العَهْدِ بِهِ I have known it for a long time; لا عَهْدَ لَهُ بِهِ he has no knowledge of it; ظَلَّ كَعَهْدي بِهِ it is just like I remember 5 ◀ [مُدّة الحُكْم] government; regime; في عَهْدِ شَخْصٍ under the regime of sb; وَليّ العَهْدِ crown prince; heir to the throne 6 ◀ (Chr) Testament; العَهْد القَديم \ الجَديد the Old/New Testament

عُهْدة *n* care; custody; في عُهْدةِ شَخْصٍ under the custody of sb

تَعَهُّد *n* 1 ◀ [الْتِزام] |تَعَهُّدات| obligation; promise, pledge 2 ◀ [رِعاية] care

تَعْهيد *n* تَعْهيد جَماعيّ crowdsourcing

مُتَعاهِد *adj* contracting

مُتَعَهِّد *n* 1 ◀ [صاحِب مَشْروع] organizer; initiator; مُتَعَهِّد حَفَلاتٍ event organizer; party planner 2 ◀ [مُقاوِل] contractor; مُتَعَهِّد بِناءٍ building contractor, property developer

مُعاهَدة *n* agreement, treaty, pact, convention; مُعاهَدة دُوَلِيّة an international treaty; مُعاهَدة سَلامٍ peace treaty; مُعاهَدة نَوَوِيّة nuclear arms treaty; مُعاهَدة تِجارِيّة trade agreement; commercial treaty; مُعاهَدة التِجارةِ الحُرّةِ free trade agreement; مُعاهَدة ثَقافِيّة a cultural agreement; مُعاهَدة مَنْعِ الانْتِشارِ النَوَويِّ non-proliferation treaty; مُعاهَدة جِنيف the Geneva Convention; مُعاهَدة روما the Treaty of Rome; مُعاهَدة بين دَوْلَتَيْنِ an agreement between two countries; عَقَدَ مُعاهَدةً to enter into/conclude a pact; وَقَّعَ على مُعاهَدةٍ to sign a pact; أَقَرَّ مُعاهَدةً ,صَدَّقَ على مُعاهَدةٍ to ratify a treaty; أَلْغى مُعاهَدةً to cancel an agreement, to abrogate a pact

مَعْهَد *n* |مَعاهِدُ| institute, academy, school; مَعْهَد موسيقيّ music school, conservatory; دَرَسَ في المَعْهَدِ الموسيقيِّ to study at the music school; مَعْهَد عالٍ college, academy; مَعْهَد الدِفاعِ للُغاتِ Defense Language Institute; مَعْهَد في الجامِعةِ an institute/school at a university

من مَعْنًى in the broadest/largest sense of the word; بِكُلِّ مَعْنى الكَلِمةِ in every sense of the word; مَعْنى هذه الكَلِمةِ the meaning of this word; عِلْم المَعاني semantics; تَغَيُّر المَعْنى change of meaning; اخْتِلاف في المَعْنى difference in meaning; تَعَدُّد المَعاني polysemy; قالَ ما مَعْناهُ ... what he said was to the effect that ...; أَدّى مَعْنًى to render a meaning; ما مَعْنى كَلامِكَ؟ what do you mean?; اسْم المَعْنى abstract noun 2 ◀ [هَدَف] meaning; importance; مَعْنى الحَياةِ the meaning of life; غَيْر ذي مَعْنًى ,بِلا \ بِدونِ مَعْنًى meaningless; unimportant; حادِث ذو مَعْنًى an event of great importance

مَعْنِيّ A *adj* 1 ◀ [مَقْصود] concerned, intended, in question; الشَخْص المَعْنِيّ the intended person; المادّة \ التَقْرير المَعْنِيّ(ة) the article/decision in question 2 ◀ [صاحِب الشَأْنِ] concerned, interested, involved; مَعْنِيّ بالأَمْرِ the person/party concerned; الأَطْراف المَعْنِيّة the interested parties; المُوَظَّف المَعْنِيّ the official concerned 3 ◀ [مُهْتَمّ] concerned; اللَجْنة المَعْنِيّة بِحُقوقِ الإِنْسانِ the commission on human rights

B *n* the person concerned

‹ **عِهْ** *v* see وَعى

‹ **عَهِدَ** *v* |a; عَهْد| 1 ◀ [كَلَّفَ] to charge, to assign, to entrust; عَهِدَ إلى شَخْصٍ بِشَيْءٍ to entrust sb with sth; عَهِدَ إلى شَخْصٍ بِمَهَمّةٍ to charge sb with a task; عَهِدَ بِحَقيبةِ وِزارةٍ to appoint as head of a ministry; عَهِدَ بِحَقيبةِ الخارِجيّة (إلى شَخْصٍ) to appoint (sb) foreign minister 2 ◀ [عَرَفَ] to know; to be acquainted with; فيما أَعْهَدُ to my knowledge, as far as I know; ما زالَ كَما عَهِدْتُهُ he is still the same

عاهَدَ *v* |على| to promise; to commit oneself (to); عاهَدَ زَوْجَتَهُ على الإِخْلاصِ to promise one's wife to be faithful

تَعَهَّدَ *v* 1 ◀ [الْتَزَمَ] to assume, to take upon oneself; to pledge, to vow, to promise; تَعَهَّدَ إلى شَخْصٍ بِشَيْءٍ to promise sb sth; تَعَهَّدَ بِفِعْلِ شَيْءٍ to vow to do sth 2 ◀ [رَعى] to take care of; to pay attention to; تَعَهَّدَ شَخْصاً to take care of sb; تَعَهَّدَ الحَديقةَ to take care of the garden

تَعاهَدَ *v* to make a treaty; to promise each other

عَهْد *n* |عُهود| 1 ◀ [اتِّفاقيّة] treaty, agreement; convention, pact; نَقَضَ عَهْداً to break a contract 2 ◀ [وَعْد] promise, vow; وَفى

تَعْويج *n* bending

مُعْوَجّ *adj* crooked; ساقانِ مُعْوَجَّتانِ crooked legs; knock-knees

مُعْوَجّة *n* (Chem) retort (*glass vessel with a long narrow neck used for distilling liquids*)

عادَ *v* |u| ❶ [رَجَعَ] |مَعاد ,عَوْدة ,عَوْد| to come back, to go back, to return; عادَ إلى الوَطَنِ to return to one's country, to repatriate; عادَ من أمْريكا to return from America; عادَت المِياهُ إلى مَجاريها everything's back to normal; عادَ الهُدوءُ إلى القَرْيةِ peace was restored in the village; عادَت العَلاقاتُ إلى طَبيعَتِها relations were normalized; عادَ خائِباً to return empty-handed; عادَ أدْراجَهُ to retrace one's steps, to turn back; عادَ عن قَرارِهِ to reconsider one's decision; عادَ بِشَيْءٍ to bring/take sth back, to return sth; عادَ بِشَخْصٍ إلى نُقْطةِ الصِفْرِ to take sb back to square one; عادَ بِعَوائِدَ to bring in revenues; عادَ عَلَيْهِ بالأرْباحِ that yielded him a profit ❷ [فَعَلَ] |عَوْد| to do again; عادَ يَنْظُرُ he looked again; عادَتْ ووافَقَتْ she agreed again; أعودُ وأقولُ \ فأقولُ I repeat, once again, I say; عادَ فَلَبِسَ حِذاءَهُ he put his shoes back on; عادَت العَلاقاتُ تَتَوَتَّرُ من جَديدٍ relations have become strained again; لم يَعُدْ يَفْعَلُ شَيْئاً to not do sth anymore, to no longer do sth; لم نَعُدْ نَرى شَيْئاً we didn't see anything anymore; لم يَعُدِ الأمْرُ يُثيرُ اهْتِمامَهُ he was no longer interested in the case; لم يَعُدْ قادِراً على العَمَلِ he was no longer able to work; لم يَعُدْ وَزيراً he is no longer minister ❸ [إلى فَتْرةٍ مُعَيَّنةٍ] |عَوْد, مَعاد ,عَوْدة| إلى to go back to, date (back) to/from; to stem from; يَعودُ اللِقاءُ إلى السِتّينيّاتِ to stem from the sixties; عادَ إلى العاشِرِ من شَهْرِ نَيْسانَ the meeting took place on 10 April ❹ [كانَ نَتيجةً] |عَوْدة ,عَوْد| to go back (to), to be due (to); to be attributable to; تَعودُ المَسْألةُ إلى خُصومةٍ قَديمةٍ the matter goes back to an old feud ❺ [آلَ] |عَوْدة ,عَوْد| to belong (to); عادَ إلى الشَعْبِ to belong to the people ❻ [زارَ] |عِيادة| to visit; عادَ الطَبيبُ المَريضَ the doctor visited the patient ❼ (Gram) |عَوْدة ,عَوْد| to refer (to); يَعودُ الضَميرُ على الفاعِلِ the personal pronoun refers to the subject

عَوَّدَ *v* to accustom, to habituate; عَوَّدَ طِفْلاً على الطاعةِ to train a child to be obedient; عَوَّدَ نَفْسَهُ على شَيْءٍ to get used to sth

مَعْهود *adj* ❶ [مَعْروف] familiar, usual, customary; well-known; صورة مَعْهودة a familiar picture; غَير مَعْهودٍ unusual, unconventional ❷ [مُخَوَّل] entrusted

عُهْر ,عِهْر *n* adultery; prostitution

عاهِر Ⓐ *adj* |عُهّار; f pl عَواهِرُ| adulterous; whoring Ⓑ *n* |عُهّار; f pl عَواهِرُ| adulterer

عاهِرة *n* |عَواهِرُ ,عاهِرات| ❶ [مومِس] prostitute, whore (vulg) ❷ [زانِية] adulteress; whore (vulg), slut (vulg)

عاهِل *n* |عَواهِل| sovereign, monarch; king; العاهِل الأُرْدُنّي the Jordanian king

عِهْن *n* (coloured) wool

عاهِن *n* |عَواهِنُ| limb, extremity; ألْقى \ رَمى الكَلامَ \ القَوْلَ على عَواهِنِهِ to ramble, to talk without restraint

عاجَ *v* |u| ;عَوْج| ب ,على| to stay; عاجَ بِمَكانٍ to stay somewhere

عَوِجَ *v* |a; عَوَج| to be/become crooked, to be/become twisted, to be/become warped

عَوَّجَ *v* to bend, to warp, to curve; عَوَّجَ شَيْئاً to bend sth

تَعَوَّجَ *v* to be/become crooked, to be/become twisted, to be/become warped

اعْوَجَّ *v* to be/become crooked, to be/become twisted, to be/become warped; يَعْوَجُّ الخَشَبُ wood warps

عِوَج *n* crookedness; twist, kink, bend; شَيْء لا عِوَجَ فيه sth that is right and true

عاج *n* ivory; تِمْثال من العاجِ an ivory statue; ساحِل العاجِ Côte d'Ivoire, Ivory Coast

عاجيّ *adj* ❶ ivory (*before n*); قِطَع شِطْرَنْجٍ عاجيّة ivory chess pieces; بُرْج عاجيّ an ivory tower ❷ [مَنْسوب إلى ساحِلِ العاجِ] *relating to Côte d'Ivoire*; ياموسوكْرو، العاصِمة العاجيّة Yamoussoukro, the capital of Côte d'Ivoire

أَعْوَج *adj* |dipt; عوج| ❶ [مائِل] crooked, bent; عود أعْوَج a crooked stick ❷ (fig) crooked, bad; تَفْكير أعْوَج crooked thinking; سُلوك أعْوَج bad behaviour; الطَبْعُ الأعْوَجُ لا يُقَوِّمُهُ التَهْذيبُ *crooked by nature is never made straight by education*

اعْوِجاج *n* |اعْوِجاجات| warping, curving; kink, bend, twist; curvature

عَوْد *n* 1 [رُجوع] return; عَوْداً على بَدْءٍ ,عَوْداً وَبَدْءاً from the beginning; all over again; عَوْداً على بَدْءٍ back to the start 2 (Law) recidivism

عائِد A *adj* |عائِدونَ| returning; المِصْريّونَ العائِدونَ من الخارِجِ Egyptians returning from abroad
B *n* 1 [رِبْح] |عائِدات ,عَوائِدُ| profit, revenue, return; عائِدات الاسْتِثْمارِ the return on an investment; عائِدات نَفْطِيّة \ البِتْرولِ oil revenue 2 (Gram) *pronoun referring to an antecedent*
3 (Law) |عائِدونَ| reoffender, recidivist

عاد *n* listed alphabetically

عادة *n* |عَوائِدُ ,عادات| habit; custom, practice; usage; عادة سَيِّئة \ كَريهة a bad/nasty habit; العادة الشَهْرِيّة menstruation, period; تَأَخَّرَتْ عادَتُها الشَهْرِيّةُ her period's late; العادة السِرِّيّة masturbation; مارَسَ العادةَ السِرِّيّةَ to masturbate; عادات بَلَدٍ \ شَعْبٍ وَتَقاليدُهُ the ways/customs and traditions of a people/country; عادةً (ما) ,في العادةِ normally, usually, as a rule; كالعادةِ as usual; كَما هي العادةُ according to custom; على غَيْرِ عادَتِهِ as was customary; كَما جَرَتْ \ دَرَجَت العادةُ contrary to his usual practice; خارِق العادةِ \ فوق العادةِ extraordinary; إنّها لَعادةٌ قَديمةٌ أنْ ... للعادةِ it's an old custom that ...; عادَ إلى عادَتِهِ القَديمةِ to fall back into old habits; كانَ من عادَتِهِ أنْ ... to be in the habit of ...; جَرَت العادةُ أنْ ... it was customary/the practice/the custom to ...; فَعَلَ شَيْئاً جَرْياً على عادَتِهِ ,فَعَلَ شَيْئاً بِحُكْمِ العادةِ to do sth out of/by habit; اتَّخَذَهُ عادةً to make a habit of it; اكْتَسَبَ عاداتٍ سَيِّئةً to acquire/adopt bad habits; لم يَكُنْ من عادَتِهِ it was not a habit of his; تَقَيَّدَ بالعاداتِ to observe the customs; أَبْطَلَ عادةً ,تَخَلَّصَ من عادةٍ to kick/break a habit; to get out of a habit; أَقْلَعَ عن عادةٍ to give up a habit; نَبَذَ العادةَ to break with the custom

عادِيّ *adj* usual, common, normal, ordinary; يَوْم عادِيّ an ordinary day; المُواطِن \ الإِنْسان العادِيّ the common man; أَشْياء عادِيّة normal things; خِلافات عادِيّة normal differences; غَيْر عادِيٍّ unusual, uncommon; abnormal; extraordinary; أُسْلوب غَيْر عادِيٍّ an unusual method; حادِث غَيْر عادِيٍّ an extraordinary event

عاوَدَ *v* 1 [واصَلَ] to resume; عاوَدَ المُفاوَضاتِ to resume/reopen negotiations; عاوَدَ نَشاطَهُ to resume one's activities
2 [رَجَعَ] to return to, to come back to; عاوَدَهُ الخَوْفُ \ الأَلَمُ his fear/pain came back; يُعاوِدُ اللاعِبونَ التَمارينَ the players are returning to training

أَعادَ *v* 1 [كَرَّرَ] to repeat; to do again; أَعادَ الفِعْلَ \ القَوْلَ to do/say again; أَعادَ البِناءَ to reconstruct, to rebuild; أَعادَ النَظَرَ to reconsider; to re-examine, to revise; أَعادَ النَظَرَ في شَيْءٍ to reconsider sth; أَعادَ قَوْلَ شَخْصٍ to repeat sb's words; أَعادَ الكَرّةَ to try again; أَعادَ امْتِحاناً to resit an examination (BrE), to retake a test (AmE); أَعادَ طَبْعَ كِتابٍ to reprint a book; أَعادَ فَتْحَ الطُرُقِ to reopen the roads 2 [أَرْجَعَ] to return, to bring/take back, to give/send back; أَعادَ كِتاباً إلى المَكْتَبةِ العُموميّةِ to return a book to the library; أَعادَ كِتاباً لِشَخْصٍ to give sb back a book; أَعادَ طَرْداً إلى المُرْسِلِ to return a parcel to the sender; أَعادَ الدَقيقَ في الكيسِ to put the flour back in the bag; أَعادَ اللاجِئينَ to turn back refugees; أَعادَ شَيْئاً إلى جَوْهَرِهِ to reduce sth to its essence 3 [أَصْلَحَ] to restore; أَعادَ السَلامَ \ الأَمْنَ to restore peace/security; أَعادَ المَبانِيَ إلى ما كانَتْ عَلَيْهِ to restore the buildings to their original state; أَعادَ شَيْئاً إلى حَجْمِهِ الأَصْلِيِّ to restore something to its original size

تَعَوَّدَ *v* to get used/accustomed (to); to habituate oneself (to); تَعَوَّدَ على تَعَوَّدَ شَيْئاً \ على شَيْءٍ to get/become used to sth; تَعَوَّدَ عاداتٍ سَيِّئةٍ to get into bad habits

اعْتادَ *v* |a| to get used/accustomed; اعْتادَ على \ أنْ ... to be used to ..., to be in the habit of ...

اسْتَعادَ *v* to get back, to retrieve; to ask back, to reclaim; اسْتَعادَ أَرْضَهُ to get one's land back; اسْتَعادَ أَنْفاسَهُ to catch one's breath; to calm down; اسْتَعادَ وَعْيَهُ to come to/round; اسْتَعادَ قُواهُ to recover, to recuperate; اسْتَعادَ عافِيَتَهُ to regain (one's) health; اسْتَعادَ الحَديثَ حول مَوْضوعٍ to return to a subject; اسْتَعادَ تَقْديرَ \ ثِقةَ شَخْصٍ to win back sb's esteem/trust

عود *n* |عيدان ,أَعْواد| 1 (Mus) oud, lute 2 [النَباتِ] stalk, stem
3 [خَشَبة] stick; عود ثِقابٍ match

عاديّة *n* (Egypt) antiquity; عاديّات antiques; مَتْجَر عاديّاتٍ antique shop

عَوّاد *n* lute player

عَوْدة *n* return; repatriation; حَقّ العَوْدةِ the (Palestinian) right of return (*to their former homes within the current state of Israel*)

عِيادة *n* 1 [مُسْتَشْفى] clinic; عِيادة خارِجيّة an outpatient clinic 2 [طَبيب] (medical) practice; في عِيادَتِهِ in his practice; فَتَحَ عِيادة to open a practice; أدارَ عِيادةً لِطِبِّ الأَسْنانِ to manage a dental practice

عِياديّ *adj* clinical; مُعالَجة عِياديّة clinical treatment

اسْتِعادة *n* recovery, restoration, restoring; recapture, reconquest; اسْتِعادة المَدينةِ the recapture of the city; اسْتِعادة سِيادةِ الوَطَنِ restoration of national sovereignty

إعادة *n* 1 [رَدّ] giving back; sending back; restitution, restoration; إعادة الأراضي المُحْتَلّةِ restitution of the occupied territories; طَلَبَ من شَخْصٍ إعادةَ شَيْءٍ to ask sb to give sth back 2 [إرْجاع] restoration; إعادة العَلاقاتِ الدِبْلوماسيّةِ restoration of diplomatic relations; الإعادة إلى الوَطَنِ repatriation 3 [تَرْديد] re-; إعادة النظَرِ revision; reconsideration; إعادة التَنْظيم reorganization; إعادة فَتْحِ المِلَفِّ reopening of the case

اعْتِياد *n* familiarity; being used/accustomed; اعْتِياد على شَيْءٍ familiarity with sth; being used to sth

اعْتِياديّ *adj* usual, common, normal; على نَحْوٍ غَيْرِ اعْتِياديٍّ in an unusual way

تَعَوُّد *n* familiarization, habituation; acclimatization

تَعْوِيد *n* accustoming; تَعْوِيد الطُلّابِ على اسْتِعْمالِ الحاسوبِ letting the students get used to the use of the computer

مُتَعَوِّد *adj* used, accustomed; كانَ مُتَعَوِّداً على شَيْءٍ to be used to sth

مَعاد *n* hereafter

مُعاد *adj* repeated; مُباراة مُعادة a rematch

مُعْتاد *adj* 1 [عاديّ] usual, common, normal; المَكان المُعْتاد the usual place; كالمُعْتادِ as usual; على غَيْرِ المُعْتادِ unusually; وَضْع غَيْر مُعْتادٍ an unusual situation 2 [مَأْلوف] used, accustomed, habituated; كانَ مُعْتاداً على \ أنْ ... to be used to ..., to be in the habit of ...

مُعيد *n* 1 (Educ) teaching assistant 2 (Islam) المُعيد the Restorer (*one of the names of God*)

عاذَ *v* |u; عِياذة ,عَوْذ| to seek protection, to take refuge; أَعوذُ باللهِ (من شَرِّ ذلك) God help me!, God forbid!

عَوَّذَ *v* to charm, to protect (*with an amulet or a charm*)

أَعاذَ *v* to place under God's protection

تَعَوَّذَ *v* 1 |ب| [احْتَمى] to seek the protection of 2 قال أَعوذُ [باللهِ] to say the formula أَعوذُ باللهِ

اسْتَعاذَ *v* to seek protection

عِياذ *n* refuge; العِياذ باللهِ God help us!

تَعْويذ *n* 1 [تَعْزيم] exorcism 2 [تَميمة] amulet, talisman

تَعْويذة *n* |تَعاويذُ| 1 [تَميمة] amulet, talisman 2 [رُقْية] charm, spell

مَعاذ *n* |مَعاوِذُ| refuge; مَعاذَ اللهِ God forbid!

عَوِرَ *v* |a; عَوَر| to be one-eyed

أَعارَ *v* to lend, to loan (AmE); أَعارَ شَخْصاً شَيْئاً to lend sb sth; أعارَ شَيْئاً اهْتِماماً to pay attention to sth; أعارَ شَخْصاً سَمْعَهُ to lend sb one's ear

تَعاوَرَ *v* to take turns, to take alternately

اسْتَعارَ *v* to borrow, to have on loan; اسْتَعارَ سَيّارة شَخْصٍ to borrow sb's car; اسْتَعارَ كُتُباً من المَكْتَبة العامّةِ to borrow books from the public library

عَوار *n* blemish, defect

عَوْرة *n* 1 (Islam) *the parts of the body, for both men and women, which must be covered with clothing* 2 [عَيْب] defect, imperfection

اسْتِعارة *n* 1 [تَسَلُّف] borrowing 2 (Literat) metaphor, figure of speech

إعارة *n* lending; فَتْرة الإعارة lending period

أَعْوَر *adj* |dipt; عور| one-eyed; المِعى الأَعْوَر (Anat) caecum, blind gut; الأَعْوَرُ بين العُمْيانِ مَلِكٌ in the country of the blind, the one-eyed man is king

مُسْتَعار *adj* borrowed; اسْم مُسْتَعار pseudonym; شَعْر مُسْتَعار artificial hair, wig, hairpiece

مُسْتَعِير *n* borrower

مُعِير *n* lender

‹ **عازَ** *v* |u; عَوْز| to need, to require

عَوِزَ *v* |a; عَوَز| (1) [اِفْتَقَرَ] to be/become poor (2) [لم يوجَدْ] to be lacking

أعازَ, أَعْوَزَ *v* (1) [عوِزَ] to be lacking; أَعْوَزَهُ to lack; to need; أَعْوَزَهُ المالُ he was short of money, he needed money; تُعْوِزُهُ الشَّجاعةُ he lacks courage; تُعْوِزُهُ الأَدِلَّةُ he has no evidence (2) [كانَ مُعْوِزاً] to be/become poor

عَوَز *n* (1) [نَقْص] deficiency; lack, need; عَوَز الحَديدِ iron deficiency, anaemia; مَرَض العَوَز المَناعيِّ المُكْتَسَب acquired immunodeficiency syndrome, AIDS (2) [فَقْر] poverty; عاشَ في عَوَزٍ to live in poverty

مُعْوِز *adj* poor, needy

‹ **عَوْسَج** *n* (Bot) boxthorn (*Lycium*)

‹ **عَوِصَ** *v* |a; عَوَص, عِياص| to be/become difficult

اعْتاصَ *v* to be/become difficult; اعْتاصَ عَلَيْهِ الأَمْرُ it was difficult for him

عَوِيص *adj* |عِواص| difficult, complicated; obscure; مُشْكِلة عَوِيصة a difficult problem

‹ **عاضَ** *v* |u; عَوْض, عِوَض, عِياض| to compensate; عاضَ شَخْصاً بِشَيْءٍ to give sb sth as a compensation

عَوَّضَ *v* to make up; to compensate, to refund, to reimburse; to replace; عَوَّضَ عن الخَسارةِ to make up for the loss; عَوَّضَ عن الضَرَرِ to compensate/pay for the damage; عَوَّضَ عن خَسائِرِ شَخْصٍ to cover sb's losses; عَوَّضَ ٨٠ في المِائةِ من التَكاليفِ to pay 80% of the expenses; عَوَّضَ زَميلاً مَريضاً to replace a sick colleague; لا يُعَوَّضُ irreplaceable; ضَرَر لا يُعَوَّضُ irreparable damage; فُرْصة لا تُعَوَّضُ a once-in-a-lifetime chance

تَعَوَّضَ *v* to be compensated; تَعَوَّضَ من شَيْءٍ to be compensated for sth

اسْتَعاضَ *v* to replace, to substitute; to use as a substitute; اسْتَعاضَ عن الحَبْسِ بِغَرامةٍ to replace a prison sentence with a fine; صُنْدوق اُسْتُعِيضَ بِهِ عن بَرْميلِ الزُبالةِ a box that was used as a dustbin (BrE) garbage can (AmE)

عِوَض *n* |أَعْواض| compensation, recompense; substitute, replacement; عِوَضاً عن \ من عِوَض as a substitute for, in replacement of, in compensation for; instead of

اسْتِعاضة *n* substitute, replacement

تَعْوِيض *n* |تَعْوِيضات| (1) [تَرْضِية] compensation, reimbursement, refund; تَعْوِيض عن الضَرَرِ (الحاصِلِ) damages, compensation; تَعْوِيض قَدْرُهُ عِشْرونَ رِيالاً compensation of twenty riyal; مُقابِلَ تَعْوِيضٍ زَهِيدٍ for a small fee; قَدَّمَ إلى شَخْصٍ تَعْوِيضاً مالِيًّا \ مادِّيًّا (لِشَيْءٍ) to offer sb a financial compensation (for sth), to compensate sb financially (for sth); طالَبَ بِتَعْوِيضٍ, طَلَبَ تَعْوِيضاً to ask for compensation/a fee; دَفَعَ تَعْوِيضاً to pay compensation; حَصَلَ على تَعْوِيضٍ عن شَيْءٍ to get compensation for sth; مَنَحَ تَعْوِيضاً إلى \ ل to make a refund to (2) [مَعاش] allowance; تَعْوِيضات عائِلِيّة (Mor) child allowance (3) [مَبْلَغ خارِج عن الراتِبِ] bonus

تَعْوِيضِيّ *adj* compensational, compensatory, restitutive; عِلاج تَعْوِيضِيّ compensatory treatment; تَرْبِية تَعْوِيضِيّة compensatory education

‹ **عاقَ** *v* |u; عَوْق| to hinder, to impede; to prevent, to withhold; عاقَ شَخْصاً عن شَيْءٍ to prevent sb from sth

عَوَّقَ *v* to obstruct; to hinder, to impede; to delay; عَوَّقَ شَخْصاً \ شَيْئاً to obstruct sb/sth, to delay sth

أَعاقَ *v* to obstruct, to block; to hinder, to impede; أَعاقَ شَخْصاً \ شَيْئاً to obstruct sb/sth; أَعاقَ قانوناً \ اتِّفاقاً to block a law/agreement; أَعاقَ حَرَكةَ المُرورِ to obstruct traffic; أَعاقَ قافِلةً to hold up a convoy; أَعاقَ نُمُوَّ شَخْصٍ to stunt sb's growth; أَعاقَهُ مَرَضُهُ عن القُدومِ his illness prevented him from coming

تَعَوَّقَ *v* to be obstructed, to be delayed

عائِق *n* (1) [عَرْقَلة] |عَوائِقُ| hindrance, impediment; obstacle; عائِق في طَرِيقِ النُمُوِّ \ التَطَوُّرِ an impediment to growth; شَكَّلَ عائِقاً أمامَ شَيْءٍ \ شَخْصٍ to be a hindrance to sth/sb, to stand in the way of sth/sb; أَزالَ \ ذَلَّلَ \ جاوَزَ عائِقاً, تَغَلَّبَ على عائِقٍ to overcome an obstacle; بِدونِ عَوائِقَ unobstructed, unhampered (2) (Bot) larkspur (*Delphinium*)

إعاقة *n* 1 [عَرْقَلة] obstacle; hindrance, impediment; delay; إعاقة التَطَوُّرِ an impediment to development 2 [عَجْز] disability; إعاقة عَقْلِيّة a mental disability 3 (Sport) obstruction, blocking

تَعْوِيق *n* hindrance, impediment

مُعاق A *adj* disabled; مُعاق عَقْلِيًّا mentally disabled B *n* disabled person; مُعاق عَقْلِيًّا a developmentally disabled person

مَعوق *adj* disabled

مُعَوَّق A *adj* disabled; مُعَوَّق جَسَدِيًّا \ عَقْلِيًّا physically/mentally disabled B *n* disabled person; المُعَوَّقونَ the disabled

مُعَوِّق A *adj* hindering B *n* |مُعَوِّقات| obstacle, impediment; أزالَ مُعَوِّقاتٍ to remove obstacles; حاوَلَ تَجَنُّبَ المُعَوِّقاتِ to try to avoid the obstacles

‹ **عالَ** *v* |u; عَوْل, عِيالة| 1 [كَفَلَ] to provide for, to support; عالَ شَخْصاً to support sb 2 [فَقُرَ] see **عيل**

Idiom عيلَ صَبْرُهُ his patience is/was exhausted

عَوَّلَ *v* 1 [ناحَ] to lament, to moan, to whine 2 [اعْتَمَدَ] to rely, to depend; هو رَجُلٌ يُعَوَّلُ عَلَيْهِ he is sb you can rely on

أعالَ *v* to provide for, to support; أعالَ أُسْرَتَهُ to provide for one's family

عَوْل *n* support

عائِل *n* provider, breadwinner; العائِلُ الوَحيد للأُسْرةِ the sole provider for the family; حَيَوان عائِل (Bio) host

عائِلة *n* |عائِلات, عَوائِلُ| family; حَلْقة العائِلةِ family circle; اسْم العائِلةِ family name; العائِلة المالِكة \ المَلَكِيّة the Royal Family; شَجَرة عائِلةٍ family tree; كانَ من عائِلةٍ غَنِيّةٍ \ شَريفةٍ to be from a rich/noble family; ابْن \ بِنْت عائِلةٍ a respectable person

عائِلِيّ *adj* family (*before n*), domestic; عَلاقة عائِلِيّة family relationship; جَوّ عائِلِيّ a domestic atmosphere; شَرِكة عائِلِيّة a family company; حَياة عائِلِيّة family life; رَوابِط عائِلِيّة family ties; اسْم عائِلِيّ family name, surname; تَخْطيط عائِلِيّ family planning, birth control

عَويل *n* lament, wailing, moaning

عَيِّل *n* |عِيال| 1 [أُسْرة] family, household 2 [طِفْل] child

إعالة *n* support; عَجَزَ عن إعالةِ أُسْرَتِهِ not to be able to support one's family

مُعال *adj, n* dependent

مُعَوَّل *adj* reliable

مِعْوَل *n* |مَعاوِلُ| pickaxe

مُعيل *n* provider; breadwinner

‹ **مُعَوْلَم, عَوْلَمة** see **علم**

‹ **عامَ** *v* |u; عَوْم| 1 [طَفا] to float; عامَ على ظَهْرِهِ to float on one's back; عامَ على الماءِ to float on the water 2 [سَبَحَ] to swim; عامَ في البَحْرِ \ المَسْبَحِ to swim in the sea/swimming pool

عَوَّمَ *v* to launch; to set afloat; عَوَّمَ سَفينةً to launch a ship

عائِم *adj* floating, afloat; swimming

عام *n* |أعْوام| year; عام دِراسِيّ school year; academic year; العام المُنْصَرِم \ الماضي last year, the past year; العام القادِم \ المُقْبِل next year, the coming year; عام جَيِّد \ مُثْمِر a good/productive year; عام سَيِّئ \ نَحْس a bad year; حُلول \ مَطْلَع العام the beginning of the year; عام جَديد New Year; عاماً سَعيداً! Happy New Year!; كُلّ عامٍ وَأَنْتُمْ \ أَنْتَ بِخَيْرٍ *greeting which can be used for any holiday, including New Year's, birthdays, and Ramadan*; في عام ٢٠٠٠ in the year 2000

عامة *n* raft; عَبَّرَ النَهْرَ بِعامةٍ to raft across the river

عَوّام *n* swimmer

عَوّامة *n* 1 (Naut) buoy; float 2 [أداة عائمة] float; swim tube/board 3 [بَيْت على الماءِ] houseboat

تَعْويم *n* launching; floating; تَعْويم غَوّاصةٍ launching a submarine; تَعْويم عُمْلةٍ floating a currency

‹ **عَوَّنَ** *v* to help, to assist, to support

عاوَنَ *v* to help, to assist, to support; عاوَنَ شَخْصاً في شَيْءٍ to help sb in/with sth

أعانَ *v* to help, to assist, to support; أعانَ مَريضاً \ جَريحاً to help a patient/wounded person

تَعاوَنَ *v* to work together, to cooperate; to collaborate; تَعاوَنَ مع شَخْصٍ to work/cooperate with sb; تَعاوَنَ مع العَدُوِّ to collaborate with the enemy; تَعاوَنَ مع المُفَتِّشينَ

to cooperate with the inspectors; تعاوَنَ بِشَكْلٍ وَثِيقٍ to work/act in close cooperation

اسْتَعانَ *v* [1] [اسْتَعْمَلَ] |ب| to make use, to draw upon, to employ, to utilize; اسْتَعانَ بِخِبْرةِ شَخْصٍ to employ sb's expertise; اسْتَعانَ بِسِكّينٍ to use a knife [2] [طَلَبَ مُساعَدةً] |ب| to ask/call for help; اسْتَعانَ بِشَخْصٍ to ask for sb's help, to call on sb; اسْتَعانَ بِاللهِ to call on God

عَوْن *n* [1] [مُساعَدة] help, aid, assistance; مُؤَسَّسة عَوْنٍ relief organization; بِعَوْنِ اللهِ (سَيَنْجَحُ الأَمْرُ) with help of God (it will succeed); قَدَّمَ \ بَذَلَ العَوْنَ to offer/extend help; طَلَبَ عَوْناً to ask for help; مَدَّ يَدَ العَوْنِ لِشَخْصٍ to lend sb a (helping) hand [2] [مُساعِد] |أَعْوان| assistant, helper, aid

عانة *n* genital area; pubic hair; شَعْر العانةِ pubic hair; عَظْم العانةِ pubis; قَمْل العانةِ pubic lice, crabs

اسْتِعانة *n* [1] [اسْتِعْمال] |ب| use, utilization; الاسْتِعانة بِخِبْرةِ شَخْصٍ utilizing sb's expertise [2] [نِداء لِلْمُساعَدةِ] |ب| call for help; appeal; اسْتِعانة بِشَخْصٍ \ بِشَيْءٍ an appeal to sb/sth

إعانة *n* help, aid, assistance, support; subsidy; إعانة حُكوميّة government support; إعانة غِذائيّة food aid; إعانات زِراعيّة agricultural subsidies

تَعاوُن *n* cooperation, collaboration; تَعاوُن كامِل \ تامّ full cooperation; تَعاوُن مع العَدُوِّ collaboration with the enemy; التَعاوُن بين الدَوْلَتَيْنِ cooperation between two countries; بِتَعاوُنٍ (وَثِيقٍ) مع شَخْصٍ in (close) collaboration with sb; مُنَظَّمة التَعاوُنِ الإِسْلاميِّ Organization of Islamic Cooperation, OIC; مُنَظَّمة التَعاوُنِ الاقْتِصاديِّ والتَنْمِيةِ Organization for Economic Co-operation and Development, OECD; لَقِيَ تَعاوُناً to be met with cooperation; عَمَّقَ التَعاوُنَ العِلْمِيَّ والتِقْنِيَّ المُشْتَرَكَ مع ... to deepen the scientific and technical cooperation with ...

تَعاوُنيّ *adj* cooperative, cooperation (*before n*), collaboration (*before n*); جَمْعيّة تَعاوُنيّة a cooperative society; إِنْتاج تَعاوُنيّ co-production; مُنَظَّم على أَساسٍ تَعاوُنيٍّ cooperatively organized

تَعاوُنيّة *n* cooperation; cooperative, co-op

مُتَعاوِن **A** *adj* cooperative, cooperating; collaborating **B** *n* collaborator; مُتَعاوِن مع العَدُوِّ an enemy collaborator

مُسْتَعِين *adj* |ب| asking/requesting help from; getting help from

مُعاوِن *n* helper, aid; associate, assistant; مُعاوِن العَمِيدِ associate dean

مُعاوَنة *n* help, assistance, aid

مِعْوان **A** *adj* |مَعاوِينُ| helpful **B** *n* |مَعاوِينُ| helper, assistant, aid

مَعونة *n* help, aid, assistance; welfare; allowance; مَعونات (عاجِلة) (emergency) aid; مَعونة قَضائيّة legal assistance; مَعونة أَجْنَبيّة foreign aid; مَعونة مَشْروطة conditional aid

مُعِين *n* helper, assistant, aid

‹ **عاهة** *n* defect, disorder; عاهة جَسَديّة a physical disability; عاهة خِلْقيّة a congenital defect; عاهة مُزْعِجة \ مُعِيقة a disturbing defect; عاهة دائِمة \ مُسْتَديمة a permanent disorder

‹ **عَوَى** *v* |i; عُواء| to howl; عَوَى كالذِئْبِ to howl like a wolf; تَعْوِي الرِيحُ the wind is howling

عاوَى *v* to howl (at)

عُواء *n* howling; عُواء الكَلْبِ \ الذِئْبِ the howling of a dog/wolf

‹ **عابَ** *v* |i; عَيْب| [1] [الشَيْءَ] to condemn, to censure; عابَ على شَخْصٍ سُلوكَهُ to censure sb for his behaviour [2] [الشَيْءُ] to be defective; لا يَعِيبُهُ شَيْءٌ there is nothing wrong with it

عَيَّبَ *v* to condemn, to reprehend; to reproach; عَيَّبَ شَيْئاً to condemn sth

عَيْب *n* |عُيوب| fault, imperfection, shortcoming, flaw, defect; عُيوب خُلُقيّة weaknesses, vices; عُيوب جَسِيمة serious shortcomings; بَعْض العُيوبِ الصَغِيرة a few minor imperfections; لا عَيْبَ فِيهِ perfect, flawless, impeccable, faultless; irreproachable; there's nothing wrong with it; كانَتْ بِهِ عُيوبٌ to have faults; نَبَّهَ شَخْصاً إلى عُيوبِهِ to point out sb's faults; اكْتَشَفَ عُيوباً في شَيْءٍ to discover defects in sth; مِن العَيْبِ أَنْ تَغْضَبَ it's wrong to get angry; وَما العَيْبُ في ذلِكَ؟ what is wrong with that?, so what?; عَيْب! shame on you!

مَعاب *n* |مَعايِبُ| fault, flaw

مَعيب *n* disgraceful, shameful, reprehensible; imperfect, defective

مُعيب *adj* shameful, outrageous

‹ **عاث** *v* |i; عَيْث| to damage, to do harm; عاثَ فَساداً to wreak havoc, to make trouble, to damage; عاث في مالِهِ to squander one's money

‹ **عيَّدَ** *v* to celebrate

عايَدَ *v* |على| to wish (sb) a merry feast

عيد *n* |أَعْياد| Eid; feast, celebration, festival; holiday; العيد الصَغير the Lesser Eid (*Eid al-Fitr*); عيد الفِطْر Eid al-Fitr (*breaking of the fast after Ramadan*); العيد الكَبير the Greater Eid (*Eid al-Adha*); عيد الأَضْحى Eid al-Adha, Feast of the Sacrifice; عيد المَوْلِد النَبَوِيّ *the birthday of the Prophet Muhammad (12 Rabi' ul-Awwal)*; عيد الثَوْرةِ the Celebration of the Revolution; عيد ميلادٍ birthday; عيد ميلادِ المَسيحِ \ الميلادِ Christmas; العيد الوَطَنِيّ الفَرَنْسِيّ the French National Day; (أَتَمَنّى لَكُمْ) عيداً سَعيداً (I wish you a) Happy Eid!; عيدٌ مُبارَكٌ Happy Eid!; خلال \ في أَيّامِ العيدِ in the holiday season; اِحْتَفَلَ بِعيدٍ to celebrate a feast

عيدية *n* present (*for a feast*)

‹ **عارَ** *v* |i; عَيْر| ❶ [هامَ] to stray, to wander ❷ [لامَ] to blame

عَيَّرَ *v* to insult, to abuse; عَيَّرَ شَخْصاً بالجَهْلِ to call sb ignorant

عايَرَ *v* to calibrate, to gauge

عير *n* |f; عيرات| caravan

Idiom هو لا في العيرِ وَلا في النَفيرِ *he is unimportant*

عَيْر *n* |أَعْيار| wild ass, onager

عار *n* |أَعْيار| shame, disgrace; عار كَبير a total disgrace; وَصْمة عارٍ (على جَبينِ شَخْصٍ) a black mark (on sb), a mark of shame (on sb); جَلَبَ \ سَبَّبَ العارَ لِشَخْصٍ to bring shame upon sb, to discredit sb; جَلَبَ العارَ لِنَفْسِهِ to disgrace oneself; لَحِقَهُ العارُ to be shamed; من العارِ أَنْ... it's a shame that ...; هذا عارٌ عَلَيْهِ it's a shame for him

عَيّار Ⓐ *adj* straying

Ⓑ *n* vagabond, bum

عِيار *n* |أَعْيِرة ,عِيارات| ❶ [الكَيْلِ أو الوَزْنِ] measure, gauge; unit; عِيار الكَيْلِ measure of capacity; عِيار الوَزْنِ weight ❷ [الذَهَبِ] standard; ذَهَب من عِيارِ ٢٤ \ ١٨ قيراطاً 18/24-carat gold ❸ [رَصاصة] calibre; bullet; shot, round; عِيار ناريّ gunshot; مُسَدَّس من عِيارِ ٩ ملم a 9mm pistol

مُعايَرة *n* standardization; calibration, gauging

مِعْيار *n* |مَعاييرُ| standard, measure, criterion; norm; حَسْبَ مَعاييرَ مُعَيَّنةٍ according to certain standards; تَوْحيد المَعايير standardization; اِتَّخَذَ مِعْياراً \ كَمِعْيارٍ to take/use as a standard/measure; وَضَعَ مَعايير to standardize; اِسْتَوْفى المِعْيارَ to come up to the standard; طَبَّقَ مَعايير مُزْدَوِجةً, تَعامَلَ بِمِعْيارَيْنِ to have a double standard

مِعْيارِيّ *adj* normative; standard; وَحْدة مِعْيارِيّة unit; لُغة مِعْيارِيّة standard language

‹ **عَيْسَلان** *n* hyacinth

‹ **عيسى** *n* ❶ [اسْم شَخْصِيّ] Isa (*male given name*) ❷ [المَسيح] Jesus; عيسى عَلَيْهِ السَلامُ Jesus, peace be upon him

‹ **عاش** *v* |i; عَيْش ,عيشة ,مَعيش ,مَعيشة ,مَعاش| ❶ [حَيَّ] to live, to be alive; عاشَت المَلِكةُ! long live the Queen!; عاشَ من أَجْلِ شَيْءٍ \ شَخْصٍ to live for sth/sb ❷ [أَمْضى حَياتَهُ] to live, to reside; عاشَ في الماءِ \ الغابةِ to live in the water/woods; عاشَ في بِلادٍ كَلاجِئٍ to live in a country as a refugee; عاشَ في المَدينةِ to live in the city; عاشَ في خَوْفٍ to live in fear ❸ [شَيْئاً] to live, to live/go through; عاشَ الحَرْبَ to live through the war; عاشَ سَنَواتٍ طَويلةً to live many years; عاشَ عيشةً رائِعةً to live a beautiful life; عاشَ مَأْزِقاً to have a problem ❹ [مَوْرِد رِزْقٍ] to live off, to make a living; عاش على الزِراعةِ to make a living farming; عاش على الجَريمةِ to live off crime

عايَشَ *v* to live together; عايَشَ شَخْصاً to live with sb

أَعاشَ *v* to keep alive

تَعَيَّشَ *v* to live off, to make a living; تَعَيَّشَ من زِراعةِ البُنِّ to make a living farming coffee

تَعايَشَ *v* to coexist; to live/go together; تَعايَشَ مع ناسٍ to live with people; تَعايَشَ مع شَيْءٍ to coexist with sth

عَيْش *n* ❶ [وُجود] life, existence, living; عَيْش كَريم \ آمِن a respectable/safe living; عَيْش مُشْتَرَك بين المُسْلِمين والمَسيحيّين coexistence of Muslims and Christians; طَريقة \ أُسْلوب العَيْشِ way of life; وَسائِل العَيْشِ livelihood; عاشَ عَيْشاً رَغيداً to have a good life; رَخا عَيْشُهُ to have an easy life; نَعِمَ عَيْشُهُ to be well-off, to live in comfort; نَكِدَ عَيْشُهُ

to be unhappy; نَكَّدَ عَيْشَ شَخْصٍ to make sb's life miserable; لا يُمْكِنُ العَيْشُ ضاقَتْ في وَجْهِهِ سُبُلُ العَيْشِ he was poor; عَيْش الغُرابِ فيهِ uninhabitable ② [خُبْز] (Egypt) bread; عَيْش الغُرابِ mushroom

عائِش *adj* ① [حَيّ] living, alive ② [موسِر] well-off

عائِشة *n* |dipt| Aisha (*female given name*)

عيشة *n* life; عاشَ عيشَتَهُ العاديّةَ to live one's normal life

إعاشة *n* sustenance; ration

تَعايُش *n* |تَعايُشات| living together, coexistence, cohabitation; تَعايُش سِلْميّ (مع الدُوَلِ المُجاوِرةِ) a peaceful coexistence (with neighbouring countries)

تَعَيُّش *n* livelihood

مَعاش *n* |مَعاشات| ① [راتِب] pension; allowance; مَعاش التَقاعُدِ \ تَقاعُديّ pension; مَعاش بَسيط a small pension; أَصْحاب المَعاشاتِ pensioners; صُنْدوق المَعاشاتِ pension fund; بَلَغَ سِنَّ المَعاش to reach retirement age; تَقاضى المَعاشَ to receive a pension; أُحيلَ على المَعاشِ to retire ② [مَطْعَم ومَشْرَب] livelihood, living

مُعاش *adj* real-life; الواقِع المُعاش real life, reality

مَعاشيّ *adj* living (*before n*); الحالة \ الأَوْضاع المَعاشيّة living conditions

مُعايَشة *n* coexistence; living; real

مَعيشة *n* |مَعايِش| living; غَلاء \ تَكاليف المَعيشةِ the cost of living; مُسْتوى المَعيشةِ living standard; أُسْلوب \ نَمَط المَعيشةِ lifestyle, way of life; الحَدّ الأَدْنى للمَعيشةِ subsistence level

مَعيشيّ *adj* living (*before n*); livelihood (*before n*); ظُروف مَعيشيّة living conditions; أَزْمة مَعيشيّة a cost of living crisis

عَيَّطَ *v* ① [صاحَ] to scream, to yell ② [بَكى] to cry

عِياط *n* screaming; crying

عافَ *v* |a-i; عَيْف, عِياف, عِيَفان| to loathe, to detest; عافَ شَيْئاً to detest sth

عالَ *v* |i; عَيْلة| ① [فَقُرَ] to be/become poor ② [كَفَلَ] see **عول**

عَيَّلَ *v* to provide for

أَعْيَلَ *v* to have a numerous family

عالة *n* load, burden; كانَ عالةً على شَخْصٍ to live off of sb, to leech/sponge off sb; يَعيشُ عالةً على أَبيهِ he lives off of his father; كانَ عالةً على المُجْتَمَعِ to be on public assistance, to be on welfare (AmE)

عَيَّنَ *v* ① [حَدَّدَ] to determine, to fix, to set; عَيَّنَ تاريخاً to set a date; عَيَّنَ تاريخ حَفْريّاتٍ to determine the age of fossils; عَيَّنَ أَسْبابَ مُشْكِلةٍ to determine the causes of a problem ② [خَصَّصَ] to allot, to assign; عَيَّنَ لِشَخْصٍ مَبْلَغاً to allot a sum to sb ③ [وَظَّفَ] to appoint, to assign, to nominate; عَيَّنَ لَجْنةَ تَحْقيقٍ to appoint a committee of inquiry; عَيَّنَ شَخْصاً مَدى الحَياةِ to appoint sb for life; عَيَّنَ شَخْصاً كَأُسْتاذٍ جامِعيٍّ to appoint sb professor; عَيَّنَ شَخْصاً قاضِياً to appoint sb as a judge; عَيَّنَ شَخْصاً وَريثاً لَهُ to designate sb one's heir; عَيَّنَ شَخْصاً في وَظيفةٍ to assign sb to a post/an office

عايَنَ *v* to view, to inspect; to examine; عايَنَ شَيْئاً to view sth; عايَنَ البِضاعةَ to inspect the goods; عايَنَ جُثّةً to examine a body

تَعَيَّنَ *v* ① [وَجَبَ] |على| to be obligatory, to be one's duty; must, should; يَتَعَيَّنُ عَلَيَّ أَنْ أَقولَ شَيْئاً I must say sth ② [تَحَدَّدَ] to be reserved/set aside; تَعَيَّنَتْ هذه الأَرْضُ للزِراعةِ this land is reserved for agriculture

عَيْن *n* |f| ① (Anat) |أَعْيُن, عُيون| eye; عَيْن سَمَكةٍ corn (*on one's foot, etc.*); مِحْجَر العَيْنِ eye socket; زاوِية عَيْنٍ corner of the eye; عَصَب عَيْنٍ optic nerve; طَبيب العُيونِ ophthalmologist; اِلْتِهاب العَيْنِ inflammation of the eye; بُؤْبُؤ \ حَدَقة العَيْنِ pupil; تَلَأْلُؤ \ تَأَلُّق \ بَريق عَيْنَيْهِ the twinkle in his eye; في طَرْفةِ \ غَمْضة عَيْنٍ in the blink of an eye; تحت عُيونِنا before our very eyes; العَيْنُ بالعَيْنِ والسِنُّ بالسِنِّ an eye for an eye and a tooth for a tooth; البَعيدُ عن العَيْنِ بَعيدٌ عن القَلْبِ out of sight, out of mind; وَقَعَت العَيْنُ على العَيْنِ a fight broke out; أَصْبَحَ أَثَراً بعد عَيْنٍ no trace has been left; رَأى شَيْئاً رَأْيَ العَيْنِ \ بِأُمِّ عَيْنِهِ to see sth with one's own eyes; فَرَكَ عَيْنَيْهِ to rub one's eyes; فَتَحَ عَيْنَيْ شَخْصٍ على الحَقيقةِ to open sb's eyes to the truth; طَرَفَتْ عَيْناهُ to blink one's eyes; عَصَبَ العَيْنَيْنِ to blindfold; أَبْصَرَ \ رَأى بالعَيْنِ المُجَرَّدةِ to see with the naked eye; قَرَّتْ عَيْنُهُ to be delighted; مَلَأَ عَيْنَ شَخْصٍ to win/

command sb's respect; سَقَطَ من عَيْنِ شَخْصٍ to go down in sb's esteem **2** [جاسوس] |أَعْيُن, عُيون| spy; كانَتْ لَهُ عَيْنٌ عَلَيَّ he had sb spying on me **3** [الحَسَد] the evil eye; مَخافَةَ العَيْنِ out of fear for the evil eye; أَصابَتْهُ العَيْنُ to be afflicted by the evil eye **4** [ثُقْب] |أَعْيُن, عُيون| eye; mesh; opening; عَيْن الإِبْرَةِ the eye of the needle; عُيون الشَبَكَةِ the meshes of the net **5** [بِئْر] |أَعْيُن, عُيون| well; spring; عَيْن مَعْدَنِيّة a mineral spring **6** [مَسْؤول] |أَعْيان| dignitary; أَعْيان القَرْيَةِ \ المَدينَةِ the dignitaries of the village/city **7** [ذات] |أَعْيُن, عُيون| (هو) بِعَيْنِهِ he himself; هُمْ بِعَيْنِهِمْ they themselves; عَيْنَ المَكانِ the very same place; فَرْض عَيْنٍ (Isl Law) individual obligation; اسْم العَيْنِ concrete noun; ضَرَبَ وَجْهَ الأَمْرِ وَعَيْنَهُ ≈ to go to the heart of the matter **8** [حَرْف] *name of the letter* ع **9** [حَبيب] darling, sweetheart; يا عَيْني! my darling!

عِيان *n* viewing, seeing; أَظْهَرَ شَيْئاً للعِيانِ to show off sth; واضِح للعِيانِ clearly visible; شاهِد عِيانٍ eyewitness

عَيِّنة *n* **1** [نَموذَج] sample, sampling; عَيِّنة عَشْوائيّة a random sample; أَخَذَ عَيِّنةً to take a sample **2** (Med) specimen; عَيِّنة الدمِ \ البَوْلِ a blood/urine sample

عَيْنيّ *adj* **1** [غَيْر نَقْديّ] material; tangible, concrete, real; مُساعَدات عَيْنيّة material help; تَطْبيق عَيْنيّ real-world application; رَأْسمال عَيْنيّ real capital; دَفْع عَيْنيّ payment in kind **2** [بِعَيْنَيْهِ] ocular, ophthalmic, eye (*before n*); المُشاهَدة \ المُلاحَظة العَيْنيّة seeing with one's own eyes

عَيْنيّة *n* **1** [عَدَسة] eyepiece **2** [هُويّة] identity

تَعْيين *n* |تَعْيينات| **1** [تَحْديد] determination, setting, appointment; تَعْيين المَكانِ \ المَوْضِعِ localization/positioning; إعادة تَعْيينِ كَلِمةِ مُرورٍ \ سِرٍّ resetting a password **2** [تَخْصيص] assignment, allocation; تَعْيين الأَراضي land allocation **3** [مُوَظَّفٍ] appointment, nomination; التَعْيين في مَنْصِبٍ appointment to a post; تَعْيين شَخْصٍ كَمُدَرِّبٍ \ مُدَرِّباً sb's appointment as coach; قَبِلَ \ رَفَضَ تَعْييناً to accept/turn down an appointment

مُعايَنة *n* viewing; inspection; examination

مُعَيَّن **A** *adj* fixed, determined; particular, specific; مُشْكِلة \ ظاهِرة مُعَيَّنة a particular problem/phenomenon; مَبْلَغ \ وَقْت مُعَيَّن a fixed sum/time; في لَحْظةٍ مُعَيَّنةٍ at a certain point; غَيْر مُعَيَّنٍ indefinite

B *n* (Geom) rhombus

عَيَّ *v* |a; عَياء| to be incapable/unable; عَيَّ ب \ عن شَيْءٍ to be incapable of sth; عَيَّ في كَلامِهِ to be unable to express oneself; to stammer, to stutter

عَيِيَ *v* |a; عِيًا, عَيًّا| to fail, to falter

أَعْيا *v* to render incapable, to defeat; to tire, to exhaust; أَعْيا الداءُ الطَبيبَ the disease has stumped the doctor; أَعْيا عَلَيْهِ الأَمْرُ he couldn't work it out; أَعْيَتْهُ الحيلةُ he didn't know what to do, he saw no way out

عِيّ *n* **1** [عَجْز] incapacity; helplessness **2** [في الكَلامِ] stammering, stuttering **3** [تَعَب] exhaustion, fatigue

عَياء *n* **1** [تَعَب] exhaustion, fatigue; داء عَياء an incurable illness **2** [عَجْز] helplessness, incapacity

إِعْياء *n* **1** [ضَعْف] helplessness **2** [تَعَب] exhaustion, fatigue; إِعْياء مُزْمِن chronic fatigue; شَعَرَ بالإِعْياءِ to feel tired, to be fatigued

‹ **غاب** *n* غاب هِنْديّ bamboo; إِنْسان الغاب orang-utan

‹ **الغابون** *n* |f| Gabon

‹ **غاز, كاز** *n* |غازات| gas; غاز طَبيعيّ natural gas; غاز سائِل liquid gas; غاز البوتان butane; زَيْت الغازِ kerosene; غاز سامّ poison gas; غاز الأَعْصابِ nerve gas; غاز الضَحِكِ laughing gas; غاز مُسيل للدُموعِ tear gas; هُجوم بالغازِ gas attack; رائِحة غازٍ gas smell; ضَغْط الغازِ gas pressure; شَبَكة غازٍ gas piping/pipework; مَخْزون \ احْتياطيّ الغازِ gas supplies/reserves; بِئْر للغازِ gas well; حَقْل غازٍ gas field; حُقول الغازِ الجَزائِريّة the Algerian gas fields; انْبعاث الغازاتِ gas emission; اسْتِخْراج الغازِ من بَحْرِ الشَمالِ the extraction of gas from the North Sea; اسْتِهْلاك ضَخْم للغازِ a high gas consumption; هُجوم بِغازِ الأَعْصابِ a nerve gas attack; القَتْل بالغازِ gassing; تَحْويل إلى غازٍ gasification; حَوَّلَ إلى غازٍ to gasify; حَوَّلَ الفَحْمَ إلى غازٍ to convert coal into gas; شَمَّ \ اسْتَنْشَقَ غازاً to smell gas; مَدَّ شَبَكَةَ غازٍ to install gas piping; اسْتَغَلَّ حَقْلَ غازٍ to exploit a gas field; نَظَّمَ ضَغْطَ الغازِ to adjust the gas pressure; انْفَجَرَ خَزّانُ الغازِ the gas tank exploded; يَنْخَفِضُ \ يَرْتَفِعُ ضَغْطُ الغازِ the gas pressure is decreasing/increasing

غازيّ *adj* carbonated; gaseous, gas (*before n*); انْفِجار غازيّ gas explosion; عَصير غَيْر غازيٍّ non-carbonated juice; ماء غازيّ soda water; sparkling water

‹ **غازوزة** *n* soda, pop

‹ **غاق** *n coll* (Zool) cormorant

‹ **غاليري** *n* gallery

‹ **غاما** *n* gamma; أَشِعّة غاما gamma rays; gamma radiation

‹ **غامْبيا** *n* Gambia

‹ **غانا** *n* Ghana

غانيّ *n* Ghanaian

‹ **غَبَّ** *v* |i; غَبّ| to appear/occur intermittently

غَبَب *n* |أَغْباب| double chin; wattle; dewlap

غِبّ *n* consequence

غِبَّ *prep* after; زارَ غِبًّا to visit intermittently; ≈ زُرْ غِبًّا تَزْدَدْ حُبًّا absence makes the heart grow fonder

مَغَبّة *n* effect; consequence; result

‹ **غَبَرَ** *v* |u; غُبور| to pass; to elapse

غَبِرَ *v* |a; غَبَر| to become dusty

غَبَّرَ *v* to make/raise dust; to cover with dust

أَغْبَرَ *v* to make/raise dust

تَغَبَّرَ *v* to be/become dusty

اغْبَرَّ *v* to become dusty

أَغْبَرَّ *v* to be/become sand-coloured; to become dusty

غابِر *adj* |غابِرونَ, غُبَّر, غَوابِرُ| past; ancient; immemorial; أَمْجاد غابِرة lost/faded glory; من الزَمَنِ الغابِرِ ancient, from ancient times; منذ أَزْمِنةٍ غابِرةٍ from time immemorial

غُبار *n* |أَغْبِرة| dust; سَحابة من الغُبارِ cloud of dust; غُبار رَمْليّ shifting sand; لا غُبارَ عَلَيْهِ impeccable; neat; هذا أَمْرٌ لا غُبارَ عَلَيْهِ that's impeccable; نَفَضَ \ أَزالَ الغُبارَ to dust; نَفَضَ غُبارَ الأَحْزانِ to shake off sadness; نَفَضَ الغُبارَ عن شَيْءٍ to shake the dust from sth; (fig) to make a clean sweep of something

غَبَرة *n* dust

غُبْرة *n* sand colour

أَغْبَر *adj* |غُبْر| dusty; sand-coloured

مُغْبَرّ *adj* dusty; طَريق مُغْبَرّ a dusty road

مُغَبَّر *adj* dusty

‹ **غَبَش** *n* |أَغْباش| darkness; twilight

‹ **غُدَّة** *n* |غُدَد| (Anat) gland; غُدّة هُرْمونيّة hormonal gland; غُدّة مُتَورِّمة swollen gland; غُدّة حُلْوة pancreas; غُدّة دَرَقيّة thyroid gland; تَضَخُّم الغُدّة الدَرَقيّة struma; غُدّة لُعابيّة salivary gland; غُدّة سَعْتَريّة thymus gland; غُدّة لِمْفاويّة lymph node; غُدّة عَرَقيّة sweat gland

غُدّيّ *adj* glandular

‹ **غَدَرَ** *v* |i-u; غَدْر| to betray; to deceive; غَدَرَ شَخْصاً \ بِشَخْصٍ to betray sb

غادَرَ *v* to leave; to depart; غادَرَ شَيْئاً to leave sth; غادَرَ (ذاهِباً) إلى شَيْءٍ to leave for sth; غادَرَ الغُرْفةَ \ البِلادَ to leave the room/the country; لَقَدْ غادَروا الساعةَ ١٢ تماماً they departed at 12 o'clock sharp; غادَرَ القاهِرةَ إلى لُبْنانَ to depart from Cairo to Lebanon

غَدْر *n* treason; disloyalty; أَحَسَّ بالغَدْرِ to feel cheated

غادِر *adj* |غادِرونَ, غُدّار, غَدَرة|; f pl |غادِرات, غَوادِرُ| unreliable

غَدّار *adj* treacherous; perfidious

غَدّارة *n* musket

غَدير *n* |غُدُر, غُدْران| brook; stream

غَديرة *n* |غَدائِرُ| braid

مُغادِر *adj* leaving; departing

مُغادَرة *n* departure

‹ **غُداف** *n* |غِدْفان| (Zool) rook; raven; *Corvus*

‹ **غَدَقَ, غَدِقَ** *v* |a-i; غَدَق| to be abundant

أَغْدَقَ *v* to shower; to heap; أَغْدَقَ على شَخْصٍ الهَدايا to shower sb with gifts; أَغْدَقَ المَطَرُ to pour down; to shower

غَدَق *n* torrent

غَدِق *adj* abundant; copious

‹ **اغْدَوْدَنَ** *v* to grow luxuriantly/be lush (*said of hair*)

‹ **غَدا** *v* |u; غُدوّ| **1** [غادَرَ في الصَباحِ] to leave/depart in the morning **2** [أَصْبَحَ] to become; غَدا المَكانُ أَخْضَرَ the place became green **3** [بَدَأَ] to start; to begin; غَدا يَفْعَلُ شَيْئاً to begin to do sth

‹ **غَدِيَ** *v* |a; غَدٍ, غَداء| **1** [ظُهْراً] to (have) lunch **2** [صَباحاً] to (have) breakfast

غَدّى *v* to offer lunch; غَدّى ضَيْفاً to offer a guest lunch

أَغْبَش *adj* |dipt| dark; obscure

مُغَبَّش *adj* frosted

‹ **غَبَطَ** *v* |i; غَبْط| to envy; to be envious/jealous; غَبَطَ شَخْصاً على نَجاحِهِ to envy sb his success; لا يُغْبَطُ على حالِهِ not to be envied

اغْتَبَطَ *v* to be elated/delighted

غِبْطة *n* euphoria; bliss; في غايةِ الغِبْطةِ euphoric

اغْتِباط *n* |اغْتِباطات| euphoria; well-being

مُغْتَبِط *adj* elated; delighted

‹ **غَبَنَ** *v* |i; غَبْن| to cheat; to mislead; to harm; to wrong

تَغابَنَ *v* to mislead each other

غَبْن *n* injustice; deceit; fraud

تَغابُن *n* cheating; سورة التَغابُن The Mutual Deceit (*Sura 64*)

مَغْبَن *n* groin

‹ **غَبِيَ** *v* |a; غَباء, غَباوة| to be ignorant/unaware

تَغابى *v* to feign ignorance

اسْتَغْبى *v* to treat like a fool; to fool

غَبيّ **A** *adj* |أَغْبِياءُ| stupid; ignorant; foolish; رَجُل غَبيّ a foolish man; سُؤال غَبيّ a stupid question
B *n* |أَغْبِياءُ| fool; idiot

غَباء *n* stupidity; ignorance; foolishness

غَباوة *n* stupidity; ignorance; foolishness

‹ **غُتْرة** *n* |غُتْرات, غُتُرات| (Gulf) *scarf-like head covering worn by Arab men*

‹ **غَثَّ** *v* |i; غَثّ| **1** [فَسَدَ] to fester; يَغِثُّ حَديثُهُ he has an unpleasant way of speaking **2** [نَحُفَ] to be thin/meagre

غَثّ *adj* thin; meagre; rotten; طَعام غَثّ rotten food

‹ **غَثِيَ** *v* |i; غَثَيان| to be nauseous/sick; غَثِيَتْ نَفْسُهُ to be nauseous/sick

غُثاء *n coll* |أَغْثاء| scum (*froth*)

غَثَيان *n* disgust; nausea; غَثَيان الصَباحِ morning sickness; مُصاب بالغَثَيانِ nauseous/sick; شَعَرَ بِغَثَيانٍ to feel nauseous; هذا يُسَبِّبُ لي غَثَياناً that disgusts me

‹ **غَجَريّ** **A** *adj* |غَجَر| Romani, gypsy (pej)
B *n* |غَجَر| Romani, gypsy (pej); شَعْب الغَجَرِ the Romani, gypsies (pej)

غرام, غِرام, جْرام *n* |غِرامات| gram, g; مِائَتا غْرامٍ من الدَّقيقِ two hundred grams of flour

غَرَبَ *v* |u| [ذَهَبَ] ◀1 |غَرْب| to go; to leave; to depart; to get out; غَرَبَ هذا عن بالِهِ get out of here!; أُغْرُبْ عن وَجْهي ! it escaped his attention ◀2 [غَرَبَت الشَّمْسُ] |غُروب| to set

غَرُبَ *v* |u; غَرابة| to be/become strange; غَرُبَ كَلامُهُ to speak strangely

مَغْرَبَ *v* |i; مَغْرَبة| to Moroccanize

غَرَّبَ *v* ◀1 [ذَهَبَ] to travel west; شَرَّقَ وَغَرَّبَ to travel anywhere ◀2 [جَعَلَهُ غَريباً] to estrange; غَرَّبَ شَخْصاً عن بَلَدِهِ to estrange sb from his country ◀3 [أَبْعَدَ] to banish

أَغْرَبَ *v* ◀1 [بالَغَ] to exaggerate; أَغْرَبَ في الضَحِك to laugh in an exaggerated way ◀2 [سافَرَ غَرْباً] to go/travel west

تَغَرَّبَ *v* ◀1 [هاجَرَ] to emigrate; تَغَرَّبَ عن بِلادِهِ لِفَتْرةٍ طَويلةٍ he lived abroad for a long time ◀2 [أَصْبَحَ غَرْبِيًّا] to become westernized

اغْتَرَبَ *v* to emigrate; *to be far away from one's home/country*

اسْتَغْرَبَ *v* ◀1 [تَعَجَّبَ] to be amazed; to be surprised; اسْتَغْرَبَ شَيْئاً to be amazed about sth; اسْتَغْرَبَ أنّ ... to be surprised that ...; أَسْتَغْرِبُ أَنَّهُ لم يَأْتِ I'm surprised that he did not turn up ◀2 [تَشَبَّهَ بالغَرْبِ] to become westernized

غَرْب *n* ◀1 [جِهة] |غُروب| west; غَرْباً westward; الغَرْب the West; al-Gharb (*plain in the north of Morocco*); في الغَرْبِ in the west; أقْصى الغَرْبِ the Wild West; غَرْبَ باريس west of Paris; من الشَرْقِ إلى الغَرْبِ from east to west; خطّ طولٍ غَرْباً longitude west ◀2 [حِدّة] tempestuousness

غَرَب *n* (Syria) weeping willow

غارِب *n* ◀1 [حَيوانٍ] |غَوارِبُ| shoulder ◀2 [كاهِل] shoulder; أَلْقى حَبْلَ شَخْصٍ على غارِبِهِ to keep a loose rein on someone; رَمى بِرَسَنِ شَخْصٍ على غارِبِهِ *to leave someone to their own devices*

غرائِبيّ *adj* exotic; extraordinary; الأَدَب الغَرائِبيّ fantasy literature

غرائِبيّة *n* exoticism

غُراب *n* |غِرْبان| (Zool) crow; raven; غُراب الماءِ cormorant; أَسْوَد كالغُرابِ raven-black

تَغَدّى *v* to (have) lunch; تَغَدّى مع شَخْصٍ to have lunch with sb; تَغَدّى سَمَكاً to eat fish for lunch

غادٍ *n* coming; غادٍ وَرائِح coming and going

غد *n* the following day; غَداً \ يَوْمَ غَدٍ tomorrow; في الغَدِ tomorrow; the following day; في الغَدِ القَريبِ tomorrow; في غَدِ ذلك اليَوْمِ the day after; بعد غَدٍ the day after tomorrow; جيل الغَدِ the next generation; إنّ غَداً لِناظِرِهِ قَريبٌ it could happen again; tomorrow is another day

غَداء *n* |أَغْدِية| lunch; breakfast; اسْتِراحة الغَداءِ lunch break; خلال \ أَثْناءَ الغَداءِ during lunch; تَناوَلَ \ أَكَلَ الغَداءَ to eat lunch; (حانَ) وَقْتُ الغَداءِ (it's) lunch time

غَداة *n* early morning

غُدْوة *n* |غُدًا, غُدًى, غُدوّ| early morning

غَذَّ *v* |i; غَذّ| to fester; to suppurate

أَغَذَّ *v* to quicken; أَغَذَّ سَيْرَهُ to quicken one's step

غَذّى *v* to feed; غَذّى شَخْصاً بِشَيْءٍ to feed sb with sth

تَغَذّى *v* to eat; to feed on; تَغَذّى بِشَيْءٍ to feed on sth

اغْتَذى *v* to feed on

غِذاء *n* |أَغْذِية| food; nourishment; meal; أَغْذِية foods; أَغْذِية فاسِدة rotten foods; أَغْذِية سائِلة liquid food; غِذاء صِحّيّ health food; الغِذاء العُضْويّ organic food; أَغْذِية بَحْرِيّة seafood; غِذاء للعَقْلِ food for thought; سِلْسِلة الغِذاءِ food chain; أَزْمة غِذاءٍ food crisis; نَقْص \ قِلّة في الغِذاءِ lack of food

غِذائيّ *adj* nutritional, nutritious; edible; food (*before n*); زَيْت غِذائيّ cooking oil; قيمة غِذائيّة nutritional value; مُكَوِّن غِذائيّ a nutritious substance; مَوادّ غِذائيّة nutrients; تَسَمُّم غِذائيّ food poisoning; سِلْسِلة غِذائيّة food chain; نِظام غِذائيّ diet; مُساعَدة \ إعانة غِذائيّة food aid; قَدَّمَ مُساعَدةً غِذائيّةً to offer food aid

تَغْذِية *n* feeding; nutrition; تَغْذِية اصْطِناعيّة artificial feeding; تَغْذِية اسْتِرْجاعيّة feedback; RSS تَغْذِية (Comput) RSS feed; دَوْرة التَغْذِية food chain; نَقْص \ سوء التَغْذِيةِ malnutrition; مُصاب بِسوءِ التَغْذِية undernourished; تُوُفِّيَ نَتيجة سوءِ \ عانى من التَغْذِية to suffer/die from malnutrition

مُغَذٍّ *adj* nutritious; أَطْعِمة مُغَذِّية nutritious food; البَطاطِسُ مُغَذِّيةٌ جِدًّا potatoes are very nutritious

مَغْرِب *n* |مَغارِبُ| west; *time or place of sunset*; صَلاة المَغْرِبِ sunset prayer; مَشارِق الأَرْضِ وَمَغارِبُها the whole world; من المَشْرِقِ إلى المَغْرِب in the entire Arab world

مَغْرِبيّ **A** *adj* |مَغارِبة| **1** [من المَغْرِبِ الأَقْصى] Moroccan; المَمْلَكة المَغْرِبيّة (the Kingdom of) Morocco; المُهاجِرونَ المَغارِبة Moroccan emigrants **2** [من شَمالِ إفْرِيقيا] of/from the Maghreb

B *n* |مَغارِبة| Moroccan

› **غَرْبَلَ** *v* |i; غَرْبَلة| to sift; to sieve

غِرْبال *n* |غَرابيلُ| sieve; أبو غَرابيل dragonfly

غَرْبَلة *n* sifting

› **غَرَّدَ** *v* **1** [طَيْر] to tweet, to chirp; to sing, to warble **2** (Comput) to tweet

تَغَرَّدَ *v* to sing

أُغْرودة *n* |أَغاريدُ| chirping; twitter; song, warble

تَغْريد *n* **1** [العَصافير] song; singing; warbling; تَغْريد العَصافير the singing of the birds **2** (Comput) tweet; إعادة تَغْريدٍ retweet

تغريدة *n* tweet (*on Twitter*); أرْسَلَ \ وَضَعَ تَغْريدةً to tweet, to twitter (*on Twitter*)

مُغَرِّد *n* **1** [طَيْر] singing, tweeting, warbling; عُصْفور مُغَرِّد singing birds **2** (Comput) twitterer

› **الغَرْدَقة** *n* Hurghada (*city in Egypt*)

› **غَرَّ** *v* |u; غُرور| to deceive; to mislead; غَرَّهُ الشَّيْطانُ to be deceived by the devil

غَرَّرَ *v* to endanger; to delude; غَرَّرَ بِهِ أَصْحابُهُ his friends deluded him; غَرَّرَ بِنَفْسِهِ وَمالِهِ to jeopardize oneself and one's possessions

اغْتَرَّ *v* to be mislead; to be fooled; اغْتَرَّ بالمَظْهَرِ to be fooled by appearances

غَرَر *n* risk; danger; jeopardy

غِرّ **A** *adj* |أَغْرار| inexperienced; callow; green; ما زالَ غِرًّا to be wet behind the ears

B *n* |أَغْرار| novice, rookie (AmE)

غِرار *n* |أَغِرّة| manner; way; على غِرارِ ... following ...; in the manner of ...; على هذا الغِرارِ in this manner; على غِرارٍ ما one way or another

غَرابة *n* peculiarity; strangeness; تَصَرَّفَ بِغَرابةٍ to behave curiously/strangely; لا غَرابةَ في ذلك there's nothing unusual about that

غُرْبة *n* ≈ exile; في الغُرْبةِ abroad; الغُرْبة عن الأَهْلِ alienation from the family; أَكَلَتْهُ الغُرْبةُ to be/feel homesick

غَرْبيّ **A** *adj* west (*before n*); westerly; western; westward; ريح غَرْبيّة west wind; الحَضارة \ الاقْتِصاد الغَرْبيّ(ة) Western civilization/economy; فَكَّرَ تَفْكيراً غَرْبيًّا to be Western-oriented

B *n* westerner

غَرْبيَّ *adv* to the west of; غَرْبيَّ باريس to the west of Paris

غُروب *n* setting (*of the sun*)

غَريب **A** *adj* |غُرَباءُ| **1** [شاذّ] strange; odd; unusual; peculiar; surprising; crazy; عادة غَريبة an odd habit; قِصّة غَريبة a strange story; مَنْظَر غَريب an unusual sight; من الغَريبِ أنْ ... it's surprising that ...; كانَ غَريبَ الأَطْوارِ to act crazy **2** [من مَكانٍ آخَرَ] strange; unfamiliar; شَخْص غَريب stranger

B *n* |غُرَباءُ, أَغْراب| stranger; foreigner; إنَّهُ غَريبٌ في بَلَدِه he's a stranger in his own country; أنا غَريبٌ عن هُنا I'm a stranger here; لا تَتَحَدَّثْ مع الغُرَباءِ don't talk to strangers

غَريبة *n* |غَرائِبُ| oddity; strange matter; غَرائِب الطَّبيعة the wonders of nature

اسْتِغْراب *n* surprise; astonishment; amazement; هذا ما يَدْعو إلى الاسْتِغْرابِ this is astonishing

اغْتِراب *n* exile; alienation

اغْتِرابيّ *adj* emigrant (*before n*)

الغَرْبيّة *n* al-Gharbiyah (*governorate in Egypt*)

المَغْرِب *n* **1** [البَلَد] Morocco; المَغْرِب الأَقْصى Morocco **2** [المِنْطَقة] the Maghreb, North Africa

مُسْتَغْرَب *adj* strange; surprising; لَيْسَ من المُسْتَغْرَبِ أنّ ... it's not surprising that ...

مُسْتَغْرِب *adj* **1** [مَدْهوش] surprised; astonished; amazed **2** [قد أَصْبَحَ غَرْبيًّا] westernized

مَغارِبيّ *adj* Maghrebian

مُغْتَرِب *n* expatriate; migrant; foreigner

مَغْرِز *n* |مَغارِزُ| socket; مَغْرِز الضِرْسِ tooth socket

غَرَسَ *v* |i; غَرْس ,غِراسة| to plant; to cultivate; غَرَسَ شَجَرةً to plant a tree; غَرَسَ في طِفْلٍ مَبادِئَ حَميدةً to teach a child values

أَغْرَسَ *v* to plant

انْغَرَسَ *v* to be planted; to be embedded

غَرْس, غِرْس *n* |غِراس ,أَغْراس| planting; plant; crop; cutting

غِراس *n* plant; planting; crop

غِراسة *n* planting; cultivation

غَرْسة *n* cutting

غَريس *adj* planted

مَغْرِس *n* |مَغارِسُ| plantation; nursery

مَغْروس *adj* planted

أَغْرَضَ *v* to achieve; أَغْرَضَ غَرَضَهُ to achieve one's aim

تَغَرَّضَ *v* to be partial; to be biased; تَغَرَّضَ ل \ ضِدّ شَيْءٍ to side with/against sth

غَرَض *n* |أَغْراض| ① [هَدَف] goal; objective; أَغْراض خَفيّة hidden goals ② [نِيّة] aim; intention ③ [شَيْء] object; أَغْراض things, stuff; possessions; أَغْراض شَخْصيّة personal belongings

تَغَرُّض *n* bias; prejudice

مُغْرِض *adj* biased; partial; prejudiced; مَوْقِف مُغْرِض a prejudiced stand/position

غَرْغَرَ *v* |i; غَرْغَرة| to gargle

تَغَرْغَرَ *v* ① [غَرْغَرَ] to gargle ② [العَيْنُ] to be bathed in tears

غِرْغِر *n coll* guinea fowl

غَرَفَ *v* |i-u; غَرْف| to dish up; to scoop up; غَرَفَ الطَعامَ to dish up food

اغْتَرَفَ *v* to ladle, to scoop

غَرّافة *n* carafe; decanter

غَرْفة *n* scoop

غُرْفة *n* |غُرُفات ,غُرَف| ① [حُجْرة] room; غُرْفة واسِعة \ مُظْلِمة \ بَسيطة a spacious/dark/simple room; غُرْفة كَبيرة \ صَغيرة a big/small room; في غُرْفةِ الدِراسةِ in the study ② [مَصْلَحة] Chamber; الغُرْفة التِجاريّة \ غُرْفة التِجارة

غَرارة *n* inexperience; ignorance

غِرارة *n* |غَرائِرُ| *sack for straw or grain*

غُرّة *n* |غُرَر| ① [طَيْر] (Zool) coot ② [بَياض في جَبْهةِ الفَرَسِ] blaze (*white stripe on a horse*) ③ [أَوّل] beginning (*of a year or month*); غُرّة العامِ الجَديدِ the beginning of the new year

غِرّة *n* |غِرَر| carelessness; inattention; على (حين) غِرّةٍ unexpected; unforeseen; sudden; أَخَذَ شَخْصاً على غِرّةٍ to surprise sb; أُخِذ على غِرّةٍ to be surprised

غَرور *adj* |mf| deceptive; misleading

غُرور *n* conceit, pride, vanity, arrogance; نَظْرة غُرورٍ a conceited look; الغُرور بالنَفْسِ self-importance

غَرير *adj* |أَغِرّة ,أَغْرّاء| inexperienced; silly; naive

غُرَيْر *n* listed alphabetically

أَغَرّ *adj* |dipt; غُرّ; f غَرّاءُ| esteemed; respectable; distinguished; memorable; أَيّام غَرّاء memorable days

مُغْتَرّ *adj* conceited; vain

مَغْرور *adj* conceited; self-satisfied; arrogant; vain; pompous; شَخْص مَغْرور a conceited person; يا لَهُ من مَغْرورٍ he is so conceited!

غَرَزَ *v* |i; غَرْز| to prick; to stick; غَرَزَ الإبْرةَ في الثَوْبِ to thread a needle

أَغْرَزَ *v* to be covered by new plantings; أَغْرَزَ الوادي the valley turned green

انْغَرَزَ *v* to be/become stuck; to be inserted; to sink; انْغَرَزَ المِفْتاحُ في القُفْلِ the key is in the lock; انْغَرَزَتْ قَدَمُهُ في الطينِ his foot sank in the mud

غَرائِزيّ *adj* instinctive; intuitive

غُرْزة *n* |غُرَز| stitch; suture

غَريزة *n* |غَرائِزُ| instinct; urge; drive; غَريزة جِنْسيّة sexual urge, sex drive; غَريزة تِجاريّة business/commercial instinct; غَريزة أُنْثَويّة female intuition; غَريزة حَيَوانيّة animal instinct; انْقادَ لِغَرائِزِهِ he was guided by his instinct; أَشْبَعَ الغَرائِزَ to satisfy one's (sexual) needs

غَريزيّ *adj* instinctive; intuitive; نُفور غَريزيّ an instinctive aversion

Chamber of Commerce ❸ [في السَفينةِ] cabin; غُرْفة لِشَخْصَيْنِ a two-berth cabin

مِغْرَفة *n* |مَغارِفُ| scoop; soup ladle; tablespoon

‹ **غَرِقَ** *v* |a; غَرَق| to sink; to drown; غرِق في شَيْءٍ to sink into sth; غرِق في الدُيونِ \ الهُمومِ \ البُؤْسِ to be deep in debt/ trouble/misery; غرِق في النَوْمِ to sleep soundly/deeply; غرِق في أَفْكارِهِ to be deep in thought; غرِق في المالِ to be rolling in money; غرِقَتْ عَيْناهُ في الدُموعِ to cry one's eyes out; غرِق في العَمَلِ to be up to one's ears in work; غرِقَت السَفينةُ the ship sank; غرِق عَشَرةُ رُكّابٍ ten passengers drowned

غَرَّقَ *v* to drown; to submerge

أَغْرَقَ *v* ❶ [جَعَلَهُ يَغْرَقُ] to drown; to sink, to submerge; to flood; أَغْرَقَ السوقَ to dump; to flood the market; أُغْرِقَ to be flooded; أَغْرَقَ سَفينةً to sink a ship ❷ [أَعْطى بِكَثْرةٍ] to swamp, to overload; أَغْرَقَ شَخْصاً في التَعاسةِ to cause misery for sb; أَغْرَقَ شَخْصاً في العَمَلِ to swamp sb with work; أَغْرَقَ شَخْصاً بالهَدايا to shower sb with gifts; أَغْرَقَ نَفْسَهُ في الدُيونِ to get deep into debt ❸ [بالَغَ] to exaggerate; أَغْرَقَ في الضَحِكِ to laugh uncontrollably

اِسْتَغْرَقَ *v* |i| ❶ [دامَ] to last, to take; يَسْتَغْرِقُ الفيلْمُ ساعَتَيْنِ the film lasts two hours; اِسْتَغْرَقَ مُدّةً to span a period of time; قَدْرَ ما يَسْتَغْرِقُ الأَمْرُ من وَقْتٍ as long as it takes ❷ [اِنْشَغَلَ] to sink; اِسْتَغْرَقَ في العَمَلِ to be swamped with work; اِسْتَغْرَقَ في النَوْمِ to sleep soundly

اِغْرَوْرَقَ *v* |Form XII; اِغْريراق| to fill (*with water*); اِغْرَوْرَقَتْ عَيْنُهُ بالدُموعِ his eyes were watering

غَرَق *n* drowning; المَوْت غَرَقاً death by drowning; ماتَ غَرَقاً to drown; نَجا من الغَرَقِ to escape from drowning

غارِق *adj* drowned; immersed; كانَ غارِقاً في العَمَلِ to be swamped with work; غارِق في الدُيونِ to be up to one's neck in debts; غارِق في النَوْمِ fast asleep

غَريق *n* |غَرْقى| drowning/drowned person

اِسْتِغْراق *n* plunging into; absorption in

إِغْراق *n* |إِغْراقات| ❶ [غَمْر] flooding; إِغْراق السوقِ dumping; إِغْراق السوقِ الأوروبّيّةِ بالإِلِكْتْرونيّاتِ اليابانيّةِ the dumping of Japanese electronics on the European market ❷ [تَغْريق] sinking

مُسْتَغْرِق *adj* immersed; engrossed; كانَ مُسْتَغْرِقاً في التَفْكيرِ to be deep in thought

مُغْرَوْرِق *adj* filled (*with water*); مُغْرَوْرِق بالدَمْعِ tear-filled; بِعَيْنَيْنِ مُغْرَوْرِقَتَيْنِ بالدُموعِ with tear-filled eyes

‹ **غُرْلة** *n* |غُرَل| foreskin

‹ **غَرِمَ** *v* |a; غُرْم, غَرامة| ❶ [دَفَعَ غَرامةً] to pay; غَرِمَ دَيْناً to pay a debt ❷ [خَسِرَ] to suffer a loss; غَرِمَ في تِجارَتِهِ to suffer a business loss

غَرَّمَ *v* to fine; to book; غَرَّمَ سائِقاً to fine a driver

أَغْرَمَ *v* ❶ (Law) to fine; to book ❷ [أَحَبَّ] أُغْرِمَ بِشَخْصٍ to love/ adore sb

غُرْم *n* damage; loss

غَرام *n* infatuation; رِسالة غَرامٍ love letter; وَقَعَ في غَرامِ شَخْصٍ to fall in love with sb

غَرامة *n* fine; penalty; ticket; غَرامة على شَيْءٍ a fine on sth; دَفَعَ غَرامةً to pay a ticket; فَرَضَ على شَخْصٍ غَرامةً to impose a penalty on sb; حَكَمَ على شَخْصٍ بِغَرامةٍ to fine sb; حُكِمَ عَلَيْهِ بِغَرامةٍ, عوقِبَ بِدَفْعِ غَرامةٍ to be fined

غَراميّ *adj* amorous, love (*before n*); رِسالة غَراميّة love letter; قَصيدة غَراميّة love poem

غَريم *n* |غُرَماءُ, غُرّام| ❶ [نِدّ] adversary; opponent ❷ [دائِن] creditor

مَغْرَم *n* |مَغارِمُ| damage; cost

مُغْرَم *adj* infatuated; in love; mad; كانَ مُغْرَماً بِشَيْءٍ \ شَخْصٍ to be in love with sth/sb; مُغْرَم بِكُرةِ القَدَمِ to be mad about soccer

‹ **غَرين** *n* sludge

‹ **غَرْناطة** *n* Granada (*city in Spain*)

‹ **غُرْنوق** *n* |غَرانيقُ| (Zool) common crane

غُرْنوقيّ *n* (Bot) geranium

‹ **غَرّى** *v* to glue

أَغْرى *v* ❶ [جَذَبَ] to seduce; to charm; to tempt; أُغْرِيَ to be seduced/tempted; أَغْرى شَخْصاً to seduce sb; أَغْرى شَخْصاً

بِشَيْءٍ to lure sb with sth ② [حَثَّ] to incite; to encourage; أَغْرى جِنْسيّاً to seduce

غَرْو *n* surprise; amazement; لا غَرْوَ! (that's) no wonder/surprise!

غِراً *n* glue; adhesive

غِراء *n* glue; adhesive

غَرَوِيّ *adj* sticky; gluey; slimy

إغْراء *n* |إغْراءات| temptation; seduction; appeal; attraction; إغْراءات المُدُنِ الكُبْرى the temptations of the big cities; نَظْرة إغْراءٍ a seductive look

مُغْرٍ *adj* tempting; seductive; appealing; attractive; اقْتِراح \ عَرْض مُغْرٍ an attractive proposition/offer; كانَ ذلك الاقْتِراحُ \ العَرْضُ مُغْرِياً that's an attractive proposition/offer; جَعَلَ شَيْئاً مُغْرِياً to make sth appealing; صَمَدَ أمام المُغْرِياتِ to resist temptations; تَعَرَّضَ لِمُخْتَلَفِ المُغْرِياتِ to be exposed to many temptations

غُرَيْر *n* (Zool) badger

غَرينِيّ *adj* deposited; silted (up); راسِب غَرينِيّ deposited sediment

غَزُرَ *v* |u; غَزْر ,غَزارة| to be abundant; غَزُرَ المَطَرُ it was pouring *(rain)*

غَزارة *n* abundance; excess; بِغَزارةٍ amply; يَتَساقَطُ المَطَرُ بِغَزارةٍ it's pouring *(rain)*

غَزير *adj* |غِزار| abundant; inexhaustible; luxuriant; مَطَر غَزير a heavy downpour; مَخْزون غَزير an inexhaustible source/supply; شَعْر غَزير luxuriant hair; إنْتاج غَزير mass production

غَزّة *n* |dipt| Gaza *(city in Palestine)*

غَزَلَ *v* |i; غَزْل| to spin

غازَلَ *v* to court; to flirt; غازَلَ شَخْصاً to court sb

تَغَزَّلَ *v to celebrate in love poems; to sing the praises;* تَغَزَّلَ الشاعِرُ بِحَبيبَتِهِ the poet sang the praises of his beloved

تَغازَلَ *v* to flirt with each other

غَزْل *n* ① |غُزول| [خُيوط مَغْزولة] spun thread/yarn; غَزْل البَناتِ spun sugar ② [عَمَليّة الغَزْلِ] spinning

غَزَل *n* ① [تَحَبُّب] flirtation ② (Literat) ghazal *(lyric love poetry)*

غَزال *n* |غِزْلان ,غِزْلة| (Zool) gazelle; قَطيع من الغِزْلانِ a herd of gazelle(s)

غَزّال *n* spinner

غَزَلِيّ *adj* amorous

تَغَزُّل *n* flirtation

مُغازَلة *n* flirtation; مُغازَلة شَخْصٍ a flirtation with sb

مِغْزَل *n* |مَغازِلُ| spinning wheel

غَزا *v* |u| ① [أَغارَ على] |غَزْو| to invade; to conquer; غَزا بَلَداً مُجاوِراً to invade a neighbouring country; غَزَت القُوّاتُ المِنْطَقةَ the armed forces conquered the area; غَزَت البَضائعُ الغَرْبيّةُ الأَسْواقَ the market was overrun with western products ② [نَوى] |غَزْو ,غَزَوان| to mean; to intend; ما يَغْزو من كَلامِهِ هذا؟ what does he mean by that?

غَزْو *n* conquest; invasion; غَزْو أَفْغانِسْتان invasion of Afghanistan; غَزْو الكُمْبْيوتَر للمَدارِسِ the advance of computers in schools

غازٍ *n* |غُزاة| ① [مُغير] conqueror; invader; oppressor; الغُزاة الأَلْمان the German oppressors ② (Hist) Ghazi *(title given to Muslim warriors or champions)* ③ [اِسْم شَخْصِيّ] Ghazi *(male given name)*

غَزْوة *n* |غَزَوات| campaign; conquest; invasion; attack; الغَزَوات الإِسْلامِيّة the Muslim conquests

مَغْزاة *n* |مَغازٍ| military expedition; المَغازي the Muslim campaigns *(of the Prophet and his successors)*

مَغْزًى *n* |مَغازٍ| meaning; significance; tenor; مَغْزًى عَميق a deep(er) meaning; مَغْزى القِصّةِ the moral of the story

غَسَق *n* twilight; dusk; عند الغَسَقِ in the dusk; ساعةَ الغَسَقِ in the twilight hour

غَسَلَ *v* |i; غَسْل| ① [نَظَّفَ] to wash; to clean; to bathe; to rinse (out); غَسَلَ يَدَيْهِ to wash one's hands; غَسَلَ الغَسيلَ \ المَلابِسَ to do the wash/laundry; غَسَلَ الأَوانِيَ \ الصُحونَ to do/wash the dishes; غَسَلَ الكُؤوسَ to rinse (out) the glasses ② [النُقودَ] to launder; غَسَلَ أَمْوالاً to launder money

غَسَّلَ *v* to wash; to clean; غَسَّلَ مَيِّتاً to lay out a deceased person

اِنْغَسَلَ *v* to be washed

اِغْتَسَلَ *v* ① (Islam) to perform the ghusl *(full ablution)* ② [اِسْتَحَمَّ] to wash; to bathe; to rinse; اِغْتَسَلَ (بالماءِ) to rinse (with water)

غَسْل *n* **1** [تَغْسيل] washing; bathing; غَسْل الأَواني \ الصُحونِ \ المَواعينِ washing the dishes; غَسْل الدِماغ brainwashing **2** (Med) irrigation **3** (Islam) ablution

غُسْل *n* ghusl (*full ablution*)

غاسول *n* soap, lye

غَسّالة *n* **1** [آلة] washing machine; غَسّالة صُحونٍ \ أَطْباقٍ \ مَواعينَ dishwasher; غَسّالة كَهْرَبائيّة, غَسّالة مَلابِسَ \ ثِيابٍ washing machine; شَغَّلَ الغَسّالةَ to turn on the washing machine **2** [امْرَأة] laundry woman

غَسول *n* detergent; lotion

غَسيل *n* |غَسْلى, غُسَلاءُ| wash; laundry; غَسيل الصُحونِ \ المَواعينِ washing dishes; مِشْبَك \ مِلْقَط الغَسيلِ clothes peg (BrE), clothespin (AmE); حَبْل الغَسيلِ clothesline; مَسْحوق غَسيلٍ detergent; washing powder; عُلْبة مَسْحوقِ الغَسيلِ a box of detergent; حَوْض الغَسيلِ washroom; حُجْرة الغَسيلِ washbasin; مُنَعِّم الغَسيلِ fabric softener; قابل للغَسيلِ washable; غَسَلَ الغَسيلَ to do the wash/laundry; نَشَرَ الغَسيلَ على الحَبْلِ to hang out the wash/laundry (to dry); غَسيل الأَمْوالِ money laundering

اغْتِسال *n* washing; bath

مُغْتَسَل *n* washroom

مَغْسَل, مَغْسِل *n* |مَغاسِلُ| washroom

مَغْسَلة *n* |مَغاسِلُ| washbasin; washbowl; sink; مَغْسَلة عامّة laundry; launderette; *public washing accommodation*

مِغْسَلة *n* |مَغاسِلُ| washing machine

غَسانيّ *adj relating to the Ghassanids*

غُشْت *n* (Mor) August

غَشَّ *v* |u; غَشّ, غِشّ| **1** [خَدَعَ] to commit fraud; to swindle; to cheat; to deceive; غَشَّ شَخْصاً to cheat sb; غَشَّ في الامْتِحانِ to cheat on a test **2** [زَغَلَ] to adulterate; غَشَّ الهِرُوينَ to adulterate heroin

انْغَشَّ *v* to be cheated; to be deceived

غِشّ *n* fraud; swindle; malversation; بِغِشٍّ fraudulent; الغِشّ في قِطاعِ البِناءِ fraud in the construction industry; الغِشّ في التَأْميناتِ \ الضَرائِبِ insurance/tax fraud; تَصَرُّفات \ مُمارَسات غِشٍّ fraudulent acts/practices; الاشْتِراك في عَمَلِيّةِ غِشٍّ accessory to fraud; مُحارَبة الغِشِّ combatting fraud; تَصَرَّفَ بِغِشٍّ to commit/practise fraud; كافَحَ \ حارَبَ الغِشَّ to fight fraud

غَشّاش *n* fraud; swindler; cheat

مَغْشوش *adj* **1** deceived **2** forged; fake; counterfeit; سِلَع مَغْشوشة counterfeit commodities

غَشَمَ *v* |i; غَشْم| to oppress; to treat unjustly

غاشِم **A** *adj* |غَواشِمُ| brutal; رَجُل غاشِم a brutal man; اعْتِداء غاشِم a brutal attack

B *n* |غَواشِمُ| brute

غَشِيَ *v* |a| **1** |غَشا, غَشْي| [غَطّى] to cover; to veil; غَشِيَ اللَيْلُ the night fell; غَشِيَهُ النُعاسُ to be overcome by sleep; غُشِيَ عَلَيْهِ to faint **2** [زارَ] |غِشْيان| to visit; to pay a visit **3** [جامَعَ] |غِشْيان| to have sexual intercourse; غَشِيَ زَوْجَتَهُ to have sexual intercourse with one's wife

غَشّى *v* to cover; to veil; to surround; غَشّاهُ الظَلامُ to be surrounded by darkness; غَشّى الدَمْعُ عَيْنَيْهِ to get a mist of tears before one's eyes

أَغْشى *v* to cover; to envelop

تَغَشّى *v* **1** [زُجاجُ النافِذة] to mist (up); to steam up; يَتَغَشّى زُجاجُ النَوافِذِ the windows are misted/steamed up **2** [تَغَطّى] to cover oneself; تَغَشّى بِثَوْبٍ ثَقيلٍ to dress warmly **3** [جامَعَ] to have sexual intercourse; تَغَشّى زَوْجَتَهُ to have sexual intercourse with one's wife

غاشٍ *n* سورة الغاشية The Pall (*Sura 88*)

غاشِية *n* |غَواشٍ| **1** (Anat) pericardium **2** [مُصيبة] calamity, disaster **3** [قيامة] resurrection

غِشاء *n* |أَغْشِية| **1** [غِلاف] cover; skin; غِشاء واقٍ protective covering; condom **2** (Anat) film; membrane; diaphragm; غِشاء مُخاطيّ mucous membrane; غِشاء البَكارة hymen; maidenhead

غِشائيّ *adj* مَيْز غِشائيّ dialysis

غَشاوة, غِشاوة *n* mist; haze; veil; غَشاوة على البَصَرِ a mist before one's eyes

غَشَيان, غِشْيان *n* trance; faint; unconsciousness

غَشْية *n* faint; fainting fit

مُغَشَّى *adj* misted; steamed up

مَغْشيّ *adj* مَغْشيّ عَلَيْهِ unconscious

غَصَبَ *v* |i; غَصْب| ❶ [أَجْبَرَ] to force; to compel; غَصَبَ شَخْصاً على شَيْءٍ to force sb to do sth ❷ [سَرَقَ] to steal; غَصَبَ شَيْئاً من \ على شَخْصٍ to steal sth from sb; غَصَبَ شَخْصاً مِلْكَهُ to steal sb's possessions ❸ [اِغْتَصَبَ] to rape; to assault; to violate

اِغْتَصَبَ *v* ❶ [اِعْتَدى جِنْسيًّا] to rape; to assault; اِغْتَصَبَ امرَأةً to rape/assault a woman ❷ [اِنْتَزَعَ] to seize; to take (away); اِغْتَصَبَ السُّلْطةَ to seize power

غَصْب *n* compulsion; pressure; بالغَصْبِ under pressure; (فَعَلَ شَيْئاً) غَصْباً عَنْهُ (to do sth) against one's will

غاصِب *n* |غاصِبون, غُصّاب| blackmailer; extortioner

اِغْتِصاب *n* |اِغْتِصابات| ❶ [امْرَأةٍ] rape ❷ [اِنْتِزاع] forcible/violent/unlawful seizure

مُغْتَصِب *n* rapist; violator

غَصَّ *v* |a; غَصَص, غَصّ, غُصّة| ❶ [بالطَّعامِ] to choke; غَصَّ بِقِطْعةِ تُفّاحٍ to choke on a piece of apple ❷ [اِزْدَحَمَ] to be crowded; غَصَّت القاعةُ بالناسِ the hall was packed

غاصّ *adj* overcrowded; packed

غُصّة *n* |غُصّات, غُصَص| lump (*in one's throat*); كانَت في حَلْقِهِ غُصّةٌ he had a lump in his throat

غُصْن *n* |غُصون, أَغْصان| branch; twig; أَغْصان خَضْراء \ يابِسة green/dead branches; شَرْخ غُصْنٍ نَضيرٍ (Med) greenstick fracture; قَلَّمَ \ قَضَبَ أَغْصاناً to trim branches

غُصَيْن *n* |غُصَيْنات| shoot; graft; cutting

غَضِبَ *v* |a; غَضَب| to be/become angry; to be/become enraged; to be/become furious; غَضِبَ من \ على شَخْصٍ to be angry with/at sb; غَضِبَ لِشَيْءٍ \ من شَيْءٍ to be furious at/over sth

غاضَبَ *v* to be/become angry; to be angry with each other

أَغْضَبَ *v* to enrage; to irritate

تَغَضَّبَ *v* |على| to be/become angry (at)

غَضَب *n* anger; rage; fury; frenzy; wrath; غَضَباً \ من الغَضَبِ with anger; out of anger; اِسْتَشاطَ \ اِنْفَجَرَ غَضَباً to explode in anger; غَضَب أَعْمى blind rage; سَريع الغَضَبِ short-tempered; نَوْبة \ سَوْرة غَضَبٍ فَوْرة غَضَبٍ tantrum; fit of anger; أَصابَتْهُ نَوْبةُ غَضَبٍ an angry outburst; كانَ يَغْلي to be furious; من الغَضَبِ to boil with rage; أَثارَ غَضَبَ شَخْصٍ to incur/arouse sb's wrath; أَغْضَبَ شَخْصاً غَضَباً شَديداً to infuriate someone; صَبَّ جامَ غَضَبِهِ على شَخْصٍ \ شَيْءٍ to vent one's fury on sb/sth

غَضِب *adj* |غِضاب| angry; furious; enraged

غاضِب *adj* angry; furious; enraged; infuriated; غاضِب من \ على شَخْصٍ furious at sb; رِسالة غاضِبة an angry letter; رَدّ غاضِب a furious reaction; رَدَّ غاضِباً to react angrily

غَضْبان *adj* |dipt; غَضْبى; f pl غَضابى, غِضاب| angry; furious; cross

غَضوب *adj* |mf| irascible; touchy

مُغْضَب *adj* angry; furious; enraged

مُغْضِب *adj* annoying; infuriating; enraging

مَغْضوب *adj* المَغْضوب عَلَيْهِمْ من شَخْصٍ the target of sb's anger

غَضِرَ *v* |a; غَضَر| to be/become rich; to be abundant

غَضار *n* |f| clay; loam

غَضير *adj* fresh

غُضْروف *n* |غَضاريف| cartilage; غُضْروف هِلاليّ \ مَفْصِليّ meniscus

غَضَّ I *v* |u; غِضاض, غَضاضة, غَضّ| ❶ [البَصَرَ \ النَّظَرَ] to lower; to cast down; غَضَّ بَصَرَهُ \ من بَصَرِهِ to cast down/lower one's eyes; غَضَّ النَّظَرَ \ الطَّرْفَ عن شَخْصٍ to avoid looking at sb; to pay no attention to sb ❷ [اِسْتَهانَ] to belittle; غَضَّ شَخْصاً \ من شَأْنِ شَخْصٍ to belittle sb

غَضَّ II *v* |i; غَضاضة| to be soft; to be fresh; غَضَّت المَرْأةُ the woman had soft skin

غَضّ *adj* juicy; tender; فاكِهة \ لَحْم غَضّ(ة) juicy fruit/meat

غَضاضة *n* ❶ [طَراوة] freshness; tenderness ❷ [عَيْب] shortcoming; disgrace; shame; لا غَضاضةَ في ذلك there's no shame in that, there's nothing wrong with that

غُضّة *n* |غُضَض| shortcoming; inadequacy

غضيض *adj* tender; fresh; juicy

مَغَضّة *n* |مَغاضُ| shame; disgrace

‹ **غَضَّنَ** *v* to wrinkle; غَضَّنَ جَبْهَتَهُ to frown

تَغَضَّنَ *v* to wrinkle; to rumple; to get wrinkled; to get rumpled; تَغَضَّنَ وَجْهُهُ his face was wrinkled

غَضْن ,**غَضَن** *n* |غُضون| wrinkle; crease; fold

(Idiom) في غُضونِ ذلك meanwhile, in the meantime

تَغَضُّن *n* ripple; undulation

مُغَضَّن *adj* wrinkled; furrowed

‹ **أَغْضى** *v* to keep silent about; to withhold; أَغْضى الطَرْفَ عن شَيْءٍ to close/shut one's eyes to sth; أَغْضى حَياءً to be silent out of modesty/embarrassment

تَغاضى *v* to ignore; to pass over; to be blind to; to deny the existence of; تَغاضى عن شَيْءٍ to turn a blind eye to sth

تَغاضٍ *n* indifference; التَغاضي عن شَيْءٍ indifference to sth

‹ **غَطْرَسَ** *v* |i; غَطْرَسة| to be arrogant

تَغَطْرَسَ *v* to be arrogant; to be haughty; تَغَطْرَسَ في مِشْيَتِهِ to show off

غَطْرَسة *n* arrogance; haughtiness; snobbery

مُتَغَطْرِس **A** *adj* arrogant; haughty; presumptuous; snobbish **B** *n* snob

‹ **غِطْريف** *n* |غَطاريفُ ,غَطارِفة| noble man; potentate

‹ **غَطَسَ** *v* |i; غَطْس| to dive; to plunge; to go under; غَطَسَ في الماءِ to dive in the water; غَطَسَ في نَوْمٍ عَميقٍ to sink into a deep sleep; غَطَسَ في العَتَمةِ to disappear into the darkness

غَطَّسَ *v* **1** [غَمَسَ] to immerse; to dip; غَطَّسَ يَدَهُ في الماءِ to dip one's hand in the water **2** [عَمَّدَ] to baptize

غَطْس *n* (Sport) dive; diving

غاطِس *n* (Naut) draught (BrE), draft (AmE)

غَطّاس *n* **1** [غَوّاص] diver **2** (Zool) grebe (*Podicipedidae*); غَطّاس أَسْوَد الرَقَبة black-necked grebe (*Podiceps nigricollis*)

غِطاس *n* baptism; (عيد) الغِطاسِ (feast of) the Epiphany

غَطْسة *n* dip, dive

مَغْطِس ,**مِغْطَس** *n* |مَغاطِسُ| bath; bathtub

‹ **غَطَشَ** *v* |i; غَطْش| to be dark (*night*)

غَطِشَ *v* |a; غَطَش| to be weak/feeble (*eyes*)

‹ **غَطَّ** *v* |i| **1** [خَرَّ] |غَطيط| to snore; غَطَّ في النَوْمِ to snore in one's sleep; to sleep soundly **2** [غَمَسَ] |غَطّ| to immerse

غَطيط *n* snore; snoring

‹ **غَطا** *v* |u; غَطْو| to cover; to report on

غَطّى *v* **1** [جَلَّلَ] to cover (up); to conceal; to tuck in; to roof; غَطّى شَيْئاً بـ ... to cover sth with ...; غَطّى طِفْلاً to tuck a child in; غَطّى على الحَقيقةِ to disguise/veil the truth; غَطّى ظَهْرَ شَخْصٍ to back (up)/support sb; تُغَطّي السُحُبُ \ الغُيومُ السَماءَ the sky has clouded over; غَطّى المُشْتَبَهُ فيهِمْ بَعْضُهُمْ على بَعْضٍ the suspects covered for each other; غَطَّت الأَشْجارُ المَنْزِلَ the trees hid the house from view **2** [تَكاليفَ] to cover; to fund; غَطّى تَكاليفَ \ مَصاريفَ شَيْءٍ to fund sth; غَطّى تَكاليفَ شَيْءٍ بِقَرْضٍ to cover the cost of sth with borrowed money **3** [مِنْطَقةً \ فَتْرةً] to cover; to command; غَطّى فَتْرةً to cover a period; غَطّى مِنْطَقةً to command an area **4** [إِعْلامِيّاً] to cover; to report; غَطّى حادِثةً إِعْلامِيّاً to cover an event **5** [تَفَوَّقَ] to surpass; to be excel; to overshadow; غَطَّتْ بِجَمالِها الآخَرينَ \ على الآخَرينَ she surpassed the others in beauty

تَغَطّى *v* to be covered; to be snowed under; تَغَطّى بالنَباتِ \ بِغِطاءٍ to be covered with plants/a blanket

غِطاء *n* **1** |أَغْطِية| [غِلاف] cover; canvas; spread; cloak; veil; تحت غِطاءِ شَيْءٍ under cover/the veil of sth; غِطاء الرَأْسِ head covering; كَشَفَ الغِطاءَ عن شَخْصٍ to expose sb **2** [صِمام] lid; cover; cap; hood; غِطاء مُحَرِّكٍ bonnet (BrE), hood (AmE); غِطاء بِئْرٍ well cover **3** [سرير] blanket

تَغْطِية *n* **1** [سَتْر] covering; تَغْطِية الرَأْسِ covering the head **2** (Busn) cover, covering; fund; تَغْطِية شامِلة full cover; تَغْطِية تَكاليفَ \ مَصاريفَ \ نَفَقاتٍ (financial) funding; تَغْطِية العَجْزِ المالِيِّ covering the deficit **3** (Journ) coverage; report; تَغْطِية مَوْضوعِيّة an objective report; تَغْطِية إِعْلامِيّة press coverage; تَغْطِية مُسْتَمِرّة rolling coverage **4** (Sport) marking; cover; تَغْطِية لاعِبٍ man-to-man marking

مُغَطّى *adj* covered; roofed; veiled; camouflaged; مُغَطّى بالثَلْجِ snow-covered; حَوْض سِباحةٍ مُغَطّى an indoor swimming pool

1 ‹ **غَفَرَ** *v* |i; |غُفْران| to forgive; to pardon; to absolve; غَفَرَ شَيْئاً لِشَخْصٍ to forgive sb sth

اغْتَفَرَ *v* to forgive; لا يُغْتَفَرُ unforgivable; inexcusable; هذا خطأٌ لا يُغْتَفَرُ this is an unforgivable mistake; اغْتَفَرَ شَيْئاً لِشَخْصٍ to forgive sb sth

اسْتَغْفَرَ *v* to ask forgiveness; to beg forgiveness; أَسْتَغْفِرُ اللهَ I ask God's forgiveness; good gracious/heavens; سَوْفَ أَسْتَغْفِرُ لَكُمْ رَبّي I'll ask God to forgive you

غافِر *n* سورة غافِر The Forgiver (*Sura 40*)

غَفّار **A** *adj* merciful; clement

B *n* الغَفّار the Repeatedly Forgiving (*one of the names of God*)

غَفْر *n* mercy; forgiveness; pardon

غُفْران *n* mercy; forgiveness; absolution; عيد الغُفْرانِ Yom Kippur, Day of Atonement; نَسْأَلُ اللهَ الغُفْرانَ we ask God's forgiveness

غفور **A** *adj* merciful; clement

B *n* الغفور the Much-Forgiving (*one of the names of God*)

اسْتِغْفار *n* forgiveness; *the act of seeking forgiveness from God*

مَغْفِرة *n* forgiveness; pardon; absolution; مَغْفِرة ذُنوبِهِ forgiveness of his sins; طَلَبَ المَغْفِرةَ من اللهِ to ask God for his forgiveness

مَغْفور *adj* |ل| forgiven; exonerated; المَغْفور لَهُ the deceased; السَّيِّد فُلانٌ المَغْفورُ لَهُ the late Mr X; غَير مَغْفور لَهُ unforgiven

2 **انْغَفَرَ** *v* to open

غَفير **A** *adj* numerous; abundant; large; جَمْع غَفير a large crowd; عَدَد غَفير a large number

B (Egypt) *n* police station

‹ **غَفَلَ** *v* |u; |غُفول ,غَفْلة| to neglect; to ignore; غَفَلَ عن شَيْءٍ to neglect/ignore sth

غَفَّلَ *v* to numb; to stultify

غافَلَ *v* to take unawares, to take by surprise; غافَلَهُ الزَمَنُ he ran out of time unawares

أَغْفَلَ *v* to neglect; to overlook; أَغْفَلَ شَيْئاً to neglect/overlook sth

تَغَفَّلَ *v* to take by surprises; to take unawares; تَغَفَّلَهُ خَصْمُهُ his opponent took him by surprise

تَغافَلَ *v* to neglect; to disregard; تَغافَلَ شَيْئاً \ عن شَيْءٍ to neglect sth

اسْتَغْفَلَ *v* to consider stupid/a fool; to make a fool of

غُفْل *adj* |أَغْفال| devoid of; غُفْل من unsigned; غُفْل من التَوْقيع التاريخ undated

غافِل **A** *adj* |غُفَّل ,غُفول ,غافِلونَ| negligent; inattentive; غافِل عن شَيْءٍ to be negligent with regard to sth; to be inattentive to/on sth

B *n* |غُفَّل ,غُفول ,غافِلونَ| scatterbrain

غَفْلة *n* negligence; inattention; oblivion; مَوْت الغَفْلَةِ a sudden death; على حين غَفْلَةٍ ,على \ في غَفْلَةٍ unawares; by surprise; على غَفْلَةٍ مِنْهُ without him knowing; كانَ على غَفْلَةٍ من ... to be unaware/unsuspecting of ...

إغْفال *n* |إغْفالات| omission; neglect

تَغافُل *n* neglect

مُغَفَّل *adj* foolish; stupid

‹ **غَفا** *v* |u; |غُفُوّ ,غَفْو| غَفِيَ to slumber; to nap; to doze (off)

غَفِيَ *v* |a; |غَفًى| to be/get sleepy; to be/get drowsy

أَغْفى *v* to doze (off); to nap; أَغْفى قَليلاً to take/have a nap

غافٍ *n* asleep

غَفْوة *n* nap

إغْفاءة *n* nap

‹ **غَلَبَ** *v* |i; |غَلَبة ,غَلْب| to beat; to defeat; to triumph; to be victorious; لا يُغْلَبُ invincible; غَلَبَ فريقاً to beat a team; غَلَبَ خَصْمَهُ to defeat one's opponent; غَلَبَ شَخْصاً to triumph over sb; غَلَبَ عَلَيْهِ النَوْمُ to be overcome by sleep; غُلِبَ على أَمْرِهِ to suffer defeat; قالَ بِصَوْتٍ يَغْلِبُ عَلَيْهِ النُعاسُ to say in a sleepy voice

غَلَّبَ *v* to let prevail; غَلَّبَ المَصْلَحَةَ العامّةَ على المَصْلَحة الخاصّةِ to let the public interest prevail over the individual interest

غالَبَ *v* to fight; to combat; غالَبَ النَوْمَ to fight off sleep

تَغَلَّبَ *v* |على| to overcome; to overpower; تَغَلَّبَ على نَفْسِهِ to brace oneself; تَغَلَّبَ على مُشْكِلةٍ \ إحساسٍ بالخَجَلِ to overcome a problem/feeling of shame; تَغلَّبَ عَلَيْهِ اليَأْسُ \ النُعاسُ to be overcome by despair/sleep

تغالَبَ *v* to wrestle each other

غالِب **A** *adj* |غَوالِبُ| dominant; (ما) في الغالِبِ \ غالِبِه ,غالِباً usually; mostly, predominantly; في الغالِبِ الأَعَمِّ nearly always

B *n* |غالِبونَ ,غَلَبة| winner; victor

غالِبيّة *n* majority; تظَلُّ غالِبيّةُ الناسِ في البُيوتِ the majority of the people stay at home; زَعيم الغالِبيّة السِياسيّةِ the leader of the political majority; غالِبيّة كاسِحة an overwhelming majority

غَلاّب *adj* almighty

غَلَبة *n* victory; triumph; prevalence; predominance; غَلَبة الحَقِّ the prevalence of justice; لَهُ الغَلَبةُ he has the upper hand; غَلَبة في الانْتِخاباتِ election victory

أَغْلَب *adj* |dipt; غُلْب| most; major; أَغْلَب الناسِ most people; أَغْلَبُهُمْ لَيسَ عُضْواً most of them aren't members; أَغْلَب الظَنِّ على \ في most likely; most probably; in all probability; في أَغْلَبِ الأَحْيانِ ,الأَغْلَبِ usually; generally; primarily

أَغْلَبيّة *n* majority; bulk; الأَغْلَبيّة الساحِقة the overwhelming majority; الأَغْلَبيّة الصامِتة the silent majority; الأَغْلَبيّة المُطْلَقة the absolute majority; أَغْلَبيّة السُكّانِ the bulk of the population; بِأَغْلَبيّةِ الأَصْواتِ by a majority of votes; وُجْهة نَظَرِ الأَغْلَبيّةِ majority view; مَوْقِف الأَغْلَبيّة majority position; قَرار بالأَغْلَبيّةِ majority decision; شَكَّلَ الأَغْلَبيّةَ to be in the majority; اتَّخَذَ قَراراً بالأَغْلَبيّةِ to decide by majority

تَغَلُّب *n* surmounting; overcoming; لا يُمْكِنُ التَغَلُّبُ عَلَيْهِ insurmountable; صُعوبات لا يُمْكِنُ التَغَلُّبُ عَلَيْها insurmountable difficulties

تَغْليب *n* granting victory

مَغْلوب *adj* defeated; beaten; conquered; subdued; مَغْلوب على أَمْرِهِ weak; defenceless

غَلَس *n* darkness; dusk

غَلْصَمة *n* |غَلاصِمُ| palate; uvula

غَلِطَ *v* |a; غَلَط| to be mistaken; to err, to make a mistake; غَلِطَ في الحِسابِ to miscalculate

غَلَّطَ *v* to cause to commit a mistake; to accuse of an error or mistake

غالَطَ *v* to fool; to cause to commit a mistake; to mislead/misguide

أَغْلَطَ *v* to cause to commit a mistake

غَلَط **A** *adj* wrong; incorrect; mistaken; erroneous

B *n* |أَغْلاط| mistake; error; fault; inaccuracy; غَلَط إمْلائيّ a spelling mistake; بِدونِ أَغْلاطٍ faultless; وَقَع في الغَلَطِ to make a mistake

غَلْطان *adj* |dipt| wrong; erring; mistaken; كانَ غَلْطانَ to be wrong

غَلْطة *n* |أَغْلاط ,غَلَطات| mistake; error; fault; blunder; غَلْطة فادِحة a gross error; غَلْطة مَطْبَعيّة a misprint; غَلْطة لِسانٍ a slip of the tongue; ارْتَكَبَ غَلْطةً to make a mistake

مُغالَطة *n* error; misconception; fallacy

مَغْلوط *adj* incorrect; false; wrong

غَلُظَ *v* |u; غِلَظ ,غِلْظة| to thicken; to be harsh/difficult; يَغْلُظُ العَيْشُ life is difficult; غَلُظَ قَلْبُهُ to have a heart of stone; غَلُظَ على شَخْصٍ to treat sb harshly

غَلَّظَ *v* to make thick; غَلَّظَ يَميناً to take an oath; to swear

غالَظَ *v* to be harsh

أَغْلَظَ *v* to speak rudely; to use harsh language; أَغْلَظَ لِشَخْصٍ القَوْلَ \ في القَوْلِ to use rude/harsh language with sb

اسْتَغْلَظَ *v* to find harsh; to find crude

غِلَظ *n* thickening; غِلَظ الجِلْدِ a thickening of the skin

غِلاظة *n* harshness; coarseness

غِلْظة *n* rudeness; تَصَرَّفَ بِغِلْظةٍ to be rude

غَليظ **A** *adj* |غِلاظ| **1** [فَظّ] ill-mannered; rude; uncivil; blunt; curt; مُلاحَظة غَليظة a blunt/curt remark **2** [سَميك] thick; غَليظ البِنْية heavily built **3** [خَشِن] coarse **4** [وَقور] holy; يَمين غَليظة a solemn oath

B *n* |غِلاظ| lout

مُغَلَّظ *adj* solemn; ceremonious

غَلْغَلَ *v* |i; غَلْغَلة| **1** [دَخَلَ] to penetrate, to enter; to become immersed in **2** [أَدْخَلَ] |في| to put in

تَغَلْغَلَ *v* to penetrate; to pervade; تَغَلْغَلَ في الغابةِ to penetrate the forest; تَغَلْغَلَت الشَرِكةُ في السوقِ the company has penetrated the market; تَغَلْغَلَ الفَسادُ في المُؤَسَّسةِ corruption has pervaded the organisation; تَغَلْغَلَت الجَريمةُ المُنَظَّمةُ في المُجْتَمَع organized crime has pervaded society

غَلَفَ *v* |i; غَلْف| to wrap; to envelop; to cover

غَلِفَ *v* |a; غَلَف| to be uncircumcised

غَلَّفَ *v* **1** [غطّى] to wrap; to envelop; to cover; غَلَّفَ هَدِيّةً to wrap a gift/present **2** (P&P) to bind; to cover; غَلَّفَ كِتاباً to bind/cover a book

تَغَلَّفَ *v* to be covered; to be cloaked; تَغَلَّفَ بِغِلافِ البَراءةِ to be cloaked in innocence

غِلاف *n* |أَغْلِفة| **1** [غِطاء] cover; packing; غِلاف جَوّي atmosphere; تحت غِلافِ شَيْءٍ under cover of sth; فَتَحَ غِلافَ هَدِيّةٍ to unwrap a present **2** (P&P) cover; binding; غِلاف وَرَقيّ a soft/paper cover; غلاف من الجِلْد a leather cover; على الغِلافِ on the cover **3** [أَجْهِزة] covering; case **4** [ظَرْف] envelope; وَضَعَ رِسالةً في غِلافٍ to put a letter in an envelope

غُلْفة *n* |غُلَف| foreskin

أَغْلَف *adj* |dipt; غُلْف| **1** [فظّ] rude, uncivilized **2** [أَقْلَف] uncircumcised

تَغْليف *n* **1** [في الوَرَقِ أو الخَشَبِ...] packing; مَوادّ التَغْليفِ packing material **2** (P&P) covering; wrapping; وَرَق تَغْليفٍ wrapping-paper; تَغْليف الكُتُبِ bookbinding

مُغَلَّف **A** *adj* wrapped; covered
B *n* envelope

غَلْفَنَ *v* |i; غَلْفَنة| to galvanize; to zinc

غَلَقَ *v* |i; غَلْق| to close; to lock

غَلَّقَ *v* to close with force

أَغْلَقَ *v* to close, to shut; to lock; to fence in; أَغْلَقَ البابَ \ النافِذةَ \ الطَريقَ to close the door/window/road; أَغْلَقَ البابَ (بالمِفْتاحِ) to lock the door (with the key); أَغْلَقَ مِعْطَفَهُ to close one's coat; أَغْلَقَ الرادِيو to turn off the radio; أَغْلَقَ بابَ المُناقَشةِ to cut off debate; سَتُغْلِقُ الدَكاكينُ أَبْوابَها the shops will close their doors

انْغَلَقَ *v* to close; to be closed; to be locked; انْغَلَقَ على نَفْسِهِ to be introverted; to keep to oneself

اسْتَغْلَقَ *v* to be impenetrable; to be inaccessible; اسْتَغْلَقَ عَلَيْهِ الفَهْمُ to be struck dumb/dumbfounded

غَلَق *n* |أَغْلاق| **1** (Phot) shutter **2** [قُفْل] lock; fastening

إغْلاق *n* locking; closing; closure; مَوْعِد الإغْلاقِ closing time/hour; بعد مَوْعِدِ الإغْلاقِ after hours; إغْلاق الشَرِكاتِ the closing of companies; أَحْكَمَ إغْلاقَ البابِ to lock the door properly

انْغِلاق *n* blockage; isolation; هذه الدَوْلة في حالةِ انْغِلاقٍ this country is in a state of isolation; الانْغِلاق على الذاتِ introversion; نِظام الفَرامِلِ \ المَكابِحِ المانِع للانْغِلاقِ ABS, anti-lock braking system

انْغِلاقيّ *adj* closed, secluded; نِظام انْغِلاقيّ a closed system

مِغْلاق *n* |مَغاليقُ| lock; latch

مُغْلَق *adj* closed; locked; shut; باب مُغْلَق a locked door; اجْتِماع مُغْلَق a closed meeting; قَلْب \ عَقْل مُغْلَق an introverted nature; وَصَلَت المُفاوَضاتُ إلى طَريقٍ مُغْلَقٍ negotiations have reached an impass

مِغْلَق *n* |مَغالِقُ| lock

مُنْغَلِق *adj* closed; introvert

غَلَّ I *v* |u; غَلّ| to shackle; to chain; to fetter; غَلَّ شَخْصاً to chain sb; غَلَّ يَدَيْ شَخْصٍ to handcuff sb

غَلَّ II *v* |i; غِلّ| غَلَّ صَدْرُهُ to harbour/bear a grudge

غَلَّلَ *v* to handcuff, to fetter, to enchain

أَغَلَّ *v* to yield; to produce; أَغَلَّت الأَرْضُ كثيراً هذا العامَ the land has produced high yields this year

انْغَلَّ *v* |في| to enter, to penetrate (into)

اسْتَغَلَّ *v* **1** [انْتَهَزَ] to exploit; to utilize; اسْتَغَلَّ الفُرْصةَ to take the opportunity; اسْتَغَلَّ نُفوذَهُ to abuse one's position; اسْتَغَلَّ وَقْتَهُ to use one's time well; اسْتَغَلَّ الوَضْعَ to exploit the situation; لم يَسْتَغِلَّ شَيْئاً to not utilize sth **2** [اسْتَثْمَرَ] to exploit; to invest; to run; اسْتَغَلَّ أَمْوالَهُ في بِناءِ الجامِعاتِ he invested his money in building universities **3** [انْتَهَزَ] to exploit; to take advantage of; to abuse; اسْتَغَلَّ شَيْئاً \ شَخْصاً to take advantage of sth/sb; اسْتَغَلَّ العُمّالَ to exploit the workers; اسْتَغَلَّ طيبةَ قَلْبِ شَخْصٍ to take advantage of sb's good nature

غَلّ *n* |أَغْلال ,غُلول| 1 [قَيْد] chain; shackle; handcuff; تَخَلَّصَ من أَغْلالِ الماضي to break the chains of the past 2 [عَطَش] a raging thirst

غِلّ *n* hate; rancor

غِلال *n* yield

غِلالة *n* a thin, long gown; غِلالة نَوْمٍ nightgown

غَلّة *n* |غِلال ,غَلّات| crops; yield; produce; غَلّة عالِية high yields

غُلّة *n* thirst

غليل *n* 1 [عَطَش] a raging thirst 2 [غَيْظ] rage; anger; شَفى غَليلَهُ to vent one's rage (on); فَشَّ غَليلَهُ to relieve one's anger

اسْتِغْلال *n* 1 [تَسْخير] exploitation; misuse; abuse; اسْتِغْلال فاحِش shameless exploitation; اسْتِغْلال جِنْسيّ sexual abuse; أَساءَ اسْتِغْلالَ شَيْءٍ to abuse sth 2 [اسْتِثْمار] exploitation; utilization

اسْتِغْلاليّ *n* exploiter; leech

مُسْتَغَلّ *adj* exploited; utilised; غَيْر مُسْتَغَلٍّ unexploited; unutilised

مُسْتَغِلّ *n* exploiter; proprietor, manager; مُسْتَغِلّ فُنْدُقٍ hotel manager

مُغِلّ *adj* fruitful; productive

مَغْلول *adj* 1 [مُقَيَّد] shackled; cuffed; مَغْلول اليَدَيْنِ powerless, impotent 2 [مُتَعَطِّش] thirsty

غَلِم *adj* (old use) aroused; in heat

غُلام *n* |غِلْمان ,غِلْمة| 1 [شابّ] boy, lad; young man, youth 2 [خادِم] servant

غُلْمة *n* lust, sensuous desire

غَلْموت *n* (Zool) guillemot

غَلا *v* |u| 1 [ثَمَنٌ] |غَلاء| to be/become expensive; غَلَت الأَسْعارُ غَلاءً فاحِشاً the prices have risen dramatically; حَبيبي غَلا في عَيْني my beloved is precious to me 2 [بالَغَ] |غُلوّ| to exaggerate

غَلّى *v* 1 [أَغْلى] to make more expensive 2 [فَوَّرَ] see غلي

غالى *v* to boast; to exaggerate; to overdo

أَغْلى *v* 1 [غَلّى] to make more expensive; أَغْلى السِعْرَ to increase the price 2 [جَعَلَهُ يَغْلي] see غلي

اسْتَغْلى *v* to regard as expensive

غُلوّ *n* excess; exaggeration; hyperbole

غالٍ A *adj* expensive; costly; precious; valuable; هَدايا \ لَوْحات غالِية valuable gifts/paintings; غالٍ على القَلْبِ precious to the heart; دَفَعَ ثَمَناً غالِياً من أَجْلِ شَيْءٍ to pay dearly for something

B *n* |غُلاة| extremist; *a term used in the theology of Shia Islam to describe some minority Muslim groups who hold beliefs deemed deviant by mainstream Shi'i theology*

غَلاء *n* being expensive; غَلاء المَعيشةِ the high costs of living; غَلاء فاحِش exorbitant prices

غُلْواء *n* |dipt f| excess; extravagance

مُغالاة *n* exaggeration; excess

مُغالٍ *adj* مُغالًى فيهِ exaggerated; excessive; كَلام مُغالًى فيه exaggerated words

جْلوكوز ,غْلوكوز *n* glucose

غْلوكوما *n* (Med) glaucoma

غَلى *v* |i| |غَلَيان ,غَلْي| 1 [وَصَلَ إلى دَرَجةِ الغَلَيانِ] to boil; غَلى من شِدّةِ الغَضَبِ to boil with rage; يَغْلي الماءُ عند دَرَجةِ ١٠٠ سِلْسِيوس water boils at 100° C 2 [أَوْصَلَ إلى دَرَجةِ الغَلَيانِ] to boil; to bring to a boil; غَلى الماءَ to boil water

غَلّى *v* 1 [فَوَّرَ] to boil; to bring to a boil; غَلّى الماءَ to boil water 2 [أَغْلى] see غلو

أَغْلى *v* 1 [جَعَلَهُ يَغْلي] to boil; to bring to the boil; أَغْلى الماءَ to boil water 2 [غَلّى] see غلو

غَلّاية *n* 1 [إبْريق] (tea) kettle; الغَلّايةُ على النارِ the kettle is on 2 [جِهاز] boiler; water heater

غَلَيان *n* boiling; دَرَجة \ نُقْطة الغَلَيانِ boiling point; تَجاوَزَ دَرَجةَ \ نُقْطةَ الغَلَيانِ to exceed the boiling point

غَلْيون *n* |غَلاوينُ ,غَلايينُ| 1 [لِلتَّدْخينِ] (tobacco) pipe; أَشْعَلَ \ دَخَّنَ غَلْيوناً to light/smoke a pipe 2 [نارْجيلة] water pipe

غْليسَرين *n* glycerine

غِليسين *n* (Bot) wisteria

غَلْيون *n* |غَلايينُ| galleon

غَمَدَ *v* |u| |غَمْد| to sheathe

أَغْمَدَ *v* **1** [طَعَنَ] to stab; أَغْمَدَ السِكّينَ في صَدْرِ شَخْصٍ to stab sb in the chest **2** [السَيْفَ] to sheathe

تغَمَّدَ *v* to cover; تَغَمَّدَهُ اللهُ بِرَحْمَتِهِ God had mercy on him

غِمْد *n* |أَغْماد, غُمود| sheath; غِمْد وَتَرِيّ tendon sheath; أَخْرَجَ \ سَحَبَ \ جَرَّدَ سَيْفاً من غِمْدِهِ to unsheathe a sword

غَمَرَ *v* |u; غَمْر| to immerse; to flood; to shower; to overwhelm; غَمَرَ الماءُ الأَرْضَ the land was flooded by water; غَمَرَهُ شُعورُ الحُبِّ to be overwhelmed by feelings of love; غَمَرَ شَخْصاً بالهَدايا \ بِشَهائِدِ الشَرَفِ to shower sb with gifts/honours; يَغْمُرُ السُيّاحُ المَدينةَ tourists overran the city

غَمُرَ *v* |u; غُمورة, غَمارة| to overflow; to be abundant

غامَرَ *v* to venture; to risk; غامَرَ بِنَفْسِهِ to dive into an adventure

انْغَمَرَ *v* to be/become flooded; to be/become immersed; انْغَمَرَتِ الحُقولُ the fields were flooded

غَمْر *adj* **1** [فائِض] |غُمور| abundant; غَمْر الرِداءِ generous **2** [ساذَج] |أَغْمار| unsuspecting; naïve

غِمْر *n* |غُمور| envy; hatred

غامِر *adj* |غُمور| overwhelming; immense; tremendous; فَرَح غامِر immense joy

غِمار *n* disaster; calamity

غَمْرة *n* |غِمار, غَمَرات| vehemence; adversity; غَمَرات المَوْتِ death agonies; death-struggle; غِمار الحَياة the struggles of life; في غَمْرةِ المَعْرَكةِ in the heat of the battle

مُغامِر **A** *adj* adventurous

B *n* adventurer

مُغامَرة *n* **1** [حادِث مُثير] adventure; روح المُغامَرةِ an adventurous spirit; التَطَلُّع إلى المُغامَرةِ longing for adventure **2** [عَمَلِيّة خَطيرة] a risky enterprise

مَغْمور *adj* **1** [غامِض] unknown; obscure; inglorious; شاعِر مَغْمور an obscure poet; اخْتَفَى مَغْموراً to fade into obscurity **2** [غارِق] flooded; inundated; مَناطِق مَغْمورة flooded areas

غَمَزَ *v* |i; غَمْز| **1** [بالعَيْنِ] to wink; to blink; غَمَزَ بِعَيْنِهِ إلى شَخْصٍ to wink at sb **2** [شَنَّعَ] to slander; to defame; غَمَزَ ب \ على شَخْصٍ to defame sb **3** [ضَوْء] to flash

تَغامَزَ *v* to wink at one another

غَمْز *n* eye contact

غَمّاز *n* |غَمّازات| flashing light; غَمّاز السَيّارةِ turn signal, blinker

غَمّازة *n* dimple; غَمّازة في الخَدِّ dimple in the cheek

غَمْزة *n* wink

غَمَسَ *v* |i; غَمْس| to immerse; to dip; to sop

غَمَّسَ *v* to dip; to soak; غَمَّس ريشةً في الحِبْرِ to dip a pen in ink; غَمَّس الخُبْزَ بالمَرَقِ to soak the bread in sauce

انْغَمَسَ *v* to sink; to subside; انْغَمَس في المَلَذّاتِ to indulge in pleasures

غموس **A** *adj* **1** [مُخْتَرِق] penetrating **2** [كارِثِيّ] disastrous; catastrophic

B *n* [يُؤْكَلُ مع الخُبْزِ] (sandwich) filling; dip

(Idiom) يَمين غَموس perjury

انْغِماس *n* plunge; immersion

مَغْموس *adj* immersed; dipped

مُنْغَمِس *adj* preoccupied

غَمَصَ *v* |i; غَمْص| to despise

غَمَضَ, غَمُضَ *v* |u; غُموض| **1** [الكَلامُ] to be/become obscure; to be/become indistinct; غَمُضَ كَلامُهُ to speak indistinctly **2** [العَيْنُ] to close (*eyes*); لم تَغْمُضْ لَهُ عَيْنٌ to not get a wink of sleep

غَمَّضَ *v* غَمَّض عَيْنَيْهِ to close one's eyes

أَغْمَضَ *v* أَغْمَض طَرْفَهُ \ عَيْنَهُ عن شَيْءٍ to turn a blind eye to sth; أَغْمَض عَيْنَيْهِ عن الحَقيقةِ to close one's eyes to the truth

غامِض *adj* |غَوامِض| obscure, vague, indefinable; ambiguous; mysterious, puzzling; إِحْساس غامِض an indefinable feeling; قَرار \ إِجْراء غامِض a half-hearted decision/measure; شَخْصِيّة غامِضة a shady character; مَفْهوم \ سُؤال غامِض a vague definition/question; كَلام غامِض vague language; أَحْداث غامِضة mysterious events; قَضايا غامِضة shady business; مَعْلومات غامِضة ambiguous information; غَوامِض القَضِيّةِ the obscure aspects of the matter; غَوامِضُ أَفْكارِهِ his most intimate thoughts; لِأَسْبابٍ غامِضةٍ for obscure reasons

غامِضة *n* |غَوامِض| enigma; mystery; riddle

غَمْضة *n* blink, blinking; في غَمْضةِ عَيْنٍ in the blink of an eye

غُموض *n* 1 [سِرِّيّة] mystery; اكْتَنَفَ الغُموضُ الاجْتِماعَ a shroud of mystery surrounded the meeting; اكْتَنَفَ الغُموضُ تَصَرُّفاتِهِ to act mysteriously 2 [عَدَم وُضوحٍ] uncertainty; ambiguity; vagueness; غُموض في القانونِ an ambiguity in the law; تَكَلَّمَ بِغُموضٍ to speak cryptically; كَشَفَ الغُموضَ to take away the uncertainty; خَيَّمَ الغُموضُ على … there was some uncertainty about ...

غُمَّيْضة *n* hide and seek; لَعِبَ لُعْبَةَ الغُمَّيْضةِ to play hide and seek

‹ **غَمَطَ** *v* |i; غَمْط| to despise; to disdain; غَمَطَ شَخْصاً حَقَّهُ to violate sb's rights; غَمَطَ خَصْمَهُ to look down on one's opponent

‹ **غَمْغَمَ** *v* |i; غَمْغَمة| to mumble; to mutter

غَمْغَمة *n* mumbling; muttering

‹ **غَمِقَ** *v* |a; غَمْق| to be moist/wet

غَمَّقَ *v* to deepen (*a colour*)

اغْمَقَّ *v* to deepen (*colour*)

غامِق *adj* dark; dusky; gloomy; لَوْن غامِق a dark colour; أَخْضَر غامِق dark/deep green

‹ **غَمَّ** *v* |u; غَمّ| to sadden; to grieve; to distress; غَمَّنا هذا أَشَدَّ الغَمِّ that caused us great distress

أَغَمَّ *v* 1 [أَحْزَنَ] to sadden; to grieve; to distress 2 [السَماءُ] to become overcast; أَغَمَّت السَماءُ the sky became overcast

انْغَمَّ *v* to be/become worried; to be/become distressed; to grieve

اغْتَمَّ *v* to be/become depressed; to be/become sad

غَمّ *n* |غُموم| distress; sorrow; grief; gloom; كَرَبَهُ الغَمُّ to be burdened with sorrow

غَمام *n coll* |غَمائِمُ| cloud; حَبّ \ حَبّة الغَمامِ hail, hailstone

غِمامة *n* |غَمائِمُ| blinker (BrE), blinder (AmE); muzzle

غُمّة *n* distress; sorrow; grief

مُغْتَمّ *adj* sad; sombre; gloomy; depressed

مُغِمّ *adj* sad; depressing; musty; stuffy; sultry; مَكان مُغِمّ a musty place; غُرْفة \ صالة مُغِمّة a stuffy room/hall; جَوّ مُغِمّ a stale atmosphere; sultry weather; انْطِباع مُغِمّ a depressing impression

مَغْموم *adj* sad; sombre; distressed; afflicted; depressed; مِزاج مَغْموم a black mood

‹ **غَمى** *v* |passive only; غُمِيَ عَلَيْهِ |غَمْي| to faint; to lose consciousness

غَمّى *v* 1 [غَطّى] to cover; to hide 2 [عَصَبَ العَيْنَيْنِ] to blindfold

أَغْمى *v* أُغْمِيَ عَلَيْهِ to faint; to lose consciousness

إغْماء *n* |إغْماءات| unconsciousness; faint

مُغْمًى *n* مُغْمًى عَلَيْهِ unconscious; fainted

مَغْميّ *n* مَغْميّ عَلَيْهِ unconscious; fainted; سَقَطَ مَغْميًّا عَلَيْهِ to faint; كانَ مَغْميًّا عَلَيْهِ to be in a dead faint

‹ **غَنِجَ** *v* |a; غَنْج| to be coquettish; to flirt

تَغَنَّجَ *v* to be coquettish; to flirt

غَنِج *adj* coquettish

مِغْناج *adj* flirtatious

‹ **غَنْدور** *n* |غَنادِرة| (Egypt) dandy

‹ **غُنوصيّ** *adj* gnostic

غُنوصيّة *n* Gnosticism

‹ **غَرْغَرينا ,غَنْغَرينا** *n* (Med) gangrene; mortification; أَعْضاء مُصابة بالغَنْغَرينا gangrenous limbs

‹ **غَنِمَ** *v* |a; غُنْم ,غَنْم ,غَنَم ,غَنيمة| to seize; to capture; غَنِمَ أَسْلِحةً to capture weapons; غَنِمَت المُقاوَمةُ دَبّابَتَيْنِ the resistance seized two tanks

أَغْنَمَ *v* to give as booty

اغْتَنَمَ *v* to seize; to capture; اغْتَنَمَ الفُرْصةَ to seize the opportunity

غَنَم *n coll* |أَغْنام| sheep; راعي الغَنَمِ shepherd; رَبّى الغَنَمَ to keep sheep; جَزَّ صوفَ الغَنَمِ to shear the sheep

غانِم *adj* successful; عادَ سالِماً غانِماً to return safe and sound

غَنّام *n* shepherd

غَنيمة *n* |غَنائِمُ| booty; spoils; غَنيمة ضَخْمة rich booty; غَنيمة بارِدة easy target/prey; تَشْتَمِلُ الغَنيمةُ ١٠٠٠٠ دولار the spoils amount to 10,000 dollars; اقْتَسَمَ الغَنائِمَ to divide up the booty; خَرَجَ من الوَليمةِ بِدونِ غَنيمةٍ to come off badly

اغْتِنام *n* taking/seizing an opportunity

مُسْتَغانِم *n* listed alphabetically

مَغْنَم *n* |مَغانِم| advantage

غَنَّ *v* |a; غَنّ| to twang

غُنَّة *n* nasal pronunciation (*when reciting the Koran*); في صَوْتِهِ غُنَّةٌ his voice has a twang

أَغَنّ *adj* |dipt| [1] [أَخَنّ] nasal; حَرْف أَغَنّ (Ling) nasal letter [2] [كَثير الشَجَر] luxuriant; lush

غَنِيَ *v* |a; غِنًى ,غَناء| [1] [صارَ غَنِيًّا] to be/become rich [2] [اِكْتَفى] |ب| to be content with; to be satisfied with; غَنِيَ بِشَيْءٍ to be satisfied with sth; غَنِيَت المَرْأَةُ بِوَلَدٍ واحِدٍ the woman was content with one child [3] [لم يُحْتَجْ إِلَيْهِ] |عن| to not need, to be able to do without; غَنِيَ عن شَيْءٍ to not need sth

غَنّى *v* to sing; غَنّى أُغْنِيةً to sing a song

أَغْنى *v* [1] [أَثْرى] to enrich [2] [كَفى] to be enough; to be sufficient; to render superfluous/redundant; الحالُ يُغْني عن السُؤالِ the situation is self-explanatory [3] [نابَ] |عن| to replace; to substitute; أَغْنى عن شَخْصٍ to replace sb [4] [نَفَعَ] to help; أَغْنى شَخْصاً عن الشَقاءِ to keep sb from misery

تَغَنّى *v* to sing; تَغَنّى بالجَمالِ to sing of beauty

اِغْتَنى *v* to be/become rich; اِغْتَنى على حِسابِ شَخْصٍ \ شَيْءٍ to get rich at the expense of sb/sth

اِسْتَغْنى *v* [1] [غَنِيَ] to be/become rich [2] [لا يَحْتاجُ إلى] |عن| to not need, to be able to do without; اِسْتَغْنى عن شَيْءٍ to be able to do without sth; يُسْتَغْنى عَنْهُ redundant; إضافة يُسْتَغْنى عَنها a redundant addition; لا يُسْتَغْنى عَنْهُ indispensable; لا يُمْكِنُهُ أَنْ يَسْتَغْنِيَ عن نَظّارَتِهِ he can't do without his glasses; بعد انْتِقالِهِ سَيَسْتَغْني عن سَيّارَتِهِ he'll be able to get by without a car after moving; هذا العُضْوُ لا يُسْتَغْنى عَنْهُ في الجَمْعِيّةِ this member is indispensable for the society

غَنِيّ [A] *adj* |أَغْنِياء| rich; wealthy; well-to-do; رَجُل غَنِيّ a wealthy man; البِلاد الغَنِيّة developed nations; غَنِيّ بالنَفْطِ rich in oil; شَخْص غَنِيّ عن التَعْريفِ sb who needs no introduction; كانَ غَنِيًّا عن البَيانِ to be self-evident [B] *n* |أَغْنِياء| [1] [ثَرِيّ] rich person; الأَغْنِياء rich people, the wealthy [2] (Islam) الغَنِيّ the Rich (*one of the names of God*)

غانِية *n* |غانِيات ,غَوانٍ| [1] [حَسْناء] beautiful girl/woman; belle [2] [مومِس] prostitute

غَناء *n* [1] [ثَرْوة] wealth, luxury; richness [2] [بِلا حاجة] |عن| doing without; لا غَناءَ عن ذلك that's indispensable [3] [اِسْتِعمال] use; لا غَناءَ في ذلك that's useless

غِناء *n* [1] [تَغَنٍّ] song; singing; مَشاهير الغِناءِ العَرَبِيِّ Arab star singers [2] [أَلْحان] song; tune

غِنائِيّ *adj* vocal; lyrical; singing; أَلْبوم غِنائِيّ album; موسيقى غِنائِيّة vocal music; مَسْرَحيّة غِنائِيّة opera; musical

غِنائِيّة *n* opera; musical

غِنًى *n* [1] [ثَرْوة] wealth; richness; luxury; غِنى لُغَتِنا the richness of our language; يَزْدادُ الفُقَراءُ فَقْراً والأَغْنِياءُ غِنًى the rich get richer and the poor get poorer [2] [لا حاجةَ] |عن| doing without; لا غِنى لَهُ عن indispensable; essential; لا غِنى عَنْهُ he can't do without it; هذا الكِتابُ لا غِنى عَنْهُ لِفَهْمِ التاريخِ this book is essential to understanding history; إِنَّهُ في غِنًى عن ذلك he needs that like a hole in the head

اِسْتِغْناء *n* being able to do without; لا يُمْكِنُ الاسْتِغْناءُ عن شَيْءٍ \ شَخْصٍ to not be able to do without sth/sb; to have to rely on sth/sb; لا يَسْتَطيعُ الاسْتِغْناءَ عن ذلك he can't do without it; عَدَم الاسْتِغْناءِ عَنْهُ indispensability

إِغْناء *n* enrichment; إِغْناء روحِيّ spiritual enrichment

أُغْنِية ,**أُغْنِيّة** *n* |أَغانِيّ ,أُغْنِيات ,أَغانٍ| song; أُغْنِية جَديدة \ جَميلة a new/beautiful song; أُغْنِية شَعْبِيّة a folk song; أُغْنِية مُصَوَّرة a music video; أَسْمَعُ أُغْنِيةً to listen to a song; غَنّى \ رَدَّدَ أُغْنِيةً to sing a song; أُغْنِية عن الحُبِّ a song about love; لَحَّنَ \ كَتَبَ أُغْنِيةً to write a song; تَمَرَّنَ على أَداءِ أُغْنِيةٍ to practise a song

مُسْتَغْنًى *adj* مُسْتَغْنًى عَنْهُ dispensable; useless

مُغْنٍ *n* المُغْني the Enricher (*one of the names of God*)

مُغَنٍّ *n* [1] [مَنْ يُغَنّي] singer; vocalist; مُغَنٍّ مُغَنّي صَدْحٍ tenor; مُغَنٍّ مَشْهور a famous singer [2] (Bio) chiffchaff

مَغْنًى *n* |مَغانٍ| (Egypt) villa

غْواتيمالا *n* Guatemala

غاثَ *v* |u; غَوْث| to help; to support

أَغاثَ *v* to help; to aid; to relieve; أَغاثَ الجَرْحى to aid the wounded

اسْتَغاثَ *v* |ب| to ask for help; to seek aid; اسْتَغاثَ بِشَخْصٍ to ask sb for help

غَوْث *n* aid; relief; وِكالة غَوْثِ اللاجِئين refugee relief organization

اسْتِغاثة *n* appeal for aid; call for help; اسْتِغاثة بِشَخْصٍ \ بِشَيْءٍ to appeal to sb/sth; نِداء اسْتِغاثةٍ cry for help; distress call; SOS

إغاثة *n* emergency aid/relief; إغاثة إنْسانيّة humanitarian aid; إغاثة دُوَليّة an international relief action; إغاثة المَنْكوبينَ the relief of victims; مُنَظَّمة \ عَمَليّة إغاثةٍ relief organization/mission; مَوادّ إغاثةٍ عاجلة (emergency) relief supplies

مَغُوثة *n* |مَغاوِثُ| (emergency) relief supplies

مُغيث *n* rescuer; saviour

غارَ *v* |u; غَوْر| ① ◀ [خَسَفَ] to collapse; to cave in ② ◀ [غاصَ] to seep; غارَ الماءُ الأَرْضَ the water seeped into the earth ③ ◀ [حَسَدَ] see **غير**

أغارَ *v* ① ◀ [غَزا] to raid; to attack; to invade; أغارَ على مِنْطَقةٍ to invade a territory; أغارَ على الثَلاّجةِ to raid the fridge ② ◀ [أثارَ الحَسَدَ] see **غير**

غَوْر *n* |أَغْوار| ① ◀ [عُمْق] depth; bottom; لا يُسْبَرُ, عَميق الغَوْرِ غَوْرُهُ incomprehensible; mysterious ② ◀ [مُنْخَفَض] depression; غَوْر الأُرْدُنِ Jordan Valley ③ ◀ [مَصْدَر] raiding; bursting in on

غائِر *adj* deep; hollow; submerged

غار *n* |غيران, أَغْوار| ① ◀ [كَهْف] cave; cavern ② (Bot) bay, laurel; شَجَر الغارِ bay tree; وَرَقة شَجَرِ الغارِ bay/laurel leaf; إكْليل الغارِ laurel wreath

غارة *n* raid; attack; invasion; غارة جَوّيّة an air raid; غارة بَحْريّة an attack from sea; شَنَّ غارةً to launch/mount an attack

مَغار *n* |مَغارات| cave; cavern

مَغارة *n* |مَغاوِرُ, مَغارات| cave; cavern

مِغْوار Ⓐ *adj* |مَغاوير| brave; courageous Ⓑ *n* |مَغاويرُ| (Mil) commando; مَغاوير commandos; مَغاوير حِزْبِ اللهِ a Hezbollah commando

مُغير *n* raider

غورو *n* guru

غوريلاّ *n* |غوريلاّت| (Zool) gorilla

غاصَ *v* |u; غَوْص, مَغاص, غِياص, غِياصة| to dive; to plunge; غاصَ في الماءِ \ المَسْبَحِ to dive into the water/pool; غاصَ في العَمَلِ to drown in work; غاصَ في مَوْضوعٍ to be immersed in a subject; غاصَ في الوَحْلِ to sink in the mud; غاصَ في المَشاكِلِ to be in deep trouble

غَوَّصَ *v* to dive; to plunge

غَوْص *n* dive; plunge

غائِص *n* diver

غَوّاص *n* diver

غَوّاصة *n* submarine; غَوّاصة نَوَويّة \ ذَرّيّة nuclear submarine

تَغَوَّطَ *v* to defecate; to move one's bowels

غائِط *n* excrement, faeces, stool

غوطة *n* oasis; fertile valley

تَغَوُّط *n* defecation; bowel motion

غَوْغاء *n* |dipt f| riff-raff; mob

غَوْغائيّ Ⓐ *adj* demagogic Ⓑ *n* demagogue

غَوْغائيّة *n* demagogy

تَغَوَّلَ *v* ① ◀ [كانَ مُتَفَشِّياً] to be predominant ② ◀ [كانَ فَظيعاً] |على| to behave horribly towards

اغْتالَ *v* to murder; to assassinate; اغْتالَ شَخْصاً to murder sb

غول *n* |أَغْوال, غيلان| ghoul; bogeyman; demon

غائِلة *n* |غَوائِلُ| calamity; disaster; catastrophe

غولة *n* (female) ghoul; حَليب الغولةِ ≈ hen's teeth; جَلَبَ حَليبَ الغولةِ ≈ to get blood from a stone

غيلة *n* assassination

اغْتِيال *n* |اغْتِيالات| assassination; murder; عَمَليّة اغْتِيالٍ assault; attack; نَفَّذَ عَمَليّةَ اغْتِيالٍ to commit an assault; مُحاوَلة اغْتِيالٍ assassination attempt; قامَ ب \ نَجا من مُحاوَلةِ اغْتِيالٍ to commit/survive an assassination attempt; اغْتِيال السادات the assassination of Sadat; دَبَّرَ \ أَفْشَلَ مُحاوَلةَ اغْتِيالِ شَخْصٍ to plot/thwart an attempt on sb's life

مُغول, مُغوليّ *adj* see **مغول**

غَوى *v* |i; غَيّ, غَواية| ① ◀ [ضَلَّ] to stray ② ◀ [أَضَلَّ] to seduce; to tempt; غَوى الشَيْطانُ الإنْسانَ the devil tempted the man

أغْوى *v* 1 [أغْرى] to seduce; to tempt; أغْوى فَتاةً to seduce a girl; أغْوى شَخْصاً لِفِعْلِ شَيْءٍ to tempt sb to do sth 2 [أَضَلَّ] to mislead; to lead astray

غاوٍ *n* seducer

غَواية *n* seduction; temptation

إغْواء *n* |إغْواءات| seduction; temptation

مُغْوٍ *adj* seductive; tempting; attractive

‹ **غويانا** *n* Guyana; Guiana

‹ **غاب** *v* |i; غَيْب, غَيْبة, غِياب, غَيْبوبة, مَغيب| 1 [لم يَحْضُرْ] to be absent; to fail to attend; to stay away; غابَ عن المَدْرَسةِ \ الدَّرْسِ اليَوْمَ he skipped school/class today; غابَ ثَلاثةَ أشْهُرٍ he stayed away for three months 2 [اخْتَفى] to disappear; to go away; غابَت الشَّمْسُ the sun set; قد غابَ ذلك عن ذاكِرَتِه \ بالِهِ that has slipped his mind

غَيَّبَ *v* to cause to disappear; to remove

تَغَيَّبَ *v* |عن| to be absent; to stay away; تَغَيَّبَ عن شَيْءٍ to stay away from sth; تَغَيَّبَ عن المَدْرَسةِ to skip school; تَغَيَّبَ الكاتِبُ بِسَبَبِ المَرَضِ the secretary was absent due to illness; نادِراً ما يَتَغَيَّبُ he's rarely absent

اغْتابَ *v* to gossip; to slander; اغْتابَ شَخْصاً to gossip about sb

غَيْب *n* |غُيوب| absence; invisibility; the unseen; غَيْباً by heart; عن ظَهْرِ غَيْبٍ from memory; عالَم الغَيْبِ the unseen world; عِلْم الغَيْبِ knowledge of the unseen (*said of God*); هذا في عِلْمِ الغَيْبِ God only knows; الإنْسانُ لا يَعْلَمُ الغَيْبَ humans do not know the unseen; قَرَأَ الغَيْبَ to predict the future

غائِب A *adj* 1 [غَيْر حاضِرٍ] absent; كانَ غائِباً to be absent 2 (Gram) صيغة الغائِبِ third person B *n* absentee

غاب *n* (Bot) listed alphabetically

غابة *n* |غاب, غابات| forest, woods; jungle; غابة مَداريّة \ اسْتِوائيّة jungle; rain forest; حارِس الغابة forester; حَريق الغابةِ forest fire; كَثير الغاباتِ woody; قانون \ شَريعة الغابة the law of the jungle

غِياب *n* absence; non-attendance; non-appearance; غِياب قصير \ طَويل a short/long absence; في \ عند غِيابِ شَخْصٍ in the absence of sb; حَكَمَ على شَخْصٍ بالغِيابِ to sentence sb by default/in absentia

غِيابيّ *adj* absent; غِيابيًّا in absentia; حُكْم غِيابيّ judgement by default/in absentia

غيبة *n* slander; gossip; scandalmongering

غَيْبَة *n* absence; non-attendance; طالَتْ غَيْبَتُهُ he was absent for a long time

غَيْبوبة *n* (Med) unconsciousness; coma; في حالةِ غَيْبوبةٍ comatose; أُصيبَ بِغَيْبوبةٍ to go into a coma; to pass out; كانَ في غَيْبوبةٍ to be in a coma; to be unconscious; صَحا \ أفاقَ من غَيْبوبةٍ to wake from a coma; to regain consciousness

غَيْبيّ *adj* metaphysical; supernatural; occult

اغْتِياب *n* gossip

تَغَيُّب *n* |تَغَيُّبات| absence; non-attendance; تَغَيُّب عن المَدْرَسةِ absence from school

تَغْييب *n* removal

مُتَغَيِّب *adj* absent

مُغْتاب *n* gossiper

مَغيب *n* setting (*of the sun*)

‹ **غيتو** *n* |غيتوات| ghetto; عاشَ طُفولَتَهُ في غيتو as a child, he lived in a ghetto

‹ **غَيْث** *n* |غُيوث, أغْياث| rain

‹ **تَغايَدَ** *v* to sway; to walk gracefully

أغْيَد *adj* |dipt; غيد| flexible; delicate, refined

‹ **غار** *v* |a; غَيْرة| 1 [حَسَدَ] to be jealous; to protect, to guard jealously; غارَ من \ على شَخْصٍ to be jealous of/over sb; غارَتْ على زَوْجِها من زَميلَتِهِ الجَديدةِ she was jealous of her husband's new female colleague; غارَ على مَصالِحِ الوَطَنِ to protect the national interests 2 [خَسَفَ \ غاصَ] see **غور**

غَيَّرَ *v* to change; to alter; to modify; to replace; to move around; غَيَّرَ الأثْمِنةَ to change the prices; غَيَّرَ وَظيفَتَهُ \ رَأْيَهُ to change one's job/opinion; غَيَّرَ ثَوْباً to alter a garment; غَيَّرَ المَلابِسَ to change clothes; غَيَّرَ شَيْئاً في الوَضْعِ to change/alter sth in the situation; غَيَّرَ الزَّيْتَ \ إطارَ سَيّارةٍ to change the oil/a tyre; غَيَّرَ مَكانَ خِزانةٍ to move a cupboard; غَيَّرَ مَوْعِداً to change

غَيْريّ A *adj* altruistic

B *n* altruist

غَيْريّة *n* altruism

غيور *adj* |غُيُر| jealous; envious; زَوْج غيور a jealous husband

إغارة *n* raid; incursion

تَغاير *n* variety; diversity; heterogeneity

تغَيُّر *n* |تغَيُّرات| change; transformation; modification; turnover; تَغَيُّر مُفاجِئ \ واضِح a sudden/clear transformation; غَيْر قابِلٍ للتَغَيُّرِ unchanging; تغَيُّر جِذْريّ \ جَوْهَريّ a structural/fundamental change; تَغَيُّرات عميقة \ مَلْحوظة drastic/radical changes; تَغَيُّر بَسيط \ طَفيف a small/simple modification; تَغَيُّر مُناخيّ climate change; تَغَيُّر دَرَجةِ الحَرارةِ a change of temperature; تَغَيُّر للأَحْسَنِ a change for the better; تَغَيُّر الفُصولِ the change of seasons; عَمَليّة التَغَيُّر change process; كانَ هذا نُقْطةَ تَغَيُّرٍ في حَياتي that was a turning point in my life

تَغْيير *n* |تَغْييرات| 1 [تَبْديل] change; alteration, modification; replacement; قابل للتَغْيير replaceable; قِطَع قابِلة للتَغْيير replaceable parts; تَغْيير جِذْريّ a radical change; تَغْيير إطارٍ changing a tyre; تَغْيير مَواعيدِ الانْطِلاقِ a change in departure times; أَحْدَثَ تَغْييراً to make an alteration; أَدْخَلَ تَغْييراً على شَيْءٍ to make a modification to sth; دَخَلَ عَلَيْهِ تَغْيير to undergo a change 2 [تَنْويع] change; variation; أَحَبَّ التَغْييرَ to be fond of variation

مُتَغاير *adj* heterogeneous; varying; جَماعة مُتَغايِرة a heterogeneous group; تَرْكيبة مُتَغايِرة a varying composition

مُتَغَيِّر A *adj* changing; changeable; alternating; irregular; نَموذَج مُتَغَيِّر an irregular pattern

B *n* (Math) quantity; parameter; variable; مُتَغَيِّر مَعْلوم \ مَجْهول a known/unknown quantity

مُغاير *adj* different (from)

مُغَيَّر *adj* modified; changed; اقْتِراح مُغَيَّر a modified proposal

غاضَ *v* |i; غَيْض, مَغاض| to decrease; to diminish; to drop; غاضَ الماءُ the water leaked away

غَيْض *n* decline, decrease; small amount; هذا غَيْضٌ من فَيْضٍ this is just the tip of the iceberg

an appointment; غَيَّرَ الخُطَطَ \ السِياسةَ to change the plans/policy; غَيَّرَ اسْماً to rename; غَيَّرَ التَرْتيبَ to change the order; غَيَّرَ القِطارَ \ الطائِرةَ to transfer to a train/aircraft; لا يُغَيِّرُ ذلك في الأَمْرِ شَيْئاً that doesn't change a thing

غايَرَ *v* to differ from, to diverge from

أَغارَ *v* 1 [أَثارَ الحَسَدَ] to make jealous 2 [غزا] see غور

تَغَيَّرَ *v* 1 [تَبَدَّلَ] to change; to be changed; to be modified; لَقَدْ تَغَيَّرَ الوَضْعُ تَماماً the situation has changed completely; تَغَيَّرَت الأَحْوالُ بالنِسْبةِ للماضي the circumstances have changed, compared to the past 2 (Bio) to mutate

تَغايَرَ *v* to differ; to be different; اتَّفَقوا في صِفاتٍ وَتَغايَروا في صِفاتٍ أُخْرى they were the same in some ways and different in others

غَيْر A *adj* 1 [سِوى] except; على \ ب \ من غَيْرِ without; على غَيْرِ مَعْرِفةٍ مِنْهُ without him knowing; غَيْرَ أَنَّ ... except (for) ...; but ... 2 [أَكْثَر من] more than; غَيْرَ مَرّةٍ more than once; غَيْر واحِدٍ more than one; لا غَيْرُ خَمْسونَ جُنَيْهاً فَقَطْ لا غَيْرُ not more than fifty pounds 3 [لا] not; non-; غَيْر شَرْعيٍّ illegal; غَيْر مَحْدودٍ unlimited; غَيْر مَعْروفٍ unknown; هو على غَيْرِ عادَتِهِ he's not his usual/normal self; كانَ رَفْضُهُ غَيْرَ مُقْنِعٍ his refusal wasn't convincing

B *n* [آخَر] other; الغَيْر third party; the others; شُؤون الغَيْرِ other people's business; غَيْرُ ذلك sth else; إلى غَيْرِ ذلك and the like; et cetera; الكُتُب والدَفاتِر وغَيْرُها books, notebooks and the like; أَنْتَ رَجُلُ الدارِ ولا أَحَدَ غَيْرُكَ you are the man of the house, nobody else; يُريدُ تَسْليمَ السُلْطةِ إلى الرَئيسِ دون غَيْرِهِ he wants to transfer power to the president only

غِيار *n* exchange; replacement; قِطْعة غِيارٍ spare part; حَرَّرَ غِيارَ السَيّارةِ to put the car in neutral

غَيْران *adj* jealous; zealous

غيرة, غَيْرة *n* 1 [إِحْساس بالشَرَفِ] (sense of) honour/pride; حَرَّكَ غَيْرةَ شَخْصٍ to appeal to sb's honour 2 [حَسَد] jealousy; envy; نَظْرة غَيْرةٍ envious glances; غَيْرة من \ على شَخْصٍ jealousy of/over sb; أَحَسَّ بالغَيْرةِ من شَخْصٍ to be be jealous of sb; أَثارَ غَيْرةَ شَخْصٍ to arouse sb's envy; أَحْرَقَت الغَيْرةُ قَلْبَها she was eaten up with jealousy

غَيْضة *n* bushes; thicket

‹ **غَيْط** *n* |غيطان| field; land

‹ **غاظَ** *v* |i; غَيْظ| to irritate; to enrage; to infuriate; to annoy

أَغاظَ *v* to irritate; to enrage; to infuriate; أَغاظَ شَخصاً إلى حَدٍّ كَبيرٍ to irritate sb intensely

اغْتاظَ *v* |من| to be/become furious; to be/become enraged; to lose one's temper; to rant; اغْتاظَ من شَيْءٍ \ شَخصٍ to be furious at sth/with sb

غَيْظ *n* anger; fury; wrath; irritation; غَيْظ من شَيْءٍ fury over/about sth; من غَيْظِهِ out of anger; غَيْظ مَكْظوم \ مَكْبوت restrained/bottled up anger; نَظْرة غَيْظٍ a wrathful look; اسْتَشاط غَيْظاً to flame up with rage; تَمَيَّزَ غَيْظاً to boil/burn with rage; كَظَمَ غَيْظَهُ to suppress one's anger; أَفْرَغَ غَيْظَهُ to vent one's anger; أَثارَ ذلك غَيْظَهُ that raised/provoked his wrath

إغاظة *n* enraging, infuriation, irritation

اغْتِياظ *n* anger; fury; rage; رَدَّ باغْتِياظٍ to react angrily

مُغْتاظ *adj* angry; furious; enraged; outraged; wrathful; مُغْتاظ من شَيْءٍ enraged by/with sth

مُغيظ *adj* annoying; irritating; infuriating

‹ **غيل** *n* |غُيول, أَغْيال| undergrowth; brushwood

‹ **غَيْلَم** *n* |غَيالِمُ| tortoise

‹ **غامَ** *v* |i; غَيْم| to become overcast; to cloud over; غامَت السَماءُ the sky clouded over/up

غَيَّمَ *v* to become overcast; to cloud over

أَغامَ *v* to become cloudy

غَيْم *n coll* |غُيوم| cloud, clouds; clouding; غَيْمة من الغُبارِ a cloud of dust; مُتَلَبِّد بالغُيومِ overcast; cloudy; طَبَقة غُيومٍ clouds; غُيوم كَثيفةٍ \ مُتَلَبِّدةٍ a thick/dense layer of clouds; احْتِمال ظُهورِ غُيومٍ a chance of clouds; لا غَيْمةَ في السَماءِ not a cloud in the sky; تَلَبَّدَت السَماءُ بالغُيومِ the sky clouded over/up; تُشْرِقُ الشَمْسُ وراء الغُيومِ ≈ every cloud has a silver lining

غائِم *adj* cloudy; overcast; غَيْر غائِم cloudless; يَوْم غائِم a cloudy day; سَماء غائِمة a cloudy/overcast sky; كَلام غائِم vague language; غائِم بِشِدّةٍ (with) heavy clouds/clouding

مُغَيِّم *adj* cloudy, overcast

‹ **غَيْن** *n* |f| *name of the letter* غ

‹ **غينيا** *n* Guinea; غينيا الجَديدة New Guinea; غينيا بيساو Guinea-Bissau

‹ **غَيْهَب** *n* |غَياهِبُ| darkness; gloom; أَلْقى بِشَخْصٍ في غَياهِبِ السِجْنِ to throw sb in the darkness of prison

‹ **غاية** **A** *n* **1** [هَدَف] goal, objective, purpose; intention; لِغاية ... for the benefit/purpose of ...; أَدْرَكَ غايَتَهُ to achieve one's aim; to reach one's goal; الغايةُ تُبَرِّرُ الوَسيلةَ the end justifies the means; إرْضاءُ الناسِ غايةٌ لا تُدْرَكُ it's impossible to satisfy people **2** [حَدّ] extreme; للغايةِ to the limit; extreme; utmost; شَخْصيّ \ سِرّيّ للغايةِ strictly personal/confidential; في غايةِ الأَهَمّيّةِ extremely important; imperative; الأَمْر في غايةِ السُهولةِ the matter is extremely simple

B *prep* until; بَقِيَ في مِصْرَ لغايةِ عامِ ١٩٩٠ he stayed in Egypt until 1990; إلى غايةِ تَحْقيقِهِ لأَهْدافِه until he has realized his goals

غَيّ *n* sin

‹ **ف** *conj* [1] [نَسَق فِعْلَيْن] and; قالَ لي ... فَقُلْتُ لَهُ ... he said to me ... and then I said to him ...; اسْتَيْقَظَ فَوَجَدَ ساعَتَهُ واقِفةً he woke up to discover his watch had stopped [2] [بعد ذلك] afterwards, thereafter; يَنْشَأُ الإنْسانُ طِفْلاً فَشابًّا فَكَهْلاً فَشَيْخاً a person grows up from a child into a young man, then an adult then an elder [3] [في تَعابيرَ ظَرْفِيّة] واحِداً فَواحِداً one by one; شَيْئاً فَشَيْئاً piece by piece; أَكْثَر فَأَكْثَر more and more [4] [... فَقالَ] تَحَدَّثَ \ رَدَّ فَقالَ ... he spoke/replied, saying ...; [5] [لِتَخْصيص ما سَبَق] أَعودُ فَأَقولُ ... I will say once again ... أَسْرَعْتُ فَأَقْفَلْتُ بابَ المَوْضوعِ I hurried to close the topic [6] [قبل اسْتِنْتاجٍ] therefore, so; then; أنا أُفَكِّرُ فَأَنا مَوْجودٌ I think, therefore I am; مَرِضَ الأُسْتاذُ فَأُلْغِيَت المُحاضَرةُ the teacher fell ill, so the lecture was cancelled; مَنْ لَيْسَ مَعي فَهُوَ ضِدّي you're either with me or against me [7] [لِسَبَبٍ] because, since; لَقَدْ حَزِنَ كَثيراً على مَوْتِ صَديقَتِهِ فَقَدْ أَحَبَّها كَثيراً he was saddened by the death of his friend, because he loved her very much [8] [لِلتَوَقُّعِ] as expected; سَمِعَ هذا الكَلامَ فَلَمْ يُصَدِّقْ he heard what was said, but (as expected) did not believe it [9] [فَإنَّ] لِذا فَإنَّ مُسْتَوى المَعيشةِ مُرْتَفِعٌ جِدًّا and that's the reason why the living standards are very high; وَرَغْمَ ذلك فَإنَّ هُناكَ شَيْئاً هامًّا يُمْكِنُ أَنْ يُقالَ nevertheless there's something important to be said [10] [جُمْلة شَرْطِيّة] then; إذا كُنْتَ لم تَفْهَمْني فَقُلْ لي ذلك if you didn't understand me, then tell me; إذا حَضَرْتُم غداً فَسَوْفَ تَجِدونَ كُلَّ المَشاكِلِ قد حُلَّتْ if you come tomorrow then you'll find all the problems have been solved [11] [أَمّا ... فَ ...] أَمّا عِلْمُ الإنْسانِ فَمَحْدودٌ as for the knowledge of people, it's limited; أَمّا السُكّانُ فَهُمْ على ما يُرامُ with regard to the residents, they're fine [12] [قبل سُؤالٍ] فَلِماذا يَمْنَعُ الناسُ الخُبْزَ مِنّي؟ why are they refusing to give me bread? [13] [لِنَصْبِ الفِعْلِ] لِماذا لم تَأْتِني فَأُكْرِمَكَ why didn't you come to me so that I could have honoured you [14] [بما ... ف ...] بِما أَنَّني مَشْغولةٌ جِدًّا فَلَنْ أُسافِرَ غداً given that I'm extremely busy, I won't be travelling tomorrow [15] [أَفَ ...] maybe, perhaps; أَفَتَظُنُّ أنّ ...؟ perhaps you believe that ...?

‹ **فا** *n* (Mus) fah

‹ **فاء** *n* |f| *name of the letter* ف

‹ **افْتَأَتَ** *v* |على| to think up, to invent, to fabricate; to tell lies (about)

‹ **فاتورة** *n* |فَواتيرُ| invoice, bill; حَرَّرَ \ كَتَبَ فاتورةً to issue an invoice

‹ **الفاتيكان** *n* |f| the Vatican, Vatican City; في الفاتيكان in the Vatican

‹ **فُؤاد** *n* |أَفْئِدة| [1] [قَلْب] heart; فارِغ الفُؤادِ carefree [2] [اسْم شَخْصيّ] Fuad (*male given name*)

‹ **فَأْر** *n coll* |فِئْران| [1] [حَيَوان] mouse; rat; مِصْيَدة الفِئْرانِ mousetrap; أُذُن الفَأْرِ (Bot) forget-me-not; ذَيْل الفَأْرِ (Bot) rat-tail; وَقَعَ كالفَأْرِ في المِصْيَدةِ to be trapped like a rat; غابَ القِطُّ الْعَبْ يا فَأْرُ when the cat's away the mice will play; هُما كالقِطِّ والفَأْرِ they fight like cats and dogs [2] (Comput) فَأْرة mouse; ضَغَطَ على الفَأْرة to click the mouse; حَرَّكَ الفَأْرةَ to move the mouse [3] (Tools) فَأْرة plane

فارة *n* [1] (Zool) mouse [2] (Tools) plane

‹ **فازْلين** *n* Vaseline

‹ **فَأْس** *n* |f; فُؤوس, أَفْؤُس| axe; pickaxe

‹ **فاس** *n* |f| Fez (*city in Morocco*)

‹ **فاشِسْتيّ** *adj, n* fascist

فاشِسْتيّة *n* fascism

فاشيّ **A** *adj* fascist; فاشيّ جَديد neo-fascist
B *n* fascist

فاشيّة *n* fascism; فاشيّة جَديدة neo-fascism; مُقاوَمة الفاشيّةِ the fight against fascism

فاصولية, **فاصوليا**, **فاصولْيا** *n* French bean, green bean; فاصولِية بَيْضاء white bean

فَأْفَأَ *v* |i; فَأْفَأة| to stutter, to stammer, to splutter

فاكْس *n* fax (*machine*); بِواسِطةِ \ رِسالة \ بَيان فاكْس fax (*message*); عن طَريقِ \ عَبْرَ الفاكْس by fax; رَقْم الفاكْس fax number; تَلَقّى رِسالة فاكْس to receive a fax; أَرْسَلَ \ بَعَثَ رِسالةً بالفاكْس to send a fax; أَرْسَلَ عَبْرَ الفاكْس to fax

فاكْسْمِيْل *n* fax (*machine*)

تَفاءَلَ *v* to regard as a good omen; to be optimistic; تَفاءَلَ بِشَيْءٍ to regard sth as a good omen

فَأْل *n* |أَفْؤُل, فُؤول| good omen; فَأْل حَسَن \ خَيْرٍ a good omen

تَفاؤُل *n* optimism, sanguineness; تَفاؤُل شَديد great optimism; تَفاؤُل حَذِر moderate optimism; بِتَفاؤُلٍ with optimism; دائِم التَفاؤُلِ an eternal optimist; دَعا \ دَفَعَ إلى التَفاؤُلِ to call for/incite optimism; هذا لا يُشَجِّعُ على التَفاؤُلِ this doesn't call for optimism; أَبْدى تَفاؤُلَهُ بِشَيْءٍ to express an optimistic view of sth; فاقَ أَكْثَرَ التَوَقُّعاتِ تَفاؤُلاً to exceed the most optimistic expectations

تَفاؤُليّ *adj* optimistic, sanguine

مُتَفائِل **A** *adj* optimistic, sanguine; تَقْدير مُتَفائِل an optimistic estimate; كانَ مُتَفائِلاً بِشَيْءٍ to be optimistic about sth
B *n* optimist

فالْس *n* waltz

فاليوم *n* Valium®; اسْتَعْمَلَ الفاليوم to take Valium

فانْتازيا *n* **1** (Mus) fantasia **2** [فراسة] fantasia (*Arabic horse show*)

فانلاّ, **فانِلّة** *n* **1** [قُماش] flannel **2** [قميص] flannel shirt

فانوس *n* |فَوانيسُ| oil lamp, lantern

فانيلا *n* vanilla

فِئة *n* **1** [مَجْموعة] group, class, order; category; انْتَمى إلى فِئةٍ to belong to a category; في \ من كُلِّ فِئاتِ (الشَعْبِ) in/from all (social) classes **2** (Sport) division, league; الفِئة الأولى the first division

فِئَوي *adj* categorial, group (*before n*); factional; نَشاطات فِئَويّة group activities

فِئَويّة *n* factionalism

فاوانيا *n* peony

فايْكِنْج *n* Viking, Norseman

فِبْراير *n* (Mor, Egypt, Gulf) February

فَبْرَكَ *v* to fabricate

فَبْرَكة *n* fabrication; فَبْرَكة الأَخْبارِ fabricating (false) news

مُفَبْرَك *adj* fabricated, manufactured; قِصّة مُفَبْرَكة a fabricated story

فَتِئَ *v* |a; فَتْء| to refrain, to abstain; ما فَتِئَ يَفْعَلُ ... he never ceased doing ...

فَتَّ *v* |u; فَتّ| to crumble; فَتَّ الخُبْزَ to crumble the bread

فَتَّتَ *v* to shred, to crumble; to pulverize, to shatter, to fragment; فَتَّتَ البِسْكوت to crumble a biscuit (BrE) cookie (AmE); فَتَّتَ وَرَقاً to shred paper; مَنْظَر يُفَتِّتُ الأَكْبادَ a heart-rending scene; فَتَّتَ حصى الكُلى to pulverize kidney stones

تَفَتَّتَ *v* to fall apart, to crumble (away), to disintegrate; يَتَفَتَّتُ الصَخْرُ the rock is crumbling

فُتات *n* |mf; فَتائِتُ| remains, remnants; morsels, crumbs; فُتات الطَعام leftovers

فَتّة *n a dish made of bread crumbs, meat stock and fava beans*

تَفَتُّت *n* disintegration, crumbling, fragmentation; تَفَتُّتٌ اجْتِماعيّ social disintegration; تَفَتُّتُ الخَشَبِ the crumbling of wood

فَتَحَ *v* |a; فَتْح| **1** [عَكْس أَغْلَقَ] to open; فَتَحَ عَيْنَيْهِ to open one's eyes; فَتَحَ عُلْبةً to open a can; فَتَحَ زُجاجة نَبيذٍ to uncork a bottle of wine; فَتَحَ باباً \ صِواناً \ نافذة to open a door/cupboard/window; فَتَحَ السَتائِرَ to open the curtains; فَتَحَ رِسالةً to open a letter; فَتَحَ كِتاباً to open a book; فَتَحَ مِنْطَقةً to open (up) an area; فَتَحَ شَهِيّةَ شَخْصٍ to whet sb's appetite; يَفْتَحُ المَحَلُّ أَبْوابَهُ في التاسِعةِ the shop opens at nine o'clock **2** [انْتَصَرَ] to conquer, to capture; فَتَحَ مَدينةً to conquer a city **3** [شَغَّلَ جِهازًا] to turn on, to switch on; فَتَحَ الرادِيو to turn on the radio **4** [مَوْضوعاً] to bring up, to enter upon; فَتَحَ مَوْضوعاً to bring up a topic **5** [بَدَأَ] to open, to start;

فَتَحَ حِساباً مَصْرِفيّاً to open a bank account; فَتَحَ الاجْتِماعَ to open the meeting

فَتَّحَ *v* to open; فَتَّحَ البابَ to open the door

فاتَحَ *v* to address first, to speak first to

تَفَتَّحَ *v* to come out, to open; تَتَفَتَّحُ الزُهورُ the flowers are coming out

اِنْفَتَحَ *v* to be open; to open (up); اِنْفَتَحَ على العالَمِ to open up to the outside world; اِنْفَتَحَ على أَفْكارٍ جَديدةٍ to be open to new ideas

اِفْتَتَحَ *v* to open, to inaugurate; to begin, to start; اِفْتَتَحَ مَدْرَسةً to open a school; اِفْتَتَحَ نَدْوةً to open a symposium

اِسْتَفْتَحَ *v* to start, to begin

فَتْح *n* 1 [عَكْس إغْلاق] opening; إعادة الفَتْحِ reopening 2 [اِسْتيلاء] |فُتوحات, فُتوح| conquest, capture; فَتْح مَدينةٍ the conquest of a city; كانَ فَتْحُ مَكّةَ فَتْحَ الفُتوحِ the conquest of Mecca was the biggest conquest; فُتوحات البُلْدانِ (Hist) the conquests of the (non-Islamic) countries; سورة الفَتْح The Victory (*Sura 48*); حَرَكة فَتْح Fatah (*Palestinian political party*)

فاتِح A *adj* |فَواتِحُ| light; لَوْن فاتِح light colour, pastel colour; أَخْضَر فاتِح light green
B *n* 1 [الأَوَّل] first; فاتِح يَنايِر the first of January 2 [مَنْ فَتَحَ] |فاتِحونَ| conqueror 3 [شَهْر] شَهْر الفاتِح (Hist) September (*Libya under Gaddafi*)

فاتِحة *n* |فَواتِحُ| beginning, start, opening; Fatiha; سورة الفاتِحة The Opening (*Sura 1*)

فَتّاح *n* الفَتّاح the Opener (*one of the names of God*)

فَتّاحة *n* opener; can opener; bottle opener; فَتّاحة زُجاجاتٍ bottle opener

فَتْحة *n* fatha (*the vowel sign for a*)

فُتْحة *n* |فُتَح, فُتْحات| opening, hole; فُتْحة في الحائطِ an opening in the wall; فُتْحة سَقْفٍ sliding roof, sun roof

اِفْتِتاح *n* 1 [تَدْشين] inauguration 2 [فَتْح] opening; اِفْتِتاح المَعْرِضِ the opening of the exhibition; اِفْتِتاح البَرْنامَجِ the opening of the programme; حَفْلة الافْتِتاحِ الرَسْميِّ للبُطولةِ the opening ceremony of the championship

اِفْتِتاحيّ *adj* inaugural, opening (*before n*); مَقال اِفْتِتاحيّ editorial, leading article; عَرْض اِفْتِتاحيّ premiere, opening performance; كَلِمة اِفْتِتاحيّة opening word; خِطاب اِفْتِتاحيّ an inaugural speech

اِفْتِتاحيّة *n* 1 (Mus) overture 2 (Journ) editorial, leading article

اِنْفِتاح *n* openness, opening, public nature; اِنْفِتاح اِقْتِصاديّ economic openness; سِياسة الانْفِتاح opening-up policy; open-door policy

مُتَفَتِّح *adj* 1 [مَفْتوح] open, accessible 2 (Bot) flowering, blooming

مِفْتاح *n* |مَفاتيحُ| 1 [لِفَتْحِ الأَقْفال] key; مِفْتاح بابِ البَيْتِ front-door key, house key; عَلّاقة \ حَلْقة مَفاتيحَ key ring; مِفْتاح عُموميّ master key; public key; أَدْخَلَ المِفْتاحَ في القُفْلِ to put the key in the lock; أَدارَ المِفْتاحَ to turn the key 2 (Tools) spanner (BrE), wrench (AmE); مِفْتاح إنْجْليزيّ adjustable spanner (BrE), screw wrench (AmE) 3 (Elec) switch, button; مِفْتاح رَئيسيّ main switch 4 (Mus) clef 5 (fig) key, secret; مِفْتاح السَعادةِ the secret of happiness; مِفْتاح اللُغْزِ the key to the mystery; مِفْتاح الإجابةِ على السُؤالِ the key to the answer to the question 6 [جُزْء آلةٍ] key; مِفْتاح العالي shift key; مِفْتاح العَوْدةِ backspace key; لَوْحة مَفاتيحَ keyboard; ضَرَبَ مِفْتاحاً \ ضَغَطَ على مِفْتاحٍ to hit/press a key 7 [في سِكّة حَديدٍ] points (BrE), switch (AmE)

مِفْتاحيّ *adj* key (*before n*); كَلِمة مِفْتاحيّة key word

مَفْتوح *adj* 1 [عَكْس مُغْلَق] open, opened, accessible; جُرْح مَفْتوح an open wound; يَوْم مَفْتوح an open day; رِسالة مَفْتوحة an open letter; نِهاية مَفْتوحة an open ending; النافِذةُ مَفْتوحةٌ the window is open; الدُكّانُ مَفْتوحٌ the shop is open; لا يَزالُ الطَريقُ مَفْتوحاً أَمامَهُ the road is still open to him; مَفْتوح للجَماهيرِ \ للجَميعِ open to the public; أَبْوابُ التَسْجيلِ مَفْتوحةٌ للجَميعِ registration is open to all; كانَ مَفْتوحاً to be open; تَرَكَ البابَ مَفْتوحاً to leave the door open 2 [بِلاد وَقَعَ فَتْحُها] conquered

مُنْفَتِح *adj* open, receptive, amenable; كانَ مُنْفَتِحاً على شَيْءٍ to be open to sth; كانَ مُنْفَتِحاً للأَفْكارِ الجَديدةِ to be open to new ideas

فَتَرَ *v* |u; فُتور| to cool off; to slacken, to flag, to wane; فَتَرَت الصَداقةُ the friendship has flagged; فَتَرَت العَلاقاتُ relations have cooled; فَتَرَ الحَماسُ enthusiasm has waned

فَتَّرَ *v* to cool (down); to slacken, to enfeeble, to sap; فَتَّرَتْ هذه الأَحْداثُ من عَزيمَتي these events have sapped my determination

أَفْتَرَ *v* to weaken, to enfeeble

فِتْر *n* small span (*the distance between thumb and index finger*)

فاتِر *adj* |فَواتِرُ| 1 [بين الحارِّ والبارِدِ] tepid, lukewarm; شاي فاتِر lukewarm tea 2 [خَفيف] lukewarm; chilly, cool; flat, tame; جَوّ فاتِر a bleak atmosphere; رَدّ فِعْلٍ فاتِر a lukewarm response; اسْتِقْبال فاتِر a cool reception

فَتْرة *n* |فَتَرات| period, while, spell; (interval of) time; فَتْرة قَصيرة \ طَويلة a short/long period; لِفَتْرةٍ قَصيرةٍ for a moment; فَتْرة تَمْهيديّة initial period; فَتْرة نَقاهةٍ period of recovery; فَتْرة انْتِقاليّة transitional period; (كانَ) في فَتْرةٍ انْتِقاليّةٍ (to be) in a transitional period; تَسْتَغْرِقُ الفَتْرةُ الانْتِقاليّةُ شَهْرَيْنِ the transition period will last two months; في \ خلال الفَتْرةِ الانْتِقاليّةِ during the transitional period; فَتَرات مُتَباعِدة wide intervals; الفَتْرة الماضِية the past period; خلال فَتْرةِ سَنَتَيْنِ in a period of two years; الفَتْرة ما بين ١١٠٠ و١٣٠٠ the period 1100 - 1300; الفَتْرة ما بين القَرْنِ ال١٢ والقَرْنِ ال١٤ the period from the 12th till the 14th century; فَتْرة مَجيدة \ مُظْلِمة في تاريخِنا a glorious/dark period in our history; تُعَدُّ هذه الفَتْرةُ من أَحْلَكِ الفَتَراتِ this period is considered one of the darkest periods; فَتْرة (قَصيرة) من الزَمَنِ a (short) period of time; في \ خلال فَتْرةِ يَوْمٍ (واحِدٍ) within a period of a day; منذ فَتْرةٍ طَويلةٍ since a long time; (في) الفَتْرةِ الأَخيرةِ lately, recently; بعد فَتْرةٍ (وَجيزةٍ) after a (short) while; انْقَضَت الفَتْرةُ the period has elapsed; من فَتْرةٍ لِأُخْرى ,بين فَتْرةٍ وأُخْرى from time to time; في فَتْرةٍ بعد فَتْرةٍ now and then

فُتور *n* 1 [بُرودة] chilliness; slackening, flagging; فُتور في العَلاقةِ a chilliness in the relationship 2 [خُمول] indifference, nonchalance, laxity

فَتَّشَ *v* 1 |عن| [بَحَثَ] to search for, to look for; to look up; فَتَّشَ عن شَيْءٍ to search for sth; فَتَش عن سَعادَتِهِ to seek one's fortune 2 [تَفَحَّصَ] to search; to examine, to inspect, to check; فَتَّشَ مَنْزِلَ شَخْصٍ to conduct a search of sb's house; فَتَّشَ المُسافِرينَ to search travellers

فَتّوش *n* a salad with bread, onions and parsley

تَفْتيش *n* |تَفْتيشات, تَفاتيشُ| inspection, examination; search; تَفْتيش مَنْزِلٍ house search; أَمْر التَفْتيشِ search warrant; نُقْطة تَفْتيشٍ checkpoint; تَفْتيش جَسَديّ body search; تَفْتيش دَقيق thorough inspection; أَجْرى عَمَليّةَ تَفْتيشٍ شامِلة \ واسِعة \ دَقيقة to conduct a comprehensive/large-scale/thorough inspection

مُفَتِّش *n* inspector, investigator; مُفَتِّش الضَرائِبِ tax inspector; مُفَتِّش في الحافِلةِ \ القِطارِ ticket inspector on bus/train; مُفَتِّش مَباحِثَ detective

مُفَتِّشيّة *n* inspectorate; مُفَتِّشيّة العَمَلِ labour inspectorate

فَتَفَتَ *v* |i| 1 [هَمَسَ] to speak secretly; فَتَفَت إلى شَخْصٍ to speak secretly to sb 2 [فَتَّتَ] to crumble

فَتْفوتة *n* |فَتافيتُ| crumb, morsel

فَتَقَ *v* |u; فَتْق| to unstitch

فَتَّقَ *v* to unstitch; to rip (open)

تَفَتَّقَ *v* to come loose; to tear (apart)

انْفَتَقَ *v* to come loose; to tear (apart)

فَتْق *n* |فُتوق| 1 (Med) rupture, hernia; فَتْق الظَهْرِ disc hernia, slipped disc; فَتْق الأُرْبيّة inguinal hernia 2 [مَلابِس] split, rip; tear

فِتاق *n* rupture, hernia

فَتَكَ *v* |i-u; فَتْك| ب| to kill, to murder, to assassinate; فَتَكَ بالعَدُوِّ to kill the enemy

فَتْك *n* murder, killing; destruction, annihilation

فاتِك A *adj* |فُتّاك| fatal, deadly, lethal; سَمّ فاتِك deadly poison; مَرَض فاتِك a deadly disease

B *n* |فُتّاك| murderer, killer

فَتّاك *adj* murderous, deadly; fatal; مَرَض فَتّاك a deadly disease; سِلاح فَتّاك a lethal/deadly weapon

فَتَلَ *v* |i; فَتْل| to braid, to plait; to twist, to twine

فَتْلة *n* |فَتَلات| thread; شَمَّعَ الفَتْلةَ (colloq Egypt) to sneak off

فتيل [A] *adj* twisted, twined

[B] *n* |فتائِلُ, فتيلات| fuse, slow match; أَشْعَلَ الفَتيلَ to light the fuse; اشْتَعَلَ فَتيلُ الحَرْبِ war has broken out; أَشْعَلَ فَتيلَ الانْفِجارِ to spark an explosion; هذا لا يُجْدي \ يُغْني فَتيلاً this is of no use at all; لا فَتيلَ ولا نَقيرَ absolutely nothing

فتيلة *n* |فتائِلُ, فَتيلات| wick, taper

مَفْتول *adj* twisted, twined; مَفْتول العَضَلاتِ muscular; جِسْم مَفْتول العَضَلاتِ a muscular body

‹ **فَتَنَ** *v* |i; فُتون, فَتْن| [1] [أغرى] to seduce, to charm, to enchant; to intrigue, to captivate, to fascinate; فَتَنَ النِساءَ to charm women; فَتَنَهُ عن عَمَلِهِ حُبُّهُ للقِمارِ his gambling fever kept him from his work [2] [اخْتَبَرَ] to test, to try, to put to the test

أَفْتَنَ *v* to enchant, to fascinate

افْتَتَنَ *v* to be/become fascinated; افْتَتَنَ بِشَخْصٍ \ بِشَيْءٍ to be enchanted by sb/sth

فاتِن [A] *adj* |فَواتِنُ| tempting, charming, graceful; ابْتِسامة \ فَتاة فاتِنة a charming smile/girl; امْرَأة فاتِنة femme fatale; فاتِن الجَمالِ ravishingly beautiful

[B] *n* |فَواتِنُ| فاتِن النِساءِ seducer, ladies' man

فَتّان *adj* fascinating, enchanting; جَمال فَتّان a ravishing beauty

فِتْنة *n* |فِتَن| [1] [سِحْر] charm, attractiveness; temptation, enticement; فِتْنة المَرْأةِ the charm of women [2] [فَوْضى] revolt, sedition; riot, unrest, commotion; أَخْمَدَ فِتْنةً to suppress a revolt; مُثير الفِتَنِ agitator [3] [اخْتِبار] testing (*of man by God*)

افْتِتان *n* fascination, captivation

مَفاتِن *n pl* |dipt| charms, charming qualities

مَفْتون *adj* fascinated, captivated; كانَ مَفْتوناً بِشَخْصٍ \ بِشَيْءٍ to be captivated by sb/sth

‹ **فَتِيَ** *v* |a; فَتاء| to be young, to be youthful

أَفْتى *v* (Isl Law) to give a formal legal opinion, to deliver a fatwa

اسْتَفْتى *v* [1] [سَأَلَ عن الرَأْيِ] to canvass opinion; to ask for an opinion [2] (Isl Law) to ask for a formal legal opinion (fatwa)

فَتِيّ *adj* youthful, young

فَتاة *n* |فَتَيات| girl; young woman; فَتاة حَمْقاء a silly girl; فَتاة جَميلة a beautiful girl

فُتُوّة *n* [1] [شَباب] adolescence [2] [مُروءة] noble manliness (*magnanimity and chivalry*)

فَتْوى *n* |f; فَتاوى, فَتاوٍ| fatwa (*formal legal opinion in answer to a legal question*)

فَتًى *n* |فِتْية, فِتْيان| boy, young man, youth; فَتى الأَحْلامِ Prince Charming

اسْتِفْتاء *n* |اسْتِفْتاءات| referendum; اسْتِفْتاء في شَيْءٍ a referendum on sth; أَجْرى اسْتِفْتاءً (شَعْبيًّا) to hold a referendum; اسْتِفْتاء الرَأْيِ العامِّ a canvass of (the) public opinion

إِفْتاء *n deliverance of formal legal opinions (fatwas)*; دار الإِفْتاءِ office of the mufti

مُفْتٍ *n* mufti (*official expounder of Islamic law*); سَماحة المُفْتي His Eminence the Mufti; أَصْدَرَ المُفْتي فَتْوى the mufti issued a fatwa

‹ **فَثَأَ** *v* |a; فَثْء| to quench, to still, to satisfy

‹ **فَجَأَ, فَجِئَ** *v* |a; فَجْء, فَجْأة, فُجاءة| to (take by) surprise, to come suddenly, to confront unexpectedly; فَجَأَتْنا العاصِفةُ we were caught in a storm

فَجِئَ *v* |a; فَجْء, فَجْأة, فُجاءة| to surprise

فاجَأَ *v* to (take by) surprise, to come suddenly, to confront unexpectedly; فاجَأَ شَخْصاً بِشَيْءٍ to surprise sb with sth

فُجاءة *n* surprise, unexpected event; فُجاءةً unexpectedly, suddenly; مَوْت الفُجاءةِ sudden death

فُجائيّ *adj* sudden, unexpected; حَرَكة فُجائيّة an unexpected move

فَجْأة, فُجْأة *n* surprise; فَجْأةً suddenly, unexpectedly; حَدَثَ الانْفِجارُ فَجْأةً the explosion happened unexpectedly

مُتَفاجِئ *adj* surprised

مُفاجِئ *adj* surprising, sudden, unexpected; جاءَ مَوْتُها مُفاجِئاً her death came unexpectedly; هُجوم مُفاجِئ a surprise attack; المَوْت المُفاجِئ sudden death; تَطَوُّر مُفاجِئ an unexpected development; كانَ مُفاجِئاً to come as a surprise

مُفاجَأة *n* surprise; مُفاجَأة لِشَخْصٍ a surprise for sb; مُفاجَأة جَميلة \ سارّة a pleasant surprise

‹ **أَفَجَّ** *v* to hurry

فَجّ *n* |فِجاج| mountain pass

فِجّ *adj* 1▸ [غَيْر ناضِجٍ] unripe, immature 2▸ [فَظّ] blunt, rude

فُجاج *n* (mountain) pass

فَجاجة *n* unripeness, immaturity; فَجاجة الفاكِهةِ the unripeness of the fruit

فَجَرَ *v* |u; فُجور| 1▸ [فَسَقَ] to lead a loose life, to live licentiously 2▸ [الماءَ] to let flow

فَجَّرَ *v* 1▸ [نَسَفَ] to blow up, to explode; فَجَّرَ شَيْئاً to blow sth up; فَجَّرَ بِنايةً to blow up a building; فَجَّرَ مَوْقِفاً \ مُشْكِلةً to let a situation/problem erupt 2▸ [الماءَ] to let flow

تَفَجَّرَ *v* 1▸ [القُنْبُلَةُ] to explode, to blow up 2▸ [تَدَفَّقَ] to erupt, to break out, to burst out; تَفَجَّرَ الوَضْعُ the situation has come to a head; تَفَجَّرَت الأَزْمةُ the crisis has erupted 3▸ [الماءُ] to flow, to stream, to gush

اِنْفَجَرَ *v* 1▸ [تَفَجَّرَ] to bang, to burst; to erupt, to burst out, to break out; اِنْفَجَرَ بالضَحْكِ \ بالبُكاءِ ,اِنْفَجَرَ ضاحِكاً \ باكِياً to burst into laughter/tears; اِنْفَجَرَ البُرْكانُ the volcano erupted; اِنْفَجَرَت عَجَلَةُ السَيّارة the tyre of the car has blown out; اِنْفَجَرَت الأَزْمةُ the crisis has come to a head 2▸ [مُتَفَجِّراتٌ] to blow up, to explode; to go off, to detonate; اِنْفَجَرَ المَبْنَى the building has exploded

فَجْر *n* dawn, daybreak, early morning; اِنْبلاج الفَجْرِ break of dawn; صَلاة الفَجْرِ morning prayer; سورة الفَجْر The Break of Day (*Sura 89*); عند طُلوع الفَجْرِ ,في الفَجْرِ at daybreak, at the break of day; خُيوط الفَجْرِ الأولى the first light of day; طَلَعَ الفَجْرُ morning has broken

فاجِر *adj* |فَجَرة ,فُجّار| depraved, profligate

فاجِرة *n* |فَواجِرُ| loose woman, adulteress

فُجور *n* licentiousness, debauchery; مَشَى في طَرِيقِ الفِسْقِ والفُجورِ to lead a dissolute life

الفُجَيْرة *n* Fujairah (*one of the United Arab Emirates*)

اِنْفِجار *n* |اِنْفِجارات| 1▸ [اِخْتِراق، فَرْقَعة] explosion; eruption, outbreak, outburst; اِنْفِجار نَوَوِيّ nuclear explosion; اِنْفِجار ضَخْم \ عَنِيف a huge explosion; اِنْفِجار بُرْكانٍ volcanic eruption; قابِل للانْفِجارِ explosive; أَصْداء الانْفِجاراتِ the sound of the explosions; الانْفِجار العَظِيم the Big Bang 2▸ (*fig*) outburst, burst; اِنْفِجار غَضَبٍ \ عُنْفٍ an outburst of rage/violence; اِنْفِجار سُكّانِيّ \ دِيموغْرافِيّ population explosion

اِنْفِجارِيّ *adj* explosive; صَوْت اِنْفِجارِيّ (*Ling*) occlusive, plosive; مُحَرِّك اِنْفِجارِيّ internal combustion engine

تَفَجُّر *n* explosion; outbreak, outburst, eruption; تَفَجُّر الاضْطِراباتِ \ الأَحْداثِ the outbreak of disturbances/incidents

تَفْجير *n* |تَفْجيرات| blowing up, detonation

تَفْجيرِيّ *adj* explosive, bombing; مادّة تَفْجيرِيّة explosive material

مُتَفَجِّر A *adj* explosive; مَوادّ مُتَفَجِّرة explosives; وَضْع مُتَفَجِّر an explosive situation B *n* |مُتَفَجِّرات| explosive; شِحْنة مُتَفَجِّراتٍ an explosive charge; وَضَعَ مُتَفَجِّراتٍ to place explosives; قامَ بِتَفْجِيرِ المُتَفَجِّراتِ to detonate explosives

مُفَجِّر *n* 1▸ [آلة] detonator, switch 2▸ [شَخْص] bomber

فَجَعَ *v* |a; فَجْع| to afflict, to distress, to hurt; فَجَعَهُ مَوْتُ أَبِيهِ he was stricken by the death of his father

أَفْجَعَ *v* to torment, to agonize; to distress, to grieve; أَفْجَعَ أَخِي خَبَرُ وَفاةِ المَلِكِ news of the king's death distressed my brother

تَفَجَّعَ *v* to be tormented, to be agonized; to be afflicted, to be distressed; تَفَجَّعْتُ للمُصِيبةِ التي حَصَلَتْ I was painfully afflicted by the disaster

فاجِع *adj* painful, distressing, grievous; خَبَر فاجِع tragic news

فاجِعة *n* |فَواجِعُ| misfortune, disaster, catastrophe; drama, tragedy

فَجِيعة *n* |فَجائِعُ| misfortune, disaster, catastrophe; drama, tragedy

مُفْجِع *adj* painful, grievous; tragic; حادِث مُفْجِع a tragic accident; خَبَر مُفْجِع tragic news

مَفْجوع *adj* tormented, distressed

فُجْل ,فِجْل *n* |فُجول| radish; فُجْل الخَيْلِ horseradish

فَجا *v* |u; فَجْو| to open (up)

وَضَعَ شَخْصاً \ شَيْئاً مَوْضِعَ ,أَخْضَعَ شَخْصاً \ شَيْئاً للفَحْصِ فَحْصٍ to put sb/sth to the test

فاحِص *n* investigator, researcher

اِسْتَفْحَلَ *v* to escalate; to worsen, to become worse, to deteriorate; to increase; اِسْتَفْحَلَ المَرَضُ the illness has grown worse; اِسْتَفْحَلَت المُشْكِلةُ the problem has escalated

فَحْل *n* |فُحول, فُحولة| stud, stallion; potent male

فُحولة *n* potency, manliness, virility

اِسْتِفْحال *n* escalation; worsening, deterioration; increase; اِسْتِفْحال العُنْفِ the escalation of violence; اِسْتِفْحال الجَريمةِ an increase in crime (rates); اِسْتِفْحال الوَضْعِ \ المَرَضِ the seriousness of the situation/illness

مُسْتَفْحِل *adj* serious, grave; overwhelming

فَحِمَ *v* |a; فَحْم| to be dumbfounded, to be beyond speech

فَحُمَ *v* |u; فُحومة, فُحوم| to be/become black

فَحَّمَ *v* to char, to carbonize; فَحَّمَت النارُ الخَشَبَ the fire has charred the wood

أَفْحَمَ *v* to refute, to score off; to silence with arguments

تَفَحَّمَ *v* to char, to carbonize; تَفَحَّمَتْ أَجْسامُ الضَحايا the bodies of the casualties were completely charred

فَحْم *n* |فُحومات| coal; charcoal; فَحْم حَجَرِيّ coal; فَحْم نَباتِيّ peat; فَحْم مُنَشَّط activated carbon; فَحْم الخَشَبِ \ الحَطَبِ charcoal; مَنْجَم فَحْمٍ coal mine; أَحْرَقَ \ اِسْتَعْمَلَ الفَحْمَ to burn coal; عَمِلَ بالفَحْمِ to run on coal

فاحِم *adj* coal-black, pitch-black

فَحّام *n* coalman

فَحْمِيّ *adj* coal (*before n*)

مُفَحِّم *n* carburetter (BrE), carburetor (AmE)

فَحْوى *n* |f; فَحاوى, فَحاوٍ| meaning, sense, connotation; import, tenor, purport; فَحْوى إيجابِيّة \ سَلْبِيّة a positive/negative connotation; فَحْوى الرِسالةِ the tenor of the letter; أَعْطى كَلامَهُ فَحْوى مُعَيَّنةً to give one's words a certain meaning

فَخَتَ *v* |a; فَخْت| to drill through, to perforate, to pierce

فَخَّخَ *v* to rig with explosives; to booby-trap

فَجْوة *n* |فَجَوات, فِجاء| ① [شَقّ] gap, opening, aperture; distance; فَجْوة حَضارِيّة cultural gap; الفَجْوة التِقْنِيّة the technological gap; الفَجْوة الرَقْمِيّة the digital divide; الفَجْوة بين الأَغْنِياءِ والفُقَراءِ the gap between rich and poor; أَغْلَقَ فَجْوةً to close a gap; سَدَّ فَجْوةً to fill a gap; قَلَّصَ \ ضَيَّقَ الفَجْوة to narrow the gap; زادَ الفَجْوةَ اتِّساعاً to widen the gap ② [اِنْقِسام] rift, split

أَفْحَج *adj* |dipt; فُحْج| bow-legged

فَحَّ *v* |i-u; فَحّ, فَحيح| to hiss; to blow

فَحيح *n* hiss, hissing; فَحيح الأَفْعى the hissing of a snake; هَمَسَ بِفَحيحٍ \ كالفَحيحِ to whisper in a hiss

فَحَشَ *v* |u; فُحْش| to be excessive, to be exorbitant, to be extravagant

فَحُشَ *v* |u; فُحْش| to be obscene, to be vulgar

أَفْحَشَ *v* to behave in an obscene way; أَفْحَشَ في قَوْلِهِ to use obscene language

فُحْش *n* obscenity

فاحِش *adj* ① [بَذيء] obscene, indecent, vulgar; shameless; قَوْل فاحِش obscene language; شَيْء فاحِش obscenity ② [مُتَجاوِز الحَدَّ] obscene, exorbitant, excessive, extravagant; مَبْلَغ فاحِش an outrageous sum (of money); ثَراء فاحِش obscene wealth

فاحِشة *n* |فَواحِشُ| ① [اِمْرَأة سَيِّئة الأَخْلاقِ] harlot, prostitute ② [قَوْل أو فِعْل شَنيع] outrage, indecent behaviour

فَحْشاء *n* |dipt f| indecent behaviour; الفَحْشاء والمُنْكَر obscenity and evil

فَحَصَ *v* |a; فَحْص| to examine, to test, to check; فَحَصَ مَريضاً to examine a patient; فَحَصَ البِضاعة to examine the merchandise; فَحَصَ فَحْصاً دَقيقاً to perform a detailed examination

تَفَحَّصَ *v* to examine, to check; تَفَحَّصَ إِمْكانِيّةً to explore a possibility; تَفَحَّصَ جَوازَ سَفَرٍ to check a passport

فَحْص *n* |فُحوص| examination, investigation, test; فَحْص طِبِّيّ a medical examination; فَحْص شامِل a thorough investigation; فَحْص مَخْبَرِيّ lab test; نَتيجة فَحْصٍ the result of a test; حُجْرة فَحْصٍ examination room; إِعادة الفَحْصِ re-examination; أَجْرى فَحْصاً to carry out an investigation;

فَخّ *n* |فُخوخ ,فِخاخ| trap, snare, catch; وَقَعَ في فَخٍّ to fall into a trap; نَصَبَ فَخًّا to set a trap

تَفْخيخ *n* booby trap

مُفَخَّخ *adj* rigged with explosives; booby-trapped; سَيّارة مُفَخَّخة car bomb

‹ **فَخْذ ,فَخِذ** *n* |f; أَفْخاذ| thigh, upper leg; الفَخِذ اليُسْرى \ اليُمْنى the left/right upper leg; المِنْطَقة ما بين الفَخِذَيْن crotch

‹ **فَخَر** *v* |a; فَخْر| to be proud, to pride oneself; to brag, to boast; فَخَرَ بِشَيْءٍ to be proud of sth; فَخَرَ بِابْنِهِ to be proud of one's son; فَخَرَ بِتَجْرِبَتِهِ (الطَويلةِ) to pride oneself on one's (extensive) experience

فاخَرَ *v* to brag, to boast; to be proud, to pride oneself; فَخَرَ بِمَعْرِفَتِهِ to boast about one's knowledge

تَفَخَّرَ *v* to be proud, to be haughty

تَفاخَرَ *v* to boast, to brag; to show off; to be proud, to pride oneself; تَفاخَرَ بِشَيْءٍ to take pride in sth

افْتَخَرَ *v* to be proud, to pride oneself; to boast, to brag

فَخْر *n* pride; لَيْسَ هُناكَ مَدْعاةٌ لِلفَخْرِ there's nothing to be proud of; بِكُلِّ فَخْرٍ وَاعْتِزازٍ with pride, proudly

فاخِر *adj* |فَواخِرُ| excellent, magnificent, superb; luxury, exquisite; شِقّة فاخِرة a luxury apartment; أَطْعِمة فاخِرة exquisite food; بَيْت \ بِناية فاخِر(ة) a stately house/building; وَجْبة فاخِرة a fancy meal

فاخورة *n* |فاخورات ,فَواخير| pottery

فاخوريّ *n* potter

فَخّار *n* ceramics, pottery, earthenware; صانِع الفَخّارِ potter

فِخارة *n* pottery, ceramics

فَخّاريّ **A** *adj* earthen, ceramic
B *n* potter

فَخّاريّات *n pl* earthenware, pottery

فَخْريّ *adj* honorary; لَقَب فَخْريّ honorary title; دُكْتور فَخْريّ honorary doctor; دُكْتوراه فَخْرِيّة honorary doctorate; قُنْصُل فَخْريّ honorary consul

فَخور *adj* proud; كانَ فَخوراً بِشَيْءٍ to be proud of sth; كانَ فَخوراً بِابْنِهِ to be proud of one's son

افْتِخار *n* pride; بِكُلِّ افْتِخارٍ with pride, proudly; قالَ لي بِافْتِخارٍ إنّ ... he told me proudly that ...

أَفْخَر *adj* |dipt| most beautiful, best; ارْتَدَت أَفْخَرَ ما لَدَيْها من ثِيابٍ she put on her best clothes; قارورة من أَفْخَرِ أَنْواعِ النَبيذِ a bottle of the very best wine

مُتَفاخِر **A** *adj* proud
B *n* boaster, braggart

مُفاخَرة *n* bragging, boasting

مُفْتَخِر *adj* proud; chic, exquisite

مَفْخَرة *n* |مَفاخِرُ| showpiece, object of pride; إنَّهُ مَفْخَرةُ أُمِّهِ he is the pride of his mother

‹ **فَخْفَخَ** *v* |i; فَخْفَخة| to boast, to brag

فَخْفَخة *n* bragging, boasting; ostentation, show

‹ **فَخُمَ** *v* |u; فَخامة| to have style, to have elegance; to be stately, to be imposing

فَخَّمَ *v* **1** [عَظَّمَ] to glorify, to praise, to honour **2** (Ling) to pronounce emphatically

فَخْم *adj* |فِخام| stately, majestic, luxury

فَخامة *n* **1** (Title) Excellency; صاحِب الفَخامةِ His Excellency; فَخامة الرَئيسِ His Excellency, the President **2** [عِظَم] style, grandeur; luxury

تَفْخيم *n* **1** [تَعْظيم] glorification **2** (Ling) velarization

مُفَخَّم *adj* **1** [طَنّان] bombastic, pompous, swollen; لُغة مُفَخَّمة inflated language, bombast **2** (Ling) emphatic, velarized

‹ **فَدَحَ** *v* |a; فَدْح| to weigh (heavily), to oppress; فَدَحَهُ الدَيْنُ the debt weighed heavily on him

فادِح *adj* sizeable, substantial, enormous; خَسارة فادِحة a heavy loss; أَضْرار فادِحة substantial damage; كَذِب فادِح a blatant lie; ثَمَن فادِح an exorbitant price; ارْتَكَبَ خَطأً فادِحاً to be greatly mistaken

فادِحة *n* |فَوادِحُ| catastrophe, disaster

فَداحة *n* voluminosity, largeness

‹ **فَدَخَ** *v* |a; فَدْخ| to break, to crush

‹ **فَدَمَ** *v* |i; فَدْم| to muzzle, to gag

فَدْم *adj* |فِدام| stupid, dumb

فِدام *n* clamp, brace, clasp

فَدامة *n* cretinism

فَدَّنَ *v* to fatten (up)

فادِن *n* |فَوادِنُ| **1** (Naut) plumb line, lead line, sounding line **2** (Tools) plumb line

فَدّان *n* |فَدادينُ| **1** (Meas) feddan (*a square measure of about 4,200 square metres*) **2** [ثَوْرانِ] a yoke of two oxen (*pulling a plough*)

فَدى *v* |i; فِداء ,فِدًى| to ransom, to redeem, to buy freedom; to buy off; to (set) free; فدى عَبْداً to buy a slave's freedom; فدى سَجيناً to ransom a prisoner

فادى *v* to buy freedom, to ransom, to redeem

تَفادى *v* to avoid, to evade, to steer clear; to prevent, to avert; تَفادى أنْ ... to avoid ...; تَفادى وُقوعَ حادِثٍ to avoid an accident; تَفادى الضَرائِبَ to evade taxes

افْتَدى *v* to buy (one's) freedom, to redeem (oneself), to ransom (oneself); to buy off; افْتَداهُ بِنَفْسِهِ \ بِحَياتِهِ he paid for it with his life

فادٍ *n* **1** [مُخَلِّص] redeemer **2** [اسْم شَخْصيّ] فادي Fadi

فِداء *n* buying off, redemption; ransom; كَبْش الفِداء scapegoat; كانَ كَبْشَ الفِداءِ to be a scapegoat; ماتَ فِداءً لِلوَطَنِ \ لِلقَضِيَّةِ to die for one's country/cause

فِدائيّ *n* guerrilla, resistance fighter; الفِدائيّونَ الفِلَسْطينيّونَ Palestinian fedayeen

فِدًى ,فَدًى *n* ransom; جُعِلْتُ فِداكَ! could I but sacrifice myself for you!

فِدْية *n* |فِدًى ,فِدْيات| buying off; ransom (money), redemption money; فِدْية كَبيرة \ ضَخْمة a large ransom; فِدْية مِقْدارُها ٢٥٠٠٠٠ دولار a $250,000 ransom; طالَبَ بِفِدْيةٍ \ دَفَعَ فِدْيةً to demand/pay a ransom; طَلَبَ فِدْيةً لِإطْلاقِ سَراحِ شَخْصٍ to demand a ransom for sb's release

تَفادٍ *n* avoidance; prevention; تَفادِياً لِشَيْءٍ in order to avoid sth

فَذّ *adj* |أَفْذاذ| unique, only, singular; شَخْصيّة فَذّة a great mind; هو فَذٌّ في شَجاعَتِهِ he is unique in his courage

فَذْلَكَ *v* |i; فَذْلَكة| to nag, to harp, to whine

فَذْلَكة *n* **1** [تَذَمُّر] nagging, harping; فَذْلَكة لُغَويّة linguistic nitpicking **2** [تَلْخيص] recapitulation; فَذْلَكة المُوازَنة draft budget

الفُرات *n* the Euphrates (River)

فَرانْدة *n* veranda

الفْرانْكو *n* Franco-Arabic (*Arabic written with Latin characters and numbers on the Internet and phones*)

فَراوْلة *n* (Egypt, NA) strawberry

فَرْبَيون *n* (Bot) spurge

فَرَجَ *v* |i; فَرْج| **1** [فَتَحَ] to open; to make an opening **2** [أَراحَ] |عن| to relieve, to solace, to lighten; فَرَجَ عن شَخْصٍ الأَحْزانَ to relieve sb's distress

فَرَّجَ *v* to open

أَفْرَجَ *v* |عن| to release, to set free, to discharge; أَفْرَجَ عن الأَسْرى to release the prisoners of war; أَفْرَجَ القاضي عن المُتَّهَم بِكَفالةٍ ماليّةٍ the judge released the suspect on bail; أَفْرَجَ عن بَضائِعَ to release goods (*from customs*)

تَفَرَّجَ *v* **1** [نَظَرَ] |على| to look (at/on), to view, to watch; تَفَرَّجَ على التِلْفاز to watch television; تَفَرَّجَ على الصُوَرِ to look at pictures; تَفَرَّجَ على ما في المَحَلِّ to look round (in) the shop **2** [زالَ] to disappear; قد تَفَرَّجَ الهَمُّ والغَمُّ the worries have disappeared **3** [شَقَّ] to split, to crack

انْفَرَجَ *v* **1** [انْفَتَحَ] to open **2** [زالَ] to disappear; انْفَرَجَت الأَزْمةُ the crisis has come to an end

فَرْج *n* |فُروج| **1** (Anat) vagina **2** [شَقّ] crack, split; opening

فَرَج *n* **1** [انْفِراج] relief, solace; بعد كُلِّ شِدّةٍ فَرَجٌ ,الفَرَجُ بعد الشِدّةِ the darkest hour is that before the dawn **2** [اسْم شَخْصيّ] Faraj (*male given name*)

فُرْجة *n* |فُرَج| **1** [مَصْدَر] watching, viewing, onlooking **2** [مَنْظَر] spectacle, sight, scene **3** [شَقّ] crack, split; opening

فَرّوج *n coll* |فَراريجُ| chick, young chicken

إفْراج *n* |إفْراجات| release, discharge, unblocking; الإفْراج من السِجْنِ release from prison; الإفْراج عن بَضائِعَ مُحْتَجَزةٍ the release of confiscated goods; إذْن إفْراجٍ release permit (*of goods by customs*); شَهادة إفْراجٍ ضَريبيٍّ tax exemption certificate

انْفِراج *n* |انْفِراجات| **1** (Pol) political thaw, détente; الانْفِراج في العَلاقاتِ بين الشَرْقِ والغَرْبِ the détente in relations between East and West **2** [فَرَج] relief; انْفِراج حول شَيْءٍ relief about sth

تَفاريج *n pl* |dipt| openings, gaps; تَفاريج الأَصابِعِ the gaps between the fingers

تَفْريج *n* relief, solace

مُتَفَرِّج *n* spectator, viewer, watcher; تَواجَدَ بين المُتَفَرِّجِينَ to be among the audience; وَقَفَ مَوْقِفَ المُتَفَرِّجِ to assume the attitude of an onlooker

مُنْفَرِج *adj* **1** [مَفْتوح] (wide) open; كانَتْ عَيْناهُ مُنْفَرِجَتَيْنِ his eyes were open; زاوِية مُنْفَرِجة an obtuse angle **2** [مُسْتَريح] relaxed

فِرْجار *n* |فَراجيرُ| (pair of) compasses

فِرْجَوْن *n* brush

فَرِحَ *v* |a; فَرَح| to rejoice, to be/become happy; فَرِحَ بِشَيْءٍ to be happy with sth

فَرَّحَ *v* to make happy, to gladden

أَفْرَحَ *v* to make happy, to gladden; to delight, to rejoice, to cheer (up); يُفْرِحُني أَنْ أَسْمَعَ هذا I'm glad to hear that; أَفْرَحَ شَخْصاً to cheer sb (up); أَفْرَحَ شَخْصاً بِشَيْءٍ to make sb happy with sth

فَرَح *n* |أَفْراح| **1** [سُرور] joy, gladness, elation; happiness, merriment; فَرَح بِشَيْءٍ joy over sth; من الفَرَحِ out of joy; شارَكَ شَخْصاً أَفْراحَهُ to share in sb's joy; أَطْلَقَ صَيْحةَ الفَرَحِ to utter a cry of joy; ضَحِكَ بِفَرَحٍ to laugh cheerfully; كادَ يَطيرُ من شِدّةِ الفَرَحِ to be practically leaping for joy; لا تَكادُ الدُنْيا تَسَعُهُ من شِدّةِ الفَرَحِ to be beside oneself with joy **2** [زِفاف] wedding (party)

فَرِح *adj* cheerful, merry, happy; أَنا فَرِحٌ لَكَ! I'm happy for you!; كانَ فَرِحاً بِشَيْءٍ to be pleased with sth

فَرْحان *adj* |dipt; فَرْحى، فَراحى| glad, happy, pleased; عادَ فَرْحانَ to return happily

فَرْحة *n* |فَرَحات| joy, delight, pleasure; قَضى على فَرْحة شَخْصٍ to rain on sb's parade

مُفْرِح *adj* joyful, happy, pleasant; خَبَر مُفْرِح good news, glad tidings

فَرَّخَ *v* **1** [البَيْضَ] to hatch **2** [الدَجاجةُ] to incubate; to have chicks; فَرَّخَ الإرْهابَ to breed terrorism

أَفْرَخَ *v* **1** [البَيْضُ] to hatch **2** [الدَجاجةُ] to incubate; to have chicks

فَرْخ *n* |أَفْراخ، فُروخ، فِراخ| **1** [صَغير الطائِرِ] chick, chicken **2** (Bot) shoot, stolon, sprout **3** [نَوْع من السَمَكِ] bass

فَرّاخة *n* incubator, hatcher, brooder

فَرَدَ، فَرُدَ *v* |u; فَرْد، فُرود| **1** [تَوَحَّدَ] to withdraw, to retire; to be single, to be alone; to do alone; فَرَدَ بالرَأْيِ to be alone in one's opinion; فَرَدَ عن شَيْءٍ to withdraw from sth **2** [نَشَرَ] to unfold; to spread (out); فَرَدَ الصَحيفةَ to open the newspaper

أَفْرَدَ *v* **1** [خَصَّصَ] to allot, to allocate, to devote; أَفْرَدَ صَفْحةً كامِلةً لِخَبَرٍ to devote an entire page to a news **2** [عَزَلَ] to select; to isolate, to set aside; أَفْرَدوا المُجْرِمَ في زِنْزانةٍ they put the criminal in an isolation cell

تَفَرَّدَ *v* to be alone; to do alone; تَفَرَّدَ بِفِعْلِ شَيْءٍ to do sth by oneself

انْفَرَدَ *v* **1** [انْعَزَلَ] to separate, to isolate, to segregate **2** [تَوَحَّدَ] to be alone; to do alone; انْفَرَدَتْ هذه الصَحيفةُ بِنَشْرِ الخَبَرِ this newspaper had exclusive coverage of the news

اسْتَفْرَدَ *v* **1** [تَوَحَّدَ] to be alone; to do alone **2** [اخْتارَ] to select, to single out

فَرْد **A** *n* |أَفْراد، فُرادى| **1** [شَخْص] individual, person; هذا يَنْطَبِقُ على الفَرْدِ والمُجْتَمَعِ this applies to the individual and the society; أَفْراد الأُسْرةِ family members; فَرْداً فَرْداً one by one **2** [حِذاء، جَوْرَب، إلخ] twin, single (*of a pair*) **B** *adj* |أَفْراد، فُرادى| solitary, lone; single; الرَجُل الفَرْد the solitary man

فَرادة *n* uniqueness; ذو الفَرادةِ unique

فُرادى *adv* see فَرْدان

فَرْدان *adj* |فُرادى| apart, separate, single; فُرادى one at a time, one by one

فَرْداني *adj* single, individual

مُفْرَدة *n* vocabulary item; جَدْوَل مُفْرَداتٍ list of words, word list; مُفْرَدات vocabulary; مُفْرَدات اللُغةِ العَرَبيّةِ the Arabic lexicon; دِراسة المُفْرَداتِ lexicology; حَفِظَ المُفْرَداتِ to memorize words

مُنْفَرِد *adj* single, individual; isolated, detached, separate; حالة مُنْفَرِدة an isolated incident; اتِّفاق مُنْفَرِد a unilateral agreement; عَزَفَ مُنْفَرِداً to play solo

فِرْدَوْس *n* |فَراديسُ| ⟨1⟩ [جَنّة] paradise ⟨2⟩ [اِسْم شَخْصيّ] Firadaus (*female given name*)

فِرْدَوْسيّ *adj* heavenly, paradisal; حُلْم فِرْدَوْسيّ heavenly dream

فَرَّ *v* |i; فَرّ, فِرار, مَفَرّ| to flee, to escape (from), to run off; فَرَّ السُكّانُ the inhabitants have fled; فَرَّ من السِجْنِ to escape from prison; فَرَّ من البِلادِ to flee the country; فَرَّ من وَجْهِ العَدالةِ to be on the run from justice

أَفَرَّ *v* to put to flight

افْتَرَّ *v* ⟨1⟩ [تَلَأْلَأَ] to glitter, to shimmer, to flash ⟨2⟩ [تَبَسَّمَ] *to show one's teeth when smiling*

فارّ *adj* fugitive, fleeing

فَرّ *n* escape, flight; بين الكَرِّ والفَرِّ in fits and starts

فِرار *n* flight, escape; لاذَ بالفِرارِ to flee, to seek safety in flight; أَجْبَرَ شَخْصاً على الفِرارِ to put sb to flight

مَفَرّ *n* way out; لا مَفَرَّ مِنْهُ unavoidable, inevitable; لم يَعُدْ هُناكَ مَفَرٌّ there's no way out; كانَ ضَروريًّا لا مَفَرَّ مِنْهُ it was an inevitable necessity; إنَّهُ قَدَرٌ لا مَفَرَّ مِنْهُ it is an inevitable fate

فَرَزَ *v* |i; فَرْز| ⟨1⟩ [صَنَّفَ] to sort (out), to sift, to classify; فَرَزَ الرَسائِلَ الوارِدةَ to sort the incoming mail; فَرَزَ حَسَبَ اللَوْنِ to sort by colour; فَرَزَ الصُوَرَ to sort pictures; فَرَزَ أَصْواتَ الناخِبينَ to sort through the votes ⟨2⟩ [فَصَلَ] to secrete, to excrete; to separate; فَرَزَ القِشْدةَ to skim the cream off

أَفْرَزَ *v* to secrete, to excrete; أَفْرَزَ سائِلاً \ اللُعابَ to secrete fluid/mucus; أَفْرَزَ الحَليبَ to lactate; أَفْرَزَ هُرْموناتٍ to produce hormones; أَفْرَزَ عَرَقاً to sweat, to perspire

فَرْز *n* sorting, sifting; فَرْز الأَصْواتِ the sorting of votes

فارِزة *n* |فَوارِزُ| comma

فَرّازة *n* sorting machine, sorter

فَرْدانيّة *n* individualism

فَرْدة *n* twin, single (*of a pair*); فَرْدة حِذاءٍ a (single) shoe; فَرْدة وَلَقِيَتْ أُخْتَها (Tunisia) ≈ two peas in a pod (*a single that has found its twin*)

فَرْديّ **A** *adj* ⟨1⟩ [خاصّ] individual, personal; تَرْتيب فَرْديّ individual ranking; تَعْليم فَرْديّ individual teaching; عَمَليّة فَرْديّة an individual action; حَقّ فَرْديّ an individual right; حُكْم \ سُلْطة فَرْديّ(ة) absolute power ⟨2⟩ [مُنْفَرِد] single; لُعْبة فَرْديّة singles; single-player game; أَداء فَرْديّ solo performance, one-man performance ⟨3⟩ [رَقْم] odd; عَدَد فَرْديّ an odd number

B *n* ⟨1⟩ [شَخْص مُنْعَزِل] (solitary) individual, individualist ⟨2⟩ (Sport) singles; فَرْديّ سَيِّداتٍ \ رِجالٍ ladies'/men's singles

فَرْديّة *n* individuality

فَريد *adj* |فَرائِدُ| only, single, unique; مُناسَبة \ فُرْصة فَريدة a unique opportunity; فَريد من نَوْعِهِ one of a kind

فَريدة *n* |فَرائِدُ| jewel, gem, precious stone

إفْراد *n* individualization

أَفْراديّ, إفْراديّ *adj* individual, personal; زِنْزانة إفْراديّة isolation cell; قَيْد إفْراديّ personal identification registration

الفَرْديّة *n* individualism, individuality; الفَرْديّة في الأَداءِ individualism

انْفِراد *n* solitude, loneliness; isolation, seclusion; على انْفِرادٍ alone, in private; individually; كُلّ قَضيّةٍ على انْفِرادٍ each case individually

انْفِراديّ *adj* individualistic, solitary; one-sided, unilateral; solo (*before n*); حَبْس انْفِراديّ solitary confinement; سُلوك انْفِراديّ individualistic behaviour; قامَ بِعَمَليّةٍ انْفِراديّةٍ to act alone

انْفِراديّة *n* individualism

مُتَفَرِّد *adj* unique, only, single

مُفْرَد **A** *adj* ⟨1⟩ (Gram) singular; كَلِمة مُفْرَدة a singular word ⟨2⟩ [فَرْد] single; بِمُفْرَدِهِ alone, by oneself; تُقيمُ \ تَسْكُنُ بِمُفْرَدِها she lives alone ⟨3⟩ [رَقْم] odd

B *n* ⟨1⟩ (Gram) singular; مُفْرَد كَلِمةِ "أَطْفالٍ" هو "طِفْلٌ" the singular of 'children' is 'child'; في صيغةِ المُفْرَدِ in the singular (form) ⟨2⟩ [بَنْد] item, topic

إفراز *n* |إفرازات| **1** (Med) production; secretion, excretion, discharge; إفْرازات secretion **2** [نتيجة] result

مُفْرَز *adj* secreted

مَفْرَزة *n* |مَفارِزُ| party, group, team; مَفْرَزة من الشُرْطةِ a squad of policemen

‹ **فِرْزان** *n* queen (*in chess*)

‹ **فِرْزَجة** *n* diaphragm, pessary

1‹ **فَرَسَ** *v* |i; فَرْس| to kill, to tear (*prey*); فَرَسَ الأَسَدُ فريسَتَهُ the lion mauled its prey

تَفَرَّسَ *v* |في| to gaze at; to look at, to eye; تَفَرَّسَ في شَيْءٍ \ شَخْصٍ to gaze at sth/sb

اِفْتَرَسَ *v* to catch prey (*and tear it up*); اِفْتَرَسَ الأَسَدُ فريسَتَهُ the lion mauled its prey

فارِس *n* |فَوارِسُ, فُرْسان| horseman, rider; knight; فُرْسان cavalry; المُمارِسُ يَغْلِبُ الفارِسَ practice makes perfect

فارسة *n* horsewoman

فِراسة *n* acuteness, discernment

فَرَس *n* |أَفْراس| horse; mare; فَرَس جافِل a skittish horse; فَرَس النَبيِّ hippopotamus; فَرَس البَحْرِ sea horse; فَرَس النَهْرِ praying mantis; يَصْهَلُ الفَرَسُ the horse neighs

فُروسيّة *n* **1** (Sport) horsemanship, equitation, riding; نادي \ مَدْرَسة الفُروسيّةِ riding school, manege **2** [وسام] knighthood

فَريسة *n* |فَرائِسُ| **1** [حَيَوان] prey, game; طارَدَ فَريسةً to stalk prey; اِلْتَهَمَ التِمْساحُ فَريسَتَهُ the crocodile devoured its prey **2** [ضَحيّة] prey, victim; وَقَعَ فَريسةً سَهْلةً to be an easy prey; وَقَعَ فَريسةً لليَأْسِ to fall prey to despair; وَقَعَ فَريسةً بِيَدِ الأَعْداءِ to fall victim to the enemy

مُفْتَرِس *adj* predatory, rapacious; نَباتات مُفْتَرِسة carnivorous plants; حَيَوان مُفْتَرِس predator

مِفْراس *n* scanner

2‹ **فارِس** *n* |dipt| Persia

فارِسيّ **A** *adj* |فُرْس| Persian; (اللُغة) الفارِسيّة Persian-Farsi (*language*)

B *n* |فُرْس| Persian (*person*)

فارسيّة *n* Persian (*language*)

الفُرْس *n* |f| Persia; بِلادُ الفُرْسِ Persia

‹ **فَرْسَخ** *n* |فَراسِخُ| parasang (*linear measurement, 6 to 8 kilometres*)

‹ **فَرَشَ** *v* |i; فَرْش| **1** [بَسَطَ] to spread (out); فَرَشَ شَيْئاً to spread sth (out); فَرَشَ الطائِرُ جَناحَيْه the bird spread its wings **2** [أَثَّثَ] to equip, to furnish **3** [بَلَّطَ] to pave

فَرَّشَ *v* **1** [بَسَطَ] to spread (out); فَرَّشَ الطائِرُ the bird spread its wings **2** [أَثَّثَ] to equip, to furnish; فَرَّشَ البَيْتَ بالسَجّادِ to furnish the house with carpets

اِفْتَرَشَ *v* to stretch out on; اِفْتَرَشَ الأَرْضَ to sleep on the floor

فَرْش *n* |فُروش| **1** [أَثاث] furnishing; interior, (suite of) furniture; فَرْش حَديث \ عَصْريّ a modern interior **2** [سَجّادة] carpet, rug

فَراش **A** *n* [الطاحونِ] mill wheel

B *n coll* (Zool) butterfly; فَراشة لَيْليّة moth; دودة الفَراشةِ caterpillar; اِصْطادَ الفَراشَ to catch butterflies; أَطْيَش من فَراشةٍ reckless

فَرّاش *n* (Egypt) manservant, cleaner

فِراش *n* |أَفْرِشة, فُرُش| bed; فِراش وَثير \ مُريح a soft/comfortable bed; فِراش المَرَضِ sickbed; فِراش المَوْتِ deathbed; لَوازِم الفِراشِ bedclothes; فِراش الزَوْجيّةِ the conjugal bed; مُلازِم الفِراشِ bedridden; لَزِمَ الفِراشَ, كانَ مُلْزَماً بالفِراشِ to be confined to bed; أَوى إلى فِراشِهِ to go to bed; رَقَدَ في الفِراشِ to lay in bed; اِسْتَلْقى على الفِراشِ to lay stretched out on the bed

فَرّاشة *n* housekeeper

فُرْشاة *n* **1** [للتَنْظيفِ] brush; فُرْشاة الأَسْنانِ toothbrush; فُرْشاة وَجاروف, وَمِجْرَفة dustpan and brush **2** [رَسْمٍ] paintbrush; فُرْشاة الرَسْمِ paintbrush

فُرْشة *n* |فُرَش| **1** [للتَنْظيفِ] brush; فُرْشة مَلابِسَ clothes brush; فُرْشة الشَعْرِ hairbrush; فُرْشة أَسْنانٍ toothbrush; فُرْشة حِلاقةٍ shaving brush **2** [رَسْمٍ] paintbrush

مِفْرَش *n* |مَفارِشُ| tablecloth, cloth

مَفْروش *adj* furnished; شَقّة مَفْروشة a furnished apartment; مَفْروشات furniture, household effects

‹ **فَرْشَحَ** *v* |i; فَرْشَحة| to stand straddle-legged, to straddle

افْتَرَضَ أنْ يَكونَ ...; افْتَرَضَ أنّ \ أنْ ... to assume that ...; يُفْتَرَضُ أنْ تَعْرِفَ ذلك صَحيحاً to assume that it is right; you're supposed to know that **2** [أَجْبَرَ] |على| to impose on/upon; افْتَرَضَ شَيْئاً على شَخْصٍ to impose sth upon sb

فَرْض *n* |فُروض| **1** [افْتِراض] assumption, supposition; presupposition; على فَرْضِ أنّ ... assuming that ..., on the assumption that ...; فَرْضاً presupposing (that); على أَحْسَنِ الفُروضِ at the best of times **2** (Islam) religious duty **3** [حِصّة] inheritance, portion

فُرْضة *n* |فُرَض| notch, nick

فَرْضيّ *adj* hypothetical

فَرْضيّة *n* supposition, assumption; hypothesis, theory, proposition; presupposition; فَرْضيّة صَحيحة \ خاطِئة a correct/an incorrect assumption; فَرْضيّة راجِحة a plausible hypothesis; أَثْبَتَ \ أَكَّدَ فَرْضيّةً to confirm a hypothesis; اسْتَبْعَدَ \ رَفَضَ فَرْضيّةً to reject a hypothesis; انْطَلَقَ من الفَرْضيّةِ أنّ ... to start from the assumption that ...

فَريضة *n* |فَرائِضُ| **1** (Islam) (religious) duty; أَدّى فَريضةً to perform a religious duty **2** [حِصّة] inheritance, portion; أَصْحاب الفَرائِضِ heirs; عِلْم الفَرائِضِ law of succession

افْتِراض *n* |افْتِراضات| **1** [احْتِمال] assumption, supposition, hypothesis; presupposition; افْتِراضاً أنّ ...، على افْتِراضِ أنّ ... under the assumption that ..., assuming that ... **2** [فِكْرة مُسَلَّمة] proposition, postulate, hypothesis; افْتِراض جُزافيّ \ جَريء a bold proposition; وَضَعَ \ طَرَحَ افْتِراضاً to put forward a proposition

افْتِراضيّ *adj* hypothetical; virtual; أَمْر افْتِراضيّ a hypothetical case; سُؤال افْتِراضيّ a hypothetical question; لَوْحة مَفاتيحَ افْتِراضيّة virtual keyboard; مَكْتَب \ فَصْل افْتِراضيّ virtual office/classroom; افْتِراضيّ مَحْض purely hypothetical

مُفْتَرَض *adj* supposed, alleged, presumed; الوَريث المُفْتَرَض the alleged heir; من المُفْتَرَضِ أنّ ... it can be assumed that ...

مَفْروض *adj* **1** [إِلْزاميّ] prescribed, obliged, enforced; من المَفْروضِ أنّ ... it's necessary that ...; لَيْسَ من المَفْروضِ أنْ ... it's (really) not necessary that ...; لَيْسَ من المَفْروضِ

فُرْصة *n* |فُرَص| chance, opportunity; فُرْصة سانِحة \ مُواتِية a good opportunity; فُرْصة سَعيدة! pleased to meet you; فُرْصة تَسْجيلٍ a scoring opportunity; فُرَص عَمَلٍ job opportunities, employment; فُرْصة العُمْرِ the chance of a lifetime; تكافُؤ الفُرَصِ equal opportunities; خَلَقَ فُرَصاً to create opportunities; اغْتَنَمَ \ انْتَهَزَ \ اسْتَغَلَّ الفُرْصةَ ل ... to seize the opportunity to ...; فَوَّتَ الفُرْصةَ to let the opportunity go by; فاتَتْهُ الفُرْصةُ، تَرَكَ الفُرْصةَ تَضيعُ (مِنْهُ) he missed the opportunity; أَتاحَ لِشَخْصٍ فُرْصةَ ... \ الفُرْصةَ ل ... to give sb the opportunity to ...; لدى حُلولِ الفُرْصةِ، إنْ سَنَحَت الفُرْصةُ، إنْ أُتيحَت الفُرْصةُ when the opportunity presents itself; وَجَدَ أُتيحَتْ (لَهُ) الفُرْصةُ ل ... to get the opportunity to ...; الفُرْصةَ ل ... to find the opportunity to ...; تَحَيَّنَ الفُرْصةَ to wait for the right moment; حانَتْ فُرْصَتُكَ this is your chance, your chance has come; قد لا تَكونُ هُناكَ فُرْصةٌ أُخْرى there may not be another opportunity; في أَوَّلِ فُرْصةٍ تَسْنَحُ (لي) at the first available opportunity (for me); كانَتْ عِنْدَهُ فُرْصةٌ جَيِّدةٌ في ... he had a good chance to ...

فَريصة *n* |فَرائِصُ| pectoral muscle; جاءَ وَفَرائِصُهُ تَرْتَجِفُ \ تَرْتَعِدُ he came with shaking knees

مِفْراص *n* hacksaw

فِرْصاد *n* mulberry (tree)

فَرَضَ *v* |i; فَرْض| **1** [أَوْجَبَ] to impose, to prescribe; to oblige, to make, to force; فَرَضَ على شَخْصٍ فِعْلَ شَيْءٍ to make sb do sth; فَرَضَ شَيْئاً على شَخْصٍ to prescribe sth to sb; فَرَضَ عُقوبةً على شَخْصٍ to impose a punishment on sb; فَرَضَ ضَرائِبَ \ رُسومَ المُرورِ to levy taxes/toll; فَرَضَ نَفْسَهُ to impose oneself; فَرَضَ إرادَتَهُ على شَخْصٍ to impose one's will on sb **2** [قَدَّرَ] to assume, to presume, to suppose; فَرَضَ جَدَلاً to suppose (*as a basis for discussion*); لِنَفْرِضْ أنّ ... let's assume that ...; لِنَفْرِضْ أنّ هذه الفَرْضيّةَ صَحيحةٌ let's assume that this theory is right **3** [عَيَّنَ] to allot, to allocate, to assign **4** [حَزَّ] to cut out; فَرَضَ العودَ \ في العودِ to cut notches in a stick

أَفْرَضَ *v* to impose, to enforce

افْتَرَضَ *v* **1** [فِكْرةً مُسَلَّمةً] to assume, to presume, to suppose; to presuppose, to postulate; افْتَرَضَ شَيْئاً to suppose sth;

تَصِلَ الأُمورُ إلى هذا الحَدّ it needn't go that far ❷ [مُفْتَرَض] supposed, assumed, hypothetical

‹ **فَرَطَ** *v* |u; فَرْط| ❶ [سَبَقَ] to go ahead, to precede ❷ [أَفْلَتَ] to slip, to escape

فَرَّطَ *v* to ignore, to neglect, to omit; to waste, to squander; فَرَّطَ أَرْضَهُ to let one's land go to waste

أَفْرَطَ *v* to exaggerate, to go too far, to be excessive; أَفْرَطَ (في شَيْءٍ) to be excessive (in sth); أَفْرَطَ في تَأْنيبِ صاحِبِهِ he was excessive in rebuking his friend; أَفْرَطَ في الطَعامِ to eat to excess; أَفْرَطَ في شُرْبِ الخَمْرِ to drink too much (alcohol)

اِنْفَرَطَ *v* to come loose, to become untied; انْفَرَطَ عِقْدُهُمْ they broke up

فَرْط *n* surplus, excess; فَرْط التَفَهُّمِ a surplus of understanding; فَرْط التَنَفُّسِ hyperventilation; من فَرْطِ تَرَدُّدِهِ because of his excessive reluctance

فارِط *adj* (Mor) past, last, previous; الأُسْبوع \ السَنة الفارِط(ة) last week/year

إِفْراط *n* profusion, excess, splurge; بِإِفْراطٍ excessively; إفْراط في صَيْدِ السَمَكِ overfishing; الإفْراط في الحَسّاسيّةِ hypersensitivity; دون إفْراطٍ أو تَفْريطٍ ,لا إفْراطَ ولا تَفْريطَ (neither) too much nor too little; إفْراط في اسْتِخْدامِ الأَدْوِيةِ excessive use of medicine

تَفْريط *n* negligence, neglect, carelessness; wastefulness, squandering; دون تَفْريطٍ أو تَنازُلٍ without (any) concessions; دون إفْراطٍ أو تَفْريطٍ ,لا إفْراطَ ولا تَفْريطَ (neither) too much nor too little

مُفْرِط *adj* excessive, exaggerated, extravagant; شُرْب كُحولٍ مُفْرِط في الشَرابِ ,مُفْرِط drinking to excess; كَمّيّة مُفْرِطة an excessive amount

مُفَرِّط *adj* prodigal, extravagant, wasteful

‹ **فَرْطَحَ** *v* |i; فَرْطَحة| to broaden, to make broad, to widen

‹ **فَرَعَ** *v* |a; فَرْع ,فُروع| to stand out, to excel; to exceed, to surpass; to be long; فَرَعَ شَعْرُها his hair was long

فَرَّعَ *v* to branch, to subdivide, to split (up)

تَفَرَّعَ *v* ❶ [تَشَعَّبَ] to split (up), to branch (off); تَفَرَّعَ إلى to split into; تَفَرَّعَتْ أَغْصانُ الشَجَرةِ the tree branched out; تَفَرَّعَت المَشاكِلُ the problems expanded ❷ [كانَ فَرْعاً لَهُ] to spring, to arise; تَفَرَّعَ من \ عن to stem from

اِفْتَرَعَ *v* to deflower

فَرْع *n* |أَفْرُع ,فُروع| ❶ [شَجَرة] branch ❷ [شُعْبة] branch, arm; انْقَسَمَ إلى فُروعٍ to be split into branches; فَرْع من النَهْرِ a branch of the river; فَرْع من فُروعِ العائِلةِ a branch of the family ❸ [وكالة، مَتْجَر] branch (office), establishment; فَرْع لِشَرِكةٍ a branch office of a company; لِهَذِهِ الشَرِكةِ سِتّةُ فُروعٍ this company has six establishments; فَتَحَ \ أَغْلَقَ فَرْعاً (جَديداً) to open/close a (new) branch ❹ [مَجال] discipline, industry, division; فُروع الرِياضةِ varieties of sport; فُروع العِلْمِ branches of science

فارِع *adj* tall, big; فارِع القامةِ tall and slender

فَرْعِيّ *adj* secondary, minor, local; مَوْضوع فَرْعِيّ a minor issue; انْتِخابات فَرْعِيّة district elections; لَجْنة فَرْعِيّة sub-commission; مَجْموعة فَرْعِيّة subset; مَكْتَب فَرْعِيّ district office; سُلُطات فَرْعِيّة local authorities

تَفَرُّع *n* |تَفَرُّعات| branching, ramification, bifurcation

مُتَفَرِّع *adj* derived

‹ **فِرْعَوْن** *n* |فَراعِنة| pharaoh

فِرْعَوْنِيّ *n* pharaonic

‹ **فَرَغَ ,فَرِغَ** *v* |a; فَراغ ,فُروغ| to be done, to be finished; to be empty, to be void; فَرَغَ صَبْري I am out of patience; فَرَغَ الخَزّانُ the tank is empty; فَرَغَ من عَمَلِهِ to be finished with one's work

فَرَّغَ *v* ❶ [أَخْلى] to empty, to void; to unload, to discharge; فَرَّغَ شاحِنةً to unload a lorry (BrE) truck (AmE); فَرَّغَ بُنْدُقيّةً to empty a rifle ❷ [أَخْرَجَ] to unload, to discharge; فَرَّغَ شَحْنةً to unload cargo; فَرَّغَ البَضائِعَ to unload goods ❸ [صَبَّ] to pour out

أَفْرَغَ *v* ❶ [أَخْلى] to empty, to void, to unpack; to unload, to discharge; أَفْرَغَ كَأْساً to empty a glass; أَفْرَغَ شَنْطَتَهُ to empty one's bag; أَفْرَغَ غَيْظَهُ to vent one's anger; أَفْرَغَ حَقيبَتَهُ to unpack one's suitcase; أَفْرَغَ بُنْدُقيّةً to empty a rifle; أَفْرَغَ بَطّاريّةً to discharge a battery; أَفْرَغَ سَفينةً to discharge a ship ❷ [أَخْرَجَ] to unload, to discharge; أَفْرَغَ العُلَبَ من العَرَبةِ to unload the boxes from the cart

تفرّق *v* to spread (out), to disperse, to break up; تفرّقوا في جميعِ الجهاتِ they spread in all directions

تفارق *v* to part, to separate, to break up; هذانِ الصديقانِ لا يكادانِ يتفارقانِ these two friends are practically inseparable

افترق *v* to part, to separate, to break up; افترقنا بعد وُصولِنا we parted after our arrival

فرْق *n* |فُروق| 1 [اختِلاف] difference, distinction, contrast; فرْق كبير \ جوهريّ \ شاسع a major/substantial/an enormous difference; فرْق دقيق nuance; الفرْق بين هذا وذلك the difference between this and that; فرْق زمنيّ time difference; فرْق في السِنّ age difference; لَيْسَ هُناكَ فرْقٌ ,لا يوجَدُ فرْقٌ it makes no difference, there's no difference; لَيْسَ هُناكَ فرْقٌ لا فرْقَ بين ... و... there's no difference between ... and ...; لا فرْقَ عِنْدي بين الاخْتِيارَيْنِ I see no difference between both options 2 [مَوْضِع افتِراقِ الشعْرِ] parting

فَرَق *n* fear, fright

فِرْق *n* |فُروق| swarm, drove, herd

فارِق A *adj* distinctive, distinguishing
B *n* |فوارِق| difference, distinction; فارق شاسع an enormous difference; فارِق زمَنيّ time difference; يَبْلُغ الفارِقُ الزَمَنيُّ ثَلاثَ ساعاتٍ the time difference is three hours; عَوَّضَ فارِقاً to eliminate a difference

فاروق, فروق *n* Farouk (*male given name*)

فِراق *n* separation, parting, leave-taking; لم يَقْدِرْ على فِراقِ شَخْصٍ not to be able to part from sb

فُرْقان *n* distinction, discernment; يَوْم الفُرْقانِ the Day of Distinction (*between believers and non-believers*); سورة الفُرْقان The Criterion (*Sura 25*)

فُرْقة *n* separation, parting

فِرْقة *n* |فِرَق| 1 [مَجْموعة] ensemble, troupe, band; brigade, squad, team; فِرْقة مَسْرَحيّة \ تَمْثيلٍ theater troupe; فِرْقة رِياضيّة sports team; فِرْقة رَقْصٍ dance troupe; فِرْقة موسيقيّة \ موسيقى music group, band; فِرْقة سِمْفونيّة symphony orchestra, philharmonic orchestra; فِرْقة الباليه ballet (company) 2 (Mil) division; legion; brigade; فِرْقة من الجُنودِ

تفرّغ *v* |لِ| to devote oneself to; تَفَرَّغَ للعِلْمِ to throw oneself into science; تَفَرَّغَ للفَنِّ \ للرياضةِ to devote oneself to arts/sports

اسْتفْرغ *v* to vomit, to throw up

فارِغ *adj* |فُراغ| empty, void, blank; بَطّاريّة فارِغة an empty battery; صَفْحة فارِغة a blank page; مَكان فارِغ an open space; كَلام فارِغ nonsense; جَواب فارِغ a meaningless answer; بِفارِغِ الصَبْرِ impatiently فارِغ العَقْلِ \ الرَأْسِ empty-headed;

فَراغ *n* |فَراغات| 1 [خَلاء] void, vacuum, vacuity; خَلَفَ فَراغاً (كَبيراً) to leave a (great) emptiness; وَقْت فَراغ spare time, time off; فَراغ سِياسيّ \ إداريّ a political/administrative vacuum; وَقَعَت البِلادُ في فَراغٍ سِياسيٍّ the country was left with a political vacuum 2 [فَجْوة] space, clearance; gap, blank; الفَراغ بين عارِضَتَيْنِ the space between two beams; مَلَأَ الفَراغَ to fill the space; سَدَّ فَراغاً to fill a gap

فُروغ *n* void, emptiness, vacuity

إفْراغ *n* emptying, unloading

تَفْريغ *n* 1 (Elec) discharge 2 [مَصْدَر] unloading, emptying

مُفْرَغ *adj* vicious; حَلْقة \ دائِرة مُفْرَغة a vicious cycle

مُفَرَّغ *adj* vacuum (*before n*); كيس مُفَرَّغ (من الهَواءِ) a vacuum bag

مَفْروغ *adj* أَمْر مَفْروغ مِنْهُ a foregone conclusion

فَرْفَر *v* |i| |فَرْفَرة| to flap, to flutter; to be unstable

فُرْفُر *n* see فُرْفور

فُرْفُر, فُرْفور *n* |فَرافير| small bird

فَرَق *v* |u| |فَرْق, فُرْقان| to separate, to divide; to differentiate, to distinguish; فَرَقَ الشَعْرَ to part one's hair; فَرَقَ بين شَيْئَيْنِ to distinguish one thing from the other

فَرِق *v* |a| |فَرَق| to be afraid; to fear, to dread; لَهُ شَكْلٌ يَفْرَقُ مِنْهُ الأَطْفالُ he has an appearance that frightens children

فَرَّق *v* 1 [شَتَّتَ] to scatter, to disperse; فَرَّقَ المُتَظاهِرينَ to disperse the demonstrators 2 [بين] to divide, to separate, to part; to distinguish, to differentiate; فَرِّقْ تَسُدْ divide and rule; فَرَّقَ بين أَوْلادِهِ to treat one's children differently 3 [فَزَعَ] to startle, to be/become afraid

فارَق *v* to part, to separate; to leave; فارَقَ الحَياةَ to die; فارَقَنا he has passed away; فارَقَ الحَياةَ قبل أنْ يَصِلَ إلى المُسْتَشْفى he died before he could reach the hospital a troop of soldiers **3** [طائِفة] sect; grouping, faction; فِرَق دينيّة religious factions

فَريق *n* |فِرَق| **1** (Sport) (sports) team, side, crew; الفَريق الوَطَنيّ \ القَوْميّ the national team; الفَريق (الوَطَنيّ) التونسيّ the Tunisian (national) team; فَريق كُرة القَدَم football (BrE) soccer (AmE) team; فَريق كُرةِ القَدَمِ الوَطَنيّ the national football (BrE) soccer (AmE) team; الفَريق الضَّيْف the visiting team; الفَريق المُضيف the home team; فَريق مُنافِس opposing team; شَكَّلَ فَريقاً to make up a team; (لا) يَلْعَبُ الفَريقُ جَيِّداً the team is (not) playing well **2** [جَماعة] team, party, shift; فَريق طِبّيّ a medical team; فَريق عَمَلٍ team, squad; روح الفَريق team spirit; فَريق من خُبَراءَ a team of experts; عَمِلَ في فَريق to work in a team **3** (Mil) lieutenant general; vice admiral; فَريق أَوَّل general; admiral

افْتِراق *n* departure; separation, division

المَفْرَق *n* |f| Mafraq (*city in Jordan*)

تَفَرُّق *n* separation, dispersion

تَفْرِقة *n* **1** [عُنْصُريّة] discrimination, segregation; تَفْرِقة عُنْصُريّة racism, racial discrimination; تَفْرِقة دينيّة religious discrimination **2** [اخْتِلاف] difference, distinction; بِلا تَفْرِقةٍ without distinction **3** [تَفْريق] division, partition, separation; تَفْرِقة في المَرْقَدِ والمَأْكَلِ (legal) separation

تَفْريق *n* **1** [تَوْزيع] distribution **2** [تَمْييز] differentiation, distinction **3** [فَصْل] separation, dispersal; تَفْريق المُتَظاهِرين the dispersal of demonstrators; تَفْريق جُسْمانيّ (legal) separation

مُتَفَرِّق *adj* various, different, diverse; scattered; مُتَفَرِّقات sundries, miscellaneous (items); من أَنْحاءٍ مُتَفَرِّقةٍ from various directions

مُفارَقة *n* departure; difference, distinction; contradiction, paradox; مُفارَقة تاريخيّة anachronism

مُفْتَرَق *n* |مُفْتَرَقات| مُفْتَرَق الطُرُق crossing, junction

مَفْرِق *n* |مَفارِقُ| parting (*of the hair*); مَفْرِق الطَريقِ bifurcation, fork

مُفَرَّق *adj* **1** [مَفْصول] separated **2** [مُشَتَّت] scattered, dispersed **3** [مُوَزَّع] distributed **4** (Busn) بائِع \ تاجِر المُفَرَّق retailer, retail merchant

مُفَرِّق *adj* separating, parting

‹ **فَرْقاطة** *n* frigate

‹ **فَرْقَعَ** *v* |i| فَرْقَعة| **1** [سُمِعَ لَهُ دَويٌّ] to bang, to crack, to pop; to sputter **2** [فَجَّرَ] to crack, to pop; فَرْقَعَ أَصابِعَهُ to crack one's knuckles; فَرْقَعَ بالوناً to pop a balloon

تَفَرْقَعَ *v* to bang, to crack, to snap

فَرْقَعة *n* |فَرْقَعات, فَراقِعُ| **1** [انْفِجار] bang, pop **2** [أَطيط] cracking

مُفَرْقِعة *n* explosive; firework; خُبَراء المُفَرْقِعاتِ explosives experts

‹ **فَرَكَ** *v* |u; فَرْك| to rub; to scrub; فَرَكَ الأَرْضَ to scrub the floor; فَرَكَ عَيْنَيْهِ \ يَدَيْهِ to rub one's eyes/hands

فَريك *n cooked green wheat*

‹ **فَرَمَ** *v* |i; فَرْم| to chop finely, to mince, to hash; فَرَمَ اللَحْمَ to grind meat

فَرّامة *n* mincing machine, mincer; فَرّامة لَحْمٍ meat mincer

مِفْرَمة *n* (meat) mincer, mincing machine

مَفْروم *adj* chopped, finely cut; بَصَلة مَفْرومة a (finely) chopped onion; لَحْم مَفْروم minced meat

‹ **فَرَمان** *n* |فَرَمانات, فَرامينُ| decree, ordinance

‹ **فَرْمَلَ** *v* |i; فَرْمَلة| to brake

فَرْمَلة *n* |فَرامِلُ| **1** [مِكْبَح] brake; فَرْمَلة اضْطِراريّة emergency brake; دَوّاسة الفَرْمَلةِ brake pedal; داسَ على الفَرامِلِ to step on the brakes **2** [مَصْدَر كَبَحَ] braking

‹ **فُرْن** *n* |أَفْران| **1** [آلة] oven, cooker; فُرْن الصَهْرِ العالي blast furnace; فُرْن كَهْرَبائيّ electric cooker; وَضَعَ شَيْئاً في الفُرْنِ to put sth in the oven **2** [مَخْبَز] baker's (shop)

فَرّان *n* baker

‹ **تَفَرْنَجَ** *v* to become westernized/Europeanized

إفْرَنْجيّ *n* see أفرنج

إفْرَنْجيّ **A** *adj* |إفْرِنْج, إفْرَنْجة| European; (Hist) Frankish; خُبْز إفْرَنْجيّ bread (loaf); French bread, baguettes

B *n* |إفْرِنْج, إفْرَنْجة| European; (Hist) Frank; بِلاد الإفْرِنْجِ Europe

‹ **فَرَنْسا, فِرَنْسا** *n* France

فَرَنْساويّ, فَرَنْساوِيّ **A** *adj* French; (اللُغة) الفَرَنْساوِيّة French (*language*)

B *n* French man/person, Frenchman; الفَرَنْساوِيّونَ the French, French people

فَرَنْساوِيّة *n* French (*language*)

فَرَنْسِيّ **A** *adj* French; (اللُغة) الفَرَنْسِيّة French (*language*)

B *n* French man/person, Frenchman; الفَرَنْسِيّونَ the French, French people

‹ فَرَنْك, فِرَنْك *n* |فَرَنْكات| franc; وَرَقة نَقْدِيّة من فِئة ٢٠٠٠ فَرَنْك a two thousand franc note (BrE) bill (AmE)

‹ فَرَنْكوفونِيّ *adj* francophone, French-speaking

فَرَنْكوفونِيّة *n* francophones, French-speakers

‹ فارِه *adj* active, lively, agile

‹ فَرْو *n coll* |فِراء| fur, pelt, fleece; فَرْوة الذِئْبِ wolfskin; فَرْوة بَيْضاء \ بُنّيّة a white/brown coat (of fur); فَرْوة سَميكة a thick coat (of fur); أَبو فَرْوةٍ chestnut

فَرّاء *n* furrier

‹ فَرَى *v* |i; فَرْي| to split, to cleave, to cut open

أَفْرَى *v* to split, to cut

اِفْتَرَى *v* |على| to slander, to libel, to calumniate; اِفْتَرَى على شَخْصٍ to tell lies about sb; اِفْتَرَى الكَذِبَ to lie

فَرِيّ *adj* new, unprecedented; أَتى \ جاءَ شَيْئاً فَرِيًّا to do an unprecedented thing

اِفْتِراء *n* |اِفْتِراءات| slander, calumny, defamation; lie

‹ فِرِيزَر, فْرِيزَر *n* freezer; deep freeze

‹ فَزَرَ *v* |u; فَزْر| to tear, to rip; فَزَرَ الثَوْبَ to tear the cloth

فِزْر *n* (tiger) cub

فازورة, فَزّورة *n* |فَوازيرُ| riddle, puzzle

فَزارة *n* leopardess

‹ فَزَّ *v* |i; فَزّ| to startle, to start

أَفَزَّ *v* to frighten, to startle; to scare off

اِسْتَفَزَّ *v* to challenge, to provoke, to dare; اِسْتَفَزَّ الشُرْطةَ to provoke the police

اِسْتِفْزاز *n* |اِسْتِفْزازات| provocation, defiance; نَظَرَ إلى شَخْصٍ بِاسْتِفْزازٍ to look at sb defiantly; اِسْتِفْزاز مَشاعِرِ الآخَرينَ provoking other people's feelings

اِسْتِفْزازِيّ *adj* provocative, defiant; نَظْرة \ سُلوك اِسْتِفْزازِيّ(ة) a defiant look/attitude; عَمَل اِسْتِفْزازِيّ a provocative action

مُسْتَفِزّ *adj* provocative, provoking

‹ فَزِعَ *v* |a; فَزَع| to startle, to start, to be shocked; to be scared, to be afraid; فَزِعَ من شَيْءٍ \ شَخْصٍ to be afraid of sth/sb; فَزِعَ من نَوْمِهِ to wake with a start

فَزَّعَ *v* to frighten, to scare, to alarm

أَفْزَعَ *v* to frighten, to scare, to alarm; أَفْزَعَ شَخْصاً to scare sb

فَزَع *n* |أَفْزاع| fear, fright, terror; dismay, horror; اِرْتَجَفَ من شِدّة الفَزَع to tremble with fear; بَثَّ, أَثارَ الفَزَعَ لدى شَخْصٍ, الفَزَعَ في نَفْسِ شَخْصٍ to strike terror into sb; اِنْتابَهُ الفَزَعُ he was paralyzed with fear

فَزِع *adj* terrified, afraid, frightened; نَظْرة فَزِعة an anxious look; صاحَ \ صَرَخَ فَزِعاً to give a cry of fear

فَزّاعة *n* |فَزازيعُ| فَزّاعة الطُيور scarecrow

مُفْزَع *adj* panic, frantic, terror-stricken

مُفْزِع *adj* terrifying, frightening, scary; alarming, shocking; فيلْم مُفْزِع a scary movie; صُوَر مُفْزِعة terrifying images

‹ فُسْتان *n* |فَساتينُ| dress, gown, frock (BrE); لَبِسَ \ اِرْتَدى فُسْتاناً to wear a dress

‹ فُسْتُق *n* pistachio (nut); فُسْتُق العَبيدِ peanut; فُسْتُق حَلَبِيّ pistachio nut

فُسْتُقِيّ *adj* pistachio (*a pale green colour*)

‹ فَسَحَ *v* |a; فَسْح| to make room, to make space

فَسُحَ *v* |u; فَساحة, فُسْحة| to be/become spacious, to be/become roomy

فَسَّحَ *v* to broaden, to widen, to make space; فَسَّحَ شارِعاً \ طَرِيقاً to broaden a street/road; فَسَّحَ المَجالَ \ في المَجال أمام \ ل ... to clear the way for ...

أَفْسَحَ *v* to widen, to broaden, to make room; أَفْسَحَ مَكاناً to go out of the way, to move over; أَفْسَحَ المَكانَ لِشَيْءٍ to make room for sth

تَفَسَّحَ *v* **1** [اِتَّسَعَ] to be/become wide, to be/become spacious **2** [تَنَزَّهَ] to walk, to take a walk

انْفَسَحَ *v* to be/become wide/spacious/roomy

فُسْحة *n* |فُسْحات ,فُسَح| 1 [فَراغ] space, room, (small) clearance; فُسْحة من الوَقْتِ a little time, some time; فُسْحة من الراحةِ some rest; فُسْحة للتَداوُلِ room for discussion 2 [نُزْهة] walk, stroll

فَسِيح *adj* |فِساح| broad, wide; spacious, ample, roomy; مَنْزِل \ شِقّة \ غُرْفة فَسِيح(ة) a spacious house/apartment/room

‹ **فَسَخَ** *v* |a; فَسْخ| 1 [أَلْغى] to dissolve, to withdraw, to revoke; فَسَخَ الخِطْبةَ \ العَلاقةَ to break off the engagement/relationship; فَسَخَ عَقْداً to cancel a contract 2 (Med) to disjoint, to dislocate

فَسَّخَ *v* to tear (to pieces)

تَفَسَّخَ *v* to fall apart, to disintegrate, to fall to pieces; to rot, to decay, to decompose; to be dislocated; قد تَفَسَّخَ الطَعامُ the food has gone bad; قد تَفَسَّخت الجُثّةُ the corpse was decomposed

انْفَسَخَ *v* to be/become invalid; to be revoked, to be cancelled, to be dissolved; انْفَسَخَ العَقْدُ the contract was cancelled

فَسْخ *n* dissolving, cancellation, withdrawal; فَسْخ الخُطوبةِ calling-off of the engagement

فَسْخة *n* splinter, sliver

فَسِيخ *n* (Egypt) salted fish

تَفَسُّخ *n* disintegration, fragmentation; تَفَسُّخ المُجْتَمَعِ the fragmentation of society

مُتَفَسِّخ *adj* rotten, decayed; decadent

‹ **فَسَدَ** *v* |i-u; فُسود ,فَساد| to rot, to decay, to be/go bad; to degenerate, to deteriorate; فَسَدت الأَخْلاقُ the morals were corrupted; فَسَدَ الطَعامُ the food went bad

أَفْسَدَ *v* to spoil, to botch (up), to ruin; أَفْسَدَ العَلاقةَ to ruin the relationship; أَفْسَدَ مَذاقَ حَياةِ شَخْصٍ to embitter sb's life; أَفْسَدَ البيئةَ to spoil the environment; أَفْسَدَ لَوحةً to ruin a painting; أَفْسَدَ المُفاوَضاتِ to blow the negotiations; أَفْسَدَ عَلَينا خُطّتَنا he spoiled our plan

فاسِد *adj* |فَسْدى| 1 [تالِف] rotten, spoilt, bad; depraved, immoral; تُفّاح فاسِد rotten apples; طَعام \ حَليب \ بَيْض فاسِد bad food/milk/eggs; مُجْتَمَع فاسِد a decadent society; جَوّ فاسِد a spoilt atmosphere 2 [باطِل] invalid, (null and) void; عَقْد فاسِد a void contract 3 [الأَخْلاقِ] corrupt, bribable

فَساد *n* decay, rot, decomposition; deterioration, corruption; فَساد خُلُقيّ \ الأَخْلاقِ moral decay, perversion; قابِل للفَسادِ perishable; فَساد اللُغةِ language corruption; مُكافَحة الفَسادِ the fight against corruption; عَمَّ الفَسادُ دَوائِرَ الدَوْلةِ corruption is widespread among the government; عاثَ فَساداً to wreak havoc

إفْساد *n* deterioration; decay, rot

مَفْسَدة *n* |مَفاسِد| a devastating thing, a cause of ruin

‹ **فَسَّرَ** *v* to interpret, to explain, to expound; to comment (*on the Koran*); فَسَّرَ شَيْئاً to explain sth; فَسَّرَ حُلْماً to interpret a dream; فَسَّرَ الإنجيلَ \ القُرْآنَ to interpret the Bible/Koran; هذا يُفَسِّرُ عَدَمَ مَجيئِهِ that explains why he didn't come; فَسَّرَ شَيْئاً بطَريقةٍ مُعَيَّنةٍ to interpret sth in a certain way

اسْتَفْسَرَ *v* to inquire, to ask for an explanation; اسْتَفْسَرَ عن المَقْصودِ to inquire about the intention; اسْتَفْسَرَ شخصاً عن اسْمِهِ to inquire (after) sb's name

اسْتِفْسار *n* |اسْتِفْسارات| inquiry, question

تَفْسير *n* |تَفاسيرُ| explanation, explication, interpretation; exegesis; تَفْسير واضِح a clear explanation; تَفْسير حَرْفيّ a literal interpretation; تَفْسير القُرْآنِ commentary on the Koran, Koranic exegesis; طَلَبَ تَفْسيراً \ طالَبَ بِتَفْسيرٍ to demand an explanation; أَعْطى تَفْسيراً to give an interpretation

تَفْسيريّ *adj* explanatory, exegetic

مُفَسِّر *n* exegete

‹ **فُسْطاط ,فِسْطاط** *n* |فَساطيطُ| (large) tent, pavilion; الفُسْطاط Fustat (*first capital of Egypt under Arab rule*)

‹ **فَسْفَس** *n coll* |فَسافِسُ| bedbug

فُسَيْفِساء *n* |dipt f| mosaic

‹ **فوسفور ,فُسْفور** *n* phosphorus

‹ **فَسَقَ** *v* |i-u; فِسْق ,فُسوق| to lead a dissolute life; to stray (*from the right path*)

فِسْق *n* licentiousness, sinfulness; مَشى في طَريقِ الفِسْقِ والفُجورِ to lead a dissolute life

فاسِق A *adj* |فَسَقة, فُسّاق| depraved, licentious
B *n* |فَسَقة, فُسّاق| wrongdoer (*Koran*)

فَسْقيّة *n* |فَسْقيّات, فَساقيّ| fountain

فِسْكوز *n* viscose

فَسْل *n* |فُسول, أَفْسُل| cutting, slip

فسيلة *n* |فَسائِل| shoot, sprout

فَسا *v* |u; فَسْو, فُساء| to break wind, to fart

فَسْو *n* wind, fart

فاسٍ *adj* windy, flatulent

فُساء *n* wind, fart

فِسيولوجي A *adj* physiological
B *n* physiologist

فِسيولوجيّة *n* فِسيولوجيا, physiology

فَشَخ *v* |a; فَشْخ| to stride, to take large steps

فَشّار *n* liar

فُشار *n* popcorn

فَشّ *v* |u; فَشّ| 1 ▸ [نَفَّس] to deflate, to vent, to bleed; فَشَّ غليلَهُ to vent one's anger 2 ▸ [خَلَعَ] to blow up, to crack; فَشَّ خَزينةً to crack a safe

انْفَشّ *v* to (become) empty, to become deflated

فَشَك *n coll* cartridge; فَشَك فارِغ empty cartridge, shell

فَشِلَ *v* |a; فَشَل| to fail, to be unsuccessful; to go wrong, to fall through; فَشِلَ زَواجُهُ his marriage failed; فَشِلَ في شَيْءٍ to fail in sth, to be unsuccessful in sth; فَشِلَت المُحادَثاتُ the talks have broken down; فَشِلَت الخُطّةُ the plan failed; فَشِلَت المُحاوَلاتُ the attempts have fallen through; فَشِلَت المُبادَرةُ the initiative fell through; فَشِلَ فَشَلاً ذَريعاً to fail spectacularly; فَشِلَ كِتابُهُ الأَخيرُ فَشَلاً ذَريعاً his latest book totally flopped

أَفْشَلَ *v* to frustrate, to thwart, to foil; أَفْشَلَ عَمَليّةَ الانْتِخاباتِ to sabotage the elections

فَشَل *n* failure, fiasco, flop; فَشَل تامّ \ ذَريع a complete failure; فَشَل مَحْتوم an inevitable failure; فَشَل سِياسيّ a political failure; فَشَل السِياسةِ الحُكوميّة the collapse of government policy; فَشَل كُلْويّ kidney failure; الخَوْف من الفَشَلِ fear of failure; آلَ إلى الفَشَلِ, انْتَهى بالفَشَلِ to end in failure, to lead to nothing; آلَتْ كُلُّ مُحاوَلةٍ للتَجْديدِ إلى الفَشَلِ every attempt at modernization ended in failure; باءَ بالفَشَلِ to fail; باءَتْ مُحاوَلَتُهُ بالفَشَلِ his attempt failed

فاشِل *adj* failing; مُحاوَلة فاشِلة a failed attempt; شَخْص فاشِل failure

إفْشال *n* thwarting, foiling

فَشا *v* |u; فَشْو, فُشوّ| to spread (about); to be prevalent, to prevail

أَفْشى *v* to reveal, to disclose, to divulge; to give away, to betray; أَفْشى شَيْئاً to divulge sth; أَفْشى سِرًّا to reveal a secret

تَفَشّى *v* to break out, to spread (about); to be prevalent, to prevail, to rage; تَفَشّى الفَسادُ corruption is widespread; يَتَفَشّى وَباءٌ there's an epidemic, an epidemic is raging; تَفَشّى المَرَضُ the disease spread

إفْشاء *n* publication, disclosure

تَفَشٍّ *n* spreading, raging, outbreak; تَفَشّي وَباءٍ the raging of an epidemic

مُتَفَشّ *adj* epidemic, widespread; مَرَض مُتَفَشّ an epidemic disease

فَصُحَ *v* |u; فَصاحة| to be eloquent

أَفْصَحَ *v* 1 ▸ [صَرَّحَ] |عن| *to express oneself in flawless Arabic*; to express, to put into words; أَفْصَحَ عن شَيْءٍ to make sth known; أَفْصَحَ عن نَواياهُ to declare one's intentions 2 ▸ [صَفا] to be/become clear

تَفَصَّحَ *v* to affect eloquence

فِصْح *n* |فُصوح| 1 ▸ (Chr) عيد الفِصْح Easter, paschal feast 2 ▸ [صَحْو] clearness, clarity

فَصاحة *n* eloquence; correct (linguistic) usage; تَكَلَّمَ العَرَبيّةَ بِفَصاحةٍ to speak Arabic correctly; عَبَّرَ عن مَشاعِرِهِ بِفَصاحةٍ to express one's feelings clearly

فُصْحى *n* see أَفْصَح

فَصيح *adj* |فُصَحاءُ, فِصاح, فُصُح| 1 ▸ [خالِص] pure, clear; عَرَبيّ فَصيح in correct Arabic; باللُغةِ العَرَبيّةِ الفَصيحة Standard Arabic 2 ▸ [بَليغ] eloquent, fluent; فَصيح اللِسانِ eloquent

إفْصاح *n* expression; statement, declaration

أَفْصَح *adj* |dipt| purer, purest; اللُغة العَرَبيّة الفُصْحى ,الفُصْحى classical Arabic; Modern Standard Arabic, MSA; في اللُغة الفُصْحى in classical Arabic

فَصَدَ *v* |i; فَصْد ,فِصاد| to bleed, to let blood, to phlebotomize; فَصَدَ مَريضاً to bleed a patient

تَفَصَّدَ *v* to stream, to flow, to pour

اِنْفَصَدَ *v* to stream, to flow, to pour

فَصْد *n* bleeding, bloodletting, phlebotomy

فاصِدة *n* |فَواصِدُ| sand fly

مِفْصَد *n* |مَفاصِدُ| lancet

فَصَّصَ *v* to peel and divide into segments

فَصّ *n* |فُصوص| 1 ◀ (Anat) lobe; فَصّ الدماغ lobe of the brain 2 ◀ [فِلْقة] segment, clove, lobe; فَصّ ثومٍ a clove of garlic 3 ◀ [حَجَر] (precious) stone, gem; خاتَم بِفَصٍّ من الياقوتِ الأَحْمَرِ a ring with a ruby; بِنَصِّهِ وَفَصِّهِ literally

فِصّة *n* alfalfa

فَصَلَ *v* |i; فَصْل| 1 ◀ [فَرَّقَ] to separate, to part, to divide; to disconnect, to disjoin; فَصَلَ بين جَيْشَيْنِ مُتَحارِبَيْنِ to separate two fighting armies; فَصَلَ رَأْسَ شَخْصٍ عن جَسَدِهِ to behead sb 2 ◀ [طَرَدَ] to fire, to dismiss, to expel; فَصَلَ شَخْصاً من وَظيفَتِهِ to fire sb; فَصَلَ مُسْتَخْدِماً to fire an employee; فَصَلَ تِلْميذاً من المَدْرَسةِ to expel a student from school 3 ◀ [حَكَمَ] to pass judgment, to decide; فَصَلَ في قَضيّةٍ to pass judgment in a matter

فَصَّلَ *v* 1 ◀ [شَرَحَ بالتَفْصيلِ] to work out, to elaborate, to go into details; فَصَّلَ اقْتِراحاً to work out a proposal 2 ◀ [أَوْضَحَ] to make clear, to clarify, to specify; فَصَّلَ خُطَطاً to clarify plans; سورة فُصِّلَتْ Explained in Detail (*Sura 41*) 3 ◀ [صَنَّفَ] to group, to categorize, to classify 4 ◀ [قَطَعَ] to cut (out); فَصَّلَ فُسْتاناً to cut out a dress

فاصَلَ *v* 1 ◀ [انْفَصَلَ] to break with, to part with; فاصَلَ شَريكاً to break with a partner 2 ◀ [ساوَمَ] to bargain, to haggle

اِنْفَصَلَ *v* to separate, to part, to break; to split off, to secede; اِنْفَصَلَ عن ... to separate oneself from ...; اِنْفَصَلَ عن حِزْبٍ (سِياسيٍّ) to leave a (political) party

فَصْل *n* 1 ◀ [مَصْدَر] separation, disconnection, segregation; فَصْل السُلُطاتِ the separation of powers; فَصْل تامّ a strict separation 2 ◀ [صَفّ] |فُصول| class, classroom; طَرَدَ شَخْصاً من الفَصْلِ to send sb out of the classroom 3 ◀ [مَوْسِم] |فُصول| season; الفُصول الأَرْبَعة the four seasons; دُخول فَصْلِ الشِتاءِ the beginning of winter; فَصْل الأَمْطارِ rainy season; الفَصْل الأَوَّل من العامِ الدِراسيِّ the first semester of the school year 4 ◀ [طَرْد من العَمَلِ] dismissal, release, discharge; فَصْل ٤٠٠ من المُوَظَّفين the dismissal of 400 staff members; فَصْل جَماعيّ mass lay-offs 5 ◀ [من مَسْرَحيّةٍ] |فُصول| act; الفَصْل الأَوَّل \ الثاني the first/second act; المَشْهَد الثالِث من الفَصْلِ الأَوَّلِ the third scene of the first act; مَسْرَحيّة هَزْليّة في خَمْسةِ فُصولٍ a comedy in five acts 6 ◀ [من كِتاب] |فُصول| chapter; الفَصْل الثاني \ التاسِع chapter two/nine

فاصِل A *adj* separating, dividing; جِدار فاصِل dividing wall; خَطّ \ حَدّ فاصِل dividing line, boundary
B *n* 1 ◀ [اسْتِراحة] interval, pause, interruption; فاصِل إعْلانيّ commercial break; فاصِل موسيقيّ a musical interlude 2 ◀ [حاجِز] separation, division

فاصِلة *n* |فَواصِلُ| 1 ◀ [عَلامة] comma; أَرْقام قبل \ بعد الفاصِلةِ digits before/after the comma; فاصِلة مَنْقوطة semicolon; ثَلاثة فاصِلة خَمْسة three point five 2 ◀ (Mus) فاصِلة موسيقيّة interval

فَصائِليّ *adj* factional

فِصال *n* weaning

فَصْلة *n* offprint

فَصْليّ *adj* quarterly; مَجَلّة فَصْليّة quarterly (magazine); تَقْرير فَصْليّ quarterly report

فَصيل *n* |فُصْلان| young camel

فَصيلة *n* |فَصائِلُ| 1 ◀ [فِئة] faction; group; platoon; فَصيلة دَمٍ blood type 2 ◀ (Bio) family; اسْم فَصيلةٍ family name; الفَصيلة القَرْنيّة legumes; فَصيلة لُغَويّة language family; كانَ من فَصيلةِ الفِئْرانِ to belong to the mouse/*Muridae* family

فَيْصَل *n* |فَياصِلُ| 1 ◀ [مِعْيار] standard, criterion, decisive argument 2 ◀ [حَكَم] arbitrator, arbiter 3 ◀ [اسْم شَخْصيّ] Faisal (*male given name*)

انْفِصال *n* |انْفِصالات| separation; secession; انْفِصال الزَوْجَيْنِ the separation of the married couple; خَوْف من الانْفِصالِ separation anxiety

انْفِصاليّ [A] *adj* separatist; حَرَكة انْفِصاليّة separatist movement [B] *n* separatist, separationist

انْفِصاليّة *n* separatism

تَفْصيل *n* |تَفْصيلات| ,تَفاصيلُ| detail, specification, itemization; بالتَفْصيلِ in detail; جُمْلةً وتَفْصيلاً entirely, fully; أَعْطى \ دَخَلَ \ خاضَ في التَفاصيلِ ,التَفاصيلَ to go into details; أَوْضَحَ اقْتِراحاً \ خُطّةً بالتَفْصيلِ to detail a proposal/plan

تَفْصيلة *n* cut, fit, tailoring; تَفْصيلة جَيِّدة \ جَميلة a nice cut

تَفْصيليّ *adj* detailed, minute; وَصْف تَفْصيليّ a detailed description

مَفْصِل *n* |مَفاصِلُ| [1]▸ (Anat) joint, articulation; مَفْصِل كُرَويّ حُقّيّ ball-and-socket joint; الْتِهاب المَفاصِلِ arthritis; أُصيب بالْتِهابِ المَفاصِلِ to suffer from arthritis; داء المَفاصِلِ disease of the joints [2]▸ (Tech) articulation, joint, hinge

مُفْصَل *adj* jointed, articulate, hinged

مُفَصَّل *adj* detailed, minute, elaborate; خُطّة \ اقْتِراح مُفَصَّل(ة) a detailed plan/proposal; خَريطة مُفَصَّلة a detailed map

مُفَصِّلة *n* hinge

مَفْصِليّ *adj* articular; مَفْصِليّات arthropods, arthropoda; الْتِواء مَفْصِليّ sprain

مَفْصول *adj* [1]▸ [مُفَرَّق] separate, apart [2]▸ [مَصْروف] dismissed, sent away, fired; مَفْصول من الوَظيفةِ fired

مُنْفَصِل *adj* separate, apart, detached; حُروف مُنْفَصِلة separate letters

فَصَمَ *v* |i; فَصْم| to split, to crack, to cleave

انْفَصَمَ *v* to crack, to split, to break; انْفَصَمَ الجِدارُ the wall was cracked

فاصِمة *n* (Elec) fuse

فُصام *n* schizophrenia

فُصاميّ *adj* schizophrenic; اضْطِراب فُصاميّ schizophrenic disorder

انْفِصام *n* separation, split, division; انْفِصام الشَخْصيّةِ schizophrenia; عانى من انْفِصامِ الشَخْصيّةِ to be schizophrenic

انْفِصاميّ *adj, n* schizophrenic

مَفْصوم *adj* schizophrenic

مُنْفَصِم *adj* split; مُنْفَصِم الشَخْصيّةِ schizophrenic, having a split personality

فَضَحَ *v* |a; فَضْح| [1]▸ [أَخْزى] to dishonour, to compromise, to disgrace; فَضَحَ شَخْصاً to make a fool of sb [2]▸ [كَشَفَ] to reveal, to expose, to betray; فَضَحَ شَيْئاً to bring sth to light; فَضَحَ مُؤامَرةً to uncover a conspiracy; فَضَحَ أَسْراراً حُكوميّةً to divulge state secrets

انْفَضَحَ *v* to be exposed, to be revealed; انْفَضَحَ الأَمْرُ the matter has come to light

افْتَضَحَ *v* to be exposed, to be revealed; افْتَضَحَ الأَمْرُ the matter has come to light; افْتَضَحَ أَمْرُهُ he was exposed

فَضْح *n* exposure, uncovering

فاضِح *adj* scandalous, shameful, indecent; serious, severe; فِعْل فاضِح a shameful deed; انْتِهاك فاضِح a serious violation

فَضيحة *n* |فَضائِحُ| scandal, shame, disgrace; فَضيحة سِياسيّة \ جِنْسيّة a political/sex scandal; فَضيحة كَبيرة \ كُبْرى a big scandal; تَسَبَّبَ في فَضيحةٍ to cause a scandal; كانَ مُتَوَرِّطاً في فَضيحةٍ to be involved in a scandal

افْتِضاح *n* revelation, disclosure, exposure

افْتِضاحيّ *n* exhibitionist

مَفْضوح *adj* shameful, disgraceful, scandalous

فَضَّ *v* |u; فَضّ| [1]▸ [سَوّى] to settle, to solve, to appease; فَضَّ نِزاعاً to settle an argument [2]▸ [فَتَحَ] to open (up), to break open, to break up; to pierce, to perforate; فَضَّ رِسالةً to open a letter; فَضَّ بَكارة فَتاةٍ to deflower a girl [3]▸ [فَرَّقَ] to discontinue, to dissolve, to disperse; فَضَّ الاجْتِماعَ to adjourn the meeting

فَضَّضَ *v* to silver-plate, to (plate with) silver; فَضَّضَ سِواراً \ ساعةً to silver-plate a bracelet/watch

انْفَضَّ *v* [1]▸ [انْتَشَرَ] to scatter, to disperse, to separate [2]▸ [انْفَتَحَ] to be opened, to open [3]▸ [سُوِّيَ] to be settled; انْفَضَّ الخِلافُ بين الطَرَفَيْنِ the conflict between the two parties was settled

اجْلِسْ من فَضْلِكَ (if you) please; can continue his studies; من فَضْلِكَ! please, take a seat!; يَرْجِعُ الفَضْلُ في ذلك إِلَيْكَ you deserve all credit for this **2** [فائِض] surplus, rest, remainder; فَضْلاً عن ... aside from ...; فَضْلاً عن ذلك besides, moreover

فاضِل *adj* |فُضَلاءُ, فاضِلونَ| **1** [ذو فَضِيلةٍ] honest, virtuous, kind-hearted; رَجُل فاضِل a man of virtue, a sincere man **2** [باقٍ] remaining; هذا هو المَبْلَغُ الفاضِلُ لَدَيَّ بعد التَسَوُّق this is the amount of money that remains after shopping

فُضالة *n* waste (product)

فَضْلة *n* |فَضَلات| rest, remainder, residue; waste (product); فَضَلات waste (matter); فَضْلة من القُماش remnant; فَضَلات مَنْزِليّة rubbish (BrE) garbage (AmE); فَضَلات الطَعامِ leftovers; فَضَلات عُضْوِيّة organic waste

فُضول *n* **1** [تَدَخُّل] curiosity, meddlesomeness, interference; الفُضول حول شَيْءٍ curiosity of sth; بِدافِعِ الفُضولِ out of curiosity; مُجَرَّد فُضولٍ mere curiosity; أَشْبَعَ \ قَمَعَ فُضولَهُ to satisfy one's curiosity; أَثارَ فُضولَ شَخْصٍ to arouse sb's curiosity; دَفَعَهُ الفُضولُ he was prompted by curiosity **2** [ما لا فائِدةَ فيهِ] superfluity, redundancy; من فُضولِ القَوْلِ needless to say

فُضوليّ **A** *adj* curious, meddlesome, interfering; نَظَرات فُضوليّة prying eyes
B *n* snoop

فُضوليّة *n* curiosity, inquisitiveness

فَضيل *adj* |فُضَلاءُ| superior, virtuous, respectable; الشَهْر الفَضيل the month of Ramadan

فَضيلة *n* |فَضائِلُ| **1** [حصانة] virtue; advantage; الصِدْقُ من الفَضائِلِ sincerity is a virtue **2** [لَقَب] respectable, honourable; فَضيلة الشَيْخ the honourable sheikh; صاحِب الفَضيلةِ His Eminence

أَفْضَل *adj* |dipt; أَفْضَلونَ, أَفاضِلُ; f فُضْلى; f pl فُضْلَيات| better; best

أَفْضَليّة *n* priority, preference; superiority; أَعْطى الأَفْضَلِيّةَ لِشَيْءٍ to give preference to sth; لَيْسَ لَدَيَّ أَفْضَلِيّةٌ I have no preference

4 [أُنْهِيَ] to be/become dissolved; انْفَضَّ الاجْتِماعُ the meeting broke up

افْتَضَّ *v* افْتَضَّ بَكارةَ شَخْصٍ to deflower sb

فِضّة *n* silver; من الفِضّةِ (made of) silver; فِضّة خالِصة pure silver; إذا كانَ الكَلامُ من فِضّةٍ فَإنَّ السُكوتَ من ذَهَبٍ speech is silver but silence is golden; طَلى سِواراً \ ساعةً بالفِضّةِ to silver-plate a bracelet/watch

فِضّيّ *adj* made of silver, silvery, silver (*before n*); خاتَم فِضّيّ a silver ring; فِضّيّات silverware; الشاشة الفِضّيّة the silver screen

مُفَضَّض *adj* silver-plated, plated with silver

فَضْفَضَ *v* |i; فَضْفَضة| to hang loosely, to bag, to sag

فَضْفاض *adj* **1** [واسِع] baggy, loose, wide; فُسْتان فَضْفاض a loose dress **2** [طَنّان] bombastic, inflated, pompous

فَضَلَ *v* |u; فَضْل| to be left (over), to remain, to be surplus; فَضَلَ عِنْدَهُ مالٌ he had money left

فَضُلَ *v* |u; فُضول| to be good, to be honest, to be sincere

فَضَّلَ *v* to prefer, to choose; to give preference, to privilege, to favour; فَضَّلَ حَلاًّ to prefer a solution; فَضَّلَ أنْ ... to prefer that ...; وَيُفَضَّلُ preferably; فَضَّلَ شَيْئاً على شَيْءٍ to prefer sth to sth else; فَضَّلَ الشايَ على القَهْوة to prefer tea to coffee; إنّني أُفَضِّلُ الشايَ I prefer tea; فَضَّلَ شَخْصاً (على شخصٍ) to favour sb (above sb else); فَضَّلَ عَدَمَ الحُضورِ to choose not to come; أُفَضِّلُ أنْ أَبْقى في البَيْتِ I prefer to stay home

فاضَلَ *v* to compare; فاضَلَ بين شَيْئَيْنِ to compare two things (*in order to determine which deserves preference*)

أَفْضَلَ *v* to oblige, to do a favour; أَفْضَلَ على شَخْصٍ to oblige sb, to do sb a favour

تَفَضَّلَ *v* to do a favour, to oblige; تَفَضَّلْ (if you) please, go ahead, there you go; تَفَضَّلْ بالجُلوسِ take a seat; تَفَضَّلَ بِزِيارَتِنا he favoured us with a visit

تَفاضَلَ *v* to pretend to be greater, to pretend to be better

فَضْل *n* |فُضول, أَفْضال| **1** [إِحْسان] merit, grace, favour; kindness, amiability; بِفَضْلِ ... by the grace of ..., thanks to ...; بِفَضْلِ اللهِ by the grace of God; يَسْتَطيعُ أنْ يُتابِعَ دِراسَتَهُ بِفَضْلِ هذه المِنْحةِ الدِراسيّةِ thanks to this scholarship he

تَفاضُل *n* (Maths) differential; حِساب التَفاضُلِ differential calculus

تَفاضُليّ *adj* (Maths) differential; الحِساب التَفاضُليّ differential calculus

تَفْضيل *n* [1] [تَمْييز] favouring, preference, privilege; تَفْضيلُهُ شَيْئاً \ لِشَيْءٍ his preference for sth [2] (Gram) صيغة التَفْضيلِ comparative; صيغة التَفْضيلِ العُلْيا superlative

تَفْضيليّ *adj* privileged, preferential, priority (*before n*); مُعامَلة تَفْضيليّة preferential treatment

مُفَضَّل *adj* privileged; favourite, preferable, best; صَديقي المُفَضَّل my best friend; الموسيقى المُفَضَّلة لَدَيَّ my favourite music; كُتُبُها المُفَضَّلة her favourite books; أُغْنِية مُفَضَّلة favourite song; الشَخْصيّة المُفَضَّلة favourite; من المُفَضَّلِ preferably

فَضا *v* |u; فُضوّ, فَضاء| to be/become empty, to be/become void

فَضّى *v* to (make) empty, to (make) void

أَفْضى *v* [1] [أَدّى] |إلى| to lead to, to result in, to end in; أَفْضى إلى حَلٍّ to lead to a solution; أَفْضى إلى اتِّفاقٍ to result in an agreement [2] [أَعْلَمَ] |بِ| to announce, to notify, to divulge; أَفْضى بِسِرٍّ to divulge a secret

فاضٍ *adj* empty, void, vacant; المَكانُ فاضٍ the place is empty

فَضاء *n* |أَفْضِية| cosmos, universe, space; atmosphere, air; سَفينة فَضاءٍ space travel; رِيادة الفَضاءِ astronaut; رائِد فَضاءٍ spacecraft, spaceship; الفَضاء الإلِكْتْرونيّ \ الافْتِراضيّ cyberspace; وَكالة الفَضاءِ والطَيَرانِ الأَميركيّة NASA, National Aeronautics and Space Administration; حَمْلَقَ في الفَضاءِ to stare (off) into space; قامَ بِرِحْلةٍ في الفَضاءِ to make a journey into space

فَضائيّ *adj* spatial, spacial, space (*before n*); سَفينة فَضائيّة spacecraft; الأَبْحاث الفَضائيّة space research, space exploration; اتِّصالات فَضائيّة satellite communications; تِلِفِزْيون فَضائيّ satellite television

تَفَضّى *v* to have free time

فِطَحْل *n* |فَطاحِلُ| a great scholar

فَطَرَ *v* |u; فَطْر| [1] [خَلَقَ] to create, to bring into being; فُطِرَ عَلَيْهِ it's in his nature [2] [شَقَّ] to cleave, to split, to break apart; يَفْطُرُ القُلوبَ heartbreaking; حُزْن يَفْطُرُ القُلوبَ heartbreaking grief

أَفْطَرَ *v* to break one's fast; to (have) breakfast

تَفَطَّرَ *v* to break, to be broken

انْفَطَرَ *v* to break, to split, to crack

فُطْر *n coll* |فُطور; sing n فُطْر| mushroom, fungus, toadstool; فُطْر سامّ \ صالِح للأَكْلِ poisonous/edible mushrooms

فِطْر *n* fast breaking; عيد الفِطْرِ Eid ul-Fitr (*feast of breaking the Ramadan fast on 1 Shawwal*)

فاطِر *n* سورة فاطِر The Originator (*Sura 35*)

فُطار *n* mycosis

فِطْرة *n* |فِطَر| [1] [خَليقة] nature, character, disposition; حَسَن الفِطْرة good-natured; فِطْرةً by nature; الفِطْرة السَليمة common sense [2] [صَدَقة] alms

فُطْريّ *adj* fungoid, fungal, fungus (*before n*); mouldy; مَرَض فُطْريّ fungal infection, mycosis; فُطْريّات mushrooms, fungi; نَبات فُطْريّ mushroom

فِطْريّ *adj* instinctive, intuitive, natural; سُلوك فِطْريّ instinctive behaviour; رَدّ فِعْلٍ فِطْريّ an instinctive reaction

فُطور *n* breakfast

فَطير *adj* [1] [غَيْر ناضِجٍ] not well done, not well-cooked [2] [طازَج] fresh, new

فَطيرة *n* |فَطائِرُ| pie, tart; pancake; *sweet or salty pastry made of water, flour and shortening*

إفْطار *n* breakfast; fast breaking (*after sunset during the month of Ramadan*)

انْفِطار *n* splitting, cleaving; سورة الانْفِطار The Cleaving Asunder (*Sura 82*)

مَفْطور *adj* |على| naturally inclined to; الإنْسانُ مَفْطورٌ على الخَيْرِ man is good by nature

فَطيس *adj* (Islam) *not ritually slaughtered and therefore not fit for consumption*

أَفْطَس *adj* |dipt; فُطْس| flat-nosed, snub-nosed

فَطَمَ *v* |i; فِطام, فَطْم| to wean (off), to stop breastfeeding

انْفَطَمَ *v* to be off the breast, to be weaned

فاطِمة *n* |dipt| Fatima (*female given name*)

فاطِميّ *adj* Fatimid; الدَوْلة الفاطِميّة the Fatimid dynasty

فَطيم *adj* |فُطُم| (recently) weaned

فَطِنَ, فَطَنَ, فَطُنَ *v* |a-u; فِطْنة, فَطانة| 1 [أَدْرَكَ] to realize, to see (through), to become aware; فَطِنَ إلى \ لِنَوايا شَخْصٍ to see what sb is up to 2 [صارَ ذا فِطْنةٍ] to be/become clever

فَطَّنَ *v* to make aware, to make alert; فَطَّنَ الأَبُ ابْنَهُ بالمَوْضوعِ the father explained the topic to his son

تَفَطَّنَ *v* |إلى| to realize, to become aware of, to see (through); تَفَطَّنَ إلى خُطورةِ المَوْقِفِ he realized the seriousness of the situation

فَطِن *adj* clever, bright, sharp; شابّ \ إنْسان فَطِن a clever boy/person

فَطانة *n* acuteness, discernment, cleverness; نَجَحَ في أَعْمالِهِ لِأَنَّهُ كانَ ذا فَطانةٍ he was successful in his work because he was clever

فِطْنة *n* |فِطَن| acuteness, discernment, cleverness; أَنْقَذَتْهُ فِطْنَتُهُ من ذلك المَوْقِفِ الحَرِجِ his cleverness saved him from that awkward situation; البِطْنَةُ تَأْفِنُ الفِطْنَةَ *a full stomach dulls the mind*

فَطين *adj* |فُطَناءُ| intelligent

فَظَّ *v* |a; فَظاظة| to be rude, to be uncivil

فَظّ A *adj* |أَفْظاظ| rude, ill-mannered, boorish; شَخْص فَظّ a boor; جَواب فَظّ an abrupt answer; مُلاحَظة فَظّة a snappy remark; بِطَريقةٍ فَظّةٍ in a rude way; roughly

B *n* |أَفْظاظ| 1 [عِلْج] lout, boor 2 (Zool) walrus

فَظاظة *n* rudeness, coarseness, incivility; فَظاظة تِجاهَ شَخْصٍ rudeness towards sb; عامَلَ شَخْصاً بِفَظاظةٍ to treat sb discourteously

فَظُعَ *v* |u; فَظاعة| to be horrible, to be terrible, to be disgusting

أَفْظَعَ *v* to make awful, to make terrible, to make horrible

اسْتَفْظَعَ *v* to loathe, to detest

فَظاعة *n* |فَظائِعُ| atrocity, terror, horror; فَظائِع الحَرْبِ the horrors of war; تَحَمَّلَ فَظائِعَ to endure terror; يا لَلْفَظاعةِ! how awful!; ارْتَكَبَ فَظائِعَ to commit atrocities

فَظيع *adj* |فُظَعاءُ| 1 [رَهيب] terrible, awful, atrocious; جَريمة \ قَتْلٍ فَظيعة a gruesome murder; حادِث \ مَنْظَر \ كارِثة فَظيع (ة) a terrible accident/sight/disaster; جَوّ فَظيع atrocious weather; نَتانة فَظيعة a horrible stench; الحَقيقة الفَظيعة the terrible truth; صُداع فَظيع a terrible headache; كانَت الضَوْضاءُ فَظيعةً the noise was horrible; كانَت العَواقِبُ فَظيعةً the consequences were horrible; بِشَكْلٍ فَظيعٍ terribly, awfully 2 [رائع] terrific, awesome, excellent; فيلْم فَظيع a wonderful film; رِواية فَظيعة an amazing novel

أَفْظَع *adj* ugliest, most horrible

فَعَلَ *v* |a; فِعْل, فَعْل| to do; to make; to perform; to act; ماذا تَفْعَلُ في غُرْفَتي؟ what are you doing in my room?; أَفْعَلُ ما أُريدُ I'll do whatever I want

فَعَّلَ *v* 1 [أَنْشَطَ] to activate 2 [وَزَنَ] to scan *(a verse)*

فاعَلَ *v* to react, to respond

تَفاعَلَ *v* to react, to respond; to interact; تَفاعَلَ مع الفيلْمِ to immerse in a film (BrE) movie (AmE)

انْفَعَلَ *v* to be moved, to be affected; to be/become agitated, to get excited; انْفَعَلَ بِشَيْءٍ to be moved by sth; to become agitated by sth

افْتَعَلَ *v* to make up, to invent, to fabricate; افْتَعَلَ حُجَّةً to fabricate an argument

فِعْل *n* 1 [عَمَل] |أَفْعال, فِعال, أَفاعيلُ| act, action, deed; فِعْل خَيْرٍ a good deed; فِعْل مُنْعَكِس reflex; الفِعْل وَرَدّ الفِعْلِ action and reaction; بالفِعْلِ, فِعْلاً indeed, actually, really; لَقَدْ حَدَثَ هذا ما حَدَثَ فِعْلاً this is what actually happened; ذلك بالفِعْلِ that has really happened; قَرَنَ القَوْلَ بالفِعْلِ to suit the action to the word; أَفاعيل great deeds, feats; أَفْعال إجْراميّة criminal acts; (نُريدُ) أَفْعالاً لا أَقْوالاً actions speak louder than words 2 [أَثَر] |أَفْعال, فِعال| effect, result; doing; بِفِعْلِ أنّ ... due to/as a result of the fact that ...; بِفِعْلِ مُرورِ الوَقْتِ with the passing of time 3 (Gram) |أَفْعال| verb; فِعْل مُساعِد auxiliary verb; فِعْل مُطاوِع \ غَيْر مُطاوِعٍ reflexive/non-reflexive verb; فِعْل ناقِص defective verb *(verb with a weak third radical)*; أَفْعال مُتَعَدِّية transitive verbs; أَفْعال غَيْر مُتَعَدِّيةٍ intransitive verbs; فِعْل مُعْتَلّ weak verb; فِعْل صَحيح strong verb; جِذْر الفِعْلِ verb stem; صيغة الفِعْلِ verb form; اسْم الفِعْلِ verbal noun; صَرَّفَ فِعْلاً to conjugate a verb

مُتَفاعِل *adj* interactive

مُفاعِل *n* |مُفاعِلات| (Phys) reactor; مُفاعِل نَوَوِيّ \ ذَرِّيّ nuclear reactor

مُفْتَعَل *adj* artificial, fabricated; اتِّهامات مُفْتَعَلة false accusations; ابْتِسامة مُفْتَعَلة a forced smile

مَفْعول *n* |مَفاعيلُ| ① [أَثَر] effect, impact; مَفْعول إِدْماني an addictive effect; مَفْعول دَواءٍ the effect of a medicine; مَفْعول قَرارٍ the effect of a decision; كانَ مَفْعولُهُ بَعيدَ المَدى it had far-reaching effects ② [نَفاذ] effectiveness, validity, operation; كانَ سارِيَ ,سَرى مَفْعولُهُ ساري المَفْعولِ valid, effective; المَفْعولِ to be valid/effective; يَسْري مَفْعولُ القانونِ the law is going into effect; غَيْر ساري المَفْعول invalid, void; أَصْبَحَ \ أَبْطَلَ مَفْعولَ كانَ غَيْرَ ساري المَفْعولِ to be/become invalid; شَيْءٍ to render sth invalid; جَواز سَفَرٍ غَيْر ساري المَفْعولِ an invalid passport; بِمَفْعولٍ رَجْعِيٍّ with retrospective effect; مَفْعول سَرَيان \ نَفاذ المَفْعول coming into force ③ (Gram) اسْم مَفْعول بِهِ (direct) object; مَفْعول بِهِ غَيْر مُباشِرٍ indirect object; المَفْعول past participle

مَفْعوليّة *n* passivity

مُنْفَعِل *adj* ① [مُهْتاج] agitated, upset, moved; ما زالَ أَبي مُنْفَعِلاً من جَرّاءِ الصَدْمةِ my father is still upset by the trauma ② [خامِل] passive

فَعَمَ *v* |a; فَعْم| to fill (up), to cram, to stuff; فَعَمَ الإِبْريقَ ماءً to fill the jug with water

فَعُمَ *v* |u; فُعومة ,فَعامة| to be/become full

فَعَّمَ *v* to fill (up); فَعَّمَ الكَأْسَ شَراباً he filled the glass with a beverage

أَفْعَمَ *v* to cram, to stuff, to pack; to overload

مُفْعَم *adj* full, filled; مُفْعَم بالحُبِّ loving; مُفْعَم بالحَيَوِيّة lively

أُفْعُوان *n* |أَفاعٍ| male viper

أُفْعُوانيّة *n* roller coaster

أَفْعى *n* |f; أَفاعٍ| ① (Zool) (venomous) snake, viper, adder ② (fig) shrew, bitch

فَغَرَ *v* |a-u; فَغْر| to open (the mouth) wide; فَغَرَ فَمَهُ \ فاهُ to open one's mouth wide

فَغْر *n* colostomy; fistula

فاعِل *n* ① [شَخْص] doer; فاعِل خَيْرٍ benefactor ② (Gram) subject; اسْم الفاعِلِ present participle; فاعِل الجُمْلةِ the subject of the sentence

فاعِليّة *n* ① [مُطابَقة الهَدَفِ] effectiveness, suitability, efficiency; فاعِليّة الدَواءِ the effectiveness of the medicine ② [نَشاط] activity; فاعِليّة إِشْعاعيّة radioactivity; فاعِليّة المُخِّ brain activity

فَعّال *adj* effective, efficient, suitable; active; المُكَوِّنات \ المَوادّ الفَعّالة the active ingredients/substances; دَواء فَعّال an effective medicine; غَيْر فَعّالٍ ineffective; إِجْراءات فَعّالة effective measures; اتَّخَذَ إِجْراءاتٍ فَعّالةً to take effective measures; لَعِبَ دَوْراً فَعّالاً في شَيْءٍ to play an active role in sth

فَعّاليّة *n* effectiveness, suitability, efficiency; functionality; فَعّاليّة الدَواءِ the effectiveness of the medicine

فَعْلة *n* deed, action, act

فِعْليّ *adj* ① [حَقيقيّ] real, actual, factual; فِعْلِيًّا actually, really; التَكاليف الفِعْليّة the actual costs; السُلْطة الفِعْليّة the real power; مُساهَمة فِعْليّة a substantial contribution; القيمة \ الدَخْل الفِعْليّ(ة) the real value/income ② (Gram) verbal; جُمْلة فِعْليّة verbal sentence

افْتِعال *n* fabricating, making up, inventing

انْفِعال *n* |انْفِعالات| emotion; agitation, excitement; سَريع الانْفِعالِ irritable, excitable; رَدَّ بِانْفِعالٍ to react emotionally; تَصَرَّفَ بِانْفِعالٍ to act excitedly; ضَبَطَ انْفِعالاتِ to keep one's emotions under control

انْفِعاليّ *adj* emotional, sentimental

انْفِعاليّة *n* sentimentality, emotionalism

تَفاعُل *n* |تَفاعُلات| interaction, interplay; (chemical) reaction; تَفاعُل كيماويّ chemical reaction; تَفاعُل مُتَسَلْسِل chain reaction; التَفاعُل بين ... the interaction between ...; تَفاعُل فُلانٍ مع فُلانٍ the interaction of X with Y

تَفاعُليّ *adj* interactive; مَوْقِع تَفاعُليّ an interactive website

تَفاعُليّة *n* interactivity

تَفْعيل *n* |تَفاعيلُ| activation, stimulation

تَفْعيلة *n* |تَفاعيلُ| (Literat) metrical foot

تَفَقُّد *n* test, inspection, examination

تَفَقُّدِيّ *adj* inspection (*before n*); جَوْلة تَفَقُّدِيّة inspection round; قائمة تَفَقُّدِيّة checklist

مَفْقُود **A** *adj* lost, missing, gone; كانَ مَفْقُوداً to be missing; زَوْجُها مَفْقودٌ منذ الحَرْبِ her husband has been missing since the war

B *n* missing person; بَحَثَ عن المَفْقُودين to search for missing persons; مَفْقُودات lost and found

فَقُرَ *v* |u; فَقارة| to be/become poor, to become impoverished

أَفْقَرَ *v* to impoverish, to reduce to poverty, to ruin; أَفْقَرَت الحَرْبُ الأَهْلِيَّةُ هذا البَلَدَ the civil war impoverished that country

افْتَقَرَ *v* **1** [احْتاجَ] to lack, to do without, to be in want; افْتَقَرَ إلى شَيْءٍ to be lacking in sth, to be in want of sth; افْتَقَرَ إلى الوَسائِلِ to lack means; افْتَقَرَ إلى الوَقْتِ to lack time **2** [فَقُرَ] to be/become needy, to be/become poor

فَقْر *n* poverty; فَقْر مُدْقِع abject poverty; فَقْر الدَم anaemia; خطّ \ حَدّ \ مُسْتَوى الفَقْرِ poverty line; دون \ تحت خَطِّ الفَقْرِ below the poverty line; عاش في فَقْرٍ to live in poverty; عانى فَقْراً to suffer poverty; أَشَدّ بُلْدانِ العالَمِ فَقْراً the poorest countries of the world; يَزْدادُ الفُقَراءُ فَقْراً والأَغْنِياءُ غِنًى the rich are getting richer and the poor are getting poorer

فاقِرة *n* |فَواقِرُ| catastrophe, disaster

فَقارة *n* |فَقار| vertebra

(Idiom) ذو الفَقار *nickname of the fourth caliph Ali*

فَقارِيّ *adj* vertebrate; الفَقارِيّات \ الحَيَوانات الفَقارِيّة vertebrates; لا فَقارِيّ invertebrate; اللافَقارِيّات \ الحَيَوانات اللافَقارِيّة invertebrates

فَقْرة, فِقْرة *n* |فِقْرات, فِقَرات, فِقَر| **1** [مَقْطَع نَصٍّ] paragraph, section, passage; في فِقْرةٍ in a paragraph; الفِقْرة الرابِعة section 4 **2** (Law) paragraph, clause; section **3** (Anat) vertebra

فِقْرِيّ *adj* spinal, vertebrate; سِلْسِلة \ عمود فِقْرِيّ(ة) vertebral column, spine

فَقير **A** *adj* |فُقَراءُ| poor, destitute; poverty-stricken; أُسْرة \ بَلَد \ حَيّ فَقير(ة) a poor family/country/neighbourhood; فَقير إلى (المَوادِّ الأَوَّلِيّةِ) short of (raw materials)

فاغِر *adj* gaping, wide open; فاغِرَ الفَمِ with mouth wide open

فاغِية *n* henna blossom

فَقَأَ *v* |a; فَقْء| to (cut) open, to lance; to gouge out (*eye*); فَقَأَ الطَبيبُ البَثْرةَ the doctor cut the pustule open

تَفَقَّأَ *v* to burst, to pop

انْفَقَأَ *v* to burst open; انْفَقَأَت البَثْرةُ the pustule burst open

فَقَدَ *v* |i; فِقْدان, فَقْد| to lose; فَقَدَ مِصْداقِيَّتَهُ to lose one's credibility; فَقَدَ والِدَيْهِ to lose one's parents; فَقَدَ صَوابَهُ to lose one's mind; فَقَدَ السَيْطَرةَ على نَفْسِهِ to lose control of oneself

أَفْقَدَ *v* to take away from, to bereave of, to deprive of; أَفْقَدَ شَخْصاً الرَغْبةَ to spoil sb's appetite

تَفَقَّدَ *v* **1** [فَتَّشَ] to inspect, to examine, to investigate; to check; تَفَقَّدَ حَرَسَ الشَرَفِ to inspect the honour guard; تَفَقَّدَ الجُيُوشَ to inspect the troops; تَفَقَّدَ المُدَرِّسُ أَحوالَ تَلامِيذِهِ the teacher kept apprised of the situation of his students **2** [بَحَثَ] to seek, to look for

افْتَقَدَ *v* to miss, to lack, to be deprived of; يَفْتَقِدُ القُدْرةَ على التَعْبِيرِ he lacks the ability to express himself; افْتَقَدَ شَيْئاً (بِشِدَّةٍ) to miss sth (greatly)

فَقْد *n* loss, bereavement

فاقِد **A** *adj* |فاقِدونَ| destitute, devoid, lacking; فاقِد الضَمِيرِ unscrupulous; فاقِد الأَمَلِ without hope; هو فاقِدٌ لِبَصَرِهِ he's blind

B *n* **1** [ضَياع] |فَواقِدُ| wasting, spilling; التَقْلِيل من فاقِدِ الماءِ reduction of water waste; بَدَل فاقِد replacement **2** [شَخْص] |فاقِدونَ| loser; فاقِد الشَيْءِ لا يُعْطِيهِ you can't give what you don't have

فِقْدان *n* loss, bereavement; lack; يَخْشَونَ فِقْدانَ وَظائِفِهِمْ they fear the loss of their jobs; أَحَسَّ بالفِقْدانِ to experience a loss; عانى من فِقْدانِ الذاكِرةِ to suffer from loss of memory; مَرَض فِقْدانِ المَناعةِ المُكْتَسَبةِ acquired immunodeficiency syndrome (AIDS)

فَقيد **A** *adj* lost, missing; dead

B *n* dead person, deceased; عائِلة الفَقيدِ the family of the deceased

افْتِقاد *n* lack, loss, want; افْتِقاد الثِقةِ the lack of confidence

تَفاقُم *n* worsening, deterioration; تَفاقُم الأَوْضاعِ a worsening of the situation; حَدّ من تَفاقُمِ الأَزْمةِ a stop to the escalation of the crisis; هذا يَزيدُ الوَضْعَ تَفاقُماً that makes the situation even worse

مُفاقَمة *n* aggravation

‹ **فَقُهَ** *v* |u; فَقاهة| to have legal knowledge; فَقُهَ في دينِهِ he had much knowledge of his religion

فَقِهَ *v* |a; فِقْه| to understand, to grasp, to realize; فَقِهَ الأَمْرَ he got it; لم أَفْقَهْ ما قُلْتَهُ I haven't understood what you said

فَقَّهَ *v* to teach, to instruct; فَقَّهَ الأُسْتاذُ الطالِبَ the teacher instructed the student; فَقَّهَ المُعَلِّمُ طُلّابَهُ عُلومَ اللُغةِ the teacher taught his students linguistics

أَفْقَهَ *v* to teach, to instruct

تَفَقَّهَ *v* to go (deeply) into, to study thoroughly; تَفَقَّهَ في شَيْءٍ to have (a) thorough knowledge of sth

فِقْه *n* fiqh (*Islamic jurisprudence*); عِلْم الفِقْهِ jurisprudence; الفِقْه الإسْلاميّ Islamic jurisprudence, fiqh; فِقْه اللُغةِ philology, linguistics; أُصول الفِقْهِ the principles of jurisprudence

فِقْهيّ *adj* (religiously) juristic; *relating to (Islamic) jurisprudence*

فَقيه *n* |فُقَهاءُ| (Islamic) legist, (Islamic) jurisprudent, expert of fiqh

‹ **فَكَّرَ** *v* **1** [تَفَكَّرَ] to think over, to reflect, to consider; to ponder, to brood, to contemplate; to think; فَكَّرَ أنّ ... to think that ...; فَكَّرَ في شَخْصٍ to think of sb; فَكَّرَ في شَيْءٍ to think about sth; فَكَّرَ بطَريقةٍ مَنْطِقيّةٍ to think logically; فَكِّرْ ثُمَّ دَبِّرْ look before you leap; أُفَكِّرُ في أنْ أُسافِرَ I'm considering going on a journey; سَيُفَكِّرُ أَلْفَ مَرّةٍ قبل أنْ ... he'll think twice before ... **2** [ذَكَّرَ] to remind, to put in mind; فَكَّرَ شَخْصاً بالماضي to remind sb of the past

تَفَكَّرَ *v* to think; to reflect, to consider, to think over; to ponder, to brood, to contemplate; تَفَكَّرَ في شَيْءٍ to deliberate over sth; تَفَكَّرَ في قَضيّةٍ to reflect on a matter; تَفَكَّرَ في وَضْعِهِ \ حالَتِهِ to consider one's position

افْتَكَرَ *v* to remember, to recall, to recollect

فِكْر *n* |أَفْكار| **1** [تَفْكير] (way of) thinking; reflection, musing, pondering; فِكْر مُسْتَقِلّ independent thinking; ثاقِب الفِكْرِ

B *n* |فُقَراءُ| **1** [شَخْص فَقير] poor person, pauper; الفَجْوة بين الفُقَراءِ والأَغْنِياءِ the gap between the poor and the rich **2** (Islam) Sufi; fakir

افْتِقار *n* poverty, impoverishment; need, want, lack; الافْتِقار إلى الإرادةِ السِياسيّةِ a lack of political will

‹ **فَقَسَ** *v* |i; فَقْس| to hatch (out)

فَقّوس *n coll* **1** (Egypt, NA) *a kind of cucumber* **2** (Syria) *a kind of melon*

تَفْقيس *n* see تَفْقيص

‹ **فَقَشَ** *v* |i; فَقْش| to break (open)

‹ **فَقَصَ** *v* |i; فَقْص| to hatch (out), to break (open)

فَقَّصَ *v* to hatch (out), to incubate; فَقَّصَ بَيْضةً to incubate an egg

فَقّوص *n coll* cucumber

تَفْقيص, تَفْقيس *n* incubation; آلة التَفْقيصِ incubator

مِفْقَص, مِفْقَس *n* incubator, hatcher, brooder

‹ **فَقَطْ** *particle* only, solely, merely; للاسْتِهْلاكِ المَحَلّيِّ فَقَطْ for local consumption only; لَيْسَ ... فَقَطْ بَلْ ... not only ..., but also ...; ٥٠٠ جُنَيْه فَقَطْ (لا غَيْرُ) 500 Egyptian pounds exactly; هُناكَ مَكانٌ لِثَلاثةِ أَشْخاصٍ فَقَطْ there's only room for three people

‹ **فَقَعَ** *v* |a; فَقْع, فُقوع| to burst, to pop; فَقَعَ ضَحْكةً to burst into laughter

فَقَّعَ *v* to snap; فَقَّعَ أَصابِعَهُ to snap one's fingers

انْفَقَعَ *v* to burst (open), to pop (open); يَنْفَقِعُ البَيْضُ the eggs burst open

فاقِع *adj* |فَواقِعُ| bright, vivid, garish; أَحْمَر فاقِع bright red

فُقّاعة *n* |فَقاقيعُ| bubble; فُقّاعة صابونٍ (soap) bubble; فُقّاعة عَقاريّة real estate bubble; فُقّاعة الإنْتَرْنِت dot-com bubble

‹ **فَقُمَ** *v* |u; فَقْم, فَقَم, فُقوم, فَقامة| to worsen, to become worse, to deteriorate; فَقُمَ الأَمْرُ the matter got worse

فاقَمَ *v* to worsen, to make worse, to aggravate; فاقَمَ المَوْقِفَ to aggravate the situation; فاقَمَ الاتِّفاقُ الأَزْمةَ the agreement has worsened the crisis

تَفاقَمَ *v* to escalate, to worsen, to deteriorate; يَتَفاقَمُ الخِلافُ the conflict is escalating

فُقْمة *n* |فُقَم| (Zool) seal

on ...; أَرْفُضُ مُجَرَّدَ التَفْكِيرِ فيهِ I won't even consider it

مُفَكِّر *n* thinker; مُفَكِّر بارِز a great thinker

مُفَكِّرة *n* diary, notebook

فَكَّ *v* |u; فَكّ| 1 [فَصَلَ أَجْزاءَهُ] to disassemble, to take apart; to unfasten, to twist off; فَكَّ شَيْئاً to disassemble sth; فَكَّ الغِطاءَ to twist off the lid; فَكَّ زِرّاً to undo a button; فَكَّ خِطْبَتَهُ to break one's engagement; فَكَّ لَوالِبَ to loosen screws 2 [حَلَّ] to disentangle, to unravel; to dislocate, to disjoint; فَكَّ خَيْطاً to disentangle a thread; فَكَّ عُقْدَةً to unravel a tangle 3 [النُقودَ] to change, to give change; فَكَّ وَرَقَةً نَقْدِيَّةً من فِئَةِ مائةِ أورو to give change for a hundred euro note (BrE) bill (AmE) 4 [فَسَّرَ] to decode, to decipher, to unravel; فَكَّ شِفْرَةً to decipher a code; فَكَّ لُغْزاً to unravel a mystery 5 [حَرَّرَ] to lift, to raise; to redeem, to pay off; فَكَّ الرَهْنَ to take (sth) out of pawn; فَكَّ حِصاراً to lift an embargo

فَكَّكَ *v* 1 [فَصَلَ وَفَرَّقَ] to dismantle, to disassemble, to take apart; to unfasten, to loosen; فَكَّكَ أَسْلِحَةً نَوَوِيَّةً to dismantle nuclear weapons; فَكَّكَ مَصْنَعاً to dismantle a factory 2 (Literat) to deconstruct

تَفَكَّكَ *v* to fall apart, to crumble, to break into pieces; to come loose; تَفَكَّكَ إلى مَجْموعاتٍ صَغيرةٍ to break up into small groups; تَفَكَّكَت العائلةُ the family fell apart

اِنْفَكَّ *v* to be/come loose, to become untied, to come off; ما انْفَكَّ يَفْعَلُ شَيْئاً to keep doing sth; انْفَكَّ الحِزامُ the belt came loose; انْفَكَّت العُقْدةُ the knot slipped

اِفْتَكَّ *v* to redeem; to snatch away

فَكّ *n* 1 [تَفْكيك] disassembling, taking apart 2 (Anat) |فُكوك| jaw; فَكّ عُلْوِيّ upper jaw; فَكّ سُفْلِيّ lower jaw

فَكاك, فِكاك *n* ransom (money); release; escape; لا فِكاكَ مِنْهُ it is inevitable

فَكّة *n* (Egypt) (small) change, coins

تَفَكُّك *n* |تَفَكُّكات| disintegration, fragmentation, falling apart; التَفَكُّك الأُسْرِيّ the breaking up of the family; تَفَكُّك العَلاقاتِ الاجْتِماعِيَّةِ disintegration of social relations

تَفْكيك *n* disassembling, dismantlement, taking apart; unraveling; تَفْكيك أَسْلِحةٍ نَوَوِيَّةٍ dismantling of nuclear

sharp-witted; شارِدُ الفِكْرِ distracted; كانَ شارِدَ الفِكْرِ to be absent-minded; رِجالُ الفِكْرِ the thinkers; أَهْلُ الفِكْرِ the intelligentsia; أَعْمَلَ فِكْرَهُ to use one's brains, to think; قَدَحَ زِنادَ فِكْرِهِ to rack one's brains 2 [رَأْي] thought, idea; opinion, view; أَفْكار body of thought, ideas; أَفْكار شُيوعِيّة communist ideas; أَفْكار هذا العالِمِ ideas of this scholar; تَسَلْسُلُ أَفْكارٍ train of thought; تَبادُلُ الأَفْكارِ exchange of thoughts; تَبادَلَ الأَفْكارَ حَوْلَ ... to exchange ideas on ...; عَبَّرَ عن أَفْكارِهِ to express one's thoughts; أَطْلَقَ العِنانَ لِأَفْكارِهِ to give one's thoughts free rein

فِكْرة *n* |فِكَر, أَفْكار| idea, concept, notion; thought, view; فِكْرة أَساسِيّة a basic idea; فِكْرة رائِعة \ نَيِّرة a brilliant idea; فِكْرة مَهْجورة an outmoded idea; صاحِبُ الفِكْرةِ deviser, originator; فِكْرة عن الناسِ view of mankind; فِكْرة بِخُصوصِ \ حول شَيْءٍ an idea about sth; كانَتْ عِنْدَهُ فِكْرةٌ he had an idea; عَنَّتْ لَهُ فِكْرةٌ, خَطَرَتْ على بالِهِ فِكْرةٌ an idea came to his mind, an idea occurred to him; ساهَمَ في تَكْوينِ فِكْرةٍ عن شَيْءٍ to contribute to the thinking on sth; أَوْحى إلى شَخْصٍ بالفِكْرةِ ... to inspire sb with the idea that ...; لَيْسَتْ لَدَيْهِ أَدْنى فِكْرةٍ he hasn't got the faintest idea; غَيَّرَ فِكْرَتَهُ عن شَخْصٍ to adjust one's image of sb; على فِكْرةٍ ... by the way ..., speaking of ...; على فِكْرةٍ، لَقَدْ حَصَلْتُ على تَرْقِيةٍ by the way, I got a promotion

فِكْرِيّ *adj* mental; intellectual; الكِتابةُ عَمَلٌ فِكْرِيٌّ writing is an intellectual activity; حَقّ المِلْكِيّةِ الفِكْرِيّةِ intellectual property rights

تَفْكير *n* thought; thinking, pondering, reflection; reasoning; التَفْكير في شَيْءٍ \ شَخْصٍ the thought of sth/sb; تَفْكير عَميق musing, pondering; تَفْكير سَليم common sense; بِدونِ تَفْكيرٍ unthinking, thoughtless; عَمَلِيّة تَفْكيرٍ thought process; طَريقة التَفْكيرِ way of thinking; أُسْلوب تَفْكيرٍ pattern of thought, line of thinking; فَريق تَفْكيرٍ think tank; تَغْيير في أُسْلوبِ التَفْكيرِ a shift in the pattern of thought; بعد تَفْكيرٍ طَويلٍ after much deliberation; أَمْعَنَ التَفْكيرَ to ponder; أَمْعَنَ التَفْكيرَ في سُؤالٍ to ponder a question; اسْتَغْرَقَ في التَفْكيرِ to be lost in thought; كانَ تَفْكيري مُرَكَّزٌ في ... my thoughts concentrated weapons; تَفْكيك المُسْتَوْطَنات sectional; قابِل للتَفْكيك dismantlement of settlements

تفْكيكيّ *adj* (Literat) deconstructionist

تفْكيكيّة *n* (Literat) deconstruction; deconstructionism

مُتَفَكِّك *adj* incoherent; unfastened, fallen apart

مِفَكّ *n* |مِفَكّات| screwdriver

مُفَكَّك *adj* disjointed; أُسْرة مُفَكَّكة a broken home

مَفْكوك *adj* loose, unfastened

‹ **فَكِهَ** *v* |a; فَكَه ,فكاهة| to be funny, to be humorous

فَكَّهَ *v* to entertain with jokes

فاكَهَ *v* to joke, to jest, to make jokes

تَفَكَّهَ *v* to have fun, to amuse oneself, to be amused

تفاكَهَ *v* to exchange jokes, to tell jokes to one another

فكِه *adj* funny, witty, humorous

فاكِهانيّ *n* fruit seller

فاكِهة *n* |فَواكِهُ| fruit; فاكِهة مَدارية \ اسْتِوائيّة tropical fruit; فاكِهة فِجّة \ غَيْر ناضِجةٍ unripe fruit; فاكِهة طازَجة fresh fruit; الخُضَر والفَواكِه vegetables and fruit; سَلّة فَواكِهَ basket of fruit; زِراعة الفاكِهةِ fruit growing; فَواكِه البَحْرِ shellfish, fruits de mer; سُكَّر الفَواكِهِ fructose

فُكاهة *n* humour; joke, jest, fun; تَمَتَّعَ بِروحِ الفُكاهةِ to have a sense of humour

فُكاهيّ **A** *adj* humorous, humoristic, comic

B *n* humorist

‹ **فِلاش** *n* flash (bulb), flashlight

‹ **فْلامِنْجو** *n* flamingo

‹ **فْلامَنْكيّ** **A** *adj* |فْلامَنْك| Flemish; (اللُغة) الفْلامَنْكيّة Flemish (*language*)

B *n* |فْلامَنْك| Fleming

‹ **فُلان** *n* so-and-so, someone (or other), what's-his-name; اِبْن فُلانٍ the son of so-and-so; فُلان الفُلانيّ Mr/Mrs So-and-So; قالَ لي فُلانٌ someone told me

فُلانيّ *adj* such-and-such; في الشارِعِ الفُلانيِّ in such-and-such a street; في الساعةِ الفُلانيّة at such-and-such an hour; فُلان الفُلانيّ Mr/Mrs So-and-So

‹ **فْلانْدَرا** *n* Flanders

‹ **فِلِبِّينيّ ,فِليبّينيّ** **A** *adj* Philippine, Filipino; (اللُغة) الفيليبّينيّة Filipino (*language*)

B *n* Filipino (*person*)

الفيليبّين ,الفِلِبِّين *n* |f| (the) Philippines, (the) Philippine Islands

‹ **فَلَتَ** *v* |i; فَلْت| to escape, to run/get away, to slip (away); فَلَتَت الزُجاجةُ من (بَيْنِ) يَدَيْهِ the bottle slipped from his hands; فَلَتَ الحِصانُ من مَرْبِطه the horse ran away from the place where it was tied up

أَفْلَتَ *v* **1** [هَرَبَ] to break out/free, to get away, to escape; أَفْلَتَ من شَخْصٍ to escape (from) sb; أَفْلَتَ من عُقوبةٍ to escape (from) punishment; أَفْلَتَ من الأَنْظارِ to escape attention; أَفْلَتَ من انْتِباهِ شَخْصٍ to elude sb's notice; اسْتَطاعَ أنْ يُفْلِتَ to manage to escape; أَفْلَتَت الزُجاجةُ من يَدِهِ the bottle slipped from his hands; أَفْلَتَتْ مِنْهُ الكَلِماتُ the words slipped from his mouth; تُفْلِتُ الحَيَواناتُ the animals are breaking free; أَفْلَتَ من يَدِ العَدالةِ to be on the run from the police **2** [أَطْلَقَ] to release, to (set) free, to liberate; أَفْلَتَ شَيْئاً to let sth slip

تَفَلَّتَ *v* to break loose, to escape

انْفَلَتَ *v* to escape, to slip, to get away; to come loose, to come off; انْفَلَتَتْ هذه الكَلِماتُ من شَفَتَيْهِ the words slipped from his mouth; انْفَلَتَ عن كُلِّ مُراقَبةٍ to escape every inspection

فَلْتان *n* |dipt| chaos, disarray; recklessness; فَلْتان أَمْنيّ security chaos

فَلْتة *n* **1** |فَلَتات| [أَمْر غَيْر مُتَوَقَّعٍ] unexpected event; فَلْتةً unexpectedly, suddenly; خَرَجَ الطالِبُ من الصَفِّ فَلْتةً the student suddenly left the classroom; أُغْلِقَ البابُ فَلْتةً the door was suddenly closed **2** [هَفْوة] error, mistake

إفْلات *n* escape

انْفِلات *n* escape; صِمام الانْفِلاتِ escape valve, exhaust valve

مُنْفَلِت *adj* unbridled, unrestrained, free

‹ **فِلْتِر** *n* filter (tip); سَجائِر بِدونِ فِلْتِرٍ unfiltered cigarettes

‹ **فَلَجَ** *v* |i-u; فَلْج| to split, to cleave

فَلْج *n* |فُلوج| crack, split, crevice

فالِج *n* hemiplegia, unilateral paralysis

مَفْلوج *adj* hemiplegic, unilaterally paralysed

فَلَحَ v |a; فَلْح| ⓵ [الأَرْضَ] to plough, to till, to cultivate; فَلَحَ الأَرْضَ to turn over the soil, to cultivate the land ⓶ [شَقَّ] to split, to cleave; إنّ الحَديدَ بالحَديدِ يُفْلَحُ to fight fire with fire

أَفْلَحَ v to succeed, to be successful; to thrive, to prosper; أَفْلَحَ في أَعْمالِهِ to do good business

فَلْح n split, crack, cleft; فَلْح شَرَجيّ anal cleft

فَلاح n prosperity; success; bliss; أَرْجو لَكَ الفَلاحَ I wish you all the best

فَلاّح n |فَلاّحة, فَلاّحون| farmer, peasant

فِلاحة n farming, agriculture; ploughing, cultivation; فِلاحة البَساتين horticulture

فَلاّحيّ adj agricultural, rustic, rural; نُموّ فَلاّحيّ agricultural growth

فِلاحيّ adj agrarian, agricultural

مُفْلِح adj prosperous, thriving, successful; تِجارة مُفْلِحة successful trade

فِلْذة n |فِلَذات, فِلَذ| piece, lump

فولاذ n listed alphabetically

فِلِزّ n |فِلِزّات| فِلِزّ, فِلَزّ metal

فَلَّسَ v to declare bankrupt; فَلَّسَ شَرِكةً to declare a company bankrupt

أَفْلَسَ v to go bankrupt, to fail; أَفْلَسَتْ تِلْكَ الشَرِكةُ that company has gone bankrupt; أَفْلَسَتْ حيلَتُهُ to be at the end of one's wits

فَلْس n |فُلوس| ⓵ [وَحْدة نَقْدِيّة] fils (*0.001 Jordanian dinar*); فُلوس (colloq) money; أَعادَ إِلَيَّ الفُلوسَ he returned the money to me ⓶ [سَمَكٍ] scale

إِفْلاس n bankruptcy, failure; إِفْلاس الشَرِكة التِجارِيّة bankruptcy of the company's business; يوشِكُ على الإِفْلاسِ to be close to bankruptcy; أَعْلَنَ إِفْلاسَ شَرِكةٍ to declare a company bankrupt

تَفْليسة n bankruptcy; وَكيل التَفْليسة bankruptcy trustee

مُفْلِس adj |مَفاليسُ| bankrupt; كانَ مُفْلِساً to be bankrupt

فِلَسْطين n |dipt f| Palestine

فِلَسْطينيّ Ⓐ adj Palestinian; القَضِيّة الفِلَسْطينِيّة the Palestinian issue; مُنَظَّمة التَحْريرِ الفِلَسْطينِيّة Palestine Liberation Organization, PLO; حَرَكة التَحْريرِ الفِلَسْطينِيّة (فَتح) Fatah; السُلْطة (الوَطَنِيّة) الفِلَسْطينِيّة the Palestinian (National) Authority

Ⓑ n Palestinian (*person*)

فَلْسَفَ v |i; فَلْسَفة| to philosophize; فَلْسَفَ شَيْئاً to philosophize on sth

تَفَلْسَفَ v to philosophize

فَلْسَفة n philosophy; فَلْسَفة أَخْلاقِيّة ethics; فَلْسَفة الحَياةِ philosophy of life; فَلْسَفة كانْت the philosophy of Kant; كُلِّيّة الفَلْسَفةِ the Faculty of Philosophy

فَلْسَفيّ adj philosophical; اعْتِبارات \ تَأَمُّلات فَلْسَفية philosophical reflections; نَظْرة فَلْسَفِيّة a philosophical view

فَيْلَسوف n |فَلاسِفة| philosopher

فَلْطَحَ v |i; فَلْطَحة| to flatten, to make flat

مُفَلْطَح adj flat, flattened, level; سَمَك مُفَلْطَح flatfish; وَجْه مُفَلْطَح a flat face

فَلَعَ v |a; فَلْع| to cleave (in half), to split; فَلَعَ رَأْسَ عَدُوِّهِ بِسَيْفِهِ he clove the head of his enemy in half with his sword

تَفَلَّعَ v to burst (open), to split, to crack; قد تَفَلَّعَتْ قَدَماهُ his feet have cracked

انْفَلَعَ v to burst (open), to crack, to break (open)

فَلْفَلَ v |i; فَلْفَلة| to pepper

فُلْفُل n |فَلافِل| فِلْفِل, فُلْفُل ⓵ [حُلْو] (sweet) pepper; فُلْفُل بارِد \ رومِيّ (sweet) pepper; فُلْفُل مَحْشوّ stuffed pepper; فُلْفُل مَسْحوق paprika ⓶ [حارّ] pepper; فُلْفُل أَسْوَد black pepper; فُلْفُل أَبْيَض white pepper; فُلْفُل أَحْمَر red pepper; فُلْفُل حارّ \ حِرّيف hot pepper, chilli pepper

فَلافِل n |dipt| falafel

فُلَيْفِلة n (sweet) pepper; فُلَيْفِلة خَضْراء \ صَفْراء \ حَمْراء green/yellow/red pepper

مُفَلْفَل adj peppered, peppery

فَلَقَ v |i; فَلْق| to cleave, to split, to rend; فَلَقَ خَشَبةً to split a block of wood horror film; شَرِكة أَفْلامٍ film company; رَقابة الأَفْلامِ film censorship; طاقِم فيلْمٍ film crew; موسيقى فيلْمٍ soundtrack; عَرْض فيلْمٍ film (showing); مَهْرَجان أَفْلامٍ film festival; تَدورُ أَحْداثُ هذا الفيلْمِ حول ... this film is about ...; صَوَّرَ فيلْماً to make a film 2 [شَريط] film 3 (Phot) (roll of) film

‹ **فُلان** *n* listed alphabetically

فِلّين *n* cork

فِلّينة *n* 1 [سدادة] cork 2 (Fishg) fishing float

فِلّيني *adj* cork; نَعْل \ حائط فِلّينيّ a cork sole/wall

‹ **فْلوت** *n* (transverse) flute

‹ **فُلور** *n* fluorine

فَلْوَرة *n* fluorite content; fluorescence

فُلوريّ *adj* fluorescent; انْسِمام فِلوريّ fluorosis

مُفَلْوِر *adj* fluorescent

‹ **فْلوريد** *n* fluoride

‹ **فْلوريدا** *n* Florida (*US state*)

‹ **فْلورين** *n* |فْلورينات| guilder, florin

‹ **فَلوكة** *n* |فَلائِكُ| felucca (*small boat with a sail*)

‹ **فَلّى** *v* to delouse, to louse, to rid of lice

‹ **فَم** *n* |أَفْواه| 1 [إِنْسانٍ] mouth; فاغِرَ الفَمِ with open mouth; أَعْلَنَ شَيْئاً بِمِلْءِ فَمِهِ loudly; بِمِلْءِ فَمِهِ to proclaim something loudly; سَمِعَ شَيْئاً من فَمِ شَخْصٍ to hear sth from sb's own mouth; كانَ مُضْغَةً في أَفْواهِ الناسِ to be the talk of the town 2 [حَيَوانٍ] beak, bill; snout, muzzle, jaws 3 [أَشْياءَ] mouth, muzzle; embouchure, estuary, mouth; mouthpiece, embouchure; فَم زُجاجةٍ bottle mouth; فَم نَهْرٍ river mouth

فَمَويّ *adj* oral; صَوْت فَمَويّ oral sound

‹ **فيميه** *adj* listed alphabetically

‹ **فَنار** *n* |فَنارات| lighthouse

‹ **فِنْجال** *n* see فِنْجان

‹ **فِنْجان**, **فِنْجال** *n* |فَناجينُ| (coffee) cup; فِنْجان من القَهْوةِ a cup of coffee; قَرَأَ فِنْجاناً to predict the future from reading coffee grounds

‹ **فَنِدَ** *v* |a; فَنَد| to be senile

فَنَّدَ *v* to refute, to rebut, to disprove; فَنَّدَ شَيْئاً to disallow sth; فَنَّدَ ادِّعاءً to dispute a claim

فَلَقَ *v* to split, to cleave, to rend

تَفَلَّقَ *v* to split, to crack; قد تَفَلَّقَتْ قَدَماهُ his feet have cracked (open)

انْفَلَقَ *v* to split, to crack; انْفَلَقَ البابُ the door has cracked

فَلْق *n* |فُلوق| crack, split, cleft; هُناكَ عِدّةُ فُلوقٍ في البابِ there are several cracks in the door

فَلَق *n* daybreak, dawn

فِلْق *n* |فُلوق| half

فالِق *n* (Geol) fault

فِلْقة *n* piece; lobe; نَحْتاجُ إلى فِلْقةٍ أُخْرى من الخَشَبِ لِإِتْمامِ صُنْعِ الصُنْدوقِ we need another piece of wood to finish the chest

فَيْلَق *n* |فَيالِقُ| regiment; (army) corps; الفَيْلَق الرابِع في الجَيْشِ المِصْريِّ the fourth corps of the Egyptian army

انْفِلاق *n* splitting, fission; انْفِلاق الذَرّةِ nuclear fission

تَفْلِيق *n* listed alphabetically

‹ **فَلَك** *n* |أَفْلاك| (Astron) orbit; عِلْم الفَلَكِ astronomy; سورة الفَلَقِ The Daybreak (*Sura 113*); فيزياء الفَلَكِ astrophysics; يَدورُ في فَلَكِ أَصْدِقائِهِ he joins in with his friends

فُلْك *n* ship; ark; فُلْك نوحٍ Noah's ark

فَلَكيّ A *adj* astronomical, astronomic; أَرْصاد فَلَكيّة astronomical observations; عالِم \ راصِد فَلَكيّ astronomer B *n* astronomer

‹ **فُلْكْلور** *n* see فولْكْلور

‹ **فَلَّ** *v* |u; فَلّ| to blunt, to dull; فَلَّ سِكّيناً to blunt a knife

فَلَّلَ *v* to notch, to indent

انْفَلَّ *v* to become blunt, to become dull

فَلّ *n* |فُلول| notch, indentation, small crack

فُلّ *n* jasmine; صَباحَ الفُلِّ good morning

فِلّة *n* |فِلَل| see فيلا

مَفْلول *adj* blunt, dull

‹ **فيلْم**, **فِلْم** *n* |أَفْلام| 1 [سينَمائيّ] film (BrE), movie (AmE); picture (BrE), motion picture (AmE); فيلْم جَيِّد \ جَميل a good/beautiful film; فيلْم سينَمائيّ (cinema) film; فيلْم وَثائِقيّ \ تَسْجيليّ documentary; فيلْم جِنْسيّ \ جِنْسٍ sex film, porno; فيلْم رُعْبٍ

تَفْنيد *n* refutation, rebuttal, disproof

‹ **فُنْدُق** *n* |فَنادِق| hotel; فُنْدُق غالٍ \ رَخيص an expensive/cheap hotel; فُنْدُق راقٍ \ فاخِر a luxurious hotel; فُنْدُق الدَرَجة الأولى \ المُمْتازة a first-class hotel; صاحِب فُنْدُق hotelier; سِلْسِلة فَنادِق hotel chain; نَزَلَ \ أقامَ في فُنْدُق to stay in a hotel; حَجَزَ حُجْرةً (لِمُدّةِ لَيْلةٍ) في فُنْدُق to book a hotel room (for a night)

فَنْدَقة *n* hotel business, hotel sector

فُنْدُقيّ *adj* hotel (*before n*); مُؤَسَّسة فُنْدُقيّة hotel chain, hotel group; القِطاع الفُنْدُقيّ hotel sector; مَدْرَسة فُنْدُقيّة hotel management school

‹ **فِنِزْويلا** *n* Venezuela

فِنِزْويليّ *adj, n* Venezuelan

‹ **فِنْطاس** *n* |فَناطيس| (water) tank, cistern, reservoir; barrel, cask, vat

‹ **فِنيقيّ** *adj, n* see فينيقيّ

‹ **فَنَك** *n coll* fennec (fox) (*Fennecus zerda*)

‹ **فانِلّة** *n* see فانل

‹ **فِنْلَنْدا** *n* Finland

فِنْلَنْديّ **A** *adj* Finnish; (اللُغة) الفِنْلَنْديّة Finnish (*language*) **B** *n* Finn (*person*)

‹ **فَنَّنَ** *v* to diversify, to vary, to bring variety; to mix, to mingle; فَنَّنَ الكَلامَ to embellish one's words (*with various figures of speech*)

تَفَنَّنَ *v* to be an expert; to excel; يَتَفَنَّنُ في لَعِبِه he excels in his area

اِفْتَنَّ *v* to be a specialist/expert/master

فَنَن *n* |أَفْنان| branch, twig

فَنّ *n* 1 [عَمَل إبْداعيّ] |فُنون| art; technique, skill, science; فَنّ العِمارة \ الفَنّ المِعْماريّ architecture; الفَنّ المِعْماريّ الإسْلاميّ Islamic architecture; الفُنون الجَميلة the fine arts; الفَنّ التَشْكيليّ the visual arts; مَعْهَد الفُنونِ التَشْكيليّة \ الجَميلة art academy; فَنّ صِناعيّ industrial art; فُنون القِتال martial arts; تِجارة الفَنّ art trade; تاريخ الفُنونِ art history; عاشِق لِلفَنّ art-loving 2 [نَوْع] |أَفانين| kind, specimen, variety; أَفانين من ... various kinds of ...

فَنّان *n* artist; فَنّان مَشْهور \ مَعْروف a famous artist; فَنّان مَوْهوب a gifted artist; فَنّان تَشْكيليّ a visual artist

فَنّيّ **A** *adj* 1 [تَقْنيّ] technical; خَلَل فَنّيّ a technical malfunction; مَدْرَسة فَنّيّة a technical school; دَعْم فَنّيّ technical/tech support 2 [مَنْسوب إلى الفَنّ] artistic; مَواهِب فَنّيّة artistic talents **B** *n* technician

مُتَفَنِّن *n* expert, specialist

‹ **فَنِيَ** *v* |a; فَناء| to perish, to pass away; to vanish, to disappear, to cease to exist; العالَمُ سَيَفْنى في يَوْمٍ من الأَيّام the world will perish some day; فَنِيَ في عَمَلِه to be totally absorbed in one's work

أَفْنى *v* to destroy, to ruin, to devastate; to spend, to pass; أَفْنى عُمْرَه مع شَخْصٍ to spend one's life with sb

تَفانى *v* |في| to be wrapped up in; to devote oneself to, to dedicate oneself to, to be devoted to; تَفانى في شَيْءٍ to dedicate oneself to sth

فانٍ *adj* mortal; transient, transitory, passing

فَناء *n* 1 [هَلاك] disappearance, vanishing; passing away 2 (Islam) disappearance into God (*mystical*)

فِناء *n* |أَفْنِية| court, courtyard, patio; في الفِناءِ in the courtyard; فِناء القَصْرِ the court of the palace

تَفانٍ *n* dedication, devotion, effort; التَفاني في سَبيلِ شَيْءٍ \ شَخْصٍ devotion to sth/sb

مُتَفانٍ *adj* devoted, dedicated; كانَ مُتَفانياً في خِدْمةِ أُسْرَتِه to be devoted to one's family

‹ **فِنيك** *n* carbolic acid, phenol

‹ **فِهْ** *v* see وَفى

‹ **فَهْد** *n* |أَفْهُد, فُهود| cheetah; leopard, panther

‹ **فَهْرَسَ** *v* |i; فَهْرَسة| to index; to catalogue; to make a table of contents; فَهْرَسَ كِتاباً to index a book

فِهْرِس, فِهْرِسْت *n* |فَهارِس| table of contents, index; catalogue; فِهْرِس المُحْتَوَيات \ المَوْضوعاتِ table of contents; في الفِهْرِسِ in the table of contents; فِهْرِس أَسْماءِ الأَعْلام \ المَوْضوعاتِ name/subject index; فِهْرِس القُرْآنِ Koran concordance; فِهْرِس مَوْضوعيّ subject catalogue; فِهْرِس

أَبْجَديّ alphabetical catalogue; رَجَعَ إلى الفِهْرِسِ to consult the catalogue; أَعَدَّ فِهْرِساً to compile a catalogue

فَهْرَسة *n* indexing

مُفَهْرَس *adj* indexed

‹ **فَهْقَة** *n* atlas (*vertebra*)

‹ **فَهِمَ** *v* |a; فَهْم, فَهَم| to understand, to comprehend, to realize; to see (through), to be on to, to grasp; فَهِمَ شَخْصاً \ شَيْئاً to understand sb/sth; فَهِمَ في شَيْءٍ to know about sth; فَهِمَ شَرْحَ شَخْصٍ to grasp sb's explanation; لا أَفْهَمُكَ I don't understand you, I don't follow you; لا أَفْهَمُ ذلك I don't see it, I don't get it; فَهِمَ نُكْتَةً to get a joke; لم يَفْهَمْ he didn't get it, he didn't understand it; فَهِمَ شَيْئاً من كَلام شَخْصٍ to gather sth from sb's words; فَهِمَ من كَلامِ \ تَصَرُّفِ \ رِسالَةِ شَخْصٍ أنّ ... to understand from sb's words/behaviour/letter that ...

فَهَّمَ *v* to instruct, to make understand; to persuade, to convince

أَفْهَمَ *v* to make understand, to explain

تَفَهَّمَ *v* to understand, to comprehend

تَفاهَمَ *v* to understand one another, to get along; تَفاهَمَ مع شَخْصٍ to get along well with sb; تَفاهَمَ على شَيْءٍ \ بِشَأْنِ شَيْءٍ to reach agreement on sth

اسْتَفْهَمَ *v* to enquire, to make enquiries, to ask; اسْتَفْهَمَ شَخْصاً \ من شَخْصٍ عن شَيْءٍ to ask sb about sth

فَهْم *n* |أَفْهام| understanding, comprehension; insight, perception; سوء الفَهْمِ misunderstanding; صُعوبة الفَهْمِ difficulty in understanding; لا يُمْكِنُ فَهْمُهُ incomprehensible; أساءَ الفَهْمَ to misunderstand; أَساءَ فَهْمَ قَصْدِ شَخْصٍ to misunderstand sb's intention; كانَ سَريعَ الفَهْمِ to be quick-witted; أَخْطَأْتُ الفَهْمَ I misunderstood it, I got it wrong

فَهِم *adj* |فِهام| quick-witted, quick on the uptake

فَهّامة *adj* quick-witted, keen; رَجُل فَهّامة a quick-witted man

فَهيم *adj* |فُهَماءُ| acute, discerning, quick-witted

اسْتِفْهام *n* inquiry, questioning, question; أَداة \ حَرْف الاسْتِفْهامِ interrogative particle; جُمْلة اسْتِفْهامٍ interrogative sentence; عَلامة الاسْتِفْهامِ question mark; وَضَعَ \ طَرَحَ عَلاماتِ الاسْتِفْهامِ حول \ على شَيْءٍ to have doubts about sth

تَفاهُم *n* mutual understanding, mutual agreement; agreement, arrangement; مُذَكِّرة تَفاهُمٍ مع \ في شَأْنِ ... an agreement with/on ...; تَوَصَّلَ إلى التَفاهُمِ to reach an agreement; التَفاهُم بين المَسيحيّينَ والمُسْلِمينَ mutual understanding between Christians and Muslims; سوء تَفاهُمٍ misunderstanding; سوء تَفاهُمٍ حول \ بِشَأْنِ شَيْءٍ a misunderstanding about sth; تَسَبَّبَ في \ أَدّى إلى سوءِ تَفاهُمٍ to give rise to misunderstandings; نَجَمَ عن سوءِ تَفاهُمٍ to be based on a misunderstanding; أَزالَ سوءَ تَفاهُمٍ to eliminate a cause of misunderstanding; لا يُمْكِنُ التَفاهُمُ مَعَهُ he's not open to reason

تَفَهُّم *n* understanding, comprehension; أَبْدى تَفَهُّماً لِشَيْءٍ to have sympathy for sth, to appreciate sth

مُتَفَهِّم *adj* understanding, sympathetic; غَيْر مُتَفَهِّمٍ ل ... unsympathetic to ...

مَفاهيميّ *adj* conceptual

مَفْهوم **A** *adj* |مَفاهيمُ| understandable, comprehensible, intelligible; understood; غَيْر مَفْهوم incomprehensible, unintelligible; كَلام غَيْر مَفْهوم an incomprehensible story; تَمْتَمَ بِكَلِماتٍ غَيْر مَفْهومةٍ to mumble unintelligible words; بِكَلِماتٍ مَفْهومةٍ in comprehensible language; من المَفْهوم understandably, obviously; من المَفْهوم أنّ المُعارَضةَ تَقِفُ ضِدّ خُطّةِ الحُكومةِ it's obvious that the opposition is against the government plan

B *n* |مَفاهيمُ| idea, concept, notion; مَفاهيم عامّة universals; مَفاهيم أَساسيّة \ أَوَّليّة fundamental concepts; حَسَبَ المَفاهيمِ الفَرَنْسيّةِ by French standards; في مَفْهومي in my concept; اخْتِلاط المَفاهيمِ \ اخْتِلالات في المَفاهيمِ confusion of concepts; هذا مَفْهومٌ بِحَدِّ ذاتِهِ that's a concept in itself

‹ **فو** *n* |أَفْواه| mouth (*construct state of* فَم); لا فُضَّ فوكَ! how well you have spoken!

‹ **فوبْيا** *n* phobia; فوبْيا العَناكِبِ arachnophobia

‹ **فاتَ** *v* |u; فَوْت, فَوات| [1] ‹ [تَجاوَزَ] to escape, to elude, to pass by; to miss; لَقَدْ لم يَفُتْهُ أنّ ... he didn't fail to notice that ...; فاتَتْني تِلْكَ المُلاحَظةُ that remark passed me by; فاتَهُ العَرْضُ he missed the performance; فاتَهُ القِطارُ \ الباصُ he missed

أَفْيَح *adj* |dipt| ❶ [واسِع] big, roomy, spacious ❷ [فَوّاح] fragrant

فَوْد *n* |أَفْواد| (Anat) temple

فودْكا *n* vodka

فودو *n* voodoo

فارَ *v* |u; فَوَران ,فَوْر| to foam, to effervesce, to fizz; to bubble (up), to boil (over); to squirt, to gush; يَفورُ الحَليبُ the milk is boiling over; فارَ غَضَبُهُ to boil with rage

فَوَّرَ *v* to (make) boil, to bring to the boil; فَوَّرَ الماءَ to boil water

أَفارَ *v* to (make) boil, to bring to the boil; أَفارَ الماءَ to boil water

فَوْر *n* فَوْرَ immediately after; فَوْرَ ذلك immediately after this; فَوْرَ هُبوطِ الطائِرةِ immediately after the airplane landed; على الفَوْرِ ,من فَوْرِه ,فَوْراً immediately, at once, right away; اِذْهَبْ إِلَيْهِ على الفَوْرِ go to him right away; رَدَّ فَوْراً to react without delay; سَأَفْعَلُ هذا فَوْراً I'll do it right away; يَجِبُ إِيقافُهُ فَوْراً he must be stopped at once

فَوّار *adj* bubbling, effervescent, foaming; حَبّة فَوّارة effervescent tablet

فَوّارة *n* فَوّارة ماءٍ ساخِنٍ geyser, hot spring

فَوَران *n* outburst; bubbling, effervescence

فَوْرة *n* ❶ [تَفَجُّر] fit, outburst, impulse; فَوْرة غَضَبٍ tantrum ❷ [اِزْدِهار] bloom, flowering ❸ [شِدّة] intensity

فَوْرِيّ *adj* prompt, immediate, instant; دَفْع فَوْرِيّ a prompt payment; مُراسَلة \ تَراسُل فَوْرِيّ(ة) (Comput) instant messaging, IM; تَرْجَمة فَوْرِيّة simultaneous translation; تَرْجَمَ تَرْجَمةً فَوْرِيّةً to interpret simultaneously

فورْمالين *n* formalin, spirits

فورْمولا *n* (Sport) formula; فورْمولا واحِد Formula One (racing)

فورْمَيْكا *n* formica

فازَ *v* |u; فَوْز| to win; to defeat; to triumph, to be victorious, to gain the victory; فازَ بِجائِزةٍ to win a prize; فازَ على شَخْصٍ to defeat sb; فازَ بِقَلْبِ فَتاةٍ to win the heart of a girl

فَوْز *n* victory, triumph, win; حَقَّقَ الفَوْزَ to achieve victory; فَوْز ساحِق \ كاسِح an overwhelming victory; فَوْز على فَريقٍ آخَر defeat of the other team; فَوْز بِأَرْبَعةِ أَهْدافٍ مُقابِلَ هَدَفَيْنِ a 4-2 win

the train/bus; لا أَحَدَ يُريدُ أَنْ يَفوتَهُ القِطارُ nobody wants to miss the train; لا تَفوتُهُ صَغيرةٌ وَلا ,لا تفوتُهُ شارِدةٌ وَلا وارِدةٌ كَبيرةٌ he doesn't miss a thing ❷ [مَضى] to pass (by), to go by, to pass over; to be over, to be past; ما فاتَ ماتَ let bygones be bygones; فاتَتْكَ الفُرْصةُ your chance has gone by, you missed the opportunity; فاتَ الأَوانُ \ الوَقْتُ it's too late, time is up

فَوَّتَ *v* to miss (out on); to cause to miss; فَوَّتَ عَلَيَّ الفُرْصةَ he made me miss the opportunity; فَوَّتَ الفُرْصةَ to let an opportunity go by

تَفاوَتَ *v* to differ, to be different, to vary; تَفاوَتَ تَفاوُتاً كَبيراً to differ widely; تَتَفاوَتُ قيمةُ الدولار the value of the dollar varies

افْتاتَ *v* ❶ [اِخْتَلَقَ] to invent, to think up, to fabricate ❷ [اِسْتَبَدَّ] to reign supreme, to act autocratically

فائِت *adj* past, last; الأُسْبوع \ العام الفائِت last week/year

فَوات *n* passage, lapse, expiration; قبل فَواتِ الوَقْتِ before it's too late; أَدْرَكَ شَيْئاً قبل فَواتِ الوَقْتِ to realize sth before it's too late

تَفاوُت *n* discrepancy, difference; variety, diversity

مُتَفاوِت *adj* different; other; آراء مُتَفاوِتة different opinions; مُتَفاوِت السَماكةِ of varying thickness

فَوْتَرَ *v* to invoice, to bill

فوتوغْرافِيّ **A** *adj* photographic **B** *n* photographer

فوتوغْرافِيا *n* photography

فوتون *n* photon

فَوَّجَ *v to send/dispatch in groups*

فَوْج *n* |أَفْواج| ❶ (Mil) battalion; فَوْج عَسْكَرِيّ a battalion of soldiers ❷ [فَريق] team, troop, group; نِظام الأَفْواجِ shift work; فَوْج من الطُيورِ a flock of birds

فاحَ *v* |u; فَوْح ,فَوَحان| to smell, to be fragrant; تَفوحُ (مِنْهُ) رائِحةٌ طَيِّبةٌ it smells lovely; فاحَتْ مِنْهُ رائِحةُ الطيبِ it smelt of perfume; فاحَتْ مِنْهُ رائِحةُ السَجائِرِ he smelt of cigarettes

فَوّاح *adj* fragrant, sweet-smelling, aromatic

تَفْويض *n* |تَفْويضات| authorization, empowerment; mandate, power of attorney, authority; أَعطى \ مَنَح تَفْويضاً to grant authority; تَفْويض مُطْلَق unlimited authority

مُتَفاوِض *n* negotiator

مُفاوِض *n* negotiator

مُفاوَضة *n* ⟨1⟩ [تَفاوُض] negotiation, talk; مُفاوَضات مُكَثَّفة intense negotiations; مُفاوَضات عَسيرة \ شاقّة tough negotiations; المُفاوَضات بين مُنَظَّمةِ التَحْريرِ الفِلَسْطينيّةِ وَإسْرائيلَ the negotiations between the PLO and Israel; مَوْقِف قَويّ \ ضَعيف في المُفاوَضاتِ a strong/weak negotiating position; طاوِلة المُفاوَضاتِ negotiating table; جَلَسَ على طاوِلةِ المُفاوَضاتِ to sit down at the negotiating table; أَجْرى مُفاوَضاتٍ مع شَخْصٍ to carry on negotiations with sb ⟨2⟩ (Isl Law) commercial partnership

مُفَوَّض **A** *adj* authorized, having power of attorney; الوَزير المُفَوَّض the minister plenipotentiary

B *n* delegate, representative; commissioner; authorized agent, deputy; مُفَوَّض سامٍ high commissioner

مُفَوِّض *n* secretary

مُفَوَّضيّة *n* ⟨1⟩ [وَظيفة] *the office or position of commissioner; the office or position of envoy* ⟨2⟩ [لَجْنة] commission; المُفَوَّضيّة الأوروبيّة the European Commission, the EC ⟨3⟩ [مَكْتَب] commissioner's office; المُفَوَّضيّة العُلْيا للاجِئينَ Office of the High Commissioner for Refugees ⟨4⟩ [مَرْكَز الشُرْطة] (Mor) police station

فَوّاطة *n* towel rail

فوطة *n* |فُوَط| ⟨1⟩ [مِنْشَفة] towel ⟨2⟩ [مَرْيَلة] bib, feeder ⟨3⟩ [مِنْديل] napkin, serviette; فوطة صِحّيّة sanitary towel (BrE) napkin (AmE), (menstrual/maxi) pad

فَوْعة *n* smell, scent; في فَوْعةِ الشَبابِ in the prime of youth

فاقَ *v* |u| ⟨1⟩ [بَرَّز على] |فَوْق ,فُواق| to stand out, to tower; to exceed, to surpass, to transcend; فاقَ شَخْصاً to surpass sb, to be superior to sb; فاقَ شَخْصاً عِلْماً to surpass sb in knowledge; فاقَ شَيْئاً to exceed sth; فاقَ كُلَّ التَوَقُّعاتِ to exceed all expectations; فاقَ كُلَّ الحُدودِ to exceed all bounds ⟨2⟩ [شَهِقَ] |فُواق| شَهْقةً عالِيةً to have the hiccups, to hiccup

فائِز **A** *adj* winning, triumphant, victorious; الفَريق الفائِز بِكَأْسِ العالَمِ the team that won the World Cup

B *n* winner, victor

فَوْزيّ *n* Fawzi (*male given name*)

فَوْزيّة *n* |dipt| Fawzia (*female given name*)

مَفازة *n* |مَفازات ,مَفاوِزُ| ⟨1⟩ [فَوْز] victory, triumph ⟨2⟩ [صَحْراء] desert

فوسْفات ,فُسْفات *n* phosphate; خالٍ من الفوسْفاتِ phosphate-free; مَساحيق غَسيلٍ خالِية من الفوسْفاتِ non-phosphate detergents

فوسْفور *n* see فُسْفور

فوشْيا ,فوشِية *adj, n* fuchsia

فَوَّضَ *v* ⟨1⟩ [عَهِدَ] to delegate, to hand over, to consign; فَوَّضَ مَهامَّ to delegate tasks; فَوَّضَ عَمَلاً إلى شَخْصٍ to delegate work to sb; فَوَّضَ الرِئاسةَ to hand over (the) chairmanship; فَوَّضَ أَمْرَهُ للهِ to dedicate oneself to God ⟨2⟩ [وَكَّلَ] to empower, to authorize; فَوَّضَ شَخْصاً في فِعْلِ شَيْءٍ to authorize sb to do sth

فاوَضَ *v* to negotiate, to bargain, to treat; فاوَضَ شَخْصاً على شَيْءٍ to negotiate with sb on sth

تَفاوَضَ *v* to negotiate, to bargain; تَفاوَضَ مع شَخْصٍ حول مَسْألةٍ to negotiate with sb on a matter

فَوْضَويّ **A** *adj* anarchicistic; chaotic, disorderly, confused

B *n* anarchist

فَوْضَويّة *n* anarchism

فَوْضى *n* |f| anarchy; chaos, disorder, mess; فَوْضى شامِلة \ تامّة total chaos; فَوْضى عارِمة a real mess; يا لَها من فَوْضى! what a mess (in here)!; فَوْضى سِياسيّة \ اقْتِصاديّة \ ماليّة political/economic/financial chaos; تَعُمُّ \ تَسودُ الفَوْضى chaos rules; بَلَد تَعْصِفُ بِهِ الفَوْضى a country where chaos rules; أَحْدَثَ الفَوْضى, أَدّى إلى الفَوْضى to make a mess, to create chaos; رُكام فَوْضى a heap of rubble; (fig) a big mess

تَفاوُض *n* |تَفاوُضات| negotiation; غَيْر قابِلٍ للتَفاوُضِ non-negotiable

تَفاوُضيّ *adj* negotiating, negotiation (*before n*)

أفاق *v* to wake up, to awake; to come to, to recover, to regain consciousness; أفاق من التَخْدير to recover from anesthesia; أفاق من الغَيْبوبة to wake from a coma

تَفَوَّقَ *v* |على| to exceed, to surpass, to outstrip; to outdo, to overshadow; تَفَوَّقَ على شَخْصٍ (في شَيْءٍ) to surpass sb (in sth); تَفَوَّقَ على مُنافِسيهِ he outstripped his competitors; تَفَوَّقَ على خَصْمِهِ to outplay one's opponent; تَفَوَّقَ على سَلَفِهِ to excel one's predecessor; تَفَوَّقَ في مادّةٍ to excel in a (school) subject

اسْتَفاقَ *v* to get up, to rise; to wake up, to awaken

فَوْقَ *prep* above, over; on, on top of; فَوْقَ الأَراضي المِصْرِيّةِ over Egyptian territory (*in Egyptian airspace*); تُحَلِّقُ الطائِرةُ فَوْقَ البَحْرِ the airplane is flying over the sea; فَما فَوْقَهُ and more, and upward; عِشْرونَ فَما فَوْقَ twenty and older, over twenty; فَوْقَ العِشْرينَ over twenty, more than twenty; تَتَراوَحُ أَعْمارُهُمْ بين الثَلاثينَ وَما فَوْقَ السَبْعينَ their age varies from thirty to over seventy; فَوْقَ أَيِّ شُبْهةٍ \ شَكٍّ above all suspicion/doubt; فَوْقَ بَنَفْسَجِيٍّ ultraviolet; فَوْقَ صَوْتِيٍّ ultrasonic, supersonic; فَوْقَ ذَلِكَ moreover, beyond that; فَوْقَ العادةِ extraordinary; وَضَعْتُهُ فَوْقَ رَأْسي I placed it on my head

فَوْقُ *adv* up, upstairs; above, on top; إلى فَوْقُ upwards; من فَوْقِ الطاوِلةِ from atop the table

فائِق *adj* excellent, surpassing, exquisite; superior, unrivalled, unequalled; سُرْعة فائِقة a tremendous speed; عِناية فائِقة excellent care; حاسوب فائِق supercomputer; نَصّ فائِق hypertext; بُروتوكول نَقْلِ النَصِّ الفائِقِ hypertext transfer protocol, HTTP; مع فائِقِ الشُكْرِ والاحْتِرامِ with many thanks; هذا عَمَلٌ فائِقٌ this is excellent work; فائِق الجَمالِ gorgeous; فائِق الصُغْرِ very small

فاقة *n* poverty, want, need; عانى من الفاقة to be in want/need

فُواق *n* hiccup, hiccups

فَوْقانيّ *adj* upper, higher, located above; الطَبَقة الفَوْقانيّة the upper layer

فَوْقيّ *adj* top, topmost, upper

إفاقة *n* awakening; recovery; غُرْفة الإفاقةِ recovery room

تَفَوُّق *n* ascendancy, supremacy, excellence; superiority; تَفَوُّق عَسْكَريّ military supremacy; تَفَوُّق عَدَديّ superior numbers; تَفَوُّق عِلْميّ scientific superiority; إحْساس بالتَفَوُّقِ feeling of superiority

مُتَفَوِّق **A** *adj* superior; excellent, outstanding; مُتَفَوِّق في الرِياضةِ \ الشِطْرَنْجِ brilliant at sports/chess
B *n* brilliant person, virtuoso

‹ **فول** *n coll* |فولات| (broad) bean; marrowfat (pea); فول سودانيّ peanut; فول مُدَمَّس *a dish of cooked beans with oil*; كُلُّ فولةٍ لَها كَيّالٌ ≈ every Jack must have his Jill

فَوّال *n* seller of cooked fava beans

‹ **فولاذ** *n* steel; فولاذ مَطْليّ بالزِنْكِ galvanized steel; فولاذ مُضادّ للصَدَأ، فولاذ غَيْر قابِلٍ للصَدَأ stainless steel

فولاذيّ *adj* steel (*before n*), (made) of steel; فولاذيّ الهَيْكَلِ with a steel frame

‹ **فولْت**, **فولْط** *n* volt; تَوَتُّر قَدْرُهُ ٢٢٠ فولْت a voltage of 220 volts

فولْتيّة, **فولْطيّة** *n* voltage; فولْتيّة قَدْرُها ٢٢٠ فولْت a voltage of 220 volts

‹ **فولْسْكاب** *n* foolscap

‹ **فولْكْلور**, **فُلْكْلور** *n* folklore

فولْكْلوريّ *adj* folkloric, folkloristic; موسيقى فولْكْلوريّة folkloric music

‹ **فونوغْراف** *n* |فونوغْرافات| record-player, gramophone (BrE), phonograph (AmE)

‹ **فونولوجيّ** *adj* phonological

‹ **فونولوجِيا** *n* phonology

‹ **فونيم** *n* phoneme

‹ **فاهَ** *v* |u; فَوْه| |ب| to say, to utter, to voice; لم يَفُهْ بِكَلِمةٍ (عن المَوْضوعِ) he kept silent (about the matter)

تَفَوَّهَ *v* to say, to utter, to voice; تَفَوَّهَ بِعِباراتٍ عُنْصُريّةٍ to make racist statements

فوه *n* **1** [فَم] |أَفْواه| mouth; فَتَحَ فاهُ to open one's mouth; وَضَعَ الطَعامَ في فيهِ to put the food in one's mouth; دارَ الخَبَرُ على الأَفْواهِ the news was on everyone's lips **2** [تابَل] |أَفاويهُ| spice; herb

〈 **فيتْنام** *n* |f| Vietnam

〈 **فيتو** *n* veto; حَقّ الفيتو (right of) veto; اسْتَخْدَمَ الفيتو ضدّ شَيْءٍ to exercise one's veto against sth

〈 **فيجي** *n* |f| Fiji

〈 **فاحَ** *v* |i; فَيْح ,فَيَحان| to smell, to be fragrant

〈 **أفادَ** *v* 1 [صَرَّحَ] to inform; to report, to mention; to state, to certify; أفادَ … بأنّ \ أنّ … أفادَت المَصادِرُ الرَسْميّةُ أنّ official sources have reported that … 2 [نَفَع] to be of use, to avail, to help; أفادَ لِشَيْءٍ to be of use for sth; أفادَ شَخصاً \ شَيْئاً to benefit sb/sth; لن يُفيدَ بِشَيْءٍ it won't do any good; أفادَ خِبْرةً to acquire experience 3 [اسْتَفادَ |من|] to profit from, to make use of; أفادَ من شَيْءٍ to profit from sth 4 [عَنى] to mean

اسْتَفادَ *v* |من ,ب| to benefit from, to make use of; اسْتَفادَ من شَيْءٍ to benefit from sth; اسْتَفادَ بِما لَدَيْهِ من وَقْتٍ to make the most of one's time

فائِدة *n* |فَوائِدُ| 1 [نَفْع] use, usefulness; benefit; purpose; لا فائِدةَ منه ,عَديم الفائِدةِ useless, pointless; لا فائِدة من ذلك there's no use in that; عادَ عَلَيْهِ بالفائِدةِ he benefits from that 2 (Busn) interest; returns; سِعْر \ مُعَدَّل \ نِسْبة الفائِدةِ interest rate; مُعَدَّلُ الفائِدةِ مُرْتَفِعٌ \ مُنْخَفِضٌ the interest rate is high/low; خَفض قيمةِ الفائِدةِ reduction of interest; مُغَلّ لِفائِدةٍ profitable; بِدونِ فائِدةٍ \ فَوائِدَ interest-free; قَرْض بِدونِ فَوائِدَ an interest-free loan; يَحْمِلُ فَوائِدَ ,بِفَوائِدَ interest-bearing; قَرْض بِفَوائِدَ an interest-bearing loan; فائِدة على قَرْضٍ debit interest; دَفَعَ فائِدةً على قَرْضٍ to pay debit interest; فائِدة مُرَكَّبة compound interest; فائِدة على القُروضِ \ الوَدائِعِ interest on loans/deposits; احْتَسَبَ فَوائِدَ \ فَرَض to calculate interest; ارْتَفَعَ \ انْخَفَضَ مُعَدَّلُ الفائِدة the interest rate has gone up/down; حَمَلَ فَوائِدَ ,عادَ بِفائِدةٍ to yield interest; جَنى فائِدةً to collect returns 3 [مَعْنًى] meaning

اسْتِفادة *n* profit, benefit

إفادة *n* 1 [نَفْع] use, usefulness; advantage, benefit, profit; قِلّة الإفادةِ uselessness 2 [إعْلام] notification, communication, statement; إفادة الشاهِدِ testimony, (statement of) evidence

مُسْتَفيد *n* beneficiary

فوَّهة *n* opening, hole, aperture; mouth, muzzle; crater; فوَّهة المِدْفَع the muzzle of a cannon

فَوْهة ,فوهة *n* opening, aperture, orifice

أفْوَه *adj* |dipt| broad-mouthed, having a broad mouth

تَفوُّه *n* utterance, voicing; لم يَقْدِرْ على التَفوُّهِ بِهِ he couldn't bring himself to say it

مُفَوَّه *adj* well-spoken, eloquent

〈 **في** *prep* 1 [مَكان] in, within; at; on; نَسْكُنُ في قَرْيةٍ we live in a village; في القاهرة \ العراق in Cairo/Iraq; في الشارعِ in the street; في الجامِعةِ at the university; في البَلْكونة on the balcony; في التِلِفِزْيونِ on television; بِما فيه including, among 2 [حول] about; ماذا تَقولُ في هذا؟ what do you say about that?; نَتَكَلَّمُ في السِياسةِ we talk about politics 3 [وَقْت، تاريخ] on; at; in; في يَوْمِ الأَحَدِ on Sunday; في أيِّ وَقْتٍ؟ at what time?; في (الساعةِ) العاشِرة at ten o'clock; في سَنةِ ٢٠٠٢ in the year 2002; في السابِقِ in the past; في الصَباح in the morning; في نَفْسِ الوَقْتِ at the same time; في يَوْمٍ من الأيّام one day; تَدْخُلُ عائِشةُ في هذه اللَحْظةِ Aisha comes in at this moment; في مُخْتَلِفِ المُناسَباتِ at various occasions; في زِيارةٍ رَسْميّةٍ during an official visit 4 [فيما] فيما بَعْدُ afterwards, later 5 [طَريقة] ابْتَسَمَ لي في أدَبٍ he smiled politely at me 6 [اتِّجاه] وَقَفَتْ في النافِذةِ she stood in the window; نَظَرَ في ساعَتِهِ he looked at his watch; هَمَسَ في أُذُني he whispered in my ear 7 (Math) times, by; خَمْسة أمْتارٍ في عَشَرةٍ five metres by ten; ٥٠ في المِائةِ 50%; ثَلاثة في خَمْسةٍ three times five

(Idioms) هل لَكَ في …؟ would you like to …?; في حاجةٍ إلى … in need of …

فيمَ *pron* see فيما

〈 **فَيَّأ** *v* to give shade

أفاءَ *v* to bestow, to grant; to give as booty

فَيْء *n* (war) booty; shade; return; في فَيْءِ الشَجَرةِ in the shade of the tree; الفَيْء الى الحَقِّ the return to justice

تَفَيَّأ *v* to seek shade

〈 **فيتامين** *n* |فيتامينات| vitamin; غَنيّ بالفيتاميناتِ rich in vitamins; فيتامين أ \ ب \ ج vitamin A/B/C

مُفاد *n* tenor, purport; خَبَر مُفادُهُ أنّ ... a message to the effect that ...

مُفيد *adj* 1 [نافِع] useful, advantageous, beneficial; غَيْر مُفيدٍ useless; مَوادّ \ مُعْطَيات \ مَعْلومات مُفيدة useful material/data/information; كانَتْ لَهُ تَجْرِبةٌ مُفيدةٌ he had a useful experience 2 [ذو مَعْنًى] meaningful, significant; كَلام مُفيد meaningful words

‹ **فيدِراليّ** *adj* federal; جُمْهوريّة فيدِراليّة a federal republic; على مُسْتَوًى فيدِراليٍّ on a federal level; الحُكومة الفيدِراليّة the federal government; نِظام فيدِراليّ federalism

فِدْراليّة, فيدْراليّة *n* federation

‹ **فيدِيو** *n* video; تَصْوير فيدِيو video recording; جِهاز فيدِيو video (recorder); بِطاقة فيدِيو video card; كاميرا فيدِيو video camera; شَريط فيدِيو, كاسيت فيديو videotape; شَريط فيدِيو فارِغ a blank videotape; أَجْهِزة فيديو video equipment; لُعْبة فيديو video game; مُؤْتَمَر فيديو videoconference; مَحَلّ أَفْلام فيديو video store; اسْتَأْجَرَ فيلْمَ فيديو to rent a video; أُسْطُوانات الفيديو الرَقْميّة DVDs; سَجَّلَ شَيْئاً بالفيديو to record sth on video; سَجَّلَ شَيْئاً على شَريطِ فيديو to videotape sth

‹ **فيرْجينيا** *n* Virginia (*US state*)

فيرْجينِيا الغَرْبيّة *n* West Virginia (*US state*)

‹ **فيرْمونْت** *n* |f| Vermont (*US state*)

‹ **فَيْروز** *n* 1 [حَجَر ثَمين] turquoise 2 [اسْم شَخْصيّ] |dipt| Fairuz (*female given name*)

فَيْروزيّ *adj* turquoise

‹ **فَيْروس** *n* |فَيْروسات| virus; فَيْروس الكُمْبيوتَر computer virus; فَيْروس فَتّاك a deadly virus; فَيْروس نَقْصِ المَناعةِ البَشَريّةِ human immunodeficiency virus, HIV; دَواء ضِدّ فَيْروسٍ antiviral medication; انْتِشار فَيْروسٍ the spread of a virus

فَيْروسيّ *adj* viral; عَدْوى فَيْروسيّة a viral infection; الْتِهاب فَيْروسيّ a viral inflammation; مَرَض فَيْروسيّ a viral disease; ماتَ بِسَبَبِ \ كانَ مُصاباً بِمَرَضٍ فَيْروسيٍّ to die from/have a viral disease

‹ **فيزا** *n* visa

‹ **فيزْياء, فيزِياء** *n* |f| physics; فيزياء نَوَوِيّة nuclear physics; فيزياء الأَجْسامِ الصُلْبةِ the physics of solids; عالِم فيزياءِ physicist

فيزيائيّ A *adj* physical; قانون فيزِيائيّ a physical law; ظَواهِر فيزِيائيّة physical phenomena

B *n* physicist

‹ **فيزيولوجيّ** *adj* physiological

فيزِيولوجِيا *n* physiology

‹ **فيسْبوك, فيس بوك, فايْسْبوك, فايْس بوك** *n* Facebook®

فيسْبوكيّ, فايْسْبوكيّ A *adj* relating to Facebook

B *n* Facebook user

‹ **فيشة** *n* |فيشات, فِيَش| 1 [في القِمارِ] token, counter 2 (Elec) socket, outlet

‹ **فاضَ** *v* |i; فَيْض, فَيَضان| to overflow, to flow over, to run over; فاضَ النَهْرُ the river overflowed; يَفيضُ البانْيو the bath tub is overflowing; فاضَتْ عَيْنُهُ دَمْعاً he cried his eyes out; فاضَ بِهِ الحُزْنُ he was overwhelmed by grief; فاضَ امْتِناناً to brim with gratitude; فاضَ ثِقةً to overflow with confidence; فاضَ عن الحاجةِ to be remaining, to be left; فاضَ عن شَيْءٍ to result from sth; فاضَ عن الحُدود to exceed the boundaries; فاضَ الإِنْتاجُ عن الحاجةِ المَحَلّيّة the production exceeds the local need; فاضَتْ أَنْفاسُهُ to give up the ghost

أَفاضَ *v* to dwell, to enlarge; أَفاضَ عن التَفاصيلِ to dwell on the details

اسْتَفاضَ *v* to be superabundant; اسْتَفاضَ بِضَوْءِ الشَمْسِ to be bathed in sunlight

فَيْض *n* stream, flood, torrent; tidal wave, tide; فَيْض من الدُموع a flood of tears; فَيْض من الكَلِماتِ a waterfall of words; فَيْض من نورٍ a flood of light; فَيْض من الحُزْنِ a wave of grief; هذا غَيْضٌ من فَيْضٍ this is just the tip of the iceberg

فائِض A *adj* surplus, excess; abundant, plentiful; وَزْن فائِض excess weight

B *n* 1 [زِيادة] |فَوائِضُ| surplus, overplus, excess; فائِض المِيزانِ التِجاريِّ trade surplus; فائِض من الوَقْتِ a surplus of time; فائِض الإِنْتاج overproduction 2 [رِبْح] profit

فَيّاض *adj* abundant, plentiful; generous

فَيَضان *n* |فَيَضانات| flood, flooding, inundation; فَيَضان جارِف a torrential flood; فَيَضانات عارِمة \ شَديدة huge floods;

فَيَضانات كاسِحة devastating floods; خطر الفَيَضاناتِ danger of flooding

اسْتِفاضة *n* elaboration, enlarging, expanding; بِاسْتِفاضةٍ elaborately, verbosely; لا داعِيَ للاسْتِفاضة في الحَديثِ there's no cause for elaboration

مُسْتَفيض *adj* elaborate, detailed, verbose; مُناقَشة مُسْتَفيضة an elaborate discussion

‹ فَيْفاء *n* |dipt f; فَيافٍ| desert

‹ فيفْريّ *n* (Algeria, Tunisia) February

‹ فيكْتوريّ *adj*, *n* Victorian

‹ فيل *n* |أَفْيال, فِيَلة, فُيول| 1 (Zool) elephant; سورة الفيل The Elephant (*Sura 105*) 2 [شِطْرَنْج] bishop

‹ فيلاّ, فِلّة *n* |f; فيلاّت, فِلَل| villa (*Western-style house*); فيلاّ فَخْمة a spacious villa

‹ فَيْلَجة *n* |فَيالِجُ| cocoon, pod

‹ فيما *conj* see ما

‹ فيميه *adj* smoked; زُجاج فيميه smoked glass

‹ فَيْنة *n* moment, instant; بين الفَيْنةِ والأُخْرى from time to time, now and again

‹ فينيسِيا *n* Venice

‹ فينيقيّ *adj*, *n* Phoenician

فينيقِيا, فنيقِيا *n* |dipt| Phoenicia

‹ فينيل *n* vinyl

‹ فِيورْد *n* fjord

‹ فْيوز *n* |فْيوزات| fuse

‹ الفَيّوم *n* |f| Fayum (*province/city in Egypt*)

‹ فِيينا *n* Vienna

‹ **ق** *n* سورة ق Qaf (*Sura 50*)

‹ **قات** *n* khat (*a stimulant derived from a shrub of the same name*)

‹ **قادِس** *n* |قَوادِسُ| galley

‹ **قارورة** *n* |قَواريرُ| bottle

‹ **قاروس**, **قاروص** *n coll* sea bass

‹ **قازوزة** *n* soft drink, fizzy drink (BrE), soda (AmE)

‹ **قاطور** *n* |قَواطيرُ| alligator

‹ **قاف** *n* |f| *name of the letter* ق

‹ **قاقُم** *n* stoat, ermine

‹ **قاوَنْد** *n* kingfisher

‹ **قَبَّ** *v* |u; قَبّ| ① [قَطَعَ] to chop off; to amputate ② [بَنى قُبَّةً] to build (a dome)

قَبَّبَ *v to shape like a dome*

قَبّ *n* |أَقْبَاب| hub (*of a wheel*); lever (*of a balance*)

قَبّة *n* collar

قُبّة *n* |قِباب, قُبَب| dome; *type of domed shrine* (NA); قُبّة سَماويّة planetarium; القُبّة الزَرْقاء heavens, firmament; القُبّة الخَضْراء the Green Dome (*dome over the Prophet Muhammad's grave in the Mosque of the Prophet in Medina*); قُبّة الصَخْرةِ the Dome of the Rock (*in Jerusalem*); جَعَلَ من الحَبّةِ قُبّةً to make a mountain out of a molehill

مُقَبَّب *adj* dome-shaped

‹ **قَبُحَ** *v* |u; قُبْح, قَباحة| ① [في الصورةِ] to be/become ugly ② [في الفِعْلِ] to be objectionable/reprehensible

قَبَّحَ *v* ① [بَشَّعَ] to make ugly; قَبَّحَ اللهُ وَجْهَهُ, قَبَّحَهُ اللهُ *God curse him* ② [أدانَ] to condemn; to disapprove of; قَبَّحَ على شَخْصٍ فِعْلَهُ to condemn sb's actions

اسْتَقْبَحَ *v* to disapprove of

قُبْح *n* ugliness; disgrace

قَباحة *n* ugliness; disgrace

قَبيح *adj* |قِباح| ① [بَشِع] ugly; hideous, repulsive; وَحْش قَبيح horrible monster ② [شائِن] nasty; shameless; offensive; كَلِمات قَبيحة offensive words ③ (Isl Law) objectionable, reprehensible

1‹ **قَبَرَ** *v* |i-u; قَبْر, مَقْبَر| to bury, to inter

أَقْبَرَ *v* to bury

قَبّار *n* gravedigger

قَبْر *n* |قُبور| grave; قَبْر جَماعيّ mass grave; حَفَرَ قَبْراً to dig a grave; شَيَّعَ شَخْصاً إلى القَبْرِ to escort sb to his grave; قَبْر الجُنْديِّ المَجْهولِ the tomb of the Unknown Soldier; بَلاطة قَبْرٍ headstone, tombstone

مَقْبَرة *n* |مَقابِرُ| cemetery, graveyard; مَقْبَرة عائِليّة family grave; مَقْبَرة جَماعيّة mass grave; مَقْبَرة عَسْكَريّة military cemetery, war cemetery (BrE); مَقْبَرة الشُهَداءِ *cemetery for soldiers killed in battle*; انْتِهاك حُرْمةِ مَقابِرَ grave desecration

2‹ **قُبَّر** *n coll* lark

3‹ **قُبّار** *n* caper

‹ **قُبْرُص** *n* |f| Cyprus

قُبْرُصيّ *adj, n* |قَبارِصة| Cypriot

‹ **قَبَسَ** *v* |i; قَبْس| to acquire; قَبَسَ العِلْمَ to acquire knowledge; قَبَسَ نورَ شَيْءٍ to be enlightened by sth

اقْتَبَسَ *v* ① [كَلاماً] to quote, to cite; اقْتَبَسَ مَقْطَعاً to quote an excerpt ② [اسْتَوْحى] to adapt; اقْتَبَسَ مَسْرَحيّةً من تَأْليفِ شِكْسْبير to adapt a Shakespeare play

قَبَس *n* flame

قابِس I *n* |قَوابِسُ| (Elec) (power) plug; أَدْخَلَ \ وَضَعَ القابِسَ في المِقْبَسِ to insert the plug into the socket

قِباضة *n* raising, collecting, levying (*of funds or taxes*)

قَبَضاي *n* listed alphabetically

قَبْضة *n* |قَبَضات| ❶ [سَيْطَرة] grip, grasp; قَبْضة حَديديّة iron grip; قَبْضة مُحْكَمة firm grip; ... في قَبْضةِ in the grip of ..., in the grasp of ...; وَقَعَ في قَبْضةِ شَخْصٍ to fall into sb's hands; أَحْكَمَ قَبْضَتَهُ على شَيْءٍ to have a firm grip on sth ❷ [حَفْنة] fistful; قَبْضة من الأَرُزِّ fistful of rice ❸ [كَفّ] قَبْضة اليَدِ fist ❹ [مِقْياس] *linear measurement (approx 12 centimetres)*

انْقِباض *n* ❶ [تَقَلُّص] contraction ❷ [كَآبة] depression

مِقْبَض, مَقْبِض *n* |مَقابِض| knob, handle, grip, pull; مِقْبَض بابٍ door knob/handle; مِقْبَض مُسَدَّسٍ \ بُنْدُقيّةٍ butt of a gun/rifle

مَقْبوض *adj* مَقْبوض عَلَيْهِ detainee; قَلْبُهُ مَقْبوضٌ to be worried, to be distressed

مُنْقَبِض *adj* ❶ [مُتَقَلِّص] contracted ❷ [مُكْتَئِب] depressed

‹ **قَبَضاي** *n* bodyguard

‹ **قُبْطِيّ, قِبْطِي** 🅰 *adj* |أَقْباط, قِبْط| Coptic

🅱 *n* |أَقْباط, قِبْط| Copt

‹ **قُبْطان** *n* |قَباطِنة, قَباطينُ| captain; commander

قَبَعَ *v* |a| ❶ [في مَكانٍ] |قُبوع| to remain; to languish; قَبَعَ في السِجْنِ to be in jail/prison ❷ [الحَيَوانُ] |قُباع, قِباع, قَبْع| to grunt; يَقْبَعُ الخِنْزيرُ the pig grunts ❸ [القُنْفُذُ] |قُبوع| *to pull in/withdraw its head (hedgehog)*

قابِع *adj* ❶ [مَوْجود] being, remaining; languishing; قابِع وراء القُضْبانِ languishing behind bars; فَريق قابِع على قاعِ \ ذَيْلِ التَرْتيبِ a team languishing at the bottom of the rankings; نِظام قابِع على صَدْرِ الشَعْبِ a regime oppressing its people ❷ [مُخْتَبِئ] withdrawn

قُبَّعة *n* hat; cap; لَبِسَ قُبَّعةً to put on a hat; القُبَّعات الزَرْقاء the blue helmets (*UN forces*)

‹ **قَبْقاب** *n* |قَباقيبُ| clog, wooden shoe

‹ **قَبِلَ** *v* |a; قُبول, قَبول| ❶ [رَضِيَ ب] to accept, to receive; قَبِلَ to approve (of); قَبِلَ شَخْصاً \ شَيْئاً to accept sb/sth; قَبِلَ التَعازِيَ to receive condolences; قَبِلَ العَواقِبَ to accept the consequences; قَبِلَ هِبةً من شَخْصٍ to accept a donation from sb; قَبِلَ اسْتِقالةَ شَخْصٍ to accept sb's resignation; قَبِلَ شَيْئاً

قابِس II *n* |dipt f| Gabès (*city in Tunisia*)

اقْتِباس *n* |اقْتِباسات| ❶ [اسْتِشْهاد] quotation, quote; عَلامة اقْتِباسٍ quotation mark ❷ [تَحْوير] adaptation; اقْتِباس سينَمائيّ من قِصّةِ "البُؤَساءِ" film adaptation of Les Misérables

مُقابَسة *n* (scholarly) debate

مِقْبَس, مَقْبِس *n* |مَقابِسُ| ❶ (Elec) socket ❷ (Comput) plug-in; يُمْكِنُكَ تَحْميلُ المَقْبِسِ هُنا you can download the plug-in here

مُقْتَبَس *adj* derived; مُقْتَبَس من الواقِعِ based on reality; عِبارة مُقْتَبَسة quote

‹ **قُبْصة, قَبْصة** *n* pinch; قَبْصة مِلْحٍ a pinch of salt

‹ **قَبَضَ** *v* |i; قَبْض| ❶ [أَمْسَكَ] to grab; to hold; قَبَضَ شَيْئاً \ على شَيْءٍ to grab sth; قَبَضَ الصَدْرَ \ النَفْسَ to be depressing; قَبَضَ يَدَهُ عن النَفَقةِ to keep a tight hand on one's purse, to not spend anything; قَبَضَ على الجَمْرِ(ة) to be fervently committed; قَبَضَ على جَمْرِ(ة) الإصْلاحِ \ الحَقِّ \ إلخ to be committed to reform/truth/etc.; قُبِضَتْ روحُهُ to die ❷ [اعْتَقَلَ] |على| to arrest; to capture, to seize, to apprehend; قَبَضَ على شَخْصٍ to arrest sb; قَبَضَ على شَخْصٍ في حالةِ التَلَبُّسِ to catch sb in the act; قَبَضَ على عِصابةِ مُجْرِمينَ to round up a gang of criminals; قَبَضَ على الحَرامِيّةِ \ المُجْرِمينَ \ المُداهِمينَ to apprehend the thieves/criminals/ burglars ❸ [حَصَلَ على] to receive; قَبَضَ مالاً \ مُرَتَّباً to receive money/payment

تَقَبَّضَ *v* to contract

انْقَبَضَ *v* to contract; انْقَبَضَ قَلْبُهُ \ صَدْرُهُ to be/become sad; انْقَبَضَتْ عَضَلاتُهُ to flex one's muscles

قَبْض *n* ❶ [اعْتِقال] arrest; detention; إلْقاء القَبْضِ arrest; apprehension; أَمْر بِإلْقاءِ القَبْضِ arrest warrant; أَصْدَرَ أَمْراً بِإلْقاءِ القَبْضِ to issue an arrest warrant; أَلْقى القَبْضَ على شَخْصٍ to arrest sb, to capture sb; أَلْقى القَبْضَ على عِصابةٍ to round up a gang; أُلْقِيَ القَبْضُ عَلَيْهِ to be arrested ❷ (Med) constipation

قابِض 🅰 *adj* grabbing, holding, clutching; شَرِكة قابِضة holding company

🅱 *n* ❶ [سَيّارةٍ] clutch; مَداس القابِضِ clutch pedal ❷ (Islam) القابِض the Restrainer (*one of the names of God*)

تَقَبَّلْ تَعازِينا الصادِقةَ للعيدِ to receive holiday greetings; please accept our sincere condolences 2 (Relig) to answer; تَقَبَّلَ to accept; تَقَبَّلَ اللهُ دُعاءَهُ God has answered his prayers; تَقَبَّلَ اللهُ صِيامَكَ may God accept your fast

تَقابَلَ *v* to meet each other; تَقابَلَ اللاعِبانِ the two players met

اِسْتَقْبَلَ *v* 1 [لاقَ] to receive; to welcome; اِسْتَقْبَلَ ضَيْفاً to receive a guest; اِسْتَقْبَلَ البَطْرِيَرْكُ \ الأَميرُ \ الوَزيرُ الوُفودَ the patriarch/prince/minister received the delegations; اِسْتَقْبَلَ شَخْصاً اِسْتِقْبالاً حارًّا to give sb a warm welcome; اِسْتَقْبَلَ مَوْلوداً جَديداً to welcome a new baby 2 [البَثَّ] to receive; اِسْتَقْبَلَ البَثَّ to receive a broadcast

قَبْلَ *prep* before; قَبْلَ ذلك before that, previously; قَبْلَ كُلِّ شَيْءٍ especially, above all, most importantly; قَبْلَ العَصْرِ before evening prayers, ≈ in the late afternoon; من الواحِدةِ بعد الظُهْرِ حتّى الثالِثةِ قَبْلَ العَصْرِ from 1 pm to 3 p.m.; قَبْلَ الظُهْرِ before noon/midday prayers, ≈ in the late morning; قَبْلَ عِدَّةِ أَيّامٍ \ سَنَواتٍ a few days/years ago; a few days/years before; العام قَبْلَ الماضي the year before last; الدَوْر قَبْلَ النِهائيِّ the penultimate round; الحَلْقة قَبْلَ الأَخيرةِ the second to last episode; قَبْلَ الميلادِ Before Christ, BC; Before Common Era, BCE; وَصَلَ قَبْلي he arrived before me; أَدْرَكَ شَيْئاً قَبْلَ فَواتِ الوَقْتِ \ الأَوانِ to realize sth before it's too late; قَبْلَ أَنْ ... before ...; صَمَتَ لَحْظةً قَبْلَ أَنْ يَقولَ شَيْئاً he was silent for a moment before saying anything; من قَبْلِ أَنْ ... before ...; قَدْرُهُ مَكْتوبٌ من قَبْلِ أَنْ يَأْتِيَ إلى الحَياةِ his fate was written before he was born; قَبْلَ قَليلٍ just now, a moment ago; قَبْلَ شَيْءٍ بِدَقيقةٍ \ بِساعةٍ \ بِيَوْمٍ a minute/hour/day before sth; قَبْلاً before, previously; already

قَبْلُ *adv* من قَبْلُ previously, formerly; earlier, before that; لم يَكُنْ ذلك مُباحاً من قَبْلُ that was not allowed previously; لم يَحْدُثْ من قَبْلُ it hasn't happened before; أَكْثَر من ذي قَبْلُ more than before

قُبُل *n* |أَقْبال| (old use) front (side); كانَ قَميصُهُ قُدَّ من قُبُلٍ his shirt was torn from the front (*from Surat Yusuf*)

قِبَل *n* 1 [من قِبَلِ] من قِبَلِ by; from; تَعَرَّضوا لِإطْلاقِ نارٍ من قِبَلِ جَماعةٍ مُسَلَّحةٍ they were fired upon by an armed group

قَبِلَ اعْتِذاراً to accept sth without reservation; قَبِلَ بِدونِ تَحَفُّظٍ to accept an apology; قَبِلَ شَخْصاً عُضْواً to accept sb as a member; لن نَقْبَلَ بِهذا الشَرْطِ we will not accept this condition; قَبِلَ بالاقْتِراحِ to agree with the proposal; لا أَقْبَلُ بِهذا التَصَرُّفِ I don't approve of this behavior; قُبِلَ مَطْلَبُكَ your application/request has been approved 2 [كانَ في إمْكانِهِ] to be able to; لا يَقْبَلُ الشَكَّ to be unquestionable/indisputable 3 [المَوْلودَ] (old use) to deliver (*a baby*); قَبِلَت القابِلةُ المَوْلودَ the midwife delivered the baby

قَبَّلَ *v* to kiss; قَبَّلَ شَخْصاً to kiss sb; قُبِّلَ to be kissed; قَبَّلَ حَبيبَتَهُ to kiss one's beloved; قَبَّلَ بِحَرارةٍ to kiss passionately; قَبَّلَ يَدَ شَخْصٍ to kiss sb's hand; قَبَّلَ فَمَ \ خَدَّيْ شَخْصٍ to kiss sb on the mouth/cheeks

قابَلَ *v* 1 [لاقى] to meet, to encounter; to interview; قابَلَ شَخْصاً to meet/encounter sb; to interview sb; قابَلَ شَخْصاً لِأَوَّلِ مَرّةٍ to meet sb for the first time; قوبِلَ طَلَبُهُمْ بالرَفْضِ their request was met with a refusal 2 [واجَهَ] to face; سَيُقابِلُ الفَريقُ الفائِزَ من المُباراةِ المُقْبِلةِ the team will face the winner of the next match 3 [الشَيْءَ بالشَيْءِ] to pay back; قابَلَ العُنْفَ بالعُنْفِ to repay violence with violence; قابَلَ شَيْئاً بالمِثْلِ to return sth like for like 4 [ماثَلَ] to be equal to, to be the equivalent of; الدولارُ يُقابِلُ حَوالَيْ ٥٠ ليرةً سوريّةً a dollar is equal to about 50 Syrian pounds 5 [قارَنَ] to compare; قابَلَ شَيْئاً بِشَيْءٍ to compare sth to sth; قابَلَ شَيْئَيْنِ to compare two things

أَقْبَلَ *v* 1 [قَرُبَ] to arrive; to approach; to show up; أَقْبَلَت الحافِلةُ the bus arrived; أَقْبَلَ الناخِبونَ بِكَثافةٍ the voters turned out in great numbers; قد أَقْبَلَ العامُ the year has begun 2 [كَرَّسَ] |على| to dedicate/devote oneself to; to occupy oneself with; to start; أَقْبَلَ على العَمَلِ to set to work; أَقْبَلَ على دُروسِهِ to devote oneself to one's studies; أَقْبَلَ على الشِراءِ to buy enthusiastically, to go on a shopping spree; أَقْبَلَ المُسْتَثْمِرونَ على شِراءِ الأَسْهُمِ the investors went on a stock-buying spree

تَقَبَّلَ *v* 1 [قَبِلَ] to accept; to receive; تَقَبَّلَ النَصيحةَ to take advice; تَقَبَّلَ التَهانِيَ to receive congratulations;

سِياسة القَبولِ قاسِية stringent/strict admission requirements; نالَ قَبولَ شَخْصٍ admittance policy; immigration policy; حَظِيَ بِقَبولِ شَخْصٍ to be accepted by sb; to gain the approval of sb; اعْتَذَرَ عن قَبولِ شَيْءٍ to decline to accept sth; لا يُمْكِنُ قَبولُهُ \ القَبولُ بِهِ to be unacceptable; لَقِيَ قَبولاً to be well received (art, ideas, etc.); هذا الكِتابُ لم يَلْقَ قَبولاً من الجُمْهورِ this book was not well received by the people; تَفَضَّلوا بِقَبولِ فائِقِ الاحْتِرامِ yours sincerely, sincerely (yours) (AmE); yours faithfully (BrE) (used when you don't know the addressee's name)

قَبيل *n* type; kind; species; من قَبيل like; as; (شَيْء) من هذا القَبيلِ (sth) like this; (sth) similar, similarly; كَلِمات من نَفْسِ القَبيلِ words of similar meaning; لَيْسَ من قَبيلِ المُصادَفةِ أنْ … it's not a coincidence that …; لَيْسَ من قَبيلِ المُبالَغةِ القَوْلُ إنّ … it's no exaggeration to say that …; هذا من قَبيلِ ذَرِّ الرَمادِ في العُيونِ that's nothing but a smoke screen

قُبَيْلَ *prep* just/shortly before; قُبَيْلَ أنْ just before; shortly before; قُبَيْلَ هُبوطِ الطائِرةِ في المَطارِ shortly before the plane landed at the airport

قَبيلة *n* |قَبائِل| tribe; clan; قَبائِل رُحَّل nomadic tribes

اسْتِقْبال *n* |اسْتِقْبالات| ⟨1⟩ [شَخْصٍ] welcome; reception; accommodation; اسْتِقْبال حارّ \ حافِل \ حاشِد a warm welcome; اسْتِقْبال فاتِر a lukewarm welcome; لَقِيَ اسْتِقْبالاً حارًّا to receive a warm welcome; رَفَضَ اسْتِقْبالَ شَخْصٍ to refuse to receive sb; تَهَيَّأَ لِاسْتِقْبالِ شَيْءٍ \ شَخْصٍ to welcome the coming of sth/sb's arrival; شَكَرَ شَخْصاً على حُسْنِ \ حَفاوةِ الاسْتِقْبالِ (fml) to thank sb for the warm reception; في اسْتِقْبالِ شَخْصٍ waiting/present to receive sb; أقامَ حَفْلَ \ حَفْلةَ اسْتِقْبالٍ to give a reception; مَراسِم اسْتِقْبالٍ official reception ceremonies; صالة \ قاعة \ غُرْفة اسْتِقْبالٍ living room; reception room; lobby; صَفْحة الاسْتِقْبالِ home page; مَرْكَز اسْتِقْبالٍ shelter; اسْتِقْبال اللاجِئينَ the reception of refugees; مَرْكَز اسْتِقْبالِ اللاجِئينَ Refugee Processing Centre ⟨2⟩ [البَثِّ] reception

إقْبال *n* ⟨1⟩ [حُضور] attendance; turnout; إقْبال جَماهيرِيّ popularity; إقْبال كَثيف \ ضَعيف high/low turnout; لاقى إقْبالاً شَديداً \ كَبيراً to be well received ⟨2⟩ [اهْتِمام] interest;

⟨2⟩ [طاقة] ability, capability; لا قِبَلَ لَهُ على \ بِذَلِكَ he can't do that; he's not capable of doing that, he couldn't do that

قِبَلَ *prep* facing, opposite; in the proximity of

قابِل *adj* |ل| susceptible to; subject to; receptive to; قابِل للتَنْفيذِ feasible, achievable, attainable; قابِل للتَجْديدِ renewable; قابِل للتَطْبيقِ applicable; قابِل للتَحْويلِ convertible; transferable; غَيْر قابِلٍ للتَفاوُضِ non-negotiable; غَيْر قابِلٍ للتَرْجَمةِ untranslatable; كانَ قابِلاً لِشَيْءٍ to be susceptible to sth

قابِلة *n* |قابِلات, قَوابِلُ| midwife; قابِلة مَأْذونة (ME) ≈ registered midwife

قابِلِيّة *n* ability; readiness, willingness; susceptibility; الأكْثَر \ الأقَلّ قابِلِيّةً ل … the best/least able to …; عَدَم قابِلِيّةٍ inability; قابِلِيّة للاسْتِعْمارِ vulnerability to colonization; قابِلِيّة عُمْلةٍ للتَحْويلِ convertibility of a currency; قابِلِيّة للتَكَيُّفِ adaptability

قُبالةَ *prep* opposite, facing, across from; in front of; المَبْنى قُبالةَ الجامِعةِ the building is opposite the university; قُبالةَ شَواطِئِ جَنوبِ لُبْنانَ off the coast of South Lebanon; العَشَراتُ يَعْتَصِمونَ قُبالةَ السِفارةِ dozens are demonstrating in front of the embassy

قِبالة *n* midwifery

قُبْلة *n* |قُبَل, قُبُلات, قُبْلات| kiss; peck; قُبْلة حارّة passionate kiss; قُبْلاتي الحارّة ≈ hugs and kisses (endearment to friends or family, as in a letter); قُبْلة الحَياةِ mouth-to-mouth resuscitation; طَبَعَ قُبْلةً على خَدِّ شَخْصٍ to plant a kiss on sb's cheek; قُبْلة على اليَدِ kiss on the hand; أرْسَلَ \ رَمى قُبْلةً في الهَواءِ لِشَخْصٍ to blow sb a kiss

قِبْلة *n* ⟨1⟩ (Islam) qiblah (the direction faced in prayer); القِبْلة الأولى Jerusalem ⟨2⟩ [شَيْء جَذّاب] magnet, attraction; قِبْلة للسُيّاحِ tourist attraction

قَبَلِيّ *adj* tribal; مُجْتَمَع قَبَلِيّ tribal society; عُرْف قَبَلِيّ tribal law

قَبَلِيّة *n* tribalism

قَبول, قُبول *n* acceptance; admission; امْتِحان \ اخْتِبار القَبولِ entrance examination; شَرْط القَبولِ admission requirement; entry requirement; شُروط القَبولِ في جامِعةٍ \ كُلّيّةٍ admission requirements for a university/college; شُروط قَبولٍ صَعْبة \

demand; انْتَعَشَ الإقْبالُ على شِراءِ الأَسْهُمِ stock trading recovered sharply

تَقَبُّل *n* acceptance; كانَ مُهَيَّأً لِتَقَبُّلِ شَيْءٍ to be prepared to accept sth

مُتَقابِل *adj* opposite

مُتَقَبِّل *adj* receptive

مُسْتَقْبَل *n* ① [الزَمَن القادِم] future; perspective; المُسْتَقْبَل القَريب the near future; المُسْتَقْبَل البَعيد the distant future; آفاق المُسْتَقْبَلِ the far/distant future; the long term; المُسْتَقْبَل المَنْظور the foreseeable future; مُسْتَقْبَل مُشْرِق \ زاهِر \ باهِر a bright future; مُسْتَقْبَل أَفْضَل a better future; مُسْتَقْبَل واعِد a promising future; مُسْتَقْبَل مُظْلِم a dark future; في المُسْتَقْبَلِ, مُسْتَقْبَلاً in the future; اسْتَشْرَفَ المُسْتَقْبَلَ to forecast/predict the future; تَنَبَّأَ بالمُسْتَقْبَلِ to foresee/divine the future; هَدَّدَ مُسْتَقْبَلَ شَيْءٍ to threaten sth's future; رَهَنَ مُسْتَقْبَلَ شَيْءٍ to hold sth's future hostage; تَطَلُّع نحو مُسْتَقْبَلٍ أَفْضَلَ striving towards a better future; صَنَعَ \ بَنَى مُسْتَقْبَلاً أَفْضَلَ to build a better future; فَكَّرَ في المُسْتَقْبَلِ to think of/consider the future; خَطَّطَ للمُسْتَقْبَلِ to plan for the future; أَسَّسَ للمُسْتَقْبَلِ to build a foundation for the future; تَفاؤُل \ تَشاؤُم بالمُسْتَقْبَلِ optimism/pessimism about the future; لا مُسْتَقْبَلَ لَهُ he has no future; لَهُ مُسْتَقْبَلٌ بارِزٌ he has a bright future; مُسْتَقْبَلُنا على المِحَكِّ our future is on the line; ماذا يُخَبِّئُ لَنا المُسْتَقْبَلُ؟ what will the future bring us? ② (Gram) future tense

مُسْتَقْبِل *n* receiver

مُسْتَقْبَلِيّ *adj* future (*before n*); upcoming; زَوْجَتي المُسْتَقْبَلِيّة my future wife; رُؤْيَة \ صورة مُسْتَقْبَلِيّة لِشَيْءٍ vision for the future of sth; أَحْلام مُسْتَقْبَلِيّة dreams for the future

مُقابِل Ⓐ *adj* opposite, facing; *on the other side*; الاتِّجاه المُقابِل the opposite direction

Ⓑ *n* ① [مُعادِل] equivalent; compensation; *sth done in exchange*; مُقابِل ذلك فَإِنَّ ... on the other hand ...; مُقابِل مادّيّ financial compensation; بِمُقابِلٍ (ماليٍّ) for (monetary) compensation; بِدونِ مُقابِلٍ free; voluntary; مُساعَدة بِدونِ مُقابِلٍ voluntary cooperation; في مُقابِلِ إفْراجٍ عن أَسْرى in exchange for the release of prisoners; لِكُلِّ شَيْءٍ مُقابِلٌ everything has a price; there's no such thing as a free lunch ② [مُسْتَجوِب] interviewer

مُقابِلَ *prep* opposite, facing; in exchange for, for; instead of; against; مُقابِلَ ذلك فَإِنَّ ... on the other hand ...; مُقابِلَ تَعْويضٍ for a fee; مُقابِلَ مَبْلَغٍ ماليٍّ in exchange for a sum of money; الأَرْض مُقابِلَ السَلامِ land for peace; سِعْر اليَن مُقابِلَ الجُنَيْهِ the exchange rate between the yen and the pound; ارْتِفاع سِعْرِ شَيْءٍ مُقابِلَ تَراجُع سِعْرِ شَيْءٍ آخَرَ rise of the price of sth versus a decrease in the price of sth else (*stocks*); ثَمانِية أَهْدافٍ مُقابِلَ لاشَيْءٍ 8-0 (*score*)

مُقابَلة *n* ① [اجْتِماع] interview; meeting; dialogue; أَجْرى مُقابَلةً مع شَخْصٍ to conduct an interview with sb; to hold a meeting with sb ② [مُباراة] game, match

مُقْبِل *adj* next, coming; future; following, subsequent; الأُسْبوع \ الشَهْر المُقْبِل next week/month; الثُلاثاء المُقْبِل next Tuesday; the following Tuesday; الأَجْيال المُقْبِلة future generations; المَرْحَلة المُقْبِلة the next phase; إِنْتَرْنِت الجيل المُقْبِل next-generation Internet; الرَئيس المُقْبِل the next president

مُقَبِّلات *n pl* appetizers, starters, hors-d'oeuvres; first course

مَقْبول *adj* ① [سائغ] acceptable, reasonable; credible, plausible; تَقْدير مَقْبول pass mark (BrE), passing grade (AmE); صيغة مَقْبولة لِجَميع الأَطْرافِ a plan acceptable to all sides; لا يوجَدُ عُذْرٌ مَقْبولٌ لِذلِكَ there's no excuse for that; حَلّ مَقْبول acceptable solution; غَيْر مَقْبولٍ unacceptable, intolerable; objectionable; تَصَرُّف غَيْر مَقْبولٍ intolerable behaviour; طَلَب غَيْر مَقْبولٍ an unacceptable demand ② [مُعْتَمَد] recognized ③ (Law) admissible; غَيْر مَقْبولٍ inadmissible

مَقْبولِيّة *n* acceptability; شَخْص أَكْثَر مَقْبولِيّةً a more acceptable person; عَدَم مَقْبولِيّةٍ unacceptability

مُقْتَبَل *n* في مُقْتَبَلِ العُمْرِ in the prime of life

‹ **قَبّان** *n* scale; weighbridge (BrE), truck scale (AmE); بَيْضة القَبّانِ counterweight, counterbalance

‹ **قَبْو** *n* |أَقْبِية| basement, cellar; في القَبْوِ in the basement; قَبْو مُعْتِم \ مُظْلِم dark cellar; قَبْو رَطْب dank/damp cellar

‹ **قَتاد** *n* (Bot) tragacanth

حَقَّق في قَضِيّة قَتْلِ شَخْصٍ involvement in the killing of sb; قَتْلٍ to investigate a murder; ارْتَكَبَ جَرِيمةَ قَتْلٍ to commit murder; أَسْفَرَ عن قَتْلِ شَخْصٍ to result in sb's death; أَباحَ \ بَرَّرَ القَتْلَ to allow/justify killing; هَدَّدَ شَخْصاً بالقَتْلِ to threaten to kill sb; أَمَرَ بِقَتْلِ شَخْصٍ to order sb to be killed; خَطَّطَ \ تآمَرَ لِقَتْلِ شَخْصٍ to plan/conspire to kill sb; لم يَتَوَرَّعْ عن قَتْلِ شَخْصٍ to not hesitate to kill sb

قاتِل **A** *adj* |قاتِلونَ, قَتَلة, قُتّال| **1** [مُميت] deadly, fatal, mortal; lethal; murderous; فَيْروس \ عَدْوى \ مَرَض قاتِل(ة) deadly virus/infection/disease; رَصاصة \ طَعْنة قاتِلة fatal shot/stab; أُصيبَ إصابةً قاتِلةً to be mortally wounded; ارْتَكَبَ خَطأً قاتِلاً to commit a fatal mistake **2** [شَديد] terrible, awful, unbearable; أَجْواء يَأْسٍ قاتِلٍ a state of deep despair; الرُطوبةُ قاتِلةٌ! the humidity is unbearable! **3** [رائع] amazing, incredible; هَدَف قاتِل *dramatic match-winning goal*; جَمال قاتِل stunning beauty

B *n* |قاتِلونَ, قَتَلة, قُتّال| killer; murderer; قاتِل مَأْجور (hired) assassin

قَتّال *adj* deadly, fatal; lethal

قِتال *n* battle, combat; fighting, hostilities; fight; قِتال دائِر ongoing hostilities; قِتال ضارٍ \ عَنيف \ شَرِس savage/violent/ fierce fighting; مَيْدان \ ساحة القِتالِ battlefield; arena; احْتِدام \ انْدِلاع القِتالِ outbreak of hostilities; تَجَدُّد القِتالِ resumption of hostilities; وَقْف القِتالِ ceasefire; جَبْهة القِتالِ front (*line of contact between two armies*); رِياضة فُنونِ القِتالِ martial arts; مُتَطَوِّع لِقِتالٍ volunteer fighter; تَدْريب على القِتالِ combat training; مُسْتَعِدّ \ جاهِز للقِتالِ ready for battle

قِتاليّ *adj* military; martial; fighting, combat; فُنون قِتاليّة martial arts; مِرْوَحيّة قِتاليّة combat helicopter; عَقيدة قِتاليّة warrior ethos; كَفاءة قِتاليّة military capability; روح قِتاليّة fighting spirit

قَتيل **A** *adj* |قَتالى, قُتَلاءُ, قَتْلى| killed; سَقَطَ \ أُرْدِيَ قَتيلاً to be struck down; الرَئيس الّذي أُرْدِيَ قَتيلاً the president who was killed

B *n* |قَتالى, قُتَلاءُ, قَتْلى| victim, casualty; *person killed*; أَدّى إلى سُقوطِ قَتيلٍ to lead to one death; أَوْقَعَت المَذْبَحةُ ١١ قتيلاً

‹ **قَتَرَ** *v* |u; قَتْر| to be a miser

قَتَّرَ *v* to be a miser; to be/become stingy; قَتَّرَ على عِيالِهِ to be stingy with one's family

قُتار *n* smell, scent, fragrance

تَقْتير *n* stinginess, miserliness

مُقَتِّر *adj* stingy, miserly

‹ **قَتَلَ** *v* |u; قَتْل| to kill; to murder; قَتَلَ شَخْصاً \ حَيَواناً to kill sb/ an animal; قَتَلَ شَخْصاً عَمْداً \ عن عَمْدٍ to murder sb; قُتِلَ بالرَصاصِ to be shot dead; قَتَلَ شَخْصاً بِوَحْشيّةٍ to kill sb savagely; قَتَلَ شَخْصاً بِدَمٍ بارِدٍ to murder sb in cold blood; قُتِلَ بِ \ على يَدِ شَخْصٍ to die at sb's hands; قَتَلَ الوَقْتَ to kill time; قُتِلَ في المَعارِكِ to be killed in battle; قَتَلَهُ الجوعُ to die from hunger

Idiom قَتَلَ شَيْئاً بَحْثاً to study sth thoroughly

قَتَّلَ *v* to kill; to slaughter

قاتَلَ *v* to fight; to battle; to combat; to struggle; قاتَلَ العَدُوَّ to fight the enemy; قاتَلَ بِشَراسةٍ (لِفِعْلِ شَيْءٍ) to fight fiercely (to do sth); قاتَلَ بِبَسالةٍ \ بِشَجاعةٍ to fight bravely; قاتَلَ حتّى الرَمَقِ الأَخيرِ to fight to the bitter end; قاتَلَ حتّى المَوْتِ to fight to the death; قاتَلَ في سَبيلِ شَيْءٍ to fight for the cause of sth; قاتَلَهُ اللهُ *may God fight him*; ≈ the bastard!

تَقاتَلَ *v* to battle; to fight each other

اقْتَتَلَ *v* to battle; to fight

اسْتَقْتَلَ *v* to risk one's life, to defy death

قَتْل *n* killing; murder; قَتْل مع سَبْقِ الإِصْرارِ premeditated murder; قَتْل على الهُوِيّةِ sectarian killing; قَتْل رَحيم euthanasia; mercy killing; قَتْل جَماعيّ mass murder; قَتْل عَمْد \ عَمْداً murder, homicide (AmE); القَتْل الخَطأ manslaughter; جِناية قَتْلٍ (عَمْدٍ) murder (*without mitigating circumstances*); ≈ aggravated (BrE) first-degree (AmE) murder; عَمَليّات قَتْلٍ murderous acts; قَضيّة قَتْلٍ murder case; murder trial; تُهْمة القَتْلِ murder charge; accusation of murder; إدانة بِتُهْمةِ القَتْلِ العَمْدِ murder conviction; شُروع في \ مُحاوَلة قَتْلٍ attempted murder; تَحْريض على القَتْلِ incitement of murder; تَواطُؤ في قَتْلٍ conspiracy to commit murder; ضُلوع في قَتْلِ شَخْصٍ accessory to the murder of sb; التَوَرُّط في

eleven people were killed in the carnage; قَتْلى الحَرْبِ casualties of war; حَصيلة قَتْلى (زِلْزالٍ، فَيَضاناتٍ، إلخ) death toll (from an earthquake, flood, etc.)

اقْتِتال *n* fighting, conflict; combat; اقْتِتال داخِليّ civil conflict; اقْتِتال مَذْهَبيّ \ طائِفيّ sectarian violence

مُتَقاتِل *adj* fighting; struggling

مُقاتِل **A** *adj* combat (*before n*), fighter (*before n*); طائِرة مُقاتِلة fighter, fighter jet/plane

B *n* fighter; مُقاتِل انْفِصاليّ separatist fighter; مُقاتِل مُناهِض resistance/opposition fighter; مُقاتِل أَجْنَبيّ foreign fighter; مُقاتِلونَ مُوالونَ \ تابِعونَ ل ... fighters loyal to/belonging to ...; تَجْنيد المُقاتِلينَ recruitment of fighters; تَسَلُّل المُقاتِلينَ عَبْرَ الحُدودِ infiltration of fighters over the border

مُقاتَلة *n* fighting; fight, struggle; combat

مَقْتَل *n* |مَقاتِلُ| **1▸** [قَتْل] murder, killing; أَدّى إلى \ أَسْفَرَ عن مَقْتَلِ شَخْصٍ to lead to sb's killing; تَسَبَّبَ بِمَقْتَلِ شَخْصٍ to cause sb to be killed (outright); غَداةَ مَقْتَلِ (على الفَوْرِ) شَخْصٍ in the aftermath of the killing of sb; انْتِقاماً \ ثَأْراً لِمَقْتَلِ شَخْصٍ in retaliation/revenge for sb's killing; أَدانَ مَقْتَل مَدَنِيّين to condemn the killing of civilians; مُلابَسات مَقْتَل شَخْصٍ the circumstances of sb's murder; مَقْتَل شَخْصٍ في انْفِجارٍ \ كَمينٍ \ غارةٍ killing of sb in an explosion/ambush/raid; مَقْتَل شَخْصٍ بِرَصاصٍ sb's fatal shooting **2▸** [مَكان قَتْلٍ] murder scene **3▸** [عُضْو حَسّاس] Achilles' heel; weakness; أَصابَ من شَخْصٍ المَقْتَلَ to cut sb to the quick

مَقْتول *adj* killed; murdered

‹ **قَتَمَ** *v* |u; قُتوم| to cloud over; to darken

قاتِم *adj* |قَواتِمُ| dark; gloomy; رَسَمَ صورةً قاتِمةً عن شَيْءٍ to paint a bleak picture of sth; لَوْن قاتِم a dark colour

قَتام *n* dark, darkness

قَتامة *n* darkness; gloom; bleakness

أَقْتَم *adj* |dipt| darker; darkest

‹ **قِثّاء** *n coll* cucumber

‹ **قَثْطَرة**, **قِثْطار** *n* catheter

‹ **قَحْبة** *n* |قِحاب| (vulg) prostitute; promiscuous woman; whore (vulg)

‹ **قِحة** *n* see **وقح**

‹ **قُحّ** *adj* |أَقْحاح| pure, unadulterated; true, genuine; عَرَب أَقْحاح pure-blooded Arabs

‹ **قَحَطَ** *v* |a; قُحوط, قَحْط| to fail to happen; to fail to appear; قَحَطَ المَطَرُ the rain held off; إذا قَسا القَلْبُ قَحَطَت العَيْنُ *a hard heart sheds no tears*

قَحْط *n* **1▸** [جَفاف] drought; famine; قَحْط ثَقافيّ \ فِكْريّ cultural/intellectual stagnation; القَحْط الشِعْريّ writer's block **2▸** (Med) curettage; عَمَلِيّة التَوْسيع والقَحْط dilatation and curettage, D&C (*abortion*)

‹ **قَحْطان** *n* |dipt| Qahtan (*legendary progenitor of the Qahtanis (the inhabitants of the southern Arabian peninsula)*)

‹ **قَحَفَ** *v* |a; قَحْف| to swallow; to absorb

قِحْف *n* |قِحَفة, أَقْحاف, قُحوف| skull; cranium

‹ **قَحِلَ** *v* |a; قَحْل| to dry up; to dry out; قد قَحِلَت الأَرْضُ the soil has dried up

قَحْل *n* desolation

قاحِل *adj* dry, arid; barren, poor; صَحْراء قاحِلة barren desert

‹ **أَقْحَمَ** *v* to involve; to intrude; أَقْحَمَ نَفْسَهُ في شَيْءٍ to get involved in sth; أَقْحَمَ نَفْسَهُ في النِقاشِ to insinuate oneself into a conversation; لا أُريدُ أنْ أُقْحِمَ عائِلَتي في ذلك I don't want to involve my family in this

اقْتَحَمَ *v* **1▸** to break in, to break into, to penetrate; to intrude; to infringe on; اقْتَحَمَ مَنْزِلاً to break into a house **2▸** (Comput) to hack; to infect (*of a virus*)

اقْتِحام *n* break-in, forcible entry; incursion, invasion; اقْتِحام المَنْزِلِ break-in, unlawful entry; نَفَّذَ الجَيْشُ عَمَلِيّةَ اقْتِحامٍ لِلبَلَدِ the army made an incursion into the town

مُقْتَحِم *n* intruder

مُقْحَم *adj* imposed; forced, artificial; superfluous, unnecessary, irrelevant; مُقْحَم في شَيْءٍ involuntarily/unwittingly involved in sth; غَيْر مُقْحَم indigenous; authentic; تَيّار لِيبِراليّ غَرْبيّ مُقْحَم في مُجْتَمَعِنا a liberal Western framework imposed on our society; آخِرُ مَشْهَدٍ مُتَكَلَّفٌ ومُقْحَمٌ على الفيلْم the last scene feels artificial and forced into the film; الكَلِمةُ لَيْسَتْ مُقْحَمةً بَلْ إنَّها لازِمةٌ the word isn't superfluous; it's necessary (*grammar*)

‹ **قَدْ** *particle* ❶ [الماضي] already; yet; *equivalent to perfect "have/has"*; قَدْ حانَ الوَقْتُ it's time, time's up; قَدْ فَعَلْتُ ذلك I've (already) done that; قَدْ عَرَفْتُ \ عَلِمْتُ ذلك I already knew that; قَدْ بَدَأَ العَمَلُ بالفِعْلِ the work has begun in earnest; ما حَصَلَ قَدْ حَصَلَ what's done is done; كانَ قَدْ قالَ من قَبْلُ إنّ ... he had said before that ...; سَيَكونُ قَدْ حَلَّ المُشْكِلَةَ he will have solved the problem; عِنْدَما وَصَلَ كانَ الصَباحُ قَدْ طَلَعَ when he arrived, it was already morning ❷ [المُضارِع] may, might; maybe, possibly, likely; قَدْ يُؤَدّي إلى ... it could lead to ...; قَدْ يَكونُ مُفيداً it might be beneficial; قَدْ يَحْصُلُ خلافٌ there could be an argument; كُلُّ شَخْصٍ قَدْ يُخْطِئُ everybody makes mistakes; قَدْ يَأْتي وَقَدْ لا يَأْتي he might come, he might not; قَدْ لا تَكونُ هُناكَ فُرْصةٌ أُخْرى there might not be another chance

‹ **قَدَحَ** *v* |a; قَدْح| ❶ [النارَ] to strike, to spark (*flint*); قَدَحَ النارَ to make fire (*with flint*); قَدَحَ شَرَراً to spark, to make sparks; عَيْناها تَقْدَحانِ شَرَراً her eyes are flashing (*from anger, passion*); قَدَحَ زِنادَ فِكْرِهِ to think hard, to rack one's brains ❷ [ذَمَّ] |في| to defame, to malign, to vilify, to cast aspersions on; to reject; قَدَحَ في عِرْضِ شَخْصٍ to defame sb, to speak ill about sb; قَدَحَ في نَتائِجِ الانْتِخاباتِ to reject the election results

قَدْح *n* defamation, vilification, aspersion; قَدْح وَذَمّ (Law) defamation; libel; slander; رَفَعَ دَعْوى \ قَضِيّةَ قَدْحٍ وذَمٍّ to file a defamation suit; اتُّهِمَ بِجُرْمِ القَدْحِ والذَمِّ to be charged with criminal defamation

قَدَح *n* |أَقْداح| ❶ [كَأْس] cup, glass; mug; قَدَح القَهْوة \ الشايِ coffee cup/teacup; cup of coffee/tea; قَدَح نَبيذٍ \ خَمْرٍ wine glass; glass of wine ❷ [مِقْياس] *liquid measure, approx 2 litres*

قَدّاح *n* flint

قَدّاحة *n* lighter

‹ **قَدَّ** *v* |u; قَدّ| to cut/slice into strips; قُدَّ to be made/designed; يُقَدُّ قُدَّ الثَوْبُ على قَدِّ لابِسِهِ the robe is made to fit the wearer; قُدَّ من شَيْءٍ to be made of sth; قُدَّ قَلْبُهُ من صَخْرٍ he has a heart of stone

قَدَّدَ *v to cut into strips and dry; to make sun-dried jerky*

قَدّ *n* |قُدود| ❶ [حَجْم] size; scope, extent; quantity, amount; على قَدِّ شَيْءٍ fitting sth; of the same size as sth; to the same extent as sth; هذا الفُسْتانُ على قَدّي this dress fits me; على قَدِّ المَقامِ appropriate to the situation; على قَدِّ الحالِ of limited means, humble; ordinary, average, unremarkable; على قَدِّ لِحافِكَ مُدَّ رِجْلَيْكَ ≈ cut your coat to suit your cloth (*your actions should be in accordance with your means*) ❷ [قامة] figure; لَها قَدٌّ مَيّاسٌ \ رَشيقٌ \ مَمْشوقٌ she has an elegant figure

قُدّ *n* cod, codfish

قِدّة *n* |قِدَد| lath; batten

قَديد *n sun-dried strips of meat, usually lamb*

مُقَدَّد *adj* sliced, cut into strips (*meat/fish*)

‹ **قَدَرَ** *v* |i; قُدْرة, مَقْدُرة, مَقْدَرة, مَقْدِرة| ❶ [اسْتَطاعَ] |على| to be able to; to be capable of; قَدَرَ على السِباحةِ \ المَشْيِ to be able to swim/walk; قَدَرَ على تَحَمُّلِ شَيْءٍ to be able to bear/handle sth; لا أَقْدِرُ على العَمَلِ I'm not able to work ❷ (Islam) to will/ordain (*said of God*)

قَدَّرَ *v* ❶ [خَمَّنَ] to assess, to estimate, to appraise, to value, to judge; قَدَّرَ نِسَبَ النَجاحِ to estimate the chances of success; قَدَّرَ قيمةَ شَيْءٍ بِخَمْسينَ دولار to estimate the value of something at fifty dollars; قَدَّرَ قيمةَ العَقارِ to value (BrE) appraise (AmE) real estate; يُقَدِّرُ الخُبَراءُ أنّ ... experts estimate/consider that ...; يُقَدِّرُ الخُبَراءُ الخَسائِرَ ب ... experts estimate the losses at ...; الإنْسانُ يُقَدِّرُ واللهُ يُدَبِّرُ man proposes, God disposes; لا يُقَدَّرُ بِثَمَنٍ \ بِمالٍ priceless; invaluable; لَوْحة لا تُقَدَّرُ بِثَمَنٍ a priceless painting; كِتاب لا يُقَدَّرُ بِثَمَنٍ للطُلّابِ an invaluable book for students; قُدِّرَتْ كُلْفةُ المَشْروعِ بِمِلْيارَيْ دولار the cost of the project was estimated at $2 billion; تُقَدَّرُ قيمةُ الصَفْقةِ ب ... the deal is valued at ...; يُقَدَّرُ احْتِياطيُّها من النَفْطِ ب ... its oil reserves are valued at ...; قُدِّرَ بِنَحْوِ \ بِحَوالَيْ ... to be worth approximately ...; نِسْبةُ الإنْفاقِ على التَعْليمِ تُقَدَّرُ بِنَحْوِ ٩,٥ في المِائةِ education spending makes up approximately 9.5%; تُقَدَّرُ ثَرْوَتُهُ بِنَحْوِ ١٠٠ مِلْيون دولار his net worth is around $100 million ❷ [اسْتَحْسَنَ] to appreciate, to value, to respect, to esteem; قَدَّرَ شَيْئاً \ شَخْصاً to appreciate sth/sb; to respect whim of fate; شاءَت الأَقْدارُ أنْ ... it was predestined that ...; it so happened that ...; آمَنَ بالقَضاءِ والقَدَرِ to believe in predestination; اسْتَسْلَمَ لِقَدَرِهِ to resign oneself to one's fate; إنْ شاءَت الأَقْدارُ if fate allows, ≈ hopefully

قِدْر *n* |قُدور| pot, pan

قادِر **A** *adj* |قَوادِرُ| capable; able; غَيْر قادِرٍ incapable, unable; كانَ قادِراً على شَيْءٍ to be capable of sth, to be able to do sth; هو وَحْدُهُ القادِرُ على شَيْءٍ he is the only one who can do sth; لم يُعَدْ قادِراً على شَيْءٍ to no longer be capable of sth **B** *n* القادِر the Omnipotent (*one of the names of God*)

قُدْرة *n* |قُدُرات| ability, capacity, potential; power, force, strength; القُدْرة على فِعْلِ شَيْءٍ the ability to do sth; قُدْرة عالِية \ هائِلة high/low ability; قُدْرة فائِقة \ خارِقة extraordinary ability; قُدْرة جِنْسيّة (sexual) potency; قُدْرة حِصانيّة horsepower; قُدْرة تَنافُسيّة competitiveness; قُدْرة شِرائيّة purchasing power; قُدْرة إنْتاجيّة production capacity, productivity; قُدْرة كُلِّيّة total capacity; قُدْرة ماليّة financial capability/capacity; قُدْرة دِفاعيّة defensibility; قُدْرة قِتاليّة fighting ability; قُدْرة ذاتيّة self-sufficiency; inner strength; قُدْرة عَقْلِيّة \ ذِهْنِيّة mental capacity; قُدْرة اسْتيعابيّة capacity (*storage*); قُدْرة مُحَرِّكة drive; عَدَم القُدْرةِ inability; عَدَم القُدْرةِ (الجِنْسيّةِ \ على الانْتِصابِ) impotence; مَدى قُدُراتِ شَخْصٍ the extent of sb's abilities; زِيادة قُدْرةٍ improved ability, increased capability; تَنْخَفِضُ \ تَرْتَفِعُ القُدْرةُ الشِرائيّةُ purchasing power is declining/increasing; عَزَّزَ \ حَسَّنَ قُدُراتِهِ to strengthen one's capacity; to improve one's abilities; امْتَلَكَ \ مَلَكَ قُدْرةً to have an ability; أثْبَتَ قُدْرَتَها to prove its abilities; فاقَ قُدْرةَ شَيْءٍ \ شَخْصٍ to exceed sth's capacity/ sb's abilities; أَضْعَفَ قُدْرةَ شَيْءٍ to degrade sth's capability; طَوَّرَ قُدْرةً to develop a capability; أظْهَرَ قُدْرةً to demonstrate a capability; اسْتَغَلَّ قُدْرةَ شَيْءٍ \ شَخْصٍ to use sth/sb's capability; to take advantage of sth/sb's ability; قُدْرة على تَحَمُّلِ شَيْءٍ ability to handle sth; قُدْرة على اتِّخاذِ القَراراتِ decisiveness; قُدْرة على اسْتيعابِ شَيْءٍ ability to absorb sth/ take sth in; قُدْرة على الصُمودِ resilience; resistance; قُدْرة كُلِّيّة omnipotence; اللهُ الكُلِّيّ القُدْرةِ God the Omnipotent

sth/sb; قَدَّرَ قيمةَ شَخْصٍ \ شَيْءٍ to appreciate the value of sb/sth; قَدَّرَ شَيْئاً \ شَخْصاً بالِغَ \ حَقَّ التَقْديرِ to value sth/sb highly, to have great respect for sth/sb; قَدَّرَ شَيْئاً \ شَخْصاً حَقَّ قَدْرِهِ to appreciate the true worth of sth/sb **3** [اللهُ] to predestine, to preordain; لا قَدَّرَ اللهُ God forbid

أَقْدَرَ *v* **1** [جَعَلَهُ قادِراً] to enable **2** [رَآهُ قَديراً] to consider capable

تَقَدَّرَ *v* **1** [بِقَدَرٍ] to be predestined; to be predetermined; تَقَدَّرَ لَهُ أنْ ... to be predestined to ... **2** [تَمَّ تَقْديرُهُ] to be estimated; to be appraised

اقْتَدَرَ *v* to be capable; to be able; اقْتَدَرَ على شَيْءٍ to be capable of sth

قَدْر *n* |أَقْدار| **1** [كَمِّيّة] extent, amount; قَدْرَ طاقَتِهِ \ إمْكانِهِ as best as he can; أكْبَر قَدْرٍ مُمْكِنٍ من الشَفّافيّة as much transparency as possible; على قَدْرِ in proportion to, to the extent that; على قَدْرٍ ما to a certain extent; قَدْرَ \ ب \ على قَدْرِ المُسْتَطاعِ \ الإمْكانِ as much as possible; to the best of one's ability; يَفْعَلُ ذلك على قَدْرِ ما يَسْتَطيعُ he will do that as best as he can; حاوَلَ قَدْرَ الإمْكانِ فِعْلَ شَيْءٍ to try as hard as possible to do sth; تَجَنَّبَ قَدْرَ الإمْكانِ شَيْئاً to avoid sth as much as possible **2** [قيمة] amount, quantity; value, worth; قَدْر كَبير \ عالٍ من شَيْءٍ a lot of sth, a large amount of sth; قَدْر كافٍ من شَيْءٍ enough of sth; قَدْر هائِل \ ضَئيل من شَيْءٍ a very small amount of sth; قَدْر مَعْقول من شَيْءٍ a reasonable amount of sth; بالقَدْرِ نَفْسِهِ \ بِنَفْسِ القَدْرِ in the same amount, to the same extent; مَبْلَغ \ زَمَن قَدْرُهُ ... an amount / time of ...; مَبْلَغ قَدْرُهُ ٢٠٠٠ دولار a sum amounting to 2,000 dollars; سَجَّلَ زَمَناً قَدْرُهُ ١٨.٣١ دَقيقة (Sport) he set a time of 18:31; تَطَلَّبَ قَدْراً كَبيراً \ مُعَيَّناً من شَيْءٍ to require a large/certain amount of sth; القَدْر الظاهِرِيّ (Astron) apparent magnitude; عَرَفوا قَدْرَهُ (Mor) *they were familiar with its contents (said of a declaration)* **3** (Relig) predestination, destiny; omnipotence (*of God*); سورة القَدْر Power (*Sura 97*); لَيْلَة القَدْرِ the Night of Power (*the night the first verses of the Koran were revealed*)

قَدَر *n* |أَقْدار| fate, destiny, predestination; قَدَر مَحْتوم \ مَقْدور inevitable fate; سُخْرِيّة القَدَرِ the irony of fate; مَشيئة الأَقْدارِ

قَدَريّ **A** *adj* fatalistic

B *n* **1** [جَبْرِيّ] fatalist **2** (Islam) Qadarite (*follower of theological movement in early Islam asserting humanity's free will*)

قَدَريّة *n* **1** [جَبْريّة] fatalism **2** (Islam) القَدَريّة Qadariyya (*theological movement in early Islam asserting humanity's free will*)

قَدير *adj* skilled; competent; powerful

اقْتِدار *n* capability

تَقْدير *n* |تَقْديرات، تَقاديرُ| **1** [تَقْييم] evaluation, assessment; estimate, appraisal; في تَقْديري in my opinion; على أَقْصى تَقْديرٍ at least; تَقْدير مُمْتاز A, excellent (BrE); تَقْدير مَقْبول C, pass mark (BrE), passing grade (AmE); التَقْدير التَراكُميّ overall grade average, cumulative GPA (AmE); تَقْديرات أَوَّليّة \ مَبْدَئيّة preliminary estimates; تَقْدير خاطِئ miscalculation; تَقْديرات ماليّة financial estimates; budget, appropriations; تَقْدير تَقْريبيّ rough estimate; تَقْدير السَنَد bond rating; تَقْدير الجَمارِكِ customs valuation; بالَغَ في التَقْديرِ to overvalue, to overrate; تَقْدير المَصْروفاتِ للعامِ ٢٠١٤ cost estimates for 2014; تَقْديرات النُموّ الاقْتِصاديّ economic growth estimates; حَسَبَ \ بِحَسَبِ التَقْديراتِ according to estimates; نَجَحَ بِتَقْديرِ جَيِّدٍ \ جَيِّدٍ جِدًّا to pass with a grade of 'good'/'very good' (BrE), ≈ to get a C/B (AmE); أَخْطَأَ \ أَساءَ (في) التَقْديرَ to misjudge/miscalculate; تَتَفاوَتُ التَقْديراتُ (بين) estimates vary (between); قامَ بِتَقْديرِ المَصاريفِ to estimate the costs; تَقْدير اسْتِقْرائيّ extrapolation; تُشيرُ التَقْديراتُ إلى أنَّ ...، تُفيدُ التَقْديراتُ بِأَنَّ ... estimates indicate that ...; اسْتِناداً إلى تَقْديراتٍ based on estimates; التَقْدير الدائِريّ (Geom) radian **2** [احْتِرام] esteem, regard, appreciation, recognition; تَقْديراً لِ in appreciation/recognition of; تَقْديراً لِعَطاءِ \ لِجُهودِ شَخْصٍ in recognition of sb's contribution/efforts; تَقْدير عَميق \ عالٍ deep/high appreciation; تَقْدير الذاتِ self-esteem; شَهادة تَقْديرٍ a certificate of appreciation; مع فائِقِ التَقْديرِ yours sincerely, sincerely yours (AmE) (*in a letter*); أَعْرَبَ \ عَبَّرَ عن تَقْديرٍ to express appreciation; أَظْهَرَ تَقْديراً لِشَيْءٍ to appreciate sth; نالَ تَقْديراً to be appreciated; حَظِيَ بِتَقْديرٍ من شَخْصٍ to gain/earn sb's respect; وَجَّهَ تَحيّةَ تَقْديرٍ إلى شَخْصٍ to salute sb; اسْتَحَقَّ التَقْديرَ to deserve respect; كانَ مَحَلَّ \ مَوْضِعَ تَقْديرِ شَخْصٍ to be held in high regard by sb; أَخْطَأَ في تَقْديرِ شَخْصٍ to misjudge sb **3** (Ling) *underlying structure*

تَقْديريّ *adj* **1** [تَخْمينيّ] estimated, approximate; ميزانيّة \ مُوازَنة تَقْديريّة estimated budget **2** [تَكْريميّ] appreciative, grateful; جائِزة تَقْديريّة special prize **3** [وَفْقاً لِحَصافَتِهِ] discretionary

مُتَقَدِّرة *n* mitochondrion

مُقْتَدِر *adj* capable, competent, skillful

مِقْدار *n* |مَقاديرُ| quantity, amount; dose, dosage; magnitude (Math); المِقْدار الصَحيح correct dosage; مِقْدار من الوَقْتِ period of time; بِمِقْدارٍ كافٍ adequately; بِهٰذا المِقْدارِ to that extent; أَكْبَر مِقْدارٍ مُمْكِنٍ (من ...) the most (...) possible; تَحْديد مَقادير الأَدْوِيةِ determining medication dosage; زادَ عَدَدُ السُكّانِ بِمِقْدارِ مِلْيونِ نَسَمةٍ the population increased by one million people; ارْتَفَعَ صافي الأَرْباحِ بِمِقْدارِ الضِعْفِ \ الضِعْفَيْنِ net profits doubled; انْخَفَضَتِ الأَسْعارُ بِمِقْدارِ الثُلْثِ \ النِصْفِ prices decreased by a third/half; تَراجَعَ مُتَوَسِّطُ المَرْدودِ بِمِقْدارِ نُقْطَتَيْنِ average yields fell by two points; مَبْحَث مَقادير الأَدْوِيةِ (Med) posology

مُقَدَّر **A** *adj* estimated; predestined; قيمة مُقَدَّرة valuation price; العَجْز المُقَدَّر بِعِشْرينَ مِلْيونَ دولار the estimated deficit of $20 million; كانَ مُقَدَّراً أنْ ... to be predestined to ...

B *n* estimate, budget; wealth, resources; مُقَدَّرات الوَطَنِ \ الشَعْبِ the country's/people's wealth; الهَيْمَنة \ السَيْطَرة الأَجْنَبيّة على مُقَدَّراتِها foreign control of its resources

مَقْدِرة *n* ability, capability; في مَقْدِرَتِهِ أنْ يَنْجَحَ he is capable of success; العَفْو عند المَقْدِرة *a pardon in spite of one's power (to punish)*

مَقْدور **A** *adj* |مَقاديرُ| predestined

B *n* **1** [قَدَر] |مَقاديرُ| fate, destiny; مَقْدورُكَ أنْ ... your destiny is to ... **2** [إمْكان] |مَقْدورات| capability, ability; كانَ في مَقْدورِهِ أنْ ... to be capable of ..., to be able to; لَيْسَ في مَقْدورِ الحُكومةِ أنْ تَفْعَلَ ذلك the government is incapable of doing that; هل في مَقْدورِكَ أنْ ... are you able to ..., can you ...

قَدُسَ *v* |u; قُدْس، قُدُس| to be/become holy

قَدَّسَ *v* to consecrate; to hallow; قَدَّسَ اللهُ سِرَّهُ God bless his soul (*formula used after mentioning a saint*); قَدَّسَ شَيْئاً (الحُرِّيّة، الحَياةَ، إلخ) to hold sth sacred (*freedom, life, etc*)

تَقَدَّسَ *v* to be/become holy; (الله) تَقَدَّسَ في عُلاهُ God on high

قُدْس *n* |mf; أَقْداس| ◆1 [مَكان مُقَدَّس] sanctuary; قُدْس الأَقْداسِ Holy of Holies; inner sanctum ◆2 [المَدينة] (مَدينة) القُدْس Jerusalem; القُدْس الشَريف the holy city of Jerusalem; القُدْس المُحْتَلّة East Jerusalem (*occupied portion of Jerusalem*); القُدْس الشَرْقيّة \ العَرَبيّة East/Arab Jerusalem; القُدْس الغَرْبيّة West Jerusalem; تَهْويد \ عُروبة القُدْسِ Judaization/Arabization of Jerusalem; مِلَفّ \ قَضيّة القُدْسِ the Jerusalem issue; تَقْسيم القُدْسِ the division of Jerusalem; الشَطْر الشَرْقيّ بالقُدْسِ the eastern sector of Jerusalem

قُدُس *n* holiness; sacredness; الروح القُدُس (Islam) the archangel Gabriel; (Chr) the Holy Spirit

قادِس *n* listed alphabetically

قادوس *n* |قَواديسُ| hopper; bucket; container

قُدّاس *n* |قَداديسُ, قُدّاسات| (Chr) church service, religious service; Mass; Eucharist; قُدّاس إلَهيّ ,صَلاة قُدّاسٍ Mass; قُدّاس احْتِفاليّ celebratory Mass; قُدّاس حَبْريّ pontifical Mass; قُدّاس الميلادِ Christmas Mass; قُدّاس الفِصْحِ Easter Mass; قُدّاس جَنائِزيّ ,قُدّاس لِراحةِ نَفْسٍ requiem, funeral Mass; كِتاب القُدّاسِ missal; خادِم القُدّاسِ altar boy, acolyte; أَقامَ \ تَرَأَّسَ قُدّاساً to hold Mass; حَضَرَ القُدّاسَ to go to church; to attend Mass; to celebrate the Eucharist; خَدَمَ القُدّاسَ to serve as an altar boy; to sing during Mass/services (*choir*)

قَداسة *n* holiness; sanctity; هالة القَداسةِ halo; قَداسة البابا \ صاحِب القَداسةِ الحَبْرَ الأَعْظَمِ His Holiness the Pope; His Holiness

قُدْسيّ *adj* holy, sacred; الحَرَم القُدْسيّ (الشَريف) Temple Mount; حَديث قُدْسيّ sacred hadith (*the words of God as repeated by Muhammad*)

قُدْسيّة *n* holiness, sacredness

قُدّوس *n* most holy; القُدّوس the Holy (*one of the names of God*)

قِدّيس *n* saint; القِدّيس يوحَنّا Saint John; قِدّيس شَفيع patron saint; ذَخيرة قِدّيسٍ relic (*of a saint*); كَرَّمَ قِدّيساً to venerate a saint; عيد كُلِّ \ جَميعِ القِدّيسينَ All Saints' Day, All Hallows

تَقْديس *n* consecration, sanctification; devotion, reverence, veneration; تَقْديس خُبْزٍ وَخَمْرٍ consecration of bread and wine (*for the Eucharist*); تَقْديس شَخْصٍ canonization of sb; تَقْديس الأَوْلياءِ saint cults

مَقْدِس *n* sanctuary; بَيْت المَقْدِسِ Jerusalem

مُقَدَّس A *adj* holy; sacred; الأَماكِن \ الدِيار المُقَدَّسة the holy places; العَتَبات المُقَدَّسة the Holy Gateway (*shrines of Najaf and Karbala in Iraq*); المَشاعِر المُقَدَّسة *ritual sites* (*in or near Mecca*) *involved in the rites of Hajj*; الكِتاب المُقَدَّس the Bible; الإنْجيل المُقَدَّس the New Testament; الأَراضي المُقَدَّسة the Holy Land; المَدينة المُقَدَّسة the Holy City; المَجْمَع المُقَدَّس the Holy Synod (*of the Coptic church*); البَيْت المُقَدَّس Jerusalem
B *n* sanctuary; sacred place

قَدَمَ *v* |u; قُدوم ,قَدْم| to precede

قَدُمَ *v* |u; قِدَم| to be old

قَدِمَ *v* |a; قُدوم| to come, to arrive, to approach

قَدَّمَ *v* ◆1 [عَرَضَ] to offer, to give, to present; to submit; قَدَّمَ اسْتِقالةً to tender a resignation; قَدَّمَ تَنازُلاتٍ to make concessions; قَدَّمَ تَعْزِيَتَهُ to offer one's condolences; قَدَّمَ مُساعَدةً \ الدَعْمَ to give help/support; قَدَّمَ اقْتِراحاً to submit a proposal; قَدَّمَ خِدْمةً to render/provide a service; قَدَّمَ طَلَباً to submit a request; to place an order; قَدَّمَ تَقْريراً to issue a report; قَدَّمَ مَعْلوماتٍ \ دَليلاً to provide information/proof; قَدَّمَ طَعْناً (Law) to lodge an appeal; قَدَّمَ تَضْحِياتٍ to make sacrifices; قَدَّمَ اعْتِراضاً to raise an objection; قَدَّمَ الحُجَجَ \ الوَثائِقَ to submit evidence/documents; قَدَّمَ حَفْلةً \ عَرْضاً to give a performance, to put on a show; قَدَّمَ مَسْرَحيّةً to perform/stage a play; قَدَّمَ لِشَخْصٍ وَجْبةً to serve a meal to sb; قَدَّمَ لِشَخْصٍ الحِسابَ to give sb the bill; قَدَّمَ الشُكْرَ لِشَخْصٍ to extend one's thanks to sb; قَدَّمَ نَفْسَهُ إلى الشُرْطةِ to turn oneself in to the police; دون أنْ يُقَدِّمَ مَزيداً من الإيضاحاتِ without offering further clarification ◆2 [عَرَّفَ] to present; to introduce; قَدَّمَ ضَيْفاً to introduce a guest; قَدَّمَ مُحاضِراً to present a speaker; قَدَّمَ مَوْضوعاً to introduce a subject; قَدَّمَ كِتاباً to write an introduction to a book ◆3 (Journ) to present;

قَدَّمَ بَرْنامَجاً وَثائِقِيّاً to present a documentary **4** [مَوْعِداً] to move up, to bring forward; قَدَّمَ تاريخَ الانْتِخاباتِ to bring forward (BrE) move up (AmE) elections; قَدَّمَ ساعَتَهُ بِخَمْسِ دَقائِقَ to set one's watch five minutes ahead **5** [جَعَلَهُ قُدّامَهُ] to let go first, to send ahead

أَقْدَمَ *v* |على| to risk, to dare; to commit, to carry out; أَقْدَمَ على فِعْلِ شَيْءٍ to do sth; to carry out sth; أَقْدَمَ على الانْتِحارِ to commit suicide; أَقْدَمَ على فَعْلَتِهِ لِأَنَّ ... he did what he did because ...; أَقْدَمَ على خَطْوَةٍ to take a step; أَقْدَمَ على مُجازَفَةٍ to take a risk

تَقَدَّمَ *v* **1** [تَطَوَّرَ] to advance, to progress, to make progress; تَقَدَّمَ خَطْوَةً to take a step forward; تَقَدَّمَ بِاطِّرادٍ to progress steadily; تَقَدَّمَ إلى الأَمامِ to move forward, to progress; تَقَدَّمَ في السِنِّ, تَقَدَّمَتْ بِهِ السِنُّ to grow old; to get older; رَجُل تَقَدَّمَتْ بِهِ السِنُّ an elderly man **2** [كانَ \ صارَ قُدّامَهُ] to lead (the way); تَقَدَّمَ على شَيْءٍ \ شَخْصٍ to be ahead of sth/sb; يَتَقَدَّمُهُمْ ... the foremost of whom is ...; تَقَدَّمَتْ المُشَيِّعينَ أَرْمَلَةُ الفَقيدِ the deceased's widow led the funeral procession; تَقَدَّمَ الضُيوفُ بِهَدَفٍ the away team was ahead by one goal; تَقَدَّمَ بِفارِقٍ ضَئيلٍ \ كَبيرٍ to be slightly/far ahead; تَقَدَّمَ على المُنافِسِ to be ahead of the competition **3** [سارَ] to advance, to proceed; تَقَدَّمَ الجَيْشُ the army advanced; تَقَدَّمَ بِبُطْءٍ to advance slowly, to make slow progress; تَقَدَّمَ على المُفاوَضاتِ to pursue negotiations **4** [قَدَّمَ] to submit, to present; تَقَدَّمَ بِشَكْوى to lodge a complaint; تَقَدَّمَ بِطَلَبٍ to submit an application; to place an order; تَقَدَّمَ بالشُكْرِ to extend one's thanks; تَقَدَّمَ بِدَعْوى ضدّ شَخْصٍ to file a lawsuit against sb; تَقَدَّمَ بِاقْتِراحٍ to make a proposal; تَقَدَّمَ بِطَعْنٍ to file an appeal; تَقَدَّمَ بِتَعْزِيَةٍ لِشَخْصٍ to offer one's condolences to sb; تَقَدَّمَ بِاسْتِقالَتِهِ to tender one's resignation; تَقَدَّمَ بِاعْتِراضٍ to raise an objection; تَقَدَّمَ للامْتِحانِ to sit/take an exam

تَقادَمَ *v* to go by, to pass; to become antiquated/obsolete; to expire; تَقادَمَ الزَمَنُ time has passed; شَيْء تَقادَمَ الزَمَنُ عَلَيْهِ sth obsolete/antiquated; نِظام تَقادَمَ الزَمَنُ عَلَيْهِ an antiquated regime; تَقادَمَت الدَعْوى the statute of limitations on the case has expired

اسْتَقْدَمَ *v* to summon, to send for; to recruit; اسْتَقْدَمَ التَعْزيزاتِ to send for reinforcements; اسْتَقْدَمَ لاعِباً \ مُدَرِّباً من الخارِجِ to recruit a player/coach from abroad

قَدَم *n* |f; أَقْدام| **1** (Anat) foot; حافي القَدَمَيْنِ, بِقَدَمَيْنِ حافِيَتَيْنِ barefoot; قَدَم حَنْفاء \ عَرْجاء club foot, talipes; قَدَم مُسَطَّحة flatfoot; كُرة القَدَمِ football (BrE), soccer (AmE); وَقْع \ وَطْء الأَقْدامِ step, footstep; مَوْطِئ قَدَمٍ foothold, influence; pied-à-terre; أَثَر قَدَمٍ \ الأَقْدامِ footprint; أَخْمَص \ باطِن القَدَمِ sole (*of the foot*); إِصْبَع القَدَمِ toe; ظَهْر القَدَمِ top of the foot; كاحِل القَدَمِ ankle; كَعْب القَدَمِ heel; مُشْط القَدَمِ instep; إِبْهام القَدَمِ big toe; وَطِئَتْ قَدَماهُ مَكاناً to set foot somewhere; ثَبَّتَ \ رَسَّخَ قَدَمَهُ في مَكانٍ to gain a (firm) foothold somewhere; وَقَفَ على قَدَمَيْهِ \ أَقْدامِهِ (بِثَباتٍ) to stand (firmly) on one's own two feet; اقْتَفى آثارَ أَقْدامِ شَخْصٍ to follow in sb's footsteps; قد جَرى على قَدَمٍ وَساقٍ to be well under way; ثَبَّتَ أَقْدامَهُ على الأَرْضِ to fall/land on one's feet; مَشْياً \ سَيْراً على الأَقْدامِ going on foot; من (قِمّةِ) رَأْسِهِ إلى أَخْمَصِ قَدَمَيْهِ from top/head to toe **2** (Meas) foot (*linear measurement*); قَدَم مُرَبَّع square foot; قَدَم مُكَعَّب cubic foot; مَرْكَبي طولُهُ ١٣ قَدَماً my boat is 13 feet long **3** [أَساس] footing, basis; على قَدَمِ المُساواةِ on an equal footing, on equal terms; عامَلَ شَخْصاً على قَدَمِ المُساواةِ to treat sb fairly

قِدَم *n* antiquity, ancient times; منذ القِدَمِ from/since time immemorial; ضارِب في القِدَمِ ancient; بالِغ القِدَمِ very old

قادِم *adj* |قادِمونَ, قُدوم, قُدّام| next, coming, future, following; السَنة القادِمة next year; the following year; الحَلْقة القادِمة the following episode/broadcast; خلال \ في الفَتْرةِ القادِمةِ in the future; أَجْيال قادِمة future generations

قُدّامَ *prep* before, in front of

قُدُماً *adv* forwards, forward; onwards; مَضى \ سارَ قُدُماً to move forward

قَدوم **A** *adj* |قُدُم| brave, courageous

B *n* |قُدُم, قَدائِمُ| hammer

قَدّوم *n* |قُدُم, قَدائِمُ| adze

قُدوم *n* arrival; انْتَظَرَ قُدومَ شَخْصٍ to await sb's arrival

قَديم *adj* |قُدامى, قُدَماءُ| ① [عَكْس حَديث] old; ancient; قَديماً previously; قَديم الطِرازِ obsolete, out-of-date; مِن الطِرازِ القَديمِ old-fashioned; في قَديم الزَمانِ previously, in olden times; once upon a time; أُسْلوب قَديم old-fashioned style; لُغات قَديمة classical languages; المِصْريّونَ القُدَماء ancient Egyptians; عادة قَديمة ancient custom; حَيّ قَديم historic part of town; بِناية قَديمة old building; صَديق قَديم old friend; وَرَق قَديم waste paper; العَهْد القَديم the Old Testament; موسيقى قَديمة ancient music; لِهَذا المُؤَلِّف أُسْلوبٌ قَديمٌ في الكِتابة this writer has an old-fashioned style (of writing) ② [سابِق] former, ex-; بَيْتُنا القَديم our former house; رَقْم قِياسيّ قَديم previous record

اِسْتِقْدام *n* bringing in; recruiting; اِسْتِقْدام العَمالة (الأَجْنَبيّة) importing (foreign) workers; اِسْتِقْدام مُدَرِّب جَديد recruitment of a new coach

إِقْدام *n* boldness, daring; recklessness, audacity, temerity

أَقْدَميّة *n* seniority

تَقادُم *n* |تَقادُمات| ageing, obsolescence; سَقَطَت هذه الجَريمةُ بالتَقادُمِ the statute of limitations on this crime has expired; تَقادُم الزَمَنِ passage of time

تَقَدُّم *n* ① [تَطَوُّر] progress, advancement, headway; شَريط تَقَدُّمٍ (Comput) progress bar; أَحْرَزَ \ حَقَّقَ تَقَدُّماً to make progress/headway, to move forward; تَقَدُّم مَلْموس \ مَلْحوظ tangible/noteworthy progress; لَم يُحْرِزْ أَيَّ تَقَدُّمٍ يُذْكَر he made no appreciable progress; رَغْمَ تَقَدُّمِه في السِنِّ in spite of his advanced age ② [سَيْر] march, advance ③ [سَبْق] head start, advantage

تَقَدُّميّ *adj* advanced, progressive; حِزْب تَقَدُّميّ progressive party; هو تَقَدُّميٌّ في أَفْكارِه he has progressive ideas; فَكَّرَ تَفْكيراً تَقَدُّمِيًّا to have progressive thoughts

تَقَدُّميّة *n* progressiveness

تَقْديم *n* |تَقْديمات| ① [تَسْليم] presentation, offer; giving, presenting, offering; تَقْديم تَقْريرٍ presentation of a report; تَقْديم مُساعَدةٍ offering assistance; helping ② (Art) performance; تَقْديم مَسْرَحيّةٍ performance of a play ③ (Journ) presentation; تَقْديم تَقْريرٍ report, coverage

مُتَقَدِّم **A** *adj* advanced, developed; مُتَقَدِّم في الطابورِ at the front of the line/queue; المُتَقَدِّم ذِكْرُهُ aforementioned, mentioned above; بُلْدان مُتَقَدِّمة developed countries; تَقْنيات مُتَقَدِّمة advanced technology; مُتَقَدِّم في السِنِّ elderly, old; في سِنٍّ مُتَقَدِّمةٍ at an advanced age, in old age; في مَرْحَلةٍ \ حالةٍ مُتَقَدِّمةٍ at an advanced stage **B** *n* candidate, applicant; مُتَقَدِّم للاِمْتِحانِ exam candidate, test taker (AmE); مُتَقَدِّم لاِنْتِخاباتِ الرِئاسة presidential candidate

مِقْدام *adj* |مَقاديمُ| brave, courageous

مُقَدَّم **A** *adj* ① [سابِقاً] مُقَدَّماً beforehand, in advance, previously ② [ما قُدِّمَ] presented, submitted; رُفِضَ الطَعْنُ المُقَدَّمُ من قِبَلِ المُتَّهَمِ the defendant's appeal was denied **B** *n* ① (Busn) down payment, prepayment ② [رُتْبة] (Mor) *district chief/head* ③ (Mil) lieutenant-colonel

مُقَدِّم *n* ① [مَنْ يُقَدِّمُ] speaker, announcer, narrator ② (Comput) مُقَدِّم الخِدْمةِ service provider ③ (Islam) المُقَدِّم *He who brings forward* (*one of the names of God*)

مُقَدِّمة *n* مُقَدِّمة القِياسِ premise

مُقَدِّمة *n* ① [طَليعة] front, face, head; مُقَدِّمة طائِرةٍ nose of an aircraft; في مُقَدِّمة الأَوْلَويّاتِ a top priority; كانَ في مُقَدِّمة السِباقِ to be in the lead, to be in front ② [تَمْهيد] introduction, preface, foreword; مُقَدِّمة كِتابٍ introduction to a book; مُقَدِّمة موسيقيّة prelude, overture

‹ **اِقْتَدى** *v* to emulate, to copy, to follow; اِقْتَدى بالمُعَلِّمِ to follow the teacher's example

قُدْوة *n* example, model; كانَ قُدْوةً لِشَخْصٍ to be an example to sb

اِقْتِداء *n* copying, following; emulation, imitation; اِقْتِداء بِنَموذَجِ شَخْصٍ following sb's example; اِقْتِداءً بـ ... following ..., in emulation of ...

مُقْتَدٍ *n* follower

‹ **قَذُرَ, قَذِرَ** *v* |a-u; قَذَر, قَذارة| to be/get dirty

قَذَّرَ *v* to make dirty, to soil

اِسْتَقْذَرَ *v* to deem dirty; اِسْتَقْذَرَ شَيْئاً \ شَخْصاً to find sth/sb dirty

قَذَر *n* |أَقْذار| filth, dirt

قَذِر **A** *adj* dirty, filthy; نِكات \ مُحادَثات قَذِرة dirty jokes/talk; أيْدٍ \ مَلابِس قَذِرة dirty hands/clothes; نَشَرَ الغَسيلَ القَذِرَ to air one's dirty laundry; حيلة قَذِرة dirty/mean trick **B** *n* pig, slob

قاذورة *n* rubbish, filth; قاذورات trash, garbage

قَذارة *n* dirtiness, filth; littering

قَذَعَ *v* |a; قَذْع| to slander, to malign, to defame; قَذَعَ شَخْصاً to speak ill/badly of sb

أقْذَعَ *v* to disparage; أقْذَعَ شَخْصاً to speak ill/badly of sb

مُقْذِع *adj* biting, stinging, cutting; نَقْد مُقْذِع stinging criticism; هِجاء مُقْذِع cruel mockery; شَتيمة مُقْذِعة a cutting insult

قَذَفَ *v* |i; قَذْف| to throw, to pitch, to shoot; قَذَفَ كُرةً to shoot a ball; قَذَفَ مَدينةً بالقَنابِلِ to bomb a city; قَذَفَ شَخْصاً بالشَتائِمِ to hurl insults at sb; قَذَفَ شَخْصاً بالحِجارةِ to throw rocks at sb; قَذَفَ البُرْكانُ الرَمادَ والحُمَمَ the volcano spewed ash and lava

قَذَّفَ *v* to row, to paddle

تَقاذَفَ *v* to throw at each other; تَقاذَفَ الاتِّهاماتِ to hurl accusations back and forth

انْقَذَفَ *v* to be thrown/launched

قَذْف *n* **1** [وِشاية] defamation, slander; القَذْف العَلَنِيّ libel **2** [قَصْف] bombing, shelling, bombardment **3** [مَنِيّ] ejaculation; قَذْف مُبَكِّر premature ejaculation **4** [كُرةً] shooting *(a ball)*

قاذِف *adj* throwing, pitching; bombing; طائِرة قاذِفة bomber

قاذِفة *n* bomber; launcher; قاذِفة اللَهَبِ \ النار flame thrower; قاذِفة الصَواريخ rocket launcher, RPG

قَذّاف *n* catapult; howitzer; grenade launcher

قَذْفة *n* shot, attempt *(ball games)*

قَذْفِيّ *adj* slanderous, libellous

قَذيفة *n* |قَذائِفُ| bomb; missile, projectile; grenade; قَذيفة مُوَجَّهة guided missile; أطْلَقَ قَذيفةً to fire a missile; رَمى شَخْصاً بِقَذائِفَ to fire projectiles at sb

مِقْذاف *n* |مَقاذيفُ| paddle, oar

مَقْذوف *n* |مَقاذيفُ| projectile, missile; bullet, round

قَذال *n* |قُذُل, أقْذِلة| back of the head

قَذِيَ *v* |i; قَذْي| to have sth in one's eye; قَذَتْ عَيْنُهُ to have sleep in one's eye

قَذّى *v* to rub *(eyes)*; قَذّى عَيْنَهُ to rub sleep from one's eyes

قَذًى *n* |قُذِيّ, أقْذاء| sleep, sand *(in the eye upon waking)*

قَرَأَ *v* |a; قِراءة| to recite; to read; to study; قَرَأَ نَصّاً to read a text; قَرَأَ نَصّاً جَهْراً to recite a text, to read a text out loud; قَرَأَ جَرائِدَ \ كُتُباً to read newspapers/books; قَرَأَ فِنْجاناً to read tea leaves/coffee grounds; قَرَأَ كَفَّ شَخْصٍ to read sb's palm; قَرَأَ قِصّةً لِطِفْلٍ to read a story to a child; قَرَأَ أفْكارَ شَخْصٍ to read sb's thoughts; قَرَأَ عن مَوْضوعٍ to read about a subject; قَرَأَ في الجَريدةِ (أنّ ...) to read in the newspaper (that ...); قَرَأَ على شَخْصٍ to serve one's apprenticeship with sb; لا يُقْرَأُ illegible; خَطّ لا يُقْرَأُ illegible handwriting

أقْرَأَ *v* to tell, to pass a message; أقْرَأَ شَخْصاً السَلامَ to extend greetings to sb

اسْتَقْرَأَ *v* to study, to research; اسْتَقْرَأَ جَوانِبَ المَوْضوعِ to study the issue from all sides; اسْتَقْرَأَ المُسْتَقْبَلَ to envision/anticipate the future

قُرْء *n* |قُروء| menstruation, menstrual cycle

قارِئ *n* |قارِئونَ, قُرّاء| reader; reciter of the Koran; قارِئ مُنْتَبِه \ واعي observant/attentive reader; قارِئ كُتُبٍ إلِكْتْرونيّةٍ e-book reader; بَريد القُرّاءِ letters to the editor; نِسْبة القُرّاءِ readership, circulation

قِراءة *n* **1** [مُطالَعة] reading; قِراءة صامِتة \ جَهْرِيّة reading to oneself/out loud; قاعة القِراءةِ public library; مَهارة القِراءةِ reading skill; نَهَم في \ تَعَطُّش إلى القِراءةِ appetite for reading; اسْتَطاعَ قِراءةَ أفْكارِ شَخْصٍ to be able to read sb's mind; إنَّهُ مولَعٌ بالقِراءةِ he's an avid reader; نَصَحَ شَخْصاً بِقِراءةِ شَيْءٍ to recommend that sb read sth; عند القِراءةِ الدَقيقةِ \ السَطْحِيّة on a careful/cursory reading **2** (Relig) recitation; *variant reading of the Koran*; عِلْم القِراءاتِ *the study of variant readings of the Koran*

قُرْآن *n* |قَرائينُ| Koran; القُرْآن الكَريم the Holy Koran; تَفْسير القُرْآنِ commentary on the Koran; شاهِد من القُرْآنِ quotation from the Koran; حَفِظَ القُرْآنَ to learn the Koran by heart

قُرْآنِيّ *adj* Koranic; آية قُرْآنيّة Koranic verse

تَقْتَرِبُ دَرَجةً face close to sb; تَقْتَرِبُ النِهايةُ the end is nigh; الحَرارةِ من الثَلاثينَ دَرَجةً the temperature is approaching thirty degrees

اسْتَقْرَبَ *v to find sth near*

قُرْب *n* |أَقْراب| proximity, nearness, closeness; قُرْبَ in the proximity, nearby; بالقُرْبِ in (close) proximity; بالقُرْبِ من near, close to/by, in (close) proximity of, in the neighbourhood/vicinity of; تَقَعُ القَرْيةُ قُرْبَ مَدينةِ دِمَشْقَ the village is near Damascus

قارِب *n* |قَوارِبُ| boat; sloop; barge; قارِب نَجاةٍ \ إِنْقاذٍ lifeboat; قارِب مَطاطيّ \ خَشَبيّ rubber/wooden boat; قارِب شِراعيّ sailboat; قارِب إِنْقاذٍ lifeboat

قِراب *n* |قُرُب, أَقْرِبة| 1 [غِمْد] case, holder, sheath 2 [المُسافِرِ] knapsack

قَرابة *n* kinship; (blood) relationship; relation; قَرابة العَصَبِ \ الدَمِ blood relationship; قَرابة بين نَوْعَيْنِ relationship between two species; يَرْتَبِطونَ بِصِلةِ القَرابةِ to be connected by blood

قُرابةَ *prep* approximately, almost, about, around; اسْتَمَرَّتِ الحَرْبُ قُرابةَ عِقْدٍ من الزَمانِ the war lasted almost a century; قُرابةَ الساعةِ العاشِرةِ صَباحاً around 10 a.m.

قُرْبان *n* |قَرابينُ| 1 (Chr) host; Eucharist; سِرّ القُرْبانِ المُقَدَّسِ Eucharist; the Holy Sacrament; تَناوَلَ القُرْبانَ to take Communion; خُبْزُ القُرْبانِ المُقَدَّسِ host; عيد القُرْبانِ Corpus Christi 2 [ذَبيحة] offering, sacrifice; قَدَّمَ قُرْباناً للآلِهةِ to make a sacrifice to the gods

قُرْبانة *n* (Chr) Communion

قِرْبة *n* |قِرَب, قِرْبات| waterskin; قِرْبة ساخِنة hot-water bottle; مِزْمار القِرْبةِ bagpipe

قُرْبى *n* |f| kinship; (blood) relationship; ذو القُرْبى relative

قَريب A *adj* |قَرائِبُ, أَقارِبُ, أَقْرِباءُ| 1 [مَكان] close, near, beside; قَريب من \ إلى close to; قَريب من \ إلى هُنا nearby; قَريب من \ إلى المَنْزِلِ close to home; من مَسافةٍ قَريبةٍ, من قَريبٍ nearby, close by; كانَ قَريباً to be close; في مَدينةٍ قَريبةٍ in a nearby city; بَقِيَ قَريباً to stay close; إِطْلاق النارِ عَلَيْهِ من مَسافةٍ قَريبةٍ to be shot at close range; تَقَعُ الرِباطُ قَريباً من الدارِ البَيْضاءِ Rabat is close to Casablanca; في قَرْيةٍ قَريبةٍ

اسْتِقْراء *n* 1 [تَقْدير] extrapolation 2 [فَلْسَفة] induction; أَثْبَتَ شَيْئاً عن طَريقِ الاسْتِقْراءِ to prove sth by induction

اسْتِقْرائيّ *adj* inductive; تَقْدير اسْتِقْرائيّ estimate based on extrapolation

مُقْرِئ *n* Koranic reciter

مِقْرَأ *n* |مَقارِئ| lectern

مَقْروء *adj* legible, readable; widely read; جَريدة مَقْروءة a widely read newspaper; خَطّ مَقْروء legible handwriting; إِعْلام مَقْروء print media

‹ **قَرُبَ** *v* |u; قُرْب| to approach, to be/come closer; ما يَقْرُبُ من ... about ..., around ..., approximately ...; almost ...; ما يَقْرُبُ من ٥٠٠ دولار about 500 dollars

قَرِبَ *v* |a; قُرْبان, قُرْب| to approach, to be/come closer; قَرِبَ شَيْئاً to approach sth; قَرِبَ مَسافةً to close a distance

قَرَّبَ *v* 1 [أَدْنى] |إلى| to bring closer/nearer; قَرَّبَ شَخْصاً إِلَيْهِ to become close to sb 2 [جَعَلَ مَفْهوماً] to explain; قَرَّبَ مَسْأَلةً to make an issue understandable 3 [عَدَداً] to round (off); قَرِّب العَدَدَ ٨٩٣٤ لِأَقْرَب ١٠٠ round 8,934 to the nearest hundred 4 [ضَحّى] to sacrifice

قارَبَ *v* to approach; قارَبَ شَخْصاً to come towards sb; قارَبَ الاسْتِحالةَ to verge on the impossible; قارَبَ النِهايةَ to near the end; قارَبَ مَسْأَلةً (من زاويةٍ مُعَيَّنةٍ) to approach an issue (from a certain angle); قارَبَ شَخْصاً في الرَأْيِ to have similar views to sb; قارَبَ الرَقْمَ العالَميَّ to get close to the world record; عُمْرُهُ يُقارِبُ السِتّينَ he's sixtyish

تَقَرَّبَ *v* 1 [حاوَلَ القُرْبَ مِنْهُ] to try to approach; to curry favour; تَقَرَّبَ إلى شَخْصٍ to try to approach sb; to seek sb's favour 2 (Chr) to take Communion

تَقارَبَ *v* to approach each other, to get/come together; to be close, to be related; تَتَقارَبُ وِجْهاتُ نَظَرِهم they are closing the gap between their positions

اقْتَرَبَ *v* to approach, to come closer; to be on the way; اقْتَرَبَ من حَيَوانٍ to approach an animal; اقْتَرَبَ من سِنِّ السَبْعينَ to be going on seventy; اقْتَرَبَ من هَدَفِهِ to get close to one's goal; اقْتَرَبَ شَيْئاً فَشَيْئاً to gradually approach, to come closer and closer; اقْتَرَبَ بِوَجْهِهِ من شَخْصٍ to bring one's

من الطَريقِ in a village close to the road **2** [وَقْت] recent; soon; قَريباً soon, shortly; presently; قَريب العَهْدِ recent; منذ (عَهْدٍ) قَريبٍ recently, lately; في المُسْتَقْبَلِ القَريبِ in the near future; في الماضي القَريبِ in the recent past; في أَمَدٍ \ عن \ عَمّا قَريبٍ soon, before long, shortly; في القَريبِ العاجِلِ very soon; سَتَنْتَهي الحَرْبُ قَريباً جدًّا the war will end very soon **3** [تَقْريباً] close, approximate; رَأْيُكَ قَريبٌ من المَعْقولِ your opinion is somewhat sensible

B *n* |قَرائِبُ ,أَقارِبُ ,أَقْرِباءُ| relative, family member, blood relation; أَقارِب \ أَقْرِباء family; إنَّها قَريبَتي \ من أَقارِبي she's family, she's related to me; الأَقارِبُ عَقارِبُ *one's relatives are one's worst enemies*; well, that's relatives for you; أَحْبِبْ قَريبَكَ كَنَفْسِكَ love thy kin as thyself

اقْتِراب *n* |اقْتِرابات| **1** [دُنوّ] approach; proximity, nearness; اقْتِراب الأَجَلِ the proximity/nearness of death; يَصْعُبُ الاقْتِرابُ مِنْهُ it's hard to get close to; he's unapproachable; it's difficult to discuss (*topic*) **2** (Sport) run-up

أَقْرَب *adj* |dipt; أَقارِبُ ,أَقْرَبونَ| nearer; nearest; مَكْتَب البَريد الأَقْرَب the nearest post office; في أَقْرَبِ وَقْتٍ (مُمْكِنٍ) as soon as possible, without delay; الأَقْرَبونَ أَوْلى بالمَعْروفِ ≈ blood is thicker than water; *give charity to relatives before strangers*; ... أَقْرَب ما يَكونُ إلى more like ..., almost equivalent to ...; قِصّة أَقْرَب ما تكونُ إلى الخَيالِ a hard-to-believe story; أَقْرَب الأَقْرِباء close relatives

تَقارُب *n* |تَقارُبات| **1** [تَقَرُّب] rapprochement; مُحاوَلة تَقارُبٍ attempt at a rapprochement **2** [تَشابُه] affinity; شَعَرَ بالتَقارُبِ مع شَخْصٍ to feel an affinity for/with sb; تَقارُب لُغَويّ \ ثَقافيّ \ سِياسيّ linguistic/cultural/political affinity; التَقارُب بين شَخْصَيْنِ affinity between two people

تَقَرُّب *n* approaching; currying favor; التَقَرُّب من \ إلى شَيْءٍ \ شَخْصٍ getting close to sth/sb; currying favor with sth/sb; يُحاوِلُ التَقَرُّبَ من الأَحْزابِ الدينيّةِ he's pandering to the religious parties

تَقْريب *n* bringing closer; تَقْريب وِجْهاتِ النَظَرِ narrowing the gap between opinions/positions; تَقْريباً ,على التَقْريبِ \ بـ approximately, about, around, roughly; almost, nearly

تَقْريبيّ *adj* approximate; rough; تَقْدير \ رَسْم تَقْريبيّ rough estimate/outline; أَرْقام تَقْريبيّة estimated figures/numbers

مُتَقارِب *adj* related, similar; close together; لُغات مُتَقارِبة related languages; هُما مُتَقارِبانِ في السِنِّ they are almost the same age; على فَتَراتٍ مُتَقارِبةٍ at short intervals

مُقارِب **A** *adj* approximately; similar; هذا مُقارِبٌ لِدَخْلِ العامِ السابِقِ this is roughly the same as last year's income

B *n* (Geom) asymptote

مُقارَبة *n* **1** [أُسْلوب] approach; مُقارَبة جَديدة لِشَيْءٍ a new approach to sth **2** [تَقْريب] approximation; مُقارَبة مُتَتابِعة successive approximation **3** [نَسْق] juxtaposition

مِقْراب *n* |مَقارِبُ| telescope

مُقَرَّب **A** *adj* close; favourite; intimate; أَصْدِقاؤُهُ المُقَرَّبونَ his close/closest friends; مَصادِر مُقَرَّبة من الرَئيسِ sources close to the president

B *n* confidant; المُقَرَّبونَ مِنْهُ those close/closest to him

مَقْرُبة ,مَقْرَبة *n* |مَقارِبُ| short distance; على مَقْرُبةٍ من close to, near, not far from; تَقَعُ القَرْيةُ على مَقْرُبةٍ من مَدينة دِمَشْقَ the village is near Damascus

قارِت *n* omnivore

قَرَحَ *v* |a; قَرْح| to wound, to injure

قَرِحَ *v* |a; قَرَح| to ulcerate

قَرَّحَ *v* to wound, to injure

تَقَرَّحَ *v* to ulcerate; to be covered with ulcers

اقْتَرَحَ *v* **1** [قَدَّمَ لِلبَحْثِ] to suggest, to propose; اقْتَرَح تَعْديلاً to propose an amendment; اقْتَرَح على شَخْصٍ شَيْئاً to suggest sth to sb; اقْتَرَحَ (على شَخْصٍ) أنْ \ أنّ ... to suggest (to sb) that ...; أَقْتَرِحُ أنْ نُغادِرَ غَداً I propose we leave tomorrow; أَقْتَرِحُ أنْ نَأْخُذَ اسْتِراحةً قَصيرةً I propose that we take a short break **2** [أَتى بِفِكْرةٍ] to invent, to make up

قَرْح *n* |قُروح| ulcer, abscess, sore

قَراح *adj* |أَقْرِحة| pure, clear; ماء قَراح pure water

قَرْحة ,قُرْحة *n* |قِرَح| ulcer, abscess, sore; قَرْحة مَعِديّة \ في المَعِدةِ stomach ulcer, peptic ulcer; قَرْحة الفَمِ canker sore; قَرْحة في العَيْنِ corneal ulcer, eyesore; قَرْحة القَدَمِ الناتِجة عن السُكَّريّ diabetic foot ulcer

قَريحة *n* |قَرائِح| talent, gift, genius; قَريحة فَنّيّة artistry; artistic talent

اقْتِراح *n* |اقْتِراحات| suggestion, proposal, offer; motion, resolution; اقْتِراح بَديل counterproposal; اقْتِراح نِهائيّ final proposal; اقْتِراح على شَخْصٍ suggestion to sb; مَشْروع اقْتِراحٍ draft proposal; صاغَ \ قَدَّمَ مَشْروعَ اقْتِراحٍ to draw up/submit a draft proposal; تَقَدَّمَ بِاقْتِراحٍ ,طَرَحَ \ قَدَّمَ اقْتِراحاً to make a proposition; تَبَنّى اقْتِراحاً to pass/carry/adopt a motion/ resolution; to accept a proposal; رَفَضَ اقْتِراحاً to reject/defeat a motion/resolution; to reject a proposal; بِناءً على اقْتِراحِ شَخْصٍ at the suggestion of sb

مُتَقَرِّح *adj* ulcerous

مُقْتَرَح **A** *adj* proposed; تَعْديل مُقْتَرَح proposed amendment **B** *n* proposal, proposition

مُقَرَّح *adj* ulcerous

‹ **قِرْد** *n* |قِرَدة ,قُرود| monkey; كُلُّ قِرْدٍ في عَيْنِ أُمِّهِ غَزالٌ *every mother thinks her child is beautiful*

قُراد *n coll* |قِرْدان| tick

‹ **قَرْدَحة** *n* |قَرادِح| Adam's apple

قُرْدوح *n* baboon

‹ **قُرَيْدِس** *n* (Syria) shrimp

‹ **قَرَّ** *v* |i; قَرّ ,قَرار| **1** ◀ [اسْتَقَرَّ] to settle (down); قَرَّ بِمَكانٍ to settle in a place; قَرَّ رَأْيُهُ قَرَّ الرَّأْيُ على أَنْ ... it was decided that ...; قَرَّ رَأْيُهُ على فِعْلِ ذلك he decided to do that; قَرَّتْ ,قَرَّ عَيْناً (بِشَيْءٍ) عَيْنُهُ (بِشَيْءٍ) to be delighted (by sth) **2** ◀ [بَرَدَ] to be cold/chilly

قَرَّرَ *v* to decide, to determine, to resolve; قَرَّرَ مَصيرَهُ بِنَفْسِهِ to determine one's own fate; قَرَّرَ أَنْ يُؤَجِّلَ شَيْئاً to decide to delay sth; قَرَّرَ اتِّخاذَ إِجْراءاتٍ to decide to take measures

أَقَرَّ *v* **1** ◀ [أَبْرَمَ] to accept, to approve; to ratify; to sanction; to confirm; أَقَرَّ مُعاهَدةً to ratify a treaty; أَقَرَّ تَوْصِيةً to approve a recommendation **2** ◀ [اعْتَرَفَ |ب|] to admit, to confess, to acknowledge; أَقَرَّ بِذَنْبِهِ to confess one's guilt; أَقَرَّ شَخْصاً بالحَقِّ to agree with sb **3** ◀ [ثَبَّتَ] to seal; to consolidate; أَقَرَّ صَفْقةً to seal a deal

تَقَرَّرَ *v* to be decided

اسْتَقَرَّ *v* **1** ◀ [في مَكانٍ] to settle; اسْتَقَرَّ في عُمانَ to settle in Oman **2** ◀ [ثَبَتَ] to stabilize; اسْتَقَرَّ رَأْيُهُ على فِعْلِ ذلك to decide to do that; قد اسْتَقَرَّ سِعْرُ الدولارِ the value of the dollar has stabilized

قارّ *adj* **1** ◀ [مُسْتَقِرّ] permanent, steady, fixed; دَخْل قارّ fixed income; لَجْنة قارّة permanent committee; هاتِف قارّ landline **2** ◀ [بارِد] cold

قارّة *n* continent; mainland; القارّة الإفْريقيّة the African continent/mainland; القارّة الأوروبّيّة the European mainland; القارّة السَوْداء Africa; مِن جَميعِ القارّاتِ from all continents; شِبْه قارّةٍ subcontinent; عابِر لِ \ عَبْرَ القارّاتِ \ السَمْراء intercontinental

قارّيّ *adj* continental; مُناخ قارّيّ continental climate; تَصادُم قارّيّ (Geol) continental collision; لَوْح قارّيّ (Geol) (tectonic) plate; الجُرُف القارّيّ (Geog) neritic zone, coastal waters

قُرّ *n* cold, coldness; chill, chilliness

قَرار *n* |قَرارات| decision; verdict, judgement; قَرار سَليم right decision; قَرار نِهائيّ final verdict; قَرار حُكوميّ government decision; قَرار اسْتِئْنافيّ decree; appellate decision; قَرار حازِم resolute decision; قَرار دُوَليّ \ الأُمَمِ المُتَّحِدةِ UN resolution; قَرار مَجْلِسِ الأَمْنِ (التابِعِ للأُمَمِ المُتَّحِدةِ) (UN) Security Council resolution; قَرار يَتَعَلَّقُ ,قَرار خاصّ ب \ بِشَأْنِ شَيْءٍ بِشَيْءٍ a decision about/regarding sth; قَرار تَشْكيلِ لَجْنةٍ a decision to form a committee; قَرار بِرَفْعِ الحَظْرِ a decision to end the embargo; القَرار القاضي بِجَمْعِ الأَسْلِحةِ the decision to confiscate the weapons; بِقَرارٍ وِزاريٍّ by ministerial order; صانِعُ القَرارِ decision-maker; مَشْروع قَرارٍ draft resolution; القَرارُ ثابِتٌ the decision is final; اتَّخَذَ قَراراً to decide, to make a decision; اتِّخاذ قَرارٍ decision-making; تَمَّ \ اتُّخِذَ القَرارُ the decision has been made; تَوَصَّلَ إلى قَرارٍ to reach a decision; تَبَنّى \ أَقَرَّ قَراراً to adopt a resolution; راعى القَرارَ to abide by the verdict; راعى شَيْئاً في اتِّخاذِ القَرارِ to take sth into consideration when making a decision; أَيَّدَ قَراراً حُكومِيًّا to support a government decree

قَرارة *n* **1** ◀ [عُمْق] depth; bottom; في قَرارةِ نَفْسِهِ deep down inside, in one's heart **2** ◀ [مُنْخَفِض] low-lying place

قُرارة *n* deposit, sediment

قُرّة *n* ① ◂ [شَخْص مُفَضَّل] قُرَّة العَيْن darling, apple of one's eye; كانَ قُرَّةَ عَيْنِ الأُسْرةِ to be the darling of the family ② ◂ (Bot) قُرَّة العَيْن watercress

قِرّة *n* cold, coldness

قَرير *adj* قَرير العَيْنِ satisfied, happy; نامَ قَريرَ العَيْنِ to sleep in peace

اِسْتِقْرار *n* ① ◂ [اِسْتِتْباب] اسْتِقْرار stability; stabilization; اسْتِقْرار أَسْعار صَرْفِ العُمْلاتِ economic stability; اقْتِصاديّ stabilization of the exchange rates; عَدَم اسْتِقْرار instability, transience; عَدَم الاسْتِقْرار السِياسيِّ political instability; اسْتَتَبَّ الاسْتِقْرارَ to enhance stability; زادَ في الاسْتِقْرارِ to maintain stability; زَعْزَعَ الاسْتِقْرارَ to disrupt stability ② ◂ [إقامة] staying, residing

إِقْرار *n* ① ◂ [شَهادة] statement, affidavit, certificate, declaration; إقْرار ضَريبيّ tax form/return/declaration; إقْرار طِبّيّ doctor's certificate; مَلأَ إقْراراً ضَريبيّاً to complete a tax form ② ◂ [مُصادَقة] ratification, approval; تأخير إقْرارِ المُوازَنةِ delay in approving the budget; إقْرار ضِمْنيّ tacit approval/ acknowledgment

تَقْرير *n* |تَقارير| report; account; (news) report, coverage; تَقرير سَنَويّ annual report/survey/review; تَقْرير نِهائيّ final report; تَقْرير إخْباريّ press release, communiqué; تَقْرير صُحُفيّ news report; نَشَرَ تَقْريراً صُحُفيّاً to issue a press release; تَقْرير عن الاجْتِماعِ \ الجَلْسةِ report on the meeting/session; رَفَعَ \ أَعَدَّ \ قَدَّمَ تَقْريراً to report, to make a report of; to give an account of; قَدَّمَ تَقْريراً عن الوَضْعِ to report on the situation; وَضَعَ تَقْريراً to draw up a report

مُسْتَقَرّ *n* seat; residence; مُسْتَقَرّ الحُكومةِ seat of government

مُسْتَقِرّ *adj* stable, balanced, steady; regular; جَوّ مُسْتَقِرّ calm weather; ضَغْط مُسْتَقِرّ steady pressure; غَيْر مُسْتَقِرّ unstable, insecure; وَضْع غَيْر مُسْتَقِرّ an unstable situation; حالة صِحّيّة غَيْر مُسْتَقِرّةٍ unstable condition

مَقَرّ *n* |مَقارّ| headquarters, seat; residence; مَقَرّ رَئيسيّ headquarters, head office; مَقَرّ رَسْميّ official headquarters; official residence; مَقَرّ العَمَلِ post, workplace; مَقَرّ شَرِكةٍ company headquarters; place of business; اتَّخَذَ مَقَرّاً (في مَكانٍ) to take up residence (somewhere), to move in (somewhere); وَقَعَ مَقَرُّهُ في العاصِمةِ to be headquartered in the capital

مُقَرَّر **A** *adj* decided, set; المَوْعِد المُقَرَّر (سابِقاً) the (previously) established deadline; كانَ من المُقَرَّرِ أنْ ... to be decided that ...; to be intended that ...
B *n* |مُقَرَّرات| ① ◂ [قرار] decision; resolution; قَرارات مُؤْتَمر باريس the Paris Conference resolutions ② ◂ [مَنْهَج] curriculum, syllabus; handbook, textbook; مُقَرَّرات دِراسيّة academic curricula

مُقَرِّر *n* committee secretary, reporter; ≈ chairman; أَعْلَنَ مُقَرِّرُ اللَجْنةِ الماليّةِ أنّ ... the chairman of the finance committee announced that ...

مَقْرور *adj* cold, chilly

قَرِسَ *v* |a; قَرَس| to freeze; to be bitterly cold

أَقْرَسَ *v* to freeze

قارِس *adj* ice-cold, icy, freezing; bleak; dry, cutting (*wind*); بَرْد قارِس freezing cold; bitter cold; شِتاء قارِس harsh winter; رِياح قارِسة freezing/cutting wind

قِرْش *n* ① ◂ [فُلوس] |قُروش| piastre; cent, penny (*any small amount of money*); لن أَدْفَعَ قِرْشاً واحِداً I won't pay a single cent; القِرْشُ الأَبْيَضُ يَنْفَعُ في اليَوْمِ الأَسْوَدِ ≈ save your pennies for a rainy day ② ◂ (Zool) shark

قَريش, **قَريشة** *n dry, low-fat cheese*; جُبْن قَريش cottage cheese

قُرَيْش *n* |dipt| Quraysh (*the prophet Muhammad's tribe*); سورة قُرَيْش Quraysh (*Sura 106*)

قَرَصَ *v* |u; قَرْص| ① ◂ [لَدَغَ] to sting; to bite; قَرَصَهُ البُرْغوثُ to be bitten by a flea; قَرَصَهُ الجوعُ to suffer from hunger ② ◂ [بِأَصابِعِهِ] to pinch; to squeeze; قَرَصَ ذِراعَ \ وَجْنةَ شَخْصٍ to pinch sb's arm/cheek

قَرَّصَ *v* قَرَّصَ العَجينَ *to divide dough into round breads*

قُرْص *n* |أَقْراص| ① ◂ [شَيْء مُسْتَدير] disc; *disc-shaped object*; قُرْص (الخُبْزِ) flatbread, pitta bread; قُرْص الشَمْسِ solar disk; قُرْص عَقيليّ Bundt cake; قُرْص العَسَلِ honeycomb; قُرْص أَرْقامِ الهاتِفِ rotary dial ② ◂ (Comput) disk; مُحَرِّكُ أَقْراصٍ (disk) drive;

قُرْص hard disk; قُرْص مَرِن \ لَيِّن floppy disk; قُرْص صُلْب compact disc, CD, CD-ROM ❸ (Med) (coated) مُدَمَّج \ مَضْغوط tablet, pill ❹ (Sport) discus; رَمْي القُرْصِ discus throw

قارِص *adj* stinging, biting; sour; ذُباب قارِص gadfly; كَلام قارِص biting remarks; ريح قارِصة freezing/biting wind; قَوارِص (NA) citrus fruits

قاروص *n* see قاروس

قُرّاص *n* ❶ (Bot) nettle; stinging nettle; قُرّاص (مُحْرِق) stinging nettle ❷ (Med) طَفْح القُرّاصِ nettle rash, hives

قَرْصة *n* bite; sting; pinch

‹ **قَرْصَنَ** *v* |i; قَرْصَنة| ❶ [اِخْتَرَقَ] to hack; قَرْصَنَ مَوْقِعاً \ صَفْحةً to hack a site/page ❷ [نَسَخَ] to pirate

قُرْصان *n* |قَراصِنة| ❶ [في البَحْرِ] pirate; hijacker ❷ (Comput) hacker; قُرْصان مَعْلوماتيّ hacker

قَرْصَنة *n* ❶ [في البَحْرِ] piracy ❷ (Comput) piracy; hacking

مُقَرْصَن *adj* ❶ [مُخْتَرَق] hacked; حاسوب مُقَرْصَن a hacked computer ❷ [مَنْسوخ] pirated; فيلْم مُقَرْصَن a pirated film; بَرامِج مُقَرْصَنة pirated software

‹ **قَرَضَ** *v* |i; قَرْض| to gnaw, to nibble; قَرَضَ شَيْئاً to nibble (on) sth; قَرَضَ الفَأْرُ الوَرَقَ mice gnawed at the paper

قارَضَ *v* to lend; قارَضَ شَخْصاً to grant/issue sb a loan

أَقْرَضَ *v* to lend (out); أَقْرَضَ شَخْصاً مَبْلَغاً من المالِ to lend sb money

انْقَرَضَ *v* to become extinct; انْقَرَضَت الدَيْناصوراتُ the dinosaurs became extinct

اقْتَرَضَ *v* to borrow; اقْتَرَضَ مالاً من شَخْصٍ to borrow money from sb

اسْتَقْرَضَ *v* to ask for a loan

قَرْض, **قِرْض** *n* |قُروض| loan; credit; قَرْض حُكوميّ public/government loan; قَرْض بِفائِدةٍ \ بِدونِ فائِدةٍ interest-bearing/interest-free credit; قَرْض بِضَمانةٍ حُكومِيّةٍ government-backed loan; قَرْض قيمَتُهُ ١٠.٠٠٠ أورو loan of 10,000 euros; أَخَذَ قَرْضاً, حَصَلَ على قَرْضٍ to secure/obtain a loan; مَنَحَ \ قَدَّمَ \ أَعْطى قَرْضاً لِشَخْصٍ to grant/issue/give sb a loan; سَدَّدَ قَرْضاً to pay off a loan

قارِض *n* |قَوارِضُ| (Zool) rodent; (رُتْبة \ فَصيلة) القَوارِض the rodent order (*Rodentia*); الجَرْبوعُ يَنْتَمي إلى رُتْبةِ القَوارِضِ the jerboa is a (kind of) rodent

(Idiom) ذُبابة قارِض horsefly

قُرّاضة *n* (Zool) clothes moth

قَريض *n* poetry

اسْتِقْراض *n* loan request

اقْتِراض *n* borrowing; loan; زِيادة تَكْليفِ الاقْتِراضِ increased borrowing costs

إقْراضيّ *adj* lending (*before n*); بَرْنامَج إقْراضيّ lending program

انْقِراض *n* extinction; حَيَوان مُهَدَّد بالانْقِراضِ endangered species

مُقْتَرِض *n* borrower

مِقْراض *n* |مَقاريضُ| (nail) clippers, scissors; trimming/pruning shears, hedge shears; wire-cutters

مِقْرَض *n* |مَقارِضُ| scissors; ابْن مِقْرَضٍ ferret

مُنْقَرِض *adj* extinct; حَيَوانات \ نَباتات مُنْقَرِضة extinct animal/plant species

‹ **قُرْط** *n* |أَقْراط, قِراط, قُروط| earring

‹ **قَرْطاج**, **قَرْطاجة** *n* |dipt f| Carthage (*city in Tunisia*); Carthage (*ancient city on the coast of North Africa*)

‹ **قِرْطاس** *n* |قَراطيسُ| ❶ [صَحيفة] (sheet of) paper; papyrus ❷ [وَرَقة تُلَفُّ] *bag rolled from paper*

‹ **قُرْطُبة** *n* Cordoba (*city in Spain*)

‹ **قُرْطُم**, **قِرْطِم** *n* (Bot) safflower; Carthamus

‹ **قَرَّظَ** *v* to praise, to commend

قَرَظ *n* *type of acacia*

تَقْريظ *n* praise, commendation

‹ **قَرَعَ** *v* |a; قَرْع| to bang, to pound, to hammer; to sound, to ring; قَرَعَ باباً to bang on a door; قَرَعَ جَرَساً to ring a bell; قَرَعَ طَبْلاً to bang a drum; قَرَعَ الكَأْسَ to toast; to clink glasses; قَرَعَ سِنَّهُ to gnash/grind one's teeth

قَرِعَ *v* |a; قَرَع| to go bald

قَرَّعَ *v* ❶ [وَبَّخَ] to reprimand, to reprove, to rebuke ❷ [قَصَّ] to cut off completely; قَرَّعَ شَعْرَهُ to shave one's head

قرَّفَ *v* to nauseate, to disgust; قرَّفَ شَخْصاً to disgust sb

قارَفَ *v* to yield (to), to submit (to); to be seduced (by); قارَفَ الذَنْبَ to be seduced by sin

اقْتَرَفَ *v* to commit; to perpetrate; اقْتَرَفَ ذَنْباً to commit a sin; اقْتَرَفَ جَريمةً to commit a crime

قَرَف *n* distaste, disgust, revulsion; شَعَرَ بالقَرَفِ من شخْصٍ to be disgusted with sb, to be revolted by sb

قَرافة *n* cemetery, graveyard

قِرْفة *n* |قِرَف| ◀1 [نَوْع من البَهارِ] cinnamon; عود قِرْفةٍ cinnamon stick; قَبْصة قِرْفةٍ pinch of cinnamon ◀2 (Zool) أُمّ قِرْفةٍ pangolin

قِرْفيّ *adj smelling/tasting of cinnamon*; cinnamon-brown

مُقْرِف *adj* loathsome; horrible; disgusting, repulsive; رَجُل مُقْرِف loathsome man; مَنْظَر مُقْرِف disgusting sight

‹ **قَرْفَصَ** *v* |i; قَرْفَصة| to squat, to crouch

قُرْفُصاء *n* |dipt f| crouch, squatting position; جَلَسَ القُرْفُصاءَ to crouch, to squat

‹ **قَرَقَ** *v* |i; قَرْق| to talk nonsense

‹ **قِرْقَدنّ** *n* European dormouse

‹ **قَرْقَذان** *n* squirrel

‹ **قَرْقَرَ** *v* |i; قَرْقَرة| to growl; to rumble, to grumble; to purr; *to make a rumbling growl (camel)*; يُقَرْقِرُ بَطْنُهُ his stomach is growling; تُقَرْقِرُ القِطّةُ the cat is purring

قَرْقَرة *n* |قَراقِرُ| growl; rumbling; purring

‹ **قَرْقَشَ** *v* |i; قَرْقَشة| to crunch

‹ **قَرْقَعَ** *v* |i; قَرْقَعة| to clatter; to creak

قَرْقَعة *n* rumbling; beating; banging; clanging; سَمِعَ قَرْقَعةَ طُبول الحَرْبِ to hear the beating of the war drums; قَرْقَعة السِلاح the clash of weapons; (fig) war, fighting

‹ **قَرْقَفَ** *v* |i; قَرْقَفة| to chatter (*teeth*); to shiver with cold

قُرْقُف *n* (Zool) tit; القُرْقُف الأَزْرَق blue tit (*Parus caeruleus*)

‹ **قَرَقوز** *n* puppet (*from a puppet show /play*)

‹ **قُرْقوش** *n* |قَراقيش| cartilage; قَراقيش (Egypt) *wafer-thin biscuit*

قِرِلّى *n* (Zool) kingfisher

‹ **قَرَمَ** *v* |i; قَرْم| to nibble, to munch

قُرْم *n* mangrove (*Avicennia marina*)

قارَعَ *v* ◀1 [ضارَبَ] to challenge; to contest; to fight; قارَعَ الحُجّةَ بالحُجّةِ to counter one argument with another ◀2 [ساهَمَ] to draw lots

تَقارَعَ *v* ◀1 [تَضارَبَ] to strike one another ◀2 [أَلْقى القُرْعةَ] to strike lots

اقْتَرَعَ *v* ◀1 [انْتَخَبَ] to vote; اقْتَرَعَ لِمُرَشَّحٍ \ حِزْبٍ to vote for a candidate/party ◀2 [أَجْرى قُرْعةً] to put up for raffle; to draw lots; اقْتَرَعَ من أَجْلِ شَيْءٍ to draw lots for sth

قَرْع A *n* percussion; knocking, rapping; ringing; قَرْع طَبْلٍ percussion drum; قَرْع ناقوسِ الخَطَرِ ringing of alarm bells
B *n coll* pumpkin; قَرْع صَيْفيّ courgette (BrE), zucchini (AmE); دودة القَرْعِ round worm

قارِعة *n* ◀1 [وَسَط] middle; على \ في قارِعةِ الطَريقِ in the middle of the road ◀2 [كارِثة] catastrophe; سورة القارِعة The Striking Hour (*Sura 101*)

قُرْعة *n* |قُرَع| raffle, lot; بالقُرْعةِ appointed by lot; قَرَّرَ شَيْئاً بالقُرْعةِ to determine sth by drawing lots; إجْراء القُرْعةِ raffling; أَجْرى القُرْعةَ to raffle (off); أَجْرى \ سَحَبَ قُرْعةً to raffle (off); أَجْرى قُرْعةً للفَوْزِ بِتَذاكِرَ مَجّانيّةٍ to raffle off free tickets

اقْتِراع *n* |اقْتِراعات| ◀1 [تَصْويت] election; vote, voting; صُنْدوق اقْتِراعٍ ballot box; حَقّ الاقْتِراعِ suffrage, voting rights; مَرْكَز \ مَقَرّ اقْتِراعٍ polling station (BrE) place (AmE); أَجْرى اقْتِراعاً to take a vote/ballot/poll ◀2 [قُرْعة] raffle, drawing lots; أَجْرى الاقْتِراعَ to raffle (off); قَرَّرَ شَيْئاً بالاقْتِراعِ to determine sth by drawing lots; الاقْتِراع للدَوْرِ رُبْعِ النِهائيّ the draw for the quarter finals

أَقْرَع *adj* |dipt| bare; أَرْض قَرْعاء bare soil

تَقْريع *n* scolding, dressing-down, admonition; تَعَرَّضَ للتَقْريعِ to get a dressing-down

مُقْتَرِع *n* voter; نِسْبة المُقْتَرِعينَ voter turnout

مِقْرَعة *n* |مَقارِعُ| ◀1 [بابٍ] knocker ◀2 [أَداة من خَشَبٍ] hammer

‹ **قِرْغيزْسْتان** *n* |f| Kyrgyzstan

‹ **قَرَفَ** *v* |i; قَرْف| to peel

قَرِفَ *v* |a; قَرَف| من| to loathe, to detest; قَرِفَ من شَخْصٍ to have an aversion to sb; to loathe sb

قُرْمة *n* |قُرَم| (Egypt) tree stump; woodblock, log

قَرْمَدَ *v* |i; قَرْمَدة| to plaster; to tile

قِرْميد *n* |قَراميدُ| ⓵ [حِجارة] roofing tile; tile; brick; سَقْف من القِرْميدِ الأَحْمَرِ red tile roof ⓶ [ما يُطْلى بِهِ] plaster, stucco

قِرْميديّ *adj* tile; brick

قِرْمِز *n* crimson, scarlet

قِرْمِزيّ *adj* crimson, scarlet; حُمّى قِرْمِزيّة scarlet fever

قَرْمَشَ *v* |i; قَرْمَشة| to crunch; طَعام يَقَرْمِشُ بين الأَسْنانِ food that crunches in your mouth

تَقَرْمَشَ *v* to be crunchy; to make a funny noise

مُقَرْمِش *adj* crispy, crunchy

مُقَرْمِشات *n pl* snacks, nibbles (infml)

قَرْموط *n* |قَراميطُ| catfish

قَرَنَ *v* |i; قَرْن| to unite, to combine; to connect, to attach; قَرَنَ القَوْلَ بالفِعْلِ \ بالعَمَلِ to suit the action to the word; ≈ actions speak louder than words; قَرَنَ بين عَمَلَيْنِ to combine two jobs; قَرَنَ شَيْئاً بِشُروطٍ to attach conditions to sth

قارَنَ *v* ⓵ [قابَلَ] to compare; to draw an analogy/a parallel; قارَنَ اللُغَةَ العَرَبيّةَ ب \ مع اللُغةِ الروسيّةِ to compare Arabic to/with Russian; لا يُقارَنُ بما أَنْجَزْتَ it's not comparable to what you've accomplished; قارَنَ نَفْسَهُ بِشَخْصٍ to compare oneself to sb; إذا ما قورِنَ بالماضي compared with the past ⓶ [صاحَبَ] to join (in)

أَقْرَنَ *v* to combine, to unite; أَقْرَنَ القَوْلَ بالفِعْلِ \ بالعَمَلِ to suit the action to the word; ≈ actions speak louder than words

اقْتَرَنَ *v* ⓵ [تَزَوَّجَ] |ب| to marry; اقْتَرَنَتْ أُخْتي بِرَجُلٍ يابانيٍّ my sister married a Japanese man ⓶ [ارْتَبَطَ] |ب| to be connected, to be linked; to coincide; اقْتَرَنَ بِشَيْءٍ to be connected with sth; اقْتَرَنَ بِمُوافقةِ شَخْصٍ to have sb's consent; اقْتَرَنَتْ زِيارَتُهُ بعيدِ الأَضْحى his visit coincided with Eid ul-Adha

تَقارَنَ *v* to form a pair, to be a couple; to be linked

قَرْن *n* |قُرون| ⓵ [مِائة سَنةٍ] century; القُرون الوُسْطى Middle Ages; من القُرونِ الوُسْطى medieval; قُرون غابِرة past centuries ⓶ [حَيَوانٍ] horn; قَرْن اسْتِشْعارٍ antenna, feeler (*of an insect*); القَرْنِ الإفْريقيّ the Horn of Africa; وَحيد القَرْنِ rhinoceros; قَرْن وَحيدِ القَرْنِ rhinoceros horn; ذو القَرْنَيْنِ he who has horns (*epithet of Alexander the Great*) ⓷ [مادّة] horn; مُشْط مَصْنوع من قَرْنِ الغَزالِ a comb made of gazelle horn

قِرْن *n* |أَقْران| equal; peer; لَقِيَ قِرْنَهُ he has met his match

قِران *n* ⓵ [زَواج] marriage, matrimony; يَوْم عَقْدِ القِرانِ wedding day; عَقَدَ القِرانَ to be joined in matrimony; عَقَدَ قِرانَهُ على الآنِسةِ ... he was joined in matrimony with Miss ... ⓶ (Astrol) conjunction

قَرْنيّة *n* cornea

قَرين *n* |قُرَناءُ| ⓵ [زَوْج] husband, spouse, consort; قَرين المَلِكةِ the (Prince) Consort ⓶ [مُناظِر] equal, peer; وَجَدَ قَرينَهُ في شَيْءٍ \ شَخْصٍ to find one's match in sth/sb; لا قَرينَ لَهُ without equal, unparalleled

قَرينة *n* |قَرائِنُ| ⓵ [زَوْجة] wife, spouse, consort; الرَئيس وَقَرينَتُهُ the president and his wife ⓶ [دَليل] indication, sign, clue; قَرينة على شَيْءٍ an indication of sth; تَوَصَّلَت الشُرْطةُ إلى قَرائِنَ تُؤَكِّدُ أنّ ... the police have indications that confirm that ... ⓷ [صِلة] connection, relationship; قَرينة الكَلامِ context ⓸ (Law) presumption; قَرينة البَراءةِ \ الشَكِّ presumption of innocence; the benefit of the doubt

اقْتِران *n* ⓵ [ارْتِباط] link, connection ⓶ (Astrol) conjunction ⓷ (Psych) association

أَقْرَن *adj* |dipt; قُرْن; f قَرْناءُ| ⓵ [ذو قَرْنٍ] horned ⓶ [لا مُقاطَعة بين حاجِبَيْهِ] *having a unibrow*

مُقارَن *adj* comparative; عِلْم اللُغةِ المُقارَن comparative linguistics

مُقارِن *adj* comparative; إطار مُقارِن comparative framework; مُقارِناً ب ... in/by comparison with ..., compared with ...

مُقارَنة *n* comparison; قابِل للمُقارَنةِ comparable; مُقارَنة غَيْر عادِلةٍ an unfair comparison; مُقارَنة بين فيلْمَيْنِ comparison between two films; مُقارَنة لُغةٍ ب \ مع لُغةٍ أُخْرى comparison between one language and another; بالمُقارَنةِ مع شَيْءٍ \ شَخْصٍ compared with sth/sb, in comparison with sth/sb; مُقارَنةً ب \ مع العامِ الماضي compared with last year; على وَجْهِ المُقارَنةِ by way of comparison; لا يوجَدُ وَجْهُ مُقارَنةٍ there is no comparison

مِقْرَن *n* yoke

مَقْرون *adj* connected, linked; حَواجِب مَقْرونة unibrow

مَقَرونة, مَكَرونة *n* pasta

‹ **قَرْنَبيط** *n* cauliflower

‹ **مُقَرْنَص** *n* muqarnas (*type of corbel used in Islamic architecture*)

‹ **قَرَنْفُل, قُرُنْفُل** *n* 1 [تابِل] clove; كَبْش قَرَنْفُلٍ a (single) clove 2 carnation; قَرَنْفُل الشاعِرِ Sweet William (*Dianthus barbatus*)

‹ **قَرَوْسَطيّ** *adj* medieval; فَلْسَفة قَرَوْسَطيّة medieval philosophy

‹ **قَرَى** *v* |i; قِرًى| to receive hospitably; to accommodate; قَرَى شَخْصاً to receive sb hospitably; to accommodate sb

تَقَرَّى *v* to investigate

قَرَوِيّ A *adj* rural; village (*before n*); *of/from Kairouan*; مُجْتَمَع قَرَوِيّ rural community; مَجْلِس قَرَوِيّ village council B *n* villager; *resident of Kairouan*; جامِعة القَرَوِيّين al-Karaouine (*mosque and university of Fez*)

قِرًى *n* hospitality; hospitable welcome

قَرْية *n* |قُرًى| village; سُكّان \ أَهْل القَرْيةِ village residents

‹ **قُزَح** *n* rainbow; قَوْس قُزَحٍ rainbow

قُزَحيّة *n* (*Anat*) iris

‹ **قَزَّ** *v* |u; قَزّ| to detest; to have an aversion to; قَزَّتْ نَفْسُهُ شَيْئاً \ عن \ من شَيْءٍ to detest sth; to have an aversion to sth

تَقَزَّزَ *v* to be disgusted; to feel aversion; تَقَزَّزَ من شَخْصٍ \ شَيْءٍ to to be disgusted by sb/sth; to have an aversion to sb/sth; تَقَزَّزَ من رائِحةِ \ مَنْظَرِ شَيْءٍ to be disgusted by the smell/sight of sth

قَزّ *n* silk; دودة القَزِّ silkworm

قَزّاز *n* silk merchant

تَقَزُّز *n* revulsion, distaste, disgust; تَقَزُّز من شَيْءٍ \ شَخْصٍ aversion to sth/sb; شَيْء يُثير التَقَزُّزَ sth detestable/disgusting

مُتَقَزِّز *adj* sick, disgusted

مُقَزِّز *adj* disgusting, repulsive, revolting; مَنْظَر مُقَزِّز a disgusting sight

‹ **قَزَع** *n coll* billowing clouds

‹ **قَزُمَ** *v* |u; قَزامة| *to be a dwarf*

قَزَّمَ *v* to belittle, to trivialize

تَقَزَّمَ *v* to suffer from dwarfism

قَزَم, قَزْم *n* A |أَقْزام| 1 [خُرافيّ] dwarf; gnome; الأَميرة والأَقْزام السَّبْعة Snow White and the Seven Dwarfs 2 [من شَعْبٍ إفْريقيّ] pygmy 3 [شَخْص قَصير] midget, little person B *adj* |أَقْزام| miniature, pygmy, dwarf (*before n*); حِصان قَزَم miniature horse; نَجْم \ كَوْكَب قَزَم dwarf star/planet

قَزَميّ *adj* dwarf (*before n*), pygmy (*before n*); كَوْكَب قَزَميّ dwarf planet

تَقَزُّم *n* dwarfism; *becoming shorter*

تَقْزيم *n* belittlement, belittling; تَقْزيم دَوْرِ شَخْصٍ belittling sb's involvement

‹ **قَزْوين** *n* |dipt f| Qazvin (*province in Iran and its capital*); بَحْر قَزْوينَ Caspian Sea

‹ **قَسَرَ** *v* |i; قَسْر| to force, to compel; قَسَرَ شَخْصاً على شَيْءٍ to force sb to do sth

قَسْر *n* force, compulsion, coercion; قَسْراً under duress/pressure, involuntarily; هُجِّرَ قَسْراً to be displaced/forced out

قَسْريّ *adj* forced, enforced, compulsory; تَهْجير قَسْريّ forced migration, displacement; اخْتِفاء قَسْريّ forced disappearance; غِياب قَسْريّ enforced absence

‹ **قَسَّ** *v* |u; قُسوسة| to enter the priesthood

قَسّ, قِسّ *n* |قُسوس, قُسُس| priest; clergyman, preacher, pastor

قُسوسة *n* priesthood; ministry

قِسّيس *n* |أَقِسّة, قُسّان, قَساوِسة, قِسّيسونَ| priest; clergyman, preacher, pastor; رَسَمَ شَخْصاً قِسّيساً to ordain someone as a priest; مَنْصِب قِسّيسٍ priesthood

‹ **قَسَطَ** *v* |i; قِسْط| to act righteously; to be fair/just

قَسَّطَ *v* 1 [قَسَّمَ] to divide; to ration 2 [الدَّيْنَ] to pay off; to pay in installments; قَسَّطَ ثَمَنَ بَيْتٍ to pay for a house

أَقْسَطَ *v* to act righteously; to be fair/just

قِسْط *n* |أَقْساط| 1 [مَرْحَلة] instalment, payment; على أَقْساطٍ in instalments; قِسْط شَهْريّ monthly payment; دَفَع \ سَدَّدَ ثَمَنَ شَيْءٍ على أَقْساطٍ to pay sth in instalments; سَدَّدَ آخِرَ قِسْطٍ من الدَّيْنِ to pay the last instalment of a debt; أَقْساط مَدْرَسيّة school tuition; the cost of schooling 2 [تأمينٍ] premium; contribution 3 [نَصيب] portion, share; قِسْط

كَبير \ وافِر من شَيْءٍ a generous portion of sth; نالَ قِسْطاً كَبيراً من المَجْدِ والشُهْرةِ to gain a great deal of fame; أَخَذَ قِسْطَهُ من الراحةِ to take a well-earned rest; تَحَمَّلَ قِسْطاً كَبيراً من المَسْؤوليّةِ to bear a great deal of responsibility ❹ [عَدْل] fairness

تَقْسيط *n* payment in instalments, payment plan; اشْتَرى شَيْئاً بالتَقْسيطِ to buy sth on an instalment/a payment plan; to buy sth on credit; طَلَبَ تَقْسيطَ الدَيْنِ to request a payment plan

مُقْسِط Ⓐ *adj* equitable; الْتِهاب الفَقارِ المُقْسِطِ (Med) ankylosing spondylitis

Ⓑ *n* المُقْسِط the Equitable (*one of the names of God*)

قِسْطاس *n* |قَساطيسُ| (pair of) scales, balance

قَسْطَرة *n* catheter

قَسْطَل *n* |قَساطِلُ| chestnut

القُسْطَنْطينيّة *n* Constantinople

قَسَمَ *v* |i; قَسْم| ❶ [جَزَّأَ] to divide, to split; to share out; قَسَمَ مُناصَفةً to split evenly; قَسَمَ شَيْئاً إلى \ في جُزْأَيْنِ to divide sth into two; قَسَمَ مَجْموعةً إلى مَجْموعَتَيْنِ to split a group into two groups; قَسَمَ شَيْئاً (مُناصَفةً) بين طَرَفَيْنِ to divide sth (evenly) between two parties ❷ (Math) to divide; قَسَمَ عِشْرينَ على أَرْبَعةٍ to divide twenty by four

قَسَّمَ *v* to divide, to split; to distribute, to share out; قَسَّمَ الأَرْباحَ to share out the profits; قَسَّمَ التَلاميذَ إلى مَجْموعَتَيْنِ to divide the students into two groups; قَسَّمَ شَيْئاً إلى أَقْسامٍ to divide sth into pieces

قاسَمَ *v* to share; قاسَمَ شَخْصاً شَيْئاً to share sth with sb

أَقْسَمَ *v* to swear; to take an oath; أَقْسَمَ باللهِ to swear to God; أَقْسَمَ يَميناً to swear an oath; أَقْسَمَ أَلاّ يَقولَ إلاّ الحَقيقةَ to swear to tell the truth

تَقَسَّمَ *v* ❶ [تَفَرَّقَ] to be divided; to be be partitioned; تَقَسَّمَ الطَلَبةُ فِرَقاً the students were divided into teams ❷ [اقْتَسَمَ] to distribute between themselves; تَقَسَّموا الطَعامَ they divided the food among themselves

تَقاسَمَ *v* to share with each other, to distribute between themselves; تَقاسَمَ التَرْكةَ مع إِخْوَتِهِ to share the inheritance with one's siblings; تَقاسَمَ الصَدارةَ to share the lead (position); تَقاسَمَ شَيْئاً بالتَساوي to share in sth equally

انْقَسَمَ *v* to be/become divided; انْقَسَمَت الآراءُ the views differed; انْقَسَمَ الفَريقُ إلى مَجْموعَتَيْنِ the team was split into two groups

اقْتَسَمَ *v* to share, to distribute between themselves; اقْتَسَمَ الغَنائِمَ to share the spoils

قَسَم *n* |أَقْسام| oath; قَسَم بُقْراط Hippocratic oath; أَدّى قَسَماً to make/take/swear an oath; to swear; تَصْريح مَشْفوع بالقَسَمِ sworn statement, affidavit; قَسَم الوَظيفةِ oath of office

قِسْم *n* |أَقْسام| ❶ [جُزْء] part, portion, section; القِسْم الشَرْقيّ من القُدْسِ the eastern part of Jerusalem; يَقَعُ الكِتابُ في خَمْسةِ أَقْسامٍ the book consists of five volumes/parts; سَيْطَرَ الجَيْشُ على قِسْمٍ كَبيرٍ من المَدينةِ the army controlled a large part of the city; قِسْم الكَلامِ part of speech ❷ [مِنْطَقة] district; department ❸ (Admin) department, section; قِسْم التاريخِ the history department ❹ (Sport) division, league; القِسْم الأَوَّل the first division ❺ (Educ NA) classroom; class; year; القِسْم الابْتِدائيّ first/second grade; القِسْم الأَوَّل \ الثاني (SA) elementary school

قاسِم *n* |قَواسِمُ| ❶ (Math) denominator, divisor; القاسِم المُشْتَرَك الأَعْظَم the greatest common denominator; القاسِم المُشْتَرَك بين كُلِّ الفِئاتِ (fig) the common denominator among all the factions ❷ [اسْم شَخْصيّ] Qasim (*male given name*)

قَسامة *n* beauty

قِسْمة *n* |قِسَم| ❶ [تَقْسيم] allotment, distribution; قِسْمة عادِلة a fair distribution; هذه هي قِسْمَتُهُ من الغَنيمةِ this is his share of the spoils ❷ [قَدَر] fate, destiny; كُلُّ شَيْءٍ قِسْمةٌ وَنَصيبٌ ≈ what can you do?, ≈ *c'est la vie* ❸ (Math) division; قِسْمة على ثَلاثةٍ division by three; قابِل للقِسْمةِ divisible; غَيْر قابِلٍ للقِسْمةِ indivisible; بِلادي لا تَقْبَلُ القِسْمةَ my country cannot be divided

قَسيم *n* |أَقْسِماءُ| partner; participant

قَسيمة *n* |قَسائِمُ| voucher, coupon; ticket; receipt; قَسيمة الاشْتِراكِ subscription card; دَفْعَ قيمةِ قَسيمةٍ to pay the value of voucher; وَزَّعَ قَسائِمَ المَوادِّ الغِذائيّةِ to distribute food-aid vouchers

اقْتِسام *n* |اقْتِسامات| distribution, division; dividing; اقْتِسام الغَنائِمِ \ الثَّرْوةِ division of the spoils/wealth

انْقِسام *n* |انْقِسامات| division, schism; انْقِسام الذَّرّاتِ splitting atoms; انْقِسام داخِلَ \ في الحِزْبِ a rift in the party; سَبَّبَ انْقِساماً to cause a schism; كَرَّسَ \ عَمَّقَ الانْقِسامَ (بين الجانِبَيْنِ) to entrench/deepen divisions (between the two sides)

تَقْسيم *n* |تَقْسيمات| **1** [تَجْزِئة] division; district; classification; تَقْسيم إداريّ administrative district; تَقْسيم الدَوائِرِ \ الانْتِخابيّ electoral district, constituency (BrE), district (AmE); defining electoral districts, districting (AmE); تَقْسيم كِتابٍ (إلى أبْوابٍ) division of a book (in chapters); تَقْسيم إلى أجْزاءٍ division into sections; التَقْسيم إلى فُصولٍ classification; إعادة التَقْسيم redivision, rearrangement; إعادة تَقْسيم الدَوائِرِ redrawing electoral districts, redistricting (AmE) **2** [تَوْزيع] distribution; proportion

تَقْسيمة *n* |تَقاسيمُ| (Mus) *instrumental solo*

مُقاسِم *n* partner

مُقاسَمة *n* sharing; مُقاسَمة الأَرْباحِ profit sharing

مُقَسَّم *adj* divided; غير مُقَسَّمٍ undivided; قُبْرُص مُقَسَّمةٌ إلى شَطْرَيْنِ Cyprus is divided into two parts

مُقَسِّم *n* distributor

مَقْسوم **A** *adj* divisible; divided; مَقْسوم على ٣ divisible by three; مِنْطَقة مَقْسومة بين بَلَدَيْنِ a region divided between two countries

B *n* (Math) |مَقاسيمُ| dividend; مَقْسوم عَلَيْهِ divisor, denominator

مُنْقَسِم *adj* divided, shared; divisible

‹ **قُسَنْطينة** *n* |dipt| Constantine (*city in Algeria*)

‹ **قَسا** *v* |u; قَساوة, قَسْوة| to be stern/strict/cruel; قَسا على شَخْصٍ to be stern/strict with sb; قَسا قَلْبُهُ to be/become cruel; ... مَهْما قَسَت الظُروفُ no matter how difficult the circumstances ...

قَسّى *v* to harden

قاسى *v* to suffer, to endure; قاسى آلاماً to be in pain; قاسى المِحَنَ to endure hardship

أَقْسى *v* to harden; أَقْسى قَلْبَهُ to be/become cruel

قاسٍ **A** *adj* |قُساة| **1** [صُلْب] hard, solid, stiff, tough; غِطاء قاسٍ solid cover; hard top (*car*) **2** [عَنيف] harsh, strict, cruel, merciless; مُعامَلة قاسِية cruel treatment; كَلام قاسٍ harsh words; نِظام قاسٍ a brutal regime; إجْراءات \ تَدابير قاسِية strict measures; draconian measures; بِنَبْرةٍ قاسِيةٍ in a harsh tone; تَعَلَّمَ دَرْساً قاسِياً to learn a hard lesson; الحَياةُ مَدْرَسةٌ قاسِيةٌ life is a cruel teacher **3** [شَديد] extreme; hard, tough; heavy; جوع قاسٍ extreme hunger; بَرْد قاسٍ bitter cold; عُقوبة قاسِية a harsh punishment; ضَرْبة قاسِية a heavy blow; في \ تحت ظُروفٍ قاسِيةٍ under difficult circumstances

B *n* |قُساة| brute; monster

قَساوة *n* cruelty; harshness; قَساوة على شَخْصٍ cruelty against sb; عامَلَ شَخْصاً \ شَيْئاً بِقَساوةٍ to handle sth/sb harshly/ roughly; بِقَساوةٍ cruelly, harshly

قَسْوة *n* cruelty, harshness; difficulty, extremity; قَسْوة القَلْبِ hardness of heart; قَسْوة الطَبيعةِ \ المَناخِ the harshness of nature/the climate; قَسْوة الظُروفِ (الاقْتِصاديّة) the difficulty of the (economic) conditions; بِقَسْوةٍ cruelly, harshly

مُقاساة *n* hardship, deprivation

‹ **قَشيب** *adj* |قُشُب| new; clean

‹ **قَشْتالة** *n* (Geog) Castile

‹ **قَشْتاليّ** *adj, n* Castilian

‹ **قَشَدَ** *v* |i-u; قَشْد| to skim off

قِشْدة *n* cream; whipping cream; خَفَقَ القِشْدةَ to whip cream

قِشْديّ *adj* **1** [اللَوْنِ] cream (*before n*); cream-coloured; فُسْتان قِشْديّ a cream-coloured dress **2** [الطَعام] creamy

مَقْشود *adj* lean, low-fat; حَليب مَقْشود skimmed (BrE) skim (AmE) milk; جُبْنة مَقْشودة low-fat cheese

‹ **قَشَرَ** *v* |i-u; قَشْر| **1** [فَواكِهَ وَخُضَراً] to peel, to pare; to rasp, to scrape; قَشَرَ تُفّاحاً to peel apples **2** [سَلَخَ] to skin

قَشَّرَ *v* to peel, to pare, to shell, to husk; قَشَّرَ بُرْتُقالةً \ بَيْضةً to peel an orange/egg; قَشَّرَ تُفّاحاً to peel apples; قَشَّرَ الجَمْبَريَّ to peel/shell shrimps

تَقَشَّرَ *v* to peel (off), to flake (off), to scale; يَتَقَشَّرُ جِلْدُ الثُعْبانِ the snake is shedding its skin; يَتَقَشَّرُ الطِلاءُ the paint is peeling off

انْقَشَرَ *v* to peel/flake (off)

قِشْر *n* |قُشور| 1 [بَيْض] shell; كَسَرَ قِشْرَ بَيْضةٍ to break an eggshell 2 [ثَمَر] peel, rind; pod; قِشْر البُرْتُقالِ orange peel/rind 3 [شَجَر] bark 4 [قَمْح] chaff 5 [الجِلْد] flake; قِشْر الرَّأْسِ dandruff 6 [السَّمَك] scale

قَشّارة *n* peeler

قُشارة *n* peel, peelings

قِشْرة *n* |قِشَر| skin, crust, shell; القِشْرة الأَرْضيّة the earth's crust; قِشْرة على الحَليبِ skin on milk; قِشْرة فولٍ سودانيٍّ peanut shell; قِشْرة بَيْضٍ eggshell; قِشْرة المُخِّ \ الدماغ, القِشْرة الخارِجيّة للمُخّ cerebral cortex; قِشْرة كِلْسيّة crust of lime (*soil*); scale, boiler scale (*pipes*)

قِشْريّ A *adj* scaly, flaky
B *n* قِشْريّات crustaceans

تَقْشير *n* peeling; تَقْشير البَصَلِ peeling onions; تَقْشير الجِلْدِ skin peel/resurfacing

مُقَشِّر *n* مُقَشِّر للجِلْدِ exfoliator

مِقْشَرة *n* |مَقاشِرُ| peeler

‹ **قَشَّ** *v* |i-u; قَشّ| 1 [بَحَثَ] to collect, to gather; to search, to scour; قَشَّ الذاكِرةَ الجَماعيّةَ to search the collective memory; قَشَّ المَكانَ to scratch about/around somewhere looking for food 2 [يَبِسَ] to dry up; to be/become dry

قَشّ *n* |قُشوش| straw; hay; كَوْم قَشٍّ haystack; قَشّ الأَرُزّ rice hulls; من قَشٍّ (made of) straw; بَيْت \ كوخ من قَشٍّ straw hut; بَحَثَ عن إبْرةٍ في كَوْمةِ قَشٍّ to look for a needle in a haystack; حُمّى القَشّ hay fever

قَشّة *n* straw, a stalk of straw; القَشّة الّتي قَصَمَتْ ظَهْرَ البَعيرِ the straw that broke the camel's back; كانَ كالقَشّةِ في مَهَبِّ الريحِ to be like a straw in the wind (*to be at the mercy of fate*)

تَقْشيش *n* upholstering (*with bamboo, hay, straw*); تَقْشيش الكَراسيِّ chair upholstering

مِقَشّة *n* broom, brush; عَصا مِقَشّةٍ broomstick, broom handle

‹ **قَشَطَ** *v* |i; قَشْط| to slice; to scrape off, to strip off; to skim off

قَشَّطَ *v* to rob; to plunder

قُشاط *n* *flaky hard candy*; piece, chip; قُشاط السِمْسِمِ sesame candy; قُشاط الفولِ السودانيِّ peanut brittle

قِشاط *n* string, chord, belt

قِشْطة *n* 1 (Bot) Annona (*Annonaceae*) 2 (Culin) cream, whipping cream

مِقْشَط *n* |مَقاشِطُ| plane, file

‹ **قَشَعَ** *v* |a; قَشْع| to drive away, to disperse; قَشَعَ الظَلامَ to dispel the darkness

أَقْشَعَ *v* to dispel, to drive away, to scatter

انْقَشَعَ *v* to brighten/clear up; to disperse; يَنْقَشِعُ السَحابُ the sky's clearing up; انْقَشَعَ الغُبارُ \ الدُخانُ the dust/smoke cleared

قَشَع *n* (Med) sputum

‹ **اقْشَعَرَّ** *v* to shiver, to tremble; اقْشَعَرَّ بَدَنُهُ \ جِلْدُهُ to shiver; اقْشَعَرَّتْ من البَرْدِ she shivered from the cold

قُشَعْريرة *n* goose bumps; shiver; شَعَرَ بِقُشَعْريرةٍ من شَيْءٍ to shiver/get goose bumps from sth; جاءَتْني قُشَعْريرةٌ من الفيلْمِ the movie gave me goose bumps

‹ **قَشُفَ** *v* |u; قَشافة| to live in squalor

تَقَشَّفَ *v* 1 [اقْتَصَدَ] to economize, to reduce; to stretch (*meagre resources*); تَقَشَّفَ في الاسْتِهْلاكِ to reduce consumption 2 [اكْتَفى بالضَروريِّ] to be austere; to live austerely

تَقَشُّف *n* 1 [اقْتِصاديّ] austerity, cutbacks, retrenchment; عَمَليّة \ سِياسة التَقَشُّفِ austerity measures/policy; عَمَليّة تَقَشُّفٍ شاملة \ على مُسْتَوًى واسِعٍ wide-ranging austerity measures; اتَّخَذَ إجْراءاتِ تَقَشُّفٍ to take austerity measures; تَقَشُّفات اقْتِصاديّة economic retrenchment 2 [زُهْد] abstinence

تَقَشُّفيّ *adj* austere; austerity (*before n*); سِياسة تَقَشُّفيّة austerity policy

مُتَقَشِّف A *adj* ascetic; austere; مُوازَنة مُتَقَشِّفة an austere budget
B *n* ascetic

‹ **قِشْلة** *n* |قِشَل| qishla (*ancient military fort*)

‹ **قَصَبَ** *v* |i; قَصْب| to butcher, to carve

قَصَّبَ *v* 1 [شَعْراً] to curl 2 [طَرَّزَ] to embroider

قَصَب *n* coll cane; قَصَب السُكَّرِ sugar cane; سُكَّر القَصَبِ cane sugar

(Idiom) نال \ أحرَزَ قَصَبَ السَبْقِ to play a pioneering role, to be a trailblazer; to achieve great success

قَصّاب *n* butcher

قِصابة *n* butchery

قَصَبة *n* **1** [أُنبوب] pipe, tube, reed; قَصَبة هوائيّة \ الرِئة windpipe; bronchi **2** [بَلْدة] (NA) citadel; kasbah **3** [عظْم] marrowbone; قَصَبة الساقِ shin bone, tibia **4** [قلم] reed pen **5** (Mus) *a type of wind instrument* **6** [مِقْياس] *linear measurement, approx 3.5 meters*

قَصَبيّ *adj* reed (*before n*)

قَصَدَ *v* |i; قَصْد| **1** [تَوَجَّهَ] to go to; to proceed towards; قَصَدَ المَدينةَ to go to the city **2** [نَوى] to mean, to intend, to plan (*actions*); قَصَدَ شَيْئاً to intend sth; لم يَقْصِدْ بِهِ سوءاً to not mean any harm; قَصَدَ السَفَرَ إلى وَطَنِهِ to plan to travel to one's homeland **3** [عَنى] to mean, to intend (*speech*); قَصَدَ من كَلامِهِ شَيْئاً to intend to say sth; ماذا تَقْصِدُ؟ what do you mean?; what are you trying to say?; ماذا تَقْصِدُ بِهَذِهِ المُلاحَظةِ؟ what do you mean by that remark?

قَصَّدَ *v* to write poetry

أَقْصَدَ *v* to write poetry

تَقَصَّدَ *v* to intend, to aim; to economize, to save; مَنْ يَتَقَصَّدُ تَشْويهَ صورَتِنا those who aim to tarnish our image

اقْتَصَدَ *v* to economize; to save; اقْتَصَدَ في نَفَقاتِ الدَوْلة to cut back on government spending; يَقْتَصِدُ الجِهازُ في اسْتِخْدامِ الماءِ والطاقةِ the machine saves water and energy; سَيّارة تَقْتَصِدُ في اسْتِهْلاكِ الوَقود a fuel-efficient car

قَصْد *n* goal, purpose, intention; meaning; قَصْد خَفيّ ulterior motive; عن قَصْدٍ, قَصْداً intentionally, deliberately, well-considered, knowingly; عن غَيْرِ قَصْدٍ unintentionally, inadvertently, accidentally; بِقَصْدِ فِعْلِ شَيْءٍ with the intention to do sth; لم يَكُنْ قَصْدي that was not my intention; فَهِمْتُ قَصْدَكَ I know what you mean; اللهُ وراء القَصْدِ *God supports our goal*

قاصِد *adj* going, intending; resolute; قاصِداً in the direction of, with the intention to; resolutely; مَسيرة قاصِدة forward march; عَدَد السُيّاحِ القاصِدينَ تِلْكَ المَناطِقِ the number of tourists headed for those regions

قُصادَ *prep* opposite, in front of

قَصْديّ *adj* intentional, deliberate; جَريمة قَصْديّة intentional crime

قَصيد *n genre of Arabic poetry*; بَيْتُ القَصيدِ essence

قَصيدة *n* |قَصائِدُ| poem; qasida (*classical Arabic poem*); قَصيدة مَدْحٍ ode, laudatory poem; قَصيدة غَزَليّة love poem; كَتَبَ قَصيدةً to write a poem; أَلْقى قَصيدةً to recite a poem

اقْتِصاد *n* **1** [تَدْبير الحَياةِ الاقْتِصاديّة] economy; اقْتِصاد حُرّ open economy; اقْتِصاد جُزْئيّ microeconomics; اقْتِصاد كُلّيّ macroeconomics; الاقْتِصاد العالَميّ \ الوَطَنيّ the global/national economy; اقْتِصاد مُخَطَّط \ مُوَجَّه planned economy; عِلْم الاقْتِصادِ economics; اقْتِصاد قِياسيّ econometrics; عالِم اقْتِصادٍ economist; إنْعاش الاقْتِصادِ stimulating the economy; أَحْيا الاقْتِصادَ to revive the economy; دَمَّرَ الاقْتِصادَ to destroy the economy **2** [تَوْفير] retrenchment

اقْتِصاديّ **A** *adj* **1** [مَنْسوب إلى الاقْتِصادِ] economic; اقْتِصاديّات economy; اقْتِصاديّ كُلّيّ macroeconomic; اقْتِصاديّ جُزْئيّ microeconomic; السِياسة الاقْتِصاديّة economic policy; وِزارة الشُؤونِ الاقْتِصاديّةِ Ministry of Economic Affairs, Department of Trade and Industry (BrE), Department of Commerce (AmE); فَتْرة ازْدِهارٍ \ رُكودٍ اقْتِصاديٍّ period of economic boom/recession **2** [مُقْتَصِد] economical; frugal; thrifty; غَيْر اقْتِصاديّ uneconomical; سَيّارة اقْتِصاديّة economical car; مِصْباح اقْتِصاديّ energy-efficient light bulb **B** *n* economist

مُقْتَصِد *adj* economical, thrifty

مَقْصَد *n* destination

مَقْصِد *n* |مَقاصِدُ| **1** [وِجْهة] destination; مَقْصِد سياحيّ a tourist destination **2** [غاية] goal, intention; مَقاصِد الشَريعةِ *principal objectives of Islamic law*

مَقْصود **A** *adj* deliberate, intentional; غَيْر مَقْصودٍ unintentional; unintended; تَأْثير غَيْر مَقْصودٍ unintended consequence, side effect; إهانة مَقْصودة deliberate insult **B** *n* **1** [مَعْنًى] meaning; فَهِمَ المَقْصودَ to understand the intended meaning; ... المَقْصودُ بذلِكَ هو what's meant by that is ... **2** ◀ [هَدَف] aim, goal

قَصْدير *n* tin

قَصْديريّ *adj* tin (*before n*); tin-coloured

قَصَرَ *v* |u| **1** ◀ [عَجَزَ] |قُصور| to be remiss; قَصَرَ عن واجِباتِهِ to be remiss in one's duties; قَصَرَ عن تَسْديدِ دَيْنِهِ to fail to repay one's debts **2** ◀ [أَخَذَ من طولِهِ] |قِصَر| to shorten, to curtail **3** ◀ [حَصَرَ] |قَصْر| to limit, to restrict; قَصَرَ نَفْسَهُ على فِعْلِ الخَيْرِ to limit oneself to doing good; قَصَرَ المُحادَثَةَ على مَوْضوعٍ واحِدٍ to limit the conversation to one subject; قَصَرَ نَفَقاتِهِ to restrict one's expenses

قَصُرَ *v* |u|; قَصَر, قِصَر, قَصْر, قَصارة| to be/become short; تَقْصُرُ الأَيّامُ the days are shortening

قَصَّرَ *v* **1** ◀ [أَهْمَلَ] to fail, to fall short; to neglect; to omit; قَصَّرَ في شَيْءٍ to neglect sth; قَصَّرَ في واجِبِهِ \ مُهِمَّتِهِ \ عَمَلِهِ to fail in one's duty/task/work; قَصَّرَ في الأَداءِ to fail to perform; قَصَّرَ في حَقِّ شَخْصٍ to disrespect sb, to do sb wrong **2** ◀ [جَعَلَهُ قصيراً] to shorten; to curtail, to reduce; قَصَّرَ سِرْوالاً to take up a pair of trousers (BrE), to hem a pair of pants (AmE); قَصَّرَ لِشَخْصٍ مُدَّةَ العُقوبةِ to reduce sb's sentence; قَصَّرَ المَسافةَ بين شَيْئَيْنِ to shorten the distance between two things; قَصَّرَ عُمْرَ شَخْصٍ \ شَيْءٍ to shorten sb's/sth's life; (fig) to be the death of sb/sth **3** ◀ [غَسَلَ وبَيَّضَ] to bleach

أَقْصَرَ *v* **1** ◀ [جَعَلَهُ قصيراً] to shorten, to cut short **2** ◀ [امْتَنَعَ] |عن| to refrain from, to abstain from; أَقْصَرَ عن شَيْءٍ to refrain from sth; أَقْصَرَ عن القُمارِ to abstain from gambling

تَقاصَرَ *v* **1** ◀ [قَصُرَ] to become shorter **2** ◀ [أَمْسَكَ] |عن| to stop; to refrain from; تَقاصَرَ عن شَيْءٍ to refrain from sth

اقْتَصَرَ *v* |على| to be restricted (to), to be limited (to); to limit (oneself) (to); ... اقْتَصَرَ الأَمْرُ على the matter was restricted to ...; ... لا يَقْتَصِرُ الضَرَرُ على (مُجَرَّدِ) the damage is not limited (solely) to ...; يَقْتَصِرُ دَوْرُ اللَجْنَةِ على تَقْديمِ المَشورةِ the council's role is limited to offering advice; اقْتَصَرَ الإمامُ في القَراءةِ على الفاتِحةِ فَقَطْ the imam limited his readings to just the Fatiha

قَصْر *n* **1** ◀ [قَلْعة] |قُصور| castle, palace; القَصْر المَلَكيّ the royal palace; القَصْر الكَبير Ksar El Kebir (*city in Morocco*); قَصْر العَدالةِ \ العَدْلِ Palace of Justice, courthouse; قَصْر السَلامِ the Peace Palace (*home of the International Court of Justice in The Hague*); قَصْر الرِئاسةِ presidential palace; قَصْر في الهَواءِ, قَصْر أَحْلامٍ castles in the air/sky; (fig) dream **2** ◀ [حَصْر] limitation, reduction; قَصْر عَدَدِ القوّاتِ reduction in the number of troops; قَصْر الصَلاةِ shortening of the prayer

قِصَر *n* shortness, brevity; قِصَر النَظَرِ nearsightedness, myopia; (fig) narrow-mindedness, lack of foresight

قاصِر **A** *adj* **1** ◀ [غَيْر قادِر] unable, incapable; كانَ قاصِراً عن الحَرَكَةِ to be unable to move **2** ◀ [غَيْر بالِغ] minor, underage **B** *n* minor

قَصّار *n* |قُصّار| bleacher (*obsolete profession*)

قُصارى *adj* utmost; بَذَلَ قُصارى جُهْدِهِ to do one's utmost, to try as hard as one can; ... قُصارى القَوْلِ أنّ the bottom line is ..., suffice to say that...

قَصْريّة *n* |قَصارٍ| (Egypt) chamber pot; flower pot

قُصور *n* **1** ◀ [عَجْز] shortcomings, insufficiency; deficiency, lack; أَوْجُه القُصورِ shortcomings; قُصور عَقْليّ mental deficiency; قُصور في الأَداءِ unsatisfactory performance, failure **2** ◀ [كَسَل] passivity, laziness; قُصور ذاتيّ lethargy, inertia **3** ◀ [في السِنِّ] minority

قَصير *adj* |قِصار| **1** ◀ [المُدّة] short; في فَتْرةٍ \ مُدّةٍ قَصيرةٍ in a short space of time; من \ منذ فَتْرةٍ قَصيرةٍ recently, lately; في الأَجَلِ \ الأَمَدِ القَصيرِ in the short term; مُهْلة قَصيرة short notice **2** ◀ [عَكْس طَويل] short; small; شَعْر قَصير short hair; سِرْوال قَصير shorts; تَنّورة قَصيرة short skirt; كانَ قَصيرَ القامةِ to be of short stature; to be of small build

اقْتِصار *n* limitation; restriction; اقْتِصار الطَلَبِ limited/short supply; (فَقَطْ) ... عَدَم الاقْتِصارِ على not being limited (just) to ...; كانَ اقْتِصاراً على الضَروريِّ to be limited to the bare essentials

الأُقْصُر *n* |f| Luxor (*city in Egypt*)

تَقْصير *n* **1** ◀ [إهْمال] negligence; omissions; shortcomings; اتَّهَمَ شَخْصاً بالتَقْصيرِ في أَداءِ التَقْصيرِ to accuse sb of negligence;

الواجبِ failure in the performance of one's duties **2** [عَكْس تَطْويلٍ] shortening, curtailment; خِدْمة تَقْصيرِ الرَّوابِطِ URL shortening service; تَقْصير المُدّةِ \ المُهْلةِ shortening the time frame/limit; تَقْصير وِلايةِ الرَّئيسِ \ المَجْلِسِ shortening the president's/council's term in office

مُقْتَصَر *adj* short, concise, succinct

مُقَصِّر **A** *adj* negligent, remiss; كانَ مُقَصِّراً في شَيْءٍ to be negligent/remiss in sth

B *n* culprit; *(criminally) negligent person*; مُحاسَبة المُقَصِّرينَ bringing the culprits to justice

مَقْصور *adj* limited; كانَ مَقْصوراً على to be limited to; مَقْصور على الزَّبائِنِ for customers only; أَلِف مَقْصورة alif maqsura *(word-final alif, written as a dotless ya)*

مَقْصورة *n* |مَقْصورات, مَقاصيرُ| **1** [غُرْفة] room; compartment; مَقْصورة مَلابِسَ dressing room **2** [في سَيّارةٍ] interior; مَقْصورة (داخِليّة) interior *(of a car)*; المَقْصورة الخَلْفيّة \ الأَمامِيّة back/front seat; مَقْصورة الرُّكّابِ \ التَحْميلِ passenger/cargo compartment **3** [في سَفينةٍ \ طائرةٍ] cabin; مَقْصورة القِيادةِ cockpit **4** [في المَسْرَحِ] box, loge **5** [في قِطارٍ] compartment; مَقْصورة الدَرَجةِ الأولى first-class compartment **6** (Sport) dugout **7** [في الجامِعِ] *chamber of the imam in a mosque; separate room for women in a mosque*

‹ **قَصَّ** *v* |u| **1** [قَطَعَ] |قَصّ| to cut (off), to trim, to snip, to mow; قَصَّ شَعْرَهُ to cut one's hair; قَصَّ أَظافِرَهُ to clip one's nails; قَصَّ وَرَقاً to cut paper; قَصَّ الشَريطَ to cut the ribbon *(officially opening a place or event)* **2** [رَوى] |قَصَص| to narrate, to tell; قَصَّ على شَخْصٍ قِصّةً to tell sb a story; قَصَّ الأَكاذيبَ to tell lies

قَصَّصَ *v* to cut (off), to trim

قاصَّ *v* to settle *(one's debts)*

اقْتَصَّ *v* |من| to take revenge (on), to repay; اقْتَصَّ من شَخْصٍ to take revenge on sb

قَصَص *n* tale, narration; سورة القَصَص The Stories *(Sura 28)*

قاصّ *n* |قُصّاص| narrator, storyteller; أَديب قاصّ literary storyteller

قَصّ *n* **1** [ما تَمَّ قَصُّهُ] cutting, clipping; إجْهاد القَصِّ shear stress **2** [سَرْد] storytelling, narration; فَنّ القَصِّ the art of storytelling **3** (Anat) عَظْم القَصِّ breastbone, sternum

قَصّاص *n* |قُصّاص| novelist, storyteller

قِصاص *n* redress, retribution, revenge; طالَبَ بالقِصاصِ من القاتِلِ to demand that the killer be brought to justice; نالَ قِصاصَهُ العادِلَ he received his just deserts

قُصاصة *n* clipping, scrap paper, flyer; قُصاصة صَحيفةٍ \ جَريدةٍ newspaper/press cutting; قُصاصات وَرَقٍ (small) pieces of paper; وَزَّعَ قُصاصاتٍ to hand out flyers; قُصاصات فَنّيّة (Comput) clip art

قَصّة *n* cut; قَصّة شَعْرٍ a haircut

قُصّة *n* fringe (BrE), bangs (AmE), lock of hair

قِصّة *n* |قِصَص| story, tale, narrative; قِصّة عن ... a story about ...; قِصّة قَصيرة short story, novella; قِصّة حُبٍّ \ غَرامٍ love story; قِصّة خُرافيّة fairy tale; قِصّة رَمْزيّة allegory; قِصّة حَقيقيّة \ واقِعيّة a true story; قِصّة رُعْبٍ thriller; مَغْزى القِصّةِ the moral of the story; مَجْموعة قِصَصٍ a collection of stories; حَكى \ رَوى قِصّةً to tell a story; سَرَدَ قِصّةً to narrate a story; اخْتَرَعَ قِصّةً to make up a story

قَصَصيّ, قِصَصيّ **A** *adj* narrative; epic; شِعْر قَصَصيّ epic poem; مَجْموعة قَصَصيّة a collection of stories, collected works; فَنّ قَصَصيّ the art of storytelling

B *n* novelist, storyteller

أُقْصوصة *n* |أَقاصيصُ| novella, short story

مُقاصّة *n* settlement of accounts, compensation; غُرْفة المُقاصّةِ clearing house

مِقَصّ *n* |مِقَصّات, مَقاصُّ| scissors; قَصَّ بِمِقَصٍّ to cut with scissors; أَبو مِقَصٍّ earwig; مِقَصّ الرَّقيبِ censorship; المِقَصّ الأَيْسَر \ الأَيْمَن the left/right goalpost

مَقْصوص *adj* |مَقاصيصُ| cut, clipped; صورة مَقْصوصة a cropped image/picture

مَقْصوصة *n* skimmer *(utensil)*

مِقَصّيّ *adj* scissor *(before n)*; سَدَّدَ الكُرةَ بِطَريقةٍ مِقَصّيّةٍ to scissor-kick the ball *(football/soccer)*

‹ **قَصْعة** *n* |قَصَعات, قِصَع, قِصاع| *large (wooden) bowl*

‹ **قَصَفَ** *v* |i| **1** [ضَرَبَ بالقَنابِلِ] |قَصْف| to bomb, to bombard, to shell; to shoot at; قَصَفَ العَدُوَّ to shoot at the enemy;

قَصَفَ مَدينةً to bomb a city; قَصَفَ بالمِدْفَعيّة \ الصَواريخ to bombard with artillery/missiles **2** [كَسَرَ] to break **3** [الرَعْدُ] to rumble

تَقَصَّفَ *v* to break

تَقاصَفَ *v* to criticize/attack each other

انْقَصَفَ *v* to be broken

قَصْف *n* **1** [قَذْف] bombardment, bombing, shelling; قَصْف مِدْفَعيّ artillery bombardment; قَصْف عَنيف heavy shelling; قَصْف صاروخيّ bombardment with missiles; نَفَّذَ قَصْفاً to carry out a bombardment; عَمَليّة قَصْفٍ bombardment; تَشْديد القَصْفِ escalation of the bombing **2** [صَوْت] thunder, thundering; rumble

قَصِف *adj* breakable; delicate; fragile; frail

قاصِف *adj* **1** [ضارِب] bombing, firing; طائِرة قاصِفة bomber (plane) **2** [شَديد] intense, strong; رِياح قاصِفة strong wind

قَصْفة *n* |قَصَفات| **1** [قَذْف] bombardment, bombarding **2** [صَوْت] thunder clap

مَقْصِف *n* |مَقاصِفُ| cafeteria, canteen (BrE); مَقْصِف المَدْرَسةِ school canteen

قَصْقَصَ *v* |i; قَصْقَصة| to cut up

قَصَلَ *v* |i; قَصْل| to chop off, to cut off

قَصَل *n* chaff

مِقْصَلة *n* |مِقْصَلات, مَقاصِلُ| guillotine; scaffold

قَصَمَ *v* |i; قَصْم| to break, to shatter; قَصَمَ شَيْئاً to break sth; القَشّة التي قَصَمَتْ ظَهْرَ البَعير the straw that broke the camel's back

تَقَصَّمَ *v* to break

انْقَصَمَ *v* to break

قَصِم *adj* tender; fragile, frail

قاصِم *adj* |قَواصِمُ| fatal, disastrous, devastating; الضَرْبة القاصِمة للمُنَظَّمة the fatal blow for the organization

قاصِمة *n* قاصِمة الظَهْرِ fatal blow

قَصا, قَصِيَ *v* |a-u; قَصْو, قُصو, قَصا, قَصًى| to be distant, to be far (away)

قَصِيَ *v* |a; قَصاً| to be distant, to be far (away)

أَقْصى *v* to send away, to remove; أَقْصى شَخْصاً من عَمَلِهِ to dismiss sb; أَقْصى شَخْصاً بِنَفْسِهِ to personally remove sb

تَقَصّى *v* to examine, to investigate, to study; تَقَصّى الحَقائِقَ to examine the facts

اسْتَقْصى *v* to examine, to investigate, to study; اسْتَقْصى الحَقائِقَ \ المَعْلوماتِ to investigate the facts

قَصيّ *adj* distant, remote; مَكان قَصيّ a faraway place

قاصٍ *adj* distant, remote; يَعْرِفُ القاصي والداني أنّ ... everybody knows that ...

اسْتِقْصاء *n* investigation, research; الاسْتِقْصاء عن شَيْءٍ the investigation of/into sth; مَفْرَزة الاسْتِقْصاءِ (Leb) detention centre

اسْتِقْصائيّ *adj* exploratory

إقْصاء *n* removal, elimination, exclusion; إقْصاء الأَقَلّيّاتِ the exclusion of minorities; إقْصاء فَريقٍ the elimination of a team (*from a tournament*); إقْصاء شَخْصٍ عن مَنْصِبِهِ the removal of sb from their office/position; إقْصاء شَخْصٍ عن السُلْطةِ the exclusion of sb from power; سِياسة الإقْصاءِ والتَهْميشِ a policy of exclusion and marginalization

إقْصائيّ *adj* dismissing, removing; دَوْرة إقْصائيّة play-off

أَقْصى **A** *adj* |f قُصْوى| extreme, utmost; أَقْصى اليَسارِ \ اليَمينِ the extreme left/right; أَقْصى مِقْدارٍ \ كَمّيّةٍ maximum dose/amount; أَقْصى الحُدودِ the outer borders/limits; مُحاوَلة قُصْوى all-out effort; المَسْجِد الأَقْصى al-Aqsa Mosque (*in Jerusalem*); الشَمال الأَقْصى the extreme north; الشَرْق الأَقْصى the Far East; إلّا في الضَرورةِ القُصْوى unless absolutely necessary; إلى أَقْصى حَدٍّ to the extreme, utmost; في أَقْصى الأَحْوالِ in extreme situations; من أَدْناهُ إلى أَقْصاهُ from top to bottom, completely; تَوَخّى أَقْصى دَرَجاتِ الحَذَرِ to exercise extreme caution; بِأَقْصى جُهْدٍ with a supreme effort

B *n* |أَقاصٍ| ultimate, maximum; أَقاصي الأَرْضِ the farthest corners of the earth

تَقَصٍّ *n* |تَقَصّيات| investigation, enquiry; لَجْنة تَقَصّي الحَقائِقِ committee/board of enquiry, fact-finding committee

قَضَبَ *v* |i; قَضْب| to cut off, to trim

قَضَمَ، قَضِمَ *v* |a-i; قَضْم| to gnaw, to nibble, to bite; قَضَمَ شَيْئاً to nibble (on) sth; قَضَمَ أَظافِرَهُ to bite one's nails; قَضَمَ أَرْضَ شَخْصٍ to nibble away at sb's land

قاضِم *n* |قَواضِمُ| (Zool) rodent

قَضَى *v* |i; قَضاء| ① [أَزالَ |على|] to kill, to eradicate, to eliminate; to avert; قَضى على to kill sb; قَضى على شَخْصٍ to eradicate evil/corruption; قَضى على آمالِ الشَرِّ \ الفَسادِ to dash sb's hope; قَضى على عائِلَةٍ بِأَكْمَلِها شَخْصٍ to wipe out an entire family; قَضى على الخَطَرِ to avert danger; قُضِيَ عَلَيْهِ he's done for ② [وَقْتاً] to spend; to kill, to while away; قَضى لَيْلَتَهُ (في فُنْدُقٍ) to spend the night (in a hotel); قَضى إجازَتَهُ \ عُطْلَتَهُ في مَكانٍ to spend one's vacation somewhere; قَضى الوَقْتَ في مُشاهَدَةِ التَلْفَزة to kill time by watching television; قَضى عُقوبَةَ خَمْسِ سَنَواتٍ في السِجْنِ to spend five years in prison ③ [أَتَمَّ] to finish, to fulfil; to do, to carry out, to perform; قَضى واجِبَهُ to do/perform one's duty; قُضِيَ الأَمْرُ the case has been decided; it is done, the matter has been settled; قَضى الصَلاةَ to finish praying; قَضى حاجَتَهُ to relieve oneself; قَضى وَطَرَهُ \ حاجَتَهُ (من شَخْصٍ) to have one's sexual needs met (by sb) ④ [ماتَ] to die; قَضى نَحْبَهُ to fulfil a vow; to die; قَضى غَرَقاً to drown ⑤ [فَرَضَ] to determine, to ordain; to prescribe, to stipulate; قَضى بِشَيْءٍ to prescribe sth; يَقْضي الاقْتِراحُ بِأَنْ ... the proposal stipulates that ...; يَقْضي القانونُ بِأَنْ ... the law regulates that ...; قَضى اللهُ أَنْ لا نَعْبُدَ إلّا إيّاهُ God has ordained that we should worship only Him ⑥ [حَكَمَ قَضائِيًّا] to judge, to sentence; قَضى بين شَخْصَيْنِ to mediate between two people; قُضِيَ بالسِجْنِ \ بالإعْدامِ to be sentenced to prison/death; قَضى لِشَخْصٍ to judge in favour of sb; قُضِيَ الأَمْرُ the case has been decided

قَضّى *v* to carry out, to execute

قاضى *v* (Law) to prosecute, to try; قاضى شَخْصاً to prosecute sb; قاضى مُجْرِماً to try a criminal

تَقَضّى *v* to be finished, to be completed; to pass, to go by

تَقاضى *v* ① [قَبَضَ] to receive; تَقاضى مالاً \ راتِباً to earn money/a salary ② (Law) to litigate

اقْتَضَبَ *v* ① [قَطَعَ] to shorten, to trim ② [الكَلامُ] to improvise, to extemporize ③ [أَوْجَزَ] to summarize, to abridge, to cut short

قَضيب *n* |قُضْبان| ① [حَديديّ] bar, rod, rail; قَضيب حَديديّ iron bar; قُضْبان قَفَصٍ the bars of a cage; قُضْبان الوَقودِ النَوَويِّ nuclear fuel rods; وراء \ خَلْفَ القُضْبانِ behind bars, in jail; قَبَعَ وراء القُضْبانِ to languish behind bars; خَرَجَ القِطارُ عن القُضْبانِ the train (was) derailed ② (Anat) penis; قَضيب الذَكَرِ the male member; انْتَصَبَ قَضيبُهُ to get an erection ③ [الشَجَرة] stick, twig

اقْتِضاب *n* abridgement, summary; brevity, succinctness; بِاقْتِضابٍ in short/brief; أَجابَ بِاقْتِضابٍ (شَديد) to answer (very) briefly

مُقْتَضَب *adj* short, brief, concise, terse; بَيان مُقْتَضَب summary report; تَصْريح مُقْتَضَب concise answer; جَواب مُقْتَضَب short statement; مُلَخَّص مُقْتَضَب brief summary

قَضَّ I *v* |u; قَضّ| ① [هَدَمَ] to demolish, to tear down ② [قَلَعَ] to tear out, to pull out; قَضَّ وَتَداً to pull out a plug ③ [ثَقَبَ] to drill (through)

قَضَّ II *v* |a; قَضَض| to be rough, to be crude

أَقَضَّ *v* أَقَضَّ مَضْجَعَ شَخْصٍ to keep sb awake, to give sb sleepless nights

انْقَضَّ *v* ① [هَجَمَ] to jump, to charge, to throw oneself; انْقَضَّ على شَخْصٍ to jump/attack sb; to fly at/go for someone's throat; انْقَضَّ على العَدوِّ to charge at the enemy; انْقَضَّ على فَريسَتِهِ to pounce/swoop down on its prey ② [سَقَطَ] to fall, to collapse

قَضّ *n coll* gravel, pebbles; بِقَضِّهِ وَقَضيضِهِ as a whole, in its entirety; الناس بِقَضِّهِمْ وَقَضيضِهِمْ every single one of the people

قَضيض *n* gravel; pebble; بِقَضِّهِ وَقَضيضِهِ as a whole, in its entirety; الناس بِقَضِّهِمْ وَقَضيضِهِمْ every single one of the people

انْقِضاض *n* |انْقِضاضات| ① [هُجوم] assault, attack, onslaught; انْقِضاض على الصَدارة surging into the lead ② (Aviat) nosedive

قُضاعة *n* otter

رَفَعَ حِفْظَ قَضيّةً criminal case/trial; جنائيّة to adjourn a case; رَبَحَ \ قَضيّةً على شَخْصٍ to take legal action against sb; كَسَبَ قَضيّةً to win a case; طَرَحَ قَضيّةً على المَحْكَمةِ to bring a case before the court; طَرَحَ قَضيّةً على الرَأْيِ العامِّ to try a case in the court of public opinion; قَضيّة خاسِرة a lost case

اقْتِضاء *n* necessity, emergency; عند الاقْتِضاءِ if necessary, if need be; in case of emergency

انْقِضاء *n* expiration; قبل انْقِضاءِ الشَهْرِ before the end of the month; انْقِضاء المُهْلَةِ passing/expiration of the deadline

تقاضٍ *n* 1 [تَسَلُّم] receiving 2 (Law) litigation

مُتَقاضٍ *n* litigant, plaintiff/defendant (*in a civil suit*); defendant (*in a criminal case*); حُقوق المُتَقاضينَ the rights of the parties; the defendant's rights

مُقاضاة *n* prosecution, trial; bringing suit, suing; مُقاضاة مُجْرِمٍ prosecution of a criminal; اعْتَزَمَ \ نَوى مُقاضاةَ شَخْصٍ to intend to sue sb

مُقْتَضى A *adj* required, necessary, imperative

B *n* |مُقْتَضَيات| requirement, necessity; clause; مُقْتَضَيات necessities; مُقْتَضَيات العَصْرِ modernity; *modern values/ways of life*; مُقْتَضى شَرَفٍ debt of honour; حَسَبَ ,بِمُقْتَضى شَيْءٍ بِمُقْتَضى مُقْتَضَياتِ شَيْءٍ in accordance/conformity with sth; المادّةِ الرابِعةِ من هذا القانونِ in accordance with article four of this law; ل \ حتّى يَبْنِيَ على الشَيْءِ مُقْتَضاهُ to take the necessary steps

مُنْقَضٍ *adj* last, previous; expired; الأُسْبوع \ العام المُنْقَضي last week/year; مُنْقَضِية العِدّةِ *a divorced/widowed woman whose required waiting period has passed*

‹ **قَطْ** *adv* see فَقَطْ

‹ **قطا** *n coll* |قَطَيات ,قَطَوات| sandgrouse

‹ **قَطَبَ** *v* |i; قُطوب ,قَطْب| to frown; قَطَبَ حاجِبَيْه to furrow one's brows

قَطَّبَ *v* to frown; قَطَّبَ الجَبينَ to wrinkle one's forehead; قَطَّبَ الحاجِبَيْنِ to furrow one's brows

اسْتَقْطَبَ *v* 1 [جَذَبَ] to pull, to attract; اسْتَقْطَبَ الاهْتِمامَ \ النَظَرَ to draw attention 2 (Phys) to polarize

انْقَضى *v* to end, to conclude, to pass; انْقَضَت المُدّةُ \ الفَتْرةُ the period ended; قد انْقَضى الأَمْرُ the matter has come to an end; ... إذا انْقَضَت المُهْلَةُ if the deadline passes ...; قد انْقَضى عُمْرُهُ his days are numbered

اقْتَضى *v* to demand, to require, to need; اقْتَضَت الظُروفُ أنْ يَرْحَلَ circumstances forced him to leave; اقْتَضى عِنايةً كَبيرةً to require much care/attention; إذا اقْتَضَت ,إنْ اقْتَضى الحالُ الحاجةُ ,إذا اقْتَضى الأَمْرُ ذلك if/when needed

اسْتَقْضى *v* to demand, to claim

قاضٍ A *adj* deadly, lethal, fatal; سُمٌّ قاضٍ deadly poison

B *n* |قُضاة| judge, magistrate; قاضٍ مُحايِد a neutral judge; قاضي التَحْقيقِ examining judge/magistrate; قاضي القُضاةِ Lord Chief Justice (BrE), Supreme Court Judge (AmE); سَعادة القاضي the Honourable Judge; Your Honour; هَيْئة القُضاةِ court (of justice/law); قاضي الأَحْداثِ magistrate of a juvenile court

قَضاء *n* 1 [إزالة] elimination; removal; القَضاء على المُعارَضةِ السِياسيّةِ elimination of political opposition 2 [تأْدِية] performance, fulfilment, accomplishment, taking care of; قَضاء الواجِبِ performance of one's duty; قَضاء الحاجةِ relieving oneself; قَضاء وَطَرٍ \ حاجةٍ fulfilment of one's sexual needs 3 [الوَقْتِ] spending; قَضاء العُطْلةِ في مِصْرَ spending the holiday in Egypt 4 (Law) judiciary, magistracy, administration of justice; دار القَضاءِ court/courthouse; رَجُل القَضاءِ magistrate; رِجال القَضاءِ the magistracy; أُحيلَ إلى القَضاءِ to be handed over to the judiciary 5 (Admin) |أَقْضِية| district 6 [قَدَر] fate; divine will; قَضاءً وَقَدْراً by will of God; لا رادَّ لِقَضاءِ اللهِ it is God's will

قَضائيّ *adj* judicial, legal, court (*before n*); إجْراءات قَضائيّة (court) procedures; خطأ \ مُلاحَقة قَضائيّ(ة) a miscarriage of justice; تَحْقيق \ حُكْم قَضائيّ a judicial inquiry/decision; بِأَمْرٍ قَضائيٍّ by court order

قَضيّة *n* |قَضايا| 1 [مَسْأَلة] case, matter, issue, question; قَضيّة مُؤْلِمة painful matter; قَضيّة بِشَأْنِ شَيْءٍ \ شَخْصٍ issue regarding sth/sb; تَوَكَّلَ \ اعْتَنى بِقَضايا شَخْصٍ to look after/manage sb's affairs 2 [دَعْوى] case; lawsuit; trial; قَضيّة

قَطْر *n* 1 (Med) drip, infusion 2 [تَقَطُّر] dripping 3 [سَحْب] pulling, towing

قَطَر *n* |dipt f| Qatar; دَوْلة قَطَرَ the state of Qatar; أَمير قَطَرَ the prince/emir of Qatar

قُطْر *n* |أَقْطار| 1 (Geog) country; region; district; جَوْلة في الأَقْطارِ العَرَبِيّةِ a tour of the Arab countries; القُطْر السوريّ Syria 2 [بُنْدُقِيّة] calibre 3 (Math) diameter, centre line; نِصْف القُطْرِ radius

قاطِرة *n* locomotive; قاطِرة بُخاريّة \ بُخارٍ steam locomotive; قاطِرة ديزِل diesel locomotive; قاطِرة كَهْرَبائيّة electric locomotive

قاطور *n* |قَواطيرُ| listed alphabetically

قِطار *n* |قُطُرات ,قُطُر ,قِطارات| train; قِطار سَريع express train; قِطار فائِق السُّرعةِ high-speed train; قِطار كَهْرَبائيّ electric train; قِطار رُكّابٍ passenger train; قِطار شَحْنٍ \ بِضاعةٍ freight/goods train; قِطار أَنْفاقٍ underground (railway) (BrE), subway (AmE); سائِق قِطارٍ train driver; اصْطِدام \ حادِثة قِطارٍ train collision/accident; مَحَطّة قِطارٍ train/railway station; حَرَكة قِطاراتٍ train/rail traffic; راكِب القِطارِ train/rail passenger; تَغْيير القِطارِ transfer; (سافَرَ) بالقِطارِ (to travel) by train; فاتَهُ القِطارُ to miss the train; (fig) to miss the boat; اسْتَقَلَّ \ رَكِبَ القِطارَ to take the train; أَدْرَكَ القِطارَ to catch the train

قَطّارة *n* pipette, dropper

قُطارة *n* distillate

قَطْرة *n* |قَطَرات| drop, drip; قَطْرةً قَطْرةً drop by drop; قَطْرة ماءٍ \ نَفْطٍ \ حَليبٍ drop of water/oil/milk; قَطْرة نَدًى dewdrop; قَطْرة الأُذُنِ \ العَيْنِ ear drops/eye drops; حتّى آخِرِ قَطْرةِ دَمٍ ... to the last drop of blood

قَطَرِيّ *adj, n* Qatari

قُطْرِيّ *adj* 1 (Math) diametral; diagonal 2 [إِقْليميّ] regional

قُطْرِيّة *n* regionalism

اسْتِقْطار *n* (Chem) distillation

تَقَطُّر *n* trickle, drip, dribble

تَقْطير *n* 1 distillation, percolation, refinement; distillate; تَقْطير النَفْطِ oil/petroleum refinement; الرَيّ بالتَقْطيرِ

قُطْب *n* |أَقْطاب| 1 (Elec) pole; قُطْب كَهْرَبائيّ electrode; قُطْب سالِب \ موجَب cathode/anode; negative/positive pole 2 (Pol) top figure, leader; centre of power; أَقْطاب السِيّاسةِ political leaders; عالَم مُتَعَدِّد الأَقْطابِ a multipolar world 3 (Geog) pole; القُطْب الجَنوبيّ \ الشَماليّ the South/North Pole; في القُطْبِ الشَماليِّ at the North Pole; رِحْلة اسْتِكْشافيّة إلى القُطْبِ الجَنوبيِّ expedition to the South Pole; دائِرة القُطْبِ الجَنوبيِّ the Antarctic Circle; مِنْطَقة القُطْبِ الجَنوبيِّ the Antarctic (region); نَجْم القُطْبِ الشَماليِّ the Pole Star, Polaris 4 [مِحْوَر] axis, hub; قُطْب تِكْنولوجيّ technology hub

قاطِبة *n* all, whole; العَرَب قاطِبةً all the Arabs; العالَم قاطِبةً the whole world

قُطْبِيّ *adj* polar; مِنْطَقة قُطْبيّة polar region; القارّة القُطْبيّة الجَنوبيّة Antarctica; التَعَدُّديّة القُطْبيّة multipolarity; دائِرة قُطْبيّة polar circle; مِحْوَر قُطْبيّ polar axis; المُحيط القُطْبيّ الشَماليّ the Arctic Ocean; هَواء قُطْبيّ (بارِد) polar cold front

اسْتِقْطاب *n* |اسْتِقْطابات| 1 polarization; اسْتِقْطاب طائِفيّ sectarian polarization 2 [جَذْب] attraction; نَجَحَ في اسْتِقْطابِ الاسْتِثْماراتِ to be successful in attracting investment

اسْتِقْطابِيّ *adj* polarizing

تَقْطيب *n* wrinkle; تَقْطيب الحاجِبَيْنِ frowning, with knitted brows

مُقَطِّب *adj* مُقَطِّب الحاجِبَيْنِ frowning, with knitted brows

قَطَرَ *v* |u| قَطْر| 1 [سالَ قَطْرةً قَطْرةً] to drip, to trickle; قُلوبُنا تَقْطُرُ دَماً our hearts are breaking, we are greatly saddened 2 [سَحَبَ] to drag, to tow; قَطَرَ سَيّارةً to tow a car

قَطَّرَ *v* 1 [أَسالَ قَطْرةً قَطْرةً] to drip, to trickle; قَطَّرَ قَطْرةً في العَيْنِ to put drops in one's eye 2 [اسْتَخْرَجَ] to distil; قَطَّرَ الكُحولَ to distil alcohol

تَقَطَّرَ *v* to drip, to trickle, to dribble; تَقَطَّرَ العَرَقُ من جَبينِهِ the sweat ran down his forehead; يَتَقَطَّرُ الماءُ من الحَنَفيّةِ water is dripping from the tap (BrE) faucet (AmE)

تَقاطَرَ *v* to trickle (down); to stream; تَقاطَرَ الناسُ إلى الساحةِ people streamed into the square

اسْتَقْطَرَ *v* to distill; to drip

drip irrigation; تَقْطير جافّ (Chem) dry distillation 2▸ (Med) drip, infusion

مَقْطورة *n* 1▸ [للشَحْنِ] trailer, semi-trailer; wagon; railway/railroad carriage 2▸ [للتَخْييمِ] mobile home, caravan (BrE), trailer (AmE)

قُطْرُب *n* |قَطارِبُ| glow-worm, firefly

قَطْرَس *n* albatross

قَطْرَنَ *v* |i; قَطْرَنة| to tar; يُقَطْرِنونَ السَقْفَ they are tarring the roof

قَطْران *n* tar; قَطْران في السَجائِرِ cigarette tar; طَلَى بالقَطْرانِ to tar; زِفْت وَقَطْران awful

فَطَسَ *v* |i; فُطوس, فَطْس| to die

قَطاس *n* yak

قَطَّ *v* |u; قَطّ| to sharpen

قَطُّ *adv* ever; (*with negative:*) never; هل رَأَيْتَ مِثْلَ هذا قَطُّ؟ did you ever see anything like this?; لا ... قَطُّ never (before); لم أَرَ مِثْلَ ذلك قَطُّ I've never seen anything like it; لم أَفْعَلْ هذا قَطُّ I've never done that (before); لم يَتَغَيَّرْ تَصَرُّفُهُ قَطُّ his behaviour never changed

قِطّ *n* |قِطَط, قِطاط, قِطَطَة| [سِنَّوْر] cat; قِطّ أَرْقَط tabby-and-white cat (BrE), calico cat (AmE); قِطّ مُتَوَحِّش wildcat; ذَكَر القِطِّ tomcat; قِطّ مَخْصِيّ neutered cat; غابَ القِطُّ الْعَبْ يا فَأْرُ when the cat's away the mice will play; هُما كالقِطِّ والفَأْرِ ≈ there is bad blood between them

قَطَعَ *v* |a; قَطْع| 1▸ [قَصَّ] to cut (through), to bisect, to cut in two; to slice, to chop; قَطَعَ أَشْجاراً to chop wood; to cut down/fell trees; قَطَعَ يَدَ شَخْصٍ to cut off sb's hand; قَطَعَ قِطْعَةً من اللَحْمِ to cut off a piece of meat; قَطَعَ غُصْناً من شَجَرةٍ to cut a branch off a tree; قَطَعَ مَعْدِناً to cut metal; قَطَعَ الطَريقَ على شَخْصٍ to block/bar sb's way 2▸ [أَوْقَفَ] to break off, to halt, to interrupt; قَطَعَ الأَمَلَ to give up/abandon hope; قَطَعَ الطَريقَ to block the road; قَطَعَ خَطَّ الهاتِفِ to cut the phone line; قَطَعَ الكَهْرَباءَ \ التَيّارَ عن شَخْصٍ to cut sb's electricity off; قَطَعَ الحَديثَ to stop talking; قَطَعَ حَديثَ شَخْصٍ to interrupt sb; قَطَعَ جَدْوَلَ أَعْمالِ شَخْصٍ to interrupt sb's work; قَطَعَ زِيارَتَهُ to cut one's trip short; قَطَعَ الإِرْسالَ الإِذاعِيَّ to interrupt a broadcast; قَطَعَ عَلاقَتَهُ مع شَخْصٍ to break up with sb; قَطَعَ العَلاقاتِ \ الصِلاتِ to break off relations; قَطَعَ عَلاقَتَهُ بِوالِدَيْهِ to break off relations with one's parents; قَطَعَ الخُيوطَ to sever ties; قَطَعَ دِراساتِهِ to discontinue one's studies; قَطَعَ المُساعَداتِ to stop helping 3▸ [عَبَرَ] to traverse, to cross; to follow; قَطَعَ شارِعاً \ طَريقاً to cross a street/road; قَطَعَ مَسافةً to cover a distance; to close a gap; قَطَعَ شَوْطاً كَبيراً (fig) to make significant progress; قَطَعَ مَسافاتٍ طَويلةً to cross great distances; (fig) to (have) come a long way; قَطَعَ مَساراً to follow a route; قَطَعَ مَرْحَلةً to go through a phase; قَطَعَ وَعْداً to make a promise; قَطَعَ على نَفْسِهِ عَهْداً to take a vow

(Idiom) قَطَعَ تَذْكِرةً to buy a ticket

قَطَّعَ *v* to cut up, to slice/chop up; to bisect; قَطَّعَ شَيْئاً to cut sth up (into pieces); قَطَّعَ الوَرَقَ قِطَعاً صَغيرةً to tear/cut up paper into little pieces; قَطَّعَ شَيْئاً إِرْباً إِرْباً to cut sth to/into pieces

قاطَعَ *v* 1▸ [رَفَضَ التَعامُلَ] to boycott; قاطَعَ الانْتِخاباتِ to boycott the elections; قاطَعَ المُنْتَجاتِ الفَرَنْسيّةَ to boycott French products 2▸ [الكَلامَ] to interrupt; قاطَعَ حَديثَ شَخْصٍ to interrupt sb

أَقْطَعَ *v* 1▸ [مَنَحَ] to grant, to give 2▸ [سَكَتَ] to be/become silent 3▸ [انْقَطَعَ] to sever; أَقْطَعَ عن أَهْلِهِ to break off relations with one's family

تَقَطَّعَ *v* to be/become severed; to be interrupted; تَقَطَّعَ قَلْبُهُ أَلَماً his heart was torn apart by grief; تَقَطَّعَ الطَريقُ the road was blocked; تَقَطَّعَتْ بِهِ السُبُلُ to be stranded

تَقاطَعَ *v* 1▸ [افْتَرَقَ] to separate, to part; to break off relations 2▸ [تَصالَبَ] to cross; to intersect; تَقاطَعَتْ مَصالِحُ الجانِبَيْنِ the two sides had mutual interests

انْقَطَعَ *v* 1▸ [انْفَصَمَ] to be interrupted, to be cut off, to be disconnected; to stop, to be finished; انْقَطَعَ الحَبْلُ the rope broke; انْقَطَعَتْ أَخْبارُهُ there was no more news from him, he was not heard from again; انْقَطَعَ(ت) الصورةُ \ الصَوْتُ the picture/audio cut out; انْقَطَعَ التَيّارُ there was a power failure/cut; انْقَطَعَتْ عَلاقَتُهُما they broke up 2▸ [تَوَقَّفَ|عن] to cease, to stop; انْقَطَعَ عن العَمَلِ to stop working; انْقَطَعَ عن

الدِراسةِ to quit school ❸ [تَفَرَّغَ] |إلى| to dedicate to; to dive/plunge into; انْقَطَعَ إلى شَيْءٍ to dedicate oneself to sth

اقْتَطَعَ *v* ❶ [مالاً] to withhold, to deduct, to debit; to claim, to eat up; اقْتَطَعَ مَبْلَغاً to deduct an amount; اقْتَطَعَ نِسْبةً مِئَويّةً من الراتِبِ to deduct a certain percentage of the wages; يَقْتَطِعُ تَعْليمُ أَبْنائِنا جُزْءاً كَبيراً من دَخْلِنا educating our children eats up a large portion of our income ❷ [فَصَلَ] to chop off, to cut off, to rip off; to cut out, to cut away; اقْتَطَعَ الحَجَرَ من جَبَلٍ to quarry stone from a mountain ❸ [احْتَلَّ] to occupy; اقْتَطَعَ الأَرْضَ to occupy land ❹ [اشْتَرى] اقْتَطَعَ تَذْكِرةً to reserve/buy a ticket

اسْتَقْطَعَ *v* to withhold, to deduct

قَطْع *n* ❶ [قَصّ] cutting; قَطْع شَجَرٍ cutting down trees; هَمْزة القَطْعِ hamzat al-qat' (*phonemic glottal stop*); قَطْع الجُسورِ burning bridges; قَطْع مُكافِئ parabola; قَطْع زائِد hyperbola ❷ [انْقِطاع] interruption, stopping, breaking off; دون قَطْعِ النَظَرِ عن شَيْءٍ without looking away from sth; قَطْع العَلاقاتِ severing ties; قَطْع الحِساباتِ (Levant) settling the bills; لا يُمْكِنُ قَطْعُهُ inseparable ❸ [أَكيد] certainty; قَطْعاً, بالقَطْعِ certainly, absolutely, positively, by all means; لا ... قَطْعاً certainly not, by no means; مُسْتَحيل قَطْعاً absolutely impossible ❹ [عُبور] crossing

قاطِع **A** *adj* ❶ [مُقْنِع] convincing; decisive, conclusive; explicit; إجابة قاطِعة conclusive answer; حُجّة قاطِعة convincing argument; تَحْريم قاطِع explicit ban; دَليل قاطِع conclusive proof; رَفَض بِشَكْلٍ قاطِعٍ to refuse outright; نفى شَيْئاً نَفْياً قاطِعاً to deny sth categorically ❷ [حادّ] sharp, cutting **B** *n* |قُطّاع, قَطَعة| cutter; قاطِع الطَريق *person who sets up a roadblock to rob or attack travellers*; robber; (Hist) highwayman, footpad; قاطِع التَذاكِرِ ticket seller

قاطِعة *n* |قَواطِعُ| ❶ [سِنّ] front tooth, incisor ❷ [سِكّين] cutter ❸ (Elec) circuit breaker

قِطاع *n* |قِطاعات| ❶ [مِنْطَقة] district; قِطاع غَزّةَ the Gaza Strip ❷ [شُعْبة] sector; القِطاع العامّ \ الخاصّ the public/private sector; القِطاع الزِراعيّ the agricultural sector, agriculture; القِطاع الصِناعيّ the industrial sector; القِطاع المَصْرِفيّ \ البَنْكيّ banking; قِطاع الخِدْماتِ the service sector; قِطاع اقْتِصاديّ a sector of industry

قِطْعة *n* |قِطَع| ❶ [جُزْء] piece, portion, fragment, segment; قِطْعة فَنّيّة work of art; قِطْعة موسيقيّة piece of music, composition; قِطْعة دائِريّة segment of a circle; قِطْعة أَثاثٍ piece of furniture; قِطْعة سِلاحٍ weapon; قِطَع غِيارٍ replacement parts; قِطْعة غِيارٍ للسَيّارةِ car part; قِطَع نَقْديّة coins, cash; سوق القِطَعِ the currency market; قِطْعة من الخَشَبِ woodblock, log; قِطْعة أَرْضٍ piece of land; plot, parcel; قِطْعة قُماشٍ \ جِلْدٍ \ لَحْمٍ piece of cloth/leather/meat; باعَ بالقِطْعةِ to sell by the piece/individually ❷ [شِطْرَنْج إلخ] piece; قِطْعة شِطْرَنْجٍ piece, chessman

قَطْعيّ *adj* convincing, definite, definitive, absolute; مَوْقِف قَطْعيّ definitive stand(point); أَثْبَتَ شَيْئاً بالدَليلِ القَطْعيِّ to prove sth with convincing evidence

قَطْعيّة *n* certainty, decisiveness

قَطيع *n* |قُطْعان| group, herd, flock; قَطيع من البَقَرِ herd of cows; رَعى قَطيعاً من الخِرافِ to herd a flock of sheep

قَطيعة *n* ❶ [انْفِصام] breach, rift, split; القَطيعة بين الحَبيبَيْنِ rift/split between two lovers; قَطيعة مَعْرِفيّة cognitive dissonance ❷ [الرَحِم] *animosity within the family*

اقْتِطاع *n* deduction, reduction, withholding; اقْتِطاع ضَريبيّ withholding of tax

إقْطاع *n* feudal system, feudalism; allotment; ذو الإقْطاعِ liege

إقْطاعيّ **A** *adj* feudal; النِظام الإقْطاعيّ the feudal system, feudalism **B** *n* large landowner

إقْطاعيّة *n* feudalism; الإقْطاعيّة في القُرونِ الوُسْطى medieval feudalism

انْقِطاع *n* discontinuity, interruption; cessation; بِدونِ \ بلا انْقِطاعٍ uninterrupted, continuous; انْقِطاع التَيّارِ \ الكَهْرَباءِ power outage/cut; انْقِطاع الحَيْضِ amenorrhea; menopause; بعد انْقِطاعٍ طَويلٍ after a long hiatus/break; كانَت السَماءُ تُمْطِرُ بِدونِ انْقِطاعٍ to rain continuously

تَقاطُع *n* intersection, crossing, junction; تَقاطُع الطُرُقِ intersection, junction; في نُقْطةِ تَقاطُعِ الخُطوطِ at the intersection of two lines; نُقْطة تَقاطُعٍ (بين مُجْتَمَعَيْنِ) a meeting point (between two societies)

تَقْطيع *n* |تَقاطيعُ| ⟨1⟩ [قَطْع] division, cutting; ripping, shredding; تَقْطيع الأَوْصالِ dismemberment; تَقْطيع الوَقْتِ stalling, playing for time ⟨2⟩ [مَغْص] colic; stomach/abdominal cramp ⟨3⟩ [الوَجْهِ] تَقاطيع الوَجْهِ facial features ⟨4⟩ [في الشِعْرِ] chanting

مُتَقاطِع *adj* intersecting, crosswise; كَلِمات مُتَقاطِعة crossword (puzzle); خُطوط مُتَقاطِعة intersecting lines

مُتَقَطِّع *adj* disrupted, discontinuous, intermittent; غَيْر مُتَقَطِّع continuous; خَطّ مُتَقَطِّع dashed/dotted line; اشْتِباكات مُتَقَطِّعة intermittent clashes; بِصَوْتٍ مُتَقَطِّعٍ with a faltering voice; على فَتَراتٍ \ في أَوْقاتٍ مُتَقَطِّعةٍ at intervals, intermittently, now and again; بِصورةٍ مُتَقَطِّعةٍ, بِشَكْلٍ مُتَقَطِّعٍ by fits and starts

مُسْتَقْطَع *adj* وَقْت مُسْتَقْطَع time-out

مُقاطَعة *n* ⟨1⟩ [امْتِناع] boycott; مُقاطَعة الانْتِخاباتِ boycott of the elections; عَمَلِيّة مُقاطَعةٍ boycott; أَعْلَنَ مُقاطَعةً to announce a boycott; هَدَّدَ بِمُقاطَعةٍ to threaten a boycott; رَفَعَ المُقاطَعةَ عن بَلَدٍ to end the boycott of a country ⟨2⟩ [في الحَديثِ] interruption; مُقاطَعة قَصيرة brief interruption ⟨3⟩ (Admin) region, province, county

مَقْطَع *n* |مَقاطِعُ| ⟨1⟩ [تَقاطُع] section; sectional plane; profile; مَقْطَع عَرْضيّ cross section; مَقْطَع طولِيّ lengthwise section ⟨2⟩ [جُزْء] excerpt, section, passage, selection; قَرَأَ مَقاطِعَ من كِتابِهِ he read selections from his book; قَرَأَ مَقْطَعاً من قَصيدةٍ to read an excerpt from a poem ⟨3⟩ (Literat) verse, stanza; مَقْطَع غِنائيّ \ شِعْريّ stanza of a song/poem; المَقْطَع الأَوَّل \ الثاني من أُغْنِيةٍ the first/second verse of a song ⟨4⟩ (Ling) syllable; مَقْطَع صَوْتيّ \ لَفْظيّ syllable ⟨5⟩ [فيلْم] clip; مَقْطَع فيديو video clip

مُقْطَع *n* vassal, feudal tenant

مُقَطَّع Ⓐ *adj* sliced, disjointed, isolated; مُقَطَّع الأَوْصالِ fragmented, dismembered; مُقَطَّع بالطولِ إلى شَرائِحَ sliced lengthwise into strips/slivers

Ⓑ *n* المُقَطَّعات (الحُروف) *isolated letters of unknown significance heading 29 Quranic suras*

مِقْطَع *n* |مَقاطِعُ| opener, instrument

مَقْطَعِيّ *adj* cross-sectional, cross section (*before n*); دِراسة مَقْطَعِيّة cross-sectional study; صورة مَقْطَعِيّة scan; تَصْوير مَقْطَعِيّ مُحَوْسَب CT scan

مَقْطوع *adj* cut off, disconnected, singular, isolated; severed; كانَ مَقْطوعَ الصِلةِ مع شَيْءٍ to be cut off from sth; رَأْس مَقْطوع a severed head; مَبْلَغ مَقْطوع lump sum; رَسْم مَقْطوع flat fee

مَقْطوعة *n* |مَقْطوعات, مَقاطيعُ| (Mus) piece, selection; مَقْطوعة موسيقيّة piece of music, composition

مُنْقَطِع *adj* closed off, cut off; مُنْقَطِع النَفَسِ breathless; مُنْقَطِع عن العالَمِ cut off from the outside world; غَيْر مُنْقَطِعٍ fixed; مُنْقَطِع النَظيرِ unprecedented, unrivalled; نَجاح \ إِقْبال مُنْقَطِع النَظيرِ unprecedented success/turnout

› **قَطَفَ** *v* |i; قَطْف, قُطوف| to pick, to harvest; قَطَفَ زُهوراً \ عِنَباً to pick flowers/grapes; قَطَفَ ثِمارَ شَيْءٍ to reap the benefits of sth

اقْتَطَفَ *v* ⟨1⟩ [قَطَفَ] to harvest, to pick ⟨2⟩ [اخْتارَ] to pick, to select; اقْتَطَفَ فِقْرةً to select a paragraph

قَطْف *n* pick, picking; harvest; قَطْف الزَيْتونِ the olive harvest; قَطْف ثِمارِ شَيْءٍ reaping the benefits of sth

قاطِف *n* fruit picker

قَطائِف *n pl* |dipt| *pancakes stuffed with nuts and topped with syrup*

قِطاف *n* harvest, picking; قِطاف العِنَبِ \ الزَيْتونِ the grape/olive harvest

قَطيفة *n* ⟨1⟩ [قُماش] velvet; velour; قَطيفة مُضَلَّعة \ قُطْنٍ corduroy, needlecord (BrE) ⟨2⟩ (Bot) |قَطائِفُ| African marigold

اقْتِطاف *n* picking, gathering

مُقْتَطَف Ⓐ *adj* chosen, selected

Ⓑ *n* |مُقْتَطَفات| selection, piece; مَجْموعة من مُقْتَطَفاتِ الكِتابةِ anthology; مُقْتَطَفات من كِتابٍ selections from a book

مِقْطَف *n* |مَقاطِفُ| basket

› **قَطْقاط** *n* plover

› **قِطْقِط** *n* ⟨1⟩ [شَفْشاف] sleet ⟨2⟩ [قِطّ] (infml) kitty

› **قَطَلَ** *v* |i-u; قَطْل| to cut (off)

‹ **قُطاميّ، قُطام** *n* sparrowhawk

‹ **قِطْمار** *n* **1** [فاكِهةٍ] pericarp **2** [شَيْء تافِه] insignificant matter

‹ **قَطَنَ** *v* |u; قُطون| to live (in), to reside (at); قَطَنَ في شِقّةٍ to live in an apartment; قَرْية يَقْطُنُها أَلْفُ نَسَمةٍ a village inhabited by a thousand people

قَطَن *n* |أَقْطان| lumbar region; loin

قُطْن *n* |أَقْطان| cotton; قُطْن طِبّيّ cotton balls; قُطْن الأُذُنِ cotton bud (BrE) swab (AmE); من القُطْنِ (made of) cotton; قُطْن خام raw cotton; لَبِسَ لِباساً مَصْنوعاً من القُطْنِ to put on/wear cotton clothes; نَدَفَ القُطْنَ to card/comb cotton

قاطِن **A** *adj* |قُطّان| residing, living **B** *n* |قُطّان| resident

قَطانيّ *n* legume

قُطْنيّ *adj* cotton; شَراشِف قُطْنِيّة cotton sheets

يَقْطين *n coll* winter squash, gourd

‹ **قَطَوِيّات** *n pl* Pteroclididae, sandgrouse *(family)*

‹ **ق.ع.** *abbr* قِطاع عامّ *(public sector)*

‹ **قَعَدَ** *v* |u; قُعود| **1** [جَلَسَ] to sit (down), to be seated; قَعَدَ على كُرْسيٍّ to sit down on a chair; قَعَدَ يَتَفَرَّجُ على شَيْءٍ to sit watching sth **2** [امْتَنَعَ] |عن| to refrain from; قَعَدَ عن التَعْليم he didn't get an education; قَعَدَ عن الانْطِلاقِ to refrain from leaving **3** [مَنَعَ] |بِـ| to keep off/out **4** [أَقْعَدَ] to seat; قَعَدَتْ بِهِ رُكْبَتاهُ his knees were shaky **5** [بَدَأَ] to start, to begin; قَعَدَ يَكْتُبُ رِسالةً to start to write a letter

أَقْعَدَ *v* **1** [مَنَعَ] to keep out, to hold back; أَقْعَدَ شَخْصاً عن شَيْءٍ to keep sb from sth; أَقْعَدَني المَرَضُ عن العَمَلِ the illness kept me from work **2** [أَجْلَسَ] to seat, to settle; to make stay; أَقامَ الدُنْيا وَلَمْ يُقْعِدْها to make a scene; أَقْعَدَني المَرَضُ في الفِراشِ the illness confined me to bed; أُقْعِدَ to become paralyzed

تَقَعَّدَ *v* |عن| to not wish for; تَقَعَّدَ عن شَيْءٍ to not wish for sth

تَقاعَدَ *v* **1** [أُحيلَ إلى المَعاشِ] |عن| to retire (from); تَقاعَدَ عن التَدْريسِ to retire from teaching; لن يَتَقاعَدَ أَبَداً he will never retire **2** [لم يَهْتَمّ] |عن| to keep aloof (from)

اقْتَعَدَ *v* to sit (down) on; اقْتَعَدَ صَخْرةً to sit (down) on a rock

قاعِد *adj* sitting, seated; قاعِد عن العَمَلِ unemployed, idle

قاعِدة *n* |قَواعِدُ| **1** [أَساس] base, foundation, foot; قاعِدة بُرْجٍ base of a tower; قاعِدة اتِّفاقٍ foundation of an agreement; قاعِدة تِمْثالٍ pedestal, base; قاعِدة من الإسْمَنْت concrete foundation; قاعِدة مُثَلَّثٍ base of a triangle; قاعِدة ثُلاثيّة tripod; وَسَّعَ القاعِدةَ to broaden the base **2** [تَنْظيم إرْهابيّ] (تَنْظيم) القاعِدة al-Qaeda *(militant Islamic fundamentalist group)* **3** [مَبْدَأ] regulation; basic principle; قَواعِد ثابِتة fixed/set rules; قاعِدة أَساسيّة \ جَوْهَرِيّة basic/fundamental rule; قاعِدة قانونيّة rule of law; قاعِدة مُرورٍ traffic regulation; قَواعِد اللُغةِ grammar (rules); كِتاب القَواعِدِ grammar book; كِتاب قَواعِد اللُغةِ العَرَبيّةِ Arabic grammar book; وَفْقاً للقَواعِدِ according to the rules; راعى القَواعِدَ to observe the rules; اتَّبَعَ \ طَبَّقَ \ وَضَعَ قاعِدةً to follow/implement/prescribe a rule; الْتَزَمَ بالقَواعِدِ to abide by/follow the rules; وَضَعَ \ راجَعَ \ عَدَّلَ القَواعِدَ to draw up/review/modify the regulations **4** [مِقْياس] criterion, standard; القَواعِد المَرْعِيّة statutory criteria/standards; راعى قَواعِدَ قِياسيّةً to apply/follow criteria; صاغَ \ أَعَدَّ \ وَضَعَ قَواعِدَ قِياسيّةً to formulate/draw up/lay down criteria **5** (Comput) قاعِدة بَياناتٍ database **6** (Chem) base **7** (Mil) base; قاعِدة عَسْكَرِيّة military/army base; قاعِدة بَحْرِيّة marine base; قاعِدة جَوِّيّة air base; قاعِدة إطْلاقِ صَواريخَ missile/rocket base **8** (Sport) base

قاعِديّ *adj* **1** [أَساسيّ] basic, fundamental; الهَيْكَل القاعِديّ infrastructure; زَوْج قاعِديّ (Bio) base pair **2** [نِظاميّ] systematic, regular

قَعْدة *n* **1** [مَصْدَر] sitting; seat; ذو القَعْدةِ Dhu al-Qaada *(the eleventh month of the year in the Islamic calendar)* **2** [مَقْعَد] seat

قِعْدة *n* sitting, seated position

قَعود *n* |قُعُد، أَقْعِدة| *young camel*

قَعيد *n* |قُعَداءُ| companion

تَقاعُد *n* retirement, pension; تَقاعُد مُبَكِّر early retirement; سِنّ التَقاعُدِ pensionable/retirement age; مَعاش \ راتِب التَقاعُدِ retirement pension; صُنْدوق (مَعاشاتِ) التَقاعُدِ pension/retirement fund; قانون التَقاعُدِ المُبَكِّرِ early retirement scheme; الإحالة إلى \ على التَقاعُدِ retirement; كانَ لَهُ حَقٌّ في مَعاشِ التَقاعُدِ to have a right to a pension; أَحالَ شَخْصاً

أُحيلَ على التَقاعُدِ to be pensioned off; أحالَ إلى \ على التَقاعُدِ to pension sb off

تَقاعُديّ *adj* retirement (*before n*), pensionary; مَعاش تَقاعُديّ retirement pension

مُتَقاعِد **A** *adj* retired; كانَ مُتَقاعِداً to be retired

B *n* retiree, pensioner

مَقْعَد *n* |مَقاعِدُ| **1** ◀ [كُرْسيّ] chair, seat, place; مَقْعَد خَلْفيّ back seat; مَقْعَد مَدْرَسيّ school desk; عادَ إلى مَقاعِدِ الدِراسة to go back to school; نَهَضَ \ قامَ من مَقْعَدِهِ to get out of one's chair; حَجَزَ مَقْعَداً to reserve a seat/place **2** ◀ (Pol) seat; حازَ \ حَصَلَ على ٥ مَقاعِدَ to win/get five seats; تَوْزيع مَقاعِدِ البَرْلَمانِ distribution/division of seats; مَقْعَد في البَرْلَمانِ parliamentary seat; شَغَلَ \ مَلأَ مَقْعَداً to fill a seat **3** ◀ [دَرّاجة إلخ] saddle, seat **4** ◀ [جُزْء من الكُرْسيِّ] seat; مَقْعَد من الخَيْزُرانِ \ المُخْمَلِ cane/velvet seat

مُقْعَد **A** *adj* disabled

B *n* disabled person

مُقْعِد *adj* crippling

مَقْعَدة *n* buttocks, bottom; الجيئة بالمَقْعَدةِ (Med) breech presentation

‹ **قَعُرَ** *v* |u; قَعارة| to be or become deep/hollow, to be hollowed out

قَعَّرَ *v* to excavate, to hollow out, to deepen

تَقَعَّرَ *v* to be deep; to be hollowed out; تَقَعَّرَ في كَلامِهِ to talk posh/fancy

قَعْر *n* |قُعور| **1** ◀ [قاع] bottom, depths; في قَعْرِ البَحْرِ at the bottom/in the depths of the sea; قَعْر فِنْجانٍ the bottom of a cup; في قَعْرِ دارِنا in our own backyard **2** ◀ [جَوْف] cavity

مُقَعَّر *adj* **1** ◀ [عَكْس مُحَدَّب] concave; deep, hollow; مِرْآة مُقَعَّرة concave mirror; (fig) distorted image, funhouse mirror (AmE); عَدَسة مُقَعَّرة concave lens **2** ◀ [طَريقة لَفْظ] stuck-up, posh

‹ **قَعِسَ** *v* |a; قَعَس| to be sway-backed, to be saddlebacked

تَقاعَسَ *v* |عن| to be negligent (in), to be remiss (in); to omit; تَقاعَسَ عن شَيْءٍ to be negligent in sth; تَقاعَسَ عن أداءِ واجِبِهِ to be remiss in the performance of one's duty

قَعَس *n* lordosis, swayback, saddleback

أَقْعَس *adj* |dipt; قُعْس| sway-backed

تَقاعُس *n* negligence, neglect, laxity; تَقاعُسُهُ عن (القِيامِ بـ) واجِبِهِ his neglect of duty

‹ **قَعْقَعَ** *v* |i; قَعْقَعة| to clatter, to rattle, to click, to crack

قُعْقُع *n coll* magpie

قَعْقَعة *n* rattle, clatter

‹ **أَقْعى** *v* to sit (*said of a dog*); أَقْعى الكَلْبُ the dog sat

‹ **قِفْ** *v* see وقف

‹ **قَفَرَ** *v* |u; قَفْر| to follow

قَفُرَ *v* |u; قَفارة| to be desolate; to be uninhabitable

أَقْفَرَ *v* to be deserted; to be desolate, to be uninhabitable; أَقْفَرَت الشَوارِعُ the streets emptied out/became deserted

قَفْر **A** *adj* inhospitable, uninhabitable

B *n* |قِفار| wasteland, wilderness, desert

قَفير *n* |قَفائِرُ, قُفْران| beehive

إِقْفار *n* desolation

مُقْفِر *adj* empty, deserted; inhospitable, uninhabitable; شارع مُقْفِر a deserted street

‹ **قَفَزَ** *v* |i; قَفْزان, قَفْز| to jump (up), to leap (up); قَفَزَ عالياً \ طَويلاً to jump high/far; قَفَزَ مُؤَشِّرُ \ سِعْرُ الأَسْهُمِ the stock index/price jumped; قَفَزَ على \ فوق شَيْءٍ to leap on/over sth; قَفَزَ من كُرْسيِّهِ to leap from one's chair; قَفَزَ فوق الحَقائِقِ to ignore the facts

قَفْز *n* (Sport) jumping, jump; قَفْز طَويل long jump; قَفْز عالٍ high jump; قَفْز بالزانة pole vault; قَفْز عن \ على الحَواجِز hurdles; قَفْز ثُلاثيّ triple jump; قَفْز على الحَبْلِ rope skipping

قُفّاز *n* |قَفافيزُ, قُفّازات| glove, mitten; قُفّازانِ a pair of gloves; قُفّاز من الجِلْدِ \ الصوفِ \ الحَريرِ a leather/woolen/silk glove; عُلْبة القُفّازاتِ the glove compartment; رَمى \ الْتَقى قُفّازَ التَحَدّي to throw down/take up the gauntlet (*to issue/accept a challenge:*)

قَفْزة *n* |قَفَزات| jump, leap; قَفْزة بِطولِ ثَمانيةِ أَمْتارٍ an eight-metre jump; حَقَّقَ قَفْزةً نَوْعيّةً to make/take a quantum leap; حَقَّقَ قَفَزاتٍ كَبيرةً to improve by leaps and bounds

قَفيز *n* |أَقْفِزة| *dry measurement (approx 500 litres)*

مِقْفَز *n* |مَقافِزُ| diving board

‹ **قَفَصَ** *v* |i; قَفْص| to cage

قَفَص *n* |أَقْفاص| **1** [للحَيَواناتِ] cage, crate; وَضَعَ \ حَشَرَ في قَفَصٍ to put in a cage; في قَفَصِ الاتِّهامِ in the dock **2** [للشَحْنِ] crate **3** (Anat) قَفَص صَدْرِيّ rib cage, chest

قَفْصة *n* |dipt| Gafsa (*city in Tunisia*)

‹ **قُفْطان** *n* |قَفاطِين| caftan

‹ **قَفَّ** *v* |i; قُفوف| **1** [تَقَبَّضَ] to shrimp **2** [الشَّعْرُ] to stand on end; قَفَّ شَعْرُهُ his hair stood on end

قُفَّة *n* |قُفَف| basket

‹ **القَفْقاس** *n* Caucasus

‹ **قَفْقَفَ** *v* |i; قَفْقَفة| to shiver with cold

‹ **قَفَلَ** *v* |i| **1** [أَغْلَقَ] |قَفْل| to close, to lock (up) **2** [رَجَعَ] |قُفول| to return home

قَفَّلَ *v* to close (up), to lock (up)

أَقْفَلَ *v* **1** to close (up), to lock (up); أَقْفَلَ البابَ (بالمِفْتاحِ) to lock the door (with a key); أُقْفِلَتِ المَحالُّ the stores were closed/shuttered **2** to finish, to conclude; أَقْفَلَ النقاشَ \ المَلَفَّ to close the debate/file; أَقْفَلَ المُؤَشِّرُ \ البورْصةُ على ارْتِفاعٍ the index/market closed higher

قُفْل *n* |أَقْفال، قُفول| lock, padlock; ثُقْبُ القُفْلِ keyhole; كَسَرَ قُفْلاً to force/break a lock; أَغْلَقَ أَقْفالَ البابِ to close the door tightly

قافِلة *n* |قَوافِلُ| **1** [جِمالٍ] caravan; الكِلابُ تَنْبَحُ والقافِلةُ تَسِيرُ dogs bark but the caravan moves on (*progress cannot be stopped by the criticism of the small-minded*) **2** (Mil) convoy; قافلة عَسْكَرِيّة military convoy; قافِلة سُفُنٍ convoy of ships; قافلة إغاثةٍ convoy of emergency supplies

قَفّال *n* locksmith

إِقْفال *n* closing, close, closure; locking; عند إقْفالِ البورْصةِ at the market's close; سِعْر إقْفالِ الأَسْهُمِ the stock's closing price; إقْفال مِلَفٍّ the closure of a case; إقْفال بابٍ closing of a door; (fig) loss of an opportunity; تَمَّ إقْفالُ بابِ المُناقَشةِ the time for discussion has passed

مُقْفَل *adj* closed, locked, shut; قاعة مُقْفَلة ,مَلْعَب مُقْفَل dome stadium

مَقْفول **A** *adj* closed, shut; locked **B** *n* (NA) *the base of a kiskas/couscoussière*

‹ **قُفْلوط** *n* shallots, green onions

‹ **قَفا** *v* |u; قَفْو| to follow, to track, to trace; قَفا أَثَرَ شَخْصٍ to track sb

قَفَّى *v* to rhyme, to make rhyme

تَقَفَّى *v* to follow, to track, trace

اقْتَفَى *v* to follow, to track, to trace; اقْتَفَى أَثَراً to follow a track; اقْتَفَى أَثَرَ شَخْصٍ to hunt/track sb down; to follow in sb's footsteps, to follow sb's example; اقْتَفَى أَثَرَ المُجْرِمينَ to track down the criminals; اقْتَفَى أَثَرَ المالِ to follow the money; تَقْتَفي الدُوَلُ الخليجيّةُ أَثَرَ الكُوَيْتِ the Gulf countries are following Kuwait's example

قافِية *n* |قَوافٍ| rhyme

قَفاً *n* |mf; أَقْفاء ,أَقْفِية| neck; back of the head; buttocks

اقْتِفاء *n* following, tracking; اقْتِفاء أَثَرٍ tracking, tracing; نَجَحوا في اقْتِفاءِ أَثَرِ المُجْرِمينَ they successfully tracked down the criminals

مُقَفًّى *adj* rhyming; شِعْر مُقَفًّى rhyming verse/poetry

‹ **قَلاووز ,قَلاووظ** *n* screw; propeller

‹ **قَلَبَ** *v* |i; قَلْب| **1** [أَدارَ] to turn (around/over), overturn, to upset; قَلَبَ كَأْساً to turn a glass over; قَلَبَ صَفْحةً to turn a page; قَلَبَ المَوازينَ to upset the balance; قَلَبَ الطاوِلةَ على شَخْصٍ to turn the tables on sb; قَلَبَ شَيْئاً رَأْساً على عَقِبٍ to turn sth upside down, to twist sth around completely; (fig) to inspect sth thoroughly **2** [الحُكومةَ] to overthrow; قَلَبَ الجَيْشُ الحُكومةَ the army has overthrown the government **3** [أَوْقَعَ] to knock (over/down); قَلَبَ القِدْرَ على الأَرْضِ to knock the kettle to the floor

قَوْلَبَ *v* |i; قَوْلَبة| to cast

قَلَّبَ *v* **1** [دَوَّرَ] to tilt, to turn (around/over) **2** [فَتَّشَ] to inspect, to investigate; قَلَّبَ صُنْدوقاً to search a box; قَلَّبَ القَضِيّةَ to look at sth from every angle **3** (Med) to examine; قَلَّبَ مَريضاً to examine a patient

تَقَلَّبَ *v* **1** [انْقَلَبَ] to be turned (around/over); to turn/roll (around/over); تَقَلَّبَ على السَرِيرِ to turn/roll over in bed;

تَقَلَّبَ كُلَّ اللَّيْلِ to toss and turn all night; تَقَلَّبَ في النِعْمةِ to be rolling in money 2▸ [تَغَيَّرَ] to fluctuate, to vary; تَتَقَلَّبُ الأَسْعارُ the prices vary; تَقَلَّبَ نُزولاً \ صُعوداً to tumble/jump; تَقَلَّبَ في وَظائِفَ مُتَعَدِّدةٍ he's bounced around several jobs

انْقَلَبَ *v* 1▸ [تَقَلَّبَ] to turn (around/over); to be turned (around/over); to capsize; to be overthrown; انْقَلَبَ رَأْساً على عَقِب to flip head over heels; (fig) to be radically changed; انْقَلَبَ على شَخْصٍ to turn against sb; انْقَلَبَ السِحْرُ على الساحِرِ ≈ to create a monster; انْقَلَبَت السَفينةُ the ship capsized; انْقَلَبَ على ظَهْرِهِ في الماءِ to flip over on one's back in the water; انْقَلَبَ الحُكْمُ the government was overthrown 2▸ [تَغَيَّرَ] to change, to take a turn; انْقَلَبَ إلى شَيْءٍ to change into sth; انْقَلَبَ إلى النَقيضِ to become the opposite; انْقَلَبَ إلى كابوسٍ \ جَحيم to become a nightmare/a living hell

قَلْب *n* |قُلوب| 1▸ [مَصْدَر] reversal, inversion 2▸ (Anat) heart; جِراحة القَلْبِ cardiac/heart surgery; صِمام قَلْبٍ heart valve; ضَرْبة \ نَبْضة \ دَقّة القَلْبِ heartbeat; مَرَض قَلْبٍ (عُضال) an (incurable) heart condition; عانى من مَرَضِ قَلْبٍ to have a heart condition; مريض قَلْبٍ a cardiac/heart patient; (fig) a lovesick person; عِلْم أَمْراضِ القَلْبِ cardiology; أَخِصّائيّ أَمْراضِ القَلْبِ cardiologist; قِسْم أَمْراضِ القَلْبِ the cardiology department; رَسْم \ تَخْطيط القَلْبِ cardiogram, electrocardiogram, ECG; أَجْرى رَسْمَ القَلْبِ to do an ECG; تَدْليك القَلْبِ heart massage; عِنْدَهُ قَلْبٌ ضَعيفٌ he has a weak heart; يَخْفِقُ قَلْبُهُ his heart is pounding 3▸ [مَشاعِر] heart; قَلْب مَكْسور a broken heart; قَلْبٌ من ذَهَبٍ a heart of gold; قَلْبُهُ أَبْيَضُ \ أَسْوَدُ he has a good/bad character; قَلْباً وَقالَباً with heart and soul, through and through; فَنّان قَلْباً وَقالَباً a born artist; بِقَلْبٍ دامٍ with a heavy heart; من القَلْبِ from the heart; من كُلِّ قَلْبي with all my heart, wholeheartedly; من صَميمِ \ أَعْماقِ قَلْبي from the bottom of my heart; قَلْبُهُ كَبيرٌ \ نَقيٌّ he's got a big/pure heart; طيبة قَلْبٍ kind-heartedness; عِنْدَهُ قَلْبٌ من الحَجَرِ he has a heart of stone; نَغِلَ قَلْبُهُ على شَخْصٍ to hold/bear a grudge against sb; سَلَبَ \ سَرَقَ قَلْبَ شَخْصٍ to steal sb's heart; كانَ ما في قَلْبِهِ على لِسانِهِ to wear one's heart on one's sleeve; يَتَمَزَّقُ القَلْبُ على مَشْهَدِهِ it's heartbreaking to see; اسْتَمَعَ إلى نِداءِ قَلْبِهِ to listen to one's heart; فَتَحَ قَلْبَهُ لِشَخْصٍ to open one's heart to sb; to confide in sb; أُسْتُهيمَ قَلْبُهُ to be infatuated; قَسا \ أَقْسى قَلْبُهُ to become cruel; كَسَرَ قَلْبَ شَخْصٍ to break sb's heart; انْكَسَرَ قَلْبي my heart is broken; عَقَدَ قَلْبَهُ على شَيْءٍ to lose one's heart to sth; البَعيدُ عن العَيْنِ بَعيدٌ عن القَلْبِ out of sight, out of mind; قَوّى قَلْبَ شَخْصٍ to hearten someone; مَنْظَر تَتَصَدَّعُ لَهُ القُلوبُ a heartbreaking scene; مَنْظَر يُدْمي \ يُفْرِحُ القَلْبَ sth heartbreaking/heart-warming 4▸ [وَسَط] centre, middle, heart; قَلْب المَوْضوعِ \ المُشْكِلةِ the (very) heart of the matter/problem; قَلْب الهُجوم the centre forward; وَقَعَ في قَلْبِ مِنْطَقةِ الخَطَرِ to land in the middle of the danger zone

قُلَّب *adj* inconstant, capricious; إنَّهُ رَجُلٌ حَوَّلٌ قُلَّبٌ his moods are volatile, he is moody

قالَب, **قالِب** *n* |قَوالِبُ| 1▸ [نَموذَج] mould, template, form; stencil; baking/cake pan; قالَب لِشَيْءٍ a mould for sth; قالَب الأَحْذِيةِ last (*shoemaker's tool*); وَضَعَ شَيْئاً في قالَبٍ to cast/mould sth in a mould; فَنّان قَلْباً وَقالَباً a born artist 2▸ [إطار] mould, type, form; في قالَبٍ كوميديٍّ \ روائيٍّ in the form of a comedy/novel; قالَب نَمَطيّ stereotype 3▸ [قِطْعة] piece, bar; قالَب فَحْمٍ briquette; قالَب صابونٍ bar of soap; قالَب حَلْوى a cake; قالَب شوكولاتةٍ chocolate bar; قالَب مُحَرِّكٍ engine block

قَلّاب *n* 1▸ (Transp) dumper (BrE) dump (AmE) truck 2▸ (Aviat) flap

قَلْبيّ *adj* cardiac, heart (*before n*); heartfelt; تَحِيّاتي القَلْبيّة affectionately yours; مَرَض قَلْبيّ heart condition, heart disease; ذَبْحة قَلْبيّة angina; نَوْبة \ سَكْتة قَلْبيّة heart attack, cardiac arrest; أُصيبَ بِنَوْبةٍ قَلْبيّةٍ to have a heart attack

انْقِلاب *n* |انْقِلابات| 1▸ [تَغَيُّر] change, turn, reversal; overturning, capsizing; انْقِلابات اجْتِماعيّة \ سِياسيّة social/political changes; انْقِلاب سَفينةٍ the capsizing of a boat; حادِث انْقِلابِ شاحِنةٍ \ حافِلةٍ accident involving an overturned truck/bus 2▸ [إسْقاط] coup, revolution; انْقِلاب عَسْكَريّ military coup; انْقِلاب فاشِل \ ناجِح unsuccessful/

successful coup; انْقِلاب دَمَوِيّ \ أَبْيَض bloody/bloodless coup; حَرَكة انْقِلابٍ revolutionary movement; مُحاوَلة انْقِلابٍ attempted coup; أَحْبَطَ مُحاوَلةَ انْقِلابٍ to thwart an attempted coup; قامَ بِانْقِلابٍ to launch a coup

انْقِلابيّ *adj* revolutionary, coup (*before n*); مُحاوَلة انْقِلابيّة a coup attempt

تَقَلُّب *n* |تَقَلُّبات| change, fluctuation, variation, volatility; تَقَلُّب مَناخيّ climatic change; تَقَلُّبات سِياسيّة political upheaval; تَقَلُّبات جَوّيّة severe weather; تَقَلُّبات حادّة sharp fluctuations; تَقَلُّب سِعْرِ العُمْلةِ the volatility of the exchange rate

تَقْليب *n* [1] ◀ [قَلْب] reversal, inversion [2] ◀ [فَحْص] inspection, examination

مُتَقَلِّب *adj* changing, varying; changeable, variable; flexible; unstable, volatile, turbulent; هو مُتَقَلِّبُ المزاج his moods are volatile, he is moody; الجَوُّ \ الطَقْسُ مُتَقَلِّبٌ the weather is changeable; فَتْرة زَمَنيّة مُتَقَلِّبة turbulent times

مَقْلَب *n* |مَقالِب| [1] ◀ [وَجْه] side, facet, face; المَقْلَب الشَرْقيّ من الجَبَلِ the eastern face of the mountain; في المَقْلَبِ الآخَرِ ... on the other hand ..., on the other side ... [2] ◀ [مَزْبَلة] dump, landfill; مَقْلَب القُمامةِ dump [3] ◀ [مَكيدة] joke, trick; دَبَّرَ مَقْلَباً لِشَخْصٍ to play a trick on sb

مِقْلَب *n* |مَقالِبُ| hoe

مَقْلوب *adj* upside down, inverted; opposite, reversed; بالمَقْلوبِ backwards; turned around; inside out; هَرَم \ مُثَلَّث مَقْلوب an inverted pyramid/triangle

‹ **قَلَح** *n* tartar; قَلَح الأَسْنانِ tartar

قُلاح *n* tartar; أَزالَ القُلاحَ to remove tartar

‹ **قَلَّدَ** *v* [1] ◀ [حاكى] to imitate, to copy, to mimic, to follow; قَلَّدَ شَخْصاً to imitate sb; قَلَّدَ صَوْتَ العَصافيرِ to mimic birdsong; قَلَّدَ صَوْتَ شَخْصٍ to mimic sb's voice [2] ◀ [نَسَخَ] to copy, to reproduce; قَلَّدَ لَوْحةً فَنّيّةً to reproduce a painting [3] ◀ [مَنْصِباً] to appoint; قَلَّدَ شَخْصاً الوِزارة to appoint sb minister [4] ◀ [عَلَّقَ] to hang on/over/around; to decorate; قَلَّدَ شَخْصاً وِساماً \ سِلْسِلةً to hang a medal/necklace around sb's neck

تَقَلَّدَ *v* [1] ◀ [المَنْصِبَ] to hold, to occupy; تَقَلَّدَ مَنْصِباً to hold a position [2] ◀ [لَبِسَ] to put on; تَقَلَّدَ وِساماً to be decorated (*with a medal*); تَقَلَّدَ سِلْسِلةً to put on a necklace

قِلادة *n* |قَلائِدُ| necklace, chain, collar; قِلادة ذَهَبيّة a gold necklace; ارْتَدى قِلادةً to wear a necklace

تَقْليد *n* |تَقاليدُ| [1] ◀ [عُرْف] convention, tradition, custom; تَقاليد traditions, customs; تَقْليد مُتَّبَع tradition, established practice; تَقْليد عَريق an age-old tradition; حَسَبَ التَقاليدِ traditionally, according to tradition; مُنافٍ للتَقاليدِ contrary to tradition; حافَظَ على التَقاليدِ to preserve tradition; أَخَلَّ بالتَقاليدِ to go against tradition; احْتَرَمَ التَقاليدَ (الاجْتِماعيّةَ) to observe (social) convention [2] ◀ [مُحاكاة] imitation, copy; forgery, counterfeit; تَقْليد جَيِّد \ مُتْقَن good/perfect imitation; تَقْليد ساخِر parody [3] ◀ [تَنْصيب] installation, inauguration; تَقْليد شَخْصٍ مَنْصِباً installation of sb in office

تَقْليديّ A *adj* traditional, conventional; أَسْلِحة تَقْليديّة conventional weapons; غَريمُهُ التَقْليديّ his arch-rival; بِشَكْلٍ تَقْليديٍّ in the traditional way; صِناعات تَقْليديّة old trades/crafts

B *n* traditionalist

تَقْليديّة *n* traditionalism; conformism

مِقْلاد *n* |مَقاليدُ| rein; key; مَقاليد الأُمورِ the reins, control; مَقاليد الحُكْمِ \ السُلْطةِ (the reins of) power, authority; تَسَلَّمَ \ تَوَلّى مَقاليدَ الحُكْمِ to take (the reins of) power; تَسَلَّمَ \ تَوَلّى مَقاليدَ الأُمورِ to take the reins, to take control

مُقَلِّد *n* imitator, mimic

‹ **قُلُزّ، قِلِزّ** *n* bronze

‹ **قُلْزُم** *n* بَحْر القُلْزُم the Red Sea

‹ **قَلْس** *n* |قُلوس| [1] ◀ (*Med*) regurgitation, reflux; القَلْس المَعِديّ المَريئيّ gastroesophageal reflux, acid reflux [2] ◀ (*Naut*) cable

‹ **قَلَصَ** *v* |i; قُلوص| to shrink, to diminish, to contract

قَلَّصَ *v* [1] ◀ [نَقَّصَ] to reduce, to decrease, to lower; قَلَّصَ الفارِقَ (بَيْنَهُما) to reduce the differences (between them), to close the distance (between them); قَلَّصَ شَيْئاً بِمِقْدارِ النِصْفِ to decrease sth by half; قَلَّصَ العَجْزَ في ميزانيّةِ الدَوْلةِ to reduce the budget deficit; قَلَّصَ النَفَقاتِ to lower the costs [2] ◀ [شَنَّجَ] to squeeze/press together; to contract; قَلَّصَ أَصابِعَ قَدَمَيْهِ to curl one's toes

تَقَلَّصَ *v* ① [انْكَمَشَ] to shrink, to shrivel (up); to contract; يَتَقَلَّصُ القَلْبُ \ تَتَقَلَّصُ العَضَلةُ the heart/muscle is contracting; تَقَلَّصَتْ مِساحاتُ الغاباتِ forested areas are in decline ② [قَلَّ] to diminish, to decrease; يَتَقَلَّصُ نُفوذُهُ his influence is diminishing; تَقَلَّصَتْ مِساحاتُ الأَمَلِ \ الحُرِّيّةِ hope/freedom has been curtailed

تَقَلُّص *n* |تَقَلُّصات| ① [حَجْم] shrinking, shrinkage; تَقَلُّص حَجْمِ الوارِداتِ shrinking of imports; تَقَلُّص الفارِقِ (بَيْنَهُما) closing the gap (between them) ② [انْكِماش] contraction, cramp; تَقَلُّص عَضَليّ muscle spasm, muscle cramp; أُصيبَ بِتَقَلُّصٍ عَضَليٍّ في فَخِذِهِ he got a cramp in his thigh ③ [انْخِفاض] recession; decline

تَقْليص *n* reduction, decrease; shrinking; تَقْليص الفارِقِ \ الفَجْوةِ (بَيْنَهُما) closing the gap (between them); ضَرورة تَقْليصِ حَجْمِ الحُكومةِ the need to shrink the size of government; تَقْليص عَدَدِ الطُّلّابِ reduction in the number of students; أَدّى إلى تَقْليصِ العُنْفِ to result in a decrease of violence

مُقَلَّص *adj* restricted, limited; تَشْكيل حُكومةٍ مُقَلَّصةٍ the formation of a small government/cabinet

مُقَلِّص *adj* contracting

‹ **قَلَعَ** *v* |a; قَلْع| to pull out, to extract; to uproot; قَلَعَ أَشْجاراً to uproot trees; قَلَعَ ضِرْساً to pull out/extract a molar

قَلَّعَ *v* to pull out, to extract; to uproot

أَقْلَعَ *v* ① [انْطَلَقَ] to leave, to depart; to take off; to set sail; تُقْلِعُ الطائِرةُ the aircraft is taking off; سَتُقْلِعُ السَفينةُ بعد ساعةٍ the ship will set sail in an hour ② [تَرَكَ] |عن| to quit, to stop, to give up, to abandon; أَقْلَعَ عن التَدْخينِ \ شُرْبِ الكُحولِ to quit smoking/drinking; أَقْلَعَ عن عادةٍ to kick a habit; أَقْلَعَتْ عَنْهُ الحُمّى his fever broke

اقْتَلَعَ *v* ① [نَبات] to uproot, to pull out; اقْتَلَعَ أَشْجاراً من جُذورِها to uproot trees; اقْتَلَعَ شَيْئاً من الأَرْضِ to pull sth out from the soil; اقْتَلَعَ الأَعْشابَ الطُّفَيْلِيّةَ to weed; to pull up weeds ② [مَشاكِل] to eradicate; اقْتَلَعَ الفَسادَ من جُذورِهِ to root out corruption; اقْتَلَعَ مُشْكِلةً to eradicate a problem

قِلْع *n* |قُلوع, إقلاع| sail

قَلاع *n* |قُلُع| sail

قُلاع *n* (Med) aphtha, oral ulcers

قُلاعيّ *adj* حُمّى قُلاعيّة foot-and-mouth disease

قَلْعة *n* |قِلاع, قُلوع| ① [بُرْج] castle, citadel, fort, fortress, stronghold; قَلْعة حَصينة impregnable fortress; قَلْعة مُسَوَّرة walled castle; اسْتَوْلى على قَلْعةٍ to capture a stronghold ② [شِطْرَنْج] rook, castle

اقْتِلاع *n* uprooting; eradication; اقْتِلاع الأَشْجارِ uprooting trees; اقْتِلاع الإِرْهابِ من جُذورِهِ rooting out terrorism, eradication of terrorism

إِقْلاع *n* ① [انْطِلاق] start, departure; take-off; مَوْعِد إِقْلاعِ الطائِرةِ the plane's scheduled take-off ② [تَرْك] cessation, stopping; الإِقْلاع عن التَدْخينِ smoking cessation

تَقْليعة *n* rage, craze; آخِر تَقْليعةٍ the latest rage

مِقْلاع *n* |مَقاليعُ| catapult (BrE), slingshot (AmE)

مَقْلَع *n* |مَقالِعُ| quarry, stone quarry; مَقْلَع للرُخام marble quarry; مَقْلَع للحَجَرِ الرَمْليِّ sandstone quarry

‹ **قَلْف** *n* bark; rind

قُلْفة *n* |قُلَف| (Anat) foreskin, prepuce; قُلْفة الذَكَرِ foreskin; قُلْفة البَظْرِ clitoral hood

‹ **قَلِقَ** *v* |a; قَلَق| |على| to be/become worried (about); to be/become concerned (about); قَلِقَ على شَيْءٍ to worry about sth

أَقْلَقَ *v* ① [أَهَمَّ] to worry, to alarm/concern; أَقْلَقَني هذا الخَبَرُ I was alarmed by this news; أَقْلَقَ راحةَ شَخْصٍ to disturb sb; أَمْر يُقْلِقُ البالَ a disturbing/worrying matter ② [أَزْعَجَ] to be/get annoyed; أَقْلَقَهُ الضَجيجُ to be annoyed by the noise

قَلَق *n* concern, worry; alarm, anxiety; قَلَق شَديد great anxiety; مَصْدَر قَلَقٍ a source of concern; قَلَق على \ من شَيْءٍ \ شَخْصٍ concern for sth/sb; مُثير للقَلَقِ worrisome, alarming; شُعور بالقَلَقِ concern, anxiety; عَبَّرَ عن قَلَقِهِ ,أَبْدى قَلَقَهُ to express one's concern; أَحَسَّ بالقَلَقِ to worry; to be concerned; دَعا للقَلَقِ ,أَثارَ \ بَعَثَ \ سَبَّبَ القَلَقَ to cause concern/alarm; لا داعِيَ للقَلَقِ there's no cause for concern/alarm; بِوَجْهٍ يَبْدو عَلَيْهِ القَلَقُ with a worried face; هذا أَمْرٌ لا يُثيرُ القَلَقَ لَدَيَّ I'm not worried about that

قَلِق *adj* worried, concerned; alarmed; كانَ قَلِقاً to be concerned; قَلِق على \ من شَخْصٍ \ شَيْءٍ to be worried about sb/sth

مِقْلاق *adj* overanxious; شَخْص مِقْلاق worrier

مُقْلِق *adj* disturbing, worrisome, alarming; تَطَوُّر مُقْلِق disturbing development

قُلْقاس *n* taro, elephant's ear (*Colocasia esculenta*)

قَلْقَل *v* |i; قَلْقَلة| to shock, to offend, to agitate; قَلْقَلَ مَشاعِرَ المُشاهِدينَ to shock the viewers

تَقَلْقَل *v* to be agitated, to be shocked; to rock, to begin to move; تَقَلْقَلَ القِطارُ the train began to move; تَقَلْقَلَت الحَرَكَةُ الاقْتِصادِيّةُ the economy has suffered a shock

قَلْقَلة *n* |قَلاقِلُ| unrest, agitation, disturbance, commotion; مُثير القَلاقِل troublemaker, agitator

تَقَلْقُل *n* instability

مُتَقَلْقِل *adj* crumbling; rickety, unstable, insecure

قَلّ *v* |قِلّة, قُلّ, قِلّ| [1] [عَكْس كَثُرَ] to decrease, to diminish, to lessen, to decline; يَقِلُّ الاهْتِمامُ (بِشَيْءٍ) interest (in sth) is waning; لا يَقِلُّ عن أَلْفَيْنِ to not be less than 2,000; ما لا يَقِلُّ عن … at (the) least …; لا يَقِلُّ أَهَمِّيّةً (عن ذلك) … no less important (than that) is … [2] [نَدَرَ] to be rare, to be unusual; قَلَّ أنْ أَراهُ I rarely see him; قَلَّ أنْ يَأتِيَ في الوَقتِ he's seldom on time

قَلَّل *v* to reduce, to minimize, to diminish, to cut back; قَلَّلَ العَدَدَ to reduce the numbers; قَلَّلَ من شَيْءٍ to play down sth; قَلَّلَ من فاعِلِيّةِ شَيْءٍ to reduce the effect of sth; قَلَّلَ من أَهَمّيّةِ \ قيمةِ \ شَأنِ شَيْءٍ to minimize the importance of sth

أَقَلّ *v* [1] [نَقَلَ] to transport, to move, to carry; كانَت الطائِرةُ تُقِلُّ مِئةَ راكِبٍ the plane was carrying one hundred passengers [2] [أَنْقَصَ] to reduce, to minimize

تَقَلَّل *v* to consider little/small

اسْتَقَلّ *v* [1] [رَكِبَ] to ride (in), to take, to use; اسْتَقَلَّ الطائِرةَ to take a plane; مُسَلَّحونَ يَسْتَقِلّونَ سَيّارةً مَدَنيّةً gunmen in a civilian car [2] [صارَ مُسْتَقِلّاً] to be/become independent; to be/become autonomous; اسْتَقَلَّ عن العائِلةِ to become independent of the family [3] [حَمَلَ] to take on; اسْتَقَلَّ بإدارة الشَرِكةِ to take on the management of the company; اسْتَقَلَّ بواجِبٍ to take on a duty [4] [اسْتَخَفَّ] to underestimate; to underrate

قُلّة *n* |قُلَل| jug, pitcher

قِلّة *n* |قِلَل| scarcity, shortage, lack; قِلّة الوُجودِ rarity, rare occurrence; قِلّة الصَبْرِ impatience; قِلّة الأَدَبِ rudeness; قِلّة الحَياءِ impudence, shamelessness; قِلّة قَليلة من … a tiny bit of …, very, very few …

قَلَّما *conj* rarely, seldom, hardly; قَلَّما يَزورُنا he seldom visits us

قَليل [A] *adj* |قِلال, قَلائِلُ, أَقِلّاءُ| little, few; single; عَدَد قَليل a small number; مَعْلومات قَليلة little information; قبل أَيّامٍ قَليلةٍ a few days ago; إنْسان قَليل المَعْرِفةِ a person with little knowledge; قَليلاً a little, somewhat, slightly; just; خِفْتُ قَليلاً I got a bit scared; تَجاوَزَ المِائةَ بِقَليلٍ to slightly exceed one hundred; قَليلاً قَليلاً gradually; وَقْت \ مال قَليل little time/money; بِصَوْتٍ مُنْخَفِضٍ قَليلاً in a slightly lowered voice; الرِجالُ أَمْثالُكَ قَليلونَ there are few men like you; قَليل الأَدَبِ ill-mannered, impolite, rude; قَليل الحَياءِ shameless; قَليل الصَبْرِ impatient

[B] *n* [1] [كَمّيّة صَغيرة] little; bit; قَليل من a little (of), (a little) bit of; قَليل من المِلْحِ a pinch of salt; قَليل من الصَبْرِ a little patience; قَليل من السُكَّرِ \ الحَليبِ a little sugar/milk; قَليلاً ما rarely; بِقَليلٍ little, just [2] [فَتْرة قَصيرة] قبل قَليلٍ just (now); بعد قَليلٍ soon; منذ قَليلٍ recently; lately; عَمّا قَليلٍ shortly; قبل \ بعد ذلك بِقَليلٍ just before/after that

اسْتِقْلال *n* independence; autonomy; اسْتِقْلال القَضاءِ the independence of the judicial system; عيد الاسْتِقْلالِ Independence Day; النِضال من أَجْلِ الاسْتِقْلالِ the struggle for independence; أَعْلَنَ اسْتِقْلالَهُ to declare one's independence; نالَت تونِسُ اسْتِقْلالَها من فَرَنْسا Tunisia won its independence from France

اسْتِقْلالِيّ *adj* regarding independence; حَرَكة اسْتِقْلالِيّة independence movement

اسْتِقْلالِيّة *n* independence; الاسْتِقْلالِيّة عن النُخْبةِ السِياسِيّةِ independence from the political elite

أَقَلّ *adj* |dipt| less, least; smaller, smallest; أَقَلّ بِكَثيرٍ a lot less; أَقَلّ ما يُمْكِنُ as few/little as possible; أَقَلّ واقِعِيّةً less realistic;

مَقْلَمة, مِقْلَمة *n* pencil case

‹ قَلَنْسوة *n* |قَلانِس, قَلانيس| 1 [لِباس الرَّأْسِ] cap, hood, bonnet; 2 [قِطْعة] قَلَنْسُوة يَهودِيّة kippa (*cap worn by observant male Jews*) [الفِطْرِ] (mushroom) cap

‹ قَلا *v* |u; قَلْو| to fry, to deep-fry

قَلى *v* |i; قَلْي| to fry, to deep-fry; قَلى السَمَكَ \ البَطاطِسَ to fry fish/potatoes

قِلْو *n* base, alkali

قِلْويّ, قَلَويّ *adj* basic, alkaline

قِلًى *n* base, alkali

مِقْلاة *n* |مَقالٍ| frying pan, skillet (AmE); قَلى البَيْضَ في المِقْلاةِ to fry eggs in a frying pan; مِقْلاة كَهْرَبائيّة (electric) deep fryer

مِقْلى *n* |مَقالٍ| frying pan, skillet (AmE)

مَقْليّ *adj* fried; بَيْضة مَقْليّة fried egg

‹ قَلْوَظَ *v* to screw on

[1]‹ قُم *n* |f| Qom (*city in Iran*)

[2]‹ ق.م. *abbr* BC (*abbreviation of* قبل الميلادِ)

‹ قَميء *adj* despicable; unattractive

‹ قُمْباز *n* robe (*for men*)

‹ قَمْح *n* |قُموح| wheat, grain; دَقيق القَمْحِ wheat flour; سُنْبُل القَمْحِ an ear of wheat; حَبّة القَمْحِ a grain of wheat; مَحْصول القَمْحِ wheat crop

قَمْحة *n* qamha (*weight measure, approx 0.05 grammes*)

قَمْحيّ *adj* light brown, golden; بَشْرة قَمْحيّة (light) olive skin tone; شَعْر قَمْحيّ light brown hair

[1]‹ قَمَرَ *v* |u; قَمْر| to gamble

قَمِرَ *v* |a; قَمَر| 1 [أَضاءَ بنورِ القَمَرِ] to be moonlit 2 [اِشْتَدَّ بَياضُهُ] to be pale 3 [تَحَيَّرَ بَصَرُهُ] to be blinded (by snow)

قَمَّرَ *v* to toast

قامَرَ *v* to bet, to gamble; قامَرَ بِشَيْءٍ to bet sth, to gamble with sth; قامَرَ بِمَصير \ بِمُسْتَقْبَلِ البَلَدِ to gamble with the fate/future of the country; قامَرَ على حِصانٍ to bet on a horse

أَقْمَرَ *v* to be moonlit; أَقْمَرَت اللَيْلَةُ the moon is shining

تَقامَرَ *v* to bet, to gamble; تَقامَرَ على سِباقِ الخَيْلِ to bet on horse racing

(أو) على الأَقَلِّ at least; نِصْفَ ساعةٍ على الأَقَلِّ at least half an hour; ... لَيسَ أَقَلُّهُ not the least of which is ...; دَخْلي أَقَلُّ من دَخْلِهِ I earn less than he does

أَقَلّيّة *n* minority (group); أَقَلّيّة صَغيرة a small minority; أَقَلّيّة عِرْقيّة \ أَثْنيّة ethnic minority; أَقَلّيّة ثَقافيّة cultural minority; حُكومة أَقَلّيّةٍ minority government; وُجْهة نَظَرِ الأَقَلّيّةِ minority opinion/point of view; شَكَّلَ الأَقَلّيّةَ to be in the minority

تَقْليل *n* reduction, cutting; decrease; تَقْليل الانْبِعاثاتِ emissions reductions; تَقْليل الفَجْوة (مع شَيْءٍ \ بين شَيْئَيْنِ) closing the gap (with sth/between two things); تَقْليل من أَهَمّيّةِ شَيْءٍ minimizing the importance of sth

تَقْليليّة *n* minimalism

مُسْتَقِلّ *adj* independent, autonomous; دَوْلة مُسْتَقِلّة independent state; إِقْليم مُسْتَقِلّ بِذاتِهِ autonomous region/district

‹ قَلَمَ *v* |u; قَلْم| to cut, to trim, to clip

قَلَّمَ *v* to cut, to trim, to clip, to prune; قَلَّمَ أَظافِرَهُ to cut one's nails; قَلَّمَ أَظافِرَ شَخْصٍ to clip sb's wings, to limit sb's power

قَلَم *n* |أَقْلام| 1 [أَداة الكِتابة] pen; قَلَم حِبْرٍ fountain pen; قَلَم حِبْرٍ جافٍّ ballpoint pen; قَلَم رَصاصٍ pencil; سورة القَلَمِ The Pen (*Sura 68*); ... بِقَلَمِ written by...; بِجَرّة قَلَمٍ with a stroke of the pen; بَرى قَلَمَ رَصاصٍ to sharpen a pencil; كَتَبَ بِقَلَمٍ to write with a pen; كَتَبَ الرِسالةَ بِقَلَمِهِ to write a letter by hand; حُرِّرَت المَقالةُ بِقَلَمِ رَئيسِ التَحْريرِ the article was drawn up by the chief editor 2 [مَكْتَب] office; قَلَم الاقْتِراعِ polling station; قَلَم المَحْكَمةِ registry; registrar

قُلامة *n* nail cuttings

قَلَميّ *adj* handwritten, by pen, ink (*before n*); صورة قَلَميّة a written portrait

أَقْلَمة, إِقْليم, تَأَقْلُم *n* see أقلم

تَقْليم *n* trimming, clipping, pruning; مِقَصّ التَقْليمِ pruning shears; تَقْليم أَظافِرِ شَخْصٍ ≈ clipping sb's wings, limiting sb's power

مِقْلام *n* |مَقاليمُ| pruning shears

مُقَلَّم *n* striped; pinstripe

قِمار *n* gamble; gambling; لُعْبة قِمارٍ game of chance; كازينو قِمارٍ casino; مائِدة القِمارِ gaming table

قَمَر *n* |أَقْمار| moon; satellite; قَمَر صِناعيّ \ اصْطِناعيّ satellite; قَمَر تَجَسُّسيّ spy satellite; وَجْه القَمَرِ lunar phase; سَطْح القَمَرِ the surface of the moon; (في) ضَوْءِ القَمَرِ (by) moonlight; سورة القَمَر The Moon (*Sura 54*); أَطْلَقَ قَمَراً صِناعيًّا to launch a satellite

قُمُر *n* جُزُر القُمُرِ Comoros

قَمْراء *n* |dipt f| moonlight; في القَمْراءِ by moonlight

قَمَريّ *adj* moon (*before n*); lunar; سَنة قَمَرِيّة lunar year; تَقْويم قَمَريّ lunar calendar; الحُروف القَمَرِيّة (Gram) the moon letters (*that do not assimilate the preceding lam of the article*)

قُمْريّ *n* turtle dove

قَمَرِيّة *n moon-shaped window*

أَقْمَر *adj* |dipt| 1 ◀ [مُضاء] moonlit; لَيْلة قَمْراء moonlit night 2 ◀ [أَبْيَض] pale

مُقامِر *n* gambler

مَقْمَر *n* |مَقامِرُ| gambling house

مُقْمِر *adj* moonlit; لَيْلة مُقْمِرة moonlit night

مُقَمَّر *adj* toasted

[2] **قَمْرة** *n* cabin; saloon; قَمْرة القِيادةِ cockpit

‹ **قاموس** *n* |قَواميسُ| 1 ◀ [مُعْجَم] dictionary; قاموس عَرَبيّ – هولَنْديّ an Arabic-Dutch dictionary; قاموس جَيْبٍ pocket dictionary; قاموس ثُنائيّ اللُغةِ \ إِلِكْترونيّ bilingual/ electronic dictionary; بَحَثَ عن شَيْءٍ في القاموس to look sth up in the dictionary 2 ◀ [مُحيط] ocean

‹ **قَمّاش** *n* cloth merchant

قُماش *n* |أَقْمِشة| cloth, fabric, material, textile; أَقْمِشة قُطْنيّة \ كَتّانيّة cotton/linen fabrics; قُماش خَيْمةٍ tent canvas; قِطْعة قُماشٍ piece of material

قُماشيّ *adj* cloth, fabric, textile

‹ **قَمَصَ** *v* |i-u; قَمْص, قِماص| to gallop

تَقَمَّصَ *v* 1 ◀ [لَبِسَ قَميصاً] to put on a shirt 2 ◀ [انْتَقَلَ] to throw/ project oneself into; to reincarnate; تَقَمَّصَ المُمَثِّل الشَخْصيّةَ \ الدَوْرَ the actor threw himself into the role; تَتَقَمَّصُ الروحُ the soul reincarnates

قَميص *n* |قُمْصان, أَقْمِصة| shirt, undershirt, blouse; قَميص داخِليّ undershirt, vest (BrE); قَميص نَوْمٍ nightgown, chemise; قَميص بِأَكْمامٍ طَويلةٍ \ قَصيرةٍ long-/short-sleeved shirt; رَقْم القَميصِ (player's) number; لَبِسَ \ ارْتَدى \ خَلَعَ قَميصاً to put on/wear/take off a shirt

تَقَمُّص *n* 1 ◀ [انْتِقال] throwing/projecting oneself into, inhabiting; transmigration of the soul; قُدْرَتُهُ على تَقَمُّصِ شَخْصيّاتٍ \ أَدْوارٍ مُخْتَلِفةٍ his ability to inhabit different characters/roles 2 ◀ [ارْتِداء] to wear (*a shirt*); يَسْتَحِقُّ تَقَمُّصَ الزِيِّ الوَطَنيِّ he deserves to wear the nation's uniform

‹ **قَمَطَ** *v* |i-u; قَمْط| to wrap (up); قَمَطَ مَوْلوداً to swaddle a baby

قِماط *n* |قُمُط, أَقْمِطة| 1 ◀ [لِفافة] swaddle blanket 2 ◀ [حِفاض] nappy (BrE), diaper (AmE)

‹ **قِمَطْر** *n* |قَماطِرُ| school bag

‹ **قَمَعَ** *v* |a; قَمْع| to oppress, to suppress, to put down; قَمَعَ شَعْباً to oppress a people; قَمَعَ التَظاهُراتِ بالعُنْفِ to violently suppress demonstrations

أَقْمَعَ *v* to suppress, to submit

قَمْع *n* oppression, suppression; قَمْع عَنيف \ دَمَويّ violent/ bloody oppression; قَمْع التَظاهُراتِ \ التَمَرُّدِ suppression of the demonstrations/rebellion; حُكومة تُمارِسُ القَمْعَ an oppressive government

قِمْع *n* |أَقْماع| funnel

قامِع *n* oppressor

قَمْعيّ *adj* repressive; نِظام قَمْعيّ a repressive regime

قِمَعِيّة *n* foxglove (*Digitalis*)

‹ **قُمْقُم, قُمْقُمة** *n* |قَماقِمُ| perfume bottle; أَخْرَجَ المارِدَ من قُمْقُمِه (السِحْريِّ) ≈ to let the genie out of the bottle (*to unleash events which cannot then be controlled*)

‹ **قَمِلَ** *v* |a; قَمَل| to have lice, to be infested with lice

قَمَّلَ *v* to have lice, to be infested with lice

قَمْل *n coll* louse; قَمْل الرَأْسِ head lice; قَمْل نَباتٍ aphid; فَلى \ فَلّى القَمْلَ to search/comb for lice; to scrutinize carefully

قُمَّليّات *n pl* mites

مُقَمِّل *adj* lice-infested; كانَ مُقَمِّلاً to have lice

‹ **قُمامة** *n* |قُمام, قُمامات| refuse (BrE), rubbish (BrE), garbage (AmE); صُنْدوق \ وِعاء القُمامةِ dustbin (BrE), trash can (AmE); عَرَبة القُمامةِ dustcart (BrE), garbage truck (AmE); سَلّة القُمامةِ waste-paper basket (BrE), wastebasket (AmE); كيس القُمامةِ bin liner (BrE), garbage/trash bag (AmE); كَوْم القُمامةِ rubbish dump (BrE), (garbage) dump (AmE); لَمَّ \ جَمَّعَ القُمامة to collect refuse

‹ **قِمّة** *n* |قِمَم| [1] [أَعْلى] peak, summit; top; قِمَم جَبَلِيّة mountain ridge; قِمّة شَيْءٍ the height of sth; the peak of sth; قِمّة الرَأْسِ crown of the head; قِمّة جَبَلٍ mountain peak; قِمّة شَجَرةٍ treetop; قِمّة الإِنْجازِ the highest achievement; وَصَلَ إلى القِمّةِ to reach the summit [2] [مُؤْتَمَر] summit, conference; قِمّة \ مُؤْتَمَر مُصَغَّرة a mini-conference; القِمّة العَرَبِيّة Arab summit; قِمّة الدُوَلِ قِمّة مَجْموعةِ الثَمانِيةِ G-8 summit; لِقاء قِمّةٍ summit; قِمّة (الدُوَلِ) العِشْرينَ, الغَنِيّة G-20 summit; مُؤْتَمَر قِمّةٍ أوروبّيّ European summit; تُعْقَدُ \ تُقامُ القِمّةُ في ... the conference is being held in ... [3] [قِيادة] top

‹ **قَمِن** *adj* worthy, deserving

قَمين, قَمينة *n* |قَمينات| kiln, furnace

‹ **قَنَأَ** *v* |a; قُنوء| to be bright red

‹ **قِنا** *n* Qina (*city/governorate in Egypt*)

‹ **قَنال** *n* canal, channel; القَنال الإِنْجليزيّ the English Channel

‹ **قُنَّب, قِنَّب** *n* hemp, cannabis; قِنَّب هِنْديّ Indian hemp, marijuana; زَرَعَ القِنَّبَ to grow hemp

‹ **قُنْبَر** *n coll* lark

‹ **قُنْبُلة** *n* |قَنابِل| bomb; shell; grenade; قُنْبُلة نَوَوِيّة \ ذَرِّيّة nuclear bomb, atom bomb; فَجَّرَ قُنْبُلَةً نَوَوِيّةً to detonate a nuclear bomb; قُنْبُلة هَيْدروجينيّة hydrogen bomb; قُنْبُلة يَدَوِيّة hand grenade; قُنْبُلة حارِقة firebomb; قُنْبُلة مَوْقوتة \ زَمَنِيّة time bomb; زَرَعَ قُنْبُلَةً مَوْقوتَةً to plant a time bomb; انْفَجَرَت القُنْبُلةُ المَوْقوتةُ the time bomb went off; قُنْبُلة عُنْقودِيّة cluster bomb; قُنْبُلة انْشِطارِيّة fragmentation grenade; القُنْبُلة المُسَيِّلة للدُموعِ tear gas; قاذِفة قَنابِل bomber; انْفِجار قُنْبُلةٍ explosion of a bomb; أَلْقى \ رَمى \ أَطْلَقَ قَنابِلَ to throw bombs; أَبْطَلَ مَفْعولَ قُنْبُلةٍ to defuse/deactivate a bomb

‹ **قُنَّبيط** *n* cauliflower

‹ **قَنَتَ** *v* |u; قُنوت| to be submissive

‹ **قَنْد** *n* |قُنود| hard candy

‹ **قُنْدُس** *n* |قَنادِس| (*Zool*) beaver

‹ **قَنْدول** *n* broom (*Calycotome*)

قِنْديل *n* |قَناديل| lamp; lantern; oil lamp; قِنْديل البَحْرِ jellyfish

‹ **قَنْدَلَفْت** *n* |قَنْدَلَفْتِيّة| (*Chr*) sexton

‹ **قُنْزُعة** *n* |قَنازِع| crest, tuft (*of feathers*); forelock (*of hair*)

‹ **قَنَصَ** *v* |i; قَنْص| to hunt; قَنَصَ البَطَّ to hunt ducks

اقْتَنَصَ *v* to grab, to snatch (up), to clinch; to hunt, to chase; اقْتَنَصَ فُرْصةً to seize an opportunity

قَنْص *n* hunt

قَنّاص *n* |قَنّاصة| [1] [قاتِل] sniper, sharpshooter, assassin; شَخْص قُتِلَ بِرَصاصِ \ بِنيرانِ قَنّاصٍ a person killed by sniper fire [2] [صائِد] hunter

قَنيص *n* game

اقْتِناص *n* seizure, seizing, grabbing; hunt, hunting; اقْتِناص فُرْصةٍ seizing an opportunity

‹ **قُنْصُل** *n* |قَناصِل| consul; قُنْصُل عامّ consul general; قُنْصُل فَخْرِيّ honorary consul

(Idiom) بِنْت القُنْصُلِ poinsettia (*Euphorbia pulcherrima*)

قُنْصُليّ *adj* consular; تَمْثيل قُنْصُليّ consular representation; السِلْك القُنْصُليّ consular corps

قُنْصُلِيّة *n* consulate; القُنْصُلِيّة المَغْرِبِيّة في لَنْدَن the Moroccan consulate in London

‹ **قَنِطَ** *v* |a; قَنَط, قُنوط, قَناطة| to despair; عَلَيْكَ أَلاّ تَقْنَطَ أَمامَ المَصائِبِ you shouldn't despair over misfortune

أَقْنَطَ *v* to drive to despair, to discourage

قانِط *adj* desperate, despondent, despairing

قُنوط *n* despair, desperation; اسْتَسْلَمَ لِلقُنوطِ to give in to despair

‹ **قِنْطار** *n* |قَناطيرُ| qantar (*unit of weight which has varied between 45 to 150 kg at different places and times*)

قَنْطَرة *n* |قَناطِرُ| [1] [قَوْس] arch [2] [جِسْر] bridge, arched bridge [3] [قَناة اصْطِناعِيّة] aqueduct [4] [سَدّ] dam

قنوع *adj* |قُنُع| satisfied, content, fulfilled; رَجُل قَنوع a content man

اقْتِناع *n* conviction, belief; اقْتِناع راسِخ a firm conviction; كانَ على اقْتِناع (تامٍّ) بِشَيْءٍ to be (completely) convinced of sth; كانَ على اقْتِناعٍ بِضَرورةِ \ أَهَمّيّةِ شَيْءٍ to be convinced of the necessity/importance of sth

إقْناع *n* persuasion; convincing, persuading; شَخْص سَهْل الإقْناع an easily convinced person, a pushover; القُدْرة على الإقْناع persuasive powers

مُقْتَنِع *adj* convinced; كانَ مُقْتَنِعاً بِشَيْءٍ to be convinced of sth; كانَ غَيْرَ مُقْتَنِعٍ بِشَيْءٍ to be unconvinced by sth; هو مُقْتَنِعٌ بِأَنَّهُ على حَقٍّ he's convinced he's right

مُقْنِع *adj* convincing, persuasive; إجابة مُقْنِعة a convincing answer; مُبَرِّر مُقْنِع persuasive justification; أَدِلّة \ حُجَج مُقْنِعة convincing evidence

مُقَنَّع *adj* masked; لِصّ مُقَنَّع a masked robber

‹ **قَنْغَر** *n* kangaroo

‹ **قُنْفُذ** *n* |قَنافِذُ| hedgehog; قُنْفُذ البَحْرِ sea urchin

‹ **قَنْقَر** *n* kangaroo

‹ **قَنِمَ** *v* |a; قَنَم| to become rancid; قَنِمَ اللَحْمُ the meat has gone bad

‹ **قَنَّنَ** *v* 1 [اقْتَصَدَ] to ration; قَنَّنَ اسْتِخْدامَ الكَهْرَباءِ to ration electricity 2 [دَوَّنَ] to regulate, to legislate, to codify; قَنَّنَ حُقوقَ شَخْصٍ to codify sb's rights

قانون *n* |قَوانينُ| 1 (Law) law, legislation, code; القانون الجِنائيّ, قانون العُقوبات criminal law, the penal code; قانون إداريّ administrative law; القانون المَدَنيّ civil law; قانون خاصّ a specific law; private law; قانون خاصّ بِإقامةِ دينٍ a law establishing a religion; فَرَضَت الميلِشيا قَوانينَها الخاصّةَ the militia imposed its own laws; قانون عامّ public law; القانون التِجاريّ commercial law; القانون العَسْكَريّ \ البَحْريّ military/maritime law; قانون الضَرائِب \ الهِجْرة tax/immigration law; قانون دُسْتوريّ constitutional law; القَوانين السارِية (المَفْعولِ) applicable laws, the laws in force; القانون الأوروبّيّ European legislation; القانون الدُوَليّ international law; قانون تأديبيّ disciplinary rules; قانون تَأْديبيّ طِبّيّ medical code of practice; قانون انْتِقاليّ

مُقَنْطَر *adj* arched, vaulted

‹ **قَنْطَريون** *n* knapweed, star thistle (*Centaurea*); قَنْطَريون عَنْبَريّ cornflower (*Centaurea cyanus*)

‹ **قَنِعَ** *v* |a; قَنَع, قُنْعان, قَناعة| 1 |ب| to be satisfied/content (with); قَنِعَ بِما عِنْدَهُ (من مالٍ) to be content with what one has (financially) 2 |ب| to be convinced (by); قَنِعَ بِشَيْءٍ to be convinced by sth

قَنَّعَ *v* 1 [بِقِناع] to veil, to mask 2 [أَقْنَعَ] to convince, to persuade

أَقْنَعَ *v* to persuade, to convince; أَقْنَعَ شَخْصاً بِشَيْءٍ to persuade sb of sth; أَقْنَعَ شَخْصاً بِأَنْ... to convince sb that ...; أَقْنَعَ شَخْصاً بِأَنْ يَفْعَلَ شَيْئاً to convince sb to do sth; أَقْنَعَ شَخْصاً بالبَقاءِ to convince sb to stay; حاوَلَ أَنْ يُقْنِعَ شَخْصاً to try to persuade sb; أَقْنَعَ الناخِبين to canvass voters

تَقَنَّعَ *v* to be masked, to be disguised; تَقَنَّعَ بِقِناعٍ to hide behind a mask; سِياسيّ يَتَقَنَّعُ بِقِناعِ الدينِ a politician hiding behind the mask of religion

اقْتَنَعَ *v* |ب| to be/become convinced (of), to see, to recognize, to admit; اقْتَنَعَ بِخَطِئِه to recognize one's mistake; اقْتَنَعَ بِشَيْءٍ to admit sth; اقْتَنَعَ بِوِجْهةِ نَظَرِ شَخْصٍ to be convinced of sb's point of view; to come around to sb's point of view; اقْتَنَعَ بِضَرورةِ شَيْءٍ to be/become convinced of the necessity of sth

قَنِع *adj* satisfied, content

قانِع *adj* |قُنَّع| satisfied, content

قِناع *n* |قِناعات, أَقْنِعة| 1 [وَجْهٍ] mask; guise; قِناع واقٍ gas mask; قِناع غَطْسٍ diving mask; تحت \ وراء قِناعِ شَيْءٍ under the guise of sth; تحت قِناعِ الدينِ under the guise of religion; كَشْف القِناعِ exposure; وَضَعَ \ لَبِسَ قِناعاً to put on/wear a mask; كَشَفَ القِناعَ عن to unmask, to expose; كَشَفَ القِناعَ عن جاسوسٍ to expose a spy 2 [للتَجْميل] mask; قِناع الطينِ clay mask 3 [للمَرْأة] veil

قَناعة *n* 1 [رِضى] satisfaction, contentment; القَناعةُ كَنْزٌ لا يُفْنى contentment is an everlasting treasure 2 [يَقين] belief, conviction; كانَ على قَناعةٍ (تامّةٍ) بِشَيْءٍ to be (completely) convinced of sth; قَناعة راسِخة a firm belief transitional provisions; قانون أَساسيّ (لِشَرِكةٍ أو مُؤَسَّسةٍ) statutes (of an organization or institution); قَوانين صارِمة strict laws; مَشْروع قانونٍ bill; رَجُل قانونٍ lawyer, jurist; نَصّ القانونِ the text of the law; the letter of the law; دَوْلة قانونٍ constitutional state; شَخْصيّة اعْتِباريّة في القانونِ legal person under the law; تَعْديل القانونِ amendment; خارِج عن القانونِ outlaw; في قانونِ العُقوباتِ in criminal law, in the penal code; في المادّةِ ٨ من هذا القانونِ in article 8 of this law; بِاسْمِ القانونِ in the name of the law; وَفْقاً \ طِبْقاً للقانونِ المَدَنيِّ in accordance with civil law; بِموجِبِ القانونِ by law; حَسَبَ القَوانينِ according to the law; ضدّ القانونِ against the law; طَبَّقَ قانوناً to enforce the law; راعى \ احْتَرَمَ القانونَ to observe/respect the law; خالَفَ \ خَرَقَ القانونَ to break the law; خَرَجَ على \ عن القانونِ to break the law; تَحايَلَ على القانونِ to circumvent/elude the law; سَنَّ \ أَصْدَرَ قانوناً to enact/issue a law; تَبَنّى قانوناً to pass legislation; أَدْخَلَ قانوناً حَيِّزَ التَنْفيذِ to bring a law into effect; قَدَّمَ \ رَفَضَ مَشْروعَ قانونٍ to introduce/reject a bill; داسَ على القانونِ to trample on the law; انْتَهَكَ القَوانينَ الدُوَلِيّةَ to violate international law; اسْتَحْدَثَ قانوناً جَديداً to introduce new legislation; كانَ فوق القانونِ to be above the law; القانونُ الانْتِقاليُّ ساري المَفْعولِ the transitional provisions are in effect **2** [قاعِدة] law, rule; قانون الغابة the law of the jungle; قَوانين سَماوِيّة \ إلاهيّة divine laws **3** (Sci) law; قانون العَرْضِ والطَلَبِ the law of supply and demand; قانون الجاذِبِيّةِ the law of gravity; قوانين فيزيائيّة \ اقْتِصاديّة laws of physics/economics; قَوانين نْيوتُن للحَرَكةِ Newton's laws of motion; قانون الطَبيعةِ the law of nature **4** (Mus) zither

قانونيّ **A** *adj* legal, statutory; lawful, legitimate, allowed; قانونيًّا by law, rightly; غَيْر قانونيٍّ illegal, illegitimate, unlawful; clandestine; نِصاب قانونيّ quorum; إجْراءات قانونيّة legal measures; مُسْتَنَد \ نَصّ قانونيّ legal document/text; السِنّ القانونيّة the legal age; مُهْلة قانونيّة statutory time limit, legal deadline; اسْتِشارة قانونيّة legal advice; مُسْتَشار قانونيّ legal advisor; مُسَوِّغ قانونيّ legal justification; حُكْم قانونيّ legal provision; مَبْدَأ قانونيّ a principle of the law; مُعْتَرَف بِهِ \ مَنْصوص عَلَيْهِ قانونيًّا acknowledged/stipulated by law; مَسْؤول قانونيًّا liable, legally responsible; من الناحِيةِ القانونيّةِ ... from a legal standpoint ...; عَبْرَ طُرُقٍ قانونيّةٍ in a legal manner; مُساعَدة قانونيّة legal aid; دَليل قانونيّ legal guide; legal evidence; حِماية قانونيّة legal protection; أَدّى اليَمينَ القانونيّةَ to be sworn in; أَخَذَ إجْراءاتٍ قانونيّةً to take legal steps/measures; بَلَغَ السِنَّ القانونيّةَ (لِفِعْلِ شَيْءٍ) to reach the legal age (to do sth)
B *n* lawyer

قانونيّة *n* legality, lawfulness; عَدَم قانونيّةِ شَيْءٍ the illegality of sth

قُنّ *n* |قِنان| chicken coop, henhouse; قُنّ الدَجاجِ chicken coop

قِنّ *n* |أَقْنان, أَقِنّة| serf

قِنانة *n* serfdom, bondage; القِنانة الإِقْطاعيّة feudal serfdom

قُنّة *n* |قُنَن, قِنان| (old use) top, pinnacle

قِنّينة *n* |قَنانٍ| bottle, flask; قِنّينة غازٍ, قِنّينة مولوتوف Molotov cocktail, petrol bomb (BrE); أَلْقى بِقِنّينةِ مولوتوف to throw a Molotov cocktail

قَوْنَنة *n* codification

تَقْنين *n* rationing, regulation, regulating; legislation; تَقْنين الكَهْرَباءِ electricity rationing; ساعات تَقْنينِ الكَهْرَباءِ rolling blackouts

لاقانونيّ *adj* unlawful, illegal

‹ **قَنا, قَنى** *v* |u; قَنْو, قُنُوّ, قُنْو| to acquire

قَنّى *v* to dig; قَنّى قَناةً to dig a canal

اقْتَنى *v* to acquire, to get; اقْتَنى سَيّارةً to get a car

قانٍ *adj* blood red, bright red; reddish; دَم قانٍ bright-red blood; الأَحْمَر القاني deep red, blood red; الأَزْرَق \ الأَسْوَد القاني purple/reddish-black

قَناة *n* **1** [تُرْعة] |قَنَوات, أَقْنِية| canal, channel, waterway; قَناة رَيٍّ irrigation channel; قَناة السُوَيْسِ Suez Canal; قَناة مائيّة waterway; قَنَوات مائيّة طَبيعيّة \ اصْطِناعيّة natural/artificial waterways **2** [إذاعة] channel; قَناة فَضائيّة satellite channel; على القَناةِ الثانِيةِ on channel two **3** (Anat) |قَنَوات, قِناء, قُنِيّ|

قَهْقَرة *n* decline, regression; retreat

قَهْقَرى *n* |f| retreat, withdrawal; رَجَعَ \ عادَ القَهْقَرى to retreat

قَهْقَرِيّ *adj* فَيْروس قَهْقَرِيّ (Bio) retrovirus

تَقَهْقُر *n* decline, deterioration; التَقَهْقُر الحَضاريّ \ الاجْتِماعيّ cultural/social decay; تَقَهْقُرُ الاقْتِصادِ economic decline

‹ **قَهْقاع** *n* roar (*of a bear*)

‹ **قَهْقَهَ** *v* |i; قَهْقَهة| to guffaw, to roar; قَهْقَهَ من الفَرَح to roar with pleasure; قَهْقَهَ بِصَوْتٍ عالٍ to guffaw loudly

قَهْقَهة *n* guffaw, roar (of laughter); قَهْقَهة عالِية a loud guffaw

‹ **قَهَم** *n* anorexia; قَهَم عُصابيّ anorexia nervosa

‹ **قَهْوة** *n* 1 [شَراب البُنّ] coffee; قَهْوة سادة black coffee; فِنْجان قَهْوةٍ coffee cup; فِنْجانٌ من القَهْوة cup of coffee; احْتَسى \ شَرِبَ القَهْوة to drink coffee 2 [مَقْهًى] |قَهَوات, قَهاوِيّ| cafe, coffee house, coffee shop

قَهْوَجيّ *n person who makes/sells coffee*; coffee shop proprietor

مَقْهًى *n* |مَقاهٍ| cafe, coffee house, coffee shop; صاحِب مَقْهًى coffee shop owner; مَقْهى الإِنْتَرْنِت Internet cafe; جَلَسَ في مَقْهًى to sit in a cafe

‹ **قابَ** *v* |u; قَوْب| to dig

قاب *n* على قابِ قَوْسَيْنِ (أو أَدْنى) very near, just around the corner, imminent; باتَ على \ كانَ قابَ قَوْسَيْنِ من شَيْءٍ to be very close to sth; كانَ قابَ قَوْسَيْنِ أو أَدْنى من المَوْتِ to be a hair's breadth from death; باتَ على قابِ قَوْسَيْنِ أو أَدْنى من الحَرْبِ to be on the brink of war

قوباء *n* eczema; قوباء حَلَقِيّة ringworm (*dermatophytosis*)

‹ **قاتَ** *v* |u; قوت, قَوْت| to nourish, to feed

قَوَّتَ *v* to nourish, to feed

تَقَوَّتَ *v* to eat, to feed

اقْتاتَ *v* to eat, to feed; اقْتاتَ على الحَشَراتِ to feed on insects

قوت *n* |أَقْوات| 1 [طَعام] food, nourishment; لا يَمْتَلِكُ قوتَ يَوْمِهِ to have nothing to eat 2 [مَدْخول] living, livelihood; كَسَبَ قوتَهُ بِعَرَقِ جَبينِهِ to make an honest living

مُقيت *n* المُقيت the Nourisher (*one of the names of God*)

‹ **تَقَوَّحَ** *v* to be infected, to fester; يَتَقَوَّحُ إِصْبَعي my finger is infected

قُنوة, قِنْوة *n* |قَنَيات| tube, tract; قَناة هَضْمِيّة digestive tract; قَناة أوسْتاكيوس Eustachian tube; القَناة المَنَوِيّة vas deferens

قِنْوة, قُنْوة *n* acquisition; possession

قِنْية, قُنْية *n* acquisition; possession

اقْتِناء *n* acquisition, purchase; اقْتِناء الأَسْلِحةِ acquiring weapons

مُقْتَنًى *n* |مُقْتَنَيات| acquisition; possession, property; collection; مُقْتَنَيات المَتْحَفِ the museum's acquisitions/collections; مُقْتَنَيات شَخْصِيّة personal possessions

‹ **قِهْ** *v* see وَقى

‹ **قَهَرَ** *v* |a; قَهْر| 1 [غَلَبَ] to conquer, to defeat; قَهَرَ شَخْصاً \ شَيْئاً to defeat sb/sth; قَهَرَ الصِعابَ to overcome difficulties; جَيْش لا يُقْهَرُ an invincible army 2 [أَجْبَرَ] to force; قَهَرَ شَخْصاً على شَيْءٍ to force sb to do sth

قَهْر *n* 1 [إِخْضاع] subjugation, victory, oppression; ماتَ قَهْراً *to die as a result of great injustice or grief*; قَهْر الشَعْبِ subjugation of the people; قَهْر النَفْسِ self-conquest 2 [إِجْبار] compulsion, coercion; قَهْراً forcibly, compulsory

قاهِر *adj* strong, powerful, overwhelming; قوّة قاهِرة superior strength; overwhelming force; سَبَب قاهِر a compelling reason; ظُروف قاهِرة extreme circumstances

القاهِرة *n* Cairo

قاهِرِيّ *adj, n* Cairene

قَهّار A *adj* powerful, almighty

B *n* القَهّار the Subduer (*one of the names of God*)

قَهْرِيّ *adj* forced, compulsory; الوَسْواس القَهْرِيّ obsessive-compulsive disorder, OCD; سَبَب قَهْرِيّ a compelling reason

مَقْهور *adj* defeated, oppressed; شَعْب مَقْهور an oppressed people

‹ **قَهْرَمان** *n* |قَهارِمة| butler; housekeeper

‹ **قَهْقَرَ** *v* |i; قَهْقَرة| to retreat, to withdraw

تَقَهْقَرَ *v* 1 [تَراجَعَ] to withdraw, to recoil; تَقَهْقَرَ مَذْعوراً to recoil in horror 2 [هَبَطَ] to decline, to deteriorate, to regress; to retreat, to give/lose ground, to fall behind; تَقَهْقَرَ إلى الوَراءِ to regress; to fall behind; تَقَهْقَرَ في الدِراسةِ to decline academically; تَقَهْقَرَت الأَرْيافُ اقْتِصاديًّا the countryside has declined economically

قادَ *v* |u; قِياد ,قِيادة| **1** [رَأَس] to lead, to command; to chair, to govern; قادَ جَيْشاً to command an army; قادَ جَوْقةً موسيقيّةً to front a band; قادَ تَنْظيماً إرْهابيًّا to lead a terrorist group; قادَ المُباراةَ الحَكَمُ الجَزائِريُّ the Algerian referee presided over the tournament **2** [ساقَ] to drive; to steer, to operate; قادَ سَيّارةً \ قِطاراً to drive a car/train; قادَ السَيّارةَ إلى اليَسارِ to steer the car to the left; قادَ السَفينةَ إلى الضِفّةِ to steer the ship to shore; قادَ حِصاناً to steer a horse **3** [أَرْشَدَ] to lead (away/off), to carry away/along, to drive (away); قادَ إلى حَلٍّ to lead to a solution; قادَ شَخْصاً to lead sb away; قادَ فَريقَهُ إلى الفَوْزِ to lead one's team to victory

انْقادَ *v* to obey, to submit, to be led; انْقادَ لِشَخْصٍ to obey sb; انْقادَ إلى هَزيمةٍ to be led to defeat

اقْتادَ *v* to lead (away); اقْتادَتْهُ الشُرْطةُ the police led him away

قائِد *n* |قوّاد ,قوَّد ,قادة ,قادات| **1** [زَعيم] leader, head, commander, captain; قائِد فِرْقةٍ موسيقيّةٍ conductor; قائِد مَجْموعةٍ group leader; قادة الحِزْبِ party leaders **2** [سائِق] driver; pilot; قائِد سَيّارةٍ driver; قائِد طائِرةٍ pilot **3** (Mil) army commander/leader; general; قائِد أَعْلى \ عامّ commander-in-chief; قائِد عَسْكَريّ military leader; قائِد القوّاتِ commander of the troops

قَوّاد *n* **1** [في البِغاءِ] pimp, procurer **2** [إهانة] *dishonourable man (used as a term of abuse)*

قِوادة *n* pimping, procurement

قِياد *n* **1** [زَعامة] leadership **2** [مِقْوَد] rein, halter; سَهْل القِيادِ compliant; أَسْلَسَ قِيادَهُ لِشَخْصٍ to submit oneself to sb

قِيادة *n* **1** [زَعامة] leadership, command, management, government; تحت قِيادة ... under the leadership of ...; القُدْرة على قِيادةِ فَريقٍ executive ability, leadership skills **2** [وَسيلة نَقْلٍ] steering, drive; قِيادة سَيّارةٍ driving a car; بُرْج قِيادةٍ control tower; bridge (*of a ship*); رُخْصة قِيادةٍ (خاصّة) (non-commercial) driving licence; امْتِحان قِيادةٍ driving test; عَجَلة قِيادةٍ steering wheel; لَوْحة قِيادةٍ dashboard; عَصا قِيادةٍ control stick; حُجْرة \ غُرْفة قِيادةٍ cabin, cockpit; أَخَذَ زِمامَ قِيادةٍ to take control **3** (Mil) command; قِيادة الجَيْشِ \ عَسْكَريّة army command; قِيادة عُلْيا \ عامّة high command; general staff; مَقَرّ \ مَرْكَز قِيادةٍ headquarters, command post; تحت قِيادةِ شَخْصٍ under sb's command; سَفينة قِيادةٍ flagship

قِياديّ *adj* leading, commanding; شَخْصيّة قِياديّة a leader; مَنْصِب قِياديّ an executive position

انْقِياد *n* compliance, submission; سَهْل الانْقِيادِ compliant, acquiescent; عَدَم الانْقِيادِ unwillingness, intractability, non-compliance

مِقْوَد *n* |مَقاوِدُ| **1** [مَرْكَبة] steering wheel; مِقْوَد سَيّارةٍ steering wheel; مِقْوَد سَفينةٍ wheel, helm; مِقْوَد طائِرةٍ control stick; مِقْوَد درّاجةٍ handlebars; فَقَدَ السَيْطَرةَ على المِقْوَدِ to lose control of the steering wheel **2** [الحِصانُ] halter, rein, leash

قَوَّرَ *v* to gouge, to hollow out

قار *n* asphalt, tar, pitch, bitumen

تَقْوير *n* excavation

تَقْويرة *n* (low) neckline, décolletage

مُقَوَّر *adj* décolleté, low-necked

قَوِسَ *v* |a; قَوَس| to be/become curved/bent; قَوِسَ ظَهْرُهُ to have a crooked back

قَوَّسَ *v* **1** [الشَيْءَ] to bend, to curve; قَوَّسَ ظَهْرَهُ to arch one's back; it made his back crooked; قَوَّسَ غُصْناً to bend a branch; قَوَّسَ السَقْفَ to construct an arched roof **2** [قَوِسَ] to be/become arched/curved/bent

تَقَوَّسَ *v* to bend, to curve, to arch; تَقَوَّسَ ظَهْرُهُ he became hunched

قَوْس *n* |أَقْواس| **1** [شَكْل هَنْدَسيّ] arc, bow; arch, vault; قَوْس قُزَحٍ rainbow; بِكُلِّ أَلْوانِ قَوْسِ قُزَحٍ in all the colors of the rainbow; قَوْس الكَمانِ bow (*music*); قَوْس نَصْرٍ triumphal arch; Arc de Triomphe (*in Paris*); كانَ تحت \ أمام قَوْسِ المَحْكَمةِ to be before the court, to be on trial **2** [في الكِتابةِ] parenthesis; bracket; قَوْس مُزْدَوِج bracket; بين قَوْسَيْنِ ... incidentally ..., by the way ...; وَضَعَ شَيْئاً بين قَوْسَيْنِ to put sth in parentheses **3** (Mil) bow; قَوْس وَنُشّاب bow and arrow; على قابِ قَوْسَيْنِ (أو أَدْنى) very near, just around the corner, imminent; باتَ على \ كانَ قابَ قَوْسَيْنِ من شَيْءٍ to be very close to sth, to come within a whisker of sth; كانَ قابَ قَوْسَيْنِ أو أَدْنى من المَوْتِ to be a hair's breadth from death;

قَوْقَع *n coll* mollusc; snail, slug

قَوْقَعة *n* |قواقِعُ| ⬚1 shell; قواقع بَحْرِيّة seashells; خَرَجَ من قَوْقَعَتِهِ to come out of one's shell; انْطَوى في قَوْقَعَتِهِ to withdraw into one's shell ⬚2 (Anat) cochlea; قَوْقَعة الأُذُنِ cochlea; زَرْع \ زِراعة قَوْقَعةٍ cochlear implant

‹ **قالَ** *v* |u; قَوْل| ⬚1 [تَفَوَّهَ] to say, to speak, to tell; قالَ لِشَخْصٍ إنّ ... to tell sb (that) ...; قالَ شَيْئاً عن شَيْءٍ to say sth about sth; قالَ بِرَأْيٍ to voice an opinion; قالَتْ مَصادِرُ إنّ ... sources report that ...; قالَ مُتَحَدِّثٌ بِاسْمِ الوِزارةِ إنّ ... a spokesman for the ministry said that ...; كَما يَقولُ المَثَلُ ... as the saying goes, ...; قد يَقولُ قائلٌ ... word has it that ...; قيلَ \ يُقالُ إنّ ... one could say (that) ...; على ما \ حَسْبَما \ كَما يُقالُ \ قيلَ according to reports; حتّى لا يُقالَ إنّ ... so that it won't be said (that) ...; وَقيلَ ... it's said ... (too); قيلَ كَلامٌ كَثيرٌ عن ... much has been said about ...; أو قُلْ ... or rather ..., that is to say ...; مَدْعوماً من الغَرْبِ، أو قُلْ أَمْريكا supported by the West, or rather America ⬚2 [نامَ] see قيل

قَوَّلَ *v* to make say; قَوَّلَ شَخْصاً ما لم يَقُلْهُ to put words into sb's mouth; قَوَّلَ شَخْصاً الحَقَّ to make sb speak the truth

قاوَلَ *v* ⬚1 [فاوَضَ] to negotiate ⬚2 [جادَلَ] to discuss, to debate ⬚3 [تَعاقَدَ] to contract, to run a business

تَقَوَّلَ *v* |على| to talk about; to gossip; تَقَوَّلَ على شَخْصٍ أَكاذيبَ to spread rumours about sb

قَوْل *n* |أَقْوال, أَقاويلُ| saying, proverb; statement, remark; أَقاويل gossip; قَوْل مَأْثور motto; قَوْل شائع \ قَديم a well-known/old saying; قَوْل عن \ في شَيْءٍ a statement about sth; خُلاصة القَوْلِ in brief, in a word; من الصَعْبِ القَوْلُ إنّ ... it is difficult to say that ...; من نافِلةِ القَوْلِ إنّ ... it goes without saying that ...; قَوْلُهُ تَعالى the word of God (*in the Koran*); قَوْلاً وَعَمَلاً \ فِعْلاً in words and actions; (نُريدُ) أَفْعالاً \ أَعْمالاً لا أَقْوالاً actions speak louder than words; هذه زُبْدةُ القَوْلِ this is the moral of the proverb; مُقْتَطَفات من أَقْوالِ شَخْصٍ selected quotes of sb; أَفْحَشَ في قَوْلِهِ to use obscene language; أَخَذَ أَقْوالَ شَخْصٍ to take sb's statement; كَرَّرَ القَوْلَ إنّ ... to state repeatedly that ...; اكْتَفى بالقَوْلِ إنّ ... to merely say that ...; خَلَصَ إلى القَوْلِ ... خَتَمَ القَوْلَ ... to wrap up by saying ...;

باتَ على قابِ قَوْسَيْنِ أو أَدْنى من الحَرْبِ to be on the brink of war ⬚4 (Astrol) (بُرْج) القَوْسِ Sagittarius

قَوّاس *n* archer

قُوَيْسة *n* sage

أَقْوَس *adj* |dipt| *with a crooked/hunched/bent back*

تَقَوُّس *n* curve, bend, arch; تَقَوُّس الساقَيْنِ bow-leggedness, genu varum

مُقَوَّس *adj* curved, arched; سَقْف مُقَوَّس domed roof

‹ **قاضَ** *v* |u; قَوْض| ⬚1 [هَدَمَ] to destroy, to demolish, to tear down; قاضَ بِناءً to demolish a building ⬚2 [انْكَسَرَ] see قيض

قَوَّضَ *v* to destroy, to demolish, to tear down; قَوَّضَ عَمَلِيّةَ السَلامِ to destroy the peace process; قَوَّضَ دَوْلَةً to destroy a state

تَقَوَّضَ *v* to collapse, to be destroyed, to be demolished

تَقْويض *n* |تَقْويضات| undermining, subverting; subversion; destruction, demolition, devastation; تَقْويض اسْتِقْرارِ شَيْءٍ destabilizing sth; تَقْويض جُهودِ شَخْصٍ undermining sb's efforts; اتِّهام بِتَقْويضِ السُلْطةِ \ النِظامِ subversion charges

‹ **قوطة** *n* tomato

قوطيّ, غوطيّ *adj* Gothic; العِمارة القوطيّة Gothic architecture

‹ **قاع** *n* |قيعان| bottom, base; depth; في قاعِ البَحْرِ at the bottom of the sea

قاعة *n* hall, room; قاعة مُقْفَلة closed-roof stadium; قاعة المُحاضَرات lecture hall; قاعة المَحْكَمة courtroom; قاعة الاحْتِفالات reception room; قاعة عَرْضٍ gallery; قاعة المَطارِ \ المَحَطّة arrivals/departure lounge; الوُصولِ \ المُغادَرةِ station/airport concourse; قاعة المَدْرَسة classroom; قاعة المُؤْتَمَرات conference hall

‹ **قاقَ** *v* |u; قَوْق| to cackle, to cluck (*chicken*)

قَوَّقَ *v* to cackle, to cluck (*chicken*)

قَوْق *n* cackle, cluck (*chicken*)

قاق *n* crow; قاق الماءِ cormorant

‹ **قَوْقَس** *n* ring-necked dove

‹ **تَقَوْقَعَ** *v* to withdraw/retreat into its shell (*turtle*); (fig) to retire/withdraw; تَقَوْقَعَ على نَفْسِهِ to withdraw into oneself; to curl up into a ball

نَسْتَطيعُ القَوْلَ إنّ ... يُمْكِنُ القَوْلُ إنّ ... it can be said that ...; we can say that ..., one might say that ...

قائِل *adj* saying, stating; المَثَل القائِل ... the proverb which says ...; مَضى قائِلاً ... he continued, saying ...; أجابَني قائِلاً ... he answered me with the words ...

قال *n* talk; القيل والقال rumour, gossip, talk

قَوّال *adj* talkative, loquacious

قيل *n* القيل والقال rumour, gossip, talk

مَقال, **مَقالة** *n* article, treatise, essay; مَقالة عِلْمِيّة a scholarly article; كاتِب مَقالاتٍ essayist; مَقال رَئيسيّ \ افْتِتاحيّ editorial; مَقال بِعُنْوانِ ... an article entitled ...; مَقال عن \ على \ حول ... an essay on ...; مَقالة عن ديكارْت an essay on Descartes; كَتَبَ \ نَشَرَ مَقالاً to write/publish a paper

مُقاوِل *n* 1 [قِطاع البِناءِ] contractor; مُقاوِلونَ مَحَلِّيّونَ \ أَجانِب local/foreign contractors; نِقابة \ اتِّحاد المُقاوِلينَ contractors association/federation 2 [مُتَعَهِّد] entrepreneur

مُقاوَلة *n* 1 [شَرِكة] contracting firm, enterprise; مُقاوَلة البِناءِ \ النَفْطِ construction/oil contracting firm 2 [كَوْن شَخْصٍ مُقاوِلاً] entrepreneurship

مَقول *n* |مَقولات| utterance

مَقولة *n* utterance, saying, quote, words; talk, rumour; مَقولة كاذِبة deceitful words; في مَقولَتِهِ الشَهيرةِ ... in his famous quote ..., as he famously said ...; مَقولة مَشْهورة a well-known saying, a proverb; دَحَضَ المَقولةَ الرَسْمِيّةَ to refute the official story

قَوْلَبَ *v* see قلب

قولون *n* (Anat) colon; سَرَطان القولون colon cancer; (عَمَلِيّة) تَنْظير القولون colonoscopy; القولون العَصَبِيّ irritable bowel syndrome

قامَ *v* |u; قِيام, قَوْمة| 1 [نَهَضَ] to rise, to stand up; قامَ من المَوْتِ \ القَبْرِ to rise from the dead; قامَ من الفِراشِ to get up, to get out of bed; قامَ من مَقْعَدِهِ to get out of one's chair; قامَ مَقامَ شَخْصٍ to fill in for sb 2 [أَدّى |ب|] to perform, to carry out, to undertake, to do; قامَ بِواجِبِهِ to carry out one's duty; قامَ بِزِيارةٍ to pay a visit; قامَ بِدَوْرٍ to play a role; قامَ بِعَمَلِيّةٍ (جِراحِيّةٍ) to perform a (surgical) operation; قامَ بِعَمَلِيّةٍ (عَسْكَرِيّةٍ) to carry out a (military) operation; قامَ بالدِفاعِ عن الوَطَنِ to defend one's country; قامَ بِأَشْغالِ البَيْتِ to do housework; قامَ بِنُزْهةٍ to take a walk 3 [تَأَسَّسَ] to come into being; قامَتْ بَيْنَهُما عَلاقةٌ a relationship developed between them; قامَ على أَنْقاضِ شَيْءٍ to be founded on the ruins of sth, to rise from the ashes of sth 4 [اعْتَمَدَ |على|] قامَ على to be based on sth; قامَ على شَيْءٍ to be based on sth; قامَ على مَبادِئِ الاحْتِرامِ to be based on respect; قامَ على أَساسِ الشَريعةِ الإسْلامِيّةِ to be based on the principles of Islamic law 5 [راقَبَ |على|] to take care of, to look after; قامَ على شَيْءٍ to take care of sth

قَوَّمَ *v* 1 [قَيَّمَ] to evaluate, to assess; قَوَّمَ الوَضْعَ to evaluate the situation; قَوَّمَ النَتائِجَ to assess the results 2 [أَصْلَحَ] to correct, to rectify; to adjust; قَوَّمَ خَطَأً to correct a mistake; قَوَّمَ الوَضْعَ to rectify the situation; قَوَّمَ الخِطَط to adjust the plans

قَيَّمَ *v* to evaluate, to assess, to judge, to value; قَيَّمَ النَتائِجَ to evaluate the results; قَيَّمَ شَخْصاً وَفْقاً لِمَهاراتِهِ التِقْنِيّةِ to judge sb on his technical skills

قاوَمَ *v* to resist, to oppose, to fight; to withstand, to persevere, to endure; قاوَمَ شَخْصاً \ شَيْئاً to resist sb/sth; قاوَمَ الشَرَّ to fight evil; قاوَمَ البَرْدَ to endure the cold; قاوَمَ بِشِدّةٍ to strenuously oppose; قاوَمَ بِكُلِّ قُواهُ to resist with all of one's might; قاوَمَ الإغْراءَ to resist temptation; قاوَمَ العَدُوَّ to hold off the enemy; لا يُقاوَمُ irresistible, unstoppable; رَغْبة لا تُقاوَمُ an irresistible urge

أَقامَ *v* 1 [نَظَّمَ] to organize, to effect, to bring about; أَقامَ حَفْلةً \ احْتِفالاً to throw a party; أَقامَ مُباراةً to organize a tournament; أَقامَ قُدّاساً to hold Mass; أَقامَ حَديثاً to strike up a conversation; أَقامَ دَعْوى على شَخْصٍ to bring a case against sb; أَقامَ الصَلاةَ to perform the prayer; أَقامَ مَأْدُبةً \ حَفْلَ العَشاءِ على شَرَفِ شَخْصٍ to hold a banquet/dinner in sb's honor 2 [أَسَّسَ] to establish, to found; أَقامَ حَواجِزَ \ مَتاريسَ to erect barricades; to place obstacles; أَقامَ مَتْحَفاً to open a museum; أَقامَ عَلاقةً to establish relations 3 [أَثارَ] to agitate, to rouse, to rile up; أَقامَ الدُنْيا وَلَمْ يُقْعِدْها to make a scene

[4] [مَكَثَ] to stay, to remain, to reside; أقامَ في الخارِجِ \ بَلَدٍ آخَرَ \ فُنْدُقٍ to reside abroad/in another country/in a hotel; أقامَ في مَكانٍ to remain somewhere; أقامَ في مُخَيَّمٍ to stay in a camp [5] [أَظْهَرَ] to produce; أقامَ دَليلاً to produce evidence [6] [من المَوْتِ] to resurrect (*said of God*)

تَقَوَّمَ *v* to rectify

اسْتَقامَ *v* to be straight/erect; to straighten up; to be fair/honest, to act correctly; اسْتَقامَ في جَلْسَتِهِ to sit up straight; اسْتَقامَتْ أُمورُهُ to be on the right track; to get on the right track; اسْتَقامَ الطَريقُ the road is straight; هذا الكَلامُ لا يَسْتَقيمُ this statement is not correct

قَوْم *n coll* |no singular noun; أَقْوام| [1] [شَعْب] people; tribe; بَنو قَوْمِهِ one's people [2] [ناس] people; عِلْيَة القَوْمِ the elite, the upper class; قالَ قَوْمٌ إنّ ... some people said that ...; مَصائِبُ قَوْمٍ عند قَوْمٍ فَوائِدُ one man's misery is another man's fortune

قائِم [A] *adj* |قُيّام, قُوّام, قُيَّم| upright, standing; established; قائِم بِذاتِهِ \ بِنَفْسِهِ established; حَقيقة قائِمة بِذاتِها an established fact; زاوِية قائِمة a right angle; النِظام القائِم the establishment; لا يَزالُ قائِماً to be still standing

[B] *n* |قُيّام, قُوّام, قُيَّم| [1] [عَمود] (goal) post; (tent) pole; مَرَّت الكُرةُ قُرْبَ القائِمِ الأَيْمَنِ the ball passed by the right post [2] [مُوَظَّف] قائِم بالأَعْمالِ delegate; القائِم بِأَعْمالِ السَفير ambassador; acting ambassador

قائِمة *n* [1] [لائِحة] |قائِمات, قَوائِمُ| list, record, table; قائِمة انْتِخابِيّة electoral list, ballot; القائِمة السَوْداء the blacklist; وَضَعَ شَخْصاً على القائِمةِ السَوْداءِ to blacklist sb; قائِمة جَرْدٍ inventory; قائِمة طَعامٍ menu; قائِمة المُشْتَرِكينَ \ المُكْتَسَباتِ the list of participants/acquisitions; قائِمة بَريدٍ mailing list; الثالِث على القائِمةِ third up; وَرَدَ (اسْمُهُ) في القائِمةِ to appear on the list; أَعَدَّ قائِمةً to draw up a list; وَضَعَ \ سَجَّلَ اسْمَ شَخْصٍ في القائِمةِ أُدْرِجَ اسْمُهُ ضِمْنَ to put sb on the list; قائِمةِ شَيْءٍ to be included in the list of sth; شَطَبَ اسْمَ شَخْصٍ من القائِمةِ to remove sb from the list, to scratch sb off the list; كانَ على رَأْسِ \ في ذَيْلِ القائِمةِ to be at the top/bottom of the list; احْتَلَّ الأَوَّلِيّةَ على القائِمةِ to occupy the top spot [2] (Comput) |قائِمات, قَوائِمُ| menu; قائِمة مُنْسَدِلة drop-down menu [3] [الحَيَوانِ] |قَوائِمُ| paw; leg; قَوائِم العَنْكَبوتِ spiders' legs [4] [عَمود] |قَوائِمُ| post; leg; قَوائِم الكُرْسيِّ chair legs

قائِمَّقام, قائِمَقام *n* leader, mayor, commissioner

قائِمَقامِيّة *n* (Iraq) *administrative district*

قامة *n* stature, figure, build; كانَ قَصيرَ القامةِ to be of small stature, to be short; كانَ فارِعَ القامةِ to be tall and slender; قامة مَمْشوقة \ طَويلة tall stature; رَجُل ذو قامةٍ نَحيلةٍ a slender man

قَوام *n* figure, build, stature; قَوام فارِع \ رَشيق a tall/slim figure; امْرَأة مَمْشوقة القَوام a slender woman

قَوّام *n* support, one who supports; الرِجالُ قَوّامونَ على النِساءِ men are the protectors and maintainers of women (*Koran 8:67*)

قِوام *n* size, value; foundation, support, pillar; بَلَغَ قِوامُهُ ... to reach a size of ...; قوّات يَبْلُغُ قِوامُها ثَمانِيةَ آلافِ جُنْديٍّ a force numbering eight thousand soldiers; قِطاع يَبْلُغُ قِوامُهُ أَرْبَعةَ مِلْياراتِ دولار a sector worth four billion dollars

قِوامة *n* guardianship, custody

قَوْميّ [A] *adj* state (*before n*), national; nationalist; الأَمْن القَوْميّ national security; السِياسة القَوْمِيّة state politics; الدَوْلة القَوْمِيّة nation state; الدَخْل القَوْميّ national income; الناتِج القَوْميّ (الإجْماليّ) gross national product (*GNP*); حِزْب قَوْميّ nationalist party; عيد قَوْميّ national holiday; على المُسْتَوى القَوْميِّ nationally, on a national level

[B] *n* nationalist; قَوْميّ مُتَطَرِّف ultra-nationalist

قَوْمِيّة *n* nationalism; القَوْمِيّة العَرَبِيّة Arab nationalism

قَويم *adj* straight, upright, righteous; على الطَريقِ القَويمِ on the right path, on the straight and narrow; سُلوك قَويم proper behaviour

قِيام *n* [1] [تَأْدِية] performance, execution, undertaking; القِيام بالواجِباتِ performance of duties; القِيام بِدَوْرٍ playing a role; القِيام بِعَمَلِهِ doing his work, performing his function; نوى \ اعْتَزَمَ القِيامَ بِشَيْءٍ to intend to do sth; ما يَنْبَغي \ يَجِبُ القِيامُ بِهِ what must/should be done; قبل قِيامِ الثَوْرةِ before the revolution took place [2] [تَأْسيس] establishment, founding; قِيام الدَوْلةِ the country's founding [3] [انْطِلاق] (Egypt) residence, address, domicile; مَحَلّ إقامةٍ مُؤَقَّت \ دائِم a temporary/permanent address; بِدونِ مَحَلِّ إقامةٍ ثابِتٍ without a fixed address/permanent residence; (Law) of/with no fixed abode; حَقّ الإقامةِ legal residency; إقامة جَبْرِيّة house arrest; وُضِعَ في الإقامةِ الجَبْرِيّةِ to be under house arrest; فَرَضَ على شَخْصٍ الإقامةَ الجَبْرِيّةَ to place sb under house arrest; رُخْصة \ تَصْريح إقامةٍ residence permit, residence visa (AmE); رُخْصة إقامةٍ دائِمةٍ a permanent residence permit; حَصَلَ على رُخْصةِ إقامةٍ to get a residence permit **2** [تَأْسيس] establishment, founding; erecting; إقامة العَلاقاتِ establishment of relations; إقامة الدَوْلةِ the nation's founding; إقامة حَواجِزَ putting up barriers **3** [تَنْظيم] holding, organizing; إقامة مَعْرِضٍ holding an exhibition **4** [قِيام ب] undertaking, executing; إقامة مَشْروعٍ undertaking a project

تَقْويم *n* |تَقاويمُ| **1** [زَمَنِيّ] calendar, chronology; era; التَقْويم الميلاديّ \ الجْريجوريّ the Gregorian calendar, the Western calendar, the Christian calendar; التَقْويم الهِجْرِيّ the Islamic calendar **2** [تَقْييم] assessment, evaluation; إعادة التَقْويمِ re-evaluation; تَقْويم مَوْضوعِيّ an objective assessment; تَقْويم الأَداءِ performance evaluation; تَقْويم إيجابِيّ للوَضْعِ a positive assessment of the situation; أَجْرى تَقْويماً شامِلاً to conduct a comprehensive evaluation **3** [تَحْسين] reform, improvement, amendment **4** (Med) correcting, straightening; تَقْويم الأَسْنانِ orthodontics; طَبيب تَقْويمٍ orthodontist; جِهاز تَقْويمٍ brace(s); تَقْويم النُطْقِ speech therapy **5** [إنْشاء] establishment

تَقْويمِيّ *adj* evaluative, evaluation (*before n*), estimative; corrective, reformative; orthopedic; اجْتِماع تَقْويمِيّ evaluation meeting

تَقْييم *n* |تَقْييمات| **1** [تَقْدير] valuation, estimation, appraisal; تَقْييم مالِيّ financial assessment; تَقْييم العَقارِ real estate appraisal; إعادة التَقْييمِ revaluation; إعادة تَقْييمٍ للسَهْمِ a revaluation of the stock; أَعادَ تَقْييمَ شَيْءٍ to revaluate sth **2** [تَقْويم] evaluation, assessment; تَقْييم المَشْروعِ evaluation of the project; تَقْييمات المُسْتَخْدِمينَ user ratings; تَقْييم

departure; مَوْعِد قِيامٍ departure date/time **4** [نُهوض] rising, resurrection; قِيام الساعةِ the Apocalypse, Judgement Day

قِيامة *n* resurrection; يَوْم القِيامةِ Judgement Day; قِيامة السَيِّدِ المَسيحِ the resurrection of Christ; قِيامة (من بَعْدِ المَوْتِ) المَوْتى the resurrection of the dead; سورة القِيامة The Rising of the Dead (*Sura 75*)

(Idiom) قامَتْ قِيامَتُهُ to be up in arms, all hell broke loose

قَيِّم **A** *adj* **1** [ثَمين] valuable, expensive, precious; مَعْلومات قَيِّمة valuable information **2** [مُسْتَقيم] honest, sincere
B *n* curator, guardian, custodian

قيمة *n* |قِيَم| **1** [ثَمَن] value, worth; قيمة مُضافة value added, added value; ضَريبة (على) القيمةِ المُضافةِ value added tax, VAT; قيمة اسْمِيّة nominal value; قيمة حَقيقِيّة true/fair value; قيمة آنِيّة current value, actual cash value; قيمة تِجارِيّة \ سوقِيّة market value; إجْماليّ القيمةِ الرَأْسماليّةِ total capital value, market capitalization/cap; قيمة مُقابِلة corresponding value; قيمة زائِدة surplus value; الزِيادة في القيمةِ, قيمة جَوْهَرِيّة intrinsic value; قيمة فَنِّيّة artistic value; انْخِفاض \ هُبوط القيمةِ devaluation; هَدِيّة قيمَتُها مائةُ دولار a gift worth a hundred dollars; عَديم القيمةِ, بِدونِ قيمةٍ worthless; ثابِت القيمةِ stable in value; رَفْع قيمةِ العُمْلةِ (currency) revaluation; انْخَفَضَتْ \ ارْتَفَعَتْ قيمَتُهُ to decrease/increase in value; بَلَغَتْ قيمَتُهُ ..., وَصَلَتْ قيمَتُهُ إلى ... its value has reached ...; حَدَّدَ \ قَدَّرَ قيمةَ شَيْءٍ to determine/estimate the value of sth; ما قيمةُ ذلك؟ how much is that worth?; لا قيمةَ لَهُ it has no value, it is worthless **2** [مَبْدَأ] value, principle; القِيَم الروحِيّة القِيَم moral values; القِيَم الإنْسانِيّة human values; والأَخْلاقِيّة والأَخْلاق values; تَمَسَّكَ بالقِيَمِ to uphold one's values

قيمِيّ *adj* value-based

قَيّوم *n* القَيّوم the Guardian (*one of the names of God*)

اسْتِقامة *n* honesty, integrity, virtue, righteousness; اسْتِقامة خُلُقِيّة \ أَخْلاقِيّة moral integrity; اسْتِقامة سِياسِيّة political righteousness; تُهْمة عَدَمِ الاسْتِقامةِ corruption charges

إقامة *n* **1** [مُكوث] residency, stay; إقامة قَصيرة \ طَويلة a short/long stay; إقامة في الخارِجِ a stay abroad; تَكاليف الإقامةِ accommodation expenses; مَحَلّ إقامةٍ (place of)

شامِل وَمَوْضوعيّ a thorough and objective evaluation; إعادة التَقْييم reassessment, re-evaluation; إعادة تَقْييم للسِياسةِ a reassessment of the policy; أَجْرى تَقْييماً للوَضْعِ to evaluate the situation

تَقْييميّ *n* evaluative; بَحْث تَقْييميّ evaluative study

مُسْتَقيم **A** *adj* 1 [غَيْر مُعْوَجّ] straight, upright; خَطّ \ ظَهْر مُسْتَقيم a straight line/back; مُسْتَقيماً straight ahead 2 [في السُلوكِ] righteous, correct; إِنْسان مُسْتَقيم a righteous person; الصِراط المُسْتَقيم the path of righteousness; ظَلَّ في الطَرِيقِ المُسْتَقيمِ to keep to the straight and narrow **B** *n* |مُسْتَقيمات| (Anat) rectum

مُسْتَقيميّ *adj* rectal; فَحْص مُسْتَقيميّ rectal examination; السَرَطان القولونيّ المُسْتَقيميّ colorectal cancer

مَقام **A** *n* |مَقامات| 1 [مَكانة] place, location; position, rank; قامَ مَقامَ شَيْءٍ to substitute for sth; صاحِب المَقام incumbent; هو عِنْدي في مَقام والِدي he's like a father to me; في المَقام الأَوَّلِ ... in the first place ..., firstly ... 2 [مَدْفَن] shrine, tomb, resting place; مَقام وَليٍّ صالِحٍ \ نَبيٍّ a saint/prophet's shrine 3 (Math) denominator; البَسْط والمَقام the numerator and the denominator; تَوْحيد المَقاماتِ finding the lowest common denominator 4 (Mus) tonality, key, scales; المَقامات الموسيقيّة (العَرَبيّة) maqamat (*the Arab melodic modes*) **B** *adj* being held, ongoing; المَعْرِض المُقام حاليًّا the exhibit currently being held

مُقام *n* 1 [إقامة] stay 2 [مَوْضِع الإقامة] (place of) residence

مَقامة *n* maqama (*literary genre of rhymed prose*)

مُقاوِم **A** *adj* resistant, repellent; فولاذ مُقاوِم للصَدَأ stainless steel; مُقاوِم للحَرارةِ heat-resistant; مُقاوِم للماءِ waterproof; مُقاوِم للأَدْوِيَةِ resistant to medicines; مُقاوِم للإِنْفِلْوَنْزا effective against the flu **B** *n* resistance fighter; adversary; مُقاوِم بَطَل a heroic resistance fighter; مُقاوِم للاحْتِلالِ a fighter resisting the occupation

مُقاوَمة *n* 1 [مُعارَضة] resistance, revolt; opposition, protest; مُقاوَمة عَنيفة \ شَرِسة \ ضارِية violent/strong/fierce resistance; مُقاوَمة مُسَلَّحة armed resistance; عَمَلِيّة المُقاوَمةِ act of resistance; مُقاوَمة (ضِدّ) شَيْءٍ protest against sth; حَرَكة مُقاوَمةٍ resistance movement; تَشْتَدُّ المُقاوَمةُ the opposition is growing; واجَهَ مُقاوَمةً to meet with opposition; قَهَرَ المُقاوَمة to break the resistance 2 (Elec) resistance; مُقاوَمة كَهْرَبائيّة electrical resistance; resistor

مُقاوَميّة *n* (Elec) resistivity

مُقَوِّم *n* |مُقَوِّمات| 1 [مُكَوِّن] component, constituent, element; requirement, necessity; مُقَوِّمات أَساسيّة basic elements; مُقَوِّمات النَجاحِ keys to success; مُقَوِّمات الزَواجِ الناجِحِ what makes a successful marriage; أَدْنى مُقَوِّماتِ العَيْشِ the minimum necessities of life 2 (Gram) constituent 3 (Med) مُقَوِّم الأَسْنانِ orthodontist

مُقيم **A** *adj* 1 [ساكِن] living, residing, resident; مُقيم بِسورِيا residing in Syria 2 [دائِم] permanent, lasting **B** *n* resident

قَوِيَ *v* |a; قُوّة| 1 [اِشْتَدَّ] to increase, to rise; to become strong/powerful; تَقْوى الريحُ the wind is picking up 2 [اِسْتَطاعَ] |على| to be able to, to be capable of; قَوِيَ على شَيْءٍ to be able to do sth; قَوِيَ على تَحَمُّلِ شَيْءٍ to be capable of enduring sth; قَوِيَ على مُواجَهةِ الصِعابِ to be able to face difficulties

قَوّى *v* to raise, to strengthen, to consolidate, to reinforce; قَوّى مَرْكَزَهُ to consolidate one's position; قَوّى عَضَلاتِهِ to strengthen one's muscles; (fig) to flex one's muscles (*in challenge or threat*); قَوّى عَزيمَتَهُ to strengthen one's resolve; قَوّى أَمَلَ شَخْصٍ to raise sb's hope; قَوّى قَلْبَ شَخْصٍ to hearten sb; قَوّى رَأْيَ \ اِعْتِقادَ شَخْصٍ to reinforce sb's opinion/conviction

قاوى *v* to vie/compete in strength

أَقْوى *v* to be/become desolate; to be/become depopulated

تَقَوّى *v* to be/become strong, to harden

اِسْتَقْوى *v* to be strong; to become strengthened

قَوِيّ **A** *adj* |أَقْوِياءُ| [عَكْس ضَعيف] strong, powerful; خَصْم قَوِيّ a strong opponent; بَلَد \ جَيْش قَوِيّ a powerful country/army; ريح قَوِيّة a stiff wind; إرادة \ شُعور قَوِيّ(ة) a strong will/feeling; امْرَأة ذات إرادةٍ قويّةٍ a strong-willed woman; صَوْت قويّ a loud voice; انْفِجار \ فَرْقعة قويّ(ة) a powerful explosion/blast; ضَرْبة قويّة a heavy blow; تَسْديدة قويّة (Sport) a powerful kick/shot; حُجّة قويّة a strong argument; ذاكِرة قويّة a good memory; شَخْصيّة قويّة a forceful personality; مُحرِّك \ مَغْنَطيس قويّ a powerful motor/magnet; مَوْقِف قويّ a strong position; رِسالة قويّة a strongly worded letter; بِلَهْجةٍ قويّةٍ in forceful language; هو قويُّ الجِسْمِ he has a strong build

B *n* القويّ the Strong (*one of the names of God*)

قوّة *n* |قوّات, قُوًى| [1] [جَسَديّة] strength, power; بِقوّةٍ strongly; ضَرَبَ شَخْصاً بِقوّةٍ to hit sb hard; وَقَعَ بِقوّةٍ to come down hard; بالقوّةِ forcibly, by force; قوّة بِنْية physique; قُوًى عَقْليّة intellectual powers; مَنْهوك القوى with no strength left; فَعَلَ شَيْئاً بِكُلِّ قُواهُ to do sth with all one's might; بَدَّدَ قُواهُ to waste one's energies [2] [قُدْرة] strength, power, force; قوّة عَدَديّة numerical strength; قوّة شِرائيّة purchasing power; قوّة الكَلِماتِ the power of words; تَوْزيع القُوى the distribution of power; ميزان \ تَوازُن القُوى the balance of power; اخْتِلال ميزانِ القُوى a deterioration in the balance of power; تكافُؤ \ تفاوُت مَوازينِ القُوى an equal/unequal balance of power; مَوْقِع قوّةٍ position of power; احْتَلَّ مَوْقِعَ قوّةٍ to take up/have a position of power [3] [دَوْلة] power; قوّة نَوَويّة \ ذَرّيّة nuclear/atomic power; قوّة عُظْمى superpower; قوّة اقْتِصاديّة عالَميّة world economic power; قوّة أَجْنَبيّة a foreign power [4] (Math) power [5] (Phys) power; قوّة دافِعة momentum; قوّة مُسَيِّرة driving force; قوّة الجاذِبيّةِ gravity; قوّة طارِدة مَرْكَزيّة, قوّة نابِذة centrifugal force; قوّة مُضادّة \ مُعاكِسة counterforce [6] (Mil) force, troop; قوّات (مُسَلَّحة) (military) forces; قوّات خاصّة elite troops, special forces; قوّات دُوَليّة international (military) forces; قوّات مُتَعَدِّدة الجِنْسيّاتِ multi-national forces; قوّة مُدَرَّعة \ المُدَرَّعاتِ armoured force, (mechanized) cavalry; قوّات مُساعِدة auxiliary troops; قوّات الأُمَمِ المُتَّحِدةِ UN forces; قوّات أَمْنيّة, قوّات الأَمْنِ security forces; قوّات حِفْظِ السَلامِ peacekeeping forces; قوّات جَوّيّة air force; قوّات بَرّيّة army, land forces; قوّات بَحْريّة navy; أَرْسَلَ \ نَشَرَ قوّاتٍ to send/deploy troops; سَحَبَ قوّاتِهِ to withdraw one's troops; وَضَعَ قوّاتٍ to station troops

تَقْوِية *n* strengthening; تَقْوِية العَلاقاتِ \ الأَواصِرِ strengthening relations/ties; تَقْوِية عَضَلاتِهِ strengthening one's muscles

مُقَوٍّ **A** *adj* intensifying, strengthening, stimulating; مادّة مُقَوِّية stimulant; حُقْنة مُقَوِّية (fig) stimulant, shot in the arm (infml); تَأْثير مُقَوٍّ stimulating effect

B *n* |مُقَوِّيات| stimulant; tonic; مُقَوِّيات supplements; مُقَوِّيات جِنْسيّة aphrodisiacs; *treatment for sexual dysfunction*

مُقَوًّى *adj* strengthened, reinforced; وَرَق مُقَوًّى cardboard, paperboard

‹ **قاءَ** *v* |i; قَيْء| to vomit, to throw up

قَيَّأَ *v* to make vomit

تَقَيَّأَ *v* to vomit, to throw up; تَقَيَّأَ دَماً to vomit blood

قَيْء *n* vomit; vomiting; المَيْل إلى القَيْءِ nausea

قُياء *n* vomit; vomiting

تَقَيُّؤ *n* vomiting; شَعَرَ بالتَقَيُّؤِ to feel queasy, to be nauseous

مُقَيِّئ **A** *adj* nauseating, nauseous, sickly; رائِحة مُقَيِّئة a nauseating smell

B *n* |مُقَيِّئات| emetic

‹ **قيثارة, قيثار, قيتارة, قيتار** *n* guitar; harp; عازِف قيثارةٍ guitarist, guitar player; عَزَفَ على القيثارة to play the guitar; مَعْزوفة القيثارة, عَزْف على القيثارةِ guitar-playing

‹ **قاحَ** *v* |i; قَيْح| to fester; to ulcerate

قَيَّحَ *v* to fester; to ulcerate

تَقَيَّحَ *v* to fester; to ulcerate

قَيْح *n* |قُيوح| pus

تَقَيُّح *n* sepsis

مُتَقَيِّح *adj* septic

‹ **قَيَّدَ** *v* [1] [كَبَّلَ] to chain, to bind; to handcuff; قَيَّدَ شَخْصاً to bind/chain/handcuff someone; قَيَّدَ مُعْتَقَلاً to bind/chain/handcuff a detainee [2] [حَصَرَ] to restrict, to curb, to limit; قَيَّدَ حُرّيّةَ شَخْصٍ to restrict sb's freedom [3] [دَوَّنَ] to register, to record, to stipulate, to write down; قَيَّدَ شُروطاً to stipulate conditions **4** (Busn) to record, to enter into the books; قَيَّدَ مَبْلَغاً تحت التكاليفِ to record an amount as expenses

تَقَيَّدَ *v* **1** [اِحْتَرَمَ|ب] to observe, to comply with; تَقَيَّدَ بِقانونٍ \ بِاتِّفاقٍ \ بِشَرْطٍ to observe a law/agreement/regulation **2** [صُفِّدَ] to be bound, to be chained **3** [حُصِرَ] to be/become limited

قيد، قَيْد (NA) *n* قيدَ أُنْمُلةٍ \ شَعْرةٍ a tiny bit; لن يُؤَثِّرَ عَلَيْهِ قيدَ شَعْرةٍ it will have no influence whatsoever on him; لم يَتَزَحْزَحْ قيدَ شَعْرةٍ to not give/budge an inch

قَيْد *n* |قُيود| **1** [غُلّ] chain, shackle; handcuff, cuff; تَخَلَّصَ من قُيودِ العُبوديّةِ to cast off the yoke of slavery; وَضَعَ قُيوداً في يَدَيْ شَخْصٍ to handcuff sb **2** [شَرْط] condition, restriction; قُيود جُمْرُكيّة import/export restrictions; قُيود مَفْروضة على شَيْءٍ restrictions imposed on sth; قُيود على تَصْديرِ سِلَعٍ export restrictions; بدونِ قَيْدٍ أو شَرْطٍ unconditionally; قُيود على الحُرِّيّةِ restrictions of freedom; وَضَعَ \ فَرَضَ قُيوداً على شَخْصٍ to impose restrictions on sb **3** [تَسْجيل] registration; رَقْم القَيْدِ registration number; إخْراج قَيْد (Leb) identity certificate

قَيْدَ *prep* under; على قَيْدِ الحَياةِ alive; على قَيْدِ البَصَرِ in sight; قَيْدَ الاعْتِقالِ \ الحَبْسِ in detention; الأَمْرُ قَيْدَ المُعالَجةِ \ الدَّرْسِ the matter is under consideration; الجِسْرُ قَيْدَ الإنْشاءِ the bridge is under construction; خلال الفَتْرةِ قَيْدَ المُقارَنةِ during the period in question; ما زالَ \ بَقِيَ \ ظَلَّ ... قَيْدَ (على) ... to remain ...., to still be ... (*in a state or condition*); ما زالَ على قَيْدِ الحَياةِ to be still alive, to survive; ما زالَ قَيْدَ الدِّراسةِ \ البَحْثِ to still be under study; ما زالَ قَيْدَ التَّنْفيذِ to still be being implemented

تَقَيُّد *n* |تَقَيُّدات| observation, compliance, adherence; تَقَيُّد صارِم \ تامّ strict/complete compliance; تَقَيُّد بالقانونِ compliance with the law; تَقَيُّد بِإرْشاداتٍ \ بِتَعْليماتٍ following guidelines/teachings; تَقَيُّد صارِم بالنُّصوصِ strict adherence to the text

تَقْييد *n* |تَقاييدُ، تَقْييدات| **1** [تَحْديد] restriction, limitation; تَقْييد حُرِّيّةِ التَّعْبيرِ limiting freedom of speech; تَقْييد حَرَكاتِ شَخْصٍ restricting sb's movements **2** [تَدْوين] registration, entry, enrollment

تَقْييديّ *adj* restrictive, limiting; سِياسة تَقْييديّة a restrictive policy; أَحْكام \ شُروط تَقْييديّة restrictive measures/conditions

مُقَيَّد *adj* **1** [مَحْصور] limited, bounded; bound, handcuffed; تَعَدُّديّة مُقَيَّدة limited pluralism; مُقَيَّد الأَيْدي handcuffed; القَوانين المُقَيِّدة لِلحُرِّيّاتِ freedom-restricting laws; غَيْر مُقَيَّدٍ unlimited; غَيْر مُقَيَّدٍ بِحُدودٍ not bound by borders **2** [مُسَجَّل] registered

مُقَيِّد *adj* restrictive

‹ **قَيْدوم** *n* **1** [رَئيس كُلِّيّةٍ] (Mor) dean **2** [مُقَدِّمة سَفينةٍ] prow, bow **3** [الأَكْبَر سِنّاً] *oldest or most senior member of a group*; قَيْدوم الفَريقِ the most senior member of the team; قَيْدوم الأَسْرى the prisoner who has been imprisoned for the longest

‹ **قير** *n* tar

‹ **قيراط** *n* |قَراريطُ| **1** [وَزْن] carat (*weight measure, approx 0.2 grams*); مُرَصَّع بِعَشَرةِ قَراريطَ من الأَلْماسِ inlaid with 10-carat diamonds **2** [صَفاء] carat (*unit of purity for gold alloys*); الذَّهَب عِيارَ ٢٤ قيراطاً 24-carat gold, 24k gold **3** [مِساحة] qirat (*area measure, approx 175 square metres*) **4** [كَمِّيّة] qirat (*dry measurement, approx 0.06 litres*)

‹ **القَيْرَوان** *n* |f| Kairouan (*city in Tunisia*)

‹ **قاسَ** *v* |i; قَيْس، قِياس| **1** [أَخَذَ قِياسَ شَيْءٍ] to measure, to weigh; قاسَ الطولَ \ العَرْضَ to measure the length/width; قاسَ شَيْئاً بِشَيْءٍ to weigh sth against sth; قاسَ أَداءَ الأَسْهُمِ to track the performance of stocks **2** [جَرَّبَ مَلابِسَ] to try on, to fit; قاسَ سِرْوالاً \ مِعْطَفاً \ حِذاءً to try on a pair of trousers/a coat/shoes

قَيَّسَ *v* to standardize

قايَسَ *v* to compare; قايَسَ شَيْئاً بِشَيْءٍ آخَرَ to compare sth with sth else; قايَسَ بين شَيْئَيْنِ to make comparisons between two things

قَيّاس *n* land surveyor

قِياس *n* |أَقْيِسة، قِياسات| **1** [مِساحة، حَجْم] measurement, dimension, proportion; أَخَذَ قِياسَ شَخْصٍ to take someone's measurements **2** [شَبَه] analogy, relation; قِياساً على شَيْءٍ by analogy with sth; in relation to sth; قِياساً \ بالقِياسِ إلى شَيْءٍ \ شَخْصٍ compared to sth/sb **3** [مِعْيار] measure; قِياس مِعْيارِيّ standard measure; standard size; شَريط قِياسٍ

قَيْصَرِيّ *adj* imperial; tsarist; وِلادة \ عَمَلِيّة قَيْصَرِيّة a caesarean (section), a C-section; روسِيا القَيْصَرِيّة Tsarist Russia

قَيْصَرِيّة *n* ⟦1⟧ [حُكْم] empire, tsardom; القَيْصَرِيّة الروسِيّة the Tsardom of Russia ⟦2⟧ (Med) caesarean

‹ **قَيْصوم** *n* yarrow (*Achillea*); القَيْصوم العِطْرِيّ lavender cotton (*Achillea fragrantissima*)

‹ **قاضَ** *v* |i; قَيْض| ⟦1⟧ [انْكَسَرَ] to break, to crack, to tear; قاضَ الجِدارُ the wall came down ⟦2⟧ [هَدَمَ] see قوض

قَيَّضَ *v* to send (*said of God*); قَيَّضَ اللهُ لَهُمْ حاكِماً عادِلاً God sent them a righteous leader

قايَضَ *v* to exchange; قايَضَ شَخْصاً to exchange with sb; قايَضَ الزَيْتَ بالقَمْحِ to exchange oil for grain

تَقَيَّضَ *v* to break, to crack, to collapse

انْقاضَ *v* to collapse

مُقايَضة *n* exchange, barter; مُقايَضة تِجارِيّة bartering, barter; مُقايَضة الأرْضِ بالسَلام land for peace

‹ **قاظَ** *v* |i; قَيْظ| to be blisteringly hot (*weather*)

قَيْظ *n* |أقْياظ| heat; في قَيْظِ اليَوْمِ in the heat of the day; مَوْجة قَيْظٍ heat wave

قائِظ *adj* scorching; صَيْف قائِظ a scorching hot summer

‹ **قافَ** *v* |u; قَوْف| to follow; قافَ أثَرَ شَخْصٍ to follow in sb's footsteps

قَيَّفَ *v* to follow

اقْتافَ *v* to follow; اقْتافَ أثَرَ شَخْصٍ to follow in sb's footsteps

قائِف *n* |قافة| tracker

قِيافة *n* tracking, pursuit (*of a track*)

‹ **قَيْقَب** *n* maple (tree) (*Acer*)

‹ **قالَ** *v* |i; قَيْل ,قائِلة ,قَيْلولة ,قيل| ⟦1⟧ [نامَ] to (take a) nap ⟦2⟧ [تَفَوَّهَ] see قول

قَيَّلَ *v* to cause to take a midday nap

أقالَ *v* ⟦1⟧ [طَرَدَ] to dismiss, to fire; أقالَ الحُكومةَ \ وَزيراً to dismiss the government/a minister; أقالَ شَخْصاً من مَنْصِبِهِ to remove sb from office/from his job ⟦2⟧ [ألْغى] to cancel, to annul; أقالَ البَيْعَ to cancel the purchase

تَقَيَّلَ *v* to nap

measuring tape; أجْهِزة قِياسٍ دَقيقة \ حَسّاسة precise/sensitive measurement equipment; مِسْطَرة قِياسٍ ruler; تَوْحيد القِياسِ standardization ⟦4⟧ [أخْذ القِياسِ] measurement, measuring ⟦5⟧ (Philos) analogy, syllogism; reasoning; قِياس فاسِد faulty reasoning; a false analogy

قِياسِيّ *adj* ⟦1⟧ [أعْلى رَقْم مُسَجَّل] record (*before n*); رَقْم قِياسِيّ record; بَلَغَ مُعَدَّلاتٍ قِياسِيّةً to reach record levels; وَقْت \ زَمَن قِياسِيّ record time ⟦2⟧ [عِيارِيّ] standard, comparable; مُواصَفات قِياسِيّة standard specifications; حاوِية قِياسِيّة twenty-foot equivalent units, TEU (*standard container measurement*)

تَقْيِيس *n* standardization; تَقْيِيس الاتِّصالات telecommunication standardization

مَقاس *n* |مَقاسات| measurement, size; أخَذَ المَقاساتِ to take the measurements; المَقاس المُناسِب لَهُ one's size (*clothing*); على \ حَسَبَ مَقاسِهِ in one's size, to fit; فَصَّلَ شَيْئاً على مَقاسِ شَخْصٍ to custom fit sth for sb; قانون مُفَصَّل على مَقاسِ شَخْصٍ a law tailored to benefit sb

مِقْياس *n* |مَقاييس| ⟦1⟧ [مِعْيار] standard, criterion, norm; مَقاييس عامّة \ خُلُقِيّة \ إنْسانِيّة common/moral/human standards; مِقْياس شَيْءٍ the norm for sth; مَقاييس حَيَوِيّة biometric specifications; مِقْياس الرَسْمِ scale (*map*); مِقْياس ريخْتِر Richter scale; مِقْياس السُمْكِ calliper rule; مِقْياس الطولِ rule, ruler; على مِقْياسٍ كَبيرٍ on a large scale; المُنَظَّمة الدُوَلِيّة لِتَوْحيدِ المَقاييسِ International Standards Organization, ISO; بِكُلِّ المَقاييسِ in every respect, by any measure; وِفْقاً لِلمَقاييسِ ,حَسَبَ المَقاييسِ according to the standard; هُناكَ مَقاييسُ مَعْمولٌ بِها there are standards in place; وَضَعَ \ طَبَّقَ مَقاييسَ مُعَيَّنةً to apply a fixed standard ⟦2⟧ (Mus) time ⟦3⟧ [آلة] clock, meter, gauge; مِقْياس الحَرارة thermometer; مِقْياس الارْتِفاع altimeter; مِقْياس الضَغْطِ manometer; مِقْياس الفولْت voltmeter; مِقْياس الزَلازِلِ seismograph

‹ **قِيشانِيّ** *n* faience

‹ **قَيْصَر** *n* |قَياصِرُ ,قَياصِرة| emperor; Caesar; tsar; kaiser; عَصْر \ عَهْد القَياصِرة imperial age; أعْطوا ما لِقَيْصَرَ لِقَيْصَرَ وَما للهِ للهِ render unto Caesar the things which are Caesar's, and unto God the things that are God's (*phrase attributed to Jesus in the synoptic gospels*)

resign; طالَبَ بِاسْتِقالةِ شَخْصٍ to ask sb to resign, to demand sb's resignation

إقالة *n* dismissal, firing; إقالة المُدَرِّب the firing of the coach; إقالة الحُكومةِ the dismissal of the government

مُسْتَقيل *adj* outgoing, recently resigned; الحُكومة المُسْتَقيلة the outgoing government

‹ **قوم** see تَقْييميّ ,تَقْييم ,قَيّوم ,قيمة ,قَيِّم ,قيامة ,قِيام ,قَيِّمَ

‹ **قَيْنة** *n* |قِيان| **1** [مُغَنِّية] female singer **2** [أَمة] female slave **3** [ماشِطة] maid

‹ **قَيّوط** *n* coyote, prairie wolf

‹ **أُمّ القَيْوَيْن** *n* |f| (Geog) Umm al-Qaiwain (*one of the United Arab Emirates*)

اسْتَقالَ *v* to resign, to retire, to step down; اسْتَقالَ من مَنْصِبِهِ \ وَظيفَتِهِ to resign from one's post/job; اسْتَقالَ احْتِجاجاً to resign in protest; اسْتَقالَ بعد خَسارةٍ \ فَضيحةٍ to resign following a loss/scandal

قيل *n* see قول

قَيْلولة *n* siesta; أَخَذ قَيْلولةً to (take a) nap, to take a siesta; وَقْت \ فَتْرة \ ساعة القَيْلولةِ midday; *the hottest part of the day*

اسْتِقالة *n* resignation; اسْتِقالة طَوْعيّة voluntary resignation; اسْتِقالة جَماعيّة mass resignation; اسْتِقالة من مَنْصِبِهِ resignation from one's post; قَدَّمَ اسْتِقالَتَهُ to hand in one's resignation; قَبِلَ \ رَفَضَ اسْتِقالةَ شَخْصٍ to accept/refuse to accept sb's resignation; اُضْطُرَّ إلى الاسْتِقالةِ to be forced to

ك prep (such) as, like; يَعْمَلُ كَمُهَنْدِسٍ he works as an engineer; قالَ كالمُعْتَذِرِ ... he said apologetically ...; he said, as an excuse, ...; تَماماً كَ ... exactly like ...; كالعادةِ as usual; كَمِثْلِهِ like him

كَأَنَّما *conj* as if

كَذَلِكَ *adv* see ذا

كَئِبَ *v* |a; كَآبة| to be/become depressed

أَكْأَبَ *v* to depress; to sadden

اكْتَأَبَ *v* to be/become depressed

كَآبة *n* melancholy, depression, gloom; sadness, sorrow; بِكَآبةٍ sadly; مُصاب بالكَآبةِ depressed, dejected; مَشاعِر الكَآبةِ feelings of depression; مَرَض الكَآبةِ depression

كَئِيب *adj* 1 [حَزِين] depressed, dejected, melancholy; في حالةٍ كَئِيبةٍ in a depressed state; انْطِباع كَئِيب a melancholy impression 2 [مُحْزِن] depressing, miserable, dismal; مَنْظَر كَئِيب a depressing sight; بَيْت كَئِيب a dingy house; جَوّ كَئِيب miserable weather

اكْتِئاب *n* |اكْتِئابات| (Psych) depression; اكْتِئاب مُزْمِن chronic depression; اكْتِئاب بعد الوِلادةِ postnatal (BrE) post-partum (AmE) depression; مُضادّ اكْتِئابٍ antidepressant; عانى من الاكْتِئابِ to suffer from depression

مُكْتَئِب *adj* depressed, dejected, melancholy; جَوّ مُكْتَئِب a dejected mood

كاب *n* cap

كاباشينو *n* cappuccino

كابوك *n* (Agric) kapok

كابول *n* |f| Kabul (*the capital of Afghanistan*)

كاتِدْرائِيّة *n* cathedral

كاثود *n* cathode

كاثوليكيّ A *adj* |كاثوليك| (Roman) Catholic; الكَنِيسة الكاثوليكيّة (الرومِيّة) the (Roman) Catholic church; العَقِيدة الكاثوليكيّة the Catholic faith; تَرْبِية كاثوليكيّة a Catholic education
B *n* |كاثوليك| (Roman) Catholic

كاثوليكيّة *n* Catholicism

كَأْداء *n* |dipt f| sadness, grief, distress

كادِر *n* |كَوادِرُ| cadre, staff; كَوادِر مُتَوَسِّطة middle management; كَوادِر حِزْبِيّة party officials

كادْمِيوم *n* cadmium

كاراتيه, كاراتي *n* karate; مارَسَ رِياضةَ الكاراتيه to practise karate

كاراج *n* see كَراج

كارْبراتير *n* carburettor

كارْتِل *n* cartel; إنْشاء كارْتِل formation of a cartel

كارو *n* (NA, Egypt) cart

كارولايْنا الجَنوبِيّة *n* South Carolina (*US state*)

كارولايْنا الشَمالِيّة *n* North Carolina (*US state*)

كاروه *n* |كاروهات| (ذو) كاروهاتٍ \ كاروهٍ chequered

كاري, كَري *n* curry

كاريبِيّ A *adj* Caribbean
B *n* الكاريبِيّ the Caribbean

كاريزْما *n* charisma

كاريزْمِيّ *adj* charismatic

كاريكاتور, كاريكاتير *n* caricature; cartoon; رَسّام الكاريكاتيرِ caricaturist; cartoonist; رَسَمَ كاريكاتيراً to draw a caricature

كاريكاتوريّ, كاريكاتيريّ *adj* caricatural; صورة كاريكاتوريّة caricatural picture

كازاخْستان *n* |f| Kazakhstan

› قازوزة, كازوزة n (Egypt, NA) fizzy drink (BrE), soda (pop) (AmE)

› كازينو n |كازينوهات| ❶ [نادٍ للقِمارِ] casino ❷ [نادٍ لَيْليٌّ] night club

› كَأْس n |mf; كُؤُوس| ❶ [للشُرْبِ] glass; cup; كَأْس من الخَمْرِ \ الماءِ a glass of wine/water; أَفْرَغَ كَأْساً to empty a glass ❷ (Sport) cup; كَأْس أَنْدِيةِ أَبْطالِ الدَوْرِيِّ cup winner; الفائِز بالكَأْسِ national champions cup; كَأْس العالَمِ World Cup; المُنافَسة على كَأْسِ العالَمِ the World Cup competition; فازَ بالكَأْسِ \ بِكَأْسِ العالَمِ to win the cup/World Cup; سَلَّمَ كَأْساً to present a cup

› كاسيت n (music) cassette

› كاجو, كاشو n cashew (nut)

› كاف n |f| name of the letter ك

› كافور n |كَوافِرُ, كَوافيرُ| ❶ [رائِحة] camphor ❷ [شَجَر] eucalyptus (tree) (Eucalyptus)

› كافِيار n caviar

› كافِيين n caffeine

› كاكاو n ❶ [مادّة] cocoa (powder); عُلْبة كاكاو a box of cocoa ❷ [مَشْروب] cocoa, (drinking) chocolate; كاكاو بالحَليبِ (drinking) chocolate, cocoa; فِنْجان من الكاكاو a cup of cocoa; شَرِبَ الكاكاو to drink cocoa

› كاكي n (Bot) kaki, Japanese persimmon (Diospyros kaki)

كاكيّ adj khaki

› كالْسيوم n calcium

› كالّو n |كالوهات| (Med) corn

› كالوري, كالوريه n calorie

› كاليفورْنْيا n California (US state)

› كامة n (Aut) cam

› كامْبودْيا n Cambodia

كامْبوديّ **A** adj Cambodian; الكامْبوديّة (اللُغة) Cambodian (language)
B n Cambodian (person)

› كاميرا n |كاميرات| camera, film camera (BrE), movie camera (AmE); الكاميرا الخَفيّة hidden camera; كاميرا الإنْتَرْنِت \ الويب webcam; تَدورُ الكاميرا the camera is rolling

› الكاميرون n |f| Cameroon

› كَأَنَّ conj see أنن

› كانبَرا n (Geog) Canberra

› كانْتون n ❶ [مُقاطَعة] canton ❷ [مَدينة] |f| Canton (old name for Guangzhou (city in China))

› كانْتين, كَنْتين n canteen (restaurant)

› كانْساس n |f| Kansas (US state)

› كانو n canoe

› كَباريه n cabaret

› كَبَّ v |u; كَبّ| ❶ [جَعَلَ كُبَباً] to wind ❷ [قَلَبَ] to overthrow, to tip over, to upset

كَبَّبَ v ❶ [جَعَلَ كَباباً] to make kebab ❷ [جَعَلَ كُبَباً] to wind into a ball

أَكَبَّ v ❶ [انْقَلَبَ] أَكَبَّ رَأْسَهُ he looked down ❷ [انْكَبَّ |على|] to apply oneself to, to devote oneself to; أَكَبَّ على شَيْءٍ to devote oneself to sth

انْكَبَّ v ❶ [أَقْبَلَ |على|] to apply oneself to, to occupy oneself with; to throw oneself into; انْكَبَّ على شَيْءٍ to throw oneself into sth; انْكَبَّ على القِراءةِ \ الموسيقى to occupy oneself with reading/music ❷ [انْقَلَبَ] to overturn, to topple

كَباب n kebab

كُبّة n |كُبَب| ❶ [لَفيفة خَيْطٍ] ball; كُبّة صوفٍ a ball of wool ❷ [في وَرَقِ اللَعِبِ] hearts ❸ (Culin) meatball

إكْباب n preoccupation; devotion, dedication, perseverance

انْكِباب n dedication, devotion; الانْكِباب على شَيْءٍ \ شَخْصٍ devotion to sth/sb

مَكَبّ n مَكَبّ النُفايات rubbish dump (BrE), garbage dump (AmE); landfill

مُكِبّ adj |على| dedicated, devoted; كانَ مُكِبًّا على المُطالَعةِ he was absorbed in his reading

مِكَبّ n |مَكابّ, مِكَبّات| bobbin, spool, reel

مُنْكَبّ adj |على| dedicated, devoted

› كَبَتَ v |i; كَبْت| to restrain, to suppress, to bottle up; كَبَتَ مَشاعِرَ \ عَواطِفَ to suppress feelings/emotions; كَبَتَ رَغَباتِهِ to suppress one's desires; كَبَتَ حَماسَهُ to restrain one's enthusiasm

كَبْت *n* inhibition, restraint; كَبْت نَفْسيّ mental restraint

كَبّوت، كَبّود *n* |كَبابيتُ| 1▸ [سَيّارة] bonnet (BrE), hood (AmE) 2▸ [واقٍ] condom 3▸ [مِعْطَف] cloak

مَكْبوت *adj* inhibited, restrained, suppressed; غَيْظ مَكْبوت pent-up rage; ضَحْكة مَكْبوتة stifled laughter, titter; غَيْر مَكْبوتٍ uninhibited

كَبَحَ *v* |a; كَبْح| 1▸ [فَرْمَلَ] to stop, to hold up; to brake; كَبَحَ السَّيّارةَ to brake the car 2▸ [قَمَعَ] to curb, to control, to suppress; كَبَحَ تَطَوُّراً to curb progression; كَبَحَ غَيْظَهُ to control one's anger; كَبَحَ لِسانَهُ to hold one's tongue; كَبَحَ جِماحَ المُقاوِمينَ to keep the rebels under control; كَبَحَ حُرِّيّةَ الصِحافةِ to restrict the freedom of the press

كَبْح *n* braking; curbing; restraint, control; مُضاعِف الكَبْح power-assisted brakes; دَوّاسة الكَبْح brake pedal

كابِح *n* |كَوابِحُ| control, restraint; لا كابِحَ لَهُ he cannot be stopped

كابِحة *n* |كَوابِحُ| brake

كَبّاحة *n* brake

كَبْحيّ *adj* brake (*before n*); نِظام مَنْع انْزِلاقٍ كَبْحيّ *anti-lock breaking system (ABS)*

مِكْبَح *n* |مَكابِحُ| brake; مِكْبَح يَدَويّ handbrake; زَيْت المِكْبَح brake fluid

كَبَّدَ *v* to cause; كَبَّدَ شَخْصاً خَسائِرَ كَبيرةً to cause sb great loss

كابَدَ *v* to undergo, to suffer, to endure; كابَدَ الشَوْقَ to harbour desires; كابَدَ الأَلَمَ to endure pain

تَكَبَّدَ *v* to suffer, to undergo, to endure; تَكَبَّدَ هَزيمةً \ خَسارةً to suffer defeat/damage; تَكَبَّدَ جَرْحى to suffer casualties

كَبِد، كَبْد، كِبْد *n* |f; أَكْباد، كُبود| 1▸ (Anat) liver; سَنْدَويتْش كَبِدٍ a liver sandwich; كَبِد الإِوَزِّ goose liver, foie gras; زَيْت كَبِدِ الحوتِ cod liver oil; الْتِهاب الكَبِد hepatitis; مَرَض الكَبِدِ liver disease; أُصيبَ بِمَرَضِ الكَبِد to have liver disease; مَريض بالكَبِدِ liver patient 2▸ [باطِن] interior, inside; مَنْظَر يُفَتِّتُ الأَكْبادَ a heartrending scene 3▸ [وَسَط] center, middle; في كَبِدِ السَماءِ high in the sky

كَبّاد *n* lemon tree (*Citrus limon*)

كُباد *n* hepatosis

كَبِديّ *adj* liver (*before n*); الْتِهاب كَبِديّ hepatitis; تَلَيُّف كَبِديّ cirrhosis

كَبّود *n* |كَبابيدُ| see كَبّوت

كَبَرَ *v* |u; كَبْر| to be older than; يَكْبُرُني أَخي my brother is older than me; كَبَرَ شَخْصاً بِخَمْسِ سَنَواتٍ to be older than sb by five years

كَبُرَ *v* |u; كُبْر، كِبار، كَبارة| to grow, to be/become big; تَكْبُرُ العائِلةُ the family is expanding; كَبُرَ في عَيْني he rose in my opinion

كَبِرَ *v* |a; كِبَر| to outgrow; to grow old/older; كَبِرَ على اللَعِبِ to outgrow playing

كَبَّرَ *v* 1▸ (Islam) *to say* **اللهُ أَكْبَرُ** (*God is great*) 2▸ [صورةً] to make bigger, to enlarge, to magnify; كَبَّرَ صورةً to enlarge a photo

كابَرَ *v* to be stubborn, to be obstinate; كابَرَ في الإِنْكارِ to persistently deny

أَكْبَرَ *v* 1▸ [تَعَجَّبَ] to admire, to regard as formidable 2▸ [بالَغَ] أَكْبَرَ مُشْكِلةً to exaggerate a problem

تَكَبَّرَ *v* |على| to be arrogant, to be haughty; to look down on; تَكَبَّرَ على شَخْصٍ to look down on sb

تَكابَرَ *v* to be haughty, to swagger

اسْتَكْبَرَ *v* 1▸ [تَكَبَّرَ] to be arrogant, to be haughty 2▸ [عَدَّ شَيْئاً كَبيراً] to deem sth important

كَباريه *n* listed alphabetically

كُبْر *n* greatness, grandeur

كِبْر *n* pride, arrogance, conceit

كِبَر *n* 1▸ [السِنّ] (old) age; كِبَر السِنِّ old age 2▸ [ضَخامة] largeness

كِبْرياء *n* |dipt| arrogance, haughtiness, pride

كَبير **A** *adj* |كِبار، كُبَراءُ| 1▸ [الحَجْم] great, big, large; حَجْم كَبير large size; غَرامة \ حِساب كَبير(ة) a hefty fine/bill; مُشاجَرة كَبيرة a huge row; مَبْلَغ كَبير a considerable sum; عَدَد كَبير a large amount; لُقْمة \ جُرْعة كَبيرة a good bite/gulp; خَطَر كَبير a substantial risk; أَغْلَبيّة كَبيرة a large majority; آمال كَبيرة great expectations; العيد الكَبير Eid ul-Kabir (*festival marking the culmination of the annual pilgrimage to Mecca. Also called Eid ul-Adha*) 2▸ [في السِنّ] old; الكِبار والصِغار the old and the young; يَبْدو كَبيراً بالنِسْبةِ لِسِنِّهِ he looks old for his age; أَخي الكَبير my older brother 3▸ [بارِز] eminent, prominent, leading;

a great writer; كاتِب كَبير the leading expert; كَبير الخُبَراءِ senior officials/officers; كِبار المَسْؤولينَ \ الضُبّاطِ المَسْؤولونَ the senior officials, bigwigs الكِبار

B *n* الكَبير the Great (*one of the names of God*)

اِسْتِكْبار *n* arrogance, haughtiness, pride

إكْبار *n* **1** [اِحْتِرام] respect, esteem, regard **2** [إعْجاب] admiration

أكْبَر *adj* |dipt; أكابِرُ, أكْبَرونَ| greater, bigger, larger; older; أخي أكْبَرُ مِنّي بِتِسْعِ سَنَواتٍ my brother is nine years older than me; الاِبْن الأكْبَر the eldest son; ذو أهَمِّيّةٍ كُبْرى of the utmost importance; في كُبْرَياتِ الصُحُفِ in the major newspapers; ثاني أكْبَرِ دِيانةٍ بعد المَسيحيّةِ the second largest religion after Christianity; اللهُ أكْبَرُ God is great; أكابِرُ leading persons; seniors

تَكَبُّر *n* arrogance, haughtiness, pride; vanity; snobbery

تَكْبير *n* |تَكْبيرات| **1** [صورةٍ] enlargement, magnification **2** (Islam) *saying* اللهُ أكْبَرُ (*God is great*)

مُتَكَبِّر **A** *adj* proud, haughty, snobbish; سُلوك \ نَظْرة \ حَرَكة مُتَكَبِّر(ة) a haughty air/look/gesture

B *n* **1** [مُخْتال] snob **2** (Islam) المُتَكَبِّر the Majestic (*one of the names of God*)

مُكابَرة *n* stubbornness, obstinacy

مُكَبَّر *adj* enlarged, magnified; صورة مُكَبَّرة enlarged photo, blow-up

مُكَبِّر **A** *adj* enlarging, magnifying; عَدَسة مُكَبِّرة magnifying glass; نَظّارة مُكَبِّرة binoculars

B *n* |مُكَبِّرات| amplifier; مُكَبِّر صَوْتٍ loudspeaker, speaker

2 **كَبَر** *n* (Bot) capers (*Capparis spinosa*)

‹ **كَبْرَتَ** *v* to vulcanize

كِبْريت *n* **1** (Chem) sulphur; كِبْريت حُرّ pure sulphur; كِبْريت غير مُتَبَلْوِرٍ amorphous sulphur; حَمْض الكِبْريتِ sulphuric acid, vitriol; حَمْض الكِبْريتِ المُخَفَّف \ المُرَكَّز diluted/concentrated sulphuric acid **2** [ثِقاب] match

كِبْريتات *n* sulphate

كِبْريتيّ *adj* sulphuric, sulphur (*before n*); حامِض كِبْريتيّ sulphuric acid

كِبْريتيت *n* sulphite

كِبْريتيد *n* sulphide

‹ **كُبْري** *n* |كَباري| (Egypt) see كوبْري

‹ **كَبَسَ** *v* |i; كَبْس| **1** [ضَغَطَ] to press, to push in; to squeeze; to click (*with a mouse*); كَبَسَ الوَرَقَ to press paper **2** [هَجَمَ] to attack, to raid; كَبَسَت الشُرْطةُ على المَنْزِلِ the police raided the house

كَبَّسَ *v* to massage

كَبْس *n* compression; pressure

كابوس *n* |كَوابيسُ| nightmare; رَأى كابوساً to have a nightmare

كَبّاس *n* |كَبابيسُ| piston

كَبْسة *n* |كَبَسات| **1** [هُجوم مُفاجِئ] surprise attack, raid **2** (Sport) overhead smash **3** [ضَغْط] pushing, pressing; كَبْسة زِرٍّ a press of the button

كَبيس **A** *adj* يَوْم كَبيس leap day, intercalary day; سَنة كَبيسة leap year

B *n* horseradish (*Armoracia rusticana*)

مِكْبَس *n* |مَكابِسُ| piston, plunger; press; (Jordan) stapler

مَكْبوس *adj* compressed, pressed

‹ **كَبْسولة** *n* **1** (Med) capsule; أخَذَ كَبْسولةً to take a capsule **2** (Aerosp) capsule; كَبْسولة فَضاءٍ space capsule

‹ **كَبَشَ** *v* |i; كَبْش| to grasp, to clench; to take a handful of; كَبَشَ شَيْئاً to take a handful of sth

كَبْش *n* |أكْباش, كِباش| **1** (Zool) ram, male sheep; كَبْش الفِداءِ scapegoat; جَعَلَ شَخْصاً كَبْشَ فِداءٍ to make sb a scapegoat **2** [آلة حَرْبيّة] battering ram

كَبْشة *n* |كَبَشات| **1** [مِلْعَقة] serving spoon **2** [مِقْدار] handful

كُبْشة *n* |كُبَش| hook

‹ **كَبْكَبَ** *v* |i; كَبْكَبة| to turn over; to spill

‹ **كَبَّلَ** *v* to chain (up), to shackle, to fetter; كَبَّلَ شَخْصاً to shackle sb; كَبَّلَ يَدَيْ شَخْصٍ to handcuff sb

كابَلَ *v* to put off, to postpone

كَبْل *n* |كُبول| **1** [قَيْد] chain, shackle, fetter **2** [سِلْك سَميك] cable, rope **3** (Elec) wire, cable; كَبْل مُفْرَد القَلْبِ \ مُتَعَدِّد القُلوبِ single-core/multi-core cable

كابِل *n* |كَوابِلُ| [1] [سِلْك سَميك] cable; rope [2] (Elec) wire, cable; كابِل بَحْرِيّ submarine cable

مُكَبَّل *adj* chained, shackled, fettered

كَبا *v* |u; كَبْو, كُبُوّ| to stumble, to trip; to fall

أَكْبى *v* to fail, to miss

كَبْوة *n* |كَبَوات| fall, tumble; لِكُلِّ جَوادٍ كَبْوةٌ ≈ to err is human

كِتابْخانة *n* see كتب

كَتالوج *n* |كَتالوجات| catalogue

كَتَبَ *v* |u; كِتابة| [1] [دَوَّنَ] to write (down); كَتَبَ رِسالةً to write a letter; كَتَبَ شَيْئاً لِشَخْصٍ to write sth to sb; كَتَبَ اسْمَهُ to write (down) one's name; كَتَبَ اسْمَهُ وَعُنْوانَهُ to fill in one's name and address; كَتَبَ (شَيْئاً) على وَرَقة to write (sth) on a piece of paper; كَتَبَ كَلِماته الأَخيرة to write down one's last words; كَتَبَ هذا الكتابَ كاتِبٌ مَشْهورٌ this book is written by a famous writer [2] [قَدَّرَ] to predestine, to preordain, to foreordain; كَتَبَ لِشَخْصٍ شَيْئاً to predestine sb to sth; كُتِبَ عَلَيْهِ ذلك he was predestined to that

كاتَبَ *v* to correspond with, to write to; كاتَبَ شَخْصاً to correspond with sb

أَكْتَبَ *v* to dictate, to make write

تَكاتَبَ *v* to write to each other, to keep up a correspondence

اكْتَتَبَ *v* to subscribe, to register, to put one's name down; اكْتَتَبَ ب \ في \ على أَسْهُم to subscribe for shares

اسْتَكْتَبَ *v* to dictate, to make write; to ask to write; اسْتَكْتَبَ شَخْصاً شَيْئاً to dictate sth to sb

كاتِب [A] *adj* |كاتِبونَ, كُتّاب, كَتَبة| writing; آلة كاتِبة typewriter; تَعَلَّمَ الضَرْبَ على الآلةِ الكاتِبةِ to learn to type
[B] *n* |كُتّاب, كاتِبون, كَتَبة| [1] [أَدبيّ] writer, author; كاتِب كُتُب الأَطْفالِ a writer of children's books; كاتِب رِوائيّ novelist [2] [مُوَظَّف] clerk, writer; كاتِبُ الدَوْلةِ (NA) Minister of State (BrE), Undersecretary of State (AmE); كاتِبُ المَحْضَرِ \ الجَلْسةِ secretary, clerk; كاتِبُ المَحْكَمةِ court clerk; كاتِب سِرٍّ private secretary; كاتِب العَدْلِ notary (public) [3] [من كَتَبَ شَيْئاً] writer

كاتِبة *n* [1] [مُؤَلِّفة] (female) writer [2] [سِكْرِتيرة] (female) secretary

كَتائِبيّ [A] *adj* Phalangist
[B] *n* Phalangist

كُتّاب *n* |كَتاتيبُ| Koranic school

كِتاب *n* |كُتُب| [1] [مَطْبوع] book; كِتاب شَيِّق \ جَيِّد a fascinating/good book; كِتاب رائِج best seller; كِتاب إِلِكْتْرونيّ e-book; كِتاب مَسْموع audio book; كُتُب رَخيصة \ نادِرة \ رائِجة cheap/rare/popular books; كِتاب مَدْرَسيّ \ دِراسيّ school book, textbook; كِتاب أَطْفالٍ children's book; كِتاب طَبْخٍ cookbook, cookery book (BrE); كِتاب مِن \ في ٣٠٠ صَفْحةٍ a three-hundred page book; الكِتاب المُبين, كِتاب اللهِ, الكِتاب الكَريم the Koran; أَهْل الكِتابِ the People of the Book (*Christians and Jews*); الكِتاب المُقَدَّس the Bible; جاءَ في الكِتابِ المُقَدَّسِ to be written in the Bible; تَلا من الكِتابِ المُقَدَّسِ to recite from the Bible; مَعْرِض الكِتابِ book fair; بائِع كُتُبٍ bookseller; دار الكُتُبِ library; *publishing house in Egypt*; رَفّ \ خِزانة كُتُبٍ bookshelf; حَقيبة كُتُبٍ school bag; أَلَّفَ \ كَتَبَ كِتاباً to write a book [2] [رِسالة] letter [3] [عَقْد] contract; deed; كِتاب الزَواجِ \ الطَلاقِ marriage/divorce certificate; كَتَبَ كِتابَهُ to marry; كَتَبَ كِتابَ الزَواجِ to join in matrimony

كِتابة *n* [1] [تَحْرير] (act of) writing; piece of writing, text; كِتابةً in writing; آلة كِتابةٍ typewriter; لَوازِم الكِتابةِ stationary, writing materials; وَرَق الكِتابةِ writing paper; اسْم الكِتابةِ pen name; مَهارة الكِتابةِ writing skill; تَعَلَّمَ الكِتابةَ to learn to write [2] [خَطّ] script; writing system; كِتابة هيروغْليفيّة Egyptian hieroglyphs; كِتابة مِسْماريّة cuneiform script; الكِتابة السيريليّة \ العَرَبيّة Cyrillic/Arabic script [3] [سِكْرِتاريّة] secretariat; عَمِلَ في قِسْمِ الكِتابة to work in the secretariat

كِتابْخانة, كُتُبْخانة *n* library

كِتابيّ *adj* written, in writing; كِتابيًّا in writing; امْتِحان \ تَصْريح كِتابيّ a written exam/statement; خَطَأ \ غَلْطة كِتابيّ(ة) writing error, typing error; لُغة كِتابيّة written language

كُتُبيّ *n* |كُتُبيّة| bookseller, book dealer

كُتُبيّة *n* bookshop (BrE), bookstore (AmE)

كُتَيِّب *n* |كُتَيِّبات| booklet, pamphlet, leaflet

كَتيبة *n* |كَتائِبُ| squadron, battalion, regiment; militia; كَتيبة مُشاةٍ an infantry regiment; كَتيبة انْتِحاريّة suicide squad

اكْتِتاب *n* |اكْتِتابات| registration, enrolment; subscription

مَكْتَب *n* |مَكاتِبُ| ⟨1⟩ [طاوِلة للكِتابةِ] (writing) desk, bureau, secretaire; جلَس \ عمِل على مَكْتَبِهِ to sit/work at one's desk; سَطْح المَكْتَبِ desktop ⟨2⟩ (Admin) office, bureau, department; مَكْتَب فَرْعيّ \ تَمْثيليّ branch (office); مَكْتَب رَئيسيّ head office; في المَكْتَبِ الرَئيسيِّ at the head office; في مَكْتَبِ فُلانٍ at sb's office; كانَ في المَكْتَبِ to be at the office; مَكْتَب اسْتِعْلاماتٍ information bureau, inquiry desk; مَكْتَب مَعْلوماتٍ سِياحيّةٍ tourist information office; مَكْتَب الحالةِ المَدَنيّةِ register office (BrE), county clerk's office (AmE); مَكْتَب بَريدٍ post office; مَكْتَب صِحّةٍ (Egypt) (public) health service ⟨3⟩ [غُرْفة] study; مَكْتَب الإدارةِ boardroom

مَكْتَبة *n* |مَكْتَبات, مَكاتِبُ| ⟨1⟩ [خِزانة كُتُبٍ] bookcase ⟨2⟩ [لاسْتِعارةِ الكُتُبِ] library; مَكْتَبة عُموميّة public library; مَكْتَبة جامِعيّة \ الجامِعةِ university library; أَمين مَكْتَبةٍ librarian; اسْتَعارَ كِتاباً من المَكْتَبةِ to borrow a book from the library; هو مَكْتَبةٌ مُتَنَقِّلةٌ he's a walking encyclopedia ⟨3⟩ [كُتُبيّة] bookshop (BrE), bookstore (AmE)

مَكْتَبيّ *adj* أَدَوات مَكْتَبيّة office supplies, stationery; حاسوب مَكْتَبيّ desktop (computer); حُزْمة مَكْتَبيّة office suite

مَكْتوب ⟨A⟩ *adj* ⟨1⟩ [كِتابيّ] written (down), in writing; مَكْتوب بِخَطِّ اليَدِ handwritten; الصِحافة المَكْتوبة the printed press ⟨2⟩ [مُقَدَّر] destined, foreordained; كانَ مَكْتوباً to be destined ⟨3⟩ [مُدَوَّن] registered, recorded; اتِّفاق غَيْر مَكْتوبٍ unwritten agreement

⟨B⟩ *n* |مَكاتيبُ| [رِسالة] letter; (piece of) writing

‹ **أَكْتَع** *adj* |dipt| *having (partially) paralysed fingers; one-armed*

‹ **كَتَفَ** *v* |u; كَتْف| to tie the hands behind the back

كَتَّفَ *v* to tie the hands behind the back; كَتَّفَ شَخْصاً to tie sb's hands behind his back

تَكَتَّفَ *v* to cross one's arms

تَكاتَفَ *v* to support, to assist, to aid; to rally round, to stand together

كَتِف, كَتْف, كِتْف *n* |mf; أَكْتاف, كِتَفة| (Anat) shoulder; عَظْم الكَتِفِ \ لَوْح الكَتِفِ shoulder blade, scapula; رَبَّتَ على كَتِفِ شَخْصٍ to pat sb on the shoulder; وَضَعَ ذِراعَهُ حول كَتِفِ شَخْصٍ to wrap one's arm around sb's shoulder; هَزَّ كَتِفَيْهِ to shrug one's shoulders; كانَ عَريضَ الكَتِفَيْنِ to be broad-shouldered; حَمَلَ شَخْصاً على كَتِفَيْهِ to carry sb on one's shoulders; يَعْرِفُ \ يَعْلَمُ من أَيْنَ تُؤْكَلُ الكَتِفُ he knows his stuff, he's been around; صَعِدَ على أَكْتافِ شَخْصٍ to make use of sb's influence

كَتّافة *n* shoulder pad

كَتّافيّة *n* epaulette

كَتيفة *n* |كَتائِفُ| pillar; buttress, prop

مَكْتوف *adj* shackled, fettered, chained; وَقَفَ \ ظَلَّ مَكْتوفَ اليَدَيْنِ to stand by helplessly; نَظَرَ مَكْتوفَ اليَدَيْنِ to look on helplessly

‹ **تَكْتيك** *n* listed alphabetically

‹ **كَتْكوت** *n* |كَتاكيتُ| chick

‹ **كَتَّلَ** *v* to ball

تَكَتَّلَ *v* to agglomerate, to conglomerate, to clot

كُتْلة *n* |كُتَل| ⟨1⟩ lump, clod, chunk; mass, bulk; stub; كُتْلة صَخْريّة boulder; massif; كُتْلة تُرابٍ clod; كُتْلة لَزِجة a sticky mass; كُتْلة حَيَويّة biomass ⟨2⟩ (Pol) power block; شَكَّلَ كُتْلةً to form a power block; الكُتْلة الشُيوعيّة the Communist bloc ⟨3⟩ (Meas) mass

تَكَتُّل *n* |تَكَتُّلات| (Pol) formation of a bloc; تَكَتُّل حِزْبيّ party bloc

مُتَكَتِّل *adj* agglomerate, conglomerate, clotted

‹ **كَتَمَ** *v* |u; كَتْم, كِتْمان| to keep secret, to keep quiet; to conceal, to hide, to obscure; to suppress; كَتَمَ شَيْئاً to hush sth up, to keep sth secret; كَتَمَ أَخْباراً to withhold news; كَتَمَ مُشْكِلةً to hide a problem; كَتَمَ أَنَّهُ فَعَلَ شَيْئاً he hid that he had done sth; كَتَمَ حَقائِقَ \ الحَقيقة to obscure facts/the truth

كَتَّمَ *v* to hide, to conceal

كاتَمَ *v* to hide, to conceal, to keep secret

تَكَتَّمَ *v* |على| to keep secret, to keep quiet, to conceal; تَكَتَّمَ على شَيْءٍ to keep sth quiet

اكْتَتَمَ *v* to hide, to conceal; to suppress

اسْتَكْتَمَ *v* to confide; اسْتَكْتَمَ شَخْصاً سِرًّا to confide a secret to sb

كاتِم *n* |كَواتِمُ| *person who conceals sth*; كاتِم الصَوْتِ silencer (BrE), muffler (AmE)

كِتْمان *n* discretion, secrecy; confidentiality; concealment; كِتْمان السِرِّ confidentiality; في طَيِّ الكِتْمانِ under the seal of secrecy; أَبْقى مَوْضوعاً طَيَّ الكِتْمانِ to keep sth secret; اِلْتَزَمَ بِكِتْمانِ السِرِّ to be sworn to secrecy; عالَجَ شَيْئاً بِكِتْمانٍ to treat sth discreetly

كَتوم *adj* |كُتُم| discreet; reticent, taciturn; secretive; غَيْر كَتومٍ indiscreet

كَتيم *adj* compact, dense; impenetrable

تَكَتُّم *n* |تَكَتُّمات| discretion, secrecy

مَكْتوم *adj* hidden, concealed; stifled, smothered; ضَحْكَة مَكْتومة stifled laughter, chuckle

كَتّان *n* flax (*Linum usitatissimum*); linen; كَتّان خام \ غَيْر مُبَيَّضٍ \ أَبْيَض coarse/unbleached/white linen; بِزْر كَتّانٍ flaxseed, linseed; زَيْت الكَتّانِ flaxseed oil, linseed oil; قِطْعَة قُماشٍ من الكَتّانِ a linen cloth

كَتّانيّ *adj* linen (*before n*)

كَثَب *n* nearness, closeness, proximity; عن كَثَبٍ at close quarters, at a short distance

كَثيب *n* |كُثْبان, كُثُب, أَكْثِبة| dune, sandhill

كَثّ, كَثيث *adj* thick, dense (*said of beard or hair*); شَعْر كَثّ thick hair

كَثُرَ *v* |u; كَثْرة| to be many, to be numerous; to increase, to grow

كَثَّرَ *v* to multiply, to increase, to augment; كَثَّرَ اللهُ خَيْرَكَ may God increase your well-being (*expression of gratitude*)

كاثَرَ *v* to outnumber

أَكْثَرَ *v* 1 [كَثَّرَ] to increase, to augment 2 [أَتى بِكَثيرٍ مِنْهُ] to do frequently, to do a lot; أَكْثَرَ من مَدْحِ شَخْصٍ to always speak well of sb; أَكْثَرَ من الصَدَقةِ he does a lot of charity work; يُكْثِرُ الوَلَدُ من الاِبْتِسامِ the boy smiles a lot; أَكْثَرَ الطالِبُ من المُطالَعةِ the student read a lot

تَكَثَّرَ *v* to increase, to grow

تَكاثَرَ *v* 1 [اِزْدادَ] to increase, to multiply; تَكاثَرَ بِسُرْعةٍ \ بِشِدّةٍ to multiply quickly, to proliferate; يَتَكاثَرُ الجُمْهورُ the crowd increases; تَتَكاثَرُ الأَسْئِلةُ more questions arise 2 [تَناسَلَ] to reproduce

اِسْتَكْثَرَ *v* to regard as too much, to deem excessive

كَثْرة *n* abundance; multitude; بِكَثْرةٍ abundantly, lavishly

كَثير *adj* |كِثار, كَثيرونَ| (*with uncountable noun*) much, a lot of; (*with countable noun*) many, a lot of; سُكَّر كَثير much/a lot of sugar; سَيّارات كَثيرة many cars, a lot of cars; (ال)كَثير من ... much, many, a lot of ...; كَثير من النَبيذِ much/a lot of wine; كَثير من الناسِ, أُناس كَثيرونَ many people, a lot of people; قَرَأْتُ الكَثيرَ من الكُتُبِ I've read many books; بِكَثيرٍ much, (by) far; أَحْسَن بِكَثيرٍ \ كَثيراً much better; هو أَحْسَنُ مِنّي بِكَثيرٍ he is much better than me; هذا كَثيرٌ! that is over the top!; كَثيراً very, to a large extent; أَتَأَسَّفُ كَثيراً لِعَدَمِ حُضوري I'm very sorry that I cannot come; أَدْهَشَني كَثيراً ما رَأَيْتُهُ I was very surprised by what I saw; كَثيراً ما often, frequently; كَثيراً ما يَبْكي he cries often

كَوْثَر *n* 1 [اِسْم شَخْصيّ] |f dipt| Kawthar (*female given name*) 2 (Islam) Kawthar (*name of a river in Paradise*); سورة الكَوْثَرِ Abundance (*Sura 108*)

إِكْثار *n* increase, augmentation, growth

أَكْثَر *adj* |dipt| more; most; several; أَكْثَر من نِصْفِ ساعةٍ more than half an hour; أَكْثَر من مَرّةٍ more than once; أَكْثَر من اللازِمِ \ اللُزومِ more than necessary, too much; أَكْثَر فَأَكْثَر more and more; أَكْثَر من, أَكْثَر عَمّا كانَ عَلَيْهِ أَكْثَر تَطَوُّراً more developed; أَكْثَر من أَيِّ وَقْتٍ مَضى more than ever; أَكْثَر الناسِ most of the people; أَكْثَر ما at most; أَكْثَرَ الوَقْتِ (for) most of the time; على الأَكْثَرِ mostly; أَكْثَر ما يُعْجِبُني what pleases me most; النَتيجة الأَكْثَر اِحْتِمالاً the most probable result; الأَكْثَرونَ the majority; ما أَكْثَرَهُمْ! there are so many!

أَكْثَريّة *n* majority, bulk; most; أَكْثَريّة السُكّانِ the majority of the population; في أَكْثَريّةِ الأَحْيانِ most times

تَكاثُر *n* |تَكاثُرات| 1 increase, augmentation; سورة التَكاثُرِ The Piling Up (*Sura 102*) 2 reproduction; تَكاثُر جِنْسيّ \ غَيْر جِنْسيٍّ sexual/asexual reproduction

تَكْثير *n* increase, augmentation, multiplication

كَثُفَ *v* |u; كَثافة| to be thick, to be dense

‹ **كَحَلَ** *v* |a-u; كَحْل| *to make (the eyelids) black with kohl*; كَحَلَتْ عَيْنَيْها she lined her eyes with kohl

كَحَّلَ *v to make (the eyelids) black with kohl*

تَكَحَّلَ *v to make (the eyelids) black with kohl*

اكْتَحَلَ *v to make (the eyelids) black with kohl*

كُحْل *n* kohl (*eyeliner for making the eyelids black*)

كاحِل *n* |كَواحِلُ| ankle; كاحِل مَكْسور a broken ankle; الْتِواء كاحِلٍ a sprained ankle

كَحّال *n* (old use) ophthalmologist, eye doctor

كُحْليّ *adj* dark blue, deep blue

كُحول *n* **1** [شَراب] drink, liquor, alcohol; الكُحول والمُخَدِّرات alcohol and drugs; الإدْمان على الكُحولِ alcoholism; شُرْب \ اسْتِهْلاك الكُحول alcohol consumption; فَحْص نِسْبةِ الكُحول alcohol test; مُدْمِن كُحولٍ alcoholic; خالٍ من الكُحولِ non-alcoholic, alcohol-free **2** (Chem) alcohol (*ethanol*); نِسْبة الكُحول alcohol content; نِسْبة كُحولٍ عالِية \ مُنْخَفِضة a high/low alcohol content; كُحول ميثيلي methylated spirits

كُحوليّ *adj* alcoholic; مَشْروبات كُحوليّة alcoholic beverages, spirits; شَراب كُحوليّ drink, liquor

كَحيل *adj* |كَحائِلُ| black

أَكْحَل *adj* |dipt; كُحْل| **1** [كُحْليّ] made up with kohl (*eyes*) **2** [أَسْوَد] (Tunisia) black

مُكَحَّلة *n* hyacinth (*Hyacinthus orientalis*)

‹ **كَدَحَ** *v* |a; كَدْح| to toil, to labour; كَدَحَ كَدْحاً to sweat blood; كَدَحَ طولَ حَياتِهِ to toil one's life away

كادِح **A** *adj* hard-working, diligent **B** *n* (manual) labourer

‹ **كَدَّ** *v* |u; كَدّ| **1** [اجْتَهَدَ] to toil, to labour; كَدَّ في العَمَلِ to work one's fingers to the bone **2** [أَتْعَبَ] to fatigue, to exhaust, to wear out

كادّ *adj* hard-working, industrious

كَدّ *n* effort, exertion

مَكْدود *adj* overworked, overtired, exhausted

‹ **كَدِرَ** *v* |a; كَدَر| to be/become troubled/turbid

كَثَّفَ *v* **1** [جَعَلَهُ كَثيفاً] to condense, to concentrate, to thicken; كَثَّفَ الحَليبَ to condense milk **2** [كَثَّرَ] to intensify, to increase; كَثَّفَ زِياراتِهِ to increase one's visits

تَكَثَّفَ *v* to condense, to thicken; to become concentrated

تَكاثَفَ *v* to condense, to thicken; to become concentrated; تَكاثَفَ الضَبابُ \ السَحابُ the fog/clouds thickened

كَثافة *n* density, thickness; consistency; كَثافة سُكّانيّة population density; كَثافة سُكّانيّة كَبيرة \ عالِية \ مُتَزايِدة a large/high/increasing population density; كَثافة نَوْعيّة relative density; كَثافة مادّةٍ \ غازٍ concentration of a substance/gas; كَثافة الاسْتِخْدام intensity of use; خَفَّفَ كَثافةَ الدَمِ to lower blood viscosity

كَثيف *adj* |كِثاف| **1** [غَليظ] thick, dense; نَبات كَثيف lush vegetation; لِحْية \ شارِب كَثيف(ة) a thick beard/moustache; ضَباب \ سَحاب كَثيف thick fog/clouds; سائِل كَثيف a thick liquid **2** [قَويّ] intensive; لِقاءات كَثيفة frequent encounters; مُراقَبة كَثيفة intensive surveillance; حُضور كَثيف large attendance

تَكاثُف *n* condensation

تَكَثُّف *n* (Chem) concentration

تَكْثيف *n* condensation; intensification; ناتِج التَكْثيفِ condensate

مُتَكاثِف *adj* concentrated; thick, dense

مُكَثَّف *adj* **1** [مُرَكَّز] intensive; تَدْريب \ مُراقَبة \ مُشاوَرات مُكَثَّف(ة) intensive training/control/consultations; اتِّصالات مُكَثَّفة close contacts; تَرْبية الماشِية المُكَثَّفة intensive cattle breeding **2** [مُتَكاثِف] concentrated; حَليب مُكَثَّف evaporated milk

مُكَثِّف *n* |مُكَثِّفات| capacitor, condenser

‹ **تَكَثْلَكَ** *v* to become (a) Catholic

‹ **كجم** *abbr* kg, kilogram

‹ **كَحَتَ** *v* |a; كَحْت| to scrape (off), to scratch off; كَحَتَ الدِهانَ to strip (off) paint

كَحْت *n* curettage

‹ **كَحَّ** *v* |u; كُحّة| to cough

كُحّة *n* cough

تَكاذَبَ *v* to lie to each other

كَذِب *n* lie, falsehood, untruth; جِهاز كَشْفِ الكَذِبِ polygraph, lie detector

كِذْب *n* lie, untruth, falsehood; inaccuracy; حَبْلُ الكِذْبِ قَصيرٌ a lie never lives to be old; كِذْبٌ في كِذْبٍ lie after lie

كاذِب **A** *adj* false, untrue; fake, sham; قِصّة كاذِبة a false story; حَمْل كاذِب phantom pregnancy; شَهادة كاذِبة false testimony; بَيانات كاذِبة incorrect data; مَظْهَر كاذِب disguise; أَمَل كاذِب false hope; إِنْذار كاذِب false alarm
B *n* liar

كَذّاب *n* liar

كِذْبة *n* lie; كِذْبة بَيْضاء a white lie

كَذوب *n* liar

أَكْذَب *adj* |dipt| falser, more untruthful

أُكْذوبة *n* |أَكاذيبُ| lie; أُكْذوبة أَبْريلَ \ نَيْسانَ April Fool's joke; حَكى أُكْذوبة كَبيرة a big lie; هذه كُلُّها أَكاذيبُ! it's all lies!; اخْتَلَقَ \ افْتَعَلَ أُكْذوبةً to fabricate a lie أَكاذيبَ to tell lies;

تَكْذيب *n* denial; contradiction

‹ **كَراتْشي** *n* |f| Karachi (*largest city in Pakistan*)

‹ **كَراج, كاراج** *n* |كَراجات| garage

‹ **كَرار** *n* |كَرارات| pantry, larder

‹ **كُرافَت, كُرافات** *n* |كُرافَتات| tie, cravat

‹ **كَراوْيا** *n* see كَرَوْيا

‹ **كَرَبَ** *v* |u; كَرْب| **1** [اشْتَدَّ] to sadden, to grief, to afflict **2** [كادَ] كَرَبَ أَنْ يَفْعَلَ شَيْئاً to almost do sth

أَكْرَبَ *v* to run

اكْتَرَبَ *v* to be dejected, to be down, to be worried; اكْتَرَبَ لِشَيْءٍ to be worried about sth

كَرْب *n* |كُروب| grief, distress, sorrow; أَزالَ الكَرْبَ to cheer up

كُرْبة *n* |كُرَب| concern, worry, anxiety; grief

مَكْروب *adj* dejected, depressed

مِكْروب *n* see ميكروب

‹ **كُرْباج** *n* |كَرابيجُ| (riding) whip; lash; ضَرَبَ شَخْصاً بالكُرْباجِ to whip sb

‹ **كِرْباس** *n a cotton fabric*

كَدَّرَ *v* to trouble, to disturb; كَدَّرَ عَيْشَ شَخْصٍ to disturb sb's life

تَكَدَّرَ *v* to be/become troubled; تَكَدَّرَ عَيْشُهُ he had many troubles

كَدَر *n* |أَكْدار| annoyance; trouble, problem

كَدِر *adj* **1** [غَيْر صافٍ] turbid, muddy, roily; ماء كَدِر muddy water **2** [صَعْب] troubled; حَياتُهُ كَدِرةٌ he lives a troubled life

كَدَرة *n* ooze, mud

كُدْرة *n* muddiness, turbidity

تَكْدير *n* **1** [إِخْلال] disturbing, disturbance, troubling; تَكْدير الأَمْنِ العامِّ disturbing the public safety **2** [تَحْقير] affront, provocation, offence

مُتَكَدِّر *adj* vexed, annoyed, irritated

مُكَدَّر *adj* restless, upset, troubled

‹ **كَدَسَ** *v* |i; كَدْس| to pile up, to accumulate

كَدَّسَ *v* to pile up, to accumulate; to press together

تَكَدَّسَ *v* to pile up, to accumulate; to stack; to be piled up

كُدْس *n* |أَكْداس| pile, heap, stack

كُدّاس *n* haystack; pile of straw

تَكَدُّس *n* |تَكَدُّسات| pile-up, build-up, accumulation

تَكْديس *n* |تَكْديسات| accumulation; stacking, piling up

مُتَكَدِّس *adj* cumulative, accumulative; stacked

مُكَدَّس *adj* piled up, stacked, heaped up

‹ **كَديش** *n* |كُدْش| (Zool) carthorse

‹ **كَدَمَ** *v* |i-u; كَدْم| to bruise, to cause a bruise

كَدْم *n* |كُدوم| bruise, contusion; كَدْم في ساقِهِ a bruise on one's leg

كَدْمة *n* |كَدَمات| bruise, contusion

‹ **أَكْدى** *v* to skimp, to stint, to cut back

كُدْية *n* |كُدًى| begging, mendicancy

‹ **كَذا** *adv* see ذا

‹ **كَذَبَ** *v* |i; كَذِب, كِذْب| to lie (to); كَذَبَ عن ماضيه to lie about one's past; كَذَبَ على شَخْصٍ to lie to sb

كَذَّبَ *v* **1** [أَنْكَرَ] to deny, to refute; كَذَّبَ كَلامَ شَخْصٍ to refute sb's words; كَذَّبَ شائِعةً to refute a rumour **2** [اتَّهَمَ بالكَذِبِ] to call a liar

أَكْذَبَ *v* to call a liar, to refute

مُكْتَرِث *adj* |ل ,ب| attentive; مُكْتَرِث بِشَيْءٍ attentive to sth; غَيْر مُكْتَرِثٍ indifferent, uninterested

‹ **كَرَخانة** *n* |كَراخينُ| (ME) factory, workshop; brothel, whorehouse

‹ **كُرْديّ** **A** *adj* |أَكْراد ,كُرْد| Kurdish; (اللُغة) الكُرْديّة Kurdish (*language*)

B *n* |أَكْراد ,كُرْد| Kurd (*person*)

الكُرْد *n* the Kurds

‹ **كُرْدِسْتان** *n* |f| Kurdistan; كُرْدِسْتان العِراقِ *Kurdish region in North Iraq*

كُرْدِسْتانيّ *adj* Kurdish, Kurdistan (*before n*)

‹ **كُرْدون** *n* cordon; كُرْدون الشُرْطةِ police cordon

‹ **كَرْدينال ,كارْدينال** *n* |كَرادِلة| (Relig) cardinal

‹ **كَرَّ** *v* |u; كَرّ| **1** [هَجَمَ] to attack; كَرَّ على شَخْصٍ to attack sb **2** [تَراجَعَ] to withdraw, to retreat

كَرَّرَ *v* **1** [أَعادَ] to repeat, to do again, to redo; كَرَّرَ قَوْلَ شَخْصٍ to repeat what sb says; كَرَّرَ جُمْلةً to repeat a sentence; كَرَّرَ سَنةً دِراسيّةً to repeat a (school) year **2** [صَفّى] to refine; كَرَّرَ النَفْطَ to refine oil; كَرَّرَ السُكَّرَ to refine sugar

تَكَرَّرَ *v* **1** [حَدَثَ مَرّةً بعد الأُخْرى] to repeat (itself), to be repeated, to recur **2** [تَمَّتْ تَصْفِيَتُهُ] to be refined

كَرّ *n* attack, offensive, charge; على كَرِّ الزَمَنِ over the course of time; بين الكَرِّ والفَرِّ in fits and starts; دَرَسَ بِكَرٍّ to study hard

كَرّة *n* **1** [هُجوم] attack **2** [مَرّة] (one) time; كَرّةً بعد كَرّةٍ time after time; كَرّةً أُخْرى some other time; once more; أَعادَ الكَرّةَ to try one more time

كُرور *n* succession, sequence

كَرير *n* (Med) croup

تَكْرار *n* repetition, reiteration; مِراراً وتَكْراراً ,تَكْراراً repeatedly, time and again

تَكْراريّ *adj* repeated, frequent; frequency (*before n*); repetitious; حَرَكة \ دَوْرة تَكْراريّة repeated movement/cycle; جَدْوَل تَكْراريّ frequency table

تَكَرُّر *n* recurrence, repetition; frequency

تَكْرير *n* |تَكْريرات| **1** [إعادة] repetition, reiteration **2** [تَنْقِية] refining; مَعْمَل تَكْريرٍ refinery

‹ **كَرْبَلاء** *n* |dipt f| Karbala (*city in Iraq*)

‹ **كَرْبَنَ** *v* |i; كَرْبَنة| to char, to carbonize

مُكَرْبِن *n* carburettor

‹ **كَرْبون** *n* carbon; وَرَقة كَرْبون a (sheet of) carbon paper; أَوَّل أوكْسيدِ الكَرْبون carbon monoxide; ثاني أوكْسيدِ الكَرْبون carbon dioxide, carbonic acid gas; التَأْريخ بالكَرْبون المُشِعِّ carbon dating, radiocarbon dating

كَرْبونيّ *adj* carbon (*before n*); نُسْخة كَرْبونيّة carbon copy

‹ **كَرْبوهيدْرات** *n* carbohydrate; غَنيّ بالكَرْبوهيدْراتِ high in carbohydrates

‹ **كَرْتون** *n* |كَراتينُ| cardboard, paperboard

كَرْتونة *n* carton, cardboard box

كَرْتونيّ *adj* cardboard (*before n*)

‹ **كَرَثَ** *v* |u; كَرْث| to distress, to trouble; كَرَثَهُ الحُزْنُ على مَوْتِ اِبْنِهِ he was torn with grief over the death of his son

أَكْرَثَ *v* to distress

اكْتَرَثَ *v* |ل ,ب| to care (for), to be concerned (about); to pay attention (to); اكْتَرَثَ ل \ بِمَصيرِ شَخْصٍ to be concerned about sb's fate; اكْتَرَثَ ل \ بالنَتيجةِ to be concerned about the result; لم يَكْتَرِثْ بِشَيْءٍ \ بِشَخْصٍ not to care about sth/sb; اكْتَرَثَ ل \ بِشَيْءٍ to take sth to heart; لا تَكْتَرِثْ للأَمْرِ! don't take it too hard!

كارِث *adj* disastrous, catastrophic

كارِثة *n* |كَوارِثُ| disaster, catastrophe, calamity; كارِثة بيئيّة environmental disaster; كارِثة طَبيعيّة natural disaster; كارِثة نَفْطيّة oil spill; كارِثة مائيّة flood; مِنْطَقة الكَوارِثِ disaster area; كارِثة مَحْتومة an inevitable disaster; عام الكَوارِثِ year of disasters; كارِثة رَهيبة \ كُبْرى a major catastrophe; تَفادى \ تَجَنَّبَ وُقوعَ كارِثةٍ to avert a catastrophe; تَقَعُ \ تَحْدُثُ كارِثةٌ a calamity occurs

كارِثيّ *adj* disastrous, catastrophic; عَواقِب كارِثيّة disastrous consequences

كُرّاث ,كَرّاث *n* leek (*Allium*); كُرّاث أَنْدَلُسيّ shallot, scallion (AmE)

اكْتِراث *n* care, concern, attention; عَدَم الاكْتِراثِ lack of interest; قِلّة الاكْتِراثِ indifference; عَمِلَ بِدونِ اكْتِراثٍ to go about things in a careless manner

‹ **كَرِشَ** *v* |a; كَرَش| to be wrinkled

تَكَرَّشَ *v* to be wrinkled

كِرْش *n* |أكْراش, كُروش| ◀1 [(الإِنْسانِ)] (pot) belly, paunch; قد صارَ لَهُ كِرْشٌ he grew a pot belly; كِرْش كَبِير a big belly ◀2 [(المُجْتَرِّ)] rumen

أَكْرَش *adj* |dipt; كُرْش; f كَرْشاءُ; f pl كَرْشاوات, كُرْش| pot-bellied, paunchy

‹ **كَرَعَ** *v* |a; كَرْع| to sip; to slurp

تَكَرَّعَ *v* ◀1 [تَجَشَّأَ] to burp, to belch ◀2 [غَسَلَ أَكارِعَهُ] *to perform the partial ablution of one's lower legs (for prayer)*

كُراع *n* |أَكارِعُ, أَكْرُع| paw; foot; (lower) leg

تَكَرُّع *n* |تَكَرُّعات| burp, belch

‹ **كَرَفان, كَرَفانة** *n* |كَرَفانات| caravan, mobile home

‹ **كَرَفْس** *n* celery (*Apium graveolens dulce*); celeriac (*Apium graveolens rapaceum*)

1‹ **كُرْكِيّ** *n* |كَراكِيّ| (common) crane (*Grus grus*); سَمَك الكَراكِيّ pike (*Esox lucius*)

2‹ **كَرّاكة** *n* ◀1 [جِهاز لِتَعْمِيق المِياهِ] dredge, dredger ◀2 [عَصا بِخُطّافٍ] grappling hook, drag

‹ **كَرْكار** *n* limestone

‹ **كَرْكَبَ** *v* |i; كَرْكَبة| to clutter, to jumble; to confuse, to disturb

‹ **كَرْكَدَنّ** *n* rhinoceros (*Rhinocerotidae*); كَرْكَدَنّ بَحْرِيّ \ البَحْرِ narwhal (*Monodon monoceros*)

‹ **كَرْكَدِيه, كَرْكَدِية** *n* ◀1 (Bot) hibiscus (*Hibiscus*) ◀2 [شَراب] karkadeh (*infusion made of a variety of hibiscus*)

‹ **كَرْكَرَ** *v* |i; كَرْكَرة| كَرْكَرَ في الضَحِكِ to roar with laughter

‹ **كُرْكُم** *n Curcuma*; turmeric; كُرْكُم طَوِيل turmeric (*Curcuma longa*)

‹ **كَرْكَنْد** *n* lobster (*Homarus*)

‹ **كَرْكُوك** *n* |dipt f| Kirkuk (*city in Iraq*)

‹ **كَرُمَ** *v* |u; كَرامة, كَرَم| to be generous, to be noble, to be magnanimous

كَرَّمَ *v* to honour, to revere, to venerate; كَرَّمَ شَخْصاً to honour sb; كَرَّمَ ذِكْرى شَخْصٍ to honour sb's memory; كَرَّمَ اللهُ وَجْهَهُ *may God bless him*

كارَمَ *v* to treat generously

مُتَكَرِّر *adj* repeated, frequent; بِطَلَبٍ مُتَكَرِّرٍ by frequent request; بعد تَحْذِيراتٍ مُتَكَرِّرةٍ after repeated warnings

مُكَرَّر *adj* repeated, reiterated; bis (*as a direction in a musical score, indicating that a section is to be repeated*)

‹ **كَرْز** *n* preaching, evangelization

كَرَز *n* cherry (*Prunus avium*); قَطَفَ كَرَزاً to pick cherries; شَجَرة الكَرَزِ cherry tree

كارِز *n* preacher

‹ **كَرَّسَ** *v* ◀1 [خَصَّصَ] to devote, to dedicate; كَرَّسَ وَقْتَهُ ل ... to devote one's time to ...; كَرَّسَ اهْتِمامَهُ لِشَيْءٍ \ لِشَخْصٍ to devote one's attention to sth/sb; كَرَّسَ جُهْدَهُ من أَجْلِ شَيْءٍ \ شَخْصٍ to devote one's effort to sth/sb; كَرَّسَ نَفْسَهُ لأُسْرَتِهِ to be devoted to one's family; تُكَرِّسُ هذه الجَرِيدةُ صَفْحةً كامِلةً للبِيئةِ this newspaper devotes an entire page to the environment; كَرَّسَ حَياتَهُ للدِفاعِ عن الوَطَنِ to devote one's life to defending one's country ◀2 [قَدَّسَ] to consecrate, to dedicate ◀3 [أَسَّسَ] to lay the foundation

تَكَرَّسَ *v* to be devoted, to be dedicated; to be consecrated

كُرّاسة *n* |كُرّاسات, كَرارِيس| notebook, exercise book

كُرْسِيّ *n* |كَراسِيُّ, كَراسٍ| ◀1 [مَقْعَد] chair, seat; الكُرْسِيّ الكَهْرَبائِيّ the electric chair; كُرْسِيّ هَزّاز \ مُتَأَرْجِح rocking chair; كُرْسِيّ المُقْعَدِينَ \ مُتَحَرِّك wheelchair, invalid chair; كُرْسِيّ دائِر swivel chair; كُرْسِيّ مَقْذوف ejection seat; كُرْسِيّ مُصْحَفٍ *reading table (and chair) for the Koran*; آية الكُرْسِيّ the Throne Verse (*Koran*) ◀2 [حامِلة] pedestal, base ◀3 (Educ) chair, professorate, professorship; كُرْسِيّ الأَدَبِ العَرَبِيِّ the chair in Arabic literature; أُسْتاذ كُرْسِيّ professor ◀4 (Gram) seat; كُرْسِيّ الهَمْزةِ seat of the hamza ◀5 (Tech) bearing; كُرْسِيّ التَحْمِيلِ bearing

(Idiom) ذات الكُرْسِيّ Cassiopeia (*constellation*)

كَرّوسة *n* (Transp) carriage, coach

تَكْرِيس *n* devotion, dedication; consecration

مُكَرَّس *adj* devoted, dedicated; consecrated

‹ **كُرْسوع** *n* |كَراسِيعُ| *the carpal end of the ulnar bone*

‹ **كِرْسِنّة** *n* (Bot) vetch (*Vicia*)

أَكْرَمَ *v* to honour; أَكْرَمَ والِدَيْه he honoured his parents

تَكَرَّمَ *v* [1] [تَلَطَّفَ] to be so kind (*as to do sth*); أَرْجو أَنْ تَتَكَرَّمَ وَتُغْلِقَ الشُبّاكَ would you be so kind as to close the window; تَكَرَّمَ بالرَدِّ to be kind enough to answer [2] [أَعْطى] to present; تَكَرَّمَ على شَخْصٍ بِشَيْءٍ to present sb with sth

كَرْم *n* |كُروم| [1] [عِنَب] (wine) grape; زِراعة الكَرْمِ viniculture [2] [نَبات] vine, grapevine [3] [مَكان زِراعةِ الكَرْمِ] vineyard; باعَ كَرْمَهُ واشْتَرى مَعْصَرةً (*to sell one's vineyard and buy a press*); ≈ to kill the goose that lays the golden eggs

كَرَم *n* [1] [قِرى] hospitality; تَعْبيراً عن شُكْرِنا على حُسْنِ كَرَمِكَ an expression of our gratitude for your hospitality [2] [سَخاء] generosity, magnanimity; كَرَم الأَخْلاقِ noble-mindedness

كَرّام *n* winegrower

كَرامة *n* [1] [شَرَف] dignity, worth; إهانةً \ اِعْتَبَرَ شَيْئاً انْتِهاكاً لِكَرامَتِهِ to think sth beneath one's dignity; حِفظ كَرامَتَهُ to preserve one's dignity; لا كَرامةَ لِنَبيٍّ بين قَوْمِهِ a prophet is not without honour, save in his own country [2] [مُعْجِزة] miracle (*worked by a marabout*); صاحِب كَراماتٍ miracle worker

كَرْمة *n* vine, grapevine; كَرْمة عَذْراء grapevine

كَريم [A] *adj* |كِرام, كُرَماءُ| [1] [نَبيل] noble; حَجَر كَريم a precious stone; عائِلة \ أَصْل كَريم(ة) a noble family/descent; رَجُل كَريم a noble man; حِصان كَريم a thoroughbred; القُرّاء الكِرام the esteemed readers; القُرْآن الكَريم the Holy Koran; مَرَّ على شَيْءٍ مُرورَ الكِرامِ to generously overlook sth [2] [مِعْطاء] generous, magnanimous, hospitable
[B] *n* [1] (Islam) الكَريم the Bountiful (*one of the names of God*) [2] [اسْم شَخْصيّ] Karim (*male given name*)

كَريمة *n* |كَرائِمُ| |dipt| [1] [بِنْت] daughter [2] [اسْم شَخْصيّ] Karima (*female given name*) [3] [شَيْء نَفيس] precious object

إِكْرام *n* honour, homage; إِكْراماً لِ ... in honour of ...; إِكْراماً لِهَذا الفَنّانِ الكَبيرِ in honour of this great artist; إِكْرام لِشَخْصٍ an homage to sb

إِكْرامِيّة *n* tip, gratuity; أَعْطى إِكْرامِيّةً to leave a tip; أَخَذ إِكْرامِيّةً to get a tip; إِكْرامِيّة بَسيطة a modest tip; إِكْرامِيّة كَبيرة a large tip

تَكْريم *n* honouring, homage, tribute; تَكْريم الأَبْطالِ الرِياضيّينَ the tribute to the champions; حَفْلة تَكْريمٍ لِشَخْصٍ a party in honour of sb; شَمَلَ كُلَّ الأَعْضاءِ بالتَكْريمِ he thanked all the members

تَكْريميّ *adj* honouring, in honour of; اِحْتِفال تَكْريميّ a honouring party

مُكَرَّم *adj* respectable, venerable; مَكّة المُكَرَّمة *common name for Mecca*

مَكْرُمة *n* good deed

‹ **كَرْما** *n* karma

‹ **كَرَمِلاً** *n* caramel

‹ **كَرَنْب, كُرُنْب** *n* cabbage; كُرُنْب ساقيّ kohlrabi; كُرُنْب سافوي savoy (cabbage); كُرُنْب بْروكْسِل (Brussels) sprout; كُرُنْب مُحَمَّض sauerkraut; مَحْشوّ كُرُنْبٍ stuffed cabbage leaves

كَرْنيب *n* gourd, calabash

‹ **كَرْنَفال** *n* carnival

‹ **كُرْنيش** *n* see كورْنيش

‹ **كَرُهَ** *v* |u; كَراهة| to be offensive, to be nasty, to be loathsome; to be loathsome

كَرِهَ *v* |a; كَراهيّة, كَراهة, كُرْه| to hate, to loathe, to detest; كَرِهَ شَيْئاً \ شَخْصاً to hate sth/sb

كَرَّهَ *v* to arouse aversion

أَكْرَهَ *v* |على| to force (to), to compel (to), to oblige (to); أَكْرَهَ شَخْصاً على شَيْءٍ to force sb to (do) sth

تَكَرَّهَ *v* to have an aversion to, to loathe, to detest

اِسْتَكْرَهَ *v* [1] [وَجَدَهُ كَريهاً] to find nasty, to find loathsome [2] [أَجْبَرَ] to force, to compel, to oblige; اِسْتَكْرَهَ شَخْصاً على (فِعْلِ) شَيْءٍ to force sb to (do) sth

كُرْه *n* hatred, disgust; aversion; كُرْهاً, (مِنْهُ) على كُرْهٍ under duress; unwillingly; فَعَلَ شَيْئاً على كُرْهٍ مِنْهُ to do sth reluctantly; كُرْهاً بِ ... out of hatred for ...; كَرِهَ شَيْئاً كُرْهاً أَعْمى to hate sth deeply; طَوْعاً أو كَرْهاً willingly or unwillingly

كارِه *adj* averse; abhorrent; كارِهاً unwillingly; قُلْتُ كارِهاً: ... I said with distaste: ...; راضِياً أو كارِهاً willingly or unwillingly;

يَجِبُ أنْ تَقومَ بِواجِباتِكَ المَدْرَسِيّةِ طائِعاً أو كارِهاً you have to do your homework, willingly or not

كاروه *n* listed alphabetically

كَراهة *n* hatred, dislike

كَراهِية *n* hatred, disgust; aversion; كَراهِية عَميقة \ مُتَأَصِّلة a deep hatred; كَراهِية عَمْياء blind hate; كَراهِية عُنْصُرِيّة racial hatred, racism; كَراهِية الأَجانِب hatred of foreigners, xenophobia; كَراهِية بين الفَريقَيْن hatred between the two groups; كَراهِية ل \ تِجاهَ شَخْصٍ \ شَيْءٍ hatred for/towards sb/sth; مَشاعِر كَراهِيةٍ feelings of hatred; على كَراهِيةٍ with regret

كَريه *adj* nasty, unpleasant, offensive; مَذاق \ طَعْم كَريه a nasty taste; رائِحة كَريهة an unpleasant smell

إكْراه *n* pressure, compulsion, coercion; إكْراه بَدَنيّ imprisonment (*for debt or contempt*); إكْراه جِنْسيّ sexual assault; سَرِقة بالإكْراهِ robbery; لا إكْراهَ في الدين there's no compulsion in religion; بالإكْراهِ by force

مُكْرَه *adj* involuntary, forced; مُكْرَهٌ أخاكَ لا بَطَلَ *forced by circumstances, rather than led by courage*

مَكْروه **A** *adj* **1** [كَريه] hated, detested **2** (Isl Law) condemnable, reprehensible

B *n* |مَكْروهات| discomfort, inconvenience; adversity; دون أنْ يَنالَهُم مَكْروهٌ without them experiencing adversity; نَزَلَ بِه مَكْروهٌ he faced adversity

‹ **كُرة** *n* |كُرات, كُرًى| **1** [جِسْم كُرَويّ] ball; globe, sphere; كُرة أرْضيّة (terrestrial) globe; نِصْف الكُرة الأَرْضيّةِ hemisphere; نِصْف الكُرةِ الأَرْضيّةِ الشَمالِيّ \ الجَنوبِيّ the Northern/Southern Hemisphere; كُرة زُجاجيّة \ بِلَّوْريّة a crystal ball; كُرة القَدَمِ football (BrE), soccer (AmE); football (BrE), soccer ball (AmE); دَوْرِيّ كُرةِ القَدَمِ football (BrE) soccer (AmE) league; كُرة الطاوِلةِ table tennis; لَعِبَ كُرةَ الطاوِلةِ to play table tennis; كُرة اليَدِ handball; الكُرة الطائِرة volleyball; لَعِبَ الكُرةَ الطائِرةَ to play volleyball; كُرة المِضْرَبِ tennis; كُرة القاعِدةِ baseball; الكُرة الحَديديّة shot-put; كُرة الماءِ water polo; رَمْي الكُرةِ boules; مَرَّرَ الكُرةَ to pass the ball (on); انْقَضَّ على كُرةٍ to dive for a ball **2** (Geom) sphere

كُرَويّ *adj* round, spherical; الأَرْض كُرَوِيّةٌ the earth is round

كُرَوِيّة *n* roundness, sphericity

كُرَيّة *n* **1** [جِسْم كُرَويّ] globule; pellet; bubble **2** (Anat) كُرَيّة دَمَوِيّة (blood) corpuscle; كُرَيّات حَمْراء \ بَيْضاء red/white corpuscles

‹ **كُرْواتي** **A** *adj* Croatian; (اللُغة) الكُرْواتيّة Croatian (*language*) **B** *n* Croatian (*person*)

‹ **كُرُواتيا** *n* Croatia

‹ **كُرْواسان** *n* croissant

‹ **كَرَوان** *n* |كِرْوان, كَراوينُ| كَرَوان الماءِ whimbrel (*Numenius phaeopus*); curlew (*Numenius*)

‹ **كَرْوان سَراي** *n* caravanserai; caravan

‹ **كُرْوشيه** *n* crochet; من نَسيجِ الكُروشيه crocheted

‹ **كْرُوكيت** *n* croquette

‹ **كْروم** *n* chromium, chrome

‹ **كْرُوموسْفير** *n* chromosphere

‹ **كُروموسوم, كْرُوموزوم** *n* |كْرُوموسومات| chromosome

‹ **كْرُون, كْرُونا** *n* (Fin) crown

‹ **كْرُونولوجيّ** *adj* chronological

‹ **كَراوْيا, كَرَوْيا** *n* caraway (*Carum carvi*)

‹ **كَرِيَ** *v* |a; كَرًى| to sleep, to be asleep

كارى *v* to let (out), to rent (out), to hire out; كارى شَخْصاً شَيْئاً to hire out sth to sb

أَكْرى *v* to let (out), to rent (out), to hire out

اكْتَرى *v* to hire, to rent; to hire, to employ; اكْتَرى سَيّارةً to rent a car

كِراء *n* hire, rent, hiring

كَرًى *n* sleep

مُسْتَكْرٍ *n* renter, tenant

مُكارٍ *n* donkey driver

مُكْتَرٍ *n* renter, tenant

مُكْرٍ *n* lessor, landlord

‹ **كْريب فْرُوْت** *n* grapefruit

‹ **كْريت, كِريد** *n* |f| Crete

مَكْسَب *n* |مَكاسِبُ| profit, gain; مَكْسَب كَبير a large profit; مَكْسَب مالِيّ \ عادَ عَلَيْهِ بالمَكْسَب he made a profit on it; أَدَبِيّ financial/moral gain; مَكْسَب سِياسِيّ \ اِنْتِخابِيّ political/ electoral gain

مُكْسِب *adj* profitable, remunerative, lucrative; عَمَل مُكْسِب a lucrative job

‹ **كُسْبَرة** *n* see كُزْبَرة

‹ **كُسْتُلِيتة** *n* cutlet, chop

‹ **كَسْتَناء** , **كَسْتَنة** *n* chestnut (tree) (*Castanea*); ثَمَرة الكَسْتَناءِ chestnut

كَسْتَنائِيّ *adj* chestnut (*before n*), auburn

‹ **كَسَحَ** *v* |a; كَسْح| ❶ [كنس] to sweep; كَسَحَ البَيْتَ to sweep the house ❷ [أَذْهَبَ] to wipe out, to sweep away

كَسِحَ *v* |a; كَسَح| to be crippled, to limp

اكْتَسَحَ *v* to wipe out, to sweep away; to overflow, to flood; اِكْتَسَحَ قَرْيَةً to sweep away a village; اِكْتَسَحَ العَدُوَّ to wipe out the enemy; يَكْتَسِحُ الإِعْصارُ المِنْطَقة the tornado sweeps the area

كاسِح *adj* overwhelming, crushing; غالِبِيّة كاسِحة an overwhelming majority; فَوْز كاسِح a sweeping victory

كاسِحة *n* dredger; كاسِحة جَليد icebreaker; كاسِحة أَلْغام minesweeper

كُساح *n* rickets

كَسِيح *adj* |كُسْحان| lame; paralysed

اكْتِساح *n* wipeout; flooding, overflowing

أَكْسَح *adj* |dipt; f كَسْحاءُ| كُسْح, كُسْحان| lame; paralysed

مِكْسَحة *n* broom

‹ **كَسَدَ** *v* |u; كُسود, كَساد| to sell poorly, to be unmerchantable; to stagnate, to halt

كاسِد *adj* stagnant, slack, dull; سوق كاسِدة a stagnant market; مَوْسِم كاسِد a slack season

كَساد *n* depression, recession, stagnation; كَساد التِجارة slump in trade; كَساد اقْتِصادِيّ economic recession

‹ **كَسَرَ** *v* |i; كَسْر| ❶ [حَطَّمَ] to break (open), to break in pieces, to force (open); كَسَرَ كَأْساً to break a glass; كَسَرَ رِجْلَيْهِ

‹ **كْرِيسْتال** *n* crystal; شاشة من الكْرِيسْتال السائِلِ liquid crystal display, LCD

‹ **كْرِيفون** *n* grapefruit

‹ **كْرِيكِت** *n* (Sport) لُعْبة الكْرِيكِت cricket

‹ **كْرِيم** *n* |mf| cream; كْرِيم الأَساسِ foundation; كْرِيم الحِلاقةِ shaving cream; دَهَنَ الكْرِيم to apply a cream

كْرِيمة *n* (Culin) cream

‹ **كُزْبَرة** , **كُسْبَرة** *n* coriander (*Coriandrum sativum*); كُزْبَرة خَضْراء chervil (*Anthriscus cerefolium*)

‹ **كَزَّ** *v* |u; كُزوزة, كَزازة| ❶ [تَقَلَّصَ] to shrivel, to wither, to dry out ❷ [بَخُلَ] to be miserly ❸ [كُزَّ أُصيبَ بالكُزاز] to get tetanus

كَزَز *n* miserliness, stinginess

كَزّ *adj* |كُزّ| ❶ [يابِس] dry, withered; rigid, stiff ❷ [بَخيل] miserly, stingy

كُزّاز , **كُزاز** *n* tetanus

‹ **كَسَبَ** *v* |i; كَسْب| to win, to gain, to acquire; to earn; كَسَبَ ٣٠٠٠ أورو صافِياً في الشَهْرِ to earn 3,000 euros net per month; يَكْسِبُ جَيِّداً لدى تِلْكَ الشَرِكةِ he earns good money with that company; كَسَبَ رِزْقَهُ to support oneself, to earn a living; كَسَبَ وُدَّ \ حُبَّ شَخْصٍ to win sb's sympathy/love; كَسَبَ نُفوذاً \ سُلْطةً to acquire influence/authority

كَسَّبَ *v* to yield, to pay; هذه الوَظيفةُ تُكَسِّبُ جَيِّداً that job pays well; كَسَّبَ شَخْصاً مالاً كَبيراً to yield sb a lot of money

أَكْسَبَ *v* to impart, to grant, to confer

تَكَسَّبَ *v* to make a living, to live; تَكَسَّبَ من الغِناءِ والرَقْصِ to make a living from singing and dancing

اكْتَسَبَ *v* to acquire, to obtain, to gain; اكْتَسَبَ مَهاراتٍ to acquire skills; اكْتَسَبَ الخِبْرةَ \ مَعْرِفةً to gain experience/ knowledge; اكْتَسَبَ حَقًّا to earn a right

كَسْب *n* profit, gain; earnings; كَسْب ثَلاثِ نُقَطٍ \ مَقاعِدَ a gain of three points/seats; كَسْب مَشْروع legal earnings

اكْتِساب *n* acquisition, obtaining, procurement; اكْتِساب قِطْعةِ أَرْضٍ the acquisition of a piece of land; اكْتِساب الشُهْرةِ \ المَعْرِفةِ the acquisition of fame/knowledge

مُكْتَسَب *adj* acquired, learned; سُلوك مُكْتَسَب learned behaviour; خِبْرة \ حَقّ مُكْتَسَب(ة) acquired expertise/right to break one's legs; كَسَرَ مَعْنَوِيّاتِ شَخْصٍ to break sb's morale; كَسَرَ الصَّمْتَ to break the silence; كَسَرَ حِصاراً to break an embargo; كَسَرَ التَّقاليدَ to break with tradition; كَسَرَ قُفْلاً to force open a lock; كَسَرَ حاجِزَ الخَوْفِ to dispel fear; كَسَرَ قَلْبَ شَخْصٍ to break sb's heart ② (Gram) to provide with a kasra (*the vowel 'i'*)

كَسَّرَ *v* to break (into pieces), to destroy; to shatter, to crush; كَسَّرَ زُجاجاً to shatter glass; كَسَّرَ اللَّوْزَ \ الجَوْزَ to crack almonds/nuts

تَكَسَّرَ *v* to be broken (in pieces); to break; تَتَكَسَّرُ الأَمْواجُ على الشاطِئِ waves are breaking on the shore

انْكَسَرَ *v* to break (down), to break apart; to be refracted; انْكَسَرَت الكَأْسُ the glass broke; يَنْكَسِرُ السَّدُّ the levy is bursting; يَنْكَسِرُ الضَّوْءُ the light is being refracted; انْكَسَرَتْ ساقُهُ he broke his leg; انْكَسَرَ قَلْبي my heart is broken

كَسْر *n* ① [عَظْمٍ \ شَيْءٍ] |كُسور| fracture, break; كَسْر خَطير a serious fracture; كَسْر مُضاعَف a compound fracture; كَسْر مُزْدَوِج \ مُتَعَدِّد a double/multiple fracture; كَسْر في الساقِ broken leg; أُصيبَ بِكَسْرٍ to suffer a fracture; نُقْطة الكَسْرِ breaking point; قابِل لِلكَسْرِ breakable, fragile; أَدَوات \ بَضائِع قابِلة لِلكَسْرِ breakables ② (Math) |كُسورات، كُسور| fraction; كَسْر بَسيط simple fraction

كاسِر *adj* breaking; طَيْر كاسِر bird of prey; كَواسِر الطَّيْرِ birds of prey

كَسّارة *n* ① [آلة] pulverizer; كَسّارة جَوْزٍ (pair of) nutcrackers ② (Sport) shin guard

كَسْرة *n* |كَسَرات| ① (Gram) kasra (*the short vowel 'i'*) ② [هَزيمة] defeat

كِسْرة *n* |كِسَرا، كِسْرات| fragment, (small) piece, splinter; crumb; كِسْرة من الخُبْزِ a crumb of bread

كَسْرِيّ *adj* (Math) fractional; عَدَد كَسْرِيّ fraction

كَسير *adj* |كَسْرى، كَسارى| broken, fractured

انْكِسار *n* ① [تَحَطُّم] fracture, break; سُهولة الانْكِسارِ fragility; خَطّ الانْكِسارِ line of fracture ② (Phys) refraction; انْكِسار الضَّوْءِ في الماءِ the refraction of light in water

تَكْسير *n* breaking, fracturing; جَمْع التَّكْسيرِ (Gram) broken plural

مُتَكَسِّر *adj* broken, fractured

مُكَسَّر *adj* broken; جَمْع مُكَسَّر (Gram) broken plural; بِعَرَبِيّةٍ مُكَسَّرةٍ in broken Arabic

مُكَسَّرات *n pl* mixed nuts

مَكْسور *adj* broken; كَأْس مَكْسور الحافةِ a chipped glass

مُنْكَسِر *adj* broken, defeated

‹ **كَسَرولة** *n* casserole

‹ **كَسَعَ** *v* |a; كَسْع| to kick in the rear; to chase away; كَسَعَ ذَنَبَهُ to put its tail between its legs (*dog*)

‹ **كَسَفَ** *v* |i; كُسوف| to darken, to become dark; to eclipse; كَسَفَت الشَّمْسُ there was a solar eclipse

انْكَسَفَ *v* to darken, to become dark

كاسِف *adj* dark, gloomy; sad, downcast; يَوْم كاسِف a black day

كُسوف *n* (solar) eclipse; كُسوف الشَّمْسِ eclipse of the sun; كُسوف جُزْئِيّ a partial eclipse of the sun; كُسوف كامِل \ تامّ \ كُلِّيّ a total eclipse of the sun

‹ **كُسْكُس، كُسْكُسي، كُسْكُسو** *n* couscous

كَسْكاس *n* |كَساكِس| couscoussier (*couscous cooker*)

‹ **كَسِلَ** *v* |a; كَسَل| to be lazy; to laze/hang around

تَكاسَلَ *v* to be idle, to laze (around)

كَسَل *n* laziness, idleness

كَسِل *adj* lazy, idle

كَسْلان Ⓐ *adj* |dipt; كَسالى، كُسالى، كَسْلى| lazy, idle Ⓑ *n* |dipt; كَسالى، كُسالى، كَسْلى| (Zool) sloth; دُبّ كَسْلان sloth

كَسول Ⓐ *adj* lazy, idle Ⓑ *n* lazybones, sluggard

تَكاسُل *n* laziness, idleness

مُتَكاسِل *adj* lazy, idle

‹ **كَسَمَ** *v* |i; كَسْم| to make a living

كَسَّمَ *v* to fashion clothing, to make clothes

كَسْم *n* cut, style, tailoring

مُكَسَّم *adj* shapely, well-shaped

‹ **كَسا** *v* |u; كَسْو| ① [أَلْبَسَ] to put on clothes, to dress; كَسا شَخْصاً ثَوْباً to put a robe on sb ② [غَطّى] to cover

كَسِيَ *v* |a; كَسًا| to be/get dressed

كَسَى *v* ① [أَلْبَسَ] to dress ② [غَطَّى] to cover

أَكْسَى *v* to dress, to clothe, to garb

اكْتَسَى *v* to dress, to clothe, to garb

كِساء *n* |أَكْسِية| (article of) clothing, garment, garb

كُسْوة, كِسْوة *n* |كُسًى, كِسًى, كَساوٍ| ① [لِباس] clothing, garment ② (Islam) kiswah (*the cloth that covers the Kaaba*); الكِسْوة المُشَرَّفة kiswah

تَكْسِية *n* panelling, wainscoting

مَكْسوّ *adj* dressed, clothed

كُشّة *n* a lock of hair

كُشْتُبان, كُشْتِبان *n* |كَشاتِبينُ| thimble; زَهْر الكَشاتِبينِ foxglove (*Digitalis*)

كَشَحَ *v* |a; كَشْح| ① [فَرَّقَ] to disperse, to scatter, to chase away ② [بِعَداوةٍ] to harbour; كَشَحَ لِشَخْصٍ بالعَداوةِ to harbour enmity toward sb

كَشْح *n* |كُشوح| side, flank

كَشَّرَ *v* to make faces, to grimace; كَشَّرَ وَجْهَهُ to make faces; كَشَّرَ الأَسَدُ عن أَسْنانِهِ \ أَنْيابِهِ the lion bared its fangs

كُشَري *n* (Egypt) *a dish made of lentils, rice and macaroni*

تَكْشيرة *n* grimace

كَشَطَ *v* |i; كَشْط| ① [حَكَّ] to scratch (off), to scrape (off), to chafe; كَشَطَ الطِلاءَ من الحائطِ to scrape paint off the wall ② [مَحا] to cross off, to remove, to delete; كَشَطَ التِلْميذُ كَلِماتٍ كَثيرةً the student deleted a lot of words

انْكَشَطَ *v* to be chafed, to be scraped

كَشْط *n* ① [جُرْح] chafing, scrape; أُصيبَ بِكَشْطٍ to get a scrape ② (Med) curettage

كاشِط *adj* abrasive

مِكْشَط *n* |مَكاشِطُ| scraper

مِكْشَطة *n* |مَكاشِطُ| scraper

كَشَفَ *v* |i; كَشْف| ① [أَظْهَرَ] to reveal, to disclose, to uncover; to lay open, to lay bare; to betray, to give away; to solve; كَشَفَ عن شَيْءٍ to bring sth to light; كَشَفَ أنّ ... to reveal that ...; لم يُكْشَفْ شَيْءٌ عن مَضْمونِ الاتِّفاقِ nothing has been revealed about the contents of the agreement; كَشَفَ عن خُطّةٍ \ سِرٍّ (عن سِرٍّ) كَشَفَ النِقابَ to divulge a secret/plan; كَشَفَ عن مَكْنونِ صَدْرِهِ to uncover (a secret); to unburden oneself; كَشَفَ عن أُسُسٍ قَديمةٍ لِمَعْبَدٍ to lay bare the old foundation of a temple; كَشَفَ عن مَقابِرَ جَماعيّةٍ to uncover mass graves; كَشَفَ أَسْرارَ الكَوْنِ to solve the mysteries of the universe; كَشَفَ نَفْسَهُ to give oneself away; كَشَفَ عن الحَقيقةِ to find out the truth; كَشَفَ الغِطاءَ عن شَخْصٍ to tell the truth about sb; كَشَفَ شَيْئاً \ شَخْصاً على حَقيقَتِهِ to expose sth/sb ② [فَحَصَ] to examine, to investigate; كَشَفَ على مَريضٍ to examine a patient

كاشَفَ *v* to reveal, to disclose, to divulge; كاشَفَ شَخْصاً بِأَمْرٍ to reveal sth to sb

تَكَشَّفَ *v* to be revealed, to be uncovered; to come to light

انْكَشَفَ *v* to be revealed, to be uncovered; to come to light; انْكَشَفَ الأَمْرُ the matter was revealed

اكْتَشَفَ *v* to discover, to find out, to detect; اكْتَشَفَ شَيْئاً to discover sth; اكْتَشَفَ أنّ ... to find out that ...; اكْتَشَفَ خَطأً في نَصٍّ to detect an error in a text

اسْتَكْشَفَ *v* to explore, to investigate; to discover; اسْتَكْشَفَ الطَريقَ \ المِنْطَقةَ to explore the route/terrain; لم يَسْتَكْشِفْ بَعْدُ unexplored; اسْتَكْشَفَ إِمْكانيّةً to explore a possibility

كَشْف *n* |كُشوف| ① [بَيان] overview, summary; list, register, inventory; كَشْف حِسابٍ bank statement; كَشْف بِأَسْماءِ الطُلّابِ a list of students' names ② [مَصْدَر] revelation, disclosure, divulgence; الكَشْف عن تِمْثالٍ \ نُصْبٍ تِذْكاريٍّ the unveiling of a statue/monument ③ (Med) examination, investigation; كَشْف طِبّيّ medical examination

كاشِف **A** *adj* ضَوْء كاشِف torch (BrE), flashlight (AmE) **B** *n* |كَشَفة| detector; كاشِف المَعادِنِ metal detector

كَشّاف *n* |كَشّافة| ① [في حَرَكةٍ كَشْفيّةٍ] Scout; رَئيس كَشّافةٍ Scoutmaster, Scout leader ② [جِهاز] floodlight; كَشّاف ضَوْئيّ torch (BrE), flashlight (AmE); floodlight ③ (Mil) scout

كِشافة, كَشّافة *n* scouting

كَشْفيّة *n* scouting, scout movement/association

اسْتِكْشاف *n* |اسْتِكْشافات| reconnaissance, scouting, exploration; خَرَجَ للاسْتِكْشافِ to go out scouting

السُجونُ مُكْتَظّةٌ an overpopulated area; مِنْطَقة مُكْتَظّة بالسُكّانِ بالسُجَناءِ the prisons are overcrowded

‹ **كَظَمَ** *v* |i; كُظُوم ,كَظْم| to control (oneself), to restrain, to suppress; كَظَمَ غَيْظَهُ to control one's anger; كَظَمَ ضَحْكةً \ ابْتِسامةً to suppress a laugh/smile

كَظيم *adj* angry; irritated, agitated

كَظيمة *n* vacuum flask, Thermos®

مَكْظوم *adj* suppressed, restrained

‹ **كَعَّبَ** *v* to raise to the third power, to cube

كَعْب *n* |كُعوب ,كِعاب| ❶ [عَظْم الكاحِلِ] ankle ❷ [عَقِب] heel ❸ [حِذاء] heel; حِذاء بِكَعْبٍ عالٍ high-heel shoes

كاعِب *adj* |كَواعِبُ| with full breasts, well-formed (*girl*)

الكَعْبة *n* Kaaba (*sanctuary in Mecca*); الكَعْبة المُشَرَّفة the Holy Kaaba

تَكْعيبيّ *adj* cubist

تَكْعيبيّة *n* cubism

مُكَعَّب **A** *adj* cubic; مِتْر مُكَعَّب من الماءِ \ الغازِ \ الأَرْضِ a cubic metre of water/gas/soil

B *n* |مُكَعَّبات| ❶ (*Math*) cube, third power ❷ (*Geom*) cube ❸ [كُتْلة] block, chunk, lump; عُلْبة من المُكَعَّباتِ box of (building) blocks; مُكَعَّب سُكَّرٍ lump of sugar, sugar cube; مُكَعَّب مَرَقةٍ stock cube

‹ **كُعْبُرِيّ** *adj* الشِرْيان الكُعْبُرِيّ radial artery

‹ **كَعْك** *n coll* cake; pie, pastry; الكَعْكة الصَفْراء yellowcake (*uranium*); خَبَزَ كَعْكةً to bake a cake

‹ **كَعَمَ** *v* |a; كَعْم| to muzzle (*a camel*)

‹ **كغ** *abbr* kg, kilogram

‹ **كَفَأَ** *v* |a; كَفْء| ❶ [قَلَبَ] to tip over, to turn over ❷ [انْصَرَفَ] to turn away, to turn aside; كَفَأَ عن شَخصٍ \ شَيْءٍ to turn away from sb/sth

كافَأَ *v* ❶ [جازى] to reward, to repay, to recompense; كافَأَ شَخْصاً على شَيْءٍ to reward sb for sth; كافَأَ شَخْصاً بِمَبْلَغٍ ماليٍّ to reward sb with a sum of money; كافَأَ شَخْصاً بِسَخاءٍ to reward sb handsomely ❷ [ساوى] to equal, to be equal, to be similar; كافَأَ شَخْصاً في الرُتْبة to rank equal with sb

أَكْفَأَ *v* to turn over, to capsize

اسْتِكْشافيّ *adj* explorative, reconnaissance (*before n*); رِحْلة اسْتِكْشافيّة explorative expedition; reconnaissance flight; طائِرة اسْتِكْشافيّة reconnaissance plane

اكْتِشاف *n* |اكْتِشافات| discovery, find; اكْتِشاف مُذْهِل \ مُدْهِش a startling/surprising discovery; اكْتِشاف أَمْريكا the discovery of America; مَكان اكْتِشافِ (شَيْءٍ) site of (sth's) discovery

انْكِشاف *n* revelation, disclosure

مُكاشَفة *n* frankness, openness; confession, revelation; مُكاشَفة الشَعْبِ بالحَقيقةِ telling the people the truth

مُكْتَشَف *n* مُكْتَشَفات discoveries

مُكْتَشِف *n* discoverer, explorer

مِكْشاف *n* detector

مَكْشوف *adj* unveiled, uncovered; مَكْشوف الرَأْسِ bareheaded; ب \ على المَكْشوفِ openly, publicly; لَعِبَ على المَكْشوفِ to show one's cards

‹ **كُشْك** *n* |أَكْشاك| kiosk; booth; stand, stall

كِشْك *n* gruel made of burghul and curdled milk

‹ **كَشْكَشَ** *v* |i; كَشْكَشة| to pleat, to fold

كَشْكَش *n* |كَشاكِشُ| frill, furbelow

‹ **كَشْكول** *n* mishmash, jumble

‹ **كِشْمِش** *n* currant; gooseberry (*Ribes uva-crispa*); كِشْمِش أَحْمَر redcurrant (*Ribes rudrum*); كِشْمِش أَسْوَد blackcurrant (*Ribes nigrum*)

‹ **كَشْمير** *n* |f| Kashmir (*region between India and Pakistan*)

‹ **كُظْر** *n* |كُظور| adrenal gland

‹ **كُظْرين** *n* adrenaline; أَفْرَزَ كُظْريناً to produce adrenaline

‹ **كَظَّ** *v* |u; كَظّ| to fill (up)

اكْتَظَّ *v* to be filled (up), to be full, to be packed; اكْتَظَّ بِشَيْءٍ to be filled (up) with sth

اكْتِظاظ *n* congestion, overcrowding; اكْتِظاظ السُكّانِ overpopulation; اكْتِظاظ المُدُنِ بالسُكّانِ the overcrowding of the cities

مُكْتَظّ *adj* crammed, packed, overfull; صالة مُكْتَظّة a crowded hall; كانَت القاعة مُكْتَظّةً the hall was packed; قِطار مُكْتَظّ بالرُكّابِ a jam-packed train; مُكْتَظّ بالسُكّانِ overpopulated;

تكافح *v* to fight one another

كِفاح *n* |كِفاحات| fight, battle, struggle; كِفاح مُسَلَّح armed conflict; كِفاح مُشْتَرَك ضدّ الاسْتِعْمارِ joint struggle against colonialism; خاضَ الكِفاحَ (ضدّ شَخْصٍ) to enter into combat (with sb)

مُكافِح *n* opponent, adversary, fighter; مُكافِح للإجْرامِ crime-fighter

مُكافَحة *n* fight, combat; مُكافَحة البِطالةِ \ الإرْهابِ \ مَرَضِ السَّرَطانِ the fight against unemployment/terrorism/cancer

كَفَرَ *v* |u; كُفْر, كُفْران| to be an infidel, to not believe; to be ungrateful; كَفَرَ باللهِ to not believe in God

كَفَّرَ *v* 1 [أعْطى الكَفّارةَ] |عن| to do penance (for), to atone (for), to make amends (for); كَفَّرَ عن شَيْءٍ to do penance for sth; كَفَّرَ عن خَطأٍ to make amends for a mistake 2 [أكْفَرَ] to charge with heresy, to charge with unbelief 3 [غَفَرَ] to forgive; كَفَّرَ اللهُ لَهُ ذُنوبَهُ God forgave him his sins

أكْفَرَ *v* 1 [كَفَّرَ] to charge with heresy, to charge with unbelief 2 [صَيَّرَ كافِراً] to make an infidel

كَفْر *n* |كُفور| hamlet, settlement

كُفْر *n* unbelief; atheism

كافِر A *adj* |كِفار, كَفَرة, كُفّار, كافِرونَ| unbelieving; كافِر بالنِعْمةِ ungrateful

B *n* |كِفار, كَفَرة, كُفّار, كافِرونَ| unbeliever, disbeliever; مُؤْمِنونَ وَكُفّار believers and unbelievers; كافِر باللهِ atheist; سورة الكافِرونَ The Disbelievers (*Sura 109*); الجوعُ كافِرٌ a hungry man has no conscience

كَفّارة *n* penance, atonement; يَوْمُ الكَفّارةِ Day of Atonement, Yom Kippur (*in Jewish calendar*)

كُفْران *n* atheism; infidelity, unbelief

تَكْفير *n* 1 [عن] atonement, penance, expiation; تَكْفير عن شَيْءٍ penance for sth 2 [إكْفار] charge of heresy, charge of unbelief

تَكْفيريّ *adj* expiatory, atoning; الفِكْر التَكْفيريّ Takfirism

كَفَّ *v* |u; كَفّ| 1 [انْصَرَفَ] |عن| to stop, to give up, to cease; to abandon; كَفَّ عن البُكاءِ to stop crying; كَفَّ المُنْشِدُ عن الإنْشادِ the singer stopped singing; كَفَّ شَخْصاً عن (فِعْلٍ)

تَكافَأَ *v* to match, to be similar, to be equal; تَتَكافأُ حُقوقُ الجَميع all people have equal rights

انْكَفَأَ *v* to withdraw, to retreat; to be reversed, to be inverted

كُفْء , كَفْء , كِفْء *adj* |أكْفاء , كِفاء| competent, qualified, capable; طَبيب كُفْء a competent doctor; مُوَظَّف كُفْء a qualified employee; غَيْر كُفْءٍ incompetent; كانَ كُفْئاً لِعَمَلِهِ to be equal to one's job

كُفُؤ , كُفوء *adj* |أكْفاء , كِفاء| equal, equivalent, matching; غَيْر كُفُؤ incompetent; مُدير غَيْر كُفُؤ an incompetent manager

كَفاءة *n* 1 [أهْلِيّة] qualification, skill, competence, ability; عَدَم الكَفاءةِ incompetence; كَفاءة عالِية a high qualification; مُدَرِّس ذو كَفاءةٍ a qualified teacher; كَفاءة قِياديّة executive ability; عند تَواجُدِ الكَفاءةِ if found suitable; كَفاءات بَشَرِيّة human skills; حُكومة كَفاءاتٍ غَيْر حِزْبِيّةٍ technocracy 2 [فَعّالِيّة] efficiency, effectiveness

انْكِفاء *n* relapse, reversion; withdrawal, retreat

انْكِفائيّ A *adj* regressive

B *n* (Pol) isolationist

تَكافُؤ *n* equality, parity, equivalence; تَكافُؤ الفُرَصِ equality of opportunities; عَدَم التَكافُؤِ inequality

تَكافُئيّة *n* valency (BrE), valence (AmE)

مُتَكافِئ *adj* equivalent, equal, alike; غَيْر مُتَكافِئٍ unequal; صِراع غَيْر مُتَكافِئٍ an unequal struggle; مُنافَسة غَيْر مُتَكافِئةٍ unfair competition; على أساسٍ مُتَكافِئٍ on equal footing; كانَ مُتَكافِئاً مع شَيْءٍ to keep in step with sth

مُكافَأة *n* reward, remuneration, recompense; bonus, gratuity, premium; تَسَلَّمَ \ مَنَحَ مُكافَأةً to get/give a reward; مُكافَأة شَرَفِيّة \ فَخْرِيّة fee, honorarium; تَلَقّى مُكافَأةً to receive a gratuity

كُفْتة *n* kofta/kefta (*spicy meatball*)

كافَحَ *v* to struggle, to (wage a) fight, to battle; to combat; كافَحَ شَيْئاً to battle sth; كافَحَ أزْمةَ السَّكَنِ to fight the housing shortage; كافَحَ مَرَضاً (بالأدْوِيةِ) to fight a disease (with medicine); كافَحَ تِجارةَ المُخَدِّراتِ to fight the drug trade; كافَحَ من أجْلِ العَدالةِ to fight for justice; كافَحَ أُمورَهُ to manage one's own affairs

شَيْءٍ to stop sb from (doing) sth **2▸** [عَمِيَ] to be/become blind; كَفَّ بَصَرُهُ he was/became blind

تَكَفَّفَ *v* to beg

اسْتَكَفَّ *v* **1▸** [اسْتَدارَ] to be curled up, to be coiled up **2▸** [أحاطَ] to surround **3▸** [تَسَوَّلَ] to hold out one's hand (*begging*)

كافّة *n* all; كافّةً entirely, fully; كافّة السُّكّانِ ,السُّكّان كافّةً all the inhabitants; تَمَتَّعَ بِكافّةِ حُقوقِهِ he enjoyed all his rights

كَفّ *n* |mf| **1▸** (Anat) |كُفوف ,أَكُفّ| palm (of the hand); hand; باطِنِ الكَفِّ palm of the hand; ظاهِر الكَفّ back of the hand; كَفّ يُسْرى left hand; كَفّ يُمْنى right hand; قَرَأَ كَفَّ شَخْصٍ to read sb's palm; وَضَعَ شَيْئاً على كَفِّ عِفريتٍ to jeopardize sth; بَسَطَ كَفَّهُ to hold out one's hand; وَضَعَ حَياتَهُ على كَفِّهِ to risk one's life **2▸** [امْتِناع] refraining, resistance; لم يَسْتَطِعِ الكَفَّ عن النَظَرِ he couldn't resist looking

(Idiom) كَفّ مَرْيَم chaste tree (*Vitex agnus-castus*)

كَفاف *n* sufficient means for a living; عاشَ عَيْشَةَ الكَفافِ to live a bare subsistence

كِفاف *n* |أَكِفّة| edge, border, hem

كُفّة *n* |كُفَف| hem, edge, border; الكُفّة فوق \ تحت الرُكْبةِ the hem above/under the knee

كِفّة ,كَفّة *n* |كِفاف ,كِفَف| **1▸** [الميزانِ] scale (*of a balance*) **2▸** (Anat) palm (of the hand)

كَفيف **A** *adj* |أَكِفّاءُ| blind, sightless

B *n* |أَكِفّاءُ| blind person

مَكْفوف **A** *adj* |مَكافيفُ ,مَكْفوفونَ| blind, sightless; وُلِدَ مَكْفوفاً to be born blind

B *n* |مَكافيفُ ,مَكْفوفونَ| blind person

كَفْكَفَ *v* |i; كَفْكَفة| كَفْكَفَ دُموعَهُ to dry one's tears

كَفَلَ ,كَفِلَ ,كَفُلَ *v* |a-u| **1▸** [ضَمِنَ] |كَفالة ,كُفول ,كَفْل| to guarantee, to warrant, to vouch; كَفَلَ شَيْئاً to stand surety for sth **2▸** [أعالَ] |كَفالة| to support, to provide for, to maintain

كَفَّلَ *v* to support, to provide for, to maintain; to (release on) bail

أَكْفَلَ *v* to guarantee; to give as security, to appoint as security

تَكَفَّلَ *v* to warrant, to guarantee, to vouch; to stand surety; تَكَفَّلَ بِشَيْءٍ to be answerable for sth; تَكَفَّلَ بِنَفْسِهِ to look after oneself

تَكافَلَ *v* to vouch for each other; to stand by each other

كَفَل *n* |أَكْفال| bottom, behind, buttocks

كافِل *n* |كُفّل| breadwinner, provider

كَفالة *n* **1▸** [ضَمان] guaranty, security, bail; كَفالة الأَمْنِ ensuring security; لِقاءَ كَفالةٍ to get bail; (خَرَجَ) بِكَفالةٍ (to be out) on bail; أَفْرَجَ عن شَخْصٍ ,أَخْلى سَبيلَ شَخْصٍ بِكَفالةٍ ,أَطْلَقَ سَراحَ شَخْصٍ بِكَفالةٍ to release sb on bail

2▸ (Busn) guarantee, warranty; guarantee (card), certificate of guarantee; كَفالة مَدى الحَياةِ lifetime guarantee; دَرّاجة مع كَفالةٍ لِسَنةٍ واحِدةٍ a bicycle with a year's guarantee

كَفيل **A** *adj* |كُفَلاءُ| guaranteeing, ensuring; السُبُل الكَفيلة بِتَنْفيذِ الاتِّفاقِ the means that ensure execution of the agreement; إِجْراءات كَفيلة بِوَقْفِ المَعْرَكةِ procedures that guarantee to end the battle

B *n* |كُفَلاءُ| surety, guarantor; sponsor

تَكافُل *n* **1▸** [تَعايُش] symbiosis **2▸** [تَضامُن] solidarity, mutual responsibility; تَكافُل اجْتِماعيّ social solidarity

تَكافُليّ *adj* تَكافُليّ مُتَعَضّ symbiotic; عَلاقة تَكافُليّة مُتَعَضّية symbiotic relation

مُتَكافِل *adj* vouching (*for each other*)

مَكْفول *adj* guaranteed, warranted

كَفَنَ *v* |i; كَفْن| to (wrap in a) shroud

كَفَّنَ *v* to (wrap in a) shroud

كَفَن *n* |أَكْفان| shroud, winding sheet

اكْفَهَرَّ *v* to darken, to cloud over, to grow gloomy; اكْفَهَرَّ وَجْهُهُ عِنْدَما سَمِعَ الأَخْبارَ السَّيِّئةَ his face darkened when he heard the bad news; اكْفَهَرَّتِ السَّماءُ the sky clouded over

مُكْفَهِرّ *adj* surly, stern, sullen; dark; وَجْه مُكْفَهِرّ a surly expression; سَماء مُكْفَهِرّة a dark sky

كَفى *v* |i; كِفاية| to be enough, to be sufficient, to suffice; يَكْفيهِ enough ...; هذا يَكْفي! that's enough!; ما يَكْفي من مالِهِ he has enough money; تَكْفي بَيْضةٌ واحِدةٌ لِهَذِهِ الوَصْفةِ one egg will do for this recipe; لم يَحْصُل الحِزْبُ على ما يَكْفي من مَقاعِدَ the party hasn't won enough seats; يَكْفي إِرْسالُ رِسالةٍ a letter will do; جَمَعْتُ ما يَكْفي من النُّقودِ لِلسَفَرِ إِلَيْكَ I saved enough money to come visit you; المَبْنى

كَبيرٌ بِما يَكْفي the building is big enough; كَفى بِاللهِ شَهيداً God is witness enough

Idiom كَفى شَخْصاً العَناءَ to save sb the trouble

اِكْتَفى *v* |i| to have/be enough, to make do; to content oneself; اِكْتَفى بِمَبْلَغٍ مُعَيَّنٍ to content oneself with a certain amount; اِكْتَفى بِهِ to content oneself with it; اِكْتَفى بِما عِنْدَهُ مِنَ المالِ to make do with one's money; لَمْ يَكْتَفِ بِذلِكَ، بَلْ ... he did not content himself with that, but ... as well

كَفِيّ *adj* enough, sufficient; لَيْسَتِ الوَسائِلُ (المادِّيَّةُ) كَفِيَّةً the (financial) means aren't sufficient

كافٍ *adj* |كُفاة| enough, sufficient, adequate; غَيْر كافٍ insufficient, inadequate; مَكان \ طَعام كافٍ enough room/food; إِمْكانِيّات كافِية enough possibilities; مَؤونة \ إِجْراءات كافِية adequate provisions/measures; جَواب كافٍ an adequate answer; طاقة \ وَسائِل غَيْر كافِيَة insufficient capacity/means; كَمِّيَّة غَيْر كافِيَة an insufficient quantity

كِفاية *n* enough; ما فيهِ الكِفايةُ enough

اِكْتِفاء *n* contentment, satisfaction; اِكْتِفاء ذاتِيّ self-sufficiency

مُكْتَفٍ *adj* satisfied, contented; مُكْتَفٍ ذاتِيًّا self-sufficient

كَلَأَ *v* |a; كِلاء، كَلْء| to protect, to guard, to preserve; كَلَأَ اللهُ وَلَدي may God protect my child

كَلّا *excl* (oh) no, not at all, certainly not

كِلا *particle* |f كِلْتا| both; either; كِلا الجُزْئَيْنِ both parts; في كِلا الجانِبَيْنِ on both sides; في كِلْتا الحالَتَيْنِ in either case; كِلانا both of us; ذَهَبَ كِلاهُما they both went; رَأَيْتُ كِلَيْهِما I saw them both; أُلْقِيَ القَبْضُ على كِلْتَيْهِما they (*f*) were both arrested

كْلارينيت *n* clarinet

كْلاسيكِيّ، كِلاسيكِيّ *adj* classic, classical; موسيقى كْلاسيكِيّة classical music; نَموذَج كْلاسيكِيّ a classic model; سَيّارة كْلاسيكِيّة a classic car

كْلاسيكِيّة *n* classicism, classicalism

كَلِبَ *v* |a; كَلَب| 1 [أُصيبَ بِداءِ الكَلْبِ] to have/get rabies; to be/become rabid 2 [طَمِعَ] |على| to covet, to desire; كَلِبَ على شَيْءٍ to covet sth

تَكالَبَ *v* to be out for, to be after, to be bent on; تَكالَبَ على جَمْعِ المالِ to be bent on amassing wealth

كَلْب *n* |كِلاب| dog; كَلْب ضالّ cur, mutt; كَلْب أَصيل a purebred dog; كَلْب وَفِيّ a faithful dog; كَلْب بوليسِيّ police dog; كَلْب الرّاعي sheepdog; كَلْب حِراسةٍ watchdog; كَلْب إِثْرٍ tracker (dog); كَلْب هامِل stray dog; كَلْب شَرِس vicious dog; كَلْب جَحود ungrateful dog; كَلْب صَيْدٍ hound, sporting dog; تيفوس الكِلابِ Weil's disease; عيشة الكِلابِ dog's life; داء الكَلْبِ rabies; كَلْب الماءِ otter; اِبْنُ الكَلْبِ son of a bitch; تَنْبَحُ الكِلابُ (the) dogs bark; اِحْتَرِسْ مِنَ الكَلْبِ beware of the dog; تَصَرَّفَ مِثْلَ الكَلْبِ المَسْعورِ to behave like a mad dog; لا يَضيرُ السَّحابَ عُواءُ الكِلابِ *the clouds aren't disturbed by the dog's barking*; إِنْ كانَتْ لَكَ حاجةٌ عِنْدَ كَلْبٍ فَقُلْ لَهُ: يا سَيِّدي ≈ you can catch more flies with honey than with vinegar; كُلّ كَلْبٍ بِبابِهِ نَبّاحٌ every cock will crow upon his own dunghill

كَلَب *n* rabies, canine madness, hydrophobia

كَلِب *adj* rabid, affected with rabies

كُلّاب *n* |كَلاليبُ| (pair of) pincers; cramp

كَلْبة *n* female dog, bitch

كَلْبِيّ A *adj* cynical; canine, doggish; شَهْوة كَلْبِيّة bulimia B *n* cynic; Cynic (*a member of a school of ancient Greek philosophers*)

كَلْبِيّة *n* (Philos) Cynicism

كَليب *adj* |كَلْبى| rabid, affected with rabies

مَكْلوب *adj* rabid, affected with rabies

كَلَبْشة *n* handcuffs, manacles

كُلْثوم *adj* 1 [مُمْتَلِئ] round, full 2 [الوَجْهِ] round-cheeked 3 [اسْم شَخْصِيّ] Kalthum (*female given name*)

مُكَلْثَم *adj* round-cheeked; وَجْه مُكَلْثَم a round-cheeked face

كَلَحَ *v* |a; كُلوح، كُلاح| to frown, to scowl

كالَحَ *v* to treat hostilely

كالِح *adj* 1 [لَوْن] grey, pale, pallid; وَجْه كالِح a pale face; مَبْنًى كالِح a grey building 2 [صَعْب] hard, heavy, difficult; زَمَن كالِح a hard time

كَلَسَ *v* |i; كَلْس| to plaster, to whitewash, to stucco

كَلَّسَ *v* to plaster, to whitewash, to stucco; كَلَّسَ حائِطاً to plaster a wall

تَكَلَّسَ v to calcify

كِلْس n lime; (lime) mortar; حَجَر الكِلْسِ limestone; أزالَ الكِلْسَ to decalcify, to descale

كَلّاسة n limekiln

كِلْسيّ adj calcareous, calciferous; أَرْض كِلْسيّة calcareous soil; حَجَر كِلْسيّ limestone

تَكَلُّس n |تكلُّسات| calcification

‹ **كالْسِيوم**, **كَلْسِيوم** n see كالْسِيوم

‹ **كَلِفَ** v |a; كَلَف| 1 [أَحَبَّ] |ب| to be (very) fond of; to love; كَلِفَ بِشَيْءٍ \ بِشَخْصٍ to be fond of sth/sb 2 [الوَجْهُ] to be freckled

كَلَّفَ v 1 [تطَلَّبَ] to cost; كَلَّفَ (مالاً) كَثيراً to cost a lot (of money); كَلَّفَ ١٢ دولار to cost twelve dollars; كَلَّفَ قوّةً كَبيرةً \ جُهْداً كَبيراً \ وَقْتاً كَثيراً to take a lot of time; to require a lot of strength/trouble; يُكَلِّفُهُ هذا ثَمَناً باهِظاً that is costing him dearly; سَيُكَلِّفُهُ كثيراً that is going to cost him; كَلَّفَ شَخْصاً حَياتَهُ to cost sb his life; مَهْما كَلَّفَهُ الأَمْرُ at any cost 2 [فَرَضَ] to charge, to order, to commission; كَلَّفَ شَخْصاً بِمُهِمّةٍ to charge sb with a task; كَلَّفَ نَفْسَهُ بِمُهِمّةٍ to take charge of a task; كُلِّفَ بِشَيْءٍ to be commissioned with sth; كَلَّفَ شَخْصاً أَنْ يَفْعَلَ شَيْئاً to assign sb to do sth

تَكَلَّفَ v 1 [تَحَمَّلَ] |ب| to see to, to take care of, to take upon oneself; تَكَلَّفَ بِعَمَلٍ to take care of a job 2 [اِصْطَنَعَ] to feign, to simulate, to pretend; تَكَلَّفَ الضِحْكَ to force a laugh 3 [كَلَّفَ] to cost; تَكَلَّفَ (مالاً) كَثيراً to cost a lot (of money)

كَلَف n coll freckle

كَلِف adj fond, mad, crazy; كانَ كَلِفاً بِشَيْءٍ \ بِشَخْصٍ to be crazy about sth/sb

كُلْفة n |كُلَف| 1 [نَفَقة] cost, expense, expenditure; كُلْفة مُتَدَنِّية low cost 2 [رَسْميّات] ceremony; formality; من دونِ كُلْفةٍ without ceremony; رَفَعَ الكُلْفةَ مع شَخْصٍ to treat sb in an informal way 3 [نَسيج] *a thin fabric*

تَكَلُّف n pretence, show, mannerism

تَكْلِفة n |تَكاليفُ| cost, expense; تَكاليف expenses; تَكاليف باهِظة \ بَسيطة high/low costs; تَكاليف إدارِيّة administrative costs; تَكاليف العَمَلِ labour costs; التَكاليف والأَرْباح costs and benefits; سِعْر التَكْلِفةِ cost, purchase price; تحت \ دون سِعْرِ التَكْلِفةِ below cost; سِعْر تَكْلِفةٍ يَبْلُغُ ٥ دولاراتٍ a purchase price of five dollars; باعَ شَيْئاً بِسِعْرِ التَكْلِفةِ to sell sth at cost; بِدونِ تَكاليف free of charge; تَحَمَّلَ التَكاليفَ to bear the expenses; دَفَعَ تَكاليفَ to defray the costs; ساهَمَ في التَكاليف to contribute towards the costs; غَطّى التَكاليفَ to cover the costs; تَرْتَفِعُ \ تَنْخَفِضُ التَكاليفُ the costs rise/fall; خَفَّضَ التَكاليفَ to reduce the costs

تَكْليف n 1 [واجِب] commissioning, charging 2 [رَسْميّات] ceremony, formality; بِدونِ تَكْليفٍ informal, informally

مُتَكَلِّف adj affected, mannered, forced; كَلام مُتَكَلِّف affected speech; مَجاز مُتَكَلِّف strained imagery; غَيْر مُتَكَلِّفٍ unaffected, relaxed

مُكَلَّف A adj commissioned, charged; كانَ مُكَلَّفاً بِشَيْءٍ to be in charge of sth

B n delegate

مُكَلِّف adj costly, expensive; عَمَليّة مُكَلِّفة an expensive operation

‹ **كَلْفيني** A adj Calvinistic

B n Calvinist

كَلْفينيّة n Calvinism

‹ **تَكَلْكَلَ** v to become callous

كَلْكَلة n callous

‹ **كَلَّ** v |i; كَلّ, كِلّة, كَلال, كَلالة| 1 [تَعِبَ] to be/become tired, to be/become fatigued; لم يَكِلّ عن فِعْلِ شَيْءٍ to keep doing sth tirelessly 2 [ضَعُفَ] to weaken, to grow weak

كَلَّلَ v 1 [جَعَلَهُ إكْليلاً] to crown; to laurel 2 (Chr) to join in matrimony

تَكَلَّلَ v to be crowned; to be rewarded; تَكَلَّلَ بالنَجاحِ to be rewarded with success; تَكَلَّلَتْ جُهودُهُ his efforts paid off

كَلَل n tiredness, fatigue; عَمِلَ بِدونِ كَلَلٍ وَلا مَلَلٍ to work tirelessly; كَلَل المَعادِنِ metal fatigue

كُلّ n 1 [وَحْدة] whole, entirety; everyone, all; الكُلّ everyone, all; الكُلّ يُريدُ السَلامَ everyone wants peace; على كُلٍّ in any case; مَثَّلَ كُلاً to form a whole; الكُلّ في واحِدٍ all together

كَليل *adj* |كِلال| ① [مُتْعَب] tired, weary; exhausted ② [غَيْر حادٍّ] dull, blunt ③ [ضَعيف] weak, feeble

إكْليل *n* |أَكِلّة, أكاليل| ① [رُعْلة] wreath, garland; إكْليل من الزُهورِ floral wreath ② [تاج] crown; diadem ③ (Bot) spiraea (*Spiraea*); إكْليل الجَبَلِ rosemary (*Rosmarinus officinalis*)

إكْليليّ *adj* شِرْيان إكْليليّ coronary artery

تَكْليل *n* coronation, crowning

مُكَلَّل *adj* crowned

كَلَمَ *v* |i| |كَلْم| to wound, to injure; كَلَمَ شَخْصاً to injure sb

كَلَّمَ *v* to talk, to speak, to address; to communicate, to lecture; كَلَّمَ شَخْصاً (في شَيْءٍ) to speak to sb (about sth); كَلَّمَ شَخْصاً بالهاتِفِ to talk to sb on the telephone

كالَمَ *v* to address, to speak to, to talk to; كالَمَ شَخْصاً to address sb

تَكَلَّمَ *v* to speak, to talk; to say, to utter; تَكَلَّمَ إلى \ مع شَخْصٍ to talk to/with sb; تَكَلَّمَ عن شَيْءٍ \ شَخْصٍ to speak about sth/sb; تَكَلَّمَ الإنْجليزيّةَ بِطَلاقةٍ to speak English fluently; لم يَتَكَلَّمْ عن الخُطّةِ he said nothing about the plan

كَلْم *n* |كِلام, كُلوم| cut, gash, slash

كَلام *n coll* |no singular noun| speech, talk; remark, utterance; word, words; كَلام فارِغ idle talk, nonsense; هذا كُلُّهُ كَلامٌ فارِغٌ! that's all nonsense!; تَكَلَّمَ كَلاماً فارِغا to talk nonsense; كَلام مُبْتَذَل banality; كَلام غَريب silly talk; كَلام بَذيء \ فاحِش foul language; عِلْم الكَلامِ discourse (*Islamic philosophical discipline of seeking theological principles through dialectic*); قَوارِص الكَلامِ biting words; قُدْرة على الكَلامِ power of speech; حُرّيّة الكَلامِ freedom of speech; قِسْم الكَلامِ part of speech; كَلام اللهِ تَعالى the Word of God; قَليل الكَلامِ curt; تَعَلَّمَ الكَلامَ to learn to talk; سَحَبَ كَلامَهُ to swallow one's words; لم يَتَسَنَّ لَهُ الكَلامُ he wasn't able to get a word in; وَجَّهَ الكَلامَ إلى شَخْصٍ to address sb; كَلامُ اللَيْلِ يَمْحوهُ النَهارُ nighttime promises evaporate in the light of day; كَذَّبَ كَلامَ شَخْصٍ to disprove sb's words; كانَ مَحَطَّ الكَلامِ he was the topic of conversation

كَلاميّ *adj* verbal

كَلِمة *n* ① [لَفْظ] word; كَلِمة دَخيلة loan word; كَلِمة مُعاكِسة antonym; كَلِمة مُرادِفة synonym; كَلِمات رَقيقة \ حُلْوة

② [كُلّ شَيْءٍ] each; every; كُلّ شَخْصٍ \ واحِدٍ everyone; كُلّ شَيْءٍ everything, all; كُلّ رَجُلٍ جَيِّدٍ every good man; كُلّ واحِدٍ (مِنْهُمْ \ مِنْكُمْ \ ...) every one (of them/you/...); على كُلّ حالٍ anyhow, anyway, at least; كُلّ سَنَتَيْنِ every two years ③ [كُلّ الشَيْءِ] all; the whole; كُلّ العالَمِ, العالَمُ كُلُّهُ the whole world; اليَوْمَ كُلُّهُ all day; هذا كُلُّهُ all this ④ [كُلّ الأَشْياءِ] all; كُلّ العَرَبِ all (the) Arabs; كُلّ الأَعْضاءِ المَوْجودين all members present; كُلُّ الأثاثِ جَديدةٌ all the furniture is new; في كُلِّ الظُروفِ in all circumstances; كُلّ الحُقوقِ الّتي تَتَمَتَّعُ بِها ... all the rights you have ...; كُلُّهُمْ all of them; لم يَكونوا كُلُّهُمْ مُوافِقين not all of them agreed; كُلّ مُمْتَلَكاتِها all her possessions ⑤ [كُلّ مِن] كُلّ من الدُوَلِ السِتِّ each of the six countries; في كُلٍّ من مِصْرَ والمَغْرِبِ in Egypt as well as in Morocco, in both Egypt and Morocco ⑥ [كُلّ مَنْ \ ما] كُلّ مَنْ رَأَيْتُ everyone I saw; كُلّ ما فَعَلْتَهُ everything you did; كُلّ ما في جَيْبِهِ everything in his pocket; كُلّ ما حَدَثَ في العالَمِ من تَغَيُّراتٍ all the changes that took place in the world

كُلّة *n* |كُلَل| marble, taw

كِلّة *n* |كِلَل, كِلّات| mosquito net

كُلَّما *conj* whenever; as; the more ... the ...; كُلَّما أَمْكَنَ ذلك whenever (it's) possible; كُلَّما يَشاءُ whenever he wants; سَأزورُكَ كُلَّما أَتاحَتْ لي الظُروفُ لِذَلِكَ I will visit you as often as circumstances allow for; يَسْتَعينُ بِصَديقِهِ كُلَّما مَرَّ بِأَزْمةٍ whenever he's in a crisis, he will turn to his friend for help; كُلَّما ازْدادَ دَخْلُكَ كُلَما دَفَعْتَ ضَرائِبَ أَكْثَرَ the more you earn, the more tax you will pay

كُلّيّ *adj* entire, total, complete; المَبْلَغ الكُلّيّ the total amount; تَشابُه كُلّيّ perfect resemblance; مُسْتَوًى كُلّيّ overall level; كُلّيًّا in its entirety, totally; مُرْهَق كُلّيًّا totally exhausted; نَسيتُ كُلّيًّا أنْ ... I completely forgot to ...; كُلّيًّا أو جُزْئيًّا wholly or partly; كُلّيّات universals

كُلّيانيّة *n* totality, entirety

كُلّيّة *n* ① (Educ) faculty; academy; كُلّيّة حَرْبيّة \ عَسْكَريّة military academy; مَجْلِس الكُلّيّةِ faculty board; أُسْتاذ في كُلّيّةِ الآدابِ a professor in the Faculty of Arts ② [تَمام] بِكُلّيّتِهِ in its entirety

مَعْسولة sweet words; كَلِمة بَذيئة \ قَبيحة a dirty word; كَلِمات فارِغة \ جَوْفاء nonsense; كَلِمة شُكْرٍ a word of thanks; أَعْطى شَخْصاً كَلِمة شَرَفٍ word of honour; كَلِمة شَرَفٍ to give sb one's word of honour; كَلِمة مُرَكَّبة a compound; كَلِمة صَعْبة \ مُزْدَوِجة المَعْنى a difficult/ambiguous word; كَلِمة سِرٍّ \ سِرّيّة password; قالَ كَلِمةَ السِرِّ to give the password; كَلِمة سِحْرِيّة magic word; كَلِمة رَئيسيّة key word; بِكُلِّ ما في الكَلِمةِ من مَعْنًى meaning of a word; مَعْنى كَلِمةٍ in every sense of the word; رَجُل بِمَعْنى الكَلِمة a man in the true sense of the word; قائمة \ لائحة كَلِماتٍ list of words; اخْتِيار الكَلِماتِ choice of words; اسْتِعْمال كَلِماتٍ use of words; تَصْريف الكَلِماتِ formation of words; تَلاعُب بالكَلِماتِ play on words; فَيْض من الكَلِماتِ a flood of words; حَلَّ كَلِماتٍ مُتَقاطِعةً crossword (puzzle); كَلِمات مُتَقاطِعة to solve a crossword (puzzle); قالَ الكَلِمةَ الحاسِمةَ to say the decisive word; احْتَرَمَ كَلِمَتَهُ to keep one's word; حَفِظَ كَلِماتٍ to memorize words; شَطَبَ كَلِمةً to strike out a word; أَيَّدَ الكَلِماتِ بالأَفْعالِ to suit the action to the word; كَلِمةً كَلِمةً word by word; بِكَلِمةٍ واحِدةٍ in one word; بِكَلِماتٍ أُخْرى in other words; يَجِبُ إعْطاءُ الكَلِمةِ للشَعْبِ the people should be given a voice; رَدَّدَ كَلِماتِ شَخْصٍ حَرْفِيًّا to repeat sb's words literally; لَهُ الكَلِمةُ الأَخيرةُ he has the final word **2** [خُطْبة] address, speech, talk; كَلِمة افْتِتاحيّة opening word; في كَلِمَتِه الافْتِتاحيّةِ in his opening words; أَلْقى كَلِمةً to make a speech; ... الكَلِمةُ الآنَ لـ I now give the floor to ...; أَعْطى شَخْصاً الكَلِمةَ to give sb the floor; تَناوَلَ الكَلِمةَ to take the floor

كَلِيم *n* **1** [سَجّادة] kilim (*woollen carpet*) **2** [مَجْروح] wounded **3** [مُتَكَلِّم] speaker

Idiom كَليم اللهِ Moses

تَكَلُّم *n* speaking, talking

مُتَكَلِّم *n* **1** [مُتَحَدِّث] speaker **2** [عالِم] theologian (*who practises* عِلْم الكَلام) **3** (Gram) first person

مُكالَمة *n* conversation, talk, discussion; (phone) call; مُكالَمة هاتِفيّة phone call; مُكالَمة هاتِفيّة مَحَلِّيّة \ داخِلِيّة \ خارِجيّة local/long-distance/international phone call; مُكالَمة مَجهولة المَصْدَرِ an anonymous phone call; سِعْر المُكالَمةِ الهاتِفيّةِ call charge; رَدَّ على \ تَلَقّى \ اسْتَقْبَلَ مُكالَمةً هاتِفيّةً to receive a phone call; أَجرى مُكالَمةً هاتِفيّةً to answer a phone call; مُكالَمةٍ هاتِفيّةٍ to have a telephone conversation; تَنَصَّتَ على مُكالَماتٍ هاتِفيّةٍ to tap the telephone; سَجَّلَ مُكالَماتٍ هاتِفيّةً to record phone calls

مَكْلوم **A** *adj* stricken, afflicted **B** *n* victim

‹ **كُلَّما** *conj* see كلل

‹ **كولونيا** *n* |f| Cologne (*city in Germany*)

‹ **كُلْوِيّ** *adj* renal, nephritic, kidney (*before n*); فَشَل كُلْوِيّ renal failure

كُلْية ,كُلْوة *n* |كُلًى| (Anat) kidney; مَرَض الكُلى kidney disease; أُصيبَ بِمَرَضِ الكُلى to suffer from kidney disease; غَسْل الكُلْيةِ dialysis, haemodialysis

‹ **كْلور** *n* chlorine; chloride

‹ **كْلوروفورم** *n* chloroform

‹ **كْلوريد** *n* chloride; كْلوريد الصوديوم sodium chloride

‹ **كْليب** *n* (music) video, video clip

‹ **كْليشيه** *n* (P&P) plate, block; كْليشيه حَفْرِيّ, طَبْعة عن كْليشيه حَفْرِيّ etching

كَمْ *adv* **1** [اسْتِفْهام] how much, how many; كَم الساعةُ؟ what time is it?; كَمْ هي دَرَجةُ الحَرارةِ؟ what is the temperature?; كَمْ مَرّةً how many times, how often; كَمْ بَيْتاً, كَمْ من البُيوتِ how many houses; كَمْ كِتاباً \ مِن الكُتُبِ قَرَأْتَ؟ how many books have you read?; كَمْ من الوَقْتِ (for) how long; بِكَمْ؟ (for) how much?; مع كَمْ صَديقاً \ صَديقٍ with how many friends **2** [تعَجُّب] *expression of amazement at the quantity of sth*; كَمْ كِتاباً قَرَأْتَ! you've read so many books!; كَمْ أَسْعَدُ في قُدومِكَ! I'm so happy with your visit!

كَمّ *n* **1** [كَمِّيّة] quantity, amount; الكَمّ والكَيْف quantity and quality; من حَيْثِ الكَمِّ والكَيْفِ, كَمًّا وَكَيْفاً quantitatively and qualitatively **2** (Phys) quantum; ميكانيكا الكَمِّ quantum mechanics; نَظَرِيّة الكَمِّ quantum theory

كَمِّيّ *adj* **1** [مُتَعَلِّق بِعَدَدٍ] quantitative; حَسَّنَ شَيْئاً كَمِّيًّا to improve sth quantitatively; تَحْليل كَمِّيّ a quantitative

‹ **كَمَر** *n* |أَكْمار| belt

كَمَرة *n* beam, (iron) girder

‹ **كُمْسارِيّ** *n* |كُمْسارِيّة| (Egypt) conductor, ticket collector

‹ **كَمُش** *v* |u; كَماشة| to be brave

تَكَمَّش *v* to contract, to shrink, to pull together

انْكَمَش *v* to shrink, to contract, to curl up; سَتَنْكَمِشُ هذه المادّةُ this material will shrink; انْكَمَشَ خَوْفاً to shrink with fear; يَنْكَمِشُ الاقْتِصادُ the economy is contracting; انْكَمَشَ على نَفْسِهِ to shrink in the wash; انْكَمَشَ بعد الغَسِيل to withdraw into oneself

كَمّاشة *n* (pair of) pincers, (pair of) tongs

انْكِماش *n* 1 (Econ) deflation; decrease, reduction 2 [بعد الغَسْل] shrinkage, shrinking

مُنْكَمِش *adj* contracted, shrunk; مُنْكَمِش على نَفْسِهِ withdrawn within oneself

‹ **كَمُلَ** *v* |u; كُمول, كَمال| to be/become complete, to be/become whole; to be perfect; تَكْمُلُ أَخْلاقُهُ he has perfect manners

كَمَّلَ *v* to complete, to settle, to wind up; كَمَّلَ دِراسَتَهُ to finish one's study; يُكَمِّلُ كُلٌّ مِنْهُما الآخَرَ they complement one another

أَكْمَلَ *v* to finish, to wind up, to complete; أَكْمَلَ كَلامَهُ to finish speaking; تَرَكَ شَخْصاً يُكْمِلُ كَلامَهُ to let sb finish speaking; دَعْني أُكْمِلُ كَلامي (will you) let me finish; أَكْمَلَ عَمَلَهُ to finish one's work; أَكْمَلَ الطالِبُ دِراسَتَهُ في أَمْرِيكا the student completed his studies in America

تَكَمَّلَ *v* to be/become complete

تَكامَلَ *v* to complement, to complete, to make up; يَتَكامَلان جَيِّداً they complement each other well

اكْتَمَلَ *v* to be/become complete; to be finished, to be concluded; اكْتَمَلَ بِناءُ المَدْرَسةِ في العامِ الماضي the construction of the school was finished last year; قد اكْتَمَلَتْ تَرْجَمةُ الكِتابِ أَخيراً the translation of the book has recently been completed

اسْتَكْمَلَ *v* to finish, to complete, to wind up; اسْتَكْمَلَ مِلَفًّا to close a file

كامِل *adj* |كَمَلة| entire, total, whole; complete, full; غَيْر كامِلٍ incomplete; ساعة كامِلة a full hour; بِكامِلِ وَزْنِهِ with his full

analysis 2 (Phys) quantum (*before n*); كِيمِياء كَمِّيّة quantum chemistry; عَدَد كَمّيّ a quantum number

كَمِّيّة *n* quantity, amount; quantum, batch, bunch; كَمِّيّة كَبِيرة \ صَغِيرة a large/small quantity; بِكَمِّيّاتٍ كَبِيرةٍ in large quantities; كَمِّيّة من الطاقةِ \ الكُتُبِ \ القَهْوةِ an amount of energy/books/coffee; حَدَّدَ كَمِّيّةً to quantify; تَحْدِيد كَمِّيّةٍ quantification

‹ **كَمْء** *n* |كَمْأ, أَكْمُؤ| desert truffles (*Terfeziaceae*)

‹ **كَما** *conj* see ما

‹ **كَمان** *n* violin; كَمان أَوْسَط viola; كَمان أَجْهَر (double) bass, contrabass (violin); عازِف كَمانٍ violin case; صُنْدوق الكَمانِ violinist; عَزَفَ الكَمانَ \ على الكَمانِ to play the violin

‹ **كَمْبِيالة** *n* postal order, money order, bill of exchange

‹ **كُمْبْيوتَر**, **كومْبيوتَر** *n* computer; كُمْبْيوتَر شَخْصِيّ personal computer; كُمْبْيوتَر قَوِيّ a powerful computer; كُمْبْيوتَر نَقّال portable computer, laptop (computer), notebook (computer); شَبَكة كُمْبْيوتَر computer network; (computer) terminal; بَرْنامَج كُمْبْيوتَر computer program; عِلْم الكُمْبْيوتَر information science, computer science; دَرَسَ هَنْدَسة الكُمْبْيوتَر to study computer engineering; اسْتَخْدَمَ الكُمْبْيوتَر to use the computer

‹ **كَمَتَ** *v* |u; كَمْت| to hide, to conceal

كُمَيْت *adj* reddish-brown, auburn, maroon

‹ **كُمَّثْرى** *n coll* |f; sing n كُمَّثْراة| pear; شَجَرة الكُمَّثْرى pear tree (*Pyrus*)

‹ **كَمَحَ** *v* |a; كَمْح| to rein in (*riding or pack animal*)

‹ **كامِخ** *n* |كَوامِخُ| pickled gherkins (BrE), pickles (AmE)

‹ **كَمِدَ** *v* |a; كَمْد| 1 [حَزُنَ] to be/become sad 2 [اللَّوْنُ] to become pale, to fade, to lose colour

كَمَّدَ *v* to apply a compress

أَكْمَدَ *v* to sadden, to grieve

كَمِد *n* (intensely) sad/grief-stricken

كامِد *adj* sad, unhappy, sorrowful

كِماد *n* compress; كِماد ساخِن a hot compress

كِمادة *n* compress; وَضَعَ كِمادةً على وَرَمٍ to place a compress on swelling weight; فريق كامِل a whole team; مُفاجأة كامِلة a complete surprise; سِلْسِلة كامِلة a complete series; رَجُل كامِل a perfect man; وَقْت كامِل full-time; وَظيفة كامِلة a full-time job; بِكامِلِهِ بالكامِلِ totally, entirely; بِشَكْلٍ شِبْهِ كامِلٍ nearly, almost

كَمال *n* |كَمالات| **1** [تَمام] perfection; completeness; الكَمالُ لله only God is perfect; لا كَمالَ إلاّ لَوَجْهِ الله nobody's perfect; بِتَمامِهِ وَكَمالِهِ to perfection **2** [اِسْم شَخْصِيّ] Kamal (*male given name*)

كَمالِيّ *adj* extra, accessory; luxurious, luxury; سِلَع كَمالِيّات, كَمالِيّة luxury goods

اسْتِكْمال *n* completion, finish

اكْتِمال *n* completion, finishing, completeness

إكْمال *n* completion, finishing; الإكْمال التِلْقائِيّ autocomplete

أكْمَل *adj* |dipt| بِأَكْمَلِهِ completely, entirely; لَقَدْ احْتَرَقَ المَنْزِلُ بِأَكْمَلِهِ the house burned down completely; مَجْلِس الإدارةِ بِأَكْمَلِهِ the entire board; على أكْمَلِ وَجْهٍ to the fullest

تَكامُل *n* **1** (Pol) unification, integration; التَكامُل الأوروبّيّ the European unification; تَكامُل اقْتِصادِيّ economic integration **2** (Math) integral

تَكامُلِيّ *adj* integral, integrative, all-inclusive; عَلاقة تَكامُلِيّة integrative relationship

تَكْمِلة *n* completion; complement, supplement; كَتَبَ تَكْمِلةَ القِصّةِ to write an end to the story; تَكْمِلة دِراسةٍ completion of a study

تَكْميل *n* |تَكْميلات| supplement, addition, complement; completion

تَكْميلِيّ *adj* supplementary, additional, complementary; دُروس تَكْميلِيّة an additional course

مُتَكامِل *adj* integral, entire, complete; supplementary, additional, complementary; نِظام مُتَكامِل an integrated system

مُكْتَمِل *adj* complete, full, plenary

مُكَمِّل *adj* complementary, additional, supplementary; مُكَمِّلات accessories

› **كَمَّ** *v* |u; كَمّ| to muzzle; to silence; كَمَّ كَلْباً to muzzle a dog; كَمَّ فَمَ شَخْصٍ to silence sb

كَمَّمَ *v* to muzzle; to silence; كَمَّمَ أَفْواهَ المُعارِضينَ to silence dissidents

كَمّ, كَمِّيّ, كَمِّيّة see كم

كُمّ *n* |أكْمام, كِمَمة| sleeve; قَميص بِأَكْمام طَوِيلةٍ \ قَصيرةٍ a shirt with long/short sleeves; شَمَّرَ كُمَّهُ to roll up one's sleeves

كِمامة *n* |كِمامات, كَمائِمُ| muzzle, gag; mask

كُمّة *n* kumma (*traditional headgear in the Gulf states*)

كُمومِيّ *adj* quantum (*before n*); طاقة كُمومِيّة quantum energy; نَظَرِيّة كُمومِيّة quantum theory

› **كَمَنَ** *v* |u; كُمون| **1** [الشَخْصُ] to hide, to conceal oneself, to take cover **2** [الشَيْءُ] to be found, to lie, to be dormant; يَكْمُنُ الحَلّ في ... the solution is to be found in ...; رَوْعَتُها يَكْمُنُ في بَساطَتِها its greatness lies in its simplicity

كامِن *adj* |كَوامِنُ| hidden, latent, underlying; فَيْروس كامِن a latent virus; قُوَى كامِنة hidden powers; أَلَم كامِن a hidden pain; لِسَبَبٍ كامِنٍ for an obscure reason; ثائِر كامِن في الجِبالِ a revolutionary hiding in the mountains

كَمّون *n* cumin (*Cuminum cyminum*); كَمّون حُلْو anise, aniseed (*Pimpinella anisum*)

كَمين **A** *adj* secret; رَغْبة كَمينة a secret desire **B** *n* ambush, pitfall, trap; نَصَبَ كَميناً لِشَخْصٍ to prepare an ambush for sb; وَقَعَ في كَمينٍ to fall into a trap

مَكْمَن *n* |مَكامِنُ| hideaway, hiding place, ambush

› **كَمَنْجة** *n* violin

› **أَكْمَه** *adj* |dipt| blind (*from birth*)

› **كَمِيّ** *adj* |كُماة, أَكْماء| fully armoured, heavily armed

› **كَنّارة** *n* |كَنّارات, كَنانيرُ| lyre

› **كَنارِيّ** *n* canary (*Serinus canaria*)

› **كَنَب** *n* callous

كَنَبة *n* couch, sofa

› **كُنْتْرَباس** *n* contrabass, (double) bass

› **كِنْدة** *n* Kindah (*kingdom in Arabia before the rise of Islam*)

كِنْدِيّ *adj* *from or pertaining to Kindah (a kingdom in Arabia before the rise of Islam)*

كَنود *adj* ungrateful

كُنود *n* ingratitude, ungratefulness

كَنَدا *n* Canada

كَنَديّ *adj, n* Canadian

كُنْدُش *n* (Zool) magpie (*Corvidae*); عَقْعَق الكُنْدُشِ oystercatcher (*Haematopus*)

كَنّارة *n* listed alphabetically

كَنَزَ *v* |i; كَنْز| to hoard (up), to save; كَنَزَ مالَهُ to hoard one's money

اكْتَنَزَ *v* 1 [امْتلأ] to be thick, to be compact, to be sturdy 2 [ادَّخَرَ] to hoard (up)

كَنْز *n* |كُنوز| treasure; كَنْز مَدْفون a hidden treasure; غُرْفة كَنْزٍ treasury; صُنْدوق كَنْزٍ treasure chest; بَحَثَ عن كَنْزٍ to seek a treasure; عَثَرَ على كَنْزٍ to find a treasure

كَنْزة *n* 1 [مَلابِس] sweater, pullover; كَنْزة سَميكة a thick sweater; كَنْزة من الصوفِ a woollen sweater; نَسَجَ كَنْزةً to knit a sweater; لَبِسَ كَنْزةً to wear a pullover 2 [اسْم شَخْصيّ] |dipt| Kenza (*female given name*)

مُكْتَنِز *adj* sturdy, compact, thick; plump, voluptuous; ample, generous; جِسْم مُكْتَنِز a voluptuous body; صَدْر مُكْتَنِز an ample bosom

مَكْنَز *n* |مَكانِزُ| thesaurus

كَنَسَ *v* |u; كَنْس| to sweep (clean); كَنَسَ الشارِعَ to sweep the street

كَنَّسَ *v* to sweep, to brush

كَنائِسيّ *adj* ecclesiastical, church (*before n*); موسيقى كَنائِسيّة church music

كَنّاس *n* sweeper; street sweeper

كُناسة *n* sweepings

كَنَسيّ *adj* ecclesiastical, church (*before n*); مَجْمَع كَنَسيّ synod; زَواج كَنَسيّ a church wedding; السُلْطة الكَنَسيّة ecclesiastical power

كَنيس *n* synagogue

كْنيسِت *n* Knesset

كَنيسة *n* |كَنائِسُ| 1 [مَبْنًى] church (building); بُرْج كَنيسةٍ church tower 2 [جَماعة] church, religious denomination; الكَنيسة الكاثوليكيّة the Catholic Church; أَبو الكَنيسةِ Church Father

مَكْناس *n* listed alphabetically

مِكْنَسة *n* |مَكانِسُ| broom; مِكْنَسة كَهْرَبائيّة vacuum cleaner

كُنّاش *n* |كَنانيشُ| (Mor) notebook; register; كُنّاش الحالةِ المَدَنيّةِ ≈ marriage certificate; (municipal) register; كُنّاش الزَواجِ marriage register

كَنْغَر *n* kangaroo (*Macropus*)

كَنَفَ *v* |u; كَنْف| 1 [صانَ] to protect, to guard, to preserve; كَنَفَ شَخْصاً to take sb under one's protection 2 [جَعَلَهُ في عائِلَتِهِ] to receive, to take in, to take up; كَنَفَ يَتيماً في بَيْتِهِ to take an orphan into one's home

اكْتَنَفَ *v* 1 [أَحاطَ ب] to surround, to enclose; لا يَكْتَنِفُ ذلك أَيُّ سوءٍ there's no harm in that; هذا المَوْضوع يَكْتَنِفُهُ الغُموضُ this subject is surrounded by obscurity 2 [شَخْصاً] to take charge of

كَنَف *n* |أَكْناف| 1 [جانِب] side, flank 2 [صَدْر] chest; breasts, bosom 3 [قَلْب] bosom, heart

كُنافة *n* kunafa (*cheese pastry made of shredded dough and soaked in sweet syrup*)

كَنيف *n* |كُنُف| toilet (bowl), lavatory (bowl)

كَنكة *n* (Egypt) Turkish coffee pot

كُنْكان *n a card game*

كَنْكَنَ *v* |i; كَنْكَنة| to stay at home; to nestle, to cuddle up

كَنَّ *v* |u; كُنون, كَنّ| to hide, to conceal; to harbour, to nourish; كَنَّ مَوَدّةً to feel sympathy

أَكَنَّ *v* to keep secret, to hide, to conceal; أَكَنَّ لِشَخْصٍ الخَيْرَ to be well disposed towards sb

اسْتَكَنَّ *v* to calm down; to nestle

كانون *n* |dipt| |كَوانينُ| 1 [شَهْر] كانون الأَوَّل (Levant, Iraq) December; كانون الثاني (Levant, Iraq) January; شَهْر الكانونِ (Hist) December (*Libya under Gaddafi*) 2 [مَوْقِد] brazier, stove

كِنّ *n* |أَكِنّة, أَكْنان| shelter, refuge, hiding place; house

كِنان *n* |أَكِنّة| awning; pent roof, shed roof

كِنانة *n* |كَنائِنُ, كِنانات| quiver (*for holding arrows*)

كَنّة *n* |كَنائِنُ| 1 [زَوْجة الابْنِ] daughter-in-law 2 [زَوْجة الأَخِ] sister-in-law

‹ كَهْرَمان *n* amber
‹ كَهْروضَوْئي *adj* photovoltaic
‹ كَهْرومائيّ, كَهْرَمائيّ *adj* hydroelectric; طاقة كَهْرومائيّة hydroelectricity; مَحَطّة كَهْرَمائيّة hydroelectric power station
‹ كَهْرومَغْناطيسيّ *adj* electromagnetic; مَجال \ حَقْل كَهْرومَغْناطيسيّ an electromagnetic field; مَوْجات \ إشْعاع كَهْرومَغْناطيسيّ(ة) electromagnetic waves/radiation
‹ اكْتَهَفَ *v* to live in a cave
كَهْف *n* |كُهوف| cave, cavern; سورة الكَهْف The Cave (*Sura 18*); ساكِن الكُهوف caveman
‹ كَهُلَ *v* |u; كُهولة| to be middle-aged
اكْتَهَلَ *v* to be middle-aged
كَهْل *adj* |كُهول| middle-aged
كاهِل *n* |كَواهِل| shoulder; upper back; أَلْقى شَيْئاً على كاهِلِ شَخْصٍ to burden sb with sth; أَثْقَلَ كاهِلَ شَخْصٍ to overburden sb; تَقَعُ المَسْؤوليّةُ على كاهِلِ شَخْصٍ the responsibility falls on sb's shoulders
كُهولة *n* middle age
‹ كَهُنَ *v* |u; كَهانة| to be/become a priest
تَكَهَّنَ *v* |ب| to predict, to foretell, to prophesy; تَكَهَّنَ بِشَيْءٍ to predict sth
كاهِن *n* |كَهَنة, كُهّان| ❶ [الكَهَنوت] priest ❷ [عَرّاف] fortune teller, seer, clairvoyant
كاهِنة *n* priestess
كِهانة *n* priesthood
كَهَنوت *n* priesthood; ministry; رِجال الكَهَنوتِ the clergy
كَهَنوتيّ *adj* priestly, sacerdotal
تَكَهُّن *n* |تَكَهُّنات| prognosis, prediction, prophecy
مُتَكَهِّن *n* fortune teller
‹ كَوّة *n* |كَوّات, كُوىً, كِواء| opening, aperture, hole; كَوّة سَفينةٍ porthole
‹ كَوارْتْز *n* quartz
‹ كَوارْك *n* quark
‹ كُوالا, كُوال *n* koala (*Phascolarctus cinereus*)
‹ كَواليني *n* |كَوَلينيّة| locksmith

كُنّة *n* |كِنان, كُنّات| lean-to, shed, awning
مَكْنون **A** *adj* hidden, concealed
B *n* مَكْنونات النَّفْسِ the hidden content of the psyche
‹ اكْتَنَهَ *v* to capture the essence, to (try to) understand thoroughly
كُنْه *n* essence, quintessence
‹ كَنى *v* |i; كِناية| to call, to name; to denote
كَنّى *v* to give a kunya; to call by the kunya
تَكَنّى *v* *to be known by a certain kunya*
كِناية *n* metaphor
كُنْية *n* |كُنىً| kunya (*a name for an adult derived from his/her eldest child's name*); كُنْيَتُهُ أَبو عَليّ his kunya is Abu Ali
‹ كَهْرَبَ *v* |i; كَهْرَبة| to electrify, to charge with electricity
تَكَهْرَبَ *v* to be electrified, to be charged with electricity
كَهْرَب *n* |كَهارِبُ| electron
كَهْرَباء *n* |f| electricity; (electric) current; مَصْلَحة الكَهْرَباءِ electric company; شَبَكة تَوْزيع الكَهْرَباءِ electricity grid; اسْتِهْلاك الكَهْرَباءِ electricity supply; التَزْويد بالكَهْرَباءِ power consumption; انْخِفاض \ ارْتِفاع اسْتِهْلاكِ الكَهْرَباءِ a decrease/increase in power consumption; اسْتَهْلَكَ كَثيراً من الكَهْرَباءِ to consume a lot of power; وَلَّدَ الكَهْرَباءَ to generate electricity; قَطَعَ الكَهْرَباءَ to cut the electricity off; انْقَطَعَت الكَهْرَباءُ the power supply has failed; وَفَّرَ الكَهْرَباءَ to save electricity; صَعَقَ بالكَهْرَباءِ to electrocute
كَهْرَبائيّ **A** *adj* electric, electrical; دائِرة كَهْرَبائيّة electrical circuit; طاقة كَهْرَبائيّة electrical energy, electrical power; فُرْن \ مِدْفَأة كَهْرَبائيّ(ة) an electric stove/heater; ضَوْء \ نور كَهْرَبائيّ electric light; قيثارة كَهْرَبائيّة an electric guitar; أَسْلاك \ آلات كَهْرَبائيّة electrical wires/appliances; تَيّار كَهْرَبائيّ electric current; جُهْد \ تَوَتُّر كَهْرَبائيّ voltage, tension; مُنْتَجات كَهْرَبائيّة electrics; مُحَرِّك كَهْرَبائيّ (electric) motor
B *n* electrician
كَهْرَبائيّة *n* كَهْرَبائيّة ساكِنة static electricity
كُهَيْرِب *n* |كُهَيْرِبات| electron
مُكَهْرَب *adj* electrically charged, electrified, live; كانَ مُكَهْرَباً it was (electrically) charged

‹ **كوب** *n* |أَكْواب| cup, mug, (drinking) glass; كوب حَليبٍ \ من الحَليبِ a cup of milk; كوب الماءِ hydrangea (*Hydrangea*)

كاب *n* listed alphabetically

كوبة *n* hearts (*in playing cards*); أَرْبَعة كوبة four of hearts

كوبيّ **A** *adj* Cuban

B *n* **1** [شَخْص من كوبا] Cuban **2** (*Zool*) guinea pig, cavy (*Cavia porcellus*)

كوبيّة *n* hydrangea (*Hydrangea*)

‹ **كوبا** *n* Cuba

‹ **كوبالْت** *n* cobalt; أَزْرَق الكوبالْت cobalt blue

‹ **كوبْرا** *n* |كوبْرات| cobra

‹ **كوبْري**, **كُبْري** *n* |كَباريّ| bridge; flyover (BrE), overpass (AmE)

‹ **كوبون** *n* |كوبونات| coupon; دَفَعَ قيمة كوبون to pay (out) a coupon

‹ **كوتة** *n* quota

‹ **كَوْثَر** *n* see كثر

مُكَوْثَر *n* |مُكَوْثَرات| polymer

‹ **مَكْوَجيّ** *n* see كوي

‹ **كوخ** *n* |أَكْواخ| hut, cabin; كوخ طينيّ a mud hut; كوخ خَشَبيّ a log cabin; كوخ بائِس a shabby hut; بَنَى كوخاً to build a hut

1 ‹ **كادَ** *v* |a; كَوْد| **1** [أَوْشَكَ] to be about, to be on the point; كادَ يَموتُ he almost died; كادَ الأَمْرُ يَتَسَبَّبُ بِأَزْمةٍ the issue almost caused a crisis; يَكادُ لا يُطاقُ it's almost unbearable; ما كادَ \ لم يَكَدْ يَخْرُجُ حتّى ... no sooner had he left, than ...; ما كادَ يَخْرُجُ من البَيْتِ وإذا بِجَرَس الهاتِفِ يَرِنُّ as soon as he left the house, the phone rang; لا يَكادُ أَحَدٌ يَفْهَمُ ما يَقولُهُ hardly anybody understands what he's saying **2** [أَرادَهُ بِسوءٍ \ خَدَعَ] see كيد

كاد *n* بالكاد scarcely, hardly

2 ‹ **كود** *n* code; كود مَصْدَريّ source code

كوديّ *adj* encoded, enciphered; اسْم كوديّ code name

‹ **كودين** *n* codeine

‹ **كَوَّرَ** *v* **1** [شَدَّ] to make round, to form into a ball; to clench; كَوَّرَ عَجيناً to form dough into a ball **2** [لَفَّ] to wind, to coil

تَكَوَّرَ *v* to be/become round, to be/become ball-shaped; to conglomerate

كور *n* |كيران ,أَكْوُر ,أَكْوار| forge, smithy

كِوار *n* beehive, hive

كورة *n* |كُوَر| district; village; town

تَكْوير *n* winding, coiling; سورة التَكْوير The Folding Up (*Sura 81*)

مُكَوَّر *adj* round, spherical; خَدّانِ مُكَوَّرانِ round cheeks; وَجْه مُكَوَّر a round face; الأَرْضُ مُكَوَّرةٌ the Earth is round

‹ **كورَس** *n* (church) choir; chorus

‹ **كورْسيه** *n* |كورْسيهات| corset, bodice

‹ **كورْنيش**, **كُرْنيش** *n* corniche, costal road

‹ **كوري** *n* curie

‹ **كوريّ** **A** *adj* Korean; (اللُغة) الكوريّة Korean (*language*)

B *n* Korean (*person*)

كورِيا *n* Korea; كورِيا الجَنوبيّة South Korea; كورِيا الشَماليّة North Korea

كوز *n* |كيزان ,أَكْواز| **1** (*Bot*) spadix; كوز صَنَوْبَرٍ pine cone **2** [إناء] mug

‹ **كوزْموبوليتانيّ**, **كوسْموبوليتانيّ** *adj* cosmopolitan

‹ **كاسَ** *v* |u; كَوْس| **1** [عَرَجَ] to limp, to hobble **2** [أَدُبَ] see كيس

كوس *n* |كوسات| (*Geom*) square; T-square, set square

كوسة, **كوسى**, **كوسا** *n* courgette (BrE), zucchini (AmE)

‹ **كوسْتاريكا** *n* Costa Rica

‹ **كَوْسَج** *n* swordfish (*Xiphias gladius*)

كوشَر *adj* kosher

‹ **كوع**, **كاع** *n* |أَكْواع ,كيعان| **1** [اليَد] wrist, carpus **2** [مِرْفَق] elbow; ارْتَكَزَ بِكوعِهِ على شَيْءٍ to lean one's elbow on sth

‹ **كوفيّ** *adj* Kufic; خَطّ كوفيّ Kufic script

كوفيّة *n* keffiyeh (*traditional Arab headdress fashioned from a square, usually cotton, scarf*)

الكوفة *n* Kufa (*city in Iraq*)

‹ **كوك** *n* (*Geol*) coke; فَحْم الكوكِ coke

‹ **كوكا** *n* coca (*Erythroxylum coca*); وَرَق الكوكا coca leaves

‹ **كوكايين**, **كوكائين** *n* cocaine, coke; تَعاطى الكوكايين to use cocaine; اسْتَنْشَقَ \ شَمَّ الكوكايين to snort cocaine

‹ **كَوْكَب** *n* |كَواكِبُ| planet; star; كَوْكَب سَيّار planet; الكَوْكَب الأَحْمَر the red planet (*Mars*); نِظام كَواكِبَ planetary system; star system

كَوْكَبة *n* **1** [جَماعة] group, party; كَوْكَبة من المُفَكِّرينَ a group of intellectuals **2** (Astron) constellation **3** (Mil) squadron

كَوْكَبيّ *adj* planetary, planet (*before n*); starry, starlike, star (*before n*); نِظام كَوْكَبيّ star system; planetary system

كُوَيْكِب *n* asteroid

‹ **كوكْتيل** *n* cocktail; شَرِبَ كوكْتيل to drink a cocktail; خَلَّطَ كوكْتيل to mix a cocktail; كوكْتيل غِنائيّ *a mix of songs by various artists*

‹ **كوكي** *n* |كوكيز| (Comput) cookie

‹ **كولِسْترول** *n* cholesterol

‹ **كولورادو** *n* |f| Colorado (*US state*)

‹ **كولومْبِيا** *n* Colombia; قِطاع كولومْبِيا District of Columbia, DC

‹ **كولونيل** *n* colonel

‹ **كوليرا** *n* cholera; تَتَفَشّى \ تَنْتَشِرُ الكوليرا cholera is spreading; أُصيبَ بالكوليرا to have cholera

‹ **كوليس** *n* |كَواليسُ| (Theat) coulisse, wing; وراء الكَواليسِ behind the scenes

‹ **كَوَّمَ** *v* to pile (up), to heap (up), to stack (up); كَوَّمَ الصَّناديقَ to stack up crates

تَكَوَّمَ *v* to accumulate, to pile up, to amass; تَكَوَّمَت المَلابِسُ على الأَرْضِ the clothes were piled on the floor

كَوْم *n* |أَكْوام, كيمان| **1** [كُدْس] pile, heap, mound; كَوْم من الأَوْراقِ \ الكُتُبِ a pile of papers/books; كَوْم حِجارةٍ a pile of stones; كَوْم تِبْنٍ a bale of hay **2** [تَلّ] hill

كامة *n* listed alphabetically

كَوْمة *n* |كُوَم| heap, pile; mass; كَوْمة من الأَحْجارِ a pile of rocks

تَكَوُّم *n* accumulation, pile-up, build-up

‹ **كومْبارْس** *n* (Cin) extra, walk-on

‹ **كوميديّ** *adj* comic, comical; فيلْم كوميديّ a comedy; أوبيرا كوميديّة a comic opera; مُمَثِّل كوميديّ comedian

‹ **كانَ** *v* |u; كَوْن, كَيْنونة| **1** [فِعْل الوُجودِ] to be; كانَ أبي مُعَلِّماً my father was a teacher; كانَ البِناءُ في حالةٍ سَيِّئةٍ the building was in bad condition; كانَ يا ما كانَ ... once upon a time, there was ...; أَحْسَن \ أَشَدّ ما يَكونُ as good/severe as possible; كانَ أَبي من الذين هاجَروا my father was among the people who emigrated; كانَ من أَوْلَويّاتِ سِياسَتِهِ تَحْسينُ الوَضْعِ الاقْتِصاديِّ improving the economic situation was one of the his policies' priorities; الواحِد، فَرْداً كانَ أم مَجْموعةً people, individually or in a group **2** [المَوْقِع] to be (located), to lie, to stand; كانَ على الطاوِلةِ to lie on the table; كانَ مَعَهُ أَخوهُ his brother was with him; لم أَكُنْ أَبَداً في بَغْدادَ I've never been in Baghdad; مَنْ كانَ هُناكَ من الرِجالِ the men who were present there **3** [مع فِعْلٍ آخَرَ] *modal verb which, in combination with present-tense verb, forms the past progressive and past habitual aspects*; كانوا يَلْعَبونَ they were playing; كانَ صَديقي يَسْبَحُ my friend was swimming; كانَ يَشْرَبُ فِنْجاناً من القَهْوةِ كُلَّ يَوْمٍ he used to drink a cup of coffee each day; كانَ (دائِماً) يَشْرَبُ كَأْساً من النَبيذِ مع الطَعامِ he would (always) drink a glass of wine with his meal **4** [تَمَكَّنَ |ل|] to be able, to be capable; ما كانَ لَهُ أَنْ ... he was not capable of ... **5** [امْتَلَكَ |ل|] to have; كانَ لي أَصْدِقاءُ في الخارِجِ I had friends abroad; كانَ لَهُ مالٌ to have money; كانَ عِنْدَهُ أَطْفالٌ to have children **6** [كانَ عَلَيْهِ |على|] to have to, to need; كانَ على الوَزيرِ أَنْ يَتَّخِذَ قَراراً the minister needed to make a decision **7** (Gram) (the verb) kaana; كانَ وَأَخَواتُها kaana and her sisters (*verbs of being, becoming, remaining, and seeming*); خَبَر كانَ *the predicate of an equational sentence with kaana*; أَصْبَحَ في خَبَرِ كانَ to become a thing of the past **8** [اسْتَسْلَمَ] see **كين**

كَوَّنَ *v* **1** [شَكَّلَ] to form, to shape, to mould; كَوَّنَ شَخْصيّةَ شَخْصٍ to mould sb's character **2** [رَكَّبَ] to build (up), to compound, to construct; كَوَّنَ رِسالةً to compose a message **3** (Educ) to school, to train, to educate; كَوَّنَ مُتَرْجِمينَ to train interpreters; كَوَّنَ شَخْصاً مُعَلِّماً to train sb to be a teacher

تَكَوَّنَ *v* |من| to come into existence, to arise; to consist of, to be formed (by), to be composed (of); تَكَوَّنَ من شَيْءٍ to consist of sth

اسْتَكانَ *v* to surrender, to submit, to yield

كَوْن *n* |أَكْوان| **1** [عالَم] cosmos, universe; عِلْم الكَوْنِ cosmology **2** [وُجود] existence, being; كَوْنُهُ خارِجَ الوِزارةِ لا يَعْني أَنَّهُ لَيْسَ لَهُ تَأْثيرٌ the fact that he is outside of the ministry doesn't mean that he has no influence

كائِن [A] *adj* [مَوْجود] being, existing, existent; كائِناً ما كانَ whatever it may be; يَعْمَلُ في شَرِكةِ اسْتِثْمارٍ كائِنةٍ في بَيْروتَ he works in some investiment company in Beirut [B] *n* |كائِنات| [مَخْلوق] being, creature; كائِنات حَيّة \ عاقِلة living/intelligent beings; كائِنات غَريبة \ غَيْر أَرْضيّة alien/extraterrestrial beings; كائِن أُحاديّ الخَلِيّةِ a single-celled organism; كائِنات دَقيقة microorganisms

كَوْنيّ *adj* cosmic, universal, cosmo-; أَشِعّة كَوْنيّة cosmic radiation

كِيان *n* |كِيانات| entity, existence, being; كِيان مُسْتَقِلّ \ مُنْفَصِل a separate entity; الكِيان الفِلَسْطينيّ the Palestinian entity; شَكَّلَ كِياناً to form an entity; في أَعْماقِ كِيانِهِ in his innermost being

كَيْنونة *n* existence, being, entity

التَكْوين *n* Genesis (*book of the Bible*)

تَكَوُّن *n* origin, genesis, formation

تَكْوين *n* [1] [إِنْشاء] construction, formation, compounding; بَدْء تَكْوينٍ birth [2] (Educ) education, schooling, training; تَكْوين مِهْنيّ vocational training; تَكْوين روحيّ spiritual education; تَكْوين الشَبابِ the education of the young; تَلَقّى تَكْويناً to receive an education [3] [بِنْية] constitution, condition, configuration

تَكْوينيّ *adj* educational, educative, formative

مُتَكَوِّن *adj* compound, composite, composed; فَريق مُتَكَوِّن من ثَمانِيَةِ أَشْخاصٍ a team consisting of eight people

مَكان *n* |أَماكِنُ, أَمْكِنة| [1] [مَوْضِع] place, location, spot; أَماكِن بَعيدة distant places; مَكان قَفْر an inhospitable place; مَكان مُناسِب \ رائِع a suitable/splendid location; اسْم مَكانٍ place name, toponym; ظَرْف مَكانٍ adverb of place; في كُلِّ مَكانٍ everywhere; في مَكانٍ آخَرَ elsewhere; من الأَهَمّيّةِ بِمَكانٍ very important; مَكانَكَ! stop!; مَكانَهُ in his/its place; وَضَعَ شَيْئاً في مَكانِهِ to put sth in its place; لو كُنْتُ مَكانَكَ if I were you; لو كُنْتُ مَكانَكَ لَما أَتَيْتُ if I were you, I wouldn't have come; اسْتَكْشَفَ المَكانَ to explore the place; أَخَذَ مَكانَ شَخْصٍ to take sb's place [2] [مِساحة] space, room; لِضيقِ المَكانِ due to lack of space; أَفْسَحَ المَكانَ لِشَيْءٍ to make room for sth; لا مَكانَ لَهُ في هذه الفَتْرةِ there's no place for him in these times [3] [مَنْزِلة] position, status, standing; مَكان بارِز \ مَرْموق a prominent position

مَكانة *n* standing, status, position; مَكانة رَئيسيّة a key position; مَكانة عالِية a high status; ذو مَكانةٍ عالِيةٍ highly placed; تَمَتَّعَ بِمَكانةٍ مَرْموقةٍ to hold a high position; لَهُ مَكانةٌ كَبيرةٌ في الحُكومةِ he holds a high position within the government

مُكَوَّن *adj* formed, composed

مُكَوِّن [A] *adj* formative, constituting [B] *n* |مُكَوِّنات| component, ingredient, constituent; مُكَوِّن أَساسيّ (essential) component; مُكَوِّنات شَيْءٍ ingredients of sth; مُكَوِّنات غِذائيّة ingredients

‹ **كونْت** *n* count

‹ **كونْتوار** *n* bar

‹ **كَوْنِج** *n* (Zool) Eurasian hobby (*Falco subbuteo*)

‹ **كونشِرْتو** *n* concerto

‹ **كونْفِدراليّ** *adj* confederal; Confederate

كونْفِدراليّة *n* confederation

‹ **كونْياك** *n* cognac, (French) brandy; كَأْس من الكونْياك a glass of cognac; كونْياك مُعَتَّق vintage cognac; شَرِبَ الكونْياك to drink cognac

‹ **كونيتيكَت** *n* |f| Connecticut (*US state*)

‹ **كَوى** *v* |i| كَيّ [1] [مَلابِسَ] to iron; to press; كَوى سِرْوالاً to iron a pair of trousers [2] (Med) to cauterize, to burn away, to sear up; كَوى قَلْبَ شَخْصٍ to spurn sb's affection

اكْتَوى *v* [1] [بِمِكْواةٍ] to be pressed, to be ironed [2] [بالنارِ] to be burned; to suffer (intensely); اكْتَوى بِنارِ \ بِنيرانِ شَيْءٍ to be caused (great) suffering by sth

كاوٍ *adj* biting, corrosive, caustic; سائِل \ حَمْض \ غاز كاوٍ a corrosive liquid/acid/gas; مادّة تَنْظيف كاوية a corrosive cleaning agent; صودا كاوية caustic soda

كَوّاء *n* ironer (*person who irons laundry*)

كَيّ *n* [1] [مَلابِسَ] ironing; طاوِلة \ مائِدة \ لَوْح الكَيِّ ironing board [2] (Med) cauterization

مِكْواة *n* |مَكاوٍ| (flat) iron; مِكْواة الشَعْرِ curling iron

مَكْوَجيّ *n* ironer (*person who irons laundry*)

مَكْوِيّ *adj* ironed; branded

كُوَيْتِيّ *adj, n* Kuwaiti

الكُوَيْت *n* |f| Kuwait; دَوْلة الكُوَيْتِ the State of Kuwait; مَدِينة الكُوَيْتِ, الكُوَيْت العاصِمة Kuwait City

كُوَيِّس *adj* (colloq Egypt) good, nice, okay

كَيْ *conj* so that, in order that, (in order) to; جاءَ كَيْ يُساعِدَكَ he came to help you; حَذَّرْتُكَ كَيْ لا تَفْعَلَ ما فَعَلْتُهُ I warned you not to do what I did

كَيْلا *conj* in order not to, lest; كَيْلا يَضُرَّ أَوْلادَهُ in order not to damage his children

كَيْما *conj* so that, in order that, in order to; كَيْما لا تَذْهَبَ جُهودُنا سُدًى so that our efforts will not be in vain

لِكَيْ *conj* so that, in order that, (in order) to; جاءَ لِكَيْ يُساعِدَكَ he came to help you; فَعَلَ ذلك لِكَيْ يَتَنَصَّلَ من مَسْؤوليَّتِهِ he did that in order to shirk his responsibility

لِكَيْلا *conj* in order not to, lest; طَلَبَ حَصْرَ النِقاشِ لِكَيْلا تَطولَ الجَلْسَةُ he requested to shorten the discussion lest the session be too long

لِكَيْما *conj* so that, in order that, (in order) to; يَجِبُ أَنْ نَنْطَلِقَ الآنَ لِكَيْما يَتَسَنّى لَنا أَنْ نَصِلَ في الوَقْتِ المُحَدَّدِ we must leave now in order to arrive on time

كَيْتَ *n* كَيْتَ وَكَيْتَ so-and-so, such-and-such; كَذا وَكَيْتَ so-and-so

مَكْيَج, مَكِياج, ماكِياج see مكيج

كادَ *v* |i; كَيْد| [1] [أَرادَهُ بِسوءٍ] to conspire, to plot, to scheme; كادَ لِشَخْصٍ to conspire against sb [2] [خدَعَ] to deceive; كادَ شَخْصاً to deceive sb; كادَ لِشَخْصٍ مَكيدةً to play a (dirty) trick on sb [3] [أَوْشَكَ] see كود

كايَدَ *v* to deceive, to double-cross

كَيْد *n* |كِياد| deceit, deception; trick, intrigue

كائِد *n* intriguer, schemer, plotter

مُكايَدة *n* [1] [عَرْقَلة] inconveniencing; vexing [2] [مُناوَرة] manoeuvring; مُكايَدة سِياسيّة political manoeuvring [3] [خَدْع] tricking

مَكيدة *n* |مَكائِدُ, مَكايِدُ| machinations, intrigue, plot; trick, ruse; مَكيدة شَريرة a dirty trick; كادَ لِشَخْصٍ مَكيدةً to play a (dirty) trick on sb; دَبَّرَ مَكيدةً لِشَخْصٍ to hatch a plot against sb

كير *n* |أَكْيار| bellows

كيروسين *n* kerosene

كاسَ *v* |i; كِياسة, كَيْس| [1] [أَدُبَ] to be courteous, to be polite [2] [عَرَجَ] see كوس

كيس *n* |mf; أَكْياس, كِيَسة| [1] [جِراب] bag, sack; pouch; كيس وَرَقيّ \ من الوَرَقِ paper bag; كيس بِلاسْتيكيّ \ من البِلاسْتيكِ plastic bag; كيس هَوائيّ airbag; كيس رُزٍّ \ من الرُزِّ a bag of rice; كيس المِخَدّةِ \ الوِسادةِ pillowcase; (مَسْحوق) في أَكْياسٍ (powder) in sachets [2] (Med) cyst

كَيِّس *adj* |أَكْياس, كَيْسى; f pl كِياس| polite, courteous, well-mannered

كِياسة *n* courtesy, politeness; قَليل الكِياسةِ impolite

مُكَيَّس *adj* packed in bags

كيش *n* (Zool) shoveler (*Anas clypeata*)

كَيَّفَ *v* [1] [عَدَّلَ] to adapt, to conform, to assimilate; كَيَّفَ شَيْئاً مع شَيْءٍ to adapt sth to sth; كَيَّفَ نَفْسَهُ مع الظُروفِ to adjust oneself to circumstances [2] [شَكَّلَ] to form, to shape, to mould [3] [الهَواءَ] to air-condition (*a room*) [4] [دَخَّنَ] to smoke

تَكَيَّفَ *v* |مع| to adapt oneself (to), to conform (to), to assimilate (with); تَكَيَّفَ مع الأَغْلَبيّةِ to conform to the majority; تَكَيَّفَ مع عاداتِ بَلَدٍ to follow the customs of a country

كَيْف *n* [1] [نَوْعيّة] quality; الكَمّ والكَيْف quantity and quality; كَمًّا وَكَيْفاً, من حَيْثُ الكَمِّ والكَيْفِ quantitatively and qualitatively [2] [حَشيش] cannabis; weed; hashish

كَيْفَ *adv* how; كَيْفَ الحالُ \ حالُكَ؟ how do you do?, how are you?; أَعْرِفُ كَيْفَ يَفْعَلُ ذلك I know how he does that; كَيْفَ عَرَفْتَ ذلك؟ how did you know that?; كَيْفَ لا تُنَفَّذُ قَراراتُ الحُكومةِ how is it that government decisions are not being carried out?

كَيْفَما *conj* however; كَيْفَما كانَ الحالُ whatever the case may be; كَيْفَما كانَ (الأَمْرُ) anyhow, anyway

كَيْفِيّ *adj* qualitative

كَيْفيّة *n* [1] [حالة] character, quality, nature [2] [طَريقة] way, manner, mode; كَيْفيّة الاسْتِعْمالِ directions for use; كَيْفيّة الدَفْعِ means of payment

تَكَيُّف *n* |تَكَيُّفات| adjustment, adaptation, assimilation

‹ **كيلومتر** *n* |كيلومترات| kilometre; جَرى ١٥ كيلومِتراً to run 15 kilometres; قَطَعَ ٢٥ كيلومتْراً to cover (a distance of) 25 kilometres; يُشيرُ العَدّادُ إلى ١٠٠ كيلومِترٍ في الساعةِ the speedometer is at 100 kph

‹ **كيلوواط** *n* kilowatt; كيلوواط ساعة kilowatt-hour; ١٠٠ كيلوواط ساعة 100 kilowatt-hours

‹ **كَيْما** *conj* see **كي**

‹ **كيمياء** *n* |f| chemistry; الكيمياء العُضْويّة \ اللاعُضْويّة organic/inorganic chemistry; كيمِياء أَحْيائيّة \ حَيَويّة biochemistry; اخْتِصاصيّ في الكيمِياءِ الحَيَويّةِ biochemist; دَرَسَ الكيمِياءَ to study chemistry

كيماويّ **A** *adj* chemical; كيماويّات chemicals, chemical products; تَفاعُل كيماويّ a chemical reaction; الصِناعة الكيماويّة the chemical industry **B** *n* chemist

كيميائيّ **A** *adj* chemical; كيميائيّ حَيَويّ biochemical; تَفاعُل \ تَجْرِبة \ صيغة كيميائيّ(ة) chemical reaction/experiment/formula; الصِناعة الكيميائيّة the chemical industry **B** *n* chemist

‹ **كانَ** *v* |i; كَيْن| **1** [اسْتَسْلَمَ] to submit, to surrender, to yield **2** [وُجِدَ] see **كون**

اسْتكانَ *v* to submit, to surrender, to yield

اسْتِكانة *n* humility, submissiveness

مُسْتكين *adj* submissive, humble

‹ **كينْتاكي** *n* |f| Kentucky (*US state*)

‹ **كينِيا** *n* Kenya

‹ **كينين** *n* quinine

‹ **كيهَك** *n* Koiak (*the fourth month of the Coptic calendar*)

‹ **كيوي** *n* **1** [فاكِهة] kiwi (fruit) **2** (Zool) kiwi (*Apteryx*)

تَكْييف *n* **1** [تَهْيئة] adaptation, modification, adjustment **2** [تَبْريد] air conditioning; تَكْييف الهَواءِ air conditioning; جِهاز \ نِظام التَكْييفِ air conditioner

مُكَيَّف *adj* adapted, adjusted, conditioned; غُرْفة مُكَيَّفة an air-conditioned room

مُكَيِّف *n* air conditioning; air conditioner; مُكَيِّف هَواءٍ air conditioning, air conditioner

‹ **كالَ** *v* |i; كَيْل| to measure (out); to weigh; to mete out; كالَ الزَيْتَ to check the oil level; كالَ اللَبَنَ \ القَمْحَ to measure out the milk/wheat; كالَ لِشَخْصٍ الشَتائِمَ to heap abuse on sb

كَيَّلَ *v* to measure

كايَلَ *v* to return like for like, to repay in kind

كَيْل *n* |أكْيال| measure, measuring jug, measuring cup; كالَ لِشَخْصٍ بِكَيْلِهِ to pay sb back in his own coin; طَفَحَ الكَيْلُ enough is enough, that's the limit

كَيْلا *conj* see **كي**

كَيْلة *n* **1** [مِقْياس] *a dry measure of about 17 litres* **2** [وِعاء] measuring jug

مِكْيال *n* |مَكاييلُ| measure; المَوازِين والمَكاييل weights and measures; كالَ بِمِكْيالَيْن to apply double standards

‹ **كيلو** *n* kilo, kilogram; كيلو سُكَّرٍ \ من السُكَّرِ a kilo of sugar; ٦٨ كيلو 68 kilos; نِصْف كيلو pound; أَخَفّ \ أَثْقَل بِخَمْسةِ كيلوغْرامات five kilos lighter/heavier; سَمِنَ خَمْسةَ كيلوغْرامات to put on five kilograms

‹ **كيلوبايْت** *n* kilobyte

‹ **كيلوجول** *n* kilojoule

‹ **كيلوغْرام**, **كيلوجْرام** *n* |كيلوغْرامات| kilogram, kilo; كيلوغْرام سُكَّرٍ \ من السُكَّرِ a kilogram of sugar; كانَ وَزْنُهُ ٧٠ كيلوغْراماً he weighed 70 kilograms

ل

لا I *particle* 1 [عَكْس نَعَمْ] no; قالَ: لا he said: no; قَطْعاً لا absolutely not 2 [نَفْي] not; بلا see بِلا ;2 إنْ لا see إنْ لا \ أنْ لا he doesn't لا يَكْتُبُ ;God forbid! لا سَمَحَ اللهُ ;... that not ألاّ ... write; لا تَكْتُبْ! don't write!; لا تَثِقوا بِأَحَدٍ وَلا حتّى بي trust no one, not even me 3 [النافية للجِنْس] لا حاجةَ لِذِكْرِهِ (there's) no need to mention it; لا سَبيلَ إلى ... (there's) no possibility to ...; لا عَمَلَ لي الآنَ at the moment I have no work; لا بُدَّ مِنْهُ (أنْ \ أنّ) ... it's necessary (that) ...; it should ...; رَجُل لا مَثيلَ لَهُ a man like no other 4 [لا ... إلاّ] لا إلَهَ إلاّ اللهُ there is no god but God; لا يُمْكِنُ أنْ يَتَحَقَّقَ السَلامُ إلاّ في إطارِ قَراراتِ الأُمَمِ المُتَّحِدةِ peace can only be realized within the framework of UN resolutions 5 [لا ... وَلا ...] لا ... وَلا ... neither ... nor ...; لا هذا وَلا ذاكَ neither this nor that 6 [نَحْت] دَعْم لا مَحْدود unlimited support

لا II *n* (*Mus*) la

لااجْتِماعيّ *adj* see جمع

لاأَخْلاقيّ *adj* see خلق

لائِكيّ *adj* secular

لائِكيّة *n* secularism

لابة *n* lava

لابْ توبْ *n* laptop

لاتْفِيا *n* Latvia

لاتْفيّ A *adj* Latvian; (اللُغة) اللاتْفيّة Latvian (*language*)
B *n* Latvian (*person*)

لاتينيّ *adj* (اللُغة) اللاتينيّة Latin

لادُسْتوريّ *adj* see دستر

لاريكْس *n* larch

لازُوَرْد *n* lapis (lazuli)

لازُوَرْديّة *n* azure

لَ *particle* 1 [تَوْكيد] indeed; really, truly; إنَّهُ لَكَبيرٌ he's really big; يا لَكَ من بَغْلٍ! you're such a mule!; لَشَدَّ ما ... how much/very ...; لَشَدَّ ما كانَ سُروري إذْ ... how happy I was when ..., I was so happy when ... 2 [تَوْطِئة للجَوابِ] لو لاهُ لَمُتْنا جوعاً if it hadn't been for him, we would have starved

لِ A *prep* 1 [مِلْكيّة] of, belonging to; by; هذا لي this is mine; كِتاب لِنَجيب مَحْفوظ a book by Naguib Mahfouz; أَوَّلُ كِتابٍ لَهُ his first book; زَميل سابِق لَهُ a former colleague of his; لَهُ سَيّارةٌ جَميلةٌ he has a beautiful car; لَهُ عِنْدي ١٠٠ دولار I owe him $100 2 [مُوَجَّه إلى] to, directed/aimed at; قالَ شَيْئاً لِشَخْصٍ to say sth to sb 3 [خلال] for, during, through (*time*); لِأَوَّلِ مَرّةٍ for the first time; لِمُدّةِ سَنَتَيْنِ during (a period of) two years 4 [حَقّ] لَهُ أنْ ... he has the right to ...; لَيْسَ لَكَ أنْ ... you are not allowed to ... 5 [عَلامة المَفْعول] زِيارَتُهُ لَها his visit to/with her; دَوْلة مُنْتِجة لِلبِتْرولِ an oil-producing country 6 [لِصالِح] for, for the benefit/purpose of; because of, to; لِسَبَبٍ ما for some reason or another; اليَوْمُ العالَميّ لِلمَرْأةِ International Women's Day; فَعَلَ ذلك لِأَبيهِ he did it for his father; أَتَتْ لِمُناقَشةِ المَشْروعِ she came to discuss the project 7 [تابِع لِ] آخِر مُقابَلةٍ لي مَعَهُ my last encounter with him; على الجانِبِ الآخَرِ لِلطَريقِ on the other side of the road 8 [اسْم شَرِكةٍ] شَرِكة النيلِ لِلتَأْمينِ Nile Insurance Company
B *conj* 1 [كَيْ] so that, in order that; because (of), for, to; لِكَيْ see كَي; لِهَذا for this reason 2 [هَيّا] فَلْنَذْهَبْ \ لِنَذْهَبْ let's go; لِيَخْرُجْ let him leave!; لِيَتَخَلَّصْ من الشُعورِ بالذَنْبِ let him stop feeling guilty!

لِمَ *adv* see ما

لِما, لِماذا see ما

لُؤْم *n* meanness, vileness

لَئِيم *adj* |لُؤْمان, لُؤَماءُ, لِئام| vile, mean, depraved, wicked

تَلاؤُم *n* agreement, harmony, compatibility; correspondence; تَلاؤُم الأَلْوانِ harmony of colours; التَلاؤُم مع المُسْتَجِدّاتِ compatibility with the recent developments

مُتَلائِم *adj* matching, compatible, harmonious; similar; أَلْوان مُتَلائِمة matching colours

مُلائِم *adj* suitable, appropriate, favourable; fitting, convenient, matching; right, proper; consistent; حَلّ مُلائِم an appropriate solution; في مِزاجٍ مُلائِمٍ in the right mood; وَفَّر المُناخَ المُلائِمَ to create a favourable climate; كانَ مُلائِماً لِشَيْءٍ \ شَخْصٍ to be suitable for sth/sb

مُلاءَمة *n* 1 [مُناسَبة] suitability, appropriateness; هو الأَكْثَرُ مُلاءَمةً ل ... he's most suitable for ... 2 [صُلْح] agreement, harmony

‹ **لام** *n* |f| *name of the letter* ل

‹ **لاما, لامة** *n* (Zool) llama (*Lama glama*)

‹ **لامُبالاة, لامُبالي** see بلوابلي

‹ **لامَحْدودِيّة** *n* see حدد

‹ **لامَرْكَزِيّ, لامَرْكَزِيّة** see ركز

‹ **لامُنْتَمٍ** *n* see نموانمي

‹ **لاموس** *n* lemming

‹ **اللامِيون الأَبْيَض** *n* white dead-nettle (*Lamium album*)

‹ **لأَنَّ** *conj* see أنن

‹ **لانِهائِيّ, لانِهائِيّة** see نهوانهي

‹ **لاهاي** *n* |f| The Hague

‹ **لاهوتِيّ** A *adj* theological; مَسائِل لاهوتِيّة theological issues B *n* theologian

‹ **لاهور** *n* |f| Lahore (*city in Pakistan*)

‹ **لاوُس** *n* |f| Laos

‹ **لاوَعْي** *n* see وعي

‹ **لاوَنْدة** *n* lavender (*Lavandula*)

‹ **لَبْوة, لَبُؤة** *n* lioness

‹ **لَبَّ** *v* |u; لَبّ, لُبوب, لَبابة| 1 [بَقِيَ] to stay, to remain 2 [حَكُمَ] to become wise

‹ **لاسامِيّ, لاسامِيّة** see سام

‹ **لاسِلْكِيّ** *adj* see سلك

‹ **لاشَرْعِيّة** *n* see شرع

‹ **لاشُعور** *n* see شعر

‹ **لاشَيْء** *n* see شيأ

‹ **لاكْتوز** *n* lactose; عَدَم تَحَمُّلِ اللاكْتوز lactose intolerance

‹ **لَأْلَأَ** *v* |i; لَأْلَأة| to twinkle, to glitter, to sparkle; to flash, to shine

تَلَأْلَأَ *v* to twinkle, to glitter, to sparkle; to flash, to shine, to gleam; تَلَأْلَأَ في الشَّمْسِ to gleam in the sunlight

لُؤْلُؤ *n coll* |لَآلِئُ| pearl; لُؤْلُؤة مُزَيَّفة a fake pearl; عِقْد من اللُؤْلُؤ a pearl necklace; أُمّ اللُؤْلُؤ mother-of-pearl; صَيْد اللُؤْلُؤ pearling

لُؤْلُؤِيّ *adj* pearly

تَلَأْلُؤ *n* |تَلَأْلُؤات| sparkle, glitter, twinkle; flash, shine; brightness, radiance; تَلَأْلُؤ المُجَوْهَراتِ the glitter of jewelry; تَلَأْلُؤ النُجوم the twinkling of the stars

‹ **لالّة** *n* (NA) madam, lady

‹ **لَأَمَ** *v* |a; لَأْم| to bandage, to dress, to bind (up); لَأَمَ جُرْحاً to dress a wound

لَؤُمَ *v* |u; لَآمة, لُؤْمة| to be wicked/mean

لاءَمَ *v* 1 [ناسَبَ] to suit, to be suitable/appropriate/adequate; to be convenient; to fit, to match, to agree; لاءَمَ شَيْئاً \ شَخْصاً to match sth/sb; (لا) يُلائِمُ it is (not) convenient 2 [كَيَّفَ] to adapt, to fit; to arrange, to regulate 3 [صالَحَ |بين] to reconcile, to conciliate, to harmonize, to bring together

أَلْأَمَ *v* 1 [تَصَرَّفَ بِلُؤْمٍ] to act meanly 2 [أَصْلَحَ] to repair, to mend

تَلاءَمَ *v* to fit, to match, to suit; to be consistent, to be in agreement/harmony with; تَلاءَمَ مع شَيْءٍ to be consistent with sth

الْتَأَمَ *v* 1 [شُفِيَ] to heal; to be healed/cured; to be repaired/mended; الْتَأَمَ الجُرْحُ the wound has healed 2 [اجْتَمَعَ] to meet, to convene, to gather, to assemble; الْتَأَمَ مَجْلِسُ الوُزَراءِ اليَوْمَ the cabinet met today 3 [اتَّفَقَ] to match, to agree, to suit

لُبّ *n* |أَلْباب| ① [جَوْهَر] core, essence, quintessence, heart; لُبّ المَوْضوع \ المُشْكِلةِ the core of the matter/problem; لُبّ النِقاشِ the heart of the debate ② [عَقْل] reason, intellect, mind ③ [ثَمَرة] pulp, flesh; pith; لُبّ الثَمَرةِ fruit pith

لُباب *n* kernel, core, inner part, pith

لَبيب **A** *adj* |أَلِبّاءُ| rational, sensible, reasonable; intelligent, bright; wise, knowledgeable

B *n* |أَلِبّاءُ| an intelligent/rational/wise person; اللَبيب بالإشارةِ يَفْهَمُ a nod is as good as a wink

تَلْبيب *n* |تلابيبُ| collar; أَمْسَكَ بِتَلابيبِ شَخْصٍ to grab sb by the collar

لَبِثَ *v* |a; لُباث, لَبَث, لُبْث, لَبْث| to stay, to remain, to sojourn; to linger; لَبِثَ في السِجْنِ أَرْبَعَ سَنَواتٍ he was in prison for four years; لم يَلْبَثْ ... , ما لَبِثَ أَنْ \ حتّى ... it didn't take long before ..., in no time ..., soon ...; ما لَبِثَ أَنْ عادَ it didn't take long before he returned

تَلَبَّثَ *v* to hesitate, to linger; to stay, to sojourn; to stay put, to stand still

تِلْباثيّة, تِلْباثيّ listed alphabetically

لَبَخ *n* (Bot) Albizzia (*Albizia lebbeck*)

لَبْخة *n* compress, poultice

لَبَدَ *v* |u; لُبود| ① [أَقامَ] to stay, to remain ② [الصوفُ] to cling, to adhere, to stick

لَبَّدَ *v* to cause to adhere to, to stick on; لَبَّدَت الغُيومُ السَماءَ the sky was overcast

تَلَبَّدَ *v* to tangle, to mat; to become/get entangled; to cling, to adhere; to compress; قد تَلَبَّدَت السَماءُ بالغُيومِ the sky was overcast

لِبْد *n* |لُبود, أَلْباد| felt

لابِد *adj* situated, located; سَرَطانة لابدة carcinoma in situ

لُبّادة *n* |لَبابيدُ| ① [قُبَّعة] a felt cap ② [للحِصانِ] saddlecloth

لُبْدة, لِبْدة *n* |لِبَد| ① [الأَسَدِ] mane ② [شَعْر أو صوف مُتَلَبِّد] tangle

مُتَلبِّد *adj* entangled, stuck together; compact, compressed; covered; شَعْر مُتَلَبِّد tangled hair; مُتَلَبِّد بالغُيومِ overcast

مُلَبَّد *adj* tangled, matted; compact, compressed, pressed together; covered; شَعْر مُلَبَّد tangled hair; مُلَبَّد بالغُيومِ overcast; السَماءُ مُلَبَّدةٌ بالغُيومِ the sky is overcast

لَبِسَ *v* |a; لُبْس| to dress, to put on, to wear; لَبِسَ قُبَّعةً \ قلادةً to wear a hat/necklace; لَبِسَ حِذاءَهُ to put on one's shoes; لَبِسَ نظّارَتَهُ الشَمْسيّةَ to put on one's sunglasses; لَبِسَ معْطَفاً \ جَوارِبَ to put on a coat/socks

لَبَّسَ *v* ① [كَسا] to dress, to put on; to wear ② [غَطّى] to cover, to coat, to cloak ③ [خَلَطَ] to make obscure/vague, to twist, to distort; لَبَّسَ القِصّةَ to distort the story

لابَسَ *v* ① [ارْتَبَطَ ب] to associate with, to be in close contact with; to accompany; لابَسَ شَيْئاً to be associated with sb ② [أَحاطَ] to surround

أَلْبَسَ *v* ① [كَسا] to clothe, to dress; أَلْبَسَ أَطْفالَهُ to dress one's children ② [غَطّى] to cover, to coat, to cloak

تَلَبَّسَ *v* ① [ارْتَدى] to wear, to put on; to dress oneself, to get dressed ② [الأَمْرُ] to be obscure/vague/unclear; to be ambiguous ③ [بالأَمْرِ |ب|] to get involved/embroiled in, to be drawn into; to be absorbed/engrossed in; تَلَبَّسَ بِجَريمةٍ to be involved in a crime; تَلَبَّسَ بِدَوْرٍ to be absorbed in a role

الْتَبَسَ *v* to be obscure/vague/unclear; to be dubious/questionable; to be ambiguous; الْتَبَسَ عَلَيْهِ الأَمْرُ the issue confused him

لُبْس, لَبْس *n* ambiguity, vagueness, obscurity; وَضَّحَ اللَبْسَ to clarify the ambiguities

لِبْس *n* clothes, attire

لابِس *adj* wearing, dressed in, clothed in

لِباس *n* |أَلْبِسة| clothing, clothes, dress; لِباس عَصْريّ modern/old-fashioned clothes; لِباس تَقْليديّ a traditional costume; لِباس مُحْتَشِم modest clothing; أَلْبِسة جاهزة ready-to-wear clothing; لِباس الشُرْطةِ a police uniform; لِباس رَسْميّ uniform; مُرْتَدِياً لِباسَهُ الرَسْميَّ to be in uniform

لِبْسان *n* (Bot) listed alphabetically

لَبوس *n* |لُبُس| ① [مَلابِس] clothing, attire; garment, dress ② (Med) suppository

لَبّيسة *n* لَبّيسة الأَحْذِيةِ shoehorn

الْتِباس *n* ambiguity, equivocality; confusion

تَلَبُّس *n* ❶ [في جَريمةٍ] في حالةِ التَلَبُّسِ in the act, red-handed ❷ [تَوَرُّط] involvement

تَلْبيس *n* ❶ [تَغْطِية] covering, coating, lining, upholstery; dressing, clothing ❷ [احْتِيال] deception, fraud

مُتَلَبِّس *adj* ❶ [بالجَريمة] مُتَلَبِّساً in the act, red-handed; أُلْقِيَ القَبْضُ عَلَيْه مُتَلَبِّساً he was caught red-handed ❷ [مُتَوَرِّط |ب] involved

مُلابَسة *n* ❶ [مُعاشَرة] association, contact ❷ [ظُروف] مُلابَسات circumstances; مُلابَسات مَجْهولة unknown circumstances; مُلابَسات الحادِثةِ the circumstances of the accident

مَلْبَس *n* |مَلابِسُ| piece of clothing, dress, costume, garment; مَلابِس clothes; مَلابِس مُسْتَعْمَلة second-hand clothes; مَلابِس داخِليّة underwear; مَلابِس رِياضيّة sportswear; مَلابِس نِسائيّة women's clothing; ارْتَدى مَلابِسَ نِسائيّةً to wear women's clothing; مَحَلّ مَلابِسَ clothes shop; شَرِكة مَلابِسَ clothing manufacturer; غُرْفة تَغْيير المَلابِسِ dressing room; لَبِسَ \ خَلَعَ المَلابِسَ to put on/take off clothing

مُلَبَّس *adj* ❶ [مُغَطًى] covered, coated, upholstered; هذا المَقْعَدُ مُلَبَّسٌ بالجِلْدِ this couch is upholstered in leather ❷ [مَشْكوك فيهِ] dubious

مَلْبوس *adj* worn; مَلْبوسات clothes

مُلْتَبِس *adj* obscure, vague, unclear, ambiguous; dubious, questionable, uncertain; intricate, complex, confusing; فِكْرة مُلْتَبِسة a vague notion; جُمْلة مُلْتَبِسة an ambiguous sentence

‹ **لِبْسان** *n* black mustard seeds; white mustard seeds

‹ **لَبَطَ** *v* |i-u; لَبْط| to kick; to strike/knock down

‹ **لَبِق** *adj* tactful, diplomatic, polite; قَرار لَبِق a diplomatic decision; شَخْص لَبِق a diplomatic person; مُتَحَدِّث لَبِق a tactful speaker

لَباقة *n* tact, diplomacy; بِلَباقةٍ tactfully; اللَباقة في الحَديثِ \ الكَلامِ tactfulness in speaking; عامَلَ شَخْصاً بِلَباقةٍ to treat sb tactfully; تَعامَلَ مع الأَمْرِ بِلَباقةٍ to handle sth tactfully

‹ **لَبَكَ** *v* |u; لَبْك| to mix, to blend

تَلَبَّكَ *v* to be confused/disorganized; تَلَبَّكَتْ مَعِدَتُهُ he had an upset stomach

‹ **لَبْلَبَ** *v* |i; اللَبْلَبة| على، ب| to fondle, to caress

لَبْلاب *n* (Bot) ivy (*Hedera*); bindweed; لَبْلاب أَرْضيّ ground ivy (*Glechoma hederacea*); رابِطة اللَبْلابِ the Ivy League (*a group of some of the oldest and most prestigious universities in the US*)

‹ **لَبَنَ** *v* |a; لَبْن| to give a lot of milk

أَلْبَنَ *v* to lactate

الْتَبَنَ *v* to suckle

لَبَن *n* ❶ [حَليب] |أَلْبان، لِبان| milk; لَبَن رائِب \ زَباديّ yoghurt; لَبَن مُرَكَّز condensed milk; لَبَن بَقَريّ cow's milk; لَبَن ماعِزٍ goat's milk; لَبَن الأُمِّ breast milk; مُشْتَقّات \ مُنْتَجات الأَلْبانِ dairy products; لَبَن كامِل الدَسَم whole milk; سُكَّر اللَبَنِ lactose; زَهْرة اللَبَنِ الثَلْجيّة snowdrop (*Galanthus*); لا تَبْكِ على اللَبَنِ المَسْكوبِ it's no use crying over spilt milk ❷ [لَبَن مَمْخوض] buttermilk; كَأْس من اللَبَنِ a glass of buttermilk ❸ [يوغورت] yoghurt

لِبْن، لَبِن *n* loam, clay; طوب لَبِنٍ clay brick

لَبّان *n* (Egypt) milkman

لُبان *n* ❶ [عِلْك] chewing gum ❷ [بَخور] frankincense ❸ (Bot) incense tree

لَبْنة *n* lebneh, strained/Greek yoghurt

لَبِنة *n* clay brick, adobe

لُبْنى *n* |f| Lubna (*female given name*)

لَبَنيّة *n* labaniya (*sweet dish made of milk*)

لَبون *n* |لَبائِنُ، لُبْن، لِبان| mammal

مَلْبَن *n* (Egypt) Turkish delight

مَلْبَنة *n* |مَلابِنُ| ❶ [مَصْنَع الأَلْبانِ] creamery, dairy factory ❷ [دُكّان لِبَيْع الأَلْبانِ] dairy store

مِلْبَنة *n* |مَلابِنُ| milk jug

‹ **تَلَبْنَنَ** *v* to become Lebanese

لُبْنان *n* |dipt f| Lebanon; جَبَل لُبْنان Mount Lebanon

لُبْنانيّ Ⓐ *adj* Lebanese; الجُمْهوريّة اللُبْنانيّة the Lebanese Republic Ⓑ *n* Lebanese (*person*)

‹ **لَبْوة** *n* |لَبَوات| see لَبُؤة

‹ **لَبّى** *v* to comply with, to agree/consent to; to accept; to grant, to meet; لَبّى شَيْئاً to agree to sth; لَبّى حاجةً to meet a need;

اِلْتَجَأَ *v* to take refuge, to seek shelter/sanctuary; اِلْتَجَأَ إلى شَيْءٍ to seek refuge in sth; اِلْتَجَأَ إلى شَخْصٍ to take shelter with sb

لاجِئ *n* refugee; asylum seeker; fugitive; لاجِئونَ سِياسِيّونَ political refugees; تَدَفُّق اللاجِئين a stream of refugees; مُخَيَّم اللاجِئينَ refugee camp; اِسْتِقْبال اللاجِئينَ the reception of refugees; عَرَضَ \ مَنَحَ اللُجوءَ السِياسيَّ للاجِئينَ to grant refugees political asylum

لُجوء *n* asylum, refuge; لُجوء سِياسيّ political asylum; سِياسَة اللُجوءِ asylum/refugee policy; طالِب اللُجوءِ asylum seeker; refugee; قانون اللُجوءِ refugee law; حَقّ اللُجوءِ right of asylum; طَلَب اللُجوءِ asylum application; قَدَّمَ طَلَبَ اللُجوءِ \ طَلَباً لِلُّجوءِ to apply for asylum; إجْراءات طَلَبِ اللُجوءِ asylum procedure; بَدَأَ إجْراءاتِ طَلَبِ اللُجوءِ to initiate an asylum procedure; مَنَحَ \ رَفَضَ اللُجوءَ to grant/refuse asylum

اِلْتِجاء *n* seeking refuge/shelter/sanctuary; asylum; أَمْكَنَ الاِلْتِجاءَ إلى مَكانٍ to find refuge somewhere

مُلْتَجَأ *n* refuge, sanctuary; shelter

مَلْجَأ *n* |مَلاجِئُ| refuge, sanctuary; hiding place, shelter; مَلْجَأ أَطْفالٍ a children's home; هو مَلْجَؤُنا الوَحيدُ he's our only resort; مَلْجَأ ضِدّ غاراتٍ جَوِّيَّةٍ an air-raid shelter; وَفَّرَ \ قَدَّمَ مَلْجَأً لِشَخْصٍ to give sb shelter

‹ **لَجَب** *n* noise, tumult

‹ **لَجَّ** *v* |i; لَجَج, لَجاج, لَجاجة| **1** [أَصَرَّ] to insist, to persist; to press, to urge; لَجَّ في طَلَبٍ to keep asking; لَجَّ على شَخْصٍ في شَيْءٍ to press sb for sth **2** [عَنَد] to be stubborn/obstinate

لاجَّ *v* to dispute/argue with

تَلاجَّ *v* to argue obstinately

اِلْتَجَّ *v* to be noisy

لُجّ *n* abyss, depth (*of the sea*)

لَجاجة *n* obstinacy

لَجَّة *n* clamour, noise, tumult; بِلَجَّةٍ وَضَجَّةٍ with a lot of noise

لَجوج *adj* insistent, persistent, pressing

‹ **لِجاف** *n* crosspiece, railway sleeper (BrE), cross tie (AmE)

‹ **لَجْلَجَ** *v* |i; لَجْلَجة| to stammer, to stutter

لَبّى دَعْوةً to accept an invitation; لَبّى الرَغَباتِ \ الطَلَباتِ to comply with the wishes/demands; لَبّى نِداءَ الوَطَنِ to serve one's country

لَبَّيْكَ *excl* here I am!, at your service!; لَبَّيْكَ اللّهُمَّ لَبَّيْكَ here I am at thy service O Lord (*invoked by pilgrims at the hajj*)

تَلْبِية *n* compliance with, agreement to, accession to; acceptance of; granting of, responding to; تَلْبِيةً لِ ... in reaction to ...; تَلْبِية حاجاتِ الشَعْبِ meeting the needs of the people

مُلَبٍّ *adj* compliant, consenting, accepting; granting, obliging; responsive, responding

‹ **لَتَّ** *v* |u; لَتّ| to chatter, to prattle

‹ **لِتْر, لِيتَر** *n* |لِتْرات| litre; لِتْر \ أَرْبَعونَ لِتْراً من الماءِ one litre/forty litres of water

‹ **الَّتي** *pron* see الَّذي

‹ **لَثِغَ** *v* |a; لَثَغ| to mispronounce; لَثِغَ بالراءِ *to be unable to pronounce the letter* ر; لَثِغَ بالسينِ to lisp

لُثْغة *n* lisp; *inability to pronounce the letter* ر

‹ **لَثَمَ** *v* |i; لَثْم| to kiss

لَثَّمَ *v* to veil, to cover

تَلَثَّمَ *v* to be covered/veiled; to be hidden/concealed

لِثام *n* |لُثُم| veil, cover; أَماطَ اللِثامَ عن شَيْءٍ to lift the veil on sth

لَثْمة *n* |لَثَمات| kiss

مُلَثَّم *adj* veiled; masked

‹ **لِثَة, لِثّة** *n* |لِثات, لِثًى| gums; لِثة مُلْتَهِبة \ دامِية inflamed/bleeding gums; فَساد اللِثةِ periodontitis

لِثَوِيّ *adj* interdental; gingival; صَوْت لِثَوِيّ (Ling) an interdental consonant

‹ **لَجَأَ** *v* |a; لُجوء| |إلى| to take/seek refuge/shelter in, to flee to; to resort to; to refer/turn to; لَجَأَ إلى شَيْءٍ to seek refuge in sth; لَجَأَ إلى الخارِجِ to take refuge abroad; لَجَأَ إلى مَدينةٍ أُخْرى to flee to another city; لَجَأَ إلى المَحْكَمةِ to go to court; لَجَأَ إلى اسْتِخْدامِ العُنْفِ to resort to violence

أَلْجَأَ *v* **1** [اضْطَرَّ] |إلى| to force; أَلْجَأَ شَخْصاً إلى فِعْلِ شَيْءٍ to force sb to do sth **2** [حَمى] to protect, to shelter; to defend

تَلَجْلَجَ *v* to stammer, to stutter; to falter

لَجْلَج *adj* insincere; الحَقُّ أَبْلَجُ والباطِلُ لَجْلَجٌ honesty is the best policy

لَجَمَ *v* |u; لَجْم| to bridle, to rein in; to control, to restrain, to keep in check, to hold back; لَجَمَ حِصاناً to keep/hold a horse under control; لَجَمَ لِسانَ شَخْصٍ to silence sb

أَلْجَمَ *v* to restrain, to bridle

لِجام *n* |لُجُم, أَلْجِمة| [1] ◀ [رُكوب] rein, bridle [2] ◀ (Anat) frenulum

لَجْنة *n* |لِجَن, لِجان, لَجْنات| committee, commission, board, panel; لَجْنة دائِمة standing committee; لَجْنة اسْتِشارِيّة advisory board; لَجْنة إدارِيّة board of directors; لَجْنة بَرْلَمانيّة parliamentary committee; اللَجْنة المَرْكَزِيّة the central committee; اللَجْنة الأوروبّيّة the European Commission; اللَجْنة الأولِمْبيّة الدَوْليّة the International Olympic Committee; لَجْنة عَمَلٍ action committee; لَجْنة تَفْتيشٍ \ تَحْكيمٍ inspection/arbitration committee; لَجْنة إشْرافٍ \ إدارةٍ \ تَحْقيقٍ supervision/management/research committee; لَجْنة تأْديبيّة disciplinary committee; مَثَلَ أمامَ اللَجْنة التأْديبيّة to appear before a disciplinary committee; شَكَّلَ \ أَلَّفَ \ نَصَّبَ \ أَحْدَثَ لَجْنةً to form a committee; كانَ عُضْواً في اللَجْنةِ to be on the board; تَجْتَمِعُ اللَجْنةُ في جَلْسةٍ مُغْلَقةٍ the committee convened behind closed doors

لُجَيْن *adj* silver, silvery

لَحَّ *v* |i; لَحّ| to be close (*relationship*)

أَلَحَّ *v* to insist, to urge, to press; to persist, to persevere; أَلَحَّ على \ في شَيْءٍ to insist on sth; أَلَحَّ على شَخْصٍ لِفِعْلِ شَيْءٍ to urge sb to do sth

لَحوح *adj* obstinate, persistent; obtrusive, intrusive, pushy

إلْحاح *n* |إلْحاحات| insistence, emphasis; urgency; بِإلْحاحٍ insistently; بِناءً على إلْحاحٍ من شَخْصٍ at sb's insistence; قالَ شَيْئاً بِإلْحاحٍ to emphasize sth; طالَبَ شَخْصاً بِإلْحاحٍ أنْ ... to urge sb to ...

مُلِحّ *adj* [1] ◀ [ضَروريّ] urgent, pressing, acute, dire; ضَرورة مُلِحّة dire need; رِسالة مُلِحّة a pressing letter; حالة مُلِحّة an urgent situation; أُمور مُلِحّة urgent matters; سُؤال مُلِحّ a pressing question; مُشْكِلة \ حاجة \ مَسْألة مُلِحّة a pressing problem/necessity/issue; كانَت الحاجةُ إلَيْهِ مُلِحّةً he was urgently needed [2] ◀ [مُصِرّ] tenacious, persistent, insistent; intrusive, pushy

مِلْحاح *adj* tenacious, persistent, insistent

لَحَدَ *v* |a; لَحْد| [1] ◀ [دَفَنَ] to bury; لَحَدَ المَيِّتَ to bury the deceased [2] ◀ [حَفَرَ] to dig, to excavate; لَحَدَ قَبْراً to dig a grave [3] ◀ [كَفَرَ] to deny God

أَلْحَدَ *v* [1] ◀ [كَفَرَ] to apostatize, to be/become a heretic; to be/become an atheist [2] ◀ [حَفَرَ قَبْراً ل] to bury

اِلْتَحَدَ *v* [1] ◀ [مالَ] to deviate, to digress [2] ◀ [في الدينِ] to become an infidel, to abandon one's faith

لَحْد *n* |أَلْحاد, لُحود| grave, tomb; من المَهْدِ إلى اللَحْدِ from the cradle to the grave

إلْحاد *n* atheism; apostasy

إلْحاديّ **A** *adj* atheistic, apostate

B *n* atheist, apostate

مُلْحِد **A** *adj* |مُلْحِدونَ, مَلاحِدة| heretical, apostate; atheistic

B *n* |مُلْحِدونَ, مَلاحِدة| heretic, apostate; atheist

لَحِسَ *v* |a; لَحْس, لَحْسة, لُحْسة, مَلْحَس| to lick (off), to lap (up)

لَحْسة *n* lick, lap

لَحَظَ *v* |a; لَحْظ, لَحَظان| to look at, to observe; to notice, to perceive; to regard, to consider

لاحَظَ *v* to look at, to observe; to notice, to perceive, to be/become aware of; لاحَظَ أنّ ... to observe that ...; لاحَظَ شَيْئاً to observe sth; لاحَظَ وُجودَ شَخْصٍ to be aware of sb's presence; لاحَظَ تَجْرِبةً عِلْميّةً to observe a scientific experiment; لاحَظَ على شَخْصٍ عَلاماتَ الخَوْفِ to notice sb's fear

لَحْظ *n* |أَلْحاظ| look, glance

لَحْظة *n* |لَحَظات| moment, instant, minute, second; لَحْظةً! one minute!; لَحْظة من فَضْلِكَ one moment, please; قبل لَحْظةٍ just now; في لَحْظةٍ in an instant; في لَحْظةٍ مُعَيَّنةٍ at a specific moment; في لَحْظةِ ضَعْفٍ in a moment of weakness; في آخِرِ لَحْظةٍ at the eleventh hour; في أيِّ لَحْظةٍ at any given time; في مِثْلِ هذه اللَحَظاتِ in such moments; لَحْظة من الراحةِ \ الوَقْتِ a moment of peace/time; سَكَتَ عن الكَلامِ

لَحْظةً he was silent for a minute; سَأعودُ بعد لَحَظاتٍ I'll be back in a moment

مُلاحَظ *adj* obvious, evident, clear; noticeable, remarkable

مُلاحِظ *n* observer, supervisor, controller; مُلاحِظ عُمّالٍ overseer

مُلاحَظة *n* ⓵ [رَصْد] observation; perception, awareness; المُلاحَظة بالمُشارَكةِ participant observation ⓶ [تَعْليق] remark, observation; comment, note, annotation; مُلاحَظة عَرَضيّة a casual remark; مُلاحَظة هامِشيّة a marginal note, a side note; a footnote; مُلاحَظات على شَيْءٍ comments on sth; مُلاحَظة على \ حول شَيْءٍ \ شَخْصٍ a remark about sth/sb; جَدير بالمُلاحَظةِ remarkable, noteworthy; أَبْدى \ وَضَعَ مُلاحَظةً to make a comment; أَبْدى مُلاحَظاتٍ to make notes; سَجَّلَ مُلاحَظةً حول مَسْأَلةٍ to jot down a note about sth

مَلْحوظ *adj* noticeable, observable; remarkable, considerable; غَيْر مَلْحوظٍ unobserved; unnoticeable; تَشابُه مَلْحوظ a remarkable similarity; فارِق \ فَرْق غَيْر مَلْحوظٍ an unnoticeable difference; تَحَسُّن \ تَناقُص مَلْحوظ a substantial improvement/decrease; قد ازْدادَ بِشَكْلٍ مَلْحوظٍ it has increased remarkably

مَلْحوظة *n* ⓵ [تَعْليق] comment, remark; note, annotation; postscript, PS; ذَيَّلَ \ زَوَّدَ نَصًّا to make a note; دَوَّنَ مَلْحوظةً بِمَلْحوظاتٍ to annotate a text ⓶ [مُلاحَظة] observation

لَحَفَ *v* |a; **لَحْف**| to cover; to hide

أَلْحَفَ *v* to insist, to press

تَلَحَّفَ *v* |ب| to wrap oneself (in), to cover oneself (with)

الْتَحَفَ *v* to wrap oneself (in)

لِحاف *n* |**أَلْحِفة, لُحُف**| quilt, duvet; blanket, cover; لِحاف مُرَقَّع patchwork quilt

مِلْحَفة *n* quilt, duvet

لَحِقَ *v* |a; **لَحْق, لَحاق**| ⓵ [تَبِعَ] to follow, to go/chase after; لَحِقَ بِفَتاةٍ to follow a girl ⓶ [ارْتَبَطَ |ب|] to be attached to, to adhere/cling to; to be connected with ⓷ [انْضَمَّ إلى] to join; to keep close to, to hang on to; لَحِقَ بالجُمْهورِ to be part of the audience; لَحِقَ بِأَهْلِهِ في هولَنْدا he joined his family in the Netherlands; الضَرَر الذي لَحِقَ the damage that followed ⓸ [أَدْرَكَ] to reach, to catch, to get; لَحِقَ القِطارَ to catch the train

لاحَقَ *v* ⓵ [تَبِعَ] to follow; to go after, to chase, to pursue; to persecute; لاحَقَ شَخْصاً to chase sb ⓶ (Law) to prosecute

أَلْحَقَ *v* ⓵ [تَسَبَّبَ في] to inflict, to administer; to cause; أَلْحَقَ هَزيمةً بالعَدوِّ to inflict a defeat on the enemy; أَلْحَقَ خَسائِرَ كَبيرةً بِشَخْصٍ to cause sb severe losses ⓶ [أَضافَ] to attach, to append, to enclose; to add, to supplement ⓷ [أَوْفَدَ] to assign (*as an attaché*)

تَلاحَقَ *v* to succeed, to follow/come successively

الْتَحَقَ *v* to join, to become a member of; to enrol, to enlist; الْتَحَقَ بالمَدْرَسةِ الثانويّةِ to start secondary school; الْتَحَقَ بِكُلّيّةِ الطِبِّ to enrol in the Faculty of Medicine (BrE) medical school (AmE); الْتَحَقَ بِحِزْبِ الاسْتِقْلالِ to join the Independence Party; الْتَحَقَ بِأُسْرَتِهِ to join one's family; الْتَحَقَ بالقوّاتِ المُسَلَّحةِ to join the army

اسْتَلْحَقَ *v* ⓵ [أَلْحَقَ] to annex, to append, to attach ⓶ [تَبَنّى] to adopt (*a child*)

لاحِق Ⓐ *adj* later, future, coming; following, next, subsequent; لاحِقاً later (on); في وَقْتٍ لاحِقٍ at a later time; دِراسات لاحِقة further research; المَرْحَلة اللاحِقة the next stage Ⓑ *n* accessory, attachment; لَواحِق الكَلِماتِ (Gram) word suffixes

لاحِقة *n* |**لَواحِقُ**| ⓵ [شَيْء إضافيّ] supplement, adjunct, appendage; addendum, appendix, annex ⓶ (Gram) suffix, ending; لاحِقة الجَمْعِ plural ending

لِحاق *n* ⓵ [انْضِمام] membership, enrollment ⓶ [إدْراك] catching; اللِحاق بالقِطارِ catching a train

الْتِحاق *n* joining, entry; enrollment; مُعَدَّل الالْتِحاقِ بالمَدارِسِ the average number of children attending school

إلْحاق *n* ⓵ [إضافة] appendage, attachment ⓶ (Pol) annexation

مُتَلاحِق *adj* ⓵ [مُتَتابِع] successive, consecutive; continuous; في أَيّامٍ مُتَلاحِقةٍ on consecutive days ⓶ [أَبَديّ] permanent, lasting, everlasting

مُلاحِق *n* pursuer, chaser

مُلاحَقة *n* ① [مُطارَدة] pursuit, chase ② (Law) prosecution; مُلاحَقة قضائيّة \ قانونيّة judicial proceedings; legal prosecution; أعْفى شَخْصاً من المُلاحَقةِ القَضائيّة to acquit sb

مُلْحَق *n* ① [كِتابٍ] |مُلْحَقات, مَلاحِقُ| appendix, addendum, pull-out, supplement; مُلْحَق كِتابٍ supplement to the book; مُلْحَق رِسالةٍ enclosure to the letter; مُلْحَق بِأَسْماءِ الأَعْلامِ appendix with a list of given names ② [بِنايةٍ] |مَلاحِقُ| annex; extension ③ [مُوظَّف في السِفارة] |مُلْحَقونَ| attaché, envoy; مُلْحَق عَسْكَريّ \ تِجاريّ \ زِراعيّ military/commercial/agricultural attaché ④ [إضافة] |مُلْحَقات, مَلاحِقُ| addition, supplement; مُلْحَق وَصيّةٍ codicil ⑤ [جَريدةٍ] |مُلْحَقات, مَلاحِقُ| section, supplement; المُلْحَق العِلْميّ the science section

لَحَمَ *v* |u; لَحْم, لِحام| to weld, to solder; to fuse, to join; لَحَمَ بالكَهْرَباءِ to weld electrically; لَحَمَ الفولاذَ to weld steel; لَحَمَ أَجْزاءً to weld pieces together

لاحَمَ *v* to weld/solder together

تَلاحَمَ *v* to put together, to fasten, to stick/cling together; to be connected/linked, to be fused together

الْتَحَمَ *v* ① [الْتَصَقَ] to come together, to unite; to cling/stick together ② [لَحَمَ] to weld, to solder; to fuse, to join ③ [جُرْحٌ] to heal, to mend; التَحَمَ الجُرْحُ the wound has healed ④ [تَقاتَلَ] to fight/battle/combat with

لَحْم *n coll* |لِحام, لُحوم| meat, flesh; لَحْم نَيِّء \ قاسٍ raw/dry meat; لَحْم مَفْروم \ مُدَخَّن \ مُمَلَّح minced/smoked/salted meat; لَحْم قَليل \ كَثير الدُهْنِ lean/fat meat; لَحْم بَقَريّ beef; لَحْم الخِنْزيرِ pork; لُحوم meat products; آكِل لُحومٍ carnivore; آكِل لُحومِ البَشرِ cannibal; طَبَق من اللَحْمِ meat dish; بِلَحْمِهِ وَشَحْمِهِ in person; من لَحْمي وَدَمي my own flesh and blood; إنْسان من لَحْمٍ وَدَمٍ a person of flesh and blood; هو لَحْمٌ على وَضَمٍ he's lost, there's no hope for him; قَلى \ شَوى لَحْماً to roast meat

لاحِم A *adj* |لَواحِمُ| carnivorous; النَباتات اللَواحِم carnivorous plants
B *n* |لَواحِمُ| carnivore

لَحّام *n* ① [عامِل اللِحامِ] welder ② [جَزّار] butcher

لِحام *n* |لِحامات| welding, soldering; مِكْواة \ كاوِية لِحامٍ soldering iron; ماكِنة لِحامٍ welding apparatus

لِحامة *n* welding

لُحْمة *n* |لُحَم| ① [نَسيج] weft ② [قَرابة] bond of union

لَحْميّة *n* adenoids

لَحيم *adj* corpulent, plump; fleshy, meaty

لُحَيْمة *n* outgrowth

الْتِحام *n* ① [رابِطة] connection, attachment; union; الْتِحام السَفينةِ الفَضائيّةِ بالمَحَطّةِ المَداريّةِ the connection of the spacecraft to the space station ② [انْدِماج] fusion, joining; coherence, cohesion; الْتِحام نَوَويّ nuclear fusion ③ [مَعْرَكة] battle, combat, fight; confrontation, encounter

تَلاحُم *n* ① [تَماسُك] coherence, cohesion ② [مَعْرَكة] battle, combat, fight, clash

مُلْتَحِم *adj* ① [مُتَماسِك] coherence, cohesion ② [مُوَحَّد] merged, coalesced; fused, united ③ [في قِتالٍ] clashing, battling

مَلْحَمة *n* ① [شِعْريّة] epic, saga ② [مَسْلَخ] slaughterhouse ③ [مُقاتَلة] fierce battle

مَلْحَميّ *adj* heroic, epic

لَحَنَ *v* |a; لَحْن| to make a grammatical mistake

لَحَّنَ *v* to make/compose music; to set to music; لَحَّنَ أغانِيَ to compose a song

أَلْحَنَ *v* to make mistakes (*in speech*)

لَحْن *n* ① [نَغَم] |أَلْحان| tune, melody; لَحْن مَرِح a merry tune; غَنّى \ عَزَفَ لَحْناً to sing/play a tune ② [خَطَأ لُغَويّ] |لُحون| grammatical mistake; لَحْن العامّةِ common mistake

تَلْحين *n* |تَلاحينُ| composition (*music*)

مُلَحِّن *n* composer

مَلْحون *adj* ungrammatical, incorrect; colloquial

لَحى *v* |i; لَحْي| to insult, to abuse

الْتَحى *v* to grow a beard

لَحْي *n* |لُحِيّ, أَلْحٍ| jaw, jawbone

لِحاء *n* |أَلْحِية| ① (Bot) bark ② (Anat) cortex; لِحاء الدِماغِ cerebral cortex

‹ **لِحْية** *n* |لِحىً, لُحىً| beard; لِحْية كَثيفة \ كَثّة a full beard; أَطْلَقَ لِحْيَتَهُ to grow one's beard

مُلْتَحٍ *adj* bearded

مَلْحاء *n* deciduous tree

‹ **لَخْبَطَ** *v* |i; لَخْبَطَة| to disorganize, to disarrange; to shuffle

لَخْبَطَة *n* disorder

مُلَخْبَط *adj* disorganized, disordered; mixed up, muddled

‹ **لَخَّصَ** *v* to summarize, to outline; to sum up, to recap; لَخَّصَ بِاقْتِضابٍ to briefly outline; لَخَّصَ مُحاضَرةً to summarize a lecture; لَخَّصَ كِتاباً to summarize a book; لَخَّصَ أَقْوالَ شَخْصٍ to recap sb's statements

تَلَخَّصَ *v* to be abridged/summarized

تَلْخيص *n* |تَلْخيصات| summary, outline

مُلَخَّص [A] *adj* concise, brief; abridged, summary (*before n*) [B] *n* |مُلَخَّصات| excerpt, abstract, extract, outline; مُلَخَّص مُقْتَضَب a short extract; مُلَخَّص مُخْتَصَر a brief outline; مُلَخَّص لِمَقالةٍ an excerpt from an article

‹ **لَخِنَ** *v* |a; لَخَن| to stink; to be/become rotten/decayed/rancid

‹ **لَدَّ** *v* |u; لَدّ| to quarrel/fight with, to dispute violently with

لَدود *adj* |أَلِدّاء, أَلِدّة| implacable; خَصْم لَدود a fierce opponent; عَدوّانِ لَدودانِ two sworn enemies

أَلَدّ *adj* |dipt; لَدود, لُدّ| implacable

‹ **لَدَغَ** *v* |u; لَدْغ| to bite; to sting

لَدْغة *n* |لَدَغات| bite; sting

مَلْدوغ *adj* bitten; stung; كالمَلْدوغ as if stung

‹ **لَدُنَ** *v* |u; لُدونة, لَدانة| to be soft/flexible

لَدَّنَ *v* to make soft/flexible

لَدُن *prep* من لَدُنِ from (the side of); من لَدُنِ بُلْدانِ الخَليجِ from the side of the Gulf countries; وَجَدَ مُقاوَمةً من لَدُنِ الدُوَلِ العَرَبِيّةِ to encounter resistance from the Arab countries

لَدائِنُ *n* synthetics, plastics; من اللَدائِنِ synthetic (*before n*), plastic (*before n*)

لَدانة *n* softness, flexibility, pliability

لُدونة *n* softness, flexibility, pliability

‹ **لَدى** *prep* [1] [عِنْدَ] with, near, by; لَدَيَّ الكِتابُ I have the book with me; لَدَيْهِ أَدِلّةٌ كَثيرةٌ he has a lot of proof; السَفير اليَمَنِيّ لَدى الأُمَمِ المُتَّحِدةِ the Yemeni ambassador to the United Nations [2] [في] at, on, upon; لَدى سُقوطِ الطائِرةِ at the plane crash site [3] [مِنْ قِبَلِ] مَقْبول لَدى وِزارةِ العَدْلِ acknowledged by the Ministry of Justice

‹ **لِذا** *pron* see ذا

‹ **لَذَّ** *v* |a; لَذاذة, لَذاذ| to taste good, to be delicious/tasty; to be lovely/wonderful/delightful; لَذَّ لَها العَيْشُ في لُنْدُن she loved living in London

لَذَّذَ *v* to gratify, to please, to give pleasure to

تَلَذَّذَ *v* to find tasty/delicious; to like, to enjoy, to take pleasure in; to be pleased/delighted, to get pleasure from; تَلَذَّذَ شَيْئاً \ بِشَيْءٍ to enjoy sth

الْتَذَّ *v* to find tasty/delicious; to enjoy; to be pleased/delighted

اسْتَلَذَّ *v* to enjoy, to like, to find pleasant; to take pleasure/delight in

لَذاذة *n* |لَذائِذُ| sweetness, charm; enjoyment, pleasure

لَذّة *n* pleasure, delight, joy; لَذّة الحَواسّ thrill of the senses, sensual pleasure; لَذّة الصَلاةِ \ الأَكْلِ \ الجِنْسِ the pleasure of prayer/food/sex; في مُنْتَهى اللَذّةِ absolutely delicious; أَعْطى لَذّةً to give joy, to give a thrill; وَجَدَ لَذّةً في شَيْءٍ to take pleasure in sth

لَذيذ *adj* |لِذاذ, لُذّ| delicious, tasty, nice; delightful, pleasant, comfortable; وَجْبة لَذيذة a delicious meal; طَعْم لَذيذ a nice taste; دِفْء لَذيذ pleasant warmth; رائِحة لَذيذة a pleasant aroma

مُتَلَذِّذ *n* epicure

مَلَذّة *n* |مَلاذُّ, مَلَذّات| pleasure, delight, joy; fun, amusement, enjoyment; مَلَذّات الحَياةِ the pleasures of life

‹ **لَذَعَ** *v* |a; لَذْع| to sting, to smart, to burn; لَذَعَهُ الحُبُّ he burned with love

لاذِع *adj* |لَواذِعُ| [1] [كَلِمات] biting, sharp; stinging, snappy; نَقْد \ تَهَكُّم لاذِع stinging criticism/mockery; مُلاحَظة لاذِعة a snappy remark; بِكَلِماتٍ لاذِعةٍ with harsh words [2] [طَعام] spicy, pungent; طَعْم لاذِع spicy food

‹ **لِذَلِكَ** *adv* see ذا

‹ **لَذِيَ** *v* |a; لَذًى |ب| to stick, to adhere

الَّذي *pron* |الَّذينَ; f الَّتي; f pl الَّواتي, اللاَّتي; m du اللَّذانِ; f du اللَّتانِ|

① [نَعْت الصِلَةِ] ◂ who; which; that; الرَجُل الَّذي يَسْكُنُ في هذا البَيْتِ the man who lives in this house; ما الَّذي which (is it that)

② [اسْم الصِلَةِ] ◂ what; that which; the one who; الَّتي أَحْبَبْتُها لم أَتَزَوَّجْها I didn't marry the one (that) I loved; كُنْتُ الأَوَّلَ بين الَّذينَ لَبَّوْا الدَعْوة I was the first (one) to respond to the appeal

‹ **لَزَبَ** *v* |u; لُزوب| to adhere, to stick

‹ **لَزِجَ** *v* |a; لَزَج, لُزوج| to stick to, to cling to; to be sticky

تَلَزَّجَ *v* to be sticky

لَزِج *adj* sticky, tacky, adhesive; viscous, syrupy; مادّة لَزِجة a sticky substance

لُزوجة *n* stickiness, adhesiveness; viscosity

‹ **لَزَّ** *v* |u; لَزّ, لِزاز| ① [أُجْبِرَ] ◂ to be forced ② [تَرابَطَ] ◂ to stick together; to unite; to connect

‹ **لَزِقَ** *v* |a; لُزوق| to stick, to cling, to adhere

أَلْزَقَ *v* to stick, to paste; أَلْزَق صورةً بالحائط to stick a picture on the wall

الْتَزَقَ *v* to attach, to adhere

لازِق *adj* sticky, adhesive

لِزاق *n* glue, adhesive

لَزْقة *n* |لَزَقات| plaster (BrE), Band-Aid® (AmE); compress

‹ **لَزِمَ** *v* |a; لُزوم| ① [وَجَبَ] ◂ to be necessary/imperative; to be required/obligatory; ما يَلْزَمُ من إجْراءاتٍ necessary measures; إذا لَزِمَ الأَمْرُ if required; يَلْزَمُ التَوَصُّلُ إلى حَلٍّ a solution must be found ② [لم يُفارِقْهُ] ◂ to continue, to keep on; to persevere, to persist; لَزِمَ الصَمْتَ to observe the silence; لَزِمَ غُرْفَتَهُ to remain in one's room; لَزِمَ الفِراشَ to be confined to bed

لازَمَ *v* ① [صاحَبَ] ◂ to accompany, to escort; to be inseparable from, to keep close to; لازَمَ الفِراشَ to be confined to bed; لازَمَ الطالِبُ مُدَرِّسَهُ the student accompanied his teacher ② [لم يُفارِقْهُ] ◂ to continue, to keep on; to persevere, to persist; لازَمَ المُطالَعةَ he was constantly reading; لازَمَهُ المَرَضُ he was always sick

أَلْزَمَ *v* to bind, to hold; to force, to obligate, to oblige; أَلْزَمَ شَخْصاً شَيْئاً \ بِشَيْءٍ to hold sb to sth; أَلْزَمَ شَخْصاً بِقَوْلِهِ to hold sb to a statement; أَلْزَمَ شَخْصاً البَيْتَ to force sb to stay at home

تَلازَمَ *v* to be connected/linked, to go together; to be inseparable, to be attached to; تَلازَمَ مع شَيْءٍ to go together with sth

الْتَزَمَ *v* ① [تَعَهَّدَ] ◂ to take on; to practice, to exercise; الْتَزَمَ شَيْئاً \ بِشَيْءٍ to take on sth; الْتَزَمَ الصَبْرَ to practice patience ② [احْتَرَمَ] ◂ to observe, to follow; to obey, to respect, to comply with, to adhere; الْتَزَمَ شَيْئاً \ بِشَيْءٍ to comply with sth; الْتَزَمَ بِمَبادِئِهِ to adhere to one's principles; الْتَزَمَ أَوامِرَ to follow orders; يَلْتَزِمُ بما يَعِظُ he practices what he preaches

اسْتَلْزَمَ *v* to require, to need; to demand, to ask; اسْتَلْزَمَ عِنايةً خاصّةً to require much attention; إذا اسْتَلْزَمَ الأَمْرُ if need be

لازِم *adj* necessary, needed, imperative; required, obligatory; غَيْر لازِم unnecessary; فِعْل لازِم intransitive verb; أَكْثَر من اللازِم more than necessary

لازِمة *n* |لَوازِمُ| ① [موسيقيّ] ◂ refrain, chorus; لازِمة أُغْنِية refrain ② [عادة قَوْليّة] ◂ filler

لِزام *adj* necessary, needed; required, obligatory; لَقَدْ باتَ لِزاماً عَلَيْنا أَنْ ... it has become necessary for us to/that ...

لُزوم *n* necessity, need, requirement, demand; عَدَم اللُزوم redundancy, sth unnecessary; زائِد عن اللُزوم more than necessary; عند اللُزوم if need be; حَسَبَ اللُزوم according to the needs, as much as needed; أَكْثَر من اللُزوم more than necessary, too much

لَوازِم *n* necessities, needs, requirements; supplies, utensils; لَوازِم شَيْءٍ the requirements of/for sth; لَوازِم مَدْرَسيّة school supplies, stationery; لَوازِم البِناءِ building supplies

الْتِزام *n* |الْتِزامات| ① [مُراعاة] ◂ compliance, accordance, observance; الْتِزام بالعَقْدِ \ الاتِّفاقِ observance of the contract/agreement; أَوْصَت الشُرْطةُ الناسَ بالتِزامِ مَنازِلِهِمْ the police advised the people to stay at home ② [واجِب] ◂ commitment; duty, obligation; الْتِزام سِياسيّ a political commitment; الْتِزام مَعْنَويّ \ اجْتِماعيّ a moral/social duty; الْتِزامات ماليّة \ قانونيّة financial/legal obligations; بِلا الْتِزامٍ without obligation; دون أَيِّ الْتِزام without any commitment; تَعَهَّدَ \ وَفى بالتِزاماتِهِ

to assume/meet one's obligations **3** [وَعْد] contract, agreement; الْتِزام كِتابيّ a written contract; وَفى بالِتزام to observe an agreement; أخَذَ على نَفْسِهِ الْتِزاماً to enter into an agreement

إلْزام *n* coercion, compulsion; force; من دونِ إلْزامٍ without force

إلْزاميّ *adj* compulsory, obligatory, imperative; compelled, obliged, forced; خِدْمة إلْزاميّة conscription; فَرَضَ شَيْئاً بصورةٍ إلْزاميّةٍ to impose an obligation on sb

تَلْزيم *n* subcontracting, farming out; the granting of a concession/franchise

مُتَلازِم *adj* inseparable, inextricable; correlative; مُتَلازِم مع شَيْءٍ inextricably bound up with sth

مُتَلازِمة *n* syndrome; مُتَلازِمة داوْن Down's syndrome

مُسْتَلْزَم *n* |مُسْتَلْزَمات| مُسْتَلْزَمات requirements, supplies, utensils

مُلازِم **A** *adj* inherent, innate; bound; مُلازِم لِشَيْءٍ inherent in sth; كانَ مُلازِماً الفِراش to be bedridden

B *n* lieutenant; مُلازِم أوَّل \ ثانٍ first/second lieutenant

مُلْتَزِم **A** *adj* committed, dedicated; consistent; حِزْب مُلْتَزِم a dedicated party; كاتِب مُلْتَزِم a committed writer

B *n* entrepreneur, contractor

مُلْزَم *adj* obligated, bound; liable; ... كانَ مُلْزَماً ب liable for/to ...; كانَ مُلْزَماً بالفِراش to be confined to bed

مُلْزِم *adj* binding, imperative; obligatory, requisite; غَيْر مُلْزِم non-committal; اتِّفاق \ قاعِدة \ نَصيحة مُلْزِم(ة) a binding agreement/rule/advice

مَلْزَمة *n* |مَلازِمُ| course book; book section

مِلْزَمة *n* |مَلازِمُ| vice (metal tool)

لَسَعَ *v* |a; لَسْع| to sting, to prick; to bite; لَسَعَهُ عَقْرَبٌ he was stung by a scorpion; يَلْسَعُ البَعوضُ mosquitoes bite

لَسْعة *n* sting, prick; bite; لَسْعة عَقْرَبٍ \ زُنْبورٍ a scorpion's/wasp's sting

لاساميّ, لاساميّة see سام

لاسَنَ *v* to argue with

تَلاسَنَ *v* to argue, to quarrel, to debate; to exchange insults

لَسِن *adj* eloquent, articulate

لِسان *n* |mf; أَلْسُن, أَلْسِنة| **1** (Anat) tongue; ... على لِسانِ \ ب as related by ...; ناطِقة بِلِسانِ الحُكومةِ the government spokeswoman; نَطَقَ بِلِسانِ الحُكومةِ to speak on behalf of the government; لِسان أَرْضيّ headland; لِسان الحَمَلِ plantain; لِسان نارٍ flame; لِسان العُصْفور type of pasta; فيكُس لِسانِ العُصْفورِ bo tree (Ficus religiosa); لِسان الحِذاءِ tongue (shoe); لِجام اللِسانِ frenulum; طَليق اللِسانِ eloquent; كانَ طَويلَ اللِسانِ to have a big mouth; كانَ سَليطَ اللِسانِ to have a sharp tongue; كانَ على طَرَفِ لِسانِهِ to be on the tip of one's tongue; كانَ على كُلِّ لِسانٍ to be on everyone's lips; كانَ ما في قَلْبِهِ على لِسانِهِ to wear one's heart on one's sleeve; كَبَحَ لِسانَهُ to mind one's words; مَدَّ لِسانَهُ لِشَخْصٍ to stick one's tongue out at sb; أَحْرَقَ شَخْصاً باللِسانِ to tell sb off; عَقَلَت الدَهْشَةُ لِسانَهُ to be dumbfounded; لَجَمَ لِسانَ شَخْصٍ to silence sb; تناقَلَت الأَلْسُنُ الخَبَرَ the news spread; تَداوَلَتْهُ الأَلْسُنُ it went from mouth to mouth; تَعَقَّدَ \ انْعَقَدَ لِسانُهُ to be tongue-tied

2 [لُغة] speech; كانَتْ فَصيحة اللِسانِ she spoke eloquently

3 [مُتَحَدِّث] spokesman, spokesperson; لِسان حالِ حَرَكةِ التَحْرير the spokesman for the liberation movement

4 (Mus) reed

لِسانيّ **A** *adj* **1** [لُغَويّ] linguistic; lingual **2** [شَفَهيّ] verbal, oral

B *n* linguist

لِسانيّات *n pl* linguistics; دَرَسَ اللِسانيّاتِ to study linguistics; لِسانيّات تَوْليديّة generative linguistics; لِسانيّات اجْتِماعيّة sociolinguistics; لِسانيّات حاسوبيّة computational linguistics; لِسانيّات نَظَرِيّة theoretical linguistics; لِسانيّات مُقارَنة comparative linguistics

أَلْسُنيّ **A** *adj* linguistic; أَلْسُنيّات linguistics

B *n* linguist

مُلاسَنة *n* argument, altercation

لاشى *v* to annihilate, to wipe out, to decimate; to destroy, to ruin

تَلاشى *v* to be destroyed/ruined, to be wiped out/annihilated; to vanish, to disappear, to fade away; to blur, to become unclear; to disperse, to evaporate; يَتَلاشى الأَمَلُ all hope

إلْصاق *n* sticking

مُتَلاصِق *adj* near, close; bordering, neighbouring, adjacent

مُلْتَصِق *adj* |ب| attached, stuck, sticking, clinging; التُهْمَةُ مُلْتَصِقَةٌ بِهِ the accusation stuck to him; كانَ الطِفْلُ مُلْتَصِقاً بِأُمِّهِ the child clung to his mother

مُلْصَق *n* |مُلْصَقات| poster, placard, playbill; sticker; في \ على مُلْصَقٍ on a placard

مُلْصَقة *n* (Ling) affix

مُلَصَّقة *n* collage

‹ **لَطَخَ** *v* |a; لَطْخ| to stain, to smear, to soil, to dirty

لَطَّخَ *v* to stain, to smear, to soil, to dirty; لَطَّخ شَيْئاً to dirty sth; لَطَّخ شَرَفَ \ سُمْعة شَخْصٍ to tarnish sb's honour/reputation; لَطَّخ يَدَيْهِ بالدَمِّ to have blood on one's hands

تَلَطَّخَ *v* to be/become stained/soiled/smeared; to spot, to smudge

لُطاخة *n* smear; لُطاخة عُنُق الرَحِم, لُطاخة باب cervical smear test, Pap test

لَطْخة *n* |لَطَخات| stain, spot, smudge, smear; لَطْخة سَوْداء a black stain

تَلْطيخ *n* mess, bungle; كَفاكَ تَلْطيخاً! stop making a mess!

مُلَطَّخ *adj* stained, blotched, smeared, smudged; مُلَطَّخ بالدِماء bloodstained; أَيْديهِمْ مُلَطَّخةٌ بالدِماء they have blood on their hands

‹ **لَطَعَ** *v* |a; لَطْع| لَطَعَ شَخْصاً (Egypt) to keep sb waiting

‹ **لَطَفَ** *v* |u; لُطْف, لَطَف| |ب| to have mercy on; لَطَفَ اللهُ بِهِ may God have mercy on him

لَطُفَ *v* |u; لُطْف, لَطافة| to be kind/nice/friendly, to be sympathetic/lovable/amiable; to be polite/courteous

لَطَّفَ *v* to alleviate, to relieve, to soften, to ease; لَطَّفَ من الأَلَمِ to ease the pain

لاطَفَ *v* **1** [عامَلَ بلُطْفٍ] to treat kindly/affectionately; to be polite/courteous with; لاطَفَ شَخْصاً to treat sb with affection **2** [دَلَّل] to stroke, to caress; to pet **3** [سايَرَ] to humour

أَلْطَفَ *v* أَلْطَفَ لِشَخْصٍ في القَوْلِ to speak kindly to sb

تَلَطَّفَ *v* to be kind/affectionate/compassionate/soft-hearted

vanishes; تَتَلاشى سُلْطَتُهُ his authority is fading; تَتَلاشى الفَواصِلُ بين الخَيالِ والحَقيقةِ the boundary between fiction and reality is blurred; قد تَلاشى الصَوْتُ \ تَلاشَت الموسيقى the sound/music has faded

‹ **لَصَّ** *v* |u; لَصّ| to steal, to rob, to pilfer; to do on the sly

تَلَصَّصَ *v* to peek, to peep, to leer; to spy; تَلَصَّص على شَخْصٍ to spy on sb; تَلَصَّص على الفَتَياتِ to peep at the girls

لِصّ *n* |لُصوص, أَلْصاص| thief

لُصوصيّة *n* banditry, thievery

مُتَلَصِّص *n* voyeur, peeping Tom

‹ **لَصَفَ** *v* |u; لَصف| to fluoresce

لاصِف *adj* fluorescent

‹ **لَصِقَ** *v* |a; لُصوق, لَصْق| to stick, to adhere; to cling, to attach; لَصِق بِشَيْءٍ to cling to sth; يَلْصَقُ شَيْءٌ بأَصابِعي sth is sticking to my fingers

لَصَّقَ *v* to paste/stick together

لاصَقَ *v* to border on, to adjoin, to be next to

أَلْصَقَ *v* to stick, to adhere, to glue; to attach, to affix; أَلْصَقَ شَيْئاً ب \ على شَيْءٍ to glue sth to/on sth; أَلْصَق صُوَراً في أَلْبومٍ to stick photos in an album; أَلْصَق طابِعَ بَريدٍ على ظَرْفٍ to stamp an envelope; أَلْصَق تُهمةً بِشخصٍ to accuse sb

تَلاصَقَ *v* to stick/paste together

الْتَصَقَ *v* |ب| to stick to, to cling to, to adhere to; to be attached to, to be affixed to; الْتَصَقَ بِشَيْءٍ to stick to sth; الْتَصَقَ بِشَخْصٍ to cling to sb

لاصِق *adj* sticky; adhesive, cohesive

لاصِقة *n* sticker, label

لِصاق *n* glue, adhesive

لَصْقة *n* plaster

لَصوق *n* plaster (BrE), Band-Aid® (AmE)

لَصيق *adj* near, close; bordering, adjacent, neighbouring, touching; رَقابة لَصيقة close surveillance

لَصيقة *n* sticker, label

الْتِصاق *n* sticking, adhesion; مِقْلاة مُضادّة للالْتِصاقِ non-stick frying pan

اِسْتَلْطَفَ *v* to like; to find sympathetic; اِسْتَلْطَفَ شَخْصاً to find sb sympathetic

لُطْف *n* |أَلْطاف| kindness, gentleness, friendliness, benevolence; consideration; mercy; لُطْف القَدَرِ providence; بِلُطْفٍ gently; اِبْتَسَمَ بِلُطْفٍ to smile kindly; قالَ شَيْئاً بِلُطْفٍ to say sth in a friendly way; هذا لُطْفٌ من ماري that is nice of Mary

لَطافة *n* kindness, friendliness; politeness

لَطيف **A** *adj* |لُطَفاءُ ,لِطاف| friendly, kind, nice, sympathetic; sweet, gentle, amiable, pleasant; polite, courteous; elegant, charming; يا لَطيفُ! good heavens!; رَجُل \ امرأة لَطيف(ة) a friendly man/woman; طَبْع لَطيف a sweet character; اِبْتِسامة لَطيفة an amiable smile; وَجْه \ صَوْت لَطيف a sympathetic face/voice; الجَوُّ لَطيفٌ the weather is nice; كانَ لَطيفاً to be kind

B *n* اللَطيف the Gentle (*one of the names of God*)

لَطيفة *n* |لَطائِفُ| **1** [نُكْتة] joke, jest, gag **2** [اِسْم شَخْصيّ] |dipt| Latifa (*female given name*)

تَلْطيف *n* softening, easing; تَلْطيف العِبارةِ euphemism

مُلاطَفة *n* **1** [مُحاسَنة] friendliness, kindness, courtesy **2** [تَدْليل] caress, touch **3** [مُجامَلة] flattery

مُلَطِّف *adj* sedative; palliative; دَواء مُلَطِّف sedative

لَطَمَ *v* |i; لَطْم| to hit, to slap; to beat, to knock, to strike

تَلاطَمَ *v* **1** [تَضارَبَ] to exchange blows, to brawl, to clash **2** [الأَمْواجُ] to pound (*waves*)

لَطْمة *n* |لَطَمات| hit, slap, smack, blow; shove; تَلَقّى لَطْمةً to be hit in the face

مَلْطَم *n* |مَلاطِمُ| cheek

لَظِيَ *v* |a; لَظًى| to be ablaze, to burn brightly; to catch fire; to set fire to

تَلَظّى *v* to be ablaze, to blaze fiercely, to burn brightly; to catch fire

لَظًى *n* flame; blazing fire, blaze; bright light

لَعِبَ *v* |a; لَعْب ,لِعْب ,لَعِب| to play; لَعِبَ كُرةَ القَدَمِ to play football (BrE) soccer (AmE); لَعِبَ الوَرَقَ to play cards; لَعِبَ دَوْرَ البَطَلِ في فيلْمٍ to play the leading part in a film; لَعِبَ دَوْراً حاسِماً to play a decisive part; لَعِبَ دَوْراً في اتِّخاذِ قَرارٍ to play a part in the decision; لَعِبَ بِأَعْصابِ شَخْصٍ to play on sb's nerves; لَعِبَ مع أَطْفالِهِ to play with one's children; لَعِبَ الطِفْلُ بالكُرةِ the child played with the ball; لَعِبَ لِنادٍ to play for a club; لَعِبَ في المُنْتَخَبِ الوَطَنيِّ to play for the national team; تَلْعَبُ السَعوديّةُ ضدّ الجَزائِرِ Saudi Arabia is playing Algeria

لاعَبَ *v* **1** [لَعِبَ] to play with; لاعَبَ القِطّةَ to play with the cat; لاعَبَ أَطْفالَهُ to play with one's children **2** [جِنْسيّاً] to fool around with, to play with (*sexually*); لاعَبَ زَوْجَتَهُ to fool around with one's wife

أَلْعَبَ *v* **1** [جَعَلَهُ يَلْعَبُ] to cause to play, to make play **2** [لَعِبَ] to play **3** [سالَ لُعابُهُ] to dribble, to slaver, to slobber

تَلَعَّبَ *v* to play, to be playful; to trifle

تَلاعَبَ *v* to commit/practise/perpetrate fraud; to cheat, to swindle; تَلاعَبَ بالحِساباتِ to tamper with the accounts

لَعِب ,لِعْب *n* |أَلْعاب| **1** [مَصْدَر لَعِبَ] game; أَلْعاب الإِنْتَرْنِت online games; أَوْراق لَعِبٍ playing cards; اِلْتَزَمَ بِقَواعِدِ اللَعِبِ to play by the rules; لَعِب نَظيف fair play **2** (Sport) game, match; أَلْعاب رِياضيّة sports; أَلْعاب القُوى athletics; الأَلْعاب الأولِمْبيّة the Olympic Games; الأَلْعاب الأولِمْبيّة الشَتْويّة the Winter Olympics

لاعِب *n* player, athlete, sportsman; لاعِب هاوٍ amateur; لاعِب مُحْتَرِف professional (player); لاعِب دُوَليّ international; لاعِب كُرةِ القَدَمِ soccer player; لاعِب أَساسيّ stringer; لاعِب جَناحٍ winger; لاعِب اِحْتِياطيّ substitute; مُتَعَدِّد اللاعِبينَ (Comput) multiplayer

لُعاب *n* saliva, drivel, dribble; سالَ لُعابي my mouth is watering

لُعْبة *n* |لُعَب| **1** [ما يُلْعَبُ بِهِ] game, toy, plaything; لُعْبة الضاما draughts (BrE), checkers (AmE); لُعْبة جَماعيّة \ فَرْديّة team/individual game; لُعْبة ذَكاءٍ mental exercise; لُعْبة أَطْفالٍ children's game; اِلْتَزَمَ بِقَواعِدِ اللُعْبةِ to stick to the rules of the game; غَيَّرَ قَوانينَ \ قَواعِدَ اللُعْبةِ to change the rules of the game **2** [مُباراة] game, match; لُعْبة سِياسيّة a political game; رَبِحَ \ خَسِرَ في لُعْبةٍ to win/lose a match; لَعِبَ لُعْبةً to play a game **3** [دُمْية] doll

لَعوب *adj* |f; لَعائِبُ| **1** [يُحِبُّ اللَهْوَ] playful, frisky **2** [مِغْناج] coquettish, flirtatious; فَتاة لَعوب coquette

أُلْعوبة *n* |أَلاعيبُ| plaything; doll, puppet

تلاعُب *n* |تَلاعُبات| manipulation, tampering; fraud, deceit, swindle; تَلاعُب بِنَتائِجِ الانْتِخاباتِ fix the election results; تَلاعُب لَفْظيّ \ بالأَلْفاظِ \ بالكَلِماتِ pun; تَلاعُب بالصُوَرِ photoshopping, photo manipulation

مُلاعِب *n* playmate, playfellow

مَلْعَب *n* |مَلاعِبُ| playing field, sports ground, court, pitch; stadium; في المَلْعَبِ on the playing field; مَلْعَب مُزْدَحِم \ خالٍ a(n) full/empty stadium; المَلْعَب الأولِمْبيّ the Olympic stadium; مَلْعَب كُرةِ القَدَمِ football (BrE) soccer (AmE) stadium; مَلْعَب التِنِسِ tennis court; نِصْف المَلْعَبِ half court, half field; طَرَد لاعِبًا من المَلْعَبِ to send a player off the field

لَعْثَمَ *v* |i; لَعْثَمة| to stutter, to stammer

تَلَعْثَمَ *v* to stutter, to stammer; تَلَعْثَمَ في كَلامِهِ to fumble for words

تَلَعْثُم *n* hesitation; stuttering, stutter

مُتَلَعْثِم *n* stutterer, stammerer

لاعِج *n* |لَواعِجُ| ardent love

لُعاع، لُعاعة *n* endive

لَعِقَ *v* |a; لَعْق، لَعْقة، لُعْقة| to lick (off); to lap up; لَعِقَ شَفَتَيْهِ to lick one's lips

مِلْعَقة *n* |مَلاعِقُ| spoon; مِلْعَقة طَعامٍ tablespoon; مِلْعَقة صَغيرة \ شايٍ teaspoon; مِلْعَقة عَسَلٍ a spoonful of honey; أبو مِلْعَقةٍ (Zool) spoonbill (*Plataleinae*); أَكَلَ بِمِلْعَقةٍ to eat with a spoon

لَعْل *n* (Geol) garnet

لَعَلَّ *particle* maybe, perhaps; لَعَلَّهُ يَكْفي أنْ ... maybe it's sufficient to/that ...; لَعَلَّ الطَقْسَ بارِدٌ it might be cold outside

لَعْلَعَ *v* |i; لَعْلَعة| to boom

تَلَعْلَعَ *v* to flicker, to shimmer

لَعَنَ *v* |a; لَعْن| to curse, to damn; لَعَنَ شَخْصًا \ شَيْئًا to curse sb/sth; لَعَنَكَ اللهُ! God damn you!

لاعَنَ *v* **1** [لَعَنَ] to curse, to damn **2** (Islam) *to accuse a woman of adultery*

تلاعَنَ *v* to curse/damn each other

لَعْن *n* curse

لِعان *n* curse, imprecation; (Isl Law) *sworn allegation of adultery committed by one's spouse*

لَعْنة *n* |لَعَنات، لِعان| **1** [شَرّ] curse; لَعْنة الفَراعِنةِ the Pharaoh's curse; لَعْنة اللهِ عَلَيْكَ God damn you **2** [شَتيمة] curse, swear word, expletive; oath

لَعين *adj* |لُعَناءُ| cursed, damned, detested; تِلْكَ الحَرْب اللَعينة that damned war!

مُلاعَنة *n* (Isl Law) *conditional self-imprecation (the case of permanent divorce and separation between a couple when the husband accuses his wife of adultery)*

مَلْعون *adj* |مَلاعينُ| cursed, damned; شَيْء مَلْعون damned thing, bloody thing (BrE); هذه التِكْنولوجِيا المَلْعونة! this damned technology!

لاغِب *adj* |لُغَّب| tired, exhausted, weary, languid

لُغوب *n* tiredness, exhaustion, weariness, fatigue

لُغْد *n* |أَلْغاد، لُغْدود، لُغاديد| double chin; dewlap, wattle

لَغَزَ *v* |u; لَغْز| to speak in riddles

أَلْغَزَ *v* to mystify; to equivocate, to speak in riddles; أَلْغَزَ في كَلامِهِ to speak in riddles

لُغْز *n* |أَلْغاز| riddle, puzzle; mystery, enigma; حَلَّ \ فَكَّ لُغْزًا to solve/unravel a mystery

مُلْغَز *adj* mysterious, enigmatic, cryptic; vague, ambiguous, obscure

لَغَطَ *v* |a; لَغْط، لِغاط| to be noisy/clamorous; to whoop

لَغْط *n* |أَلْغاط| noise, clamor, tumult; crying, yelling, shouting; أَثارَ لَغْطًا كَثيرًا to make a lot of noise

لَغَمَ *v* |a; لَغْم| to lay/plant mines, to mine; لَغَمَ الطَريقَ to lay mines on the road

لَغَّمَ *v* to lay/plant mines, to mine

أَلْغَمَ *v* to amalgamate

لَغَم *n* |أَلْغام| mine, booby-trap; لَغَم أَرْضيّ landmine; لَغَم بَحْريّ sea mine; داسَ على لَغَمٍ أَرْضيٍّ to step on a landmine; اصْطَدَمَ بِلَغَمٍ بَحْريٍّ to hit a sea mine; حَقْل أَلْغامٍ minefield; كاسِحة أَلْغامٍ minesweeper; أَزالَ أَلْغامًا \ كَسَحَ to sweep/clear mines; زَرَعَ \ أَلْغامًا to lay mines

مُلْغَم *n* amalgam

مُلَغَّم *adj* mined, booby-trapped; سَيّارة مُلَغَّمة booby-trapped car

مَلْغوم *adj* mined, booby-trapped; explosive; سَيّارة مَلْغومة car bomb; رِسالة مَلْغومة letter bomb; سُؤال مَلْغوم a loaded question

لَغا *v* |u; لَغْو| 1 ◀ [تَكَلَّمَ] to talk, to speak; to chatter 2 ◀ [بَطَلَ] to be/become null/void/invalid

أَلْغى *v* to cancel, to terminate, to annul; to abolish; to reverse, to undo; أُلْغِيَ to expire; أَلْغى شَيْئاً to terminate sth; أَلْغى مُباراةً \ سَفراً to cancel a match/trip; أَلْغى اتِّفاقيّةً \ مُعاهَدةً to terminate a treaty; أَلْغى إجْراءً \ قَراراً to reverse a measure/decision; أَلْغى الحُكْمَ بالإعدام to abolish capital punishment; أَلْغى زِيارَتَهُ to cancel one's visit; أَلْغى اشْتِراكَهُ to cancel one's membership; أَلْغى اشْتِراكَهُ في مَجَلّةٍ to cancel one's subscription to a magazine; أَلْغى مَشْروعاً to abandon a project; أُلْغِيَ المَوْعِدُ the appointment has been cancelled

لَغْو *n* nonsense, rubbish; chatter

لاغٍ *adj* invalid, void, false; اتِّفاق لاغٍ an invalid agreement; عَقْد لاغٍ a void contract

لُغة *n* language, tongue; لُغة أَجْنَبيّة a foreign language; لُغة حَيّة a modern language; لُغة مَيِّتة \ مَهْجورة a dead language; لُغة عامّيّة \ مَحْكيّة \ دارِجة colloquial language; لُغة العامّةِ vernacular; لُغة عالَميّة world language; لُغة مُسْتَعْمَلة language of communication; لُغة صارِمة forceful language; اللُّغة المُحادثةِ \ الكِتابةِ the spoken/written language; لُغة الإنْجْليزيّة \ العَرَبيّة the English/Arabic language; لُغة الإشارةِ sign language; لُغة البَلَدِ national language; بِلُغةِ البَلَدِ in the national language; لُغة أُمّ mother tongue; ابْن اللُّغةِ native speaker; ثُنائيّ اللُّغةِ bilingual; تَعَدُّد اللُّغاتِ multilingualism; عِلْم اللُّغةِ linguistics; فِقه اللُّغةِ philology; تَعْليم اللُّغةِ language teaching; مَتْن اللُّغةِ lexicon; مَعْرِفة باللُّغاتِ knowledge of languages; مُتَعَلِّق باللُّغةِ linguistic; دَوْرة لُغةٍ (Mor) language course; تابَعَ دَوْرة \ دُروس لُغةٍ to take a language course; تَكَلَّمَ لُغةً, تَمَكَّنَ من لُغةٍ to speak a language; أَتْقَنَ لُغةً to have mastery of a language; أَتْقَنَ لُغةً أَجادَ لُغةً to have good command of a language; أَجادَ لُغةً كِتابةً وَمُحادَثةً to have written and verbal command of a language; اللُّغةُ الانْجْليزيّةُ لُغةٌ عالَميّةٌ English is a world language

لُغَويّ **A** *adj* linguistic, language (*before n*), lingual; صَحيح \ خاطِئ لُغَويًّا linguistically correct/incorrect; مَعْرِفة لُغَويّة linguistic knowledge; مَسْأَلة لُغَويّة language issue; حُدود لُغَويّة linguistic boundaries; بَحْث لُغَويّ a linguistic study; اقْتِراض لُغَويّ borrowing words (*from other languages*)
B *n* linguist

لُغَويّات *n pl* linguistics; لُغَويّات تَطْبيقيّة applied linguistics

إلْغاء *n* |إلْغاءات| cancellation, discontinuation; annulment, repeal; termination, abolition; إلْغاء حَظْرٍ lifting the embargo; إلْغاء قانونٍ repealing a law; إلْغاء مُعاهَدةٍ the termination of a treaty; إلْغاء اشْتِراكٍ the discontinuation of a subscription

مُلْغًى *adj* invalid, void, null; canceled, annulled, repealed

لَغِيَ *v* |a; لَغًى| to talk nonsense

لَفَتَ *v* |i; لَفْت| to attract attention; لَفَتَ إلى أنّ ... to point out that ...; لَفَتَ الانْتِباهَ \ النَّظَرَ to attract attention; ما لَفَتَ انْتِباهي أنّ ... what attracted my attention, is/was ...; لَفَتَ انْتِباهَ شَخْصٍ إلى شَيْءٍ to bring sth to sb's attention

تَلَفَّتَ *v* to look around

الْتَفَتَ *v* 1 ◀ [أَدارَ] to turn (around); الْتَفَتَ حَوْلَهُ to look around; الْتَفَتَ إلى الوَراءِ to turn around; الْتَفَتَ إلى اليَسارِ \ اليَمين to turn to the left/right; الْتَفَتَ بِوَجْهِهِ إلى شَخْصٍ to turn to face sb; الْتَفَتَ إلى رَئيسةِ المَجْلِسِ to address the chairwoman
2 ◀ [اهْتَمَّ] to heed, to consider, to pay attention to

اسْتَلْفَتَ *v* to attract (*attention*)

لِفْت *n* turnip (*Brassica rapa*)

لافِت *adj* remarkable, noticeable, striking; لافِت لِلنَّظَرِ eye-catching; غَيْر لافِتٍ لِلنَّظَرِ inconspicuous; على نَحْوٍ لافِتٍ remarkably

لافِتة *n* |لافِتات, لَوافِتُ| billboard, sign, placard; banner; لافِتة إعْلانيّة advertising board

لَفْتة *n* 1 ◀ [اسْتِدارة] turning, rotation, revolution 2 ◀ [تَعْبيرٌ عن عاطِفةٍ] gesture

الْتِفاتة *n* 1 ◀ [اسْتِدارة] turn, rotation 2 ◀ [تَعْبيرٌ عن عاطِفةٍ] gesture; الْتِفاتة كَريمة a grand gesture

لَفّة *n* ① [دَوْرة] rotation, revolution, turn; سُرْعةُ المُحَرِّكِ ١٠٠٠ لَفّةٍ في الدَقيقةِ the engine is running at 1,000 revolutions per minute ② [عُلْبة] roll, cylinder; coil, reel; لَفّة من القُماشِ a roll of cloth

لَفيف *n* ① [جَماعة] group; gathering, crowd ② (Law Mor) *a group of witnesses who confirm sb's statement in court* ③ (Gram) فِعْل لَفيف *an irregular verb with two weak letters, such as* وَفى *and* نَوى

لَفيفة *n* roll, scroll; bundle, package

تَلافيف *n* |dipt| twist, coil, convolution; في تَلافيفِ شَيْءٍ in the depth of sth; في تَلافيفِ الدِماغِ within the brain

مُلْتَفّ *adj* twisted, coiled, winding; الأَشْجار المُلْتَفّة winding trees

مِلَفّ *n* |مِلَفّات| ① [لِحِفْظِ الأَوْراقِ] folder, (document) file; وَضَعَ \ حَفِظَ شَيْئاً في مِلَفٍّ to file sth ② [مَجْموعة وَثائِق] file, dossier, records; مِلَفّ كامِل a complete file; مِلَفّ شائِك a delicate dossier; مِلَفّ صِحّيّ \ طِبّيّ medical records; مِلَفّ (فُلان) (sb's) dossier; مِلَفّ القَضيّةِ الفِلَسْطينيّة the Palestine issue ③ [كُمْبيوتر] file; حَفِظَ \ غَيَّرَ \ حَذَفَ مِلَفّاً to save/edit/delete a file; بُروتوكول نَقْلِ المِلَفّاتِ file transfer protocol, FTP

مَلْفوف A *adj* wrapped, coiled, enveloped B *n* cabbage

لَفَّقَ *v* to make up, to concoct, to fabricate; to falsify, to counterfeit; to feign, to simulate; لَفَّقَ رِوايةً to make up a story

تَلْفيق *n* concoction, fabrication; falsification; تَلْفيق تُهْمةٍ fabricating charges

مُلَفَّق *adj* made up, fabricated; counterfeited, falsified; قِصّة مُلَفَّقة fabricated story

لَفْلَفَ *v* |i; لَفْلَفة| ① [ثَوْباً] to wrap, to envelop ② [أَخْفى] to cover up, to conceal

تَلَفْلَفَ *v* to be wrapped/enveloped

أَلْفى *v* to find, to discover; أَلْفى صَديقَهُ يَسْقي الأَزْهارَ he found his friend watering the flowers

تَلافى *v* ① [تَدارَكَ] to correct, to rectify; تَلافى الآثارَ to erase tracks ② [تَجَنَّبَ] to prevent, to avoid, to avert; تَلافى أَخْطاءً to prevent mistakes; تَلافى الآثارَ to avoid effects

مُلْفِت *adj* remarkable, attractive, striking; كَلام مُلْفِت a remarkable statement

لَفَحَ *v* |a; لَفْح, لَفَحان| to scorch, to singe, to sear, to burn

لافِح *adj* scorching, searing, burning; sweltering; حَرّ لافِح a sweltering heat

لَفْحة *n* blight; لَفْحة الشَمْسِ sunburn

لَفَظَ *v* |i; لَفْظ| ① [نَطَقَ] to pronounce; to utter, to express ② [أَخْرَجَ] to throw out, to eject, to expel; to emit, to discharge; لَفَظَ أَنْفاسَهُ الأَخيرة to breathe one's last

تَلَفَّظَ *v* to pronounce; to utter, to express, to say

لَفْظ *n* |أَلْفاظ| ① [تَعْبير] word, term, expression; لَفْظ وَمَعْنًى form and content; لَفْظ نابٍ swear word; لَفْظ الجَلالةِ *the word* الله *(God)*; تَلاعُب بالأَلْفاظِ pun ② [نُطْق] pronunciation

لَفْظة *n* word, utterance, expression

لَفْظيّ *adj* verbal, phonetic; literal; اشْتِراك لَفْظيّ homonym; تَلاعُب لَفْظيّ pun

تَلَفُّظ *n* pronunciation, articulation

مَلْفوظ *adj* expressed, voiced, declared; pronounced

لَفَّعَ *v* to cover, to wrap

تَلَفَّعَ *v* to be wrapped/covered; تَلَفَّعَ بِعَباءَتِهِ to be wrapped in one's cloak

مِلْفَع *n* (Islam) *a scarf used to cover the head*

لَفَّ *v* |u; لَفّ| ① [طَوى] to roll up; لَفَّ سيجارةً to roll a cigarette; لَفَّ السَجّادةَ to roll up the carpet ② [أَدارَ] to wind, to coil, to reel, to spool; لَفَّ خَيْطاً على بَكَرةٍ to wind thread on to a spool ③ [غَلَّفَ] to fold, to wrap

تَلَفَّفَ *v* to be wrapped; to wrap oneself

الْتَفَّ *v* ① [اسْتَدارَ] to curl, to coil, to convolute; to twist, to turn, to wind; الْتَفَّ حول ... to wind around ... ② [تَغَطّى] to be wrapped; to wrap oneself; الْتَفَّ بِلِحافٍ to wrap oneself in a blanket ③ [ناصَرَ] to gather, to cluster; الْتَفَّ حول شَخْصٍ to gather around sb ④ [تَحايَلَ] |على| to get around; الْتَفَّ على القانونِ to get around the law

لَفّ *n* winding, wrapping; بِدونِ لَفٍّ وَدَوَرانٍ in plain terms

لِفافة *n* |لِفافات, لَفائِف| ① [عِصابة] bandage; swathe ② [قِماط] wrapper, cover ③ [سيجارة] cigarette

لَقَّبَ *v* to call, to address as; to nickname, to dub; to describe, to label; لَقَّبَ شَخْصاً بالحِمارِ to call sb a donkey

تَلَقَّبَ *v* to be nicknamed, to be called

لَقَب *n* |أَلْقاب| **1** [كُنْيَة] nickname; epithet; سَمَّى شَخْصاً بِلَقَبٍ, أَعْطى شَخْصاً لَقَباً to give sb a nickname; لُقِّبَ \ سُمِّيَ بِلَقَبٍ to be nicknamed **2** [اِسْم العائِلَة] family name, surname, last name **3** [مِيزة] title; لَقَب فَخْرِيّ honorary title; لَقَب جامِعِيّ a university degree; لَقَب بارون \ أُسْتاذ جامِعِيّ the title of baron/professor; لَقَب شَرَفٍ a noble title; حَمَلَ \ اِسْتَعْمَلَ لَقَباً to bear/use a title; أَحْرَزَ \ اِكْتَسَبَ لَقَباً to win/gain a title **4** (Sport) title; صِراع على اللَّقَبِ championship match; لَقَب البُطولَةِ الوَطَنِيّةِ the title of national champion; حامِل \ صاحِب اللَّقَبِ title-holder; مُدافِع عن اللَّقَبِ title defender; حَمَلَ اللَّقَبَ to hold the title; دافَعَ عن اللَّقَبِ to defend the title; فازَ بِلَقَبِ البُطولَةِ to win the title; أَحْرَزَ لَقَبَ البُطولَةِ to win the champion's title; خَسِرَ \ أَضاعَ اللَّقَبَ to lose the title; حافَظَ على اللَّقَبِ to retain the title; مُنِحَ لَقَبُ ... to be granted the title of ...

مُلَقَّب *adj* nicknamed, called; المُلَقَّب ب ... alias ..., aka ...; أبو حامِد المُلَقَّب بالغَزالِيِّ Abu Hamid aka al-Ghazzali

لَقَّحَ *v* **1** [طَعَّمَ] to vaccinate, to inoculate; لَقَّحَ شَخْصاً ضِدّ مَرَضٍ \ الإنْفلونْزا to vaccinate sb against a disease/the flu **2** (Bio) to pollinate; to impregnate, to inseminate; لَقَّحَ اِصْطِناعِيّاً to artificially inseminate; لَقَّحَ أَزْهاراً to pollinate flowers; لَقَّحَ بُوَيْضَةً to fertilize an ovum; لَقَّحَ أُنْثى to impregnate a woman

أَلْقَحَ *v* to pollinate; to impregnate, to cover, to inseminate; يُلْقِحُ الثَّوْرُ البَقَرَةَ the bull impregnates the cow

تَلَقَّحَ *v* **1** [شَخْصٌ] to be vaccinated; تَلَقَّحَ الوَلَدُ ضِدّ الجُدَرِيِّ the boy was vaccinated against the smallpox; يَجِبُ أنْ يَتَلَقَّحَ الطِفْلُ ثَلاثَ مَرّاتٍ a child must be vaccinated three times **2** [شَيْءٌ] to be pollinated, to be fertilized; to be enriched; تَلَقَّحَت البُوَيْضَةُ the egg was fertilized; تَتَلَقَّحُ اللُغَةُ بِما حَوْلَها من ثَقافَةٍ a language is enriched by the surrounding culture

لَقاح, لِقاح *n* **1** (Med) vaccine; لَقاح ضِدّ السُلِّ a vaccine against tuberculosis **2** (Bio) pollen **3** (Zool) semen (*from animal*)

تَلاقُح *n* cross-fertilization, cross-pollination; تَلاقُح الأَفْكارِ exchanging ideas

تَلْقِيح *n* **1** (Med) vaccination, inoculation; تَلْقِيح إجْبارِيّ mandatory vaccination; تَلْقِيح ضِدّ الحَصْبَةِ الأَلْمانِيّةِ \ الجُدَرِيِّ a vaccination against rubella/smallpox; تَمَّ تَلْقِيحُهُ he's been vaccinated **2** (Bio) pollination; insemination, impregnation; تَلْقِيح اِصْطِناعِيّ artificial insemination

مُلَقَّح *adj* **1** (Med) vaccinated, inoculated **2** (Bio) inseminated, impregnated; fertilized

لَقَدْ *particle* yet, already; لَقَدْ فَهِمْتُهُ الآنَ now I understand

لَقَطَ *v* |u; لَقْط| **1** [جَمَعَ] to gather, to collect, to pick up, to glean; to pick, to peck at **2** (Phot) لَقَطَ صورةً to take a picture

تَلَقَّطَ *v* to gather, to pick up

اِلْتَقَطَ *v* **1** [جَمَعَ] to gather, to collect; to pick up, to glean; اِلْتَقَطَ شَيْئاً من الأَرْضِ to pick sth up from the floor; اِلْتَقَطَ فِكْرَةً \ إشاراتٍ من شَخْصٍ to get an idea/information from sb **2** (Phot) اِلْتَقَطَ صورةً to take a picture **3** [البَثَّ] to obtain, to receive; اِلْتَقَطَ بَثّاً to receive a broadcast

لاقِط *n* |لَواقِطُ| لاقِط الصَوْتِ microphone; receiver; لاقِط أَرْضِيّ ground receiver; لاقِط شَمْسِيّ solar panel; لِكُلِّ ساقِطةٍ لاقِطةٌ every Jack has his Jill

لاقِطة *n* **1** (Tech) detector **2** [كَلِمة] a spoken word

لَقْطة *n* |لَقَطات| photograph, picture, shot; لَقْطة شاشةٍ (Comput) screenshot; صَوَّرَ لَقْطةً to take a picture

لُقْطة *n* |لُقَطات| find, catch

لَقِيط *n* |لُقَطاء| foundling

اِلْتِقاط *n* **1** [جَمْع] gathering, collecting **2** [البَثّ] reception; اِلْتِقاط البَثِّ التِلِفِزْيونِيِّ television reception **3** (Phot) photographing

مِلْقَط *n* |مَلاقِطُ| tweezers; a pair of pincers/pliers, forceps; pin, peg; clamp; tongs; مِلْقَط الغَسِيلِ clothes peg; سَحَبَ طِفْلاً بالمِلْقَطِ to deliver a baby by forceps

لَقِفَ *v* |a; لَقْف, لَقَفان| to seize, to catch, to grab

لَقَّفَ *v* to throw/fling/cast/toss at/to

تَلَقَّفَ *v* to seize, to catch, to grab, to snatch; to pick up, to gather

أَلْقى *v* ❶ [رَمى] to throw, to cast, to fling, to hurl; أَلْقى قَنابِلَ to throw bombs; أَلْقى إلى شَخْصٍ بِكُرةٍ to throw a ball at sb; أَلْقى نَظْرةً على شَيْءٍ \ شَخْصٍ to take a look at sth/sb; أَلْقى بِنَفْسِهِ to put oneself in danger; أَلْقى بِنَفْسِه إلى الخَطَرِ to jump out the window; أَلْقى القَبْضَ على من النافِذةِ to arrest sb; أَلْقى المَسْؤوليّةَ على شَخْصٍ to hold sb responsible ❷ [أَلْقى مُحاضَرةً] to recite; أَلْقى قَصيدةً to recite a poem; أَلْقى خِطاباً \ خُطْبةً to give a lecture; أَلْقى مُحاضَرةً to make a speech

تَلَقّى *v* to receive, to get; to take; تَلَقّى كَدْمةً عَنيفةً to take a blow; تَلَقّى دَرْساً to take lessons; تَلَقّى أَمْراً to get an order; تَلَقّى نَقْداً \ to receive a letter/assignment; تَلَقّى رِسالةً \ واجِباً شُكْراً to receive criticism/thanks; تَلَقّى تَرْحيباً to win support; تَلَقّى هَديّةً من شَخْصٍ to receive a gift from sb

تلاقى *v* to meet each other, to assemble

اِلْتَقى *v* |ب| to meet, to encounter, to come together; to gather, to assemble, to bring/call together; اِلْتَقى بِشَخْصٍ to meet sb; اِلْتَقى بِشَخْصٍ في الشارِعِ to meet sb on the street; يَلْتَقي اِلْتَقى بِشَخْصٍ صُدْفةً النَهْرانِ هُناكَ the two rivers meet there; to run into sb; اِلْتَقَيا في المَحَطّةِ the two met at the station; اِلْتَقَتْ وُجْهاتُ النَظَرِ the opinions overlapped

اِسْتَلْقى *v* to lie (down); اِسْتَلْقى في السَريرِ to lie in bed

لِقاء *n* |لِقاءات| ❶ [اِلْتِقاء] meeting, encounter, assembly; reunion; interview; إلى اللِقاءِ goodbye; مَكانُ اللِقاءِ meeting place; لِقاء مع شَخْصٍ a reunion with sb ❷ [مُباراة] لِقاء وُدّيّ \ ساخِن a friendly/competitive match

لَقيّة *n* find, discovery

اِسْتِلْقاء *n* lying (down), resting; rest, peace, tranquility

اِلْتِقاء *n* meeting, encounter, assembly; reunion; مَكان \ نُقْطة اِلْتِقاءِ meeting place/point; نُقْطة اِلْتِقاءِ نَهْرَي النيلِ الأَزْرَقِ والنيلِ الأَبْيَضِ the confluence of the Blue Nile and the White Nile

إِلْقاء *n* ❶ [نَثْر \ شِعْر] delivering, reciting (*speech, lecture, poetry, etc.*) ❷ [رَمْي] throwing, casting, tossing ❸ [إيقاف] إِلْقاء القَبْضِ arrest

تَلاقٍ *n* meeting, encounter, assembly

اِلْتَقَفَ *v* to seize, to catch, to grab, to snatch

لَقْلَقَ *v* |i; لَقْلَقة| to clatter (*stork*); to chatter; to rumble

لَقْلَق, لَقلاق *n* |لَقالِقُ| stork (*Ciconiidae*)

لَقَمَ *v* |u; لَقْم| to obstruct, to block, to clog; لَقَمَ الطَريقَ to block a road

لَقِمَ *v* |a; لَقْم| to devour, to gobble (up), to guzzle; لَقِمَ الطَعامَ to devour food

لَقَّمَ *v* ❶ [أَكَّلَ] to feed; to supply ❷ [السِلاحَ] (Syria) to load, to upload

أَلْقَمَ *v* to feed, to make swallow

اِلْتَقَمَ *v* to swallow; to devour, to gobble (up)

لُقْمة *n* |لُقَم| bite, mouthful, morsel; لُقْمة العَيْشِ daily bread; livelihood; كَسَبَ لُقْمةَ عَيْشِهِ to earn one's livelihood; أَكَلَ لُقْمةً to take a bite

تَلْقيم *n* feed, feeding; تَلْقيم ويب Web feed

مُلَقِّم *n* ❶ (Comput) server ❷ [لِطابِعةٍ إلخ] feeder

لُقْمان *n* |dipt| سورة لُقْمان Luqman (*Sura 31*)

لَقِنَ *v* |a; لَقانة, لَقانية| ❶ [فَهِمَ] to understand, to infer ❷ [تَعَلَّمَ] to learn, to pick up

لَقَّنَ *v* ❶ [عَلَّمَ] to teach, to instruct, to coach; to dictate; لَقَّنَ شَخْصاً دَرْساً to teach sb a lesson ❷ [في المَسْرَحِ] to prompt ❸ (Islam) لَقِّنوا مَوْتاكُم الشَهادةَ *remind the dying to say the shahada*

تَلَقَّنَ *v* to understand, to grasp

تَلْقين *n* ❶ [عَلَّمَ] teaching, instruction; briefing ❷ [في المَسْرَحِ] prompting

مُلَقِّن *n* prompter

لَقْوة *n* لَقْوة الوَجْهِ facial paralysis

لَقِيَ *v* |a; لُقْية, لُقْيان, لِقاء| to meet (with), to encounter, to come across, to find; to get, to receive; لَقِيَ دَعْماً to get support; لَقِيَ نَجاحاً to have success; لَقِيَ مُعامَلةً حَسَنةً to be treated well; لَقِيَ قَبولاً عَظيماً to be well received; لَقيتُهُ في الشارِعِ I encountered him in the street

لاقى *v* to meet (with), to encounter, to come across, to find; to experience; لاقى مُعارَضةً to meet with opposition; لاقى شَخْصاً to meet sb; لاقى اهْتِماماً واسِعاً to get attention

تلقٍّ *n* reception; acquisition

تِلْقاء *n* من تِلْقاءِ نفْسِهِ \ ذاتِهِ of one's own accord

تِلْقائيّ *adj* automatic; spontaneous, impulsive; الإكْمال التِلْقائيّ autocomplete; ردّ فِعْلٍ تِلْقائيّ \ ردّ a spontaneous reaction; تصرّف تِلْقائيًّا to answer/act impulsively

تِلْقائيّة *n* automatism; spontaneity

مُتلقٍّ *n* recipient

مُلاقاة *n* meeting, encounter

مُلْتقًى *n* |مُلْتقَيات| [1] [الْتِقاء] meeting, conference [2] [مكان] meeting point/place [3] (Comput) forum [4] (Transp) junction, intersection

‹ **لكأ** *v* |a; لكْء| to strike, to hit; لكأ شخصاً بالسَوْطِ to whip sb

لكِئ *v* |a; لكأ| ب| to stay, to sojourn

تلكّأ *v* to loiter, to linger

‹ **لكز** *v* |u; لكْز| to punch, to thump, to pound; to poke, to jab; لكز شخْصاً بِكوعِهِ to nudge sb

لكْزة *n* |لُكز| punch, thump, knock; jab, prod

‹ **لوكْسمْبورْغ** *n* |f| Luxembourg

‹ **ألْكع** *adj* |dipt; لُكْع; f لكْعاء| [1] [لئيم] mean, low, base [2] [أحْمق] stupid, silly, foolish

‹ **لكّ** *v* |u; لكّ| to punch, to thump, to pound; to jab, to poke

لكّ, لُكّ *n* |ألْكاك, لُكوك| (sealing) wax; varnish

‹ **لِكَيْلا** *conj* see كي

لِكَيْلا *conj* see كي

‹ **لكم** *v* |u; لكْم| to punch, to strike, to box; لكم شخْصاً to punch sb

لاكم *v* to box, to fight (with); لاكم بطلَ العالَم to box the world champion

تلاكم *v* to box, to fight (with), to have a fist fight with

لكْمة *n* |لكَمات| punch, swipe

لِكَيْما *conj* see كي

مُلاكِم *n* (Sport) boxer

مُلاكَمة *n* boxing, fist fight; حلْبة المُلاكَمةِ boxing ring; مُباراة مُلاكَمةٍ boxing match

¹‹ **لكِن** *v* |a; لكَن, لُكْنة| to stammer, to falter; to speak/pronounce incorrectly

لُكْنة *n* accent; incorrect pronunciation; بِلُكْنةٍ with an accent; يتكلّمُ العربيّةَ بِلُكْنةٍ فرنْسيّةٍ he speaks Arabic with a French accent

ألْكن *adj* |dipt; لُكْن; f لكْناء| stammering, stuttering

²‹ **لكِنْ** *conj* but, however, nevertheless; yet, still; ولكِنْ but

لكِنّ *conj* but, however, nevertheless; yet, still; ولكِنّ but

‹ **لِكَيْ, لِكَيْلا, لِكَيْما** see كي

‹ **لمْ** *particle* not; لمْ يكْتُبْ he didn't write; لمْ أرَهُ I didn't see him; لمْ أرَ شيْئًا I didn't see anything; لمْ أكُنْ أعْلَمُ ذلك I didn't know; لمْ ألْقَهُ بعْدُ I haven't met him yet; إنْ لمْ يكُنْ ذلك مُمْكِناً فيَجِبُ ... if that isn't possible, then it's necessary that/to ...

‹ **لمّا** *conj* [1] [عِنْدَما] when; as, while [2] [لم ... بعْدُ] لمّا يعُدْ he hasn't returned yet

‹ **لِماذا** *adv* see ما

‹ **لمْبة** *n* lamp; light; bulb

‹ **لمَج** *v* |u; لمْج| to eat

لمّج *v* to give a snack/bite to eat; لمّج شخْصاً خُبْزاً to give sb a snack/bite to eat

لُمْجة *n* |لُمَج| snack, appetizer

‹ **لمَح** *v* |a; لمْح| to become aware of, to (take) notice of, to sense, to perceive; to glance at, to see, to observe; لمَح شخْصاً \ شيْئاً to catch a glimpse of sb/sth

لمّح *v* |إلى| to hint at, to allude to; to insinuate, to suggest; لمّح إلى شخْصٍ to allude to sb; لمّح إلى شيْءٍ to hint at sth; لمّح إلى أنّ ... to insinuate that ...

لمْح *n* flash, split second, instant, moment; في لمْحِ البصَرِ \ ب in a split second, in a blink of an eye; في أقلّ من لمْحِ البصَرِ in no time, in less than a blink of an eye

لمْحة *n* |لمَحات| [1] [نظْرة] glance, glimpse; picture, image; لمْحة سريعة a quick glance; لمْحة تاريخيّة إلى ... a look back at ... [2] [صورة] picture, image; لمْحة شامِلة a complete picture

ألْمَح *v* [1] [إلى | رأى] to glance at, to see [2] [أشار | إلى] to point/refer to, to indicate; to hint at, to allude to; to mention

مُلْتَمِس *n* applicant; مُلْتَمِس اللُجوءِ asylum seeker

مَلْمَس *n* |مَلامِس| ⟦1⟧ [لَمْس] touch; كانَ ناعِمَ المَلْمَسِ to feel soft ⟦2⟧ (Mus) fret; مَلامِس القيثارةِ the frets of a guitar ⟦3⟧ (Bio) tentacle

مَلْموس *adj* |مَلْموسات| concrete; tangible, palpable; noticeable, perceivable; غَيْر مَلْموسٍ intangible; بِشَكْلٍ \ بِصورةٍ مَلْموس (ةٍ) in a tangible way; واقِع مَلْموس a palpable reality; دَليل مَلْموس tangible proof; نَتائِج مَلْموسة tangible results; لم يُسْفِرْ عن نَتائِج مَلْموسةٍ to not produce tangible results

لَمَظ *v* |u; لَمْظ| to smack one's lips

تَلَمَّظ *v* to slurp, to smack

لَمَعَ *v* |a; لَمْع , لَمَعان| to sparkle, to twinkle, to glitter; to shine, to gleam, to beam; يَلْمَعُ شَعْرُها her hair shines; لَمَعَتْ في عَيْنَيْهِ دُموعٌ tears were glistening in his eyes; لَمَع بَريقُ الأَمَلِ في عَيْنَيْها a glimmer of hope flickered in her eyes

لَمَّعَ *v* to polish, to shine; لَمَّعَ الفِضَّةَ to polish the silver; لَمَّعَ حِذاءَهُ to polish one's shoes; لَمَّعَ الزُجاجَ \ النَوافِذَ to clean the windows

أَلْمَعَ *v* to allude to, to hint at; to insinuate, to imply; to point out

الْتَمَعَ *v* to sparkle, to twinkle, to glitter; to shine, to gleam

لَمْع *n* sparkle, glitter; shine, flash; لَمْع العَيْنَيْنِ a glimmer in the eyes; لَمْع جَوْهَرةٍ the sparkling of a jewel

لامِع *adj* |لَوامِعُ| radiant, shining, shiny, bright; brilliant, sparkling, glittering, twinkling; غَيْر لامِعٍ matt; نُجوم لامِعة twinkling stars; فِكْرة لامِعة a brilliant idea; تِلْميذ لامِع a brilliant student; أَسْماء لامِعة big names

لامِعة *n* |لَوامِعُ| fontanelle, soft spot (*on a baby's head*)

لَمّاع *adj* shining, shiny, glossy

لَمَعان *n* shine, gleam, sheen; sparkle, glitter; لَمَعان ساطِع \ مُبْهِر a strong/blinding gleam; لَمَعان شَعْرِها the shine of her hair

لُمْعة *n* shine, gloss; glitter; جَديد بِلُمْعَتِهِ brand new; لُمْعة الذَهَبِ the glitter of gold

أَلْمَع *adj* |dipt| bright, brilliant

أَلْمَعيّ *adj* bright, brilliant; الكاتِب الأَلْمَعيّ the brilliant writer

تَلْميح *n* |تَلاميحُ, تَلْميحات| ⟦1⟧ [إشارة] insinuation, suggestion, hint; allusion, reference; تَلْميح إلى شَيْءٍ an allusion to sth ⟦2⟧ (Comput) tooltip

مَلْمَح *n* |مَلامِحُ| feature, line; مَلامِح countenance; مَلامِح كَريمة \ رَقيقة noble/soft features; مَلامِح بارِزة \ مُمَيِّزة prominent/distinguishing features

لَمَزَ *v* |i-u; لَمْز| ⟦1⟧ [غَمَزَ] to wink, to signal ⟦2⟧ [عابَ] to slander; to criticize, to rebuke

لُمَزة *n* fault-finder, hair-splitter

لَمَسَ *v* |i-u; لَمْس| ⟦1⟧ [مَسَّ] to touch; لَمَسَ شَيْئاً \ شَخْصاً to touch sth/sb; لم يَلْمَس الأَكْلَ he didn't touch the food; لَمَسَني بِيَدِهِ he touched me with his hand; لا تَلْمُسْني ! don't touch me! ⟦2⟧ [أَحَسَّ] to feel, to sense, to perceive

لامَسَ *v* to touch, to graze, to brush; لامَسَ شَيْئاً \ شَخْصاً to touch sth/sb

تَلَمَّسَ *v* to touch, to feel, to grope; to sense; تَلَمَّسَ طَريقَهُ to feel one's way; تَلَمَّسَ في شَخْصٍ شَيْئاً to sense sth in sb; تَلَمَّسَ جَبْهةَ شَخْصٍ to feel sb's forehead; تَلَمَّسَ أَخْبارَ شَخْصٍ to find out information about sb

تَلامَسَ *v* to touch each other; to be contiguous; to be adjacent

الْتَمَسَ *v* to solicit, to request; to search/look for; الْتَمَسَ العِلْمَ to study; الْتَمَسَ عُذْراً to look for an excuse

لَمْس *n* touch, contact; حاسّة اللَمْسِ sense of touch; شاشة لَمْسٍ touch screen

لاموس *n* listed alphabetically

لَمْسة *n* وَضَعَ اللَمَساتِ الأَخيرةَ على شَيْءٍ to put the finishing touches on sth

لَمْسيّ *adj* touch-; لَوْحة لَمْسِيّة touchpad

الْتِماس *n* |الْتِماسات| petition, appeal; request, solicitation; طَلَب الْتِماسٍ appeal; وَجَّهَ الْتِماساً إلى شَخْصٍ to address a petition to sb; قَدَّمَ الْتِماساً to submit an appeal

تَلامُس *n* |تَلامُسات| (Elec) contact

تَلَمُّس *n* touch, feeling

مُلامَسة *n* contact; touch, caress

مُلْتَمَس *n* |مُلْتَمَسات| petition, appeal; request

اِلْتِهاب *n* |اِلْتِهابات| inflammation, infection; اِلْتِهاب مِعَوِيّ gastroenteritis; اِلْتِهاب رِئَوِيّ pneumonia; اِلْتِهاب مَفْصِلِيّ \ اِلْتِهاب مَفْصِلِيّ مُزْمِن \ حادّ chronic/acute arthritis; اِلْتِهاب المَفاصِلِ arthritis; اِلْتِهاب مُزْمِن (في الأَمْعاءِ الغَليظَةِ) a chronic inflammation (of the large intestines); أُصيبَ بالتِهابٍ to get an infection; كافَحَ \ عالَجَ الْتِهاباً to fight off/treat an infection

اِلْتِهابِيّ *adj* inflammatory; مَرَض اِلْتِهابِيّ an inflammatory disease

إِلْهاب *n* inflaming, provoking, stirring up, inciting; إِلْهاب الشارِعِ inciting chaos in the streets

مُلْتَهِب *adj* ① [مُشْتَعِل] burning, ablaze; flaming, fiery; كَلِمات مُلْتَهِبة fierce words; تحت أَشِعّةِ الشَمْسِ المُلْتَهِبةِ in the blazing sun ② (Med) inflamed, infected; حَلْق مُلْتَهِب a sore throat; جُرْح مُلْتَهِب an infected wound

‹ **لاهوت** *n* see أله

‹ **لَهِثَ, لَهَثَ** *v* |a; لُهاث ,لَهْث| ① [إِنْسانٌ] to pant, to gasp, to wheeze ② [كَلْبٌ] to hang its tongue out

لاهِث *adj* panting, gasping, breathless, wheezing

لُهاث *n* pant, gasp

‹ **لَهِجَ** *v* |a; اَلْهَج| ب| to be dedicated/attached/devoted to, to be fond of; لَهِجَ بِشَيْءٍ \ شَخْصٍ to be devoted to sth/sb

لَهْجة *n* |لَهَجات| ① [دارِجة] dialect, vernacular, language; تَكَلَّمَ لَهْجةً to speak a dialect; اللَهْجة التونِسِيّة Tunisian Arabic; لَهْجة التُجّارِ the language of the merchants; عِلْم اللَهَجاتِ dialectology ② [طَريقة نُطْقٍ] accent, tone, voice; لَهْجة صارِمة \ قَوِيّة forceful language; بِلَهْجةٍ عاطِفِيّةٍ \ عَنيفةٍ in a sweet/harsh voice; كانَتْ تَتَكَلَّمُ بِلَهْجةٍ غَريبةٍ she spoke with a strange accent

لَهْجِيّ *adj* dialectal, dialect (*before n*)

‹ **لَهَدَ** *v* |a; لَهْد| to overload/overburden

‹ **لَهْذَم** *adj* pointed, sharp

‹ **لَهِفَ** *v* |a; لَهَف| على| to long/yearn/pine for; to regret; لَهِفَ على شَيْءٍ to long for sth

تَلَهَّفَ *v* |على| to long/yearn/pine for; to be impatient for, to be eager to; to be anxious to; تَلَهَّفَ على شَيْءٍ \ شَخْصٍ to long for sth/sb

أَلْمَعِيّة *n* intelligence, cleverness, genius

مُلَمِّع *n* polish; مُلَمِّع شَمْعِيّ polishing wax

‹ **لِمْفا, لِمْف** *n* lymph

لِيمْفاوِيّ, لِمْفاوِيّ *n* lymphatic, lymphoid; غُدّة لِمْفاوِيّة lymph gland

‹ **لَمْلَمَ** *v* |i; لَمْلَمة| to gather, to collect; to come together; لَمْلَمَ أَفْكارَهُ to collect one's thoughts

تَلَمْلَمَ *v* to gather, to collect; to bring together

‹ **لَمَّ** *v* |u; لَمّ| to gather, to collect; to bring/come together

أَلَمَّ *v* ① [أَصابَ] to be hit/stricken, to suffer; أَلَمَّ بِهِ مَرَضٌ شَديدٌ he was stricken with a severe illness ② [عَرَفَ] to know, to understand; to be acquainted; أَلَمَّ بِشَيْءٍ to understand sth

لامّ *n* collector; reaper, harvester

لِمام *adv* لِماماً rarely, seldom; infrequently, occasionally

إِلْمام *n* |إِلْمامات| familiarity, knowledge, awareness; الإِلْمام بِمَوْضوعٍ مُعَيَّنٍ familiarity with a certain subject

مُلِمّ *adj* educated, knowledgeable, well grounded, familiar; expert; مُلِمّ باللُغاتِ language expert

مُلِمّة *n* disaster, calamity, catastrophe; misfortune

‹ **لَنْ** *particle* will not; won't; لَنْ أَكْذِبَ I won't lie

‹ **لَنْدُن** *n* |f| London

‹ **لانْش, لَنْش** *n* |لَنْشات| motor boat

‹ **لَهِبَ** *v* |a; لَهَب, لَهيب| to burn, to flame

لَهَّبَ *v* to kindle, to light; to provoke, to inflame

أَلْهَبَ *v* to kindle, to light; to provoke, to inflame; to arouse, to inspire; أَلْهَبَ الحَمِيّةَ to arouse enthusiasm; أَلْهَبَ النارَ to light the fire

تَلَهَّبَ *v* to burn, to be on fire, to be ablaze

اِلْتَهَبَ *v* ① [اِشْتَعَلَ] to ignite; to flare up, to burn ② (Med) to be/become inflamed/infected; to ulcerate; to fester; اِلْتَهَبَ الجُرْحُ the wound has become inflamed

لَهَب *n* flame; blaze

لَهْبان *adj* |dipt| eager, longing; thirsty

لَهوب *adj* flammable

لَهيب *n* flame; blaze

لَهاة *n* |لُهِيّ, لَهاً, لَهَيات, لَهَوات| (Anat) uvula; epiglottis

لَهَوِيّ *adj* uvular; velar; صَوْت لَهَوِيّ an uvular/velar sound

تَلْهِية *n* distraction, diversion; amusement, entertainment

مَلْهاة *n* comedy

مَلْهًى *n* |مَلاهٍ| attraction, entertainment centre; مَلْهًى لَيْلِيّ nightclub; مَدينة \ حَديقة مَلاهٍ amusement park, funfair (BrE)

تَلَهْوَجَ *v* to hurry, to haste

لَوْ *conj* ❶ [لَوْ تَحَقَّقَ ذلك] if, in case (that); فيما لَوْ if; لَوْ كانَ بِيَدي لَفَدَيْتُكَ بِعُمْري if it were in my hands, I would give my life for you ❷ [لَوْلا] لَوْلا مُحَمَّدٌ، لَما أَنْهَيْنا العَمَلَ if it hadn't been for Muhammad, we wouldn't have finished the work; لَوْلاهُ لَمُتْنا جوعاً if it hadn't been for him, we would have starved ❸ [وَلَوْ] ... وَلَوْ (أَنَّ) ... even if ..., even though ..., although ..., albeit; وَلَو صَغيرا even if he's young; اُطْلُب العِلْمَ وَلَو في الصين *search for knowledge even as far as China*; وَنَحْنُ نَسْتَفيدُ أَيْضاً، وَلَوْ بِصورةٍ أَقَلّ we profit as well, albeit to a lesser degree ❹ [كَما لَوْ] as if, as though; تُخاطِبُني كَما لَوْ كُنْتَ ... you talk to me as if you were ... ❺ [وَدَّ لَوْ] وَدِدْتُ لَوْ لَم يَتَغَيَّرْ أَيُّ شَيْءٍ I wished nothing had changed

لوبي *n* lobby; اللوبي الصِناعيّ the manufacturing lobby

لوبيا, لوبياء *n* |dipt f| bean; green bean, French bean; string bean

لوت *n* lute

لاثَ *v* |u; لَوْث| ❶ [لَطَخَ] to stain, to soil ❷ [أَبْطَأَ] to be slow, to hesitate

لَوَّثَ *v* to pollute, to contaminate; to soil; to infect; لَوَّثَ البيئة \ الأَرْضَ \ المِياهَ الجَوْفِيّة \ الهَواء to pollute the environment/soil/groundwater/air; لَوَّثَ سُمْعةً to damage a reputation; لَوَّثَ جُرْحاً to infect a wound

تَلَوَّثَ *v* to be/become polluted/contaminated; to be/become infected; to be/become soiled; تَلَوَّثُ المِياهُ the water is contaminated; تَلَوَّثَ الجُرْحُ the wound became infected

تَلَوُّث *n* pollution, contamination; تَلَوُّث نَفْطِيّ oil pollution; تَلَوُّث سَمْعِيّ radioactive contamination; تَلَوُّث إشْعاعِيّ interference; تَلَوُّث كَبير \ خَطير serious pollution; تَلَوُّث هَواءٍ air pollution; تَلَوُّث هَواءٍ كَبير \ خَطير serious air pollution; تَلَوُّث مِياهِ الأَنْهارِ river water pollution; تَلَوُّث البيئة

لَهْف *n* يا لَهْفَ شَخْصٍ! what a shame!, too bad! (*for sb*); يا لَهْفي عَلَيْكَ I'm sorry for you

لَهْفة *n* |لَهَفات| longing, yearning; apprehension; انْتَظَرَ شَيْئاً بِلَهْفةٍ to eagerly look forward to sth

تَلَهُّف *n* |تَلَهُّفات| longing, yearning; بِتَلَهُّفٍ longingly; eagerly, anxiously

مَلْهوف *adj* ❶ [تَوّاق] desiring, longing, yearning; eager ❷ [مُتَحَسِّر] sad, unhappy, sorrowful; worried

أَلْهَمَ *v* to inspire; أَلْهَمَ شَخْصاً شَيْئاً to inspire sb to do sth

الْتَهَمَ *v* to consume, to swallow; to wolf/gulp down, to devour; الْتَهَمَ الطَعامَ to wolf down food; الْتَهَمَ فَريسَتَهُ to swallow its prey; الْتَهَمَها بِعَيْنَيْه he devoured her with his eyes

اسْتَلْهَمَ *v* to get inspiration, to be inspired; to seek inspiration; اسْتَلْهَمَ القَصيدةَ من جَمالِ عَيْنَيْها the poem was inspired by the beauty of her eyes

إلْهام *n* |إلْهامات| ❶ [إيحاء] inspiration ❷ (Relig) revelation

مُلْهِم **A** *adj* inspiring; مِثال مُلْهِم an inspiring example **B** *n someone who inspires*; muse; أُمّي مُلْهِمَتي my mother inspires me

لَها *v* |u; لَهْو| ❶ [تَسَلّى] to be amused, to enjoy oneself, to have fun; لَها بِشَيْءٍ to have fun with sth ❷ [لَعِبَ] to play

لَهِيَ *v* |a; لَهاً| ❶ [غَفِلَ] |عن| to neglect, to ignore; لَهِيَ عن شَيْءٍ to neglect sth ❷ [أَحَبَّ] |ب| to like, to love, to care; لَهِيَ بِشَخْصٍ to care for sb

لَهّى *v* to distract, to divert; to entertain, to amuse

لاهى *v* to approach, to come near

أَلْهى *v* to distract, to divert; to keep; أَلْهى شَخْصاً to distract sb; أَلْهى شَخْصاً عن to keep sb from sth; أَلْهى شَخْصاً عن شَيْءٍ عَمَلِهِ to distract sb from his work

تَلَهّى *v* to be amused/entertained, to take pleasure in, to enjoy oneself, to delight in

الْتَهى *v* |ب| to amuse oneself (with), to play (with)

لَهْو *n* entertainment, amusement; distraction, diversion

لاهٍ *adj* ❶ [لاعِب] playful, jolly ❷ [غَيْر مُهْتَمٍّ] oblivious, heedless; inattentive, inconsiderate

لُشُهَداءِ الحَرْبِ a plaque to commemorate the war victims; لَوْحة رَقْمٍ billboard; لَوْحة النُقاطِ scoreboard; لَوْحة إعْلاناتٍ السَيّارةِ number plate (BrE), license plate (AmE)

لَوْحيّ *n* tabular; plate (*before n*); tablet (*before n*); حاسوب لَوْحيّ tablet (computer)

لُوَيْحة *n* لُوَيْحة الأَسْنانِ dental plaque

‹ **لاذَ** *v* |u; لَوْذ ,لِواذ ,لِياذ| 1 [ب| اِلْتَجأَ] to seek refuge/shelter/ sanctuary in/with; to resort to; لاذَ بِشَيْءٍ to resort to sth; لاذَ بِشَخْصٍ to seek refuge with sb; لاذَ بالفِرارِ to escape 2 [اِلْتَزَمَ] to practice, to observe; لاذَ بالصَمْتِ to keep silent

مَلاذ *n* refuge, shelter, sanctuary; hiding place, hideout; المَلاذ الأَخير the last resort

‹ **لورْد** *n* lord

‹ **لوري** *n* lorry, truck, van

‹ **لَوْز** *n coll* 1 (Anat) tonsil; اِلْتِهاب اللَوْزَتَيْنِ tonsillitis; بَضْع اللَوْزة tonsillectomy; اسْتَأْصَلَ اللَوْزَتَيْنِ to remove the tonsils 2 [فاكِهة] almond; شَجَرة لَوْزٍ almond tree

لَوْزيّ *adj* almond-shaped, almond (*before n*); عَيْنانِ لَوْزِيَّتانِ almond eyes

لَوْزِيّة *n* almond paste

‹ **لوسْيون** *n* |لوسْيونات| lotion

‹ **لاصَ** *v* |u; لَوْص| to peep, to peek

لاوَصَ *v* to peep, to peek

‹ **لِواط** ,**لِواطة** *n* homosexuality

لوطيّ (pej) A *adj* homosexual, gay; عَلاقة لوطيّة a homosexual relationship; كانَ لوطيًّا to be gay
B *n* homosexual, gay; queer (*offensive*)

لوطيّة *n* homosexuality

‹ **لوطُس** ,**لوتس** *n* lotus (*Lotus*)

‹ **لاعَ** *v* |u; لَوْع| to be tormented; to be impatient/tense/restless; to become ill; لاعَهُ الشَوْقُ \ الحُزْنُ to be tormented by desire/ grief

لَوَّعَ *v* to make sick; to hurt, to torment, to trouble; لَوَّعَهُ فِراقُ حَبيبَتِهِ the separation from his beloved made him sick

لاوَعْي *n* see وعي

environmental pollution; التَلَوُّث بِسَبَبِ الأَسْمِدةِ pollution from fertilizers; سَبَّبَ التَلَوُّثَ to cause pollution

تَلْويث *n* pollution, contamination; تَلْويث البيئةِ environmental pollution; مَصْدَر تَلْويثٍ a source of contamination

مُلَوَّث *adj* polluted, contaminated; dirty, filthy; infected

مُلَوِّث *n* polluter, contaminator; pollutant, contaminant; مُلَوِّث كَبير a big polluter

‹ **لوجِسْتيّ** *adj* logistic, logistical

لوجِسْتيّة *n* logistics

‹ **لاحَ** *v* |u; لَوْح| to appear, to emerge, to manifest; to seem; يَلوحُ لي أنّ ... it seems to me that ...; لاحَ في الأُفُقِ to loom on the horizon

لَوَّحَ *v* 1 [بِيَدِهِ] to wave; to beckon, to signal; to gesticulate, to gesture; لَوَّحَ بِشَيْءٍ ل \ إلى شَخْصٍ to wave at sb with sth; لَوَّحَ إلى شُرْطيٍّ \ سَيّارةِ أُجْرةٍ to signal a police officer/ taxi 2 [لَمَّحَ] to refer, to reference; to hint, to insinuate; لَوَّحَ باتِّخاذِ تَدابيرَ to threaten to take measures

أَلاحَ *v* to appear, to emerge

لَوْح *n* |أَلْواح| 1 [صَفيحة] board, plank, slat; panel, pane; لَوْح خَشَبيّ wooden plank; لَوْح شَمْسيّ solar panel; لَوْح شِراعيّ sailboard; لَوْح رُكوبِ الأَمْواجِ surfboard 2 [سَبّورة] blackboard, tablet, slate; اللَوْح المَحْفوظ (Islam) the Preserved Tablet (*the divine tablet on which God has written all that has happened and will happen*)

لائِحة *n* |لائِحات ,لَوائِحُ| 1 [قائِمة] list, table, schedule; وَرَدَ اسْمُهُ في رَأْسِ اللائِحةِ to be on the top of the list 2 (Law) لائِحة تَنْفيذيّة an implementing order; أَصْدَرَ لائِحةً تَنْفيذيّةً to issue an implementing order

لَوْحة *n* |لَوْحات ,أَلْواح| 1 (Art) painting, picture, canvas; panel; لَوْحة زَيْتيّة oil painting; لَوْحة مائيّة aquarelle, watercolour; رَسَمَ \ زَوَّرَ لَوْحةً to make/forge a painting 2 [لائحة] لَوْحة شَرَفٍ honour list 3 [جِهاز] لَوْحة مَفاتيحَ keyboard; لَوْحة رَقْميّة tablet (computer); لَوْحة تَحَكُّمٍ control panel; لَوْحة قِيادةٍ dashboard 4 [لافِتة] board, panel, plate; لَوْحة إرْشاديّة noticeboard; لَوْحة تَذْكاريّة plaque; لَوْحة تَذْكاريّة

لَوْعة *n* grief, pain; sorrow, misery; suffering, torture, torment; لَوْعة الحُبِّ lovesickness; في قَلْبِها لَوْعةٌ she's heartbroken

‹ **لوغاريتْم, لوغارِتْم** *n* logarithm

لوغاريتْميّ, لوغارِتْميّ *adj* logarithmic; مِقْياس لوغارِتْميّ a logarithmic scale

‹ **لوف** *n* (Bot) arum (*Arum*)

‹ **مِلْوَق** *n* |مَلاوِقُ| spatula

‹ **لاكَ** *v* |u; لَوْك| **1** [مَضَغَ] to chew **2** [عابَ] to slander, to discredit, speak ill/badly of; ما تَلوكُهُ الأَلْسِنةُ what is being whispered

‹ **لوكيميا** *n* leukaemia; لوكيمْيا حادّة \ مُزْمِنة acute/chronic leukaemia

‹ **لَوْلَب** *n* |لَوالِبُ| **1** [حَلَزون] spiral, coil; لَوْلَب مَنْع الحَمْلِ IUD (*intrauterine device*), coil (BrE) **2** (Tools) screw; سِنّ اللَوْلَبِ screw thread; فَكَّ لَوالِبَ to unscrew the screws

لَوْلَبيّ *adj* spiral, coil (*before n*), whorled

‹ **لامَ** *v* |u; لَوْم, مَلام, مَلامة| to blame, to reproach; to reprimand, to criticize, to rebuke; لامَ شَخْصاً على شَيْءٍ to blame sb for sth

لَوَّمَ *v* to reprimand, to criticize, to rebuke; to blame, to reproach; لَوَّمَ شَيْئاً \ شَخْصاً to criticize sth/sb

تَلَوَّمَ *v* to tarry, to linger

الْتامَ *v* to be blamed; to be censured

لَوْم, لَوْمة *n* blame, reproach; reprimand, rebuke; censure; لا لَوْمَ عَلَيْه he's not to blame; أَلْقى باللَوْم على شَخْصٍ to blame sb; تَعَرَّضَ لِلَوْمٍ to receive a reprimand; لا يَخافُ لَوْمةَ لائِم he doesn't mince his words

لائِمة *n* |لَوائِمُ| blame; reproach; أَنْحى على نَفْسه باللائِمةِ to blame oneself

مَلامة *n* reprimand, rebuke; admonition, warning

‹ **لَوَّنَ** *v* to colour (in); لَوَّنَ صورةً to colour a picture

تَلَوَّنَ *v* to colour; to be coloured; تَلَوَّنَ حَسَبَ الظُروفِ to swim with the tides

لَوْن *n* |أَلْوان| **1** [أَحْمَر، أَخْضَر، ...] colour, shade, hue, tone; لَوْن دافِئ \ بارِد \ صارِخ \ خافِت a warm/cold/garish/subdued colour; لَوْن غامِق \ داكِن a dark colour; أَلْوان هادِئة soft tones; أَلْوان فاتِحة pastel/light colours; أَلْوان أَساسيّة primary colours; مُتَعَدِّد الأَلْوانِ, غَنيّ بالأَلْوانِ colourful; باقة \ قَميص مُتَعَدِّد(ة) الأَلْوانِ a colourful bouquet/shirt; عَديم اللَوْنِ colourless; سائِل عَديم اللَوْنِ a clear fluid; يَبْهَتُ اللَوْنُ the colour fades **2** [لِلرَسْمِ] paint, dye, colour; أَلْوان زَيْتيّة oil paint; أَلْوان مائيّة watercolour **3** [نَوْع] kind, type, sort; shape, form; category, class; أَلْوان من العَذابِ all kinds of hardship; أَلْوان من الطَعامِ all sorts of food

تَلَوُّن *n* coloration

مُتَلَوِّن *adj* **1** [مُتَقَلِّب] capricious; fickle **2** [مُلَوَّن] colourful, multicoloured

مُلَوَّن *adj* coloured, tinted; colourful, multicoloured; فيلْم مُلَوَّن colour film; قَلَم مُلَوَّن coloured pencil; أَعْلام \ فَراشات مُلَوَّنة coloured flags/butterflies

مُلَوِّن *n* paint, dye, colouring (matter/substance); مُلَوِّن طَبيعيّ \ غَيْر طَبيعيٍّ natural/unnatural dye; مُلَوِّن اصْطِناعيّ synthetic dye

‹ **لَوى** *v* |i; لَيّ, لُويّ| to turn, to bend, to twist; لَوى رَقَبَتَهُ to crane one's neck; لَوى ذِراعَ شَخْصٍ to twist sb's arm; خَرَجَ وَهُوَ لا يَلْوي على شَيْءٍ he left without worrying about anything

لَوّى *v* to bend, to twist; to coil, to wriggle

أَلْوى *v* **1** [اللِواءَ] to hoist a flag **2** [أَمالَ] to bend, to turn **3** [بِيَدِه] to wave

تَلَوّى *v* to wriggle, to writhe; to be bent/twisted; تَلَوّى أَلَماً to writhe in pain

الْتَوى *v* to bend, to twist; to be bent/twisted; to wind; يَلْتَوي الطَريقُ حول الجَبَلِ the path winds around the mountain

لِواء *n* |أَلْوِية| **1** (Admin) district, province **2** [عَلَم] banner, flag **3** [رُتْبة عَسْكَريّة] major general; لِواء بَحْريّ vice admiral **4** [وَحْدة عَسْكَريّة] brigade; اللِواء الجَوّيّ the air brigade

لَيّ *n* bend, curve; distortion, contortion; لَيّ الشيشةِ shisha pipe; لا يَعْرِفُ الحَيّ من اللَيِّ he mixes up everything

الْتِواء *n* |الْتِواءات| **1** [اعْوِجاج] curve, curvature; bend, twist, turn; الْتِواء مَفْصِليّ sprain; الْتِواء الخَشَبِ warping of wood **2** (Phys) torque

مُتَلَوٍّ *adj* bending, curving, twisting, turning

مُلْتَوٍ *adj* bent, curved, twisted; crooked, warped; نَهْر مُلْتَوٍ a meandering river

مَلْوِيّ *adj* bent, curved, twisted; crooked, warped

‹ **لُويزِيانا** *n* Louisiana (*US state*)

‹ **لِيبرالِيّ** **A** *adj* **1** [مُتَحَرِّر] liberal **2** (Pol) Liberal; الحِزْب اللِيبرالِيّ the Liberal Party

B *n* liberal; اللِيبرالِيُّونَ البريطانيُّون the British liberals

لِيبِرالِيّة *n* (Pol) liberalism

‹ **لِيبْيا**, لِيبيا *n* Libya

لِيبِيّ **A** *adj* Libyan; الجماهيريّة العَرَبيّة اللِيبيّة الشَّعْبيّة الاشْتِراكيّة العُظْمى Great Socialist People's Libyan Arab Jamahiriya (*official name of Libya until 2011*)

B *n* Libyan

‹ **لِيبِيرِيا** *n* Liberia

‹ **لَيْتَ** *particle* if only, would that; لَيْتَ شِعْري if I only knew; لَيْتَهُ كانَ هُنا if only he were here

‹ **لِيتَر** *n* see لِتْر

‹ **لِيتُوانِيا** *n* Lithuania

‹ **لِيتُوانِيّ** **A** *adj* Lithuanian; (اللُغة) اللِيتُوانيّة Lithuanian (*language*)

B *n* Lithuanian (*person*)

‹ **لَيْث** *n* |لُيوث| lion

‹ **لِيثِيوم** *n* lithium; بَطّاريّة اللِيثِيوم أيُون a lithium-ion battery

‹ **لِيخْتِنْشْتَيْن** *n* |f| Liechtenstein

‹ **لِيرة** *n* pound; lira; اللِيرة السوريّة the Syrian pound

‹ **لِيزَر** *n* laser; شُعاع \ ضوء اللِيزَرِ laser beam/light

‹ **لِيزُول** *n* Lysol

‹ **لَيْسَ** *v* |no imperfect| **1** not; not to be; لَيْسَ لَهُ أنْ ... he's not allowed to ...; أَلَيْس كَذَلِكَ؟ isn't that so?; لَسْتُ أَدْري I don't know; لَسْتُ طَويلاً \ بِطَويلٍ I'm not tall; لَسْتُ ضِدّ السَلامِ I'm not against peace; لَيْسَ هُناكَ مَكانٌ أَفْضَلَ there's no better place; لَيْسَ في البَيْتِ he's not at home; هذا الرَجُلُ لَيْسَ بِفَقيهٍ this man is no legal expert **2** [امْتَلَكَ] لَيْسَ لي الحَقُّ I'm wrong

‹ **لِيسانْس** *n* licentiate; licence; حاصِل على اللِيسانْسِ licentiate; حامِل (شَهادةِ) اللِيسانْسِ licentiate

‹ **لِيسِتِين** *n* lecithin

‹ **لِيسوتو** *n* |f| Lesotho

‹ **تَلَيَّفَ** *v* to become fibrous, to form fibers

لِيف *n* |أَلْياف| fibre; bast; لِيف زُجاجيّ \ بَصَريّ \ ضَوْئيّ glass fibre; احْتَوى على الكَثيرِ من الأَلْيافِ to be high in fibres

لِيفة *n* (bath) sponge

لِيفِيّ *adj* زُجاج لِيفيّ fibreglass

تَلَيُّف *n* cirrhosis; fibrosis; تَلَيُّف الكَبِدِ cirrhosis of the liver

‹ **لاقَ** *v* |i; لِياقة| to be proper/suitable/appropriate, to suit, to befit; to fit, to match; to be decent; لاقَ بِشَيْءٍ \ بِشَخْصٍ to match sth/sb; كَما يَليقُ بِصُحُفيٍّ as is fitting for a journalist; لا يَليقُ أنْ ... it's improper that ...; يَليقُ بِهِ أنّ ... it is decent of him that ...

لائِق *adj* proper, suitable, appropriate; fitting, matching; decent, becoming; سَكَن لائِق a suitable accommodation; مَنْزِلة لائِقة a suitable position; غَيْر لائِقٍ inappropriate; نُكْتة غَيْر لائِقةٍ an inappropriate joke; سُؤال غَيْر لائِقٍ an improper question; مُلاحَظة غَيْر لائِقةٍ an impertinent remark; تَصَرُّف غَيْر لائِقٍ improper behaviour; أَعْمال غَيْر لائِقةٍ objectionable practices; لَبِسَ مَلابِسَ لائِقةً to wear suitable clothes; تَصَرَّفَ بِشَكْلٍ لائِقٍ to act appropriately; لَيْسَ من اللائِقِ أنْ ... it's inappropriate to ...

لِياقة *n* **1** [السُلوك] etiquette, propriety, decorum; courtesy, decency; لِياقة سِياسيّة \ اجْتِماعيّة political/social decency; آداب اللِياقة decorum; قَواعِد اللِياقةِ the rules of etiquette; الْتَزمَ بِقَواعِدِ \ احْتَرَمَ قَواعِدَ اللِياقة (الاجْتِماعيّة) to observe the rules of (social) etiquette; خَرَجَ عن حُدودِ اللِياقةِ to overstep the bounds of propriety **2** (Sport) fitness, condition, shape, form; لِياقة مُمْتازة top form; لِياقة بَدَنيّة physical condition; لِياقة الرِياضِيّينَ البَدَنيّة the physical condition of the sportsmen; تَمارين اللِياقةِ البَدَنيّة fitness training; رَفَعَ لِياقةً to improve one's fitness; لم يَكُنْ في لِياقَتِهِ الكامِلةِ to be in bad shape

‹ **لَيْل** *n* |لَيالٍ| evening, night; لَيْلاً, باللَيْلِ at/by night; لَيْلَ نَهارَ, لَيْلاً نَهاراً, آناءَ اللَيْلِ وَأَطْرافِ النَهارِ day and night; ثَلاثة أَيّامٍ بِلَيالِيها three days and nights; سورة اللَيْل The Night (*Sura 92*); طوال اللَيْلِ the whole night; في جَوْفِ \ ظَلامِ اللَيْلِ in the middle/dead of the night; في \ عند مُنْتَصَفِ اللَيْلِ at midnight;

لَيمونيّ *adj* lemon

‹ **ليموناضة**, **ليمونادة** *n* lemonade; قِنّينة ليمونادةٍ a bottle of lemonade

‹ **لانَ** *v* |i; لين, لَيان| to be/become flexible/pliable/supple, to relax, to ease; to be/become soft/tender/smooth; رَأْسُهُ لا يَلينُ to be stubborn; لانَتْ أَفْكارُهُ he's become open-minded

لَيَّنَ *v* to make flexible/pliable/supple, to relax; to make soft/tender/smooth, to soften; لَيَّنَ السِّياسةَ to ease the policy; لَيَّنَ الحِذاءَ to break in shoes

لايَنَ *v* to be lenient/gentle with; to be kind/friendly to

أَلانَ *v* to make flexible/supple; to make soft, to soften

تَلَيَّنَ *v* to give in/way, to yield, to be/become flexible/pliable/soft

لين *n* flexibility, pliability, suppleness; softness, tenderness, smoothness; لين الطَبْع \ الجانِبِ accommodating; حُروف اللين the weak consonants

لَيِّن *adj* |لَيِّنون, أَلْيناء| **1** [لَطيف] relaxed, kind; لَيِّن الجانِبِ lenient; لَيِّن الطَبْعِ \ العَريكةِ compliant **2** [مَرِن] flexible, yielding; supple, soft; elastic; مَعْدِن لَيِّن soft metal

لُيونة *n* **1** [مُرونة] flexibility, suppleness **2** [سَماحة] leniency, clemency, kindness; عامَلَ شَخْصاً بِلُيونةٍ to treat sb leniently

مُلايَنة *n* friendliness, kindness

مُلَيِّن *n* |مُلَيِّنات| laxative, purgative

يَسْقُطُ اللَيْلُ night is falling; يَقْتَرِبُ اللَيْلُ the evening approaches; عند سَقْطِ اللَيْلِ at nightfall; جَنَّ اللَيْلُ the night fell; كَلامُ اللَيْلِ يَمْحوهُ النَهارُ promises made by night will not last in the daytime

لَيْلاء *adj* لَيْلة لَيْلاء a long dark night

لَيْلة *n* |لَيْلات, لَيالٍ| night; هذه اللَيْلةَ, اللَيْلةَ tonight; لَيْلة سَعيدة good night; لَيْلةَ أَمْسِ last night; لَيْلة العيدِ eve of Eid; لَيْلة الزِفافِ wedding night; لَيْلة رَأْسِ السَنةِ New Year's Eve; لَيْلة السَبْتِ Friday night; في لَيْلةِ الجُمْعةِ on Thursday night; أَلْف لَيْلةٍ وَلَيْلة A Thousand and One Nights, The Arabian Nights; تَمَنّى لِشَخْصٍ لَيْلةً سَعيدةً to wish sb a good night

لَيْلى *n* |f| Layla (*female given name*)

لَيْليّ **A** *adj* nightly, nocturnal, night (*before n*); ساعة لَيْليّة a nocturnal hour; هُجوم لَيْليّ a night attack
B *n* night person

‹ **لَيْلَك**, **لَيْلَج** *n* lilac (*Syringa vulgaris*)

لَيْلَكيّ *adj* lilac

‹ **ليمان** *n* |ليمانات| prison, jail

‹ **ليموزين** *n* limousine

‹ **لَيْمون** *n coll* lemon; لَيْمون الجَنّة grapefruit; لَيْمون حامِض lime; عَصير لَيْمونٍ lemon juice; عَصَرَ لَيْمونةً to squeeze a lemon

م

‹ **م** *abbr* 1 [تاريخ ميلاديّ] AD (*Anno Domini*) 2 [مِتر] m (*metre*) 3 [مَساءً] in the evening (*short for* مَساءً) 4 [مُهَندِس] ≈ M.Sc. (*Master of Science*)

‹ **ما** A *pron* 1 [ماذا] what; ما لَكَ؟ what's the matter with you?; what is it to you?; ما الّذي what; ما الّذي بِكَ؟ what's the matter with you?; إذا ما see إذا 2 [الّذي] what, that which; ما يَقْرَأُه من الكُتُب the books he reads; بما فيه including, inclusive of; أكْثَر ما يُعْجِبُني what pleases me most 3 [للتعَجُّب] how, what; ما أحْسَنَهُ! how good he is!; ما أجْمَلَ ذلك الفيلْمَ! what a beautiful film!
B *particle* 1 [نَفْي] not; ما كَتَبَ he didn't write; ما زالَ قائماً he is still standing/there; ما من أحَدٍ nobody 2 [غَيْر مَعْروف] some, any; رَجُل ما some man; لِسَبَب ما for some reason; في يَوْمٍ ما one/some day; كِتاب \ بَيْت ما any book/house

ماذا *pron* what; ماذا تُريدُ منّي؟ what do you want from me?; ماذا يوجَدُ في ذلك الصُندوقِ؟ what's in that box?; ماذا نَعْمَلُ؟ what do we do?

مِثْلَما *conj* as, like; فَعَلْتُ مِثْلَما فَعَلَ مُحَمَّدٌ I did it as Muhammad (did)

مِمّا, **مِمَّ** *pron* 1 [من ماذا؟] from/of what; مِمَّ تَخافُ؟ what are you scared of? 2 [الّذي] which; ... مِمّا أدّى إلى ... which led to ... 3 [من ما] than; أكْثَر مِمّا كُنْتُ أظُنُّ more than I thought

بَعْدَما *conj* after; بَعْدَما دَخَلَ في غَيْبوبةٍ after falling unconscious

بِما, **بِمَ** *pron* بِما أنّ since, as, now (that), considering the fact that; بِما في ذلك inclusive of; ... تَعَلَّمْتُ الكَثيرَ بِما في ذلك I learned a lot, among other things ...

بَيْنَما *conj* while; whereas

عَمّا, **عَمَّ** *pron* about ... what; لا يَعْلَمُ عَمّا يَتَكلَّمُ he doesn't know what he is talking about; عَمّا هو عَلَيْهِ الآنَ compared to what it is now; عن \ عَمّا قليل soon; عن \ عَمّا قريب soon, in a minute; عَمَّ تَتَكَلَّمُ؟ what are you talking about?

عِنْدَما *conj* when, as, while; as soon as; عِنْدَما كُنْتُ طِفْلاً عَلَّموني أنْ لا أكْذِبَ when I was a child they taught me not to lie; غادَرَتْ عِنْدَما كُنْتُ نائماً she left while I was sleeping

فيما, **فيمَ** *conj* while; فيما أعْرِفُ as far as I know; فيما يَلي below, hereinafter; فيما أعْتَقِد in my opinion; فيما بَعْدُ hereafter, after that, afterwards; فيمَ تُفكّرينَ يا حَبيبَتي؟ what are you thinking about, honey?; ما حَدَثَ فيما بَعْدُ كانَ أسْوأَ what happened after that was worse; نَظَرَ فيما حَوْلَهُ to look around; قالَ فيما قالَ he said among other things; فيما إذا, فيما لو if

كُلَّما *conj* see كلل

كَما *conj* as, like; likewise, as well; furthermore; كَما هي العادةُ \ كَما هو الحالُ as usual; كَما هو مُقَرَّرٌ as has been decided; كَما هو الأمْرُ as is the case; البَيْتُ يَبْقى كَما هو the house remains as it is; كَما لو as if; كَما لو كُنْتُ مَعَكَ as if I were with you; كَما تَعْرِفونَ ... as you all know ...

لِما, **لِمَ** *adv* why; because of, for; لِمَ فَعَلْتَ ذلك؟ why did you do that?; why not?; انْتَقَلْنا إلى العاصِمةِ لِما يَتَوَفَّرُ فيها من خَدَماتٍ we moved to the capital because of all the services it offers

لِماذا *adv* why, for what reason; لِماذا فَعَلْتَ هذا؟ why did you do this?; أتَعْرِفُ لِماذا؟ do you know why?

‹ **مِئة**, **مِائة** *n* see مأي

‹ **ماجِسْتير** *n* Master; رِسالة ماجِسْتير Master's thesis; ماجِسْتير في الآدابِ Master of Arts; ماجِسْتير في العُلومِ Master of Science

‹ **مادَبا** *n* Madaba (*city in Jordan*)

‹ **ماديرا** *n* Madeira

‹ **مار** *n* saint, St; كَنيسة مارِ يوسُفَ the church of St Joseph

ماراثون *n* marathon

ماراثونيّ *adj* marathon (*before n*); مُفاوَضات ماراثونيّة marathon negotiations

مارِس *n* (NA, Gulf) March; في (شَهْرِ) مارِس in March

مارِسْتان *n* lunatic asylum

مارْشال، مارِشال *n* (field) marshal

مارْك *n* |مارْكات| mark; المارْك الأَلْمانيّ Deutschmark

مارْكة *n* brand; مارْكة تِجاريّة trademark; مارْكة تِجاريّة مُسَجَّلة a registered trademark; مارْكة غَيْر مَعْروفةٍ an unknown brand; مارْكة جَيِّدة \ رَديئة a good/bad brand

مارْكسيّ **A** *adj* Marxist

B *n* Marxist

مارْكْسيّة *n* Marxism

مارونيّ *adj, n* Maronite

مارينا *n* marina

مازوت *n* mazut

مازوشيّ **A** *adj* masochistic

B *n* masochist

مازوشيّة *n* masochism

ماس *n* diamond; ماس حُرّ a pure diamond; قاطِع الماس diamond cutter

ماسيّ *adj* diamond (*before n*); خاتَم ماسيّ a diamond ring; يوبيل ماسيّ a diamond jubilee

ماساتْشوسِتْس *n* |f| Massachusetts (*US state*)

ماسْتِر *n* master's

ماسورة *n* |مَواسيرُ| **1** [بُنْدُقيّة] barrel (*of a gun*) **2** [أُنْبوب] tube, pipe; شَبَكة مَواسيرَ a network of pipes

ماسونيّ **A** *adj* Masonic, Freemason's; مَحْفِل ماسونيّ Masonic Lodge, Constituent Lodge

B *n* Freemason, Mason

ماسونيّة *n* Freemasonry

ماغْما *n* magma

مافِيا *n* Mafia

مَئِق *v* |مَأَق| sobbing

مَأْقة *n* sob

ماكْرو *n* macro

ماكْروبِيوتيك *n* macrobiotics

ماكْريل *n* mackerel

ماكِياج *n* see مكيج

ماكِينة، ماكِنة *n* |ماكينات، مَكائِنُ| machine

ماكْيير *n* make-up artist

مالاوي *n* |f| Malawi

مالْديف *n* جُزُر المالْديف the Maldives

مالْديفيّ **A** *adj* Maldivian; (اللُغة) المالْديفيّة Maldivian (*language*)

B *n* Maldivian (*person*)

مالْطا، مالْطة *n* Malta

مالْطيّ **A** *adj* Maltese; (اللُغة) المالْطيّة Maltese; حُمّى مالْطيّة brucellosis

B *n* Maltese

مالَقة *n* Malaga

مالي *n* |f| Mali

ماليّ **A** *adj, n* Malian

B *adj* see مول

ماليزيا *n* Malaysia

ماليزيّ *adj, n* Malay

مَأْمَأَ *v* |i; مَأْمَأة| to bleat

ماما *n* mama, mummy (BrE), mommy (AmE), mum (BrE), mom (AmE)

ماموث *n* mammoth

مَأَنَ *v* |a; مَأْن| to sustain; to provide

مُؤْنة *n* |مُؤَن| provisions, food supplies

مَؤونة *n* |مُؤَن| provisions, food supplies; قامَ بِجَمْعِ المَؤونةِ to stock up on provisions; مَؤونة الجَيْشِ army provisions

مانْجو *n* see مَنْجو

مانولِيا *n* magnolia (*Magnolia*)

مانيفِسْتو *n* **1** [إِعْلان] manifesto **2** (Naut, Aviat) waybill

مانيكير *n* manicure

ماهيّة *n* essence, core; nature; ماهيّة الأَمْرِ \ المُشْكِلةِ the essence of the matter/problem; ماهيّة الفَنِّ the nature of art; فَكَّرَ في ماهيّةِ الحَياةِ to reflect on the essence of life; أَفْصَحَ عن ماهيّة الحَلّ to articulate the right solution

ماوْريّ *adj, n* Maori

ماوْس *n* (Comput) mouse; نَقَر بالماوْس to click the mouse

مائة, مِئة *num* |مِئات| hundred; مِائة كِتابٍ one hundred books; مِئات من الأشْخاصِ \ السِنينَ \ الأمْتارِ \ المَلايينَ hundreds of people/years/metres/millions; خانة المِئاتِ (Math) hundreds column; سَبْعة في المِئةِ seven per cent; أَرْبَعة في المِئةِ من السُكّانِ \ الأسْهُمِ \ الأصْواتِ four per cent of the population/shares/votes; مِئة ب \ في المِئةِ a hundred per cent; أكيد \ مُتأكِّد مِئة بالمِئةِ a hundred per cent sure; واحِد من مِئةٍ من الثانِيةِ a hundredth of a second

مِئَويّ *adj* in terms of percentage; Celsius; خَمْس دَرَجاتٍ مِئويّةٍ five degrees Celsius; نِسْبة مِئويّة عالِية \ مُرْتَفِعة a high percentage

ماي *n* (Algeria, Tunisia) May

مايْسْترو *n* maestro

مايو *n* (Mor, Egypt, Gulf) May

مَيورْقة, مايورْكا *n* Majorca

مايونيز *n* mayonnaise; صَلْصة مايونيز mayonnaise

مايوه *n* |مايوهات| (Egypt) swimming suit; لَبِسَ مايوهاً to wear a swimming suit

مَتّ *v* |u; مَتّ| **1** [رَبَطَ] إلى to be/become connected with, to be/become related to; مَتَّ إلى شَيْءٍ بِصِلةٍ to be/become connected with sth **2** [صاهَرَ] to become related by marriage to, to marry into the family of

مَتَحَ *v* |a; مَتْح| to draw from a well

مِتْر *n* |أمْتار| metre; مِتْر شَرِيطيّ tape measure; مِتْر مُرَبَّع \ مُكَعَّب a square/cubic metre; مِتْرانِ مُكَعَّبانِ من الرَمْلِ two cubic metres of sand; المَسافة \ الطول بالأمْتارِ the distance/length in metres; طولُهُ \ ارْتِفاعُهُ \ عَرْضُهُ \ عُمْقُهُ مِترانِ it's two metres long/high/wide/deep

مِتْريّ *adj* metric; النِظام المِتْريّ the metric system

تَمَتْرَسَ *v* see ترس

مِتْرو *n* Underground (BrE), tube (BrE), subway (AmE), metro; مِتْرو أَنْفاقٍ tube (BrE), subway (AmE); اسْتَقَلَّ \ بالمِتْرو by tube; رَكِبَ مِتْرو الأَنْفاقِ to take/ride the tube

مَتَعَ *v* |a; مُتوع| to take along; مَتَعَ بِشَيْءٍ to take sth along

مَتَّعَ *v* **1** [جَعَلَ شَخْصاً يَتَمَتَّعُ] to make enjoy; to entertain, to amuse **2** [زَوَّدَ] to furnish; مَتَّعَ شَخْصاً بِشَيْءٍ to furnish sb with sth **3** (Law) مَتَّعَ مُطْلَّقَتَهُ *to pay a compensation to a divorced woman*

أَمْتَعَ *v* to make enjoy, to please

تَمَتَّعَ *v* **1** [حَظِيَ] |ب| to enjoy; تَمَتَّعَ بِشَيْءٍ to enjoy sth; تَمَتَّعَ بِصِحّةٍ كامِلةٍ to enjoy perfect health; تَمَتَّعَ بِشَعْبِيّةٍ كَبيرةٍ to be very popular; تَمَتَّعَ بِحَقٍّ to enjoy a right; تَمَتَّعَ بِمَوْهِبةٍ كَبيرةٍ to be blessed with great talent **2** [تَلَذَّذَ] to enjoy oneself

اسْتَمْتَعَ *v* to enjoy oneself; اسْتَمْتَعَ بِشَيْءٍ to enjoy sth

مَتاع *n* **1** [تَمَتُّع] |أَمْتِعة| enjoyment, pleasure **2** [شَيْء] thing **3** [مُمْتَلَكات] utensil; الأَمْتِعة الشَخْصِيّة personal belongings; أَمْتِعة (البَيْتِ) household effects; أَمْتِعة (السَفَرِ) luggage, baggage (AmE); مُسْتَوْدَع الأَمْتِعةِ left luggage office (BrE), unclaimed baggage office (AmE); رَفّ \ حامِل الأَمْتِعةِ luggage rack; سَقَط المَتاعِ waste

مُتْعة *n* |مُتَع| enjoyment, pleasure, delight; مُتْعة للأَنْظارِ a pleasure for the eyes; وَجَدَ مُتْعةً في شَيْءٍ to find pleasure in sth; مُتْعة سَكَنٍ enjoyment of residence; زَواج \ نِكاح مُتْعةٍ mut'ah marriage (*fixed-term or short-term contractual marriage in Shia Islam*)

مُمْتِع *adj* pleasant, nice, agreeable; enjoyable, amusing; فيلْم مُمْتِع a nice film; يَوْم مُمْتِع a pleasant day; قِصّة مُمْتِعة an amusing story

اسْتِمْتاع *n* pleasure; بِاسْتِمْتاعٍ with pleasure, with relish; نَظَرَ \ تَفَرَّجَ بِاسْتِمْتاعٍ to watch in amusement

تَمَتُّع *n* pleasure

مُتَّقٍ *adj* see وقي

مَتُنَ *v* |u; مَتانة| to be/become firm/strong

مَتَّنَ *v* to make strong, to strengthen

مَتْن *n* |مِتان, مُتون| **1** [سَطْح] على مَتْنِ سَفينةٍ \ طائِرةٍ on board/aboard a ship/plane; على مَتْنِ السَيّارة in the car **2** [نَصّ] corpus; text; مَتْن اللُغةِ lexicon; مُتون القَوانينِ Corpus Juris, body of law **3** [ظَهْر] back

مَتانة *n* firmness, strength; durability

مَتين **A** *adj* |مِتان| [صُلْب] strong, firm, solid; فِراش مَتين a firm bed/pillow; عَلاقة مَتينة a strong relationship; أَحْذِية مَتينة sturdy shoes; صَداقة \ عائِلة مَتينة a close friendship/family;

مِثْل *n the same thing*; equal, counterpart; أَمْثال حَسَن people like Hassan; بالمِثْل in the same manner; مَبْدأ المُعامَلةِ بالمِثْلِ the principle of reciprocity; رَدَّ على شَخْصٍ بالمِثْلِ to talk back to sb; عامَلَ شَخْصاً بالمِثْلِ to pay sb back; كَمِثْلِهِ like him; مِثْلَ like, (such) as; مِثْلُهُ such (a), like that/him, of that kind; مِثْلُهُ تَماماً exactly the same; مِثْل هذه القَضايا \ التَغيُّراتِ such matters/changes; هل رَأَيْتَ مِثْلَ هذا قَطُّ ؟ did you ever see such a thing?; لَيْسَتْ مِثْلَ أَخيها she is not like her brother; لِماذا تَفْعَلُ مِثْلَهُمْ ؟ why are you acting like them?

مُتَماثِل *adj* similar, homogeneous, analogous; symmetrical

مُتَمَثِّل *adj* **1** [مُكَوَّن] consisting (of) **2** [تَمَّ تَمْثيلُهُ] represented; الأَحْزاب المُتَمَثِّلة في المَجْلِسِ the parties that are represented in the council

مِثال *n* |مُثُل ,أَمْثِلة| example; model; مِثال نَموذَجيّ classic example, textbook case; مِثال نَموذَجيّ في الصَبْرِ \ المُواظَبةِ a model of patience/perseverance; كانَ المِثالَ النَموذَجيَّ لِشَيْءٍ to be exemplary for sth; مِثال مُضادّ counterexample; مِثال أَعْلى ideal; نادِر المِثالِ unequalled; مِثالٌ على ذلك أنّ ... an example of this is that ...; خَيْر \ أَفْضَل مِثالٍ على ذلك أنّ ... the best example of this is that ...; على مِثالِ ... after the model of ...; على سَبيلِ المِثالِ for example, for instance; على سَبيلِ \ أَعْطى المِثالِ لا الحَصْرِ as an example and not exhaustively; ضَرَبَ مِثالاً to give an example; انْتَهَجَ مِثالاً to pursue an ideal; كانَ مِثالاً لِشَيْءٍ to serve as a model for sth

مِثاليّ **A** *adj* ideal, idealistic; exemplary; proverbial; زَوْج مِثاليّ an ideal husband; رَجُل \ سَيِّدة مِثاليّ(ة) a true gentleman/lady; المَرْأة المِثاليّة the perfect woman; صُورة مِثاليّة an idealized image; حَلّ مِثاليّ a perfect solution; تَصَرُّفاتُهُ مِثاليّةٌ his behaviour is exemplary; مِثاليًّا \ بِشَكْلٍ مِثاليٍّ ideally; كانَ مِثاليًّا to set a good example

B *n* idealist

مِثاليّة *n* idealism

مِثْلَما *conj* see ما

مِثْليّ **A** *adj* homosexual, gay (infml); مِثْليّ جِنْسيًّا homosexual; عَلاقة جِنْسيّة مِثْليّة a homosexual relationship

B *n* homosexual; زَواج المِثْليّين gay marriage

أَساس مَتين a solid base; بِناء \ طاوِلة مَتين(ة) a solid structure/table; مَبْنيّ بِناءً مَتيناً solidly constructed

B *n* المَتين the Firm (*one of the names of God*)

مَتى *adv* when; إلى \ حتّى مَتى until when?; مُنْذُ مَتى ؟ since when?

مَثَل *v* |u; مُثول| **1** [شابَهَ] to look like, to resemble; مَثَلَ شَخْصاً to resemble sb **2** [شَبَّهَ] to compare; مَثَلَ شَخْصاً بِشَخْصٍ to compare sb with sb **3** [فَضُلَ] to be good

مَثُل *v* |u; مَثالة| to appear, to present oneself; مَثُلَ أمام مَحْكَمةٍ to appear in court, to stand trial; مَثُلَ أمامَ القاضي to appear before the judge; مَثُلَ بين يَدَي المَلِكِ to have an audience with the king

مَثَّل *v* **1** [نابَ] to represent; مَثَّلَ بَلَداً to represent a country **2** [مَسْرَحيّة] to act, to play, to perform; مَثَّلَ (شَخْصيّة) جيمْس بونْد to play James Bond; مَثَّلَ لِأَوَّلِ مَرّةٍ في مَسْرَحيّةٍ to make one's first appearance in a play; مَثَّلَ وَقائِعَ جَريمةٍ to reconstruct a crime **3** [تَظاهَرَ] to put on an act **4** [شَبَّهَ] to compare **5** [نَكَّلَ |ب|] to give as an example

ماثَل *v* **1** [شابَهَ] to resemble, to be/look like, to be similar **2** [قارَنَ] to compare; ماثَلَ شَخْصاً بِأَبيهِ to compare sb with his father

تَمَثَّل *v* **1** [قَلَّدَ] to imitate, to (try to) become like; تَمَثَّلَ شَخْصيّةَ أبيهِ to imitate one's father **2** [تَصَوَّرَ] to imagine, to fancy **3** [تَجَسَّدَ |في|] to be embodied by, to be personified in; to be represented by

تَماثَل *v* to resemble each other, to look alike; تَماثَلَ مع شَخْصٍ في كُلِّ شَيْءٍ to resemble sb in everything; تَماثَلَ للشِفاءِ to get better, to recuperate

امْتَثَل *v* to obey, to submit oneself to; امْتَثَلَ لِقانونٍ \ أَمْرٍ to obey a law/an order

مَثَل *n* |أَمْثال| **1** [حِكْمة] proverb, saying; مَثَل شَعْبيّ a a popular saying **2** [مِثال] example; مَثَلاً for example/instance; مَثَل أَعْلى a good example, ideal, a role model; مَضْرِب المَثَلِ a classic example; أَقامَ لِشَخْصٍ مَثَلاً to set an example to sb; أُفَكِّرُ مَثَلاً في ... for instance I'm thinking of ...; ضَرَبَ اللهُ مَثَلاً God gave as an example **3** [قِصّة] parable

مِثْليّة *n* مِثْليّة جِنسيّة homosexuality

مُثول *n* ❶ [بين يَدَيْ المَلِكِ] audience ❷ [أمام المَحْكَمةِ] appearance

مَثيل 🅐 *adj* |أَمْثال, مُثُل| same, similar, analogous 🅑 *n* |أَمْثال, مُثُل| equal, match, peer; لا مَثيلَ لَهُ unequalled, incomparable; لَيْسَ لَهُ مَثيلٌ he has no equal; جَمال \ شَجاعة \ فَخامة لا مَثيلَ لَهُ \ لَها unparalleled beauty/courage/ luxury; إلى مُسْتَوًى لم يَسْبِقْ لَهُ مَثيلٌ to an unrivalled level

مُماثِل *adj* similar, comparable; analogous, corresponding; حالة \ ظاهِرة مُماثِلة a similar case/phenomenon; مَوْقِع مُماثِل mirror site; مُماثِل لِشَيْءٍ corresponding to sth; بِشَكْلٍ مُماثِلٍ in the same way, similarly

مُماثَلة *n* similarity, correspondence, resemblance; parallel, analogy

مُمْتَثِل *adj* conformist, compliant; غَيْر مُمْتَثِلٍ nonconformist

مُمَثِّل *n* ❶ [نائِب] representative, delegate; مُمَثِّل الشَعْبِ representative (of the people); مُمَثِّل الرَئيسِ the representative of the president; مُمَثِّل شَرِكةٍ كَبيرةٍ a representative of a major company; بَعَثَ مُمَثِّلاً to send a representative; النوّابُ هُمْ مُمَثِّلو الشَعْبِ the delegates are the representatives of the people ❷ (Theat) actor; مُمَثِّل مَسْرَحيّ actor; مُمَثِّل بَديل stand-in; مُمَثِّل مُساعِد supporting actor

مُمَثِّليّة *n* representation

امْتِثال *n* compliance, conformity

أَمْثَل *adj* |dipt; أَماثِل; f مُثْلى; f pl مُثْلَيات| optimal; الاسْتِخْدام \ الاسْتِغْلال الأَمْثَل optimal use; نَتيجة مُثْلى an optimal result

أُمْثولة *n* |أَماثيلُ| example, lesson

تَماثُل *n* |تَماثُلات| symmetry; similarity; تَماثُل بين أَشْياء symmetry between things

تِمْثال *n* |تَماثيلُ| statue, sculpture, figure; تِمْثال نِصْفيّ bust; تَماثيل بْرونْزيّة bronze sculptures; تِمْثال من المَرْمَرِ a marble statue; تِمْثال الحُرّيّةِ Statue of Liberty; نَصَبَ تِمْثالاً to erect a statue

تَمْثيل *n* ❶ [مَسْرَح] acting, performance; تَمْثيل إيمائيّ pantomime, mime; فِرْقة تَمْثيلٍ theatre group/troupe; إعادة تَمْثيلِ شَيْءٍ a reconstruction of sth; تَمْثيل وَقائِع الجَريمةِ the reconstruction of a crime ❷ [نِيابة] representation; تَمْثيل دِبْلوماسيّ diplomatic representation ❸ [الطَعام] التَمثيل الغَذائيّ metabolism ❹ [تَصَنُّع] comedy, play-acting ❺ [تَصْوير] depiction, representation ❻ [تَنْكيل] torture, atrocity

تَمْثيليّ *adj* ❶ theatrical, dramatic; إيماءات تَمْثيليّة theatrical gestures ❷ representative

تَمْثيليّة *n* (stage) play; تَمْثيليّة هَزْليّة \ فُكاهيّة comedy, farce

‹ **مَثانة** *n* (Anat) bladder; الْتِهاب المَثانةِ bladder infection; أُصيبَ بِالْتِهاب المَثانةِ to suffer from a bladder infection; أُصيبَ بِحَصًى في المَثانةِ to suffer from bladder stones

‹ **مَجَّ** *v* |u; مَجّ| to spit out

‹ **مَجَدَ, مَجُدَ** *v* |u; مَجْد| to be glorious

مَجَّدَ *v* to praise, to commend, to glorify

أَمْجَدَ *v* to praise, to commend, to glorify

تَمَجَّدَ *v* to be praised, to be glorified

مَجْد *n* |أَمْجاد| glory, fame; مَجْد زائِل past glory; ذُرْوة المَجْدِ heyday; كانَ في ذُرْوةِ مَجْدِهِ he was in his heyday; في ذُرْوةِ المَجْدِ in full glory; أَعادَ شَيْئاً من مَجْدِهِ القَديمِ to restore sth to its old glory; كانَ في أَوْجِ مَجْدِهِ to be at the height of one's fame

ماجِد 🅐 *adj* |أَمْجاد| glorious, illustrious 🅑 *n* ❶ (Islam) الماجِد the Illustrious (*one of the names of God*) ❷ [اِسْم شَخْصيّ] Majid (*male given name*)

مَجْديّ *n* Majdi (*male given name*)

مَجيد 🅐 *adj* |أَمْجاد, مُجَداءُ| glorious, illustrious, magnificent; ماضٍ \ نَصْر مَجيد a glorious past/victory; تاريخ مَجيد an illustrious history; الميلاد المَجيد the Birth of Christ 🅑 *n* المَجيد the All-Glorious (*one of the names of God*)

تَمْجيد *n* |تَمْجيدات| glorification; تَمْجيد النَفْسِ self-glorification; تَمْجيداً لِشَيْءٍ \ شَخْصٍ in praise of sth/sb

‹ **مَجَريّ** 🅐 *adj* |مَجَر| Hungarian; (اللُغة) المَجَريّة Hungarian (*language*) 🅑 *n* |مَجَر, حَجَرْيّون| Hungarian (*person*)

المَجَر *n* |f| Hungary

‹ **مَجْريط** *n* *old name for Madrid*

انْمَحَق *v* to be destroyed

امْتَحَق *v* to wane

مُحاق *n* waning moon

ماحَكَ *v* to quarrel, to row, to wrangle

تَماحَكَ *v* to quarrel

مَحِلَ *v* |a; مُحول ,مَحْل| to be barren, to be infertile (*land*)

أَمْحَلَ *v* to be barren/sterile

ماحِل *adj* sterile, infertile; barren, bleak; dry, arid

امْتَحَنَ *v* to examine, to give an exam; to (put to the) test, to try; امْتَحَنَ طُلّاباً to examine students; امْتَحَنَ صَبْرَ شَخْصٍ to put sb's patience to the test; أُمْتُحِنَ to be tested (*in an exam*); to be tested (*emotionally or morally*)

مِحْنة *n* |مِحَن| ❶ [بَلِيّة] trial, ordeal, affliction; suffering, misfortune; مِحْنة عَصيبة a terrible ordeal; مَرَّ بِمِحْنةٍ عَصيبةٍ to undergo a terrible ordeal; أُبْتُلِيَ بمِحْنة to suffer misfortune; قاسى المِحَنَ to suffer afflictions ❷ (Relig) inquisition; Mihna (*Islamic inquisitional court in the ninth century AD*)

مُمْتَحَن *n* examinee, examination candidate; سورة المُمْتَحَنة The Examined One (*Sura 60*)

مُمْتَحِن *n* (Educ) examiner

امْتِحان *n* |امْتِحانات| ❶ [اخْتِبار] examination, exam, test; امْتِحان شَفَوِيّ \ تَحْريرِيّ oral/written examination; امْتِحان نِهائِيّ final examination; امْتِحان جُزْئِيّ partial examination; امْتِحان دُخولٍ entrance examination; مُتَقَدِّم لِلامْتِحانِ examination candidate; مَوادّ الامْتِحانِ examination subjects; examination materials; إعادة الامْتِحانِ a resit; قامَ بِامْتِحانٍ جُزْئِيّ to take a partial examination; اسْتَعَدَّ لِلامْتِحانِ to prepare for an exam; أَدّى \ أَنْجَزَ امْتِحاناً to take an exam; خاضَ امْتِحاناً to undergo an exam; نَجَحَ في، اجْتازَ امْتِحاناً to pass an exam; رَسَبَ في امْتِحانٍ to fail an exam; أَعادَ الامْتِحانَ to resit (an exam) ❷ [مِحْنة] ordeal, trial; امْتِحان من اللهِ a trial from God; تَعَرَّضَ لِامْتِحانٍ قاسٍ to face a terrible ordeal

مَحا *v* |u; مَحْو| to erase, to rub out, to wipe out; مَحا ذِكْرى to erase a memory; مَحا مِلَفًّا to delete a file; كَلامُ اللَّيْلِ يَمْحوهُ النَّهارُ promises made by night will not last in the daytime

مَجَلَ, مَجِلَ *v* |a-u; مُجول ,مَجْل| to develop blisters; مَجَلَتْ يَدُهُ his hand is blistered

مَجْل *n coll* |إمجال| blister

مَجال *n* see جول

مُمَجْمَج *adj* indistinct, vague, unclear

مَجَنَ *v* |u; مَجانة ,مُجون ,مُجْن| to joke, to jest

ماجِن *adj* |مَواجِنُ| impudent, shameless, rude; حَفْلة ماجِنة orgy

مَجّان *n* مَجّاناً ,بالمَجّانِ free; الدُّخول مَجّاناً free admission; وَزَّعَ شَيْئاً بالمَجّانِ to distribute sth free of charge; كانَ مُتَوَفِّراً بالمَجّانِ to be available for free; حَصَلَ على شَيْءٍ مَجّاناً to get sth for free

مَجّانِيّ *adj* free (of charge), gratuitous; بِطاقة مَجّانِيّة a free ticket; نُسْخة مَجّانِيّة من شَيْءٍ a free copy of sth

مُجون *n* shamelessness, impudence, impertinence

مَجوس *n* Magi, Magians (*adherents of Mazdaism*); المَجوس the Magi (*the Wise Men of the East*)

(Idiom) لِبْلاب المَجوس (Bot) veronica (*Veronica*)

المَجوسيّة *n* Mazdaism

مُحّ *n* |أَمْحاح| ❶ [صَفار البَيْضِ] (egg) yolk; مُحّ البَيْضِ egg yolk ❷ [لُبّ] core; choice part

مَحَّصَ *v* ❶ [طَهَّرَ] to purify, to clarify ❷ [اخْتَبَرَ] to examine closely, to scrutinize

أَمْحَصَ *v* to reappear, to come out again

تَمَحَّصَ *v* to be/become purified, to be/become clarified

تَمْحيص *n* |تَمْحيصات| ❶ [تَطْهير] clarification; بِحاجةٍ إلى مَزيدٍ من التَمْحيصِ in need of more clarification ❷ [اخْتِبار] thorough examination; بدونِ تَمْحيصٍ unthinkingly

مَحُضَ *v* |u; مَحْض| to be pure

أَمْحَضَ *v* to be sincere

مَحْض *adj* pure, sheer, utter; mere; مَحْضاً merely; مَحْض صُدْفةٍ pure chance; بِمَحْضِ الصُّدْفةِ by pure chance; هُراء مَحْض utter nonsense; بِمَحْضِ إرادَتِهِ by one's own will, freely

مَحَقَ *v* |a; مَحْق| to wipe out, to erase, to efface; to destroy; مَحَقَ شَيْئاً to erase sth

أَمْحَقَ *v* to wane

مَحى *v* |i; مَحْي| to wipe out, to erase, to wipe away

انْمَحى ,امَّحى *v* to be wiped out, to be effaced

مَحْو *n* eradication, erasure; حَمْلة مَحْوِ الأُمِّيّة a campaign to eradicate illiteracy; غَيْر قابِلٍ للمَحْوِ ineradicable

ماحِيَة *n* 1 [مِمْحاة] eraser, rubber (BrE) 2 [مَسّاحة] wiper

مِمْحاة *n* |مَماحٍ| 1 [ماحِيَة] eraser, rubber (BrE) 2 [مَسّاحة] wiper

تَمَحْوَرَ *v* see حور

المُخا *n* Mocha (*city in Yemen*)

مُخّ *n* |مِخاخ, مِخَخة| brain, brains; المُخّ البَشَرِيّ the human brain; المُخ والمُخَيْخ the cerebrum and the cerebellum; فاعِلِيّة المُخِّ brain activity; ارْتِجاج في المُخ concussion; أُصيبَ بِارْتِجاجٍ في المُخِّ to suffer a concussion; اسْتَعْمَلَ مُخَّهُ to use one's brain

مُخِّيّ *adj* cerebral, brain (*before n*); قِشْرة مُخِّيّة cerebral cortex

مُخَيْخ *n* cerebellum; المُخ والمُخَيْخ the cerebrum and the cerebellum

مَخَرَ *v* |a-u; مَخْر ,مُخور| to plough; مَخَرَ الأَرْضَ to plough the land

مَخْر *n* (Naut) wake, wash

ماخور *n* |مَواخيرُ| brothel

مَخْرَقَ *v* |i; مَخْرَقة| to invent, to think up, to fabricate

مَخَضَ *v* |a-i-u; مَخْض| to churn; to shake violently; مَخَضَ اللَبَنَ to churn milk

مَخِضَ *v* |a; مَخاض ,مِخاض| to be in labour, to be parturient; مَخِضَتْ she was in labour

تَمَخَّضَ *v* to result; to bring forth, to produce; تَمَخَّضَ الاجْتِماعُ عن قَرارَيْنِ the meeting resulted in two resolutions

مَخاض *n* contractions, labour pains; أَلَم المَخاضِ contractions, labour pains; مَخاض عَسير strong contractions; حالة المَخاضِ labour; كانَتْ في مَرْحَلةِ ,جاءَها المَخاضُ المَخاضِ she was in labour

مَخيض *n* buttermilk

مِمْخَضة *n* |مَماخِضُ| (milk) churn

مَمْخوض *adj* churned

مَخَطَ *v* |a-u; مَخْط ,مُخوط| to blow (one's nose)

تَمَخَّطَ *v* to blow (*one's nose*)

مُخاط *n* |أَمْخِطة| (nasal) mucus, snot

مُخاطِيّ *adj* غِشاء مُخاطِيّ mucous membrane, mucosa

مُخْل *n* |أَمْخال| lever

مِخْلة *n* |مِخَل ,مَخالي| nosebag

مَدام *n* madam, Madame

مَدَحَ *v* |a; مَدْح ,مِدْحة| to praise, to commend, to laud; مَدَحَ شَخْصاً (لِشَيْءٍ) to praise sb (for sth); مَدَحَ كِتاباً \ فيلْماً to review a book/film (BrE) movie (AmE) favourably; مَدَحَ إِنْجازاتِ شَخْصٍ to celebrate sb's accomplishments

امْتَدَحَ *v* to praise, to commend, to laud; امْتَدَحَ عَمَلَ شَخْصٍ to praise sb's work

مَدْح *n* compliment; praise, eulogy, laudation

مادِح *adj* laudatory, panegyric

مَدّاح *n* eulogist, panegyrist

مِدْحَت *n* Midhat (*male given name*)

مَديح *n* |مَدائِحُ ,أَمْداح| compliment; praise, laudation; ode, laudatory poem; يَسْتَحِقُّ المَديحَ laudable, praiseworthy; فِرْقة أَمْداحٍ choir; مَديح (على) شَخْصٍ \ شَيْءٍ an ode to sb/sth; المَدائِح النَبَوِيّة odes to the prophet Muhammad; كالَ المَديحَ (ل \ على شَيْءٍ \ شَخْصٍ) to be full of praise (for sth/sb)

مَمْدوح A *adj* praised, celebrated

B *n* Mamdouh (*male given name*)

مَدَّ *v* |u; مَدّ| 1 [بَسَطَ] to extend, to stretch (out); to spread (out); to hold out; مَدَّ لِشَخْصٍ يَدَ العَوْنِ to lend sb a helping hand; مَدَّ ساقَيْهِ \ ذِراعَيْهِ to stretch one's legs/arms; مَدَّ يَدَهُ إِلى شَيْءٍ to reach for sth, to extend one's hand to sth 2 [زَوَّدَ] to supply, to provide 3 [أَطالَ] to prolong, to lengthen; مَدَّ اللهُ عُمْرَهُ may God prolong his life 4 [شَقَّ (طَريقاً)] to construct, to build; مَدَّ جِسْراً to construct a bridge; مَدَّ خَطَّ سِكّةٍ حَديدِيّةٍ to build a railway

مَدَّدَ *v* 1 [بَسَطَ] to stretch (out); to spread (out) 2 [أَطالَ] to lengthen, to prolong, to extend; مَدَّدَ عَقْداً to extend a contract; مَدَّدوا جَوازَ سَفَرِهِ they have renewed his passport

مادَّ *v* to tarry, to linger

أَمَدَّ *v* to provide, to supply, to furnish; أَمَدَّ شَخْصاً بِشَيْءٍ to supply sb with sth; أَمَدَّ شَخْصاً بالمَعْلوماتِ to supply sb with information

تَمَدَّدَ *v* **1** [تَمَطَّى] to lie (down), to sprawl, to stretch (oneself) out **2** [انْبَسَطَ] to expand, to swell, to stretch; يَتَمَدَّدُ الحَديدُ بالحَرارة iron expands with heat

امْتَدَّ *v* to extend, to stretch (out)

اسْتَمَدَّ *v* to derive, to take; اسْتَمَدَّ شُهْرَتَهُ من شَيْءٍ to derive one's fame from sth

مَدَد *n* **1** [دَعْم] reinforcement **2** [مَوارِد] provisioning, supply

مادّة *n* |مَوادُّ| **1** [عُنْصُر مُكَوِّن لِشَيْءٍ] material, matter, substance; مادّة اصْطِناعيّة synthetic (material); مادّة خام \ أَوَّليّة raw material; مادّة نِصْف مَصْنوعةٍ semi-finished product; مادّة مُصَنَّعة final product, ready-made good; مَوادّ كيمِيائيّة (خَطِرة) (dangerous) chemicals; أَنْتَجَ مَوادَّ كيمِيائيّةً to produce chemicals; مادّة سامّة \ كاوية \ نَتِنة a poisonous/corrosive/stinky substance; مادّة ثَمينة \ قَوِيّة valuable/strong material; مادّة عُضْويّة organic material; مادّة صَلْبة solid (substance); مادّة مَناعيّة antibody; مادّة حافِظة preservative; مَوادّ غِذائيّة \ مُغَذِّية food products, food **2** [جُزْء] component, part **3** [قانونٍ] article, clause, section; مادّة قانونيّة \ في القانونِ section of the law **4** [في المَدْرَسةِ] (school) subject, field (of study); مادّة صَعْبة \ مُمِلّة a difficult/boring subject; مادّة إجْباريّة a compulsory subject; مَوادّ تِقْنِيّة \ عِلْمِيّة technical/scientific subjects; مادّة الدَّرْسِ subject matter

مادّيّ **A** *adj* material; materialistic; financial; ضَرَر \ مُساعَدة \ أَمْلاك مادّيّ(ة) material damage/help/property; مَشاكِل مادّيّة financial problems; عَقْليّة \ مُجْتَمَع مادّيّ(ة) a materialistic mentality/society; عاشَ في ظُروفٍ مادّيّةٍ صَعْبةٍ to experience difficult financial circumstances

B *n* materialist

مادّيّة *n* **1** [التَعَلُّق بالمادّيّاتِ] materialism **2** (Philos) materialism

مُتَمَدِّد *adj* lying

مَدّ *n* |مُدود| **1** [تَجْهيز] construction, building **2** [عَكْس جَزْر] high tide, rising tide, flood (tide); مَدّ وَجَزْر high tide and low tide, ebb and flow; حَرَكة \ فَتْرة المَدِّ أو الجَزْرِ tide; مَدّ بَحْريّ عِمْلاق tsunami **3** [إطالة] lengthening, elongation, stretching; مَدّ البَصَرِ \ النَظَرِ range of vision; على مَدِّ البَصَرِ \ النَظَرِ within seeing distance **4** (Gram) lengthening of a vowel; حُروف المَدِّ consonants indicating a long vowel (*alif, waw, ya'*)

مُدّ *n* |أَمْداد, مِداد| *a dry measure (appr. 18 l in the eastern Arab world and appr. 47 l in the western Arab world)*

مَدّاد *n* fountain pen

مِداد *n* **1** [حِبْر] ink **2** [سَماد] manure, dung, fertilizer

مَدّة *n* madda (*sign over alif that indicates a glottal stop followed by long a*)

مُدّة *n* |مُدَد| period (of time), while, duration; مُدّة طَويلة a good while; دامَ مُدّةً طَويلةً to take a long time; مُدّة زَمَنيّة length of time; مُدّةً من الزَمَنِ for a while; لِمُدّةِ سَنَتَيْنِ for a period of two years

مِدّة *n* pus, (purulent) matter

مَديد *adj* |مُدُد| long, extended; deep

مُسْتَمَدّ *adj* derived, taken; هذه الكَلِمةُ مُسْتَمَدّةٌ من الإنْجْليزيّةِ this word is derived from English

مُمْتَدّ *adj* stretched, outstretched; extensive; extended, prolonged

مُمَدَّد *adj* extensive, spread out, expansive

مَمْدود *adj* **1** [مُوَسَّع] stretched, outstretched; extensive; بِذِراعَيْنِ مَمْدودَتَيْنِ with outstretched arms **2** (Gram) lengthened; أَلِف مَمْدودة *long vowel a followed by a hamza*

امْتِداد *n* |امْتِدادات| expansion; extent, expanse; length; على امْتِدادِ ... along ...; during ...; على امْتِدادِ الشارِعِ along the street; في امْتِداد هذا الشارِع in this stretch of the street; على امْتِدادِ العالَمِ around the world; على امْتِدادِ البَصَرِ as far as the eye can see; على امْتِدادِ فَتْرةٍ طَويلةٍ for a long time; على امْتِدادِ أَشْهُرِ السَنةِ the whole year long, throughout the year; على امْتِدادِ ٢٠ مِتْراً for a distance of 20 metres

إمْداد *n* |إمْدادات| **1** [تَزْويد] supply, provision; delivery; إمْدادات supplies; إمْدادات غِذائيّة food supplies; الإمْداد بالمَوادِّ الغِذائيّةِ the supply of foodstuffs; الإمْداد بالغازِ والماءِ the gas and water supply; الإمْداد والتَمْوين logistics **2** [عَوْن] help, assistance, aid; قَطَعَ الإمْداداتِ الماليّةَ to cut off financial aid

تَمَدُّد *n* **1**▸ [تَوَسُّع] extension, expansion; increase **2**▸ (*Phys*) expansion, extension; قابلِيَّة التَمَدُّدِ expandability; تَمَدُّد حَجْمِيّ cubic expansion; تَمَدُّد الكَوْنِ the expansion of the universe

تَمْديد *n* |تَمْديدات| lengthening, prolongation, extension; تَمْديد مُدَّة الاسْتِعارةِ extension of the lending period; تَمْديد صَلاحِيَّة جَوازِ سَفَرٍ renewal of a passport

تَمْديدة *n* extension (piece)

لامادِّيّة *n* immaterialism

‹ **مَدَر** *n* clod (of earth), lump (of earth)

مَدَرة *n* clod of earth

‹ **مَدْريد** *n* |f| Madrid

‹ **مَدَغَشْقَر** *n* |f| Madagascar

‹ **مَدَّنَ** *v* to civilize, to urbanize

تَمَدَّنَ *v* to urbanize; to become civilized

مَدَنيّ **A** *adj* **1**▸ [غَيْر عَسْكَرِيّ] civil, civic, civilian; urban; مُجْتَمَع مَدَنيّ civil society; السُلْطة المَدَنيّة (والعَسْكَرِيّة) the civil (and the military) authorities; مَحْكَمة مَدَنيّة a civil court; دَعْوى \ حُكْم مَدَنيّ(ة) a civil lawsuit/verdict; زَواج مَدَنيّ civil marriage; دِفاع مَدَنيّ civil defence; مُهَنْدِس مَدَنيّ civil engineer **2**▸ [من المَدينة المُنَوَّرة] Medinan, of/from Medina; سورة مَدَنيّة *sura revealed in Medina*
B *n* civilian, citizen; المَدَنيّونَ the civilian population

مَدَنيّة *n* civilization

مَدينة *n* |مَدائِنُ, مُدُن| city, town; مَدينة عُظْمى metropolis; المَدينة Medina (*city in Saudi Arabia*); مَدينة النَبِيّ City of the Prophet (*epithet for Medina*); المَدينة المُنَوَّرة the Radiant City (*epithet for Medina*); مَدينة القُدْسِ Jerusalem; المَدينة المُقَدَّسة the Holy City; المَدينة الفاضِلة Utopia, El Dorado; مَدينة نَصْر Nasr City (*district in Cairo*); المُدُن الكُبْرى the big cities; مَرْكَز \ وَسَط المَدينةِ town centre, city centre, downtown (AmE)

مُدَيْنة *n* small town

مَدينِيّ *adj* urban, municipal, city (*before n*)

تَمَدُّن *n* urbanization; civilization

تَمْدين *n* urbanization; تَمْدين الريفِ the urbanization of the countryside

‹ **مادى** *v* to grant a respite

أَمْدى *v* to grant a respite

تَمادى *v* **1**▸ [دامَ] to persist, to persevere, to go on; تَمادى في الكَذِبِ to persist in lying **2**▸ [تَطاوَلَ] to last (too) long

مَدًى *n* range, reach, scope; radius, extent; مَدى عَمَلٍ extent of work; مَدى بُنْدُقيّة the range of a rifle; في \ ضِمْنَ مَدى إطْلاقِ نارٍ within shooting range; صَواريخ طَوِيلة \ قَصيرة \ مُتَوَسِّطة المَدى long/short/medium-range missiles; مَدى الحَياةِ lifelong, for life; على مَدى الوَقْتِ in the course of time; على مَدى البَصَرِ as far as the eye can see; على المَدى القَريبِ \ البَعيدِ in the short/long run; على مَدى مِائة مِتْرٍ at a distance of 100 metres; على مَدى العام بِأَكْمَلِه throughout the year; سُئِلَ عن مَدى صِحّة هذا people asked to what extent this was correct; لا يَعْرِفونَ مَدى خُطورةِ هذه الخُطْوة they don't know how dangerous this step is; سَيَنْظُرُ في مَدى إمْكانيّةِ الاسْتِفادةِ مِنْهُ he will investigate to what extent he can profit from it

مُدْية *n* |مُدًى| knife

تَمادٍ *n* perseverance, persistence; مع التَمادي in the long run

‹ **مُذْ** *prep* since; مُذ كانَ في الثالِثة من عُمْرِه since he was three years old; مُذْ ذاكَ since (then)

‹ **مَذِر** *adj* rotten, putrid; بَيْضة مَذِرة a rotten egg

‹ **مَذَقَ** *v* |u; مَذْق| to thin, to dilute

‹ **تَمَذْهَبَ** *v* see ذهب

‹ **مَرَأَ** *v* |a; مَراءة| to be palatable; to be wholesome

مَرُؤَ *v* |u; مُروءة| to be humane/civilized

مَرِئَ *v* |a; مَراءة| to be palatable; to be wholesome

اسْتَمْرَأَ *v* to savour (*a meal*)

مُروءة *n* chivalry

مَريء *n* |أَمْرِئة, مُروء| gullet, oesophagus

امْرُؤ *n* |gen امْرِئ; acc امْرَءاً| man; المَرْء one, they

امْرَأة *n* |definite المَرْأة; نِساء| woman, lady; امْرَأة مُسِنّة an elderly lady; تَحْرير \ تَحَرُّر المَرْأةِ emancipation of women, women's liberation; طَبيب أَمْراضِ النِساءِ gynaecologist

‹ **مَرّاكُش** *n* |dipt f| Marrakech (*city in Morocco*)

‹ **مَرَّ** *v* |u; مَرّ, مُرور, مَمَرّ| [اِجْتازَ] ⓵ ‹ |ب| to pass (by/through), to go by; مَرَّ على شَيْءٍ; مَرَّ بِجِسْرٍ \ بِشارِعٍ to pass a bridge/street; مُرورَ الكِرامِ to not mention sth; مَرَّ بِمَراحِلَ مُتَعَدِّدةٍ to pass through several phases ⓶ ‹ [مَضى] to go by, to pass (by), to elapse; مَرَّ بدونِ مَشاكِلَ to pass off without problems; مَرَّتْ أَرْبَعُ دَقائِقَ \ ساعاتٍ four minutes/hours went by; مَرَّ بِسُرْعةٍ \ على خَيْرٍ to go quickly/smoothly; مَرَّ الوَقْتُ بِسُرْعةٍ time flew by; مَرَّ ذِكْرُهُ to be mentioned before ⓷ ‹ [زارَ] to call by, to drop by; مَرَّ على شَخْصٍ to pay a call on sb ⓸ ‹ [صارَ مُرًّا] to be in a bitter mood

مَرَّرَ *v* ⓵ ‹ [أَعْطى] to pass on, to hand over ⓶ ‹ (Sport) to (make a) pass; مَرَّرَ الكُرةَ إلى شَخْصٍ to pass the ball to sb ⓷ ‹ (Comput) to forward; مَرَّرَ رِسالةً to forward a message

أَمَرَّ *v* ⓵ ‹ [جَعَلَهُ يَمُرُّ] to make pass; to let pass, to let go by ⓶ ‹ [صارَ مُرًّا] to become bitter, to become embittered ⓷ ‹ [صَيَّرَهُ مُرًّا] to make bitter, to embitter

اسْتَمَرَّ *v* to last, to go on, to continue; اسْتَمَرَّ في الكَلامِ to continue talking; اسْتَمَرَّ في الدِراسةِ to continue (with) one's studies; يَسْتَمِرُّ الجَوُّ الحارُّ the warm weather lasts; اسْتَمَرَّ الصَقيعُ the frost persisted; يَسْتَمِرُّ تَأْثيرُ هذا الدَواءِ لِمُدّةِ ... the effect of this medicine lasts for ...; اسْتَمَرَّ في مَنْحِ الدَعْمِ الحُكوميِّ \ التَعْويضِ to continue (paying) the subsidy/allowance; يَسْتَمِرُّ الوَضْعُ على ما هو عَلَيْهِ the situation continues as is

مارّ *n* |مارّة, مارّونَ| passer-by, pedestrian

مَرّ *n* ⓵ ‹ [مِسْحاة] |أَمْرار, مُرور| shovel, spade ⓶ ‹ [مَضى] passing, going by; على مَرِّ الأَيّامِ \ الزَمانِ over the course of days/time; على مَرِّ السِنينَ over the years

مُرّ Ⓐ *adj* |أَمْرار| bitter; nasty; الحَقيقة المُرّة the harsh reality, the bitter truth; مَذاق مُرّ a nasty taste; أَحْلى المُرَّيْنِ the lesser of two evils; كانَ أمامَ أَمْرَيْنِ أَحْلاهُما مُرٌّ he had to choose the lesser of two evils

Ⓑ *n* |أَمْرار| ⓵ ‹ [صَمْغ] myrrh (*Commiphora*) ⓶ ‹ [عُفوصة] bitterness; قاسَمَ شَخْصاً الحَياةَ بِحُلْوِها وَمُرِّها to share the sweet and the bitter with sb

مِرار *n* (ما) مِراراً often; مِراراً وَتَكْراراً again and again

‹ **مُرّان** *n* beech (*Fagus*)

‹ **مَرَثَ** *v* |u; مَرْث| to soak, to macerate

‹ **مَرِجَ** *v* |a; مَرَج| to be confused, to be disturbed, to be disordered

مَرْج *n* |مُروج| ⓵ ‹ [مَرْعًى] meadow, pasture, grassland; lawn, field (of grass); لَعِبَ في المَرْجِ to play in the field ⓶ ‹ [هَرْج] commotion; هَرْج وَمَرْج chaos; يا لَلْهَرْجِ والمَرْجِ! oh, what chaos!

مَرَج *n* disorder, disturbance

‹ **مَرْجان** *n coll* coral; مَرْجان أَحْمَر red coral

مَرْجانيّ *adj* coralline, coral (*before n*); جَزيرة مَرْجانيّة atoll; سِوار \ سِلْسِلة مَرْجانيّ(ة) a coral bracelet/chain

‹ **مَرِحَ** *v* |a; مَرَح| to have a laugh, to have fun; to horse around; سَرَحَ وَمَرِحَ to do as one likes

مَرَح *n* fun, cheerfulness, mirth; من أَجْلِ المَرَحِ for fun

مَرِح *adj* |مَراحى, مَرْحى| cheerful, merry, lively; مِزاج مَرِح a cheerful mood; كانَ مِزاجُهُ مَرِحاً he was in high spirits; طَبْع مَرِح a cheerful disposition; موسيقى مَرِحة lively music

مَرْحى *excl* hooray; bravo

مِمْراح *adj* cheerful, blithe

‹ **المِرِّيخ** *n* Mars (*planet*)

‹ **مَرَدَ** *v* |u; مُرود| to be rebellious, to rebel

تَمَرَّدَ *v* to rebel, to revolt, to mutiny; تَمَرَّدَ على شَخْصٍ \ شَيْءٍ to rise (in revolt) against sb/sth; تَمَرَّدَ على حُكومةٍ to rebel against a government

مارِد Ⓐ *adj* |مُرّاد, مَرَدة, مارِدونَ| rebellious, mutinous, defiant

Ⓑ *n* |مُرّاد, مَرَدة, مارِدونَ| giant; devil

مُتَمَرِّد Ⓐ *adj* rebellious, mutinous, subversive

Ⓑ *n* rebel, insurgent

أَمْرَد *adj* ⓵ ‹ [دون لِحْيةٍ] beardless ⓶ ‹ [دون وَرَقٍ] leafless (*tree*)

تِمْراد *n* |تَماريدُ| dovecote, pigeon house

تَمَرُّد *n* uprising, rebellion, revolt; تَمَرُّد مُسَلَّح \ عَسْكَريّ armed/military rebellion; قامَ بِتَمَرُّدٍ to commit (an act of) insubordination

تَمَرُّديّ *adj* rebellion (*before n*); حَرَكة تَمَرُّديّة guerrilla movement

‹ **مَرْدَقوش** *n* (sweet) marjoram (*Origanum majorana*)

مُرورِيّ *adj* traffic (*before n*); سَلامة مُرورِيّة traffic safety, road safety; اخْتِناق مُرورِيّ traffic jam; حادِث مُرورِيّ (خطير) a (serious) traffic accident; مُخالَفة مُرورِيّة traffic offence

مَرير *adj* |مَرائِرُ| bitter, harsh, sour; كَلِمات مَريرة bitter words; قِتال \ عِراك مَرير a bitter fight; تَجْرِبة مَريرة a bitter experience

مَريرة *n* determination, resoluteness

مُسْتَمِرّ *adj* lasting, permanent; continuous, constant, uninterrupted; تَهْديد مُسْتَمِرّ a constant threat; عَرْض مُسْتَمِرّ a continuous performance; جَفاف مُسْتَمِرّ prolonged drought; طَلَقات مُسْتَمِرّة continuous shooting; تَيّار مُسْتَمِرّ direct current

مَمَرّ *n* |مَمَرّات| ❶ [للمُرور] passage, corridor, aisle; path; gallery, walkway; track, course; مَمَرّ خاصّ private road; مَمَرّ ضَيِّق \ خَطِر a narrow/dangerous passage; مَمَرّ مائيّ waterway; مَمَرّ الراجِلين footpath; مَمَرّ المُشاة pedestrian crossing ❷ (Transp) (traffic) lane; المَمَرّ الأَيْسَر \ الأَيْمَن من الطَريقِ the left/right lane ❸ [جَبَليّ] (mountain) pass; مَمَرّ جَبَليّ mountain pass

اسْتِمْرار *n* continuation; بِاسْتِمْرارٍ continually, constantly; إنَّه مَريضٌ بِاسْتِمْرارٍ he is constantly ill; تَرْتَفِعُ أَسْعارُ البَنْزين بِاسْتِمْرارٍ petrol prices continue to go up

اسْتِمْرارِيّ *adj* continuous

اسْتِمْرارِيّة *n* continuation, continuity; اسْتِمْرارِيّة السِياسةِ the continuity of policy

أَمَرّ *adj* |dipt| more bitter, bitterer; الأَمَرّانِ the two bitter things (*poverty and old age*); عانى الأَمَرَّيْنِ to suffer badly (*from poverty and old age*); أَذاقَ شَخْصاً الأَمَرَّيْنِ to cause sb misery

تَمْرير *n* ❶ (Sport) passing, making a pass ❷ (Comput) scrolling

تَمْريرة, **تَمْرير** *n* (Sport) pass; تَمْريرة عَرْضِيّة a cross pass; تَمْريرة طَويلة a long pass

‹ **مُرْزة** *n* (Zool) harrier (*Circus*)

‹ **مَرْزُبان** *n* |مَرازِبة| satrap (*a provincial governor in the ancient Persian empire*)

‹ **مارَسَ** *v* to practise, to exercise; to pursue; to do; مارَسَ رِياضةً to practise a sport; مارَسَ التَمارينَ الرِياضيّةَ to do gymnastics; مارَسَ الجِنْسَ to have sex; مارَسَ السِياسةَ to apply oneself to politics; مارَسَ هِواياتٍ to pursue hobbies; مارَسَ ضَغْطاً

مَرارة *n* ❶ gall bladder; حَصاة في المَرارةِ gallstone; اسْتَأْصَلَ الحَصاةَ من المَرارة to (surgically) remove a gallstone ❷ [عَكْس حَلاوةٍ] bitterness; ذاقَ مَرارةَ العَيْشِ to taste the bitterness of life

مَرّة *n* |مَرّات, مِرار| time; مَرّةً once; مَرّةً في السَنةِ once a year; مَرَّتَيْنِ twice; مَرّةً ... ومَرّةً ... the one time ... and the other ...; مَرّاتٍ عَديدةً often, frequently; مَرّةً واحِدةً one time, once; لِمَرّةٍ واحِدةٍ for one time; هذه المَرّةَ this time, this once; مَرّةً أُخْرى once again, once more; مَرّةً ثانِيةً another time, a second time; للمَرّةِ الثانِيةِ for the second time; المَرّةَ الأَخيرةَ the last time; للمَرّةِ الأَخيرةِ for the last time; المَرّةَ تِلْوَ المَرّةِ, مَرّةً تِلْوَ الأُخْرى ذاتَ مَرّةٍ time after time, time and again; ذاتَ مَرّةٍ once, one day; لِلمَرّةِ الأولى, لِأَوَّلِ مَرّةٍ for the first time; كُلَّ مَرّةٍ each time, every time; أَكْثَر من مَرّةٍ, غَيْرَ مَرّةٍ more than once; عِدّةَ مَرّاتٍ many times, repeatedly; بالمَرّةِ at all; لا \ لَيْسَ ... بالمَرّةِ not ... at all, by no means; كانَ لا يَدْرُسُ بالمَرّةِ he didn't study at all; هذا الاتِّهامُ غَيْرُ صَحيحٍ بالمَرّةِ this accusation is by no means correct

مُرّة *n* في الحُلْوةِ والمُرّةِ for better or (for) worse

مِرّة *n* |مِرَر| bile, gall

مُرور *n* ❶ [مَمَرّ] passage, crossing; حُرِّيّة المُرورِ free passage; سَمَحَ بالمُرورِ to allow to pass; جَواز المُرورِ pass ❷ [مُواصَلات] traffic; حَرَكة المُرورِ (flow of) traffic; شُرْطة \ قِسْم المُرورِ traffic police/department; شُرْطيّ مُرورٍ traffic policeman; لَوْحة مُرورٍ road sign, traffic sign; نِظام مُرورٍ traffic regulations; تَنْظيم حَرَكةِ المُرورِ the regulation of traffic; ازْدِحام المُرورِ traffic congestion; حَرَكة مُرورٍ مُزْدَحِمة heavy traffic; إشارة المُرورِ traffic light; حَرَكة المُرورِ الجَوّيّ air traffic; السَلامة في المُرورِ road safety; مَنَعَ \ عَرْقَلَ المُرورَ to obstruct traffic; الْتَزَمَ بِقَواعِدِ المُرورِ to observe the traffic rules; فَتَحَ طَريقاً \ جِسْراً للمُرورِ to open a road/bridge for traffic ❸ [زَمَن] course, lapse; ب \ مع مُرورِ الوَقْتِ in the course of time; بعد مُرورِ الوَقْتِ with the passing of time ❹ (Busn) transit ❺ [دَوْرة] passing, tour; أَثْناءَ مُرورِهِ على الأَقْسامِ during his tour of the departments ❻ (Comput) كَلِمة مُرورٍ password

على شَخْصٍ to exert pressure on sb; مارَسَ مِهْنَتَهُ to practise one's profession

تَمَرَّسَ *v* to get used, to become accustomed; تَمَرَّسَ في تَجارِبَ to acquire experience

مُتَمَرِّس *adj* experienced, practised, seasoned; مُتَمَرِّس في الرِياضةِ seasoned in the sport

مِراس *n* صَعْبُ المِراسِ unruly; كانَ أَطْفالُها صِعابَ المِراسِ her children were (rather) unmanageable

مَرَسة *n* |أَمْراس ,مَرَس| cord, rope

مُمارِس 🅰 *adj* sitting, incumbent, practising; المُدير المُمارِس the sitting manager; أَعْضاء اللَجْنةِ المُمارسونَ the sitting councillors; طَبيب مُمارِس عامّ a medical practitioner 🅱 *n* practitioner; مُمارِس فُنونِ القِتالِ a practitioner of martial arts, martial artist; المُمارِسُ يَغْلِبُ الفارِسَ practice makes perfect

مُمارَسة *n* exercise, practice, practising; مُمارَسة السُلْطةِ the exercise of power; مُمارَسة رِياضةٍ the practice of sport; أَفْضَل عند مُمارَسةِ مِهْنَتِهِ in pursuance of one's profession; مُمارِساتٍ best practice; مَنْع مُمارَسةِ المِهْنةِ occupational ban

تَمَرُّس *n* practice, exercise; performance

مَرْسيليا *n* Marseilles (*city in France*)

مَرْسين *n* myrtle (*Myrtus*)

مَرَشَ *v* |u; مَرْش| to scratch

مَرِضَ *v* |a; مَرَض| to be/become sick, to fall ill

مَرَّضَ *v* ⓵ [اعتنى بالمَريضِ] to nurse, to care for ⓶ [أَمْرَض] to make sick, to make ill

أَمْرَضَ *v* to make sick, to make ill

تَمارَضَ *v* to feign illness, to malinger; تَمارَضَ المَريضُ the patient feigned illness

مَرَض *n* |أَمْراض| disease, disorder; illness, sickness; مَرَض فاتِك \ مُزْمِن \ عُضال a chronic/incurable illness; مَرَض قاتِل a terminal illness; (مُعْدٍ) مَرَض جِنْسيّ \ تَناسُليّ sexually transmitted disease, venereal disease; تَجَنُّب الأَمْراض التَناسُلِيّة to prevent venereal diseases; مَرَض جِلْديّ skin disease; أَمْراض باطِنِيّة internal diseases; مَرَض مُعْدٍ an infectious disease; مَرَض خَطير a serious illness; المَرَض الخَبيث the malignant disease (*cancer*); مَرَض عَقْليّ mental illness; أَمْراض القَلْبِ والشَرايينِ cardiovascular diseases; الأَمْراض الشائِعة common diseases; مَرَض سَريع الانْتِشارِ a rapidly spreading disease; عِلْم الأَمْراضِ pathology; اخْتِصاصيّ في عِلْمِ الأَمْراضِ pathologist; عِلْم أَمْراضِ النِساءِ gynaecology; طَبيب \ أَخِصّائيّ أَمْراضِ النِساءِ gynaecologist; فِراش المَرَضِ sickbed; أَعْراض مَرَضٍ symptoms of a disease, syndrome; جُرْثومة حامِلة لِمَرَضٍ disease-carrying germ; حَدَّدَ أَعْراضَ مَرَضٍ to diagnose a syndrome; أُصيبَ بِمَرَضٍ to contract a disease, to develop a disease; عانى من مَرَضٍ to suffer from a disease; أَقْعَدَهُ المَرَضُ disease has struck him; شَعَرَ بالمَرَضِ to feel ill; اسْتَفْحَلَ المَرَضُ the illness has grown worse; أَثْناءَ مَرَضِه during his illness

مَرَضيّ *adj* morbid, pathological, patho-; sick; تَعْويض مَرَضيّ sick pay; إجازة مَرَضِيّة sick leave

مَريض 🅰 *adj* |مَرْضى| sick, ill, diseased; كانَ مَريضاً to be ill 🅱 *n* |مَرْضى| sick person, patient; مَريض مُزْمِن a chronically sick patient; مَريض القَلْبِ cardiac (patient); مَريض بالرِئة lung patient

مُمَرِّض *n* (male) nurse

مُمَرِّضة *n* (female) nurse; مُمَرِّضة لَيْلِيّة night nurse

تَمْريض *n* nursing, care; عِلْم التَمْريضِ nursing; مِهْنة التَمْريضِ nursing profession; دار تَمْريضٍ nursing home

تَمْريضيّ *adj* nursing

مَرْع *n* |أَمْرُع ,أَمْراع| pasture

مَريع *adj* fruitful, productive, fertile

مَرَّغَ *v* to roll (*in the dust*); to rub

تَمَرَّغَ *v* to roll (*in the dust*)

مَرْغاريتا *n* marguerite (*Argyranthemum*)

مَرْغَرين *n* margarine; مَرْغَرين نَباتيّ vegetable margarine

مِرْفَت *n* |dipt f| Merfet (*female given name*)

مُرْفيم ,مورْفيم *n* morpheme

مُرْفين *n* see مورْفين

مَرَقَ *v* |u; مُروق| ⓵ [ارْتَدَّ] to renounce; مَرَقَ من الدينِ to renounce faith ⓶ [اخْتَرَقَ] to drill through, to pierce, to penetrate

مَرَق, مَرَقة *n* broth, stock, bouillon

مارِق *adj* |مَرَقة, مُرّاق| renegade; heretical, apostate; دَوْلة مارِقة rogue state

مُراق *n* hypochondria

مُروق *n* apostasy; heresy

‹ **مُرْقُص** *n* |dipt| Marcus (*male given name*)

‹ **مَرْكَز** *v* see ركز

تَمَرْكَز *v* see ركز

مُتَمَرْكِز *adj* see ركز

تَمَرْكُز *n* see ركز

‹ **مَرْكيز** *n* marquess, marquis

‹ **مَرْمَطون, مَرْمَتون** *n* kitchen boy, cook's boy

‹ **تَمَرْمَرَ** *v* to mumble, to murmur

مَرْمَر *n* marble, alabaster; عَمود من المَرْمَرِ a marble pillar

مَرْمَريّ *adj* marble (*before n*); alabaster (*before n*)

‹ **مَرْموط** *n* marmot (*Marmota*)

‹ **مَرَنَ** *v* |u; مُرون, مُرونة, مَرانة| **1** [كانَ مَرِناً] to be elastic, to be flexible **2** [تَعَوَّدَ] to become accustomed, to get used

مَرَّنَ *v* to train, to practise, to coach; مَرَّنَ عَضَلاتِهِ to exercise one's muscles; مَرَّنَ ذاكِرَتَهُ to train one's memory

تَمَرَّنَ *v* to practise, to rehearse, to train; تَمَرَّنَ على امْتِحانٍ to practise for an exam

مَرِن *adj* elastic; flexible, pliable, supple; مادّة مَرِنة elastic material; سِياسة قَبولٍ مَرِنة a flexible admittance policy

مُتَمَرِّن *adj* experienced, trained, practised

مِران *n* training, practice, exercise

مَرانة *n* see مُرونة

مُرونة, مَرانة *n* elasticity; flexibility, suppleness; resilience; انْعِدام المُرونةِ a lack of flexibility

مَرين *n* listed alphabetically

مُمَرِّن *n* trainer, coach

تَمَرُّن *n* exercise, practice

تَمْرين *n* |تَمارينُ, تَمْرينات| exercise, practice, training; تَمارين تَمْرينات رِياضيّة gymnastics; تَمارين ذِهْنيّة mental training; أدّى \ أَجْرى تَمْريناً, قامَ بِتَمْرينٍ عَسْكَريّة military exercises; to do an exercise; حَلَّ تَمارينَ الحِسابِ to solve math problems

‹ **مَرْو** *n* **1** [حَجَر] quartz **2** [مَدينة] |f| Merv (*town in Turkmenistan*)

مُرْوّة *n* see مُروءة

‹ **مَرْوان** *n* Marwan (*male given name*)

‹ **ماری** *v* to dispute, to argue

تَماری *v* to argue, to debate

امْتَرى *v* |في| to doubt, to suspect

مِراء *n* لا مِراءَ فيهِ indisputable; ... لا مِراءَ في أنّ it's an undeniable fact that ...

مُرْية *n* doubt; quarrel

‹ **ماريجُوانا** *n* marijuana

‹ **مَرْيَم** *n* |dipt f| **1** [اسْم شَخْصيّ] Maryam, Mary (*female given name*) **2** [العَذْراء] Mary (*mother of Jesus*); مَرْيَم العَذْراء the Virgin Mary; سورة مَرْيَم Maryam (*Sura 19*)

‹ **مَرْيَميّة** *n* sage (*Salvia officinalis*)

‹ **مَرين** بَنو مَرين the Marinid dynasty

‹ **مَزَجَ** *v* |u; مَزْج, امْتِزاج| to mix, to mingle, to blend; مَزَجَ الشايَ بالعَسَلِ to mix honey into tea

مازَجَ *v* to mix, to mingle, to blend; مازَجَ بين أَشْياءَ to mix things up

تَمازَجَ *v* to be mixed, to be mingled, to be blended

امْتَزَجَ *v* to be mixed, to be mingled, to be blended; to mix, to mingle, to blend; امْتَزَجَتْ دِماؤُهُم their bloodlines mixed

مَزْج *n* hybrid; mongrel; blend, mix

مازِج *n* carburettor

مِزاج *n* |أَمْزِجة| **1** [حالة نَفْسيّة] mood; temper; مزاج سَوْداويّ \ صافٍ a melancholy/cheerful mood; مِزاج مُتَقَلِّب a whimsical mood; مِزاج رائِق \ مُعَكَّر a good/bad mood; كانَ رائِقَ \ مُعَكَّرَ المِزاجِ to be in a good/bad mood; صَعْبُ المِزاجِ moody, grumpy **2** [طَبيعة] temperament, disposition, character; مِزاج هادِئ \ كَئيب a calm/melancholic nature **3** (Med) مِزاج نَزْفيّ haemophilia

مِزاجيّ *adj* temperamental, unpredictable

مَزيج *n* |مُزُج| mixture, blend, mix

مُمْتَزِج *adj* mixed, blended

مَمْزوج *adj* mixed, blended

امْتِزاج *n* mixture, mix, blend

تَمازُج *n* mixing, blending; mixture

‹ **مَزَحَ** *v* |a; مَزْح| to joke, to jest, to make fun; أَنت تَمْزَحُ you're joking, you must be joking

مازَحَ *v* to tease; to fool around with, to banter with; مازَحَ شَخْصاً to fool sb

تَمازَحَ *v* to poke fun at each other, to tease one another

مَزْح *n* joke, jest, fun; على سَبيلِ المَزْحِ for the fun of it; بِلا مَزْحٍ seriously, no kidding

مازِح **A** *adj* funny, comic, comical **B** *n* joker, jester

مَزّاح *n* joker, jester

مِزاح, مُزاح *n* joke, jest, fun; قَصَدْتُ المُزاحَ I was only joking

مَزْحة *n* joke; prank; مَزْحة ثَقيلة practical joke; لَيْسَتْ مَزْحةً it's no joke

مُمازَحة *n* teasing, banter

‹ **مِزْر** *n* ale (*a kind of beer*)

‹ **مَزَّ** *v* |u; مَزّ| to suck

مُزّ *adj* slightly sour, slightly tart, acidy

مَزّة *n* mezze (*assorted starters and appetizers*)

‹ **مَزَّعَ** *v* to tear, to rip, to rend; مَزَّعَ القُطْنَ to card cotton

‹ **مَزَّقَ** *v* to tear (up), to rip (up), to shred; مَزَّقَ وَرَقةً \ رِسالةً \ جَريدةً to tear up a piece of paper/letter/newspaper; مَزَّقَ شَيْئاً نِصْفَيْنِ to tear sth apart; مَزَّقَ إِرْباً إِرْباً to tear sth to pieces; مَزَّقَ شَيْئاً قِسْمَيْنِ \ ثَلاثةَ أَقْسام to tear sth in two/three pieces; مَزَّقَ فَريسَتَهُ to maul its prey; مَنْظَر يُمَزِّقُ القَلْبَ a heart-rending scene

تَمَزَّقَ *v* to tear (apart), to rip

مَزْق *n* tear, rip

مِزْقة *n* |مِزَق| shred

مُمَزَّق *adj* torn, ripped, rent; سِرْوال مُمَزَّق torn trousers

تَمَزُّق *n* tear, rip; حَدَثَ تَمَزُّقٌ (في المَهْبَلِ) أَثْناءَ الوَضْعِ to suffer tearing during childbirth

تَمْزيق *n* tearing, ripping

‹ **مُزْن** *n coll* |مُزَن| rain cloud

‹ **مَزِيّة** *n* |مَزايا| **1** [امْتِياز] privilege; advantage; تَمَتَّعَ بِمَزايا to enjoy privileges **2** [سِمة] characteristic, feature

‹ **مُسْتَحِية** *n* sensitive plant (*Mimosa pudica*); touch-me-not (*Impatiens noli-tangere*)

‹ **مُسْتَغانِم** *n* |dipt f| Mostaganem (*city in Algeria*)

‹ **مَسَحَ** *v* |a| **1** [نَظَّفَ بالمَسْح] |مَسْح| to wipe, to rub; to clear, to clean; مَسَحَ الأَرْضَ بِشَخْصٍ to wipe the floor with sb **2** [مَحا] |مَسْح| to wipe off, to brush/wipe away; to polish; مَسَح فَمَهُ \ يَدَيْهِ to wipe off one's mouth/hands; مَسَحَ نَظّارَتَهُ to wipe one's glasses; مَسَحَ الدُموعَ to wipe away the tears; مَسَحَ الأَثاثَ (بِمِنْديلٍ) to go over the furniture (with a cloth); مَسَحَ جَبينَهُ to mop one's forehead; مَسَحَ العَرَقَ من جَبينِهِ to wipe the sweat from one's forehead; مَسَحَ السَبّورةَ to erase the blackboard; مَسَحَ كَلِمةً من السَبّورة to erase a word on the blackboard **3** [قاسَ] |إِمْساحة, مَسْح| to survey; مَسَحَ مِنْطَقةً to survey an area **4** (Chr) |مَسْح| to anoint

تَمَسَّحَ *v* |بـ| to curry favour with; *to seek a blessing by touching a holy object*

مَسْح *n* **1** (Chr) المَسْح بالزَيْتِ المُقَدَّسِ anointing **2** (Med) مَسْح [بَحْث] scan; مَسْح الدِماغ a brain scan **3** مَسْح إِلِكْتروني مَيْداني fieldwork; field survey

مِسْح *n* |مُسوح| (monk's) habit

ماسِح *n* **1** (Tech) scanner; ماسِح ضَوْئيّ scanner **2** [مَسّاح] |ماسِحون, مُسّاح, مَسَحة| surveyor; ماسِح الأَرْضِ land surveyor **3** [الأَحْذِيةِ] |ماسِحون, مُسّاح, مَسَحة| shoeshine; ماسِح أَحْذِيةٍ shoeshine

مَسّاح *n* surveyor; مَسّاح الأَرْضِ land surveyor

مَسّاحة *n* **1** [للمَسْحِ] board duster **2** [زُجاجِ سَيّارةٍ] windscreen wiper (BrE), windshield wiper (AmE)

مِساحة *n* **1** [الأَراضي] surveying; مَعْلومات المِساحةِ cadastral data; مَكْتَب المِساحاتِ Land Registry (BrE), cadastre (AmE); خَريطة \ أَطْلَس المِساحةِ cadastral map/atlas **2** (Geom) surface; مِقْياس المِساحةِ square measure; مِساحة الكُرةِ الأَرْضيّةِ earth's surface; حَسَبَ مِساحة شَكْلٍ to calculate the (surface) area of a figure; غطّى مِساحةً كبيرةً to cover a lot of area; قِطْعة أَرْضٍ مِساحَتُها ٢٥ كيلومتْراً مُرَبَّعاً a piece of land with a surface area of 25 square kilometre

مَسْحة *n* |**مَسَحات**| ① (Med) smear (test); أَخَذَ مَسْحةً to take a smear test ② (fig) touch; مَسْحة شَخْصِيّة a personal touch; مَسْحة من الرومانسيّةِ a touch of romance ③ (Chr) المَسْحة الأخيرة the extreme unction; مَسْحة المَرْضى the last rites

مَسيح *n* |**مُسَحاءُ, مَسْحى**| messiah; المَسيح the Messiah (*Christ*); السَيِّد المَسيح the Lord Jesus; عيد ميلادِ المَسيحِ Christmas

مَسيحيّ **A** *adj* Christian; مَدْرَسة \ حِزْب \ اتِّحاد مَسيحيّ(ة) a Christian school/party/association

B *n* Christian

مَسيحيّة *n* Christianity; Christendom; اعْتَنَقَ المَسيحيّةَ to embrace Christianity

مِمْسَحة *n* |**مِمْسَحات, مَماسِحُ**| floorcloth; mop; مِمْسَحة زُجاج wiper

تِمْساح *n* listed alphabetically

مَسَخَ *v* |a; **مَسْخ**| ① [شَوَّهَ] to deform, to disfigure ② [حَوَّلَ] to transform, to metamorphose

مَسْخ *n* |**مُسوخ**| ① [تَحْريف] distortion; disfigurement ② [تَغْيير المَظْهَر] metamorphosis ③ [وَحْش] monstrosity; monster

مَسيخ *adj* ① [من الطَعامِ] insipid, tasteless ② [الشَكْل] deformed

مَسَّدَ *v* to massage; to stroke

مَسَد *n coll* |**إِمْساد, أَمْساد**| (palm) fibre; raffia; سورة المَسَد The Palm Fibre (*Sura 111*)

تَمْسيد *n* massage

مِسْرى *n* Mesra (*the twelfth month of the Coptic calendar*)

مَسَّ *v* |u; **مَسّ, مَسيس**| ① [لَمَسَ] to touch, to feel; مَسَّ يَدَ شَخْصٍ to touch sb's hand ② [خالَفَ] |ب| مَسَّ بِشَيْءٍ to harm sth ③ [كانَ ماسًّا] |إِلَيْهِ| مَسَّت الحاجّةُ إِلَيْهِ there was urgent need of it ④ [أَصابَ] to befall, to hit; مَسَّهُ المَرَضُ he became ill

ماسَّ *v* to touch, to brush; ماسَّ شَيْئاً to brush against sth

تَماسَّ *v* to touch each other; to be contiguous

ماسّ **A** *adj* urgent, pressing; حاجة ماسّة an urgent need; كانَ في حاجةٍ ماسّةٍ إلى شَيْءٍ to have an urgent need for sth; كانَت الرَغْبةُ فيهِ \ الحاجةُ إِلَيْهِ ماسّةً it/he was urgently wanted/needed

B *n* (Elec) ماسّ كَهْرَبائيّ short circuit

مَسّ *n* contact; touch; مَسّ الحُمّى attack of fever; أَصابَهُ مَسٌّ من الجُنونِ he's gone crazy

مَساس *n* لا مَساسَ لَهُ بالمَوْضوعِ that's got nothing to do with it

مِساس *n* touch; المِساس بالنِظامِ والأَمْنِ العامِّ breach of the peace

مَسيس *adj* كانَ في مَسيسِ الحاجةِ إلى ... to be in urgent need of ...

مُماسّ *n* (Math) tangent

مَمْسوس *adj* ① [مَلْموس] touched; tangible; غَيْر مَمْسوسٍ untouched ② [مَجْنون] insane

أَمَسّ *adj* |dipt| كانَ في أَمَسِّ الحاجةِ إلى شَيْءٍ to be in urgent need of sth

تَماسّ *n* contact; تَماسّ مُباشِر direct contact; خَطّ تَماسٍّ line of demarcation; نُقْطة تَماسٍّ point of contact; نُقْطة تَماسٍّ دائِرةٍ the point of tangency of a circle; كانَ على تَماسٍّ مع شَيْءٍ to be in contact with sth

مُسْطَرين *n* see سطر

مُصَقَّعة, مُسَقَّعة *n* moussaka (*a layered aubergine/eggplant casserole*)

مَسَكَ *v* |i-u; **مَسْك**| ① [قَبَضَ] to grasp, to grab, to clasp, to seize; مَسَكَ الحَبْلَ to grab the rope; مَسَكَ بِيَدِ شَخْصٍ to clasp sb's hand ② [اعْتَقَلَ] to catch ③ [أَشْرَفَ على] to supervise; مَسَكَ الحِساباتِ to keep the books; مَسَكَ الدَفاتِرَ to do the accounts

مَسَّكَ *v* to grasp, to grab

أَمْسَكَ *v* ① [قَبَضَ] to grasp, to grab, to clasp, to seize, to grip, to hold; أَمْسَكَ قَلَماً to grab a pen; أَمْسَكَ بِقَلَمٍ ووَرَقةٍ to get a pen and paper; أَمْسَكَ بِحَبْلٍ \ بِكِتابٍ to hold a rope/book; أَمْسَكَ شَخْصاً من يَدِهِ to take a person by the hand; أَمْسَكَ شَخْصاً من مِعْطَفِهِ to grab sb by his coat ② [مَنَعَ] |عن| to abstain, to refrain; to restrain; أَمْسَكَ المَريضُ عن الطَعامِ the patient refrained from eating ③ [كَفَّ] |عن| to cease, to stop; أَمْسَكَ عن العَمَلِ to cease work ④ (Med) أَمْسَكَ

البَطْن \ الأَمْعاء to cause constipation

تَمَسَّكَ *v* to adhere, to stick; to persist; تَمَسَّكَ بِمَبادِئِه \ مُعْتَقَداتِه \ آرائِه to stick to one's principles/convictions/opinions; تَمَسَّكَ بِغُصْنٍ to cling to a branch

تَماسَكَ *v* to bond, to hold together; to consolidate

اسْتَمْسَكَ *v* ① [ب| تَمَسَّكَ ب] to cling ② [عن| كَفَّ عن] to refrain

مَسْك *n* grip; مَسْك الدَفاتِرِ accounting, bookkeeping

مِسْك *n* musk; مِسْك الخِتامِ the perfect conclusion

ماسِك *adj* grasping

مُتَماسِك *adj* ① [مُتَرابِط] coherent, consistent, connected; قِصّة \ سِياسة مُتَماسِكة a coherent story/policy; غَيْر مُتَماسِكٍ inconsistent ② [صُلْب] solid

مُتَمَسِّك *adj* tenacious

مَسْكة *n* grip, handle

مُسْكة *n* |مُسَك| avarice, greed

مُمْسِك *adj* constipated

إِمْساك *n* ① (Med) constipation; إِمْساك مُزْمِن chronic constipation; أَثار الإِمْساكَ to cause constipation; عانى من الإِمْساكِ to suffer from constipation ② (Islam) *start of the fasting time*; مِدْفَع الإِمْساكِ *cannon shot indicating the start of the fasting time during Ramadan* ③ [امْتِناع] abstinence

إِمْساكيّة *n calendar indicating fasting and prayer times during Ramadan*

تَماسُك *n* ① [تَرابُط] coherence, consistency ② (Phys) cohesion; تَماسُك مَوادَّ the cohesion between substances

تَمَسُّك *n* ① [مَصْدَر] attachment; adherence ② (Busn) bond; IOU

مَسْكَرة *n* mascara

مِسْكين, تَمَسْكَنَ see سكن

مَسّى *v to wish (sb) a good evening*; مَسّاكَ اللهُ بالخَيْرِ good evening

أَمْسى *v to enter into evening; to spend the evening*

مَساء *n* |مَساءات, أَمْساء, أَمْسيّات| evening; مَساءً at night; مَساء السَبْتِ Saturday evening; مَساءَ الخَيْرِ good evening/afternoon; مَساءَ الأَمْسِ yesterday evening; مَساء الغَدِ tomorrow evening; مَساءَ اليَوْمِ tonight; حَلَّ المَساءُ the night descended; في المَساءِ during the evening

مَسائيّ *adj* evening (*before n*); دَوام مَسائيّ evening shift

أُمْسِيّة *n* |أَماسِيّ| evening; أُمْسِيّة إِعْلاميّة an information evening; أُمْسِيّة ثَقافيّة cultural evening

مَشيج *n* |أَمْشاج| gamete, germ cell

مَشَحَ *v* |a; مَشْح| *to administer extreme unction*

مَشَّ *v* |u; مَشّ| *to suck (marrow from) a bone*; مَشَّ عَظْما to suck marrow from a bone

مَشَطَ *v* |i-u; مَشْط| ① [الشَعْر] to comb ② [بَحَثَ] to comb, to search

مَشَّطَ *v* ① [الشَعْرَ] to comb ② [فَتَّشَ] to search, to comb; مَشَّطَ المِنْطَقة to comb the area

مُشْط *n* |أَمْشاط, مِشاط| ① [لِلشَعْر] comb; مُشْط دَقيق \ غَليظ a fine-tooth/wide-toothed comb ② (Mus) bridge ③ [الغَزْل] reed ④ [جَرّافة] rake ⑤ (Anat) مُشْط القَدَمِ metatarsus; instep

ماشِطة *n* |ماشِطات, مَواشِط| ① [حَلّاقة] hairdresser ② [قَيْنة] lady's maid ③ [مُغَنِّيّة] (female) singer

مِمْشَط *n* |مَماشِط| comb

تَمْشيط *n* ① [الشَعْر] combing ② [بَحْث] combing, searching

مَشَقَ *v* |u; مَشْق| to stretch

امْتَشَقَ *v* ① [خَطِفَ] to snatch ② [جَرَّدَ] to draw, to pull out

مَشْق *n* |أَمْشاق| ochre

مَمْشوق *adj* slender, slim; امْرَأة مَمْشوقة a slim woman

مِشْمِش *n* apricot

مَشى *v* |i; مَشْي| to go; to walk, to stroll; امْشِ! get away!; مَشى وراء شَخْصٍ to walk behind sb; مَشى مع شَخْصٍ مَسافةً to accompany sb part of the way

ماشى *v* ① [سايَرَ] to keep pace/up; لم يَسْتَطِعْ أَنْ يُماشِيَ شَخْصاً he was unable to keep up with sb ② [مَشى] to walk/go along

تَمَشّى *v* ① [مَشى] to walk, to stroll; to pace; تَمَشّى قَليلاً \ ساعةً to go for a short/an hour's walk; تَمَشّى في الشَوارِعِ to wander the streets ② [سايَرَ] to keep up/pace ③ [وافَقَ] to accord, to harmonize

تَماشى *v* ① [مع] to walk together ② [وافَقَ] to accord, to correspond, to agree, to harmonize; تَماشى مع شَيْءٍ to be proportionate to sth; تَماشى مع الوَقائِعِ to fit in with the

‹ **مَصَّ** *v* |a-u; مَصّ| to suck; to suck up; to suck out; مَصَّ شَيْئاً to suck sth; مَصَّ الإصْبَعَ to suck one's thumb; مَصَّ سُمَّ ثُعْبانٍ to suck out snake poison; مَصَّ مَصّاصةً to suck on a dummy (BrE) pacifier (AmE)

امْتَصَّ *v* to absorb, to soak up; to suck; امْتَصَّ الماءَ to absorb water; امْتَصَّ هواءً مَسْموماً to suction out toxic air; يَمْتَصُّ الإسْفَنْجُ الماءَ the sponge soaks up water

ماصّ *adj* absorbent

مَصّاص *n* bloodsucker; vampire; مَصّاص دِماءٍ vampire

مَصّاصة *n* **1** [حَلَمة من المَطاطِ] (rubber) teat (BrE), nipple (AmE); dummy (BrE), pacifier (AmE) **2** [حَلْوى] lollipop

مُمْتَصّ *adj* absorbent; مُمْتَصّ صَدَماتٍ shock absorber

مِمَصّ *n* |مِمَصّات| siphon, pipette

امْتِصاص *n* |امْتِصاصات| absorption; قابليّة الامْتِصاصِ absorbency

‹ **مِصْطَبة** *n* see مَسْطَبة

‹ **مُصْطَكاء**, **مُصْطَكّى**, **مَصْطَكّى** *n* mastic (*Pistacia lentiscus*); صَمْغ المُصْطَكاءِ mastic (*plant resin*)

‹ **مَصْع** *n* whiplash

‹ **مَصَلَ** *v* |u; مَصْل, مُصول| to curdle

مَصْل *n* |مُصول| serum; مَصْل الجُدَريّ smallpox vaccine

مَصالة, مُصالة *n* serum

‹ **مَصْمَصَ** *v* |مَصْمَصة| to suck up, to sip

‹ **مَضُرَ** *v* |u; مُضور| to sour

مُضَر *n* |dipt| Mudar (*Arab ancestor*); لُغة مُضَرَ Arabic

ماضِر *adj* sour

‹ **أَمَضَّ** *v* to hurt, to pain

مَضَض *n* pain, torment; على مَضَضٍ unwillingly, grudgingly; unwilling, reluctant

مُضاض *n* spindle tree (*Euonymus*)

‹ **مَضَغَ** *v* |a-u; مَضْغ| to chew; to gnaw; مَضَغَ طَعامَهُ to chew one's food

مَضْغ *n* chewing

مُضْغة *n* |مُضَغ| **1** [لُقْمة] bite, morsel; كانَ مُضْغةً في أَفْواهِ الناسِ he was on everyone's lips **2** [جَنين] embryo

facts; لم يَتَماشَ مع رَغْبة شَخْصٍ تَماشى to meet sb's wishes; لم يَتَماشَ مع السِياسةِ المُتَّبَعةِ to be inconsistent with the policy

مَشْي *n* walk; march; عَصا \ حِذاء المَشْيِ walking stick/shoe; رِياضة المَشْيِ hiking

ماشٍ **A** *adj* |مُشاة| [سائِر] walking; ماشِياً on foot **B** *n* |مُشاة| **1** [مارّ] pedestrian; مَمَرّ المُشاةِ pedestrian crossing; مَكان مُخَصَّص للمُشاةِ pedestrian zone **2** (Mil) infantryman; مُشاة infantry; مُشاة البَحْرِيّة marines

ماشي *excl* (colloq Egypt, Levant) OK, okay, fine

ماشِية *n* |مَواشٍ| cattle, stock; سوق الماشِيةِ cattle market; طاعون الماشِيةِ cattle plague, rinderpest; تَرْبِية الماشِية cattle breeding; مُرَبّي ماشِيةٍ stockbreeder; رَبّى الماشِيةَ to keep cattle; قِطاع تَرْبِيةِ الماشِيةِ stockbreeding; رَأْس من الماشِيةِ a head of cattle; تَرْعى الماشِيةُ في المَرْجِ the cattle are grazing in the pasture

مَشّاء *n* walker

مَشّاية *n* slipper, mule

مِشْية *n* walk, gait; سَرَّعَ \ أَبْطَأَ مِشْيَتَهُ to quicken/slow one's pace; تَعَرَّفَ على شَخْصٍ من مِشْيَتِهِ to recognize sb's walk

مُماشاة *n* keeping pace/up; keeping company

مَمْشى *n* |مَماشٍ| passage, corridor, passageway; alley

تَمَشٍّ *n* **1** [مَشْي] walk, stroll **2** [مُجاراة] conformity, harmony; تَمَشِّياً مع \ على in line with

تَمْشِية *n* walking; running; تَمْشِية الكِلابِ dog walking; تَمْشِية أُمورِه the running of one's affairs

‹ **مَصَّرَ** *v* to Egyptianize

تَمَصَّرَ *v to become an Egyptian*

مِصْر *n* |dipt f| **1** [البَلَد] Egypt; مِصْر القَديمة ancient Egypt; مِصْر الجَديدة Heliopolis (*district in Egypt*); جُمْهوريّة مِصْر العَرَبيّة Arab Republic of Egypt **2** [قُطْر] |أَمْصار| country; الأَمْصار الإسْلاميّة the Islamic countries

مُصْران *n* |مَصارينُ| gut; المُصْران الأَعْوَر blind gut, caecum; المُصْران الغَليظ the large intestine

مِصْريّ **A** *adj* Egyptian **B** *n* Egyptian (*person*)

مَصير *n* |مَصارينُ, مُصْران| **1** [مِعىً] intestine **2** [قَدَر] see صير

تَمْضِية *n* spending (*of time*); تَمْضِية الوَقْت pastime

أَمْطَر *v* 1 [السَماءُ] to rain; تُمْطِرُ السَماءُ it's pouring 2 [بِشَيْءٍ] to pelt, to bombard; أَمْطَرَ مَدينةً بالقَذائِفِ to bombard a city with missiles; أَمْطَرَ شَخْصاً بوابِلٍ من الشَتائِم to call sb everything under the sun; أَمْطَرَ شَخْصاً بالأَسْئِلَةِ to bombard sb with questions

اِسْتَمْطَر *v* to invoke; *to ask for rain*

مَطَر *n* |أَمْطار| rain; مَطَر مَحَلّيّ a local rain shower; مَطَر حَمْضيّ acid rain; مَطَر غَزير downpour; أَمْطار غَزيرة a heavy downpour; أَمْطار خَفيفة monsoon rains; أَمْطار مَوْسِمِيّة drizzle; سُقوط \ هُطول \ نُزول أَمْطار رَعْدِيّة thunderstorm; الأَمْطارِ rainfall; نَوْبات مَطَرٍ showers; مَوْسِم الأَمْطارِ rainy season; فَصْل الأَمْطارِ the rains; المَطَرُ مُنْعِشٌ the rain is refreshing; احْتِمال سُقوطِ الأَمْطارِ a chance of rain; غُيوم مُحَمَّلة بالأَمْطار storm clouds; في \ تحت المَطَرِ in/through the rain; يَتَناثَرُ المَطَرُ it's pouring; يَنْزِلُ \ يَسْقُطُ \ يَنْهَمِرُ المَطَرُ it's raining; تَتَساقَطُ الأَمْطارُ بِغَزارةٍ ,تَهْطِلُ الأَمْطارُ ≈ it's raining cats and dogs

ماطِر *adj* rainy

مَطْرة *n* (rain) shower

مَطَرة *n* water bottle

مَطَرِيّ *adj* pluvial (*relating to rain*)

مَطَرِيّة *n* (NA) umbrella

مَطير *adj* rainy, wet

مُمْطِر *adj* rainy, wet, showery; جَوّ مُمْطِر rainy weather; يَوْم مُمْطِر a wet day; يَوْم \ صَيْف غَيْر مُمْطِر a dry day/summer

مِمْطَر, مِمْطَرة *n* |مَماطِر| raincoat

مُطْران, مِطْران, مَطْران *n* |مَطارِنة| archbishop; bishop

مَطْرانِيّة *n* archbishopric; diocese

مَطَّ *v* |u; مَطّ| to stretch, to pull out

تَمَطَّط *v* to expand; to stretch; to be elastic

مَطّاط A *adj* rubber; قُماش مَطّاط an elastic material; قانون مَطّاط a law open to interpretation
B *n* rubber; مَطّاط اصْطِناعِيّ \ صِناعِيّ synthetic rubber; من المَطّاطِ rubber

مَضْمَض *v* |i; مَضْمَضة| to rinse the mouth

تَمَضْمَض *v* to rinse the mouth

مَضى *v* |i; مُضِيّ| 1 [انْقَضى] to pass, to elapse, to go by; to expire; يَمْضي الوَقْتُ بِسُرْعةٍ time flies; فيما مَضى in the past; لَقَدْ مَضى شَهْرٌ على الحادِثِ months ago; من شُهورٍ مَضَتْ a month has passed since the accident; أَكْثَر من أيِّ وَقْتٍ مَضى more than ever before 2 [اسْتَمَرَّ] to proceed; مَضى في الكَلامِ he continued talking 3 [غادَرَ] to leave; مَضى إلى حالِ سَبيلِهِ to go away 4 [شَرَعَ في] *to proceed to do sth*

مَضّى *v* to spend; مَضّى وَقْتَهُ في شَيْءٍ to spend one's time doing sth

أَمْضى *v* 1 [وَقَّعَ] to sign; to autograph; أَمْضى عَقْداً \ رِسالةً to sign a contract/letter 2 [قَضى الوَقْتَ] to spend; أَمْضى ما عَلَيْهِ (من السَجْن) to serve one's time (in prison) 3 [نَفَّذَ] to execute, to carry out; أَمْضى حُكْماً to carry out a sentence

مُضِيّ *n* 1 [انْقِضاء] lapse, passing; على مُضِيِّ الزَمانِ permanently 2 [ذَهاب] departure 3 [اسْتِمْرار] |في| continuation

ماضٍ A *adj* 1 [مُنْصَرِم] past, bygone; last; المَرّة الماضية last time; الأُسْبوع \ العام الماضي the past week/year; الأَعْوام \ الأَسابيع \ الأَيّام الماضِية the previous years/weeks/days; يَوْم الاثْنَيْنِ الماضي last Monday 2 [حادّ] sharp; acute
B *n* |مَواضٍ| 1 [عَكْس الحاضِرِ] past; ماضٍ مَجيد a glorious past; ماضي شَخْصٍ sb's past; الماضي المَرير the bitter past; اسْتِرْجاع \ اسْتِذْكار الماضي flashback; دَفَنَ الماضِيَ to bury the past; انْتمى إلى الماضي to belong to the past; يَعيشُ في الماضي he lives in the past; طَوى (صَفْحة) الماضي to turn over a new leaf; في الماضي in the past; في الماضي القَريب in the recent past; في \ من الماضي البَعيدِ \ السَحيقِ in/from the distant past; الماضي والحاضِر past and present 2 (Gram) perfect; past; الماضي التامّ the past perfect; صيغة الماضي the past tense

مَضاء *n* sharpness, acuteness; vigorousness

إِمْضاء *n* 1 [تَوْقيع] signature; signing; وَضَعَ إِمْضاءَهُ على شَيْءٍ to put one's signature on sth 2 [مَصْدَر] spending (*of time*); إِمْضاء الوَقْتِ spending time

‹ **مَعْجَن** *v* see عجن

‹ **مَعِدة, مِعْدة** *n* |مِعَد| stomach; مَعِدة خاوِية an empty stomach; عَضَلة المَعِدة stomach muscle; مِنْطَقة المَعِدةِ gastric region; الْتِهاب المَعِدة gastritis; عانى من الْتِهابِ المَعِدةِ to suffer from gastritis; قَرْحة في المَعِدةِ stomach ulcer; حُموضة في المَعِدةِ acidity (of the stomach); حُرْقة وَحُموضة في المَعِدةِ heartburn

مِعْدة *n* stomach

مَعِديّ *adj* gastric; *relating to the stomach*; قَرْحة مَعِديّة stomach ulcer

‹ **مَعْز, مَعَز** *n coll* |مَعيز, أَمْعُز| goat

ماعِز *n* |مَواعِزُ| goat; راعي الماعِزِ goatherd; قَطيع من الماعِزِ a herd of goats

مِعْزاة *n* nanny goat

‹ **مَعِص** *v* |a; مَعَص, مَعْص| to have cramp

‹ **امْتَعَض** *v* to be/become angry/annoyed; امْتَعَض من شَيْءٍ to be annoyed at sth

مُمْتَعِض *adj* angry, annoyed, irritated; resentful

امْتِعاض *n* |امْتِعاضات| irritation; indignation; resentment; بِامْتِعاضٍ unwilling

‹ **مَعَط** *v* |a; مَعْط| to pull out

‹ **مَعَك** *v* |a; مَعْك| to rub

‹ **مَعْكَرونة, مَكَرونة** *n* macaroni; pasta

‹ **مَعْمَعة** *n* |مَعامِعُ| tumult, commotion

‹ **أَمْعَنَ** *v* to overdo; to scrutinize; to dwell; أَمْعَنَ التَّفْكيرَ to ponder; أَمْعَنَ النَّظَرَ في شَيْءٍ to scrutinize sth

تَمَعَّنَ *v* to scrutinize; to think through; تَمَعَّنَ في شَيْءٍ to examine sth carefully

ماعون *n* |مَواعينُ| utensil, implement; سورة الماعون The Small Kindnesses (*Sura 107*)

مَعان *n* |f| Ma'an (*city in Jordan*)

مَعين *n* spring, source

إِمْعان *n* **1** [جِدّ] devotion, attentiveness; قَرَأَ شَيْئاً بِإِمْعانٍ to read sth thoroughly/with full attention **2** [إِفْراط] excessiveness; إِمْعان في السرّيّة \ الدقّة utmost secrecy/precision

تَمَعُّن *n* |تَمَعُّنات| *close examination*; هذا بِحاجةٍ إلى تَمَعُّنٍ that needs careful consideration

مَطّاطيّ *adj* rubber (*of rubber*); elastic; إطارات \ رَصاص مَطّاطيّ(ة) rubber bullets/tires; رِباط مَطّاطيّ rubber band

تَمَطُّط *n* elasticity; flexibility

‹ **تَمَطَّق** *v* to taste; *to smack one's lips*

‹ **مَطَلَ** *v* |u; مَطْل| to stretch

ماطَلَ *v* to procrastinate, to delay

مُماطِل **A** *adj* delaying
B *n* procrastinator

مُماطَلة *n* delay, postponement; procrastination; hesitation

تَماطُل *n* procrastinating

‹ **مَطا** *v* |u; مَطْو| *to quicken one's step*

أَمْطى *v* to ride (*an animal*)

تَمَطّى *v* to stretch; تَمَطّى في مِشْيَتِهِ to strut

امْتَطى *v* **1** [مَطِيّةً] to ride; امْتَطى حِصاناً to ride a horse **2** [وَسيلة نَقْلٍ] to board; to get in; امْتَطى السَّيّارةَ to get in the car

مَطِيّة *n* |مَطايا, مَطِيّ| mount

‹ **مَعَ** *prep* **1** [مُصاحَبة] with; مَعاً together; إِنَّهُمْ يَعْمَلونَ مَعاً من أَجْلِ أَهْدافٍ مُشْتَرَكةٍ they work together towards common goals; كانَ الشَّيْءُ مَعَهُ he had it at hand; كانَ يُسافِرُ مَعَ صَديقَتِهِ he travelled together with his friend; لَيْسَ مَعَنا مالٌ we have no money with us; لو أَنَّهُ كانَ مَعَنا اليَوْمَ if only he could be with us today **2** [بالرَّغْمِ من] in spite of, despite; مَعَ هَذا \ ذَلِكَ in spite of this; مَعَ كُلِّ هذا for all this; مَعَ كَوْنِهِ مَأْخوذاً من نَصٍّ آخَرَ despite the fact that it has been taken from another text **3** [وَقْت] مَعَ الفَجْرِ at dawn; في آنٍ مَعاً at the same time **4** [بِمُحاذاةِ شَيْءٍ] مَعَ الحائِطِ along the wall **5** [مُعامَلة] كانَ لَطيفاً مَعَها he was good to her **6** [تَعْبير عن إِحْساساتٍ] مَعَ تَحِيّاتي المُخْلِصةِ with my sincere greetings; مَعَ خالِصِ الشُّكْرِ with sincere thanks **7** [مُوافَقة] هل هو مَعَ قَرارِ الوَزيرِ أو ضِدَّهُ؟ is he for or against the minister's decision?; مَنْ ليس مَعي فَهُوَ ضِدّي whoever is not with me, is against me **8** [مَعَ أَنَّ] مَعَ أَنَّهُ كانَ قَدْ سَأَلَني مَرّاتٍ كَثيرةً although he had asked me several times

مَعِيّة *n* entourage; company

‹ **تَمَعَّجَ** *v* to wind, to twine

‹ **مَعا** *v* |u; مُعاء| to miaow

‹ **مِعَوِيّ** *adj relating to the intestines*; الْتِهاب مِعَوِيّ enteritis; حُمّى مِعَوِيّة enteric fever; عانى من مَغَصٍ مِعَوِيٍّ to have an upset stomach

مِعًى, مِعْي *n* |أَمْعاء, أَمْعِية| intestine; المِعى المُسْتَقيم rectum; المِعى الدَقيق \ الغَليظ the small/large intestine; المِعى الأَعْوَر blind gut; المِعى الاثْنا عَشَرِيّ duodenum

‹ **مَغْد** *n* nightshade (*Solanum*)

‹ **مُغْرة** *n* ochre

‹ **مَغْرَبَ** *v* see **غرب**

‹ **مَغْص, مَغَص** *n* |أَمْغاص| colic; stomach cramp

مَمْغوص *adj* كانَ مَمْغوصاً to suffer from a stomach cramp

‹ **تَمَغَّطَ** *v* to stretch; to be expanded

مُتَمَغِّط *adj* elastic, stretchy

تَمَغُّط *n* elasticity, stretchiness

‹ **مُغْنة, مُغْنى** *n* خَشَب المُغْنة mahogany

‹ **مَغْنِيسيوم** *n* magnesium

‹ **مَغْنَطَ** *v* |i; مَغْنَطة| to magnetize

‹ **مَغْنِطْرون** *n* magnetron

‹ **مَغْنَطيس, مَغْناطيس, مِغْنَطيس** *n* magnet; مَغْنَطيس كَهْرَبائيّ electromagnet; مَغْنَطيس قَوِيّ a strong magnet

مَغْنَطيسيّ, مَغْناطيسيّ *adj* magnetic; طاقة \ قوّة مَغْنَطيسيّة magnetic energy/force; حَقْل مَغْنَطيسيّ a magnetic field

مَغْنَطيسيّة, مَغناطيسيّة, مِغْنَطيسيّة *n* magnetism

‹ **مَغْنولِيا** *n* magnolia (*Magnolia*)

‹ **مُغوليّ, مُنْغوليّ** **A** *adj* |مُغول| Mongolian, Mongol; (اللُغة) المُغوليّة Mongolian, Mongol (*language*); غَزْو مُغوليّ a brutal attack

B *n* |مُغول| Mongolian, Mongol (*person*)

المُغول *n* the Mongols; the Moguls; بِلاد المُغول Mongolia

‹ **مَقَتَ** *v* |u; مَقْت| to detest, to loathe, to hate; مَقَتَ شَخْصاً to hate sb

مَقْت *n* abhorrence, loathing, hatred

مَقيت *adj* |مُقَتاءُ| repulsive, loathsome; شَخْص مَقيت a repulsive person

‹ **مَقْدونِس, بَقْدونِس** *n* parsley; مَقْدونِس إِفْرَنْجيّ chervil (*Anthriscus cerefolium*)

‹ **مَقْدونِيا** *n* Macedonia

‹ **مَقْديشو** *n* |f| Mogadishu

‹ **مَقَرَ** *v* |u; مَقْر| to marinate

مَقِر *n* aloe

امْتَقَعَ *v* اُمْتُقِعَ to turn pale

مُمْتَقَع *adj* pale

‹ **مُقْلة** *n* |مُقَل| eye, eyeball; مُقْلة العَيْنِ eyeball

‹ **مُقامِق** *n* ventriloquist

‹ **مَكَثَ** *v* |u; مُكْث, مُكوث| to remain, to stay, to live; مَكَثَ مع شَخْصٍ طَوِيلاً to stay for long with sb

مُكوث *n* stay

‹ **مَكَرَ** *v* |u; مَكْر| to deceive, to cheat; مَكَرَ بِشَخْصٍ to deceive sb

ماكَرَ *v* to deceive

مَكْر *n* cunning, slyness; deception; بالمَكْرِ والخِداعِ by tricks and devices; بِمَكْرٍ by devious means

ماكِر **A** *adj* |مَكَرة| sly, cunning, crafty, wily; artful, guileful; ضَحْكة ماكِرة a sly grin; خُطّة ماكِرة a cunning plan; بِشَكْلٍ ماكِرٍ sneaky

B *n* |مَكَرة| sly person

مَكّار **A** *adj* sly, cunning, crafty, wily

B *n* sly person

‹ **مِكْروب** *n* see ميكْروب

‹ **مِكْروباص** *n* minibus

مَكْرونة *n* see مَعكَرون

‹ **مَكَسَ** *v* |i; مَكْس| *to collect taxes/tolls*

ماكَسَ *v* to bargain, to haggle

مَكْس *n* |مُكوس| toll; tax

‹ **مَكْسيكيّ** **A** *adj* Mexican

B *n* Mexican (*person*)

المَكْسيك *n* |f| Mexico

‹ **مَكّة** *n* |dipt| Mecca; مَكّة المُكَرَّمة (sacred) Mecca

مَكّوك *n* |مَكاكيكُ| ❶ (*Aerosp*) مَكّوك فَضائيّ (space) shuttle; أَطْلَقَ مَكّوكاً فَضائيًّا to launch a space shuttle ❷ [بَكَرة] bobbin

مَكّوكيّ *adj* shuttle (*diplomacy, bus*)

مَكّيّ *adj* Meccan; سورة مَكّيّة *Sura of the Koran revealed in Mecca*

‹ **مَكُنَ** *v* |u; مَكانة| to be/become strong

مَكَّنَ *v* [1] [قَدَّرَ على] to enable; مَكَّنَ شَخصاً من شَيْءٍ to provide sb with sth; مَكَّنَ شَخصاً من أنْ ... to enable sb to ... [2] [ثَبَّتَ] to strengthen, to consolidate

أَمْكَنَ *v* [1] [كانَ مُمْكِناً] to be possible/feasible; يُمْكِنُهُ أنْ يَفْعَلَ ذلك he can do that; لا يُمْكِنُهُ أنْ ... it is not possible to ...; يُمْكِنُ القَوْلُ إنَّ ... it may be said that ...; أَكْثَر ما يُمْكِنُ as much as possible [2] [جَعَلَ قادِراً] to enable; أَمْكَنَ شَخْصاً من شَيْءٍ to enable sb to do sth

تَمَكَّنَ *v* [1] [اِسْتَطاعَ] |من| to be able/capable; تَمَكَّنَ من شَيْءٍ to be in a position to do sth [2] [حَكَمَ] |من| to have/gain power; to seize

اِسْتَمْكَنَ *v* to be able/capable; اِسْتَمْكَنَ من شَيْءٍ to be able to do sth

مُتَمَكِّن *adj* [1] [راسِخ] expert; skilled, adept; كانَ مُتَمَكِّناً من شَيْءٍ to be adept at sth [2] (*Gram*) declinable; غَيْر مُتَمَكِّنٍ indeclinable

مُكْنة *n* power; capacity; لَيْسَ في مُكْنَتِهِ أنْ ... he is unable to ...

مَكْنَنَ *v* listed alphabetically

مَكين *adj* |مُكَناءُ| strong, solid

مُمْكِن *adj* possible, feasible, viable; من المُمْكِنِ أنْ ... it is possible that ...; غَيْر مُمْكِنٍ impossible; هذا غَيْرُ مُمْكِنٍ it's impossible

مُمْكِنات *n pl* possibilities

إمْكان *n* |إمْكانات| [1] [اِحْتِمال] possibility; عَدَم الإمْكانِ impossibility; كانَ بالإمْكانِ أنْ ... it was possible to ...; عند الإمْكانِ if possible; ب \ على قَدْرِ الإمْكانِ as much as possible [2] [قُدْرة] ability; كانَ في إمْكانِهِ (أنْ يَفْعَلَ شَيْئاً) he was able (to do sth); لَيْسَ في إمْكاني أنْ ... it's not in my power to ...

إمْكانيّة *n* |إمْكانات, إمْكانيّات| [1] [اِحْتِمال] possibility, chance, likelihood, probability; إمْكانيّة كَبيرة a big chance; وَفَّرَ الإمْكانيّاتِ لِشَيْءٍ to create opportunities for sth [2] [فُرْصة] opportunity, chance; إمْكانيّات مُسْتَقْبَليّة prospects; تَوْسيع الإمْكانيّاتِ a broadening of the possibilities; وَفَّرَ \ أَتاحَ إمْكانيّةً to offer a chance

تَمَكُّن *n* [1] [قُدْرة] ability, capacity [2] [سَيْطَرة] control; mastery

تَمْكين *n* strengthening, consolidation

تَمْكينيّ *adj* enabling; بيئة تَمْكينيّة enabling environment

‹ **مَكْناس** *n* |dipt f| Meknès (*city in Morocco*)

‹ **مَكْنَنَ** *v* |i; مَكْنَنة| to mechanize; مَكْنَنَ الزِراعةَ to mechanize agriculture

مَكْنَنة *n* mechanization

‹ **مَكْيَجَ** *v* |i; مَكْيَجة| to make up (*one's face*)

ماكْياج, ماكِياج, مَكْياج, مَكِياج *n* make-up, cosmetics; greasepaint; وَضَعَ المَكِياجَ to put on make-up; اِسْتَعْمَلَ المَكِياجَ to use make-up; طَلَى شَخْصاً بالمَكِياجِ to slather make-up on sb; طَلَى وَجْهَهُ بالمَكِياجِ to slather on make-up; حَقيبة المَكِياج cosmetic bag, beauty case

‹ **مَلَأَ** *v* |u; مَلْء, مَلْأة, مِلْأة| to fill (up); to fill out; مَلَأَ اسْتِمارةً to fill out a form; مَلَأَ ساعةً to wind a clock; مَلَأَ فَراغاً to fill a gap; مَلَأَ المَخْزونَ to replenish stocks; مَلَأَ الكُؤوسَ to fill the glasses; مَلَأَ كَأْساً بالنَبيذِ to fill up a glass with wine; مَلَأَ خَزينةً بالبِنْزينِ to fill up a tank with petrol (BrE) gas (AmE); مَلَأَ شَخْصاً بالفَرَحِ \ الحُبِّ to fill sb with joy/love; مَلَأَ شَخْصاً رُعْباً to frighten sb

مالَأَ *v* to support; to help

أَمْلَأَ *v* to fill up/in

تَمَلَّأَ *v* to be full (of), to be filled (with); تَمَلَّأَ غَيْظًا to be filled with anger

اِمْتَلَأَ *v* to fill, to become full; to be filled; اِمْتَلَأَ بِشَيْءٍ to be filled with sth

مَلْء *n* filling

مَلَأ *n* |أَمْلاء| [1] [جُمْهور] crowd; audience; على المَلَأِ in public [2] [أَشْراف] notables; council of elders

مِلْء *n* |أَمْلاء| content; مِلْء اليَدِ handful; صَوْت مِلْؤُهُ الشَفَقةُ a voice full of compassion

مَلاءة *n* solvency

مُلاءة *n* sheet; مُلاءات linen, bedding

مَلْآن *adj* |مِلاء| f pl |مَلْأَنة ,مَلْأى| fat, plump, stout

مَلِيء *adj* **1** [مُمْتَلِئ] full, filled; fat; كَأْس مَلِيئة a full glass; قاعة مَلِيء بالناسِ a full house; حافِظة نُقودٍ مَلِيئة a fat purse; مَلِيئة full of people; مَلِيء بالأَوْراقِ \ الأَفْكارِ full of paper/ideas; مَلِيء بالسَعادةِ \ الأَمَلِ \ الرَغْبةِ filled with joy/hope/longing; حَقيبة مَلِيئة بالهَدايا a bag full of gifts; سَتكونُ الأَشْهُرُ المُقْبِلةُ مَلِيئةً بالمُفاجَآتِ the coming months will be full of surprises **2** (Busn) solvent

مُمالِئ **A** *adj* partial, biased **B** *n* supporter; collaborator

مُمالأة *n* partiality; collaboration

مُمْتَلِئ *adj* full, filled; مَعِدة مُمْتَلِئة a full stomach; رَجُل مُمْتَلِئ a plump man; مُمْتَلِئ الجِسْمِ plump, stocky; نِصْف مُمْتَلِئ half-full; مُمْتَلِئ للرَأْسِ full to the brim

مَمْلوء *adj* filled; غَيْر مَمْلوءٍ blank, empty; اسْتِمارة غَيْر مَمْلوءةٍ a blank form

امْتِلاء *n* fullness, repletion; امْتِلاء الجِسْمِ corpulence, plumpness

‹ **مَلاريا** *n* malaria; بَعوضة المَلاريا malaria mosquito

‹ **مَلايو** *n* لُغة المَلايو Malay, Malayan (*language*)

مَلايُويّ *adj* Malay, Malayan; (اللُغة) المَلايُويّة Malay, Malayan (*language*)

‹ **مالَج** *n* |مَوالِجُ| trowel

‹ **مَلُحَ** *v* |u| **1** |مَلاحة ,مُلوحة| [صارَ مِلحاً] to be/become salty **2** |مَلاحة| [حَسُنَ مَنْظَرُهُ] to be handsome

مَلَّحَ *v* to salt; to pickle

أَمْلَحَ *v* to be salty

مِلْح *n* |mf| |مِلاح ,أَمْلاح| salt; مِلْح بَحْرِيّ sea salt; أَمْلاح مَعْدِنيّة mineral salts; أَضافَ مِلْحاً إلى الطَعامِ to season the food with salt; بِدونِ مِلْحٍ salt-free; حِمْية بِدونِ مِلْحٍ a salt-free diet; المِلْح والفُلْفُل salt and pepper

مالِح *adj* salt, salty; ماء مالِح salt water; marinade; مَوالِح savoury snacks

مالِحة *n* |مَوالِحُ| مَوالِح citrus fruit

مَلّاح *n* **1** [رُبّان] sailor, seaman; مَلّاح فَضائيّ astronaut; مَلّاح جَوّيّ pilot; مَلّاحون seamen **2** [حَيّ اليَهودِ] (Morocco) Jewish quarter

مَلاحة *n* **1** [حُسْن] beauty; kindness **2** [مُلوحة] saltiness **3** [مَخْزَن المِلْحِ] salt mine

مِلاحة *n* navigation; shipping; مِلاحة ساحِلِيّة coastal navigation; مِلاحة تِجارِيّة merchant navy; مِلاحة داخِلِيّة inland navigation; مِلاحة نَهْرِيّة river traffic; مِلاحة جَوّيّة aviation; مِلاحة فَضائيّة astronautics; مِلاحة بَحْرِيّة دُوَلِيّة international shipping; شَرِكة مِلاحةٍ shipping company; قِطاع المِلاحةِ the maritime industry; خطّ المِلاحةِ the course (of navigation); صالِح للمِلاحةِ navigable

مِلاحيّ *adj* nautical; آلة مِلاحيّة a nautical instrument

مُلْحة *n* |مُلَح| anecdote; joke

مِلْحيّ *adj* salt, salty

مُلوحة *n* saltiness; salinity

مَليح *adj* |مِلاح ,أَمْلاح| pretty, handsome; nice; فَتاة مَليحة a pretty girl

مُمَلَّح *adj* salted; cured

مَمْلَحة *n* |مَمالِحُ| salt mine; salt pan

مِمْلَحة *n* |مَمالِحُ| salt cellar

تَمَلُّح *n* salinization

‹ **مُلوخيّة** *n* Jew's mallow (*Corchorus olitorius*); mulukhiyya (*the leaves of Jew's mallow, used as a vegetable, or a thick green stew made with meat and dried or chopped mulukhiyya leaves*)

مَليخ *adj* tasteless

‹ **أَمْلَد** *adj* |dipt| tender

‹ **مَلَّسَ** *v* **1** [جَعَلَهُ أَمْلَسَ] to smooth, to polish **2** [الأَرْضَ] to level (*the ground*)

مَلاسة *n* smoothness; مَلاسة العاجِ the smooth texture of ivory

أَمْلَس *adj* |dipt| |مُلْس| smooth, sleek

‹ **تَمَلَّصَ** *v* |مِن| to avoid, to evade, to dodge; تَمَلَّصَ من مَسْؤوليَّتِهِ to back out of one's responsibility; تَمَلَّصَ من حُكْمٍ to escape the execution of a sentence

مَلِص *adj* smooth

مَليص A *adj* slippery

B *n* |مَلْصى ,مِلاص| [وُلِدَ مَيِّتاً] stillborn baby

تَمَلُّص *n* evasion, elusion

مَلَطَ *v* |u; مَلْط| *to shave off hair*

مَلَّطَ *v* to plaster; مَلَّطَ حائِطاً to plaster a wall

مِلْط *n* |أَمْلاط| rogue

مِلاط *n* |مُلُط| 1 [الأَسْنانِ] cement 2 [طين] mortar, cement

مَلِقَ *v* |a; مَلَق| to flatter

أَمْلَقَ *v* to be reduced to poverty, to be very poor

تَمَلَّقَ *v* to flatter, to sweet-talk, to butter up; تَمَلَّقَ شَخْصاً to flatter sb

مُتَمَلَّق *adj* flattered

مُتَمَلِّق A *adj* smarmy, unctuous

B *n* toady, bootlicker; wheedler

مُمالِق *adj* sycophantic; flattering, smooth

مِمْلَق *n* planer

إِمْلاق *n* poverty

تَمَلُّق *n* |تَمَلُّقات| flattery

مَلَكَ *v* |i; مَلْك ,مُلْك ,مِلْك ,إِمْلاك| 1 [حازَ] to own, to possess; مَلَكَ مالاً to have money; مَلَكَ مالاً كَثيراً to have plenty of money; ما مَلَكَتْ يَمينُهُ one's possessions 2 [سَيْطَرَ] to rule, to reign; مَلَكَ نَفْسَهُ to control oneself; مَلَكَ زِمامَ الأُمور to be pulling the strings 3 [تَمَكَّنَ] to be able

مَلَّكَ *v to transfer ownership; to make the owner*

أَمْلَكَ *v* 1 [جَعَلَ الشَيْءَ مِلْكًا ل] to make the owner of 2 [مَلَّكَ] to make king

تَمَلَّكَ *v* to own, to possess; to appropriate; تَمَلَّكَهُ الخَوْفُ he was seized with fear

تَمالَكَ *v* to restrain, to check; تَمالَكَ أَعْصابَهُ to check one's nerves; تَمالَكَ نَفْسَهُ to restrain oneself; لم يَتَمالَكْ نَفْسَهُ to lose control of oneself

امْتَلَكَ *v* to own, to possess; امْتَلَكَ بَيْتاً to own a house; امْتَلَكَ مَوْهِبةً \ ميزةً to have a gift/quality

اسْتَمْلَكَ *v* to appropriate; to control

مَلَك *n* see مَلاك

مَلِك *n* |مُلوك ,أَمْلاك| 1 [عاهِل] king, sovereign, monarch; مَلِكُ الحَيَواناتِ the king of beasts; نائِب المَلِكِ viceroy; داء المُلوكِ gout; جَلالة المَلِك(ة) Majesty; عاشَ مِثْلَ المَلِكِ to live like a king 2 [في الشَطْرَنْج] king *(in chess)*

مُلْك *n* 1 [مُمْتَلَكات] right of ownership; possession; أَنا مُلْكُ يَدَيْكَ I'm at your disposal 2 [سُلْطة] kingship; rule, power; صاحِب المُلْكِ God 3 (Islam) سورة المُلْك The Sovereignty (*Sura 67*); مالِك المُلْك the Owner of Sovereignty (*one of the names of God*)

مِلْك *n* |أَمْلاك| 1 [ما يَمْلِكُهُ الإِنْسانُ] property, possession; أَمْلاك goods; مِلْك ثَمين a precious possession; أَمْلاك أَميريّة crown property; أَمْلاك الحُكومةِ state property; ضَريبة الأَمْلاك property tax; بَيْت مِلْك owner-occupied property; في مِلْك الدَوْلةِ in public ownership 2 (Isl Law) *private property*

مالِك *n* |مُلّاك ,مُلَّك| 1 [صاحِب] owner, possessor, holder; المالِك الشَرْعيّ the rightful owner 2 [اسْم شَخْصيّ] Malik (*male given name*) 3 (Islam) مالِك المُلْك the Owner of Sovereignty (*one of the names of God*)

مالِكة *n* |dipt| Malika (*female given name*)

مالِكيّ A *adj* Maliki; المَذْهَب المالِكيّ the Maliki school (*one of the four major schools of jurisprudence in Sunni Islam*)

B *n* Maliki

مالِكيّة *n* (Isl Law) *the Maliki school of jurisprudence*

مَلائِكيّ *adj* angelic

مَلاك *n* |مَلائِكة| 1 [روح سَماويّة] angel; المَلاك جِبْريل the angel Gabriel; المَلاك الحارِس ,مَلاك الصِيانةِ guardian angel 2 [إِنْسان] angel, dear; أَطْفال كالمَلائِكةِ angelic children

مَلّاك *n* owner, possessor

مَلّاكيّ *adj* private

مَلَكة *n* gift, talent, aptitude; مَلَكة لُغَويّة linguistic talent

مَلِكة *n* 1 [رَئيسة الدَوْلةِ أو زَوْجة المَلِكِ] queen, monarch; مَلِكة جَمالٍ a beauty queen; زَوْج المَلِكةِ the prince consort 2 (Zool) queen; مَلِكة النَحْلِ the queen bee 3 [في لُعْبة الشِطْرَنْج] queen

مَلَكوت *n* realm, kingdom; مَلَكوت السَماواتِ the kingdom of heaven

B *n* |مَماليكُ| slave; Mameluke (*a member of a regime descended from Turkish, Mongol, and Circassian slaves which ruled Syria and Egypt*)

مَمْلوكيّ *adj* Mameluke

اسْتِمْلاك *n* |اسْتِمْلاكات| appropriation; expropriation

امْتِلاك *n* |امْتِلاكات| possession; امْتِلاك مَنْزِلٍ \ مَنازِلَ home ownership

تَمَلُّك *n* possession; التَمَلُّك بالتَأْجير leasing

تَمْليك *n* conveyance/transfer of property; بَيْت تَمْليكٍ owner-occupied property

مَلّ ¹ *v* |a; مَلالة, مَلال, مَلَل| to be/become bored; to be/become weary; مَلَّ شَيْئاً to be fed up with sth

أَمَلّ *v* to bore; to annoy

تَمَلَّل *v* **1** [مَلّ] to be bored; to fidget **2** [اعْتَنَق] to embrace a religion

امْتَلّ *v* to embrace (*a religion*)

مَلالة *n* boredom; tedium

مِلّة *n* |مِلَل| religion, faith; sect

مَلَل *n* boredom; weariness; dullness; شَعَرَ بالمَلَلِ to feel bored; عَمِلَ بدونِ كَلَلٍ وَلا مَلَلٍ to work with unflagging zeal

مَلول *adj* bored, fed up

مَليلية *n* listed alphabetically

مُمِلّ *adj* boring, tedious, dull, monotonous; فيلم \ مُحاضرة مُمِلّ(ة) a boring film/lecture; عَمل مُمِلّ monotonous work; كِتاب مُمِلّ a dull book; شَخص مُمِلّ a dull person

مُلاّ ² *n* mullah

مِلّيم *n* listed alphabetically

مَلْمَلَ *v* |i; مَلْمَلة| to hurry, to hasten

تَمَلْمَلَ *v* to be restless; to fidget

مُتَمَلْمِل *n* fidget

مَلْمَلة *n* unrest, restlessness

تَمَلْمُل *n* restlessness

أَمْلى *v* to dictate

تَمَلّى *v* to enjoy

مَلْوة *n a dry measure, approx. 4 l*

مَلَكوتيّ *adj* heavenly, divine

مَلَكيّ *adj* royal, regal, kingly; اسْتِقْبال مَلَكيّ a royal welcome; الحِزْب المَلَكيّ the royalist party; القَصْر المَلَكيّ the royal palace; العائِلة المَلَكيّة the royal family; زِيارة مَلَكيّة a royal visit; اسْتَقْبَلَ شَخْصاً اسْتِقْبالاً مَلَكيًّا to give sb a royal welcome; القوّات الجَوّيّة \ البَحْريّة المَلَكيّة the royal air force/navy

مِلْكيّ *adj* proprietary

مَلَكيّة *n* monarchy, kingship; مَلَكيّة مُطْلَقة an absolute monarchy; المَلَكيّة الدُسْتوريّة \ الحَديثة the constitutional/modern monarchy

مِلْكيّة *n* property, possession; ownership; مِلْكيّة خاصّة private property; مِلْكيّة مُشْتَرَكة joint ownership; مِلْكيّة فِكْريّة intellectual property; حَقّ المِلْكيّةِ the right of ownership; حَقّ المِلْكيّةِ الفِكْريّةِ the intellectual right of ownership; مُسْتَنَد \ سَنَد \ صَكّ \ عَقْد مِلْكيّةٍ title deed; نَقْل المِلْكيّةِ property transfer; عَقْد نَقْل المِلْكيّة property transfer contract; نَقَلَ المِلْكيّةَ (التامّة) إلى ... to transfer the (full) ownership to ...; نَزْع مِلْكيّةٍ expropriation; نَزْع المِلْكيّةِ الأَرْضِ \ المَساكِنِ the expropriation of land/houses

مُلوكيّ *adj* royal, monarchic; عُرْس مُلوكيّ royal wedding

مُلوكيّة *n* royalty, monarchy

مَليك *n* |مُلَكاءُ| **1** [عاهِل] king **2** [مالِك] owner

مُمْتَلَك **A** *adj* owned

B *n* |مُمْتَلَكات| property, possession, belongings; مُمْتَلَكات شَخْصيّة \ فَرْديّة personal possessions; مُمْتَلَكات عَقاريّة real property; مُمْتَلَكات مَنْقولة \ ثابتة movable/immovable property; مُمْتَلَكات الدَوْلةِ state property

مُمْتَلِك *n* owner

مَمْلَكة *n* |مَمالِكُ| kingdom; المَمْلَكة المَغْرِبيّة the Kingdom of Morocco; المَمْلَكة المُتّحِدة the United Kingdom; المَمْلَكة الهولَنْديّة the Kingdom of the Netherlands; مَمْلَكة الحَيَواناتِ the animal kingdom

مَمْلوك **A** *adj* owned; كانَ مَمْلوكاً to be owned; كانَ مَمْلوكاً لِعائِلةٍ to be owned by a family; صِناعات مَمْلوكة للدَوْلةِ state-owned industries

مِنْ *prep* 1 [اِبْتداءً مِنْ مَكانٍ] from, off; (out) of; مِنْ دِمَشْقَ إلى بَيْروتَ from Damascus to Beirut; إلى الجَنوبِ مِن العاصِمةِ south of the capital; أَخَذَ المِخَدّةَ مِنْ على الكُرْسيِّ he took the cushion off the chair 2 [اِبْتِداءً مِنْ زَمانٍ] (as) from; مِن السّاعةِ العاشِرةِ إلى الخامِسةِ from ten o'clock till five o'clock; مِنْ أَوَّلِ يَنايِرَ from 1 January; مِنْ يَوْمِهِ on the (very) same day; مِنْ ساعَتِهِ at that moment; مِنْ شَهْرٍ since one month (ago); مِنْ زَمانٍ from way back, of old 3 [مادّة] of; مِن الخَشَبِ (made) of wood, wooden; بَيْت \ طاوِلة مِن الخَشَبِ a wooden house/table 4 [بِسَبَب] of, with; تَجَمَّدَ مِن البَرْدِ to freeze with cold; كادَتْ أَنْ تُجَنَّ مِنْ شِدّةِ الفَرَحِ she almost went crazy with joy 5 [عَبْرَ] out (of), from; نَظَرَ مِن النافِذةِ to look out (of) the window 6 [تَبْعيض] of, among; قَدَح مِن الماءِ a cup of water; كَثير مِن المَشاكِلِ lots of problems; عالِم مِن العُلَماءِ a scientist; عُضْو مِنْ أَعْضاءِ المَجْلِسِ a member of the council; كِتاب مِنْ كُتُبي one of my books; (وَ)مِنْها ... including ..., among which ...; الأَكْراد مِنْهُمْ the Kurds among them; هذا الجُزْء مِن العالَمِ this part of the world; كُلٌّ مِنْهُما each one of the two; ما مِنْ أَحَدٍ nobody; الجُزْء الأَكْبَر مِنْها the biggest part of it; مِنْ بَيْنِهِمْ ضابِطٌ سابِقٌ among them is a former officer; ما قَرَأْتُهُ مِنْ كُتُبٍ whatever books I have read 7 [مُقارَنة] than; هو أَكْبَرُ مِنّي he's older than I; ضَرَرُهُ أَكْثَرُ مِنْ نَفْعِهِ it does more harm than good 8 [مع صيغة المَجْهول] by, on the part of; خَطَوات تَمَّ اتِّخاذُها مِنْ مَجْموعةٍ مِن الدُّوَلِ steps that have been taken by a bloc of states 9 [يا] يا لَكَ مِنْ أَنانيٍّ you are so selfish; يا لَهُ مِنْ بَخيلٍ what a miser he is 10 [عُضْو جَسَديّ] by, at; سَحَبَتْهُ مِنْ ذِراعِهِ إلى الخارِجِ she pulled him outside by his arm

مِمَّنْ *pron* among those who; لَسْتُ مِمَّنْ يُحِبّونَ ذلك I'm not among those who like that

المَنامة *n* Manama (*the capital of Bahrain*)

مِنْتول *n* menthol

مَنْجة *n* see مَنْجو

مَنْجَنيز *n* manganese

مَنْجَنيق *n* |مَنْجَنيقات, مَجانِقُ| catapult

مَنْجو, مانْغو, مَنْجة, مَنْجا, مَنْجاة, مَنْغا *n* |مَنْجات| mango

مَليّ *n* long period of time; فَكَّرَ مَلِيًّا to ponder, to consider, to contemplate

مِمْلاة *n* dictating machine

إِمْلاء *n* |أَمالٍ, أَماليُّ| spelling; dictating; dictation; إِمْلاء الشُّروطِ dictating conditions; طَبَّقَ قَواعِدَ الإِمْلاءِ to apply spelling rules

إِمْلائيّ *adj* orthographic, spelling (*before n*); خَطَأ \ تَصْحيح إِمْلائيّ spelling mistake/correction; تَدْقيق إِمْلائيّ spellchecker

مِلْيار *n* |مِلْيارات| billion, thousand million

مِلْيارْدير *n* |مِلْيارْديرات| billionaire

مِلّيبار *n* millibar

مِلّيغْرام *n* |مِلّيغْرامات| milligram

مِلّيلِتْر *n* millilitre

مَليلية *n* Melilla (*exclave and autonomous city of Spain located on the north coast of Africa*)

مِليم *n* |مِلّيمات, مَلاليمُ| millieme (*the smallest monetary unit in Egypt that equals 1/1000 of an Egyptian pound*); لا مِلّيمَ واحِدَ not a single penny

مِلّيمِتْر *n* |مِلّيمِتْرات| millimetre

مِلْيون, مَلْيون *n* |مَلايينُ| million; صاحِب مَلايينَ millionaire

مِلْيونيّ *adj* million-strong; millions-strong; مُظاهَرة مِلْيونيّة a demonstration of millions

مِلْيونير *n* |مِلْيونيرات| millionaire

مِمَّ *pron* see مِمّا

مِمّا *pron* see ما

مِمَّنْ *pron* see من

مَنْ *pron* 1 [اسْم اسْتِفْهامٍ] who, which one; لِمَنْ؟ whose?; مع مَنْ؟ with whom?; لِمَنْ هذا المِعْطَفُ؟, مِعْطَفُ مَنْ هذا؟ whose coat is this?; مَنْ هو رَئيسُ مِصْرَ؟ who is the president of Egypt?; مَنْ مِنْكُمْ قَرَأَ هذا الكِتابَ؟ which one of you has read this book? 2 [الّذي] (everyone) who, whoever; he/she who, the one who, those who; بِمَنْ فيهِ included, inclusive; احْتَرَقَ البَيْتُ بِمَنْ فيهِ the house burned down, along with everyone in it; مِن النّاسِ مَنْ يَقولُ some people say; مَنْ وَعَدَ وَفى promise is debt

‹ **مَنَحَ** *v* |a; مَنْح| to give, to award, to grant; to bestow, to confer; مَنَحَ شَخْصاً جائِزةً to award sb a prize; مَنَحَ شَخْصاً رُخْصةً to grant sb a licence

مَنْح *n* award, awarding, granting; مَنْح جائِزةٍ awarding of a prize; مَنْح عَقْدٍ لِشَرِكةٍ awarding of a contract to a company

مانِح *n* 1 [واهِب] giver, donor 2 (Med) donor

مَمْنوح *adj* awarded, granted, given

مِنْحة *n* |مِنَح| scholarship, (study) grant; gift, donation; allowance; مِنْحة دِراسيّة scholarship; نِظام المِنَح (الدِراسيّة) scholarship system; مَنَحَ مِنْحةً دِراسيّةً to award a scholarship; حَصَلَ على مِنْحةٍ to receive a scholarship; أَقَرَّ مِنْحةً to grant an allowance; صَرَفَ مِنْحةً to pay out an allowance

‹ **مَنْدَب** *n* see باب المَنْدَب

باب المَنْدَب *n* Bab al-Mandeb (*strait near Djibouti*)

‹ **مَنْدَرين** *n* mandarin, tangerine

‹ **مِنْديل**, **مَنْديل** *n* |مَناديلُ| 1 [مَحْرَمة] handkerchief; napkin; مِنْديل وَرَقيّ tissue 2 [حِجاب] (Mor) headscarf; مِنْديل رَأْسٍ headscarf

‹ **مَنْدولين**, **مَنْدولينة** *n* mandolin; عَزَفَ على المَنْدولين to play (the) mandolin

‹ **مُنْذُ** *prep* since, for; ago; مُنْذُ ذلك الوَقْتِ since then; مُنْذُ ذلك اليَوْم since that day, from that day on; مُنْذُ قَريبٍ (only) just, recently; مُنْذُ وَقْتٍ طَويلٍ \ قصيرٍ for a long/short time; مُنْذُ فَتْرةٍ \ مُدّةٍ طَويلةٍ for a long time; a long time ago; مُنْذُ شَهْرٍ وَهُوَ مَريضٌ he has been ill for a month; مُنْذُ أَنْ since

مُنْذُئِذٍ *adv* since (then), ever since

‹ **تَمَنْطَقَ** *v* see نطق

‹ **مَنَعَ** *v* |a; مَنْع| 1 [حالَ دونَ] to prevent, to restrain, to hinder; to stop, to obstruct; مَنَعَ شَخْصاً من الحُضورِ ,مَنَعَ قُدومَ شَخْصٍ to prevent sb from coming; مَنَعَ شَخْصاً من (فِعْلِ) شَيْءٍ to keep sb from (doing) sth; لَيْسَ هُناكَ ما يَمْنَعُكَ من فِعْلِ ذلك nothing keeps you from doing that; مَنَعَ المُرورَ to obstruct (free) passage; مَنَعَ شَخْصاً من مُمارَسةِ عَمَلِه to obstruct sb from doing his job 2 [حَرَّمَ] to forbid, to interdict, to prohibit; مَنَعَ شَخْصاً من مُزاوَلةِ مِهْنةِ المُحاماةِ to suspend sb from practicing law; مَنَعَ شَخْصاً من دُخولِ شَيْءٍ to deny sb admission to sth

مانَعَ *v* |في| to resist, to rebel (against), to protest (against); مانَعَ في شَيْءٍ to object to sth; مانَعَ في أَنْ ... to protest (the fact) that ...

تَمَنَّعَ *v* to abstain, to refrain, to forbear

امْتَنَعَ *v* to refrain, to abstain, to forbear; امْتَنَعَ عن أيِّ تَعْليقٍ to decline to comment; امْتَنَعَ عن التَصْويتِ to abstain from voting

مَنْع *n* 1 [حَظْر] ban, prohibition; مَنْع قانونيّ a legal ban; مَنْع صَريح an explicit ban; مَنْع اسْتيرادٍ import ban; مَنْع تِجاريّ trade embargo; مَنْع تِجارةِ العاجِ a trade embargo on ivory; فَرَضَ مَنْعاً to impose a ban 2 [حَيْلولة] prevention; مَنْع الحَمْلِ contraception, birth control

مانِع A *adj* forbidding, prohibitive; حُكْم \ شَرْط مانِع prohibitive order; مانِع لِلحَرارةِ heat-resistant

B *n* |مَوانِعُ| 1 [عائِق] hindrance, obstacle, impediment; مَوانِع شَرْعيّة legal obstacles; مَوانِع الزَواجِ marriage obstacles; هي خالِيةٌ من مَوانِعِ النِكاحِ there are no impediments to (a) marriage for her; مانِع مائيّ water barrier; مانِع الاسْتِعْمالِ contraindication 2 [اعْتِراض] objection; لا مانِعَ no objection; لا مانِعَ لَيْسَ عِنْدي مانِعٌ I have no objection, I don't mind; لا مانِعَ لَكَ عن \ في فِعْلِ ذلك nothing keeps you from doing that 3 (Islam) المانِع the Withholder (*one of the names of God*)

مُمانِع A *adj* opposing, rejecting

B *n* rejectionist

مُمانَعة *n* opposition; resistance; reluctance

مَمْنوع *adj* forbidden, prohibited, banned; illegal, illicit, unlawful; وَسائِل مَمْنوعة illegal means; مَمْنوعٌ الدُخولُ no entry; مَمْنوعٌ الدُخولُ على الكِلابِ no dogs allowed; مَمْنوعٌ التَدْخينُ ,التَدْخينُ مَمْنوعٌ no smoking; كُلُّ مَمْنوعٍ مَتْبوعٌ \ مَرْغوبٌ فيه forbidden fruit is sweetest

مَناعة *n* 1 (Med) immunity, resistance, defence; مَناعة طَبيعيّة natural immunity; جِهاز المَناعةِ (الطَبيعيّة) the (natural) immune system; نَشَّطَ جِهازَ المَناعةِ to activate the immune system; قَوّى جِهازَ المَناعةِ to strengthen the immune system;

اكْتَسَبَ مَناعةً to gain immunity; ذو مَناعةٍ resistant, immune; مَناعة ضدّ immunity against diseases; مَناعة ضدّ الأَمْراضِ resistance against المُضادّاتِ الحَيَويّةِ \ المُبيداتِ الحَشَريّةِ antibiotics/pesticides; فِقْدان المَناعةِ loss of resistance, immunodeficiency; مَرَض نَقْصِ \ فِقْدانِ المَناعةِ المُكْتَسَبةِ acquired immunodeficiency syndrome, AIDS; مُصاب بِمَرَضِ فِقْدانِ المَناعةِ المُكْتَسَبةِ afflicted by AIDS; AIDS patient **2** [دِبْلوماسيّة] immunity; مَناعة دِبْلوماسيّة diplomatic immunity

مَناعيّ *adj* immunity (*before n*), immuno-, resistance (*before n*); جِهاز مَناعيّ immune system; مادّة مَناعيّة antibody

مَنيع *adj* |مُنَعاءُ| immune, resistant; inaccessible, impregnable; كانَ مَنيعاً immune to a certain disease; مَنيع على مَرَضٍ مُعَيَّنٍ ضدّ شَيْءٍ to be resistant to sth; زُجاج مَنيع bulletproof glass

امْتِناع *n* |امْتِناعات| abstention, refraining; restraint, forbearance; الامْتِناع عن الدَفْعِ default, non-payment; الامْتِناع عن التَصْويتِ abstention (from voting)

مُنْغوليّ *adj, n* see مُغوليّ ‹

مُنْغوليا *n* Mongolia ‹

مِنْك *n* سُرْعوب المِنْكِ mink (*Neovison, Mustela*) ‹

مَنَّ *v* |u; مَنّ| to give, to present, to impart; مَنَّ على شَخْصٍ بِشَيْءٍ to impart sth to sb ‹

امْتَنَّ *v* to bestow blessings; امْتَنَّ اللهُ عَلَيْنا بِنِعَمٍ كَثيرةٍ God has bestowed many blessings upon us; امْتَنَّ لِشَخْصٍ to be grateful to sb

مُمْتَنّ *adj* grateful, thankful; كانَ مُمْتَنًّا لِشَخْصٍ to be grateful to sb

مَمْنون *adj* grateful, thankful

مَنّ *n* **1** [ما يُنْعَمُ بِهِ] gift, donation, present; manna **2** [حَشَرة] aphid (*Aphididae*) **3** [وَزْن] |أَمْنان| *a weight of approx 900 grams*

مَنّان **A** *adj* generous, liberal, magnanimous
B *n* generous donor

مِنّة *n* |مِنَن| favour, grace

امْتِنان *n* gratitude, appreciation; قَبِلَ بِامْتِنانٍ to accept with gratitude; أَبْدى امْتِنانَهُ to show one's gratitude; دَليل على الامْتِنانِ a token of appreciation

مَنْهَج, مُمَنْهَج see نهج ‹

مَنى *v* |i; مَنْي| مُنِيَ بِهَزيمةٍ to suffer a defeat ‹

مَنّى *v* |بِ| to make hope (for), to give reason to hope (for)

أَمْنى *v* to ejaculate

تَمَنّى *v* to wish (for), to desire; to hope; تَمَنّى شَيْئاً to wish for sth; أَتَمَنّى أنْ ... I hope that ....; أَتَمَنّى أنْ يَفْعَلَ ذلك I hope that he will do that; لا أَتَمَنّى I hope not; تَمَنّى لِشَخْصٍ أنْ ... to wish for sb to ....; تَمَنّى لِشَخْصٍ التَوْفيقَ \ الحَظَّ السَعيدَ to wish sb success/good luck; أَتَمَنّى لَكَ كَثيراً من السَعادةِ \ العافِيةِ I wish you lots of happiness/good health

اسْتَمْنى *v* to masturbate

مَنيّ *n* |مُنْي| sperm, semen, seed; قَذَفَ \ أَطْلَقَ المَنيَّ to ejaculate, to discharge one's seed

مَنَويّ *adj* sperm (*before n*); حَيَوان مَنَويّ sperm (cell); سائِل مَنَويّ sperm, semen

مَنًى *n* fate, destiny; death

مِنى *n* |f| Mina (*valley near Mecca*)

مِنًى *n* sperm, semen

مَنِيّة *n* |مَنايا| fate, destiny; death

مُنْية *n* |مُنًى| wish, desire

اسْتِمْناء *n* masturbation, onanism

إِمْناء *n* ejaculation, seminal discharge

أُمْنِيّة *n* |أَمانٍ, أَمانيّ| **1** [رَجاء] wish, desire; fantasy; أُمْنِيّة مُتَواضِعة a modest wish; أُمْنِيّة طِفْلٍ a child's wish; قائِمة أُمْنِيّاتٍ wish list; أَعَزّ الأَماني heart's desire; حَقَّقَ أُمْنِيّةً to grant a wish **2** [اسْم شَخْصيّ] |dipt| Oumniya (*female given name*)

تَمَنٍّ *n* |تَمَنِّيات| wish; desire; تَمَنِّيات طَيِّبة (بالعامِ الجَديدِ) best wishes (for the new year); أَطْيَب التَمَنِّياتِ hearty congratulations

مُنى *n* |f| Mona (*female given name*) ‹

المِنْيا *n* al-Minya (*city in Egypt*) ‹

مَهاة *n* |مَهًا, مَهَوات| oryx (*Oryx*) ‹

مُهْجة *n* |مُهَج, مُهَجات| **1** [قَلْب] heart **2** [اسْم شَخْصيّ] |dipt| Muhja (*female given name*) ‹

‹ **مَهَّدَ** *v* **1** [بَسَطَ] to pave; to smooth, to level, to make even; مَهَّدَ فِراشَهُ to make one's bed **2** [سَهَّلَ] to facilitate, to make easy, to ease; مَهَّدَ الطَريقَ لِشَيْءٍ \ لِشَخْصٍ to pave the way for sth/sb; مَهَّدَ الطَريقَ لِشَخْصٍ لِ ... to prepare the way for sb to ... **3** [رَتَّبَ] to prepare, to arrange, to make ready **4** [قَدَّمَ] to introduce

تَمَهَّدَ *v* to be paved, to be cleared; to be in order; to be arranged, to be settled

مَهْد *n* |مُهود| **1** [سَرير طِفْلٍ] crib, cradle; في المَهْدِ in the cradle; من المَهْدِ إلى اللَحْدِ from the cradle to the grave **2** (fig) cradle, origin; مَهْد الحَضارة the cradle of civilization; وَأَدَ الديموقْراطيّةَ في مَهْدِها to nip democracy in the bud

مُمَهَّد *adj* paved; smoothed, leveled; غَيْر مُمَهَّدٍ unpaved; طَريق مُمَهَّد a paved road; وَجَدَ الطَريقَ أَمامَهُ مُمَهَّدةً the way was paved for him

مِهاد *n* |مُهُد, أَمْهِدة| bed

تَمْهيد *n* **1** [تَسْوية] smoothing, leveling **2** [تَهْيِئة] introduction, preparation; تَمْهيداً لِ ... in preparation of ... **3** [مُقَدِّمة] |تَمْهيدات| preface, foreword; تَمْهيد بِقَلَمِ المُحَرِّرِ foreword by the editor

تَمْهيديّ *adj* preparatory, introductory, preliminary; فَصْل تَمْهيديّ an introductory chapter; مُحادَثات تَمْهيديّة preliminary talks; بَحْث \ دِراسة تَمْهيديّ(ة) preliminary study; بَرْنامَج تَمْهيديّ introductory programme; مَرْحَلة تَمْهيديّة preliminary stage

‹ **مَهَرَ** *v* |u| **1** |مَهارة| [كانَ ماهِراً] to be skilful; to stand out, to excel; مَهَرَ في شَيْءٍ to be skilled in sth **2** |مَهارة| [خَتَمَ] to stamp **3** |مَهْر| [المَرْأَةَ] to pay a dowry; مَهَرَ امْرَأَةً to pay a dowry to a woman

أَمْهَرَ *v* to give a dower (*to the bride*)

مَهْر *n* |مُهور| dowry, bride's portion

مُهْر *n* |أَمْهار, مِهارة| foal, colt

ماهِر *adj* |مَهَرة| **1** [بارِع] skilful, dexterous; proficient; حِرَفيّ \ عامِل ماهِر a skilled craftsman/worker; شَخْص غَيْر ماهِرٍ bungler; عامِل غَيْر ماهِرٍ an unskilled labourer; كانَ ماهِراً to be skilled **2** [اسْم شَخْصيّ] Maher (*male given name*)

مَهارة *n* skill, skilfulness, dexterity; مَهارة يَدَويّة manual skill; مَهارات عَمَليّة practical skills; مَهارات فَنّيّة \ تِقْنيّة technical skills; مَهارة في شَيْءٍ proficiency at sth; مَهارة في الكِتابة writing skill; اكْتَسَبَ مَهارةً to acquire a skill; صَقَلَ مَهاراتِهِ to refine one's skills; فَعَلَ شَيْئاً بِمَهارةٍ to do sth skilfully; لَدَيْها قَدْرٌ من المَهارة she has a certain degree of skill; هذا يَتَطَلَّبُ مَهارةً this requires skill

مُهْرة *n* |مُهَر| filly, female foal; cutie (infml), babe (infml) (*pretty young woman*)

مَهْريّ *adj* اللُغة المَهْريّة Mehri (*South Arabian language*)

‹ **مَهْرَجان** *n* see هرج

‹ **مَهَق** *n* albinism

أَمْهَق *adj* |dipt; مُهْق; f pl مَهْقاوات| albino (*before n*)

‹ **مَهَلَ** *v* |a; مَهْل, مُهْلة| to dawdle, to tarry, to linger

مَهَّلَ *v* to make slow down

أَمْهَلَ *v* to give respite; أَمْهَلَ شَخْصاً to give sb (a) respite

تَمَهَّلَ *v* to slow down, to slacken; تَمَهَّلَ في خُطاهُ to slow down one's pace

اسْتَمْهَلَ *v* to ask for a respite

مَهْل *n* **1** [راحة] ease, leisure; على مَهْلِكَ take it easy; مَهْلاً, على مَهْلٍ slowly, leisurely; على أَقَلَّ من مَهْلِهِ at one's leisure **2** [تَأْجيل] postponement

مُتَمَهِّل **A** *adj* slow, deliberate **B** *n* dawdler, laggard

مُهْلة *n* |مُهَل| **1** [تَأْجيل] postponement, delay; extension; مُهْلة كافية للتَفْكير enough time to reflect; حَدَّدَ لِشَخْصٍ مُهْلةً to grant sb a respite; أَعْطى \ مَنَحَ شَخْصاً مُهْلةَ بِضْعةِ أَيّامٍ to give sb a few days' grace **2** [فَتْرة] time limit, deadline; interval; مُهْلة يَوْمَيْنِ a two day deadline

إمْهال *n* delay

إمْهاليّ *adj* dilatory

تَمَهُّل *n* slowness, deliberateness

‹ **مَهْما** *conj* whatever; however; مَهْما كانَ الأَمْرُ whatever the case may be; مَهْما تَكُن الأَسْبابُ whatever the reasons may be; مَهْما طالَ الوَقْتُ no matter how long it may last

اسْتَمات *v* to risk one's life, to defy death, to show contempt for death

مَوْت *n* death, decease, demise; مَوْت جَماعيّ mass death; مَوْت أَبْيَض natural death; مَوْت زُؤام a sudden death; المَوْت جوعاً death by starvation; خطَر المَوْتِ mortal danger; مُعَرَّض ل \ بَعيد عن خطَرِ المَوْتِ in/out of (mortal) danger; الخَوْف من المَوْتِ fear of death; فِراش المَوْتِ deathbed; مُؤَدٍّ إلى المَوْتِ fatal, lethal; عند \ بعد المَوْتِ at/after death; بين الحَياةِ والمَوْتِ between life and death; المَوْت بِسَبَبِ شَيْءٍ death due to sth; واجَهَ المَوْتَ to face death; حَصَدَ المَوْتُ ١٩ شَخْصاً 19 people died; صارَعَ المَوْتَ to struggle with death; نَجا من المَوْتِ to escape death; أَدْرَكَهُ المَوْتُ death overtook him; غَيَّبَهُ المَوْتُ death took him; حَدَّ على مَوْتِ شَخْصٍ to mourn over sb's death; المَوْتُ يَدْنو مِنْكَ death is imminent; كانَ على وَشْكِ المَوْتِ to have one foot in the grave; كانَ مُشْرِفاً على المَوْتِ to be on one's deathbed, to be on the verge of death

مُسْتَميت *adj* heroic, death-defying; دِفاع مُسْتَميت a heroic defence

مَمات *n* death

مُميت A *adj* [مُهْلِك] deadly, fatal, mortal; terminal; حادِث مُميت a fatal accident; خَطيئة مُميتة a mortal sin

B *n* المُميت the Destroyer (*one of the names of God*)

مَوات *n* inanimate object; wasteland

مَوَتان *n* death

مَيِّت, مَيْت A *adj* |مَوْتى, أَمْوات| dead, lifeless, deceased; إنَّهُ مَيِّتٌ he is dead; شِبْه مَيِّتٍ half-dead; (صَبيّ) مَوْلود مَيِّتاً stillborn (child)

B *n* |مَوْتى, أَمْوات| dead person, deceased; مُسْتَوْدَع المَوْتى mortuary; عَدَد المَوْتى number of dead; سَيّارة المَوْتى hearse; قامَ بِإحْياءِ ذِكْرى المَوْتى to commemorate the dead; سَقَطَ مَوْتى there were casualties; واذْكُروا مَوْتاكُمْ بِخَيْرٍ speak well of the dead

ميتة *n* death; ميتة هادِئة a quiet death

مَيْتة *n* (Isl Law) dead animal (*which is not slaughtered ritually*)

اسْتِماتة *n* contempt for death

مَهَنَ *v* |a-u; مَهْنة, مَهْن| to practise a profession

مَهُنَ *v* |u; مَهانة| to be despicable; to be humiliated

امْتَهَنَ *v* 1 [مِهْنةً] to practise professionally; امْتَهَنَ التِجارةَ to be in business 2 [احْتَقَرَ] to despise, to disdain

مُمْتَهِن *n* professional, expert

مِهْنة *n* |مِهَن| 1 [حِرْفة] profession, trade, occupation; مِهْنة حُرّة a free profession; مِهْنة جَميلة a beautiful profession; أَقْدَم مِهْنةٍ في العالَمِ the world's oldest profession; أَسْرار المِهْنةِ the tricks of the trade; مَجال المِهْنةِ field; أجادَ مِهْنَتَهُ to understand one's profession; مارَسَ \ زاوَلَ مِهْنةً to practise a profession; عادَ إلى مِهْنةٍ to resume one's profession; أَفْشى سِرَّ المِهْنةِ to breach one's professional confidentiality 2 [حَياة عَمَلٍ] career

مِهْنيّ *adj* professional, vocational; تَكْوين مِهْنيّ professional training

مِهْنيّة *n* professionalism; productivity

مَهين *adj* |مُهَناءُ| despicable, contemptible; offensive

امْتِهان *n* contempt, disdain

تَماهى *v* 1 [تَوافَقَ] |مع| to be congruent with 2 [شَعَرَ بالتَماثُلِ] |مع| to identify oneself with

ماءَ *v* |u; مُواء| to mew, to miaow

مِائة see مأي

مُواء *n* |مُواءات| mewing, miaowing

موبايل *n* |موبايلات| mobile (phone)

ماتَ *v* |u; مَوْت| to die, to decease, to pass away; ماتَ بِسَبَبِ شَيْءٍ to die of sth; ماتَ جوعاً \ عَطَشاً to die of starvation/thirst; ماتَ خَوْفاً to die of fear, to be scared to death; ماتَ من شِدَّةِ البَرْدِ to freeze to death; ماتَ بِمَرَضِ السَرَطانِ to die of cancer; ماتَ عن عِشْرينَ سَنةً he died at the age of twenty; ماتَ عن زَوْجةٍ وَثَلاثِ بَناتٍ he left (behind) a wife and three daughters; كادَ يَموتُ to almost die; to choke; ما فاتَ ماتَ let bygones be bygones, what's done is done

مَوَّتَ *v* to kill, to put to death

أَماتَ *v* to kill

تَماوَتَ *v* to pretend to be dead; to feign weakness

إماتة *n* إماتة رَحيمة euthanasia

‹ **موتور** *n* motor; engine

‹ **موتوسيكِل** *n* |موتوسيكِلات| motorcycle, motorbike; moped

‹ **موتيف** *n* motif

‹ **موتيل** *n* motel

‹ **موثة**, **مَوْثة** *n* prostate (gland)

‹ **ماجَ** *v* |u; مَوْج, مَوَجان| ⟨1⟩ [هاجَ] to well up, to rise; to be agitated; to be excited ⟨2⟩ [البَحْرُ] to heave, to surge; to well up, to rise

مَوَّجَ *v* to ripple, to ruffle; to wave

تَمَوَّجَ *v* to undulate, to wave, to heave; يَتَمَوَّجُ سَطْحُ الماءِ the surface of the water ripples

تَماوَجَ *v* to undulate; to swell; to fluctuate

مَوْج *n coll* |أَمْواج| ⟨1⟩ [في الماءِ] wave, breaker; surf; swell, heave; أَمْواج مُرْتَفِعة high waves; راكِب الأَمْواجِ surfer; حاجِز أَمْواجٍ breakwater, jetty; تَمايَلَ مَعَ الأَمْواجِ to roll with the waves ⟨2⟩ (Phys) wave, undulation; طول مَوْجةٍ wave length; مَوْجة مُتَوَسِّطة \ قصيرة \ طَويلة medium/short/long wave; مَوْجات ضَوْئيّة \ صَوْتيّة \ كَهْرَبائيّة light/sound/electrical waves ⟨3⟩ (fig) wave, surge, boom; مَوْجة أَعْمالٍ إِرْهابِيّةٍ a wave of terrorism; مَوْجة من السُخْطِ \ الانْتِقاداتِ a wave of indignation/criticism; مَوْجة حَرٍّ heatwave; اكْتَسَحَتْ مَوْجةُ حَرٍّ المَدينةَ a heatwave struck the city; رَكِبَ المَوْجةَ to join the bandwagon

مائِج *adj* swelling, surging

مُتَمَوِّج *adj* undulating; wavy; سَطْح مُتَمَوِّج a corrugated surface; حُمّى مُتَمَوِّجة brucellosis

مُمَوَّج *adj* undulating; wavy, curled

تَماوُج *n* wave motion, undulation; swell

تَمَوُّج *n* |تَمَوُّجات| ⟨1⟩ [تَماوُج] wave motion, undulation, swell; تَمَوُّج قَوِيّ a heavy swell ⟨2⟩ [مَوْجة] wave; تَمَوُّج في الشَعْرِ a wave in the hair

تَمَوُّجِيّ *adj* undulating, wavy, waving; حَرَكة تَمَوُّجِيّة undulatory movement

‹ **موح** *adj* see وحي

‹ **مودة** *n* see موضة

‹ **مودِم** *n* modem

‹ **موديل** *n* |موديلات| ⟨1⟩ [طِراز] model, design; موديل مُصَغَّر miniature ⟨2⟩ [للرَسّامِ] model

‹ **مارَ** *v* |u; مَوْر| to move from side to side, to move back and forth

تَمَوَّرَ *v* to move from side to side, to move back and forth

مُتَمَوِّرة *n* amoeba

‹ **موراتوريوم** *n* moratorium

‹ **مورْس** *n* Morse; شَفْرة مورْس Morse code

‹ **مورْفولوجيّ** *adj* morphologic, morphological

‹ **مورْفولوجِيا** *n* morphology

‹ **مورْفين**, **مُرْفين** *n* morphine

‹ **مورْمونيّ** *adj*, *n* Mormon

‹ **موريتانيّ** *adj*, *n* Mauritanian

‹ **موريتانِيا** *n* Mauritania (*country in West Africa*)

‹ **موريشِيوس** *n* |f| Mauritius

‹ **مَوْز** *n coll* banana; سُباطة مَوْزٍ a bunch of bananas; قَشَّرَ مَوْزةً to peel a banana

‹ **موزَمْبيق**, **موزامْبيق** *n* |f| Mozambique

‹ **موسْكو** *n* |f| Moscow

‹ **موسْكوفيّ** *adj*, *n* Muscovite

‹ **موسْلين** *n* muslin

‹ **موسى** *n* |مَواسٍ, أَمْواس| ⟨1⟩ [آلة الحِلاقةِ] razor ⟨2⟩ [اسْم شَخْصيّ] Musa, Moses (*male given name*) ⟨3⟩ [النَبِيّ] Moses (*the prophet*); جَبَل موسى (Egypt) Mount Sinai; (Mor) Jebel Musa

Idiom سَمَك موسى sole (*Solea solea*)

‹ **موسيقار** *n* musician; composer

‹ **موسيقى** *n* |f| music; فَنّ الموسيقى (the art of) music; موسيقى خَلْفِيّة background music; موسيقى عَصْرِيّة \ كْلاسيكيّة modern/classical music; موسيقى شَعْبِيّة folk music, traditional music; موسيقى الراب rap music; مَدْرَسة موسيقى music school; عَزَفَ الموسيقى to make music

موسيقيّ **A** *adj* musical; قِطْعة موسيقِيّة piece of music; concerto; فِرْقة موسيقِيّة (brass) band

B *n* musician

‹ **مَوْص** *n* straw

الموصُل, المَوْصِل *n* |f| Mosul (*city in Iraq*)

موضة *n* fashion, vogue, trend; موضة نِسائيّة ladies' fashion; آخِر صَيْحاتِ الموضةِ the latest fashion; تَبَعاً ,على الموضةِ للموضةِ fashionable, in vogue; موسيقى \ مَلابِس على الموضةِ fashionable music/clothes; باتَ موضةً to come into fashion; أَصْبَحَ موضةً قديمةً to go out of fashion; تَماشى مع الموضةِ to keep up with fashion

تَمَوْضُع ,تَمَوْضَعَ ,مَوْضَعَ see وضع

موظ *n* moose

موف *adj*, *n* mauve

موكيت *n* wall-to-wall carpeting; moquette

مَوَّلَ *v* to finance, to fund; to sponsor; مَوَّلَ مَشْروعاً \ بَحْثاً to finance a project/research

تَمَوَّلَ *v* to be financed, to be funded

مول *n* |مولات| mall, shopping centre

مال *n* |أَمْوال| ❶ [نُقود] money; fortune, wealth, riches; أَمْوال finances, funds; المال العامّ public funds; أَمْوال الدَوْلة government funds; رَأْس مالٍ capital; انْتِقال رُؤوسِ الأَمْوالِ movement of capital; سوق رُؤوس أَمْوالٍ capital market; سُلْطان المالِ the power of money; تَبْذير الأَمْوالِ waste of money; كَثير المالِ rich, wealthy; بَيْت المالِ treasury; من أَمْوالٍ خاصّةٍ out of private means; من مالِهِ الخاصِّ of his own money; بَذَّرَ \ أَسْرَفَ مالَهُ to squander one's money; اسْتَثْمَرَ مالاً to invest money; وَظَّفَ \ وَضَعَ مالاً في شيْءٍ to invest money in sth; أَرْجَعَ مالاً to pay back money; أَنْفَقَ أَمْوالاً طائِلةً to spend a fortune; المالُ السائبُ يُعَلِّمُ السَرِقةَ opportunity makes the thief ❷ [مِلْك] property, asset; أَمْوال مَنْقولة movable properties, movables; أَمْوال ثابِتة immovable properties; fixed funds

ماليّ 🅐 *adj* financial, monetary; اسْتِقْرار ماليّ monetary stability; الْتِزامات ماليّة financial obligations; قِطاع ماليّ finance, financial sector; مَسْأَلة ماليّة financial matter; قَدَّمَ مُساعَدةً ماليّةً لِشَخْصٍ to provide sb with financial support 🅑 *adj*, *n* see مالي

ماليّة *n* finance, monetary affairs; وَزير الماليّةِ minister of finance, Chancellor of the Exchequer (BrE), Secretary of the Treasury (AmE); وِزارة الماليّة ministry of finance, Treasury (BrE), Treasury Department (AmE)

مُمَوِّل *n* financier, moneylender; sponsor

مَوّال *n* |مَواويلُ| *a ballad in colloquial language*

تَمْويل *n* financing, funding; sponsoring; تَمْويل خارِجيّ external financing; تَمْويل جَماعيّ crowdfunding; مَصْدَر تَمْويلٍ source of financing; نظام التَمْويل financing system; تَكَفَّلَ بِتَمْويلِ حَدَثٍ to sponsor an event

تَمْويليّ *adj* financial; احْتِياج \ حاجة تَمْويليّة financial need

مولْدوفا *n* Moldova

مومِياء *n* |dipt f; موميات| mummy

مانَ *v* |u; مَوْن ,مُؤْنة| ❶ [وَفَّرَ] to provision, to supply (with provisions) ❷ [كَذَبَ] see مين

مَوَّنَ *v* to provision, to supply (with provisions)

تَمَوَّنَ *v* to stock up (on provisions)

مُمَوِّن *n* supplier, deliverer; (domestic) caterer

مونة *n* provisions

تَمْوين *n* provisioning, supply; الإِمْداد والتَمْوين logistics; وِزارة التَمْوينِ ministry of supply

تَمْوينيّ *adj* supplying, providing; مُساعَدة تَمْوينيّة government food aid

مونا *n* Mona (*female given name*)

موناكو *n* |f| Monaco

مونْتاج *n* (Cin) montage, editing

مونْتانا *n* Montana (*US state*)

مونَسْتيرة *n* (Bot) monstera (*Monstera deliciosa*)

مونولوج *n* monologue, soliloquy

ماهَ *v* |u; مَوْه| to abound in water

مَوَّهَ *v* ❶ [حَرَّفَ] to conceal, to veil; to misrepresent, to falsify; مَوَّهَ الحَقيقةَ to conceal the truth ❷ [رَقَّقَ] to thin, to dilute, to water down ❸ (Mil) to camouflage

مَوْه *n* مَوْه الرَأْسِ hydrocephalus

ماء *n* |مِياه ,أَمْواه| ❶ [سائِل] water; ماء ساخِن \ بارِد \ فاتِر hot/cold/lukewarm water; ماء مَعْدِنيّ mineral water, spring water; زُجاجة \ كَأْس من الماءِ المَعْدِنيِّ a bottle/glass of mineral water; ماء غازيّ soda (water), carbonated water; ماء مُقَدَّس holy water; ماء عَذْب \ مالِح fresh/salt water; ماء أُجاج \ آسِن brackish water; ماء جارٍ running water; كالماءِ الجاري fluently; يَجْري الماءُ the water is running; ماء صافٍ \ نَقيّ clear water; ماء عَكِر troubled water; ماء ثَقيل heavy water; مِياه جَوْفيّة groundwater; مِياه سَطْحيّة surface water; مِياه صالِحة للشُرْبِ ,الشُرْبِ drinking water, potable water; ماء أُكْسيجينيّ hydrogen peroxide; ماء الرَأْسِ amniotic fluid; دَوْرة المِياهِ toilet (BrE), lavatory (BrE), bathroom (AmE), restroom (AmE); مَصْرَف مِياهٍ drainpipe; تَصْريف المِياهِ drainage; قَطْرة \ سَطْل \ كَأْس ماءٍ a drop/bucket/glass of water; التَبْريد بالماءِ water cooling; مَصْلَحة الماءِ waterworks; أُنْبوب ماءٍ water pipe; بُرْج ماءٍ water tower; اسْتِهْلاك الماءِ water consumption; تَلَوُّث الماءِ water pollution; تَوْزيع المِياهِ water supply; الإمْداد بِمِياهِ الشُرْبِ the supply of drinking water; تَصْفِية \ تَنْقِية المِياهِ water purification/treatment; دولابُ الماءِ waterwheel; ضِدُّ الماءِ, مُقاوِم للماءِ waterproof, watertight; غَنيّ بالماءِ abounding in water; مِنْطَقة غَنيّة بالماءِ an area with abundant water; شَهْر الماء (Hist) May (*Libya under Gaddafi*) ❷ [مَجْرى ماءٍ] water, المِياه waterway, watercourse; المِياه الداخِليّة inland waterways; المِياه الإقْليميّة territorial waters; مِياه ساحِليّة coastal waters; هَنْدَسة المِياهِ hydraulic engineering, hydraulics; خَريطة \ خارِطة المِياهِ water map, hydrographic map; خَطّ الماءِ waterline; حَيّة الماءِ water snake; جار الماءِ alder (*Alnus*); سَطْح \ وَجْه الماءِ water surface; مُسْتَوى الماءِ water level; يَرْتَفِعُ مُسْتَوى الماءِ the water level rises; يَنْزِلُ \ يَنْخَفِضُ مُسْتَوى الماءِ the water level drops; تَفيضُ مِياهُ النَهْرِ the river overflows; عادَت المِياهُ إلى مَجاريها things have returned to normal; حَرَثَ في الماءِ *to waste time and effort*

(Idioms) الماء (الأَبْيَض) (Med) cataract; ماء الوَجْهِ self-respect

مائيّ *adj* watery, aquatic, water (*before n*); عَلامة مائيّة watermark; أَلْوان مائيّة watercolours; رَسْم مائيّ watercolour, aquarelle; عِلْم الأَحْياءِ المائيّةِ marine biology

ماهيّ *adj* watery, aqueous

مُمَوَّه *adj* gold-plated

تَمْويه *n* camouflage

تَمْويهيّ *adj* feigned, sham, mock; هُجوم تَمْويهيّ feint, mock attack

‹ **ماوِيّة** *n* juice, sap

‹ **مي** *n* (Mus) mi

‹ **مْيانْمار** *n* |f| Myanmar

‹ **ميتافيزِياء, ميتافيزيقا** *n* metaphysics

‹ **ميتافيزيقيّ** *adj* metaphysical

‹ **ميتالِك** *adj* metallic

‹ **ميتْروبول** *n* metropolis

‹ **ميثادون** *n* methadone

‹ **ميثان** *n* methane; غاز الميثان methane

‹ **ميثانول** *n* methanol, methyl alcohol

‹ **ميثوديّ** *n* Methodist

‹ **ميثوديّة** *n* Methodism

‹ **ميثولوجِيا** *n* mythology; الميثولوجيا اليونانيّة Greek mythology

‹ **ميثولوجيّ** *adj* mythological

‹ **ميغابايْت, ميجابايْت** *n* megabyte, MB

‹ **ماحَ** *v* |i; مَيْح| to boast, to brag, to swagger

اسْتَماحَ *v* to ask; أَسْتَميحُكَ عُذراً I beg your pardon

‹ **مادَ** *v* |i; مَيَدان, مَيْد| to be moved, to be shocked, to be upset

مائِدة *n* table; مائِدة مُسْتَديرة round table discussion; مائِدة المُؤْتَمَر conference table; مائِدة مُفَضَّلة table (reserved) for regulars; مائِدة حائِطٍ console (table); مائِدة الطَعام dining table; مفْرَش مائِدةٍ tablecloth; آداب المائِدةِ table manners; طَقْم \ أَدَوات المائِدةِ tableware; حَجَزَ مائِدةً to reserve a table; جَلَسَ على المائِدةِ to sit down at the table; سورة المائِدة The Table (*Sura 5*)

مَيْدان *n* |مَيادينُ| ❶ [ساحة] open place, square; في مَيْدانٍ in a square; في مَيْدانِ سُلَيْمان باشا in Suleiman Pasha square; مَيْدان القِتالِ \ المَعْرَكةِ theatre of war; مَيْدان الحَرْبِ battlefield, battleground ❷ [مَلْعَب] circuit, track, course; مَيْدان سِباقٍ racetrack; مَيْدان سِباقِ الدَرّاجاتِ bicycle track, velodrome; مَيْدان الرِمايةِ shooting range; وَسَط المَيْدانِ midfield, centre circle; لاعِب وَسَطِ المَيْدانِ midfielder, midfield player ❸ [رومانيّ] arena ❹ (fig) domain, field,

كانَ ... من المُمَيِّزاتِ أنّ ... it is typical that ...; characteristics;
مُمَيِّزاً لِشَيْءٍ \ لِشَخْصٍ to be characteristic of sth/sb

مُمَيِّزة *n* 1 [خاصّيّة] distinguishing feature, peculiarity 2 [وِسام الشَرَفِ] (mark of) honour

ميزة *n* 1 [خاصية] distinguishing feature, characteristic 2 [نَفْع] advantage, plus; preference; ميزة تَفْضيليّة privilege; ميزات إداريّة administrative features; تَمَتَّعَ بِميزاتٍ to enjoy benefits

امْتِياز *n* |امْتِيازات| 1 [نُبوغ] distinction, cachet; بامْتِيازٍ (مع مَرْتَبةِ الشَرَفِ) with (high) distinction 2 (Econ) concession; هو صاحِبُ امْتِيازٍ he is a concessionaire; عَقْد امْتِيازٍ deed of concession; مَنَحَ امْتِيازاً to grant a concession 3 [تَفْضيل] privilege, advantage; امْتِياز ضَريبيّ tax advantage; الامْتِيازات الأَجْنَبيّة (Hist) the Capitulations (*exceptional provisions granted to foreigners by the Ottoman Empire*); مَنْح امْتِيازاتٍ favouritism; مَنَحَ امْتِيازاً to grant a privilege; تَمَتَّعَ بِامْتِيازٍ to enjoy a privilege; كانَ لَدَيْه امْتِيازُ ... he had the privilege of ... 4 (Law) preference

أَمْيَز *adj* |dipt| better; more unique/special

تَمْييز *n* |تَمْييزات| 1 [تَفْريق] differentiation, distinction; دون تَمْييزٍ without differentiation; سِنّ التَمْييزِ age of discretion; مَحْكَمة التَمْييزِ court of cassation 2 [عُنْصُريّ] discrimination; تَمْييز عُنْصُريّ racial discrimination, racism; تَمْييز على أَساسِ الجِنْسِ sex discrimination, gender discrimination; تَمْييز إيجابيّ positive discrimination (BrE), affirmative action (AmE) 3 (Gram) *accusative of specification*

تَمْييزيّ *adj* discriminatory; مُعامَلة تَمْييزيّة discriminatory treatment

‹ **ماسَ** *v* |i; مَيْس, مَيَسان| to strut, to flaunt

‹ **ميسوري** *n* |f| Missouri (*US state*); نَهْر ميسوري the Missouri (River)

‹ **ميسيسيبي** *n* |f| Mississippi (*US state*); نَهْر ميسيسيبي the Mississippi (River)

‹ **ميشيغان** *n* |f| Michigan (*US state*)

‹ **ماطَ** *v* |i; مَيْط, مَيَطان| [عن] to withdraw, to move away

أَماطَ *v* to remove, to put away; أَماطَ اللِثامَ عن شَيْءٍ to reveal sth

في مَيْدانِ ... in the field of ...; area; في مُخْتَلِفِ المَيادينِ in many areas

مَيْدانيّ *adj* field (*before n*); دِراسة \ بَحْث مَيْدانيّ(ة) field study/research; الباحِثونَ المَيْدانيّونَ field researchers

‹ **ميدالِية** *n* medal; ميدالِية ذَهَبيّة \ فِضّيّة \ بُرُنْزيّة a gold/silver/bronze medal; فازَ بِميدالِيةٍ to win a medal; سَلَّمَ الميدالِياتِ to present medals

‹ **ميرة** *n* provisions, victuals, supplies

‹ **ميرانْغ** *n* meringue

‹ **مَيْرون** *n* (Chr) chrism; سِرّ المَيْرون confirmation

‹ **ميريلانْد** *n* |f| Maryland (*US state*)

‹ **مازَ** *v* |i; مَيْز| to distinguish

مَيَّزَ *v* 1 [فَرَّقَ] to distinguish, to differentiate; to characterize, to typify; مَيَّزَ شَخْصاً \ شَيْئاً to characterize sb/sth; ذلك (ما) يُمَيِّزُهُ that is typical of him 2 [عُنْصُريًّا] to discriminate 3 [فَضَّلَ] |على, عن| to give preference over, to prefer to

تَمَيَّزَ *v* to be distinguished, to be marked, to be characterized; to distinguish oneself; تَتَمَيَّزُ المَدينةُ بِعَدَدٍ كَبيرٍ من ... the city is characterized by a great number of ...; تَمَيَّزَ في شَيْءٍ to excel in sth

تَمايَزَ *v* to differ from one another; to distinguish oneself from another

امْتازَ *v* to distinguish oneself; امْتازَ بِشَيْءٍ to distinguish oneself by/for sth

مَيْز *n* distinction; مَيْز غِشائيّ dialysis; مَيْز عُنْصُريّ racial discrimination

مُتَمَيِّز *adj* separate, different; extraordinary; مَوْهِبة مُتَمَيِّزة an exceptional talent

مُمْتاز *adj* excellent, outstanding, perfect; مَراجِع مُمْتازة excellent references; ذو جَوْدةٍ مُمْتازةٍ of outstanding quality; طَبَخَ \ غَنّى بِصِفةٍ مُمْتازةٍ to cook/sing superbly; عَدَد مُمْتاز (من مَجَلّةٍ) special issue (of a magazine); بِشَكْلٍ مُمْتازٍ excellently

مُمَيَّز *adj* special; إنَّهُ شَخْصٌ مُمَيَّزٌ he is a special person

مُمَيِّز *adj* characteristic, typical, distinguishing; صِفة \ خاصّة مُمَيِّزة a characteristic feature; خاصّيّات مُمَيِّزة distinguishing

ماعَ *v* |i; مَيْع| to melt, to dissolve

مَيَّعَ *v* to melt, to liquefy

تَمَيَّعَ *v* to melt, to dissolve

مائِع *adj* |مَوائِعُ| liquid, fluid

مَيْعة *n* مَيْعة الشَباب prime of youth

مُيوعة *n* instability; fluidity

تَمْييع *n* melting, dissolving; liquefaction

ميغابيكْسِل *n* megapixel, MP

ميغاهيرْتْز *n* megahertz, MHz

ميغاواط, ميجاوات *n* megawatt, MW

ميكا *n* mica

ميكانيك *n* mechanics

ميكانيكا *n* mechanics; عِلْم الميكانيكا mechanics

ميكانيكيّ **A** *adj* mechanical; ساعة ميكانيكيّة a mechanical clock
B *n* (car) mechanic

ميكْروب, ميكْروبة, مِكْروب *n* |ميكْروبات| microbe

ميكْروباص *n* |ميكْروباصات| microbus (*small minibus*)

ميكْروسْكوب *n* |ميكْروسْكوبات| microscope

ميكْروفون *n* |ميكْروفونات| microphone; من خِلالِ الميكْروفون by microphone; (تَحَدَّثَ) في الميكْروفون (to talk) in the microphone

ميكْروفيلْم *n* microfilm

ميكْرون *n* micron

مَيْكَنة *n* mechanization; مَيْكَنة الزِراعةِ agricultural mechanization

مالَ *v* |i; مَيْل, مَيَلان| **1** [جَنَحَ إلى] to slope, to slant, to lean (over); مالَ إلى الأمامِ \ الخَلْفِ to lean forward/backward; يَميلُ الجِدارُ \ تَميلُ الصَخْرةُ the wall/rock leans (over) **2** [كَرِهَ] |عن| to be disinclined to, to be averse to **3** [تَحَيَّزَ ل] to incline, to tend; مالَ إلى فِعْلِ شَيْءٍ to be inclined to do sth; مالَ إلى الخِداعِ to lean towards deception; مالَ إلى الشُيوعيّةِ to incline towards communism; مالَ إلى رَأْيِ غَيْرِهِ to incline to someone else's opinion; مالَ إلى مَزيدٍ من الحُرّيّةِ to lean towards more freedom

مَيَّلَ *v* to bend, to incline; مَيَّلَ بين أَمْرَيْنِ to choose between two things

أَمالَ *v* **1** [حَرَّفَ] to bend, to tilt; أَمالَ رَأْسَهُ to tilt one's head **2** [نَفَّرَ] |عن| to make averse to, to make disinclined to **3** (Ling) to pronounce with imala (*vowel shift where the [a] tends to be pronounced as [e]*)

تَمَيَّلَ *v* to reel, to totter, to waver

تَمايَلَ *v* to swing, to sway, to swerve; to totter; يَتَمايَلُ القارِبُ the boat sways; تَمايَلَ في الطَريقِ to swerve on the road; تَمايَلَ إلى اليَسارِ \ اليَمينِ to swerve to the left/right

اسْتَمالَ *v* to persuade; to trap, to rope; اسْتَمالَ الجُمْهورَ to win over the public

ميل *n* |أَمْيال| mile; على بُعْدِ ١٠ أَمْيالٍ من الشاطِئِ 10 miles off the coast

مَيْل *n* |مُيول, أَمْيال| **1** [نُزوع] tendency, inclination; predilection; مَيْل شَديد \ خَفيف a strong/slight inclination; المَيْل إلى شَيْءٍ a tendency towards sth; مُيول إلى الرِياضيّاتِ an aptitude for mathematics; كانَ شَديدَ المَيْلِ إلى البَقاءِ he was strongly inclined to stay **2** [انْحِدار] inclination, tilt; مَيْل مِحْوَر الأَرْضِ the tilt of the earth's axis

مائِل *adj* slanting, sloping, oblique; diagonal; خَطّ \ شَريط مائِل a diagonal line; حُروف مائِلة italic letters, italics; سَقْف مائِل a pitched roof; مائِل إلى الأَسْفَلِ \ إلى الأَعْلى slanting down/up

مُتَمايِل *adj* tottering, staggering; swinging, swaying

مَيّال *adj* inclined, disposed; prone; كانَ مَيّالاً إلى شَيْءٍ to be disposed to sth

مُيول *n* **1** [نُزوع] tendency, inclination **2** [غُروب] setting, sinking

اسْتِمالة *n* persuasion

إمالة *n* (Ling) imala (*a vowel shift exhibited in many varieties of Arabic, where the [a] is raised towards [e] in certain contexts*)

أَمْيَل *adj* |dipt| more inclined; أنا أَمْيَلُ إلى الاعْتِقادِ أنّ ... I am more inclined to believe that ...

تَمايُل *n* stagger, lurch

ميلانوما *n* melanoma

مينا, مينى, ميناء *n* ① [طِلاء] enamel, glaze, glazing; فُخار مَطْليّ بالمينا glazed pottery; طَلى بالمينا to glaze ② [الأَسْنانِ] (dental) enamel; مينا الأَسْنانِ dental enamel ‹

ميناء *n* see وني ‹

ميني *adj* mini-; ميني باص minibus ‹

مينيسوتا *n* Minnesota (*US state*) ‹

مِياه *n* see ماء ‹

مْيونِخ *n* |f| Munich (*city in Germany*) ‹

ميلودْراما *n* melodrama ‹

ميلودْراميّ *adj* melodramatic

ميليشِيا *n* militia; ميليشِيات طائِفيّة sectarian militias ‹

ميم *n* |f| *name of the letter* م ‹

ميم *n* |ميمات| meme; ميم الإنْتَرْنِت Internet meme

ميموزا *n* mimosa (*Mimosa*) ‹

مانَ *v* |i; مَيْن| ① [كَذَبَ] to lie ② [وَرَّدَ] see مون ‹

مَيْن *n* |f| Maine (*US state*)

تناءى *v* to be far apart

انْتَأَى *v* to go/be away

ناءٍ *adj* far; distant, remote; بَلَد ناءٍ a faraway country; مِنْطَقة نائية a remote area

مَنْأًى *n* distant place; ب \ في مَنْأًى عن far away from; بَقِيَ ب \ في مَنْأًى عن شَيْءٍ to stay away from sth; كانَ بِمَنْأًى عن المَوْضوعِ he had nothing to do with it

‹ **ناي** *n* |نايات| flute, reed pipe; عازِف النايِ flautist (BrE), flutist (AmE); عَزَفَ على النايِ to play the flute

‹ **نَبَأَ** *v* |a; نُبوء، نَبْأ| to rise, to be/become elevated

نَبَّأَ *v* to inform; to report; نَبَّأَ شَخْصاً بِشَيْءٍ to inform sb about sth; نَبَّأَ عن شَيْءٍ to report sth

أَنْبَأَ *v* to announce; to inform; to report; أَنْبَأَ شَخْصاً بِشَيْءٍ to inform sb about sth

تَنَبَّأَ *v* to predict, to forecast; تَنَبَّأَ لِشَخْصٍ بِمُسْتَقْبَلٍ زاهِر to predict a bright future for sb; ... تَنَبَّأَ أَنَّ \ بِأَنَّ to forecast that ...

اسْتَنْبَأَ *v* to inquire, to ask for information

نَبَأ *n* |أَنْباء| news; report; announcement, message; أَنْباء حَسَنة \ سَيِّئة good/bad news; أَحْدَث الأَنْباءِ the latest news; وَكالة \ نَشْرة الأَنْباءِ a news agency/broadcast; سورة النَبَأ The Tidings (*Sura 78*); أَكَّدَ نَبَأً to confirm a message; نَشَرَ أَنْباءً to spread news; ... نَقَلَ النَبَأَ الّذي to bring the news that ...; بَلَغَهُ النَبَأُ أَنّ ... the news reached him that ...; ... أَفادَت الأَنْباءُ أَنّ it was reported that ...

نُبوءة *n* prophecy; prognosis; prediction, forecast

تَنَبُّؤ *n* |تَنَبُّؤات| prediction, forecast; prognosis; قابِل لِلتَنَبُّؤِ predictable; غَيْر قابِلٍ لِلتَنَبُّؤِ unpredictable; تَنَبُّؤات جَوِّيّة weather forecast; تَنَبُّؤ أَحْوالِ الجَوِّ weather forecast; لم يَتَحَقَّق ذلك التَنَبُّؤ that prediction didn't come true

‹ **نابُلُس**, **نابْلُس** *n* |f| Nablus (*city in Palestine*)

‹ **نادِية** *n* |dipt| Nadia (*female given name*)

‹ **نارَجيلة** *n* see نرجل

‹ **ناردين** *n* (Bot) valerian (*Valeriana*)

‹ **نارَنْج** *n* (Bot) bitter orange (*Citrus × aurantium*)

‹ **نازِيّ** *adj*, *n* Nazi; نازِيّ جَديد neo-Nazi

نازِيّة *n* Nazism; النازِيّة الجَديدة neo-Nazism

‹ **ناس** *n* see أنس

‹ **الناظور** *n* |f| Nador (*city in Morocco*)

‹ **ناقوبة** *n* woodpecker

‹ **نَأَمَ** *v* |a-i; نَئيم| to moan

‹ **ناموس** *n* |نَواميسُ| [1] [حَشَرة] mosquito; سِرْب من الناموسِ a swarm of mosquitoes [2] [قانون] law, code, norm; الناموس الأَكْبَر archangel Gabriel; ناموس الطَبيعةِ law of nature; النَواميس الاجْتِماعيّة social norms

ناموسِيّة *n* mosquito net

‹ **نامِيبِيّ** *adj*, *n* Namibian

نامِيبِيا *n* Namibia

‹ **نانو** *n* nano; عِلْم النانو nanoscience; تِكْنولوجيا النانو nanotechnology; نانو ثانية nanosecond

‹ **نانوتِكْنولوجِيا** *n* nanotechnology

‹ **نانومِتْر** *n* nanometre

نانومِتْرِيّ *adj* nanometric

‹ **ناهيكَ** *excl* see ناهٍ

‹ **نَأَى** *v* |a; نَأْي| to be/remain far/distant; نَأَى عن بَيْتِهِ to be far from home; نَأَى بِنَفْسِهِ عن to distance/dissociate oneself from

ناءَى *v* to keep far away, to keep at a distance

أَنْأَى *v* to remove

تَنَبُّؤِيّ *adj* prophetic; predictive; إدْخال نَصّ تَنَبُّؤِيّ (Tech) predictive text input

مُتَنَبِّئ *n* fortune-teller; *a person claiming to be a prophet*; المُتَنَبّي Al-Mutanabbi (*Abu at-Tayyib Ahmad ibn al-Husayn, a 10th century Iraqi who is considered to be one of the greatest classical Arab poets*)

‹ **أُنْبوب, أُنْبوبة** *n* |أَنابيبُ| **1** [ماسورة] pipe, tube; hose; أُنْبوب الرَّشّ garden hose; أنابيب المِياهِ water pipes; أُنْبوب النَفْط oil pipeline; شَبَكة أنابيب \ خطّ piping; pipeline; شَبَكة أنابيبِ المِياهِ water (supply) system; مَدَّ \ أَنْشأَ خطَّ أَنابيبَ to lay a pipeline **2** [لِلتَعْبئة] tube; cylinder; أُنْبوب أُكسِجينٍ \ غازٍ oxygen/gas cylinder; أُنْبوبة مَعْجونِ الأَسْنانِ a tube of toothpaste **3** (Med) test tube; أُنْبوب اخْتِبارٍ a test tube; طِفْل الأنابيبِ a test-tube baby; تَخْصيب الأَنابيبِ in vitro fertilization

أُنْبوبيّ *adj* tubular, cylindrical, pipe (*before n*); قُنْبُلة أُنْبوبيّة pipe bomb

‹ **نَبَتَ** *v* |u; نَبْت| to sprout, to come up, to germinate; to grow; نَبَتَت الأَرْضُ the earth was overgrown; تَنْبُتُ البُذورُ \ الزَرْعُ the seed/crop is sprouting; نَبَتَتْ فِكْرةٌ an idea was born

نَبَّتَ *v* to sow; to plant

أَنْبَتَ *v* **1** [نَبَتَ] to sprout, to come up, to germinate **2** [أَخْرَجَ النَّباتَ] to cause to sprout

اسْتَنْبَتَ *v* to plant, to set; to cultivate; to culture; اسْتَنْبَتَ البَكْتيريا to culture bacteria

نَبْت *n coll* |نُبوت| **1** (Bot) plant; vegetation **2** [نُموّ] germination; growth

نَبات *n coll* (Bot) plant; vegetation; crop; نَبات مُتَسَلِّق climber, climbing plant/vine; نَبات مائيّ \ صَخْريّ a water/rock plant; نَبات لَحيم a succulent; نَبات حَوْليّ an annual; نَبات طِبّي a medicinal plant; نَبات الزينة an ornamental plant; عِلْم النَباتِ botany; عالِم النَباتِ botanist

نَباتيّ **A** *adj* [مَصْنوع من النَباتِ] vegetable (*before n*), botanical; vegetarian; زُبْدة نَباتيّة margarine; وَجْبة نَباتيّة a vegetarian meal; الغِطاء النَباتيّ vegetation; زَخارِف نَباتيّة وَهَنْدَسيّة floral and geometric designs **B** *n* **1** [شَخص لا يَأْكُل اللُحومَ] vegetarian **2** [مُتَخَصِّص بالنَباتاتِ] botanist

نَباتيّة *n* vegetarianism

اسْتِنْبات *n* (Bio) culture; planting, cultivating; اسْتِنْبات بُذورٍ planting seeds; اسْتِنْبات البَكْتيريا a bacterial culture

إنْبات *n* germination

تَنْبيت *n* |تَنْبيتات| cultivation

مُسْتَنْبَت *n* |مُسْتَنْبَتات| (Bio) culture; مُسْتَنْبَت بَكْتيريا a bacterial culture

مَنْبِت, مَنْبَت *n* |مَنابِتُ| **1** [مَشْتَل] nursery; arboretum; مَنْبِت الشَعْرِ (hair) follicle **2** [مَنْشَأ] source, origin; المَنْبِت الاجْتِماعيّ the social environment

‹ **نِبْتون** *n* Neptune

‹ **نَبَحَ** *v* |a; نَبْح, نُباح, نَبيح| to bark; تَنْبَحُ الكِلابُ dogs bark; the dogs are barking; الكِلابُ تَنْبَحُ والقافِلةُ تَسيرُ the dogs bark but the caravan moves on (*progress cannot be stopped by the criticism of the small-minded*)

نَبْح *n* bark; نَبْحُ الكِلابِ لا يُضِرُّ السَحابَ *a dog's bark does not injure its owner*

نَبّاح *adj* barking; yelping; كَلْب نَبّاح a barking dog

نُباح *n* bark, barking

‹ **نَبَذَ** *v* |i; نَبْذ| **1** [تَخَلّى] to renounce; to refrain from; نَبَذَ الإرْهابَ \ التَطَرُّفَ \ العُنْفَ to renounce terrorism/extremism/violence; نَبَذَ اسْتِخْدامَ السِلاحِ to refrain from using weapons; نَبَذَ الاقْتِتالَ to give up fighting **2** [رَمى] to throw away, to dump, to discard; to expel **3** [خَرَقَ] to break; نَبَذَ العادةَ to break with the tradition **4** [أَهْمَلَ] to neglect, to disregard **5** [أَنْتَجَ النَبيذَ] to make wine

نَبَّذَ *v* to make wine

نابَذَ *v* **1** [خالَفَ] to oppose, to resist **2** [فارَقَ] to part from, to separate from, to break (up) with

تَنابَذَ *v* to fight, to quarrel

انْتَبَذَ *v* **1** [اعْتَزَلَ] to withdraw, to retreat, to seclude oneself **2** [العِنَبَ] to make wine; انْتَبَذَ العِنَبَ to make wine from grapes

نَبْذ *n* |أَنْباذ| ❶ [تافِهة] trifle ❷ [إِهْمال] renunciation, refraining from; وَجَّهَ دَعْوةً إلى نَبْذِ العُنْفِ to call for the renunciation of violence

نابِذ *adj* centrifugal; قوّة نابِذة centrifugal force

نابِذة *n* centrifuge

نُبْذة *n* |نُبَذ| overview, profile, summary; fragment, section; نُبذة عن النِقاط الأَساسيّة an overview of the main points

نَبيذ *n* |أَنبِذة| wine; نَبيذ أَحمَر \ أَبيَض red/white wine; زُجاجة نَبيذ a bottle of wine; a wine bottle; كَأْس \ زُجاجة من النَبيذ a glass/bottle of wine; ذاقَ نَبيذاً to taste wine

مَنْبوذ **A** *adj* rejected, unwelcome
B *n* pariah, outcast; persona non grata; untouchable (*a low-caste or casteless member of Hindu society*)

‹ **نَبَرَ** *v* |i;| نَبْر to lay the stress/emphasis/accent on; to sing in a high-pitched voice

اِنْتَبَرَ *v* ❶ [تَوَرَّمَ] to swell ❷ [صَعِدَ إلى المِنبَر] to ascend the pulpit

نَبْر *n* (Ling) intonation; accent, stress

نَبْرة *n* ❶ [صَوْت] tone; voice; timbre; بِنَبْرةٍ ساخِرةٍ in a sarcastic tone ❷ [وَرَم] swelling ❸ (Ling) accent, stress; النَبْرةُ على المَقطَعِ الأَوَّلِ the stress is on the first syllable

مِنْبَر *n* |مَنابِرُ| minbar, pulpit, rostrum; من على المِنْبَر from the pulpit; مِنْبَر حُرّ an open forum; اعْتَلى المِنبَرَ to ascend the minbar

‹ **نِبْريج** *n* |نَباريجُ| hose, pipe, tube

‹ **نِبْراسْكا** *n* Nebraska (*US state*)

‹ **نِبْراس** *n* |نَبارِسُ| lantern; lamp, light; (fig) model, example; نِبْراس للأَجْيالِ القادِمةِ a shining light for future generations

‹ **نَبَزَ** *v* |i;| نَبْز to dub, to give a nickname to; نَبَزَ شَخْصاً to give sb a nickname

نَبَز *n* |أَنْباز| nickname; title

‹ **نَبَسَ** *v* |i;| نَبْس, نُبْسة to speak, to say; to utter; to stammer; لم يَنْبِسْ بِبِنْتِ شَفةٍ ,لم يَنبِس بِكَلِمةٍ to not say a word

‹ **نَبَشَ** *v* |u;| نَبْش ❶ [أَخْرَجَ من الأَرْضِ] to excavate, to exhume; نَبَشَ قَبْراً to exhume a grave; لا تَنْبِشِ القُبورَ leave the dead alone ❷ [كَشَفَ] to reveal, to uncover, to unearth; نَبَشَ فَضيحةً to reveal a scandal

نَبْش *n* ❶ [إخراج من الأَرْضِ] excavation ❷ [كَشْف] revelation, uncovering, disclosure

نَبّاش *n* desecrator

‹ **نَبَضَ** *v* |i;| نَبْض, نَبَضان to beat, to throb; to pulsate; يَنْبِضُ العِرْقُ the vain is throbbing; يَنْبِضُ قَلْبُهُ his heart is pounding

نَبْض *n coll* |أَنْباض| heartbeat; pulse (rate); نَبْض مُضْطَرِب an irregular heartbeat; نَبْض سَريع \ بَطيء a rapid/slow pulse (rate); جَسَّ نَبْضَ شَخْصٍ to take sb's pulse

نابِض **A** *adj* beating, throbbing; pulsating; نابِض بالحَياة lively; وَصْف نابِض بالحَيَويّة a vivid description
B *n* |نَوابِضُ| spring; spiral; نابِض حَلَزونيّ \ لَوْلَبيّ a coil spring

مَنْبِض *n* |مَنابِضُ| pulse, heartbeat; مَنْبِض القَلْب pulse, heartbeat

‹ **نَبَطَ** *v* |i-u;| نَبْط, نُبوط to stream; to well up

اِسْتَنْبَطَ *v* ❶ [اسْتَنْتَجَ] to deduce, to gather; اسْتَنْبَطَ نَتائِجَ من ... to draw conclusions from ... ❷ [ابْتَكَرَ] to invent, to think of/up, to come up with; اسْتَنْبَطَ طُرُقاً \ وَسائِلَ جَديدةً to think of new ways ❸ [حَصَلَ على] to get, to receive; اسْتَنْبَطَ تَصَوُّراً أَميناً عن شَيْءٍ to get a reliable impression of sth

نَبَط *n* |أَنْباط| Nabataean

نَبَطيّ *adj* Nabataean

اِسْتِنْباط *n* |اِسْتِنْباطات| ❶ [اِسْتِنْتاج] deduction; اسْتِنْباط فِكْريّ deduction ❷ [اِبْتِكار] invention

‹ **نَبَعَ** *v* |a-i-u;| نَبْع, نُبوع, نَبَعان to originate, to come (from); to rise, to well up; نَبَعَ من شَيْءٍ to originate from sth; يَنبُعُ نَهْرُ الفُراتِ من الأَراضي التُرْكيّة the river Euphrates rises in Turkey; تَنْبُعُ أَهَمّيّةُ هذا البَحْثِ من ... the importance of this study comes from ...

نَبْع *n* |نُبوع| well, spring; جَلَبَ المِياهَ من النَبْع to dip water out of the well

مَنْبَع *n* |مَنابِعُ| source, origin; well, spring; مَنابِع نَهْرِ النيلِ the sources of the Nile; مَنْبَع نَفْطٍ an oil well; مَنْبَع فَسادٍ a source of corruption; أَخَذَ مَنْبَعَهُ من ... to have its origin in ...

يَنْبوع *n* |يَنابيعُ| source, origin; well, spring; يَنابيع نَهْرِ النيلِ the sources of the Nile

‹ **نَبَغَ** *v* |a-i-u; نُبوغ, نَبْغ| ⟨1⟩ [بَرَزَ] to excel; to be a genius; نَبَغَ في الرِياضيّاتِ to excel at mathematics ⟨2⟩ [ظَهَرَ] to appear, to emerge

نابِغ *adj* |نَوابِغُ| brilliant, bright; excellent, outstanding; talented

نابِغة *n* |نَوابِغُ| genius; talent; نابِغة في الموسيقى \ التِقْنيّة a musical/technical genius; نابِغة في الحِسابِ a genius in mathematics

نُبوغ *n* excellence, eminence; talent

‹ **نَبْق** *n* (Bot) buckthorn (*Rhamnus*)

‹ **نَبْكة, نَبَكة** *n* hill, elevation

‹ **نَبَلَ** *v* |u; نَبْل| to shoot arrows at; نَبَلَ الهَدَفَ to shoot arrows at the target

نَبُلَ *v* |u; نُبْل| to be noble

نَبْل *n coll* |نِبال| arrow; أَمْطَرَ شَخْصاً بِوابِلٍ من النِبالِ to shower the enemy with arrows

نُبْل *n* ⟨1⟩ [أَخْلاق] nobility, generosity of spirit ⟨2⟩ [نَسَب] nobility, the aristocracy, peerage (BrE)

نابِل *n* archer; اخْتَلَطَ الحابِلُ بالنابِلِ everything was mixed up

نَبّال *n* |نَبّالة| archer

نَبالة *n* nobility, the aristocracy, peerage (BrE)

نَبيل **A** *adj* |نُبَلاءُ| noble, generous; chivalrous, gallant; عَمَل نَبيل a generous deed; طَبْع نَبيل a noble character; رَجُل نَبيل a gallant man; لَقَب نَبيلٍ a title of nobility; عائِلة نَبيلة an aristocratic family; من عائِلةٍ نَبيلةٍ of noble birth; الحِصانُ حَيَوانٌ نَبيلٌ horses are noble animals

B *n* |نُبَلاءُ| ⟨1⟩ [شَريف الأَصْل] a noble, a nobleman ⟨2⟩ [اسْم شَخْصيّ] Nabil (*male given name*)

‹ **نَبُهَ, نَبَهَ, نَبِهَ** *v* |u; نَباهة| to be famous/well-known

نَبِهَ *v* |a; نَبَه| to notice; to observe; to (take) heed, to pay attention; نَبِهَ لِشَيْءٍ to heed sth

نَبَّهَ *v* ⟨1⟩ [أَطْلَعَ] to warn; to alarm; to indicate; نَبَّهَ إلى خَطَرٍ to warn for danger; نَبَّهَ مُسْتَعْمِلي الطَريقِ إلى أنّ ... to warn road users that ...; نَبَّهَ شَخْصاً إلى شَيْءٍ to indicate sth to sb ⟨2⟩ [أَيْقَظَ] to wake up, to awaken

أَنْبَهَ *v* to awaken, to arouse from sleep

تَنَبَّهَ *v* ⟨1⟩ [فَطِنَ] to notice, to be aware; to (take) heed, to pay attention; to be alert; تَنَبَّهَ إلى \ ل to pay attention to; تَنَبَّهَ لِخُطورةِ المَوْقِفِ to be aware of the danger of the situation ⟨2⟩ [اسْتَيْقَظَ] to come round; to wake up, to awaken

انْتَبَهَ *v* |إلى| to pay attention (to), to notice, to take heed (of); to be careful (of), to watch out (for), to be alert (for); to consider, to take into consideration; انْتَبَهَ جَيِّداً to watch carefully; انْتَبَهَ إذا حَدَثَ شَيْءٌ to watch if sth happens; انْتَبَهَ إلى شَيْءٍ to notice sth; لم أَنْتَبِهْ إلَيْهِ I didn't pay attention to it; لم أَنْتَبِهْ للمُكالَمةِ I didn't hear the phone (*after missing a call*); انْتَبِهْ! attention!; انْتَبِهْ إلى كَلامِكَ! watch your words!; كانَ الشَيْءُ الوَحيدُ الّذي لم يَنْتَبِهوا إلَيْهِ ... the one thing they did not consider was ...; لا يَنْتَبِهُ أَحَدٌ إلى حُقوقِ المَرْأةِ no one takes women's rights into consideration

نُبْه *n* insight, understanding

نابِه *adj* |نُبَهاءُ| ⟨1⟩ [نَبيل] noble; renowned ⟨2⟩ [ذَكيّ] intelligent, bright; طالِب نابِه an apt pupil

نَباهة *n* cleverness, brightness

نَبيه **A** *adj* |نُبَهاءُ| intelligent, bright; quick-witted; طِفْل نَبيه a bright child

B *n* Nabih (*male given name*)

نَبيهة *n* |dipt| Nabiha (*female given name*)

انْتِباه *n* ⟨1⟩ [اهْتِمام] attention; concentration; انْتِباه! look out!, be careful!; attention!; عدم انْتِباهٍ inattention; بِانْتِباهٍ attentive; مُثير للانْتِباهِ noticeable, interesting; أشياء لا تُثيرُ الانْتِباهَ uninteresting things; أَعارَ شَيْئًا انْتِباهاً to pay attention to; أَعْطى كُلَّ انْتِباهِهِ \ اسْتَرْعى \ لَفَتَ to focus all attention; جَذَبَ \ جَلَبَ الانْتِباهَ to attract attention; صَرَفَ الانْتِباهَ (عن شَيْءٍ) \ رَكَّزَ انْتِباهَهُ to distract attention from (sth); الانْتِباهَ على شَيْءٍ to concentrate on sth; لم يَعْرِ شَخْصاً انْتِباهاً to not pay attention to sb ⟨2⟩ [حَذَر] alertness, attentiveness; caution

تَنْبيه *n* |تَنْبيهات| ⟨1⟩ [إعْلام] notification; warning, alarm; آلة تَنْبيهٍ (car) horn, hooter (BrE) ⟨2⟩ [مُلاحَظة] remark; NB

مُتَنَبِّه *adj* alert, vigilant; observant; mindful; كانَ مُتَنَبِّهاً لِشَيْءٍ to be mindful of sth

اسْتَنْتَجَ *v* to conclude, to gather; to deduce, to derive, to infer; اسْتَنْتَجَ شَيْئاً من شَيْءٍ to deduce sth from sth; اسْتَنْتَجَ أنّ ... to conclude that ...; اسْتَنْتَجَ من كَلامِ شَخْصٍ أنّ ... to gather from sb's words that ...

ناتِج *n* ❶ (Econ) product; إجْماليّ الناتِج القَوْميّ الإجْماليّ, الناتِج القَوْميّ gross national product, GNP; الناتِج المَحَلّيّ الإجْماليّ, إجْماليّ الناتِج المَحَلّيّ gross domestic product, GDP ❷ (Comput) output

نِتاج *n* ❶ [حاصِل] product, production; yield, harvest, proceeds; result; نِتاج طَبيعيّ لِشَيْءٍ a natural result of sth; نِتاج أَدَبيّ a literary work; نِتاج فِكْريّ \ ثَقافيّ an intellectual/cultural production; جاءَ نِتاجاً لِشَيْءٍ to be the result of sth ❷ (Zool) offspring (*animal*); نِتاج الخَيْل foal

نَتيجة *n* |نَتائِجُ| ❶ [عاقِبة] result, outcome; consequence, effect; finding; نَتيجةً ل, نَتيجةً as a result of, because of, due to, owing to; بالنَتيجة, نَتيجةً لِذَلِكَ consequently; بِدونِ نَتيجةٍ with no results; الأَسْباب والنَتائِج cause and effect; نَتيجة مُباشِرة \ مَنْطِقيّة a direct/logical effect; نَتيجة جَيِّدة \ مُمْتازة \ سَيِّئة a good/excellent/bad result; نَتائِج مُرْضِية \ مُخَيِّبة satisfactory/disappointing results; نَتيجة مَلْموسة a tangible result; نَتائِج عِلْميّة scientific findings; النَتائِج المُبْتَغاة \ المَنْشودة the desired effect; نَتيجة بَحْثٍ \ اخْتِبار research/test result; نَتيجة الانْتِخاباتِ \ الاسْتِفْتاءِ the outcome of the elections/referendum; ماتَ نَتيجةَ شَيْءٍ to die from to the effects of sth; قَبِلَ النَتائِجَ to accept the consequences; اسْتَخْلَصَ نَتائِجَ to draw conclusions; أَعْلَنَ النَتيجةَ to announce the results; أَحْرَزَ \ حَصَلَ على \ تَوَصَّلَ إلى نَتائِجَ to achieve/get/obtain results; أَسْفَرَ عن نَتائِجَ to lead to results; النَتيجةُ أنّ ... the result is that ...; أيّا كانَت النَتيجةُ regardless of the result ❷ [حاصِل] score; result; نَتائِج رِياضيّة sports scores; نَتيجة ١٨٦ نُقْطةً a score of 186 (points); نَتيجة عالية \ ضَعيفة \ نِهائيّة a high/low/final score; حَصَلَ على نَتيجةٍ جَيِّدةٍ \ سَيِّئةٍ to have a good/bad score ❸ [يَوْميّة] calendar; نَتيجة الحائِطِ wall calendar ❹ [إنْتاج] production; yield, profit

اسْتِنْتاج *n* |اسْتِنْتاجات| conclusion; deduction, inference; اسْتِنْتاج خاطِئ \ غَيْر صَحيح \ غَيْر مَنْطِقيّ a wrong/incorrect/

مُنَبِّه *n* |مُنَبِّهات| ❶ [مادّة مُثيرة] stimulant (*drug*); مُنَبِّهات stimulants; اسْتَخْدَمَ مُنَبِّهاتٍ to use stimulants ❷ [آلة] alarm (clock); وَقَّتَ المُنَبِّهَ to set the alarm; يَرِنُّ المُنَبِّهُ the alarm is going off ❸ [سَيّارة] (car) horn, hooter (BrE); ضَغَطَ على المُنَبِّهِ to sound the horn

مُنْتَبِه *adj* alert, attentive; vigilant; مُسْتَمِعونَ مُنْتَبِهونَ attentive listeners; جُمْهور مُنْتَبِه an attentive audience

‹ **نَبا** *v* |u; نَبْو, نُبُوّ| to shun; to dislike; نَبا عن شَيْءٍ to dislike sth; نَبا بِهِ المَكانُ the place was not convenient for him

تَنَبّى *v* to claim to be a prophet

ناب *adj* ugly, nasty; كَلِمات نابِية nasty words

نُبُوّة *n* prophethood; prophecy

نَبَويّ *adj* prophetic; *of the Prophet Muhammad*; السيرة النَبَويّة the life of the Prophet Muhammad

نَبيّ *n* |أَنْبِياء, نَبِيّون| prophet; النَبيّ the Prophet (*Muhammad*); خاتَم النَبِيّينَ the Seal of the Prophets (*the last prophet, Muhammad*); سورة الأَنْبِياء The Prophets (*Sura 21*); سُنّة النَبيّ the Sunna; *the customs and practices of the Prophet Muhammad*; مَدينة النَبيّ the city of the Prophet (*Medina*); فَرَس النَبيّ a praying mantis; لا كَرامةَ لِنَبيٍّ بين قَوْمِهِ a prophet is not without honour, save in his own country; صَلِّ على النَبيّ *a polite way of expressing disagreement with what was just said, or urging sb to calm down or think more positively*

‹ **النِت** *n* the Net

‹ **نَتَأَ** *v* |a; نُتوء| to protrude; to stick up; تَنْتَأُ الصَخْرةُ the rock sticks up

ناتِئ *adj* protruding; swollen, bulging

نُتوء *n* protrusion, projection, outcrop; lump, bump; swelling, bulge; نُتوء صَخْريّ a rocky outcrop

‹ **نَتَجَ** *v* |i; إنْتاج| عن| to result from, to be the result of; to arise from, to follow from; نَتَجَ هذا الخِلافُ عن سوءِ فَهْمٍ this conflict is the result of a misunderstanding

أَنْتَجَ *v* ❶ [صَنَعَ] to produce; to yield; to generate, to bring forth; to make, to cause; أَنْتَجَ كَثيراً \ قَليلاً to produce much/little; أَنْتَجَ مُنْتَجاتٍ زِراعيّةً to yield agricultural products ❷ (Zool) to give birth; to produce (*animals*) ❸ (Theat, Cin) to produce; أَنْتَجَ فيلْماً \ مَسْرَحيّةً to produce a film/play

مِنْتاش *n* (a pair of) tweezers

‹ **نَتَعَ** *v* |i-u; نُتوع| to drip, to trickle; to seep; نَتَعَ الدمُ من الجُرْحِ blood dripped from the wound

‹ **نَتَفَ** *v* |i; نَتْف| to pull out, to pluck; to pick; نَتَفَ رِيشَ دَجاجةٍ to pluck a chicken; نَتَفَ الحاجِبَيْنِ \ شَعْرَ الحَواجِبِ to pluck one's eyebrows

نَتَّفَ *v* to pull/pluck out

نُتْفة *n* |نُتَف| ❶ [من الشَعْرِ] tuft, knot ❷ [قَليل] bit, little; pinch, touch

مِنْتاف *n* |مَناتيفُ| (a pair of) tweezers

‹ **مِنْتول** *n* listed alphabetically

‹ **نَتَنَ, نَتِنَ, نَتُنَ** *v* |a-i-u; نَتْن, نَتانة, نُتونة| to stink, to smell (bad); to rot, to decay

نَتَّنَ *v* ❶ [نَتَنَ] to stink, to smell (bad); to rot, to decay ❷ [جَعْلَهُ مُنْتِناً] to make stink

أَنْتَنَ *v* to stink, to smell (bad); to rot, to decay

نَتْن *n* stench

نَتِن *adj* rotten; stinking; رائِحة نَتِنة a putrid smell

نَتانة *n* stench; decay, rottenness

إِنْتان *n* sepsis

مُنْتِن *adj* stinking; rotten

‹ **نَثَّ** *v* |u; نَثيث| to sweat (out)

نَثيث *n* sweat

‹ **نَثَرَ** *v* |i-u; نَثْر, نِثار| ❶ [ذَرَّ] to scatter, to spread, to disperse; نَثَرَ شَيْئاً على شَيْءٍ to scatter sth on sth ❷ (Literat) to write prose

تَناثَرَ *v* to be scattered/dispersed; to splatter

اِنْتَثَرَ *v* to be scattered/dispersed

اِسْتَنْثَرَ *v* to sniff, to inhale (*through the nose*); *to rinse one's nose*

نَثْر *n* prose; النَثْرُ العَرَبيّ المُعاصِر modern Arabic prose; قَصيدة النَثْر prose poetry

ناثِر *n* a prose writer

نِثار *n* confetti; *candy or money that is scattered at parties*

نَثْرِيّ *adj* in prose, prosaic; في قالِبٍ نَثْرِيٍّ in the form of prose

مُتَناثِر *adj* scattered, dispersed; شَظايا مُتَناثِرة scattered shrapnel

illogical conclusion; وَصَلَ \ تَوَصَّلَ إلى اسْتِنْتاجٍ to reach a conclusion; يُمْكِنُ الاسْتِنْتاجُ بِأَنَّ ... one may conclude that ...

اِسْتِنْتاجِيّ *adj* deductive

إِنْتاج *n* production, manufacture; make, brand; إِنْتاج كَثيف intensive production; إِنْتاج أَلْبانٍ the production of dairy products; إِنْتاج سَيّاراتٍ the production of cars; إِنْتاج سينَمائِيّ \ فيلْمٍ a film production; شَرِكة إِنْتاجِ الأَفْلامِ a film production company; إِنْتاج مُشْتَرَك a co-production; كَثيرُ الإِنْتاجِ productive; وَسيلة الإِنْتاجِ a production method; تَحْديد \ وَقْف الإِنْتاجِ a production restriction/stop; عَمَلِيّة الإِنْتاجِ the production process; خَطّ الإِنْتاجِ a production line; أَنْشَأَ خَطَّ إِنْتاجٍ to set up a production line; تَكاليف الإِنْتاجِ the costs of production; هذا إِنْتاجٌ أَمْريكِيٌّ this is made in the USA

إِنْتاجِيّ *adj* production (*before n*), productive; قُدْرة \ طاقة إِنْتاجِيّة productive capacity, productivity

إِنْتاجِيّة *n* productivity, productive capacity/power; مَحْصول ذو إِنْتاجِيّةٍ عالِيةٍ a high-yielding crop; زِيادة الإِنْتاجِيّة increased productivity

مُنْتَج *n* |مُنْتَجات| product; مُنْتَج ثانَوِيّ by-product; مُنْتَج زِراعِيّ agricultural product; مُنْتَجات اسْتِهلاكِيّة consumer goods

مُنْتِج **A** *adj* productive; producing; غَيْر مُنْتِجٍ unproductive; دُوَل مُنْتِجة لِلنَفْطِ oil producing countries
B *n* ❶ [صانِع] manufacturer, producer, maker ❷ [عَمَلٍ فَنِّيٍّ] producer

مَنْتوج *n* |مَنْتوجات| product; مَنْتوج وَطَنِيّ national product; المَنْتوجات الفَلّاحِيّة \ الزِراعِيّة agricultural products

‹ **نَتَحَ** *v* |a; نَتْح| to transpire; to sweat; to exude

‹ **نَتَرَ** *v* |u; نَتْر| to pull/tear away

‹ **نِتْرات** *n* nitrate; سَماد نِتْرات الأَمونيوم ammonium nitrate fertilizer

‹ **نِتْروجين** *n* nitrogen

‹ **نِتْريك** *n* nitrite; حامِض النِتْريك nitric acid

‹ **نَتَشَ** *v* |i; نَتْش| to pull/pluck out; to extract; نَتَشَ الشَعْرَ to pull out hair(s)

مَنْثور **A** *adj* **1** [مُفَرَّق] scattered, dispersed; هَباء مَنْثور dust in the wind **2** (Literat) in prose, prosaic; شِعْر مَنْثور prose poetry **B** *n* (Bot) stock (*Matthiola*)

‹ **نَجاشِيّ** *n* Negus (*a title bestowed on kings in the Afro-Asiatic Ge'ez, Tigrinya, Tigre and Amharic languages*); *a ruler, or the supreme ruler, of Ethiopia*

‹ **نَجُبَ** *v* |u; نَجابة| **1** [كانَ كَريمَ الأَصْلِ] to be of noble birth **2** [تَفَوَّقَ] to be excellent/outstanding

أَنْجَبَ *v* to give birth, to bear; to sire, to father, to beget; to have; to produce, to bring forth; أَنْجَبَتْ طِفْلاً to give birth to a child; أَنْجَبَتْ تَوْأماً she had twins; أَنْجَبَ سَبْعَ بَناتٍ he had seven daughters; أَنْجَبَ أَطْفالاً من امْرَأةٍ to father children by a woman; أَنْجَبَتْ أَطْفالاً من رَجُلٍ to bear a man's children; قد أَنْجَبَتْ هذه المَدينةُ الكَثيرَ من الأُدَباءِ this city has brought forth many writers

نَجْب *adj* noble

نَجابة *n* nobility

نَجيب *adj* |أَنْجاب ,نُجَباءُ ,نُجُب| **1** [نَبيل] aristocratic, of noble birth **2** [مُمْتاز] excellent, outstanding **3** [اِسْم شَخْصيّ] Najib (*male given name*)

إِنْجاب *n* reproduction; breeding; مُعَدَّل الإِنْجابِ the birth rate; سَنّ الإِنْجابِ child-bearing age; هو غَيْرُ قادِرٍ على الإِنْجابِ he can't have children

إِنْجابيّ *adj* birth (*before n*), birthing (*before n*); reproductive; صِحّة إِنْجابيّة reproductive health

‹ **نَجَحَ** *v* |a; نَجاح| **1** [الشَخْصُ] to succeed, to be successful; to pass; نَجَحَ في امْتِحانٍ to pass an exam; نَجَحَ بِتَفَوُّقٍ to pass with distinction, to pass cum laude (AmE); نَجَحَ في إِقْناعِ شَخْصٍ بِشَيْءٍ to successfully convince sb of sth **2** [الأَمْرُ] to be successful; to work; نَجَحَت العَمَليّةُ the operation was successful

نَجَّحَ *v* to make successful/succeed; to make pass

أَنْجَحَ *v* to make successful/succeed; to make pass

ناجِح *adj* successful; prosperous; حَفْلة ناجِحة a successful party; شَرِكة ناجِحة a prosperous company; سَيِّدة أَعْمالٍ ناجِحة a successful businesswoman

نَجاح *n* |نَجاحات| success; prosperity; بِنَجاحٍ successfully; نَجاح كَبير \ عَظيم \ باهِر a big/great/tremendous success; نَجاح شَخْصيّ a personal success; طَريقة أُثْبِتَ نَجاحُها a proven method; لَقِيَ \ حَقَّقَ \ سَجَّلَ \ أَحْرَزَ نَجاحاً to achieve success; نَجاحاً في شَيْءٍ to be successful in sth; أَتَمَنّى لَكَ النَجاحَ الكامِلَ I wish you every success; كانَ النَجاحُ حَليفَهُمْ they were successful; النَجاحُ حَليفُ كُلِّ مُثابِرٍ those who work hard will be successful

‹ **نَجَدَ** *v* |u; نَجْد| to help, to assist; to save

نَجِدَ *v* |a; نَجَد| to sweat, to perspire

نَجَّدَ *v* to upholster; to furnish; نَجَّدَ غُرْفةً to furnish a room; نَجَّدَ وِسادةً to upholster a cushion

ناجَدَ *v* to save; to help, to assist

أَنْجَدَ *v* to save; to help, to assist

اِسْتَنْجَدَ *v* to ask for help/assistance; اِسْتَنْجَدَ صَديقَهُ \ بِصَديقِهِ to ask one's friend for help

نَجْد *n* |نُجود ,نِجاد| **1** [مُرْتَفَع] highland, plateau **2** (Geog) نَجْد Najd (*plateau in the central region of the Arabian Peninsula*) **3** [أَثاث] piece of furniture

نَجّاد *n* upholsterer

نِجاد *n* belt, sword belt

نَجْدة *n* |نَجَدات| help, assistance, relief; rescue; النَجْدةَ! النَجْدةَ! help! help!; شُرْطة النَجْدةِ *a specialized police unit which responds to emergencies*; مُؤَسَّسة النَجْدةِ relief organization; طَلَبَ النَجْدةَ to request help

تَنْجيد *n* upholstery, covering; قُماش التَنْجيدِ upholstery fabric

مُنْجِد *n* rescuer

مُنَجَّد *adj* upholstered; مَقْعَد مُنَجَّد an upholstered chair

‹ **نَجَذَ** *v* |u; نَجْذ| to bite/chew (*with the molars*)

ناجِذ *n* |نَواجِذُ| molar; عَضَّ بالنَواجِذِ على شَيْءٍ ≈ to grab sth with both hands; to wholeheartedly embrace sth; عَضَّ على ناجِذَيْهِ to grit one's teeth, to grin and bear it; ضَحِكَ بِكُلِّ نَواجِذِهِ to grin from ear to ear

‹ **نَجَرَ** *v* |u; نَجْر| **1** [صَنَعَ من الخَشَبِ] to build/make from wood **2** [قَطَعَ] to hew; to carve **3** [كَشَطَ] to plane

نجّار *n* carpenter, woodworker; cabinetmaker; يَعْمَلُ نَجّاراً he's a carpenter by trade

نُجارة *n* wood shavings

نِجارة *n* carpentry, woodwork; وَرْشة النِجارة carpentry workshop; مِهْنة النجارة carpentry (*as a trade/occupation*)

مَنْجَر, مَنْجَرة *n* |مَناجِرُ| woodwork shop

مِنْجَر *n* |مَناجِرُ| (Tools) plane, jointer

مَنْجور *n* woodwork, panelling

‹ **نَجَزَ** *v* |u| ⓵ [أَتَمَّ] |نَجْز| to accomplish, to achieve; to do, to carry out; to complete ⓶ [تَمَّ] |نَجْز| to be accomplished/completed

نَجِزَ *v* |a; نَجَز| to be accomplished/completed

ناجَزَ *v* to fight (with/against), to combat (with/against); ناجَزَ شَخْصاً to fight sb

أَنْجَزَ *v* to accomplish, to achieve; to do, to perform, to carry out; to complete, to realize; أَنْجَزَ مُهِمّةً to perform a task; أَنْجَزَ دِراسةً to complete a study; أَنْجَزَ تَرْجَمةً to do a translation; أَنْجَزَ العَديدَ من الأَعْمالِ to do a lot of work

ناجِز *adj* ⓵ [مَقْضِيّ] accomplished, completed ⓶ [تامّ] complete, total; اسْتِقْلال ناجِز complete independence

إِنْجاز *n* |إِنْجازات| achievement, accomplishment, success; performance; completion; قَيْدَ الإِنْجازِ under construction; إِنْجاز عَظيم quite an achievement; إِنْجاز المُعامَلاتِ completion of transactions; حَقَّقَ إِنْجازاً to realize a success; قامَ بِإِنْجازٍ جَيِّدٍ to put on a good performance

مُنْجَز *adj* achieved, accomplished; completed, done

مُنْجِز *n* achiever

‹ **نَجُسَ, نَجِسَ** *v* |a-u; نَجاسة| to be/become impure

نَجَّسَ *v* to befoul, to pollute, to contaminate; to make unclean

أَنْجَسَ *v* to soil, to stain

تَنَجَّسَ *v* to be/become impure; to be/become contaminated

نَجَس *n* impurity, uncleanliness, filth

نَجِس *adj* |أَنْجاس| ⓵ [غَيْر طاهِر] impure, unclean; لَحْمُ الخِنْزيرِ نَجِسٌ بالنِسْبةِ للمُسْلِمينَ pork is considered unclean by Muslims ⓶ [مُسَبِّب للنَجاسةِ] *causing impurity*

نَجاسة *n* impurity, uncleanness

نَجيس *adj* incurable

‹ **نَجَعَ** *v* |a; نَجْع, نُجوع| to be useful/effective; to be curative// beneficial; نَجَعَ الدَواءُ the medicine was effective

أَنْجَعَ *v* ⓵ [أَفْلَحَ] to succeed ⓶ [نَفَعَ] to be useful

انْتَجَعَ *v* to take/seek refuge with; انْتَجَعَ الرَجُلُ أَخاهُ the man sought refuge with his brother

ناجِع *adj* effective, useful; beneficial; constructive; غَيْر ناجِعٍ ineffective; inefficient; إِجْراء غَيْر ناجِعٍ an inefficient measure; أَدْوِية ناجِعة \ غَيْر ناجِعةٍ effective/ineffective medicines; حَلّ ناجِع للمُشْكِلةِ an effective solution to the problem

نَجاعة *n* usefulness, efficacy, effectiveness; benefit; effect; النَجاعة العِلاجيّة therapeutic efficacy; أَثْبَتَ نَجاعة شَيْءٍ to prove/demonstrate sth's effectiveness

نَجيع *adj* useful; beneficial

مُنْتَجَع *n* |مُنْتَجَعات| resort; spa; مُنْتَجَع شَتْويّ winter resort; مُنْتَجَع سِياحيّ holiday resort, tourist resort; مُنْتَجَع صِحّيّ spa; health resort

‹ **نَجَف** *n* |نِجاف| hill, mound; dune

نَجَفة *n* |نَجَف, نَجَفات| chandelier

النَجَف *n* |f| Najaf (*city in Iraq*)

‹ **نَجَلَ** *v* |u; نَجْل| to beget, to father

نَجْل *n* |أَنْجال| son; offspring, progeny; نَجْل الأَميرِ the son of the prince

نَجْلاء *n* |dipt f| Najla (*female given name*)

نَجيل *n* |نُجُل| grass; نَجيل صِناعيّ artificial grass, AstroTurf®

أَنْجَل *adj* |dipt| wide-eyed; gaping; طَعْنة نَجْلاء a fatal stab

إِنْجيل *n* listed alphabetically

مِنْجَل *n* |مَناجِلُ| sickle, scythe

مَنْجَلة *n* (Tools) (bench) vise

‹ **نَجَمَ** *v* |u; نُجوم| ⓵ [نَتَجَ] |عن| to result from; to be caused by; نَجَمَ عن سوءِ التَفاهُم to result from a misunderstanding; نَجَمَتْ عن الفَيَضانِ خَسائِرُ مادّيّةٌ كَبيرةٌ the flood resulted in large financial losses; إِنّ الانْفِجارَ نَجَمَ عن تَسَرُّبٍ للغازِ the explosion was caused by a gas leak ⓶ [طَلَعَ] to rise, to ascend

نَجّى *v* to rescue, to save; نَجّى شَخصاً من شَيْءٍ to rescue sb from sth

ناجى *v* to confide in/to; to whisper to; ناجى نَفْسَهُ to talk to oneself

أَنْجى *v* to rescue, to save; أَنْجى شَخْصاً to rescue sb

تَناجى *v* to whisper to each other; to confide in each other

اِسْتَنْجى *v* ◀1▶ [سَلِمَ] to be saved/rescued; to cope, to manage; to escape; اِسْتَنْجى من شَيْءٍ to be saved from sth ◀2▶ [تَطَهَّرَ] to clean oneself

ناجٍ *n* |ناجونَ| survivor; الناجونَ من حادِثةٍ \ كارِثةٍ \ حَرْبٍ the survivors of an accident/disaster/war; بَحَثَ عن ناجين to search for survivors

نَجاة *n* ◀1▶ [إنْقاذ] rescue, salvation; survival; escape; طَوْق النَجاةِ lifebuoy, lifesaver (AmE); زَوْرَق \ قارِب النَجاةِ lifeboat; صَدْرِيّة \ حِزام النَجاةِ a life jacket; النَجاة من المَوْتِ an escape from death ◀2▶ [اِسْم شَخْصيّ] |dipt| Najat (*female given name*)

نَجْوة *n* highland, plateau; في نَجْوةٍ من \ ب far from; free from

نَجْوى *n* ◀1▶ [مُناجاة] a confidential talk; a secret conversation ◀2▶ [اِسْم شَخْصيّ] |f| Najwa (*female given name*)

نَجيّ *n* |أَنْجِية| confidant, close friend

اِسْتِنْجاء *n* ◀1▶ [خَلاص] escape, deliverance ◀2▶ [طَهارة] cleaning, washing

مُناجاة *n* a confidential talk, a secret conversation; monologue, soliloquy

مُنْجٍ *n* rescuer, savior

مُنَجٍّ *n* |مُنَجّونَ| rescuer, savior

مَنْجاة *n* |مَناجٍ| refuge, shelter; protection, safety; كانَ بِمَنْجاةٍ من الزِلْزالِ to be protected from the earthquake

مَنْجًى *n* |مَناجٍ| refuge, shelter; protection, safety

نَحَبَ *v* |a-i; نَحيب, نَحْب| to lament, to wail; to weep

اِنْتَحَبَ *v* to lament, to wail; to weep; اِنْتَحَبَ بِمَرارةٍ \ بِصَمْتٍ to weep bitterly/silently

نَحْب *n* ◀1▶ [بُكاء] lamentation, wailing ◀2▶ [مَوْت] death; قضى نَحْبَهُ to die ◀3▶ [مُدّة من الزَمَن] period, time

نَحيب *n* lamentation, wailing; weeping

نَجَّمَ *v* ◀1▶ [راقَبَ النُجومَ] to observe the stars; to practise astrology, to predict the future (*through astrology*) ◀2▶ (old use) [قَسَّطَ] to pay in instalments

تَنَجَّمَ *v* to practise astrology

نَجْم *n coll* |أَنْجُم, نُجوم| ◀1▶ (Astron) star; نَجْم مُذَنَّب \ هاوٍ comet, shooting star; النَجْم القُطْبيّ the Pole Star, the North Star, Polaris; نُجوم ثابِتة fixed stars; مَجْموعة نُجومٍ constellation; نَجْمة الميلادِ Christmas star; poinsettia (*Euphorbia pulcherrima*); سورة النَجْم The Star (*Sura 53*) ◀2▶ [شَكْل] star; نَجْمة داوودَ Star of David; نَجْم البَحْرِ starfish; زَهْرة النَجْمةِ (Bot) *Aster* ◀3▶ [شَخْص مَشْهور] star, celebrity; نَجْم سينَمائيّ a film star; نَجْم صاعِد an up-and-coming star; نَجْمة التَمْثيلِ \ الغِناءِ a famous actress/singer; أَفَلَ نَجْمُهُ his star faded ◀4▶ [تَصْنيف فُنْدُقٍ أو مَطْعَمٍ] star; فُنْدُق ثَلاثةِ نُجومٍ a three-star hotel ◀5▶ (P&P) asterisk, star

ناجِم *adj* |عن| resulting; originating, arising; خَسائِر \ أَضْرار ناجِمة عن الحَريقِ losses/damages resulting from the fire; تَلَوُّث ناجِم عن الصِناعةِ pollution from industry

نَجّام *n* astrologer

نَجْميّ *adj* stellar, star (*before n*)

نُجوميّة *n* stardom

تَنْجيم *n* ◀1▶ [العِرافة] astrology; prediction, divination; عِلْم التَنْجيم astrology ◀2▶ (old use) [تَقْسيط] payment by instalments

تَنْجيميّ *adj* astrological

مَنْجَم *n* |مَناجِمُ| mine, quarry, pit; mining; مَنْجَم الفَحْمِ coal mine; عامِل مَنْجَمٍ miner; مُهَنْدِس مَناجِمَ mining engineer; اسْتِثْمار المَناجِمِ the mining industry; عَمِلَ في المَناجِمِ to work in the mines

مُنَجِّم *n* astrologer

نَجا *v* |u| ◀1▶ [خَلَصَ] |نَجاة, نَجاء| to escape; to save oneself; to be rescued/saved; to survive; نَجا من كارِثةٍ \ حادِثةٍ to survive a disaster/accident; نَجا من الخَطَرِ \ المَوْتِ to escape from danger/death; نَجا بِنَفْسِهِ \ بِجِلْدِهِ to save one's skin; نَجا بِأُعْجوبةٍ to be saved by a miracle ◀2▶ [أَسَرَّ] |نَجْو, نَجْوى| to confide in/to; نَجا شَخْصاً to confide in sb; نَجا شَخْصاً بِشَيْءٍ to confide sth to sb

نَحْس *n* |نُحوس| misfortune, disaster, bad luck; يَوم نَحْسٍ an unlucky day; جَلَبَ لِشَخْصٍ النَحْسَ to bring sb bad luck; لازَمَهُ النَحْسُ to be dogged by misfortune; فَكَّ النَحْسَ to break the spell/curse

نَحْس *n* an evil/bad omen

نَحّاس *n* coppersmith

نُحاس *n* copper; نُحاس أَحْمَر \ أَصْفَر copper/brass; أُكْسيد النُحاسِ الثُنائيّ copper (II) oxide, CuO

نُحاسيّ *adj* copper (*before n*), brass (*before n*); أَنابيب نُحاسيّة copper pipes; أَدَوات نُحاسيّة brassware, copperware; الآلات النُحاسيّة brass wind instruments

نَحيس *adj* |نُحَساءُ| unlucky, ill-fated; عام نَحيس a catastrophic year

مَنْحوس *adj* unlucky, ill-fated

‹ **نَحُفَ** *v* |u; نَحافة| to lose weight, to slim; نَحُفَ جِسْمُهُ to lose weight; نَحُفَ جِدًّا to lose a lot of weight

أَنْحَفَ *v* to make thin/lean; أَنْحَفَتْهُ الحُمّى to lose weight from fever

نَحافة *n* leanness, thinness; emaciation

نَحيف *adj* |نُحَفاءُ, نِحاف| thin, lean, slender, slim; skinny; fragile; نَحيف البِنْيَةِ \ القَوامِ of slender build

‹ **نَحَلَ, نَحُلَ, نَحِلَ** *v* |a-u; نُحول| ① [هُزِلَ] to be/become emaciated/thin; to lose weight; to pine/waste away; نَحَلَ من الحُزْنِ to pine away from grief ② [نَسَبَ إِلَيْهِ] to mistakenly ascribe/attribute to; نَحَلَ شَخْصاً القَوْلَ to mistakenly ascribe the statement to sb

نَحَلَ, نَحُلَ, نَحِلَ *v* |a; نُحول| to pine/waste away

أَنْحَلَ *v* to make lean/thin

تَنَحَّلَ *v* to ascribe to oneself

انْتَحَلَ *v* ① [تَنَحَّلَ] to plagiarize, to commit plagiarism; to impersonate, to pose as, to pass oneself off as; انْتَحَلَ شِعْراً to plagiarize a poem; انْتَحَلَ شَخْصيّةَ \ صِفةَ شَخْصٍ to impersonate sb; انْتَحَلَ صِفةَ شُرْطيٍّ to pose as a police officer; انْتَحَلَ اسْمَ ... to assume the name of ... ② [انْتَسَبَ] to convert to, to embrace, to adopt; انْتَحَلَ الإِسْلامَ to convert to Islam; انْتَحَلَ الدينَ المَسيحيَّ to embrace Christianity;

‹ **نَحَتَ** *v* |i-u; نَحْت| to sculpt, to chisel; to carve, engrave; to cut; نَحَتَ تِمْثالاً to make a sculpture; نَحَتَ خَشَباً to carve wood

نَحْت *n* ① (Art) sculpture; carving; نَحْت حَجَريّ a stone sculpture; نَحْت خَشَبيّ a wood carving ② (Ling) portmanteau, compound; إنّ البَسْمَلَةَ هي نَحْتٌ من عِبارةِ بِسْمِ اللهِ *al-basmala* is a portmanteau of the phrase *b-ism Allah*, 'in the name of God'

نَحّات *n* sculptor

مِنْحات *n* |مَناحيتُ| chisel

مَنْحوت A *adj* (Art) sculpted, chiseled; carved
B *n* (Ling) compound

مَنْحوتة *n* statue, sculpture

‹ **نَحَرَ** *v* |u; نَحْر| to slaughter, to butcher; نَحَرَ خَروفاً to slaughter a lamb

ناحَرَ *v* to fight, to battle; to quarrel, to argue; ناحَرَ شَخْصاً على شَيْءٍ to fight with sb over sth

تَناحَرَ *v* to fight each other; to fight, to struggle; to compete

انْتَحَرَ *v* to commit suicide, to kill oneself; انْتَحَرَ شَنْقاً to hang oneself; انْتَحَرَ يَأْساً to kill oneself in despair

نَحْر *n* ① [ذَبْح] slaughtering, butchering ② (Anat) throat, neck; windpipe, gullet

انْتِحار *n* |انْتِحارات| suicide; انْتِحار جَماعيّ mass suicide; انْتِحار سِياسيّ political suicide; مُحاوَلة انْتِحارٍ فاشِلة a failed suicide attempt; حاوَلَ الانْتِحارَ to attempt suicide

انْتِحاريّ *adj* suicidal, suicide (*before n*); هُجوم \ عَمَليّة انْتِحاريّ(ة) a suicide attack/operation; تَفْجير انْتِحاريّ suicide bombing

مُتَناحِر *adj* warring, fighting; الأَطْراف المُتَناحِرة the warring parties

مُنْتَحِر *n* suicide (*sb who commits suicide*); ماتَ مُنْتَحِراً to kill oneself

مَنْحَر *n* |مَناحِرُ| throat; neck

‹ **نَحيزة** *n* diathesis; natural disposition

‹ **نَحَسَ** *v* |a; نَحْس| to cause bad luck, to bring bad luck to; نُحِسَ to be struck by disaster

نَحُسَ *v* |u; نُحوسة, نَحْس| to be struck by disaster

نَحَّسَ *v* to coat with copper

تَنَحّى عن العَرْشِ مَنْصِبِهِ \ وَظيفَتِهِ to resign from one's job; to step down from the throne, to abdicate the throne; لن يَتَنَحّى طَوْعاً he will not step down willingly

انْتَحى *v* انْتَحى جانِباً to step aside

نَحْو *n* |أَنْحاء| ◆1 [اتِّجاه] direction, side; corner; في \ إلى \ من جَميع أَنْحاءِ العالَمِ in/to/from all corners of the world ◆2 [تقْريباً] approximately, about, around; منذ نَحْوِ سَنَةٍ since approximately a year ago; من نَحْوِ ٤٠ في المِائَةِ about 40%; في نَحْوِ الساعةِ الخامِسةِ around five o'clock ◆3 [مِثْل] like; هو وَنَحْوُهُ وَنَحْوُ ذلك and the like, and things like that; he and people like him; أو نَحْو ذلك or something similar ◆4 [طَريقة] way, manner; على نَحْوٍ ما one way or another; على نَحْوِ ما ذُكِر in the above-mentioned way; على النَحْوِ مُعَيَّنٍ \ مُخْتَلِفٍ in a certain/different manner; وَعلى هذا النَحْوِ التالي in the following way; على هذا النَحْوِ in this way; et cetera, etc.; لَيْسَت المَسْأَلةُ على هذا النَحْوِ that isn't the issue ◆5 (Ling) grammar, syntax; النَحْو التَوْليديّ \ التَحْويليّ generative/transformational grammar; النَحْو والصَرْف syntax and morphology

نَحْوَ *prep* to, toward; in the direction of; اتَّجِهْ نَحْوَ مَكانٍ to go to a place

ناحِية *n* |نَواحٍ| ◆1 [جانِب] side; aspect, facet; direction; ناحِيَةَ in the direction of; نَظَرَ ناحِيَةَ النافِذَةِ to look towards the window; نَواحٍ surroundings; من ناحِيَةٍ ... وَمِنْ ناحِيَةٍ أُخْرى ... on the one hand ..., on the other (hand) ...; من ناحِيَةٍ اقْتِصاديّةٍ from an economic point of view; من كُلِّ \ جَميعِ النَواحي in every respect; from every angle; مُتَعَدِّد النَواحي many-sided; multifaceted ◆2 (Admin) district, region

نَحْويّ **A** *adj* grammatical; syntactic; أَخْطاء نَحْوِيّة grammatical errors

B *n* |نَحْوِيّونَ, نُحاة| grammarian

مُتَنَحّ *adj* recessive; جين مُتَنَحٍّ a recessive gene

مَنْحًى *n* |مَناحٍ| ◆1 [اتِّجاه] course, direction; trend, tendency; مَنْحًى جَديد a new course; مَنْحًى تَصاعُديّ an upward trend; أَخَذَ مَنْحًى آخَرَ to take a different course; نَحا مَنْحى التَطَرُّفِ

انْتَحَلَ رَأْيَ شَخْصٍ to adopt sb's opinion; انْتَحَلَ الأَعْذارَ to make up excuses

نَحْل *n coll* (Zool) bee; عَسَل النَحْلِ honey; شَمْع النَحْلِ beeswax; شَجَرة النَحْلِ (Bot) *Tetradium daniellii*; سورة النَحْلِ The Bee (*Sura 16*)

ناحِل *adj* |نُحول, نَواحِلُ| slim; weak, fragile; narrow

نَحّال *n* beekeeper, apiarist

نِحالة *n* beekeeping, apiculture

نِحْلة *n* creed, belief

نُحول *n* leanness, slimness; emaciation

نَحيل *adj* |نُحَّل, نَحْلى| slim, thin, skinny; emaciated; خصر نَحيل a slim waist; نَحيل الجِسْمِ \ الجَسَدِ thin, skinny

انْتِحال *n* impersonation; plagiarism; انْتِحال الصِفةِ \ الشَخْصيّةِ \ الهُويّة impersonation; انْتِحال صِفة طَبيبٍ impersonating a doctor

مُنْتَحَل *adj* false, fake; spurious, unauthentic; plagiarized; اسْم مُنْتَحَل pseudonym

مُنْتَحِل *n* impersonator; plagiarist; مُنْتَحِل الصِفة impersonator

مَنْحَل *n* |مَناحِلُ| beehive, apiary

مَنْحول *adj* spurious, apocryphal

‹ **نُحام** *n* flamingo

‹ **نَحْنُ** *pron* we, us; نَحْنُ كَمُسْلِمينَ us Muslims; نَحْنُ خِرّيجي كُلّيّةِ الآدابِ we as graduates of the Faculty of Arts

‹ **نَحْنَحَ** *v* |i; نَحْنَحة| to clear the throat

تَنَحْنَحَ *v* to clear the throat

‹ **نَحا** *v* |a-u; نَحْو| ◆1 [ذَهَب] to go, to move; to lean, to tend; الرَأْيُ العامُّ يَنْحو في اتِّجاهِ اليَمينِ public opinion is moving to the right; نَحا مَنْحى \ نحو التَطَرُّفِ to be trending towards extremism ◆2 [قَلَّدَ] to follow; to imitate, to copy; نَحا نحو شَخْصٍ to follow (in sb's footsteps)

نَحّى *v* to remove, to put aside; to eliminate; نَحّى حِجارةً من الطَريقِ to remove a stone from the road

أَنْحى *v* ◆1 [أَلْقى] to turn; أَنْحى باللائِمةِ على شَخْصٍ to lay blame on sb, to heap reproach on sb ◆2 [أَمالَ] to turn away, to avert; أَنْحى بَصَرَهُ to avert one's eyes

تَنَحّى *v* to give up, to forego; to resign, to step down; to give way to, to step aside; تَنَحّى جانِباً to step aside; تَنَحّى عن

to be trending towards extremism ❷ [مَجال] field, domain, area; في جَميعِ مَناحي الحَياةِ in all areas of life; دِراسة ذات مَنحًى اقْتِصاديٍّ a study in the field of economics

نَخَبَ *v* |u; نَخْب| ❶ [اخْتارَ] to choose, to select ❷ [صَوَّتَ] to vote

انْتَخَبَ *v* ❶ [اخْتارَ] to choose, to select, to pick ❷ [اقْتَرَعَ] to vote, to elect; انْتَخَبَ شَخْصاً رَئِيساً to elect sb (as) president

نَخْب *n* |أَنْخاب| toast; شَرِبَ نَخْبَ \ على نَخْبِ شَخْصٍ to drink a toast to sb; تَبادَلَ النَخْبَ to exchange a toast; على نَخْبِكَ! to your health!

ناخِب *n* voter, constituent; النَاخِبونَ الجُمْهورِيّونَ Republican voters; ٣٣٪ من أَصْواتِ النَاخِبينَ 33% of the votes

نُخْبة *n* |نُخَب| elite, top; selection; نُخْبة صَغيرة a small elite; النُخْبة العَسْكَرِيّة \ السِياسِيّة the military/political elite; نُخْبة الأَفْلامِ the best films; النُخْبة الحاكِمة the ruling elite; نُخْبة من العُلَماءِ والمُفَكِّرينَ a select group of scientists and philosophers

نُخْبَوِيّ *adj* elitist

نُخْبَوِيّة *n* elitism

انْتِخاب *n* |انْتِخابات| ❶ [مَصْدَر] choice, selection; عَمَلِيّة انْتِخاب selection procedure; الانْتِخاب الطَبيعِيّ natural selection ❷ (Pol) election; انْتِخابات عامّة general elections; انْتِخابات بَرْلَمانِيّة \ نِيابِيّة parliamentary elections; انْتِخابات حُرّة free elections; انْتِخابات سِرِّيّة \ عَلَنِيّة secret/public elections; انْتِخابات مُبَكِّرة early elections, by-elections (BrE); انْتِخابات وَطَنِيّة \ مَحَلِّيّة national/local elections; انْتِخابات مُباشِرة \ غَيْر مُباشِرةٍ direct/indirect elections; انْتِخابات تَشْرِيعِيّة legislative elections; انْتِخاب أَوَّلِيّ \ الرَئِيس primary/presidential election; حَقّ الانْتِخابِ suffrage; قانون الانْتِخابِ electoral law; نِظام الانْتِخابِ voting system; وَرَقة \ بِطاقة انْتِخابٍ ballot; مَرْكَز \ مَقَرّ انْتِخابٍ polling station; صُنْدوق انْتِخاب ballot box; إِعادة الانْتِخابِ re-election; إِعادة انْتِخابِهِ رَئِيساً his re-election as president; لا يُمْكِنُ انْتِخابُهُ ineligible for election; تَمَتَّعَ بِحَقِّ الانْتِخابِ to have the right to vote; قاطَعَ الانْتِخاباتِ to boycott the elections; أَجْرى انْتِخاباتٍ to hold elections; فازَ \ خَسِرَ في الانْتِخاباتِ to win/lose the elections

انْتِخابِيّ *adj* electoral, election (*before n*); نَجاح انْتِخابِيّ electoral success; حَمْلة انْتِخابِيّة election campaign; دائِرة انْتِخابِيّة constituency; تَجَمُّع انْتِخابِيّ election rally; بَرْنامَج انْتِخابِيّ platform

مُنْتَخَب *n* |مُنْتَخَبات| ❶ [نُخْبة] selection; مُنْتَخَبات anthology; مُنْتَخَبات من أَعْمالِ ... an anthology of the work of ...; مُنْتَخَب من شَيْءٍ a selection of sth ❷ (Sport) selection, team; المُنْتَخَب الوَطَنِيّ the national team; المُنْتَخَب السَعودِيّ the Saudi national team

مُنْتَخِب *n* voter, constituent

نَخَرَ *v* |i-u; نَخْر, نَخير| ❶ [فَتَّ] to gnaw (on), to nibble (at); to eat away (at); to riddle, to perforate, to spread throughout; نَخَرَ شَخْصاً \ شَيْئاً من الداخِلِ to eat away at sb/sth from the inside; نَخَرَهُ الفَسادُ حتّى العَظْمِ to be riddled to the core with corruption; جُثّة نَخَرَها الرَصاصُ a body riddled with bullets ❷ [مَدَّ الصَوْتَ في خَياشيمِهِ] to sniff; to snort

نَخِرَ *v* |a; نَخَر| to decay, to disintegrate

نَخَر *n* necrosis, decay; نَخَر الأَسْنانِ cavities, caries

نَخِر *adj* rotten, decayed; ضِرْس نَخِر a decayed molar

ناخِر, نَخِر *adj* having a snoring sound

نَخير *n* snort; grunt

مِنْخار *n* nostril

مِنْخَر, مَنْخَر, مَنْخِر *n* |مَناخِر| nostril

مَنْخور *adj* rotten, decayed; riddled, perforated; سِنّ مَنْخورة a rotten tooth; مَنْخور بالرَصاص riddled with bullets

نَخْرَبَ *v* |i; نَخْرَبة| to riddle, to perforate, to make holes in

نُخْروب *n* |نَخاريب| hole; cavity; نَخاريب النَحْلِ honeycomb

مُنَخْرَب *adj* riddled; honeycombed (*texture*)

نَخَزَ *v* |a; نَخْز| to poke, to prod, to nudge; to sting, to hurt; to goad, to urge on/forward; يَنْخَزُ الجُنْدِيُّ بِبُنْدُقِيَّتِهِ المُعْتَقَلَ the soldier pokes the prisoner with his rifle

نَخَسَ *v* |a-u; نَخْس| to poke; to goad, to urge on/forward; نَخَسَ حِماراً بِعَصاً to urge a donkey forward with a stick

نَخّاس *n* ❶ [بائِع العَبيدِ] slave trader ❷ [بائِع الدَوابِّ] cattle dealer

نِخاسة *n* ➊ [تِجارة الرَقيق] slave trade; سوق النِخاسةِ slave market ➋ [تِجارة الماشِية] cattle trade

نُخط *n* amniotic fluid; سائِل النُخْطِ amniotic fluid

نَخَعَ *v* |a; نُخوع| to cough/spit up phlegm, to expectorate

تَنَخَّعَ *v* to cough/spit up phlegm, to expectorate

نُخاع *n* |نُخُع| marrow, bone marrow; نُخاع شَوْكي spinal cord; عَمَليّة زَرْع النُخاعِ bone marrow transplant; حتّى النُخاعِ to the core

نُخاعة *n* expectoration, mucus, phlegm

نُخاعيّ *adj relating to bone marrow or the spinal cord*; عَظْم نُخاعيّ marrowbone; (Sci) medullary bone (*in birds and dinosaurs*)

نَخَلَ *v* |u; نَخْل| to sift, to sieve, to strain; نَخَلَ الرَمْلَ to sift sand

تَنَخَّلَ *v* to sift, to sieve, to strain

انْتَخَلَ *v* to sift, to sieve, to strain

نَخْل *n coll* |نَخيل| palm, palm tree, date palm; زَيْت نَخيلٍ palm oil; سَعَف نَخيلٍ palm fronds

نُخالة *n* bran, chaff; خُبْز النُخالةِ wholewheat bread

نَخيل *n* see نَخْل

مُنْخَل, مُنْخُل *n* |مَناخِل| sieve, sifter, strainer; مُنْخُل الدَقيقِ flour sifter

نَخَمَ *v* |a; نَخْم| to cough/spit up phlegm, to expectorate

تَنَخَّمَ *v* to cough/spit up phlegm, to expectorate

نُخامة *n* expectoration, mucus, phlegm; رَمى بِنُخامَتِهِ to cough up phlegm

نُخاميّ *adj* غُدّة نُخاميّة pituitary gland

نَخا *v* |u; نَخْوة| ب| to be proud of; نَخا بِشَيْءٍ to be proud of sth

نَخْوة *n* ➊ [حَماسة] fervour, ardour ➋ [شَهامة] nobility, dignity; pride, honour

نَدَبَ *v* |u; نَدْب| ➊ [ناحَ] to lament, to mourn (for); نَدَبَ المَيِّتَ to mourn the deceased ➋ [أَوْفَدَ] to delegate, to depute; to authorize, to commission; to appoint, to assign; نَدَبَ شَخْصاً إلى القِيامِ بِشَيْءٍ to appoint sb to do sth

أَنْدَبَ *v* to scar over

انْتَدَبَ *v* to assign, to commission, to appoint; to delegate, to deputize; انْتَدَبَ شَخْصاً للقِيامِ بِشَيْءٍ to assign sb to do sth; انْتَدَبَت المَحْكَمةُ مُحامِياً للدِفاعِ عن المُتَّهَمِ the court appointed a lawyer to defend the accused

نَدَب *n* |نُدوب, أَنْداب| scar

نَدّابة *n* wailing woman, mourner

نَدْبة, نَدَبة *n* |أَنْداب, نُدوب| scar; تَرَكَ نَدَبَةً to leave a scar

انْتِداب *n* |انْتِدابات| ➊ [حِماية سِياسيّة] mandate; إقْليم تحت الانْتِدابِ mandated territory; الانْتِداب البَريطانيّ the British Mandate ➋ [إيفاد] delegate, deputy

باب المَنْدَب *n* see مندب

مُنْتَدَب **A** *adj* assigned, mandated; authorized, empowered; عُضْو مُنْتَدَب representative; managing director, CEO
B *n* representative, delegate

مَنْدوب **A** *adj* (Isl Law) recommended
B *n* ➊ [مَبْعوث] representative, delegate, agent, envoy; commissioner, deputy; المَنْدوب السامي High Commissioner; مَنْدوب خاصّ special envoy; مَنْدوب دائِم permanent delegate; مَنْدوب التَأْمينِ insurance agent; بَعَثَ مَنْدوباً to send a representative ➋ [صَحَفيّ] reporter, journalist; مَنْدوب جَريدةٍ a reporter for a newspaper

مَنْدوبيّة *n* ➊ [وَظيفة] position of commissioner ➋ [مَكْتَب] commissioner's office

مُنْتَدَح *n* alternative, option, choice

مَنْدوحة *n* alternative, option, choice; لا مَنْدوحةَ مِنْهُ \ عَنْهُ it is inevitable; لا مَنْدوحةَ من الإقْرارِ أنّ ... it must be admitted that ...; لا مَنْدوحةَ لَكَ عَنْهُ you have no choice

نَدَّ *v* |i; نَدّ, نَدَد, نِداد, نُدود, نَديد| to escape; to flee; نَدَّتْ عَنْهُ ضَحْكةٌ a laugh escaped him

نَدَّدَ *v* |ب| to denounce, to criticize; نَدَّدَ بِشَيْءٍ \ شَخْصٍ to denounce sth/sb

نَدّ *n* incense; عود النَدِّ aloeswood

نِدّ *n* |أَنْداد| peer, equal, match; النِدّ للنِدِّ (Comput) peer-to-peer; شَبَكة النِدِّ للنِدِّ (Comput) peer-to-peer network; تَعامُل النِدِّ للنِدِّ treating everybody equally; وَجَدَ نِدَّهُ to find one's match; كانَ نِدًّا لِشَخْصٍ to be sb's equal

تَنْديد *n* |تَنْديدات| condemnation, denouncement, criticism; تَنْديد بِشَيْءٍ condemnation of sth

نَدَرَ *v* |u; نُدور, نَدْر| to be rare/unusual; to be scarce; فيما نَدَرَ seldom; يَنْدُرُ أنْ … it's rare that …; يَنْدُرُ أنْ تَجِدَ نظيراً لَهُ you rarely find sb like him

تَنَدَّرَ *v* to jest, to joke

نادِر *adj* [1] ◀ [قليل الوُجودِ] rare, unusual, scarce; شَيْء نادِر rarity; سِلْعة نادِرة a rare commodity; نباتات نادِرة rare plants; نادِر المِثالِ unparalleled; نادِراً seldom; كانَ نادِراً to be rare; نادِراً ما حَدَثَ it rarely happens; من النادِرِ أنْ … it's rare that …
[2] ◀ [اسْم شَخْصيّ] Nadir (*male given name*)

نادِرة *n* |نَوادِر| [1] ◀ [نُكْتة] anecdote; نادِرة ظَرِيفة a funny anecdote
[2] ◀ [اسْم شَخْصيّ] Nadira (*female given name*)

نُدْرة *n* rarity; scarcity, shortage; واجَهَ مُشْكِلةَ نُدْرةِ المِياهِ to face a water shortage

نَدْغ *n* (Bot) *Satureja*; نَدْغ بُسْتانيّ summer savory (*Satureja hortensis*)

نَدَفَ *v* |i; نَدْف| to comb, to card; to make flakes, to clump; نَدَفَ القُطْنَ to comb cotton; نَدَفَ ثَلْجاً to snow

نُدْفة *n* |نُدَف| flake; flock; tuft; نُدْفة الثَلْجِ snowflake; نُدْفة صوفٍ a tuft of wool

نَديف *adj* carded, teased

نَدَلَ *v* |u; نَدْل| to snatch, to take away

نَدِلَ *v* |a; نَدَل| to be dirty

نادِل *n* |نُدُل| waiter; نادى النادِلَ to summon the waiter

مَنْدَل *n* fragrant wood

مِنْديل *n* see مندل

نَدِمَ *v* |a; نَدَم, نَدامة| |على| to regret, to repent, to be sorry; نَدِمَ على شَيْءٍ to regret sth; نَدِمَ على فِعْلَتِهِ to regret what one has done

نادَمَ *v* نادَمَ شَخْصاً على الشَرابِ to have a drink with sb

أَنْدَمَ *v* to make regret

تَنَدَّمَ *v* |على| to repent, to regret, to be sorry; to mourn; تَنَدَّمَ على مَوْتِ زَميلٍ to mourn the death of a colleague

نَدَم *n* remorse, regret; إبْداء النَدَمِ, إعْراب \ تَعْبير عن النَدَمِ an expression of regret; أبْدى نَدَمَهُ to show remorse; عَضَّ أصابِعَهُ نَدَماً to be overcome with regret; لا يَنْفَعُ النَدَمُ regret is of no use

نادِم [A] *adj* |نُدّام| remorseful, regretful, repentant, sorry; كانَ نادِماً على شَيْءٍ to regret sth; كانَ غَيْرَ نادِمٍ على شَيْءٍ to be unrepentant about sth
[B] *n* |نُدّام| penitent

نَدامة *n* remorse; regret; repentance; شَرِبَ كَأْسَ النَدامةِ to be deeply sorry; في التَأَنّي السَلامةُ وَفي العَجَلةِ النَدامةُ ≈ act in haste, repent at leisure

نَدْمان *adj* |نَدامى| remorseful, contrite

نَديم *n* |نِدام, نُدَماءُ| confidant; companion; drinking buddy

مُنادَمة *n* *drinking together/in company*

نادى *v* [1] ◀ [صاحَ] to call (out), to cry (out), to shout, to exclaim; الواجِبُ يُناديني duty calls [2] ◀ [طَلَبَ] |ل, ب| to call for, to demand; to advocate; نادى بالديمُقْراطيّة \ بالمُساواةِ to call for democracy/equality; نادى بالاسْتِقْلالِ to call for independence [3] ◀ [دَعا] to declare, to proclaim; نودِيَ به رَئيساً he was proclaimed president

تَنادى *v* to call out to each other

انْتَدى *v* to convene, to assemble

نادٍ *n* |نَوادٍ, أَنْدِية| club, society, association; نادي الحَيِّ community centre; نادي الشُرْطةِ police association; نادٍ رِياضيّ sports club; نادٍ صِحّيّ fitness centre; نادي كُرةِ القَدَمِ football (BrE) soccer (AmE) club; لَعِبَ في نادٍ to play at a club; انْتَسَبَ إلى نادٍ to join a club; كانَ عُضْواً في نادٍ to be a member of a club

نِداء *n* |نِداءات| [1] ◀ [اسْتِعانة] call, appeal; invitation; نِداء عاجِل an urgent appeal; نِداء اسْتِغاثةٍ a distress call, SOS; مَرْكَز نِداءٍ a call centre; وَجَّهَ نِداءً إلى شَخْصٍ to make an appeal to sb; وَجَّهَ نِداءً لِوَقْفِ القِتالِ to appeal to stop the fighting
[2] ◀ [صَيْحة] call, calling, cry; نِداء القَلْبِ the voice of the heart
[3] (Gram) أداة نِداءٍ vocative particle

نَدْوة *n* |نَدَوات| seminar, conference, symposium; نَدْوة صِحافيّة a press conference; نَظَّمَ \ عَقَدَ نَدْوةً to organize/hold a conference; نَدْوة عن \ حول مُسْتَقْبَلِ الزِراعةِ a symposium on the future of agriculture

مُنادٍ *n* herald, crier; *person who calls*; المُنادونَ بالديمُقْراطيّةِ those calling for democracy

مُناداة *n* call, appeal; المُناداة بالتَغْيير a call for change; المُناداة بِخَلْقِ فُرَصِ عَمَلٍ \ بالحُكْمِ الذاتيِّ the call for job opportunities/autonomy

مُنادًى *n* (Gram) *a noun in the vocative case*

مُنْتَدًى *n* |مُنْتَدَيات| ① [مَكان الاجْتِماع] meeting place ② (Comput) forum; مُنْتَدى إِنْتَرْنِت Internet forum; مُنْتَدى دَعْم support forum ③ [نَدْوة] forum, seminar; عَقَدَ مُنْتَدًى to hold a seminar

‹ **نَدِيَ** *v* |a; نُدوّة, نَداوة, نَدًى| to be moist/damp; to be dewy; نَدِيَت الحُقولُ the fields were covered in dew

نَدّى *v* to moisten, to make damp

أَنْدى *v* to moisten, to wet

تَنَدّى *v* to be moist/damp; to be dewy

نَديّ *adj* moist, damp, dewy; نَديّ الكَفِّ generous; مُغَنٍّ نَديّ الصَوْتِ *a singer with a beautiful, strong voice*

نَدى *n* |f| Nada (*female given name*)

نَدًى *n* |أَنْداء, أَنْدِية| dew

نَدْيان *adj* |dipt| moist, damp, dewy

‹ **نَذَرَ** *v* |i-u; نَذْر, نُذور| to take/make a vow; نَذَرَ نَفْسَهُ \ حَياتَهُ للهِ to devote oneself/dedicate one's life to God

نَذِرَ *v* |a; ب| إنْذر| to be on one's guard against; نَذِرَ بِشَيْءٍ to be on one's guard against sth

أَنْذَرَ *v* ① [حَذَّرَ] to warn, to alarm, to caution; أَنْذَرَ شَخْصاً to caution sb; أَنْذَرَ بِخَطَرٍ to warn of danger ② [أَخْطَرَ] to urge, to press; to order, to instruct; أَنْذَرَ شَخْصاً بِتَسْليمِ نَفْسِهِ to urge sb to turn himself in

نَذْر *n* |نُذورات, نُذور| (Chr) vow, oath, pledge; نَذْر الفَقْرِ a vow of poverty

نَذير *n* |نُذُر| omen, herald; نَذير سوءٍ \ شُؤْمٍ a bad omen

إنْذار *n* |إنْذارات| ① [إخْطار] warning, cautioning; admonition, summons, exhortation; إنْذار مُبَكِّر an early warning; إنْذار ل \ إلى شَخْصٍ a warning to sb; إنْذار نِهائيّ ultimatum; وَجَّهَ إنْذاراً نِهائيًّا to give an ultimatum; تَلَقّى إنْذاراً to receive an admonition ② [عَلامة] alarm; إنْذار كاذِب a false alarm; صَفّارة الإنْذار (warning) siren; جِهاز إنْذارٍ fire alarm, smoke detector; pager; إنْذار ضِدّ السَرِقةِ burglar alarm; مَرْكَز الإنْذارِ warning centre; حالة إنْذار state of emergency; جَرَس \ إشارة \ جِهاز إنْذارٍ alarm bell/signal/system; دَقَّ جَرَسَ الإنْذارِ to ring the alarm bell ③ (Sport) a yellow card

تَناذُر *n* syndrome

مُنْذِر Ⓐ *adj* portentous; مُنْذِر بالخَطَرِ, مُنْذِر بالشَرِّ ominous; alarming

Ⓑ *n* monitor

‹ **نَذُلَ** *v* |u; نَذالة| to be despicable/without honour

نَذْل Ⓐ *adj* |نُذول, أَنْذال| despicable, mean, vile

Ⓑ *n* |نُذول, أَنْذال| scoundrel, villain, rogue

نَذالة *n* depravity, meanness

‹ **نَرْجِس** *n* ① (Bot) *Narcissus* ② [اِسْم شَخْصيّ] |f dipt| Narjis (*female given name*)

نَرْجِسيّة *n* narcissism

‹ **نارَجيل** *n* coconut palm/tree (*Cocos*)

نَرْجيلة, نارَجيلة *n* ① [شيشة] |نَراجيلُ| water pipe, hookah; دَخَّنَ النَرْجيلةَ to smoke hookah ② (Bot) coconut

‹ **نَرْد** *n* backgammon; لَعِبَ النَرْدَ to play backgammon

‹ **نَرْفَزَ** *v* |i; نَرْفَزة| ① [أَقْلَقَ] to make nervous, to distress ② [أَغْضَبَ] to bother, to annoy; يُنَرْفِزُني it/he bothers me

تَنَرْفَزَ *v* to be bothered, to be annoyed

نَرْفَزة *n* nervousness; شَعَرَ بالنَرْفَزة to be nervous

مُنَرْفَز *adj* nervous

‹ **نُرْويجيّ** Ⓐ *adj* Norwegian; (اللُغة) النُرْويجيّة Norwegian (*language*)

Ⓑ *n* Norwegian (*person*)

النُرْويج *n* |f| Norway

‹ **نَزَحَ** *v* |a-i; نُزوح| ① [هاجَرَ] to emigrate, to go abroad; to migrate, to move (away), to depart; نَزَحَ من الريفِ إلى المَدينةِ to move from the country to the city; نَزَحَ عن دارِهِ to leave one's house ② [فَرَّغَ] to empty, to bail out (*water*); نَزَحَ البِئْرَ to empty water from the well

نازِح *n* emigrant; migrant

نُزوح *n* emigration; migration; exodus; حَرَكة النُزوحِ من القُرى إلى المُدُنِ the migration from the villages to the cities

نَزْر *n* trifle, trace, bit; نَزْر يَسير \ قَليل a little bit

نَزير *adj* little, insignificant, small; نَزْر نَزير a little bit

نَزَّ *v* |i| نَزّ, نَزيز| 1 ▸ [المَكانُ] to leak, to trickle 2 ▸ [الجُرْحُ] to discharge fluid

نَزّ *n* welling up; excretion

نَزَعَ *v* |i| 1 ▸ [قَلَعَ] |نَزْع| to remove, to take away; to tear/pull out, to extract; to take off; نَزَعَ مِسْماراً to pull out a nail; نَزَعَ مَلابِسَ to undress; نَزَعَ يَدَهُ من جَيْبِهِ to take one's hand out of one's pocket; نَزَعَ شَيْئاً عن شَخْصٍ to take sth away from sb; نَزَعَ السِلاحَ to disarm; نَزَعَ فَتيلَ شَيْءٍ to defuse sth, to disarm sth; نَزَعَ المِلْكيَّةَ to expropriate 2 ▸ [حَنَّ وَاشْتاقَ] |نُزوع| to long for, to desire; نَزَعَ إلى شَيْءٍ to long for sth 3 ▸ [مالَ] |نُزوع| to be inclined, to lean, to tend; نَزَعَ إلى شَيْءٍ to be inclined towards sth; نَزَعَ عن شَيْءٍ to be disinclined to sth

نَزَّعَ *v* to remove, to take away; to tear/pull out, to extract

نازَعَ *v* to argue with, to dispute; to fight/contend (with/against); نازَعَ شَخْصاً شَيْئاً \ في شَيْءٍ to fight with sb over sth

تَنازَعَ *v* |على| to argue with, to dispute; to fight/contend (with/against); to struggle; تَنازَعَ على مِنْطَقةٍ to fight over a territory; تَنازَعَ على السُلْطةِ to struggle for power

اِنْتَزَعَ *v* 1 ▸ [أَخَذَ قَهْراً] to take away, to confiscate; to grab, to seize; to wring, to extract; اِنْتَزَعَ أَراضِيَ to confiscate land; اِنْتَزَعَ الصَدارةَ من شَخْصٍ to snatch the lead from sb; اِنْتَزَعَ من الشَعْبِ حُقوقَهُ to deprive the people of their rights; اِنْتَزَعَ تَصْريحاً \ اعْتِرافاً من شَخْصٍ to extract a statement/confession from sb 2 ▸ [اِنْقَلَعَ] to be snatched/torn away; اِنْتَزَعَت الشَجَرةُ من شِدّةِ الريح the tree was uprooted by the strong wind

نَزْع *n* removal, extraction; نَزْع السِلاحِ disarmament; نَزْع الأَلْغامِ demining, mine removal; نَزْع المِلْكيّةِ expropriation

نازِع *adj* سورة النازِعات Those Who Drag Forth (*Sura 79*)

نَزّاع *adj* |إلى| tending (toward)

نِزاع *n* |نِزاعات| conflict, quarrel, dispute; discord, disagreement, controversy; fight, struggle; نِزاع قانونيّ lawsuit; نِزاع حُدوديّ a border dispute; نِزاع مُسَلَّح an armed conflict; نِزاع دينيّ \ طائِفيّ a religious/sectarian conflict; نِزاع دامٍ a bloody conflict; نِزاع حادّ a grim struggle; نِزاع مع شَخْصٍ \ بين طَرَفَيْنِ a disagreement with sb/between two parties; نِزاع بين زَوْجَيْنِ a domestic quarrel; نُقْطة \ مَوْضِع نِزاعٍ a point of difference; حالة نِزاعٍ a state of conflict; فَضَّ \ سَوّى \ حَسَمَ \ اِحْتَدَّ نِزاعاً to settle a dispute; أَثارَ النِزاعَ to provoke a fight; اِحْتَدَمَ النِزاعُ the controversy flared up; لا نِزاعَ في هذا الأَمْرِ that's indisputable

نَزْعة *n* |نَزَعات| inclination, tendency; propensity, disposition; attitude; -ism; نَزْعة طَبيعيّة natural propensity; نَزْعة عُنْصُريّة racist tendencies; النَزْعة الإِنْسانيّة humanism; نَزْعة فَرْديّة individualism; نَزْعة قَوْميّة nationalism; ذو نَزْعةٍ يَساريّةٍ left-leaning

نُزوع *n* |نُزوعات| 1 ▸ [رَغْبة] endeavor, striving; hunger, desire; drive; النُزوع إلى الاسْتِقْلالِ the drive for independence 2 ▸ [مُيول] tendency, trend; ثَمّةَ نُزوعٌ إلى الانْتِقالِ إلى المَرْكَزيّةِ there's a tendency towards centralization

تَنازُع *n* |تَنازُعات| struggle, conflict; dispute; تَنازُع البَقاءِ the struggle for life; التَنازُع على السُلْطةِ the struggle for power

مُتَنازَع *adj* |على| challenged, disputed, contested; controversial; الجُزُر \ المَناطِق المُتَنازَع عَلَيْها the disputed islands/territories; أَرْض مُتَنازَع على مِلْكيَّتِها disputed land

مُتَنازِع *adj* conflicting, contending, warring; الأَطْراف المُتَنازِعة the conflicting/warring parties

مُنازِع A *adj* struggling, contending B *n* adversary, opponent; contender; enemy; من دونِ مُنازِعٍ undisputed; الزَعيم من دونِ مُنازِعٍ the undisputed leader

مُنازَعة *n* conflict, struggle; dispute, disagreement; controversy; مُنازَعة عَسْكَريّة a military conflict; مُنازَعة قَضائيّة a legal dispute; مُنازَعة ماليّة a financial disagreement

مَنْزَع *adj* |مَنازِع| 1 ▸ goal, aim 2 ▸ tendency, trend 3 ▸ behaviour

مَنْزوع *adj* taken away, moved, removed; مِنْطَقة مَنْزوعة السِلاحِ demilitarized zone

نَزْغ *n* |نَزَغات| incitement to evil; نَزْغ الشَيْطانِ satanic temptations

نَزْغة *n* |نَزَغات| incitement to evil

نَزَفَ *v* |i| نَزْف| to bleed; to haemorrhage; نَزَفَ بِغَزارةٍ \ بِشِدّةٍ to bleed profusely; نَزَفَ المُصابُ the injured person was the train/out of the car ③ [حَلَّ بِمَكانٍ] to stay (over/with), to move into; نَزَلَ ضَيفاً عند شَخْصٍ to stay with sb as a guest; نَزَلَ في فُنْدُقٍ to stay at a hotel; نَزَلَ ب \ في مَنْزِلٍ ,نَزَلَ مَنْزِلاً to move into a house ④ [وافَقَ] |عند| to yield/submit to, to comply with, to meet; نَزَلَ عند مَطْلَبِ المُعارَضةِ to meet the demand of the opposition; نَزَلَ عند إرادةِ شَخْصٍ to comply with sb's wish ⑤ [تَرَكَ] to renounce, to disclaim; نَزَلَ عن شَيْءٍ to renounce sth ⑥ (Islam) to be revealed

نَزَّلَ *v* ① [خَفَضَ] to lower, to drop, to let/bring down; نَزَّلَ الحَقائِبَ to bring the suitcases down; هذا لا يُنَزِّلُ من قيمَتِهِ that doesn't diminish its value ② [أَنْزَلَ] to drop (off), to let off; نَزَّلَ شَخْصاً عند المُسْتَشْفى to drop sb off at the hospital ③ [أَوْحى] to reveal ④ (Comput) to download; نَزَّلَ أُغْنِيةً من الإنْتَرْنِت to download a song from the Internet

نازَلَ *v* to compete/struggle/fight with; نازَلَ شَخْصاً to compete with sb

أَنْزَلَ *v* ① [جَعَلَهُ يَنْزِلُ] to lower, to bring/take down; to demote; أَنْزَلَ العَلَمَ to lower the flag; أَنْزَلَ من رُتْبةِ شَخْصٍ to demote sb; أَنْزَلَ شَيْئاً إلى السوقِ to bring sth to market; أَنْزَلَ ناساً إلى الشارِعِ to bring people to the streets; أَنْزَلَ عُقوبةً بِشَخْصٍ to impose a punishment on sb; أَنْزَلَ خَسائِرَ to cause damage ② [كاشَفَ ب] to reveal; أَنْزَلَ اللهُ القُرْآنَ على مُحَمَّدٍ God revealed the Koran to Muhammad

تَنَزَّلَ *v* ① [نَزَلَ] to come down, to descend, to drop ② [تَرَكَ] to give up, to abandon; to waive; تَنَزَّلَ عن حَقِّهِ to waive one's right

تَنازَلَ *v* |عن| to give up, to abandon, to relinquish; to waive, to disclaim, to renounce; to resign; تَنازَلَ عن شَيْءٍ to give sth up; تَنازَلَ عن الأَراضي to give up one's land; تَنازَلَ عن العَرْشِ to renounce the throne; تَنازَلَ عن حَقِّهِ في شَيْءٍ to waive one's right to sth; تَنازَلَ عن مَطْلَبِهِ to drop one's demand; لم يَتَنازَلْ عن شِبْرٍ (واحِدٍ) من شَيْءٍ to not give up a (single) piece of sth; تَنازَلَ عن مَبادِئِهِ to abandon one's principles; تَنازَلَ عن مَنْصِبٍ في الحُكومةِ to resign one's government post

اسْتَنْزَلَ *v* to ask to forgo

bleeding; نَزَفَ دَماً من جُرْحٍ \ الأَنْفِ to bleed from a wound/ the nose; يَنْزِفُ الجُرْحُ the wound is bleeding; نَزَفَ عِرْقاً \ دُموعاً to sweat/cry profusely

أَنْزَفَ *v* to exhaust, to empty

اسْتَنْزَفَ *v* to exhaust, to finish, to drain, to deplete; to consume, to spend; اسْتَنْزَفَ مَوارِدَ to deplete resources; اسْتَنْزَفَ طاقَتَهُ to drain all one's energy

نَزْف *n* bleeding, haemorrhage; نَزْف أَنْفِيّ a bloody nose; نَزْف داخِلِيّ internal bleeding; نَزْف دِماغِيّ خَطير a massive brain haemorrhage

نَزْفِيّ *adj* مِزاج نَزْفِيّ haemophilia

نَزيف *n* bleeding, haemorrhage; نَزيف داخِلِيّ internal bleeding; نَزيف دِماغِيّ \ في الدِماغِ a brain haemorrhage; نَزيف مِعَوِيّ \ مَعِدِيّ gastrointestinal bleeding; نَزيف الدَمِ bleeding; bloodshed; نَزيف الدَمِ في العِراقِ the bloodshed in Iraq; نَزيف الأَنْفِ a bloody nose; أَوْقَفَ النَزيفَ to stop the bleeding

اسْتِنْزاف *n* exhaustion, drainage, depletion; attrition; اسْتِنْزاف المَوارِدِ resource depletion; حَرْب اسْتِنْزافٍ a war of attrition; شَنَّ حَرْبَ اسْتِنْزافٍ to wage a war of attrition

اسْتِنْزافِيّ *adj* attritional; حَرْب اسْتِنْزافِيّة war of attrition

مُسْتَنْزَف *adj* exhausted, consumed, drained, depleted; مَوارِد مُسْتَنْزَفة depleted resources

نَزِقَ, نَزَقَ *v* |a-i; نَزَق, نُزوق, نَزْق| to be/become foolishly bold, to behave recklessly

نَزَق *n* thoughtlessness, recklessness, impetuosity

نَزِق *adj* thoughtless, reckless, impetuous

نَزَلَ *v* |i; نُزول| ① [هَبَطَ] to descend, to go/come down; to fall, to drop (down); to land; نَزَلَ الدَرَجَ, نَزَلَ على السَلالِمِ to go down the stairs; نَزَلَ من الجَبَلِ to come down from the mountains; نَزَلَ إلى المَرْتَبةِ العاشِرةِ to drop back to tenth place; نَزَلَ إلى الشارِعِ to take to the streets; نَزَلَ بِهِ مَكْروهٌ an accident befell him; يَنْزِلُ المِصْعَدُ the lift (BrE) elevator (AmE) is going down; يَنْزِلُ المَطَرُ it is raining; تَنْزِلُ الحَرارةُ the temperature is dropping ② [تَرَجَّلَ] to get off/down/out, to step down, to disembark, to dismount; نَزَلَ من دَرّاجَتِهِ to get off one's bicycle; نَزَلَ من القِطارِ \ السَيّارةِ to get off

نُزُل *n* |أَنْزال| hotel, guest house, inn; صاحِب نُزُلٍ innkeeper; نُزُل للسُيّاحِ a hotel for tourists

نازِل **A** *adj* **1** [هُبوط] descending, coming down, going down; downward; مَلاك نازِل من السَماءِ an angel descending from heaven; المَشيمة النازِلة (Med) placenta previa **2** [ساكِن] staying, residing

B *n* resident; lodger, guest; نازِل في الفُنْدُقِ a guest at the hotel

نازِلة *n* |نَوازِلُ| **1** [مُصيبة] disaster, calamity, catastrophe **2** (Geol) stalactite

نازِليّ *n* (Zool) hake

نِزال *n* hand-to-hand combat; bout, fight

نَزْلة *n* |نَزَلات| infection of the mucous membranes; نَزْلة شُعَبيّة \ صَدْريّة bronchitis; نَزْلة بَرْدٍ cold; نَزْلة وافِدة flu

نُزول *n* **1** [انْحِدار] descent; نُزول مَطَرٍ \ أَمْطارٍ rainfall; نُزولاً down, downwards; اتَّجَهَ نُزولاً to be headed downwards; طُلوعاً \ صُعوداً وَنُزولاً up and down **2** [طائِرة] landing **3** [مُوافَقة] agreement, accordance; نُزولاً عند رَغْبةِ الأَهْلِ in accordance with the family's wishes, at the behest of the family **4** [إقامة] residency

نَزيل *n* |نُزَلاءُ| resident, boarder, lodger, guest; نَزيل فُنْدُقٍ hotel guest; نَزيل مُسْتَشْفًى inpatient; نَزيل سِجْنٍ prisoner, inmate

اسْتِنْزال *n* deduction; discount

إِنْزال *n* |إِنْزالات| lowering, landing; إِنْزال القُرْآنِ the Koranic revelation; إِنْزال السَفينةِ launching a ship; إِنْزال عُقوبةٍ punishing, handing down punishment; قوّات إِنْزالٍ landing forces

تَنازُل *n* |تَنازُلات| **1** |عن| [عن حَقِّهِ] waiving, yielding; تَنازُل عن حُقوقِهِ waiving one's rights **2** [عن مَطالِبِه] concession, accommodation; تَنازُلات مُؤْلِمة painful concessions; دون أَيِّ تَنازُلٍ without any concessions; تَنازُلات إِقْليميّة territorial concessions; قَدَّمَ تَنازُلاتٍ to make concessions

تَنازُليّ *adj* descending, decreasing; بَدَأَ العَدُّ التَنازُليُّ the countdown has begun

تَنْزيل *n* |تَنْزيلات| **1** [تَخْفيض] demotion; reduction, lowering; تَنْزيلات sale; cut, decrease; تَنْزيلات ضَريبيّة tax cut; تَنْزيل إلى رُتْبةٍ أَدْنى a demotion to a lower rank **2** [وَحْي] revelation; تَنْزيل القُرْآنِ the revelation of the Koran **3** (Comput) download, downloading; التَنْزيل والتَحْميل downloading and uploading; خِيارات التَنْزيل download options

مُنازَلة *n* clash, conflict

مَنْزِل *n* |مَنازِلُ| house, home; residence; في مَنْزِلِ السَفيرِ at the ambassador's residence; مَنْزِل أَهْلِهِ \ عائِلَتِهِ his parental home; رَقْم المَنْزِلِ house number; أَهْل المَنْزِلِ the occupants of the house; اقْتِحام المَنْزِلِ unlawful entry; سوق المَنازِلِ housing market; بَنى \ امْتَلَكَ مَنْزِلاً to build/own a house; غادَرَ المَنْزِلَ to leave the house

مُنْزَل *adj* revealed (*Koran*)

مَنْزِلة *n* |مَنازِلُ| **1** [مَكانة] place, position; status, rank; مَنْزِلة خاصّة a special place; مَنْزِلة سامِية a high position **2** (Islam) *1/7 part of the Koran*

مَنْزِليّ *adj* domestic, household (*before n*), home (*before n*); دِراسة مَنْزِليّة home study; واجِب مَنْزِليّ homework; أَدَوات \ أَجْهِزة مَنْزِليّة home appliances; عَمَل \ خِدْمة مَنْزِليّ(ة) household work; للاسْتِعْمالِ المَنْزِليِّ for household use

‹ **نَزُهَ** *v* |u| نَزاهة; **1** [تَباعَدَ] to forbear **2** [كانَ مُسْتَقيماً] to be righteous/honest

نَزَّهَ *v* to consider oneself to be above; نَزَّهَ نَفْسَهُ عن شَيْءٍ to consider oneself to be above sth

تَنَزَّهَ *v* **1** [تَمَشّى] to walk, to take a walk/stroll; تَنَزَّهَ في الحَديقةِ to take a walk in the park **2** [تَرَفَّعَ] to be far above; تَنَزَّهَ عن القُبْحِ to be far above immorality

نَزاهة *n* **1** [اسْتِقامة] integrity, sincerity, honesty; righteousness; impartiality; قِلّة النَزاهةِ dishonesty; ضِمنَ نَزاهةَ الانْتِخاباتِ to ensure the integrity of the elections; حافَظَ على نَزاهَتِهِ to maintain one's integrity **2** [عِفّة] chastity

نُزْهة *n* |نُزَه, نُزْهات| trip, excursion, tour; outing, picnic; walk; نُزْهة بَحْريّة boat trip; كانَ مُجَرَّدَ نُزْهةٍ to be a walk in the park; قامَ بِنُزْهةٍ to make a trip

نَزيه *adj* |نُزَهاءُ, نِزاه| **1** honest, sound; righteous, honourable; impartial, unprejudiced; وَسيط نَزيه an honest broker; an impartial mediator; انْتِخابات نَزيهة fair elections **2** [عَفيف] chaste

تنزُّه *n* |تنزُّهات| stroll, walk

تنزيه *n* (Theol) transcendence, incomparability; *God's transcendent distance from humanity*

مُتنزَّه *n* |مُتنزَّهات| park

مُتنزِّه *n* walker

مُنتزَه *n* |مُنتزَهات| park

مُنزَّه *adj* مُنزَّه عن الخَطَأ infallible

نزا *v* |u; نزوان, نزوّ, نزو| to leap, to jump; نزا بِهِ قَلْبُهُ إلى شيْءٍ to long for sth

نَزْوة *n* |نزوات| whim, fancy; نَزْوة عابِرة a passing fancy; نَزْوة غريبة a strange whim; صاحِب نزواتٍ an capricious person

نَزْويّ *adj* whimsical

نَسَأ *v* |a; مَنْسَأة, نَسْأ| 1 [أَخَّرَ] to postpone, to delay 2 (Busn) to sell on credit

نَسيئة *n* credit, delayed payment; اشْتَرى شَيْئاً نَسيئةً \ بنَسيئةٍ to buy sth on credit

مِنْسَأة *n* stick, staff

نَسَبَ *v* |i-u; نِسْبة, نَسَب| |إلى| to attribute, to ascribe; نَسَبَ شَيْئاً ل \ إلى شَخْصٍ to ascribe sth to sb; نَسَبَ أَقْوالاً مُعَيَّنةً إلى شَخْصٍ to attribute particular statements to sb; نَسَبَ لَوْحةً إلى رَسّامٍ to attribute a painting to an artist; نَسَبَ صِفةً ل \ إلى شَخْصٍ to attribute a quality to sb; نُسِبَ إلى to be attributed to

ناسَبَ *v* 1 [لاءَمَ] to suit, to fit, to be suitable; to be compatible with, to match; to be consistent with; ناسَبَ شَيْئاً \ شَخْصاً to suit sth/sb; عِنْدَما يُناسِبُهُ when it suits him; هذا لا يُناسِبُني this is not very convenient for me; ما يُناسِبُهُ من الأَدْوية medication that's appropriate for him; ناسَبَ ذَوْقَهُ to suit one's taste 2 [كانَ قَريباً] to be family/related 3 [صاهَرَ] to be related by marriage

تَناسَبَ *v* |مع| to be in agreement/harmony with; to suit, to fit, to be in proportion with; to be compatible with, to match; تَناسَبَ مع شَيْءٍ \ شَخْصٍ to be a good match with sth/sb; لا يَتَناسَبُ الجُهْدُ مع النَتائِجِ the efforts are disproportionate to the results

انْتَسَبَ *v* 1 [انْتَمى] |إلى| to descend from; to belong to, to be related to; انْتَسَبَ إلى عائِلةٍ نَبيلةٍ \ شَريفةٍ to be of noble birth; انْتَسَبَ إلى قَبيلةِ قُرَيْش to descend from the Quraysh tribe 2 [الْتَحَقَ] to join, to become a member, to affiliate with; انْتَسَبَ إلى حِزْبٍ \ صُفوفِ المُعارَضةِ to join a party/the opposition; انْتَسَبَ إلى كُلّيّةِ الحُقوقِ to enroll in law school

اسْتَنْسَبَ *v* to trace back the ancestry of

نَسَب *n* |أَنْساب| descent, origin, birth; kinship, relation; lineage, genealogy; أَنْساب in-laws; family; سِلْسِلة \ شَجَرة النَسَبِ family tree; عِلْم الأَنْسابِ genealogy; عَريق النَسَبِ noble; ذو نَسَبٍ رَفيعٍ \ وَضيعٍ of noble/humble birth; ذو حَسَبٍ وَنَسَبٍ of distinguished descent

نَسّاب *n* genealogist

نِسْبة *n* |نِسَب| 1 [قَدْر] content; percentage; rate; نِسْبة مِئَويّة percentage; نِسْبة مِئَويّة عالِية \ مُرْتَفِعة a high percentage; نِسْبة مُنْخَفِضة a low percentage; نِسْبة ثابِتة a fixed percentage; نِسْبة عالِية \ مُنْخَفِضة من الدُهْنِ a high/low fat content; نِسْبة من السُكّانِ a percentage of the population; نِسْبة البِطالةِ \ الحَوادِثِ the unemployment/accident rate; نِسْبة النُموِّ rate of growth; نِسْبة الرِجالِ the percentage of men; عَلامة النِسْبةِ المِئَويّةِ a per cent sign; حَصَلَ على نِسْبةٍ من الأَرْباحِ to get one's share in the profit 2 [تَماثُل بين عَلاقاتِ الأَشْياءِ] relation; proportion, ratio; النِسْبة بين الطولِ والوَزْنِ the ratio between height and weight; بِنِسْبةِ اثْنَيْنِ إلى ثَلاثةٍ a ratio of 2 to 3; النِسْبةُ بين الطولِ والعَرْضِ كَنِسْبةِ ٣:٢ the length-to-width ratio is 3:2 3 [ارْتِباط] link, relation, connection; بالنِسْبةِ ل \ إلى in relation to, concerning, regarding; بالنِسْبةِ لي in my opinion; as far as I'm concerned; بالنِسْبةِ إلى هذا المَوْضوعِ regarding this subject; نِسْبةً إلى الماضي compared with the past 4 (Gram) *an adjective of relation or pertinence, formed by the suffix -iyy*

نِسْبيّ *adj* proportional; relative, comparative; *in terms of percentage*; نِسْبيًّا relatively; كَبير \ غالٍ نِسْبيًّا relatively big/expensive; غَيْر نِسْبيٍّ disproportionate; مَفْهوم نِسْبيّ a relative notion; الرُطوبة \ السُرْعة النِسْبيّة the relative humidity/speed; حَقَّقَ نَجاحاً نِسْبيًّا to achieve a relative success; هذا نِسْبيٌّ it depends

نِسْبِيّة *n* [1] [قَدْر] relativity, relativism; proportion [2] [نَظَرِيّة] relativity, relativism; نَظَرِيّة النِّسْبِيّة the theory of relativity

نسيب *n* |أَنْسِباءُ| [1] [قَريب] relative, kinsman; أَنْسِباؤُهُ في الوَطَنِ والمَهْجَرِ one's kin at home and abroad [2] [صِهْر] brother-in-law; son-in-law [3] (Literat) *the nostalgic opening of a traditional ode in which the poet reflects on what has passed*

انْتِساب *n* affiliation, association, belonging; membership; انْتِساب إلى جَماعةٍ affiliation with a group; انْتِساب إلى نِقابةٍ membership in a union

تَناسُب *n* agreement, correspondence; proportion, relation, ratio; عَدَم التَناسُبِ disproportion; تَناسُب بين شَيْئَيْنِ a correspondence between two things

تَناسُبِيّ *adj* proportional; تَقْسيم تَناسُبِيّ a proportional division

تَناسُبِيّة *n* proportion; proportionality; مَبْدَأ التَناسُبِيّةِ the principle of proportionality

مُتَناسِب *adj* proportionate; matching, analogous, consistent; مُتَناسِب مع proportionate to; غَيْر مُتَناسِبٍ disproportionate; غَيْر مُتَناسِبٍ مع الواقِعِ inconsistent with reality

مُناسِب *adj* suitable, appropriate, convenient; adequate, satisfactory; غَيْر مُناسِبٍ unsuitable, inconvenient; هذا مُناسِبٌ \ غَيْرُ مُناسِبٍ this is convenient/inconvenient; حَلّ مُناسِب a satisfactory solution; عِلاج مُناسِب an appropriate treatment; رَدّ فِعْلٍ مُناسِب an appropriate reaction; وَقْت مُناسِب a convenient time; جاءَ \ حَدَثَ في وَقْتٍ مُناسِبٍ to be convenient; كانَ مُناسِباً لِفِعْلِ شَيْءٍ to be suited to do sth

مُناسَبة *n* occasion, event; opportunity; بِهذِهِ المُناسَبةِ in this respect/context; بالمُناسَبةِ on/for the occasion; by the way; بِمُناسَبةِ شَيْءٍ on the occasion of sth; أَقامَ حَفْلةً بِمُناسَبةِ عيدِ ميلادِهِ to throw a party for one's birthday; مُناسَبة سَعيدة a happy occasion; في المُناسَباتِ الكُبْرى at major events; في كُلِّ مُناسَبةٍ at every opportunity; في أَكْثَرِ من مُناسَبةٍ, في مُناسَباتٍ عِدّةٍ on several occasions

مُنْتَسِب [A] *adj* associated; registered, enrolled; طالِب مُنْتَسِب إلى كُلِّيّةِ الطِبِّ an enrolled medical student [B] *n* member; a registered student

مَنْسوب [A] *adj* related; attributed, assigned; مَنْسوب لِ \ إلى related to; التُهَم المَنْسوبة إلَيْهِ the charges against him; الكَلام المَنْسوب إلَيْهِ the words attributed to him [B] *n* |مَناسيبُ| level; ارْتِفاع مَنْسوبِ مِياهِ البِحارِ a rise in sea level

نَسَجَ *v* |i-u; نَسْج| to knit; to weave; to spin; نَسَجَ كَنْزةً \ جَوارِبَ to knit a sweater/socks; نَسَجَ خُيوطَ شَيْءٍ to weave sth; (fig) to create/build sth; نَسَجَ خُيوطاً عَنْكَبوتيّةً to spin a web; نَسَجَ قِصّةً to spin a tale

نَسْج *n* weaving, spinning; من نَسْجِ الخَيالِ imaginary

نَسّاج *n* [1] [مَنْ يَنْسِجُ] weaver; knitter [2] (Zool) weaver (bird) (*Ploceus*)

نَسيج *n* |نُسُج، أَنْسِجة| [1] [قُماش] textile, fabric, material; أَنْسِجة سَميكة \ رَهيفة a coarsely/finely woven fabric; صِناعة النَسيجِ the textile industry; فَنّ النَسيجِ textile art; قِطْعة من النَسيجِ a piece of fabric [2] [تَرْكيب] structure, texture; composition, constitution; النَسيج الاجْتِماعيّ the fabric of society; النَسيج الروائيّ (لِقِصّةٍ) the narrative structure (of a story); نَسيج وَحْدِهِ unique [3] [العَنْكَبوتِ] web, cobweb; نَسيج العَنْكَبوتِ a spider's web, a cobweb; نَسيج من الأَكاذيبِ a web of lies [4] (Anat) tissue; أَنْسِجة دِماغيّة brain tissue; أَمْراض النُسُجِ الداعِمةِ periodontitis; نَسيج شَحْمِيّ \ عَضَليّ fatty/muscular tissue; نَسيج ضامّ connective tissue; نَسيج تالِف damaged tissue

نَسيجِيّ *adj* textile (*before n*), fabric (*before n*)

مَنْسَج، مَنْسِج *n* |مَناسِجُ| weaving mill

مِنْسَج *n* |مَناسِجُ| loom

مَنْسوج [A] *adj* woven; knitted; سَجّاد مَنْسوج a woven carpet [B] *n* |مَنْسوجات| fabric, textile; مَنْسوجات textiles; تِجارة المَنْسوجاتِ the textiles business

نَسَخَ *v* |a; نَسْخ| [1] [صَوَّرَ] to copy; to photocopy; نَسَخَ مِلَفّاً to copy a file; نَسَخَ نَصّاً ٢٠ مَرّةً to make 20 copies of a text [2] [أَزالَ] to cancel, to abrogate, to invalidate; نَسَخَ اللهُ الآيةَ بِآيةٍ أُخْرى God has abrogated the verse by another verse

تَناسَخَ *v* [1] [تَتابَعَ] to follow successively; to follow/succeed each other [2] [الأَرْواحُ] to be reincarnated

‹ **نُسْطوريّ** *adj* Nestorian

نُسْغ *n* sap; نُسْغ شَجَرةٍ tree sap; نُسْغ الحَياةِ lifeblood

‹ **نَسَفَ** *v* |i; نَسْف| ❶ [فَجَّرَ] to bomb, to blow up, to shell ❷ [أَفْسَدَ] to torpedo, to wreck, to destroy; نَسَفَ المُفاوَضاتِ to torpedo the negotiations

أَنْسَفَ *v* to blow up

ناسِف *adj* explosive, dynamite (*before n*); قُنْبُلة ناسِفة bomb; عُبوّة ناسِفة IED (*improvised explosive device*); bomb

نَسّافة *n* torpedo boat

نُسافة *n* chaff

نَسيفة *n* ❶ [قَذيفة] torpedo ❷ (Geol) pumice, pumice stone

مِنْسَف *n* |مَناسِفُ| ❶ [غِرْبال] winnower, sieve ❷ [الأَكْلة] mansaf (*a traditional Jordanian dish made of lamb cooked in a sauce of fermented dried yogurt and served with rice or bulgur*)

‹ **نَسَقَ** *v* |u; نَسْق| to thread; to arrange in a row; نَسَقَ قِلادةً to string a necklace

نَسَّقَ *v* to order, to arrange, to array; to coordinate, to regulate; to align, to gear/tailor to; نَسَّقَ نَصًّا to format a text; نَسَّقَ مَواقِفَ الطَرَفَيْنِ to align the two parties' positions; نَسَّقَ بين حِزْبَيْنِ to coordinate between two parties; نَسَّقَ سِياسَتَهُ مع to align one's policy with; نَسَّقَ الأَعْمالَ \ الجُهودَ to coordinate the activities/efforts; نَسَّقَ بين العَمَلِ والواجِباتِ المَنْزِليّةِ to balance work and home responsibilities

تَنَسَّقَ *v* to be coordinated; to be in order, to be arranged

تَناسَقَ *v* to be/become coordinated; to be/become arranged

نَسْق *n* ordering, arrangement

نَسَق *n* ❶ [نِظام] system; format, layout, pattern; نَسَق سِياسيّ \ اِقْتِصاديّ a political/economic system; نَسَق ثَقافيّ a cultural pattern; على نَسَقِ in accordance with; على هذا النَسَقِ ... along these lines ...; على نَسَقٍ واحِدٍ following the same pattern, cut from the same cloth ❷ [سُرْعة السَيْرِ] pace; نَسَق بَطيء \ مُرْتَفِع a slow/quick pace; نَسَق النُموِّ الاقْتِصاديّ the pace of economic growth; بِدايةُ المُباراةِ عَرَفَتْ نَسَقاً بَطيئاً the beginning of the match was slow-paced; ارْتَفَعَ النَسَقَ to pick up the pace

نَسيق *adj* arranged, organized; regular, uniform; aligned

انْتَسَخَ *v* to cancel, to abrogate, to discontinue

اسْتَنْسَخَ *v* to copy; to clone; اسْتَنْسَخَ أَجِنّةً to clone embryos

نَسْخ *n* ❶ [تَصْوير] copying; آلة نَسْخٍ photocopier; حُقوق نَسْخٍ copyright ❷ (Islam) *abrogation of a Koranic verse by a later Koranic verse* ❸ [خَطّ] naskh (*a style of Arabic calligraphy; also a font variety*)

ناسِخ *n* |نُسّاخ| ❶ [مَنْ يَنْسَخُ] copyist; آلة الناسِخ \ ناسِخة copy machine, copier ❷ (Islam) آية ناسِخة *a Koranic verse that abrogates an earlier Koranic verse*

ناسِخة *n* |نَواسِخُ, ناسِخات| copy machine, copier

نَسّاخ *n* |نَسّاخة| copyist, scribe

نُسْخة *n* |نُسَخ| ❶ [صورة] copy, photocopy, duplicate; print, reprint, reproduction; نُسْخة أَصْليّة original; نُسْخة طِبْقَ الأَصْلِ an identical copy; نُسْخة مُصَوَّرة photocopy; اسْتَخْرَجَ نُسْخةً مُصَوَّرةً to make a photocopy; تَسَلَّمَ الوَثيقةَ في نُسْخَتَيْنِ to receive the document in duplicate ❷ (P&P) edition, print, version; نُسَخ مَطْبوعة edition; نُسْخة مُحْدَثة an updated version; النُسْخة الأولى original print; نُسْخة بيتا beta version; طَبْعة مَحْدودة النُسَخِ a limited edition ❸ [تَقْليد] copy, reproduction, replica

نَسْخيّ *adj* written in naskh (*script/font*)

اسْتِنْساخ *n* copying, transcription; cloning; الاسْتِنْساخ البَشَريّ human cloning

تَناسُخ *n* reincarnation; rebirth; تَناسُخ الأَرْواحِ reincarnation

مُسْتَنْسَخ *adj* cloned, copied; إِنْسان \ حَيَوان مُسْتَنْسَخ a clone

مَنْسوخ 🅐 *adj* ❶ [مَنْقول] copied, duplicated; شَريط مَنْسوخ a copied tape/video; قُرْص مَنْسوخ a burned disk; مَنْسوخ بِطَريقةٍ غَيْرِ قانونيّةٍ pirated, copied illegally ❷ [مُلْغًى] abrogated 🅑 *n* *a Koranic verse that has been abrogated by a later verse*

‹ **نَسَرَ** *v* |i; نَسْر| to cut, to tear, to lacerate

نَسْر *n* |نُسور, نُسورة| eagle; vulture

ناسور, ناصور *n* |نَواسيرُ| fistula; cyst, abscess; ناسور الوِلادةِ obstetric fistula; ناسور شَعْريّ pilonidal cyst

مِنْسَر *n* |مَناسِرُ| beak (*of a predatory bird*)

‹ **نِسْرين** *n* ❶ sweet briar, eglantine (*Rosa rubiginosa*) ❷ [اسْم شَخْصيّ] |f dipt| Nasreen (*female given name*)

شَخْصٍ to descend from sb

نُسالة *n* a frayed/loose end

اسْتِنْسِل *n* see **ستنسل**

إِنْسال *n* reproduction, procreation

تَناسُل *n* reproduction, procreation; التَناسُل البَشَريّ human reproduction; مَوْقِع التَناسُلِ (للسَمَكِ) spawning ground

تَناسُليّ *adj* reproductive; venereal, genital; أَعْضاء تَناسُلِيّة genitals; جِهاز تَناسُليّ reproductive system; مَرَض تَناسُليّ a venereal disease

تَنَسُّل *n* snag

‹ **نَسَمَ** *v* |i; نَسْم, نَسَمان| to blow gently

نَسَّمَ *v* to begin, to start, to commence

تَنَسَّمَ *v* **1** [الريحُ] to blow gently **2** [تَنَفَّس] to breathe in, to take/draw a breath, to inhale; to smell, to sniff; تَنَسَّمَ رائِحةً to inhale a scent; تَنَسَّمَ هَواءَ الحُرِّيّة to breathe the air of freedom

نَسَم *n* |أَنْسام| breath of life

نَسَمة *n* **1** [هَواء] breeze, gentle wind; نَسَمة مُنْعِشة a refreshing breeze; نَسَمة هَواءٍ a breath of air **2** [شَخْص] person, human, individual; soul; تَحْوي هذه المَدينةُ ٧٠٠.٠٠٠ نَسَمةٍ this city has 700,000 inhabitants

نَسيم *n* |نِسام, نَسائِمُ| breeze, gentle wind; نَسيم مُنْعِش \ رَطْب a refreshing/fresh wind; نَسيم عَليل a light breeze; شَمّ النَسيم (Egypt) *Coptic festival on the first Monday after Coptic Easter, celebrating the start of spring*

‹ **نَسْناس, نِسْناس** *n* |نَسانِسُ, نَسانيسُ| little monkey

‹ **نِساء** *n pl* |sing المَرْأة| women, ladies; wives; نِساء جَميلات beautiful women, pretty ladies; النِساء الحَوامِل والمُرْضِعات pregnant and nursing women; النِساء الكاتِبات \ الأديبات (female) writers; نِساء الأَعْمالِ businesswomen; نِساء الرَسولِ the wives of the Prophet; حُقوق النِساءِ women's rights; زير نِساءٍ womanizer; سورة النِساء The Women (*Sura 4*); أَمْراض النِساءِ والوِلادةِ obstetrics/gynaecology, ob-gyn; طَبيب أَمْراضِ النِساءِ والوِلادةِ an obstetrician/gynaecologist, an ob-gyn; لِلنِساءِ فَقَطْ for women only; العُنْف ضدّ النِساءِ violence against women

تَناسُق *n* |تَناسُقات| agreement, harmony; symmetry; combination; تَناسُق الأَلْوانِ matching colors

تَنْسيق *n* **1** [تَنْظيم] coordination; harmonization, harmony; التَنْسيق والتَعاوُن close cooperation; تَنْسيق الجُهودِ \ المَواقِفِ coordinating efforts/positions; تَنْسيق وَثيق \ كامِل good/perfect harmony **2** [تَرْتيب] classification, ordering, systematic arrangement

تَنْسيقيّ *adj* coordinating, steering; systematic; لَجْنة تَنْسيقيّة coordinating committee

تَنْسيقيّة *n a coordinating committee*

مُتَناسِق *adj* symmetrical, balanced; coherent; تَصْميم مُتَناسِق a symmetrical pattern; لَوْن مُتَناسِق a matching color; تَنْمية مُتَناسِقة balanced growth

مُنَسَّق *adj* trim, neat; organized, coordinated; جَهْد مُنَسَّق coordinated effort

مُنَسِّق *n* coordinator; مُنَسِّق المَشْروعِ project coordinator

‹ **نَسَكَ** *v* |u; نَساكة| to be ascetic, to lead an ascetic life

تَنَسَّكَ *v* to be pious/devout; to lead an ascetic life

ناسِك **A** *adj* |نُسّاك| ascetic, austere **B** *n* |نُسّاك| ascetic, hermit

تَنَسُّك *n* asceticism

مَنْسَك *n* |مَناسِكُ| **1** [طُقوس] rite, ritual; ceremony; مَناسِك الحَجِّ the rituals of the hajj; أَدّى مَناسِكَ الحَجِّ to perform the rituals of the hajj **2** [صَوْمَعة] monastery cell; hermitage

‹ **نَسَلَ** *v* |u; نَسْل, نُسول| **1** [انْفَصَلَ] to drop/fall out; to fray; يَنْسُلُ السَجّادُ the carpet is fraying; يَنْسُلُ الريشُ the feathers are falling out **2** [أَنْجَبَ] to beget; to reproduce, to procreate

نَسَّلَ *v* to unravel, to shred

أَنْسَلَ *v* **1** [أَنْجَبَ] to beget; to reproduce, to procreate **2** [طَرَحَ صوفَهُ أو ريشَهُ أو شَعْرَهُ] to moult

تَنَسَّلَ *v* to unravel

تَناسَلَ *v* to reproduce, to procreate

نَسْل *n* |أَنْسال| descendants, offspring, progeny; تَحْديد \ تَنْظيم \ ضَبْط النَسْل birth control, family planning; تَحْسين النَسْلِ eugenics; نَسْل إبراهيمَ Abraham's descendants; كانَ من نَسْلِ

نِسائيّ *adj* women's, female, feminine; feminist; أَشْغال نِسائيّة female labour; تَعْليم نِسائيّ women's/female education; مَلابِس \ أَزْياء نِسائيّة women's clothing/fashion; مَجَلّات نِسائيّة women's magazines; الحَرَكة النِسائيّة the feminist movement; الجِراحة النِسائيّة والتَوْليد (Levant) obstetrics/gynaecology, ob-gyn

نِسْوة *n pl* women

نِسْويّ *adj* women's, female, feminine; feminist; الحَرَكة النِسْويّة the feminist movement

نِسْويّة *n* feminism

‹ **نَسِيَ** *v* |a; نِسْيان, نَسْي| to forget; نَسِيَ أنْ \ أنّ ... to forget to/that ...; نَسِيَ الرَقْص to forget how to dance; نَسيتُ الاسْمَ the name has slipped my mind; لا يُنْسى unforgettable; يَوْم \ حَدَث لا يُنْسى a memorable day/event; إنْسَ ذلك! forget it!; لا تَنْسَ مَوْعِدَنا don't forget our appointment

نَسّى *v* to make/let forget

أَنْسى *v* to make/let forget; to cure of; أَنْسى شَخْصاً عادةً to cure sb of a habit

تَناسى *v* to pretend to have forgotten; to attempt to forget, to repress; to put aside, to ignore; تَناسَوْا خِلافاتِهِمْ to put aside their differences

نَسِيّ *adj* |نَسْيانُ| forgetful; oblivious

نَسْي **A** *adj* forgotten; نَسْياً مَنْسيًّا completely forgotten

B *n* forgetfulness, oblivion; sth that has been forgotten

نَساً *n* |أَنْساء| sciatic nerve; عِرْق النَسا sciatica

نِسْيان *n* **1** [سَهْو] oblivion; غَياهِب \ طَيّ النِسْيانِ oblivion; اِجْتَذَبَ شَيْئاً من بَراثِنِ النِسْيانِ to rescue sth from oblivion; طَواهُ النِسْيانُ to fade into oblivion **2** [نَسيّ] forgetfulness, to have a short memory; forgetting; نِسْيان أَحْقادِ الماضي forgetting past grudges; كَثير النِسْيانِ forgetful **3** (Med) amnesia, loss of memory; أُصيبَ بالنِسْيانِ to suffer from amnesia

مَنْسيّ *adj* forgotten; نَسْياً مَنْسيًّا completely forgotten

‹ **نَسيء** *n* El Nasii (*the thirteenth month of the Coptic calendar*)

‹ **نَشَأَ** *v* |a; نَشْء, نُشوء, نَشْأة| to come into existence/being, to originate; to arise, to grow; to start; to result from; نَشَأَ من \ عن شَيْءٍ to result from sth; نَشَأَ في شَيْءٍ to result in sth; نَشَأَ في حَيٍّ فَقيرٍ to grow up in a poor neighbourhood; نَشَأَتْ مُناقَشةٌ حادّةٌ an intense debate arose; نَشَأَ حَريقٌ a fire broke out; مَتى نَشَأَتْ هذه الفِكْرةُ؟ when did this idea originate?

نَشَّأَ *v* to raise, to bring up

أَنْشَأَ *v* to establish, to set up, to found; to build, to construct; to produce, to create; أَنْشَأَ سَدًّا to build a dam; أَنْشَأَ شَرِكةً to establish a company; أُنْشِئَت الشَرِكةُ عامَ ٢٠٠٢ the company was founded in 2002; أَنْشَأَ فَرْعاً في مَكانٍ to set up a branch somewhere; أَنْشَأَ حِزْباً to found a party; أَنْشَأَ لَجْنةَ تَحْقيقٍ to establish a fact-finding committee; أَنْشَأَ مَشْروعاً to launch a project; أَنْشَأَ حِساباً to create an account; أَنْشَأَ رِسالةً to compose a message

نَشْء *n* the youth, young people; new generation

ناشِئ **A** *adj* growing, arising, emerging; اِقْتِصاديّات \ أَسْواق ناشِئة emerging economies/markets; ديمُقْراطيّة ناشِئة a fledgling democracy; النِزاعات \ الخِلافات الناشِئة عن شَيْءٍ disputes/conflicts arising from sth

B *n* beginner, newcomer; youths, young people

نَشْأة *n* emergence, beginning, start; growth, development, evolution; establishment, founding; نَشْأة الكَوْنِ the creation of the universe; نَشْأة كَنيسةٍ the founding of a church; نَشْأة الحَضارة الإنْسانيّة the emergence of human civilization

نُشوء *n* growth, development, evolution; emergence, rise; نَظَريّة النُشوء والارْتِقاء \ والتَطَوُّر the theory of evolution; نُشوء أَزْمةٍ سِياسيّةٍ the emergence of a political crisis

نُشوئيّ **A** *adj* evolutionary

B *n* evolutionist

إنْشاء *n* **1** [بِناء] |إنْشاءات| building, construction; foundation, establishment, installation; إنْشاءات construction activity; إنْشاءات بِتْروليّة oil installations; إنْشاء شَرِكةٍ the founding of a company; إنْشاءات جَديدة the construction of new buildings; كانَ قَيْدَ \ تحت الإنْشاءِ to be under construction **2** [مُؤَسَّسة] establishment, foundation, institution, organisation; إنْشاءات صِحّيّة medical institutions **3** [كِتابة] essay, paper; إنْشاء

نَشَدَ *v* |u; نَشْد ,نَشْدة ,نِشْدان| ❶ [قَصَدَ] to strive for, to aim for/at; to seek, to want; نَشَدَ المَجْدَ \ الاسْتِقْلال to strive for fame/independence ❷ [اسْتَحْلَفَ] to implore, to supplicate; أَنْشُدُكَ اللهَ I beg you in the name of God

ناشَدَ *v* to implore, to beseech; to order, to summon; to urge, to implore; ناشَدَ شَخْصاً فِعْلَ شَيْءٍ to urge sb to do sth

أَنْشَدَ *v* to sing; to recite; أَنْشَدَ لَحناً to sing a melody; أَنْشَدَ النَشيدَ الوَطَنيَّ to sing the national anthem; أَنْشَدَ قصيدةً to recite a poem

تَناشَدَ *v* to recite to one another

نِشْدان *n* seeking, searching for

نَشيد *n* |أَناشيدُ ,نَشائِدُ ,أَنْشاد| song, anthem; hymn; chant; نَشيد عَسْكَريّ military march; أَناشيد دينيّة religious hymns; نَشيد وَطَنيّ national anthem

إنْشاد *n* singing; recitation; فِرْقة إنْشادٍ choir; إنْشاد قَصيدةٍ recitation of a poem

أُنْشودة *n* |أَناشيدُ ,أَنْشاد| song, anthem; hymn; chant

مُناشَدة *n* appeal, summons, urgent request; مُناشَدات مُتَكَرِّرة \ عاجِلة repeated/urgent appeals; جَدَّدَ المُناشَدةَ to renew an appeal; مُناشَدة المُجْتَمَعِ الدُوَليِّ الضَغْطَ على ... an appeal to the international community to exert pressure on ...

مُنْشِد *n* singer; chanter

مَنْشود *adj* desired, desirable, wanted; pursued; الحَلّ المَنْشود the desired solution; الهَدَف المَنْشود the intended goal

نَشَرَ *v* |u; نَشْر| ❶ [رَوَّجَ] to spread, to disperse; to distribute; نَشَرَ إشاعاتٍ to spread rumours; نَشَرَ العُنْفَ في البِلادِ to spread violence throughout the country ❷ [أَعْلَنَ] to announce, to make public; نَشَرَ شَيْئاً to announce sth ❸ [أَصْدَرَ] to publish, to issue; نَشَرَ كِتاباً to publish a book ❹ [مَدَّ] to spread (out), to hang (out); to unfold, to unroll, to unwind; to smooth (out), to make flat; نَشَرَ الغَسيلَ to hang the laundry ❺ [جُنوداً] to deploy; نَشَرَ قُوّاتٍ to deploy forces; نَشَرَ خَمْسينَ أَلْفَ جُنْديٍّ في مِنْطَقةٍ to deploy 50,000 troops in a region ❻ [الضَوْءَ] to diffuse; to emit; نَشَرَ الضَوْءَ على شَيْءٍ to shed light on sth ❼ [الخَشَبَ] to saw; نَشَرَ لَوْحَ خَشَبٍ to saw a board

an essay on sth; كَتَبَ إنْشاءً حول \ عن شَيْءٍ to write a paper ❹ [أُسْلوب] style ❺ (Gram) *a sentence that cannot be declared factually true or false (such as a question, command, etc.)*

إنْشائيّ *adj* ❶ [بِنائيّ] structural; construction (*before n*), building (*before n*); مَشْروع إنْشائيّ a construction project; عَيْب إنْشائيّ a structural defect; شَرِكة إنْشائيّة a construction company; صِناعات إنْشائيّة the building industry ❷ [أُسْلوبيّ] stylistic, style (*before n*), composition (*before n*); قِطْعة إنْشائيّة a piece of writing; مَوْضوع إنْشائيّ essay; (مُجَرَّد) عِبارة إنْشائيّة (just) a pretty turn of phrase

مَنْشَأ *n* |مَناشِئُ| origin; source; شَهادة المَنْشَأِ certificate of origin; بَلَد المَنْشَأِ country of origin; خَلايا المَنْشَأِ stem cells

مُنْشِئ *n* founder; builder

مُنْشَأة *n* ❶ [مُؤَسَّسة] establishment, foundation, institution; company, enterprise; مُنْشَأة خَيْريّة charity ❷ [أَجْهِزة] installation, system; facility; building; مُنْشَآت عَسْكَريّة military facilities

نُشادِر, نوشادِر *n* ammonium chloride; مِلْح النُشادِرِ sal ammoniac; غاز النُشادِرِ ammonia

نَشِبَ *v* |a; نَشَب ,نُشْبة ,نُشوب| ❶ [انْدَلَعَ] to break out; نَشِبَ حَريقٌ a fire broke out; نَشِبَتْ أَحْداثُ شغب riots broke out; نَشِبَ خِلافٌ بين الطَرَفَيْنِ a dispute arose between the two parties; نَشِبَتْ حَرْبٌ بين الدَوْلَتَيْنِ a war broke out between the two countries ❷ [عَلِقَ] to be attached to, to cling/stick to; to be/get caught in, to be/get stuck in; نَشِبَ في الحِبالةِ to be stuck in a net

أَنْشَبَ *v* to attach, to fix; أَنْشَبَ أَظافِرَهُ في شَيْءٍ to dig one's nails into sth; (fig) to get a hold of sth

نَشّاب *n* archer

نُشّاب *n coll* |نَشاشيبُ| arrow; قَوْس وَنُشّاب bow and arrow

نَشّابة *n* rolling pin

نُشوب *n* outbreak; نُشوب الحَرْبِ \ الثَوْرة the outbreak of war/revolution

نَشَجَ *v* |i; نَشيج| to sob, to weep; to whimper

نَشيج *n* |نُشُج| sobbing, weeping; whimpering

مُعاهَدة مَنْع الانْتِشارِ النَوويّ a non-proliferation treaty ❷ [جُنودٍ] deployment; إعادة انْتِشارِ القوّاتِ redeployment of forces ❸ [الضَوْء] propagation; diffusion; انْتِشار الضَوْءِ the propagation of light

مُنْتَشِر *adj* ❶ [شائع] scattered, spread; فُروع مُنْتَشِرة في البِلادِ branches across the country ❷ [جُنود] deployed; الجُنود المُنْتَشِرونَ في أوروبّا soldiers deployed in Europe ❸ [الضَوْء] diffuse; نور \ ضَوْء مُنْتَشِر a diffuse light

مِنْشار *n* |مَناشيرُ| saw; مِنْشار المُنْحَنَياتِ jigsaw; أبو مِنْشارٍ sawfish

مَنْشَر *n* |مَناشِرُ| ❶ [لِنَشْر الخَشَبِ] sawmill ❷ [لِلتَجْفيفِ] drying rack; *flat place for drying grains and such*

مَنْشَرة *n* |مَناشِرُ| sawmill

مَنْشور *n* |مَناشيرُ, مَنْشورات| ❶ [بَيان] publication; leaflet, pamphlet, circular; piece of writing, text; مَنْشور وِزاريّ a government publication; مَنْشور بابَويّ papal encyclical; أَصْدَرَ مَنْشوراتٍ to publish leaflets; وَزَّعَ مَناشيرَ to distribute pamphlets ❷ (Geom) prism

نَشَزَ *v* |i-u; نَشْز| ❶ [اِرْتَفَعَ] to rise, to go up ❷ [في الزَواجِ] to treat one's spouse badly

ناشِز *adj* |mf| ❶ (Mus) false, out of tune ❷ [زَوْج أو زَوْجة] recalcitrant, rebellious, disobedient; امْرَأة ناشِز(ة) a disobedient wife

ناشِزة *n* |نَواشِزُ| (Med) protuberance

نَشاز *n* dissonance, discord, discordance; cacophony

نُشوز *n* discord; disobedient behaviour, bad treatment; *violation of the marital obligations by disobedience (by the wife) or maltreatment (by the husband)*

نَشَّ *v* |i; نَشّ, نَشيش| ❶ [لَوَّحَ] to swat (at); نَشَّ الذُبابَ to swat at flies; (fig) to be idle, ≈ to twiddle one's thumbs; لا يَهِشُّ وَلا يَنِشُّ *to be powerless or lacking in influence in a given situation* ❷ [جَفَّ] to become dry ❸ [صَوَّتَ] to hiss, to sizzle; to simmer

نَشّاش **A** *adj* absorbent; وَرَق نَشّاش paper towels; blotting paper **B** *n* swatter; نَشّاش ذُبابٍ fly-whisk; fly swatter

مِنَشّة *n* fly swatter

نَشَّرَ *v* to spread, to scatter

أَنْشَرَ *v* to resurrect, to bring back to life

تَنَشَّرَ *v* ❶ [اِنْتَشَرَ] to spread; to be spread ❷ [جُنودٌ] to be deployed

اِنْتَشَرَ *v* |i| ❶ [تَنَشَّرَ] to spread, to disperse; to be spread/widespread, to be dispersed; اِنْتَشَرَ في أَرْجاءِ البِلادِ to spread all over the country; اِنْتَشَرَ المَرَضُ the disease has spread; يَنْتَشِرُ الوَباءُ the epidemic is spreading; يَنْتَشِرُ داءُ الإنْفْلُونْزا there's an outbreak of flu; يَنْتَشِرُ الخَبَرُ \ تَنْتَشِرُ الإشاعةُ the news/rumour is spreading ❷ [جُنودٌ] to be deployed; اِنْتَشَرَتْ قوّاتُ الأَمْنِ في المَدينةِ security forces were deployed throughout the city ❸ [الضَوْءُ] to propagate; to be emitted; يَنْتَشِرُ الضَوْءُ مَوْجِيًّا light propagates as a wave

نَشْر *n* ❶ [تَوْزيع] distribution, spreading; نَشْر ثَقافةِ الحِوارِ \ السَلامِ promoting a culture of dialogue/peace ❷ [كُتُبٍ] publication; circulation, issue; publishing; نَشْر إلِكْترونيّ electronic publishing; دار نَشْرٍ publishing house; إعادة النَشْرِ reissue, reprinting; مَنْع النَشْرِ publication ban; حُرِّيّة النَشْرِ freedom of the press; حَقّ النَشْرِ copyright; حَظَرَ نَشْرَ كِتابٍ to ban a book ❸ (Relig) resurrection

ناشِر *n* publisher; بَحَثَ عن ناشِرٍ لِكِتابِهِ to search for a publisher for one's book

نُشارة *n* sawdust

نَشْرة *n* |نَشَرات| bulletin; publication; newspaper; نَشْرة إخْباريّة news, newscast, news bulletin; نَشْرة دَوْريّة periodical; نَشْرة جَوّيّة weather forecast; نَشْرة حِزْبيّة party newspaper; نَشْرة رِياضيّة \ الرِياضةِ sports news; نَشْرة الأَسْعارِ price list; نَشْرة الأَنْباءِ news broadcast; النَشْرة الإحْصائيّة الشَهْرِيّة monthly statistical bulletin

نُشور *n* resurrection

اِنْتِشار *n* ❶ [اِتِّساع] circulation, spreading, propagation; proliferation; أَقَلّ اِنْتِشاراً less prevalent; واسِع الانْتِشارِ widespread; فِكْرة واسِعة الانْتِشارِ a widely held opinion; اِنْتِشار إشاعةٍ \ مَرَضٍ the spreading of a rumour/disease; اِنْتِشار المَسيحيّة the spreading of Christianity; اِنْتِشار الأَسْلِحةِ النَوَوِيّة the proliferation of nuclear weapons;

اعْتِقال نُشَطاء كَتائِبِ الأقْصى human rights activists; الإنْسانِ the arrest of al-Aqsa Brigade operatives

أُنْشوطة *n* |أَناشيطُ| knot; noose, loop; عَقَدَ \ عَمِلَ أُنْشوطةً to tie/make a knot

تَنْشيط *n* activation; stimulation, promotion; تَنْشيط التَبادُلِ التِجاريّ promotion of trade; تَنْشيط المَبيعاتِ sales promotion; إعادة تَنْشيطٍ reactivation

مُنَشَّط *adj* activated; stimulated, invigorated

مُنَشِّط A *adj* activating; stimulating; مادّة \ دَواء مُنَشِّط(ة) a stimulant

B *n* 1 |مُنَشِّطات| stimulant; drug; مُنَشِّطات stimulants; amphetamines; تَناوُل \ تَعاطي المُنَشِّطاتِ amphetamine abuse; (Sport) doping 2 |مُنَشِّطونَ| activist

نَشَفَ, **نَشِفَ** *v* |a-u; نُشْف| to dry up/out, to run dry; نَشِفَ الماءُ \ البِئْرُ the water/well dried up

نَشَّفَ *v* 1 [جَفَّفَ] to dry, to make dry; نَشَّفَ شَعْرَهُ to dry one's hair 2 [الماءَ] to wipe, to mop; to wipe away/off, to mop up; نَشَّفَ العَرَقَ to wipe away the sweat

تَنَشَّفَ *v* to dry oneself

ناشِف *adj* 1 [جافّ] dry, arid 2 [خَشِن] crude, unkind

نَشّاف *n coll* dryer; absorption; وَرَق نَشّاف paper towels; blotting paper

نَشّافة *n* 1 [أداة] dryer 2 [خِرْقة] rag, cloth

مِنْشَفة *n* |مَناشِفُ| towel; مَناشِف وَرَقيّة paper towels; مِنْشَفة صِحّيّة sanitary towel (BrE) napkin (AmE), maxi pad

أَنْشَقَ *v* to make inhale; to give to smell

تَنَشَّقَ *v* to inhale, to breathe in; to smell, to sniff up; تَنَشَّقَ دُخاناً \ غازاتٍ to inhale smoke/gas

اِنْتَشَقَ *v* to inhale, to breathe in; to sniff up; اِنْتَشَقَ رائحةَ شَيْءٍ to inhale the fragrance of sth

اِسْتَنْشَقَ *v* to inhale, to breathe in; to smell; to sniff up; to sniff, to snort; اِسْتَنْشَقَ الهَواءَ to breathe in the air; اِسْتَنْشَقَ الماءَ to sniff up water

نَشوق *n* snuff

نَشَطَ *v* |i; نَشْط| to knot, to tie with/in a knot; نَشَطَ حَبْلاً to tie a rope in a knot

نَشِطَ *v* |a; نَشاط| to be active/energetic; to be enthusiastic; نَشِطَ لِشَيْءٍ to be enthusiastic about sth; نَشِطَ في العَمَلِ to work enthusiastically

نَشَّطَ *v* to activate; to stimulate, to encourage; نَشَّطَ الدَوْرةَ الدَمَويّةَ to stimulate blood circulation; نَشَّطَ الاقْتِصادَ \ الصِناعةَ to stimulate the economy/industry; نَشَّطَ عَمَليّةَ السَلامِ to encourage the peace process; نَشَّطَ الأَبُ ابْنَهُ لِيَعْمَلَ the father encouraged his son to work

أَنْشَطَ *v* to activate; to stimulate, to invigorate

تَنَشَّطَ *v* to be active/energetic; to feel like, to be up for; تَنَشَّطَ لِفِعْلِ شَيْءٍ to feel like doing sth

نَشِط *adj* active, lively, brisk; دَوْر نَشِط an active role; الإطار النَشِط the active window

ناشِط A *adj* active; حَرَكة ناشِطة an active movement; دَوْر ناشِط an active role; كانَ ناشِطاً في مَجالِ ... to be active in the field of ...

B *n* activist; member, operative; ناشِطونَ عَرَب وَأوروبيّونَ Arab and European activists

نَشاط *n* |أَنْشِطة| activity, action; busyness, liveliness; energy; نَشاط اقْتِصاديّ economic activity; نَشاط بَدَنيّ exercise; نَشاط جِسْمانيّ \ فِكْريّ physical/intellectual activity; أَنْشِطة اجْتِماعيّة \ ثَقافيّة social/cultural activities; نَشاط مَحْموم feverish activity; نَشاط إشْعاعيّ radioactivity; حُمّى النَشاطِ مُفْعَم Internet activity; Internet activism; نَشاط الإنْتَرْنِت بالحَيَويّةِ والنَشاطِ energetic; يَفيضُ نَشاطاً he's full of energy

نَشاطيّة *n* 1 (Sci) activity; النَشاطيّة الإشْعاعيّة radioactivity; سِلْسِلة نَشاطيّة العَناصِرِ activity series of elements 2 [اجْتِماعيّ] activism; النَشاطيّة السِياسيّة political activism

نَشيط A *adj* |نُشَطاءُ, نِشاط| active, busy; energetic, lively; حَياة نَشيطة a busy life; مادّة نَشيطة an active substance; عُضْو نَشيط في الحِزْبِ an active member of the party; كانَ نَشيطاً في السِياسةِ to be active in politics; كانَ نَشيطاً to be energetic

B *n* |نُشَطاءُ, نِشاط| activist; member, operative; نُشَطاء حُقوقِ

اسْتِنْشاق *n* inhaling, inhalation; اسْتِنْشاق الدُخانِ smoke inhalation

تَنْشيقة *n* a pinch of snuff

نَشَلَ *v* |u; نَشْل| to steal, to pilfer; to snatch; نَشَلَ مِحْفَظَةَ شَخْصٍ من جَيْبِهِ to pick sb's pocket; نَشَلَ حَقيبةَ يَدِ شَخْصٍ to snatch sb's purse

انْتَشَلَ *v* 1 [اخْتَطَفَ] to take, to snatch 2 [أَنْقَذَ] to pick up; to save, to rescue; to extricate, to extract; انْتَشَلَ غَرْقى to rescue people from drowning; انْتَشَلَ شَخْصاً من مَأْزِقٍ to extricate sb from difficulties; أُنْتُشِلَتْ جُثَثُ الضَحايا the bodies of the victims were extracted

نَشّال *n* pickpocket; انْتَبِهْ من النَشّالينَ! beware of pickpockets!

انْتِشال *n* rescuing, saving; recovery; انْتِشال سَفينةٍ من الماءِ salvage; انْتِشال الجُثَثِ recovery of bodies

نَشْنَش *v* |i; نَشْنَشة| 1 [صَوَّتَ] to simmer, to bubble, to sizzle 2 [فارِه] to be nimble/lively

نَشِيَ *v* |a; نَشْو| to be/become intoxicated, to be/get drunk

نَشّى *v* to starch

انْتَشى *v* 1 [ابْتَهَجَ] to rejoice, to be delighted/pleased; انْتَشى بانْتِصارِهِ to revel in one's victory 2 [سَكِرَ] to become intoxicated/drunk 3 [شَمَّ] to smell

نَشاً *n* starch; نَشا الذُرةِ corn starch

نَشاء *n* starch; paste; نَشاء البَطاطِسِ potato starch; نَشاء الذُرةِ corn starch

نَشْوان *adj* |نَشاوى; f نَشْوى| tipsy, intoxicated; euphoric, ecstatic

نَشْوة *n* rapture, exaltation, bliss; intoxication; نَشْوة الانْتِصارِ flush of victory; نَشْوة الفَرَحِ euphoria; نَشْوة جِنْسيّة sexual pleasure; قِمّة النَشْوة (الجِنْسيّةِ) orgasm; شَعَرَ بِنَشْوةٍ to be euphoric

نَشَوِيّ *adj* starchy; مادّة نَشَوِيّة starchy material

نَشَوِيّات *n pl* carbohydrates

مُنْتَشٍ *adj* ecstatic

نَصَبَ *v* |u; نَصْب| 1 [أَقامَ] to raise, to put up; to install, to construct, to set; نَصَبَ جِسْراً to construct a bridge; نَصَبَ تِمْثالاً to put up a statue; نَصَبَ خَيْمةً to pitch a tent; نَصَبَ فَخًّا to set a trap; نَصَبَ مَكْمَناً \ كَميناً لِشَخْصٍ to ambush sb; نَصَبَ نَفْسَهُ لِشَيْءٍ to dedicate oneself to sth 2 [عَيَّنَ] to appoint, to assign; نَصَبَ نَفْسَهُ مَلِكاً he proclaimed himself king 3 [احْتالَ |على|] to deceive, to swindle, to cheat; نَصَبَ على شَخْصٍ to deceive sb 4 (Gram) *to put in the accusative/subjunctive*

نَصِبَ *v* |a; نَصَب| 1 [تَعِبَ] to be tired/weary/exhausted 2 [تَهالَكَ] to strive, to go out of one's way

نَصَّبَ *v* 1 [قَلَّدَ] to appoint, to assign; نَصَّبَ شَخْصاً وَزيراً to appoint sb minister 2 (Comput) to install; نَصَّبَ بَرْنامَجاً to install a program

ناصَبَ *v* to be hostile to, to oppose; ناصَبَ شَخْصاً العَداءَ to be hostile to sb; ناصَبَ شَخْصاً الحَرْبَ to declare war on sb

أَنْصَبَ *v* to exhaust, to wear out

انْتَصَبَ *v* 1 [قامَ] to stand, to be/become upright; to rise, to become erect; انْتَصَبَ شَعْرُهُ his hair stood on end; انْتَصَبَ قَضيبُهُ to get an erection 2 [عُيِّنَ] to be appointed/assigned 3 (Gram) *to be in the accusative/conjunctive*

نَصْب *n* 1 [إقامة] putting up, erecting; construction, erection; نَصْب خَيْمةٍ \ حَواجِزَ putting up a tent/roadblock 2 [غِشّ] swindle, fraud, deception; اتَّهَمَ شَخْصاً بالنَصْبِ to accuse sb of fraud 3 [تَنْصيب] appointment, assignment, nomination 4 (Gram) accusative; subjunctive; نَصْب الفِعْلِ the subjunctive mood; حالة النَصْبِ the accusative case

نَصَب *n* exhaustion, weariness, fatigue

نُصْب, نُصُب *n* |أَنْصاب| 1 [تِمْثال] statue; monument; نُصْب تَذْكارِيّ commemorative monument, memorial; أَقامَ نُصْباً تَذْكارِيًّا to erect a monument; نُصْب الجُنْدِيِّ المَجْهولِ the monument of the Unknown Soldier 2 [وَثَن] idol 3 [أَمام] نُصْبَ in front of; نُصْبَ عَيْنَيْهِ right in front of one's eyes; وَضَعَ هَدَفاً نُصْبَ عَيْنَيْهِ to have a goal in mind

ناصِب *adj* 1 [مُتْعِب] difficult, hard, severe; هَمّ ناصِب a major concern 2 (Gram) *governing the accusative/subjunctive*

نَصّاب *n* swindler, fraud, crook; cheat, impostor, deceiver

نِصاب *n* |نُصُب| 1 [أَصْل] original state/condition, origin, beginning; عادَ إلى نِصابِهِ to return to normal; سَيَعودُ الحَقُّ إلى نِصابِهِ justice will be done; وَضَعَ الأُمورَ في نِصابِها

الصَحيحَ to put affairs in order, to put things right **2** [حِصّة] quorum; عَدَم اكتِمالِ النِصابِ lack of a quorum; تَوَفَّرَ \ اكْتَمَلَ النِصابُ القانونيُّ there was a legal quorum; نِصاب الغَنَمِ \ الذَهَبِ the minimum number of sheep/amount of gold upon which zakat is due **3** [السِلاح] the handle/grip of a weapon/tool

نَصْبة *n* sapling; نَصْبة زَيْتونٍ olive sapling

نَصيب *n* |أَنْصِبة, نُصُب| **1** [حَظّ] fate, destiny; كُلُّ شَيْءٍ قِسْمةٌ وَنَصيبٌ everything is predestined **2** [حِصّة] share, quota, portion; dividend; نَصيب الأَسَدِ the lion's share; نَصيب الفَرْدِ per capita; نَصيب من الرِبْحِ a share in the profit; كانَ من نَصيبِهِ to fall to one's share; to be one's lot

اِنْتِصاب *n* |اِنْتِصابات| **1** [وُقوف] standing upright/erect; rising **2** [نُعوظ] erection; اِنْتِصاب القَضيبِ erection; ضُعْف الاِنْتِصابِ, عَدَم القُدْرةِ على الاِنْتِصابِ erectile dysfunction, impotence

تَنْصيب *n* **1** [في مَنْصِبٍ] inauguration; nomination, appointment; تَنْصيب الرَئيسِ \ المَلِكِ inauguration/coronation; اِحْتِفال \ مَراسيم التَنْصيبِ inauguration ceremony; أَعادَ تَنْصيبَ شَخْصٍ to reappoint sb, to reinstate sb **2** (Comput) installation, installing; تَنْصيب بَرْنامَجٍ installing a program

مُنْتَصِب *adj* upright, erect; standing; قامة مُنْتَصِبة an upright posture; قَضيب مُنْتَصِب an erect penis; التِمْثال المُنْتَصِب في الساحةِ the statue standing in the square

مَنْصِب *n* |مَناصِبُ| job, position; office, function, post; rank, level; مَنْصِب شَرَفيّ \ فَخْريّ an honorary post; مَنْصِب قِياديّ \ رَفيع an executive/high-level position; مَنْصِب رَفيع في الحُكومةِ a high-level government position; مُدّة مَنْصِبٍ term of office; شَغَلَ \ تَبَوَّأَ \ تَقَلَّدَ \ تَوَلّى مَنْصِباً to take office; to hold an office; تَطَلَّعَ إلى مَنْصِبٍ أَكْبَرَ \ أَعْلى مَنْصِباً to aspire to a higher office; اِسْتَقالَ من مَنْصِبِهِ to resign from one's job/office; أَقالَ شَخْصاً من مَنْصِبٍ to dismiss sb, to fire sb; عُزِلَ من مَنْصِبِهِ to be removed from office

مِنْصَب *n* |مَناصِبُ| tripod, stand

مَنْصوب *adj* |مَنْصوبات| **1** (Gram) *in the accusative case/subjunctive mood*; المُضارِع المَنْصوب subjunctive **2** [قائِم] erected, set up; خَيْمة مَنْصوبة an erected tent; فَخّ مَنْصوب a laid trap

نَصَتَ *v* |i; نَصْت| to listen

أَنْصَتَ *v* to listen; أَنْصَتَ ل \ إلى شَيْءٍ \ شَخْصٍ to listen to sth/sb

تَنَصَّتَ *v* to eavesdrop, to monitor, to listen (in); to tap; تَنَصَّتَ على المُكالَماتِ الهاتِفيّةِ to eavesdrop on a phone call; تَنَصَّتَ على هاتِفِ شَخْصٍ to tap sb's phone; تَنَصَّتَ من وَراءِ البابِ to listen at the door

تَنَصُّت, **تَصَنُّت** *n* eavesdropping; tapping; التَنَصُّت على الهاتِفِ phone tapping; جِهاز تَنَصُّتٍ a listening device, a bug; وَضَعَ جِهازَ تَنَصُّتٍ في مَكْتَبِ شَخْصٍ to bug sb's office

نَصَحَ *v* |a; نُصْح, نَصْح, نَصاحة, نَصيحة| **1** [وَصّى] to advise, to counsel, to give advice to, to recommend; نَصَحَ شَخْصاً to counsel sb; نَصَحَ شَخْصاً \ لِشَخْصٍ بِفِعْلِ شَيْءٍ to advise sb to do sth; نَصَحَ شَخْصاً بالتَوَقُّفِ عن التَدْخينِ to advise sb to stop smoking; نَصَحَ شَخْصاً \ لِشَخْصٍ بِعَدَمِ فِعْلِ شَيْءٍ to advise sb against sth **2** [خَلَصَ] to be sincere

أَنْصَحَ *v* to advise

تَناصَحَ *v* to give each other advice

اِنْتَصَحَ *v* to follow advice, to listen to advice

اِسْتَنْصَحَ *v* to ask for/seek advice

نُصْح, **نَصْح** *n* advice, counsel; نُصْح صادِق sincere advice; نُصْح ب (عَدَمِ) فِعْلِ شَيْءٍ advice to (not) do sth; قَدَّمَ لِشَخْصٍ النُصْحَ والمُساعَدةَ to advise and assist sb

ناصِح **A** *adj* |ناصِحونَ, نُصَّح, نُصّاح| advisory, consultative, counselling (*before n*)

B *n* |ناصِحونَ, نُصَّح, نُصّاح| adviser, counsellor; ناصِحو الرَئيسِ the president's advisers

نَصوح *adj* sincere, honest

نَصيحة *n* |نَصائِحُ| advice, counsel, recommendation; بِناءً على نَصيحةِ ... on the recommendation of ...; إِسْداء النَصائِحِ recommendation; وَجَّهَ \ قَدَّمَ \ أَسْدى نَصيحةً لِشَخْصٍ to give sb advice; طَلَبَ النَصيحةَ to ask for advice; اِسْتَخَفَّ بِنَصيحةٍ to disregard advice; قَبِلَ \ أَخَذَ \ تَبِعَ نَصيحةَ شَخْصٍ to accept/take/follow sb's advice

‹ **نَصَرَ** *v* |u; نَصْر ,نُصور| **1** [أعانَ] to give victory, to make triumph (*said of God*); المَلِك، نَصَرَهُ اللهُ the king, may God give him the victory; اللهُ يَنْصُرُكُمْ على أَعْدائِكُمْ! God grant you victory over your enemies! **2** [نَجّا] to save, to rescue; to release, to deliver

نَصَّرَ *v* **1** [جَعَلَهُ نَصْرانيًّا] to Christianize; نَصَّرَ شَخْصاً to Christianize sb **2** [عَمَّدَ] to baptize

ناصَرَ *v* to assist; to support, to hold; ناصَرَ فِكْرَةً \ مُعْتَقَداً to support an idea/conviction

تَنَصَّرَ *v* to become a Christian, to be converted to/adopt Christianity

تَناصَرَ *v* to support each other

اِنْتَصَرَ *v* **1** [غَلَبَ] |على| to defeat, to beat, to be victorious, to triumph/prevail over; اِنْتَصَرَ على خَصْمٍ to defeat an adversary; اِنْتَصَرَ على الشَرِّ to overcome evil **2** [اِنْتَقَمَ] |من| to take revenge/vengeance on; اِنْتَصَرَ من شَخْصٍ to take revenge on sb **3** [أَيَّدَ] to help, to assist, to support

اِسْتَنْصَرَ *v* to ask for help/assistance; اِسْتَنْصَرَ شَخْصاً to turn to sb for help

نَصْر *n* **1** [غَلَبة] victory, triumph; قَوْس نَصْرٍ triumphal arch; دَوْرة \ جَوْلة نَصْرٍ lap of honor; عَلامة النَصْرِ victory/V sign; سورة النَصْر The Divine Support (*Sura 110*); حَقَّقَ \ أَحْرَزَ نَصْراً to triumph, to achieve victory; ادَّعى النَصْرَ to declare victory; اِحْتَفَلَ بالنَصْرِ to celebrate the victory **2** [اِسْم شَخْصيّ] نَصْر الله Nasrallah (*male given name*)

ناصِر *n* |ناصِرونَ ,أَنْصار ,نُصّار| **1** [مُساعِد] helper, supporter, assistant **2** [اِسْم شَخْصيّ] Nasser (*male given name*); شَهْر ناصِر (Hist) July (*Libya under Gaddafi*)

ناصِريّ *adj* nasserist

ناصور *n* see ناسور

نَصْرانيّ **A** *adj* |نَصْرانيّونَ ,نَصارى| Christian; العَقيدة النَصْرانيّة Christian doctrine

B *n* |نَصْرانيّونَ ,نَصارى| Christian; النَصارى العَرَب Arab Christians

نَصْرانيّة *n* Christianity

نُصْرة ,نَصْرة *n* help, assistance, aid; support, backing; نُصْرة المَظْلوم defense of the oppressed

نَصير *n* |أَنْصار ,نُصَراءُ| **1** [مُؤَيِّد] helper, supporter; follower, disciple; أَنْصار followers **2** [اِسْم شَخْصيّ] Naseer (*male given name*)

نَصيرة *n* |dipt| Naseera (*female given name*)

نُصَيْرِيّة *n* Nusayria, Alawites (*religious group centred in Syria who follow a branch of the Twelver school of Shia Islam*)

النَاصِرة *n* Nazareth (*town in Israel*)

النَاصِريّة *n* Nasserism (*Arab nationalist political ideology based on the ideas of the former Egyptian president Nasser*)

اِنْتِصار *n* |اِنْتِصارات| victory, triumph; اِنْتِصار باهِر \ عَظيم a glorious/great victory; اِنْتِصارات مُتَتالِية successive victories; اِنْتِصار على الشَرِّ \ العَدوِّ victory over evil/the enemy; حَقَّقَ اِنْتِصاراً ساحِقاً to achieve an overwhelming victory, to win by a landslide

تَنْصير *n* Christianization, conversion to Christianity; تَنْصير شَخْصٍ converting sb to Christianity

مُناصِر *n* supporter, follower, adherent; مُناصِرو المُعارَضة opposition supporters; دَعا مُناصِريهِ إلى فِعْلِ شَيْءٍ to call on one's followers to do sth

مُناصَرة *n* help, aid; backing, assistance

مُنْتَصِر **A** *adj* victorious, triumphant

B *n* victor; خَرَجَ من الصِراعِ مُنْتَصِراً to emerge victorious from the battle

مَنْصور **A** *adj* victorious; supported/aided (*by God*)

B *n* victor

‹ **نَصَّ** *v* |u; نَصّ| **1** [حَدَّدَ] |على| to stipulate, to prescribe; to determine, to specify; يَنُصُّ الاتِّفاقُ على أنّ ... the contract stipulates that ...; يَنُصُّ القانونُ على أنّ ... the law prescribes that ... **2** [كَتَبَ] to write down, to draw up

نَصَّصَ *v* to write down, to draw up, to put into text

نَصّ *n* |نُصوص| text; script; wording; نَصًّا ورُوحاً in letter and spirit; النَصّ الأَصْليّ the original text; نَصّ فائِق hypertext; بُروتوكول نَقْلِ النَصِّ الفائِق hypertext transfer protocol, HTTP; بِنَصِّهِ الحَرْفيِّ ,بِنَصِّهِ وَفَصِّهِ literally; حَسَبَ نَصِّ القانونِ according to the text of the law; نَصّ مُحاضَرةٍ \ خُطْبةٍ \ قِصّةٍ the text of a lecture/speech/story; مَجْموعة نُصوصٍ

a compilation of texts; مُعالِج \ مُنَسِّق النُصوصِ word processor; كَتَبَ \ تَلا نَصًّا to write/recite a text; اِلْتَزَمَ بالنَصِّ to be faithful to the text

نَصّيّ *adj* textual; رِسالة نَصّيّة text message

تَنْصيص *n* ① [اِقْتِباس] quotation; عَلامة التَنْصيصِ quotation mark ② [وَضْع الشُروطِ] stipulation; تَنْصيص على شَيْءٍ stipulation of sth

مِنَصّة *n* |مَناصُّ ,مِنَصّات| podium, stage, dais; platform; مِنَصّة التَتْويج a victory stand; مِنَصّة نَفْطيّة \ نَفْطٍ بَحْريّة an oil rig; وَقَفَ على مِنَصّةٍ to stand on a podium

مَنْصوص *adj* described, specified, formulated; stipulated; الشُروط المَنْصوص عَلَيْها في القَرارِ the conditions stipulated in the resolution; الحُقوق المَنْصوص عَلَيْها في الدُسْتورِ the rights specified in the constitution

نَصَعَ *v* |a; نَصاعة ,نُصوع| ① [وَضَحَ] to be/become clear/bright; to be/become evident/obvious ② [أَقَرَّ |ب|] to recognize, to acknowledge, to accept; نَصَعَ بالحَقِّ to accept the law

أَنْصَعَ *v* to acknowledge, to recognize

ناصِع *adj* clear, pure, bright; immaculate, perfect; evident, obvious; أَحْمَر ناصِع bright red; أَبْيَض ناصِع ,ناصِع البَياضِ immaculate white; أَسْنان ناصِعة البَياضِ pearly white teeth; صَفْحة ناصِعة a blank slate; حَقيقة ناصِعة an evident truth; مَلَكَ سِجِلًّا ناصِعاً to have a perfect record

نَصاعة *n* brightness, clarity; نَصاعة اللَوْنِ the brightness of the colour; نَصاعة الرَأْيِ the clarity of the viewpoint

نَصَفَ *v* |i-u; نُصوف ,نَصْف| ① [بَلَغَ نِصْفَهُ] to reach the middle, to be halfway; نَصَفَ الكِتابَ to be halfway through a book; قد نَصَفَ النَهارُ it was midday ② [قَسَمَ] to bisect, to cut/divide in half

نَصَّفَ *v* to bisect, to cut/divide in half; نَصَّفَ شَيْئاً to bisect sth

ناصَفَ *v* to share equally; ناصَفَ شَخْصاً شَيْئاً to split sth in half with sb

أَنْصَفَ *v* to be impartial, to treat fairly, to do justice to; أَنْصَفَ شَخْصاً to do sb justice, to treat sb fairly

اِنْتَصَفَ *v* ① [بَلَغَ النِصْفَ] to reach the middle, to be halfway; اِنْتَصَفَ اللَيْلُ it was midnight ② [اِنْتَقَمَ |من|] to demand justice from, to seek compensation from; to take vengeance/revenge on; اِنْتَصَفَ من شَخْصٍ to demand compensation from sb

اِسْتَنْصَفَ *v* to demand justice, to seek compensation

نِصْف *n* |أَنْصاف| ① [شَطْر] half; ساعة وَنِصْف one hour and a half; في الساعةِ السادِسةِ والنِصْفِ at half past six; نِصْف سَنَويٍّ biannual; النِصْف الأَكْبَر the bigger half; نِصْف السِعْرِ half the price; نِصْف لِتْرٍ \ كيلومِتْرٍ half a liter/kilometer; نِصْف ساعةٍ \ سَنةٍ \ مِلْيونٍ half an hour/year/million; نِصْف قُطْرٍ (Math) radius ② [مُنْتَصَف] middle; في نِصْفِ الطَريقِ in the middle of the road; فى نِصْفِ اللَيْلِ in the middle of the night; حامِل في نِصْفِ الشَهْرِ الرابِعِ three and a half months pregnant

نِصْفيّ *adj* half (*before n*), semi-, demi-, mid-; تِمْثال نِصْفيّ bust; اِنْتِخابات التَجْديدِ النِصْفيّ midterm elections

اِنْتِصاف *n* ① [وَسَط] halfway point ② [تَعْويض] redress

إِنْصاف *n* justice; fairness; impartiality; بِعَدْلٍ وَإِنْصافٍ justly and fairly; روح العَدْلِ والإِنْصافِ a sense of justice

تَنْصيف *n* halving; bisection

مُناصَفة *n* divided into halves; مُناصَفةً ,على أَساسِ المُناصَفةِ fifty-fifty, in half

مُنْتَصَف *n* middle, centre, halfway; مُنْتَصَف اللَيْلِ midnight; في مُنْتَصَفِ الطَريقِ in the middle of the road; halfway (there), half-finished; في مُنْتَصَفِ شَهْرِ نوفَمْبِر mid-November; في مُنْتَصَفِ الثَمانيناتِ in the mid-80s; في مُنْتَصَفِ الصَيْفِ \ الشِتاءِ in the height of summer/depths of winter; في \ بعد مُنْتَصَفِ الكِتابِ to be at/past the mid-way point of the book; خَطّ المُنْتَصَفِ centre line

مُنْصِف *adj* just, fair, reasonable; objective, impartial; غَيْر مُنْصِفٍ unjust; حَلّ مُنْصِف a fair solution; مُراقِب مُنْصِف an objective observer

مُنَصِّف *n* (Geom) bisector

تَنَصَّلَ *v* ① [من |من|] to distance/dissociate from; to shirk, to shift/pass on to; تَنَصَّلَ من شَيْءٍ to distance oneself from sth; تَنَصَّلَ من مَسْؤوليّتِه to shirk one's responsibility; تَنَصَّلَ من تَعَهُّدِهِ \ اِلْتِزامِهِ to back out of one's promise/commitment ② [نَصَلَ] to run

مِنْضَحة *n* |مَناضِحُ| sprinkler, sprayer

نَضَدَ *v* |i; نَضْد| ❶ [رَكَمَ] to stack, to pile ❷ [نَسَّقَ] to arrange, to order

نَضَّدَ *v* ❶ [رَكَمَ] to stack, to pile ❷ (P&P) to typeset, to compose; نَضَّدَ كِتاباً to typeset a book

تَنَضَّدَ *v* ❶ [رُكِمَ] to be piled/stacked up ❷ [نُسِّقَ] to be arranged/ordered; تَنَضَّدَتْ أَسْنانُهُ to have perfect teeth

نَضيد *adj* arranged, orderly; أَسْنان نَضيدة perfect teeth

تَنَضُّد *n* stratification

تَنْضيد *n* ❶ [تَكْديس] stacking ❷ (P&P) typesetting, composition; تَنْضيد الحُروفِ typesetting

مُنَضِّد *n* typesetter, compositor

مِنْضَدة *n* |مَناضِدُ, مِنْضَدات| ❶ [طاوِلة] table, counter, desk; مِنْضَدة الطَعامِ dining/kitchen table; مِنْضَدة سَريرٍ bedside table (BrE), nightstand (AmE) ❷ [ظُلَّة] stall, booth, stand

نَضَرَ, نَضِرَ, نَضُرَ *v* |a-u; نَضْرة, نُضور, نَضارة| to shine, to radiate; to flourish, to bloom

نَضِر *adj* radiant, bright; flourishing, blooming; أَلْوان نَضِرة bright colours; بَشَرة نَضِرة a radiant/glowing complexion

ناضِر *adj* ❶ [ساطِع] radiant, bright; flourishing, blooming ❷ [طَرِيّ] fresh; verdant

نَضارة *n* ❶ [اِزْدِهار] vigour, bloom ❷ [طَراوة] freshness; youth, youthfulness; نَضارة البَشَرةِ youthful skin

نَضْرة *n* ❶ [اِزْدِهار] bloom; wealth ❷ [طَراوة] freshness

نَضير *adj* ❶ [ساطِع] radiant, bright; flourishing, blooming ❷ [طَرِيّ] fresh; youthful, young; وَجْه نَضير a young face

نَضَّ *v* |i; نَضّ, نَضيض| to drip, to trickle

ناضَلَ *v* to fight, to combat; to apply/devote oneself, to strive; ناضَلَ ضِدَّ ... to fight against ...; ناضَلَ من أَجْلِ \ في سَبيلِ ... to strive for ...; ناضَلَ من أَجْلِ حُقوقِهِ to fight for one's rights; ناضَلَ في سَبيلِ مُثُلِه \ حُقوقِه to fight for one's ideals/rights

نِضال *n* |نِضالات| fight, struggle, battle, combat; نِضال مُسَلَّح armed combat; نِضال من أَجْلِ الحُرِّيّةِ the struggle for freedom

نِضاليّ *adj* combat (*before n*); combative; مَسيرة ,عَمَل نِضاليّ نِضاليّة struggle, resistance

نَصْل *n coll* |نُصول, أَنْصُل, نِصال| blade; arrowhead, spearhead

ناصِية *n* |نَواصٍ| ❶ [شَعْر مُقَدِّمِ الرَأْسِ] fringe (BrE), bangs (AmE); قَصَّ الناصِيةَ to trim the fringe ❷ [مُقَدِّم الرَأْسِ] forehead; مِنْطَقة الناصِيةِ frontal lobe; امْتَلَكَ ناصِيَتَهُ to control oneself ❸ [رَأْس الشارِعِ] the end of the street; على ناصِيةِ الشارِعِ at the end of the street

نَضَبَ *v* |u; نُضوب| to dry up, to run out; to seep into the ground; نَضَبَتِ الحُقولُ the fields dried up; كانَتْ فَرْحَتُهُ قد نَضَبَتْ تَماماً his joy had completely faded; لا يَنْضُبُ inexhaustible

ناضِب *adj* |نُضَّب| dry, barren, arid

نُضوب *n* ❶ [نَفاد] depletion ❷ [جَدْب] aridity, barrenness, sterility

مُنَضَّب *adj* depleted; يورانِيوم مُنَضَّب depleted uranium

نَضِجَ *v* |a; نَضْج| ❶ [بَلَغَ] to ripen, to be/become ripe; to mature; تَنْضُجُ الفاكِهةُ في الخَريفِ the fruit ripens in the fall; نَضِجَتْ الظُروفُ ... conditions are ripe (for) ... ❷ [الطَعامُ] to be cooked/ready/done

نَضَّجَ *v* ❶ [بَلَغَ] to ripen; to mature ❷ [الطَعامُ] to cook well

أَنْضَجَ *v* ❶ [بَلَغَ] to ripen; to mature ❷ [الطَعامُ] to cook well

ناضِج *adj* ❶ [بالِغ] ripe, ripened; mature, matured; فاكِهة ناضِجة ripe fruit; امْرَأة ناضِجة a full-grown woman; غَيْر ناضِج unripe; immature; فَواكِه غَيْر ناضِجةٍ unripe fruit ❷ [الطَعامُ] well-cooked

نُضوج *n* ❶ [بُلوغ] ripeness; maturity; سِنّ النُضوجِ age of maturity ❷ [الطَعام] doneness (*state of being fully cooked*)

إِنْضاج *n* ❶ [الثَمَر] maturation; ripening ❷ [الطَعامَ] cooking, browning; إِنْضاج اللَحْمِ cooking of the meat (*until done*)

نَضَحَ *v* |a-i; نَضْح| ❶ [رَشَحَ] to leak, to spill; كُلّ إِناءٍ بما فيه يَنْضَحُ ≈ what's bred in the bone will come out in the flesh; *one's inner nature will always be revealed* ❷ [رَشَّ] to sprinkle, to spray, to water

نَضّاحة *n* sprinkler

نُضوح *n* leakage, spill; exudation

تَناضُح *n* osmosis

مُناضِل *n* fighter, combatant; resistance/freedom fighter; champion, advocate; مُناضِل من أَجْلِ \ في سَبيلِ شَيْءٍ a fighter for sth; مُناضِل من أَجْلِ حُقوقِ الإنْسانِ a fighter for human rights

مُناضَلة *n* fight, struggle, battle

‹ **نِضْوة** *n* |أَنْضاء| horseshoe

‹ **نَطَحَ** *v* |a; نَطْح| to butt, to ram; to thrust

ناطَحَ *v* to butt, to ram; to thrust; بُرْج يُناطِحُ السَحابَ a skyscraper; أَسْعار تُناطِحُ السَحابَ sky-high prices

تَناطَحَ *v* to butt (against) each other

ناطِح *adj* |نَواطِحُ| touching, abutting; thrusting; ناطِحة السَحابِ skyscraper

نَطْحة *n* headbutt, butt; thrust, push

‹ **نَطَرَ** *v* |u; نَطْر ,نِطارة| to guard, to watch

ناطور *n* |نَواطيرُ| doorkeeper, gatekeeper, guard; watchman (of farmland)

نُطّار *n* scarecrow

‹ **نَطْرون** *n* natron, sodium carbonate

‹ **تَنَطَّسَ** *v* to scrutinize, to examine thoroughly; to be fastidious; تَنَطَّسَ في اللَبْسِ to dress well; تَنَطَّسَ في الأَكْلِ to be a picky eater

نِطاسيّ **A** *adj* |نُطُس| skilled, proficient; experienced **B** *n* |نُطُس| expert, specialist, authority

‹ **نَطَّ** *v* |u; نَطّ| to jump, to leap; to bounce; to frolic

تَنَطَّطَ *v* to jump about

نَطّ *n* jumping, leaping, skipping; نَطّ الحَبْلِ rope skipping (BrE), jump roping (AmE)

نَطّاط **A** *adj* frisky, bouncy **B** *n* jumper; grasshopper; نَطّاط الطين mudskipper (*Oxudercinae*); نَطّاط الأَوْراقِ leafhopper (*Cicadellidae*)

نَطّة *n* jump, leap; bounce

‹ **تَنَطَّعَ** *v* **1** [في الكَلامِ] to affect eloquence **2** [في العَمَلِ] to feign skillfulness

نِطْع *n* |نُطوع| (Anat) hard palate

نِطْعيّ *adj* palatal; حَرْف نِطْعيّ (Ling) denti-alveolar sound

‹ **نَطَفَ** *v* |i-u; نَطْف ,تَنْطاف ,نَطَفان ,نِطافة| to drip, to trickle; يَنْطِفُ الماءُ the water is dripping

نُطْفة *n* |نُطَف| **1** [قَطْرة] drop **2** [مَنيّ] sperm, semen; النُطَف المَنَويّة sperm, semen; مُسْتَوى النُطَفِ المَنَويّةِ sperm count

‹ **نَطَقَ** *v* |u; نُطْق ,نُطوق ,مَنْطِق| to utter, to speak, to say; to pronounce, to articulate; نَطَقَ بِكَلِمةٍ to utter a word; نَطَقَ بِاسْمِ شَخْصٍ to speak on sb's behalf; نَطَقَ بِلُغةِ الضادِ to speak Arabic; نَطَقَ الكَلِماتِ باللُكْنةِ الأَمْريكيّةِ to pronounce words with an American accent

Idiom نَطَقَ بِحُكْمٍ to pass judgement, to sentence

تَمَنْطَقَ I *v* **1** [تَحَزَّمَ] to gird oneself **2** [تَعاطى المَنْطِقَ] to be/become a logician

نَطَّقَ *v* to make/let speak, to teach to speak

أَنْطَقَ *v* to make/let speak, to teach to speak

تَنَطَّقَ *v* to gird oneself, to put on a belt

اسْتَنْطَقَ *v* to question, to interrogate; to hear; اسْتَنْطَقَ مُتَّهَماً to interrogate a suspect

نُطْق *n* **1** [لَفْظ] pronunciation, articulation; النُطْق الصَحيح \ السَليم the correct pronunciation; عَجَزَ عن نُطْقِ شَيْءٍ to be unable to pronounce sth **2** [الكَلام] speech; قُدْرة على النُطْقِ power of speech; تَقْويم النُطْقِ speech therapy

Idiom النُطْق بالحُكْمِ verdict; sentencing

ناطِق **A** *adj* speaking, talking; able to speak, endowed with the faculty of speech; فيلْم ناطِق a talking film; دَليل ناطِق clear proof; ناطِق باللُغةِ الإنْكْليزيّة an English speaker; الناطِقونَ بالضادِ the Arabs **B** *n* speaker; spokesman, press officer; ناطِق بِاسْمِ مُنَظَّمةٍ a spokesman for an organization; ناطِق رَسْميّ بِاسْمِ الحُكومةِ a government spokesman; قالَ الناطِقُ بِاسْمِ النِقابةِ إنّ ... the trade union spokesman said (that) ...

نِطاق *n* |نُطُق| **1** [مَدًى] range, scope, extent, span; circle; نِطاق عائِليّ family circle; نِطاق قانونٍ \ قاعِدةٍ the scope of a law/measure; نِطاق الانْتِباهِ attention span; على النِطاقِ الإقْليميّ \ البَلَديّ at the regional/municipal level; على نِطاقٍ واسِعٍ, واسِع النِطاقِ large-scale; widespread; على نِطاقٍ ضَيِّقٍ, ضَيِّق النِطاقِ small-scale; وَسَّعَ نِطاقَ شَيْءٍ to expand the scope

مَنْطِقيّ **A** *adj* |مَناطِقة ,مَنْطِقيّونَ| logical, rational; غَيْر مَنْطِقيٍّ illogical; قرار غَيْر مَنْطِقيٍّ an illogical decision; نَتيجة مَنْطِقيّة a logical consequence; تَفْكير \ اسْتِنْتاج مَنْطِقيّ logical thinking/conclusion; قَرار مَنْطِقيّ a rational decision; بِصورةٍ مَنْطِقيّةٍ, بِشَكْلٍ مَنْطِقيٍّ logically; هذا من المَنْطِقيّ that's only logical **B** *n* |مَناطِقة ,مَنْطِقيّونَ| logician

مَنْطوق **A** *adj* spoken, uttered, pronounced, enunciated; غَيْر مَنْطوقٍ بِهِ unspoken; لُغة مَنْطوقة spoken language **B** *n* |مَنْطوقات| text, statement, formulation; مَنْطوق الاتِّفاق the text of an agreement; مَنْطوق حُكْمٍ the text of a judgement

〈 **نَطَل** *v* |u; نَطْل| to apply a warm compress

〈 **نَظَرَ** *v* |u; نَظَر ,مَنْظَر| **1** [رأى] to look, to see; to watch, to observe; نَظَرَ إلى شَخْصٍ \ شَيْءٍ to look at sb/sth; نَظَرَ إلى شَخْصٍ خُلْسةً to steal a glance at sb; نَظَرَ مَكْتوفَ اليَدَيْنِ to stand by helplessly; نَظَرَ إلى الخَلْفِ \ الوَراءِ to look backwards; نَظَرَ إلى شَيْءٍ بِاهْتِمام to watch sth attentively; نَظَرَ إلى شَخْصٍ بِفُضولٍ to observe sb curiously; أُنْظُرْ ما يَلي see below **2** [دَرَسَ] to look at, to study, to examine; to consider, to regard; نَظَرَ في قَضيّةٍ to take up a case; نَظَرَ إلى شَيْءٍ من وُجْهةِ نَظَرٍ أُخْرى to look at sth from another perspective; نَظَرَ إذا ما ... to consider whether ...

نَظَّرَ *v* **1** [قارَنَ] to draw a parallel/comparison **2** [نَظَريّةً] to theorize

ناظَرَ *v* **1** [كانَ نَظيراً لِ] to approach; to be equal to; ناظَرَ الأَلْفَ to approach a thousand; ناظَرَ شَخْصاً to be sb's equal **2** [ناقَشَ] to debate; ناظَرَ حول مَوْضوعٍ to debate about a subject

تَنَظَّرَ *v* to scrutinize

تَناظَرَ *v* **1** [تَقابَلَ] to face each other **2** [تَجادَلَ] to debate

انْتَظَرَ *v* **1** [تَرَقَّبَ] to wait for, to await; انْتَظَرَ شَيْئاً \ شَخْصاً to wait for sth/sb; انْتَظَرَ شَخْصاً في المَطارِ to wait for sb at the airport; انْتَظَرَ دَوْرَهُ to wait one's turn **2** [تَوَقَّعَ] to expect, to anticipate; انْتَظَرَ شَيْئاً من شَخْصٍ to expect sth from sb; أَنْتَظِرُ مَجيءَ أخي هذا المَساءَ I'm expecting my brother tonight; يَنْتَظِرُكَ مُسْتَقْبَلٌ جَميلٌ you've got a bright future ahead of you; تَنْتَظِرُ مَوْلوداً she's expecting a baby

of sth **2** [حِزام] belt **3** (Comput) domain; اسْم نِطاقٍ domain name; نِظام أَسْماءِ النِطاقاتِ DNS, Domain Name System; نِطاق فَرْعيّ subdomain

نُطْقيّ *adj* phonetic; pronunciation (*before n*); speech (*before n*); تَقْويم نُطْقيّ speech therapy

اسْتِنْطاق *n* |اسْتِنْطاقات| questioning, interrogation, examination, cross-examination; اسْتِنْطاق المُتَّهَمِ the interrogation of the suspect; اسْتِنْطاق الشُهودِ the examination of witnesses; خَضَعَ لِاسْتِنْطاقٍ to undergo interrogation

مَناطِقيّ *adj* territorial, areal, zonal; تَقْسيم مَناطِقيّ territorial division

مَنْطِق *n* **1** [التَفْكير السَليم] logic, reason; reasoning; مَنْطِق سَليم sound reasoning; مَنْطِق أَعْوَج twisted logic; مَنْطِق عَقْلانيّ \ العَقْلِ rational logic; حَسَبَ مَنْطِقِهِ ... according to his logic ..., by his reasoning ... **2** [أُسْلوب] mindset; language; مَنْطِق طائِفيّ a sectarian mindset; لا يَنْفَعُ مَعَهُمْ إلاّ مَنْطِقُ القوّةِ they don't understand anything but the language of force **3** (Philos) dialectic, logic; عِلْم المَنْطِقِ logic **4** [كَلام] speech

مِنْطَق *n* |مَناطِقُ| belt

مِنْطَقة *n* |مَناطِقُ| region, area, zone; territory; مِنْطَقة حُدوديّة border region; مِنْطَقة مُجاوِرة \ مُحاذِية adjacent area; مِنْطَقة جَبَليّة mountainous region; مِنْطَقة قُطْبيّة polar region; المَناطِق الحارّة hot regions; المَناطِق الاسْتِوائيّة \ المَداريّة the tropics; في المِنْطَقةِ الساحِلِيّةِ in the coastal area; مِنْطَقة خَصِبة a fertile area; مِنْطَقة صِناعيّة industrial zone; مِنْطَقة مُتَأَخِّرة \ مُتَخَلِّفة a backward area; مِنْطَقة (تِجارةٍ) حُرّة free-trade zone; مِنْطَقة مَنْكوبة disaster area; مِنْطَقة مُحَرَّمة forbidden territory; المِنْطَقة الحَرام no-man's-land; مِنْطَقة مَنْزوعة السِلاحِ demilitarized zone; مِنْطَقة الحُكْمِ الذاتيِّ autonomous dominion; مِنْطَقة نُفوذٍ sphere of influence; مِنْطَقة مَسْؤوليّة area of responsibility; مِنْطَقة مُحايِدة \ عَدائيّة \ مُحْتَلّة neutral/hostile/occupied territory; مِنْطَقة مَحْميّة safety zone; عَيَّنَ مِنْطَقةً مَحْميّةً to establish a safety zone; في \ خارِجَ مِنْطَقةٍ inside/outside a territory; دافَعَ عن مِنْطَقَتِهِ to defend one's territory; احْتَلَّ مِنْطَقةً to occupy a territory; اسْتَوْلى على مِنْطَقةٍ to seize a territory; رَسَمَ حُدودَ مِنْطَقةٍ to mark out a territory

نِظارة *n* supervision; management, administration

نَظْرة *n* |نَظَرات| **1** [المَرّة من النَظَر] look, glance; نَظْرة شَهْوانيّة \ قاتِلة a longing/withering look; نَظْرة مُخْتَلَسة a furtive glance; حُبّ من أَوَّلِ نَظْرةٍ love at first sight; أَلْقى نَظْرةً على شَيْءٍ \ شَخْصٍ to look at sth/sb; لم يُعَبِّرْهُ بِنَظْرةٍ to not deign to look at sb; نَظَرَ إلى شَيْءٍ نَظْرةً شُموليّةً to look thoroughly at sth **2** [وُجْهة نَظَرٍ] view, viewpoint, standpoint; نَظْرة عامّة \ شامِلة overview; نَظْرة شَخْصيّة a personal view; نَظْرة ضَيِّقة a narrow view; أَلْقى نَظْرةً مُخْتَلِفةً على شَيْءٍ to have a different view of sth; نَظَرَ إلى المُسْتَقْبَلِ نَظْرةً مُتَفائِلةً to take an optimistic view of the future

نَظَريّ *adj* **1** [عَكْس عَمَليٍّ] theoretical, academic; مَعْرِفة نَظَريّة theoretical knowledge; من الوُجْهةِ النَظَريّةِ theoretically; الامْتِحان النَظَريّ theory exam; قَدَّمَ تَفْسيراً نَظَريًّا لِشَيْءٍ to give a theoretical explanation for sth **2** [تَخْمينيّ] speculative

نَظَريّة *n* theory; نَظَريّة سائِدة a prevailing theory; نَظَريّة فيزيائيّة a physics theory; نَظَريّة المُؤامَرةِ a conspiracy theory; نَظَريّة التَطَوُّرِ the theory of evolution; طَوَّرَ نَظَريّةً to develop a theory; دافَعَ عن نَظَريّةٍ to defend a theory; دَعَّمَ \ أَيَّدَ نَظَريّةً to support a theory; صَحَّت النَظَريّةُ the theory was correct

نَظير *n* |نُظَراءُ; f pl نَظائِرُ| **1** [زَميل] counterpart; الْتَقى الرَئيسُ نَظيرَهُ الروسيَّ the president met with his Russian counterpart **2** [مِثْل] equal, peer, match; النَظير للنَظير peer-to-peer; عَزَّ نَظيرُهُ, لا نَظيرَ لَهُ, مُنْقَطِع النَظيرِ unequalled; شَجاعة \ جَمال لا نَظيرَ لَهُ \ لَها unparalleled courage/beauty; نَجاح لا نَظيرَ لَهُ unparalleled success **3** (Chem) isotope; نَظائِر مُشِعّة radioisotope

نَظيرَ *prep* in return/exchange for, against, for, at; نَظيرَ تَعْويضٍ for compensation; كانَ يَكْدَحُ طوال اليَوْمِ نَظير بِضْعةِ قُروشٍ he toiled all day for a few pennies

الناظور *n* see **ناظور**

انْتِظار *n* waiting; expectation, anticipation; على غَيْرِ انْتِظارٍ unexpected; غُرْفة \ قاعة \ حُجْرة الانْتِظارِ waiting room; فَتْرة الانْتِظارِ waiting time; قائِمة \ لائِحة الانْتِظارِ waiting list; كانَ ب \ في انْتِظارِ شَيْءٍ to be anticipating of sth, to be awaiting sth; أنا بِانْتِظارِكَ I'm waiting for you

نَظَر *n* |أَنْظار| **1** [بَصَر] eyesight, sight; look, view; بالنَظَرِ \ نَظَراً إلى in consideration of; مَدى النَظَرِ eyeshot; على مَدِّ النَظَرِ within sight; قَصير النَظَرِ short-sighted; مُلْفِت للنَظَرِ \ لافِت striking, remarkable; شَيْء لافِت \ مُلْفِت للنَظَرِ sth striking; بِغَضِّ النَظَرِ irrespective of; بِغَضِّ \ بِقَطْعِ \ بِصَرْفِ النَظَرِ عن الاسْتِثْناءاتِ irrespective of the exception; بِغَضِّ النَظَرِ عَمّا ذُكِرَ irrespective of what has been said; لَفَتَ النَظَرَ \ الأَنْظارَ to attract attention; لَفَتَ نَظَرَ شَخْصٍ إلى شَيْءٍ to bring sth to the attention of sb; غَضَّ النَظَرَ عن to shut one's eyes to; حَوَّلَ نَظَرَهُ to avert one's eyes; تَوَجَّهَت الأَنْظارُ إلى ... to look at ...; اخْتَلَسَ النَظَرَ to peep; حَجَبَ شَيْئاً عن الأَنْظارِ to put sth out of sight; اخْتَفى عن الأَنْظارِ to disappear out of sight; ظَلَّ بَعيداً عن الأَنْظارِ to stay out of sight; تابَعَ شَخْصاً بِنَظَرِه to follow sb with one's eyes; كانَ مَحَطَّ الأَنْظارِ to be the center of attention **2** [رَأْي] opinion, vision, view; أَهْل النَظَرِ theoreticians; وُجْهة نَظَرٍ point of view; من وُجْهةِ نَظَري, في نَظَري in my opinion; وُجْهة نَظَري في هذه القَضيّةِ my opinion on this issue; وُجْهة نَظَرٍ شَخْصيّة \ رَسْميّة a personal/official opinion; دافَعَ عن وُجْهةِ نَظَرٍ to defend a position; نَظَرَ إلى مَسْأَلةٍ من وُجْهةِ نَظَرٍ أُخْرى to look at sth from another angle **3** [دِراسة] consideration; إعادة النَظَرِ reconsideration; بعد إِمْعانِ النَظَرِ after careful consideration; دَقَّقَ النَظَرَ في المَعْلوماتِ to look closely at the data; أَعادَ النَظَرَ في مَسْأَلةٍ to reconsider sth; إنّ القَضيّةَ تحت النَظَرِ the case is under consideration

ناظِر *n* |نَواظِرُ| **1** [مُتَفَرِّج] observer, spectator **2** [مُتَوَلٍّ] manager, head; supervisor, foreman; ناظِر المَدْرَسةِ headmaster, (school) principal

ناظور *n* endoscope; field glasses; binoculars

نَظّاراتي *n* optician

نَظّارة *n* glasses, spectacles (BrE), eyeglasses (AmE); نَظّارة \ نَظّارات glasses, spectacles (BrE), eyeglasses (AmE); نَظّارات شَمْسيّة sunglasses; نَظّارات طِبّيّة prescription glasses; نَظّارات واقِية safety glasses; نَظّارة مُكَبِّرة binoculars; إطار نَظّارةٍ frames; لَبِسَ \ ارْتَدى نَظّاراتٍ to wear glasses; وَضَعَ \ لَبِسَ نَظّارَتَهُ to put on one's glasses; نَزَعَ نَظّارَتَهُ to take off one's glasses

نَظُفَ *v* |u; نَظافة| to be/become clean

نَظَّفَ *v* to clean; to wash; نَظَّفَ أَسْنانَهُ to brush one's teeth; نَظَّفَ أُذُنَيْهِ \ أَظافِرَهُ to clean one's ears/nails; نَظَّفَ النَوافِذَ \ الأَرْضِيَّةَ \ الطاوِلَةَ to clean the windows/floor/table; نَظَّفَ البَيْتَ \ مَبْنًى to clean the house/a building

تَنَظَّفَ *v* to become clean

نَظافة *n* cleanliness, neatness; hygiene; عامِل النَظافةِ cleaner; حافَظَ على النَظافةُ من الإيمانِ cleanliness is next to godliness; نَظافةِ شُبّاكِهِ (Sport) to not allow any goals to be scored

نَظيف *adj* |نِظاف, نُظَفاءُ| ❶ [غَيْر وَسِخٍ] clean, tidy; fresh; hygienic; مَلابِس نَظيفة clean clothes; ماء \ هَواء نَظيف clean water/air; طاقة نَظيفة clean energy ❷ [بَريء] innocent; نَظيف اليَدَيْنِ innocent ❸ (Sport) *describing a win in which no points or victories were scored by the other team*; فاز بِهَدَفَيْنِ نَظيفَيْنِ to win 2-0; بِثَلاثةِ أَشْواطٍ نَظيفةٍ to sweep three games

تَنْظيف *n* |تَنْظيفات| cleaning, clean-up; سائِل \ مادّة تَنْظيفٍ cleaning product; تَنْظيف جافّ \ كيميائيّ dry cleaning; تَنْظيف الشَوارِعِ street cleaning

مُنَظِّف *n* ❶ [شَخْص] cleaner ❷ [مادّة] |مُنَظِّفات| cleaning product

نَظَمَ *v* |i; نَظْم, نِظام| to string, to thread; to compose; نَظَمَ اللُؤْلُؤَ to string pearls; نَظَمَ قَصيدةً to write a poem

نَظَّمَ *v* ❶ [رَتَّبَ] to organize, to arrange, to put in order; نَظَّمَ كُتُبَهُ to arrange one's books; نَظَّمَ بَيْتَهُ to tidy up one's house ❷ [أَعَدَّ] to organize, to arrange; نَظَّمَ حَفْلةً \ إِضْراباً \ اِجْتِماعاً to organize a party/strike/gathering; نَظَّمَ لِقاءً to arrange a meeting; نَظَّمَ دَوْرةً دِراسيّةً to organize a course ❸ [ضَبَطَ] to organize, to manage; to regulate; نَظَّمَ حَياتَهُ to organize one's life; نَظَّمَ أُمورَهُ to manage one's affairs; نَظَّمَ الإِدارةَ to organize the administrative department; نَظَّمَ التِجارةَ to regulate trade; نَظَّمَ حَرَكةَ المُرورِ to regulate traffic

تَنَظَّمَ *v* to be organized; to be regulated

تَناظَمَ *v* to be well arranged/organized

اِنْتَظَمَ *v* to be/become organized; to be/become regulated; to be/become sorted/divided/classified; تَنْتَظِمُ العَلاقاتُ relations

تَناظُر *n* symmetry; تَناظُر فائِق supersymmetry

تَنْظير *n* ❶ [تَفْكير] theorization ❷ (Med) scope; تَنْظير داخِليّ endoscopy

تَنْظيريّ *adj* theorizing, theoretical; كِتابات تَنْظيريّة theoretical writings

مُتَناظِر *adj* corresponding, analogous; غَيْر مُتَناظِرٍ asymmetric

مُناظِر *n* ❶ [نَظير] counterpart ❷ [مُناقِش] debater

مُناظَرة *n* discussion, debate, dispute; controversy, argument, quarrel; مُناظَرة رِئاسيّة a presidential debate; مُناظَرة قانونيّة a legal battle; دَعا شَخْصاً إلى مُناظَرةٍ تِلِفِزْيونِيّةٍ to invite sb to a televised debate; جَرَت المُناظَرةُ a discussion was held

مُنْتَظَر *adj* expected, anticipated, foreseen; غَيْر مُنْتَظَرٍ unexpected; إِمْكانيّات غَيْر مُنْتَظَرةٍ unanticipated possibilities; من المُنْتَظَرِ أنْ ... it's to be expected that ...

مِنْظار *n* |مَناظيرُ| ❶ [آلة يُنْظَرُ بِها] telescope, binoculars; microscope, magnifying glass; مِنْظار طِبّيّ speculum; endoscope; مِنْظار فَلَكيّ telescope; جِراحة المَناظيرِ endoscopic surgery; نَظَرَ إلى شَيْءٍ بالمِنْظارِ to look at sth with a telescope ❷ [سِلاح] sight

مَنْظَر *n* |مَناظِرُ| ❶ [مَشْهَد] view, sight; scenery; مَنْظَر عامّ panorama; مَناظِر طَبيعيّة scenery; مَنْظَر جَميل a wonderful view; مَنْظَر رائِع \ هائِل a magnificent/impressive sight ❷ [هَيْئة] appearance, sight; غَيَّرَ مَنْظَرَ الغُرْفةِ to change the appearance of the room ❸ [المَسْرَح إلْخ] scene; مَناظِر من فيلْمٍ scenes from a film

مُنَظِّر *n* theoretician

مَنْظور **A** *adj* ❶ [مَرْئيّ] foreseeable; visible; غَيْر مَنْظورٍ invisible; في مَكانٍ مَنْظورٍ in a visible place; في المُسْتَقْبَلِ \ المَدى \ الأَجَلِ المَنْظورِ in the foreseeable future; المَنْظور البَعيدِ الأَمَدِ in the distant future ❷ [مُصاب بالعَيْنِ] afflicted by the evil eye

B *n* ❶ [وُجْهة نَظَرٍ] view, viewpoint, point of view; perspective, angle; من مَنْظورٍ from an angle; من هذا المَنْظورِ from this perspective; في مَنْظورِ الكاتِبِ from the writer's point of view; من المَنْظورِ التاريخيِّ from a historical point of view ❷ (Art) perspective have been normalized; انْتَظَمَ في مَجْموعاتٍ صَغيرةٍ to be divided into small groups

نَظْم *n* poetry; composition of a poem

ناظِم **A** *adj* organizing; regulating; الهَيْئة الناظِمة للاتِّصالاتِ telecoms regulator

B *n* 1 [شاعِر] poet 2 [مُنَظِّم] organizer

نِظام *n* |نِظامات, نُظُم, أَنْظِمة| 1 [مَبادِئ مُرْتَبِطة] system, order; نِظام شَمْسيّ solar system; النِظام المِتْريّ \ العُشْريّ the metric/decimal system; نِظام ضَريبيّ \ الضَرائِبِ tax system; نِظام قَضائيّ legal system; نِظام اقْتِصاديّ \ سِياسيّ economic/political system; النِظام البَرْلَمانيّ parliamentary system; نِظام الحِزْبِ الواحِدِ one-party system; نِظام تَشْغيلٍ operating system 2 [قَواعِد] rules, regulation; system, order; نِظام أَساسيّ statutes; نِظام التَحَكُّم \ المُراقَبةِ \ المُراجَعةِ control system; النِظام الداخِليّ internal rules 3 [رِجيم] diet; نِظام غِذائيّ diet; اتَّبَعَ نِظاماً غِذائيًّا to be on a diet 4 [حُكْم] government, regime, order; النِظام الحاكِم the established order; نِظام عالَميّ world order; تَغْيير النِظام regime change; أَسْقَطَ النِظامَ to topple the regime 5 [انْضِباط] order, discipline; النِظام والانْضِباط order and discipline; النِظام العامّ public order; مُحافَظة على النِظامِ العامِّ law enforcement; أَخَلَّ بالنِظامِ العامِّ to disturb public order

نِظاميّ *adj* systematic, organized, orderly; regular; أُسْلوب \ تَرْكيبة نِظاميّ(ة) a systematic approach; القُوّات النِظاميّة the uniformed services

انْتِظام *n* order, regularity, uniformity; انْتِظام عامّ \ اجْتِماعيّ public/social order; عَدَم انْتِظامٍ irregularity; بانْتِظامٍ regularly; حَصَلَ \ حَدَثَ بانْتِظامٍ to occur regularly

تَنْظيم *n* |تَنْظيمات| 1 [تَرْتيب] organization, arrangement; control, planning, structuring; تَنْظيم الأُسْرةِ family planning; تَنْظيم العَمَلِ organization of the work; إعادة التَنْظيمِ reorganization; إعادة تَنْظيمِ الإدارةِ management reorganization; أَعادَ التَنْظيمَ to reorganize; أَعادَ تَنْظيمَ قِسْمٍ to reorganize a department; قامَ بالتَنْظيمِ to organize; تَوَلّى التَنْظيمَ to be in charge of the organization 2 [مَجْموع] organization; تَنْظيم إرْهابيّ terrorist organization; تَنْظيم القاعِدةِ al-Qaeda

تَنْظيميّ *adj* organizational, organization (*before n*); regulatory; هَيْكَل تَنْظيميّ organizational chart; قَوانين تَنْظيميّة regulatory laws

لانِظام *n* chaos; حالة اللانِظامِ a chaotic situation

مُنْتَظِم *adj* orderly, systematic; regular; بِصورةٍ \ بِصِفةٍ مُنْتَظِمةٍ, بِشَكْلٍ مُنْتَظِمٍ regularly; غَيْر مُنْتَظِمٍ irregular; دَخْل مُنْتَظِم a regular income; رِحْلات مُنْتَظِمة regular/scheduled flights; في مَواعيدَ \ أَوْقاتٍ غَيْرِ مُنْتَظِمةٍ at irregular intervals

مُنَظَّم *adj* organized, arranged; orderly; regular; غَيْر مُنَظَّمٍ unorganized; irregular; عَمَل مُنَظَّم orderly work; الإجْرام \ الجَريمة المُنَظَّم(ة) organized crime; مُعارَضة مُنَظَّمة organized opposition

مُنَظِّم *n* 1 [آلة] |مُنَظِّمات| regulator, control; مُنَظِّم الحَرارةِ thermostat 2 [شَخْص] |مُنَظِّمونَ| organizer, coordinator; مُنَظِّمو التَظاهُرةِ protest organizers

مُنَظَّمة *n* organization, institution; في \ داخِلَ المُنَظَّمةِ within the organization; مُنَظَّمة غَيْر حُكوميّة non-governmental organization, NGO; المُنَظَّمة الدَوْليّة لِتَوْحيد المَقاييس the International Organization for Standardization, the ISO; المُنَظَّمة الإسْلاميّة للتَرْبِيةِ والعُلوم والثَقافةِ (إيسيسْكو) Islamic Educational, Scientific and Cultural Organization (ISESCO); المُنَظَّمة العَرَبيّة للتَرْبِيةِ والثَقافةِ والعُلومِ (أَلِكْسو) Arab League Educational, Cultural and Scientific Organization (ALECSO); مُنَظَّمة الصِحّةِ العالَميّة the World Health Organization, the WHO; مُنَظَّمة الأَغْذِيةِ والزِراعةِ (التابِعة للأُمَمِ المُتَّحِدةِ) the (UN) Food and Agriculture Organization, the FAO; مُنَظَّمة الوَحْدةِ الإفْريقيّةِ the Organization of African Unity, the OAU; مُنَظَّمة الأُمَمِ المُتَّحِدةِ للتَرْبِيةِ والعِلْمِ والثَقافةِ the United Nations Educational, Scientific, and Cultural Organization, the UNESCO; مُنَظَّمة الأُمَمِ المُتَّحِدةِ للطُفولةِ (اليونيسِف) United Nations Children's Fund (UNICEF)

مَنْظوم **A** *adj* orderly, organized, systematic; metrical, rhythmical (*poetry*)

B *n* poetry

مَنْظومة *n* 1 [تَنْظيم] system; مَنْظومة دِفاعيّة defence system; مَنْظومة مُتَكامِلة an integrated system 2 [قَصيدة] poem

‹ **نَعَبَ** *v* |a-i; نَعْب ,نَعيب| to caw, to croak; يَنْعَبُ الغُرابُ the crow is cawing

نُعاب *n* cawing, croaking

‹ **نَعَتَ** *v* |a; نَعْت| to describe, to designate, to characterize; to brand, to label, to call; نَعَتَ شَخْصاً بالكِذْبِ \ بالغِشِّ to call sb a liar/imposter

نَعْت *n* |نُعوت| 1 [صِفَة] description, characterization; quality, characteristic, feature 2 (Gram) adjective

نَعْتيّ *adj* adjectival; descriptive

مَنْعوت A *adj* described, characterized, branded B *n* (Gram) *a noun described by an adjective*

‹ **نَعْجة** *n* |نَعَجات ,نِعاج| (Zool) ewe, female sheep

‹ **نَعَرَ** *v* |a-i; نَعير ,نُعار| 1 [الدابّةُ] to grunt, to snort 2 [العِرْقُ] to spurt, to squirt; نَعَرَ العِرْقُ بالدَمِ blood spurted from the vein

ناعور *n* |نَواعيرُ| hemophilia

ناعورة *n* |نَواعيرُ| waterwheel, noria

نُعَرة *n* |نُعَرات ,نُعَر| 1 (Zool) horsefly, gadfly 2 [عَصَبيّة] arrogance, feeling of superiority; نُعَرة وَطَنيّة chauvinism, nationalism

نَعير *n* noise, clamour; grunting, snorting

‹ **نَعَسَ** *v* |a-u; نُعْس| to be/feel sleepy, to be half asleep; to doze off

أَنْعَسَ *v* to make sleepy

ناعِس *adj* |نُعْس| sleepy, drowsy, half asleep

نُعاس *n* sleepiness, drowsiness; غَلَبَهُ النُعاسُ to be overcome by sleepiness; أَحَسَّ \ شَعَرَ بالنُعاسِ to be sleepy

نَعْسان *adj* |dipt; نِعاس; f نَعْسى| sleepy, drowsy; كانَ نَعْسانَ to be sleepy

‹ **أَنْعَشَ** *v* 1 [أَحْيا] to refresh; to activate, to stimulate; to revive, to animate; أَنْعَشَ ذاكِرةَ شَخْصٍ to refresh sb's memory; أَنْعَشَ الآمالَ to restore hope; أَنْعَشَ الاقْتِصادَ \ الصِناعةَ to revive the economy/an industry 2 (Med) to resuscitate, to reanimate; أَنْعَشَ شَخْصاً to resuscitate sb

انْتَعَشَ *v* to be invigorated/refreshed; to revive; to recover, to recuperate; انْتَعَشَت التِجارةُ trade has been revived

نَعْش *n* |نُعوش| 1 [للمَوْتى] coffin, casket; bier; حَمَلَ نَعْشاً to carry a casket 2 (Astrol) بَنات نَعْشٍ الكُبْرى \ الصُغْرى Ursa Major/Minor

انْتِعاش *n* |انْتِعاشات| revival, recovery; انْتِعاش اقْتِصاديّ economic recovery

إنْعاش *n* 1 [إحْياء] resuscitation, reanimation; revival, recovery; غُرْفة الإنْعاشِ recovery room; خُطّة الإنْعاشِ الاقْتِصاديّ economic recovery plan 2 [جَعْل شَيْئاً مُنْعِشاً] refreshment

مُنْتَعِش *adj* refreshed

مُنْعِش A *adj* fresh, refreshing; ماء مُنْعِش fresh water; شَراب \ مَشْروب مُنْعِش a refreshing beverage B *n* مُنْعِش عَقاريّ property developer

مَنْعوش *adj* carried in a coffin

‹ **نَعَظَ** *v* |a; نُعوظ| to have/get an erection

ناعوظ *n* aphrodisiac

نُعوظ *n* erection

‹ **نَعَقَ** *v* |a-i; نَعْق ,نَعيق| to croak, to caw; to hoot; يَنْعَقُ البومُ owls hoot; يَنْعَقُ الغُرابُ crows caw

‹ **نَعَّلَ** *v* 1 [الحِذاءَ] to sole, to resole 2 [الحِصانَ] to shoe; نَعَّلَ حِصاناً to shoe a horse

انْتَعَلَ *v* 1 [الحِذاءَ] to put on; to wear (*shoes*); انْتَعَلَت الكَعْبَ العالي to wear high-heels 2 [الحِصانُ] to be shod

نَعْل *n* |mf; نِعال ,أَنْعُل| 1 [حِذاء] shoe, sandal; اخْلَعْ نَعْلَيْكَ take off your shoes 2 [سُفْل الحِذاءِ] sole; نَعْل حِذائِهِ the sole of one's shoe 3 [الحِصانِ] shoe, horseshoe

‹ **نَعُمَ** *v* |u; نُعومة| to be/become soft; يَنْعُمُ عَيْشُهُ to lead a comfortable life

نَعِمَ *v* |a; نَعْمة ,مَنْعَم| 1 [سُرَّ |ب|] to enjoy; نَعِمَ بِشَيْءٍ to enjoy sth 2 [كانَ مَيْسوراً] to be prosperous; نَعِمَ عَيْشُهُ to lead a prosperous life 3 [هَدَأَ] to be calm; نَعِمَ بالُهُ to be at ease

نَعَّمَ *v* to soften, to smooth; نَعَّمَ الجِلْدَ to soften the skin

أَنْعَمَ *v* 1 [أَحْسَنَ] to give, to grant, to bestow; أَنْعَمَ على شَخْصٍ بِشَيْءٍ to give sb sth; أَنْعَمَ على شَخْصٍ بِحُبِّهِ to give sb one's love; أَنْعَمَ النَظَرَ (جَيِّداً) في شَيْءٍ to take a (good) look at sth; أَنْعَمَ اللهُ صَباحَكَ good morning; أَنْعَمَ اللهُ عَلَيْهِ بِصِحّةٍ

جيِّدةِ God gave him good health **2** [جَعَلَ مُرِيحاً] to make comfortable **3** [في الأَمْرِ |في|] to apply/devote oneself to

تَنَعَّمَ *v* |ب| to enjoy, to bask in; تَنَعَّمَ خَيْراتِ شَيْءٍ to enjoy the riches/abundance of sth; تَنَعَّمَ بِأَشِعَّةِ الشَّمْسِ to bask in the sun

نَعَم *n* |أَنْعام| cattle, livestock; سورة الأَنْعام The Cattle (*Sura 6*)

نَعَمْ *excl* **1** [عَكْس لا] yes, indeed; نَعَمْ، أنا مُتَفائِلٌ yes, I'm an optimist; هل جاءَ أَحْمَدُ؟ نَعَمْ لَقَدْ جاءَ did Ahmad come? Yes, he came **2** [ماذا قُلْتَ] what?, what did you say?

نِعْمَ *excl* good!, excellent!, outstanding; نِعْمَ الحالُ fine, good (*as an answer to* كيف حالُكَ); نِعْمَ المَوْلى God is great; نِعْمَ الرَجُلُ نَبيل! Nabeel is an outstanding man!; نِعْمَ ما فَعَلْتَ well done!

ناعِم *adj* |نَواعِمُ| **1** [عَكْس خَشِن] soft, smooth; fine; رَمْل \ تُراب ناعِم fine sand/soil; الجِنْس الناعِم the softer sex; ناعِم كالحَرِير as soft as silk **2** [حَبّات] powdered, powdery; سُكَّر ناعِم powdered sugar, confectioner's sugar

ناعِمة *n* |نَواعِمُ| (Bot) sage (*Salvia*)

نَعام *n coll* |نَعائِمُ| (Zool) ostrich; وَضَعَ \ دَفَنَ رَأْسَهُ كالنَعامةِ في الرَمْلِ to buy one's head in the sand (like an ostrich)

نُعْمان *n* **1** [دَم] blood **2** [اِسْم شَخْصيّ] No'man (*male given name*)

Idioms شَقائِقُ النُعْمانِ (poppy) anemone (*Anemone coronaria*); sea anemone (*Actiniaria*); سَمَكة شَقائِقِ النُعْمانِ clownfish, Anemonefish (*Amphiprioninae*)

نَعْمة *n* |نَعَمات| comfort, luxury

نِعْمة *n* |نِعَم, أَنْعُم, نِعْمات, إِنْعِمات| gift, donation; benefaction; blessing, grace; نِعْمة البَصَرِ the gift of sight; نِعَمُ اللهِ God's grace; بِنِعْمةِ اللهِ by the grace of God; حَديث النِعْمة upstart; nouveau-riche; هو وَلِيُّ نِعْمَتي he's my benefactor; تَحَوَّلَت النِعْمةُ إلى نَقْمةٍ the blessing turned into a curse

نُعومة *n* smoothness; delicacy

Idiom نُعومة أَظْفارِهِ childhood

نَعيم *n* bliss

نَعيمة *n* |dipt| Naima (*female given name*)

إِنْعام *n* |dipt| **1** [عَطِيّة] gift, donation; benefaction **2** [النَظَرِ] إِنْعام النَظَرِ careful study **3** [اِسْم شَخْصيّ] |f dipt| In'am (*female given name*)

مُنَعَّم *adj* **1** [لَيِّن] soft; كَلام مُنَعَّم soft words **2** [مَيْسور] well-to-do, prosperous

مُنَعِّم *adj* soothing, smoothing

نَعْناع *n* mint; peppermint; نَعْناع فِلْفِليّ peppermint; شاي بِنَعْناع mint tea

نَعى *v* |a; نَعْي, نَعِيّ, نَعْيان| **1** [الفَقِيدَ] to announce the death of; نَعى شَخْصاً to announce sb's death **2** [وَبَّخَ] to rebuke, to reprimand; نَعى على شَخْصٍ شَيْئاً to rebuke sb for sth

نَعْي *n* obituary, death announcement; بِطاقة نَعْيٍ mourning card

نَعْية *n* obituary, death announcement

مَنْعًى, مَنْعاة *n* |مَناعٍ| obituary, death announcement

نُغْبة *n* gulp, drink, draught (BrE), draft (AmE)

نُغَر *n* |نِغْران| canary; finch; النُغَرِيّات *Serinus*

نَغَز *v* |a; نَغْز| **1** [دَغْدَغَ] to tickle **2** [حَرَّكَ بَيْنَهُمْ] to cause discord

نَغَشَ *v* |a; نَغْش, نَغَشان| to be agitated

ناغَشَ *v* to tease; to flirt with

نُغاش *n* little person; dwarf

نُغاشيّ *n* little person; dwarf

نَغَصَ *v* |a; نَغْص| to spoil, to ruin

نَغَّصَ *v* to spoil, to ruin; نَغَّصَ الجَوَّ to spoil the atmosphere; نَغَّصَ حَياةَ شَخْصٍ, نَغَّصَ على شَخْصٍ حَياتَهُ to ruin sb's life

أَنْغَصَ *v* to spoil, to make loathsome; أَنْغَصَ على شَخْصٍ عَيْشَهُ to spoil sb's life

تَنَغَّصَ *v* to be spoiled/ruined

مُنَغِّص **A** *n* vexation **B** *adj* vexing

مُنَغِّصات *n pl* annoyances

نَغّاض *n* cumulus

نَغَفة *n* pupa

نَغَلَ *v* |u; نُغولة| to be illegitimate, to be a bastard

نَغِلَ *v* |a; نَغَل| to fester; كانَ النَدَمُ يَنْغَلُ في شَرايِيني regret festered in my veins

نَغْل, نَغِل *n* |نُغول| **1** [مُوَلَّد] hybrid **2** [وَلَد زِنًى] illegitimate child, bastard

نَفّاج *n* boaster, braggart

نَفَحَ *v* |a; نَفْح, نَفَحان, نُفاح| 1 [أعْطى] to give, to grant, to donate; نَفَحَهُ مالاً to give him money 2 [هَبَّ] to blow (*wind*) 3 [انْتَشَرَ] to spread (*a scent*); to be fragrant

نافَحَ *v* |عن| to defend (against), to protect (from)

نَفْحة *n* |نَفَحات| 1 [هِبة] gift, donation 2 [ريح] a gust of wind; نَفْحة الريح a gust of wind 3 [رائِحة] fragrance, scent, perfume 4 [قِطْعة] portion, piece

مِنْفَحة *n* (Zool) abomasum (*fourth stomach of ruminant*)

نَفَخَ *v* |a; نَفْخ| 1 [بالفَم] to blow, to blow/breathe into; نَفَخَ في النايِ to play the flute; نَفَخَ دُخانَ سيجارَتِهِ to blow cigarette smoke; نَفَخَ النارَ to fan the fire; نَفَخَ فيهِ من روحِهِ He breathed His spirit into him (*Koran*) 2 [مَلأ بالهَواءِ] to inflate, to pump/blow up; نَفَخَ إطارَ درّاجةٍ \ كُرةً \ بالوناً to inflate a tyre/ball/balloon; نَفَخَ شِدْقَيْهِ to be conceited

نَفَّخَ *v* to puff, to huff

انْتَفَخَ *v* 1 [تورَّمَ] to be blown up/inflated; to bulge, to expand; to be/become distended 2 [تكَبَّرَ] to be/become conceited

نَفْخ *n* blowing; آلة نَفْخٍ wind instrument

نُفاخ *n* (Med) swelling; نُفاخ رِئَويّ emphysema

نُفّاخة *n* 1 [فُقّاعة] bubble 2 [لُعْبة] balloon

نَفْخة *n* breath of air; wind, breeze

انْتِفاخ *n* |انْتِفاخات| swelling, protuberance; inflation; انْتِفاخ البَطْنِ abdominal swelling

تَنَفُّخ *n* 1 [انْتِفاخ] inflation 2 [تَصَرُّف مُتَكَبِّر] conceited behaviour

مُنْتَفِخ *adj* inflated, pumped up; swollen, bloated, puffy; وَجْه مُنْتَفِخ a puffy face

مِنْفاخ, مِنْفَخ *n* |مَنافِخُ| pump, air pump; blowpipe, bellows

مَنْفوخ *adj* 1 [مُنْتَفِخ] inflated, pumped up; swollen, bloated 2 [سَمين] plump, fat, obese

نَفِدَ *v* |a; نَفَد, نَفاد| to be/become out of stock, to be sold out, to sell out; to be/become used up, to be/become depleted; نَفِدَ صَبْري my patience is exhausted; نَفِدَ المالُ the money has run out; نَفِدَت البِضاعةُ the item has sold out; نَفِدَ الطَعامُ

نَغيل *n* illegitimate child, bastard

نَغَمَ, نَغِمَ *v* |a-i-u; نَغْم, نَغَم| to hum; to sing softly

نَغَّمَ *v* to hum; to sing softly

تناغَمَ *v* to harmonize, to be/sound harmonious; to be in agreement

نَغَم, نَغْم *n* |أنْغام| melody, tune; على أَنْغامِ النَشيدِ الوَطَنيِّ to the tune of the national anthem

نَغْمة *n* |نَغَمات| 1 [صَوْت جَميل] sound, tone; نَغْمة آلةٍ موسيقيّةٍ the sound of a musical instrument 2 [مِزاج] tone, air, spirit; نَغْمة التَفاؤُلِ a tone of optimism; عزفَ نَغْمةً جديدةً to sing a different tune; اسْتَعادَ نَغْمةَ الفَوْزِ بعد خَسارةٍ to get back on the victory train (after a loss) 3 [الهاتِف] ringtone

تَنْغيم *n* intonation

مُتَناغِم *adj* harmonious; in agreement

مُنَغَّم *adj* melodious, tuneful

نَغى *v* |i; نَغْي| to speak indistinctly

ناغى *v* to talk tenderly/gently to; to court, to woo, to speak words of love to; ناغى طِفْلاً to talk gently to a child; ناغى إمْرَأةً to woo a woman

نَفَثَ *v* |i-u; نَفْث| to spit, to spit out, to spew; to expectorate, to cough up; to exhale; يَنْفُثُ البُرْكانُ اللابة the volcano is belching out lava; نَفَثَ الدَمَ to cough up blood; نَفَثَ دُخاناً to exhale smoke

نَفْث *n* 1 [بَصْق] spit, salvia 2 [انْبِعاث] emission, ejection; spitting, belching, spewing; نَفْث الغازاتِ gas emissions; نَفْث الحِبْرِ inkjet (*printer*)

نَفّاث *adj* طائِرة نَفّاثة jet, jet aircraft; طائِرة نَفّاثة ضَخْمة jumbo jet; مُحَرِّك نَفّاث jet engine; حَبْر نَفّاث inkjet (*printer*)

نَفّاثة *n* jet, jet aircraft; وَقود النَفّاثاتِ jet fuel

نَفّاثيّ *adj* jet (*before n*); تَسْيير نَفّاثيّ jet propulsion

نَفْثة *n* |نَفَثات| spit, saliva; expectorate

نَفَجَ *v* |u; نَفْج, نَفَجان, نُفوج| 1 [ارْتَفَعَ] to rise; يَنْفُجُ العَجينُ the dough is rising 2 [فَخَرَ] |ب| to boast, to brag; نَفَجَ بِشَيْءٍ to boast about sth

اسْتَنْفَجَ *v* to take out, to produce

the food is finished; لا يَنْفَدُ inexhaustible; مَؤونة لا تَنْفَدُ an inexhaustible supply

أَنْفَدَ *v* to be/become exhausted, to come to an end

اسْتَنْفَدَ *v* to use up, to finish, to deplete, to exhaust; اسْتَنْفَدَ ذَخائِرَهُ to use up one's ammunition; اسْتَنْفَدَ مَخْزوناً to finish a supply; اسْتَنْفَدَ المَوارِدَ الطَبيعيّةَ to exhaust the natural resources

نافِد *adj* sold out; used up, finished, depleted, exhausted; هو نافِدُ الصَبْرِ his patience is exhausted

نَفاد *n* depletion, exhaustion

نَفَذَ *v* |u; نُفوذ, نَفاذ| 1 [خَرَقَ] to penetrate, to enter; to pierce; نَفَذَ السَهْمُ في صَدْرِهِ the arrow pierced his chest 2 [تَمَّ التَنْفيذُ] to be executed/implemented, to be in effect; نَفَذَ الحُكْمُ the decree was implemented 3 [مَهَرَ] to be skilled/proficient

نَفَّذَ *v* to implement, to execute, to carry out; to realize, to accomplish, to complete; نَفَّذَ حُكْماً to carry out a sentence; نَفَّذَ إضْراباً \ اعْتِصاماً to carry out a strike/sit-in; نَفَّذَ أوامِرَ to carry out orders; نَفَّذَ مُخَطَّطاتٍ \ إجْراءاتٍ to implement plans/measures

أَنْفَذَ *v* 1 [أَجْرى] to implement, to carry out; to realize, to accomplish 2 [أَدْخَلَ] to cause to penetrate

تَنَفَّذَ *v* to be carried out/implemented

نافِذ *adj* |نَوافِذُ| 1 [مُخْتَرِق] penetrating, piercing; رائِحة نافِذة a penetrating odour 2 [المَفعولِ] applicable, current, operative; valid, in effect; قانون نافِذ (المَفعولِ) a current law; التَشْريعات النافِذة the legislation in force; كانَ نافِذاً to be in effect

نافِذة *n* |نَوافِذُ| 1 [شُبّاك] window; casement; زُجاج النافِذةِ windowpane; نافِذة على العالَمِ a window on the world; فَتَحَ \ أَغْلَقَ النافِذةَ to open/close the window; فَتَحَ النافِذةَ على مِصْراعَيْها to open the window wide; أَلْقى بِشَيْءٍ من النافِذةِ to throw sth out the window; نَظَرَ من النافِذةِ to look out the window; تُطِلُّ النافِذةُ على الشارِعِ the window overlooks the street 2 (Comput) window

نَفاذ *n* 1 [انْتِهاء] depletion, exhaustion, consumption; نَفاذ الصَبْرِ impatience; نَفاذ الوَقودِ fuel shortage 2 [سَرَيان] validity, legitimacy; effectiveness; نَفاذ القانونِ legal force 3 [اخْتِراق] penetration; penetrating

نَفّاذ *adj* penetrating, piercing; رائِحة نَفّاذة a penetrating odour; بَصيرة نَفّاذة insight

نَفاذيّة *n* permeability, penetrability

نُفوذ *n* influence, impact; authority, power; ذو نُفوذٍ influential; سِياسيّ ذو نُفوذٍ an influential politician; دائِرة نُفوذٍ sphere of influence; jurisdiction; اسْتَغَلَّ نُفوذَهُ to abuse one's position; اسْتَخْدَمَ نُفوذَهُ to wield one's influence; كانَ قَويَّ \ عَديمَ النُفوذِ to have great/no influence; تَمَتَّعَ بِنُفوذٍ واسِعٍ to be widely influential

نُفوذيّة *n* permeability, penetrability

إنْفاذ *n* implementation, realization, execution; accomplishment

تَنْفيذ *n* 1 [تَطْبيق] implementation, realization; accomplishment; قابِل للتَنْفيذِ feasible; قابِليّة التَنْفيذِ feasibility; حَيِّزَ التَنْفيذِ in effect, in force; دَخَلَت الاتِّفاقيّةُ حَيِّزَ التَنْفيذ في أَيّار الماضي the agreement went into effect last May; مَرْحَلة التَنْفيذِ implementation phase; تَنْفيذ مَشْروعٍ the realization of a project; تَنْفيذ وَعْدٍ the fulfilment of a promise 2 (Law) execution, enforcement; تَنْفيذ حُكْمٍ \ عُقوبةٍ carrying out of a sentence/punishment; وَقْف \ إيقاف التَنْفيذِ suspension; عُقوبة سِجْنٍ مع إيقاف \ وَقْفِ التَنْفيذ a suspended jail sentence; عُقوبة سَجْنٍ مع التَنْفيذ an unconditional jail sentence; وَضَعَ مَوْضِعَ التَنْفيذ to put into effect, to implement

تَنْفيذيّ *adj* executive; سُلْطة تَنْفيذيّة executive authority; هَيْئة \ جِهة تَنْفيذيّة an executive agency/authority; وَظيفة \ مُهِمّة تَنْفيذيّة an executive function/task

مُتَنَفِّذ *adj* influential

مَنْفَذ *n* |مَنافِذُ| 1 [مَخْرَج] exit; passage, opening, gateway; مَنْفَذ بَحْريّ sea gate; مَنْفَذ المِياهِ floodgate; لا مَنْفَذَ لَهُ من المُشْكِلةِ there's no solution for his problem 2 (Comput) port; مَنْفَذ اليو إس بي USB port

مُنْفِذ *adj* permeable, porous; غَيْر مُنْفِذٍ للماءِ waterproof

مُنَفِّذ *n* perpetrator, responsible party; executor; هُويّة مُنَفِّذِ الهُجومِ the identity of the attacker

تَنافُرِيّ *adj* repellent, revolting; repulsive, repulsion; قوّة تَنافُرِيّة repulsive force

مُتَنافِر *adj* clashing, incompatible, conflicting; قُطْبانِ مُتَنافِرانِ two opposite poles; الأَلْوانُ مُتَنافِرةٌ the colours clash

مُنَفِّر *adj* disgusting, repulsive; رائِحة \ صورة مُنَفِّرة a repulsive smell/image

‹ **نَفُس** *v* |u; نَفاسة| to be valuable/precious; نَفُسَت الأَحْجارُ الكَرِيمةُ the jewels were valuable

نَفِس، نُفِسَتْ *v* |a; إِنْفاس| to give birth; to be post-partum

نَفَّسَ *v* ⓵ [عن| [صرَّفَ] to give/bring relief; to vent, to unload; نَفَّسَ عن غَضَبِهِ to vent one's anger ⓶ [عن| [رَفَّهَ] to cheer/brighten up; نَفَّسَ عن شَخْصٍ (كُرْبَتَهُ) to cheer sb up

نافَسَ *v* to compete with, to contend/vie for; نافَسَ شَخْصاً; نافَسَ شَخْصاً على \ في شَيْءٍ to compete with sb over sth; على اللَقَبِ to compete with sb for the title

تَنَفَّسَ *v* to breathe; تَنَفَّسَ هواءً to breathe air; تَنَفَّسَ الصُعَداءَ to breathe a sigh of relief; تَنَفَّسَ تَنَفُّساً عَميقاً to breathe deeply; تَنَفَّسَ بِصُعوبةٍ to breathe heavily

تَنافَسَ *v* to compete/vie/contend with each other, to rival; تَنافَسَ مع شَخْصٍ على شَيْءٍ to compete with sb over sth; يَتَنافَسُ المُرَشَّحونَ في الانْتِخاباتِ the candidates are vying in the election

نَفْس *n* |f; أَنْفُس، نُفوس| ⓵ [روح] soul; mind, psyche; عِلْم النَفْسِ psychology; عالِمِ النَفْسِ psychologist; تَطْوير النَفْسِ self-development; ضَبْط النَفْسِ self-control; ثِقة بالنَفْسِ \ self-confidence; بِشِقِّ النَفْسِ \ الأَنْفُسِ بالذاتِ narrowly, barely, scarcely; في قَرارةِ \ دَخيلةِ نَفْسِهِ from the bottom of one's heart; ما في نَفْسِهِ what one feels; كانَ في نَفْسِهِ أَنْ ... to intend to ...; كانَ في صِراعٍ مع النَفْسِ to be conflicted; كَلَّفَ نَفْسَهُ to take great pains; هاجَت النُفوسُ feelings ran high; صَلّى لِراحةِ نَفْسِ شَخْصٍ to pray for sb's soul ⓶ [نَفْس الشَيْءِ] same, similar; نَفْس المَكانِ، المَكان نَفْسُهُ the same place; نَفْس الشَيْءِ، الشَيْء نَفْسُهُ the same thing; يُفَكِّرونَ في نَفْسِ الشَيْءِ نَفْسِهِ they are thinking of the same thing; أُريدُ نَفْسَ الكِتابِ I want the same book ⓷ [شَخْص بِنَفْسِهِ] self; لِنَفْسِهِ (فَقَطْ) (just) for himself; بِنَفْسِهِ he personally; by himself;

‹ **نَفَرَ** *v* |i-u; نَفْر| ⓵ [من| [كَرِهَ] to be averse to, to dislike; to turn away from, to alienate oneself from; نَفَرَ من شَخْصٍ to have an aversion to sb; to alienate oneself from sb; نَفَرَ من شَيْءٍ to be averse to sth; نَفَرَتْ من زَوْجِها she turned away from her husband ⓶ [من| [الحَيَوانُ] to shy at, to shrink from ⓷ [هَرَبَ] to flee (from), to run away (from)

نَفَّرَ *v* to repulse, to revolt, to repel; to scare off, to frighten; to alienate; نَفَّرَ شَخْصاً to repulse sb; نَفَّرَ الزَبائِنَ to scare off customers

نافَرَ *v* to be averse to, to dislike, to hate; نافَرَ شَخْصاً to hate sb

تَنافَرَ *v* ⓵ [تَخاصَمَ] to repulse, to revolt, to repel ⓶ [أَلْوان] to clash, to mismatch, to be incompatible

اسْتَنْفَرَ *v* ⓵ [دَعا للقِتال] to call into battle, to mobilize; to stir up; اسْتَنْفَرَ العَصَبِيّةَ الطائِفِيّةَ to stir up sectarian tensions ⓶ [خافَ] to be frightened away ⓷ [أَهَبَّ] to alarm, to alert

نَفَر *n* | أَنْفار| ⓵ [فَرْد] person, individual, soul; مِائة نَفَرٍ a hundred people; مُقاوِل أَنْفارٍ labour contractor ⓶ [جَماعة] a small group/knot of people; نَفَر من الأَصْدِقاءِ a handful of friends

نافِر *adj* | نُفَّر، نَفْر| ⓵ [بارِز] protruding, bulging; عُنُق نافِر a long neck; عَضَلات نافِرة bulging muscles ⓶ [كارِه] averse ⓷ [هارِب] fearful, skittish, shy

نافورة *n* |نَوافيرُ| fountain; نافورة من الرُخامِ a marble fountain

نَفْرة *n* ⓵ [كُرْه] aversion, dislike ⓶ [مُغادَرة] leaving, turning away; نَفْرة الحَجيجِ من عَرَفاتٍ the pilgrims leaving Arafat

نُفور *n* aversion, dislike, antipathy; نُفور كَبير a deep antipathy; نُفور من فِعْلِ شَيْءٍ an aversion to doing sth; نُفور من شَخْصٍ a dislike of sb; أَحَسَّ بالنُفورِ من شَخْصٍ to take a dislike to sb

نَفير *n* |أَنْفِرة، أَنْفار| ⓵ [بوق] horn, trumpet, bugle; horn, hooter (BrE); دَقَّ \ أَطْلَقَ نَفيراً، نَفَخَ في نَفيرٍ to blow a horn ⓶ (Mil) a call to arms

اسْتِنْفار *n* mobilization; stirring up

تَنافُر *n* |تَنافُرات| aversion, dislike, antipathy; disagreement, discord, dissension; quarrel, debate; تَنافُر الأَصْواتِ disharmony; التَجاذُب والتَنافُر (magnetic) attraction and repulsion inhalation of a substance; ضيق \ عُسر تَنَفُّسٍ breathing difficulties; فَرْط التَنَفُّسِ hyperventilation; جِهاز تَنَفُّسٍ اصْطِناعيًّا (اصْطِناعيٍّ) respirator; أَجْرى لِشَخْصٍ تَنَفُّساً اصْطِناعيًّا to put sb on a respirator

تَنَفُّسيّ *adj* respiratory; الْتِهاب تَنَفُّسيّ respiratory infection; جِهاز تَنَفُّسيّ respirator; مَجارٍ تَنَفُّسيّة airway

تَنْفيس *n* ventilation, airing; relief, release, discharge; تَنْفيس الأَزْمةِ defusing the crisis; التَنْفيس عن التَوَتُّراتِ easing tensions; صِمام تَنْفيسٍ relief valve

مُتَنافِس *n* competitor, opponent, rival

مُتَنَفَّس *n* outlet, vent, release; وَجَدَ مُتَنَفَّساً لِشَيْءٍ to find an outlet for sth

مُنافِس **A** *adj* competing, competitive; أَسْعار مُنافسة competitive prices
B *n* competitor, rival; المُنافِسونَ the competition; أَكْبَر المُنافِسينَ the biggest competitors; قَضى على المُنافِسينَ to beat the competition; تَفَوَّقَ على كُلِّ مُنافِسيهِ to outperform all competitors

مُنافَسة *n* competition, rivalry; مُنافَسة عادِلة \ شَريفة fair competition; مُنافَسة حادّة \ شَديدة \ قَويّة \ مُتَكافِئة stiff competition; حِدّة المُنافَسةِ the fierceness of the competition; لاقى مُنافَسةً to meet competition; واجَهَ المُنافَسةَ to face the competition; توجَدُ مُنافَسةٌ بين الدَوْلَتَيْنِ المُتَجاوِرَتَيْنِ a rivalry exists between the neighbouring countries

نَفَشَ *v* |u; نَفْش| **1** [نَفَخَ] to inflate, to make swell; to puff out, to spread out; يَنْفُشُ الطاووسُ ريشَهُ the peacock spreads his feathers **2** [الصوفَ] to comb, to card; نَفَشَ الصوفَ \ القُطْنَ to comb wool/cotton **3** [الشَعْرَ] to backcomb (BrE), to tease (AmE)

انْتَفَشَ *v* **1** [الصوفُ] to be combed/carded **2** [القِطُّ] to bristle

مَنْفوش *adj* **1** [الشَعْرُ، الريشُ] fluffy, bushy; bristling; حَواجِب مَنْفوشة bushy eyebrows; كانَ مَنْفوشاً to be ruffled up
2 [الصوفُ] combed, carded; صوف مَنْفوش combed wool

نَفَضَ *v* |u; نَفْض| to shake (out/off), to beat (out); to dust (off/down); نَفَضَ شَجَرةً to shake a tree; نَفَضَ سَجّادةً to beat a rug; نَفَضَ الغُبارَ to shake off dust; نَفَضَ الغُبارَ عن شَيْءٍ

وَجَدَ نَفْسَهُ (في مَكانٍ \ حالةٍ) to find oneself (in a place/ situation); اعْتَمَدَ على نَفْسِهِ to take care of oneself; جاءَ من تِلْقاءِ نَفْسِهِ to come voluntarily; جاءَني بِنَفْسِهِ he himself came to me; غَسَلَتْ نَفْسَها she washed herself; أَخْدِمْ نَفْسَكَ بِنَفْسِكَ help yourself

نَفَس *n* |أَنْفاس| **1** [هَواء] breath; كانَ طَويلَ النَفَسِ to have stamina; كانَ قَصيرَ النَفَسِ to be short-winded; انْقَطَعَ نَفَسُهُ to be out of breath; كَتَمَ \ أَمْسَكَ نَفَسَهُ \ أَنْفاسَهُ to hold one's breath; الْتَقَطَ \ اسْتَعادَ أَنْفاسَهُ to catch one's breath; لَفَظَ أَنْفاسَهُ الأَخيرةَ to breathe one's last; فاضَتْ أَنْفاسُهُ to die
2 [دَخَّنَ] puff, draw, drag; أَخَذَ \ جَذَبَ نَفَساً من سيجارَتِهِ to take a drag from one's cigarette

نِفاس *n* childbirth; puerperium; حُمّى النِفاسِ puerperal fever

نُفَساء *n* |dipt f; نِفاس, نُفَساوات| a woman in childbirth

نَفْسانيّ *adj* psychological; psychiatric; mental; طَبيب نَفْسانيّ psychiatrist; مَريض \ عِلاج نَفْسانيّ a psychiatric patient/ treatment; مُسْتَشْفى أَمْراضٍ نَفْسانيّة a psychiatric hospital

نَفْسيّ *adj* psychological, mental; psychiatric; spiritual; حالة نَفْسيّة mental health; أَلَم نَفْسيّ mental suffering; مَريض نَفْسيّ mentally disturbed; a psychiatric patient; صِراع نَفْسيّ inner struggle; راحة نَفْسيّة inner calm; تَحْليل نَفْسيّ psychoanalysis; مُحَلِّل نَفْسيّ psychoanalyst; جَسَديّ – نَفْسيّ, نَفْسيّ بَدَنيّ psychosomatic

نَفْسيّة *n* state/frame of mind, mood

نَفيس *adj* |نِفاس| valuable, precious; priceless; مَعادِن نَفيسة precious metals; ضَحّى بالنَفْسِ والنَفيسِ to sacrifice everything

نَفيسة *n* |نَفائِسُ| an object of value

تَنافُس *n* |تَنافُسات| competition, rivalry; تَنافُس بين الأَشْخاصِ competition between people

تَنافُسيّ *adj* competitive, competing; صِراع تَنافُسيّ competition; قُدْرة تَنافُسيّة competitiveness; أَسْعار تَنافُسيّة competitive prices

تَنافُسيّة *n* competitiveness

تَنَفُّس *n* respiration, breathing; inhalation; تَنَفُّس مُنْتَظِم regular breathing; تَنَفُّس اصْطِناعيّ artificial respiration; تَنَفُّس مادّةٍ

to dust sth off; نَفَض عَنْهُ غُبارَ الكَسَل to shake off one's laziness; نَفَض يَدَهُ من شَيْءٍ \ شَخْصٍ to wash one's hands of sth/sb

نَفَّضَ *v* to shake off dust

أَنْفَضَ *v* to use up, to exhaust

انْتَفَضَ *v* 1 [ارْتَعَش] to shiver, to shake, to tremble, to quiver; انْتَفَض فَزَعاً \ من الفَزَعِ to shake with fear 2 [ثارَ] to rise up, to revolt, to rebel; انْتَفَض ضدّ شَخْصٍ to rebel against sb 3 [عادَ] to make a comeback; انْتَفَضَ الفَرِيقُ في الشَوْطِ الثاني the team made a comeback in the second half

انْتِفاض *n* shiver, shake, tremor, tremble

انْتِفاضة *n* intifada, uprising, revolt; انْتِفاضة شَعْبِيّة a popular revolt; الانْتِفاضة (الفِلَسْطِينِيّة) the (Palestinian) intifada

مِنْفَضة *n* |مَنافِضُ| 1 [صَحْن السَجائِرِ] ashtray; رَمى \ وَضَعَ سيجارةً في مِنْفَضةٍ to put a cigarette in an ashtray 2 [لِلتَنْظِيفِ] duster; مِنْفَضة رِيشٍ feather duster

نِفْط، نَفْط *n* oil, petroleum; بِئْر \ حَقْل \ مِنَصّة \ ناقِلة نَفْطٍ oil well/field/rig/tanker; بِئْر نَفْطٍ غَزِير a rich oil well; أُنْبوب \ أَنابِيب نَفْطٍ oil pipeline; تَنْقِيب عن النَفْطِ oil drilling; اسْتِخْراج النَفْطِ oil recovery; إِنْتاج النَفْطِ petroleum production; شَرِكة نَفْطٍ oil company; شَرِكات \ دُوَل مُنْتِجة لِلنَفْطِ oil-producing companies/countries; صِناعة النَفْطِ petroleum industry; سوق النَفْطِ العالَمِيّة the international oil market; تَصْدِير النَفْطِ oil export; حِصار على النَفْطِ oil boycott; أَزْمة النَفْطِ oil crisis; اسْتِهْلاك النَفْطِ oil consumption; مُشْتَقّات النَفْطِ oil derivatives, petroleum products; غَنِيّ بالنَفْطِ rich in oil; (عَمِلَ) في قِطاعِ النَفْطِ (to work) in the oil industry; نَقَّبَ عن النَفْطِ to drill for oil; يَرْتَفِعُ \ يَزِيدُ سِعْرُ النَفْطِ the price of oil is rising

نافِطة *n* |نَوافِطُ| blister

نَفّاطة *n* 1 [مَكان اسْتِخْراج نَفْطٍ] oil well 2 [بَثْرة] blister

نَفْطِيّ *adj* oil (*before n*), petroleum (*before n*); حَظْر نَفْطِيّ oil boycott; مِنَصّة نَفْطِيّة oil rig

نَفَعَ *v* |a; نَفْع| to be useful, to help; to be beneficial/profitable/advantageous; نَفَعَ شَخْصاً to be useful to sb; نَفَعَ في شَيْءٍ to help with sth; لا يَنْفَعُنِي شَيْئاً \ في شَيْءٍ it's useless to me; لا يَنْفَعُ! it's no use!, it's no good!; سَتَنْدَمُ يَوْمَ لا يَنْفَعُ النَدَمُ you'll be sorry but it'll be too late; القِرْشُ الأَبْيَضُ يَنْفَعُ في اليَوْمِ الأَسْوَدِ one should save for a rainy day

انْتَفَعَ *v* to use, to utilize; to profit/benefit from, to take advantage of; انْتَفَعَ ب \ من شَيْءٍ to profit from sth

اسْتَنْفَعَ *v* to use, to make use of, to utilize; to exploit; to profit/benefit from

نَفْع *n* use; benefit, advantage; النَفْع العامّ the common good; عادَ على شَخْصٍ بالنَفْعِ to be beneficial to sb; أَجْدى نَفْعاً to be useful, to work; هذا لا يُجْدي نَفْعاً that's useless, that's not working; لا نَفْعَ لَهُ useless; لا نَفْعَ لي في ذلك that's useless to me; ما نَفْعُ هذا؟ what's the point of that?

نافِع A *adj* useful; beneficial, advantageous; غَيْر نافِعٍ useless; حَلّ نافِع للجَمِيعِ a solution for everybody

B *n* 1 (Islam) النافِع the Benefactor, the Source of Good (*one of the names of God*) 2 [اسْم شَخْصِيّ] Nafi' (*male given name*)

نافِعة *n* benefit; useful/helpful thing; رُبَّ ضارّةٍ نافِعةٌ it's a blessing in disguise; ما نَفَعَنِي بِنافِعةٍ it does me no good

نَفّاع *adj* useful

نَفْعِيّ A *adj* opportunistic, expedient; utilitarian

B *n* opportunist

نَفْعِيّة *n* opportunism

انْتِفاع *n* use, exploitation; benefit; حَقّ الانْتِفاعِ right of use, usufruct

انْتِفاعِيّ A *adj* opportunistic

B *n* opportunist

مُنْتَفِع *n* beneficiary; user; usufructuary; المُنْتَفِعونَ بالعَفْوِ those receiving amnesty

مَنْفَعة *n* |مَنافِعُ| use; benefit, advantage; profit, gain; مَنافِع صِحِّيّة health benefits; المَنْفَعة العامّة the common good; عَلاقات مُتَبادَلة المَنْفَعةِ mutually beneficial relations

مَنْفَعِيّ *adj, n* utilitarian

نَفَقَ *v* |u| 1 [ماتَ] |نُفوق| to die, to perish (*animals*); نَفَقَتْ مَواشِيهِمْ بِسَبَبِ الجَفافِ their livestock died on account of the drought 2 [نَفِدَ] |نَفَق| to be exhausted/used up

نافَقَ *v* to be hypocritical; to feign, to dissemble, to dissimulate

أَنْفَقَ *v* to spend; أَنْفَقَ المالَ على سَيَّارةٍ جَديدةٍ to spend money on a new car; أَنْفَقَ وَقْتَهُ على \ في شَيْءٍ to spend time on sth; أَنْفَقَ على شَخْصٍ to provide for sb

نَفَق *n* |أَنْفاق| tunnel, subway (BrE); نَفَق طَويل \ مُظْلِم a long/dark tunnel; (fig) a difficult situation; دَخَلَ في \ خَرَجَ من نَفَقٍ مُظْلِمٍ to get into/out of a difficult situation; نَفَق أَرْضيّ an underground passageway; نَفَق هَوائيّ wind tunnel; مِتْرو \ قِطار أَنْفاقٍ metro, underground (BrE), subway (AmE); حَفَرَ نَفَقاً to dig a tunnel

نافِق *adj* dead (animals); دَجاجة نافِقة a dead chicken

نِفاق *n* hypocrisy; dissimulation; نِفاق سِياسيّ \ أَخْلاقيّ political/moral hypocrisy

نَفَقة *n* |نَفَقات، إنفاق| ⟦1⟧ [مَصْروف] cost; spending, expense, expenditure; support, sustenance; على نَفَقةِ ... at the expense of ...; هذا على نَفَقتي this is on me; نَفَقات عامّة overhead costs; نَفَقات باهِظة exorbitant costs; نَفَقات المَعيشةِ the cost of living; نَفَقات حُكوميّة government spending; غَطّى نَفَقاتٍ to cover expenses ⟦2⟧ [بعد الطَلاقِ] maintenance (BrE), alimony (AmE); دَفَعَ النَفَقةَ to pay maintenance

إِنْفاق *n* spending, expense, expenditure; spending; إِنْفاق عَسْكَريّ military spending; الإِفْراط \ الإِهْدار في الإِنْفاقِ overspending/wasteful spending

مُنافِق **A** *adj* hypocritical, insincere
B *n* ⟦1⟧ [مُراء] hypocrite; dissembler ⟦2⟧ (Islam) *sb who acted as a supporter of the Prophet Muhammad in Medina but sabotaged him secretly*; سورة المُنافِقونَ The Hypocrites (*Sura 63*)

مُنافَقة *n* hypocrisy; dissimulation

مِنْفاق *n* |مَنافيقُ| spendthrift

〈 **نَفَّلَ** *v* to give extra

تَنَفَّلَ *v* to do more than necessary; to perform more prayers than necessary

نَفْل *n* a voluntary act of worship (*prayer, fasting, etc., above and beyond what is required by duty*)

نَفَل *n* |أَنْفال، نُفول، إِنفال| ⟦1⟧ [غَنيمة] spoils, booty, loot; سورة الأَنْفالِ The Spoils of War (*Sura 8*); (حَمْلة \ قَضيّة \ عَمَليّة) الأَنْفالِ al-Anfal (campaign/case/operation), the Kurdish genocide (*killing of Kurds and other ethnic minorities in northern Iraq by Saddam Hussein's regime, 1986–9*) ⟦2⟧ (Bot) clover, trefoil (*Trifolium*)

نافِل *adj* superfluous, redundant; من نافِلِ القَوْلِ إنّ ... needless to say that ...

نافِلة *n* a voluntary act of worship (*prayer, fasting, etc., above and beyond what is required by duty*); صَلاة النافِلةِ additional prayers

(Idiom) من نافِلةِ القَوْلِ أنّ ... it goes without saying that ...

نَوْفَل *n* |نَوافِلُ| ⟦1⟧ [كَريم] benefactor ⟦2⟧ [اِسْم شَخْصيّ] Nawfal (*male given name*)

〈 **نَفى** *v* |i; نَفْي| ⟦1⟧ [أَنْكَرَ] to deny, to disavow, to contradict; to refute, to disprove; نَفى تُهْمةً to deny an accusation; نَفى زَعْماً \ خَبَراً to refute a claim/report; نَفى شَيْئاً نَفْياً قاطِعاً to deny sth categorically ⟦2⟧ [أَبْعَدَ] to banish, to exile; to deport, to expel; نُفِيَ to be banished; نَفى شَخْصاً إلى \ من مَكانٍ to deport sb to/from somewhere

نافى *v* to conflict with, to contravene, to be contradictory/inconsistent with; نافى شَيْئاً to be conflict with sth

تَنافى *v* to conflict, to be contradictory/inconsistent; تَنافى مع شَيْءٍ to conflict with sth

انْتَفى *v* ⟦1⟧ [انْعَدَمَ] to be eliminated, to be negated, to no longer exist; انْتَفَت الحاجةُ إلى شَيْءٍ sth was no longer needed ⟦2⟧ [أُبْعِدَ] to be exiled/banished; to deport, to expel

نَفْي *n* ⟦1⟧ [إِنْكار] denial, refusal; جواب بالنَفْيِ a negative answer; شاهِد نَفْيٍ a defense witness; نَفى شَيْئاً نَفْياً قاطِعاً to deny sth categorically; رَفَضَ النَفْيَ أو التَأْكيدَ to neither confirm nor deny ⟦2⟧ [تَرْحيل] exile, banishment; deportation; نَفْي نابوليون Napoleon's exile; النَفْي مَدى الحَياةِ a lifelong exile ⟦3⟧ (Gram) negation; حَرْف \ أَداة النَفْيِ negative particle

نُفاية *n* waste, refuse, rubbish (BrE), garbage (AmE), trash (AmE); نُفايات waste; نُفايات مَنْزِليّة household rubbish; نُفايات نَوَويّة \ مُشِعّة nuclear/radioactive waste; خَزَّنَ النُفاياتِ النَوَويّةَ to store nuclear waste; نُفايات مُضِرّة \ سامّة hazardous/toxic waste; نُفايات كيماويّة \ كيميائيّة chemical waste; جَمْع النُفاياتِ refuse collection; مَكَبّ النُفاياتِ the dump; إعادة اسْتِعْمالِ النُفاياتِ recycling

تَنْقِيب *n* |تَنْقيبات| drilling; التَنْقيب الأَثَريّ \ عن الآثارِ excavation, archeological dig; عَمَليّات التَنْقيبِ عن النَفْطِ oil drilling

مَناقِب *n pl* |dipt| virtues, qualities

مُنَقِّب *n* prospector; excavator

نَقَحَ *v* |a; نَقْح| to cherry-pick; to extract (*the best part*); نَقَحَ العُلَماءُ العَرَبُ الحَضارةَ اليونانيّةَ Arab scholars took the best parts of Greek culture

نَقَّحَ *v* to revise, to correct; to edit; نَقَّحَ نَصًّا to edit a text

أَنْقَحَ *v* to rectify

تَنْقيح *n* |تَنْقيحات| revision, correction, editing

مُنَقَّح *adj* revised, corrected; edited; طَبْعة مُنَقَّحة a revised edition

نَقَدَ *v* |u; نَقْد| 1 [أَظْهَرَ العُيوبَ] to criticize, to find fault with; نَقَدَ شَيْئاً \ شَخْصاً to criticize sth/sb; نَقَدَ اقْتِراحاً to criticize a proposal 2 [كِتاباً إلخ] to review, to critique; نَقَدَ كِتاباً \ فيلْماً to review a book/film 3 [دَفَعَ] to pay in cash

أَنْقَدَ *v* to pay in cash

انْتَقَدَ *v* to criticize, to find fault with; انْتَقَدَ شَيْئاً \ شَخْصاً to criticize sth/sb; انْتَقَدَ لِباسَ شَخْصٍ to criticize sb's clothes

نَقْد *n* 1 [مال] |نُقود| cash, money; نُقود money; نَقْداً in cash; نَقْد سائِل cash; نُقود مُزَيَّفة counterfeit money; صُنْدوق نُقودٍ strongbox; صُنْدوق النَقْدِ الدُوَليّ the International Monetary Fund, the IMF; كيس نُقودٍ change purse; تَداوُل النُقودِ money circulation; صَرَّفَ \ بَدَّلَ \ اسْتَبْدَلَ نُقوداً في الخارِجِ to exchange money abroad; دَفَعَ (شَيْئاً) نَقْداً to pay (sth) in cash 2 [تَحْليل] criticism, disapproval, comment; review, critique; نَقْد لاذِع \ هَدّام \ بَنّاء sharp/destructive/constructive criticism; نَقْد ذاتيّ self-criticism; نَقْد إيجابيّ \ سَلْبيّ a good/bad review; النَقْد الأَدَبيّ literary criticism; نَقْد كِتابٍ a book review; كانَ مَحَطَّ نَقْدٍ to be subject to criticism; قَبِلَ شَيْئاً بِدونِ نَقْدٍ to accept sth uncritically

ناقِد A *adj* |نَقَدة ,نُقّاد ,ناقِدونَ| critical, discerning
B *n* |نُقّاد ,ناقِدونَ| critic, reviewer; ناقِد فَنّيّ \ سينَمائيّ \ أَدَبيّ art/film/literary critic; ناقِد سِياسيّ political critic; أَخْرَسَ النُقّادَ to silence the critics

نَقْديّ *adj* 1 [ماليّ] financial, monetary; وَحْدة نَقْديّة monetary unit; قِطْعة نَقْديّة coin; وَرَقة نَقْديّة bank note, bill (AmE);

انْتِفاء *n* absence, lack; انْتِفاء الحاجةِ إلى شَيْءٍ the lack of necessity for sth

مُتَنافٍ *adj* contradictory, inconsistent

مُنافٍ *adj* contradictory, conflicting, inconsistent; incompatible; كانَ مُنافِياً للأَخْلاقِ to be contrary to morality; كانَ مُنافِياً لِمَبْدَأِ المُساواةِ to conflict with the principle of equality

مَنْفًى *n* |مَنافٍ| 1 [اغْتِراب] exile, banishment; الحُكومة في المَنْفى the government in exile 2 [مَكان] place of exile

مَنْفيّ A *adj* 1 [مُبْعَد] exiled, banished; deported, expelled
2 [مُنْكَر] denied, rejected, discarded
B *n* exile; deportee

نَقَبَ *v* |u; نَقْب| 1 [خَرَقَ] to perforate, to make a hole 2 [بَحَثَ] |عن| to search/look for; نَقَبَ عن شَيْءٍ to look for sth

نَقَّبَ *v* 1 [حَفَرَ] to drill; to dig, to excavate; نَقَّبَ عن الآثارِ to undertake an an (archeological) excavation; نَقَّبَ عن النَفْطِ to drill for oil; نَقَّبَ في الأَرْشيفِ \ الماضي to dig in the archives/the past 2 [بَحَثَ] |عن| to search/look for

تَنَقَّبَ *v* 1 [شَدَّ النِقابَ على الوَجْهِ] to wear a niqab (*covering one's face*) 2 [صارَتْ بِهِ ثُقَبٌ] to be perforated 3 [بالَغَ في البَحْثِ] to search/look for; to scrutinize

نَقَب *n* (صَحْراء) النَقَب the Negev (Desert)

ناقوبة *n* listed alphabetically

نِقاب *n* |أَنْقِبة ,نُقُب| veil; niqab (*a veil covering all of the face apart from the eyes*); لَبِسَ النِقابَ to wear the niqab; كَشَفَ النِقابَ عن شَيْءٍ to unveil sth; كَشَفَ النِقابَ عن سِرٍّ \ خُطّةٍ to unveil a secret/plan

نِقابة *n* union, association, syndicate; نِقابة مِهْنيّة trade union; نِقابة المُعَلِّمينَ teachers' union; نِقابة المُحامينَ the bar association; عُضْو نِقابةٍ union member; اتِّحاد نِقاباتٍ a union federation; انْضَمَّ إلى نِقابة to join a union

نِقابَويّ *adj* corporate

نِقابَويّة *n* corporatism

نِقابيّ A *adj* union (*before n*); حَرَكة نِقابيّة union movement
B *n* union member

نَقيب *n* |نُقَباءُ| 1 [رَئيس] leader, head, chief 2 [نِقابةٍ] union leader 3 (Mil) captain

نَقْرة *n* |نَقَرات| ◀1▶ [دَقّة] blow, knock; tap ◀2▶ (Comput) click (*with a mouse*)

نُقْرة *n* |نُقَر| ◀1▶ [دَقّة] knock, tap; سَمِعَ نُقْرةَ البابِ to hear a knock at the door ◀2▶ (Comput) click; نُقْرة على الفَأْرةِ a click of the mouse ◀3▶ [حُفْرة] cavity, hole ◀4▶ (Anat) socket, eye socket; نُقْرة العَيْنِ eye socket

نَقير *n a worthless thing*; لا يَمْلِكُ شَرْوى نَقيرٍ he hasn't got a cent to his name

مِنْقار *n* |مَناقيرُ| ◀1▶ [مِنْقاد] beak, bill; مِنْقار البَطِّ platypus (*Ornithorhynchus anatinus*) ◀2▶ [مِعْوَل] axe, mattock

نِقْرِس *n* |نَقارِسُ| (Med) gout; أُصيبَ بالنِقْرِسِ to have gout

نَقَزَ *v* |i-u; نَقْز, نِقاز, نَقَزان| to frolic, to gambol; to hop, to skip

نَقَّزَ *v* ◀1▶ [الطائِر] to hop, to skip; to jump, to leap ◀2▶ [الطِفْلَ] to rock

نَقَسَ *v* |u; نَقْس| to sound, to ring

ناقوس *n* |نَواقيسُ| bell; gong; بُرْج الناقوسِ clock tower; ناقوس الخَطَرِ alarm bell; دَقَّ \ قَرَعَ ناقوسَ الخَطَرِ to sound the alarm

نَقَشَ *v* |u; نَقْش| to carve, to engrave, to inscribe; to sculpt; نَقَشَ كِتابةً في \ على شَيْءٍ to carve letters in/on sth

ناقَشَ *v* to discuss, to argue, to raise; ناقَشَ مَوْضوعاً \ مَسْأَلةً to discuss a topic/issue; ناقَشَ شَيْئاً مع شَخْصٍ to discuss sth with sb; ناقَشَ رِسالةً \ أُطْروحةً to defend a thesis

تَناقَشَ *v* to discuss, to debate; تَناقَشَ في مَسْأَلةٍ to discuss an issue

نَقْش *n* |نُقوش| carving, engraving, inscription; sculpture; mural, fresco; نُقوش فِرْعَوْنيّة pharaonic inscriptions; العِلْمُ في الصِغَرِ كالنَقْشِ في الحَجَرِ as the twig is bent so the tree inclines

نَقّاش *n* carver, engraver; sculptor; painter, artist

نِقاش *n* |نِقاشات| discussion, controversy, debate; quarrel, argument; لا نِقاشَ فيهِ undisputed; نِقاش حادّ \ ساخِن a heated discussion; نِقاش مُعَمَّق \ صَريح \ جِدّيّ \ مَفْتوح a deep/candid/serious/open discussion; نِقاش حَيّ (Comput) live chat; مَوْضوع نِقاشٍ a subject for debate; مَدار النِقاشِ the central issue of the debate; أَجْرى نِقاشاً to have a debate; طَرَحَ شَيْئاً للنِقاشِ to bring sth up for discussion

دَفْع نَقْديّ financial crisis ◀2▶ [نَقْداً] cash (*before n*); أَزْمة نَقْديّة cash payment; جائِزة نَقْديّة cash prize ◀3▶ [مُنْتَقِد] critical, discerning; رُوح نَقْديّة \ وَعْي نَقْديّ a critical mind; قَرَأَ شَيْئاً بِعَيْنٍ نَقْديّةٍ to read sth critically

اِنْتِقاد *n* |اِنْتِقادات| criticism, disapproval; اِنْتِقاد لاذِع sharp criticism; أَثارَ اِنْتِقاداً to arouse criticism

اِنْتِقاديّ *adj* critical; تَصْريحات اِنْتِقاديّة critical remarks

مُنْتَقِد ■A *adj* critical, discerning
■B *n* critic

مِنْقاد *n* |مَناقيدُ| beak, bill (*of a bird*)

نَقِذَ *v* |a; نَقَذ| to be saved/rescued

أَنْقَذَ *v* to save, to rescue; أَنْقَذَ شَخْصاً من شَيْءٍ to rescue sb from sth; أَنْقَذَ حَياةَ شَخْصٍ to save sb's life; أَنْقَذَ ما يُمْكِنُ إِنْقاذُهُ to save what can be saved; to make the best of sth

اِسْتَنْقَذَ *v* to save, to rescue

إِنْقاذ *n* rescue, salvation, relief; رَجُل إِنْقاذٍ rescue worker; عَمَلِيّات الإِنْقاذِ rescue operations; قارِب إِنْقاذٍ lifeboat; مُحاوَلة إِنْقاذٍ rescue attempt; مُحاوَلة إِنْقاذٍ ناجِحة \ فاشِلة a successful/unsuccessful rescue attempt; الجَبْهة الإِسْلامِيّة لِلإِنْقاذِ Islamic Salvation Front

مُنْقِذ *n* ◀1▶ [مُنَجٍّ] rescuer, saver; protector, guardian; لا مُنْقِذَ لَهُ he's beyond help ◀2▶ [في المَسْبَحِ] lifeguard, pool attendant

نَقَرَ *v* |u; نَقْر| ◀1▶ [دَقَّ] to drum, to tap; to knock; نَقَرَ (بِأَصابِعِهِ) على المائِدةِ to drum (one's fingers) on the table ◀2▶ (Comput) to click; نَقَرَ بالماوْس \ بالفأْرةِ to click with the mouse; نَقَرَ على زِرٍّ to click a button ◀3▶ [الطائِرُ] to peck ◀4▶ (Mus) to pick, to pluck, to strum; نَقَرَ العودَ to strum an oud ◀5▶ [حَفَرَ] to engrave, to carve

نَقَّرَ *v* to peck

ناقَرَ *v* to wrangle/bicker with; to quarrel/argue with; ناقَرَ شَخْصاً to bicker with sb

تَناقَرَ *v* to bicker with each other

ناقِر *n* ناقِر الخَشَبِ woodpecker (*Picidae*)

ناقور *n* |نَواقيرُ| *a musical wind instrument of copper or brass*; horn, trumpet, bugle

نَقّار *n* |نَقّارة| engraver, carver; نَقّار الخَشَبِ woodpecker (*Picidae*)

نِقاشيّ *adj* discussion (*before n*), debate (*before n*); بَرْنامَج نِقاشيّ discussion programme

مُناقِش *n* debater, discussant; disputant

مُناقَشة *n* debate, discussion, dispute; قابِل للمُناقَشةِ debatable; غَيْر قابِلٍ للمُناقَشةِ not open to discussion; مُناقَشة حادّة \ حامِية an intense/heated argument; مُناقَشة عامّة a public debate; مُناقَشة حول مَوْضوعٍ a debate on a subject; حَلْقة مُناقَشةٍ a panel discussion; مُناقَشة رِسالةِ الدُكْتوراه \ أُطْروحةٍ a thesis defence; دَخَلَ في مُناقَشةٍ to enter into debate; شارَكَ في مُناقَشةٍ to join in a discussion; عَرَضَ قَضيّةً للمُناقَشةِ to bring a matter up for discussion; كانَ قَيْدَ \ على بِساطِ المُناقَشةِ to be up for discussion

مِنْقاش *n* |مَناقيش| chisel

مَنْقوش *adj* engraved, carved, chiselled; sculptured; painted; حَجَر مَنْقوش carved stone; كانَ مَنْقوشاً في ذاكِرَتِهِ to be engraved on one's memory

‹ **نَقَصَ** *v* |u; نَقْص, نُقْصان| ❶ [أَعْوَزَ] to lack; to be lacking/missing; تَنْقُصُهُ الخِبْرةُ \ الشَجاعةُ to lack experience/courage; نَقَصَهُ المالُ to not have any money ❷ [صَيَّرَهُ ناقِصاً] to reduce, to decrease, to curtail; نَقَصَ وَزْنُهُ to lose weight ❸ [ضَعُفَ] to be weak; to be inadequate/insufficient; تَنْقُصُهُ المَعْرِفةُ to have insufficient knowledge

نَقَّصَ *v* to reduce, to decrease, to curtail; نَقَّصَ شَيْئاً to curtail sth; نَقَّصَ من ساعاتِ العَمَلِ to reduce working hours; نَقَّصَ في الأَسْعارِ to cut prices

أَنْقَصَ *v* to reduce, to decrease; أُنْقِصَ (من الثَمَنِ) to be reduced (in price)

تَناقَصَ *v* to decline, to decrease, to diminish; تَناقَصَ تَدْريجيًّا \ باسْتِمْرارٍ to gradually/steadily decline; يَتَناقَصُ الإِنْتاجُ production is declining

انْتَقَصَ *v* to decrease, to reduce; to detract, to derogate; to belittle, to abase; انْتَقَصَ من شَيْءٍ to detract from sth; انْتَقَصَ من حُقوقِ شَخْصٍ to detract from sb's rights

اسْتَنْقَصَ *v* ❶ [عَدَّ ناقِصاً] to find incomplete/deficient ❷ [الثَمَنَ] to ask for a reduction of the price

نَقْص *n* ❶ [عَيْب] deficiency, shortcoming, defect; flaw, fault, blemish; inferiority, inadequacy, insufficiency; عُقْدة \ مُرَكَّب النَقْصِ inferiority complex; عانى من عُقْدة \ مُرَكَّبِ النَقْصِ to have an inferiority complex; إِحْساس \ شُعور بالنَقْصِ a feeling of inferiority; شَعَرَ بِنَقْصٍ to feel inferior ❷ [عَجْز] deficit, shortage, lack; نَقْص في عَدَدِ العامِلينَ undermanning; نَقْص في المَوادِّ الغِذائيّةِ a food shortage; نَقْص شَديد a severe shortage; نَقْص مُلِحّ \ حادّ an acute shortage; نَقْص المَناعةِ a lack of resistance; نَقْص الخِبْرةِ a lack of experience; سَدَّ النَقْصَ to make up a deficit ❸ [انْخِفاض] decline, decrease; نَقْص المَواليدِ a decline in the birth rate

ناقِص **A** *adj* |نُقَّص| ❶ [غَيْر كامِلٍ] incomplete, lacking, insufficient; defective, faulty; مَجْموعة ناقِصة an incomplete collection; وَصْف ناقِص an incomplete description; مَعْلومات ناقِصة incomplete information ❷ (Gram) defective, weak; فِعْل ناقِص a defective verb (*with a weak third radical*) **B** *n* |نُقَّص| (Math) minus, less; عَلامة ناقِص minus sign; سَبْعةٌ ناقِصٌ ثَلاثةٌ يُساوي أَرْبَعةً seven minus three equals four

نُقْصان *n* decrease, lessening; omission; lack, shortage; ناقِص نُقْصاناً شَديداً severely lacking; in very short supply; بِلا زِيادةٍ أو نُقْصانٍ without addition or omission

نَقيصة *n* |نَقائِص| fault, defect; shortcoming, lack

انْتِقاص *n* |انْتِقاصات| decrease, lessening; impairment; انْتِقاص من شَيْءٍ a decrease in sth

تَناقُص *n* |تَناقُصات| decrease, decline, reduction; تَناقُص الإِنْتاجِ a production decline

مُناقَصة *n* bid, bidding, tender; مُناقَصة عامّة \ خاصّة a public/private bid; طَرَحَ مُناقَصةً to solicit bids

مَنْقوص *adj* reduced, decreased; inadequate, insufficient; incomplete, imperfect; كامِل غَيْر مَنْقوصٍ complete

‹ **نَقَضَ** *v* |u; نَقْض| ❶ [هَدَمَ] to destroy, to demolish, to knock/tear/pull down; نَقَضَ مَصْنَعاً قَديماً to tear down an old factory ❷ [نَكَثَ] to break, to violate, to breach; نَقَضَ يَمينَهُ to break one's oath; نَقَضَ عَهْداً to renege on an pledge ❸ [أَبْطَلَ] to nullify, to annul, to invalidate, to cancel; to reverse, to quash; to veto; نَقَضَ قَراراً \ إِجْراءً to reverse a decision/measure; نَقَضَ حُكْماً to reverse a judgement

مُناقِض *adj* contradictory, conflicting, inconsistent, incompatible; مَوْقِف مُناقِض a contradictory position; كانَ مُناقِضاً to be contradictory; مُناقِض للواقِع inconsistent with reality

مُناقَضة *n* contradiction, incoherence, inconsistency; opposition, difference

نَقَطَ *v* |u; نَقْط| to dot, to point, to punctuate; نَقَطَ الزايَ to dot the zay

نَقَّطَ *v* 1 [لَطخ] to dot, to spot, to fleck 2 [الحَرْف] to dot 3 [الماء] to drip, to trickle; كَلام يُنَقِّطُ عَسَلاً *sweet but empty words*

نَقّاطة *n* pipette

نُقْطة *n* |نُقَط، نِقاط| 1 [رَقْطة] point, dot, spot, speck; blotch; نُقَط حَمْراء على الجِلْدِ red blotches on the skin 2 [عَلامة] point (BrE), full stop (BrE), period (AmE); decimal (point), dot; نُقْطَتانِ colon; وَضَعَ نُقْطةً to dot; وَضَعَ النُقَطَ على الحُروفِ to point consonants; (fig) to make things perfectly clear 3 (Sport) point; فازَ \ رَبِحَ بالنِقاطِ to score points; سَجَّلَ \ أَحْرَزَ \ حَقَّقَ نِقاطاً to win on points 4 [مَكان] post, station; point, location, position; نُقْطة جُمْرُكيّة checkpoint; نُقْطة البوليسِ \ الشُرْطةِ police post; نُقْطة مُراقَبةٍ observation post; نُقْطة انْطِلاقٍ point of departure; نُقْطة اللاعَوْدةِ point of no return 5 [مَوْضوع] point, matter, question, issue; نُقْطة أَساسيّة a fundamental question; نُقْطة حَسّاسة a sensitive issue; نُقْطة ضَعْفِهِ one's weak point; عالَجَ شَيْئاً نُقْطةً بِنُقْطةٍ to treat sth point by point 6 [سائِل] drop, droplet, drip

نُقْطيّ *n* dot (*before n*), point (*before n*); رَمْز نُقْطيّ bullet point

تَنْقيط *n* 1 [تَقَطُّر] dripping, trickling; الرَيّ بالتَنْقيطِ drip irrigation 2 [تَلْطيخ بِنُقَطٍ] pointing, dotting; تَنْقيط الحُروفِ pointing letters (*writing the dots on and under Arabic letters to distinguish them*)

مُنَقَّط *adj* speckled, dotted, spotted; punctuated; قُماش مُنَقَّط polka dot fabric

مَنْقوط *adj* punctuated; فاصِلة مَنْقوطة semicolon

نَقَعَ *v* |a; نَقْع| to soak; to marinate (*meat*); to steep, to infuse (*tea*); نَقَعَ شَيْئاً في الماءِ to soak sth in water; نَقَعَ الغَسيلَ to soak the

ناقَضَ *v* to contradict, to be contradictory to, to be inconsistent with; to be in conflict with, to be incompatible with; هذا الكَلامُ يُناقِضُ تَصْريحاتِ الوَزيرِ this contradicts the minister's statements

تَنَقَّضَ *v* 1 [هُدِمَ] to be destroyed 2 [نُكِثَ] to be breached/violated 3 [بَطَلَ] to be cancelled, to be annulled/invalidated; to be reversed

تَناقَضَ *v* to contradict, to be contradictory/inconsistent; to be in conflict, to be incompatible; تَناقَضَ مع شَيْءٍ to be inconsistent with sth; تَناقَضَ مع نَفْسِهِ to contradict oneself; تَناقَضَ في الأَهْدافِ to have conflicting goals

انْتَقَضَ *v* to be cancelled, to be annulled/invalidated

نَقْض *n* 1 (Law) cancellation, annulment, invalidation; veto; حَقّ النَقْضِ veto (power); اسْتَخْدَمَ حَقَّ النَقْضِ to veto, to exercise one's veto power; نَقْض حُكْمِ المَحْكَمةِ الابْتِدائيّةِ reversal of the lower court's ruling; مَحْكَمة النَقْضِ court of cassation, supreme court; حُكْم قابِل \ غَيْر قابِلٍ للنَقْضِ a revocable/irrevocable judgement 2 [هَدْم] |أَنْقاض| debris; أَنْقاض مَبْنًى (مَهْدومٍ) debris of a (ruined) building

نَقيض *n* 1 [عَكْس] opposite, contrary, antipode; contrast; على النَقيضِ on the contrary; هو نَقيضُ أَخيهِ he and his brother are complete opposites; يَبْدو هذا على النَقيضِ من ذلك this seems to contradict that 2 (Rhet) antithesis

تَناقُض *n* |تَناقُضات| contradiction, conflict; incompatibility; inconsistency, paradox; opposite, antithesis; تَناقُض وِجْدانيّ ambivalence; تَناقُض ظاهِريّ a paradox; تَناقُض الأَهْدافِ conflicting goals; تَناقُض بين ... a contradiction between ...; في أَقْوالِهِ تَناقُضاتٌ عَديدةٌ there are many inconsistencies in his statements

تَناقُضيّ *adj* contradictory; paradoxical

مُتَناقِض *adj* contradictory, conflicting, incompatible, inconsistent; paradoxical; opposite; أَخْبار \ مَواقِف مُتَناقِضة conflicting reports/positions; اتِّجاهات مُتَناقِضة opposite directions; كانَ مُتَناقِضاً to be inconsistent; كانَ مُتَناقِضاً مع شَيْءٍ to be incompatible with sth

4 [الخَبَرَ] to convey, to carry, to communicate; to pass on/down, to quote; to report; نَقَلَ خَبَراً to pass on a message; نَقَلَ عن مَصْدَرٍ عَسْكَرِيٍّ to report from a military source; نَقَلَ عن الوَزِيرِ قَوْلَهُ to quote the minister **5** [في الإذاعةِ] to report on, to cover; نَقَلَ مُباراةً to cover a match **6** (Elec) to conduct, to transmit; نَقَلَ الكَهْرَباءَ to conduct electricity

ناقَلَ *v* to exchange words with

تَنَقَّلَ *v* to move; to travel, to wander; to be transferred/transmitted/conveyed; تَنَقَّلَ من مَكانٍ إلى آخَرَ to travel from one place to another; تَنَقَّلَ بين شَتّى البُلْدانِ to travel through several countries; تَنَقَّلَ الخَبَرُ the news travelled

تَناقَلَ *v* to hand down, to pass on, to transmit; تَناقَلَ قِصَصاً to hand down stories; تَناقَلَ خَبَراً to pass on a news; تَناقَلَ شَفَوِيًّا to transmit orally

اِنْتَقَلَ *v* **1** [إلى مَكانٍ آخَرَ] to move, to relocate; to shift, to pass; اِنْتَقَلَ إلى مَدينةٍ أُخْرى to move to another city; اِنْتَقَلَ إلى شارِعٍ to turn on to a street; اِنْتَقَلَ الاهْتِمامُ \ الانْتِباهُ إلى شَيْءٍ آخَرَ the attention shifted to sth else; يَنْتَقِلُ الحَريقُ إلى العِماراتِ المُجاوِرةِ the fire is spreading to the adjacent buildings **2** [إلى الصَفِّ التالي] to move up; اِنْتَقَلَ إلى الصَفِّ الثاني to move up to the second grade **3** [تَحَوَّلَ] to change, to switch; to proceed; to transfer; اِنْتَقَلَ إلى التَصْويتِ to proceed to the vote; اِنْتَقَلَ إلى (مُعالَجةِ) الأُمورِ العادِيّةِ to proceed to the order of the day; اِنْتَقَلَ إلى مَوْضوعٍ آخَرَ to change the subject; اِنْتَقَلَ إلى وَظيفةٍ أُخْرى to transfer to another job; اِنْتَقَلَ إلى المُراسِلِ في مَكانِ الحَدَثِ to go over to the reporter on the scene **4** (Sport) to transfer; اِنْتَقَلَ إلى نادٍ آخَرَ to transfer to another club

Idiom اِنْتَقَلَ إلى رَحْمةِ اللهِ to die

نَقْل *n* **1** [إيصال] transport (BrE), transportation (AmE); transfer, relocation, move; النَقْل العُموميّ \ العامّ public transport; نَقْل حَضَريّ (Mor) urban traffic; النَقْل البَرّيّ \ بَرًّا road transport; النَقْل البَحْرِيّ sea transport; النَقْل الجَوّيّ air traffic; air transport; النَقْل الجَوّيّ الداخِليّ \ الدُوَليّ domestic/international air traffic; النَقْل بالقِطارِ \ السَفينةِ transport by train/boat; نَقْل البَضائِعِ freight traffic; نَقْل السَوائِلِ

laundry; نَقَعَ الزَبيبَ to soak raisins; نَقَعَ أَوْراقَ الشايِ to steep tea leaves; نَقَعَ اللَحْمَ في الزَيْتِ to marinate meat in oil

أَنْقَعَ *v* to soak; to steep

اِنْتَقَعَ *v* to soak; to steep; يَنْتَقِعُ الغَسيلُ the laundry is soaking

اِسْتَنْقَعَ *v* to be/become stagnant; to be/become swampy

نَقْع *n* |أَنْقُع| **1** [مَصْدَر] soaking; steeping, infusion **2** [مُسْتَنْقَع] stagnant water; swamp

نُقوع *n* dried fruit

نَقيع *n* |أَنْقِعة| infusion

مُسْتَنْقَع *n* |مُسْتَنْقَعات| **1** [أَرْض سَبِخة] swamp, bog, marsh **2** [وَرْطة] quagmire; مُسْتَنْقَع سِياسيّ a political quagmire; مُسْتَنْقَع دَمٍ a bloody quagmire; أَصْبَحَتْ حَرْبُ العِراقِ مُسْتَنْقَعاً the Iraq war turned into a quagmire

مَنْقوع *adj* soaked, saturated, drenched

نَقَفَ *v* |u; نَقْف| **1** [بالأَصابِعِ] to knock, to tap, to rap **2** [الكَتْكوت] to hatch out

نِقْف *n* |أَنْقاف| chick

نَقْفة *n* a snap of the fingers

مَنْقوف *adj* broken (*eggshell, bone, e.g.*)

نَقَّ *v* |i; نَقيق| to croak; to cluck; to rumble, to grumble; تَنِقُّ الضَفادِعُ frogs croak; تَنِقُّ ضَفادِعُ بَطْنِهِ his stomach is rumbling

نَقّاق *n* grumbler

نَقيق *n* cluck, clucking, cackle; croak, croaking; نَقيق الدَجاجِ the clucking of a chicken; نَقيق الضُفْدَعِ the croaking of frogs

نَقَلَ *v* |u; نَقْل| **1** [حَوَّلَ] to transport, to carry, to move; to transfer, to transmit; to ship, to fly; نَقَلَ بالطائِرةِ to transport by air; نَقَلَ الفَحْمَ \ النَفْطَ to transport coal/oil; نَقَلَ مُسافِرينَ to carry passengers; نَقَلَ الأُكْسِجينَ to carry oxygen; نَقَلَ خِزانةً to move a cupboard; نَقَلَ سُلُطاتِهِ to hand over one's powers; نَقَلَ شَيْئاً \ شَخْصاً إلى ... to transport sth/sb to ...; نَقَلَ شَخْصاً إلى قِسْمٍ \ سِجْنٍ آخَرَ to transfer sb to another department/prison; نَقَلَ مَرَضاً إلى شَخْصٍ to transmit a disease to sb; نَقَلَ البَياناتِ الرَقْمِيّةَ to transmit digital data **2** [نَسَخَ] to copy, to reproduce; نَقَلَ شَيْئاً حَرْفِيًّا من كِتابٍ to reproduce sth word for word **3** [تَرْجَمَ] to translate, to render; نَقَلَ إلى لُغةٍ أُخْرى to translate into another language

انْتِقال *n* |انْتِقالات| transfer, relocation, move; switching; انْتِقال إلى من شَيْءٍ إلى آخَر switching from sth to sth else; عيد انْتِقالِ العَذْراءِ a relocation to The Hague; مَدينةِ لاهاي (Chr) Assumption

انْتِقاليّ *adj* ① intermediate, transitional, interim; فَتْرة \ مَرْحَلة انْتِقاليّة transition period/phase; حُكومة انْتِقاليّة interim government; شَكْل انْتِقاليّ intermediate form ② [مُعْدٍ] communicable, transmittable; أَمْراض انْتِقاليّة communicable diseases

تَنَقُّل *n* |تَنَقُّلات| movement, transportation, transfer; حُرّيّة التَنَقُّل freedom of movement

مُتَنَقِّل *adj* mobile, portable; travelling; هاتِف مُتَنَقِّل mobile phone, mobile (BrE), cell phone (AmE)

مُناقَلة *n* relocation

مِنْقَلة *n* |مَناقِلُ| ① [أَداة] protractor ② [لُعْبة] *a board game popular in Africa, the Middle East and Central Asia*

مَنْقول *adj* |مَنْقولات| ① [نَقّال] movable, portable, transportable, mobile; مُمْتَلَكات \ أَمْلاك مَنْقولة, مَنْقولات moveables, personal property/effects; أَمْلاك مَنْقولة وَغَيْر مَنْقولةٍ movable and immovable property, personal property and real estate ② [مَحْمول] transported; بَضائِع مَنْقولة goods transported ③ [من شَخْصٍ إلى آخَر] transmitted; أَمْراض مَنْقولة جِنْسيًّا sexually transmitted diseases

نَقَمَ, نَقِمَ *v* |i; نَقْم, نَقَم| |على| to hate, to grudge, to harbor malice against; to be angry at; نَقَمَ على شَخْصٍ to hate sb; to be angry at sb; نَقَمَ على شَخْصٍ شَيْئاً to begrudge sb sth

انْتَقَمَ *v* to avenge, to take revenge, to retaliate; انْتَقَمَ لِشَيْءٍ to avenge sth, to take revenge for sth; انْتَقَمَ لِهَزيمةٍ to avenge a defeat; انْتَقَمَ من شَخْصٍ to take revenge on sb; انْتَقَمَ من خَصْمٍ to retaliate against an opponent

ناقِم *adj* angry, furious; resentful, revengeful, vindictive; indignant, discontent; ناقِم على شَخْصٍ angry at sb

نِقْمة, نَقْمة *n* |نِقْمات, نِقَم| resentment, grudge, spite; punishment, curse; أَثارَ النِقْمةَ to cause resentment; تَحَوَّلَت النِعْمةُ إلى نِقْمةٍ the blessing turned into a curse

transport of fluids; نَقْل المَوادِّ الخَطيرةِ transport of hazardous materials; نَقْل الدَمِ a blood transfusion; نَقْل المَرَضِ transmission of the disease; نَقْل البَياناتِ data transmission; نَقْل شَرِكةٍ إلى بَلَدٍ آخَرَ the relocation of a company to another country; وَسيلة نَقْلٍ means of transport; شَرِكة نَقْلٍ transport company; وَثيقة النَقْلِ waybill; مُتَعَهِّد النَقْلِ carrier; مَنْع النَقْلِ a ban on transport; خِدْمة النَقْلِ shuttle service; خِدْمة النَقْلِ بين لُنْدُن وَبَيْروتَ shuttle service between London and Beirut; قابِل للنَقْلِ transferable; قُرْص قابِل للنَقْلِ a removable disk ② (Phys) conductivity; نَقْل حَراريّ \ كَهْرَبائيّ thermal/electrical conductivity; نَقْل جَيِّد للحَرارةِ high heat conductivity ③ (Mech) transmission ④ [أَحاديث] conveying, passing on; نَقْلاً عن ... on the authority of ..., as passed on by ...

ناقِل Ⓐ *adj* conducting, conductive; سِلْك ناقِل للكَهْرَباءِ electric cable
Ⓑ *n* |نُقّال, نَقَلة, ناقِلونَ| ① [حَمّال] carrier, courier; conveyor ② [ناسِخ] copier, copyist, transcriber; transmitter ③ [مُتَرْجِم] translator ④ (Phys) conductor; ناقِل تَسَلْسُليّ عامّ USB port; ناقِل حَرَكةٍ gear lever (BrE), gear shift (AmE); ناقِل السُرْعةِ transmission; ناقِل حَرَكةٍ أوتوماتيكيّ \ يَدَويّ an automatic/manual transmission; ناقِل للحَرارةِ a conductor of heat

ناقِلة *n* carrier, transporter; tanker; ناقِلة طائِراتٍ aircraft carrier; ناقِلة نَفْطٍ oil tanker; ناقِلة نَفْطٍ ضَخْمة supertanker

نَقّال *adj* portable, transportable; mobile; هاتِف نَقّال mobile phone, mobile (BrE), cell (phone) (AmE); حاسوب نَقّال laptop; كُرْسيّ نَقّال wheelchair; عِيادة \ مَنْزِل نَقّال(ة) a mobile clinic/home

نَقّالة *n* ① [للجَرْحى] stretcher, gurney (AmE); نَقّالة طِبّيّة stretcher; على نَقّالةٍ on a stretcher; وَضَعَ \ حُمِلَ على نَقّالةٍ to place/be transported on a stretcher ② [عَرَبة يَدٍ] wheelbarrow ③ [سَيّارة] truck, lorry (BrE)

نَقْلة *n* move, step; بِنَقْلةٍ واحِدةٍ in one move; نَقْلة نَوْعيّة a quantum leap, a qualitative step

نُقْلة *n* |نُقَل| ① [نَقْل] move, removal, relocation, transfer ② [نَميمة] slander, gossip

انْتِقام *n* revenge, vengeance; reprisal, retaliation, retribution; انْتِقاماً لِ ... in retaliation for ...; انْتِقام لِقَتْلِ قَرِيبٍ revenge for the murder of a relative; عَمَلِيّة انْتِقام retaliatory action; تَعَطُّش إلى الانْتِقامِ ,مَشاعِر \ روح الانْتِقامِ vindictiveness; قامَ بالانْتِقامِ to take revenge; دَعا إلى الانْتِقامِ to call for revenge; نوى \ اسْتَهْدَفَ \ تَعَمَّدَ الانْتِقامَ ,رَغِبَ في الانْتِقامِ to be intent on revenge

انْتِقاميّ *adj* revengeful, retaliatory, vindictive, retributive; عَمَلِيّة انْتِقامية ,رَدّ \ عَمَل \ هُجوم انْتِقاميّ retaliatory action

مُنْتَقِم **A** *adj* revengeful, retaliatory, vindictive, retributive **B** *n* 1 [ثائِر] avenger, revenger 2 (Islam) المُنْتَقِم the Avenger (*one of the names of God*)

‹ **نَقْنَق** *v* |i; نَقْنَقة| to croak; تُنَقْنِقُ الضَفادِعُ frogs croak

‹ **نَقَهَ ,نَقِهَ** *v* |a; نَقْه ,نُقوه| to recover, to recuperate, to convalesce; نَقِهَ من مَرَضٍ to recover from a disease

نَقاهة *n* recovery, recuperation, convalescence; دار النَقاهةِ nursing home; recovery center; فَتْرة النَقاهةِ recovery period

‹ **نَقِيَ** *v* |a; نُقاوة ,نَقاوة ,نَقاء| to be pure/clean

نَقّى *v* 1 [خَلَّصَ من الشَوائِبِ] to clean; to purify, to clarify; نَقّى الماءَ to purify water; نَقّى الأَجْواءَ to clear the air 2 [اخْتارَ] to choose, to select; to elect

انْتَقى *v* to choose, to select; to elect; انْتَقى عِباراتِهِ \ كَلِماتِهِ بِدِقّةٍ to choose one's words carefully

نَقِيّ *adj* |أَنْقِياءُ ,نِقاء| clean, pure, undiluted; هَواء نَقِيّ fresh air; ضَمير نَقِيّ a clear conscience

نَقاء *n* purity, cleanness; clarity, clearness; نَقاء عِرْقِيّ \ العِرْق racial purity; نَقاء الضَميرِ clarity of conscience; نَقاء الهَواءِ \ الماءِ cleanness of the air/water

نَقاوة *n* purity, cleanness; clarity, clearness

انْتِقاء *n* selection, choice; انْتِقاء طَبيعيّ natural selection

انْتِقائيّ *adj* selective; إجْهاض انْتِقائيّ selective abortion; سِياسة قُبولٍ انْتِقائيّة a selective admission policy

انْتِقائيّة *n* selectivity

تَنْقِية *n* purification, cleaning, cleansing; clearing, clarifying; تَنْقِية الأَجْواءِ clearing the air; تَنْقِية الماءِ water purification

مُنْتَقًى **A** *adj* chosen, selected **B** *n* chosen one

‹ **أَنْقى** *v* to clean, to purify

‹ **نَكَبَ** *v* |u; نُكوب ,نَكْب| 1 [مالَ] to deviate, to swerve; نَكَبَت الريحُ the wind changed 2 [أَصابَ بِنَكْبةٍ] to aflict, to affect; to be ill-affected; نَكَبَهُ الدَهْرُ fate has been unkind to him

نَكَّبَ *v* to divert, to deflect

تَنَكَّبَ *v* 1 [أَخَذَ على عاتِقِهِ] to take on, to shoulder; تَنَكَّبَ شَيْئاً to take on sth; تَنَكَّبَ مَسْؤوليّةَ شَيْءٍ to take responsibility for sth; تَنَكَّبَ بُنْدُقيّةً to shoulder a rifle 2 [اتَّكَأَ] |على| to lean/recline/rest on; تَنَكَّبَ على شَيْءٍ to lean on sth 3 [تَجَنَّبَ] to avoid; to prevent; تَنَكَّبَ الخَطَرَ to avoid danger 4 [مالَ] to bend away, to turn off; تَنَكَّبَ عن الطَريقِ to turn off the road

نَكْب *n* |نُكوب| disaster, catastrophe, calamity

نَكْبة *n* |نَكَبات| disaster, catastrophe, calamity; نَكَبات disaster; نَكْبة فِلَسْطينَ ,النَكْبة (الفِلَسْطينيّة) al-Nakba, the Catastrophe (*the events of 1948, when many Palestinians were displaced from their homeland by the creation of the new state of Israel*)

مَنْكِب *n* |مَناكِبُ| 1 (Anat) shoulder; مَنْكِبانِ عَريضانِ broad shoulders 2 [مُرْتَفَع] highland, upland

مَنْكوب **A** *adj* afflicted, affected, stricken; duped; المِنْطَقة \ الأُسْرة المَنْكوبة the stricken area/family; السُكّان المَنْكوبونَ the affected population **B** *n* victim; مَنْكوبو الفَيَضانِ \ الزِلْزالِ the victims of the flood/earthquake; عَوَّضَ المَنْكوبينَ to compensate the victims

‹ **نَكَتَ** *v* |u; نَكْت| to scratch (off); to scrape (off)

نَكَّتَ *v* to joke, to jest; نَكَّتَ على شَخْصٍ to joke about sb

نَكّات **A** *adj* funny, witty, amusing **B** *n* 1 [شَخْص] joker, jester 2 (Zool) avocet (*Recurvirostra*)

نُكْتة *n* |نِكات ,نُكَت| joke, jest, gag, anecdote; نُكْتة جَميلة \ جَيِّدة a good joke; نُكْتة بارِدة \ سَمِجة a stupid joke; نُكْتة مُبْتَذَلة \ ظَريفة a dirty joke; نُكَت على البُخَلاءِ jokes about misers; حَكى \ رَوى \ أَلْقى نُكَتاً to tell jokes; أَفْسَدَ النُكْتةَ to ruin a joke

‹ **نِكْتارين** *n* nectarine

نَكَثَ *v* |i-u; **نَكْث**| to violate, to breach, to break; نَكَثَ وَعْدَهُ to break one's promise

نَكَحَ *v* |a-i-u; **نِكاح**| **1** [تَزَوَّجَ] to marry, to wed **2** [جامَعَ] to have sex with, to make love to

أَنْكَحَ *v* to marry off, to give in marriage; أَنْكَحَهُ إيّاها والِدُها her father married her off to him

نِكاح *n* **1** [زَواج] marriage, matrimony, wedlock; عَقْد نِكاحٍ marriage certificate **2** [جِماع] sex, intercourse, lovemaking

نَكِدَ, **نَكَدَ** *v* |a; **نَكَد**, **نَكاد**| to be unhappy/miserable; نَكِدَ عَيْشُهُ his life was unhappy

نَكَّدَ *v* to spoil, to mar; نَكَّدَ عَيْشَ شَخْصٍ to make sb's life difficult

ناكَدَ *v* to harass

نَكْد *n* |أَنْكاد| hardship, trouble, misery

نَكَد *n* |إنْكاد| misfortune, trouble, misery

نَكِد *adj* |أَنْكاد| **1** [شَكِس] grumpy, bad-tempered, irritable, cantankerous; رَجُل عَجوز نَكِد grumpy old man **2** [شاقّ] difficult, hard, complex

نَكَديّ *adj* moody

مَنْكود *adj* |مَناكيدُ| unhappy, miserable; (شَخْص) مَنْكود الحَظِّ unlucky (person)

نَكِرَ *v* |a; **نَكير**, **نُكور**, **نُكْر**, **نَكَر**, **نُكُر**| to be ignorant/unknowing/ unaware of; نَكِرَ شَيْئاً to be ignorant of sth

نَكَّرَ *v* **1** [قَنَّعَ] to disguise, to mask **2** (Gram) *to use a noun in its indefinite form*

أَنْكَرَ *v* **1** [نفى] to deny; to refute, to disprove; أَنْكَرَ تُهْمَةً to refute an accusation; أَنْكَرَ الحَقائِقَ to deny the facts; ... أَنْكَرَ أَنّ to deny that ...; أَنْكَرَ أَنَّهُ عُضْوٌ في تَجَمُّعٍ to deny membership of a group; لم يُثْبِتْ ولم يُنْكِرْ شَيْئاً to neither confirm nor deny sth **2** [لم يَعْتَرِفْ بِهِ] to disavow, to renounce, to repudiate; أَنْكَرَ مَبادِئَهُ \ مَوْقِفَهُ to disavow one's principles/position; أَنْكَرَ جَميلَ شَخْصٍ to deny sb their right; أَنْكَرَ على شَخْصٍ حَقَّهُ to be ungrateful to sb **3** [عابَ] to denounce

تَنَكَّرَ *v* **1** [تَغَيَّرَ] to disguise, to mask, to dress up; to be disguised/ masked; تَنَكَّرَ في لِباسِ امْرَأَةٍ to be disguised in women's clothing; تَنَكَّرَ في زِيِّ الشُّرْطَةِ to be dressed in police uniforms **2** [ل|أَنْكَرَ] to deny; to treat with contempt or neglect; تَنَكَّرَ للحُقوقِ المَشْروعةِ لِشَخْصٍ to deny sb's lawful rights

اسْتَنْكَرَ *v* to disapprove of; to criticize, to rebuke; to denounce, to condemn; اسْتَنْكَرَ شَيْئاً to disapprove of sth; اسْتَنْكَرَ شَيْئاً بِشِدَّةٍ to strongly condemn sth; اسْتَنْكَرَ سُلوكَ \ تَصَرُّفاتِ شَخْصٍ to criticize sb's behaviour

ناكِر *adj* denying; ناكِر المَعْروفِ unappreciative, ungrateful

نُكْران *n* denial; disavowal; نُكْران الجَميلِ ingratitude; نُكْران الذاتِ selflessness; شَيْء لا يُمْكِنُ نُكْرانُهُ sth that can not be denied

نَكِرة *adj* indefinite (*noun*)

نَكير **A** *adj* difficult, hard

B *n* **1** [إنْكار] denial **2** (Islam) Nakir (*one of the two angels who test the faith of the dead in their tombs*)

اسْتِنْكار *n* |اسْتِنْكارات| disapproval, condemnation, denunciation; اسْتِنْكار شَديد اللَهْجة a strongly worded denunciation; أَبْدى اسْتِنْكارَهُ to show one's disapproval; أَعْرَبَ عن اسْتِنْكارِهِ لِشَيْءٍ to express one's condemnation of sth

إنْكار *n* |إنْكارات| **1** [نَفْي] denial; refutation, disproof; إنْكار الذاتِ self-denial, selflessness; إنْكار المَحْرَقةِ Holocaust denial; كابَرَ في الإنْكارِ to deny persistently; لا يُمْكِنُ إنْكارُهُ undeniable; كانَ هذا لا يُمْكِنُ إنْكارُهُ there's no denying this; في حالةِ إنْكارٍ to be in a state of denial **2** [رَفْض] disavowal, renunciation, repudiation

إنْكاريّ *adj* denying; negative; مَوْقِف إنْكاريّ a negative standpoint

أَنْكَر *adj* |dipt| reprehensible, horrible, awful; جَريمة نَكْراء a heinous crime; هَزيمة نَكْراء a crushing defeat

تَنَكُّر *n* |تَنَكُّرات| **1** [تَخَفٍّ] disguise **2** [ل|إنْكار] denial, denying; تَنَكُّر للحَقيقةِ denial of the truth

تَنَكُّريّ *adj* masked, disguised, dressed up; حَفْلة تَنَكُّريّة a fancy dress party (BrE), a costume party (AmE)

تَنْكير *n* indefiniteness; أَداة التَنْكير the indefinite article

مُتَنَكِّر *adj* masked, disguised, dressed up; جاءَ مُتَنَكِّراً في مَلابِسِ إمْرَأةٍ he arrived, dressed up as a woman

مُسْتَنْكَر *adj* objectionable, reprehensible, condemnable

مُنْكَر **A** *adj* **1** [فَظيع] reprehensible, detestable, objectionable; هَزيمة مُنْكَرة a rout, a humiliating defeat **2** [مَنْفيّ] denied, refuted **3** [مَرْفوض] disavowed, renounced **4** (Isl Law) *not prohibited but discouraged*

B *n* **1** [عَمَل وَحْشيّ] atrocity; الفَحْشاء والمُنْكَر indecency and evil; ارْتَكَبَ مُنْكَراً to commit an atrocity **2** (Islam) Munkar (*one of the two angels who test the faith of the dead in their tombs*)

مُنَكَّر *adj* indefinite; اسْم مُنَكَّر indefinite noun

‹ **نَكَزَ** *v* |u; نَكْز| to goad on, to urge on, to incite

نَكْزة *n* poke

‹ **نَكَسَ** *v* |u; نَكْس| **1** [العَلَمَ] to fly at half-mast (*flags*) **2** [قَلَبَ] to reverse, to turn (around), to invert; نُكِسَ to relapse **3** [طَأْطَأَ] to bow, to bend, to incline; نَكَسَ رَأْسَهُ to bow one's head

نَكَّسَ *v* **1** [العَلَمَ] to fly at half-mast (*flags*); نُكِّسَت الأَعْلامُ the flags were flown at half-mast **2** [قَلَّبَ] to reverse, to turn (around), to invert; نَكَّسَ عائِداً إلى البَيْتِ he turned around and went back home **3** [طَأْطَأَ] to bow, to bend, to incline; نَكَّسَ رَأْسَهُ to bow one's head

انْتَكَسَ *v* **1** [المَريضُ] to relapse, to have a relapse **2** [انْقَلَبَ] to be reversed/inverted

نُكْس *n* relapse; deterioration

ناكِس *adj* relapsing, recurrent

نَكْسة *n* |نَكَسات| relapse, setback; recession, stagnation; deterioration; النَكْسة the Six Day War, the War of 1967 (*between Arab states and Israel*); نَكْسة عَسْكَرِيّة a military defeat; نَكْسة اقْتِصادِيّة an economic recession; نَكْسة مَريضٍ a relapse of the patient; أُصيبَ ب \ تَعَرَّضَ لِنَكْسةٍ to experience a setback

انْتِكاس *n* setback; relapse; deterioration

انْتِكاسة *n* setback, regression; انْتِكاسة خَطيرة a dangerous setback

تَنَكُّس *n* degeneration; regression

مُنَكَّس *adj* **1** [مُقَلَّب] lowered, bowed; reversed, inverted; مُنَكَّس الرَأْسِ with head bowed **2** [العَلَم] كانَ العَلَمُ مُنَكَّساً the flag flew at half mast

‹ **نَكَشَ** *v* |u; نَكْش| **1** [بِئْراً] to dredge; to clear out **2** [الأَرْضَ] to spade, to turn over; نَكَشَ التُرْبةَ to turn (over) the soil

مِنْكاش *n* |مَناكيش| dredge; hoe

مِنْكَش *n* |مَناكِش| pickaxe; hoe

مَنْكوش *n* unruly

‹ **نَكَصَ** *v* |u; نَكْص, نُكوص, مَنْكَص| to withdraw, to recoil, to retreat; to recede, to regress, to decrease; نَكَصَ على عَقِبَيْهِ to turn on one's heels

نُكوص *n* withdrawal, retreat; regression, decrease; reneging, going back on; النُكوص عن وَعْدِهِ reneging on one's promise

‹ **نَكْعة** *n* نَكْعة فُطْرٍ mushroom cap

‹ **نَكَفَ** *v* |u; نَكْف| [عن] to condescend to, to look down on, to disdain; to reject, to dismiss; نَكَفَ عن شَيْءٍ to look down on sth; to reject sth

اسْتَنْكَفَ *v* **1** [من, عن] to decline, to reject, to refuse **2** [من, عن] to be vain/pompous, to consider oneself above; يَسْتَنْكِفُ من العَمَلِ اليَدَويِّ he thinks he's too good to do manual labour

نُكاف *n* (Med) mumps; كانَ مُصاباً بالنُكافِ to have the mumps

نُكافيّ *adj* parotid; غُدّة نُكافيّة parotid gland; الْتِهاب الغُدّةِ النُكافيّةِ mumps

نَكَفة *n* parotid gland

مُناكَفة *n* **1** [خِلاف] argument; مُناكَفة بين الوَزيرِ والرَئيسِ an argument between the minister and the president **2** [إزْعاج] annoyance **3** [مُعارَضة] opposition; provocation; مُناكَفة للحُكومةِ opposing/provoking the government

‹ **نَكَّلَ** *v* |ب| to torture; to punish; to maltreat; نَكَّلَ بِمُعارِضينَ سِياسيّينَ \ بالسُجَناءِ to torture political opponents/the prisoners

أَنْكَلَ *v* to drive/force back

نِكْل *n* |أَنْكال, نُكول| **1** [حَديدة اللِجامِ] bit **2** [قَيْد] chain, shackle **3** [مَعْدِن] see نَيْكَل

نَكال *n* exemplary punishment, example

تَنْكيل *n* torture; abuse; التَنْكيل بِشَخْصٍ the torture of sb; تَعَرَّضَ للتَنْكيلِ to be tortured; ارْتَكَبَ عَمَليّاتِ التَنْكيلِ to commit torture

لانَمَطيّ *adj* atypical; اِلْتِهاب رِئَويّ لانَمَطيّ atypical pneumonia

‹ **نَمَّق** *v* 1 [زَيَّنَ] to embellish, to decorate, to adorn 2 [الصورةَ] to retouch (*photos*)

تَنْميق *n* 1 [تَزْيين] flowery prose 2 [صورة] retouching (*photos*)

مُنَمَّق *adj* elegant, flowery, ornate; embellished, decorated, adorned; حُروف مُنَمَّقة decorative letters; كَلام مُنَمَّق flowery words, bombast

‹ **نَمِلَ** *v* |a; نَمَل| to tingle, to prickle; تَنْمَلُ أَنامِلي my fingertips are tingling

نَمْل *n coll* |نِمال| ant; مُسْتَعْمَرة نَمْلٍ anthill; آكِل نَمْلٍ anteater; سورة النَمْل The Ant (*Sura 27*); لا يُؤْذي نَمْلة he wouldn't hurt a fly

نَمَل *n* tingle, prickle; أَحَسَّ بِنَمَلٍ to feel a tingle

نَمْلة *n* |نَمْل, نَمْلات| 1 (Med) eczema 2 (Zool) see نَمْل

نَمْليّة *n* pantry, larder (*a cupboard to protect food from insects*)

أَنْمُلة, أَنْمَلة *n* |أَنامِل| fingertip; أَنامِل رَشيقة nimble fingers; قَيْد أُنْمُلةٍ a very small amount, just a little bit; لم يَتَقَدَّم قَيدَ أُنْمُلةٍ to not get anywhere; لم يَتَغَيَّرْ قَيْدَ أُنْمُلةٍ he hasn't changed one bit; تَنْمَلُ أَنامِلي my fingertips are tingling

تَنْميل *n* tingle

‹ **نَمَّ** *v* |i-u; نَمّ| 1 [عن] [أَشارَ] to show, to reflect, to indicate, to betray; نَمَّ عن شَيْءٍ to indicate sth; نَمَّ عن جَهْلٍ عَميق to betray a deep ignorance 2 [ثَرْثَرَ] to stir up/make trouble; to slander, to gossip, to tattle; نَمَّ بين الناس to stir up trouble between people

نَمّ *n* slander, gossip

نَمّام *n* informer; slanderer, gossip

نَميمة *n* |نَمائِم| slander, gossip

‹ **نَمْنَمَ** *v* |i; نَمْنَمة| to adorn, to decorate, to embellish

نَمْنَمة *n* wren (*Troglodytidae*)

مُنَمْنَم *adj* adorned, decorated, embellished

مُنَمْنَمة *n* miniature

‹ **نَما** *v* |u; نُموّ| to grow; to develop; to increase, to rise; نَما نُمُوًّا طَبيعيًّا to develop naturally; نَما بِنِسْبة ١٠ في المِائة to increase by 10%; يَنْمو الأَطْفالُ the children are growing up

‹ **نَكَّهَ** *v* to flavour

نَكْهة *n* 1 [رائِحة] aroma, flavour 2 [مادّة] flavouring, seasoning

‹ **نَكى** *v* |i; إِنكاية| to defeat, to subdue; to hurt, to harm, to injure

نِكاية *n* annoyance, irritation; discontent, dissatisfaction; نِكايةً بِشَخْصٍ out of dissatisfaction with sb; to spite sb

‹ **نَمْذَجَ** *v* |i; نَمْذَجة| see نموذج

‹ **نَمِرَ** *v* |a; نَمَر, نُمْرة| to become furious

نَمَّرَ *v* 1 [رَقَّمَ] to number 2 [عَبَسَ] to become furious

تَنَمَّرَ *v* to become furious

نَمِر, نِمْر, نَمِر *n* |أَنْمار, نُمُر, نُمور| tiger; leopard; panther; النَمِر الآسْيَويّ Asian tiger

نِمْرة *n* number; النِمْرةُ غَلَطٌ the number's wrong

أَنْمَر *adj* |dipt; نُمْر| speckled; striped

مُتَنَمِّر *n* bully

‹ **نُمْرُقة, نُمْرُق** *n* |نَمارِقُ| cushion, pillow

‹ **نامَسَ** *v* 1 [الصائِدُ] to hide in a hunting lodge 2 [سارَّ] to confide a secret to

نِمْس *n coll* |نُموس| ferret (*Mustela putorius furo*); mongoose

ناموس *n* listed alphabetically

نِمْساويّ *adj*, *n* Austrian

النِمْسا *n* Austria

‹ **نَمِشَ** *v* |a; نَمَش| to be freckled

نَمَش *n* freckle

نَمِش *adj* freckled; وَجْه نَمِش a freckled face

أَنْمَش *adj* |dipt; نُمْش| freckled

تَنْميش *n* etching

مُنَمَّش *adj* freckled

‹ **نَمَط** *n* |أَنْماط, نِماط| manner, way, method, style; نَمَط فِكْريّ \ من التَفْكير way of thinking; نَمَط الحَياة lifestyle; على النَمَطِ التَقْليديّ in the traditional way; على النَمَطِ الغَرْبيّ in Western style; على هذا النَمَطِ in this manner

نَمَطيّ *adj* characteristic, typical, stereotypical, distinctive; صورة نَمَطيّة stereotype; شَخْصيّة نَمَطيّة a distinctive personality; حاوِية نَمَطيّة (Meas) TEU, standard container

تَنْميط *n* standardization; typology, classification

نمى *v* |i; نَمْي ,نَماء ,نَمِيّة| ⟨1⟩ [زادَ] to increase, to rise, to grow; to expand; to make progress; نَمى المالُ the capital increased ⟨2⟩ [شاعَ] to be spread/propagated; to become known; نَمى الحَديثُ the news spread ⟨3⟩ [رَفَعَهُ في الإسْنادِ إلى] to attribute, to ascribe

نَمّى *v* to develop, to stimulate; to increase, to make grow/advance/expand; نَمّى قُدْرَتَهُ to increase one's capacity/capability; نَمّى عَلاقةً to develop a relationship; نَمّى الاقْتِصادَ to stimulate the economy

أَنْمى *v* to increase, to make grow/advance/expand; to develop; أَنْمى ثَرْوَتَهُ to increase one's wealth; أَنْمى المَناطِقَ الرِيفيّةَ to develop the countryside

تَنامى *v* to grow, to increase; to develop, to advance; تَنامى تَدْريجاً to increase gradually; تَنامَتْ مَشاعِرُ خَيْبةِ أَمَلٍ feelings of disappointment grew

انْتَمى *v* |إلى| to belong to, to be a part of; to join, to be/become a member of, to be/become affiliated with; انْتَمى إلى حِزْبٍ to join a party; انْتَمى إلى الثَدْيِيّاتِ to be a mammal

نُمُوّ *n* growth, increase; progress; development; نُمُوّ اقْتِصاديّ economic growth; نُمُوّ عَقْلِيّ intellectual development; نُمُوّ عَشْوائيّ indiscriminate growth; نُمُوّ سُكّانيّ \ ديموغرافيّ population growth; أَرْقام النُمُوّ growth figures; نِسْبة \ مُعَدَّل النُمُوّ growth rate; هُرْمون النُمُوّ growth hormone; كامِل النُمُوّ full-grown; أَكْمَلَ نُمُوَّهُ to reach full growth; في طَوْرِ النُمُوّ growing, developing; سَجَّلَتْ أَرْباحُ الشَرِكةِ نُمُوّاً نِسْبَتُهُ ٣٠ في المِائةِ the company's profit experienced a growth of 30 per cent; تَشْهَدُ هذه المِنْطَقةُ نُمُوّاً اقْتِصاديّاً this region is flourishing economically

نامٍ *adj* developing, advancing; growing, increasing; دَوْلة نامِية developing country; أَسْواق نامِية emerging markets

نَماء *n* growth, increase; development; نَماء اقْتِصاديّ economic development

نَمائيّ *adj* developmental; أَهْداف نَمائيّة development goals

انْتِماء *n* membership, affiliation, association; belonging; انْتِماء عِرْقيّ ethnicity; انْتِماء إلى تَنْظيمٍ إرْهابيٍّ membership of a terrorist organization

إنْماء *n* development, advancement, growth; إنْماء مُتَوازِن balanced growth

إنْمائيّ *adj* development *(before n)*; مَشْروع إنْمائيّ development project; بَرْنامَج الأُمَمِ المُتَّحِدةِ الإنْمائيّ United Nations Development Programme, UNDP

تَنْمَويّ *adj* developmental, growth-related; مَشْروع تَنْمَويّ development project

تَنْمِية *n* development, growth; تَنْمِية مُسْتَدامة \ مُسْتَديمة sustainable development; مُساعَدات التَنْمِيةِ development aid

لامُنْتَمٍ *adj* |اللامُنْتَمون| ideologically independent

مُتَنامٍ *adj* gradually growing/developing/increasing; غَضَب مُتَنامٍ growing anger; لَعِبَ دَوْراً مُتَنامِياً to play a growing role

مُنْتَمٍ **A** *adj* belonging, affiliated; committed; غَيْر مُنْتَمٍ إلى حِزْبٍ non-partisan **B** *n* member; المُنْتَمون إلى النِقابةِ the members of the union

نَمْذَجَ *v* |i; نَمْذَجة| to model

نَموذَج، نُموذَج، أُنْموذَج *n* |نَماذِج| model, type; shape, form; paradigm, pattern; example, sample; نَموذَج أَصْليّ \ أَوَّل archetype; prototype

نَموذَجيّ *adj* ⟨1⟩ [مَنْسوب إلى النَموذَج] model *(before n)*; exemplary, characteristic, typical; مِثال نَموذَجيّ a classic example; مَزْرَعة نَموذَجيّة a model farm ⟨2⟩ [مِثاليّ] ideal, perfect; ظُروف نَموذَجيّة ideal conditions

نَهْ *v* see ونى

نَهَبَ *v* |a-u; نَهْب| to loot, to plunder, to ransack; to steal from, to rob; نَهَب بَيْتاً to steal from a house; نَهَب بَنْكاً to rob a bank

تَناهَبَ *v* to race, to run

انْتَهَبَ *v* to steal, to rob; to seize; انْتَهَبَ شَيْئاً to steal sth

نَهْب *n* |إنْهاب| ⟨1⟩ [سَرِقة] robbery; looting, plundering; عَمَلِيّة نَهْبٍ robbery; سَلْب وَنَهْب looting ⟨2⟩ [ما يُؤْخَذُ] loot, booty, plunder ⟨3⟩ [الحِصانِ] gallop

ناهِب *n* thief, robber, plunderer; ناهِب البُنوكِ bank robber; ناهِبو ثَرَواتِ بُلْدانِهِمْ those who plunder their countries' riches

نَهّاب **A** *adj* looting, plundering **B** *n* robber; looter, plunderer

تَنَهُّد *n* |تَنَهُّدات| sigh; كَتَم \ حَبَسَ تَنَهُّداً to suppress a sigh

تَنْهيدة *n* sigh; تَنَهَّدَ تَنْهيدةً عَميقةً to sigh deeply

〈 **نَهَرَ** *v* |a; نَهْر| ◻1 [زَجَرَ] to rebuff, to rebuke; to rant at, to rage against; نَهَرَ شَخْصاً بِشِدّةٍ to severely rebuke sb ◻2 [جَرى] to flow, to stream; نَهَرَ الماءُ الأَرْضَ the water flowed over the land

اِنْتَهَرَ *v* ◻1 [زَجَرَ] to scold, to rebuke; to rebuff ◻2 [جَرى] to stream, to flow

نَهْر *n* |أَنْهُر ,أَنْهار ,نُهور| river; نَهْر جَليديّ glacier; نَهْر النيلِ the Nile River; مَجْرى نَهْرٍ riverbed; river course; ضِفّة \ مَصَبّ النَّهْرِ river bank/mouth; فَرَس النَّهْرِ hippopotamus; في النَّهْرِ on the river; عند \ على طولِ النَّهْرِ by/along the river; ما بين النَّهْرَيْنِ Mesopotamia; سارَ في نَهْرٍ to navigate a river; عَبَرَ نَهْراً to cross a river

نَهار *n* |أَنْهُر ,نُهُر| day, daytime; نَهار أَمْسِ \ السَّبْتِ yesterday/Saturday; نِصْف نَهارٍ noon; في النَّهارِ ,نَهاراً in the daytime, during the day, by day; لَيْلَ نَهارَ ,لَيْلاً نَهاراً day and night; في وَضَحِ \ عِزِّ النَّهارِ ,جِهاراً نَهاراً in broad daylight; نَهارُكَ سَعيدٌ! good day!; طَلَعَ النَّهارُ day was breaking

نَهارِيّ *adj* diurnal, daytime (*before n*), daylight (*before n*), day (*before n*); مَرْكَز الرِّعايةِ النَّهارِيّة day care centre

نَهْرِيّ *adj* river (*before n*); (Geol) fluvial; نَقْل \ مِلاحة نَهْرِيّ(ة) river transportation

نُهَيْر *n* |نُهَيْرات| small river, creek, brook; tributary; rivulet

〈 **نَهَزَ** *v* |a; نَهْز| to push, to shove; to urge on

ناهَزَ *v* to approach; to reach; ناهَزَ السَّبْعينَ من عُمْرِه to be nearing seventy; ناهَزَ عَدَدُهُم المِلْيونَيْنِ they numbered nearly two million

اِنْتَهَزَ *v* to seize, to grab; اِنْتَهَزَ الفُرْصةَ to seize the opportunity

نُهْزة *n* |نُهَز| chance, opportunity

اِنْتِهازِيّ **A** *adj* opportunistic; Machiavellian; سُلوك اِنْتِهازِيّ opportunistic behaviour

B *n* opportunist; profiteer

اِنْتِهازيّة *n* opportunism

〈 **نُهَس** *n* |نِهْسان| shrike (*Laniidae*); butcherbird (*Cracticidae*)

〈 **مَنْهَجَ** *v* |i; مَنْهَجة| to programme, to schedule

نَهَجَ *v* |a; نَهْج| ◻1 [سَلَكَ] to follow, to pursue; to proceed; نَهَجَ الطَّريقَ to follow the road; نَهَجَ على مِنْوالِ شَخْصٍ to proceed in the same manner as sb ◻2 [أَوْضَحَ] to clarify, to explain

نَهِجَ *v* |a; نَهَج| to pant; to have difficulty breathing

أَنْهَجَ *v* to put out of breath

اِنْتَهَجَ *v* to follow, to pursue; اِنْتَهَجَ طَريقاً to follow a road; اِنْتَهَجَ سِياسةً to pursue a policy

نَهْج *n* |نُهوج| ◻1 [سَبيل] way, approach; method, procedure; نَهْج مُتَشَدِّد a hard-line approach ◻2 [طَريق] road, street; way, path

نَهَج *n* gasp, pant, panting

مُمَنْهَج *adj* systematic

مِنْهاج *n* |مَناهيجُ| ◻1 [بَرْنامَج] curriculum; مِنْهاج التَّرْبِيةِ اللُّغَوِيّةِ language curriculum ◻2 [سَبيل] method, program, approach

مَنْهَج *n* |مَناهِجُ| ◻1 [بَرْنامَج] curriculum; مَنْهَج دِراسِيّ curriculum; syllabus ◻2 [نِظام] method, approach; program, system; مَناهِج البَحْثِ research method; اِنْتَهَجَ \ اِتَّبَعَ مَنْهَجاً to follow an approach

مَنْهَجِيّ *adj* ◻1 [نِظامِيّ] methodical, systematic, orderly; formal; طَريقة مَنْهَجِيّة a systematic approach; تَعْذيب \ تَدْمير مَنْهَجِيّ systematic torture/destruction; رَفْض مَنْهَجِيّ a consistent refusal ◻2 (Relig) Methodist; الكَنيسة المَنْهَجِيّة the Methodist church

مَنْهَجِيّة *n* ◻1 [طَريقة] methodology, systematics; system ◻2 (Relig) Methodism

〈 **نَهَدَ** *v* |a; نُهود| ◻1 [المَرْأةُ] to have large breasts, to be buxom ◻2 [قامَ] to rise, to get up

ناهَدَ *v* ◻1 [خاصَمَ] to fight/quarrel with, to combat; to resist, to oppose ◻2 [قامَ] to rise, to get up

تَنَهَّدَ *v* to sigh, to heave a sigh; تَنَهَّدَ تَنَهُّداً عَميقاً ,تَنَهَّدَ بِعُمْقٍ to sigh deeply

نَهْد *n* |نُهود| breast; نَهْدانِ breasts; bust, bosom; نَهْدانِ كَبيرانِ \ مُمْتَلِئانِ \ نافِرانِ large/full/prominent breasts

ناهِد *adj* |نَواهِدُ| buxom

|ب| assuming, taking on; نُهوض بِمَسْؤولِيّة assuming responsibility

مُناهِض **A** *adj* resisting, opposing, fighting; مُناهِض ل against, anti-; تَظاهُرات مُناهضة للحُكومة anti-government protests **B** *n* opponent; fighter; مُناهِض للعَوْلَمة globalization opponent, anti-globalization activist

مُناهَضة *n* resistance; opposition, antagonism; اتِّفاقيّة مُناهَضة التَعْذيب Convention Against Torture

نَهَق *v* |a; نَهيق ,نُهاق ,نَهْق| to bray; يَنْهَقُ الحِمارُ donkeys bray

تَناهَق *v* to bray

نَهيق *n* bray, braying

نَهَك *v* |a; نَهْكة ,نَهْك| to wear/tire out, to exhaust, to fatigue; نُهِك to be exhausted

أَنْهَك *v* to wear/tire out, to exhaust, to fatigue; to drain; أَنْهَك شَخْصاً to exhaust sb; أَنْهَك فَريقاً to overwork a team; أُنْهِك to be exhausted

انْتَهَك *v* to violate, to infringe on; to defile, to desecrate; انْتَهَك عِرْض \ حُرْمة شَخصٍ to defile sb's honour; انْتَهَك حُقوق شَخصٍ to infringe on sb's rights; انْتَهَك قانوناً to break a law; انْتَهَك حُرْمة قَبْرٍ \ كَنيسةٍ to desecrate a grave/church; انْتَهَك الحَظْرَ الجَوّيَّ to violate a no-fly zone

نَهْكة *n* exhaustion, fatigue

انْتِهاك *n* |انْتِهاكات| violation, infringement; defilement, desecration; انْتِهاك حُقوقِ الإنْسانِ the violation of human rights

إنْهاك *n* exhaustion, burnout; إنْهاك جَسَديّ physical exhaustion; مَلامِح الإنْهاكِ signs of exhaustion

مُنْتَهَك *adj* defiled, desecrated

مُنْهَك *adj* exhausted, worn out, burned out; جَسَد مُنْهَك a worn-out body; كانَ مُنْهَكاً to be worn out; كانَ مُنْهَكاً جِسْميًّا وعَقْليًّا to be physically and mentally exhausted

مُنْهِك *adj* exhausting, tiring, fatiguing

مَنْهوك *adj* exhausted, worn out, tired out; مَنْهوك القُوى to have no strength left

نَهِل *v* |a; نَهَل ,مَنْهَل| **1** [شَرِبَ] to drink, to slake, to quench **2** [أَخَذَ] |من| to draw from/on; to build upon; نَهِلَ من ثَقافاتٍ

نَهَش *v* |a; نَهْش| to bite, to snap; نَهَش شَيْئاً \ في شَيْءٍ to bite sth; نَهَش شَخْصاً to bite sb; نَهَش عِرْضَ شَخْصٍ to disgrace sb; نَهَش لَحْمَ شَخْصٍ to speak ill of sb, to bad-mouth sb; نَهَش جَسَد شَخصٍ \ شَيْءٍ to eat away at sb/sth; يَنْهَشُ الكَلْبُ \ تَنْهَشُ الحَيّةُ the dog/snake bites

مَنْهوش *adj* lean

نَهَض *v* |a; نَهْض ,نُهوض| **1** [قامَ] to rise, to stand up, to get up; نَهَض مُبَكِّراً \ مُتَأَخِّراً to get up early/late; نَهَض من القَبْرِ to rise from the grave; نَهَض من كَبْوةٍ to recover/rebound from a misfortune; نَهَض من غَفْوَتِه to wake from one's nap; نَهَض مُجَدَّداً \ من جَديدٍ to rise again **2** [تَحَمَّل] |ب| to take on, to assume; نَهَض بِشَيْءٍ to take on sth; نَهَض بِأَعْباءٍ \ بِمَسْؤولِيّةٍ to take on burdens/responsibility **3** [أَسْرَع] |إلى| to go/proceed/rush towards, to head for, to advance on; نَهَض إلى العَدوِّ to advance on the enemy

ناهَض *v* to oppose, to resist, to rebel against; ناهَض الإجْراءاتِ to oppose the measures

أَنْهَض *v* to wake, to awaken; to raise

اسْتَنْهَض *v* to encourage, to stimulate, to motivate; to incite, to urge/goad/spur on; اسْتَنْهَض هِمَمَ شَخْصٍ to encourage sb's ambitions

ناهِض *adj* **1** [قائِم] standing, upright, erect; conclusive, indisputable; دَليل ناهِض conclusive evidence **2** [مُرْتَفِع] rising; اقْتِصادات ناهِضة emerging economies **3** [نَشيط] energetic, active; diligent

نَهْضة *n* renaissance; rebirth, revival, recovery; advancement, promotion; نَهْضة اقْتِصاديّة economic recovery; النَهْضة الأوروبّيّة the Renaissance (*in Europe*); عَصْر النَهْضةِ العَرَبيّةِ al-Nahda (*the Arabic renaissance of the nineteenth century*); النَهْضة الإسْلاميّة the Islamic revival

نَهْضَويّ *adj* renaissance (*before n*); *relating to al-Nahda (the Arabic renaissance of the nineteenth century)*; تَيّار نَهْضَويّ renaissance movement

نُهوض *n* **1** [صُعود] advancement; recovery, revival; النُهوض الاقْتِصاديّ \ بالاقْتِصادِ economic recovery **2** [تَحَمُّل]

انْتَهى *v* 1 [تَمَّ] to be concluded/finished, to end, to be over/past; to be completed; to expire; انْتَهى من شَيْءٍ to be finished with sth; انْتَهَتْ عَلاقَتُهُما their relationship is over; انْتَهى الفيلْمُ the film has ended; انْتَهَتْ مُدَّةُ تَأْشيرَتي my visa has expired; يَنْتَهي العَرْضُ في الحادِيَةَ عَشْرَةَ the show ends at eleven; لن يَنْتَهِيَ العَمَلُ the work will not be completed 2 [خَلَصَ إلى] |ب| to end in, to come to, to turn out to; to lead to, to result in, to turn into; انْتَهى بِفَشَلٍ to end in failure; انْتَهى بِعِراكٍ \ بِمُشاجَرَةٍ to end in a fight; انْتَهى بِهِ المَطافُ إلى مَكانٍ \ هُنا to end up somewhere/here; انْتَهى بِهِ الأَمْرُ إلى أنْ ... it resulted in ... 3 [كَفَّ] |عن| to abandon, to give up

نَهْي *n* ban, prohibition; هو صاحِبُ الأَمْرِ والنَهْيِ he lays down the law

ناهٍ *adj* prohibitive, forbidding; ناهيكَ عن besides; ناهيكَ عن دَوْرِ المُعارَضةِ apart from the role of the opposition; كانَ الآمِرَ الناهِيَ to be the absolute leader

ناهِية *n* |نَواهٍ| ban, prohibition

نِهائيّ *adj* 1 [أَخير] final; ultimate; نِهائيًّا finally; لا نِهائيّ endless; قبل النِهائيِّ penultimate; إنْذار نِهائيّ ultimatum; الهَدَف \ النَتيجة النِهائيّ(ة) the ultimate goal/result; الدَوْر \ دَوْر قبل \ نِصْف النِهائيِّ quarter-final; مُباراة رُبْع نِهائيٍّ(ةٍ) semi-final; مُباراة نِهائيّة final 2 [لا رُجوعَ عَنْهُ] final, ultimate, definitive, irreversible; القَرار \ الحُكْم النِهائيّ the final decision/judgment; الصيغة النِهائيّة the definitive version

نِهاية *n* 1 [آخِر] end, ending, conclusion; finish; final; في نِهايةِ in conclusion; في نِهاية الأَمْرِ finally; النِهايةِ نِهاية مَفْتوحة open-ended; نِهاية سَعيدة a happy ending; نِهاية السَنةِ New Year's eve; خَطّ النِهايةِ finish (line); إلى ما لا نِهايةَ لَهُ ad infinitum, indefinitely 2 [غاية] limit, utmost

نُهْية *n* |نُهًى| intellect

انْتِهاء *n* end, conclusion; انْتِهاء الحَرْبِ the end of the war

إنْهاء *n* ending, end, conclusion; completion; termination; إنْهاء الاحْتِلالِ ending the occupation

تَناهٍ *n* finiteness

نَهِلَ من مَعينِ العِلْمِ to drink from the fountain of knowledge; عِدّةٍ to draw from many cultures;

أَنْهَلَ *v* to water

مَنْهَل *n* |مَناهِلُ| 1 [بِئْر] watering place; spring, well; شَرِبَ من مَناهِلِ المِياهِ to drink from springs 2 [مَصْدَر] source; مَنْهَل عِلْمٍ a source of knowledge

نَهِمَ *v* |a; نَهَم, نَهامة| to hunger, to crave; to be greedy/gluttonous/voracious; نَهِمَ بِشَيْءٍ to crave sth; نَهِمَ في العِلْمِ to hunger for knowledge; نَهِمَ في الأكْلِ to have a voracious appetite

نَهَم *n* hunger, craving; greed, gluttony; بِنَهَمٍ gluttonous; نَهَم في الأَكْلِ \ القِراءةِ voracious eating/reading

نَهِم, **نَهيم** A *adj* greedy, gluttonous, voracious

B *n* glutton

نُهام *n* bulimia; نُهام عَصَبيّ bulimia nervosa

نُهاميّ *adj, n* bulimic

نَهيم *adj* see نَهِم

مَنْهوم A *adj* 1 [نَهِم] greedy, gluttonous, voracious 2 [نُهاميّ] bulimic

B *n* bulimic

نَهْنَهَ *v* 1 [نَشَجَ] to sob 2 [امْتَنَعَ] |عن| to abstain/refrain from

نَهى, **نَها** *v* |u; نَهْي| to forbid; to restrain; نَهى شَخْصاً عن شَيْءٍ to forbid sth for sb; نُهِيَ اللهُ عَنْهُ to be forbidden by God

أَنْهى *v* 1 [أَبْلَغَهُ غايَتَهُ] to conclude, to end, to finish, to complete; أَنْهى شَيْئاً to end sth; أَنْهى دَوْرةً دراسيّةً بِنَجاحٍ to complete a course successfully; أَنْهى الخِطْبَةَ \ العَلاقةَ to break off the engagement/relationship; أَنْهى العَلاقةَ مع شَخْصٍ to break up with sb 2 [كَفَّ] |عن| to stop, to quit; أَنْهى عن شُرْبِ الخَمْرِ to quit drinking 3 [أَوْصَلَ] to bring, to send; أَنْهى إلَيْهِ الكِتابَ to send him the book; أَنْهى الأَمْرَ إلى الحاكِمِ to bring the case to court

تَناهى *v* 1 [بَلَغَ نِهايَتَهُ] to be concluded/finished, to end, to be completed 2 [كَفَّ] |عن| to stop, to quit; تَناهى عن شُرْبِ الخَمْرِ to quit drinking 3 [بَلَغَ] to reach, to arrive; تَناهى الخَبَرُ إلى أَسْماعِهِ the news reached him; تَناهى إلى عِلْمي أنّ ... I learned that ...

ناوَبَ *v* to take turns with, to alternate with, to rotate; ناوَبَ شَخْصاً to take turns with sb

أَنابَ *v* 1 [أَوْفَدَ] to deputize, to appoint as deputy, to make/let replace; to authorize; to be replaced/substituted; أَنابَ شَخْصاً عَنْهُ to be replaced by sb; أَنابَ المُديرُ وَكيلَهُ في المُؤْتَمَرِ the director appointed his representative to replace him at the conference 2 [تابَ] to regret, to repent; أَنابَ إلى اللهِ to repent before God

تَناوَبَ *v* to take turns with, to alternate with; to rotate; تَناوَبَ الخِدْمَةَ مع شَخْصٍ to take turns working with sb; خَمْسة أَهْدافٍ تَناوَبَ على تَسْجيلها ... five goals scored in turn by ...; تَناوَبَتْ جُيوشُ الطَرَفَيْنِ السَيْطَرَةَ على المِنْطَقةِ the two armies traded control of the area back and forth

انْتابَ *v* to happen, to befall, to afflict; to be overcome with/beset by; انْتابَهُ شُعورٌ بالشَكِّ he was overcome with doubt; انْتابَتْني الدَهْشَةُ I was taken by surprise; انْتابَني الخَوْفُ I was frightened

نائِب *n* |نوّاب| representative, substitute, delegate; vice-, deputy, agent, adjunct; نائِب المَلِكِ viceroy; نائِب الرَئيسِ vice-president; نائِب رَئيسِ الوُزَراءِ Vice Prime Minister; نائِب المُدير \ النائِب العُموميّ deputy/assistant director; نائِب العامّ the public prosecutor, the attorney general (AmE); مَجْلِس النوّابِ Member of Parliament, MP; في البَرْلَمانِ parliament; (AmE) the House (of Representatives)

(Idiom) نائِب الفاعِلِ *the subject of a passive verb*

نائِبة *n* |نائِبات, نَوائِبُ| disaster, calamity, catastrophe; مَنْ نَظَرَ في العَواقِبِ سَلِمَ من النوائِبِ ≈ look before you leap

نوبة A *n* |نُوَب| disaster, calamity, catastrophe; crisis, emergency; mishap

B *n pl* see نوبيّ

نَوْبة *n* 1 (Med) attack, fit, seizure; نَوْبة صَرْعٍ an epileptic seizure; نَوْبة من الحُمّى a bout of fever; نَوْبة من الرَبْوِ an asthma attack; نَوْبة قَلْبيّة a heart attack; نَوْبة عَصَبيّة a nervous breakdown; في نَوْبةِ جُنونٍ \ غَيْرةٍ in a fit of insanity/jealousy; أُصيبَ بِنَوْبةٍ to have a seizure; أَصابَتْهُ نَوْبةٌ من الضَحِكِ he had a laughing fit; انْتابَتْهُ نَوْبةُ سُعالٍ he had a coughing fit

لامُتَناهٍ *adj* infinite, eternal; unlimited, endless; الفَضاء اللامُتَناهي infinite space; الحُبّ اللامُتَناهي endless love; مُناقَشة لامُتَناهِية an endless discussion

لانِهائيّ *adj* infinite, eternal; unlimited, endless

لانِهائيّة *n* infinity, eternity

لانِهاية *n* 1 (Math) infiniteness 2 [أَبَد] infinity, eternity

مُتَناهٍ *adj* 1 [نِهائيّ] finite; limited; خَيال غَيْر مُتَناهٍ an unbridled imagination 2 [لِلغاية] extreme, utmost; بِدِقّةٍ مُتَناهِيةٍ accurately, precisely, meticulously

مُنْتَهٍ *adj* finished, terminated; expired; خِلالَ الوِلايةِ المُنْتَهِية during the final term (of office)

مُنْتَهًى *n* 1 [حَدّ] utmost, extreme; في مُنْتَهى السُهولةِ \ البَساطةِ extremely simple 2 [آخِر] end, close; بَلَغَ مُنْتَهاهُ to come to an end

ناءَ *v* |u; نَوْء| 1 [سَقَطَ] to collapse; to yield, to succumb; ناءَ بِ \ تحت الحِمْلِ to collapse under a load 2 [أَثْقَلَ] to weigh heavily upon; ناءَ بِهِ الحِمْلُ the load weighed heavily upon him 3 [كانَ غَيْرَ مَطْبوخٍ] see نيأ

ناوَأَ *v* to resist, to oppose, to withstand

نَوْء *n* |أَنْواء| 1 [إِثْقال] overburdening 2 [مَطَر] rain; storm, hurricane

مُناوِئ A *adj* resisting, opposing; anti-; تَظاهُرة مُناوِئة للحَرْبِ an anti-war protest

B *n* opponent, antagonist

نُواكْشوط *n* |f| Nouakchott (*capital and district of Mauritania*)

نابَ *v* |u| 1 [بَدَّلَ] |عن; نِيابة, مَناب| to replace, to substitute; to take over; نابَ عن شَخْصٍ to replace sb; نابَ عن شَخْصٍ في شَيْءٍ to take over sth from sb 2 [مَثَّلَ] |عن; نِيابة, مَناب| to represent, to act for, to stand in for; to fill in for; نابَ عن شَخْصٍ (في شَيْءٍ) to represent sb (in sth); يَنوبُ عن المَلِكِ أثناء غِيابِهِ he is filling in for the king during his absence; نابَ عن المَلِكِ في طاوِلةِ الحِوارِ he represented the king at the talks 3 [أَصابَ] |نَوْب| to afflict, to strike; نابَهُ دُوارٌ to have a dizzy spell

نَوَّبَ *v* to deputize, to appoint as deputy, to make/let replace; نَوَّبَ شَخصاً في الاجْتِماعِ to appoint sb to replace him in the meeting

نائِح A *adj* plaintive, weeping; صَوْت نائِح a weeping voice B *n* mourner

نائِحة *n* a hired female mourner

نُواح *n* lamentation, mourning; crying, weeping

مَناحة *n* lamentation, mourning, wailing

‹ **أَناخَ** *v* 1 [أقامَ] to stay, to remain; أناخَ بِمَكانٍ to stay somewhere 2 [الجَمَلَ] to make kneel down (*a camel*)

مَناخ, مُناخ *n* 1 [حالة الجوّ] climate; weather conditions; مَناخ دافِئ \ جافّ \ رَطْب \ بارِد a dry/humid/cold climate; مَناخ مَداريّ \ اسْتِوائيّ حارّ a warm/hot climate; مَناخ مَداريّ \ اسْتِوائيّ a tropical climate; تَغَيُّر المَناخِ climate change 2 [بيئة] climate, atmosphere; المَناخ الاقْتِصاديّ \ السِياسيّ the economic/political climate; مَناخ فِكْريّ an intellectual atmosphere; مَناخ اسْتِثْمارٍ \ اسْتِثْماريّ investment climate; مَناخ مُلائِم \ مُناسِب ل ... a favourable climate for ...

مَناخيّ, مُناخيّ *adj* climatic, climate (*before n*); weather (*before n*); ظُروف \ أَحْوال مُناخيّة weather conditions; تَغَيُّرات مُناخيّة climate change; ظَواهِر مُناخيّة climatic phenomena

‹ **نَوَّرَ** *v* 1 [الصُبْحُ] to dawn; نَوَّرَ الصُبْحُ the day dawned 2 [أَضاءَ] to light, to illuminate, to fill with light; to light up, to make bright; نَوَّرَ الغُرْفةَ to light up the room 3 [أَزْهَرَ] to blossom, to bloom, to flower; نَوَّرَ الشَجَرُ the trees are blooming

ناوَرَ *v* to manoeuvre; ناوَرَ وَداوَرَ to wriggle every which way

أَنارَ *v* 1 [أَضاءَ] to light, to illuminate, to fill with light; أَنارَ الغُرْفةَ to light up the room; أَنارَ شَمْعةً to light a candle; أَنارَ الطَريقَ للأَجْيالِ القادِمةِ to light the way for future generations 2 [أَوْضَحَ] to shed light on, to elucidate; أَنارَ أَمْراً to shed light on a matter

اسْتَنارَ *v* 1 [تَثَقَّفَ] |ب| to seek/obtain enlightenment, to be guided by; اسْتَنارَ بِرَأْيِ شَخْصٍ في أَمْرٍ to seek sb's opinion in a matter 2 [اسْتَضاءَ] |ب| to be lit/illuminated by; اسْتَنارَ بِمِصْباحٍ to be lit by a lamp

نور *n* |أَنْوار| 1 [ضَوْء] light; ray of light; نور ساطِع a bright light; نور كَشّاف searchlight; عاكِس النور lampshade; reflector; أَضاءَ \ أَشْعَلَ النورَ to turn on the light; أَطْفَأَ النورَ

نُوَب 2 [دَوْر] |نُوَب| turn, rotation, alternation; بالنَوْبةِ alternately; in turn; نَوْبات مَطَرٍ rain showers; كانَ في نَوْبةِ الحِراسةِ to be on guard 3 (Mus) suite

نوبيّ A *adj* |نوبة, نوبيّونَ| Nubian; (اللُغة) النوبيّة Nubian (*language*) B *n* |نوبة, نوبيّونَ| Nubian (*person*); بِلاد النوبةِ Nubia

نِيابة *n* representation, proxy, substitution; deputyship, replacement; النِيابة العامّة the public prosecutor, the attorney general (AmE); بالنِيابةِ deputy, acting; بالنِيابةِ \ نِيابةً عن on behalf of; حَضَرَ نِيابةً عن شَخْصٍ to attend on behalf of sb

نِيابيّ *adj* parliamentary; مَجْلِس نِيابيّ parliament; انْتِخابات نِيابيّة parliamentary elections; وَفْد نِيابيّ a parliamentary delegation

إنابة *n* substitution, representation; accreditation, authorization; إنابة قَضائيّة letters rogatory, letter of request (*from a court to a foreign court*); بالإنابة acting (on behalf); المُدير العامّ بالإنابةِ acting general manager

تَناوُب *n* 1 [تَبادُل] alternation, rotation; بالتَناوُبِ alternately, by turns; العَمَل بالتَناوُبِ shift work 2 [تَعاقُب] succession; بالتَناوُبِ successively, in turns

مُتَناوِب *adj* 1 [مُتَبادِل] alternating, rotating; تَيّار مُتَناوِب alternating current, AC 2 [مُتَعاقِب] successive, consecutive

مُناوِب *adj* on duty/call, acting; الطَبيب المُناوِب the attending physician; كانَ مُناوِباً لَيْلاً to have the night duty/shift

مُناوَبة *n* alternation, rotation; مُناوَبة لَيْليّة night shift; جَدْوَل المُناوَبةِ duty/rotation schedule

‹ **نوبِل** *n* Nobel; جائِزةِ نوبل Nobel (prize); فائِز بجائِزةِ نوبل Nobel laureate; حَصَلَ على جائِزةِ نوبل to win a Nobel prize

‹ **نوتة** *n* |نُوَت| 1 (Mus) notes; notation; النوتة الموسيقيّة musical notation; اسْتَطاعَ قِراءةَ النوتةِ to be able to read music 2 [كُرّاسة] notebook

نوتيّ *n* |نوتيّة, نَواتيّ| sailor, mariner

‹ **ناحَ** *v* |u| نَوْح, نُواح, نِياح, نِياحة, مَناح| 1 [نَحَبَ] to lament, to mourn; to cry, to weep; ناحَ على المَيِّتِ to mourn for the deceased 2 [هَدَرَ] to coo

نوح *n* Noah (*male given name*); سورة نوح Noah (*Sura 71*)

to turn off the light; خَرَجَ إلى النورِ ,رَأى \ أَبْصَرَ النورَ to see the light, to realize the truth **2** [خَيْر] goodness, light, blessing; صَباح النورِ! good morning!; سورة النور The Light (Sura 24); سَبْت النورِ Holy Saturday; أُمّ النورِ the Virgin Mary; عَلَيْكَ نورٌ! bravo! **3** (Islam) النور the Light (*one of the names of God*) **4** [اِسْم شَخْصيّ] Nour (*male/female given name*)

نَوْر *n coll* |أَنْوار| blossoms, flowers

نَوَر *n coll* gypsies; tramps, vagabonds

نار *n* |f; نيران| **1** [حَريق] fire, flames; جَبَل نارٍ volcano; كُتْلة من النيرانِ blaze, conflagration, inferno; أَشْهَر من نارٍ على عَلَمٍ widely known, very famous; قَدَحَ النارَ to make fire (*with flint*); كانَ بين نارَيْنِ to be between a rock and a hard place; لَعِبَ بالنارِ to play with fire; كانَ على نارٍ to be on tenterhooks; اِسْتَضاءَ بِنارِ شَخْصٍ to be enlightened by sb; أَوْقَدَ \ أَشْعَلَ \ أَضْرَمَ النارَ في شَيْءٍ to set sth on fire; شَبَّت النارُ the fire flared up; اِنْتَشَرَت النارُ سَريعاً the fire spread rapidly; اِرْتَفَعَتْ أَلْسِنةُ النارِ من السَقْفِ the flames shot up through the roof **2** [في المَطْبَخِ] flame, heat; stove, stovetop, burner; على نارٍ هادِئةٍ on low (heat); وَضَعَ طَنْجَرةً على النارِ to put a pan on the stove **3** [من أَسْلِحةٍ] fire, firing; نيران حامية heavy fire; مَرْمى نيرانٍ crossfire; وَقْف إِطْلاقِ النارِ ceasefire; أَعْلَنَ وَقْفَ إِطْلاقِ النارِ to declare a ceasefire; أَطْلَقَ النارَ to fire **4** (Relig) hell; أَصْحاب أَهْلِ النارِ those who are condemned to hell **5** [شَهْر] (شَهْر) آي النار (Hist) January (*Libya under Gaddafi*)

ناريّ *adj* of fire, fiery, fire (*before n*); دَرّاجة ناريّة motorcycle, motorbike (BrE); خُطْبة ناريّة a fiery speech; عِيار \ طَلْقة ناريّ(ة) shot, round; أَطْلَقَ عِياراتٍ ناريّةً في الهَواءِ to fire shots in the air; جُثَث عَلَيْها آثارُ أَعيرةٍ ناريّةٍ bodies with gunshot wounds; سِلاح ناريّ firearm; أَلْعاب ناريّة fireworks; أَشْعَلَ أَلْعاباً ناريّةً to light fireworks; جِدار \ حاجِز ناريّ firewall

نوّار *n coll* blossom, flower; (شَهْر) النوّار (Hist) February (*Libya under Gaddafi*)

نورانيّ *adj* **1** [مُضيء] luminous, light (*before n*) **2** [مُوَضِّح] enlightening; كَلِمات نورانيّة enlightening words

نَيِّر *adj* **1** [مُضيء] luminous, radiant, bright **2** [مُثَقَّف] enlightened, brilliant; فِكْرة نَيِّرة a brilliant thought

اِسْتِنارة *n* enlightenment

إنارة *n* **1** [إضاءة] lighting, illumination; إنارة الشَوارِعِ street lighting **2** [تَنْوير] enlightenment

أَنْوَر *n* |dipt| Anwar (*male given name*)

تَنْوير *n* enlightenment

تَنْويريّ *adj* enlightening

مُسْتَنير *adj* **1** [مُضاء] illuminated, lightened **2** [مُثَقَّف] enlightened; الفِكْر المُسْتَنير enlightened thinking; تَيّار مُسْتَنير an enlightened movement

مَنار *n* |مَنائِرُ ,مَناوِرُ| **1** [مِئْذَنة] minaret **2** [مَعْلَم] lighthouse; beacon, marker, landmark

مَنارة *n* |مَنائِرُ ,مَناوِرُ| **1** [مِئْذَنة] minaret **2** [لِلسُفُنِ] lighthouse

مُناوَرة *n* manoeuvre, move; مُناوَرات exercise; مُناوَرة ذَكيّة \ تَكْتيكيّة a clever/tactical manoeuvre; مُناوَرة عَسْكَريّة a military manoeuvre; قامَ بِمُناوَرةٍ to perform a manoeuvre

مَنْوَر *n* skylight

مُنَوَّر *n* illuminated; المَدينة المُنَوَّرة Medina

مُنير **A** *adj* radiant, shining, luminous **B** *n* Munir (*male given name*)

نَوْرَج *n* |نَوارِجُ| (Agric) thresher

نَوْروز ,نَيْروز *n* Persian New Year

نَوْرَس *n* |نَوارِسُ| (Zool) gull, seagull (*Laridae*); نَوْرَس البَحْرِ seagull

ناسَ *v* |u; نَوْس ,نَوَسان| to dangle, to hang; to swing

ناس *n* see أنس

ناووس *n* |نَواويسُ| sarcophagus

ناوَشَ *v* to skirmish

تَناوَشَ *v* to spar

مُناوَشة *n* skirmish; تَجْري مُناوَشاتٌ بَسيطةٌ بين \ مع ... there are minor skirmishes between ...

ناصَ *v* |u; نَوْص ,مَناص ,مَنيص| |عن| to avoid, to dodge, to evade; to withdraw from; ناصَ عن شَيْءٍ to avoid sth

مَناص *n* escape, way out, getaway; avoidance; alternative; لا مَناصَ مِنْهُ unavoidable; obligatory, mandatory

نَوْعيّة *n* quality; characteristic; نَوْعيّة عالِية good quality; تَحْسين نَوْعيّةِ الماءِ water quality; نَوْعيّة الحَياة quality of life; تَحْسين نَوْعيّةِ شَيْءٍ improving the quality of sth

تَنَوُّع *n* |تَنَوُّعات| variety, diversity; عَدَم تَنَوُّع a lack of diversity; تَنَوُّع شَديد a huge variety; تَنَوُّع ثَقافيّ cultural diversity; تَنَوُّع حَيَويّ \ أَحْيائيّ \ بيئيّ biodiversity

تَنْويع *n* |تَنْويعات| variation, differentiation; inconsistency; diversification; تَنْويع الإنْتاج product differentiation; تَنْويع الاقْتِصادِ economic diversification; تَنْويع النَشاطِ الاقْتِصاديّ the diversification of economic activities; تَنْويع في الأَداءِ inconsistent performance

تَنْويعة *n* variant, variation

مُتَنَوِّع **A** *adj* varied, diverse, diversified, different; miscellaneous, various; حُلول مُتَنَوِّعة a variety of solutions; سِلَع مُتَنَوِّعة various goods; أَسْباب مُتَنَوِّعة different reasons; عَرْض مُتَنَوِّع a diverse supply; بَرْنامَج مُتَنَوِّع a varied programme

B *n* مُتَنَوِّعات miscellanies, sundries

مُنَوَّع *adj* varied, diverse, diversified, different

نوغة *n* nougat

ناف *v* |u; نَوْف| **1** [اِرْتَفَعَ] to be high/elevated **2** [زادَ] to exceed, to surpass; نافَ على المِائة to be over a hundred

أَناف *v* **1** [اِرْتَفَعَ] to be high/elevated **2** [زادَ] to exceed, to surpass; مُنذ ما يُنيفُ خَمْسَ سَنَواتٍ over five years; مُنذ ما يُنيفُ على قَرْنٍ over a century ago

نَيِّف *n* more than, over, above; ثَلاثونَ وَنَيِّف ,نَيِّف وَثَلاثونَ over thirty

نِيافة *n* صاحِب النِيافة His Excellency (*the title of a Coptic cardinal-bishop*)

مُنيف *adj* high, lofty; exalted, eminent, outstanding

نَوْفَل *n* see نفل

نوفَمْبر *n* (NA, Gulf) November; في (شَهْرِ) نوفَمْبر in November

ناقة *n* |ناقات ,نِياق ,نوق| female camel; لا ناقةَ لَهُ في الأَمْرِ وَلا جَمَلَ *he doesn't have anything to do with it*

نَيِّق *adj* fastidious; picky, finicky; prissy

ناطَ *v* |u; نَوْط ,نِياط| to entrust, to assign, to make responsible (for); كُلُّ شاةٍ من رِجْلِها تُناطُ each person is responsible for his own actions

أَناطَ *v* |ب| to entrust with, to allot to; to make dependent/conditional on; أَناطَ بِشَخْصٍ مُهِمّةً to allot a task to sb; أَناطَ شَيْئاً بِعُهْدةِ شَخْصٍ to leave sth in the care of someone

نَوْط *n* |أَنْواط| medal, badge

نوطة *n* (Mus) note

نِياط *n* |أَنْوِطة ,نوط| aorta; قَطَّعَ \ مَزَّقَ نِياطَ قَلْبِ شَخْصٍ to cut sb to the core

مَناط *n* point; هو مِنّي مَناطُ الثُرَيّا he's out of my reach

مُناط *adj* assigned; الصَلاحيّات المُناطة بِها the authorities assigned to her

مَنوط *adj* **1** [مُفَوَّض |ب|] responsible for, in charge of, entrusted with; assigned to; الدَوْر المَنوط بِلُبْنان the role assigned to Lebanon **2** [مُعَلَّق |ب|] dependent on, conditional on; الحَلُّ مَنوطٌ بِهِ the solution depends on him

مُنَوَّط *adj* |ب| entrusted with, commissioned with

نَوَّعَ *v* to diversify, to vary; to be changeable, to be inconsistent; نَوَّعَ الأَطْعِمةَ to vary the diet; يُنَوِّعُ في أَدائِهِ his performance is inconsistent

تَنَوَّعَ *v* to be diverse, to vary; تَنَوَّعَ أَشْكالُهُ the form varies; تَنَوَّعَ بِحَسَبِ شَيْءٍ to vary according to sth

نَوْع *n* |أَنْواع| **1** [ضَرْب] type, kind; form, shape; نَوْعاً ما somewhat; من نَوْعٍ آخَرَ of a different form; من أَيِّ نَوْعٍ كانَ of any kind; وَحيد من نَوْعِهِ one of a kind; الأَوَّل من نَوْعِهِ the first of his kind; نَوْع فَريد من ... a unique kind of ...; نَوْع مُعَيَّن من الناسِ a particular type of people **2** [جِنْس] category, class, order; sort, species, variety; نَوْع آكِلاتِ الحَشَراتِ the order of insectivores; نَوْع نادِر من الطُيور a rare species of bird

نَوْعيّ *adj* characteristic, specific; qualitative; تَحْليل نَوْعيّ a qualitative analysis; نَقْلة \ قَفْزة نَوْعيّة a quantum leap; الثِقْل النَوْعيّ specific gravity; الخَصائِص النَوْعيّة the specific features

‹ **نالَ** *v* |u; نَوْل| **1** [أَعْطى] to give, to grant; نالَ على شَخْصٍ بِشَيْءٍ to give sb sth; نالَ شَخْصاً بِسوءٍ to cause sb harm **2** [حَصَلَ على] see **نيل**

نَوَّلَ *v* to give, to grant; نَوَّلَ شَخْصاً شَيْئاً to give sb sth

ناوَلَ *v* **1** [أَعْطى] to give, to hand (on/over), to pass (on); to present; to donate; ناوِلْني ذلك الكِتابَ hand me that book **2** [الدَواءَ] to give, to administer

تَناوَلَ *v* **1** [عالَجَ] to discuss, to treat, to deal with; to examine, to pursue, to address; تَناوَلَ مَوْضوعاً بالحَديثِ to discuss a subject; تَناوَلَ مَوْضوعاً بِعُمْقٍ \ بِشَكْلٍ مُفَصَّلٍ to address a subject in depth/in detail; ماذا يَتَناوَلُ هذا الكِتابُ؟ what's this book about? **2** [تَعاطى] to eat, to consume; to have, to take; تَناوَلَ حَبَّةً to take a pill; تَناوَلَ وَجْبةَ الطَعامِ to have a meal; تَناوَلَ الكَلِمةَ to take the floor

نَوْل *n* |أَنْوال| loom

نَوال *n* **1** [هَدِيّة] gift, present; favour, benefit **2** [اسْم شَخْصيّ] |f dipt| Nawal, Noelle (*female given name*)

نَوْلون *n* freight; أَسْعار النَوْلونِ البَحْريِّ the prices of sea freight

تَناوُل *n* **1** [مَوْضوع] treatment, discussion **2** [طَعام] consumption; eating; drinking; taking

مُتَناوَل *n* reach, range; خارِجَ مُتَناوَلِ اليَدِ unreachable; كانَ في مُتَناوَلِ اليَدِ to be near at hand; كانَ \ لم يَكُنْ في مُتَناوَلِ شَخْصٍ to be within/beyond sb's reach

مُتَناوِل *n* communicant

مُناوَلة *n* **1** (Chr) communion **2** [تَسْليم] handling, delivery; مُناوَلة أَرْضيّة ground handling

مِنْوال *n* **1** [آلة] loom **2** [طَريقة] method, manner, way, fashion; على هذا المِنْوالِ in this way; هُمْ على مِنْوالٍ واحِدٍ they're birds of a feather; اسْتَمَرَّ على نَفْسِ المِنْوالِ to continue in the same fashion; نَهَجَ على مِنْوالِ شَخْصٍ to proceed in the same manner as sb

‹ **نامَ** *v* |a; نَوْم, نِيام| to sleep; to go to sleep, to fall asleep; نامَ جَيِّداً to sleep well; نامَ نَوْماً خَفيفاً \ عَميقاً to sleep soundly/lightly; نامَ نَوْماً هادِئاً \ قَلِقاً to sleep peacefully/fitfully; نامَ مِلْءَ جَفْنَيْهِ to sleep like a log

نَوَّمَ *v* **1** [أَنامَ] to lay down, to put to bed, to lull to sleep; نَوَّمَ طِفْلاً to put a child to bed **2** (Med) to anaesthetize, to narcotize; نَوَّمَ شَخْصاً to anaesthetize sb **3** (Psych) to hypnotize; نَوَّمَ شَخْصاً to hypnotize sb

أَنامَ *v* to lay down, to put to bed, to make sleep

تَناوَمَ *v* to pretend to be asleep

اسْتَنامَ *v* to be lulled to sleep; to trust, to rely on; اسْتَنامَ إلى شَيْءٍ to rely on sth

نَوْم *n* sleep; نَوْم عَميق \ هَنيء a deep/refreshing sleep; نَوْم مَغْنَطيسيّ hypnosis; نَوْم اليَقْظةِ sleepwalking; غُرْفة \ حُجْرة نَوْمٍ bedroom; وَقْت النَوْمِ bedtime; ثَوْب \ قَميص نَوْمٍ nightgown; أَبو النَوْمِ poppy; ذَهَبَ للنَوْمِ to go to bed; اسْتَيْقَظَ من النَوْمِ to wake up; أَغْرَقَ \ اسْتَغْرَقَ في النَوْمِ to sleep soundly; أَقْلَقَ نَوْمَ شَخْصٍ to disturb sb's sleep; لم يَذُقِ النَوْمَ he didn't sleep

نائِم **A** *adj* |نِيام| asleep, sleeping **B** *n* |نِيام| sleeper

نَوّام *n* sleeper; sleepyhead

الأَنام *n* see **أنام**

تَنْويم *n* **1** [مَغْنَطيسيّ] hypnosis; تَنْويم مَغْنَطيسيّ hypnosis **2** (Med) anaesthesia

مَنام *n* |مَنامات| dream; رَأى شَيْئاً \ شَخْصاً في مَنامِهِ to dream about sth/sb

مَنامة *n* **1** [مَلابِس النَوْمِ] nightgown **2** [مَوْضِع النَوْمِ] bedroom, dormitory **3** (Geog) listed alphabetically

مُنَوِّم **A** *adj* sleep-inducing; حَبّة مُنَوِّمة sleeping pill **B** *n* **1** [دَواء] |مُنَوِّمات| sedative; تَناوَلَ مُنَوِّماً to take a sedative **2** [مَغْنَطيسيّ] hypnotist

‹ **نَوَّنَ** *v* (Gram) to add nunation to a noun

نون *n* **1** [حَرْف] |f| *name of the letter* ن **2** [حوت] whale; ذو النونِ Jonah (*the prophet*)

نونة *n* dimple (*in cheek/chin*)

نونيّة *n* chamber pot, potty (infml)

تَنْوين *n* (Gram) nunation

مُنَوَّن *adj* (Gram) nunated

‹ **نُوَنْبِر** *n* (Mor) November

‹ **نَوَّهَ** *v* ① [دَعا] to call ② [ذَكَرَ] to mention, to note, to point out, to indicate; to state; to stress; نَوَّهَ ب \ إلى أَهَمِّيَّةِ شَيْءٍ to stress the importance of sth ③ [مَدَحَ] to praise, to commend; نَوَّهَ بِجُهودِ \ دَوْرِ شَخْصٍ to praise sb's efforts/role

تَنْويه *n* ① [ذِكْر] mention, reference; clue, hint, allusion ② [مَدْح] praise, commendation, laudation; عِبارة التَنْويه words of praise

مُنَوَّه *adj* المُنَوَّه عَنْهُ the above mentioned

‹ **نَوّ** *n* ① [زَوْبَعة] storm ② [حَيَوان] wildebeest, gnu (*Connochaetes*)

‹ **نَوى** *v* |i; نَواة ,نِيّة| to mean, to intend, to plan; to resolve, to decide; to consider; نَوى أنْ ... to plan to ...; نَوى شَيْئاً to intend sth; نَوى الانْتِقامَ to be intent on revenge; نَوى التَوَقُّفَ عن التَدْخينِ to resolve to quit smoking; نَوى الخَيْرَ \ الشَرَّ لِشَخْصٍ to mean well/ill towards sb

انْتَوى *v* to intend, to mean, to plan; to consider; انْتَوى شَيْئاً to intend sth

نَواة *n* |نَوًى ,نَوَيات| ① [ثَمْر] kernel, stone; pip, seed; غَيْرُ ذي نَواةٍ seedless ② [جَوْهَر] core, nucleus; نَواة ذَرّة atomic nucleus

نَوَوِيّ *adj* atomic; nuclear; أَسْلَحة نَوَوِيّة nuclear weapons; العَصْر النَوَوِيّ the nuclear age; طِبّ نَوَوِيّ nuclear medicine; مِنْطَقة خالِية من الأَسْلِحةِ النَوَوِيّةِ nuclear-free zone; إشْعاع نَوَوِيّ nuclear radiation; صاروخ نَوَوِيّ nuclear missile

نِيّة *n* |نِيّات ,نَوايا| intention, plan, purpose; desire, will; نِيّة ثابتة a firm intention; بِحُسْنِ \ بسوءِ نِيّة ,بِنِيّةٍ حَسَنةٍ \ سَيِّئةٍ with good/bad intentions, in good/bad faith; حَسَن \ صافي النِيّةِ sincere; عَقَدَ نِيَّتَهُ على شَيْءٍ to get sth into one's head; كانَ حَسَنَ النِيّةِ to mean well; to be sincere; كانَ في نِيَّتِهِ أنْ ... to have the intention to ...; كانَ الأَمْرُ في نِيَّتِهِ to have the intention to do sth; كانَتْ نِيَّتُهُ حَسَنةً his intentions were good; صَدَقَتْ نَواياها her intentions were sincere; إنَّما الأَعْمالُ بالنِيّاتِ it's the thought that counts

‹ **ناءَ** *v* |i; نَيْء ,نُيوء| ① [كانَ غَيْرَ مَطْبوخٍ] to be raw/uncooked ② [سَقَطَ \ أَثْقَلَ] see نوأ

نِيء ,نِيّ ,نَيِّئ *adj* raw, uncooked; خَضْراوات نَيِّئة raw vegetables

‹ **ناب** *n* |أَنْياب ,نُيوب| ① [حَيَوانٍ] fang; tusk; أَنْياب سامّة poisonous fangs; أَنْياب عاجٍ \ من عاجٍ ivory tusks; نابا الفيلِ elephant tusk ② [إنْسانٍ] incisor, canine tooth; كَشَّرَ عن أَنْيابِهِ to bare one's teeth

‹ **نيبال** *n* |f| Nepal

‹ **نيباليّ** *adj, n* Nepalese

‹ **نِتْروغْليسِرين** *n* nitroglycerine

‹ **النيجِر** *n* |f| Niger

‹ **نَيْجيرِيا** *n* Nigeria

‹ **نير** *n* |أَنْيار ,نيران| yoke; رَزَحَ تحت نيرِ الاسْتِعْمارِ to suffer under the yoke of colonialism

‹ **نَيْروز** *n* Persian New Year; Coptic New Year

‹ **نَيْزَك** *n* |نَيازِكُ| meteor, meteorite

نَيْزَكيّ *adj* meteoric; حَجَر نَيْزَكيّ meteorite

‹ **نَيْسان ,نيسان** *n* |dipt| (Levant, Iraq) April

‹ **نيشان** *n* |نَياشينُ| ① [وِسام] award, medal; badge of honour, sign; نالَ \ قُلِّدَ نيشاناً to be decorated ② [هَدَف] goal, aim; target, mark

نَيْص *n* porcupine

‹ **نيفادا** *n* Nevada (*US state*)

‹ **نيفاديّ** *adj* Nevadan

‹ **نَيِّق** *adj* see نوق

‹ **نيقوسِيا** *n* Nicosia

‹ **ناكَ** *v* |i; نَيْك| to fuck (*vulg*); ناكَ شَخْصاً to fuck sb

‹ **نيكاراغْوا** *n* Nicaragua

‹ **نَيْكَل** *n* nickel

‹ **نيكوتين** *n* nicotine; خالٍ من النيكوتين nicotine-free

‹ **نالَ** *v* |a; نَيْل ,مَنال| ① [أَحْرَزَ] to get, to receive; to acquire, to gain, to obtain; to achieve, to attain; نالَ جائِزةً to get a prize; نالَ تَقْديراً \ إعْجاباً to be appreciated/admired; نالَ ثَلاثَ نِقاطٍ to gain three points; نالَ ثِقةَ الناخِبينَ to win the trust of the voters; نالَ مَبْلَغاً على حِسابِهِ to receive a sum of money in one's bank account ② [شَتَمَ] to abuse, to insult; to discredit; نالَ من شَخْصٍ to insult sb; to discredit sb ③ [أَثَّرَ] to impress; to affect, to influence; نالَ من شَخْصٍ to impress sb ④ [أَعْطى] see نول

نَيَّلَ *v* to dye with indigo/blue

‹ **نَيْلوفَر ,نيلوفر ,نيلَوْفَر** *n* water lily; lotus

‹ **نَيْلون ,نايْلون** *n* nylon; من النَّيْلونِ nylon

‹ **نِتْرون ,نُيوتْرون ,نْيوتْرون** *n* neutron

‹ **نْيو جيرْسي** *n* |f| New Jersey (*US state*)

‹ **نْيودِلْهي** *n* |f| New Delhi

‹ **نيوزيلَنْدا** *n* New Zealand

‹ **نْيو مَكْسيكو** *n* |f| New Mexico (*US state*)

‹ **نيون** *n* neon; fluorescent; مِصْباح نيون neon light; ضَوْء النِيون fluorescent light; neon lamp

‹ **نْيو هامْشير** *n* |f| New Hampshire (*US state*)

‹ **نِيويورْك** *n* |f| New York (*US city and state*)

نيّ *n* see **نيأ**

أنالَ *v* to make/let attain

نيل *n* 1 [لَوْن] indigo 2 [مادّة مُلَوِّنة] indigo 3 [نَهْر] Nile; النيل the Nile (river); نَهْر النيلِ الأَبْيَض the White Nile

نَيْل *n* acquisition, obtainment; accomplishment, achievement

نيليّ *adj* 1 [اللَّوْنِ] indigo; dark blue 2 [مَنْسوب لِنَهْرِ النيلِ] *belonging/related to the Nile*; تِمْساح نيليّ Nile crocodile (*Crocodylus niloticus*)

مَنال *n* 1 [إحْراز] achievement, attainment; acquisition, obtaining; سَهْل \ قَريب المَنالِ achievable; available; عَسير \ صَعْب المَنالِ unattainable; unavailable; ما زالَ بَعيدَ المَنالِ it's far from reality 2 [اسْم شَخْصيّ] |f dipt| Manal (*female given name*)

‹ **نيلَج** *n* indigo

ه

هـ *abbr* (Islam) *Hijri calendar*

ها *excl* هاكَ! here, take it!; ها أنا ذا here I am; ها أنا أُمٌّ! I am a mother!; ... ها نَحْنُ نرى كيف here we see how ...; ها! ها! ha! ha! (*indicating laughter*)

هاء *n* |f| *name of the letter* ه

هاتِ *excl* |هاتوا; f هاتي| give me, bring me; هاتِ الفِنْجانَ! bring me the cup!

هاتانِ *pron* see هَذا

هاتور *n* Hatour (*the third month of the Coptic calendar*)

هارْب *n* harp

هارْمونيكا *n* harmonica, mouth organ; عَزَفَ على هارْمونيكا to play harmonica

هارون, هَرون *n* |dipt| Harun (*male given name*); Aaron (*male given name*)

هافانا *n* Havana

هَؤُلاءِ *pron* see هَذا

هانِم *n* (Egypt) madam (*term of address for a lady*)

هانيبال *n* شَهْر هانيبال (Hist) August (*Libya under Gaddafi*)

هاهُنا *adv* here

هاواي *n* |f| Hawaii (*US state*)

هاوايِيّ *adj* Hawaiian

هاوُن, هاوون *n* |أَهْوان, هَواوينُ| mortar; هاوُن وَمدَقّة mortar and pestle; مِدْفَع الهاوُنِ (Mil) mortar

هايتي *n* |f| Haiti

هايتِيّ *adj, n* Haitian

هَبَّ *v* |u; هُبوب, هَبّ| ❶ [الريح] to blow; to rage; تَهُبُّ الريحُ (بِقوّةٍ) the wind is blowing (hard); يَهُبُّ النَسيمُ there's a gentle breeze ❷ [قامَ] to rise (up), to get up; to wake up; هَبَّ لِلدِفاعِ عن وَطَنِهِ to rise up to defend one's country; هَبَّ لِلقِتالِ to throw oneself into battle ❸ [بَدَأَ] to start, to begin; هَبَّ يَفْعَلُ شَيْئاً to start doing sth, to up and do sth

هَبَّبَ *v* to tear (up)

تَهَبَّبَ *v* to be worn, to be torn

هَباب *n* fine dust, soot

هِباب *n* soot

هَبّة *n* gust of wind

هُبوب *n* the blowing of the wind; هُبوب الرِياحِ the blowing of the wind

مَهَبّ *n* مَهَبّ الريحِ windward; أَصْبَحَ كالقَشّةِ في مَهَبِّ الريحِ to become like a reed in the wind

هَبَتَ *v* |i; هَبْت| to make fall, to knock down; هَبَتَ شَخْصاً to knock sb down; هُبِتَ to be faint-hearted

مَهْبوت *adj* ❶ [جَبان] cowardly, faint-hearted ❷ [مَعْتوه] dim-witted

هِبة *n* see وهب

هَبَرَ *v* |u; هَبْر| to cut into large pieces; هَبَرَ اللَحْمَ to cut the meat into pieces

هَبِرَ *v* |a; هَبَر| to be fleshy, to be meaty

هَبْرة *n* piece of boneless meat

هُبَيْرة *n* hyena, hyaena

هَبَشَ *v* |i; هَبْش| to grab, to seize; to gather, to collect

هَبَطَ *v* |i-u; هُبوط| ❶ [نَزَلَ] to descend, to drop, to fall; to collapse, to come down; to sag, to subside; يَهْبِطُ اللَيْلُ night is falling; يَهْبِطُ المِصْعَدُ إلى الطابَقِ الأَرْضيِّ the elevator is going down to the ground floor; هَبَطَتْ قيمَتُهُ to decrease in value; هَبَطَ سِعْرُهُ إلى ٣ دَراهِم to fall in price to 3 dirhams ❷ [طائِرة] to land, to touch down; هَبَطَتِ الطائِرةُ the airplane has landed; هَبَطَ في مَطار to land at an airport

أَهْبَطَ *v* to lower; to bring down, to cause to descend

انْهَبَطَ *v* to drop, to fall, to descend

هابِط *adj* descending, falling, dropping; downward; مُعَدَّل هابِط a low average; حَرَكة هابِطة a downward movement; صاعِداً هابِطاً up and down

هُبوط *n* **1** [الطائِرةِ] landing, touchdown; هُبوط اضطِراريّ emergency landing; جِهاز الهُبوطِ landing gear; الهُبوط في مَطارِ بَيْروتَ the landing at the Beirut airport; الهُبوط على القَمَرِ the moon landing; بَدَأَ بالهُبوطِ to start the landing (sequence); قامَ بِهُبوطٍ to make a landing; قامَ بِهُبوطٍ اضْطِراريٍّ to make an emergency landing **2** [انْخِفاض] fall, descent, drop; هُبوط في القَلْبِ a drop in pulse rate; هُبوط الدولارِ the fall of the dollar; هُبوط دَرَجةِ الحَرارة a drop in temperature

مَهْبِط *n* |مَهابِطُ| **1** (Elec) cathode **2** [مَكان الهُبوطِ] landing place; مَهْبِط طائِراتٍ runway, airstrip

مَهْبَطة *n* |مَهابِطُ| parachute

‹ **هَبِلَ** *v* |a; هَبَل| (old use) to lose a child (*of mother*); to go insane

اهْتَبَلَ *v* **1** [كَذِبَ واحْتالَ] to plot, to scheme; اهْتَبِلْ هَبَلَكَ mind your own business **2** [فُرْصةً] to seize, to grab; اهْتَبَلَ الفُرْصةَ ل ... to seize the opportunity to ...

هَبَل *n* اهْتَبِلْ هَبَلَكَ mind your own business

أَهْبَل *adj* |dipt; هُبْل| idiotic, stupid; طِفْل أَهْبَل an idiotic child

مَهْبِل, مَهْبَل *n* |مَهابِلُ| vagina; مِنْظار المَهْبَلِ (Med) duckbill speculum, colposcope

مَهْبَليّ *n* vaginal; إفْرازات مَهْبَلِيّة vaginal discharge

مَهْبول **A** *adj* crazy, nuts, idiotic, nuts
B *n* fool

‹ **هِبْلَع** *n* greyhound

‹ **هَبْهَبَ** *v* to bark

هَبْهاب *n* fata morgana, mirage

‹ **هَبا** *v* |u; هُبوّ| to rise up; to whirl up (*dust*)

هَباء *n* |أَهْباء| fine dust (*floating dust particles that can only be seen in the sunlight*)

هَبْوة *n* |هَبَوات| dust particle

‹ **هَتَرَ** *v* |u; هَتْر| to rip up, to tear to pieces

هاتَرَ *v* to slander, to insult

تَهاتَرَ *v* **1** [الخَصْمانِ] to contradict one another; to accuse one another falsely **2** [الشَهاداتُ] to be contradictory

اسْتَهْتَرَ *v* |ب| to behave irresponsibly, to be reckless; to snub; اسْتَهْتَرَ بِمَشاعِرِ الآخَرِينَ to not care about others' feelings

اسْتِهْتار *n* |اسْتِهْتارات| disregard; carelessness

تَهاتُر *n* contradiction, conflict

مُسْتَهْتِر *adj* careless, reckless; inconsiderate

مُهاتَرة *n* **1** [تُهْمة] accusation **2** [إهانة] insult **3** [شِجار] altercation, quarrel

‹ **هَتَفَ** *v* |i; هُتاف| **1** [صاحَ] to shout, to cry out, to exclaim; to chant; هَتَفَ بِشِعاراتٍ to chant slogans **2** [تَلْفَنَ] to telephone, to ring (up); هَتَفَ إلى شَخْصٍ to ring sb **3** [أَشادَ] to cheer, to applaud; هَتَفَ بِحَياةِ الزَعيمِ to cheer on the leader **4** [الحَمامةُ] to coo

هاتَفَ *v* to phone, to call

هاتِف *n* |هَواتِفُ| **1** [تِلفون] telephone; هاتِف عُموميّ public phone; هاتِف لاسِلْكِيّ wireless phone; هاتِف ذَكِيّ smartphone; هاتِف مَحْمول \ نَقّال mobile (phone) (BrE), cell (phone) (AmE); جِهاز الهاتِف telephone, handset; دَليل الهاتِف phone book; شَبَكة الهاتِفِ telephone network; حَرارة الهاتِف dial tone; رَقْم الهاتِف phone number; ما هو رَقْمُ هاتِفِكَ؟ what is your phone number?; طَلَبَ رَقْمَ هاتِفٍ to ask for a phone number; to dial a phone number; هل عِنْدَكَ هاتِفٌ؟ do you have a telephone?; على الهاتِفِ on the phone; قالَ شَيْئاً على \ عَبْرَ الهاتِفِ to say sth over the telephone; رَفَعَ \ وَضَعَ سَمّاعة الهاتِف to answer/put down the telephone; يَرِنُّ جَرَسُ الهاتِفِ the phone is ringing **2** [صَوْت باطِنِيّ] inner voice; هاتِف القَلْبِ inner voice

هاتِفيّ *adj* telephonic; هاتِفيًّا by telephone; مُكالَمة هاتِفيّة phone call; تَلَقّى اتِّصالاً هاتِفيًّا to receive a phone call; اتَّصَلَ هاتِفيًّا to call (up); طَلَب هاتِفيّ dial-up Internet; أَجْرَى اتِّصالاً هاتِفيًّا بِشَخْصٍ, اتَّصَلَ بِشَخْصٍ هاتِفيًّا to contact sb by telephone; يُمْكِنُ الاتِّصالُ بِهِ هاتِفيًّا he's reachable by phone

هُتاف *n* |هُتافات| **1** [الجمهور] cheer, applause; بِعاصِفةٍ من الهُتافِ with a storm of applause; هُتاف عالٍ \ هائِل \ صاخِب \ حَماسيّ loud/enormous/deafening/enthusiastic cheer; دَوَّت الهُتافاتُ there were cheers; هُتافات الجُمْهورِ cheers from the crowd **2** [نِداء] exclamation, cry, shout; slogan

‹ **هَتَكَ** *v* |i; هَتْك| **1** [شَقَّ] to tear apart **2** [فَضَحَ] to assault, to violate, to dishonour; هَتَكَ عِرْضَ شَخْصٍ to rape sb; هَتَكَ عِرْضَ امْرَأةٍ to violate a woman

هَتَّكَ *v* to tear to shreds

تَهَتَّكَ *v* **1** [كانَ قَليلَ الحَياءِ] to be shameless; to be licentious **2** [مَزَّقَ] to tear, to rip

هَتْك *n* violation, rape

تَهَتُّك *n* |تَهَتُّكات| shamelessness, impudence; immorality

مُتَهَتِّك **A** *adj* debauched, immoral
B *n* beast, brute

‹ **أَهْتَم** *adj* |dipt; هُتْم| toothless

‹ **هَتَنَ** *v* |i; هُتون, هَتْن| to rain hard, to pour

‹ **هَجَأَ** *v* |a; هُجوء, هَجْء| to be stopped, to be appeased (*hunger*)

أَهْجَأَ *v* to appease (*sb 's hunger*)

‹ **هَجَّ** *v* |i; هَجيج, هَجّ| **1** [اتّقدَ] to burn, to be on fire; هَجَّت النارُ the fire was burning **2** [هدَمَ] to demolish

هَجيج *n* flame; هَجيج النارِ the crackling of the fire

‹ **هَجَدَ** *v* |u; هُجود| to stay awake at night

تَهَجُّد *n* (Islam) tahajjud (*voluntary additional night prayers*)

‹ **هَجَرَ** *v* |u; هِجْران, هَجْر| to leave (behind), to abandon; to give up, to renounce; هَجَرَ زَوْجَتَهُ وَأَوْلادَهُ he left his wife and children; هَجَرَ شَخْصاً to abandon sb; هَجَرَ وَطَنَهُ to leave one's country; هَجَرَ الدِراسةَ to give up studying

هَجَّرَ *v* to banish, to deport; to drive away, to dispel

هاجَرَ *v* to emigrate; to migrate; to immigrate; هاجَرَ إلى كَندا to emigrate to Canada

أَهْجَرَ *v* to desert, to abandon

تَهاجَرَ *v* to desert one another, to separate

هاجِرة *n* midday, noon

هِجْران *n* abandonment

هِجْرة *n* **1** [الناسِ] emigration; migration; immigration; الهِجْرة النَبَوِيّة the Hijra (*the prophet Muhammad's departure from Mecca to Medina*); الهِجْرة من ... the migration from ...; الهِجْرة من الريفِ the rural migration; الهِجْرة إلى القَرَوِيّة الهِجْرة إلى المَدينة \ المُدُنِ urban migration; الهِجْرة إلى الجَنوب \ المَدينة the migration to the south/city; حَرَكة هِجْرة جَماعِيّة exodus; هِجْرة العُقول \ الأَدْمِغة brain drain; مَوْجة هِجْرةٍ a wave of migration **2** [الطَيْر] migration; مَوْسِم هِجْرة الطُيورِ bird migration season; هِجْرة الخُطّاف swallow migration; سِياسة الهِجْرة immigration policy

هِجْرِيّ *adj relating/pertaining to the Hegira*; سَنة هِجْرِيّة Islamic year; سَنة ١٤٢٣ هِجْرِيّة the Islamic year 1423

هَجير *n* midday heat

تَهْجير *n* banishment; deportation; تَهْجير قَسْرِيّ forced deportation, forced displacement

مُهاجِر *n* **1** [مَنْ يُهاجِرُ] emigrant; migrant; immigrant; مُهاجِرونَ من شَرْق أوروبّا \ إفْريقيا immigrants from Eastern Europe/Africa **2** [أَحَد أَنْصارِ النَبِيِّ] *companion of the prophet Muhammad during his migration to Medina*

مُهاجَرة *n* migration; emigration

مَهْجَر *n* |مَهاجِرُ| *country where one emigrates to*; في المَهْجَرِ abroad (*in case of migration*); المَغارِبة في المَهْجَرِ Moroccans living abroad

مَهْجَرِيّ *adj* migrant, living overseas; exiled; أَدَب مَهْجَرِيّ migrant literature

مَهْجور *adj* desolate; abandoned, deserted; obsolete; لُغة مَهْجورة a dead language; مِنْطَقة مَهْجورة a desolate area; أَرْض مَهْجورة wasteland; بَيْت مَهْجور an abandoned house; كَلِمة مَهْجورة an obsolete word

‹ **هِجْرِس, هَجْرَس** *n* |هَجارِسُ| (fox) cub

‹ **هَجَسَ** *v* |i-u; هَجْس| to occur, to come to mind; هَجَسَ في نَفْسِهِ أنْ... it occurred to him to...

هاجِس *n* |هَواجِسُ| idea; obsession, fixed idea; premonition; هاجِس شَيْءٍ \ شَخْصٍ an obsession with sth/sb

‹ **هَجَعَ** *v* |a; هُجوع, هَجْع| to sleep, to slumber; to doze

هُجْنة *n* |هُجُن| fault, incorrect language

هَجين **A** *n* |هُجُن, هُجَناءُ, مَهاجينُ, مَهاجِنة| **1** (Bio) cross, cross-breed, hybrid **2** [مُخْتَلِط النَسْلِ] mixed race **B** *adj* |هُجُن, هُجَناءُ, مَهاجينُ, مَهاجِنة| **1** (Bio) cross-breed, hybrid; حِصان هَجين a non-thoroughbred horse **2** [مُخْتَلِط النَسْلِ] mixed race **3** (Aut) hybrid; سَيّارة هَجينة hybrid car; مُحَرِّك هَجين hybrid engine

اسْتِهْجان *n* |اسْتِهْجانات| disapproval, condemnation

تَهْجين *n* **1** [مَزْج السُلالاتِ] crossing, cross-breeding; تَهْجين فَصيلَتَيْن cross-breeding of two species **2** (Ling) pidginisation; تَهْجين اللُغةِ pidginisation (*mixture between two or more languages*)

مُسْتَهْجَن *adj* reprehensible, condemnable

هَجا *v* |u; هِجاء, هَجْو| to taunt, to abuse; to ridicule ‹

هَجّى *v* to spell

هاجى *v* to taunt, to ridicule

تَهَجّى *v* to spell; تَهَجّى اسْماً to spell a name; تَهَجّى حُروفَ الهِجاءِ to recite the alphabet

هَجْو *n* satire

هَجّاء *adj* satirical, biting

هِجاء *n* **1** [أَلِفْباء] spelling; حُروف الهِجاءِ alphabet **2** [هَجْو] satire; كَتَبَ هِجاءً في شَيْءٍ to write a satire on sth

هِجائيّ *adj* **1** [أَلِفْبائيّ] alphabetical; تَرْتيب هِجائيّ alphabetical order **2** [عَكْس مَدْحيٍّ] satirical; قَصيدة هِجائيّة satirical poem

هَجْوي *adj* satirical

تَهَجٍّ *n* spelling; أَصابَ \ أَخْطَأَ في تَهَجّي كَلِمةٍ to spell a word right/wrong

تَهْجِية *n* spelling

هَدَأَ *v* |a; هُدوء, هَدْء| to be/become calm; to calm down, to quiet down, to die down; هَدَأَ ضَجيجُ الشارِعِ the street noise died down; قد هَدَأَت العاصِفةُ the storm had abated; اهْدَأْ take it easy, calm down; هَدَأَ الأَلَمُ عَنْهُ his pain had subsided ‹

هَدَّأَ *v* to calm (down), to quiet; to temper; هَدَّأَ شَخْصاً to calm sb down; هَدَّأَ من رَوْعِ شَخْصٍ to dispel sb's fear; هَدَّأَ الخَواطِرَ to calm people's nerves; هَدَّأَ سُرْعَتَهُ to slow down

هاجِع *adj* sleeping; dormant

مَهْجَع *adj* |مَهاجِعُ| dormitory, sleeping quarters

هَجَمَ *v* |u; هُجوم| to attack, to raid; to storm, to assail; هَجَمَ على العَدُوِّ to attack the enemy ‹

هاجَمَ *v* to attack, to raid; to storm, to assail; هاجَمَ شَخْصاً \ مَدينةً to attack sb/a city

أَهْجَمَ *v* to make attack

تَهَجَّمَ *v* to attack; تَهَجَّمَ على شَخْصٍ to attack sb

تَهاجَمَ *v* to attack one another

هَجْمة *n* |هَجَمات| charge, attack; هَجْمة مُعاكِسة \ مُضادّة counter attack; صَدَّ هَجْمةً to repel an attack; واجَهَ \ شَنَّ هَجْمةً على الحُكومةِ to launch an attack on the government

هُجوم *n* attack, charge; storming, raid; offensive; هُجوم مُفاجِئ surprise attack; هُجوم مُسَلَّح \ عَنيف an armed/a violent raid; هُجوم كَبير \ واسِع a major/massive offensive; هُجوم مُضادّ \ مُعاكِس counter-attack; هُجوم جَوّيّ air raid; قَلْب الهُجومِ (Sport) centre forward; شَنَّ هُجوماً to launch an attack; صَدَّ هُجوماً to ward off an attack; هُجوم انْتِقاميّ retaliatory attack; شَنَّ هُجوماً \ نَفَّذَ هُجوماً انْتِقامِيًّا to launch a retaliatory attack; نَفَّذَ هُجوماً مُضادًّا \ مُعاكِساً to counter-attack; نَفَّذَ هُجوماً جَوِّيًّا to carry out an air raid; هُجوم بالقَنابِلِ bombing raid, bomb attack

هُجوميّ *adj* aggressive; offensive; اسْتْراتيجيّة هُجوميّة an offensive strategy; تَكْتيك هُجوميّ offensive tactic; خُطّة هُجوميّة plan of attack

تَهَجُّم *n* attack, assault

مُهاجِم *n* **1** [مُعْتَدٍ] attacker, assailant, aggressor **2** (Sport) attacker, forward

مُهاجَمة *n* attack, charge; offensive; مُهاجَمة شَيْءٍ \ شَخْصٍ an attack on sth/sb

هَجَّنَ *v* to cross-breed, to interbreed; هَجَّنَ أَصْنافاً مُخْتَلِفةً to cross-breed different varieties ‹

اسْتَهْجَنَ *v* to disapprove, to condemn; to object to, to denounce

هَجّان *n* camel rider

هِجان *n* |هُجُن, هَجائِنُ| white camel; سِباق الهُجُنِ camel race

أَهْدَأَ *v* to calm down, to quiet down; أَهْدَأَ الرَضيعَ to lull the baby to sleep

هادِئ *adj* quiet, calm, peaceful; جَوّ هادِئ calm weather; بيئة \ a relaxed atmosphere; بَحْر \ نَهْر هادِئ a calm sea/river; لَيْلة هادِئة a quiet environment/night; شارِع \ مَكان هادِئ a quiet street/place; عاشَ حَياةً هادِئةً to lead a quiet life; بَقِيَ هادِئًا to keep quiet

هَدْأة *n* 1 [سُكون] calm, quiet; stillness, tranquillity 2 (Ling) pause

هُدوء *n* stillness, quiet, calm; peace, tranquillity; هُدوء وادِع a peaceful tranquillity; بِهُدوءٍ quietly; بِكُلِّ هُدوءٍ quite calmly; الهُدوء! silence!, quiet!; يُرْجى الْتِزامُ الهُدوءِ silence please; طَلَبَ الهُدوءَ to ask for silence; حافَظَ ,الْتَزَمَ الهُدوءَ على الهُدوءِ (والنِظامِ) to keep quiet; أَعادَ النِظامَ والهُدوءَ to restore the peace and quiet; مَرَّ بِهُدوءٍ to pass by quietly; عادَ الهُدوءُ إلى المِنْطَقةِ peace has returned to the area; عَكَّرَ الهُدوءَ to disturb the peace

تَهْدِئة *n* calming, quieting, pacification

مُهَدِّئ *n* |مُهَدِّئات| tranquillizer, calmative, sedative; دَواء مُهَدِّئ للأَعْصابِ tranquillizer

هَدِبَ *v* |a; هَدَب| *to have long eyelashes*

هَدَّبَ *v* to fringe, to trim with fringes

تَهَدَّبَ *v* to droop (*branches*); تَهَدَّبَت الأَغْصانُ the branches were drooping

هُدْب *n* |أَهْداب| 1 (Anat) eyelash 2 [ثَوْبٍ] fringe; frayed end

هُدّاب *n* frayed end; fringe

أَهْدَب *adj* |dipt| أَهْدَب العَيْنَيْنِ *having long eyelashes*

هَدَجَ *v* |i; هَدْج| to shuffle, to shamble; to stagger, to totter

تَهَدَّجَ *v* to tremble, to shake; تَهَدَّجَ صَوْتُهُ his voice quavered

تَهَدُّج *n* vibration, trembling, shaking

مُتَهَدِّج *adj* unsteady, shaky, quivering; تَكَلَّمَ بِصَوْتٍ مُتَهَدِّجٍ to speak with a shaky voice

هَدَّ *v* |u; هَدّ| 1 [هَدَمَ] to demolish, to destroy, to pull down 2 [أَضْعَفَ] to weaken, to undermine

هَدَّدَ *v* to threaten, to menace; هَدَّدَ شَخْصاً \ شَيْئاً to threaten sb/sth; هَدَّدَ شَخْصاً بِسِلاحٍ to threaten sb with a weapon; هَدَّدَ شَخْصاً بالضَرْبِ to threaten to beat sb; هَدَّدَ سَلامةَ شَيْءٍ to jeopardize sth

تَهَدَّدَ *v* to threaten; تَهَدَّدَ شَخْصاً بالسَجْنِ to threaten sb with imprisonment

انْهَدَّ *v* to be demolished, to be/get torn down

هَدّ *n* destruction, demolition

هَدّة *n* thud

تَهْديد *n* |تَهْديدات| threat, menace; تَهْديد بالتَشْهيرِ blackmail; تَهْديد بالقوّة threat of force; تَهْديد للأَمْنِ a security threat; تحت التَهْديدِ رِسالة \ خِطاب تَهْديدٍ threatening letter; بِمُسَدَّسٍ at gunpoint; شَكَّلَ تَهْديداً لِشَيْءٍ to constitute a threat to sth; وَجَّهَ \ أَطْلَقَ تَهْديداتٍ to utter threats; نَفَّذَ تَهْديداتٍ to carry out threats

تَهْديديّ *adj* threatening, menacing, intimidating; لَهْجة تَهْديديّة threatening tone

مُهَدَّد *adj* threatened, menaced; مُهَدَّد بالانْقِراضِ endangered, threatened with extinction; حَيَوان مُهَدَّد بالانْقِراضِ an endangered animal

مُهَدِّد *adj* threatening, menacing

مَهْدود *adj* demolished, wrecked, destroyed; مَهْدود القُوى exhausted

هَدَرَ *v* |i; هَدير ,هَدْر| 1 [رَدَّدَ صَوْتَهُ] to hum; to roar (*lion*); to thunder, to roll; تَهْدِرُ الأَمْواجُ the waves are foaming; هَدَرَ البَحْرُ \ النَهْرُ \ الماءُ the sea/river/water roared 2 [بَذَّرَ] to waste, to squander; هَدَرَ المالَ والوَقْتَ to waste time and money

أَهْدَرَ *v* to waste, to squander

هَدْر *adj* هَدْراً in vain; ذَهَبَ دَمُهُ هَدْراً to sacrifice oneself in vain; ذَهَبَ سَعْيُهُ هَدْراً his efforts were in vain

هادِر *adj* |هَوادِرُ| noisy, loud, boisterous; ماء هادِر roaring water

هَدير *n* hum; grumbling, growling; roar; thunder, roll, rumble; هَدير البَحْرِ \ الأَمْواجِ the roar of the sea/waves; هَدير المَدافِعِ the booming of cannons; هَدير الآلاتِ the din of machinery

إهْدار *n* waste; إهْدار الأَمْوالِ العامّةِ squandering public money

مُهْدَر A *adj* invalid

B *n* مُهْدَر الدَمِ outcast (*no longer under the protection of one's tribe*)

مَهْدور *adj* lost, useless; الوَقْت المَهْدور lost time, time wasted; مَهْدور الدَم *cast out from one's tribe*

‹ **هَدْرَجَ** *v* |i; هَدْرَجة| to hydrogenate (*to cause to combine with hydrogen*)

‹ **هيدْروجين** *n* hydrogen

‹ **هَدَفَ** *v* |u; هَدْف| to aim at, to intend; هَدَفَ إلى نَتيجةٍ to aim at a result

أَهْدَفَ *v* to approach

اسْتَهْدَفَ *v* [1] [قَصَدَ] to aim at, to intend, to have in mind; اسْتَهْدَفَ شَيْئاً to have sth in mind; اسْتَهْدَفَ شَخْصاً to have it in for sb [2] [تَعَرَّضَ] to be exposed, to be a target; أُسْتُهْدِفَ بالنَقْد to be the target of criticism

هَدَف *n* |أَهْداف| [1] [غَرَض] target, aim; intention, objective, object; هَدَف نِهائيّ ultimate goal, final objective; هَدَف مُضادّ cross-purpose; counter goal; الهَدَف المَرْجوّ \ المَنْشود the desired outcome; وَصَلَ إلى هَدَفِه, حَقَّق هَدَفَهُ to achieve one's aim; جَعَلَ شَيْئاً هَدَفاً لَهُ to make sth one's aim; بِهَدَفِ (فِعْلِ شَيْءٍ) with the intention of (doing sth); بِلا هَدَفٍ aimless; ما هي الأَهْدافُ المَرْجوّة؟ what is the objective?; مُحَدَّد الهَدَفِ determined [2] [سِلاح] target; هَدَف الاعْتِداءِ the target of the attack; هَدَف مَدَنيّ civilian target; هَدَف بَرّيّ ground target; أصابَ الهَدَفَ to hit the target [3] (Sport) goal; هَدَف التَعادُلِ equalizer; هَدَف مُضادّ counter goal; فارِق الأَهْدافِ, نِسْبة الأَهْدافِ goal difference; سَجَّلَ \ أَحْرَزَ هَدَفاً to score/kick a goal; فازَ بِثَلاثةِ أَهْدافٍ نَظيفةٍ to win by three goals to zero; فازَ بِهَدَفٍ مُقابِلَ لا شَيْءَ to win one to zero

هادِف *adj* determined, aimed, purposeful; إجْراءات هادِفة specific measures, meaningful action; فيلْم هادِف a movie with a message

هَدّاف *n* striker, centre forward; top scorer; لائِحة الهَدّافينَ the list of top scorers

اسْتِهْداف *n* targeting

تَهْديف *n* scoring; فُرْصة التَهْديفِ \ لِلتَهْديفِ the chance to score

مُسْتَهْدَف [A] *adj* exposed, open; مَجْموعة مُسْتَهْدَفة target group [B] *n* target

مِهْداف *n* sight (*on a gun*)

‹ **هَدَلَ** *v* |i; هَديل| [1] [دَلّى] to let hang; هَدَلَتْ شَعْرَها she let her hair down [2] [الحَمامُ] to coo

تَهَدَّلَ *v* to dangle, to hang

هَديل *n* cooing (*of a pigeon*)

مُتَهَدِّل *adj* hanging

‹ **هَدَمَ** *v* |i; هَدْم| to pull down, to demolish, to tear down; to destroy, to wreck; هَدَمَ مَصْنَعاً قَديماً to demolish an old factory; هَدَمَ جِداراً to tear down a wall; هَدَمَ حُجّةً to tear apart an argument; هَدَمَ مَنازِلَ \ مَبانِيَ to wreck houses/buildings

هَدَّمَ *v* to demolish, to tear down, to destroy

تَهَدَّمَ *v* to be destroyed, to be demolished; to be/become dilapidated; to collapse, to fall down

انْهَدَمَ *v* to collapse, to fall to pieces, to fall down

هَدْم *n* demolition, destruction

هَدّام *adj* destructive, devastating; noxious, harmful

هُدام *n* seasickness; مُصاب بالهُدامِ seasick

تَهَدُّم *n* collapse, decay

تَهْديم *n* |تَهْديمات| demolition, destruction, wrecking

مُتَهَدِّم *adj* torn down, destroyed, wrecked; dilapidated, run down

مُهَدَّم *adj* torn down, destroyed, wrecked

مُهَدِّم *n* demolisher, demolition contractor; wrecker

مَهْدوم *adj* destroyed, demolished, wrecked

‹ **هَدَنَ** *v* |i; هُدون| to calm down, to become quiet

هَدَّنَ *v* to calm down, to quiet down

هادَنَ *v* to reconcile; to conclude a truce

هُدْنة *n* |هُدَن, هُدْنات| [1] [وَقْف القِتالِ] truce, armistice, ceasefire; هُدْنة بين بَلَدَيْنِ a truce between two countries; انْتَهَكَ \ خَرَقَ هُدْنةً to break/violate a truce; أَعْلَنَ هُدْنةً to call a truce; اتِّفاق هُدْنةٍ truce agreement; خَطّ الهُدْنة demarcation line; هُدْنة مُؤَقَّتة \ دائِمة a temporary/long-term truce [2] [سُكون] quiet, calm

مُهادِن *adj* tame, meek, docile; submissive

مُهادَنة *n* truce, armistice, ceasefire

‹ **هَدْهَدَ** *v* |i; هَدْهَدة| to rock, to cradle; هَدْهَدَ (طِفْلاً) حتّى يَنامَ to rock (a child) to sleep; هَدْهَدَ مَشاعِرَ شَخْصٍ to flatter sb

هُدْهُد *n* |هَداهِدُ| hoopoe (*Upupa epops*)

‹ **هَدَى** *v* |i; هَدْي| to lead, to guide, to show the way; هَدَى شَخْصاً الطَريقَ \ إلى الطَريقِ to show sb the way

هادى *v* to exchange presents

أَهْدى *v* ⟦1⟧ [أَعْطى] to give, to gift; أَهْدى شَيْئاً to give sth as a present; أَهْدى شَيْئاً ل \ إلى شَخْصٍ to make sb a gift of sth; أَهْدى شَخْصاً هَدِيّةً to give sb a present ⟦2⟧ [تَكْريماً] to dedicate; أَهْدى كِتاباً إلى شَخْصٍ to dedicate a book to sb

تَهادى *v* ⟦1⟧ [تَبادَلَ الهَدايا] to exchange presents ⟦2⟧ [في مَشْيَتِهِ] to sway

اهْتَدى *v to be led on the right path by God*; to be led; لم يَهْتَدِ إلى الطَريقِ to not find the (right) way; اهْتَدى بِتَعاليمِ الإِسْلامِ to follow the teachings of Islam

اسْتَهْدى *v* to ask for guidance; اسْتَهْدى باللهِ to ask God for guidance

هَدْي *n* guidance, direction

هادٍ *n* ⟦1⟧ [مُرْشِد] spiritual guide; leader ⟦2⟧ (Islam) الهادي the Guide (*one of the names of God*)

هِداية *n* spiritual guidance; الهِداية من اللهِ the guidance comes from God

هُدًى *n* spiritual guidance, guidance on the right path (*according to the Koran*); على غَيْرِ هُدًى without guidance

هَدِيّة *n* |هَدايا| gift, present; أَعْطى \ أَهْدى هَدِيّةً to give a present; أُعْطِيَ \ تَلَقّى هَدِيّةً to receive a present; قَدَّمَ \ قَبِلَ هَدِيّةً to present/accept a gift; قَدَّمَ لِشَخْصٍ هَدِيّةً to present a gift to sb

إهْداء *n* |إهْداءات| dedication; إهْداء ل \ إلى شَخْصٍ a dedication to sb

أَهْدى *adj travelling a better (spiritual) path*

مُهْتَدٍ *n* convert, proselyte

مَهْدَوِيّ *adj* Mahdist; الحَرَكة المَهْدَوِيّة the Mahdi movement

مَهْدِي *n* (Islam) Mahdi (*a leader prophesied to rule for a proscribed period before Judgement Day*); a person who is rightly guided

مَهْدِيّ *adj* Mahdist; الحَرَكة المَهْدِيّة the Mahdi movement (*in 19th century Sudan*)

‹ **هَذا** *pron* see ذا

‹ **هَذانِ** *pron* see هَذا

‹ **هَذَبَ** *v* |i; هَذْب| to prune, to trim; هَذَبَ شَجَرةً to prune a tree

هَذَّبَ *v* ⟦1⟧ [أَصْلَحَ] to refine, to polish, to touch up; هَذَّبَ نَصًّا to polish a text ⟦2⟧ [قَلَّمَ] to prune, to trim ⟦3⟧ [أَدَّبَ] to educate; to discipline; هَذَّبَ أَوْلادَهُ to teach one's children good manners

تَهَذَّبَ *v* to be well mannered, to be civilized, to be well educated

تَهْذيب *n* politeness; refinement; discipline; تَهْذيب النَفْسِ moral improvement; self-control

مُهَذَّب *adj* well mannered, civilized, refined; غير مُهَذَّبٍ uncivilized

مُهَذِّب *adj* edifying, corrective

‹ **هَذَرَ** *v* |i-u; هَذْر ,هَذَر| to talk nonsense, to babble

هَذِرَ *v* |a; هَذَر| to babble; يَهْذُرُ كَلامُهُ he talks nonsense

أَهْذَرَ *v* to twaddle, to drivel; مَنْ أَكْثَرَ أَهْذَرَ ≈ silence is golden (*too much talk leads to nonsense*)

هَذْر *n* nonsense, rubbish; هَذْر سِياسيّ political nonsense

هَذَر *n* babble, drivel

مِهْذار *n* |مَهاذيرُ| prattler, chatterbox

هَذْرَمَ *v* |i; هَذْرَمة| to jabber

‹ **هُذْلوليّ** *adj* hyperbolic; خَطّ هُذْلوليّ hyperbola

هَذِهِ *pron* see هَذا

‹ **هَذى** *v* |i; هَذَيان ,هَذْي| to be delirious, to hallucinate; to ramble, to rave

هاذٍ *adj* raving, delirious

هُذاء *n* ravings

هَذَيان *n* delirium, hallucination, illusion; كانَ في حالةِ هَذَيانٍ to experience a delirium

‹ **هَرَأَ** *v* |a; هَرْء| *to talk in a slipshod and ugly way*; هَرَأَ في كَلامِهِ to talk slovenly

هَرَّأَ *v* to damage; to weaken; هَرَّأَ جَسَدَ شَخْصٍ to damage sb's body

أَهْرَأَ *v* to overcook, to overdo; أَهْرَأَ البَطاطِسَ to overcook potatoes

تَهَرَّأَ *v* to fall apart; to be overcooked

اهْتَرَأَ *v* to wear (out); اهْتَرَأَ الحِذاءُ the shoes were worn out

هُراء *n* nonsense, rubbish, twaddle; هذا هُراءٌ that's nonsense; هُراء في هُراءٍ ,هُراء مَحْض plain nonsense

مُهْتَرِئ *adj* worn, tatty

‹ **هَرَبَ** *v* |u; هُروب| to flee, to run away; to escape; to elope; هَرَبَ من to be on the run from sb; هَرَبَ من شَخْصٍ الاضْطِهادِ \ الحَرْبِ \ الحَقيقةِ to escape oppression/war/reality; هَرَبَ من السِجْنِ to desert the army; هَرَبَ من الجَيْشِ to escape from prison; هَرَبَ من المَدْرَسة to skip school

هَرَّبَ *v* 1 [بَضائِعَ] to smuggle; هَرَّبَ السَجائِرَ \ المَخَدِّراتِ to smuggle cigarettes/drugs 2 [شَخْصاً] to let escape; to force to flee; هَرَّبَ شَخْصاً to help sb to escape; to force sb to flee

أَهْرَبَ *v* 1 [شَخْصاً] to force to flee 2 [بالِغَ] to be drowned; أَهْرَبَ في العَمَلِ to be drowned in one's work

تَهَرَّبَ *v* |من| to evade, to elude, to dodge; to escape; to run away; تَهَرَّبَ من الحَقيقةِ to escape from reality; تَهَرَّبَ من العُقوباتِ \ الضَرائِبِ to evade sanctions/taxes; تَهَرَّبَ من شَخْصٍ to avoid sb; تَهَرَّبَ من مَسْؤوليَّتِهِ to shirk one's responsibility; تَهَرَّبَ من الواجِبِ to avoid obligations

هَرَب *n* escape; break, jailbreak; مُحاوَلة الهَرَبِ escape attempt; هَرَب من السِجْنِ jailbreak

هارِب A *adj* fugitive; هارِب من وَجْهِ العَدالةِ on the run from the law
B *n* fugitive, escapee; هارِب من الجَيْشِ army deserter; هارِب من خِدمةِ العَلَمِ fugitive from military service

هُروب *n* break, jailbreak; escape; مُحاوَلة هُروبٍ escape attempt; أَثْناءَ \ عند مُحاوَلةِ هُروبٍ during an escape attempt; أَحْبَطَ مُحاوَلةَ الهُروبِ to thwart an escape attempt; حاوَلَ الهُروبَ من السِجْنِ to attempt to escape from prison; هُروب من السِجْنِ an escape from prison; طَريق الهُروبِ escape route; الهُروب من الجُنْدِيَّةِ (Mil) desertion

تَهَرُّب *n* evasion, elusion; شَرْط التَهَرُّبِ escape clause; تَهَرُّب من الضَرائِبِ tax evasion

تَهْريب *n* |تَهْريبات| smuggling, trafficking; contraband; تَهْريب الأَشْخاصِ trafficking of people

مُتَهَرِّب *adj* evasive, elusive

مَهْرَب *n* |مَهارِبُ| 1 [مَخْرَج] escape, way out; لا مَهْرَبَ مِنْهُ there's no escape from it; unavoidable, inescapable 2 [مَلْجَأ] refuge, retreat

مُهَرَّب *adj* smuggled; مُهَرَّبات contraband

مُهَرِّب *n* smuggler, trafficker; مُهَرِّب مُخَدِّراتٍ a drugs smuggler

‹ **هُرْبول** *n* blindworm, slow-worm

‹ **هَرْبيس** *n* herpes

‹ **هيرْتْز ,هِرْتْز** *n* (Phys) hertz (*unit of frequency*)

‹ **هَرَجَ** *v* |i; هَرْج| to be/become agitated

هَرَّجَ *v* to clown about, to lark about; هَرَّجَ مع شَخْصٍ to lark about with sb

هَرْج *n* bedlam, commotion, hubbub; هَرْج وَمَرْج chaos; سَبَّبَ الهَرْجَ to cause commotion

تَهْريج *n* clowning, joking

تَهْريجيّ *adj* clownish; comical

مُهَرِّج *n* comedian, joker; clown, buffoon

مَهْرَجان ,مِهْرَجان *n* |مَهْرَجانات| festival, carnival; gala; مَهْرَجان سينَمائيّ film festival

‹ **هَرْجَلة** *n* disorder, disarray, chaos

‹ **هَرَّ** *v* |i; هَرير| to growl

هِرّ *n* |هِررة| cat; tomcat (*male cat*)

هِرّة *n* |هِرَر| kitten

هَرير *n* growling, growl

هُرَيْرة *n* kitten

‹ **هَرَسَ** *v* |u; هَرْس| to purée, to mash; to crush, to pound; هَرَسَ شَيْئاً to mash sth

هَريس A *adj* grounded, crushed, mashed
B *n* pulp, purée

هَريسة *n* 1 (NA) *spicy red pepper paste used in Tunisian cuisine and as a condiment* 2 (ME) *a sweet cake made of cooked semolina or farina soaked in simple syrup*

مِهْراس *n* |مَهاريسُ| (NA) mortar and pestle

هَرون n see هارون ‹
هُرْي n |أَهْراء| granary ‹
هَزَأَ v |a; هُزْء ,هَزْء| to scoff (at), to jeer (at), to mock; هَزَأَ ب \ هَزَأَ من شَخْصٍ على شَيْءٍ to mock sb/sth; هَزَأَ من شَخْصٍ \ شَيْءٍ to jeer at sb for sth ‹
هَزِئَ v |a; مَهْزَأة ,هُزوء ,هُزُؤ ,هُزْء ,هَزْء| to mock, to jeer, to scoff
اسْتَهْزَأَ v |ب| to jeer at, to scoff at, to mock; اسْتَهْزَأَ بِشَخْصٍ \ شَيْءٍ to scoff at sb/sth
هازِئ adj sarcastic; ironic
هُزْأة n رَجُل هُزْأةٍ; object of derision, laughing stock
اسْتِهْزاء |اسْتِهْزاءات| derision, scorn; sarcasm; mockery
اسْتِهْزائيّ adj mocking, jeering; sarcastic
مُسْتَهْزِئ adj disparaging, mocking
هِزَبْر ,هِزْبِر n |هَزابِر| lion ‹
هَزَج v |a; هَزَج| to sing ‹
هازِجة n reed warbler, chiffchaff
أُهْزوجة n |أَهازيج| song; أُهْزوجة شَعْبيّة folk song
هَزَر v |i; هَزْر| to joke; هَزَرَ مع شَخْصٍ to play a joke on sb ‹
هَزار n |هَزارات| nightingale (*Luscinia megarhynchos*)
هَزَّ v |u; هَزّ| to shake, to jolt, to agitate; هَزَّ شَيْئاً to shake sth; هَزَّ دَعائِمَ شَيْءٍ to shake the foundations of sth; هَزَّ الكَتِفَيْن to shrug one's shoulders; هَزَّ رَأْسَهُ to nod; هَزَّ ذَيْلَهُ to wag its tail ‹
هَزْهَزَ v to shake
اهْتَزَّ v to shake, to tremble, to shiver; to quake; اهْتَزَّت ثِقَتُهُ his confidence was shaken; اهْتَزَّ قَلْبُهُ his heart skipped a beat; تَهْتَزُّ الأَرْض تحت قَدَمَيْه the ground trembles under his feet
هَزّاز n كُرْسيّ هَزّاز rocking chair
هَزّة n shock; هَزّة أَرْضيّة earthquake; هَزّة خَفيفة \ عَنيفة a mild/severe shock; هَزّة الجِماع orgasm; هَزّة ارْتِداديّة aftershock
هِزّة n liveliness, vivacity
اهْتِزاز n |اهْتِزازات| shock, quake; tremor, vibration; اهْتِزازات هَوائيّة \ أَرْضيّة air/ground vibrations
اهْتِزازيّ adj vibrating, trembling; شَلَل اهْتِزازيّ Parkinson's disease

مَهْروس adj grounded, mashed; مَهْروس البَطاطِس mashed potatoes
هَرَشَ v |u; هَرْش| to scratch ‹
هَرِشَ v |a; هَرْش| to be touchy, to be prickly
هَرَّشَ v to sow discord; to goad, to provoke
هَرْطَقة n heresy ‹
هَرْطوقيّ A adj |هَراطِقة| heretical; أَفْكار هَرْطوقيّة heretical ideas
B n |هَراطِقة| heretic
هَرِعَ v |a; هَرَع| to hurry, to hasten, to rush; هَرِعَ إلى مَكانٍ to hurry to a place ‹
أَهْرَعَ v to hurry, to rush
هَرَع n hysteria
هَرَفَ v |i; هَرْف |ب| to rave (about), to praise excessively; يَهْرِفُ بما لا يَعْرِفُ he is talking nonsense ‹
هَرَقَ v |a; هَرْق| to pour; هَرَقَ الماءَ to pour water ‹
أَهْرَقَ v to pour, to shed; أَهْرَقَ الدِماءَ to shed blood
مُهْرَق n |مَهارِقُ| parchment
هَرِمَ v |a; مَهْرَم ,هَرَم| to grow very old ‹
هَرَم n |أَهْرامات ,أَهْرام| pyramid
هَرِم adj ancient
هَرَميّ adj hierarchical; pyramidal, pyramidical; تَنْظيم هَرَميّ hierarchy; تَسْويق هَرَميّ pyramid scheme
هَرَميّة n hierarchy
أَهْراميّ adj pyramidal, pyramidical; الأَرْقام الأَهْراميّة pyramidal numbers
هُرْمون ,هورْمون n |هُرْمونات| hormone; هُرْمونات ذُكوريّة \ أُنْثَويّة male/female hormones; اضْطِراب في الهُرْموناتِ hormonal disorder ‹
هُرْمونيّ adj hormonal; تَأْثير هُرْمونيّ hormonal influence
هَرْهَرَ v |i; هَرْهَرة| to make a sound, to laugh, to roar ‹
هِراوة n |هَراوى ,هِراوات| 1 [عَصا] club, bludgeon, cudgel 2 [عَصا الشُرْطيّ] baton, truncheon ‹
هَرْوَلَ v |i; هَرْوَلة| to run, to scurry ‹
هَرْوَلة n jog, run
مُهَرْوِل adj running, jogging; مُهَرْوِلاً at a jog

مُهْتَزّ *adj* moved, shaken; unstable; صورة مُهْتَزّة a blurry picture; شَخْصِيّة مُهْتَزّة an unstable character

مَهْزوز *adj* shaken, moved; صورة مَهْزوزة a blurry picture

‹ **هَزَعَ** *v* |a; هَزْع| to hurry, to hasten

هَزيع *n* a part of the night

‹ **هَزَلَ, هَزِلَ** *v* |a-i; هَزْل| **1** [مَزَحَ] to joke, to jest; to tease **2** [صارَ نَحيلاً] to lose weight, to become thin; to waste away

هَزَّلَ *v* to cause to lose weight, to enervate

هازَلَ *v* to tease; to jest, to joke

أَهْزَلَ *v* to weaken, to cause to lose weight

هَزْل *n* joke, jest; على سَبيلِ الهَزْلِ in jest

هازِل **A** *adj* humorous, playful **B** *n* joker, jester

هُزال *n* thinness, leanness, skinniness; مَرَض الهُزالِ anorexia nervosa

هَزْلِيّ *adj* comic, humorous, funny; مُلاحَظة هَزْلِيّة a humorous remark

هَزيل *adj* |هَزْلى| thin, skinny, lean; scrawny, gaunt

مَهْزَلة *n* |مَهازِلُ| farce

مَهْزول *adj* skinny, scrawny, thin, emaciated

‹ **هَزَمَ** *v* |i; هَزيمة, هَزْم| **1** [كَسَرَ] to defeat, to conquer, to vanquish; هَزَمَ الخَصْمَ \ العَدُوَّ to defeat the opponent/enemy; هَزَمَ هَزيمةً ساحِقةً to gain a sweeping victory, to win by a landslide **2** [الرَّعْدُ] to thunder, to roll; to whistle (*wind*); to buzz, to hum; هَزَمَ الرَّعْدُ the thunder rumbled

انْهَزَمَ *v* to suffer a defeat, to be defeated

هَزيم *n* thunder; هَزيم الرَّعْدِ thunderclap

هَزيمة *n* |هَزائِمُ| defeat; هَزيمة كُبْرى \ قاسية \ ثَقيلة a heavy defeat; هَزيمة ساحِقة \ ماحِقة \ نَكْراء a crushing defeat; مُنِيَ \ باءَ بِهَزيمةٍ to suffer a defeat; أَلْحَقَ هَزيمةً بِشَخْصٍ to inflict (a) defeat upon sb; اسْتَسْلَمَ للهَزيمةِ to acknowledge defeat

انْهِزام *n* defeat

انْهِزامِيّ *adj* defeatist

انْهِزامِيّة *n* defeatism

مَهْزوم *adj* defeated; جَيْش مَهْزوم a defeated army

‹ **تَهَزْهَزَ** *v* to bump, to jolt, to rock

‹ **هَسَّ** *v* |i; هَسّ| to whisper

هُسّ *excl* shh, hush

هَسيس *n* whisper, whispering

‹ **هَسْهَسَ** *v* |i; هَسْهَسة| to gurgle (*brook*)

هَسْهَسة *n* whisper, whispering; هَسْهَسة النارِ hissing of the fire

‹ **هَشَّ** *v* |i; هُشوشة| **1** [تَبَسَّمَ] to smile, to wear a smile **2** [كانَ هَشًّا] to be crisp; to be brittle, to be crumbly; هَشَّ الغُصْنُ the branch has dried out; هَشَّ الخُبْزُ the bread has become crisp

هَشّ *adj* **1** [قابِل للكَسْرِ] breakable, fragile, brittle; السَلام الهَشّ the fragile peace; عِظام هَشّة brittle bones; مادّة هَشّة fragile material **2** [فَرِح] happy, cheerful **3** [طَرِيّ] crisp, fresh

هَشاش *adj* breakable, fragile, brittle

هَشاشة *n* fragility, brittleness

‹ **هَشَمَ** *v* |i; هَشْم| to break into pieces; هَشَمَ الحَطَبَ to chop wood

هَشَّمَ *v* to smash, to destroy, to shatter; هَشَّمَ الزُجاجَ to shatter glass

تَهَشَّمَ *v* to break, to fall to pieces; to be shattered, to be smashed

هاشِم *n* Hashem (*male given name*)

هاشِمِيّ *adj* Hashemite; المَمْلَكة الأُرْدُنِّيّة الهاشِمِيّة the Hashemite Kingdom of Jordan (*the official name of Jordan*)

هِشام *n* Hisham (*male given name*)

هَشيم **A** *adj* dry, fragile **B** *n* kindling; انْتَشَرَ انْتِشارَ النارِ في الهَشيمِ to spread like wildfire

مُتَهَشِّم *adj* broken (into pieces)

‹ **هَصَرَ** *v* |i; هَصْر| to crush, to squeeze

‹ **هَضْبة** *n* |هِضاب| hill, height, highland; plateau, tableland; في الهِضابِ in the hills; على الهَضْبةِ on the hill; هَضْبة الجولانِ Golan Heights; سِلْسِلة هِضابٍ a range of hills

‹ **هَضَمَ** *v* |i; هَضْم| **1** [الطَعامَ] to digest **2** [تَحَمَّلَ] to deal with, to cope with; to endure, to bear; to accept; هَضَمَ خَبَراً to cope with the news; هَضَمَ فِكْرةً to accept an idea **3** [ظَلَمَ] to violate, to infringe (on); هَضَمَ حَقَّ شَخْصٍ to wrong sb

‹ **هَفا** *v* |u; هَفو| ◆1 [خفق] to pound, to throb; هَفا قَلْبُهُ his heart pounded ◆2 [زَلّ] to make a mistake, to err; هَفا لِسانُهُ he made a slip (of the tongue) ◆3 [أَسْرَعَ] to rush, to be eager for

هَفْوة *n* |هَفوات| error, mistake, blunder; هَفْوة لِسانٍ slip of the tongue; ارْتَكَبَ هَفْوةً to commit a gaffe; لِكُلِّ عالِمٍ هَفْوةٌ *even scholars make mistakes*

‹ **هِكْتار** *n* |هِكْتارات| hectare; ١٠ هِكْتاراتٍ من الأَرْضِ 10 hectares of land

‹ **هِكْتوغْرام** *n* هِكْتوجْرام hectogram

هِكْتولِتْر *n* hectolitre

هِكْتومِتْر *n* hectometre

‹ **هٰكَذا** *adv* see ذا

‹ **هَكَر** *n* hacker

هَكَّرَ *n* (Comput) to hack; هَكَّرَ مَوْقِعاً \ حِساباً to hack a site/account

‹ **تَهَكَّمَ** *v* to mock, to taunt, to ridicule; تَهَكَّمَ على شَخْصٍ \ شَيْءٍ to mock sb/sth

تَهَكُّم *n* |تَهَكُّمات| sarcasm, mockery; caricature, parody

تَهَكُّميّ *adj* sarcastic, cynical, mocking; مُلاحَظة \ ضَحْكة \ نَبْرة تَهَكُّمِيّة a sarcastic remark/laugh/tone

مُتَهَكِّم ◼A *adj* sarcastic, cynical

◼B *n* sarcastic person; scoffer

‹ **هَلْ** *particle* ◆1 [أَ] *question particle*; هَلْ هذا صَحيحٌ؟ is this true?; هَلْ فَعَلْتَ ذلك فِعْلاً؟ did you really do that? ◆2 [إذا ما] if; لا أَعْرِفُ هَلْ هذا صَحيحٌ I don't know if this is right

هَلاّ *particle* why not; هَلاّ جَلَسْتَ؟ why don't you sit down?

‹ **هَلِبَ** *v* |a; هَلَب| to be hairy

هُلْب *n coll* stubble, bristle

هلْب *n* |أَهْلاب| anchor

أَهْلَب *adj* |dipt| hairy, shaggy

مُهَلَّبِيّة *n a sweet dessert made of rice flour, milk and sugar*

‹ **هَلْبوت** *n* سَمَك هَلْبوت halibut (*Hippoglossus*)

‹ **هَلَسَ** *v* |i; هَلْس| to exhaust, to waste away

هَلَّسَ *v* to pine away, to become emaciated

أَهْلَسَ *v* to smile faintly

هَلْس *n* ◆1 [سُلّ] tuberculosis ◆2 [هُزال] emaciation, exhaustion

انْهَضَمَ *v* to digest, to be digested

هَضْم *n* digestion; سوء \ عُسْر الهَضْمِ poor digestion, indigestion; عَسِر \ صَعْب الهَضْمِ hard to digest, indigestible; غِذاء صَعْب الهَضْمِ indigestible food; سُهولة الهَضْمِ easy digestion, ease of digestion; غِذاء سَهْل الهَضْمِ easily digestible food; الأَرُزُّ سَهْلُ الهَضْمِ easily digestible rice; سَهَّلَ \ ساعَدَ على الهَضْمِ to ease digestion; قابل للهَضْم digestible

هَضْميّ *adj* digestive, digestion (*before n*); جهاز هَضْميّ digestive system; اخْتِصاصيّ الجهاز الهَضْميّ gastroenterologist; قَناة هَضْميّة digestive tract

مَهْضوم *adj* حُقوق مَهْضومة violated rights; مَهْضوم الحَقِّ treated unjustly, aggrieved

‹ **هَطَلَ** *v* |i; هَطْلان, هُطول, هَطْل| to stream, to pour down, to gush; يَهْطِلُ المَطَرُ بِغَزارةٍ it's raining cats and dogs

تَهاطَلَ *v* to stream

هُطول *n* precipitation; هُطول الأَمْطار rainfall

تَهاطُل *n* stream; تَهاطُل نَوَويّ nuclear fallout; تَهاطُل الأَمْطارِ rainfall

‹ **هَفَتَ** *v* |i; هُفات, هَفْت| ◆1 [انْخَفَضَ] to decrease, to diminish, to abate ◆2 [تَطايَرَ] to twirl, to swirl; to fly, to flutter

تَهافَتَ *v* to rush at, to charge; تَهافَتَ على شَيْءٍ to charge at sth; تَهافَتَتِ الأَحْداثُ the events happened in rapid succession

تَهافُت *n* |تَهافُتات| rush, run; تَهافُت على المَحَلاّتِ a dash to the shops; التَهافُت على التَذاكِرِ \ المَساكِنِ a scramble for tickets/houses; التَهافُت على بَيْعِ الدولارِ the rush to sell dollars

مُتَهافِت *adj* packed; أَشْخاص مُتَهافِتونَ على السُلْطةِ people jostling for power

‹ **هَفَّ** *v* |i; هَفيف, هَفّ| ◆1 [الريحُ] to blow; هَفَّت الريحُ the wind was blowing ◆2 [أَسْرَعَ] to rush past, to run past; هَفَّ على بالِهِ أَنّ ... it suddenly occurred to him that ...

هِفّ ◼A *adj* empty; trifling

◼B *n* smelt, sparling

هَفّاف *adj* transparent

‹ **هَفْهاف** *adj* translucent; light, airy

اِسْتِهْلاكِيّ *adj* consumer (*before n*), consumption (*before n*); مُجْتَمَع اسْتِهْلاكِيّ consumer society; سِلَع \ مُنْتَجات اسْتِهْلاكِيّة consumer goods

اِهْتِلاك *n* depreciation

إِهْلاك *n* depreciation

تَهْلُكة *n* risk, danger; destruction, ruin

مُتَهالِك *adj* rickety, wobbly; كُرْسِيّ مُتَهالِك a rickety chair

مُسْتَهْلَك *adj* consumed, used (up); paid off; فِكْرة مُسْتَهْلَكة an outmoded idea; آلات مُسْتَهْلَكة used equipment; مَوْضوع مُسْتَهْلَك an over discussed topic

مُسْتَهْلِك *n* consumer, user; سِعْر المُسْتَهْلِك retail price, consumer price; صِغار \ كِبار المُسْتَهْلِكين small/large consumers; سوق المُسْتَهْلِكين consumer market

مُهْلِك *adj* destructive, fatal, deadly; سُرْعة مُهْلِكة a deadly speed; عَواقِب مُهْلِكة fatal consequences

مَهْلَكة *n* |مَهالِكُ| pitfall, trap; danger

هَلَّ *v* |i; هَلّ| 1 [ظَهَرَ] to come up, to appear (*new moon*); هَلَّ هِلالُ العيد the new moon of Eid has appeared 2 [بَدَأَ] to begin, to start; هَلَّ الشَهْرُ the month has begun; هَلَّ عَلَيْنا الشِتاءُ winter has set in; هَلَّ عَلَيْنا الخَيْرُ a good thing happened to us

هَلَّلَ *v* 1 [شَهَدَ] *to say* لا إِلَهَ إِلاّ الله (*there is no god but God*) 2 [صاحَ فَرَحاً] to shout with joy; to cheer; هَلَّلَ لِلبَطَل to cheer the champion

أَهَلَّ *v* 1 [حَمِدَ اللّهَ] to praise God 2 [الشَهْرُ] to begin (*a new month*)

تَهَلَّلَ *v* to beam with joy; to shine; تَهَلَّلَ وَجْهُهُ his face beamed with joy

اِنْهَلَّ *v* to fall down; انْهَلَّ المَطَرُ the rain was pouring down

اِسْتَهَلَّ *v* 1 [بَدَأَ] to begin, to start, to open; اسْتَهَلَّ شَهْرُ رَمَضانَ the month of Ramadan has begun; اسْتَهَلَّ المُؤْتَمَرَ بِكَلِمةٍ to open the conference with a speech 2 [تَهَلَّلَ] to radiate, to shine

هِلال *n* |أَهِلّة, أَهاليلُ| new moon; half-moon, crescent moon; الهِلال الأَحْمَر the Red Crescent; الهِلال الخَصيب the fertile crescent; رُؤْية الهِلال sighting of the new moon (*at the beginning of Ramadan*)

هَلِعَ *v* |a; هَلَع| to be/become anxious, to panic; to be/become terrified

هَلَع *n* alarm, panic, dismay; بِحالةٍ من الهَلَع in (a) panic

هَلِع *adj* anxious, worried, uneasy

هَلوع *adj* anxious, nervous, panicky

هَلْفوت *adj* |هَلافيتُ| loafer, layabout (BrE), bum (AmE)

هَلْقَمَ *v* |i; هَلْقَمة| to gobble (down), to gulp (down); هَلْقَمَ ما في فَمِهِ من طَعام بِسُرْعةٍ he gobbled down the food in his mouth

هَلَكَ *v* |i; تَهْلُكة, هَلاك| to die, to perish, to be killed; هَلَكَ في حادِثِ مُرور to die in a traffic accident

أَهْلَكَ *v* to destroy, to ruin, to wreck; أَهْلَكَ صِحَّتَهُ to ruin one's health; أَهْلَكَ المالَ to spend too much money

تَهالَكَ *v* 1 [جَدَّ] |في| to exert oneself (in), to do one's best (in); to be worn out 2 [ارْتَمى] |على| to throw oneself (into/upon), to pounce (on)

اِهْتَلَكَ *v* to put oneself in danger

اِسْتَهْلَكَ *v* to consume, to use (up); اسْتَهْلَكَ البَضائِعَ to consume goods; اسْتَهْلَكَ الكَثيرَ من الكَهْرباءِ \ الماءِ \ الطاقةِ to use a lot of electricity/water/energy; يَسْتَهْلِكُ المُحَرِّكُ الكَثيرَ من البَنْزينِ the engine guzzles petrol (BrE) gas (AmE); اسْتَهْلَكَ مَبالِغَ ضَخْمةً to consume large amounts of money

هالِك *adj* |هَوالِكُ, هَلْكى| transitory, mortal; perishable; destructible; dying

هَلاك *n* ruin, destruction; damnation; أَدّى إلى هَلاكِ شَخْصٍ to bring ruin upon sb; to destroy sb; الهَلاك الأَبَدِيّ eternal damnation

اِسْتِهْلاك *n* |اسْتِهْلاكات| consumption, using up; الاسْتِهْلاك المَحَلِّيّ domestic consumption; الاسْتِهْلاك الخاصّ private consumption; آخِر تاريخ الاسْتِهْلاكِ use-by date; ضَريبة على الاسْتِهْلاكِ, ضَرائِب \ رُسوم الاسْتِهْلاكِ consumption tax, excise; ضَريبة على اسْتِهْلاكِ الطاقةِ energy tax; اسْتِهْلاك الغازِ \ الوَقودِ gas/fuel consumption; مُعَدَّل الاسْتِهْلاكِ the average consumption; اسْتِهْلاك مُرْتَفِع \ مُنْخَفِض للماءِ high/low water consumption; زِيادة الاسْتِهْلاكِ an increase in consumption

هِلاليّ *adj* سَطح هِلاليّ (Phys) meniscus (*curved upper surface of a liquid in a tube*)

اسْتِهْلال *n* beginning, start, opening; initiation, inception

اسْتِهْلاليّ *adj* starting, opening; حَرْف اسْتِهْلاليّ capital letter

تَهْليل *n* |تَهاليلُ| **1** [تَصْفيق] cheers, cheering, applause; (Islam) saying لا إلَهَ إلاّ اللهُ (*there is no god but God*) **2** [هَدْهَدة] lullaby; تَهْليلة للطِفْل

مُتَهَلِّل *adj* joyful, cheerful; radiant, beaming

مُسْتَهَلّ *n* start, beginning, opening; في مُسْتَهَلِّ الجَلْسةِ at the opening of the session

مُهَلَّل *adj* crescent-shaped

‹ **هَلِّلويا** *excl* hallelujah

‹ **هَلُمَّ** *particle* come (on), let's ...; هَلُمَّ بِنا! come on!, let's go!; وَهَلُمَّ جَرًّا and so on

هُلام *n* gel, gelatine, jelly

هُلاميّ *adj* **1** [جيلاتينيّ] gelatinous, jelly-like; هُلاميّات البَحْرِ sea molluscs (*Mollusca*) **2** [غير واضِح] vague, indefinable; فِكْرة هُلاميّة a vague idea

‹ **هَلْهَلَ** *v* |i; هَلْهَلة| to weave finely

مُهَلْهَل *adj* flimsy, paper-thin; dilapidated; scruffy, shabby; مُهَلْهَل الثِياب scruffy

‹ **هَلْوَسَ** *v* |i; هَلْوَسة| to hallucinate

هَلْوَسة *n* |هَلاوِسُ| hallucination, delusion

مُهَلْوِس *adj* psychedelic

‹ **هِليكوبْتِر** *n* helicopter

‹ **هيلْيوم**, **هِلْيوم** *n* helium

‹ **هَلْيون**, **هِلْيَوْن** *n* asparagus

‹ **هُمْ** *pron* they (*m*)

‹ **هُما** *pron* the two of them, they (*two*)

‹ **هَمْبورْجَر**, **هَمْبَرْغَر** *n* hamburger

‹ **هَمَج** *n coll* barbarian

هَمَجيّ **A** *adj* |هَمَج| wild, uncivilized; barbarian, barbaric; قَبائِل هَمَجيّة barbarian tribes; تَصَرُّف هَمَجيّ barbaric behaviour **B** *n* |هَمَج| barbarian, savage

هَمَجيّة *n* barbarism, barbarity, savagery

‹ **هَمَدَ** *v* |u; هُمود| to quiet down, to subside, to fade away; هَمَدَت الأَصْواتُ the noise died down; هَمَدَت النارُ the fire has gone out

أَهْمَدَ *v* to extinguish, to put out

هامِد *adj* |هَوامِدُ| quiet; lifeless; جُثّة هامِدة a lifeless body, corpse; شَجَرة هامِدة a dead tree

هُمود *n* passivity, inaction; extinction

‹ **هَمَرَ** *v* |u; هَمْر| to pour down

انْهَمَرَ *v* to rain; to stream, to flow; يَنْهَمِرُ المَطَرُ it's pouring; تَنْهَمِرُ القَذائِفُ bombs are raining down; تَنْهَمِرُ الأَسْئِلةُ questions stream forth

هَمْرة *n* |هَمَرات| shower (of rain)

مُنْهَمِر *adj* pouring, streaming

‹ **هَمَزَ** *v* |i-u; هَمْز| to urge on, to incite, to drive; to spur on; هَمَزَ فَرَساً to spur on a horse

هَمْزة *n* |هَمَزات| glottal stop; hamza (*Arabic consonant*); هَمْزة القَطْع disjunctive hamza; هَمْزة الوَصْل conjunctive hamza; كانَ هَمْزةَ الوَصْلِ بين الطَرَفَيْنِ he was the link between both parties

هُمَزة *n* سورة الهُمَزة (Islam) The Scandalmonger (*Sura 104*)

مِهْماز, **مِهْمَز** *n* |مَهاميزُ| spur

مَهْموز *adj* with a hamza; فِعْل مَهْموز *verb containing a hamza*

‹ **هَمَسَ** *v* |i; هَمْس| to whisper; هَمَسَ إلى شَخْصٍ بِشَيْءٍ to whisper sth to sb

تَهامَسَ *v* to whisper to each other, to exchange whispers

هَمْس *n* whisper, whispering; هَمْساً in whispers

هَمْسة *n* whisper, whispering; تَبادَلَ الهَمَساتِ to exchange whispers

مَهْموس *adj* (Gram) voiceless, unvoiced, surd; حَرْف مَهْموس a voiceless consonant

‹ **هَمْسْتَر** *n* hamster (*Cricetinae*)

هَمَّشَ *v* to marginalize; to margin, to marginate

هامِش *n* |هَوامِشُ| **1** [جانِب الصَفْحةِ] margin; خطّ الهامِشِ margin; على الهامِشِ in the margin **2** (fig) fringe, periphery; على هامِشِ المُجْتَمَعِ on the margins of society; على هامِشِ

مُهْمَل **A** *adj* **1** [مَهْجور] neglected, uncared for; كَمّيّة مُهْمَلة a negligible amount; صارَ مُهْمَلاً to become obsolete **2** [حَرْف] *without a diacritical point*; حُروف مُهْمَلة letters without diacritical points

B *n* |مُهْمَلات| مُهْمَلات waste; سَلّة المُهْمَلاتِ waste-paper basket (BrE) trash can (AmE); أَلْقى شَيْئاً في سَلّةِ المُهْمَلاتِ to throw sth in the waste-paper basket

مُهْمِل **A** *adj* careless; negligent, neglectful; مُهْمِل في عَمَلِهِ careless in one's work

B *n* loafer

هَمْلَجة *n* amble (*horse*)

هَمَّ *v* |u; هَمّ| **1** [عَناهُ الأَمْرُ] to concern, to interest, to occupy; لم يَهُمَّهُ الأَمْرُ (أَبَداً) it doesn't concern me; لا يَهُمُّني he couldn't care less; هذا لا يَهُمُّ this is not important **2** [عَزَمَ] to have in mind, to intend, to plan **3** [أَقْلَقَ] to distress, to disquiet; هَمَّني هذا الخَبَرُ this message distressed me

أَهَمَّ *v* **1** [اهْتَمَّ] to interest, to concern; هذا لا يُهِمُّني that doesn't concern me; هذا يُهِمُّني كَثيراً that really matters to me; لِمَنْ يُهِمُّهُ الأَمْرُ to whom it may concern; (لا) يُهِمُّني أَمْرُكَ I (don't) care about you **2** [أَقْلَقَ] to distress, to disquiet

اهْتَمَّ *v* **1** [بالى] |ب| to be interested in, to care about; to concern oneself with, to trouble oneself about; اهْتَمَّ بِشَخْصٍ \ بِشَيْءٍ to care about sb/sth **2** [اغْتَمَّ] |ل, ب| to be anxious about, to worry about; اهْتَمَّ لِشَيْءٍ to be anxious about sth

هامّ *adj* important, weighty, significant; شَخْص هامّ an important person; مَسْأَلة غَيْر هامّةٍ an unimportant matter

هامّة *n* |هَوامّ| pest, vermin; poisonous animal, venomous animal

هَمّ *n* |هُموم| **1** [اهْتِمام] concern, worry; حَمَلَ هُموماً كَثيرةً \ قَليلةً to have many/few worries; كانَ كُلُّ هَمِّهِ أَنْ ... his only concern was that ....; قَلْبُهُ مُثْقَلٌ بالهُمومِ he is burdened with worries; هُمْ في الهَمِّ سَواءٌ they're in the same boat; كانَتْ حَياتُهُ خالِيةً من الهُمومِ he had no worries, he was carefree; خالٍ من الهَمِّ carefree **2** [حُزْن] sadness, sorrow

هَمّام *adj* brave

هُمام *adj* |هِمام| magnanimous, generous; gallant, chivalrous

الأَخْبارِ on the periphery of the news **3** [عَدَد نِسْبيّ] margin; هامِش ضَيِّق a narrow margin; هامِش أَرْباحٍ profit margin; هامِش رِبْحٍ كَبير a big profit margin; هامِش خَطَأٍ, نِسْبة هامِشٍ margin of error; هامِش الخَطَأِ المَقْبول an acceptable margin of error; هامِش خَطَأٍ أَقَلّ من ٢٪ a margin of error of less than 2%

هامِشيّ *adj* marginal; حَياة \ ظاهِرة هامِشيّة a marginal existence/phenomenon; مُلاحَظة هامِشيّة a casual remark, a marginal note; لَعِبَ دَوْراً هامِشيًّا to play a marginal role

تَهْميش *n* marginalization

مُهَمَّش *adj* marginal, in the margin

هَمَعَ *v* |a-u; هُموع| هَمَعَتْ عَيْنُها she cried

هَمَكَ *v* |u; هَمْك| to urge, to press, to keep after; هَمَكَ شَخْصاً في شَيْءٍ to urge sb to do sth properly

انْهَمَكَ *v* to be absorbed, to be wrapped up, to be dedicated; to be busy; انْهَمَكَ في عَمَلِهِ to be wrapped up in one's work; انْهَمَكَ في الفَسادِ to be engaged in corruption

انْهِماك *n* |انْهِماكات| preoccupation, involvement

مُنْهَمِك *adj* absorbed, preoccupied; كانَ مُنْهَمِكاً في شَيْءٍ to be completely preoccupied by sth

أَهْمَلَ *v* **1** [تَهاوَنَ] to ignore, to forsake; to overlook, to leave out, to neglect; أَهْمَلَ شَيْئاً to be negligent in sth; أَهْمَلَ شَيْئاً \ شَخْصاً to ignore sth/sb; أَهْمَلَ مَظْهَرَهُ \ لِياقَتَهُ البَدَنيّةَ to neglect one's appearance/physical fitness; أَهْمَلَ صِحَّتَهُ to neglect one's health; أَهْمَلَ الأَطْفالَ \ الحَيَواناتِ to neglect the children/animals; أَهْمَلَ نَصيحةً to ignore advice **2** (Law) to be in default

انْهَمَلَ *v* to stream, to flow, to pour; يَنْهَمِلُ المَطَرُ غَزيراً the rain is pouring down

هَمَل *adj* neglected, left to oneself; الهَمَل من الشَّبابِ homeless youth

هامِل *adj* |هُمّال, هُمَّل| كَلْب هامِل stray dog

إِهْمال *n* neglect, negligence; carelessness; disregard; عن إِهْمالِهِ out of carelessness; وَقَعَ الخَطَأُ نَتيجةَ إِهْمالٍ the error was caused by negligence; إِهْمال في تَأْدِيةِ الواجِبِ carelessness in the performance of a duty; يُمْكِنُ إِهْمالُهُ negligible

هِمّة *n* |هِمَم| 1 [عَزْم] ambition, aspiration; motivation, determination, decisiveness; ضُعف الهِمّةِ lack of ambition, lack of interest; عالي الهِمّةِ with high ambitions; كانَ بَعيدَ الهِمّةِ to be highly ambitious; ثَبَّطَ هِمّةَ شَخْصٍ to discourage sb 2 [انْدفاع] endeavour, effort; اسْتَنْهَضَ هِمَمَ شَخْصٍ to encourage sb 3 [نَشاط] energy; شَخْص لا هِمّةَ لَهُ a listless person

اهْتِمام *n* |اهتِمامات| 1 [انْتِباه] interest, attention; عَدَم الاهْتِمامِ lack of interest; مَجال الاهْتِمامِ field of interest; مَوْضِع اهْتِمامٍ point of interest; أعارَ (شَيْئاً) اهْتِماماً to pay attention (to sth); وَجَّهَ اهْتِمامَهُ على \ إلى شَيْءٍ to focus one's attention on sth; أبْدى \ أظْهَرَ اهْتِماماً to show (an) interest; اهْتِمام ب \ ل ... interest in ...; اسْتَمَعَ \ أنْصَتَ إلى شَيْءٍ باهْتِمامٍ to listen to sth attentively; كانَ مَحَلَّ \ مَوْضِعَ اهْتِمامٍ to receive a lot of attention; مُثير للاهْتِمامِ interesting; اسْتَعْلَمَ \ سَأَلَ عن شَيْءٍ باهْتِمامٍ to enquire with interest after sth; أثارَ اهْتِمامَ (شَخْصٍ) to arouse (sb's) interest; كِتاب مُثير للاهْتِمامِ an interesting book; أُمور ذات اهْتِمامٍ مُشْتَرَكٍ matters of common interest 2 [رِعاية] care, concern

أَهَمّيّة *n* importance, significance, consequence; ذو أَهَمّيّةٍ important, weighty; ذو أَهَمّيّةٍ أساسيّةٍ \ جَوْهَرِيّةٍ of great importance; مَسْأَلة ذات أَهَمّيّة فائِقةٍ ,أمْر بالِغ الأَهَمّيّةِ a matter of great importance; حُجَج ذات أَهَمّيّةٍ weighty arguments; كانَ ذا أَهَمّيّةٍ to be of importance; كانَ ذا أَهَمّيّةٍ كَبيرةٍ بالنِسْبةِ لِشَخْصٍ \ لِشَيْءٍ to be of great consequence to sth/sb; فَقَدَ من أَهَمّيّتِهِ to become less important; اكْتَسَبَ أَهَمّيّةً to become more important; عَلَّقَ أَهَمّيّةً على شَيْءٍ to attach importance to sth; فَهِمَ \ لم يُقَدِّرْ أَهَمّيّةَ شَيْءٍ to realize/underestimate the importance of sth; كَبير \ قَليل الأَهَمّيّةِ of great/little importance; لا يَقِلُّ أَهَمّيّةً عن ... no less important than ...; قَلَّلَ من أَهَمّيّةِ المَشاكِلِ to simplify problems; لا أَهَمّيّةَ لَهُ insignificant; اسْتَوى في الأَهَمّيّةِ مع ... to be equally important as ...; على دَرَجةٍ من الأَهَمّيّةِ to a significant extent; على دَرَجةٍ كَبيرةٍ من الأَهَمّيّةِ very important

مُهْتَمّ A *adj* interested, attentive; كانَ مُهْتَمًّا (جِدًّا) بِشَيْءٍ to be (very) interested in sth; غَيْر مُهْتَمٍّ indifferent B *n* interested person

مُهِمّ *adj* important, significant; main, principal; interesting; مَكان مُهِمّ a prominent place; اخْتِلاف \ فَرْق مُهِمّ a significant difference; مُباراة \ اجْتِماع مُهِمّ(ة) an important match/meeting; مَعْلومات مُهِمّة important information; عامِل \ دَوْر مُهِمّ an important factor/role; مَوْضوع مُهِمّ a main topic; شَخْصيّة مُهِمّة an important person; شَخْص مُهِمّ جِدًّا very important person, VIP; نُقْطة مُهِمّة (في تَطَوُّرٍ أو تَحَوُّلٍ) milestone (in development or change); غَيْر مُهِمٍّ unimportant; مَسْأَلة غَيْر مُهِمّةٍ a matter of little importance; من المُهِمِّ جِدًّا أنْ... it's very important that ...; لَعِبَ دَوْراً مُهِمًّا he played a prominent role

مَهَمّة *n* |مَهامّ| see مُهِمّة

مُهِمّة, مَهَمّة *n* |مُهِمّات, مَهامّ| task, duty; mission, assignment, commission; مُهِمّة سِلْمِيّة peace mission; مُهِمّة ناجِحة a successful mission; شَريط المَهامِّ (Comput) taskbar; مَجْموعة مُهِمّاتٍ range of duties; مُتَعَدِّد المَهامِّ multitasking; تَأْدِية المَهامِّ performance of tasks; قامَ بِمُهِمّةٍ, أدّى \ نَفَّذَ مُهِمّةً to perform a task; أنْجَزَ مُهِمّةً to accomplish a mission; فَوَّضَ مَهامَّ to delegate duties

مَهْموم *adj* concerned, worried; وَجْه مَهْموم a worried face; مَهْموم بِشَخْصٍ \ بِشَيْءٍ concerned about sb/sth

هَمْهَمَ *v* |i; هَمْهَمة| to murmur, to mumble, to mutter; to hum, to growl, to rumble

هَمْهَمة *n* |هَمْهَمات, هَماهِم| murmur, muttering; هَمْهَمة غَيْر مَفْهومة unintelligible muttering

هَنُؤَ *v* |u; هَناءة| to be easy

هَنِئَ *v* |a; هَناءة, هَنَأ| to do good (*food and drinks*); هَنِئَ لَهُ الطَعامُ the meal did him good; هَنِئَ من الطَعامِ to have had enough to eat; هَنِئَ بِشَيْءٍ to enjoy sth

هَنَّأَ *v* to congratulate; هَنَّأَ شَخْصاً (بِشَيْءٍ) to congratulate sb (on sth)

تَهَنَّأَ *v* to enjoy, to take pleasure

هانِئ *adj* happy, glad; carefree

هَناء *n* |هَناءات| happiness, bliss; بالهَناءِ والشِفاءِ enjoy your meal, bon appétit

هَنِيء *adj* pleasant, nice; wholesome; هَنِيئاً (لَكَ) congratulations; *an expression used at the end of a meal or after a great success*; هَنِيئاً مَرِيئاً *an expression used at the end of a meal or after a great success*

تَهْنِئَة *n* |تَهانِئُ, تَهانٍ| congratulations, felicitations; بَرْقِيّة تَهْنِئَةٍ congratulatory message; أَسْعَد التَهاني heartfelt congratulations; التَهاني القَلْبِيّة sincerest congratulations; مع أَحَرِّ التَهانِئِ with best wishes; قَدَّمَ التَهانِئَ لِشَخْصٍ to congratulate sb; هذا جَدِيرٌ بالتَهْنِئَةِ this deserves congratulations

مُهَنِّئ *n* well-wisher

‹ هُنا *adv* here, over here, in this place; يَسْكُنُونَ هُنا they live here; من هُنا إلى هُناكَ back and forth

هُناكَ, هُنالِكَ *adv* **1** [في ذلك المَكانِ] there, over there, in that place; إلى هُناكَ to there; كانَ يَسْكُنُ هُناكَ لِمُدّةِ سَنَتَيْنِ he lived there for two years **2** [يوجَدُ] there is/are; هُناكَ سَبَبانِ لِهَذا there are two causes for this

هُنالِكَ *adv* see هُناكَ

‹ هِنْد *n* |dipt f| **1** [اسْم شَخْصِيّ] Hind (*female given name*) **2** [بِلاد] see الهِنْد

هِنْدِيّ **A** *adj* |هُنود| Indian; (اللُّغة) الهِنْدِيّة Hindi (*language*); المُحيط الهِنْدِيّ the Indian Ocean; تَمْر هِنْدِيّ tamarind (*Tamarindus indica*) **B** *n* |هُنود| Indian (*person*); الهُنود الحُمْر Native Americans; أَحَد الهُنودِ الحُمْرِ a Native American

الهِنْد *n* India; بِلاد الهِنْدِ India

‹ هِنْدِباء, هِنْدِبا *n* |f| هِنْدِباء أَنْدِيفِيّة endive (*Cichorium endivia*); هِنْدِباء بَرِّيّة chicory (*Cichorium intybus*)

‹ هِنْداز *n* measure

‹ هَنْدَسَ *v* |i; هَنْدَسة| to design, to engineer (*structurally or architecturally*)

هَنْدَسة *n* geometry; architecture; الجَبْر والهَنْدَسة algebra and geometry; هَنْدَسة مِعْمارِيّة \ العِمارةِ architecture, building; هَنْدَسة ميكانيكِيّة mechanical engineering; هَنْدَسة تَحْلِيلِيّة analytic geometry; هَنْدَسة وَصْفِيّة descriptive geometry; هَنْدَسة فَنِّيّة engineering; هَنْدَسة كَهْرَبائِيّة electrical engineering; هَنْدَسة جينِيّة \ وِراثِيّة genetic engineering; هَنْدَسة إِلِكْتْرونِيّة electronic engineering, electronics

هَنْدَسِيّ *adj* geometric; أَشْكال هَنْدَسِيّة geometric figures; القُوّات الهَنْدَسِيّة the Royal Engineers

مُهَنْدِس *n* engineer; technician; مُهَنْدِس مِعْمارِيّ architect; مُهَنْدِس ميكانيكِيّ mechanical engineer; مُهَنْدِس مَدَنِيّ civil engineer; مُهَنْدِس فَنِّيّ technical engineer; مُهَنْدِس زِراعِيّ agricultural engineer; مُهَنْدِس كَهْرَبائِيّ electrical engineer; مُهَنْدِس ديكورٍ interior designer

‹ هَنْدَمَ *v* |i; هَنْدَمة| to arrange, to put in order; to tidy up

تَهَنْدَمَ *v* to be arranged/adjusted; to preen oneself, to smarten up

هِنْدام *n* neatness, tidiness; groomed appearance; أَصْلَحَ هِنْدامَهُ to adjust one's clothes

مُهَنْدَم *adj* neat, tidy, well-groomed

‹ هُنْدوراس *n* |f| Honduras

هُنْدوراسِيّ, هُنْدورِيّ *adj*, *n* Honduran

‹ هِنْدوسِيّ *adj*, *n* Hindu

هِنْدوسِيّة *n* Hinduism

‹ هُنْغاريا *n* Hungary

هُنْغارِيّ **A** *adj* Hungarian; (اللُّغة) الهُنْغارِيّة Hungarian (*language*) **B** *n* Hungarian (*person*)

‹ تَهَنَّفَ *v* to sniff

‹ هَنَّ *v* |i; هَنين, هُنّ| إلى to long (for), to yearn (for)

هُنَّ *pron* they (*f*)

‹ هُنَيْهة *n* moment, a little while

‹ هَهُنا *adv* here; هَهُنا نَجِدُ أنّ ... here we find that ...

‹ هُوَ *pron* he; it; هُوَ صَدِيقِي he is my friend; كِتابُهُ هُوَ *his* book; بَقِيَ هُوَ هُوَ he remained the same; وَهُوَ namely (*before an enumeration*)

هُوِيّة *n* **1** [شَخْصِيّة] identity; إِثْبات الهُوِيّة identification, proof of identity; مَجْهول الهُوِيّة of unknown identity, anonymous; عَدَم كَشْفِ الهُوِيّة anonymity; سَرِقة الهُوِيّةِ identity theft; اضْطِراب الهُوِيّةِ الجِنْسِيّة gender identity disorder; غَيَّرَ هُوِيَّتَهُ to change one's identity; أَثْبَتَ هُوِيَّتَهُ to prove one's identity; حَدَّدَ الهُوِيّة to establish the identity **2** [بِطاقة] identity card

‹ هَوِجَ *v* |a; هَوَج| to be rash

هَوْجاء *n* |dipt f; هُوج| cyclone, hurricane

أَهْوَج *adj* |dipt| reckless, thoughtless, rash

‹ هادَ *v* |u; هَوْد| **1** [تابَ] to repent **2** [كانَ يَهودِيًّا] to be a Jew

هورمون *n* see **هُرْمون**

هَوِس *v* |a; هَوَس| to be mad, to be crazy, to be possessed

هَوَّس *v* to drive crazy, to make mad

تَهَوَّس *v* to go mad, to go crazy

هَوَس *n* mania, obsession, craze; أَصابَهُ الهَوَسُ to go manic; مُصاب بهوسِ السَرِقةِ kleptomania; هَوَس السَرِقةِ kleptomaniac; مُصاب بِهَوَسِ الإحْراقِ pyromaniac; هَوَس بالسَيّاراتِ an obsession with cars

هَوِس *adj* mad, crazy, insane

هَوَسِيّ *adj* manic

هَوِيس *n* |أَهْوِسة| lock; sluice

مُهَوَّس *adj* maniacal, obsessed

مَهْووس **A** *adj* maniacal, obsessed; مَهْووس بِكُرة القَدَمِ mad about football (BrE) soccer (AmE)

B *n* maniac, obsessed person

هاش *v* |u; هَوْش| to be agitated; to be in a muddle

هَوَّش *v* to incite, to stir up; هَوَّش بين الناسِ to incite the people

تَهْويش *n* provocation, agitation

مُهَوِّش *n* agitator, instigator

هاعَ *v* |u; هَوْع| to gag, to retch

هوكي *n* hockey; هوكي (على) الجَليدِ ice hockey; عَصا الهوكي hockey stick; لَعِبَ الهوكي to play hockey

هالَ *v* |u; هَوْل| **1** to frighten, to scare **2** [نَتَرَ] see **هيل**

هَوَّلَ *v* **1** [بالَغَ] to dramatize, to exaggerate; هَوَّلَ حادِثاً to dramatize an accident; هَوَّلَ أَمْراً to exaggerate an issue

2 [أَفْزَعَ |على] to frighten, to scare; to daunt, to intimidate; هَوَّلَ على شَخْصٍ to intimidate sb

اسْتَهالَ *v* to consider tremendous, to be horrified at

هَوْل *n* |أَهْوال| atrociousness, terror, horror; يا لَلْهَوْلِ! how dreadful!; أَبو الهَوْلِ the Sphinx; هَوْل المَنْظَرِ the gruesomeness of the scene

هائِل *adj* |هَوائِلُ| **1** [ضَخْم] tremendous, formidable; gigantic, colossal, enormous; بِسُرْعةٍ هائِلةٍ at a tremendous speed; مَشاكِل هائِلة huge problems; نَجاح هائِل a tremendous

هَوَّدَ *v* **1** [مَشى بِبُطْءٍ] to proceed slowly **2** [جَعَلَ يَهوديًّا] to make Jewish

هاوَدَ *v* to be compliant, to be lenient

تَهَوَّدَ *v* to be converted to Judaism

هود *n* **1** Hud (*name of a prophet in the Koran*); سورة هود Hud (*Sura 11*)

2 الهود the Jews

هَوادة *n* tolerance; kindliness; بِلا هَوادةٍ merciless, ruthless

تَهْويد *n* Judaization

تَهْويدة *n* lullaby; غَنّى تَهْويدةً to sing a lullaby

يَهوديّ **A** *adj* |يَهود| Jewish; المُؤْتَمَر اليَهوديّ العالَميّ World Jewish Congress, WJC

B *n* |يَهود| Jewish person, Jew

يَهوديّة *n* Judaism

هَوْدَج *n* |هَوادِجُ| canopy

هَوَّرَ *v* to demolish, to pull down

تَهَوَّرَ *v* **1** [تَهَدَّمَ] to collapse, to fall down **2** [كانَ طائِشاً] to act rashly, to be reckless

انْهارَ *v* **1** [سَقَطَ] to collapse, to fall down; to sink; انْهارَ الجِسْرُ the bridge has collapsed; يَنْهارُ المَبْنى the building is falling in

2 (fig) to collapse, to break down; انْهارَت المُباحَثاتُ the negotiations have broken down; انْهارَتْ أَعْصابُهُ he had a nervous breakdown

هَوْر *n* |أَهْوار| lake, lagoon; marsh

انْهِيار *n* |انْهِيارات| collapse, breakdown, degeneration; fall, downfall; انْهِيار ثَلْجيّ avalanche; انْهِيار شديد \ عَصَبيّ a total/nervous breakdown; انْهِيار حائِط بَرْلين the fall of the Berlin wall; انْهِيار الإمْبَراطوريّة الرومانيّة the fall of the Roman empire; خطَر انْهِيارٍ danger of collapse; انْهِيار السوقِ الماليّةِ (Fin) crash; انْهِيار ائْتِلافٍ حُكوميٍّ the collapse of a government coalition

تَهَوُّر *n* boisterousness; rashness, impulsiveness

مُتَهَوِّر **A** *adj* boisterous; thoughtless, reckless, rash; شَباب مُتَهَوِّرونَ reckless youth

B *n* daredevil, foolhardy person

مُنْهار *n* **1** [ساقِط] collapsed, fallen down **2** (fig) collapsed, broken down; مُنْهار نَفْسيًّا mentally wrecked success; كَمّيّة هائِلة astronomical figures; أَرْقام هائِلة an enormous amount **2** [مُخيف] terrifying, frightening, horrible; دَويّ هائِل a terrifying sound

هالة *n* **1** [حول الرَّأْسِ] aureole, halo **2** (Astron) corona, halo **3** [اسْم شَخْصيّ] |dipt| Hala (*female given name*)

تَهْويل *n* |تَهاويلُ, تَهْويلات| **1** [أَفْزَع] intimidation, threat, browbeating **2** [بالَغَ] exaggeration

مَهول *adj* horrible, atrocious; tremendous; عَدَد مَهول a tremendous amount

مُهَوِّل *adj* frightening, terrifying

هولَنْدا, هولَنْدة, هولانْدا *n* Holland, the Netherlands

هولَنْديّ **A** *adj* Dutch, Netherlands (*before n*); (اللُغة) الهولَنْديّة Dutch (*language*)
B *n* Dutch person

هولوغرام *n* hologram

هَوَّمَ *v* to doze, to nap

هامة *n* |هام, هامات| **1** [أَعْلى الرَّأْسِ] crown, vertex, top **2** [رَأْس] head

هَوْمة *n* desert

هانَ *v* |u; هَوْن| to be easy; هانَ عَلَيْهِم الأَمْرُ it was easy for them

هَوَّنَ *v* to make easy, to facilitate; هَوِّنْ عَلَيْكَ take it easy

هاوَنَ *v* to be compliant

أَهانَ *v* to offend, to insult; to humiliate; أَهانَ شَخْصاً (إهانةً كَبيرةً) to offend sb (seriously)

تَهاوَنَ *v* |ب| to neglect, to be negligent (in), to fail to do; تَهاوَنَ بِشَيْءٍ to neglect sth

اسْتَهانَ *v* |ب| to disdain, to despise; to undervalue, to underestimate; اسْتَهانَ بِشَيْءٍ \ بِشَخْصٍ to feel contempt for sth/sb; لا يُسْتَهانُ بِهِ significant; هذا شَيْءٌ لا يُسْتَهانُ بِهِ this is no small thing; هذا مَبْلَغٌ لا يُسْتَهانُ بِهِ this is a significant sum; اسْتَهانَ بالعَواقِبِ to underestimate the consequences

هون *n* humiliation, indignity

هَوْن *n* ease; يَسيرُ على هَوْنِهِ he walks slowly; على هَوْنِكَ! slow down!

هاوُن *n listed alphabetically*

هَوان *n* degradation; humiliation, offence

هُوَيْنى *n* |f| rest, relaxation, ease; مَشى الهُوَيْنى to stroll, to amble

هَيِّن, هَيْن *adj* |أَهْوِناءُ, هَيِّنونَ| easy, simple

هينة *n* ease; يَمْشي على هينَتِهِ he walks slowly

اسْتِهانة *n* contempt, disdain; disregard; بِاسْتِهانةٍ disdainfully; اسْتِهانة بالمَوْتِ disregard for death; تَكَلَّمَ بِاسْتِهانةٍ to speak scornfully;

إهانة *n* insult, humiliation; defamation, derision; إهانة كَبيرة a serious insult; إهانة المَلِك(ةِ) lese-majesty; إهانة لِشَخْصٍ an insult to sb; شَكَّلَ إهانةً to be an insult; وَجَّهَ إهانةً إلى شَخْصٍ to insult sb; تَعَرَّضَ لِإهاناتٍ to (have to) take insults; اعْتَبَرَ شَيْئاً إهانةً to take sth as an insult; أَحَسَّ بالإهانةِ to feel insulted

أَهْوَن *adj* |dipt| easier; أَهْوَن الشَّرَّيْنِ the lesser of two evils, the lesser evil

تَهاوُن *n* |تَهاوُنات| laxity; negligence, neglect

مُتَهاوِن *adj* negligent, careless, lax

مُهان *adj* offended, hurt

مَهانة *n* disgrace, humiliation

مُهين *adj* humiliating, ignominious; مُلاحَظة مُهينة a derogatory remark; هَزيمة مُهينة a humiliating defeat

هَوى *v* |i; هُوِيّ| **1** [سَقَطَ] to crash down, to fall down, to tumble down; هَوى من السُلَّم to tumble from the stairs; هَوَت الطائِرةُ the airplane crashed **2** [ماتَ] to die

هَوِيَ *v* |a; هَوىً| to love, to be in love with; to like, to be fond of; هَوِيَ بِنْتاً to be in love with a girl

هَوّى *v* to air, to ventilate; هَوّى مَلابِسَ \ غُرْفةً to air clothes/a room

هاوى *v* to humor, to flatter

أَهْوى *v* **1** [سَقَطَ] to crash down, to fall down **2** [أَلْقى] to throw down; to drop **3** [مَدَّ] to reach out; أَهْوى بِيَدِه إلى شَيْءٍ to extend one's hand to sth **4** [وَثَبَ |على|] to pounce (on)

تَهاوى *v* to throw oneself down; to collapse, to break down; to fall

انْهوى *v* to fall down

اسْتَهْوى *v* to attract; to fascinate, to charm, to win over; to seduce, to tempt; اسْتَهْوى شَخْصاً to win sb over

هاوٍ *n* |هُواة| ① [عَكْس مُحْتَرِف] amateur; مَسْرَح الهُواةِ amateur theatre; مُلاكِم هاوٍ amateur boxer; لاعِب هاوٍ amateur (*non-professional player*) ② [مُحِبّ] lover, fan; هُواة السَيّاراتِ car enthusiasts

هاوِية *n* abyss, chasm; hell; كانَ على حافةِ الهاوِيةِ to be on the brink of disaster

هَواء *n* |أَهْواء, أَهْوِية| ① [جَوّ] atmosphere; air; الهَواء الطَلْق the open/fresh air; في الهَواءِ الطَلْقِ in the open, outdoors; باتَ في الهَواءِ الطَلْقِ to sleep in the open air; هَواء جافّ \ رَطْب dry/humid air; اسْتَنْشَقَ الهَواءَ الطَلْقَ to breathe fresh air; أَزالَ الهَواءَ to ventilate; تَكْييف الهَواءِ air conditioning; يَبْني قُصوراً في الهَواءِ he builds castles in the air (*he daydreams of sth highly unpractical*) ② [ريح] wind; نَسمة هَواءٍ breeze ③ [بَثّ] air; كانَ على الهَواءِ to be on the air

هَوائيّ **A** *adj* pneumatic; aerial, air (*before n*); كيس هَوائيّ airbag **B** *n* aerial (BrE), antenna (AmE); هَوائيّ فَضائيّ satellite dish

هَوّاية *n* ventilator, fan

هِواية *n* hobby, pastime; amateurism; كَهِوايةٍ as a hobby; من بابِ الهِوايةِ for pleasure

هوّة *n* |هُوًى, هوّات| abyss; gap, chasm, gulf; crevice; هوّة عَميقة a deep gulf; هوّة واسِعة a wide gap; على حافةِ الهوّةِ on the brink of the abyss; ضاقَت الهوّةُ the gap narrowed; رَدَمَ الهوّةَ to bridge the gap; الهوّة الرَقْميّة the digital divide; اتَّسَعَت الهوّةُ بَيْنَهُما the gap between them has widened; تَفْصِلُ بَيْنَهُما هوّةٌ there's a gap that separates them

هَوًى *n* |أَهْواء, هَوايا| ① [مَيْل] love; passion; بائِعة الهَوى prostitute ② [نَزْوة] caprice, whim; inclination; على هَواهُ at one's whim; تَصَرَّفَ على هَواهُ to act at one's whim; اتَّبَعَ هَواهُ to follow one's inclination

اسْتِهْواء *n* fascination; temptation, appeal

تَهْوِية *n* ventilation, airing; نِظام التَهْوِيةِ ventilation system; تَهْوِية المَكانِ the ventilation of a space

مِهْواة *n* |مَهاوٍ| ventilator, fan

مَهْوًى, مَهْواة *n* |مَهاوٍ| shaft; abyss, chasm; crevice; مَهْوًى عَميق a deep shaft

‹ **هِيَ** *pron* she; هِيَ صَديقَتي she is my girlfriend; she is my friend; الحالة تَبْقى هِيَ هِيَ the situation remains the same

‹ **هاءَ** *v* |a-i; هَيْئة| ① [كانَ وَسيماً] to be/become good-looking, to be/become beautiful ② [اسْتَعَدَّ] to be ready, to be prepared

هَيَّأَ *v* ① [أَعَدَّ] to prepare, to get ready, to make ready; هَيَّأَ نَفْسَهُ لِشَيْءٍ to prepare oneself for sth; هَيَّأَ التَلاميذَ لامْتِحانٍ to get the pupils ready for an exam ② (Comput) to format

تَهَيَّأَ *v* ① [اسْتَعَدَّ] to prepare oneself, to get oneself ready; تَهَيَّأَ لِشَيْءٍ to get oneself ready for sth ② [أَمْكَنَ] تَهَيَّأَتْ لَهُ الفُرْصةُ لِفِعْلِ شَيْءٍ he got the chance to do sth

تَهايَأَ *v* to adapt oneself, to adjust oneself

هَيِّئ *adj* elegant, refined; good-looking

هَيْئة *n* ① [مُؤَسَّسة، جَمْعيّة] body, authority, organ; institution, institute, organization, corps; هَيْئة حُكوميّة government body; الهَيْئة المَعْنيّة \ المَسْؤولة the competent/proper authority; هَيْئة رَسْميّة an official body; هَيْئة عامّة a public authority; هَيْئة دِبْلوماسيّة \ سِياسيّة diplomatic/political corps; هَيْئة التَدْريس \ التَحْرير \ الأَطِبّاء teaching/editorial/medical staff ② [مَظْهَر] appearance, aspect; shape, form; تَغَيُّر الهَيْئةِ transformation; غَيَّر هَيْئَتَهُ to change one's form; على \ في هَيْئةِ ... in the shape of ...; هَيْئَتُها جَميلةٌ she has a pretty appearance; تَعَدُّد الهَيْئاتِ multiformity ③ [حال] state, condition

تَهايُؤ *n* adaptation, adjustment

تَهْيِئة *n* setting up, preparation; تَهْيِئة مَناخٍ مُناسِبٍ creating a favourable climate; عَمَليّة تَهْيِئةِ الرَأْيِ العامِّ preparing public opinion

مُهايِئ *n* |مُهايِئات| adaptor

مُهايَأة *n* ① [تَعْديل] adaptation, adjustment ② (Isl Law) joint usufruct

مُهَيَّأ *adj* ready, set; prepared

‹ **هابَ** *v* |a; مَهابة, هَيْبة| ① [خافَ] to fear, to dread, to be afraid of ② [احْتَرَمَ] to look up to, to think highly of; هابَ شَيْئاً \ شَخْصاً to stand in awe of sth/sb

هَيَّبَ *v* to make dread; هَيَّبَ شَيْئاً إلى شَخْصٍ to make sb fear sth

أَهابَ *v* to call on, to incite, to encourage; أَهابَ بِشَخْصٍ إِلى عَمَلِ شَيْءٍ to call on sb to do sth

تَهَيَّبَ *v* 1 [خافَ] to fear, to dread, to be afraid of 2 [اِحْتَرَمَ] to look up to, to think highly of; تَهَيَّبَ فِي شَخْصٍ to think highly of sb

هَيّاب *adj* timid, shy, bashful

هَيْبَة *n* 1 [مَقام] standing, prestige; فَقَدَ هَيْبَتَهُ to lose one's prestige 2 [خَوْف] awe; fear, dread

مَهابة *n* dignity; prestige, standing

مَهيب *adj* 1 [وَقور] prestigious; charismatic; مَشْروع مَهيب a prestigious project; قائِد مَهيب a charismatic leader 2 [مُخيف] frightening, terrifying, fearsome

مُهيب *adj* frightening, terrifying, fearsome

‹ **هيبيّ** *n* |هيبيز| hippie

‹ **هاجَ** *v* |i; هَيَجان ,هَيْج| to rant; to be/become agitated, to get enraged; هاجَت النُّفوسُ feelings were running high

هَيَّجَ *v* to irritate, to agitate, to provoke; to incite, to stir up, to excite; هَيَّجَ أَعْصابَ شَخْصٍ to get on sb's nerves

أَهاجَ *v* to incite, to stir up, to agitate

تَهَيَّجَ *v* to be/become agitated, to get enraged; to rant

اِهْتاجَ *v* to be/become agitated; to rant

هَيْج *n* tension; excitement; commotion

هائِج *adj* agitated, excited; wild, turbulent; بَحْر هائِج a rough sea; نَهْر هائِج a wild river; المِياه الهائِجة the turbulent water; عاصِفة هائِجة a heavy storm; هائِج جِنْسِيًّا sexually aroused

هِياج *n* excitement, frenzy; tumult, commotion; هِياج مَحْموم great excitement, feverish frenzy

هَيْجاء *n* |dipt f| combat, battle, fight

هَيَجان *n* excitement, frenzy; upheaval, disturbance; outburst; أَثارَ \ أَحْدَثَ هَيَجاناً to stir up/make trouble; كانَ في حالةِ هَيَجانٍ to be (sexually) excited, to be horny (infml)

اِهْتِياج *n* agitation, unrest; uproar, commotion

تَهَيُّج *n* |تَهَيُّجات| 1 [إثارة] excitement; commotion, upheaval; agitation, trouble 2 (Med) irritation; تَهَيُّج جِلْديّ skin irritation

تَهْييج *n* agitation, stimulation, incitement

مُتَهَيِّج *adj* agitated; frenzied, excited

مُهْتاج *adj* excited; agitated

مُهَيِّج A *adj* exciting, stimulating, rousing; compelling; inciting; عَقاقير مُهَيِّجة stimulants

B *n* instigator, agitator, rioter

‹ **هيدْروكَرْبون** *n* hydrocarbon; هيدْروكَرْبونات عُضْويّة organic hydrocarbons

‹ **هيدْروكْلوريد** *n* hydrochloride

‹ **هَيْدْروكَهْرَبائيّ** *adj* hydroelectric

‹ **هيدْروليّ** *adj* hydraulic

‹ **هيدْروليكيّ** *adj* hydraulic; رافِعة \ أُسْطُوانة هيدْروليكيّة a hydraulic crane/cylinder

‹ **هيرْتْز** *n* see هِرْتْز

‹ **هيروغْليفيّ** *adj* حَرْف هيروغْليفيّ hieroglyph; كِتابة هيروغْليفيّة hieroglyphs

‹ **هيرُوين** *n* heroin; هيرُوين خالِص pure heroin; تِجارة الهيرُوين heroin trade; اسْتَعْمَلَ الهيرُوين to use heroin

‹ **هِسْتِريا ,هيسْتيريا** *n* hysteria

هيسْتيريّ *adj* hysterical; نَوْبة هيسْتيريّة a hysterical fit

‹ **هَيْشة** *n* commotion, tumult

‹ **هاضَ** *v* |i; هَيْض| to break

هَيَّضَ *v* to annoy, to irritate

هَيْضة *n* cholera

مَهيض *adj* shattered, broken

‹ **هَيْطَل** *n* see هطل

‹ **هافَ** *v* |هَيْف| 1 [طَمِئَ] to thirst, to be parched 2 [هَرَبَ] to run away (slave) 3 [كانَ نَحيلاً] to be slim, to be frail

هَيِفَ *v* |a; هَيَف ,هِياف| to be slim, to be slender

أَهْيَف *adj* |dipt| slim, slender; slight

‹ **هَيْكَلَ** *v* |i; هَيْكَلة| to structure

هَيْكَل *n* |هَياكِلُ| 1 [بِنْية] body, fuselage; frame, framework; chassis; هَيْكَل مُدْمَج \ مَتين a sturdy frame; هَيْكَل فولاذيّ \ حَديديّ a steel/an iron frame; هَيْكَل دَرّاجةٍ a bicycle frame; هَيْكَل بِنايةٍ a building frame; هَيْكَل سَفينةٍ a ship's hull;

هَيْكَل السَّيّارةِ car chassis 2 (Anat) carcass; هَيْكَل عَظْميّ skeleton; carcass; هَيْكَل إنْسانٍ human skeleton; هَيْكَل السَّمَكةِ fish bone 3 [مَعْبَد] temple; هَيْكَل سُلَيْمانَ the temple of Salomon

هَيْكَلة *n* structuring; إعادة الهَيْكَلةِ restructuring

هَيْكَليّ *adj* structural; skeleton (*before n*); مَشاكِل هَيْكَليّة structural problems

هَيْكَليّة *n* structure; هَيْكَليّة واضِحة a clear structure

‹ **هالَ** *v* |i; هَيْل| 1 [نَثَرَ] to strew, to scatter, to sprinkle 2 [أخافَ] see هول

انْهالَ *v* انْهالَ على شَخْصٍ to attack sb, to fall upon sb

هَيْل *n* piled-up sand; الهَيْل والهَيْلَمان tons of money

هَيْلَمان *n* الهَيْل والهَيْلَمان tons of money

انْهِيال *n* collapse, subsidence; انْهِيال الأَرْضِ landslide

‹ **هامَ** *v* |i| 1 [طافَ] هَيْم |هَيَمان to wander, to roam, to rove; هامَ على وَجْهِهِ to wander aimlessly; هامَ في المَدينةِ to wander through the city 2 [أَحَبَّ] هُيام ,هِيام| to love, to be in love, to fall in love; هامَ بِشَخْصٍ to fall in love with sb

هَيَّمَ *v* to make crazy/blind (*love*)

اسْتَهامَ *v* أُسْتُهيمَ he was besotted

هائِم *adj* هُيَّم ,هُيّام| 1 [شارِد] roaming; confused 2 [عاشِق] مَجْنون] desperately in love

هائِمات *n pl* plankton

هُيام *n* passion, passionate love

هَيْمان *adj* |dipt; هِيام; f هَيْمى| desperately in love

هَيوم *adj* mystified, bewildered, perplexed, confused

‹ **هَيْمَنَ** *v* |i; هَيْمَنة| 1 [سَيْطَرَ] to dominate, to control, to manage; هَيْمَنَ على بَلَدٍ to control a region; هَيْمَنَ على مِنْطَقةٍ to control a country; هَيْمَنَ على أَمْلاكِ شَخْصٍ to manage sb's possessions 2 [قالَ آمين] to say 'amen'

هَيْمَنة *n* dominion, control, dominance; hegemony, supremacy; فَرَض هَيْمَنَتَهُ to establish one's supremacy

مُهَيْمِن A *adj* dominant, predominant; overbearing B *n* 1 [خَفير] administrator, guardian 2 (Islam) المُهَيْمِن the Guardian (*one of the names of God*)

‹ **هيموغْلوبين ,هيموجْلوبين** *n* haemoglobin

‹ **هيموفيلِيا** *n* haemophilia

‹ **هَيْهات ,هَيْهاتَ** *excl* how impossible!; هَيْهاتَ أَنْ ... it's out of the question that ..., it's impossible that ...

‹ **هَيولى ,هَيُولى** *n* substance, matter; protoplasm

‹ **هَيّا** *excl* let's go!, come on!; هَيّا بنا ,هَيّا نَذْهَبْ let's go

و

وَ **A** *conj* **1** [الجَمْع] and; أَكَلْنا وَشَرِبْنا we ate and drank; وَقْتَما تَشاءُ وَأَيْنَما تَشاءُ whenever and wherever you want it; لا ... وَلا ... neither ...nor ... **2** [تعاقُب] سَلَّمَ عَلَيَّ وَانْصَرَفَ he said hello to me and left **3** [مع] with; لا يَتماشى والسِياسةَ المُتَّبَعةَ it doesn't agree with the observed policy **4** [وَلا] even; وَلا واحِدَ not even one, nobody at all; وَلا مَرَّةً not even once **5** [حال: تَزامُن] while, when; مَشَوْا إلى البَيْتِ وَهُمْ يَتَحَدَّثونَ they walked home talking **6** [حال: +قد] أجابَ وَقَدْ غَطَّتْ وَجْهَهُ ابْتِسامةٌ he answered smiling **7** [بَدَل] نَسْأَلُ وَبِحَقٍّ we wonder, with good reason; رغم وُجودِهِ وِبوَفْرةٍ even though it exists, and in abundance **8** [بين] عَلاقات الجَزائِرِ وَمِصْرَ the relations between Algeria and Egypt

B *prep* واللهِ I swear to God; والنَبيِّ I swear by the Prophet

وا *excl* oh; وا أَسَفاهُ how awful

وَأَدَ *v* |i; وَأْد| **1** [بِنتاً] to bury alive (*a newborn girl*); وَأَدَ الديموقراطيّةَ to stamp out democracy **2** [قَيَّدَ] to restrict; وَأَدَ الحُرِّيّاتِ to restrict liberties

اتَّأَدَ *v* to be slow

وَئيد *adj* slow, deliberate

تُؤَدة *n* deliberation; في تُؤَدةٍ consciously; deliberately, carefully; slowly

وارسو *n* |f| Warsaw

واشِنْطُن *n* |f| **1** Washington, DC (*capital of the United States*) **2** Washington (state) (*US state*)

واط *n* watt; مِصْباح قُدْرَتُهُ ٦٠ واط a 60 watt lamp; قُدْرَتُهُ ٦٠ واط with a capacity of 60 watts; اسْتَهْلَكَ ٢٠٠ واط to consume 200 watts

وافِل *n* waffle

واق *n* (Zool) bittern (*Ixobrychus*)

وقي *adj* see **واقٍ**

مَوْئِل *n* |مَوائِلُ| refuge, shelter

والونيا *n* Wallonia (*southern region of Belgium*)

واءَمَ *v* to adapt oneself to; to harmonize with

تَواءَمَ *v* to be in harmony; to agree; تَواءَمَ مع شَيْءٍ to be in harmony with sth

وِئام *n* harmony, accord; في وِئامٍ مع شَيْءٍ in harmony with sth

تَوْأَم *n* see **تأم**

مُوائِم **A** *adj* consistent; suitable; مُوائِم لِشَيْءٍ consistent with sth

B *n* (Elec) adaptor

مُواءَمة *n* adaptation; harmonization

واو *n* |f| *name of the letter* و

وايومِنْغ *n* |f| Wyoming (*US state*)

وَبِئَ *v* |a; وَبَأ| to be stricken (*by an epidemic*)

وَباء *n* |أَوْبِئة| (Med) epidemic; انْدلاع \ انْتِشار وَباءٍ the outbreak/spread of an epidemic; أَوْدى الوَباءُ بِحَياةِ أَكْثَرَ من ٢٠٠٠٠ شَخْصٍ the epidemic claimed the lives of more than 20,000 people

وَبائِيّ *adj* epidemic; مَرَض وَبائِيّ an epidemic disease

مَوْبوء *adj* stricken, contaminated, infected; بَلَد مَوْبوء a contaminated area; مَوْبوء بالفَسادِ plagued by corruption

وَبَّخَ *v* to reprimand, to rebuke, to scold; وَبَّخ شَخْصاً على شَيْءٍ to reprimand sb for sth; وَبَّخ مُوَظَّفاً to reprimand an employee; وَبَّخ شَخْصاً تَوْبيخاً لاذِعاً to scold sb severely

تَوْبيخ *n* |تَوْبيخات| reprimand, reproof, rebuke, scolding; تَوْبيخ لاذِع a severe/harsh reprimand; تَعَرَّضَ للتَوْبيخِ to be reprimanded

وَبَر *n* |أَوْبار| hair (*usually of camel*); fur, down; أَهْل الوَبَرِ *the Bedouins*

وَبَرِيّ *adj* hairy, downy

وَتَرِيّ *adj* stringed, string (*before n*); وَتَرِيّات stringed instruments; آلة وَتَرِيّة stringed instrument

وَتيرة *n* |وَتائِر| tempo, pace; بِوَتيرةٍ سَريعةٍ \ عالِيةٍ \ هادِئةٍ \ بَطيئةٍ at a great/high/calm/slow pace; رَفَعَ \ صَعَّدَ الوَتيرةَ to increase the tempo; اسْتَمَرَّ \ حافَظَ على نَفْسِ الوَتيرةِ to keep up the pace; يَتَكَلَّمُ على وَتيرةٍ واحِدةٍ he speaks in a monotone

تَتْرى *adv* one after the other, in succession; المُبادَراتُ تَتْرى one initiative followed the other

تَواتُر *n* succession; على \ بالتَواتُرِ in succession, one after the other; تَواتُرُ الأَحْداثِ the succession of events

تَوَتُّر *n* |تَوَتُّرات| ⓵ [تَأَزُّم] tension; تَوَتُّر عَصَبيّ nervousness; تَوَتُّر نَفسيّ psychological stress; تَوَتُّر مَلْموس a palpable tension; التَوَتُّر المُتَصاعِد the increasing tension; بُؤْرة تَوَتُّر flashpoint, centre of tension; خَفَّفَ \ قَلَّلَ التَوَتُّرَ to relieve/reduce the tension; أَنْهى \ بَدَّدَ التَوَتُّرَ to put an end to the tension; تَزْدادُ حِدّةُ التَوَتُّرِ the tension rises; خَيَّمَ التَوَتُّرُ على البِلادِ the country was fraught with tension ⓶ (Elec) tension; تَوَتُّر عالٍ high tension

تَوْتير *n* تَوْتير الوَضْعِ aggravating the situation

مُتَواتِر *adj* successive, consecutive; frequent, recurring; أَخْبار \ أَنْباء مُتَواتِرة recurring messages/reports

مُتَوَتِّر *adj* tense, nervous; أَعْصاب مُتَوَتِّرة tense nerves; ضِحْكة مُتَوَتِّرة a nervous laugh; مُتَوَتِّر الأَعْصابِ nervous, tense; كانَ مُتَوَتِّراً to be in suspense

مَوْتور *n* sb who lost a relative by murder and has yet to avenge him

‹ **وَتين** *n* |أَوْتِنة, وُتُن| aorta

‹ **واتى** *v* ⓵ [حاقَ] to befall; واتَتْني فِكْرةٌ I got an idea; واتاني الحَظُّ I was lucky ⓶ [لاءَمَ] to go well with, to be suitable for ⓷ [زَوَّدَ] to provide; واتى شَخْصاً بِشَيْءٍ to provide sb with sth

مُواتٍ *adj* see أتي

‹ **وَثَأَ** *v* |a; وَثْء| to sprain, to twist

وَثْء *n* sprain, pain

مَوْثوء *adj* sprained, twisted, strained; كاحِل مَوْثوء a sprained ankle

أَوْبَر *adj* |dipt| hairy, downy

‹ **وَبَش** *n* |أَوْباش| أَوْباش rabble, scum

‹ **وَبَقَ** *v* |i; وَبْق, وُبوق| to go to ruin

أَوْبَقَ *v* to ruin

موبِقات *n pl* mortal sins

موبِقة *n* |مَوابِقُ| grave sin

‹ **وَبَلَ** *v* |i; وَبْل| to pour (rain); تَبِلُ السَماءُ the rain is pouring down

وابِل *n* ⓵ [مَطَر] downpour, shower; وابِل من المَطَرِ a heavy shower, heavy rain, cloudburst ⓶ (fig) flood; وابِل من الشَتائِمِ a stream of abuse; وابِل من الرَصاصِ a hail of bullets; وابِل من الأَسْئِلةِ a barrage of questions; وابِل من الشَكاوى a flood of complaints

وَبال *n* evil, scourge

وَبيل *adj* ⓵ [كارِثيّ] disastrous, catastrophic ⓶ [غَيْر صِحّيّ] unhealthy

‹ **وَبِهَ, وَبَهَ** *v* |a; وَبْه| |ل, ب| to pay attention (to), to take notice (of)

‹ **وَتَدَ** *v* |i; وَتْد| to fasten, to secure

وَتَّدَ *v* to fasten; drive in firmly

وَتَد, وَتِد *n* |أَوْتاد| tent peg, stake, pin

‹ **وَتَرَ** *v* |i; وَتْر| to stretch

وَتَّرَ *v* to stretch; وَتَّرَ قَوْساً to draw a bow; وَتَّرَ أَعْصابَ شَخْص to make sb nervous

واتَرَ *v* to do sth at intervals

أَوْتَرَ *v* to provide with a string

تَوَتَّرَ *v* to be/become strained; تَوَتَّرَت العَلاقاتُ بَيْنَهُما the relations between them were strained

تَواتَرَ *v* to follow, to happen in succession; تَواتَرَت الأَحْداثُ بِشَكْلٍ مُتَسارِعٍ the events happened in quick succession

وَتْر, وِتْر *adj* odd, uneven; رَقْم وَتْر an odd number

وَتَر *n* |أَوْتار| ⓵ [للآلة] string; وَتَر القَوْسِ string; شَدَّ الأَوْتارَ to string; ضَرَبَ على الوَتَرِ الحَسّاسِ ≈ to hit a nerve ⓶ (Anat) tendon; وَتَر مُمَزَّق \ مُلْتَهِب a torn/inflamed tendon; الأَوْتار الصَوْتيّة the vocal cords

وَثيق *adj* |وِثاق| firm, solid, close; عَلاقات \ ارْتِباطات وَثيقة close relations/ties; تعاوُن وَثيق close cooperation; مَصادِر وَثيقة الصِلةِ reliable sources; تقارَبَ تَقارُباً وَثيقاً to be closely related

وَثيقة *n* |وَثائِق| ❶ [مُسْتَنَد] document, paper, deed, certificate; وَثائِق records, papers, documents; وَثيقة رَسْميّة an official document; وَثيقة عَدْليّة a notarial deed; وَثائِق مَخْتومة deeds under seal; سَلَّمَ \ قَدَّمَ وَثيقةً to hand over/present a document; أَمْضى \ وَقَّعَ وَثيقةً to sign a document; تَفَحَّصَ الوَثائِق to go through the documents ❷ (Comput) document

تَواثَقَ *v* to agree

تَوْثيق *n* |تَوْثيقات| ❶ [تَثْبيت] authentication, homologation; ratification ❷ [تَعْزيز] strengthening; تَوْثيق العَلاقاتِ \ الرَوابِطِ strengthening of the relations/ties ❸ [التَزْويد بالوَثائِق] documentation; مَرْكَز التَوْثيقِ والمَعْلوماتِ documentation and information centre

تَوْثيقيّ *adj* documentary; authenticated; فيلْم تَوْثيقيّ documentary film; مَعْلومات تَوْثيقيّة documentary information

ثِقة **A** *adj* [مَوْثوق بِهِ] reliable; مَصادِر ثِقة reliable sources; شاهِد \ مُخْبِر ثِقة a reliable witness/informer
B *n* [إيمان] trust, confidence, faith; ثِقة تامّة complete trust; ثِقة عَمْياء blind faith; overconfidence; ثِقة مُتَبادَلة mutual trust; ثِقة مُطْلَقة في شَيْءٍ absolute faith in sth; على مَبْدَأ الثِقةِ on the basis of trust; عَدَم \ انْعِدام الثِقةِ lack of faith, distrust; ثِقة بالنَفْسِ \ بالذاتِ self-confidence, self-assurance; عَدَم الثِقةِ بالنَفْسِ lack of self-confidence, insecurity; شَعَرَ بِعَدَمِ الثِقةِ بِنَفْسِهِ to feel insecure, to lack self-confidence; أَزْمة ثِقةٍ crisis of confidence; عَلاقة ثِقةٍ *a relationship based on mutual trust*; جَدير بالثِقةِ trustworthy; كانَ على ثِقةٍ من أَنْ ... to trust that ...; كانَتْ لَدَيْهِ ثِقةٌ في شَيْءٍ \ شَخْصٍ to have faith in sth/sb, to trust sth/sb; فَقَدَ \ عَزَّزَ ثِقَتَهُ بِنَفْسِهِ to lose/boost one's self-confidence; اقْتِراع ثِقةٍ vote of confidence; طَرْح الثِقةِ في وَزيرٍ a vote of confidence in a minister; طَرَحَ الثِقةَ بالحُكومةِ to ask for a vote of confidence in the government; وَضَعَ الثِقةَ في شَخْصٍ \ شَيْءٍ to put one's faith in sb/sth; نالَ \ كَسَبَ

‹ **وَثَبَ** *v* |i| |وَثْب, وُثوب, وَثيب, وَثَبان| to jump, to leap; to pounce; وَثَبَ على فَريسَتِهِ to pounce on its prey; وَثَبَ على \ فوق شَيْءٍ to jump on sth

واثَبَ *v* to throw oneself at, to pounce upon

أَوْثَبَ *v* to make jump, to bounce

تَوَثَّبَ *v* to jump; to pounce

تَواثَبَ *v* to jump

وَثْب *n* leap(ing), jump(ing); وَثْب طَويل (Sport) long jump; وَثْب عالٍ (Sport) high jump

وَثْبة *n* |وَثَبات| leap; وَثْبة ثُلاثيّة (Sport) triple jump

مُتَوَثِّب *adj* lively, vigorous; روح مُتَوَثِّبة a brilliant mind

‹ **وِثار** *n* bed

وَثير *adj* soft, comfortable

‹ **وَثُقَ** *v* |u; وَثاقة| |من| to be sure; وَثُقَ من شَيْءٍ to be sure of sth

وَثِقَ *v* |i; ثِقة, وُثوق| to trust, to believe; to rely; وَثِقَ بِنَفْسِهِ to have self-confidence; وَثِقَ بِشَخْصٍ to trust sb; to rely on sb; لا يوثَقُ بِهِ unreliable, untrustworthy; وَثِقَ من أَنْ ... to be confident that ..., to rest assured that...

وَثَّقَ *v* ❶ [أَحْكَمَ] to strengthen; وَثَّقَ الصَداقةَ to strengthen the friendship ❷ [صَدَّقَ] to ratify; to authenticate, to certify; وَثَّقَ مُعاهَدةً دُوَلِيّةً to ratify an international treaty ❸ [زَوَّدَ بالوَثائِق] to document

واثَقَ *v* to agree

أَوْثَقَ *v* to tie up, to fetter; أَوْثَقَ شَخْصاً to tie sb up

تَوَثَّقَ *v* ❶ [في الأَمْرِ] to act honestly ❷ [تَشَدَّدَ] to be firm/solid; to be strengthened; تَوَثَّقَت الصَداقةُ the friendship became stronger

اسْتَوْثَقَ *v* |من| to make sure, to check, to verify; اسْتَوْثَقَ من شَيْءٍ to check sth, to make sure of sth

واثِق *adj* confident, sure, convinced; واثِق من نَفْسِهِ self-confident, self-assured; واثِق بالنَجاحِ confident to win; واثِق من فَوْزِه convinced to succeed; غَيْر واثِقٍ بِنَفْسِهِ insecure

وَثائِقيّ *adj* documental; فيلْم وَثائِقيّ \ تَسْجيليّ documentary

وِثاق, وَثاق *n* |وُثُق| handcuffs; fetter

وُثوق *n* confidence, trust, faith

اسْتَوْجَبَ *v* ⓵ ◀[اسْتَلْزَمَ] to require, to demand, to make compulsory; يَسْتَوْجِبُ تَفْكيراً it requires some thought; اسْتَوْجَبَ على شَخْصٍ أنْ ... to demand from sb that ...
⓶ ◀[اسْتَحَقَّ] to deserve, to be worthy of

واجِب Ⓐ *adj* obligatory, imperative, necessary; الرِعاية الواجِبة the necessary care; الصَوْمُ واجِبٌ fasting is obligatory; حُضورُهُ واجِبٌ his attendance is imperative
Ⓑ *n* |واجِبات| ⓵ ◀[الْتِزام] duty, obligation; الشُعور بالواجِبِ sense of duty; واجِباتُهُ وَحُقوقُهُ his duties and rights; من واجِبي أنْ أُساعِدَها it is my duty to help her, I have to help her; أدّى واجِبَهُ to perform/fulfil one's duty; قامَ بِواجِبِهِ to do/perform one's duty; تَخَلّى عن \ قَصَّرَ في واجِبِهِ to forsake/neglect one's duty; من الواجِبِ أنْ ... it is necessary that ...
⓶ ◀[عَمَل] assignment, task; واجِب البَيْت, واجِب مَنْزِلِيّ, واجِبات homework

وَجْبة *n* |وَجَبات| meal; dish; وَجْبة جَيِّدة \ لَذيذة \ شَهيّة a good/nice/tasty meal; وَجْبة قَوِيّة \ مُغَذِّية a substantial/nutritious meal; وَجْبة خَفيفة a light meal, snack; وَجْبة دَسِمة a high-fat meal; وَجَبات سَريعة fast food; وَجْبة العَشاء dinner; ثَلاث وَجَباتٍ في اليَوْم three meals a day; تَناوَلَ وَجْبَةَ الطَعام to take/have a meal

وُجوب *n* obligation; necessity

وُجوبِيّ *adj* necessary

إيجاب *n* ⓵ ◀[إلْزام] obligation ⓶ ◀[إثْبات] affirmation, confirmation; أجابَ بالإيجابِ to answer in the affirmative

إيجابِيّ *adj* positive; affirmative; نَتيجة إيجابيّة a positive result; صِفة إيجابيّة a positive trait; جَواب إيجابِيّ an affirmative answer; رَأى شَيْئاً بِطَريقةٍ إيجابيّةٍ to consider sth positively; اتَّخَذَ مَوْقِفاً إيجابيّاً to take a positive stance

إيجابِيّات *n pl* positive aspects; الإيجابيّات والسَلْبيّات the pros and cons; إيجابيّاتُهُ أكْثَرُ من سَلْبِيّاتِهِ it has more advantages then disadvantages

موجَب *adj* ⓵ ◀[إيجابِيّ] affirmative ⓶ (Math) positive; عَدَد موجَب a positive number ⓷ (Elec) positive

موجِب Ⓐ *adj* obligating; أسْباب موجِبة compelling reasons

ثِقة شَخْصٍ to gain sb's trust; تَمَتَّعَ بِثِقةِ شَخْصٍ to enjoy sb's trust; تَزَعْزَعَتْ ثِقَتي my trust was shaken; تَحَدَّثَ بِثِقةٍ to speak with confidence

مُوَثَّق *adj* documented, registered; attested; تَقْرير مُوَثَّق بِشَكْلٍ جَيِّدٍ a well-documented report; مُوَثَّق بالأَسْماءِ والأَماكِنِ documented with names and places

مُوَثِّق *n* notary

مَوْثوق *adj* reliable, trustworthy; مَوْثوق بِهِ reliable; مُخْبِر مَوْثوق بِهِ a reliable informant; تَقْدير مَوْثوق بِهِ a reliable estimate; من مَصْدَرٍ مَوْثوقٍ بِهِ from a reliable source; مَعْلومات غَيْر مَوْثوقٍ بها \ غَيْر مَوْثوقةٍ unreliable information; شُهَداء مَوْثوق بِهِمْ reliable witnesses

مَوْثوقيّة *n* reliability; authenticity; مَوْثوقيّة الأَخْبارِ the reliability of the news; عَدَم مَوْثوقيّةٍ unreliability

ميثاق *n* |مَواثيقُ| ⓵ ◀[مُعاهَدة] treaty, pact, charter; ميثاق شَرَفٍ gentleman's/gentlemen's agreement; code of conduct; ميثاق الأُمَمِ المُتَّحِدةِ United Nations Charter; انْتَهَكَ ميثاقاً to violate a treaty ⓶ (Comput) protocol; ميثاق الإنْتَرْنِت Internet Protocol, IP

ميثاقِيّ *adj* treaty (*before n*), pact (*before n*); مادّة ميثاقيّة a treaty article

وَثَن *n* |أَوْثان, وُثُن| idol, god; عَبَدَ الأَوْثانَ to worship idols

وَثَنِيّ Ⓐ *adj* heathen, pagan
Ⓑ *n* idolater, heathen

وَثَنِيّة *n* idolatry, paganism

وَجَبَ *v* |i; وُجوب| to be/become obligatory, to be necessary; يَجِبُ ألاّ تَتَسَرَّعَ it has to remain a secret; يَجِبُ أنْ يَبْقى سِرّيًّا you must not judge too quickly; يَجِبُ الاسْتِفادةُ من دُروسِ الماضي we have to learn from the past; وَجَبَ على to have to, must, to be obliged; يَجِبُ عَلَيْها فِعْلُهُ she has to do it; لا يَجِبُ عَلَيْها فِعْلُهُ she doesn't have/need to do it

وَجَّبَ *v* to obligate, to impose

أَوْجَبَ *v* to make necessary, to obligate, to impose; أَوْجَبَ لِشَخْصٍ الدَفْعَ to obligate sb to pay

تَوَجَّبَ *v* to be necessary; تَوَجَّبَ عَلَيْهِ أنْ ... he had to ...

وُجوديّة *n* (Philos) existentialism

إيجاد *n* creation; إيجاد وَظائِفَ جَديدةٍ the creation of new jobs; إيجاد حَلٍّ \ تَسْوِيةٍ the creation of a solution/settlement

تواجُد *n* presence; تَواجُد عَسْكَرِيّ military presence

مُتواجِد *adj* existing, available

مَوْجود **A** *adj* **1** [حاضِر] present; كانَ مَوْجوداً to be present; لَيْسَ مَوْجوداً he's not there/here/in **2** [مُتَوفِّر] existing, present; available; المَوادُّ مَوْجودةٌ the materials are there; المَشاكِل المَوْجودة the existing problems; غَيْر مَوْجودٍ non-existent

B *n* (Busn) مَوْجودات assets

‹ **وَجْدة** *n* Oujda (*town in eastern Morocco*)

‹ **وِجار** *n* |أَوْجِرة| den, burrow; cave

وَجْرة *n* |أَوْجار| pitfall

ميجار *n* |مَياجير| club

‹ **وَجَزَ** *v* |i; وَجْز, وُجوز| to be brief, to summarize

أَوْجَزَ *v* to summarize, to outline; أَوْجَزَ كَلامَهُ to summarize his words

وَجيز *adj* short, brief, concise; pithy; عِبارة وَجيزة a pithy saying

إيجاز *n* shortness, conciseness, brevity; بِإيجازٍ briefly; اخْتَصَرَ شَيْئاً بِإيجازٍ to summarize sth briefly

موجَز **A** *adj* summarized, concise, succinct; جَواب موجَز a succinct reply; وَصْف موجَز a short description; تَحَدَّثَ عن شَيْءٍ بِشَكْلٍ موجَز to speak briefly about sth

B *n* |مَواجِز| summary, excerpt, abstract; موجَز النَّصِّ a summary of the text; موجَز الأَخْبارِ news brief; موجَز نَحْوٍ a grammar compendium

‹ **وَجَسَ** *v* |i; وَجْس, وَجَسان| to be/become afraid; وَجَسَ خيفَةً من شَيْءٍ to be/become afraid of sth

أَوْجَسَ *v* **1** [خافَ] to fear **2** [أَحَسَّ] to feel

تَوَجَّسَ *v* to fear; تَوَجَّسَ من شَيْءٍ \ شَخْصٍ to fear sth/sb; تَوَجَّسَ من شَيْءٍ شَرًّا to have a bad feeling about sth

‹ **وَجِعَ** *v* |a; وَجَع| to feel pain, to be in pain

أَوْجَعَ *v* to hurt; أَوْجَعَ شَخْصاً to hurt sb

تَوَجَّعَ *v* to be in pain; تَوَجَّعَ لِشَخْصٍ to feel compassion for sb

B *n* |موجِبات| necessity; motive, reason; بِموجِبِ ... according to, in accordance with; on the basis of, by virtue of; بِموجِبِهِ whereby, by which; بِموجِبِ القَواعِدِ in accordance with the rules; بِموجِبِ قَرارٍ وِزارِيٍّ by virtue of a ministerial decree

‹ **وَجَدَ** *v* |i| **1** [لَقِيَ] |وُجود| to find, to come across; وُجِدَ to be found, to exist, to be; وَجَدَ عَمَلاً \ بَيْتاً to find a job/home; وَجَدَ أَخْطاءً to find errors; وَجَدَ حَلاً لِشَيْءٍ to find a solution for sth; لم يَجِدِ الطَريقَ he couldn't find the way; وَجَدْتُهُ نائِماً I found him sleeping; وَجَدَ نَفْسَهُ to find oneself, to be; وَجَدَ نَفْسَهُ في مَأْزِقٍ to find oneself in a difficult position; يوجَدُ there is; ... توجَدُ مَتاحِفُ كَثيرةٌ في there are many museums in ...; إنْ وُجِدَ if present/available; ابْحَثْ تَجِدْ seek and you will find; مَنْ طَلَبَ وَجَدَ he who seeks will find **2** [رَأَى] |وُجود| to find, to think; ... وَجَدَ أنْ to think that ...; وَجَدَ شَيْئاً غَيْرَ مُناسِبٍ to find sth inappropriate; وَجَدَ شَيْئاً ضَرورِيًّا to find sth necessary **3** [عَشِقَ] |وَجْد| to love; وَجَدَ بِشَخْصٍ to love sb

أَوْجَدَ *v* |i| **1** [أَبْدَعَ] to create, to produce; أَوْجَدَ فُرَصَ عَمَلٍ to create job opportunities **2** [أَحْدَثَ] to cause, to bring about **3** [وَجَدَ] to find, to obtain; أَوْجَدَ بَدائِلَ لِشَيْءٍ to find alternatives for sth

تَواجَدَ *v* to be, to exist, to be present; تَواجَدَ في مَكانِ الجَريمة to be at the site of the crime

وَجْد *n* love

واجِد *n* **1** [مَنْ وَجَدَ] finder **2** (Islam) الواجِد the Finder (*one of the names of God*)

وِجْدان *n* feeling, sentiment

وِجْدانِيّ *adj* emotional, sentimental; الشِعْر الوِجْدانِيّ love poetry; لَحَظات وِجْدانِيّة emotional moments

وُجود *n* **1** [حُضور] presence; كُلِّيّ الوُجودِ omnipresent; قَبِلَ بِوُجودِ مُراقِبينَ دُوَلِيّينَ to accept the presence of foreign observers; اعْتَرَفَ بِوُجودِ خِلافاتٍ to admit that there are differences **2** [حَياة] existence, being, life; حَقّ الوُجودِ the right to exist; مَعْرَكة الوُجودِ the struggle for life; أَساس الوُجودِ raison d'être; بَحْث عن مَعْنًى لِلوُجودِ to look for the meaning of life; جاءَ إلى الوُجودِ to come into being

وُجودِيّ *adj* existential

to face reality/the truth; واجهَ مَشاكِلَ (ماليّةً) to be confronted with financial problems

تَوَجَّهَ *v* ① [ذَهَبَ] to go, to head; تَوَجَّهَ إلى جِهةٍ أُخرى to go (in) another direction; تَوَجَّهَ إلى شَخْصٍ to head for sb; to turn to sb; تَوَجَّهَ إلى شَيْءٍ to head for sth; تَوَجَّهَ إلى المُديرِ \ المَدْخَلِ to go to the manager/entrance ② [اتَّجَهَ] to turn; تَوَجَّهَ إلى شَخْصٍ to turn to sb; تَوَجَّهَ إلى مَجْلِسِ الشَّعْبِ \ الرَئيسِ to turn to the parliament/chairman; تَوَجَّهَت الأَنْظارُ إلَيْهِ all eyes were on him; تَوَجَّهَ بِسُؤالٍ \ بِطَلَبٍ إلى شَخْصٍ to turn to sb with a question/request

تَواجَهَ *v* to face each other

اتَّجَهَ *v* |i| ① [قَصَدَ] to go, to head; اتَّجَهَ إلى شَيْءٍ \ شَخْصٍ to head for sth/sb; اتَّجَهَ إلى قاعةِ الدَرْسِ to go to the classroom ② [عَكَفَ] to be oriented; اتَّجَهَ إلى المُسْتَقْبَلِ to head for the future

وَجْه *n* ① (Anat) |وُجوه| face; وَجْه مُعَبِّر an expressive face; وُجوه مَأْلوفة \ غَيْر مَأْلوفةٍ familiar/strange faces; وَجْه مُحْتَقِن \ شاحِب a red/pale face; سِمات \ أساريرِ الوَجْهِ features; صَفْعة على الوَجْهِ a slap in the face; وَجْهاً لِوَجْهٍ face to face; وَجْهاً لِوَجْهٍ مع عَدوِهِ face to face with his enemy; شَخْص بِوَجْهَيْنِ a two-faced person; احْمَرَّ وَجْهُهُ to blush; أَشْرَقَ \ تَطَلَّقَ وَجْهُهُ his face lit up; كَشَفَ عن وَجْهِهِ الحَقيقيِّ to show one's true face; حَفِظَ \ صانَ ماءَ وَجْهِهِ to save face; عَلا وَجْهَهُ الحُزْنُ ,بَدَتْ على وَجْهِهِ أماراتُ الحُزْنِ ≈ his face was grief-stricken; أَغْلَقَ البابَ في وَجْهِ شَخْصٍ to slam the door in sb's face; ابْتَسَمَ في وَجْهِ شَخْصٍ to smile at sb; ضَحِكَ في وَجْهِ شَخْصٍ to laugh in sb's face ② [جانِب] |وُجوه ,أَوْجُه| side, surface; front; وَجْه آخَر other/reverse side; الوَجْه الآخَر للعُمْلةِ the other side of the medal; كانَ لَهُ وَجْهٌ آخَرُ he had another side, he had another side to him; مُتَعَدِّد الأَوْجُهِ multifaceted; لِكُلِّ مَسْأَلةٍ وَجْهانِ every case has two sides; من كُلِّ الأَوْجُه from all sides; inside and outside; في وَجْهِهِ in his presence; ضَرَبَ وَجْهَ الأَمْرِ وَعَيْنَهُ to hit the nail on the head (*to touch on the very essence of the matter*) ③ [مَظْهَر] |وُجوه ,أَوْجُه| aspect, respect, facet; كَلام ذو بِوَجْهَيْنِ two-faced talk; وَجْه الشَبَهِ common ground; وَجْهَيْنِ

وَجَع *n* |أَوْجاع ,وِجاع| pain; وَجَع مِعَويّ intestinal pain; وَجَع الأَسْنانِ toothache; وَجَع الظَهْرِ backache, back pain; سَبَّبَ أَوْجاعَ الظَهْرِ to cause/give backaches; عانى من وَجَعٍ في المَعِدةِ to have a stomach ache

وَجيع *adj* painful

موجع Ⓐ *adj* painful; ضَرْبة موجعة a painful blow; الحَقيقة الموجِعة the painful truth

Ⓑ *n* |مَواجِعُ| pain, ache

مَوْجوع *adj* in pain

‹ **وَجَفَ** *v* |i| |وَجيف ,وُجوف ,وَجْف| ① [خَفَقَ] to throb, to beat; يَجِفُ القَلْبُ the heart beats ② [اضْطَرَبَ] to be agitated

أَوْجَفَ *v* to disturb, to agitate

‹ **وُجاق** *n* |وُجاقات| stove

‹ **وَجِلَ** *v* |مَوْجَل ,وَجَل|; imperf يَوْجَلُ| to be/become afraid, to fear; وَجِلَ من شَيْءٍ \ شَخْصٍ to be/become afraid of sth/sb

وَجَل *n* |أَوْجال| fear, dread

وَجِل *adj* |وِجال ,وَجِلون| fearful; كانَ وَجِلاً من شَيْءٍ \ شَخْص to be afraid of sth/sb

‹ **وَجَمَ** *v* |i| |وُجوم ,وَجْم| to be speechless (*with indignation*); to be silent (*from grief*)

واجِم *adj* speechless, silent

وُجوم *n* speechlessness (*from indignation*)

‹ **وَجْنة** *n* |وَجَنات| (Anat) cheek; عَظْم الوَجْنةِ cheekbone; احْمَرَّتْ وَجْنَتاهُ to have rosy cheeks

‹ **وَجَّهَ** *v* ① [قادَ] to direct, to steer ② [أَرْسَلَ] to send, to dispatch; to address; وَجَّهَ رِسالةً \ طَلَباً إلى شَخْصٍ to send a letter/request to sb; وَجَّهَ الكَلامَ \ الخِطابَ إلى شَخْصٍ to address sb ③ [صَوَّبَ] to aim; وَجَّهَ مُسَدَّساً إلى شَخْصٍ to aim a pistol at sb ④ [أَدارَ] to turn; وَجَّهَ وَجْهَهُ \ ظَهْرَهُ إلى شَخْصٍ to turn one's face to/back on sb; وَجَّهَ خُطاهُ نحو شَيْءٍ to turn one's steps to(wards) sth; وَجَّهَ اهْتِمامَهُ إلى شَيْءٍ \ شَخْصٍ to turn one's attention to sth/sb ⑤ [عَبَّرَ] to utter; وَجَّهَ تُهْمةً إلى شَخْصٍ to accuse sb; وَجَّهَ تَحْذيراتٍ إلى شَخْصٍ to warn sb

واجَهَ *v* to face, to confront, to be confronted with; to fight, to defy; واجَهَ شَخْصاً \ شَيْئاً to confront sb/sth; واجَهَ شَخْصاً بالحَقيقةِ to confront sb with the truth; واجَهَ الواقِعَ \ الحَقيقةَ

عامٍّ \ خاصٍّ in general/particular; على وَجْهِ الخُصوصِ in particular; بِوَجْهٍ واسِعٍ on a large scale; من كُلِّ الوُجوهِ in all aspects, in every way; من وُجوهٍ كَثيرةٍ \ عِدّةٍ in many/several aspects; من عِدّةِ أَوْجُهٍ in many respects; لا وَجْهَ لَهُ من الصِحّةِ it's all wrong ④ (Astron) |أَوْجُه| phase; أَوْجُه القَمَرِ الأَرْبَعة the four lunar phases ⑤ [طَريقة] way, manner; على وَجْهِ … in the way of …; على أَحْسَنِ وَجْهٍ as good as possible ⑥ [سُمْعة] ابْيَضَّ وَجْهُ شَخْصٍ to bring sb honour; سَوَّدَ وَجْهَ شَخْصٍ to bring sb into discredit, to blacken sb's good name/character

(Idiom) لِوَجْهِ اللهِ free of charge

واجِهة *n* ① [مُقَدَّم الشَيْءِ] front, outside; واجِهة مَبْنًى, واجِهة أَماميّة front, facade; واجِهة عَرْضٍ showcase, display case; واجِهة دُكّانٍ shopfront, show window; واجِهة خَلْفيّة back, background ② (Comput) interface; واجِهة بَرْمَجةِ تَطْبيقاتٍ API, application programming interface; واجِهة مُسْتَخْدِمٍ \ اسْتِخْدامٍ (رُسوميّة) (graphical) user interface

وَجاهة *n* distinction, prominence, prestige

وِجْهة, وُجْهة *n* ① [جِهة] direction; وُجْهة نَظَرٍ point of view; تَباعُد في وُجْهاتِ النَظَرِ diversity of opinion; تَقْريب وُجْهاتِ النَظَرِ bringing together the points of view ② [مَقْصَد] destination; وُجْهة نِهائيّة final destination

وَجْهيّ *adj* facial; تَعْبير وَجْهيّ facial expression

وَجيه Ⓐ *adj* |وُجَهاءُ| good, sound; مُبَرِّر \ سَبَب \ سُؤال وَجيه a good excuse/reason/question Ⓑ *n* |وُجَهاءُ| notable, dignitary

اتِّجاه *n* |اتِّجاهات| ① [جِهة] direction, course; بِاتِّجاهِ in the direction of; بِاتِّجاهِ الغَرْبِ westward(s); خَطْوة في الاتِّجاه الصَحيحِ a step in the right direction; في اتِّجاهَيْنِ مُخْتَلِفَيْنِ in two different directions; طَريق بِاتِّجاهٍ واحِدٍ a one-way road; اتَّخَذَ اتِّجاهاً to take a direction; غَيَّرَ الاتِّجاهَ to change direction, to take a different course ② [تَيّار] opinion; trend; اتِّجاه فِكْريّ line/school of thought

تِجاهَ, تُجاهَ *prep* in front of, opposite; to(wards); with respect to; عَواطِفُهُ \ مَشاعِرُهُ تُجاهَها his feelings for her; الْتِزاماتُهُ تُجاهَها his obligations to(wards) her

تَوَجُّه *n* inclination, tendency; view, mentality

تَوْجيه *n* |تَوْجيهات| ① [إلى جِهةٍ مُعَيَّنةٍ] directing, orientating; إعادة تَوْجيهٍ redirection; forwarding; أَعادَ تَوْجيهَ رِسالةٍ to forward a message; ذِراع تَوْجيهٍ control stick, joystick; قِسْم تَوْجيهٍ orientation class; التَوْجيه المِهْنيّ career guidance; تَوْجيه نِداءٍ sending out a call; تَوْجيه دَعْوةٍ extending an invitation ② [إرْشاد] guidance; تَوْجيهات instructions, directives; تَوْجيه دِراسيّ study advice, academic coaching ③ [تَحَكُّم] direction, instruction

تَوْجيهيّ *adj* instructional, guiding; فيلْم تَوْجيهيّ an instructional film; شَهادة تَوْجيهيّة *diploma after secondary school entitling admittance to university*

جِهة *n* ① [جانِب] side; direction; جِهة عُلْويّة top; في الجِهةِ العُلْويّةِ at the top; جِهة تَحْتيّة \ سُفْلى bottom; جِهة أَماميّة front; في الجِهةِ الأَماميّةِ at/in the front; جِهة داخِليّة inside; الجِهة المُقابِلة other/opposite side; الجِهة الغَرْبيّة west side; في الجِهةِ الغَرْبيّةِ on the west side; في \ إلى \ من كُلِّ الجِهاتِ in/to/from all directions; من الجِهَتَيْنِ from both sides; من جِهةِ الشَمالِ from the north; من جِهةِ الفَلاّحينَ from the part of the farmers; من جِهَتي on/for my part; من جِهةٍ …. وَمِنْ جِهةٍ أُخْرى on the one hand … on the other hand; تَبادُل من جِهةٍ واحِدةٍ one-way exchange; اتَّجَهَ إلى جِهةٍ مُعَيَّنةٍ to head in a certain direction; إلى جِهةٍ أُخْرى in another direction ② [مِنْطَقة] district, area; الجِهة الغَرْبيّة لِلمَدينة the western area of the city ③ [صاحِب السُلْطةِ] authority; الجِهات المُخْتَصّة the relevant authorities ④ (Geog) الجِهات الأَرْبَعة the four points (*of a compass*)

جِهَويّ *adj* regional; نَقْل جِهَويّ (Mor) regional transport; جَريدة جِهَويّة a provincial newspaper

مُتَّجَه *n* direction; في كُلِّ مُتَّجَهٍ in all directions

مُتَّجِه Ⓐ *adj* heading; القِطار المُتَّجِه إلى لُنْدُن the train to London Ⓑ *n* (Math) vector; كَمِّيّة مُتَّجِهة vector

مُواجِه *adj* opposite; مُواجِه لِشَيْءٍ opposite sth; الباب المُواجِه لِلجِدارِ the door opposite the wall

مُواجَهة *n* ① [مُقابَلة] confrontation; مُواجَهة قَوِيّة \ عَنيفة a harsh/violent confrontation; مُواجَهة عَسْكَريّة a military confrontation; مُواجَهة مع العَدوّ a confrontation with the enemy; في مُواجَهةِ opposite; دُوَل خطّ المُواجَهةِ the Front-line States [2] [مُعالَجة] approach; مُواجَهة المَشاكِلِ confronting problems

مُوَجَّه *adj* directed, guided; مُوَجَّه إلى \ ضدّ شَخْصٍ directed to/against sb; كانَ مُوَجَّهاً لِشَيْءٍ to be oriented towards sth

مُوَجِّه *n* supervisor, instructor, counsellor

وَحَدَ *v* |i; وَحْد, وَحِدة, وَحْدة, حِدة| to be alone, to be unique

وَحَّدَ *v* [1] [جَمَّعَ] to unite, to unify; to integrate; وَحَّدَ الجُهُود to join forces; وَحَّدَ بَلَداً to unite a country [2] (Relig) *to believe in the unity of God; to be a monotheist*

تَوَحَّدَ *v* [1] [اتَّحَدَ] to be united; يَتَوَحَّدُ في الرَدِّ to have the same reaction; تَتَوَحَّدُ الصُفوفُ the ranks are closing [2] [انْعَزَلَ] to be alone; تَوَحَّدَ بِرَأْيِهِ to stand alone with one's opinion

اتَّحَدَ *v* [1] [تَوَحَّدَ] to form a union, to unite; to join; اتَّحَدَ في النِضالِ to join forces [2] [ضَمَّ] to combine; يَتَّحِدُ الكِبْرِيت مع الأُكْسِجين sulphur combines with oxygen

وَحْد *n* وَحْدَهُ, لِوَحْدِهِ alone, by himself; هي وَحْدَها تَعْرِفُ she alone knows; نَسيج وَحْدِهِ one of a kind; لَسْنا وَحْدَنا في المَعْرَكةِ we are not alone in the struggle; كُلُّ واحِدٍ لِوَحْدِهِ every man for himself

واحِد [A] *num* [رَقْم] one; رَقْم واحِد number one; واحِد وَعِشْرونَ twenty one; الساعة الواحِدة one o'clock; في حَوالي الساعةِ الواحِدةِ at about one o'clock; في يَوْم واحِدٍ in one day; في مَوْضِع واحِدٍ in one place; واحِد من كُلِّ خَمْسةِ أَشْخاصٍ one out of five people; واحِد من المُعَلِّمين one of the teachers, a teacher; غَيْر واحِدٍ more than one

[B] *adj* [فَريد] only; the same; النَتيجةُ واحِدةٌ the result is the same

[C] *n* [1] [شَيْء] واحِداً بعد الآخَرِ, واحِداً فَواحِداً one after the other, one by one [2] [المَرْء] الواحِد one, people, you; قد يَتَساءَلُ الواحِدُ لِماذا one may wonder why; كُلّ واحِدٍ everyone, everybody; كُلّ واحِدٍ مِنْهُمْ each/every one of them [3] (Islam) الواحِد the Only One (*one of the names of God*)

وَحْدانيّ [A] *adj* solitary

[B] *n* loner

وَحْدانيّة *n* singleness, oneness; وَحْدانيّة اللهِ the unity of God

وَحْدة, وِحْدة *n* [1] [عَكْس الاخْتِلافِ] unity; uniformity; مَذْهَب وَحْدةِ الوُجودِ pantheism [2] [عُزْلة] loneliness, desolation; أَحَسَّ بالوَحْدةِ to feel lonely [3] [اتِّحاد] union, unity; community; الوَحْدة العَرَبيّة Arab unity; الْتَحَقَ بِوَحْدةٍ to join a union; مُنَظَّمة الوَحْدةِ الإفْريقيّة Organisation of African Unity, OAU [4] [قِسْم] unit, group; وَحْدة صَرْفيّة (Ling) morpheme; وَحْدة حَرْبيّة, وَحْدة عَسْكَريّة military/army unit [5] [قياس] unit; وَحْدة قِياسِ شِدّةِ التَيّارِ the unit of electric current; وَحْدة نَقْديّة monetary/currency unit; وَحْدة حِسابيّة unit of account; وَحْدة زَمَنيّة unit of time; سِعْر الوَحْدةِ unit price

وَحْدَويّ *adj* unitary

وَحيد *adj* [1] [فَريد] only, sole; unique; وَحيد أَبَوَيْهِ only child; ابْنُهُ الوَحيد his only son; الطَريقة الوَحيدة the only way; هو المُرَشَّحُ الوَحيدُ he is the only candidate; وَحيد من نَوْعِهِ one of a kind [2] [مُنْفَرِد] alone, solitary; lonely, lost; وَحيداً alone; بَقِيَ وَحيداً to stay behind alone

اتِّحاد *n* |اتِّحادات| [1] [انْضِمام] unification; unity, harmony; الاتِّحادُ قُوّةٌ united we stand [2] [جَمْعيّة] unity; association, union; federation, confederacy, league; الاتِّحاد الأوروبّيّ the European Union, EU; the European Community; الاتِّحاد النَقْديّ الأوروبيّ the European Monetary Union; الاتِّحاد الروسيّ the Russian Federation; اتِّحاد عامّ umbrella organization; اتِّحاد شَرِكاتٍ consortium; اتِّحاد مَصارِفَ banking association, a consortium of banks; اتِّحاد الأَطِبّاءِ العَرَبِ the Union of Arab Doctors; أَعْضاء الاتِّحادِ association members; رَئيس الاتِّحادِ the union chairman/president; أَسَّسَ اتِّحاداً to found a union; شَكَّلَ اتِّحاداً to form a confederation

اتِّحاديّ *adj* federal, unionist

أَوْحَد *adj* |dipt| unique, singular

تَوَحُّد *n* [1] [عُزْلة] isolation; loneliness [2] (Med) autism; مُصاب بالتَوَحُّدِ autistic

تَوَحُّديّ *adj* autistic

تَوْحيد *n* [1] [المَعايير] uniforming; standardization; تَوْحيد القَواعِدِ \ القَوانينِ standardization of the rules/laws [2] [مَصْدَر] unification, combination; تَوْحيد أوروبا the unification of

Europe; تَوْحيد القُوى combining forces; تَوْحيد الجُهودِ the joining of the efforts; إعادة التَوْحيدِ reunification; إعادة تَوْحيد أَلْمانيا the German reunification [3] (Relig) monotheism; *belief in the unity of God*

تَوْحيديّ *adj* monotheistic

حِدة *n* solitude; على حِدةٍ alone, isolated; separate, separately

مُتَّحِد *adj* united; harmonious; الأُمَم المُتَّحِدة the United Nations, UN; الوِلايات المُتَّحِدة (الأَمْريكيّة) the United States (of America), US

مُتَوَحِّد *adj* lonely; solitary

مُوَحَّد *adj* [1] ◀ [حَسَبَ المَعاييرِ] uniform; تَرْكيب \ لِباس مُوَحَّد uniform composition/clothing; سِعْر مُوَحَّد a uniform price; اسْتِخْدام مَعايير مُوَحَّدةٍ the use of uniform standards [2] ◀ [مُشْتَرَك] united; القُدْس المُوَحَّدة united Jerusalem; اتَّخَذوا مَوْقِفاً مُوَحَّداً they shared the same point of view; اليورو هو العُمْلةُ الأوروبيّةُ المُوَحَّدةُ the euro is the common European currency

مُوَحِّد *n* *sb who believes in the unity of God*; المُوَحِّدونَ (Hist) the Almohads

‹ **أَوْحَشَ** *v* [1] ◀ [إحْساس] *to make sb feel lonely*; أَوْحَشَتْهُ أُمُّهُ he missed his mother [2] ◀ [المَكانُ] to be deserted

تَوَحَّشَ *v* [1] ◀ [صارَ كالوَحْشِ] to be/become wild [2] ◀ صارَ قَفْراً [خالِياً] to be deserted

اسْتَوْحَشَ *v* [1] ◀ [الشَخْصُ] to become/feel lonely [2] ◀ [المَكانُ] to be deserted [3] ◀ [افْتَقَدَ] to miss; اسْتَوْحَشَ لِشَخْصٍ to miss sb

وَحْش [A] *adj* desolate; مَكان وَحْش a desolate place, waste land [B] *n* |وُحْشان ,وُحوش| wild animal; monster; وُحوش ضارية wild animals, predatory animals; حِمار الوَحْشِ zebra

وَحْشة *n* loneliness, desolation; أَحَسَّ بالوَحْشةِ to feel lonely; إحْساس بالوَحْشةِ loneliness

وَحْشيّ *adj* [1] ◀ [هَمَجيّ] wild, savage; قَبائِل وَحْشيّة savage tribes [2] ◀ [قاسٍ] brutal, cruel, barbaric; جَريمة وَحْشيّة a brutal crime; عَمَل وَحْشيّ cruelty, atrocity; بِعُنْفٍ وَحْشيٍّ with brute force, barbarically

وَحْشيّة *n* cruelty

اسْتيحاش *n* estrangement, alienation

تَوَحُّش *n* |تَوَحُّشات| brutality

مُتَوَحِّش *adj* wild; barbaric

مُسْتَوْحِش *adj* [1] ◀ [الشَخْصُ] lonesome [2] ◀ [المَكانُ] savage, barbaric

موحِش *adj* deserted, lonely, desolate; مَكان موحِش a deserted place; بَدا الطَريقُ موحِشاً the street looked deserted

‹ **أَوْحَلَ** *v* to throw/drop in the mud

تَوَحَّلَ *v* to become muddy

وَحْل ,وَحَل *n* |أَوْحال ,وُحول| mud, mire, sludge; لَطَّخَ اسْمَ \ سُمْعَةَ شَخْصٍ بالوَحْلِ to drag sb's name through the mud

وَحِل *adj* muddy

موحِل *adj* muddy; مِنْطَقة موحِلة muddy ground

‹ **وَحِمَ** *v* |وَحَم|; imperf |يَوْحِمُ| (old use) to have a strong appetite for *(concerning pregnant women)*

وَحَم *n* craving of a pregnant woman

وِحام *n* appetite

‹ **وَحى** *v* |i; وَحْي| to inspire

أَوْحى *v* [1] ◀ [أَشارَ] to give an impression, to suggest; أَوْحى بِأَنَّ... to give the impression that... [2] ◀ [أَلْهَمَ] to inspire; to suggest; أَوْحى بِشَيْءٍ to inspire sth; أَوْحى لِشَخْصٍ بِشَيْءٍ to suggest to sb sth; أوحِيَ إِلَيْهِ it came to him [3] ◀ [الله] to reveal

اسْتَوْحى *v* [1] ◀ [اسْتَلْهَمَ] to be inspired; to seek inspiration [2] ◀ [اشْتَقَّ] |من| to derive, to deduce; اسْتَوْحى رَأْيَهُ من شَيْءٍ to derive one's opinion from sth

وَحْي *n* revelation; inspiration; وَحْي إلهيّ a divine revelation; وَسيط الوَحْيِ oracle

إيحاء *n* |إيحاءات| suggestion, insinuation; أَدّى ,أَعْطى إيحاءً ... إلى الإيحاءِ بِأَنَّ ... to imply that ...

إيحائيّ *adj* suggestive; سُؤال إيحائيّ a suggestive/leading question

موحٍ *adj* inspiring; suggestive; عَبَّرَ \ تَحَدَّثَ عن شَيْءٍ بِشَكْلٍ موحٍ to tell sth in a suggestive manner

‹ **وَخَزَ** *v* |i; وَخْز| to sting, to prick; وَخَزَ شَخْصاً بِدَبّوسٍ to prick sb with a pin

ودود A *adj* 1 [مَحْبوب] dear, loved, beloved; likeable; غَيْر وَدودٍ unsympathetic 2 [كَثير الحُبّ] loving, tender

B *n* الوَدود the Loving (*one of the names of God*)

وِدّي ,وُدّي ,وَدّي *adj* friendly, amicable; مُباراة وِدّيّة a friendly match; a training match; مُصالَحة وِدّيّة an amicable arrangement

مَوَدّة *n* 1 [حَنان] friendship, affection; رَمْز مَوَدّةٍ a token of affection; كَنَّ المَوَدّةَ لِشَخْصٍ to feel affection for sb 2 [حُبّ] love, infatuation 3 [أُلْفة] intimacy

وَدَعَ *v* |a; وَدْع| 1 [أَوْدَعَ] to put down, to deposit 2 [تَرَكَ] to let, to leave; دَعْهُ عَنْكَ! stop that!; دَعْنا من هذا! enough about that! 3 [أَمْر] دَعْنا نَذْهَبْ let's go!; دَعْنا نَذْهَبُ بِسَلامٍ! let us go in peace!; دَعْنا نَفْرَحُ بالفَوْز let's rejoice at our victory

وَدَّعَ *v* to say goodbye/farewell, to see off; وَدَّعَ شَخْصاً \ شَيْئاً to say farewell to sb/sth; وَدَّعَ شَخْصاً الوَداعَ الأَخيرَ to pay one's last respects to sb

أَوْدَعَ *v* to put/lay down; to deposit, to entrust; أَوْدَعَ شَيْئاً to deposit sth, to entrust sth; أَوْدَعَ نُقوداً في البَنْكِ to deposit money into a bank; أَوْدَعَ مَبْلَغاً في حِسابٍ بَنْكيٍّ to deposit an amount into a bank account; أَوْدَعَ شَخْصاً السِجْنَ to throw sb in prison

اِسْتَوْدَعَ *v* to entrust, to deposit; أَسْتَوْدِعُكَ اللهَ farewell, God be with you

وَدَع *n coll* seashells

وادِع *n* depositor

وَداع *n* farewell; كَلِمة \ خُطْبة وَداعٍ farewell speech; رِسالة وَداعٍ farewell letter; هَدِيّة وَداعٍ farewell present; حَفْلة وَداعٍ farewell party; حِجّة الوَداع the farewell pilgrimage (*the last hajj of the Prophet Muhammad*); تَبادَلَ تَحيّةَ الوَداع to take leave of each other; وَداعاً! farewell!, goodbye!

وَداعيّ *adj* farewell (*before n*); كَلِمة وَداعيّة farewell speech

وَديع *adj* |وُدَعاءُ| peaceful, peaceable; tame, meek; كانَ كالحَمَلِ الوَديع to be as meek as a lamb

وَديعة *n* |وَدائِعُ| 1 (Busn) deposit, down payment 2 [أَمانة] *sth entrusted to sb's custody*; تَرَكَ عند شَخْصٍ شَيْئاً وَديعةً to deposit sth with sb

وَخْز A *n* 1 [وَجَع] twinge, shooting pain; وَخز مُؤْلِم a shooting pain; a stab of pain; وَخْز في الظَهْرِ twinge in the back; وَخْز الضَميرِ pangs of conscience; وَخْز بالإبَرِ acupuncture 2 [قَليل] bit; وَخْز قَليل a little bit

B *n coll* [شَكّة] sting, prick; وَخْزة إِبْرةٍ a needle prick

وَخَطَ *v* |i; وَخْط| to turn grey

وَخُمَ *v* |u; وَخامة| to be unhealthy

وَخَم *n* drowsiness (*after eating*); feeling of being full

وَخِم *adj* unhealthy, bad

وَخيم *adj* unhealthy, harmful; bad, evil; وَخيم العاقِبة disastrous, fatal; عَواقِب وَخيمة dire consequences; العَواقِب الوَخيمة للتَدْخينِ the bad effects of smoking

تُخَمة ,تُخْمة *n* |تُخَم, تُخَمات| indigestion

وَخى *v* |i; وَخْي| to intend, to aim at

تَوَخّى *v* to intend, to aim; كانَ يتوَخّى ... he intended to ...

وَخْي *n* intention, plan; goal, aim

وَدَجَ *v* |i; وَدْج| to slaughter; وَدَجَ الذَبيحةَ to slaughter the sacrificial animal

وَدَج *n* |أَوْداج| carotid artery

وَدَّ *v* |a; وَدّ ,وُدّ ,وِدّ ,وِداد ,مَوَدّة| 1 [تَمَنّى] to want, to wish; وَدِدْتُ لَوْ ... I wished that ...; وَدِدْتُ أَنْ أُسافِرَ مَعَكَ I wished I could travel with you 2 [فَضَّلَ] to love; وَدَّ شَخْصاً \ شَيْئاً to love sb/sth

تَوَدَّدَ *v* to (try to) be loved, to try to win favor/friendship; to show love; تَوَدَّدَ إلى صَديقِه he tried to make his friend like him

تَوادَّ *v* to be friends

وِدّ ,وُدّ *n* love, affection; attachment; عِبارة وِدٍّ a token of affection; بوِدِّه أَنْ ... he wants to...; بوِدّي أَنْ أُسافِرَ I would like to travel; بوِدّي لو أُسافِرُ I wished I could travel

وِداد ,وُداد ,وَداد *n* 1 [مَوَدّة] affection, friendship, love 2 [اِسْم شَخْصيّ] Wedad (*female given name*)

وِداديّ *n* supporter

وِداديّة *n* (NA) association

استيداع *n* 1 [إيداع] deposit 2 [تقاعُد] early retirement; أُحيلَ على الاسْتيداعِ he was forced into retirement

إيداع *n* deposit; إيداع على حِسابٍ, إيداع مَصْرِفي bank deposit; وَصْل \ إيصال إيداع deposit receipt

تَوْديع *n* farewell

دَعة *n* gentleness; kindness

مُسْتَوْدَع *n* |مُسْتَوْدَعات| warehouse, stockroom, depot; في المُسْتَوْدَع in the warehouse

مودَع *adj* deposited; المودَع لَدَيْه depositary

مودِع *n* depositor

ميدَعة *n* |مَوادِعُ| apron

‹ **وَدَفة** *n* thistle

‹ **وادِق** *adj* rainy

وِداق *n* فَتْرة الوِداقِ mating season

وَديق *adj* rutting; in heat

‹ **وَدَك** *n* fat (*in meat*)

‹ **مودم** *n* listed alphabetically

‹ **وَدى** *v* |i; وَدْي, دِيَة| to pay blood money

أَوْدى *v* 1 [أَخَذَ] |ب| to take; to kill; أَوْدى الاعْتِداءُ بِحَياة شَخْصَيْن two persons died in the attack 2 [ماتَ] to die

وادٍ *n* |وِدْيان, أَوْدِية| 1 [مَكان مُنْخَفِض بين جَبَلَيْن] valley; وادي المُلوك the Valley of the Kings; صَرْخة في وادٍ a cry in the desert; ذَهَبَتْ صَيْحَتُهُ في وادٍ his shout went unheard 2 [نَهْر] river bed, wadi

دِية *n* blood money

‹ **وَذَرَ** *v* |i; وَذْر| to cut

وَذِرَ *v* |imperfect or imperative only; وَذَر| to let, to leave

‹ **وَرَّبَ** *v* to equivocate, to tergiversate

وارَبَ *v* 1 [الباب] to set ajar 2 [خاتَلَ] to outsmart, to trick; وارَبَ شَخْصاً to outsmart sb

مُوارَبة *n* wordiness; بِدونِ مُوارَبةٍ without wasting words, straight out; قالَ \ سَأَلَ شَيْئاً بِدونِ مُوارَبةٍ to say/ask sth straight out

‹ **وَرِثَ** *v* |i; وِرْث, إِرْث, وِراثة, تُراث| to inherit, to be heir; وَرِثَ شَخْصاً \ من \ عن شَخْصٍ to inherit from sb; وَرِثَ صِفاتِ أَبيهِ he inherited his father's qualities; وَرِثَ ثَرْوةً to inherit a fortune

وَرَّثَ *v* 1 [شَخْصاً] to appoint as heir; وَرَّثَ شَخْصاً to appoint sb as one's heir 2 [مالاً] to leave, to bequeath; وَرَّثَ شَخْصاً مالاً to leave sb money

أَوْرَثَ *v* 1 [تَرَكَ] to leave, to bequeath; أَوْرَثَ مُمْتَلَكاتِهِ لِشَخْصٍ to leave one's possessions to sb; أَوْرَثَ شَخْصاً حُزْناً to make sb sad 2 [شَخْصاً] to appoint as heir; أَوْرَثَ شَخْصاً to appoint sb as one's heir

تَوارَثَ *v* to inherit; تَوارَثَ مَرَضاً to inherit a disease

وارِث *n* |وَرَثة, وُرّاث| 1 [مَنْ يَرِثُ] heir 2 (Islam) الوارث the Inheritor (*one of the names of God*)

وِراثة *n* heredity; وِراثة سَرَطانِ الثَدْيِ breast cancer heredity; عِلْم الوِراثة genetics; عِلْم الوِراثة الجُزَيْئِيّة molecular genetics

وِراثيّ *adj* hereditary; مَرَض وِراثيّ a hereditary disease; تَرْكيب وِراثيّ genotype; هَنْدَسة وِراثيّة genetic engineering; صِفات وِراثيّة hereditary qualities; مُنْتَجات غِذائيّة مُعَدَّلة وِراثيًّا genetically modified foods, GM foods

وِراثيّات *n pl* genetics; عالِم الوِراثيّاتِ geneticist

وَريث *n* |وُرَثاءُ| heir, inheritor; وَريث شَرْعيّ \ قانونيّ lawful heir; وَريث طَبيعيّ natural heir; الوَريث الوَحيد sole inheritor; التَقْسيم على الوُرَثاءِ the division among the heirs (*of the legacy*); رَجَعَ إلى الوَريثِ to fall to the heir

إِرْث *n* inheritance, legacy; heritage; قانون الإرْثِ law of inheritance/succession; طِبْقاً \ بِموجِبِ قانونِ الإرْثِ according to the law of succession; حَقّ الإرْثِ right of inheritance/succession; ضَريبة الإرْثِ inheritance tax; الحِرْمان من الإرْثِ disinheritance; تَرَكَ إرْثاً to leave an inheritance

تُراث *n* inheritance, legacy; التُراث الثَقافيّ \ الحَضاريّ cultural legacy

تُراثيّ *adj* historical, inherited; مَعْرِض تُراثيّ historical exhibition

تَوارُث *n* heredity

تَوْريث *n* (Law) bequest

مُتَوارَث *adj* inherited, hereditary

وِرْد *n* |أَوْراد| **1** [مَوْرِد] watering place **2** (Islam) *a set portion of the Koran which the worshipper commits himself to recite; a practice of repeating the name of God*

وارِد **A** *adj* **1** [مَوْجود] found; mentioned; هذا أَمرٌ غَيْرُ وارِدٍ this doesn't exist; this is out of the question **2** [داخِل] incoming; صُنْدوق البَريدِ الوارِدِ inbox رَسائِل وارِدة incoming messages;

B **1** (Econ) واردات imports, imported goods; returns, incomings **2** [مَنْ وَرَدَ]

(Idiom) لَيْسَ في الوارِدِ إجْراءُ تَغْيير he has no intention of changing

وارِدة *n* لا تَفوتُهُ شارِدةٌ وَلا وارِدةٌ he doesn't miss a thing

وِرْدان *n* بِنْت وِرْدان cockroach

وَرْدِيّ *adj* pink; خَشَب وَرْدِيّ rosewood

وَرْدِيّة *n* **1** [شُغْل] وَرْدِيّة لَيْلِيّة (Egypt) night shift **2** (Bot) rhododendron (*Rhododendron*)

وَرِيد *n* |أَوْرِدة، وُرُد، وُرود| blood vessel, vein; تَوَسُّع الأَوْرِدةِ varicose vein; أُصيبَ بِتَوَسُّعِ الأَوْرِدةِ to suffer from varicose veins; مُنْتَفِخ الوَريدِ with swollen veins; عَبْرَ، عن طَرِيق الوَريدِ \ الأَوْرِدةِ intravenous, intravenously

اسْتيراد *n* import, importation; الاسْتيراد والتَّصْدير import and export; اسْتيراد النَفْطِ \ الأَسْلِحةِ import of oil/weapons; اسْتيراد من ... import from...; مَنْع اسْتيرادٍ import ban; مَنْع فَرْض \ رَفْع مَنْعِ اسْتيرادٍ an import ban on sth; اسْتيرادِ شَيْءٍ to impose/lift an import ban; يَرْتَفِعُ \ يَزيدُ الاسْتيرادُ imports are up; انْخَفَضَ الاسْتيرادُ imports are down

اسْتيرادِيّ *adj* importing, import (*before n*); اقْتِصاد اسْتيرادِيّ وَلَيْسَ تَصْديرِيًّا an importing rather than exporting economy

إيراد *n* |إيرادات| revenue, income, returns; إيراد العَمَلِ earnings; إيرادات الدَّوْلة state revenues; إيرادات فيلْمٍ the box-office receipts; صافي الإيراد the net profit; جَنى إيراداتٍ عالِيةً to gain high profits

تَوارُد *n* succession; تَوارُد الخَواطِر telepathy

تَوْريد *n* |تَوْريدات| **1** [تَزْويد] supply; تَوْريد الأَدْوِيةِ the supply of medicines **2** [اسْتيراد] import; التَوْريد إلى غَزّةَ import into Gaza

مُتَوَرِّد *adj* red, reddish, blushing

مُوَرِّث *n* (Law) testator; عند وَفاةِ المُوَرِّثِ at the time of death of the testator

مُوَرِّثة *n* (Bio) gene

مَوْروث **A** *adj* inherited

B *n* مَوْروث جينيّ genome

ميراث *n* |مَواريثُ| inheritance, legacy; heritage; الميراث الفِكْرِيّ لِشَخْصٍ the intellectual legacy of sb; قانون الميراثِ law of inheritance/succession; ضَريبة الميراثِ inheritance tax; الحِرْمان من الميراثِ disinheritance; حَرَمَ ابْناً من الميراثِ to disinherit a son; نَصيب \ حِصّة في الميراثِ inheritance, portion; طالَبَ بِنَصيبِهِ في الميراثِ to claim one's inheritance; نَصيبُهُ الشَرْعِيّ \ القانونيّ في الميراثِ his legal portion; بَدَّدَ ميراثاً to squander an inheritance; حَصَلَ على ميراثٍ to obtain an inheritance; قَبِلَ ميراثاً to accept an inheritance

وَرَدَ *v* |i; وُرود| **1** [بَلَغَ] to reach, to arrive, to come **2** [جاءَ في] to be said/mentioned (*in a book/letter/newspaper*); وَرَدَ في كِتابٍ \ مَخْطوطةٍ to be mentioned in a book/manuscript

وَرَّدَ *v* **1** [زَوَّدَ] to supply, to furnish, to provide; to deliver **2** [اسْتَوْرَدَ] to import, to bring in **3** [الشَّجَرُ] to bloom, to blossom; وَرَّدَت الشَجَرةُ the tree bloomed **4** [لَوَّنَ] to redden; وَرَّدَت خَدَّها she rouged her cheeks

أَوْرَدَ *v* **1** [ذَكَرَ] to mention, to state; to quote; to put in a newspaper, to publish; أَوْرَدَت الصَحيفةُ أنّ ... the newspaper said that ...; أَوْرَدَ مَعْلوماتٍ to publish data **2** [اسْتَوْرَدَ] to import, to bring in

تَوَرَّدَ *v* to be/become red

تَوارَدَ *v* **1** [اتَّفَقَ] to correspond, to be similar; تَوارَدَت الأَفْكارُ \ الخَواطِرُ the ideas were similar **2** [وَصَلَ الواحِدُ تِلْوَ الآخَرِ] to come one after the other, to succeed one another; تَوارَدَت الأَخْبارُ ≈ news streamed in

اسْتَوْرَدَ *v* to import, to bring in

وَرْد *n coll* |وُرود| (Bot) rose (*Rosa*); flower; باقة من الوَرْدِ الأَحْمَرِ a bunch of red roses; ماء \ عِطْر الوَرْدِ rose water; وَرْد الحِمارِ oleander (*Nerium oleander*)

‹ **وَرَفَ** *v* |i; وَرْف| 1 [اِمْتَدَّ] to stretch, to be long 2 [خَضِرَ] to be green

أَوْرَفَ *v* to stretch, become long (*shadow*)

وارِف *adj* 1 [مُمْتَدّ] extending; ظِلّ وارِف a long shadow 2 [أَخْضَر] lush, green

‹ **وَرَقَ** *v* |i; وَرْق| to leaf

وَرَّقَ *v* 1 [الشَجَرُ] to leaf 2 [الكِتابَ] to leaf through, to thumb through

أَوْرَقَ *v* to leaf

وَرَق *n* |أَوْراق| 1 (Bot) leaves; تَتَساقَطُ أَوْراقُ الأَشْجارِ the leaves are falling from the trees 2 [رَقائِق] paper; وَرَق رَسائِلَ writing paper, stationery; وَرَق تَواليت toilet paper; وَرَق الجُدْرانِ wallpaper; وَرَق صُوَر photo paper; وَرَق نَشّاف blotting paper; وَرَق مُقَوًّى cardboard; عُلْبة \ غِلاف من الوَرَق المُقَوّى a cardboard box/cover; قِطْعة وَرَقٍ a piece of paper, sheet; قِطْعة وَرَقِ الصَنْفَرةِ a piece of sandpaper; مُجَرَّد حِبْر على وَرَقٍ just ink on paper; أَوْراق نَقْدِيّة \ مالِيّة paper money, banknotes; زَوَّرَ أَوْراقاً مالِيَّةً to counterfeit banknotes; وَضَعَ أَفْكارَهُ على الوَرَقِ to put one's thoughts on paper; كَبَسَ الوَرَقَ to press paper; نَفِدَ الوَرَقُ the paper has run out 3 [وَثيقة] document, paper; أَوْراق papers, documents; الأَوْراق، من فَضْلِك! your papers, please! 4 [اللَعِب] (playing) cards; وَزَّعَ وَرَقَ اللَعِبِ to deal the cards

وَرِق *adj* leafy

وارِق *adj* leafy

وَرّاق *n* 1 [بائِع أَوْراقٍ] paper goods dealer 2 [كاتِب] writer

وِراقة *n* paper making, paper trade

وَرَقة *n* |أَوْراق ,وَرَقات| 1 [قِطْعة وَرَقٍ] piece of paper, leaf, sheet; note; وَرَقة نَقْدِيّة banknote; وَرَقة نَقْدِيّة من فِئة خَمْسينَ جُنَيْهاً a fifty pound banknote; وَرَقة مالِيّة security; denomination; وَرَقة عَمَلٍ agenda, work schedule; worksheet; وَرَقة يانَصيبٍ lottery ticket; وَرَقة وَقَلَم pen and paper; كَتَبَ شَيْئاً على وَرَقةٍ to write sth on a piece of paper; قَدَّمَ وَرَقةً بَحْثِيّةً في مُؤْتَمَرٍ to present a paper at a conference 2 [نَباتٍ] leaf; أَوْراق الشَجَرِ tree leaves, foliage 3 [لَعِبٍ] playing card, card; وَرَقة لَعِبٍ playing card; وَرَقة رابِحة trump (card); سَحَبَ وَرَقةً

مُسْتَوْرِد *n* importer

مَوْرِد *n* |مَوارِدُ| 1 [مَنْهَل] well, spring 2 [مَصْدَر] source, resource; مَوْرِد طاقةٍ energy source; مَوارِد مَعْدِنِيّة mineral resources; مَوارِد طَبيعِيّة natural resources; مَوْرِد مالِيّ a source of income; مَوارِد بَشَرِيّة human resources; المَوارِد الحُكومِيّة government revenues; مَوارِد الدَوْلةِ state revenues; المَوارِد المائِيّة water resources; إدارة المَوارِدِ المائِيّةِ water resource management; قَلَّلَ الضَغْطَ على المَوارِدِ المائِيّةِ to ease the pressure on water resources

مُوَرِّد A *adj* شَرِكة مُوَرِّدة supply company B *n* supplier, furnisher; مُوَرِّد مَوادِّ البِناءِ building materials supplier

‹ **وَرْزازات** *n* |dipt f| Ouarzazate (*city in Morocco*)

‹ **مورْس** *n* listed alphabetically

‹ **وَرِش** *adj* frisky, playful

وَرَشان *n* |وِرْشان| wood pigeon (*Columba palumbus*)

وَرْشة *n* |وِرَش ,وَرْشات| 1 [مَشْغَل] workshop; studio; وَرْشة إصْلاحٍ repair shop, garage 2 [في نَدْوةٍ أو مُؤْتَمَرٍ] workshop

‹ **وَرَّطَ** *v* to involve, to entangle; وَرَّطَ شَخْصاً في نِزاعٍ to involve sb in a fight

أَوْرَطَ *v* to involve, to entangle

تَوَرَّطَ *v* تَوَرَّطَ في شَيْءٍ to become involved in sth, to become mixed up in sth

وَرْطة *n* |وِراط ,وَرَطات| difficulty, problem, dilemma; كانَ في وَرْطةٍ to have a problem, to be in trouble; وَقَعَ في وَرْطةٍ to get into a difficult situation, to be in a difficult situation; أَوْقَعَ نَفْسَهُ في وَرْطةٍ to get oneself into trouble; أَنْقَذَ شَخْصاً من وَرْطةٍ to get sb out of a difficult situation; تَخَلَّصَ من وَرْطةٍ to get out of trouble; to solve a problem

مُتَوَرِّط *adj* involved, entangled, embroiled; كانَ مُتَوَرِّطاً في جَريمةٍ \ فَضيحةٍ to be embroiled in a crime/scandal

‹ **وَرِعَ ,وَرُعَ** *v* |وَرَع; imperf يَرِعُ ,يَوْرُعُ| to be pious

تَوَرَّعَ *v* |عن| to abstain (from), to refrain (from); تَوَرَّعَ عن \ من الإِثْمِ to abstain from sin

وَرِع *adj* |أَوْراع| pious, god-fearing

تَرَكَ شَيْئاً وَراءَهُ to leave sth behind; شَخْصٍ to stand behind sb; وَضَعَ النِزاعَ وَراءَهُ to leave the conflict behind; ما وَراءَ البِحارِ overseas; ما وَراءَ النَهْرِ (Hist) Transoxania; إلى ما وَراءَ الحُدودِ over the border; من الوَراءِ from behind; مِنْ وَراءِ البابِ from behind the door; القَصْد من وَراءِ ذلك the intention behind it; هو وَراءَ الحُكومة he supports the government

تَوْرِية *n* ① [تَلاعُب بالأَلْفاظِ] pun, double entendre ② [دَفْن] burial; تَوْرِية الجُثْمانِ burial of the body

ماوَرائيّ *adj* supernatural; metaphysical

ماوَرائيّة *n* supernatural

وَزَبَ *v* |i; وُزوب| to flow

ميزاب *n* |مَيازيبُ| roof gutter

وَزَرَ *v* |i; وِزْر| ① [حَمَلَ] to carry ② [أَثِمَ] to commit a sin

تَوَزَّرَ *v* to become a minister

اتَّزَرَ *v* ① [أَثِمَ] to sin, to commit a sin ② [لَبِسَ إزاراً] to put on a cloak

اسْتَوْزَرَ *v to try to become a minister*

وِزْر *n* |أَوْزار| burden; وَضَعَت الحَرْبُ أَوْزارَها the war has come to an end; عَلَيْهِ وِزْرٌ he is to blame

وِزارة, وَزارة *n* ① [هَيْئة حُكوميّة] department, ministry; وِزارة الداخِليّة Ministry/Department of the Interior, Home Office (BrE); وِزارة الإعْلام Ministry of Information; وِزارة الشُؤونِ الاقْتِصاديّة Ministry of Economics; وِزارة الدِفاع Ministry of Defence; وِزارة العَمَلِ Ministry of Work/Employment; وِزارة المالِيّة Ministry of Finance; وِزارة الأَوْقافِ والشُؤونِ الإسْلاميّة Ministry of Religious Endowments and Islamic Affairs; وِزارة التَمْوينِ Ministry of Supply; وِزارة النَفْطِ والثَروة المَعْدِنيّة Ministry of Oil and Mineral Resources; وِزارة الشَبيبةِ والرِياضة Ministry of Youth and Sports; وِزارة التَرْبِيةِ والتَعْليم Ministry of Education; وَكيل الوِزارةِ undersecretary; وَزير بِلا وِزارةٍ minister without portfolio ② [مَنْصِب] ministership ③ [حُكومة] government; أَلَّفَ \ شَكَّلَ وِزارةً to form a government

وِزاريّ *adj* ministerial, departmental; قَرار وِزاريّ a ministerial decree; سُلْطة \ مَسْؤوليّة وِزاريّة ministerial power/ responsibility; تَشْكيل وِزاريّ cabinet

to draw/take a card; لَعِبَ الوَرَقةَ الأَخيرةَ to play one's last trump; في أَيْديهِم وَرَقةٌ قَويّةٌ ≈ to be in a strong position

وَرَقيّ *adj* paper (*before n*); الصِحافة الوَرَقيّة printed media

مورِق *adj* leafy

وَرِك, وِرْك *n* |f; أَوْراك| (Anat) hip; haunch; مَفْصِل الوِرْكِ hip joint; كانَ عَريضَ \ نَحيفَ الوِرْكِ to be broad/narrow-hipped; انْكَسَرَتْ وِرْكُهُ he broke his hip

وِرْكيّ *adj* sciatic; أَلَم العَصَبِ الوِرْكيِّ sciatica

أَوْرَك *adj* |dipt; وُرْك| broad-hipped

وَرَل *n* |أَوْرال| monitor lizard (*Varanus*)

وَرِمَ *v* |i; وَرَم| to swell, to be/become swollen

وَرَّمَ *v* to cause to swell; to inflate

تَوَرَّمَ *v* to swell, to be/become swollen; يَتَوَرَّمُ كاحِلُهُ his ankle is swollen

وَرَم *n* |أَوْرام| swelling; tumour; bump, lump, growth; وَرَم سَرَطانيّ cancerous tumour; وَرَم دَمَويّ haematoma; وَرَم دِماغيّ \ في المُخِّ brain tumour; وَرَم عَضَليّ myoma; عِلْم الأَوْرام oncology; وَرَم حَميد \ خَبيث a benign/malignant tumour; وَرَم داخِلَ الجِسْم an internal swelling; وَرَم في الثَدْيِ a lump in the breast; اسْتَأْصَلَ وَرَماً (بواسِطةِ \ عن طَريقِ عَمَليّةٍ) to (surgically) remove a tumour

مُتَوَرِّم *adj* swollen; رُكْبة مُتَوَرِّمة a swollen knee

وَرْنَشَ *v* |i; وَرْنَشة| to varnish

وَرْنيش *n* ① [طِلاء] varnish; lacquer; وَرْنيش الخَشَبِ wood varnish; وَرْنيش الأَظافِرِ nail polish ② [للأَحْذِية] shoe polish

وَرَنْك *n* skate (*type of fish*)

وَرْوار *n* bee-eater (*Meropidae*)

وَرّى *v* to hide

وارى *v* ① [أَخْفى] to hide ② [دَفَنَ] to bury

تَوارى *v* to hide oneself, to conceal oneself, to disappear; تَوارى عن الأَنْظارِ to disappear from sight

وَراءَ *prep* behind; at the back of; beyond; وَراءَ البَيْتِ at the back of the house; إلى الوَراءِ backwards, back, to the rear; نَظْرة إلى الوَراءِ flashback; حَرَكة إلى الوَراءِ a backward movement; مَنْ وَراءَ هذا الهُجوم؟ who is behind this attack?; وَقَفَ وَراءَ

توْزيعيّ *n* distributional

مُوَزِّع *n* delivery man; dealer; distributor, supplier; مُوَزِّع الجَرائِدِ newspaper man/boy; مُوَزِّع بَرِيدٍ postman (BrE), mailman (AmE); مُوَزِّع سَيّاراتٍ car dealer; مُوَزِّع آليّ dispenser

‹ **وَزَغ** *n coll* |أَوْزاغ| gecko (*Pachydactylus*)

‹ **وَزّال** *n* (Bot) broom (*Fabaceae*)

‹ **وَزَنَ** *v* |i; إِزنة ,وَزْن| 1 [قاسَ وَزْنَ شيْءٍ] to weigh; وَزَنَ اللُّحومَ \ الأَمْتِعةَ to weigh meat/luggage; وَزَنَ كيلوغراماً من التُّفّاحِ to weigh a kilo of apples; وَزَنَ الكَلامَ to weigh one's words 2 [بَلَغَ وَزْنُهُ] to weigh; وَزَنَ خَمْسةً وَسَبْعينَ كيلو he weighed seventy five kilos; قُنْبُلة تَزِنُ أَلْفَ كيلوغْرام a 1,000 kg bomb

وازَنَ *v* 1 [عادَلَ] to balance, to equilibrate; وازَنَ شَيْئًا to keep sth in balance 2 [قارَنَ] to compare; to weigh; وازَنَ بين شَيْءٍ وَشَيْءٍ to compare something with something, to compare one thing to another

تَوازَنَ *v* to be balanced, to be in equilibrium

اِتَّزَنَ *v* to be in equilibrium

وَزْن *n* |أَوْزان| 1 [تَحْديد الوَزْنِ] weighing 2 [ثِقْل] weight, mass; وَزْن صافٍ net weight; وَزْن قائِم \ إِجْماليّ gross weight; الوَزْن الفارِغ tare weight; وَزْن أَقْصى maximum weight; وَزْن نَوْعيّ specific gravity, density; تَحْديد الوَزْنِ النَّوْعيِّ determination of the specific gravity; وَزْن جُزَيْئيّ molecular weight/mass; وَزْن زائِد overweight; extra weight; وَزْن الريشةِ featherweight; وَزْن خَفيف lightweight; وَزْن الديكِ (Sport) lightweight; وَزْن الذُّبابةِ (Sport) flyweight; اِنْعِدام الوَزْنِ weightlessness, zero-gravity; بَلَغَ وَزْنُهُ خَمْسةً وَسَبْعينَ كيلو غراماً he weighed seventy-five kilos; اِزْدادَ وَزْنُهُ خَمْسةَ كيلوغراماتٍ he gained five kilos; هَبَطَ \ خَفَضَ وَزْنُهُ he lost weight; كانَ ثَقيلَ \ خَفيفَ الوَزْنِ to be heavy/light 3 [مِثْقال] weight; وَزْن مِقْدارُهُ خَمْسةُ غراماتٍ a five gram weight 4 [أَهَمِّيّة] weight, importance; أَقامَ لِشَيْءٍ وَزْناً to attach importance to sth; لا وَزْنَ لَهُ insignificant; اِكْتَسَبَ وَزْناً إِضافيًّا to gain importance 5 [شِعْريّ] metre; وَزْن قَصيدةٍ \ بَيْتٍ the metre of a poem/line 6 (Gram) pattern, form, measure; وَزْن الفِعْلِ verb pattern

وِزْرة *n* |وِزَرات| apron; loincloth

وَزير *n* |وُزَراءُ| 1 (Pol) minister, Secretary of State; vizier; الوَزير المُفَوَّض the minister plenipotentiary; رَئيس الوُزَراءِ ,الأَوَّل prime minister; وَزير الخَليفةِ the vizier of the caliph; وَزير الخارِجيّةِ Minister of Foreign Affairs/Relations, Secretary of State for the Home Department, Home Secretary (BrE), Secretary of State (AmE); وَزير الدِفاع Minister of Defence, Defence Secretary, Secretary of State for Defence (BrE), Secretary of Defence (AmE); وَزير العَدْلِ Minister of Justice, ≈ Lord (High) Chancellor (BrE), ≈ Attorney General (AmE); وَزير الماليّةِ Minister of Finance, Chancellor of the Exchequer (BrE), Secretary of the Treasury (AmE); رِئاسة الوُزَراءِ prime ministership; رَئيس الوُزَراءِ الحاليّ the current prime minister; نائِب وَزيرٍ deputy secretary, deputy minister; مَجْلِس الوُزَراءِ cabinet, council of ministers; اِجْتِماع مَجْلِسِ الوُزَراءِ cabinet meeting; مَنْصِب وَزيرٍ ministerial post; اِحْتَلَّ \ تَقَلَّدَ مَنْصِبَ وَزيرٍ to hold a ministerial post; سِيادة \ مَعالي الوَزيرِ His Excellency the Minister 2 [في الشِطْرَنْج] queen

‹ **وَزّ** *n coll* goose (*Anatidae*)

‹ **وَزَعَ** *v* |a; وَزْع| to restrain

وَزَّعَ *v* to distribute, to hand out, to spread; to deliver; to divide, to allot; وَزَّعَ مَنْشوراتٍ to distribute pamphlets; وَزَّعَ الجَريدةَ to distribute the newspaper; وَزَّعَ بَضائِعَ \ رَسائِلَ \ البَريدَ to deliver goods/letters/the mail; وَزَّعَ أَدْوِيةً \ أَغْذِيةً to distribute medicines/food; وَزَّعَ جَوائِزَ to hand out prizes; وَزَّعَ الأَدْوارَ to assign the roles; وَزَّعَ الرِبْحَ على الأَعْضاءِ to share the profit amongst the members

تَوَزَّعَ *v* to be divided; to be distributed, to be handed out

وازِع *n* |وُزّاع ,وَزَعة| objection; sanction; وازِع أَخْلاقيّ moral objection

تَوْزيع *n* |تَوْزيعات| distribution, allocation, allotment; division; presentation; تَوْزيع موسيقيّ instrumentation, musical arrangement; تَوْزيع الشَهاداتِ \ الجَوائِزِ certificate/prize presentation; تَوْزيع المَجَلّاتِ \ الصُحُفِ magazine/newspaper distribution; تَوْزيع المَهامِّ task allocation; إِعادة التَوْزيعِ redistribution; مَرْكَز تَوْزيعٍ distribution centre

آلة] 3◀ statement of profit and loss ميزان الربْحِ والخسارةِ
ميزان [توازُن] 4◀ see-saw [لعِبٍ] 5◀ (Astrol) (بُرْج) الميزان Libra
القُوى balance of power

ميزانيّة *n* budget, balance; ميزانيّة سَنَويّة annual budget; ميزانيّة الدَوْلةِ state/national budget; سَنةِ ٢٠١٤ the budget for 2014; عَجْز الميزانيّة \ في الميزانيّةِ budget deficit; قَلّصَ \ خفَضَ العَجْزَ في الميزانيّةِ to cut the budget deficit; قَدّمَ ميزانيّةً to present a budget; وَضعَ \ أَعَدّ ميزانيّةً to make/prepare an estimate; to budget; وَضعَ ميزانيّةَ التكاليفِ to make an estimate of the costs; حَدّدَ الميزانيّةَ to determine the budget; to budget; تَحْديد ميزانيّةٍ budgeting

وازى *v* 1◀ [شابَهَ] to be equal to; يُوازي هذا سِعْرَ سَيّارةٍ that equals the price of a car 2◀ [حاذى] to be parallel to; وازى شَيْئاً to run parallel to sth 3◀ [بيّنَ خَطّيْنِ] to make parallel

توازى *v* to run side by side, to go together; توازى مع شَيْءٍ to run parallel to sth; to coincide with sth

تَوازٍ *n* (Math) parallelism; تَوازٍ مع شَيْءٍ a parallel with sth

مُتَوازٍ A *adj* parallel; مُتَوازي الأَضْلاعِ parallelogram; خُطوط مُتَوازِية parallel lines
B *n* مُتَوازِيانِ (Sport) parallel bars

مُوازٍ *adj, n* parallel

مُوازاة *n* 1◀ [تَشابُه] parallel; مُوازاة بين شَيْءٍ وَشَيْءٍ a parallel between sth and sth 2◀ (Math) parallelism

وَسِخَ *v* |وَسَخ; imperf يَوْسَخُ| to be/become dirty

وَسَّخَ *v* to dirty, to make dirty; to pollute; وَسَّخَ شَيْئاً to make sth dirty; وَسَّخ نَفْسَهُ to get dirty

أَوْسَخَ *v* to dirty, to soil, to stain

تَوَسَّخَ *v* to be/become dirty

اتَّسَخَ *v* to be/become dirty; اتَّسَخَ وَجْهُهُ his face became dirty

وَسَخ *n* |أَوْساخ| dirt, filth; كانَ مُغَطّى بالأَوْساخِ to be covered in dirt

وَسِخ A *adj* dirty, filthy, soiled, unclean; بُقَع وَسِخة dirty stains
B *n* dirty person; ابْن الوَسِخةِ son of a bitch, bastard

وَساخة *n* dirt, filth, muck

تَوْسيخ *n* making dirty, soiling; تَوْسيخ يَدَيْه to get one's hands dirty

وَزْنيّ *adj* weight (*before n*), weighty; حُمولة وَزْنيّة carrying capacity

وَزين *adj* weighty, ponderous

تَوازُن *n* stability; balance, equilibrium; تَوازُن القُوى balance of power; حالة عَدَمِ التَوازُنِ, حالة اللاتَوازُنِ an unstable situation, unbalance; جِهاز التَوازُنِ (Anat) organ of balance; اخْتِلال \ عَدَم التَوازُنِ lack of balance, unbalance; نُقْطة تَحْقيق التَوازُنِ break-even point; حافَظَ على تَوازُنِهِ to keep one's balance; فَقَدَ تَوازُنَهُ to lose (one's) balance; أَوْجَدَ \ خَلَقَ تَوازُناً to bring balance; أَحْدَثَ \ أَقامَ تَوازُناً to provide balance; اسْتَعادَ تَوازُنَهُ to regain/recover one's balance; أَخَلَّ بالتَوازُنِ to upset/disturb the balance; راعى التَوازُناتِ to maintain the balance of power

زِنة *n* weight

مُتَّزِن *adj* well-balanced, balanced, stable; طَبْع مُتَّزِن a well-balanced nature; حُكْم مُتَّزِن a balanced judgment; غَيْر مُتَّزِنٍ unbalanced, unstable; تَفْكير مُتَّزِن balanced thinking

مُتَوازِن *adj* well-balanced, balanced, stable; مُتَوازِن \ غَيْر مُتَوازِنٍ balanced/off balance; غَيْر مُتَوازِنٍ unbalanced; قَرار غَيْر مُتَوازِنٍ a poor decision

مُوازِن *n* (Elec) stabilizer

مُوازَنة *n* 1◀ [مُعادَلة] weighing, comparison; مُوازَنة بين السِعْرِ والجَوْدةِ a comparison between price and quality; مُوازَنة بين المَصالِحِ المُخْتَلِفةِ weighing of the different interests 2◀ [ميزانيّة] budget, balance; المُوازَنة العامّة للدَوْلةِ state/national budget 3◀ [تَثْبيت] balance, stabilization; المُوازَنة بين الطَلَبِ والعَرْضِ the balance between supply and demand

مَوْزون *adj* 1◀ [مَدْروس] well-considered; كَلام مَوْزون measured words 2◀ [مُتَوازِن] balanced 3◀ [مَنْظوم] rhythmic, rhythmical, metrical

ميزان *n* |مَوازينُ| 1◀ [آلة] (pair of) scales, balance; ميزان حَرارةٍ thermometer; ميزان ماءٍ spirit level (BrE), level (AmE); ميزان الذَهَبِ gold scale; وَقَفَ على الميزانِ to stand on the scales 2◀ (Busn) balance; budget; ميزان المَدْفوعاتِ balance of payments, BOP; ميزان تِجاريّ balance of trade; العَجْز \ الفائِض في الميزانِ التِجاريّ balance of trade deficit/surplus;

وَسَطِيّ *adj* middle (*before n*), in the middle; حَلّ وَسَطِيّ compromise; شَكْل وَسَطِيّ intermediate form; المُحَرِّكُ وَسَطِيّ الوَضْعِيّةِ the engine is in the middle

وَسِيط **A** *adj* |وُسَطاءُ| intermediate; ; الحَلَقة الوَسِيطة the intermediate link

B *n* |وُسَطاءُ| **1** [بين شَخْصٍ وآخَرَ] intermediary; mediator; وَسِيط بين ... an intermediary between...; عن طَرِيقِ وَسِيطٍ through an intermediary **2** [في تَحْضِيرِ الأَرْواحِ] medium; وَسِيط الوَحْي oracle

أَوْسَط **A** *adj* |dipt; أَواسِطُ| middle (*before n*), central; الشَّرْق الأَوْسَط the Middle East; آسِيا الوُسْطى Central Asia; أوروبّا الوُسْطى Central Europe; جُمْهورِيّة إفْرِيقِيا الوُسْطى the Central African Republic; الإصْبَع الوُسْطى the middle finger; العُصور الوُسْطى the Middle Ages; مَدِينة من القُرونِ الوُسْطى a medieval city

B *n* |dipt; أَواسِطُ| middle; أَواسِط إفْرِيقِيا Central Africa; أَواسِط الأُسْبوعِ the middle of the week; في أَواسِطِ الثَمانِيناتِ in the mid-eighties; خَيْرُ الأُمور أَوْسَطُها the middle ground is best

أَوْسَطِيّ *adj* شَرْق أَوْسَطِيّ Middle Eastern; السوق الشَّرْق أَوْسَطِيّة the Middle Eastern market

مُتَوَسِّط **A** *adj* intermediate; medium; average; مُتَوَسِّط الحَجْمِ medium-sized; مُتَوَسِّط الطول medium length; مُتَوَسِّط الدَخْلِ with an average income; مُتَوَسِّط العُمْرِ middle-aged; السِعْر المُتَوَسِّط the average price; (Tech) مَوْجة مُتَوَسِّطة medium wave; البَحْر الأَبْيَض المُتَوَسِّط the Mediterranean, the Mediterranean Sea; البُلْدان المُطِلّة على البَحْرِ (الأَبْيَضِ) المُتَوَسِّطِ, بُلْدان حَوْضِ البَحْرِ (الأَبْيَضِ) المُتَوَسِّطِ the Mediterranean countries; في مِنْطَقةِ المُتَوَسِّطِ in the Mediterranean; شَرْق المُتَوَسِّطِ the Eastern Mediterranean

B *n* average; mean; في المُتَوَسِّطِ on average

مُتَوَسِّطِيّ *adj* Mediterranean; مُناخ مُتَوَسِّطِيّ a Mediterranean climate

‹ **وَسُعَ** *v* |يَوْسُعُ; وَساعة| imperf to be/become wide, to be/become spacious

وَسِعَ *v* |a| **1** [اِحْتَوى] |سَعة| to contain, to comprise; to have room for, to be large enough for; يَسَعُ المَلْعَبُ خَمْسِينَ أَلْفَ

مُتَّسِخ *adj* dirty, filthy, soiled, grubby; يَدانِ مُتَّسِختانِ \ مَلابِس مُتَّسِخة dirty hands/clothes

‹ **وَسَّدَ** *v* to put a pillow under the head

تَوَسَّدَ *v* to use as a pillow; to rest on

وِسادة *n* |وَسائِدُ, وِسادات| pillow, cushion; وِسادة وَثِيرة a soft pillow; وِسادة هَوائِيّة air bag; غِطاء \ كِيس وِسادةٍ pillowcase

‹ **وَسَّطَ** *v* **1** [جَعَلَ في الوَسَطِ] to put/set in the middle **2** [صَيَّرَ وَسِيطاً] to appoint as mediator

تَوَسَّطَ *v* **1** [كانَ في الوَسَطِ] to be in the middle **2** [عَمِلَ وَسِيطاً] to mediate; تَوَسَّطَ في نِزاعٍ to mediate in a conflict; تَوَسَّطَ بين الحُكومةِ والمُتَمَرِّدِينَ to mediate between the government and the rebels

وَسْطَ *prep* in the middle of, amidst, among; وَسْطَ الدارِ in the middle of the house; وَسْطَ أَصْدِقائِهِ among his friends

وَسَط *n* |أَوْساط| **1** [مُنْتَصَف] middle, centre; وَسَط المَدِينةِ city centre; تَقَعُ مَدِينةُ مَدْرِيد في وَسَطِ اسْبانْيا Madrid is in the middle of Spain; مَشى \ وَقَفَ \ جَلَسَ في الوَسَطِ to walk/stand/sit in the middle; وَسَط أوروبّا Central Europe; خَيْرُ الأُمورِ أَوْساطُها the middle ground is the best; خَطّ الوَسَطِ centre line; دون الوَسَطِ mediocre, moderate; أَحْزاب الوَسَطِ centrist parties; وَسَط المَيْدانِ centre circle; midfield **2** [خَصْر] waist **3** [بِيئة] environment, milieu; community; أَوْساط مُطَّلِعة diplomatic circles; الأَوْساط الدِبْلوماسِيّة informed circles; الأَوْساط الراقِية \ الشَعْبِيّة the higher/lower social classes; the higher/lower spheres; في وَسَطِنا in our midst; انْحَدَرَ من وَسَطٍ فَقِيرٍ to come from a poor background

واسِطة *n* |وَسائِطُ| means; الوَسائِط المُتَعَدِّدة multimedia; واسِطة العِقْدِ the most important part; بِواسِطةِ by means of, through, by, with; بِواسِطةِ شَخْصٍ by using sb's connections; بالواسِطةِ indirectly

وَساطة *n* mediation, intervention; مُحاوَلة وَساطةٍ mediation attempt; وَساطة العَمَلِ employment mediation; ب \ عن وَساطةِ شَخْصٍ mediation; intercession; قامَ بِوَساطةٍ to mediate, to act as mediator

وَسْطانِيّ *adj* middle, central, intermediate; باب وَسْطانِيّ a central door

صَحْراء واسِعة a vast desert; شارِع واسِع a wide street 2 [شامِل] صَلاحيّات واسِعة extensive powers, wide authority; تَجْرِبة واسِعة a broad experience; واسِع النِطاقِ large-scale, widespread; على نِطاقٍ واسِعٍ on a large scale; إمْكانيّات واسِعة many possibilities; خَيال واسِع a rich imagination; في مَعْناهُ الواسِع in the broadest sense; مَصْدَر واسِع الاطِّلاع a well-informed source; واسِع الانْتِشارِ widespread; هُجوم واسِع a massive attack; هو واسِعُ الحيلةِ he has many tricks

B *n* الواسع the All-Embracing (*one of the names of God*)

وَسيع *adj* wide; large; vast

اتِّساع *n* |اتِّساعات| 1 [سَعة] width; extent; اتِّساع الصِراع the extent of the struggle; زادَ اتِّساعاً to expand in size, to become broader/wider; اتِّساع الإمْبراطوريّة البَريطانيّةِ the extent of the British Empire 2 [امْتِداد] expansion, enlargement; extension; growth; اتِّساع الضَغْط increasing pressure 3 (Phys) amplitude

تَوَسُّع *n* |تَوَسُّعات| expansion, extension; enlargement; تَوَسُّع صِناعيّ \ اقْتِصاديّ industrial/economic expansion; تَوَسُّع على المُسْتَوى الدُوَليّ \ العالَميّ international expansion; تَوَسُّع اسْتِعْماريّ colonial expansion; تَوَسُّع سُكّانيّ population growth; تَوَسُّع اسْتيطانيّ settlement expansion; تَوَسُّع في الاتِّجاهِ الجَنوبيّ expansion to the south; تَوَسُّع الأَوْرِدةِ varicose veins

تَوَسُّعيّ *adj* expansionist; سِياسة تَوَسُّعيّة expansionist policy

تَوَسُّعيّة *n* expansionism

تَوْسيع *n* |تَوْسيعات| widening, broadening; expansion, extension; enlargement; تَوْسيع نَهْرٍ river widening; تَوْسيع الإمْكانيّاتِ expansion of the possibilities; مَشْروع \ خُطّة تَوْسيعٍ expansion plan

سَعة, سِعة *n* 1 [قُدْرة] size; capacity; volume; power; سَعة عالِية \ مُنْخَفِضة a high/low capacity; سَعة ماليّة financial capacity; سَعة كَهْرَبائيّة capacitance, electrical capacity; سَعة مُسْتَشْفًى hospital capacity; سَعة المُحَرِّكِ engine capacity/size; على قَدْرِ سَعَتي to the best of my ability, as best as I can; اسْتَقْبَلَ شَخْصاً على الرَحْبِ والسَعةِ welcome!;

وَسِعَ مَقْعَدٍ the stadium has a seating capacity of 50,000; وَسِعَ لِكُلِّ المُتَفَرِّجينَ to offer enough space for all the spectators 2 [وَسُعَ] |سَعة| to be/become wide, to be/become spacious 3 [قَدَرَ] |وُسْع| to be possible; لا يَسَعُهُ أَنْ ... he is not able to ..., it is not in his power to ...; لا يَسَعُني إلاّ أَنْ أَقولَ ... I can only say ...

وَسَّعَ *v* 1 [أَوْسَعَ] to make wider/more spacious, to broaden; to enlarge, to expand; to extend; وَسَّعَ مَعْرِفَتَهُ to increase one's knowledge; وَسَّعَ غُرْفةً \ مَطاراً to extend a room/an airport; وَسَّعَ شارِعاً \ طَريقاً to widen a street/road; وَسَّعَ الشِرْيانَ التاجيَّ to dilate the coronary artery 2 [سَخِيَ] |على| to be generous; وَسَّعَ اللهُ عَلَيْهِ God made him rich, God blessed him

أَوْسَعَ *v* 1 [وَسَّعَ] to make wider/more spacious, to broaden; to enlarge; to extend 2 [أَشْبَعَ] to give in abundance; أَوْسَعَ شَخْصاً شَتْماً to heap abuse on sb; أَوْسَعَ شَخْصاً ضَرْباً to give sb a sound beating

تَوَسَّعَ *v* 1 [امْتَدَّ] to extend, to expand; to be extended/expanded; to grow, to spread; تَوَسَّعَ بِسُرْعةٍ فائِقةٍ to expand rapidly; تَوَسَّعَ على مِساحةٍ to extend over an area 2 [أَكْثَرَ] to do sth extensively; تَوَسَّعَ في فِعْلِ شَيْءٍ to do sth extensively; تَوَسَّعَ في النَفَقةِ to incur great expenses; تَوَسَّعَ في تَصْديرِ شَيْءٍ to export sth on a large scale

اتَّسَعَ *v* 1 [تَوَسَّعَ] to extend, to stretch out; to grow; اتَّسَعَت الحَلْقةُ the circle expanded; اتَّسَعَت ابْتِسامَتُهُ his smile widened, his smile grew 2 [امْتَدَّ] to have room for, to hold; اتَّسَعَ لِأَرْبَعةِ رُكّابٍ to be able to seat up to four passengers

وُسْع *n* power, capacity; وُسْع حَيَويّ lung capacity; كانَ بِوُسْعِهِ أَنْ... it was in his power to ...; لم يَعُدْ في وُسْعِنا إلاّ أَنْ ... all we can do is ...; بَذَلَ كُلَّ ما في وُسْعِهِ to do all in one's power, to do one's utmost; لم يَدَّخِرْ وُسْعاً to spare no trouble or expense

واسِع **A** *adj* 1 [فَسيح] wide, spacious; extensive, extended; broad; large; غُرْفة واسِعة a large room; سِرْوال \ تَنّورة واسِع(ة) wide trousers/a wide skirt; حَلْقة \ فُتْحة واسِعة a wide circle/opening; نَظْرة واسِعة a broad view/vision;

والسَعةِ to extend a warm welcome to sb (2) [كَثْرة] plenty, abundance; عن سَعةٍ abundantly, amply (3) (Phys) amplitude

مُتَّسَع *n* (1) [أَرْض] piece of land (2) [كَثير] ample, plenty; لَدَيْه مُتَّسَعٌ من الوَقْتِ he has enough time

مُتَّسِع *adj* extensive; wide, spacious; large; ثُغْرة مُتَّسِعة a large hole

مُوَسَّع *adj* extensive; comprehensive; دِراسة مُوَسَّعة an extensive study

مَوْسوعة *n* encyclopedia; lexicon; مَوْسوعة طِبِّيّة \ فَنِّيّة a medical/technical encyclopedia

مَوْسوعيّ *adj* encyclopedic

‹ **وَسَقَ** *v* |i; وَسْق| to load

اتَّسَقَ *v* to be consistent

اتّساق *n* coherence; consistency

مُتَّسِق *adj* consistent, coherent; خُطّة مُتَّسِقة a consistent plan; غَيْر مُتَّسِقٍ incoherent; inconsistent

‹ **وِسْكي** *n* see ويسْكي

‹ **تَوَسَّلَ** *v* (1) [اسْتَجْدى] |إلى| to implore, to beg; to ask for help; تَوَسَّل إلى شَخْصٍ to beg sb (2) [تَذَرَّعَ] to use as a means

وَسيلة *n* |وَسائِلُ| means, device; aid; وَسائِل تِقْنِيّة technical means; وَسائِل بَصَرِيّة visual aids; وَسائِل مَشْروعة \ غَيْر مَشْروعةٍ legal/illegal means; من وَسائِل خاصّةٍ of private means; عَمِلَ ب \ الْتَجأَ إلى وَسيلةٍ to use/resort to a means; وَسائِل مُساعَدةٍ aids; وَسائِل الإعْلامِ (mass) media; means of communication; وَسائِل الاتِّصالاتِ means of communication; أَلَيْسَ هُناكَ وَسيلةٌ أُخْرى؟ is there no other way?; الغايةُ تُبَرِّرُ الوَسيلةَ the end justifies the means

تَوَسُّل *n* |تَوَسُّلات| request, supplication, solicitation; تَوَسُّل للعَفْوِ petition for pardon

مُتَوَسِّل *n* beggar

موسْلين *n* listed alphabetically

‹ **وَسَمَ** *v* |i; وَسْم, سِمة| to brand, to mark, to stamp; to stigmatise; وَسَمَ البَقَرَ to brand cows; وَسَمَ شَخْصاً بالخِيانة \ بالكَذِبِ to brand sb as a traitor/liar

وَسُمَ *v* |وَسْم, سِمة; imperf يَوْسُمُ| to be pretty/handsome

تَوَسَّمَ *v* to expect; تَوَسَّمَ الخَيْرَ to have high hopes

اتَّسَمَ *v* to be marked, to be characterized; اتَّسَمَ هذا القَرْنُ بالتَقَدُّمِ this century was characterized by progression; يَتَّسِمُ تَصَرُّفُهُ ب ... his behaviour is characterized by ...

وَسْم *n* |وُسوم| (1) [الماشيةِ] brand, mark (2) (Comput) tag (*html etc.*)

وِسام *n* |أَوْسِمة| badge of honour, decoration, medal; وِسام مَلَكِيّ royal honour; وِسام رَفيع high honour; قَلَّدَ شَخْصاً وِساماً to award sb a decoration; مَنَحَ لِشَخْصٍ وِساماً to decorate sb, to invest sb with an order; حَصَلَ على وِسام, تَسَلَّمَ \ تَقَلَّدَ وِساماً to receive a decoration

وَسامة *n* charm, beauty

وَسيم *adj* |وِسام, وُسَماءُ| pretty, handsome; شابّ وَسيم a handsome young man

تَوْسيم *n* branding, marking

سِمة *n* (1) [خاصّيّة] characteristic, feature; sign; سِمةُ الإرْهابِ signs of terrorism; من أَبْرَزِ سِماتِهِ one of its most important characteristics (2) (Bot) stigma

مَوْسِم *n* |مَواسِمُ| (1) [أَوان] season, time of the year; مَوْسِم السِياحةِ tourist season, high season; مَوْسِم الزِراعةِ agricultural season; مَوْسِم الحَصادِ harvest season; مَوْسِم القُطْنِ cotton season; مَوْسِم الإجازةِ holiday season; خُضْراوات المَوْسِمِ seasonal vegetables; حُلول المَوْسِمِ الجَديدِ the arrival of the new season; في المَوْسِمِ الثاني [تَلْفِزيون] in the second season (2) [مَهْرَجان] festival (3) [عيد] feast day

مَوْسِميّ *adj* seasonal; عَمَل مَوْسِميّ seasonal work; رِياح مَوْسِمِيّة seasonal winds

مَوْسوم *adj* branded, marked

‹ **وَسِنَ** *v* |وَسَن, سِنة; imperf يَوْسَنُ| to slumber, to nap, to doze off

وَسَن *n* sleepiness

وَسْنان *adj* sleepy

سِنة *n* |سِنَن| nap, slumber, doze

‹ **وَسْوَسَ** *v* |i; وَسْوَسة| (1) [هَمَسَ] to whisper; وَسْوَسَ لَهُ الشَيْطانُ the devil whispered evil in his heart (2) [أَغْرى] to tempt

وَسْواس *n* |وَساوِسُ| doubt; anxiety; الوَسْواس the Whisperer (*the Devil*); وَسْواس المَرَضِ hypochondria

وَسْواسِيّ *adj* obsessive

وَسْوَسة *n* ① [هَمْس] whisper ② [إغْراء] temptation

مُوَسْوَس *adj* obsessed, obsessive

‹ **واسى** *v* to comfort, to console

أَوْسى *v* to shave (*the head*)

مُؤاسٍ, مُواسٍ *adj* compassionate; comforting

مُواساة *n* comfort; sympathy, condolence; تَعْبِيراً عن مُواساتِهِ as an expression of his sympathy

موسى *n* listed alphabetically

‹ **وَشَجَ** *v* |i; وَشْج, وَشيج| to be entangled

تَواشَجَ *v* to merge, to integrate

وَشيجة *n* |وَشائِجُ| entanglement

‹ **وَشَّحَ** *v* to adorn, to embellish; وَشَّحَ شَخْصاً بِوِسامٍ to decorate sb

تَوَشَّحَ *v* |بـ| to put on, to garb oneself (with)

اتَّشَحَ *v* to put on

وِشاح *n* |وَشائِحُ, أَوْشِحة, وُشُح| sash; ornamented belt

مُوَشَّح *n* Arabic poetic form

‹ **وَشَرَ** *v* |i; وَشْر| to saw

مَوْشور *n* |مَواشيرُ| ① (Geom) prism ② [لِلتَّحْليل الضَوْءِ] prism

‹ **وَشيش** *n* rustling; وَشيش البَحْرِ rustling of the sea

‹ **وَشَّعَ** *v* to reel, to spool

وَشيعة *n* |وَشائِعُ| (Elec) coil

‹ **وَشَق** *n* (Zool) lynx (*Lynx*)

‹ **أَوْشَكَ** *v* to be on the point/verge of, to be about to; أَوْشَكَ أنْ يَخْرُجَ to be on the point of leaving; أَوْشَكَ على الانْهِيارِ to threaten to collapse; توشِكُ (السَماءُ) أنْ تُمْطِرَ it's about to rain; أَوْشَكْتُ أنْ أَنْسى الأَمْرَ I almost forgot it; يوشِكُ أنْ يَكونَ مُسْتَحيلاً that is nearly impossible; لَحْظةُ الوَداعِ it's almost time to say goodbye

وَشْك *n* hurry; speed; كانَ على وَشْكِ ... ,على وَشْكِ ... to be on the point/verge of ...; كانَ على وَشْكِ الخُروجِ \ أنْ يَخْرُجَ to be on the point of going out; هو على وَشْكِ الانْطِلاقِ he is about to leave; هو على وَشْكِ الإفْلاسِ he is nearly bankrupt

وَشيك *adj* imminent, near; خَطَر \ نِزاع وَشيك an imminent danger/conflict; الاتِّفاقُ وَشيكٌ agreement is imminent

موشِك *adj* on the point/verge of; هو موشِكٌ على الإفْلاسِ he is nearly bankrupt; كانَ موشِكاً على البُكاءِ to be near tears

‹ **وَشَل** *n* |أَوْشال| tears; trickle, thin stream

‹ **وَشَّمَ** *v* to tattoo

وَشْم *n* |وُشوم, وِشام| tattoo; وَضَعَ وَشْماً to put a tattoo

‹ **وَشْوَشَ** *v* |i; وَشْوَشة| to whisper

تَوَشْوَشَ *v* to whisper

وَشْوَشة *n* whisper

‹ **وَشى** *v* |i| ① [طَرَّزَ] |وَشْي| to embroider; to embellish ② [نَمَّ] |وِشاية, وَشْي| to betray; to tell on; وَشى بِشَخْصٍ إلى الشُرْطَةِ to tell on sb to the police ③ [سَعى] |وِشاية, وَشْي| to slander, to defame

وَشّى *v* to embroider, to embellish

واشٍ *n* |وُشاة, واشونَ| traitor, informer

وِشاية *n* slander, defamation; وِشاية كاذِبة slander

تَوْشِية *n* embroidery, embellishment

شِية *n* mark; mole

‹ **وَصِبَ** *v* |وَصَب; imperf يَوْصَبُ| to be (chronically) ill

وَصَب *n* |أَوْصاب| illness; fatigue

‹ **وَصَدَ** *v* |i; وَصْد| to be firm

أَوْصَدَ *v* to close, to shut

وَصيد *n* |وَصائِدُ| threshold, doorstep

موصَد *adj* closed, shut; باب موصَد a closed door

‹ **وَصَع** *n* (Zool) wren (*Troglodytidae*)

‹ **وَصَفَ** *v* |i; وَصْف| ① [نَعَتَ] to describe, to depict, to characterize; to picture; وَصَفَ شَيْئاً to describe sth; وَصَفَ شَخْصاً بأنَّهُ to describe sb as; وَصَفَ شَخْصاً بالكَرَمِ to describe sb as generous; وَصَفَ ما حَدَثَ to describe what happened; وَصَفَ شُعوراً to describe a feeling; لا يوصَفُ indescribable, beyond words; فَرْحة لا توصَفُ indescribable joy ② [فَرَضَ] to prescribe; وَصَفَ الراحةَ to prescribe rest; وَصَفَ لِلْمَريضِ دَواءً to prescribe the patient medicine

اتَّصَفَ *v* |بـ| to be characterized; اتَّصَفَ بِشَيْءٍ to be characterized by sth

اسْتَوْصَفَ *v* to consult

وَصْف *n* |أَوْصاف| description, depiction, characterization; وَصْف دَقيق an accurate description; وَصْف مُوَسَّع a lengthy/comprehensive description; أَوْصاف description (*of a person*); أَوْصاف المُتَّهَم the description of the perpetrator; أَعْطى أَوْصافاً to give a description; طابَقَ الأَوْصافَ to answer to/fit the description

وَصّاف *n* describer, depicter

وَصْفة *n* |وَصَفات| ① (Culin) recipe ② (Med) prescription; وَصْفة طَبيبٍ doctor's prescription; وَصْفة طِبِّيّة medical prescription

وَصْفيّ *adj* descriptive, depictive

وَصيف *n* |وُصَفاءُ| servant, valet, page

وَصيفة *n* |وَصائِفُ| servant, maid; lady-in-waiting; وَصيفة شَرَفٍ maid of honour

تَوْصيف *n* |تَوْصيفات| classification, specification, description; تَوْصيف وَظيفيّ job description

صِفة *n* ① [خاصّيّة] property, quality; capacity; بِصِفةٍ عامّةٍ in general, by and large; بِصِفةٍ خاصّةٍ in particular, particularly, especially; صِفة غالِبة dominant quality; بِصِفةٍ غَيْر رَسْميّةٍ unofficially; بِصِفَتِه وَزيراً in his capacity as minister; تَصَرَّفَ بِصِفَتِه ... to act in his capacity as ...; تَمَتَّعَ بِصِفةِ ... to be characterised as ... ② (Gram) adjective; asyndetic relative clause ③ (Law) title

مُتَّصِف *adj* |ب| characterized by

مُسْتَوْصَف *n* |مُسْتَوْصَفات| clinic, infirmary, dispensary

مُواصَفة *n* specification, description; qualification; المُواصَفات المَطْلوبة requirements, qualifications; المُواصَفات الفَنِّيّة \ التِّقْنِيّة the technical specifications

مَوْصوف *adj* ① [مُتَّصِف] |ب| characterized by; described ② (Med) prescribed ③ (Gram) *noun followed by an adjective or asyndetic relative clause*

وَصَلَ *v* |i| ① [جاءَ] |وُصول| إلى to arrive at/in, to reach; وَصَلَ إلى مَكانٍ to arrive at a place; وَصَلَ إلى المَحَطّةِ \ المَدينةِ \ البابِ to arrive at the station/in the city/at the door; وَصَلَ إلى مَقْصِدِه to reach one's destination; وَصَلَ بِشَيْءٍ to bring sth ② [بَلَغَ] |وُصول| إلى to reach; to amount to; وَصَلَ إلى سِنٍّ مُعَيَّنةٍ to reach a certain age; وَصَلَني الخَبَرُ I received the news; تَصِلُ سُرْعةُ هذه السَيّارةِ إلى ٢٠٠ كم في الساعةِ this car can reach a speed of 200 kph; وَصَلَت الحالةُ إلى حَدٍّ لا يُطاقُ the situation has become unbearable; يَصِلُ عَدَدُ القوّاتِ العَسْكَرِيّةِ إلى أَلْفَيْ جُنْديٍّ the number of troops comes to two thousand; يَصِلُ سِعْرُ هذه الآلةِ إلى أَلْفِ دولار the price of this device is one thousand dollars ③ [ضَمَّ] |صِلة, وَصْل| to connect, to join, to link; وَصَلَ بين أَمْرَيْنِ to make a connection between two cases; صِلْ رَحِمَكَ! stay in contact with your relatives!

وَصَّلَ *v* ① [رَبَطَ] to connect, to join, to link, to link up, to attach; وَصَّلَ شَيْئاً بِشَيْءٍ to connect two things; وَصَّلَ أَسْلاكَ الكَهْرباءِ to connect electric wires ② [أَوْصَلَ] to bring, to take; وَصَّلَ الأَطْفالَ إلى المَدْرَسةِ to take the children to school

واصَلَ *v* to continue, to proceed; واصَلَ سَفَرَهُ to continue one's journey; واصَلَ بَحْثَهُ \ دِراسَتَهُ \ تَعْليمَهُ to continue (with) one's research/studies/education; واصَلَ بِنَفَسٍ واحِدٍ to do in one breath; فاصِل وَنُواصِلُ (Media) ≈ we'll be back after the break

أَوْصَلَ *v* ① [نَقَلَ] to bring, to take, to deliver; أَوْصَلَ شَخْصاً إلى مَنْزِلِه \ بَيْتِه to take sb home; أَوْصَلَ شَيْئاً إلى شَخْصٍ to bring sb sth; أَوْصَلَ بَرْقِيّةً \ رِسالةً to deliver a telegram/letter; أَوْصِلْ \ بَلِّغْ تَحِيّاتي إلى ... give my (kind) regards to ... ② [أَدّى] to lead; يوصِلُ الطَريقُ إلى أَسْوانَ the road leads to Aswan ③ (Phys) to conduct, to transmit

تَوَصَّلَ *v* ① [وَصَلَ] |إلى| to reach; to gain access (to); تَوَصَّلَ إلى اتِّفاقٍ to reach an agreement ② [تَلَقّى] |ب| to receive (*by mail*); تَوَصَّلَ بِرِسالةٍ to receive a letter

تَواصَلَ *v* ① [اِجْتَمَعَ] to be interconnected; تَواصَلَ مع شَخْصٍ \ شَيْءٍ to be connected with sb/sth; to get through to sb/sth ② [تَتابَعَ] to follow each other; تَواصَلَت الاعْتِداءاتُ the attacks came one after another ③ [اِسْتَمَرَّ] to continue, to be continued; سَيَتَواصَلُ التَعاوُنُ the cooperation will continue

اِتَّصَلَ *v* ① [خاطَبَ] |بِ| to contact, to get in touch with, to reach; اِتَّصَلَ بِشَخْصٍ to contact sb, to get in touch with sb; اتَّصَلَ بِشَخْصٍ هاتِفيًّا to call sb, to phone sb, to give sb a ring; اتَّصَلَ بِشخصٍ على رَقْمِ … to reach sb by telephone at …; اتَّصَلَ بِمَنْزِلِ \ عَمَلِ شَخْصٍ to phone sb's house/work ❷ (Comput) |بـ| to connect; اتَّصَلَ بالإنْتَرْنِت to connect to the Internet ❸ [الْتَأَمَ] to be connected ❹ [انْتَسَبَ] |إلى| to be allied to; to join; to belong to; اتَّصَلَ إلى مَجْموعةٍ to belong to a group

وَصْل *n* ❶ [رَبْط] |أَوْصال| connection, coupling; junction; خَطّ وَصْلٍ hyphen; طَريق وَصْلٍ connecting road; هَمْزة الوَصْلِ (Ling) *conjunctive hamza* ❷ [قَسيمة دَفْعٍ] |وُصولات| receipt, voucher

واصِل *n* clutch

وِصال *n* union, communion; وِصال الحَبيبَيْنِ the union of lovers

وَصْلة *n* (Gram) *symbol on the alif which indicates deletion of the glottal stop and liaison between the previous vowel and the following consonant*

وُصْلة *n* |وُصَل ,وُصْلات| ❶ [بين شَيْئَيْنِ] joint, connection ❷ [سِلْك] extension cord ❸ (Elec) connector ❹ (Comput) link

وُصول *n* arrival; الوُصول المَفْتوح (Comput) open access; بعد \ عند الوُصولِ after/at arrival; قاعة \ صالة الوُصولِ arrival hall, arrivals hall; ساعة \ تَوْقيت الوُصولِ arrival time; إمْكانيّة الوُصولِ accessibility

وُصوليّ *n* opportunist

وُصوليّة *n* opportunism

وَصيلة *n* adaptor

اتِّصال *n* |اتِّصالات| ❶ [تَخابُر] contact, communication; connection, link; اتِّصال داخِليّ \ خارِجيّ internal/external communication; اتِّصالات وَثيقة close contacts; اتِّصال مُباشِر direct contact, a direct connection; اتِّصال جِنْسيّ sexual contact/intercourse; اتِّصال لاسِلْكيّ radio contact, a wireless connection; اتِّصالات لاسِلْكيّة wireless communication; اتِّصال هاتِفيّ contact by telephone, phone call; اتِّصالات هاتِفيّة telephone communication; الاتِّصالُ سَيِّئٌ the line is bad; الاتِّصال بالعالَمِ الخارِجيِّ communication with the external world; وَسيلة اتِّصالٍ means of communication; نُقْطة اتِّصالٍ meeting point; مَسْؤول اتِّصال contact, contact person; خطّ الاتِّصالِ communication line; كانَ على اتِّصالٍ to be in contact; كانَ على اتِّصالٍ بِشَخْصٍ \ شَيْءٍ to be in connection with sb/sth; بَقِيَ على اتِّصالٍ بِشَخْصٍ to keep in contact with sb; قَطَعَ الاتِّصالَ to disconnect; تَلَقّى اتِّصالاً هاتِفيًّا to receive a phone call; أَجْرى اتِّصالاً to make contact, to establish/make a connection; أَجْرى اتِّصالاً هاتِفيًّا مَحَلِّيًّا \ داخِليًّا to make a local phone call; أَجْرى اتِّصالاً هاتِفيًّا خارِجيًّا \ دُوَليًّا to make a long distance/international phone call; يُمْكِنُ الاتِّصالُ بِهِ he can be reached; لم يَسْتَطِعِ الاتِّصالَ he wasn't be able to get through ❷ (Comput) connection; الاتِّصال بالإنْتَرْنِت Internet access; شَبَكة اتِّصالٍ network; سُرْعة الاتِّصالِ connection speed; شَبَكة اتِّصالاتٍ لاسِلْكيّةٍ واسِعة النِطاق wireless broadband (communications) network; صِناعة تِكْنولوجِيا المَعْلوماتِ والاتِّصالاتِ information and communication technology, ICT

اتِّصالاتيّ *adj* communication (*before n*)

اتِّصالي *adj* communication (*before n*)

المَوْصِل *n* see موصل

إيصال *n* |إيصالات| receipt, voucher

تَواصُل *n* ❶ [اجْتِماع] connection, communication; مَوْقِع تَواصُلٍ اجْتِماعيٍّ social networking site ❷ [تَتابُع] succession; alternation ❸ [اسْتِمْرار] continuation

تَوْصيل *n* ❶ [رَبْط] connecting, joining ❷ (Elec) |تَوْصيلات| wire, cable; تَوْصيل كَهْرَبائيّ electrical resistivity; wiring; تَوْصيلات تحت الأَرْضِ underground pipes/cables

تَوْصيلة *n* connection; تَوْصيلة الهاتِفِ a phone connection; تَوْصيلة بِسَيّارةٍ lift, ride

صِلة *n* ❶ [عَلاقة] connection, relation, link; contact; tie, bond, relationship; الصِلة بين التَدْخينِ وَمَرَضِ السَرَطانِ the link between smoking and cancer; ذو صِلةٍ بِشَيْءٍ related to sth; رَوابِط ذات صِلةٍ related links; وَثيق الصِلةِ بِشَيْءٍ closely associated with sth; لا صِلةَ لَهُ بالقَضيّةِ \ بالمَوْضوعِ that has no relevance to the matter/subject; كانَ على صِلةٍ بِشَيْءٍ to be in connection to sth, to have a connection with sth; كانَ على صِلةٍ وَطيدةٍ \ وَثيقةٍ بِشَخْصٍ to have a strong relationship with sb, to have close ties with sb; جَمَّدَ الصِلاتِ to freeze/

suspend the contacts; وَثَّقَ الصِلاتِ to strengthen relations; قَطَعَ الصِلاتِ to break off relations ② (Gram) صِلة المَوْصولِ relative clause

مُتَّصِل *adj* ① [مُسْتَمِرّ] continuous ② [مَرْبوط] connected; مُتَّصِل بالأرْضِ earthed (BrE), grounded (AmE) ③ (Comput) online; غَيْر مُتَّصِل offline ④ (Gram) ضَمير مُتَّصِل pronominal suffix

مُتَواصِل *adj* consecutive; continuous, constant; خَطّ مُتَواصِل a continuous line; سَيْل مُتَواصِل a steady stream; عَرْض مُتَواصِل non-stop performance/show; الانْتِقادات المُتَواصِلة constant criticism; التَدْخين المُتَواصِل chain smoking

مُواصَلة *n* ① (Transp) connection; المُواصَلات العامّة public transport (BrE) transportation (AmE); المُواصَلات السِلْكيّة واللاسِلْكيّة telecommunications ② [مُتابَعة] continuation, continuity; مُواصَلة الحَرَكةِ follow-through

مُوَصِّل A *adj* leading; مادّة مُوَصِّلة conductor; مادّة مُوَصِّلة للكَهْرَباءِ electrical conductor B *n* conductor; مُوَصِّل فائِق التَوْصيلِ superconductor; شِبْه مُوَصِّلٍ semiconductor

مَوْصول *adj* connected; اسْم مَوْصول (Gram) relative pronoun

‹ **وَصَمَ** *v* |i; وَصْم, صِمة| to stigmatize, to brand; to disgrace; وَصَمَ شَخْصاً بالإجْرامِ \ بالعُنْصُريّة to brand sb as a criminal/racist

تَوَصَّمَ *v* to be stigmatized

وَصْمة *n* |وَصَمات| brand, mark; stigma; وَصْمة عارٍ blot, stain; حَمَلَ وَصْمةً to carry a stigma

‹ **وَصْوَصَ** *v* |i; وَصْوَصة| to peep

وَصْواص *n* |وَصاوِص| peephole

‹ **وَصّى** *v* ① [نَصَحَ |ب|] to recommend, to commend; to advise; وَصّى شَخْصاً بِشَيْءٍ to recommend sb sth ② [وَرَّثَ بِوَصيّةٍ] to leave, to bequeath; وَصّى لِشَخْصٍ شَيْئاً to leave sb sth, to bequeath sth to sb ③ [عَيَّنَ وَصِيًّا] to appoint as a guardian ④ [عَهِدَ |ب|] to entrust

أَوْصى *v* ① [أَوْرَثَ] to bequeath, to leave; أَوْصى بِأَمْوالٍ لِشَخْصٍ to bequeath money to sb; أَوْصى لِشَخْصٍ to put sb in his will; أَوْصى إِلى شَخْصٍ to appoint sb as guardian/executor (*in one's will*) ② [عَهِدَ] to entrust; أَوْصى شَخْصاً بِشَيْءٍ to entrust sb with sth ③ [أَمَرَ] to order, to charge, to commission ④ [نَصَحَ |ب|] to recommend, to commend, to advise; أَوْصى بِشَخْصٍ to recommend sb; أَوْصى شَخْصاً بِشَيْءٍ to advise sb sth

اسْتَوْصى *v* اسْتَوْصى بِشَخْصٍ خَيْراً to have the best intentions with sb

وَصِيّ *n* |أَوْصِياءُ| custodian, guardian; trustee; عَيَّنَ وَصِيًّا to appoint a guardian

وِصاية *n* |وَصايا| legal restraint; guardianship, custody; tutelage; الوِصاية على شَخْصٍ guardianship over sb; فَرَضَ على شَخْصٍ الوِصايةَ to place sb under legal restraint; وُضِعَ \ كانَ تحت الوِصايةِ to be under legal restraint; to be under guardianship

وَصيّة *n* |وَصايا| ① [تَوْريث] will; كَتَبَ وَصيَّتَهُ to make one's will; أَدْرَجَ شَخْصاً في وَصيَّتِه to remember sb in one's will ② [أَمْر] command, order; الوَصايا العَشْر the Ten Commandments; اتَّبَعَ وَصيّةً to obey a command; الْتَزَمَ بِوَصيّةٍ to follow an order; نَفَّذَ وَصيّةَ شَخْصٍ to act on sb's orders

إيصاء *n* ① [ميراث] bequest ② [نَصيحة] recommendation; advice, counsel ③ [دين] preaching

إيصائيّ *adj* testamentary; وارِث إيصائيّ testamentary heir

تَوْصِية *n* |تَوْصِيات, تَواصٍ| recommendation, advice; خِطاب تَوْصِيةٍ letter of recommendation; أَصْدَرَ تَوْصِيةً to advise

مُوصٍ *n* testator

مُوَصًّى *n* principal, client

‹ **تَوَضَّأَ** *v* (Islam) *to perform the ritual ablution before prayer*

وُضوء *n* (Islam) *ritual ablution before prayer*

مِيضَأة *n* basin (*for the ritual ablution*)

‹ **وَضَّبَ** *v* to tidy (up), to organize; to prepare

تَوْضيب *n* packaging

‹ **وَضَحَ** *v* |i; وُضوح| to be/become clear/evident; to appear

وَضَّحَ *v* to make clear/plain, to elucidate, to clarify; to explain, to illustrate; وَضَّحَ شَيْئاً to make sth clear; وَضَّحَ أَمْراً \ مَسْأَلةً to elucidate a matter, to shed light on a matter; وَضَّحَ مُشْكِلةً to clarify a problem

أَوْضَحَ *v* to make clear, to elucidate, to clarify; to explain, to illustrate; أَوْضَحَ أَمْراً \ مَسْأَلةً to elucidate a matter, to shed

تَوْضيحيّ *adj* explanatory, clarifying, illustrative; مُذَكِّرة \ مِثال \ نَموذَج تَوْضيحيّة an explanatory memorandum; تَوْضيحيّ an illustrative example/model

مُوَضَّح *adj* explained, clarified; المَفاهيم المُوَضَّحة أَعْلاهُ the above explained concepts

وَضَر *n* |أَوْضار| dirt

مَوْضَعَ *v* |i; مَوْضَعة| to locate

وَضَعَ *v* |a; وَضْع| ⟦1⟧ [حَطَّ] to put down, to place; to deposit; to lay down, to set down; وَضَعَ كِتاباً على المائِدةِ to place a book on the table; وَضَعَ السَّمّاعَةَ على الجِهازِ to hang up, to put the receiver down; وَضَعَ ماءً على النارِ to put some water on, to boil water; وَضَعَ رَأْسَهُ على كَتِفِ شَخْصٍ to lay one's head on sb's shoulder; وَضَعَ نَفْسَهُ مَكانَ شَخْصٍ to put oneself in sb's place/shoes; وَضَعَ قوّاتٍ to station troops; وَضَعَ شَيْئاً في غَيْرِ مَوْضِعِهِ to put sth in the wrong place; وَضَعَ شَخْصاً مَوْضِعَ شَخْصٍ to let sb take sb else's position; وَضَعَ يَدَهُ على شَيْءٍ lay hands on sth ⟦2⟧ [وَلَدَ] to give birth, to bear; وَضَعَ طِفْلاً to give birth to a child ⟦3⟧ [أَنْشَأَ] to make, to draw up; وَضَعَ أَساسَ شَيْءٍ to lay the foundation for sth; وَضَعَ قانوناً \ قَواعِدَ to make a law/rules; وَضَعَ شُروطاً to lay down conditions; وَضَعَ حَدًّا لِشَيْءٍ to put an end to sth; وَضَعَ رَسْماً بَيانيًّا to lay out a scheme; وَضَعَ لائِحةً to make a list; وَضَعَ اقْتِراحاً to make a proposal; وَضَعَ تَقْريراً to draw up a report ⟦4⟧ [أَسْقَطَ] to discharge; وَضَعَ عن شَخْصٍ الدَّيْنَ to discharge sb from his debt ⟦5⟧ [لَبِسَ] to put on; وَضَعَ قُبَّعةً على رَأْسِهِ to put on a hat; وَضَعَ نَظّارَتَهُ to put on one's glasses; وَضَعَ قِناعاً to put on a mask ⟦6⟧ [تَذَلَّلَ] to humble; وَضَعَ نَفْسَهُ to humble oneself

تَمَوْضَعَ *v* to be situated

واضَعَ *v* to reach an agreement

أَوْضَعَ *v* to hurry

تَواضَعَ *v* to be modest, to behave modestly; to be/become humble

اتَّضَعَ *v* to humble oneself

وَضْع *n* |أَوْضاع| ⟦1⟧ [حال] situation, state; position; الوَضْع الاقْتِصاديّ \ السِياسيّ \ الماليّ the economic/political/

light on a matter; أَوْضَحَ قَراراً \ مُقْتَرَحاً to explain a decision/proposal

تَوَضَّحَ *v* to be/become clear, to come to light

اتَّضَحَ *v* to be/become clear; to appear, to become obvious; اتَّضَحَ أَنّ ... it turned out that ...; اتَّضَحَ من المُسْتَنَداتِ أَنّ ... from the documents it appeared that ...

اِسْتَوْضَحَ *v* to ask for a clarification; اسْتَوْضَحَ شَخْصاً (عن شَيْءٍ) to ask sb for an explanation (about sth)

وَضَح *n* light; في وَضَحِ النَهارِ in broad daylight

واضِح *adj* clear, lucid; plain, obvious, evident; خَطّ واضِح clear handwriting; تَعْليمات واضِحة clear instructions; كِذْبة واضِحة an obvious lie; واضِح وُضوحَ الشَمْسِ (في رابِعةِ النَهارِ) clear as day, crystal clear; بِتَعابير واضِحةٍ in clear terms; بِصَوْتٍ واضِحٍ in a clear voice; غَيْر واضِحٍ unclear, vague, hazy; شَيْء غَيْر واضِحٍ sth unclear; من الواضِحِ أَنّ ... it is obvious that...; لِيَكُن الأَمْرُ واضِحاً let it be clear; الفَرْقُ واضِحٌ جِدًّا the difference is very clear; لَيْسَ واضِحاً بَعْدُ ما إذا ... it is not clear yet whether...; واضِح بِذاتِهِ it speaks for itself

وَضّاح *adj* ⟦1⟧ [واضِح] clear, obvious, evident ⟦2⟧ [ساطِع] shining

وُضوح *n* clarity, clearness; بِوُضوحٍ clearly, distinctly; عَدَم الوُضوحِ vagueness, obscurity; عالي الوُضوحِ high definition, HD; شَرَحَ شَيْئاً بِوُضوحٍ to make sth clear; في مُنْتَهى الوُضوحِ abundantly clear; وُضوح النِظامِ clarity of arrangement

اِسْتيضاح *n* |اسْتيضاحات| enquiry, investigation

إيضاح *n* |إيضاحات| explanation, clarification, elucidation; simplification

إيضاحيّ *adj* explanatory, illustrative, clarifying; رَسْم إيضاحيّ illustrative drawing

تَوْضيح *n* |تَوْضيحات| explanation, elucidation; illustration; طَلَبَ تَوْضيحاً to ask for an explanation; لِتَوْضيحِ وُجْهةِ نَظَري to illustrate my point of view; تَوْضيحاً ل ... by way of illustration of...; أَعْطى \ قَدَّمَ المَزيدَ من التَوْضيحِ to make sth clearer, to throw more light on sth

مَوْضِع *n* |مَواضِعُ| ◀1 [مَكان] place, spot; location, position; كانَ في مَوْضِعِهِ to be in the right place; في غَيْرِ مَوْضِعِهِ out of place, in the wrong place; نَقْد في غَيْرِ مَوْضِعِهِ undeserved criticism; هذا الخَوْفُ في مَوْضِعِهِ this fear is justified; وَضَعَ شَيْئاً مَوْضِعَ التَنْفيذ to carry out sth; تَحْديد المَوْضِع orientation, positioning; حَدَّدَ مَوْضِعَهُ to position oneself ◀2 [مَوْضوع] object, subject; مَوْضِع بَحْثٍ the object of research; كانَ مَوْضِعَ سُخْرِيّة \ إعْجاب to be the object of mockery/admiration; كانَ مَوْضِعَ الاهْتِمام to be the centre of attention; كانَ مَوْضِعَ جَدَل to be the subject of controversy

مَوْضِعِيّ *adj* local, topical; تَخْدير مَوْضِعِيّ local anaesthesia

مَوْضوع ◀A *adj* put down

◀B *n* |مَواضيعُ ,مَوْضوعات| [مَسْأَلة] subject, theme, topic; matter; مَوْضوع رَئيسِيّ \ مَرْكَزِيّ a central theme; مَوْضوع البَحْثِ research topic; مَوْضوع الساعةِ topic of the hour; فِهْرِس المَوْضوعاتِ table of contents; مُتَعَلِّق بالمَوْضوع relevant; هذا خارِجٌ عن المَوْضوعِ ≈ that is besides the point; عالَجَ مَوْضوعاً to treat a subject; تَطَرَّقَ ,أثارَ \ فَتَحَ مَوْضوعاً to bring up a subject, to address a topic; دَخَل في لِمَوْضوعِ to get to the point; طَرَقَ لُبَّ المَوْضوعِ to get to the point, to get to the core of the matter; المَوْضوع رَتَّبَ \ بَوَّبَ الكُتُبَ حَسَبَ مَوْضوعاتِها to arrange books by subject

مَوْضوعِيّ *adj* ◀1 [نِسْبة للمَوْضوع] with respect to content ◀2 [مُحايِد] objective

مَوْضوعِيّة *n* objectivity; نَظَرَ إلى الأمْرِ بِمَوْضوعِيّةٍ to look at the case objectively

وَضَم *n* |أَوْضِمة ,أوْضام| butcher's/slaughtering block; كانَ مِثْلَ لَحْمٍ على وَضَمٍ to be vulnerable

وَطِئَ *v* |a; وَطْء| ◀1 [دَخَلَ] to tread on, to set foot on; وَطِئَ أَرْضَ المَلْعَبِ to set foot on the playground; أَوَّل مَنْ وَطِئَتْ قَدَماهُ القَمَرَ the first man to set foot on the moon ◀2 [جامَعَ] to have sexual intercourse; وَطِئَ امْرَأةً to have sex with a woman ◀3 [داسَ] to trample underfoot

وَطَّأَ *v* ◀1 [مَهَّدَ] to level ◀2 [سَهَّلَ] to fluff up ◀3 [أَعَدَّ] to prepare ◀4 [خَفَضَ] to lower

واطَأَ *v* to agree; واطَأَ شَخْصاً على شَيْءٍ to agree with sb on sth

financial situation; وَضْع حَرِج a difficult/awkward position; وَضْع قانونِيّ legal position; وَضْع خاصّ special position; الوَضْع الحالي the present situation; الوَضْع الراهِن the present condition, the status quo; أَبْقى على الوَضْعِ الراهِنِ to maintain the status quo; الأَوْضاع السِياسِيّة the political situation; أَوْضاع مَعيشِيّة living conditions; وَضْع الجَوّ the weather condition; كانَ في وَضْعٍ صَعْبٍ to be in a difficult position; يَسْتَمِرُّ الوَضْعُ على ما هو عَلَيْه the situation remains as it is ◀2 [وِلادة] childbirth, delivery; آلام الوَضْعِ contractions ◀3 [حَطّ] putting down, laying down; stationing; وَضْع اليَد sealing; وَضْع القَواعِد regulation; وَضْع الأخْتام seizure

واضِع *n* maker, founder; author, drafter; واضِع عِلْم الجَبْر the founder of algebra; واضِع النَصِّ the author of the text; واضِعو السِياساتِ policymakers

وَضاعة *n* lowliness, humbleness

وَضْعِيّة *n* ◀1 [حال] situation, position, state; وَضْعِيّة شائكة a difficult situation ◀2 (Philos) positivism ◀3 [وَضْع] position

وَضيع *adj* |وُضَعاءُ| base, low, humble; نَسَب وَضيع humble origins; وَضيع المَوْلِدِ low class

وَضيعة *n* |وَضائِعُ| deposit

اتِّضاع *n* humility, humbleness, modesty

تَمَوْضُع *n* stationing; positioning; تَمَوْضُع قوّاتٍ عَسْكَرِيّةٍ the stationing of military troops; نِظام التَمَوْضُع العالَمِيّ Global Positioning System, GPS

تَواضُع *n* humility, humbleness, modesty; بِكُلِّ تَواضُعٍ in all humility; تَواضُع كاذِب false modesty

ضَعة ,ضِعة *n* humbleness, humility; inferiority

مُتَواضِع *adj* modest, humble, simple; insignificant, small; أُناس مُتَواضِعونَ simple people; دَخْل \ ثَمَن مُتَواضِع a modest income/price; شابّ مُتَواضِع a humble young man; إنْجازات مُتَواضِعة modest achievements; غَيْر مُتَواضِعٍ immodest; عاشَ حَياةً مُتَواضِعةً to live modestly

مُواضَعة *n* agreement; convention

مَواضيعِيّ *adj* thematic; تَرْتيب مَواضيعِيّ thematic ordering

توَاطَأَ *v* ❶ [تآمَرَ] |مع| to plot together, to conspire; to collaborate, to cooperate; تواطأَ مع شَخْصٍ to conspire with sb; تواطأَ مع المافيا \ العَدوّ to collaborate with the Mafia/the enemy ❷ [وافَقَ] |على| to agree; تَواطأَ على ... to agree with ...

وَطْء *n* ❶ [دَوْس] footsteps ❷ [جِماع] sexual intercourse

واطِئ *adj* low; مائِدة واطِئة a low table; صَوْت واطِئ a deep voice

وَطْأة *n* pressure, weight; intensity; شَديد الوَطْأةِ oppressive, heavy; حَرّ شَديد الوَطْأةِ an oppressive heat; تحت وطْأةِ ... under pressure of...; عانى من وَطْأةِ الاحْتِلالِ ≈ to bear the brunt of the occupation; خفَّف من الوَطْأةِ to ease the pressure

أَوْطَأ *adj* |dipt| lower

تواطُؤ *n* conspiracy, collusion; complicity

تَوْطِئة *n* ❶ [تَمْهيد] preparation; تَوْطِئةً ل ... in preparation for ... ❷ [مُقَدِّمة] introduction, prologue, preface

مُتَواطِئ **A** *adj* conspiring **B** *n* conspirator; accomplice, collaborator

مَوْطِئ *n* |مَواطِئ| footstep; footprint; حَصَلَ على مَوْطِئ قَدَم في المِنْطَقةِ to gain a foothold in the region

وَطَدَ *v* |i; وَطْد| ❶ [ثَبَّتَ] to strengthen, to consolidate ❷ [مَهَّدَ] to level, to flatten

وَطَّدَ *v* ❶ [ثَبَّتَ] to strengthen, to consolidate; to intensify; وَطَّدَ الصِلاتِ \ العَلاقاتِ to strengthen the bonds/the relationship; وَطَّدَ العَزْمَ ... to be determined to ...; وَطَّدَ أَقْدامَهُ في ... to gain a foothold in ... ❷ [مَهَّدَ] to level, to make even; وَطَّدَ الأَرْضَ to level the ground

تَوَطَّدَ *v* to be strengthened

وَطيد *adj* strong, firm, stable; صِلة وَطيدة strong bond; عَلاقة وَطيدة a strong relationship

تَوْطيد *n* strengthening, consolidation; تَوْطيد العَلاقاتِ بين مِصْرَ وَأَلْمانيا consolidation of the relations between Egypt and Germany

مُتَوَطِّد *adj* strong, firm

وَطَر *n* |أَوْطار| wish

وَطَسَ *v* |i; وَطْس| to pulverize

وَطيس *n* |وُطُس, أَوْطِسة| fight, struggle; حامي الوَطيسِ fierce; حَمِيَ الوَطيسُ fierce fighting broke out

وَطَشَ *v* |i; وَطْش| to hit

وَطَنَ *v* |i; وَطْن| |ب| to dwell

وَطَّنَ *v* to settle down, to get settled; وَطَّنَ نَفْسَهُ ل \ على شَيْءٍ to prepare oneself for sth; to adjust oneself to sth

تَوَطَّنَ *v* to choose for a residence

اسْتَوْطَنَ *v* to settle down, to take up one's residence; to acclimatize

وَطَن *n* |أَوْطان| homeland, nation, country; الوَطَن العَرَبِيّ the Arab world; وطَن الأُمّ motherland, mother country; وَطَن جَديد \ ثانٍ a new/adopted country; حُبّ الوَطَنِ patriotism; من أَجْلِ الوَطَنِ for one's country; قامَ بِخِدْمةِ وَطَنِهِ to serve one's country; خائِن لِلْوَطَنِ traitor to one's country; خِيانة الوَطَنِ high treason

وَطَنِيّ **A** *adj* national; home (*before n*); patriotic, nationalistic; على المُسْتَوى الوَطَنِيّ nationwide; التاريخ الوَطَنِيّ national history; الحُكومة الوَطَنيّة the national government; السِياسة الوَطَنِيّة national politics; بُطولة وَطَنِيّة national championship; الراية \ العَلَم الوَطَنِيّ(ة) the national flag; عيد وَطَنِيّ a national holiday; حَقّ وَطَنِيّ civil right; نُعْرة وَطَنِيّة national pride **B** *n* patriot, nationalist

وَطَنِيّة *n* patriotism, nationalism

اسْتيطان *n* establishment of settlements

اسْتيطانِيّ *adj* colonist (*before n*); سِياسة اسْتيطانِيّة settlement policy

تَوْطين *n* ❶ [إِسْكان] settlement ❷ [مُواطَنة] nationalization

مُتَوَطِّن *adj* endemic; مَرَض مُتَوَطِّن an endemic disease

مُسْتَوْطِن **A** *adj* native, indigenous, endemic; مَرَض مُسْتَوْطِن an endemic disease **B** *n* colonist; settler

مُسْتَوْطَنة *n* settlement; المُسْتَوْطَنات الإِسْرائيلِيّة في الضِفّةِ الغَرْبِيّةِ the Israeli settlements in the West Bank; فَكَّكَ مُسْتَوْطَناتٍ to dismantle settlements

مُواطِن *n* **1** [ساكِن] citizen, national; resident; مُواطِن بَحْرَيْنيّ a Bahraini citizen; مُواطِن عالَميّ global citizen **2** [شَخْص من نَفْسِ البَلَد] fellow citizen, countryman

مُواطَنة *n* citizenship; حَقّ المُواطَنةِ right to citizenship; حُرِمَ من حَقِّ المُواطَنةِ to be denied the right to citizenship

مَوْطِن *n* |مَواطِنُ| **1** [مَحَلّ سُكْنى] residence **2** [وَطَن] native country; فَرَّ من مَوْطِنِهِ to flee one's home country **3** [بيئة] habitat, environment **4** [مَكان] place, spot, point; مَوْطِن الضُعْفِ weak spot; وَضَعَ يَدَهُ على مَوْطِنِ العِلّةِ to lay one's finger on the sore spot

وَطْواط *n* |وَطاوِطُ, وَطاويطُ| bat (*Chiroptera*)

واظَبَ *v* |على| to persevere (in), to persist (in), to keep on; واظَبَ على الدِراسة to persevere in one's studies

مُواظِب **A** *adj* persistent, persevering; studious, diligent **B** *n* go-getter

مُواظَبة *n* persistence, perseverance

وَظَّفَ *v* **1** [عَيَّنَ] to employ, to hire; وَظَّفَ شَخْصاً to hire sb **2** [اِسْتَثْمَرَ] to invest; وَظَّفَ أَمْوالاً to invest money **3** [اِسْتَخْدَمَ] to use; to apply; وَظَّفَ كُلَّ ما لَدَيْهِ لِ ... to use all he has in order to...; وَظَّفَ إِمْكاناتِهِ to harness/use his potential

تَوَظَّفَ *v* to work, to be employed; تَوَظَّفَ في بَنْكٍ to work in a bank

وَظائِفيّ *adj* occupational; تَقْسيم وَظائِفيّ division of jobs

وَظيفة *n* |وَظائِفُ| **1** [عَمَل] job, position, function, post, office; وَظيفة حُكوميّة a government job; وَظيفة عامّة \ عُموميّة a public sector job; وَظيفة إداريّة a management position; وَظيفة ثابِتة \ مُؤَقَّتة a steady/temporary job; وَظيفة جَيِّدة a good job; وَظيفة حَسّاسة a security sensitive position; وَظيفة شاغِرة vacancy; وَظيفة كامِلة a full-time job; قَسَم الوَظيفةِ oath of office; تَفاصيل الوَظيفةِ job specification; مُواصَفات وَظيفةٍ job description; طَلَبَ وَظيفةً to apply for a job; طَلَب وَظيفةٍ job application; طالِب وَظيفةٍ applicant; إِعْلان عن وَظيفةٍ job ad; أَدّى \ شَغَّلَ وَظيفةً to perform a job; حَصَلَ على وَظيفةٍ to get a job; قَبِلَ وَظيفةً to accept a job; اِسْتَقالَ من وَظيفةٍ to resign from one's job; هذه الوَظيفةُ شاغِرةٌ this job is vacant; تَقَلَّدَ وَظيفةً to fill a position; أثناء قِيامِهِ بِوَظيفَتِهِ in the course of one's work; فَصَلَ شَخْصاً من وَظيفَتِهِ to fire sb **2** [مُهِمّة] function; وَظيفة دِماغيّة brain function; وَظيفة مُكَثِّفٍ (Elec) the function of a capacitor; وَظائِف رَئيسيّة \ ثانَويّة primary/secondary functions; مُتَعَدِّد الوَظائِفِ multifunctional; عِلْم وَظائِفِ الأَعْضاءِ physiology **3** [واجِب البَيْتِ] (Syr) homework

وَظيفيّ *adj* **1** [ما يَتَعَلَّقُ بالوَظيفة] functional; اضْطِرابات وَظيفيّة functional disorders **2** [عَمَليّ] functional; دَوْر وَظيفيّ a functional role **3** [مِهْنيّ] occupational; عِلاج وَظيفيّ occupational therapy

تَوْظيف *n* |تَوْظيفات| **1** [تَعْيين] employment; تَوْظيف النِساءِ the employment of women **2** [اِسْتِثْمار] investment **3** [اِسْتِخْدام] use; تَوْظيف الجَيْشِ في أَمْرٍ the use of the army in sth; تَوْظيف المَوارِدِ use of the resources

تَوْظيفيّ *adj* functional

مُوَظَّف *n* **1** [عامِل في إدارةٍ] employee, worker; clerk; مُوَظَّف ثابِت a permanent staff member; مُوَظَّف إداريّ an administrative assistant; مُوَظَّف في بَنْكٍ bank employee; شُؤون المُوَظَّفينَ personnel matters; مَكْتَب \ قِسْم \ دائِرة شُؤونِ المُوَظَّفينَ personnel department (BrE), human resources (HR) department (AmE); هَيْئة المُوَظَّفينَ personnel, staff; عُضْو من هَيْئةِ المُوَظَّفينَ staff member **2** [حُكوميّ] civil servant, official; officer; مُوَظَّف بَسيط \ سامٍ a minor/high official; مُوَظَّف حُكوميّ a civil/public servant, a government official; مُوَظَّف من \ في \ لدى وِزارةِ الماليّةِ an official of the Finance Department

وَعَبَ *v* |i; وَعْب| to take the whole/all

اِسْتَوْعَبَ *v* **1** [فَهِمَ] to understand, to comprehend; اِسْتَوْعَبَ نَصًّا to understand a text; اِسْتَوْعَبَ الوَضْعَ to understand the situation **2** [وَسِعَ] to be able to take in, to have room for; to contain; تَسْتَوْعِبُ السَيّارةُ حتّى سَبْعةِ رُكّابٍ the car can seat up to seven people **3** [اِسْتَأْصَلَ] to root out, to exterminate

اِسْتيعاب *n* **1** [اِمْتِصاص] understanding, comprehension; قُدْرة على الاسْتيعابِ comprehension ability; صَعْب الاسْتيعابِ difficult to understand; وَجَدَ صُعوبةً في

حَدَّدَ مَوْعِداً appointment; كانَ على مَوْعِدٍ to be on time; أَخْلَفَ مَوْعِداً to make an appointment, to set a date; أَجَّلَ مَوْعِداً to fail to keep an appointment; to postpone an appointment

ميعاد *n* |مَواعيدُ| appointment, appointed time; ميعاد الوُصولِ time of arrival; ميعاد السَفَرِ time of departure; مَواعيد القِطارِ train times, train departures; مَواعيد الصَلاةِ prayer times; من غَيْرِ ميعادٍ early; في ميعادِهِ on time; قبل ميعادِهِ without appointment; على غَيْرِ ميعادٍ untimely; حَدَّدَ ميعاداً to set a date

(Idiom) رُبَّ صُدْفةٍ خيرٌ من أَلْفِ ميعادٍ a spontaneous encounter is often better than an appointment

〈 **وَعُرَ** *v* |يَوْعُرُ| imperf; |وُعورة ,وَعارة| to be inaccessible

وَعْر *adj* |أَوْعار ,وُعور| 1 [يَصْعُبُ سَلْكُهُ] inaccessible; rough, rugged; مَكان \ مِنْطَقة وَعْر(ة) rugged terrain, rough territory; طَريق وَعْر an inaccessible road 2 [صَعْب] difficult, hard

وُعورة *n* roughness; وُعورة الأَرْضِ the difficulty of the terrain

〈 **وَعَزَ** *v* |i; وَعْز| to instruct, to order

أَوْعَزَ *v* 1 [نَصَحَ] to advise, to recommend; أَوْعَزَ إلى شَخْصٍ بِفِعْلِ شَيْءٍ to advise sb to do sth 2 [أَمَرَ] to instruct, to order, to command; أَوْعَزَ إلى شَخْصٍ بِفِعْلِ شَيْءٍ to instruct sb to do sth

إيعاز *n* |إيعازات| 1 [اقتراح] advice, recommendation; suggestion 2 [أَمْر] instruction, order, command

〈 **وَعَظَ** *v* |i; عِظة ,وَعْظ| to preach; to exhort; to warn; to admonish; وَعَظَ شَخْصاً to preach to sb

اتَّعَظَ *v* to heed a warning; اتَّعَظَ بِشَيْءٍ to let sth be a warning; اتَّعَظَ من الماضي to learn from the past

وَعْظ *n* admonition, warning; sermon

واعِظ *n* |وُعّاظ| preacher

عِظة *n* sermon; exhortation

مَوْعِظة *n* |مَواعِظُ| sermon; admonition; exhortation; أَلْقى مَوْعِظةً to preach fire and brimstone; مَوْعِظة أَخْلاقيّة a sermon on morality; moral admonition

〈 **تَوَعَّكَ** *v* to be unwell, to be indisposed

[سِعة] 2 to find sth hard to understand اسْتيعابِ شَيْءٍ accommodation; طاقة الاسْتيعابِ accommodation capacity 3 [إبادة] extermination, eradication

〈 **وَعَدَ** *v* |i; وَعْد| to promise, to make a promise; وَعَدَ شَخْصاً بِشَيْءٍ to promise sb sth; وَعَدَ شَخْصاً بالتَأْييدِ to promise sb support; وَعَدَ أَنْ … to promise to...; وَعَدَ بِفِعْلِ شَيْءٍ to promise to do sth; وَعَدَ بِأَنَّهُ سَيَبْذِلُ جُهوداً to promise to do one's best; عِدْني بِوَفائِكَ! promise me!; مَنْ وَعَدَ وَفى ≈ a promise made is a debt unpaid

واعَدَ *v* to make an appointment with; to promise each other

أَوْعَدَ *v* to promise

تَوَعَّدَ *v* to threaten, to menace

تَواعَدَ *v* to make an appointment; to promise each other; تَواعَدَ على اللِقاءِ to make an appointment to meet each other

وَعْد *n* |وُعود| promise, vow, word; رَجُل صادِق الوَعْدِ a man of his word; وَعَدَ وَعْداً to make a promise; أَطْلَقَ وُعوداً to make promises; وَفى بِوَعْدِهِ to stay true to/keep one's word, to fulfil one's promise; أَخْلَفَ \ نَكَثَ وَعْدَهُ to break one's promise; ذَكَّرَ شَخْصاً بِوَعْدِهِ to keep/hold someone to his promise; وَعْدُ الحُرِّ دَيْنٌ عَلَيْهِ ≈ a promise made is a debt unpaid

واعِد *adj* promising, hopeful; مُسْتَقْبَل واعِد a bright future; تَطَوُّرات واعِدة promising developments; فُرْصة واعِدة a promising opportunity; سوق واعِدة a promising market

وَعيد *n* threat, menace; نَظْرة وَعيدٍ a threatening look

تَوَعُّديّ *adj* threatening

عِدة *n* promise

مُتَوَعِّد *adj* threatening, menacing

مَوْعِد *n* |مَواعِدُ| 1 [أَجَل] appointed time; آخِر مَوْعِدٍ ,مَوْعِد أَخير deadline; مَوْعِد نِهائيّ final date, deadline; في مَوْعِدٍ غايَتُهُ \ أَقْصاهُ شَهْرُ مارِس not later than March; في مَوْعِدِه on time, at the appointed time; جاءَ \ حَضَرَ في المَوْعِدِ to come/ arrive on time; قبل المَوْعِدِ early, before the appointed time, in advance 2 [وَقْت لِقاءٍ] appointment, date, rendezvous; مَوْعِد مع شَخْصٍ an appointment with sb; المَوْعِد المُحَدَّد the set date; مَوْعِد غَداءٍ lunch appointment; حَسَبَ المَوْعِدِ by appointment; بِناءً على مَوْعِدٍ سابِقٍ based on a previous

وَعْكة *n* indisposition, malaise; nausea

تَوَعُّك *n* |تَوَعُّكات| indisposition; شَعَرَ بالتَوَعُّكِ to feel sick/unwell

مُتَوَعِّك *adj* ill, unwell

‹ **وَعْل** *n* |وُعول, أَوْعال| (Zool) ibex (*Capra*); chamois

‹ **وَعْوَع** *v* |i; وَعْوَعة| to howl, to whine (*fox*); to cry, to whine (*children*); to complain

‹ **وَعى** *v* |i; وَعْي| ⓵ [أَدْرَكَ] to realize, to be/become aware of; وَعى شَيْئاً to realize sth; وَعى الخَطَرَ \ إلى الخَطَرِ to be aware of the danger; لا يَعي أنّ... he doesn't understand that...; لا يَكادُ يَعي he is hardly aware ⓶ [حَوى] to comprise ⓷ [تَذَكَّرَ] to remember; to know by heart

وَعّى *v* to make aware, to inform; to give advice

أَوْعى *v* to put into a vessel

وَعْي *n* ⓵ [إدْراك] awareness, understanding; consciousness; الوَعْي القَوْميّ national consciousness; وَعْي تاريخيّ historical consciousness; وَعْي بيئيّ environmental awareness; وَعْي مَعْلوماتيّ information literacy; زِيادة الوَعْي, رَفْع مُسْتَوى الوَعْي an increasing awareness; عَمِلَ شَيْئاً عن وَعْيٍ to do sth consciously ⓶ [عَكْس غَيْبوبةٍ] consciousness; ما وراء الوَعْي subconsciousness; فُقْدان الوَعْي unconsciousness; فَقَدَ الوَعْيَ to lose consciousness, to faint; عادَ إلَيْه وَعْيُهُ, اسْتَعادَ \ اسْتَرْجَعَ وَعْيَهُ to regain consciousness; كانَ في كامِلِ وَعْيِه to be fully conscious

واعٍ *adj* |وُعاة, واعون| aware, conscious; كانَ واعِياً لِشَيْءٍ to be aware of sth; اخْتِيار واعٍ a conscious choice; دِراسة واعِية an attentive study; غَيْر واعٍ لِشَيْءٍ unaware of sth; واعِياً ل \ ب... aware of ...

وِعاء *n* |أَوْعِية, أَواعٍ| ⓵ [إناء] vessel, pot ⓶ (Anat) vessel; وِعاء دَمَوِيّ blood vessel; وِعاء شَعْرِيّ capillary; تَوَسُّع \ تَضَيُّق الأَوْعِية الدَمَوِيّةِ vascular dilatation/constriction

وِعائيّ *adj* vascular; نَسيج وِعائيّ vascular tissue; مَرَض وِعائيّ vascular disease

تَوْعَوِيّ *adj* educational, awareness-raising, enlightening; حَمْلة تَوْعَوِيّة awareness-raising campaign

تَوْعِية *n* information, awareness; تَوْعِية صِحّيّة health education; تَوْعِية بيئيّة environmental awareness; حَمْلة تَوْعِيةٍ للجَماهيرِ a public awareness campaign

لاواعٍ *adj* unaware, unconscious

لاوَعْي *n* (Psych) subconscious, unconscious; اللاوَعْي الجَماعيّ the collective unconscious

‹ **وَغْد** *n* |وُغْدان, أَوْغاد| scoundrel, rascal, villain

‹ **وَغَرَ, وَغِرَ** *v* |a-i; وَغْر, وَغَر| ⓵ [اشْتَدَّ حَرُّهُ] to become very hot ⓶ [اغْتاظَ] to resent

أَوْغَرَ *v* to arouse anger

‹ **وَغَلَ** *v* |i; وُغول| to penetrate

أَوْغَلَ *v* ⓵ [تَعَمَّقَ في الدِراسةِ] to go deeply (into); to study/treat thoroughly; to apply oneself (to); أَوْغَلَ في مَوْضوعٍ to delve deeply into a subject ⓶ [دَخَلَ] to penetrate deeply into; أَوْغَلَ في الغابةِ to penetrate deeply into the forest ⓷ [في السَيْرِ] أَوْغَلَ في السَيْر to walk quickly

تَوَغَّلَ *v* to penetrate deeply; تَوَغَّلَ الجَيْشُ في المِنْطَقةِ the army penetrated deeply into the region

موغِل *adj* deep-rooted; in-depth; موغِل في القِدَم very old; تاريخ موغِل في القِدَم ancient history

‹ **وَغًى, وَغْي** *n* battle; ساحة وَغًى battlefield, battleground

‹ **وَفَدَ** *v* |i; وَفْد, وُفود, وِفادة| to arrive; to visit; وَفَدَ إلى مَكانٍ to arrive somewhere

أَوْفَدَ *v* to delegate, to depute; أَوْفَدَ شَخْصاً to delegate sb; أَوْفَدَ شَخْصاً إلى مُؤْتَمَرٍ to send sb as delegate to a conference

تَوافَدَ *v* to flock; to arrive together; تَوافَدَ العَشَراتُ للميدانِ dozens of people flocked to the square; تَوافَدَ رُؤَساءُ الدُوَلِ إلى القِمّة heads of state arrived the summit

وَفْد *n* |وُفود| delegation, deputation; حِزْب الوَفْدِ (Egypt) the Wafd party; وَفْد مُرافِق accompanying delegation; شَكَّلَ وَفْداً to form a delegation

وافِد *n* |وُفود, أَوْفاد, وُفّاد| expatriate; وافِد جَديد newcomer; debutant; foreign worker (*in Gulf countries*)

وِفادة *n* arrival; حُسْن الوِفادةِ hospitality; أَكْرَمَ \ أَحْسَنَ وِفادةَ شَخْصٍ to receive sb hospitably

تَوْفير في النَفَقاتِ **2** [ادِّخار] saving; economizing, cutback; دَفْتَر التَوْفير deposit book; صُنْدوق التَوْفير savings bank; مَكَّنَت الإجْراءاتُ الحُكومةَ من تَوْفير ٥٠ مَلْيون دولار the measures gave a saving of 50 million dollars

مُتَوافِر *adj* available, obtainable; abundant; مُتَوافِر في الأَسْواقِ on the market

مُتَوَفِّر *adj* available, in stock, at hand; مُتَوَفِّر في الأَسْواقِ on the market; لم يَعُدْ مُتَوَفِّراً to be no longer available, to be out of stock; المَنْتوجات المُتَوَفِّرة the products in stock; المَعْرِفة المُتَوَفِّرة the knowledge at hand; المَوارِد \ الوَسائِل المُتَوَفِّرة the available means/resources

مُوَفِّر **A** *adj* saving; مُوَفِّر للوَقْتِ time-saving; مُوَفِّر للطاقة energy saving

B *n* provider; مُوَفِّر خِدْماتِ إنْتَرْنت Internet provider

مَوْفور *adj* abundant, ample; مَوْفور الصِحّةِ in perfect health

وَفَضَ *v* |i; وَفْض| to run, to hurry

وفاض *n* bag; لم يَأْتِ خاليَ الوِفاضِ he didn't come empty-handed

وَفَّقَ *v* **1** [بين شَيْئَيْنِ] to reconcile; to bring together, to combine; وَفَّق بين شَيْئَيْنِ to reconcile two things **2** [أَنْجَحَ] to make successful; وَفَّقَهُ اللهُ may God grant him success; وُفِّقَ to be successful, to succeed; وُفِّقَ في عَمَلِهِ \ مَسْعاهُ to be successful in one's job/effort **3** [جَعَلَ شَيْئاً مُوافِقاً] to make suitable, to adjust; وَفَّقَ شَيْئاً to make sth suitable

وافَقَ *v* **1** [لاءَمَ] to be convenient for, to suit; وافَقَ شَخْصاً to be convenient for sb **2** [على| قَبِلَ بِشَيْءٍ] to agree with/on/to; to accept, to consent to, to ratify; approve of; وافَقَ على شَيْءٍ to accept sth; to agree on sth; وافَقَ شَخْصاً على رَأْيِهِ \ قَوْلِهِ to agree with sb; وافَقَ على كَلامِ شَخْصٍ to agree with what sb says; وافَقَ على أنَّ \ أنْ... to approve that ...; وافَقَ على طَلَبٍ to comply with a request **3** [طابَقَ] to fit in with, to correspond with, to be consistent with; وافَقَ شَيْئاً to fit in with sth

تَوَفَّقَ *v* to succeed

إيفاد *n* delegation, deputation

موفَد *n* delegate, deputy; representative, envoy; عَيَّنَ موفَداً to appoint a delegate

وَفَرَ *v* |وَفْر, وُفور|; imperf يَفِرُ| to be abundant

وَفُرَ *v* |وَفارة|; imperf يَوْفُرُ| see وَفَرَ

وَفَّرَ *v* **1** [زَوَّدَ] to provide, to supply, to furnish, to give; وَفَّرَ العَمَلَ to supply jobs; وَفَّرَ المَزيدَ من الأَمْنِ to provide more safety; وَفَّرَ القوّةَ to give strength; وَفَّرَ السِلاحَ to supply weapons; وَفَّرَ الأَجْواءَ المُناسِبةَ to create the right atmosphere; وَفَّرَ حَلاً to provide a solution **2** [اقْتَصَدَ] to save, to spare; to economize; وَفَّرَ مِساحةً to save space; وَفَّرَ مالاً to save money; وَفَّرَ مَبْلَغاً to save an amount **3** [أَغْنى] spare; وَفَّرَ على شَخْصٍ التَفاصيلَ to spare sb the details

أَوْفَرَ *v* to augment, to multiply

تَوَفَّرَ *v* **1** [وُجِدَ] to be available; to be sufficient; to be abundant; تَتَوَفَّرُ المَعْلوماتُ there is enough information; تَوَفَّرَتْ فيه الشُروطُ to fulfil the conditions; تَوَفَّرَ بِكَثْرةٍ to be plentiful **2** [انْكَبَّ] to devote oneself to; تَوَفَّرَ على الشَيْءِ to devote oneself to sth **3** [امْتَلَكَ] have at one's disposal; تَوَفَّرَ على نُقودٍ to have money at one's disposal; يَتَوَفَّرُ على كُلِّ شَيْءٍ he has everything

تَوافَرَ *v* to be abundant

وَفْر *n* |وُفور, وَفَرات| **1** [اقْتِصاد] saving **2** [فائِض] surplus

وافِر *adj* abundant, plentiful; large, wide, huge; قِسْط وافِر a large portion; تَنَوُّع وافِر a wide variety; تَشْكيلة وافِرة a wide selection; أُعْرِبُ عن وافِرِ الامْتِنانِ لَكُمْ I would like to express my deepest gratitude to you

وَفْرة *n* abundance, profusion; بِوَفْرةٍ in abundance, plenty

وَفير *adj* abundant, ample, plentiful; wide, large; كانَ وَفيراً to be abundant; مَحْصول وَفير a rich harvest; أَمْوال وَفيرة lots of money, ample funds

تَوافُر *n* عند تَوافُرِ الظُروفِ when the conditions are right

تَوَفُّر *n* availability

تَوْفير *n* **1** [تَزْويد] supply, provision; تَوْفير الأَدْوِيةِ \ الغِذاءِ supply of medicines/food; تَوْفير الحِمايةِ offer of protection a contract; يَقْضِي الاتِّفاقُ بما يَلي the agreement reads as follows 2 [مُطابَقة] similarity; اتِّفاق المَعاني similarity in meaning; اتِّفاق في المَعْنى synonymy 3 [مُصادَفة] coincidence; اتِّفاقاً by coincidence

اتِّفاقيّ *adj* 1 [تَصادُفيّ] accidental 2 [عُرْفيّ] conventional

اتِّفاقيّة *n* agreement, contract, pact, covenant; اتِّفاقيّة نَوَويّة nuclear arms treaty; اتِّفاقيّة تِجاريّة trade agreement; اتِّفاقيّة دُوَليّة an international agreement; اتِّفاقيّة ثُنائيّة a bilateral agreement; اتِّفاقيّة التِجارةِ الحُرّةِ free trade agreement; اتِّفاقيّة تَعاوُنٍ cooperation treaty; اتِّفاقيّة وارْسو the Warsaw Pact; اتِّفاقيّة مع الوِلاياتِ المُتَّحِدةِ a pact with the United States; اتِّفاقيّة خِدمةٍ terms of use; أَبْرَمَ اتِّفاقيّةً to conclude a pact; وَقَّعَ اتِّفاقيّةً to sign a treaty

تَوافُق *n* 1 [الأَشْياءِ] compatibility; congruence 2 (Mus) chord 3 (Gram) agreement; تَوافُق الفِعْلِ والفاعِلِ في العَدَدِ the agreement between subject and verb in number

تَوافُقيّ *adj* حَلّ تَوافُقيّ compromise solution; مُرَشَّح تَوافُقيّ consensus candidate

تَوْفيق *n* 1 [نَجاح] success, good luck, prosperity; بالتَوْفيقِ good luck!; أَتَمَنّى لَكَ التَوْفيقَ I wish you success 2 [مُصالَحة] reconciliation; harmonization; unification; التَوْفيق بين مَصالِحَ the reconciliation of interests 3 [اِسْم شَخْصيّ] Tawfiq (*male given name*)

تَوْفيقيّ *adj based on compromise*; التَحْليل التَوْفيقيّ combinational analysis; دَوْر تَوْفيقيّ *a role of bringing the parties together for a compromise*

مُتَّفَق *adj* agreed; كَما هو مُتَّفَقٌ عَلَيْهِ as agreed upon

مُتَّفِق *adj* agreed; كانَ مُتَّفِقاً على شَيْءٍ to agree on/about something; غَيْر مُتَّفِقٍ in disagreement

مُتَوافِق *adj* 1 [قابِل للتَوافُقِ] compatible, similar; consistent; مَصالِح مُتَوافِقة similar interests 2 [بالإِجْماعِ] united

مُوافِق *adj* 1 [قابِل] agreeing; approving; أنا مُوافِقٌ I agree, OK; هَزَّ رَأْسَهُ مُوافِقاً to nod one's head in agreement 2 [مُصادِف] consistent; مُوافِق ل consistent with 3 [مُلائِم] suitable

مُوافَقة *n* approval, consent, authorization; مُوافَقة ضِمْنيّة tacit approval, implied consent; مُوافَقة مَجْلِسِ الوُزَراءِ Cabinet

تَوافَقَ *v* to be in agreement, to be in accordance, to agree; to be consistent; to correspond; تَوافَقَ مع شَيْءٍ to be in agreement with sth; to correspond with sth

اتَّفَقَ *v* 1 [تَفاهَمَ] |على| to agree on/to; to reach an agreement on; اتَّفَقَ على شَيْءٍ to agree on/to sth; اتَّفَقَ مع شَخْصٍ على شَيْءٍ to agree with sb on sth; اتَّفَقَ على أنْ ... to agree that ...; لم يَتَّفِقْ مع شَخْصٍ to disagree with sb; اتَّفَقْنا! agreed!, it's a deal! 2 [اِنْسَجَمَ] to correspond, to be in agreement; تَتَّفِقُ الآراءُ it is agreed upon 3 [صادَفَ] to come to pass; اتَّفَقَ لَهُ it fell to him unexpectedly; كَيْفَما اتَّفَقَ whatever may come; at random, haphazardly; no matter how

وَفْقَ *prep* according to, in accordance with; وَفْقاً ل according to, in accordance with, in agreement with; on the basis of; وَفْقَ القانونِ, وَفْقاً للقانونِ according to the law; سارَ وَفْقاً للخُطّةِ to go according to plan; وَفْقَ الشَريعةِ الإِسْلاميّةِ according to Islamic law; وَفْقاً للتَوَقُّعاتِ in line with expectations; وَفْقَ الأَصْلِ true copy of the original

وِفاق *n* accordance, concord; unity; الوِفاق الوَطَنيّ national accord

وِفاقيّ *adj* agreed, consensual, agreement (*before n*), accord (*before n*); حَلّ وِفاقيّ a consensual solution

اتِّفاق *n* |اتِّفاقات| 1 [اتِّفاقيّة] agreement, arrangement; contract, treaty; اتِّفاق جَماعيّ collective agreement; اتِّفاق نَوَويّ nuclear agreement; اتِّفاق وِدّيّ gentleman's agreement, an amicable settlement; اتِّفاق حُكوميّ coalition agreement, governmental agreement; اتِّفاق مَبْدَئيّ tentative agreement; اتِّفاق بين طَرَفَيْنِ an agreement between two parties; اتِّفاق على القَضيّةِ agreement on the matter; عَقَدَ \ أَبْرَمَ اتِّفاقاً مع شَخْصٍ to conclude a contract with sb, to make a deal with sb; تَوَصَّلَ إلى اتِّفاقٍ to come to an agreement, to reach an agreement; وَقَّعَ اتِّفاقاً \ على اتِّفاقٍ to sign a contract; نَفَّذَ اتِّفاقاً to implement an agreement; الْتَزَمَ بالاتِّفاقِ to stick to an agreement; هذا حَسَبَ الاتِّفاقِ that is as agreed; هذا مُخالِفٌ للاتِّفاقِ that is contrary to the agreement; تَعارَضَ مع اتِّفاقٍ to be contrary/adverse to the agreement; طَبَّقَ اتِّفاقاً to execute an agreement; أَخَلَّ بِاتِّفاقٍ \ خَرَقَ اتِّفاقاً to violate approval; بِمُوافَقةِ الحُكومةِ with approval of the government; بِمُوافَقةِ الطَرَفَيْنِ by mutual consent; مُوافقة على شَيْءٍ approval to/for/with/of; صَرَّحَ \ أَظْهَرَ مُوافَقَتَهُ على شَيْءٍ to express one's approval of sth; عَبَّرَ عن مُوافَقَتِهِ المَبْدَئيّةِ to agree in principle; حَصَلَ على المُوافَقةِ to get permission; حازَ على مُوافَقةِ شَخْصٍ to get sb's consent, to receive sb's approval; أَعْطى \ مَنَحَ مُوافَقَتَهُ على شَيْءٍ to give one's permission for/to sth

مُوَفَّق *adj* successful, prospering; fortunate; صَفْقة مُوَفَّقة a successful deal; إِنَّهُ مُوَفَّقٌ في عَمَلِهِ he is successful in his job

وافِل *n* listed alphabetically

وَفَى *v* |i; |وَفاء| ب| to keep, to live up to; to fulfil; وَفَى بِشَيْءٍ to live up to sth; وَفَى بِوَعْدِهِ to keep one's promise; لم يَفِ بِوَعْدِهِ to fail to keep one's promise; وَفَى بِعَهْدٍ \ عَقْدٍ to fulfil a promise/contract; وَفَى بالالْتِزاماتِ to meet one's obligations; مَنْ وَعَدَ وَفَى a promise is a promise

وَفَّى *v* to give to the full extent; وَفَّى شَخْصاً حَقَّهُ to give sb what he is entitled to; وَفَّى المَوْضوعَ حَقَّهُ to treat a subject exhaustively

وافَى *v* 1 ◀ [فاجَأَ] to overtake; وافاهُ المَوْتُ \ الأَجَلُ death overtook him 2 ◀ [وَفَّى] to give, to deliver; وافَى شَخْصاً حَقَّهُ to give sb what he is entitled to 3 ◀ [أَتى] to come; وافَى ب to bring

أَوْفَى I *v* 1 ◀ [بِعَهْدٍ] |ب| to fulfil, to keep, to live up to; أَوْفَى بالتِزامِهِ to fulfil one's obligation; أَوْفَى بِمَطالِبِ شَخْصٍ to meet sb's demands 2 ◀ [زادَ] to exceed; أَوْفَى على المِائةِ to exceed one hundred

تَوَفَّى *v* 1 ◀ [أَماتَ] to let die; تُوُفِّيَ to die, to pass away, to perish; تَوَفّاهُ اللهُ God has taken him unto himself; تُوُفِّيَ بِحادِثِ سَيْرٍ to be killed in a traffic accident 2 ◀ [أَخَذَ] to take; تَوَفَّى حَقَّهُ to take one's share

اسْتَوْفَى *v* 1 ◀ [أَخَذَ] to receive in full 2 ◀ [اسْتَجابَ] to fulfil; اسْتَوْفَى الشَروطَ to meet the conditions 3 ◀ [تَعَمَّقَ] to treat exhaustively

وَفِيّ *adj* |أَوْفِياءُ| loyal, faithful, true; زَوْج وَفِيّ a faithful husband; وَفِيّ لِشَيْءٍ \ شَخْصٍ loyal to sth/sb صَديق وَفِيّ a true friend;

وافٍ *adj* sufficient, enough; مَعْلومات وافية sufficient information; تَحْقيق وافٍ a full investigation

وَفاء *n* 1 ◀ [تَنْفيذ] fulfilment; الوَفاء بالْتِزامٍ \ بِتَعَهُّدٍ the fulfilment of an obligation; الوَفاء بالحاجاتِ fulfilment of needs, meeting the needs; وَفاءً in fulfilment of 2 ◀ [إِخْلاص] loyalty, faithfulness, fidelity; عَدَم الوَفاءِ قِلّة الوَفاءِ unfaithfulness; disloyalty; تَعَهَّدَ بالوَفاءِ to swear allegiance; الوَفاء لِمَبادِئِهِ staying true to one's principles; وَفاءً لِأَبي out of respect for my father's wish

وَفاة *n* |وَفَيات| death, decease; الوَفاة المُفاجِئة \ غَيْر المُتَوَقَّعة the sudden/unexpected death; سَبَب الوَفاةِ cause of death; حَتّى في صَباحِ \ يَوْمِ وَفاتِهِ the morning/day of his death; يَوْمِ وَفاتِهِ until his dying day; شَهادة وَفاةٍ death certificate; حَرَّرَ شَهادةَ وَفاةٍ to draw up a death certificate; مُعَدَّل \ نِسْبة الوَفَياتِ death rate; مُعَدَّل وَفَياتِ الأَطْفالِ الرُضَّعِ infant mortality rate; حادِث \ حالة وَفاةٍ death; حالة وَفاةٍ مَأْساوِيّة a tragic death

اسْتيفاء *n* fulfilment; الاسْتيفاء بالشُروطِ القانونيّةِ fulfilment of the legal conditions; مُدّة اسْتيفاءٍ (Fin) deferment of amortization

أَوْفَى II *adj* more faithful, more loyal

إيفاء *n* |إيفاءات| 1 ◀ [دَفْع] payment; إيفاء القَرْضِ loan payment 2 ◀ [الْتِزام] keeping, fulfilment

مُتَوَفًّى *n* deceased, dead person

مُسْتَوْفٍ *adj* fulfilling; كانَ مُسْتَوْفِياً للمَعاييرِ to meet the standards

مُوافاة *n* giving; طَلَبَ مُوافاتَهُ بِمَعْلوماتٍ to ask for information

مُوَفٍّ *adj* completing; مُوَفِّي الشَهْرِ the last day of the month

وَقْب *n* |أَوْقاب| socket

وَقَّتَ *v* to set a time, to time

تَواقَتَ *v* to coincide, to occur simultaneously

وَقْت *n* |أَوْقات| 1 ◀ [فَتْرة زَمَنيّة] time; period; أَوْقات عَصيبة hard times; أَوْقات شِدّةٍ times of hardship; وَقْت فَراغٍ spare/free time; وَقْت السَرّاءِ \ الضَرّاءِ good/bad times; وَقْت ضائِع lost time; (Sport) injury time; وَقْت إِضافيّ extra time; أَوْقات العَمَلِ office/working hours; خارِجَ أَوْقاتِ العَمَلِ outside office hours; خلال \ أثناء أوْقاتِ العَمَلِ during office hours; قِلّة \ ضِيق الوَقْتِ lack of time, limited time; إضاعة \ مَضْيَعة وَقْتٍ waste of time; بِمُرورِ الوَقْتِ as time went on; in time; في أوْقاتِ الحَرْبِ \ المَجاعةِ in times of war/famine; طوال الوَقْتِ the whole time, all the time; كانَ عِنْدَهُ الوَقْتُ to have enough time; لَيْسَ عِنْدَهُ وَقْتٌ he has no time; لا وَقْتَ لَدَيْهِ لِلتَفْكيرِ he has no time to think; لم يَتَّسِعْ لَهُ الوَقْتُ لِشَيْءٍ to have no time for sth; يَمُرُّ الوَقْتُ time goes by/passes; يَمْضي الوَقْتُ بِسُرْعةٍ time passes quickly, time flies; اسْتَغْرَقَ وَقْتاً طَويلاً to take a long time; قاسَ الوَقْتَ to measure the time; أمْضى \ قَتَلَ الوَقْتَ to pass/kill time; كَرَّسَ وَقْتَهُ ل... to spend/devote one's time on...; أضاعَ وَقْتَهُ to waste one's time, to fool around; أضاعَ وَقْتاً ثَميناً to lose precious time; وَجَدَ وَقْتاً لِشَيْءٍ to find the time for sth; أخَذَ الوَقْتَ الكافي لِشَيْءٍ to take one's time for/over sth; تَجاوَزَ الوَقْتَ المُخَصَّصَ لَهُ to exceed the appointed time; هذا يَحْتاجُ لِلوَقْتِ this needs time; لم يَمْنَحْ شَخْصاً الوَقْتَ to leave someone no time; رَبِحَ \ كَسَبَ الوَقْتَ to gain time; ضاقَ بِهِ الوَقْتُ to run out of time; فاتَ الوَقْتُ it is too late; ما زالَ هُناكَ مُتَّسَعٌ من الوَقْتِ there is enough time left; المَسْألةُ مَسْألةُ وَقْتٍ it's a question of time; الوَقْتُ من ذَهَبٍ time is money 2 [ميقات] time; moment; وَقْتَ in the time of; وَقْتَها then, at the time; في وَقْتٍ غَيْرِ مُناسِبٍ at the wrong time; وَقْت الصَّيْفِ summertime; وَقْت قِياسيّ record time; في غَيْرِ وَقْتِهِ at the wrong time; مع الوَقْتِ in time; في ذاتِ الوَقْتِ at the same time, at that very moment; في أيِّ وَقْتٍ at any time, whenever; في أقْصَرِ \ أسْرَعِ \ أقْرَبِ وَقْتٍ مُمْكِنٍ as soon as possible; في نَفْسِ الوَقْتِ at the same time, simultaneously; في وَقْتٍ سابِقٍ at a previous time; في وَقْتٍ لاحِقٍ later, at a later time; في بَعْضِ الأوْقاتِ sometimes; من وَقْتٍ لِآخَرَ, بين وَقْتٍ وآخَرَ from time to time, now and then; في كَثيرٍ من الأوْقاتِ often, many times; في الوَقْتِ الراهِنِ \ الحاضِرِ at this moment, at the present time; في الوَقْتِ المُحَدَّدِ on time; يَجِبُ الحُضورُ في الوَقْتِ المُحَدَّدِ you must attend on time; حتّى \ إلى وَقْتٍ قَريبٍ until recently; منذ ذلك الوَقْتِ since; في الوَقْتِ المُناسِبِ, في وَقْتِه in due course, in good time, at the right moment; في وَقْتٍ قَرِيبٍ in the near future; الوَقْت المُناسِب لِفِعْلِ شَيْءٍ the right moment to do sth; أكْثَر من أيِّ وَقْتٍ مَضى more than ever; ما زالَ الوَقْتُ مُبَكِّراً ل... it's still too early to...; حانَ الوَقْتُ the time has come

وَقْتَئِذٍ *adv* then, at the time, at that time

وَقْتَذاكَ *adv* then, at the time, at that time; in those days; كُنْتُ وَقْتَذاكَ أعيشُ في القاهِرةِ I was living in Cairo then

وَقْتَما *conj* when; whenever; وَقْتَما تُرِيدُ whenever you want

وَقْتيّ *adj* temporary, transient; temporal

تَواقُت *n* concurrence, conjunction, synchronization

تَوْقيت *n* 1 [وَقْت] time; تَوْقيت شَتْويّ wintertime; تَوْقيت صَيْفيّ summer time, Daylight Saving Time; تَوْقيت مَحَلّيّ local time; تَوْقيت غْرينيتْش Greenwich Mean Time; تَوْقيت العَمَلِ working hours 2 [تَقْدير الوَقْتِ] timing; أحْسَنَ تَوْقيتَ شَيْءٍ to time sth well 3 (Sport) finish time

مُؤَقَّت *adj* temporary, provisional; وَظيفة \ عَمَل مُؤَقَّت(ة) a temporary job; قَرار مُؤَقَّت a provisional decision; عُقوبة مُؤَقَّتة a temporary punishment; إجْراء \ تَعْويض مُؤَقَّت a provisional measure/compensation; أجازَ شَيْئًا مُؤَقَّتاً to allow sth on an interim basis; أوْقَفَ شَيْئًا بِصورةٍ مُؤَقَّتةٍ to suspend sth temporarily

مُوَقَّت *adj* temporary

مُوَقِّت *n* chronometer; stopwatch

مَوْقوت *adj* timed; قُنْبُلة مَوْقوتة time bomb

ميقات *n* |مَواقيتُ| 1 [وَقْت] time; ميقات الصَّلاةِ (Islam) prayer times 2 (Islam) *the stations during the Hajj where pilgrims put on their pilgrimage garment*

وَقَحَ, وَقِحَ, وَقُحَ *v* |a-i-u; وُقوح, وُقوحة, وَقاحة, قَحة, قِحة| to be cheeky; to be shameless; to be rude

تَواقَحَ *v* to behave in an insolent manner

وَقِح *adj* |وُقُح| impolite, insolent, impertinent, cheeky; تَصَرُّف وَقِح shameless behaviour; جَواب وَقِح an insolent reply; سُؤال وَقِح an impertinent question

وَقاحة *n* impudence, insolence, impertinence, cheek; يا لَها من وَقاحةٍ! of all the nerve!; أجابَ بِوَقاحةٍ to answer insolently

قِحة *n* impudence, insolence, impertinence, cheek

‹ **وَقَدَ** *v* |i; وُقود ,وَقْد ,وَقَد| to burn; to ignite

أَوْقَدَ *v* to kindle, to light; أَوْقَدَ شَمْعَةً to light a candle

تَوَقَّدَ *v* to glow; to burn; تَوَقَّدَتْ عَيْناهُ his eyes were glowing (*with excitement/rage*)

اِتَّقَدَ *v* to blaze, to burn; اِتَّقَدَ حَماساً to burn with zeal

اِسْتَوْقَدَ *v* to kindle, to light

وَقّاد **A** *adj* burning, glowing; bright **B** *n* stoker

وَقْدة *n* fire, blaze; في وَقْدةِ القَيْظِ in the burning heat of the sun

وَقود *n* fuel; وَقود حَفْرِيّ \ أُحْفوريّ fossil fuel; وَقود حَيَويّ biofuel; وَقود الطائِراتِ paraffin (BrE), kerosene (AmE); خَزّان وَقودٍ fuel tank; اِسْتِهْلاك الوَقودِ fuel consumption; اِسْتِهْلاك قَليل \ أَقَلّ لِلوَقودِ low/lower fuel consumption; دَوّاسة الوَقودِ gas pedal; throttle; تَزَوَّدَ بالوَقودِ to refuel

وَقيد *n* fuel

اِتِّقاد *n* **1** [اِحْتِدام] glow, burning, flame **2** [حَماسة] passion, ardour, zeal

إيقاد *n* kindling, lighting

تَوَقُّد *n* glowing; تَوَقُّد الذَكاءِ sparkling intelligence

مُتَّقِد *adj* glowing; burning, flaming

مُسْتَوْقِد *n* hearth, fireplace

مَوْقِد *n* |مَواقِدُ| hearth, fireplace; cooker, stove; مَوْقِد غازٍ gas cooker, gas burner; مَوْقِد نَفْطٍ oil burner; مَوْقِد كَهْرَبائيّ an electric cooker; شُعْلة \ رَأْس المَوْقِدِ gas ring; طَبَخَ على مَوْقِدٍ to cook on a cooker

‹ **وَقَّرَ** *v* to respect, to revere

أَوْقَرَ *v* to overburden

وَقار *n* dignity, poise; veneration, respect; مَشى بِوَقارٍ to walk with dignity

وِقار *n* grouper, serranid

وَقور *adj* |وُقُر| sober, solemn, sedate

مُوَقَّر *adj* venerable, respectable, honourable

‹ **وَقَصَ** *v* |i; وَقْص| to break someone's neck

‹ **وَقَعَ** *v* |a; وُقوع| **1** [سَقَطَ] to fall, to tumble; وَقَعَ من السُلَّمِ to fall down the stairs; وَقَعَت الزَهْرِيّةُ \ الخِزانةُ the vase/closet fell down; وَقَعَ في غَرامِها he fell in love with her **2** [حَدَثَ] to happen, to take place, to occur; وَقَعَ حادِثٌ there was an accident; وَقَعَ انْقِلابٌ عَسْكَرِيٌّ a military coup took place **3** [كانَ] to be located, to lie; to be subject (to); وَقَعَ على البَحْرِ to lie on the sea; تَقَعُ مَدينةُ طَنْجة في شَمالِ المَغْرِبِ Tanger lies in the north of Morocco; وَقَعَ تحت طائِلةِ القانونِ to be punishable by law **4** [عَثَرَ] to get into; to end up in; وَقَعَ في فَخٍّ to walk into a trap; وَقَعَ في الغَلَطِ to make a mistake; وَقَعَ في قَضيّةٍ to get involved in a matter; وَقَعَ في مَشاكِلَ to get into trouble; وَقَعَ في يَدِ العَدوِّ to fall into the hands of the enemy

وَقَّعَ *v* **1** [أَمْضى] to sign, put one's signature; وَقَّعَ وَثيقةً to sign a document; وَقَّعَ على مُعاهَدةٍ \ اتِّفاقيّةٍ \ تَصْريحٍ to sign a pact/agreement/statement; وَقَّعَ على الاِسْتِلام to sign for delivery; وَقَّعَ بالأَحْرُفِ الأولى to initial, to put one's initials **2** [نَفَّذَ] to perform, to carry out

واقَعَ *v* to have sex with

أَوْقَعَ *v* **1** [أَسْقَطَ] to cause to fall; to bring down; أَوْقَعَ زُجاجةً to knock over a bottle; أَوْقَعَت الحَرْبُ أَكْثَرَ من ٣٠ أَلْفَ قَتيلٍ the war cost more than 30,000 lives **2** [فَرَّقَ] to sow seeds of discord; أَوْقَعَ بين شَخْصَيْنِ to drive a wedge between two people **3** [سَبَّبَ] to cause **4** [جَعَلَ شَخْصاً يَقَعُ في] to make, to allow; أَوْقَعَ شَخْصاً في كَمينٍ to let sb to walk into an ambush; أَوْقَعَ شَخْصاً في وَرْطةٍ to get sb into trouble

تَوَقَّعَ *v* to expect, to anticipate, to foresee; يَتَوَقَّعُ أَنْ يَرْبَحَ he expects to win; تَوَقَّعَ حُدوثَ مَشاكِلَ to foresee problems; تُتَوَقَّعُ أَمْطارٌ رَعْدِيّةٌ a thunderstorm is expected; لم أَتَوَقَّعْ هذا مِنْكَ! I didn't expect this from you!

وَقْع *n* **1** [سُقوط] falling; وَقْع أَقْدامٍ the sound of footsteps; وَقْع الصاعِقةِ a stroke of lightning, thunderbolt; كانَ لِلخَبَرِ وَقْعُ الصاعِقةِ عَلَيْهِ the news hit him like a thunderbolt **2** [تَأْثير] impact, impression

واقِع **A** *adj* **1** [ساقِط] falling **2** [حاصِل] happening; أَمْر واقِع a fait accompli; وَضَعَ شَخْصاً أمامَ الأَمْرِ الواقِعِ to confront sb with a reality **3** [كائِن] located; الجِبال الواقِعة في جَنوبِ المَغْرِبِ the mountains in the south of Morocco

تَوْقيع *n* |تَوْقيعات| signing; signature; تَوْقيع على عَقْدٍ a signature on a contract; تَوْقيع رِسالةٍ \ مُعاهَدةٍ the signing of a letter/treaty; تَوْقيع بالأَحْرُفِ الأولى initialled; تَوْقيع مُخْتَصَر initials; تَوْقيع رَقْميّ \ إلِكْترونيّ a digital/electronic signature

مُتَوَقَّع *adj* expected; predictable; غَيْر مُتَوَقَّعٍ unexpected, unforeseen; مَصاريف غَيْر مُتَوَقَّعةٍ unforeseen expenses, incidental expenditure; نِهاية مُتَوَقَّعة a predictable ending; من المُتَوَقَّع أنْ ... it is expected that ...; رَدّ فِعْلٍ غَيْر مُتَوَقَّعٍ an unexpected reaction; أَقَلّ من المُتَوَقَّعِ less than expected

مَوْقِع *n* |مَواقِعُ| ◆1 [مَكان \ مَوْقِف] place, location, position, site; المَوْقِع الجُغْرافيّ the location, the geographic location; مَوْقِع مَرْكَزيّ \ مُنْعَزِل \ إسْتراتيجيّ a central/isolated/strategic location; مَوْقِع أَثَريّ an archaeological site; مَوْقِع مُتَقَدِّم an advanced position; مَوْقِع سَفينةٍ the position of a ship; حَدَّدَ مَوْقِعَهُ to define one's position; نِظام تَحْديدِ المَواقِعِ navigation system; نِظام تَحْديدِ المَواقِعِ العالَميّ Global Positioning System, GPS; احْتَلَّ \ اتَّخَذَ مَوْقِعَهُ to take up one's position; تَكَبَّدَ خَسارةَ مَواقِعَ to suffer loss of territory; مَوْقِع قُوّةٍ position of power ◆2 (Comput) website, site; home page; مَوْقِع تَفاعُليّ an interactive website; مَوْقِع مَحْجوب \ مَحْظور a blocked website; مَوْقِع إلِكْترونيّ, مَوْقِع على الإنْتَرْنِت website; مَوْقِع مُشارَكةِ الصُوَرِ \ المِلَفّاتِ photo/file sharing site; صاحِب مَوْقِعٍ webmaster; تَعْيين مَوْقِعٍ site designation; خَريطة مَوْقِعٍ site map; زارَ مَوْقِعاً to visit a website; أَطْلَقَ مَوْقِعاً to launch a website

مُوَقَّع *adj* ◆1 [تَمَّ تَوْقيعُهُ] signed, initialled ◆2 [تَمَّ تَنْفيذُهُ] carried out

مُوَقِّع *n* signer; المُوَقِّع أَدْناهُ \ أَسْفَلَهُ the undersigned

مَوْقِعة *n* |مَواقِعُ| battle

ميقاع *n* metronome

وَقَفَ *v* |i; وُقوف, وَقْف| ◆1 [قامَ] to stand; to place oneself, to post oneself; وَقَفَ مع \ وراء \ إلى جانِبِ شَخْصٍ to stand behind sb; مَنْ يَقِفُ وراء هذه الجَريمةِ؟ who is behind this crime?; وَقَفَ على المَدْخَلِ \ البابِ to stand at the entrance/door ◆2 [سَكَنَ] to stop, to come to a standstill;

◆B *n* |وُقوع, وُقَّع, وَقائِعُ| [حَقيقة] reality; truth; واقِع مَفْروض imposed reality; الواقِع المُعاش \ اليَوْميّ the everyday reality; الواقِع السِياسيّ \ الاقْتِصاديّ the political/economic reality; في الواقِعِ, في واقِعِ الأَمْرِ in fact, in reality, actually; دون الواقِعِ far from reality; مُخالِف للواقِعِ contrary to the truth; أَدْرَكَ الواقِعَ to face reality; تَرْجَمَ شَيْئاً إلى الواقِعِ to translate sth to reality

واقِعة *n* event, happening, incident; fact; سورة الواقِعة (Islam) The Event (*Sura 56*)

واقِعيّ *adj* realistic; real, actual; نَظْرة واقِعيّة a realistic view; تَقْدير واقِعيّ a realistic estimation; إنْسان واقِعيّ a realistic person, a realist; سِياسة واقِعيّة realpolitik; حالة واقِعيّة real case; غَيْر واقِعيٍّ unreal; unrealistic; الفِكْر الواقِعيّ realism; تَوَقُّعات غَيْر واقِعيّةٍ unrealistic expectations

واقِعيّة *n* reality; realism; ما فوق الواقِعيّةِ surrealism

وَقْعة *n* |وَقَعات| ◆1 [سَقْطة] fall ◆2 [اشْتِباك] battle

وُقوع *n* ◆1 [سُقوط] falling ◆2 [حُدوث] incidence

وَقيعة *n* |وَقائِعُ| ◆1 [حَدَث] incident, happening; fact; وَقائِع facts, proceedings; الوَقائِع الصَحيحة \ الحَقيقيّة the real facts; عَرَضَ الوَقائِعَ to present the facts; وَقائِع الجَلْسةِ the proceedings of the session ◆2 [خِلاف] battle

إيقاع *n* |إيقاعات| ◆1 (Mus) rhythm, time, beat, cadence; عازِف إيقاعٍ drummer; ضابِط الإيقاعِ drummer; الْتَزَمَ بالإيقاعِ to keep the rhythm; قادَ الإيقاعَ to keep time ◆2 [إسْقاط] bringing down ◆3 [تَسْبيب] causing

إيقاعيّ *adj* rhythmic, rhythmical; آلة إيقاعيّة percussion instrument

تَوَقُّع *n* expectation, anticipation; prospect; forecast; تَوَقُّعات حَسَنة \ سَيِّئة good/bad prospects; تَوَقُّعات العُمْرِ life expectancy; مُحْبِط للتَوَقُّعاتِ not living up to the expectations, disappointing; حَسَبَ التَوَقُّعاتِ ... expectations are that ...; خِلافاً لِكُلِّ التَوَقُّعاتِ other than expected, against all expectations; صَحَّتْ تَوَقُّعاتي my expectations came true; حَقَّقَ \ أَرْضى التَوَقُّعاتِ to live up to the expectations; فاقَ \ تَجاوَزَ التَوَقُّعاتِ to exceed/surpass expectations; فاقَ كُلَّ التَوَقُّعاتِ to go beyond all expectations; أَكَّدَ \ أَثْبَتَ التَوَقُّعاتِ to confirm expectations

قِفْ stop!; وَقَفَ عند شَيْءٍ to stop at sth; وَقَفْتُ عند هذا الحَدِّ I stopped here, I stopped at this point; وَقَفَ يَشْرَبُ to stop drinking **3** [اِكْتَشَفَ] to discover, to find out; وَقَفَ على السِرِّ to discover the secret **4** [وَقَّفَ] to bring to a standstill **5** [نَهَضَ] to stand up, to rise; وَقَفَ لِشَخْصٍ to stand up for sb **6** [قاوَمَ] to withstand; وَقَفَ في وَجْهِ شَخْصٍ to withstand sb, to oppose sb **7** [اِتَّخَذَ] to take; وَقَفَ مَوْقِفاً to take a standpoint **8** (Gram) |على| *to pronounce a word in the pausal form*

وَقَّفَ *v* **1** [جَعَلَهُ يَقِفُ] to stop, to bring to a standstill, to halt, to hold up; to arrest; وَقَّفَ سَيّارةً to stop a car **2** [أَسَّسَ وَقْفاً] |على| to found a waqf

أَوْقَفَ *v* **1** [جَعَلَهُ يَقِفُ] to stop, to bring to a standstill, to halt, to hold up; أَوْقَفَ شَخْصاً to stop sb; أَوْقَفَ آلَةً to turn off a machine; أَوْقَفَ العَمَلَ to stop work; أَوْقَفَ اللُعْبَةَ \ المُباراةَ to stop the game/match; أَوْقَفَ الدَعْمَ الحُكوميَّ to cut off government support; أَوْقَفَ تَنْفيذَ الحُكْمِ to stay the execution of a verdict; أَوْقَفَ جَريدةً عن الصُدورِ to ban a newspaper from publication **2** [أَطْلَعَ] to inform; أَوْقَفَ شَخْصاً على شَيْءٍ |على| to inform sb of sth **3** [أَسَّسَ وَقْفاً] to found a waqf **4** [أَجَّلَ] to suspend; أَوْقَفَ شَخْصاً عن العَمَلِ to suspend sb from his work

تَوَقَّفَ *v* **1** [وَقَفَ] to stop, to come to a standstill, to stand still; تَوَقَّفَ عند الحُدودِ to stop at the border **2** [اِنْتَهى] to stop, to end; تَتَوَقَّفُ الآلَةُ the machine stops; سَيَتَوَقَّفُ الأَلَمُ the pain will pass **3** [كَفَّ] |عن| to quit, to discontinue; to refrain from; to cease, to stop; تَوَقَّفَ عن شَيْءٍ to stop doing sth; تَوَقَّفَ عن العَمَلِ to stop working; تَوَقَّفَ عن التَدْخينِ to stop smoking **4** [تَعَلَّقَ] |على| to depend on; تَوَقَّفَ على شَيْءٍ to depend on sth; ... يَتَوَقَّفُ هذا أَوَّلاً وَأَخيراً على this completely depends on...

اِسْتَوْقَفَ *v* to stop, to bring to a stop; اِسْتَوْقَفَ سَيّارةً to stop a car

وَقْف *n* **1** [تَوَقُّف] stop, stopping; وَقْف التَجارِبِ النَوَوِيَّةِ the end of nuclear tests; وَقْف إِطْلاقِ النارِ ceasefire, truce **2** (Islam) |أَوْقاف| waqf (*religious foundation, endowment fund*); وِزارة الأَوْقافِ Ministry of Awqaf (*of religious foundations*) **3** (Gram) *pausal ending* (Idioms) كانَ وَقْفاً على to be dependent on; وَقْفاً ل \ على restricted to

واقِف *adj* |واقِفون، وُقوف| standing; stopping

وَقْفة *n* **1** [وُقوف] stop, halt **2** [اِسْتِراحة] pause **3** (Mus) rest **4** [وَضْعة] position, attitude; وَقْفة جادّة a serious attitude; وَقَفَ مَعي وَقْفةَ الرِجالِ he stood behind me like a real man **5** [العيد] eve; وَقْفة العيدِ the eve of the holiday, the day before the holiday

وَقْفيّ *adj* religious endowment (*before n*); مِلْك وَقْفيّ public religious property

وُقوف *n* **1** [تَوَقُّف] parking; stopping; مَمْنوعُ الوُقوفُ no parking **2** (Islam) *the rite of standing at certain places, specifically Mount Arafat, during the Hajj pilgrimage in Mecca*

إيقاف *n* **1** [كَفّ] stopping; حاوَلَ إيقافَ شَيْءٍ to try to stop sth; لا يُمْكِنُ إيقافُهُ there is no stopping him; إيقاف التَجارِبِ النَوَوِيّةِ the ending of nuclear tests **2** [حَبْس] arrest, detention **3** [تَعْطيل] suspension; تَمَّ إيقافُهُ عن العَمَلِ he is suspended

تَوَقُّف *n* **1** [وُقوف] stopping, stop; standstill **2** [اِنْقِطاع] stoppage; stopover; التَوَقُّف عن العَمَلِ off work, out of business; تَوَقُّف في الطَريقِ stopover, pit stop; بِدونِ \ بِلا تَوَقُّفٍ non-stop; تَوَقُّف لِمُدّةِ سِتِّ ساعاتٍ a six-hour stopover

تَوْقيف *n* |تَوْقيفات| **1** [تَعْطيل] stopping; suspension; blocking; تَوْقيف حِسابٍ بَنْكيٍّ the closing of a bank account **2** [اِعْتِقال] arrest, detention; تَوْقيف اِحْتِياطيّ preventive custody

مُتَوَقِّف *adj* **1** [واقِف] standing still; سَيّارة مُتَوَقِّفة a stationary car **2** [مُنْتَهٍ] interrupted; مُفاوَضات مُتَوَقِّفة interrupted negotiations **3** [مُتَعَلِّق] dependent

مَوْقِف *n* |مَواقِفُ| **1** [مَحَطّة] stop, station, stopping place; مَوْقِف حافِلةٍ bus stop; مَوْقِف سَيّارةٍ \ سَيّاراتٍ parking space; car park; بَحَثَ عن مَوْقِفٍ للسَيّارةِ to look for a parking space; وَجَدَ مَوْقِفاً للسَيّارةِ to find a parking place **2** [رَأْي] position; stance, opinion, standpoint, viewpoint; attitude; مَوْقِف حازِم \ صُلْب \ مُتَشَدِّد a firm/strong/rigorous stand; مَوْقِف عَدائيّ a hostile attitude; مَوْقِف مُتَوَسِّط a middle position; مَوْقِف إيجابيّ \ سَلْبيّ a positive/negative attitude;

واقِية *n* واقِية صَدَماتٍ bumper; واقِية مُبَرِّدٍ grille

وِقائيّ *adj* preventive; تَوْجيهات \ تَعْليمات وِقائيّة safety regulations; إجْراءات وِقائيّة preventive measures

وِقاية *n* prevention, precaution; للوِقايةِ من for the prevention of; الوِقايةُ خَيْرٌ من العِلاجِ prevention is better than cure, ≈ an ounce of prevention is worth a pound of cure (AmE)

اتِّقاء *n* prevention

تَقْوى *n* |f| devoutness, piety

تَقيّ *adj* |أتْقِياءُ| pious, God-fearing; رَجُل تَقيّ a God-fearing man

تَقِيّة *n* (Islam) dissimulation (*hiding one's religious affiliation*)

مُتَّقٍ *adj* pious, God-fearing

‹ **تَوَكَّأَ** *v* to lean; تَوَكَّأَ على عُكّازَيْنِ to walk with crutches

اتَّكَأَ *v* to lean; اتَّكَأَ على حائِطٍ te lean against a wall

مُتَّكَأ *n* |مُتَّكَآت| armchair, lounge chair; sofa; ottoman

مُتَّكِئ *adj* |على| leaning

‹ **وَكَبَ** *v* |i; وُكوب, وَكْب| to walk slowly

واكَبَ *v* **1** [رافَقَ] to go along with, to accompany, to escort; to keep up with; واكَبَتْهُ الشُرْطةُ he was escorted by the police; واكَبَ العَصْرَ to keep up with the times **2** [ماشى] to go together with; واكَبَهُ شَيْءٌ to go together with sth, to correlate with sth

مُواكَبة *n* escort

مَوْكِب *n* |مَواكِبُ| parade; procession; مَوْكِب احْتِفاليّ a festive parade; مَوْكِب جِنازةٍ a funeral procession; مَوْكِبٍ من الأطْفال a parade of children

‹ **وَكَّدَ** *v* to affirm, to confirm

تَوَكَّدَ *v* to be affirmed

تَوْكيد *n* |تَواكيد, تَوْكيدات| affirmation, confirmation

‹ **وَكْر** *n* |وُكور, أوْكار| **1** [طَيْر] nest **2** [مَقَرّ] hotbed; وَكْر الإجْرامِ a hotbed of crime; وَكْر اللُصوصِ robbers' den

‹ **وَكَزَ** *v* |i; وَكْز| to punch

‹ **وَكَسَ** *v* |i; وَكْس| to decrease in value

‹ **وَكَفَ** *v* |i; وَكْف, وَكَفان| to drip, to trickle; to leak; يَكِفُ الماءُ water drips

‹ **وَكَلَ** *v* |i; وَكْل, وُكول| to entrust

مَوْقِف إنْكاريّ a negative viewpoint; مَوْقِف قَويّ a strong position; مَوْقِف مُعْتَدِل a moderate position; مَوْقِف قَطْعيّ a final stance; مَوْقِف شَخْصٍ من شَيْءٍ \ شَخْصٍ sb's attitude towards sth/sb; مَوْقِفُهُ حِيالَ الأزْمةِ his opinion about the crisis; تَحْديد مَوْقِفٍ making a stand; مَوْقِف سِياسيّ a political stance; وَقَفَ \ اتَّخَذَ مَوْقِفاً (من شَيْءٍ) to take a stand (on sth); تَبَنّى مَوْقِفاً مُحايِداً to take a neutral position; مَوْقِفاً جَديداً to take a new stance; غَيَّرَ مَوْقِفَهُ to change one's position; تَراجَعَ \ تَخَلّى تَمَسَّكَ \ الْتَزَمَ بِمَوْقِفِهِ to hold one's ground; عن مَوْقِفِهِ to reconsider one's opinion; لَيَّنَ مَوْقِفاً to moderate an opinion; هو مَعْروفٌ بالثَباتِ في مَواقِفِهِ he's known for his tenacity **3** [الجَسَد] position, attitude **4** [حالة] situation, position; مَوْقِف صَعْب \ حَرِج \ مُحْرِج a difficult/awkward/embarrassing situation **5** [مَسْرَح] scene

مُوَقَّف *adj* |عن| مُوَقَّف عن العَمَلِ out of work

مَوْقوف **A** *adj* **1** [مُتَعَلِّق] dependent; مَوْقوف على dependent on **2** [سَجين] detained, in custody; مَوْقوف على ذِمّةِ التَحْقيقِ in preventive custody **3** [سَيّارة] parked
B *n* **1** [أسير] detainee, prisoner **2** (Islam) مَوْقوف عَلَيْهِ *beneficiary or usufructuary of a waqf*

‹ **وَقْوَقَ** *v* |i; وَقْوَقة| to cuckoo

وَقْوَق *n* (Zool) cuckoo (*Cuculidae*)

‹ **وَقى** *v* |i; وِقاية, وَقْي| to protect, to shield, to guard; وَقى شَخْصاً من البَرْدِ to protect sb against the cold; وَقى نَفْسَهُ من المَشاكِلِ to protect oneself from trouble

وَقّى *v* to protect, to guard

تَوَقّى *v* to prevent; to avoid

اتَّقى *v* **1** [احْتَمى] to shelter oneself from, to protect oneself against; اتَّقى المَطَرَ \ الثَلْجَ \ البَرْدَ to shelter oneself from the rain/snow/cold **2** [خافَ] to be on one's guard against, to beware of **3** [الله] to fear; اتَّقى اللهَ to fear God (*to follow and remain in harmony with the laws of God*); اتَّقِ اللهَ! fear God!

واقٍ **A** *adj* preventive; protective; دِرْع واقٍ a protective shield; كْريم واقٍ من الشَمْسِ sunscreen; قِناع واقٍ gas mask
B *n* condom

وَكَّلَ *v* to authorize, to empower; to give/grant authority, to give/grant a mandate; to appoint as representative; وَكَّلَ شَخْصاً في \ على فِعْلِ شَيْءٍ to authorize sb to do sth; وَكَّلَ مُحامِياً to appoint a solicitor

أَوْكَلَ *v* to assign, to entrust; أَوْكَلَ أَمْراً إلى شَخْصٍ to entrust sth to sb

تَوَكَّلَ *v* 1 [اِعْتَمَدَ] to trust; تَوَكَّلَ على اللهِ to trust in God 2 [صارَ وَكيلاً] to be authorized; to be responsible; to act as a representative 3 [ضَمِنَ] to guarantee; تَوَكَّلَ بِشَيْءٍ to guarantee sth

تواكَلَ *v* to depend on each other, to trust each other

اتَّكَلَ *v* to trust; to rely; اتَّكَلَ على شَيْءٍ \ شَخْصٍ to trust in sth/sb; اتَّكِلْ على اللهِ! rely on God!

وَكالة, وِكالة *n* 1 (Busn) agency; representation; وَكالة الأَنْباءِ press/news agency; وَكالة سِياحيّة travel agency 2 (Law) power of attorney, authorization, mandate; procuration, proxy; وَكالة عامّة general power(s) of attorney; تزوّجَ بوكالةٍ to marry by proxy 3 [مُؤَسَّسة] agency; وَكالة الأُمَمِ المُتَّحِدةِ لإِغاثةِ وَتَشْغيلِ اللاجِئينَ (الفِلَسْطينيّينَ) United Nations Relief and Works Agency (for Palestine Refugees in the Near East) (*UNRWA*); الوَكالة الدُوَليّة للطاقةِ الذَرّيّة International Atomic Energy Agency (*IAEA*)

وَكيل *n* |وُكَلاءُ| 1 (Busn) representative, agent; deputy; وَكيل تِجاريّ dealer; وَكيل لِشَرِكةِ التَأْمينات agent of an insurance company 2 (Law) representative; procurator, solicitor (BrE), attorney (AmE); وَكيل شَرْعيّ a legal representative; الوَكيل العامّ attorney general; وَكيل المَلِكِ (Mor) the public prosecutor; وَكيل النِيابةِ العامّةِ (Egypt) the public prosecutor; وَكيل الوِزارة (Egypt) Deputy Secretary 3 (Islam) الوَكيل the Trustee (*one of the names of God*)

(Idiom) وَكَفى باللهِ وَكيلاً God is enough as a Disposer of affairs

اتِّكال *n* trust; reliance, dependency

اتِّكاليّة *n* inertia, passiveness

إيكال *n* entrusting, assigning, authorizing

تَوْكيل *n* |تَوْكيلات| power (of attorney), authorization; حَصَلَ على تَوْكيلٍ to be authorized/empowered, to acquire authorization; to receive a mandate; مَنَحَ تَوْكيلاً to give power, to grant authority; to give a mandate; سَيَنْتَهي التَوْكيلُ بعد أُسْبوعٍ the mandate will expire a week from now; تَوْكيل كامِل full power of attorney; تَوْكيل عامّ a general power of attorney; بالتَوْكيلِ by proxy; by attorney

مُوَكَّل A *adj* authorized; assigned; العَمَل المُوَكَّل إلَيْهِ the work that was assigned to him
B *n* representative

مُوَكِّل *n* client; مُوَكِّل مُحامٍ the client of a solicitor

مَوْكول *adj* entrusted, assigned; العَمَل المَوْكول إلَيْهِ the work that was assigned to him

وَلَجَ *v* |i; وُلوج, لِجة| to enter; وَلَجَ عِمارةٍ \ إلى عِمارةٍ to enter a building; وَلَجَ مَرْحَلةً to enter a phase; وَلَجَ البابَ to go through the door

أَوْلَجَ *v* to put in, to insert

وُلوج *n* entry; امْتِحان الوُلوج (Mor) entrance examination

مولَج *adj* entrusted; اللَجْنة المولَجة بِشُؤونِ المال the commission that is entrusted with finances

وَلَدَ *v* |i; مَوْلِد, لِدة, وِلادة| 1 [إنْسان] to bear, to give birth; وُلِدَ to be born 2 [حَيَوان] to have young 3 [نَشَأَ] to bring forth; مَتى وُلِدَتْ هذه الفِكْرةُ؟ when did this idea come about?

وَلَّدَ *v* 1 [كَوَّنَ] to generate, to produce; وَلَّدَ التَيّارَ to generate electricity 2 [ساعَدَ على الوِلادةِ] to assist in childbirth

تَوَلَّدَ *v* 1 [وُلِدَ] to be born 2 [نَشَأَ] to originate; to be brought forth, to be generated; تَوَلَّدَ من شَيْءٍ to originate from sth

تَوالَدَ *v* to reproduce, to propagate, to multiply

اسْتَوْلَدَ *v* to impregnate

وَلَد *n* |أَوْلاد, وُلْد| 1 [خَلَف] son, child, descendant; حِصّة \ نَصيب وَلَدٍ child's portion; عِنْدَهُ ثَلاثةُ أَوْلادٍ he has three children 2 [صَبيّ] boy, guy, lad 3 [وَرَقة اللَعِبِ] jack

والِد *n* father; parent; procreator; والِدانِ parents

والِدة *n* mother

وِلادة *n* 1 [وَضْع] birth; delivery; parturition; وِلادة عَسيرة a difficult delivery; وِلادة قَيْصَريّة a caesarean delivery; وِلادة مُعَجَّلة \ قبل الأَوانِ premature birth; يَوْم الوِلادةِ day of birth, birthday; تاريخ الوِلادةِ date of birth; سَنة الوِلادةِ year of

مَوْلود A *adj* |مَواليدُ| born

B *n* |مَواليدُ| newborn child, baby; مَوْلود جَديد \ حَديث a new baby; مَوْلود قبل الأَوانِ a premature baby; نِسْبة المَواليدِ birth rate; هو من مَواليد ١٩٥٧ he was born in 1957; رُزِقَ مَوْلوداً to have a baby; الوالِدةُ والمَوْلودُ في صِحّةٍ جَيِّدةٍ mother and child are doing well

ميلاد *n* 1 [وِلادة] birth; يَوْم الميلادِ birthday; تاريخ الميلادِ date of birth; مَكان \ مَحَلّ الميلادِ place of birth; شَهادة \ قَيْد الميلادِ birth certificate; عيد ميلادٍ birthday; حَفْل عيدِ ميلادٍ birthday party; احْتَفَلَ بعيدِ ميلادِهِ to celebrate one's birthday; أَجْمَل التَهاني بِمُناسَبةِ عيد ميلادِكَ best wishes on your birthday; عيدَ ميلادٍ سَعيداً happy birthday; تَمَنّى لِشَخْصٍ عيدَ ميلادٍ سَعيداً to wish sb a happy birthday; ميلاد السَيِّد المَسيح the birth of Christ; قبل الميلادِ BC (*before Christ*); بعد الميلادِ AD (*Anno Domini*); عيد الميلادِ \ ميلادِ المَسيحِ Christmas; احْتَفَلَ بعيدِ ميلادِ المَسيحِ to celebrate Christmas 2 [اسْم شَخْصيّ] Milad, Miled (*male given name*)

ميلاديّ *adj* of the Christian era, AD; سَنة ميلاديّة calendar year (*Gregorian*); القَرْن السابِع الميلاديّ seventh century AD

وَلَسَ *v* |i; وَلْس| to deceive; to commit fraud

والَسَ *v* to cheat

أَوْلَسَ *v* |ب| to misrepresent

مُوالَسة *n* deceit; fraud

وَلِعَ *v* |وَلَع, وَلوع; imperf يَوْلَعُ| ب| to be passionately fond of, to be crazy about; وَلِع بِشَيْءٍ \ شَخْصٍ to be passionate about sth/sb

وَلَّعَ *v* to enamour

أَوْلَعَ *v* to enamour, to kindle love; أولِعَ بِشَيْءٍ \ شَخْصٍ to be crazy/mad about sth/sb, to have a passion for sth/sb

تَوَلَّعَ *v* |ب| to be passionate about

وَلَع *n* passion; infatuation, crush

وَلّاعة *n* (Egypt) lighter

وَلوع *adj* passionate, mad; infatuated

مولَع *adj* passionate, enthusiastic, ardent; crazy, mad, wild; كانَ مولَعاً بِشَيْءٍ \ شَخْصٍ to be passionate about sth/sb, to be crazy/mad about sth/sb; كانَ مولَعًا بالسَمَكِ \ بالسِباحةِ to love

birth; عِلْم الوِلادةِ obstetrics, midwifery; مَكان \ مَحَلّ الوِلادةِ place of birth, native city; تَنْظيم الوِلادةِ birth control, family planning; غُرْفة الوِلادةِ delivery room; مُسْتَشْفى الوِلادةِ obstetric/maternity clinic; جَناح \ قِسْم الوِلادةِ maternity ward/department, obstetric(al) ward; شَهادة وِلادةٍ birth certificate; إجازة الوِلادةِ maternity/confinement leave; عَدَد الوِلاداتِ birth rate; يَرْتَفِعُ عَدَدُ الوِلاداتِ \ يَنْخَفِضُ the birth rate falls/grows; قبل الوِلادةِ prenatal; عند \ منذ الوِلادةِ at/from birth; ماتَتْ عند الوِلادةِ to die in childbirth 2 [الحَيَواناتِ] birth, litter 3 (fig) birth, origin; وِلادة جَديدة rebirth; وِلادة الكِتابةِ the origin of writing

وَلود *adj* |f| fertile, bearing many children; امْرَأة وَلود a woman with many children

وَليد *n* |وِلْدان| 1 [مَوْلود] newborn child, baby 2 [اسْم شَخْصيّ] Walid (*male given name*)

اسْتيلاد *n* breeding, propagation; production

تَوالُد *n* reproduction, multiplication; breeding, generation; تَوالُد ذاتيّ \ تِلْقائيّ spontaneous generation

تَوْليد *n* 1 [مُساعَدة عند الوِلادةِ] assistance at childbirth; عِلْم التَوْليدِ obstetrics, midwifery; جَناح \ قِسْم التَوْليدِ maternity ward/department; أَخِصّائيّ التَوْليدِ obstetrician; midwife 2 [إنْتاج] generation; تَوْليد كَهْرَباءٍ \ طاقةٍ electricity/energy generation; مَحَطّة تَوْليدِ الكَهْرَباءِ power plant, power station

تَوْليديّ *adj* generative; النَحْو التَوْليديّ generative grammar

لِدة *n* |لِدات, لِدون| contemporary

مَوْلِد *n* |مَوالِدُ| 1 [يَوْم الوِلادةِ] birthday; مَوْلِد النَبيِّ birthday of the Prophet Muhammad 2 [مَكان الوِلادةِ] هو مِصْريُّ المَوْلِدِ he is Egyptian by birth 3 [وِلادة] birth; يَوْم مَوْلِدٍ day of birth; تاريخ المَوْلِدِ date of birth; عند \ منذ المَوْلِدِ at/from birth

مُوَلَّد A *adj* generated, produced

B *n* (Ling) neologism

مُوَلِّد *n* |مُوَلِّدات| generator; مُوَلِّد كَهْرَبائيّ \ كَهْرَباءٍ electric generator, dynamo; مُوَلِّد غازٍ gas generator; مُوَلِّد نَوَويّ \ ذَرّيّ nuclear/atomic power station

مُوَلِّدة *n* midwife

تَوَلّى *v* ⓵ [قامَ بِـ] to take upon oneself, to take charge of; to occupy, to hold; تَوَلّى أَمْراً to take sth upon oneself, to take charge of sth, to assume the responsibility of sth, to be in control of sth; تَوَلّى الحُكْمَ \ زِمامَ الحُكْمِ to come into power, to seize power; تَوَلّى السُّلْطةَ to take over the government, to seize control; تَوَلّى الإشْرافَ to supervise, to monitor; تَوَلّى وَظائِفَ مُخْتَلِفةً to hold different jobs; تَوَلّى مَنْصِبَ أُسْتاذٍ to hold a professorship ⓶ [أدارَ] to manage, to be in charge of; to administer; to arrange; تَوَلّى شُؤُونَهُ to arrange one's affairs; تَوَلّى الأَعْمالَ to be in charge of the work ⓷ [أَعْرَضَ] to turn away; تَوَلّى عن شَخْصٍ \ شَيْءٍ to turn away from sb/sth

تَوالى *v* to follow in succession; تَوالَت المَصائِبُ disasters occurred one after the other

اسْتَوْلى *v* |على| to take possession of, to seize, to confiscate, to capture; to conquer, to occupy; اسْتَوْلى على شَيْءٍ to take possession of sth; اسْتَوْلى على الحُكْمِ to seize power; اسْتَوْلى على بَلَدٍ to occupy a country; اسْتَوْلى على الجائِزةِ he took the prize; اسْتَوْلى عَلَيْهِ الحُزْنُ he was overcome by grief

وَليّ *n* |أَوْلياءُ| ⓵ [مالِك] owner; وَلِيّ العَهْدِ crown prince, heir to the throne; وَلِيّ النِعْمةِ benefactor ⓶ [وَصيّ] guardian; وَلِيّ الأَمْرِ guardian to sb; وَلِيّ شَخْصٍ legal guardian; عَيَّنَ وَلِيًّا to appoint a guardian ⓷ (Islam) saint; marabout; الوَلِيّ the Patron (*one of the names of God*) ⓸ [نَصير] follower; helper; friend

والٍ *n* |وُلاة| ⓵ [حاكِم] governor, ruler; viceroy ⓶ (Islam) الوالي the Governor (*one of the names of God*)

وَلاء *n* ⓵ [وَفاء] loyalty, allegiance; devotion; وَلاء لِشَخْصٍ loyalty to sb; أَدانَ بالوَلاءِ لِشَخْصٍ to owe allegiance to sb; أَقْسَمَ يَمينَ الوَلاءِ لِ ... to swear (an oath of) allegiance to ⓶ [تَتابُع] succession

وِلائيّ *adj* state (*before n*), government (*before n*); اخْتِصاص وِلائيّ state jurisdiction

وَلاية *n* help; friendship; supervision

وِلاية *n* ⓵ [مَنْصِب] governorship, regency; term of office; تَمْديد \ تَجْديد الوِلايةِ extension/renewal of the term of fish/swimming; مولَع بلَعِبِ الشِطْرَنْج a passionate chess player; مولَع بالشِراءِ acquisitive; مولَع بالنِساءِ womanizer, ladykiller; إنَّهُ مولَعٌ بالقِراءةِ he is an avid reader, he is fond of reading

وَلَغَ *v* |a; وَلْغ, وُلوغ| to lap, to lick; to slobber

والَفَ *v* (NA) to become attached

تَوْليفة *n* mixture, blend, combination

مُوالِف *n* tuner; مُوالف الراديو \ التلِفِزْيون radio/television tuner

أَوْلَمَ *v* to prepare a feast

وَليمة *n* |وَلائِمُ| banquet, feast; wedding dinner

وَلَهَ, وَلِهَ *v* |وَلَه|; imperf يَوْلَهُ, يَلِهُ to become mad (*with love/grief*)

وَلَّهَ *v* to throw into misery

أَوْلَهَ *v* to make crazy, to drive insane

واله *adj* bewildered, confused

وَلْهان *adj* |dipt; وُلَّه| ⓵ [حُبًّا] infatuated, passionate, crazy in love ⓶ [حُزْناً] deeply distressed, heartbroken

وَلْوَلَ *v* |i; وَلْوَلة, وِلْوال| to lament, to wail

وَلْوَلة *n* wailing

وَلِيَ *v* |i; وَلاية, وِلاية| ⓵ [تَبِعَ] to follow; ما يَلي what follows; فيما يَلي in what follows; فيما يَلي بَعْضُ الإرْشاداتِ in what follows are some guidelines; كَما يَلي as follows ⓶ [حَكَمَ] to govern, to rule; to run; to be in charge; وَلِيَ البَلَدَ \ على البَلَدِ to rule the country/over the country ⓷ [جاوَرَ] to be adjacent to, to lie next to

وَلّى *v* |i| ⓵ [عَيَّنَ] to appoint as ruler/governor; to put in charge ⓶ [الوَجْهَ] to turn away; وَلّى وَجْهَهُ عن شَخْصٍ \ شَيْءٍ to turn away from sb/sth; وَلّى اهْتِماماً بِشَيْءٍ \ شَخْصٍ to give attention to sth/sb

والى *v* ⓵ [أَيَّدَ] to support, to back, to be an adherent; والى شَخْصاً to support sb ⓶ [تابَعَ] to continue, to go on

أَوْلى *v* ⓵ [أَعْطى] to give; أَوْلى اهْتِماماً to give attention; أَوْلى ثِقةً to have confidence ⓶ [جَعَلَهُ والِياً] to commission; to put in charge; to appoint as ruler/governor; أَوْلى شَخْصاً أَمْراً to commission sth to sb office **2** [خِلافة] succession; وِلاية العَهْدِ succession to the throne **3** [إقْليم] (federal) state; vilayet (*a province of the Ottoman Empire, governed by a vali*); الوِلايات المُتَّحِدة (الأَمْريكيّة) the United States (of America), US **4** (Law) guardianship

اسْتيلاء *n* occupation, capture; seizure, confiscation; اسْتيلاء على حِصْنٍ the capture of a fortress; الاسْتيلاء على مُمْتَلَكاتِ الغَيْرِ the confiscation of other people's possessions; الاسْتيلاء على السُلْطةِ takeover, coup

أَوْلَويّة *n* priority; precedence; حَدَّدَ أَوْلَويّاتٍ to establish priorities; أَعْطى الأَوْلَويّةَ لِشَيْءٍ to give priority to sth; كانَ \ مَثَّلَ أَعْلى أَوْلَويّةٍ to be the highest priority

أَوْلى *adj* |ب| more entitled to; more appropriate for; كانَ أَوْلى بِشَيْءٍ to be more entitled to sth; الأَوْلى بِكَ أَنْ ... first you should have to...

إيلاء *n* (Islam) *annulment of a marriage by the husband's vow to have refrained from intercourse*

تَوالٍ *n* succession; sequence; على التَوالي one after the other, successively; in a row; لِليَوْمِ الثالِثِ على التَوالي for the third day in a row; على تَوالي السِنينَ as the years went by, with the years; تَوْصيل على التَوالي (Elec) series connection

تَوْلِية *n* appointment (*to a position, as governor or as successor*); inauguration

مُتَوالٍ *adj* successive, consecutive; uninterrupted; أَرْبَع مَرّاتٍ مُتَوالِيةٍ four times in a row

مُتَوَلٍّ *adj* entrusted, in charge; مُتَوَلّي التَحْقيقِ the person in charge of the investigation

مُوالٍ **A** *adj* loyal; faithful; مُوالٍ لِشَخْصٍ loyal to sb **B** *n* friend; supporter, partisan; follower

مُوالاة *n* **1** [تَأْييد] support; بِمُوالاةِ ... with the support of... **2** [مُتابَعة] continuation

مَوْلَويّة *n* Mawlawiyya (*the Sufi order of Mawla Jalal al-Din Rumi*)

مَوْلًى *n* |مَوالٍ| **1** [سَيِّد] lord, patron; مَوْلايَ \ مَوْلانا *form of address to a religious person, teacher or ruler* **2** [عَبْد] client; servant

‹ **أَوْمَأَ** *v* to make a gesture, to signal, to beckon; أَوْمَأَ بِرَأْسِهِ to nod one's head

إيماء *n* making gestures; فَنّ الإيماءِ pantomime, mime

إيماءة *n* gesture; sign, signal

إيمائيّ *adj* pantomimic; تَمْثيل إيمائيّ pantomime

‹ **مومِس** *n* |مومِسات| prostitute, whore (vulg)

‹ **وَمَضَ** *v* |i; وَمْض, وَميض, وَمَضان| to flash

أَوْمَضَ *v* to flash; to flicker; to gleam, to glimmer; to glance furtively

وَمْضة *n* flash (of light); flicker; glimmer; في وَمْضةِ عَيْنٍ in a blink of an eye; هُناكَ وَمْضةٌ من الأَمَلِ there is a glimmer of hope

وَميض *n* twinkle, sparkle, glint

‹ **وَمَقَ** *v* |i; وَمْق| to love tenderly

‹ **وِنْش** *n* |وِنْشات, أَوْناش| (Egypt Constr) crane

‹ **وَنى, وَنِيَ** *v* |i; وَنْي| to be/become tired, to be/become faint/weak, to be/become lazy; لا يَني unflagging; لا يَني يُكَرِّرُ he does not tire of repeating

تَوانى *v* to be laid-back; تَوانى عن أَداءِ عَمَلِهِ to be laid-back in one's work

وانٍ *adj* weak, feeble

تَوانٍ *n* laziness; negligence

مُتَوانٍ *adj* laid-back; lazy; negligent

ميناء *n* |f; مَوانٍ, مَوانِئُ| **1** [مَرْسًى] harbour, port; ميناء دُوَليّ international port; ميناء حُرّ free port; ميناء تَرانْزيت \ عُبورٍ transit port; خِدْمة المَواني harbour service; رُسوم الميناءِ harbour dues; دَفَعَ رُسومَ الميناءِ to pay the harbour dues; عَبَرَ ميناءً to call in at a port, to pass through a harbour **2** [مَدينة] seaport, seaport town; ميناء الإسْكَنْدَرِيّةِ the seaport of Alexandria **3** [الساعةِ] dial

‹ **وَهَبَ** *v* |a; وَهْب| **1** [مَنَحَ] to give away, to donate; to grant; وَهَبَ شَخْصاً المالَ \ المَلابِسَ to give money/clothes to sb; وَهَبَ شَخْصاً حُبَّهُ to give sb one's love **2** [افْتَرَضَ] to suppose; هَبْ ... suppose that...; هَبْني فَعَلْتُ ذلك assuming that I did it, suppose I had done it

واهِب *n* giver, donor

وَهّاب *n* الوَهّاب the Bestower (*one of the names of God*)

وَهّابيّ *adj, n* Wahhabi

وَهّابيّة *n* Wahhabism (*Islamic movement in Saudi Arabia*)

مَوْهِبة *n* |مَواهِبُ| [1] ◄ [مَلَكة] talent, gift, giftedness; مَوْهبة كَبيرة \ مُفْرِطة \ مُتَميِّزة a great/enormous/extraordinary talent; مَوْهِبة موسيقيّة musical talent; مَوْهِبة سِياسيّة \ رِياضيّة \ أَدَبيّة a talent for politics/sports/writing; مَوْهِبة الرِياضيّات a gift for mathematics; ذو مَوْهِبةٍ طَبيعيّةٍ a naturally talented person; رَجُل ذو مَواهِبَ كَبيرةٍ a very talented man; أَظْهَرَ مَوْهِبةً to show talent; مَلَكَ مَوْهِبةً لُغَويّةً to have a flair for languages; تَوَفَّرَ على مَوْهِبةٍ في شَيْءٍ to have a talent for sth [2] ◄ [شَخْص] مَواهِب شابّة young talents

مَوْهوب [A] *adj* talented, gifted; موسيقيّ \ خَطيب مَوْهوب a gifted musician/speaker; بِنْت مَوْهوبة a talented girl

[B] *n* talent

هِبة *n* [1] ◄ [عَطِيّة] present, gift, donation, grant; هِبة من السَماء godsend; مَنَحَ \ هِبة بِقيمةِ ٦٠٠ دينار a donation of 600 dinars; قَدَّمَ هِبةً to make a donation [2] ◄ [اسم شَخْصيّ] |dipt| Hiba (*female given name*)

‹ **وَهَجَ** *v* |i; وَهْج, وَهيج, وَهَجان| to glow; to burn

أَوْهَجَ *v* to light

تَوَهَّجَ *v* to glow; to burn; يَتَوَهَّجُ الأَمَلُ ≈ hope persists, hope flickers

وَهْج *n* glowing; burning

وَهَج *n* blaze, heat

وَهّاج *adj* glowing; burning

مُتَوَهِّج *adj* glowing; burning

‹ **وَهْدة** *n* |وُهَد, وِهاد| [1] ◄ [أَرْض مُنْخَفِضة] lowland, lowlands [2] ◄ [هوّة] ravine, gorge

‹ **وَهْران** *n* |dipt f| Oran (*city in Algeria*)

‹ **وَهْق** *n* |أَوْهاق| lasso

‹ **وَهِلَ** *v* |وَهَل; imperf يَوْهَلُ| to be frightened

وَهَل *n* fear

وَهْلة *n* |وَهَلات| moment, instant; short while; مُنْذُ الوَهْلةِ الأولى from the beginning; للوَهْلةِ الأولى at first, initially; لِأَوَّلِ وَهْلةٍ at first, initially; at first sight; بَدا لِوَهْلةٍ أنّ ... for a short while it seemed that ...

‹ **وَهَمَ** *v* |i; وَهْم| to think, to believe, to suppose

وَهِمَ *v* |وَهَم; imperf يَوْهَمُ| to make a mistake; to be mistaken

وَهَّمَ *v* to fool; to make believe

أَوْهَمَ *v* |ب| to make believe; to fool into; أَوْهَمَ شَخْصاً بِشَيْءٍ to make sb believe sth; to fool sb into sth; أَوْهَمَ نَفْسَهُ بِأَنَّ ... to deceive oneself into thinking that ...; to imagine that ...

تَوَهَّمَ *v* to imagine; to think; تَوَهَّمَ أنّ ... to imagine that ...; to have the delusion that ...

اتَّهَمَ *v* to suspect; to accuse, to charge, to indict; اتَّهَمَ شَخْصاً بِشَيْءٍ to suspect sb of sth; to accuse sb of sth; to charge sb with sth; اتَّهَمَ شَخْصاً بِفِعْلِ شَيْءٍ to suspect sb of doing sth; to accuse sb of doing sth; اتَّهَمَ شَخْصاً بالكَسَلِ to accuse sb of being lazy; اتَّهَمَ شَخْصاً بالغِشِّ \ بالقَتْلِ \ بالابْتِزازِ to charge sb with fraud/murder/blackmail; اتَّهَمَ شَخْصاً صَراحةً to accuse sb openly

وَهْم *n* |أَوْهام| fantasy; illusion; delusion; زَوال وَهْمٍ disillusionment, disappointment; كانَتْ لَدَيْهِ أَوْهامٌ عن شَيْءٍ, خَلَّصَ to have illusions about sth; عَلَّقَ أَوْهاماً على شَيْءٍ أَزالَ أَوْهامَ شَخْصٍ, شَخْصاً من أَوْهامِهِ to rob sb of his illusions, to shatter sb's illusions; تَخَلَّصَ من أَوْهامِهِ to be robbed of one's illusions

واهِم *adj* wrong, false; deluded; مُعْتَقَد واهِم delusion; إِنَّكَ واهِمٌ you are wrong

وَهْميّ *adj* imaginary, illusory, unreal; fictitious; الحَقيقة الوَهْميّة virtual reality; خَطّ وَهْميّ an imaginary line; مَرَض وَهْميّ an imaginary disease; عَقار \ دَواء وَهْميّ placebo

اتِّهام *n* |اتِّهامات| accusation; charge, indictment; suspicion; اتِّهام كاذِب \ باطِل a false/empty accusation; اتِّهام صَريح a strong accusation; قَفَص الاتِّهام prisoner's dock; قَرار الاتِّهامِ indictment; غُرْفة اتِّهام ≈ criminal division (*of a court*); وَجَّهَ أَصابِعَ الاتِّهامِ إلى شَخْصٍ \ شَيْءٍ to point a finger at sb/sth

اسْتيهام *n* phantasm

إِيهام *n* illusion; delusion

تُهْمة *n* |تُهَم, تُهْمات| accusation, charge, indictment; تُهْمة كاذِبة \ باطِلة a false/empty accusation; التُهْمةُ جَريمةُ قَتْلٍ the charge is murder; أَنْكَرَ التُهْمةَ to deny the accusation; أَسْقَطَ تُهْمةً to drop a charge; وَجَّهَ تُهْمةً إلى شَخْصٍ to bring

وهى *v* |i; وَهْي| to be weak

أَوْهى *v* to weaken

واهٍ *adj* |وُهاة| 1 [ضَعيف] weak; حُجّة واهية \ ذَريعة a weak excuse, flimsy excuse 2 [جِداليّ] contestable

وَيْ *excl expression of surprise*

ويب *n* Web; صَفْحة ويب web page

وَيْح *excl* وَيْحاً لَكَ، وَيْحَكَ how terrible for you

واحة *n* oasis; واحة من الهُدوء an oasis of peace

ويسْكونْسن *n* |f| Wisconsin (*US state*)

ويسْكي, وِسْكي *n* whisky; كَأْس \ زُجاجة من الويسْكي a glass/bottle of whisky

وَيْل *n* woe; وَيْلَكَ \ وَيْلٌ لَكَ woe unto you; ذاقَ الوَيْلَ to go through misery

وَيْلة *n* woe

ويلْز *n* |f| Wales

ويلينْغْتون *n* |f| Wellington (*capital of New Zealand*)

charges against sb; قُبِضَ عَلَيْهِ بِتُهْمةِ السَرِقةِ to be arrested on suspicion of robbery

تَوَهُّم *n* fantasy; delusion

مُتَّهَم **A** *adj* accused; suspected; كانَ مُتَّهَماً بِشَيْءٍ to be suspected of sth

B *n* suspect; accused, defendant; مُتَّهَم رَئيسيّ main/chief suspect; بَلَّغَ المُتَّهَمَ بالحُكْمِ to issue the accused a sentence; حَقَّقَت الشُرْطةُ مع المُتَّهَم the police interrogated the suspect

مُتَّهِم *n* accuser

مُتَوَهَّم *adj* delusional

وَهَنَ *v* |i; وَهَن, وَهْن| to be/become weak, to grow feeble

أَوْهَنَ *v* to weaken; أَوْهَنَ الروحَ المَعْنَويّة to demoralize

وَهْن, وَهَن *n* weakness, feebleness; وَهْن عَصَبيّ nervous breakdown; وَهْن نَفْسيّ mental exhaustion; شَعَرَ بالوَهْنِ to feel weak

واهِن *adj* |وُهُن| weak, feeble; ضَوْء واهِن a faint light; شَيْخ واهِن a feeble old man

يا *particle* 1 [نداء] O (old use) (*vocative particle*); يا حَسَنُ! (O) Hassan!; يا عَبْدَ المَلِكِ! hey, Abdalmalik!; يا أَيُّها المُؤْمِنونَ O ye faithful
2 [تَعَجُّب] what, how; يا لَصَفاءِ السَماءِ! what good fortune!; يا لَلْهَوْلِ how awful; يا لَهُ من بَخيلٍ what a miser (he is); يا خَسارةً \ لَلْخَسارةِ! what a pity!, too bad!; يا سَلامُ! how wonderful!

ياء *n* |f| *name of the letter* ي

يابانيّ A *adj* Japanese; (اللُغة) اليابانيّة Japanese (language); اليِن اليابانيّ the Japanese yen
B *n* Japanese

اليابان *n* |f| Japan; بَحْر اليابان the Sea of Japan

يارْدة *n* yard (*unit of linear measure equal to 3 feet (0.9144 metres)*); على مَسافةِ خَمْسِ يارْداتٍ من المَرْمى five yards from the goal

يَئِسَ *v* |a-i; يَأْس, يَآسة| to despair; to give up; يَئِسَ من حالةِ شَخْصٍ to give up on sb; يَئِسَ من الحَياةِ to be tired of life; لا تَيْأَسْ don't give up/despair

أَيْأَسَ *v* to deprive of hope

اسْتَيْأَسَ *v* to despair

يَأْس *n* despair, desperation; يَأْساً out of despair; سِنّ اليَأْسِ menopause; مَرَّتْ بِسِنِّ اليَأْسِ to go through menopause; دَفَعَ شَخْصاً إلى اليَأْسِ to drive sb to despair; عاشَ بين اليَأْسِ والأَمَلِ to live between fear and hope; لا يَأْسَ مع الحَياةِ وَلا حَياةَ مع اليَأْسِ while there's life, there's hope; أُصيبَ بِحالةٍ من اليَأْسِ to feel despair; تَمَلَّكَهُ \ أَدْرَكَهُ اليَأْسُ تَماماً to be overcome by utter despair

يائِس *adj* desperate; مُحاوَلة يائِسة a desperate attempt; حُبّ يائِس desperate love; يائِس من الحَياةِ tired of life

مَيْؤوس *adj* مَيْؤوس مِنْهُ hopeless; lost; حالة مَيْؤوس مِنْها a hopeless situation; مَريض مَيْؤوس من حالَتِهِ a patient who has been given up

ياسَمين *n* jasmine; ياسَمين البَرِّ clematis; ثَوْرة الياسَمينِ the Jasmine Revolution (*Tunisia, 2010-11*)

ياسِنْت *n* (Bot) hyacinth (*Hyacinthus*)

يافوخ *n* |يَوافيخ| crown, top (*of an infant's head*); fontanelle, soft spot

ياقة *n* collar; roll-neck, turtleneck; border, band

ياقوت *n* |يَواقيتُ| ruby; ياقوت أَحْمَر ruby; ياقوت أَزْرَق sapphire

ياقوتيّة *n* (Bot) hyacinth; ياقوتيّة الماءِ water hyacinth (*Eichhornia*)

ياك *n* yak

يام *n* yam (*Dioscorea*)

يانْسون, يَنْسون, يانِسون *n* anise, aniseed; بُذور \ حَبّ اليانِسونِ anise seeds

يانَصيب *n* lottery; السَحْب الأَوَّل \ الأَخير لليانَصيبِ the first/last draw of the lottery; رَبِحَ الجائِزةَ الكُبْرى في اليانَصيبِ to win the lottery; لَعِبَ اليانَصيبَ to play the lottery; وَرَقة يانَصيبٍ lottery ticket

ياه *excl* oh!

ياهو *n* Yahoo!®

يَباب *adj* |mf| deserted; devastated; أَرْض يَباب a wasteland; خَراب يَباب complete devastation

يَبْروح, يَبْروج *n* (Bot) mandrake (*Mandragora*)

يَبِسَ *v* |a; يُبْس, يَبْس| to be/become dry, to dry out, to have run dry

يَبَّسَ *v* to dry; يَبَّسَ خُبْزاً to dry bread

أَيْبَسَ *v* to dry

تَيَبَّسَ *v* to dry (out/up), to shrivel (up); to be/become stiff; to harden, to set; تَيَبَّسَت الحُقولُ the fields are parched; قد تَيَبَّسَتْ ذِراعُهُ his arm is stiff

يُبْس *n* drought, dryness

يابِس *adj* |يَبْس ,يُبَّس| dry, desiccated; خُبْز يابِس dried bread *(used in recipes or as croutons)*; stale bread; غُصْن \ شَجَرة يابِس(ة) a dead branch/tree; أَعْشاب \ أَوْراق يابِسة withered grass/leaves

يابِسة *n* (dry) land; على اليابِسةِ on dry land; اليابِسة ! land ahoy!; أَنْزَلَ شَيْئاً إلى اليابسةِ to put sth ashore

يَباس *n* dryness

يُبوسة *n* dryness

مُتَيَبِّس *adj* stiff, rigid; desiccated

‹ **يَتِمَ ,يَتَمَ ,يَتُمَ** *v* |a-i-u; يُتْم| to be orphaned, to lose one's parents; to lose a parent

يَتَّمَ *v* to orphan; *to deprive a child of one or both parents;* أَرْمَلوا زَوْجَتَهُ وَيَتَّموا أَطْفالَهُ they made his wife a widow and his children orphans

أَيْتَمَ *v* to orphan

تَيَتَّمَ *v* to be/become an orphan

يَتيم **A** *n* |أَيْتام ,يَتامى| orphan; *a child who has lost one of their parents;* يَتيم الأُمِّ *a child who has lost his mother;* يَتيم الأَبَوَيْنِ an orphan; دار \ مَأْوى \ مَلْجأ الأَيْتامِ orphanage; تَبَنّى يَتيماً to adopt an orphan **B** *adj* |أَيْتام ,يَتامى| **1** [فاقِد الوالِدَيْنِ] orphaned; *having lost a parent;* طِفْل يَتيم an orphaned child **2** lone, sole, single; unique; فازوا بِهَدَفٍ يَتيمٍ they won by a just a single goal

مَيْتَم *n* |مَياتِمُ| orphanage

‹ **يَتوع** *n* (Bot) spurge *(Euphorbia)*

‹ **يَثْرِب** *n* |dipt| Yathrib *(original name of Medina)*

‹ **يَحْمور** *n* see حمر

‹ **يَحْيى** *n* Yahya *(male given name)*

‹ **يَخْت** *n* |يُخوت| yacht, (cabin) cruiser; نادي اليَخْتِ yacht club, sailing club; يَخْت شِراعيّ sailboat; سِياحة اليُخوتِ (pleasure) cruise

‹ **يَخْنة** *n* stew, casserole; يَخْنة البَطاطا بالدَجاجِ chicken and potato stew

‹ **يَد** *n* |f; أَيْدٍ ,أَيادٍ| **1** (Anat) hand; يَد يُمْنى \ يُسْرى right/left hand; ب \ في يَدِهِ اليُسْرى with/in his left hand; يَد بَيْضاء benefaction; يَد عامِلة labour, manpower; يَد عامِلة (غَيْر) كافِية sufficient/insufficient manpower; ظَهْر اليَد the back of the hand; مِلْء اليَد handful; كُرة اليَد handball; لَمْسة يَد (Sport) hands; فارِغ \ صِفْر اليَدَيْنِ empty-handed; خَرَجَ من شَيْءٍ صِفْرَ اليَدَيْنِ to come away empty-handed; باليَدِ manually; بِيَدٍ من حَديدٍ with an iron fist; في مُتَناوِلِ يَدِ شَخْصٍ within sb's reach/grasp; يَداً ب \ في يَدٍ hand in hand; على يَدِ شَخْصٍ by sb, at the hands of sb; كِتاب على يَدِ شَخْصٍ a book (written) by sb; قُتِلَ على يَدِ مَجْهولينَ to be killed by unknown persons; كانَ \ لم يَكُن الأَمْرُ بِيَدِهِ to have control/no control over the matter; خَرَجَ الأَمْرُ من يَدِهِ to let things get out of hand, to lose control of the matter; كانَتْ لَهُ يَدٌ في الأَمْرِ to have a hand in sth; أنا مَكْتوفُ اليَدَيْنِ my hands are tied; كانَ في مُتَناوَلِ يَدِهِ to be on hand, to be within reach; طَلَبَ يَدَ (شَخْصٍ) to propose (to sb); مَدَّ يَدَ العَوْنِ \ المُساعَدةِ to give a helping hand; كانَ في أَيادٍ أَمينةٍ to be in good hands; زَحَفَ على يَدَيْهِ وَرِجْلَيْهِ to crawl on all fours; انْتَقَلَ من يَدٍ إلى يَدٍ to pass into other hands; to be passed from hand to hand; تَداوَلَتْهُ الأَيْدي it was passed from hand to hand; وَقَعَ \ سَقَطَ في يَدَيْ شَخْصٍ to fall into the hands of sb; وَضَعَ يَدَهُ على شَيْءٍ to lay one's hands on sth, to touch sth; to get one's hands on sth, to take/claim ownership of sth; وَضَعَ يَدَهُ على الجَرْحِ to put one's finger on the problem, to hit the nail on the head; أَطْلَقَ يَدَ شَخْصٍ في شَيْءٍ to give sb a free hand in sth; وَضَعَ يَدَهُ في يَدِ شَخْصٍ to join together, to form a coalition; هُمْ يَدٌ واحِدةٌ they are hand in glove; يَدُ اللهِ مع الجَماعةِ many hands make light work; ضَمَّ يَدَيْهِ to clasp one's hands; كانَ خفيفَ اليَدِ to work fast; كانَ طَويلَ اليَدِ to have sticky fingers *(thief)*; to be noble *(generosity)*; رَفَعَ يَدَهُ على شَخْصٍ to raise one's hand against sb; يَداهُ مُلَطَّخَتانِ بالدَمِ he has blood on his hands; أَفْلَتَ الشَيْءُ من يَدِهِ he let it slip from his hands; مَدَّ يَدَهُ ل ... to extend one's hand to ...; مَدَّ يَدَ العَوْنِ لِشَخْصٍ to offer sb a helping hand; كانَتْ يَدُهُ مَمْدودةً لِشَيْءٍ to be open to sth, to be willing to try sth; أَهْوى بِيَدِهِ إلى شَيْءٍ to reach out one's hand for sth; بين يَدَيْهِ in his presence, in front of him; أَخَذَ حَقَّهُ بِيَدِهِ to take the law into one's own hands; نَظيفُ اليَدَيْنِ clean,

بِكُلِّ العُسْرِ يُسْراً after a storm comes a calm 2 [راحة] ease; أَدّى فَرِيضةَ الحَجِّ في يُسْرٍ وَسُهولةٍ with great ease; يُسْرٍ وَسُهولةٍ he performed the hajj with ease

يَسار *n* 1 [عَكْس يمين] left side; يَميناً وَيَساراً right and left; يَساراً \ على اليَسارِ on the left, left; إلى اليَسارِ (to the) left; على يَسارِهِ to/on his left 2 (Pol) اليَسار the Left; أَحْزاب اليَسارِ the left-wing parties; يَسار الوَسَطِ the centre-left; اليَسار المُتَطَرِّف \ المُتَشَدِّد the far left

يَساريّ *adj* 1 (Pol) left-wing, leftist; جَناح يَساريّ left wing; حِزْب يَساريّ leftist party 2 [مَنْسوب إلى جِهة اليَسارِ] left

يَسْرة *n* left, left side

يَسير *adj* 1 [سَهْل] easy; simple 2 [قَليل] small, little; (على) مَسافة يَسيرة a short distance (away)

أَيْسَر *adj* |dipt; يُسْر| left; على الجانِبِ الأَيْسَرِ on the left (side); اليَد \ العَيْن اليُسْرى the left hand/eye; ظَهير أَيْسَر (Sport) left back; كانَ أَيْسَرَ to be left-handed; كَتَبَ بِيَدِهِ اليُسْرى to write left-handed

تَيْسير *n* 1 [تَسْهيل] lightening, easing, facilitation; promotion, stimulation; تَيْسير الشُروطِ easing requirements; تَيْسير عَوْدةِ المُهاجِرينَ facilitating repatriation; اتِّفاقيّة تَيْسيرِ وَتَنْمية التَبادُلِ التِجاريِّ an agreement to facilitate and develop trade 2 [اسْم شَخْصيّ] Taysir (*male/female given name*)

مُتَيَسِّر *adj* available, accessible; possible, feasible; easy, comfortable; كانَتْ أُمورُهُ مُتَيَسِّرةً things were going well for him (*financially*); حالَتُهُ المادّيّةُ غَيْرُ مُتَيَسِّرة his financial situation is precarious; البَثُّ غَيْرُ مُتَيَسِّرٍ حالِيًّا the broadcast is currently unavailable

موسِر A *adj* |مَياسيرُ, موسِرونَ| rich, well-to-do, affluent; الطَبَقات الموسِرة the affluent classes

B *n* |مَياسيرُ, موسِرونَ| wealthy person

مَيْسِر *n* gambling; تَحْريم الخَمْرِ والمَيْسِرِ (Islam) prohibition of alcohol and gambling

مُيَسَّر *adj* facilitated, eased; simplified; قَرْض مُيَسَّر (Econ) soft loan; شُروط مُيَسَّرة (Econ) concessional terms; القِراءة المُيَسَّرة simplified reading materials

honest, uncorrupted 2 [مِقْبَض] handle; يَد السَيْفِ the hilt of a sword; يَد المِطْرَقةِ the grip of a hammer; يَد المِكْنَسةِ the handle of a broom

يَدَويّ *adj* manual, hand (*before n*); يَدَويًّا manually; قُنْبُلة يَدَويّة hand grenade; فَرْز يَدَويّ manual counting/sorting; حِرَف \ أَشْغال يَدَويّة handicrafts; مِكْبَح يَدَويّ handbrake; من صُنْعٍ يَدَويٍّ, يَدَويّ الصُنْعِ handmade; عُبوّة يَدَويّة الصُنْعِ a home-made bomb

يِديشيّ *adj* Yiddish; (اللُغة) اليِديشيّة Yiddish (*language*)

يَرْبوع *n* |يَرابيعُ| (Zool) jerboa (*Dipodidae*); gerbil (*Gerbillus*)

يَراع *n* 1 [قَلَم] (reed) pen 2 (Zool) firefly, glow-worm 3 [جَبان] coward

يَراعة *n* (Mus) clarinet

يَرَقة *n* (Zool) larva; يَرَقات البَعوضِ mosquito larvae; يَرَقات الذُبابِ maggots

يَرَقان A *n* (Med) jaundice; hepatitis; مَرَض اليَرَقانِ jaundice; أُصيبَ باليَرَقانِ to suffer from jaundice

B *n coll* (Zool) larva; caterpillar

يَرْموك *n* (Geog) نَهْر اليَرْموكِ Yarmouk River (*in Jordan*)

يَس *n* سورة يَس Ya Sin (*Sura 36*)

يَسَرَ, يَسُرَ, يَسِرَ *v* |a-u; يَسَر, يُسْر| to be easy

يَسُرَ *v* |u; يُسْر| to be/become easy

يَسِرَ *v* |a; يَسَر| to be/become rich

يَسَّرَ *v* to ease, to facilitate; to simplify; يَسَّرَ انْدِماجَ شَخْصٍ في المُجْتَمَعِ to ease sb's integration into society; اللهُ يُيَسِّرُ God help us

ياسَرَ *v* to be indulgent; to be lenient

تَيَسَّرَ *v* 1 [تَسَهَّلَ] to be easy; to be possible; تَيَسَّرَ عَلَيْهِ \ لَهُ الحَجُّ it was easy for him to perform the hajj 2 [اسْتَعَدَّ] to be prepared, to prepare oneself; تَيَسَّرَ لِلسَفَرِ to prepare oneself for a journey

اسْتَيْسَرَ *v* to become easy

يَسِر *adj* soft (*of water*)

يُسْر *n* 1 [ثَراء] well-being, comfort; wealth; يُسْر ماليّ financial well-being; في اليُسْرِ والعُسْرِ for better or for worse; إنّ بعد

مَيْسَرة *n* [1] [غِنًى] wealth, well-being; أَهْل المَيْسَرةِ people of means [2] [الجِهة اليُسْرى] left side; left flank; port; مَيْسَرة السَّفينةِ the ship's port side; هاجَموا مَيْسَرةَ الجَيْشِ they attacked the army's left flank

مَيْسور *adj* |مَياسيرُ ,مَيْسورونَ| [1] [ثَرِيّ] rich, well-to-do, affluent; عاشَ مَيْسوراً to live in comfort; الطَّبَقات المَيْسورة the affluent classes [2] [سَهْل] easy

يَسوع *n* |dipt| (Chr) Jesus; يَسوع الناصِريّ Jesus of Nazareth

يَسوعيّ [A] *n* Jesuit
[B] *adj* Jesuit; جامِعة يَسوعيّة a Jesuit university

يَشْب *n* (Geol) jade; jasper

يَشْم *n* (Geol) jade

يَشْمَك *n* yashmak (*kind of face veil*)

يَعْسوب *n* see عسب

يَعْقوب *n* |dipt| Yaqub, Jacob (*male given name*)

يافِطة *n* (ME) sign, signboard; banner; poster

يَفَعَ *v* |a; يُفوع ,يَفْع| to have reached puberty, to be an adolescent

أَيْفَعَ *v* to have reached puberty, to be an adolescent

تَيَفَّعَ *v* to have reached puberty; to be an adolescent

يَفْع *n* adolescence

يافِع *n* |يُفْعان ,يَفعة| teenager, youth, adolescent

يَفاع *n* |يُفوع| hill

يَفاعة *n* adolescence, puberty

يَقْطين *n coll* see قطن

يَقِظَ *v* |a; يَقَظ| [1] [صَحا] to wake up [2] [تَنَبَّهَ] to pay attention, to be alert

أَيْقَظَ *v* [1] [أَفاقَ] to wake (up); أَيْقَظَ شَخْصاً to wake sb; أَيْقَظَ شَخْصاً من سُباتِهِ to shake sb out of their lethargy [2] [أَثارَ] to arouse, to awaken; أَيْقَظَ شَهيّةَ شَخْصٍ to awaken sb's appetite; to arouse sb's desire; أَيْقَظَ ضَميرَ شَخْصٍ to awaken sb's conscience; أَيْقَظَ الحَماسَ to arouse enthusiasm

تَيَقَّظَ *v* [1] [صَحا] to wake up [2] [تَنَبَّهَ] to pay attention, to be on one's guard, to be alert

اسْتَيْقَظَ *v* [1] [صَحا] to wake up, to awaken; اسْتَيْقَظَ من النَوْمِ to wake up; اسْتَيْقَظ من حُلْمٍ to wake up from a dream; اسْتَيْقَظَ من سُباتِهِ to be shaken out of one's lethargy; اسْتَيْقَظَ من \ على صَوْتٍ to be awakened by a noise; اسْتَيْقَظَ من \ على كابوسٍ to awaken from a nightmare/to be awakened by a nightmare [2] [تَنَبَّهَ] to be on one's guard, to be alert

يَقِظ *adj* |أَيْقاظ| [1] [مُنْتَبِه] attentive, alert, watchful, observant; حارِس يَقِظ a watchful guard; شَخْص ضَميرُهُ يَقِظٌ a conscientious person; بِضَميرٍ يَقِظٍ conscientiously [2] [صاحٍ] (wide) awake; كانَ يَقِظاً بعد نَوْم عَميقٍ he was awake after a deep sleep

يَقْظان *adj* |dipt; يَقاظى f ;يَقْظى| [1] [صاحٍ] awake [2] [مُنْتَبِه] alert, watchful

يَقْظة ,يَقَظة *n* waking; watchfulness, attention, vigilance; حُلْم يَقْظةٍ daydream; نَوْم اليَقْظة half-asleep, half-awake; تَوَخّى اليَقْظةَ to exercise vigilance, to be vigilant

اسْتيقاظ *n* waking (up); اسْتيقاظ مُبَكِّر waking up early

تَيَقُّظ *n* watchfulness, vigilance; تَيَقُّظ تامّ red alert; تَيَقُّظ دائم eternal vigilance

مُتَيَقِّظ *adj* [1] [مُتَنَبِّه] watchful, alert, vigilant; ظَلَّ \ بَقِيَ مُتَيَقِّظاً to remain vigilant; كانَ مُتَيَقِّظاً للخَطَرِ he was on the alert for danger [2] [صاحٍ] awake, awoken

مُسْتَيْقِظ *adj* awake; بَقِيَ مُسْتَيْقِظاً to stay awake

موقِظ *n sb who wakes people up (e.g. in the army)*

يَقِنَ *v* |a; يَقْن ,يَقين| [1] [ثَبَتَ] to be certain, to be sure [2] [تَحَقَّقَ] to know for sure, to know for certain; to be convinced

أَيْقَنَ *v* to know for certain, to be convinced; أَيْقَنَ شَيْئاً \ بِشَيْءٍ to know sth for certain; أَيْقَنَ أَنَّهُ قادِرٌ على شَيْءٍ to be sure that one is capable of sth

تَيَقَّنَ *v* to know for certain, to be convinced; to ascertain, to make sure; تَيَقَّنَ شَيْئاً \ من شَيْءٍ to know sth for certain; تَيَقَّنَ تَيَقُّناً تامًّا (من شَيْءٍ) to be absolutely convinced (of sth); تَيَقَّنَ من حَقيقةِ الأَمْرِ to ascertain the truth of the matter

اسْتَيْقَنَ *v* to know for certain, to be convinced; اسْتَيْقَنَ أَنَّ ... to be sure that ...; اسْتَيْقَنَ شَيْئاً \ من شَيْءٍ to be sure of sth; اسْتَيْقَنْتُ من صِحّةِ هذه الحَقيقةِ I was convinced of the validity of this fact; اسْتَيْقَنَ أَنَّهُمْ لا يُريدونَ السَلامَ he was positive that they do not want peace

يقين *n* certainty, conviction, sureness; يَقيناً certainly; عَدَم اليَقينِ uncertainty; على يَقينٍ assured, confident; عَلِمَ شَيْئاً عِلْمَ اليَقينِ to know sth for certain, to be convinced of sth; عَلِمَ عِلْمَ اليَقينِ أنّ ... to know for certain that ...; كانَ على يَقينٍ راسِخٍ \ جازِمٍ to be firmly convinced; كانَ على يَقينٍ من أنّ ... to be certain that ...; يُداخِلُنا يَقينٌ بِأَنَّ ... we are convinced that ...; تَزايَدَ عَدَمُ اليَقينِ حول المُسْتَقْبَلِ the uncertainty about the future increased; على دَرَجةٍ عالِيةٍ من اليَقينِ with a large measure of certainty

يَقينيّ *adj* certain, sure, positive; مَعْرِفة يَقينيّة certain knowledge; حَقيقة يَقينيّة an undeniable fact

تَيَقُّن *n* certainty; ascertaining, making sure; زَعَمَ شَيْئاً بِتَيَقُّنٍ to assert sth with certainty; لا تَيَقُّن \ عَدم التَيَقُّنِ uncertainty; من دونِ التَيَقُّنِ من صِحَّتِها without ascertaining its validity

مُتَيَقِّن *adj* certain, positive, convinced; كانَ مُتَيَقِّناً (من) أنّ ... to be convinced that ...

موقِن *adj* certain, convinced; كانَ موقِناً من شَيْءٍ to be certain of sth; كانَ موقِناً أنّ ... to be sure that ...

يَلاّ *excl* come on, hurry up, let's go; يَلاّ بنا! let's go!; يَلاّ يا شَبابُ! come on, guys!

يَمَّمَ *v* to go, to head, to make one's way; to turn; يَمَّمَ صَوْبَ \ شَطْرَ \ نحو مَكانٍ to head towards a place; يَمَّمَ وَجْهَهُ نحو القِبْلةِ he turned towards Mecca *(for the prayer)*

تَيَمَّمَ *v* **1** [للصَلاةِ] *to perform the ritual ablution with sand instead of water* **2** [هَدَفَ] to intend, to aim at

يَمّ *n* |يُموم| sea

يَمام *n coll* |يَمائِمُ| Barbary dove *(Streptopelia risoria); any of several varieties of wild pigeon*

تَيَمُّم *n ritual ablution with sand*

يَمَنَ *v* |u; يُمْن| **1** [حَظَّ] to be lucky **2** [جِهة] to come from the right; to go to the right

يَمُنَ, يَمِنَ *v* |a-u; يُمْن, مَيْمَنة| to be good; to do good; يُمِنَ to be happy, to be blessed

يَمَّنَ *v* **1** [ذَهَبَ جِهةَ اليَمينِ] to go to the right **2** [بَرَّكَ] to bless

تَيَمَّنَ *v* |ب| to call down blessings; to see a good omen; تَيَمَّنَ بِشَخْصٍ \ بِشَيْءٍ to ask for/get a blessing from sb/sth

يُمْن *n* good luck, good fortune, prosperity; اليُمْن والبَرَكة good blessings and fortune; يَوْم يُمْنٍ a lucky day

يَمْنة *n* right side; يَمْنةً (to the) right; مالَ رَأْسهُ يَمْنةً he turned his head to the right

يَمَني **A** *adj* Yemeni, Yemenite; الجُمْهوريّة العَرَبيّة اليَمَنيّة the Yemen Arab Republic

B *n* a Yemenite

يَمين *n* |f| **1** [جهة] right (side); يَميناً to/at/on the right; يَميناً وَشِمالاً to the right and left; يَمينَ (على يمينِ) شَيْءٍ \ شَخصٍ to the right of sth/sb; إلى اليَمينِ to the right; الْتَزَمَ اليَمينَ to keep to the right; الأَوْلَوِيّةُ لليَمينِ traffic from the right has right of way; تَوَجَّهَ \ انْعَطَفَ إلى اليَمينِ to turn (to the) right; ما مَلَكَتْ يَمينهُ his possessions **2** [قَسَم] |أَيْمُن, أَيْمان| oath; يَمين غَليظة a solemn oath; يَمين كاذِبة \ غَموس perjury; أَدّى \ حَلَفَ يَميناً to take/swear an oath; نَقَضَ يَمينهُ, حَنِثَ ب \ في يَمينِهِ to break one's oath; يَمين الوَلاءِ والإِخْلاصِ the oath of allegiance; البَيِّنة على مَنْ ادَّعى واليَمينُ على مَنْ أَنْكَرَ (Law) the plaintiff provides evidence and the defendant takes the oath **3** (Pol) اليَمين the Right; اليَمين المُتَطَرِّف \ المُتَشَدِّد the extreme right; تَلَقَّوْا تَأْييداً من اليَمينِ they were supported by the right (wing)

يَميني *adj* (Pol) right-wing; حِزْب \ سِياسيّ يَمينيّ a right-wing party/politician; يَمينيّ مُتَطَرِّف extreme right-wing

اليَمَن *n* (Geog) Yemen

أَيْمَن *adj* |dipt| **1** [في الجانِبِ اليَمينِ] right; الرُكْبة اليُمْنى \ الكاحِل الأَيْمَن the right knee/ankle; في الدُرْجِ الأَيْمَنِ in the right-hand drawer; كَتَبَ بِيَدِهِ اليُمْنى to write with one's right hand **2** [ذو اليُمْن] lucky, blessed

تَيَمُّن *n* blessing; سُمِّيَ تَيَمُّناً بِاسْمِ شَخْصٍ to be named in honour of sb

مُيَمَّن *adj* auspicious

مَيْمَنة *n* right side; right wing; starboard

‹ **اليوتوپيا ,يوتوبِيا ,اليوطوبيا ,يوطوبيا** *n* Utopia

‹ **يوغا** *n* yoga; مارَس اليوغا to practise yoga

‹ **يوغوسْلافيّ** *adj, n* Yugoslav

يوغوسْلافِيا *n* Yugoslavia; يوغوسْلافِيا السابِقة the former Yugoslavia

‹ **يوكا** *n* yucca (*Yucca*)

‹ **يوكالِبْتُس** *n* see أوكالِبْتوس

‹ **يولِيو** *n* (Mor, Egypt, Gulf) July

‹ **يولْيوز** *n* (Mor) July

‹ **يَوْم** *n* |أيّام| ⓵ [أَرْبَع وَعِشْرونَ ساعةً] day; twenty-four hours; يَوْم كَبيس leap day; يَوْم دِراسيّ \ مَدْرَسيّ school day; يَوْم عيدٍ holiday; اليَوْم الآخِر ,يَوْم القِيامةِ \ الدينِ (Relig) Judgement Day; اليَوْمَ today; يَوْمَهُ \ يَوْمَها then, at that time; كانَ يَوْمَها في الخارِجِ he was abroad at the time; في أيّامِ العَمَلِ on weekdays, on working days; مع الأَيّامِ in the course of time; من يَوْمٍ لآخَرَ ,بين يَوْمٍ وَلَيْلةٍ from one day to the next; يَوْماً بعد يَوْم day after day; في يَوْمٍ من الأيّامِ ,ذاتَ يَوْمٍ ,في يَوْمٍ ما ,يَوْماً ما one day, some day, once upon a time; سَوْفَ نَعودُ يَوْماً ما إلى أَرْضِنا one day we will return to our land; كُلّ يَوْم every day; مَرّةً \ مَرَّتَيْنِ في اليَوْمِ once/twice a day; 24 ساعةً في اليَوْمِ 24 hours per day; يَوْمَ (أنْ) ... on the day (that) ...; يَوْمَ الكارِثةِ (on) the day of the disaster; يَوْمَ أنْ قابَلْتُ الأُسْتاذَ on the day (that) I met the professor; أَصْبَحَتْ أُمّي مَريضةً يَوْمَ غادَرْتُها my mother fell ill the day I left her; من اليَوْمِ from now on; لليَوْمِ الثاني على التَوالي for the second day in a row ⓶ [عَصْر] day, age; أيّامَ ... in the days of ..., during ...; حَصَلَ ذلك أيّامَ السُلْطانِ عَبْدِ الحَميدِ that happened in the days of Sultan Abdelhamid; اليَوْمَ today, nowadays; كانَ ابْنَ اليَوْمِ to be modern; في يَوْمِنا هذا \ أيّامِنا هذه nowadays, these days; أيّام العَرَبِ Days of the Arabs (*legendary battles between pre-Islamic Arab tribes, as well as the literary genre of epic martial prose narrating those battles*)

يَوْمَئِذٍ *adv* then, (on) that day; كانَ يَوْمَئِذٍ جالِساً في مَكْتَبِهِ he sat in his office that day

يَوْمَذاكَ *adv* then, (on) that day; يَوْمَذاكَ لم تَكُنْ هُناكَ حُدودٌ there weren't any borders then

مَيْمون *adj* fortunate, lucky; blessed; العَهْد المَيْمون the prosperous period (*of sb's reign*); على الطائِرِ المَيْمونِ have a good journey

‹ **يَنايِر** *n* (Mor, Egypt, Gulf) January

‹ **يَنْبوع** *n* see نبع

‹ **يَنْسون** *n* see يانِسون

‹ **يَنَعَ** *v* |a-i; يَنْع ,يُنْع ,يُنوع| to be ripe, to ripen; to grow up

أَيْنَعَ *v* to be ripe, to ripen; to grow up; قد أَيْنَعَتْ ثِمارُها its fruit has ripened; (fig) it is ripe for the taking

يانِع *adj* |يُنْع| ripe, mature; ثِمار يانِعة ripe fruit; شاب \ صَبيّة يانِع(ة) a mature youth/girl

‹ **يَنّ** *n* yen; يَنّ يابانيّ Japanese yen

‹ **يَهود** *n* see هود

‹ **يَهْوَه** *n* Yahweh, Jehova (*name of God in the Hebrew Bible*)

‹ **يُوان** *n* yuan (*Chinese currency*)

‹ **يوبيل** *n* jubilee, anniversary; احْتَفَلَ بِيوبيل to celebrate an anniversary; اليوبيل الخامِس والعِشْرونَ \ الفِضّيّ لِتَأْسيسِ شَيْءٍ the 25th/silver anniversary of the founding of sth; يوبيل ذَهَبيّ a golden jubilee; يوبيل المَلِكةِ الماسيّ the Queen's diamond jubilee

‹ **يوتا** *n* Utah (*US state*)

‹ **يوحَنّا** *n* |m| Yuhanna, John (*Christian male given name*)

‹ **يود** *n* (Chem) iodine; صِبْغة اليودِ tincture of iodine

‹ **يورانِيوم ,أورانِيوم** *n* uranium; يورانِيوم مُخَصَّب enriched uranium; يورانِيوم مُسْتَنْفَد \ مُنَضَّب depleted uranium; خامات اليورانيوم uranium ore; تَخْصيب اليورانِيوم uranium enrichment

‹ **يورو ,أورو** *n* euro; عَجْز قَدْرُهُ ثَلاثُمِائةِ أَلْفِ يورو a deficit of 300,000 euros; دَفَعَ 5 يورو إضافيّةً to pay another 5 euros

‹ **يوسُف** *n* |dipt| Yusuf, Joseph (*male given name*); سورة يوسُف Joseph (*Sura 12*); هو بَريءٌ بَراءةَ الذِئْبِ من دَمِ يوسُفَ he is completely innocent

(Idiom) يوسُف أَفَنْدي mandarin, tangerine, clementine (*Citrus reticulata*)

يوسُفيّ *n* mandarin, tangerine, clementine (*Citrus reticulata*)

يَوْميّ *adj* daily; الحَياة \ الرَّتابة اليَوْميّة daily life/routine; صَحيفة \ جَريدة يَوْميّة daily paper; للاسْتِعْمالِ اليَوْميِّ for daily use; الواقِع اليَوْميّ everyday reality; اتِّصالات شِبْه يَوْميّة near-daily contact

يَوْميّات *n pl* diary; journal; دَفْتَر اليَوْميّاتِ log, logbook; كَتَبَ \ ذَكَرَ شَيْئاً في يَوْميّاتِهِ to write sth in one's diary

يَوْميّة *n* 1 [روزْنامة] calendar; diary, journal; accounts book, ledger 2 [أُجْرة] a day's wages

مُياوَم A *adj* per diem, daily, day (*before n*)

B *n* day laborer

يوناني A *adj* |يونان, يونانيّونَ| Greek; (اللُغة) اليونانيّة Greek (*language*)

B *n* |يونان, يونانيّونَ| Greek (*person*)

اليونان *n* |f| (Geog) Greece; اليونان القَديمة ancient Greece

يونُس *n* |dipt| Yunus, Jonah (*male given name*); سورة يونُس Jonah (*Sura 10*)

يونِسْكو *n* |f| UNESCO (*United Nations Educational, Scientific and Cultural Organization*)

يونيسِف *n* |f| UNICEF (*United Nations Children's Fund*)

يونِيو *n* (Mor, Egypt, Gulf) June; في (شَهْرِ) يونْيو in June

يويو *n* yo-yo

English irregular verbs

قائمة الأفعال الشاذة في اللغة الإنجليزية

infinitive مصدر	past tense الماضي	past participle المفعول
arise	arose	arisen
awake	awoke	awoken
babysit	babysat	babysat
be	*was/were	been
bear	bore	borne
beat	beat	beaten
become	became	become
befall	befell	befallen
beget	begot, *old use* begat	begotten
begin	began	begun
behold	beheld	beheld
bend	bent	bent
beseech	besought, beseeched	besought, beseeched
beset	beset	beset
bet	bet	bet
bid[1]	bid	bid
bid[2]	*bid, bade,	*bid, bidden
bind	bound	bound
bite	bit	bitten
bleed	bled	bled
blow	blew	blown
break	broke	broken
breed	bred	bred
bring	brought	brought
broadcast	broadcast, broadcasted	broadcast, broadcasted
browbeat	browbeat	browbeaten
build	built	built
burn	burned, *Brit* burnt	burned, *Brit* burnt
burst	burst	burst
bust	bust, busted	bust, busted
buy	bought	bought
cast	cast	cast
catch	caught	caught
choose	chose	chosen
cling	clung	clung
come	came	come
cost	*cost, costed	*cost, costed
creep	crept	crept
cut	cut	cut
deal	dealt	dealt
dig	dug	dug
dive	dived, *Amer* dove	dived
do	did	done
draw	drew	drawn
dream	dreamed, *Brit* dreamt	dreamed, *Brit* dreamt
drink	drank	drunk
drive	drove	driven
dwell	dwelt, dwelled	dwelt, dwelled
eat	ate	eaten
fall	fell	fallen
feed	fed	fed
feel	felt	felt
fight	fought	fought
find	found	found
fit	fitted, *Amer* fit	fitted, *Amer* fit
flee	fled	fled

infinitive مصدر	past tense الماضي	past participle المفعول
fling	flung	flung
fly	flew	flown
forbid	forbade, forbad	forbidden
forecast	forecast, forecasted	forecast, forecasted
foresee	foresaw	foreseen
foretell	foretold	foretold
forget	forgot	forgotten
forgive	forgave	forgiven
forego	forwent	foregone
forsake	forsook	forsaken
freeze	froze	frozen
get	got	got, *Amer* gotten
give	gave	given
go	went	gone
grind	ground	ground
grow	grew	grown
hang	*hung, hanged	*hung, hanged
have	had	had
hear	heard	heard
heave	*heaved, hove	*heaved, hove
hide	hid	hidden
hit	hit	hit
hold	held	held
hurt	hurt	hurt
inlay	inlaid	inlaid
input	input, inputted	input, inputted
keep	kept	kept
kneel	knelt, kneeled	knelt, kneeled
knit	knitted, knit	knitted, knit
know	knew	known
lay	laid	laid
lead	led	led
lean	leaned, *Brit* leant	leaned, *Brit* leant
leap	leaped, *Brit* leapt	leaped, *Brit* leapt
learn	learned, *Brit* learnt	learned, *Brit* learnt
leave	left	left
lend	lent	lent
let	let	let
lie	lay	lain
light	lit, lighted	lit, lighted
lose	lost	lost
make	made	made
mean	meant	meant
meet	met	met
mishear	misheard	misheard
mislay	mislaid	mislaid
mislead	misled	misled
misread	misread	misread
mistake	mistook	mistaken
misunderstand	misunderstood	misunderstood
mow	mowed	mowed, mown
offset	offset	offset
outdo	outdid	outdone
overcome	overcame	overcome
overdo	overdid	overdone
overdraw	overdrew	overdrawn

infinitive مصدر	past tense الماضي	past participle المفعول
overhang	overhung	overhung
overhear	overheard	overheard
override	overrode	overridden
overrun	overran	overrun
oversee	oversaw	overseen
overshoot	overshot	overshot
oversleep	overslept	overslept
overtake	overtook	overtaken
overthrow	overthrew	overthrown
pay	paid	paid
plead	pleaded, *Amer* pled	pleaded, *Amer* pled
preset	preset	preset
proofread	proofread	proofread
prove	proved	proved, proven
put	put	put
quit	quit	quit
read	read	read
rebuild	rebuilt	rebuilt
recast	recast	recast
redo	redid	redone
remake	remade	remade
repay	repaid	repaid
reset	reset	reset
resit	resat	resat
retake	retook	retaken
rewind	rewound	rewound
rewrite	rewrote	rewritten
rid	rid	rid
ride	rode	ridden
ring	rang	rung
rise	rose	risen
run	ran	run
saw	sawed	sawn *Brit*, sawed *Amer*
say	said	said
see	saw	seen
seek	sought	sought
sell	sold	sold
send	sent	sent
set	set	set
sew	sewed	sewed, sewn
shake	shook	shaken
shed	shed	shed
shine	*shone, shined	*shone, shined
shoe	shod	shod
shoot	shot	shot
show	showed	shown, showed
shrink	shrank	shrunk, shrunken
shut	shut	shut
sing	sang	sung
sink	sank	sunk
sit	sat	sat
slay	slew	slain
sleep	slept	slept
slide	slid	slid
sling	slung	slung
slink	slunk	slunk
slit	slit	slit
smell	smelled, *Brit* smelt	smelled, *Brit* smelt
sow	sowed	sown, sowed
speak	spoke	spoken
speed	*sped, speeded	*sped, speeded
spell	spelled, *Brit* spelt	spelled, *Brit* spelt
spend	spent	spent
spill	spilt, spilled	spilt, spilled
spin	spun	spun
spit	spat, *Amer* spit	spat, *Amer* spit
split	split	split
spoil	spoiled, *Brit* spoilt	spoiled, *Brit* spoilt
spread	spread	spread
spring	sprang, sprung	sprung
stand	stood	stood
steal	stole	stolen
stick	stuck	stuck
sting	stung	stung
stink	stank, stunk	stunk
strew	strewed	strewed, strewn
stride	strode	stridden
strike	struck	struck
string	strung	strung
strive	strove, strived	striven, strived
swear	swore	sworn
sweep	swept	swept
swell	swelled	swollen, swelled
swim	swam	swum
swing	swung	swung
take	took	taken
teach	taught	taught
tear	tore	torn
tell	told	told
think	thought	thought
thrive	throve, thrived	thriven, thrived
throw	threw	thrown
thrust	thrust	thrust
tread	trod	trodden, trod
typecast	typecast	typecast
typeset	typeset	typeset
undercut	undercut	undercut
undergo	underwent	undergone
underlie	underlay	underlain
understand	understood	understood
undertake	undertook	undertaken
underwrite	underwrote	underwritten
undo	undid	undone
unwind	unwound	unwound
uphold	upheld	upheld
upset	upset	upset
wake	woke	woken
waylay	waylaid	waylaid
wear	wore	worn
weave	wove	woven
wed	wedded, wed	wedded, wed
weep	wept	wept
wet	wet, wetted	wet, wetted
win	won	won
wind	wound	wound
withdraw	withdrew	withdrawn
withhold	withheld	withheld
withstand	withstood	withstood
wring	wrung	wrung
write	wrote	written

* used according to context متعلق بسياق الكلام

Conjugations of Arabic verbs

تصريفات الأفعال العربية

Contents

Form I - sound فعل

Imperative		Jussive	Subjunctive	Indicative	Perfect	
	Active	يَفْعَلْ	يَفْعَلَ	يَفْعَلُ	فَعَلَ	هو
		تَفْعَلْ	تَفْعَلَ	تَفْعَلُ	فَعَلَتْ	هي
افْعَلْ		تَفْعَلْ	تَفْعَلَ	تَفْعَلُ	فَعَلْتَ	أنتَ
افْعَلي		تَفْعَلي	تَفْعَلي	تَفْعَلينَ	فَعَلْتِ	أنتِ
		أَفْعَلْ	أَفْعَلَ	أَفْعَلُ	فَعَلْتُ	أنا
		يَفْعَلا	يَفْعَلا	يَفْعَلانِ	فَعَلا	هما-m
		تَفْعَلا	تَفْعَلا	تَفْعَلانِ	فَعَلَتا	هما-f
افْعَلا		تَفْعَلا	تَفْعَلا	تَفْعَلانِ	فَعَلْتُما	أنتما
		يَفْعَلوا	يَفْعَلوا	يَفْعَلونَ	فَعَلوا	هم
		يَفْعَلْنَ	يَفْعَلْنَ	يَفْعَلْنَ	فَعَلْنَ	هنّ
افْعَلوا		تَفْعَلوا	تَفْعَلوا	تَفْعَلونَ	فَعَلْتُمْ	أنتم
افْعَلْنَ		تَفْعَلْنَ	تَفْعَلْنَ	تَفْعَلْنَ	فَعَلْتُنَّ	أنتنّ
		نَفْعَلْ	نَفْعَلَ	نَفْعَلُ	فَعَلْنا	نحن
	Passive	يُفْعَلْ	يُفْعَلَ	يُفْعَلُ	فُعِلَ	هو
				PP مَفْعول	AP فاعِل	

Form I - R2=R3 مرّ

Imperative		Jussive	Subjunctive	Indicative	Perfect	
	Active	يَمْرُرْ	يَمُرَّ	يَمُرُّ	مَرَّ	هو
		تَمْرُرْ	تَمُرَّ	تَمُرُّ	مَرَّتْ	هي
اُمْرُرْ		تَمْرُرْ	تَمُرَّ	تَمُرُّ	مَرَرْتَ	أنتَ
مُرّي		تَمُرّي	تَمُرّي	تَمُرّين	مَرَرْتِ	أنتِ
		أَمْرُرْ	أَمُرَّ	أَمُرُّ	مَرَرْتُ	أنا
		يَمُرّا	يَمُرّا	يَمُرّانِ	مَرّا	هما-m
		تَمُرّا	تَمُرّا	تَمُرّانِ	مَرَّتا	هما-f
مُرّا		تَمُرّا	تَمُرّا	تَمُرّانِ	مَرَرْتُما	أنتما
		يَمُرّوا	يَمُرّوا	يَمُرّون	مَرّوا	هم
		يَمْرُرْنَ	يَمْرُرْنَ	يَمْرُرْنَ	مَرَرْنَ	هنّ
مُرّوا		تَمُرّوا	تَمُرّوا	تَمُرّون	مَرَرْتُمْ	أنتم
اُمْرُرْنَ		تَمْرُرْنَ	تَمْرُرْنَ	تَمْرُرْنَ	مَرَرْتُنَّ	أنتنّ
		نَمْرُرْ	نَمُرَّ	نَمُرُّ	مَرَرْنا	نحن
	Passive	يُمْرَرْ	يُمَرَّ	يُمَرُّ	مُرَّ	هو
				PP مَمْرور	AP مارّ	

Form I - R1=و: وصل

Imperative		Jussive	Subjunctive	Indicative	Perfect	
	Active	يَصِلْ	يَصِلَ	يَصِلُ	وَصَلَ	هو
		تَصِلْ	تَصِلَ	تَصِلُ	وَصَلَتْ	هي
صِلْ		تَصِلْ	تَصِلَ	تَصِلُ	وَصَلْتَ	أنتَ
صِلي		تَصِلي	تَصِلي	تَصِلينَ	وَصَلْتِ	أنتِ
		أَصِلْ	أَصِلَ	أَصِلُ	وَصَلْتُ	أنا
		يَصِلا	يَصِلا	يَصِلانِ	وَصَلا	هما-m
		تَصِلا	تَصِلا	تَصِلانِ	وَصَلَتا	هما-f
صِلا		تَصِلا	تَصِلا	تَصِلانِ	وَصَلْتُما	أنتما
		يَصِلوا	يَصِلوا	يَصِلونَ	وَصَلوا	هم
		يَصِلْنَ	يَصِلْنَ	يَصِلْنَ	وَصَلْنَ	هنّ
صِلوا		تَصِلوا	تَصِلوا	تَصِلونَ	وَصَلْتُمْ	أنتم
صِلْنَ		تَصِلْنَ	تَصِلْنَ	تَصِلْنَ	وَصَلْتُنَّ	أنتنّ
		نَصِلْ	نَصِلَ	نَصِلُ	وَصَلْنا	نحن
	Passive	يوصَلْ	يوصَلَ	يوصَلُ	وُصِلَ	
			PP مَوْصول		AP واصِل	

Form I - R1=ي: يسر

Imperative		Jussive	Subjunctive	Indicative	Perfect	
	Active	يَيْسَرْ	يَيْسَرَ	يَيْسَرُ	يَسِرَ	هو
		تَيْسَرْ	تَيْسَرَ	تَيْسَرُ	يَسِرَتْ	هي
ايسَرْ		تَيْسَرْ	تَيْسَرَ	تَيْسَرُ	يَسِرْتَ	أنتَ
ايسَري		تَيْسَري	تَيْسَري	تَيْسَرينَ	يَسِرْتِ	أنتِ
		أَيْسَرْ	أَيْسَرَ	أَيْسَرُ	يَسِرْتُ	أنا
		يَيْسَرا	يَيْسَرا	يَيْسَرانِ	يَسِرا	هما-m
		تَيْسَرا	تَيْسَرا	تَيْسَرانِ	يَسِرَتا	هما-f
ايسَرا		تَيْسَرا	تَيْسَرا	تَيْسَرانِ	يَسِرْتُما	أنتما
		يَيْسَروا	يَيْسَروا	يَيْسَرونَ	يَسِروا	هم
		يَيْسَرْنَ	يَيْسَرْنَ	يَيْسَرْنَ	يَسِرْنَ	هنّ
ايسَروا		تَيْسَروا	تَيْسَروا	تَيْسَرونَ	يَسِرْتُمْ	أنتم
ايسَرْنَ		تَيْسَرْنَ	تَيْسَرْنَ	تَيْسَرْنَ	يَسِرْتُنَّ	أنتنّ
		نَيْسَرْ	نَيْسَرَ	نَيْسَرُ	يَسِرْنا	نحن
	Passive	يوسَرْ	يوسَرَ	يوسَرُ	يُسِرَ	
			PP مَيْسور		AP ياسِر	

Form I - R2=و, imperf with عاد :و

Imperative		Jussive	Subjunctive	Indicative	Perfect	
	Active	يَعُدْ	يَعودَ	يَعودُ	عادَ	هو
		تَعُدْ	تَعودَ	تَعودُ	عادَتْ	هي
عُدْ		تَعُدْ	تَعودَ	تَعودُ	عُدْتَ	أنتَ
عودي		تَعودي	تَعودي	تَعودينَ	عُدْتِ	أنتِ
		أَعُدْ	أَعودَ	أَعودُ	عُدْتُ	أنا
		يَعودا	يَعودا	يَعودانِ	عادا	هما-m
		تَعودا	تَعودا	تَعودانِ	عادَتا	هما-f
عودا		تَعودا	تَعودا	تَعودانِ	عُدْتُما	أنتما
		يَعودوا	يَعودوا	يَعودونَ	عادوا	هم
		يَعُدْنَ	يَعُدْنَ	يَعُدْنَ	عُدْنَ	هنّ
عودوا		تَعودوا	تَعودوا	تَعودونَ	عُدْتُمْ	أنتم
عُدْنَ		تَعُدْنَ	تَعُدْنَ	تَعُدْنَ	عُدْتُنَّ	أنتنّ
		نَعُدْ	نَعودَ	نَعودُ	عُدْنا	نحن
	Passive	يُعَدْ	يُعادَ	يُعادُ	عيدَ	هو
				PP مَعود	AP عائِد	

Form I - R2=و\ي, imperf with نام :ا

Imperative		Jussive	Subjunctive	Indicative	Perfect	
	Active	يَنَمْ	يَنامَ	يَنامُ	نامَ	هو
		تَنَمْ	تَنامَ	تَنامُ	نامَتْ	هي
نَمْ		تَنَمْ	تَنامَ	تَنامُ	نِمْتَ	أنتَ
نامي		تَنامي	تَنامي	تَنامينَ	نِمْتِ	أنتِ
		أَنَمْ	أَنامَ	أَنامُ	نِمْتُ	أنا
		يَناما	يَناما	يَنامانِ	ناما	هما-m
		تَناما	تَناما	تَنامانِ	نامَتا	هما-f
ناما		تَناما	تَناما	تَنامانِ	نِمْتُما	أنتما
		يَناموا	يَناموا	يَنامونَ	ناموا	هم
		يَنَمْنَ	يَنَمْنَ	يَنَمْنَ	نِمْنَ	هنّ
ناموا		تَناموا	تَناموا	تَنامونَ	نِمْتُمْ	أنتم
نَمْنَ		تَنَمْنَ	تَنَمْنَ	تَنَمْنَ	نِمْتُنَّ	أنتنّ
		نَنَمْ	نَنامَ	نَنامُ	نِمْنا	نحن
	Passive	يُنَمْ	يُنامَ	يُنامُ	نيمَ	هو
				PP مَنوم	AP نائِم	

Form I - R2=ي, imperf with باع :ي

Imperative		Jussive	Subjunctive	Indicative	Perfect	
	Active	يَبعْ	يَبيعَ	يَبيعُ	باعَ	هو
		تَبعْ	تَبيعَ	تَبيعُ	باعَتْ	هي
بِعْ		تَبعْ	تَبيعَ	تَبيعُ	بِعْتَ	أنتَ
بيعي		تَبيعي	تَبيعي	تَبيعينَ	بِعْتِ	أنتِ
		أَبعْ	أَبيعَ	أَبيعُ	بِعْتُ	أنا
		يَبيعا	يَبيعا	يَبيعانِ	باعا	هما-m
		تَبيعا	تَبيعا	تَبيعانِ	باعَتا	هما-f
بيعا		تَبيعا	تَبيعا	تَبيعانِ	بِعْتُما	أنتما
		يَبيعوا	يَبيعوا	يَبيعونَ	باعوا	هم
		يَبِعْنَ	يَبِعْنَ	يَبِعْنَ	بِعْنَ	هنّ
بيعوا		تَبيعوا	تَبيعوا	تَبيعونَ	بِعْتُمْ	أنتم
بِعْنَ		تَبِعْنَ	تَبِعْنَ	تَبِعْنَ	بِعْتُنَّ	أنتنّ
		نَبعْ	نَبيعَ	نَبيعُ	بِعْنا	نحن
	Passive	يُبَعْ	يُباعَ	يُباعُ	بيعَ	هو

	PP	AP
	مَبيع	بائِع

Form I - R3=و: دعا

Imperative		Jussive	Subjunctive	Indicative	Perfect	
	Active	يَدْعُ	يَدْعُوَ	يَدْعو	دَعا	هو
		تَدْعُ	تَدْعُوَ	تَدْعو	دَعَتْ	هي
اُدْعُ		تَدْعُ	تَدْعُوَ	تَدْعو	دَعَوْتَ	أنتَ
اُدْعي		تَدْعي	تَدْعي	تَدْعينَ	دَعَوْتِ	أنتِ
		أَدْعُ	أَدْعُوَ	أَدْعو	دَعَوْتُ	أنا
		يَدْعُوا	يَدْعُوا	يَدْعُوانِ	دَعَوا	هما-m
		تَدْعُوا	تَدْعُوا	تَدْعُوانِ	دَعَتا	هما-f
اُدْعُوا		تَدْعُوا	تَدْعُوا	تَدْعُوانِ	دَعَوْتُما	أنتما
		يَدْعوا	يَدْعوا	يَدْعونَ	دَعَوْا	هم
		يَدْعونَ	يَدْعونَ	يَدْعونَ	دَعَوْنَ	هنّ
اُدْعوا		تَدْعوا	تَدْعوا	تَدْعونَ	دَعَوْتُمْ	أنتم
اُدْعونَ		تَدْعونَ	تَدْعونَ	تَدْعونَ	دَعَوْتُنَّ	أنتنّ
		نَدْعُ	نَدْعُوَ	نَدْعو	دَعَوْنا	نحن
	Passive	يُدْعَ	يُدْعى	يُدْعى	دُعِيَ	هو

	PP	AP
	مَدْعوّ	داعٍ

Form I - R3=ي, perf ends in مضى :ى

Imperative		Jussive	Subjunctive	Indicative	Perfect	
	Active	يَمْضِ	يَمْضِيَ	يَمْضي	مَضى	هو
		تَمْضِ	تَمْضِيَ	تَمْضي	مَضَتْ	هي
امْضِ		تَمْضِ	تَمْضِيَ	تَمْضي	مَضَيْتَ	أنتَ
امْضي		تَمْضي	تَمْضي	تَمْضينَ	مَضَيْتِ	أنتِ
		أَمْضِ	أَمْضِيَ	أَمْضي	مَضَيْتُ	أنا
		يَمْضِيا	يَمْضِيا	يَمْضِيانِ	مَضَيا	m-هما
		تَمْضِيا	تَمْضِيا	تَمْضِيانِ	مَضَتا	f-هما
امْضِيا		تَمْضِيا	تَمْضِيا	تَمْضِيانِ	مَضَيْتُما	أنتما
		يَمْضوا	يَمْضوا	يَمْضونَ	مَضَوْا	هم
		يَمْضينَ	يَمْضينَ	يَمْضينَ	مَضَيْنَ	هنّ
امْضوا		تَمْضوا	تَمْضوا	تَمْضونَ	مَضَيْتُمْ	أنتم
امْضينَ		تَمْضينَ	تَمْضينَ	تَمْضينَ	مَضَيْتُنَّ	أنتنّ
		نَمْضِ	نَمْضِيَ	نَمْضي	مَضَيْنا	نحن
	Passive	يُمْضَ	يُمْضى	يُمْضى	مُضِيَ	هو
				PP مَمْضيّ	AP ماضٍ	

Form I - R3=ي, perf ends in بقي :ي

Imperative		Jussive	Subjunctive	Indicative	Perfect	
	Active	يَبْقَ	يَبْقى	يَبْقى	بَقِيَ	هو
		تَبْقَ	تَبْقى	تَبْقى	بَقِيَتْ	هي
ابْقَ		تَبْقَ	تَبْقى	تَبْقى	بَقيتَ	أنتَ
ابْقَيْ		تَبْقَيْ	تَبْقَيْ	تَبْقَيْنَ	بَقيتِ	أنتِ
		أَبْقَ	أَبْقى	أَبْقى	بَقيتُ	أنا
		يَبْقَيا	يَبْقَيا	يَبْقَيانِ	بَقِيا	m-هما
		تَبْقَيا	تَبْقَيا	تَبْقَيانِ	بَقِيَتا	f-هما
ابْقَيا		تَبْقَيا	تَبْقَيا	تَبْقَيانِ	بَقيتُما	أنتما
		يَبْقَوْا	يَبْقَوْا	يَبْقَوْنَ	بَقوا	هم
		يَبْقَيْنَ	يَبْقَيْنَ	يَبْقَيْنَ	بَقينَ	هنّ
ابْقَوْا		تَبْقَوْا	تَبْقَوْا	تَبْقَوْنَ	بَقيتُمْ	أنتم
ابْقَيْنَ		تَبْقَيْنَ	تَبْقَيْنَ	تَبْقَيْنَ	بَقيتُنَّ	أنتنّ
		نَبْقَ	نَبْقى	نَبْقى	بَقينا	نحن
	Passive	يُبْقَ	يُبْقى	يُبْقى	بُقِيَ	هو
				PP مَبْقيّ	AP باقٍ	

Form I - R1=ء: أمر

Imperative		Jussive	Subjunctive	Indicative	Perfect	
	Active	يَأْمُرْ	يَأْمُرَ	يَأْمُرُ	أَمَرَ	هو
		تَأْمُرْ	تَأْمُرَ	تَأْمُرُ	أَمَرَتْ	هي
مُرْ		تَأْمُرْ	تَأْمُرَ	تَأْمُرُ	أَمَرْتَ	أنتَ
مُري		تَأْمُري	تَأْمُري	تَأْمُرينَ	أَمَرْتِ	أنتِ
		آمُرْ	آمُرَ	آمُرُ	أَمَرْتُ	أنا
		يَأْمُرا	يَأْمُرا	يَأْمُرانِ	أَمَرا	هما-m
		تَأْمُرا	تَأْمُرا	تَأْمُرانِ	أَمَرَتا	هما-f
مُرا		تَأْمُرا	تَأْمُرا	تَأْمُرانِ	أَمَرْتُما	أنتما
		يَأْمُروا	يَأْمُروا	يَأْمُرونَ	أَمَروا	هم
		يَأْمُرْنَ	يَأْمُرْنَ	يَأْمُرْنَ	أَمَرْنَ	هنّ
مُروا		تَأْمُروا	تَأْمُروا	تَأْمُرونَ	أَمَرْتُمْ	أنتم
مُرْنَ		تَأْمُرْنَ	تَأْمُرْنَ	تَأْمُرْنَ	أَمَرْتُنَّ	أنتنّ
		نَأْمُرْ	نَأْمُرَ	نَأْمُرُ	أَمَرْنا	نحن
	Passive	يُؤْمَرْ	يُؤْمَرَ	يُؤْمَرُ	أُمِرَ	هو

	PP	AP
	مَأْمور	آمِر

Form I - R2=ء: سأل

Imperative		Jussive	Subjunctive	Indicative	Perfect	
	Active	يَسْأَلْ	يَسْأَلَ	يَسْأَلُ	سَأَلَ	هو
		تَسْأَلْ	تَسْأَلَ	تَسْأَلُ	سَأَلَتْ	هي
اسْأَلْ		تَسْأَلْ	تَسْأَلَ	تَسْأَلُ	سَأَلْتَ	أنتَ
اسْأَلي		تَسْأَلي	تَسْأَلي	تَسْأَلينَ	سَأَلْتِ	أنتِ
		أَسْأَلْ	أَسْأَلَ	أَسْأَلُ	سَأَلْتُ	أنا
		يَسْأَلا	يَسْأَلا	يَسْأَلانِ	سَأَلا	هما-m
		تَسْأَلا	تَسْأَلا	تَسْأَلانِ	سَأَلَتا	هما-f
اسْأَلا		تَسْأَلا	تَسْأَلا	تَسْأَلانِ	سَأَلْتُما	أنتما
		يَسْأَلوا	يَسْأَلوا	يَسْأَلونَ	سَأَلوا	هم
		يَسْأَلْنَ	يَسْأَلْنَ	يَسْأَلْنَ	سَأَلْنَ	هنّ
اسْأَلوا		تَسْأَلوا	تَسْأَلوا	تَسْأَلونَ	سَأَلْتُمْ	أنتم
اسْأَلْنَ		تَسْأَلْنَ	تَسْأَلْنَ	تَسْأَلْنَ	سَأَلْتُنَّ	أنتنّ
		نَسْأَلْ	نَسْأَلَ	نَسْأَلُ	سَأَلْنا	نحن
	Passive	يُسْأَلْ	يُسْأَلَ	يُسْأَلُ	سُئِلَ	هو

	PP	AP
	مَسْؤول	سائِل

Form I - R3=ء: بدأ

Imperative		Jussive	Subjunctive	Indicative	Perfect	
	Active	يَبْدَأْ	يَبْدَأَ	يَبْدَأُ	بَدَأَ	هو
		تَبْدَأْ	تَبْدَأَ	تَبْدَأُ	بَدَأَتْ	هي
ابْدَأْ		تَبْدَأْ	تَبْدَأَ	تَبْدَأُ	بَدَأْتَ	أنتَ
ابْدَئي		تَبْدَئي	تَبْدَئي	تَبْدَئينَ	بَدَأْتِ	أنتِ
		أَبْدَأْ	أَبْدَأَ	أَبْدَأُ	بَدَأْتُ	أنا
		يَبْدَآ	يَبْدَآ	يَبْدَآنِ	بَدَآ	m-هما
		تَبْدَآ	تَبْدَآ	تَبْدَآنِ	بَدَأَتا	f-هما
ابْدَآ		تَبْدَآ	تَبْدَآ	تَبْدَآنِ	بَدَأْتُما	أنتما
		يَبْدَؤوا	يَبْدَؤوا	يَبْدَؤونَ	بَدَؤوا	هم
		يَبْدَأْنَ	يَبْدَأْنَ	يَبْدَأْنَ	بَدَأْنَ	هنّ
ابْدَؤوا		تَبْدَؤوا	تَبْدَؤوا	تَبْدَؤونَ	بَدَأْتُمْ	أنتم
ابْدَأْنَ		تَبْدَأْنَ	تَبْدَأْنَ	تَبْدَأْنَ	بَدَأْتُنَّ	أنتنّ
		نَبْدَأْ	نَبْدَأَ	نَبْدَأُ	بَدَأْنا	نحن
	Passive	يُبْدَأْ	يُبْدَأَ	يُبْدَأُ	بُدِئَ	هو

	PP مَبْدوء	AP بادِئ

Form I - 4R ترجم

Imperative		Jussive	Subjunctive	Indicative	Perfect	
	Active	يُتَرْجِمْ	يُتَرْجِمَ	يُتَرْجِمُ	تَرْجَمَ	هو
		تُتَرْجِمْ	تُتَرْجِمَ	تُتَرْجِمُ	تَرْجَمَتْ	هي
تَرْجِمْ		تُتَرْجِمْ	تُتَرْجِمَ	تُتَرْجِمُ	تَرْجَمْتَ	أنتَ
تَرْجِمي		تُتَرْجِمي	تُتَرْجِمي	تُتَرْجِمينَ	تَرْجَمْتِ	أنتِ
		أُتَرْجِمْ	أُتَرْجِمَ	أُتَرْجِمُ	تَرْجَمْتُ	أنا
		يُتَرْجِما	يُتَرْجِما	يُتَرْجِمانِ	تَرْجَما	m-هما
		تُتَرْجِما	تُتَرْجِما	تُتَرْجِمانِ	تَرْجَمَتا	f-هما
تَرْجِما		تُتَرْجِما	تُتَرْجِما	تُتَرْجِمانِ	تَرْجَمْتُما	أنتما
		يُتَرْجِموا	يُتَرْجِموا	يُتَرْجِمونَ	تَرْجَموا	هم
		يُتَرْجِمْنَ	يُتَرْجِمْنَ	يُتَرْجِمْنَ	تَرْجَمْنَ	هنّ
تَرْجِموا		تُتَرْجِموا	تُتَرْجِموا	تُتَرْجِمونَ	تَرْجَمْتُمْ	أنتم
تَرْجِمْنَ		تُتَرْجِمْنَ	تُتَرْجِمْنَ	تُتَرْجِمْنَ	تَرْجَمْتُنَّ	أنتنّ
		نُتَرْجِمْ	نُتَرْجِمَ	نُتَرْجِمُ	تَرْجَمْنا	نحن
	Passive	يُتَرْجَمْ	يُتَرْجَمَ	يُتَرْجَمُ	تُرْجِمَ	هو

VN تَرْجَمة	PP مُتَرْجَم	AP مُتَرْجِم

Form II - sound درّس

Imperative		Jussive	Subjunctive	Indicative	Perfect	
	Active	يُدَرِّسْ	يُدَرِّسَ	يُدَرِّسُ	دَرَّسَ	هو
		تُدَرِّسْ	تُدَرِّسَ	تُدَرِّسُ	دَرَّسَتْ	هي
دَرِّسْ		تُدَرِّسْ	تُدَرِّسَ	تُدَرِّسُ	دَرَّسْتَ	أنتَ
دَرِّسي		تُدَرِّسي	تُدَرِّسي	تُدَرِّسينَ	دَرَّسْتِ	أنتِ
		أُدَرِّسْ	أُدَرِّسَ	أُدَرِّسُ	دَرَّسْتُ	أنا
		يُدَرِّسا	يُدَرِّسا	يُدَرِّسانِ	دَرَّسا	هما-m
		تُدَرِّسا	تُدَرِّسا	تُدَرِّسانِ	دَرَّسَتا	هما-f
دَرِّسا		تُدَرِّسا	تُدَرِّسا	تُدَرِّسانِ	دَرَّسْتُما	أنتما
		يُدَرِّسوا	يُدَرِّسوا	يُدَرِّسونَ	دَرَّسوا	هم
		يُدَرِّسْنَ	يُدَرِّسْنَ	يُدَرِّسْنَ	دَرَّسْنَ	هنّ
دَرِّسوا		تُدَرِّسوا	تُدَرِّسوا	تُدَرِّسونَ	دَرَّسْتُمْ	أنتم
دَرِّسْنَ		تُدَرِّسْنَ	تُدَرِّسْنَ	تُدَرِّسْنَ	دَرَّسْتُنَّ	أنتنّ
		نُدَرِّسْ	نُدَرِّسَ	نُدَرِّسُ	دَرَّسْنا	نحن
	Passive	يُدَرَّسْ	يُدَرَّسَ	يُدَرَّسُ	دُرِّسَ	هو

VN	PP	AP
تَدْريس	مُدَرَّس	مُدَرِّس

Form II - R2=R3 برّر

Imperative		Jussive	Subjunctive	Indicative	Perfect	
	Active	يُبَرِّرْ	يُبَرِّرَ	يُبَرِّرُ	بَرَّرَ	هو
		تُبَرِّرْ	تُبَرِّرَ	تُبَرِّرُ	بَرَّرَتْ	هي
بَرِّرْ		تُبَرِّرْ	تُبَرِّرَ	تُبَرِّرُ	بَرَّرْتَ	أنتَ
بَرِّري		تُبَرِّري	تُبَرِّري	تُبَرِّرينَ	بَرَّرْتِ	أنتِ
		أُبَرِّرْ	أُبَرِّرَ	أُبَرِّرُ	بَرَّرْتُ	أنا
		يُبَرِّرا	يُبَرِّرا	يُبَرِّرانِ	بَرَّرا	هما-m
		تُبَرِّرا	تُبَرِّرا	تُبَرِّرانِ	بَرَّرَتا	هما-f
بَرِّرا		تُبَرِّرا	تُبَرِّرا	تُبَرِّرانِ	بَرَّرْتُما	أنتما
		يُبَرِّروا	يُبَرِّروا	يُبَرِّرونَ	بَرَّروا	هم
		يُبَرِّرْنَ	يُبَرِّرْنَ	يُبَرِّرْنَ	بَرَّرْنَ	هنّ
بَرِّروا		تُبَرِّروا	تُبَرِّروا	تُبَرِّرونَ	بَرَّرْتُمْ	أنتم
بَرِّرْنَ		تُبَرِّرْنَ	تُبَرِّرْنَ	تُبَرِّرْنَ	بَرَّرْتُنَّ	أنتنّ
		نُبَرِّرْ	نُبَرِّرَ	نُبَرِّرُ	بَرَّرْنا	نحن
	Passive	يُبَرَّرْ	يُبَرَّرَ	يُبَرَّرُ	بُرِّرَ	هو

VN	PP	AP
تَبْرير	مُبَرَّر	مُبَرِّر

Form II - R1=و: وجّه

Imperative		Jussive	Subjunctive	Indicative	Perfect	
	Active	يُوَجِّهْ	يُوَجِّهَ	يُوَجِّهُ	وَجَّهَ	هو
		تُوَجِّهْ	تُوَجِّهَ	تُوَجِّهُ	وَجَّهَتْ	هي
وَجِّهْ		تُوَجِّهْ	تُوَجِّهَ	تُوَجِّهُ	وَجَّهْتَ	أنتَ
وَجِّهي		تُوَجِّهي	تُوَجِّهي	تُوَجِّهينَ	وَجَّهْتِ	أنتِ
		أُوَجِّهْ	أُوَجِّهَ	أُوَجِّهُ	وَجَّهْتُ	أنا
		يُوَجِّها	يُوَجِّها	يُوَجِّهانِ	وَجَّها	هما-m
		تُوَجِّها	تُوَجِّها	تُوَجِّهانِ	وَجَّهَتا	هما-f
وَجِّها		تُوَجِّها	تُوَجِّها	تُوَجِّهانِ	وَجَّهْتُما	أنتما
		يُوَجِّهوا	يُوَجِّهوا	يُوَجِّهونَ	وَجَّهوا	هم
		يُوَجِّهْنَ	يُوَجِّهْنَ	يُوَجِّهْنَ	وَجَّهْنَ	هنّ
وَجِّهوا		تُوَجِّهوا	تُوَجِّهوا	تُوَجِّهونَ	وَجَّهْتُمْ	أنتم
وَجِّهْنَ		تُوَجِّهْنَ	تُوَجِّهْنَ	تُوَجِّهْنَ	وَجَّهْتُنَّ	أنتنّ
		نُوَجِّهْ	نُوَجِّهَ	نُوَجِّهُ	وَجَّهْنا	نحن
	Passive	يُوَجَّهْ	يُوَجَّهَ	يُوَجَّهُ	وُجِّهَ	هو

VN تَوْجيه	PP مُوَجَّه	AP مُوَجِّه

Form II - R1=ي: يسّر

Imperative		Jussive	Subjunctive	Indicative	Perfect	
	Active	يُيَسِّرْ	يُيَسِّرَ	يُيَسِّرُ	يَسَّرَ	هو
		تُيَسِّرْ	تُيَسِّرَ	تُيَسِّرُ	يَسَّرَتْ	هي
يَسِّرْ		تُيَسِّرْ	تُيَسِّرَ	تُيَسِّرُ	يَسَّرْتَ	أنتَ
يَسِّري		تُيَسِّري	تُيَسِّري	تُيَسِّرينَ	يَسَّرْتِ	أنتِ
		أُيَسِّرْ	أُيَسِّرَ	أُيَسِّرُ	يَسَّرْتُ	أنا
		يُيَسِّرا	يُيَسِّرا	يُيَسِّرانِ	يَسَّرا	هما-m
		تُيَسِّرا	تُيَسِّرا	تُيَسِّرانِ	يَسَّرَتا	هما-f
يَسِّرا		تُيَسِّرا	تُيَسِّرا	تُيَسِّرانِ	يَسَّرْتُما	أنتما
		يُيَسِّروا	يُيَسِّروا	يُيَسِّرونَ	يَسَّروا	هم
		يُيَسِّرْنَ	يُيَسِّرْنَ	يُيَسِّرْنَ	يَسَّرْنَ	هنّ
يَسِّروا		تُيَسِّروا	تُيَسِّروا	تُيَسِّرونَ	يَسَّرْتُمْ	أنتم
يَسِّرْنَ		تُيَسِّرْنَ	تُيَسِّرْنَ	تُيَسِّرْنَ	يَسَّرْتُنَّ	أنتنّ
		نُيَسِّرْ	نُيَسِّرَ	نُيَسِّرُ	يَسَّرْنا	نحن
	Passive	يُيَسَّرْ	يُيَسَّرَ	يُيَسَّرُ	يُسِّرَ	هو

VN تَيْسير	PP مُيَسَّر	AP مُيَسِّر

Form II - R2=و: زوّد

Imperative		Jussive	Subjunctive	Indicative	Perfect	
	Active	يُزَوِّدْ	يُزَوِّدَ	يُزَوِّدُ	زَوَّدَ	هو
		تُزَوِّدْ	تُزَوِّدَ	تُزَوِّدُ	زَوَّدَتْ	هي
زَوِّدْ		تُزَوِّدْ	تُزَوِّدَ	تُزَوِّدُ	زَوَّدْتَ	أنتَ
زَوِّدي		تُزَوِّدي	تُزَوِّدي	تُزَوِّدينَ	زَوَّدْتِ	أنتِ
		أُزَوِّدْ	أُزَوِّدَ	أُزَوِّدُ	زَوَّدْتُ	أنا
		يُزَوِّدا	يُزَوِّدا	يُزَوِّدانِ	زَوَّدا	هما-m
		تُزَوِّدا	تُزَوِّدا	تُزَوِّدانِ	زَوَّدَتا	هما-f
زَوِّدا		تُزَوِّدا	تُزَوِّدا	تُزَوِّدانِ	زَوَّدْتُما	أنتما
		يُزَوِّدوا	يُزَوِّدوا	يُزَوِّدونَ	زَوَّدوا	هم
		يُزَوِّدْنَ	يُزَوِّدْنَ	يُزَوِّدْنَ	زَوَّدْنَ	هنّ
زَوِّدوا		تُزَوِّدوا	تُزَوِّدوا	تُزَوِّدونَ	زَوَّدْتُمْ	أنتم
زَوِّدْنَ		تُزَوِّدْنَ	تُزَوِّدْنَ	تُزَوِّدْنَ	زَوَّدْتُنَّ	أنتنّ
		نُزَوِّدْ	نُزَوِّدَ	نُزَوِّدُ	زَوَّدْنا	نحن
	Passive	يُزَوَّدْ	يُزَوَّدَ	يُزَوَّدُ	زُوِّدَ	هو

VN	PP	AP
تَزْويد	مُزَوَّد	مُزَوِّد

Form II - R2=ي: غيّر

Imperative		Jussive	Subjunctive	Indicative	Perfect	
	Active	يُغَيِّرْ	يُغَيِّرَ	يُغَيِّرُ	غَيَّرَ	هو
		تُغَيِّرْ	تُغَيِّرَ	تُغَيِّرُ	غَيَّرَتْ	هي
غَيِّرْ		تُغَيِّرْ	تُغَيِّرَ	تُغَيِّرُ	غَيَّرْتَ	أنتَ
غَيِّري		تُغَيِّري	تُغَيِّري	تُغَيِّرينَ	غَيَّرْتِ	أنتِ
		أُغَيِّرْ	أُغَيِّرَ	أُغَيِّرُ	غَيَّرْتُ	أنا
		يُغَيِّرا	يُغَيِّرا	يُغَيِّرانِ	غَيَّرا	هما-m
		تُغَيِّرا	تُغَيِّرا	تُغَيِّرانِ	غَيَّرَتا	هما-f
غَيِّرا		تُغَيِّرا	تُغَيِّرا	تُغَيِّرانِ	غَيَّرْتُما	أنتما
		يُغَيِّروا	يُغَيِّروا	يُغَيِّرونَ	غَيَّروا	هم
		يُغَيِّرْنَ	يُغَيِّرْنَ	يُغَيِّرْنَ	غَيَّرْنَ	هنّ
غَيِّروا		تُغَيِّروا	تُغَيِّروا	تُغَيِّرونَ	غَيَّرْتُمْ	أنتم
غَيِّرْنَ		تُغَيِّرْنَ	تُغَيِّرْنَ	تُغَيِّرْنَ	غَيَّرْتُنَّ	أنتنّ
		نُغَيِّرْ	نُغَيِّرَ	نُغَيِّرُ	غَيَّرْنا	نحن
	Passive	يُغَيَّرْ	يُغَيَّرَ	يُغَيَّرُ	غُيِّرَ	هو

VN	PP	AP
تَغْيير	مُغَيَّر	مُغَيِّر

Form II - R3=غطّى :و\ي

Imperative		Jussive	Subjunctive	Indicative	Perfect	
	Active	يُغَطِّ	يُغَطِّي	يُغَطِّي	غَطّى	هو
		تُغَطِّ	تُغَطِّي	تُغَطِّي	غَطَّتْ	هي
غَطِّ		تُغَطِّ	تُغَطِّي	تُغَطِّي	غَطَّيْتَ	أنتَ
غَطِّي		تُغَطِّي	تُغَطِّي	تُغَطِّينَ	غَطَّيْتِ	أنتِ
		أُغَطِّ	أُغَطِّي	أُغَطِّي	غَطَّيْتُ	أنا
		يُغَطِّيا	يُغَطِّيا	يُغَطِّيانِ	غَطَّيا	هما-m
		تُغَطِّيا	تُغَطِّيا	تُغَطِّيانِ	غَطَّتا	هما-f
غَطِّيا		تُغَطِّيا	تُغَطِّيا	تُغَطِّيانِ	غَطَّيْتُما	أنتما
		يُغَطّوا	يُغَطّوا	يُغَطّونَ	غَطَّوْا	هم
		يُغَطِّينَ	يُغَطِّينَ	يُغَطِّينَ	غَطَّيْنَ	هنّ
غَطّوا		تُغَطّوا	تُغَطّوا	تُغَطّونَ	غَطَّيْتُمْ	أنتم
غَطِّينَ		تُغَطِّينَ	تُغَطِّينَ	تُغَطِّينَ	غَطَّيْتُنَّ	أنتنّ
		نُغَطِّ	نُغَطِّي	نُغَطِّي	غَطَّيْنا	نحن
	Passive	يُغَطَّ	يُغَطّى	يُغَطّى	غُطِّيَ	هو

VN	PP	AP
تَغْطِيَة	مُغَطًّى	مُغَطٍّ

Form II - R1=أكّد :ء

Imperative		Jussive	Subjunctive	Indicative	Perfect	
	Active	يُؤَكِّدْ	يُؤَكِّدَ	يُؤَكِّدُ	أَكَّدَ	هو
		تُؤَكِّدْ	تُؤَكِّدَ	تُؤَكِّدُ	أَكَّدَتْ	هي
أَكِّدْ		تُؤَكِّدْ	تُؤَكِّدَ	تُؤَكِّدُ	أَكَّدْتَ	أنتَ
أَكِّدي		تُؤَكِّدي	تُؤَكِّدي	تُؤَكِّدينَ	أَكَّدْتِ	أنتِ
		أُؤَكِّدْ	أُؤَكِّدَ	أُؤَكِّدُ	أَكَّدْتُ	أنا
		يُؤَكِّدا	يُؤَكِّدا	يُؤَكِّدانِ	أَكَّدا	هما-m
		تُؤَكِّدا	تُؤَكِّدا	تُؤَكِّدانِ	أَكَّدَتا	هما-f
أَكِّدا		تُؤَكِّدا	تُؤَكِّدا	تُؤَكِّدانِ	أَكَّدْتُما	أنتما
		يُؤَكِّدوا	يُؤَكِّدوا	يُؤَكِّدونَ	أَكَّدوا	هم
		يُؤَكِّدْنَ	يُؤَكِّدْنَ	يُؤَكِّدْنَ	أَكَّدْنَ	هنّ
أَكِّدوا		تُؤَكِّدوا	تُؤَكِّدوا	تُؤَكِّدونَ	أَكَّدْتُمْ	أنتم
أَكِّدْنَ		تُؤَكِّدْنَ	تُؤَكِّدْنَ	تُؤَكِّدْنَ	أَكَّدْتُنَّ	أنتنّ
		نُؤَكِّدْ	نُؤَكِّدَ	نُؤَكِّدُ	أَكَّدْنا	نحن
	Passive	يُؤَكَّدْ	يُؤَكَّدَ	يُؤَكَّدُ	أُكِّدَ	هو

VN	PP	AP
تَأْكيد	مُؤَكَّد	مُؤَكِّد

Form II - R3=ء: لجّأ

Imperative		Jussive	Subjunctive	Indicative	Perfect	
	Active	يُلَجِّئْ	يُلَجِّئَ	يُلَجِّئُ	لَجَّأَ	هو
		تُلَجِّئْ	تُلَجِّئَ	تُلَجِّئُ	لَجَّأَتْ	هي
لَجِّئْ		تُلَجِّئْ	تُلَجِّئَ	تُلَجِّئُ	لَجَّأْتَ	أنتَ
لَجِّئي		تُلَجِّئي	تُلَجِّئي	تُلَجِّئين	لَجَّأْتِ	أنتِ
		أُلَجِّئْ	أُلَجِّئَ	أُلَجِّئُ	لَجَّأْتُ	أنا
		يُلَجِّئا	يُلَجِّئا	يُلَجِّئانِ	لَجَّآ	هما-m
		تُلَجِّئا	تُلَجِّئا	تُلَجِّئانِ	لَجَّأَتا	هما-f
لَجِّئا		تُلَجِّئا	تُلَجِّئا	تُلَجِّئانِ	لَجَّأْتُما	أنتما
		يُلَجِّئوا	يُلَجِّئوا	يُلَجِّئونَ	لَجَّؤوا	هم
		يُلَجِّئْنَ	يُلَجِّئْنَ	يُلَجِّئْنَ	لَجَّأْنَ	هنّ
لَجِّئوا		تُلَجِّئوا	تُلَجِّئوا	تُلَجِّئونَ	لَجَّأْتُمْ	أنتم
لَجِّئْنَ		تُلَجِّئْنَ	تُلَجِّئْنَ	تُلَجِّئْنَ	لَجَّأْتُنَّ	أنتنّ
		نُلَجِّئْ	نُلَجِّئَ	نُلَجِّئُ	لَجَّأْنا	نحن
	Passive	يُلَجَّأْ	يُلَجَّأَ	يُلَجَّأُ	لُجِّئَ	هو

VN تَلْجِئة	**PP** مُلَجَّأ	**AP** مُلَجِّئ

Form II - 4R تدحرج

Imperative		Jussive	Subjunctive	Indicative	Perfect	
	Active	يَتَدَحْرَجْ	يَتَدَحْرَجَ	يَتَدَحْرَجُ	تَدَحْرَجَ	هو
		تَتَدَحْرَجْ	تَتَدَحْرَجَ	تَتَدَحْرَجُ	تَدَحْرَجَتْ	هي
تَدَحْرَجْ		تَتَدَحْرَجْ	تَتَدَحْرَجَ	تَتَدَحْرَجُ	تَدَحْرَجْتَ	أنتَ
تَدَحْرَجي		تَتَدَحْرَجي	تَتَدَحْرَجي	تَتَدَحْرَجين	تَدَحْرَجْتِ	أنتِ
		أَتَدَحْرَجْ	أَتَدَحْرَجَ	أَتَدَحْرَجُ	تَدَحْرَجْتُ	أنا
		يَتَدَحْرَجا	يَتَدَحْرَجا	يَتَدَحْرَجانِ	تَدَحْرَجا	هما-m
		تَتَدَحْرَجا	تَتَدَحْرَجا	تَتَدَحْرَجانِ	تَدَحْرَجَتا	هما-f
تَدَحْرَجا		تَتَدَحْرَجا	تَتَدَحْرَجا	تَتَدَحْرَجانِ	تَدَحْرَجْتُما	أنتما
		يَتَدَحْرَجوا	يَتَدَحْرَجوا	يَتَدَحْرَجونَ	تَدَحْرَجوا	هم
		يَتَدَحْرَجْنَ	يَتَدَحْرَجْنَ	يَتَدَحْرَجْنَ	تَدَحْرَجْنَ	هنّ
تَدَحْرَجوا		تَتَدَحْرَجوا	تَتَدَحْرَجوا	تَتَدَحْرَجونَ	تَدَحْرَجْتُمْ	أنتم
تَدَحْرَجْنَ		تَتَدَحْرَجْنَ	تَتَدَحْرَجْنَ	تَتَدَحْرَجْنَ	تَدَحْرَجْتُنَّ	أنتنّ
		نَتَدَحْرَجْ	نَتَدَحْرَجَ	نَتَدَحْرَجُ	تَدَحْرَجْنا	نحن
	Passive	يُتَدَحْرَجْ	يُتَدَحْرَجَ	يُتَدَحْرَجُ	تُدُحْرِجَ	هو

VN تَدَحْرُج	**PP** مُتَدَحْرَج	**AP** مُتَدَحْرِج

Form III - sound سالم

	Perfect	Indicative	Subjunctive	Jussive	Imperative
Active					
هو	سالَمَ	يُسالِمُ	يُسالِمَ	يُسالِمْ	
هي	سالَمَتْ	تُسالِمُ	تُسالِمَ	تُسالِمْ	
أنتَ	سالَمْتَ	تُسالِمُ	تُسالِمَ	تُسالِمْ	سالِمْ
أنتِ	سالَمْتِ	تُسالِمينَ	تُسالِمي	تُسالِمي	سالِمي
أنا	سالَمْتُ	أُسالِمُ	أُسالِمَ	أُسالِمْ	
هما-m	سالَما	يُسالِمانِ	يُسالِما	يُسالِما	
هما-f	سالَمَتا	تُسالِمانِ	تُسالِما	تُسالِما	
أنتما	سالَمْتُما	تُسالِمانِ	تُسالِما	تُسالِما	سالِما
هم	سالَموا	يُسالِمونَ	يُسالِموا	يُسالِموا	
هنّ	سالَمْنَ	يُسالِمْنَ	يُسالِمْنَ	يُسالِمْنَ	
أنتم	سالَمْتُمْ	تُسالِمونَ	تُسالِموا	تُسالِموا	سالِموا
أنتنّ	سالَمْتُنَّ	تُسالِمْنَ	تُسالِمْنَ	تُسالِمْنَ	سالِمْنَ
نحن	سالَمْنا	نُسالِمُ	نُسالِمَ	نُسالِمْ	
Passive					
هو	سولِمَ	يُسالَمُ	يُسالَمَ	يُسالَمْ	

AP	PP	VN
مُسالِم	مُسالَم	مُسالَمة

Form III - R2=R3 حاجّ

	Perfect	Indicative	Subjunctive	Jussive	Imperative
Active					
هو	حاجَّ	يُحاجُّ	يُحاجَّ	يُحاجِجْ	
هي	حاجَّتْ	تُحاجُّ	تُحاجَّ	تُحاجِجْ	
أنتَ	حاجَجْتَ	تُحاجُّ	تُحاجَّ	تُحاجِجْ	حاجِجْ
أنتِ	حاجَجْتِ	تُحاجّينَ	تُحاجّي	تُحاجّي	حاجّي
أنا	حاجَجْتُ	أُحاجُّ	أُحاجَّ	أُحاجِجْ	
هما-m	حاجّا	يُحاجّانِ	يُحاجّا	يُحاجّا	
هما-f	حاجَّتا	تُحاجّانِ	تُحاجّا	تُحاجّا	
أنتما	حاجَجْتُما	تُحاجّانِ	تُحاجّا	تُحاجّا	حاجّا
هم	حاجّوا	يُحاجّونَ	يُحاجّوا	يُحاجّوا	
هنّ	حاجَجْنَ	يُحاجِجْنَ	يُحاجِجْنَ	يُحاجِجْنَ	
أنتم	حاجَجْتُمْ	تُحاجّونَ	تُحاجّوا	تُحاجّوا	حاجّوا
أنتنّ	حاجَجْتُنَّ	تُحاجِجْنَ	تُحاجِجْنَ	تُحاجِجْنَ	حاجِجْنَ
نحن	حاجَجْنا	نُحاجُّ	نُحاجَّ	نُحاجِجْ	
Passive					
هو	حوجَّ	يُحاجُّ	يُحاجَّ	يُحاجَجْ	

AP	PP	VN
مُحاجّ	مُحاجّ	مُحاجّة

Form III - R1=و: وافق

Imperative		Jussive	Subjunctive	Indicative	Perfect	
	Active	يُوافِقْ	يُوافِقَ	يُوافِقُ	وافَقَ	هو
		تُوافِقْ	تُوافِقَ	تُوافِقُ	وافَقَتْ	هي
وافِقْ		تُوافِقْ	تُوافِقَ	تُوافِقُ	وافَقْتَ	أنتَ
وافِقي		تُوافِقي	تُوافِقي	تُوافِقينَ	وافَقْتِ	أنتِ
		أُوافِقْ	أُوافِقَ	أُوافِقُ	وافَقْتُ	أنا
		يُوافِقا	يُوافِقا	يُوافِقانِ	وافَقا	هما-m
		تُوافِقا	تُوافِقا	تُوافِقانِ	وافَقَتا	هما-f
وافِقا		تُوافِقا	تُوافِقا	تُوافِقانِ	وافَقْتُما	أنتما
		يُوافِقوا	يُوافِقوا	يُوافِقونَ	وافَقوا	هم
		يُوافِقْنَ	يُوافِقْنَ	يُوافِقْنَ	وافَقْنَ	هنّ
وافِقوا		تُوافِقوا	تُوافِقوا	تُوافِقونَ	وافَقْتُمْ	أنتم
وافِقْنَ		تُوافِقْنَ	تُوافِقْنَ	تُوافِقْنَ	وافَقْتُنَّ	أنتنّ
		نُوافِقْ	نُوافِقَ	نُوافِقُ	وافَقْنا	نحن
	Passive	يُوافَقْ	يُوافَقَ	يُوافَقُ	ووفِقَ	هو

VN	PP	AP
مُوافَقة \ وِفاق	مُوافَق	مُوافِق

Form III - R1=ي: ياسر

Imperative		Jussive	Subjunctive	Indicative	Perfect	
	Active	يُياسِرْ	يُياسِرَ	يُياسِرُ	ياسَرَ	هو
		تُياسِرْ	تُياسِرَ	تُياسِرُ	ياسَرَتْ	هي
ياسِرْ		تُياسِرْ	تُياسِرَ	تُياسِرُ	ياسَرْتَ	أنتَ
ياسِري		تُياسِري	تُياسِري	تُياسِرينَ	ياسَرْتِ	أنتِ
		أُياسِرْ	أُياسِرَ	أُياسِرُ	ياسَرْتُ	أنا
		يُياسِرا	يُياسِرا	يُياسِرانِ	ياسَرا	هما-m
		تُياسِرا	تُياسِرا	تُياسِرانِ	ياسَرَتا	هما-f
ياسِرا		تُياسِرا	تُياسِرا	تُياسِرانِ	ياسَرْتُما	أنتما
		يُياسِروا	يُياسِروا	يُياسِرونَ	ياسَروا	هم
		يُياسِرْنَ	يُياسِرْنَ	يُياسِرْنَ	ياسَرْنَ	هنّ
ياسِروا		تُياسِروا	تُياسِروا	تُياسِرونَ	ياسَرْتُمْ	أنتم
ياسِرْنَ		تُياسِرْنَ	تُياسِرْنَ	تُياسِرْنَ	ياسَرْتُنَّ	أنتنّ
		نُياسِرْ	نُياسِرَ	نُياسِرُ	ياسَرْنا	نحن
	Passive	يُياسَرْ	يُياسَرَ	يُياسَرُ	يوسِرَ	هو

VN	PP	AP
مُياسَرة	مُياسَر	مُياسِر

Form III - R2=و: حاول

Imperative		Jussive	Subjunctive	Indicative	Perfect	
	Active	يُحاوِلْ	يُحاوِلَ	يُحاوِلُ	حاوَلَ	هو
		تُحاوِلْ	تُحاوِلَ	تُحاوِلُ	حاوَلَتْ	هي
حاوِلْ		تُحاوِلْ	تُحاوِلَ	تُحاوِلُ	حاوَلْتَ	أنتَ
حاوِلي		تُحاوِلي	تُحاوِلي	تُحاوِلينَ	حاوَلْتِ	أنتِ
		أُحاوِلْ	أُحاوِلَ	أُحاوِلُ	حاوَلْتُ	أنا
		يُحاوِلا	يُحاوِلا	يُحاوِلانِ	حاوَلا	هما-m
		تُحاوِلا	تُحاوِلا	تُحاوِلانِ	حاوَلَتا	هما-f
حاوِلا		تُحاوِلا	تُحاوِلا	تُحاوِلانِ	حاوَلْتُما	أنتما
		يُحاوِلوا	يُحاوِلوا	يُحاوِلونَ	حاوَلوا	هم
		يُحاوِلْنَ	يُحاوِلْنَ	يُحاوِلْنَ	حاوَلْنَ	هنّ
حاوِلوا		تُحاوِلوا	تُحاوِلوا	تُحاوِلونَ	حاوَلْتُمْ	أنتم
حاوِلْنَ		تُحاوِلْنَ	تُحاوِلْنَ	تُحاوِلْنَ	حاوَلْتُنَّ	أنتنّ
		نُحاوِلْ	نُحاوِلَ	نُحاوِلُ	حاوَلْنا	نحن
	Passive	يُحاوَلْ	يُحاوَلَ	يُحاوَلُ	حووِلَ	هو

VN مُحاوَلَة	PP مُحاوَل	AP مُحاوِل

Form III - R2=ي: زايد

Imperative		Jussive	Subjunctive	Indicative	Perfect	
	Active	يُزايِدْ	يُزايِدَ	يُزايِدُ	زايَدَ	هو
		تُزايِدْ	تُزايِدَ	تُزايِدُ	زايَدَتْ	هي
زايِدْ		تُزايِدْ	تُزايِدَ	تُزايِدُ	زايَدْتَ	أنتَ
زايِدي		تُزايِدي	تُزايِدي	تُزايِدينَ	زايَدْتِ	أنتِ
		أُزايِدْ	أُزايِدَ	أُزايِدُ	زايَدْتُ	أنا
		يُزايِدا	يُزايِدا	يُزايِدانِ	زايَدا	هما-m
		تُزايِدا	تُزايِدا	تُزايِدانِ	زايَدَتا	هما-f
زايِدا		تُزايِدا	تُزايِدا	تُزايِدانِ	زايَدْتُما	أنتما
		يُزايِدوا	يُزايِدوا	يُزايِدونَ	زايَدوا	هم
		يُزايِدْنَ	يُزايِدْنَ	يُزايِدْنَ	زايَدْنَ	هنّ
زايِدوا		تُزايِدوا	تُزايِدوا	تُزايِدونَ	زايَدْتُمْ	أنتم
زايِدْنَ		تُزايِدْنَ	تُزايِدْنَ	تُزايِدْنَ	زايَدْتُنَّ	أنتنّ
		نُزايِدْ	نُزايِدَ	نُزايِدُ	زايَدْنا	نحن
	Passive	يُزايَدْ	يُزايَدَ	يُزايَدُ	زويِدَ	هو

VN مُزايَدة	PP مُزايَد	AP مُزايِد

Form III - R3=و\ي: نادى

Imperative		Jussive	Subjunctive	Indicative	Perfect	
	Active	يُنادِ	يُنادِيَ	يُنادي	نادى	هو
		تُنادِ	تُنادِيَ	تُنادي	نادَتْ	هي
نادِ		تُنادِ	تُنادِيَ	تُنادي	نادَيْتَ	أنتَ
نادي		تُنادي	تُنادي	تُنادينَ	نادَيْتِ	أنتِ
		أُنادِ	أُنادِيَ	أُنادي	نادَيْتُ	أنا
		يُنادِيا	يُنادِيا	يُنادِيانِ	نادَيا	هما-m
		تُنادِيا	تُنادِيا	تُنادِيانِ	نادَتا	هما-f
نادِيا		تُنادِيا	تُنادِيا	تُنادِيانِ	نادَيْتُما	أنتما
		يُنادوا	يُنادوا	يُنادونَ	نادَوْا	هم
		يُنادينَ	يُنادينَ	يُنادينَ	نادَيْنَ	هنّ
نادوا		تُنادوا	تُنادوا	تُنادونَ	نادَيْتُمْ	أنتم
نادينَ		تُنادينَ	تُنادينَ	تُنادينَ	نادَيْتُنَّ	أنتنّ
		نُنادِ	نُنادِيَ	نُنادي	نادَيْنا	نحن
	Passive	يُنادَ	يُنادى	يُنادى	نودِيَ	هو

VN	PP	AP
مُناداة\نِداء	مُنادًى	مُنادٍ

Form III - R1=ء: آزر

Imperative		Jussive	Subjunctive	Indicative	Perfect	
	Active	يُؤازِرْ	يُؤازِرَ	يُؤازِرُ	آزَرَ	هو
		تُؤازِرْ	تُؤازِرَ	تُؤازِرُ	آزَرَتْ	هي
آزِرْ		تُؤازِرْ	تُؤازِرَ	تُؤازِرُ	آزَرْتَ	أنتَ
آزِري		تُؤازِري	تُؤازِري	تُؤازِرينَ	آزَرْتِ	أنتِ
		أُؤازِرْ	أُؤازِرَ	أُؤازِرُ	آزَرْتُ	أنا
		يُؤازِرا	يُؤازِرا	يُؤازِرانِ	آزَرا	هما-m
		تُؤازِرا	تُؤازِرا	تُؤازِرانِ	آزَرَتا	هما-f
آزِرا		تُؤازِرا	تُؤازِرا	تُؤازِرانِ	آزَرْتُما	أنتما
		يُؤازِروا	يُؤازِروا	يُؤازِرونَ	آزَروا	هم
		يُؤازِرْنَ	يُؤازِرْنَ	يُؤازِرْنَ	آزَرْنَ	هنّ
آزِروا		تُؤازِروا	تُؤازِروا	تُؤازِرونَ	آزَرْتُمْ	أنتم
آزِرْنَ		تُؤازِرْنَ	تُؤازِرْنَ	تُؤازِرْنَ	آزَرْتُنَّ	أنتنّ
		نُؤازِرْ	نُؤازِرَ	نُؤازِرُ	آزَرْنا	نحن
	Passive	يُؤازَرْ	يُؤازَرَ	يُؤازَرُ	أوزِرَ	هو

VN	PP	AP
مُؤازَرة	مُؤازَر	مُؤازِر

Form III - R2=ء: ساءل

Imperative		Jussive	Subjunctive	Indicative	Perfect	
	Active	يُسائِلْ	يُسائِلَ	يُسائِلُ	ساءَلَ	هو
		تُسائِلْ	تُسائِلَ	تُسائِلُ	ساءَلَتْ	هي
سائِلْ		تُسائِلْ	تُسائِلَ	تُسائِلُ	ساءَلْتَ	أنتَ
سائِلي		تُسائِلي	تُسائِلي	تُسائِلينَ	ساءَلْتِ	أنتِ
		أُسائِلْ	أُسائِلَ	أُسائِلُ	ساءَلْتُ	أنا
		يُسائِلا	يُسائِلا	يُسائِلانِ	ساءَلا	هما-m
		تُسائِلا	تُسائِلا	تُسائِلانِ	ساءَلَتا	هما-f
سائِلا		تُسائِلا	تُسائِلا	تُسائِلانِ	ساءَلْتُما	أنتما
		يُسائِلوا	يُسائِلوا	يُسائِلونَ	ساءَلوا	هم
		يُسائِلْنَ	يُسائِلْنَ	يُسائِلْنَ	ساءَلْنَ	هنّ
سائِلوا		تُسائِلوا	تُسائِلوا	تُسائِلونَ	ساءَلْتُمْ	أنتم
سائِلْنَ		تُسائِلْنَ	تُسائِلْنَ	تُسائِلْنَ	ساءَلْتُنَّ	أنتنّ
		نُسائِلْ	نُسائِلَ	نُسائِلُ	ساءَلْنا	نحن
	Passive	يُساءَلْ	يُساءَلَ	يُساءَلُ	سوئِلَ	هو

VN	PP	AP
مُساءَلة	مُساءَل	مُسائِل

Form III - R3=ء: فاجأ

Imperative		Jussive	Subjunctive	Indicative	Perfect	
	Active	يُفاجِئْ	يُفاجِئَ	يُفاجِئُ	فاجَأَ	هو
		تُفاجِئْ	تُفاجِئَ	تُفاجِئُ	فاجَأَتْ	هي
فاجِئْ		تُفاجِئْ	تُفاجِئَ	تُفاجِئُ	فاجَأْتَ	أنتَ
فاجِئي		تُفاجِئي	تُفاجِئي	تُفاجِئينَ	فاجَأْتِ	أنتِ
		أُفاجِئْ	أُفاجِئَ	أُفاجِئُ	فاجَأْتُ	أنا
		يُفاجِئا	يُفاجِئا	يُفاجِئانِ	فاجَآ	هما-m
		تُفاجِئا	تُفاجِئا	تُفاجِئانِ	فاجَأَتا	هما-f
فاجِئا		تُفاجِئا	تُفاجِئا	تُفاجِئانِ	فاجَأْتُما	أنتما
		يُفاجِئوا	يُفاجِئوا	يُفاجِئونَ	فاجَؤوا	هم
		يُفاجِئْنَ	يُفاجِئْنَ	يُفاجِئْنَ	فاجَأْنَ	هنّ
فاجِئوا		تُفاجِئوا	تُفاجِئوا	تُفاجِئونَ	فاجَأْتُمْ	أنتم
فاجِئْنَ		تُفاجِئْنَ	تُفاجِئْنَ	تُفاجِئْنَ	فاجَأْتُنَّ	أنتنّ
		نُفاجِئْ	نُفاجِئَ	نُفاجِئُ	فاجَأْنا	نحن
	Passive	يُفاجَأْ	يُفاجَأَ	يُفاجَأُ	فوجِئَ	هو

VN	PP	AP
مُفاجَأة	مُفاجَأ	مُفاجِئ

Form IV - sound أنجز

Imperative		Jussive	Subjunctive	Indicative	Perfect	
	Active	يُنْجِزْ	يُنْجِزَ	يُنْجِزُ	أَنْجَزَ	هو
		تُنْجِزْ	تُنْجِزَ	تُنْجِزُ	أَنْجَزَتْ	هي
أَنْجِزْ		تُنْجِزْ	تُنْجِزَ	تُنْجِزُ	أَنْجَزْتَ	أنتَ
أَنْجِزي		تُنْجِزي	تُنْجِزي	تُنْجِزينَ	أَنْجَزْتِ	أنتِ
		أُنْجِزْ	أُنْجِزَ	أُنْجِزُ	أَنْجَزْتُ	أنا
		يُنْجِزا	يُنْجِزا	يُنْجِزانِ	أَنْجَزا	هما-m
		تُنْجِزا	تُنْجِزا	تُنْجِزانِ	أَنْجَزَتا	هما-f
أَنْجِزا		تُنْجِزا	تُنْجِزا	تُنْجِزانِ	أَنْجَزْتُما	أنتما
		يُنْجِزوا	يُنْجِزوا	يُنْجِزونَ	أَنْجَزوا	هم
		يُنْجِزْنَ	يُنْجِزْنَ	يُنْجِزْنَ	أَنْجَزْنَ	هنّ
أَنْجِزوا		تُنْجِزوا	تُنْجِزوا	تُنْجِزونَ	أَنْجَزْتُمْ	أنتم
أَنْجِزْنَ		تُنْجِزْنَ	تُنْجِزْنَ	تُنْجِزْنَ	أَنْجَزْتُنَّ	أنتنّ
		نُنْجِزْ	نُنْجِزَ	نُنْجِزُ	أَنْجَزْنا	نحن
	Passive	يُنْجَزْ	يُنْجَزَ	يُنْجَزُ	أُنْجِزَ	هو

VN إِنْجاز	PP مُنْجَز	AP مُنْجِز

Form IV - R2=R3 أقرّ

Imperative		Jussive	Subjunctive	Indicative	Perfect	
	Active	يُقْرِرْ	يُقِرَّ	يُقِرُّ	أَقَرَّ	هو
		تُقْرِرْ	تُقِرَّ	تُقِرُّ	أَقَرَّتْ	هي
أَقْرِرْ		تُقْرِرْ	تُقِرَّ	تُقِرُّ	أَقْرَرْتَ	أنتَ
أَقِرّي		تُقِرّي	تُقِرّي	تُقِرّينَ	أَقْرَرْتِ	أنتِ
		أُقْرِرْ	أُقِرَّ	أُقِرُّ	أَقْرَرْتُ	أنا
		يُقِرّا	يُقِرّا	يُقِرّانِ	أَقَرّا	هما-m
		تُقِرّا	تُقِرّا	تُقِرّانِ	أَقَرَّتا	هما-f
أَقِرّا		تُقِرّا	تُقِرّا	تُقِرّانِ	أَقْرَرْتُما	أنتما
		يُقِرّوا	يُقِرّوا	يُقِرّونَ	أَقَرّوا	هم
		يُقْرِرْنَ	يُقْرِرْنَ	يُقْرِرْنَ	أَقْرَرْنَ	هنّ
أَقِرّوا		تُقِرّوا	تُقِرّوا	تُقِرّونَ	أَقْرَرْتُمْ	أنتم
أَقْرِرْنَ		تُقْرِرْنَ	تُقْرِرْنَ	تُقْرِرْنَ	أَقْرَرْتُنَّ	أنتنّ
		نُقْرِرْ	نُقِرَّ	نُقِرُّ	أَقْرَرْنا	نحن
	Passive	يُقْرَرْ	يُقَرَّ	يُقَرُّ	أُقِرَّ	هو

VN إِقْرار	PP مُقَرّ	AP مُقِرّ

Form IV - R1=و: أوقف

Imperative		Jussive	Subjunctive	Indicative	Perfect	
	Active	يوقِفْ	يوقِفَ	يوقِفُ	أَوْقَفَ	هو
		توقِفْ	توقِفَ	توقِفُ	أَوْقَفَتْ	هي
أَوْقِفْ		توقِفْ	توقِفَ	توقِفُ	أَوْقَفْتَ	أنتَ
أَوْقِفي		توقِفي	توقِفي	توقِفينَ	أَوْقَفْتِ	أنتِ
		أوقِفْ	أوقِفَ	أوقِفُ	أَوْقَفْتُ	أنا
		يوقِفا	يوقِفا	يوقِفانِ	أَوْقَفا	هما-m
		توقِفا	توقِفا	توقِفانِ	أَوْقَفَتا	هما-f
أَوْقِفا		توقِفا	توقِفا	توقِفانِ	أَوْقَفْتُما	أنتما
		يوقِفوا	يوقِفوا	يوقِفونَ	أَوْقَفوا	هم
		يوقِفْنَ	يوقِفْنَ	يوقِفْنَ	أَوْقَفْنَ	هنّ
أَوْقِفوا		توقِفوا	توقِفوا	توقِفونَ	أَوْقَفْتُمْ	أنتم
أَوْقِفْنَ		توقِفْنَ	توقِفْنَ	توقِفْنَ	أَوْقَفْتُنَّ	أنتنّ
		نوقِفْ	نوقِفَ	نوقِفُ	أَوْقَفْنا	نحن
	Passive	يوقَفْ	يوقَفَ	يوقَفُ	أوقِفَ	هو

VN إيقاف	PP موقَف	AP موقِف

Form IV - R1=ي: أيقظ

Imperative		Jussive	Subjunctive	Indicative	Perfect	
	Active	يوقِظْ	يوقِظَ	يوقِظُ	أَيْقَظَ	هو
		توقِظْ	توقِظَ	توقِظُ	أَيْقَظَتْ	هي
أَيْقِظْ		توقِظْ	توقِظَ	توقِظُ	أَيْقَظْتَ	أنتَ
أَيْقِظي		توقِظي	توقِظي	توقِظينَ	أَيْقَظْتِ	أنتِ
		أوقِظْ	أوقِظَ	أوقِظُ	أَيْقَظْتُ	أنا
		يوقِظا	يوقِظا	يوقِظانِ	أَيْقَظا	هما-m
		توقِظا	توقِظا	توقِظانِ	أَيْقَظَتا	هما-f
أَيْقِظا		توقِظا	توقِظا	توقِظانِ	أَيْقَظْتُما	أنتما
		يوقِظوا	يوقِظوا	يوقِظونَ	أَيْقَظوا	هم
		يوقِظْنَ	يوقِظْنَ	يوقِظْنَ	أَيْقَظْنَ	هنّ
أَيْقِظوا		توقِظوا	توقِظوا	توقِظونَ	أَيْقَظْتُمْ	أنتم
أَيْقِظْنَ		توقِظْنَ	توقِظْنَ	توقِظْنَ	أَيْقَظْتُنَّ	أنتنّ
		نوقِظْ	نوقِظَ	نوقِظُ	أَيْقَظْنا	نحن
	Passive	يوقَظْ	يوقَظَ	يوقَظُ	أوقِظَ	هو

VN إيقاظ	PP موقَظ	AP موقِظ

Form IV - R2=أقام :و\ي

Imperative		Jussive	Subjunctive	Indicative	Perfect	
	Active	يُقِمْ	يُقيمَ	يُقيمُ	أَقامَ	هو
		تُقِمْ	تُقيمَ	تُقيمُ	أَقامَتْ	هي
أَقِمْ		تُقِمْ	تُقيمَ	تُقيمُ	أَقَمْتَ	أنتَ
أَقيمي		تُقيمي	تُقيمي	تُقيمينَ	أَقَمْتِ	أنتِ
		أُقِمْ	أُقيمَ	أُقيمُ	أَقَمْتُ	أنا
		يُقيما	يُقيما	يُقيمانِ	أَقاما	هما-m
		تُقيما	تُقيما	تُقيمانِ	أَقامَتا	هما-f
أَقيما		تُقيما	تُقيما	تُقيمانِ	أَقَمْتُما	أنتما
		يُقيموا	يُقيموا	يُقيمونَ	أَقاموا	هم
		يُقِمْنَ	يُقِمْنَ	يُقِمْنَ	أَقَمْنَ	هنّ
أَقيموا		تُقيموا	تُقيموا	تُقيمونَ	أَقَمْتُمْ	أنتم
أَقِمْنَ		تُقِمْنَ	تُقِمْنَ	تُقِمْنَ	أَقَمْتُنَّ	أنتنّ
		نُقِمْ	نُقيمَ	نُقيمُ	أَقَمْنا	نحن
	Passive	يُقَمْ	يُقامَ	يُقامُ	أُقيمَ	هو

VN إقامة	**PP** مُقام	**AP** مُقيم

Form IV - R3=أجرى :و\ي

Imperative		Jussive	Subjunctive	Indicative	Perfect	
	Active	يُجْرِ	يُجْرِيَ	يُجْري	أَجْرى	هو
		تُجْرِ	تُجْرِيَ	تُجْري	أَجْرَتْ	هي
أَجْرِ		تُجْرِ	تُجْرِيَ	تُجْري	أَجْرَيْتَ	أنتَ
أَجْري		تُجْري	تُجْري	تُجْرينَ	أَجْرَيْتِ	أنتِ
		أُجْرِ	أُجْرِيَ	أُجْري	أَجْرَيْتُ	أنا
		يُجْرِيا	يُجْرِيا	يُجْرِيانِ	أَجْرَيا	هما-m
		تُجْرِيا	تُجْرِيا	تُجْرِيانِ	أَجْرَتا	هما-f
أَجْرِيا		تُجْرِيا	تُجْرِيا	تُجْرِيانِ	أَجْرَيْتُما	أنتما
		يُجْروا	يُجْروا	يُجْرونَ	أَجْرَوْا	هم
		يُجْرينَ	يُجْرينَ	يُجْرينَ	أَجْرَيْنَ	هنّ
أَجْروا		تُجْروا	تُجْروا	تُجْرونَ	أَجْرَيْتُمْ	أنتم
أَجْرينَ		تُجْرينَ	تُجْرينَ	تُجْرينَ	أَجْرَيْتُنَّ	أنتنّ
		نُجْرِ	نُجْرِيَ	نُجْري	أَجْرَيْنا	نحن
	Passive	يُجْرَ	يُجْرى	يُجْرى	أُجْرِيَ	هو

VN إجْراء	**PP** مُجْرًى	**AP** مُجْرٍ

Form IV - R1=ء: آلم

	Imperative	Jussive	Subjunctive	Indicative	Perfect	
Active		يُؤْلِمْ	يُؤْلِمَ	يُؤْلِمُ	آلَمَ	هو
		تُؤْلِمْ	تُؤْلِمَ	تُؤْلِمُ	آلَمَتْ	هي
	آلِمْ	تُؤْلِمْ	تُؤْلِمَ	تُؤْلِمُ	آلَمْتَ	أنتَ
	آلِمي	تُؤْلِمي	تُؤْلِمي	تُؤْلِمينَ	آلَمْتِ	أنتِ
		أولِمْ	أولِمَ	أولِمُ	آلَمْتُ	أنا
		يُؤْلِما	يُؤْلِما	يُؤْلِمانِ	آلَما	هما-m
		تُؤْلِما	تُؤْلِما	تُؤْلِمانِ	آلَمَتا	هما-f
	آلِما	تُؤْلِما	تُؤْلِما	تُؤْلِمانِ	آلَمْتُما	أنتما
		يُؤْلِموا	يُؤْلِموا	يُؤْلِمونَ	آلَموا	هم
		يُؤْلِمْنَ	يُؤْلِمْنَ	يُؤْلِمْنَ	آلَمْنَ	هنّ
	آلِموا	تُؤْلِموا	تُؤْلِموا	تُؤْلِمونَ	آلَمْتُمْ	أنتم
	آلِمْنَ	تُؤْلِمْنَ	تُؤْلِمْنَ	تُؤْلِمْنَ	آلَمْتُنَّ	أنتنّ
		نُؤْلِمْ	نُؤْلِمَ	نُؤْلِمُ	آلَمْنا	نحن
Passive		يُؤْلَمْ	يُؤْلَمَ	يُؤْلَمُ	أولِمَ	هو

VN	PP	AP
إيلام	مُؤْلَم	مُؤْلِم

Form IV - R2=ء: أسأل

	Imperative	Jussive	Subjunctive	Indicative	Perfect	
Active		يُسْئِلْ	يُسْئِلَ	يُسْئِلُ	أَسْأَلَ	هو
		تُسْئِلْ	تُسْئِلَ	تُسْئِلُ	أَسْأَلَتْ	هي
	أَسْئِلْ	تُسْئِلْ	تُسْئِلَ	تُسْئِلُ	أَسْأَلْتَ	أنتَ
	أَسْئِلي	تُسْئِلي	تُسْئِلي	تُسْئِلينَ	أَسْأَلْتِ	أنتِ
		أُسْئِلْ	أُسْئِلَ	أُسْئِلُ	أَسْأَلْتُ	أنا
		يُسْئِلا	يُسْئِلا	يُسْئِلانِ	أَسْأَلا	هما-m
		تُسْئِلا	تُسْئِلا	تُسْئِلانِ	أَسْأَلَتا	هما-f
	أَسْئِلا	تُسْئِلا	تُسْئِلا	تُسْئِلانِ	أَسْأَلْتُما	أنتما
		يُسْئِلوا	يُسْئِلوا	يُسْئِلونَ	أَسْأَلوا	هم
		يُسْئِلْنَ	يُسْئِلْنَ	يُسْئِلْنَ	أَسْأَلْنَ	هنّ
	أَسْئِلوا	تُسْئِلوا	تُسْئِلوا	تُسْئِلونَ	أَسْأَلْتُمْ	أنتم
	أَسْئِلْنَ	تُسْئِلْنَ	تُسْئِلْنَ	تُسْئِلْنَ	أَسْأَلْتُنَّ	أنتنّ
		نُسْئِلْ	نُسْئِلَ	نُسْئِلُ	أَسْأَلْنا	نحن
Passive		يُسْأَلْ	يُسْأَلَ	يُسْأَلُ	أُسْئِلَ	هو

VN	PP	AP
إِسْآل	مُسْأَل	مُسْئِل

Form IV - R3=ء: أخطأ

Imperative		Jussive	Subjunctive	Indicative	Perfect	
	Active	يُخْطِئْ	يُخْطِئَ	يُخْطِئُ	أَخْطَأَ	هو
		تُخْطِئْ	تُخْطِئَ	تُخْطِئُ	أَخْطَأَتْ	هي
أَخْطِئْ		تُخْطِئْ	تُخْطِئَ	تُخْطِئُ	أَخْطَأْتَ	أنتَ
أَخْطِئي		تُخْطِئي	تُخْطِئي	تُخْطِئينَ	أَخْطَأْتِ	أنتِ
		أُخْطِئْ	أُخْطِئَ	أُخْطِئُ	أَخْطَأْتُ	أنا
		يُخْطِئا	يُخْطِئا	يُخْطِئانِ	أَخْطَآ	هما-m
		تُخْطِئا	تُخْطِئا	تُخْطِئانِ	أَخْطَأَتا	هما-f
أَخْطِئا		تُخْطِئا	تُخْطِئا	تُخْطِئانِ	أَخْطَأْتُما	أنتما
		يُخْطِئوا	يُخْطِئوا	يُخْطِئونَ	أَخْطَؤوا	هم
		يُخْطِئْنَ	يُخْطِئْنَ	يُخْطِئْنَ	أَخْطَأْنَ	هنّ
أَخْطِئوا		تُخْطِئوا	تُخْطِئوا	تُخْطِئونَ	أَخْطَأْتُمْ	أنتم
أَخْطِئْنَ		تُخْطِئْنَ	تُخْطِئْنَ	تُخْطِئْنَ	أَخْطَأْتُنَّ	أنتنّ
		نُخْطِئْ	نُخْطِئَ	نُخْطِئُ	أَخْطَأْنا	نحن
	Passive	يُخْطَأْ	يُخْطَأَ	يُخْطَأُ	أُخْطِئَ	هو

VN	PP	AP
إِخْطاء	مُخْطَأ	مُخْطِئ

Form IV - 4R اطمأنّ

Imperative		Jussive	Subjunctive	Indicative	Perfect	
	Active	يَطْمَأْنِنْ	يَطْمَئِنَّ	يَطْمَئِنُّ	اطْمَأَنَّ	هو
		تَطْمَأْنِنْ	تَطْمَئِنَّ	تَطْمَئِنُّ	اطْمَأَنَّتْ	هي
اطْمَأْنِنْ		تَطْمَأْنِنْ	تَطْمَئِنَّ	تَطْمَئِنُّ	اطْمَأْنَنْتَ	أنتَ
اطْمَئِنّي		تَطْمَئِنّي	تَطْمَئِنّي	تَطْمَئِنّينَ	اطْمَأْنَنْتِ	أنتِ
		أَطْمَأْنِنْ	أَطْمَئِنَّ	أَطْمَئِنُّ	اطْمَأْنَنْتُ	أنا
		يَطْمَئِنّا	يَطْمَئِنّا	يَطْمَئِنّانِ	اطْمَأَنّا	هما-m
		تَطْمَئِنّا	تَطْمَئِنّا	تَطْمَئِنّانِ	اطْمَأَنَّتا	هما-f
اطْمَئِنّا		تَطْمَئِنّا	تَطْمَئِنّا	تَطْمَئِنّانِ	اطْمَأْنَنْتُما	أنتما
		يَطْمَئِنّوا	يَطْمَئِنّوا	يَطْمَئِنّونَ	اطْمَأَنّوا	هم
		يَطْمَأْنِنَّ	يَطْمَأْنِنَّ	يَطْمَأْنِنَّ	اطْمَأْنَنَّ	هنّ
اطْمَئِنّوا		تَطْمَئِنّوا	تَطْمَئِنّوا	تَطْمَئِنّونَ	اطْمَأْنَنْتُمْ	أنتم
اطْمَأْنِنَّ		تَطْمَأْنِنَّ	تَطْمَأْنِنَّ	تَطْمَأْنِنَّ	اطْمَأْنَنْتُنَّ	أنتنّ
		نَطْمَأْنِنْ	نَطْمَئِنَّ	نَطْمَئِنُّ	اطْمَأْنَنّا	نحن
	Passive	يُطْمَأْنَنْ	يُطْمَأَنَّ	يُطْمَأَنُّ	اُطْمُئِنَّ	هو

VN	PP	AP
اطْمِئْنان	مُطْمَأَنّ	مُطْمَئِنّ

Form V - sound تحدث

Imperative		Jussive	Subjunctive	Indicative	Perfect	
	Active	يَتَحَدَّثْ	يَتَحَدَّثَ	يَتَحَدَّثُ	تَحَدَّثَ	هو
		تَتَحَدَّثْ	تَتَحَدَّثَ	تَتَحَدَّثُ	تَحَدَّثَتْ	هي
تَحَدَّثْ		تَتَحَدَّثْ	تَتَحَدَّثَ	تَتَحَدَّثُ	تَحَدَّثْتَ	أنتَ
تَحَدَّثي		تَتَحَدَّثي	تَتَحَدَّثي	تَتَحَدَّثينَ	تَحَدَّثْتِ	أنتِ
		أَتَحَدَّثْ	أَتَحَدَّثَ	أَتَحَدَّثُ	تَحَدَّثْتُ	أنا
		يَتَحَدَّثا	يَتَحَدَّثا	يَتَحَدَّثانِ	تَحَدَّثا	هما-m
		تَتَحَدَّثا	تَتَحَدَّثا	تَتَحَدَّثانِ	تَحَدَّثَتا	هما-f
تَحَدَّثا		تَتَحَدَّثا	تَتَحَدَّثا	تَتَحَدَّثانِ	تَحَدَّثْتُما	أنتما
		يَتَحَدَّثوا	يَتَحَدَّثوا	يَتَحَدَّثونَ	تَحَدَّثوا	هم
		يَتَحَدَّثْنَ	يَتَحَدَّثْنَ	يَتَحَدَّثْنَ	تَحَدَّثْنَ	هنّ
تَحَدَّثوا		تَتَحَدَّثوا	تَتَحَدَّثوا	تَتَحَدَّثونَ	تَحَدَّثْتُمْ	أنتم
تَحَدَّثْنَ		تَتَحَدَّثْنَ	تَتَحَدَّثْنَ	تَتَحَدَّثْنَ	تَحَدَّثْتُنَّ	أنتنّ
		نَتَحَدَّثْ	نَتَحَدَّثَ	نَتَحَدَّثُ	تَحَدَّثْنا	نحن
	Passive	يُتَحَدَّثْ	يُتَحَدَّثَ	يُتَحَدَّثُ	تُحُدِّثَ	هو

VN	PP	AP
تَحَدُّث	مُتَحَدَّث	مُتَحَدِّث

Form V - R2=R3 تردّد

Imperative		Jussive	Subjunctive	Indicative	Perfect	
	Active	يَتَرَدَّدْ	يَتَرَدَّدَ	يَتَرَدَّدُ	تَرَدَّدَ	هو
		تَتَرَدَّدْ	تَتَرَدَّدَ	تَتَرَدَّدُ	تَرَدَّدَتْ	هي
تَرَدَّدْ		تَتَرَدَّدْ	تَتَرَدَّدَ	تَتَرَدَّدُ	تَرَدَّدْتَ	أنتَ
تَرَدَّدي		تَتَرَدَّدي	تَتَرَدَّدي	تَتَرَدَّدينَ	تَرَدَّدْتِ	أنتِ
		أَتَرَدَّدْ	أَتَرَدَّدَ	أَتَرَدَّدُ	تَرَدَّدْتُ	أنا
		يَتَرَدَّدا	يَتَرَدَّدا	يَتَرَدَّدانِ	تَرَدَّدا	هما-m
		تَتَرَدَّدا	تَتَرَدَّدا	تَتَرَدَّدانِ	تَرَدَّدَتا	هما-f
تَرَدَّدا		تَتَرَدَّدا	تَتَرَدَّدا	تَتَرَدَّدانِ	تَرَدَّدْتُما	أنتما
		يَتَرَدَّدوا	يَتَرَدَّدوا	يَتَرَدَّدونَ	تَرَدَّدوا	هم
		يَتَرَدَّدْنَ	يَتَرَدَّدْنَ	يَتَرَدَّدْنَ	تَرَدَّدْنَ	هنّ
تَرَدَّدوا		تَتَرَدَّدوا	تَتَرَدَّدوا	تَتَرَدَّدونَ	تَرَدَّدْتُمْ	أنتم
تَرَدَّدْنَ		تَتَرَدَّدْنَ	تَتَرَدَّدْنَ	تَتَرَدَّدْنَ	تَرَدَّدْتُنَّ	أنتنّ
		نَتَرَدَّدْ	نَتَرَدَّدَ	نَتَرَدَّدُ	تَرَدَّدْنا	نحن
	Passive	يُتَرَدَّدْ	يُتَرَدَّدَ	يُتَرَدَّدُ	تُرُدِّدَ	هو

VN	PP	AP
تَرَدُّد	مُتَرَدَّد	مُتَرَدِّد

Form V - R1=و: توقّف

Imperative		Jussive	Subjunctive	Indicative	Perfect	
	Active	يَتَوَقَّفْ	يَتَوَقَّفَ	يَتَوَقَّفُ	تَوَقَّفَ	هو
		تَتَوَقَّفْ	تَتَوَقَّفَ	تَتَوَقَّفُ	تَوَقَّفَتْ	هي
تَوَقَّفْ		تَتَوَقَّفْ	تَتَوَقَّفَ	تَتَوَقَّفُ	تَوَقَّفْتَ	أنتَ
تَوَقَّفِي		تَتَوَقَّفِي	تَتَوَقَّفِي	تَتَوَقَّفِينَ	تَوَقَّفْتِ	أنتِ
		أَتَوَقَّفْ	أَتَوَقَّفَ	أَتَوَقَّفُ	تَوَقَّفْتُ	أنا
		يَتَوَقَّفَا	يَتَوَقَّفَا	يَتَوَقَّفَانِ	تَوَقَّفَا	هما-m
		تَتَوَقَّفَا	تَتَوَقَّفَا	تَتَوَقَّفَانِ	تَوَقَّفَتَا	هما-f
تَوَقَّفَا		تَتَوَقَّفَا	تَتَوَقَّفَا	تَتَوَقَّفَانِ	تَوَقَّفْتُمَا	أنتما
		يَتَوَقَّفُوا	يَتَوَقَّفُوا	يَتَوَقَّفُونَ	تَوَقَّفُوا	هم
		يَتَوَقَّفْنَ	يَتَوَقَّفْنَ	يَتَوَقَّفْنَ	تَوَقَّفْنَ	هنّ
تَوَقَّفُوا		تَتَوَقَّفُوا	تَتَوَقَّفُوا	تَتَوَقَّفُونَ	تَوَقَّفْتُمْ	أنتم
تَوَقَّفْنَ		تَتَوَقَّفْنَ	تَتَوَقَّفْنَ	تَتَوَقَّفْنَ	تَوَقَّفْتُنَّ	أنتنّ
		نَتَوَقَّفْ	نَتَوَقَّفَ	نَتَوَقَّفُ	تَوَقَّفْنَا	نحن
	Passive	يُتَوَقَّفْ	يُتَوَقَّفَ	يُتَوَقَّفُ	تُوُقِّفَ	هو

VN تَوَقُّف	PP مُتَوَقَّف	AP مُتَوَقِّف

Form V - R1=ي: تيسّر

Imperative		Jussive	Subjunctive	Indicative	Perfect	
	Active	يَتَيَسَّرْ	يَتَيَسَّرَ	يَتَيَسَّرُ	تَيَسَّرَ	هو
		تَتَيَسَّرْ	تَتَيَسَّرَ	تَتَيَسَّرُ	تَيَسَّرَتْ	هي
تَيَسَّرْ		تَتَيَسَّرْ	تَتَيَسَّرَ	تَتَيَسَّرُ	تَيَسَّرْتَ	أنتَ
تَيَسَّرِي		تَتَيَسَّرِي	تَتَيَسَّرِي	تَتَيَسَّرِينَ	تَيَسَّرْتِ	أنتِ
		أَتَيَسَّرْ	أَتَيَسَّرَ	أَتَيَسَّرُ	تَيَسَّرْتُ	أنا
		يَتَيَسَّرَا	يَتَيَسَّرَا	يَتَيَسَّرَانِ	تَيَسَّرَا	هما-m
		تَتَيَسَّرَا	تَتَيَسَّرَا	تَتَيَسَّرَانِ	تَيَسَّرَتَا	هما-f
تَيَسَّرَا		تَتَيَسَّرَا	تَتَيَسَّرَا	تَتَيَسَّرَانِ	تَيَسَّرْتُمَا	أنتما
		يَتَيَسَّرُوا	يَتَيَسَّرُوا	يَتَيَسَّرُونَ	تَيَسَّرُوا	هم
		يَتَيَسَّرْنَ	يَتَيَسَّرْنَ	يَتَيَسَّرْنَ	تَيَسَّرْنَ	هنّ
تَيَسَّرُوا		تَتَيَسَّرُوا	تَتَيَسَّرُوا	تَتَيَسَّرُونَ	تَيَسَّرْتُمْ	أنتم
تَيَسَّرْنَ		تَتَيَسَّرْنَ	تَتَيَسَّرْنَ	تَتَيَسَّرْنَ	تَيَسَّرْتُنَّ	أنتنّ
		نَتَيَسَّرْ	نَتَيَسَّرَ	نَتَيَسَّرُ	تَيَسَّرْنَا	نحن
	Passive	يُتَيَسَّرْ	يُتَيَسَّرَ	يُتَيَسَّرُ	تُيُسِّرَ	هو

VN تَيَسُّر	PP مُتَيَسَّر	AP مُتَيَسِّر

Form V - R2=و: تصوّر

Imperative		Jussive	Subjunctive	Indicative	Perfect	
	Active	يَتَصَوَّرْ	يَتَصَوَّرَ	يَتَصَوَّرُ	تَصَوَّرَ	هو
		تَتَصَوَّرْ	تَتَصَوَّرَ	تَتَصَوَّرُ	تَصَوَّرَتْ	هي
تَصَوَّرْ		تَتَصَوَّرْ	تَتَصَوَّرَ	تَتَصَوَّرُ	تَصَوَّرْتَ	أنتَ
تَصَوَّرِي		تَتَصَوَّرِي	تَتَصَوَّرِي	تَتَصَوَّرِينَ	تَصَوَّرْتِ	أنتِ
		أَتَصَوَّرْ	أَتَصَوَّرَ	أَتَصَوَّرُ	تَصَوَّرْتُ	أنا
		يَتَصَوَّرَا	يَتَصَوَّرَا	يَتَصَوَّرَانِ	تَصَوَّرَا	هما-m
		تَتَصَوَّرَا	تَتَصَوَّرَا	تَتَصَوَّرَانِ	تَصَوَّرَتَا	هما-f
تَصَوَّرَا		تَتَصَوَّرَا	تَتَصَوَّرَا	تَتَصَوَّرَانِ	تَصَوَّرْتُمَا	أنتما
		يَتَصَوَّرُوا	يَتَصَوَّرُوا	يَتَصَوَّرُونَ	تَصَوَّرُوا	هم
		يَتَصَوَّرْنَ	يَتَصَوَّرْنَ	يَتَصَوَّرْنَ	تَصَوَّرْنَ	هنّ
تَصَوَّرُوا		تَتَصَوَّرُوا	تَتَصَوَّرُوا	تَتَصَوَّرُونَ	تَصَوَّرْتُمْ	أنتم
تَصَوَّرْنَ		تَتَصَوَّرْنَ	تَتَصَوَّرْنَ	تَتَصَوَّرْنَ	تَصَوَّرْتُنَّ	أنتنّ
		نَتَصَوَّرْ	نَتَصَوَّرَ	نَتَصَوَّرُ	تَصَوَّرْنَا	نحن
	Passive	يُتَصَوَّرْ	يُتَصَوَّرَ	يُتَصَوَّرُ	تُصُوِّرَ	هو

VN تَصَوُّر	PP مُتَصَوَّر	AP مُتَصَوِّر

Form V - R2=ي: تغيّر

Imperative		Jussive	Subjunctive	Indicative	Perfect	
	Active	يَتَغَيَّرْ	يَتَغَيَّرَ	يَتَغَيَّرُ	تَغَيَّرَ	هو
		تَتَغَيَّرْ	تَتَغَيَّرَ	تَتَغَيَّرُ	تَغَيَّرَتْ	هي
تَغَيَّرْ		تَتَغَيَّرْ	تَتَغَيَّرَ	تَتَغَيَّرُ	تَغَيَّرْتَ	أنتَ
تَغَيَّرِي		تَتَغَيَّرِي	تَتَغَيَّرِي	تَتَغَيَّرِينَ	تَغَيَّرْتِ	أنتِ
		أَتَغَيَّرْ	أَتَغَيَّرَ	أَتَغَيَّرُ	تَغَيَّرْتُ	أنا
		يَتَغَيَّرَا	يَتَغَيَّرَا	يَتَغَيَّرَانِ	تَغَيَّرَا	هما-m
		تَتَغَيَّرَا	تَتَغَيَّرَا	تَتَغَيَّرَانِ	تَغَيَّرَتَا	هما-f
تَغَيَّرَا		تَتَغَيَّرَا	تَتَغَيَّرَا	تَتَغَيَّرَانِ	تَغَيَّرْتُمَا	أنتما
		يَتَغَيَّرُوا	يَتَغَيَّرُوا	يَتَغَيَّرُونَ	تَغَيَّرُوا	هم
		يَتَغَيَّرْنَ	يَتَغَيَّرْنَ	يَتَغَيَّرْنَ	تَغَيَّرْنَ	هنّ
تَغَيَّرُوا		تَتَغَيَّرُوا	تَتَغَيَّرُوا	تَتَغَيَّرُونَ	تَغَيَّرْتُمْ	أنتم
تَغَيَّرْنَ		تَتَغَيَّرْنَ	تَتَغَيَّرْنَ	تَتَغَيَّرْنَ	تَغَيَّرْتُنَّ	أنتنّ
		نَتَغَيَّرْ	نَتَغَيَّرَ	نَتَغَيَّرُ	تَغَيَّرْنَا	نحن
	Passive	يُتَغَيَّرْ	يُتَغَيَّرَ	يُتَغَيَّرُ	تُغُيِّرَ	هو

VN تَغَيُّر	PP مُتَغَيَّر	AP مُتَغَيِّر

Form V - R3=و\ي: تبقّى

Imperative		Jussive	Subjunctive	Indicative	Perfect	
	Active	يَتَبَقَّ	يَتَبَقّى	يَتَبَقّى	تَبَقّى	هو
		تَتَبَقَّ	تَتَبَقّى	تَتَبَقّى	تَبَقَّتْ	هي
تَبَقَّ		تَتَبَقَّ	تَتَبَقّى	تَتَبَقّى	تَبَقَّيْتَ	أنتَ
تَبَقَّيْ		تَتَبَقَّيْ	تَتَبَقَّيْ	تَتَبَقَّيْنَ	تَبَقَّيْتِ	أنتِ
		أَتَبَقَّ	أَتَبَقّى	أَتَبَقّى	تَبَقَّيْتُ	أنا
		يَتَبَقَّيا	يَتَبَقَّيا	يَتَبَقَّيانِ	تَبَقَّيا	هما-m
		تَتَبَقَّيا	تَتَبَقَّيا	تَتَبَقَّيانِ	تَبَقَّتا	هما-f
تَبَقَّيا		تَتَبَقَّيا	تَتَبَقَّيا	تَتَبَقَّيانِ	تَبَقَّيْتُما	أنتما
		يَتَبَقَّوْا	يَتَبَقَّوْا	يَتَبَقَّوْنَ	تَبَقَّوْا	هم
		يَتَبَقَّيْنَ	يَتَبَقَّيْنَ	يَتَبَقَّيْنَ	تَبَقَّيْنَ	هنّ
تَبَقَّوْا		تَتَبَقَّوْا	تَتَبَقَّوْا	تَتَبَقَّوْنَ	تَبَقَّيْتُمْ	أنتم
تَبَقَّيْنَ		تَتَبَقَّيْنَ	تَتَبَقَّيْنَ	تَتَبَقَّيْنَ	تَبَقَّيْتُنَّ	أنتنّ
		نَتَبَقَّ	نَتَبَقّى	نَتَبَقّى	تَبَقَّيْنا	نحن
	Passive	يُتَبَقَّ	يُتَبَقّى	يُتَبَقّى	تُبُقِّيَ	هو

VN	PP	AP
تَبَقٍّ	مُتَبَقًّى	مُتَبَقٍّ

Form V - R1=ء: تأهّل

Imperative		Jussive	Subjunctive	Indicative	Perfect	
	Active	يَتَأَهَّلْ	يَتَأَهَّلَ	يَتَأَهَّلُ	تَأَهَّلَ	هو
		تَتَأَهَّلْ	تَتَأَهَّلَ	تَتَأَهَّلُ	تَأَهَّلَتْ	هي
تَأَهَّلْ		تَتَأَهَّلْ	تَتَأَهَّلَ	تَتَأَهَّلُ	تَأَهَّلْتَ	أنتَ
تَأَهَّلي		تَتَأَهَّلي	تَتَأَهَّلي	تَتَأَهَّلينَ	تَأَهَّلْتِ	أنتِ
		أَتَأَهَّلْ	أَتَأَهَّلَ	أَتَأَهَّلُ	تَأَهَّلْتُ	أنا
		يَتَأَهَّلا	يَتَأَهَّلا	يَتَأَهَّلانِ	تَأَهَّلا	هما-m
		تَتَأَهَّلا	تَتَأَهَّلا	تَتَأَهَّلانِ	تَأَهَّلَتا	هما-f
تَأَهَّلا		تَتَأَهَّلا	تَتَأَهَّلا	تَتَأَهَّلانِ	تَأَهَّلْتُما	أنتما
		يَتَأَهَّلوا	يَتَأَهَّلوا	يَتَأَهَّلونَ	تَأَهَّلوا	هم
		يَتَأَهَّلْنَ	يَتَأَهَّلْنَ	يَتَأَهَّلْنَ	تَأَهَّلْنَ	هنّ
تَأَهَّلوا		تَتَأَهَّلوا	تَتَأَهَّلوا	تَتَأَهَّلونَ	تَأَهَّلْتُمْ	أنتم
تَأَهَّلْنَ		تَتَأَهَّلْنَ	تَتَأَهَّلْنَ	تَتَأَهَّلْنَ	تَأَهَّلْتُنَّ	أنتنّ
		نَتَأَهَّلْ	نَتَأَهَّلَ	نَتَأَهَّلُ	تَأَهَّلْنا	نحن
	Passive	يُتَأَهَّلْ	يُتَأَهَّلَ	يُتَأَهَّلُ	تُؤُهِّلَ	هو

VN	PP	AP
تَأَهُّل	مُتَأَهَّل	مُتَأَهِّل

Form V - R2=ء: تراّس

Imperative		Jussive	Subjunctive	Indicative	Perfect	
	Active	يَتَرَأَّسْ	يَتَرَأَّسَ	يَتَرَأَّسُ	تَرَأَّسَ	هو
		تَتَرَأَّسْ	تَتَرَأَّسَ	تَتَرَأَّسُ	تَرَأَّسَتْ	هي
تَرَأَّسْ		تَتَرَأَّسْ	تَتَرَأَّسَ	تَتَرَأَّسُ	تَرَأَّسْتَ	أنتَ
تَرَأَّسي		تَتَرَأَّسي	تَتَرَأَّسي	تَتَرَأَّسينَ	تَرَأَّسْتِ	أنتِ
		أَتَرَأَّسْ	أَتَرَأَّسَ	أَتَرَأَّسُ	تَرَأَّسْتُ	أنا
		يَتَرَأَّسا	يَتَرَأَّسا	يَتَرَأَّسانِ	تَرَأَّسا	m–هما
		تَتَرَأَّسا	تَتَرَأَّسا	تَتَرَأَّسانِ	تَرَأَّسَتا	f–هما
تَرَأَّسا		تَتَرَأَّسا	تَتَرَأَّسا	تَتَرَأَّسانِ	تَرَأَّسْتُما	أنتما
		يَتَرَأَّسوا	يَتَرَأَّسوا	يَتَرَأَّسونَ	تَرَأَّسوا	هم
		يَتَرَأَّسْنَ	يَتَرَأَّسْنَ	يَتَرَأَّسْنَ	تَرَأَّسْنَ	هنّ
تَرَأَّسوا		تَتَرَأَّسوا	تَتَرَأَّسوا	تَتَرَأَّسونَ	تَرَأَّسْتُمْ	أنتم
تَرَأَّسْنَ		تَتَرَأَّسْنَ	تَتَرَأَّسْنَ	تَتَرَأَّسْنَ	تَرَأَّسْتُنَّ	أنتنّ
		نَتَرَأَّسْ	نَتَرَأَّسَ	نَتَرَأَّسُ	تَرَأَّسْنا	نحن
	Passive	يُتَرَأَّسْ	يُتَرَأَّسَ	يُتَرَأَّسُ	تُرُؤِّسَ	هو

VN	PP	AP
تَرَؤُّس	مُتَرَأَّس	مُتَرَئِّس

Form V - R3=ء: تجرّأ

Imperative		Jussive	Subjunctive	Indicative	Perfect	
	Active	يَتَجَرَّأْ	يَتَجَرَّأَ	يَتَجَرَّأُ	تَجَرَّأَ	هو
		تَتَجَرَّأْ	تَتَجَرَّأَ	تَتَجَرَّأُ	تَجَرَّأَتْ	هي
تَجَرَّأْ		تَتَجَرَّأْ	تَتَجَرَّأَ	تَتَجَرَّأُ	تَجَرَّأْتَ	أنتَ
تَجَرَّئي		تَتَجَرَّئي	تَتَجَرَّئي	تَتَجَرَّئينَ	تَجَرَّأْتِ	أنتِ
		أَتَجَرَّأْ	أَتَجَرَّأَ	أَتَجَرَّأُ	تَجَرَّأْتُ	أنا
		يَتَجَرَّآ	يَتَجَرَّآ	يَتَجَرَّآنِ	تَجَرَّآ	m–هما
		تَتَجَرَّآ	تَتَجَرَّآ	تَتَجَرَّآنِ	تَجَرَّأَتا	f–هما
تَجَرَّآ		تَتَجَرَّآ	تَتَجَرَّآ	تَتَجَرَّآنِ	تَجَرَّأْتُما	أنتما
		يَتَجَرَّؤوا	يَتَجَرَّؤوا	يَتَجَرَّؤونَ	تَجَرَّؤوا	هم
		يَتَجَرَّأْنَ	يَتَجَرَّأْنَ	يَتَجَرَّأْنَ	تَجَرَّأْنَ	هنّ
تَجَرَّؤوا		تَتَجَرَّؤوا	تَتَجَرَّؤوا	تَتَجَرَّؤونَ	تَجَرَّأْتُمْ	أنتم
تَجَرَّأْنَ		تَتَجَرَّأْنَ	تَتَجَرَّأْنَ	تَتَجَرَّأْنَ	تَجَرَّأْتُنَّ	أنتنّ
		نَتَجَرَّأْ	نَتَجَرَّأَ	نَتَجَرَّأُ	تَجَرَّأْنا	نحن
	Passive	يُتَجَرَّأْ	يُتَجَرَّأَ	يُتَجَرَّأُ	تُجُرِّئَ	هو

VN	PP	AP
تَجَرُّؤ	مُتَجَرَّأ	مُتَجَرِّئ

Form VI - sound تبادل

Imperative		Jussive	Subjunctive	Indicative	Perfect	
	Active	يَتَبادَلْ	يَتَبادَلَ	يَتَبادَلُ	تَبادَلَ	هو
		تَتَبادَلْ	تَتَبادَلَ	تَتَبادَلُ	تَبادَلَتْ	هي
تَبادَلْ		تَتَبادَلْ	تَتَبادَلَ	تَتَبادَلُ	تَبادَلْتَ	أنتَ
تَبادَلي		تَتَبادَلي	تَتَبادَلي	تَتَبادَلينَ	تَبادَلْتِ	أنتِ
		أَتَبادَلْ	أَتَبادَلَ	أَتَبادَلُ	تَبادَلْتُ	أنا
		يَتَبادَلا	يَتَبادَلا	يَتَبادَلانِ	تَبادَلا	هما-m
		تَتَبادَلا	تَتَبادَلا	تَتَبادَلانِ	تَبادَلَتا	هما-f
تَبادَلا		تَتَبادَلا	تَتَبادَلا	تَتَبادَلانِ	تَبادَلْتُما	أنتما
		يَتَبادَلوا	يَتَبادَلوا	يَتَبادَلونَ	تَبادَلوا	هم
		يَتَبادَلْنَ	يَتَبادَلْنَ	يَتَبادَلْنَ	تَبادَلْنَ	هنّ
تَبادَلوا		تَتَبادَلوا	تَتَبادَلوا	تَتَبادَلونَ	تَبادَلْتُمْ	أنتم
تَبادَلْنَ		تَتَبادَلْنَ	تَتَبادَلْنَ	تَتَبادَلْنَ	تَبادَلْتُنَّ	أنتنّ
		نَتَبادَلْ	نَتَبادَلَ	نَتَبادَلُ	تَبادَلْنا	نحن
	Passive	يُتَبادَلْ	يُتَبادَلَ	يُتَبادَلُ	تُبودِلَ	هو

VN تَبادُل	PP مُتَبادَل	AP مُتَبادِل

Form VI - R2=R3 تحابّ

Imperative		Jussive	Subjunctive	Indicative	Perfect	
	Active	يَتَحابَبْ	يَتَحابَّ	يَتَحابُّ	تَحابَّ	هو
		تَتَحابَبْ	تَتَحابَّ	تَتَحابُّ	تَحابَّتْ	هي
تَحابَبْ		تَتَحابَبْ	تَتَحابَّ	تَتَحابُّ	تَحابَبْتَ	أنتَ
تَحابّي		تَتَحابّي	تَتَحابّي	تَتَحابّينَ	تَحابَبْتِ	أنتِ
		أَتَحابَبْ	أَتَحابَّ	أَتَحابُّ	تَحابَبْتُ	أنا
		يَتَحابّا	يَتَحابّا	يَتَحابّانِ	تَحابّا	هما-m
		تَتَحابّا	تَتَحابّا	تَتَحابّانِ	تَحابَّتا	هما-f
تَحابّا		تَتَحابّا	تَتَحابّا	تَتَحابّانِ	تَحابَبْتُما	أنتما
		يَتَحابّوا	يَتَحابّوا	يَتَحابّونَ	تَحابّوا	هم
		يَتَحابَبْنَ	يَتَحابَبْنَ	يَتَحابَبْنَ	تَحابَبْنَ	هنّ
تَحابّوا		تَتَحابّوا	تَتَحابّوا	تَتَحابّونَ	تَحابَبْتُمْ	أنتم
تَحابَبْنَ		تَتَحابَبْنَ	تَتَحابَبْنَ	تَتَحابَبْنَ	تَحابَبْتُنَّ	أنتنّ
		نَتَحابَبْ	نَتَحابَّ	نَتَحابُّ	تَحابَبْنا	نحن
	Passive	يُتَحابَبْ	يُتَحابَّ	يُتَحابُّ	تُحوبَّ	هو

VN تَجابّ	PP مُتَجابّ	AP مُتَجابّ

Form VI - R1=و: تواصل

Imperative		Jussive	Subjunctive	Indicative	Perfect	
	Active	يَتواصَلْ	يَتواصَلَ	يَتواصَلُ	تَواصَلَ	هو
		تَتواصَلْ	تَتواصَلَ	تَتواصَلُ	تَواصَلَتْ	هي
تَواصَلْ		تَتواصَلْ	تَتواصَلَ	تَتواصَلُ	تَواصَلْتَ	أنتَ
تَواصَلي		تَتواصَلي	تَتواصَلي	تَتواصَلينَ	تَواصَلْتِ	أنتِ
		أَتواصَلْ	أَتواصَلَ	أَتواصَلُ	تَواصَلْتُ	أنا
		يَتَواصَلا	يَتَواصَلا	يَتَواصَلانِ	تَواصَلا	m-هما
		تَتَواصَلا	تَتَواصَلا	تَتَواصَلانِ	تَواصَلَتا	f-هما
تَواصَلا		تَتَواصَلا	تَتَواصَلا	تَتَواصَلانِ	تَواصَلْتُما	أنتما
		يَتَواصَلوا	يَتَواصَلوا	يَتَواصَلونَ	تَواصَلوا	هم
		يَتَواصَلْنَ	يَتَواصَلْنَ	يَتَواصَلْنَ	تَواصَلْنَ	هنّ
تَواصَلوا		تَتَواصَلوا	تَتَواصَلوا	تَتَواصَلونَ	تَواصَلْتُمْ	أنتم
تَواصَلْنَ		تَتَواصَلْنَ	تَتَواصَلْنَ	تَتَواصَلْنَ	تَواصَلْتُنَّ	أنتنّ
		نَتَواصَلْ	نَتَواصَلَ	نَتَواصَلُ	تَواصَلْنا	نحن
	Passive	يُتَواصَلْ	يُتَواصَلَ	يُتَواصَلُ	تُووصِلَ	هو

VN	PP	AP
تَواصُل	مُتَواصَل	مُتَواصِل

Form VI - R2=و: تجاوز

Imperative		Jussive	Subjunctive	Indicative	Perfect	
	Active	يَتَجاوَزْ	يَتَجاوَزَ	يَتَجاوَزُ	تَجاوَزَ	هو
		تَتَجاوَزْ	تَتَجاوَزَ	تَتَجاوَزُ	تَجاوَزَتْ	هي
تَجاوَزْ		تَتَجاوَزْ	تَتَجاوَزَ	تَتَجاوَزُ	تَجاوَزْتَ	أنتَ
تَجاوَزي		تَتَجاوَزي	تَتَجاوَزي	تَتَجاوَزينَ	تَجاوَزْتِ	أنتِ
		أَتَجاوَزْ	أَتَجاوَزَ	أَتَجاوَزُ	تَجاوَزْتُ	أنا
		يَتَجاوَزا	يَتَجاوَزا	يَتَجاوَزانِ	تَجاوَزا	m-هما
		تَتَجاوَزا	تَتَجاوَزا	تَتَجاوَزانِ	تَجاوَزَتا	f-هما
تَجاوَزا		تَتَجاوَزا	تَتَجاوَزا	تَتَجاوَزانِ	تَجاوَزْتُما	أنتما
		يَتَجاوَزوا	يَتَجاوَزوا	يَتَجاوَزونَ	تَجاوَزوا	هم
		يَتَجاوَزْنَ	يَتَجاوَزْنَ	يَتَجاوَزْنَ	تَجاوَزْنَ	هنّ
تَجاوَزوا		تَتَجاوَزوا	تَتَجاوَزوا	تَتَجاوَزونَ	تَجاوَزْتُمْ	أنتم
تَجاوَزْنَ		تَتَجاوَزْنَ	تَتَجاوَزْنَ	تَتَجاوَزْنَ	تَجاوَزْتُنَّ	أنتنّ
		نَتَجاوَزْ	نَتَجاوَزَ	نَتَجاوَزُ	تَجاوَزْنا	نحن
	Passive	يُتَجاوَزْ	يُتَجاوَزَ	يُتَجاوَزُ	تُجووِزَ	هو

VN	PP	AP
تَجاوُز	مُتَجاوَز	مُتَجاوِز

Form VI - R2=ي: تزايد

Imperative		Jussive	Subjunctive	Indicative	Perfect	
	Active	يتزايَدْ	يتزايَدَ	يتزايَدُ	تزايَدَ	هو
		تتزايَدْ	تتزايَدَ	تتزايَدُ	تزايَدَتْ	هي
تزايَدْ		تتزايَدْ	تتزايَدَ	تتزايَدُ	تَزايَدْتَ	أنتَ
تزايَدي		تتزايَدي	تتزايَدي	تتزايَدين	تَزايَدْتِ	أنتِ
		أتزايَدْ	أتزايَدَ	أتزايَدُ	تَزايَدْتُ	أنا
		يتزايَدا	يتزايَدا	يتزايَدانِ	تزايَدا	هما-m
		تتزايَدا	تتزايَدا	تتزايَدانِ	تزايَدَتا	هما-f
تزايَدا		تتزايَدا	تتزايَدا	تتزايَدانِ	تَزايَدْتُما	أنتما
		يتزايَدوا	يتزايَدوا	يتزايَدونَ	تزايَدوا	هم
		يتزايَدْنَ	يتزايَدْنَ	يتزايَدْنَ	تزايَدْنَ	هنّ
تَزايَدوا		تتزايَدوا	تتزايَدوا	تتزايَدونَ	تزايَدْتُمْ	أنتم
تَزايَدْنَ		تتزايَدْنَ	تتزايَدْنَ	تتزايَدْنَ	تزايَدْتُنَّ	أنتنّ
		نتزايَدْ	نتزايَدَ	نتزايَدُ	تزايَدْنا	نحن
	Passive	يُتزايَدْ	يُتزايَدَ	يُتزايَدُ	تُزويِدَ	هو

VN تزايُد	PP مُتزايَد	AP مُتزايِد

Form VI - R3=و\ي: تمادى

Imperative		Jussive	Subjunctive	Indicative	Perfect	
	Active	يَتمادَ	يَتمادى	يَتمادى	تمادى	هو
		تَتمادَ	تتمادى	تتمادى	تمادَتْ	هي
تَمادَ		تَتمادَ	تتمادى	تتمادى	تَمادَيْتَ	أنتَ
تَماديْ		تَتماديْ	تَتماديْ	تَتمادَيْنَ	تَمادَيْتِ	أنتِ
		أتمادَ	أتمادى	أتمادى	تَمادَيْتُ	أنا
		يَتمادَيا	يَتمادَيا	يَتمادَيانِ	تمادَيا	هما-m
		تَتمادَيا	تَتمادَيا	تَتمادَيانِ	تمادَتا	هما-f
تمادَيا		تَتمادَيا	تَتمادَيا	تَتمادَيانِ	تمادَيْتُما	أنتما
		يَتمادَوْا	يَتمادَوْا	يَتمادَوْنَ	تمادَوْا	هم
		يَتمادَيْنَ	يَتمادَيْنَ	يَتمادَيْنَ	تمادَيْنَ	هنّ
تمادَوْا		تَتمادَوْا	تَتمادَوْا	تَتمادَوْنَ	تمادَيْتُم	أنتم
تَمادَيْنَ		تَتمادَيْنَ	تَتمادَيْنَ	تَتمادَيْنَ	تَمادَيْتُنَّ	أنتنّ
		نَتمادَ	نَتمادى	نَتمادى	تمادَيْنا	نحن
	Passive	يُتَمادَ	يُتمادى	يُتمادى	تُمودِيَ	هو

VN تَمادٍ	PP مُتمادًى	AP مُتمادٍ

Form VI - R1=ء: تآمر

Imperative		Jussive	Subjunctive	Indicative	Perfect	
	Active	يَتآمَرْ	يَتآمَرَ	يَتآمَرُ	تآمَرَ	هو
		تَتآمَرْ	تَتآمَرَ	تَتآمَرُ	تآمَرَتْ	هي
تَآمَرْ		تَتآمَرْ	تَتآمَرَ	تَتآمَرُ	تآمَرْتَ	أنتَ
تَآمَري		تَتآمَري	تَتآمَري	تَتآمَرينَ	تآمَرْتِ	أنتِ
		أَتآمَرْ	أَتآمَرَ	أَتآمَرُ	تآمَرْتُ	أنا
		يَتآمَرا	يَتآمَرا	يَتآمَرانِ	تآمَرا	هما-m
		تَتآمَرا	تَتآمَرا	تَتآمَرانِ	تآمَرَتا	هما-f
تآمَرا		تَتآمَرا	تَتآمَرا	تَتآمَرانِ	تآمَرْتُما	أنتما
		يَتآمَروا	يَتآمَروا	يَتآمَرونَ	تآمَروا	هم
		يَتآمَرْنَ	يَتآمَرْنَ	يَتآمَرْنَ	تآمَرْنَ	هنّ
تآمَروا		تَتآمَروا	تَتآمَروا	تَتآمَرونَ	تآمَرْتُمْ	أنتم
تآمَرْنَ		تَتآمَرْنَ	تَتآمَرْنَ	تَتآمَرْنَ	تآمَرْتُنَّ	أنتنّ
		نَتآمَرْ	نَتآمَرَ	نَتآمَرُ	تآمَرْنا	نحن
	Passive	يُتآمَرْ	يُتآمَرَ	يُتآمَرُ	تُؤومِرَ	هو

VN تآمُر	PP مُتآمَر	AP مُتآمِر

Form VI - R2=ء: تساءل

Imperative		Jussive	Subjunctive	Indicative	Perfect	
	Active	يَتَساءَلْ	يَتَساءَلَ	يَتَساءَلُ	تَساءَلَ	هو
		تَتَساءَلْ	تَتَساءَلَ	تَتَساءَلُ	تَساءَلَتْ	هي
تَساءَلْ		تَتَساءَلْ	تَتَساءَلَ	تَتَساءَلُ	تَساءَلْتَ	أنتَ
تَساءَلي		تَتَساءَلي	تَتَساءَلي	تَتَساءَلينَ	تَساءَلْتِ	أنتِ
		أَتَساءَلْ	أَتَساءَلَ	أَتَساءَلُ	تَساءَلْتُ	أنا
		يَتَساءَلا	يَتَساءَلا	يَتَساءَلانِ	تَساءَلا	هما-m
		تَتَساءَلا	تَتَساءَلا	تَتَساءَلانِ	تَساءَلَتا	هما-f
تَساءَلا		تَتَساءَلا	تَتَساءَلا	تَتَساءَلانِ	تَساءَلْتُما	أنتما
		يَتَساءَلوا	يَتَساءَلوا	يَتَساءَلونَ	تَساءَلوا	هم
		يَتَساءَلْنَ	يَتَساءَلْنَ	يَتَساءَلْنَ	تَساءَلْنَ	هنّ
تَساءَلوا		تَتَساءَلوا	تَتَساءَلوا	تَتَساءَلونَ	تَساءَلْتُمْ	أنتم
تَساءَلْنَ		تَتَساءَلْنَ	تَتَساءَلْنَ	تَتَساءَلْنَ	تَساءَلْتُنَّ	أنتنّ
		نَتَساءَلْ	نَتَساءَلَ	نَتَساءَلُ	تَساءَلْنا	نحن
	Passive	يُتَساءَلْ	يُتَساءَلَ	يُتَساءَلُ	تُسوئِلَ	هو

VN تَساؤُل	PP مُتَساءَل	AP مُتَسائِل

Form VI - R3=تباطأ :ء

Imperative		Jussive	Subjunctive	Indicative	Perfect	
	Active	يَتَباطَأْ	يَتَباطَأَ	يَتَباطَأُ	تَباطَأَ	هو
		تَتَباطَأْ	تَتَباطَأَ	تَتَباطَأُ	تَباطَأَتْ	هي
تَباطَأْ		تَتَباطَأْ	تَتَباطَأَ	تَتَباطَأُ	تَباطَأْتَ	أنتَ
تَباطَئي		تَتَباطَئي	تَتَباطَئي	تَتَباطَئينَ	تَباطَأْتِ	أنتِ
		أَتَباطَأْ	أَتَباطَأَ	أَتَباطَأُ	تَباطَأْتُ	أنا
		يَتَباطَآ	يَتَباطَآ	يَتَباطَآنِ	تَباطَآ	هما-m
		تَتَباطَآ	تَتَباطَآ	تَتَباطَآنِ	تَباطَأَتا	هما-f
تَباطَآ		تَتَباطَآ	تَتَباطَآ	تَتَباطَآنِ	تَباطَأْتُما	أنتما
		يَتَباطَؤوا	يَتَباطَؤوا	يَتَباطَؤونَ	تَباطَؤوا	هم
		يَتَباطَأْنَ	يَتَباطَأْنَ	يَتَباطَأْنَ	تَباطَأْنَ	هنّ
تَباطَؤوا		تَتَباطَؤوا	تَتَباطَؤوا	تَتَباطَؤونَ	تَباطَأْتُمْ	أنتم
تَباطَأْنَ		تَتَباطَأْنَ	تَتَباطَأْنَ	تَتَباطَأْنَ	تَباطَأْتُنَّ	أنتنّ
		نَتَباطَأْ	نَتَباطَأَ	نَتَباطَأُ	تَباطَأْنا	نحن
	Passive	يُتَباطَأْ	يُتَباطَأَ	يُتَباطَأُ	تُبوطِئَ	هو

VN تَباطُؤ	**PP** مُتَباطَأ	**AP** مُتَباطِئ

Form VII - sound انخفض

Imperative		Jussive	Subjunctive	Indicative	Perfect	
	Active	يَنْخَفِضْ	يَنْخَفِضَ	يَنْخَفِضُ	انْخَفَضَ	هو
		تَنْخَفِضْ	تَنْخَفِضَ	تَنْخَفِضُ	انْخَفَضَتْ	هي
انْخَفِضْ		تَنْخَفِضْ	تَنْخَفِضَ	تَنْخَفِضُ	انْخَفَضْتَ	أنتَ
انْخَفِضي		تَنْخَفِضي	تَنْخَفِضي	تَنْخَفِضينَ	انْخَفَضْتِ	أنتِ
		أَنْخَفِضْ	أَنْخَفِضَ	أَنْخَفِضُ	انْخَفَضْتُ	أنا
		يَنْخَفِضا	يَنْخَفِضا	يَنْخَفِضانِ	انْخَفَضا	هما-m
		تَنْخَفِضا	تَنْخَفِضا	تَنْخَفِضانِ	انْخَفَضَتا	هما-f
انْخَفِضا		تَنْخَفِضا	تَنْخَفِضا	تَنْخَفِضانِ	انْخَفَضْتُما	أنتما
		يَنْخَفِضوا	يَنْخَفِضوا	يَنْخَفِضونَ	انْخَفَضوا	هم
		يَنْخَفِضْنَ	يَنْخَفِضْنَ	يَنْخَفِضْنَ	انْخَفَضْنَ	هنّ
انْخَفِضوا		تَنْخَفِضوا	تَنْخَفِضوا	تَنْخَفِضونَ	انْخَفَضْتُمْ	أنتم
انْخَفِضْنَ		تَنْخَفِضْنَ	تَنْخَفِضْنَ	تَنْخَفِضْنَ	انْخَفَضْتُنَّ	أنتنّ
		نَنْخَفِضْ	نَنْخَفِضَ	نَنْخَفِضُ	انْخَفَضْنا	نحن
	Passive	يُنْخَفَضْ	يُنْخَفَضَ	يُنْخَفَضُ	انْخُفِضَ	هو

VN انْخِفاض	**PP** مُنْخَفَض	**AP** مُنْخَفِض

Form VII - R2=R3 انشقّ

Imperative		Jussive	Subjunctive	Indicative	Perfect	
	Active	يَنْشَقِقْ	يَنْشَقَّ	يَنْشَقُّ	انْشَقَّ	هو
		تَنْشَقِقْ	تَنْشَقَّ	تَنْشَقُّ	انْشَقَّتْ	هي
انْشَقِقْ		تَنْشَقِقْ	تَنْشَقَّ	تَنْشَقُّ	انْشَقَقْتَ	أنتَ
انْشَقّي		تَنْشَقّي	تَنْشَقّي	تَنْشَقّينَ	انْشَقَقْتِ	أنتِ
		أَنْشَقِقْ	أَنْشَقَّ	أَنْشَقُّ	انْشَقَقْتُ	أنا
		يَنْشَقّا	يَنْشَقّا	يَنْشَقّانِ	انْشَقّا	هما-m
		تَنْشَقّا	تَنْشَقّا	تَنْشَقّانِ	انْشَقَّتا	هما-f
انْشَقّا		تَنْشَقّا	تَنْشَقّا	تَنْشَقّانِ	انْشَقَقْتُما	أنتما
		يَنْشَقّوا	يَنْشَقّوا	يَنْشَقّونَ	انْشَقّوا	هم
		يَنْشَقِقْنَ	يَنْشَقِقْنَ	يَنْشَقِقْنَ	انْشَقَقْنَ	هنّ
انْشَقّوا		تَنْشَقّوا	تَنْشَقّوا	تَنْشَقّونَ	انْشَقَقْتُمْ	أنتم
انْشَقِقْنَ		تَنْشَقِقْنَ	تَنْشَقِقْنَ	تَنْشَقِقْنَ	انْشَقَقْتُنَّ	أنتنّ
		نَنْشَقِقْ	نَنْشَقَّ	نَنْشَقُّ	انْشَقَقْنا	نحن
	Passive	يُنْشَقَقْ	يُنْشَقَّ	يُنْشَقُّ	انْشُقَّ	هو

VN	PP	AP
انْشِقاق	مُنْشَقّ	مُنْشَقّ

Form VII - R2=و\ي: انساق

Imperative		Jussive	Subjunctive	Indicative	Perfect	
	Active	يَنْسَقْ	يَنْساقَ	يَنْساقُ	انْساقَ	هو
		تَنْسَقْ	تَنْساقَ	تَنْساقُ	انْساقَتْ	هي
انْسَقْ		تَنْسَقْ	تَنْساقَ	تَنْساقُ	انْسَقْتَ	أنتَ
انْساقي		تَنْساقي	تَنْساقي	تَنْساقينَ	انْسَقْتِ	أنتِ
		أَنْسَقْ	أَنْساقَ	أَنْساقُ	انْسَقْتُ	أنا
		يَنْساقا	يَنْساقا	يَنْساقانِ	انْساقا	هما-m
		تَنْساقا	تَنْساقا	تَنْساقانِ	انْساقَتا	هما-f
انْساقا		تَنْساقا	تَنْساقا	تَنْساقانِ	انْسَقْتُما	أنتما
		يَنْساقوا	يَنْساقوا	يَنْساقونَ	انْساقوا	هم
		يَنْسَقْنَ	يَنْسَقْنَ	يَنْسَقْنَ	انْسَقْنَ	هنّ
انْساقوا		تَنْساقوا	تَنْساقوا	تَنْساقونَ	انْسَقْتُمْ	أنتم
انْسَقْنَ		تَنْسَقْنَ	تَنْسَقْنَ	تَنْسَقْنَ	انْسَقْتُنَّ	أنتنّ
		نَنْسَقْ	نَنْساقَ	نَنْساقُ	انْسَقْنا	نحن
	Passive	يُنْسَقْ	يُنْساقَ	يُنْساقُ	اُنْسيقَ	هو

VN	PP	AP
انْسِياق	مُنْساق	مُنْساق

Form VII - R3=انبغى :واي

Imperative		Jussive	Subjunctive	Indicative	Perfect	
	Active	يَنْبَغِ	يَنْبَغِيَ	يَنْبَغي	انْبَغى	هو
		تَنْبَغِ	تَنْبَغِيَ	تَنْبَغي	انْبَغَتْ	هي
انْبَغِ		تَنْبَغِ	تَنْبَغِيَ	تَنْبَغي	انْبَغَيْتَ	أنتَ
انْبَغي		تَنْبَغي	تَنْبَغي	تَنْبَغِينَ	انْبَغَيْتِ	أنتِ
		أَنْبَغِ	أَنْبَغِيَ	أَنْبَغي	انْبَغَيْتُ	أنا
		يَنْبَغِيا	يَنْبَغِيا	يَنْبَغِيانِ	انْبَغَيا	هما-m
		تَنْبَغِيا	تَنْبَغِيا	تَنْبَغِيانِ	انْبَغَتا	هما-f
انْبَغِيا		تَنْبَغِيا	تَنْبَغِيا	تَنْبَغِيانِ	انْبَغَيْتُما	أنتما
		يَنْبَغوا	يَنْبَغوا	يَنْبَغونَ	انْبَغَوْا	هم
		يَنْبَغِينَ	يَنْبَغِينَ	يَنْبَغِينَ	انْبَغَيْنَ	هنّ
انْبَغوا		تَنْبَغوا	تَنْبَغوا	تَنْبَغونَ	انْبَغَيْتُمْ	أنتم
انْبَغِينَ		تَنْبَغِينَ	تَنْبَغِينَ	تَنْبَغِينَ	انْبَغَيْتُنَّ	أنتنّ
		نَنْبَغِ	نَنْبَغِيَ	نَنْبَغي	انْبَغَيْنا	نحن
	Passive	يُنْبَغَ	يُنْبَغى	يُنْبَغى	انْبُغِيَ	هو

VN انْبِغاء	PP مُنْبَغًى	AP مُنْبَغٍ

Form VII - R3=انطفأ :ء

Imperative		Jussive	Subjunctive	Indicative	Perfect	
	Active	يَنْطَفِئْ	يَنْطَفِئَ	يَنْطَفِئُ	انْطَفَأَ	هو
		تَنْطَفِئْ	تَنْطَفِئَ	تَنْطَفِئُ	انْطَفَأَتْ	هي
انْطَفِئْ		تَنْطَفِئْ	تَنْطَفِئَ	تَنْطَفِئُ	انْطَفَأْتَ	أنتَ
انْطَفِئي		تَنْطَفِئي	تَنْطَفِئي	تَنْطَفِئِينَ	انْطَفَأْتِ	أنتِ
		أَنْطَفِئْ	أَنْطَفِئَ	أَنْطَفِئُ	انْطَفَأْتُ	أنا
		يَنْطَفِئا	يَنْطَفِئا	يَنْطَفِئانِ	انْطَفَآ	هما-m
		تَنْطَفِئا	تَنْطَفِئا	تَنْطَفِئانِ	انْطَفَأَتا	هما-f
انْطَفِئا		تَنْطَفِئا	تَنْطَفِئا	تَنْطَفِئانِ	انْطَفَأْتُما	أنتما
		يَنْطَفِئوا	يَنْطَفِئوا	يَنْطَفِئونَ	انْطَفَؤوا	هم
		يَنْطَفِئْنَ	يَنْطَفِئْنَ	يَنْطَفِئْنَ	انْطَفَأْنَ	هنّ
انْطَفِئوا		تَنْطَفِئوا	تَنْطَفِئوا	تَنْطَفِئونَ	انْطَفَأْتُمْ	أنتم
انْطَفِئْنَ		تَنْطَفِئْنَ	تَنْطَفِئْنَ	تَنْطَفِئْنَ	انْطَفَأْتُنَّ	أنتنّ
		نَنْطَفِئْ	نَنْطَفِئَ	نَنْطَفِئُ	انْطَفَأْنا	نحن
	Passive	يُنْطَفَأْ	يُنْطَفَأَ	يُنْطَفَأُ	انْطُفِئَ	هو

VN انْطِفاء	PP مُنْطَفَأ	AP مُنْطَفِئ

Form VIII - sound اعترف

Imperative		Jussive	Subjunctive	Indicative	Perfect	
	Active	يَعْتَرِفْ	يَعْتَرِفَ	يَعْتَرِفُ	اعْتَرَفَ	هو
		تَعْتَرِفْ	تَعْتَرِفَ	تَعْتَرِفُ	اعْتَرَفَتْ	هي
اعْتَرِفْ		تَعْتَرِفْ	تَعْتَرِفَ	تَعْتَرِفُ	اعْتَرَفْتَ	أنتَ
اعْتَرِفي		تَعْتَرِفي	تَعْتَرِفي	تَعْتَرِفينَ	اعْتَرَفْتِ	أنتِ
		أَعْتَرِفْ	أَعْتَرِفَ	أَعْتَرِفُ	اعْتَرَفْتُ	أنا
		يَعْتَرِفا	يَعْتَرِفا	يَعْتَرِفانِ	اعْتَرَفا	هما–m
		تَعْتَرِفا	تَعْتَرِفا	تَعْتَرِفانِ	اعْتَرَفَتا	هما–f
اعْتَرِفا		تَعْتَرِفا	تَعْتَرِفا	تَعْتَرِفانِ	اعْتَرَفْتُما	أنتما
		يَعْتَرِفوا	يَعْتَرِفوا	يَعْتَرِفونَ	اعْتَرَفوا	هم
		يَعْتَرِفْنَ	يَعْتَرِفْنَ	يَعْتَرِفْنَ	اعْتَرَفْنَ	هنّ
اعْتَرِفوا		تَعْتَرِفوا	تَعْتَرِفوا	تَعْتَرِفونَ	اعْتَرَفْتُم	أنتم
اعْتَرِفْنَ		تَعْتَرِفْنَ	تَعْتَرِفْنَ	تَعْتَرِفْنَ	اعْتَرَفْتُنَّ	أنتنّ
		نَعْتَرِفْ	نَعْتَرِفَ	نَعْتَرِفُ	اعْتَرَفْنا	نحن
	Passive	يُعْتَرَفْ	يُعْتَرَفَ	يُعْتَرَفُ	اُعْتُرِفَ	هو

VN اعْتِراف	PP مُعْتَرَف	AP مُعْتَرِف

Form VIII - R2=R3 امتدّ

Imperative		Jussive	Subjunctive	Indicative	Perfect	
	Active	يَمْتَدِدْ	يَمْتَدَّ	يَمْتَدُّ	امْتَدَّ	هو
		تَمْتَدِدْ	تَمْتَدَّ	تَمْتَدُّ	امْتَدَّتْ	هي
امْتَدِدْ		تَمْتَدِدْ	تَمْتَدَّ	تَمْتَدُّ	امْتَدَدْتَ	أنتَ
امْتَدّي		تَمْتَدّي	تَمْتَدّي	تَمْتَدّينَ	امْتَدَدْتِ	أنتِ
		أَمْتَدِدْ	أَمْتَدَّ	أَمْتَدُّ	امْتَدَدْتُ	أنا
		يَمْتَدّا	يَمْتَدّا	يَمْتَدّانِ	امْتَدّا	هما–m
		تَمْتَدّا	تَمْتَدّا	تَمْتَدّانِ	امْتَدَّتا	هما–f
امْتَدّا		تَمْتَدّا	تَمْتَدّا	تَمْتَدّانِ	امْتَدَدْتُما	أنتما
		يَمْتَدّوا	يَمْتَدّوا	يَمْتَدّونَ	امْتَدّوا	هم
		يَمْتَدِدْنَ	يَمْتَدِدْنَ	يَمْتَدِدْنَ	امْتَدَدْنَ	هنّ
امْتَدّوا		تَمْتَدّوا	تَمْتَدّوا	تَمْتَدّونَ	امْتَدَدْتُم	أنتم
امْتَدِدْنَ		تَمْتَدِدْنَ	تَمْتَدِدْنَ	تَمْتَدِدْنَ	امْتَدَدْتُنَّ	أنتنّ
		نَمْتَدِدْ	نَمْتَدَّ	نَمْتَدُّ	امْتَدَدْنا	نحن
	Passive	يُمْتَدَدْ	يُمْتَدَّ	يُمْتَدُّ	اُمْتُدَّ	هو

VN امْتِداد	PP مُمْتَدّ	AP مُمْتَدّ

Form VIII - R1=و: اتّهم

Imperative	Jussive	Subjunctive	Indicative	Perfect	
Active					
	يَتَّهِمْ	يَتَّهِمَ	يَتَّهِمُ	اتَّهَمَ	هو
	تَتَّهِمْ	تَتَّهِمَ	تَتَّهِمُ	اتَّهَمَتْ	هي
اتَّهِمْ	تَتَّهِمْ	تَتَّهِمَ	تَتَّهِمُ	اتَّهَمْتَ	أنتَ
اتَّهِمي	تَتَّهِمي	تَتَّهِمي	تَتَّهِمينَ	اتَّهَمْتِ	أنتِ
	أَتَّهِمْ	أَتَّهِمَ	أَتَّهِمُ	اتَّهَمْتُ	أنا
	يَتَّهِما	يَتَّهِما	يَتَّهِمانِ	اتَّهَما	هما-m
	تَتَّهِما	تَتَّهِما	تَتَّهِمانِ	اتَّهَمَتا	هما-f
اتَّهِما	تَتَّهِما	تَتَّهِما	تَتَّهِمانِ	اتَّهَمْتُما	أنتما
	يَتَّهِموا	يَتَّهِموا	يَتَّهِمونَ	اتَّهَموا	هم
	يَتَّهِمْنَ	يَتَّهِمْنَ	يَتَّهِمْنَ	اتَّهَمْنَ	هنّ
اتَّهِموا	تَتَّهِموا	تَتَّهِموا	تَتَّهِمونَ	اتَّهَمْتُمْ	أنتم
اتَّهِمْنَ	تَتَّهِمْنَ	تَتَّهِمْنَ	تَتَّهِمْنَ	اتَّهَمْتُنَّ	أنتنّ
	نَتَّهِمْ	نَتَّهِمَ	نَتَّهِمُ	اتَّهَمْنا	نحن
Passive	يُتَّهَمْ	يُتَّهَمَ	يُتَّهَمُ	اُتُّهِمَ	هو

VN	PP	AP
اتِّهام	مُتَّهَم	مُتَّهِم

Form VIII - R2=و\ي: احتاج

Imperative	Jussive	Subjunctive	Indicative	Perfect	
Active					
	يَحْتَجْ	يَحْتاجَ	يَحْتاجُ	احْتاجَ	هو
	تَحْتَجْ	تَحْتاجَ	تَحْتاجُ	احْتاجَتْ	هي
احْتَجْ	تَحْتَجْ	تَحْتاجَ	تَحْتاجُ	احْتَجْتَ	أنتَ
احْتاجي	تَحْتاجي	تَحْتاجي	تَحْتاجينَ	احْتَجْتِ	أنتِ
	أَحْتَجْ	أَحْتاجَ	أَحْتاجُ	احْتَجْتُ	أنا
	يَحْتاجا	يَحْتاجا	يَحْتاجانِ	احْتاجا	هما-m
	تَحْتاجا	تَحْتاجا	تَحْتاجانِ	احْتاجَتا	هما-f
احْتاجا	تَحْتاجا	تَحْتاجا	تَحْتاجانِ	احْتَجْتُما	أنتما
	يَحْتاجوا	يَحْتاجوا	يَحْتاجونَ	احْتاجوا	هم
	يَحْتَجْنَ	يَحْتَجْنَ	يَحْتَجْنَ	احْتَجْنَ	هنّ
احْتاجوا	تَحْتاجوا	تَحْتاجوا	تَحْتاجونَ	احْتَجْتُمْ	أنتم
احْتَجْنَ	تَحْتَجْنَ	تَحْتَجْنَ	تَحْتَجْنَ	احْتَجْتُنَّ	أنتنّ
	نَحْتَجْ	نَحْتاجَ	نَحْتاجُ	احْتَجْنا	نحن
Passive	يُحْتَجْ	يُحْتاجَ	يُحْتاجُ	اُحْتيجَ	هو

VN	PP	AP
احْتِياج	مُحْتاج	مُحْتاج

Form VIII - R3=التقى :و\ي

Imperative		Jussive	Subjunctive	Indicative	Perfect	
	Active	يَلْتَقِ	يَلْتَقِيَ	يَلْتَقي	اِلْتَقى	هو
		تَلْتَقِ	تَلْتَقِيَ	تَلْتَقي	اِلْتَقَتْ	هي
اِلْتَقِ		تَلْتَقِ	تَلْتَقِيَ	تَلْتَقي	اِلْتَقَيْتَ	أنتَ
اِلْتَقي		تَلْتَقي	تَلْتَقي	تَلْتَقينَ	اِلْتَقَيْتِ	أنتِ
		أَلْتَقِ	أَلْتَقِيَ	أَلْتَقي	اِلْتَقَيْتُ	أنا
		يَلْتَقِيا	يَلْتَقِيا	يَلْتَقِيانِ	اِلْتَقَيا	هما-m
		تَلْتَقِيا	تَلْتَقِيا	تَلْتَقِيانِ	اِلْتَقَتا	هما-f
اِلْتَقِيا		تَلْتَقِيا	تَلْتَقِيا	تَلْتَقِيانِ	اِلْتَقَيْتُما	أنتما
		يَلْتَقوا	يَلْتَقوا	يَلْتَقونَ	اِلْتَقَوْا	هم
		يَلْتَقينَ	يَلْتَقينَ	يَلْتَقينَ	اِلْتَقَيْنَ	هنّ
اِلْتَقوا		تَلْتَقوا	تَلْتَقوا	تَلْتَقونَ	اِلْتَقَيْتُم	أنتم
اِلْتَقينَ		تَلْتَقينَ	تَلْتَقينَ	تَلْتَقينَ	اِلْتَقَيْتُنَّ	أنتنّ
		نَلْتَقِ	نَلْتَقِيَ	نَلْتَقي	اِلْتَقَيْنا	نحن
	Passive	يُلْتَقَ	يُلْتَقى	يُلْتَقى	اُلْتُقِيَ	هو

VN	PP	AP
اِلْتِقاء	مُلْتَقًى	مُلْتَقٍ

Form VIII - R1=ائتمر :ء

Imperative		Jussive	Subjunctive	Indicative	Perfect	
	Active	يَأْتَمِرْ	يَأْتَمِرَ	يَأْتَمِرُ	اِئْتَمَرَ	هو
		تَأْتَمِرْ	تَأْتَمِرَ	تَأْتَمِرُ	اِئْتَمَرَتْ	هي
اِئْتَمِرْ		تَأْتَمِرْ	تَأْتَمِرَ	تَأْتَمِرُ	اِئْتَمَرْتَ	أنتَ
اِئْتَمِري		تَأْتَمِري	تَأْتَمِري	تَأْتَمِرينَ	اِئْتَمَرْتِ	أنتِ
		آتَمِرْ	آتَمِرَ	آتَمِرُ	اِئْتَمَرْتُ	أنا
		يَأْتَمِرا	يَأْتَمِرا	يَأْتَمِرانِ	اِئْتَمَرا	هما-m
		تَأْتَمِرا	تَأْتَمِرا	تَأْتَمِرانِ	اِئْتَمَرَتا	هما-f
اِئْتَمِرا		تَأْتَمِرا	تَأْتَمِرا	تَأْتَمِرانِ	اِئْتَمَرْتُما	أنتما
		يَأْتَمِروا	يَأْتَمِروا	يَأْتَمِرونَ	اِئْتَمَروا	هم
		يَأْتَمِرْنَ	يَأْتَمِرْنَ	يَأْتَمِرْنَ	اِئْتَمَرْنَ	هنّ
اِئْتَمِروا		تَأْتَمِروا	تَأْتَمِروا	تَأْتَمِرونَ	اِئْتَمَرْتُم	أنتم
اِئْتَمِرْنَ		تَأْتَمِرْنَ	تَأْتَمِرْنَ	تَأْتَمِرْنَ	اِئْتَمَرْتُنَّ	أنتنّ
		نَأْتَمِرْ	نَأْتَمِرَ	نَأْتَمِرُ	اِئْتَمَرْنا	نحن
	Passive	يُؤْتَمَرْ	يُؤْتَمَرَ	يُؤْتَمَرُ	اُؤْتُمِرَ	هو

VN	PP	AP
اِئْتِمار	مُؤْتَمَر	مُؤْتَمِر

Form VIII - R2=ء: التأم

	Imperative	Jussive	Subjunctive	Indicative	Perfect
Active هو		يَلْتَئِمْ	يَلْتَئِمَ	يَلْتَئِمُ	الْتَأَمَ
هي		تَلْتَئِمْ	تَلْتَئِمَ	تَلْتَئِمُ	الْتَأَمَتْ
أنتَ	الْتَئِمْ	تَلْتَئِمْ	تَلْتَئِمَ	تَلْتَئِمُ	الْتَأَمْتَ
أنتِ	الْتَئِمِي	تَلْتَئِمِي	تَلْتَئِمِي	تَلْتَئِمِينَ	الْتَأَمْتِ
أنا		أَلْتَئِمْ	أَلْتَئِمَ	أَلْتَئِمُ	الْتَأَمْتُ
هما-m		يَلْتَئِما	يَلْتَئِما	يَلْتَئِمانِ	الْتَأَما
هما-f		تَلْتَئِما	تَلْتَئِما	تَلْتَئِمانِ	الْتَأَمَتا
أنتما	الْتَئِما	تَلْتَئِما	تَلْتَئِما	تَلْتَئِمانِ	الْتَأَمْتُما
هم		يَلْتَئِمُوا	يَلْتَئِمُوا	يَلْتَئِمُونَ	الْتَأَمُوا
هنّ		يَلْتَئِمْنَ	يَلْتَئِمْنَ	يَلْتَئِمْنَ	الْتَأَمْنَ
أنتم	الْتَئِمُوا	تَلْتَئِمُوا	تَلْتَئِمُوا	تَلْتَئِمُونَ	الْتَأَمْتُمْ
أنتنّ	الْتَئِمْنَ	تَلْتَئِمْنَ	تَلْتَئِمْنَ	تَلْتَئِمْنَ	الْتَأَمْتُنَّ
نحن		نَلْتَئِمْ	نَلْتَئِمَ	نَلْتَئِمُ	الْتَأَمْنا
Passive هو		يُلْتَأَمْ	يُلْتَأَمَ	يُلْتَأَمُ	الْتُئِمَ

VN	PP	AP
الْتِئام	مُلْتَأَم	مُلْتَئِم

Form VIII - R3=ء: اختبأ

	Imperative	Jussive	Subjunctive	Indicative	Perfect
Active هو		يَخْتَبِئْ	يَخْتَبِئَ	يَخْتَبِئُ	اخْتَبَأَ
هي		تَخْتَبِئْ	تَخْتَبِئَ	تَخْتَبِئُ	اخْتَبَأَتْ
أنتَ	اخْتَبِئْ	تَخْتَبِئْ	تَخْتَبِئَ	تَخْتَبِئُ	اخْتَبَأْتَ
أنتِ	اخْتَبِئِي	تَخْتَبِئِي	تَخْتَبِئِي	تَخْتَبِئِينَ	اخْتَبَأْتِ
أنا		أَخْتَبِئْ	أَخْتَبِئَ	أَخْتَبِئُ	اخْتَبَأْتُ
هما-m		يَخْتَبِئا	يَخْتَبِئا	يَخْتَبِئانِ	اخْتَبَآ
هما-f		تَخْتَبِئا	تَخْتَبِئا	تَخْتَبِئانِ	اخْتَبَأَتا
أنتما	اخْتَبِئا	تَخْتَبِئا	تَخْتَبِئا	تَخْتَبِئانِ	اخْتَبَأْتُما
هم		يَخْتَبِئُوا	يَخْتَبِئُوا	يَخْتَبِئُونَ	اخْتَبَؤُوا
هنّ		يَخْتَبِئْنَ	يَخْتَبِئْنَ	يَخْتَبِئْنَ	اخْتَبَأْنَ
أنتم	اخْتَبِئُوا	تَخْتَبِئُوا	تَخْتَبِئُوا	تَخْتَبِئُونَ	اخْتَبَأْتُمْ
أنتنّ	اخْتَبِئْنَ	تَخْتَبِئْنَ	تَخْتَبِئْنَ	تَخْتَبِئْنَ	اخْتَبَأْتُنَّ
نحن		نَخْتَبِئْ	نَخْتَبِئَ	نَخْتَبِئُ	اخْتَبَأْنا
Passive هو		يُخْتَبَأْ	يُخْتَبَأَ	يُخْتَبَأُ	اُخْتُبِئَ

VN	PP	AP
اخْتِباء	مُخْتَبَأ	مُخْتَبِئ

Form IX - sound اخضر

Imperative		Jussive	Subjunctive	Indicative	Perfect	
	Active	يَخْضَرِرْ	يَخْضَرَّ	يَخْضَرُّ	اخْضَرَّ	هو
		تَخْضَرِرْ	تَخْضَرَّ	تَخْضَرُّ	اخْضَرَّتْ	هي
اخْضَرِرْ		تَخْضَرِرْ	تَخْضَرَّ	تَخْضَرُّ	اخْضَرَرْتَ	أنتَ
اخْضَرّي		تَخْضَرّي	تَخْضَرّي	تَخْضَرّينَ	اخْضَرَرْتِ	أنتِ
		أَخْضَرِرْ	أَخْضَرَّ	أَخْضَرُّ	اخْضَرَرْتُ	أنا
		يَخْضَرّا	يَخْضَرّا	يَخْضَرّانِ	اخْضَرّا	هما-m
		تَخْضَرّا	تَخْضَرّا	تَخْضَرّانِ	اخْضَرَّتا	هما-f
اخْضَرّا		تَخْضَرّا	تَخْضَرّا	تَخْضَرّانِ	اخْضَرَرْتُما	أنتما
		يَخْضَرّوا	يَخْضَرّوا	يَخْضَرّونَ	اخْضَرّوا	هم
		يَخْضَرِرْنَ	يَخْضَرِرْنَ	يَخْضَرِرْنَ	اخْضَرَرْنَ	هنّ
اخْضَرّوا		تَخْضَرّوا	تَخْضَرّوا	تَخْضَرّونَ	اخْضَرَرْتُمْ	أنتم
اخْضَرِرْنَ		تَخْضَرِرْنَ	تَخْضَرِرْنَ	تَخْضَرِرْنَ	اخْضَرَرْتُنَّ	أنتنّ
		نَخْضَرِرْ	نَخْضَرَّ	نَخْضَرُّ	اخْضَرَرْنا	نحن
	Passive	يُخْضَرَرْ	يُخْضَرَّ	يُخْضَرُّ	اُخْضُرَّ	هو

VN	PP	AP
اخْضِرار	مُخْضَرّ	مُخْضَرّ

Form X - sound استخدم

Imperative		Jussive	Subjunctive	Indicative	Perfect	
	Active	يَسْتَخْدِمْ	يَسْتَخْدِمَ	يَسْتَخْدِمُ	اسْتَخْدَمَ	هو
		تَسْتَخْدِمْ	تَسْتَخْدِمَ	تَسْتَخْدِمُ	اسْتَخْدَمَتْ	هي
اسْتَخْدِمْ		تَسْتَخْدِمْ	تَسْتَخْدِمَ	تَسْتَخْدِمُ	اسْتَخْدَمْتَ	أنتَ
اسْتَخْدِمي		تَسْتَخْدِمي	تَسْتَخْدِمي	تَسْتَخْدِمينَ	اسْتَخْدَمْتِ	أنتِ
		أَسْتَخْدِمْ	أَسْتَخْدِمَ	أَسْتَخْدِمُ	اسْتَخْدَمْتُ	أنا
		يَسْتَخْدِما	يَسْتَخْدِما	يَسْتَخْدِمانِ	اسْتَخْدَما	هما-m
		تَسْتَخْدِما	تَسْتَخْدِما	تَسْتَخْدِمانِ	اسْتَخْدَمَتا	هما-f
اسْتَخْدِما		تَسْتَخْدِما	تَسْتَخْدِما	تَسْتَخْدِمانِ	اسْتَخْدَمْتُما	أنتما
		يَسْتَخْدِموا	يَسْتَخْدِموا	يَسْتَخْدِمونَ	اسْتَخْدَموا	هم
		يَسْتَخْدِمْنَ	يَسْتَخْدِمْنَ	يَسْتَخْدِمْنَ	اسْتَخْدَمْنَ	هنّ
اسْتَخْدِموا		تَسْتَخْدِموا	تَسْتَخْدِموا	تَسْتَخْدِمونَ	اسْتَخْدَمْتُمْ	أنتم
اسْتَخْدِمْنَ		تَسْتَخْدِمْنَ	تَسْتَخْدِمْنَ	تَسْتَخْدِمْنَ	اسْتَخْدَمْتُنَّ	أنتنّ
		نَسْتَخْدِمْ	نَسْتَخْدِمَ	نَسْتَخْدِمُ	اسْتَخْدَمْنا	نحن
	Passive	يُسْتَخْدَمْ	يُسْتَخْدَمَ	يُسْتَخْدَمُ	اُسْتُخْدِمَ	هو

VN	PP	AP
اسْتِخْدام	مُسْتَخْدَم	مُسْتَخْدِم

Form X - R2=R3 استقرّ

Imperative		Jussive	Subjunctive	Indicative	Perfect	
	Active	يَسْتَقْرِرْ	يَسْتَقِرَّ	يَسْتَقِرُّ	اسْتَقَرَّ	هو
		تَسْتَقْرِرْ	تَسْتَقِرَّ	تَسْتَقِرُّ	اسْتَقَرَّتْ	هي
اسْتَقْرِرْ		تَسْتَقْرِرْ	تَسْتَقِرَّ	تَسْتَقِرُّ	اسْتَقْرَرْتَ	أنتَ
اسْتَقِرّي		تَسْتَقِرّي	تَسْتَقِرّي	تَسْتَقِرّينَ	اسْتَقْرَرْتِ	أنتِ
		أَسْتَقْرِرْ	أَسْتَقِرَّ	أَسْتَقِرُّ	اسْتَقْرَرْتُ	أنا
		يَسْتَقِرّا	يَسْتَقِرّا	يَسْتَقِرّانِ	اسْتَقَرّا	هما-m
		تَسْتَقِرّا	تَسْتَقِرّا	تَسْتَقِرّانِ	اسْتَقَرَّتا	هما-f
اسْتَقِرّا		تَسْتَقِرّا	تَسْتَقِرّا	تَسْتَقِرّانِ	اسْتَقْرَرْتُما	أنتما
		يَسْتَقِرّوا	يَسْتَقِرّوا	يَسْتَقِرّونَ	اسْتَقَرّوا	هم
		يَسْتَقْرِرْنَ	يَسْتَقْرِرْنَ	يَسْتَقْرِرْنَ	اسْتَقْرَرْنَ	هنّ
اسْتَقِرّوا		تَسْتَقِرّوا	تَسْتَقِرّوا	تَسْتَقِرّونَ	اسْتَقْرَرْتُم	أنتم
اسْتَقْرِرْنَ		تَسْتَقْرِرْنَ	تَسْتَقْرِرْنَ	تَسْتَقْرِرْنَ	اسْتَقْرَرْتُنَّ	أنتنّ
		نَسْتَقْرِرْ	نَسْتَقِرَّ	نَسْتَقِرُّ	اسْتَقْرَرْنا	نحن
	Passive	يُسْتَقْرَرْ	يُسْتَقَرَّ	يُسْتَقَرُّ	اُسْتُقِرَّ	هو

VN اسْتِقْرار	**PP** مُسْتَقَرّ	**AP** مُسْتَقِرّ

Form X - R1=و: استوعب

Imperative		Jussive	Subjunctive	Indicative	Perfect	
	Active	يَسْتَوْعِبْ	يَسْتَوْعِبَ	يَسْتَوْعِبُ	اسْتَوْعَبَ	هو
		تَسْتَوْعِبْ	تَسْتَوْعِبَ	تَسْتَوْعِبُ	اسْتَوْعَبَتْ	هي
اسْتَوْعِبْ		تَسْتَوْعِبْ	تَسْتَوْعِبَ	تَسْتَوْعِبُ	اسْتَوْعَبْتَ	أنتَ
اسْتَوْعِبي		تَسْتَوْعِبي	تَسْتَوْعِبي	تَسْتَوْعِبينَ	اسْتَوْعَبْتِ	أنتِ
		أَسْتَوْعِبْ	أَسْتَوْعِبَ	أَسْتَوْعِبُ	اسْتَوْعَبْتُ	أنا
		يَسْتَوْعِبا	يَسْتَوْعِبا	يَسْتَوْعِبانِ	اسْتَوْعَبا	هما-m
		تَسْتَوْعِبا	تَسْتَوْعِبا	تَسْتَوْعِبانِ	اسْتَوْعَبَتا	هما-f
اسْتَوْعِبا		تَسْتَوْعِبا	تَسْتَوْعِبا	تَسْتَوْعِبانِ	اسْتَوْعَبْتُما	أنتما
		يَسْتَوْعِبوا	يَسْتَوْعِبوا	يَسْتَوْعِبونَ	اسْتَوْعَبوا	هم
		يَسْتَوْعِبْنَ	يَسْتَوْعِبْنَ	يَسْتَوْعِبْنَ	اسْتَوْعَبْنَ	هنّ
اسْتَوْعِبوا		تَسْتَوْعِبوا	تَسْتَوْعِبوا	تَسْتَوْعِبونَ	اسْتَوْعَبْتُم	أنتم
اسْتَوْعِبْنَ		تَسْتَوْعِبْنَ	تَسْتَوْعِبْنَ	تَسْتَوْعِبْنَ	اسْتَوْعَبْتُنَّ	أنتنّ
		نَسْتَوْعِبْ	نَسْتَوْعِبَ	نَسْتَوْعِبُ	اسْتَوْعَبْنا	نحن
	Passive	يُسْتَوْعَبْ	يُسْتَوْعَبَ	يُسْتَوْعَبُ	اُسْتوعِبَ	هو

VN اسْتيعاب	**PP** مُسْتَوْعَب	**AP** مُسْتَوْعِب

Form X - R1=ي: استيقظ

Imperative		Jussive	Subjunctive	Indicative	Perfect	
	Active	يَسْتَيْقِظْ	يَسْتَيْقِظَ	يَسْتَيْقِظُ	اسْتَيْقَظَ	هو
		تَسْتَيْقِظْ	تَسْتَيْقِظَ	تَسْتَيْقِظُ	اسْتَيْقَظَتْ	هي
اسْتَيْقِظْ		تَسْتَيْقِظْ	تَسْتَيْقِظَ	تَسْتَيْقِظُ	اسْتَيْقَظْتَ	أنتَ
اسْتَيْقِظي		تَسْتَيْقِظي	تَسْتَيْقِظي	تَسْتَيْقِظينَ	اسْتَيْقَظْتِ	أنتِ
		أَسْتَيْقِظْ	أَسْتَيْقِظَ	أَسْتَيْقِظُ	اسْتَيْقَظْتُ	أنا
		يَسْتَيْقِظا	يَسْتَيْقِظا	يَسْتَيْقِظانِ	اسْتَيْقَظا	هما-m
		تَسْتَيْقِظا	تَسْتَيْقِظا	تَسْتَيْقِظانِ	اسْتَيْقَظَتا	هما-f
اسْتَيْقِظا		تَسْتَيْقِظا	تَسْتَيْقِظا	تَسْتَيْقِظانِ	اسْتَيْقَظْتُما	أنتما
		يَسْتَيْقِظوا	يَسْتَيْقِظوا	يَسْتَيْقِظونَ	اسْتَيْقَظوا	هم
		يَسْتَيْقِظْنَ	يَسْتَيْقِظْنَ	يَسْتَيْقِظْنَ	اسْتَيْقَظْنَ	هنّ
اسْتَيْقِظوا		تَسْتَيْقِظوا	تَسْتَيْقِظوا	تَسْتَيْقِظونَ	اسْتَيْقَظْتُم	أنتم
اسْتَيْقِظْنَ		تَسْتَيْقِظْنَ	تَسْتَيْقِظْنَ	تَسْتَيْقِظْنَ	اسْتَيْقَظْتُنَّ	أنتنّ
		نَسْتَيْقِظْ	نَسْتَيْقِظَ	نَسْتَيْقِظُ	اسْتَيْقَظْنا	نحن
	Passive	يُسْتَيْقَظْ	يُسْتَيْقَظَ	يُسْتَيْقَظُ	اُسْتوقِظَ	هو

VN	PP	AP
اسْتيقاظ	مُسْتَيْقَظ	مُسْتَيْقِظ

Form X - R2=و\ي: استفاد

Imperative		Jussive	Subjunctive	Indicative	Perfect	
	Active	يَسْتَفِدْ	يَسْتَفيدَ	يَسْتَفيدُ	اسْتَفادَ	هو
		تَسْتَفِدْ	تَسْتَفيدَ	تَسْتَفيدُ	اسْتَفادَتْ	هي
اسْتَفِدْ		تَسْتَفِدْ	تَسْتَفيدَ	تَسْتَفيدُ	اسْتَفَدْتَ	أنتَ
اسْتَفيدي		تَسْتَفيدي	تَسْتَفيدي	تَسْتَفيدينَ	اسْتَفَدْتِ	أنتِ
		أَسْتَفِدْ	أَسْتَفيدَ	أَسْتَفيدُ	اسْتَفَدْتُ	أنا
		يَسْتَفيدا	يَسْتَفيدا	يَسْتَفيدانِ	اسْتَفادا	هما-m
		تَسْتَفيدا	تَسْتَفيدا	تَسْتَفيدانِ	اسْتَفادَتا	هما-f
اسْتَفيدا		تَسْتَفيدا	تَسْتَفيدا	تَسْتَفيدانِ	اسْتَفَدْتُما	أنتما
		يَسْتَفيدوا	يَسْتَفيدوا	يَسْتَفيدونَ	اسْتَفادوا	هم
		يَسْتَفِدْنَ	يَسْتَفِدْنَ	يَسْتَفِدْنَ	اسْتَفَدْنَ	هنّ
اسْتَفيدوا		تَسْتَفيدوا	تَسْتَفيدوا	تَسْتَفيدونَ	اسْتَفَدْتُم	أنتم
اسْتَفِدْنَ		تَسْتَفِدْنَ	تَسْتَفِدْنَ	تَسْتَفِدْنَ	اسْتَفَدْتُنَّ	أنتنّ
		نَسْتَفِدْ	نَسْتَفيدَ	نَسْتَفيدُ	اسْتَفَدْنا	نحن
	Passive	يُسْتَفَدْ	يُسْتَفادَ	يُسْتَفادُ	اُسْتُفيدَ	هو

VN	PP	AP
اسْتِفادة	مُسْتَفاد	مُسْتَفيد

Form X - R3=و\ي: استغنى

Imperative		Jussive	Subjunctive	Indicative	Perfect	
	Active	يَسْتَغْنِ	يَسْتَغْنِيَ	يَسْتَغْنِي	اسْتَغْنَى	هو
		تَسْتَغْنِ	تَسْتَغْنِيَ	تَسْتَغْنِي	اسْتَغْنَتْ	هي
اسْتَغْنِ		تَسْتَغْنِ	تَسْتَغْنِيَ	تَسْتَغْنِي	اسْتَغْنَيْتَ	أنتَ
اسْتَغْنِي		تَسْتَغْنِي	تَسْتَغْنِي	تَسْتَغْنِينَ	اسْتَغْنَيْتِ	أنتِ
		أَسْتَغْنِ	أَسْتَغْنِيَ	أَسْتَغْنِي	اسْتَغْنَيْتُ	أنا
		يَسْتَغْنِيا	يَسْتَغْنِيا	يَسْتَغْنِيانِ	اسْتَغْنَيا	هما-m
		تَسْتَغْنِيا	تَسْتَغْنِيا	تَسْتَغْنِيانِ	اسْتَغْنَتا	هما-f
اسْتَغْنِيا		تَسْتَغْنِيا	تَسْتَغْنِيا	تَسْتَغْنِيانِ	اسْتَغْنَيْتُما	أنتما
		يَسْتَغْنُوا	يَسْتَغْنُوا	يَسْتَغْنُونَ	اسْتَغْنَوْا	هم
		يَسْتَغْنِينَ	يَسْتَغْنِينَ	يَسْتَغْنِينَ	اسْتَغْنَيْنَ	هنّ
اسْتَغْنُوا		تَسْتَغْنُوا	تَسْتَغْنُوا	تَسْتَغْنُونَ	اسْتَغْنَيْتُمْ	أنتم
اسْتَغْنِينَ		تَسْتَغْنِينَ	تَسْتَغْنِينَ	تَسْتَغْنِينَ	اسْتَغْنَيْتُنَّ	أنتنّ
		نَسْتَغْنِ	نَسْتَغْنِيَ	نَسْتَغْنِي	اسْتَغْنَيْنا	نحن
	Passive	يُسْتَغْنَ	يُسْتَغْنَى	يُسْتَغْنَى	اُسْتُغْنِيَ	هو

VN	PP	AP
اسْتِغْناء	مُسْتَغْنًى	مُسْتَغْنٍ

Form X - R1=ء: استأثر

Imperative		Jussive	Subjunctive	Indicative	Perfect	
	Active	يَسْتَأْثِرْ	يَسْتَأْثِرَ	يَسْتَأْثِرُ	اسْتَأْثَرَ	هو
		تَسْتَأْثِرْ	تَسْتَأْثِرَ	تَسْتَأْثِرُ	اسْتَأْثَرَتْ	هي
اسْتَأْثِرْ		تَسْتَأْثِرْ	تَسْتَأْثِرَ	تَسْتَأْثِرُ	اسْتَأْثَرْتَ	أنتَ
اسْتَأْثِري		تَسْتَأْثِري	تَسْتَأْثِري	تَسْتَأْثِرينَ	اسْتَأْثَرْتِ	أنتِ
		أَسْتَأْثِرْ	أَسْتَأْثِرَ	أَسْتَأْثِرُ	اسْتَأْثَرْتُ	أنا
		يَسْتَأْثِرا	يَسْتَأْثِرا	يَسْتَأْثِرانِ	اسْتَأْثَرا	هما-m
		تَسْتَأْثِرا	تَسْتَأْثِرا	تَسْتَأْثِرانِ	اسْتَأْثَرَتا	هما-f
اسْتَأْثِرا		تَسْتَأْثِرا	تَسْتَأْثِرا	تَسْتَأْثِرانِ	اسْتَأْثَرْتُما	أنتما
		يَسْتَأْثِروا	يَسْتَأْثِروا	يَسْتَأْثِرونَ	اسْتَأْثَروا	هم
		يَسْتَأْثِرْنَ	يَسْتَأْثِرْنَ	يَسْتَأْثِرْنَ	اسْتَأْثَرْنَ	هنّ
اسْتَأْثِروا		تَسْتَأْثِروا	تَسْتَأْثِروا	تَسْتَأْثِرونَ	اسْتَأْثَرْتُم	أنتم
اسْتَأْثِرْنَ		تَسْتَأْثِرْنَ	تَسْتَأْثِرْنَ	تَسْتَأْثِرْنَ	اسْتَأْثَرْتُنَّ	أنتنّ
		نَسْتَأْثِرْ	نَسْتَأْثِرَ	نَسْتَأْثِرُ	اسْتَأْثَرْنا	نحن
	Passive	يُسْتَأْثَرْ	يُسْتَأْثَرَ	يُسْتَأْثَرُ	اُسْتُؤْثِرَ	هو

VN	PP	AP
اسْتِئْثار	مُسْتَأْثَر	مُسْتَأْثِر

Form X - R2=ء: استيأس

Imperative		Jussive	Subjunctive	Indicative	Perfect	
	Active	يَسْتَيْئِسْ	يَسْتَيْئِسَ	يَسْتَيْئِسُ	اسْتَيْئَسَ	هو
		تَسْتَيْئِسْ	تَسْتَيْئِسَ	تَسْتَيْئِسُ	اسْتَيْئَسَتْ	هي
اسْتَيْئِسْ		تَسْتَيْئِسْ	تَسْتَيْئِسَ	تَسْتَيْئِسُ	اسْتَيْئَسْتَ	أنتَ
اسْتَيْئِسي		تَسْتَيْئِسي	تَسْتَيْئِسي	تَسْتَيْئِسينَ	اسْتَيْئَسْتِ	أنتِ
		أَسْتَيْئِسْ	أَسْتَيْئِسَ	أَسْتَيْئِسُ	اسْتَيْئَسْتُ	أنا
		يَسْتَيْئِسا	يَسْتَيْئِسا	يَسْتَيْئِسانِ	اسْتَيْئَسا	هما-m
		تَسْتَيْئِسا	تَسْتَيْئِسا	تَسْتَيْئِسانِ	اسْتَيْئَسَتا	هما-f
اسْتَيْئِسا		تَسْتَيْئِسا	تَسْتَيْئِسا	تَسْتَيْئِسانِ	اسْتَيْئَسْتُما	أنتما
		يَسْتَيْئِسوا	يَسْتَيْئِسوا	يَسْتَيْئِسونَ	اسْتَيْئَسوا	هم
		يَسْتَيْئِسْنَ	يَسْتَيْئِسْنَ	يَسْتَيْئِسْنَ	اسْتَيْئَسْنَ	هنّ
اسْتَيْئِسوا		تَسْتَيْئِسوا	تَسْتَيْئِسوا	تَسْتَيْئِسونَ	اسْتَيْئَسْتُمْ	أنتم
اسْتَيْئِسْنَ		تَسْتَيْئِسْنَ	تَسْتَيْئِسْنَ	تَسْتَيْئِسْنَ	اسْتَيْئَسْتُنَّ	أنتنّ
		نَسْتَيْئِسْ	نَسْتَيْئِسَ	نَسْتَيْئِسُ	اسْتَيْئَسْنا	نحن
	Passive	يُسْتَيْئَسْ	يُسْتَيْئَسَ	يُسْتَيْئَسُ	أُسْتوئِسَ	هو

VN	PP	AP
اسْتِيآس	مُسْتَيْئَس	مُسْتَيْئِس

Form X - R3=ء: استمرأ

Imperative		Jussive	Subjunctive	Indicative	Perfect	
	Active	يَسْتَمْرِئْ	يَسْتَمْرِئَ	يَسْتَمْرِئُ	اسْتَمْرَأَ	هو
		تَسْتَمْرِئْ	تَسْتَمْرِئَ	تَسْتَمْرِئُ	اسْتَمْرَأَتْ	هي
اسْتَمْرِئْ		تَسْتَمْرِئْ	تَسْتَمْرِئَ	تَسْتَمْرِئُ	اسْتَمْرَأْتَ	أنتَ
اسْتَمْرِئي		تَسْتَمْرِئي	تَسْتَمْرِئي	تَسْتَمْرِئينَ	اسْتَمْرَأْتِ	أنتِ
		أَسْتَمْرِئْ	أَسْتَمْرِئَ	أَسْتَمْرِئُ	اسْتَمْرَأْتُ	أنا
		يَسْتَمْرِئا	يَسْتَمْرِئا	يَسْتَمْرِئانِ	اسْتَمْرَآ	هما-m
		تَسْتَمْرِئا	تَسْتَمْرِئا	تَسْتَمْرِئانِ	اسْتَمْرَأَتا	هما-f
اسْتَمْرِئا		تَسْتَمْرِئا	تَسْتَمْرِئا	تَسْتَمْرِئانِ	اسْتَمْرَأْتُما	أنتما
		يَسْتَمْرِئوا	يَسْتَمْرِئوا	يَسْتَمْرِئونَ	اسْتَمْرَؤوا	هم
		يَسْتَمْرِئْنَ	يَسْتَمْرِئْنَ	يَسْتَمْرِئْنَ	اسْتَمْرَأْنَ	هنّ
اسْتَمْرِئوا		تَسْتَمْرِئوا	تَسْتَمْرِئوا	تَسْتَمْرِئونَ	اسْتَمْرَأْتُمْ	أنتم
اسْتَمْرِئْنَ		تَسْتَمْرِئْنَ	تَسْتَمْرِئْنَ	تَسْتَمْرِئْنَ	اسْتَمْرَأْتُنَّ	أنتنّ
		نَسْتَمْرِئْ	نَسْتَمْرِئَ	نَسْتَمْرِئُ	اسْتَمْرَأْنا	نحن
	Passive	يُسْتَمْرَأْ	يُسْتَمْرَأَ	يُسْتَمْرَأُ	أُسْتُمْرِئَ	هو

VN	PP	AP
اسْتِمْراء	مُسْتَمْرَأ	مُسْتَمْرِئ

Arabic cases

حالات الإعراب العربية

Singular مفرد

Definite معرف	*masculine* مذكر	*feminine* مؤنث
nominative الرفع	المُدَرِّسُ الجَديدُ	المُدَرِّسةُ الجَديدةُ
genitive الجرّ	المُدَرِّسِ الجَديدِ	المُدَرِّسةِ الجَديدةِ
accusative النصب	المُدَرِّسَ الجَديدَ	المُدَرِّسةَ الجَديدةَ

Indefinite غير معرف	*masculine*	*feminine*
nominative	مُدَرِّسٌ جَديدٌ	مُدَرِّسةٌ جَديدةٌ
genitive	مُدَرِّسٍ جَديدٍ	مُدَرِّسةٍ جَديدةٍ
accusative	مُدَرِّساً جَديداً	لمُدَرِّسةً جَديدةً

Sound masculine plural جمع مذكر سالم

	definite	*indefinite*
nominative	المُدَرِّسونَ المِصْريّونَ	مُدَرِّسونَ مِصْريّونَ
genitive	المُدَرِّسينَ المِصْريّينَ	مُدَرِّسينَ مِصْريّينَ
accusative	المُدَرِّسينَ المِصْريّينَ	مُدَرِّسينَ مِصْريّينَ

Sound feminine plural جمع مؤنث سالم

	definite	*indefinite*
nominative	المُدَرِّساتُ المِصْريّاتُ	مُدَرِّساتٌ مِصْريّاتٌ
genitive	المُدَرِّساتِ المِصْريّاتِ	مُدَرِّساتٍ مِصْريّاتٍ
accusative	المُدَرِّساتِ المِصْريّاتِ	مُدَرِّساتٍ مِصْريّاتٍ

Broken plural جمع التكسير

	definite	*indefinite*
nominative	الرِجالُ الجُدُدُ	رِجالٌ جُدُدٌ
genitive	الرِجالِ الجُدُدِ	رِجالٍ جُدُدٍ
accusative	الرِجالَ الجُدُدَ	رِجالاً جُدُداً

Dual (definite/indefinite) مثنى (معرف \ غير معرف)

	masculine	feminine
nominative	(ال)مُدَرِّسانِ (ال)جَديدانِ	(ال)مُدَرِّستانِ (ال)جَديدَتانِ
genitive	(ال)مُدَرِّسَيْنِ (ال)جَديدَيْنِ	(ال)مُدَرِّستَيْنِ (ال)جَديدَتَيْنِ
accusative	(ال)مُدَرِّسَيْنِ (ال)جَديدَيْنِ	(ال)مُدَرِّستَيْنِ (ال)جَديدَتَيْنِ

Diptotes ممنوع من الصرف

	definite	indefinite
nominative	الدَنانيرُ	دَنانيرُ
genitive	الدَنانيرِ	دَنانيرَ
accusative	الدَنانيرَ	دَنانيرَ

Words ending in كلمات تنتهي بـٍ ٍ

Indefinite	*masculine*	*feminine*
nominative	داعٍ	داعِيةٌ
genitive	داعٍ	داعِيةٍ
accusative	داعِياً	داعِيةً

Definite	*masculine*	*feminine*
nominative	الداعي	الداعِيةُ
genitive	الداعي	الداعِيةِ
accusative	الداعِيَ	الداعِيةَ

Words ending in كلمات تنتهي بـًى ًى

Indefinite	*masculine*	*feminine*
nominative	مُرْتَضًى	مُرْتَضاةٌ
genitive	مُرْتَضًى	مُرْتَضاةٍ
accusative	مُرْتَضًى	مُرْتَضاةً

Definite	*masculine*	*feminine*
nominative	المُرْتَضى	المُرْتَضاةُ
genitive	المُرْتَضى	المُرْتَضاةِ
accusative	المُرْتَضى	المُرْتَضاةَ

Full forms of numbers in Arabic

العدد والمعدود في العربية

Cardinal numbers الأعداد الأصلية

	with masculine noun قبل اسم مذكر	with feminine noun قبل اسم مؤنث		with masculine noun قبل اسم مذكر	with feminine noun قبل اسم مؤنث
1	كِتابٌ واحِدٌ	كُرةٌ واحِدةٌ	50	خَمْسونَ كِتاباً	خَمْسونَ كُرةً
2	كِتابانِ اثْنانِ	كُرتانِ اثْنَتانِ	60	سِتّونَ كِتاباً	سِتّونَ كُرةً
3	ثَلاثةُ كُتُبٍ	ثَلاثُ كُراتٍ	70	سَبْعونَ كِتاباً	سَبْعونَ كُرةً
4	أَرْبَعةُ كُتُبٍ	أَرْبَعُ كُراتٍ	80	ثَمانونَ كِتاباً	ثَمانونَ كُرةً
5	خَمْسةُ كُتُبٍ	خَمْسُ كُراتٍ	90	تِسْعونَ كِتاباً	تِسْعونَ كُرةً
6	سِتّةُ كُتُبٍ	سِتُّ كُراتٍ	100	مِائةُ كِتابٍ	مِائةُ كُرةٍ
7	سَبْعةُ كُتُبٍ	سَبْعُ كُراتٍ	101	مِائةُ كِتابٍ وَكِتابٌ	مِائةُ كُرةٍ وَكُرةٌ
8	ثَمانِيةُ كُتُبٍ	ثَماني كُراتٍ	102	مِائةُ كِتابٍ وَكِتابانِ	مِائةُ كُرةٍ وَكُرتانِ
9	تِسْعةُ كُتُبٍ	تِسْعُ كُراتٍ	103	مِائةٌ وَثَلاثةُ كُتُبٍ	مِائةٌ وَثَلاثُ كُراتٍ
10	عَشَرةُ كُتُبٍ	عَشْرُ كُراتٍ	112	مِائةٌ وَاثْنا عَشَرَ كِتاباً	مِائةٌ وَاثْنَتا عَشْرةَ كُرةً
11	أَحَدَ عَشَرَ كِتاباً	إِحْدى عَشْرةَ كُرةً	120	مِائةٌ وَعِشْرونَ كِتاباً	مِائةٌ وَعِشْرونَ كُرةً
12	اثْنا عَشَرَ كِتاباً	اثْنَتا عَشْرةَ كُرةً	200	مِائَتا كِتابٍ	مِائَتا كُرةٍ
13	ثَلاثةَ عَشَرَ كِتاباً	ثَلاثَ عَشْرةَ كُرةً	210	مِائَتانِ وَعَشَرةُ كُتُبٍ	مِائَتانِ وَعَشْرُ كُراتٍ
14	أَرْبَعةَ عَشَرَ كِتاباً	أَرْبَعَ عَشْرةَ كُرةً	300	ثَلاثُمِائةِ كِتابٍ	ثَلاثُمِائةِ كُرةٍ
15	خَمْسةَ عَشَرَ كِتاباً	خَمْسَ عَشْرةَ كُرةً	365	ثَلاثُمِائةٍ وَخَمْسةٌ وَسِتّونَ كِتاباً	ثَلاثُمِائةٍ وَخَمْسٌ وَسِتّونَ كُرةً
16	سِتّةَ عَشَرَ كِتاباً	سِتَّ عَشْرةَ كُرةً			
17	سَبْعةَ عَشَرَ كِتاباً	سَبْعَ عَشْرةَ كُرةً	400	أَرْبَعُمِائةِ كِتابٍ	أَرْبَعُمِائةِ كُرةٍ
18	ثَمانِيةَ عَشَرَ كِتاباً	ثَمانِيَ عَشْرةَ كُرةً	486	أَرْبَعُمِائةٍ وَسِتّةٌ وَثَمانونَ كِتاباً	أَرْبَعُمِائةٍ وَسِتٌّ وَثَمانونَ كُرةً
19	تِسْعةَ عَشَرَ كِتاباً	تِسْعَ عَشْرةَ كُرةً			
20	عِشْرونَ كِتاباً	عِشْرونَ كُرةً	900	تِسْعُمِائةِ كِتابٍ	تِسْعُمِائةِ كُرةٍ
21	واحِدٌ وَعِشْرونَ كِتاباً	إِحْدى وَعِشْرونَ كُرةً	1,000	أَلْفُ كِتابٍ	أَلْفُ كُرةٍ
22	اثْنانِ وَعِشْرونَ كِتاباً	اثْنَتانِ وَعِشْرونَ كُرةً	1,001	أَلْفُ كِتابٍ وَكِتابٌ	أَلْفُ كُرةٍ وَكُرةٌ
23	ثَلاثةٌ وَعِشْرونَ كِتاباً	ثَلاثٌ وَعِشْرونَ كُرةً	1,002	أَلْفُ كِتابٍ وَكِتابانِ	أَلْفُ كُرةٍ وَكُرتانِ
24	أَرْبَعةٌ وَعِشْرونَ كِتاباً	أَرْبَعٌ وَعِشْرونَ كُرةً	1,003	أَلْفٌ وَثَلاثةُ كُتُبٍ	أَلْفٌ وَثَلاثُ كُراتٍ
28	ثَمانِيةٌ وَعِشْرونَ كِتاباً	ثَمانٍ وَعِشْرونَ كُرةً	1,004	أَلْفٌ وَأَرْبَعةُ كُتُبٍ	أَلْفٌ وَأَرْبَعُ كُراتٍ
30	ثَلاثونَ كِتاباً	ثَلاثونَ كُرةً	1,492	أَلْفٌ وَأَرْبَعُمِائةٍ وَاثْنانِ وَتِسْعونَ كِتاباً	أَلْفٌ وَأَرْبَعُمِائةٍ وَاثْنَتانِ وَتِسْعونَ كُرةً
31	واحِد وَثَلاثونَ كِتاباً	إِحْدى وَثَلاثونَ كُرةً			
32	اثْنانِ وَثَلاثونَ كِتاباً	اثْنَتانِ وَثَلاثونَ كُرةً	1,759	أَلْفٌ وَسَبْعُمِائةٍ وَتِسْعةٌ وَخَمْسونَ كِتاباً	أَلْفٌ وَسَبْعُمِائةٍ وَتِسْعٌ وَخَمْسونَ كُرةً
33	ثَلاثةٌ وَثَلاثونَ كِتاباً	ثَلاثٌ وَثَلاثونَ كُرةً			
40	أَرْبَعونَ كِتاباً	أَرْبَعونَ كُرةً			

	with masculine noun قبل اسم مذكر	with feminine noun قبل اسم مؤنث
2,000	أَلْفا كِتابٍ	أَلْفا كُرةٍ
2,017	أَلْفانِ وَسَبْعةَ عَشَرَ كِتاباً	أَلْفانِ وَسَبْعَ عَشْرةَ كُرةً
3,000	ثَلاثةُ آلافِ كِتابٍ	ثَلاثةُ آلافِ كُرةٍ
3,072	ثَلاثةُ آلافٍ وَاثْنانِ وَسَبْعونَ كِتاباً	ثَلاثةُ آلافٍ وَاثْنَتانِ وَسَبْعونَ كُرةً
8,000	ثَمانيةُ آلافِ كِتابٍ	ثَمانيةُ آلافِ كُرةٍ
11,000	أَحَدَ عَشَرَ أَلْفَ كِتابٍ	أَحَدَ عَشَرَ أَلْفَ كُرةٍ
11,500	أَحَدَ عَشَرَ أَلْفاً وَخَمْسُمِائةِ كِتابٍ	أَحَدَ عَشَرَ أَلْفاً وَخَمْسُمِائةِ كُرةٍ

	with masculine noun قبل اسم مذكر	with feminine noun قبل اسم مؤنث
21,000	واحِدٌ وَعِشْرونَ أَلْفَ كِتابٍ	واحِدٌ وَعِشْرونَ أَلْفَ كُرةٍ
200,000	مِائَتا أَلْفِ كِتابٍ	مِائَتا أَلْفِ كُرةٍ
325,000	ثَلاثُمِائةٍ وَخَمْسةٌ وَعِشْرونَ أَلْفَ كِتابٍ	ثَلاثُمِائةٍ وَخَمْسةٌ وَعِشْرونَ أَلْفَ كُرةٍ
1,000,000	مَلْيونُ كِتابٍ	مَلْيونُ كُرةٍ

Ordinal numbers الأعداد الترتيبية

	with masculine noun قبل اسم مذكر	with feminine noun قبل اسم مؤنث
1	الكِتابُ الأَوَّلُ	الكُرةُ الأولى
2	الكِتابُ الثاني	الكُرةُ الثانيةُ
3	الكِتابُ الثالِثُ	الكُرةُ الثالِثةُ
4	الكِتابُ الرابِعُ	الكُرةُ الرابِعةُ
5	الكِتابُ الخامِسُ	الكُرةُ الخامِسةُ
6	الكِتابُ السادِسُ	الكُرةُ السادِسةُ
7	الكِتابُ السابِعُ	الكُرةُ السابِعةُ
8	الكِتابُ الثامِنُ	الكُرةُ الثامِنةُ
9	الكِتابُ التاسِعُ	الكُرةُ التاسِعةُ
10	الكِتابُ العاشِرُ	الكُرةُ العاشِرةُ
11	الكِتابُ الحادِيَ عَشَرَ	الكُرةُ الحادِيةَ عَشْرةَ
12	الكِتابُ الثانِيَ عَشَرَ	الكُرةُ الثانِيةَ عَشْرةَ
13	الكِتابُ الثالِثَ عَشَرَ	الكُرةُ الثالِثةَ عَشْرةَ
14	الكِتابُ الرابِعَ عَشَرَ	الكُرةُ الرابِعةَ عَشْرةَ
15	الكِتابُ الخامِسَ عَشَرَ	الكُرةُ الخامِسةَ عَشْرةَ
16	الكِتابُ السادِسَ عَشَرَ	الكُرةُ السادِسةَ عَشْرةَ
17	الكِتابُ السابِعَ عَشَرَ	الكُرةُ السابِعةَ عَشْرةَ
18	الكِتابُ الثامِنَ عَشَرَ	الكُرةُ الثامِنةَ عَشْرةَ
19	الكِتابُ التاسِعَ عَشَرَ	الكُرةُ التاسِعةَ عَشْرةَ

	with masculine noun قبل اسم مذكر	with feminine noun قبل اسم مؤنث
20	الكِتابُ العِشْرونَ	الكُرةُ العِشْرونَ
21	الكِتابُ الحادي والعِشْرونَ	الكُرةُ الحادِيةُ والعِشْرونَ
22	الكِتابُ الثاني والعِشْرونَ	الكُرةُ الثانِيةُ والعِشْرونَ
23	الكِتابُ الثالِثُ والعِشْرونَ	الكُرةُ الثالِثةُ والعِشْرونَ
24	الكِتابُ الرابِعُ والعِشْرونَ	الكُرةُ الرابِعةُ والعِشْرونَ
31	الكِتابُ الحادي والثَلاثونَ	الكُرةُ الحادِيةُ والثَلاثونَ
38	الكِتابُ الثامِنُ والثَلاثونَ	الكُرةُ الثامِنةُ والثَلاثونَ
250	الكِتابُ المِائَتانِ والخَمْسونَ	الكُرةُ المِائَتانِ والخَمْسونَ
871	الكِتابُ الثَمانِمِائةِ والحادي والسَبْعونَ	الكُرةُ الثَمانِمِائةِ والحادِيةُ والسَبْعونَ
1,000	الكِتابُ الأَلْفُ	الكُرةُ الأَلْفُ

Full forms of dates and years in Arabic

التواريخ والسنين في العربية

In 1973:

فِي سَنةِ أَلْفٍ وَتِسْعِمِائةٍ وَثَلاثٍ وَسَبْعينَ

In 2014:

في عامِ أَلْفَيْنِ وَأَرْبَعةَ عَشَرَ

In 1492:

في عامِ أَلْفٍ وَأَرْبَعِمِائةٍ وَاثْنَيْنِ وَتِسْعينَ

On the first of May:

في الأَوَّلِ من أَيّارَ

8 May 1975:

الثامِنُ من أَيّارَ سَنةَ أَلْفٍ وَتِسْعِمِائةٍ وَخَمْسٍ وَسَبْعينَ

Today is 9 February 1995:

اليَوْمَ التاسِعُ من شُباطَ عامَ أَلْفٍ وَتِسْعِمِائةٍ وَخَمْسةٍ وَتِسْعينَ

On 5 May 2005:

في الخامِسِ من مايو سَنةَ أَلْفَيْنِ وَخَمْسٍ

On 23 July 1838:

في الثالِثِ والعِشْرينَ من يوليو سَنةَ أَلْفٍ وَثَمانِمِائةٍ وَثَمانٍ وَثَلاثينَ

On 12 August 1991:

في الثانِيَ عَشَرَ من آبَ عامَ أَلْفٍ وَتِسْعِمِائةٍ وَواحِدٍ وَتِسْعينَ

Names of months in Arabic

أسماء الشهور في العربية

	Egypt and the Gulf	Iraq and the Levant	Tunisia and Algeria	Morocco
	مصر والخليج	العراق وبلاد الشام	تونس والجزائر	المغرب
January	يَناير	كانون الثاني	جانْفيّ	يَنايِر
February	فِبْراير	شُباط	فيفْريّ	فِبْراير
March	مارِس	آذار	مارِس	مارِس
April	أَبْريل	نَيْسان	أَفْريل	أَبْريل
May	مايو	أَيار	ماي	مايو
June	يونيو	حُزَيْران	جُوان	يونيو
July	يوليو	تمّوز	جُويلِية	يولِيو
August	أَغُسْطُس	آب	أوت	غُشْت
September	سِبْتَمْبِر	أَيْلول	سِبْتَمْبر	شُتَمْبِر
October	أُكْتوبِر	تِشْرين الأَوَّل	أُكْتوبِر	أُكْتوبر
November	نوفَمْبِر	تِشْرين الثاني	نوفَمْبِر	نُونْبِر
December	ديسَمْبِر	كانون الأَوَّل	ديسَمْبِر	دُجَمْبِر

Islamic months الشهور الإسلامية

مُحَرَّم	Muharram
صَفَر	Safar
رَبيع الأَوَّل	Rabi al-Awwal
رَبيع الثاني \ الآخِر	Rabi al-Thani/al-Akhir
جُمادى الأولى \ الأَوَّل	Jumada l-Ula/l-Awwal
جُمادى الثانِية \ الآخِرة	Jumada l-Thaniya/l-Akhira
رَجَب	Rajab
شَعْبان	Shaaban
رَمَضان	Ramadan
شَوّال	Shawwal
ذو القَعْدةِ	Dhu al-Qada
ذو الحِجّةِ	Dhu al-Hijja

Aa

a /eɪ, ə/, **an** /ən/ *determiner* [أداة التَّنْكير]; **~ man/horse/unit** رَجُل \ حِصان \ وِحْدة; **~n aunt/egg/hour/X-ray** خالة \ بَيْضة \ ساعة \ صورة بالأَشِعّةِ السينيّةِ

A, a /eɪ/ *n* **1** (letter) [أَوَّل حَرْفٍ من الأَبْجَديّةِ الإِنْكليزيّةِ]; **from A to Z** من الأَلِفِ إلى الياءِ; **the A to Z of cooking** فَنّ الطَّبْخِ من أَلِفِه إلى يائِهِ **2** (A) (Mus) لا ≈ (نَغْمة من نَغَماتِ السُّلَّمِ الموسيقيِّ) **3** (A) (place) **to get from A to B** انْتَقَلَ من نُقْطةِ أَلِفٍ إلى نُقْطةِ باءٍ **4** (A) (Med) **blood group A** فَصيلة الدَم أ \ أ **5** (in house numbers) **47a** 47 أ **6** (A) (major road in UK) **an accident on the A68** حادِث على طَريق A68

AA /eɪ'eɪ/ *abbr* **1** (BrE) = **Automobile Association** جَمْعيّة السَّيّاراتِ **2** = **Alcoholics Anonymous** الكُحوليّونَ المَجْهولونَ

AAA /eɪeɪ'eɪ/ *abbr* **1** (BrE) = **Amateur Athletics Association** جَمْعيّة هُواةِ أَلْعابِ القُوى **2** (AmE) = **American Automobile Association** جَمْعيّة السَّيّاراتِ الأَمْريكيّة

aback /ə'bak/ *adv* **to be taken ~** انْدَهَشَ; **I was taken ~ by his answer** انْدَهَشْتُ من جَوابِه

abacus /'abəkəs/ *n* (*pl* **abacuses**) مِعْداد (مَعاديدُ)

abandon /ə'band(ə)n/ *vt* **1** (to leave behind) تَخَلّى (عن)، هَجَرَ (u; هَجْر) ‹*the baby, dog*›; **his mother had ~ed him as a child** تَخَلَّتْ عَنْهُ أُمُّهُ عِنْدَما كانَ طِفْلاً; **to ~ ship** فارَقَ السَفينةَ **2** (to give up) تَوَقَّفَ (عن) ‹*the plan, attempt*›

abandoned /ə'band(ə)nd/ *adj* **1** ‹*car, building*› مَهْجور; ‹*baby*› مُتَخَلًّى عَنْهُ **2** (uninhibited) ‹*movements, dancing*› غَيْر مُقَيَّدٍ

abandonment /ə'band(ə)nm(ə)nt/ *n* **1** (of spouse, family) هَجْر **2** (of a place) هَجْر

abase /ə'beɪs/ *v refl* (**abases, abasing, abased**) (fml) **to ~ oneself** أَهانَ نَفْسَهُ, حَطَّ من نَفْسِهِ

abashed /ə'baʃt/ *adj* خَجْلان (خَجْلى, خَجالى)

abate /ə'beɪt/ *vi* «storm, anger» هَدَأَ (a; هُدوء, هَدْء); «fever» انْخَفَضَ

abattoir /'abətwɑː/ *n* مَجْزَرة (مَجازِرُ)

Abba /'abə/ *n* **1** (name for God) أب **2** (title of bishops and patriarchs) أب (آباء) **3** (**abba**) (infml) (father) أب

abbey /'abi/ *n* (*pl* **abbeys**) **1** (community) دَيْر ≈ (كَنيسة كَبيرة مع دَيْرٍ للرُّهْبانِ أو للراهِباتِ) **2** (church) كَنيسة (كانَتْ دَيْراً في الماضي)

abbot /'abət/ *n* رَئيس الدَيْرِ, دَيْرانيّ

abbreviate /ə'briːvɪeɪt/ *vt* اخْتَصَرَ ‹*a phrase, word*›

abbreviation /əbriːvɪ'eɪʃ(ə)n/ *n* اخْتِصار

ABC /eɪbiː'siː/ *n* **1** (alphabet) أَبْجَديّة, الحُروف الأَبْجَديّة **2** (rudiments) **the ~ of sth** أَبْجَديّات شَيْءٍ **3** (AmE) = **American Broadcasting Company** [شَرِكة إذاعةٍ أَمْريكيّة]

abdicate /'abdɪkeɪt/ **A** *vt* **1** **to ~ the throne** «king, queen» تَنازَلَ عن العَرْشِ **2** (not to fulfil) تَخَلّى (عن) ‹*a responsibility, role*›
B *vi* «king, queen» اعْتَزَلَ

abdication /ˌabdɪ'keɪʃ(ə)n/ *n* **1** (of the throne) تَنازُل عن العَرْشِ, اعْتِزال العَرْشِ **2** (of a responsibility) تَخَلٍّ

abdomen /'abdəmən/ *n* بَطْن (بُطون, أَبْطُن)

abdominal /ab'dɒmɪn(ə)l/ *adj* ‹*muscles, pain, regions*› بَطْنيّ, في مِنْطَقة البَطْنِ

abduct /əb'dʌkt/ *vt* اخْتَطَفَ, خَطَفَ (i; خَطْف) ‹*a victim, woman*›

abduction /əb'dʌkʃ(ə)n/ *n* خَطْف, اخْتِطاف (اخْتِطافات)

abet /ə'bɛt/ *vt* (**-tt-**) حَرَّضَ (على) ‹*terrorism, murder*›; **aid and ~** حَرَّضَ على جَريمةٍ

abeyance /əˈbeɪəns/ *n* **to be in ~** [كانَ مُعَلَّقاً \ غَيْرَ مُسْتَخْدَمٍ]

abhor /əbˈhɔː/ *vt* **(-rr-)** (fml) مَقَتَ (u; مَقْت)، كَرِهَ (a; كُرْه، كَرِه، كَراهيّة، كَراهة) اشْمَأَزَّ (من) ‹*violence, an idea*›

abide /əˈbʌɪd/ *vi* (*past tense, past participle* **abode** or **abided**)
1 **can't ~ sb/sth** لم يَطِقْ شَخْصاً \ شَيْئاً; **I can't ~ his arrogance/behaviour** لا أُطيقُ غَطْرَسَتَهُ \ سُلوكَهُ 2 **to ~ by the rules** الْتَزَمَ بالقَوانينِ

ability /əˈbɪlɪti/ *n* (*pl* **abilities**) 1 (capability) قُدرة، مَقْدِرة (قُدُرات)، قابِليّة; **she did the task to the best of her ~** بَذَلَتْ كُلَّ جُهْدِها لِإِنْجازِ المُهِمّةِ; **he had lost the ~ to speak** كانَ قد فَقَدَ قابِليَّتَهُ على النُطْقِ 2 (talent) قُدْرة (قُدُرات)، كَفاءة; **children of differing abilities** أَطْفال بِقُدُراتٍ مُخْتَلِفةٍ

abject /ˈabdʒɛkt/ *adj* 1 ‹*failure, poverty*› مُدْقِع 2 ‹*apology, coward*› ذَليل (أَذِلّة، أَذِلّاءُ)

ablaze /əˈbleɪz/ *adj pred* 1 (burning) **to be ~** «buildings, town» كانَ مُشْتَعِلاً \ مُلْتَهِباً \ مُتَوَقِّداً 2 (liter) (bright) وَهّاج; **to be ~ with colour** كانَ مُشْتَعِلاً بالأَلْوانِ

able /ˈeɪb(ə)l/ *adj* (**abler, ablest**) 1 (having ability to) **to be ~ to do sth** اِسْتَطاعَ أَنْ يَفْعَلَ شَيْئاً; **he was/wasn't ~ to read it** كانَ \ لم يَكُنْ قادِراً على قِراءَتِهِ; **I'll be ~ to give you more information after the meeting** سَوْفَ يَكونُ بِمَقْدوري أَنْ أُعْطِيَكَ مَزيداً من المَعْلوماتِ بعد الاجْتِماعِ 2 (skilled) ‹*lawyer, student*› ماهِر (مَهَرة)، كُفْء (أَكْفاء); **she's a very ~ lawyer** هي مُحامِيةٌ ماهِرةٌ جِدّاً

able-bodied /eɪb(ə)lˈbɒdɪd/ *adj* ‹*man, adult*› مُعافًى، في صِحّةٍ جَيِّدةٍ

abnormal /əbˈnɔːm(ə)l/ *adj* ‹*behaviour, child*› غَيْرُ طَبيعيٍّ

abnormality /abnɔːˈmalɪti/ *n* (*pl* **abnormalities**) خلل (خِلال)

aboard /əˈbɔːd/ **A** *adv* **to go ~** ‹*a plane, ship, train*› صَعِدَ (a; صُعود) على مَتْنٍ
B *prep* ‹*a plane, ship, train*› على مَتْنِ

abode /əˈbəʊd/ *n* (liter hum) سَكَن، مَسْكَن (مَساكِنُ); **of no fixed ~** (Law) لَيْسَ لَهُ مَأْوًى

abolish /əˈbɒlɪʃ/ *vt* أَلْغى ‹*a tax, slavery*›; أَوْقَفَ ‹*allowance*›; **the president has ~ed compulsory military service** أَلْغى الرَئيسُ الخِدْمةَ العَسْكَريّةَ الإلْزاميّةَ

abolition /abəˈlɪʃ(ə)n/ *n* إلْغاء (إلْغاءات); **the ~ of monarchy/the death penalty** إلْغاء المَلَكيّةِ \ عُقوبةِ المَوْتِ

abominable /əˈbɒm(ə)nəb(ə)l/ *adj* ‹*treatment*› فَظيع; ‹*behaviour*› مَقيت

abomination /əbɒmɪˈneɪʃ(ə)n/ *n* مَقْت

aboriginal /abəˈrɪdʒɪn(ə)l/ **A** *adj* ‹*community, population*› أَصْليّ
B *n* (native of a place) ساكِن أَصْليّ

aborigine /abəˈrɪdʒɪniː/ *n* **the Australian A~s** سُكّان أُسْتُراليا الأَصْليّون; **he is an ~** هو من السُكّانِ الأَصْليّين

abort /əˈbɔːt/ *vt* 1 أَجْهَضَ ‹*a foetus, baby*› 2 أَجْهَضَ ‹*a mission, project*›; أَوْقَفَ ‹*a program, test*›

abortion /əˈbɔːʃ(ə)n/ *n* إجْهاض (إجْهاضات); **to have an ~** تَعَرَّضَ للإجْهاضِ

abortive /əˈbɔːtɪv/ *adj* ‹*attempt, coup*› مُجْهَض

abound /əˈbaʊnd/ *vi* 1 «wildlife, rumours» كَثُرَ (u; كَثْرة) 2 **to ~ in** *or* **with sth** اكْتَظَّ \ امْتَلأَ بِشَيْءٍ

about /əˈbaʊt/ **A** *adj* 1 (expressing future intention) **to be ~ to do sth** أَوْشَكَ \ كانَ على وَشْكِ أَنْ يَفْعَلَ شَيْئاً; **we're (just) ~ to start** نَحْنُ على وَشْكِ أَنْ نَبْدَأَ; **I was just ~ to ask you the same thing** كُنْتُ على وَشْكِ أَنْ أَسْأَلَكَ نَفْسَ السُؤالِ 2 (active) نَشِط، نَشيط (نِشاط); **you were (up and) ~ early this morning** لَقد كُنْتَ مُتَيَقِّظاً مُبَكِّراً هذا الصَباحَ
B *prep* 1 (concerning, regarding) **a documentary ~ Nasser/the oil industry** فيلْم وَثائِقيّ عن ناصِرٍ \ صِناعةِ النِفْطِ; **what's it ~?** ما مَوْضوعُهُ؟; **it's ~ ...** هو بِخُصوصِ ...; **now, ~ your overdraft ...** والآنَ، بِخُصوصِ سَحْبِكَ على المَكْشوفِ ... 2 (in the nature of) **there's something weird ~ him** هُناكَ شَيْءٌ غَريبٌ فيه; **what I like ~ her is ...** ما يُعْجِبُني فيها هو ... 3 (bound up with) **business is ~ profit** التِجارةُ تَتَعَلَّقُ بالرِبْحِ 4 (occupied with) **to know what one is ~** عَرَفَ ما هو مُقْبِلٌ عَلَيْهِ; **while you're ~ it ...** بَيْنَما أَنْتَ تَشْتَغِلُ فيه ...; **and be quick ~ it!** وأَسْرِعْ في القِيامِ بِهِ! 5 (around) **to wander ~ the streets** سارَ هائِماً على وَجْهِهِ في الشَوارِعِ; **strewn ~ the floor** مُتَناثِر على الأَرْضيّةِ 6 (in suggestions) **how** *or* **what ~ some tea?** ماذا عن بَعْضِ الشايِ؟; **how ~ it?** ما رَأْيُكَ في هذا؟ 7 (in asking opinions) **what ~ the tax implications?** ما رَأْيُكَ

ماذا عَنْكَ؟ في الآثارِ المُتَرَتِّبَة على الضَريبةِ؟; **what ~ you?** ⑧ (fml) (on) **to have drugs/a weapon hidden ~ one's person** خَبَّأَ مُخَدِّراتٍ \ سِلاحاً عِنْدَهُ

C *adv* ① (approximately) حَوالَيْ, تَقْريباً; **it's ~ the same as yesterday** هو نَفْسُ ما كانَ عَلَيْهِ بالأَمْسِ تَقْريباً; **at ~ 6 p.m.** عند حَوالَي ال6 مَساءً ② (almost) تَقْريباً; **that seems ~ right** يَبْدو ذلك صَحيحاً تَقْريباً; **I've had just ~ enough of her!** تَحَمَّلْتُ مِنْها بِما فيه الكِفايةُ! ③ (in circulation) **there was no one ~** لم يَكُنْ هُناكَ أَحَدٌ في الجِوارِ; **a lot of flu is going ~** هُناكَ الكَثيرُ من الناسِ يُعانونَ من الإِنْفِلْوَنْزا ④ (near) **ask Jack, he's somewhere ~** اسْأَلْ جاك، هو في مَكانٍ ما قَريبٍ على مَقْرُبةٍ

Idioms **it's about time (that)** آنَ الأَوانُ (أَنْ); **that's about it** هذا هو كُلُّ شَيْءٍ

about-turn /əbaʊt'tɛːn/ *n* تَغْيير شامِل

above /ə'bʌv/ **A** *prep* ① (over) فَوْقَ; **~ sea level** فوق مُسْتَوى سَطْحِ البَحْرِ; **~ the surface** فوق السَطْح; **the apartment ~ ours** الشَقّة الّتي فوق شَقّتِنا ② (in number, degree) فَوْقَ; **5° ~ zero** خَمْس دَرَجاتٍ فوق الصِفْرِ; **~ the age of 21** فوق سِنِّ الحادي والعِشْرينَ ③ (superior in rank) ما فَوْقَ; **officers ~ the rank of captain** الضُبّاط ما فوق رُتْبَةِ النَقيبِ; **the teams ~ them in the table** ما فَوْقَهُمْ من الفِرَقِ في الجَدْوَلِ

B *adv* ① (higher up) **the apartment ~** الشَقّة الّتي تَعْلو شَقّتَنا ② (in texts) **see ~** أُنْظُرْ أَعْلاهُ

C (above all) *adv phr* الأَهَمّ من هذا وَذاكَ; **~ all, stay out of debt** الأَهَمُّ من هذا وَذاكَ، ابْقَ بَعيداً عن الدُيونِ

above board *adj pred* ‹deal, operations› سَليم

above-mentioned /əˌbʌv'mɛnʃ(ə)nd/ *adj* ‹article, fact› مَذْكور أَعْلاهُ

abrasive /ə'breɪsɪv/ *adj* ① ‹cleaner, pad› كاشِط, حاكّ ② ‹manner, personality› قاسٍ, خَشِن

abreast /ə'brɛst/ *adv* ① (side by side) **to walk three ~** مَشَوا ثَلاثَتُهُمْ إلى جانِبِ بَعْضِهِم البَعْضِ ② (up to date) **to keep ~ of the news** بَقِيَ مُطَّلِعاً على الأَخْبارِ

abridge /ə'brɪdʒ/ *vt* ‹a novel, text› اخْتَصَرَ; **an ~d edition** طَبْعَة مُخْتَصَرة

abroad /ə'brɔːd/ *adv* ① ‹to travel, move› خارِجَ البِلادِ ② ‹to study, live› في الخارِجِ

abrupt /ə'brʌpt/ *adj* ① ‹halt, departure› مُفاجِئ ② ‹manner, question› جاف, فَظّ

abruptly /ə'brʌptli/ *adv* ① (suddenly) ‹to end, leave› فَجْأَةً ② (curtly) ‹to speak, gesture› بِفَظاظةٍ ③ (steeply) ‹to rise, fall› بِشَكْلٍ حادٍّ

ABS /eɪbiː'ɛs/ *n* = **anti-lock braking system** نِظام مَنْعِ انْغِلاقِ المَكابِحِ

abscess /'absɪs/ *n* خُرّاج (خَراريجُ)

abscond /əb'skɒnd/ *vi* «prisoners, detainees» هَرَبَ (هُروب), فَرَّ (i; فَرّ, فِرار, مَفَرّ) (u;

abseiling /'abseɪlɪŋ/ *n* (BrE) [عَمَليّة الهُبوطِ من الارْتِفاعاتِ بالحِبالِ]

absence /'abs(ə)ns/ *n* غِياب

Idiom **to be conspicuous by one's absence** [كانَ عَدَمُ وُجودِهِ مُلْفِتاً للانْتِباهِ]

absent /'abs(ə)nt/ *adj* ① (from school, work) ‹colleague, boss› غائِب (غائِبونَ, غُيَّب, غُيّاب); **to be ~ from school/the office** غابَ عن المَدْرَسةِ \ من المَكْتَبِ ② (missing) ‹name, place› غَيْر مَوْجودٍ; **Russia was ~ from the list** غابَ اسْمُ روسْيا عن القائِمةِ

absentee /ˌabs(ə)n'tiː/ *n* غائِب (غائِبونَ, غُيَّب, غُيّاب)

absentee ballot *n* (AmE) اقْتِراع غِيابيّ

absenteeism /abs(ə)n'tiːɪz(ə)m/ *n* غِياب

absent-minded /ˌabs(ə)nt'maɪndɪd/ *adj* شارِد الذِهْنِ

absolute /'absəluːt/ *adj* ‹necessity, truth› مُطْلَق; **in ~ silence** في صَمْتٍ تامٍّ

absolutely /'absəluːtli/ *adv* ‹fantastic, right› مُطْلَقاً; **she ~ loved/hated it** حَبَّتْهُ \ كَرِهَتْهُ إلى حَدِّ العَظْمِ

absolute pitch *n* [القُدْرة على التَعَرُّف على \ ضَبْطِ النَغَماتِ]

absolution /absə'luːʃ(ə)n/ *n* غُفْران, حِلّة

absolve /əb'zɒlv/ *vt* ① (fml) ‹a defendant, company› بَرَّأَ; **to ~ sb from** *or* **of sth** بَرَّأَ شَخْصاً من شَيْءٍ ② «priest» غَفَرَ ‹a sinner› (i; غُفْران ,ل)

absorb /əbˈzɔːb/ *vt* [1] (to take in) امْتَصَّ ‹*heat, water*› [2] (to captivate) شَدَّ (i-u; شَدّ) ‹*a student, an audience*›; **to be ~ed in one's work** اسْتَغْرَقَ في عَمَلِهِ

absorbent /əbˈzɔːb(ə)nt/ *adj* ‹*cotton, material*› مُمْتَصّ

absorbent cotton *n* (AmE) قُطْن ماصّ

absorption /əbˈzɔːpʃ(ə)n/ *n* [1] (of heat, liquids) امْتِصاص (امْتِصاصات) [2] (engrossment) انْهِماك, اسْتِغْراق (انْهِماكات)

abstain /əbˈsteɪn/ *vi* [1] (in a vote) امْتَنَعَ عن التَصْويت [2] (from eating, drinking) امْتَنَعَ (عن)

abstention /əbˈstɛnʃ(ə)n/ *n* (from vote) امْتِناع (امْتِناعات); **ten votes for, two against and three ~s** عَشَرة أَصْواتٍ مع، وَصَوْتَيْنِ ضدّ، وثَلاثة مُمْتَنِعين

abstinence /ˈabstɪnəns/ *n* زُهْد, تَقَشُّف

abstract /ˈabstrakt/ *adj* [1] ‹*idea, concept*› مُجَرَّد [2] ‹*art, painting*› تَجْريديّ

abstraction /əbˈstrakʃ(ə)n/ *n* [1] (vagueness) شُرود الذِهْنِ \ الفِكْرِ [2] (concept) تَجْريد

absurd /əbˈsəːd/ *adj* ‹*idea*› عَبَثِيّ

absurdity /əbˈsəːdɪti/ *n* سَخافة

Abu Dhabi /ˌabuː ˈdɑːbi/ *pr n* أبو ظَبْي (f)

abundance /əˈbʌnd(ə)ns/ *n* غَزارة, كَثْرة, وَفْرة

abundant /əˈbʌnd(ə)nt/ *adj* ‹*rain, supplies*› غَزير, وافِر (غِزار); **an ~ supply of sth** مَخْزون وافِر من شَيْءٍ

abuse **A** /əˈbjuːz/ *vt* [1] (sexually, physically) اعْتَدى (على), أساءَ, اسْتَغَلَّ ‹*a patient, child*› [2] (to exploit) اسْتَباحَ حُرْمةً الاسْتِعْمال ‹*a position, one's power*› [3] (to insult) سَبَّ (u; سَبّ), شَتَمَ (i-u; شَتْم) ‹*a customer, soldier*›

B /əˈbjuːs/ *n* [1] (insults) شَتْم, سِباب; **to be subjected to racial ~** تَعَرَّضَ لِسِبابٍ عُنْصُريٍّ [2] (of power) اسْتِغْلال, إساءة الاسْتِعْمالِ [3] (of a child, an elderly person) إساءة المُعامَلةِ

abusive /əˈbjuːsɪv/ *adj* [1] (insulting) ‹*customer*› سَيِّئ الطَبْعِ; ‹*language*› مُسيء, بَذيء [2] (violent, cruel) ‹*relationship*› يَتَميَّزُ بالعُنْفِ \ بِسوءِ المُعامَلةِ; ‹*husband*› مُتَعَسِّف

abysmal /əˈbɪzm(ə)l/ *adj* ‹*failure, performance*› سَيِّئ جِدًّا

abyss /əˈbɪs/ *n* هاوِية

AC /eɪˈsiː/ *abbr* [1] = **air conditioning** تَكْييف الهَواءِ [2] = **alternating current** تَيّار مُتَرَدِّد \ مُتَناوِب

a/c /eɪˈsiː/ *abbr* = **account** حِساب (حِسابات), حِساب مَصْرِفيّ \ بَنْكيّ

academia /ˌakəˈdiːmɪə/ *n* الأكاديميا, المُجْتَمَع الأكاديميّ

academic /akəˈdɛmɪk/ **A** *adj* [1] ‹*year, staff*› أكاديميّ, جامِعيّ [2] (theoretical) ‹*question, debate*› نَظَريّ

B *n* جامِعيّ (أُسْتاذ \ باحِث جامِعيّ)

academy /əˈkadəmi/ *n* (*pl* **academies**) [1] (school) أكاديمية [2] (learned society) أكاديمية

accede /əkˈsiːd/ *vi* (fml) [1] (to a demand, request) لَبّى, اسْتَجابَ [2] (to the throne) ارْتَقى

accelerate /əkˈsɛləreɪt/ *vi* «driver, car» أَسْرَعَ; «events» تَسارَعَ

acceleration /əksɛləˈreɪʃ(ə)n/ *n* تَسارُع

accelerator /əkˈsɛləreɪtə/ *n* [1] (Aut) دَوّاسة البَنْزينِ [2] (Phys) مُعَجِّل, مُسَرِّع

accent /ˈaksɛnt, ˈaks(ə)nt/ *n* لُكْنة; **a foreign ~** لُكْنة أَجْنَبِيّة

accentuate /əkˈsɛntʃueɪt/ *vt* أَبْرَزَ

accept /əkˈsɛpt/ *vt* [1] (when sth is offered) قَبِلَ (a; قَبول, قُبول) ‹*an invitation, a job*› [2] (to take on) قَبِلَ (a; قَبول, قُبول) ‹*a challenge, responsibility*›

acceptable /əkˈsɛptəb(ə)l/ *adj* [1] (satisfactory) ‹*explanation, progress*› مَقْبول [2] (tolerable) ‹*behaviour*› مَقْبول

acceptance /əkˈsɛpt(ə)ns/ *n* [1] (of an invitation, a gift, job) قُبول [2] (of a practice, custom) قُبول

access /ˈaksɛs/ **A** *n* دُخول; **to have ~ to sth** (to a building, data) اسْتَطاعَ الدُخولَ إلى شَيْءٍ; (to funds) تَمَكَّنَ من الحُصولِ على شَيْءٍ

B *vt* [1] (to enter) دَخَلَ (u; دُخول) ‹*a room, building*› [2] (to retrieve) اسْتَرْجَعَ ‹*data*›; (to obtain) تَحَصَّلَ (على) ‹*funds*›

access course *n* (BrE) دَوْرة تَأْهيلِيّة

accessibility /əksɛsɪˈbɪlɪti/ *n* (of a place) سُهولة الوُصولِ; (of a person) سُهولة التَقارُبِ; (of a topic, material) سُهولة المَنالِ

accessible /əkˈsɛsɪb(ə)l/ *adj* [1] ‹*area, beach*› مَفْتوح [2] ‹*data, funds*› مُتاح

accession /ək'sɛʃ(ə)n/ *n* (to power, the throne) ارْتِقاء; (to a treaty, an organization) انْضِمام

accessory /ək'sɛs(ə)ri/ *n* (*pl* **accessories**) لاحِقة (لَواحِقُ), تابِع (تَوابِعُ)

accident /'aksɪd(ə)nt/ *n* 1 (mishap) حادِث; **car/road ~** حادِثُ سَيّارةٍ / طَريقٍ; **to have an ~** تَعَرَّضَ إلى حادِثٍ 2 (chance event) صُدْفة (صُدَف); **I found it by ~** وَجَدْتُهُ بالصُدْفةِ

accidental /aksɪ'dɛnt(ə)l/ *adj* 1 ‹*death, collision*› عَرَضيّ; ‹*overdose*› بالخَطَأِ 2 ‹*meeting*› بالصُدْفةِ

accidentally /aksɪ'dɛnt(ə)li/ *adv* 1 (by accident) ‹*to collide*› عَرَضيًّا; ‹*to shoot, delete*› بالخَطَأِ 2 (by chance) ‹*to meet*› مُصادَفةً

accident and emergency *n* (BrE) قِسْم الحَوادِثِ والطَوارِئِ

accident-prone /,aksɪd(ə)nt'prəʊn/ *adj* [كَثير \ سَريع التَعَرُّضِ للحَوادِثِ]; **don't let him into the kitchen, he's so ~** لا تَدَعْهُ يَدْخُلُ المَطْبَخ، فَهُوَ يَتَعَثَّرُ حتّى في رِجْلَيْهِ

acclaim /ə'kleɪm/ A *vt* نَوَّهَ (ب), أَثْنى (على), مَدَحَ (a; مَدْح, مِدْحة) ‹*an author, album*›

B *n* ثَناء (أَثْنِية), تَنْويه, مَدْح

acclimate /'aklɪmeɪt, ə'klʌɪmət/ *vi* (AmE) ▸ **acclimatize**

acclimatize, -ise (BrE) /ə'klʌɪmətʌɪz/ *vi* «settlers, plants» تَأَقْلَمَ; **to ~** *or* **become ~d to sth** تَأَقْلَمَ مع شَيْءٍ

accolade /'akəleɪd/ *n* وِسام (أَوْسِمة), نيشان (نَياشينُ)

accommodate /ə'kɒmədeɪt/ *vt* 1 (to provide a room for) ‹*guests*› بَيَّتَ 2 (to provide space for) ‹*passengers, wheelchairs*› اسْتَوْعَبَ 3 (to satisfy) ‹*a need*› أَشْبَعَ; ‹*wish*› حَقَّقَ

accommodating /ə'kɒmədeɪtɪŋ/ *adj* ‹*attitude, approach*› طَيِّع

accommodation /əkɒmə'deɪʃ(ə)n/ *n* 1 (also **accommodations** AmE) (lodgings) مَسْكَن (مَساكِنُ), مَحَلّ إقامةٍ; **to find ~** وَجَدَ مَسْكَناً \ مَحَلَّ إقامةٍ; **to look for ~** بَحَثَ عن مَسْكَنٍ \ مَحَلِّ إقامةٍ 2 (compromise) تَسْوِية

accommodation officer, accommodations officer (AmE) *n* مَسْؤول سَكَنٍ

accompaniment /ə'kʌmp(ə)nɪm(ə)nt/ *n* مُرافَقة, مُصاحَبة

accompanist /ə'kʌmp(ə)nɪst/ *n* مُرافِق, مُصاحِب

accompany /ə'kʌmp(ə)ni/ *vt* (**accompanies, accompanying, accompanied**) 1 (to go with) رافَقَ; **I accompanied her to the station** رافَقْتُها إلى المَحَطّةِ 2 (to play with) رافَقَ

accomplice /ə'kʌmplɪs/ *n* شَريك في جَريمةٍ

accomplish /ə'kʌmplɪʃ/ *vt* ‹*a task, an objective*› أَنْجَزَ; **mission ~ed!** تَمَّ إنْجازُ المُهِمّةِ!

accomplished /ə'kʌmplɪʃt/ *adj* ‹*musician, athlete, liar, thief*› ماهِر (مَهَرة), بارِع

accomplishment /ə'kʌmplɪʃm(ə)nt/ *n* 1 (of an aim) إنْجاز مُنْجَز (إنْجازات) 2 (skill)

accord /ə'kɔːd/ *n* اتِّفاق (اتِّفاقات); **to reach an ~ with sb** تَوَصَّلَ إلى اتِّفاقٍ مع شَخْصٍ; **I volunteered of my own ~** تَطَوَّعْتُ من نَفْسي

accordance /ə'kɔːd(ə)ns/ *phr* (**in accordance with**) بموجب; **in ~ with the rules/law** بموجب القَواعِدِ \ القانونِ

according /ə'kɔːdɪŋ/ *phr* (**according to**) 1 (as stated by) ‹*newspaper, police*› وَفْقاً ل, بِحَسَب; **~ to reports, nine people were killed** وَفْقاً للتَقاريرِ، قُتِلَ تِسْعةُ أَشْخاصٍ 2 (depending on) ‹*ability, size*› وَفْقاً ل, بموجِبِ, حَسَبَ; **students are graded ~ to ability** يُصَنَّفُ الطُلّابُ حَسَبَ قُدُراتِهِمْ 3 (in agreement with) ‹*law, act*› حَسَبَ; ‹*principles*› وَفْقَ; **everything went ~ to plan** مَرَّ كُلُّ شَيْءٍ حَسَبَ الخُطّةِ

accordingly /ə'kɔːdɪŋli/ *adv* ‹*to adjust, amend*› وَفْقاً لِذلِكَ; **in wet weather the speed must be reduced ~** عِنْدَما يَكونُ الطَقسُ مُمْطِراً، يَجِبُ أنْ تُخَفَّضَ السُرْعةُ وَفْقاً لِذلِكَ

accordion /ə'kɔːdɪən/ *n* أَكورْدِيون

accost /ə'kɒst/ *vt* ‹*a passer-by*› أَوْقَفَ

account /ə'kaʊnt/ A *n* 1 (in a bank, post office, store) حِساب (حِسابات) 2 **to take sth into ~** أَخَذَ شَيْئاً في \ بِعَيْنِ الاعْتِبارِ 3 (description) وَصْف (أَوْصاف) 4 **on ~ of sth** بِسَبَبِ شَيْءٍ, نَظَراً إلى \ لِشَيْءٍ; **on my/his ~** بِسَبَبي \ بِسَبَبِهِ; **on no ~** لا ... بِأَيِّ حالٍ من الأَحْوالِ, لا ... على الإطْلاقِ

B (**accounts**) *n pl* (records) حِسابات, دَفاتِر

C (**accounts**) *n sing* or *n pl* (department) قِسْم المُحاسَبةِ

(Idiom) **there is no accounting for taste** لِكُلٍّ ذَوْقُهُ

(Phrasal verb) **account for**: **~ for [sth/sb]** 1 (to explain) عَلَّلَ [شَيْئاً] ‹events, a fact, an expense›; (to locate) تَبَيَّنَ مَكانَ [شَيْءٍ \ شَخْصٍ] ‹a passenger, vehicle› 2 (to represent, make up) مَثَّلَ [شَيْئاً] ‹a proportion, percentage›; **exports ~ for 10% of our trade** تُمَثِّلُ الصادِراتُ ٪10 من تِجارَتِنا 3 (to destroy, kill) دَمَّرَ [شَيْئاً] ‹a vehicle, plane›; قَتَلَ [شَخْصاً] ‹a soldier, fighter› 4 (to defeat) غَلَبَ [شَيْئاً \ شَخْصاً] ‹an opponent, a team›

accountability /əˌkaʊntəˈbɪlɪti/ *n* مُساءَلة

accountable /əˈkaʊntəb(ə)l/ *adj* **to be ~ to sb for sth** كانَ مَسْؤولاً أمامَ شَخْصٍ عن شَيْءٍ

accountancy /əˈkaʊnt(ə)nsi/ *n* مُحاسَبة

accountant /əˈkaʊnt(ə)nt/ *n* مُحاسِب (مُحاسِبون)

account holder *n* صاحِب الحِسابِ

accounting /əˈkaʊntɪŋ/ *n* مُحاسَبة

account manager *n* مُدير الحِساباتِ

account number *n* رَقَم الحِسابِ

accredit /əˈkrɛdɪt/ *vt* 1 (to appoint) اعْتَمَدَ, فَوَّضَ ‹a diplomat, representative› 2 (to sanction) أَقَرَّ (على), صَدَّقَ ‹a course, an organization›

accreditation /əkrɛdɪˈteɪʃ(ə)n/ *n* 1 (by an institution) إقْرار, اعْتِماد 2 (to an organization) تَفْويض (تَفْويضات)

accrue /əˈkruː/ **A** *vi* «benefits, interest» دَرَّ (i-u; دَرّ)
B *vt* 1 جَمَّعَ ‹interest, a debt› 2 [احْتَسَبَ نَفَقاتٍ غَيْرَ مُدْرَجةٍ في قائِمة حِسابِ آخِرِ السَنةِ] ‹expenditure›

accumulate /əˈkjuːmjʊleɪt/ **A** *vt* جَمَعَ (a; جَمْع) ‹interest, wealth›
B *vi* «fluid» تَجَمَّعَ; «sediment» تَرَسَّبَ; «possessions» تَراكَمَ, تَكَدَّسَ

accumulation /əkjuːmjʊˈleɪʃ(ə)n/ *n* [u] تَكْديس

accuracy /ˈakjʊrəsi/ *n* دِقّة

accurate /ˈakjʊrət/ *adj* دَقيق

accurately /ˈakjərətli/ *adv* بِدِقّةٍ

accusation /akjʊˈzeɪʃ(ə)n/ *n* تُهْمة (تُهَم), اتِّهام (اتِّهامات); **to admit/deny the ~** اعْتَرَفَ بالتُهْمةِ المُوَجَّهةِ إلَيْهِ \ أَنْكَرَ التُهْمةَ المُوَجَّهةَ إلَيْهِ

accusative /əˈkjuːzətɪv/ **A** *adj* ‹case, ending› النَصْبِ; **a noun in the ~ case** اسْم مَنْصوب
B *n* نَصْب

accuse /əˈkjuːz/ *vt* (in general) اتَّهَمَ; (in court) وَجَّهَ اتِّهاماً إلى; **to ~ sb of doing sth** اتَّهَمَ شَخْصاً بِفِعْلِ شَيْءٍ

accused /əˈkjuːzd/ *n* (*pl* **accused**) **the ~** المُتَّهَم

accuser /əˈkjuːzə/ *n* مُتَّهِم

accusing /əˈkjʊːzɪŋ/ *adj* ‹look, tone› اتِّهامٍ

accustom /əˈkʌstəm/ *vt* **to ~ sb to sth/to doing sth** عَوَّدَ شَخْصاً على شَيْءٍ \ على عَمَلِ شَيْءٍ

accustomed /əˈkʌstəmd/ *adj* 1 **to be ~ to doing sth** اعْتادَ على القِيامِ بِشَيْءٍ 2 (usual) ‹role, tone› مُعْتاد

ace /eɪs/ *n* 1 (in cards) آس (آسات) 2 (in tennis) ضَرْبة ساحِقة

ache /eɪk/ **A** *n* أَلَم (آلام)
B *vi* «head, stomach» آلَمَ (Form IV; imperf يُؤْلِمُ)

achieve /əˈtʃiːv/ *vt* حَقَّقَ ‹a goal, victory›

achievement /əˈtʃiːvm(ə)nt/ *n* إنْجاز (إنْجازات)

Achilles heel /əˌkɪliːz ˈhiːl/ *n* كَعْب أَخيلِ (نُقْطة ضُعْفٍ)

aching /ˈeɪkɪŋ/ *adj* ‹body› مُؤْلِم

acid /ˈasɪd/ **A** *n* حَمْض (أَحْماض), حامِض (حَوامِض); **hydrochloric/citric ~** حامِض الهيدْروكْلوريد \ السِتْريك
B *adj* ‹solution, taste› حَمْضيّ

acidic /əˈsɪdɪk/ *adj* 1 ‹solution, substance› حَمْضيّ, حامِض
2 (bitter) ‹taste, wine› حامِض

acidity /əˈsɪdɪti/ *n* 1 (Chem) (of a substance) حُموضة, حَمْضيّة
2 (of a remark) فَظاظة

acid rain *n* مَطَر حَمْضيّ

acid test *n* اخْتِبار حَقيقيّ

acknowledge /əkˈnɒlɪdʒ/ *vt* 1 (to accept) أَقَرَّ (ب) ‹a fact›; اعْتَرَفَ (ب) ‹a mistake, responsibility, an error, problem›; **to ~ defeat** أَقَرَّ بِهَزيمَتِهِ 2 (to confirm receipt of) أَقَرَّ باسْتِلامِ ‹a letter›

acknowledgement /əkˈnɒlɪdʒm(ə)nt/ **A** *n* 1 (of a fact, problem, responsibility, an error) إقْرار 2 (of a letter) إقْرار باسْتِلامٍ

B (**acknowledgements**) *n pl* (in a book) كَلِمة شُكْرٍ

acne /'akni/ *n* بُثور ,حَبّ الشَّبابِ

acorn /'eɪkɔːn/ *n* بَلّوط (n coll)

acoustic /ə'kuːstɪk/ *adj* **1** ‹*range, effects*› سَمْعيّ ,صَوْتيّ **2** ‹*instrument, guitarist*› تَقْليديّ (غَيْر كَهْرَبائيٍّ)

acoustic guitar *n* [قيثارة عاديّة]

acoustics /ə'kuːstɪks/ *n pl* صَوتيّات

acquaint /ə'kweɪnt/ **A** *vt* **to get** *or* **become ~ed with sb** تَعَرَّفَ على شَخْصٍ; **they've been ~ed for a long time** يَعْرِفُ بَعْضُهُم البَعْضَ منذ زَمَنٍ بَعيدٍ **B** *v refl* **to ~ oneself with the facts/procedure** اطَّلَعَ على الحَقائِقِ \ الإِجْراءاتِ

acquaintance /ə'kweɪnt(ə)ns/ *n* **1** (relationship) مَعْرِفة (مَعارِفُ) **2** (person) مَعْرِفة (مَعارِفُ)

acquainted /ə'kweɪntɪd/ *adj* **to be ~** كانا من مَعارِفِ بَعْضِهِما البَعْضِ; **to get ~ with sb** تَعَرَّفَ على شَخْصٍ

acquiesce /,akwɪ'ɛs/ *vi* أَذْعَنَ للأَمْرِ

acquire /ə'kwʌɪə/ *vt* **1** (to obtain) حَصَلَ (u; حُصول ;على) ‹*land, information, shares, a right*› **2** (to develop) اكْتَسَبَ ‹*a skill, expertise*›

acquired /ə'kwʌɪəd/ *adj* ‹*habit, skill*› مُكْتَسَب; **it's an ~ taste** إِنَّهُ ذَوْقٌ مُكْتَسَبٌ

acquisition /,akwɪ'zɪʃ(ə)n/ *n* **1** (item obtained) مُقْتَنًى (مُقْتَنَيات) **2** (obtaining) تَمَلُّك ,اقْتِناء

acquit /ə'kwɪt/ *vt* (**-tt-**) بَرَّأَ ‹*a prisoner, the accused*›; **to be ~ted of sth** بُرِّئَ من شَيْءٍ

acquittal /ə'kwɪt(ə)l/ *n* (Law) تَبْرِئة

acre /'eɪkə/ *n* (measure of land) [وَحْدة لِقِياسِ الأَرْضِ تُعادِلُ 4840 يارْدةً مُرَبَّعةً]

acreage /'eɪk(ə)rɪdʒ/ *n* مساحة أَكْريّة

acrid /'akrɪd/ *adj* ‹*smell, taste*› حادّ

acrobat /'akrəbat/ *n* بَهْلَوان (بَهْلَوانات)

acrobatic /akrə'batɪk/ *adj* ‹*dancer, movements*› بَهْلَوانيّ

acrobatics /akrə'batɪks/ *n pl* أَلْعاب بَهْلَوانيّة

across /ə'krɒs/ **A** *prep* **1** (from one side to the other) **to go** *or* **travel ~ sth** عَبَرَ شَيْئاً; **the bridge ~ the river** الجِسْر المُمْتَدّ عَبْرَ النَهْرِ; **the scar ~ his face** النَدَبة على وَجْهِهِ; **to travel ~ country** عَبَرَ البَلَدَ ,سافَرَ عَبْرَ البَلَدِ; **she leaned ~ the table** انْحَنَتْ على الطاوِلةِ **2** (opposite) في الناحِيةِ \ الجِهةِ الأُخْرى; **he lives ~ the street** يَسْكُنُ في الناحِيةِ الأُخْرى من الشارِعِ **3** (throughout) **~ the world** عَبْرَ العالَمِ

B *adv* **1** (from one side to the other) **the lake is two miles ~** عَرْض البُحَيْرةِ مِيلَيْنِ; **to help sb ~** ساعَدَ شَخْصاً في العُبورِ **2** (on, to the other side) **to go ~ to sb** ذَهَبَ باتِّجاهِ شَخْصٍ; **to look ~ at sb** نَظَرَ باتِّجاهِ شَخْصٍ **C** (**across from**) *prep phr* في الناحِيةِ المُقابِلةِ

acrylic /ə'krɪlɪk/ *n* **1** (textile) أَكْريليك **2** (paint) صِبْغ أَكْريليك

act /akt/ **A** *vt* (in plays, movies) أَدّى ,مَثَّلَ ‹*a part, role*›

B *vi* **1** (to take action) «rescuers, governments» تَصَرَّفَ, عَمِلَ (a; عَمَل); **we must ~ quickly** لا بُدَّ أنْ نَتَصَرَّفَ بِسُرْعةٍ; **she still believes she was ~ing for the best** ما زالَتْ تَعْتَقِدُ أَنَّها كانَتْ تَعْمَلُ ما فيهِ الصالِحُ **2** (to represent) **to ~ for sb, to ~ on behalf of sb** تَصَرَّفَ بالنِيابة عن ,نابَ عن شَخْصٍ **3** (to behave) «person» تَصَرَّفَ **4** (in plays, movies) «actor» مَثَّلَ **5** (to pretend) «person» تَظاهَرَ **6** (to take effect) «drugs, medicines» قامَ بِمَفْعولِهِ **7** (to serve as) **to ~ as sth** «people, things» أَدّى وَظيفةَ شَيْءٍ ,قامَ بِدَوْرِ شَيْءٍ; **he ~ed as our interpreter** قامَ بِدَوْرِ المُتَرْجِمِ لَنا

C *n* **1** (action, deed) فِعْل ,(تَصَرُّفات) تَصَرُّف ,(أَعْمال) عَمَل (أَفْعال); **an ~ of cruelty/kindness** عَمَل وَحْشيّ \ طَيِّب **2** (also **Act**) (law) قانون (قَوانينُ) ,قَرار (قَرارات); **an act of Parliament/Congress** قانون صادِر عن البَرْلَمانِ \ الكونْجْرِس; **Transportation of Dangerous Goods A~, 1992** قانون نَقْلِ البَضائِعِ الخَطِرةِ لِعامِ 1992 **3** (of a play) فَصْل (فُصول) **4** (entertainment routine) عَرْض تَرْفيهيّ

Idioms **to be caught in the act** ضُبِطَ مُتَلَبِّساً; **to get in on the act** لَحِقَ بالرَكْبِ; **to get one's act together** نَظَّمَ نَفْسَهُ

Phrasal verbs **act out: ~ out [sth], ~ [sth] out** مَثَّلَ [شَيْئاً] ‹*a role, fantasy*›

• **act up** (infml) (to misbehave) «child» أَساءَ السُلوكَ; (to hurt)

«part of the body» آلَمَ (Form IV; imperf يُؤْلِمُ); (to malfunction) «machine» تَعَطَّلَ

acting /'aktɪŋ/ **A** *n* تَمْثيل **B** *adj* ‹*manager, director*› مُناوِب

action /'akʃ(ə)n/ *n* **1** [u] (practical measures) إجْراء; **this requires immediate ~** يَتَطَلَّبُ هذا الأَمْرُ اتِّخاذَ إجْراءٍ فَوْرِيٍّ; **to take ~ against sb** اتَّخَذَ إجْراءً ضدّ شَخْصٍ; **to put a plan into ~** وَضَعَ خُطَّةً مَوْضِعَ التَنْفيذِ; **to be out of ~** «machinery, equipment» تَعَطَّلَ; «player» تَوَقَّفَ عن اللَعِبِ **2** (deed) فِعْل (أَفْعال); **~s speak louder than words** الأَفْعالُ صَوْتُها أَعْلى من الكَلِماتِ **3** [u] (of a film, play) أَحْداث **4** [u] (fighting) اشْتِباك, قِتال; **he saw ~ in several theatres of war** اشْتَرَكَ في عَمَليّاتٍ قِتاليّةٍ في عَدَدٍ من مَسارِحِ المَعارِكِ **5** [u] (infml) (excitement) إثارة, تَشْويق **6** (lawsuit) قَضيّة (قَضايا), دَعْوى قَضائيّة; **to bring an ~ against sb** رَفَعَ قَضيّةً على شَخْصٍ **7** [u] (operation) طَريقة عَمَلٍ

(Idiom) **a piece** *or* **slice of the action** (infml) نَصيب من التورْتة, جُزْء من المَكْسَبِ \ الإثارة

actionable /'akʃ(ə)nəb(ə)l/ *adj* ‹*offence, statement*› يُعاقِبُ عَلَيْهِ القانونُ

action film, action movie *n* فيلْم أَكْشِن

action group *n* مَجْموعة عَمَلٍ

action-packed /'akʃ(ə)npakt/ *adj* ‹*film, holiday, programme*› مَليء بالأَحْداثِ

action replay *n* (BrE) إعادة بَطيئة

activate /'aktɪveɪt/ *vt* شَغَّلَ ‹*a system, an alarm*›

activation /aktɪ'veɪʃ(ə)n/ *n* (of a device) تَشْغيل, تَنْشيط; (of a clause) تَفْعيل (تَفاعيلُ)

active /'aktɪv/ *adj* ‹*member, life, volcano*› نَشِط; **he was killed on ~ service** قُتِلَ أثناء فَتْرة خِدْمَتِهِ في الجَيْشِ

actively /'aktɪvli/ *adv* ‹*to participate, encourage*› بِنَشاطٍ

activism /'aktɪvɪz(ə)m/ *n* نَشاطيّة [حَمْلة حازِمة لِإحْداثِ تَغْيير سِياسيٍّ \ اجْتِماعيٍّ]

activist /'aktɪvɪst/ *n* ناشِط

activity /ak'tɪvɪti/ *n* (*pl* **activities**) **1** (busy situation) فَعّاليّة (ME), نَشاط (أَنْشِطة) (NA); **the market was a hive of ~** كانَ السوقُ مُكْتَظًّا **2** (pursuit or task) نَشاط (أَنْشِطة)

activity holiday *n* (BrE) [عُطْلة مُخَصَّصة للأَنْشِطةِ الرياضيّةِ]

activity week *n* (BrE) أُسْبوع فَعّاليّاتٍ

actor /'aktə/ *n* مُمَثِّل

actress /'aktrɪs/ *n* مُمَثِّلة

actual /'aktʃʊəl/ *adj before n* **1** (real, specific) ‹*price, size*› فِعْليّ; **I don't remember his ~ words** لا أَتَذَكَّرُ كَلِماتِه الفِعْليّةَ; **in ~ fact** في الواقِعِ **2** (precise) ذاته; **on the ~ day of the election** في يَوْمِ الانْتِخاباتِ ذاتِهِ; **this is the ~ room that she worked in** هذه هي الحُجْرةُ ذاتُها الّتي كانَتْ تَعْمَلُ فيها

actually /'aktjʊəli/ *adv* **1** (in fact) في حَقيقةِ الأَمْرِ; **~, I prefer the blue one** أنا في حَقيقةِ الأَمْرِ أُفَضِّلُ الأَزْرَقَ **2** (really) فِعْلاً; **yes, it ~ happened!** نَعَم، لَقَدْ حَدَثَ ذلك فِعْلاً!

actuary /'aktʃʊəri/ *n* (*pl* **actuaries**) [مُحاسِب خَبير في إحْصاءاتِ التَأْمين]

acumen /'akjʊmən, ə'kju:mən/ *n* ذَكاء, فِطْنة, حِذْق; **business ~** فِطْنة رِجالِ الأَعْمالِ

acupuncture /'akjʊˌpʌŋ(k)tʃə/ *n* العِلاج بالوَخز بالإبَرِ

acupuncturist /'akjʊpʌŋkʃərɪst/ *n* مُعالِج بالإبَرِ الصينيّة

acute /ə'kju:t/ *adj* **1** (severe) ‹*anxiety, pain*› حادّ **2** (sudden) ‹*case, illness*› حادّ **3** (sharp) ‹*mind, sense*› حادّ **4** ‹*angle*› حادّ **5** (also **acute accent**) [عَلامة ´ توضَعُ فوق حُروفِ العِلّةِ في بَعْضِ اللُغاتِ لِتَوْضيحِ نُطْقِها]

acutely /ə'kju:tli/ *adv* (intensely) ‹*embarrassed, aware*› بِشِدّةٍ, بِشَكْلٍ قاطِعٍ

ad /ad/ *n* = **advertisement** **1** (in a newspaper) **(small) ~** إعْلان (صَغير) **2** (on radio, TV) ▸ **advertisement**

AD /eɪ'di:/ *abbr* = **Anno Domini** (ميلاديّ) م; **in ~ 450** في عامِ 450 م

Adam /'adəm/ *pr n* آدَم (dipt)

adamant /'adəm(ə)nt/ *adj* ‹*stance, attitude*› مُصِرّ

Adam's apple *n* تُفّاحة آدَمَ

adapt /ə'dapt/ **A** *vt* كَيَّفَ ‹*a technique, method*›; عَدَّلَ ‹*a novel, play*›; **to ~ a story for a modern audience** عَدَّلَ قِصّةً لِتُناسِبَ الجُمْهورَ المُعاصِرَ

B *vi* «children, animals» تَكَيَّفَ; **my children are ~ing to their new environment** يَتَكَيَّفُ أَطْفالي مع بيئَتِهِم الجَديدةِ

adaptable /əˈdaptəb(ə)l/ *adj* ‹worker› قابِل للتَكَيُّفِ, قابِل للتَأَقْلُمِ; ‹machine› قابِل للتَعْديلِ

adaptation /adəpˈteɪʃ(ə)n/ *n* اقْتِباس (اقْتِباسات)

adaptor, **adapter** /əˈdaptə/ *n* مُهايِئ (مُهايِئات)

add /ad/ *vt* ➊ (to put with sth) أَضافَ ‹emphasis, colour›; **~ your name to the list** أَضِف اسْمَكَ إلى القائِمةِ ➋ (Math) (to count) **to ~ together** جَمَعَ (a; جَمْع) ‹numbers›; **to ~ the figure to the total** أَضافَ الرَقْمَ إلى المَجْموعِ

(Phrasal verbs) **add in**: **~ [sth] in, ~ in [sth]** أَضافَ [شَيْئاً] ‹the butter, costs›
• **add on**: **~ [sth] on, ~ on [sth]** أَضافَ [شَيْئاً] ‹an item, a room›
• **add to**: **~ to [sth]** زادَ من [شَيْءٍ] ‹the problems, confusion›
• **add up**: **A** **~ up** «the story, facts» كانَ مَعْقولاً; **it doesn't ~ up** لَيْسَ مَعْقولاً **B** **~ up [sth], ~ [sth] up** جَمَعَ [شَيْئاً] ‹the cost, numbers›

adder /ˈadə/ *n* أَفْعى (f; أَفاعٍ)

addict /ˈadɪkt/ *n* ➊ (drug-user) مُدْمِن; **a cocaine ~** مُدْمِن كوكايين ➋ (infml) (to TV, coffee) مُدْمِن

addicted /əˈdɪktɪd/ *adj* **to be ~ to alcohol/drugs** كانَ مُدْمِناً على الكُحولِ \ المُخَدِّراتِ

addiction /əˈdɪkʃ(ə)n/ *n* ➊ (to a drug) إدْمان; **heroin ~** *or* **~ to heroin** إدْمان الهيرُوين ➋ (infml) (to TV, coffee) وَلَع

addictive /əˈdɪktɪv/ *adj* ‹drug, substance› مُسَبِّب للإدْمانِ, إدْمانيّ; **power is ~** السُلْطةُ تُسَبِّبُ إدْمانَها

addition /əˈdɪʃ(ə)n/ **A** *n* ➊ (to list, house) إضافة; **the latest ~ to the family** آخِر إضافةٍ إلى الأُسْرةِ ➋ (of numbers) جَمْع **B** (**in addition**) *phr* بالإضافةِ إلى ذلك; **the bus broke down and in ~ we had to pay for a taxi** تَعَطَّلَت الحافِلةُ وَإضافةً إلى ذلك اضْطَرَرْنا إلى دَفْعِ أُجْرةِ التَكْسي

additional /əˈdɪʃ(ə)n(ə)l/ *adj* ‹information, charges› إضافيّ

additionally /əˈdɪʃ(ə)n(ə)li/ *adv* إضافةً \ بالإضافةِ إلى ذلك, زِيادةً \ عِلاوةً على ذلك

additive /ˈadɪtɪv/ *n* مادّة مُضافة

add-on /ˈadɒn/ **A** *adj* ‹module› إضافيّ **B** *n* أَداة إضافيّة (مُلْحَقات), مُلْحَق

address /əˈdrɛs/ **A** *n* ➊ عُنْوان (عَناوينُ); **a forwarding/return ~** عُنْوان جَديد \ المُرْسِلِ ➋ (Comput) عُنْوان (عَناوينُ) **B** *vt* ➊ (to write the destination on) عَنْوَنَ (i; عَنْوَنة) ‹a parcel, letter› ➋ (to speak to) خاطَبَ ‹a rally, an audience› ➌ (to direct) وَجَّهَ ‹a remark, complaint›

address book *n* دَفْتَر العَناوينِ

addressee /ˌadrɛˈsiː/ *n* مُرْسَل إلَيْهِ

Aden /ˈeɪd(ə)n/ *pr n* عَدَن (dipt f)

adenoids /ˈadɪnɔɪdz/ *n pl* لَحْميّة, زَوائِد أَنْفيّة

adept /əˈdɛpt/ *adj* ‹performer, politician› ماهِر (مَهَرة)

adequate /ˈadɪkwət/ *adj* ➊ (sufficient) ‹supply, funds› وافٍ ➋ (satisfactory) ‹explanation› وافٍ

adequately /ˈadɪkwətli/ *adv* ‹prepared, to pay, explain› كَما يَنْبَغي, على نَحْوٍ مُلائِمٍ

ADHD /eɪdiːeɪtʃˈdiː/ *n* = **attention deficit hyperactivity disorder** اضْطِراب فَرْطِ الحَرَكةِ وَقُصورِ الانْتِباهِ

adhere /ədˈhɪə/ *vi* ➊ (to stick) «sticker, label» الْتَصَقَ (ب); **to ~ to sth** الْتَصَقَ بِشَيْءٍ ➋ (to follow, observe) تَقَيَّدَ (ب); **to ~ to sth** تَقَيَّدَ بِشَيْءٍ; **you must ~ to the rules** يَجِبُ أنْ تَتَقَيَّدَ بالقَواعِدِ

adherence /ədˈhɪərəns/ *n* (to an ideology, a deadline) الْتِزام

adherent /ədˈhɪər(ə)nt/ *n* تَبَع (أَتْباع), تابِع (أَتْباع), مُشايِع

adhesion /ədˈhiːʒ(ə)n/ *n* الْتِصاق

adhesive /ədˈhiːsɪv/ **A** *adj* ‹label, tape› لاصِق **B** *n* لِصاق, مادّة لاصِقة

ad hoc /ad ˈhɒk/ *adj* ‹arrangement› [بِناءً على \ تَبَعاً للحالةِ المُعَيَّنةِ]; **on an ~ basis** بِناءً على الحالةِ المُعَيَّنةِ

adjacent /əˈdʒeɪs(ə)nt/ *adj* ‹building, land› مُلاصِق, مُتاخِم, مُجاوِر; **~ to sth** مُلاصِق لِشَيْءٍ

adjective /ˈadʒɪktɪv/ *n* صِفة

adjoin /əˈdʒɔɪn/ *vt* جاوَرَ, تاخَمَ, حاذى ‹a room, field›

adjoining /əˈdʒɔɪnɪŋ/ *adj* ‹office, land› مُجاوِر; **the ~ room** الغُرْفة المُجاوِرة

adjourn /ə'dʒɜːn/ *vt* أَجَّلَ ‹*a meeting, session, trial*›

adjournment /ə'dʒɜːnm(ə)nt/ *n* (of a trial, meeting) تَأْجيل

adjudicate /ə'dʒuːdɪkeɪt/ **A** *vt* «commission» قامَ بالتَّحْكيمِ في ‹*a contest*›; «judge» أَصْدَرَ حُكْماً في ‹*a case*›

B *vi* حَكَمَ (u; حُكْم); **to ~ on a matter/dispute** حَكَمَ في قَضيَّةٍ \ نِزاعٍ

adjust /ə'dʒʌst/ **A** *vt* ضَبَطَ (i-u; ضَبْط) ‹*the position, a screw*›; عَدَّلَ ‹*a price, figures*›

B *vi* تَأَقْلَمَ, تَكَيَّفَ (مع); **I ~ed to the new system** تَكَيَّفْتُ \ تَأَقْلَمْتُ مع النِظامِ الجَديدِ

adjustable /ə'dʒʌstəb(ə)l/ *adj* ‹*angle, position, spanner*› قابل للضَبْطِ \ للتَعْديلِ

adjustment /ə'dʒʌs(t)m(ə)nt/ *n* **1** (of a screw, machine, volume) ضَبْط; (of a price) تَعْديل (تَعْديلات) **2** (to a new environment) تَأَقْلُم, تَكَيُّف

adjutant /'adʒʊt(ə)nt/ *n* (Mil) مُساعِد

ad-lib /ad'lɪb/ **A** *vi* (**-bb-**) «actor» ارْتَجَلَ

B *vt* (**-bb-**) ارْتَجَلَ ‹*jokes, lines*›

administer /əd'mɪnɪstə/ *vt* **1** أَدارَ ‹*a company, funds, a territory*› **2** أَعْطى ‹*a medicine, treatment*›; أَقامَ ‹*justice*›; طَبَّقَ ‹*a punishment*›

administration /ədmɪnɪ'streɪʃ(ə)n/ *n* **1** (of a school, hospital) إدارة **2** (BrE) (of a failing company) [عَمَليّة إدارة شَرِكةٍ تُعاني مِن مَشاكِلَ ماليّةٍ]; **to go into ~** وُضِعَ تحت الحِراسةِ القَضائيّةِ **3** (of a medicine, treatment) إعْطاء; (of justice, discipline) إقامة **4** (AmE) (government) إدارة

administrative /əd'mɪnɪstrətɪv/ *adj* ‹*error, staff*› إداريّ

administrator /əd'mɪnɪstreɪtə/ *n* **1** (in a department, office) مُوَظَّف الإدارةِ **2** (BrE) (of a failing company) [شَخْص يُديرُ شَرِكةً تُعاني من مَشاكِلَ ماليّةٍ]

admirable /'adm(ə)rəb(ə)l/ *adj* ‹*quality, behaviour*› يَسْتَحِقُّ الإعْجابَ

admiral /'adm(ə)r(ə)l/ *n* أَميرال

admiration /admə'reɪʃ(ə)n/ *n* إعْجاب; **to win people's ~** فازَ بِإعْجابِ الناسِ

admire /əd'mʌɪə/ *vt* أُعْجِبَ بـ ‹*a hat, sb's work*›

admirer /əd'mʌɪərə/ *n* **1** (of a feat, politician) مُعْجَب **2** (suitor) مُعْجَب

admission /əd'mɪʃ(ə)n/ *n* **1** (recognition) اعْتِراف, إقْرار **2** (entry) سَماح بِدُخولٍ; **'no ~'** 'مَمْنوعٌ الدُخولُ'; **~ to a building/an organization** سَماح بِدُخولِ بِنايةٍ \ مُنَظَّمةٍ **3** (price of entry) رَسْمُ الدُخولِ; **to charge ~** طالَبَ بِثَمَنٍ \ رَسْمِ الدُخولِ **4** (to hospital) إدْخال

admissions office /əd'mɪʃ(ə)nz ,ɒfɪs/ *n* دائِرة القُبولِ والتَسْجيلِ

admit /əd'mɪt/ *vt* (**-tt-**) **1** (to recognize) أَقَرَّ (ب), اعْتَرَفَ (ب) ‹*a mistake, one's guilt, fact*› **2** (to allow in) سَمَحَ بالدُخولِ ‹*a concertgoer, ticket holder*› **3** (to a hospital) أَدْخَلَ ‹*a patient, child*›

(Phrasal verb) **admit to**: **~ to [sth]** (to confess to) أَقَرَّ بـ [شَيْءٍ] ‹*a crime, mistake*›

admittance /əd'mɪt(ə)ns/ *n* حَقّ الدُخولِ; **'no ~'** 'مَمْنوعٌ الدُخولُ'

admittedly /əd'mɪtɪdli/ *adv* حَقيقةً; **~, it wasn't easy** حَقيقةً، لم يَكُن الأَمْرُ هَيِّناً

admonish /əd'mɒnɪʃ/ *vt* (fml) وَبَّخَ, أَنَّبَ ‹*a child, witness*›; **to ~ sb for sth/for doing sth** وَبَّخَ شَخْصاً على فِعْلِ شَيْءٍ

ado /ə'duː/ *n* **without further ~** [مِن غَيْرِ مَزيدٍ من الضَجّةِ \ التَأْخيرِ]

adolescence /adə'lɛs(ə)ns/ *n* مُراهَقة

adolescent /adə'lɛs(ə)nt/ **A** *adj* **1** ‹*girl, boy*› مُراهِق **2** (childish) ‹*behaviour*› مُراهِق

B *n* مُراهِق

adopt /ə'dɒpt/ *vt* تَبَنّى ‹*a baby, child*›

adopted /ə'dɒptɪd/ *adj* **1** ‹*son, daughter*› مُتَبَنّى **2** ‹*country*› بالتَبَنّي

adoption /ə'dɒpʃ(ə)n/ *n* تَبَنٍّ

adoptive /ə'dɒptɪv/ *adj* ‹*parent, home*› بالتَبَنّي

adorable /ə'dɔːrəb(ə)l/ *adj* ‹*baby, kitten*› فاتِن

adoration /adə'reɪʃ(ə)n/ *n* إعْجاب, تَوْقير

adore /ə'dɔː/ *vt* ‹*son, mother*› عَشِقَ (a; عِشْق); **I ~ cooking for friends** أَعْشَقُ الطَّبْخَ للأَصْدِقاءِ

adoring /ə'dɔːrɪŋ/ *adj* ‹*parent*› مُتَيَّم; ‹*fan, crowd*› مولَع

adorn /ə'dɔːn/ *vt* زَيَّنَ ‹*a room, one's hair*›

adornment /ə'dɔːnm(ə)nt/ *n* زينة

adrenaline, **adrenalin** /ə'drɛn(ə)lɪn/ *n* أَدْرينالين

Adriatic /ˌeɪdrɪ'atɪk/ *pr n* **the Adriatic (Sea)** البَحْر الأَدْرِياتيكيّ

adrift /ə'drɪft/ *adj*, *adv* **1** ‹*sailor, boat*› دونَ تَوْجيهٍ, هائِم (هُيَّم, هُيّام); **to cast sb ~** تَرَكَ شَخْصاً لِمَصيرِهِ **2** (without purpose) هائِم (هُيَّم, هُيّام) **3** ‹*screw, wheel*› مُنْفَصِل, مَفْكوك; **to come ~** انْفَصَلَ, انْفَكَّ

adroit /ə'drɔɪt/ *adj* **1** ‹*politician*› بارِع, حاذِق (حُذّاق) **2** ‹*movement, footwork*› بارِع, مُحْكَم

ADSL /eɪdiːɛs'ɛl/ *n* = **asymmetrical digital subscriber line** خطّ المُشْتَرِكِ الرَقْميّ غَيْر المُتَماثِل

adulation /adjʊ'leɪʃ(ə)n/ *n* إطْراء

adult /'adʌlt, ə'dʌlt/ **A** *n* راشِد, بالِغ
B *adj* **1** (mature) راشِد; **all her ~ life** كُلّ حَياتِها الراشِدةِ
2 (suitable for adults) مُناسِب للكِبارِ ‹*film, magazine*›

adultery /ə'dʌlt(ə)ri/ *n* زِنًى, خِيانة زَوْجيّة; **to commit ~** زَنى (i; زِنًى, زِناء)

adulthood /'adʌlthʊd/ *n* رُشْد, بُلوغ; **to reach ~** وَصَلَ سِنَّ البُلوغِ \ الرُشْدِ

advance /əd'vɑːns/ **A** *vt* **1** **to ~ sb twenty pounds** أَسْلَفَ شَخْصاً عِشْرينَ جُنَيْهاً **2** ‹*sb's career, interests*› دَفَعَ إلى الأمامِ
B *vi* **1** (to move forward) «troops, lions» تَقَدَّمَ **2** (to make progress) «society, students» تَقَدَّمَ
C *n* **1** (of troops, vehicles) تَقَدُّم **2** (in science, knowledge) تَقَدُّم **3** (sum of money) سُلْفة (سُلَف) **4** **to make ~s to sb** تَوَدَّدَ إلى شَخْصٍ (لِغَرَضٍ جِنْسيٍّ)
D **(in advance)** *phr* مُقَدَّماً

advance booking *n* حَجْز مُقَدَّم

advanced /əd'vɑːnst/ *adj* **1** (not elementary) ‹*course, class*› مُتَقَدِّم **2** (progressive) ‹*technology*› مُتَقَدِّم; (progressive) ‹*equipment*› مُتَطَوِّر **3** (ahead in development) ‹*stage, age*› مُتَقَدِّم

advance guard, **advance party** *n* طَليعة (طَلائِعُ)

advancement /əd'vɑːnsm(ə)nt/ *n* **1** (furthering of a cause, science) تَقَدُّم **2** (fml) (promotion at work) تَرْقِية; (in society) رُقيّ

advance warning *n* إنْذار مُتَقَدِّم

advantage /əd'vɑːntɪdʒ/ *n* **1** (favourable factor) ميزة; **the ~s of a university education** ميزات التَعْليمِ الجامِعيِّ; **to have an ~ over a competitor** كانَ لَهُ ميزةٌ على مُنافِسِهِ; **'programming experience an ~'** 'يُفَضَّلُ مَنْ لَدَيْهِ خِبْرةٌ في البَرْمَجةِ' **2** [u] (benefit) مَنْفَعة, فائِدة; **there is no ~ in waiting** لا فائِدةَ من الانْتِظارِ; **there is some ~ in going early** هُناكَ مَنْفَعةٌ في الذَهابِ مُبَكِّراً; **what ~ would that give us?** ما الفائِدةُ الّتي سَيَعودُ بِها ذلك عَلَيْنا؟; **it would be to our ~ to sell/keep it** سَوْفَ يَكونُ من مَصْلَحَتِنا أنْ نَبيعَها \ نَحْتَفِظَ بها; **to turn the situation to one's ~** حَوَّلَ الأَمْرَ لِصالِحِهِ **3** **to take ~ of a situation/an offer** اسْتَغَلَّ مَوْقِفاً \ عَرْضاً; **we took ~ of the sale to buy new curtains** انْتَهَزْنا فُرْصةَ التَنْزيلاتِ وَاشْتَرَيْنا سَتائِرَ جَديدةً; **they took ~ of our hospitality** اسْتَغَلّوا كَرَمَنا مَعَهُمْ **4** [u] (in tennis) نُقْطة تَقَدُّم (أَوَّل نُقْطةٍ يَتِمُّ إحْرازُها بعد تَعادُلِ اللاعِبَيْنِ ب40 نُقْطةً لِكُلٍّ مِنْهُما)

advantageous /adv(ə)n'teɪdʒəs/ *adj* ‹*position, terms*› مُفيد

advent /'advɛnt/ *n* **1** (coming) مَجيء **2** **(Advent)** (season) الآحاد الأَرْبَعة الّتي تَسْبِقُ عيدَ الميلادِ

adventure /əd'vɛntʃə/ *n* مُغامَرة

adventure holiday *n* عُطْلة مَليئة بالمُغامَراتِ

adventure playground *n* (BrE) مَلْعَب مُغامَراتٍ (للأَطْفالِ)

adventurous /əd'vɛntʃ(ə)rəs/ *adj* **1** ‹*traveller*› مُغامِر **2** ‹*policy*› مُغامِر **3** ‹*journey*› مُتَّسِم بالمُغامَراتِ

adverb /'advəːb/ *n* ظَرْف (ظُروف)

adversary /'advəs(ə)ri/ *n* (*pl* **adversaries**) خَصْم (خُصوم, أَخْصام), غَريم (غُرَماءُ, غُرّام)

adverse /'advəːs/ *adj* **1** (negative) ‹*effect, reaction, criticism*› سَلْبيّ **2** ‹*conditions*› غَيْر مُلائِم

adversely /'advəːsli/ *adv* ‹*to affect, influence*› بِشَكْلٍ غَيْر مُلائِمٍ, سَلْبيًّا; **output has been ~ affected by the shortage of raw materials** تَأَثَّرَ المَحْصولُ سَلْبيًّا بِنُقْصانِ مَوادَّ خامةٍ

adversity /əd'və:sɪti/ *n* (*pl* **adversities**) شِدّة (مِحَن), مِحْنة

advert /'advə:t/ *n* (BrE infml) إعْلان (إعْلانات)

advertise /'advətʌɪz/ **A** *vt* **1** ‹*a product, event*› قامَ بالإعْلانِ (عن), أَعْلَنَ (عن) **2** ‹*a vacancy*› أَعْلَنَ (عن) **3** (to draw attention to) ‹*a fact*› أَعْلَنَ (عن)
B *vi* **1** (for publicity) نَشَرَ إعْلاناتٍ **2** (in small ads) قامَ بالإعْلانِ; **to ~ for sth** وَضَعَ إعْلاناً لِشَيْءٍ

advertisement /əd'və:tɪsm(ə)nt/ *n* **1** (for a product, an event) إعْلان (إعْلانات) (ME), إشْهار (NA); **an ~ for washing powder** إعْلان عن مَسْحوقِ غسيلٍ **2** (for a vacancy) إعْلان (إعْلانات) **3** (recommendation) دِعاية; **a good/poor ~ for sth** دِعاية جَيِّدة \ سَيِّئة لِشَيْءٍ

advertiser /'advətʌɪzə/ *n* مُعْلِن

advertising /'advətʌɪzɪŋ/ *n* **1** صِناعة الإعْلاناتِ **2** إعْلانات; **to go into ~** امْتَهَنَ صِناعةَ الإعْلاناتِ

advertising agency *n* مَكْتَب إعْلاناتٍ

advertising campaign *n* حَمْلة إعْلاناتٍ

advertising executive *n* مُدير إعْلاناتٍ

advice /əd'vʌɪs/ *n* **1** (informal) نَصيحة (نَصائِح); **a piece of ~** نَصيحة; **it was good/bad ~** كانَتْ نَصيحةً جَيِّدةً / سَيِّئةً; **I need ~ on pension planning** أَحْتاجُ إلى نَصيحةٍ بِخُصوصِ تَخْطيطٍ تَقاعُدي **2** (from an expert) اسْتِشارة; **to take professional ~** اسْتَشارَ جِهةً مُخْتَصّةً

advisable /əd'vʌɪzəb(ə)l/ *adj* ‹*booking, warm clothing*› مُسْتَحْسَن; **it is ~ to arrive early** من المُسْتَحْسَنِ الوُصولُ باكِراً

advise /əd'vʌɪz/ *vt* **1** (to give advice to) نَصَحَ (a; نُصْح, نَصْح, نَصيحة) ‹*a client, patient*›; **to ~ sb to do sth** نَصَحَ شَخْصاً بِأَنْ يَقومَ بِشَيْءٍ; **to ~ sb against doing sth** نَصَحَ شَخْصاً بِعَدَمِ القِيامِ بِشَيْءٍ; **he ~d us to take out car insurance** نَصَحَنا بِأَنْ نُؤَمِّنَ سَيّارَتَنا **2** (to recommend) نَصَحَ (a; نُصْح, نَصْح, نَصيحة ب) ‹*rest, a course of action*›; **the doctor ~d daily exercise** نَصَحَ الطَبيبُ بِتَمارينَ يَوْميّةٍ **3** (to inform) أَخْطَرَ ‹*a company, candidate, parents*›; **to ~ sb (of sth)** أَخْطَرَ شَخْصاً (بِشَيْءٍ)

adviser, advisor /əd'vʌɪzə/ *n* مُسْتَشار

advisory /əd'vʌɪz(ə)ri/ *adj* ‹*committee, role*› اسْتِشاريّ

advocacy /'advəkəsi/ *n* **1** (of a cause) دَعْم, تَأْييد **2** (Law) مُحاماة

advocate **A** /'advəkət/ *n* **1** (Law) مُحامٍ (مُحامونَ) **2** (supporter) مُسانِد; **to be an ~ of acupuncture** كانَ مُسانِداً للوَخْزِ بالإبَرِ
B /'advəkeɪt/ *vt* ‹*reform, abolition*› سانَدَ, ناصَرَ

Aegean Sea, Aegean /iːˌdʒiːən 'siː/ *pr n* **the ~** بَحْر إيجة

aerial /'ɛːriəl/ **A** *n* هَوائيّ; **a radio/TV ~** هَوائيّ المِذْياعِ / التِلْفازِ
B *adj* ‹*bombardment, survey*› جَوّيّ

aerobics /ɛː'rəʊbɪks/ *n sing* إيروبيك (رِياضة بَدَنيّة مَبْنيّة على تَمارينَ شَديدةٍ لِزِيادةِ قوّةِ القَلْبِ); **to do ~** مارَسَ الإيروبيك

aerodynamic /ɛːrəʊdʌɪ'namɪk/ *adj* ‹*design, efficiency*› أيرودِيناميكيّ

aeroplane /'ɛːrəpleɪn/ *n* (BrE) طائِرة

aerosol /'ɛːrəsɒl/ *n* **1** (substance) أيْروسول **2** (container) عُبوّة أيْروسول

aerospace /'ɛːrəspeɪs/ **A** *n* الطَيَران والفَضاء الجَوّيّ
B *modifier* ‹*industry, company*› الطَيَرانِ والفَضاءِ الجَوّيّ

aesthetic, esthetic (AmE) /iːs'θɛtɪk/ *adj* ‹*judgement, value*› جَماليّ

afar /ə'fɑː/ *adv* (liter) بَعيد

affable /'afəb(ə)l/ *adj* ‹*personality, host*› أنيس

affair /ə'fɛː/ **A** *n* **1** (case) قَضيّة (قَضايا); **the Helmsley ~** قَضيّة هِلْمْزْلي **2** (event) حَدَث (أَحْداث); **the wedding was an informal ~** اتَّسَمَ الزِفافُ بِعَدَمِ رَسْميّتِهِ **3** (relationship) عَلاقة غَراميّة
B (**affairs**) *n pl* (matters) شُؤون; **her lawyer looked after her ~s while she was ill** تَوَلّى مُحاميها شُؤونَها أثناء مَرَضِها

affect /ə'fɛkt/ *vt* **1** (physically) أَثَّرَ (على) ‹*a region, an outcome*›; **the reforms ~ us all** تُؤَثِّرُ الإصْلاحاتُ عَلَيْنا جَميعاً **2** (emotionally) أَثَّرَ (على) ‹*a child, relative*›; **his death has ~ed us all** أَثَّرَتْ وَفاتُهُ عَلَيْنا جَميعاً **3** أَثَّرَ (على), أصابَ ‹*a patient, sb's health*›; **a high percentage of people are ~ed by cancer** نِسْبةٌ عاليةٌ من الناسِ مُصابةٌ بِمَرَضِ السَرَطانِ; **smoking ~s the lungs** التَدْخينُ يُؤَثِّرُ على الرِئَتَيْنِ

affected /əˈfɛktɪd/ *adj* (pej) ‹*manner, person*› مُتَكَلَّف

affection /əˈfɛkʃ(ə)n/ *n* مَوَدَّة; **to have an ~ for sb** كَنَّ المَوَدَّةَ لِشَخْصٍ

affectionate /əˈfɛkʃ(ə)nət/ *adj* ‹*brother*› عَطوف (عُطُف); ‹*hug*› حارّ

affidavit /ˌafɪˈdeɪvɪt/ *n* [إقْرار مَشْفوع بالقَسَم]; **to swear an ~** [أَقْسَمَ يَميناً بِحَقيقةِ ما أَقَرَّهُ كِتابيًّا]

affiliate **A** *vt* /əˈfɪlɪeɪt/ ضَمَّ (u; ضَمّ) ‹*an organization, a club*›

B *vi* (combine) «groups, individuals» انْضَمَّ

C *n* /əˈfɪlɪət/ فَرْع (فُروع, أَفْرُع)

affiliation /əfɪlɪˈeɪʃ(ə)n/ *n* انْتِساب; **my religious/political ~s** انْتِسابي الدينيّ \ السِياسيّ

affinity /əˈfɪnɪti/ *n* (*pl* **affinities**) (empathy) مَيْل (مُيول)

affinity card *n* [بِطاقة ائْتِمانٍ تَسْمَحُ لِلبَنْكِ بِالتَبَرُّعِ لِجَمْعِيّةٍ خَيْرِيّةٍ \ مُنَظَّمةٍ]

affirm /əˈfəːm/ *vt* **1** (to state) أكَّد ‹*a commitment, one's innocence*›

2 (to confirm) أَثْبَتَ ‹*a decision, sb's popularity*›

affirmation /afəˈmeɪʃ(ə)n/ *n* إقْرار, تأْكيد (تأْكيدات)

affirmative /əˈfəːmətɪv/ **A** *adj* **1** ‹*answer, vote*› إيجابيّ

2 ‹*action, policy*› جازِم

B *n* إيجاب; **to answer in the ~** جاوَبَ بالإيجابِ

affix /əˈfɪks/ *vt* (fml) أَلْصَقَ ‹*a stamp, label*›

afflict /əˈflɪkt/ *vt* أَصابَ ‹*a patient, country*›

affliction /əˈflɪkʃ(ə)n/ *n* **1** (condition, ailment) مُعاناة, إصابة

2 [u] (suffering) بَلْوى

affluence /ˈafluəns/ *n* غِنًى

affluent /ˈafluənt/ *adj* ‹*suburb, lifestyle*› ثَرِيّ (أَثْرِياءُ)

afford /əˈfɔːd/ *vt* **1** (financially) تَحَمَّلَ النَفَقاتِ ‹*a car, holiday*›

2 (to spare) مَلَكَ (i; مَلْك, مُلْك, مِلْك) ‹*the effort, time*›

3 (to risk) تَحَمَّلَ ‹*the scandal*›; **this government can't ~ any more mistakes** لَيْسَ بِإمْكانِ هذه الحُكومةِ تَحَمُّلُ ارْتِكابِ أَخْطاءٍ أُخْرى

affordable /əˈfɔːdəb(ə)l/ *adj* ‹*price*› مُناسِب; ‹*housing*› مَيْسور التَكْلِفةِ

affront /əˈfrʌnt/ *n* إهانة

Afghan /ˈafgan/ **A** *n* **1** (also **Afghani**) (citizen) أَفْغانيّ (أَفْغان)

2 (language) (اللُغة) الأَفْغانيّة

B *adj* (also **Afghani**) ‹*politics, rug*› أَفْغانيّ

Afghanistan /afˈganɪstɑːn, afˈganɪstan/ *pr n* أَفْغانِسْتان (f)

afield /əˈfiːld/ *adv* **to go far/further ~** ذَهَبَ بَعيداً \ أَبْعَدَ

afloat /əˈfləʊt/ **A** *adj* (in water) ‹*ship, survivors*› طافٍ, عائِم

B *adv* (in water) **to stay ~** «ship» بَقِيَ طافِياً

afoot /əˈfʊt/ *adj pred* **to be ~** «plans, changes» كانَ على قَدَمٍ وَساقٍ

aforementioned /əfɔːˈmɛnʃ(ə)nd/ *adj* (fml) ‹*article, incident*› آنِف \ سابِق الذِكْرِ; **the ~ John Simmons** جون سيمونْز الآنِف الذِكْرِ

afraid /əˈfreɪd/ *adj* **1** (scared) **to be too ~ to go out** «children, prisoners» مَنَعَهُ خَوْفُهُ من الذَهابِ إلى الخارِجِ; **to be ~ of sb/sth** خافَ من شَخْصٍ \ شَيْءٍ; **the children are ~ of the dark/their uncle** الأَطْفالُ خائِفونَ من الظَلامِ \ عَمِّهِمْ; **to be ~ of doing sth** خَشِيَ من فِعْلِ شَيْءٍ; **I'm ~ of breaking it** أَخْشى أَنْ أَكْسِرَهُ; **to be ~ to do sth** خَشِيَ أَنْ يَفْعَلَ شَيْئاً; **he was ~ to jump** لم يَتَجَرَّأْ على القَفْزِ **2** (expressing regret) **to be ~ that ...** خَشِيَ أنَّ . . .; **I'm ~ I can't come** أَخْشى أَنّني لن أَسْتَطيعَ المَجيءَ

afreet /ˈafriːt/ *n* عِفْريت (عَفاريتُ)

afresh /əˈfrɛʃ/ *adv* ‹*start, look*› مُجَدَّداً

Africa /ˈafrɪkə/ *pr n* إفْريقيا

African /ˈafrɪk(ə)n/ *n, adj* إفْريقيّ

African American *n, adj* أَمْريكيّ إفْريقيّ

African Union *n* الاتِّحاد الإفْريقيّ

Afro-American /afrəʊəˈmɛrɪk(ə)n/ *n, adj* إفْريقي–أَمْريكيّ

Afro-Caribbean /ˌafrəʊkarɪˈbiːən/ *n, adj* أَفْرو–كاريبيّ

after /ˈɑːftə/ **A** *prep* **1** (later than) بَعْدَ; **the day ~ tomorrow** بعد غَدٍ; **it was ~ six o'clock** كانَت الساعةُ قد تَجاوَزَت السادِسةَ; **immediately** *or* **shortly ~ their arrival** مُباشَرةً بعد \ فَوْرَ وُصولِهِمْ; **any applications received ~ that date will be rejected** سَيُرْفَضُ أَيُّ طَلَبٍ يَصِلُ بعد ذلك التاريخِ **2** (given) بَعْدَ; **~ all we did for you!** بعد كُلِّ ما فَعَلْناهُ من أَجْلِكَ!; **~ what she's been through, she's no longer interested**

بعد التَجْرِبةِ الّتي مَرَّتْ بِها، لم تَعُدْ مُهْتَمّةً **3** (expressing contrast) مُقارَنةً ب; **it's boring here ~ Cairo** مُقارَنةً بالقاهِرةِ الجَوُّ هُنا مُمِلٌّ **4** (in order) عَقِبَ ,بَعْدَ; **the adjective comes ~ the noun** تَأْتي الصِفةُ بعد الاسْمِ; **~ you!** [تَفَضَّلْ أَنْتَ أَوَّلاً!] **5** (in priority) بَعْدَ; **for him, family comes ~ his career** بالنِسْبةِ لَهُ، العَمَلُ أَهَمُّ من الأُسْرةِ **6** (behind) **to chase ~ sb/sth** حاوَلَ اللَحاقَ بِشَخْصٍ \ بِشَيْءٍ; **please shut the door ~ you** أَغْلِقِ البابَ وَراءَكَ; **I'm not tidying up ~ you!** لن أُنَظِّفَ وَراءَكَ! **7** (in the direction of) **to stare ~ sb** حَدَّقَ إلى شَخْصٍ مُغادِرٍ; **'don't forget!' Mimi called ~ her** 'لا تَنْسى!' صاحَتْ وَراءَهُ ميمي **8** (in pursuit of) **that's the house they're ~** ذلك هو البَيْتُ الّذي يُحاوِلونَ الحُصولَ عَلَيْهِ; **the police are ~ him** تُحاوِلُ الشُرْطةُ الإمْساكَ بِهِ; **he's ~ your job** يُريدُ أنْ يَأْخُذَ وَظيفَتَكَ **9** (beyond) بَعْدَ **10** (stressing continuity, repetitiveness) **generation ~ generation** جيلاً بعد جيلٍ; **year ~ year** سَنةً بعد سَنةٍ; **it was one disaster ~ another** كانَتْ كارِثةً تَلْوَ الأُخْرى **11** (in honour/memory of) **to be named ~ sb/sth** سُمِّيَ على اسْمِ شَخْصٍ \ شَيْءٍ **12** (AmE) (past) **it's twenty ~ eleven** الساعةُ الآنَ الحادِيةَ عَشَرَ وَعِشْرونَ دَقيقةً **13** (in the manner of) **'~ Millet'** 'على طَريقةِ ميليه'

B *conj* (in time) بعد ما; **~ we had left we realized that ...** بعد ما غادَرْنا أَدْرَكْنا أنّ ...; **they didn't call the police ~ you explained the situation** لم يَتَّصِلوا بالشُرْطةِ بعد ما شَرَحْتَ المَوْقِفَ; **why did he do that ~ we'd warned him of the consequences?** لماذا فَعَلَ ذلك بعد ما حَذَّرْناهُ من العَواقِبِ؟

C *adv* (following an event) **the week/year ~** الأُسْبوعَ \ العامَ التالي; **he left a day/week ~** رَحَلَ بعد يَوْمٍ \ أُسْبوعٍ; **soon** *or* **not long ~** بعد وَقْتٍ قَصيرٍ

D (**afters** BrE infml) *n pl* تَحْلِية (تُقَدَّمُ في آخِرِ الطَعامِ)

E (**after all**) *adv, prep* **1** (in reiterations) على أَيِّ حالٍ; **he should have paid: he suggested it ~ all** كانَ عَلَيْهِ أنْ يَدْفَعَ: فَهُوَ مَنْ اقْتَرَحَ ذلك على أَيِّ حالٍ **2** (all things considered) في النِهايةِ; **it wasn't such a bad idea ~ all** لم تَكُنْ فِكْرةً سَيِّئةً أَبَداً في النِهايةِ

afterbirth /ˈɑːftəbəːθ/ *n* سُخْد ,مَشيمة

aftercare /ˈɑːftəkɛː/ *n* عِناية لاحِقة

after-effect /ˈɑːftərɪfɛkt/ *n* (of a drug) تَأْثير لاحِق; (of an accident, storm) تَبِعة; **the ~s of the hurricane** تَبِعات الإعْصارِ

aftermath /ˈɑːftəmaθ, ˈɑːftəmɑːθ/ *n* أَعْقاب; **in the ~ of the war/scandal** في أَعْقابِ الحَرْبِ \ الفَضيحةِ

afternoon /ɑːftəˈnuːn/ *n* (from 12 to 3) ظَهيرة; (from 3 to sunset) عَصْر; **in the ~** بعد الظُهْرِ, في العَصْرِ; **on Friday ~** في ظَهيرةِ \ عَصْرِ يَوْمِ الجُمْعةِ; **good ~!** مَساءُ الخَيْرِ!

afterpains /ˈɑːftəpeɪnz/ *n pl* أَلَم بعد الوِلادةِ

after-sales service /ˈɑːftəseɪlz ˌsəːvɪs/ *n* خِدْمة ما بعد البَيْعِ

aftershave /ˈɑːftəʃeɪv/ *n* آفْتَر شَيْف (مُسْتَحْضَر يُسْتَعْمَلُ بعد الحِلاقةِ)

aftershock /ˈɑːftəʃɒk/ *n* تابِع زِلْزاليّ

aftersun /ˈɑːftəsʌn/ *adj* *<care, cream>* [يُسْتَخْدَمُ بعد التَعَرُّضِ للشَمْسِ]

aftertaste /ˈɑːftəteɪst/ *n* مَذاق عالِق

afterthought /ˈɑːftəθɔːt/ *n* [فِكْرة تَخْطُرُ على البالِ لاحِقاً]

afterwards /ˈɑːftəwədz/, **afterward** (AmE) /ˈɑːftəwəd/ *adv* **1** (later) فيما بَعْدُ; **it was only ~ that I noticed ...** لم أُلاحِظْ إلاّ فيما بَعْدُ أنّ ...; **I regretted it ~** نَدِمْتُ عَلَيْهِ فيما بَعْدُ **2** (in sequences) بعد ذلك; **soon** *or* **shortly** *or* **not long ~** بعد ذلك بِقَليلٍ; **immediately** *or* **directly ~** فَوْراً بعد ذلك, بعد ذلك مُباشَرةً

again /əˈgeɪn/ *adv* ثانِيةً ,مَرّةً أُخْرى; **sing it ~!** غَنّيها مَرّةً أُخْرى!; **never ~!** لآخِرِ مَرّةٍ!; **once ~** مَرّةً أُخْرى

against /əˈgeɪnst, əˈgɛnst/ *prep* **1** (opposed to) **to be ~ sb/sth** كانَ ضِدّ شَخْصٍ \ شَيْءٍ; **they are campaigning ~ Donald Reegan** يَقومونَ بِحَمْلةٍ ضِدّ دونالْد ريغان; **I have nothing ~ taxation** لَيْسَ لَدَيَّ أَيُّ شَيْءٍ ضِدّ الضَرائِبِ; **they are ~ the idea** هُمْ ضِدّ الفِكْرةِ; **100 votes for and 20 votes ~** 100 صَوْتٍ مع و20 صَوْتاً ضِدّ; **to be ~ doing sth** كانَ ضِدّ فِعْلِ شَيْءٍ; **the fight ~ inflation is being lost/won** المَعْرَكةُ ضِدّ التَضَخُّمِ في طَريقِها للرِبْحِ \ للخَسارةِ **2** (physically) عَلى; **put it ~ the wall** ضَعْهُ على الحائِطِ **3** (counter to) **to go ~ tradition/one's beliefs** لم يَتَماشَ مع التَقاليدِ \ اعْتِقاداتِهِ; **the conditions are ~ us** الظُروفُ ضِدَّنا; **the decision went ~ us** لم يَكُنِ القَرارُ

4 (compared to) **the pound fell/rose ~ the dollar** في صالِحِنا **5** (in contrasts) انْخَفَض \ ارْتَفَع سِعْرُ الجُنَيْهِ الاسْتِرْلينيِّ أمام الدولار **the blue looks pretty ~ the yellow** يَبْدو الأَزْرَقُ جَميلاً مُقابِلَ الأَصْفَرِ؛ **hold it up ~ the light** ارْفَعْهُ في الاتِّجاهِ المُقابِلِ للضَوْءِ **6** (in exchange for) مُقابِل؛ **could I have an advance ~ my first month's salary?** هل يُمْكِنُني الحُصولُ على سُلْفَةِ راتِبِ أَوَّلِ شَهْرٍ؟

age /eɪdʒ/ **A** *n* **1** (point in sb's life) سِنّ (أَعْمار)، عُمْر (mf); **at the ~ of six/at six years of ~** في سِنِّ السادِسةِ؛ **she's twice/half his ~** عُمْرُها ضِعْفُ / نِصْفُ عُمْرِهِ؛ **he doesn't look his ~** لم يَبْلُغِ السِنَّ ~ يَبْدو أَصْغَرَ من عُمْرِهِ الحَقيقيِّ؛ **to be under ~** لم يَبْلُغِ السِنَّ القانونيّةَ؛ **to come of ~** بَلَغَ السِنَّ القانونيّةَ؛ **~ of consent** السِنّ القانونيّة للزَواجِ **2** [u] (state of being old) شَيْخوخة؛ **with ~** مع تَقَدُّمِ العُمْرِ **3** (era) عَصْر (عُصور)؛ **the information ~** عَصْر المَعْلوماتِ؛ **in this day and ~** في الزَمَنِ الحاليِّ؛ **the golden ~ of Hollywood** العَصْر الذَهَبيّ لِهوليوود
B (**ages**) *n pl* (infml) (long time) **we haven't been out for ~s** لم نَخْرُجْ منذ زَمَنٍ طَويلٍ
C *vt* (*present participle* **ageing**, **aging** AmE; *past participle* **aged**) جَعَلَهُ يَشيخُ \ يَهْرَمُ ‹*a person*›
D *vi* (*present participle* **ageing**, **aging** AmE; *past participle* **aged**) «person, population» شاخَ (a; هَرَم)، هَرِمَ (a; هَرَم) كَبُرَ (u)

aged *adj* **1** /eɪdʒd/ عُمْرُهُ، يَبْلُغُ من العُمْرِ؛ **a boy ~ 12** وَلَد في الثانِيةَ عَشْرةَ من عُمْرِهِ؛ **you must be ~ 18 or over** يَجِبُ أَنْ تكونَ ثَمانِيةَ عَشَرَ عاماً أو أَكْبَرَ **2** /eɪdʒɪd/ (old) ‹*pensioner*› عَجوز (mf; عُجُز، عَجائِزُ)

age group *n* فِئة عُمْرِيّة

ageing, **aging** (AmE) /ˈeɪdʒɪŋ/ **A** *n* تَقَدُّم في السِنِّ
B *adj attrib* مُتَقَدِّم في السِنِّ، مُسِنّ

ageism /ˈeɪdʒɪz(ə)m/ *n* تَمْييز ضدّ كِبارِ السِنِّ

ageist /ˈeɪdʒɪst/ *adj* ‹*policy, remark*› مُتَحَيِّز ضدّ المُسِنّينَ

agency /ˈeɪdʒ(ə)nsi/ *n* (*pl* **agencies**) **1** (Busn) وَكالة **2** (government department) هَيْئة

agenda /əˈdʒɛndə/ *n* جَدْوَل أَعْمالٍ، أَجِنْدة؛ **to be on the ~** انْدَرَجَ في جَدْوَلِ الأَعْمالِ؛ **the minister has a hidden** *or* **secret ~** الوَزيرُ لَهُ أَجِنْدةٌ خَفِيّةٌ

agent /ˈeɪdʒ(ə)nt/ *n* **1** (for a company, group) وَكيل (وُكَلاءُ) **2** (intelligence officer) عَميل (عُمَلاءُ)

aggravate /ˈagrəveɪt/ *vt* **1** (to make worse) فاقَمَ ‹*condition, situation*›; **I ~d an old knee injury** فاقَمْتُ من وَضْعِ جُرْحٍ قَديمٍ في الرُكْبةِ **2** (to annoy) أَغاظَ ‹*a friend, brother*›

aggregate **A** /ˈagrɪgət/ *n* **1** (total amount) مَجْموع (مَجاميعُ)، إجْمال؛ **in ~ the results are positive** بالإجْمالِ النَتائِجُ إيجابِيّةٌ **2** (in scores) مَجْموع النِقاطِ؛ **United won on ~** رَبِحَ اليونايْتِد بِناءً على مَجْموعِ النِقاطِ **3** (for building) حَصْباء (dipt f)
B /ˈagrɪgət/ *adj* **1** ‹*losses, demand*› إجْماليّ **2** ‹*score*› مَجْموع، حاصِل
C /ˈagrɪgeɪt/ *vt* (to combine) جَمَعَ (a; جَمْع) ‹*figures, points, scores*›

aggression /əˈgrɛʃ(ə)n/ *n* **1** [u] (hostility) عُدْوانِيّة **2** (attack) عُدْوان

aggressive /əˈgrɛsɪv/ *adj* **1** (hostile, violent) ‹*dog*› عُدْوانِيّ؛ ‹*fighter*› شَرِس **2** (forceful, determined) ‹*salesperson*› مُنْدَفِع، شَرِس؛ ‹*campaign*› مُتَحَمِّس

aggressively /əˈgrɛsɪvli/ *adv* **1** ‹*to behave, react*› بِعُدْوانِيّةٍ، بِضَراوةٍ **2** (Fin) ‹*to promote, market*› بِقُوّةٍ

aggro /ˈagrəʊ/ *n* (infml) **1** (violence) عُدْوانِيّة **2** (difficulties) مَتاعِب

aghast /əˈgɑːst/ *adj pred* مَذْعور

agile /ˈadʒʌɪl/ *adj* **1** (flexible) ‹*cat, gymnast*› مَرِن **2** (mentally aware) ‹*mind, thinking*› يَقِظ

agility /əˈdʒɪlɪti/ *n* (physical) خِفّة حَرَكةٍ؛ (mental) فِطْنة

aging *n*, *adj* ▸ **ageing**

agitate /ˈadʒɪteɪt/ *vi* «activist» أَثارَ \ أَجَّجَ الرَأْيَ العامَّ؛ **to ~ for/against reform** أَثارَ \ أَجَّجَ الرَأْيَ العامَّ لِصالِحِ \ ضِدّ الإصْلاحاتِ

agitated /ˈadʒɪteɪtɪd/ *adj* ‹*voice, state*› مُنْفَعِل

agitation /adʒɪˈteɪʃ(ə)n/ *n* **1** (anxiety) هِياج **2** (Pol) إثارة الشَغَبِ

AGM /eɪdʒiːˈɛm/ *n* = **annual general meeting** جَمْعِيّة عُمومِيّة سَنَوِيّة

agnostic /ag'nɒstɪk/ **A** *n* مُعْتَنِق اللاأَدْرِيَّة **B** *adj* ‹*view, interpretation*› لاأَدْرِيّ

ago /ə'gəʊ/ *adv* **three weeks ~** قبل ثَلاثةِ أَسابيعَ; **a few minutes ~** قبل بِضْعِ دَقائِقَ; **that was long ~, that was a long time ~** كانَ ذلك منذ زَمَنٍ بَعيدٍ; **how long ~ was that?** كم مَضى من الوَقْتِ على ذلك؟; **not long ~** قبل فَتْرةٍ لَيْسَتْ بالبَعيدةِ

agog /ə'gɒg/ *adj pred* **to be ~ at sth** (with excitement) كانَ مُتَحَمِّساً لِشَيْءٍ; (with expectation) كانَ مُتَلَهِّفاً لِشَيْءٍ

agonize, -ise (BrE) /'ag(ə)nʌɪz/ *vi* «parent, judges» تَعَذَّبَ; **the panel ~d over the decision** تَعَذَّبَ المُجْتَمِعونَ خلال سَعْيِهِم للتَوَصُّلِ إلى قَرارٍ

agonizing, -ising (BrE) /'ag(ə)nʌɪzɪŋ/ *adj* ‹*decision*› مُؤْلِم جِدّاً; ‹*pain*› مُبَرِّح

agony /'ag(ə)ni/ *n* (*pl* **agonies**) (physical) أَلَم مُبَرِّح; (mental) مُعاناة ,(عَذابات) عَذاب

agony aunt *n* [مُحَرِّرة عَمود قُلوبٍ حائرةٍ]

agony column *n* عَمود قُلوبٍ حائرةٍ ≈ (في صَحيفةٍ \ مَجَلّةٍ)

agoraphobia /ˌag(ə)rə'fəʊbɪə/ *n* رُهاب الخَلاءِ

agrarian /ə'grɛːrɪən/ *adj* ‹*law, reform*› زِراعِيّ

agree /ə'griː/ **A** *vt* (*past tense, past participle* **agreed**) ① (to be in agreement) وافَقَ; **I ~ (that) it sounds unlikely** أُوافِقُ أَنَّهُ يَبْدو بَعيدَ الاحْتِمالِ ② (to come to an agreement) **to ~ to do sth** وافَقَ على فِعْلِ شَيْءٍ; **they ~d to extend the deadline** وافَقوا على تَمْديدِ المَوْعِدِ النِهائِيِّ; **he ~d to meet us at six o'clock** وافَقَ أَنْ يُقابِلَنا في الساعةِ السادِسةِ ③ (to decide) اتَّفَقَ (على) ‹*a date, price, the terms*›; **no conditions have been ~d** لم يَتِمَّ الاتِّفاقُ على أَيّةِ شُروطٍ

B *vi* (*past tense, past participle* **agreed**) ① (to have the same opinion) «friends» اتَّفَقَ, وافَقَ; **I ~ with you** أُوافِقُكَ الرَأْيَ; **we ~ about most things** نَتَّفِقُ حول مُعْظَمِ الأُمورِ; **I couldn't ~ more!** أَتَّفِقُ مَعَكَ تَماماً! ② (to reach an understanding) «panel, judges» اتَّفَقَ; **the jury failed to ~** لم تَتَّفِقْ هَيْئةُ المُحَلَّفينَ ③ (to consent) «people, person» قَبِلَ, وافَقَ (قُبول, قَبول ;a); **did he ~?** هل وافَقَ؟; **to ~ to a decision/proposal** وافَقَ على قَرارٍ \ اقْتِراحٍ; **they won't ~ to her going alone** لن يُوافِقوا على ذَهابِها وَحْدَها ④ (to approve of) **to ~ with a practice/belief** وافَقَ على مُمارَسةٍ \ اعْتِقادٍ ⑤ (to tally) «figures, statements» تَوافَقَ ⑥ (to suit) **to ~ with sb** ناسَبَ شَخْصاً; **city life ~s with me** تُناسِبُني الحَياةُ في المَدينةِ; **I ate something that didn't ~ with me** أَكَلْتُ شَيْئاً لم يُرِحْني ⑦ (in grammar) «adjective, verb» طابَقَ

C (**agreed**) *adj* ‹*date, budget*› مُتَّفَق عَلَيْهِ; **as ~d, we shall meet on ...** حَسَبَ الاتِّفاقِ، سَنَتَقابَلُ يَوْمَ . . . ; **it has been ~d that compensation will be paid** تَمَّ الاتِّفاقُ على دَفْعِ تَعْويضٍ; **we are ~d on future policy** نَحْنُ مُتَّفِقونَ على السِياسةِ المُسْتَقْبَلِيّةِ

agreeable /ə'griːəb(ə)l/ *adj* ① ‹*trip, climate*› مُمْتِع ② ‹*personality*› عَذْب (عِذاب); ‹*manner*› لَطيف (لُطَفاءُ, لِطاف)

agreement /ə'griːm(ə)nt/ *n* ① (between parties) اتِّفاق; **to reach ~ on a problem** تَوَصَّلَ إلى اتِّفاقٍ بِشَأْنِ مُشْكِلةٍ; **we are in ~ on all points** نَحْنُ مُتَّفِقونَ على كُلِ النِقاطِ ② (undertaking) اتِّفاق (اتِّفاقات); **an ~ to repay the loan** اتِّفاق على سَدادِ القَرْضِ ③ (consent) **to give one's ~ to a proposal** أَعْطى مُوافَقَتَهُ على المُقْتَرَحِ ④ (treaty) اتِّفاقيّة, مُعاهَدة; **under the terms of the Lisbon ~** وَفْقاً لِأَحْكامِ مُعاهَدةِ لِشْبونة ⑤ (contract) عَقْد (عُقود); **under the terms of the ~** وَفْقاً لِأَحْكامِ العَقْدِ ⑥ (in grammar) مُطابَقة

agricultural /agrɪ'kʌltʃ(ə)rəl/ *adj* ‹*produce, implements*› زِراعِيّ

agriculture /'agrɪkʌltʃə/ *n* زِراعة

agronomist /ə'grɒnəmɪst/ *n* خَبير زِراعِيّ

agronomy /ə'grɒnəmi/ *n* عِلْم الزِراعةِ

aground /ə'graʊnd/ *adv* جانِحاً

ah /ɑː/ *excl* آه; **~ yes, of course!** آه نَعَمْ، طَبْعاً!; **~ well!** آه حَسَناً, فَلْيَكُنْ!

AH /eɪ'eɪtʃ/ *abbr* (هِجْرِيّ) هـ; **this Koran is dated 556 ~** يَعودُ هذا القُرْآنُ إلى 556 هـ

ahead /ə'hed/ **A** *adv* ① (in space) ‹*to go on, run*› إلى الأَمامِ; **we've sent Jo on ~** أَرْسَلْنا جو في الطَليعةِ; **a few kilometres ~** بَعْض الكيلومِتْراتِ إلى الأَمامِ; **the road ~ is blocked** الطَريقُ إلى الأَمامِ مَسْدودٌ; ▸ **straight** ② (in time) **in the months ~** في الشُهورِ القادِمةِ; **who knows what lies ~?**

مَنْ يَعْلَمُ ما يَحْمِلُهُ المُسْتَقْبَلُ؟; **he's good/bad at looking ~** يُجيدُ \ لا يُجيدُ التَخْطيطَ المُسْتَقْبَلِيَّ ③ (in a leading position) **to be ~ in the polls** تَقَدَّمَ في اسْتِطْلاعاتِ الرَأْيِ; **to be 30 points ~** كانَ في المُقَدِّمةِ بِـ30 نُقْطةً; **to be 3% ~** تَقَدَّمَ بِـ 3٪ ④ (more advanced) **to be ~ in physics/geography** «students, class» كانَ مُتَقَدِّماً في الفيزياءِ \ الجُغْرافيا

B (**ahead of**) *prep phr* ① (in front of) قَبْلَ ‹*a person, vehicle*›; **to be three metres ~ of sb** كانَ قبل شَخْصٍ بِثَلاثةِ أَمْتارٍ ② (in time) **to arrive ~ of time** وَصَلَ قبل الوَقْتِ; **to arrive ~ of sb** وَصَلَ قبل شَخْصٍ; **to be three seconds ~ of the next competitor** كانَ مُتَقَدِّماً بِثَلاثِ ثَوانٍ على المُنافِسِ التالي; **to be ~ of one's time** كانَ سابقاً لِزَمانِهِ \ لِعَصْرِهِ ③ (in polls, ratings) **to be ~ of sb** تَقَدَّمَ على شَخْصٍ ④ (more advanced) **to be (way) ~ of the others** «students, class» تَفَوَّقَ (بِكَثيرٍ) على الآخَرينَ; **our researchers are ~ of the field** باحِثونا مُتَفَوِّقونَ في مَجالِهِمْ

aid /eɪd/ **A** *n* (to a person, country) مُساعَدة, إعانة
B *vt* ① ساعَدَ, أَعانَ ‹*a colleague, child*› ② أَعانَ ‹*digestion, a recovery*›

aid agency *n* وكالة مَعونةٍ

aide /eɪd/ *n* مُساعِد

aide-de-camp /ˌeɪddəˈkɒ̃/ *n* (*pl* **aides-de-camp**) ضابِط مُعاوِن

AIDS, **Aids** /eɪdz/ *n* = **Acquired Immune Deficiency Syndrome** (مَرَض نَقْصِ المَناعةِ المُكْتَسَبةِ) سيدا إيدْز (ME), (NA)

AIDS awareness *n* تَوْعِية بِمَرَضِ الإيدْز

AIDS sufferer *n* مَريض الإيدْز

AIDS vaccine *n* مَصْل مُضادّ لِمَرَضِ الإيدْز

AIDS virus *n* فَيْروس الإيدْز

aid worker *n* [عامِل في مَجال تَقْديمِ المَعونةِ]

ail /eɪl/ **A** *vt* آلَمَ (Form IV; imperf يُؤْلِمُ) آذى (Form IV; imperf يُؤْذي) ‹*the economy, society*›
B *vi* **to be ~ing** دَنِفَ (a; دَنَف)

ailing /ˈeɪlɪŋ/ *adj* ① ‹*parent, relative*› مَريض, مُعْتَلّ, مُتَوَعِّك ② ‹*economy, company*› مُعْتَلّ (مَرْضى)

ailment /ˈeɪlm(ə)nt/ *n* عِلّة (عِلَل), مَرَض, وَعْكة (أَمْراض)

aim /eɪm/ **A** *vt* ① (to point) وَجَّهَ ‹*a gun, camera*›; **he ~ed the pistol at me** وَجَّهَ المُسَدَّسَ إلَيَّ ② (to direct) سَدَّدَ ‹*a kick, blow*›; **he ~ed a punch at me** سَدَّدَ لَكْمةً إلَيَّ ③ (to orientate) وَجَّهَ ‹*a campaign, film*›; **the programme is ~ed at teenagers** البَرْنامجُ مُوَجَّهٌ للمُراهِقينَ
B *vi* ① (to direct a gun, stone) سَدَّدَ; **to ~ at sb/sth** سَدَّدَ إلى شَخْصٍ \ شَيْءٍ ② (to intend) هَدَفَ (u; هَدْف); **to ~ to do sth** هَدَفَ إلى فِعْلِ شَيْءٍ
C *n* ① (with a gun) **to take ~ at sb/sth** سَدَّدَ إلى شَخْصٍ \ شَيْءٍ ② (objective) هَدَف (أَهْداف), غَرَض (أَغْراض); **my ~ is to finish it tomorrow** هَدَفي أنْ أُنْهيهِ غَداً

aimless /ˈeɪmləs/ *adj* ① ‹*existence, youth*› طائِش, بِلا هَدَفٍ ② ‹*walk*› بِلا هَدَفٍ

ain't /eɪnt/ (infml) *abbr* ① = **am not**, = **are not**, = **is not** ▸ **be** ② = **has not**, = **have not** ▸ **have**

air /ɛː/ **A** *n* ① (substance) هَواء; **in the open ~** في الهَواءِ الطَلْقِ; **the diver came up for ~** صَعِدَ الغَطّاسُ للسَطْحِ لاسْتِنْشاقِ بَعْضِ الهَواءِ; **check the ~ in the tyres** تَحَقَّقْ من مُسْتَوى الهَواءِ في الإطاراتِ ② (in flying) جَوّ; **to travel by ~** سافَرَ جَوًّا; **Cairo from the ~** القاهِرة من الجَوِّ ③ (in broadcasting) **to be/go on (the) ~** «programmes, interview» تَمَّ \ بَدَأَ بَثُّهُ على الهَواءِ; **the series will be back on the ~ in January** سَوْفَ يَعودُ المُسَلْسَلُ إلى الشاشةِ في شَهْرِ يَنايِر; **the show goes on (the) ~ from 7.00 a.m.** يَبْدَأُ بَثُّ البَرْنامَجِ في السابِعةِ صَباحاً; **the channel goes off the ~ at midnight** يَنْتَهي بَثُّ القَناةِ عند مُنْتَصَفِ اللَيْلِ ④ (image projected) انْطِباع; **she met us with an ~ of indifference** [أَعْطَتْنا انْطِباعاً بِعَدَمِ المُبالاةِ حينَ قابَلَتْنا] ⑤ (tune) نَغَم (أَنْغام)
B *vt* ① (to freshen) هَوّى ‹*the sheets, bed*› ② (to let air into) هَوّى ‹*a room, house*› ③ (to express) عَبَّرَ (عن) ‹*an opinion, one's views*›; **to ~ one's grievances** عَبَّرَ عن أَحْزانِهِ ④ (AmE) (to broadcast) بَثَّ (i-u; بَثّ), أَذاعَ ‹*a show*›

Idioms **there is something in the air** يَلوحُ في الأُفُقِ شَبَحُ شَيْءٍ; **to vanish into thin air** اخْتَفى دون أنْ يَتْرُكَ أَدْنى أَثَرٍ

air ambulance *n* إسْعاف جَوِّيّ

airbag /ˈɛːbag/ *n* وِسادة هَوائيّة

airbase *n* قاعِدة جَوِّيّة

airbed /ˈɛːbɛd/ *n* (BrE) فِراش هَوائيّ

airborne /ˈɛːbɔːn/ *adj* **1** <*particles, seeds*> مَنْقول جَوًّا **2** <*plane, helicopter*> مُحَلِّق في الهَواءِ **3** (Mil) <*troops, division*> مَحْمول جَوًّا

airbrush /ˈɛːbrʌʃ/ *vt* عَدَّلَ <*a photo, wrinkles*>

air-conditioned *adj* <*room, bus*> مُكَيَّف

air conditioning *n* تَكْييف الهَواءِ

aircraft /ˈɛːkrɑːft/ *n* (*pl* **aircraft**) طائِرة

aircraft carrier *n* حامِلة طائِراتٍ

aircrew /ˈɛːkruː/ *n* طاقِم جَوّيّ

airfare /ˈɛːfɛː/ *n* سِعْر تَذْكِرة طَيَرانٍ

airfield /ˈɛːfiːld/ *n* مَهْبِط طائِراتٍ

air force *n* سِلاح جَوّيّ, قُوّات جَوّيّة

air freshener *n* مُعَطِّر الجَوِّ

airgun /ˈɛːgʌn/ *n* بُنْدُقيّة ضَغْطٍ

airhead /ˈɛːhɛd/ *n* (infml) غَبيّ (أَغْبياءُ)

air hostess *n* مُضيفة طَيَرانٍ, مُضيفة جَوّيّة

air letter *n* رِسالة جَوّيّة

airlift /ˈɛːlɪft/ **A** *n* جِسْر جَوّيّ; **an ~ of supplies** جِسْر جَوّيّ لِلإمْداداتِ

B *vt* نَقَلَ جَوًّا <*supplies, troops*>

airline /ˈɛːlʌɪn/ *n* خَطّ جَوّيّ, شَرِكة طَيَرانٍ

airmail /ˈɛːmeɪl/ *n* بَريد جَوّيّ; **by ~** بالبَريدِ الجَوّيِّ

airman /ˈɛːmən/ *n* (*pl* **-men**) [طَيّار \ مَلاّح جَوّيّ في القُوّاتِ الجَوّيّةِ]

airplane /ˈɛːpleɪn/ *n* (AmE) طائِرة

air pollution *n* تَلَوُّث الهَواءِ \ الجَوِّ

airport /ˈɛːpɔːt/ *n* مَطار (مَطارات), ميناء جَوّيّ

air raid *n* غارة جَوّيّة

airship /ˈɛːʃɪp/ *n* سَفينة هَوائيّة

airsick /ˈɛːsɪk/ *adj* **to be/get ~** أُصيبَ بِدُوارِ الجَوِّ

airsickness /ˈɛːsɪknəs/ *n* دُوار الجَوِّ

airspace /ˈɛːspeɪs/ *n* مَجال جَوّيّ

air strike *n* ضَرْبة جَوّيّة

airstrip /ˈɛːstrɪp/ *n* مَهْبِط \ مَدْرَج طائِراتٍ

air terminal *n* مَبْنى الرُّكّابِ

airtight /ˈɛːtʌɪt/ *adj* **1** <*container, seal*> مُحْكَم الغَلْقِ **2** <*alibi, argument*> قاطِع

air-to-air /ˌɛːtuːˈɛː/ *adj* <*missile, refuelling*> جَوّ جَوّ

air traffic control *n* مُراقَبة الحَرَكةِ الجَوّيّةِ

air traffic controller *n* مُراقِب الحَرَكةِ الجَوّيّةِ

air travel *n* السَفَر جَوًّا

air vent *n* فَتْحة تَهْوِيةٍ

airwaves /ˈɛːweɪvz/ *n pl* مَوْجات الأثيرِ

airway /ˈɛːweɪ/ *n* **1** (air route) مَمَرّ جَوّيّ **2** (airline) شَرِكة خُطوطِ الطَيَرانِ **3** (air passage) مَسْلَك هَوائيّ

airworthy /ˈɛːwəːði/ *adj* <*plane, helicopter*> صالِح لِلطَيَرانِ

airy /ˈɛːri/ *adj* (**airier, airiest**) <*room, apartment*> طَلِق الهَواءِ

airy-fairy /ˌɛːriˈfɛːri/ *adj* (infml) <*theory, ideas*> [مِثاليّ وَغَيْر عَمَليّ \ واقِعيّ]

aisle /ʌɪl/ *n* **1** (on a train, plane) مَمَرّ (مَمَرّات) **2** (in a supermarket) مَمَرّ (مَمَرّات) **3** (in a cinema) مَمَرّ (مَمَرّات) **4** (in a church) مَمَرّ (مَمَرّات)

ajar /əˈdʒɑː/ **A** *adv* **to leave sth ~** تَرَكَ شَيْئاً مُوارَباً <*door, gate*>

B *adj* <*door, gate*> مُوارَب

AK *abbr* ▸ **Alaska**

aka /eɪkeɪˈeɪ/ *abbr* = **also known as** مَعْروف كَذَلِكَ بِ

akin /əˈkɪn/ *adj pred* (similar) **to be ~ to sth** كانَ شَبيهاً بِشَيْءٍ

AL *abbr* **1** ▸ **Albania** **2** ▸ **Alabama**

Alabama /ˌaləˈbamə/ *pr n* أَلاباما

Alabaman /ˌaləˈbamən/ *n, adj* [(شَخْص) من أَلاباما]

alarm /əˈlɑːm/ **A** *n* **1** (warning in emergencies) إِنْذار (إِنْذارات); (warning to wake up) صَوْت مُنَبِّهٍ **2** (device in emergencies) جِهاز إِنْذارٍ; (alarm clock) مُنَبِّه **3** [u] (fear, worry) قَلَق

B *vt* **1** (to worry) أَقْلَقَ **2** (to fit a warning system to) جَهَّزَ بِجِهازِ إِنْذارٍ <*a house, vehicle*>

alarm clock *n* مُنَبِّه

alarmed /əˈlɑːmd/ *adj* **1** (worried) قَلِق **2** <*door, vehicle*> مُجَهَّز بِجِهازِ إِنْذارٍ

alarming /əˈlɑːmɪŋ/ *adj* ‹*increase, news*› مُثير للقَلَق, مُقْلِق

alas /əˈlas/ *excl* (liter) مع الأَسَفِ, للأَسَفِ

Alaska /əˈlaskə/ *pr n* ألاسْكا

Alaskan /əˈlask(ə)n/ *pr n, adj* (شَخْص) من ألاسْكا

Albania /alˈbeɪnɪə/ *pr n* ألْبانِيا

Albanian /alˈbeɪnɪən/ **A** *n* **1** (citizen) ألْبانيّ (ألْبان) **2** (language) (اللُغة) الألْبانيّة **B** *adj* ‹*class, teacher*› ألْبانيّ (ألْبان)

albatross /ˈalbətrɒs/ *n* قَطْرَس

albeit /ɔːlˈbiːɪt/ *conj* (fml) وَلَوْ (أنّ), رَغْمَ (أنّ)

albino /alˈbiːnəʊ/ **A** *n* (*pl* **albinos**) أَمْهَق (dipt; مُهْق) **B** *modifier* ‹*mouse, gorilla*› أَمْهَق (dipt; مُهْق)

album /ˈalbəm/ *n* **1** (for stamps, photos) ألْبوم (ألْبومات) **2** (Mus) ألْبوم (ألْبومات)

alchemist /ˈalkəmɪst/ *n* كيمِيائيّ

alcohol /ˈalkəhɒl/ *n* **1** (as a drink) كُحول; **I don't drink ~** أنا لا أَتَناوَلُ الكُحولَ **2** (Chem) كُحول

alcoholic /alkəˈhɒlɪk/ **A** *adj* ‹*drink, content*› كُحولي **B** *n* مُدْمِن كُحولٍ

alcoholism /ˈalkəhɒlɪz(ə)m/ *n* إدْمان الكُحولِ

alcopop /ˈalkəʊpɒp/ *n* ألْكوبوب (مَشْروب كُحوليّ حُلْو)

alcove /ˈalkəʊv/ *n* تَجْويف (تَجاويفُ)

alderman /ˈɔːldəmən/ *n* (*pl* **-men**) **1** (AmE) (councilman) عُضْو مَجْلِسٍ بَلَديٍّ **2** (BrE) (senior councillor) [عُضْو سامٍ في مَجْلِسٍ بَلَديٍّ (قبل 1972)]

ale /eɪl/ *n* مِزْر (نَوْع من الجِعةِ)

Aleppo /əˈlɛpəʊ/ *pr n* حَلَب (dipt f)

alert /əˈləːt/ **A** *adj* **1** (lively) ‹*child, dog*› يَقِظ **2** (attentive) يَقِظ **B** *n* **1** (state of watchfulness) **to be on the ~ for sth** تَحَسَّبَ من شَيْءٍ **2** (warning) تَحْذير (تَحْذيرات); **a security ~** تَحْذير أَمْنيّ; **the manufacturer issued a safety ~** أَصْدَرَ المُنْتِجُ تَحْذيراً بِخُصوصِ سَلامةِ مُنْتَج **C** *vt* (to warn) حَذَّرَ (من) ‹*the authorities, police*›; **to ~ sb to a danger/situation** حَذَّرَ شَخْصاً من خَطَرٍ \ وَضْعٍ

A level *n* (in UK) = **Advanced level** البَكالوريا ≈ (مُسْتَوًى دِراسيّ يَسْمَحُ بالدُخولِ إلى الجامِعةِ)

Alexandria /alɪgˈzɑːndrɪə/ *pr n* الإسْكَنْدَرِيّة

algebra /ˈaldʒɪbrə/ *n* جَبْر

Algeria /alˈdʒɪərɪə/ *pr n* الجَزائِر (f)

Algerian /alˈdʒɪərɪən/ *n, adj* جَزائِريّ

Algiers /alˈdʒɪəz/ *pr n* الجَزائِر العاصِمة

algorithm /ˈalgərɪð(ə)m/ *n* خُوارِزْمِيّة

alias /ˈeɪlɪəs/ **A** *adv* المُلَقَّب ب; **Marshall Mathers ~ rapper Eminem** مارْشَل ماذَرْز المُلَقَّبُ بِمُغَنّي الراب إمينيم **B** *n* **1** (assumed name) اسْم مُسْتَعار **2** (Comput) اسْم مُسْتَعار

alibi /ˈalɪbʌɪ/ *n* دَفْع بالغَيْبة (حُجّة غِيابٍ ساعةَ وُقوعِ جَريمةٍ); **she had a good ~** كانَتْ تَمْلِكُ حُجّةَ غِيابٍ مُقْنِعةٍ ساعةَ وُقوعِ الجَريمةِ

alien /ˈeɪlɪən/ **A** *adj* **1** (from another country) ‹*agent, government*› أَجْنَبيّ **2** (unknown) ‹*concept*› غَيْر مَعْروفٍ; **to be ~ to sb** كانَ غَيْرَ مَعْروفٍ لدى شَخْصٍ **3** (from space) ‹*spacecraft, invasion*› فَضائيّ **B** *n* **1** (Law) (foreigner) أَجْنَبيّ (أَجانِبُ, أَجْنَبيّونَ); **an illegal ~** أَجْنَبيّ يُقيمُ بِطَريقةٍ غَيْرِ شَرْعيّةٍ **2** (creature from space) مَخْلوق فَضائيّ

alien abduction *n* اخْتِطاف من قِبَلِ مَخْلوقاتٍ فَضائيّةٍ

alienate /ˈeɪlɪəneɪt/ *vt* ‹*a supporter, colleague*› نَفَّرَ

alienation /eɪlɪəˈneɪʃ(ə)n/ *n* **1** (Psych) عُزْلة **2** (of property) نَقْل \ تَحْويل المِلْكيّة

alight /əˈlʌɪt/ **A** *adj* مُتَّقِد, مُتَوَهِّج; **to be ~** كانَ مُتَّقِداً **B** *adv* **to set sth ~** أَشْعَلَ \ أَوْقَدَ شَيْئاً **C** *vi* «passengers» نَزَلَ (i; نُزول)

align /əˈlʌɪn/ *vt* صَفَّ (u; صَفّ) ‹*wheels*›; حاذَى ‹*text*›

alignment /əˈlʌɪnm(ə)nt/ *n* **1** (Tech) تَراصّ; **to be in/out of ~** كانَ مُتَراصًّا \ غَيْرَ مُتَراصٍّ **2** (Pol) تَحالُف

alike /əˈlʌɪk/ **A** *adj* **to look ~** كانوا مُتَشابِهينَ **B** *adv* **1** ‹*to think, to dress*› بِطَريقةٍ مُتَشابِهةٍ; **they think ~** هُمْ يُفَكِّرونَ بِطَريقةٍ مُتَشابِهةٍ **2** ‹*to appeal to, to affect*› كَما; **these regulations apply to teachers and students ~** تَنْطَبِقُ هذه القَوانينُ على المُدَرِّسينَ كَما على الطُلّابِ

alimony /ˈalɪməni/ *n* نَفَقة (نَفَقات)

A-list /ˈeɪlɪst/ *n* أَكْبَر \ أَشْهَر نُجوم; **an ~ celebrity** من أَكْبَرِ النُجومِ \ المَشاهير

alive /əˈlaɪv/ *adj* 1 (living) ‹*victim, prisoner*› حَيّ (أَحْياء); **to be burned/buried ~** أُحْرِقَ \ دُفِنَ حَيًّا 2 (in existence) ‹*tradition*› حَيّ; ‹*interest*› حاضِر 3 (lively) **to come ~** ‹*party, history, city*› بَدَأَ يَنْبِضُ بالحَياةِ, رَجَعَتْ إلَيْهِ الحَياةُ 4 (crowded) **to be ~ with insects** غَصَّ بالحَشَراتِ

alkali /ˈalkəlaɪ/ *n* (*pl* **alkalis**) مادّة قَلَوِيّة

alkaline /ˈalkəlaɪn/ *adj* ‹*solution, soil*› قَلْوِيّ

all /ɔːl/ **A** *determiner* 1 (each one of) كُلّ, جَميع; **~ questions must be answered** يَجِبُ الإجابةُ على جَميعِ الأَسْئِلةِ; **~ those who ..., ~ those people who ...** كُلّ أُولَئِكَ الَّذينَ ...; **in ~ three movies** في كُلٍّ من الأَفْلامِ الثَلاثةِ 2 (the whole of) جَميع, كُلّ; **~ his life** كُلّ حَياتِهِ; **~ the time** كُلّ الوَقْتِ; **~ day/evening** كُلّ النَهارِ \ المَساءِ; **~ year round** على مَدارِ العامِ; **I had ~ the work!** أُلْقِيَ على عاتِقي كُلُّ العَمَلِ!; **you are ~ the family I have!** أَنْتَ كُلُّ مَنْ تَبَقّى من أُسْرَتي! 3 (total) **in ~ honesty/innocence** بِكُلِّ صَراحةٍ \ براءةٍ; **in ~ honesty, I think his dismissal was justified** بِكُلِّ صَراحةٍ، أَعْتَقِدُ أنّ طَرْدَهُ كانَ مُبَرَّراً; **she asked in ~ innocence what was happening** سَأَلَتْ بِكُلِّ بَراءةٍ عَمّا كانَ يَحْدُثُ 4 (any) **beyond ~ expectations** فوق كُلِّ التَوَقُّعاتِ; **to deny ~ knowledge of sth** أَنْكَرَ أَيَّ مَعْرِفةٍ بِشَيْءٍ; **he is guilty beyond ~ doubt** هو مُذْنِبٌ بِدونِ أَيِّ شَكٍّ

B *pron* 1 (everything) كُلّ شَيْءٍ; **to risk ~** خاطَرَ بِكُلِّ شَيْءٍ; **~ is not lost** ما زالَ الأَمَلُ قائِماً; **~ was well** كانَ كُلُّ شَيْءٍ على ما يُرامُ; **~ or nothing** كُلّ شَيْءٍ أو لا شَيْءَ; **will that be ~?** هل سَيَكونُ ذلك كُلَّ شَيْءٍ؟; **that's ~** هذا كُلُّ شَيْءٍ; **speed/safety is ~** السُرْعةُ \ السَلامةُ هي أَهَمُّ شَيْءٍ; **and that's not ~** وَذلِكَ لَيْسَ كُلَّ شَيْءٍ; **500 in ~** 500 إجْمالاً; **after ~ that has happened** بعد كُلِّ ما حَدَثَ 2 (the only thing) كُلّ; **that's ~ I want** ذلك كُلُّ ما أُريدُ; **~ I know is that ...** كُلُّ ما أَعْرِفُهُ هو أنّ ...; **~ you need is ...** كُلُّ ما تَحْتاجُ إلَيْهِ هو ... 3 (everyone) الكُلّ, الجَميع; **'~ welcome'** 'الدَعْوة عامّة'; **~ of the employees** كُلّ المُوَظَّفينَ; **~ of us want ...** جَميعُنا يُريدُ ...; **not ~ of them came** لم يَحْضُروا جَميعَهُمْ; **we want ~ of them back** نُريدُهُمْ أنْ يَعودوا جَميعاً; **thank you, one and ~** شُكْراً للجَميعِ، فَرْداً فَرْداً 4 (indicating wholeness) **~ of our belongings** كُلّ مُمْتَلَكاتِنا; **I ate it ~** أَكَلْتُهُ كُلَّهُ; **~ of this land is ours** كُلُّ هذه الأَرْضِ مِلْكُنا; **not ~ of the time** لَيْسَ كُلَّ الوَقْتِ; **these are ~ valid points** هذه كُلُّها نِقاطٌ صَحيحةٌ

C *adv* 1 (completely) تَماماً; **~ alone** *or* **on one's own** وَحيد تَماماً; **to be ~ wet** كانَ مُبْتَلاً تَماماً; **dressed ~ in white** يَرْتَدي مَلابِسَ كُلُّها بَيْضاءُ; **~ around the garden/along the canal** حَول الحَديقةِ \ على طولِ القَناةِ كُلِّها; **to be ~ for sth** كانَ مُؤَيِّداً تَماماً لِشَيْءٍ; **it's ~ about ...** الأَمْرُ كُلُّهُ يَتَعَلَّقُ ب ...; **tell me ~ about it!** أَخْبِرْني كُلَّ شَيْءٍ عَنْهُ!; **she asked ~ about you** سَأَلَتْ عَنْكَ أَسْئِلةً كَثيرةً 2 (nothing but) **to be ~ talk** كانَ مُجَرَّدَ كَلامٍ; **that stew was ~ water!** تِلْكَ اليَخْنةُ كانَتْ كُلُّها ماءً! 3 (in scoring) **(they are) six ~** سِتُّ نِقاطٍ لِكُلٍّ مِنْهُمْ; **the final score is three ~** النَتيجةُ النِهائيّةُ هي ثَلاثةٌ لِكُلٍّ مِنْهُمْ

D *n* **to give one's ~** بَذَلَ قُصارى جُهْدِهِ; **he gave his ~, but was beaten in the final** بَذَلَ قُصارى جُهْدِهِ، وَلَكِنَّهُ خَسِرَ في النِهائيِّ

E (*in combination* **all+**) (completely) **~-concrete/-glass/-metal** مَصْنوع بالكامِلِ من الخَرَسانةِ \ الزُجاجِ \ المَعْدِنِ; **an ~-female cast/group** طاقِم نِسْوِيّ \ مَجْموعة نِسْوِيّة; **~-male team/jury** فَريق ذُكوريّ \ هَيْئة مُحَلَّفينَ ذُكوريّة

F (**all that**) *adv phr* **he's not ~ that strong** هو لَيْسَ بِكُلِّ تِلْكَ القُوّةِ; **it's not as far as ~ that!** هو لَيْسَ بِكُلِّ ذلك البُعْدِ!; **I don't know her ~ that well** لا أَعْرِفُها بِشَكْلٍ جَيِّدٍ

G (**all the**) *adv phr* **~ the more difficult/effective** أَكْثَر صُعوبةٍ \ فاعِلِيّةٍ بِكَثيرٍ; **~ the better!** أَحْسَنُ وَأَحْسَنُ!; **to laugh ~ the more** ضَحِكَ كَثيراً جِدًّا

H (**at all**) *adv phr* 1 (intensifying possibility) بِأَيِّ حالٍ من الأَحْوالِ; **if it's at ~ possible, if at ~ possible** إذا كانَ هذا مُمْكِناً بِأَيِّ حالٍ من الأَحْوالِ; **anything at ~ will do** أَيُّ شَيْءٍ مَهْما كانَ سَيَفي بالغَرَضِ 2 (intensifying negativity) على الإطْلاقِ, بَتاتاً; **there's nothing at ~ here** لَيْسَ هُناكَ أَيُّ شَيْءٍ على الإطْلاقِ هُنا; **we know nothing at ~** *or* **we don't**

know anything at ~ about ... لا نَعْلَمُ أَيَّ شَيْءٍ على الإطْلاقِ بِخُصُوصِ ...

2 (**of all**) *prep phr* **1▸** (in rankings) **the easiest of ~** الأَسْهَل; **first/last of ~** الأَوَّل \ الآخِر فيهِمْ; **best of ~, we could go home early** أَفْضَلُ ما هُنالِكَ أَنَّهُ يُمْكِنُنا العَوْدَةُ إلى بُيوتِنا مُبَكِّراً; **the last question was the easiest of ~** آخِرُ سُؤالٍ كانَ الأَسْهَلَ فيهِمْ **2▸** (emphatic) **why today of ~ days?** لِماذا اليَوْمَ من بين كُلِّ الأَيّامِ؟; **not now of ~ times!** لَيْسَ الآنَ هو الوَقْتُ المُناسِبُ!; **we met George, of ~ people!** قابَلْنا جورْج، من بين كُلِّ الناسِ!

(Idioms) **all along** طوال الوَقْتِ; **they knew it ~ along** كانوا يَعْلَمونَهُ طوال الوَقْتِ; **all but ~** الكُلّ \ الجَميع فيما عَدا; **all but us were told** أُخْبِرَ الجَميعُ فيما عَدانا; **all in all** بِشَكْلٍ عامٍّ، عُموماً; **~ in ~, it's a good result** بِشَكْلٍ عامٍّ، هي نَتيجةٌ جَيِّدةٌ; **all of** على الأَقَلِّ; **he must be ~ of 50** لا بُدَّ أنّ عُمْرَهُ على الأَقَلِّ 50 عاماً; **all too** تَماماً; **it is ~ too obvious that ...** من الواضِحِ تَماماً أنّ ...; **she saw ~ too clearly that ...** رَأَتْ بِكُلِّ وُضوحٍ أنّ ...; **~ too often** في كَثيرٍ من الأَحْيانِ; **for all** (in as far as) على حَدِّ, بِقَدْرِ; **for ~ I know** على حَدِّ عِلْمي; **they could be dead for ~ the difference it would make!** قد يَكونونَ مَيِّتينَ وَلَكِنَّ هذا لن يُشَكِّلَ أَيَّ فَرْقٍ!; **that's all very well, that's all well and good** كُلُّ هذا جَيِّدٌ; **to be all smiles** مَلأَت الابْتِساماتُ وَجْهَهُ

Allah /ˈalə/ *pr n* الله

all-American /ˌɔːləˈmɛrɪk(ə)n/ *adj* ‹*girl, hero*› يَمْتَلِكُ كُلَّ الصِفاتِ المُمَيِّزة للمُثُلِ الأَمْريكيّةِ

allay /əˈleɪ/ *vt* (fml) قَلَّلَ (من) ‹*a fear, concern*›

all-clear /ɔːlˈklɪə/ *n* **to give the ~** أَعْطى إشارةَ زَوالِ الخَطَرِ

allegation /alɪˈgeɪʃ(ə)n/ *n* ادِّعاء (ادِّعاءات)

allege /əˈlɛdʒ/ *vt* زَعَمَ (u; زَعْم), ادَّعى ‹*abuse, fraud*›

alleged /əˈlɛdʒd/ *adj* ‹*culprit, illness, negligence*› مَزْعوم

allegedly /əˈlɛdʒɪdli/ *adv* كَما يُقالُ; **~ he stole over 10,000 pounds** يُقالُ بِأَنَّهُ سَرَقَ ما يَزيدُ عن 10,000 جُنَيْهٍ اسْتِرْلينيٍّ

allegiance /əˈliːdʒ(ə)ns/ *n* وَلاء

alleluia /ˌalɪˈluːjə/ ▸**hallelujah**

allergic /əˈləːdʒɪk/ *adj* مُصاب بِحَسّاسيّةٍ; **are you ~ to cats?** هل تُعاني من حَسّاسيّةٍ من القِطَطِ؟

allergist /ˈalədʒɪst/ *n* أَخِصّائيّ حَسّاسيّةٍ

allergy /ˈalədʒi/ *n* (*pl* **allergies**) حَسّاسيّة; **I have an ~ to dust** لَدَيَّ حَسّاسيّةٌ ضِدّ \ من الغُبارِ

alleviate /əˈliːvieɪt/ *vt* خَفَّفَ ‹*symptoms, stress*›

alley /ˈali/ *n* (*pl* **alleys**) زُقاق (mf; أَزِقّة), مَمَرّ (مَمَرّات)

(Idiom) **to be right up sb's alley** (infml) [دَخل ضِمْنَ اهْتِماماتِ شَخْصٍ]

alleyway /ˈaliweɪ/ *n* زُقاق (mf; أَزِقّة)

alliance /əˈlʌɪəns/ *n* تَحالُف

allied /ˈalʌɪd/ *adj* ‹*nations, forces*› مُتَحالِف

alligator /ˈalɪgeɪtə/ *n* قاطور, تِمْساح أَمْريكيّ \ اسْتِوائيّ

all-important /ɔːlɪmˈpɔːt(ə)nt/ *adj* ‹*goal, statistic*› شَديد الأَهَمِّيّةِ

all-inclusive /ɔːlɪnˈkluːsɪv/ *adj* ‹*fee, holiday*› شامِل كُلَّ شَيْءٍ

all-in-one /ɔːlɪnˈwʌn/ *adj* ‹*garment, printer*› مُتَكامِل

all-in wrestling /ˌɔːlɪn ˈrɛslɪŋ/ *n* [نَوْع من المُصارَعةِ الحُرّةِ]

all-night /ɔːlˈnʌɪt/ *adj* ‹*radio station, negotiations*› طوال اللَيْلِ

allocate /ˈaləkeɪt/ *vt* خَصَّصَ ‹*funds, tasks*›

allocation /aləˈkeɪʃ(ə)n/ *n* **1▸** (amount) (food) حِصّة (حِصَص); (money) مُخَصَّص; **our student ~ will increase/decrease next year** سَتَزْدادُ \ سَتَقِلُّ مُخَصَّصاتُ طُلّابِنا في السَنةِ القادِمةِ **2▸** (process) تَخْصيص

allot /əˈlɒt/ *vt* (**-tt-**) خَصَّصَ ‹*a share, resources*›

allotment /əˈlɒtm(ə)nt/ *n* (BrE) [قِطْعة أَرْضٍ مُسْتَأْجَرة للبَسْتَنةِ]

all out *adj* ‹*strike, effort*› شامِل

all over *adv* **1▸** (finished) مُنْتَهٍ إلى غَيْرِ رَجْعةٍ; **it's all over between us** انْتَهى ما بَيْنَنا إلى غَيْرِ رَجْعةٍ **2▸** (everywhere) في كُلِّ مَكانٍ; **to be trembling all over** ارْتَجَفَ من أَعْلى رَأْسِهِ إلى أَخْمَصِ قَدَمَيْهِ **3▸** (typically of someone) كالمُعْتادِ; **that's Helen all over; she's always been generous** تِلْكَ هي هيلين، كالمُعْتادِ، كَريمةٌ

allow /əˈlaʊ/ **A** *vt* **1▸** (to authorize) سَمَحَ (a; سَماح ل), صَرَّحَ (ل), أَذِنَ (a; إذْن ل) ‹*a person, an organization*›; **to ~ sb to do sth** سَمَحَ لِشَخْصٍ بِأَنْ يَفْعَلَ شَيْئاً; **she is ~ed to drive the**

car مَسْموحٌ لَها بِقِيادةِ السَّيّارة; he ~ed them into the house سَمَحَ لَهُمْ بالدُخولِ إلى المَنْزِلِ; you are ~ed three chances مَسْموحٌ لَكَ بِثَلاثِ فُرَصٍ **2** (to let) تَرَكَ (تَرْك; u) ,سَمَحَ (ل; a) ‹a situation, person›; he ~ed the situation to get worse تَرَكَ الوَضْعَ يَزْدادُ سوءاً; to ~ a building to be altered/ demolished أَجازَ تَغْيِيرَ \ هَدْمَ مَبْنًى **3** (to enable) to ~ sb/sth to do sth مَكَّنَ شَخْصاً \ شَيْئاً أَنْ يَفْعَلَ شَيْئاً ‹an improvement, a development› **4** (to allocate) خَصَّصَ ,أَفْرَدَ; to ~ two days for the job خَصَّصَ يَوْمَيْنِ للمُهِمَّةِ **5** (to approve) «referee» احْتَسَبَ ‹a goal› **6** (to admit) سَمَحَ بالدُخول (ل) ‹children, a non-member›; 'no dogs ~ed' 'مَمْنوعٌ دُخولُ الكِلابِ'

B *v refl* to ~ oneself **1** (to grant) سَمَحَ لِنَفْسِهِ ب ‹a drink, treat› **2** (to allocate) أَعْطى \ أَمْهَلَ نَفْسَهُ ‹time›; ~ yourself enough time أَمْهِلْ نَفْسَكَ وَقْتاً كافِياً **3** (to let) تَرَكَ نَفْسَهُ; I ~ed myself to be persuaded تَرَكْتُ نَفْسي أَقْتَنِعُ

(Phrasal verb) **allow for**: ~ for [sth] أَخَذَ \ وَضَعَ [شَيْئاً] في الحُسْبانِ ‹delays, wastage›

allowance /ə'laʊəns/ *n* **1** (grant) مُخَصَّص (مُخَصَّصات) **2** (from an employer) بَدَل (بَدَلات) **3** (against tax) مِقْدار الدَخْلِ الّذي لا تُسْتَحَقُّ عَلَيْهِ ضَريبةٌ **4** (spending money: for a child) مَصْروف جَيْبٍ; (for a spouse) مَصْروف شَخْصيّ; (for a student) مِنْحة; (from a trust, guardian) مَعونة (مَعونات) **5** (entitlement) your baggage ~ is 40 kgs وَزْنُ الأَمْتِعةِ المَسْموحُ بِهِ هو 40 كج **6** (concession) to make ~s for sth أَخَذَ شَيْئاً بِعَيْنِ الاعْتِبارِ; to make ~s for sb راعى ظُروفَ شَخْصٍ

alloy /'alɔɪ/ *n* خَليط مَعْدِنيّ ,أُشابة (أَشائِبُ)

alloy wheel *n* جُنْط (جُنوط)

all-powerful /ɔːl'paʊəfʊl/ *adj* ‹God, ruler› جَبّار

all right, alright **A** *adj* **1** (expressing satisfaction) to be all right كانَ جَيِّداً \ حَسَناً; the interview/trip was all right كانَت المُقابَلةُ \ الرِحْلةُ جَيِّدةً; (infml) sounds all right to me! حَسَناً! ,أنا مُوافِقٌ! **2** (well) to feel all right شَعَرَ أَنَّهُ بِخَيْرٍ \ على ما يُرامُ; she's all right هي على ما يُرامُ **3** (able to manage) will you be all right? هل سَتكونُ على ما يُرامُ؟ **4** (permissible) is it all right if ...? هَل هُناكَ مانِعٌ لو ...؟; would it be all right to leave early? هل هُناكَ مانِعٌ في المُغادَرةِ باكِراً؟; that's (quite) all right! لا بَأْسَ! ,لا عَلَيْكَ!

B *adv* (quite well) ‹to work, hear› مَقبولاً ,لا بَأْسَ بِهِ; she's doing all right هي بِخَيْرٍ \ على ما يُرامُ;

C *excl* **1** (expressing agreement) نَعَمْ ,حَسَناً; 'Would you like to help?' - 'all right' 'هل يُمْكِنُكَ المُساعَدةُ؟' – 'حَسَناً'; I want you to answer the questions, all right? أُريدُكَ أَنْ تُجيبَ على الأَسْئِلةِ، حَسَناً؟ **2** (introducing topic) إذاً ,حَسَناً; all right, let's move on to ... حَسَناً، لِنَنْتَقِلْ إلى ...

all-round (BrE) /ɔːl'raʊnd/, **all-around** (AmE) /ɔːlə'raʊnd/ *adj* ‹athlete, improvement› شامِل; he was a skilled ~ musician كانَ عازِفاً ماهِراً شامِلاً

all-rounder /ɔːl'raʊndə/ *n* to be a good ~ كانَ مُتَعَدِّدَ المَواهِبِ

All Saints' Day /ɔːl 'seɪnts deɪ/ *n* عيد جَميعِ القِدّيسينَ

all-terrain vehicle /ɔːltə,reɪn 'viːk(ə)l/ *n* سَيّارة للطُرُقِ الوَعْرةِ

all-time /ɔːl'tʌɪm/ *adj* ‹record› [أَبَداً]; he was one of Hollywood's ~ greats كانَ واحِداً من أَعْظَمِ عُظَماءِ هوليوود; this is an ~ record for the 100 metres هذا أَفْضَلُ رَقْمٍ مُسَجَّلٍ في سِباقِ المِائةِ مِترٍ أَبَداً

all told *adv* (in total) بِأَجْمَعِهِ ,كُلِّيّاً

allude /ə'l(j)uːd/ *vi* to ~ to sth/sb «article, author» لَمَّحَ إلى شَيْءٍ \ شَخْصٍ

alluring /ə'l(j)ʊərɪŋ/ *adj* ‹prospect, charm› مُغْوٍ ,مُغْرٍ

allusion /ə'luːʒ(ə)n/ *n* تَلْميح ,تَلْميحات (تَلاميحُ); to make (an) ~ to sth لَمَّحَ إلى شَيْءٍ

ally /'alʌɪ/ **A** *n* (*pl* allies) حَليف (حُلَفاءُ)

B /ə'lʌɪ/ *v refl* (allies, allying, allied) to ~ oneself with sb حالَفَ شَخْصاً

al-Madinah /almə'diːnə/ *pr n* المَدينة (المُنَوَّرة)

almanac, almanack /'ɔːlmənak/ *n* روزْنامة

almighty /ɔːl'mʌɪti/ *adj* **1** (omnipotent) ‹God, Allah› جَبّار (جَبابِرة ,جَبابِرُ ,جَبّارونَ) **2** (infml) (huge) ‹crash› هائِل; ‹row› عَنيف

Almohad /'alməhad/ *n* مُوَحِّد (من رَعايا دَوْلةِ المُوَحِّدينَ)

almond /'ɑːmənd/ *n* **1** (nut) لَوْز (n coll) **2** (also **almond tree**) شَجَرة لَوْزٍ

Almoravid /al'mɔːrəvɪd/ *n* مُرابط (من رَعايا دَوْلَةِ المُرابطين)

almost /ɔːlməʊst/ *adv* **1** (nearly) تَقْريباً; **~ any train will do** سَوْفَ يَفي أيُّ قِطارٍ تَقْريباً بالغَرَضِ; **we're ~ there** نَحْنُ على وَشْكِ الوُصولِ **2** (implying narrow escape) **he ~ died** كادَ أنْ يَموتَ

alms /ɑːmz/ *n pl* (old use) (donations to the poor) صَدَقة; (zakat) زَكاة

al-Nakba /al'nakbə/ *n* النَّكْبة

aloft /ə'lɒft/ *adv* ‹*to hold, stay*› عالِياً

alone /ə'ləʊn/ **A** *adj* **1** (on one's own) وَحْدَهُ, بِمُفْرَدِهِ; **he was ~ in Paris** كانَ في باريس بِمُفْرَدِهِ; **she was all ~ in the house** كانَتْ وَحْدَها تَماماً في المَنْزِلِ; **I'll leave you ~ now** سَوْفَ أتْرُكُكَ وَحْدَكَ الآنَ; **please leave him ~** من فَضْلِكَ، دَعْهُ في حالِهِ; **leave it ~!** اتْرُكْهُ وَشَأْنَهُ! **2** (for emphasis) **she ~ believed in him** وَحْدَهُ فَقَط; هي وَحْدَها فَقَطْ مَنْ كانَتْ تُؤْمِنُ بِهِ; **she is not ~ in thinking that ...** لَيْسَتْ هي فَقَطْ مَنْ تَعْتَقِدُ أنّ ...; **the house stands ~ in its own grounds** يَقِفُ المَنْزِلُ مُنْفَرِداً على أرْضِهِ الخاصّةِ; **I can't afford a bicycle, let ~ a car** لا أسْتَطيعُ شِراءَ دَرّاجةٍ، فما بالُكَ بِسَيّارةٍ

B *adv* **1** (on one's own) ‹*to live, travel*› وَحيداً, مُنْفَرِداً **2** (unaided) ‹*to manage, act*› بِمُفْرَدِهِ **3** (exclusively) **for this reason ~** لِهَذا السَّبَبِ فَقَطْ; **this figure ~ shows ...** هذا الشَّكْلُ وَحْدَهُ يُبَيِّنُ ...

Idiom **to go it alone** شَقّ طَريقَهُ بِنَفْسِهِ

along /ə'lɒŋ/ **A** *prep* بِمُحاذاةِ; **there were chairs ~ the wall** كانَتْ هُناكَ كَراسٍ بِمُحاذاةِ الجِدارِ; **to walk ~ the beach** مَشى على الشاطِئِ

B *adv* **1** (onwards) إلى الأمامِ; **the bakery is further ~, past the bank** المَخْبَزُ إلى الأمامِ، بعد البَنْكِ; **she told me the story as we walked ~** حَكَتْ لي القِصّةَ وَنَحْنُ نَمْشي **2** (with sb) **I'll be ~ in a minute** سَأكونُ عِنْدَكَ خلال دَقيقةٍ; **bring a friend ~ if you like** اصْطَحِبْ صَديقاً إنْ أحْبَبْتَ; **to come ~** وَصَلَ (وُصول); **come ~, we haven't got all day!** تَعالَ، لَيْس لَدَيْنا اليَوْمُ كُلُّهُ!

C (**along with**) *phr* (accompanied by) مَعَ

alongside /əlɒŋ'sʌɪd/ **A** *prep* **1** (next to) إلى \ بِجانِبِ, بِمُحاذاةِ; **to draw up ~ sb** مَرَّ إلى جانِبِ شَخْصٍ **2** (together with) مع; **to work ~ sb** عَمِلَ مع شَخْصٍ

B *adv* بِمُحاذاتِهِ, إلى \ بِجانِبِهِ; **to come ~** مَرَّ إلى جانِبِهِ

aloof /ə'luːf/ *adj* ‹*manner, politician*› مُتَحَفِّظ

aloud /ə'laʊd/ *adv* (audibly) بِصَوْتٍ مَسْموعٍ; **to read (sth) ~** قَرَأ (شَيْئاً) بِصَوْتٍ مَسْموعٍ

alpaca /al'pakə/ *n* (حَيَوان) الألْبَكة

alpha /'alfə/ *n* **1** (letter) ألْفا **2** (BrE Educ) (grade) امْتِياز; **to get an ~** حَصَلَ على دَرَجةِ امْتِيازٍ

alphabet /'alfəbɛt/ *n* ألِفْباء (f), أبْجَديّة, حُروف الهِجاءِ

alphabetical /alfə'bɛtɪk(ə)l/ *adj* ‹*list, index*› هِجائيّ, ألِفْبائيّ; **in ~ order** بِتَرْتيبٍ ألِفْبائيٍّ \ هِجائيٍّ

alphabetically /,alfə'bɛtɪkli/ *adv* أبْجَدِيًّا

alpha male *n* فَحْل (فُحول, فُحولة)

alpha particle *n* جُسَيْم ألْفا

alpha radiation *n* إشْعاع ألْفا

alpine, **Alpine** /'alpʌɪn/ *adj* ‹*scenery, flowers*› ألْبيّ

Alps /alps/ *pr n pl* (**the Alps**) جِبال الألْب

al-Qaeda /al'kʌɪdə/ *n* القاعِدة

already /ɔːl'rɛdi/ *adv* قَدْ; **it's 10 o'clock ~** قد حَلّت الساعةُ العاشِرةُ; **I've ~ had breakfast** قد تَناوَلْتُ فُطوري

alright /ɔːl'rʌɪt/ ▸ **all right**

Alsatian /al'seɪʃ(ə)n/ *n* (BrE) كَلْب الراعي الألْمانيّ

also /'ɔːlsəʊ/ *adv* **1** (as well) أيْضاً, كَذَلِكَ; **~ available in red** مُتوفِّر أيْضاً باللَّوْنِ الأحْمَرِ; **it is ~ worth remembering that ...** يَجْدُرُ كَذَلِكَ التَذَكُّر أنّ ... **2** (furthermore) عِلاوةً على ذلك, إضافةً \ بالإضافةِ إلى ذلك; **~, there wasn't enough to eat** عِلاوةً على ذلك، لم يَكُنْ هُناكَ ما يَكْفي من الطَّعامِ

altar /'ɔːltə/ *n* مَذْبَح (مَذابِحُ)

alter /'ɔːltə/ **A** *vt* **1** (to change) غَيَّرَ ‹*a text, sb's behaviour*›; **that doesn't ~ the fact that he lied** ذلك لا يُغَيِّرُ من حَقيقةِ كَوْنِهِ قد كَذَبَ **2** عَدَّلَ ‹*a garment*›; **you can have the trousers ~ed** يُمْكِنُكَ إجْراءُ تَعْديلاتٍ على السِّرْوالِ

B *vi* «places, people» تَغَيَّرَ

alteration /ɔːltəˈreɪʃ(ə)n/ **A** *n* **1** (of a text, to sb's plans) تَغْيير (تَغْييرات); **to make ~s (to sth)** أَدْخَل تَغْييراتٍ (على شَيْءٍ) **2** ‹*of a garment*› تَعْديل (تَعْديلات) **B** (**alterations**) *n pl* تَرْميمات

alternate **A** /ˈɔːltəneɪt/ *vt* ناوَبَ; **to ~ sth and** *or* **with sth** ناوَبَ بين شَيْءٍ وشَيْءٍ **B** /ˈɔːltəneɪt/ *vi* «worker, chairperson» تَناوَبَ; «colours, events» تَلاحَقَ **C** /ɔːlˈtəːnət/ *adj* **1** (successive) مُتَناوِب **2** (every other) مُتَناوِب; **on ~ days** في أَيّامٍ مُتَناوِبةٍ **3** (AmE) (alternative) بَديل (بَدائِل)

alternately /ɔːlˈtəːnətli/ *adv* بالتَناوُبِ; **we were ~ angry and amazed** غَضِبْنا مَرّةً وَانْدَهَشْنا مَرّةً أُخْرى

alternating /ˈɔːltəneɪtɪŋ/ *adj* ‹*layers, colours*› مُتَناوِب

alternating current *n* تَيّار مُتَرَدِّد \ مُتَناوِب

alternative /ɔːlˈtəːnətɪv/ **A** *adj* **1** (different) ‹*route, method, source*› آخَر, بَديل; **to make ~ arrangements** قامَ بِتَرْتيباتٍ بَديلةٍ \ أُخْرى **2** (unconventional) ‹*lifestyle, values*› بَديل, مُخالِف, مُغاير; **the interest in ~ medicine** الاهْتِمامُ بالطِبِّ البَديلِ **B** *n* بَديل (بَدائِل), خِيار; **what is the ~ to legal action?** ما هو البَديلُ عن الإجْراءِ القانونيِّ؟; **she had no ~ but to pay** لم يَكُنْ لَدَيْها خِيارٌ سِوى الدَفْعِ

alternative energy *n* طاقة بَديلة

alternatively /ɔːlˈtəːnətɪvli/ *adv* أَوْ, بَدَلاً من ذلك; **~, you can book by phone** أو بِإمْكانِكَ أَنْ تَحْجِزَ هاتِفيًّا

alternative medicine *n* طِبّ بَديل

although /ɔːlˈðəʊ/ *conj* **1** (despite the fact that) بالرَغْمِ من أَنّ, مع أنّ; **~ large, the apartment is too small for them** بالرَغْمِ من أنّ الشَقّةَ كَبيرةٌ، إلاّ أَنّها صَغيرةٌ بالنِسْبةِ لَهُمْ; **~ it may seem strange, it's true** على الرَغْمِ من أَنَّهُ قد يَبْدو غَريباً، إلاّ أَنَّهُ صَحيحٌ; **they are poor, ~ very generous** هُمْ فُقَراءُ، وبالرَغْمِ من ذلك فَهُمْ كُرَماءُ **2** (however) وَلَكِنْ, وَمَعَ ذلك; **you don't have to attend, ~ we do advise you to** لَسْتَ مُطالَباً بالحُضورِ، وَمَعَ ذلك نَنْصَحُكَ بالحُضورِ

altitude /ˈaltɪtjuːd/ *n* (of an aircraft, a mountain) الارْتِفاع فوق مُسْتَوى سَطْحِ البَحْرِ; **at an ~ of 20,000 ft** على ارْتِفاعِ 20,000 قَدَمٍ

alto /ˈaltəʊ/ *n* (*pl* **altos**) ألْتو (أَعْلى الأَصْواتِ في غِناءِ الرِجالِ)

altogether /ɔːltəˈgeðə/ *adv* **1** (completely) ‹*ridiculous, different*› تَماماً, كُلِّيّةً; **that's another matter ~** هذه مَسْأَلةٌ أُخْرى تَماماً; **that's not ~ true** لَيْسَ هذا صَحيحاً على الإطْلاقِ **2** (in total) إجْمالاً; **how much is that ~?** كم السِعْرُ إجْمالاً؟ **3** (all things considered) في مُجْمَلِهِ, على الإجْمالِ; **~, it was a mistake** كانَ هذا في مُجْمَلِهِ خَطَأً

aluminium (BrE) /aləˈmɪnɪəm/, **aluminum** (AmE) /əˈluːmɪnəm/ *n* ألومِنيوم

aluminium foil (BrE), **aluminum foil** (AmE) *n* وَرَق ألومِنيوم

alumna /əˈlʌmnə/ *n* (*pl* **alumnae**) (AmE) خِرّيجة

alumnus /əˈlʌmnəs/ *n* (*pl* **alumni** AmE) خِرّيج

always /ˈɔːlweɪz/ *adv* دائِما, على الدَوام, باسْتِمْرارٍ; **he's ~ complaining** هو يَشْكو \ يَتَذَمَّرُ على الدَوامِ

Alzheimer's, **Alzheimer's disease** /ˈaltshʌɪməz dɪˌziːz/ *n* مَرَض ألْزِهايْمَر

am /am/ ▸ **be**

a.m. /eɪˈem/ *adv* = **ante meridiem**; **three ~** الثالثة صَباحاً

Amal /əˈmɑːl/ *pr n* أَمَل (أَفْواج المُقاوَمةِ اللُبْنانيّةِ)

amalgamate /əˈmalgəmeɪt/ **A** *vt* ‹*companies, schools*› أَدْمَجَ **B** *vi* «companies, trade unions» انْدَمَجَ

amass /əˈmas/ *vt* (a; جَمْع) جَمَعَ ‹*information, a collection*›; كَدَّسَ ‹*a fortune*›; راكَمَ ‹*debts*›

amateur /ˈamətə/ **A** *n* **1** (athlete, musician) هاوٍ (هُواة) **2** (unskilled person) شَخْص تَعوزُهُ المَهارةُ \ الخِبْرةُ **B** *adj* ‹*footballer*› هاوٍ (هُواة); ‹*competition*› لِلْهُواةِ

amateur dramatics *n pl* المَسْرَح الهاوي

amaze /əˈmeɪz/ *vt* ‹*an audience, onlookers*› أَدْهَشَ

amazed /əˈmeɪzd/ *adj* ‹*expression, look*› انْدِهاشٍ, تَعَجُّبٍ; **I'm ~ (that)...** أنا مُنْدَهِشٌ (أَنّ) ...

amazement /əˈmeɪzm(ə)nt/ *n* دَهْشة

amazing /əˈmeɪzɪŋ/ *adj* ‹*story, player*› مُدْهِش

amazingly /əˈmeɪzɪŋli/ *adv* ‹*good, ignorant*› بِشَكْلٍ مُذْهِلٍ \ مُثير للدَهْشةِ; **to be ~ honest/simple** كانَ صادِقاً \ بَسيطاً بِشَكْلٍ مُثيرٍ للدَهْشةِ

Amazon /ˈaməz(ə)n/ *pr n* (**the Amazon**) الآمازون

ambassador /amˈbasədə/ *n* سَفير (سُفَراءُ); **the British A~ to the UAE** السفير البريطانيّ لدى الإماراتِ العَرَبيّةِ المُتَّحِدةِ

ambassador-at-large /amˈbasədərət,lɑːdʒ/ *n* (*pl* **ambassadors-at-large**) سَفير فوق العادةِ

amber /ˈambə/ *n* **1** (resin) كَهْرَمان **2** (BrE) (traffic signal) ضَوْء أَصْفَر

ambidextrous /,ambɪˈdɛkstrəs/ *adj* [قادِر على اسْتِخْدام اليَدَيْنِ بِنَفسِ المَهارة]

ambience /ˈambɪəns/ *n* (fml) جَوّ (أَجْواء)

ambient /ˈambɪənt/ *adj* ‹*temperature*› الجَوِّ المُحيطِ; ‹*noise*› مُحيط

ambiguity /ambɪˈgjuːɪti/ *n* (*pl* **ambiguities**) غُموض, اِلْتِباس

ambiguous /amˈbɪgjʊəs/ *adj* ‹*sentence, phrase*› مُلْتَبِس

ambition /amˈbɪʃ(ə)n/ *n* **1** [u] (characteristic) طُموح **2** (aim) طُموح (طُموحات)

ambitious /amˈbɪʃəs/ *adj* **1** ‹*politician, executive*› طَموح **2** ‹*plan, attempt*› طَموح

ambivalent /amˈbɪv(ə)l(ə)nt/ *adj* ‹*attitude, response*› مُتَضارِب

amble /ˈamb(ə)l/ *vi* **to ~ along** تَمَشّى

ambulance /ˈambjʊl(ə)ns/ *n* سَيّارة إسْعافٍ; **to call an ~** اتَّصَلَ بِسَيّارةِ إسْعافٍ

ambulance crew *n* طاقِم سَيّارةِ إسْعافٍ

ambulance driver *n* سائِق سَيّارةِ إسْعافٍ

ambulance man *n* سائِق سَيّارةِ إسْعافٍ

ambulance woman *n* [عامِلة في طاقِمِ سَيّارةِ إسْعافٍ]

ambush /ˈambʊʃ/ **A** *n* كَمين; **to lie in ~** كانَ في كَمينٍ **B** *vt* نَصَبَ كَميناً لِ ‹*a patrol, tourists*›

ameba (AmE) *n* (*pl* **amebae, amebas**) ▸ **amoeba**

amen /ɑːˈmɛn, eɪˈmɛn/ *excl* آمين

amenable /əˈmiːnəb(ə)l/ *adj* سَهْل الإقْناعِ; **to be ~ to an idea/a proposal** سَهُلَ إقْناعُهُ بِفِكْرةٍ \ باقْتِراحٍ

amend /əˈmɛnd/ *vt* عَدَّلَ ‹*a law, clause*›

amendment /əˈmɛn(d)m(ə)nt/ *n* (to a law, contract) تَعْديل (تَعْديلات)

amends /əˈmɛn(d)z/ *n pl* **to make ~ (to sb)** قامَ بِإرْضاءِ (شَخْصٍ); **to make ~ for the damage/suffering** عَوَّضَ عن الضَرَرِ \ المُعاناةِ

amenities /əˈmiːnɪtiːz/ *n pl* مَرافِق

America /əˈmɛrɪkə/ *pr n* **1** (country) أَمْريكا **2** (continental land mass) الأَمْريكَتانِ

American /əˈmɛrɪk(ə)n/ **A** *adj* **1** (of the US) ‹*embassy, troops*› أَمْريكيّ; **a slight ~ accent** لُكْنة أَمْريكيّة خَفيفة **2** (of the Americas) ‹*continent, tribes*› أَمْريكيّ
B *n* **1** (person) أَمْريكيّ **2** (also **American English**) الإنْجْليزيّة الأَمْريكيّة

American dream *n* (**the American dream**) الحُلْم الأَمْريكيّ

American football *n* كُرة القَدَمِ الأَمْريكيّة

American Indian *n* هِنْديّ أَحْمَر

amethyst /ˈaməθɪst/ *n* جَمَشْت, بَنَفْش

amiable /ˈeɪmɪəb(ə)l/ *adj* ‹*chat, gentleman*› لَطيف (لُطَفاءُ, لِطاف)

amicable /ˈamɪkəb(ə)l/ *adj* ‹*solution, agreement*› وِدّيّ

amid /əˈmɪd/, **amidst** /əˈmɪdst/ *prep* في ظِلِّ, وَسْطَ ‹*allegations, rumours*›; بَيْنَ, وَسْطَ ‹*wreckage, trees*›

amiss /əˈmɪs/ **A** *adj* **there is something ~, something is ~** هُناكَ شَيْءٌ خَطأٌ
B *adv* **to take sth ~** عَدَّ شَيْئاً إهانةً

Amman /əˈmɑːn/ *pr n* عَمّان (dipt f)

ammunition /amjʊˈnɪʃ(ə)n/ *n* ذَخيرة (ذَخائِرُ); **we ran out of ~** نَفِدَتْ ذَخيرَتُنا

ammunition dump *n* مَخْزَن ذَخيرةٍ

amnesia /amˈniːzɪə/ *n* فِقْدان الذاكِرةِ

amnesty /ˈamnɪsti/ *n* (*pl* **amnesties**) عَفْو عامّ

amniocentesis /,amnɪəʊsɛnˈtiːsɪs/ *n* (*pl* **amniocenteses** /-ˈtiːsiːz/) بَزْل السائِلِ الأَمْنِيوسيِّ

amniotic /amnɪ'ɒtɪk/ *adj* سَلَويّ

amoeba (BrE), **ameba** (AmE) /ə'mi:bə/ *n* (*pl* **amoebae, amoebas**) أميبا ,مُتَمَوِّرة ,مُتَحَوِّلة

amok /ə'mɒk/ *adv* **to run ~** «dogs, children» هاجَ (i; هَيْج, هَيَجان)

among /ə'mʌŋ/, **amongst** /ə'mʌŋst/ *prep* 1▸ (in the middle of, surrounded by) وَسْطَ; **~ the crowd** وَسْطَ الجُمْهورِ; **you're ~ friends** أَنْتَ وَسْطَ أَصْدِقاءَ 2▸ (one of) **~ the longest rivers in Asia** من بَيْنِ أَطْوَلِ الأَنْهارِ في آسْيا; **to be ~ the first to do sth** كانَ من بَيْنِ أوائِلِ القائِمينَ بِشَيْءٍ 3▸ (between) بَيْنَ; **sort it out ~ yourselves** تَصَرَّفوا فيما بَيْنَكُمْ 4▸ (affecting) وَسْطَ; **unemployment ~ young people** البَطالة وَسْطَ الشَبابِ

amortization, -isation (BrE) /ə,mɔ:tʌɪz'eɪʃ(ə)n/ *n* إطْفاء

amortize, -ise (BrE) /ə'mɔ:tʌɪz/ *vt* أَطْفَأَ, أَهْلَكَ ‹*an investment, cost*›

amount /ə'maʊnt/ *n* 1▸ (quantity: of goods, food) قَدْر (أَقْدار), كَمّيّة; **an enormous ~ of work remains to be done** لا يَزالُ هُناكَ قَدْرٌ \ كَمٌّ هائِلٌ من العَمَلِ يَجِبُ القِيامُ بِهِ; **add a small ~ of sugar** أَضِفْ مِقْداراً صَغيراً من السُكَّرِ; **small ~s of aid go a long way** كَمّيّاتٌ صَغيرةٌ من المُساعَداتِ تَكْفي لِمُدّةٍ مُعَيَّنةٍ; **I'm entitled to a certain ~ of recognition** أَسْتَحِقُّ قَدْراً مُعَيَّناً من التَقْديرِ 2▸ (infml) (number: of people, objects) عَدَد (أَعْداد); **a huge ~ of claims is processed each day** تَتِمُّ مُعايَنةُ عَدَدٍ كَبيرٍ من الشَكاوى كُلَّ يَوْمٍ 3▸ (of money) قيمة (قِيَم), مَبْلَغ (مَبالِغُ); **to charge sb the full ~** طَلَبَ من شَخْصٍ دَفْعَ المَبْلَغِ كامِلاً; **what is the outstanding ~?** ما هو المَبْلَغُ المُسْتَحَقُّ؟

(Phrasal verb) **amount to**: **~ to [sth]** 1▸ (to add up to) بَلَغَ [شَيْئاً] ‹*a total*›; **the costs ~ to $2000** وَصَلَت التَكاليفُ إلى $2000 2▸ (to equal) ساوى \ عادَلَ [شَيْئاً] ‹*a confession, triumph*›; **it ~s to the same thing** في كِلْتا الحالَتَيْنِ سَتَكونُ النَتيجةُ واحِدةً; **it doesn't ~ to much** لا يُساوي الكَثيرَ

amp /amp/ *n* 1▸ also = **ampere** أَمْبير 2▸ (infml) = **amplifier** مُكَبِّر (مُكَبِّرات), مُضَخِّم (مُضَخِّمات)

amphetamine /am'fɛtəmi:n/ *n* أَمْفيتامين

amphibian /am'fɪbɪən/ **A** *n* 1▸ (Zool) بَرْمائيّ (بَرْمائيّات) 2▸ (Aviat) طائِرة بَرْمائيّة; **the Catalina was a popular ~** كانَتْ طائِرةُ كاتالينا البَرْمائيّةُ تَحْظى بالشَعْبيّةِ **B** *adj* ▸ **amphibious**

amphibious /am'fɪbɪəs/ *adj* ‹*vehicle, animal*› بَرْمائيّ; **the frog is an ~ creature** الضِفْدَعُ مَخْلوقٌ بَرْمائيٌّ

amphitheatre (BrE), **amphitheater** (AmE) /'amfɪθi:ətə/ *n* مُدَرَّج (مُدَرَّجات)

ample /'amp(ə)l/ *adj* 1▸ ‹*evidence, supply*› وَفير; **there's ~ room** كانَتْ هُناكَ مُتَّسَعٌ من المَكانِ; **to have ~ opportunity to do sth** لَدَيْهِ فُرَصٌ كَثيرةٌ لِعَمَلِ شَيْءٍ 2▸ ‹*figure, bust*› ضَخْم (ضِخام), كَبير (كِبار, كُبَراءُ)

amplification /,amplɪfɪ'keɪʃ(ə)n/ *n* تَكْبير (تَكْبيرات), تَضْخيم

amplifier /'amplɪfʌɪə/ *n* مُكَبِّر (مُكَبِّرات), مُضَخِّم (مُضَخِّمات)

amplify /'amplɪfʌɪ/ *vt* (**amplifies, amplifying, amplified**) قَوّى ‹*electric current*›; كَبَّر, ضَخَّمَ ‹*a signal, sound*›

ampoule (BrE), **ampule** (AmE) /'ampu:l/ *n* أُمْبولة

amputate /'ampjʊteɪt/ *vt* بَتَرَ (u; بَتْر) ‹*a leg, limb*›

Amsterdam /,amstə'dam/ *pr n* أَمْسْتِرْدام (f)

Amtrak® /'amtrak/ *n* (AmE) شَرِكة أَمْتراك (للسِكَكِ الحَديديّةِ الأَمْريكيّةِ)

amulet /'amjʊlɪt/ *n* تَعْويذة (تَعاويذُ), تَميمة (تَمائِمُ), طِلَسْم (طَلاسِمُ)

amuse /ə'mju:z/ **A** *vt* 1▸ (to cause to laugh) سَلّى; **to be ~d at or by sth** تَسَلّى بِشَيْءٍ 2▸ (to entertain) «games, stories» سَلّى **B** *v refl* **to ~ oneself** تَسَلّى

amusement /ə'mju:zm(ə)nt/ *n* 1▸ (mirth) اسْتِمْتاع; **a look of ~** نَظْرة اسْتِمْتاعٍ 2▸ (entertainment) تَسْلِية; **for ~** لِلتَسْلِيةِ

amusement arcade *n* (BrE) صالة أَلْعابٍ

amusement park *n* مَدينة مَلاهٍ

amusing /ə'mju:zɪŋ/ *adj* 1▸ (funny) ‹*story, speaker*› مُسَلٍّ 2▸ (entertaining) ‹*pastime, activity*› مُسَلٍّ

an /an, ən/ ▸ **a**

anabolic steroids /,anəbɒlɪk 'stɪərɔɪds/ *n pl* اسْتيرويْدات ابْتِنائيّة

anachronism /ə'nakrənɪz(ə)m/ *n* مُفارَقة تاريخيّة

anaemia (BrE), **anemia** (AmE) /ə'ni:mɪə/ *n* أنيمْيا, فَقْر الدَمِ

anaemic (BrE), **anemic** (AmE) /əˈniːmɪk/ ***adj*** *‹patient, infant›* مُصاب بِفَقْرِ الدَمِ

anaesthesia (BrE), **anesthesia** (AmE) /ˌanɪsˈθiːzɪə/ ***n*** تَخْدير

anaesthetic (BrE), **anesthetic** (AmE) /ˌanɪsˈθɛtɪk/ ***n, adj*** مُخَدِّر; **to give sb a local/general ~** أَعْطى شَخْصاً مُخَدِّراً مَوْضِعِيًّا \ كُلِّيًّا

anaesthetist (BrE), **anesthetist** (AmE) /əˈniːsθətɪst/ ***n*** أَخِصّائيّ تَخْديرٍ

anaesthetize (BrE), **anesthetize** (AmE), **-ise** (BrE) /əˈniːsθətʌɪz/ ***vt*** بَنَّجَ, خَدَّرَ *‹a patient, an animal›*

anagram /ˈanəgram/ ***n*** جِناس تَصْحيفيّ

anal /ˈeɪn(ə)l/ ***adj*** ① (Anat) *‹region›* شَرَجيّ ② (Psych) *‹stage›* شَرَجيّ

analgesia /ˌan(ə)lˈdʒiːzɪə/ ***n*** فِقْدان الإحْساسِ بالألَم

analgesic /ˌan(ə)lˈdʒiːzɪk/ ***n*** مُسَكِّن (مُسَكِّنات)

analog (AmE) ▸ **analogue**

analogous /əˈnaləgəs/ ***adj*** *‹process, system›* مُماثِل

analogue (BrE), **analog** (AmE) /ˈanəlɒg/ ***n*** نَظير (نُظَراءُ; f pl نَظائِرُ), شَبيه (أشْباه), مَثيل (أَمْثال, مُثُل)

analogy /əˈnalədʒi/ ***n*** مُماثَلة, قِياس (قِياسات)

anal-retentive /eɪnəlrəˈtɛntɪv/ ***adj*** *‹personality›* أنيق بِشَكْلٍ مُبالَغ فيه

analyse (BrE), **analyze** (AmE) /ˈan(ə)lʌɪz/ ***vt*** ① حَلَّلَ *‹data, result, a sample›* ② (Psych) قامَ بِتَحْليلٍ نَفْسيٍّ لـ *‹a patient, client›*

analysis /əˈnalɪsɪs/ ***n*** (*pl* **analyses** /əˈnalɪsiːz/) تَحْليل (تَحْليلات, تَحاليل)

analyst /ˈan(ə)lɪst/ ***n*** ① (of data) مُحَلِّل (مُحَلِّلونَ) ② (Psych infml) مُحَلِّل (مُحَلِّلونَ)

analytic /anəˈlɪtɪk/, **analytical** /anəˈlɪtək(ə)l/ ***adj*** *‹tool, method›* تَحْليليّ

analyze (AmE) ***vt*** ▸ **analyse**

anaphylaxis /ˌanəfɪˈlaksɪs/ ***n*** حَسّاسيّة مُفْرِطة

anarchic /əˈnɑːkɪk/ ***adj*** ① (chaotic) *‹situation, society›* فَوْضَويّ ② (unconventional) *‹comedy, genius›* غَيْر مَأْلوفٍ

anarchism /ˈanəkɪz(ə)m/ ***n*** فَوْضَويّة

anarchist /ˈanəkɪst/ ***n, adj*** فَوْضَويّ

anarchy /ˈanəki/ ***n*** ① (chaos) فَوْضى (f) ② (Pol) فَوْضى (f)

Anatolia /ˌanəˈtəʊlɪə/ ***pr n*** الأناضول (f)

anatomy /əˈnatəmi/ ***n*** (*pl* **anatomies**) عِلْم التَشْريحِ

ancestor /ˈansɛstə/ ***n*** سَلَف (أَسْلاف)

ancestral /anˈsɛstr(ə)l/ ***adj*** *‹home, rights›* مَوْروث

ancestry /ˈansɛstri/ ***n*** أَسْلاف

anchor /ˈaŋkə/ **A** ***n*** ① (on a ship) مِرْساة (مَراسٍ), هِلْب (أَهْلاب); **to drop/weigh ~** أَلْقى \ رَفَع مِرْساةً ② (of TV show) مُقَدِّم بَرْنامَجٍ, مُذيع

B ***vi*** (Naut) رَسا (u; رُسُوّ)

C ***vt*** (Radio, TV) قَدَّمَ *‹a programme, show›*

anchorman /ˈaŋkəmən/ ***n*** (*pl* **-men**) مُذيع

anchorwoman /ˈaŋkəwʊmən/ ***n*** (*pl* **-women**) مُذيعة

anchovy /ˈantʃəvi/ ***n*** (*pl* **anchovies** or **anchovy**) بَلَم, سَنَمورة

ancient /ˈeɪnʃ(ə)nt/ ***adj*** ① *‹civilization, custom›* قَديم (قُدَماءُ, قُدامى); **the ~ Greeks** الإغْريق القُدَماء; **to study ~ history** دَرَسَ التاريخَ القَديمَ; **that's ~ history!** (infml) تِلْكَ قِصّةٌ أَكَلَ عَلَيْها الدَهْرُ وَشَرِبَ! ② (infml) *‹car, clothes›* مُهْتَرِئ

and /and, ənd/ ***conj*** و, فَ; **bread ~ butter** خُبْزٌ وَزُبْدة; **he stood up ~ walked out** قامَ وَخَرَجَ; **two hundred ~ sixty-two** مِائَتانِ وَاثْنانِ وَسِتّون; **faster ~ faster** أَسْرَع فَأَسْرَع

Andes /ˈandiːz/ ***n pl*** **the ~** جِبال الأَنْديز

Andorra /anˈdɔːrə/ ***pr n*** أَنْدورا

anecdotal /ˌanɪkˈdəʊt(ə)l/ ***adj*** *‹memoirs, account›* حَكائيّ; **~ evidence suggests that ...** توحي الأَدِلّةُ القَصَصيّةُ بِأَنَّ ...

anecdote /ˈanɪkdəʊt/ ***n*** نادِرة (نَوادِرُ), مُلْحة (مُلَح), طُرْفة (طُرَف)

anemia (AmE) /əˈniːmɪə/ ***n*** ▸ **anaemia**

anemic (AmE) ***adj*** ▸ **anaemic**

anemone /əˈnɛməni/ ***n*** شَقيق (n coll; شَقائِقُ)

anesthesia (AmE) ▸ **anaesthesia**

anesthetic (AmE) ***n, adj*** ▸ **anaesthetic**

anesthetist (AmE) ***n*** ▸ **anaesthetist**

anesthetize (AmE) ***vt*** ▸ **anaesthetize**

anew /əˈnjuː/ ***adv*** (liter) *‹to start, spring›* مِن جَديدٍ, مُجَدَّداً

angel /ˈeɪndʒ(ə)l/ *n* ① (of God) مَلاك (مَلائِكة) ② (kind person) مَلاك (مَلائِكة)

angelic /anˈdʒɛlɪk/ *adj* ‹voice, face› مَلائِكيّ

anger /ˈaŋɡə/ **A** *n* غَضَب; **words spoken in ~** كَلِمات قيلَتْ في لَحْظةِ غَضَبٍ

B *vt* أَغْضَبَ ‹a partner, colleague›

angina /anˈdʒʌɪnə/, **angina pectoris** /anˌdʒʌɪnə ˈpɛktərɪs/ *n* ذَبْحة صَدْريّة

angiogram /ˈandʒɪə(ʊ)ɡram/ *n* صورة وِعائيّة

angiography /ˌandʒɪˈɒɡrəfi/ *n* تَخْطيط \ تَصْوير الأَوْعِية

angioplasty /ˈandʒɪə(ʊ)ˌplasti/ *n* (*pl* **angioplasties**) رَأْب قَسْطَرة القَلْبِ, الوِعاءِ

angle /ˈaŋɡ(ə)l/ **A** *n* ① (between lines) زاوية (زَوايا); **a 60° ~** زاوية مِقْدارُها 60 دَرَجةً; **he was wearing his cap at an ~** كانَ يَرْتَدي قُبَّعَتَهُ بِشَكْلٍ مائِلٍ ② (point of view) زاوية (زَوايا), وِجْهة نَظَر; **we've looked at the problem from every ~** تَناوَلْنا المُشْكِلةَ من كُلِّ وِجْهةِ نَظَرٍ \ زاوِيةٍ ③ (of shot, kick) ضَرْبة زاوِيةٍ

B *vt* ① (to tilt) حَرَّفَ, أَمالَ ‹a camera, light› ② (to hit) سَدَّدَ في اتِّجاهٍ مُنْحَرِفٍ ‹the ball, a shot› ③ (to slant) [قَدَّمَ من وِجْهةِ نَظَرٍ مُعَيَّنةٍ] ‹an article, a programme›; **the programme is ~d at a middle-aged audience** البَرْنامَجُ مُوَجَّهٌ إلى جُمْهورٍ في مُتَوَسِّطِ العُمْرِ

C *vi* (infml) (to try to get) **to ~ for compliments/work** سَعى إلى سَماعِ الإِطْراءاتِ \ الحُصولِ على عَمَلٍ

angler /ˈaŋɡlə/ *n* صَيّاد سَمَكٍ

anglerfish /ˈaŋɡləfɪʃ/ *n* أَبو الشَّصّ

Anglican /ˈaŋɡlɪk(ə)n/ *n, adj* أَنْجْليكانيّ

angling /ˈaŋɡlɪŋ/ *n* رِياضة صَيْدِ السَّمَكِ

Anglo-French /ˌaŋɡləʊˈfrɛntʃ/ *adj* ‹team, relations› إِنْجْليزيّ – فَرَنْسيّ

Anglo-Saxon /aŋɡləʊˈsaks(ə)n/ **A** *adj* ‹times, England› أَنْجلوساكْسونيّ

B *n* ① (person) أَنْجلوساكْسونيّ ② (language) (اللُّغة) الأَنْجلوساكْسونيّة

Angola /aŋˈɡəʊlə/ *pr n* أَنْغولا

Angolan /aŋˈɡəʊlən/ *n, adj* أَنْغوليّ

angrily /ˈaŋɡrɪli/ *adv* ‹to react, speak› بِغَضَبٍ; **they were all shouting ~** كانوا كُلُّهُمْ يَصْرُخونَ بِغَضَبٍ

angry /ˈaŋɡri/ *adj* (**angrier, angriest**) ‹mob, scene, look› غاضِب; **to get ~** غَضِبَ (a; غَضَب); **to be ~ with sb** كانَ غاضِباً من شَخْصٍ

anguish /ˈaŋɡwɪʃ/ *n* كَرْب (كُروب), عَذاب (عَذابات, أَعْذِبة)

angular /ˈaŋɡjʊlə/ *adj* ‹features, shape› ذو زَوايا

animal /ˈanɪm(ə)l/ *n* ① (living creature) حَيَوان (حَيَوانات) ② (violent person) حَيَوان (حَيَوانات)

animal activist *n* ناشِط في مَجالِ حُقوقِ الحَيَوانِ

animal rights *n* حُقوق الحَيَوانِ

animal testing *n* إِجْراء التَّجارِبِ على الحَيَواناتِ

animate /ˈanɪmeɪt/ *vt* ① (Cin) حَرَّكَ ‹a film, character› ② (to enliven) أَحْيا ‹an evening, a debate›

animated /ˈanɪmeɪtɪd/ *adj* ① ‹film, cartoon› مُتَحَرِّك ② ‹conversation, face› حَيَويّ

animation /anɪˈmeɪʃ(ə)n/ *n* ① (Cin) رُسوم مُتَحَرِّكة ② (vivacity) حَيَويّة

animator /ˈanɪmeɪtə/ *n* رَسّام الرُسومِ المُتَحَرِّكةِ

animosity /ˌanɪˈmɒsɪti/ *n* (*pl* **animosities**) عَداء (عَداءات)

aniseed /ˈanɪsiːd/ *n* ① (flavour) نَكْهة اليانْسونِ ② (seed) بُذور اليانْسونِ

Ankara /ˈaŋk(ə)rə/ *pr n* أَنْقَرة

ankle /ˈaŋk(ə)l/ *n* كاحِل (كَواحِلُ); **to have a broken ~** كانَ لَدَيْهِ كَسْرٌ في الكاحِلِ

ankle chain *n* خَلْخال (خَلاخيلُ)

ankle sock *n* [جَوْرَب قَصير]

annex **A** /əˈnɛks/ *vt* ضَمَّ (u; ضَمّ), أَلْحَقَ ‹a country, territory›

B /ˈanɛks/ *n* (also **annexe** BrE) مُلْحَق (مُلْحَقات, مَلاحِقُ)

annihilate /əˈnʌɪleɪt/ *vt* دَمَّرَ ‹an enemy, a city›

anniversary /anɪˈvəːs(ə)ri/ *n* (*pl* **anniversaries**) ① (of an event) ذِكْرى سَنَويّة ② (of sb's wedding) ذِكْرى زَواجٍ

annotate /ˈanəteɪt/ *vt* عَلَّقَ بالحَواشي على ‹a text, manuscript›

announce /əˈnaʊns/ *vt* أَعْلَنَ ‹an intention, a result›

announcement /əˈnaʊnsm(ə)nt/ *n* 1 (spoken) إعلان (إعْلانات); **to make an ~** أَصْدَرَ إعْلاناً 2 (written) إعلان (إعْلانات)

announcer /əˈnaʊnsə/ *n* مُذيع, مُعْلِن

annoy /əˈnɔɪ/ *vt* أَزْعَجَ, ضايَقَ ‹*a customer, neighbour*›

annoyance /əˈnɔɪəns/ *n* 1 (feeling) ضيق, انْزِعاج; **her ~ at the committee's decision was obvious** كانَ انْزِعاجُها من قرارِ اللَجْنةِ واضِحاً 2 (nuisance) إزْعاج

annoyed /əˈnɔɪd/ *adj* ‹*look, tone*› مُنْزَعِج; **to get ~ with sb** انْزَعَجَ من شَخْصٍ

annoying /əˈnɔɪɪŋ/ *adj* ‹*habit, noise*› مُزْعِج

annual /ˈanjʊəl/ **A** *adj* سَنَوِيّ
B *n* 1 (plant) نَبات حَوْلِيّ 2 (book) حَوْلِيّة (كِتاب \ دَوْرِيّة سَنَوِيّ(ة))

annually /ˈanjʊəli/ *adv* ‹*to publish, review*› سَنَوِيًّا

annul /əˈnʌl/ *vt* (**-ll-**) أَلْغى ‹*an agreement*›; فَسَخَ (a; فَسْخ) ‹*a marriage*›

annulment /əˈnʌlm(ə)nt/ *n* (of an agreement) إلْغاء; (of a marriage) فَسْخ

anoint /əˈnɔɪnt/ *vt* مَسَحَ بالزَيْتِ المُقَدَّسِ ‹*a king, sb's feet*›

anomaly /əˈnɒm(ə)li/ *n* (*pl* **anomalies**) انْحِراف, شُذوذ (انْحِرافات), خُروج عن المَأْلوفِ

anonymity /anəˈnɪmɪti/ *n* مَجْهولِيّة

anonymous /əˈnɒnɪməs/ *adj* ‹*source, donor, letter*› مَجْهول

anorak /ˈanərak/ *n* [مِعْطَف مُشَمَّع]

anorexia /ˌanəˈrɛksɪə/, **anorexia nervosa** /anəˌrɛksɪə nəːˈvəʊsə/ *n* قَهَم, فِقْدان الشَهِيّةِ

anorexic /anəˈrɛksɪk/ **A** *adj* مُصاب بالقَهَمِ العُصابِيِّ; **she displayed classic ~ symptoms** ظَهَرَتْ عَلَيْها الأَعْراضُ الكْلاسيكيّةُ للقَهَمِ العُصابِيِّ
B *n* شَخْص مُصاب بالقَهَمِ العُصابِيِّ

another /əˈnʌðə/ **A** *determiner* 1 (additional) آخَر (f pl أُخْرَيات); **would you like ~ drink?** هَل تُريدُ مَشْروباً آخَرَ؟; **have ~ coffee** تَناوَلْ كوباً آخَرَ من القَهْوة; **we have received yet ~ bill** تَلَقَّيْنا فوق ذلك فاتورةً أُخْرى; **that will cost you ~ £50** سَيُكَلِّفُكَ ذلك 50 جُنَيْهاً أُخْرى; **they stayed ~ three hours** مَكَثوا لِثَلاثِ ساعاتٍ أُخْرى; **in ~ five weeks** خلال خَمْسةِ أَسابيعَ أُخْرى 2 (different) آخَر (f pl أُخْرَيات); **~ time** وَقْت آخَر; **he's found ~ job** لَقَدْ وَجَدَ وَظيفةً أُخْرى; **there's ~ way of doing it** هُناكَ طَريقةٌ أُخْرى لِفِعْلِه; **that's quite ~ matter** ذلك أَمْرٌ مُخْتَلِفٌ تَماماً 3 (new) **~ Garbo** [فَنّانة جَديدة مِثْل غاربو]; **~ Vietnam** [في مِثْلِ مَوْهِبةِ جارْبو فيتْنام أُخْرى]
B *pron* 1 (additional one) واحد آخَر; **can I have ~?** هل يُمْكِنُني أنْ أَحْصُلَ على واحِدٍ آخَرَ؟; **one after ~** واحد تِلْوَ الآخَرِ; **she tried on one hat after ~** جَرَّبَتْ قُبَّعةً تِلْوَ الأُخْرى 2 (different one) آخَر (f pl أُخْرَيات); **errors of one kind or ~** أَخْطاء من نَوْعٍ أو آخَرَ; **for one reason or ~ she won't ...** لِسَبَبٍ أو لآخَرَ هي لن ...; **~ of the witnesses said that ...** قالَ واحِدٌ آخَرُ من الشُهودِ إنّ ...

answer /ˈɑːnsə/ **A** *n* 1 (reply) جَواب, إجابة (أَجْوِبة), رَدّ (رُدود); **to get/give an ~** اسْتَلَمَ \ أَعْطى جَواباً; **there's no ~** (on the telephone) ما من رَدٍّ \ جَوابٍ; (to the door) ما من مُجيب; **in ~ to your question** رَدًّا على سُؤالِكَ 2 (in exams, tests) جَواب, إجابة (أَجْوِبة); **that is the right/wrong ~** ذلك هو الجَوابُ الصَحيحُ \ الخاطِئُ 3 (solution) حَلّ (حُلول); **there's no easy ~ to the problem** لَيْسَ هُناكَ حَلٌّ سَهْلٌ للمُشْكِلةِ
B *vt* 1 أَجابَ (على), رَدَّ (u; رَدّ; على) ‹*a question, letter, the telephone*›; **could you ~ the door?** هل يُمْكِنُكَ فَتْحُ البابِ؟ 2 رَدَّ (u; رَدّ; على) ‹*a charge, criticism*› 3 (to meet) وَفى (i; وَفاء; ب) ‹*a need, description*›
C *vi* 1 (to reply) أَجابَ 2 (to correspond) **to ~ to a description** طابَقَ الوَصْفَ

Phrasal verbs **answer back** (BrE) جاوَبَ بِفَظاظةٍ

• **answer for**: **~ for [sth]** (to account for) بَرَّرَ [شَيْئاً] ‹*one's action, crimes*›; **they have a lot to ~ for!** عَلَيْهِمْ تَبْريرُ الكَثيرِ من الأَشْياءِ!

• **answer to**: **~ to [sb]** (to be responsible to) كانَ مَسْؤولاً أمام [شَخْصٍ]

answerable /ˈɑːns(ə)rəb(ə)l/ *adj* مَسْؤول; **to be ~ to sb for sth** كانَ مَسْؤولاً أمام شَخْصٍ عن شَيْءٍ

answering machine /'ɑːnsərɪŋ məʃiːn/, **answerphone** /'ɑːnsəfəʊn/ (BrE) *n* جِهاز الرَدِّ الآليّ

ant /ant/ *n* نَمْل (n coll; نمال)

antagonize, -ise (BrE) /an'tag(ə)nʌɪz/ *vt* اسْتَعْدَى ‹*a government, colleague*›

Antarctic /an'tɑːktɪk/ **A** *pr n* (**the Antarctic**) القُطْب الجَنوبيّ **B** *adj* ‹*winter, ice cap*› قُطْبيّ جَنوبيّ

Antarctica /ant'ɑːktɪkə/ *pr n* أَنْتَرْكْتِكا

anteater /'antiːtə/ *n* آكِل نَمْلٍ

antecedent /,antɪ'siːd(ə)nt/ *n* سابِقة (سَوابِق, سابِقات)

antelope /'antɪləʊp/ *n* (*pl* **antelopes** or **antelope**) ريم

antenatal /antɪ'neɪt(ə)l/ *adj* ‹*care, clinic*› ما قبل الوِلادةِ

antenatal class *n* (BrE) دَرْس ما قبل الوِلادةِ

antenna /an'tɛnə/ *n* **1** (*pl* **antennae**) (of insects, crustaceans) مِجَسّ (مَجاسُّ, مِجَسّات) **2** (*pl* **antennas**) (for radio, TV) هَوائيّ

anterior /an'tɪərɪə/ *adj* أَماميّ

anthem /'anθəm/ *n* **1** (theme tune) نَشيد (أَناشيدُ) **2** (choral music) تَرْنيمة (تَرانيمُ)

anthology /an'θɒlədʒi/ *n* (*pl* **anthologies**) مُخْتارات

anthrax /'anθraks/ *n* الجَمْرة الخَبيثة

anthropologist /,anθrə'pɒlədʒɪst/ *n* مُخْتَصّ بالأَنْثروبولوجيا

anthropology /,anθrə'pɒlədʒi/ *n* عِلْم الإِنْسانِ, أَنْثروبولوجيا

anti /'anti/ *prep* ضِدَّ

anti- /'anti/ *prefix* **1** (opposed to) مُضادّ **2** (preventing) مُضادّ

anti-aircraft /,anti'ɛːkrɑːft/ *adj* ‹*gun, missile*› مُضادّ للطائِراتِ

antibacterial /,antɪbak'tɪərɪəl/ *adj* ‹*agent, soap*› مُضادّ للبَكْتيرْيا

antibiotic /,antɪbʌɪ'ɒtɪk/ *n* مُضادّ حَيَويّ; **to be on ~s** كانَ يَتَناوَلُ مُضادّاتٍ حَيَويّةً

antibody /'antɪbɒdi/ *n* (*pl* **antibodies**) جِسْم مُضادّ

anticipate /an'tɪsɪpeɪt/ *vt* **1** (to foresee) اسْتَبَقَ ‹*problems, delay*› **2** (to guess in advance) تَنَبَّأَ (ب) ‹*needs, consequences*›; **we can't ~ every possible outcome** لا نَسْتَطيعُ التَنَبُّأَ بِكُلِّ نَتيجةٍ مُمْكِنةٍ **3** (to pre-empt) اسْتَبَقَ ‹*a colleague, an event*›

anticipation /antɪsɪ'peɪʃ(ə)n/ *n* **1** (excitement) تَرَقُّب **2** (expectation) اسْتِباق; **thanking you in ~** أَشْكُرُكَ مُقَدَّماً

anticlimax /antɪ'klʌɪmaks/ *n* خَيْبة أَمَلٍ

anticlockwise /antɪ'klɒkwʌɪz/ *adj, adv* (BrE) عَكْسَ اتِّجاهِ عَقارِبِ الساعةِ

antics /'antɪks/ *n pl* (comical behaviour) تَصَرُّفات هَزْلِيّة \ تُثيرُ الضَحِكَ; (unpleasant behaviour) تَصَرُّفات سَخيفة

antidepressant /,antɪdɪ'prɛs(ə)nt/ *n* مُضادّ للاكْتِئابِ

antidote /'antɪdəʊt/ *n* تِرْياق

antifreeze /'antɪfriːz/ *n* مُضادّ للتَجَمُّدِ

antigen /'antɪdʒ(ə)n/ *n* مُسْتَضِدّ

antiglobalization, -isation (BrE) /anti,gləʊbəlʌɪ'zeɪʃ(ə)n/ *n* مُناهَضة العَوْلَمةِ

anti-hero /'antihiːrəʊ/ *n* (*pl* **-roes**) بَطَل مُزَيَّف

antihistamine /antɪ'hɪstəmɪn/ *n* مُضادّ الهيسْتامين

anti-nuclear /antɪ'njuːklɪə/ *adj* مُناهِض للأَسْلِحةِ النَوَوِيّةِ; **~ protests/protestors** احْتِجاجات \ مُحْتَجّونَ ضدَّ الأَسْلِحةِ النَوَوِيّةِ

antipathy /an'tɪpəθi/ *n* (*pl* **antipathies**) نُفور

anti-personnel /antipəːsə'nɛl/ *adj* (Mil) مُضادّ للأَشْخاصِ; **an ~ mine** لَغَم مُضادّ للأَشْخاصِ

antiperspirant /antɪ'pəːspɪrənt/ *n* مُضادّ التَعَرُّقِ

antipruritic /,antɪprʊ'rɪtɪk/ *adj* ‹*agent*› مُضادّ للحِكّةِ

antiquarian /,antɪ'kwɛːrɪən/ **A** *adj* أَثَريّ; **~ bookshop** مَتْجَر كُتُبٍ أَثَرِيّةٍ \ نادِرةٍ **B** *n* (dealer in antiques) تاجِر عادِيّاتٍ, بائِع أَثَرِيّاتٍ; (dealer in books) تاجِر كُتُبٍ قَديمةٍ \ نادِرةٍ; (collector) جامِع أَثَرِيّاتٍ

antique /an'tiːk/ **A** *n* عادِيّة **B** *adj* ‹*furniture, jewellery*› عَتيق

antique dealer *n* تاجِر عادِيّاتٍ

antique shop *n* مَتْجَر عادِيّاتٍ

antiquity /an'tɪkwɪti/ *n* (*pl* **antiquities**) **1** [u] (ancient times) العُصور القَديمة **2** [u] (age) قِدَم, عِتْق **3** (relic) أَثَر (آثار), عادِيّة

anti-roll bar /anti'rəʊl bɑː/ *n* قَضيب مانِع للانْقِلابِ \ للتَدَحْرُجِ

anti-Semitic /ˌantɪsɪˈmɪtɪk/ *adj* ‹*remarks, incident*› لاساميّ

anti-Semitism /antiˈsɛmətiz(ə)m/ *n* مُعاداة اليَهودِ, لاساميّة

antiseptic /antɪˈsɛptɪk/ *n* مُطَهِّر

antisocial /antɪˈsəʊʃ(ə)l/ *adj* 1 (unacceptable) ‹*behaviour*› غَيْر اجْتِماعيّ 2 (reclusive) ‹*person*› مُضادّ \ مُعادٍ للمُجْتَمَعِ

anti-theft /ˌantɪˈθɛft/ *adj* ‹*lock, device*› مُضادّ للسَرِقةِ

antithesis /anˈtɪθəsɪs/ *n* (*pl* **antitheses**) نَقيض

antiviral /antɪˈvʌɪr(ə)l/ *adj* ‹*agent, drug*› مُضادّ للفَيْروساتِ; **four ~ drugs have been approved for the treatment of influenza** تَمَّت المُوافَقةُ على أَرْبَعةِ أَدْوِيةٍ مُضادّةٍ للفَيْروساتِ لِمُعالَجةِ الإنْفِلوَنْزا

anti-virus software /antiˈvʌɪrəs sɒftwɛː/ *n* برامِج الحِمايةِ من \ مُكافَحةِ الفَيْروساتِ

anti-war /ˌantiˈwɔː/ *adj* ‹*protesters, movement*› مُناهِض للحَرْبِ

antlers /ˈantləz/ *n pl* قُرون الأيِّل

anus /ˈeɪnəs/ *n* فُتْحة الشَرَج

anvil /ˈanvɪl/ *n* سِنْدان (سَنادينُ)

anxiety /aŋˈzʌɪəti/ *n* (*pl* **anxieties**) 1 (worry) قَلَق 2 [u] (eagerness) **~ to do sth** تَوْق \ تَلَهُّف لِفِعْلِ شَيْءٍ 3 (in psychology) حَصْر نَفْسيّ

anxiety attack *n* نَوْبة حَصْرٍ نَفْسيٍّ

anxious /ˈaŋ(k)ʃəs/ *adj* 1 (worried) ‹*parents, passengers*› قَلِق; **to be ~ about doing sth** قَلِقَ بِشَأْنِ القِيامِ بِشَيْءٍ 2 (worrying) ‹*moment, thoughts*› مُقْلِق 3 (eager) تَوّاق; **to be ~ to do sth** تاقَ إلى القِيامِ بِشَيْءٍ

anxiously /ˈaŋkʃəsli/ *adv* ‹*to wait, look*› بِقَلَقٍ

any /ˈɛni/ **A** *determiner* 1 **I don't want ~ breakfast** لا أُريدُ أَيَّ إفْطارٍ; (with negative, implied negative) **he hasn't got ~ money/coins** لَيْسَ لَدَيْهِ أَيُّ مالٍ \ عُمْلاتٍ مَعْدَنيّةٍ; **they hardly ate ~ cake/biscuits** بالكادِ أَكَلوا من الكَعْكةِ \ البَسْكويت 2 (in questions, conditional sentences) **is there ~ tea/bread?** هل هُناكَ أَيُّ شايٍ \ خُبْزٍ؟; **are there ~ eggs/figs?** هل هُناكَ أَيُّ بَيْضٍ \ تينٍ؟; **if you have ~ doubts, contact ...** إذا كانَ لَدَيْكَ أَيُّ شَكٍّ، اتَّصِلْ ب ... 3 (no matter which) أَيّ; **~ kind/pencil will do** أَيُّ نَوْعٍ \ قَلَمِ رَصاصٍ سَيَفي بالغَرَضِ; **you can have ~ cup** *or* **cups you like** يُمْكِنُكَ أنْ تَحْصُلَ على أَيِّ كوبٍ \ أَكْوابٍ تُريدُ; **~ information would be very useful** أَيُّ مَعْلوماتٍ سَتكونُ مُفيدةً جدًّا; **~ teacher will tell you the same thing** أَيُّ مُدَرِّسٍ سَيقولُ لَكَ نَفْسَ الشَيْءِ; **he might return at ~ time, he might return ~ time** قد يَعودُ في أَيِّ وَقْتٍ; **~ one of you could have done it** كانَ بِإمْكانِ أَيٍّ واحِدٍ مِنْكُمْ أنْ يَفْعَلَهُ; **you can only withdraw $400 at ~ one time** يُمْكِنُكَ أنْ تَسْحَبَ 400 دولاراً فَقَطْ في أَيِّ عَمَليّةِ سَحْبٍ واحِدةٍ

B *pron* 1 (with negative, implied negative) **he doesn't have ~, he hasn't got ~** لَيْسَ لَدَيْهِ أَيٌّ مِنْهُ; **there is hardly ~ left** لم يَتَبَقَّ تَقْريباً أَيٌّ مِنْهُ; **there aren't ~ others** لا يوجَدُ غَيْرُهُمْ; **she doesn't like ~ of them** لا يُعْجِبُها أَيٌّ مِنْهُمْ 2 (in questions, conditional sentences) **I'd like some tea, if you have ~** أُريدُ بَعْضَ الشاي، إذا كانَ لَدَيْكَ أَيٌّ مِنْهُ; **have you got ~?** هل لَدَيْكَ أَيٌّ مِنْهُ؟; **have ~ of you got a car?** هل لدى أَيٍّ مِنْكُمْ سَيّارةٌ؟; **are ~ of them blue?** هل أَيٌّ مِنْهُم أَزْرَقُ؟; **we have very few left, if ~** بَقِيَ لَدَيْنا القَليلُ جِدًّا، هذا إذا بَقِيَ شَيْءٌ أَصْلاً; **if we have ~, they'll be over there** إذا كانَ لَدَيْنا أَيٌّ مِنْهُمْ، فَسَيَكونونَ هُنالِكَ 3 (no matter which) أَيّ; **~ of them could do it** يُمْكِنُ لِأَيٍّ مِنْهُمْ أنْ يَفْعَلَهُ; **~ of those pencils** أَيّ من أَقْلامِ الرَصاصِ تِلْكَ; **'which colour would you like?'—'~'** 'أَيَّ لَوْنٍ تُريدُ؟' — 'أَيَّ واحِدٍ'

C *adv* 1 (with comparatives) **can't you walk ~ faster?** أَلا يُمْكِنُكَ السَيْرُ أَسْرَعَ من ذلك؟; **there isn't ~ better lawyer in the country** لَيْسَ هُناكَ أَيُّ مُحامٍ أَفْضَلَ مِنْهُ في البَلَدِ; **is he feeling ~ better?** هل يَشْعُرُ بِأَيِّ تَحَسُّنٍ؟; **have you got ~ more of these?** هل لَدَيْكَ المَزيدُ من هذه؟; **do you want ~ more wine?** هل تُريدُ المَزيدَ من الخَمْرِ؟; **we can't pay you ~ more than $15 an hour** لا يُمْكِنُنا أنْ نَدْفَعَ لَكَ أَكْثَرَ من 15 دولاراً في الساعةِ; **I don't like him ~ more than you do** كُرْهي لَهُ لا يَقِلُّ عن كُرْهِكَ إيّاهُ; **he doesn't live here ~ more** *or* **longer** لم يَعُدْ يَعيشُ هُنا; **if it gets ~ hotter in here I shall have to leave** إذا اشْتَدَّتِ الحَرارةُ هُنا سَأُضْطَرُّ للمُغادَرةِ; **I can't leave ~ later than 6 o'clock** لا أَسْتَطيعُ التَأَخُّرَ أَكْثَرَ من ال6 تَماماً 2 (infml) (at all) على الإطْلاقِ; **that doesn't help me ~** ذلك لا يُساعِدُني على الإطْلاقِ

anybody /ˈɛnɪbɒdi/ *pron* 1▸ (with negative, implied negative) أَيّ شَخصٍ ,أَحَد; **there wasn't ~ in the house/car** لم يَكُنْ هُناكَ أَحَدٌ في البَيْتِ \ السَّيّارةِ; **there's never ~ at home** لَيْسَ هُناكَ أَبَداً أَيُّ شَخصٍ في البَيْتِ; **without ~ knowing** دون أنْ يَعْلَمَ أَحَدٌ; **I didn't have ~ to talk to** لم يَكُنْ لَدَيَّ أَيُّ شَخْصٍ أَتَحَدَّثُ مَعَهُ; **hardly ~ came** تَقْريباً لم يَأْتِ أَحَدٌ; **there wasn't ~ there** لم يَكُنْ هُنالِكَ أَحَدٌ 2▸ (in questions, conditional sentences) أَحَد; **is there ~ in the house?** هل هُناكَ أَحَدٌ في البَيْتِ؟; **did ~ see him?** هل رَآهُ أَحَدٌ؟; **if ~ asks, tell them I've gone out** إذا سَأَلَ أَحَدٌ، فَقُلْ إنّي قد خَرَجْتُ; **is ~ nice/interesting coming?** هل سَيأْتي أَحَدٌ لَطيفٌ \ مُثيرٌ للاهْتِمام؟ 3▸ (no matter who) **~ could do it** يُمْكِنُ لِأَيِّ شَخْصٍ أنْ يَفْعَلَهُ; **~ but him/you/his wife** أَيّ شَخْصٍ إلاّ هو \ أَنْتَ \ زَوْجَتَهُ; **~ can make a mistake** يُمْكِنُ لأيِّ شَخْصٍ أنْ يُخْطِئَ; **~ would think you were deaf** أَيُّ شَخْصٍ سَيَعْتَقِدُ أَنَّكَ كُنْتَ أَصَمًّا; **you can invite ~ you like** يُمْكِنُكَ أنْ تَدْعُوَ أَيَّ شَخْصٍ تُريدُ 4▸ (somebody unimportant) **she's not just ~: she's the boss** هي لَيْسَتْ أَيَّ شَخْصٍ: إنّما هي الرَّئيسةُ; **we can't ask just ~ to do it: we need an electrician** لا يُمْكِنُنا أنْ نَسْأَلَ أَيَّ شَخْصٍ أنْ يَفْعَلَهُ: بَلْ نَحْتاجُ كَهْرَبائِيًّا 5▸ (somebody important) **~ who was ~ was at the ceremony** كُلُّ الأَشْخاصِ ذَوي المَكانةِ الرَّفيعةِ كانوا في الحَفْلِ ▸ **guess**

anyhow /ˈɛnɪhaʊ/ *adv* 1▸ (in any case) ▸ **anyway** 2▸ (in a disorderly way) كَيْفَما اتَّفَقَ ,بِشَكْلٍ غَيْرِ مُنَظَّمٍ; **papers were scattered ~ over the desk** كانَتِ الأَوْراقُ مُتَناثِرةً على المَكْتَبِ بِشَكْلٍ غَيْرِ مُنَظَّمٍ; **they slapped the paint on just ~** لَطَّخوهُ بالطِلاءِ بِشَكْلٍ عَشْوائِيٍّ

anyone /ˈɛnɪwʌn/ *pron* ▸ **anybody**

anyplace /ˈɛnɪpleɪs/ *adv* (AmE) ▸ **anywhere**

anything /ˈɛnɪθɪŋ/ *pron* 1▸ (with negative, implied negative) أَيّ شَيْءٍ; **she didn't say/do ~** لم تَقُلْ \ تَفْعَلْ أَيَّ شَيْءٍ; **they never do ~** لا يَفْعَلونَ أَيَّ شَيْءٍ مُطْلَقاً; **he didn't have ~ to do** لم يَكُنْ لَدَيْهِ أَيُّ شَيْءٍ يَفْعَلُهُ; **she doesn't want ~ (too) expensive/cheap** هي لا تُريدُ أَيَّ شَيْءٍ غالٍ \ رَخيصٍ (جِدًّا); **there was hardly ~ left** لم يَتَبَقَّ هُناكَ تَقْريباً أَيُّ شَيْءٍ; **don't believe ~ he says** لا تُصَدِّقْ أَيَّ شَيْءٍ يَقولُهُ 2▸ (in questions, conditional sentences) أَيّ شَيْءٍ; **is there ~ in the fridge?** هل هُناكَ أَيُّ شَيْءٍ في الثَلاّجةِ؟; **is ~ the matter?** ما الخَطْبُ؟; **have you got ~ in blue/red?** هل لَدَيْكَ أَيُّ شَيْءٍ لَوْنُهُ أَزْرَقُ \ أَحْمَرُ؟; **if ~ happens** *or* **should happen to her** إذا حَدَثَ أَيُّ شَيْءٍ لَها; **is there ~ to be done?** هل هُناكَ أَيُّ شَيْءٍ يُمْكِنُ فِعْلُهُ؟; **is there ~ in the rumour that ...?** هل هُناكَ أَيُّ أَساسٍ للإشاعةِ الّتي تَقولُ إنّ ...؟ 3▸ (no matter what) أَيّ شَيْءٍ; **we eat ~** نَحْنُ نَأْكُلُ أَيَّ شَيْءٍ; **they'd do ~ for you** سَيَفْعَلونَ أَيَّ شَيْءٍ من أَجْلِكَ; **~ is possible** أَيُّ شَيْءٍ مُمْكِنٌ; **you can have ~ you like** يُمْكِنُكَ أنْ تَحْصُلَ على أَيِّ شَيْءٍ يُعْجِبُكَ; **I'd do** *or* **give ~ to get that job** سَأَفْعَلُ أَيَّ شَيْءٍ لِأَحْصُلَ على تِلْكَ الوَظيفةِ; **she likes ~ to do with horses** هي تُحِبُّ أَيَّ شَيْءٍ لَهُ عَلاقةٌ بالخَيْلِ; **it could cost ~ between $150 and $250** سَيَكونُ سِعْرُهُ أَيَّ مَبْلَغٍ بين 150$ وَ250$; **he was ~ but happy/a liar** لم يَكُنْ سَعيداً \ كَذّاباً أَبداً; **'was it interesting?'—'~ but!'** 'هل كانَ مُثيراً للاهْتِمام؟' — 'لا، على الإطْلاقِ!'; **he wasn't annoyed, if ~, he was quite pleased** لم يَكُنْ مُتَضايقاً، بَلْ كانَ سَعيداً جِدًّا

(Idiom) **anything goes** أَيُّ شَيْءٍ مُباحٌ

anytime /ˈɛnɪtʌɪm/ *adv* (also **any time**) مَتى ما; **come ~ you like** تَعالَ مَتى ما أَحْبَبْتَ

anyway /ˈɛnɪweɪ/ *adv* 1▸ (in any case, besides) على أَيِّ حالٍ; **I was planning to do that ~** كُنْتُ أُخَطِّطُ للقِيامِ بِذَلِكَ على أَيِّ حالٍ; **I don't want to go, and ~ I have to look after Dad** لا أُريدُ أنْ أَذْهَبَ، وَعلى أَيِّ حالٍ يَجِبُ عَلَيَّ أنْ أَرْعى والِدي; **why do you want to know, ~?** وَعَلى أَيِّ حالٍ، لِماذا تُريدُ أنْ تَعْرِفَ؟ 2▸ (nevertheless) على أَيِّ حالٍ; **thanks ~** شُكْراً على أَيِّ حالٍ; **you may not like it, but I'm going ~** قد لا يُعْجِبُكَ هذا، وَلَكِنّي ذاهِبٌ على أَيِّ حالٍ 3▸ (at least, at any rate) على الأَقَلِّ; **we can't go, not yet ~** لا يُمْكِنُنا أنْ نَذْهَبَ، لَيْسَ بَعْدُ على الأَقَلِّ; **until recently ~, the accepted view was ...** حَتّى وَقْتٍ قَريبٍ على الأَقَلِّ، كانَ الرَّأْيُ المَقْبولُ هو ... 4▸ (well: as sentence adverb) **~, we got to the departure lounge ...** وَعَلى كُلِّ حالٍ، وَصَلْنا إلى صالةِ المُغادَرةِ ...; **~, I'd better go now** وَعَلى كُلِّ حالٍ، من الأَفْضَلِ أنْ أُغادِرَ الآنَ

anywhere /ˈɛnɪwɛː/ *adv* **1** (with negative, implied negative) **you can't go ~** لا يُمْكِنُكَ الذَهابُ إلى أيِّ مَكانٍ; **there isn't ~ to sit/sleep** لَيْسَ هُناكَ أيُّ مَكانٍ للجُلوسِ \ للنَوْمِ; **we didn't go ~ special/interesting** لم نَذْهَبْ إلى أيِّ مَكانٍ خاصٍّ \ مُثيرٍ للاهْتِمامِ; **I can't find my keys ~** لا أَسْتَطيعُ العُثورَ على مَفاتيحي في أيِّ مَكانٍ; **complaining isn't going to get you ~** لن تُجْديكَ الشَكْوى شَيْئاً **2** (in questions, conditional sentences) في \ إلى أيِّ مَكانٍ; **have you seen Andrew ~?** هل رَأَيْتَ أَنْدرو في أيِّ مَكانٍ؟; **have you got a screwdriver/a comb ~?** هل لَدَيْكَ مِفَكٌّ \ مُشْطٌ في أيِّ مَكانٍ؟; **did you go ~ nice?** هل ذَهَبْتَ إلى أيِّ مَكانٍ جَميلٍ؟; **we're going to Spain, if ~** إذا ذَهَبْنا إلى أيِّ مَكانٍ، فَسَيَكونُ إسْبانيا **3** (no matter where) **~ you like** أَيْنَما تُحِبُّ; **you can buy it ~** يُمْكِنُكَ أنْ تَشْتَرِيَهُ من أيِّ مَكانٍ; **~ in the world/in Europe** أيّ مَكانٍ في العالَمِ \ أوروبّا; **~ except** *or* **but Birmingham** أيّ مَكانٍ إلا بِرْمِنْجْهام; **~ she goes, he follows her** يَتْبَعُها أَيْنَما تَذْهَبُ; **~ between 50 and 100 people** فيما بين 50 و100 شَخْصٍ

aorta /eɪˈɔːtə/ *n* وَتين, أَوْرْطى

apace /əˈpeɪs/ *adv* (liter) ‹*to continue, grow*› بِسُرْعةٍ

apart /əˈpɑːt/ **A** *adj, adv* **1** (at a distance in time or space) **place the posts three metres ~** ضَع العَواميدَ على بُعْدِ ثَلاثةِ أَمْتارٍ عن بَعْضِها البَعْض; **the babies were born 2 weeks ~** وُلِدَ الأَطْفالُ بِفارِقِ أُسْبوعَيْنِ; **the houses were far ~** كانَت البُيوتُ بَعيدةً عن بَعْضِها; **he stood ~ from the group** وَقَفَ بِمَعْزِلٍ عن المَجْموعةِ **2** (separated) مُنْفَصِل; **we hate being ~** نَكْرَهُ البُعْدَ عن بَعْضِنا البَعْض; **keep them ~** افْصِلْهُمْ; **they live in a world ~** يَعيشونَ في عالَمٍ مُخْتَلِفٍ تماماً (يَتَمَيَّزُ بِمُنْتَهى الرَفاهِيةِ) **3** (leaving aside) بِصَرْفِ \ بِغَضِّ النَظَرِ عن; **cats ~, I don't like animals** باسْتِثْناءِ القِطَطِ، فَأَنا لا أُحِبُّ الحَيَواناتِ

B (**apart from**) *prep phr* **1** (separate from) بِمَعْزِلٍ عن; **it stands ~ from the other houses** يَقَعُ بِمَعْزِلٍ عن البُيوتِ الأُخْرى; **he lives ~ from his wife** يَعيشُ مُنْفَصِلاً عن زَوْجَتِهِ **2** (except for) باسْتِثْناءِ; **~ from swimming, no other sports are available** باسْتِثْناءِ السِباحةِ، لا تَتَوَفَّرُ أيُّ رِياضاتٍ أُخْرى **3** (leaving aside) إلى جانِبِ; **~ from being illegal, it's also dangerous** إلى جانِبِ عَدَمِ شَرْعِيَّتِهِ، فَهُوَ أَيْضاً خَطيرٌ

apartheid /əˈpɑːtheɪt/ *n* عَزْل عُنْصُريّ, أَبارتْهايْد

apartment /əˈpɑːtm(ə)nt/ *n* شِقّة (شِقَق)

apartment building, **apartment house** (AmE) *n* عِمارة (عَمائِرُ, عِمارات)

apathetic /apəˈθɛtɪk/ *adj* ‹*voters, attitude*› لا \ غَيْر مُبالٍ

apathy /ˈapəθi/ *n* عَدَم الاكْتِراثِ \ الاهْتِمامِ, لامُبالاة, هُمود

ape /eɪp/ **A** *n* **1** قِرْد (قِرَدة, قُرود); **female ~** أُنْثى القِرْدِ; **the higher ~s** القِرَدة العُلْيا **2** (person) قِرْد (قِرَدة, قُرود)

B *vt* قَلَّدَ ‹*speech, behaviour, manners*›; **she ~s the manners of her friends** هي تُقَلِّدُ أَساليبَ أَصْدِقائِها

aperitif /əˈpɛrɪtiːf/ *n* [مَشْروب مُشَهٍّ]

aperture /ˈapətʃə/ *n* **1** (in a wall, door) فُتْحة (فُتَح, فُتْحات) **2** (Phot) فُتْحة (فُتَح, فُتْحات), مَنْفَذ (مَنافِذُ), ثُقْب (أَثْقاب, ثُقوب) ثُقْب (ثُقوب)

apex /ˈeɪpɛks/ *n* (*pl* **apexes, apices**) قِمّة (قِمَم)

Apex /ˈeɪpɛks/ *n* = **Advance Purchase Excursion** أَبيكْس (رِحْلات مُخَفَّضة مَدْفوعة مُقَدَّماً)

aphid /ˈeɪfɪd/ *n* قَمْل نَباتٍ, مَنّ; **now is the time to spray against ~s** حانَ الآنَ وَقْتُ الرَشِّ ضِدّ المَنِّ

aphis /ˈeɪfɪs/ *n* (*pl* **aphides**) قَمْل نَباتٍ, مَنّ

aphrodisiac /afrəˈdɪzɪak/ *n* ناعوظ

apiece /əˈpiːs/ *adv* **1** (for each person) لِكُلِّ فَرْدٍ **2** (with prices) للقِطْعة الواحدة

apocalypse /əˈpɒkəlɪps/ *n* أَحْداث جِسام; **the A~** (Chr) سِفْر الرُؤْيا; (Islam) رُؤْيا غَيْبيّة

apolitical /eɪpəˈlɪtɪk(ə)l/ *adj* ‹*writing, publication, person*› غَيْر مُهْتَمٍّ \ لا يَهْتَمُّ بالسِياسةِ; **I'm completely ~** أنا لا أَهْتَمُّ مُطْلَقاً بالسِياسةِ; **the campaign is ~** الحَمْلةُ لَيْسَتْ سِياسيّةً

apologetic /əpɒləˈdʒɛtɪk/ *adj* ‹*smile, letter*› اعْتِذارٍ; **to be ~ about the delay** أَبْدى اعْتِذارَهُ بِشَأْنِ التَأْخيرِ; **she gave me an ~ smile** ابْتَسَمَتْ لي ابْتِسامةَ اعْتِذارٍ

apologize, -ise (BrE) /əˈpɒlədʒʌɪz/ *vi* «speaker, letter» اعْتَذَرَ; **to ~ for arriving late** اعْتَذَرَ لِوُصولِهِ مُتَأَخِّراً

apology /əˈpɒlədʒi/ *n* (*pl* **apologies**) اعْتِذار (اعْتِذارات); **to make an ~** قَدَّمَ اعْتِذاراً; **I think I owe you an ~** أَعْتَقِدُ بِأَنَّني مَدينٌ لَكَ باعْتِذارٍ

apostasy /əˈpɒstəsi/ *n* رِدّة

apostate /ˈapəsteɪt/ *n* مُرْتَدّ

apostle /əˈpɒs(ə)l/ *n* حَوارِيّ

apostrophe /əˈpɒstrəfi/ *n* فاصِلة عُلْيا

app /ap/ (infml) *n* ▸ **application** 2

appal (BrE), **appall** (AmE) /əˈpɔːl/ *vt* (**-ll-**) «behaviour, attitude» صَعَقَ (a; صَعْق); **to be ~led at** *or* **by sth** صُعِقَ بِشَيْءٍ; **I was ~led by their ignorance** صَعَقَني جَهْلُهُمْ

appalling /əˈpɔːlɪŋ/ *adj* 1 ‹conditions, crime› فَظيع 2 ‹weather, manners› فَظيع

apparatus /ˌapəˈreɪtəs/ *n* 1 (instruments, equipment) أَجْهِزة 2 (of government) جِهاز (أَجْهِزة)

apparel /əˈpar(ə)l/ *n* مَلابِس, أَزْياء

apparent /əˈpar(ə)nt/ *adj* 1 (obvious) ‹error, ease› واضِح; **to become ~** أَصْبَحَ واضِحاً; **he lost his temper for no ~ reason** فَقَدَ أَعْصابَهُ بِدونِ أَسْبابٍ واضِحةٍ 2 (seeming) ‹contradiction, lack› ظاهِرِيّ

apparently /əˈparəntli/ *adv* 1 (according to reports) كَما يَبْدو; **~, the blood test was negative** يَبْدو أَنَّ نَتيجةَ تَحْليلِ الدَمِ كانَتْ سَلْبيّةً 2 (outwardly) ‹healthy, positive› ظاهِرِيًّا

apparition /apəˈrɪʃ(ə)n/ *n* طَيْف (أَطْياف)

appeal /əˈpiːl/ **A** *vt* (AmE) ‹a decision, ruling› طَعَنَ (a-u; طَعْن) (في)
B *vi* 1 (to request) «police, governments» ناشَدَ, اِلْتَمَسَ; **to ~ for calm/information** اِلْتَمَسَ الهُدوءَ \ مَعْلوماتٍ; **the police ~ed for witnesses to come forward** ناشَدَتِ الشُرْطةُ الشُهودَ الاِتِّصالَ بِها 2 (against a verdict) «defendant, lawyers» طَعَنَ (a-u; طَعْن) (في); **to ~ against a sentence/conviction** طَعَنَ في حُكْمٍ \ إدانةٍ; **to ~ to a higher court** تَقَدَّمَ بِطَعْنٍ \ رَفَعَ طَعْناً لِمَحْكَمةٍ عُلْيا 3 (to be attractive) **to ~ to sb** «idea, activity» راقَ لِشَخْصٍ
C *n* 1 (call) نِداء (نِداءات), اِلْتِماس (اِلْتِماسات), اِسْتِغاثة, مُناشَدة; **to make an ~ for help/funds** وَجَّهَ نِداءً لِطَلَبِ المُساعَدةِ \ الأَمْوالِ 2 (for donations) نِداء (نِداءات), مُناشَدة 3 (against a decision, verdict) طَعْن; **the court allowed the ~** وافَقَتِ المَحْكَمةُ على الطَعْنِ; **the ~ was dismissed** أُلْغِيَ الطَعْنُ 4 [u] (attraction, interest) جاذِبيّة; **a sport with a wide ~** رِياضة ذات شَعْبيّةٍ كَبيرةٍ; **it has no ~ for me** لا يَجْتَذِبُني, لَيْسَ مِن اهْتِماماتي

appeal court (BrE), **appeals court** (AmE) *n* مَحْكَمة اسْتِئْنافٍ

appealing /əˈpiːlɪŋ/ *adj* 1 (attractive) ‹prospect, feature› جَذّاب 2 (beseeching) ‹look› مُسْتَعْطِف

appear /əˈpɪə/ *vi* 1 (to become visible) «person, symptoms» ظَهَرَ (a; ظُهور), بانَ (i; بَيان); **her name ~s on the list** يَظْهَرُ اسْمُها على اللائحةِ; **a man ~ed at the window** ظَهَرَ \ بانَ رَجُلٌ على النافِذةِ 2 (to seem) «person, situation» بَدا (u; بُدوّ, بَداء); **they ~ to have forgotten** يَبْدو أَنَّهُمْ قد نسوا; **there ~s to be some mistake** يَبْدو أَنَّ هُناكَ خَطَأً ما; **so it ~s, so it would ~** على ما يَبْدو 3 (to perform) «actor, singer» ظَهَرَ (a; ظُهور), أَدّى (على); **to ~ on TV/on Broadway** ظَهَرَ على التِلْفازِ \ مَسْرَحِ بْرودْواي 4 (to be published) «article, book» صَدَرَ (i-u; صُدور), نُشِرَ; **to ~ in print** صَدَرَ (i-u; صُدور), نُشِرَ 5 (in court) «defendant, witness» مَثَلَ (u; مُثول); **to ~ in court** مَثَلَ أمامَ المَحْكَمةِ

appearance /əˈpɪər(ə)ns/ **A** *n* 1 [u] (look) مَظْهَر; **they are similar in ~** هُمْ مُتَشابِهونَ في المَظْهَرِ; **he takes a lot of care with his ~** يَعْتَني كَثيراً بِمَظْهَرِهِ 2 [u] (impression) اِنْطِباع; **she gave the ~ of being in complete control of the situation** بَدَتْ \ ظَهَرَتْ وَكَأَنَّها مُتَحَكِّمةٌ تَماماً في الوَضْعِ; **the state may seek to give the ~ of neutrality** قد تَسْعى الدَوْلةُ لإِعْطاءِ انْطِباعٍ بالحِيادِيّةِ 3 (in public) حُضور, ظُهور; **to make an ~** حَضَرَ حَدَثاً; **I'd better put in an ~** مِن الأَفْضَلِ أَنْ أُسَجِّلَ حُضوري 4 (on TV, in a play) ظُهور; **she made a guest ~ on his TV show** ظَهَرَتْ كَضَيْفةٍ في بَرْنامَجِهِ التِلِفِزْيونِيِّ; **his last ~ in the team** آخِر ظُهورٍ لَهُ في الفَريقِ 5 (in court) مُثول
B (**appearances**) *n pl* مَظاهِر; **you shouldn't judge by ~s** لا يَجِبُ أَنْ تَحْكُمَ على المَظاهِرِ

Idiom **to keep up appearances** حافَظَ على المَظاهِرِ

appease /əˈpiːz/ *vt* 1 (to placate) ‹a government, one's critics› اِسْتَرْضى 2 (to satisfy) ‹one's conscience› أَراحَ, أَرْضى; ‹sb's anger› كَبَحَ جِماحَ

appellant /əˈpel(ə)nt/ *n* مُسْتَأْنِف

appendectomy /ˌap(ə)nˈdɛktəmi/, **appendicectomy** /əpɛndɪˈsɛktəmɪ/ *n* (*pl* **appendectomies**) اسْتِئْصال الزائِدةِ الدوديّةِ

appendicitis /əˌpɛndɪˈsʌɪtɪs/ *n* الْتِهاب الزائِدةِ الدوديّةِ

appendix /əˈpɛndɪks/ *n* **1** (*pl* **appendixes**) (Anat) الزائِدة الدوديّة **2** (*pl* **appendices**) (of a book) مُلْحَق (مَلاحِقُ, مُلْحَقات)

appetite /ˈapɪtʌɪt/ *n* **1** (for food) شَهيّة; **to work up an ~** عَمِلَ على فَتْحِ الشَهيّةِ; **you'll spoil your ~** سَتُفْسِدُ شَهيّتَكَ **2** (for adventure, information) رَغْبة (رَغَبات, رِغاب); **he no longer had any ~ for life** لم تَبْقَ لَدَيْهِ أيّةُ رَغْبةٍ في الحَياةِ

appetite suppressant *n* مُثَبِّط للشَهيّة

appetizer, -iser (BrE) /ˈapɪtʌɪzə/ *n* مُشَهٍّ (مُشَهِّيات)

appetizing, -ising (BrE) /ˈapɪtʌɪzɪŋ/ *adj* ‹*meal, dish*› شَهِيّ

applaud /əˈplɔːd/ *vt, vi* ‹*a speech, sb's efforts*› (على) أَثْنى

applause /əˈplɔːz/ *n* تَصْفيق; **let's give a round of ~ for Paul!** دَعْنا نُصَفِّقْ لِبول!

apple /ˈap(ə)l/ *n* (fruit) تُفّاح (n coll); (tree) شَجَرة تُفّاحٍ

(Idiom) **to be the apple of sb's eye** كانَ قُرّةَ عَيْنِهِ

apple core *n* لُبّ تُفّاحةٍ

apple pie *n* فَطيرة تُفّاحٍ

applet /ˈaplɪt/ *n* (Comput) أَبْليت (تَطْبيق \ بَرْنامَج صَغير)

apple tree *n* شَجَرة تُفّاحٍ

appliance /əˈplʌɪəns/ *n* آلة (أَجْهِزة), جِهاز; **household ~s** أَجْهِزة مَنْزِليّة; **electrical ~s** أَجْهِزة كَهْرَبائيّة

applicable /əˈplɪkəb(ə)l, ˈaplɪkəb(ə)l/ *adj* ‹*theory, law*› قابِل للتَطْبيقِ, مَعْمول بِهِ, ساري المَفْعولِ; **this is ~ to all employees** هذا يَنْطَبِقُ على جَميعِ المُوَظَّفينَ

applicant /ˈaplɪk(ə)nt/ *n* مُقَدِّم طَلَبٍ

application /aplɪˈkeɪʃ(ə)n/ *n* **1** طَلَب (طَلَبات) **2** (Comput) تَطْبيق (تَطْبيقات), بَرْنامَج (بَرامِجُ) **3** [u] (of ointment, varnish) دَهْن **4** [u] (of a law, penalty, rule) تَطْبيق

application form *n* اسْتِمارة تَقْديمِ طَلَبٍ (ME), نَموذَج تَقْديمِ طَلَبٍ (NA)

applied /əˈplʌɪd/ *adj* ‹*science, linguistics*› تَطْبيقيّ

apply /əˈplʌɪ/ **A** *vt* (**applies, applying, applied**) **1** (to put on) وَضَعَ (a; وَضْع) ‹*one's make-up, paint*› **2** (to use) اسْتَعْمَلَ, اسْتَخْدَمَ ‹*a method, theory*›; **to ~ the brakes** اسْتَخْدَمَ المَكابِحَ **3** (to implement) طَبَّقَ, نَفَّذَ ‹*the law, rules*› **4** (to exert) اسْتَعْمَلَ ‹*pressure, force*›

B *vi* **1** (to have force) «rules, laws» سَرى (i; سَرَيان, سُرًى, مَسْرًى); **the same rules ~ to everyone** تَسْري نَفْسُ القَوانينِ على الجَميعِ **2** **to ~ for a loan/passport** قَدَّمَ طَلَباً للحُصولِ على قَرْضٍ \ جَوازِ سَفَرٍ; **to ~ for a job** قَدَّمَ طَلَبَ عَمَلٍ; **to ~ for citizenship** تَقَدَّمَ بِطَلَبِ الحُصولِ على الجِنْسيّةِ; **to ~ for a divorce** تَقَدَّمَ بِطَلَبِ طَلاقٍ; **to ~ for membership of an organization** قَدَّمَ طَلَبَ عُضْويّةٍ في مُنَظَّمةٍ

C *v refl* **to ~ oneself** صَبَّ مُجْمَلَ اهْتِمامِهِ على شَيْءٍ

appoint /əˈpɔɪnt/ *vt* **1** عَيَّنَ ‹*a committee, representative*› **2** حَدَّدَ, عَيَّنَ ‹*a date, place*›

appointment /əˈpɔɪntm(ə)nt/ *n* **1** (meeting) مَوْعِد (مَواعِدُ); **to make an ~ with the dentist** حَدَّدَ مَوْعِداً مع طَبيبِ الأَسْنانِ **2** (to a post) عَيَّنَ

appraisal /əˈpreɪz(ə)l/ *n* **1** (of a situation, evidence) تَقْدير (تَقادِيرُ, تَقْديرات) **2** (of an employee) تَقْييم

appraise /əˈpreɪz/ *vt* **1** (to assess) قَيَّمَ ‹*a situation, sb's performance*› **2** (to value) ثَمَّنَ ‹*a painting, property*›

appraiser /əˈpreɪzə/ *n* (AmE) مُثَمِّن

appreciable /əˈpriːʃəb(ə)l/ *adj* ‹*effect, difference*› مَحْسوس, مَلْحوظ; ‹*amount, increase*› مَلْموس

appreciate /əˈpriːʃɪeɪt/ **A** *vt* **1** (to be grateful for) كانَ مُمْتَنّاً لِ; (to be appreciative of) قَدَّرَ ‹*sb's support, effort*›; **your hard work is much ~d by the public** يُقَدِّرُ الجُمْهورُ جِدّاً عَمَلَكَ الشاقَّ **2** (to enjoy) تَذَوَّقَ ‹*music, art*› **3** (to understand) قَدَّرَ ‹*the importance, fact*›

B *vi* «antiques, property» ارْتَفَعَتْ قيمَتُهُ

appreciation /əpriːʃɪˈeɪʃ(ə)n/ *n* **1** (gratitude) امْتِنان; (recognition) تَقْدير; **to express/show one's ~** عَبَّرَ عن \ أَظْهَرَ تَقْديرَهُ; **in ~ of sth** امْتِناناً \ تَقْديراً لِشَيْءٍ **2** (of art, food) تَذَوُّق **3** (of the facts) فَهْم, تَقْدير **4** (in value) ارْتِفاع القيمةِ

appreciative /əˈpriːʃətɪv/ *adj* **1** (grateful) <*letter, smile*> اِمْتِنانٍ; **I was very ~ of the support they gave me** كُنْتُ مُمْتَنًّا جِدًّا للدَعْمِ الّذي قَدَّموهُ لي **2** (admiring) <*comments*> إعْجابٍ; <*audience*> مُعْجَب

apprehend /aprɪˈhɛnd/ *vt* قَبَضَ (i; قَبْض) (على) <*a suspect, culprit*>

apprehension /aprɪˈhɛnʃ(ə)n/ *n* **1** (fear) قَلَق, هَمّ (هُموم) **2** (arrest) إلْقاء القَبْضِ

apprehensive /aprɪˈhɛnsɪv/ *adj* <*look, tone*> قَلِق; **to be/feel ~ about sth** كانَ قَلِقاً بِشأْنِ شَيْءٍ

apprentice /əˈprɛntɪs/ *n* مُتَدَرِّب; **an ~ electrician** كَهْرَبائيّ تحت التَدْريبِ

apprenticeship /əˈprɛntɪ(s)ʃɪp/ *n* تَدْريب مِهَنيّ

approach /əˈprəʊtʃ/ **A** *vt* **1** (to draw near to) اقْتَرَبَ (من), دَنا (u; دُنوّ) (من) <*a person, place*>; **he is ~ing sixty** يَقْتَرِبُ من سِنِّ السِتّينَ; **we ~ed the city from the north** اقْتَرَبْنا من المَدينةِ من جِهةِ الشَمالِ; **it was ~ing dawn** اقْتَرَبَ الوَقْتُ من الفَجْرِ **2** (to deal with) تَعامَلَ (مع), عالَجَ <*a problem, subject*> **3** (to engage with) تَوَجَّهَ (إلى, نحو), فاتَحَ <*a person, an organization*>; **she was ~ed by a man in the street** تَوَجَّهَ إلَيْها رَجُلٌ في الشارِعِ; **they ~ed several organizations for help** تَوَجَّهوا إلى عِدّةِ شَركاتٍ لِطَلَبِ المُساعَدةِ

B *vi* «person, car, deadline» اقْتَرَبَ, دَنا (u; دُنوّ); **winter is ~ing** يَقْتَرِبُ الشتاءُ

C *n* **1** (drawing near) اقْتِراب, دُنوّ; **the ~ of winter/death** اقْتِراب الشِتاءِ \ المَوْتِ **2** (route of access) مَدْخَل (مَداخِل) **3** (way of dealing) نَهْج, أُسْلوب (أَساليبُ); **he takes a pragmatic ~ to the problem** يَتَّخِذُ نَهْجاً عَمَليًّا في التَعامُلِ مع المُشْكِلةِ **4** (contact) مُفاتَحة, اتِّصال مَبْدَئيّ; **to make ~es to sb** أَجْرى اتِّصالاً مَبْدَئيًّا مع شَخْصٍ

approachable /əˈprəʊtʃəb(ə)l/ *adj* <*headteacher, boss*> مُنْفَتِح

approach road *n* [طَريق مُؤَدٍّ لِمَكانٍ ما]

appropriate **A** /əˈprəʊprɪət/ *adj* **1** (suitable) مُناسِب, مُلائِم; **books ~ for children** كُتُب مُلائِمة للأَطْفالِ **2** (relevant) <*authority, department*> مَعْنيّ

B /əˈprəʊprɪeɪt/ *vt* **1** (to seize) اسْتَوْلى (على) <*the property*> **2** (to earmark) خَصَّصَ <*funds*>

appropriately /əˈprəʊprɪətli/ *adv* <*to behave, dress*> بِشَكْلٍ صَحيحٍ

appropriation /əˌprəʊprɪˈeɪʃ(ə)n/ *n* **1** (of assets) اسْتيلاء **2** (AmE) (allocation) مَبْلَغ مَرْصود

approval /əˈpruːv(ə)l/ *n* **1** (agreement) مُوافَقة, اسْتِحْسان **2** **to buy sth on ~** [جَرَّبَ شَيْئاً قبل شِراءِه]

approve /əˈpruːv/ **A** *vt* اسْتَحْسَنَ <*a product, plan*> **B** *vi* **to ~ of sb/sth** حَبَّذَ شَخْصاً \ شَيْئاً <*sb's behaviour, action*>; **he doesn't ~ of drinking** لا يُحَبِّذُ الشُرْبَ

approving /əˈpruːvɪŋ/ *adj* <*smile, glance*> اسْتِحْسانٍ

approximate /əˈprɒksɪmət/ *adj* <*amount, value*> تَقْريبيّ

approximately /əˈprɒksɪmətli/ *adv* <*equal, correct*> تَقْريباً, بالتَقْريبِ; **to calculate a figure ~** قامَ بِحِسابِ رَقْمٍ بالتَقْريبِ

approximation /əˌprɒksɪˈmeɪʃ(ə)n/ *n* تَقْريب

apricot /ˈeɪprɪkɒt/ *n* (fruit) مِشْمِش

April /ˈeɪpr(ɪ)l/ *n* أَبْريل (Mor, Egypt, Gulf), نَيْسان (dipt; Levant, Iraq), أَفْريل (Algeria, Tunisia) ▸ **March**

April Fool's Day *n* يَوْم كِذْبةِ أَبْريل

apron /ˈeɪpr(ə)n/ *n* مَرْيَلة (مَرايِلُ), وِزْرة (وِزَرات)

apt¹ /apt/ *adj* **1** (suitable) <*choice, comment*> مُناسِب, مُلائِم; **the title is very ~** العُنْوانُ جِدُّ مُناسِبٍ; **the song was ~ for the occasion** كانَت الأُغْنيّةُ مُلائِمةً للمُناسَبةِ **2** (inclined) **to be ~ to happen** كانَ من المُرَجَّحِ أنْ يَحْدُثَ

apt² *abbr* = **apartment** شِقّة (شِقَق)

aptitude /ˈaptɪtjuːd/ *n* مَوْهِبة (مَواهِبُ), مَلَكة

aptly /ˈaptli/ *adv* <*named, described*> بِشَكْلٍ مُلائِم \ مُناسِبٍ; **as he so ~ remarked, ...** كَما أَشارَ بِدِقّةٍ \ بِوُضوحٍ, ...

Aqaba, Gulf of *n* خَليج العَقَبة

aquarium /əˈkwɛːrɪəm/ *n* (*pl* **aquariums, aquaria**) [مَرْبًى للحَيَواناتِ المائيّةِ]

Aquarius /əˈkwɛːrɪəs/ *n* **1** (sign) بُرْج الدَلْوِ **2** (person) [من مَواليدِ بُرْجِ الدَلْوِ]

aquarobics /ˌakwəˈrəʊbɪks/ *n* [تَمارين رِياضيّة مائيّة]

aquatic /əˈkwatɪk/ *adj* <*plant, habitat*> مائيّ

aqueduct /ˈakwɪdʌkt/ *n* قَنْطَرة (قَناطِرُ)

AR *abbr* ▸ **Arkansas**

Arab /ˈarəb/ **A** *n* عَرَبيّ (عَرَب)

B *adj* ‹*culture, countries*› عَرَبيّ; **the ~ League** الجامِعة العَرَبيّة

Arabia /əˈreɪbɪə/ *pr n* (شِبْه) الجزيرة العَرَبيّة

Arabian /əˈreɪbɪən/ *adj* ‹*prince, cuisine*› عَرَبيّ

Arabian camel *n* جَمَل عَرَبيّ

Arabian Desert *n* (**the Arabian Desert**) الصَحْراء العَرَبيّة

Arabian Gulf *n* (**the Arabian Gulf**) الخَليج العَرَبيّ

Arabian Peninsula *n* (**the Arabian Peninsula**) (شِبْه) جَزيرة العَرَب, الجَزيرة العَرَبيّة

Arabian Sea *n* (**the Arabian Sea**) البَحْر العَرَبيّ

Arabic /ˈarəbɪk/ **A** *n* (اللُغة) العَرَبيّة; **she speaks fluent ~** تَتَكَلَّمُ العَرَبيّةَ بِطَلاقةٍ; **Modern Standard ~** اللُغة العَرَبيّة الفُصْحى (المُعاصِرة)

B *adj* ‹*speaker, translation, numeral*› عَرَبيّ

Arab–Israeli /arəbɪzˈreɪli/ *adj* ‹*peace process, war*› عَرَبيّ إسْرائيليّ

Arabist /ˈarəbɪst/ *n* مُسْتَعْرِب

Arabize, -ise (BrE) /ˈarəbʌɪz/ *vt* عَرَّبَ ‹*a term, an expression*›; **the term has become ~d** تَمَّ تَعْريبُ المُصْطَلَح

arable /ˈarəb(ə)l/ *adj* ‹*crop, land*› زِراعيّ; **~ farmer** مُزارِع

Arab Spring *n* الرَبيع العَرَبيّ

Aramaic /ˌarəˈmeɪɪk/ *n* (اللُغة) الآراميّة

arbiter /ˈɑːbɪtə/ *n* حَكَم (حُكّام), مُحَكَّم

arbitrary /ˈɑːbɪt(rə)ri/ *adj* ‹*arrest, decision*› تَعَسُّفيّ

arbitrate /ˈɑːbɪtreɪt/ **A** *vt* حَكَمَ (u; حُكْم) (في), فَصَلَ (i; فَصْل) (في) ‹*a dispute, claim*›

B *vi* «committees, courts» حَكَمَ (u; حُكْم)

arbitration /ɑːbɪˈtreɪʃ(ə)n/ *n* تَحْكيم; **to go to ~** لَجَأَ إلى التَحْكيم

arc /ɑːk/ *n* قَوْس (أَقْواس)

arcade /ɑːˈkeɪd/ *n* **1** (Archit) رِواق مُقَنْطَر \ مَمَرّ **2** (also **shopping arcade**) سوق مُقَنْطَر

arch /ɑːtʃ/ **A** *n* قَوْس (أَقْواس)

B *vt* قَوَّسَ; **to ~ one's back** «gymnast, cat» قَوَّسَ ظَهْرَهُ

C (**arch-**) *prefix* الأَهَمّ

archaeological (BrE), **archeological** (AmE) /ɑːkɪəˈlɒdʒɪk(ə)l/ *adj* ‹*remains, evidence*› أَثَريّ, آثاريّ

archaeologist (BrE), **archeologist** (AmE) /ˌɑːkɪˈɒlədʒɪst/ *n* عالِم آثارٍ, أَثَريّ

archaeology (BrE), **archeology** (AmE) /ˌɑːkɪˈɒlədʒi/ *n* عِلْم الآثارِ

archaic /ɑːˈkeɪɪk/ *adj* ‹*language, custom*› قَديم

archangel /ˈɑːkeɪndʒ(ə)l/ *n* رَئيس المَلائِكة

archbishop /ɑːtʃˈbɪʃəp/ *n* مُطْران (مَطارِنة); **the ~s of Canterbury and York** مَطارِنة كانْتَرْبَري وَيورْكَ; **he was appointed ~ when he was only forty** عُيِّنَ مُطْراناً عِنْدَما كانَ في الأَرْبَعينَ من عُمْرِهِ فَقَطْ

arch-enemy /ˌɑːtʃˈenəmi/ *n* عَدوّ لَدود

archeological (AmE) *adj* ▸ **archaeological**

archeologist (AmE) *n* ▸ **archaeologist**

archeology (AmE) *n* ▸ **archaeology**

archer /ˈɑːtʃə/ *n* نَبّال (نَبّالة)

archery /ˈɑːtʃ(ə)ri/ *n* رِياضة القَوْسِ والنُشّاب

architect /ˈɑːkɪtɛkt/ *n* مُهَنْدِس مِعْماريّ

architectural /ɑːkɪˈtɛktʃ(ə)r(ə)l/ *adj* ‹*design, student*› مِعْماريّ

architecture /ˈɑːkɪtɛktʃə/ *n* **1** (art) العِمارة \ فَنّ مِعْماريّ **2** (style) العِمارة \ هَنْدَسة مِعْماريّة, أُسْلوب مِعْماريّ

archive /ˈɑːkʌɪv/ **A** *n* أَرْشيف (أَراشيفُ)

B *vt* (Media) أَرْشَفَ (i; أَرْشَفة) ‹*a photograph, an article*›; (Comput) أَرْشَفَ (i; أَرْشَفة) ‹*data, a file*›

archivist /ˈɑːkɪvɪst/ *n* أَمين الأَرْشيفِ; **a film ~** أَمين أَرْشيفِ الأَفْلامِ

arch-rival /ˌɑːtʃˈrʌɪv(ə)l/ *n* مُنافِس لَدود

Arctic /ˈɑːktɪk/ **A** *pr n* (**the Arctic**) القُطْب الشَماليّ

B *adj* ‹*winter*› قارِس; ‹*expedition*› قُطْبيّ

ardent /ˈɑːd(ə)nt/ *adj* ‹*fan, supporter*› حَماسيّ, حارّ

ardour (BrE), **ardor** (AmE) /ˈɑːdə/ *n* **1** (enthusiasm) حَماس, حَماسة **2** (passion) وَلَع

arduous /ˈɑːdjʊəs/ *adj* **1** ‹*task, climb*› شاقّ **2** ‹*conditions, journey*› شاقّ

are /ɑː/ ▸ **be**

area /ˈɛːrɪə/ *n* **1** (in measurements) مِساحة **2** (of a town, city, country) مِنْطَقة (مَناطِقُ) **3** (in a building) **a no-smoking ~** مِنْطَقة مَمْنوعٌ التَدْخينُ فيها; **a dining ~** صالة طَعامٍ \ حُجْرة **4** (of business, activity) مَجال (مَجالات); **that is not my ~ of expertise** لا يَدْخُلُ ذلك في مَجالِ خِبْرَتي

area code *n* مِفْتاح الاتِّصالِ بِمِنْطَقةٍ \ بِدَوْلةٍ

arena /əˈriːnə/ *n* **1** (for sports, concerts) مَلْعَب (مَلاعِبُ) **2** (scene) حَلْبة (حَلَبات)

aren't /ɑːnt/ *abbr* = **are not** ▸ **be**

Argentina /ˌɑːdʒ(ə)nˈtiːnə/ *pr n* الأَرْجَنْتين (f)

Argentinian /ˌɑːdʒ(ə)nˈtɪnɪən/ *n, adj* أَرْجَنْتينيّ

arguably /ˈɑːgjuːəbli/ *adv* يُمْكِنُ القَوْلُ; **he was ~ the best tenor of his day** يُمْكِنُ القَوْلُ بِأَنَّهُ كانَ أَفْضَلَ مُغَنّي صَدْحٍ في زَمانِهِ

argue /ˈɑːgjuː/ **A** *vt* **1** (to debate) جادَلَ (في), ناقَشَ ‹*a case, point*›; **he ~d the case for reform** قَدَّمَ حُجَجاً على أَهَمِّيّةِ الإِصْلاحِ; **a well-~d book/essay** كِتاب \ مَقال بِهِ حُجَجٌ قَوِيّةٌ **2** (to maintain) زَعَمَ (u; زَعْم), ادَّعى; **it could be ~d that ...** يُمْكِنُ الادِّعاءُ بِأَنَّ ...

B *vi* **1** (to quarrel) «partners, groups» تَشاجَرَ, تَجادَلَ, تَنازَعَ; **they're always arguing about money** دائِماً ما يَتَشاجَرونَ حول المالِ; **he ~d with her for hours** ظَلَّ يَتَجادَلُ مَعَها لِعِدّةِ ساعاتٍ; **don't ~!** لا تُجادِلْ! **2** (to give reasons) «lawyers, authors» جادَلَ; **to ~ for/against sth** جادَلَ لِصالِحِ \ ضِدَّ شَيْءٍ

argument /ˈɑːgjʊm(ə)nt/ *n* **1** (quarrel) خِلاف, جِدال, شِجار (خِلافات); **to have an ~ about** *or* **over sth** تَجادَلَ حول شَيْءٍ; **I had an ~ with my brother about it** تَجادَلْتُ مع أَخي حول هذا الأَمْرِ; **they had an ~ over the bill** حَدَثَ خِلافٌ بَيْنَهُمْ بِخُصوصِ الفاتورةِ **2** (debate) جَدَل, نِقاش; **it's open to ~** هذا الأَمْرُ مَفْتوحٌ لِلنِقاشِ; **there is a lot of ~ about this** هُناكَ الكَثيرُ من الجَدَلِ حول هذا الأَمْرِ; **for the sake of ~** على سَبيلِ الجَدَلِ **3** (case) حُجّة (حُجَج); **an ~ for** *or* **against sth** حُجّة لِإِثْباتِ \ نَفْيِ شَيْءٍ; **he made the ~ that it was too expensive** قَدَّمَ الحُجّةَ أَنَّهُ كانَ غالِياً جِدّاً **4** (line of reasoning) اسْتِدْلال (اسْتِدْلالات), سِلْسِلة من الحُجَجِ

argumentative /ɑːgjʊˈmɛntətɪv/ *adj* ‹*nature, child*› مُحِبّ للجَدَلِ

aria /ˈɑːrɪə/ *n* (*pl* **arias**) آرْيا (مَقْطوعة غِنائيّة مُطَوَّلة لِمُغَنٍّ مُنْفَرِدٍ في الأوبِرا)

arid /ˈarɪd/ *adj* ‹*desert*› قاحِل; ‹*climate*› جافّ

Aries /ˈɛːriːz/ *n* **1** (sign) بُرْج الحَمَلِ **2** (person) مِن مَواليدِ بُرْجِ الحَمَلِ

arise /əˈrʌɪz/ *vi* (*past tense* **arose**; *past participle* **arisen**) «problems, opportunities» ظَهَرَ (a; ظُهور); **if the need ~s** إذا ظَهَرَت الحاجةُ

aristocracy /ˌarɪˈstɒkrəsi/ *n* (*pl* **aristocracies**) أَرِسْتُقْراطيّة; **she married a member of the ~** تَزَوَّجَتْ من أَحَدِ أَفْرادِ الطَبَقةِ الأَرِسْتُقْراطيّةِ

aristocrat /ˈarɪstəkrat/ *n* أَرِسْتُقْراطيّ

aristocratic /ˌarɪstəˈkratɪk/ *adj* ‹*family, line*› أَرِسْتُقْراطيّ; **he has ~ connections** لَدَيْهِ عَلاقاتٌ في الوَسَطِ الأَرِسْتُقْراطيِّ

arithmetic /əˈrɪθmətɪk/ *n* عِلْم الحِسابِ

Arizona /ˌarɪˈzəʊnə/ *pr n* أريزونا

Arizonan /ˌarɪˈzəʊnən/ *pr n, adj* أَريزونيّ

ark /ɑːk/ *n* سَفينة, فُلْك (سُفُن, سَفائِنُ); **Noah's ~** سَفينة نوحٍ \ فُلْك

Arkansas /ˈɑːk(ə)nsɔː/ *pr n* أَرْكَنْساس (f)

arm /ɑːm/ **A** *n* **1** (part of the body) ذِراع (f; أَذْرُع); **~ in ~** مُتَشابِكَي \ مُتَأَبِّطَي الذِراعَيْنِ; **to give sb one's ~** سانَدَ شَخْصاً بِيَدِهِ; **to take sb's ~** اتَّكَأَ على ذِراعِ شَخْصٍ; **to have an overcoat over one's ~** حَمَلَ مِعْطَفاً على ساعِدِهِ; **to cross one's ~s** تَكَتَّفَ, عَقَدَ ذِراعَيْهِ على صَدْرِهِ; **within ~'s reach** في مُتَناوَلِ اليَدِ **2** (of a jacket, sweater) كُمّ (أَكْمام); **the ~s need shortening** تَحْتاجُ الأَكْمامُ إلى التَقْصيرِ; **the long ~ of the law** اليَدُ الطولى للقانونِ **3** (of a chair) ذِراع (f; أَذْرُع), يَد (f; أَيادٍ) **4** (of spectacles) ذِراع (f; أَذْرُع) **5** (of the sea) لِسان (بَحْريّ)

B (**arms**) *n pl* **1** (weapons) أَسْلِحة; **to be up in ~s against the reforms** عارَضَ الإِصْلاحاتِ بِشِدّةٍ **2** (in heraldry) شِعار (شِعارات)

C *vt* (to equip) سَلَّحَ *<the rebels, gang>*; **they were ~ed with Kalashnikovs** كانوا مُسَلَّحين ببَنادِقِ كْلاشِنْكوف; **~ed with the latest statistics, they easily won the argument** لِأَنَّهُمْ كانوا مُزَوَّدين بِأَحْدَثِ الإِحْصائِيّاتِ فقَدْ كَسَبوا الجِدالَ بِسُهولةٍ
D *v refl* **to ~ oneself with the statistics/best medicine** زَوَّدَ نَفْسَهُ بالإِحْصائِيّاتِ \ بِأَفْضَلِ الأَدْوِيةِ
(Idioms) **to cost an arm and a leg** كَلَّفَ ثَمَناً باهِظاً; **to keep sb at arm's length** تَحَفَّظَ في عَلاقَتِهِ مع شَخْصٍ; **to twist sb's arm** لَوى ذِراعَ شَخْصٍ (ضَغَطَ عَلَيْهِ); **with open arms** بتَرْحابٍ

armaments /ˈɑːməmənts/ *n pl* تَسَلُّح

armaments industry *n* صِناعة السِلاح

armband /ˈɑːmband/ *n* **1** (for identification) شارة; (as a sign of mourning) شَريط الحِدادِ **2** (as a swimming aid) عَوّام الذِراع (يُساعِدُ على إِبْقاءِ الذِراع طافِياً أثناء السِباحةِ)

armchair /ˈɑːmtʃɛː/ *n* [كُرْسيّ مُريح (ذو مِسْنَدَيْ ذِراع)]

armed /ɑːmd/ *adj <conflict, struggle>* مُسَلَّح; **to be convicted of ~ robbery** حُكِمَ عَلَيْهِ بتُهْمةِ السَطْوِ المُسَلَّحِ

armed forces, armed services *n pl* قوّات مُسَلَّحة

Armenia /ɑːˈmiːnɪə/ *pr n* أَرْمينِيا

Armenian /ɑːˈmiːnɪən/ **A** *n* **1** (citizen) أَرْمينيّ **2** (language) (اللُغة) الأَرْمينيّة
B *adj <ambassador, border>* أَرْمينيّ

armistice /ˈɑːmɪstɪs/ *n* هُدْنة (هُدَن, هُدْنات)

armour (BrE), **armor** (AmE) /ˈɑːmə/ *n* **1** (of a knight, warrior) دِرْع (أَدْرُع, دُروع); **a suit of ~** دِرْع (أَدْرُع, دُروع) **2** (on a vehicle, ship) دِرْع (أَدْرُع, دُروع)

armoured (BrE), **armored** (AmE) /ˈɑːməd/ *adj <truck, vehicle>* مُصَفَّح, مُدَرَّع

armoured car (BrE), **armored car** (AmE) *n* **1** سَيّارة مُصَفَّحة لِنَقْلِ الأَمْوالِ **2** (AmE) مُدَرَّعة \ مُصَفَّحة

armoured division (BrE), **armored division** (AmE) *n* فِرْقة مُدَرَّعة

armoured personnel carrier (BrE), **armored personnel carrier** (AmE) *n* ناقِلة جُنودٍ مُدَرَّعةٍ

armour-plated (BrE), **armor-plated** (AmE) /ˌɑːməˈpleɪtɪd/ *adj <vehicle, ship>* مُدَرَّع

armoury (BrE), **armory** (AmE) /ˈɑːm(ə)ri/ *n* (*pl* **armouries**) **1** (for storage) مَخْزَن \ مُسْتَوْدَع أَسْلِحةٍ **2** (AmE) (factory) مَصْنَع أَسْلِحةٍ

armpit /ˈɑːmpɪt/ *n* إِبْط (آباط)

armrest /ˈɑːmrɛst/ *n* مَسْنَد ذِراع

arms control *n* الحَدّ من (انْتِشارِ) الأَسْلِحةِ

arms race *n* سِباق تَسَلُّح

arms treaty *n* مُعاهَدة الحَدِّ من التَسَلُّحِ

arm-wrestling /ˈɑːmˌrɛs(ə)lɪŋ/ *n* [مُصارَعة الذِراعَيْنِ]

army /ˈɑːmi/ *n* (*pl* **armies**) **1** (Mil) جَيْش (جُيوش) **2** (of volunteers, thugs) جَيْش (جُيوش)

army surplus store *n* [مَتْجَر مُعَدّاتٍ وَمَلابِسَ عَسْكَرِيّةٍ فائِضةٍ]

A road *n* (BrE) [طَريق كَبير]

aroma /əˈrəʊmə/ *n* رائِحة زَكِيّة

aromatherapist /əˌrəʊməˈθɛrəpɪst/ *n* [مُمارِس طِبِّ الرَوائِحِ]

aromatherapy /ərəʊməˈθɛrəpi/ *n* (*pl* **aromatherapies**) العِلاج بالرَوائِحِ

aromatic /arəˈmatɪk/ *adj <herb, foliage>* فَوّاح, عِطْرِيّ

arose /əˈrəʊz/ *past tense* ▸ **arise**

around /əˈraʊnd/ **A** *adv* **1** (approximately) حَوالَيْ; **at ~ 3 p.m.** في حَوالي الثالِثةِ عَصْراً; **it sells for ~ £200** يُباعُ بِحَوالَيْ 200 جُنَيْهِ اسْتِرْلينيٍّ; **she must be ~ forty** لا بُدَّ أَنَّها تَبْلُغُ من العُمْرِ حَوالَيْ أَرْبَعينَ عاماً **2** (in the vicinity) قَريب; **ask Simon, he's somewhere ~** اِسْأَلْ سايْمُن، هو في مَكانٍ ما هُنا; **there's nobody ~** لَيْسَ هُناكَ أَحَدٌ قَريبٌ من هُنا **3** (on all sides) **all ~** في كُلِّ مَكانٍ; **the only shop for miles ~** الدُكّان الوَحيد في دائِرةٍ قُطْرُها أَمْيالٌ عِدّةٌ; **everyone crowded ~** تَجَمَّعَ الجَميعُ حول المَكانِ **4** (in circulation) **to be ~** تَواجَدَ; **computers have been ~ for years** الحاسوبُ مُتَواجِدٌ منذ سَنَواتٍ **5** (from one place to another) **to follow sb ~** تَبِعَ شَخْصاً في كُلِّ مَكانٍ; **to walk ~ the town** تَمَشّى في المَدينةِ **6** (to face in the opposite direction) **to turn ~** دارَ (u; دَوْر, دَوَران)
B *prep* **1** (surrounding) حَوْلَ *<the fire, table>*; **the fields ~ the village** الحُقول حول القَرْيةِ **2** (with times, dates) حَوالَيْ; **~ midnight/2005** حَوالَيْ مُنْتَصَفَ اللَيْلِ \ 2005 **3** (throughout)

في أَنْحاءِ; **clothes were scattered ~ the room** كانَت المَلابِسُ مُبَعْثَرَةً في أَنْحاءِ الغُرْفَةِ; **all ~ the world** في كُلِّ أَنْحاءِ العالَمِ

(Idiom) **to have been around** كانَ ذا خِبْرَةٍ وَمَعْرِفَةٍ

arouse /ə'raʊz/ *vt* ❶ أَثارَ ‹*suspicion, interest*› ❷ (sexually) أَثارَ

arpeggio /ɑː'pɛdʒɪəʊ/ *n* (*pl* **arpeggios**) صَوْت تَتابُعِيّ

arraign /ə'reɪn/ *vt* اسْتَدْعى ‹*a suspect, defendant*›

arrange /ə'reɪn(d)ʒ/ **A** *vt* ❶ (to place) نَسَّق, رَتَّب ‹*furniture, books*›; **she was arranging the flowers/her hair** كانَتْ تُنَسِّقُ الأَزْهارَ \ تُصَفِّفُ شَعْرَها ❷ (to organize) دَبَّر, نَظَّم ‹*a meeting, visit, transport*›; **we've ~d to meet tomorrow** اتَّفَقْنا على الاجْتِماعِ غَداً; **an ~d marriage** زَواج مُدَبَّر; **I'll ~ the accommodation** سَوْفَ أُدَبِّرُ الإقامةَ ❸ (Fin) (to set up) أَعَدَّ, رَتَّبَ ‹*a loan, the finance*› ❹ (Mus) أَعادَ التَّوْزيعَ ‹*a piece, music*›
B *vi* **to ~ for sb to do sth** «parents, companies» اتَّفَقَ مع شَخْصٍ على فِعْلِ شَيْءٍ; **we've ~d for someone to meet you at the airport** اتَّفَقْنا مع شَخْصٍ على أَنْ يَسْتَقْبِلَكَ في المَطارِ; **can you ~ for the sofa to be delivered?** هل يُمْكِنُكَ أَنْ تُرَتِّبَ تَوْصيلَ الأَريكةِ؟

arrangement /ə'reɪn(d)ʒm(ə)nt/ *n* ❶ (grouping of furniture) تَرْتيب (تَرْتيبات); (grouping of flowers) تَنْسيق; **what is the seating ~?** ما هو تَرْتيبُ أَماكِنِ الجُلوسِ؟ ❷ (agreement) اتِّفاق (اتِّفاقات); **I'm sure we can come to some ~** أنا واثِقٌ أَنَّهُ يُمْكِنُنا أَنْ نَتَوَصَّلَ إلى اتِّفاقٍ; **by ~** بالاتِّفاقِ ❸ (**arrangements** *n pl*) (plans) تَرْتيبات, خُطَط; **to make ~s for sth** قامَ بِعَمَلِ التَّرْتيباتِ لِشَيْءٍ; **the company handled the travel ~s** تَوَلَّت الشَرِكةُ شَأْنَ تَرْتيباتِ السَفَرِ ❹ (of music) [قِطْعة موسيقيّة أُعيدَ تَوْزيعُها \ تَمَّ تَكْييفُها]

array /ə'reɪ/ *n* (range) تَشْكيلة

arrears /ə'rɪəz/ *n pl* مُتَأَخِّرات

arrest /ə'rɛst/ **A** *vt* قَبَضَ (i; قَبْض على) ‹*a suspect, thief*›
B *n* قَبْض; **to be under ~** قُبِضَ عَلَيْهِ; **to make an ~** قَبَضَ على شَخْصٍ

arrival /ə'rʌɪv(ə)l/ *n* وُصول

arrivals board *n* لَوْحة وُصولٍ

arrivals lounge *n* صالة وُصولٍ

arrival time *n* مَوْعِد وُصولٍ

arrive /ə'rʌɪv/ *vi* ❶ (at a place) وَصَلَ (i; وُصول); **we ~d at the stadium** وَصَلْنا إلى المَلْعَبِ ❷ **to ~ at a conclusion/decision** وَصَلَ \ تَوَصَّلَ إلى اسْتِنْتاجٍ \ قَرارٍ

arrogance /'arəg(ə)ns/ *n* عُنْجُهِيّة, عَجْرَفة, تَكَبُّر

arrogant /'arəg(ə)nt/ *adj* ‹*swagger, statement*› مُتَعَجْرِف, مُتَكَبِّر

arrow /'arəʊ/ *n* ❶ (weapon) سَهْم (سِهام, أَسْهُم) ❷ (sign) سَهْم (سِهام, أَسْهُم)

arse /ɑːs/ *n* (BrE vulg) (anus) إِسْت; (buttocks) دُبُر, مُؤَخِّرة (أَدْبار)

arsehole /'ɑːshəʊl/ *n* (BrE vulg) أَحْمَق (dipt; حُمْق; f حَمْقى)

arsenal /'ɑːs(ə)n(ə)l/ *n* تَرْسانة أَسْلِحة; **now they can add nuclear weapons to their ~** بِإمْكانِهِم الآنَ أَنْ يُضيفوا أَسْلِحةً نَوَويّةً لِتَرْسانَتِهِمْ

arson /'ɑːs(ə)n/ *n* حَريق مُتَعَمَّد

arsonist /'ɑːs(ə)nɪst/ *n* [مُشْعِل حَرائِق]

art /ɑːt/ *n* ❶ (skill) فَنّ (فُنون); **the ~ of calligraphy** فَنّ الخَطِّ ❷ (paintings, drawings) فَنّ (فُنون); **Modern/Pre-Islamic ~** الفَنّ المُعاصِر \ الجاهِليّ; **to study ~** دَرَسَ الفَنَّ ❸ (**the Arts**) (artistic activities) الفُنون; **to be a patron of the ~s** كانَ راعِياً لِلفُنونِ

art dealer *n* تاجِر أَعْمالٍ فَنِّيّةٍ

artefact /'ɑːtɪfakt/ *n* [شَيْء من صُنْعِ الإنْسانِ]

arterial /ɑː'tɪərɪəl/ *adj before n* ❶ ‹*blood, blockage*› شِرْيانيّ ❷ ‹*road*› رَئيسيّ

arteriosclerosis /ɑːˌtɪərɪəʊsklə'rəʊsɪs/ *n* تَصَلُّب الشَرايينِ

artery /'ɑːt(ə)ri/ *n* (*pl* **arteries**) شِرْيان (شَرايينُ)

art exhibition *n* مَعْرِض فَنّيّ

art gallery *n* ❶ (museum) صالة عَرْضٍ ❷ (shop) [مَتْجَر أَعْمالٍ فَنِّيّةٍ]

arthritis /ɑː'θrʌɪtɪs/ *n* الْتِهاب المَفاصِلِ

artichoke /'ɑːtɪtʃəʊk/ *n* خُرْشوف (خَراشيفُ)

article /'ɑːtɪk(ə)l/ *n* ❶ (item) سِلْعة (سِلَع); **an ~ of clothing** قِطْعة مَلْبَسٍ ❷ (in a publication) مَقالة ❸ (Ling) [أَداة تَعْريفٍ \ تَنْكيرٍ]

articulate **A** /ɑː'tɪkjʊlət/ *adj* ‹*speaker, argument*› يُعَبِّرُ بِوُضوحٍ

B /ɑːˈtɪkjʊleɪt/ *vt* **1** (to pronounce) نطَقَ \ لَفَظَ بِوُضوحٍ ‹*words*› **2** (to express) عَبَّرَ بِوُضوحٍ عن ‹*a view, one's feelings*›

articulated lorry /ɑːˌtɪkjəleɪtɪd ˈlɒri/ *n* (BrE) شاحِنة مَقْطورة

artifact /ˈɑːtɪfakt/ (AmE) *n* ▸ **artefact**

artificial /ɑːtɪˈfɪʃ(ə)l/ *adj* ‹*flowers, sweetener*› اصْطِناعيّ ,صِناعيّ; **a dress made of ~ silk** فُسْتان مَصْنوع من حَريرٍ صِناعيٍّ

artificial limb *n* طَرَف اصْطِناعيّ

artificially /ˌɑːtɪˈfɪʃ(ə)li/ *adv* ‹*to inseminate, to incubate*› اصْطِناعيًّا; **the profits were ~ inflated** تَمَّ رَفْعُ الأَسْعارِ بِشَكْلٍ مُصْطَنَعٍ

artificial respiration *n* تَنَفُّس اصْطِناعيّ

artillery /ɑːˈtɪləri/ *n* مِدْفَعيّة

artisan /ɑːtɪˈzan/ *n* حِرَفيّ

artist /ˈɑːtɪst/ *n* فَنّان

artiste /ɑːˈtiːst/ *n* فَنّان مُحْتَرِف في [المَسْرَحِ \ السينما \ التلفِزيونِ]

artistic /ɑːˈtɪstɪk/ *adj* ‹*talent, temperament*› فَنّيّ

arts /ɑːts/ *n pl* **1** (culture) **the ~** الفُنون والآداب **2** (Educ) الآداب **3** **~ and crafts** أَشْغال فَنّيّة وَيَدَويّة

art school *n* مَدْرَسة فُنونٍ

arts student *n* طالِب آدابٍ

art student *n* طالِب فُنونٍ

artwork /ˈɑːtwəːk/ *n* **1** (objects) عَمَل فَنّيّ **2** (for books, magazines) رُسوم تَوْضيحيّة

as /az, əz/ **A** *adv* **1** (expressing degree, extent) **he is ~ intelligent ~ you** هو ذَكيٌّ مِثْلُكَ تَماماً; **she can't walk ~ fast ~ she used to** لم تَعُدْ تَسْتَطيعُ أنْ تَمْشِيَ بِسُرْعةٍ كَما في السابِقِ; **~ soon ~ possible** في أَسْرَعِ وَقْتٍ مُمْكِنٍ; **~ much ~ possible** أَقَلّ ما; **~ little ~ possible** قَدْرَ الإِمْكانِ \ المُسْتَطاعِ; **~ strong ~ an ox** قَويّ كالثَّوْرِ; **he's twice ~ strong ~ me** يُمْكِنُ قوَّتُهُ ضِعْفُ قوَّتي; **I paid ~ much ~ she did** دَفَعْتُ نَفْسَ المَبْلَغِ الّذي دَفَعَتْهُ; **the population may increase by ~ much ~ 20%** قد يَزْدادُ عَدَدُ السُكّانِ بِنِسْبةٍ تَصِلُ إلى 20٪; **~ many ~ 10,000 people attended the demonstration** حَضَرَ المُظاهَرةَ ما لا يَقِلُّ عن 10,000 شَخْصٍ; **she can play the piano ~ well ~ her sister** تُجيدُ العَزْفَ على البِيانو مِثْلَ أُخْتِها; **they have a house in Rashaya ~ well ~ an apartment in Beirut** يَمْتَلِكونَ مَنْزِلاً في راشَيّا وَكَذَلِكَ شَقّةً في بَيْروت **2** (expressing similarity) مِثْلَ; **~ before, she ...** مِثْلَما حَدَثَ من قَبْلُ، هي ...; **I thought ~ much!** كَما ظَنَنْتُ!

B *conj* **1** (in the manner that) كَما; **~ you know** كَما تَعْلَمُ; **leave it ~ it is** اتْرُكْهُ كَما هو; **~ usual** كالمُعْتادِ; **do ~ I say** افْعَلْ كَما أَقولُ لَكَ; **~ I see/understand it** كَما أَراهُ \ أَفْهَمُهُ; **~ often happens** كَما يَحْدُثُ غالِباً; **the street ~ it looked in the 1990s** الشارِع كَما كانَ يَبْدو في التِسْعيناتِ; **we're in enough trouble ~ it is** لَدَيْنا ما يَكْفينا من المَشاكِلِ في الوَضْعِ الحاليِّ; **~ one man to another** بِصَراحةٍ **2** (while, when) عِنْدَما ,بَيْنَما; **he came in ~ she was coming down the stairs** دَخَلَ بَيْنَما كانَتْ تَنْزِلُ من على الدَرَجِ; **~ she grew older, she grew richer** كُلَّما تَقَدَّمَتْ في السِنِّ، كُلَّما ازْدادَتْ ثَراءً; **~ a child, he ...** عِنْدَما كانَ طِفْلاً، كان ... **3** (because, since) بِما أَنّ; **~ you were out, I left a note** بِما أَنّكَ كُنْتَ في الخارِجِ، فَقَدْ تَرَكْتُ رِسالةً **4** (although) **strange ~ it may seem, she never returned** بالرَغْمِ من أنّ هذا يَبْدو غَريباً، لَكِنَّها لم تَعُدْ أَبَداً; **comfortable ~ the room is, it's very inexpensive** على الرَغْمِ من أنّ الحُجْرة مُريحةٌ، إلاّ أنَّها رَخيصةٌ جِدًّا; **try ~ he might, he could not forget it** بِالرَغْمِ من أَنَّهُ حاوَلَ جاهِداً، إلاّ أَنَّهُ لم يَسْتَطِعْ أنْ يَنْساهُ **5** **the same ... ~** مِثْلَ ... تَماماً; **I've got a jacket the same ~ yours** لَدَيَّ سُتْرةٌ مِثْلُ سُتْرَتِكَ تَماماً; **the same ~ always** كَما هو الحالُ دائِماً **6** (expressing purpose) **so ~ to do** حتّى يَفْعَلَ ,من أَجْلِ أنْ يَفْعَلَ

C *prep* **1** (to appear to be) مِثْلَ; **to be dressed ~ a sailor** ارْتَدى زيَّ بَحّارٍ; **he is portrayed ~ a victim** يَتِمُّ تَصْويرُهُ على أَنَّهُ ضَحيّةٌ; **it came ~ a shock** جاءَ كَصَدْمةٍ; **he was quoted ~ saying that ...** نُقِلَ عَنْهُ قَوْلُهُ أنّ ... **2** (showing status, role) كَ; **he works ~ a pilot** يَعْمَلُ كَطَيّارٍ; **a job ~ a teacher** وَظيفة مُعَلِّمٍ; **speaking ~ his closest friend, I ...** بِصِفَتي أَقْرَبُ أَصْدِقائِهِ، أَقولُ إنّ ...; **my rights ~ a parent** حُقوقي كَوالِدٍ; **with Lauren Bacall ~ Vivien** مع لورين باكال في دَوْرِ فيفْيان; **to treat sb ~ an equal** عامَلَ شَخْصاً على قَدَمِ المُساواةِ

D **(as against)** *prep phr* مُقارَنةً بِ; **75% this year ~ against 35% last year** 75٪ هذا العامَ مُقارَنةً بِ35٪ في العامِ السابِقِ

E **(as and when)** *conj phr* **~ and when the passengers arrive**

عِنْدَما يَصِلُ الرُّكّابُ; **~ and when the need arises** عِنْدَما تَقْتَضي الحاجةُ

F **(as for)** *prep phr* بالنِسْبَةِ ل, بِخُصوصِ; **~ for him, he's ailed** أمّا هو، فإنَّهُ مُتوعِّكٌ

G **(as from, as of)** *prep phr* بَدْءاً من; **~ from** *or* **of now/April** بَدْءاً من الآنِ \ أبْريل

H **(as if)** *conj phr* كَما لو أنَّ; **it looks ~ if we've lost** يَبْدو كَما لو أنَّنا قد خَسِرْنا; **~ if by accident/magic** كَما لو أنَّهُ كانَ عن طَريقِ الصُدْفةِ \ السِحْرِ; **he looked at me ~ if to say 'I told you so'** نَظَرَ إلَيَّ كَما لو أنَّهُ يُريدُ أنْ يَقولَ 'سَبَقَ وَحَذَّرْتُكَ من هذا'; **it's not ~ if she hadn't been warned!** لَيْسَ الأمْرُ كَما لو أنَّهُ لم يَسْبِقْ تَحْذيرُها!

I **(as such)** *prep phr* بِهَذا الشَكْلِ, على هذا النَحْوِ; **he doesn't believe in freedom ~ such** لا يُؤْمِنُ بالحُرِّيّةِ بِهَذا الشَكْلِ

J **(as to)** *prep phr* بِخُصوصِ; **there was no clue ~ to his whereabouts** لم يَكُنْ هُناكَ أيُّ إشارةٍ عن مَكانِهِ

asbestos /asˈbɛstɒs, azˈbɛstɒs/ *n* أَسْبَسْتوس, حَرير صَخْرِيّ

asbestosis /ˌasbɛˈstəʊsɪs, ˌazbɛˈstəʊsɪs/ *n* داء الأسْبِسْت

ASBO /ˈazbəʊ/ *n* (BrE) = **anti-social behaviour order** [حُكْم مَحْكَمةٍ لِمُكافَحةِ سُلوكٍ لااجْتِماعيٍّ]

ascend /əˈsɛnd/ **A** *vt* صَعِدَ (a; صُعود) ‹*a hill, steps*›

B *vi* «climber, path, soul» صَعِدَ (a; صُعود); «smoke» تَصاعَدَ

C **(ascending)** *present participle* ‹*scale, slope*› مُتَصاعِد

ascent /əˈsɛnt/ *n* ① (of a mountain) صُعود ② (rise) صُعود ③ (path, slope) صُعود

ascertain /ˌasəˈteɪn/ *vt* تَحَقَّقَ (من) ‹*the facts, cause*›

ascetic /əˈsɛtɪk/ *adj, n* زاهِد, مُتَقَشِّف

ASCII /ˈaski/ *n* = **American Standard Code for Information Interchange** أَسْكي (شَفْرة حاسوبٍ أمْريكيّة)

ascribe /əˈskrʌɪb/ *vt* **to ~ a meaning/value to sth** نَسَبَ مَعْنًى \ قيمةً لِشَيْءٍ; **to ~ a work of art to sb** نَسَبَ عَمَلاً فَنِّيّاً لِشَخْصٍ; **to ~ an accident/error to sth** عَزا سَبَبَ حادِثٍ \ خَطَأٍ إلى شَيْءٍ

aseptic /eɪˈsɛptɪk/ *adj* ‹*conditions, dressing, wound*› مُعَقَّم

ash /aʃ/ *n* ① (after burning) رَماد (أرْمِدة) ② **(ashes** *n pl***)** (cremated remains) رَماد (أرْمِدة) ③ (also **ash tree**) دَرْدار, كَرْكار

ashamed /əˈʃeɪmd/ *adj* خَجْلان (خَجالى), مُسْتَحٍ; **to be ~ of sth/sb** خَجِلَ من شَيْءٍ \ شَخْصٍ; **he felt ~ of his ignorance/behaviour** شَعَر بالخَجَلِ من جَهْلِهِ \ تَصَرُّفاتِهِ; **she was ~ to be seen with him** كانَتْ تَخْجَلُ من أنْ يَراها الناسُ مَعَهُ; **you ought to be ~ of yourself!** يَنْبَغي أنْ تَخْجَلَ من نَفْسِكَ!; **it's nothing to be ~ of** هذا شَيْءٌ لا يَنْبَغي أنْ تَخْجَلَ مِنْهُ

ashcan /ˈaʃkan/ *n* (AmE) ▸ **garbage can**

ashen /ˈaʃ(ə)n/ *adj* ‹*face, complexion*› شاحِب جِدًّا; ‹*sky, hair, clouds*› رَماديّ

ashore /əˈʃɔː/ *adv* **to go/come ~** نَزَلَ إلى الشاطِئِ; **the wreckage was washed ~** لُفِظَ الحُطامُ على الشاطِئِ

ashtray /ˈaʃtreɪ/ *n* طَفّاية

Ash Wednesday *n* أرْبِعاء الرَمادِ

Asia /ˈeɪʃə/ *pr n* آسِيا

Asian /ˈeɪʃ(ə)n/ **A** *adj* ① (of or from Asia) ‹*family, food*› آسِيَويّ ② (BrE) (of or from the Indian subcontinent) ‹*family, food*› [من شِبْهِ القارّةِ الهِنْديّةِ]

B *n* ① (person from Asia) آسِيَويّ ② (BrE) (person from the Indian subcontinent) [شَخْص من شِبْهِ القارّةِ الهِنْديّةِ]

aside /əˈsʌɪd/ **A** *adv* ① (to one side) **to stand/move ~** وَقَفَ \ تَحَرَّكَ جانِباً; **to step ~** تَنَحّى جانِباً; **to set/put sth ~ for sb** احْتَفَظَ بِشَيْءٍ لِشَخْصٍ; **he took me ~ to tell me** انْتَحى بي جانِباً لِيُخْبِرَني ② (leaving apart) باسْتِثْناءِ; **joking ~, it really is serious this time** بِلا مَزْحٍ، فالأمْرُ جادٌّ هذه المَرّةَ

B *n* (Theat) [كَلام فَرْديّ يُوَجِّهُهُ المُمَثِّلُ للجُمْهورِ دون باقي الشَخْصيّاتِ]

C **(aside from)** *prep phr* ① (except for) باسْتِثْناءِ; **~ from the delay at the airport, everything went very smoothly** باسْتِثْناءِ التَأْخيرِ في المَطارِ، مَرَّتِ الأمورُ بِسَلاسةٍ شَديدةٍ ② (not to mention) إلى جانِبِ; **he has a lot to worry about, ~ from financial concerns** لَدَيْهِ الكَثيرُ مِمّا يَقْلَقُ بِشَأْنِهِ، إلى جانِبِ الشُؤونِ الماليّةِ

ask /ɑːsk/ **A** *vt* ① (to enquire as to) سَأَلَ (a; سُؤال) (عن) ‹*sb's name, the reason*›; **to ~ a question** سَأَلَ سُؤالاً; **I ~ed him the time** سَأَلْتُهُ عن الوَقْتِ; **to ~ the price of sth** سَأَلَ عن سِعْرِ شَيْءٍ; **he ~ed why you did it** سَأَلَ لِماذا فَعَلْتَ ذلك; **she ~ed**

whether it was necessary سَأَلَتْ ما إذا كانَ ذلك ضَرورِيًّا

2 (to request) طَلَبَ (u; طَلَب, مَطْلَب) ‹permission, sb's opinion›; **he has ~ed permission to take the car** اِسْتَأْذَنَ لِأَخْذِ السَّيّارةِ; **I'd like to ~ a favour** أَوَدُّ أَنْ أَطْلُبَ مِنْكَ مَعْروفاً; **she ~ed a favour of** *or* **from me, she ~ed me a favour** طَلَبَتْ مِنّي مَعْروفاً; **I ~ed him for his autograph** طَلَبْتُ مِنْهُ تَوْقيعَهُ 3 (to invite) دَعا (u) ‹a person›; **I'll ~ her** سَوْفَ أَدْعوها; **I wasn't ~ed** لم يَدْعُني أَحَدٌ; **to ~ sb in** دَعا شَخْصاً إلى مَنْزِلِهِ; **to ~ sb out** دَعا شَخْصاً للخُروجِ للتَّرْفيه; **to ~ sb to dinner** دَعا شَخْصاً إلى العَشاءِ; **to ~ sb to a concert** دَعا شَخْصاً إلى حَفْلةٍ موسيقيّةٍ; **he ~ed her to marry him** عَرَضَ عَلَيْها الزَواجَ

B *vi* 1 (in requests) «person» طَلَبَ (u; طَلَب, مَطْلَب); **you only have to ~** كُلُّ ما عَلَيْكَ هو أَنْ تَطْلُبَ 2 (in finding out) «person» اِسْتَعْلَمَ; **to ~ about sb/sth** اِسْتَعْلَمَ عن شَخْصٍ \ شَيْءٍ; **we ~ed about the bus times** اِسْتَعْلَمْنا عن مَواعيدِ الحافِلةِ; **I'll ~ around** [سَوْفَ أَسْتَعْلِمُ مِمَّنْ حَوْلي]

C *v refl* **to ~ oneself the reason/question** تَفَكَّرَ في السَّبَبِ \ المَسْأَلةِ

D *n* (infml) **a big ~** مَطْلَب صَعْب

(Idiom) **to ask for it** اِسْتَحَقَّ ما حَدَثَ لَهُ

(Phrasal verbs) **ask after**: **~ after [sb]** اطْمَأَنَّ على \ سَأَلَ عن [شَخْصٍ] ‹a patient, relative›

• **ask for**: 1 **~ for [sth]** طَلَبَ [شَيْئاً] ‹a drink, money, help› 2 **~ for [sb]** طَلَبَ التَحَدُّثَ إلى [شَخْصٍ]

askance /ə'skans/ *adv* **to look ~ at sb/sth** نَظَرَ بارْتِيابٍ إلى شَخْصٍ \ شَيْءٍ

askew /ə'skju:/ *adj, adv* ‹to hang› بِشَكْلٍ مائِلٍ; ‹tie› أَعْوَجَ (dipt; عوج); ‹picture› مائِل

asking price /'ɑ:skɪŋ prʌɪs/ *n* سِعْر عَرْضٍ \ بَيْعٍ

asleep /ə'sli:p/ *adj* **to be ~** كانَ نائِماً; **to fall ~** نامَ (a; نَوْم, نِيام); **to be sound** *or* **fast ~** اسْتَغْرَقَ في النَّوْمِ

asp /asp/ *n* صِلّ (أَصْلال)

asparagus /ə'sparəgəs/ *n* هِلْيَوْن

ASPCA /eɪespi:si:'eɪ/ *n* = **American Society for the Prevention of Cruelty to Animals** الجَمْعيّة الأَمْريكيّة لِمَنْعِ القَسْوةِ ضدّ الحَيَواناتِ

aspect /'aspɛkt/ *n* 1 (feature) بُعْد (أَبْعاد) 2 (orientation) وِجْهة

aspersions /ə'spəːʃ(ə)nz, ə'spəːʒ(ə)nz/ *n pl* **to cast ~ on sth/sb** قَدَحَ في شَيْءٍ \ شَخْصٍ

asphalt /'asfalt/ *n* أَسْفَلْت

asphyxia /əs'fɪksɪə/ *n* (Med) اخْتِناق (اخْتِناقات)

asphyxiate /əs'fɪksɪeɪt/ **A** *vt* خَنَقَ (u; خَنْق) ‹a child, an animal›

B *vi* «people, animals» اخْتَنَقَ

aspic /'aspɪk/ *n* [هُلام يُصْنَعُ من مَرَقِ اللَحْمِ]

aspiration /aspə'reɪʃ(ə)n/ *n* طُموح (طُموحات)

aspire /ə'spʌɪə/ *vi* طَمَحَ (a; طُموح); **to ~ to (do) sth** طَمَحَ إلى (فِعْلِ) شَيْءٍ

aspirin /'asp(ə)rɪn/ *n* (*pl* **aspirin** or **aspirins**) أَسْبِرين

aspiring /ə'spʌɪərɪŋ/ *adj* ‹writer, actor› طَموح

ass¹ /as/ *n* 1 (animal) حِمار (حَمير, حُمُر, أَحْمِرة) 2 (infml) (fool) حِمار (حَمير, حُمُر, أَحْمِرة)

ass² /as/ *n* (AmE vulg) إِسْت, (أَدْبار, دُبُر, مُؤَخّرة)

(Idioms) **to get off one's ass** (AmE infml) تَنَشَّطَ, تَحَرَّكَ; **to kick ass** (AmE infml) [دَفَعَ الأُمورَ إلى الأَمامِ بِإِصْرارٍ \ بِفَظاظةٍ]; **to work one's ass off** (AmE infml) [عَمِلَ بِجُهْدٍ كَبيرٍ]

assailant /ə'seɪl(ə)nt/ *n* (fml) مُهاجِم, مُعْتَدٍ, مُغير

assassin /ə'sasɪn/ *n* 1 (murderer) قاتِل (قاتِلونَ, قَتَلة, قُتّال); **a hired ~** قاتِل مَأْجور 2 (Hist) (Nizari fanatic) حَشّاش

assassinate /ə'sasɪneɪt/ *vt* اغْتالَ ‹the president, a leader›

assassination /ə,sasɪ'neɪʃ(ə)n/ *n* اغْتِيال (اغْتِيالات)

assault /ə'sɔ:lt/ **A** *vt* (Law) هَجَمَ (على), اعْتَدى (u; هُجوم) ‹a woman, teacher›; **to indecently ~ sb** اعْتَدى جِنْسِيًّا على شَخْصٍ

B *n* 1 (Law) اعْتِداء (اعْتِداءات), هُجوم 2 (Mil) غارة

assault course *n* مَيْدان المَوانِعِ

assault rifle *n* بُنْدُقيّة اقْتِحامٍ

assay /ə'seɪ/ *n* (Geol) اخْتِبار (اخْتِبارات), فَحْص (فُحوص)

assemble /ə'sɛmb(ə)l/ **A** *vt* 1 (to gather) جَمَعَ (a; جَمْع) ‹a team, collection› 2 (to construct) جَمَّعَ, رَكَّبَ ‹furniture, a car›

B *vi* «crowds, passengers» تَجَمَّعَ; «Parliament, Congress» اجْتَمَعَ

assembly /əˈsɛmbli/ *n* (*pl* **assemblies**) **1** [u] (coming together) تَجَمُّع **2** (group) تَجَمُّع **3** (Pol) (institution) جَمْعِيّة (تَشْريعِيّة) **4** (at school) [اجْتِماع الطُلاّبِ والأساتِذةِ في مَدارِسِ بَريطانيا بِغَرَضِ الصَلاةِ والإعْلاناتِ إلخ] **5** [u] (of components, machines) تَرْكيب (تَرْكيبات), تَجْميع

assembly line *n* خَطّ التَجْميعِ

assembly point *n* نُقْطة اجْتِماعٍ

assent /əˈsɛnt/ **A** *n* مُوافَقة, إذْن; **to give one's ~ to the marriage/bill** مَنَحَ مُوافَقَتَهُ على الزَواجِ \ مَشْروعِ القَرارِ

B *vi* «monarchs, parents» وافَقَ (على); **to ~ to sth** وافَقَ على شَيْءٍ

assert /əˈsəːt/ *vt* **1** (to declare) أَكَّدَ ‹*one's innocence, the facts*› **2** (to demonstrate forcefully) فَرَضَ (i; فَرْض) ‹*a right, one's authority*›; **to ~ oneself** فَرَضَ نَفْسَهُ

assertion /əˈsəːʃ(ə)n/ *n* **1** (declaration) تَأْكيد (تَأْكيدات) **2** (forceful demonstration) تَأْكيد (تَأْكيدات)

assertive /əˈsəːtɪv/ *adj* ‹*personality, behaviour*› صارِم, حازِم; **she's not very ~** هي لَيْسَتْ حازِمةً جِدًّا

assess /əˈsɛs/ *vt* **1** قَدَّرَ ‹*damage, value, tax*› **2** قَيَّمَ ‹*a situation, problem*› **3** قَيَّمَ ‹*an employee, a pupil, student*›

assessment /əˈsɛsmənt/ *n* **1** (of damage, value, tax) تَقْدير (تَقاديرُ, تَقْديرات) **2** (of a situation, problem) تَقْييم **3** (of employees, pupils, students) تَقْييم

asset /ˈasɛt/ *n* أَصْل (أُصول)

asset-stripping /ˈasɛtˌstrɪpɪŋ/ *n* نَزْع الأُصولِ

asshole /ˈashəʊl/ *n* (AmE vulg) أَحْمَق (dipt; حُمْق; f حَمْقى)

assiduous /əˈsɪdjʊəs/ *adj* ‹*reader, research*› دَؤُوب

assign /əˈsʌɪn/ *vt* **1** (to appoint) عَيَّنَ ‹*an employee, an officer*› **2** (to allocate) كَلَّفَ (ب) ‹*a task, mission*›; خَصَّصَ ‹*money, a resource*›; **to ~ a task to sb** كَلَّفَ شَخْصاً بِمُهِمّةٍ

assignment /əˈsʌɪnm(ə)nt/ *n* **1** (task) مُهِمّة **2** (Educ) واجِب مَدْرَسيّ

assimilate /əˈsɪmɪleɪt/ **A** *vt* (to understand) اسْتَوْعَبَ ‹*information, an idea*›

B *vi* (to become part of) «immigrants, refugees» انْدَمَجَ; **to ~ into a community** انْدَمَجَ في مُجْتَمَعٍ

assimilation /əsɪmɪˈleɪʃ(ə)n/ *n* **1** (of information, ideas) اسْتيعاب **2** (into a society, group) انْدِماج

assist /əˈsɪst/ **A** *vt* (to give help to) ساعَدَ ‹*a client, victim*›; **to ~ sb in (doing) sth** ساعَدَ شَخْصاً في (فِعْلِ) شَيْءٍ

B *vi* (to provide help) «experts, volunteers» ساعَدَ; **to ~ in (doing) sth** ساعَدَ في (فِعْلِ) شَيْءٍ

assistance /əˈsɪst(ə)ns/ *n* مُساعدة, عَوْن

assistant /əˈsɪst(ə)nt/ **A** *n* **1** (helper) مُساعِد **2** (also **shop assistant**) بائِع (باعة, بائِعون) **3** (BrE) (in a school) (also **foreign language assistant**) [مُدَرِّس مُساعِد في اللُغاتِ الأَجْنَبيّةِ]

B *adj* ‹*editor, manager*› مُساعِد

assistant referee *n* حَكَم مُساعِد

associate **A** /əˈsəʊʃɪeɪt/ *vt* **1** (to link in the mind) رَبَطَ (i-u; رَبْط) ‹*a memory, smell*›; **to ~ sb/sth with sb/sth** رَبَطَ شَخْصاً \ شَيْئاً بِشَخْصٍ \ بِشَيْءٍ **2** **to be ~d with sth** (to be involved, connected) «costs, risks» ارْتَبَطَ بِشَيْءٍ

B /əˈsəʊʃɪət/ *n* **1** (in business, a profession) شَريك (شُرَكاءُ) **2** (of a society, professional body) عُضْو (غَيْر كامِلِ العُضْويّةِ)

C /əˈsəʊʃɪeɪt/ *vi* **to ~ with sb** عاشَرَ شَخْصاً

associate professor *n* (AmE) أُسْتاذ مُشارِك

association /əsəʊsɪˈeɪʃ(ə)n/ *n* **1** (organization, club) جَمْعِيّة **2** (cooperation) اشْتِراك (اشْتِراكات); **to do sth in ~ with sb/sth** فَعَلَ شَيْئاً بالاشْتِراكِ مع شَخْصٍ \ شَيْءٍ **3** (link, connection) عَلاقة (عَلاقات, عَلائِقُ); **the ~ between cancer and smoking** العَلاقة بين السَرَطانِ والتَدْخينِ

Association Football *n* (BrE) كُرة القَدَمِ

assorted /əˈsɔːtɪd/ *adj* ‹*biscuits, sizes*› مُتَنَوِّع

assortment /əˈsɔːtm(ə)nt/ *n* (of products, colours, sizes) تَشْكيلة

assuage /əˈsweɪdʒ/ *vt* (liter) **1** (to ease) سَكَّنَ, خَفَّفَ ‹*guilt, pain*› **2** (to satisfy) أَشْبَعَ ‹*hunger, thirst*›

assume /ə'sju:m/ *vt* ⓵ (to suppose) افْتَرَضَ; **I ~ it is safe** أَفْتَرِضُ أَنَّهُ آمِنٌ ⓶ (to adopt) تَبَنَّى *‹an expression, a stance›*; **an ~d name** اسْمٌ مُنْتَحَل ⓷ (to take on) تَوَلَّى *‹responsibility, a role›*; **to ~ command/office** تَوَلَّى القِيادةَ \ المَنْصِبَ

assumption /ə'sʌm(p)ʃ(ə)n/ *n* ⓵ (supposition) افْتِراض (افْتِراضات); **to make an ~** افْتَرَضَ ⓶ (of command, responsibility, power) تَوَلٍّ

assurance /ə'ʃʊər(ə)ns/ *n* ⓵ (confidence) ثِقة بالنَفْسِ ⓶ (statement) ضَمان (تَأْكيدات) تَأْكيد ⓷ ▸ **insurance**

assure /ə'ʃɔ:/ *vt* ⓵ (to give a guarantee to) أَكَّدَ (ل) *‹the public, customers›*; **rest ~d that ...** كُنْ على ثِقةٍ من أنّ ... ⓶ (to ensure) ضَمِنَ (a; ضَمان) *‹safety, confidentiality›* ⓷ (BrE) (to insure) أَمَّنَ (على) *‹sb's life, a sum of money›*

Assyria /ə'sɪrɪə/ *pr n* (Hist) أَشور (dipt f)

asterisk /'astərɪsk/ *n* نَجْمة (نَجْمات)

asteroid /'astərɔɪd/ *n* كُوَيْكِب

asthma /'asmə/ *n* رَبْو

asthmatic /as'matɪk/ **A** *adj ‹symptoms, patient›* الرَبْوِ **B** *n* مَريض الرَبْوِ

astonish /ə'stɒnɪʃ/ *vt* أَذْهَلَ *‹an audience, onlookers›*

astonished /ə'stɒnɪʃt/ *adj ‹look, gasp›* انْدِهاشٍ; **to be ~ at** *or* **by sth** كانَ مُنْدَهِشاً \ مُنْذَهِلاً من شَيْءٍ

astonishing /ə'stɒnɪʃɪŋ/ *adj ‹discovery, achievement›* مُثير مُذْهِل, مُدْهِش, للدَهْشة

astonishment /ə'stɒnɪʃmənt/ *n* دَهْشة; **to his ~, she decided to come back to him** أَدْهَشَهُ قَرارُها بالعَوْدة إِلَيْهِ

astound /ə'staʊnd/ *vt* (positively) أَذْهَلَ; (negatively) صَدَمَ (i; صَدْم) *‹an audience›*

astounded /ə'staʊndɪd/ *adj* مَذْهول

astounding /ə'staʊndɪŋ/ *adj ‹success, discovery›* مُثير, مُذْهِل للدَهْشة

astray /ə'streɪ/ *adv* ⓵ **to go ~** (to go missing) ضاعَ (i; ضَيْع, ضَياع); (to do wrong) أَخْطَأَ ⓶ **to lead sb ~** (to mislead) ضَلَّلَ شَخْصاً; (to corrupt) أَفْسَدَ شَخْصاً

astride /ə'strʌɪd/ *prep ‹a horse, fence›* مُنْفَرِجَ الساقَيْنِ على

astringent /ə'strɪn(d)ʒ(ə)nt/ **A** *adj* ⓵ *‹ointment, lotion›* قابِض, لَواذِعُ) لاذِع) ⓶ *‹remark, tone›* مُقَلِّص **B** *n* (مادّة قابِضة للأَنْسِجةِ) مُقَلِّص, قابِض

astrologer /ə'strɒlədʒə/, **astrologist** /ə'strɒlədʒɪst/ *n* مُنَجِّم

astrology /ə'strɒlədʒi/ *n* عِلْم التَنْجيمِ

astronaut /'astrənɔ:t/ *n* رائِد فَضاءٍ

astronomer /ə'strɒnəmə/ *n* عالِم الفَلَكِ, فَلَكيّ

astronomical /astrə'nɒmɪk(ə)l/, **astronomic** /astrə'nɒmɪk/ *adj* ⓵ (Astron) *‹observatory, telescope›* فلكيّ ⓶ (infml) (huge) *‹cost, price›* فَلَكيّ

astronomy /ə'strɒnəmi/ *n* عِلْم الفَلَكِ

astrophysicist /,astrəʊ'fɪzɪsɪst/ *n* عالِم الفيزِياءِ الفَلَكيّةِ

astute /ə'stju:t/ *adj ‹observation, politician›* ذَكيّ (أَذْكِياءُ)

Aswan /as'wɑ:n/ *pr n* أَسْوان (dipt f); **the ~ High Dam** سَدّ أَسْوانَ العالي

asylee /əsʌɪ'li:/ *n* (AmE) لاجِئ

asylum /ə'sʌɪləm/ *n* ⓵ [u] (protection) لُجوء; **to grant sb ~** مَنَحَ مَصَحّة نَفْسيّة ⓶ (institution) (old use or offensive) اللُجوءَ لِشَخصٍ

asylum seeker *n* طالِب لُجوءٍ

at /at, ət/ *prep* ⓵ (expressing location) عَلى, عِنْدَ, في; **~ school** في المَدْرَسةِ; **~ my house** عِنْدي في البَيْتِ, في بَيْتي; **~ the border** على الحُدودِ ⓶ (expressing time) في; **~ 4 o'clock** في الساعةِ الرابعةِ; **~ night** في اللَيْلِ; **~ the moment** في هذه اللَحْظةِ, حالِيًّا ⓷ (expressing a state) في; **we are ~ war/peace** نَحْنُ في حالةِ حَرْبٍ \ سَلامٍ; **to be hard ~ work** عَمِلَ بِجُهْدٍ

(Idiom) **while I'm at it** (infml) طالَما أنا بِصَدَدِ فِعْلِ هذا الأَمْرِ

ate /ɛt/ *past tense* ▸ **eat**

atheism /'eɪθɪɪz(ə)m/ *n* إِلْحاد

atheist /'eɪθɪɪst/ **A** *n* مُلْحِد (مُلْحِدونَ) **B** *adj ‹views, beliefs›* إِلْحاديّ

Athens /'aθɪnz/ *pr n* أَثينا

athlete /'aθli:t/ *n* لاعِب أَلْعابِ القُوى

athlete's foot *n* سَعْفة القَدَمِ, قَدَم الرِياضيّ

athletic /aθ'lɛtɪk/ *adj* ⓵ *‹competition, event›* رِياضيّ ⓶ *‹goalkeeper, physique›* رِياضيّ

athletics /aθ'lɛtɪks/ *n pl* (BrE) (track and field events) أَلْعاب القُوى; (AmE) (sports) أَلْعاب رِياضيّة

Atlantic /at'lantɪk/ **A** *pr n* (**the Atlantic**) المُحيط الأَطْلَسيّ \ الأَطْلَنطيّ
B *adj* ‹*coast, storm*› أَطْلَسيّ, أَطْلَنْطيّ

Atlantic Ocean *n* (**the Atlantic Ocean**) المُحيط الأَطْلَسيّ \ الأَطْلَنطيّ

atlas /'atləs/ *n* أَطْلَس, مُصَوَّر جُغْرافيّ

ATM /eɪtiː'ɛm/ *n* = **automated teller machine** صَرّاف آليّ

atmosphere /'atməsfɪə/ *n* **1** (of a planet) غِلاف جَوّيّ **2** (in a room, an environment) جَوّ (أَجْواء) **3** (mood) جَوّ (أَجْواء)

atmospheric /atməs'fɛrɪk/ *adj* **1** ‹*pressure, pollution*› جَوّيّ **2** ‹*music, film*› [يُضْفي جَوًّا جميلاً]

atom /'atəm/ *n* ذَرّة

atom bomb *n* قُنْبُلة ذَرّيّة

atomic /ə'tɒmɪk/ *adj* ‹*explosion, energy*› ذَرّيّ

atone /ə'təʊn/ *vi* **to ~ for one's sins/an error** كَفَّرَ عن سَيِّئاتِهِ \ أَخْطائِهِ

atop /ə'tɒp/ *prep* فَوْقَ

atrocious /ə'trəʊʃəs/ *adj* **1** (cruel) ‹*crime, treatment*› مُريع, فَظيع **2** (infml) (very bad) ‹*weather, spelling*› فَظيع

atrocity /ə'trɒsɪti/ *n* (*pl* **atrocities**) عَمَل وَحْشيّ

atrophy /'atrəfi/ **A** *vi* (**atrophies, atrophying, atrophied**) (Med) «muscles, limbs» ضَمَرَ (u; ضُمور, ضُمْر)
B *n* **1** (degeneration) ضُمور **2** (Med) ضُمور; **~ of the optic nerves** ضُمور الأَعْصابِ البَصَريّةِ

at sign *n* @ \ عَلامة آت

attach /ə'tatʃ/ *vt* **1** (to fix) أَلْصَقَ ‹*a label*›; رَبَطَ (i-u; رَبْط) ‹*a rope*›; **he ~ed the rope to the post** رَبَطَ الحَبْلَ بالعَمودِ **2** (to a letter, an email) أَرْفَقَ ‹*a document, file*› **3 to ~ importance to sth** أَعْطى أَهَمّيّةً لِشَيْءٍ

attaché /ə'taʃeɪ/ *n* مُلْحَق

attaché case *n* [حَقيبة أَوْراقٍ صَغيرة]

attached /ə'tatʃt/ *adj* (fond) **to be ~ to sth/sb** كانَ مُتَعَلِّقاً بِشَيْءٍ \ بِشَخصٍ

attachment /ə'tatʃm(ə)nt/ *n* **1** (affection) تَعَلُّق; **a close ~ to sb/sth** تَعَلُّق وَثيق بِشَخْصٍ \ بِشَيْءٍ **2** (tool) مُرْفَق (مُرْفَقات) **3** (in an e-mail) مُرْفَق (مُرْفَقات)

attack /ə'tak/ **A** *vt* **1** هَجَمَ (u; هُجوم; على) ‹*a victim, city*› **2** عالَجَ ‹*a task, problem*›
B *n* **1** (on a person, place) هُجوم **2** (of an illness) نَوْبة

attacker /ə'takə/ *n* **1** (assailant) مُهاجِم, مُعْتَدٍ **2** (in sport) مُهاجِم

attain /ə'teɪn/ *vt* **1** (to achieve) حَقَّقَ ‹*an ambition*›; نالَ (a; نَيْل, مَنال) ‹*a position*› **2** (to reach) بَلَغَ (u; بُلوغ) ‹*an age*›

attainment /ə'teɪnm(ə)nt/ *n* **1** [u] (of a goal) بُلوغ **2** (success) إِنْجاز (إِنْجازات)

attempt /ə'tɛm(p)t/ **A** *vt* حاوَلَ القِيامَ ب ‹*a coup*›; حاوَلَ ‹*a rescue*›; حاوَلَ الرَّدَّ على ‹*a question*›; حاوَلَ أَداءَ ‹*an exam*›; **to ~ to do sth** حاوَلَ عَمَلَ شَيْءٍ; **~ed murder/suicide** مُحاوَلة قَتْلٍ \ انْتِحارٍ
B *n* (effort) مُحاوَلة; **to make an ~ to do sth** قامَ بِمُحاوَلةٍ لِعَمَلِ شَيْءٍ; **to make an ~ on sb's life** قامَ بِمُحاوَلةِ قَتْلِ شَخْصٍ

attend /ə'tɛnd/ **A** *vt* **1** (to be present at) حَضَرَ (u; حُضور) ‹*a meeting, ceremony*› **2** (to be a member of) ذَهَبَ (a; ذَهاب; إلى) ‹*a school, class*›
B *vi* (to be present) حَضَرَ (u; حُضور)

(Phrasal verb) **attend to**: **~ to [sth/sb]** تَعامَلَ مع [شَيْءٍ \ شَخْصٍ] ‹*a problem, correspondence*›; خَدَمَ [شَخْصاً] ‹*a customer*›; اعْتَنى ب [شَخْصٍ] ‹*patient*›

attendance /ə'tɛnd(ə)ns/ *n* **1** (presence) حُضور **2** (number of people present) حُضور

attendant /ə'tɛnd(ə)nt/ *n* عامِل

attendee /atɛn'diː/ *n* حاضِر (حُضور, حُضَّر)

attention /ə'tɛnʃ(ə)n/ **A** *n* **1** (concentration) انْتِباه; **to pay ~ to sth/sb** انْتَبَهَ إلى شَيْءٍ \ شَخْصٍ; **pay ~!** انْتَبِهْ!; **to give sth/sb one's full ~** أَوْلى شَيْئاً \ شَخْصاً الانْتِباهَ الكامِلَ; **to turn one's ~ to sth** حَوَّلَ انْتِباهَهُ إلى شَيْءٍ; **~, please!** الرَجاءُ الانْتِباهُ! **2** (notice) انْتِباه, اهْتِمام; **to catch sb's ~** اسْتَرْعى انْتِباهَ \ اهْتِمامَ شَخْصٍ; **he didn't want to draw ~ to himself** لم يَرْغَبْ

في لَفْتِ الانْتِباهِ إلَيْهِ; **to be the centre of ~** كانَ مَرْكَزَ الاهْتِمامِ [3] (care) رِعاية, عِناية; **the car needs some ~** تَحْتاجُ السَّيّارةُ إلى بَعْضِ العِنايةِ; **he needs medical ~** يَحْتاجُ إلى رِعايةٍ طِبِّيّةٍ; **~ to detail** العِناية \ الاهْتِمام بالتَفاصيلِ; **for the ~ of** إلى \ لِعِناية [4] (Mil) **to stand to/at ~** وَقَفَ وَقْفةَ انْتِباهٍ
[B] *excl* انْتِباه

attention deficit disorder *n* اضْطِراب نَقْصِ الانْتِباهِ وَفَرْطِ النَشاطِ

attention span *n* فَتْرة انْتِباهٍ

attentive /əˈtentɪv/ *adj* [1] (alert) ‹*audience, pupil*› مُصْغٍ, مُنْتَبِه [2] (helpful) ‹*service*› جَيِّد; ‹*host*› مِضْياف (mf)

attenuate /əˈtenjʊeɪt/ *vt* خَفَّفَ ‹*criticism, impact*›

attic /ˈatɪk/ *n* عِلِّيّة

attire /əˈtʌɪə/ *n* (fml) ثِياب, لِبْس

attitude /ˈatɪtjuːd/ *n* مَوْقِف (مَواقِفُ)

attorney /əˈtəːni/ *n* (*pl* **attorneys**) (AmE) (at law) مُحامٍ (مُحامونَ); (representative) وَكيل (وُكَلاءُ)

attorney general *n* (*pl* **attorneys general**) [1] (in UK) نائِب عامّ [2] (in US) (at national level) وَزير العَدْلِ; (at state level) نائِب عامّ

attract /əˈtrakt/ *vt* [1] (to appeal to) جَذَبَ (i; جَذْب) ‹*people, a man*› [2] (to draw) جَذَبَ (i; جَذْب) ‹*flies, a crowd*›

attraction /əˈtrakʃ(ə)n/ *n* [1] (favourable feature) نُقْطة جَذْبٍ [2] [u] (interest) انْجِذاب; **his growing ~ to her** انْجِذابُهُ المُتَزايِد إلَيْها [3] (entertainment, sight) مَعْلَم (مَعالِمُ); **a tourist ~** مَعْلَم سِياحيّ [4] (Phys) جاذِبيّة

attractive /əˈtraktɪv/ *adj* [1] ‹*woman*› جَذّاب; ‹*village*› جَميل [2] ‹*offer, investment*› مُغْرٍ

attributable /əˈtrɪbjʊtəb(ə)l/ *adj* **to be ~ to human error/skill** نُسِبَ إلى خَطَأٍ بَشَريٍّ \ مَهارةٍ

attribute [A] /əˈtrɪbjuːt/ *vt* **to ~ sth to sth/sb** نَسَبَ شَيْئاً إلى شَيْءٍ \ شَخْصٍ ‹*a success*›; عَزا شَيْئاً إلى شَيْءٍ \ شَخْصٍ ‹*a problem*›
[B] /ˈatrɪbjuːt/ *n* (inborn) سَجيّة (سَجايا, سَجيّات); (acquired) خاصّيّة (خَصائِصُ, خاصّيّات); (character trait) خَصْلة (خِصال), صِفة

attrition /əˈtrɪʃ(ə)n/ *n* [1] (wearing down) اسْتِنْزاف; **war of ~** حَرْب الاسْتِنْزافِ [2] (in a company) [تَقْليل عَدَدِ المُوَظَّفينَ بِعَدَمِ اسْتِبْدالِ العُمّالِ المُغادِرينَ]

atypical /eɪˈtɪpɪk(ə)l/ *adj* ‹*feature, behaviour*› غَريب, شاذّ

aubergine /ˈəʊbəʒiːn/ *n* (BrE) [1] (vegetable) باذِنْجان [2] (colour) [لَوْن بَنَفْسَجيّ غامِق] (باذِنْجانات)

auburn /ˈɔːb(ə)n/ *adj* ‹*hair*› كَسْتَنائيّ

auction /ˈɔːkʃ(ə)n/ [A] *n* مَزاد (مَزادات)
[B] *vt* (also **auction off**) عَرَضَ في المَزادِ ‹*a house, painting*›

auctioneer /ɔːkʃəˈnɪə/ *n* دَلّال \ مُنادٍ بالمَزادِ

auction house /ˈɔːkʃ(ə)n ˌhaʊs/ *n* صالة المَزاداتِ

auction site *n* مَوْقِع مَزاداتٍ

audacious /ɔːˈdeɪʃəs/ *adj* [1] (bold) ‹*attempt, robbery*› جَريء [2] (impudent) ‹*behaviour, boy*› وَقِح

audacity /ɔːˈdasɪti/ *n* جُرْأة

audible /ˈɔːdɪb(ə)l/ *adj* ‹*sigh, click*› مَسْموع

audience /ˈɔːdɪəns/ *n* جُمْهور (n coll, no singul n; جَماهيرُ)

audience ratings *n* نِسَب المُشاهَدةِ

audio /ˈɔːdɪəʊ/ *n* صَوْت

audiobook /ˈɔːdɪəʊbʊk/ *n* كِتاب صَوْتيّ

audio file *n* مِلَفّ صَوْتيّ \ صَوْتٍ

audiologist /ɔːdiˈɒlədʒɪst/ *n* أخِصّائيّ سَمْعٍ

audiology /ˌɔːdiˈɒlədʒi/ *n* عِلْم السَمْعِ

audio track *n* تَسْجيل صَوْتيّ

audiovisual /ˌɔːdɪəʊˈvɪʒʊəl/ *adj* ‹*method, equipment*› سَمْعيّ بَصَريّ

audit /ˈɔːdɪt/ [A] *n* تَدْقيق حِساباتٍ
[B] *vt* دَقَّقَ (في) ‹*accounts*›; دَقَّقَ في الحِساباتِ ‹*a company*›

audition /ɔːˈdɪʃ(ə)n/ [A] *n* اخْتِبار \ تَجْرِبة أداءٍ
[B] *vi* «candidates, actors» خَضَعَ لاخْتِبارِ أداءٍ; **to ~ for a part** خَضَعَ لاخْتِبارِ أداءٍ لِدَوْرٍ
[C] *vt* «producer, director» أخْضَعَ لاخْتِبارِ أداءٍ ‹*candidates, actors*›

auditor /ˈɔːdɪtə/ *n* [1] (accountant) مُدَقِّق حِساباتٍ [2] (AmE) (student) مُسْتَمِع

auditorium /ɔːdɪˈtɔːrɪəm/ *n* (*pl* **auditoriums** or **auditoria**) قاعة (مَسْرَحٍ \ مُحاضراتٍ إلخ)

augment /ɔːgˈment/ *vt* نَمّى ‹*one's income, supplies*›

augur /ˈɔːgə/ *vi* **to ~ well/badly for sb/sth** نَبَّأَ بِخَيْرٍ \ بِشَرٍّ لِشَخْصٍ \ لِشَيْءٍ

august /ɔːˈgʌst/ *adj* ‹*organization, presence*› عَظيم

August /ˈɔːgəst/ *n* أَغُسْطُس (Egypt, Gulf), آب (dipt; Levant, Iraq), أوت (Algeria, Tunisia), غُشْت (Mor) ▸ **March**

aunt /ɑːnt/ *n* **1▸** (sister of your father) عَمّة; (sister of your mother) خالة; **A~ Kathryn** العَمّة \ الخالة كاثْرين **2▸** (wife of your father's brother) زَوْجة عَمٍّ; (wife of your mother's brother) زَوْجة خالٍ

auntie, aunty /ˈɑːnti/ *n* (infml) (father's side) عَمَّتي; (mother's side) خالَتي

au pair /əʊ ˈpɛː/ *n* [مُبْتَعَث يُقيمُ مع عائلةٍ في الخارِجِ وَيُساعِدُ في الأَعْمالِ المَنْزِلِيّةِ]

aura /ˈɔːrə/ *n* (*pl* **auras** or **aurae**) هالة

aural /ˈɔːr(ə)l/ *adj* **1▸** (Med) ‹*infection, anatomy*› أُذُنِيّ **2▸** (Educ) ‹*comprehension, test*› سَمْعِيّ

auricle /ˈɔːrɪk(ə)l/ *n* (of heart) أُذَيْن; (of ear) صِوان الأُذُنِ

auspices /ˈɔːspɪsiz/ *n pl* **under the ~ of sth/sb** تحت رِعايةِ شَيْءٍ \ شَخْصٍ

auspicious /ɔːˈspɪʃəs/ *adj* ‹*occasion*› مُواتٍ; ‹*beginning*› مُبَشِّر بالنَجاح

austere /ɒˈstɪə, ɔːˈstɪə/ *adj* ‹*building, surroundings*› بَسيط; ‹*lifestyle*› مُتَقَشِّف

austerity /ɒˈsterɪti, ɔːˈsterɪti/ *n* (of a building, an area) بَساطة; (of a lifestyle, period) تَقَشُّف

Australasia /ˌɒstrəˈleɪʒə/ *pr n* أُسْتُرالاسيا

Australia /ɒˈstreɪlɪə, ɔːˈstreɪlɪə/ *pr n* أُسْتُراليا

Australian /ɒˈstreɪlɪən, ɔːˈstreɪlɪən/ *n, adj* أُسْتُرالِيّ

Austria /ˈɒstrɪə/ *pr n* النِمْسا

Austrian /ˈɒstrɪən/ *n, adj* نِمْساوِيّ

authentic /ɔːˈθentɪk/ *adj* ‹*document, signature*› أَصْلِيّ; **an ~ Van Gogh** لَوْحة أَصْلِيّة لِفان جوخ

authenticate /ɔːˈθentɪkeɪt/ *vt* أَثْبَتَ الصِحّةَ ‹*a signature*›; تَثَبَّتَ (مِن) ‹*sb's identity*›

authenticity /ɔːθenˈtɪsɪti/ *n* أَصالة, صِحّة

author /ˈɔːθə/ *n* (كُتّاب ,كاتِبونَ) كاتِب ,مُؤَلِّف

authoritarian /ɔːˌθɒrɪˈtɛːrɪən/ *adj* ‹*government, parents*› مُتَسَلِّط, مُسْتَبِدّ

authoritative /ɔːˈθɒrɪtətɪv/ *adj* **1▸** (forceful) ‹*manner, voice*› آمِر **2▸** (reliable) ‹*work, source*› مَوْثوق بِهِ

authority /ɔːˈθɒrɪti/ *n* **1▸** [u] (power) سُلْطة; **to have the ~ to do sth** كانَ لَدَيْهِ السُلْطةُ لِفِعْلِ شَيْءٍ **2▸** (organization) سُلْطة (سُلُطات ,سُلْطات); **the local ~** السُلْطة المَحَلِّيّة; **the Algerian authorities** السُلُطات الجَزائِرِيّة **3▸** (expert) خَبير (خُبَراءُ) **4▸** [u] (forcefulness) قوّة

authorization, -isation (BrE) /ɔːθərʌɪˈzeɪʃ(ə)n/ *n* (permission) تَفْويض (تَفْويضات); (approval) مُوافقة

authorize, -ise (BrE) /ˈɔːθərʌɪz/ *vt* وافقَ (على) ‹*a loan, visit*›

autism /ˈɔːtɪz(ə)m/ *n* مَرَض التَوَحُّد

autistic /ɔːˈtɪstɪk/ *adj* ‹*child*› مُصاب بِمَرَضِ التَوَحُّدِ ,تَوَحُّدِيّ

auto /ˈɔːtəʊ/ *n* (AmE) سَيّارة

autobiographical /ɔːtəbʌɪəˈgrafɪk(ə)l/ *adj* ‹*novel, details*› سيرة ذاتِيّة

autobiography /ɔːtəbʌɪˈɒgrəfi/ *n* (*pl* **autobiographies**) سيرة ذاتيّة

autocratic /ɔːtəˈkratɪk/ *adj* ‹*regime, ruler*› اسْتِبْدادِيّ, أوتوقْراطِيّ

autocue® /ˈɔːtəʊkjuː/ *n* شاشة القِراءةِ

autograph /ˈɔːtəgrɑːf/ **A** *n* تَوْقيع (شَخْصٍ مَشْهورٍ) **B** *vt* وَقَّعَ ‹*a book, football*›

automata /ɔːˈtɒmətə/ *n pl* ▸ **automaton**

automate /ɔːtəmeɪt/ *vt* أَتْمَتَ ,شَغَّلَ آلِيًّا \ أوتوماتيكيًّا ‹*a process, task*›

automatic /ɔːtəˈmatɪk/ **A** *adj* **1▸** ‹*transmission, car wash*› آلِيّ, أوتوماتيكِيّ **2▸** ‹*reaction, reflex*› تِلْقائِيّ **B** *n* **1▸** (washing machine) غَسّالة آلِيّة **2▸** (car) سَيّارة أوتوماتيكيّة **3▸** (gun) بُنْدُقيّة أوتوماتيكيّة

automatically /ɔːtəˈmatɪkli/ *adv* ‹to switch on, wash› تِلْقائيًّا, أوتوماتيكيًّا

automatic pilot *n* طَيّار آلِيّ

automation /ɔːtəˈmeɪʃ(ə)n/ *n* تَشْغيل آلِيّ \ ذاتِيّ, أَتْمَتة

automaton /ɔːˈtɒmət(ə)n/ *n* (*pl* **automatons** *or* **automata**) آلة ذاتيّة التَشْغيلِ \ الحَرَكةِ

automobile /ˈɔːtəməbiːl/ *n* (AmE) سَيّارة

automotive /ˌɔːtəˈməʊtɪv/ *adj* ‹industry, sales› السَيّاراتِ

autonomous /ɔːˈtɒnəməs/ *adj* ‹region, state› مُسْتَقِلّ

autonomy /ɔːˈtɒnəmi/ *n* حُكْم ذاتِيّ, اسْتِقْلاليّة

autopilot /ˈɔːtəʊˌpʌɪlət/ *n* طَيّار آلِيّ

autopsy /ˈɔːtɒpsi/ *n* (*pl* **autopsies**) تَشْريح جِنائِيّ, تَشْريح جُثّةٍ

autumn /ˈɔːtəm/ *n* خَريف ▸ **summer**

auxiliary /ɔːgˈzɪlɪəri/ **A** *adj* ‹nurse, teacher› مُساعِد; ‹engine, fuel tank› إضافِيّ

B *n* (*pl* **auxiliaries**) مُساعِد

avail /əˈveɪl/ **A** *v refl* (fml) **to ~ oneself of sth** اسْتَفادَ \ اسْتَنْفَعَ مِن شَيْءٍ ‹a service, an opportunity›

B *n* **to no/little ~** دون \ بِلا جَدْوى

availability /əveɪləˈbɪlɪti/ *n* تَوَفُّر; **subject to ~** مَرْهون بالتَوَفُّرِ

available /əˈveɪləb(ə)l/ *adj* **1** ‹ticket, product› مُتَوَفِّر **2** ‹doctor, boss› مُتَواجِد

avalanche /ˈavəlɑːnʃ/ *n* انْهيار ثَلْجِيّ

avant-garde /ˌavɒ̃ˈgɑːd/ *adj* ‹artist› طَليعِيّ; ‹design› إبْداعِيّ

avarice /ˈav(ə)rɪs/ *n* جَشَع

avaricious /avəˈrɪʃəs/ *adj* ‹trader, nature› جَشِع, طَمّاع

Ave. *abbr* = **Avenue** ش. (اخْتِصار كَلِمةِ شارِعٍ)

avenge /əˈven(d)ʒ/ *vt* ثَأَرَ (ل), انْتَقَمَ (ل) (a; ثَأْر ل) ‹sb's death, a defeat›; **to ~ sb** انْتَقَمَ \ ثَأَرَ لِشَخْصٍ

avenue /ˈav(ə)njuː/ *n* **1** (street, road) طَريق \ شارِع رَئيسِيّ **2** (driveway) [طَريق مُؤَدٍّ من طَريقٍ عامٍّ إلى مَدْخَلِ بَيْتٍ] **3** (option) سَبيل (mf; سُبُل)

average /ˈav(ə)rɪdʒ/ **A** *n* مُتَوَسِّط, مُعَدَّل (مُعَدَّلات); **to be above/below ~** كانَ فوق \ دون المُتَوَسِّطِ; **to take an ~ of the results** أَخَذَ مُتَوَسِّطَ النَتائِجِ; **on ~** في المُتَوَسِّطِ; **at an ~ of 30 mph** بِمُعَدَّلِ 30 ميلاً في الساعةِ; **to work out an ~** قامَ بِحِسابِ المُتَوَسِّطِ; **by the law of ~s** طِبْقاً لِقانونِ المُتَوَسِّطاتِ

B *adj* ‹amount, cost, earnings› مُتَوَسِّط, عادِيّ; **what is the ~ age of the class?** ما هو مُتَوَسِّطُ الأَعْمارِ في الفَصْلِ؟; **on an ~ day I work seven hours** في اليَوْمِ العادِيِّ أَعْمَلُ سَبْعَ ساعاتٍ; **the ~ citizen** المُواطِن العادِيّ; **he's a very ~ writer** هو كاتِبٌ عادِيٌّ جِدًّا

C *vt* ‹80 kph› بَلَغَ المُعَدَّلَ; **I ~ seven hours' work a day** أَعْمَلُ بِمُعَدَّلِ سَبْعِ ساعاتٍ في اليَوْمِ

(Phrasal verb) **average out** وَصَلَ إلى مُعَدَّلٍ

averse /əˈvəːs/ *adj* **to be ~ to sth/to doing sth** نَفَرَ من شَيْءٍ \ فِعْلِ شَيْءٍ

aversion /əˈvəːʃ(ə)n/ *n* كُرْه, نُفور; **to have an ~ to sb/sth** نَفَرَ من شَخْصٍ \ شَيْءٍ

avert /əˈvəːt/ *vt* **1** (to prevent) دَرَأَ (a; دَرْء) ‹a disaster, war› **2** **to ~ one's eyes from sth** حَوَّلَ بَصَرَهُ عن شَيْءٍ

aviary /ˈeɪvɪəri/ *n* مَطْيَر (قَفَص \ مَبْنًى واسِع لِتَرْبِيةِ العَصافيرِ)

aviation /eɪvɪˈeɪʃ(ə)n/ *n* طَيَران

avid /ˈavɪd/ *adj* ‹fan, reader› مُتَحَمِّس

avocado /ˌavəˈkɑːdəʊ/ *n* **1** (also **avocado pear**) (fruit) أفوكادو **2** (tree) شَجَرة الأفوكادو **3** (colour) [لَوْن أَخْضَر غامِق]

avoid /əˈvɔɪd/ *vt* **1** تَجَنَّبَ ‹damage, an argument›; **in order to ~ losing more money** من أَجْلِ تَجَنُّبِ خَسارةِ المَزيدِ من المالِ **2** «vehicles, cyclists» تَفادى ‹a hole, pedestrian›

avoidable /əˈvɔɪdəb(ə)l/ *adj* ‹death, accident› يُمْكِنُ تَجَنُّبُهُ

avoidance /əˈvɔɪd(ə)ns/ *n* **1** (of a person) تَجَنُّب **2** (of a responsibility) تَهَرُّب

avowed /əˈvaʊd/ *adj attrib* ‹aim› مُعْلَن; ‹atheist› صَريح

await /əˈweɪt/ *vt* انْتَظَرَ, تَرَقَّبَ ‹instructions, a letter›

awake /əˈweɪk/ **A** *vt* (*past tense* **awoke**, *past participle* **awoken**) **1** (from sleep) أَيْقَظَ ‹a child, sleeper› **2** (to evoke) أَثارَ ‹fear, suspicion, memories›

B *vi* (*past tense* **awoke**, *past participle* **awoken**) «person, animal» اسْتَيْقَظَ; **she awoke from a deep sleep** اسْتَيْقَظَتْ من نَوْمٍ عَميقٍ

C *adj* مُسْتَيْقِظ; **he was wide ~** كانَ مُسْتَيْقِظاً تَماماً; **are you**

still ~? هل ما زِلْتَ مُسْتَيْقِظاً؟; **I couldn't stay ~** لم أَسْتَطِعْ أنْ أَبْقى مُسْتَيْقِظاً; **to lie ~** تَمَدَّدَ دون أنْ يَنامَ; **the noise kept me ~** أَبْقاني الضَجيجُ مُسْتَيْقِظاً

awaken /əˈweɪk(ə)n/ **A** *vt* (*past tense* **awoke**, *past participle* **awoken**) **1** (to stimulate) أَثارَ ‹*one's curiosity, interest*› **2** (from sleep) أَيْقَظَ ‹*a sleeper, child*›
B *vi* (*past tense* **awoke**, *past participle* **awoken**) (from sleep) «people, children» اسْتَيْقَظَ

awakening /əˈweɪk(ə)nɪŋ/ *n* صَحْوة (صَحَوات)

award /əˈwɔːd/ **A** *vt* **1** مَنَحَ (a; مَنْح) ‹*a prize, penalty, points*› **2** حَكَمَ (u; حُكْم; ب) ‹*compensation, damages*›
B *n* **1** (prize) جائِزة (جَوائِز); **to win an ~ for sth** حازَ جائِزةً في شَيْءٍ **2** (grant) مِنْحة (مِنَح)

award ceremony *n* حَفْل تَوْزيع الجَوائِزِ

award-winning /əˈwɔːdwɪnɪŋ/ *adj* ‹*film, design*› حائِز على جائِزةٍ

aware /əˈwɛː/ *adj* (conscious) مُدْرِك, واعٍ (واعون, وُعاة); **to be ~ of a problem** وَعى مُشْكِلةً; **to be ~ of a smell** انْتَبَهَ لِرائِحةٍ; **as far as I am ~** حَسَبَ \ على حَدِّ عِلْمي; **I became ~ of his plans** أَصْبَحْتُ مُدْرِكاً لِخُطَطِهِ; **the whole family is environmentally ~** كُلُّ العائِلةِ واعِيةٌ بيئيًّا

awareness /əˈwɛːnəs/ *n* وَعْي, إدْراك

awash /əˈwɒʃ/ *adj* ‹*room, deck*› غارِق \ مُغَطًّى بالماءِ; **the village is ~ with tourists** القَرْيةُ مَليئةٌ بالسُيّاحِ

away /əˈweɪ/ **A** *adv* **1** (not present) **to be ~** كانَ غائِباً; **I'll be ~ for a week** سَأَغيبُ أُسْبوعاً; **to be ~ from home** غابَ عن البَيْتِ **2** (in space) **to be fifty metres/three kilometres ~** كانَ على بُعْدِ خَمْسينَ متراً \ ثَلاثةِ كيلومترَاتٍ **3** (in time) **London is two hours ~** تَقَعُ لُنْدُن على بُعْدِ ساعَتَيْنِ; **my birthday is two months ~** تَبَقّى شَهْران على عيدِ ميلادي **4** (in the opposite direction) **to shuffle/crawl ~** دَلَفَ \ زَحَفَ في الاتِّجاهِ المُعاكِسِ **5** ‹*to play, win*› على أَرْضِ المُنافِسِ
B *adj* ‹*game, win, goal*› على أَرْضِ المُنافِسِ; **the ~ team** الفَريق الزائِر

awe /ɔː/ *n* رَهْبة, مَهابة; **to listen in ~** اسْتَمَعَ بِرَهْبةٍ; **to be in ~ of sb** هابَ شَخْصاً

awe-inspiring /ˈɔːɪnspʌɪərɪŋ/ *adj* ‹*spectacle, beauty*› مَهيب

awesome /ˈɔːs(ə)m/ *adj* **1** (daunting) ‹*power, responsibility*› رَهيب **2** (infml) (superb) مُمْتاز, رائِع

awestruck /ˈɔːstrʌk/ *adj* ‹*silence*› رَهيب; ‹*spectator*› مَذْهول

awful /ˈɔːfʊl/ *adj* **1** (unpleasant) ‹*weather*› مُقْرِف, فَظيع **2** (bad quality) ‹*film*› سَيِّءٌ جِدًّا **3** (ill) شَديد المَرَضِ; **you look ~** تَبْدو في حالةٍ يُرْثى لَها **4** (guilty) مُذْنِب; **I felt ~** أَنَّبَني ضَميري **5** (infml) (as an intensifier) فَظيع; **an ~ lot of work** كَمِّيّة فَظيعة من العَمَلِ; **she's an ~ flirt** هي لَعوبٌ جِدًّا

awfully /ˈɔːfʊli/ *adv* **1** (very badly) ‹*to sing, play*› بِشَكْلٍ سَيِّءٍ **2** جِدًّا ‹*hard, hot, nice*› بِشَكْلٍ فَظيعٍ; **she drives ~ fast!** هي تَقودُ بِسُرْعةٍ فَظيعةٍ!

awhile /əˈwʌɪl/ *adv* ‹*to wait, rest*› لِفَتْرةٍ قَصيرةٍ

awkward /ˈɔːkwəd/ *adj* **1** ‹*shape, position*› صَعْب **2** (clumsy) ‹*teenager*› أَخْرَق (dipt; خُرْق); (not graceful) ‹*movement*› غَيْر رَشيقٍ **3** (hard, problematic) ‹*issue, choice*› صَعْب (صِعاب), عَسير; **at an ~ time** في وَقْتٍ صَعْبٍ \ حَرِجٍ **4** (embarrassing) ‹*question, meeting*› مُحْرِج **5** (uncooperative) أَخْرَق (dipt; خُرْق); **you're just being ~!** أَنْتَ مُجَرَّدُ أَخْرَقٍ!

awning /ˈɔːnɪŋ/ *n* (on a shop) ظُلّة (ظُلَل); (on a tent, house) كُنّة (كِنان, كُنّات)

awoke /əˈwəʊk/ *past tense* ▸ **awake**

awoken /əˈwəʊk(ə)n/ *past participle* ▸ **awake**

AWOL /ˈeɪwɒl/ *adj* = **absent without leave** [غائِب عن الجَيْشِ بِدونِ إذْنٍ]; **to go ~** [غابَ عن الجَيْشِ بِدونِ إذْنٍ]

awry /əˈrʌɪ/ **A** *adv* **to go ~** «plans, tests» انْحَرَفَ \ خَرَجَ عن مَسارِهِ
B *adj* ‹*hair*› أَشْعَث (dipt); ‹*tie*› مائِل

axe (BrE), **ax** (AmE) /aks/ **A** *n* **1** (tool) فَأْس (f; فُؤوس, أَفْؤُس) **2** (in expenditure, jobs) سَيْف التَقَشُّفِ; **the ~ fell on public services** انْهالَ سَيْفُ التَقَشُّفِ على قِطاعِ الخِدْماتِ العامّةِ
B *vt* (to dismiss) (infml) طَرَدَ (u; طَرْد), فَصَلَ (i; فَصْل) ‹*a player, worker*›; (to do away with) أَلْغى ‹*jobs, a project*›; (to reduce drastically) خَفَّضَ ‹*funding*›

Idiom **to have an axe to grind** [كانَتْ لَهُ مَصْلَحةٌ في شَيْءٍ]

axis /ˈaksɪs/ *n* (*pl* **axes**) مِحْوَر (مَحاوِرُ)

axle /ˈaks(ə)l/ *n* جُزْء مِحْوَر العَجَلةِ; **the front/rear ~** مِحْوَر العَجَلةِ الأَماميّ \ الخَلْفِيّ

ayatollah /ˌʌɪəˈtɒlə/ *n* آية اللهِ

AZ *abbr* ▸ **Arizona**

azan /əˈzɑːn/ *n* أذان

Azerbaijan /ˌazəbʌɪˈdʒɑːn/ *pr n* أَذَرْبَيْجان

Azerbaijani /ˌazəbʌɪˈdʒɑːni/ **A** *adj* ‹*president, border*› أَذَرْبَيْجانيّ **B** *n* **1** (citizen) أَذَرْبَيْجانيّ **2** (language) (اللُغة) الأَذَرْبَيْجانيّة

Azores /əˈzɔːz/ *pr n pl* (**the Azores**) جُزُر الأَزور

Azrael /ˈazreɪl/ *pr n* عَزْرائيل

Aztec /ˈaztɛk/ *n, adj* آزْتيكيّ

azure /ˈaʒə, aˈʒj(ʊ)ə/ **A** *n* لازُوَرْدِيّة **B** *adj* ‹*sky, sea*› لازُوَرْدِيّ, سَماوِيّ

Bb

B, **b** /biː/ **A** *n* 1 (letter) باء (الحَرْف الثاني من الأَبْجَديّةِ الإِنْكْليزيّةِ) 2 (**B**) (Mus) تي ≈ (نَغْمة من نَغماتِ السُلَّم الموسيقيِّ) 3 (**B**) (Med) **blood group B** B \ فَصيلة الدَمِ ب 4 (**B**) (BrE) (secondary road in UK) **an accident on the B357** B357 حادِث على طَرِيقِ
B *abbr* (**b**) = **born** م

B & B /bi ən 'bɪ/ *n* = **bed and breakfast** 1 [u] (accommodation) المَبيت والفُطور 2 (small hotel) [بَيْت للنُزَلاءِ مع فُطورٍ]

BA /biː'eɪ/ *n* = **Bachelor of Arts** (degree) بَكالوريوس في الآدابِ (ME), ليسانْس في الآدابِ (NA); (degree holder) حاصِل على \ حامِل بَكالورِيوس في الآدابِ; **Peter Jones, ~** بيتر جونْز، بَكالورِيوس في الآدابِ

Baathist, **Ba'athist** /'bɑːθɪst/ *n*, *adj* بَعْثيّ

Baath Party, **Ba'ath Party** /'bɑːθ pɑːti/ *n* حِزْب البَعْثِ

babble /'bab(ə)l/ **A** *vi* 1 «adults» هَذَرَ (a; هَذْر); «babies» تَمْتَمَ (i; تَمْتَمة) 2 «streams» خَرَّ (i-u; خَرير)
B *vt* بَرْبَرَ (i; بَرْبَرة), هَمْهَمَ (i; هَمْهَمة) ‹*an excuse, words*›

babe /beɪb/ *n* 1 (baby) وَليد (وِلْدان) 2 (infml) (beautiful woman) حَسْناء (dipt f; حِسان)

baboon /bə'buːn/ *n* قُرْدوح

baby /'beɪbi/ **A** *n* (*pl* **babies**) 1 (infant) رَضيع (رُضَعاءُ, رَضائِعُ), صَغير (وِلْدان وَليد); **to have a ~** رُزِقَ بِوَليدٍ 2 (young animal) صَغير (صُغَراءُ, صِغار) 3 (youngest child) آخِر العُنْقودِ; (youngest member) أَصْغَر الأَعْضاءِ; **the ~ of the group** أَصْغَر أَعْضاءِ المَجْموعةِ
B *adj before n* 1 ‹*brother, sister*› صَغير (صُغَراءُ, صِغار); **a ~ boy/girl** صَبيّ وَليد \ صَبيّة وَليدة 2 ‹*animal, bird*› صَغير (صُغَراءُ, صِغار); **a ~ elephant** صَغير الفيلِ 3 (for babies) ‹*clothes, food*› أَطْفالٍ

baby buggy *n* عَرَبة أَطْفالٍ

baby carriage *n* (AmE) عَرَبة طِفْلٍ

Babylon /'babɪlɒn/ *n* بابِل (dipt f)

Babylonian /,babɪ'ləʊnɪən/ *n*, *adj* بابِليّ

babysit /'beɪbisɪt/ *vi* (*present participle* **-tt-**, *past tense, past participle* **-sat**) قامَ بِرِعايةِ أَطْفالٍ (أثناء غِيابِ الوالِدَيْنِ)

babysitter /'beɪbisɪtə/ *n* جَليس أَطْفالٍ

babysitting /'beɪbisɪtɪŋ/ *n* مُجالَسة الأَطْفالِ

baccalaureate /,bakə'lɔːrɪət/ *n* بَكالوريا

bachelor /'batʃ(ə)lə/ *n* أَعْزَب (dipt)

Bachelor of Arts *n* (degree) بَكالوريوس في الآدابِ (ME), ليسانْس في الآدابِ (NA); (degree holder) حاصِل على \ حامِل بَكالوريوس في الآدابِ

Bachelor of Medicine *n* (degree) بَكالورِيوس في الطِبِّ; (degree holder) حاصِل على \ حامِل بَكالورِيوس في الطِبِّ

Bachelor of Science *n* (degree) بَكالورِيوس في العُلومِ; (degree holder) حاصِل على \ حامِل بَكالورِيوس في العُلومِ

bacillus /bə'sɪləs/ *n* (*pl* **bacilli**) عُصَيّة

back /bak/ **A** *n* 1 (human's) ظَهْر (ظُهور, أَظْهُر); **to sleep on one's ~** نامَ على ظَهْرِهِ; **to have one's ~ to the door** كانَ ظَهْرُهُ ناحِيَةَ البابِ; **to turn one's ~ on sb/sth** أَدارَ ظَهْرَهُ لِشَخْصٍ \ لِشَيْءٍ; **you'll be glad to see the ~ of him** سَتَكونُ سَعيداً حينَ يَنْصَرِفُ; **they laugh at him behind his ~** يَضْحَكونَ عَلَيْهِ من وَراءِ ظَهْرِهِ; **to do sth behind sb's ~** فَعَلَ شَيْئاً من وَراءِ ظَهْرِ شَخْصٍ 2 (reverse side) ظَهْر (ظُهور, أَظْهُر); **sign on the ~ of the cheque** وَقِّعْ \ أَمْضِ على ظَهْرِ الشيكِ 3 (furthest away part) ظَهْر (ظُهور, أَظْهُر); **to hang one's coat on the ~ of the door** عَلَّقَ مِعْطَفَهُ على ظَهْرِ البابِ; **the answers are at the ~** الأَجْوِبةُ في آخِرِ الكِتابِ; **it's at the ~ of the class** هو في

آخِرِ الفَصْلِ \ القاعةِ; **they were riding in the ~ of the car** كانوا يَرْكَبونَ في المَقاعِدِ الخَلْفيّةِ للسيّارة; **the people at the ~ can't hear** النّاسُ الَّذينَ في الخَلْفِ لا يَسْتَطيعونَ أنْ يَسْمَعوا **4** (of buildings) جُزْء خَلْفيّ, خَلْف; **the steps at the ~ of the building** السُلَّم في الجُزْءِ الخَلْفيِّ للبِنايةِ; **the garden's round the ~** *or* **out the ~** الحَديقةُ في الخَلْفِ **5** (of a chair, sofa) ظَهْر (أظْهُر, ظُهور) **6** (in soccer, rugby) ظَهير (ظُهَراءُ, أظْهار); **he plays left/right ~** يَلْعَبُ ظَهيراً أَيْسَر \ أَيْمَن

B *adv* **1** (indicating return) **to be ~** عادَ (u; عَوْد, عَوْدة); **I'll be ~ shortly/in six weeks** سأعودُ بعد قليلٍ \ خلال سِتّة أسابيعَ; **he's ~ at work** عادَ إلى العَمَلِ; **she's ~ in the hospital** عادَتْ إلى المُسْتَشفى; **to travel to Amman and ~** سافَرَ من وإلى عَمّانَ; **long skirts are ~** عادَتْ موضةُ التَنانيرِ الطَويلة; **to get ~ to sleep** عادَ إلى النَوْمِ; **it's good to be ~ home** كم هو جَميلٌ أنْ نَعودَ إلى البَيْتِ **2** (in return) **to call** *or* **phone ~** رَدَّ على المُكالَمةِ; **he hasn't emailed me ~** لم يَرُدَّ على إيميلي **3** (backwards) ‹*to look, step*› إلى الخَلْفِ \ الوَراءِ **4** (in distance) [على مَسافةٍ إلى الوَراءِ]; **we overtook him 20 km ~** تَجاوَزْناهُ منذ عِشْرينَ كيلومِتْراً; **the house is very far ~ from the road** يَقَعُ البَيْتُ على مَسافةٍ بَعيدةٍ جِدًّا من الطَريقِ **5** (in time) مُنْذُ; **twenty-five years ~** منذ خَمْسةٍ وعِشْرينَ عاماً; **that was several weeks ~** كانَ ذلك منذ بِضْعةِ أسابيعَ; **~ in 1964/April** فيما مَضى سَنةَ 1964 \ في شَهْرِ أَبْريل; **it dates ~ to Roman times** يَعودُ إلى العُصورِ الرومانيّةِ **6** (indicating restoration) **to give/send sth ~ to sb** رَدَّ شَيْئاً إلى شَخْصٍ; **put it ~ where it belongs** أَعِدْهُ إلى مَكانِهِ \ حَيْثُ يَنْتَمي; **she wants her scissors ~** تُريدُ أنْ يُعادَ إليها مِقَصُّها **7** (in a known location) **meanwhile, ~ in Dubai, he ...** في نَفْسِ الوَقْتِ, في دُبَيّ, هو ...; **I'll see you ~ at the house** سأراكَ حينَ نَعودُ إلى البَيْتِ

C (**back and forth**) *adv phr* **to travel ~ and forth** سافَرَ ذَهاباً وإياباً

D *vt* **1** (to support) أيَّد, دَعَم (a; دَعْم), سانَدَ ‹*a candidate, proposal, project*›; **I'm ~ing the Justice Party** أُسانِدُ \ أَدْعَمُ \ أُؤَيِّدُ حِزْبَ العَدالةِ **2** (to underpin) مَوَّلَ ‹*a programme, undertaking*›; **the research is ~ed by a major pharmaceutical company** تُمَوِّلُ شَرِكةُ مَوادَّ صَيْدَليّةٍ كُبْرى البَحْثَ **3** (to substantiate) أيَّدَ ‹*an argument, claim*›; **you must ~ your claims with facts** يَجِبُ أنْ تُؤَيِّدَ ادِّعاءاتِكَ بِوَقائعَ \ بِحَقائِقَ **4** (to reverse) قادَ إلى الوَراءِ \ الخَلْفِ ‹*a car*› **5** (to bet on) راهَنَ (على) ‹*the favourite, a loser*› **6** (Mus) صاحَبَ ‹*a singer, performer*›

E *vi* (to reverse) «drivers» رَجَعَ إلى الوَراءِ; **I ~ed into the garage** رَجَعْتُ إلى الوَراءِ لأَدْخُلَ الكَراجَ

F *adj before n* (at the rear) ‹*wheel, bedroom, page*› خَلْفيّ

G (**-backed**); *in combination* **1** (of furniture) **a high-/low-~ed chair** كُرْسيّ بِظَهْرٍ طَويلٍ \ قَصيرٍ **2** (supported) **UN-~ed** بِدَعْمٍ من مُنَظَّمةِ الأُمَمِ المُتَّحِدةِ **3** (financed) **government-~ed** بِدَعْمٍ حُكوميٍّ

(Phrasal verbs) **back away** تَهَرَّبَ; **to ~ away from a problem/confrontation** تَهَرَّبَ من مُشْكِلةٍ \ مُواجَهةٍ

• **back down** (to give way) تَراجَعَ

• **back onto**: **~ onto [sth]** «house» [فَتَحَ بابُهُ الخَلْفيّ على [شَيْءٍ]]

• **back out** **A** **~ out** **1** (to emerge backwards) «drivers» [قادَ إلى الخَلْفِ للخُروجِ من بِنايةٍ] **2** (to disengage) «negotiators, competitors» انْسَحَبَ; **to ~ out of a deal/a competition** انْسَحَبَ من اتِّفاقٍ \ مُنافَسةٍ **B** **~ [sth] out** [قادَ [شَيْئاً] إلى الخَلْفِ للخُروجِ من بِنايةٍ]

• **back up** **A** **~ up** **1** (to get blocked) «drains» انْسَدَّ **2** «traffic» انْشَلَّ **B** **~ [sth] up, ~ up [sth]** **1** (to support) «facts, evidence» أيَّدَ \ دَعَمَ \ سانَدَ [شَيْئاً] ‹*a claim, case*› **2** نَسَخَ نُسْخةً احْتِياطيّةً من [شَيْءٍ] ‹*the data, file*› **C** **~ [sb] up** سانَدَ \ دَعَمَ [شَخْصاً] ‹*a colleague*›

backache /ˈbakeɪk/ *n* أَلَم ظَهْرٍ; **to have ~** كانَ عِنْدَهُ أَلَمٌ بالظَهْرِ

backbencher /bakˈbɛntʃə/ *n* (in UK) [بَرْلَمانيّ ثانَويّ في المَمْلَكةِ المُتَّحِدةِ]

backbone /ˈbakbəʊn/ *n* **1** (person's, animal's) عمود فِقْري **2** (of a system, an organization) عمود فِقْريّ

back button *n* زِرّ الخَلْفِ

backdate /bakˈdeɪt/ *vt* **1** (to bring forward) جَعَلَ لَهُ أَثَراً رَجْعيًّا ‹*an increase, payments*› **2** (to date earlier) أَرَّخَ بِتاريخٍ سابِقٍ ‹*a cheque, letter*›

back door *n* 1 (of a building) باب خَلْفِيّ 2 (of a vehicle) باب خَلْفِيّ

backdrop /'bakdrɒp/ *n* 1 (in theatres) سِتارة خَلْفِيّة 2 (for meetings, events) خَلْفِيّة

backer /'bakə/ *n* مُمَوِّل

backfire /'bakfʌɪə/ *vi* 1 (to fail) «plans, schemes» ارْتَدَّ 2 «engines, vehicles» فَرْقَعَ (i; فَرْقَعة)

backgammon /'bakgamən/ *n* نَرْد, لُعْبة الطاوِلة

background /'bakgraʊnd/ *n* 1 (social, professional) خَلْفِيّة; **she has a ~ in marketing** لَها خَلْفِيّةٌ في التَّسْويق 2 (context) خَلْفِيّة; **against a ~ of violence** على خَلْفِيّةٍ من العُنْف; **can you give me some ~ on the case?** هل يُمْكِنُ أنْ تُعْطِيَني \ تُقَدِّمَ لي خَلفيّةً عن القَضيّةِ؟ 3 (of a picture) خَلفيّة; **he preferred to stay in the ~** فَضَّلَ أنْ يَبْقى في الخَلْفِيّة

background information *n* مَعْلومات خَلْفِيّة

background music *n* موسيقى خَلْفِيّة

background noise *n* ضَجيج خَلْفِيّ

background reading *n* القِراءة حول المَوْضوع

backhand /'bakhand/ *n* [ضَرْبة بظَهْرِ المِضْرَب]

backhander /'bakhandə/ *n* (BrE infml) رَشْوة (رُشًى)

backing /'bakɪŋ/ *n* 1 (support) دَعْم 2 (for a singer) مُرافَقة

backlash /'baklaʃ/ *n* مُعارَضة

backless /'bakləs/ *adj* ‹*dress, gown*› مَفْتوح \ عاري الظَهْرِ

backlog /'baklɒg/ *n* تَراكُم (تَراكُمات)

back number *n* عدد قديم (لِجَريدةٍ \ لِمَجَلّةٍ)

backpack /'bakpak/ A *n* حَقيبة ظَهْر
B *vi* [ارْتَحَلَ حامِلاً حَقيبة ظَهْرٍ]; **to go ~ing** [ارْتَحَلَ حامِلاً حَقيبة ظَهْرٍ]

backpacker /'bakpakə/ *n* مُرْتَحِل (حامِلاً حَقيبةَ ظَهْرٍ)

back pay *n* راتِب مُتَأخِّر

back-pedal /ˌbak'pɛd(ə)l/ *vi* (**-ll-** BrE, **-l-** AmE) تَراجَعَ عن رَأْيِه

back seat *n* مَقْعَد خَلْفِيّ

Idiom **to take a back seat** كانَ لَهُ دَوْرٌ ثانَوِيٌّ

backside /'baksʌɪd/ *n* (infml) مُؤَخِّرة

backstage /bak'steɪdʒ/ A *adj before n* ‹*pass*› للكَواليسِ; ‹*crew*› خَلْفَ الكَواليسِ
B *adv* ‹*to go, work*› وراء الكَواليسِ \ السِتارِ

backstreet /'bakstriːt/ A *n* شارِع خَلْفِيّ
B *adj before n* ‹*abortion, deal*› في الخَفاءِ

backstroke /'bakstrəʊk/ *n* سِباحة الظَهْرِ

back-to-back /ˌbaktə'bak/ A *adj* (*before n* **back-to-back**) 1 ‹*houses*› مُتَلاصِق الظَهْرِ 2 ‹*defeats, championships*› مُتَتالٍ, مُتَلاحِق
B *adv* **to stand ~** «two people» وَقَفا مُتَلاصِقَي الظَهْرِ

back to front /ˌbak tə 'frʌnt/ *adv* بالعَكْسِ

backtrack /'baktrak/ *vi* 1 (to go back) رَجَعَ \ عادَ أَدْراجَهُ 2 (on a statement) (عن) تَراجَعَ

backup /'bakʌp/ *n* 1 (support) مُسانَدة, عَوْن, دَعْم 2 (replacement) **to keep the old one as a ~** احْتَفَظَ بالقديم كاحْتِياطٍ 3 (of data) نُسْخة احْتِياطيّة; **to make a ~ of one's data** عَمِلَ نُسْخةً احْتِياطيّةً لِبَياناتِهِ 4 (AmE) (of vehicles) اخْتِناق مُروريّ

backup disk *n* قُرْص النَسْخ الاحْتِياطيّ

backward /'bakwəd/ A *adj* 1 ‹*step, look*› إلى الخَلْفِ \ الوَراءِ; **she went out without so much as a ~ glance** خَرَجَتْ دون إلْقاءِ وَلَوْ نَظْرة خاطفةٍ 2 ‹*country, society*› رَجْعيّ, مُتَخَلِّف; ‹*child*› مُتَخَلِّف عَقْليًّا
B *adv* (**backwards** also **backward** BrE) 1 (in a reverse direction) ‹*to walk, step, fall*› إلى الخَلْفِ \ الوَراءِ; **to face ~s** كانَ مُواجِهاً للخَلْفِ; **the train began to go ~s** بَدَأَ القِطارُ بالسَيْرِ في الاتِّجاهِ المُعاكِسِ; **to go ~s and forwards between two places** مَرَّ ذَهاباً وَإياباً بين مَكانَيْن 2 (starting from the end) ‹*to count, wind*› عَكْسيًّا 3 (back to front) **to put sth on ~s** لَبِسَ شَيْئاً بالعَكْس

Idiom **to know sth backwards** عَرَفَ شَيْئاً حَقَّ المَعْرِفة

backwater /'bakwɔːtə/ *n* مَكان مُنْعَزِل

backyard /bak'jɑːd/ *n* 1 (BrE) (courtyard) فِناء خَلْفِيّ 2 (AmE) (back garden) حَديقة خَلْفِيّة

bacon /'beɪk(ə)n/ *n* لَحْم الخِنْزيرِ المُقَدَّدِ \ المُمَلَّح

Idioms **to bring home the bacon** (infml) كَسَبَ الرِزْق; **to save sb's bacon** (infml) أَنْقَذَ جِلْدَ شَخْصٍ

bacteria /bak'tɪərɪə/ *n pl* جَراثيم ,بَكْتيريا

bacterial /bak'tɪərɪəl/ *adj* ‹*infection, species*› جُرْثومي ,بَكْتيريّ

bacterium /bak'tɪərɪəm/ *n* (*pl* **bacteria**) بَكْتيريا (بَكْتيريات), (جَراثيمُ) جُرْثوم

bad /bad/ **A** *n* **1** (evil) شَرّ (شُرور); **there is good and ~ in everyone** يوجَدُ الخَيْرُ والشَرُّ داخِلَ كُلِّ إنْسانٍ **2** (negative aspects) عَيْب (عُيوب) ,سَلْبيّة ,سَيِّئة; **the good outweighs the ~** الإيجابيّاتُ تفوقُ السَلْبيّاتِ

B *adj* (*comparative* **worse**; *superlative* **worst**) **1** (not good) ‹*idea, decision, movie*› سَيِّئ; **to have ~ eyesight/hearing** كانَ نَظَرُهُ \ سَمْعُهُ سَيِّئاً; **I was ~ at sport/physics** كُنْتُ سَيِّئاً في الرِياضةِ \ الفيزياءِ; **it's not necessarily a ~ thing** هو لَيْسَ بالضرورةِ شَيْئاً سَيِّئاً; **'what did you think of the film?' — 'not ~'** 'ما رَأْيُكَ في الفيلْمِ؟' - 'لَيْسَ سَيِّئاً'; (infml) **as bosses go she's not ~** هي رئيسةُ عَمَلٍ لا بَأْسَ بها بالمُقارَنةِ بالآخَرينَ **2** (unfavourable) ‹*news, weather, luck*› سَيِّئ; **things are looking ~** تَبْدو الأَشْياءُ سَيِّئةً; **I've had a ~ day at work** كانَ يَوْمي في العَمَلِ سَيِّئاً; **he's in a ~ mood** مِزاجُهُ سَيِّئٌ **3** (serious) ‹*mistake, injury, accident*› شَديد ,سَيِّئ; **she has a ~ cold** تُعاني من نَزْلةِ بَرْدٍ شَديدةٍ; **how ~ is it?** إلى أيِّ دَرَجةِ الأَمْرُ سَيِّئٌ؟; **to have a ~ toothache** عانى من أَلَمِ أَسْنانٍ شَديدٍ; **there was a ~ accident with several fatalities** كانَ هُناكَ حادِثٌ سَيِّئٌ تَسَبَّبَ في وُقوعِ عِدّةِ ضَحايا **4** (harmful) سَيِّئ ,مُضِرّ ,ضارّ; **smoking is ~ for you/your health** التَدْخينُ مُضِرٌّ لَكَ \ لِصِحَّتِكَ **5** (impaired) مُصاب ,عَليل; **to have a ~ back/heart** كانَ لَهُ ظَهْرٌ \ قَلْبٌ عَليلٌ **6** (unacceptable) ‹*habit, behaviour*› سَيِّئ; **you ~ girl!** أَنْتِ بِنْتٌ سَيِّئةٌ!; **it will look ~ if we don't go** سَيَبْدو الأَمْرُ سَيِّئاً إذا لم نَذْهَبْ; **~ language** لُغة بَذيئة; **the ~ guy** الشِرّير **7** (unsuitable) ‹*time, moment*› غَيْر مُناسِبٍ ,سَيِّئ; **is this a ~ time for you?** هَل هذا وَقْتٌ غَيْرُ مُناسِبٍ لَكَ؟; **it's a ~ time for buying a house** إنَّهُ وَقْتٌ غَيْرُ مُناسِبٍ لِشِراءِ بَيْتٍ **8** (guilty) بالذَنْبِ ,بالنَدَمِ; **to feel ~ about sth** شَعَرَ بالنَدَمِ \ بالذَنْبِ بِسَبَبِ شَيْءٍ **9** (rotten) ‹*fruit, meat*› فاسِد; **to go ~** فَسَدَ (i-u; فَساد) **10** ‹*debt, loan*› مَعْدوم

C *adv* (AmE infml) ‹*to need, want*› بِشِدّةٍ; **it hurts real ~** يُؤْلِمُني بِشِدّةٍ

Idioms **he's got it bad** (infml) سَقَطَ صَريعَ الهَوى; **to be in a bad way** (ill) كانَ مَريضاً جِدّاً; (in trouble) كانَ في وَرْطةٍ; **too bad!** (infml) لِسوءِ الحَظِّ!; **'I was going to eat that!' — 'too ~!'** 'كُنْتُ سَآكُلُ ذلك!' - 'لِسوءِ الحَظِّ!'; **that's too ~!** (a shame) يا لَلْخَسارةِ!

bad debt *n* دَيْن مَعْدوم

bade /beɪd, bad/ *past tense* ▸ **bid**

badge /badʒ/ *n* شارة

badger /'badʒə/ *n* غُرَيْر

badly /'badli/ *adv* (*comparative* **worse**; *superlative* **worst**) **1** (poorly) ‹*to behave, play*› بِشَكْلٍ سَيِّئٍ; **to go ~** سارَ بِشَكْلٍ سَيِّئٍ; **to do ~** قَدَّمَ أَداءً \ مَرْدوداً سَيِّئاً; **he didn't do too ~** قَدَّمَ أداءً لا بَأْسَ بِهِ; **she took it ~** تَلَقَّتْهُ بِصَدْمةٍ; **the book was ~ written** كُتِبَ الكِتابُ بِشَكْلٍ سَيِّئٍ **2** (seriously) ‹*damaged, injured*› بِشِدّةٍ ,بِشَكْلٍ سَيِّئٍ; **the experiment went ~ wrong** فَشِلَت التَجْرِبةُ فَشَلاً ذَريعاً; **the company has been ~ hit by the recession** ضَرَبَ الكَسادُ الشَرِكةَ بِشَكْلٍ سَيِّئٍ \ بِشِدّةٍ; **he was ~ beaten in prison** ضُرِبَ بِشَكْلٍ سَيِّئٍ \ بِشِدّةٍ في السِجْنِ **3** (very much) ‹*to need, miss*› بِشِدّةٍ; **the house was ~ in need of repair** كانَ البَيْتُ يَحْتاجُ بِشِدّةٍ إلى التَصْليحِ; **she misses her brother ~** تَشْتاقُ بِشِدّةٍ إلى أَخيها; **they ~ wanted children** رَغِبا بِشِدّةٍ بِإنْجابِ أَطْفالٍ

badly off *adj* **1** (short of money) ‹*family, student*› فَقير (فُقَراءُ), مُعْوِز **2** (to be in need of) **to be ~ for clothes/ammunition** أَعْوَزَتْهُ المَلابِسُ \ الذَخيرةُ

bad-mannered /ˌbad'manəd/ *adj* ‹*child, customer*› سَيِّئ السُلوكِ ,غَيْر مُؤَدَّبٍ

badminton /'badmɪnt(ə)n/ *n* تِنِس الريشةِ

badness /'badnəs/ *n* **1** (poor quality) رَداءة **2** (wickedness) شَرّ (شُرور)

bad-tempered /ˌbad'tɛmpəd/ *adj* ‹*partner, boss*› سَيِّئ ,عَصَبيّ المِزاجِ; ‹*reply, gesture*› غاضِب

baffle /'baf(ə)l/ *vt* ‹*the police, an opponent*› أَرْبَكَ

baffled /'baf(ə)ld/ *adj* ‹*police, expert*› مُرْبَك ,مُتَحَيِّر ,مُنْذَهِل

bag /bag/ *n* **1** (for shopping) كيس (أَكْياس ,كِيسَة); **would you like a ~?** هل تُريدُ كيساً؟ **2** (contents) كيس (أَكْياس ,كِيسَة); **I added half a ~ of sugar** أَضَفْتُ نِصْفَ كيسٍ من السُكَّرِ **3** (handbag) حَقيبة يَدٍ **4** (item of luggage) حَقيبة (حَقائِبُ); **I packed my ~s and left** حَزَمْتُ حَقائِبي وَغادَرْتُ

(Idioms) **a mixed bag** مَزيج (مُزُج); **to be in the bag** كانَ في الجَيْبِ; **to have bags under one's eyes** كانَتْ هُناكَ انْتِفاخاتٌ داكِنةُ اللَوْنِ تحت عَيْنَيْهِ

baggage /ˈbagɪdʒ/ *n* **1** (luggage) حَقائِب السَفَرِ ,أَمْتِعة **2** (legacy) ماضٍ; **emotional ~** ماضٍ عاطِفيّ

baggage allowance *n* الوَزْن المَسْموح بِهِ (أثناء السَفَرِ جَوًّا)

baggage handler *n* حَمّال (حَمّالون ,حَمّالة)

baggage reclaim *n* مَكان اسْتِلامِ الأَمْتِعة

baggy /ˈbagi/ *adj* (**baggier**, **baggiest**) ‹*clothes, trousers*› واسِع

Baghdad /bagˈdad/ *pr n* بَغْداد (dipt f)

bagpipes /ˈbagpʌɪps/ *n pl* مِزْمار القِرْبة

Bahamas /bəˈhɑːməz/ *pr n* (**the Bahamas**) جُزُر البَهاما

Bahrain /bɑːˈreɪn/ *pr n* البَحْرَيْن (f)

Bahraini /bɑːˈreɪni/ *n, adj* بَحْرَيْنيّ (بَحارِنة)

bail /beɪl/ *n* كَفالة; **to be released on ~** أُطْلِقَ سَراحُهُ بِكَفالةٍ

(Phrasal verb) **bail out** **A** (from plane) [قَفَزَ من طائِرة بِمِظَلّةٍ] **B** **~ out [sb], ~ [sb] out** خَلَّصَ [شَخْصاً] من مَأْزِقٍ ‹*a person, company*› **C** **~ out [sth], ~ [sth] out** نَزَحَ [شَيْئاً] ‹*water*›; نَزَحَ الماءَ من [شَيْءٍ] ‹*a boat*›

Bailey bridge /ˈbeɪli brɪdʒ/ *n* جِسْر بَيْلي (جِسْر مُؤَقَّت يُسْتَخْدَمُ لِأَغْراضٍ عَسْكَرِيّةٍ)

bailiff /ˈbeɪlɪf/ *n* مُحْضِر

bailout /ˈbeɪlaʊt/ *n* (Fin) إِنْقاذ

Bairam /bʌɪˈrɑːm/ *n* عيد (أَعْياد); **Greater/Lesser ~** العيد الكَبير \ الصَغير

bait /beɪt/ *n* طُعْم (طُعوم)

bake /beɪk/ **A** *vt* خَبَزَ (i; خَبْز) ‹*bread, a cake*› **B** *vi* **1** (to make bread, cakes) «bakery, housewife» قامَ بالخَبْزِ **2** (to cook) «potatoes» انْشَوى **3** (infml) (to get hot) انْشَوى

baked beans *n pl* فاصوليا مَطْبوخة

baked potato *n* بَطاطا مُحَمَّرة

baker /ˈbeɪkə/ *n* خَبّاز (خَبّازونَ ,خَبّازة)

bakery /ˈbeɪk(ə)ri/ *n* (*pl* **bakeries**) مَخْبَز (مَخابِزُ)

baking /ˈbeɪkɪŋ/ **A** *n* خَبْز; **I'm going to do some ~** سَأَخْبِزُ شَيْئاً **B** *adj* (infml) (also **baking hot**) ‹*weather, room*› مُحْرِق; **I'm absolutely ~!** أنا أَحْتَرِقُ من الحَرِّ!

baking dish *n* صينيّة فُرْنٍ

baking powder *n* مَسْحوق التَخْمير

baking sheet *n* صينيّة خَبْزٍ

baking soda *n* صودا الخَبْز

baking tray *n* صينيّة خَبْزٍ

Baku /baˈkuː/ *pr n* باكو (f)

balance /ˈbal(ə)ns/ **A** *n* **1** (equilibrium) تَوازُن; **to keep/lose one's ~** حافَظَ على \ فَقَدَ تَوازُنَهُ; **aim for the right ~ between quality and price** أَهْدُفُ إلى التَوازُنِ السَليم بين الجَوْدةِ والسِعْرِ; **to throw sb off ~** (physically) أَفْقَدَ شَخْصاً تَوازُنَهُ; (to disconcert) أَرْبَكَ شَخْصاً **2** (scales) ميزان (مَوازينُ); **on ~ we had a good year** كانَت السَنةُ في نِهاية الأَمْرِ سَنةً جَيِّدةً **3** (in an account) رَصيد (أَرْصِدة) **4** (amount due) المَبْلَغ المَطْلوب; **to pay the ~** دَفَعَ المَبْلَغَ المَطْلوبَ

B *vt* **1** (to place) وَضَعَ بِشَكْلٍ مُتَوازِنٍ ‹*the plate, stick*›; **the plate was ~d on the arm of the chair** وُضِعَ الصَحْنُ بِشَكْلٍ مُتَوازِنٍ على ذِراعِ الكُرْسيِّ **2** (to compensate for) عادَلَ; **his inexperience is ~d by his enthusiasm** حَماسُهُ يُعادِلُ كَفّةَ قِلّةِ خِبْرَتِهِ **3** (to equalize) خَلَقَ التَوازُنَ بين ‹*forces, elements*› **4** (to consider) فاضَلَ (بين) ,وازَنَ (بين) ‹*interests, demands*›; **to ~ sth against sth else** فاضَلَ \ وازَنَ بين شَيْئَيْنِ **5** وازَنَ ‹*the accounts, books*›; **to ~ the budget** وازَنَ الميزانيّةَ **6** (Aut) ضَبَطَ التَوازُنَ ,وازَنَ ‹*the wheels*›

C *vi* **1** (to stay upright) حافَظَ على تَوازُنِهِ; **I can ~ on one foot** أَسْتَطيعُ أنْ أُحافِظَ على تَوازُني على رِجْلٍ واحِدةٍ **2** (to be equal) «accounts, figures» تَوازَنَ

D (**balanced**) *adj* **1** ‹*diet, budget*› مُتَوازِن **2** (unbiased) ‹*view, coverage*› مُتَوازِن

(Idioms) **to hang in the balance** كانَ مُعَلَّقاً في الميزانِ; **to strike a balance** حَقَّقَ التَوازُنَ

balance of payments *n* ميزان المَدْفوعاتِ

balance of power *n* ميزان القُوى

balance of trade *n* ميزان تِجاريّ

balance sheet *n* بَيان الميزانيّةِ

balcony /ˈbalk(ə)ni/ *n* (*pl* **balconies**) **1** (in a house, hotel) شُرْفة (شُرُفات, شُرَف) **2** (in a theatre) شُرْفة (شُرُفات, شُرَف)

bald /bɔːld/ *adj* (**balder, baldest**) **1** ‹*man, head*› أَصْلَع (dipt; صُلْع); **to go ~** أَصْبَحَ أَصْلَعَ **2** ‹*tyre*› تالف (النَّقْشِ)

bale /beɪl/ *n* (of hay, cotton, paper) حُزْمة (حُزَم)

(Phrasal verb) **bale out** (BrE) ▸ **bail out** C

Balearic Islands /ˌbalɪˌarɪk ˈʌɪləndz/, **Balearics** *pr n pl* (**the Balearic Islands**) جُزُر الباليار

baleful /ˈbeɪlfʊl/ *adj* ‹*influence, look*› مُخيف

Bali /ˈbɑːli/ *pr n* بالي (f)

Balkan /ˈbɔːlk(ə)n/ **A** *adj* ‹*states, languages*› بَلْقانيّ
B (**the Balkans**) *pr n pl* البَلْقان (f)

ball /bɔːl/ **A** *n* **1** (in games) كُرة (كُرات, كُرًى) **2** (of dough, clay, wool) كُرة (كُرات, كُرًى) **3** (dance) حَفْلة راقِصة
B (**balls**) *n pl* **1** (vulg) (testicles) خُصْيَتانِ; **he got kicked in the ~s** رُفِسَ على خُصْيَتَيْهِ **2** (infml) (nonsense) هُراء; **what ~s!** أيّ هُراء!

(Idioms) **to be on the ball** [كانَ على أَحْسَنِ حالٍ]; **to have a ball** قَضى وَقْتاً مُمْتِعاً; **to play ball** تَعاوَنَ; **to set the ball rolling** ابْتَدَرَ, أَلْقى الكُرة

ballad /ˈbaləd/ *n* **1** (poem) قِصّة شِعْريّة **2** (song) مَوّال (مَواويلُ)

ballast /ˈbaləst/ *n* **1** (for railways, roads) رَضْراض **2** (in balloons, ships) صابورة

ball bearing *n* مَحْمِل كُرَيّاتٍ

ballerina /baləˈriːnə/ *n* راقِصة باليه

ballet /ˈbaleɪ/ *n* باليه

ball game *n* **1** (any game) لُعْبة كُرةٍ **2** (AmE) (baseball) مُباراة بيسْبول

(Idiom) **to be a different ball game** هذا مَوْضوعٌ مُخْتَلِفٌ تَماماً

ballgown /ˈbɔːlgaʊn/ *n* فُسْتان سَهْرةٍ

ballistics /bəˈlɪstɪks/ *n sing* عِلْم القَذائِفِ \ المَقْذوفاتِ

balloon /bəˈluːn/ *n* **1** (as a toy, for decoration) بالون (بالونات)
2 (also **hot-air balloon**) مُنْطاد

ballooning /bəˈluːnɪŋ/ *n* **to go ~** حَلَّقَ \ رَكِبَ بالمُنْطادِ

ballot /ˈbalət/ *n* اقْتِراع (اقْتِراعات)

ballot box *n* صُنْدوق اقْتِراعٍ

ballot paper *n* وَرَقة اقْتِراعٍ

ballpark /ˈbɔːlpɑːk/ *n* (AmE) (for baseball) ساحة البيسْبول

(Idiom) **to be in the ballpark** كانَ قَريباً من الصَوابِ

ballpark figure *n* رَقْم تَقْريبيّ

ballpoint, **ballpoint pen** /ˈbɔːlpɔɪnt/ *n* قَلَم جافّ

ballroom /ˈbɔːlruːm/ *n* صالة رَقْصٍ

ballroom dancing *n* [رَقْص يَعْتَمِدُ على خَطَواتٍ ثابِتةٍ وَإيقاعاتٍ واضِحةٍ]

balm /bɑːm/ *n* بَلْسَم (بَلاسِمُ)

Baltic /ˈbɔːltɪk/ **A** *adj* **the ~ states** دُوَل البَلْطيق
B *pr n* (**the Baltic, the Baltic Sea**) بَحْر البَلْطيق

bamboo /bamˈbuː/ *n* (*pl* **bamboos**) خَيْزُران (خَيازِرُ)

bamboo shoot *n* [بُرْعُم خَيْزُرانٍ]

ban /ban/ **A** *vt* (**-nn-**) حَظَرَ (u; حَظْر) ‹*smoking, a drug, an athlete*›; **to ~ sb from doing sth** حَظَرَ على شَخْصٍ فِعْلَ شَيْءٍ
B *n* حَظْر; **a ~ on smoking** حَظْر على التَدْخينِ

banal /bəˈnɑːl/ *adj* ‹*conversation, existence, subject*› فارِغ

banana /bəˈnɑːnə/ *n* مَوْز (n coll)

(Idiom) **to go bananas** (infml) فَقَدَ عَقْلَهُ

band /band/ *n* **1** (group of people) عُصْبة (عُصَب), زُمْرة (زُمَر), جَماعة; (group of musicians) فِرْقة (فِرَق); **a jazz ~** فِرْقة جاز; **the regimental ~** فِرْقة موسيقى العَسْكَرِ **2** (stripe) شَريط (أَشْرِطة, شَرائِطُ) **3** (strip of material for a hat) رِباط (لِلقُبَّعاتِ); (for one's hair) طَوْق شَعْرٍ **4** (BrE) (for taxation, age) فِئة

(Phrasal verb) **band together** تَحالَفوا مع بَعْضِهِم البَعْضَ

bandage /ˈbandɪdʒ/ **A** *n* ضِماد (ضَمائِدُ, أَضْمِدة)
B *vt* ضَمَّدَ ‹*a wound, sb's head*›

Band-Aid® /ˈbandeɪd/ *n* (AmE) لَزْقة (لَزَقات), لَصْقة جُروحٍ

bandit /ˈbandɪt/ *n* قاطِع طَريقٍ

bandstand /ˈban(d)stand/ *n* مِنصّة (تُستَخْدَمُ من قِبَلِ فِرَقٍ موسيقيّةٍ في حَديقةٍ عامّةٍ)

bandwagon /ˈbandwag(ə)n/ *n*

Idiom **to jump** *or* **climb on the bandwagon** رَكِبَ المَوْجةَ

bandwidth /ˈbandwɪtθ/ *n* عَرْض النِطاقِ ,مُعَدَّل نَقْلِ البَياناتِ التَرَدُّديّ

bandy /ˈbandi/ **A** *adj* (**bandier, bandiest**) ‹*legs*› مُقَوَّس

B *vt* (**bandies, bandying, bandied**) **to ~ words with sb** تَجادَلَ مع شَخْصٍ

Phrasal verb **bandy about, bandy around**: **~ [sth] about** ذَكَرَ [شَيْئاً] ‹*names, figures*›

bane /beɪn/ *n* [مَصْدَر أذًى]; **to be the ~ of sb's life** [كانَ مَصْدَرَ أذًى في حَياةِ شَخْصٍ]

bang /baŋ/ **A** *n* **1▸** (noise of an explosion) دَوِيّ; (noise of a door, window) صَفْق **2▸** (blow) ضَرْبة (ضَرَبات); **a ~ on the head** ضَرْبة على الرَأْسِ

B (**bangs**) *n pl* (AmE) ناصية ,قُصّة (نَواصٍ)

C *vt* **1▸** (to strike) خَبَطَ (i; خَبْط; على) ‹*a drum, table*›; **to ~ one's fist on the table** خَبَطَ بِيَدِه على الطاوِلةِ; **she ~ed the phone down** خَبَطَتِ السَمّاعةَ **2▸** (accidentally) **she ~ed her head** اصْطَدَمَ \ ارْتَطَمَ رَأْسُها; **he ~ed his knee on the table** اصْطَدَمَتْ \ ارْتَطَمَتْ رُكْبَتُهُ بالطاوِلةِ **3▸** (to slam) صَفَقَ (i; صَفْق) ‹*a door, window*›

D *vi* **1▸** (to strike) «neighbours, children» قَرَعَ (a; قَرْع); **to ~ on the door/wall** قَرَعَ على البابِ \ الجِدارِ; **he was ~ing away at the piano** كانَ يَضْرِبُ على البيانو بِقُوّةٍ **2▸** (to make a noise) «door, shutters» اصْطَفَقَ; **the door ~ed shut** اصْطَفَقَ البابُ مُنْغَلِقاً

E *adv* (infml) **~ in the middle** تَماماً في الوَسَطِ; **to arrive ~ on time** وَصَلَ في الوَقْتِ المُحَدَّدِ تَماماً

F *excl* (imitating a gun) [صَوْت يُطْلِقُهُ الأَطْفالُ تَقْليداً لِصَوْتِ الطَلْقِ النارِيِّ]; **to go ~** [أَحْدَثَ صَوْتَ انْفِجارٍ]

Idioms **bang goes ...** (BrE infml) ذَهَبَ ... سُدًى; **~ goes my weekend** ذَهَبَتْ نِهايةُ الأُسْبوعِ سُدًى; **~ goes our dream of reaching the final** ذَهَبَتْ أَحْلامُنا في الوُصولِ إلى الدَوْرِ النِهائيِّ سُدًى; **to go/end with a bang** مَرَّ \ انْتَهى بِنَجاحٍ

Phrasal verbs **bang out**: **~ out [sth]** [عَزَفَ [شَيْئاً] عَزْفاً ناشِزاً بِصَوْتٍ عالٍ] ‹*a tune, song*›

• **bang on** (BrE infml) **to ~ on about sth** ثَرْثَرَ حول شَيْءٍ

banger /ˈbaŋə/ *n* (BrE infml) **1▸** (car) [سَيّارة مُتَهالِكة] **2▸** (firework) مُفَرْقَعة **3▸** (sausage) سُجُقّ

Bangkok /baŋˈkɒk/ *pr n* بانْكوك (f)

Bangladesh /ˌbaŋgləˈdɛʃ/ *pr n* بَنْغْلاديش (f)

Bangladeshi /ˌbaŋgləˈdɛʃi/ *n, adj* بَنْغْلاديشيّ

bangle /ˈbaŋg(ə)l/ *n* (for the ankle) خَلْخال (خَلاخيلُ); (for the wrist) سِوار (أَسْوِرة ,أَساوِرُ)

banish /ˈbanɪʃ/ *vt* **1▸** (from a country) نَفى (i; نَفْي) ,أَبْعَدَ ‹*a prince, rebel*› **2▸** (from one's mind) طَرَدَ (u; طَرْد) ‹*a thought, memory*›

banister, bannister /ˈbanɪstə/ *n* دَرْبَزين (دَرْبَزينات)

banjo /ˈbandʒəʊ/ *n* (*pl* **banjos** or **banjoes**) بانْجو

bank¹ /baŋk/ *n* **1▸** (side of a river, lake) ضِفّة (ضِفاف) **2▸** (mass of earth, snow) كُدْس (أَكْداس) ,كَوْم (أَكْوام); (of cloud, fog) كُتْلة (كُتَل) **3▸** (set of computers, lights, switches) صَفّ (صُفوف)

Phrasal verb **bank up** **A** «snow» تَكَدَّسَ ,تَكَوَّمَ **B** **~ [sth] up, ~ up [sth]** كَدَّسَ \ كَوَّمَ [شَيْئاً] ‹*the snow, earth*›

bank² /baŋk/ **A** *n* **1▸** (Fin) بَنْك (بُنوك) ,مَصْرِف (مَصارِفُ); **the B~ of Iraq/England** بَنْك العِراقِ \ إنْجِلْترا **2▸** (store, supply) بَنْك (بُنوك); **a blood/data ~** بَنْك دَمٍ \ مَعْلوماتٍ

B *vt* أَوْدَعَ ‹*money, a cheque*›; **to ~ the takings** أَوْدَعَ المَداخيلَ في البَنْكِ

C *vi* **to ~ with Banque Misr** «customers, account holders» تَعامَلَ مع بَنْكِ مِصْرَ

Idiom **it won't break the bank** (infml) لن تَقْصِمَ الظَهْرَ

Phrasal verb **bank on**: **~ on [sth]** اعْتَمَدَ على [شَيْءٍ] ‹*success, victory*›; **I wouldn't ~ on it!** لا تَعْتَمِدْ عَلَيْهِ!

bank account *n* حِساب بَنْكيّ \ مَصْرِفيّ

bank balance *n* رَصيد بَنْكيّ

bank book *n* [دَفْتَر صَفَقاتٍ بَنْكيّةٍ لِعَميلٍ]

bank card *n* بِطاقة بَنْكيّة \ مَصْرِفيّة

bank charges *n* رُسوم مَصْرِفيّة

bank clerk *n* مُوَظَّف في بَنْكٍ

banker /ˈbaŋkə/ *n* مَصْرِفِيّ

banker's draft *n* صَكٌّ بَنْكِيّ (للتعامُلاتِ بين البُنوكِ)

bank holiday *n* (BrE) يَوْم عُطْلَةٍ رَسْمِيَّةٍ

banking /ˈbaŋkɪŋ/ *n* صَيْرَفة

banking hours *n* أَوْقات فَتْحِ البَنْكِ

bank manager *n* مُدير فَرْعٍ في بَنْكٍ

banknote /ˈbaŋknəʊt/ *n* وَرَقة نَقْدِيّة

bank robber *n* سارِق بَنْكٍ

bank robbery *n* سَطْو على بَنْكٍ

bankroll /ˈbaŋkrəʊl/ *vt* مَوَّلَ *‹a campaign, candidate›*

bankrupt /ˈbaŋkrʌpt/ **A** *adj ‹debtor, company›* مُفْلِس (مَفاليسُ); **to go ~** أَفْلَسَ **B** *vt* فَلَّسَ *‹person, organization›*

bankruptcy /ˈbaŋkrʌptsi/ *n* (*pl* **bankruptcies**) إفْلاس

bank statement *n* كَشْف الحِسابِ البَنْكِيِّ

banner /ˈbanə/ *n* **1** (of cloth) لافِتة (لافِتات) **2** (on web pages) إعْلان الرايةِ

banns /banz/ *n pl* [إشْهار نِيَّةِ زَواجٍ (مِن قِبَلِ كَنيسةٍ)]

banquet /ˈbaŋkwɪt/ *n* مَأْدُبة (مَآدِبُ)

banter /ˈbantə/ *n* مُمازَحة

baptism /ˈbaptɪz(ə)m/ *n* مَعْمودِيّة, تَعْميد

baptist /ˈbaptɪst/ *n, adj* مَعْمَدانِيّ

baptize, -ise (BrE) /bapˈtʌɪz/ *vt* عَمَّدَ *‹a child, believer›*

bar /bɑː/ **A** *n* **1** (on a cage, across a door) قَضيب (قُضْبان); **to put behind ~s** سَجَنَ (u; سَجْن), وَضَعَ خَلْفَ القُضْبانِ **2** (of soap, chocolate) قالِب (قَوالِبُ); (of gold) سَبيكة (سَبائِكُ) **3** (place for drinking) حانة, بار (بارات) **4** (counter) بار (بارات), كونْتوار; **to sit at the ~** جَلَسَ على الكونْتوار \ البارِ **5** (obstacle) عَقَبة (عَقَبات, عِقاب), حاجِز (حَواجِزُ); **age is no ~ to employment** لَيْسَ التَقَدُّمُ في العُمْرِ عَقَبةً أَمامَ العَمَلِ **6** (legal profession) **the B~** مُحاماة, نِقابة المُحامينَ; **to be called to the B~** قُبِلَ في نِقابةِ المُحامينَ **7** (over the goal) **the ~** العارِضة **8** (BrE) (in an electric fire) قَضيب كَهْرَبائِيّ **9** (Mus) مِقْياس (مَقاييسُ) **B** *vt* (**-rr-**) **1** (to fasten) زَلَجَ (a; زُلوج), رَتَجَ (u; رَتْج) *‹the door, shutters›*; **the gate was ~red** أُغْلِقَ البابُ بالمِزْلاجِ **2** (to block) سَدَّ (u; سَدّ), أَوْصَدَ *‹the way, access›*; **to ~ sb's way** سَدَّ الطَريقَ على شَخْصٍ **3** (to ban) حَظَرَ (u; حَظْر) (على) *‹a person, company›*; **to ~ sb from doing sth** حَظَرَ على شَخْصٍ فِعْلَ شَيْءٍ **C** *prep* إلاّ; **all the candidates ~ one passed** كُلُّ المُرَشَّحينَ نَجَحوا إلاّ واحِداً

Idiom **to raise/lower the bar** رَفَعَ \ خَفَضَ من سَقْفِ التَوَقُّعاتِ

barb /bɑːb/ *n* شَوْكة (السِنّارةِ مَثَلاً)

Barbados /bɑːˈbeɪdɒs/ *pr n* بارْبادوس (f)

barbarian /bɑːˈbɛːrɪən/ *n* بَرْبَرِيّ (بَرابِرة)

barbaric /bɑːˈbarɪk/ *adj ‹act, practice›* بَرْبَرِيّ

barbarity /bɑːˈbarɪti/ *n* بَرْبَرِيّة

barbecue /ˈbɑːbɪkjuː/ *n* **1** (grill) مِشْواة (مَشاوٍ) **2** (gathering) حَفْلة شِواءٍ

barbed wire /ˌbɑːbd ˈwʌɪə/ *n* (BrE) أَسْلاك شائِكة

barber /ˈbɑːbə/ *n* حَلّاق

barbershop /ˈbɑːbəʃɒp/, **barber's shop** (BrE) *n* صالون حِلاقةٍ

barbiturate /bɑːˈbɪtjʊrət/ *n* بارْبيتورات

barbwire *n* (AmE) أَسْلاك شائِكة

bar chart *n* مُخَطَّط بَيانِيّ \ شَريطِيّ

barcode /bɑːˈkəʊd/ *n* شَفْرة خَيْطِيّة, بارْكود

bare /bɛː/ **A** *adj* **1** *‹foot, chest›* عارٍ (عُراة) **2** *‹walls, wire›* عارٍ (عُراة) **3** *‹facts, outline›* مُجَرَّد; **just bring the ~ essentials** لا تَجْلِبْ مَعَكَ إلاّ الأَساسِيّاتِ فَقَطْ **B** *vt* كَشَفَ (i; كَشْف) *‹breasts›*; عَبَّرَ (عن) *‹your soul›*; **the dog ~d its teeth** كَشَفَ الكَلْبُ عن أَنْيابِهِ

bareback /ˈbɛːbak/ *adv ‹to ride›* بِدونِ سَرْجٍ

barefoot /ˈbɛːfʊt/ **A** *adj ‹children, detainee›* حافٍ (حُفاة) **B** *adv ‹to run, walk›* حافِياً

barely /ˈbɛːli/ *adv* **1** *‹visible, conscious›* بالكادِ **2** *‹to manage, notice›* بالكادِ

bargain /ˈbɑːgɪn/ **A** *n* **1** (agreement) صَفْقة (صَفَقات); **to make/strike a ~** عَقَدَ \ أَبْرَمَ صَفْقةً **2** (good buy) صَفْقة (صَفَقات)

B *vi* فاوَضَ; **to ~ with sb over the price** فاصَلَ شَخْصاً على الثَّمَنِ

Idiom **into the bargain** عِلاوةً على ذلك

Phrasal verb **bargain for, bargain on: ~ for [sth], ~ on [sth]** تَوَقَّعَ [شَيْئاً]; **we got more than we ~ed for** حَصَلْنا على أَكْثَر مِمّا تَوَقَّعْنا

bargaining /ˈbɑːɡɪnɪŋ/ *n* مُفاوَضة

bargaining chip *n* وَرَقة مُساوَمةٍ

bargaining power *n* وَرَقة مُساوَمةٍ

barge /bɑːdʒ/ **A** *n* سَفينة مُسَطَّحة, صَنْدَل

B *vi* **to ~ past sb** [اِنْدَفَعَ بِشَكْلٍ أَخْرَقَ \ عَدائيٍّ بِمُحاذاةِ شَخْصٍ]

Phrasal verb **barge in** أَقْحَمَ نَفْسَهُ

baritone /ˈbærɪtəʊn/ *n* **1** [u] (voice) باريتون (دَرَجة في أَصْواتِ الرجال بين المُرْتَفِعة والمُنْخَفِضةِ) **2** (singer) جَهير أَوَّل

barium /ˈbɛːrɪəm/ *n* باريوم

bark /bɑːk/ **A** *n* **1** (of trees) لِحاء (أَلْحِية) **2** (of a dog) نَبيح

B *vi* «dogs» نَبَحَ (a; نَبْح, نُباح, نَبيح); «foxes» ضَبَحَ (a; ضَبْح)

Idiom **to be barking up the wrong tree** كانَ على خَطَأٍ

barley /ˈbɑːli/ *n* شَعير

barmaid /ˈbɑːmeɪd/ *n* ساقِية (سَواقٍ)

barman /ˈbɑːmən/ *n* (*pl* **-men**) ساقٍ (سُقاة)

barn /bɑːn/ *n* (for crops) مَخْزَن (مَخازِنُ); (for cattle) حَظيرة (حَظائِرُ)

barn dance *n* [حَفْلة رَقْصٍ ريفيٍّ]

barnyard /ˈbɑːnjɑːd/ *n* فِناء مَزْرَعةٍ

barometer /bəˈrɒmɪtə/ *n* بارومِتر, مِقْياس الضَغْطِ الجَوّيّ

baron /ˈbær(ə)n/ *n* **1** (nobleman) بارون **2** (magnate) بارون

baroness /ˈbær(ə)nəs/ *n* بارونة

baroque /bəˈrɒk, AmE bəˈrəʊk/ *adj* باروكيّ (فَنّ \ مِعْمار)

barracks /ˈbærəks/ *n + sing or pl vb* (**barracks**, *pl*) ثُكْنة (ثُكَن, ثُكُنات)

barracuda /ˌbærəˈkuːdə/ *n* (*pl* **barracudas**) بَرَكودة (صِنْف من الأَسْماكِ)

barrage /ˈbærɑːʒ, AmE bəˈrɑːʒ/ *n* **1** (dam) سَدّ (أَسْداد, سُدود) **2** (bombardment) حاجِز ناريّ

barrel /ˈbær(ə)l/ *n* **1** (for beer, wine, oil) بِرْميل (بَراميلُ) **2** (of a gun) سَبَطانة

Idiom **to have sb over a barrel** لَوى ذِراعَ شَخْصٍ

barren /ˈbær(ə)n/ *adj* **1** *‹landscape, desert›* قاحِل **2** (old use) *‹woman›* عاقِر (mf; عُقَّر; f pl عَواقِرُ)

barrette /bæˈrɛt/ *n* (AmE) مِشْبَك شَعْرٍ

barricade /ˌbærɪˈkeɪd/ **A** *n* مِتْراس (مَتاريسُ)

B *vt* *‹a road, door›* سَدَّ بِمَتاريسَ \ حَواجِزَ; **they ~d themselves in the kitchen** تَمَتْرَسوا في المَطْبَخِ

barrier /ˈbærɪə/ *n* **1** (physical) حاجِز (حَواجِزُ) **2** (emotional, ideological) حاجِز (حَواجِزُ); **language ~** عائِق لُغَويّ

barrier cream *n* كِريم عازِل

barrier reef *n* حاجِز مَرْجانيّ; **the Great Barrier Reef** الحاجِز المَرْجانيّ العَظيم

barring /ˈbɑːrɪŋ/ *prep* *‹complications, a delay›* إلاّ في حالةِ

barrister /ˈbærɪstə/ *n* مُحامي مُرافَعاتٍ

barrow /ˈbærəʊ/ *n* نَقّالة

bartender /ˈbɑːtɛndə/ *n* ساقٍ (سُقاة)

barter /ˈbɑːtə/ *vi* **1** (to exchange goods) قايَضَ **2** (to haggle) فاصَلَ

base /beɪs/ **A** *n* **1** (bottom part) قاعِدة (قَواعِدُ)

2 (headquarters for army, navy) قاعِدة (قَواعِدُ); (headquarters of a company) مَقَرّ رَئيسيّ; **an army/air force ~** قاعِدة بَرّيّة \ جَوّيّة; **she now uses London as her ~** تَتَّخِذُ الآنَ من لُنْدُن مَقَرًّا لَها **3** (basis) قاعِدة (قَواعِدُ), أَساس (أَساسات, أُسُس) **4** (of customers, fans) قاعِدة (قَواعِدُ); **our customer ~ is growing daily** تَكْبُرُ قاعِدةُ زَبائِنِنا يَوْمِيًّا **5** (Culin) [عُنْصُر أَساسيّ من مَزيجٍ للطَّبْخِ] **6** (in baseball) قاعِدة (قَواعِدُ) **7** (Chem) قاعِدة (قَواعِدُ)

B *adj* (**-er, -est**) (contemptible) *‹instincts, motives›* دَنيء (أَدْنِياءُ), وَضيع (وُضَعاءُ)

C *vt* **1** (to found) *‹a decision, film›* بَنى (i; بِناء, بُنْيان); **the film is ~d on a true story** الفيلمُ مَبْنيٌّ على قِصّةٍ واقِعيّةٍ **2** (to be located) **to be ~d in New York/Vienna** «company, person» اتَّخَذَ من نيويورك \ فيينا مَقَرًّا لَهُ

baseball /ˈbeɪsbɔːl/ *n* **1** [u] (game) بيسْبول **2** (ball) كُرة البيسْبول

baseball cap *n* قُبَّعة البيسْبول

baseline /ˈbeɪslaɪn/ *n* خطّ القاعِدةِ

baseman /ˈbeɪsmən/ *n* (*pl* **-men**) [حارِس القاعِدةِ في البيسْبول]

basement /ˈbeɪsm(ə)nt/ *n* سِرْداب (سَراديبُ, سَرادِبُ)

bash /baʃ/ (infml) **A** *vt* (to hit) ضَرَب (i; ضَرْب), خَبَطَ (i; خَبْط) <*a person, surface*>; **she ~ed her head on the shelf** ضَرَبَتْ رَأْسَها على الرَفِّ

B *n* **1** (blow) ضَرْبة (ضَرَبات), خَبْطة **2** (BrE) (attempt) مُحاوَلة; **to have a ~ at sth** حاوَلَ شَيْئاً **3** (party) حَفْلة (حَفَلات)

(Phrasal verbs) **bash in**: **~ [sth] in** [شَيْئاً] حَطَّم <*the door*>; **they threatened to ~ his head in** هَدَّدوا بِتَحْطيمِ رَأْسِهِ
• **bash into**: **~ into [sth]** [شَيْءٍ] اِصْطَدَمَ بـ <*a car, wall*>
• **bash out**: **~ [sth] out**, **~ out [sth]** [شَيْئاً] اِرْتَجَلَ <*stories, songs*>

bashful /ˈbaʃfʊl/ *adj* <*smile, schoolgirl*> خَجول

basic /ˈbeɪsɪk/ *adj* **1** (fundamental) <*principle, requirement*> أَساسيّ **2** (elementary) <*knowledge, skill*> أَساسيّ **3** (rudimentary) <*facilities, supplies*> أَساسيّ **4** (before additions) <*wage, pension*> أَساسيّ

basically /ˈbeɪsɪk(ə)li/ *adv* **1** (fundamentally) <*unchanged, sound*> من حَيْثُ الجَوْهَرِ **2** (in short) بِإيجازٍ, باخْتِصارٍ

basics /ˈbeɪsɪks/ *n pl* **1** (of a subject, skill) أَساسيّات **2** (essential items) أَساسيّات

basil /ˈbaz(ə)l/ *n* رَيْحان (رَياحينُ)

basin /ˈbeɪs(ə)n/ *n* **1** (in a bathroom) مَغْسَلة (مَغاسِلُ) **2** (for liquids, food) قَصْعة (قِصاع) **3** (of a river) حَوْض (أَحْواض, حِياض) **4** (for boats) حَوْض (أَحْواض, حِياض) **5** (low land) حَوْض (أَحْواض, حِياض)

basis /ˈbeɪsɪs/ *n* (*pl* **bases**) **1** (foundation) قِوام, أَرْضيّة, قاعِدة (قَواعِدُ); **on the ~ of this information** بِناءً على هذه المَعْلوماتِ **2** (system) شَكْل (أَشْكال, شُكول); **on a regular/daily ~** بِشَكْلٍ مُنْتَظِمٍ \ يَوْميٍّ

bask /bɑːsk/ *vi* **1** (to lie) «sunbathers, seals» تَنَعَّمَ; **to ~ in the sun** تَنَعَّمَ بِأَشِعّةِ الشَمْسِ **2** (to revel) **to ~ in the glory of sth** تَنَعَّمَ بِمَجْدِ شَيْءٍ

basket /ˈbɑːskɪt/ *n* **1** (container for carrying or storing things) سَلّة (سِلال) **2** (contents) سَلّة (سِلال); **a ~ of shopping** سَلّة من المُشْتَرَياتِ **3** (net in basketball) سَلّة (سِلال); (point scored) نُقْطة (نُقَط, نِقاط)

basketball /ˈbɑːskɪtbɔːl/ *n* **1** [u] (game) كُرة السَلّةِ **2** (ball) كُرة السَلّةِ

Basra /ˈbazrə/ *pr n* البَصْرة

bass¹ /beɪs/ *n* **1** (voice) جَهير; (singer) مُغَنٍّ جَهير الصَوْتِ **2** (instrument: double bass) كَمان أَجْهَر; (bass guitar) جيتار بيس **3** (part) [طَبَقة صَوْتٍ خَفيضٍ وَعَميقٍ]; **to sing (the) ~** [غَنّى بِطَبَقةِ صَوْتٍ خَفيضٍ وَعَميقٍ]

bass² /bas/ *n* (sea fish) قاروص; (freshwater) فَرْخ

bass clef *n* مِفْتاح 'فا'

bass drum *n* [طَبْل كَبير]

bass guitar *n* جيتار بيس

bassist /ˈbeɪsɪst/ *n* **1** (with double bass) عازِف الكَمانِ الأَجْهَرِ **2** (with bass guitar) عازِف الجيتارِ البيس

bassoon /bəˈsuːn/ *n* زَمْخَر

bastard /ˈbɑːstəd/ *n* **1** (vulg) (despicable person) ابْن العاهِرةِ **2** (Hist) (illegitimate child) طِفْل غَيْر شَرْعيٍّ

baste /beɪst/ *vt* **1** (in cooking) أَرْطَبَ, نَدّى **2** (in sewing) [خَيَّطَ تَخْييطاً مُؤَقَّتاً] <*a seam, lining*>

bastion /ˈbastɪən/ *n* **1** (of a tradition, belief) قَلْعة (قِلاع, قُلوع) **2** (of fortifications) مَعْقِل (مَعاقِلُ)

bat /bat/ **A** *n* **1** (in cricket, baseball, table tennis) مِضْرَب (مَضارِبُ) **2** (mammal) خُفّاش (خَفافيشُ), وَطْواط (وَطاوِطُ, وَطاويطُ)

B *vi* (-tt-) ضَرَبَ بالمِضْرَبِ

(Idioms) **(right) off the bat** (AmE) على الفَوْرِ, بِدونِ تَأْخيرٍ; **to bat for sb** دَعَمَ شَخْصاً

batch /batʃ/ *n* **1** (of loaves, cakes) [عَجْنة] **2** (of goods) دُفْعة (دُفُعات, دَفَعات) **3** (of trainees, prisoners) دُفْعة (دُفُعات, دَفَعات) **4** (of mail, paperwork) دُفْعة (دُفُعات, دَفَعات) **5** (Comput) (in processing) دُفْعة (دُفُعات, دَفَعات)

bated /ˈbeɪtɪd/ *adj* **with ~ breath** بِأَنْفاسٍ مَحْبوسةٍ

bath /bɑːθ/ **A** *n* **1** (wash, washing water) اِسْتِحْمام; **to have** *or* **take a ~** اِسْتَحَمَّ; **to run a ~** هَيَّأَ الحَمّامَ **2** (BrE) (bathtub) بانْيو (بانْيوهات), حَمّام (حَمّامات) **3** (AmE) (bathroom) حَمّام (حَمّامات), مِرْحاض (مَراحيضُ) **4** (in technical processes) حَوْض غَمْرٍ

B (**baths**) *n pl* **1** (BrE) (also **swimming baths**) حَوْض \ حَمّام سِباحةٍ, مَسْبَح (مَسابِحُ) **2** (in a spa) حَمّام, مُنْتَجَع صِحّيّ طَبيعيّ

C *vt* (BrE) حَمَّمَ ‹*a baby, patient*›

D *vi* (BrE) اسْتَحَمَّ

bathe /beɪð/ **A** *vt* **1** نَظَّفَ ‹*a wound, eyes*› **2** (in a bath) حَمَّمَ ‹*a baby, pet*›

B *vi* **1** (BrE) (to swim) اسْتَحَمَّ **2** (AmE) (to take a bath) اغْتَسَلَ, اسْتَحَمَّ

bather /ˈbeɪðə/ *n* سَبّاح

bathing /ˈbeɪðɪŋ/ *n* سِباحة

bathing cap *n* قَلَنْسُوة العَوْمِ

bathing suit, **bathing costume** *n* **1** (for a boy, man) تُبّان **2** (for a girl, woman) مايوه (مايوهات)

bath mat *n* حَصير حَمّامٍ

bathrobe /ˈbɑːθrəʊb/ *n* بُرْنُس (بَرانِسُ)

bathroom /ˈbɑːθruːm, ˈbɑːθrʊm/ *n* **1** (room with bath) حَمّام (حَمّامات) **2** (AmE) (lavatory) مِرْحاض (مَراحيضُ)

bathroom cabinet *n* خِزانة حَمّامٍ

bathroom scales *n* ميزان حَمّامٍ

bath towel *n* مِنْشَفة حَمّامٍ, بَشْكير (بَشاكيرُ)

bathtub /ˈbɑːθtʌb/ *n* (AmE) حَوْض اسْتِحْمامٍ, بانْيو (بانْيوهات)

baton /ˈbat(ə)n/ *n* **1** (BrE) (policeman's) هِراوة (هَراوى) **2** (conductor's) مِخْصَرة (مَخاصِرُ) **3** (in relay races) عَصا التَتابُعِ

batsman /ˈbatsmən/ *n* (*pl* **-men**) ضارِب الكُرةِ (في لُعْبةِ الكْريكِت)

battalion /bəˈtalɪən/ *n* (Mil) فَوْج (أَفْواج), كَتيبة (كَتائِبُ)

batter /ˈbatə/ **A** *n* **1** (for frying) [عَجينة سائِلة] **2** (in cricket, baseball) ضارِب الكُرةِ

B *vt* اعْتَدى بالضَرْبِ على ‹*a wife*›; دَكَّ (u; دَكّ) ‹*coast*›

battered /ˈbatəd/ *adj* **1** (worn) ‹*car, suitcase*› مُهْتَرِئ **2** (beaten) ‹*wife, baby*› مُعْتَدًى عَلَيْهِ

battering ram /ˈbatərɪŋ ˌram/ *n* مِدَقّ (مَداقّ)

battery /ˈbat(ə)ri/ *n* (*pl* **batteries**) **1** (Elec) بَطّاريّة **2** (of guns) سَريّة مِدْفَعيّة

battery charger *n* شاحِن بَطّاريّةٍ

battery farming *n* [رِعاية حَيَواناتٍ مُدَجَّنةٍ في بيئةٍ حاشِدةٍ]

battery-operated, **battery-powered** *adj* ‹*scooter, radio*› [يَعْمَلُ بالبَطّاريّةِ]

battle /ˈbat(ə)l/ **A** *n* (armed) قِتال, مَعْرَكة (مَعارِكُ); **the ~ for recognition** مَعْرَكة الاعْتِرافِ; **to fight a losing ~** حارَبَ مَعْرَكةً خاسِرةً

B *vi* «contestants» تَصارَعَ; **they ~d for control of the party** تَصارَعوا للسَيْطَرةِ على الحِزْبِ

Idiom **to be half the battle** كانَ نِصْفَ المَعْرَكةِ

battlefield /ˈbat(ə)lfiːld/ *n* مَيْدان مَعْرَكةٍ

battlements /ˈbat(ə)lmənts/ *n pl* [جِدار واطِئ على سَطْحِ القِلاعِ]

battleship /ˈbat(ə)lʃɪp/ *n* سَفينة حَرْبيّة, بارِجة (بَوارِجُ)

baud /bɔːd/ *n* بود (وَحْدة قِياسِ سُرْعةِ نَقْلِ المَعْلوماتِ)

bawdy /ˈbɔːdi/ *adj* (**bawdier**, **bawdiest**) ‹*humour, song*› بَذيء

bawl /bɔːl/ *vi* **1** (to weep) «children» نَحَبَ (بِصَوْتٍ عالٍ) **2** (to shout) «crowd, sergeant» صَرَخَ (u; صُراخ, صَريخ), زَعَقَ (a; زَعْق), زَمْجَرَ (زَمْجَرة; i), عَيَّطَ

bay /beɪ/ **A** *n* **1** (on a coast) خَليج (خُلْجان) **2** (also **bay tree**) الغارِ (شَجَرة) **3** (area) فُسْحة (فُسَح, فُسْحات) **4** **to keep sb/sth at ~** صَدَّ شَخْصاً \ شَيْئاً

B *vi* «dogs, wolves» عَوى (i; عُواء)

bay leaf *n* وَرَق الغارِ

bayonet /ˈbeɪənɪt/ *n* حَرْبة (حِراب)

bay window *n* [نافِذة غُرْفةٍ مُمْتَدّة إلى الخارِجِ]

bazaar /bəˈzɑː/ *n* **1** (market) سوق (mf; أَسْواق) **2** (charity sale) سوق خَيْريّة

BBC /biːbiːˈsiː/ *abbr* = **British Broadcasting Corporation** بي بي سي (هَيْئة الإذاعةِ البَريطانيّة)

BC /biːˈsiː/ *abbr* = **before Christ** قبل الميلادِ

bcc /biːsiːˈsiː/ *abbr* = **blind carbon copy** نُسخة كَرْبونيّة مَخفيّة (في البَريدِ الإلِكْتْرونيِّ)

BCE /biːsiːˈiː/ *abbr* = **before the Common Era** قبل الميلادِ

BCG /biːsiːˈdʒiː/ *n* لَقاح السُلِّ

be /biː/ *vi* (*present participle* **being**; *past tense* (1st & 3rd pers sing) **was** or (other subjects) **were**; *past participle* **been**) 1 (in statements) كانَ (u; كَوْن); **they are good students** هُمْ طُلّابٌ جَيِّدونَ; **it's me** هذا أنا; **it's them** إنَّهُمْ هُنا; **I preferred it as it was** أُفَضِّلُها بالشَكْلِ الّذي كانَتْ عَلَيْهِ 2 (stating probability) **if he's coming, I won't go** إذا كانَ قادِماً، فَلَنْ أَذْهَبَ; **if Henry were here, everything would be all right** لو كانَ هِنْري هُنا، لَكانَ كُلُّ شَيْءٍ على ما يُرامُ; **if I were you, I'd see a doctor** لو كُنْتُ مَكانَك، لَزُرْتُ طَبيباً; **had it not been for Frank, I'd have missed the train** لَوْلا فرانْك، لَتَأَخَّرْتُ عن القِطارِ 3 (fml) (phrases) **so ~ it** فَلْيَكُنْ; **~ that as it may ...** وَمَهْما يَكُنْ من أَمْرٍ ...; **let** *or* **leave him ~** أُتْرُكْهُ وَشَأْنَهُ; **to ~ or not to ~** أكونُ أو لا أكونُ

beach /biːtʃ/ *n* شاطِئ (شَواطِئُ,شُطْآن)

beach ball *n* كُرة شاطِئٍ

beach buggy *n* سَيّارة شاطِئٍ

beachhead /ˈbiːtʃhɛd/ *n* رَأْس جِسْرٍ ساحِليٍّ

beacon /ˈbiːk(ə)n/ *n* 1 (as a signal or warning) مَنار (مَناوِرُ), 2 (also **radio beacon**) مَنارة لاسِلْكيّة (مَنائِرُ)

bead /biːd/ *n* 1 (in jewellery) خَرَز (n coll) 2 (of sweat) قَطْرة (قَطَرات)

beady /ˈbiːdi/ *adj* (**beadier**, **beadiest**) ‹*eyes*› خَرَزيّ

beak /biːk/ *n* مِنْقار (مَناقيرُ)

beaker /ˈbiːkə/ *n* 1 (cup) قَدَح (أَقْداح) 2 (in a lab) دَوْرَق (دَوارِقُ)

beam /biːm/ A *n* 1 (of light) (single ray) شُعاع (n coll; أَشِعّة); (shaft of light) حُزْمة أَشِعّةٍ; **put the headlights on full** (BrE) *or* **high** (AmE) ~ أَشْعِلِ الأَضْواءَ العالِيَةَ (للسَيّارةِ) 2 (of wood, concrete) عارِضة

B *vt* 1 (to send) بَثَّ (i-u; بَثّ) ‹*a signal, an image*› 2 (by smiling) أَشَعَّ ‹*one's relief, thanks*›

C *vi* 1 (to smile) «couple, winners» أَشْرَقَ وَجْهُهُ 2 (to emit light) «the sun, moon» أَشْرَقَ

bean /biːn/ *n* فاصولية

bean curd *n* خَثارة الفاصولية (التوفو)

bean sprout *n* فول نابت

bear /bɛː/ A *n* دُبّ (دِبَبة)

B *vt* (*past tense* **bore**; *past participle* **borne**) 1 (fml) (to carry) حَمَلَ (i; حَمْل) ‹*a coffin, tray*› 2 (liter) (to bring) حَمَلَ (i; حَمْل) ‹*a gift, message*› 3 (to show, have) حَمَلَ (i; حَمْل) ‹*sb's name, an inscription*›; **to ~ a resemblance to sb/sth** كانَ فيهِ شَبَهٌ من شَخْصٍ \ شَيْءٍ; **it ~s no relation to reality/the facts** لَيْسَ لَهُ عَلاقةٌ بالواقِعِ \ الحَقائِقِ; **she founded the museum that ~s her name** أَسَّست المَتْحَفَ الّذي يَحْمِلُ اسْمَها 4 (to support) تَحَمَّلَ ‹*a weight, load*› 5 (to endure, tolerate) تَحَمَّلَ ‹*pain, suspense*›; **I can't ~ him** لا أَسْتَطيعُ أَنْ أَتَحَمَّلَهُ; **the pain was too much to ~** كانَ الأَلَمُ شَديداً لا يُتَحَمَّلُ 6 (to accept) تَحَمَّلَ ‹*the cost, responsibility, blame*› 7 (to withstand) تَحَمَّلَ ‹*scrutiny, examination*›; **it doesn't ~ thinking about** لا يُحْتَمَلُ التَفْكيرُ فيهِ 8 (to produce) حَمَلَ (i; حَمْل) ‹*fruit, flowers*› 9 «accounts, investments» حَمَلَ (i; حَمْل) ‹*interest*› 10 (*past participle* **borne**; *passive participle* **born**) (liter) (to give birth to) وَلَدَ (i; مَوْلِد, وِلادة) ‹*a child*›

C *vi* (*past tense* **bore**; *past participle* **borne**) 1 (to turn) **to ~ left/right** «drivers, vehicles» دارَ يَساراً \ يَميناً 2 (to have an effect) **to bring pressure to ~ on sb** «countries, organizations» ضَغَطَ على شَخْصٍ

Phrasal verbs **bear down on**: **~ down on [sb/sth]** 1 (to exert pressure on) ضَغَطَ على [شَخْصٍ \ شَيْءٍ] نحو الأَسْفَلِ ‹*a surface, body*› 2 (to approach aggressively) «storm, vehicle» اجْتاحَ [شَخْصاً \ شَيْئاً]

• **bear on**: 1 **~ on [sth]** (to affect) أَثَّرَ على [شَيْءٍ] ‹*an issue, a decision*› 2 **~ on [sb]** (to be a burden on) كانَ حِمْلاً ثَقيلاً على [شَخْصٍ], كانَ عِبْئاً على [شَخْصٍ] ‹*the poor, taxpayers*›

• **bear out**: **~ out [sth]** أَيَّدَ [شَيْئاً] ‹*a theory, claim*›

• **bear up** (to remain composed) «person» تَحَمَّلَ

• **bear upon** ▸ **bear on**

• **bear with**: **~ with [sb/sth]** صَبَرَ على ,تَحمَّلَ [شَخْصاً \ شَيْئاً] [شَخْصٍ \ شَيْءٍ] *‹a salesperson, an official›*; **please ~ with me for a moment ...** اصْبِرْ عَلَيَّ دَقيقةً من فَضْلِكَ ...

bearable /ˈbɛːrəb(ə)l/ *adj ‹heat, situation›* مُحْتَمَل

beard /bɪəd/ *n* لِحْية (لِحًى ,لُحًى)

bearded /ˈbɪədɪd/ *adj ‹man›* مُلْتَحٍ

bearer /ˈbɛːrə/ *n* 1 (of news, a gift) حامِل (حَمَلة) 2 (of a passport, cheque) حامِل (حَمَلة) 3 (at funerals) حَمّال (حَمّالة ,حَمّالون); (on expeditions) عَتّال

bearing /ˈbɛːrɪŋ/ *n* 1 (in a machine) مَحْمِل (مَحامِلُ) 2 (relevance) **to have little/a great ~ on sth** كانَ لَهُ تَأْثيرٌ ضَعيفٌ \ قَويٌّ على شَيْءٍ 3 (in navigation) **to take a compass ~** [حَدَّدَ اتِّجاهَهُ بِواسِطةِ بوصَلةٍ]; **to get/lose one's ~s** حَسَمَ \ ضَلَّ مَسارَهُ 4 [u] (of a person) وَضْعيّة

beast /biːst/ *n* 1 (animal) حَيَوان (حَيَوانات) 2 (infml) (person) شَخْص حَقير ,حَيَوان

beat /biːt/ A *vt* (*past tense* **beat**; *past participle* **beaten**) 1 (to hit) ضَرَبَ (i; ضَرْب) *‹a prisoner, an animal›*; **he ~s his wife and children** يَضْرِبُ زَوْجَتَهُ وأَطْفالَهُ; **he was ~en to death** ضُرِبَ حتّى المَوْتِ; **they ~ him with sticks** ضَرَبوهُ بالعِصِيِّ 2 (to clean) نَفَضَ (u; نَفْض) *‹a carpet, rug›* 3 (in metalworking) طَرَقَ (u; طَرْق) ,ضَرَبَ (i; ضَرْب) *‹gold, metal›* 4 «musicians» ضَرَبَ (i; ضَرْب) ,دَقَّ (u; دَقّ) *‹a drum, tambourine›*; **to ~ time** قادَ الإيقاعَ 5 (to flap) **to ~ its wings** «bird» خَفَقَ بِجَناحَيْهِ 6 (to stir) خَفَقَ (i-u; خَفْقان ,خَفْق) *‹eggs, butter›* 7 (to defeat) غَلَبَ (i; غَلَبة) ,هَزَمَ (i; هَزيمة) ,تَغَلَّبَ (على) ,تَفَوَّقَ (على) *‹a team, an opponent›*; **I ~ him at chess** هَزَمْتُهُ في الشِطْرَنْجِ; **Italy ~ Spain 2-1** *or* **by two goals to one** هَزَمَتْ إيطاليا إسْبانيا 2−1; **a new therapy/drug to ~ depression** عِلاج \ دَواء جَديد للتَغَلُّبِ على الاكْتِئابِ; **how can inflation be ~en ?** كَيفَ يُمْكِنُ التَغَلُّبُ على التَضَخُّمِ ؟ 8 (to surpass) حَطَّمَ *‹a record, score, target›*; **he ~ the world record** حَطَّمَ الرَقْمَ القِياسيَّ العالَميَّ; **they ~ all their targets** تَجاوَزوا كُلَّ أَهْدافِهِمْ; **we are hard to ~ on price** لا أَحَدَ يَسْتَطيعُ مُنافَسَتَنا في الأَسْعارِ; **you can't ~ a good book** [لا شَيْءَ يَسْتَطيعُ أَنْ يَتَفَوَّقَ على كِتابٍ جَيِّدٍ]; **for spectacular scenery Switzerland is hard to ~** سُويسْرا لا تُنافَسُ من حَيْثُ المَناظِرِ الطَبيعيّةِ الرائِعةِ 9 (infml) (to arrive before) غَلَبَ (i; غَلَبة); **she beat me to it** [غَلَبَتْني في الحُصولِ عَلَيْهِ \ الوصولِ إِلَيْهِ]; **we left early to ~ the traffic** غادَرْنا باكِراً لِنَتَجَنَّبَ الازْدِحامَ

B *vi* (*past tense* **beat**; *past participle* **beaten**) 1 ; **to ~ against sth** «rain» قَرَعَ شَيْئاً; «waves» ضَرَبَ ,تَلاطَمَ على شَيْءٍ; **to ~ on the door/a drum** قَرَعَ البابَ \ الطَبْلَ 2 «heart, pulse» دَقَّ (u; دَقّ) ,نَبَضَ (i; نَبَضان ,نَبْض) 3 «drums» دُقَّ, 4 «wings» خَفَقَ (i-u; خَفَقان ,خَفْق ,خُفوق) قُرِعَ

C *n* 1 (repeated sound) قَرْع; **they marched to the ~ of the drum** مَشَوْا على قَرْعِ الطَبْلِ 2 (rhythmic unit in music) إيقاع (إيقاعات) 3 ▸ **heartbeat** 4 (policeman's) مِنْطَقة (تحت حِراسةِ شُرْطيٍّ) 5 (Elec) (pulse) ضَرْبة (ضَرَبات) ,تَضارُب

D *adj* (infml) (tired) مُنْهَك

(Idioms) **to beat a hasty retreat** أَطْلَقَ ساقَيْهِ للريحِ (انْسَحَبَ بِسُرْعةٍ مَخافةَ سوءِ العاقِبةِ); **beat it!** (infml) أُخْرُجْ !; **if you can't beat them, join them** [الْتَحِقْ بِهِمْ إذا لم تَسْتَطِعْ أَنْ تَتَغَلَّبَ عَلَيْهِمْ]; **it beats me why/how ...** (infml) لا أَسْتَطيعُ أَنْ أَتَخَيَّلَ لِماذا \ كَيفَ ...

(Phrasal verbs) **beat back**: **~ [sb/sth] back, ~ back [sb/sth]** أَجْبَرَ [شَخْصاً \ شَيْئاً] على التَراجُعِ *‹an army, a person›*

• **beat down** 1 «rain» انْهَمَرَ; «sun» الْتَهَبَ 2 **~ [sb] down** [أَقْنَعَ [شَخْصاً] بِتَنْزيلِ السِعْرِ \ الثَمَنِ]; **I beat her down to 100 dollars** [أَقْنَعْتُها بِتَنْزيلِ السِعْرِ \ الثَمَنِ إلى 100 دولارٍ]

• **beat off**: **~ [sb/sth] off, ~ off [sb/sth]** 1 (to repel) تَصَدّى لِ [شَخْصٍ \ شَيْءٍ], صَدَّ [شَخْصاً \ شَيْئاً] *‹an attack, a challenge›* 2 (to do better than) انْتَصَرَ على [شَخْصٍ \ شَيْءٍ] *‹the competition›*

• **beat out**: **~ [sth] out, ~ out [sth]** 1 (to put out) أَطْفَأَ [شَيْئاً] *‹a fire›* 2 دَقَّ [شَيْئاً] *‹a rhythm›*

• **beat up**: 1 **~ [sb] up, ~ up [sb]** «attacker» أَشْبَعَ \ أَوْسَعَ [شَخْصاً] ضَرْباً, أَثْخَنَ *‹a victim›* 2 (infml) **to ~ oneself up** قَرَّعَ نَفْسَهُ

beaten /ˈbiːt(ə)n/ A *past participle* ▸ **beat**

B *adj* **off the ~ track** ناءٍ

beating /ˈbiːtɪŋ/ *n* 1 (punishment) ضَرْب; **he got a ~ from his father** تَعَرَّضَ إلى الضَرْبِ على يَدِ والِدِهِ 2 (damage) to take a ~ «toys, equipment» تَضَرَّرَ; «shares» تَراجَعَ بِنِسْبةٍ كَبيرةٍ; he's taken a ~ in the press تَعَرَّضَ إلى نَقْدٍ عَنيفٍ في الصِحافةِ 3 (infml) (defeat) (هَزائِمُ) هَزيمة; they'll take some ~ سَيَكونُ من الصَعْبِ إلْحاقُ الهَزيمةِ بِهِمْ 4 (of the heart) نَبْض، 5 (of drums) ضَرْب ,قَرْع نَبَضان

beautician /bju:ˈtɪʃ(ə)n/ *n* مُتَخَصِّص تَجْميلٍ

beautiful /ˈbju:tɪfʊl/ *adj* ‹*woman, voice, scenery*› جَميل

beautifully /ˈbju:tɪf(ə)li/ *adv* ‹*to sing, write*› بِشَكْلٍ جَميلٍ; a ~ furnished apartment شِقّة مَفروشة بِشَكْلٍ جَميلٍ

beauty /ˈbju:ti/ *n* (*pl* **beauties**) 1 [u] (of women, voices, scenery) جَمال 2 (attractive woman) حَسْناء (dipt f; حِسان)

beauty queen *n* مَلِكة جَمالٍ

beauty specialist *n* أخِصّائيّ تَجْميلٍ

beauty spot *n* 1 (place) مَوْقِع خَلّاب 2 (also **beauty mark** AmE) (on skin) شامة (شام ,شامات)

beaver /ˈbi:və/ *n* قُنْدُس (قَنادِسُ)

became /bɪˈkeɪm/ *past tense* ▸ **become**

because /bɪˈkɒz/ **A** *conj* لِأنَّ; **he hasn't come, ~ he's ill** لم يَأْتِ، لِأنَّهُ مَريضٌ; **~ she has a job, she's self-supporting** لِأنَّ لَدَيْها وَظيفةً، فَهِيَ تَعولُ نَفْسَها
B (**because of**) *prep phr* بِسَبَبِ; **the meeting was cancelled ~ of the floods** أُلْغِيَ الاجْتِماعُ بِسَبَبِ الفَيَضاناتِ

beck /bɛk/ *n* **to be at sb's ~ and call** كانَ رَهْنَ إشارةِ شَخْصٍ

beckon /ˈbɛk(ə)n/ **A** *vt* أوْمَأَ (إلى); **to ~ sb over** أوْمَأَ إلى شَخْصٍ بالمَجيءِ
B *vi* (to signal) أوْمَأَ; **to ~ to sb to do sth** أوْمَأَ إلى شَخْصٍ لِلقيامِ بِشَيْءٍ

become /bɪˈkʌm/ **A** *vi* (*past tense* **became**, *past participle* **become**) 1 (in development) «situation, person» أصْبَحَ; **the situation has ~ very dangerous** أصْبَحَ الوَضْعُ خَطيراً جِدّاً; **she has ~ famous** أصْبَحَتْ مَشْهورةً; **she became aware of the truth** أدْرَكَتِ الحَقيقةَ; **the house has ~ quite dilapidated** أصْبَحَ البَيْتُ مُتَهَدِّماً تَماماً 2 (in roles) أصْبَحَ; **to become queen** أصْبَحَتْ مَلِكةً; **to become a doctor** أصْبَحَ طَبيباً
B *v impers* (*past tense* **became**, *past participle* **become**) **what has ~ of your brother?** ماذا حَدَثَ لِأخيكَ؟; **what has ~ of those photos?** أيْنَ ذَهَبَتْ تِلْكَ الصُوَرُ؟
C *vt* (*past tense* **became**, *past participle* **become**) 1 (fml) «colour, style» ناسَبَ ,لاءَمَ ,لاقَ (i; لِياقة ;على) ‹*a person*›; **modern fashions do not ~ older people** الأزْياءُ الحَديثةُ لا تَليقُ على كِبارِ السِنِّ 2 (fml) «attitude, modesty» ناسَبَ ,لاقَ (i; لِياقة ;ب) ‹*a person*›

becoming /bɪˈkʌmɪŋ/ *adj* (fml) 1 (acceptable) ‹*behaviour, modesty*› لائِق 2 (attractive) ‹*dress, haircut*› جَذّاب

bed /bɛd/ *n* 1 (for sleeping) سَرير (أسِرّة); **to get into/out of ~** ذَهَبَ إلى \ قامَ من السَريرِ; **to go to ~** ذَهَبَ إلى السَريرِ; **to be in ~** كانَ في السَريرِ; **to make the ~** أعَدَّ السَريرَ; **to put the children to ~** أعَدَّ الأطْفالَ لِلنَوْمِ 2 (for plants) حَوْض (أحْواض) 3 (bottom of the sea, a lake, river) قاع (قيعان) 4 (of rice, lettuce) طَبَقة 5 (Geol) طَبَقة

(Idioms) **life is not a bed of roses** ≈ الدَهْرُ يَوْمانِ، يَوْمٌ لَكَ وَيَوْمٌ عَلَيْكَ; **to get out of bed on the wrong side** (BrE) **to get up on the wrong side of the bed** (AmE) [كانَ مِزاجُهُ مُتَعَكِّراً]; **to go to bed with sb** ذَهَبَ إلى السَريرِ مع شَخْصٍ ,ضاجَعَ شَخْصاً; **you've made your bed, now lie in it** مَنْ يَزْرَعِ الشَوْكَ يَجْنِ الجِراحَ

(Phrasal verb) **bed down** «visitors, travellers» باتَ (i; مَبيت)

BEd /bi:ˈɛd/ *n* = **Bachelor of Education** بَكالوريوس في التَرْبِيةِ

bed and breakfast *n* 1 [u] (service) [المَبيت والفُطور] 2 (small hotel) [بَيْت لِلنُزَلاءِ مع فُطورٍ]

bedbug /ˈbɛdbʌg/ *n* بَقّ الفِراشِ

bedclothes /ˈbɛdkləʊðz/ *n pl* بَياضات

bedding /ˈbɛdɪŋ/ *n* 1 (bedclothes) شَراشِف 2 (for animals) [فِراش لِلحَيَواناتِ كالتِبْنِ]

bedlam /ˈbɛdləm/ *n* (fml) صَخَب; **it was absolute ~!** كانَتْ هُناكَ فَوْضى عارِمةٌ!

bed linen *n* بَياضات السَريرِ

Bedouin /ˈbɛdʊɪn/ **A** *n* 1 (the people) بَدْو 2 (an individual) بَدَويّ (بَدْو)
B *adj* ‹*customs, culture*› بَدَويّ ,البَدْوِ

bedpan /ˈbɛdpan/ *n* [نونيّة الفِراشِ]

bedraggled /bɪˈdrag(ə)ld/ *adj* ‹*refugee, appearance*› مُلَطَّخ [بالوَحْلِ \ بالدَمِ \ بالوَسَخِ إلخ]; ‹*clothes*› رَثّ (رِثاث)

bedridden /ˈbɛdrɪd(ə)n/ *adj* ‹*patient, mother*› طَريح الفِراشِ

bedroom /ˈbɛdruːm, ˈbɛdrʊm/ *n* غُرْفة نَوْم

bedside /ˈbɛdsʌɪd/ *n* [مَوْقِع بِجانِبِ سَريرٍ (خاصّةً لِشَخْصٍ يُحْتَضَرُ \ لِمَريضٍ)]; **to be at sb's ~** كانَ بِجانِبِ سَريرِ شَخْصٍ

bedside manner *n* [طَريقة تعامُلِ الطبيبِ مع المَريضِ]

bedside table *n* طاوِلة السَريرِ الجانِبيّة

bedsit /ˈbɛdsɪt/, **bedsitter** /ˈbɛdsɪtə/ *n* (BrE) [غُرْفة تُسْتَأْجَرُ في مَسْكَنٍ مع مَنافِعَ مُشْتَرَكةٍ]

bedsore /ˈbɛdsɔː/ *n* قَرْحة الفِراشِ

bedspread /ˈbɛdsprɛd/ *n* [غِطاء سَريرٍ مُزَخْرَف]

bedtime /ˈbɛdtʌɪm/ *n* وَقْت النَوْمِ

bee /biː/ *n* نَحْل (n coll)

beech /biːtʃ/ *n* **1** (also **beech tree**) زان **2** [u] (wood) خَشَب الزان

bee-eater /ˈbiːˌiːtə/ *n* (Zool) وَرْوار

beef /biːf/ *n* لَحْم بَقَرٍ; **roast ~** لَحْم بَقَرٍ مُحَمَّر; **a joint of ~** قِطْعة لَحْم بَقَرٍ

beefburger /ˈbiːfbəːgə/ *n* (BrE) هَمْبورْجَر

beehive /ˈbiːhʌɪv/ *n* خَليّة نَحْلٍ

beekeeper /ˈbiːkiːpə/ *n* نَحّال, مُرَبّي النَحْلِ

beeline /ˈbiːlʌɪn/ *n* (infml) **to make a ~ for sb/sth** اتَّجَهَ مُباشَرةً نحو شَخْصٍ \ شَيْءٍ

been /biːn, AmE bɪn/ *past participle* ▸ **be**

beep /biːp/ **A** *n* صَوْت تَنْبيهٍ, صَفير, رَنين

B *vi* **1** «computers, alarms» أَصْدَرَ صَوْتَ تَنْبيه **2** «cars, motorbikes» أَحْدَثَ زاموراً

C *vt* **to ~ the horn** أَطْلَقَ آلةَ التَنْبيهِ

beer /bɪə/ *n* بيرة; **a glass of ~** كَأْس بيرةٍ; **two ~s, please!** من فَضْلِكَ، كَأْسَيْنِ من البيرةِ!

beer garden *n* [حَديقة مُتَّصِلة بِحانةٍ]

beer mat *n* [كَرْتونة صَغيرة توضَعُ عَلَيْها الكَأْسُ]

bee sting *n* لَسْعة نَحْلٍ

beeswax /ˈbiːzwaks/ *n* شَمْع العَسَلِ

beet /biːt/ *n* بَنْجَر

beetle /ˈbiːt(ə)l/ *n* خُنْفُساء (dipt f; خَنافِسُ)

beetroot /ˈbiːtruːt/ *n* (BrE) جِذْر الشَمَنْدَرِ, بَنْجَر

befall /bɪˈfɔːl/ *vt* (*past tense* **befell**, *past participle* **befallen**) (liter) ‹*a family, nation*› أَصابَ

before /bɪˈfɔː/ **A** *prep* **1** (earlier than) قَبْلَ; **the day ~ yesterday** قبل أَمْسِ; **it is ~ five o'clock/midday** الساعةُ تُقارِبُ الخامِسةَ \ الثانيةَ عَشَرَ ظُهْراً; **I was there the week ~ last** كُنْتُ هُناكَ الأُسْبوعَ قبل الماضي; **applications must be received ~ the due date** يَجِبُ أَنْ تَصِلَ الطَلَباتُ قبل التاريخِ المُحَدَّدِ; **~ long it will be winter** سَيَدْخُلُ فَصْلُ الشِتاءِ قَريباً; **not ~ time!** وَأَخيراً! **2** (in order) قَبْلَ; **the page ~ this one** الصَفْحة قبل هذه **3** (in priority) قَبْلَ; **for him, family comes ~ everything else** بالنِسْبةِ لَهُ، تَأْتي الأُسْرةُ قبل كُلِّ شَيْءٍ آخَرَ **4** (this side of) قَبْلَ; **turn left ~ the crossroads** انْعَطِفْ يَساراً قبل مُفْتَرَقِ الطُرُقِ **5** (in front of) أَمامَ; **she parked ~ the gate** رَكَنَتِ السَيّارةَ أمامَ البَوّابةِ; **it happened ~ our very eyes** حَدَثَ أمامَ أَعْيُنِنا; **this is the task ~ us** هذه هي المُهِمّةُ الّتي أَمامَنا **6** (in the presence of) أَمامَ; **to appear ~ a court** مَثَلَ أمامَ مَحْكَمةٍ; **to bring a bill ~ parliament** طَرَحَ مَشْروعَ قانونٍ أمامَ البَرْلَمانِ; **these are the alternatives ~ us** هذه هي الخِياراتُ المُتاحةُ أَمامَنا **7** (AmE) (in time expressions) **ten ~ six** السادِسة إلاّ عَشْرَ دَقائِقَ

B *conj* **1** (in time) **~ I go, I would like to say that ...** قبل أَنْ أَذْهَبَ، أَوَدُّ أَنْ أَقولَ إنّ...; **it was some time ~ she was able to walk again** مَضى وَقْتٌ طَويلٌ قبل أن اسْتَعادَتِ القُدْرةَ على المَشْيِ; **get out of here ~ I call the police!** اذْهَبْ من هُنا قبل أَنْ أَتَّصِلَ بالشُرْطةِ! **2** (fml) (in preference) عَلى; **he would die ~ admitting it** يُفَضِّلُ المَوْتَ على الاعْتِرافِ بِهَذا

C *adv* (at an earlier time) سابِقاً; **as ~ she refused** رَفَضَت كَما في السابِقِ; **she left the day/week ~** رَحَلَتْ قبل يَوْمٍ \ أُسْبوعٍ; **long ~** قبل فَتْرةٍ طَويلةٍ; **have you been to Egypt ~?** هل زُرْتَ مِصْرَ من قَبْلُ؟; **I've never been here/there ~** لم آتِ هُنا \ لم أَذْهَبْ هُناكَ من قَبْلُ أَبَداً; **I've never seen him ~ in my life** لم أَرَهُ في حَياتي قَطُّ

beforehand /bɪˈfɔːhand/ *adv* **1** (ahead of time) سَلَفاً ,مُسْبَقاً; **be there one hour ~** كُنْ هُناكَ ساعةً قبل الوَقْتِ; **let me know ~** أَعْلِمْني مُسْبَقاً **2** (earlier) من قَبْلُ; **we had seen them five minutes ~** كُنّا قد رَأَيْناهُمْ خَمْسَ دَقائِقَ من قَبْلُ

befriend /bɪˈfrɛnd/ *vt* صادَقَ ‹*a youngster, prisoner*›

beg /bɛg/ **A** *vt* **(-gg-)** **1** (to beseech) تَرَجّى ,تَوَسَّلَ ‹*forgiveness, permission*›; **to ~ sb to do sth** تَرَجّى شَخْصاً أَنْ يَفْعَلَ شَيْئاً; **I ~ your pardon** (in apologies) أَسْتَميحُكَ عُذْراً ,أَرْجو المَعْذِرةَ; (what?) مَعْذِرةً؟ ,عَفْواً؟; **stop, I ~ you!** تَوَقَّفْ، أَرْجوكَ! **2** (out of poverty) شَحَذَ (a; شَحْذ) ,تَسَوَّلَ ,اسْتَجْدى ‹*money, food*›

B *vi* **(-gg-)** **1** (out of poverty) «beggar» شَحَذَ (a; شَحْذ) ,تَسَوَّلَ ,اسْتَجْدى; **to ~ for money/food** تَسَوَّلَ للحُصولِ على المالِ \ الطَعامِ **2** (to plead) «person» تَوَسَّلَ (إلى); **he ~ged for mercy** اسْتَرْحَمَ; **the children ~ged to go with me** تَوَسَّلَ (إلى) الأَطْفالُ إلَيَّ أنْ يَذْهَبوا مَعي **3** «dog» تَوَسَّلَ (إلى)

Idioms **to beg the question** (to raise) طَرَحَ السُؤالَ; (to fail to consider) [اعْتَبَرَهُ تَحْصيلَ حاصِلٍ]; **to go begging** كانَ غَيْرَ مَرْغوبٍ فيهِ

began /bɪˈgan/ *past tense* ▸ **begin**

beget /bɪˈgɛt/ *vt* (*present participle* **-tt-**, *past tense* **begot** or (old use) **begat**, *past participle* **begotten**) (liter) **1** أَنْجَبَ ‹*a child, son*› **2** سَبَّبَ ‹*violence, instability*›

beggar /ˈbɛgə/ *n* **1** (poor person) شَحّاذ ,مُتَسَوِّل **2** (infml) (individual) **the lucky/poor/lazy ~** المَحْظوظ \ التَعيس \ الكَسول]

begin /bɪˈgɪn/ **A** *vt* (*present participle* **-nn-**; *past tense* **began**; *past participle* **begun**) **1** (to start) بَدَأَ (a; بَدْء) ‹*one's career, a process, journey, an investigation*›; **to ~ to do sth, to ~ doing sth** بَدَأَ يَفْعَلُ شَيْئاً; **she began work as a secretary** بَدَأَت العَمَلَ كَسِكْرِتيرةٍ; **I was ~ning to feel hungry** بَدَأْتُ أَشْعُرُ بالجوعِ; **I began looking for a new job last month** بَدَأْتُ أَبْحَثُ عن عَمَلٍ جَديدٍ الشَهْرَ الماضي; **I can't ~ to tell you how grateful I am** لا أَسْتَطيعُ أنْ أُعَبِّرَ لَكَ عن مَدى امْتِناني **2** (to cause, initiate) أَطْلَقَ ‹*a rumour, a quarrel*› **3** (to start to use) بَدَأَ يَسْتَعْمِلُ \ في الاسْتِعْمالِ ‹*a bottle, packet*›; فَتَحَ (a; فَتْح) ‹*notebook*›

B *vi* (*present participle* **-nn-**; *past tense* **began**; *past participle* **begun**) «work, story, river» بَدَأَ (a; بَدْء); **to ~ by doing sth** بَدَأَ بِفِعْلِ شَيْءٍ; **I don't know where to ~** لا أَعْرِفُ من أَيْنَ أَبْدَأُ; **to ~ again** أَسْتُؤْنِفَ; **a name ~ning with S** اسْم يَبْدَأُ بِحَرْفِ السينِ; **life ~s at 40** الحَياةُ تَبْدَأُ عند الأَرْبَعينَ; **your problems have only just begun!** [لَقَدْ بَدَأَتْ مَشاكِلُكَ للتَوِّ فَقَطْ!]

Idiom **to begin with** (at first) قبل كُلِّ شَيْءٍ; **I didn't like it to ~ with** قبل كُلِّ شَيْءٍ أنا لم أُحِبَّهُ; **he wasn't interested to ~ with** قبل كُلِّ شَيْءٍ هو لم يَكُنْ مُهْتَمّاً; (giving reasons) أَوَّلاً; **to ~ with, we like the design** أَوَّلاً، نُحِبُّ التَصْميمَ

beginner /bɪˈgɪnə/ *n* مُبْتَدِئ

beginning /bɪˈgɪnɪŋ/ **A** *n* بِداية; **in the ~** في البِدايةِ; **at the ~ of May** في بِدايةِ مايو; **from ~ to end** من البِدايةِ حتّى النِهايةِ; **it was clear from the very ~** كانَ واضِحاً منذ البِدايةِ

B **(beginnings)** *n pl* (of a person, an organization) أُصول; (of a movement, an era) بِدايات; **his family had humble ~s** كانَتْ عائِلَتُهُ من أُصولٍ مُتَواضِعةٍ; **the ~s of modern science** بِدايات العِلْمِ الحَديثِ

begot /bɪˈgɒt/ *past tense* ▸ **beget**

begotten /bɪˈgɒt(ə)n/ *past participle* ▸ **beget**

begrudge /bɪˈgrʌdʒ/ *vt* ▸ **grudge** B

beguile /bɪˈgʌɪl/ *vt* فَتَنَ (i; فَتْن ,فُتون) ,اجْتَذَبَ ‹*an audience, listeners*›

beguiling /bɪˈgʌɪlɪŋ/ *adj* ‹*charm*› ساحِر; ‹*smile*› فاتِن

begun /bɪˈgʌn/ *past participle* ▸ **begin**

behalf /bɪˈhɑːf/ *n* (**on behalf of** BrE; **in behalf of** AmE) **1** (as a representative of) ‹*to act, speak*› بالنِيابةِ عن; **I apologized on his ~** اعْتَذَرْتُ بالنِيابةِ عَنْهُ **2** (in the interests of) ‹*to negotiate, plead*› لِمَصْلَحةِ

behave /bɪˈheɪv/ **A** *vi* (**behaves, behaving, behaved**) **1** (to act) «child, group» تَصَرَّفَ; **to ~ oddly/badly** تَصَرَّفَ بِطَريقةٍ غَريبةٍ \ سَيِّئةٍ **2** (to be good) «children, animals» أَحْسَنَ التَصَرُّفَ

B *v refl* (**behaves, behaving, behaved**) «child, animal» سَلَكَ سُلوكاً حَسَناً

behaviour (BrE), **behavior** (AmE) /bɪˈheɪvjə/ *n* سُلوك

Idiom to be on one's best behaviour تَحَلّى بِأَحْسَنِ سُلوكٍ

behavioural (BrE), **behavioral** (AmE) /bɪˈheɪvjər(ə)l/ *adj* ‹*change, disorder*› سُلوكيّ

behead /bɪˈhɛd/ *vt* قَطَعَ الرَّأْسَ, ضَرَبَ العُنُقَ ‹*a prisoner, hostage*›

beheld /bɪˈhɛld/ *past tense, past participle* ▸ **behold**

behind /bɪˈhʌɪnd/ **A** *prep* **1** ‹*the chair, door, house*› وَراءَ; **there is a tennis court ~ the house** هُناكَ مَلْعَبُ تِنِس وراء المَنْزِلِ; **let's put all that ~ us now** دَعْنا نَتْرُكُ كُلَّ ذلك خَلْفَنا \ وَراءَنا الآنَ **2** (in progress) **to be ~ the others** «pupil» كانَ مُتَأَخِّراً عن الآخَرينَ; **he's way ~ the rest of the class** هو مُتَأَخِّرٌ جِدًّا عن بَقيّةِ الصَفِّ **3** (fraudulently) **to do sth ~ sb's back** فَعَلَ شَيْئاً من وَراءِ ظَهْرِ \ دون عِلْمِ شَخْصٍ **4** (supporting) **to be (solidly) ~ sb** وَقَفَ \ كانَ وَراءَ شَخْصٍ (بِقوّةٍ); **he has three years' experience ~ him** لَدَيْهِ خِبْرةُ ثَلاثِ سَنَواتٍ مَضَتْ; **the real story ~ the news** القِصّةُ الحَقيقيّةُ وراء الأَخْبارِ; **who is ~ this proposal?** مَنْ وراء هذا الاقْتِراحِ؟

B *adv* ‹*to follow on*› إلى الخَلْفِ \ الوَراءِ; ‹*to look*› في الخَلْفِ; **they followed on ~ in their car** ساروا في الخَلْفِ بِسَيّارَتِهِمْ; **he glanced ~ as he went out** أَلْقى نَظْرةً سَريعةً إلى الخَلْفِ عِنْدَما خَرَجَ

C *n* (infml) مُؤَخِّرة

D *adj* **to be ~ with one's studies/work** كانَ مُتَأَخِّراً في دِراسَتِهِ \ عَمَلِهِ; **to be too far ~** كانَ مُتَأَخِّراً لِدَرَجةٍ لا تَسْمَحُ بِتَعْويضِ ما فاتَهُ

behold /bɪˈhəʊld/ *vt* (*past tense, past participle* **beheld**) (liter) تَأَمَّلَ, شاهَدَ ‹*a sight, miracle*›

beige /beɪʒ/ **A** *n* بيج [لَوْن الصوفِ الطَبيعيِّ]

B *adj* ‹*trousers, carpet*› بيج

being /ˈbiːɪŋ/ **A** *n* **1** (creature) كائِن (كائِنات) **2** [u] (existence) **to come into ~** نَشَأَ (a; نَشْأة, نُشوء, نَشْء)

B *present participle* ▸ **be**

Beirut /beɪˈruːt/ *pr n* بَيْروت (dipt f)

Belarus /ˌbɛləˈruːs/ *pr n* بيلاروس (f)

Belarusian /ˌbɛlə(ʊ)ˈrʌʃ(ə)n/ **A** *adj* ‹*ambassador, border, food*› بيلاروسيّ

B *n* **1** (citizen) بيلاروسيّ **2** (language) (اللُغة) البيلاروسيّة

belated /bɪˈleɪtɪd/ *adj* ‹*congratulations, apology*› مُتَأَخِّر

belch /bɛltʃ/ **A** *vi* **1** «person» تَجَشَّأَ **2** «smoke, flames» انْبَعَثَ

B *vt* (to emit) أَطْلَقَ, قَذَفَ (i; قَذْف) ‹*smoke, flames*›

C *n* تَجَشُّؤ

Belfast /ˈbɛlfɑːst/ *pr n* بِلْفَسْت (f)

belfry /ˈbɛlfri/ *n* (*pl* **belfries**) بُرْج الجَرَسِ \ الناقوسِ

Belgian /ˈbɛldʒ(ə)n/ *n, adj* بَلْجيكيّ

Belgium /ˈbɛldʒəm/ *pr n* بَلْجيكا

Belgrade /bɛlˈgreɪd/ *pr n* بِلْغْراد (f)

belie /bɪˈlʌɪ/ *vt* (**belies, belying, belied**) **1** (to disguise) أَعْطى فِكْرةً خاطِئةً عن ‹*the complexity, seriousness*› **2** (to disprove) دَحَضَ (a; دَحْض, دُحوض) ‹*a claim, myth*›

belief /bɪˈliːf/ *n* **1** (conviction) اعْتِقاد (اعْتِقادات); **in the ~ that ... …** اعْتِقاداً أَنّ … ; **it's my ~ that ...** في اعْتِقادي أَنّ … ; **contrary to popular ~** على عَكْسِ الاعْتِقادِ الشائِعِ; **their arrogance/stupidity is beyond ~** غُرورُهُمْ \ غَباؤُهُمْ يَتَجاوَزُ الخَيالَ **2** (faith) إيمان, اعْتِقاد (اعْتِقادات), مُعْتَقَد (مُعْتَقَدات); **his unshakeable ~ in God** إيمانُهُ الراسِخُ باللهِ; **her unswerving ~ in democracy** إيمانُها الراسِخُ بالديمُقْراطيّةِ; **that goes against their religious ~s** ذلك يُخالِفُ مُعْتَقَداتِهِم الدينيّةَ

believable /bɪˈliːvəb(ə)l/ *adj* ‹*explanation, story*› قابِل لِلتَّصْديقِ

believe /bɪˈliːv/ **A** *vt* **1** (to accept as true) صَدَّقَ ‹*a person, story*›; **I ~ you/I don't ~ you** أُصَدِّقُكَ \ لا أُصَدِّقُكَ; **I couldn't ~ my eyes/ears** لم أَسْتَطِعْ أنْ أُصَدِّقَ عَيْنَيَّ \ أُذُنَيَّ; **I can ~ that of her!** أُصَدِّقُ أَنَّها قادِرةٌ على فِعْلِ ذلك!; **~ you me!** صَدِّقْني!; **~ it or not, I really enjoyed it** صَدِّقْ أو لا تُصَدِّقْ، لَقَد اسْتَمْتَعْتُ بِهِ حَقًّا; **if you ~ that, you'll believe anything** إذا صَدَّقْتَ ذلك فَسَتُصَدِّقُ كُلَّ شَيْءٍ **2** (to think) اعْتَقَدَ, ظَنَّ (u; ظَنّ); **I ~ that she is right, I ~ her to be right** أَعْتَقِدُ أَنَّها على حَقٍّ; **he is ~d to be dead** يُعْتَقَدُ أَنَّهُ ماتَ \ مَيِّتٌ; **I ~ so** أَظُنُّ ذلك; **I don't ~ so, I ~ not** لا أَظُنُّ \ أَعْتَقِدُ ذلك

B *vi* **1** (to have trust in) **to ~ in sb** وَثِقَ (i; ثِقة, وُثوق); **you have to ~ in yourself** يَجِبُ أنْ تَثِقَ \ تكونَ عِنْدَكَ ثِقةٌ في نَفْسِكَ **2** (to uphold) **to ~ in discipline/democracy** آمَنَ بالانْضِباطِ \

بالديمُقْراطيّةِ **3** (to have faith in) **to ~ in God** آمَنَ باللهِ

believer /bɪˈliːvə/ *n* مُؤْمِن; **to be a firm ~ in the principle of …** كانَ مُؤْمِناً بِشِدّةٍ بِمَبْدَءِ …

belittle /bɪˈlɪt(ə)l/ *vt* قَلَّلَ من الأَهَمِّيّةِ ‹an achievement›; اسْتَخَفَّ (ب) ‹a colleague›

Belize /bɛˈliːz/ *pr n* بليز (f)

bell /bɛl/ *n* جَرَس (أَجْراس)

bellboy /ˈbɛlbɔɪ/ *n* (AmE) خادِمِ فُنْدُقٍ

bellhop /ˈbɛlhɒp/ *n* (AmE) خادِمِ فُنْدُقٍ

belligerent /bəˈlɪdʒ(ə)r(ə)nt/ *adj* ‹attitude, drunk› عَنيف, عُدْوانيّ

bellow /ˈbɛləʊ/ *vi* **1** «teachers, police officers» جَأَرَ (a; جَأْر, جُؤَار) **2** «bulls, stags» خارَ (u; خُوار)

bellows /ˈbɛləʊz/ *n pl* مِنْفاخ (مَنافيخ), كير (أَكْيار)

bell pepper *n* (AmE) فُلْفُل (فَلافِل)

belly /ˈbɛli/ *n* (*pl* **bellies**) **1** (infml) (of a person) بَطْن (بُطون, أَبْطُن) **2** (of an animal) بَطْن (بُطون, أَبْطُن)

(Idiom) **to go belly up** (infml) أَفْلَس

bellyache /ˈbɛlɪeɪk/ **A** *n* (infml) مَغْص (أَمْغاص), أَلَم في المَعِدة **B** *vi* (infml) (to complain) تَذَمَّرَ (من)

belly button *n* (infml) سُرّة (سُرّات, سُرَر)

belong /bɪˈlɒŋ/ *vi* **1** (to be the property of) **to ~ to sb** «land» كانَ مِلْكاً لِشَخْصٍ; **who does this coat ~ to?** لِمَنْ هذا المِعْطَفُ؟; **the house ~s to his mother** تَمْتَلِكُ أُمُّهُ البَيْتَ **2** (to be a member) **to ~ to an organization/generation** انْتَمى إلى مُنَظَّمةٍ \ جيلٍ; **do you ~ to the club?** هل تَنْتَمي إلى النادي؟; **she ~s to the union** تَنْتَمي إلى النِقابةِ **3** (to have a place) «cutlery, linen» كانَ في مَحَلِّهِ; **where do these books ~?** أَيْنَ مَحَلُّ هذه الكُتُبِ؟; **put it back where it ~s** أَرْجِعْهُ إلى مَحَلِّهِ **4** (to fit in) «person» انْتَمى (إلى); **I feel I don't ~** لا أُحِسُّ بالانْتِماءِ

belongings /bɪˈlɒŋɪŋz/ *n pl* مُمْتَلَكات

beloved /bɪˈlʌvɪd/ **A** *adj* (fml) ‹relative, cat› عَزيز (أَعِزّة, أَعِزّاءُ), مَحْبوب **B** *n* مَحْبوب

below /bɪˈləʊ/ **A** *prep* **1** (under) تَحْتَ; **~ sea level** تَحْتَ مُسْتَوى سَطْحِ البَحْرِ; **the apartment ~ ours** الشَقّةُ الّتي تَقَعُ تَحْتَ شَقَّتِنا **2** (in number, degree etc) تَحْتَ; **5° ~ (freezing)** خَمْس دَرَجاتٍ تَحْتَ الصِفْرِ; **~ the age of 18** دون سِنِّ الثامِنةَ عَشَرَ **3** (inferior in rank) أَقَلّ (dipt); **officers ~ the rank of major** الضُبّاط أَقَلّ من رُتْبةِ رائِدٍ; **the teams ~ them in the table** الفِرَق تَحْتَهُم في الجَدْوَلِ **B** *adv* **1** (lower down) **put it on the shelf ~** ضَعْهُ على الرَفِّ الأَسْفَلِ **2** (in texts) أَدْناهُ; **see ~** أُنْظُرْ أَدْناهُ

belt /bɛlt/ **A** *n* **1** (for garments) حِزام (أَحْزِمة, حُزُم) **2** (area) حِزام (أَحْزِمة, حُزُم); **the coastal ~** حِزام الساحِلِ **3** (in karate, judo) حِزام (أَحْزِمة, حُزُم); **to be a black/brown ~** حَمَلَ حِزاماً أَسْوَدَ \ بُنِّيًّا **4** (in machinery) سَيْر (سُيور) **B** *vt* (infml) (to hit) ضَرَبَ بقوّة ‹a person, ball› **C** *vi* (to go quickly) أَسْرَعَ, انْطَلَقَ بِسُرْعةٍ; **he ~ed off down the street** انْطَلَقَ مُسْرِعاً في الشارِعِ

(Idioms) **below the belt** تحت الحِزام; **to have sth under one's belt** كانَ عِنْدَهُ شَيْءٌ في جَعْبَتِهِ; **to tighten one's belt** شَدَّ حِزامَهُ

(Phrasal verbs) **belt out: ~ out [sth], ~ [sth] out** **1** (to sing) «singers» غَنّى [شَيْئاً] بِصَوْتٍ عالٍ وَقَوِيٍّ **2** (to play) عَزَفَ [شَيْئاً] بِصَوْتٍ عالٍ وَقَوِيٍّ

• **belt up** **1** (to put on a seat belt) وَضَعَ حِزامَ الأَمانِ **2** (BrE infml) (to be quiet) صَمَتَ (u; صَمْت), سَكَتَ (u; سُكوت); **oh ~ up!** اُسْكُتْ \ اخْرَسْ!

beltway /ˈbɛltweɪ/ *n* (AmE) طَريق دائِريّ

bemoan /bɪˈməʊn/ *vt* (fml) تَحَسَّرَ (على) ‹one's fate, a loss›

bemused /bɪˈmjuːzd/ *adj* ‹onlooker› مَذْهول; ‹expression› ذُهول

bench /bɛn(t)ʃ/ *n* **1** (seat) مَقْعَد طَويل للجُلوسِ **2** (table, work surface) مِنْضَدة عَمَلٍ, طاوِلة عَمَلٍ **3** (Law) (**the Bench**) القَضاء

benchmark /ˈbɛn(t)ʃmɑːk/ *n* **1** (reference point) مِعْيار (مَعايير), نُقْطة قِياسيّة \ مَرْجِعيّة; **to set** *or* **establish a ~** وَضَعَ مِعْياراً **2** (test) اخْتِبار مِعْياريّ (بَرْنامَج لِتَقْييمِ أداءِ الكُمْبيوتَر); **to run a ~ (test)** أَجْرى اخْتِباراً مِعْيارِيًّا

bend /bɛnd/ **A** *vt* (*past tense, past participle* **bent**) **1** حَنى (i; حَنْي), ثَنى (i; ثَنْي) ‹one's knees, body› **2** لَوى (i; لَيّ, لُوِيّ) ‹a wire, pipe›

B *vi* (*past tense, past participle* **bent**) **1** «road» انْعَطَفَ, انْعَرَجَ; «river» تَعَرَّجَ **2** «tree, branch» الْتَوى **3** «person» انْحَنى; **to ~ forwards/backwards** انْحَنى إلى الأمامِ \ الخَلْفِ

C *n* **1** (curved section in a road) مُنْعَطَف (مُنْعَطَفات), مُنْعَرَج (مُنْعَرَجات); (in a river) تَعَرُّج; (in a pipe) انْحِناء; **there's a sharp ~ in the road** هُناكَ مُنْعَطَفٌ \ مُنْعَرَجٌ حادٌّ في الطَريقِ **2** (**the bends**) مَرَض الالْتِواءِ

(Idioms) (infml) **to bend over backwards to do sth** بَذَلَ كُلَّ ما في وُسْعِهِ لِيَفْعَلَ شَيْئاً; **to bend the rules** تَلاعَبَ بالقَوانينِ; (infml) **to drive sb round the bend** جَنَّنَ شَخْصاً (أَزْعَجَ شَخْصاً بِشِدَّةٍ)

(Phrasal verbs) **bend down** انْحَنى
• **bend over** انْحَنى

beneath /bɪˈniːθ/ **A** *prep* **1** (under) تَحْتَ; **the ground ~ your feet** الأَرْض الّتي تحت قَدَمَيْكَ **2** (unworthy of) دونَ; **that job is ~ me** ذاكَ العَمَلُ دون مُسْتَوايَ

B *adv* تَحْتيّ, سُفْليّ; **the floor/level ~** الطابَق \ المُسْتوى السُفْليّ

benefactor /ˈbɛnɪfaktə/ *n* مُتَبَرِّع, مُحْسِن

beneficial /bɛnɪˈfɪʃ(ə)l/ *adj* ‹effect, outcome› مُفيد; **a mutually ~ arrangement** اتِّفاق مُتَبادَل المَنْفَعةِ

beneficiary /bɛnɪˈfɪʃ(ə)ri/ *n* (*pl* **beneficiaries**) مُنْتَفِع, مُسْتَفيد

benefit /ˈbɛnɪfɪt/ **A** *n* **1** (advantage) فائِدة (فَوائِدُ), مَنْفَعة (مَنافِعُ); **the health ~s of exercise** الفَوائِدُ الصِحِّيّة للتَمارينِ الرِياضيّةِ; **to have the ~ of sth** تَمَتَّعَ بِميزةِ شَيْءٍ; **to be of ~ to sb/sth** نَفَعَ شَخْصاً \ شَيْئاً; **we work together for the ~ of the community** نَعْمَلُ مَعاً من أَجْلِ فائِدةِ المُجْتَمَعِ; **for my ~, she translated what he'd said** لِمُساعَدَتي، تَرْجَمَتْ ما قالَ; **she gave us the ~ of her expertise/knowledge** أَفادَتْنا بِخِبْرَتِها \ بِمَعْرِفَتِها **2** (payment) فائِدة (فَوائِدُ) **3** (welfare payment) إعانة, مُساعَدة اجْتِماعيّة, مَعاش (مَعاشات); **to be on ~** *or* **~s** تَقاضى مَعاشاً **4** (perk) ميزة; **salary £40,000 plus the usual ~s** الراتِبُ 40,000 جُنَيْهٍ مع الميزاتِ المُعْتادةِ **5** (charity event) حَفْلة خَيْرِيّة

B *vt* نَفَعَ (a; نَفْع), أَفادَ ‹people, the community›

C *vi* «children, companies» اسْتَفادَ (من), اسْتَنْفَعَ; **to ~ from** *or* **by sth** اسْتَفادَ من شَيْءٍ; **he ~ed from working with more experienced people** اسْتَفادَ من العَمَلِ مع أَشْخاصٍ ذَوي خِبْرةٍ أَكْثَرَ

(Idiom) **to give sb the benefit of the doubt** أَعْطى شَخْصاً فائِدةَ الشَكِّ

benefit claim *n* طَلَب إعانةٍ ماليّةٍ

benefit concert *n* حَفْلة خَيْرِيّة

benefit match *n* مُباراة خَيْرِيّة

benefit office *n* [مَكْتَب مَسْؤول عن دَفْعِ التَعْويضات]

benevolent /bɪˈnɛv(ə)l(ə)nt/ *adj* ‹smile› مَحَبّة; ‹dictator› [ذو نِيّةٍ حَسَنةٍ]

Bengali /bɛŋˈgɔːli/ **A** *n* **1** (citizen) بَنْغاليّ **2** (language) (اللُغة) البَنْغاليّة

B *adj* ‹custom, food› بَنْغاليّ

benign /bɪˈnʌɪn/ *adj* **1** ‹tumour, cell› حَميد **2** ‹expression, smile› لَطيف

Benin /bɛˈniːn/ *pr n* (country) بَنين (f)

bent /bɛnt/ **A** *past tense, past participle* ▸ **bend**

B *adj* **1** ‹needle, wire› أَعْوَج (dipt; عوج), مائِل **2** ‹old man, woman› مُنْحَنٍ

(Idiom) **to be bent on doing sth** صَمَّمَ على القِيامِ بِشَيْءٍ

bequeath /bɪˈkwiːð/ *vt* وَرَّثَ ‹one's assets, estate›

bequest /bɪˈkwɛst/ *n* تَوْريث

berate /bɪˈreɪt/ *vt* (fml) وَبَّخَ; **to ~ sb for sth** وَبَّخَ شَخْصاً على شَيْءٍ

Berber /ˈbəːbə/ **A** *n* **1** (person) أَمازيغيّ, بَرْبَريّ (بَرْبَر) **2** (Ling) (اللُغة) الأمازيغيّة \ البَرْبَرِيّة

B *adj* ‹tradition, crafts› أَمازيغيّ, البَرْبَرِ

bereaved /bɪˈriːvd/ *adj* ‹family, parent› فاقِد, مَحْروم

bereavement /bɪˈriːvm(ə)nt/ *n* فِقْدان الأَعِزّاءِ

beret /ˈbɛreɪ, AmE bəˈreɪ/ *n* [قُبَّعة مُسَطَّحة وَلَيِّنة]

beriberi /ˌbɛrɪˈbɛri/ *n* بَري بَري

Berlin /bəːˈlɪn/ *pr n* بَرْلين (f)

Bermuda /bəˈmjuːdə/ *pr n* جُزُر بَرْمودا

berry /ˈbɛri/ *n* (*pl* **berries**) كِشْمِش

berserk /bə'zɜːk/ *adj* ‹*crowd*› هائِج بِشِدَّةٍ; ‹*animal*› مَسْعور (مَساعير, مَسْعورونَ); **to go ~** أَصْبَحَ هائِجاً \ مَجْنوناً

berth /bɜːθ/ **A** *n* **1** (bunk) [سَرير في وَسيلةِ نَقْلٍ]; **a six-~ cabin** حُجْرة بِستّةِ سَرائِرَ **2** (for ships) مَرْسًى (مَراسٍ)

B *vt* «crew, captain» أَرْسى ‹*a ship*›

C *vi* «ships» رَسا (u; رَسْو)

(Idiom) **to give sb/sth a wide berth** تَجَنَّبَ شَخْصاً \ شَيْئاً

beseech /bɪ'siːtʃ/ *vt* (*past tense, past participle* **beseeched** or **besought**) تَوَسَّلَ (إلى)

beset /bɪ'sɛt/ *adj* (*past tense, past participle* **beset**) **to be ~ by strikes/natural disasters** كانَ مُتَضَرِّراً بالإضْراباتِ \ بالكَوارِثِ الطَبيعيّةِ

beside /bɪ'sʌɪd/ *prep* **1** (next to) بِجانِبِ, بِجِوارِ; **she was sitting ~ you** كانَتْ تَجلِسُ بجانِبِكَ; **they live ~ the sea** يَعيشونَ بِجِوارِ البَحْرِ **2** (in comparison with) مُقارَنةً ب, بالمُقارَنةِ مع; **my problems are minor ~ yours** مَشاكِلي بَسيطةٌ مُقارَنةً بِمَشاكِلِكَ

(Idiom) **to be beside oneself with rage/joy** لم يَتَمالَكْ نَفْسَهُ من الغَضَبِ \ الفَرَحِ

besides /bɪ'sʌɪdz/ **A** *prep* (apart from) فَضْلاً عن; **they need other things ~ money** يَحْتاجونَ إلى أَشْياءَ أُخْرى فَضْلاً عن المالِ; **~ waiting there's not a lot we can do** لَيْسَ هُناكَ الكَثيرُ مِمّا يُمْكِنُنا القِيامُ بِهِ عَدا الانْتِظارِ; **~ which, he's under contract** فَضْلاً عن ذلك، هو مُرْتَبِطٌ بعَقْدٍ

B *adv* (in addition) عِلاوةً على ذلك, بالإضافةِ إلى ذلك; **he has a car and a motorbike ~** لَدَيْهِ سَيّارةٌ وَكَذلِكَ دَرّاجةٌ نارِيّةٌ; **there is shopping to be done and much else ~** يَجِبُ القِيامُ بالتَسوُّقِ بالإضافةِ إلى أُمورٍ أُخْرى كَثيرةٍ

besiege /bɪ'siːdʒ/ *vt* «army» حاصَرَ ‹*a castle, city*›; «reporters» طَوَّقَ ‹*the hall*›

besotted /bɪ'sɒtɪd/ *adj* **to be ~ with sb** كانَ هائِماً بِشَخْصٍ

besought /bɪ'sɔːt/ *past tense, past participle* ▸ **beseech**

bespectacled /bɪ'spɛktək(ə)ld/ *adj* (fml) ‹*professor, librarian*› [ذو نَظّاراتٍ]

best /bɛst/ **A** *adj* (*superlative of* **good**) ‹*song, entry*› الأَحْسَن, الأَفْضَل; **the ~ part of a day/week** مُعْظَم اليَوْمِ \ الأُسْبوعِ; **it took the ~ part of a day to repair the car** أَخَذَ تَصْليحُ السَيّارةِ مُعْظَمَ اليَوْمِ

B *adv* (*superlative* **well**) ‹*to perform, treat*› على أَحْسَنِ وَجْهٍ; **do it as ~ you can** قُمْ بِهِ على أَحْسَنِ وَجْهٍ مُمْكِنٍ

C *n* **1** **the ~** الأَحْسَن, الأَفْضَل; **they're the ~ of friends** هُمْ أَفْضَلُ الأَصْدِقاءِ; **to do one's ~ to do sth** كَرَّسَ جُهْدَهُ لِفِعْلِ شَيْءٍ; **all the ~!** مع السَلامةِ! **2** **at ~** في أَحْسَنِ الأَحْوالِ; **at ~ we'll make £100** في أَحْسَنِ الأَحْوالِ سَنكْسِبُ 100 جُنَيْهٍ

best-before date /bɛstbɪ'fɔː deɪt/ *n* (BrE) تاريخ الصَلاحيّة

best friend *n* أَعَزّ صَديقٍ

best man *n* [وَكيل \ شاهِد العَريسِ]

bestow /bɪ'stəʊ/ *vt* (fml) «mayor, university» مَنَحَ (a; مَنْح) ‹*an honour, award*›; **to ~ an award on sb** مَنَحَ جائِزةً لِشَخْصٍ

bestseller /bɛst'sɛlə/ *n* **1** (book) كِتاب رائِج جِدًّا **2** (writer) كاتِب رائِج جِدًّا **3** (product) مَنْتوج رائِج جِدًّا

bestselling /ˌbɛs(t)'sɛlɪŋ/ *adj* ‹*book, novelist*› رائِج جِدًّا

bet /bɛt/ **A** *vt* (*present participle* **-tt-**; *past tense, past participle* **bet** or **betted**) **1** (in gambling) راهَنَ (ب), قامَرَ (ب) ‹*money*›; **he ~ £100 that his horse would win** راهَنَ ب 100 جُنَيْهٍ أنّ حِصانَهُ سَيَفوزُ **2** (infml) (to express certainty) راهَنَ; **I ~ he didn't do it by himself** أُراهِنُ أَنَّهُ لم يَفْعَلْهُ لِوَحْدِهِ; **I ~ you can't guess the answer** أُراهِنُ أَنَّكَ لن تَسْتَطيعَ أَنْ تُخَمِّنَ الجَوابَ

B *vi* (*present participle* **-tt-**; *past tense, past participle* **bet** or **betted**) **1** (in gambling) «gamblers, racegoers» راهَنَ, قامَرَ; **to ~ on a horse** راهَنَ على حِصانٍ **2** (infml) (to express certainty) راهَنَ; **I wouldn't ~ on it!** لا أُراهِنُ عَلَيْهِ!; **you bet!** بالتَأْكيد!

C *n* **1** (stake) مُراهَنة, رِهان; **to place a ~ on sth** راهَنَ على شَيْءٍ; **i had a ~ with him that Spain would win** راهَنْتُهُ على انْتِصارِ إسْبانِيا; **place your ~s!** ضَعْ رِهانَكَ! **2** (option) خِيار; **your best ~ would be to ignore him** خِيارُكَ الأَفْضَلُ أَنْ تَتَجاهَلَهُ **3** (guess) رِهان; **my ~ is that he'll love it** أُراهِنُ أَنَّهُ سَيُحِبُّهُ; **the Lions are a safe ~ to win** أُراهِنُ أَنّ فَريقَ اللايُنْز سَيَفوزُ

beta /'biːtə, AmE 'beɪtə/ *n* **1** (letter) بيتا **2** (BrE Educ) (grade) [دَرَجة \ عَلامة جَيِّدة]; **to get a ~** [حَصَلَ على دَرَجةٍ جَيِّدٍ]

beta blocker *n* حاصِر بيتا

beta test *n* اخْتِبار بيتا

beta version *n* نُسْخة بيتا

Bethlehem /ˈbɛθlɪhɛm/ *pr n* بَيْت لَحْم (f)

betray /bɪˈtreɪ/ *vt* «traitors, spies» خانَ (u; خَوْن, خِيانة) ‹*a country, sb's trust*›

betrayal /bɪˈtreɪəl/ *n* خِيانة

betrothal /bɪˈtrəʊð(ə)l/ *n* (fml) خُطوبة

better /ˈbɛtə/ **A** *adj* (*comparative of* **good**) **1** (more satisfactory or effective) أَحْسَن (dipt); **the weather was no ~** لم يَكُن الطَقْسُ أَحْسَنَ; **things are getting ~** تَتَحَسَّنُ الأَشْياءُ; **that's ~!** ذلك أَحْسَنُ!; **he looks ~ in a suit** يَبْدو أَحْسَنَ في البَدْلَةِ; **she's ~ at maths than he is** هي أَحْسَنُ مِنْهُ في الرِياضيّاتِ; **it would be ~ to do it now** من الأَحْسَنِ القِيامُ بِهِ الآنَ; **if it makes you feel any ~** لو كانَ الأَمْرُ يَجْعَلُكَ تَشْعُرُ أَحْسَنَ; **it's ~ than nothing** هو أَحْسَنُ من لا شَيْءٍ; **fish is ~ for you than meat** السَمَكُ أَحْسَنُ لِصِحَّتِكَ من اللَحْمِ; **the bigger/sooner the ~** كُلَّما كانَ أَكْبَرَ \ أَسْرَعَ كُلَّما كانَ أَحْسَنَ; **he's no ~ than a thief** هو مُجَرَّدُ لِصٍّ **2** (recovered) أَحْسَن (dipt); **to be ~** كانَ أَحْسَنَ; **you need to rest and get ~** تَحْتاجُ إلى أَنْ تَرْتاحَ وَتَتَحَسَّنَ; **is your headache/cold ~?** هل بَدَأْتَ تَتَخَلَّصُ من الصُداعِ \ البَرْدِ؟

B *adv* (*comparative* **well**) بِشَكْلٍ أَحْسَنَ \ أَفْضَلَ; **I can see ~ now** أَسْتَطيعُ أَنْ أَرى بِشَكْلٍ أَفْضَلَ الآنَ; **you can do ~ than that!** تَسْتَطيعُ أَنْ تَفْعَلَ أَحْسَنَ من ذلك!; **you'd do ~ to wait** سَيَكونُ أَفْضَلَ إذا انْتَظَرْتَ; **I like the blue one ~** أُفَضِّلُ الأَزْرَقَ; **you'd ~ go now** من الأَفْضَلِ أَنْ تَذْهَبَ الآنَ; **'will she come?' — 'she'd ~!'** 'هل سَتَأْتي ؟' – 'من الأَفْضَلِ لَها أَنْ تَفْعَلَ!'

C *n* **1** (something preferable) **the ~ of the two** أَحْسَنُهُما; **to deserve ~** اسْتَحَقَّ الأَفْضَلَ; **so much the ~, all the ~** سَيَكونُ أَحْسَنَ; **to change for the ~** تَغَيَّرَ إلى الأَحْسَنِ **2** (superior person) **one's ~s** أَسْيادُهُ

D *vt* **1** (to surpass) تَفَوَّقَ (على) ‹*a record, one's performance*› **2** (to improve) حَسَّنَ ‹*an offer, the world*›; **to ~ oneself** حَسَّنَ وَضْعِيَّتَهُ

(Idioms) **for better or for worse** في السَرّاءِ والضَرّاءِ; **to get the better of sb** تَغَلَّبَ على شَخْصٍ; **his curiosity got the ~ of him** فُضولُهُ تَغَلَّبَ عَلَيْهِ; **to go one better** تَقَدَّمَ خُطْوَةً إلى الأَمامِ

better off *adj* **1** (in wealth) أَكْثَر غِنًى; **to be ~ than sb else** كانَ أَكْثَرَ غِنًى من شَخْصٍ آخَرَ **2** (in a better situation) في حالٍ أَفْضَلَ

betting /ˈbɛtɪŋ/ *n* مُراهَنة

betting shop *n* [مَتْجَر للرِهانِ في بَريطانيا]

between /bɪˈtwiːn/ **A** *prep* **1** (in space) بَيْنَ; **just ~ ourselves** فيما بَيْنَنا فَقَطْ, السِرُّ لن يَتَجاوَزَنا **2** (in sharing) فيما بَيْنَ; **~ them they ate all the food** فيما بَيْنَهُمْ أَكَلوا كُلَّ الطَعامِ

B *adv* (also **in between**) في الوَسَطِ; **it's the one in ~** إنَّهُ الّذي في الوَسَطِ

beverage /ˈbɛv(ə)rɪdʒ/ *n* شَراب (أَشْرِبة)

beware /bɪˈwɛː/ *vi* «buyers, investors» حَذِرَ (a; حَذْر, حَذَر); احْتَرَسَ (من); **~ of the bull!** احْتَرِسْ من الثَوْرِ!

bewildered /bɪˈwɪldəd/ *adj* ‹*expression*› مُشَوَّش; ‹*old lady*› مُتَحَيِّر

bewildering /bɪˈwɪld(ə)rɪŋ/ *adj* ‹*variety, situation*› مُحَيِّر, مُرْبِك

bewitch /bɪˈwɪtʃ/ *vt* **1** (with spells) «witches» سَحَرَ (a; سِحْر) ‹*a princess, an animal*› **2** (with charm) فَتَنَ (i; فَتْن, فُتون) ‹*her, him*›

beyond /bɪˈjɒnd/ **A** *prep* **1** (in space and time) وَراءَ, فَوْقَ, إلى ما بَعْدُ; **no one is allowed ~ this point** غَيْرُ مَسْموحٍ لِأَيِّ شَخْصٍ أَنْ يَتَجاوَزَ هذه النُقْطةِ; **I live just ~ the bank** أَسْكُنُ مُباشَرةً وراءَ البَنْكِ **2** (outside the range of) في غَيْرِ المُتَناوَلِ; **to live ~ one's means** أَنْفَقَ أَكْثَرَ من إمْكاناتِهِ; **it's ~ me** لا أَسْتَطيعُ فَهْمَهُ **3** (other than) سِوى, غَيْر; **we don't know anything about it ~ the fact that ...** لا نَعْلَمُ شَيْئاً عَنْهُ سِوى أَنّ ...

B *adv* (further in space) وَراءَهُ; (in time) ما بَعْدَهُ

Bhutan /buːˈtɑːn/ *pr n* بوتان (f)

bias /ˈbʌɪəs/ *n* (*pl* **biases**) تَوَجُّه, انْحِياز, نَزْعة (نَزَعات); **the course has a scientific ~** للدَوْرةِ تَوَجُّهٌ عِلْميٌّ

biased, biassed /ˈbʌɪəst/ *adj* ‹*report, referee*› مُتَحَيِّز; **to be ~ against/in favour of sb** كانَ مُتَحَيِّزاً ضِدّ \ لِشَخْصٍ

bib /bɪb/ *n* (baby's) صَدْريّة الطِفْل; (on dungarees) [الجُزْء الأَعْلى من المِئْزَر]

Bible /ˈbʌɪb(ə)l/ *n* **(the Bible)** الكِتابُ المُقَدَّس

biblical /ˈbɪblɪk(ə)l/ *adj* ‹*account, character*› الكِتابِ المُقَدَّسِ

bibliography /ˌbɪblɪˈɒɡrəfi/ *n* (*pl* **bibliographies**) مَآخِذ

bicarbonate, **bicarbonate of soda** /bʌɪˈkɑːb(ə)neɪt/ *n* بيكَرْبونات الصوديوم

bicentenary /ˌbʌɪsenˈtiːn(ə)ri/ *n* (*pl* **bicentenaries**) ذِكْرى مِئَوِيّة ثانية

bicentennial /ˌbʌɪsenˈtenɪəl/ *n* ▸ **bicentenary**

biceps /ˈbʌɪseps/ *n* (*pl* **biceps**) عَضَلة ذات رَأْسَيْنِ

bicker /ˈbɪkə/ *vi* «children, politicians» تَشاجَرَ; **to ~ about sth** تَشاجَرَ حول شَيْءٍ

bickering /ˈbɪkərɪŋ/ *n* مُشاجَرة

bicycle /ˈbʌɪsɪk(ə)l/ *n* دَرّاجة

bicycle clip *n* [مَشْبَك سِرْوالِ راكِبِ الدَرّاجةِ]

bicycle lane *n* مَسار دَرّاجاتٍ

bid /bɪd/ **A** *vt* **1** (*present participle* **-dd-**, *past tense, past participle* **bid**) (to offer) قَدَّمَ عَطاءً \ عَرْضاً ب ,عَرَض (i; عَرْض) ‹*£100, $500*› **2** (*present participle* **-dd-**, *past tense* **bade** or **bid**, *past participle* **bid** or **bidden**) (fml) (to say) قالَ (u; قَوْل); (to request) طَلَبَ (u; طَلَب ,مَطْلَب); **to ~ sb farewell** قالَ وَداعاً لِشَخْصٍ; **she bade him wait, she bade him to wait** طَلَبَتْ مِنْهُ أنْ يَنْتَظِرَ

B *vi* (*present participle* **-dd-**, *past tense, past participle* **bid**) **1** (at auction) «bidders, buyers» عَرَضَ سِعْراً; **we were ~ding against each other** كُنّا نُزايِدُ على بَعْضِنا البَعْضَ **2** (for a contract) «companies, contractors» شارَكَ في مُناقَصةٍ; **five companies are ~ding for the contract** تُشارِكُ خَمْسُ شَرِكاتٍ في المُناقَصةِ على العَقْدِ **3** (to make an attempt) **to ~ for sth/ to do sth** «countries, players» سَعى للحُصولِ على شَيْءٍ \ لِفِعْلِ شَيْءٍ

C *n* **1** (at auction) عَرْض (عُروض); **to place a ~** قَدَّمَ \ وَضَعَ عَرْضاً **2** (offer to gain a contract) عَرْض (عُروض); (to buy a company) عَطاء (عَطاءات) **3** (attempt) سَعْي ,مُحاوَلة; **to make a ~ for freedom** قامَ بِمُحاوَلةٍ لاسْتِعادةِ حُرِّيَّتِهِ; **his failed presidential ~** سَعْيُهُ الفاشِل للتَرَشُّحِ للرِئاسةِ **4** (in card games) [عَرْض أَوَّليّ خلال مَرْحَلةِ المَزادِ]; **it's your ~** [جاءَ دَوْرُكَ للعَرْضِ]

bidden /ˈbɪd(ə)n/ *past participle* ▸ **bid**

bidder /ˈbɪdə/ *n* مُزايِد

bidding /ˈbɪdɪŋ/ *n* **1** (at auction) مُزايَدة **2** (fml) (request) أَمْر (أَوامِرُ); **to do sth at sb's ~** فَعَلَ شَيْئاً بِأَمْرٍ من شَخْصٍ

bide /bʌɪd/ *vt* **to ~ one's time** تَحَيَّنَ

bidet /ˈbiːdeɪ, AmE biːˈdeɪ/ *n* حَوْض اسْتِنْجاءٍ ,مِشْطَفة حَمّامٍ

biennial /bʌɪˈenɪəl/ *adj* ‹*conference, exhibition*› [يَقَعُ مَرّةً كُلَّ سَنَتَيْنِ]

bier /bɪə/ *n* نَعْش (نُعوش) ,تابوت (تَوابيتُ)

bifocals /bʌɪˈfəʊk(ə)lz/ *n pl* نَظّارة ثُنائيّة البُؤْرة

big /bɪɡ/ *adj* **(-gg-)** **1** (in size) ‹*garden, company, city, family*› كَبير (كِبار); **he was a ~ man** كانَ رَجُلاً كَبيراً; **how ~ is the room?** ما مَدى حَجْمِ الغُرْفة؟; **to get ~ger** «person, company, city» كَبُرَ (u; كُبْر); **she gave me a ~ smile/hug** ابْتَسَمَتْ لي ابْتِسامةً عَريضةً \ أَخَذَتْني بالأَحْضانِ; **he's a ~ eater** هو أَكولٌ **2** (important, serious) ‹*problem, difference, question*› كَبير; **you're making a ~ mistake** تَرْتَكِبُ خَطَأً كَبيراً; **tomorrow's a ~ day for me** الغَدُ يَوْمٌ كَبيرٌ لي; **I'm a ~ fan of his** أنا من مُعْجَبيهِ الكِبارِ; **to be in ~ trouble** تَعَرَّضَ إلى \ مَرَّ بِمَتاعِبَ كَبيرةٍ **3** (in age) كَبير ,كِبار ,كُبَراءُ; **his ~ brother/sister** أَخوهُ \ أُخْتُهُ الكَبير(ة); **you're a ~ boy now** أَنْتَ وَلَدٌ كَبيرٌ الآنَ **4** (infml) (successful, popular) مَشْهور ,كَبير; **the song was a ~ hit** لاقَتِ الأُغْنِيةُ نَجاحاً كَبيراً; **he's pretty ~ in Japan** هو مَشْهورٌ جِدّاً في اليابانِ **5** (infml) (generous) كَبير (كُبَراءُ ,كِبار), كَريم (كُرَماءُ ,كِرام); **to have a ~ heart** كانَ لَهُ قَلْبٌ كَبيرٌ; **well, that's ~ of you!** حَسَناً، ذلك كَرَمٌ مِنْكَ! **6** (emphatic) **you ~ baby!** أَنْتَ جَبانٌ!

Idioms **to have a big mouth** (infml) كانَ طَويلَ اللِسانِ; **me and my ~ mouth!** أَنا وَلِساني الطَويلُ!; **in a big way** (infml) إلى حَدٍّ كَبيرٍ; **to make it big** (infml) قَطَفَ ثِمارَ النَجاحِ

bigamist /ˈbɪɡəmɪst/ *n* [شَخْص مُتَزَوِّج من شَخْصَيْنِ في آنٍ واحِدٍ]

bigamy /ˈbɪɡəmi/ *n* [زَواج بِشَخْصَيْنِ في آنٍ واحِدٍ]

Big Apple *pr n* **(the Big Apple)** التُفّاحة الكَبيرة (نيويورْك)

Big Bang *n* **(the Big Bang)** الانْفِجار العَظيم

big business *n* [عَمَل كَبير وَمُرْبِح]; **to be big business** [كانَ سوقاً كَبيراً وَمُرْبِحاً]

big dipper *n* (BrE) سِكّة مَوْتٍ

big game *n* طَرائِد كَبيرة

big-headed /bɪɡˈhɛdɪd/ *adj* (infml) ‹*student, know-all*› مُغْتَرّ بِنَفْسِهِ

big mouth *n* (infml) ثَرْثار

big name *n* اسْم كَبير \ لامِع \ شَهير

bigot /ˈbɪɡət/ *n* مُتَعَصِّب

bigoted /ˈbɪɡətɪd/ *adj* ‹*remark, racist*› مُتَعَنِّت ,شَديد التَعَصُّبِ

bigotry /ˈbɪɡətri/ *n* تَعَصُّب أَعْمى

big screen *n* شاشة السينما ,الشاشة الكَبيرة

big shot *n* (infml) شَخْص ذو شَأْنٍ ,شَخْصيّة هامّة

big toe *n* إبْهام القَدَم ,إصْبَع القَدَم الكَبير

big top *n* خَيْمة سيرْك

bike /bʌɪk/ *n* (cycle) دَرّاجة (هَوائيّة); (motorbike) دَرّاجة ناريّة

(Idiom) **on your bike!** (infml) ! اُغْرُبْ عن وَجْهي

biker /ˈbʌɪkə/ *n* (infml) سائِق دَرّاجةٍ ناريّةٍ (خاصّةً عُضو في عِصابةٍ)

bikini /bɪˈkiːni/ *n* بيكيني (ثَوْب سِباحةٍ لِلنِساءِ مُكَوَّن من قِطْعَتَيْنِ)

bilateral /bʌɪˈlat(ə)r(ə)l/ *adj* ‹*relations, agreement*› ثُنائيّ

bilberry /ˈbɪlb(ə)ri/ *n* (*pl* **bilberries**) عِنَب الأَحْراج ,عِنَبيّة

bile /bʌɪl/ *n* ⬚1 (secretion) صَفْراء (dipt f), عُصارة المَرارةِ ⬚2 (fml) (anger) سوء طَبْعٍ ,غَضَب ,نَكَد; **he vented his ~ on the soldiers** صَبَّ نَكَدَهُ على الجُنودِ

bilharzia /bɪlˈhɑːtsɪə/ *n* داء البِلْهارْسِياتِ \ المُنْشَقّاتِ

bilingual /bʌɪˈlɪŋɡw(ə)l/ *adj* ⬚1 ‹*speaker, teacher*› ثُنائيّ اللُغةِ, ناطِق بِلُغَتَيْنِ ⬚2 ‹*education, document*› ثُنائيّ اللُغةِ

bill /bɪl/ **A** *n* ⬚1 (invoice) فاتورة (فَواتيرُ); **he sent me a ~ for £100** أَرْسَلَ إلَيَّ فاتورةً ب 100 جُنَيْهٍ ⬚2 (Law, Pol) (also **Bill**) مُسَوَّدة مَشْروع قانونٍ ⬚3 (poster) مُلْصَق (مُلْصَقات); **'stick no ~s'** 'لا تُعَلِّقوا المُلْصَقاتِ هُنا'; **to top the ~** تَصَدَّرَ المُلْصَقَ ⬚4 (AmE) (banknote) وَرَقة نَقْديّة; **a $20 dollar ~** وَرَقة نَقْديّة من فِئةِ 20 دولاراً ⬚5 (of a bird) مِنْقار (مَناقيرُ)

B *vt* ⬚1 (to invoice) أَرْسَلَ فاتورةً إلى ‹*a client, company*›; **to ~ sb for sth/doing sth** أَرْسَلَ فاتورةً إلى شَخْصٍ مُقابِلَ شَيْءٍ \ فِعْلِ شَيْءٍ ⬚2 (to advertise) قامَ بِإشْهارِ \ بِدِعايةٍ ل ‹*an event, a concert*›; **to be ~ed as sth** قُدِّمَ في الإعْلانِ كَشَيْءٍ; **he is ~ed to appear at the Odeon/as Hamlet** أُعْلِنَ أَنَّهُ سَيَظْهَرُ في الأُدْيون \ في دَوْرِ هَمْلِت

(Idioms) **to fit the bill** ناسَبَ المَقامَ; **this suit should fit the ~** أَظُنُّ أَنّ هذه البَدْلةَ سَتُناسِبُ المَقامَ; **to give sb/sth a clean bill of health** أَعْطى شَخْصاً \ شَيْئاً بِطاقةَ سَلامةٍ صِحّيّةٍ

billboard /ˈbɪlbɔːd/ *n* لَوْحة إعْلاناتٍ

billet /ˈbɪlɪt/ *vt* [أَمَرَ رَسْميًّا بِإيوائِهِ في بَيْتِ أَحَدِ المُواطِنينَ] ‹*a soldier, refugee*›

billfold /ˈbɪlfəʊld/ *n* (AmE) مَحْفَظة (مَحافِظُ ,مَحْفَظات)

billiards /ˈbɪljədz/ *n* لُعْبة البِلْيارْد

billing /ˈbɪlɪŋ/ *n* ⬚1 (of performers) [لائِحة مُمَثِّلي مَسْرَحيّةٍ]; **to get top ~** احْتَلَّ المَرْتَبةَ الأولى على لائِحةِ المُمَثِّلينَ ⬚2 (invoicing) كِتابة الفَواتيرِ ,فَوْتَرة

billion /ˈbɪljən/ *n, adj* بِلْيون

billionaire /bɪljəˈnɛː/ *n* بِلْيونير

bill of sale *n* عَقْد بَيْعٍ

billow /ˈbɪləʊ/ *vi* ⬚1 «clouds, smoke» انْدَفَعَ ,تَدَفَّقَ ⬚2 «fabric, curtains» انْتَفَخَ

bimbo /ˈbɪmbəʊ/ *n* (infml pej) [امْرَأة جَميلة لَكِنْ غَبيّة]

bimetallic /bʌɪmɪˈtalɪk/ *adj* ‹*strip, coin*› ثُنائيّ المَعْدِنِ

bin /bɪn/ *n* ⬚1 (BrE) (for rubbish) صُنْدوق قُمامةٍ ⬚2 (for storage) صُنْدوق (صَناديقُ)

binary /ˈbʌɪn(ə)ri/ *adj* ‹*code, digit*› ثُنائيّ

bind /bʌɪnd/ **A** *vt* (*past tense, past participle* **bound**) ⬚1 (to tie up) رَبَطَ (i-u; رَبْط), أَوْثَقَ ‹*sb's hands, a prisoner*›; **they bound the hostages hand and foot** رَبَطوا الرَهائِنَ من أَيْديهِمْ وَأَرْجُلِهِمْ ⬚2 **to bind sth into a bundle**; رَزَمَ شَيْئاً ‹*clothes, sticks*› ⬚3 (with bandages) ضَمَّدَ ‹*a wound, sb's arm*› ⬚4 (to oblige) أَلْزَمَ; **to ~ sb to secrecy** أَلْزَمَ شَخْصاً بالسِرّيّةِ; **to be bound by a law/an agreement** كانَ مُلْزَماً بِقانونٍ \ باتِّفاقٍ ⬚5 (to unite) (also **bind together**) وَحَّدَ ‹*a community, family*› ⬚6 (P&P) جَلَّدَ ‹*a book, thesis*› ⬚7 (with ingredients) شَدَّ (i-u; شَدّ) ‹*meatballs, a mixture*›

B *vi* (*past tense, past participle* **bound**) (to stick) «ingredients» تَماسَكَ

C *n* (infml) وَرْطة (وَرَطات), مَأْزِق (مَآزِقُ); **to be in a ~** كانَ في مَأْزِقٍ \ وَرْطةٍ; **what a ~!** يا لَهُ من مَأْزِقٍ!

(Phrasal verbs) **bind over**: ~ [sb] over [أَلْزَمَ [شَخْصاً *<the accused>*; **he was bound over to keep the peace** أُلْزِمَ بالحِفاظِ على الهُدوءِ

• **bind up**: ~ up [sth], ~ [sth] up [لَفَّ [شَيْئاً *<a wound, sb's ankle>*

binder /ˈbʌɪndə/ *n* **1** (for papers) مِلَفّ (مِلَفّات) **2** (for cement, paint) مادّة رابِطة

binding /ˈbʌɪndɪŋ/ **A** *n* **1** (of a book) مُجَلَّد (مُجَلَّدات) **2** (tape) حاشِية (حَواشٍ) **B** *adj* *<contract, agreement>* مُلْزِم

binge /bɪn(d)ʒ/ (infml) **A** *n* [إفراط في الأَكْلِ \ الشُرْبِ]; **to go on a drinking ~** [أفْرَطَ في شُرْبِ الكُحولِ] **B** *vi* (*present participle* **bingeing**) (infml) **to ~ on sth** [أَفْرَطَ في أَكْلِ \ شُرْبِ شَيْءٍ]

binge drinking *n* إفْراط في شُرْبِ الكُحولِ

bingo /ˈbɪŋgəʊ/ *n* بِنْجو (لُعْبة حَظٍّ)

bin liner *n* (BrE) كيس قُمامةٍ

binoculars /bɪˈnɒkjʊləz/ *n pl* (also **a pair of binoculars**) مِنْظار نَظّارة مُقَرِّبة ,ثُنائيّ \ مَيْدانيّ

biochemical /ˌbʌɪəʊˈkɛmɪk(ə)l/ *adj* *<reaction, process>* كيمْيائيّ حَيَويّ

biochemist /ˌbʌɪəʊˈkɛmɪst/ *n* اخْتِصاصيّ الكيمْياءِ الحَيَويّةِ

biochemistry /bʌɪə(ʊ)ˈkɛmɪstri/ *n* الكيمْياء الحَيَويّة

biodegradable /ˌbʌɪə(ʊ)dɪˈgreɪdəb(ə)l/ *adj* *<wrapping, substance>* قابِل للتحَلُّلِ الحَيَويِّ

biodiesel /ˈbʌɪəʊdiːz(ə)l/ *n* ديزل حَيَويّ

biodiversity /ˌbʌɪə(ʊ)dʌɪˈvəːsɪti/ *n* تَنَوُّع حَيَويّ

bioengineering /ˌbʌɪəʊɛndʒɪˈnɪərɪŋ/ *n* هَنْدَسة حَيَويّة

biographer /bʌɪˈɒgrəfə/ *n* كاتِب سيرةٍ

biographical /bʌɪəˈgrafɪk(ə)l/ *adj* *<information, details>* سيرة

biography /bʌɪˈɒgrəfi/ *n* (*pl* **biographies**) سيرة (سِيَر)

biological /bʌɪə(ʊ)ˈlɒdʒɪk(ə)l/ *adj* *<organism, age>* ,أَحْيائيّ بيولوجيّ; **a ~ detergent** مُنَظِّف بيولوجيّ

biological clock *n* ساعة بيولوجيّة

biological warfare *n* حَرْب بيولوجيّة

biologist /bʌɪˈɒlədʒɪst/ *n* عالِم بيولوجيّ \ أَحْيائيّ

biology /bʌɪˈɒlədʒi/ *n* عِلْم الأَحْياءِ

biomass /ˈbʌɪə(ʊ)mas/ *n* **1** (organisms) كُتْلة أَحْيائيّة **2** (organic matter) كُتْلة حَيَويّة

biopsy /ˈbʌɪɒpsi/ *n* (*pl* **biopsies**) خِزْعة

biotechnology /ˌbʌɪə(ʊ)tɛkˈnɒlədʒi/ *n* تِكْنولوجيا \ تِقْنيّة حَيَويّة

bipartisan /ˌbʌɪpɑːtɪˈzan/ *adj* *<agreement, policy>* مُؤَيَّد من حِزْبَيْنِ

bipolar /bʌɪˈpəʊlə/ *adj* **1** *<transistor, planet>* ثُنائيّ القُطْبِ **2** *<disorder>* ثُنائيّ القُطْبِ

birch /bəːtʃ/ *n* شَجَرة القُضْبانِ ,بَتولا

bird /bəːd/ *n* **1** (Zool) طَيْر ,طائِر (طائِرات) ,عَصافير) عُصْفور (طُيور **2** (BrE infml) (girl) عُصْفورة (colloq), قِطّة (colloq)

(Idiom) **to kill two birds with one stone** ضَرَبَ عُصْفورَيْنِ بِحَجَرٍ واحِدٍ

birdcage /ˈbəːdkeɪdʒ/ *n* قَفَص للطُيورِ

bird flu *n* إنْفلوَنْزا الطُيورِ

birdie /ˈbəːdi/ *n* **1** (in golf) بيرْدي (إنْجاز في لُعْبةِ الغولْف) **2** (infml) (bird) طُوَيْر

bird of prey *n* طائِر جارِح

bird's-eye view /bəːdzʌɪ ˈvjuː/ *n* [مَنْظَر واضِح من مَكانٍ عالٍ]

birdsong /ˈbəːdsɒŋ/ *n* غِناء العَصافيرِ

birdwatcher /ˈbəːdwɒtʃə/ *n* مُراقِب الطُيورِ

birdwatching /ˈbəːdwɒtʃɪŋ/ *n* مُراقَبة الطُيورِ

biro® /ˈbʌɪrəʊ/ *n* (BrE) (*pl* **biros**) قَلَم حِبْر جافّ

birth /bəːθ/ *n* وِلادة; **to give birth** وَلَدَتْ; **the ~ of modern genetics dates back to ...** يَعودُ ميلادُ عِلْمِ الوِراثةِ الحَديثةِ إلى ...

birth certificate *n* شَهادة ميلادٍ

birth control *n* تَحْديد النَسْلِ

birthday /ˈbəːθdeɪ/ *n* عيد ميلادٍ; **Happy B~!** عيد ميلادٍ سَعيد!

birthday cake *n* كَعْكة عيدِ ميلادٍ

birthday card *n* بِطاقة عيدِ ميلادٍ

birthday party *n* حَفْلة عيدِ ميلادٍ

birthing pool /ˈbəːθɪŋ ˌpuːl/ *n* حَمّام الوِلادةِ

birthmark /ˈbəːθmɑːk/ *n* شامة ,وَحْمة (شام ,شامات)

birth mother *n* أُمّ بيولوجيّة

birthplace /ˈbɜːθpleɪs/ *n* مَكان الميلادِ

birth rate *n* مُعَدَّل المَواليدِ

birth sign *n* بُرْج (أَبراج, بُروج)

birthweight /ˈbɜːθweɪt/ *n* الوَزْن عند الوِلادةِ

biscuit /ˈbɪskɪt/ *n* **1** (BrE) (unleavened) بَسْكوت **2** (AmE) (leavened) بَسْكوت

(Idiom) **to take the biscuit** (BrE infml) أَخذَهُ على حينِ غِرّةٍ

bisect /bʌɪˈsɛkt/ *vt* شَطَرَ (u; شَطْر), قَسَمَ نِصْفَيْنِ ‹*an area, a surface*›

bisexual /bʌɪˈsɛksjʊəl/ *n, adj* ثُنائيّ, مُزْدَوِج المُيولِ الجِنْسيّة المَيْلِ الجِنْسيِّ

bishop /ˈbɪʃəp/ *n* **1** (of diocese) أُسْقُف (أَساقِفة, أَساقِفُ) **2** (in chess) فيل (فُيول, فِيَلة, أَفْيال)

bismillah /bɪsˈmɪlə/ *excl* بِسْمِ اللهِ

bison /ˈbʌɪs(ə)n/ *n* (*pl* **bison**) ثَوْر أَمْريكيّ, بَيْسون

bit /bɪt/ **A** *past tense* ▸ **bite**

B *n* **1** (piece of food, land, paper) قِطْعة (قِطَع); **a ~ of cheese/wire** قِطْعة جُبْنٍ \ سِلْكٍ; **every ~ of dirt** كُلّ قِطْعةٍ من التُّرابِ; **to take a clock to ~s** فكَّ أَجْزاءَ ساعةٍ **2** (infml) (of time, money, information) **a ~** بَعْض; **would you like a ~ more?** هل تُريدُ المَزيدَ؟; **we need a ~ of time** نَحْنُ بحاجةٍ لِبَعْضِ الوَقْتِ; **a ~ of advice** نَصيحة (نَصائِحُ); **with a ~ of luck, we'll finish in an hour** مع بَعْضِ الحَظِّ سَنَنْتَهي بعد ساعةٍ; **we did a ~ of shopping** تَسَوَّقْنا قَليلاً; **it won't do a ~ of good** لن يَنْفَع \ يُفيدَ بِشَيْءٍ; **wait a ~!** انْتَظِرْ قَليلاً! **3** (infml) (section) جُزْء (أَجْزاء); **this ~ is brilliant!** هذا الجُزْءُ رائِعٌ!; **the ~ where the princess dies** الجُزْء الّذي تَموتُ فيه الأَميرةُ **4** (for a horse) شَكيمة (شَكائِمُ) **5** (Comput) بِت (رَقْم ثُنائيّ) **6** (for a drill) لُقْمة (لُقَم)

C (**a bit**) *adv phr* (infml) (rather) قَليلاً; **a ~ deaf/cold** أَطْرَش \ بارِد قَليلاً; **she isn't a ~ like me** لا تُشْبِهُني مُطْلَقاً \ البَتّةَ; **quite a ~ further/bigger** أَبْعَد \ أَكْبَر بِكَثيرٍ; **it's a ~ of a surprise** هي مُفاجَأةٌ نَوْعاً ما

(Idioms) **bit by bit** جُزْئاً بِجُزْءٍ, تَدْريجيًّا; **bits and bobs** (BrE) (infml) أَشْياء, أَغْراض; **bits and pieces** أَشْياء, أَغْراض; **every bit as good/clever as sb** [بِمَثابةِ شَخْصٍ في الطيبةِ \ الذَّكاءِ]; **not a bit of it!** (infml) كَلاّ!, (لا) أَبداً!; **to do one's bit** أَدّى ما عَلَيْهِ

bitch /bɪtʃ/ *n* **1** (female dog) أُنْثى الكَلْبِ, كَلْبة **2** (infml pej) (spiteful woman) شَرْموطة, قَحْبة, مومِس (colloq ME, Egypt)

bite /bʌɪt/ **A** *vt* (*past tense* **bit**; *past participle* **bitten**) قَضَمَ (a-i; قَضْم) ‹*an apple*›; **to ~ one's nails** قَضَمَ أَظافِرَهُ

B *vi* (*past tense* **bit**; *past participle* **bitten**) **1** «dogs» عَضَّ (a; عَضّ, عَضيض); «mosquitoes» لَسَعَ (a; لَسْع); «snakes» لَدَغَ (u; لَدْغ) **2** «laws, recession» ضَرَبَ (i; ضَرْب)

C *n* **1** (insect's) قَرْصة, لَسْعة; (dog's) عَضّة; (snake's) لَدْغة (لَدَغات) **2** (mouthful) عَضّة, لُقْمة; **let's have a ~ to eat** لِنَأْكُلْ لُقْمةً; **to have/take a ~ (out) of sth** أَخذَ عَضّةً من شَيْءٍ

(Idiom) **to bite one's lip** (hold back words) لَجَمَ لِسانَهُ; (hold back tears) حَبَسَ دُموعَهُ

(Phrasal verb) **bite off**: **~ off** [**sth**], **~** [**sth**] **off** نَتَش [شَيْئاً] ‹*a mouthful*›

biting /ˈbʌɪtɪŋ/ *adj* **1** ‹*insect*› لاسِع **2** ‹*wind*› قارِس **3** ‹*remark, wit*› لاذِع

bit part *n* دَوْر (تَمْثيليّ) صَغير

bitten /ˈbɪt(ə)n/ *past participle* ▸ **bite**

bitter /ˈbɪtə/ *adj* **1** ‹*taste, lemon*› مُرّ (أَمْرار) **2** ‹*cold, wind*› شَديد البُرودة, قارِس **3** ‹*disappointment, truth*› مَرير (مَرائِرُ) **4** ‹*enemy*› لَدود (لُدّ, لِداد, أَلِدّاءُ)

bitterly /ˈbɪtəli/ *adv* **1** ‹*to complain*› بِمَرارةٍ; ‹*regret*› بِحُرْقةٍ **2** ‹*cold*› جِدًّا; ‹*disappointing*› بِشِدّةٍ

bitterness /ˈbɪtənəs/ *n* **1** (of taste) مَرارة **2** (of feeling) مَرارة, أَسًى

bittersweet /ˌbɪtəˈswiːt/ *adj* **1** ‹*taste, drink*› حُلو مُرّ **2** ‹*ending, memory*› لَذيذ مُؤْلِم

bizarre /bɪˈzɑː/ *adj* ‹*incident, behaviour*› غَريب (غُرَباءُ), عُجاب, عَجيب

black /blak/ **A** *adj* **1** (in colour) ‹*car, hair*› أَسْوَد (dipt; سود, سودان; f pl سَوْداوات, سود); **to paint the gate ~** دَهَنَ البَوّابةَ باللَّوْنِ الأَسْوَدِ; **to go** *or* **turn ~** اسْوَدَّ **2** (African, Afro-Caribbean) ‹*person, community*› أَسْوَد (dipt; سود, سودان; f pl سَوْداوات, سود) **3** (without milk) ‹*coffee, tea*› سادة **4** (dirty) ‹*face, mark*› أَسْوَد (مُتَّسِخ) **5** (pessimistic) ‹*mood, future*› كَئِيب, مُعْتِم; **it was a ~ day for Britain** كانَ يَوْماً أَسْوَدَ بالنِسْبةِ لِبَريطانيا **6** (macabre) ‹*comedy, humour*› أَسْوَد (dipt) **7** (angry) ‹*look*› غاضِب

B *n* **1** (colour) أَسْوَد (dipt; سود, سودان; f pl سود, سَوْداوات); **~ is his favourite colour** الأَسْوَدُ لَوْنُهُ المُفَضَّلُ; **to be dressed in** *or* **wear ~** لَبِسَ \ ارْتَدى الأَسْوَدَ; **to beat sb ~ and blue** ضَرَبَ شَخْصاً ضَرْباً مُبَرِّحاً **2** (person) أَسْوَد (dipt; سود, سودان; f pl سود, سَوْداوات), أَسْمَر (dipt; سُمْر) **3** (in surplus) **to be in the ~** «account, company» كانَ رَصيدُهُ دائِناً **4** (in chess, draughts) أَحْجار \ قِطَع سَوْداء

C *vt* **1** (to apply black to) سَوَّدَ ‹*one's face, boots*› **2** (BrE) (to boycott) قاطَعَ ‹*goods, a cargo*›

Phrasal verb **black out A** (to lose consciousness) أُصيبَ بِحالةِ إغْماءٍ, فَقَدَ الوَعْيَ **B ~ [sth] out, ~ out [sth] 1** (to darken) أَطْفَأَ أَنْوارَ [شَيْءٍ] ‹*a stage, studio*› **2** (to censure) شَطَبَ [شَيْئاً] بالأَسْوَدِ ‹*a name, text*› **3** (to cut electricity to) قَطَعَ الكَهْرَباءَ عن [شَيْءٍ] ‹*a city, building*›

black and white A *n* أَبْيَض وأَسْوَد; **I want it in black and white** أُريدُهُ كِتابيًّا

B *adj (before n* **black-and-white***)* ‹*TV, photograph*› أَبْيَض وأَسْوَد

black belt *n* حِزام أَسْوَد

blackberry /ˈblakb(ə)ri/ *n (pl* **blackberries***)* **1** (fruit) عُلَّيْق **2** (**Blackberry®**) بْلاك بيري (جهاز اتِّصالٍ)

blackbird /ˈblakbəːd/ *n* شُحْرور (شَحارير)

blackboard /ˈblakbɔːd/ *n* سَبّورة, لَوْح أَسْوَد

black box *n* صُنْدوق أَسْوَد

blackcurrant /blakˈkʌr(ə)nt/ *n* كِشْمِش أَسْوَد

black economy *n* اقْتِصاد أَسْوَد

blacken /ˈblak(ə)n/ *vt* **1** (to make black) سَوَّدَ ‹*one's face, window*› **2** (to defame) شَوَّهَ ‹*a name, reputation*›

black eye *n* كَدْمة في \ حول العَيْنِ

blackhead /ˈblakhɛd/ *n* رَأْس أَسْوَد

black hole *n* ثُقْب أَسْوَد

black ice *n* ثَلْج \ جَليد أَسْوَد

blacklist /ˈblaklɪst/ **A** *n* لائِحة \ قائِمة سَوْداء

B *vt* أَدْرَجَ في القائِمةِ السَوْداءِ ‹*a company, product*›

black magic *n* سِحْر أَسْوَد

blackmail /ˈblakmeɪl/ **A** *n* **1** (financial) ابْتِزاز **2** (psychological) ابْتِزاز

B *vt* **1** (to extort money from) ابْتَزَّ ‹*a victim, judge*› **2** (psychologically) ابْتَزَّ ‹*a friend, lover*›

blackmailer /ˈblakmeɪlə/ *n* مُبْتَزّ

black mark *n* نُقْطة \ عَلامة سَوْداء

black market *n* سوق سَوْداء; **to buy sth on the black market** اشْتَرى شَيْئاً من السوقِ السَوْداءِ

black marketeer *n* [شَخْص يَعْمَلُ في السوقِ السَوْداءِ]

blackout /ˈblakaʊt/ *n* **1** (in wartime) إطْفاء الأَنْوارِ, تَعْتيم **2** (faint) إغْماء (إغْماءات)

Black Sea *pr n* **(the Black Sea)** البَحْر الأَسْوَد

black sheep *n* (infml) [شَخْص يُلْحِقُ الخِزْيَ \ العارَ بعائِلَتِهِ]

blacksmith /ˈblaksmɪθ/ *n* حَدّاد

black spot *n* نُقْطة سَوْداء

Black Stone *n* **(the Black Stone)** الحَجَر الأَسْوَد

black tie *n* [زِيّ رَسْميّ]

bladder /ˈbladə/ *n* مَثانة

blade /bleɪd/ *n* **1** (of a knife, razor) شَفْرة (شِفار, شَفَرات) **2** (of a propeller, oar) ريشة **3** (of grass) وَرَقة (أَوْراق, وَرَقات)

blah /blɑː/ **A** *n* (infml) (words) **~ ~ ~** كَذا وَكَذا (كَلام إضافيّ مُمِلّ فارِغ); **there is a list of restrictions, ~, ~, ~** هُناكَ قائِمةٌ من المَمْنوعاتِ، كَذا وَكَذا وَكَذا

B (the blahs) *n pl* (AmE infml) [اكْتِئاب ناتِج عن المَلَلِ]

blame /bleɪm/ **A** *vt* **(blames, blaming, blamed)** لامَ (u; لَوْم, مَلام, مَلامة) ‹*a colleague, the weather*›; **she has always ~d me** كانَتْ تَلومُني دائِماً; **to ~ sb/sth for sth** لامَ شَخْصاً \ شَيْئاً على شَيْءٍ; **to ~ sth on sb/sth** حَمَّلَ شَخْصاً \ شَيْئاً مَسْؤوليّةَ شَيْءٍ; **to be to ~ for an accident/a crisis** وَقَعَتْ عَلَيْهِ مَسْؤوليّةُ حادِثٍ \ أَزْمةٍ

B *v refl* **to ~ oneself for sth** لامَ نَفْسَهُ على شَيْءٍ; **you mustn't ~ yourself** لا تَلُمْ نَفْسَكَ; **you only have yourself to ~** لا تَلُمْ إلاّ نَفْسَكَ

C *n* **1** (responsibility) مَسْؤوليّة; **to take the ~ for sth** تَحَمَّلَ مَسْؤوليّةَ شَيْءٍ; **to put** *or* **lay the ~ for sth on sb** لامَ شَخْصاً على شَيْءٍ **2** (criticism) لَوْم; **why do I always get the ~?** لِماذا يَقَعُ عَلَيَّ اللَوْمُ دائِماً؟

blameless /'bleɪmləs/ *adj* ‹*life, victim*› بَريء (أَبْرِياءُ)

blancmange /blə'mɒnʒ/ *n* ≈ مُهَلَّبِيّة

bland /bland/ *adj* (**blander**, **blandest**) **1** ‹*food, flavour*› مَسيخ **2** ‹*manner, smile*› فاتِر (دون نَكْهةٍ)

blank /blaŋk/ **A** *adj* **1** (empty) ‹*page, screen, wall*› فارغ **2** (unrecorded) ‹*DVD, CD*› فارِغ **3** (expressionless) فارِغ; **a ~ look/stare** نَظْرة فارِغة **4** (without memory) **my mind went ~** أَصْبَحَ ذِهْني فارِغاً

B *n* **1** (empty space) فَراغ (فَراغات); **to fill in the ~s** مَلَأَ الفَراغاتِ; **my mind's a ~** ذِهْني فارِغٌ **2** (AmE) (form without writing) اسْتِمارة فارِغة **3** (dummy bullet) رَصاصة فارِغة

(Phrasal verb) **blank out**: **~ [sth] out, ~ out [sth]** مَحى [شَيْئاً] من الذاكِرةِ ‹*a memory, an event*›

blank cheque (BrE), **blank check** (AmE) *n* شيك على بَياضٍ

blanket /'blaŋkɪt/ **A** *n* **1** (for a bed) بَطّانيّة (بَطّانيّات، بَطاطينُ) **2** (layer of snow, cloud, fog) طَبَقة

B *adj before n* ‹*policy, condemnation*› شامِل

blare /bleː/ *vi* «music, alarm» دَوّى

(Phrasal verb) **blare out**: **~ out [sth]** دَوّى ب [شَيْءٍ] ‹*music, advertising*›

blaspheme /blas'fiːm/ **A** *vt* جَدَّفَ ‹*God, the prophet*›

B *vi* جَدَّفَ

blasphemous /'blasfəməs/ *adj* ‹*remark, attack*› تَجْديفيّ

blasphemy /'blasfəmi/ *n* (*pl* **blasphemies**) تَجْديف

blast /blɑːst/ **A** *n* **1** (explosion) انْفِجار (انْفِجارات) **2** (on a trumpet, car horn, whistle) [صَوْت عالٍ]; **to play music/the radio at full ~** شَغَّلَ الموسيقى \ الرادِيو بِصَوْتٍ عالٍ **3** (of air) هَبّة

B *vt* **1** (with explosives) فَجَّرَ ‹*rock, a building*›; **to ~ a hole in a wall/safe** فَجَّرَ حُفْرةً في جِدارٍ \ خَزينةٍ **2** (with gunfire, artillery) قَصَفَ (i; قَصْف) ‹*a building, convoy*› **3** «gales, winds» هَبَّ (u; هَبّ على) ‹*a tree, crop*› **4** (to hit) «strikers, batters» ضَرَبَ بِقُوّةٍ ‹*a shot, the ball*› **5** (infml) (to criticize) انْتَقَدَ بِحِدّةٍ ‹*a politician, performance*›

C *vi* **1** (with explosives) [اسْتَعْمَلَ مُفَجِّراتٍ]; **to ~ through a wall/mountain** اخْتَرَقَ حائِطاً \ جَبَلاً بِتَفْجيرٍ **2** «horns» [أَصْدَرَ صَوْتاً عالِياً]

D *excl* (infml) تَبّاً

(Phrasal verbs) **blast away** أَطْلَقَ النارَ مِراراً; **to ~ away at sth** أَطْلَقَ النارَ على شَيْءٍ مِراراً

• **blast off** «rockets» انْطَلَقَ

• **blast out** «music» دَوّى

blast-off /'blɑːstɒf/ *n* انْطِلاق, إطْلاق

blatant /'bleɪt(ə)nt/ *adj* ‹*lie, disregard*› واضِح وُضوحَ الشَمْسِ

blatantly /'bleɪt(ə)ntli/ *adv* ‹*to copy, violate*› بِشَكْلٍ واضِحٍ; **it's ~ obvious** الأَمْرُ واضِحٌ وُضوحَ الشَمْسِ

blaze /bleɪz/ **A** *n* **1** (fire) حَريق (حَرائِقُ)، لَهيب **2** (of colour, light) وَهْج; **she left in a ~ of publicity** رَحَلَتْ وَسْطَ وَهْجٍ إعْلاميٍّ **3** (on a horse) غُرّة (غُرَر)

B (**blazes**) *n pl* (infml) **what the ~s are they doing?** ماذا يَفْعَلونَ بِحَقِّ الجَحيمِ؟; **to work like ~s** عَمِلَ بِشَكْلٍ مَحْمومٍ

C *vi* **1** (to burn strongly) (also **blaze away**) «fire, house» احْتَرَقَ **2** (to shine brightly) «lights, headlights» تَوَهَّجَ; **all the lights were blazing** كانَتْ كُلُّ الأَضْواءِ تَتَوَهَّجُ **3** (to fire) (also **blaze away**) «guns, artillery» [ضَرَبَ \ أَطْلَقَ ناراً مِراراً]

(Idiom) **to blaze a trail** شَقَّ طَريقاً جَديداً

blazer /'bleɪzə/ *n* [سُتْرة خَفيفة ذات شِعارٍ مُمَيِّزٍ]

blazing /'bleɪzɪŋ/ *adj* **1** (on fire) ‹*fire, building*› مُشْتَعِل **2** (violent) ‹*argument*› حادّ **3** (very hot) ‹*sun, heat*› حارِق

bleach /bliːtʃ/ **A** *vt* **1** (to whiten) بَيَّضَ ‹*the linen, paper*›; **she ~ed her hair blonde** صَبَغَتْ شَعْرَها بِاللَوْنِ الأَصْفَرِ \ الأَشْقَرِ **2** (to disinfect) طَهَّرَ, عَقَّمَ ‹*a bathroom, floor*›

B *n* **1** (cloth whitener) مادّة تَبْييضٍ, مُبَيِّض **2** (disinfectant) مُطَهِّر

bleachers /'bliːtʃəz/ *n pl* (AmE) [مُدَرَّج مَكْشوف \ مَفْتوح]

bleak /bliːk/ *adj* (**-er, bleakest**) **1** ‹*region, landscape*› أَجْرَد (جُرْد; dipt) **2** ‹*weather, season*› [بارِد وَكَئيب] **3** ‹*outlook, prospect*› قاتِم

bleary /ˈblɪəri/ *adj* (**blearier, bleariest**) ‹*eyes, glance*› أَعْمَش (dipt; عُمْش); **to be ~-eyed** [كانَ مُتْعَبَ العَيْنَيْنِ]

bleat /bliːt/ *vi* **1** «sheep» مَأْمَأَ (i; مَأْمَأة) «goats» ثَغا (u; ثُغاء) **2** (infml) (to complain) «staff, team» تَشَكّى, تَذَمَّرَ

bleed /bliːd/ **A** *vi* (*past tense, past participle* **bled**) نَزَفَ (i; نَزْف)
B *vt* فَرَّغَ الهَواءَ من, اسْتَنْزَفَ ‹*the radiator, brakes*›

Idiom **to bleed sb dry/white** سَلَبَ شَخْصاً كُلَّ ما يَمْلِكُهُ

bleeding /ˈbliːdɪŋ/ **A** *n* نَزيف; **to stop the ~** أَوْقَفَ النَزيفَ
B *adj before n* ‹*wound, ulcers*› نازِف

bleep /bliːp/ **A** *n* صَوْت تَنْبيهٍ, صَفير, رَنين
B *vi* «alarm clocks, phones» رَنَّ (i; رَنين), صَفَّرَ, أَصْدَرَ صَوْتَ تَنْبيهٍ
C *vt* (BrE) اسْتَدْعى على جِهازِ النِداءِ الآليِّ ‹*a doctor, manager*›

bleeper /ˈbliːpə/ *n* (BrE) بَيْجَر (جِهاز النِداءِ الآليِّ)

blemish /ˈblɛmɪʃ/ *n* **1** (on skin, fruit) عَيْب (عُيوب) **2** (on reputation) شُبْهة (شُبُهات), لَطْخة (لَطَخات)

blend /blɛnd/ **A** *vt* **1** خَلَطَ (i; خَلْط) ‹*the foods, colours*› **2** جَمَعَ (a; جَمْع) بين ‹*the styles, ideas*›
B *vi* **1** «ingredients, flavours» امْتَزَجَ, اخْتَلَطَ **2** «colours, styles» تَناغَمَ
C *n* خَلْطة

Phrasal verbs **blend in**: **~ in** «colours, sounds» تَناغَمَ (مع)
• **blend into**: **~ into** [sth] تَناغَمَ مع [شَيْءٍ] ‹*a setting, crowd*›

blender /ˈblɛndə/ *n* خَلّاط

bless /blɛs/ *vt* بارَكَ ‹*a marriage, sacrament*›; **we have been ~ed with good health** أَنْعَمَ اللهُ عَلَيْنا بِصِحّةٍ جَيِّدةٍ; **~ you!** يَرْحَمُكَ اللهُ!

blessed /ˈblɛsɪd/ *adj* **1** (holy) ‹*place, name*› مُبارَك **2** (welcome) ‹*relief, silence*› عَذْب, هَنيء

blessing /ˈblɛsɪŋ/ *n* **1** (God's favour) بَرَكة **2** (good thing) نِعْمة (نِعَم, أَنْعُم); **it was a ~ in disguise** كانَتْ نِعْمةً خَفِيّةً **3** (approval) مُبارَكة

blew /bluː/ *past tense* ▸ **blow** A

blight /blʌɪt/ **A** *n* **1** (on plants) لَفْحة **2** (scourge, problem) آفة
B *vt* **1** (to infest) أَصابَ ‹*a crop*› **2** (to spoil) دَمَّرَ, أَفْسَدَ ‹*an area, a career*›

blind /blʌɪnd/ **A** *adj* **1** (sightless) ‹*child, dog*› أَعْمى (dipt; عُمْي, عُمْيان), ضَرير (أَضِرّاءُ, أَضْرار), كَفيف (أَكِفّاءُ), مَكْفوف; **to go ~** عَمِيَ (a; عَمًى), فَقَدَ بَصَرَهُ; **to be ~ in one eye** عَمِيَ في عَيْنٍ واحِدةٍ; **to be ~ to sb's faults** لم يَرَ أَخْطاءَ شَخْصٍ
2 (unquestioning) ‹*obedience, acceptance*› أَعْمى (dipt; عُمْي, عُمْيان) **3** ‹*rage, panic*› أَعْمى (dipt; عُمْي, عُمْيان) **4** ‹*corner*› أَعْمى, مَيِّت (dipt); **on my ~ side** في الزاوِيةِ العَمْياءِ \ المَيِّتةِ
5 (in research) ‹*test, trial*› [مَحْجوب البَياناتِ] **6** (Culin) ‹*tasting*› [دون مَعْرِفةٍ بالمُنْتَجِ]
B *vt* **1** أَفْقَدَ البَصَرَ, أَعْمى ‹*a person, dog*›; **he was ~ed in one eye** فَقَدَ البَصَرَ في عَيْنٍ واحِدةٍ **2** (to confuse) «lights, the sun» أَعْمى; **to be ~ed by pride/passion** أَعْمَتْهُ الكِبْرِياءُ \ أَعْماهُ الهُيامُ
C *n* **1** (**the blind** *n pl*) المَكْفوفونَ; **a school for the ~** مَدْرَسة المَكْفوفينَ **2** (on windows) سِتار (سُتُر) **3** (AmE) (for observation) مَخْبَأ (لِرَصْدِ الطُيور)
D *adv* ‹*to fly, land*› [مُسْتَعيناً بالوَسائِلِ الآلِيّةِ فَقَطْ]

Idioms **to turn a blind eye to sth** تَغاضى عن شَيْءٍ; **the blind leading the blind** أَعْمى يَقودُ أَعْمى

blind date *n* مَوْعِد غَراميّ مُرَتَّب (مَوْعِد أَوَّل بين شَخْصَيْنِ لا يَعْرِفانِ بَعْضُهُما البَعْضَ)

blindfold /ˈblʌɪn(d)fəʊld/ **A** *n* عَصْب العَيْنَيْنِ
B *vt* عَصَبَ العَيْنَيْنِ ‹*a hostage, prisoner*›
C *adv* ‹*to walk, play*› مَعْصوبَ العَيْنَيْنِ

blinding /ˈblʌɪndɪŋ/ *adj* **1** (dazzling) ‹*light*› مُبْهِر **2** (intense) ‹*headache*› أَليم; ‹*pain*› حادّ

blindly /ˈblʌɪndli/ *adv* **1** (without seeing) ‹*to grope, stumble*› بِشَكْلٍ عَشْوائيٍّ **2** (without questioning) ‹*to follow, accept*› بِشَكْلٍ أَعْمى

blindness /ˈblʌɪndnəs/ *n* عَمًى

blind spot *n* **1** (when driving) بُقْعة عَمْياء **2** (weak point) مَوْطِن جَهْلٍ, نُقْطة ضَعْفٍ

blink /blɪŋk/ **A** *vi* **1** «person» رَفَّتْ عَيْناهُ; «eyes» رَفَّ (i-u; رَفّ, رَفيف) **2** «lights» أَوْمَضَ
B *n* طَرْفة عَيْنٍ

Idiom **to be on the blink** (infml) تَعَطَّلَ

blinker /ˈblɪŋkə/ *n* ① (indicator) ضَوْء وامِض ② (**blinkers** *n pl*) (for horses) غِمامة (حِصانٍ)

blinkered /ˈblɪŋkəd/ *adj* ‹*view, approach*› ضَيِّق

blip /blɪp/ *n* ① (on a screen) وَمْضة (على شاشةِ رادار) ② (sound) إشارة صَوْتيّة, نَبْضة (على شَكْلِ رَنينٍ) ③ (in trends) [تَقَلُّب عارِض]

bliss /blɪs/ *n* هَناء (هَناءات)

blissful /ˈblɪsfʊl/ *adj* ‹*ignorance, sleep*› هَنِيء

blissfully /ˈblɪsf(ə)li/ *adv* ‹*to smile, sigh*› بِهَناءٍ; **to be ~ unaware/ignorant of sth** نَعِمَ بِجَهْلِهِ بِشَيْءٍ

blister /ˈblɪstə/ **A** *n* بَثْر (n coll; بُثُور); **his feet were covered in ~s** غَطَّت البُثورُ قَدَمَيْهِ
B *vi* «skin» بَثِرَ (a-i; بَثْر), تَنَفَّطَ; «paint» [ظَهَرَتْ فيهِ فُقّاعاتُ هَواءٍ]

blister pack *n* [نَوْع من الغِلافِ البْلاسْتيكيّ]

blithely /ˈblʌɪðli/ *adv* ① (with indifference) ‹*to ignore, assume*› بِدونِ اكْتِراثٍ ② (cheerfully) ‹*to laugh*› فارِغ, مُرْتاح البالِ, الفُؤادِ

blitz /blɪts/ *n* ① (infml) (big effort) حَمْلة (حَمَلات); **we had a ~ on the backlog** قُمْنا بِحَمْلةٍ لِإنْهاءِ \ لِأَداءِ الأَعْمالِ المُتَأَخِّرة
② (air attack) غارة جَوِّيّة

blizzard /ˈblɪzəd/ *n* [عاصِفة ثَلْجيّة شَديدة]

bloated /ˈbləʊtɪd/ *adj* ‹*stomach, corpse*› مُتَوَرِّم, مُنْتَفِخ

blob /blɒb/ *n* ① (drop) بُقْعة (بِقاع, بُقَع) ② (shape) نُقْطة (نُقَط, نِقاط)

bloc /blɒk/ *n* كُتْلة (كُتَل), تَكَتُّل (تَكَتُّلات); **to vote/act en ~** صَوَّتوا \ تَصَرَّفوا جَميعاً في نَفْسِ الوَقْتِ

block /blɒk/ **A** *n* ① (solid mass) كُتْلة (كُتَل); **a concrete/marble ~** كُتْلة إسْمَنْتٍ \ رُخامٍ ② (for chopping on) وَضَم (أَوْضام, أَوْضِمة) ③ (of houses) مُجَمَّع, مَجْموعة (مَجْموعات, مَجاميع); **a ~ of apartments** مُجَمَّع شِقَقٍ
B *vt* سَدَّ (u; سَدّ) ‹*the exit, road, drain*›; **the pass is ~ed** المَمَرُّ مَسْدودٌ

Phrasal verbs **block in**: **~ [sb/sth] in** سَدَّ سَبيلَ [شَخْصٍ \ شَيْءٍ] ‹*the cars, driver*›

• **block off**: **~ [sth] off, ~ off [sth]** سَدَّ [شَيْئاً] ‹*the street, path*›

• **block out**: **~ out [sth], ~ [sth] out** ① (to obstruct) أَعاقَ [شَيْئاً] ‹*the view, light*› ② (to suppress) كَبَتَ [شَيْئاً] ‹*a memory, problem*›

• **block up**: **~ up [sth], ~ [sth] up** سَدَّ [شَيْئاً] ‹*a hole, drain*›

blockade /blɒˈkeɪd/ **A** *n* حِصار (حُصُر)
B *vt* حاصَرَ ‹*a port, coast*›

blockage /ˈblɒkɪdʒ/ *n* انْسِداد

block-book /blɒkˈbʊk/ *vt* حَجَزَ بالجُمْلة ‹*seats*›

blockbuster /ˈblɒkbʌstə/ *n* ① (book) [كِتاب ذو رَواجٍ كَبيرٍ] ② (film) [فيلْم ذو رَواجٍ كَبيرٍ]

block capitals *n* [حُروف كَبيرة مُنْفَصِلة]

blog /blɒg/ **A** *n* مُدَوَّنة; **to keep/write a ~** كَتَبَ مُدَوَّنةً
B *vi* (**-gg-**) دَوَّنَ, كَتَبَ في مُدَوَّنةٍ

blogger /ˈblɒgə/ *n* صاحِب مُدَوَّنةٍ, مُدَوِّن

blogosphere /ˈblɒgəsfɪə/ *n* (Comput) عالَم, فَضاء المُدَوَّناتِ التَدْوينِ

bloke /bləʊk/ *n* (BrE infml) رَجُل (رِجال)

blonde /blɒnd/ **A** *adj* ‹*hair, girl*› أَشْقَر (dipt; شُقْر)
B *n* (also **blond**) شَقْراء

blood /blʌd/ *n* ① (in circulation) دَم (دِماء); **to give ~** أَعْطى دَماً ② (in kinship) قَرابة دَمٍ; **they are related by ~** هُمْ من ذَوي الأَرْحامِ; **music is in her ~** الموسيقى في دَمِها; **to be of noble ~** كانَ من سُلالةِ نُبَلاءَ ③ (personnel) **new/young ~** دِماء جَديدة

Idioms **in cold blood** بِدَمٍ بارِدٍ; **bad blood** عَداوة; **there is bad ~ between them** هُناكَ عَداوةٌ بَيْنَهُما; **to be after sb's blood** أَرادَ أَنْ يَأْخُذَ بِثَأْرِهِ \ يَنْتَقِمَ من شَخْصٍ; **to get blood out of/from a stone** or **turnip** (AmE) اسْتَحْلَبَ الصَخْرَ; **to make sb's blood boil** جَعَلَ دَمَ شَخْصٍ يَغْلي

blood bank *n* بَنْك دَمٍ

bloodbath /ˈblʌdbɑːθ/ *n* مَذْبَحة (مَذابِح); **the election turned out to be a ~ for the Liberals** تَبَيَّنَ أَنّ الانْتِخاباتِ كانَتْ كارِثةً لليبراليّينَ

blood cell *n* خَليّة \ كُرَيّة دَمٍ

blood count *n* عَدّ دَمَويّ

blood-curdling /ˈblʌdkəːdlɪŋ/ *adj* ‹*scream, tale*› مُرْعِب

blood donor *n* مُتَبَرِّع بِدَمٍ

blood group *n* فَصيلة \ زُمْرة دَمٍ

bloodless /ˈblʌdləs/ *adj* ‹coup, revolution› أَبْيَض (dipt; بيض)

blood poisoning *n* تَسَمُّم دَمٍ

blood pressure *n* ضَغْط دَمٍ

blood relation *n* قَريب قَرابةَ دَمٍ

bloodshed /ˈblʌdʃɛd/ *n* سَفْك \ إراقة الدماءِ

bloodshot /ˈblʌdʃɒt/ *adj* ‹eyes› مُحْمَرّ, مُحْتَقِن بالدَمِ

blood sport *n* رِياضة دَمَوِيّة

bloodstain /ˈblʌdsteɪn/ *n* بُقْعة دَمٍ

bloodstained /ˈblʌdsteɪnd/ *adj* ‹clothing, knife› مُلَطَّخ بالدَمِ

bloodstream /ˈblʌdstriːm/ *n* مَجْرى الدَم

blood test *n* تَحْليل \ اخْتِبار دَمٍ

bloodthirsty /ˈblʌdθəːsti/ *adj* (**bloodthirstier**, **bloodthirstiest**) ‹mob, tyrant› مُتَعَطِّش للدِماءِ

blood transfusion *n* نَقْل دَمٍ

blood type *n* فَصيلة \ زُمْرة دَمٍ

blood vessel *n* وِعاء دَمَوِيّ (عُروق), عِرْق

bloody /ˈblʌdi/ **A** *adj* (**bloodier**, **bloodiest**) **1** (covered in blood) ‹hand, rag› كانَ مُلَوَّث \ مُلَطَّخ بالدَمِ; **to have a ~ nose** عِنْدَهُ نَزيفُ أَنْفٍ **2** (violent) ‹battle, regime› دَمَوِيّ **3** (BrE infml) (expressing anger) مَلْعون (مَلاعينُ); **this ~ car!** هذه السَيّارة المَلْعونة!; **it's a ~ miracle!** إنَّها مُعْجِزةٌ حَقًّا!; **you ~ fool!** أيُّها الغَبيّ المَلْعون!

B *adv* (BrE infml) (for emphasis) ‹dangerous, expensive› جِدًّا; **the film was ~ awful** كانَ الفيلمُ سَيِّئًا جِدًّا; **a ~ good meal** وَجْبة لَذيذة جِدًّا; **what a ~ stupid idea!** يا لَها من فِكْرةٍ غَبيّةٍ!

bloom /bluːm/ **A** *n* **1** (flower) زَهْرة **2** [u] (flowering) إزْهار; **to be in ~** أَزْهَرَ

B *vi* «plants, trees» أَزْهَرَ

blossom /ˈblɒs(ə)m/ **A** *n* **1** [u] (flowers) زَهْر (n coll; زُهور) **2** (single flower) زَهْرة (أَزْهُر, أَزاهيرُ, أَزْهار)

B *vi* **1** (to flower) «trees, bushes» أَزْهَرَ **2** (to flourish) «relationship, career, romance» ازْدَهَرَ

blot /blɒt/ **A** *n* **1** (of ink) بُقْعة (بِقاع, بُقَع) **2** (blemish) لَطْخة (لَطَخات), شُبْهة (شُبُهات, شُبَهات, شُبْهات); **a ~ on the landscape** تَشْويه للمَنْظَرِ

B *vt* (**-tt-**) **1** (to dry) نَشَّفَ ‹paper, ink› **2** (to mark) لَطَّخَ ‹a page, cover›

(Phrasal verb) **blot out**: **~ out [sth]**, **~ [sth] out** **1** (to obscure) طَمَسَ [شَيْئًا] ‹a word, the sun› **2** (to obliterate) حَجَبَ [شَيْئًا] ‹pain, a memory›

blotch /blɒtʃ/ *n* بُقْعة (بِقاع, بُقَع)

blotchy /ˈblɒtʃi/ *adj* (**blotchier**, **blotchiest**) ‹skin, rash› مُبَقَّع

blotting paper /ˈblɒtɪŋ ˌpeɪpə/ *n* وَرَق نَشّاف

blouse /blaʊz/ *n* بْلوزة

blow /bləʊ/ **A** *vt* (*past tense* **blew**; *past participle* **blown**) **1** «the wind» طَيَّرَ; **the wind blew the door open/shut** فَتَحَ \ أَغْلَقَ الريحُ البابَ; **the papers were ~n out of the window** طَيَّرَت الريحُ الأَوْراقَ من الشُبّاكِ; **the ship was ~n off course** أَطاحَت الرياحُ بالسَفينةِ; **it's ~ing a gale** تَشْتَدُّ العاصِفةُ **2** نَفَخَ (a; نَفْخ) ‹smoke, a bubble›; **to ~ sb a kiss** أَشارَ بِقُبْلةٍ إلى شَخْصٍ **3** **to ~ one's nose** تَمَخَّطَ **4** نَفَخَ (a; نَفْخ) ‹a trumpet, whistle›; **to ~ the whistle for half-time** أَطْلَقَ صَفّارة انْتِهاءِ الشَوْطِ الأَوَّلِ **5** «explosions, bombs» **to ~ a hole in a wall/safe** فَجَّرَ ثُغْرةً في حائِطٍ \ خَزْنةٍ; **to be blown to pieces by an explosion** تَطايَرَتْ أَشْلاؤُهُ بِتَفْجيرٍ **6** (Elec) أَحْرَقَ ‹a fuse, gasket› **7** (infml) (to spend) **to ~ a fortune on sth** بَذَّرَ ثَرْوةً على شَيْءٍ **8** (infml) (to expose) كَشَفَ (i; كَشْف), فَضَحَ (a; فَضْح) ‹sb's cover, an operation› **9** (infml) (to ruin) ضَيَّعَ, أَضاعَ ‹a chance, deal›; **we've ~n it now!** وَضَعْنا أَنْفُسَنا في مُصيبةٍ الآنَ!; **he blew his chance** ضَيَّعَ فُرْصَتَهُ

B *vi* (*past tense* **blew**; *past participle* **blown**) **1** (through the mouth) نَفَخَ (a; نَفْخ); **to ~ into/on sth** نَفَخَ في \ على شَيْءٍ **2** «winds, breezes» هَبَّ (u; هُبوب, هَبّ), عَصَفَ (i; عَصْف, عُصوف) **3** «leaves, washing» **to ~ in the wind** اهْتَزَّ بِفِعْلِ الرِياحِ **4** (to sound) «whistles» صَفَّرَ; «trumpets» زَمَّرَ **5** (to burn out) «fuses, bulbs» احْتَرَقَ **6** (to burst) «tyre» انْفَجَرَ

C *n* **1** (hit) ضَرْبة (ضَرَبات); **he was killed by a ~ to the head** قُتِلَ بِضَرْبةٍ على الرَأْسِ; **to come to ~s** تَخانَقَ, تَشاجَرَ; **to strike a ~ for freedom** ناصَرَ الحُرِّيّةَ **2** (shock) صَدْمة

(صَدَمات); **to be a terrible ~ for sb** كانَ صَدْمةً عَنيفةً لِشَخْصٍ

3 [u] (BrE infml) (marijuana) حَشيش **4** [u] (infml) (cocaine) كوكايين

(Idiom) **to blow one's stack** *or* **top** (infml) انْفَجَرَ غَضَبُهُ

(Phrasal verbs) **blow around**, **blow about** (BrE) **A** «leaves, papers» تَطايَرَ **B** **~ [sth] around**, **~ around [sth]** ذَرّى [شَيْئاً] ‹*a leaf, piece of paper*›

• **blow away** **A** «hats, papers» طارَ (i; طَيَران) **B** **~ [sth] away**, **~ away [sth]** طَيَّرَ [شَيْئاً] بَعيداً ‹*a hat, piece of paper*› **C** **~ away [sb]**, **~ [sb] away** **1** (infml) (to kill) أَرْدى [شَخْصاً] قَتيلاً ‹*one's rival, a police officer*› **2** (infml) (to beat) أَطاحَ ب [شَخْصٍ] ‹*an opponent*›

• **blow down** **A** «fences, trees» انْهارَ **B** **~ [sth] down**, **~ down [sth]** أَطاحَ ب [شَيْءٍ] ‹*a fence, tree*›

• **blow in** **A** **1** «snow, leaves» انْدَفَعَ **2** (in explosions) «doors, windows» انْخَلَعَ, نُسِفَ **B** **~ [sth] in**, **~ in [sth]** **1** دَفَعَ [شَيْئاً] إلى الداخِلِ ‹*snow, a leaf*› **2** (in explosions) نَسَفَ [شَيْئاً] ‹*a door, window*›

• **blow off** **A** «hats, papers» تَطايَرَ **B** **~ [sth] off**, **~ off [sth]** **1** طَيَّرَ [شَيْئاً] ‹*sb's hat, a leaf*› **2** (in explosions) فَجَّرَ [شَيْئاً] ‹*sb's hand, a roof*›

• **blow out** **A** «candles, flame» انْطَفَأَ **B** **~ [sth] out**, **~ out [sth]** أَطْفَأَ [شَيْئاً] ‹*a candle, flame*›; **the storm has blown itself out** هَدَأَت العاصِفةُ

• **blow over** **A** **1** (to pass) «storms, disputes» انْحَسَرَ, تَلاشى **2** (to fall) «trees, fences» انْهارَ **B** **~ [sb/sth] over** أَطاحَ ب [شَخْصٍ \ شَيْءٍ] ‹*a tree, chair*›

• **blow up** **A** **1** (in explosions) «mines, grenades» انْفَجَرَ **2** (to develop suddenly) «winds, storms, dispute» ظَهَرَ فَجْأةً **3** (infml) (to get angry) انْفَجَرَ غَضَبُهُ **B** **~ [sb/sth] up**, **~ up [sb/sth]** (in explosions) نَسَفَ [شَخْصاً \ شَيْئاً] ‹*a building, politician*› **C** **~ [sth] up**, **~ up [sth]** **1** (to inflate) نَفَخَ [شَيْئاً] ‹*a tyre, balloon*› **2** (to enlarge) كَبَّرَ [شَيْئاً] ‹*text, an image*› **3** (to exaggerate) ضَخَّمَ [شَيْئاً] ‹*a story, an affair*›

blow-by-blow /bləʊbʌɪˈbləʊ/ *adj before n* ‹*account, description*› خَطْوةً خَطْوةً

blow-dry /ˈbləʊdrʌɪ/ **A** *vt* (**-dries**, **-drying**, **-dried**) **to ~ sb's hair** جَفَّفَ شَعْرَ شَخْصٍ

B *n* (*pl* **-dries**) تَجْفيف

blowfly /ˈbləʊflʌɪ/ *n* (*pl* **blowflies**) ذُبابة اللَحْمِ

blowgun /ˈbləʊɡʌn/ *n* (AmE) [أُنْبوبة لِرَمْيِ السِهامِ (في الصَيْدِ)]

blown /bləʊn/ *past participle* ▸ **blow** A

blowout /ˈbləʊaʊt/ *n* **1** (of a tyre) انْفِجار (انْفِجارات); **to have a ~** انْفَجَرَ إطارُ سَيّارَتِهِ **2** (of an oil well) انْفِجار (انْفِجارات) **3** (electrical) انْفِجار (انْفِجارات) **4** (infml) (meal) وَجْبة دَسِمة

blowpipe /ˈbləʊpʌɪp/ *n* [أُنْبوبة لِرَمْيِ السِهامِ (في الصَيْدِ)]

blowtorch /ˈbləʊtɔːtʃ/ *n* بوري لِحامٍ

blubber /ˈblʌbə/ **A** *n* دُهْن الحوتِ

B *vi* (infml) (to cry) انْتَحَبَ

bludgeon /ˈblʌdʒ(ə)n/ *vt* ضَرَبَ بالهِراوةِ ‹*a victim, an opponent*›; **to ~ sb to death** ضَرَبَ شَخْصاً بالهِراوةِ حتى المَوْتِ

blue /bluː/ **A** *adj* **1** (in colour) ‹*eyes, sky*› أَزْرَق (dipt; زُرْق); **to paint sth ~** لَوَّنَ شَيْئاً بالأَزْرَقِ; **to go** *or* **turn ~** ازْرَقَّ; **to be ~ with the cold** ازْرَقَّ من البَرْدِ **2** (infml) (depressed) **to feel ~** شَعَرَ بالاكْتِئاب **3** (infml) ‹*movie, joke*› جِنْسيّ

B *n* **1** (colour) أَزْرَق (dipt; زُرْق); **a dark/light ~** أَزْرَق غامِق \ فاتِح; **~ is her favourite colour** الأَزْرَقُ لَوْنُها المُفَضَّلُ; **to be dressed in** *or* **wear ~** لَبِسَ الأَزْرَقَ **2** (BrE) (in cricket, rowing, rugby) [رِياضيّ يُمَثِّل جامعةَ كامْبِريج أو أوكْسفورْد ضدّ الأُخْرى]

C (**blues**) *n pl* **1** (**the blues**) البْلوز (نَوْع من الموسيقى) **2** (infml) (to feel depressed) **to have the ~s** اكْتَأَبَ

(Idiom) **out of the blue** لا على البالِ وَلا على الخاطِرِ

blue baby *n* طِفْل مُزْرَقّ

bluebell /ˈbluːbɛl/ *n* ياقوتيّة الكَرْمِ

blueberry /ˈbluːb(ə)ri/ *n* (*pl* **blueberries**) **1** (berry) عِنَبيّة **2** (bush) شُجَيْرة العِنَبيّةِ

blue-blooded /ˌbluːˈblʌdɪd/ *adj* ‹*aristocrat, ancestor*› من النُبَلاءِ, ذو الدَمِ الأَزْرَقِ

bluebottle /ˈbluːbɒt(ə)l/ *n* [ذُباب أَزْرَق]

blue cheese *n* جُبْنة زَرْقاء

blue-chip /ˈbluːtʃɪp/ *adj* ‹*company, stock*› من الدَرَجةِ الأولى

blue-collar /ˌbluːˈkɒlə/ *adj* ‹*worker, job*› يَدَويّ

blue helmet, **blue beret** *n* قُبَّعة زَرْقاء (أَحَد أَفرادِ (قوّاتِ) حِفْظِ السَلامِ للأُمَمِ المُتَّحِدةِ)

blue jeans *n* جينْز أَزْرَق

blueprint /ˈbluːprɪnt/ *n* 1 (design, drawing) مُخَطَّط (مُخَطَّطات) 2 (for a policy) مُخَطَّط (مُخَطَّطات), تَصْميم هَنْدَسيّ

blue tit *n* حَدّاد أَزْرَق (طائِر مُغَرِّد ذو أَلْوانٍ زاهِيةٍ)

bluff /blʌf/ (infml) **A** *n* تَبَجُّح; **to call sb's ~** تَحَدّى شَخْصاً أَنْ يُنَفِّذَ ما قالَهُ

B *vi* تَحايَلَ

C *vt* خَدَعَ (a; خَديعة, خُدْعة, خَدْع)

bluish /ˈbluːɪʃ/ *adj* ‹*glow, light*› ضارِب إِلى الزُّرْقة, مُزْرَقّ; **her outfit was ~green** كانَتْ تَرْتَدي فُسْتاناً لَوْنُهُ أَخْضَرُ مُزْرَقٌّ

blunder /ˈblʌndə/ **A** *n* حَماقة

B *vi* 1 (to make a mistake) ارْتَكَبَ حَماقةً \ خَطَأً 2 (to move clumsily) **to ~ into a room** تَخَبَّطَ في مِشْيَتِهِ إلى غُرْفةٍ

blunt /blʌnt/ **A** *adj* 1 ‹*knife, pencil, scissors*› غَيْر, كَليل, مَفْلول حادٍّ 2 ‹*politician, manner*› جِلْف (أَجْلاف)

B *vt* فَلَّ (u; فَلّ), ثَلَّمَ ‹*a knife, blade*›

bluntly /ˈblʌntli/ *adv* ‹*to speak, say*› بِخُشونة, بِجَلافة

blur /bləː/ **A** *vt* (-rr-) أَبْهَمَ ‹*an outline, a boundary*›; **to ~ the distinction between right and wrong** أَبْهَمَ ما يُمَيِّزُ الصَحيحَ من الخَطَأ

B *n* [شَيْء \ شَكْل غَيْرُ واضِحِ المَعالِمِ]

blurb /bləːb/ *n* [وَصْف دِعائيّ موجَز لِكِتابٍ \ لِفيلْمٍ]

blurred /bləːd/ *adj* ‹*image, shape*› ضَبابيّ; **to have ~ vision** كانَتْ حاسّةُ الرُؤْيةِ لَدَيْهِ ضَبابيّةً

blurt out /bləːt/ *vt* **to ~ sth, to blurt sth out** انْفَلَتَ شَيْءٌ من بين شَفَتَيْهِ

blush /blʌʃ/ *vi* احْمَرَّ (وَجْهُهُ); **to ~ with embarrassment** احْمَرَّ حَرَجاً

blusher /ˈblʌʃə/ *n* أَحْمَر الخُدودِ

bluster /ˈblʌstə/ **A** *vi* «politicians, speakers» جَعْجَعَ

B *n* جَعْجَعة بِدونِ طِحْنٍ

blustery /ˈblʌst(ə)ri/ *adj* ‹*day, showers*› عاصِف

Blu-tack® /ˈbluːtak/ *n* صَمْغ (صُموغ)

BM /biːˈɛm/ *n* = **Bachelor of Medicine** (degree) بكالوريوس في الطِبِّ

BMI /ˌbiːɛmˈʌɪ/ *abbr* = **body mass index** مُؤَشِّر كُتْلةِ الجِسْمِ

B-movie /ˈbiːmuːvi/ *n* [فيلْم مُنْخَفِض الميزانيّةِ]

BMX /biːɛmˈɛks/ *n* سِباق دَرّاجاتٍ جَبَليّةٍ

BO /biːˈəʊ/ *n* (infml) = **body odour** رائِحة جِسْمٍ كَريهة

boa /ˈbəʊə/ *n* 1 (snake) بُواء 2 (scarf) **(feather) ~** شال فَرْوٍ طَويل

boar /bɔː/ *n* 1 (also **wild boar**) خِنْزير بَرّيّ 2 (male pig) ذَكَر الخِنْزيرِ

board /bɔːd/ **A** *n* 1 (plank) لَوْح (أَلْواح) 2 (committee) مَجْلِس; **~ of directors** مَجْلِس إدارةٍ, هَيْئة \ لَجْنة إداريّة, إدارة; **~ of governors** مَجْلِس حُكّامٍ; **~ of inquiry** لَجْنة \ مَجْلِس تَحْقيقٍ

3 (for games) لَوْحة لَعِبٍ 4 (in a classroom) لَوْح (أَلْواح), سَبّورة 5 (noticeboard) لَوْحة إعْلاناتٍ 6 (Electron) لَوْحة إلِكْترونيّة 7 [u] (accommodation) **~ and lodging** وَجَبات الطَعامِ والسَكَنِ; ▸**full board**, ▸**half board**

B (**boards**) *n pl* (Theat) **to tread the ~s** مَثَّلَ على خَشَبةِ المَسْرَحِ

C (**on board**) *adv phr* **to be/go on ~** كانَ \ ذَهَبَ على مَتْنِ ‹*a plane, ship*›; **to get on ~** رَكِبَ (a; رُكوب), اسْتَقَلَّ ظَهْرِ ‹*a plane, ship*›

D *vt* 1 (to get on) رَكِبَ (a; رُكوب), اسْتَقَلَّ ‹*a plane, bus*›

2 «pirates, customs officers» اقْتَحَمَ ‹*a ship, yacht*›

E *vi* 1 (at school) «pupils, students» أَقامَ بِمَدْرَسةٍ داخِليّةٍ

2 **to ~ with sb** «lodgers, guests» [حَصَلَ على المَأْكَلِ والسَكَنِ مع شَخْصٍ مُقابِلَ دَفْعِ إيجارٍ]

(Idioms) **to be above board** «schemes, clients» كانَ شَرْعيًّا \ قانونيًّا; **across the board** على, دون اسْتِثْناءٍ, بِشَكْلٍ شامِلٍ الجَميعِ; **to go by the board** فَشِلَ (a; فَشَل), أَخْفَقَ; **to take sth on board** أَخَذَ بِعَيْنِ الاعْتِبارِ

(Phrasal verb) **board up**: **~ [sth] up, ~ up [sth]** سَدَّ \ غَطّى [شَيْئاً] بِأَلْواحٍ خَشَبيّةٍ ‹*a door, house*›

boarder /ˈbɔːdə/ *n* 1 (lodger) نَزيل (نُزَلاءُ) 2 (at a school) [تِلْميذ في مَدْرَسةٍ داخِلِيّةٍ]

board game *n* لُعْبة لَوْحيّة

boarding /ˈbɔːdɪŋ/ *n* [الإقامة في مَدْرَسةٍ داخِلِيّةٍ]

boarding house *n* نُزُل (أَنْزال)

boarding pass, **boarding card** *n* بطاقة رُكوبٍ (في طائِرةٍ \ سَفينةٍ)

boarding school *n* مَدْرَسة داخِلِيّة

board meeting *n* اجْتِماع مَجْلِسِ الإدارةِ

boardroom /ˈbɔːdruːm, ˈbɔːdrʊm/ *n* قاعة اجْتِماعاتِ مَجْلِسِ الإدارة

boardwalk /ˈbɔːdwɔːk/ *n* (AmE) مَمَرّ خَشَبِيّ (بِمُحاذاةِ الشاطِئِ)

boast /bəʊst/ **A** *vt* 1 (to exaggerate) تَباهى (ب); **he ~ed that he knew the president** تَباهى بِأنّهُ يَعْرِفُ الرَّئيسَ 2 (to possess) تَباهى (ب) ‹*a library, shopping centre*›; **the city ~s a fine museum** تَتَباهى المَدينةُ بِمَتْحَفِها الرائِعِ
B *vi* تَفاخَرَ, تَباهى; **stop ~ing!** كُفَّ عَن التَباهي \ التَفاخُرِ!
C *n* تَباهٍ

boastful /ˈbəʊstfʊl/ *adj* ‹*person*› مُتَباهٍ (مُتَباهونَ), مُتَفاخِر; ‹*words*› تَباهٍ, تَفاخُر

boat /bəʊt/ *n* 1 قارِب (قَوارِبُ), زَوْرَق (زَوارِقُ), مَرْكَب (مَراكِبُ); **to row a ~** جَدَفَ قارِباً; **to sail a ~** أَبْحَرَ في قارِبٍ 2 (infml) (ship) باخِرة (بَواخِرُ), عَبّارة; **the ~ sails at six o'clock** تُبْحِرُ الباخِرةُ في الساعةِ السادِسةِ

Idioms **to be in the same boat** كانَ في الهَمِّ سَواءً; **to miss the boat** (to miss an opportunity) فاتَهُ القِطارُ; **to push the boat out** (BrE) [أَنْفَقَ الكَثيرَ من الأَمْوالِ]; **to rock the boat** تَسَبَّبَ في مَشاكِلَ]

boathouse /ˈbəʊthaʊs/ *n* [مَبْنًى على ضِفّةٍ لإيواءِ القَوارِبِ]

boating /ˈbəʊtɪŋ/ *n* رُكوب القَوارِبِ \ الزَوارِقِ (للاسْتِجْمامِ); **to go ~** ذَهَبَ في رِحْلةِ اسْتِجْمامٍ بالقارِبِ

boatman /ˈbəʊtmən/ *n* (*pl* **-men**) مَراكِبِيّ (مَراكِبِيّة)

boatswain /ˈbəʊs(ə)n/ *n* رَئيس البَحّارةِ, عَريف المَلاّحينَ

boatyard /ˈbəʊtjɑːd/ *n* حَوْض \ تَرْسانة سُفُنٍ

bob /bɒb/ **A** *vi* (**-bb-**) (also **bob up and down**) «boats, floats» اهْتَزَّ إلى الأَعْلى والأَسْفَلِ
B *n* (haircut) [قَصّة شَعْرٍ قَصيرة وَمُسْتَديرة]

bobbin /ˈbɒbɪn/ *n* مَكّوك (آلَةِ الخِياطةِ)

bobby pin /ˈbɒbi pɪn/ *n* (AmE) دَبّوس شَعْرٍ

bobby socks, **bobby sox** /ˈbɒbi sɒks/ *n pl* (AmE) [جَوارِب بَناتيّة تَصِلُ إلى أَعْلى الكاحِلِ]

bobcat /ˈbɒbkat/ *n* وَشَق

bobsled /ˈbɒbslɛd/, **bobsleigh** /ˈbɒbsleɪ/ *n* زَلاّجة جَماعيّة

bode /bəʊd/ *vi* **to ~ well/ill for sth/sb** «situation, result» كانَ فَأْلاً حَسَناً \ نَذيرَ شُؤْمٍ لِشَيْءٍ \ لِشَخْصٍ

bodice /ˈbɒdɪs/ *n* (of a dress) صَدْر (صُدور)

bodily /ˈbɒdɪli/ *adj* ‹*functions, harm*› جَسَديّ, جُسْمانيّ

body /ˈbɒdi/ *n* (*pl* **bodies**) 1 (of a person, animal) جِسْم (أَجْسام), جَسَد (أَجْساد), بَدَن (أَبْدان) 2 (also **dead body**) جُثّة (جُثَث), جُثْمان 3 (of a car, aircraft) هَيْكَل (هَياكِلُ), جِسْم (أَجْسام); **place the graph in the ~ of the text** ضَعِ الرَّسْمَ البَيانيَّ في صُلْبِ النَصِّ 4 (of evidence, opinion) مَجْموعة 5 (group) جَماعة; **the main ~ of demonstrators** الجَماعة الرَّئيسيّة من المُتَظاهِرينَ 6 (organization) هَيْئة; **an advisory/official ~** هَيْئة اسْتِشاريّة \ رَسْميّة 7 (in physics) مُجَسَّم 8 (of a wine, beer) نَكْهة 9 (of hair) كَثافة

Idioms **over my dead body!** (infml) لَن يَحْصُلَ هذا ما حَييتُ!; **to have/eat enough to keep body and soul together** (infml) كانَ لَدَيْهِ \ أَكَلَ ما يَسُدُّ رَمَقَهُ

body armour *n* دِرْع واقٍ للجِسْمِ

bodybuilder /ˈbɒdibɪldə/ *n* [مُمارِس لِرياضةِ بِناءِ \ كَمالِ الأَجْسامِ]

bodybuilding /ˈbɒdibɪldɪŋ/ *n* بِناء \ كَمال الأَجْسامِ

bodyguard /ˈbɒdigɑːd/ *n* 1 (individual) حارِس خاصّ 2 (group) حَرَس خاصّ

body language *n* لُغة الجَسَدِ

body lotion *n* مُرَطِّب جِسْمٍ

body mass index *n* مُؤَشِّر كُتْلةِ الجِسْمِ

body shop *n* وَرْشة سَمْكَرةٍ

body stocking *n* [جَوْرَب نِسائيّ كامِل للجِسْمِ]

body warmer *n* [مِعْطَف بِلا أَكْمامٍ]

bodywork /ˈbɒdiwəːk/ *n* جِسْم السَيّارةِ

bog /bɒg/ **A** *n* **1** (marshy area) مُسْتَنْقَع ,(أَهوار) هَوْر (مُسْتَنْقَعات) **2** (also **peat bog**) مُسْتَنْقَع خُثٍّ

B *vt* (-gg-)

(Phrasal verb) **bog down**: **to be/get ~ged down** عَلِقَ (a; عَلَق, عُلوق)

boggle /ˈbɒg(ə)l/ *vi* **the mind ~s!** يَنْدَهِشُ \ يَنْذَهِلُ العَقْلُ!

bog-standard /bɒgˈstandəd/ *adj* (BrE infml) ‹*computer, accommodation*› عاديّ

bogus /ˈbəʊgəs/ *adj* ‹*doctor, claim*› مُزَيَّف

Bohemian, **bohemian** /bəʊˈhiːmɪən/ *adj* ‹*lifestyle, atmosphere*› بوهيميّ

boil /bɔɪl/ **A** *vt* **1** غَلَى (i; غَلْي ,غَلَيان) ,غَلّى ‹*water, soup*›; **to ~ the kettle** غَلَى \ غَلّى الإبْرِيقَ **2** سَلَقَ (u; سَلْق) ‹*rice, meat*›; **to ~ an egg** سَلَقَ بَيْضَةً **3** غَلَى (i; غَلْي ,غَلَيان) ‹*linen, clothes*›

B *vi* «water, vegetables» غَلَى (i; غَلْي ,غَلَيان); **the water is ~ing** الماءُ يَغْلي

C *n* **1** **to bring the water/soup to the ~** غَلّى الماءَ \ الحَساءَ; **to come to the ~** بَدَأَ بالغَلَيانِ \ يَغْلي **2** (on skin) دُمَّل (دَمامِلُ), بَثْر (n coll; بُثور) ,(دَماميلُ) خُراج (أَخْرِجة)

(Phrasal verbs) **boil away** **1** (to evaporate) «liquids, water» تَبَخَّرَ **2** (to continue boiling) «liquids, saucepans» اسْتَمَرَّ في الغَلَيانِ بِشِدّةٍ

• **boil down** **A** ~ **down** «jam, sauce» قَلَّ \ تَناقَصَ بالغَلَيانِ **B** ~ **down [sth]**, ~ **[sth] down** أَنْقَصَ [شَيْئاً] بالغَلْيِ ‹*a sauce, soup*›

C ~ **down to sth** (infml) تَلَخَّصَ في شَيْءٍ

• **boil over** **1** «saucepan» فارَ (u; فَوْر ,فَوَران); «milk, soup» فارَ (u; فَوْر ,فَوَران) **2** «tension, anger» احْتَدَمَ

boiler /ˈbɔɪlə/ *n* غَلّاية ,مِرْجَل (مَراجِلُ)

boiler suit *n* (BrE) بَدْلة شُغْلٍ

boiling /ˈbɔɪlɪŋ/ *adj* **1** ‹*water, oil*› مَغْليّ **2** (infml) (very hot) حارِق; **it's ~ in here!** الجَوُّ هُنا حارِقٌ!; **this coffee's ~!** هذه القَهْوةُ تَغْلي!

boiling point *n* نُقْطة الغَلَيانِ

boisterous /ˈbɔɪst(ə)rəs/ *adj* ‹*children, laughter*› صاخِب

bold /bəʊld/ *adj* **1** (daring) ‹*adventurer, warrior*› جَريء **2** (confident) ‹*step, statement*› جَريء **3** (impudent) ‹*behaviour, look*› وَقِح **4** (strong) ‹*colour, design*› جَريء

boldly /ˈbəʊldli/ *adv* **1** (daringly) ‹*to attempt, venture*› بِجُرْأةٍ **2** (cheekily) بِجُرْأةٍ **3** (strikingly) ‹*patterned, coloured*› بِشَكْلٍ لافِتٍ \ مُلْفِتٍ للنَظَرِ

Bolivia /bəˈlɪvɪə/ *pr n* بوليفيا

Bolivian /bəˈlɪvɪən/ *n, adj* بوليفيّ

bollard /ˈbɒlɑːd/ *n* **1** (on a quay, ship) مَرْبَط (مَرابِطُ) **2** (in a road) [عمود قَصير لِمَنْع دُخولِ \ وَقْفِ المَرْكَباتِ]

bolster /ˈbəʊlstə/ **A** *n* [وِسادة \ مِخَدّة طَويلة تَمْتَدُّ على طولِ السَريرِ]

B *vt* (also **bolster up**) رَفَعَ (a; رَفْع) ‹*sb's confidence, morale*›; دَعَمَ (a; دَعْم) ‹*a claim, government*›

bolt /bəʊlt/ **A** *n* **1** (for a door, window) مِزْلاج (مَزاليجُ), تِرْباس (تَرابيسُ) **2** (screw) بُرْغيّ (بَراغيُّ), مِسْمار لَوْلَبيّ **3** (for a crossbow) سَهْم (أَسْهُم) **4** ~ **of lightning** شَرارة بَرْقٍ

B *vt* **1** (to lock) تَرْبَسَ, قَفَلَ (بِمِزْلاجٍ) ‹*a door, window*› **2** (to fasten together) ثَبَّتَ (بِبُرْغيٍّ) ‹*seats, beams*›; **the chairs are ~ed to the floor** الكَراسيُّ مُثَبَّتةٌ بِبَراغيَ إلى الأَرْضيّةِ **3** (also **bolt down**) (to eat quickly) لَقِمَ (a; لَقْم) ‹*a meal, food*›

C *vi* **1** (to run away) «horses» جَمَحَ (a; جَمْح ,جِماح ,جُموح); «deer» شَرَدَ (u; شُرود ,شِراد) **2** (to run fast) «person» رَكَضَ (u; رَكْض); **I ~ed upstairs** رَكَضْتُ إلى الأعْلى

D (**bolt upright**) *phr* بِشَكْلٍ مُسْتَقيمٍ; **he sat ~ upright in bed** جَلَسَ مُسْتَقيماً في السَرير

bomb /bɒm/ **A** *n* **1** (Mil) قُنْبُلة (قَنابِلُ); **to drop a ~ on a city** أَلْقى قُنْبُلةً على مَدينةٍ; **to detonate a ~** فَجَّرَ قُنْبُلةً; **the ~** القُنْبُلة (النَوَويّة) **2** (infml) **a ~** [كَمّيّة كَبيرة من المالِ]; **it cost a ~** كَلَّفَ كُلْفةً باهِظةً

B *vt* **1** (to drop bombs on) قَصَفَ (i; قَصْف) ‹*a city, factory*› **2** (to place a bomb in) وَضَعَ قُنْبُلةً في ‹*a train, house*›

C *vi* (infml) (to fail) «movies, projects» فَشِلَ فَشَلاً ذَريعاً

bombard /bɒmˈbɑːd/ *vt* **1** (Mil) قَصَفَ (i; قَصْف) ‹*a fort, the enemy*› **2** **to ~ sb with questions/information** أَمْطَرَ شَخْصاً بالأَسْئِلةِ \ بالمَعْلوماتِ

bombardier /ˌbɒmbəˈdɪə/ *n* **1** (BrE) (in army) عَريف في صِنْفِ المِدْفَعيّة **2** (AmE) (in air force) مُصَوِّب

bombardment /bɒmˈbɑːdm(ə)nt/ *n* قَصْف

bomb disposal expert *n* [أخِصّائيّ إبْطالِ مَفْعولِ القَنابِلِ]

bomber /ˈbɒmə/ *n* 1 (plane) قاذِفة قَنابِل 2 (terrorist) مُفَجِّر

bomber jacket *n* [سُتْرة طَيّارٍ جِلْديّة]

bombing /ˈbɒmɪŋ/ *n* 1 (by aircraft) قَذْف بالقَنابِلِ ,قَصْف 2 (by terrorists) تَفْجير (تَفْجيرات)

bomb scare *n* [هَلَع ناتِج عن نَبَأ وُجودِ قُنْبُلةٍ]

bombshell /ˈbɒmʃɛl/ *n* خَبَر صاعِق

bomb squad *n* فِرْقة القَنابِلِ (فِرْقة داخِلَ الشُّرْطةِ لِنَزْعِ فَتيلِ القَنابِلِ)

bona fide /ˌbəʊnə ˈfʌɪdi/ *adj* 1 ‹*trader, member*› سَليم الطَوِيّةِ 2 ‹*contract, offer*› بِنِيّةٍ حَسَنةٍ

bonanza /bəˈnanzə/ *n* 1 (source of wealth) فَوْرة 2 (large amount) كَمِّيّة كَبيرة ;**a movie ~** كَمِّيّة كَبيرة من الأَفْلامِ

bond /bɒnd/ **A** *n* 1 (link) عُرْوة (عُرًى), آصِرة (أواصِرُ) 2 (Fin) (in loans) سَنَد دَيْنٍ 3 (union) تَماسُك ,تَرابُط ,الْتِصاق 4 (**bonds** *n pl*) (fml) (of servitude) أغْلال ,قُيود

B *vt* رَبَطَ ,أَلْصَقَ (i-u; رَبْط) ‹*a material, the surfaces*›; **to ~ one layer to the other** أَلْصَقَ طَبَقةً بِأُخْرى

C *vi* 1 «materials, surfaces» تَماسَكَ ,تَلاصَقَ ,تَرابَطَ 2 (in relationships) «people, friends» نَشَأَتْ أَواصِرُ الصَداقةِ بَيْنَهُمْ

bondage /ˈbɒndɪdʒ/ *n* 1 (liter) (slavery) عُبوديّة 2 (sexual practice) [رَبْط الشَريكِ الجِنْسيِّ أثناءَ الجِماعِ]

bonded warehouse /ˌbɒndɪd ˈwɛːhaʊs/ *n* مُسْتَوْدَع جُمْرُكيّ

bone /bəʊn/ **A** *n* (of humans, animals) عَظْم (عِظام), عَظْمة; (of a fish) حَسَك (n coll), شَوْكة; **to break every ~ in one's body** كَسَرَ كُلَّ عَظْمةٍ في جِسْمِهِ \ جَسَدِهِ; **chicken on/off the ~** دَجاج بالعَظْمِ \ مَنْزوع العَظْمِ

B (**bones**) *n pl* هَيْكَل عَظْميّ ,عِظام

C *vt* (Culin) نَزَعَ العِظامَ من ‹*a joint, chicken*›; نَزَعَ الحَسَكَ من ‹*a fish*›

(Idioms) **bone of contention** نُقْطة خِلافٍ; **close to the bone** في الصَميمِ; **to cut sth to the bone** خَفَّضَ شَيْئاً بِشَكْلٍ جِذْريٍّ \ إلى أَقَلِّ دَرَجةٍ مُمْكِنةٍ; **to make no bones about sth** لم يَتَرَدَّدْ في فِعْلِ \ قَوْلِ شَيْءٍ

(Phrasal verb) **bone up on**: **~ up on** [**sth**] (infml) دَرَسَ [شَيْئاً] بِتَمَعُّنٍ \ باجْتِهادٍ ‹*a subject*›

bone china *n* خَزَف عَظْميّ (خَزَف صينيّ مَصْنوع بِرَمادِ العِظامِ)

bone dry *adj* (*before n* **bone-dry**) ‹*well, tank*› جافّ تَماماً

bone idle *adj* (*before n* **bone-idle**) (infml) ‹*student, clerk*› كَسول جِدّاً

bonfire /ˈbɒnfʌɪə/ *n* [نار كَبيرة مُشْتَعِلة في الهَواءِ الطَلْقِ]

Bonfire Night *n* (BrE) [لَيْلة 5 نوفَمْبِر تُشْعَلُ فيها النارُ في الخارِجِ (كَتَقْليدٍ بَريطانيٍّ)]

bonnet /ˈbɒnɪt/ *n* 1 (headgear for a baby) [قُبَّعة صَغيرة تُشَدُّ بِشَريطٍ تحت الذَقْنِ]; (for a woman) قَلَنْسُوة (قَلانِسُ, قَلانيسُ) 2 (BrE) (of a car) كَبّوت ,غِطاء المُحَرِّكِ

bonus /ˈbəʊnəs/ *n* 1 (payment) إكْراميّة ,عِلاوة 2 (advantage) فائِدة (فَوائِدُ)

bony /ˈbəʊni/ *adj* (**bonier, boniest**) 1 ‹*teenager, hand*› جِلْد على عَظْمٍ 2 ‹*fish*› مَليء بالحَسَكِ

boo /buː/ **A** *excl* [صَيْحة مُباغَتةٍ]

B *n* [صَيْحة اسْتِهْجانٍ \ ازْدِراءٍ]

C *vt* (**boos, booing, booed**) [أَطْلَقَ صَيْحةَ اسْتِهْجانٍ ضِدَّ] ‹*a performer, speaker*›

D *vi* (*3rd person present sing* **boos**; *past tense, past participle* **booed**) «crowd, spectators» [أَطْلَقَ صَيْحةَ اسْتِهْجانٍ]

boob /buːb/ **A** *n* 1 (infml) (breast) صَدْر (صُدور) 2 (BrE infml) (mistake) حَماقة 3 (AmE infml) (idiot) أَحْمَق (dipt; حُمْق ;f حَمْقى)

B *vi* (BrE) ارْتَكَبَ حَماقةً; **someone's ~ed by not sending this out in BCC** ارْتَكَبَ أَحَدُهُمْ حَماقةً بِعَدَمِ إرْسالِ هذا على شَكْلِ نُسْخةٍ كَرْبونيّةٍ مَخْفيّةٍ

boob tube *n* (AmE infml) تِلِفِزْيون (تِلِفِزْيونات)

booby /ˈbuːbi/ *n* (old use infml) أَبْلَه (dipt)

booby prize *n* [جائِزة تُمْنَحُ لِمَنْ حَلَّ أخيراً في مُسابَقةٍ]

booby trap **A** *n* 1 (Mil) فَخّ مُتَفَجِّر 2 (practical joke) [خُدْعة بِهَدَفِ المُزاحِ]

B *vt* (**booby-trap, -pp-**) 1 (Mil) فَخَّخَ ‹*a building, car*› 2 (as a joke) [نَصَبَ فَخًّا في \ على] ‹*a door, chair*›

booing /ˈbuːɪŋ/ *n* إطْلاق صَيْحة اسْتِهْجانٍ

book /bʊk/ **A** *n* 1 (publication) كِتاب (كُتُب); **a history ~** كِتاب تاريخٍ 2 (part of a larger work) جُزْء (أَجْزاء)

3 (exercise book) دَفْتَر (دَفاتِرُ) **4** (of tickets, vouchers, stamps) دَفْتَر (دَفاتِرُ); **a ~ of matches** عُلْبة ثِقابٍ رَقيقة **5** (infml) (directory) دَليل الهاتِف **6** (infml) (rulebook) **to do things by the ~** [قامَ بالأَشْياءِ حَرْفيًّا وَفْقاً للقَوانينِ \ للإِرْشاداتِ] **7** (in betting) **to keep a ~ on sth** [قَيَّدَ \ سَجَّلَ شَيْئاً في سِجِّلِ الرِهانِ]

B **(books)** *n pl* **1** (accounts) دَفاتِر حِساباتٍ; **to keep the ~s** مَسَكَ الدَفاتِرَ **2** (records) سِجِلّات; **to be on the ~s of a club/an organization** كانَ مُسَجَّلاً في سِجِلّاتِ نادٍ \ مُؤَسَّسةٍ

C *vt* **1** (to reserve) حَجَزَ (i-u; حَجْز) ‹*a table, ticket, holiday*›; **to ~ a flight/table for sb** حَجَزَ رِحْلةَ طَيَرانٍ \ طاوِلةً لِشَخْصٍ; **to ~ sb into a hotel** حَجَزَ غُرْفةً في فُنْدُقٍ لِشَخْصٍ; **the hotel was fully ~ed** كانَ الفُنْدُقُ مَحْجوزاً بِكامِلِهِ **2** (to charge) قَيَّدَ البَياناتِ (لِيُفْتَحَ لَهُ مَحْضَرُ ضَبْطٍ) ‹*an offender*›; غَرَّمَ ‹*a driver*›; **he was ~ed for speeding** عوقِبَ بِغَرامةٍ للإِفْراطِ في السُرْعةِ **3** (BrE) «referee» (أَعْطى بِطاقةً صَفْراءَ) ‹*a player*›

D *vi* حَجَزَ (i-u; حَجْز)

Idioms **to be able to read sb like a book** عَرَفَ شَخْصاً مَعْرِفةً تامّةً; **to be in sb's bad/good books** كانَ مَكْروهاً \ ذا حُظْوةٍ عِندَ شَخْصٍ; **to throw the book at sb** (to reprimand) وَبَّخَ \ أَنَّبَ شَخْصاً ‹*an employee*›; (for a crime) [أَعْطى شَخْصاً أَقْصى عُقوبةٍ] ‹*a criminal, suspect*›

Phrasal verbs **book in** (BrE) (at a hotel) سَجَّلَ اسْمَهُ
• **book up**: **~ [sth] up, ~ up [sth]** حَجَزَ [شَيْئاً] ‹*rooms, seats*›; **to be ~ed up** «hotels, restaurants» كانَ مَحْجوزاً بِكامِلِهِ; «performers» [كانَ جَدْوَلُ حَفَلاتِهِ مَليئاً تَماماً]; «doctors» [كانَتْ كُلُّ مَواعيدِهِ مَحْجوزةً]

bookcase /ˈbʊkkeɪs/ *n* خِزانة كُتُبٍ

book club *n* نادي \ مَجْموعة قِراءةٍ

bookend /ˈbʊkɛnd/ *n* مِسْنَد للكُتُبِ

booking /ˈbʊkɪŋ/ *n* **1** (reservation) حَجْز; **to make a ~** قامَ بِحَجْزٍ **2** (for a performance) حَجْز

booking clerk *n* (BrE) مُوَظَّف حَجْزِ تَذاكِرَ

booking fee *n* (BrE) رَسْم حَجْزٍ

booking form *n* (BrE) نَموذَج الحَجْزِ

booking office *n* (BrE) مَكْتَب حَجْزِ تَذاكِرَ

bookkeeper /ˈbʊkiːpə/ *n* كاتِب \ ماسِك حِساباتٍ; **he's not an accountant, he's just a ~** لَيْسَ مُحاسِباً، بَلْ مُجَرَّدُ ماسِكِ حِساباتٍ

bookkeeping /ˈbʊkiːpɪŋ/ *n* مَسْك الدَفاتِرِ

booklet /ˈbʊklɪt/ *n* كُتَيِّب (كُتَيِّبات)

book list *n* قائِمة كُتُبٍ

bookmaker /ˈbʊkmeɪkə/ *n* وَكيل المُراهَناتِ

bookmark /ˈbʊkmɑːk/ **A** *n* **1** (for books) مُؤَشِّر صَفْحةٍ **2** (for web sites) إِشارة مَرْجِعيّة

B *vt* وَضَعَ إِشارةً مَرْجِعيّةً على ‹*a web page, site*›

bookseller /ˈbʊksɛlə/ *n* بائِع كُتُبٍ

bookshelf /ˈbʊkʃɛlf/ *n* (*pl* **bookshelves**) رَفّ كُتُبٍ

bookshop /ˈbʊkʃɒp/ (BrE), **book store** (AmE) *n* مَكْتَبة \ مَحَلّ لِبَيْعِ الكُتُبِ

book token *n* (BrE) [وَرَقة بِقيمةٍ مُعَيَّنةٍ لِشِراءِ كُتُبٍ]

book value *n* قيمة دَفْتَرِيّة \ مُحاسَبيّة

bookworm /ˈbʊkwəːm/ *n* قارِئ نَهِم

boom /buːm/ **A** *n* **1** (sound of cannon, thunder) قَصْف, دَوِيّ; (of drums) دَرْداب; (of waves) هَدير **2** (period of prosperity) اِنْتِعاش (اِنْتِعاشات), اِزْدِهار (اِزْدِهارات); **the property/export ~** اِنْتِعاشُ العَقارِ \ الصادِراتِ; **a ~ in demand/oil prices** زِيادة في الطَلَبِ \ أَسْعارِ النَفْطِ **3** (increase in popularity) زِيادة \ نُموّ الشَعْبيّةِ; **a ~ in outdoor activities** رَواج للأَنْشِطةِ في الهَواءِ الطَلْقِ **4** (in sailing) عارِضة الصاري (عَمود أُفُقيّ لِرَبْطِ رَأْسِ الشِراعِ) **5** (barrier) حاجِز أَمْواجٍ طافٍ **6** (on cranes) ذِراع رافِعةٍ **7** (for a microphone) ذِراع تَطْويلِ الميكْروفون

B *vi* **1** (to make a noise) «cannons» دَوّى; «thunder» قَصَفَ (i; قَصْف), لَعْلَعَ; «voice» صاتَ (a-u; صَوْت); «drum» دَقَّ (u; دَقّ); «waves» هَدَرَ (i; هَدْر, هَدير) **2** (to prosper) «economy, trade, sales» اِزْدَهَرَ; **business is ~ing** تَشْهَدُ الحَرَكةُ التِجارِيّةُ اِزْدِهاراً **3** «hobbies, sports» راجَ (u; رَواج)

Phrasal verb **boom out**: **~ out** «music, voice, salute» لَعْلَعَ (i; لَعْلَعة)

boomerang /ˈbuːməraŋ/ *n* بومِرَنْج (عَصاً مَعْقوفة تَرْتَدُّ إلى رامِيها)

booming /ˈbuːmɪŋ/ *adj* **1** (loud) ‹*voice*› جَهْوَرِيّ; ‹*laugh*› مُدَوٍّ **2** (flourishing) ‹*economy, industry*› مُزْدَهِر

boom town *n* [مَدينة شَهِدَتْ نُموًّا وازْدِهاراً سَريعاً]

boon /buːn/ *n* نِعْمة

boost /buːst/ **A** *vt* عَزَّزَ ‹*sales, morale*›; **oil revenues ~ed the economy** عَزَّزَتْ وارِداتُ النَفْطِ الاقْتِصادَ **B** *n* دَفْعة (دَفَعات); **to give sth/sb a ~** أَعْطى شَيْئاً \ شَخْصاً دَفْعةً

booster /ˈbuːstə/ *n* 1 (Tech) جِهاز تَقْوِيةٍ, مُعَزِّز (مُعَزِّزات) 2 (Med) جُرْعة مُعَزِّزة

boot /buːt/ **A** *n* 1 (footwear for daily use) حِذاء طَويل; (for a workman, soldier) بوط; **ankle ~s** حِذاء الكاحِلِ; **climbing/hiking ~s** حِذاء تَسَلُّقٍ \ مَشْيٍ لِمَسافاتٍ طَويلةٍ; **football/rugby ~s** (BrE) حِذاء كُرةِ القَدَمِ \ الرِجْبي 2 (BrE) (of a car) صُنْدوق السَيّارة 3 (infml) (dismissal) إقالة; **to give sb the ~** أَقالَ شَخْصاً 4 (infml) (kick) **to give sb a ~ up the backside/in the head** رَكَلَ شَخْصاً على المُؤَخِّرة \ في الرَأْسِ 5 (AmE) (immobilizer) مِشْبَك (للسَيّاراتِ المُخالِفةِ) 6 (AmE infml) (recruit) مُجَنَّد في القوّاتِ البَحْريّةِ

B *vt* 1 (infml) (to kick) رَكَلَ (u; رَكْل), رَفَسَ (i-u; رَفْس) ‹*the ball*› 2 ▸ **boot up**

(Idiom) **... to boot** ...؛ وَفَوْقَ ذلكَ; **and, he got a bonus to ~** وَتَحَصَّلَ فوق ذلك على عِلاوةٍ

(Phrasal verbs) **boot out**: **~ [sb] out, ~ out [sb]** (infml) طَرَدَ [شَخْصاً] ‹*a guest, an intruder*›; **he was ~ed out at the election** أُقْصِيَ من الانْتِخاباتِ
• **boot up**: **~ [sth] up, ~ up [sth]** شَغَّلَ [شَيْئاً] ‹*a computer, system*›

boot camp *n* (AmE) 1 (for recruits) مُعَسْكَر \ مَرْكَز تَدْريبٍ 2 (for offenders) مَعْهَد إصْلاحِ الأَحْداثِ عَسْكَرِيٌّ

booth /buːð/ *n* 1 (for voting) حُجْرة تَصْويتٍ; (in a restaurant) [طاوِلة بين مَقْعَدَيْن طَويلَيْن مُتَقابِلَيْن]; **a telephone ~** حُجْرة \ كابينة هاتِفٍ عُموميٍّ; **a photo ~** حُجْرة تَصْويرٍ 2 (at a fair, market) ظُلّة (ظُلَل), كُشْك (أَكْشاك)

bootlace /ˈbuːtleɪs/ *n* رِباط جَزْمةٍ

bootstrap /ˈbuːtstrap/ *n* جِلْدة \ عُرْوة خَلْفَ حِذاءٍ طَويلٍ [تُساعِدُ على ارْتِدائِهِ]

(Idiom) **to pull oneself up by one's bootstraps** بَنى نَفْسَهُ بِنَفْسِهِ

booty /ˈbuːti/ *n* غَنيمة (غَنائِمُ)

booze /buːz/ *n* (infml) مَشْروبات كُحوليّة

border /ˈbɔːdə/ **A** *n* 1 (frontier) حَدّ (حُدود) 2 (edge) حافّة, حاشِية (حَواشٍ), طَرَف (أَطْراف) 3 (in a garden) [قِطْعة أَرْضٍ على حافّةِ الحَديقةِ تُزْرَعُ فيها الوُرودُ]

B *vt* 1 تاخَمَ, حَدَّ (u; حَدّ) ‹*a country*› 2 تاخَمَ, جاوَرَ ‹*a lake, forest*›

(Phrasal verb) **border on**: **~ on [sth]** 1 لامَسَ, تاخَمَ [شَيْئاً] ‹*a country, land*› 2 (to verge on) بَلَغَ حَدَّ [شَيْءٍ] ‹*rudeness, madness*›

border dispute *n* نِزاع على الحُدودِ

borderline /ˈbɔːdəlaɪn/ *n* خطّ فاصِل; **the ~ between reality and fantasy** الخطّ الفاصِل بين الحَقيقةِ والخيالِ

borderline case *n* [قَضيّة لا يُمْكِنُ تَحْديدُها بِدِقّةٍ]

borderline personality disorder *n* اضْطِراب الشَخْصيّةِ الحَدّيّةِ

bore¹ /bɔː/ **A** *past tense* ▸ **bear**
B *vt* 1 أَضْجَرَ, أَمَلَّ ‹*an audience, readers*› 2 حَفَرَ (i; حَفْر) ‹*a well, tunnel*›
C *n* (of a gun barrel) تَجْويف (تَجاويف)

bore² /bɔː/ *n* 1 (person) شَخْص مُمِلّ 2 (situation, task) مَصْدَر إزْعاجٍ; **what a ~!** يا لَلْمَلَلِ!

bored /bɔːd/ *adj* ‹*children*› ضَجِر, يَشْعُرُ بِمَلَلٍ ‹*expression*› مَلّ \ ضَجِرَ (من شَيْءٍ); **to be ~ (with sth)** المَلَل, الضَجَر; **to get ~ (with sth)** أُصيبَ بالمَلَلِ \ بالضَجَرِ (من شَيْءٍ)

boredom /ˈbɔːdəm/ *n* ضَجَر, مَلَل

borehole /ˈbɔːhəʊl/ *n* ثُقْب \ بِئْر الحَفْرِ

boring /ˈbɔːrɪŋ/ *adj* ‹*person, job*› مُمِلّ

born /bɔːn/ *adj* 1 **to be ~** وُلِدَ 2 (innate) **a ~ salesman/entertainer/optimist** بائِع \ مُسَلٍّ \ مُتَفائِل بالفِطْرةِ

born-again /ˌbɔːnəˈgeɪn/ *adj* مُتَجَدِّد \ يُجَدِّدُ العَهْدَ مع اليَسوعِ; **she's a ~ Christian** هي مَسيحيّةٌ مُتَجَدِّدةٌ (المَسيحيّةِ)

borne /bɔːn/ *past participle* ▸ **bear**

Borneo /ˈbɔːnɪəʊ/ *pr n* (جَزيرة) بورْنيو

borough /ˈbʌrə/ *n* 1 (in UK) مِنْطَقة إداريّة 2 (in US) بَلَديّة

borrow /ˈbɒrəʊ/ **A** *vt* اقْتَرَضَ, اسْتَدانَ, اسْتَلَفَ ‹*money*›; اسْتَعارَ ‹*a book, word*›; اقْتَبَسَ ‹*an idea*›; **may I ~ your pen?** هل أَسْتَطيعُ أَنْ أَسْتَعيرَ قَلَمَكَ؟
B *vi* حَصَلَ على قَرْضٍ, اقْتَرَضَ; **we ~ed from the bank** حَصَلْنا على قَرْضٍ \ اقْتَرَضْنا من البَنْكِ; **to ~ at a high/low rate of interest** حَصَلَ على قَرْضٍ بِنِسْبَةِ فائِدةٍ عالِيةٍ \ مُنْخَفِضةٍ

borrower /ˈbɒrəʊə/ *n* **1** (from a bank) مُقْتَرِض **2** (from a library) مُسْتَعير

borrowing /ˈbɒrəʊɪŋ/ *n* اقْتِراض

Bosnia /ˈbɒznɪə/ *pr n* البوسْنة

Bosnian /ˈbɒznɪən/ *n, adj* بوسْنيّ

bosom /ˈbʊz(ə)m/ *n* **1** (of a woman) نَهْدانِ, صَدْر (صُدور) **2** (heart, centre) قَلْب; **in the ~ of one's family** في قَلْبِ عائِلَتِه

bosom buddy, bosom pal *n* (infml) صَديق حَميم

bosom friend *n* صَديق حَميم, خِلّ (أَخلال)

boss /bɒs/ *n* (infml) **1** (superior) رَئيس (رُؤَساءُ) **2** (of a company, factory) رَئيس (رُؤَساءُ) **3** (of a party, union, gang) رَئيس (رُؤَساءُ)

Phrasal verb **boss around, boss about** (BrE): **~ [sb] around** *or* **about** تَأَمَّرَ على [شَخْصٍ]

bossy /ˈbɒsi/ *adj* (**bossier, bossiest**) (infml) ‹*brother, wife*› مُتَأَمِّر

bosun /ˈbəʊs(ə)n/ *n* ▸ **boatswain**

botanical /bəˈtanɪk(ə)l/, **botanic** /bəˈtanɪk/ *adj* ‹*specimen, medicine*› نَباتيّ; **~ gardens** حَدائق نَباتاتٍ

botanist /ˈbɒt(ə)nɪst/ *n* نَباتيّ, عالِم نَباتٍ

botany /ˈbɒt(ə)ni/ *n* عِلْم النَباتِ

botch /bɒtʃ/ *vt* (infml) أَفْسَدَ ‹*an attempt, operation*›; **a ~ed job** عَمَل سَيِّء \ فاشِل

both /bəʊθ/ **A** *adj* كِلا (f كِلْتا); **on ~ sides of the road** على كِلا جانِبَيِ الطَريقِ
B *pron* كِلا (f كِلْتا); **~ of you are wrong** كِلاكُما على خَطَأٍ; **I saw them ~ last night** رَأَيْتُ كِلَيْهِما اللَيْلَةَ الماضِيةَ
C *conj* **~ here and abroad** سَواء هُنا أم في الخارِجِ

bother /ˈbɒðə/ **A** *vt* **1** (to upset) ضايَقَ, أَزْعَجَ; **don't let it ~ you** لا تَتْرُكِ الأَمْرَ يُزْعِجُكَ \ يُضايِقُكَ; **it ~s me that he hasn't phoned** يُزْعِجُني أَنَّهُ لم يَتَّصِلْ بَعْدُ **2** (to inconvenience) ضايَقَ, أَزْعَجَ; **stop ~ing me!** تَوَقَّفْ عن إِزْعاجي!; **I wasn't ~ed by the noise** لم يُضايِقْني الضَجيجُ; **to ~ sb with details/questions** أَزْعَجَ شَخْصاً بالتَفاصيلِ \ بالأَسْئِلةِ **3** (to hurt) آلَمَ (Form IV; imperf يُؤْلِمُ), أَوْجَعَ; **her knee is still ~ing her** ما زالَتْ رُكْبَتُها تُؤْلِمُها
B *vi* **1** (to trouble oneself) أَتْعَبَ, كَلَّفَ نَفْسَهُ العَناءَ \ المَشَقّةَ; **why ~?** لِمَ نَفْسَهُ; **please don't ~** لا تُتْعِبْ نَفْسَكَ من فَضْلِكَ; **I don't think I'll ~** لا أَظُنُّ أَنّي سأُكَلِّفُ نَفْسي التَعَبَ \ الانْزِعاجَ؟; **to ~ doing sth** *or* **to do sth** كَلَّفَ نَفْسَهُ عَناءَ فِعْلِ شَيْءٍ; **don't ~ turning up tomorrow** لا تُكَلِّفْ نَفْسَكَ عَناءَ الحُضورِ غَداً; **to ~ about details/rules** كَلَّفَ نَفْسَهُ مَشَقّةَ الاعْتِناءِ بالتَفاصيلِ \ بالقَواعِدِ; **he's not ~ed about money** لَيْسَ قَلِقاً بِخُصوصِ النُقودِ; **they couldn't even be ~ed to turn up!** لم يُكَلِّفوا أَنْفُسَهُمْ حتّى عَناءَ الحُضورِ! **2** (to worry) **to ~ about sth/sb** قَلِقَ بِشَأْنِ شَيْءٍ \ شَخْصٍ; **it's/he's not worth ~ing about** لا يَسْتَحِقُّ أَنْ نَقْلَقَ بِشَأْنِهِ
C (**bothered**) *adj* (concerned) **to be ~ed that ...** كانَ مُنْزَعِجاً \ مُتَضايِقاً بِسَبَبِ...
D *n* **1** (inconvenience) مُشْكِلة, إِزْعاج, انْزِعاج; **to do sth without any ~** فَعَلَ شَيْئاً دون أَيِّ انْزِعاجٍ; **it's too much ~** إِنَّهُ مُثيرٌ للمَتاعِبِ; **to go to the ~ of doing sth** كَلَّفَ نَفْسَهُ عَناءَ فِعْلِ شَيْءٍ; **it's no ~** لَيْسَ هُناكَ مُشْكِلةٌ **2** (BrE infml) (trouble) مُشْكِلة; **to be in a bit** *or* **spot of ~** كانَ عِنْدَهُ مُشْكِلةٌ صَغيرةٌ; **she's in a spot of ~ at work** عِنْدَها مُشْكِلةٌ صَغيرةٌ في العَمَلِ
E *excl* (infml) تَبّاً

Botox® /ˈbəʊtɒks/ *n* بوتاكْس

Botswana /bɒˈtswɑːnə/ *pr n* بوتْسْوانا

bottle /ˈbɒt(ə)l/ **A** *n* **1** (for drinks, perfume, medicine) قِنّينة (قَنانٍ), زُجاجة; **beer ~** قِنّينة جِعةٍ; **a ~ of beer** قِنّينة جِعةٍ \ من الجِعةِ **2** (for a baby) قِنّينة (قَنانٍ)
B *vt* **1** عَبَّأَ في زُجاجاتٍ ‹*water, wine*›; **~d water** ماء مُعَبَّأ في زُجاجاتٍ **2** (BrE) (to preserve) عَلَّبَ (في جَرّاتٍ زُجاجيّةٍ) ‹*fruit*›

(Phrasal verb) **bottle up:** ~ [sth] up, ~ up [sth] كَظَمَ [شَيْئاً] *‹anger›*; كَتَمَ [شَيْئاً] *‹emotions›*

bottle bank *n* [حاوِية لِرَمْيِ الزُجاجاتِ]

bottle-feed /'bɒt(ə)l,fiːd/ *vt* (*past tense, past participle* **-fed**) أَرْضَعَ حَليباً اصْطِناعِيّاً *‹a baby, lamb›*

bottleneck /'bɒt(ə)lnɛk/ *n* **1** (in a road) طَرِيق ,مُخْتَنَق مُرورِيّ ضَيِّق **2** (in a process) (تَضْييقات) تَضْييق

bottle-opener /'bɒt(ə)ləʊp(ə)nə/ *n* فَتّاحة زُجاجاتٍ

bottle top *n* غِطاء قارورةٍ \ قِنّينةٍ

bottom /'bɒtəm/ **A** *n* **1** (lowest part of a hill, page) أَسْفَل (dipt; أَسافِلُ); (of a bag, a hole, the sea) قاع (قيعان), قَعْر (قُعور); **to sink** *or* **go to the ~** غَرِقَ \ نَزَلَ إلى القاعِ; **from the ~ of my heart** مِن أَعْماقِ \ صَميمِ قَلْبي **2** (underside or lowest surface) قَعْر (قُعور); **the ~ of the boat/box** قَعْرُ القارِبِ \ الصُنْدوقِ; **the ~ has fallen out of the market** انْهارَ السوقُ **3** (in classifications) أَسْفَل (dipt; أَسافِلُ), أَدْنى; **to be** *or* **come ~ of the class/league** كانَ \ جاءَ في أَسْفَلِ تَرْتيبِ الفَصْلِ \ الرابِطةِ **4** (BrE) (far end) آخِر (dipt); **at the ~ of the garden** في آخِرِ الحَديقةِ **5** (cause, root) صَميم, جَوْهَر; **to get to the ~ of a mystery/matter** وَصَلَ إلى جَوْهَرِ لُغْزٍ \ مُشْكِلةٍ **6** (infml) (buttocks) مُؤَخَّرة
B (**bottoms**) *n pl* (infml) **pyjama/tracksuit ~s** سِرْوال بيجامةٍ \ بذْلةٍ رِياضيّةٍ
C *adj* **1** (lowest) *‹shelf, sheet, layer›* سُفْلِيّ **2** (last) *‹position, team›* أَخير; **to finish/be ~** انْتَهى بِهِ المَطافُ \ كانَ في المَرْتَبةِ الأَخيرةِ

(Phrasal verb) **bottom out** «prices, recession» بَلَغَ القاعَ \ الحَضيضَ

bottomless /'bɒtəmləs/ *adj* *‹hole, pool›* عَميق جِدّاً

bottom line *n* (**the bottom line**) مَرْبِط الفَرَسِ

botulism /'bɒtjʊlɪz(ə)m/ *n* بوتيوليزْم (تَسَمُّم غِذائِيّ)

bough /baʊ/ *n* غُصْن (غُصون, أَغْصان)

bought /bɔːt/ *past tense, past participle* ▸ **buy**

boulder /'bəʊldə/ *n* جُلْمود (صَخْرة كَبيرة مَلْساء)

boulevard /'buːləvɑːd/ *n* شارِع (شَوارِعُ)

bounce /baʊns/ **A** *vt* أَوْثَبَ *‹a ball›*
B *vi* **1** «ball, hailstones» ارْتَدَّ; «children» نَطَّ (u; نَطّ); **to ~ up and down on the bed/sofa** نَطَّ على السَريرِ \ الصوفا **2** (infml) «cheques» [أُعيدَ لِعَدَمِ كِفايةِ رَصيدٍ] **3** (infml) «e-mails» [ارْتَدَّ بِسَبَبِ خطأٍ في العُنْوانِ]
C *n* **1** (of a ball) ارْتِداد (ارْتِدادات) **2** [u] (of a mattress) مُرونة; (of hair) حَيَوِيّة

(Phrasal verb) **bounce back** تَعافى

bouncer /'baʊnsə/ *n* (infml) حارِس مَلْهًى لَيْلِيٍّ

bound /baʊnd/ **A** *past tense, past participle* ▸ **bind**
B *vi* «person, animal» قَفَزَ (i; قَفْز); **he ~ed up the stairs/into the room** قَفَزَ السَلالِمَ \ إلى الغُرْفةِ
C *vt* (to border) حَدَّ (u; حَدّ); **~ed by** يَحُدُّهُ
D *n* قَفْزة (قَفَزات); **with one ~** بِقَفْزةٍ واحِدةٍ
E (**bounds**) *n pl* حُدود; **to be out of ~s** كانَتْ مِنْطَقةً مَمْنوعةً; **her imagination/energy knows no ~s** لَيْسَ لِمُخَيِّلَتِها \ طاقَتِها حُدودٌ; **it is not beyond the ~s of possibility** لَيْسَ خارِجَ حُدودِ الإمْكانِ
F *adj* **1** (certain) مُحَتَّم, مُؤَكَّد; **it was ~ to happen** كانَ من المُؤَكَّدِ أَنْ يَحْدُثَ; **it's ~ to feel strange at first** المُؤَكَّدِ أَنْ يَنْتابَكَ شُعورٌ غَريبٌ في البِدايةِ **2** (obliged) مُلْزَم; **both sides agree to be ~ by the arbitrator's decision** اتَّفَقَ الطَرَفانِ على أَنْ يَكونا مُلْزَمَيْنِ بِقَرارِ المُحَكِّمِ; **to be ~ by law to do sth** كانَ مُلْزَماً بِموجِبِ القانونِ أَنْ يَفْعَلَ شَيْئاً **3** (heading to) **a flight/ship ~ for Hong Kong** رِحْلة جَوِّيّة \ سَفينة مُتَّجِهة إلى هونْغ كونْغ **4** *‹book›* مُجَلَّد
G (**-bound**); *in combination* **1** (heading) **to be London-/homeward-~** كانَ مُتَّجِهاً إلى لُنْدُن \ البَيْتِ **2** (made non-operational) مَشْلول; **a fog-~ airport** مَطار مَشْلول بالضَبابِ

boundary /'baʊnd(ə)ri/ *n* (*pl* **boundaries**) **1** (Geog) حَدّ (حُدود) **2** (limitation) حَدّ (حُدود)

bountiful /'baʊntɪfʊl/ *adj* *‹harvest, supply›* وَفير

bounty /'baʊnti/ *n* (*pl* **bounties**) **1** (reward) مُكافَأة (لِقَتْلِ \ لاعْتِقالِ شَخْصٍ) **2** (liter) (generosity) كَرَم, سَخاء

bounty hunter *n* صَيّاد المُكافَآتِ

bouquet /bʊ'keɪ/ *n* **1** (of flowers) باقة **2** (of a wine) رائِحة (رَوائِحُ)

bourbon /'bəːb(ə)n/ *n* البورْبون (شَراب)

bourgeois /ˈbʊəʒwɑː/ *adj* <*society, values*> بُرْجُوازِيّ

bourgeoisie /ˌbʊəʒwɑːˈziː/ *n* بُرْجُوازِيّة

bout /baʊt/ *n* **1** (of fever, depression, hiccups) نَوْبة (نَوْبات); **I had a ~ of flu** أُصِبْتُ بِنَوْبةِ إِنْفِلَوَنْزا **2** (in boxing) مُباراة مُلاكَمةٍ

boutique /buːˈtiːk/ *n* بوتيك

boutonnière /ˌbuːtɒnˈjɛː/ *n* [زَهْرة توضَع في عُرْوةِ بَدْلةٍ]

bow¹ /bəʊ/ *n* **1** (for arrows) قَوْس (أَقْواس) **2** (for stringed instruments) قَوْس (أَقْواس) **3** (knot) أُرْبة (أُرَب)

bow² /baʊ/ **A** *n* **1** (movement) اِنْحِناء; **to take a ~** اِنْحَنى **2** (of ships, yachts) جُؤْجُؤ (جَآجِئ)، مُقَدِّمة، قَيْدوم **3** (crew member) [مُجَدِّف في مُقَدِّمةِ قارِبِ تَجْديفٍ]

B *vt* **to ~ one's head** حَنى \ طَأْطَأَ رَأْسَهُ

C *vi* **1** (to show respect) «servants, performers» اِنْحَنى; **to ~ to sb/sth** اِنْحَنى لِشَخْصٍ \ لِشَيْءٍ **2** (fml) (to yield) **to ~ to pressure/higher authority** خَضَعَ \ اِسْتَسْلَمَ لِلضغْطِ \ لِلسُّلْطةِ العُلْيا; **to ~ to sb's demands/wishes** خَضَعَ لِطَلَباتِ \ لِرَغَباتِ شَخْصٍ

D (**bowed**) *adj* <*head*> مَحْنِيّ، مُنْحَنٍ

(Idiom) **to bow and scrape** أَذْعَنَ وَتَذَلَّلَ

(Phrasal verbs) **bow down**: **A** **1** (to prostrate oneself) **to ~ down before sb** اِنْحَنى أمامَ شَخْصٍ **2** (to submit) **to ~ down to sb** اِنْحَنى \ رَكَعَ لِشَخْصٍ **B** **~ [sb] down** أَحْنى ظَهْرَ [شَخْصٍ]; **grief ~ed him down in his latter years** أَحْنى الحُزْنُ ظَهْرَهُ في سَنَواتِهِ الأَخيرةِ

• **bow out** (to withdraw) «competitor, politician» اِنْسَحَبَ

bowel /ˈbaʊəl/ *n* **1** (intestine) مِعًى (أَمْعاء، أَمْعِية) **2** (**bowels** *n pl*) **the ~s of the earth/building** جَوْف الأَرْضِ \ المَبْنى

bowl /bəʊl/ **A** *n* **1** (for food) سُلْطانيّة; **a ~ of soup** سُلْطانيّة من الشُّرْبةِ **2** (for washing) طَشْت (طُشوت) **3** (contents) سُلْطانيّة **4** (of a lavatory) حَوْض (أَحْواض) **5** (in bowls) كُرة البولِينْغ

B *vi* (in cricket) قَذَفَ الكُرة

(Phrasal verb) **bowl over**: **~ [sb] over** **1** (to knock down) طَرَحَ [شَخْصاً] أَرْضاً **2** (to impress) <*an audience, visitors*> أَذْهَلَ \ غَمَرَ [شَخْصاً]

bow-legged /ˌbəʊˈlɛgɪd/ *adj* <*child, gait*> مُقَوَّس الساقَيْنِ، أَفْحَج (دِّيَّة؛ فُحْج)

bowler /ˈbəʊlə/ *n* **1** (in cricket) [رامي الكُرةِ في الكْرِيكِت] **2** (also **bowler hat**) [قُبَّعة سَوْداء كُرَوِيّة]

bowling /ˈbəʊlɪŋ/ *n* **1** (in covered alley) ▸ **tenpin bowling** **2** (on grass) ▸ **bowls**

bowling alley *n* مَلْعَب البولِينْغ

bowling green *n* مَلْعَب بولِينْغ العُشْبِ الأَخْضَرِ

bowls /bəʊlz/ *n sing* لُعْبة الكُرةِ الخَشَبيّةِ

bow tie *n* رَبْطة الفَراشةِ

box /bɒks/ **A** *n* **1** صُنْدوق (صَناديقُ)، عُلْبة (عُلَب); **a ~ of matches/chocolates** عُلْبة ثِقابٍ \ شوكولاتةٍ **2** (on forms, pages) مُرَبَّع (مُرَبَّعات)، إطار (إطارات، أُطُر); **tick** *or* (AmE) **check all the ~es that apply** ضَعْ عَلامةً في كُلِّ الإِطاراتِ المُناسِبةِ

3 (on screen) صُنْدوق (صَناديقُ); **close the dialogue ~** أَغْلِقْ صُنْدوقَ الحِوارِ **4** (for spectators) مَقْصورة (مَقاصيرُ، مَقْصورات) **5** (infml) (television) **the ~** التِّلْفَزة **6** (in soccer) [مِنْطَقة يَقِفُ فيها ضارِبُ]; (in baseball) مِنْطَقة \ مُرَبَّع الجَزاءِ

7 (Sport) (for protection) [حامي الأَعْضاءِ التَناسُليّةِ] الكُرةِ **8** (at a post office) صُنْدوق (صَناديقُ); **B ~ 618** الصُّنْدوق 618 **9** (blow) صَفْعة; **a ~ on the ears** صَفْعة على الأُذُنَيْنِ **10** (shrub) بَقْس

B *vt* **1** (to pack) عَلَّبَ <*products, fruit*>; **a ~ed set** مَجْموعة في عُلْبةٍ **2** «boxers» لاكَمَ <*an opponent*>

C *vi* «boxers» لاكَمَ; **he ~ed for his country** مَثَّل بَلَدَهُ في رِياضةِ المُلاكَمةِ

(Idiom) **to think outside the box** فَكَّرَ خارِجَ الصُّنْدوقِ

(Phrasal verb) **box in**: **~ in [sth/sb]**, **~ [sth/sb] in** قَيَّدَ [شَيْئاً \ شَخْصاً] <*a car, driver*>; **to feel ~ed in** شَعَرَ أَنَّهُ مُقَيَّدٌ \ مُحاصَرٌ

box cutter *n* (AmE) سِكّين قَطْعٍ

boxer /ˈbɒksə/ *n* **1** (fighter) مُلاكِم **2** (dog) بوكْسِر

boxer shorts *n* [سِرْوال رِجاليّ داخِليّ قَصير]

boxing /ˈbɒksɪŋ/ *n* مُلاكَمة

Boxing Day *n* (BrE) [اليَوْم الثاني من أَعْيادِ الميلادِ]

boxing gloves *n* قُفّازا مُلاكَمةٍ

boxing ring *n* حَلَبة مُلاكَمةٍ

box junction *n* (BrE) [مُلْتَقى طُرُقٍ فيهِ مِنْطَقةٌ لا يَجوزُ الوُقوفُ فيها]

box number *n* رَقْم صُنْدوقِ البَريد ,رَقْم بَريديّ

box office *n* [مَحَلّ بَيْع تَذاكِرَ للسِينِما \ للمَسْرَحِ]

boy /bɔɪ/ **A** *n* **1** (young male) وَلَد (أَوْلاد), صَبِيّ (صِبْيان ,صِبْيَة), فَتًى (فِتْيَة ,فِتْيان); **a ~'s bike** دَرّاجة أَوْلادٍ; **I've known him since he was a little ~** لَقَدْ عَرَفْتُهُ مُذْ كانَ وَلَداً صَغيراً; **a group of 30 ~s and girls** مَجْموعة من 30 وَلَداً وَبِنْتاً **2** (son) ابْن (بَنون ,أَبْناء) **3** (BrE infml) (man) فَتًى (فِتْيَة ,فِتْيان), وَلَد (أَوْلاد); **to be one of the ~s** كانَ واحِداً من الفِتْيانِ; **he plays golf with the ~s** يَلْعَبُ الجولْف مع الفِتْيانِ **4** (to a dog) **down ~!** اِضْطَجِعْ على الأَرْضِ!

B *excl* (infml) **~, this tastes good!** ما شاءَ اللهُ، هذا الطَعامُ لَذيذٌ!

(Idiom) **boys will be boys** الوَلَدُ وَلَدٌ وَلَوْ حَكَمَ بَلَداً

boy band *n* فِرْقة موسيقيّة (من الشَبابِ)

boycott /ˈbɔɪkɒt/ **A** *vt* قاطَعَ ‹*a product, country*›

B *n* مُقاطَعة

boyfriend /ˈbɔɪfrɛnd/ *n* خَليل ,رَفيق ,صَديق

boyish /ˈbɔɪɪʃ/ *adj* **1** (referring to a man) ‹*charm, grin*› صِبْيانيّ **2** (referring to a woman) ‹*looks, figure*› صِبْيانيّ

Boy Scout *n* فَتى كَشّافةٍ

bra /brɑː/ *n* حَمّالة صَدْرٍ ,سوتْيان

brace /breɪs/ **A** *n* **1** (for teeth) جِهاز تَقْويمِ الأَسْنانِ **2** (for the neck, a leg) دِعامة (دَعائِمُ ,دِعامات) **3** (for a wall) دِعامة (دَعائِم ,دِعامات)

B (**braces**) *n pl* (BrE) حَمّالات البَنْطَلونِ

C *vt* (**braces, bracing, braced**) قَوّى بِدِعامةٍ ,دَعَّمَ ‹*a wall, beam*›

D *v refl* **to ~ oneself** (for an impact) أَعَدَّ نَفْسَهُ; (for a shock) شَدَّدَ عَزيمَتَهُ

bracelet /ˈbreɪslɪt/ *n* سِوار (أَساوِرُ ,أَسْوِرة ,سور), أَساوِرة

bracing /ˈbreɪsɪŋ/ *adj* ‹*air, walk*› مُنْعِش

bracken /ˈbrak(ə)n/ *n* ديشار ,سَرْخَس

bracket /ˈbrakɪt/ **A** *n* **1** (P&P) (square) قَوْس مُرَبَّع; (BrE) (round) قَوْس (أَقْواس ,قِسيّ ,قُسيّ ,قِياس); **to put a word in ~s** وَضَعَ كَلِمةً بين قَوْسَيْنِ **2** (category) فِئة; **a higher/lower price ~** شَريحة سِعْرٍ أَعْلى \ أَقَلّ **3** (for a shelf) كَتيفة (كَتائِفُ), حامِل (f: حَوامِلُ), سِناد

B *vt* **1** (in square brackets) وَضَعَ بين قَوْسَيْنِ مُرَبَّعَيْنِ ‹*a phrase, word*›; (BrE) (in round brackets) وَضَعَ بين قَوْسَيْنِ **2** (also **bracket together**) (to categorize) صَنَّفَ

brackish /ˈbrakɪʃ/ *adj* **1** (of water) أُجاج **2** (of fish) [يَعيشُ في ماءٍ أُجاجٍ]

brag /brag/ *vi* (**-gg-**) تَبَجَّحَ ,تَفاخَرَ

braggart /ˈbragət/ *n* مُتَبَجِّح ,مُتَفاخِر ,مُتَباهٍ

braid /breɪd/ *n* **1** (in one's hair) ضَفيرة (ضَفائِرُ) **2** (of silk, cotton) قَصَب

brain /breɪn/ *n* **1** (Anat) مُخّ (أَدْمِغة) ,دِماغ (مِخَخة ,مِخاخ)

2 (**brains** *n pl*) (intelligence) ذَكاء ,نَباهة; **to have ~s** كانَ نَبيهاً **3** (**brains** *n sing*) (mastermind) العَقْل المُفَكِّر \ المُدَبِّر

brainchild /ˈbreɪntʃʌɪld/ *n* [من بَناتِ أَفْكارِ]

brain damage *n* تَلَف المُخِّ

brain-dead /ˈbreɪndɛd/ *adj* ‹*patient*› مَيِّت دِماغيًّا

brain drain *n* هِجْرة العُقولِ

brain surgeon *n* جَرّاح مُخٍّ

brain surgery *n* جِراحة مُخٍّ

brain-teaser /ˈbreɪntiːzə/ *n* (infml) لُغْز ,فَزّورة (أَلْغاز)

brainwash /ˈbreɪnwɒʃ/ *vt* غَسَلَ المُخَّ \ الدِماغَ ‹*the public, children*›

brainwashing /ˈbreɪnwɒʃɪŋ/ *n* غَسيل مُخٍّ

brainwave /ˈbreɪnweɪv/ *n* فِكْرة ذَكيّة

brainy /ˈbreɪni/ *adj* (**brainier, brainiest**) (infml) ‹*child, student*› ذَكيّ (أَذْكِياءُ)

braise /breɪz/ *vt* سَبَّكَ ‹*beef, cabbage*›

brake /breɪk/ **A** *n* فَرْمَلة (فَرامِلُ), مِكْبَح (مَكابِحُ); **to apply/put on the ~s** كَبَحَ

B *vi* «car, driver» فَرْمَلَ (i; فَرْمَلة), ضَغَطَ على الفَرامِلِ

brake drum *n* طَبْلة \ أُسْطوانة الفَرامِلِ

brake fluid *n* زَيْت الفَرامِلِ

brake light *n* ضَوْء الفَرامِلِ

brake pad *n* وِسادة \ لُقْمة الفَرامِلِ

brake shoe *n* حِذاء الفَرامِل

bramble /ˈbramb(ə)l/ *n* عَوْسَج, عُلَّيْق (شُجَيْرة شائِكة)

bran /bran/ *n* نُخالة

branch /brɑːn(t)ʃ/ *n* 1 (of a tree) غُصْن (أَفْرُع, فُروع) فَرْع (غُصون, أَغْصان); (of a road, railway) تَفَرُّع (تَفَرُّعات) 2 (of a store, bank) فَرْع (فُروع, أَفْرُع)

(Phrasal verbs) **branch off** «roads, pipes» تَشَعَّبَ, تَفَرَّعَ

• **branch out** «company, trader» وَسَّعَ نَشاطَهُ; **to ~ out on one's own** وَسَّعَ نَشاطَهُ مُعْتَمِداً على نَفْسِهِ

brand /brand/ **A** *n* 1 (product) ماركة 2 (type) صِنْف (أَصْناف, صُنوف)

B *vt* 1 وَسَمَ (i; سِمة, وَسْم) ‹*an animal*› 2 **to ~ sb as irresponsible/insane** وَصَمَ شَخْصاً بِعَدَمِ المَسْؤوليّةِ \ الجُنونِ

branded /ˈbrandɪd/ *adj* ‹*products, clothing*› [حامِل ماركة تِجاريّةٍ]

brandish /ˈbrandɪʃ/ *vt* لَوَّحَ (ب) ‹*a sword, stick*›

brand leader *n* سائِد في السوق

brand loyalty *n* الوَلاء لِلْمُنْتَجاتِ

brand name *n* علامة تِجاريّة

brand new *adj* ‹*car, shoes*› [جَديد جِدّاً]

brandy /ˈbrandi/ *n* (*pl* **brandies**) بْرانْدي (مَشْروب كُحوليّ)

brash /braʃ/ *adj* ‹*businessman, manner*› مُتَهَوِّر, مُتَعَجْرِف

brass /brɑːs/ *n* 1 (metal) نُحاس أَصْفَر 2 (Mus) (also **brass section**) [قِسْم الآلاتِ النُحاسيّةِ في فِرْقة موسيقيّة]

brass band *n* [فِرْقة تَعْزِفُ آلاتِ نَفْخٍ نُحاسيّةٍ دون غَيْرِها]

brassiere /ˈbrazɪə/ *n* (old use) حَمّالة صَدْر

brass knuckles *n* (AmE) قَبْضة حَديديّة \ أَمْريكيّة

brat /brat/ *n* (infml pej) طِفْل مُزْعِج \ مُدَلَّل

Bratislava /bratɪˈslɑːvə/ *pr n* بْراتيسْلافا

bravado /brəˈvɑːdəʊ/ *n* [تَظاهُر بالجُرْأة]

brave /breɪv/ **A** *adj* ‹*soldier, deed, attempt*› شُجاع (شُجْعان)

B *n* 1 (warrior) مُحارِب 2 (liter) + *pl v* **the ~** الشُجْعان

C *vt* واجَهَ بِشَجاعةٍ ‹*a storm, bad weather*›

(Idiom) **to put on a brave face** [تَظاهَرَ بِعَدَمِ الحُزْنِ]

bravely /ˈbreɪvli/ *adv* ‹*to fight, smile*› بِشَجاعةٍ

bravery /ˈbreɪv(ə)ri/ *n* شَجاعة

bravo /brɑːˈvəʊ/ *excl* أَحْسَنْتَ, برافو

brawl /brɔːl/ **A** *n* شِجار, عِراك

B *vi* «supporters, louts» تَشاجَرَ, تَعارَكَ

brawny /ˈbrɔːni/ *adj* (**brawnier, brawniest**) ‹*arms, man*› مَفْتول العَضَلاتِ

bray /breɪ/ *vi* 1 «donkeys» نَهَقَ (a; نَهْق, نُهاق, نَهيق)

2 «people» نَهَقَ (a; نَهْق, نُهاق, نَهيق)

brazen /ˈbreɪz(ə)n/ *adj* ‹*lie, disregard*› وَقِح; **a ~ attempt to rig the result** مُحاوَلة وَقِحة لِلتَلاعُبِ بالنَتيجةِ

brazier /ˈbreɪzɪə/ *n* مِجْمَرة

Brazil /brəˈzɪl/ *pr n* برازيل (f)

Brazilian /brəˈzɪlɪən/ *n, adj* برازيليّ

Brazil nut *n* جوز البَرازيل

breach /briːtʃ/ **A** *n* 1 (of a rule, contract, agreement) إِخْلال (إِخْلالات), انْتِهاك (انْتِهاكات), نَقْض 2 (in a wall, defence) صَدْع (صُدوع), ثُغْرة

B *vt* 1 أَخَلَّ (ب) (إِخْلال), نَقَضَ (u; نَقْض), نَكَثَ (i-u; نَكْث) ‹*a contract, an agreement*› 2 صَدَعَ (a; صَدْع) ‹*a defence, wall*›

(Idiom) **to step into the breach** تَوَلّى عَمَلٍ كَبَديل

breach of contract *n* إِخْلال بالعَقْدِ

breach of the peace *n* إِخْلال بالأَمْنِ

bread /brɛd/ *n* خُبْز; **white/brown ~** خُبْز أَبْيَض \ أَسْمَر; **wholemeal/rye ~** خُبْز كامِل الحَبّةِ \ شَيْلَم

bread and butter *n* 1 (Culin) خُبْز بالزُبْدةِ 2 (source of income) رِزْق, عَيْش (أَرْزاق)

bread bin *n* (BrE) صُنْدوق الخُبْزِ

breadboard /ˈbrɛdbɔːd/ *n* [لَوْحة يُقْطَعُ عَلَيْها الخُبْزُ]

bread box *n* (AmE) [صُنْدوق يُخَزَّنُ فيه الخُبْزُ]

breadcrumbs /ˈbrɛdkrʌms/ *n pl* 1 (in cooking) بُقْصُمات

2 (fragments) فُتات الخُبْزِ

breadline /ˈbrɛdlʌɪn/ *n* **to be on the ~** [كانَ في حالةٍ من الفَقْرِ المُدْقِعِ]

bread roll *n* [خُبْزة صَغيرة]

breadth /brɛdθ/ *n* 1 (width) اتِّساع, عَرْض (اتِّساعات); **a ~ of six centimetres** عَرْض سِتّةِ سَنْتيمِتْراتٍ; **to measure the ~ of**

the cloth قاسَ عَرْضَ القُماشِ **2** (of knowledge, experience) سَعة; **the ~ of his knowledge was amazing** كانَتْ سَعةُ عِلْمِهِ مُذْهِلةً

breadwinner /ˈbrɛdwɪnə/ *n* عائِل, كاسِب العَيْشِ

break /breɪk/ **A** *vt* (*past tense* **broke**; *past participle* **broken**) **1** (in pieces) كَسَرَ (i; كَسْر) ‹*a window, plate, toy*›; **he broke his leg/arm** كَسَرَ رِجْلَهُ \ ذِراعَهُ; **to ~ a bone/tooth** كَسَرَ عَظْماً \ سِنّاً; **to ~ sth in half/two** كَسَرَ شَيْئاً إلى نِصْفَيْنِ **2** (to make inoperative) أَفْسَدَ, خَرَّبَ, عَطَّلَ ‹*a machine, camera*› **3** (to rupture) مَزَّقَ ‹*a seal*›; **the skin is not broken** الجِلْدُ غَيْرُ مُمَزَّقٍ; **the river broke its banks** اخْتَرَقَ النَهْرُ ضَفَّتَيْهِ; **to ~ the box/door open** فَتَحَ الصُنْدوقَ \ البابَ بالقوّةِ \ عُنْوةً **4** (to interrupt) كَسَرَ (i; كَسْر) ‹*the monotony, routine*›; **we broke our journey in Milan** قَطَعْنا رِحْلَتَنا للاسْتِراحة في ميلانو; **to ~ sb's concentration** قَطَعَ على شَخْصٍ حَبْلَ تَفْكيرِه **5** قَطَعَ (a; قَطْع), فَصَلَ (i; فَصْل) ‹*a circuit*› **6** (to end) قَطَعَ (a; قَطْع) ‹*ties, links*›; أَنْهى ‹*a strike, the deadlock*›; **a cough broke the silence** قَطَعَتْ كُحّةٌ حَبْلَ الصَمْتِ; **to ~ a habit** قَطَعَ عادةً; **martial law was declared to ~ the strike** أُعْلِنَت الأَحْكامُ العُرْفيّةُ لِكَسْرِ الإضْرابِ **7** (to crush) دَمَّرَ, حَطَّمَ ‹*a person, sb's resistance*›; **to ~ sb's spirit** حَطَّمَ الروحَ المَعْنَويّةَ لِشَخْصٍ; **his captors' aim was to ~ him as soon as possible** كانَ هَدَفُ آسِريهِ تَدْميرُهُ في أَسْرَعِ وَقْتٍ مُمْكِنٍ **8** (to fail to observe) خالَفَ, خَرَقَ (i-u; خَرْق), انْتَهَكَ ‹*the law, rules, an agreement*›; **he broke his word** لم يَحْتَرِمْ كَلِمَتَهُ; **he broke his promise** لم يَفِ بِوَعْدِهِ; **I can't afford to ~ this appointment** لا أَسْتَطيعُ تَحَمُّلَ عواقِبَ التَغَيُّبِ عن هذا المَوْعِدِ; **you are ~ing the speed limit** أَنْتَ تَتَجاوَزُ السُرْعةَ القانونيّةَ **9** (to exceed) حَطَّمَ ‹*a record*›; **the movie broke all records for box-office sales** حطَّمَ الفيلْمُ كُلَّ الأَرْقامِ القِياسيّةِ في مَبيعاتِ شُبّاكِ التَذاكِرِ **10** (to make known) أَذاعَ, أَعْلَنَ ‹*a news story*›; **to ~ the news to sb** أَعْلَنَ الخَبَرَ لِشَخْصٍ **11** (to lessen the impact of) كَسَرَ (i; كَسْر) ‹*the wind*›; **she managed to ~ her fall** تَمَكَّنَتْ من أنْ تُخَفِّفَ من حِدّةِ السَقْطةِ **12** (to decipher) فَكَّ (u; فَكّ), حَلَّ (u; حَلّ) ‹*a code*› **13** (in tennis) **to ~ sb's serve** كَسَرَ إرْسالَ شَخْصٍ **14** (to tame) رَوَّضَ ‹*a horse*›

B *vi* (*past tense* **broke**; *past participle* **broken**) **1** (to be damaged) «window, branch, chair, bone» تَكَسَّرَ, انْكَسَرَ; **to ~ in two** انْكَسَرَ إلى نِصْفَيْنِ; **the sound of ~ing glass** صَوْتُ البِلَّوْرِ المَكْسورِ **2** (to stop working) «machine, controller» تَعَطَّلَ, تَوَقَّفَ عن العَمَلِ **3** (boy's voice) «voice» خَشُنَ (u; خُشونة) **4** (to change) «good weather» ساءَ (u; سوء); «bad weather» تَحَسَّنَ **5** (to separate) «clouds» تَبَدَّدَ, انْقَشَعَ **6** (on the shore, rocks) «waves» تَكَسَّرَ **7** (to begin) «storm» هَبَّ (u; هُبوب); **dawn/the day was ~ing** انْبَلَجَ الفَجْرُ \ النَهارُ **8** (to become known) «the news» انْتَشَرَ; «scandal» انْفَجَرَ **9** (to stop for a rest) «workers, participants» أَخَذَ اسْتِراحةً; **we'll ~ for coffee now** سَنَأْخُذُ اسْتِراحةً لِنَتَناوَلَ قَهْوةً الآنَ **10** (to discontinue) قَطَعَ (a; قَطْع) (مع); **to ~ with tradition/the past** قَطَعَ مع التَقاليدِ \ الماضي **11** (under interrogation) انْهارَ; **to ~ under torture** انْهارَ تحت التَعْذيبِ **12** (to escape) **to ~ free** *or* **loose** «person, animal» تَحَرَّرَ; **to ~ free from convention/the past** تَحَرَّرَ من الأَعْرافِ \ الماضي

C *n* **1** فَجْوة (فَجَوات), ثُغْرة (ثُغْرات); **a ~ in the clouds** ثُغْرة في الغُيومِ **2** (in circuits) انْقِطاع **3** (pause) اسْتِراحة; **a ~ in the conversation** اسْتِراحة أثناء الحَديثِ; **I worked without a ~ for four hours** عَمِلْتُ دون اسْتِراحةٍ لِأَرْبعِ ساعاتٍ; **to take a ~** أَخَذ اسْتِراحةً; **they had a three-point lead at the ~** كانوا مُتَقَدِّمينَ بِثلاثةِ نِقاطٍ عند الاسْتِراحةِ **4** (fracture) كَسْر (كُسور), انْكِسار **5** (radical change) قَطيعة; **a ~ with tradition** قَطيعة مع التَقاليدِ; **it's good to have a ~ from routine** من الجَيِّدِ أنْ نَأْخُذَ اسْتِراحةً من الروتين; **she finally made the ~** (from a relationship, job) قامَتْ أخيراً بالقَطيعةِ; **a ~ in the weather** تَغَيُّر في حالةِ الطَقْسِ **6** (on TV) اسْتِراحة **7** (holiday) إجازة, عُطْلة (عُطَل, عُطْلات); **the Christmas ~** إجازة عيدِ الميلادِ **8** (BrE) (at school) اسْتِراحة **9** (infml) (opportunity) انْطِلاقة; **her big ~ came in 2005** جاءَت انْطِلاقَتُها الحَقيقيّةُ سَنةَ 2005; **a lucky ~** ضَرْبة حَظٍّ **10** (infml) (escape) **to make a ~ for it** قامَ بالفِرارِ **11** (in tennis) (also **break of serve, service break**) كَسْر الإرْسالِ

Idioms **at the break of day** (liter) عند انْبِلاجِ الفَجْرِ; **to break even** تَساوَت الأَرْباحُ والتَكاليفُ; **give me a break!** (infml)

(leave me alone) أُتْرُكْني وَشَأْني!; (disagreeing, disbelieving) غَيْرُ مَعْقولٍ!

(Phrasal verbs) **break away** **1** (to escape) «person, animal» فَرَّ (i; فِرار, مَفَرّ) **2** (to become detached) «piece, continent» اِنْفَصَلَ **3** (to become independent) **to ~ away from sth** «faction, state» اِنْفَصَلَ عن شَيْءٍ

• **break down** **A** **1** (to stop working) «vehicle, machine» تَعَطَّلَ, تَوَقَّفَ عن العَمَلِ **2** (to fail) «marriage, talks, system» اِنْهارَ **3** (mentally) «person» اِنْهارَ **B** **~ [sth] down, ~ down [sth]** **1** (to destroy) حَطَّمَ \ دَمَّرَ [شَيْئاً] ‹a door, barrier›; قَضى على [شَيْءٍ] ‹the opposition› **2** (into components) حَلَّلَ \ فَكَّكَ [شَيْئاً] ‹protein, food› **3** (to analyse) حَلَّلَ [شَيْئاً] ‹the numbers, data›

• **break in** **A** **1** (to enter forcibly) «thieves, intruders» دَخَلَ عُنْوةً **2** (to interrupt) «voice, person» قاطَعَ **B** **~ [sth] in** **1** رَوَّضَ \ دَجَّنَ [شَيْئاً] ‹a horse› **2** لَيَّنَ [شَيْئاً] ‹shoes, boots› **C** **~ [sb] in** عَوَّدَ [شَخْصاً] ‹a new recruit›

• **break into**: **~ into [sth]** **1** (to enter by force) اِقْتَحَمَ [شَيْئاً] ‹a building, an office›; **the car had been broken into** اُقْتُحِمَت السَيّارةُ **2** (to begin to do) **to ~ into song/a smile** بَدَأَ يُغَنّي \ يَبْتَسِمُ; **to ~ into tears/laughter** اِنْفَجَرَ بالبُكاءِ \ بالضَحْكِ; **to ~ into a run** بَدَأَ يَجْري **3** (to gain share in) حازَ على حِصّةٍ في [شَيْءٍ] ‹a market, region› **4** (to start to use) سَحَبَ من [شَيْءٍ] ‹one's savings›; فَكَّ [شَيْئاً] ‹a banknote›

• **break off** **A** **1** (to detach) «piece, handle» اِنْفَصَلَ **2** (to stop talking) «person» اِنْقَطَعَ عن الحَديثِ **B** **1** **~ off [sth], ~ [sth] off** (to detach sth) قَطَعَ \ فَصَلَ [شَيْئاً] ‹a piece, a branch› **2** **~ off [sth]** (to end) قَطَعَ \ أَنْهى [شَيْئاً] ‹an engagement, negotiations, contacts›; **the two countries broke off diplomatic relations** قَطَعَ البَلَدانِ العَلاقاتِ الدِبْلوماسيّةَ

• **break out** **1** (to start) «war, fire, violence» اِنْدَلَعَ; **to ~ out in a rash** أُصيبَ بِطَفْحٍ جِلْديٍّ; **to ~ out in a sweat** تَصَبَّبَ عَرَقاً **2** (to escape) «prisoner» فَرَّ (i; فِرار, مَفَرّ), هَرَبَ (u; هُروب); **to ~ out of prison** فَرَّ من السِجْنِ

• **break through** **A** «the sun» ظَهَرَ (a; ظُهور) **B** **~ through [sth]** اِخْتَرَقَ [شَيْئاً] ‹a barrier, wall, sb's defences›

• **break up** **A** **1** (to go to pieces) «ship, plane» تَحَطَّمَ **2** (to dissolve) «couple» اِنْفَصَلَ; «marriage, band» تَفَكَّكَ **3** (to disperse) «meeting, party» اِنْتَهى; **the clouds will ~ up in the afternoon** سَتَنْقَشِعُ السُحُبُ في المَساءِ **4** (BrE) (for holidays) «schools, children» دَخَلَ في عُطْلةٍ **B** **~ [sth] up, ~ up [sth]** **1** (to dismember) حَلَّ \ فَكَّكَ [شَيْئاً] ‹a company, monopoly› **2** (in relationships) دَمَّرَ [شَيْئاً] ‹a marriage, relationship›; فَكَّكَ [شَيْئاً] ‹a family› **3** فَرَّقَ [شَيْئاً] ‹a demonstration›; فَضَّ [شَيْئاً] ‹a fight›

breakable /ˈbreɪkəb(ə)l/ *adj* ‹object, material› قابِلٌ للكَسْرِ

breakage /ˈbreɪkɪdʒ/ *n* **1** [u] (breaking) كَسْر (كُسور) **2** (broken item) [شَيْء مَكْسور]

breakaway /ˈbreɪkəweɪ/ *n* اِنْشِقاق (اِنْشِقاقات)

breakaway republic *n* جُمْهوريّة مُنْشَقّة

breakdown /ˈbreɪkdaʊn/ *n* **1** (machine failure) عُطْل (أَعْطال), تَعَطُّل, تَوَقُّف عن العَمَلِ; **a mechanical/electrical ~** عُطْل ميكانيكيّ \ كَهْرَبائيّ **2** (collapse of discipline, a marriage) اِنْهيار (اِنْهيارات), فَشَل; **the disaster resulted in a complete ~ of law and order** أَدَّت الكارِثةُ إلى اِنْهيارٍ تامٍّ للقانونِ والنِظامِ **3** (mental collapse) اِنْهيار (اِنْهيارات); **to have a (nervous) ~** أُصيبَ بانْهيارٍ (عَصَبيٍّ) **4** (of figures, costs) بَيان تَفْصيليّ; **a ~ of the voters according to sex/age** كَشْف تَفْصيليّ للمُصَوِّتينَ على حَسَبِ أَجْناسِهِمْ \ أَعْمارِهِمْ **5** (into parts) اِنْحِلال, تَحَلُّل

breakdown recovery service *n* خِدْمة الإغاثةِ السَريعةِ (للمَرْكَباتِ)

breakdown truck *n* شاحِنة إغاثةٍ

breaker /ˈbreɪkə/ *n* [مَوْجة عالية تَتَكَسَّرُ على الشاطِئِ]

break-even point /breɪkˈiːv(ə)n ˌpɔɪnt/ *n* نُقْطة التَعادُلِ

breakfast /ˈbrɛkfəst/ *n* فُطور, إفْطار; **to have ~** تَناوَلَ الفُطورَ; **what did you have for ~?** ماذا تَناوَلْتَ في وَجْبةِ الإفْطارِ؟

breakfast television *n* بَرامِج الصَباحِ

break-in /ˈbreɪkɪn/ *n* اِقْتِحام

breaking and entering *n* سَرِقة, سَطْو على المَنازِلِ المَنازِلِ

breaking news *n* خَبَر عاجِل

breaking point *n* نُقْطة \ لَحْظة انْهِيارٍ

breakneck /ˈbreɪknɛk/ *adj* **to go at ~ speed** سارَ بِسُرْعةٍ خَطِيرةٍ

breakthrough /ˈbreɪkθruː/ *n* (discovery) اكْتِشاف (اكْتِشافات); (development) تَقَدُّم

break-up /ˈbreɪkʌp/ *n* (of an alliance) تَفَكُّك (تَفَكُّكات); (of a relationship) انْفِصال (انْفِصالات); (of a marriage) انْهِيار (انْهِيارات)

breakwater /ˈbreɪkwɔːtə/ *n* حاجِز \ كاسِر أَمْواجٍ

breast /brɛst/ *n* **1** (Anat) (of a woman) ثَدْي (أَثْداء), نَهْد (نُهود) **2** (chest) صَدْر (صُدور) **3** (of chicken, duck) صَدْر (صُدور)

breastbone /ˈbrɛs(t)bəʊn/ *n* عَظْم القَصِّ \ الصَّدْرِ

breastfeed /ˈbrɛs(t)fiːd/ **A** *vt* (*past tense, past participle* **breastfed**) أَرْضَعَ ‹*a baby, child*›
B *vi* (*past tense, past participle* **breastfed**) **1** «women, mothers» أَرْضَعَ **2** «babies» رَضَعَ (a-i; رَضْع, رَضاع, رَضاعة)

breast milk *n* لَبَن الأُمِّ

breaststroke /ˈbrɛs(t)strəʊk/ *n* سِباحة على الصَّدْرِ

breath /brɛθ/ *n* **1** [u] (air inhaled) نَفَس (أَنْفاس); **to gasp for ~** لَهَثَ (a; لَهْث, لُهاث); **to pause for ~** تَوَقَّفَ لِيَأْخُذَ نَفَساً; **to be out of ~** انْقَطَعَ نَفَسُهُ; **to get one's ~ back** اسْتَعادَ أَنْفاسَهُ; **to hold one's ~** حَبَسَ أَنْفاسَهُ **2** [u] (air exhaled) نَفَس (أَنْفاس); **I felt his warm ~ on my face** أَحْسَسْتُ بِنَفَسِهِ الدافِئِ على وَجْهي; **to have bad ~** كانَ عِنْدَهُ رائِحةُ فَمٍ كَرِيهةٌ **3** (act of breathing) تَنَفُّس; **she took a deep ~** أَخَذَتْ نَفَساً عَمِيقاً; **to go out for a ~ of fresh air** خَرَجَ لِيَأْخُذَ نَفَساً من الهَواءِ النَّقِيِّ; **in the same ~** في الآنِ نَفْسِهِ **4** (slight wind) نَسيم (نِسام, نَسائِمُ); **a ~ of air/wind** نَسيم هَواءٍ \ رِيحٍ

(Idioms) **a breath of fresh air** نَسْمة هَواءٍ مُنْعِشة; **to bring a ~ of fresh air to sth** أَضْفى روحاً جَدِيدةً على شَيْءٍ; **don't hold your breath!** (infml) لا تَتَفاءَلْ كَثِيراً!; **to take sb's breath away** خَطَفَ أَنْفاسَ شَخْصٍ; **under one's breath** بِصَوْتٍ خافِتٍ; **to mutter/curse under one's ~** تَمْتَمَ \ لَعَنَ بِصَوْتٍ خافِتٍ; **to waste one's breath** (infml) تَكَلَّمَ بِدونِ جَدْوى

breathalyse (BrE), **breathalyze** (AmE) /ˈbrɛθəlʌɪz/ *vt* حَلَّلَ [غازاتِ التَنَفُّسِ لِمَعْرِفةِ مُسْتَوى الكُحولِ] ‹*a driver*›

breathalyser (BrE), **Breathalyzer**® (AmE) /ˈbrɛθəlʌɪzə/ *n* [جِهاز قِياسِ نِسْبةِ الكُحولِ في النَّفَسِ]

breathe /briːð/ **A** *vt* **1** (to inhale) تَنَشَّقَ, تَنَفَّسَ ‹*air, fumes*› **2** (to exhale) نَفَثَ (i-u; نَفْث) ‹*smoke, germs*› **3** (to whisper) هَمَسَ (i; هَمْس); **don't ~ a word!** لا تَنْبِسْ بِبِنْتِ شَفةٍ!
B *vi* **1** «patients, singers» تَنَفَّسَ; **to ~ deeply/heavily** تَنَفَّسَ عَمِيقاً \ بِصُعوبةٍ **2** «wine» تَنَفَّسَ **3** «fabric» تَنَفَّسَ

(Idioms) **to breathe down sb's neck** (infml) (to follow closely) لازَمَ شَخْصاً مِثْلَ ظِلِّهِ; (to supervise closely) راقَبَ شَخْصاً عن كَثَبٍ; **to breathe new life into sth** بَعَثَ في شَيْءٍ حَياةً جَدِيدةً; **to breathe a sigh of relief** تَنَفَّسَ الصُعَداءَ

(Phrasal verbs) **breathe in A** «patients, singers» شَهَقَ (a; شَهِيق)
B ~ in [sth], ~ [sth] in «person» تَنَشَّقَ [شَيْئاً] ‹*air, fumes*›
• **breathe out A** «patients, singers» زَفَرَ (i; زَفِير) **B ~ out [sth], ~ [sth] out** نَفَثَ [شَيْئاً] ‹*air, smoke*›

breather /ˈbriːðə/ *n* اسْتِراحة قَصِيرة

breathing /ˈbriːðɪŋ/ *n* تَنَفُّس

breathing space *n* وَقْفة

breathless /ˈbrɛθləs/ *adj* **1** (out of breath) ‹*runner, climber*› لاهِث, مَقْطوع النَفَسِ **2** (excited) ‹*anticipation, whisper*› مَبْهور; **to be ~ with excitement** كادَ يَنْقَطِعُ نَفَسُهُ من الإثارةِ

breathtaking /ˈbrɛθteɪkɪŋ/ *adj* ‹*skill, scenery*› يَحْبِسُ الأَنْفاسَ; **you look ~** تَبْدِينَ فاتِنةً

breath test *n* [فَحْص نِسْبةِ الكُحولِ في النَّفَسِ]

bred /brɛd/ *past tense, past participle* ▸ **breed**

breed /briːd/ **A** *vt* (*past tense, past participle* **bred**) **1** «scientists, farmers» رَبّى ‹*animals*›; زَرَعَ (a; زَرْع) ‹*plants*› **2** (to lead to) وَلَّدَ ‹*resentment, violence*›
B *vi* (*past tense, past participle* **bred**) «animals, germs» تَناسَلَ
C *n* (of animals, plants) نَوْع (أَنْواع)

breeder /ˈbriːdə/ *n* مُرَبّي مَواشٍ

breeding /ˈbriːdɪŋ/ *n* **1** (reproduction) تَناسُل **2** (raising of animals) تَرْبِية; (of plants) زَرْع **3** (upbringing) تَرْبِية, نَشْأة

breeding ground *n* مَنْبَت (مَنابِتُ)

breeze /briːz/ **A** *n* نَسيم (نِسام, نَسائِمُ), نَسْمة
B *vi* **to ~ in/out** دَخَلَ \ خَرَجَ بِخِفّةٍ

breezy /ˈbriːzi/ *adj* (**breezier**, **breeziest**) 1 (windy) ‹*day, corner*› لَطيف, مُنْعِش 2 (cheerful) ‹*song, style*› مَرِح

brethren /ˈbrɛð(ə)n/ *n pl* إخْوان

brevity /ˈbrɛvɪti/ *n* قِصَر, اخْتِصار, إيجاز

brew /bruː/ **A** *vt* ‹*beer*› خَمَّرَ; ‹*tea, coffee*› حَضَّرَ, أَعَدَّ

B *vi* 1 «beer» تَخَمَّرَ; «tea, coffee» ثَقُلَ (u; ثِقْل) 2 «storm, trouble» ظَهَرَتْ بَوادِرُهُ

brewer /ˈbruːə/ *n* صانِع البيرةِ \ الجِعةِ

brewery /ˈbrʊəri/ *n* (*pl* **breweries**) مَصْنَع الجِعةِ

bribe /brʌɪb/ **A** *vt* رَشا (u; رَشْو) ‹*a witness, politician*›

B *n* رَشْوة (رُشًى)

bribery /ˈbrʌɪb(ə)ri/ *n* ارْتِشاء; **~ and corruption are rife here** الارْتِشاءُ والفَسادُ مُنْتَشِرانِ هُنا

bric-a-brac /ˈbrɪkəbrak/ *n* خُرْدَوات

brick /brɪk/ *n* طوب (n coll)

bricklayer /ˈbrɪkleɪə/ *n* بَنّاء (بالطوبِ \ بالآجُرِّ)

bridal /ˈbrʌɪd(ə)l/ *adj* ‹*gown, suite*› العَروسةِ

bride /brʌɪd/ *n* عَروس (f; عَرائِسُ), عَروسة (عَرائِسُ); **the ~ and groom** العَروس(ة) والعَريس

bridegroom /ˈbrʌɪdɡruːm, ˈbrʌɪdɡrʊm/ *n* عَريس (عِرْسان)

bridesmaid /ˈbrʌɪdzmeɪd/ *n* إشْبينة

bridge /brɪdʒ/ **A** *n* 1 (over a river, road) جِسْر (جُسور) 2 (link) جِسْر (جُسور, أَجْسُر) 3 (on a ship) بُرْج القِيادةِ 4 (of one's nose) قَصَبة 5 (on a guitar, violin) مُشْط 6 (for teeth) جِسْر 7 (game) بْريدْج

B *vt* 1 **to ~ a gap in** [**sth**] (in a conversation) سَدَّ ثُغْرةً في [شَيْءٍ]; (in a budget) سَدَّ فَجْوةً في [شَيْءٍ] 2 (to span) غَطّى ‹*two centuries, different periods*› فَتْرةً

bridging loan /ˈbrɪdʒɪŋ ˌləʊn/ *n* (BrE) قَرْض تَجْسيريّ \ مُؤَقَّت

bridle /ˈbrʌɪd(ə)l/ *n* لِجام (لُجُم, أَلْجِمة)

bridleway *n* [مَمَرّ لِراكِبِي الخَيْل]

brief /briːf/ **A** *adj* ‹*description, visit*› مُخْتَصَر; **in ~** باخْتِصارٍ

B *n* 1 (instructions) تَعْليمات 2 (responsibility) مَسْؤوليّة 3 (Law) دَعْوى (f; دَعاوٍ, دَعاوى)

C (**briefs**) *n pl* سِرْوال تَحْتيّ

D *vt* 1 (to instruct) أَعْطى تَعْليماتٍ لـ ‹*a designer, troops*› 2 (to inform) أَطْلَعَ ‹*a journalist, politician*› 3 (Law) أَطْلَعَ ‹*a barrister*›

briefcase /ˈbriːfkeɪs/ *n* حَقيبة وَثائِق

briefing /ˈbriːfɪŋ/ *n* 1 (for instructions) [اجْتِماع لِإصْدارِ أَوامِرَ] 2 (for information) [اجْتِماع لِتَقْديمِ مَعْلوماتٍ]; **a press/news ~** اجْتِماع صَحَفيّ

briefly /ˈbriːfli/ *adv* 1 (for a short time) ‹*to glance, visit*› لِمُدّةٍ قَصيرةٍ 2 (in a few words) ‹*to speak, explain*› باخْتِصارٍ 3 (in short) باخْتِصارٍ

brigade /brɪˈɡeɪd/ *n* لِواء (أَلْوِية, أَلْوِيات)

brigadier /brɪɡəˈdɪə/ *n* عَميد (عُمَداءُ)

bright /brʌɪt/ *adj* 1 (shining) ‹*light, star*› ساطِع; ‹*eyes*› لامِع 2 (full of light) ‹*room, day*› مُضيء; ‹*sky*› مُشْرِق 3 (vivid) ‹*red, colour*› فاقِع 4 (cheerful) ‹*personality*› مُبْتَهِج; ‹*conversation*› مُبْهِج; **to look on the ~ side** نَظَرَ إلى الجانِبِ المُشْرِقِ 5 (promising) ‹*future*› لامِع 6 (clever) ‹*student, child*› لامِع (لَوامِعُ); **whose ~ idea was that?** لِمَنْ هذه الفِكْرةُ اللامِعةُ؟

brighten /ˈbrʌɪt(ə)n/ **A** *vi* 1 (to become lighter) «weather» تَحَسَّنَ; «sky» أَشْرَقَ 2 (to become cheerful) «face, mood» ابْتَهَجَ 3 (to improve) «prospects, situation» تَحَسَّنَ

B *vt* 1 (to make lighter) أَضاءَ ‹*a room, the sky*› 2 (to make cheerful) أَبْهَجَ, أَسْعَدَ ‹*sb's day, life*›

Phrasal verb **brighten up** **A** **~ up** 1 (to become lighter) «weather, day» تَحَسَّنَ 2 (to become cheerful) «child, face» ابْتَهَجَ **B** **~ up** [**sth**], **~** [**sth**] **up** أَبْهَجَ [شَيْئاً] ‹*sb's day, life, a room*›

brightly /ˈbrʌɪtli/ *adv* 1 ‹*to shine, burn*› بِشَكْلٍ ساطِعٍ; **~ lit streets** شَوارِع مُضاءة بِإضاءةٍ ساطِعةٍ 2 ‹*to smile, say*› بِمَرَحٍ 3 (vividly) ‹*painted, coloured*› [بِأَلْوانٍ زاهِيةٍ]

brightness /ˈbrʌɪtnəs/ *n* 1 (of a light, the sun) سُطوع 2 (of a screen) لَمَعان 3 (vividness) زَهاء

bright spark *n* (BrE infml) شَخْص نَبيه

brill /brɪl/ **A** *n* (*pl* **brill**) (Zool) سَمَك البَريل

B *adj, excl* (BrE infml) = **brilliant** (infml) رائِع

brilliance /ˈbrɪlj(ə)ns/ *n* **1** (brightness) سُطوع, تَأَلُّق **2** (talent) أَلْمَعيّة

brilliant /ˈbrɪlj(ə)nt/ *adj* **1** (bright) ‹*sunshine, light*› مُشْرِق; ‹*colours, white*› زاهٍ **2** (talented) ‹*musician, scientist*› (لَوامِعُ) لامِع **3** (BrE infml) (fantastic) ‹*news, film*› رائع

brilliantly /ˈbrɪlɪəntli/ *adv* **1** (excellently) ‹*to play, perform*› بَتَأَلُّقٍ **2** (brightly) ‹*to shine*› بِشَكْلٍ ساطِعٍ; **~ coloured birds/clothes** طُيور \ مَلابِس زاهِية الأَلْوانِ

brim /brɪm/ **A** *n* **1** (of a hat) حَرْف (حُروف) **2** (of a glass, bowl) حَرْف (حُروف)

B *vi* **(-mm-)** **1** «eyes, glass» اِمْتَلأَ; **to ~ with tears/champagne** اِمْتَلأَ بالدُموعِ \ الشَمْبانيا **2** **to ~ with confidence/pride** اِمْتَلأَ بالثِقةِ \ الفَخْرِ

brine /braɪn/ *n* مَحْلول مِلْحيّ

bring /brɪŋ/ *vt* (*past tense, past participle* **brought**) **1** (to convey) ‹*a friend, news, supplies*› جَلَبَ (i-u; جَلْب), جاءَ (i; مَجيء ب), أَتى (i; إِتْيان ب); **to ~ sb a present, to ~ a present for sb** جَلَبَ هَدِيّةً لِشَخْصٍ; **is it all right if I ~ my son with me?** هل هُناكَ مانِعٌ أَنْ أُحْضِرَ وَلَدي مَعي؟; **cloud will spread, ~ing rain to the south** سَتَنْتَشِرُ السُحُبُ, جالِبةً الأَمْطارَ للجَنوبِ; **the game will be brought to you live** سَيَتِمُّ نَقْلُ المُباراةِ مُباشَرةً; **to ~ a child into the world** جاءَ بِطِفْلٍ إلى العالَمِ **2** (to lead, draw) ‹*a person*› أَحْضَرَ, أَتى (i; إِتْيان ب), جاءَ (i; مَجيء ب); **what ~s you here?** ما الّذي جاءَ \ أَتى بِكَ إلى هُنا؟; **the Games brought people to the city** جَلَبَت الأَلْعابُ الرِياضيّةُ النّاسَ إلى المَدينةِ; **that ~s me to the question of money** ذلك يَقودُني إلى مَسْأَلةِ النُقودِ; **her job ~s her into contact with young people** يَجْعَلُها عَمَلُها تَلْتَقي بالشَبابِ; **that ~s the total to 100** ذلك يَجْعَلُ المَجْموعَ يُساوي 100; **it brought tears to her eyes** جَعَلَ الدُموعَ تَنْهالُ من عَيْنَيْها, أَبْكاها; **to ~ sth into existence** أَوْجَدَ شَيْئاً; **to ~ oneself to do sth** أَكْرَهَ نَفْسَهُ على فِعْلِ شَيْءٍ **3** (to cause) ‹*peace, hope, destruction*› جَلَبَ (i-u; جَلْب); **his money did not ~ him happiness** لم تَجْلِبْ لَهُ أَمْوالُهُ السَعادةَ; **the case has brought him publicity** لَقَدْ جَلَبَتْ لَهُ القَضيّةُ دِعايةً **4** (Law) **to ~ a case/an action against sb** رَفَعَ قَضيّةً على شَخْصٍ; **to ~ sb to trial** قاضى شَخْصاً

(Phrasal verbs) **bring about**: **~ about [sth], ~ [sth] about** تَسَبَّبَ في [شَيْءٍ], أَحْدَثَ [شَيْئاً] ‹*change, peace*›

• **bring along**: **1** **~ along [sth], ~ [sth] along** جَلَبَ \ أَحْضَرَ [شَيْئاً] ‹*a camera, book*› **2** **~ along [sb], ~ [sb] along** جَلَبَ \ أَحْضَرَ [شَخْصاً] ‹*a friend, partner*›

• **bring back**: **~ back [sth], ~ [sth] back** **1** (to return with) جَلَبَ \ أَحْضَرَ مَعَهُ [شَيْئاً] ‹*a gift, purchase*›; **can you ~ me back some cigarettes?** هل تَسْتَطيعُ أَنْ تَجْلِبَ لي مَعَكَ بَعْضَ السَجائِرِ؟ **2** (to restore) أَعادَ [شَيْئاً] ‹*sb's sight, colour*›; **to ~ sb back to life** أَعادَ شَخْصاً إلى الحَياةِ **3** (to reintroduce) أَعادَ العَمَلَ ب [شَيْءٍ] ‹*a punishment, democracy*› **4** (to remind) أَعادَ [شَيْئاً] ‹*memories*›; **the photos brought back happy memories of childhood holidays** أَعادَت الصُوَرُ إلى الذاكِرةِ ذِكْرَياتٍ سَعيدةً من أَعْيادِ الطُفولةِ

• **bring down**: **~ down [sth], ~ [sth] down** **1** (to reduce) خَفَّضَ [شَيْئاً] ‹*prices, inflation, the temperature*› **2** (to cause to fall) أَسْقَطَ [شَيْئاً] ‹*a plane, player*› **3** (to eject) أَطاحَ ب [شَيْءٍ] ‹*a government, dictator*›

• **bring forward**: **~ forward [sth], ~ [sth] forward** **1** (to make sooner) قَدَّمَ [شَيْئاً] ‹*a date, an election*› **2** (to submit) طَرَحَ \ قَدَّمَ [شَيْئاً] ‹*a proposal, bill*›

• **bring in** **A** **~ in [sth]** جَلَبَ \ حَقَّقَ [شَيْئاً] ‹*£5 million, money*› **B** **~ in [sth], ~ [sth] in** **1** (to introduce) قَدَّمَ \ طَرَحَ [شَيْئاً] ‹*legislation*› **2** حَصَدَ \ جَمَعَ [شَيْئاً] ‹*the harvest*› **C** **~ in [sb], ~ [sb] in** **1** (to involve) جَلَبَ \ أَحْضَرَ [شَخْصاً] ‹*experts, consultants*› **2** (to call on) جَلَبَ [شَخْصاً] ‹*the police, reinforcements*› **3** (to a police station) أَحْضَرَ \ جَلَبَ [شَخْصاً] ‹*a suspect*›

• **bring off**: **~ off [sth], ~ [sth] off** حَقَّقَ \ أَنْجَزَ [شَيْئاً] ‹*deal*›

• **bring on** **A** **~ on [sth], ~ [sth] on** (to provoke) تَسَبَّبَ في [شَيْءٍ], جَلَبَ [شَيْئاً] ‹*an attack, a headache*› **B** **~ on [sb], ~ [sb] on** (in a game) أَدْخَلَ \ أَقْحَمَ [شَخْصاً] ‹*a substitute*›

• **bring out** **A** **~ out [sth], ~ [sth] out** **1** (to produce) أَصْدَرَ [شَيْئاً] ‹*a book*›; أَطْلَقَ [شَيْئاً] ‹*product*› **2** (to highlight) أَبْرَزَ \ أَظْهَرَ [شَيْئاً] ‹*the details, flavour*› **B** **~ out [sb], ~ [sb] out** (on strike) دَعا [شَخْصاً] إلى الإِضْرابِ ‹*workers*›

• **bring round**: ~ [sb] round **1** (to revive) أَنْعَشَ \ أَحْيا [شَخْصاً] *‹a patient, victim›* **2** (to convince) أَقْنَعَ [شَخْصاً]; **she brought him round to her way of thinking** أَقْنَعَتْهُ بِطَريقةِ تَفْكيرِها

• **bring together**: ~ **together** [sth/sb], ~ [sth/sb] **together** **1** (to assemble) جَمَعَ \ ضَمَّ [شَخْصاً \ شَيْئاً] *‹representatives, exhibits›* **2** (socially) جَمَعَ [شَخْصاً \ شَيْئاً] *‹a family, siblings›*

• **bring up** **A** ~ **up** [sth], ~ [sth] **up** **1** (to mention) أَثارَ [شَيْئاً] *‹a subject, question›* **2** (to vomit) تَقَيَّأَ [شَيْئاً] *‹food›* **B** ~ **up** [sb], ~ [sb] **up** رَبّى \ أَنْشَأَ [شَخْصاً] *‹a child›*; **to ~ sb up to do sth** رَبّى شَخْصاً على فِعْلِ شَيْءٍ; **she's been well/badly brought up** لَقَدْ تَرَبَّتْ تَرْبِيةً حَسَنةً \ سَيِّئةً; **he was brought up a Catholic** تَرَبّى تَرْبِيةً كاثوليكيّةً

brink /brɪŋk/ *n* **to be on the ~ of collapse/extinction/resigning** كانَ على وَشْكِ الانْهِيارِ \ الانْقِراضِ \ الاسْتِقالةِ

brisk /brɪsk/ *adj* **1** (quick) *‹walk, pace›* نَشيط ,سَريع **2** (lively) *‹business, trade›* رائِج **3** (efficient) *‹manner, salesman›* حادّ

bristle /ˈbrɪs(ə)l/ **A** *n* **1** (on an animal) هُلْب (n coll) **2** (on a person) [شَعْر قَصير خَشِن] ,شَعْر **3** (on a brush) ليف (أَلْياف ,شَعْر (شِعار ,شُعور ,أَشْعار)

B *vi* «hairs, fur» وَقَفَ (i; وُقوف ,وَقْف)

Britain /ˈbrɪt(ə)n/ *pr n* بَريطانِيا

British /ˈbrɪtɪʃ/ **A** *adj* *‹city, people›* بَريطانيّ

B *n pl* **the ~** البَريطانيّونَ

Britisher /ˈbrɪtɪʃə/ *n* (AmE) بَريطانيّ

British Isles *n pl* **(the British Isles)** الجُزُر البَريطانيّة

Briton /ˈbrɪt(ə)n/ *n* بَريطانيّ

brittle /ˈbrɪt(ə)l/ *adj* *‹bones, nails›* هَشّ

broach /brəʊtʃ/ *vt* طَرَحَ (a; طَرْح), أَثارَ *‹a subject, an issue›*

broad /brɔːd/ *adj* **1** (wide) *‹chest, back, valley›* واسِع ,عَريض; **he has ~ shoulders** لَهُ مَنْكِبانِ عَريضانِ; **the river is at its ~est here** يَبْلُغُ النَهْرُ أَقْصى اتِّساعِهِ هُنا **2** (wide) *‹smile, grin›* عَريض; **we were greeted with ~ smiles** حُيِّينا بابْتِساماتٍ رَحْب ,شاسِع ,واسِع **3** (extensive) *‹area, expanse›* عَريضة **4** (wide-ranging) *‹range, support, choice›* كَبير ,واسِع; **the choice is fairly ~** الاخْتِيارُ واسِعٌ إلى حَدٍّ كَبيرٍ **5** (general) *‹sense, outline, consensus›* عامّ; **in ~ terms** بِشَكْلٍ عامٍّ **6** (not subtle) **to drop a ~ hint** لَمَّحَ تَلْميحاً واضِحاً **7** (pronounced) *‹accent›* واضِح **8** (complete) **in ~ daylight** في وَضَحِ النَهارِ

B road *n* (BrE) [طَريق سَريع صَغير \ ثانَويّ]

broadband /ˈbrɔːdband/ **A** *n* نِطاق عَريض \ واسِع; **to have ~** كانَ عِنْدَهُ نِطاقٌ عَريضٌ

B *adj before n* *‹access, network›* عَريض \ واسِع النِطاق

broad-based /ˌbrɔːdˈbeɪst/ *adj* *‹approach, movement›* ذو قاعِدةٍ عَريضةٍ

broad bean *n* فول أَخْضَر

broadcast /ˈbrɔːdkɑːst/ **A** *n* إذاعة ,بَثّ

B *vt* (*past tense, past participle* **broadcast** or **broadcasted**) أَذاعَ *‹a programme, message›*

C *vi* (*past tense, past participle* **broadcast** or **broadcasted**) «radio stations, TV channels» بَثَّ (i-u; بَثّ)

broadcaster /ˈbrɔːdkɑːstə/ *n* مُذيع

broadcasting /ˈbrɔːdkɑːstɪŋ/ *n* إذاعة

broaden /ˈbrɔːd(ə)n/ **A** *vt* وَسَّعَ *‹one's horizons, understanding›*

B *vi* «rivers, smile» اتَّسَعَ

broadly /ˈbrɔːdli/ *adv* **1** (in general) *‹to correspond, agree›* بِشَكْلٍ \ بِصِفةٍ عامّ(ةٍ); **~ speaking** بِشَكْلٍ \ بِصِفةٍ عامّ(ةٍ) **2** *‹to grin, smile›* فاتِحاً فاهُ

broad-minded /brɔːdˈmʌɪndɪd/ *adj* *‹person, attitude›* مُنْفَتِح, واسِع الأُفُق

broadsheet /ˈbrɔːdʃiːt/ *n* [جَريدة \ صَحيفة ذات الحَجْم الكامِل]

brocade /brəˈkeɪd/ *n* بْروكار (قُماش حَريريّ مُزَرْكَش وَثَمين)

broccoli /ˈbrɒk(ə)li/ *n* قَرْنَبيط أَخْضَر ,بْروكْلي

brochure /ˈbrəʊʃə/ *n* كُتَيِّب (كُتَيِّبات)

brogue /brəʊg/ *n* **1** (shoe) [حِذاء رِجاليّ جِلْديّ] **2** (accent) [لَكْنة إقْليميّة لِمُتَحَدِّث الإنْجليزيّةِ]

broil /brɔɪl/ *vt* (AmE) شَوى (i; شَيّ) *‹meat, fish›*

broiler /ˈbrɔɪlə/ *n* **1** (chicken) فَرّوج (n coll; فَراريج) **2** (AmE) (grill) شَوّاية

broke /brəʊk/ **A** *past tense* ▸ **break**

B *adj* **to be ~** كانَ مُفْلِساً; **the system is ~** النِظامُ مُفْلِسٌ

broken /ˈbrəʊk(ə)n/ **A** *past participle* ▸ **break**
B *adj* **1** ‹*glass, leg, bone*› مَكْسور **2** (not working) ‹*radio, fridge*› مَكْسور ,مُعَطَّل **3** (beaten, exhausted) **a ~ man/woman** رَجُل مُحَطَّم \ امْرَأة مُحَطَّمة **4** (faltering) **in ~ English/French** بِلُغَةٍ إنْجليزيّةٍ \ فَرَنْسيّةٍ مَكْسورةٍ

broken-down /brəʊk(ə)nˈdaʊn/ *adj* **1** ‹*car, truck*› مُعَطَّل **2** ‹*house, wall*› مُتَهَدِّم

broken heart *n* قَلْب مَكْسور

broken-hearted /brəʊk(ə)nˈhɑːtɪd/ *adj* ‹*wife, fans*› مَكْسور القَلْبِ

broken home *n* أُسْرة مُفَكَّكة

broken marriage *n* زَواج فاشِل

broker /ˈbrəʊkə/ *n* سِمْسار (سَماسِرة ,سَماسِرُ ,سَماسيرُ) ,وَسيط (وُسَطاءُ); **commodity** *or* **commodities ~** سِمْسار سِلَعٍ

bronchiolitis /ˌbrɒŋkɪəˈlaɪtɪs/ *n* الْتِهاب الشُعَيْباتِ الهَوائيّةِ

bronchitis /brɒŋˈkaɪtɪs/ *n* الْتِهاب الشُعَبِ الهَوائيّة

bronchopneumonia /ˌbrɒŋkə(ʊ)njuːˈməʊnɪə/ *n* الْتِهاب رِئَويّ

bronze /brɒnz/ *n* **1** [u] (metal) بْرونْز **2** (Art) مَنْحوتة بْرونْزيّة **3** (Sport) (also **bronze medal**) ميدالِية بْرونْزيّة; **to win** *or* **take ~** *or* **a ~ medal** أَحْرَزَ الميداليَةَ البْرونْزيّةَ

brooch /brəʊtʃ/ *n* دَبّوس \ مِشْبَك صَدْرٍ ,بْروش

brood /bruːd/ **A** *n* (of animals) حُضْنة; (of children) صِغار
B *vi* **1** (to ponder over) «teenagers, prisoners» أَمْعَنَ التَفْكيرَ **2** «birds» حَضَنَ (u; حَضْن ,حِضانة)

brook /brʊk/ *n* جَدْوَل (جَداوِلُ) ,نُهَيْر (نُهَيْرات)

broom /bruːm/ *n* **1** (brush) مِكْنَسة (مَكانِسُ) ,مِقَشّة **2** (shrub) وَزّال

broomstick /ˈbruːmstɪk/ *n* يد \ عَصا مِكْنَسةٍ

broth /brɒθ/ *n* مَرَق ,حَساء (أَحْسِية) ,شُرْبة (شُرَب)

brothel /ˈbrɒθ(ə)l/ *n* بَيْت دَعارةٍ

brother /ˈbrʌðə/ *n* **1** (male sibling) أخ (إِخْوة) ,شَقيق (أَشِقّة ,أَشِقّاءُ); **my eldest/youngest ~** أَكْبَر \ أَصْغَر أَخٍ لي; **my elder ~** أَخي الأَكْبَر مِنّي **2** (friend, comrade) رَفيق (رُفَقاءُ ,رِفاق); **~s in arms** رُفَقاء سِلاحٍ **3** (monk, etc) أَخ (عُضْو في جَماعةٍ دينيّةٍ)

brotherhood /ˈbrʌðəhʊd/ *n* **1** (bond) أُخوّة **2** (group) أُخوّة, جَمْعيّة **3** (Rel_Chr) أَخَويّة

brother-in-law /ˈbrʌðərɪnlɔː/ *n* (*pl* **brothers-in-law**)
1 (sister's husband) زَوْج الأُخْتِ **2** (wife's brother) أَخو الزَوْجةِ; (husband's brother) أَخو الزَوْجِ **3** (wife's sister's husband) زَوْج أُخْتِ الزَوْجةِ; (husband's sister's husband) زَوْج أُخْتِ الزَوْجِ

brotherly /ˈbrʌðəli/ *adj* ‹*affection, feelings*› أَخَويّ

brought /brɔːt/ *past tense, past participle* ▸ **bring**

brow /braʊ/ *n* **1** (forehead) جَبين (جُبُن ,أَجْبِنة ,أَجْبُن) **2** (eyebrow) حاجِب (حَواجِب) **3** (of hill) حَرْف (حِرَف), حافة (حافات ,حَوافٍ)

browbeat /ˈbraʊbiːt/ (*past tense* **browbeat**, *past participle* **browbeaten**) *vt* خَوَّفَ ‹*a witness, worker*›

brown /braʊn/ **A** *adj* (**browner**, **brownest**) **1** ‹*shoes, leaves, paint, hair, eyes*› بُنّيّ; ‹*skin*› أَسْمَر (dipt; سُمْر); **light/dark ~** بُنّيّ \ اسْمَرّ فاتِح \ غامِق **2** (tanned) ‹*face, skin*› مُسْمَرّ; **to go** *or* **turn ~** اسْمَرَّ
B *n* (of an object, hair, eyes) بُنّيّ; (of skin) سُمْرة
C *vt* **1** (in cooking) حَمَّرَ ‹*meat, onions*› **2** (to tan) سَمَّرَ ‹*face, skin*›
D *vi* **1** (in cooking) «meat, potatoes» احْمَرَّ **2** (to tan) «face, skin» اسْمَرَّ

brown bread *n* خُبْز أَسْمَر

brownie /ˈbraʊni/ *n* **1** (cake) بْراوْني (كَعْكة الشُكولاتةِ والبُنْدُقِ) **2** (**Brownie**) (girl guide) فَتاة كَشّافةٍ

brown paper *n* وَرَق مُقَوّى

brown rice *n* رُزّ أَسْمَر

brown sugar *n* سُكَّر بُنّيّ

brown trout *n* سَلْمون مُرَقَّط

browse /braʊz/ **A** *vi* (in a shop) «shoppers, visitors» تَفَرَّجَ
B *vt* اسْتَعْرَضَ ,تَصَفَّحَ ‹*the Internet, a website*›
(Phrasal verb) **browse through**: **~ through [sth]** تَصَفَّحَ [شَيْئًا] ‹*a book, catalogue*›

browser /ˈbraʊzə/ *n* مُسْتَعْرِض ,مُتَصَفِّح

brucellosis /ˌbruːsəˈləʊsɪs/ *n* داء ,حُمّى مالْطيّة \ مُتَمَوِّجة البْروسيلاتِ

bruise /bruːz/ **A** *n* **1** (on skin) كَدْمة (كَدَمات) **2** (on fruit) عَطَب

B *vt* **1** (to damage a part of the body) كَدَمَ (i-u; كَدْم) ‹*a rib, leg*› **2** (to damage fruit) [تَسَبَّبَ في العَطَبِ] ‹*an apple, a peach*›

brunch /brʌn(t)ʃ/ *n* [وَجْبة صَباحيّة مُتَأَخِّرة تَحِلُّ مَحَلَّ وَجْبَتَي الفُطور والغَداءِ]

Brunei /bruːˈnʌɪ/ *pr n* بْروناي (f)

brunette /bruːˈnɛt/ *n* [امْرَأة ذات شَعْرٍ بُنّيٍّ غامِقٍ]

brunt /brʌnt/ *n* **to take the ~ of the storm/attack** تَحَمَّلَ العِبْءَ الأَكْبَرَ من العاصِفةِ \ المَعْرَكةِ

brush /brʌʃ/ **A** *n* **1** (for hair, clothes, shoes, pots, painting) فُرْشاة; (for floors) مِكْنَسة (مَكانِسُ) **2** (act of brushing) كَنْس; **to give one's hair a quick ~** مَشَّطَ شَعْرَهُ بِسُرْعةٍ **3** (encounter) مُواجَهة; **a ~ with death** مُواجَهة مع المَوْتِ; **to have a ~ with the law** كانَتْ لَدَيْهِ مَشاكِلُ مع السُّلْطةِ **4** (light touch) لَمْسة **5** (shrubs, undergrowth) أَجَم (n coll) **6** (fox's tail) [ذَيْل الثَّعْلَبِ]

B *vt* **1** (to sweep, clean) نَظَّفَ بِفُرْشاةٍ ‹*clothes, shoes*›; **to ~ one's hair** مَشَّطَ شَعْرَهُ; **to ~ one's teeth** فَرَّشَ أَسْنانَهُ **2** (with hands) كَنَّسَ ‹*the crumbs, dirt*›; رَفَعَ (a; رَفْع) ‹*one's hair*›; **she ~ed her hair out of her eyes** رَفَعَتْ شَعْرَها عن عَيْنَيْها **3** (to touch lightly) لَمَسَ بِرِفْقٍ ‹*sb's face, hand*› **4** (to apply liquid to) دَهَنَ بِفُرْشاةٍ ‹*the meat, pastry*›

C *vi* **to ~ against sth** لامَسَ شَيْئاً بِرِفْقٍ; **to ~ past sb** احْتَكَّ جَسَدُهُ بِجَسَدِ شَخْصٍ أثناء مُرورِهِ

D (**brushed**) *adj* **1** ‹*aluminium, steel*› [مَكْشوط] **2** ‹*cotton, denim*› ناعِم

(Phrasal verbs) **brush aside**: **~ aside [sth/sb], ~ [sth/sb] aside** تَجاهَلَ [شَيْئاً \ شَخْصاً] ‹*questions, criticism*›; **he ~ed his attacker aside** دَفَعَ المُعْتَدِيَ عَلَيْهِ جانِباً

• **brush away**: **~ away [sth], ~ [sth] away** مَسَحَ [شَيْئاً] ‹*tears*›; رَفَعَ [شَيْئاً] بِيَدِهِ ‹*one's hair*›

• **brush off**: **~ off [sth/sb], ~ [sth/sb] off** تَجاهَلَ [شَيْئاً \ شَخْصاً] ‹*questions, criticism*›

• **brush up** **A** **~ [sth] up** صَقَلَ [شَيْئاً] ‹*skills, knowledge*› **B** **to ~ up on sth** صَقَلَ شَيْئاً

brushwood /ˈbrʌʃwʊd/ *n* حَطَب (أَحْطاب)

brusque /brʊsk/ *adj* ‹*manner, tone*› فَظّ

Brussels /ˈbrʌs(ə)lz/ *pr n* بْروكْسِل (f)

Brussels sprout *n* كُرُنب بْروكْسِل

brutal /ˈbruːt(ə)l/ *adj* **1** ‹*murder, dictator*› وَحْشيّ **2** ‹*truth*› مُرّ; ‹*reply*› قاسٍ

brutality /brʊˈtalɪti/ *n* (*pl* **brutalities**) **1** [u] (quality) وَحْشيّة **2** (act) تَوَحُّش (تَوَحُّشات)

brutally /ˈbruːt(ə)li/ *adv* **1** ‹*to murder, beat*› بِوَحْشيّةٍ **2** **~ honest/frank** صَريح جِدًّا

brute /bruːt/ *n* **1** (man) وَحْش (وُحْشان, وُحوش) **2** (animal) وَحْش (وُحْشان, وُحوش)

brute force, **brute strength** *n* قوّة عَمْياء

BS /biːˈɛs/ *n* (degree) بَكالوريوس في العُلومِ; (degree holder) حاصِل على \ حامِل بَكالوريوس في العُلوم

BSc /biːɛsˈsiː/ *n* = **Bachelor of Science** (degree) بَكالوريوس في العُلوم; (degree holder) حاصِل على \ حامِل بَكالوريوس في العُلوم; **Mary Hughes, ~** ماري هيوز، بَكالوريوس في العُلومِ

BSE /biːɛsˈiː/ *n* = **Bovine Spongiform Encephalopathy** اعْتِلال الدِماغِ الإِسْفَنْجيّ البَقَريّ (مَرَض جُنونِ البَقَرِ)

BST /biːɛsˈtiː/ *n* = **British Summer Time** التَوْقيت الصَيْفيّ البَريطانيّ

bubble /ˈbʌb(ə)l/ **A** *n* **1** (of air, gas) فُقّاعة (فَقاقيعُ) **2** (Fin) فُقّاعة (فَقاقيعُ)

B *vi* **1** «liquids, lava» بَقْبَقَ (i; بَقْبَقة), فارَ (u; فَوْر, فَوَران) **2** «girls, students» **to ~ with enthusiasm/ideas** جاشَ بالحَماسةِ \ الأَفْكارِ

bubble bath *n* رَغْوة بانْيو

bubblegum /ˈbʌb(ə)lgʌm/ *n* عِلْك, لُبان (أَعْلاك, عُلوك)

bubble wrap *n* [غِلاف بْلاسْتيكيّ ذو فُقّاعاتٍ هَوائيّة]

bubbly /ˈbʌbli/ *adj* (**bubblier, bubbliest**) **1** ‹*personality, girl*› مَرِح (مَراحى, مَرْحى) **2** ‹*drink*› مَليء بالفَقاقيعِ

bubonic plague /bjuːbɒnɪk ˈpleɪg/ *n* طاعون دَبْليّ

Bucharest /ˌbuːkəˈrɛst/ *pr n* بوخارِسْت (f)

buck /bʌk/ **A** *n* **1** (AmE infml) (dollar) دولار أَمريكيّ **2** (male deer) ذَكَر الأَيِّلِ; (male rabbit, hare) ذَكَر الأَرْنَبِ

B *vi* «horses» [شَبَّ بِقَوائِمِهِ الأَرْبَعةِ في الهَواءِ \ إلى الأَمامِ]

(Idiom) **to pass the buck** تَهَرَّب من المَسْؤوليّة

(Phrasal verb) **buck up** **A** ~ **up** (infml) (to become happier) انْتَعَش

B ~ [**sb**] **up** (to make happier) أَفْرَح [شَخْصاً]

bucket /ˈbʌkɪt/ *n* **1** (container) جَرْدَل (جَرادِلُ) **2** (contents) جَرْدَل (جَرادِلُ)

(Idiom) **to kick the bucket** (infml) [ماتَ]

buckle /ˈbʌk(ə)l/ **A** *n* إبْزيم (أبازيمُ)

B *vt* **1** رَبَطَ (i-u; رَبْط) ‹*a belt, shoe*› **2** ثَنى (i; ثَنْي) ‹*a wheel, frame*›

C *vi* **1** «girders, shelves» انْبَعَج; **my legs ~d under me** انْهارَتْ رِجْلايَ \ ساقايَ **2** «belts, shoes» رُبِط

bud /bʌd/ **A** *n* (of leaf, flower) بُرْعُم (بَراعِمُ)

B *vi* (-dd-) (to develop leaf, flower buds) «plant, tree» بَرْعَمَ (i; بَرْعَمة)

(Idiom) **to nip sth in the bud** قَضى على شَيْءٍ قبل تَفاقُمِهِ

Budapest /buːdəˈpɛst/ *pr n* بودابِسْت (f)

Buddha /ˈbʊdə/ *pr n* بوذا

Buddhism /ˈbʊdɪz(ə)m/ *n* البوذيّة

Buddhist /ˈbʊdɪst/ *n*, *adj* بوذيّ

budding /ˈbʌdɪŋ/ *adj* ‹*athlete, actor, career*› واعِد; ‹*romance*› في بدايَتِه

buddy /ˈbʌdi/ *n* (*pl* **buddies**) (infml) **1** (friend) صَديق (أَصْدِقاءُ) **2** (form of address) أخي, صَديقي, صاحِبي

budge /bʌdʒ/ **A** *vt* حَرَّكَ ‹*the crate, handle*›

B *vi* **1** (to move) «protesters, wheels» تَحَرَّكَ **2** (to give way) «negotiators, management» غَيَّر مَوْقِفَهُ

(Phrasal verb) **budge over**, **budge up** (infml) «passengers, children» تَزَحْزَحَ

budgerigar /ˈbʌdʒ(ə)rɪgɑː/ *n* طائِر طَيِّب

budget /ˈbʌdʒɪt/ **A** *n* ميزانيّة

B *vi* **to ~ for all the costs/an increase in interest rates** أَدْخَلَ في الميزانيّة كُلَّ التَكاليفِ \ زِيادة مُعَدَّلِ الفائدةِ

budgie /ˈbʌdʒi/ *n* (BrE infml) طائِر طَيِّب

buff /bʌf/ **A** *n* **1** (infml) (enthusiast) [شَخْص مولَع (بِشَيْءٍ)]; **an opera/film ~** شَخْص مولَع بالأوبِرا \ بالأَفْلام **2** (colour) لَوْن قَمْحيّ, لَوْن أَصْفَر داكِن

B *vt* صَقَلَ, لَمَّعَ (u; صَقْل) ‹*one's shoes, metal*›

buffalo /ˈbʌfələʊ/ *n* (*pl* **buffaloes** or **buffalo**) **1** (BrE) جاموس **2** (AmE) بَيْسون (ثَوْر بَرّيّ أَمْريكيّ), ثَوْر بَرّيّ (جَواميسُ)

buffer /ˈbʌfə/ *n* **1** (protection) مَصَدّ (مَصَدّات) **2** (**buffers**) (shock absorbers) مُخَفِّفات الصَدَماتِ **3** (Comput) ذاكِرة مُؤَقَّتة

buffer state *n* دَوْلة حاجِزة

buffet[1] /ˈbʊfeɪ/ *n* **1** (meal) بوفيه, مَقْصِف (مَقاصِفُ) **2** (BrE) (in a station) مَقْصِف (مَقاصِفُ) **3** (BrE) (on a train) (also **buffet car**) بوفيه, مَقْصِف (مَقاصِفُ)

buffet[2] /ˈbʌfɪt/ *vt* **1** «winds, waves» ضَرَبَ (i; ضَرْب) ‹*a ship, coast*› **2** «misfortune, scandals» أَصابَ, ابْتَلى ‹*a politician, company*›

buffoon /bəˈfuːn/ *n* مُهَرِّج

bug /bʌg/ **A** *n* **1** (infml) (insect) بَقّ (n coll) **2** (infml) (infection) جُرْثوم (جَراثيمُ) **3** (in programs) خَطأ بَرْمَجيّ **4** (listening device) جِهاز تَنَصُّتٍ

B *vt* (-gg-) **1** زَرَعَ جِهازَ تَنَصُّتٍ في ‹*a room, building*› **2** (infml) (to annoy) أَزْعَجَ

bugger /ˈbʌgə/ *n* (BrE vulg) [شَخْص مَكْروه \ مُغيظ]

buggy /ˈbʌgi/ *n* (*pl* **buggies**) **1** (BrE) (folding pushchair) [عَرَبة أَطْفالٍ قابِلة للطَيِّ] **2** (AmE) (pram) عَرَبة أَطْفالٍ **3** (carriage) عَرَبة حَنْطورٍ **4** (for golfers) عَرَبة الجولْفِ

bugle /ˈbjuːg(ə)l/ *n* بوق (أَبْواق, بوقات)

build /bɪld/ **A** *vt* (*past tense, past participle* **built**) **1** (to construct) بَنى (i; بِناء, بُنْيان), شَيَّدَ ‹*a church, road, monument*›; **the bridge/house was built in 2008** بُنِيَ الجِسْرُ \ البَيْتُ سَنَةَ 2008; **they built a monument to him in the main square** بَنَوْا لَهُ نُصْباً تِذْكاريًّا في الساحةِ الرَئيسيّةِ **2** (to assemble) صَنَعَ (a; صِناعة) ‹*a car, ship, computer*›; **these computers are very well/badly built** هذه الحَواسيبُ مَصْنوعةٌ بِشَكْلٍ جَيِّدٍ \ سَيِّءٍ; **to ~ a shelter out of wood** بَنى مَأْوًى من الخَشَبِ **3** (to establish) بَنى (i; بِناء), أَسَّسَ ‹*a relationship, reputation*›; ‹*business*› **4** (to increase) بَنى (i; بِناء) ‹*confidence, trust*›

B *vi* (*past tense, past participle* **built**) **1** (to construct) «developers, local authorities» بَنى (i; بِناء, بُنْيان) **2** (to use as a foundation) **to ~ on one's success/experience** بَنى على نَجاحِهِ \ تَجْرِبَتِهِ **C** *n* بِنْية (بِنًى, بُنًى); **of medium/slim ~** ذو بِنْيةٍ مُتَوَسِّطةٍ \ نَحيلةٍ

Phrasal verbs **build in**: **~ [sth] in** (to construct) بَنى في [شَيْءٍ] ‹*a wardrobe, bookcase*›

• **build into**: **~ [sth] into [sth]** (to incorporate) دَمَجَ [شَيْئاً] في [شَيْءٍ] ‹*a clause, safeguard*›

• **build up** **A** 1 (to accumulate) «heat, fluid» تَراكَمَ; **traffic ~s up in the evenings** يَشْتَدُّ الازْدِحامُ في المَساءاتِ 2 (to intensify) «pressure, tension» اشْتَدَّ **B** **~ up [sth], ~ [sth] up** 1 (to develop) بَنى [شَيْئاً] ‹*a business, reputation*›; كَوَّنَ [شَيْئاً] ‹*picture*› 2 (to increase) بَنى [شَيْئاً] ‹*one's strength, confidence*›; **don't ~ your hopes up too high** لا تَبْنِ آمالاً عَريضةً **C** **~ [sth/sb] up, ~ up [sth/sb]** (to describe as) **he is being built up as a hero** يَتِمُّ تَقْديمُهُ كَبَطَلٍ

builder /ˈbɪldə/ *n* (contractor) مُتَعَهِّد بناءٍ; (worker) بَنّاء

building /ˈbɪldɪŋ/ *n* 1 (structure) مَبْنًى (مَبانٍ), عمارة (عِمارات, عَمائِرُ), بِناية 2 [u] (construction) بناء, إِنْشاء

building contractor *n* مُقاول

building site *n* مَوْقِع بِناءٍ \ إِنْشاءٍ

building society *n* (BrE) جَمْعية بِناءٍ (مُؤَسَّسة ماليّة تقومُ بِدفعِ فوائِدَ على اسْتِثماراتِ الأَعضاءِ وَتَقْديمِ قُروضٍ لِشِراءِ المَنازِلِ)

build-up /ˈbɪldʌp/ *n* 1 (of traffic) حَشْد (حُشود), تَزاحُم; (of tension, pressure) تراكُم (تراكُمات) 2 (of weapons, troops) تجَمُّع 3 (to an event) اسْتِعْداد (اسْتِعْدادات); **in the ~ to the president's visit** اسْتِعْداداً لِزيارةِ الرَّئيسِ 4 (publicity) ضَجّة

built /bɪlt/ **A** *past tense, past participle* ▸ **build**
B *adj* **powerfully/heavily ~** قَوِيّ البِنْيةِ

built-in /bɪltˈɪn/ *adj* ‹*wardrobe, oven*› جِداريّ; ‹*microphone, speaker*› مُدْمَج

built-up /bɪltˈʌp/ *adj* ‹*area*› عامِر

bulb /bʌlb/ *n* 1 (Elec) لَمْبة 2 (Bot) (of a flower) بَصَل (n coll); (of garlic) رَأْس (mf; رُؤُوس, أَرْؤُس)

bulbous /ˈbʌlbəs/ *adj* ‹*nose*› بَصَليّ (مُنْتَفِخ); ‹*eyes*› جاحِظ (جُحَّظ)

Bulgaria /bʌlˈgɛːrɪə/ *pr n* بُلْغارِيا

Bulgarian /bʌlˈgɛːrɪən/ **A** *adj* ‹*town, custom*› بُلْغاريّ
B *n* 1 (person) بُلْغاريّ (بُلْغار) 2 (language) (اللُّغة) البُلْغاريّة

bulge /bʌldʒ/ **A** *n* انْتِفاخ (انْتِفاخات)
B *vi* 1 «pockets, bags» امْتَلأَ; «stomach, muscles» انْتَفَخَ
2 (**bulging** *present participle*) ‹*eyes*› ناتِئ; ‹*pockets, bags*› مُمْتَلِئ

bulimia /bjʊˈlɪmɪə/, **bulimia nervosa** /bjʊˌlɪmɪə nəːˈvəʊsə/ *n* نُهام, شَرَه

bulimic /bjuːˈlɪmɪk/ *n, adj* نُهاميّ, شَرِه

bulk /bʌlk/ *n* 1 (large mass) كُتْلة (كُتَل) 2 (majority) **the ~ of sth** (of sales, passengers) مُعْظَم شَيْءٍ 3 **in ~** ‹*to buy, sell, transport*› بالجُمْلة

bulk buying *n* شراء بالجُمْلة

bulky /ˈbʌlki/ *adj* (**bulkier, bulkiest**) 1 (awkward) ‹*package*› ضَخْم (ضِخام) 2 (powerful) ‹*boxer, miner*› جَسيم (جِسام)

bull /bʊl/ *n* (male of the cattle species) ثَوْر (ثيران); (male elephants, whales) ذَكَر (ذُكْران, ذُكور)

Idioms **like a bull in a china shop** كَقَرَويٍّ في المَدينةِ; **to take the bull by the horns** مَسَكَ الثَّوْرَ من قَرْنَيْهِ (واجَهَ المُشْكِلةَ بِشَجاعةٍ)

bull bar *n* [مِصَدّ أَماميّ كَبير وَقَويّ]

bulldog /ˈbʊldɒg/ *n* كَلْب البولْدوج

bulldoze /ˈbʊldəʊz/ *vt* 1 (to demolish) أَزالَ \ هَدَمَ بالبُلْدوزَر ‹*a house, slum*› 2 (to clear) [أَزالَ بالبُلْدوزَر] ‹*a road, site*›

bulldozer /ˈbʊldəʊzə/ *n* بُلْدوزر (بُلْدوزرات), جَرّافة (جَرّافات)

bullet /ˈbʊlɪt/ *n* 1 (for guns) رَصاص (n coll) 2 (also **bullet point**) رَمْز نُقْطيّ

Idiom **to bite the bullet** [تَحَمَّلَ فِعْلَ شَيْءٍ بَغيضٍ]

bulletin /ˈbʊlɪtɪn/ *n* 1 (broadcast) نَشْرة (نَشَرات) 2 (newsletter) نَشْرة (نَشَرات) 3 (statement) نَشْرة (نَشَرات)

bulletin board *n* 1 (in an office, a school) لَوْحة إعْلاناتٍ \ نَشَراتٍ 2 (for computer access) نِظام لَوْحةِ البَياناتِ

bulletproof /ˈbʊlɪtpruːf/ *adj* ‹*vest, glass*› صامِد \ مُقاوِم \ عازِل للرَصاصِ

bullfight /ˈbʊlfʌɪt/ *n* مُصارَعة ثيرانٍ

bullfighter /ˈbʊlfʌɪtə/ *n* مُصارِع ثيرانٍ

bullfighting /ˈbʊlˌfʌɪtɪŋ/ *n* مُصارَعة ثيرانٍ

bullfinch /ˈbʊlfɪn(t)ʃ/ *n* دَغْناش (عُصْفور مُغَرِّد)

bullfrog /ˈbʊlfrɒɡ/ *n* [ضِفْدَع كَبير ذو صَوْتٍ عالٍ]

bullion /ˈbʊlj(ə)n/ *n* سَبيكة (سَبائِكُ); **gold/silver ~** سَبيكة ذَهَبٍ \ فِضّةٍ

bullock /ˈbʊlək/ *n* ثَوْر مَخْصيّ

bullring /ˈbʊlrɪŋ/ *n* حَلَبة \ ساحة مُصارَعةِ الثيرانِ

bullseye /ˈbʊlzʌɪ/ *n* عَيْن الهَدَفِ

bullshit /ˈbʊlʃɪt/ *n* (vulg) هُراء, كَلام فارغ

bully /ˈbʊli/ **A** *n* (*pl* **bullies**) مُتَنَمِّر

B *vt* (**bullies**, **bullying**, **bullied**) تَنَمَّرَ (على) <*a classmate, worker*>

bum /bʌm/ *n* (infml) **1** (BrE) (buttocks) مُؤَخِّرة **2** (AmE) (vagrant) مُتَشَرِّد **3** (worthless person) [شَخْص كَسول]

bumbag /ˈbʌmbaɡ/ *n* [حَقيبة صَغيرة تُرْبَط على الخَصْرِ كالحِزامِ]

bumblebee /ˈbʌmb(ə)lbiː/ *n* نَحْلة طَنّانة

bumbling /ˈbʌmb(ə)lɪŋ/ *adj* (confused) <*fool, amateur*> أَخْرَق (dipt; خُرْق)

bumf, **bumph** /bʌmf/ *n* (BrE infml) [أَوْراق مُمِلّة \ غَيْر مُهِمّةٍ]

bump /bʌmp/ **A** *n* **1** (on the head, body) تَوَرُّم (تَوَرُّمات) **2** (in a road) مَطَبّ, نُتوء; **there are some ~s in the bodywork** هُناكَ بَعْضُ النُتوءاتِ في هَيْكَلِ السَيّارةِ **3** (collision) اصْطِدام (اصْطِدامات) **4** (blow) ضَرْبة (ضَرَبات), خَبْطة **5** (sound of a fall) ارْتِطام (ارْتِطامات)

B *vt* **1** (to hit) **to ~ one's head on/against sth** ارْتَطَمَ رَأْسُهُ بِشَيْءٍ; **I accidentally ~ed the car in front** اصْطَدَمْتُ بالسَيّارةِ الّتي كانَتْ أَمامي **2** (infml) (with reservations) **to ~ sb from a flight** مَنَعَ شَخْصاً من رِحْلةِ طَيَرانٍ بِسَبَبِ الحُجوزاتِ الزائِدةِ

C *vi* **1** (to knock) **to ~ against sth/sb** اصْطَدَمَ بِشَخْصٍ \ بِشَيْءٍ **2** (to move jerkily) **we ~ed along the dirt road** كانَتْ سَيّارَتُنا تَهْتَزُّ على طولِ الطَريقِ التُرابيِّ

Phrasal verbs **bump into**: **1** **~ into [sb/sth]** (to collide with) <*a wall, car*> اصْطَدَمَ \ ارْتَطَمَ ب [شَخْصٍ \ شَيْءٍ] **2** **to ~ into [sb]** (infml) (to meet) <*an acquaintance*> الْتَقى [شَخْصاً] مُصادَفةً

• **bump off**: **~ off [sb]**, **~ [sb] off** (infml) قَتَلَ [شَخْصاً]

• **bump up**: **~ up [sth]** (infml) <*prices, the cost*> زادَ \ رَفَعَ [شَيْئاً]

bumper /ˈbʌmpə/ **A** *n* مَصَدّ (مَصَدّات), واقي الصَدَماتِ

B *adj before n* <*harvest, sales*> غَزير, وَفير

bumper car *n* (BrE) سَيّارة مَلاهٍ

bumpkin /ˈbʌm(p)kɪn/ *n* (also **country bumpkin**) (infml) [شَخْص ريفيّ غَيْر مُتَحَضِّرٍ]

bumpy /ˈbʌmpi/ *adj* (**bumpier**, **bumpiest**) **1** <*road, surface*> وَعْر **2** <*ride*> مَليء بالمَطَبّاتِ; <*flight*> بِمَطَبّاتٍ هَوائيّةٍ

bun /bʌn/ *n* **1** (cake) [رَغيف صَغير بالفَواكِهِ الجافّةِ] **2** (bread roll) [رَغيف صَغير] **3** (hairstyle) [شَعْر مَعْقود على شَكْلِ كَعْكةٍ فوق قَفا العُنُقِ]

bunch /bʌn(t)ʃ/ *n* **1** (of flowers) باقة; (of grapes) عُنْقود (عَناقيدُ); (of bananas) عِذْق (أَعْذاق, عُذوق); (of keys) حُزْمة (حُزَم) **2** (infml) (group) مَجْموعة (مَجْموعات, مَجاميعُ)

bundle /ˈbʌnd(ə)l/ **A** *n* رِزْمة (رِزَم)

B *vt* **1** (to put together) حَزَمَ (i; حَزْم) <*clothes*>; رَزَمَ (a-i-u; رَزْم) <*letters*> **2** (to push) **to ~ sb into a car/out of a room** أَقْحَمَ [شَخْصاً داخِلَ سَيّارةٍ \ أَجْبَرَ شَخْصاً على الخُروجِ من غُرْفةٍ]

bung /bʌŋ/ **A** *n* سِدادة, فِلّينة

B *vt* (BrE infml) رَمى (i; رَمْي, رِماية), قَذَفَ (i; قَذْف)

Phrasal verb **bung up**: **~ [sth] up**, **~ up [sth]** سَدَّ [شَيْئاً] <*a sink, drain*>; **my nose is ~ed up** أَنْفي مَسْدودٌ

bungalow /ˈbʌŋɡələʊ/ *n* بَنْغَل (بَيْت من طابَقٍ واحِدٍ)

bungee jumping /ˈbʌndʒiː dʒʌmpɪŋ/ *n* قَفْز البَنْجي

bungle /ˈbʌŋɡ(ə)l/ *vt* فَشِلَ (a; فَشَل) (في) <*an attempt, a robbery*>

bungling /ˈbʌŋɡlɪŋ/ *adj* <*thief, detective*> أَخْرَق (dipt; خُرْق)

bunion /ˈbʌnj(ə)n/ *n* وَكْعة (الْتِهاب في إِبْهامِ القَدَمِ)

bunk /bʌŋk/ *n* **1** (on a ship, train) سَرير (في جِدارِ سَفينةٍ أو قِطارٍ) **2** (also **bunk bed**) (in a bedroom) سَرير مُرْتَفِع

Phrasal verb **bunk off** (BrE infml) «pupils, workers» تَهَرَّبَ (من), تَسَلَّلَ (من)

bunk bed *n* سَرير ذو طابِقَيْنِ

bunker /ˈbʌŋkə/ *n* **1** (in golf) [مَوْقِع رَمْليّ يَعْتَرِضُ طَريقَ الكُرةِ في لُعْبةِ الجولْف] **2** (Mil) مَلْجَأ (مَلاجِئُ) **3** (for coal) مَخْزَن فَحْمٍ

bunny /ˈbʌni/ *n* (*pl* **bunnies**) (also **bunny rabbit**) (infml) أَرْنوب, أَرْنَب (أَرانِبُ)

bunting /ˈbʌntɪŋ/ *n* [شَرِيط أَعْلامٍ مُلَوَّنةٍ]

buoy /bɔɪ/ **A** *n* (عَوّامة (لِإرْشادِ السُفُنِ

B *vt* **1** (Naut) [وَضَعَ عَوّاماتٍ إرْشاديّةً في] ‹*a channel, wreck*›

2 (also **buoy up**) (to boost) (رَفَعَ (a; رَفْع ‹*sb's morale*›; زادَ ثِقةً ‹*a competitor*›

buoyant /ˈbɔɪənt/ *adj* **1** ‹*market, economy*› مُزْدَهِر **2** ‹*mood, spirits*› مُبْتَهِج **3** ‹*vessel, float*› قابِل للطَفْوِ

burble /ˈbəːb(ə)l/ *vi* **1** «stream, water» خَرَّ (i; خَرِير) **2** (also **burble on**) ثَرْثَرَ (i; ثَرْثَرة) بَقْبَقَ (i-u; بَقْبَقة)

burden /ˈbəːd(ə)n/ **A** *n* **1** (heavy load) حِمْل (أَحْمال) **2** (responsibility) عِبْء (أَعْباء)

B *vt* أَرْهَقَ, أَثْقَلَ; **to ~ sb with one's problems** أَثْقَلَ شَخْصاً بِمَشاكِلِهِ

bureau /ˈbjʊərəʊ/ *n* (*pl* **bureaus** or **bureaux**) **1** (agency) مَكْتَب (مَكاتِبُ) **2** (AmE) (government department) مَكْتَب (مَكاتِبُ), إدارة **3** (BrE) (desk) مَكْتَب (مَكاتِبُ) **4** (AmE) (chest of drawers) خِزانة ذات أَدْراج

bureaucracy /ˌbjʊ(ə)ˈrɒkrəsi/ *n* بِيروقْراطيّة

bureaucrat /ˈbjʊərəkrat/ *n* دِيوانيّ (عُضْو في حُكومةٍ بِيروقْراطيّة)

bureaucratic /ˌbjʊərəˈkratɪk/ *adj* ‹*rules, procedure*› بِيروقْراطيّ

burgeoning /ˈbəːdʒ(ə)nɪŋ/ *adj* ‹*economy, population*› نامٍ, مُزْدَهِر

burger /ˈbəːgə/ *n* هَمْبورْجَر

burger bar *n* [مَحَلّ لِبَيْعِ سَنْدَويْتْشاتِ البُرْجَر]

burglar /ˈbəːglə/ *n* لِصّ (لُصوص)

burglar alarm *n* جِهاز إنْذارٍ ضِدَّ السَرِقةِ

burglarize, -ise (BrE) /ˈbəːglərʌɪz/ *vt* (AmE) سَطا (u; سَطْو, سَطْوة; على) ‹*a house, an office*›

burglary /ˈbəːgləri/ *n* (*pl* **burglaries**) سَطْو, سَرِقة

burgle /ˈbəːg(ə)l/ *vt* سَطا (u; سَطْو, سَطْوة; على) ‹*a house, shop*›

burgundy /ˈbəːg(ə)ndi/ *n* **1** (wine) (also **burgundy**) [خَمْر تُصْنَعُ في بُرْغُنْدِيا] **2** [u] (colour) لَوْن خَمْريّ

burial /ˈbɛrɪəl/ *n* دَفْن

burka /ˈbʊrkɑː/ *n* بُرْقُع (بَراقِعُ)

Burkina Faso /bəːˌkiːnə ˈfasəʊ/ *pr n* بورْكِينا فاسو (f)

burlesque /bəːˈlɛsk/ *n* بورْلاسْك (عَرْض مَسْرَحيّ هَزْليّ)

burly /ˈbəːli/ *adj* (**burlier**, **burliest**) ‹*policeman, bouncer*› ضَخْم قَويّ البُنْيةِ, الجِسْمِ

Burma /ˈbəːmə/ *pr n* بورْما

Burmese /bəːˈmiːz/ **A** *n* (*pl* **Burmese**) **1** (person) بورميّ **2** (language) (اللُغة) البورْميّة

B *adj* ‹*customs, people*› بورْميّ

burn /bəːn/ **A** *vt* (*past tense, past participle* **burned** or **burnt** BrE) **1** (to destroy by fire) أَحْرَقَ ‹*a building, body, rubbish*›; **they ~ed the city/house to the ground** أَحْرَقوا المَدِينةَ \ البَيْتَ بالكامِلِ; **she ~ed a hole in her sleeve** ثَقَبَت النارُ كُمَّ ثَوْبِها; **heretics were ~ed alive** كانَ الهَراطِقةُ يُحْرَقونَ أَحْياءً; **to be ~ed to death** أُحْرِقَ حتّى المَوْتِ **2** (to injure) حَرَقَ (i; حَرْق) ‹*one's hand*›; **to ~ one's fingers** حَرَقَ أَصابِعَهُ; **the soup ~ed my mouth** حَرَقَ الحَساءُ فَمي **3** (in cooking) أَحْرَقَ ‹*the rice, toast*› **4** (to use as fuel) **to ~ coal/gas** اسْتَخْدَمَ الفَحْمَ الحَجَريَّ \ الغازَ كَوَقودٍ **5** حَرَقَ (i; حَرْق), أَحْرَقَ ‹*calories, fat*› **6** نَسَخَ (a; نَسْخ) ‹*a CD, data*›

B *vi* (*past tense, past participle* **burned** or **burnt** BrE) **1** (to produce heat) «fire» اتَّقَدَ, اشْتَعَلَ **2** (to be consumed by fire) «building, fuel» اشْتَعَلَ, احْتَرَقَ **3** (to be alight) «lights» احْتَرَقَ; «candles» احْتَرَقَ, اشْتَعَلَ **4** (in cooking) «rice, toast» احْتَرَقَ **5** (to get sunburnt) «person, skin» احْتَرَقَ (من الشَمْسِ) **6** (to feel hot) «face, cheeks» الْتَهَبَ, اشْتَعَلَ; **his face was ~ing with shame** كانَ وَجْهُهُ يَشْتَعِلُ من الخَجَلِ **7** (to be eager) **to be ~ing with desire/anger** كانَ يَتَّقِدُ شَهْوةً \ غَضَباً

C *v refl* (*past tense, past participle* **burned** or BrE, **burnt**) **to ~ oneself** حَرَقَ نَفْسَهُ

D *n* **1** (on the skin) حَرْق (حُروق) **2** (BrE) (stream) جَدْوَل (جَداوِلُ)

Idiom **to burn one's bridges** or (BrE) **boats** أَحْرَقَ الجُسورَ \ السُفُنَ

Phrasal verbs **burn down** **A** «house, village» احْتَرَقَ بالكامِلِ

B **~ down [sth], ~ [sth] down** أَحْرَقَ [شَيْئاً] بالكامِلِ ‹*a house, village*›

• **burn off: ~ off [sth], ~ [sth] off** **1** أَزالَ [شَيْئاً] بالحَرارةِ

‹*paint, varnish*› **2** اسْتَهْلَكَ [شَيْئاً] ‹*gases, fuel*› **3** حَرَقَ [شَيْئاً] ‹*calories, fat*›

• **burn out** **A** **1** «fire, candle» انْطَفَأَ **2** (through stress) أَنْهَكَهُ التَعَبُ **B** ~ **out** [sb], ~ [sb] **out** شَرَّدَ [شَخْصاً] بِإِحْراقِ بَيْتِهِ [بالكامِلِ ‹*the enemy, rebels*›

• **burn up** **A** «meteor, rocket» احْتَرَقَ **B** ~ **up** [sth], ~ [sth] **up** **1** اسْتَهْلَكَ [شَيْئاً] ‹*fuel*› **2** حَرَقَ [شَيْئاً] ‹*calories, energy*›

burner /ˈbəːnə/ *n* رَأْس مَوْقِدٍ

burning /ˈbəːnɪŋ/ *adj* **1** (very hot) ‹*sun, sand*› حارِق **2** (intense) ‹*desire, ambition*› جامِح, شَديد, مولِع **3** ‹*pain, sensation*› مُحْرِق

burnt /bəːnt/ *past tense, past participle* ▸ **burn**

burp /bəːp/ **A** *vi* تَجَشَّأَ

B *n* تَجَشُّؤ

burrow /ˈbʌrəʊ/ **A** *n* جُحْر (جُحور)

B *vi* حَفَرَ جُحْراً

bursar /ˈbəːsə/ *n* أَمين صُنْدوقٍ

bursary /ˈbəːs(ə)ri/ *n* (*pl* **bursaries**) (BrE) مِنْحة (مِنَح)

burst /bəːst/ **A** *vt* (*past tense, past participle* **burst**) فَقَعَ (a; فَقْع, فُقوع) ‹*a balloon, tyre*›; فَجَّرَ ‹*a blood vessel*›; **the river ~ its banks** اخْتَرَقَ النَهْرُ ضِفافَهُ; **a ~ pipe** أُنبوب مُنْفَجِر

B *vi* (*past tense, past participle* **burst**) **1** «balloon, tyre, dam» انْفَجَرَ; **the thaw made the pipes ~** تَسَبَّبَ ذَوَبانُ الجَليدِ في انْفِجارِ الأَنابيبِ \ المَواسيرِ **2** (to be full) **the city is ~ing at the seams** تَشْهَدُ المَدينةُ انْفِجاراً سُكّانيّاً; **to be ~ing with pride** امْتَلأَ فَخْراً **3** (to be eager) **to be ~ing to do sth** كانَ مُتَلَهِّفاً لِفِعْلِ شَيْءٍ **4** (to emerge suddenly) «people» بَرَزَ فَجْأَةً; «flames, water» انْفَجَرَ فَجْأَةً; **the sun burst through the clouds** بَرَزَت الشَمْسُ فَجْأَةً من بَيْنِ السُحُبِ; **they burst onto the music scene in 2005** بَرَزوا في المَشْهَدِ الموسيقيِّ سَنةَ 2005

C *n* **1** (outbreak of energy, activity, enthusiasm) شِحْنة; (of gunfire) وابِل; (of light, flame) دُفْقة (دُفَقات, دُفُقات); **a ~ of applause** مَوْجة من التَصْفيقِ; **a ~ of laughter** مَوْجة من الضَحِكِ; **to put on a ~ of speed** زادَ فَجْأَةً من السُرْعةِ **2** (in pipes) انْفِجار (انْفِجارات)

(Phrasal verbs) **burst in** «police, gunmen» اقْتَحَمَ; **to ~ in on sb/a meeting** اقْتَحَمَ مَكاناً على شَخْصٍ \ اجْتِماعاً

• **burst into**: ~ **into** [sth] **1** (to enter) اقْتَحَمَ [شَيْئاً] ‹*a room, meeting*› **2** (to start) **to ~ into tears** انْفَجَرَ \ أَجْهَشَ بالبُكاءِ; **to ~ into flames** انْدَلَعَتْ فيه النيرانُ; **to ~ into laughter** انْفَجَرَ بالضَحِكِ; **to ~ into song** بَدَأَ يُغَنّي \ بالغِناءِ فَجْأَةً

• **burst open** «door, suitcase, bag» انْفَتَحَ بِقوّةٍ

• **burst out** **1** (to come out) انْدَفَعَ إلى الخارِجِ; **she came ~ing out of the room** انْدَفَعَتْ خارِجَ الغُرْفةِ مُتَّجِهةً نَحْوَنا **2** (to start) **to ~ out laughing** انْفَجَرَ ضاحِكاً; **to ~ out crying** انْفَجَرَ باكِياً **3** (to exclaim) صاحَ (i; صَيْحة, صِياح), صَرَخَ (u; صُراخ, صَريخ)

Burundi /bʊˈrʊndi/ *pr n* بوروندي (f)

bury /ˈbɛri/ *vt* (**buries**, **burying**, **buried**) **1** (to put underground) دَفَنَ (i; دَفْن), طَمَرَ (i-u; طَمْر) ‹*waste, a treasure, bone*› **2** (after death) دَفَنَ (i; دَفْن), وارى التُرابَ ‹*a body, an animal*› **3** (to cover completely) دَفَنَ (i; دَفْن), طَمَرَ (i-u; طَمْر) ‹*a person, town*›; **to be buried alive** دُفِنَ حَيًّا **4** (to hide) أَخْفى ‹*a story, news*›; **to ~ one's face in one's hands** دَفَنَ وَجْهَهُ بين يَدَيْهِ; **to ~ oneself in one's work/a book** اسْتَغْرَقَ في عَمَلِهِ \ قِراءةِ كِتابٍ **5** (to plunge) غَرَزَ (i; غَرْز) ‹*a knife, one's teeth*›; **the dog buried its teeth in my ankle** غَرَزَ الكَلْبُ أَسْنانَهُ في كاحِلي

bus /bʌs/ *n* (*pl* **buses**) حافِلة (حافِلات, حَوافِل), باص (باصات), أُتوبيس

(Idiom) **to miss the bus** (infml) ضَيَّعَ الفُرْصةَ

bus conductor *n* قاطِع التَذاكِرِ (في الحافِلةِ)

bus driver *n* سائِق حافِلةٍ

bush /bʊʃ/ *n* **1** (shrub) شُجَيْرة **2** [u] (**the bush**) (bushland) الأَحْراش, الأَدْغال

(Idiom) **to beat about the bush** لَفَّ \ دارَ \ راوَغَ في الكَلامِ

bush fire *n* حَريق الغابةِ

bushy /ˈbʊʃi/ *adj* (**bushier**, **bushiest**) **1** ‹*beard, tail*› كَثيف, كَثّ **2** ‹*undergrowth, hillside*› مُدْغِل

busily /ˈbɪzɪli/ *adv* ‹*to prepare, work*› بانْكِبابٍ, بِهِمّةٍ, بِنَشاطٍ

business /ˈbɪznəs/ **A** *n* **1** [u] (commerce) تِجارة; **to be in ~** بَدَأَ العَمَلَ; **to set up in ~** بَعَثَ شَرِكةً; **she went into ~ as an**

art dealer بَدَأت العَمَلَ التِجاريَّ كَتاجِرة أَعْمالٍ فَنِّيّة; **to go out of ~** تَوَقَّفَ عن العَمَلِ التِجاريِّ; **they do a lot of ~ in Germany** يَقومونَ بالكَثيرِ من الأَعْمالِ التِجاريّةِ في أَلْمانيا; **he's away on ~** هو مُسافِرٌ في مُهِمّةِ عَمَلٍ **2** [u] (volume of trade, transactions) نَشاط \ عَمَل تِجاريّ; **to lose ~** تَراجَعَ النَشاطُ التِجاريُّ; **how's ~?** كَيف حالُ التِجارةِ؟; **~ is good/ slow** الحَرَكَةُ التِجاريّةُ جَيِّدةٌ \ بَطيئةٌ; **we are doing twice as much ~ as last summer** تَضاعَفَتْ مَبيعاتُنا بالمُقارَنةِ مع الصَيْفِ الماضي; **it's good/bad for ~** هو جَيِّدٌ \ سَيِّئٌ للتِجارةِ **3** (area of activity) حِرْفة (حِرَف), مِهْنة (مِهَن); **what's your line of ~?, what line of ~ are you in?** ما هي مِهْنَتُكَ \ حِرْفَتُكَ؟; **he's in the hotel/insurance ~** يَعْمَلُ في المَجالِ الفَنْدَقة \ التَأْمين; **the music ~** مَجال الموسيقيّ **4** (company, firm) شَرِكة; **financial help for small ~es** مُساعَدة ماديّة للشَرِكاتِ الصَغيرةِ; **it's a successful family ~** هي شَرِكةٌ عائِليّةٌ ناجِحةٌ; **small and medium ~es** شَرِكات صَغيرة وَمُتَوَسِّطة **5** [u] (matters for attention) قَضايا مُهِمّة; **let's get down to ~** لِنُرَكِّزْ على القَضايا المُهِمّةِ; **the ~ before a meeting** القَضايا المَطْروحة للنِقاشِ قبل اجْتِماعٍ; **any other ~** (on an agenda) مُتَفَرِّقات **6** [u] (concern) شَأْن; **that's her ~** ذلك شَأْنُها; **it's none of your ~!** هذا لَيْسَ من شَأْنِكَ!; **he had no ~ to be there** ما كانَ لَدَيْهِ سَبَبٌ وَجيهٌ لِيَكونَ هُناكَ **7** (situation) وَضْعيّة; **it's a dreadful/nasty ~** إنَّها وَضْعيّةٌ مُخْزِيةٌ; **the newspapers are full of this murder/drugs ~** الجَرائِدُ مَليئةٌ بِهَذِهِ الأَخْبارِ عن جَرائِمِ القَتْلِ \ المُخَدَّراتِ; **I'm fed up with the whole ~** سَئِمْتُ من الوَضْعيّةِ كُلِّها **8** (infml) (bother) مَسْأَلة مُزْعِجة; **moving house is quite a ~!** الانْتِقالُ من البَيْتِ مَسْأَلةٌ مُزْعِجةٌ جِدًّا!

B *modifier* ‹*meeting*› عَمَلٍ; ‹*letter, transaction*› تِجاريّ; **the ~ community** مُجْتَمَع الأَعْمالِ

Idioms **mind your own business!** لا تَتَدَخَّلْ في ما لا يَعْنيكَ!; **to be in the business of doing sth** كانَ يَعْمَلُ في مَجالِ شَيْءٍ; **he's not in the ~ of giving discounts** هو لَيْسَ مُهْتَمًّا بإعْطاءِ تَخْفيضاتٍ

business card *n* بِطاقة عَمَلٍ

business class *n* دَرَجة رِجالِ الأَعْمالِ

business cycle *n* دَوْرة اقْتِصاديّة

business hours *n* ساعات العَمَلِ

businesslike /ˈbɪznɪslʌɪk/ *adj* ‹*manner, discussion*› عَمَليّ

businessman /ˈbɪznɪsmən/ *n* (*pl* **-men**) رَجُل أَعْمالٍ

business park *n* مُجَمّع أَعْمالٍ, مُجَمّع إداريّ

business person, **businessperson** *n* (*pl* **-people**) رَجُل أَعْمالٍ

business plan *n* خُطّة عَمَلٍ

business school *n* كُلّيّة أَعْمالٍ

business studies *n* دِراسات تِجاريّة

business trip *n* رِحْلة عَمَلٍ

businesswoman /ˈbɪznɪswʊmən/ *n* (*pl* **-women**) سَيِّدة أَعْمالٍ

busker /ˈbʌskə/ *n* (BrE) [موسيقيّ يَعْزِفُ في الشارِعِ بِهَدَفِ جَمْعِ تَبَرُّعاتٍ من الناسِ]

bus lane *n* [مَسار مُخَصَّص للحافِلاتِ]

bus pass *n* بِطاقة رُكوبِ الحافِلةِ

busser /ˈbʌsə/ *n* ≈ نادِل

bus shelter *n* مِظَلّة انْتِظارِ الحافِلاتِ

bus station *n* مَحَطّة حافِلاتٍ

bus stop *n* مَوْقِف حافِلاتٍ

bust /bʌst/ **A** *n* **1** (bosom) صَدْر (صُدور) **2** (sculpture) تِمْثال نِصْفيّ

B *adj* (infml) **1** (broken) ‹*TV, washing machine*› مُعَطَّل **2** (bankrupt) **to go ~** «companies, traders» أَفْلَسَ

C *vt* (infml) **1** (*past tense, past participle* **busted** or **bust** BrE) (to break) ‹*a TV, washing machine*› عَطَّلَ **2** (*past tense, past participle* **busted**) (to raid) هَجَمَ (u; هُجوم; على) ‹*premises, a club*› **3** (*past tense, past participle* **busted**) (to arrest) قَبَضَ (i; قَبْض; على) ‹*a crook, thief*›

bustle /ˈbʌs(ə)l/ **A** *vi* **1** (to move busily) «servants, shoppers» [تَحَرَّكَ بِسُرْعةٍ وَنَشاطٍ]; **to ~ about** *or* **around** [تَحَرَّكَ بِسُرْعةٍ وَنَشاطٍ] **2** (to be full of activity) «streets, cities» [عَجَّ بِحَرَكةٍ \ بِنَشاطٍ]

B *n* صَخَب

bustling /ˈbʌslɪŋ/ *adj* ‹*street, city*› مُزْدَحِم

bust-up /ˈbʌstʌp/ *n* (infml) نِزاع, مُشاجَرة

busy /ˈbɪzi/ **A** *adj* (**busier, busiest**) **1** ‹*person*› مَشْغول; **she 's ~ with a customer** هي مَشْغولةٌ مع زَبونٍ; **to keep sb/oneself ~** شغَلَ شَخْصاً \ نَفْسَهُ **2** ‹*road, airport*› مُزْدَحِم; ‹*day*› حافِل; **she has a ~ schedule** لَدَيْها جَدْوَلُ أَعْمالٍ مُزْدَحِمٌ; **were the shops ~?** هل كانَتِ الدَكاكينُ مُزْدَحِمةً؟ **3** ‹*telephone line*› مَشْغول

B *v refl* (**busies, busying, busied**) **to ~ oneself with sth** شَغَلَ نَفْسَهُ \ انْشَغَلَ بِشَيْءٍ

busybody /ˈbɪzibɒdi/ *n* (*pl* **busybodies**) (infml) فُضوليّ

but /bʌt, bət/ **A** *conj* **1** (expressing reluctance, protest, surprise) **he agreed to it, ~ with reservations** وافَقَ عَلَيْه، وَلَكِنْ مع تَحَفُّظاتٍ; **~ we can't afford it!** وَلَكِنْ لا يُمْكِنُنا تَحَمُّلُ نَفَقاتِهِ!; **~ that's wonderful!** وَلَكِنْ ذلك رائِعٌ! **2** (in contradictions, contrasts) لَكِنْ, لَكِنَّ; **it's cheap ~ effective** هو رَخيصٌ وَلَكِنَّهُ فَعّالٌ; **it's not an asset ~ a disadvantage** هو لَيْسَ ميزةً بَلْ هو عَيْبٌ; **I'll do it, ~ not yet** سَوْفَ أَفْعَلُهُ وَلَكِنْ لَيْس بَعْدُ **3** (in apologies) لَكِنْ, لَكِنَّ; **excuse me, ~ ...** مَعْذِرةً، وَلَكِنْ ... **4** (for emphasis) **not twice, ~ three times** لَيْسَ مَرَّتَيْنِ، بَلْ ثَلاثَ مَرّاتٍ

B *prep* (fml) **anything ~ that** أَيُّ شَيْءٍ إلاّ ذلك; **anybody ~ him** أَيُّ شَخْصٍ إلاّ هو; **anywhere ~ Australia** أَيُّ مَكانٍ إلاّ أُسْتُراليا; **everybody ~ Paul will be there** الجَميعُ فيما عَدا بول سَيَكونونَ هُناكَ; **nobody ~ me knows how to do it** لا أَحَدَ سِوايَ يَعْلَمُ كَيْفيّةَ عَمَلِهِ; **he's nothing ~ a coward** ما هو إلاّ جَبانٌ; **there's nothing for it ~ to leave** لم يَبْقَ أيُّ خِيارٍ سوى الرَحيلِ; **where ~ in Dubai?** أَيْنَ سِوى في دُبَيّ؟; **who could do it ~ you?** مَنْ سِواكَ يُمْكِنُهُ أَنْ يَفْعَلَ هذا؟; **the last ~ one** قبل الأَخيرِ; **the next road ~ one** الشارِعُ بعد القادِمِ

C (**but for**) *prep phr* لَوْلا; **~ for you, I would have died** لَوْلاكَ، لَمُتُّ; **he would have gone ~ for me** لَوْلايَ لَذَهَبَ

D *adv* (fml) (only, just) **if I had ~ known** لو أَنّي فَقَطْ عَلِمْتُ; **I can ~ try** لَيْسَ بِوِسْعي سِوى أَنْ أُحاوِلَ; **one can't help ~ admire her** لا يَسَعُهُ سِوى أَنْ يُعْجَبَ بِها

butane /ˈbjuːteɪn/ *n* بوتان

butcher /ˈbʊtʃə/ **A** *n* **1** (profession) جَزّار (جَزّارونَ, جَزارة), لَحّام, قَصّاب; **~'s (shop)** مَلْحَمة **2** (murderer) سَفّاح, سَفّاك للدِماءِ

B *vt* **1** **to ~ a calf/lamb** ذَبَحَ عِجْلاً \ حَمَلاً **2** (to murder) قَتَّلَ ‹*civilians, a victim*›

butler /ˈbʌtlə/ *n* رَئيس الخَدَمِ, قَهْرَمان (قَهارِمة)

butt /bʌt/ **A** *vt* «animal» نَطَحَ (a; نَطْح); «person» ضَرَبَ بالرَأْسِ

B *n* **1** (of a rifle) عَقِب (أَعْقاب) **2** (of a cigarette) عَقِب (أَعْقاب) **3** (target) عُرْضة; **to be the ~ of jokes** كانَ عُرْضةً للنُكَتِ **4** (blow with the head) نَطْحة **5** (AmE infml) (buttocks) مُؤَخَّرة

Phrasal verb **butt in** قاطَعَ

butter /ˈbʌtə/ **A** *n* زُبْدة (زُبَد); **to eat bread and ~** أَكَلَ خُبْزاً وَزُبْدةً

B *vt* دَهَنَ بالزُبْدةِ ‹*bread, toast*›

Phrasal verb **butter up** (infml): **~ [sb] up, ~ up [sb]** (infml) داهَنَ \ تَزَلَّفَ إلى [شَخْصٍ], صانَعَ [شَخْصاً] ‹*one's boss, father*›

butter bean *n* (BrE) لوبيا, فاصولية

buttercup /ˈbʌtəkʌp/ *n* حَوْذان

butterfingers /ˈbʌtəfɪŋgəz/ *n* (*pl* **butterfingers**) (infml) أَخْرَق (dipt; خُرْق)

butterfly /ˈbʌtəflaɪ/ *n* (*pl* **butterflies**) **1** (insect) فَراش (n coll) **2** [u] (also **butterfly**) (in swimming) سِباحة الفَراشةِ

buttock /ˈbʌtək/ *n* رِدْف (أَرْداف)

button /ˈbʌt(ə)n/ **A** *n* **1** (on a coat, shirt) زِرّ (أَزْرار, زُرور) **2** (on a machine) زِرّ (أَزْرار, زُرور) **3** (Comput) زِرّ (أَزْرار, زُرور) **4** (AmE) (badge) شارة

B *vi* (also **button up**) «shirts, dresses» زُرِّرَ

Phrasal verb **button up**: **~ [sth] up, ~ up [sth]** **1** زَرَّرَ [شَيْئاً] ‹*one's shirt, dress*› **2** (infml) أَتَمَّ [شَيْئاً] ‹*an agreement, a deal*›

buttonhole /ˈbʌt(ə)nhəʊl/ **A** *n* **1** (on a coat, shirt) عُرْوة \ فَتْحة زِرٍّ **2** (BrE) (flower) وَرْدة صَدْرٍ

B *vt* (infml) أَجْبَرَ على التَحَدُّثِ ‹*a colleague, voter*›

buttress /ˈbʌtrɪs/ *n* (Archit) كَتِف (دِعامة خارِجيّة في جِدارٍ لِزيادةِ قُدْرة تَحَمُّلِه)

buxom /ˈbʌks(ə)m/ *adj* ناهِد, مُمْتَلِئة الثَدْيَيْنِ

buy /baɪ/ **A** *vt* (*past tense, past participle* **bought**) **1** (to purchase) اِبْتاعَ, اشْتَرى ‹*a ticket, house, car*›; **to ~ sth for sb, to ~ sb sth**

اشْتَراهُ من صَديقٍ; **he bought it from a friend** اشْتَرى شَيْئاً لِشَخْصٍ; **I've bought myself a new dress** اشْتَرَيْتُ بَدْلَةً جَديدةً لِنَفسي; **she bought it for £500** اشْتَرَتْهُ ب £500 **2** (to obtain) اشْتَرى *‹freedom, happiness›* **3** (to bribe) رَشا, اشْتَرى (رَشْو; u) *‹a politician, witness›*; **she can't be bought** لا يُمْكِنُ رَشْوَتُها **4** (infml) (to believe) صَدَّقَ *‹a story, an excuse›*

B *vi* (*past tense, past participle* **bought**) «customers, companies» اشْتَرى; **to ~ from sb** اشْتَرى من شَخْصٍ

C *n* مُشْتَرًى (مُشْتَرَيات); **a good/bad buy** صَفْقة جَيِّدة \ سَيِّئة; **an impulse ~** شِراء بِدافِعِ نَزْعةٍ اسْتِهْلاكيّةٍ

(Idiom) **to buy time** كَسَبَ \ رَبِحَ الوَقْتَ

(Phrasal verbs) **buy in** (BrE): **~ [sth] in, ~ in [sth]** اشْتَرى [شَيْئاً] بالجُمْلةِ *‹food, fuel›*

• **buy into**: **~ into [sth]** **1** اشْتَرى حِصّةً من [شَيْءٍ] *‹a company, partnership›* **2** (infml) صَدَّقَ [شَيْئاً] *‹an idea, a myth›*

• **buy off**: **~ [sb] off, ~ off [sb]** اشْتَرى ذِمّةَ [شَخْصٍ] *‹a politician, witness›*

• **buy out**: **1** **~ [sb] out, ~ out [sb]** اشْتَرى حِصّةَ [شَخْصٍ] *‹a partner, company›* **2** **to ~ oneself out of the army** [تَحَصَّلَ على إعْفاءٍ \ تَسْريحٍ من الخِدْمةِ العَسْكَريّةِ مُقابِلَ بَدَلٍ نَقْديٍّ]

• **buy up**: **~ up [sth], ~ [sth] up** اسْتَحْوَذَ على [شَيْءٍ] *‹land, shares›*

buyer /ˈbʌɪə/ *n* **1** (customer) مُشْتَرٍ (مُشْتَرونَ), شارٍ (شُراة) **2** (in a company) مَسْؤول عن المُشْتَرَياتِ

buyer's market *n* سوق المُشْتَرينَ (يَكونُ فيها العَرْضُ أكْبَرَ من الطَلَبِ فَتَنْخَفِضُ الأَسْعارُ)

buying /ˈbʌɪɪŋ/ *n* شِراء

buyout /ˈbʌɪaʊt/ *n* [اسْتِحْواذ على حِصّةِ شَرِكةٍ]

buzz /bʌz/ **A** *n* **1** (noise of an insect) أَزيز, طَنين; (of conversation) غَمْغَمة; **a ~ of excitement/anticipation** غَمْغَمة; **2** (infml) (phone call) مُكالَمة هاتِفيّة \ تِليفونيّة; إثارة \ تَرَقُّب; **to give sb a ~** هاتَفَ شَخْصاً; **3** (infml) (thrill) نَشْوة; **I get a ~ from it, it gives me a ~** يَجْعَلُني أَشْعُرُ بالنَشْوةِ \ أَنْتَشي

B *vt* **1** (to call) **to ~ sb** [أَرْسَلَ إشارةً لِشَخْصٍ بواسِطةِ الجَرَسِ الطَنّانِ]; **to ~ an apartment** ضَغَطَ على زِرِّ الجَرَسِ الكَهْرَبائيِّ **2** «plane, helicopter» طارَ قُرْبَ, حَلَّقَ على مَقْرُبةٍ من لِشَقّةٍ *‹a building, crowd, an airliner›*

C *vi* **1** «bees, flies» طَنَّ (طَنين; i) **2** (to be lively) عَجَّ بالحَيَوِيّةِ; **the house was ~ing with activity** كانَ البَيْتُ يَعُجُّ بالحَرَكةِ; **her mind ~ed with ideas** عَجَّ عَقْلُها بالأَفْكارِ

(Phrasal verb) **buzz off** (infml) انْصَرَفَ; **~ off!** انْصَرِفْ!

buzzard /ˈbʌzəd/ *n* (hawk) صَقْر حَوّام; (vulture) نَسْر (نُسور, نُسورة); (turkey vulture) بُغاث (بِغْثان)

buzzer /ˈbʌzə/ *n* جَرَس كَهْرَبائيّ

buzzword /ˈbʌzwəːd/ *n* كَلِمة \ عِبارة طَنّانة

by /bʌɪ/ **A** *prep* **1** (indicating agent, cause) بِواسِطةِ, بِ; **he was bitten ~ a snake** لُدِغَ بِأَفْعى; **a novel ~ Updike** رِواية بِقَلَمِ أوبْدِيك; **~ mistake/chance** بالخَطَأِ \ بالصُدْفةِ **2** (indicating means, method) بِ, بِواسِطةِ; **I paid ~ credit card** دَفَعْتُ بِواسِطةِ بِطاقةِ الائْتِمانِ; **to travel ~ bus/train/car** سافَرَ بالباصِ \ بالقِطارِ \ بالسَيّارةِ; **~ land/sea/air** بالبَرِّ \ بالبَحْرِ \ بالجَوِّ; **I'll begin ~ introducing myself** سَأَبْدَأُ بالتَعْريفِ عن نَفْسي **3** (near to) بِقُرْبِ, بِجانِبِ; **the telephone is ~ the window** الهاتِفُ بِجانِبِ النافِذةِ; **they have a house ~ the sea** عِنْدَهُمْ بَيْتٌ بِقُرْبِ البَحْرِ **4** (past) بِجانِبِ; **he walked straight ~ me** مَرَّ مُباشَرةً بِجانِبي **5** (not later than) عِنْدَ (في ساعةٍ مُعَيَّنةٍ أو قَبْلَها); **be back ~ midnight** عُدْ عِنْدَ مُنْتَصَفِ اللَيْلِ; **~ the time she got downstairs he had gone** في الوَقْتِ الّذي نَزَلَتْ فيهِ الدَرَجَ كانَ هو قَدْ ذَهَبَ **6** (during) خِلالَ; **~ day/night** خِلالَ النَهارِ \ اللَيْلِ **7** (according to) بِحَسَبِ, وَفْقاً لِ, بالنِسْبةِ; **~ my watch it's four o'clock** بِحَسَبِ ساعَتي إنَّها الرابِعةُ; **it's OK ~ me** هذا مُمْكِنٌ بالنِسْبةِ لي **8** (in measurements, quantities) في, بِ; **a room 8 metres ~ 10 metres** غُرْفة مِساحَتُها 8 أَمْتارٍ ب 10 أَمْتارٍ; **multiply two ~ three** اُضْرُبِ اثْنَيْنِ بِثَلاثةٍ; **prices have risen ~ 20%** ارْتَفَعَتِ الأَسْعارُ ب 20٪ **9** (indicating rate) بِ; **we are paid ~ the hour** يُدْفَعُ لَنا بالساعةِ **10** (indicating progression) بَعْدَ; **one ~ one** واحِداً بَعْدَ واحِدٍ; **day ~ day** يَوْماً بَعْدَ يَوْمٍ **11** (with reflexive pronouns) بِ; **he did it all ~ himself** قامَ بِكُلِّ ذلك بِمُفْرَدِهِ; **she lives ~ herself** هي تَعيشُ بِمُفْرَدِها

B *adv* **1** (past) مارًّا; **we watched the procession go ~** شاهَدْنا المَوْكِبَ مارًّا; **as time goes ~** بِمُرورِ الوَقْتِ **2** (to sb's house) [زائراً]; **call ~ on your way to work** قُمْ بِزيارَتنا وَأَنْتَ في طَريقكَ إلى العَمَلِ

Idioms **by and by** نِهائيًّا; **~ and ~ he came to believe her** صَدَّقَها نِهائيًّا; **by and large** في المُجْمَلِ

bye /bʌɪ/ *excl* (infml) (also **bye-bye**) وَداعاً, مع السَّلامةِ; **~, see you tomorrow!** مع السَّلامةِ، أراكَ غداً!

by-election /'bʌɪə,lɛkʃ(ə)n/ *n* (BrE) [انْتِخاب فَرْعيّ عند وَفاةِ \ مُغادَرةِ نائِبٍ]

bygone /'bʌɪgɒn/ **A** *adj* (liter) ‹*era*› غابِر; ‹*days*› (خَوالٍ) خالٍ **B** *n* **to let ~s be ~s** ≈ عَفا اللهُ عَمّا سَلَفَ

by-law, **byelaw** /'bʌɪlɔː/ *n* (BrE) قانون داخِليّ (صادِر عن سُلُطاتٍ مَحَلّيّةٍ)

bypass /'bʌɪpɑːs/ **A** *n* **1** (road) طَريق فَرْعيّ \ جانِبِيّ; **traffic in the town has eased since the ~ opened** انْحَسَرَ الازْدِحامُ في البَلْدةِ بعد افْتِتاحِ الطَرِيقِ الجانِبيّ **2** (also **bypass operation**) جِراحة المَجازة القَلْبيّة; **his father had a ~ last year** أُجْرِيَتْ لوالِدِه جِراحةُ المَجازةِ القَلْبيّةِ السَنةَ الماضِيةَ **B** *vt* **1** ‹*a superior, manager*› تَجاهَلَ, تَجاوَزَ **2** ‹*the town, city centre*› تَجاوَزَ

by-product /'bʌɪprɒdʌkt/ *n* **1** (in manufacturing) مُنْتَج ثانَويّ **2** (consequence) [نَتيجة ثانَويّة غَيْر مَقْصودةٍ]

byroad /'bʌɪrəʊd/ *n* طَريق فَرْعيّ \ جانِبيّ

bystander /'bʌɪstandə/ *n* مُتَفَرِّج

byte /bʌɪt/ *n* بايْت

byway /'bʌɪweɪ/ *n* طَريق فَرْعيّ \ جانِبِيّ

byword /'bʌɪwəːd/ *n* **to be a ~ for sth** كانَ مِثالاً نَموذَجِيًّا لِشَيْءٍ

by-your-leave /,bʌɪjɔː'liːv/ *n* **without so much as a ~** دون اسْتِئْذانٍ

Cc

C, c /siː/ **A** *n* **1** (letter) [الحَرْف الثالث من الأَبْجَدِيّة الإنْكْليزِيّة] **2** (**C**) (Mus) (نَغْمة من نَغَماتِ السُلَّم الموسيقيّ) دو ≈ **B** *abbr* **1** (**c**) = **century**; **c20th**, **C20th** القَرْن العِشْرونَ **2** (**C**) = **Celsius**, **Centigrade** مِئَوِيّ **3** (**c**) = **cent** سِنْت (جُزْء من مِئَةٍ من الدولار \ اليورو) **4** (**c**) = **circa** حَوالَيْ; **c1890** حَوالَيْ 1890

CA *abbr* ▸ **California**

cab /kab/ *n* **1** (taxi) (تاكْسيات) تاكْسي, سَيّارة أُجْرة **2** (driver's compartment) مَقْصورة القيادة, كابينة السائق

cabaret /ˈkabəreɪ/ *n* **1** (genre) [u] كَباريه **2** (nightclub) كَباريه

cabbage /ˈkabɪdʒ/ *n* كُرُنْب

cab driver *n* سائق تاكْسي

cabin /ˈkabɪn/ *n* **1** (hut) (أَكْواخ) كوخ **2** (on a ship) قَمْرة **3** (on a plane) مَقْصورة الرُكّابِ

cabin crew *n* مُضيفو الطائِرة

cabin cruiser *n* (يُخوت) يَخْت, زَوْرَق سِياحيّ

cabinet /ˈkabɪnɪt/ *n* **1** (cupboard) (خَزائِنُ, خِزانات) خِزانة **2** (also **Cabinet**) (Pol) مَجْلِس الوُزَراءِ

cabinetmaker /ˈkabɪnɪt,meɪkə/ *n* نَجّار الأَثاثِ (الفاخِرِ)

cabinet minister *n* (وُزَراءُ) وَزير

cable /ˈkeɪb(ə)l/ *n* **1** (Elec, Tel) (أَسْلاك) سِلْك, كابِل **2** (Naut) (قُلوس) قَلْس, حَبْل غَليظ **3** (Constr) (حِبال) حَبْل **4** (also **cable television** or **cable TV**) تِلِفِزْيون الكابِل

cable car *n* تيليفِريك, عَرَبة مُعَلَّقة (NA, Leb)

cable television, **cable TV** *n* تِلْفِزْيون الكابِل

caboose /kəˈbuːs/ *n* (AmE) [عَرَبة مُؤَثَّثة يَسْتَعْمِلُها طاقِمُ القِطارِ]

cab rank (BrE), **cab stand** (AmE) *n* مَوْقِف سَيّاراتِ التاكْسي

cache /kaʃ/ **A** *n* **1** (hoard) (ذَخائِرُ) ذَخيرة **2** (place) مَخْبَأ (مَخابِئُ) **3** (Comput) (for data) ذاكِرة تَخْزينٍ مُؤَقَّتٍ
B *vt* **1** خَبَّأَ ‹*a weapon, the food*› **2** (Comput) حَفِظَ في ذاكِرة تَخْزينٍ مُؤَقَّتٍ ‹*a page, file*›

cackle /ˈkak(ə)l/ *vi* **1** «hens» قاقَ (u; قَوْق) **2** «women» [ضَحِكَ بِصَوْتٍ عالٍ وَشِرّيرٍ]

cactus /ˈkaktəs/ *n* (*pl* **cacti**, **cactuses**) صَبّار

CAD /kad/ *n* = **computer-aided design** تَصْميم بِمُساعدة الحاسوب \ الكُمْبْيوتَر

CADCAM /ˈkadkam/ *n* = **computer-aided design and computer-aided manufacture** تَصْميم وَتَصْنيع بِمُساعدةِ الحاسوب \ الكُمْبْيوتَر

caddie, **caddy** /ˈkadi/ *n* (*pl* **caddies**) [شَخْص يَحْمِلُ مَضارِبَ الغولْف لِلاعِبٍ]

cadet /kəˈdɛt/ *n* طالِب عَسْكَريّ

cadge /kadʒ/ *vt* (infml) **to ~ sth off** *or* **from sb** [تَحَصَّلَ على شَيْءٍ بالتَطَفُّل على شَخْصٍ] ‹*a cigarette, lift*›

cadi /ˈkɑːdi, ˈkeɪdi/ *n* (*pl* **cadis**) (قُضاة) قاضٍ

cadre /ˈkɑːdə/ *n* كَوادِر, أُطُر

Caesarea /siːzəˈrɪə/ *pr n* قَيْسارِيّة

caesarean, **caesarian**, **cesarean** (AmE) /sɪˈzɛːrɪən/ *n* (also **caesarean section**) عَمَلِيّة قَيْصَرِيّة; **to be born by ~** وُلِدَ بِعَمَلِيّةٍ قَيْصَرِيّةٍ

cafe /ˈkafeɪ/ *n* (مَقاهٍ) مَقْهًى

cafeteria /kafɪˈtɪərɪə/ *n* كافيتيريا

caffeine /ˈkafiːn/ *n* كافِيين

cage /keɪdʒ/ **A** *n* **1** (for a bird or animal) (أَقْفاص) قَفَص **2** (of a lift) (أَقْفاص) قَفَص **3** (in baseball) [سِياج وراء ضارِبِ كُرة البيسبول]
B *vt* وَضَعَ في قَفَصٍ ‹*a bird, an animal*›

cagoule, **kagoul** /kəˈguːl/ *n* (BrE) [مِعْطَف خَفيف وَطَويل واقٍ من المَطَرِ]

cahoots /kəˈhuːts/ *n pl* (infml) **to be in ~ with sb** تَواطَأَ مع شَخْصٍ

caiman, **cayman** /ˈkeɪmən/ *n* [نَوْع من التَماسيح]

Cairo /ˈkʌɪərəʊ/ *pr n* القاهِرة

cajole /kəˈdʒəʊl/ *vt* أَقْنَعَ ‹*a colleague, an opponent*›; **to ~ sb into doing sth** أَقْنَعَ شَخْصاً بِفِعْلِ شَيْءٍ

cake /keɪk/ *n* (Culin) كَعْك (n coll)

(Idiom) **to be a piece of cake** كانَ سَهْلاً مِثْلَ شُرْبِ الماءِ

cake shop *n* مَحَلّ كَعْكٍ

cake tin *n* صينِيّة كَعْكٍ

calabrese /ˈkaləbriːs/ *n* [قُنَّبيط أَخْضر اللَوْنِ]

calamity /kəˈlamɪti/ *n* (*pl* **calamities**) كارِثة (كَوارِث)

calcium /ˈkalsɪəm/ *n* كالسِيوم

calculate /ˈkalkjʊleɪt/ *vt* **1** (by maths) حَسَبَ (u; حِساب) ‹*a value, distance*› **2** (by reasoning) قَدَّرَ ‹*a probability, an effect*›

calculated /ˈkalkjʊleɪtɪd/ *adj* ‹*risk, decision*› مَدْروس

calculating /ˈkalkjʊleɪtɪŋ/ *adj* ‹*manner, criminal*› ماكِر (مَكَرة)

calculation /kalkjʊˈleɪʃ(ə)n/ *n* حِساب (حِسابات)

calculator /ˈkalkjʊleɪtə/ *n* آلة حاسِبة

calendar /ˈkalɪndə/ *n* **1** (chart) روزْنامة, يَوْمِيّة (NA) **2** (system) تَقْويم (تَقاويم)

calendar month *n* شَهْر (أَشْهُر, شُهور)

calf /kɑːf/ *n* (*pl* **calves**) **1** عِجْل (عُجول) **2** (also **calfskin**) (leather) جِلْد العِجْلِ **3** (of leg) رَبْلة (رَبَلات), سَمانة الرِجْلِ, بَطّة الساقِ

calibration /kalɪˈbreɪʃ(ə)n/ *n* مُعايَرة

calibre (BrE), **caliber** (AmE) /ˈkalɪbə/ *n* **1** (of a firearm) عِيار (عِيارات) **2** (of an employee, athlete) مُسْتَوًى (عالٍ)

Calif *abbr* ▸ **California**

California /ˌkalɪˈfɔːnɪə/ *pr n* كاليفورْنْيا

Californian /ˌkalɪˈfɔːnɪən/ *pr n, adj* كاليفورْنِيّ

caliper, **calliper** /ˈkalɪpə/ **1** (leg support) [داعِم مَعْدِنيّ للساقِ] **2** (**calipers** *n pl*) (for measuring) مِقْياس السُمْكِ

caliph /ˈkeɪlɪf, ˈkalɪf/ *n* خَليفة (خُلَفاءُ, خَلائِفُ)

caliphate /ˈkalɪfeɪt/ *n* خِلافة

call /kɔːl/ **A** *vt* **1** (to say loudly) (also **call out**) نادى ‹*a name, number, the answer*›; **Miss Jones ~ed the register** نادَتِ الأُسْتاذةُ جونْز كَشْفَ الحُضورِ **2** (to summon by shouting) نادى ‹*a waiter, dog*›; (by phone) طَلَبَ (u; طَلَب) ‹*the police, a taxi*›; (by letter) اسْتَدْعى, طَلَبَ الحُضورَ ‹*an applicant, a witness*›; **he was ~ed before the committee** طُلِبَ مِنْهُ الحُضورُ أمام اللَجْنةِ **3** (to telephone) «callers» اتَّصَلَ (ب), اتَّصِلْ بي ‹*a number, help line*›; **~ me on 07758082928** هاتَفَ على 07758082928 **4** (to announce) أَعْلَنَ (عن) ‹*a meeting*›; أَعْلَنَ (عن), نادى (ل) ‹*an election*›; أَعْلَنَ ‹*a strike*›; دَعا (u; ل) ‹*a flight*› **5** (to name) سَمّى ‹*a baby, book, product*›; **what did they ~ the baby?** ماذا سَمَّيا الطِفْلَ؟; **she is ~ed by her maiden name** تُدْعى باسْمِها قبل الزواجِ **6** (to describe as) **are you ~ing me a liar?** هل تَقولُ إنّني كَذّابٌ؟; **I'm proud to ~ myself a democrat/Jordanian** أَشْعُرُ بالفَخْرِ عِنْدَما أَقولُ إنّني من الحِزْبِ الديمُقْراطيِّ \ أُرْدُنِّيٌّ; **I wouldn't ~ it spacious** لا أَقولُ إنَّهُ فَسيحٌ; **do you ~ that plate clean?** هل تَقولُ إنّ هذا الطَبَقَ نَظيفٌ؟; **let's ~ it £20** دَعْنا نَقولُ 20£ **7** (Sport) أَعْلَنَ, أَشارَ أنّ ‹*a ball, shot*›; **the linesman ~ed the ball out/in** أَشارَ مُساعِدُ الحَكَمِ أنّ الكُرةَ خارِجَ \ داخِلَ المَلْعَبِ; **he was ~ed offside** أُعْلِنَ أنّهُ في وَضْعِ التَسَلُّلِ

B *vi* **1** (also **call out**) (to cry out) «person» نادى; **she ~ed for the nurse** نادَتْ على المُمَرِّضةِ **2** (by telephone) اتَّصَلَ (ب), هاتَفَ; **who's ~ing?** مَنْ المُتَّصِلُ؟; **please ~ again in an hour** من فَضْلِكَ اتَّصِلْ مَرّةً أُخْرى بعد ساعةٍ **3** (to visit) «person» زارَ (u; زِيارة), مَرَّ (u; مَرّ, مُرور); **I ~ed at your house on my way home** زُرْتُ بَيْتَكَ أثناء عَوْدَتي إلى المَنْزِلِ; **this train ~s at Birmingham** هذا القِطارُ يَتَوَقَّفُ في بِرْمِنْجْهام; **all the ships ~ at Port Said** كُلُّ السُفُنِ تَتَوَقَّفُ في بورْسَعيد **4** «birds» صاحَ (i; صِياح)

C *n* **1** (by phone) مُكالَمة; **to make/receive a ~** أَجْرى \ اسْتَقْبَلَ مُكالَمةً; **to make a ~ to Syria** أَجْرى مُكالَمةً لِسوريا; **I'll give you a ~ tomorrow** سَوْفَ أَتَّصِلُ بِكَ غَداً; **to return sb's ~** اتَّصَلَ بِشَخْصٍ رَدًّا على مُكالَمَتِهِ; **to put a ~ through**

to sb وَصَّلَ مُكالَمةً لِشَخْصٍ **2** (cry) صِياح; **no one answered her ~s for help** لم يَسْتَجِبْ أَحَدٌ لاسْتِغاثاتِها **3** (summons) نِداء (نِداءات); **this is the last ~ for passengers to Berlin** هذا آخِرُ نِداءٍ للمُسافِرِينَ إلى بِرْلين; **to put out a ~ for sb** وَجَّهَ نِداءً إلى شَخْصٍ **4** (appeal) دَعْوة, مُطالَبة; **there were ~s for his resignation** كانَ هُناكَ دَعَواتٌ لَهُ للاسْتِقالةِ; **the ~ to prayer** (from a mosque) الأَذان **5** [u] (vocation) نِداء; **he felt the ~ to the priesthood** شَعَرَ بِنِداءِ الكِهانةِ **6** (demand, need) **she has many ~s on her time** لَدَيْها مَشاغِلُ كَثيرةٌ; **there's not much ~ for them at this time of year** لا يوجَدُ طَلَبٌ كَبيرٌ عَلَيْهِ في مِثْلِ هذا الوَقْتِ من العامِ; **there's no ~ for such rudeness** لا داعِيَ لِمِثْلِ هذه الوَقاحةِ; **what he did was beyond the ~ of duty** ما فَعَلَهُ تَجاوُزٌ لِمَهامِّ الوَظيفةِ **7** (visit) زِيارة قَصيرة, مُرور; **to pay a ~ on sb, to pay sb a ~** زارَ شَخْصاً, مَرَّ على شَخْصٍ **8** (on duty) **to be on ~** «doctors, engineers» كانَ في مَهَمّةٍ; **Dr Janes is out on a ~ at the moment** خَرَجَ د. جايْنز في مَهَمّةٍ حالِيًّا **9** [u] (attraction) سِحْر, جاذِبيّة; **the ~ of the wild/the big city** سِحْر البَرِّيّةِ \ المَدينةِ الكَبيرةِ **10** (decision) قَرار; **it's a tough ~** هذا قَرارٌ صَعْبٌ

(Idiom) **to be a close call** [كانَ على وَشْكِ الانْتِهاءِ بِشَكْلٍ مُخْتَلِفٍ]

(Phrasal verbs) **call away: ~ [sb] away** اسْتَدْعى [شَخْصاً]; **she was ~ed away on business** تَمَّ اسْتِدْعاؤُها في مَهَمّةِ عَمَلٍ

• **call back A 1** (by phone) عاوَدَ الاتِّصالَ **2** (to return) أَتى مَرّةً أُخرى **B ~ [sb] back 1** (by shouting) صاحَ إلى [شَخْصٍ] بالعَوْدةِ ‹*a visitor*› **2** (to call again) عاوَدَ الاتِّصالَ بـ [شَخْصٍ]; (to return sb's call) رَدَّ المُكالَمةَ لـ [شَخْصٍ]

• **call by** «visitors» مَرَّ (u; مُرور)

• **call for: ~ for [sth/sb] 1** (to demand) طالَبَ بـ [شَيْءٍ] ‹*action, an investigation*› **2** (to merit) تَطَلَّبَ \ اسْتَوْجَبَ [شَيْئاً] ‹*special treatment, a different solution*›; **this ~s for a celebration!** هذا يَسْتَوْجِبُ الاحْتِفالَ!; **that was not ~ed for** لم يَكُنْ هُناكَ داعٍ لِذَلِكَ; أَقَلَّ **3** (to collect) أَحْضَرَ [شَيْئاً] ‹*a parcel*›; [شَخْصاً] ‹*a friend*›

• **call in A 1** (to visit) زارَ (u; زِيارة), تَوَقَّفَ, مَرَّ (u; مُرور); **to ~ in on sb** زارَ شَخْصاً **2** (to telephone) «employees» أَبْلَغَ; «listeners» اتَّصَلَ; **to ~ in sick** أَبْلَغَ أَنَّهُ مَريضٌ **B ~ in [sb], ~ [sb] in 1** (to ask inside) طَلَبَ من [شَخْصٍ] الدُخولَ ‹*a patient, candidate*› **2** (to send for) اسْتَدْعى [شَخْصاً] ‹*the police, an expert*› **C ~ in [sth], ~ [sth] in 1** (to recall) طَلَبَ إرْجاعَ [شَيْءٍ] ‹*a faulty product*› **2** طالَبَ بِسَدادِ [شَيْءٍ] ‹*a loan*›

• **call off: ~ off [sth], ~ [sth] off 1** (to cancel) أَلْغى [شَيْئاً] ‹*a strike, meeting, wedding*› **2** (to halt) أَوْقَفَ [شَيْئاً] ‹*a search, an investigation*› **3** زَجَرَ \ نَهى [شَيْئاً] ‹*a dog*›

• **call on: ~ on [sb/sth] 1** (to visit) زارَ [شَخْصاً \ شَيْئاً] ‹*a friend, patient*› **2** (to invite) دَعا [شَخْصاً \ شَيْئاً] ‹*a speaker, guest*› **3** (to urge) حَثَّ \ طالَبَ [شَخْصاً \ شَيْئاً] ‹*the government, minister*›; **to ~ on sb to do sth** طالَبَ شَخْصاً أَنْ يَفْعَلَ شَيْئاً **4** (to make use of) اسْتَعانَ بـ [شَخْصٍ \ شَيْءٍ] ‹*friends, sb's services*›; **she has neighbours she can ~ on** لَدَيْها جيرانٌ يُمْكِنُها أَنْ تَسْتَعينَ بِهِمْ

• **call out A** (to cry out) «person» نادى **B ~ out [sb], ~ [sb] out 1** (to send for) اسْتَدْعى [شَخْصاً] ‹*an engineer, the doctor*›; **the government ~ed out the army** اسْتَدْعَت الحُكومةُ الجَيْشَ **2** (on strike) دَعا [شَخْصاً] إلى الإضْرابِ ‹*the workers*› **C ~ [sth] out, ~ out [sth]** نادى [شَيْئاً] ‹*a number, name*›

• **call round** (BrE) (to visit) زارَ (u; زِيارة)

• **call up A ~ up [sb], ~ [sb] up 1** (by phone) اتَّصَلَ بـ [شَخْصٍ], هاتَفَ [شَخْصاً] ‹*a friend, one's mother*› **2** (for military service) اسْتَدْعى [شَخْصاً] ‹*reservists, troops*› **3** (for a game) اخْتارَ [شَخْصاً] ‹*a player*› **B ~ up [sth], ~ [sth] up 1** (to evoke) ذَكَّرَ بـ [شَيْءٍ] ‹*a memory, an image*› **2** أَظْهَرَ [شَيْئاً] ‹*a web page, file*›

• **call upon** ▸ **call on**

call box *n* كابينة هاتِفٍ \ تِليفون

call centre *n* مَرْكَز اتِّصالٍ

caller /ˈkɔːlə/ *n* **1** (on the telephone) مُتَّصِل **2** (visitor) زائِر (زُوّار, زائِرون; f pl زُوَّر, زائِرات)

calligraphy /kəˈlɪɡrəfi/ *n* فَنّ الخَطِّ

calling /ˈkɔːlɪŋ/ *n* (vocation) مُهِمّة

calliper /ˈkælɪpə/ ▸ **caliper**

callous /ˈkaləs/ *adj* ‹*attitude*› قاسٍ; ‹*criminal*› قاسي القَلْبِ

call-out charge /ˈkɔːlaʊt tʃɑːdʒ/ *n* [أَجْر نَظيرَ مُعايَنةِ مُشْكِلةٍ \ طارِئٍ]

call-up /ˈkɔːlʌp/ *n* (of civilians) تَجْنيد

callus /ˈkaləs/ *n* (*pl* **calluses**) جُسْأة

calm /kɑːm/ **A** *adj* **1** ‹*voice, manner*› هادِئ; **to stay** *or* **keep ~** ظَلَّ هادِئاً **2** ‹*sea, surface*› هادِئ, ساكِن **3** ‹*weather, day*› هادِئ (خالٍ من الريحِ)

B *n* هُدوء

C *vt* ‹*one's nerves, a situation*› هَدَّأَ

(Phrasal verb) **calm down** **1** «people, situation» هَدَأَ (a; هَدْء, هُدوء) **2** **~ [sth/sb] down, ~ down [sth/sb]** هَدَّأَ [شَيْئاً \ شَخْصاً] ‹*a child, situation*›

calmly /ˈkɑːmli/ *adv* ‹*to speak, sit*› بِهُدوءٍ

Calor gas® /ˈkalə gas/ *n* (BrE) غاز سائِل

calorie /ˈkaləri/ *n* كالوري, سُعْر حَراريّ

calve /kɑːv/ *vi* وَلَدَت (البَقَرة)

calves /kɑːvz/ *n pl* ▸**calf**

cam /kam/ *n* كامة

camber /ˈkambə/ *n* تَحَدُّب, تَقَوُّس

Cambodia /kamˈbəʊdɪə/ *pr n* كَمْبودْيا

Cambodian /kamˈbəʊdɪən/ **A** *n* **1** (citizen) كَمْبوديّ **2** (language) (اللُغة) الكَمْبوديّة

B *adj* ‹*language, border, ambassador*› كَمْبوديّ

camcorder /ˈkamkɔːdə/ *n* كاميرا فيدْيو

came /keɪm/ *past tense* ▸**come**

camel /ˈkam(ə)l/ *n* جَمَل (جِمال, أَجْمال)

cameo /ˈkamɪəʊ/ *n* **1** (jewellery) [قِطْعة من المُجَوْهَراتِ عَلَيْها صورةٌ مَنْقوشةٌ] **2** (in a play or film) [دَوْر صَغير لِضَيْفِ شَرَفٍ]; **a ~ role** دَوْر شَرَفيّ

camera /ˈkam(ə)rə/ *n* كاميرا (كاميرات)

camera crew *n* فَريق تَصْوير

cameraman /ˈkamrəmən/ *n* (*pl* **-men**) مُصَوِّر

camera phone *n* هاتِف مَحْمول مُزَوَّد بِكاميرا

camerawork /ˈkamrəwəːk/ *n* [طَريقة تَصْوير]

Cameroon /ˌkaməˈruːn/ *pr n* الكاميرون (f)

camisole /ˈkamɪsəʊl/ *n* [قَميص نِسائيّ تَحْتيّ بِحَمّالاتِ كَتِفٍ]

camomile, chamomile (AmE) /ˈkaməmʌɪl/ *n* بابونَج

camouflage /ˈkaməflɑːʒ/ **A** *n* تَمْويه

B *vt* ‹*a tank, building*› مَوَّهَ

camp /kamp/ **A** *n* **1** (for soldiers, refugees) مُخَيَّم (مُخَيَّمات) **2** (for holidaymakers) مُخَيَّم (مُخَيَّمات)

B *vi* خَيَّمَ; **to go ~ing** ذَهَبَ للتَخْييمِ

C *adj* ‹*man*› مُخَنَّث

campaign /kamˈpeɪn/ **A** *n* حَمْلة (حَمَلات)

B *vi* «candidates, groups» قام بِحَمْلةٍ; **to ~ for/against sth** قام بِحمْلةٍ ل \ ضدّ شَيْءٍ

campaigner /kamˈpeɪnə/ *n* مُناضِل

camp bed *n* سَرير مُعَسْكَرٍ

camper /ˈkampə/ *n* **1** (person) مُخَيِّم **2** (vehicle) (also **camper van**) سَيّارة تَخْييم

campfire /ˈkampfʌɪə/ *n* نار المُخَيَّمِ

campground /ˈkampgraʊnd/ *n* (AmE) ▸**campsite**

camping /ˈkampɪŋ/ *n* تَخْييم; **to go ~** خَيَّمَ

campsite /ˈkampsʌɪt/ *n* **1** (open area) مُخَيَّم (مُخَيَّمات) **2** (AmE) (for tent, trailer) مُخَيَّم (مُخَيَّمات)

campus /ˈkampəs/ *n* (*pl* **campuses** /ˈkampəsɪz/) حَرَم جامِعيّ

camshaft /ˈkamʃɑːft/ *n* عَمود الكاماتِ

can¹ /kan, kən/ *modal aux* (*past tense, conditional* **could**; *negative in present tense* **cannot, can't**) **1** (to have the skill, knowledge to) **she can drive now** أَصْبَحَ بِإمْكانِها الآنَ أنْ تَقودَ السَيّارة; **~ you play the piano?** هل تَسْتَطيعُ أنْ تَعْزِفَ على البيانو؟; **she told us she could speak Arabic** أَخْبَرَتْنا أنّها تَسْتَطيعُ أنْ تَتَحَدَّثَ اللُغةَ العَرَبيّة; **he couldn't read or write** لا يَسْتَطيعُ القِراءةَ وَلا الكِتابةَ **2** (to have the ability to, using one's senses) **~ you see it?** هل يُمْكِنُكَ أنْ تَراهُ؟; **he can't see any more** لم يَعُدْ بِإمْكانِهِ أنْ يَرى; **we could hear them laughing** كانَ باسْتِطاعَتِنا أنْ نَسْمَعَهُمْ يَضْحَكونَ; **can you hear me now?** هل تَسْتَطيعُ أنْ تَسْمَعَني الآنَ؟ **3** (in requests) **~ I come with you?** هل يُمْكِنُني أنْ أَذْهَبَ مَعَكَ؟; **could you do me a favour?** هل بِإمْكانِكَ أنْ تُسْدِيَ

4 (to express permission) **you ~ park here** يُمكِنُكَ أنْ تَرْكِنَ سَيّارَتَكَ هُنا; **I can't leave yet** لا يُمْكِنُني أنْ أُغادِرَ بَعْدُ; **~ we leave our valuables here?** هل يُمْكِنُنا أنْ نَتْرُكَ أَشْياءَنا الثَمينةَ هُنا؟ **5** (in making offers) **~ I give you a hand?** هل يُمْكِنُني أنْ أُساعِدَكَ؟; **what ~ I get you?** ماذا تُريدُ أنْ أُحْضِرَ لَكَ؟ **6** (to express possibility) **we ~ rent a car when we arrive** يُمْكِنُنا أنْ نَسْتَأْجِرَ سَيّارةً عِنْدَما نَصِلُ; **he could be dead** قد يَكونُ مَيّتاً; **anything could happen** كُلُّ شَيْءٍ وارِدٌ; **it cannot be explained logically** لا يُمْكِنُ شَرْحُهُ بِشَكْلٍ مَنْطِقيٍّ **7** (when making suggestions) **you ~ always return it** يَبْقى بِإمْكانِكَ أنْ تَرُدَّهُ; **we could try to phone him** يُمْكِنُنا أنْ نُحاوِلَ الاتِّصالَ بِهِ **8** (to have the power to) **computers ~ process data almost instantly** تَسْتَطيعُ أَجْهِزةُ الكُمْبيوتَر أنْ تُعالِجَ البَياناتِ بِشَكْلٍ فَوْريٍّ تَقْريباً; **I'll do all I ~** سَأَفْعَلُ كُلَّ ما بِوِسْعي; **he couldn't walk for weeks** لم يَكُنْ بِاسْتِطاعَتِهِ أنْ يَمْشيَ لِعِدّةِ أَسابيعَ; **if only we could stay** أَتَمَنّى لو كانَ بِوُسْعِنا أنْ نَبْقى; **I wish I could have been there** أَتَمَنّى لو كانَ بِوِسْعي أنْ أَكونَ هُناكَ; **I can't** *or* **cannot understand why** لا يُمْكِنُني أنْ أَفْهَمَ لِماذا **9** (to indicate capability) **he ~ be quite charming** بِمَقْدورِهِ أنْ يَكونَ جَذّاباً جِدًّا; (having tendency) قد يَكونُ أَحْياناً جَذّاباً جِدًّا; **she could be very outspoken** قد تَكونُ أَحْياناً صَريحةً جِدًّا **10** (to express likelihood) **the cease-fire can't last** لَيْسَ مِنَ المُمْكِنِ أنْ يَدومَ وَقْفُ إطْلاقِ النارِ; **it can't have been easy for them** لا بُدَّ أنَّهُ لم يَكُنْ سَهْلاً عَلَيْهِمْ; **he couldn't be more than 15 years old** مِن غَيْرِ المُمْكِنِ أنْ يَكونَ عُمْرُهُ قد تَجاوَزَ ال 15 **11** (to express willingness) **we ~ take you home** يُمْكِنُنا أنْ نُوَصِّلَكَ إلى المَنْزِلِ; **I could collect you tomorrow** يُمْكِنُني أنْ أُقِلَّكَ غَداً; **I cannot give up now** لا يُمْكِنُني أنْ أَسْتَسْلِمَ الآنَ; **I couldn't possibly accept the money** ما كانَ مِنَ المُمْكِنِ بِأيِّ حالٍ مِنَ الأَحْوالِ أنْ أَقْبَلَ المالَ; **I can't say I agree** لا يُمْكِنُني أنْ أَقولَ أنّي مُوافِقٌ **12** (to express reproach) **you could have warned us** كانَ بِإمْكانِكَ أنْ تُحَذِّرَنا; **how could you!** كَيفَ جَرُؤْتَ! **13** (to express surprise) **who could it be?** يا تُرى مَنْ يَكونُ؟; **what ~ she possibly want from me?** يا تُرى ماذا تُريدُ مِنّي؟; **you can't** *or* **cannot be serious!** لا بُدَّ أنَّكَ تَمْزَحُ! **14** (for emphasis) **I couldn't agree more!** أَتَّفِقُ مَعَكَ تَماماً!; **you couldn't be more mistaken** أَنْتَ مُخْطِئٌ تَماماً! **15** (infml) (expressing strong emotion) **I was so angry I could have screamed!** كُنْتُ غاضِباً جِدًّا حتّى أنّي كُنْتُ على وَشْكِ أنْ أَصْرُخَ!; **I could murder him!** كُنْتُ على وَشْكِ أنْ أَقْتُلَهُ! **16** (avoiding repetition of verb) **'~ we borrow it?'—'of course you ~'** 'هل يُمْكِنُنا أنْ نَسْتَعيرَهُ؟' — 'بالطَبْعِ يُمْكِنُكُمْ ذلك'; **leave as soon as you ~** غادِرْ بِأَسْرَعِ وَقْتٍ مُمْكِنٍ

(Idiom) **as happy/excited** *etc.* **as can/could be** في مُنْتَهى السَعادةِ \ الحَماسِ ... إلخ; **they were as happy as could be with the present** كانوا في مُنْتَهى السَعادةِ بالهَديّةِ

can² /kan/ **A** *n* عُلْبة (عُلَب)

B *vt* **(-nn-)** (to put in cans) عَلَّبَ *<fish, fruit>*

(Idiom) **in the can** (infml) [جاهز للعَرْضِ]

Canada /ˈkanədə/ *pr n* كَنَدا

Canadian /kəˈneɪdɪən/ *n, adj* كَنَديّ

canal /kəˈnal/ *n* **1** (for ships, barges) قَناة (قَنَوات ,أَقْنِية) **2** (Anat) قَناة (قَنَوات ,أَقْنِية)

canal boat, **canal barge** *n* قارِب \ مُعَدِّية قَناةٍ

Canaries /kəˈnɛərɪz/ *pr n pl* (**the Canaries** also **the Canary Islands**) جُزُر الكَناري

canary /kəˈnɛːri/ *n* (*pl* **canaries**) (Zool) كَناريّ

Canberra /ˈkanb(ə)rə/ *pr n* كانْبَرا

cancel /ˈkans(ə)l/ *vt* **(-ll- BrE, -l- AmE)** **1** (an arrangement) أَلْغى *<an appointment, a trip>* **2** (a document) فَسَخَ (فَسْخ ;a) *<a contract>*; أَلْغى *<cheque>*

(Phrasal verb) **cancel out: ~ out [sth]** **1** (to neutralize) أَبْطَلَ *<a benefit, an effect>* **2** (Math) أَلْغى ,أَبْطَلَ *<a figure, an amount>*; **to ~ each other out** أَبْطَلَ بَعْضُهُما البَعْضَ

cancellation (BrE), **cancelation** (AmE) /ˌkansəˈleɪʃ(ə)n/ *n* **1** (of an event) إلْغاء (إلْغاءات) **2** (of a contract) إلْغاء (إلْغاءات)

cancer /ˈkansə/ *n* سَرَطان (سَرَطانات); **lung ~, ~ of the lung** سَرَطان الرِئةِ

Cancer /ˈkansə/ *n* **1** (sign) بُرْج السَرَطانِ **2** (person) [مِن مَواليدِ بُرْجِ السَرَطانِ]

cancerous /ˈkans(ə)rəs/ *adj* ‹*cells, tumour*› سَرَطانيّ

cancer patient *n* مَريض السَّرَطانِ

candid /ˈkandɪd/ *adj* ‹*interview, autobiography*› صَريح

candidacy /ˈkandɪdəsi/, **candidature** /ˈkandɪdətʃə/ (BrE) *n* (*pl* **candidacies**) تَرَشُّح

candidate /ˈkandɪdeɪt/ *n* **1** (for a job, in an election) مُرَشَّح, مُتَرَشِّح **2** (BrE) (in an exam) مُتَرَشِّح, مُمْتَحَن (NA)

candle /ˈkand(ə)l/ *n* شَمْعة (شُموع)

candlelight /ˈkand(ə)lʌɪt/ *n* ضَوْء الشُموعِ

candlestick /ˈkand(ə)lstɪk/ *n* شَمْعُدان (شَماعِدُ, شَمْعُدانات)

candy /ˈkandi/ *n* (*pl* **candies**) (AmE) **1** [u] (confectionery) حَلْوَيات **2** (item) قِطْعة حَلْوى

candyfloss /ˈkandɪflɒs/ *n* (BrE) غَزل البَناتِ

cane /keɪn/ *n* **1** (material) قَصَب **2** (of sugar, bamboo) قَصَبة, خَيْزُرانة **3** (for walking) عُكّاز (عَكاكيزُ); (of raspberry plant) [جِذْع شُجَيْرةٍ من الوَرْديّاتِ]; (for plant) ساق (f; سيقان); (BrE) (for punishment) عَصاً (f; عِصيّ)

canine /ˈkeɪnʌɪn/ *n* [حَيَوان من فَصيلةِ الكَلْبيّاتِ]

canister /ˈkanɪstə/ *n* **1** (container) عُلْبة (عُلَب) **2** (explosive) قُنْبُلة غازيّة

cannabis /ˈkanəbɪs/ *n* قِنَّب

canned /kand/ *adj* **1** (in cans) ‹*food, tuna*› مُعَلَّب **2** (pre-recorded) ‹*laughter, music*› مُسَجَّل

cannibal /ˈkanɪb(ə)l/ *n* آكِل لُحومِ البَشَرِ

cannon /ˈkanən/ *n* (*pl* **cannon** or **cannons**) مِدْفَع (مَدافِعُ)

cannonball /ˈkanənbɔːl/ *n* قَذيفة مِدْفَعٍ

cannot /ˈkanɒt/ ▸ **can¹** = **can not**

canoe /kəˈnuː/ **A** *n* كانو (قارِب تَجْديفٍ)
B *vi* (**canoes**, **canoeing**, **canoed**) [سافَرَ بالكانو]

canoeing /kəˈnuːɪŋ/ *n* [تَجْديف بالكانو]

canon /ˈkanən/ *n* **1** (complete works) الأَعْمال الكامِلة **2** (priest) كاهِن (كَهَنة, كُهّان) **3** (fml) (rule) قانون (قَوانينُ)

can opener *n* فَتّاحة

canopy /ˈkanəpi/ *n* (*pl* **canopies**) **1** (for a throne, bed) مِظَلّة (مَظالُّ, مِظَلّات) **2** (for a parachute) مِظَلّة (مَظالُّ, مِظَلّات)

cant /kant/ *n* نِفاق

can't /kɑːnt/ *abbr* = **cannot** ▸ **can¹**

cantankerous /kanˈtaŋk(ə)rəs/ *adj* ‹*grandfather, personality*› مُشاكِس

cantata /kanˈtɑːtə/ *n* كَنْتاتا (نَوْع من الموسيقى الدينيّةِ)

canteen /kanˈtiːn/ *n* **1** (BrE) (dining room) مَقْصِف (مَقاصِفُ), كانْتين **2** (bottle) زَمْزَميّة

canter /ˈkantə/ *vi* «riders, horses» خَبَّ (u; خبب)

canticle /ˈkantɪk(ə)l/ *n* نشيد (أَنْشاد, نَشائِدُ, أَناشيدُ)

canvas /ˈkanvəs/ *n* **1** (cloth) خَيْش (أَخْياش, خُيوش) **2** (work of art) لَوْحة (لَوْحات)

canvass /ˈkanvəs/ *vt* **1** [الْتَمَسَ أَصْواتاً من] ‹*voters*›; [الْتَمَسَ أَصْوات الناخِبينَ في] ‹*an area*›; **to ~ voters** الْتَمَسَ أَصْوات الناخِبينَ **2** الْتَمَسَ ‹*support*› **3** اسْتَطْلَعَ ‹*opinions*›

canvasser /ˈkanvəsə/ *n* **1** (in marketing) [شَخْص يَسْتَطْلِعُ آراءَ الناسِ حول بِضاعةٍ \ خِدْمةٍ] **2** (in politics) [شَخْص يُحاوِلُ إِقْناعَ الناسِ بالتَّصْويتِ لمُرَشَّحٍ ما]

canyon /ˈkanjən/ *n* تَلْعة (تِلاع)

canyoning /ˈkanjənɪŋ/ *n* [رِياضة القَفْزِ في المَجاري المائيّةِ الجَبَليّةِ]

cap /kap/ **A** *n* **1** (hat) قُبَّعة; **swimming** *or* **bathing ~** قُبَّعة سِباحةٍ **2** (of a pen, bottle, camera lens) غِطاء (أَغْطِية) **3** (for a tooth) غلاف
B *vt* (**-pp-**) **1** (to cover) غَطّى القِمّةَ ‹*a mountain, building*› **2** (to round off) اخْتَتَمَ ‹*a performance, career*› **3** (to limit) حَدَّ (u; حَدّ; من) ‹*spending, prices*› **4** غَلَّفَ ‹*a tooth*›
Idiom **to cap it all** وَمِمّا زادَ الطينَ بَلّةً

CAP /siːeɪˈpiː/ *n* = **Common Agricultural Policy** [السِياسة الفلاحيّة المُشْتَرَكة في أوروبّا]

capability /keɪpəˈbɪlɪti/ *n* (*pl* **capabilities**) قُدْرة (قُدُرات)

capable /ˈkeɪpəb(ə)l/ *adj* **1** (competent) ‹*leader, student*› قَدير, كُفُؤ (أَكْفاء, كِفاء) **2** (able) **to be ~ of doing sth** كانَ قادِراً على فِعْلِ شَيْءٍ

capacity /kəˈpasɪti/ *n* (*pl* **capacities**) **1** [u] (of a vehicle, stadium) سَعة; **the hall was packed to ~** امْتَلأَت القاعةُ

عن آخرِها; **the stadium has a ~ of 35,000** يَسَعُ المَلْعَبُ 35,000 شَخْصٍ; **the prison is stretched beyond ~** يَتَحَمَّلُ السِجْنُ أَكْثَرَ من طاقَتِهِ الاسْتيعابيّة **2** [u] (of a plant, factory) طاقة إِنْتاجيّة; **the factory is working at full ~/below ~** يَعْمَلُ المَصْنَعُ بكامِلِ \ تحت طاقَتِهِ الإنْتاجيّة **3** (role) دَوْر (أَدْوار), صِفة; **she works here in an advisory ~** تَعْمَلُ هُنا بصِفةٍ اسْتِشاريّة; **in his ~ as president/chairman** بِصِفَتِهِ رَئيساً \ رَئيسَ مَجْلِسِ إدارة **4** (ability) قُدْرة (قُدُرات), اسْتِطاعة; **she has a great ~ for hard work** لَدَيْها قُدْرةٌ عَظيمةٌ على العَمَلِ الشاقّ; **the task is well within his ~** المُهِمّةُ في حُدودِ اسْتطاعَتِهِ **5** (of engines) سَعة

cape /keɪp/ *n* **1** (cloak) رداء (أَرْدِية) **2** (Geog) رَأْس بَحْريّ (أَرْض داخِلة في البَحْرِ)

caper /ˈkeɪpə/ *n* **1** (Culin) قُبّار, كَبَر **2** (infml) (film) فيلْم يَمْزُج بين الجَريمةِ والفُكاهةِ] **3** (infml) (escapade) دُعابة, مَزْحة

Capernaum /kəˈpəːnjəm/ *pr n* كَفْر ناحوم (f)

Cape Town /ˈkeɪp taʊn/ *pr n* كَيْب تاوْن (f)

capillary /kəˈpɪləri/ *n* (*pl* **capillaries**) شُعَيْرة دَمَويّة

capital /ˈkapɪt(ə)l/ **A** *n* **1** (also **capital city**) عاصِمة (عَواصِمُ) **2** (also **capital letter**) حَرْف كَبير **3** [u] (Fin) رَأْسمال **B** *adj* **1** ‹*letter*› كَبير **2** ‹*offence*› اسْتِهْلالي, عَظيم

capitalism /ˈkapɪt(ə)lɪz(ə)m/ *n* رَأْسماليّة

capitalist /ˈkapɪt(ə)lɪst/ **A** *n* رَأْسماليّ **B** *adj* ‹*system, society*› رَأْسماليّ

capitalize, -ise (BrE) /ˈkapɪt(ə)lʌɪz/ **A** *vi* **to ~ on sth** «team, politician» اسْتَفادَ من شَيْءٍ **B** *vt* (Fin) مَوَّلَ ‹*a company*›

capital punishment *n* عُقوبة الإعْدام

Capitol /ˈkapɪt(ə)l/ *pr n* **the ~** (in Washington) الكابيتول

capitulate /kəˈpɪtjʊleɪt/ *vi* اسْتَسْلَمَ (ل)

Capricorn /ˈkaprɪkɔːn/ *n* **1** (sign) بُرْج الجَدْيِ **2** (person) [من مَواليد بُرْج الجَدْيِ]

caps /kaps/ *n pl* = **capital letters** حُروف كَبيرة \ اسْتِهْلاليّة

capsicum /ˈkapsɪkəm/ *n* فُلْفُل (فَلافِلُ)

capsize /kapˈsʌɪz/ *vi* «boats, yachts» انْقَلَبَ

capsule /ˈkapsjuːl/ *n* كَبْسولة

captain /ˈkaptɪn/ **A** *n* **1** (of a ship) رُبّان (رَبابينُ, رَبابِنة), قُبْطان (قَباطينُ, قَباطِنة); (of an aircraft) طَيّار, كابْتِن **2** (in the army, navy) نَقيب (نُقَباءُ) **3** (of a team) قائِد (قادة) **B** *vt* قادَ (u; قِيادة), تَرَأَّسَ, تَزَعَّمَ ‹*a team, a ship*›

caption /ˈkapʃ(ə)n/ *n* تَعْليق (تَعاليقُ, تَعْليقات)

captivate /ˈkaptɪveɪt/ *vt* أَسَرَ (i; أَسْر) ‹*an audience, sb's imagination*›

captive /ˈkaptɪv/ **A** *n* أَسير (أَسْرى, أُسَراءُ) **B** *adj* **1** (imprisoned) أَسير (أَسْرى, أُسَراءُ); **to hold sb ~** حَبَسَ شَخْصاً **2** **a ~ audience** جُمْهور أَسير

captivity /kapˈtɪvɪti/ *n* أَسْر

captor /ˈkaptə/ *n* آسِر

capture /ˈkaptʃə/ **A** *vt* **1** قَبَضَ (i; قَبْض) (على) ‹*a terrorist*›; اسْتَوْلى (على) ‹*a town*› **2** شَدَّ (i-u; شَدّ) ‹*sb's attention, interest*› **3** الْتَقَطَ ‹*an image, a mood*› **B** *n* (of a criminal, an animal) قَبْض (على); (of a town) اسْتيلاء (على)

car /kɑː/ *n* **1** (road vehicle) سَيّارة; **to travel by ~** سافَرَ بالسَيّارةِ **2** (of a train) عَرَبة; **the restaurant/dining ~** عَرَبة المَطْعَمِ

car accident *n* حادِث سَيّارةٍ

caramel /ˈkarəm(ə)l/ *n* **1** [u] (flavouring) كَراميل **2** (sweet) حَلْوى الكَراميل

carat /ˈkarət/ *n* **1** (for gold) (also **karat** AmE) قيراط (قَراريطُ); **18~ gold** الذَهَب عِيارَ 18 قيراطاً **2** (for precious stones) قيراط (قَراريطُ); **a 24~ diamond** أَلْماسة تَزِنُ 24 قيراطاً

caravan /ˈkarəvan/ *n* **1** (BrE) (towed by a car) كَرَفان, مَقْطورة **2** (horse-drawn) عَرَبة خَيْلٍ **3** (group) قافِلة (قَوافِلُ)

caravan site *n* (BrE) مَوْقِع كَرَفاناتٍ

caraway /ˈkarəweɪ/ *n* كَراوِيا

caraway seed *n* بُذور كَراوِيا

carbohydrate /kɑːbəˈhʌɪdreɪt/ *n* كَرْبوهيدْرات

car bomb *n* سَيّارة مَلْغومة \ مُفَخَّخة

carbon /ˈkɑːb(ə)n/ *n* كَرْبون

carbon copy *n* نُسْخة كَرْبونيّة

carbon dioxide *n* ثاني أوكسيدِ الكَرْبون

carbon emissions *n* انْبِعاثات الكَرْبون

carbon footprint *n* بَصْمة الكَرْبون

carbon monoxide *n* أوَّل أوكْسيد الكَرْبون

carbon-neutral /ˌkɑːb(ə)nˈnjuːtrəl/ *adj* مُحايِد الكَرْبون

carbon offsetting *n* تَعْويض الكَرْبون

car boot sale *n* (BrE) سوق السِلَعِ المُسْتَعْمَلةِ ≈ حَيْثُ تُعْرَضُ السِلَعُ في صَناديقِ السَيّاراتِ

carburettor (BrE), **carburetor** (AmE) /kɑːbəˈrɛtə/ *n* مُكَرْبِن, كارْبِراتير

carcass /ˈkɑːkəs/ *n* جُثّة (جُثَث, أَجْثاث)

carcinogen /kɑːˈsɪnədʒ(ə)n/ *n* مادّة مُسَرْطِنة

carcinogenic /ˌkɑːs(ɪ)nəˈdʒɛnɪk/ *adj* ‹*substance, by-product*› مُسَرْطِن

carcinoma /ˌkɑːsɪˈnəʊmə/ *n* وَرَم سَرَطانيّ

car crash *n* حادِث تَصادُمِ سَيّارةٍ

card /kɑːd/ *n* 1 (greeting card) بطاقة (بطاقات, بَطائِقُ) 2 (for identification) بِطاقة (بِطاقات, بَطائِقُ); **let me give you my (business) ~** دَعْني أُعْطيكَ بِطاقَتي 3 (also **credit card**) بطاقة اِئْتِمانٍ 4 (also **playing card**) وَرَقة لَعِبٍ; **to play ~s** لَعِبَ الوَرَقَ 5 (also **index card**) بِطاقة (بِطاقات, بَطائِقُ) 6 [u] (thin cardboard) وَرَق مُقَوًّى

cardamom /ˈkɑːdəməm/, **cardamon** /ˈkɑːdəmən/ *n* حَبَّهان

cardboard /ˈkɑːdbɔːd/ *n* كَرْتون (كَراتينُ), وَرَق مُقَوًّى

cardboard box *n* صُنْدوق كَرْتون \ من وَرَقٍ مُقَوًّى

cardboard city *n* [مِنْطَقة ذات بُيوتٍ من الوَرَقِ المُقَوّى يَقْطُنُ فيها المُشَرَّدونَ]

card catalogue *n* كَتالوج مَكْتَبةٍ (في بِطاقاتٍ)

card game *n* لُعْبة وَرَقٍ

cardholder /ˈkɑːdhəʊldə/ *n* صاحِب البِطاقةِ

cardiac /ˈkɑːdɪak/ *adj* ‹*surgery, disease*› قَلْبيّ, القَلْبِ

cardiac arrest *n* سَكْتة قَلْبيّة

cardigan /ˈkɑːdɪg(ə)n/ *n* سُتْرة (سُتَر)

cardinal /ˈkɑːd(ɪ)n(ə)l/ A *n* كَرْدينال (كَرادِلة)
B *adj* ‹*sin, principle*› أَساسيّ; **a ~ number** عَدَد أَصْليّ

cardiogram /ˈkɑːdɪə(ʊ)gram/ *n* رَسْم قَلْبٍ

cardiograph /ˈkɑːdɪə(ʊ)grɑːf/ *n* جِهاز رَسْمِ القَلْبِ

cardiologist /ˌkɑːdɪˈɒlədʒɪst/ *n* طَبيب قَلْبٍ, أَخِصّائيّ أَمْراضِ القَلْبِ

cardiology /kɑːdɪˈɒlədʒi/ *n* عِلْم أَمْراضِ القَلْبِ, طِبّ القَلْبِ

cardiovascular /ˌkɑːdɪəʊˈvaskjʊlə/ *adj* ‹*disease, exercise*› القَلْبِ والأَوْعِية الدَمَويّة

card trick *n* خِدْعة وَرَقٍ

care /kɛː/ A *n* 1 [u] (attention) عِناية, اِهْتِمام, حَذَر; **to take ~ to do sth** حَرَصَ على أَنْ يَفْعَلَ شَيْئاً; **he took ~ not to wake her** حَرَصَ على أَلاّ يوقِظَها; **she chose her words with ~** اِنْتَقَتْ كَلِماتِها بِعِنايةٍ; **she always takes great ~ over** *or* **with her work** دائِماً ما تُؤَدّي عَمَلَها باهْتِمامٍ بالِغٍ; **'take ~!'** (as warning) 'اِنْتَبِهْ!'; (saying goodbye) اِعْتَنِ بِنَفْسِكَ!; **'handle with ~'** 'اِحْمِلْ بِرِفْقٍ'; **he was convicted of driving without due ~ and attention** أُدينَ بِتُهْمةِ القِيادةِ بِتَهَوُّرٍ 2 [u] (supervision of a child, patient, animal) رِعاية; (of appliances, plants, clothes) عِناية; **medical ~** رِعاية طِبّيّة; **the pupils/patients in my ~** التَلاميذ \ المَرْضى تحت رِعايَتي; **to take ~ of sb** رَعى شَخْصاً ‹*a patient, a child*›; **can you take ~ of this customer?** هل يُمْكِنُكَ أَنْ تَعْتَنِيَ بِهَذا العَميلِ؟; **to take ~ of oneself** (to look after oneself) اِعْتَنى بِنَفْسِه; **I can take ~ of myself** (to cope alone) يُمْكِنُني أَنْ أَعْتَنِيَ بِنَفْسي; **to take ~ of sth** (to look after) اِعْتَنى بِشَيْءٍ ‹*the house, one's teeth*›; (to deal with) عالَجَ شَيْئاً ‹*a problem, the details*›; **take good ~ of it** اِعْتَنِ بِه جَيِّداً; **to leave sb/sth in sb's ~** تَرَكَ شَخْصاً \ شَيْئاً في رِعايةِ شَخْصٍ; **don't worry! I'll take ~ of everything** لا تَقْلَقْ! سَوْفَ أَهْتَمُّ بِكُلِّ شَيْءٍ; **John Smith, ~ of Mr and Mrs L. Smith** (on a letter) إلى جون سْميث، رِعاية السَيِّدِ والسَيِّدةِ ل. سْميث 3 [u] (BrE) (for children at risk) **to be in ~** كانَ في دارِ رِعايةِ الأَطْفالِ \ مع أُسْرةٍ حاضِنةٍ]; **to take** *or* **put a child into ~** وَضَعَ طِفْلاً في دارِ رِعايةِ الأَطْفالِ \ مع أُسْرةٍ حاضِنةٍ 4 (worry) هَمّ (هُموم), تَوَتُّر; **without a ~ in the world** لا يَحْمِلُ للدُنْيا هَمّاً

B *vt* 1 (fml) (to like) **would you ~ to sit down?** هل تَرْغَبُ في الجُلوسِ؟; **he likes her more than he ~s to admit** يُحِبُّها

بِقَدْرٍ أَكْبَرَ مِمّا يَرْغَبُ في الاعْتِرافِ بِهِ; **he would play for anyone who ~d to listen** كانَ يَعْزِفُ لِأَيِّ شَخْصٍ يَرْغَبُ في الاسْتِماعِ لَهُ **2** (to mind) **what do I ~?** لا يُهِمُّني ذلك; **I don't ~ who he marries** لا يُهِمُّني بِمَنْ سَيَتَزَوَّجُ; **I don't ~ whether she likes it or not** لا يَعْنيني ما إذا أَعْجَبَها أم لا **C** *vi* **1** (to feel concerned) بالى, اهْتَمَّ; **she ~s about other people** تَهْتَمُّ بالآخَرينَ; **it's an issue that people ~ about** هذه مَسْأَلَةٌ يَهْتَمُّ الناسُ بها; **I don't ~!** لا أُبالي!; **who ~s?** وَمَنْ يُبالي؟; **I couldn't ~ less!** لا يَعْنيني في أَيِّ شَيْءٍ!; **she couldn't ~ less about him** لا تَأْبَهُ بِهِ إطْلاقاً; **they could both be dead, for all he ~d** قد يَكونا مَيِّتَيْنِ، لَكِنَّهُ لم يَكْتَرِثْ بِهِما; **I'm past caring** لم أَعُدْ أُبالي **2** **to ~ about sb** (to feel affection) اهْتَمَّ بِشَخْصٍ

(Phrasal verb) **care for** **A** **~ for [sb/sth]** **1** (to look after) اعْتَنى بـ [شَخْصٍ \ شَيْءٍ] ‹*a child, an animal, a patient*› **2** (to be fond of) أَحَبَّ [شَخْصاً \ شَيْئاً] ‹*a friend, partner*› **B** **~ for [sth]** **1** (fml) **to ~ for sth** (to like) أَحَبَّ شَيْئاً; (to want) رَغِبَ في شَيْءٍ; **I don't much ~ for his work** لا يُعْجِبُني عَمَلُهُ كَثيراً; **would you ~ for some tea?** هل تَرْغَبُ في بَعْضِ الشاي؟ **2** (to maintain) اعْتَنى بـ [شَيْءٍ] ‹*a garden, one's skin, an appliance*›

care assistant *n* مُساعِد رِعايةِ المَرْضى

career /kəˈrɪə/ *n* مِهْنة (مِهَن)

career break *n* [انْقِطاع عن مُمارَسةِ المِهْنةِ]

careers adviser, careers officer *n* مُسْتَشار وَظيفيّ

careers office *n* [مَكْتَب اسْتِشاراتٍ وَظيفيّةٍ]

carefree /ˈkɛːfriː/ *adj* ‹*attitude, childhood*› خالي البالِ

careful /ˈkɛːfʊl/ *adj* **1** (cautious) ‹*person*› مُحْتَرِس, حَريص, حَذِر; **be ~ with that knife!** كُنْ حَذِراً مع تِلْكَ السِكّينِ!; **to be ~ with money** كانَ حَذِراً في إنْفاقِ المالِ; **be ~!** انْتَبِهْ!, احْذَرْ!; **be ~ what you say** انْتَبِهْ لِما تَقولُ; **he has to be ~ about what he eats** عَلَيْهِ أنْ يَنْتَبِهَ لِما يَأْكُلُ; **she was ~ to avoid making any noise** كانَتْ حَريصةً على ألاّ تُصْدِرَ أَيَّ ضَجيجٍ **2** (thorough) ‹*attention, planning*› دَقيق; **after ~ consideration** بعد دِراسةٍ مُتَأَنِّيةٍ

carefully /ˈkɛəf(ə)li/ *adv* **1** (paying attention) ‹*to listen, read*› بانْتِباهٍ **2** (cautiously) ‹*to walk, open*› بِحَذَرٍ

caregiver /ˈkɛːgɪvə/ *n* (AmE) مُقَدِّم رِعايةٍ

care label *n* [مُلْصَق تَعْليماتٍ \ إرْشاداتِ الغَسيلِ]

careless /ˈkɛːləs/ *adj* ‹*mistake*› طائِش; ‹*work*› غَيْر مُتْقَنٍ; ‹*remark, driving*› مُتَهَوِّر

carelessly /ˈkɛəlɪsli/ *adv* **1** (negligently) ‹*to act, drive*› دون مُبالاةٍ **2** (in carefree way) ‹*to laugh, walk*› دون مُبالاةٍ

carelessness /ˈkɛːləsnəs/ *n* لامُبالاة

carer /ˈkɛːrə/ *n* (BrE) مُقَدِّم رِعايةٍ

caress /kəˈrɛs/ *vt* داعَبَ ‹*a cheek, face*›

caretaker /ˈkɛːteɪkə/ *n* [حارِس مَبْنًى \ مُؤَسَّسةٍ]

care worker *n* مُساعِد رِعايةِ المَرْضى

cargo /ˈkɑːgəʊ/ *n* (*pl* **cargoes** or **cargos**) شَحْنة, حُمولة (شِحْنات)

cargo plane *n* طائِرة شَحْنٍ

cargo ship *n* سَفينة شَحْنٍ \ بَضائِعَ

Caribbean /ˌkarɪˈbiːən/ **A** *pr n* **(the Caribbean)** **1** (region) الكاريبيّ **2** (also **the Caribbean Sea**) البَحْر الكاريبيّ **B** *adj* ‹*island, cruise*› كاريبيّ; **the ~ Sea** البَحْر الكاريبيّ

caricature /ˈkarɪkətjʊə/ *n* كاريكاتور

caricaturist /ˈkarɪkətʃʊərɪst/ *n* رَسّام كاريكاتوريّ

caring /ˈkɛːrɪŋ/ *adj* ‹*parent, environment*› عَطوف (عُطُف)

carjacking /ˈkɑːdʒakɪŋ/ *n* سرِقة السَيّاراتِ

carnage /ˈkɑːnɪdʒ/ *n* مَجْزَرة (مَجازِر)

carnation /kɑːˈneɪʃ(ə)n/ *n* قَرَنْفُل

carnival /ˈkɑːnɪv(ə)l/ *n* كَرْنَفال

carnivorous /kɑːˈnɪv(ə)rəs/ *adj* ‹*animal, bird*› لاحِم (لَواحِمُ)

carob /ˈkarəb/ *n* **1** (tree) خَرّوب **2** (pod) خَرّوب

carol /ˈkar(ə)l/ *n* تَرْنيمة (أُغْنِية دينيّة مَسيحيّة)

carousel /ˌkarəˈsɛl/ *n* **1** (merry-go-round) أُرْجوحة دَوّامة **2** (for luggage) (في المَطارِ) حِزام ناقِل للأَمْتِعة الخَيْلِ

carp /kɑːp/ **A** *n* (*pl* **carp**) شَبّوط **B** *vi* (infml) تَذَمَّرَ (من); **to ~ about the service** تَذَمَّرَ من الخِدْمةِ

car park *n* (BrE) مَوْقِف سَيّاراتٍ

carpenter /ˈkɑːp(ə)ntə/ *n* نَجّار

carpentry /ˈkɑːp(ə)ntri/ *n* نِجارة

carpet /ˈkɑːpɪt/ *n* **1** (wall-to-wall) سَجّاد; **how much ~ is needed for the hall?** كم من السَجّادِ نَحْتاجُ للقاعةِ؟ **2** (rug) سَجّادة (سَجّادات، سَجاجيدُ)، زُرْبِيّة (زَرابِيُّ) (NA); **a ~ of flowers** سَجّادة من الزُهورِ

Idiom **to brush** *or* **sweep sth under the carpet** دَفَنَ الأَوْساخَ تحت السَجّادةِ

carpet-fitter /ˈkɑːpɪtfɪtə/ *n* مُرَكِّب سَجّادٍ

carpet shampoo *n* شامْبو السَجّادِ

car phone *n* هاتِف سَيّارةٍ

carriage /ˈkærɪdʒ/ *n* **1** (horse-drawn) عَرَبة خَيْلٍ **2** (BrE) (of a train) عَرَبة **3** (of goods) نَقْل

carriageway /ˈkærɪdʒweɪ/ *n* (BrE) [أَحَد اتِّجاهَي السَيْرِ في الطَريقِ السَريعةِ]

carrier /ˈkærɪə/ *n* **1** (company) شَرِكة نَقْلٍ; (airline) شَرِكة طَيَرانٍ **2** (of a disease) حامِل (حَمَلة)

carrier bag *n* (BrE) حَقيبة تَسَوُّق

carrion /ˈkærɪən/ *n* (also **carrion flesh**) جيفة (جِيَف، أَجْياف)

carrot /ˈkærət/ *n* جَزَر (n coll)

carry /ˈkæri/ **A** *vt* (**carries**, **carrying**, **carried**) **1** (in one's hands) حَمَلَ (i; حَمْل) ‹*a bag, child*›; **he carried the child upstairs** حَمَلَ الطِفْلَ إلى الطابَقِ العُلْوِيِّ; **could you ~ this bag for me?** هل يُمْكِنُكَ أنْ تَحْمِلَ لي هذه الحَقيبةَ؟; **she carries her camera around with her everywhere** تَحْمِلُ مَعَها كاميرَتَها في كُلِّ مَكانٍ; **he was carried off the field on a stretcher** تَمَّ حَمْلُهُ على نَقّالةٍ إلى خارِجِ المَلْعَبِ; **to ~ sth too far/to extremes** أَفْرَطَ في شَيْءٍ **2** (to convey) نَقَلَ (u; نَقْل)، حَمَلَ (i; حَمْل) ‹*passengers, cargo*›; **the seeds are carried by the wind** تَنْقُلُ الريحُ البُذورَ **3** «pipelines» نَقَلَ، وَصَّلَ (u; نَقْل) ‹*oil, blood*› **4** (to be contagious with) حَمَلَ (i; حَمْل) ‹*a disease, virus*› **5** (fml) (to be pregnant with) **to be ~ing a child** حَمَلَتْ بِطِفْلٍ **6** (to have on one) حَمَلَ، كانَ في حَوْزَتِهِ (i; حَمْل) ‹*a weapon, money, drugs*› **7** (to support) تَحَمَّلَ ‹*a weight, load*› **8** (to feature) حَمَلَ (i; حَمْل) ‹*a guarantee, warning, symbol*›; **the film carries an important social message** يَحْمِلُ الفيلْمُ رِسالةً اجْتِماعيّةً هامّةً; **to ~ conviction** كانَ لَهُ حُجِّيّةً، كانَ مُقْنِعاً **9** (to publish in a newspaper) نَشَرَ (u); (on TV, radio) أَذاعَ ‹*a story, an advertisement*› **10** (to involve) انْطَوى (على)، حَمَلَ (i; حَمْل) ‹*a risk, responsibility*› **11** (in sentencing) أَدّى (إلى) ‹*a penalty, fine*› **12** (in voting) تَبَنّى ‹*a motion, an amendment*› **13** (to stock) خَزَّنَ ‹*a product, brand*› **14** (in arithmetic) حَمَلَ (i) ‹*one, a number*›

B *vi* (**carries**, **carrying**, **carried**) «sound, voice» وَصَلَ (i; وَصْل، صِلة)، انْتَقَلَ; **her voice carries well** يَصِلُ صَوْتُها بِشَكْلٍ جَيِّدٍ; **the sound carried for miles in the still air** انْتَقَلَ الصَوْتُ لِعِدّةِ أَمْيالٍ في الهَواءِ الساكِنِ

C *v refl* (**carries**, **carrying**, **carried**) **to ~ oneself well/with confidence** وَقَفَ \ مَشى بِأَناقةٍ \ بِثِقةٍ

Idiom **to get carried away** جَمَحَ (a; جُموح، جِماح، جَمْح)، انْجَرَفَ

Phrasal verbs **carry forward**: **~ forward [sth]**, **~ [sth] forward** (Fin) رَحَّلَ [شَيْئاً] ‹*a balance, total*›

• **carry off**: **1** **~ off [sth]** (to win) نالَ [شَيْئاً]، فازَ ب [شَيْءٍ] ‹*a prize, trophy*› **2** **~ [sth] off**, **~ off [sth]** (to be successful) أَنْجَزَ \ أَدّى [شَيْئاً] ‹*the role, impersonation*›; **he carried it off with ease** أَنْجَزَهُ بِسُهولةٍ

• **carry on** **A** **1** (to continue) «person, life» اسْتَمَرَّ; **~ on with your work** اسْتَمِرَّ في عَمَلِكَ; **well, life carries on** حَسناً، الحَياةُ تَسْتَمِرُّ; **~ on down the road** اسْتَمِرَّ في السَيْرِ في الطَريقِ **2** (infml) (to behave) تَصَرَّفَ; **what a way to ~ on!** يا لَها من طَريقةٍ في التَصَرُّفِ! **B** **~ on [sth]** **1** (to conduct) أَدارَ [شَيْئاً] ‹*a business*›; أَجْرى [شَيْئاً] ‹*conversation, correspondence*› **2** (to continue) واصَلَ [شَيْئاً] ‹*a tradition, custom*›

• **carry out**: **~ out [sth]**, **~ [sth] out** **1** (to perform) أَجْرى [شَيْئاً]، قامَ ب [شَيْءٍ] ‹*research, a task, an operation, the work*›; **no one has admitted ~ing out the attack** لم يَعْتَرِفْ أَحَدٌ بِتَنْفيذِ الهُجومِ **2** (to fulfil) نَفَّذَ \ أَتَمَّ [شَيْئاً] ‹*a mission, one's duties, orders*›

• **carry over**: **~ [sth] over**, **~ over [sth]** **1** نَقَلَ [شَيْئاً] ‹*a practice, policy*› **2** رَحَّلَ [شَيْئاً] ‹*a loss, an entitlement*›

• **carry through**: **1** **~ through [sth]**, **~ [sth] through** أَكْمَلَ \ نَفَّذَ [شَيْئاً] ‹*a reform, measures*› **2** **~ [sb] through** «sense of humour, determination» أَعانَ [شَخْصاً] على تَخَطّي الظُروفِ

carryall /ˈkariɔːl/ *n* (AmE) حَقيبة (للسَفَرِ)

carrycot /ˈkarɪkɒt/ *n* (BrE) سَلّة موسى,سَرير أَطْفالٍ مَحْمولٍ (Gulf)

carry-on /ˈkariɒn/ **A** *n* (infml) (fuss) ضَجّة

B *adj before n* ‹luggage› [يُمْكِنُ حَمْلُهُ على مَتْنِ طائِرةٍ];

~ baggage أَمْتِعة اليَدِ

carry-out /ˈkariaʊt/ *n* [وَجْبة طَعامٍ تُشْتَرى من المَطْعَمِ لِتُأْكَلَ خارِجَهُ]

carsick /ˈkɑːsɪk/ *adj* **to be ~** كانَ يَشْعُرُ بِغَثَيانِ الحَرَكةِ

carsickness /ˈkɑːsɪknəs/ *n* غَثَيان الحَرَكةِ

cart /kɑːt/ **A** *n* **1** (vehicle) عَرَبة مَجْرورة **2** (also **shopping cart**) (AmE) عَرَبة تَسَوُّقٍ **3** (also **shopping cart**) (on a website) عَرَبة تَسَوُّقٍ; **add to ~** أَضِفْ إلى عَرَبةِ التَسَوُّقِ **4** (also **dessert cart**) (AmE) عَرَبة طَعامٍ

B *vt* **~ [sth] about, ~ [sth] around** (infml) حَمَلَ [شَيْئاً] (بِمَشَقّةٍ) ‹luggage, stuff›

(Idiom) **to put the cart before the horse** وَضَعَ العَرَبةَ قبل الحِصانِ

cartel /kɑːˈtel/ *n* كارْتِل

Carthage /ˈkɑːθɪdʒ/ *pr n* قَرْطاج (f)

carthorse /ˈkɑːthɔːs/ *n* بِرْذَوْن (حِصان قَويّ البِنْيةِ يُسْتَخْدَمُ في جَرِّ العَرَباتِ)

cartilage /ˈkɑːt(ɪ)lɪdʒ/ *n* غُضْروف (غَضاريفُ)

cartographer /kɑːˈtɒɡrəfə/ *n* خَرائِطيّ

carton /ˈkɑːt(ə)n/ *n* كَرْتونة

cartoon /kɑːˈtuːn/ *n* **1** (film) رُسوم مُتَحَرِّكة **2** (political) كاريكاتور; (comic strip) قِصّة مُصَوَّرة (في جَريدةٍ \ مَجَلّةٍ)

cartoonist /kɑːˈtuːnɪst/ *n* (in cinema) رَسّام رُسومٍ مُتَحَرِّكةٍ; (in print) رَسّام كاريكاتورٍ

cartridge /ˈkɑːtrɪdʒ/ *n* **1** (for a gun) خَرْطوشة (خَراطيشُ) **2** (for a printer) خَرْطوشة حِبْرٍ **3** (for a pen) خَرْطوشة حِبْرٍ **4** (for a camera) فيلْم (أَفْلام)

cartwheel /ˈkɑːtwiːl/ *n* حَرَكة العَجَلةِ (حَرَكة رِياضيّة يَأْخُذُ فيها الجِسْمُ شَكْلَ العَجَلةِ)

carve /kɑːv/ **A** *vt* **1** نَحَتَ (i-u; نَحْت) ‹wood, stone› **2** نَقَشَ (u; نَقْش) ‹initials, sb's name›; نَحَتَ (i-u; نَحْت) ‹a figure, sculpture› **3** (Culin) قَطَعَ إلى شَرائِحَ ‹meat›

B *vi* قَطَعَ اللَحْمَ إلى شَرائِحَ

(Phrasal verbs) **carve out**: **~ out [sth], ~ [sth] out** نَحَتَ [شَيْئاً] ‹a niche, name›; صَنَعَ [شَيْئاً] ‹a career, reputation›; **he ~d out a niche for himself in broadcasting** نَحَتَ لِنَفْسِهِ مَكاناً في عالَمِ البَثِّ الإذاعيِّ

• **carve up**: **~ up [sth], ~ [sth] up** (infml pej) قَسَّمَ [شَيْئاً] ‹land, spoils›

carving /ˈkɑːvɪŋ/ *n* مَنْحوتة

carving knife *n* سِكّين تَقْطيعٍ

car wash *n* مَغْسَلة سَيّاراتٍ

cascade /kasˈkeɪd/ *n* [شَلّال صَغير]

case¹ /keɪs/ **A** *n* **1** (instance) حالة; **in seven out of eight ~s** في سَبْعِ حالاتٍ من أَصْلِ ثَمانٍ; **in that ~, find an alternative** في هذه الحالةِ، أَوجِدْ بَديلاً; **in this ~, I think she is right** هذه الحالةِ، أَظُنُّها مُحِقّةً; **it's a ~ of being patient** المَطْلوبُ هو الصَبْرُ; **a ~ in point** مِثال على ذلك; **in many/most ~s** في الكَثيرِ من \ مُعْظَمِ الحالاتِ **2** (fml) (existing situation) وَضْع (أَوْضاع), حال (mf; أَحْوال); **such *or* this being the ~** بِما أَنّ الحالَ هكذا; **in fact, the opposite is the ~** في الحَقيقةِ، العَكْسُ هو الصَحيحُ; **as the ~ may be** طِبْقاً لِلحالِ; **should this be the ~ *or* if this is the ~, contact your doctor** إذا كانَ هذا هو الوَضْعَ، اتَّصِلْ بِطَبيبِكَ **3** (in a law court) قَضيّة (قَضايا); **the ~ for the defence/the prosecution** دُفوع الدِفاعِ \ الادِّعاءِ; **to win/lose one's ~** كَسَبَ \ خَسِرَ قَضيَّتَهُ; **to bring a ~ against sb/an organization** رَفَعَ قَضيّةً على شَخْصٍ \ مُنَظَّمةٍ; **to rest one's ~** خَتَمَ مُرافَعَتَهُ **4** (investigation) قَضيّة (قَضايا); **a murder ~** قَضيّة قَتْلٍ; **the ~ is closed** أُغْلِقَت القَضيّةُ; **the detectives working on the ~** المُحَقِّقونَ الَّذينَ يَعْمَلونَ في القَضيّةِ **5** (fml) (argument) حُجّة (حُجَج); **to make the ~ for sth** قَدَّمَ الحُجّةَ على شَيْءٍ; **he made a strong ~ for reform** قَدَّمَ حُجّةً قَويّةً لِلإصْلاحِ; **there is a ~ for simplifying the rules** هُناكَ مُبَرِّرٌ لِتَبْسيطِ القَواعِدِ; **she argues her ~ persuasively** تُدافِعُ عن حَقِّها بِشَكْلٍ مُقْنِعٍ **6** (Med) حالة; **five new ~s are reported each day** هُناكَ خَمْسُ حالاتٍ يَتِمُّ الإعْلانُ عَنْها كُلَّ يَوْمٍ; **it's an interesting ~** هي حالةٌ مُثيرةٌ

للاهْتِمام 7 (infml) (person) **he's a real ~!** يا لَهُ من شَخْصٍ! غَريب الأَطْوارِ; **a hopeless ~** شَخْص مَيْؤوس مِنْهُ 8 (Ling) في حالة النَّصْب ,مَنْصوب; **in the accusative ~** حالة إعْرابيّة

B **(in case)** *phr* (covering eventualities) ... فيما لو; **take it in ~ it rains** خُذْها تَحَسُّباً للمَطَر; **take the map just in ~** خُذ الخَريطة تَحَسُّباً لِأَيِّ ظَرْفٍ

C **(in any case)** *adv phr* 1 (anyway) على أيِّ حالٍ 2 (moreover) عِلاوةً على ذلك

D **(in case of)** *prep phr* (fml) في حالِ حُدوثِ

case² /keɪs/ *n* 1 (suitcase) حَقيبة (حَقائِبُ) 2 (container for glasses, binoculars) عُلْبة (عِلاب, عُلَب); (for jewellery) صُنْدوق (صَناديقُ); (for a camera) حَقيبة (حَقائِبُ); **a cigarette ~** عُلْبة سَجائِرَ 3 (crate) صُنْدوق (صَناديقُ) 4 (of wine, liquor) صُنْدوق (صَناديقُ) 5 (display cabinet) واجِهة عَرْضٍ

CASE /keɪs/ *n* = **computer-aided software engineering** هَنْدَسة البَرْمَجيّات بِمُساعَدة الحاسوب \ الكُمْبْيوتَر

casebook /ˈkeɪsbʊk/ *n* سِجِلّ الحالاتِ

case ending *n* عَلامة الإِعْراب (في القَواعِد)

case history *n* سيرة مَرَضيّة, تاريخ حالة

case law *n* قانون السَوابِق القَضائيّة

caseload /ˈkeɪsləʊd/ *n* [عَدَد الحالاتِ المَرَضيّةِ \ القَضايا الّتي يَجِبُ العَمَلُ عَلَيْها في فَتْرةٍ زَمَنيّةٍ مُعَيَّنةٍ]

case study *n* دراسة حالةٍ

caseworker /ˈkeɪswɜːkə/ *n* [مُرْشِد اجْتِماعيّ يَعْمَلُ على حالاتٍ خاصّةٍ]

cash /kæʃ/ **A** *n* 1 (notes and coins) نَقْد (نُقود); **to pay (in) ~** دَفَعَ نَقْداً; **~ on delivery** الدَّفْع عند التَّسْليمِ 2 (money in general) نُقود; **I'm a bit short of ~** لَيْسَ عِنْدي ما يَكْفي من النُقودِ

B *vt* صَرَفَ (i; صَرْف) ‹*a cheque*›

(Phrasal verb) **cash in:** 1 **~ in on [sth]** (infml) اسْتَفادَ من [شَيْءٍ] 2 **~ in [sth], ~ [sth] in** صَرَفَ [شَيْئاً] ‹*an investment, insurance policy*›

cash buyer *n* مُشْتَرٍ نَقْداً

cash card *n* بِطاقة صَرْفٍ آليٍّ

cash crop *n* مَحْصول نَقْديّ

cash desk *n* خَزينة الدَفْعِ, طاوِلة الحِسابِ

cash dispenser, **cash machine** *n* جِهاز صَرّاف آليّ, صَرْفٍ آليٍّ

cashew /ˈkæʃuː/, **cashew nut** *n* كاجو, بَلاذِر

cash flow *n* تَدَفُّق نَقْديّ

cashier /kæˈʃɪə/ *n* أَمين صُنْدوقٍ

cashless /ˈkæʃləs/ *adj* ‹*society, payment*› غَيْر نَقْديٍّ

cash machine, **cashpoint®** *n* (BrE) صَرّاف آليّ

cashmere /kæʃˈmɪə/ *n* كَشْمير

cash register *n* آلة تَسْجيلِ النَّقْدِ

casing /ˈkeɪsɪŋ/ *n* غِلاف (أَغْلِفة)

casino /kəˈsiːnəʊ/ *n* (*pl* **casinos**) كازينو (كازينوهات)

cask /kɑːsk/ *n* دَنّ (دِنان)

casket /ˈkɑːskɪt/ *n* 1 (jewel box) عُلْبة مُجَوْهَراتٍ 2 (AmE) (coffin) تابوت (تَوابيتُ)

Caspian Sea /ˌkæspɪən ˈsiː/ *pr n* (**the Caspian Sea**) بَحْر قَزْوين

cassava /kəˈsɑːvə/ *n* 1 (tree) مَنيهوت, كاسافا 2 (food) جُذور المَنيهوت

casserole /ˈkæsərəʊl/ *n* 1 (food) كَسَرولة (مَرَق يُطْبَخُ في الفُرْنِ) 2 (container) كَسَرولة (إناء لِطَبْخِ المَرَقِ على نارٍ هادِئةٍ)

cassette /kəˈset/ *n* شَريط كاسيت

cassette deck *n* جِهاز كاسيت

cassette player *n* مُشَغِّل كاسيت

cassette recorder *n* مُسَجِّل كاسيت

cassette tape *n* شَريط كاسيت

cast /kɑːst/ **A** *vt* (*past tense, past participle* **cast**) 1 (to throw) أَلْقى (رَمْي), رَمى (i; رَمْي) ‹*a stone*›; **the witch ~ a spell on her** سَحَرَتْها الساحِرةُ 2 (in fishing) رَمى (i; رَمْي) ‹*a line, net*› 3 (to cause) أَلْقى ‹*a shadow*› 4 (to direct) أَلْقى ‹*a glance, look*›; **would you ~ an eye over this?** هَلاّ أَلْقَيْتَ نَظْرةً على هذا؟; **he ~ his eyes downwards** نَظَرَ للأَسْفَلِ; **~ your mind back to last year** عُدْ بِذاكِرَتِكَ للعامِ الماضي 5 (in elections) أَدْلى (ب) ‹*a vote, ballot*›; **to ~ one's vote** أَدْلى بِصَوْتِهِ 6 (Theat) أَسْنَدَ دَوْراً إلى ‹*an actor*›; وَزَّعَ الأَدْوارَ في ‹*a play, film*›; **she was ~ in the role of Blanche** أُسْنِدَ إِلَيْها دَوْر بْلانْش 7 (to shed) «snakes» ‹skin› (من) انْسَلَخ **8** ‹a sculpture, statue› صَبَّ (u; صَبّ), سَبَكَ (i-u; سَبْك)

B *n* **1** (of actors) طاقِم تَمْثيلٍ; **members of the ~ include...** يَشْمَلُ أَعْضاءُ طاقِمِ التَمْثيلِ ...; **there is a strong supporting ~** هُناكَ عَدَدٌ من المُمَثِّلينَ المُساعِدينَ الجَيِّدينَ **2** (for a limb) (also **plaster cast**) جَبيرة (جَبائِرُ); **her arm is in a ~** يَدُها في جَبيرةٍ **3** (sculpted object) [شَيْء مَصْنوع في قالَبٍ]; (mould for sculpting) قالَب (قَوالِبُ) **4** (form, type) شَكْل, مَظْهَر; **a literary/pessimistic ~ of mind** نَزْعة أَدَبيّة \ تَشاؤُميّة **5** (of a line, net) رَمْي **6** (squint) حَوَل; **to have a ~ in one eye** كانَ لَدَيْه حَوَلٌ في إحْدى عَيْنَيْه

(Phrasal verbs) **cast about** (BrE), **cast around** بَحَث (a) فَتَّش; **she ~ about for an excuse** بَحَثَتْ عن عُذْرٍ

• **cast aside**: **1** **~ [sth] aside, ~ aside [sth]** نَحّى [شَيْئاً] جانِباً ‹one's fears, principles› **2** **~ [sb] aside, ~ aside [sb]** تَخَلّى عن [شَخْصٍ] ‹a lover, friend›

• **cast away**: **to be ~ away** [طُرِحَ على الشاطِئِ بعد غَرَقِ سَفينَتِه]

• **cast down**: **to be/feel ~ down** (to feel depressed) اغْتَمَّ, اكْتَأَبَ

• **cast off** **A** (Naut) تَحَرَّرَ, رَفَعَ المِرْساةَ **B** **~ off [sth], ~ [sth] off** تَخَلَّصَ من [شَيْءٍ] ‹shackles, chains›; تَخَلَّصَ من [شَيْءٍ] ‹an image, reputation›

castaway /'kɑːstəweɪ/ *n* [ناجٍ في حادِثِ تَحَطُّمِ سَفينةٍ \ طائرةٍ في البَحْرِ]

caste /kɑːst/ *n* طَبَقة (في النِظامِ الهِنْدوسيِّ)

caster /'kɑːstə/ *n* [عَجَلة صَغيرة مُثَبَّتة في قاعِدةِ قِطْعةِ أَثاثٍ لِتَسْهيلِ تَحْريكِها]

caster sugar *n* سُكَّر ناعِم

Castile /ka'stiːl/ *pr n* قَشْتالة

Castilian /ka'stɪliən/ **A** *n* **1** (inhabitant) قَشْتاليّ **2** (language) (اللُغة) القَشْتاليّة

B *adj* ‹wine, landscape› قَشْتاليّ

cast iron **A** *n* حَديد مَصْبوب \ مَسْبوك, حَديد الزَهْرِ

B *adj* (before *n* **cast-iron**) **1** ‹fireplace, bar› مَصْنوع من حَديدِ الزَهْرِ **2** ‹guarantee, alibi› لا مِراءَ فيه

castle /'kɑːs(ə)l/ *n* **1** (Archit) قَلْعة (قِلاع, قُلوع) **2** (in chess) قَلْعة (قِلاع, قُلوع)

cast-off /'kɑːstɒf/ *n* [شَيْء قَديم ومُهْمَل]

castrate /ka'streɪt/ *vt* خَصى (i; خِصاء) ‹a man, an animal›

casual /'kaʒjʊəl/ *adj* **1** (informal) ‹clothes› غَيْر رَسْميٍّ; ‹chat› عابِر **2** (superficial) ‹remark, observer› عابِر; **a ~ acquaintance** أَحَد المَعارِفِ العابِرينَ **3** (unconcerned) ‹attitude, gesture› غَيْر مُبالٍ **4** (chance) ‹encounter, meeting› عابِر **5** (not regular) ‹work, worker› غَيْر مُنْتَظِمٍ

casualize, -ise (BrE) /'kaʒʊəlʌɪz/ *vt* **to ~ a workforce** [حَوَّلَ عَمالةً دائِمةً إلى عَمالةٍ مُؤَقَّتةٍ]

casually /'kaʒʊəli/ *adv* **1** (informally) ‹to dress› بِشَكْلٍ غَيْرِ رَسْميٍّ; ‹to chat› بِأَرْيَحيّةٍ, بلا تَكْليفٍ **2** (unconcernedly) ‹to ask, mention› بدونِ اكْتِراثٍ

casual sex *n* عَلاقة جِنْسيّة عابِرة

casualty /'kaʒjʊəlti/ *n* (*pl* **casualties**) **1** (in a war, accident) ضَحيّة (ضَحايا) **2** (BrE) (hospital department) قِسْم الإصاباتِ

casual wear *n* مَلابِس غَيْر رَسْميّةٍ

cat /kat/ *n* **1** (domestic feline) قِطّ (قِطَط) **2** (feline) سِنَّوْر (سَنانيرُ); **the big ~s** السِنَّوْريّات الكَبيرة

(Idioms) **to let the cat out of the bag** أَفْشى سِرًّا; **to play cat and mouse with sb** لَعِبَ لُعْبةَ القِطِّ والفَأْرِ مع شَخْصٍ; **when the cat's away the mice will play** غابَ القِطُّ الْعَبْ يا فَأْرُ

CAT /kat/ *n* **1** = **computer-assisted teaching** تَعْليم بِمُساعَدةِ الحاسوبِ **2** = **computerized axial tomography** أَشِعّة مَقْطَعيّة, تَصْوير مَقْطَعيّ مُحَوْسَب

Catalan /'katəlan/ **A** *n* **1** (inhabitant) كاتالانيّ **2** (language) (اللُغة) الكاتالانيّة

B *adj* ‹language, culture› كاتالانيّ

catalepsy /'kat(ə)lɛpsi/ *n* إغْماء تَخَشُّبيّ

catalogue (BrE), **catalog** (AmE) /'kat(ə)lɒg/ *n* **1** فِهْرِس (فَهارِسُ), كَتالوج (كَتالوجات) **2** (series) سِجِلّ; **a ~ of errors** سِجِلّ أَخْطاءٍ

Catalonia /,katə'ləʊnɪə/ *pr n* كاتالونيا

catalyst /'kat(ə)lɪst/ *n* (Chem) مُحَفِّز, حَفّاز, حافِز (حَوافِزُ); **the opening of the borders was a ~ for change** كانَ فَتْحُ الحُدودِ بِمَثابةِ مُحَفِّزٍ للتَغْييرِ

catalytic converter /katə̩lɪtɪk kən'vəːtə/ *n* مُحَوِّل حَفّازٍ

catapult /'katəpʌlt/ **A** *n* (BrE) (hand-held) مِصْيادة
B *vt* أَطْلَقَ نُجوميَّةَ ‹*a performer, writer*›

cataract /'katərakt/ *n* **1** (in the eye) سادّ ,مِياه بَيْضاء **2** (waterfall) شَلّال (شَلّالات) **3** (rapids in a river) جَنْدَل (جَنادِلُ), شَلّال (شَلّالات)

catarrh /kə'tɑː/ *n* نَزْلة (نَزَلات), اِلْتِهاب (اِلْتِهابات)

catastrophe /kə'tastrəfi/ *n* كارِثة (كَوارِثُ)

catastrophic /katə'strɒfɪk/ *adj* ‹*event, flooding*› كارِثيّ

catatonia /ˌkatə'təʊnɪə/ *n* (Med) كاتاتونيا ,تَصَلُّب العَضَلاتِ

catatonic /katə'tɒnɪk/ *adj* ‹*state, schizophrenia*› تَصَلُّبيّ

catch /katʃ/ **A** *vt* (*past tense, past participle* **caught**) **1** (to hold and retain) أَمْسَكَ ,اِلْتَقَطَ ‹*a ball, fruit*›; **there was a bucket to ~ the water** كانَتْ هُناكَ دَلْوٌ لِيَسيلَ فيها الماءُ **2** (to capture criminals) قَبَضَ (i; قَبْض) (على ‹*a robber, murderer*›; (to capture animals) صادَ (i; صَيْد), اِصْطادَ ‹*a mouse, fish*›; **to get caught** ضُبِطَ; **if caught early enough, the disease can be cured** إذا تَمَّ اكْتِشافُ المَرَضِ مُبَكِّراً، كانَ العِلاجُ مُمْكِناً **3** (to take by surprise) ضَبَطَ (i-u; ضَبْط), فاجَأَ ,باغَتَ; **to ~ sb doing sth** ضَبَطَ شَخْصاً يَفْعَلُ شَيْئاً; **you wouldn't ~ me smoking!** لَن تَضْبِطَني وَأَنا أُدَخِّنُ!; **we got caught in the rain** فوجِئْنا بالمَطَرِ; **you've caught me at a bad time** جِئْتَني في وَقْتٍ سَيِّءٍ **4** (to be in time for) لَحِقَ (a; لَحْق ,لَحاق) (ب, أَدْرَكَ ‹*a bus, train, plane*›; **to ~ the post** أَدْرَكَ البَريدَ **5** (infml) (to manage to see) أَدْرَكَ ‹*a movie, show, programme*›; **I managed to ~ her in** (at home) تَمَكَّنْتُ من اللَحاقِ بِها في المَنْزِلِ **6** (to grasp) مَسَكَ (i-u; مَسْك), أَمْسَكَ ‹*sb's arm, hand*›; **to ~ hold of sth/sb** أَمْسَكَ شَيْئاً \ شَخْصاً; **to ~ sb's eye** *or* **attention** لَفَتَ \ جَذَبَ انْتِباهَ شَخْصٍ; **to ~ sb's imagination/interest** جَذَبَ اهْتِمامَ شَخْصٍ **7** (to trap, entangle) عَلِقَ (a; عَلَق ,عُلوق); **mind you don't ~ your fingers in the door** انْتَبِهْ حتّى لا تَشْتَبِكَ أَصابِعُكَ في البابِ; **I caught my sleeve on a nail** عَلِقَ كُمّي في مِسْمارٍ **8** (in perception) سَمِعَ (a; سَمْع) ‹*sb's name*›; فَهِمَ (a; فَهْم) ‹*a word*›; أَلْقى ‹*a look*›; **to ~ sight of sb/sth** لَمَحَ شَخْصاً \ شَيْئاً; **I only caught a glimpse of his face** رَأَيْتُ وَجْهَهُ في لَمْحةٍ خاطِفةٍ فَقَطْ **9** أُصيبَ ب ‹*a disease, an infection*›; **to ~ a cold** أُصيبَ بِبَرْدٍ; **you've caught the sun** (BrE) أُصِبْتَ بِحُروقِ الشَمْسِ **10** (to hit, strike) أَصابَ ‹*a person, sb's arm, head*›; **the ball caught me on the side of the head** أَصابَتْني الكُرةُ في جانِبِ رَأْسي **11** (in phrases) **to ~ fire** *or* **light** اشْتَعَلَتْ فيهِ النيرانُ; **to ~ the light** بَرَقَ في الضَوْءِ; **to ~ one's breath** الْتَقَطَ أَنْفاسَهُ

B *vi* (*past tense, past participle* **caught**) **1** (to try to grasp) **to ~ at sth** أَمْسَكَ \ حاوَلَ الإمْساكَ بِشَيْءٍ **2** (to become stuck) «sleeve, hair» عَلِقَ (a; عَلَق ,عُلوق); **my sleeve caught on a hook/in the door** عَلِقَ كُمّي في الخُطّافِ \ البابِ **3** (to start burning) «wood, fire» بَدَأَ في الاشْتِعالِ

C *n* **1** (in games) الْتِقاط; **to take** *or* (AmE) **make a ~** قامَ بالْتِقاطِ الكُرةِ; **to play ~** لَعِبَ لُعْبةَ قَذْفِ وَالْتِقاطِ الكُرةِ **2** (fastening on a necklace, box) قُفْل (أَقْفال); (on a window, door) مِزْلاج (مَزاليجُ), سَقّاطة **3** (infml) (drawback) عَيْب (خَفيّ); **it sounds good, but what's the ~?** يَبْدو جَيِّداً، وَلَكِنْ أَيْنَ يَكْمُنُ العَيْبُ؟ **4** (break in the voice) **with a ~ in his voice** بِتَهَدُّجٍ في صَوْتِهِ **5** (many fish) صَيْد وَفير; (one fish) سَمَكة **6** (marriage partner) **a good ~** عَريس لُقْطة (infml)

Phrasal verbs **catch on** **1** (to become popular) «idea, trend» انْتَشَرَ ,اشْتَهَرَ **2** (to understand) «the public, voters» اسْتَوْعَبَ, فَهِمَ (a; فَهْم); **to ~ on to sth** اسْتَوْعَبَ شَيْئاً

• **catch out**: **~ [sb] out** **1** (to take by surprise) باغَتَ \ فاجَأَ [شَخْصاً]; **we were caught out by the weather** فوجِئْنا بالطَقْسِ **2** (by questions, etc) أَوْقَعَ ب [شَخْصٍ] **3** (in cricket, baseball) أَخْرَجَ [شَخْصاً] من اللُعْبةِ بِإمْساكِ الكُرةِ قبل أَنْ تَلْمَسَ الأَرْضَ ‹*a batter*›

• **catch up** **A** **1** (to draw level) «runner, driver» لَحِقَ (a; لَحْق, لَحاق), أَدْرَكَ; **to ~ up with sb** لَحِقَ بِشَخْصٍ **2** (with work, studies) «clerk, student» عَوَّضَ ما فاتَهُ; **she has a lot of work to ~ up on** لَدَيْها الكَثيرُ من العَمَلِ المُتَأَخِّرِ لِتُنْجِزَهُ; **to ~ up on all the news** اطَّلَعَ على كُلِّ ما فاتَهُ من أَخْبارٍ **B** **1** **~ [sb/sth] up** (to get level with) لَحِقَ ب [شَخْصٍ \ شَيْءٍ] **2** **to get caught up in sth** (entangled in branches, cables) اشْتَبَكَ في شَيْءٍ; (in fighting) تَوَرَّطَ في شَيْءٍ; (in traffic) عَلِقَ في شَيْءٍ; **I got caught up in all the excitement** أَخَذَتْني غَمْرةُ الحَماسِ

catch-22 situation /katʃtwentiˈtuː sɪtjuːˌeɪʃ(ə)n/ *n* [مُعْضِلة لا مَفَرَّ مِنْها]; **to be in a ~** كانَ بين نارَيْنِ

catcher /ˈkatʃə/ *n* (Sport) ماسِك \ مُلْتَقِط الكُرةِ

catching /ˈkatʃɪŋ/ *adj* مُعْدٍ

catchment area /ˈkatʃmənt ɛːriə/ *n* **1** (of a river basin) [مِنْطَقة تابعة] **2** (for students) مُسْتَجْمَع مِياهٍ \ أَمْطارٍ [للمُؤَسَّساتِ التَعْليميّة المَحَلِّيّةِ]

catchphrase /ˈkatʃfreɪz/ *n* تَعْبير شائِع

catchword /ˈkatʃwəːd/ *n* (شِعارات) شِعار

catchy /ˈkatʃi/ *adj* (**catchier, catchiest**) ‹*tune, chorus*› يَعْلَقُ في الذِهْنِ

categorical /katɪˈɡɒrɪk(ə)l/ *adj* ‹*statement, denial*› قاطِع, قَطْعيّ

categorize, -ise (BrE) /ˈkatɪɡərʌɪz/ *vt* ‹*a patient, behaviour*› صَنَّفَ

category /ˈkatɪɡ(ə)ri/ *n* (*pl* **categories**) فِئة, (أَصْناف) صِنْف

cater /ˈkeɪtə/ *vi* «caterers» [زَوَّدَ حَفْلاً بأَطْعِمةٍ جاهِزةٍ]

(Phrasal verb) **cater for**: **~ for/to** [**sth**] ‹*an audience*› خَدَمَ [شَيْئاً]; ‹*need*› لَبّى [شَيْئاً]

caterer /ˈkeɪt(ə)rə/ *n* [مُتَعَهِّد تَجْهيز \ تَقْديمِ الأَطْعِمةِ في الحَفَلاتِ]

catering /ˈkeɪtərɪŋ/ *n* [تَجْهيز \ تَزْويد حَفْلٍ بالأَطْعِمةِ الجاهِزةِ]

caterpillar /ˈkatəpɪlə/ *n* يَرَقان

catfish /ˈkatfɪʃ/ *n* (*pl* **catfish**) (قَراميط) قَرْموط

cathedral /kəˈθiːdr(ə)l/ *n* كاتِدْرائيّة

catheter /ˈkaθɪtə/ *n* قَسْطَرة

Catholic /ˈkaθəlɪk/ *n, adj* (كاثوليك) كاثوليكيّ

Catholicism /kəˈθɒlɪsɪz(ə)m/ *n* كاثوليكيّة

catnap /ˈkatnap/ *vi* (**-pp-**) (u; غُفُوّ, غَفْو) غَفا

CAT scan *n* أَشِعّة مَقْطَعيّة, تَصْوير مَقْطَعيّ مُحَوْسَب

cat's eye® /kats ʌɪ/ *n* (BrE) (عاكِس ضَوْئيّ على الطَريقِ) عَيْن القِطِّ

catsup /ˈkatsəp/ *n* (AmE) ▸ **ketchup**

cattle /ˈkat(ə)l/ *n pl* (مَواشٍ) ماشِية

catwalk /ˈkatwɔːk/ *n* **1** (Constr) (walkway) (مَماشٍ) مَمْشى **2** (for models) مِنَصّة عَرْضِ الأَزْياءِ

Caucasian /kɔːˈkeɪʒ(ə)n, kɔːˈkeɪzɪən/ **A** *adj* **1** ‹*man, woman*› أَبْيَض **2** ‹*mountains, republics*› قَفْقاسيّ

B *n* **1** (white person) رَجُل أَبْيَض \ امْرَأة بَيْضاء **2** (person from the Caucasus) قَفْقاسيّ

caucus /ˈkɔːkəs/ **A** *n* (*pl* **caucuses**) **1** (meeting) [اجْتِماع \ مُؤْتَمَر حِزْبيّ] **2** (faction) (فُصْلان) فَصيل

B *vi* [عَقَدَ اجْتِماعاً \ مُؤْتَمَراً حِزْبيّاً]

caught /kɔːt/ *past tense, past participle* ▸ **catch**

cauliflower /ˈkɒlɪflaʊə/ *n* قَرْنَبيط

causal /ˈkɔːz(ə)l/ *adj* ‹*relationship, connection*› سَبَبيّ; **there is no ~ connection between the two** لَيْسَ هُناكَ رابِطٌ سَبَبيٌّ بين الاثْنَيْنِ

causation /kɔːˈzeɪʃ(ə)n/ *n* سَبَبيّة

cause /kɔːz/ **A** *n* **1** (origin) (أَسْباب) سَبَب, (مُسَبِّبات) مُسَبِّب; **~ and effect** السَبَب والنَتيجة **2** (fml) (reason) (أَسْباب) سَبَب, (عِلَل) عِلّة; **these statistics give ~ for concern** تَبْعَثُ هذه الإحْصائيّاتُ على القَلَقِ; **there is no ~ for alarm** لَيْسَ هُناكَ ما يَدْعو للقَلَقِ; **she never gave me any ~ to doubt her** لم أَجِدْ مِنْها أيَّ شَيْءٍ على الإطْلاقِ يَجْعَلُني أَشُكُّ فيها; **without good ~** بدونِ سَبَبٍ وَجيهٍ **3** (ideal, movement) (قَضايا) قَضيّة; **a lost ~** قَضيّة خاسِرة; **it's all in a good ~** هذا كُلُّهُ من أَجْلِ قَضيّةٍ نَبيلةٍ; **he acted in the ~ of justice/freedom** عَمِلَ من أَجْلِ قَضيّةِ العَدالةِ \ الحُرّيّةِ

B *vt* ‹*a problem, damage, injury*› (إلى) أَدّى, سَبَّبَ; **to ~ sb to do sth** دَفَعَ شَخصاً أن يَفعَلَ شَيْئاً; **to ~ sb problems** سَبَّبَ مَشاكِلَ لِشَخصٍ; **to ~ trouble** سَبَّبَ المَتاعِبَ; **to ~ cancer/migraine** سَبَّبَ سَرَطاناً \ صُداعاً نِصْفيّاً

causeway /ˈkɔːzweɪ/ *n* (جُسور) جِسْر, مَمَرّ مُرْتَفِع

caustic /ˈkɔːstɪk/ *adj* **1** ‹*chemical, substance*› حارِق, كاوٍ **2** ‹*wit, comment*› لاذِع

cauterize, -ise (BrE) /ˈkɔːtərʌɪz/ *vt* «substance, doctor, nurse» ‹*flesh, skin, wound*› (i; كَيّ) كَوى; **it used to be the practice to ~ cuts with iodine** كانَت الجُروحُ في السابِقِ تُكْوى باليودِ; **that snake bite needs to be ~d** يَجِبُ كَيُّ لَدْغةِ الأَفْعى تِلْكَ

caution /ˈkɔːʃ(ə)n/ **A** *n* **1** (fml) (care) حيطة, حِرْص, حَذَر; **to exercise ~** تَوَخّى الحَذَرَ \ الحيطةَ; **~! Low Bridge** احْذَرْ! جِسْرٌ مُنْخَفِضٌ **2** (warning) (تَحْذيرات) تَحْذير; **a word of ~** كَلِمة تَحْذيرٍ **3** (BrE) (legal warning) [إنْذار رَسْميّ بِفَرْضِ]

[تَذْكير] **4▸** (BrE) (to suspect) عُقوبةٍ في حالِ تَكْرارِ مُخالَفةٍ] رَسْميّ للمُتَّهَمِ بِحَقِّهِ في الْتِزامِ الصَمْتِ[; **he was questioned under ~** تَمَّ اسْتِجْوابُهُ بعد تَذْكيرِهِ بِحُقوقِهِ

B *vt* **1▸** (to advise) نَبَّهَ, حَذَّرَ ‹*readers, parents*›; **she ~ed parents to be vigilant** نَبَّهَت الآباءَ إلى ضَرورةِ تَوَخّي الحَذَرِ; **to ~ sb against sth/doing sth** حَذَّرَ شَخْصاً من شَيْءٍ \ فِعْلِ شَيْءٍ **2▸** (BrE) (to warn legally) أَصْدَرَ إِنْذاراً رَسْميًّا بِفَرْضِ عُقوبةٍ في حالِ تَكْرارِ مُخالَفةٍ] **3▸** (BrE) (on arrest) أَخْبَرَ بِحُقوقِهِ ‹*a suspect*›

C *vi* **to ~ against sth** حَذَّرَ من شَيْءٍ

(Idiom) **to throw caution to the wind/winds** تَصَرَّفَ بِتَهَوُّرٍ

cautionary /ˈkɔːʃ(ə)n(ə)ri/ *adj* ‹*tale, look*› تَحْذيريّ

cautious /ˈkɔːʃəs/ *adj* **1▸** (careful) ‹*driver, investor*› حَذِر, **2▸** (wary) ‹*welcome, optimism*› حَذِر مُحْتَرِس

cautiously /ˈkɔːʃəsli/ *adv* ‹*to proceed, approach*› بِحَذَرٍ, باحْتِراسٍ

cavalry /ˈkav(ə)lri/ *n* (mounted) خَيّالة, فُرْسان; (in tanks) قوّات مُدَرَّعة

cave /keɪv/ *n* كَهْف (كُهوف), مَغارة (مَغارات)

(Phrasal verb) **cave in** **A** **~ in** **1▸** (to fall down) «tunnel, roof» انْهارَ **2▸** (to submit) «negotiators, government» أَذْعَنَ **B** **~ [sth] in ~ in [sth]** هَدَمَ [شَيْئاً] ‹*roof*›; هَشَّمَ [شَيْئاً] ‹*skull, rib cage*›

caveat /ˈkavɪat/ *n* تَحَفُّظ (تَحَفُّظات); **I'm happy to approve this, with the ~ that a review will take place after six months** يُسْعِدُني أنْ أُوافِقَ على هذا، بِشَرْطِ أَنْ يَخْضَعَ للمُراجَعةِ بعد سِتّةِ أَشْهُرٍ

caveman /ˈkeɪvman/ *n* (*pl* **-men**) رَجُل \ إنْسان الكُهوفِ

cavern /ˈkav(ə)n/ *n* كَهْف (كُهوف), مَغارة (مَغارات)

caviar, **caviare** /ˈkavɪɑː/ *n* كافِيار

caving /ˈkeɪvɪŋ/ *n* رياضة اسْتِكْشافِ الكُهوفِ

cavity /ˈkavɪti/ *n* (*pl* **cavities**) (space) تَجْويف (تَجاويفُ); (in a tooth) تَسَوُّس

cavort /kəˈvɔːt/ *vi* «lambs, teenagers» قَفَزَ \ رَقَصَ فَرَحاً

caw /kɔː/ *vi* «crows» نَعَقَ (a-i; نَعْق, نَعيق)

cayenne, **cayenne pepper** /keɪˈen/ *n* فُلَيْفِلة كايين

Cayman Islands /ˈkeɪmən ʌɪləndz/ *pr n pl* (**the Cayman Islands**) جُزُر كايْمان

CBS /siːbiːˈɛs/ *n* (AmE) = **Columbia Broadcasting System** الشَبَكة التِلِفِزْيونيّة الأَمْريكيّة سي بي إس

cc /siːˈsiː/ *n* = **cubic centimetre(s)** سَنْتِمِتْر مُكَعَّب

CCTV /siːsiːtiːˈviː/ *n* = **closed-circuit television** نِظام الدَوائِرِ التِلِفِزْيونيّةِ المُغْلَقةِ

CD /siːˈdiː/ *n* = **compact disc** قُرْص مُدْمَج \ مَضْغوط, سي دي

CD player *n* مُشَغِّل سي دي

CD-ROM /siːdiːˈrɒm/ *n* قُرْص مُدْمَج \ مَضْغوط, سي دي روم

cease /siːs/ **A** *vt* أَوْقَفَ ‹*work, production*›

B *vi* «work, contact, production» تَوَقَّفَ

ceasefire /ˈsiːsfʌɪə/ *n* وَقْف إطْلاقِ النارِ

ceaseless /ˈsiːsləs/ *adj* ‹*efforts, activity*› غَيْر مُنْقَطِعٍ, مُتَواصِل

cedar /ˈsiːdə/ *n* أَرْز; **the ~ of Lebanon** أَرْز لُبْنان

cede /siːd/ *vt* تَنازَلَ (عن), تَخَلّى (عن) ‹*control, land*›

cedilla /sɪˈdɪlə/ *n* ç الإشارة تحت حَرْفِ

ceilidh /ˈkeɪli/ *n* [احْتِفال موسيقيّ شَعْبيّ]

ceiling /ˈsiːlɪŋ/ *n* **1▸** (of a room) سَقْف (أَسْقُف, سُقُف, سُقوف) **2▸** (on spending) سَقْف

celebrate /ˈsɛlɪbreɪt/ **A** *vt* احْتَفَلَ (ب) ‹*a birthday, victory*›

B *vi* «families, winners» احْتَفَلَ

celebrated /ˈsɛlɪbreɪtɪd/ *adj* ‹*pianist, sculptor*› شَهير, مَشْهور (مَشاهيرُ)

celebration /sɛlɪˈbreɪʃ(ə)n/ *n* **1▸** (celebrating) احْتِفال **2▸** (party) احْتِفال (احْتِفالات); **the ~s went on for hours** اسْتَمَرَّت الاحْتِفالاتُ لِساعاتٍ

celebrity /sɪˈlɛbrɪti/ *n* (*pl* **celebrities**) مَشْهور (مَشاهيرُ)

celeriac /sɪˈlɛrɪak/ *n* (Bot, Culin) كَرَفْس لِفْتيّ

celery /ˈsɛləri/ *n* كَرَفْس

celiac disease (AmE) *n* ▸ **coeliac disease**

celibate /ˈsɛlɪbət/ *adj* ‹*priest*› مُتَبَتِّل; ‹*life*› تَبَتُّلٍ

cell /sɛl/ *n* **1▸** (prisoner's) زِنْزانة **2▸** (Bio) خَلِيّة (خَلايا) **3▸** (Elec) خَلِيّة (خَلايا)

cellar /ˈsɛlə/ *n* (basement) قَبْو (أَقْبِية); (for wine) [قَبْو النَبيذِ]

cellist /ˈtʃɛlɪst/ *n* عازِف تْشيللو; **to be a ~** كانَ عازِفَ تْشيللو; **she's a ~ with the London Philharmonic Orchestra**

هي عازِفةُ تْشيللو في أورْكِسْترا لُنْدُن الفيلْهارْمونيّةِ

cello /'tʃeləʊ/ *n* (*pl* **cellos**) تْشيللو

cell phone *n* تِلِفون مَحْمول ,جَوّال ,موبايِل ,هاتِف نَقّال

cellular /'sɛljʊlə/ *adj* ‹*structure, mechanism*› خَلَويّ

cellular phone *n* تِلِفون مَحْمول ,جَوّال ,موبايِل ,هاتِف نَقّال

cellulite /'seljʊlʌɪt/ *n* جِلْد قِشْرِ البُرْتُقال ,السيلوليت (تراكُم للشُحومِ تحت الجِلْدِ)

cellulitis /,sɛljʊ'lʌɪtɪs/ *n* (Med) الْتِهاب ,الْتِهاب النسيجِ الخَلَويِّ الهَلَلِ

celluloid® /'seljʊlɔɪd/ *n* سِلْيولوِيْد (مادّة لَدائِنيّة صِناعيّة)

cellulose /'sɛljʊləʊs/ *n* سِلْيولوز

Celsius /'sɛlsɪəs/ *adj* مِئَويّ; **20 degrees ~** 20 دَرَجةً مِئَويّةً

Celt /kɛlt/ *n* سِلْتيّ ,كِلْتيّ

Celtic /'keltɪk/ *adj* ‹*cross, mythology*› سِلْتيّ ,كِلْتيّ

cement /sɪ'mɛnt/ **A** *n* إسْمَنْت

B *vt* وَطَّدَ ‹*a relationship*›; عَزَّزَ ‹*reputation*›

cement mixer *n* خلاّط إسْمَنْت

cemetery /'sɛmɪtri/ *n* (*pl* **cemeteries**) مَقْبَرة (مَقابِرُ)

censor /'sɛnsə/ **A** *n* رَقيب (رُقَباءُ)

B *vt* أخْضَعَ للرَقابةِ ‹*a film, publication*›; **the news was so heavily ~ed that it was not credible** خَضَعَت الأخْبارُ إلى رَقابةٍ مُشَدَّدةٍ بِحَيْثُ فقَدَتْ مِصْداقيَّتَها

censorship /'sɛnsəʃɪp/ *n* رَقابة

censure /'sɛnʃə/ **A** *vt* اسْتَهْجَنَ ‹*sb's conduct*›; انْتَقَدَ ‹*an organization*›

B *n* تَوْبيخ ,تَأْنيب ,تَقْريع

census /'sɛnsəs/ *n* (*pl* **censuses**) إحْصاء سُكّانيّ

cent /sɛnt/ *n* (of a dollar) سِنْت; (of a euro) سنت

centenary /sɛn'tiːn(ə)ri/ *n* (*pl* **centenaries**) ذِكْرى مِئَويّة

centennial /sɛn'tɛnɪəl/ *n* (AmE) ذِكْرى مِئَويّة

center (AmE) ▸ **centre**

centigrade /'sɛntɪɡreɪd/ *adj* مِئَويّ; **35 degrees ~** 35 دَرَجة مِئَويّة

centilitre (BrE), **centiliter** (AmE) /'sɛntɪliːtə/ *n* سَنْتِلِتْر

centimetre (BrE), **centimeter** (AmE) /'sɛntɪmiːtə/ *n* سَنْتِمِتْر (سَنْتِمِتْرات)

centipede /'sɛntɪpiːd/ *n* أمّ أرْبَعٍ وَأرْبَعينَ ,حَريش

central /'sɛntr(ə)l/ *adj* **1** (in the centre) ‹*arch, pillar*› مَرْكَزيّ; **~ London** وَسَط لُنْدُن **2** (conveniently situated) ‹*location*› مَرْكَزيّ **3** (key) ‹*role, theme*› مَرْكَزيّ

Central African Republic *n* (**the Central African Republic**) جُمْهوريّة إفْريقِيا الوُسْطى

Central America *n* أمْريكا الوُسْطى

Central American **A** *n* [شَخْص من أمْريكا الوُسْطى]

B *adj* ‹*rainforest, dish*› من أمْريكا الوُسْطى

central bank *n* بَنْك مَرْكَزيّ

Central Europe *n* أوروبّا الوُسْطى

central heating *n* تَدْفِئة مَرْكَزيّة

centralize, -ise (BrE) /'sɛntrəlʌɪz/ *vt* مَرْكَزَ (مَرْكَزة) ‹*power, government*›

central locking *n* قَفْل مَرْكَزيّ

central nervous system *n* جِهاز عَصَبيّ مَرْكَزيّ

central reservation *n* (BrE) رَصيف فاصِل (خطّ الوَسَطِ الفاصِل في الطُرُق ذاتِ الاتِّجاهَيْنِ)

centre (BrE), **center** (AmE) /'sɛntə/ **A** *n* **1** (mid point) وَسَط (أوْساط) ,مَرْكَز (مَراكِز); **in the ~ of the room/table** في وَسَطِ الغُرْفةِ \ الطاوِلةِ; **the ~ of Damascus** وَسَط دِمَشْقَ; **the city/town ~** وَسَط \ مَرْكَز المَدينةِ; **the ~ of the circle** مَرْكَز الدائِرةِ **2** (focal point) قَلْب ,محْوَر; **to be the ~ of attention** كانَ مِحْوَرَ الاهْتِمامِ; **to be at the ~ of a row** كانَ في قَلْبِ الصِراعِ **3** (building) مَرْكَز (مَراكِز); **a shopping/community ~** مَرْكَز تَسَوُّقٍ \ اجْتِماعيّ **4** (in politics) حِزْب \ تَيّار الوَسَطِ; **to be to the left/right of ~** كانَ يَنْتَمي إلى يَسارِ \ يَمينِ الوَسَطِ **5** (in rugby, soccer, hockey) لاعِب وَسَطٍ **6** (of a chocolate) قَلْب ,حَشْو

B *vt* **1** وَسَّطَ ‹*text, a heading*› **2** (in rugby, soccer, hockey) مَرَّرَ إلى الوَسَطِ ‹*the ball*›

C *vi* (in rugby, soccer, hockey) مَرَّرَ الكُرةَ إلى الوَسَطِ

Phrasal verbs **centre around**: **~ around [sth], be ~d around [sth]** **1** (to be located) تَمَرْكَزَ حول \ في [شَيْءٍ] ‹*a town, area*› **2** (to have as its focus) دارَ حول [شَيْءٍ] ‹*an issue, a character*›

• **centre on, centre upon**: **~ on [sth]** ▸ **centre around**

centre back (BrE), **center back** (AmE) *n* قَلْب دِفاعٍ

centre forward (BrE), **center forward** (AmE) *n* قَلْبُ هُجومٍ

centre half (BrE), **center half** (AmE) *n* قَلْب دِفاعٍ

centre of gravity (BrE), **center of gravity** (AmE) *n* مَرْكَز ثِقْلٍ

centrepiece (BrE), **centerpiece** (AmE) /ˈsɛntəpiːs/ *n* ① (on a table) [زينة وَسَطِ المائِدَةِ] ② (main feature) مِحْوَر

centre stage (BrE), **center stage** (AmE) *n* قَلْب \ وَسَط المَسْرَحِ

centrifugal /ˌsɛntrɪˈfjuːg(ə)l/ *adj* نابِذ

centrist /ˈsɛntrɪst/ *n, adj* وَسَطِيّ

century /ˈsɛntʃʊri/ *n* (*pl* **centuries**) قَرْن (قُرون); **in the 21st ~** في القَرْنِ الحادي والعِشْرينَ; **at the turn of the ~** مع إطْلالةِ القَرْنِ

CEO /siːiːˈəʊ/ *n* = **Chief Executive Officer** مُدير \ رَئيس كَبير الإداريِّينَ التَنْفيذيِّين, تَنْفيذيّ

ceramic /sɪˈramɪk/ *adj* ‹*plate, bowl*› سيراميك; **~ tile** قِطْعة كاشي سيراميك

ceramics /sɪˈramɪks/ *n* ① + *pl v* (objects) خَزَفِيّات ② + *sing v* (subject of study) خِزافة

cereal /ˈsɪərɪəl/ *n* ① (grain, plant) حَبّ (n coll; حُبوب) ② (for breakfast) [رَقائِقُ حُبوبٍ مُحَمَّصةٍ تُؤْكَل مع الحَليبِ]

cerebral /ˈsɛrɪbr(ə)l/ *adj* ① ‹*writing, music*› [يُخاطِبُ العَقْلَ (لا العاطِفةَ)] ② ‹*meningitis, haemorrhage*› دِماغيّ; **a ~ haemorrhage** نَزيف دِماغيّ

cerebral palsy *n* شَلَل دِماغيّ

ceremonial /sɛrɪˈməʊnɪəl/ *adj* ‹*occasion, dress*› رَسْميّ

ceremony /ˈsɛrɪməni/ *n* (*pl* **ceremonies**) (religious) مَنْسَك (مَناسِكُ); (non-religious) مَرْسَم (مَراسِمُ)

certain /ˈsəːt(ə)n/ **A** *adj* ① (sure, definite) واثِق, مُتَأَكِّد; **to be ~ about** *or* **of sth** كانَ واثِقاً من شَيْءٍ; **I'm ~ about** *or* **of it** أنا واثِقٌ من هذا; **they are ~ of victory** هُمْ واثِقونَ من النَصْرِ; **I'm absolutely ~ that I locked it** أنا واثِقٌ تماماً أنّني أغْلَقْتُهُ; **to make ~ that** (to ascertain) تَحَقَّقَ من أنَّ; (to ensure) تَأَكَّدَ من أنَّ; **she has made ~ of a place in the final** ضَمِنَتْ مَكاناً لَها في الدَوْرِ النِهائيِّ; **I know that for ~** أَعْلَمُ ذلك يَقيناً ② (inevitable) ‹*death, defeat*› مُؤَكَّد, حَتْميّ, مُحَقَّق; **they are heading for ~ defeat** يَتَّجِهونَ نحو هَزيمةٍ مُحَقَّقةٍ; **to be ~ of doing sth** ضَمِنَ فِعْلَ شَيْءٍ; **she's ~ to win/lose** هي مُتَأَكِّدةٌ أنّها سَتَفوزُ \ سَتَخْسَرُ ③ (specific) ‹*type, number*› مُعَيَّن; **~ people** بَعْض الناسِ, أَشْخاص مُعَيَّنونَ; **you are only allowed a ~ amount of time** لَيْسَ مَسْموحاً لَكَ إلاّ بِقَدْرٍ مُعَيَّنٍ من الوَقْتِ ④ (indeterminate) ‹*tension, satisfaction*› بَعْض; **it caused a ~ amount of confusion** سَبَّبَ قَدْراً مُعَيَّناً من اللَبْسِ; **to a ~ extent** *or* **degree** إلى حَدٍّ ما
B *pron* **~ of our members/friends** البَعْض من أَعْضائِنا \ أَصْدِقائِنا

certainly /ˈsəːt(ə)nli/ *adv* ① (definitely) بالتَأْكيد, من المُؤَكَّدِ, قَطْعاً; **he is almost ~ dead** مَوْتُهُ شِبْهُ مُؤَكَّدٍ; **I ~ won't be going there again!** قَطْعاً لن أَذْهَبَ إلى هُناكَ مَرّةً أُخْرى!; **~ not!** قَطْعاً لا! ② (expressing assent) أكيد; **'may I sit here?' — '~!'** 'هل بِإمْكاني أنْ أَجْلِسَ هُنا؟'–'أكيد!'

certainty /ˈsəːt(ə)nti/ *n* (*pl* **certainties**) ① (sureness) تَأَكُّد, تَيَقُّن ② (sure thing) أَمْر مُؤَكَّد \ مُحَتَّم; **it's a ~ that they will win** من المُؤَكَّدِ أنَّهُم سَيَفوزونَ

certificate /səˈtɪfɪkət/ *n* ① (Educ) شهادة ② (of birth, death, marriage) شهادة

certification /səːtɪfɪˈkeɪʃ(ə)n/ *n* ① (Law) شَهادة ② (of a patient) [إقرار بِضَرورةِ إدْخالِ المَريضِ إلى مَصَحّةٍ عَقْليّةٍ]

certified /ˈsəːtɪfʌɪd/ *adj* مُصَدَّق عَلَيْهِ

certified mail *n* (AmE) بَريد مُسَجَّل

certified public accountant *n* (AmE) مُحاسِب مُعْتَمَد

certify /ˈsəːtɪfʌɪ/ *vt* (**certifies**, **certifying**, **certified**) ① (to confirm) صادَقَ (على); **to ~ that** أَقَرَّ بِ ② (to declare insane) ‹*a patient*› [أَعْلَنَ إصابةَ شَخْصٍ بالجُنونِ]

cervical /ˈsəːvɪk(ə)l/ *adj* عُنُق الرَحِمِ; **~ cancer** سَرَطان عُنُقِ الرَحِمِ

cervical cancer *n* سَرَطان عُنُقِ الرَحِمِ

cervical smear *n* مَسْحة عُنُقِ الرَحِمِ

cervix /ˈsəːvɪks/ *n* (*pl* **cervices**) عُنُق الرَحِمِ

cesarean, **cesarian** (AmE) *n* ▸ **caesarean**

cessation /sɛˈseɪʃ(ə)n/ *n* (fml) <*war*> وَقْف; <*treaty*> إِلْغاء (إِلْغاءات)

cesspit /ˈsɛspɪt/, **cesspool** /ˈsɛspuːl/ *n* بالوعة مَجارٍ

cf. /siːˈɛf/ *abbr* = **confer: compare** راجِع

CFC /siːɛfˈsiː/ *n* = **chlorofluorocarbon** كْلوروفْلوروكَرْبون

ch. *abbr* = **chapter** فَصْل

Chad /tʃad/ *pr n* تْشاد (f); **Lake ~** بُحَيْرة تْشاد

chador /ˈtʃʌdə/ *n* شادور (شَمْلة تُغَطّي الرَأْسَ والبَدَنَ تَرْتَديها النِساءُ في إيران)

chafe /tʃeɪf/ **A** *vi* احْتَكَّ **B** *vt* حَكَّ (u; حَكّ)

chaff /tʃɑːf, tʃaf/ *n* قَصْل ,عُصافة

chaffinch /ˈtʃafɪn(t)ʃ/ *n* الصَغْنَج

chagrin /ˈʃagrɪn/ *n* غَمّ (غُموم) ,كَدَر (أَكْدار)

chain /tʃeɪn/ **A** *n* 1 (metal links) سِلْسِلة (سَلاسِلُ); **a length of ~** سِلْسِلة; **to put/keep sb in ~s** كَبَّلَ شَخْصاً بالسَلاسِلِ; **the dog is kept on a ~** رُبِطَ الكَلْبُ بِسِلْسِلةٍ 2 (on a door) سِلْسِلة (سَلاسِلُ) 3 (on a lavatory) سِلْسِلة (سَلاسِلُ); **to pull the ~** سَحَبَ سِلْسِلةَ السيفونِ 4 (of stores, hotels) سِلْسِلة (سَلاسِلُ); **a supermarket/hotel ~** سِلْسِلة أَسْواقٍ تِجاريّة \ فَنادِقَ 5 (series) سِلْسِلة; **the ~ of events that led to war** سِلْسِلة الأَحْداثِ الّتي أَدَّتْ إلى الحَرْبِ; **the ~ of command** سِلْسِلة القِيادة; **to make** *or* **form a human ~** شَكَّلَ سِلْسِلةً بَشَرِيّةً 6 (of mountains) سِلْسِلة (سَلاسِلُ) 7 (of atoms) سِلْسِلة (سَلاسِلُ)

B *vt* سَلْسَلَ (i; سَلْسَلة) ,قَيَّدَ \ كَبَّلَ بِسِلْسِلةٍ <*a prisoner, an animal*>; **the prisoners were ~ed together** سُلْسِلَ السُجَناءُ مَعاً; **he ~ed his bike to the post** رَبَطَ دَرّاجَتَهُ بِسِلْسِلةٍ في العامودِ; **to be ~ed to one's desk/the kitchen sink** كانَ مُضْطَرًّا للبَقاءِ في مَكْتَبِهِ \ أمامَ حَوْضِ المَطْبَخِ

chain reaction *n* تَفاعُل مُتَسَلْسِل

chainsaw /ˈtʃeɪnsɔː/ *n* مِنْشار السِلْسِلةِ \ الجَنْزيرِ (ذو أَسْنانٍ مُثَبَّتةٍ في سِلْسِلةٍ دائمة الحَرَكة)

chain-smoke /ˈtʃʌɪnsməʊk/ *vt, vi* دَخَّنَ بِشَراهةٍ

chain-smoker /ˈtʃʌɪnsməʊkə/ *n* مُدَخِّن شَرِه

chain store *n* 1 (single shop) مَتْجَر في سِلْسِلةِ مَتاجِرَ 2 (retail group) سِلْسِلة مَتاجِرَ / مَحَلاّتٍ

chair /tʃɛː/ **A** *n* 1 (seat) كُرْسيّ (كَراسٍ ,كَراسيُّ); (armchair) كُرْسيّ وَثير ذو مِسْنَدَيْ ذِراعٍ 2 (chairperson) رَئيس الجَلْسةِ; **to take the ~** تَرَأَّسَ الجَلْسةَ 3 (at a university) أُسْتاذيّة **B** *vt* تَرَأَّسَ <*a meeting*>

chairlift /ˈtʃɛːlɪft/ *n* مَعْبَر هَوائيّ

chairman /ˈtʃɛːmən/ *n* (*pl* **-men**) 1 (of a meeting) رَئيس (رُؤَساءُ) 2 (of a company, an organization) رَئيس (رُؤَساءُ)

chairperson /ˈtʃɛːpəːs(ə)n/ *n* (*pl* **-persons**) رَئيس (رُؤَساءُ)

chairwoman /ˈtʃɛːwʊmən/ *n* (*pl* **-women**) رَئيسة

chalet /ˈʃaleɪ/ *n* 1 (in mountains) شاليه 2 (in a holiday camp) شاليه

chalk /tʃɔːk/ *n* 1 (mineral) حَجَر الطَباشير 2 (for writing) طَباشير

challenge /ˈtʃalɪn(d)ʒ/ **A** *n* 1 (challenging task) تَحَدٍّ (تَحَدِّيات); **to rise to the ~** قَبِلَ تَحَدِّيًا 2 (invitation to contest) تَحَدٍّ (تَحَدِّيات) **B** *vt* 1 (to invite to a contest) تَحَدّى <*a player, combatant*>; **to ~ sb to do sth** تَحَدّى شَخْصاً في القِيامِ بِشَيْءٍ; **he ~d me to a game of chess** تَحَدّاني في الشِطْرَنْجِ 2 (to dispute the validity of) تَحَدّى <*a decision, authority*> 3 (to require identity of) أَمَرَ بالتَعْريفِ بالذاتِ <*an intruder, a suspect*>

challenger /ˈtʃalɪndʒə/ *n* مُتَحَدٍّ (مُتَحَدّيونَ)

challenging /ˈtʃalɪn(d)ʒɪŋ/ *adj* 1 <*task, environment*> شَكَّلَ تَحَدِّياً 2 <*look*> تَحَدٍّ; <*manner*> اسْتِفْزازيّ

chamber /ˈtʃeɪmbə/ *n* 1 (hall) قاعة 2 (of a parliament) مَجْلِس (مَجالِسُ); **the upper/lower ~** مَجْلِس الأَعْيانِ \ العُمومِ 3 (enclosed space) فَجْوة (فَجَوات ,فِجاء) 4 (old use) (private room) مَخْدَع (مَخادِعُ) 5 (of a gun) حُجْرة الإِطْلاقِ

chambermaid /ˈtʃeɪmbəmeɪd/ *n* عامِلة تَنْظيفِ الغُرَفِ

chamber music *n* موسيقى الحُجْرة

Chamber of Commerce *n* غُرْفة التِجارة

chamber pot *n* مِبْوَلة (كانَتْ توضَعُ في غُرَفِ النَوْمِ للاسْتِخْدامِ اللَيْليِّ)

chameleon /kəˈmiːliən/ *n* حِرْباء (f; حَرابيّ)

chamomile *n* (AmE) ▸ **camomile**

champ /tʃamp/ **A** *vi* **to be ~ing to do sth** تاقَ للقِيامِ بِشَيْءٍ; **he's ~ing to start** هو تَوّاقٌ للبَدْءِ

B *n* (infml) بَطَل (أَبْطال)

champagne /ʃamˈpeɪn/ *n* شَمْبانِيا

champion /ˈtʃampɪən/ **A** *n* **1** (Sport) بَطَل (أَبْطال) **2** (of a cause) مُناصِر, مُدافِع

B *vt* ‹a cause, sb's rights› ناصَرَ, (عن) دافَعَ

championship /ˈtʃampɪənʃɪp/ *n* بُطولة

chance /tʃɑːns/ **A** *n* **1** (opportunity) فُرْصة (فُرَص); **I haven't had a ~ to talk to him** لم أَجِدْ فُرْصةً للتَحَدُّثِ مَعَهُ; **you should go if you get the ~** يَنْبَغي أَنْ تَذْهَبَ إذا سَنَحَتْ لَكَ الفُرْصةُ; **when you get a ~, can you ...?** عِنْدَما تُتاحُ لَكَ الفُرْصةُ، هل يُمْكِنُكَ أَنْ ...؟; **give me a ~ to explain** أَعْطِني فُرْصةً حتّى أَشْرَحَ لَكَ; **you've missed your ~** فاتَتْكَ الفُرْصةُ; **now's your ~!** الآنَ هذه فُرْصَتُكَ!; **this is your last ~!** هذه هي فُرْصَتُكَ الأَخيرةُ! **2** (likelihood) احْتِمال (احْتِمالات), فُرْصة (فُرَص); **there is a ~ that he'll die** هُناكَ احْتِمالٌ أَنَّهُ سَيَموتُ; **the ~s are that she'll say yes** أَغْلَبُ الظَنِّ أَنَّها سَتَقولُ نَعَمْ; **what are her ~s of recovery?** ما هي فُرَصُها في الشِفاءِ؟; **she has a 20% ~ of survival** لَدَيْها 20٪ في المِائةِ من فُرَصِ البَقاءِ على قَيْدِ الحَياةِ; **it has little ~ of success** لَدَيْهِ فُرْصةٌ ضَئيلةٌ في النَجاحِ; **no ~!** (infml) مُسْتَحيل!; **we didn't stand a ~** لم يَكُنْ لَدَيْنا أَيُّ فُرْصةٍ; **do you have his address by any ~?** هل من المُمْكِنِ \ المُحْتَمَلِ أَنْ يَكونَ لَدَيْكَ عُنْوانُهُ؟ **3** [u] (luck) حَظّ, صُدْفة; **to meet by ~** تَقابَلَ بالصُدْفةِ; **a game of ~** لُعْبةُ حَظٍّ; **nothing is left to ~** لم يُتْرَكْ شَيْءٌ للصُدْفةِ **4** (risk) مُجازَفة, مُغامَرة, مُخاطَرة; **to take a ~** جازَفَ, خاطَرَ; **it's a ~ I'm willing to take** هي مُخاطَرةٌ أَرْغَبُ في القِيامِ بِها; **I'm taking no ~s** لن أَقومَ بِأَيِّ مُجازَفاتٍ

B *vt* **1** (fml) (to happen) **to ~ to do sth** فَعَلَ شَيْئاً بالصُدْفةِ **2** (to risk) خاطَرَ (ب), غامَرَ (ب), جازَفَ (ب); **to ~ doing sth** خاطَرَ بِفِعْلِ شَيْءٍ; **I wouldn't ~ it** لن أُخاطِرَ بِذَلِكَ

Idioms **to chance one's arm** *or* **luck** (infml) قامَ بِمُجازَفةٍ كَبيرةٍ; **to fancy one's chances** (BrE infml) مَنّى نَفْسَهُ بالفَوْزِ

Phrasal verb **chance upon, chance on**: **1** **~ upon [sb]** (fml) قابَلَ [شَخْصاً] بالصُدْفةِ **2** **~ upon [sth]** (fml) وَجَدَ [شَيْئاً] بالصُدْفةِ

chance discovery *n* اكْتِشاف بالصُدْفةِ

chancellor /ˈtʃɑːns(ə)lə/ *n* **1** (Pol) **C~ of the Exchequer** (BrE) وَزير الماليّةِ **2** (head of government) مُسْتَشار **3** (head of a university) رَئيس فَخْريّ

chance meeting *n* لِقاء بالصُدْفةِ

chandelier /ʃandəˈlɪə/ *n* ثُرَيّا (ثُرَيّات)

change /tʃeɪn(d)ʒ/ **A** *vt* **1** (to alter completely) حَوَّلَ, بَدَّلَ; (in part) غَيَّرَ, عَدَّلَ; **we have ~d the text/the shape of the lawn** غَيَّرْنا النَصَّ \ شَكْلَ المَرْجِ; **the experience ~d him completely** بَدَّلَتْهُ التَجْرِبةُ تَماماً; **to ~ one's mind** غَيَّرَ رَأْيَهُ; **I've ~d my mind about moving house** غَيَّرْتُ رَأْيي بِشَأْنِ الانْتِقالِ من المَنْزِلِ; **you've ~d the furniture round** غَيَّرْتَ تَرْتيبَ الأَثاثِ **2** (to transform) حَوَّلَ; **to ~ sth into sth else** حَوَّلَ شَيْئاً إلى شَيْءٍ آخَرَ; **sugar is ~d into alcohol** تَمَّ تَحْويلُ السُكَّرِ إلى كُحولٍ **3** ‹money› صَرَّفَ, حَوَّلَ; **to ~ euros into dollars** حَوَّلَ اليورُواتِ إلى دولاراتٍ **4** (in exchanges, upgrades) ‹one's car, a purchase, one's name› غَيَّرَ, بَدَّلَ, اسْتَبْدَلَ; **they ~d their car for a smaller one** اسْتَبْدَلوا سَيّارَتَهُمْ بِسَيّارةٍ أَصْغَرَ; **can I ~ it for a size 12?** هل يُمْكِنُني أَنْ أَسْتَبْدِلَهُ بِمَقاسِ 12؟; **if it's not suitable, we'll ~ it for you** إذا لم تَكُنْ مُناسِبةً، سَوْفَ نُبَدِّلُها لك; **she ~d her name when she divorced** غَيَّرَتْ اسْمَها بعد الطَلاقِ; **I've ~d my dentist** غَيَّرْتُ طَبيبَ أَسْناني; **to ~ places** تَبادَلَ المَقاعِدَ; **I wouldn't ~ places with the Queen** لا أُحِبُّ أَنْ أَكونَ مَكانَ المَلِكةِ; **the hotel has ~d hands** انْتَقَلَتْ مِلْكيّةُ الفُنْدُقِ إلى مالِكٍ آخَرَ; **no money ~d hands** لم يَتِمَّ دَفْعُ أَيِّ مالٍ **5** (to replace) ‹a bulb, fuse, wheel› غَيَّرَ; **to ~ the bed/sheets** غَيَّرَ مُلاءاتِ السَريرِ; **to ~ one's clothes** غَيَّرَ مَلابِسَهُ; **hurry up and get ~d!** أَسْرِعْ وَغَيِّرْ مَلابِسَكَ! **6** (with nappies, diapers) ‹a baby› غَيَّرَ الحِفاظةَ

B *vi* **1** (to alter) «situations, attitudes, people» تَغَيَّرَ; **you haven't ~d a bit!** لم تَتَغَيَّرْ مُطْلَقاً!; **the lights ~d to green** تَغَيَّرَ الضَوْءُ إلى الأَخْضَرِ; **the wind ~d** تَغَيَّرَ اتِّجاهُ الريحِ **2** (to be transformed) «person, substance» تَحَوَّلَ; **to ~ into sth**

تَحَوَّلَ إلى شَيْءٍ **3** (into different clothes) غَيَّرَ المَلابِسَ; **to ~ out of one's uniform/work clothes** غَيَّرَ زِيَّهُ \ مَلابِسَ العَمَلِ; **to ~ into a suit/jeans** غَيَّرَ مَلابِسَهُ وارْتَدى بِزَّةً \ جينْز **4** (with buses, trains) «passengers» غَيَّرَ; **~ at the next station for Westchester** غَيِّرْ في المَحَطَّةِ القادِمةِ إلى وِسْتْشِسْتَر; **all ~!** على الجَميعِ النُزولُ! **5** (when driving) غَيَّرَ تَعْشيقَ التُروسِ; **to ~ into third/fourth gear** غَيَّرَ إلى التُرْسِ الثالِثِ \ الرابِعِ

C *n* **1** (alteration) تَغْيير (تَغْييرات), تَحَوُّل (تَحَوُّلات); **a ~ in policy/the law** تَغْيير في السِياسةِ \ القانونِ; **a ~ of address** تَغْيير العُنْوانِ; **a ~ of government** تَغْيير الحُكومةِ; **there's been a ~ of plan** حَدَثَ تَغْييرٌ في الخُطَّةِ; **a ~ for the better/worse** تَغْيير للأَفْضَلِ \ للأَسْوَأِ; **to make ~s in** *or* **to sth** (to a system, structure) قامَ بِعَمَلِ تَغْييراتٍ في شَيْءٍ; (to a text) أَدْخَلَ تَعْديلاتٍ على شَيْءٍ; **they've made some ~s to the team** قاموا بِبَعْضِ التَغْييراتِ في الفَريقِ; **it makes a refreshing ~ from pasta/city life** يُعَدُّ هذا تَغْييراً مُنْعِشاً من المَعْكَرونةِ \ حَياةِ المَدينةِ; **there will have to be a ~ in your attitude** لا بُدَّ أَنْ يَكونَ هُناكَ تَغْييرٌ في مَوْقِفِكَ; **why don't you cook for a ~?** لِماذا لا تَطْبُخُ من بابِ التَغْييرِ؟ **2** [u] (alteration) تَحَوُّل, تَغْيير; **people in favour of/opposed to ~** المُؤَيِّدونَ \ المُعارِضونَ للتَغْييرِ; **a time of economic and social ~** وَقْت التَغْييرِ الاقْتِصاديِّ والاجْتِماعيِّ **3** (of clothes) **a ~ of clothes** غِيار من المَلابِسِ **4** [u] (coins) عُمْلات مَعْدِنيّة, قِطَع نَقْديّة مَعْدِنيّة; **small** *or* **loose ~** عُمْلات مَعْدِنيّة \ صَغيرة; **£5 in ~** 5 جُنَيْهاتٍ مَعْدِنيّة; **have you got ~ for £20?** هل يُمْكِنُكَ أَنْ تَسْتَبْدِلَ لي 20 جُنَيْهاً بِعُمْلاتٍ صَغيرةٍ؟ **do you have the right ~?** هل لَدَيْكَ المَبْلَغُ المَطْلوبُ بالضَبْطِ؟ **5** (money returned) باقٍ; **you won't get much ~ out of £200** لن تَحْصُلَ على باقٍ كَثيرٍ من 200 جُنَيْهٍ; **he gave me the wrong ~** أَخْطَأَ في حِسابِ الباقي الّذي أَعْطاهُ لي **6** (infml) (the menopause) **the ~, the ~ of life** سِنّ اليَأْسِ

(Phrasal verbs) **change down** (BrE Aut) نَقَلَ ناقِلَ الحَرَكةِ إلى سُرْعةٍ أَقَلَّ

• **change over** **1** (to swap roles) «drivers, guards» تَبادَلَ المَهامَّ **2** (to move) «companies, consumers» تَحَوَّلَ; **we ~d over from gas to solar heating** تَحَوَّلْنا من التَدْفِئةِ بالغازِ إلى التَدْفِئةِ بالطاقةِ الشَمْسيّةِ

• **change up** (BrE Aut) نَقَلَ ناقِلَ الحَرَكةِ إلى سُرْعةٍ أَعْلى

changeable /ˈtʃeɪn(d)ʒəb(ə)l/ *adj* ‹*weather, conditions, mood*› مُتَغَيِّر, مُتَقَلِّب

changeover /ˈtʃeɪn(d)ʒəʊvə/ *n* تَحَوُّل (تَحَوُّلات); **the ~ from analogue to digital broadcasting** التَحَوُّل من البَثِّ التَماثُليِّ إلى البَثِّ الرَقْميِّ

change purse *n* (AmE) كيس فَكّةٍ

changing /ˈtʃeɪndʒɪŋ/ *adj* ‹*world, attitudes*› مُتَغَيِّر

changing room *n* (for sport, swimming) غُرْفة تَبْديل (in a shop) غُرْفة تَجْريب المَلابِسِ

channel /ˈtʃan(ə)l/ **A** *n* **1** (waterway) قَناة (قَنَوات); **the Irish ~** قَناة الشَمالِ **2** (navigable passage) قَناة (قَنَوات), مَمَرّ مِلاحيّ **3** (for irrigation) تُرْعة (تُرَع, تُرْعات), قَناة (قَنوات) **4** (in television, radio) قَناة (قَنَوات); **to change ~s** غَيَّرَ القَنَواتِ; **it's on ~ 4** يُبَثُّ على القَناةِ الرابِعةِ **5** (of communication, diplomacy) قَناة (قَنَوات), طَريق (mf; طُرُق); **to go through official ~s** مَرَّ من خِلالِ القَنَواتِ الرَسْميّةِ; **we must keep the ~s of communication open** لا بُدَّ أَنْ نُبْقِيَ قَنَواتِ الاتِّصالِ مَفْتوحةً

B *pr n* (**the Channel** also **the English Channel**) بَحْر المانْش, القَنال الإنْجْليزيّ

C *vt* (**-ll-** BrE, **-l-** AmE) **1** (to send) نَقَلَ, وَصَّلَ (u; نَقْل) ‹*water, oil*› **2** (to direct) حَوَّلَ, وَجَّهَ ‹*one's energy, funds, efforts*›; **she ~s her creative energy into her art** وَجَّهَتْ طاقَتَها الإِبْداعيّةَ نحو فَنِّها **3** (to cut, form) حَفَرَ (i; حَفْر), شَقَّ (u; شَقّ) ‹*a groove*›

channel-hop /ˈtʃan(ə)lhɒp/ *vi* (**-pp-**) (infml) [انْتَقَلَ من قَناةٍ تِلِفِزْيونيّةٍ إلى أُخْرى مُسْتَخْدِماً جِهازَ التَحَكُّمِ عن بُعْدٍ]

Channel Tunnel *pr n* (**the Channel Tunnel**) نَفَق بَحْرِ المانْش

chant /tʃɑːnt/ **A** *n* **1** (ritual song) أُنْشودة (أَناشيدُ, أَنْشاد), تَرْتيلة (تَرْتيلات, تَراتيلُ) **2** (of demonstrators, sports fans) شِعار (شِعارات)

B *vt* **1** أَطْلَقَ ‹*slogans*›; (i) وَجَّهَ ‹*abuse*› **2** (Mus, Relig) رَتَّلَ ‹*prayers, hymns*›

C *vi* **1** «crowds, fans» أَنْشَدَ **2** (Mus, Relig) «choir, monks» أَنْشَدَ

chaos /ˈkeɪɒs/ *n* فَوْضى (f); **it was total ~** كانَت الفَوْضى عارِمةً

chaotic /keɪˈɒtɪk/ *adj* ‹*situation, lifestyle*› فَوْضَويّ

chap /tʃap/ *n* (BrE infml) (غِلْمان, غِلْمة) غُلام (رِجال) رَجُل

chap. *abbr* = **chapter** فَصْل

chapel /ˈtʃap(ə)l/ *n* كَنيسة صَغيرة

chaperone /ˈʃapərəʊn/ *n* 1 (old use) (for a young lady) وَصيفة (وَصائِف) 2 (for a group) مُرافِق

chaplain /ˈtʃaplɪn/ *n* قَسّ (قُسُس, قُسوس), قِسّيس (قِسّيسون, قَساوِسة)

chapter /ˈtʃaptə/ *n* فَصْل (فُصول)

char /tʃɑː/ *vt* (-rr-) لَفَحَ (a; لَفْح, لَفَحان), فَحَّمَ

character /ˈkarəktə/ *n* 1 (in a film, book, play) شَخْصيّة 2 (nature) شَخْصيّة; **it was out of ~ for him to be so abrupt** لم نَكُنْ قد عَهِدْنا ذلك الجَفاف مِنْهُ 3 (originality, individuality) شَخْصيّة; **a lovely old house, full of ~** بَيْت قديم جَميل, كُلُّهُ شَخصيّةٌ 4 (person) شَخْصيّة 5 (unusual person) شَخْصيّة 6 (symbol) حَرْف (حُروف)

characteristic /karəktəˈrɪstɪk/ A *adj* ‹*feature, modesty*› مُمَيِّز B *n* ميزة, خَلّة (خِلال), سِمة

characterization, **-isation** (BrE) /karaktərʌɪˈzeɪʃ(ə)n/ *n* وَصْف (أَوْصاف)

characterize, **-ise** (BrE) /ˈkarəktərʌɪz/ *vt* 1 (to typify) مَيَّزَ ‹*an era, a relationship*›; **an era ~d by globalization** عَهْد يَتَّسِمُ بالعَوْلَمةِ 2 (to depict) وَصَفَ (i; وَصْف); **to be ~d as sth** وُصِفَ بِشَيْءٍ

charade /ʃəˈrɑːd/ A *n* (pretence) تَظاهُر B (**charades**) *n pl + sing v* (game) لُعْبة تَخْمينِ الكَلِمات

charcoal /ˈtʃɑːkəʊl/ *n* 1 (fuel) فَحْم (فُحومات) 2 (for drawing) قَلَم فَحْم

charge /tʃɑːdʒ/ A *vt* 1 فَرَضَ (i; فَرْض) ‹*a fee, price*›; **to ~ sb for sth** طَلَبَ مَبْلَغاً من شَخْصٍ مُقابِلَ شَيْءٍ; **how much do you ~?** كم تَطْلُبُ مُقابِلَ هذا؟; **I ~ $50 an hour** أَطْلُبُ أَجْراً بِقيمةِ 50 دولاراً في الساعةِ; **interest is ~d at 2% per month** تُحْتَسَبُ الفائِدةُ بِمِقْدارِ 2٪ شَهْريًّا 2 (in accounts) **to ~ a cost to sth/sb** قَيَّدَ مَبْلَغاً على حِسابِ شَيْءٍ \ شَخْصٍ 3 (to accuse) اتَّهَمَ ‹*a suspect, defendant*›; **to ~ sb with an offence** اتَّهَمَ شَخْصاً بِجَريمةٍ 4 «soldiers, police» هَجَمَ, هاجَمَ (u; على) ‹*the enemy, demonstrators*› 5 (fml) (to entrust) عَهِدَ, كَلَّفَ (a; عَهْد); **to ~ sb with sth/doing sth** كَلَّفَ شَخْصاً بِشَيْءٍ \ بِفِعْلِ شَيْءٍ; **he was ~d with the task of drawing up a plan** عُهِدَ إِلَيْهِ بِمَهَمّةِ وَضْعِ خُطّةٍ 6 شَحَنَ (a; شَحْن) ‹*a battery, mobile phone*›

B *vi* 1 (for payment) **to ~ for a service** فَرَضَ رَسْماً مُقابِلَ خِدْمةٍ 2 (to rush at) **to ~ at sth/sb** «troops, police, bull» هَجَمَ على شَخْصٍ \ شَيْءٍ 3 (to run) جَرى (i; جَرْي); **he ~d into/out of the room** جَرى إلى \ خارِجَ الحُجْرة 4 «battery, mobile phone» شُحِنَ

C *n* 1 (fee) رَسْم (رُسوم), تَكْلِفة (تَكاليفُ), ثَمَن (أَثْمان, أَثْمِنة); **delivery ~s are included** رُسومُ التَّوْصيلِ مَشْمولةٌ; **free of ~** مَجّاناً; **we make a small ~ for this service** نَضَعُ رَسْماً بَسيطاً على هذه الخِدْمةِ; **there's a handling ~ of £20** هُناكَ رَسْمُ مُناوَلةٍ بِقيمةِ 20 جُنَيْهاً; **at no extra ~** بِدونِ أَيِّ تَكْلِفةٍ إِضافيّةٍ 2 (accusation) تُهْمة (تُهَم), اتِّهام (اتِّهامات); **to be held on a murder/corruption ~** قُبِضَ عَلَيْهِ بِتُهْمةِ القَتْلِ \ الفَسادِ; **he faces criminal ~s** يُواجِهُ تُهَماً جِنائيّةً; **to bring ~s against sb** وَجَّهَ تُهَماً لِشَخْصٍ; **to drop the ~s** أَسْقَطَ التُهَمَ; **he is laying himself open to ~s of bias** إِنَّهُ يَجْعَلُ نَفْسَهُ عُرْضةً للاتِّهامِ بالتَحَيُّزِ 3 [u] (control) **to be in ~ of sth** كانَ مُكَلَّفاً بِشَيْءٍ; **I wish to speak to the person in ~** أَرْغَبُ في التَحَدُّثِ إلى الشَّخْصِ المَسْؤول; **you'll be in ~ in the manager's absence** سَوْفَ تَتَوَلّى المَسْؤوليّةَ في غِيابِ المُديرِ; **to take ~** تَوَلّى أَمْراً; **to take ~ of the situation/children** تَوَلّى الوَضْعَ \ أَمْرَ الأَطْفالِ 4 (attack) هُجوم 5 (explosive) شِحْنة مُتَفَجِّرة 6 (electrical) شَحْنة (شَحْنات)

charge account *n* (AmE) حِساب ائْتِمانٍ

charge card *n* بِطاقة الدَفْعِ الآجِلِ

chargé d'affaires /ʃɑːʒeɪ daˈfɛː/ *n* (*pl* **chargés d'affaires**) القائِم بِأَعْمالِ سِفارةٍ

charge nurse *n* مُمَرِّضة مَسْؤولة

charger /ˈtʃɑːdʒə/ *n* (Electron) شاحِن

chargrilled /ˈtʃɑːgrɪld/ *adj* ‹*steak, salmon*› مَشْويّ على نارٍ قَويّةٍ

chariot /ˈtʃæriət/ *n* عَرَبة (مَفْتوحة ذات عَجَلَتَيْنِ تَجُرُّها الخُيولُ)

charisma /kəˈrɪzmə/ *n* جاذِبِيّة ,كاريزْما

charismatic /kærɪzˈmætɪk/ *adj* ‹*leader, personality*› كاريزْميّ

charitable /ˈtʃærɪtəb(ə)l/ *adj* **1** ‹*organization, donation, status*› خَيْريّ **2** (giving) ‹*person, act*› خَيِّر **3** (kind) ‹*interpretation, explanation*› مُتَسامِح

charity /ˈtʃærɪti/ *n* (*pl* **charities**) **1** (organization) مُؤَسَّسة خَيْرِيّة **2** [u] (aid) مُؤَسَّسات خَيْرِيّة; **to give to ~** تَبَرَّعَ للمُؤَسَّساتِ الخَيْرِيّةِ **3** [u] (generosity, kindness) إحْسان

charity shop *n* (BrE) مَتْجَر خَيْريّ

charity work *n* عَمَل خَيْريّ

charm /tʃɑːm/ **A** *n* **1** (attractiveness) [u] سِحْر **2** (attractive feature) (أَسْحار) سِحْر **3** (spell) (تَعاوِيذُ) تَعْويذة **4** (on a bracelet) (حُلىً ,حِلىً) حِلْية

B *vt* (a; سِحْر) ‹*an audience, a voter*› سَحَرَ

charming /ˈtʃɑːmɪŋ/ *adj* ‹*person, village*› (ساحِرونَ) ساحِر

charred /tʃɑːd/ *adj* ‹*remains, body*› مُحْتَرِق ,مُتَفَحِّم

chart /tʃɑːt/ **A** *n* **1** (map) (خَرائِطُ) خَريطة **2** (graph, diagram) شَكْل \ رَسْم بَيانيّ; (table) (جَداوِلُ) جَدْوَل **3** **the ~s** (bestselling records) الأُسْطُوانات الأَكْثَر مَبيعاً

B *vt* **1** (u; رَسْم) ‹*a course*› رَسَمَ **2** ‹*progress*› سَجَّلَ

charter /ˈtʃɑːtə/ **A** *n* **1** (constitution of a university, an organization) (مَواثيقُ) ميثاق; (of a company) قانون \ نِظام أَساسيّ **2** (grant of rights) (مَواثيقُ) ميثاق

B *vt* ‹*a plane, ship*› اسْتَأْجَرَ

chartered accountant /ˌtʃɑːtəd əˈkaʊnt(ə)nt/ *n* (BrE) مُحاسِب قانونيّ

chartered surveyor /ˌtʃɑːtəd səˈveɪə/ *n* (BrE) خَبير عَقاريّ مُعْتَمَد (يُسْدي النُّصْحَ في مَجالِ تَثْمينِ \ مُعايَنةِ العَقاراتِ والأَراضي)

charter flight *n* رِحْلة بِطائِرةٍ مُسْتَأْجَرةٍ

charter plane *n* طائِرة مُسْتَأْجَرة

chase /tʃeɪs/ **A** *vt* **1** (to pursue) تَعَقَّبَ ,لاحَقَ ,طارَدَ ‹*a thief, car*›; **to ~ sb up/down the street** طارَدَ شَخْصاً على الطَريقِ **2** (to try to attain) سَعى لِلحُصولِ ‹*a target*›; سَعى لِتَحْقيقِ ‹*title*› **3** (to make advances to) لاحَقَ ‹*women, men*› على **4** (to drive out) **to ~ sb out of somewhere** طارَدَ شَخْصاً إلى خارِجِ مَكانٍ ما

B *vi* **1** (to pursue) **to ~ after sb/sth** لاحَقَ شَخْصاً \ شَيْئاً; **he's always chasing after women** هو دائماً يُلاحِقُ النساءَ **2** (to rush) تَدافَعَ ,انْدَفَعَ; **the kids were chasing around the house** كانَ الأَطْفالُ يَتَدافعونَ في أَرْجاءِ المَنْزِلِ

C *n* **1** (pursuit) (تَعَقُّبات) تَعَقُّب ,مُلاحَقة ,مُطارَدة; **a car/police ~** مُطارَدة بالسَيّاراتِ \ بوليسيّة; **to give ~ to sb** طارَدَ شَخْصاً **2** (fml) (race) سِباق; **the ~ for the championship** السِباق للبُطولةِ

(Idiom) **to cut to the chase** دَخَلَ في المَوْضوعِ مُباشَرةً

(Phrasal verbs) **chase away**: **~ [sb/sth] away, ~ away [sb/sth]** طَرَدَ [شَخْصاً \ شَيْئاً] ‹*an intruder, a predator*›

• **chase down** (AmE) ▸ **chase up**

• **chase up** (BrE): **1** **~ [sth] up, ~ up [sth]** تَحَرّى ,تَتَبَّعَ [شَيْئاً] ‹*a debt, payment*› **2** **~ [sb] up, ~ up [sb]** لاحَقَ [شَخْصاً] عن [شَيْءٍ] ‹*a debtor, supplier, contractor*›

chasm /ˈkaz(ə)m/ *n* **1** (Geog) (هُوىً ,هوّات) هوّة ,(صُدوع) صَدْع **2** (difference) (فِجاء ,فَجَوات) فَجْوة

chassis /ˈʃasi/ *n* (*pl* **chassis**) (هَياكِلُ) هَيْكَل

chaste /tʃeɪst/ *adj* **1** (not sexual) (أَعِفّاءُ) عَفيف ,(نُزَهاءُ) نَزيه ,مُتَبَتِّل **2** (celibate) مَصون

chastise /tʃaˈstʌɪz/ *vt* (fml) عاقَبَ \ أَنَّبَ بِشِدّةٍ ‹*a child, wrongdoer*›

chastity /ˈtʃastɪti/ *n* عِفّة

chat /tʃat/ **A** *vi* (-tt-) «friends, neighbours» (دَرْدَشة ;i) دَرْدَشَ; **to ~ to** *or* **with sb** دَرْدَشَ مع شَخْصٍ

B *n* دَرْدَشة; **online/Internet ~** دَرْدَشة على الإنْتَرْنِت

(Phrasal verb) **chat up** (BrE infml): **~ [sb] up, ~ up [sb]** تَحَدَّثَ مع [شَخْصٍ] بِقَصْدِ إقامةِ عَلاقةٍ عاطِفيّةٍ \ جِنْسيّةٍ]

chatline /ˈtʃatlʌɪn/ *n* خطّ دَرْدَشةٍ

chat room *n* غُرْفة شات \ دَرْدَشةٍ

chat show *n* بَرْنامَج حِواريّ

chatter /ˈtʃatə/ **A** *vi* «people» (ثَرْثَرة ;i) ثَرْثَرَ; «birds» (زَقْزَقة ;i) زَقْزَقَ; «monkeys» (ضَحِك ,ضِحْك ,ضَحْك ;a) ضَحِكَ; **her teeth were ~ing** كانَتْ أَسْنانُها تَصْطَكُّ

B *n* **1** (of people) ثَرْثَرة **2** (of birds) زَقْزَقة

chatterbox /ˈtʃatəbɒks/ *n* (infml) ثَرْثار

chatty /ˈtʃati/ *adj* (**chattier**, **chattiest**) ‹*person*› كَثير الكَلام; ‹*letter*› [غَيْر رَسْميٍّ وَخَفيف]

chauffeur /ˈʃəʊfə/ *n* سائِق (سائِقون, سوّاق, ساقة)

chauvinism /ˈʃəʊv(ɪ)nɪz(ə)m/ *n* **1** (nationalism) شوفينيّة **2** (also **male chauvinism**) (sexism) شوفينيّة (الذُكور)

chauvinist /ˈʃəʊv(ɪ)nɪst/ *n* **1** (nationalist) شوفينيّ **2** (also **male chauvinist**) (sexist) شوفينيّ

cheap /tʃiːp/ **A** *adj* **1** (not expensive) ‹*prices, food*› رَخيص; **to be ~** كانَ رَخيصاً; **they are ~ to produce** تَكْلِفةُ إنْتاجِهِمْ رَخيصةٌ; **it works out ~er to take the train** الذَهابُ بالقِطارِ يَسْتَحِقُ أكْثَرَ مِمّا دُفِعَ; أرْخَصُ; **it's ~ at the price** (BrE) فيهِ **2** (of poor quality) ‹*shoes, wine*› رَديء; **~ and nasty** رَخيص وَرَديء **3** (easy) ‹*joke, gimmick*› رَخيص, مُبْتَذَل **4** (contemptible) ‹*person*› دَنيء, حَقير; **he made me feel ~** جَعَلَني أشْعُرُ بالحَقارةِ; **a ~ shot** هُجوم رَخيص

B *adv* (infml) ‹*to buy, sell*› بِثَمَنٍ زَهيدٍ; **weddings don't come ~** حَفلاتُ الزِفافِ لَيْسَتْ رَخيصةً; **they're going ~** يُباعون بِثَمَنٍ زَهيدٍ

(Idiom) **on the cheap** (infml pej) ‹*to buy, sell*› بِسِعْرٍ رَخيص; **to do sth on the ~** فَعَلَ شَيْئاً بِأرْخَصِ سِعْرٍ مُمْكِنٍ

cheapen /ˈtʃiːp(ə)n/ *vt* رَخَّصَ ‹*life, sb's reputation*›

cheaply /ˈtʃiːpli/ *adv* ‹*to manufacture, live*› بِتَكْلِفةٍ قَليلةٍ

cheat /tʃiːt/ **A** *vt* غَشَّ (u; غِشّ, غَشّ) ‹*a customer, the benefits system*›

B *vi* **1** (to act dishonestly) غَشَّ (u; غِشّ, غَشّ) **2** (to be unfaithful) خانَ (u; خَوْن, خِيانة); **to ~ on one's husband/wife** خانَتْ زَوْجَها \ خانَ زَوْجَتَهُ

C *n* غَشّاش; **a social security ~** شَخْص يَغُشُّ مُؤَسَّساتِ الضَمانِ الاجْتِماعيِّ

(Idiom) **to cheat death** احْتالَ على المَوْتِ

Chechen /ˈtʃetʃen/ *n, adj* (*pl* **Chechen**) شيشانيّ

Chechnya /ˌtʃetʃˈnjɑː/ *pr n* الشيشان (f)

check /tʃek/ **A** *vt* **1** (to inspect technically) فَحَصَ (a; فَحْص) ‹*the level, passport, records*›; **to ~ goods for defects** فَحَصَ البَضائِعَ لِكَشْفِ العُيوبِ; **the baggage was ~ed electronically** تَمَّ فَحْصُ الحَقائِبِ إلِكْترونيًّا **2** (to examine for accuracy) راجَعَ ‹*sb's spelling, the bill*›; **to ~ sth for errors** راجَعَ شَيْئاً لِكَشْفِ الأخْطاءِ; **~ this against the original version** قارِنْ هذا بالنُسْخةِ الأصْليّةِ; **please ~ the figures/my spelling** مِن فَضْلِكَ راجِعِ الأرْقامَ \ أخْطائي الإمْلائيّةَ **3** (to verify) تَحَقَّقَ (مِن), تَأَكَّدَ (مِن) ‹*one's facts, the time*›; **~ that the machine is turned on** تَأَكَّدْ أنّ الجِهازَ تَمَّ تَشْغيلُهُ; **I need to ~ the train times/where the station is** أحْتاجُ إلى التَحَقُّقِ من مَواعيدِ القِطارِ \ مَكانِ المَحَطّةِ **4** (to look at) تَصَفَّحَ ‹*one's email*›; نَظَرَ (u; إلى) ‹*watch*› **5** (to curb) كَبَحَ (a; كَبْح) ‹*inflation, abuses*› **6** (in chess) حاصَرَ ‹*one's opponent, sb's king*› **7** (AmE) (for safekeeping) أَوْدَعَ ‹*a coat, bag*› **8** (AmE) (before flying) سَجَّلَ ‹*one's baggage*› **9** (to mark) عَلَّمَ ‹*a box, an item*›

B *vi* **1** (to confirm) تَثَبَّتَ, تَحَقَّقَ; **I ~ed to see if anyone was watching** تَحَقَّقْتُ لِمَعْرِفةِ ما إذا كانَ أيُّ أحَدٍ يُراقِبُ; **to ~ with sb** شاوَرَ شَخْصاً **2** (to examine) **to ~ for faults/leaks** فَحَصَ شَيْئاً لِكَشْفِ العُيوبِ \ التَسْريبات

C *v refl* **to ~ oneself** كَبَحَ نَفْسَهُ

D *n* **1** (inspection) فَحْص (فُحوص), مُراقَبة; **a security ~** فَحْص أمْنيّ; **they do** *or* **run background ~s on all employees** يُجْرونَ تَحَرِّياتٍ عن جَميعِ العامِلينَ; **police were keeping a close ~ on his movements** كانَتِ الشُرْطةُ تُراقِبُ تَحَرُّكاتِهِ عن كَثَبٍ **2** (for disease, irregularity) فَحْص (فُحوص); **to have a health/medical ~** خَضَعَ لِفَحْصٍ صِحّيٍّ \ طِبّيٍّ **3** (restraint) قَيْد (قُيود), عائِق (عَوائِقُ); **~s on government power** قُيود على سُلْطةِ الحُكومةِ; **to keep** *or* **hold sth/sb in ~** وَضَعَ شَيْئاً \ شَخْصاً تحت السَيْطَرةِ; **she held her emotions in ~** سَيْطَرَتْ على مَشاعِرِها **4** (in chess) حِصار, كَشّ المَلِكِ; **~!** كُشّ!; **~ mate!** ماتَ المَلِكُ \ الشاهُ! **5** (pattern) كاروهات **6** (AmE) (in banking) شيك (شيكات); **she wrote a ~ for $570** كَتَبَتْ شيكاً بِ $570 **7** (AmE) (bill) فاتورة (فَواتيرُ); **to pick up the ~** دَفَعَ الفاتورةَ **8** (mark) عَلامة (عَلامات)

E *adj* (also **checked**) ‹*shirt, tablecloth*› كاروهاتٍ

F *excl* **1** (in chess) **~!** كُشّ! **2** (AmE infml) (expressing agreement) نَعَمْ! أجَلْ!

(Phrasal verbs) **check in** **A** **1** (for a flight) «passengers, travellers» اسَجَّلَ الدُخولَ **2** (at hotels) «guests» سَجَّلَ الدُخولَ **B** **1** **~ [sth] in, ~ in [sth]** سَجَّلَ [شَيْئاً] *‹one's baggage›* **2** **~ [sb] in, ~ in [sb]** سَجَّلَ دُخولَ [شَخْصٍ] *‹a passenger, hotel guest›*
• **check into**: **~ into [sth]**: **to ~ into a hotel** سَجَّلَ الدُخولَ إلى فُنْدُقٍ
• **check off**: **~ off [sth], ~ [sth] off** وَضَعَ عَلامةً على [شَيْءٍ] *‹names, items›*
• **check on**: **1** **~ on [sth]** (to verify) تَحَقَّقَ من [شَيْءٍ]; **to ~ on sb's progress** تَحَقَّقَ من تَقَدُّمِ شَخْصٍ **2** **~ on [sb]** (to look at) اطْمَأَنَّ على [شَخْصٍ] *‹a child, patient›*
• **check out** **A** **1** (to leave) سَجَّلَ الخُروجَ; **to ~ out of a hotel** سَجَّلَ الخُروجَ من فُنْدُقٍ **2** (to be correct) «story, information» صَحَّ (i; صِحّة), تُبُتَتْ صِحَّتُهُ **B** **~ out [sth], ~ [sth] out** **1** (to investigate) اسْتَقْصى [شَيْئاً] *‹a situation, company›* **2** (infml) (to try) جَرَّبَ [شَيْئاً] *‹a restaurant, movie›* **3** (infml) (to look at) اطَّلَعَ على [شَيْءٍ] *‹a website, an article›* **4** (AmE) (from a library) اسْتَعارَ [شَيْئاً] *‹a book›* **C** **~ [sb] out, ~ out [sb]** (to screen) اسْتَقْصى عن [شَخْصٍ] *‹a candidate, an employee›*
• **check over**: **~ [sth] over** تَفَحَّصَ [شَيْئاً] *‹a document, vehicle›*
• **check up on**: **1** **~ up on [sth]** تَثَبَّتَ من [شَيْءٍ] *‹facts›* **2** **~ up on [sb]** اسْتَقْصى عن [شَخْصٍ] *‹a person, an applicant›*

checkbook (AmE) *n* ▸ **chequebook**

checker /ˈtʃɛkə/ *n* (AmE) **1** (at checkout) صَرّاف **2** (**checkers** *n pl*) (board game) ضاما

checkered (AmE) *adj* ▸ **chequered**

checkers /ˈtʃɛkəz/ *n* (AmE) ▸ **draughts**

check-in /ˈtʃɛkɪn/ *n* **1** (procedure) تَسْجيل الدُخولِ; **use the online ~** اسْتَخْدِمْ تَسْجيلَ الدُخولِ عَبْرَ الإِنْتَرْنِت **2** (also **check-in desk**) مَكْتَب تَسْجيلِ الدُخولِ

checking account /ˈtʃɛkɪŋ əˌkaʊnt/ *n* (AmE) حِساب جارٍ

checklist /ˈtʃɛklɪst/ *n* قائِمة مُراجَعةٍ

checkmate /ˈtʃɛkmeɪt/ *n* مَوْت المَلِكِ \ الشاهِ

checkout /ˈtʃɛkaʊt/ *n* [نُقْطة دَفْعِ الحِسابِ]

checkout operator *n* مُوَظَّف كاشير

checkpoint /ˈtʃɛkpɔɪnt/ *n* نُقْطة تَفْتيشٍ

checkroom /ˈtʃɛkruːm/ *n* (AmE) (مَكْتَب) الأَمانات

check tablecloth *n* مِفْرَش ذو مُرَبَّعاتٍ

check-up /ˈtʃɛkʌp/ *n* فَحْص (فُحوص); **to go for/have a ~** ذَهَبَ لِإجْراءِ فَحْصٍ طِبِّيٍّ; **he has an annual ~ with the paediatrician** لَدَيْهِ فَحْصٌ طِبِّيٌّ سَنَوِيٌّ عند طَبيبِ الأَطْفالِ

cheek /tʃiːk/ *n* **1** (of the face) خَدّ (خُدود), وَجْنة (وَجَنات) **2** (infml) وَقاحة; **what a ~!** يا لَها من وَقاحةٍ!, يا لِوَقاحَتِهِ!

cheekbone /ˈtʃiːkbəʊn/ *n* عَظْم وَجْنِيّ

cheeky /ˈtʃiːki/ *adj* (**cheekier, cheekiest**) *‹person, grin›* وَقِح (وُقُح)

cheep /tʃiːp/ **A** *n* صَئِيّ **B** *vi* «birds, chicks» صَأى (i; صَئِيّ)

cheer /tʃɪə/ **A** *vt* شَجَّعَ *‹a team, performance›* **B** *vi* «crowds, fans» هَلَّلَ **C** *n* تَصْفيقة (هُتافات) هُتاف, (تَهاليلُ) تَهْليل; **three ~s for Tom!** لِتوم! **D** (**cheers**) *excl* **1** (as a toast) في \ بِصِحَّتِكَ **2** (BrE infml) (thanks) شُكْراً

(Phrasal verbs) **cheer on**: **~ on [sb], ~ [sb] on** شَجَّعَ [شَخْصاً] *‹a team›*
• **cheer up**: **1** **~ up** ابْتَهَجَ **2** **~ up [sb], ~ [sb] up** أَدْخَلَ البَهْجةَ على قَلْبِ [شَخْصٍ]

cheerful /ˈtʃɪəfʊl/ *adj* *‹smile, mood›* مَرِح (مَراحى, مَرْحى); *‹news›* مُبْهِج; *‹music›* سارّ

cheerleader /ˈtʃɪəliːdə/ *n* فَتاة تَشْجيعٍ

cheese /tʃiːz/ *n* جُبْن (n coll; أَجْبان)

cheeseboard /ˈtʃiːzbɔːd/ *n* [طَبَق أَجْبانٍ مُشَكَّل]

cheeseburger /ˈtʃiːzbəːgə/ *n* هَمْبَرْغر بالجُبْنِ

cheesecake /ˈtʃiːzkeɪk/ *n* كَعْكة الجُبْنِ

cheesecloth /ˈtʃiːzklɒθ/ *n* [قُماش قُطْنِيّ يُسْتَعْمَلُ لِلَفِّ الأَطْعِمةِ]

cheese mite *n* سوس جُبْنٍ

cheesy /ˈtʃiːzi/ *adj* (**cheesier, cheesiest**) **1** *‹taste, smell›* جُبْنِيّ **2** (infml) *‹grin›* أَصْفَر (dipt) **3** (infml) (tacky) *‹movie, motel›* سَيِّئ, رَديء

cheetah /ˈtʃiːtə/ *n* فَهْد (أَفْهُد, فُهود)

chef /ʃɛf/ *n* شيف ,كَبير \ رَئِيس الطُهاةِ

chemical /ˈkɛmɪk(ə)l/ **A** *adj* ‹*reaction, weapon*› كيماويّ ,كيمِيائيّ

B *n* مادّة كيميائيّة

chemical engineer *n* مُهَنْدِس كيمِيائيّ

chemist /ˈkɛmɪst/ *n* **1** (scientist) (عالِم) كيمِيائيّ **2** (BrE) (pharmacist) صَيْدَلي (صَيادِلة) **3** (BrE) (also **the chemist's**) (pharmacy) الصَيْدَلِيّة

chemistry /ˈkɛmɪstri/ *n* كيمِياء (f)

chemotherapy /ˌkiːmə(ʊ)ˈθɛrəpi/ *n* عِلاج كيميائيّ \ كيماويّ

cheque (BrE), **check** (AmE) /tʃɛk/ *n* شيك (شيكات) ,صَكّ (صُكوك)

chequebook (BrE), **checkbook** (AmE) /ˈtʃɛkbʊk/ *n* دَفْتَر شيكاتٍ

chequered (BrE), **checkered** (AmE) /ˈtʃɛkəd/ *adj* **1** ‹*flag, cloth*› ذو مُرَبَّعاتٍ \ كاروهاتٍ **2** ‹*history, career*› مُتَعَثِّر

cherish /ˈtʃɛrɪʃ/ *vt* **1** (to hold dear) أَعَزَّ ‹*a loved one, possessions*› **2** (to harbour) أَكَنَّ ‹*a hope, an ambition*›

cherry /ˈtʃɛri/ *n* (*pl* **cherries**) **1** (fruit) كَرَز **2** (also **cherry tree**) شَجَرة الكَرَز

chess /tʃɛs/ *n* شِطْرَنْج

chessboard /ˈtʃɛsbɔːd/ *n* رُقْعة \ لَوْحة شِطْرَنْجٍ

chess set *n* أَدَوات الشِطْرَنْج

chest /tʃɛst/ *n* **1** (Anat) صَدْر (صُدور) **2** (box) صُنْدوق (صَناديقُ)

(Idiom) **to get sth off one's chest** (infml) أَزاحَ شَيْئاً عن صَدْرِهِ

chestnut /ˈtʃɛsnʌt/ **A** *n* **1** (nut) كَسْتَناء ,قَسْطَل (قَساطِل) **2** (also **chestnut tree**) كَسْتَنة **3** (colour) لَوْن كَسْتَنائيّ

B *adj* ‹*hair, eyes, horse*› كَسْتَنائيّ

chevron /ˈʃɛvrən/ *n* شارة رُتْبةٍ (شَريط على شَكْلِ V لِبَيانِ رُتْبةٍ شُرْطيٍّ \ جُنْديٍّ)

chew /tʃuː/ *vt* **1** مَضَغَ (a-u; مَضْغ) ‹*food, gum*› **2** عَضَّ (a; عَضّ, عَضيض) ‹*a pencil, one's lip*›

chewing gum /ˈtʃuːɪŋ gʌm/ *n* عِلْك ,لُبان (n coll; أَعْلاك ,عُلوك)

chewy /ˈtʃuːi/ *adj* (**chewier**, **chewiest**) ‹*meat, sweets*› صَعْب المَضْغِ

chic /ʃiːk/ **A** *adj* (**chicer**, **chicest**) ‹*hairstyle, restaurant*› أَنيق

B *n* شِياكة ,أَناقة

chick /tʃɪk/ *n* كَتْكوت (كَتاكيتُ), فَرّوج (فَراريجُ) (n coll;)

chicken /ˈtʃɪkɪn/ *n* **1** (bird) دَجاج (n coll) **2** (meat) دَجاج (n coll) **3** (infml) (coward) جَبان

(Phrasal verb) **chicken out** (infml) جَبُنَ (u; جُبْن ,جَبانة)

chicken nuggets *n* ناجِتْس الدَجاجِ \ الفِراخِ

chickenpox /ˈtʃɪkɪnpɒks/ *n* جُدَريّ الماءِ

chickpea /ˈtʃɪkpiː/ *n* حِمَّص (n coll)

chicory /ˈtʃɪk(ə)ri/ *n* (vegetable) هِنْدِباء بَرِّيّة

chief /tʃiːf/ **A** *n* **1** (of a people, tribe) زَعيم (زُعَماءُ), رَئيس (رُؤَساءُ) **2** (of an organization, department) رَئيس (رُؤَساءُ)

B *adj before n* ‹*reason, rival*› رَئيسيّ

chief constable *n* (BrE) رَئيس \ مُدير الشُرْطةِ

chief executive *n* رَئيس تَنْفيذيّ

chief justice *n* **1** (BrE) (in High Court of Justice) رَئيس قاضي القُضاةِ ,المَحْكَمة العُلْيا **2** (AmE) (in Supreme Court) قاضي القُضاةِ ,رَئِيس المَحْكَمة العُلْيا

chiefly /ˈtʃiːfli/ *adv* بِشَكْلٍ رَئيسيٍّ

chief of police *n* رَئيس \ مُدير الشُرْطةِ

chief of staff *n* رَئيس الأَرْكانِ

chiffon /ˈʃɪfɒn/ *n* شيفون

chilblain /ˈtʃɪlbleɪn/ *n* تَقَرُّح في اليَدِ \ القَدَمِ بِسَبَبِ البَرْدِ

child /tʃʌɪld/ *n* (*pl* **children**) **1** (boy) طِفْل (أَطْفال), صَبيّ (صِبْية, صِبْيان), وَلَد (أَوْلاد); (girl) طِفْلة ,صَبيّة (صَبايا) **2** (son) ابْن (أَبْناء ,بَنون), وَلَد (أَوْلاد); (daughter) بِنْت (f; بَنات)

child abuse *n* إساءة مُعامَلةِ الأَطْفالِ

child abuser *n* شَخْص مُسيء للأَطْفالِ

child benefit *n* (BrE) إعانة الطِفْلِ (إعانة ماليّة من الدَوْلةِ لآباءِ الأَطْفالِ)

childbirth /ˈtʃʌɪl(d)bəːθ/ *n* وِلادة

childcare /ˈtʃʌɪl(d)kɛː/ *n* رِعاية الأَطْفالِ

childcare facilities *n* مَرافِق رِعاية الأَطْفالِ

childhood /ˈtʃʌɪldhʊd/ *n* طُفولة; **he spent his early ~ there** قَضى طُفولَتَهُ المُبَكِّرة هُناكَ

childhood friend *n* صَديق طُفولةٍ

childish /ˈtʃʌɪldɪʃ/ *adj* ‹*behaviour, comment*› طُفوليّ

childless /ˈtʃʌɪldləs/ *adj* ‹*couple, woman*› أَبْتَر (dipt)

childlike /ˈtʃʌɪl(d)lʌɪk/ *adj* ‹*innocence, enthusiasm*› طُفوليّ

childminder /ˈtʃʌɪl(d)mʌɪndə/ *n* (BrE) جَليس أَطْفالٍ

child pornography *n* مَوادّ إباحيّة عن الأَطْفالِ

children /ˈtʃɪldrən/ *n pl* ▸**child**

children's home /ˈtʃɪldrənz ˌhəʊm/ *n* مَلْجَأ أَطْفالٍ

Chile /ˈtʃɪli/ *pr n* تْشيلي (f), شيلي (f)

Chilean /ˈtʃɪlɪən/ *n, adj* شيليّ

chill /tʃɪl/ **A** *n* **1** (coldness) قُشَعْريرة, بَرْد **2** (illness) بَرْد

B *vt* بَرَّدَ ‹*wine, food*›

C *adj* ‹*wind, draught*› بارِد

(Phrasal verb) **chill out** (infml) اسْتَرْخى

chilli, chili /ˈtʃɪli/ *n* **1** (*pl* **chillies**; also **chilli pepper**) فِلْفِل حارّ

2 (also **chilli powder**) شَطّة

chilly /ˈtʃɪli/ *adj* (**chillier, chilliest**) ‹*night, air*› بارِد

chime /tʃʌɪm/ **A** *n* (of bells) رَنين; (of a clock, doorbell) دَقّ

B *vi* «bells» رَنَّ (i; رَنين); «clock» دَقَّ (u; دَقّ)

chimney /ˈtʃɪmni/ *n* (*pl* **chimneys**) مِدْخَنة (مَداخِنُ)

chimney sweep *n* مُنَظِّف مَداخِنَ

chimpanzee /tʃɪmpanˈziː/ *n* شِمْبانْزي (شَمْبَنْزِيات), بَعام

chin /tʃɪn/ *n* ذَقَن (أَذْقان, ذُقون), ذَقْن (mf; ذُقون)

(Idiom) **keep your chin up!** (infml) شُدَّ حَيْلَكَ!

china /ˈtʃʌɪnə/ *n* خَزَف صينيّ; **fine ~** خَزَف صينيّ رَقيق

China /ˈtʃʌɪnə/ *pr n* الصين (f)

chinchilla /tʃɪnˈtʃɪlə/ *n* الشانْشيلا (حَيَوان)

Chinese /tʃʌɪˈniːz/ **A** *n* (*pl* **Chinese**) **1** (citizen) صينيّ

2 (language) الصينيّة (اللُغة)

B *adj* ‹*government, restaurant*› صينيّ

chink /tʃɪŋk/ *n* (in a wall) شَقّ (شُقوق); (in curtains) فُتْحة (فُتَح, فُتُحات)

chinos /ˈtʃiːnəʊz/ *n pl* سِرْوال \ بَنْطَلون تْشينو

chip /tʃɪp/ **A** *n* **1** (splinter of wood, stone, bone) شَظِيّة (شَظايا), شُطْفة **2** (in wood, china, glass) كَسْر (كُسور), شَرْخ **3** (BrE) (fried potato) إِصْبَع بَطاطِسَ مَقْليّ **4** (AmE) (also **potato chip**) (wafer) رُقاقة بَطاطِسَ مَقْليّة **5** (in computing) رُقاقة \ شَريحة إِلِكْتْرونيّة **6** (in gambling) فيشة (فيشات, فِيَش)

B *vt* (**-pp-**) **1** (to damage) كَسَرَ جُزْءاً صَغيراً من ‹*a cup, plate, the paint*›; **to ~ a tooth** كَسَرَ طَرَفاً من سِنٍّ **2** (to shape by cutting) نَحَتَ (i-u; نَحْت) ‹*stone, wood*› **3** (in golf, football) رَفَعَ (a; رَفْع) ‹*the ball, a shot*›

C *vi* (**-pp-**) «plate, paint» تَشَقَّقَ, تَشَظّى

(Idioms) **to be a chip off the old block** (infml) شابَهَ أَباهُ; **to have a chip on one's shoulder** (infml) شَعَرَ بالظُلْمِ والمَرارةِ; **when the chips are down** (infml) في الأَوْقاتِ الصَعْبةِ

(Phrasal verbs) **chip away at**: **~ away at [sth] 1** اقْتَطَعَ من [شَيْءٍ] ‹*stone, plaster*› **2** انْتَقَصَ من [شَيْءٍ] ‹*sb's power, freedom*›

• **chip in 1** (to contribute) شارَكَ, أَسْهَمَ **2** (BrE) (infml) (in conversations) قاطَعَ

• **chip off 1** «paint, plaster» تَكَسَّرَ, تَشَظّى **2** **~ off [sth], ~ [sth] off** كَسَرَ جُزْءاً صَغيراً من [شَيْءٍ] ‹*a piece, plaster*›

chipboard /ˈtʃɪpbɔːd/ *n* خَشَب مَضْغوط

chipmunk /ˈtʃɪpmʌŋk/ *n* سِنْجاب صَيْدَنانيّ

chiropodist /kɪˈrɒpədɪst/ *n* أَخِصّائيّ مُعالَجةِ الأَقْدام

chiropody /kɪˈrɒpədi/ *n* مُعالَجة الأَقْدامِ

chiropractor /ˈkʌɪrə(ʊ)ˌpraktə/ *n* مُعالِج يَدَويّ

chirp /tʃəːp/ *vi* «birds, insects» زَقْزَقَ (i; زَقْزَقة)

chisel /ˈtʃɪz(ə)l/ **A** *n* إِزْميل (أَزاميلُ), مِنْحات (مَناحيتُ)

B *vt* (**-ll-** BrE, **-l-** AmE) نَحَتَ (i-u; نَحْت) ‹*wood, an inscription*›

chit-chat /ˈtʃɪttʃat/ *n* (infml) دَرْدَشة, ثَرْثَرة

chivalry /ˈʃɪv(ə)lri/ *n* شَهامة

chives /tʃʌɪvz/ *n pl* ثوم مُعَمَّر

chlamydia /kləˈmɪdɪə/ *n* كْلاميديا

chlorine /ˈklɔːriːn/ *n* كْلور

chlorofluorocarbon /ˌklɔːrəˌflʊərəʊˈkɑːb(ə)n/ *n* ▸**CFC**

chloroform /ˈklɔːrəfɔːm/ *n* كْلوروفورم

choc ice /ˈtʃɒk ʌɪs/ *n* (BrE) آيس كْريم مُرَبَّع مُغَطّى بالشوكولاتةِ

chock-a-block /tʃɒkəˈblɒk/ *adj* (infml) **to be ~** كانَ مُكْتَظّاً

chocolate /ˈtʃɒk(ə)lət/ **A** *n* **1** (substance) شوكولاتة **2** (sweet) شوكولاتة **3** (drink) مَشْروب شوكولاتةٍ
B *adj* ‹biscuit, cake› شوكولاتةٍ; **a ~ bar** قالِب شوكولاتةٍ

choice /tʃɔɪs/ *n* **1** (act) اخْتِيار; **we had to make a difficult ~** اضْطَرَرْنا للقِيامِ بِخِيارٍ صَعْبٍ; **it's not something I would do out of ~** هذا لَيْسَ شَيْءٌ أَفْعَلُهُ بِاخْتِياري **2** (option) خِيار; **I don't have any ~ in the matter** لَيْسَ لَدَيَّ أَيُّ خِيارٍ في الأَمْرِ **3** (variety) خِيار; **there wasn't much ~** لم تكُنْ هُناكَ خِياراتٌ كَثيرةٌ **4** (person, thing chosen) اخْتِيار; **she was the right ~ for the job** كانَتْ هي الاخْتِيارَ الصائِبَ للعَمَلِ

choir /ˈkwʌɪə/ *n* جَوْقة, كورال, خورُس

choirboy /ˈkwʌɪəbɔɪ/ *n* مُنْشِد في جَوْقةِ الكَنيسةِ

choke /tʃəʊk/ **A** *vt* **1** (to throttle) خَنَقَ (u; خَنْق) **2** (to stifle) «smoke, fumes» خَنَقَ (u; خَنْق)
B *vi* اخْتَنَقَ; **to ~ on a bone** اخْتَنَقَ بِعَظْمةٍ; **to ~ to death** اخْتَنَقَ حتّى المَوْتِ
C *n* (in car) صِمام خَنْقٍ

Phrasal verb **choke back**: **~ back [sth]** كَتَمَ \ حَبَسَ [شَيْئاً] ‹tears, a sob›

cholera /ˈkɒlərə/ *n* كوليرا

cholesterol /kəˈlɛstərɒl/ *n* كولِسْترول

choose /tʃuːz/ **A** *vt* (*past tense* **chose**, *past participle* **chosen**) **1** (to select) اخْتارَ ‹a name, candidate› **2** (to decide) اخْتارَ; **she chose to pursue a career in law** اخْتارَتْ مُزاوَلةَ مِهْنةِ المُحاماةِ
B *vi* (*past tense* **chose**, *past participle* **chosen**) (to make a choice) اخْتارَ

choosy /ˈtʃuːzi/ *adj* (**choosier, choosiest**) (infml) صَعْب الإرْضاءِ

chop /tʃɒp/ **A** *vt* (**-pp-**) (also **chop up**) قَطَّعَ ‹wood, meat, onion›
B *n* **1** (with an axe) قَطْع; (with the hand) ضَرْبة (ضَرَبات) **2** (Culin) لَحْم الضِلْعِ

Phrasal verbs **chop down**: **~ down [sth], ~ [sth] down** قَطَعَ [شَيْئاً] ‹a tree, forest›
• **chop off**: **~ off [sth], ~ [sth] off** قَطَعَ [شَيْئاً] ‹a branch, sb's head›
• **chop up** ▸ **chop** A

chopper /ˈtʃɒpə/ *n* **1** (for wood) فَأْس (f; فُؤوس); (for food) ساطور (سَواطيرُ) **2** (infml) (helicopter) هِليكوبْتِر, مِرْوَحيّة

chopping board *n* لَوْح تَقْطيعٍ

chopping knife *n* سِكّين تَقْطيعٍ

choppy /ˈtʃɒpi/ *adj* (**choppier, choppiest**) ‹sea, water› مائِج

chopstick /ˈtʃɒpstɪk/ *n* عيدان \ أَعْواد أَكْلٍ

choral /ˈkɔːr(ə)l/ *adj* ‹singing, music› كورالِيّ

chord /kɔːd/ *n* ائْتِلاف

chore /tʃɔː/ *n* **1** (routine task) شُغْل \ عَمَل البَيْتِ **2** (unpleasant task) عِبْء (أَعْباء)

choreograph /ˈkɒrɪəgrɑːf/ *vt* صَمَّمَ رَقَصاتٍ ل ‹a ballet, work›

choreographer /kɒrɪˈɒgrəfə/ *n* مُصَمِّم رَقْصٍ

choreography /ˌkɒrɪˈɒgrəfi/ *n* تَصْميم رَقْصٍ

chorister /ˈkɒrɪstə/ *n* مُنْشِد في جَوْقةِ الكَنيسةِ

chortle /ˈtʃɔːt(ə)l/ *vi* «the audience, children» ضَحِكَ من قَلْبِه

chorus /ˈkɔːrəs/ *n* **1** (group of singers) كورَس **2** (choral piece) مَقْطوعة كورال **3** (refrain) لازِمة (لَوازِمُ)

chose /tʃəʊz/ *past tense* ▸ **choose**

chosen /ˈtʃəʊz(ə)n/ *past participle* ▸ **choose**

chough /tʃʌf/ *n* غُراب أَعْصَم, زُمَّت

Christ /krʌɪst/ *pr n* **1** (Rel_Chr) المَسيح **2** (infml) (as an oath) ≈ يا إلَهي

christen /ˈkrɪs(ə)n/ *vt* عَمَّدَ ‹a baby›

christening /ˈkrɪs(ə)nɪŋ/ *n* تَعْميد

Christian /ˈkrɪstɪən/ **A** *adj* ‹faith, church› مَسيحيّ
B *n* مَسيحيّ, نَصْرانِيّ (نَصارى)

Christianity /krɪstɪˈanɪti/ *n* مَسيحيّة, نَصْرانيّة

Christian name *n* الاسْم الأَوَّل

Christmas /ˈkrɪsməs/ *n* عيد الميلادِ; **merry ~!** عيد ميلادٍ مَجيد!

Christmas card *n* بِطاقة عيد الميلادِ المَجيدِ

Christmas Day *n* يَوْم عيد الميلادِ المَجيد

Christmas Eve *n* لَيْلة \ عَشيّة عيد الميلادِ المَجيدِ

Christmas tree *n* شَجَرة عيدِ الميلادِ

chrome /krəʊm/ *n* كْروم

chromium /ˈkrəʊmɪəm/ *n* كْروم

chromosome /ˈkrəʊməsəʊm/ *n* كُروموسوم (كُروموسومات)، صِبْغِيّ (صِبْغِيّات) صِبْغِيّ

chronic /ˈkrɒnɪk/ *adj* **1** <*illness, bronchitis*> مُزْمِن **2** <*problem*> مُزْمِن؛ <*liar*> قَهْرِيّ

chronic fatigue syndrome *n* مُتلازِمة التَعَبِ المُزْمِن

chronicle /ˈkrɒnɪk(ə)l/ *n* مُدَوَّنة تاريخيّة

chronological /krɒnəˈlɒdʒɪk(ə)l/ *adj* <*order, list*> زَمَنيّ، كرونولوجيّ

chrysalis /ˈkrɪs(ə)lɪs/ *n* خادرة (خَوادِرُ)

chubby /ˈtʃʌbi/ *adj* (**chubbier, chubbiest**) <*cheeks, person*> مُمْتَلِئ

chuck /tʃʌk/ *vt* (infml) **1** (to throw) أَلْقى، رَمى (i; رَمْي، رِماية) <*a ball, stone*> **2** (also **chuck away**) (to throw away) أَلْقى، رَمى (i; رَمْي، رِماية) <*rubbish, leftovers*> **3** (to finish with) تَرَكَ (u; تَرْك) <*a boyfriend, girlfriend*> **4** (also **chuck in**) (to give up) تَرَكَ (u; تَرْك) <*a job*>

chuckle /ˈtʃʌk(ə)l/ *vi* ضَحِكَ ضَحْكَةً، ضَحِكَ بَيْنَهُ وَبَيْنَ نَفْسِهِ خافِتةً \ مَكْتومةً

chuffed /tʃʌft/ *adj* (BrE infml) **to be ~ about sth** كانَ مَسْروراً جِدًّا بِشَيْءٍ

chum /tʃʌm/ *n* (infml) صَديق (أَصْدِقاءُ)، صاحِب (أَصْحاب)

chunk /tʃʌŋk/ *n* قِطْعة (قِطَع)

chunky /ˈtʃʌŋki/ *adj* (**chunkier, chunkiest**) **1** (of food) <*stew, soup*> [يَحْتَوي على قِطَعٍ صَغيرةٍ من لَحْمٍ، خُضْرَواتٍ، ...إلخ] **2** (bulky) <*sweater*> ثَقيل؛ <*jewellery*> ضَخْم؛ <*person*> قَصير مُكْتَنِز

church /tʃɜːtʃ/ *n* (*pl* **churches**) **1** (building) كَنيسة (كَنائِسُ)؛ **they go to ~ regularly** يَذْهَبونَ إلى الكَنيسةِ بانْتِظامٍ **2** (organization) كَنيسة (كَنائِسُ)

churchgoer /ˈtʃɜːtʃgəʊə/ *n* [شَخْص مُواظِب على الذَهابِ إلى الكَنيسةِ]

church hall *n* قاعة كَنيسةٍ

churchyard /ˈtʃɜːtʃjɑːd/ *n* مَدْفِن (عند كَنيسةٍ)

churn /tʃɜːn/ **A** *n* **1** (for butter) مِمْخَضة (مَماخِضُ) **2** (BrE) (for milk) مِمْخَضة (مَماخِضُ)

B *vt* مَخَضَ (a-i-u; مَخْض) <*butter, milk*>

Phrasal verbs **churn out** (infml): ~ [sth] out, ~ out [sth] أَنْتَجَ [شَيْئاً] بِكَمّيّاتٍ كَبيرة <*products, books*>

• **churn up**: ~ [sth] up, ~ up [sth] حَرَّكَ [شَيْئاً] بِعُنْفٍ <*water*>؛ قَلَّبَ [شَيْئاً] <*turf, mud*>

chute /ʃuːt/ *n* **1** (for coal, rubbish, laundry) مَزْلَق (مَزالِقُ) **2** (at a swimming pool, theme park) مَزْلَق (مَزالِقُ)

CIA /siːʌɪˈeɪ/ *abbr* = **Central Intelligence Agency** وِكالة الاسْتِخْبارات المَرْكَزيّة (سي آي ايه)

cicada /sɪˈkɑːdə/ *n* زيز (زيزان)

cider /ˈsʌɪdə/ *n* سيدَر (عَصير تُفّاحٍ مُخَمَّر)

cigar /sɪˈgɑː/ *n* سيجار (سيجارات)

cigarette /sɪgəˈrɛt/ *n* سيجارة (سَجائِرُ، سيجارات)

cigarette end *n* عُقْب سيجارةٍ

cigarette lighter *n* قَدّاحة

cinch /sɪn(t)ʃ/ *n* (infml) أَمْر سَهْل؛ **it's a ~** الأَمْرُ سَهْلٌ

cinder /ˈsɪndə/ **A** *n* جَمْرة مُنْطَفِئة **B** (**cinders**) *n pl* رَماد (أَرْمِدة)

Cinderella /sɪndəˈrɛlə/ *pr n* **1** سينْدْريلا **2** (neglected party) مُهْمَل

cine camera *n* كاميرا سينَمائيّة

cine film *n* فيلْم \ شَريط سينَمائيّ

cinema /ˈsɪnɪmɑː, ˈsɪnɪmə/ *n* سينَما

cinemagoer /ˈsɪnɪməˌgəʊə/ *n* [شَخْص مُواظِب على الذَهابِ إلى السينَما]

cinema screen *n* شاشة سينَما

cinematic /sɪnɪˈmatɪk/ *adj* <*technique, genius*> سينَمائيّ

cinematographer /ˌsɪnəməˈtɒgrəfə/ *n* مُصَوِّر سينَمائيّ

cinnamon /ˈsɪnəmən/ *n* قِرْفة (قِرَف)

cipher /ˈsʌɪfə/ *n* **1** (code) شِفْرة **2** (nonentity) صِفْر على الشِمالِ

circa /ˈsɜːkə/ *prep* حَوالَيْ، تَقْريباً

circle /ˈsɜːk(ə)l/ **A** *n* **1** (shape) دائِرة (دَوائِرُ)؛ **to sit/stand in a ~** جَلَسَ \ وَقَفَ في حَلَقةٍ؛ **children, now form a ~** يا أَطْفالُ، والآنَ شَكِّلوا حَلَقةً \ دائِرةً؛ **to have ~s under one's eyes**

كانَتْ عِنْدَهُ هالاتٌ تحت عَيْنَيْهِ; **2** (group) دائِرة (دَوائِرُ); **his ~ of friends** دائِرة أَصْدِقائِهِ; **in business/political ~s** في الأَوْساطِ التِجاريّةِ \ السِياسيّةِ; **we don't move in the same ~s** لا نَتَواجَدُ في نفسِ الدَوائِرِ الاجْتماعيّةِ **3** (BrE) (in theatres) دَوْر (أَدْوار); **the upper/lower ~** الدَوْر العُلْويّ \ السُفْليّ

B *vt* **1** (to move around) «satellites, planets» دارَ حول ‹*the earth, sun*›; (to fly over) «planes, helicopters» حَلَّقَ فوق ‹*an airport, area*›; (to go around) «police, demonstrators» طَوَّقَ ‹*a building, prey*›; **we ~d the airport waiting for permission to land** حَلَّقْنا فوق المَطار مُنْتَظِرينَ الإِذْنَ بالهُبوطِ

2 (with a pencil, pen) وَضَعَ دائِرةً حول ‹*a number, word*›

3 (to encircle) طَوَّقَ ‹*sb's waist, a town*›

C *vi* «plane, vulture» طافَ (u; طَواف), حامَ (u; حَوْمان)

Idioms **to come full circle** عادَ إلى نُقْطةِ البِدايةِ; **to go round in circles** (infml) دارَ في حَلْقةٍ مُفْرَغةٍ

circuit /'sə:kɪt/ *n* **1** (journey around) جَوْلة **2** (Elec) دائِرة (دَوائِرُ), دارة **3** (Aut) مِضْمار (مَضاميرُ), حَلْبة (حَلَبات)

circular /'sə:kjʊlə/ **A** *adj* **1** ‹*table, room, shape*› مُسْتَدير

2 ‹*orbit, route, walk*› دائِريّ

B *n* مَنْشور

circulate /'sə:kjʊleɪt/ **A** *vt* نَشَرَ (u; نَشْر) ‹*a petition, letter*›

B *vi* **1** «rumours, documents» شاعَ (i; شَيْع, شُيوع), انْتَشَرَ

2 «blood, air» دارَ (u; دَوْر, دَوَران)

circulation /sə:kjʊ'leɪʃ(ə)n/ *n* **1** (of the blood) دَوَران **2** (of a newspaper) تَوْزيع (تَوْزيعات), نَشْر

circumcise /'sə:kəmsʌɪz/ *vt* خَتَنَ (i; خَتْن) ‹*a boy, a girl*›

circumcision /sə:kəm'sɪʒ(ə)n/ *n* (of a boy/girl) خِتان

circumference /sə'kʌmf(ə)r(ə)ns/ *n* مُحيط (دائِرةٍ)

circumflex /'sə:kəmflɛks/ *n* (also **circumflex accent**) نَبْر (عَلامة ^ توضَعُ فوق حُروفِ العِلّةِ في بَعْضِ اللُغاتِ لِتَوْضيحِ نُطْقِها)

circumstance /'sə:kəmst(ə)ns/ **A** *n* (situation) ظَرْف (ظُروف), حال (mf; أَحْوال); **in** *or* **under the ~s the expenses can be refunded** في ظِلِّ هذه الظُروفِ يُمْكِنُ رَدُّ المَصْروفاتِ; **under no ~s can this expense be justified** لا يُمْكِنُ تَبْريرُ هذه النَفَقةِ في أَيِّ حالٍ من الأَحْوالِ

B (**circumstances**) *n pl* (conditions of life) ظُروف, أَحْوال

circumstantial /sə:kəm'stanʃ(ə)l/ *adj* ‹*evidence*› ظَرْفيّ

circus /'sə:kəs/ *n* سِرْك

cirrhosis /sɪ'rəʊsɪs/ *n* (also **cirrhosis of the liver**) تَلَيُّف الكَبِدِ

CIS /si:ʌɪ'ɛs/ *pr n* = **Commonwealth of Independent States** اتِّحاد الدُوَلِ المُسْتَقِلّةِ

cistern /'sɪst(ə)n/ *n* صِهْريج (صَهاريجُ), خَزّان ماءٍ

citadel /'sɪtəd(ə)l/ *n* قَلْعة (قِلاع, قُلوع)

citation /sʌɪ'teɪʃ(ə)n/ *n* **1** (from a text) اقْتِباس (اقْتِباسات), **2** (for an award) اسْتِشْهاد (اسْتِشْهادات); شَهادة تَقْديرٍ; **the ~ recounted how he had ...** فَصَّلَتْ شَهادةُ التَقْديرِ كيف أَنَّهُ ... **3** (to appear in court) اسْتِدْعاء للمَحْكَمةِ, تَكْليف بالحُضورِ; **a ~ for reckless driving** اسْتِدْعاء للمَحْكَمةِ بِسَبَبِ القِيادةِ المُتَهَوِّرةِ

cite /sʌɪt/ *vt* (to quote) اسْتَشْهَدَ (ب) ‹*an author, a passage, book*›; (to mention) ذَكَرَ (u; ذِكْر), أَوْرَدَ ‹*an example*›

citizen /'sɪtɪz(ə)n/ *n* مُواطِن

citizenship /'sɪtɪz(ə)nʃɪp/ *n* مُواطَنة

citrus /'sɪtrəs/ *adj* ‹*juice, grove*› حَمْضيّ

citrus fruit *n* فاكِهة حَمْضيّة

citrus tree *n* شَجَرة حَمْضيّة

city /'sɪti/ *n* (*pl* **cities**) **1** مَدينة (مُدُن, مَدائِنُ) **2** (**the City**) المِنْطَقة التِجاريّة في مَدينةِ لَنْدَن

city centre, **city center** (AmE) *n* وَسَط \ مَرْكَز مَدينةٍ

city hall *n* (AmE) مَبْنى بَلَديّةٍ

city planner *n* (AmE) مُخَطِّط عُمْرانيّ

city planning *n* (AmE) تَخْطيط المُدُنِ

civet /'sɪvɪt/ *n* زَباد

civic /'sɪvɪk/ *adj* **1** ‹*leader, administration*› مَدَنيّ **2** ‹*pride, responsibility*› مَدَنيّ

civic centre, **civic center** (AmE) *n* مَبْنى إدارةٍ مَحَلّيّةٍ

civil /'sɪv(ə)l/ *adj* **1** (legal) ‹*court, offence*› مَدَنيّ **2** (polite) ‹*answer, manner*› مُهَذَّب

civil defence, **civil defense** (AmE) *n* دِفاع مَدَنيّ

civil disobedience *n* عِصْيان مَدَنيّ

civil engineer *n* مُهَندِس مَدَنيّ

civil engineering *n* هَنْدَسة مَدَنيّة

civilian /sɪˈvɪlj(ə)n/ **A** *n* مَدَنيّ **B** *adj* <*population, death*> مَدَنيّ

civilization, -isation (BrE) /ˌsɪvɪlʌɪˈzeɪʃ(ə)n/ *n* حَضارة

civilized /ˈsɪvəlʌɪzd/ *adj* **1** <*society, country*> مُتَحَضِّر **2** <*behaviour, manner*> مُهَذَّب, مُتَحَضِّر

civil law *n* قانون مَدَنيّ

civil liberty *n* حُرّيّة مَدَنيّة

civil marriage *n* زَواج مَدَنيّ

civil partnership *n* (BrE) شَراكة مَدَنيّة (عَقْد ارْتِباطٍ بين شَخْصَيْن مِثْلِيَّيْن)

civil rights *n* حُقوق مَدَنيّة

civil servant *n* مُوَظَّف مَدَنيّ

civil service *n* خِدْمة مَدَنيّة

civil war *n* حَرْب أَهْلِيّة

clad /klad/ *adj* **to be ~ in rags/fine clothes** كانَ مُرْتَدِياً ثِياباً بالِيةً \ فاخِرةً

claim /kleɪm/ **A** *vt* **1** (to assert) زَعَمَ, ادَّعَى (u; زَعْم); **he ~s that he is innocent** يَدَّعي أَنَّهُ بَريءٌ; **I don't ~ to have all the answers** لا أَدَّعي أنّ لَدَيَّ كُلَّ الأَجْوِبةِ; **no one has ~ed responsibility for the attack** لم يَدَّعِ أَحَدٌ مَسْؤوليَّتَهُ عن الهُجومِ **2** (in law) طالَبَ (ب) <*the throne, one's inheritance, a prize*>; **both parties ~ed the land** ادَّعى كِلا الطَرَفَيْنِ أَحَقِّيَّتَهُما في الأَرْضِ; **he ~ed all the credit for the work** ادَّعى أَنَّهُ صاحِبُ الفَضْلِ كُلِّهِ في إِنْجازِ العَمَلِ **3** (to apply for) طالَبَ (ب) <*damages, compensation, expenses*>; **to ~ travel expenses** طالَبَ بِمَصاريفِ السَفَرِ **4** (fml) (to cause the loss of) **the accident ~ed 50 lives** أَدّى الحادِثُ إلى مَقْتَلِ 50 شَخْصاً

B *vi* **1** (in insurance) «policyholders» طالَبَ بِتَعْويضٍ; **to ~ on one's insurance** طالَبَ شَرِكةَ تَأْمينِهِ بِتَعْويضٍ **2** (to apply for benefit) «claimants» قَدَّمَ طَلَبَ مُساعَدةٍ ماليّةٍ من الدَوْلةِ]

C *n* **1** (demand) مُطالَبة; **a pay *or* wage ~** مُطالَبة بالأَجْرِ; **he renounced his ~ to the throne** تَخَلّى عن حَقِّهِ في المُطالَبةِ بالعَرْشِ; **there are many ~s on my time** لَدَيَّ الكَثيرُ من المَشاغِلِ; **his main ~ to fame** السَبَبُ الرَئيسيّ لِشُهْرَتِهِ **2** (in insurance) مُطالَبة; **to make a ~ on one's insurance** طَلَبَ طالَبَ شَرِكةَ التَأْمينِ بِدَفْعِ مَبْلَغِ التَأْمينِ **3** (application) طَلَب (طَلَبات); **to make *or* put in a ~ for sth** قَدَّمَ طَلَباً للمُطالَبةِ بِشَيْءٍ **4** (assertion) ادِّعاء (ادِّعاءات); **despite his ~s to the contrary** رَغم ادِّعائِهِ العَكْسَ; **extraordinary ~s have been made for this drug** أُطْلِقت ادِّعاءاتٌ حول التَأْثيرِ الخارِقِ لِهَذا الدَواءِ **5** (in prospecting) قِطْعة أَرْضٍ مُخَصَّصة للتَعْدينِ

(Phrasal verb) **claim back**: **~ back** [sth], **~** [sth] **back** طالَبَ بِرَدِّ [شَيْءٍ] <*the cost, expenses*>; **to ~ one's money back** طالَبَ بِرَدِّ مالِهِ

claimant /ˈkleɪm(ə)nt/ *n* **1** (for benefit, compensation) طالِب, مُطالِب **2** (to title, estate) مُطالِب

claim form *n* اسْتِمارة \ نَموذَج مُطالَبةٍ

clairvoyant /kleːˈvɔɪənt/ *n* مُسْتَبْصِر

clam /klam/ *n* بَطْلينوس

(Phrasal verb) **clam up** «candidates, witnesses» سَكَتَ (u; صُموت, صَمْت, صَمَت, سُكات, سُكوت, سَكْت)

clamber /ˈklambə/ *vi* «hikers, children» تَسَلَّقَ بِجُهْدٍ

clammy /ˈklami/ *adj* (**clammier, clammiest**) **1** (sticky) <*hands, skin*> لَزِج, رَطْب **2** (humid) <*weather, air*> رَطْب

clamour (BrE), **clamor** (AmE) /ˈklamə/ **A** *n* **1** (noise) ضَجّة, صَخَب **2** (protest) ضَجّة **B** *vi* (to make a demand) **to ~ for sth** «crowds, public» أَحْدَثَ ضَجّةً من أَجْلِ شَيْءٍ

clamp /klamp/ **A** *n* **1** (on a bench) مِلْزَمة (مَلازِمُ) **2** (BrE) (for a car) مِشْبَك (للسَيّاراتِ المُخالِفةِ) **B** *vt* **1** <*a part, vice*> رَبَطَ \ ثَبَّتَ بِمِلْزَمةٍ **2** وَضَعَ مِشْبَكاً على عَجَلةٍ <*a car*>

(Phrasal verb) **clamp down**: **~ down** «courts, government» قَمَعَ (a; قَمْع); **to ~ down on crime/fraud** قَمَعَ الإِجْرامَ \ الاحْتِيالَ

clampdown /ˈklampdaʊn/ *n* (infml) قَمْع

clan /klan/ *n* (group of interrelated families) قَبيلة (قَبائِلُ); (large family) عَشيرة (عَشائِرُ)

clandestine /klanˈdestɪn/ *adj* <*activities*> خَفيّ, سِرّيّ; <*marriage*> عُرْفيّ

clang /klaŋ/ **A** *n* صَلْصَلة, صَليل, قَعْقَعة
B *vi* «gates, doors» قَعْقَعَ (i; قَعْقَعة); «bells» رَنَّ (i; رَنين)

clank /klaŋk/ *vi* «trains, machinery» صَلْصَلَ (i; صَلْصَلة)

clap /klap/ **A** *vt* **(-pp-) to ~ one's hands** صَفَّقَ
B *vi* **(-pp-)** «audience, crowd» صَفَّقَ
C *n* **1** **to give sb a ~** (round of applause) صَفَّقَ لِشَخْصٍ
2 (of thunder) قَصْفة (قَصَفات)

clapping /ˈklapɪŋ/ *n* تَصْفيق

claret /ˈklarət/ *n* **1** (wine) (نَبيذ) الكْلاريت **2** (colour) لَوْن أَحْمَر أُرْجُوانيّ

clarification /ˌklarɪfɪˈkeɪʃ(ə)n/ *n* **1** (explanation) تَوْضيح (تَوْضيحات) **2** (of butter) تَصْفِية

clarify /ˈklarɪfʌɪ/ *vt* **(clarifies, clarifying, clarified)** **1** وَضَّحَ ‹an issue, a statement› **2** صَفَّى ‹the butter, wine›

clarinet /klarɪˈnɛt/ *n* كْلارينَت (آلة موسيقيّة)

clarity /ˈklarɪti/ *n* **1** (clearness) وُضوح **2** (coherence) وُضوح

clash /klaʃ/ **A** *n* **1** (confrontation) تَصادُم (تَصادُمات), اشْتِباك (اشْتِباكات) **2** (contradiction) تَضارُب, تَعارُض; **a ~ of beliefs/cultures/interests** تَعارُض المُعْتَقَدات \ الثَقافات \ المَصالِح **3** (bang) قَرْع; **a ~ of cymbals** قَرْع الصُنوج
B *vt* قَرَعَ (a; قَرْع) ‹the cymbals, bin lids›
C *vi* **1** (to fight) «troops, demonstrators» اشْتَبَكَ, تَصادَمَ
2 (to be in conflict) «interests, beliefs» تَعارَضَ **3** (to coincide) «meetings, dates» تَعارَضَ **4** (to not match) «colours, patterns» تَعارَضَ, تَنافَرَ

clasp /klɑːsp/ **A** *vt* **1** أَمْسَكَ بِقوّةٍ ‹a hand, purse› **2** شَبَكَ بِمِشْبَكٍ ‹a bracelet, handbag›
B *n* **1** (on bracelet, bag, purse) مِشْبَك (مَشابِكُ); (on belt) إِبْزيم (أَبازيمُ) **2** (of hand) قَبْضة

class /klɑːs/ **A** *n* **1** (in society) طَبَقة **2** (of students) صَفّ (صُفوف) (ME), قِسْم (أَقْسام) (NA); (lesson) حِصّة (حِصَص), دَرْس (دُروس); **the ~ of 2011** دُفْعة 2011 **3** (type) فِئة **4** (in travelling) دَرَجة **5** (infml) (style) أَناقة, شِياكة
B *vt* صَنَّفَ ‹a specimen, an incident›; **~ this as a priority** صَنِّفْ هذا كَأَوْلَويّةٍ

class action *n* [دَعْوى قَضائيّة فِئويّة]

class-conscious /ˈklɑːsˌkɒnʃəs/ *adj* ‹attitudes, society› [واعٍ بالفُروقِ الطَبَقيّةِ \ بالتَدَرُّجِ الطَبَقيِّ]

classic /ˈklasɪk/ **A** *adj* **1** ‹novel, car› كْلاسيكيّ **2** ‹example, mistake› تَقْليديّ
B *n* **1** (highly regarded) عَمَل \ أَثَر كْلاسيكيّ **2** (memorable) نَموذَج كْلاسيكيّ **3** **the ~s** (ancient literary works) الآثار الأَدَبيّة الكْلاسيكيّة

classical /ˈklasɪk(ə)l/ *adj* **1** (of Greece, Rome) ‹architecture, mythology› قَديم, كْلاسيكيّ **2** (traditional) ‹music, dance› تَقْليديّ, كْلاسيكيّ

Classical Arabic /ˌklasɪkəl ˈarəbɪk/ *n* اللُغة العَرَبيّة الفُصْحى (التُراثيّة)

classics /ˈklasɪks/ *n* **1** (ancient works) أَدَب كْلاسيكيّ **2** (subject) دِراسات كْلاسيكيّة

classification /ˌklasɪfɪˈkeɪʃ(ə)n/ *n* **1** (category) صِنْف (أَصْناف, صُنوف) **2** [u] (categorization) تَصْنيف

classified /ˈklasɪfʌɪd/ **A** *adj* (categorized) ‹catalogue, directory› مُصَنَّف; **a ~ ad** إِعْلان مُبَوَّب
B *adj* (secret) ‹information, document› سِرّيّ

classify /ˈklasɪfʌɪ/ *vt* **(classifies, classifying, classified)** **1** (to file) صَنَّفَ ‹data, a book› **2** (to declare secret) صَنَّفَ تحت بَنْدِ السِرّيّةِ ‹information, a document›

classmate /ˈklɑːsmeɪt/ *n* زَميل دِراسةٍ

classroom /ˈklɑːsruːm/ *n* فَصْل (فُصول) (ME), قِسْم (أَقْسام) (NA)

classroom assistant *n* مُساعِد فَصْلٍ, مُدَرِّس مُعاوِن

class struggle *n* صِراع طَبَقيّ

class system *n* نِظام طَبَقيّ

classy /ˈklɑːsi/ *adj* **(classier, classiest)** (infml) ‹person, outfit, restaurant› راقٍ, أَنيق

clatter /ˈklatə/ **A** *n* (of dishes, pans) قَرْقَعة, صَوْت خَبْطٍ; (of hooves, a keyboard) طَقْطَقة
B *vi* «dishes, pans» قَرْقَعَ (i; قَرْقَعة); «hooves, keyboards» طَقْطَقَ (i; طَقْطَقة)

clause /klɔːz/ *n* **1** (in a contract) بَنْد (بُنود), مادّة (مَوادُّ), فِقْرة (فِقْرات) **2** (in grammar) جُمْلة (جُمَل)

claustrophobia /ˌklɔːstrəˈfəʊbɪə/ *n* رُهاب الأماكِنِ المُغْلَقةِ

claustrophobic /ˌklɔːstrəˈfəʊbɪk/ *adj* ‹*atmosphere, room*› يُسَبِّبُ رُهابَ الأماكِنِ المُغْلَقةِ; **I feel ~** أَشْعُرُ بِرُهابِ الأَماكِنِ المُغْلَقةِ

claw /klɔː/ *n* مِخْلَب (مَخالِبُ)

clay /kleɪ/ *n* **1** (soil) طَفْل, طين (أَطْيان), صَلْصال **2** (for pottery, bricks) طين (أَطْيان), صَلْصال

clay court *n* مَلْعَب تُرابيّ

clean /kliːn/ **A** *adj* **1** (not dirty) ‹*clothes, hands, dishes*› نَظيف; **to keep the house ~ and tidy** حافَظَ على البَيْتِ نَظيفاً وَمُرَتَّباً; **a ~ sheet of paper** وَرَقة فارِغة; **to wipe one's face/mouth ~** مَسَحَ وَجْهَهُ \ فَمَهُ; **keep your shoes ~** حافِظْ على حِذائِكَ نَظيفاً **2** (unpolluted) ‹*energy, fuel, water*› نَقيّ; **to develop ~er fuels** طَوَّرَ مَصادِرَ أَنْقى للطاقةِ **3** (not immoral) ‹*image, joke*› مُهَذَّب, غَيْر بَذيءٍ; **it's all good ~ fun** ما هي إلاّ مُتْعةٌ لا تَتَعَدّى حُدودَ الأَدَبِ!; **keep it ~!** حَياة نَظيفة; **~ living** بَريئةٌ **4** (free of infractions) ‹*reputation*› نَظيف; ‹*driving licence*› خالٍ من النِقاطِ \ المُخالَفاتِ; ‹*record*› خالٍ من السَوابِقِ **5** (Sport) (sportsmanlike) ‹*game*› نَظيف **6** (neat, elegant) ‹*lines*› مُنَمَّق; **to make a ~ break with the past** قَطَعَ كُلَّ صِلةٍ بَيْنَهُ وَبَيْنَ الماضي **7** (of bones) ‹*fracture, break*› بَسيط

B *adv* تَماماً; **the bullet went ~ through his shoulder** اخْتَرَقَت الرَصاصةُ كَتِفَهُ تَماماً; **to jump ~ over the wall** قَفَزَ فوق الجِدارِ تَماماً; **we're ~ out of bread** لا يوجَدُ لَدَيْنا خُبْزٌ على الإطْلاقِ

C *vt* **1** نَظَّفَ ‹*the house, a room, one's shoes*›; **I ~ed the dirt off my hands/the windscreen** نَظَّفْتُ يَدَيَّ \ زُجاجَ السَيّارةِ من الأَوْساخِ; **to have sth ~ed** أَرْسَلَ شَيْئاً إلى المَغْسَلةِ لِتَنْظيفِهِ; **to ~ one's teeth** نَظَّفَ أَسْنانَهُ; **to ~ a wound** طَهَّرَ جُرْحاً **2** نَظَّفَ ‹*fish, poultry*›

D *vi* «person, product» نَظَّفَ

E *n* (infml) تَنْظيف; **to give sth a ~** نَظَّفَ شَيْئاً

Idioms **to come clean about sth** (infml) اعْتَرَفَ بالحَقيقةِ بِخُصوصِ شَيْءٍ; **to clean up one's act** (infml) ضَبَطَ سُلوكَهُ; **to make a clean sweep** (in competitions, elections) اكْتَسَحَ; (organizations) أَجْرى تَغْييراً شامِلاً

Phrasal verbs **clean off** **A** «stain» أُزيلَ **B** **~ [sth] off, ~ off [sth]** أَزالَ [شَيْئاً] ‹*dirt, a stain*›

• **clean out**: **~ [sth] out, ~ out [sth]** نَظَّفَ [شَيْئاً] تَماماً ‹*a cupboard, fridge*›

• **clean up** **A** **1** (to clean and tidy a place) نَظَّفَ وَرَتَّبَ مَكاناً; **to ~ up after sb** نَظَّفَ وراءَ شَخْصٍ **2** (to wash oneself) تَنَظَّفَ **3** (infml) (to make a profit) حَقَّقَ رِبْحاً كَبيراً **B** **~ [sb] up** نَظَّفَ [شَخْصاً] ‹*a child, patient*›; **to ~ oneself up** تَنَظَّفَ **C** **~ [sth] up, ~ up [sth]** **1** (to make clean) نَظَّفَ [شَيْئاً] ‹*a mess, an area*› **2** (to remove crime from) طَهَّرَ [شَيْئاً] ‹*the streets, local politics*›

clean-cut /klinˈkʌt/ *adj* ‹*person, image*› مُهَنْدَم, حَسَن المَظْهَرِ

cleaner /ˈkliːnə/ *n* **1** (person) مُنَظِّف **2** (detergent) مُنَظِّف (مُنَظِّفات) **3** **the cleaner's** (shop) ▸ **dry-cleaner's** المَغْسَلة

Idiom **to take sb to the cleaner's** (infml) (to swindle) نَصَبَ على شَخْصٍ; (to defeat) هَزَمَ شَخْصاً شَرَّ هَزيمةٍ

cleaning /ˈkliːnɪŋ/ *n* تَنْظيف (تَنْظيفات)

cleaning lady *n* عامِلة نَظافةٍ

cleaning product *n* مُنَظِّف, مُنْتَج تَنْظيفٍ

cleanliness /ˈklɛnlinəs/ *n* نَظافة

cleanly¹ /ˈklɛnli/ *adj* (**cleanlier, cleanliest**) (liter) ‹*habits, animal*› طاهِر

cleanly² /ˈkliːnli/ *adv* **1** ‹*to catch, hit*› بِمَهارةٍ, بِشَكْلٍ مَضْبوطٍ; ‹*to break*› بِشَكْلٍ مُسْتَوٍ \ غَيْر مُتَعَرِّج; **to catch the ball ~** الْتَقَطَ الكُرةَ بِمَهارةٍ **2** ‹*to burn*› بدونِ شَوائِبَ

cleanse /klɛnz/ *vt* **1** نَظَّفَ ‹*skin*›; طَهَّرَ ‹*a wound*› **2** (to purify) طَهَّرَ ‹*the soul*›

cleanser /ˈklɛnzə/ *n* **1** (for skin) مُنَظِّف (مُنَظِّفات) **2** (for household use) مُنَظِّف (مُنَظِّفات)

clean-shaven /klinˈʃeɪv(ə)n/ *adj* ‹*face, man*› حَليق الذَقْنِ \ اللِحْيةِ

cleansing /ˈklɛnzɪŋ/ *adj* **1** ‹*cream, product*› مُنَظِّف للبَشَرةِ **2** ‹*action, agent*› مُنَظِّف

clean-up /ˈklinʌp/ *n* تَنْظيف (تَنْظيفات)

clear /klɪə/ **A** *adj* **1** (understandable) ‹*instructions, message, handwriting*› واضِح, مَفْهوم; **is that ~?, do I make myself ~?** هل هذا واضِحٌ؟; **let's get this ~** دَعْنا نُوَضِّحْ هذا; **I wish to**

make it ~ that I disapprove أَوَدُّ أنْ أُوَضِّحَ أنَّني غَيْرُ مُوافِقٍ **2** (obvious) ‹*evidence, indication, example*› ظاهِر ,واضِح; **it was ~ that he wasn't going to recover** كانَ واضِحاً أنَّهُ لن يَتَعافى **3** (distinct) ‹*image, sound, memory*› جَليّ ,واضِح; **she sang with a ~ voice** غَنَّتْ بِصَوْتٍ واضِحٍ **4** (transparent) ‹*plastic, glass*› شَفّاف; ‹*water*› صافٍ; **~ soup** مَرَق صافٍ **5** (unblemished) ‹*complexion, skin*› صافٍ; **she has ~ blue eyes** لَها عَيْنانِ خَضْراوانِ صافِيَتانِ **6** (with good visibility) ‹*sky, day*› صَحْو ,رائِق ,صافٍ; **on a ~ day you can see the coast of France** في يَوْمٍ صافٍ يُمْكِنُكَ أنْ تَرى ساحِلَ فَرَنْسا **7** (not confused) ‹*picture, understanding*› جَليّ ,واضِح; **there's something I'm still not ~ about** ما زالَ هُناكَ شَيْءٌ غَيْرُ واضِحٍ بالنِّسْبةِ لي; **to have a ~ head** كانَ لَهُ ذِهْنٌ صافٍ; **to keep a ~ head** حافَظَ على صَفاءِ ذِهْنِهِ; **my conscience is ~, I have a ~ conscience** ضَميري مُرْتاحٌ **8** (unobstructed) ‹*view, space*› فارِغ; ‹*road*› لا يَعوقُهُ \ يَحْجُبُهُ شَيْءٌ; **I had a ~ view of his face** رَأَيْتُ وَجْهَهُ بِوُضوحٍ; **keep Monday ~** اُتْرُكْ يَوْمَ الاثْنَيْنِ فارِغاً **9** (not touching) **to be ~ of the ground/water** كانَ غَيْرَ مُلامِسٍ لِلأَرْضِ \ للماءِ **10** (whole) ‹*week, day*› كامِل **11** (net) ‹*profit*› صافٍ

B *adv* **1** (away) بَعيداً; **to jump ~** قَفَزَ بَعيداً; **to get ~ of the traffic/town** ذَهَبَ بَعيداً عن حَرَكَةِ المُرورِ \ المَدينةِ; **stand ~ of the doors!** اِبْتَعِدوا عن الأَبْوابِ! ▸ see also **steer** **2** (completely) تَماماً; **he threw it ~ across the room** أَلْقى بِهِ إلى الجانِبِ الآخَرِ من الحُجْرةِ تَماماً

C *vt* **1** (to remove) أَزالَ ‹*the debris, snow, weeds*›; **I ~ed the papers off my desk** أَزَلْتُ الأَوْراقَ من على مَكْتَبي; **to ~ the backlog** أَنْهى الأَعْمالَ المُتَراكِمةَ **2** (to free from demonstrators) أَخْلى ‹*the streets, square*›; (from plants) اِقْتَلَعَ كُلَّ المَزْروعاتِ \ النَّباتاتِ من ‹*land*›; (from obstacles) أَزالَ العَوائِقَ من ‹*a road*›; (from clutter) رَتَّبَ ‹*a surface, desk*›; **to ~ the road of snow** أَزالَ الثَّلْجَ من الطَّريقِ; **to ~ the table** رَفَعَ الأَطْباقَ عن المائِدةِ; **to ~ one's throat** تَنَحْنَحَ; **the fresh air will ~ your head** سَوْفَ يُصَفّي الهَواءُ النَّقيُّ ذِهْنَكَ; **the building was ~ed when the alarm went off** تَمَّ إِخْلاءُ المَبْنى بعد انْطِلاقِ جَرَسِ الإنْذارِ **3** (to exonerate) بَرَّأَ ‹*the accused*›; **to ~ one's name** أَثْبَتَ بَراءَتَهُ **4** (to approve) وافَقَ (على) ‹*a request, proposal*›; **to ~ sth with sb** حَصَلَ على مُوافَقةِ شَخْصٍ على شَيْءٍ **5** (to get over) اجْتازَ ‹*a fence, hurdle*› **6** (to pass through) **to ~ customs** اجْتازَ الجَمارِكَ **7** (in football, rugby) **to ~ the ball** أَبْعَدَ الكُرَةَ عن مَرْماهُ **8** أَجْرى مُخالَصةً ‹*a cheque*› **9** (to pay off) سَدَّدَ ‹*a debt*›

D *vi* **1** (to lose clouds) «sky, weather» صَفا (u; صَفاء ,صَفْو), راقَ (u; رَوْق), صَحا (u; صَحْو ,صُحوّ) **2** (to disappear) «smoke, fog» تَبَدَّدَ ,انْكَشَفَ ,انْقَشَعَ **3** «cheque» تَمَّتْ مُخالَصَتُهُ; **'reduced to ~'** 'أسْعار مُخَفَّضة لِلتَّصْفِيةِ'

(Idioms) **to be in the clear** (out of danger) لم يَعُدْ في خَطَرٍ; (free from suspicion) لم يَعُدْ مَحَلَّ شَكٍّ; **to clear the air** (to freshen) صَفّى الهَواءَ; (to defuse the situation) نَقّى الأَجْواءَ; **to clear the way for sth** مَهَّدَ الطَّريقَ لِشَيْءٍ

(Phrasal verbs) **clear away** **1** رَتَّبَ **2** **~ [sth] away, ~ away [sth]** رَفَعَ [شَيْئاً] بعد الأَكْلِ ‹*plates*›; أَزاحَ \ أَزالَ [شَيْئاً] ‹*wreckage, snow*›

• **clear off** (BrE infml) غادَرَ \ انْصَرَفَ بِسُرْعةٍ; **~ off!** اُغْرُبْ عَنّي!

• **clear out** **A** غادَرَ مُسْرِعاً **B** **~ [sth] out, ~ out [sth]** **1** (to empty) أَفْرَغَ [شَيْئاً] ‹*a cupboard, the attic, one's desk*› **2** (to throw away) تَخَلَّصَ من [شَيْءٍ] ‹*old clothes, junk*›

• **clear up** **A** **1** (to tidy up) رَتَّبَ **2** (to brighten) «weather» صَفا (u; صَفاء ,صَفْو), راقَ (u; رَوْق), صَحا (u; صَحْو ,صُحوّ) **3** (to get better) «infection, symptoms» زالَ (a; زَوال) **B** **~ up [sth], ~ [sth] up** **1** (to tidy) رَتَّبَ [شَيْئاً] ‹*the mess, litter, toys*›; تَخَلَّصَ من [شَيْءٍ] ‹*rubbish*› **2** (to resolve) عالَجَ [شَيْئاً] ‹*a problem, the confusion, misunderstanding*›

clearance /ˈklɪərəns/ *n* **1** [u] (permission) إذْن ,تَصْريح; **to have/get ~ to do sth** حَصَلَ على تَصْريحٍ لِفِعْلِ شَيْءٍ; **to have ~ for take-off** حَصَلَ على الإذْنِ بالإقْلاعِ **2** (removal of vegetation, forest, slums) إزالة **3** [u] (by customs) تَخْليص **4** (of stock) تَصْفِية **5** [u] (of cheques) مُخالَصة **6** (gap) مَسافة فارِغة ,(فُرَج) فُرْجة; **there is 10 cm ~** هُناكَ فُرْجةٌ بِمِقْدارِ 10 سم

clearance sale *n* بَيْع تَصْفِيةٍ

clear-cut /klɪəˈkʌt/ *adj* ‹*distinction, answer, winner, victory*› واضِح

clear-headed /ˌklɪəˈhɛdɪd/ *adj* ‹*assessment, thinking*› سَليم, مَنْطِقيّ

clearing /ˈklɪərɪŋ/ *n* (in woods, forest) [مِنْطَقة أُزيلَتْ مِنْها الأَشْجارُ]

clearly /ˈklɪəli/ *adv* **1** (distinctly) ‹*to speak, hear, write*› بِوُضوح, بِشَكْلٍ واضِحٍ; **it's too dark to see ~** لا يُمْكِنُ الرُّؤْيةُ بِوُضوحٍ في هذا الظَّلامِ الشَّديدِ; **the house is ~ visible from the road** يُمْكِنُ رُؤْيةُ البَيْتِ بِوُضوحٍ من الطَّريقِ **2** (without confusion) ‹*to think*› بِوُضوحٍ **3** (obviously) ‹*related, important, upset*› بِشَكْلٍ واضِحٍ; **something was ~ wrong** كانَ من الواضِحِ أنّ هُناكَ شَيْئًا خاطِئًا; **the two incidents are ~ related** من الواضِحِ أنّ الحَدَثَيْنِ مُرْتَبِطَيْنِ; **he ~ needs psychiatric help, ~, he needs psychiatric help** من الواضِحِ أنَّهُ يَحْتاجُ إلى مُساعَدةٍ نَفْسيّةٍ

clearness /ˈklɪənəs/ *n* **1** (of liquids) نَقاء, صَفاء **2** (of the air) نَقاء **3** (of images) وُضوح **4** (of voice quality) وُضوح **5** (of thought) جَلاء, وُضوح

clear-out /ˈklɪəaʊt/ *n* (infml) حَمْلة تَنْظيفٍ, تَنْظيف شامِل (للتخَلُّصِ من الأَشْياءِ الزائِدةِ \ غَيْرِ الضَرورِيّةِ)

clearway /ˈklɪəweɪ/ *n* (BrE) [طَريق يُمْنَعُ فيهِ وُقوفُ المَرْكَباتِ إلاّ في الحالاتِ الطارِئةِ]

cleavage /ˈkliːvɪdʒ/ *n* الشَقّ بين النَهْدَيْنِ

cleave /kliːv/ *vt* (*past tense* **cleaved** or **clove**; *past participle* **cleaved** or **cleft**) فَلَقَ (i; فَلْق), فَلَجَ (i-u; فَلْج)

cleaver /ˈkliːvə/ *n* ساطور (سَواطيرُ)

clef /klɛf/ *n* (Mus) مِفْتاح (مَفاتيحُ)

cleft /klɛft/ **A** *adj* ‹*chin, lip, palate*› مَشْقوق **B** *n* شَقّ (شُقوق) فَلْق (فُلوق)

clementine /ˈklɛm(ə)ntiːn/ *n* يوسُفيّ

clench /klɛn(t)ʃ/ *vt* **1** شَدَّ (i-u; شَدّ) ‹*one's fists, teeth*› أَطْبَقَ **2** (to grasp) ‹*a knife, steering wheel*› أَمْسَكَ بِقوّةٍ \ بِشِدّةٍ

clergy /ˈkləːdʒi/ *n* رِجال الكَهَنوتِ, أَكْليروس

clergyman /ˈkləːdʒɪmən/ *n* (*pl* **-men**) قَسّ (قُسوس, قُسُس), قِسّيس (قَساوِسة, قِسّيسون)

clergywoman /ˈkləːdʒiwʊmən/ *n* (*pl* **-women**) قِسّيسة (سَيِّدة دِينٍ)

cleric /ˈklɛrɪk/ *n* رَجُل دينٍ

clerical /ˈklɛrɪk(ə)l/ *adj* **1** (Relig) ‹*establishment, clothing*› كَهَنوتيّ **2** ‹*work*› مَكْتَبيّ; ‹*error*› كِتابيّ

clerical assistant *n* كاتِب \ مُساعِد إداريّ

clerk /klɑːk/ *n* **1** (in an office, bank) مُوَظَّف **2** (AmE) (in a hotel) مُوَظَّف اسْتِقْبالٍ; (in a shop) بائِع (بائِعونَ)

clever /ˈklɛvə/ *adj* **1** (gifted) ‹*person*› ذَكيّ (أَذْكِياءُ), نَبيه (نُبَهاءُ); **to be ~ at maths/navigation** كانَ ذَكيًّا في الرِياضيّاتِ \ المِلاحةِ; **she's ~ with words** هي ماهِرةٌ في انْتِقاءِ الكَلِماتِ; **how ~ of you to work it out** لَقَدْ كانَ ذَكاءً مِنْكَ أنْ تَتَوَصَّلَ إلى الحَلِّ **2** (ingenious) ‹*idea, design, device*› مُبْتَكَر **3** (skilful) ماهِر (مَهَرة); **to be ~ at doing sth** كانَ ماهِراً في فِعْلِ شَيْءٍ; **he's ~ with his hands** هو ماهِرٌ في الأَعْمالِ اليَدَويّةِ **4** (BrE) (cunning) ماكِر (مَكَرة); **to be too ~ for sb** كانَ أَمْكَرَ من شَخْصٍ

Idiom **to be too clever by half** (infml) كانَ مَغْروراً بِذَكائِهِ

cleverly /ˈklɛvəli/ *adv* ‹*to arrange, solve*› بِذَكاءٍ

cliché /ˈkliːʃeɪ/ *n* **1** (phrase) تَعْبير مُبْتَذَل, كْليشيه **2** (in stories) كْليشيه

clichéd /ˈkliːʃeɪd/ *adj* ‹*phrase, image*› مُبْتَذَل

click /klɪk/ **A** *n* **1** (of the fingers, tongue) طَقْطَقة; (of a door, lock, switch) قَرْقَعة **2** (of a mouse, button) ضَغْطة, نَقْرة **B** *vt* **1** طَقْطَقَ (i; طَقْطَقة) ‹*one's fingers, tongue*› **2** (Comput) نَقَرَ (u; نَقْر; على), ضَغَطَ (a; ضَغْط; على) ‹*a mouse, button*› **C** *vi* **1** «door, lock» طَقْطَقَ (i; طَقْطَقة) **2 to ~ on an icon** ضَغَطَ \ نَقَرَ على أَيْقونةٍ

client /ˈklʌɪənt/ *n* (Busn) عَميل (عُمَلاءُ)

clientele /ˌkliːɒnˈtɛl/ *n* زَبائِن

cliff /klɪf/ *n* جُرُف, جُروف (أَجْراف)

cliffhanger /ˈklɪfhaŋə/ *n* [نِهاية حَلَقةٍ مُشَوِّقة \ تَحْبِسُ الأَنْفاسَ]

climate /ˈklʌɪmət/ *n* مَناخ

climate change *n* تَغَيُّرُ المُناخ

climax /ˈklʌɪmaks/ *n* (*pl* **climaxes**) ذُرْوة (ذُرًى), أَوْج

climb /klʌɪm/ **A** *vt* **1** صَعِدَ (a; صُعود), تَسَلَّقَ ‹*a mountain, ladder, tree*›; **he's still/no longer able to ~ the stairs** ما زالَ \ لم يَعُدْ قادِراً على صُعودِ الدَرَجِ **2** «plants» تَسَلَّقَ ‹*a wall, trellis*›

B *vi* **1** (with hands and feet) تَسَلَّقَ; **I ~ed onto the roof** تَسَلَّقْتُ إلى السَطْحِ; **to ~ over a fence/wall** تَسَلَّقَ السِياجَ \ السورَ; **to ~ into bed** صَعِدَ إلى السَريرِ; **to ~ up/down a ladder** صَعِدَ \ نَزَلَ السُلَّمَ **2** (in rockclimbing) تَسَلَّقَ **3** (to rise) «sun, aircraft» ارْتَفَعَ **4** (to slope up) «path, road» ارْتَفَعَ **5** (to increase) «prices, sales, temperatures» ارْتَفَعَ

C *n* **1** (by a climber) تَسَلُّق; (by car, bicycle) صُعود; **it's a steep ~ to the top of the hill** الطَريقُ المُؤَدّي إلى قِمّة التَلِّ مُرْتَفِعٌ بِشَكْلٍ حادٍّ **2** (of aircraft) صُعود

(Phrasal verb) **climb down** تَراجَعَ

climber /ˈklʌɪmə/ *n* **1** (mountaineer) مُتَسَلِّق جِبالٍ; (rock climber) مُتَسَلِّق صُخورٍ **2** (plant) نَبات مُتَسَلِّق

climbing /ˈklʌɪmɪŋ/ *n* تَسَلُّق الجِبالِ

climbing frame *n* إطار تَسَلُّقٍ

climbing lane *n* [مَسار على تَلٍّ مُخَصَّص للمَرْكَباتِ البَطيئةِ]

clinch /klɪn(t)ʃ/ *vt* عَقَدَ (i; عَقْد) ‹a deal›; أَحْرَزَ ‹a title, victory›; حَسَمَ (i; حَسْم) ‹an argument›

cling /klɪŋ/ *vi* (*past tense, past participle* **clung**) **1** (to hold on tightly) **to ~ to sb/sth** تَعَلَّقَ بِشَخْصٍ \ شَيْءٍ; **to ~ together** تَرابَطَ **2** (to stick) **to ~ (to sth)** «wet hair, clothes» الْتَصَقَ (بِشَيْءٍ) **3** (to remain faithful) **to ~ to a belief/an idea** تَشَبَّثَ بِعَقيدةٍ \ فِكْرةٍ

cling film *n* (BrE) [غِشاء شَفّاف لاصِق يُسْتَعْمَلُ لِتَغْطِيةِ الطَعامِ]

clinic /ˈklɪnɪk/ *n* **1** (for outpatients) مُسْتَوْصَف (مُسْتَوْصَفات), عِيادة **2** (AmE) (group practice) مَرْكَز طِبّيّ **3** (for coaching) جَلْسة تَدْريبٍ

clinical /ˈklɪnɪk(ə)l/ *adj* **1** ‹medicine, trial› إكْلينيكيّ, سَريريّ **2** ‹approach, precision› [مُتَجَرِّد من الإحْساسِ]

clinical depression *n* (Psych) نَوْبة الاكْتِئابِ الكُبْرى

clinically /ˈklɪnɪkli/ *adv* **1** (medically) إكْلينيكيًّا, طِبِّيًّا; **~ dead** مَيِّت طِبِّيًّا \ إكْلينيكيًّا; **~ depressed** مُكْتَئِب طِبِّيًّا \ إكْلينيكيًّا **2** (unemotionally) بِشَكْلٍ غَيْرِ عاطِفِيٍّ

clinician /klɪˈnɪʃ(ə)n/ *n* طَبيب سَريريّ

clink /klɪŋk/ **A** *vt* قَعْقَعَ (i; قَعْقَعة) ‹glasses, bottles›

B *vi* «ice cubes, jewellery» خَشْخَشَ (i; خَشْخَشة)

clip /klɪp/ **A** *n* **1** (device) مِشْبَك (مَشابِكُ) **2** (on earring) مُقْتَطَف **3** (from movie) مُقْتَطَف; (for hair) بُكْلة (بُكَل), حَبّاسة

B *vt* (**-pp-**) **1** شَبَكَ (i; شَبْك) ‹a microphone, brooch› **2** قَلَّمَ ‹a hedge, one's nails› **3** قَصَّ (u; قَصّ) ‹an article, a coupon› **4** (BrE) ثَقَبَ (u; ثَقْب) ‹a ticket›

clip art *n* قُصاصات فَنِّيّة

clipboard /ˈklɪpbɔːd/ *n* **1** (portable board) [لَوْح كِتابةٍ مَشْبَكيّ] **2** (in computing) حافِظة

clip frame *n* [إطار \ بِرْواز ذو مَلاقِطَ]

clip-on /ˈklɪpɒn/ *adj* ‹bow tie, earring› ذو مِشْبَكٍ

clip-ons /ˈklɪpɒnz/ *n pl* [حَلَق \ نَظّارات ذات المَشابِكِ]

clippers /ˈklɪpəz/ *n pl* (for nails, hair) مِقَصّ (مَقاصُّ); (for hedge, lawn) مِقْراض (مَقاريضُ)

clipping /ˈklɪpɪŋ/ *n* قُصاصة

clique /kliːk/ *n* زُمْرة (زُمَر)

clitoris /ˈklɪt(ə)rɪs/ *n* بَظْر (بُظور)

cloak /kləʊk/ **A** *n* **1** (outer garment) عَباءة (عَباء, أَعْبِئة) **2** (disguise) قِناع (قِناعات, أَقْنِعة)

B *vt* كَتَمَ (u; كَتْم, كِتْمان) ‹an intention, one's activities›

cloakroom /ˈkləʊkruːm/ *n* **1** (for coats) حُجْرة المَعاطِفِ \ الإيداعِ **2** (BrE) (lavatory) مِرْحاض (مَراحيضُ)

cloakroom attendant *n* **1** (in hotel) [مُلازِم حُجْرةِ المَعاطِفِ] **2** (BrE) (for toilets) حارِس مِرْحاضٍ

clock /klɒk/ **A** *n* **1** (timepiece) ساعة (ساعات); **to set a ~** ضَبَطَ ساعةً; **to put the ~s forward/back one hour** قَدَّمَ \ أَخَّرَ الوَقْتَ ساعةً; **to work around the ~** عَمِلَ على مَدارِ الساعةِ; **the twenty-four hour ~** نِظام الـ24 ساعةً **2** (infml) (mileometer) عَدّاد المَسافاتِ **3** (in computers) ساعة (ساعات)

B *vt* **1** (to attain) سَجَّلَ, حَقَّقَ ‹a time, speed›; **he ~ed 9.6 seconds in the 100 metres** قَطَعَ المَسافةَ في 9.6 ثانِيةٍ في سِباقِ الـ 100 مِتْرٍ **2** (to record) **the police ~ed him doing 150 km an hour** سَجَّلَتْهُ الشُرْطةُ وَهُوَ يَقودُ بِسُرْعةِ 150 كم في الساعةِ

(Idiom) **to turn the clock back** أَعادَ الزَمَنَ إلى الوَراءِ

(Phrasal verbs) **clock in** «workers» سَجَّلَ وَقْتَ الحُضورِ [للعَمَلِ]; **I ~ed in at 8.00** سَجَّلْتُ الدُخولَ الساعةَ 8:00

• **clock off** (BrE) ▸ **clock out**

• **clock on** (BrE) ▸ **clock in**

• **clock out** «workers» [سَجَّلَ وَقْتَ الانْصِرافِ من العَمَلِ]; **I ~ed off at 6.30** سَجَّلْتُ الانْصِرافَ الساعةَ 6:30

• **clock up**: ~ **up [sth]** 1 قَطَعَ [شَيْئاً] ‹*30,000 km, a distance*› 2 (infml) (to record) سَجَّلَ ‹*hours, sales, points*›

clock face *n* وَجْه ساعةٍ

clockmaker /ˈklɒkmeɪkə/ *n* صانِع \ مُصَلِّح ساعاتٍ

clock radio *n* راديو بِساعةٍ

clock tower *n* بُرْج ساعةٍ

clockwise /ˈklɒkwʌɪz/ *adj, adv* في اتِّجاهِ عَقارِبِ الساعةِ

clockwork /ˈklɒkwəːk/ **A** *n* آلَيّة الساعة; **as regular as ~** مُنْتَظِم أَشَدَّ الانْتِظامِ \ للغايةِ

B *adj* ‹*toy, radio*› أوتوماتيكيّ

clog /klɒg/ **A** *n* قَبْقاب (قَباقيبُ)

B *vt* سَدَّ (u; سَدّ) ‹*a drain, pipe*›

cloister /ˈklɔɪstə/ *n* [رِواق دَيْرٍ مَسْقوف مُحيط بِفِناءٍ]

clone /kləʊn/ **A** *n* 1 (of living being) مُسْتَنْسَخ 2 (of computer) مُسْتَنْسَخ

B *vt* اسْتَنْسَخَ ‹*an embryo, cell*›

cloning /ˈkləʊnɪŋ/ *n* اسْتِنْساخ

close¹ /kləʊs/ **A** *adj* 1 (in space, time) قَريب; **you're too ~ to the edge** أَنْتَ قَريبٌ جِدًّا من الحافّةِ; **they are very ~ in age** هُمْ مُتَقارِبونَ جِدًّا في السِنِّ; **how ~ are you to finishing it?** كم بَقِيَ لَكَ من الوَقْتِ لِإنْهائِهِ؟; **in ~ proximity to sth/sb** على مَقْرُبةٍ من شَيْءٍ \ شَخْصٍ; **to shoot sb at ~ range** أَطْلَقَ النارَ على شَخْصٍ من مَدًى قَريبٍ 2 (intimate) ‹*friend, tie*› حَميم; (nearly related) ‹*family, relative*› من الدَرَجةِ الأُولى; **to be ~ to sb** كانَ على عَلاقةٍ وَثيقةٍ بِشَخْصٍ; **to have ~ ties with** *or* **to sth** كانَ لَهُ صِلاتٌ وَثيقةٌ مع شَيْءٍ; **in ~ contact with sb/sth** على اتِّصالٍ وَثيقٍ بِشَخْصٍ \ بِشَيْءٍ 3 (in approximation) **to bear a ~ resemblance to sb/sth** شابَهَ شَخْصاً \ شَيْئاً إلى حَدٍّ كَبيرٍ; **to be ~ to doing sth** شارَفَ على فِعْلِ شَيْءٍ; **he was ~ to tears/death** شارَفَ على البُكاءِ \ المَوْتِ; **it's the ~st thing to champagne I've tasted** هو أَقْرَبُ شَيْءٍ إلى الشَمْبانيا في كُلِّ ما تَذَوَّقْتُهُ 4 (careful, thorough) ‹*inspection, examination, supervision*› دَقيق; **I took a ~r look at it** أَلْقَيْتُ عَلَيْهِ نَظْرةً أَدَقَّ; **on ~r inspection** عند الفَحْصِ بِشَكْلٍ أَدَقَّ; **to pay ~ attention to sth/sb** أَوْلى انْتِباهاً كَبيراً لِشَيْءٍ \ لِشَخْصٍ; **to keep a ~ eye** *or* **watch on sth/sb** راقَبَ شَيْئاً \ شَخْصاً عن كَثَبٍ 5 (evenly contested) ‹*race, election, contest*› مُتَقارِب; **Palmer came a ~ second** جاءَ بالْمَر في المَرْتَبةِ الثانيةِ بِفارِقٍ بَسيطٍ 6 (compact) ‹*weave, texture*› كَثيف, صَفيق; **pages of ~ print** صَفَحات كَثيفة النَصِّ; **to fly in ~ formation** حَلَّقَ في تَشْكيلاتٍ مُتَقارِبةٍ 7 (stuffy) ‹*weather*› عالي الرُطوبةِ, خانِق; **it's very ~** الجَوُّ خانِقٌ جِدًّا

B *adv* 1 (in space) عن كَثَبٍ, على مَقْرُبةٍ; **bring your chair ~r** قَرِّبْ كُرْسِيَّكَ أَكْثَرَ; **to follow ~ behind** تَبِعَ عن كَثَبٍ; **to hold sb ~** أَمْسَكَ شَخْصاً بِشِدّةٍ 2 (in approximation) على وَشْكِ; **to come ~st to an ideal/the truth** أَصْبَحَ أَقْرَبَ ما يَكونُ من كانَ مَثَلٍ أَعْلى \ الحَقيقةِ; **he came ~ to giving up/succeeding** على وَشْكِ الاسْتِسْلامِ \ النَجاحِ

C (**close by**) *adv phr* في مَكانٍ قَريبٍ, في الجِوارِ; **they live quite ~ by** يَعيشونَ في مَكانٍ قَريبٍ جِدًّا

D (**close on** also **close to**) *prep phr* ما يَقْرُبُ من; **there were ~ on 200 people** كانَ هُناكَ ما يَقْرُبُ من 200 شَخْصٍ

E (**close together**) *adv phr* على مَقْرُبةٍ من بَعْضِهِما البَعْضِ

F (**close up** also **up close**, **close to**) *adv phr* عن قُرْبٍ; **you have to look at it ~ up** يَجِبُ أَنْ تَنْظُرَ إلَيْها عن قُرْبٍ

G *n* 1 (BrE) (road) طَريق غَيْر نافِذٍ 2 (BrE) (of cathedral) فِناء الكاتِدْرائيّةِ

(Idioms) **it was a close shave** *or* **thing** (infml) نَجا بِأُعْجوبةٍ; **too close for comfort** [قَريبٌ بِشَكْلٍ يُسَبِّبُ الضَجَرَ]

close² /kləʊz/ **A** *vt* 1 (to shut) أَغْلَقَ ‹*a door, window*›; أَغْمَضَ ‹*one's eyes*› 2 (to deny access to) أَغْلَقَ ‹*a road, border, an airport*› 3 (to bring to an end) أَغْلَقَ ‹*a case, an investigation*›; خَتَمَ (i; خَتْم), أَنْهى ‹*a meeting, discussion*›; **the subject is ~d** أُغْلِقَ المَوْضوعُ 4 (to reduce) **to ~ the gap between rich and poor** ضَيَّقَ الفَجْوةَ بين الأَغْنياءِ والفُقَراءِ 5 (to conclude) أَبْرَمَ ‹*a deal*›; أَتَمَّ ‹*sale*› 6 أَغْلَقَ ‹*one's account*›

B *vi* 1 (to shut) «door» أُغْلِقَ; «eyes» أُغْمِضَ 2 (to decrease) «gap» ضاقَ (i; ضيق), قَلَّ (قِلّة) 3 (to end) «meeting, season»

انْتَهى; **the meeting will ~ at 10 pm** سَوْفَ يَنْتَهي الاجْتِماعُ 10 مَساءً **4** (to cease to operate) «factory, business» أُغْلِقَ **5** (Fin) «shares, market» أَقْفَلَ, أَغْلَقَ; **the market ~d down/up** أَقْفَلَ السوقُ على ارْتِفاعٍ \ انْخِفاضٍ; **the dollar ~d up/down against the euro** أَقْفَلَ الدولارُ على ارْتِفاعٍ \ انْخِفاضٍ مُقابِلَ اليورو **6** (to get closer) «pursuer, enemy» اقْتَرَبَ; **to ~ on sb** اقْتَرَبَ من شَخْصٍ

C *n* (end) خِتام, نِهاية; **at the ~ of trading** عند الإقْفالِ, عند نِهايةِ التَداوُلِ; **at the ~ of play** في خِتامِ المُباراةِ; **to come to** *or* **draw to a ~** وَصَلَ إلى النِهايةِ; **to bring sth to a ~** أَنْهى شَيْئاً

Phrasal verbs **close down** **A** «factory, business» أَغْلَقَ أَبْوابَهُ

B **~ down [sth]**, **~ [sth] down** أَغْلَقَ [شَيْئاً] نِهائيًّا ‹*a factory, business*›

• **close in** «enemy, pursuers» ضَيَّقَ الخِناقَ; **to ~ in on sb/sth** ضَيَّقَ الخِناقَ على شَخْصٍ \ شَيْءٍ; **darkness/winter was closing in~** اقْتَرَبَ حُلولُ الظَلامِ \ الشِتاءِ

• **close off**: **~ off [sth]**, **~ [sth] off** أَغْلَقَ [شَيْئاً] ‹*an area, a road*›

• **close up** **A** **1** «wound» الْتَأَمَ; «flower» قَفَلَ (i) **2** «trader» [أَغْلَقَ المَحَلَّ عند نِهايةِ الدَوامِ] **B** **~ up [sth]**, **~ [sth] up** **1** أَغْلَقَ [شَيْئاً] ‹*a shop, restaurant*› **2** سَدَّ [شَيْئاً] ‹*a hole, an entrance*›

• **close with**: **~ with [sb]** اشْتَبَكَ مع [شَخْصٍ] ‹*the enemy*›

closed /kləʊzd/ *adj* **1** (shut) ‹*door, eyes*› مُغْلَق; **'road ~'** 'الطَريقُ مُغْلَقٌ'; **'~ to the public'** 'مُغْلَقٌ أمامَ الجُمْهورِ'; **'~ to traffic'** 'مُغْلَقٌ أمامَ حَرَكةِ المُرورِ' **2** (restricted) ‹*system, society*› مُغْلَق; **to have a ~ mind** كانَ لَهُ عَقْلٌ مُنْغَلِقٌ \ غَيْرُ مُتَفَتِّحٍ

Idiom **behind closed doors** سِرًّا, خَلْفَ الأَبْوابِ المُغْلَقةِ, في الخَفاءِ

closed-circuit television /kləʊzd,sɜːkɪt 'telɪvɪʒ(ə)n/ *n* دائِرة تِلِفِزيونيّة مُغْلَقة

close-fitting /kləʊs'fɪtɪŋ/ *adj* ‹*shorts, blouse*› [مُنْطَبِق على مَقاييسِ الجِسْمِ بِدِقّةٍ]

close-fought /,kləʊs'fɔːt/ *adj* مُتَقارِب (من الصَعْبِ التَنَبُّؤُ بالفائِزِ)

close-knit /kləʊs'nɪt/ *adj* ‹*community, family*› مُحْكَم الأَوْصالِ

closely /'kləʊsli/ *adv* **1** (in space, time) ‹*to follow*› عن قُرْبٍ, عن كَثَبٍ **2** (in relationships) ‹*to cooperate, liaise*› بِشَكْلٍ وَثيقٍ, عن كَثَبٍ; **to work ~ with sb** عَمِلَ عن كَثَبٍ مع شَخْصٍ; **to be ~ related** «subjects, species» كانَ مُرْتَبِطاً بِشَكْلٍ وَثيقٍ; «people» كانَ مُرْتَبِطاً بِصِلةِ قَرابةٍ; **the experiments are ~ connected** التَجارِبُ مُرْتَبِطةٌ بِشَكْلٍ وَثيقٍ; **its flowers ~ resemble tulips** تُشْبِهُ زُهورُها الزَنْبَقَ إلى حَدٍّ كَبيرٍ **3** (thoroughly) ‹*to look, monitor, listen*› بِعِنايةٍ, بِدِقّةٍ; **a ~ guarded secret** سِرٌّ مَحْفوظ بِعِنايةٍ **4** (evenly) **a ~ contested election** انْتِخابات يَتَقارَبُ فيها المُتَنافِسونَ

close-run /kləʊs'rʌn/ *adj* ‹*race, contest*› [مُتَقارِب بِفارِقٍ ضَئيلٍ]

closet /'klɒzɪt/ *n* (AmE) (cupboard) خِزانة (خَزائِنُ, خِزانات); (for clothes) خِزانة مَلابِسَ

Idiom **to come out of the closet** [صَرَّحَ عن حالَتِهِ المِثْلِيّةِ الجِنْسيّةِ]

close-up /'kləʊsʌp/ *n* [صورة فوتوغرافيّة \ لَقْطة سينَمائيّة مَأْخوذة عن قُرْبٍ]

closing /'kləʊzɪŋ/ **A** *n* (of gate, door) إغْلاق; **Sunday ~** [عَدَمُ مُمارَسةِ المُتاجَرةِ يَوْمَ الأَحَدِ]

B *adj* ‹*minutes, scene*› خِتاميّ

closing date *n* تاريخ إغْلاقٍ

closing-down sale (BrE), **closing-out sale** (AmE) *n* بَيْع تَصْفِيةٍ, تَنْزيلات لِتَصْفِيةِ البَضائِعِ

closing time *n* وَقْتُ \ ميعاد إغْلاقٍ

closure /'kləʊʒə/ *n* إغْلاق

clot /klɒt/ **A** *n* جُلْطة

B *vi* (**-tt-**) «blood» تَجَمَّدَ

cloth /klɒθ/ *n* **1** [u] (fabric) قُماش **2** (for polishing, dusting) خِرْقة (خِرَق); (for floor) مِمْسَحة (مِمْسَحات, مَماسِحُ); (for drying dishes) مِنْشَفة (مَناشِفُ); (for table) مِفْرَش (مَفارِشُ)

clothe /kləʊð/ *vt* (*past tense, past participle* **clothed** or **clad**) كَسا (u; كَسْو) ‹*a child, model*›

clothes /kləʊ(ð)z/ *n pl* ثِياب, مَلابِس; **to put on/take off one's ~** لَبِسَ \ خَلَعَ ثِيابَهُ

clothes brush *n* فُرْشاة مَلابِسَ

clothes hanger *n* شَمّاعة مَلابِسَ

clothes line *n* حَبْل غَسيلٍ

clothes peg, **clothes pin** (AmE) *n* مِشْبَك \ مِلْقط غَسيلٍ

clothes shop *n* مَحَلّ مَلابِسَ

clothing /ˈkləʊðɪŋ/ *n* كِسْوة (كُسًى, كِسًى, كِساءٌ), لِباس (أَلْبِسة)

cloud /klaʊd/ **A** *n* **1** (in sky) سَحابةٌ, غَيْم (n coll; غُيوم) **2** (of smoke, dust) سَحابة **3** (of suspicion, gloom) سَحابة **B** *vt* **1** عَكَّرَ ‹*a mirror, liquid*› **2** شَوَّشَ (على) ‹*one's memory, judgement*›

(Idioms) **to be on cloud nine** كانَ في غاية السَعادةِ; **to be under a cloud** كانَ تحت الشَكِّ \ التَشْكيكِ

(Phrasal verb) **cloud over** «sky» اكْفَهَرَّ

cloud computing *n* حَوْسَبة سَحابِيّة

cloudiness /ˈklaʊdinəs/ *n* **1** (of sky) تَغَيُّم **2** (of liquids, glass) عَكَر

cloudless /ˈklaʊdləs/ *adj* ‹*sky, night*› صافٍ

cloudy /ˈklaʊdi/ *adj* (**cloudier**, **cloudiest**) **1** ‹*day, sky*› غائِم, مُلَبَّد بالغُيومِ **2** ‹*liquid*› عَكِر, غَيْر صافٍ

clout /klaʊt/ **A** *n* (infml) **1** (blow) ضَرْبة (ضَرَبات) **2** (power, influence) سَطْوة (سَطَوات) **B** *vt* ضَرَبَ بِقوّةٍ

clove /kləʊv/ *n* **1** (spice) كَبْش قَرَنْفُل **2** (of garlic) فَصّ (فُصوص), سِنّ (mf; أَسْنان)

clover /ˈkləʊvə/ *n* بِرْسيم

clown /klaʊn/ *n* مُهَرِّج

(Phrasal verb) **clown around** هَرَّجَ

cloying /ˈklɔɪɪŋ/ *adj* ‹*dessert, plot*› كَظيظ; ‹*plot*› مَعْسول

club /klʌb/ **A** *n* **1** (association) نادٍ (نَوادٍ, أَنْدِية) **2** (infml) (nightclub) نادٍ لَيْليّ **3** (for golf) عَصاً (f; عِصيّ), مِضْرَب الجولْف **4** (weapon) هِراوة (هَراوى) **5** (**clubs** *n pl*) (in cards) سَباتيّ **B** *vi* **to go ~bing** [ذَهَبَ إلى مَلاهٍ لَيْلِيّةٍ]

(Phrasal verb) **club together** «colleagues, members» تَشارَكَ

club car *n* (AmE) عَرَبة بوفيه (في القِطارِ)

club class *n* دَرَجة رِجالِ الأَعْمالِ

clubhouse /ˈklʌbhaʊs/ *n* **1** (building) مُنْتَدًى (مُنْتَدَيات) **2** (AmE) (locker rooms) غُرَف خَلْعِ المَلابِسِ

club sandwich *n* [ساندْوِتْش فاخِر بِهِ عِدّةُ طَبَقاتٍ من اللُحومِ والسَلَطاتِ]

cluck /klʌk/ *vi* «hen» قَرْقَ (i; قَرْق)

clue /kluː/ *n* **1** (hint, sign) دَليل (أَدِلّة, دَلائِلُ); **I haven't got a ~ what's going on** لَيْسَ لَدَيَّ أَدْنى فِكْرةٍ عَمّا يَدورُ **2** (in a crossword) مِفْتاح (مَفاتيحُ)

clued-up /ˌkluːdˈʌp/ *adj* (infml) **to be ~ about sth** [كانَ مُلِمّاً بِمَعْلوماتٍ كَثيرة حول شَيْءٍ]

clueless /ˈkluːləs/ *adj* (infml) بَليد

clump /klʌmp/ *n* **1** (of trees, grass, bushes, flowers) مَجْموعة (مَجاميعُ, مَجْموعات) **2** (of mud, earth) كُتْلة (كُتَل)

clumsily /ˈklʌmzɪli/ *adv* ‹*to move, dance*› بِعَدَمِ رَشاقةٍ ‹*to apologize, express sth*› دون بَراعةٍ

clumsiness /ˈklʌmzinəs/ *n* خُرْق

clumsy /ˈklʌmzi/ *adj* (**clumsier**, **clumsiest**) **1** (ungainly) ‹*person*› أَخْرَق (dipt; خُرْق); ‹*manner*› غَيْر مَصْقولٍ **2** (crude) ‹*attempt, effort*› غَيْر مُتْقَنٍ

clung /klʌŋ/ *past tense, past participle* ▸ **cling**

cluster /ˈklʌstə/ **A** *n* **1** (of buildings) مَجْموعة (مَجْموعات, مَجاميعُ); (of people) جَماعة; (of galaxies, stars) كُتْلة (كُتَل) **2** (of trees, flowers) مَجْموعة (مَجْموعات, مَجاميعُ); (of grapes, berries) عُنْقود (عَناقيدُ) **B** *vi* «people» تَجمَّعَ

clutch /klʌtʃ/ **A** *vt* أَمْسَكَ بِقوّةٍ ‹*a purse, child*› **B** *n* **1** (of a vehicle) دَوّاسة تَعْشيقٍ \ الدُبْرِياج **2** (control) **to fall into sb's ~es** وقَعَ في قَبْضةِ شَخْصٍ **3** (of eggs) حَضْنة **C** (**clutches**) *n pl* (control) بَراثِن

(Phrasal verb) **clutch at**: **~ at [sth/sb]** حاوَلَ أَنْ يُمْسِكَ ب [شَيْءٍ \ شَخْصٍ] ‹*a railing, lifebelt*› ▸ **straw**

clutch bag *n* [حَقيبة يَدٍ صَغيرة]

clutter /ˈklʌtə/ **A** *vt* (also **clutter up**) كَرْكَبَ (Egypt) (i; كَرْكَبة), كَوَّمَ ‹*a room, desk*› **B** *n* فَوْضى (f)

cluttered /ˈklʌtəd/ *adj* ‹*room, desk*› [مَمْلوء بِغَيْرِ نِظامٍ]

cm *abbr* = **centimetre(s)** سم (سَنْتِمِتر)

Co /kəʊ/ *abbr* 1 = **company** 2 = **county**

CO /siː'əʊ/ **A** *abbr* = **Colorado**

B *n* = **commanding officer** قائِد الوَحْدةِ

c/o /siː'əʊ/ *abbr* = **care of** بواسِطةِ

coach /kəʊtʃ/ **A** *n* 1 (of a team) مُدَرِّب 2 (BrE) (long-distance bus) (للمَسافاتِ الطَّويلةِ) حافِلة 3 (BrE) (of a train) عَرَبة 4 (for drama, voice) مُدَرِّس خُصوصيّ 5 (horse-drawn) عَرَبة

B *vt* 1 دَرَّب ‹a team, player› 2 مَرَّنَ ‹a pupil, child›

coach driver *n* (BrE) سائِق حافِلاتِ المَسافاتِ الطَّويلةِ

coach station *n* (BrE) مَحَطّة حافِلاتِ المَسافاتِ الطَّويلةِ

coach trip *n* (BrE) رِحْلة بِحافِلةِ المَسافاتِ الطَّويلةِ

coachwork /'kəʊtʃwɜːk/ *n* (BrE) (أَجْسام) جِسْم (هَياكِلُ), هَيْكَل

coal /kəʊl/ *n* فَحْم (فُحومات)

coalesce /ˌkəʊə'lɛs/ *vi* «substances, ideas» اِلْتَحَم, اِنْدَمَج

coalfield /'kəʊlfiːld/ *n* حَقْل فَحْمٍ

coal fire *n* نار فَحْمٍ

coalition /ˌkəʊə'lɪʃ(ə)n/ *n* اِئْتِلاف, تَحالُف

coalman /'kəʊlmən/ *n* (*pl* **-men**) فَحّام

coal mine /'kəʊl mʌɪn/ *n* مَنْجَم فَحْمٍ

coal miner *n* فَحّام

coarse /kɔːs/ *adj* (**coarser**, **coarsest**) 1 ‹texture, grass› خَشِن (خِشان); ‹cloth› غَليظ (غِلاظ); ‹sand, salt› كَثيف (كِثاف) 2 ‹person, manners› فَظّ (أَفْظاظ); ‹language› غَليظ (غِلاظ)

coast /kəʊst/ **A** *n* ساحِل (سَواحِلُ), شاطِئ (شَواطِئُ)

B *vi* (downhill) اِنْحَدَرَ, تَدَحْرَجَ; (slide) اِنْزَلَقَ

(Idiom) **the coast is clear** خَلا الجَوُّ

coastal /'kəʊst(ə)l/ *adj* ‹town, waters› ساحِليّ

coaster /'kəʊstə/ *n* 1 (drink mat) صَحْن واقٍ \ صَفيحة كَرْتونة تحت كَأْسٍ 2 (ship) سَفينة ساحِليّة

coastguard /'kəʊs(t)gɑːd/ *n* خَفَر السَواحِلِ

coastline /'kəʊs(t)lʌɪn/ *n* خَطّ الساحِلِ

coast to coast /ˌkəʊst tə 'kəʊst/ **A** *adj* (*before n* **coast-to-coast**) ‹broadcast, journey› الساحِل إلى الساحِلِ

B *adv* ‹to broadcast, advertise› على الصَعيدِ الوَطَنيِّ

coat /kəʊt/ **A** *n* 1 (garment) مِعْطَف (مَعاطِفُ) 2 (animal's) فَرْو (n coll; فِراء) 3 (of paint, varnish) طَبَقة (الطِلاءِ)

B *vt* **to ~ sth with** غَطّى شَيْئاً بـ ‹a surface, floor›

coat hanger *n* شَمّاعة مَلابِسَ

coating /'kəʊtɪŋ/ *n* غِلاف (أَغْلِفة), غِطاء (أَغْطِية)

coat of arms *n* (*n pl* **coats of arms**) شِعار نَبالةٍ

coat rack *n* شَمّاعة مَعاطِفَ

coax /kəʊks/ *vt* اِسْتَدْرَجَ, اِسْتَمالَ ‹an animal, a person›; **he had to be ~ed into telling us what happened** كانَ من الضَروريِّ أَنْ يُسْتَدْرَجَ لإِخْبارِنا عَمّا حَصَلَ

cob /kɒb/ *n* 1 (horse) [جَواد قَويّ قَصير القَوائِمِ للرُكوبِ] 2 (of maize) كوز (أَكْواز, كيزان) [وَللجَرِّ] 3 (BrE) (loaf of bread) (also **cob loaf**) [رَغيف مُسْتَدير الشَكْلِ]

cobalt /'kəʊbɔːlt/ *n* كوبالْت

cobbled /'kɒb(ə)ld/ *adj* ‹street, passage› مُرَصَّف بالحَصى

cobbler /'kɒblə/ *n* إِسْكافيّ

cobblestone /'kɒb(ə)lstəʊn/ *n* حَصاة (حَصَيات), حَصًى (n coll)

cobra /'kəʊbrə/ *n* كوبْرا (أَفْعى سامّة جِدًّا)

cobweb /'kɒbwɛb/ *n* نَسيج العَنْكَبوتِ

cocaine /kə(ʊ)'keɪn/ *n* كوكايين

coccyx /'kɒksɪks/ *n* (*pl* **coccyxes**) عُصْعُص (عَصاعِصُ)

cock /kɒk/ **A** *n* 1 (rooster) ديك (ديكة, دُيوك) 2 (male bird) ذَكَر الطَيْرِ 3 (vulg) (penis) قَضيب

B *vt* 1 (to raise) رَفَعَ (a); **to ~ an eyebrow** رَفَعَ حاجِباً; **to ~ an ear** أَرْهَفَ أُذُنَهُ; **the dog ~ed its leg** رَفَعَ الكَلْبُ رِجْلَهُ (للتَبَوُّلِ) 2 (to tilt) أَمالَ ‹one's head› 3 رَفَعَ الزِنادَ ‹a gun›

cock and bull story *n* [قِصّة مُخْتَلَقة]

cockatoo /kɒkə'tuː/ *n* (*pl* **cockatoos**) [نَوْع من البَبَّغاء ذو عُرْفٍ]

cockerel /'kɒk(ə)r(ə)l/ *n* ديك صَغير

cockeyed /'kɒkʌɪd/ *adj* (infml) (ridiculous) ‹plan, idea› سَخيف (سِخاف); (askew) ‹painting› مُنْحَرِف, مائِل

cockfighting /'kɒkfʌɪtɪŋ/ *n* مُصارَعة الدُيوكِ

cockle /'kɒk(ə)l/ *n* [مَحار قَلْبيّ الشَكْلِ صالِح للأَكْلِ]

cockney /'kɒkni/ *n* 1 (a native) [شَخْص وُلِدَ في شَرْقِ لُنْدُن] 2 [u] (dialect) [اللَهْجة الشَعْبيّة بِلُنْدُن]

cockpit /ˈkɒkpɪt/ *n* كابينة قِيادة

cockroach /ˈkɒkrəʊtʃ/ *n* صُرْصور (صَراصيرُ)

cocktail /ˈkɒkteɪl/ *n* 1▸ (drink) كوكْتيل (مَزيج من المَشْروباتِ الكُحوليّةِ وَغَيْرِ الكُحوليّة) 2▸ (food) [خَليط من الأَطْعِمةِ المُخْتَلِفةِ]

cocktail bar, **cocktail lounge** *n* حانة كوكْتيل

cocktail dress *n* فُسْتان كوكْتيل

cocktail party *n* حَفْلة كوكْتيل

cocktail stick *n* (BrE) عود كوكْتيل (عود خَشَبيّ صَغير يُشْبِهُ عودَ تَخْليل الأَسْنانِ)

cocky /ˈkɒki/ *adj* (**cockier**, **cockiest**) (infml) ‹*manner, look*› مَزْهوّ, مَغْرور

cocoa /ˈkəʊkəʊ/ *n* (powder) كاكاو; (drink) شَراب الكاكاو

coconut /ˈkəʊkənʌt/ *n* جَوْز الهِنْدِ

cocoon /kəˈkuːn/ *n* شَرْنَقة (شَرانِقُ)

cod /kɒd/ *n* (*pl* **cod**) قُدّ

COD /siːəʊˈdiː/ *n* = **cash on delivery** (BrE) = **collect on delivery** (AmE) الدَفْع عند التَسْليمِ

code /kəʊd/ **A** *n* 1▸ (cipher) شِفْرة; **a message in ~** رسالة مُشَفَّرة 2▸ (for identification) رَمْز (رُموز) 3▸ (in programming) كود 4▸ (also **dial code**) (Tel) رَمْز اتِّصالٍ 5▸ (of behaviour) مُدَوَّنة

B *vt* 1▸ شَفَّرَ ‹*an instruction, a message*› 2▸ أَعْطى رَمْزاً لِ ‹*a product, sample*›

codeine /ˈkəʊdiːn/ *n* كودين

code name *n* اسْم رَمْزيّ \ كوديّ

code word *n* كَلِمة الرَمْز

coding /ˈkəʊdɪŋ/ *n* 1▸ (of messages) تَشْفير 2▸ (for data processing) تَرْميز

coed = **coeducational** /kəʊˈed/ **A** *n* (AmE old use) [طالِبة في مَعْهَدٍ مُخْتَلَطٍ]

B *adj* ‹*college, school*› مُخْتَلَط

co-education /kəʊedjuːˈkeɪʃ(ə)n/ *n* تَعْليم مُخْتَلَط

co-educational /ˌkəʊedjuːˈkeɪʃ(ə)n(ə)l/ *adj* ‹*school, system*› مُخْتَلَط

coefficient /ˌkəʊɪˈfɪʃ(ə)nt/ *n* مُعامِل (مُعامِلات)

coeliac disease (BrE), **celiac** (AmE) /ˈsiːliak dɪziːz/ *n* ‹*disease*› مَرَض الاضْطِراباتِ الهَضْميّةِ

coerce /kəʊˈəːs/ *vt* أَجْبَرَ, أَكْرَهَ ‹*a witness, population*›; **to ~ sb into doing sth** أَكْرَهَ \ أَجْبَرَ شَخْصاً على فِعْلِ شَيْءٍ

coercion /kəʊˈəːʃ(ə)n/ *n* إجْبار, إكْراه

coexist /ˌkəʊɪgˈzɪst/ *vi* «species, peoples» تَعايَشَ

coffee /ˈkɒfi/ *n* قَهْوة; **a black/white ~** قَهْوة بِدونِ \ مع حَليبٍ

coffee break *n* اسْتِراحة قَهْوةٍ

coffee klatch *n* (AmE) حَفْلة قَهْوةٍ, اجْتِماع على قَهْوةٍ

coffee pot *n* إبْريق \ وِعاء قَهْوةٍ

coffee shop *n* 1▸ (café) مَقْهًى (مَقاهٍ) 2▸ (shop) [مَتْجَر يَبيعُ البُنَّ والقَهْوةَ]

coffee table *n* طاوِلة قَهْوةٍ

coffin /ˈkɒfɪn/ *n* تابوت (تَوابيتُ)

cog /kɒg/ *n* 1▸ (tooth) سِنّ التُرْسِ 2▸ (wheel) تُرْس (تُروس)

cognac /ˈkɒnjak/ *n* كونْياك

cognitive /ˈkɒgnɪtɪv/ *adj* ‹*theory, map, dissonance*› مَعْرِفيّ, إدْراكيّ; **a child's ~ development** نُموّ الطِفْلِ المَعْرِفيّ

cohabit /kəʊˈhabɪt/ *vi* «couples, partners» [عاش \ تعايَش عيشة الأَزْواجِ]

coherence /kə(ʊ)ˈhɪər(ə)ns/ *n* تَرابُط مَنْطِقيّ

coherent /kə(ʊ)ˈhɪər(ə)nt/ *adj* 1▸ ‹*argument, policy*› مُحْكَم, مَنْطِقيّ 2▸ ‹*speaker, patient*› مُلْتَحِم

cohesion /kə(ʊ)ˈhiːʒ(ə)n/ *n* تَماسُك

cohesive /kəʊˈhiːsɪv/ *adj* ‹*group, unit*› مُتَماسِك

cohort /ˈkəʊhɔːt/ *n* 1▸ (of a Roman legion) [كَتيبة عَسْكَريّة رومانيّة] 2▸ (in statistics) أَتْراب, أَتْرابيّة 3▸ (AmE) (friend) رَفيق (رِفاق, رُفَقاءُ)

coil /kɔɪl/ **A** *n* 1▸ (ring of rope, barbed wire) لَفّة; (of electric wire) مِلَفّ (مِلَفّات); (of hair) لَفيفة; (on a snake) لَفّة 2▸ (contraceptive) لَوْلَب (لَوالِبُ)

B *vt* لَفَّ (u; لَفّ) ‹*the wire, hair*›

C *vi* «smoke, river» الْتَوى

coin /kɔɪn/ **A** *n* قِطْعة نَقْديّة, عُمْلة مَعْدَنيّة

B *vt* ابْتَكَرَ ‹*a term, word*›; **to ~ a phrase** صاغَ \ اسْتَحْدَثَ تَعْبيراً جَديداً

(Idiom) **two sides of the same coin** وَجْهانِ لِعُمْلةٍ واحِدةٍ

coincide /ˌkəʊɪnˈsʌɪd/ *vi* «dates, events» تَصادَفَ

coincidence /kəʊˈɪnsɪd(ə)ns/ *n* صُدْفة (صُدَف)

coincidental /kəʊɪnsɪˈdɛnt(ə)l/ *adj* ‹*resemblance, occurrence*› اتِّفاقيّ, عَرَضيّ

coin-operated *adj* ‹*game, meter*› [يَعْمَلُ بِقِطَعِ النُقودِ المَعْدِنيّةِ]

coke /kəʊk/ *n* **1** (fuel) فَحْم الكوك **2** (**Coke®**) (infml) (drink) كوكا كولا **3** (infml) (cocaine) كوكايين

colander /ˈkʌləndə/ *n* مِصْفاة (مَصافٍ)

cold /kəʊld/ **A** *adj* **1** (not warm) ‹*water, air, night*› بارِد; **to be/feel ~** «person» شَعَرَ بالبَرْدِ; **it's ~ outside** الجَوُّ بارِدٌ بالخارِجِ; **the house was ~** كانَ البَيْتُ بارِداً; **the weather was very ~** كانَ الطَقْسُ بارِداً جِدًّا; **the food is getting ~** بَدَأَ الطَعامُ يَبْرُدُ **2** (distant) ‹*voice, smile, welcome*› بارِد, فاتِر; **to be ~ towards sb** كانَ فاتِراً تُجاهَ شَخْصٍ **3** ‹*colour*› بارِد **4** (infml) (unconscious) **to be out ~** كانَ فاقِدَ الوَعْيِ; **to knock sb out ~** أَفْقَدَ شَخْصاً الوَعْيَ **5** (in a guessing game) **you're ~** [أَنْتَ بَعيدٌ تَماماً عن الإجابةِ الصَحيحةِ]

B *n* **1** [u] (chilliness) بُرودة, بَرْد; **to feel the ~** شَعَرَ بالبَرْدِ \ بالبُرودةِ; **come in out of the ~** اُدْخُلْ بَعيداً عن البَرْدِ **2** (infection) زُكام, بَرْد; **a bad/heavy ~** بَرْد \ زُكام شَديد; **to have a ~** كانَ عِنْدَهُ بَرْدٌ; **to catch a ~** أُصيبَ بِنَزْلةِ بَرْدٍ

C *adv* **1** (without preparation) ‹*to speak, perform*› مُرْتَجِلاً, دون إعْدادٍ مُسْبَقٍ **2** (AmE infml) (abruptly) ‹*to stop*› فَجْأةً; **she was turned down ~** رُفِضَ طَلَبُها تَماماً

(Idioms) **in cold blood** بِلا رَحْمةٍ, بِدَمٍ بارِدٍ; **in the cold light of day** بعد تَفْكيرٍ وَتَرَوٍّ; **to get cold feet** جَبُنَ (u; جُبْن), فَقَدَ شَجاعَتَهُ; **to give sb the cold shoulder** عامَلَ شَخْصاً بِجَفاءٍ; **to leave sb cold** أَشْعَرَ شَخْصاً بالفُتورِ \ بالمَلَلِ; **to pour cold water on sth** ثَبَّطَ الهِمّةَ بِخُصوصِ شَيْءٍ

cold-blooded /ˌkəʊldˈblʌdɪd/ *adj* **1** ‹*animal*› ذو دَمٍ بارِدٍ (تَتَغَيَّرُ دَرَجةُ حَرارَتِهِ حَسَبَ دَرَجةِ حَرارةِ البيئةِ) **2** ‹*murder, killer*› عَديمُ الشَفَقةِ \ الرَحْمةِ

cold calling *n* الاتِّصال البارِد (أُسْلوب تَسْويقيّ عَبْرَ الهاتِفِ)

cold cream *n* كْريم مُرَطِّب

cold-hearted /kəʊldˈhɑːtɪd/ *adj* ‹*parent, killer*› بارِدُ القَلْبِ

coldly /ˈkəʊldli/ *adv* ‹*to reply, stare*› بِبُرودةٍ

coldness /ˈkəʊldnəs/ *n* **1** (of temperature) بُرودة **2** (of manner) فُتور, بُرودة

cold sore *n* قُرْحةُ الزُكامِ \ البَرْدِ

cold storage *n* تَخْزين بالتَبْريدِ, تَخْزين بارِد

cold store *n* مَخْزَن تَبْريدٍ

cold turkey *n* (infml) [التَوَقُّف المُفاجِئ عن المُخَدِّراتِ]

cold war *n* حَرْب بارِدة

coleslaw /ˈkəʊlslɔː/ *n* [سَلَطة الكُرُنْبِ \ المَلْفوفِ]

coley /ˈkəʊli/ *n* (BrE) [نَوْع من السَمَكِ]

colic /ˈkɒlɪk/ *n* مَغَص مِعَويّ حادّ

colitis /kəˈlʌɪtɪs/ *n* الْتِهاب القولون

collaborate /kəˈlabəreɪt/ *vi* «organizations, colleagues» تَعاوَنَ

collaboration /kəlabəˈreɪʃ(ə)n/ *n* تَعاوُن

collaborative /kəˈlab(ə)rətɪv/ *adj* ‹*research, approach*› تَعاوُنيّ

collaborator /kəˈlabəreɪtə/ *n* مُمالِئ

collage /ˈkɒlɑːʒ/ *n* (Art) فَنّ تَلْصيقيّ

collapse /kəˈlaps/ **A** *vt* (to fold up) طَوى (i; طَيّ) ‹*a pushchair, an umbrella*›

B *vi* **1** «building, tunnel, bed» تَهاوى, تَحَطَّمَ, انْهارَ; **the table ~d under the weight** تَحَطَّمَت الطاوِلةُ تحت وَطْأةِ الثِقْلِ **2** «person» سَقَطَ مَغْشيًّا عَلَيْهِ; **to ~ and die** سَقَطَ وَماتَ; **I ~d into a chair** اسْتَلْقَيْتُ على كُرْسيٍّ من شِدّةِ الإجْهادِ \ التَعَبِ **3** (to fail) «regime, negotiations, economy» فَشِلَ (a; فَشَل), انْهارَ **4** (in bankruptcy) «company, bank» انْهارَ **5** (to fold up) «pushchair, umbrella» انْطَوى **6** (to deflate) «lung» أُصيبَ باسْتِرْواحٍ

C *n* **1** (structural) انْهِيار (انْهِيارات), تَحَطُّم, تَهاوٍ **2** (of an institution, undertaking) انْهِيار (انْهِيارات); **to be on the verge of ~** كانَ على وَشْكِ الانْهِيارِ; **to be in danger of ~** واجَهَ خَطَرَ الانْهِيارِ **3** (of companies, banks) انْهِيار (انْهِيارات) **4** (physical/mental breakdown) انْهِيار; (deflation of lungs) اسْتِرْواح

collapsible /kəˈlapsəb(ə)l/ *adj ‹bed, table›* قابِل للطَّيِّ

collar /ˈkɒlə/ *n* 1 (of a shirt) قَبَّة; (of a coat) ياقة 2 (for an animal) طَوْق (أَطْواق)

collarbone /ˈkɒləbəʊn/ *n* تَرْقُوة (تَراقٍ)

collar size *n* مَقاس الياقةِ

collate /kəˈleɪt/ *vt* أَدْمَجَ *‹information, results›*

collateral /kəˈlat(ə)r(ə)l/ **A** *n* (security) ضَمانة **B** *adj ‹damage›* إضافيّ ,تَبَعِيّ ,جانِبِيّ

colleague /ˈkɒliːɡ/ *n* زَميل (زُمَلاءُ)

collect /kəˈlɛkt/ **A** *vt* 1 (to pick up) جَمَعَ (a; جَمْع) *‹firewood, eggs›*; **she ~ed up her belongings** جَمَعَتْ مُتَعَلِّقاتِها 2 (to bring together) جَمَعَ (a; جَمْع) *‹data, evidence, samples›*; **to ~ one's thoughts** اسْتَجْمَعَ أَفْكارَهُ; **over 50,000 signatures have been ~ed for the petition** تَمَّ جَمْعُ أَكْثَرَ من 50,000 تَوْقيعٍ على العَريضةِ 3 (as a hobby) جَمَعَ (a; جَمْع) *‹stamps, coins›* 4 (to accumulate) جَمَعَ (a; جَمْع) *‹rainwater, energy›*; **to ~ dust** تَراكَمَ عَلَيْهِ الغُبارُ 5 (to obtain) حَصَّلَ *‹taxes, the rent›* 6 (infml) (to win) فازَ (u; فَوْز ب) *‹an award, a prize›* 7 (to take away) جَمَعَ (a; جَمْع) *‹refuse, garbage›* 8 (to pick up) أَقَلَّ *‹a child, passenger›*; الْتَقَطَ *‹the keys›*; **to ~ a suit from the cleaners** اسْتَلَمَ بَدْلةً من مَحَلِّ التَّنْظيفِ; **I'll ~ you from the airport** سَوْفَ أُقِلُّكَ من المَطارِ

B *adv* (AmE) **to call sb ~** أَجْرى مُكالَمةً مع شَخْصٍ مَدْفوعةً من الطَّرَفِ المُتَلَقّي

C *vi* 1 (to accumulate) «dust, leaves» تَراكَمَ ,تَجَمَّعَ 2 (to assemble) «crowd» احْتَشَدَ ,تَجَمَّعَ 3 (to raise money) **to ~ for charity** جمع تَبَرُّعاتٍ خَيْرِيَّةً

D *v refl* **to ~ oneself** اسْتَجْمَعَ أَعْصابَهُ, اسْتَعادَ السَّيْطَرةَ على نَفْسِهِ

E **(collected)** *adj* 1 *‹person›* مُتَمالِك نَفْسَهُ ,رابِط الجَأْشِ, هادِئ 2 (assembled) **the ~ed works of Dickens** الأَعْمال الكامِلة لِديكِنْز

collect call *n* (AmE) مُكالَمة على حِسابِ المُتَلَقّي

collection /kəˈlɛkʃ(ə)n/ *n* 1 [u] (collecting of data, evidence) جَمْع; (of tax, rent, debts) تَحْصيل; **your car is ready for ~** سَيّارَتُكَ جاهِزةٌ للاسْتِلامِ 2 (of mail) [جَمْع البَريدِ من الصَّناديقِ] 3 (of refuse) جَمْع 4 (of records, DVDs, stamps) مَجْموعة (مَجْموعات); **a private art ~** مَجْموعة فَنِّيّة خاصّة; **a diverse ~ of people** مَجْموعة مُتَنَوِّعة من الناسِ 5 (of essays, stories) مَجْموعة (مَجْموعات) 6 (in fashion shows) مَجْموعة أَزْياءٍ 7 (collecting of money in church) جَمْع صَدَقاتٍ; (for charity) جَمْع تَبَرُّعاتٍ; (for a gift) مُساهَماتٍ; **to make** *or* **organize a ~ for sth/sb** جَمَعَ تَبَرُّعاتٍ لِشَيْءٍ \ لِشَخْصٍ

collective /kəˈlɛktɪv/ *adj ‹action, responsibility›* جَماعِيّ

collectively /kəˈlɛktɪvli/ *adv ‹to act›* بِشَكْلٍ جَماعِيٍّ; **~ we can bring a lot of pressure to bear** مَعاً نَسْتَطيعُ أَنْ نُحْدِثَ ضَغْطاً كَبيراً

collective noun *n* اسْم جَمْعٍ

collector /kəˈlɛktə/ *n* 1 (of stamps, antiques) جامِع (جامِعونَ); **a ~'s item** [نَموذَج نادِر] 2 (official) مُحَصِّل

college /ˈkɒlɪdʒ/ *n* (institution) مَعْهَد (مَعاهِدُ); (part of a university) كُلِّيّة; (AmE) (university) كُلِّيّة; (for vocational training) مَعْهَد للتَّدْريبِ المِهْنِيِّ

college of further education *n* (BrE) كُلِّيّة التَّعْليمِ المُسْتَمِرِّ

collegiate /kəˈliːdʒ(ɪ)ət/ *adj ‹life, athletics›* جامِعِيّ; *‹university›* لَدَيْهِ كُلِّيّاتٌ

collide /kəˈlaɪd/ *vi* «vehicles, planes» اصْطَدَمَ (ب)

collie /ˈkɒli/ *n* [كَلْب إِسْكُتْلَنْدِيّ ضَخْم لِرِعايةِ الغَنَمِ]

colliery /ˈkɒljəri/ *n* (*pl* **collieries**) [مَنْجَم فَحْمٍ بِمُنْشَآتِهِ وَأَجْهِزَتِهِ]

collision /kəˈlɪʒ(ə)n/ *n* اصْطِدام (اصْطِدامات)

colloquial /kəˈləʊkwɪəl/ *adj ‹term, language›* عامِّيّ; **~ Arabic** العامِّيّة العَرَبِيّة

collusion /kəˈl(j)uːʒ(ə)n/ *n* تَواطُؤ

cologne /kəˈləʊn/ *n* عِطْر (عُطور, عُطورات)

Colombia /kəˈlɒmbɪə/ *pr n* كولومْبِيا

Colombian /kəˈlɒmbɪən/ *n, adj* كولومْبِيّ

colon /ˈkəʊlən/ *n* 1 (of intestine) قولون 2 (in punctuation) نُقْطَتانِ

colonel /ˈkəːn(ə)l/ *n* (عُقَداءُ) عَقيد

colonial /kəˈləʊnɪəl/ *adj* ‹*rule, period*› اسْتِعْماريّ; (AmE) ‹*style*› اسْتِعْماريّ

colonialism /kəˈləʊnɪəlɪz(ə)m/ *n* اسْتِعْمار

colonialist /kəˈləʊnɪəlɪst/ **A** *n* مُسْتَعْمِر
B *adj* اسْتِعْماريّ

colonization, -isation (BrE) /ˌkɒlənʌɪˈzeɪʃ(ə)n/ *n* اسْتِعْمار

colonize, -ise (BrE) /ˈkɒlənʌɪz/ *vt* اسْتَعْمَرَ ‹*a territory, country*›

colonizer, -iser (BrE) /ˈkɒlənʌɪzə/ *n* مُسْتَعْمِر

colony /ˈkɒləni/ *n* (*pl* **colonies**) **1** (territory) مُسْتَعْمَرة
2 (community) (جَوالٍ, جاليات) جالية

color (AmE) ▸**colour**

Coloradan /ˌkɒləˈrɑːd(ə)n/, **Coloradoan** /ˌkɒləˈrɑːdəʊən/ *pr n, adj* [(شخص) من كولورادو]

Colorado /ˌkɒləˈrɑːdəʊ/ *pr n* **1** **the (river) ~** نَهْر كولورادو
2 (US state) كولورادو (f)

Colorado beetle *n* خُنْفُساء كولورادو

colossal /kəˈlɒs(ə)l/ *adj* ‹*statue, failure*› هائِل ,(ضِخام) ضَخْم

colour (BrE), **color** (AmE) /ˈkʌlə/ **A** *n* **1** (hue) (أَلْوان) لَوْن; **what ~ is it?** ما لَوْنُهُ؟; **the female is brown in ~** الأُنْثى بُنِّيَّةُ اللَوْنِ; **the houses were painted in bright ~s** طُلِيَت البُيوتُ بِأَلْوانٍ زاهِيةٍ; **to change ~** تَغَيَّرَ لَوْنُهُ **2** (hair dye) صِبْغة; (make-up) (أَلْوان) لَوْن; **lip ~** مُلَوِّن شِفاهٍ **3** (of skin) (أَلْوان) لَوْن; **people of all races and ~s** النّاس من كُلِّ الأَجْناس والأَلْوانِ **4** [u] (rosiness) احْمِرار; **to lose one's ~** أَصْبَحَ شاحِباً; **to put ~ into sb's cheeks** أَدّى إلى احْمِرارِ وَجْنَتَيْ شَخْصٍ **5** [u] (interesting quality) ميزة; **to give** *or* **lend ~ to sth** أَضْفى ميزةً على شَيْءٍ
B (**colours**) *n pl* **1** (of a team, jockey) أَلْوان; **the club's ~s are red and gold** أَلْوانُ النادي هي الأَحْمَرُ والذَهَبيُّ **2** (ship's flag) (أَعْلام) عَلَم; (regiment's flag) راية
C *vt* **1** (with coloured pencils, crayons) لَوَّنَ ‹*a picture*›; **to ~ one's hair** صَبَغَ شَعْرَهُ **2** (to influence) (على) أَثَّرَ ‹*one's views, judgement, perception*›
D *vi* «person, face» احْمَرَّ
(Idioms) **to show one's true colours** كَشَفَ عن وَجْهِهِ الحَقيقيِّ; **with flying colours** بِشَكْلٍ باهِرٍ

colour bar (BrE), **color bar** (AmE) *n* (BrE) تَمْييز عُنْصُريّ, تَفْرِقة عُنْصُريّة

colour-blind /ˈkʌləblʌɪnd/ (BrE), **color-blind** (AmE) *adj* مُصاب بِعَمى الأَلْوانِ

coloured (BrE), **colored** (AmE) /ˈkʌləd/ *adj* ‹*light, paper*› مُلَوَّن; **~ pencils** أَقْلام مُلَوَّنة

colourful (BrE), **colorful** (AmE) /ˈkʌləfʊl/ *adj* **1** ‹*clothes, flowers*› غَنيّ بالأَلْوانِ **2** ‹*character*› نابِض بالحَيَوِيّةِ; ‹*life, description*› مُثير

colouring (BrE), **coloring** (AmE) /ˈkʌlərɪŋ/ *n* **1** [u] (person's) لَوْن البَشَرةِ; (of animal) تَلْوين **2** (for food) مادّة مُلَوِّنة

colourless (BrE), **colorless** (AmE) /ˈkʌləlәs/ *adj* **1** (without colour) ‹*gas, liquid*› عَديم اللَوْنِ; ‹*face*› (شَواحِبُ) شاحِب
2 (bland) ‹*voice, description*› مُمِلّ

colour scheme (BrE), **color scheme** (AmE) *n* مُخَطَّط أَلْوانٍ

colour supplement (BrE), **color supplement** (AmE) *n* مُلْحَق مُلَوَّن

colt /kəʊlt/ *n* (مِهارة, أَمْهار) مُهْر

column /ˈkɒləm/ *n* **1** (pillar) (أَعْمِدة) عَمود **2** (of text) (أَعْمِدة) عَمود **3** (newspaper article) (أَعْمِدة) عَمود **4** (of tanks) (طَوابيرُ) طابور

columnist /ˈkɒləm(n)ɪst/ *n* كاتِب عَمودٍ

coma /ˈkəʊmə/ *n* غَيْبوبة

comatose /ˈkəʊmətəʊs/ *adj* ‹*state*› غَيْبوبة; ‹*patient*› في غَيْبوبةٍ

comb /kəʊm/ **A** *n* (مِشاط, أَمْشاط) مُشْط
B *vt* **1** **to ~ one's hair** مَشَطَ (i-u; مَشْط); **she's ~ing her hair** تُمَشِّطُ شَعْرَها **2** ‹*the area, wood*› مَشَّطَ
(Idiom) **to go through sth with a fine-toothed comb** مَحَّصَ شَيْئاً; **they went through the evidence with a fine-toothed ~** فَحَصوا الحُجَجَ وَمَحَّصوها

combat /ˈkɒmbat/ **A** *n* قِتال
B (**combats**) *n pl* مَلابِس مُمَوَّهة
C *vt* (-t-, -tt-) قاوَمَ, كافَحَ ‹*drugs, cancer*›

combatant /ˈkɒmbət(ə)nt/ *n, adj* مُقاتِل

combat jacket *n* سُتْرة قِتالٍ

combination /kɒmbɪˈneɪʃ(ə)n/ *n* دَمْج

combine¹ /kəmˈbʌɪn/ **A** *vt* 1 (جَمْع ;a) جَمَعَ ,أَقْرَنَ ‹*elements, activities*›; (مِزاج ,مَزْج ;u) مَزَجَ ‹*colours*›; **we ~d forces to raise funds** جَمَعْنا القُوى لِجَمْعِ الأَمْوالِ 2 (Culin) (خَلْط ;i) خَلَطَ ‹*the ingredients, flour*›

B *vi* 1 «elements, styles» انْضَمَّ 2 «firms, teams» اتَّحَدَ

combine² /ˈkɒmbʌɪn/ *n* تَحالُف

combined /kəmˈbʌɪnd/ *adj* ‹*operation, salary*› مُشْتَرَك

combo /ˈkɒmbəʊ/ *n* (infml) فِرْقة جاز \ رَقْصٍ صَغيرة

combustible /kəmˈbʌstɪb(ə)l/ *adj* قابِل للاحْتِراقِ \ للاشْتِعالِ

combustion /kəmˈbʌstʃ(ə)n/ *n* (احْتِراقات) احْتِراق

combustion engine *n* مُحَرِّك احْتِراقٍ

come /kʌm/ **A** *vt* (*past tense* **came**; *past participle* **come**) أَتى (أَتْي ,إِتْيان ;i), جاءَ (مَجيء ;i) ,أَقْبَلَ; **he's ~ a long way to see you** جاءَ مِن مَسافةٍ بَعيدةٍ لِيَراكَ

B *vi* (*past tense* **came**; *past participle* **come**) 1 (to move towards) «person, vehicle» جاءَ (مَجيء ;i) ,أَتى (أَتْي ,إِتْيان ;i); **I came on foot/by bus** جِئْتُ ماشِياً \ بالحافِلةِ; **he came into my office** أَتى إلى مَكْتَبي; **~ here!** تَعالَ هُنا!; **to ~ down the street** مَضى في الطَريقِ; **to ~ down the stairs** نَزَلَ الدَرَجَ; **to ~ running** جاءَ جَرْياً; **a woman came to the door** (inside) جاءَت امْرَأةٌ إلى البابِ; (outside) ذَهَبَت امْرَأةٌ إلى البابِ; **coming!** أنا قادِمٌ!; **the water came through the roof** تَسَرَّبَ الماءُ من السَقْفِ; **~ and have a look at this** تَعالَ وأَلْقِ نَظْرةً على هذا; **he came to me for advice** جاءَني طَلَباً للنَصيحةِ 2 «day, news, letter» (to arrive) جاءَ (مَجيء ;i) ,أَتى (أَتْي ,إِتْيان ;i), وَصَلَ (وُصول ;i); **when the time ~s** عِنْدَما يَحينُ الوَقْتُ; **~ Christmas/the summer** عِنْدَما يَأْتي عيدُ الميلادِ \ الصَيْفُ; **fashions ~ and go** المُوضةُ تَأْتي وتَذْهَبُ; **there's still the meal/speech to ~** ما زالَتْ هُناكَ الوَجْبةُ \ الكَلِمةُ الّتي سَتَأْتي لاحِقاً 3 (with purpose) «visitors, tradesmen» جاءَ (مَجيء ;i), حَضَرَ (حُضور ;u), أَتى (أَتْي ,إِتْيان ;i); **I've come for the rent** جِئْتُ لِأَخْذِ الإيجارِ; **my brother is coming for me at 10 am** سَوْفَ يَأْتي أَخي لِيَأْخُذَني في 10 صَباحاً; **they're coming for the weekend** سَوْفَ يَأْتونَ لِقَضاءِ عُطْلةِ نِهايةِ الأُسْبوعِ; **are you coming to the meeting/party?** هل سَتَحْضُرُ مَعَنا الاجْتِماعَ \ الحَفْلَ؟ 4 (to reach) «water, curtains» وَصَلَ (وُصول ;i), بَلَغَ (بُلوغ ;u); **the water came up to my knees** وَصَلَ الماءُ إلى رُكْبَتيَّ; **the curtains ~ down to the floor** تَدَلَّت \ وَصَلَت السَتائِرُ إلى الأَرْضِ 5 (to happen) حَدَثَ (حُدوث ;u), حَصَلَ (حُصول ;u); **the news came as a shock/surprise** جاءَت الأَخْبارُ كَصَدْمةٍ \ كَمُفاجَأةٍ; **to take things as they ~** لم يَسْتَبِق الأَحْداثَ; **how did you ~ to do that?** كيف تَأَتّى لَكَ أَنْ تَفْعَلَ ذلك؟; **how ~?** كيف حَدَثَ هذا؟; **that's what ~s of trying to do too much** هذا ما يَحْدُثُ عِنْدَما تُحاوِلُ أَنْ تَفْعَلَ الكَثيرَ 6 (to reach a certain state) أَصْبَحَ; **he came to know and admire him** تَعَرَّفَ عَلَيْهِ وأُعْجِبَ بِهِ; **it ~s with practice** يَأْتي بالمُمارَسةِ 7 (to be supplied) تَوَفَّرَ, يَأْتي (أَتْي ,إِتْيان ;i) أَتى; **this model ~s with a radio/sunroof** هذا الموديل مُزَوَّداً بِراديو \ بِفَتْحةِ سَقْفٍ; **the t-shirts ~ in three sizes and six colours** تَتَوَفَّرُ التي شيرْتات في ثَلاثةِ مَقاساتٍ وسِتّةِ أَلْوانٍ; **it ~s in gold or silver** يَأْتي مَصْنوعاً من الذَهَبِ أو الفِضّةِ 8 (in order) جاءَ (مَجيء ;i), أَتى (أَتْي ,إِتْيان ;i); **to ~ before/after sth** (in space, time) أَتى قبل \ بعد شَيْءٍ; **where did you ~?** ماذا كانَ تَرْتيبُكَ؟ 9 (infml) (to have an orgasm) وَصَلَ إلى هَزّةِ الجِماعِ

(Idioms) **come again?** (infml) أَعِدْ ما قُلْتَ؟; **come to that** (BrE) (infml) بالمُناسَبةِ; **come what may** مَهْما حَدَثَ; **he had it coming to him** (infml) نالَ جَزاءَهُ; **he's as stupid/honest as they come** (infml) هو غَبيٌّ \ شَريفٌ بِكُلِّ ما تَحْمِلُهُ الكَلِمةُ من مَعْنًى; **I don't know if I'm coming or going** (infml) شَعَرْتُ بالحيرةِ / بالتَوَهانِ

(Phrasal verbs) **come about** «change, situation, idea» حَدَثَ (حُدوث ;u), حَصَلَ (حُصول ;u), نَشَأَ (نَشْأة ,نُشوء ;a)

• **come across A** «message» وَصَلَ (وُصول ;i); «enthusiasm» ظَهَرَ (ظُهور ;a); **she ~s across well on TV** هي تَظْهَرُ بِشَكْلٍ جَيِّدٍ في التِلِفِزْيون **B** 1 **~ across [sth]** وَجَدَ [شَيْئاً] صُدْفةً ‹*an article, a website*› 2 **~ across [sb]** صادَفَ [شَخْصاً]

• **come after**: **~ after [sb]** تَعَقَّبَ \ طارَدَ [شَخْصاً]

• **come along** 1 (to arrive) «opportunity, bus, vendor» جاءَ

(i; مَجيء) **2** (to hurry up) **~ along!** أَسْرِعْ! **3** (to accompany sb) صاحَبَ, رافَقَ; **she came along too** جاءَتْ هي أَيْضاً; **I'm going into town - why don't you ~ along?** أنا ذاهِبٌ إلى المَدينةِ – لِماذا لا تُرافِقُني؟ **4** (to progress) «project, building work, pupil» تَقَدَّمَ; **her English is coming along well** يَتَحَسَّنُ مُسْتَواها في الإِنْجْليزيّةِ بِشَكْلٍ جَيِّدٍ

• **come apart** **1** (to fall apart) «book, shoes» تَمَزَّقَ **2** (to detach) «machine, appliance» انْفَكَّ, انْفَصَلَ

• **come around** (AmE) ▸ **come round**

• **come away** **1** (to leave) غادَرَ; **I came away very dissatisfied** غادَرْتُ وَأنا مُسْتاءٌ جِدًّا **2** (to move away) ابْتَعَدَ; **~ away from the edge** ابْتَعِدْ عن الحافّةِ **3** (to detach) «handle, part» انْفَكَّ, انْفَصَلَ

• **come back** **1** (to return) «person, letter» عادَ (u; عَوْدة), رَجَعَ (i; رُجوع); **would you like to ~ back with us?** هل تُحِبُّ أَنْ تَرْجِعَ مَعَنا؟; **they came back with a better offer** عادوا بِعَرْضٍ أَفْضَلَ **2** (to begin again) «pain, good weather» عادَ, عاوَدَ (u; عَوْدة, عَوْد) **3** (in fashion) «style, method» عادَ من جَديدٍ; **to ~ back into fashion** عادَ من جَديدٍ إلى المَوضةِ **4** (to revive) «memories» عادَ إلى الذاكِرة; **it's all coming back to me now** بَدَأْتُ أَتَذَكَّرُ كُلَّ شَيْءٍ الآنَ

• **come by** **1** (to drop in) «person» مَرَّ (u; مَمَرّ, مُرور, مَرّ), زارَ (u; زِيارة) **2** **~ by [sth]** (to get) حَصَلَ على [شَيْءٍ] ‹*money, a book*›

• **come down** **1** (to fall) «person» وَقَعَ (a; وُقوع), سَقَطَ (u; سُقوط), هَوى (i; هُوِيّ); «rain» تَساقَطَ, هَطَلَ (i; هُطول); «curtain» تَدَلّى; **he's really come down in the world** هَبَطَ مُسْتَواهُ الاجْتِماعيُّ حَقًّا **2** (to decrease) «prices, temperature» انْخَفَضَ; **car prices are coming down** أَسْعارُ السَيّاراتِ في انْخِفاضٍ **3** (to collapse) «building, ceiling, wall» تَحَطَّمَ, تَهَدَّمَ; **the bridge is coming down next month** سَوْفَ يُهْدَمُ الجِسْرُ الشَهْرَ القادِمَ **4** «plane» (to land) هَبَطَ (i-u; هُبوط); (to crash-land) هَبَطَ هُبوطاً اضْطِراريًّا

• **come down to**: **~ down to [sth]** (to be a question of) تَوَقَّفَ على [شَيْءٍ]; **when it ~s down to it** عِنْدَما يَأْتي وَقْتُ الجِدِّ

• **come down with**: **~ down with [sth]** مَرِضَ \ أُصيبَ ب [شَيْءٍ] ‹*the flu, chicken pox*›

• **come forward** «witness» تَقَدَّمَ; «volunteer» تَطَوَّعَ; **to ~ forward with a proposal** تَقَدَّمَ باقْتِراحٍ

• **come from**: **~ from [sth]** **1** (to be a native of) «person» كانَ \ انْحَدَرَ من [شَيْءٍ]; **he ~s from Morocco/New York** هو من المَغْرِبِ \ نيويورْك; **she ~s from a wealthy family/a poor background** تَنْحَدِرُ من أُسْرةٍ ثَريّةٍ \ أُصولٍ فَقيرةٍ **2** (to originate from) «money, word, noise» جاءَ \ أَتى من [شَيْءٍ]; **where does the money ~ from?** من أَيْنَ يَأْتي المالُ؟ **3** (to result from) نَجَمَ عن [شَيْءٍ]

• **come in** **1** (to enter) «person, water» دَخَلَ (u; دُخول); **~ in!** اُدْخُلْ!; **to ~ in from work/school** جاءَ من العَمَلِ \ المَدْرَسةِ **2** (to arrive) «plane, complaint, ship» وَصَلَ (i; وُصول) **3** (to be received) «money, calls, reports» أَتى (i; إِتْيان, أَتْي), جاءَ (i; مَجيء); **I didn't have any money coming in** لم يَكُنْ لَدَيَّ أَيُّ مَصْدَرٍ للدَخْلِ **4** (to be applied) «new system, rules» طُبِّقَ **5** (in fashion) «style» أَصْبَحَ موضةً \ على الموضةِ

• **come in for**: **~ in for [sth] to ~ in for criticism/praise** كانَ مَحَطَّ النَقْدِ \ المَدْحِ

• **come into**: **~ into [sth]** **1** (to inherit) وَرِثَ [شَيْئاً] ‹*money, an inheritance*› **2** (to be relevant) **money/age doesn't ~ into it** لا عَلاقةَ لَهُ بالمالِ \ بالسِنِّ

• **come off** **A** **1** (to detach) «button, wheel» انْفَكَّ; «paint» تَقَشَّرَ **2** (to be detachable) «part, panel» انْفَصَلَ **3** (infml) (to happen) «deal, trip» تَمَّ, تَحَقَّقَ (i; تَمام) **4** (infml) (to succeed) «plan, scheme» نَجَحَ (a; نَجاح) **5** (in deals, competitions) **to come off well/badly** كانَ أَداؤُهُ جَيِّداً \ سَيِّئاً; **he came off worst** خَسِرَ (a; خُسْر) **6** (to fall) «rider, cyclist» سَقَطَ (u; سُقوط), وَقَعَ (a; وُقوع) **B** **~ off [sth]** **1** (to fall off) سَقَطَ من على [شَيْءٍ] ‹*a horse, bicycle*› **2** (to stop taking) تَوَقَّفَ عن تَناوُلِ [شَيْءٍ] ‹*a drug, medication*›

• **come on** **1** **~ on!** (in disbelief) هذا غَيْرُ مَعْقولٍ!; (in exhortation) هَيّا، أَسْرِعْ! **~ on, hurry up!** أَسْرِعْ! هَيّا! **2** (to start working) «lights, heating» اشْتَغَلَ **3** (to begin) «headache, programme, night, cold» بَدَأَ (a; بَدْء) **4** (to appear) «band, actor» ظَهَرَ (a; ظُهور) **5** (to make progress) ▸ **come along** 4

• **come out** **1** (to become visible) «sun, stars» طَلَعَ (u; طُلوع), ظَهَرَ (a; ظُهور) **2** (to emerge) «person, animal, vehicle» خَرَجَ (u; خُروج); **he came out of it rather well** آلَ بِهِ الحالُ إلى وَضْعٍ جَيِّدٍ إلى حَدٍّ ما **3** (to open) «flowers, bulbs» تَفَتَّحَ **4** (to be put on the market) «book, movie, magazine» طُرِحَ في الأَسْواقِ **5** (to become known) «news, stories, reports» ظَهَرَ (a; ظُهور); **it came out that ...** اتَّضَحَ أنّ ... **6** (to result) نَتَجَ (i; نِتاج), نَجَمَ (u; نُجوم) **7** (to fall out) «hair, tooth, screw» سَقَطَ (u; سُقوط) **8** (to wash out) «stain» زالَ (a; زَوال) **9** (in calculations) نَتَجَ (i; نِتاج); **it ~s out at £750** كانَ النَاتِجُ £750 **10** (to turn out well) «photo, photocopy» ظَهَرَ واضِحاً **11** (BrE) (to strike) «workers» أَضْرَبَ; **to ~ out on strike** دَخَلَ في إضْرابٍ **12** (as being gay) «homosexual, lesbian» أَعْلَنَ أَنَّهُ مِثْليٌّ

• **come out with**: ~ **out with [sth]** تَفَوَّهَ ب [شَيْءٍ]; **whatever will she ~ out with next?** ما الّذي سَتَتَفَوَّهُ بِهِ في المَرّةِ القادِمةِ؟; **I came straight out with it** قُلْتُهُ بِطَريقةٍ مُباشِرةٍ

• **come over** **A** **1** (to drop in) زارَ (u; زِيارة) **2** (to travel) سافَرَ **3** (to convey an impression) ▸ **come across** **B** ~ **over [sb]** (to be affected by) «feeling» انْتابَ [شَخْصاً]; **what's ~ over you?** ما الّذي أصابَكَ؟

• **come round** (BrE), **come around** (AmE) **1** (to visit) زارَ (u; زِيارة) **2** (to circulate) «waiter, waitress» دارَ على الزَبائِنِ **3** (to regain consciousness) عادَ إلى وَعْيِهِ **4** (to occur) «summer, birthday» حَلَّ (i-u; حُلول) **5** (to change one's mind) غَيَّرَ رَأْيَهُ; **she eventually came round to my way of thinking** اقْتَنَعَتْ أخيراً بِطَريقَتي في التَفْكيرِ

• **come through** **A** **1** (to arrive) «news, call» وَصَلَ (i; وُصول) **2** (to be finalized) «divorce» صَدَرَ (i-u; صُدور); «funding» اعْتُمِدَ **B** ~ **through [sth]** (to survive) اجْتازَ [شَيْئاً] ‹*a crisis, an ordeal*›

• **come to** **A** (to regain consciousness) عادَ إلى وَعْيِهِ **B** ~ **to [sth]** **1** (to amount to) بَلَغَ [شَيْئاً]; **that ~s to $40** يَبْلُغُ الإجْماليُّ $40; **I never thought it would ~ to this** لم أَتَوَقَّعْ أبداً أنْ تَصِلَ الأمورُ إلى هذا الحَدِّ **2** (to be a question of) تَعَلَّقَ ب [شَيْءٍ]; **when it ~s to money/choosing wine** عِنْدَما يَتَعَلَّقُ الأَمْرُ بالمالِ \ باخْتِيارِ الخَمْرِ

• **come under**: ~ **under [sth]** **1** (to be subject to) **to ~ under attack** تَعَرَّضَ لِلهُجومِ; **to ~ under scrutiny** خَضَعَ لِلتَدْقيقِ **2** (to be classified as) انْدَرَجَ تحت [شَيْءٍ] ‹*a heading*›

• **come up** **1** (to appear) «sun, moon» طَلَعَ (u; طُلوع), بَزَغَ (u; بُزوغ) **2** (to sprout) «plants, bulbs» نَبَتَ (u; نَبْت) **3** (to approach) **to ~ up to sb** جاءَ إلى شَخْصٍ **4** (to draw near) «election, birthday» اقْتَرَبَ **5** (to arise) «problem, job, opportunity» ظَهَرَ (a; ظُهور) **6** (to be mentioned) «name, subject» وَرَدَ (i; وُرود), ذُكِرَ; **your name came up in conversation** وَرَدَ اسْمُكَ في الحَديثِ **7** (Law) «case» حانَ مَوْعِدُ النَظَرِ فيهِ

• **come up against**: ~ **up against [sth]** واجَهَ [شَيْئاً] ‹*a problem, resistance*›

• **come up for**: ~ **up for [sth]**: **to ~ up for re-election** حانَ وَقْتُ إعادةِ الانْتِخابِ; **his contract ~s up for renewal in May** سَوْفَ يَحينُ مَوْعِدُ تَجْديدِ العَقْدِ في مايو

• **come up to**: ~ **up to [sth]**: **to ~ up to sb's expectations** ارْتَقى إلى مُسْتَوى تَوَقُّعاتِ شَخْصٍ

• **come up with**: ~ **up with [sth]** **1** (to think of) فَكَّرَ في [شَيْءٍ], جاءَ ب [شَيْءٍ] ‹*an idea, a suggestion*› **2** (to produce) جاءَ \ أتى ب [شَيْءٍ] ‹*the money, information*›

• **come upon**: ~ **upon [sb/sth]** وَجَدَ [شَخْصاً \ شَيْئاً] ‹*an idea, a house*›

comeback /ˈkʌmbak/ *n* **1** (by actor, politician) عَوْدة; **to make a ~** سَجَّلَ عَوْدةً باهِرةً **2** (redress) إصْلاح (إصْلاحات); **to have no ~** لم يَمْلِكْ وَسيلةً للإصْلاحِ

comedian /kəˈmiːdɪən/ *n* مُمَثِّل كوميديّ

comedienne /kəˌmiːdɪˈɛn/ *n* مُمَثِّلة كوميديّة

comedy /ˈkɒmɪdi/ *n* (*pl* **comedies**) **1** (play, film) مَلْهاة, كوميديا **2** [u] (genre) كوميديا

comet /ˈkɒmɪt/ *n* مُذَنَّب (مُذَنَّبات)

comeuppance /kʌmˈʌp(ə)ns/ *n* (infml) **to get one's ~** نالَ عِقابَهُ \ جزاءَهُ

comfort /ˈkʌmfət/ **A** *n* **1** (ease) راحة **2** (prosperity) رَفاهِية; **to live in ~** عاشَ في رَفاهِيةٍ **3** (amenity) وَسيلة راحةٍ; **we offer every modern ~** نُقَدِّمُ كُلَّ وَسائِلِ الراحةِ الحَديثةِ; **the home ~s** وَسائِلِ الراحةِ المَنْزِليّة **4** (consolation) عَزاء, سَلْوى; **her religion/son was a great ~ to her** وَجَدَتْ عَزاءً كَبيراً في ابْنِها \ دينِها; **to take ~ from sth** وَجَدَ الطُمَأْنينةَ \ الراحةَ في شَيْءٍ; **it's a ~ to know that I am not alone** مَعْرِفَتي بِأَنّني لَسْتُ وَحيداً يَبْعَثُ على الاطْمِئْنانِ; **if it's any ~ to you** إذا كانَ هذا فيهِ عَزاءٌ لَكَ
B *vt* (to console) طَمْأَنَ (i; طَمْأَنة) ‹*a child*›; عَزّى, واسى ‹*a mourner, family*›

comfortable /ˈkʌmf(ə)təb(ə)l/ *adj* **1** ‹*sofa, hotel*› مُريح **2** ‹*guest, patient*› مُسْتَريح **3** ‹*lifestyle*› رَغْد; ‹*income*› مَيْسور **4** ‹*victory, majority*› واسع النِطاق

comfortably /ˈkʌmftəbli/ *adv* **1** ‹*to sit, dress*› بِراحةٍ **2** ‹*to live, retire*› بِيُسْرٍ

comforter /ˈkʌmfətə/ *n* **1** (AmE) (quilt) لِحاف (لُحُف) **2** (BrE) (baby's dummy) بَزّازة, مَصّاصة

comforting /ˈkʌmfətɪŋ/ *adj* ‹*words, sight*› مُواسٍ

comic /ˈkɒmɪk/ **A** *adj* ‹*event, verse*› هَزْلِيّ
B *n* **1** ▸**comedian** **2** (magazine) قِصَص مُصَوَّرة

comical /ˈkɒmɪk(ə)l/ *adj* ‹*appearance, sight*› مُضْحِك

coming /ˈkʌmɪŋ/ **A** *adj* ‹*year, election*› مُقْبِل; **this ~ Monday** الاثْنَيْنِ القادِم
B *n* **~ and going/~s and goings** مَجيء وذَهاب

comma /ˈkɒmə/ *n* فاصِلة (فَواصِلُ)

command /kəˈmɑːnd/ **A** *vt* **1** (to order) أَمَرَ (u; أَمْر); **to ~ sb to do sth** أَمَرَ شَخْصاً أَنْ يَفْعَلَ شَيْئاً; **the king ~ed that he be executed** أَمَرَ المَلِكُ بِإعْدامِهِ **2** (to have authority over) قادَ (u; قِيادة) ‹*forces, a regiment*› **3** (to inspire, obtain) حازَ (u; حِيازة; على), حَظِيَ (a; حُظْوة; ب) ‹*respect, loyalty*›; **she ~s respect in the scientific community** تَحظى باحْتِرامِ المُجْتَمَعِ العِلْمِيِّ **4** (fml) (to possess) حَصَلَ (u; حُصول; على) ‹*a majority, support*›; **to ~ a view of sth** أَطَلَّ على شَيْءٍ; **his work ~s outrageous prices** تُباعُ أَعْمالُهُ بِأَسْعارٍ فاحِشةٍ
B *n* **1** (order) أَمْر (أَوامِرُ); **to give/obey a ~** أَعْطى \ أَطاعَ أَمْراً **2** [u] (military control) قِيادة; **to be in ~** تَوَلّى القِيادةَ; **he was in ~ of land forces** كانَ قائِداً للقوّاتِ البَرّيّةِ; **the troops under his ~** القوّات تحت قِيادَتِهِ; **the enemy has ~ of the sea/air** العَدوُّ يُسَيْطِرُ على البَحْرِ \ الجَوِّ **3** [u] (mastery) سَيْطَرة; **he was in total ~ of the situation** كانَ مُسَيْطِراً على الوَضْعِ; **a good ~ of English** إجادة اللُغةِ الإنْجليزيّةِ بِشَكْلٍ تامٍّ; **she has an excellent ~ of Russian** تُجيدُ اللُغةَ الروسيّةَ بِشَكْلٍ جَيِّدٍ; **they drew on every resource at their ~** اسْتَغَلّوا كُلَّ المَصادِرِ تحت سَيْطَرَتِهِمْ **4** (in computing) أَمْر (أَوامِرُ)

commandant /ˌkɒmənˈdant/ *n* قائِد (قادات, قادة, قُوَّد, قوّاد)

commandeer /ˌkɒmənˈdɪə/ *vt* صادَرَ (لأَغْراضٍ عَسْكَريّةٍ) ‹*a vehicle, building*›

commander /kəˈmɑːndə/ *n* قائِد (قادة, قوّاد)

Commander of the Faithful *n* أَمير المُؤْمِنين

commanding /kəˈmɑːndɪŋ/ *adj* ‹*presence, lead*› مُسَيْطِر

commanding officer *n* قائِد وَحْدةٍ عَسْكَريّةٍ

commandment /kəˈmɑːndmənt/ *n* وَصيّة (وَصايا); **the Ten C~s** الوَصايا العَشْر

commando /kəˈmɑːndəʊ/ *n* (*pl* **commandos**) مِغْوار (مَغاويرُ)

commemorate /kəˈmɛməreɪt/ *vt* خلَّدَ \ أَحْيا الذِكْرى ‹*an anniversary, the victims*›

commence /kəˈmɛns/ **A** *vt* (fml) افْتَتَحَ ‹*a session, the festivities*›
B *vi* «negotiations, construction» بَدَأَ (a; بَدْء)

commencement /kəˈmɛnsm(ə)nt/ *n* **1** (fml) (beginning) بِداية **2** (AmE) (ceremony) حَفْلة تَخْريجٍ

commend /kəˈmɛnd/ *vt* **1** مَدَحَ (a; مَدْح) ‹*an act, a quality*› **2** (fml) أَوْصى (ب) ‹*a book, bill*›

commendable /kəˈmɛndəb(ə)l/ *adj* ‹*effort, performance*› جَدير بالثَناءِ, مُسْتَحْسَن

commendation /kɒmɛnˈdeɪʃ(ə)n/ *n* **1** (praise) ثَناء (أَثْنِية) **2** (Mil) (award, citation) تَنْويه **3** (in an exam, a competition) [تَقْدير جَيِّد جِدًّا]

comment /ˈkɒmɛnt/ **A** *n* **1** (remark) تَعْليق **2** [u] (discussion) تَعْقيب; **'no ~'** 'لا تَعْليقَ'
B *vi* «reviewers, judges» عَلَّقَ

commentary /ˈkɒmənt(ə)ri/ *n* (*pl* **commentaries**) **1** (in broadcast) تَعْليق (تَعاليقُ, تَعْليقات) **2** (analysis) تَحْليل (تَحْليلات, تَحاليلُ)

commentator /ˈkɒmənteɪtə/ *n* مُعَلِّق

commerce /ˈkɒmɜːs/ *n* تِجارة

commercial /kəˈmɜːʃ(ə)l/ **A** *adj* ‹*interest, success*› تِجاريّ **B** *n* إِعْلان (إِعْلانات)

commercial break *n* فاصِل إِعْلانيّ

commercialize, -ise (BrE) /kəˈmɜːʃ(ə)lʌɪz/ *vt* ‹*a product, technology*› تَجَّرَ; (pej) ‹*Christmas, society*› جَعَلَ تِجاريًّا

commercially /kəˈmɜːʃ(ə)li/ *adv* ‹*viable, successful*› تِجاريًّا

commercial traveller *n* مَنْدوب مَبيعاتٍ مُتَجَوِّل

commiserate /kəˈmɪzəreɪt/ *vi* «losers, relatives» تَعاطَفَ (مع); **to ~ with sb** تَعاطَفَ مع شَخْصٍ

commiseration /kəˌmɪzəˈreɪʃ(ə)n/ *n* شَفَقة

commission /kəˈmɪʃ(ə)n/ **A** *n* **1** (on sales, payments) عُمولة; **we charge 1% ~ on all transactions** نَتَقاضى عُمولةً قَدْرُها 1٪ على كُلِّ التَعامُلاتِ; **to work on ~** عَمِلَ بالعُمولةِ; **to earn a 10% ~ on each sale** رَبِحَ عُمولةً قَدْرُها 10٪ على كُلِّ عَمَلِيّةِ بَيْعٍ **2** (order) تَكْليف; **to give a ~ to an artist/composer** كَلَّفَ فَنّاناً \ مُلَحِّناً بِعَمَلٍ فَنّيٍّ **3** (committee) لَجْنة (لِجان); **a ~ of inquiry was appointed** تَمَّ تَعْيينُ لَجْنة تَحْقيقٍ; **to establish/appoint a ~** أَنْشَأَ \ عَيَّنَ لَجْنةً; **the United Nations High C~ for Refugees** المُفَوَّضيّة العُلْيا للأُمَمِ المُتَّحِدةِ لِشُؤونِ اللاجِئين **4** (in armed forces) تَكْليف, تَفْويض (تَفْويضات); **to receive one's ~** مُنِحَ \ قُلِّدَ رُتْبةَ ضابِطٍ في الجَيْش; **to resign one's ~** تَرَكَ العَمَلَ في الجَيْشِ **5** [u] (operational state) **to be in/out of ~** «ship, reactor, plant» كانَ في الخِدْمةِ \ خارِجَ نِطاقِ الخِدْمةِ

B *vt* **1** (to order) طَلَبَ (u; طَلَب, مَطْلَب) ‹*a report, work, portrait*›; **the council ~ed a portrait of the chairman** طَلَبَ المَجْلِسُ عَمَلَ بورْتْريه للرَّئيسِ **2** ‹*an officer*› فَوَّضَ; **a ~ed officer** ضابِط مُفَوَّض **3** (to bring into service) ‹*a ship, reactor, plant*› أَدْخَلَ في الخِدْمةِ

commissioner /kəˈmɪʃ(ə)nə/ *n* **1** (commission member) عُضْو لَجْنةٍ; **an EU C~** مُفَوَّض الاتِّحادِ الأوروبّيّ **2** (BrE) (in police) مَأْمور (شُرْطةٍ)

commit /kəˈmɪt/ *vt* (**-tt-**) **1** ارْتَكَبَ ‹*a crime, murder, sin*›; **to ~ suicide** انْتَحَرَ **2** **to ~ oneself** أَلْزَمَ نَفْسَهُ, الْتَزَمَ **3** رَصَدَ (u; رَصْد) ‹*funds, time*›

commitment /kəˈmɪtm(ə)nt/ *n* **1** (appointment) الْتِزام, تَعَهُّد (الْتِزامات) **2** [u] (to a cause) الْتِزام, تَعَهُّد

committed /kəˈmɪtɪd/ *adj* ‹*Christian, socialist*› مُلْتَزِم

committee /kəˈmɪti/ *n* لَجْنة (لَجْنات, لِجان, لِجَن)

commodity /kəˈmɒdɪti/ *n* (*pl* **commodities**) سِلْعة (سِلَع)

common /ˈkɒmən/ **A** *adj* **1** (frequent) ‹*problem, name, mistake*› شائِع; **it's ~ practice** هو مُمارَسةٌ شائِعةٌ; **a word in ~ use** كَلِمة شائِعة الاسْتِخْدام **2** (shared) ‹*interest, ancestor, aim*› مُشْتَرَك; **it's ~ knowledge** هو أَمْرٌ مَعْروفٌ; **an attempt to find ~ ground** مُحاوَلة لِإيجادِ أَرْضيّةٍ مُشْتَرَكةٍ; **the ~ good** الصالِح العامّ **3** (average, ordinary) ‹*man, woman*› عاديّ; **the ~ people** عامّة الناسِ **4** (BrE pej) (vulgar) عامّيّ, سوقيّ; **she sounds/looks so ~** تَبْدو سوقيّةً جِدًّا **5** (to be expected) ‹*courtesy, decency*› شائِع, عامّ

B *n* (public land) أَرْض عامّة \ مُشاع

C **1** (**the Commons** *n pl*) (in the UK) مَجْلِس العُموم **2** (**Commons** also **dining commons** *n sing*) [قاعة طَعام للطُلّابِ]

Idioms **as common as muck** (BrE infml) سوقيّ; **to have the common touch** كانَ يَتَمَتَّعُ بروحِ البَساطةِ; **in common** مُشْتَرَك; **to have sth in ~ with sb** كانَ هُناكَ شَيْءٌ مُشْتَرَكٌ بَيْنَهُ وبَيْنَ شَخْصٍ; **in ~ with** على غِرارِ

Common Agricultural Policy *n* السِياسة الزِراعيّة المُشْتَرَكة

common cold *n* زُكام, بَرْد, نَزْلة بَرْدٍ

common denominator *n* قاسِم مُشْتَرَك; **it is designed to appeal to the lowest common denominator** (pej) صُمِّمَت لِلجُمْهورِ السوقيِّ

common law *n* قانون مُشْتَرَك \ عامّ; **under common law** طِبْقاً للقانونِ المُشْتَرَكِ

common-law husband *n* زَوْج عُرْفيّ ≈ (زَوْج غَيْر رَسْميٍّ)

common-law marriage *n* زَواج عُرْفيّ ≈ (زَواج غَيْر رَسْميٍّ)

common-law wife *n* زَوْجة عُرْفيّة ≈ (زَوْجة غير رَسْميّة)

commonly /ˈkɒmənli/ *adv* غالِباً

Common Market *n* السوق المُشْتَرَكة

common-or-garden /ˌkɒmənɔːˈɡɑːd(ə)n/ *adj* (BrE infml) ‹*variety, plant*› عاديّ

commonplace /ˈkɒmənpleɪs/ *adj* 1 (widespread) ‹*object, occurrence*› مُبْتَذَل 2 (trite) بَديهيّ

common room *n* غُرْفة اسْتِراحةٍ

common sense *n* العَقْل \ الإدْراك السَليم

Commonwealth /ˈkɒmənwɛlθ/ *n* (**the Commonwealth**) الكومَنْوِلْث

commotion /kəˈməʊʃ(ə)n/ *n* 1 (noise) هَرْج 2 (disturbance) اضْطِراب (اضْطِرابات); **to cause a ~** سَبَّبَ اضْطِراباً

communal /ˈkɒmjʊn(ə)l, kəˈmjuːn(ə)l/ *adj* 1 (shared) ‹*area, ownership*› مُشْتَرَك; ‹*life*› جَماعيّ 2 (inter-community) ‹*violence, riots*› طائِفيّ

commune /ˈkɒmjuːn/ *n* [جَماعة من الناسِ يَعيشونَ مَعاً وَيَتَقاسَمونَ المَسْؤوليّاتِ]

communicable /kəˈmjuːnɪkəb(ə)l/ *adj* 1 ‹*idea, emotion*› قابِل للتَعْبيرِ عَنْهُ \ للشَرْحِ 2 ‹*disease, virus*› مُعْدٍ

communicate /kəˈmjuːnɪkeɪt/ A *vi* «people, devices» اتَّصَلَ (بـ)
B *vt* نَقَلَ (u; نَقْل) ‹*information, ideas*›

communication /kəmjuːnɪˈkeɪʃ(ə)n/ A *n* (of information) اتِّصال ,إعْلام (اتِّصالات)
B (**communications**) *n pl* وَسائِل نَقْل

communication skills *n* مَهارات الاتِّصالِ \ التَواصُلِ

communicative /kəˈmjuːnɪkətɪv/ *adj* ‹*speaker, style*› صَريح (صَرائِحُ, صُرَحاءُ)

communion /kəˈmjuːnjən/ *n* 1 (also **Holy communion**) العَشاء الرَبّانيّ 2 (fellowship) عِشْرة

communism /ˈkɒmjʊnɪz(ə)m/ *n* شُيوعيّة

communist /ˈkɒmjʊnɪst/ *n, adj* شُيوعيّ

community /kəˈmjuːnɪti/ *n* (*pl* **communities**) جَماعة; **the business/scientific ~** مُجْتَمَع الأَعْمالِ \ المُجْتَمَع العِلْميّ

community centre, community center (AmE) *n* مَرْكَز اجْتِماعيّ

community group *n* مَجْموعة اجْتِماعيّة

community service *n* خِدْمة المُجْتَمَعِ

commute /kəˈmjuːt/ A *vt* عَدَّلَ ‹*the sentence*›
B *vi* [سافَرَ يَوْميًّا إلى مَكانِ العَمَلِ]

commuter /kəˈmjuːtə/ *n* مُسافِر ,راكِب (شَخْص يُسافِرُ يَوْميًّا إلى مَكانِ العَمَلِ)

Comoros /ˈkɒm(ə)rəʊz/ *pr n* جُزُر القَمَرِ

compact¹ /kəmˈpakt/ *adj* 1 (compressed) ‹*snow, mass*› مَرْصوص 2 (small) ‹*building, camera*› صَغير (صِغار, صُغَراءُ)

compact² /ˈkɒmpakt/ *n* 1 (formal agreement) اتِّفاق (اتِّفاقات)
2 (also **powder compact**) (small case) بودْرة مَضْغوطة

companion /kəmˈpanjən/ *n* رَفيق (رُفَقاءُ, رِفاق)

companionship /kəmˈpanjənʃɪp/ *n* صُحْبة ,مُرافَقة

company /ˈkʌmp(ə)ni/ *n* (*pl* **companies**) 1 (business) شَرِكة; **an insurance/oil ~** شَرِكة تَأْمينٍ \ بِتْرولٍ 2 [u] (companionship) صُحْبة ,رُفْقة; **to keep sb ~** رافَقَ شَخْصاً; **I enjoy her ~** أَسْتَمْتِعُ بِرُفْقَتِها; **to be good ~** كانَ رَفيقاً جَيِّداً; **to part ~ with sb** افْتَرَقَ عن شَخْصٍ 3 [u] (society) رُفْقة; **in ~ with sb** بِرُفْقةِ شَخْصٍ; **he doesn't know how to behave properly in ~** لا يَعْلَمُ كيف يَتَصَرَّفُ بِشَكْلٍ لائِقٍ أمام الناسِ; **he got into bad ~** تَعَرَّفَ على صُحْبةٍ سَيِّئةٍ; **the assembled ~** الناس المُجْتَمِعونَ; **you're in good ~** نَحْنُ في قارِبٍ واحِدٍ 4 [u] (fml) (visitors) زُوّار; **we're expecting ~** نَتَوَقَّعُ زُوّاراً 5 (of actors, players) فِرْقة (فِرَق) 6 (of soldiers) سَرِيّة (سَرايا) 7 (of a ship) طاقِم (طَواقِمُ)

company car *n* سَيّارة شَرِكةٍ

comparable /ˈkɒmp(ə)rəb(ə)l/ *adj* ‹*level, size*› مُماثِل

comparative /kəmˈparətɪv/ A *adj* 1 ‹*analysis, literature*› مُقارَن 2 ‹*adjective, adverb*› [في صيغةِ التَفْضيلِ]
B *n* صيغة التَفْضيلِ; **'better' is the ~ of 'good'** 'أَحْسَنُ' هي صيغةُ التَفْضيلِ لِ 'جَيِّد'

comparatively /kəmˈparətɪvli/ *adv* ‹*small, easy*› نِسْبيًّا

compare /kəmˈpɛː/ A *vt* 1 (to contrast) قارَنَ ‹*results, prices*›; **~d with** *or* **to** مُقاس بِ; **to ~ notes** تَبادَلَ الآراءَ 2 (to liken)

to ~ sth/sb to sth/sb قارَنَ شَيْئاً \ شَخْصاً بِشَيْءٍ \ بِشَخْصٍ **B** *vi* «products, prices» قورِنَ; **how do they ~?** ما وَجْهُ الشَّبَهِ بَيْنَهُمْ؟; **the car's performance ~s favourably with cheaper models** أداءُ السَّيارةِ أَحْسَنُ مُقارَنةً بِنَماذِجَ أَرْخَص

comparison /kəm'parıs(ə)n/ *n* مُقارَنة; **in** *or* **by ~ with** بالمُقارَنةِ مع; **to make** *or* **draw a ~** أَجْرى مُقارَنةً

compartment /kəm'pɑːtm(ə)nt/ *n* **1** (container) قِسْم \ حَيِّز **2** (in a train) مَقْصورة (مَقْصورات ,مَقاصيرُ) للتَخْزينِ

compass /'kʌmpəs/ *n* **1** (in navigation) بوصَلة **2** (also **compasses**, *pl*) (in maths) بَرْجَل ,بِرْكار ,(فَراجيرُ) فِرْجار (بَراجِلُ); **a pair of ~es** بَرْجَل ,بِرْكار ,فِرْجار

compassion /kəm'paʃ(ə)n/ *n* عَطْف ,تَعَطُّف ,شَفَقة ,رَأْفة

compassionate /kəm'paʃ(ə)nət/ *adj* ‹person, nature› شَفيق, رَؤوف ,مُشْفِق

compass point *n* اتِّجاه البوصَلةِ

compatibility /kəm,patı'bılıti/ *n* **1** (between people) تَوافُق, **2** (between computers) انْسِجام تَوافُق

compatible /kəm'patıb(ə)l/ *adj* **1** ‹partners, policies› مُتَوافِق, مُنْسَجِم; **a donor from a ~ blood group** مُتَبَرِّع من فَصيلةِ دَمٍ مُتَوافِقةٍ مع دَمِ المَريضِ **2** (Comput) مُتَوافِق; **Mac ~ hardware** مُعَدّات مُتَوافِقة مع جِهازِ ماك

compel /kəm'pɛl/ *vt* (**-ll-**) أَجْبَرَ (على) ,أَكْرَهَ (على); **to ~ sb to do sth** أَجْبَرَ شَخْصاً على فِعْلِ شَيْءٍ

compelling /kəm'pɛlıŋ/ *adj* **1** ‹reason› قَهْرِيّ; ‹evidence› لا يُقاوَمُ **2** ‹story, performance› مُقْنِع ,مُفْحِم

compendium /kəm'pɛndıəm/ *n* (*pl* **compendiums** or **compendia**) **1** (handbook) مَرْجع (مَراجعُ) **2** (BrE) **a ~ of games** [مَجْموعة أَلْعابٍ في عُلْبةٍ واحدةٍ]

compensate /'kɒmpɛnseıt/ **A** *vt* عَوَّضَ ‹a victim, claimant› **B** *vi* **to ~ for the damage** عَوَّضَ عن الضَرَرِ

compensation /kɒmpɛn'seıʃ(ə)n/ *n* **1** (financial) تَعْويض (تَعْويضات); (moral) تَرْضِية; **he was awarded £3,000 ~ for his injuries** مُنِحَ £3,000 كَتَعْويضٍ عن إصاباتِهِ; **coming second was no ~ for all the training** لم يَكُن احْتِلالُ المَرْتَبةِ الثانيةِ تَعْويضاً عن كُلِّ التَدْريباتِ **2** (pay) أَجْر (أُجور)

compete /kəm'piːt/ **A** *vi* **1** (for a job, prize) تَنافَسَ; **to ~ for an award** تَنافَسَ على جائزةٍ **2** (in sport) تَنافَسَ ,تَبارى; **to ~ in the relay** تَبارى في سِباقِ البَدَلِ **B** (**competing**) *adj* ‹interests, claims› مُتَضارِب

competence /'kɒmpıt(ə)ns/ *n* **1** (ability) جَدارة ,كَفاءة **2** (of legal system) سُلْطة ,أَهْلِيّة

competent /'kɒmpıt(ə)nt/ *adj* **1** ‹worker› كُفْء (كِفاء ,أَكْفاء); ‹performance› مُتَمَكِّن **2** ‹court, authority› مُخْتَصّ

competition /kɒmpı'tıʃ(ə)n/ *n* **1** (rivals) [u] مُنافَسة **2** (contest) مُنافَسة ,(مُبارَيات) مُباراة; **to enter a ~** دَخَلَ مُباراةً \ مُنافَسةً; **I have decided to enter the gymnastics ~** قَرَّرْتُ دُخولَ مُنافَسةِ الجُمْباز

competitive /kəm'pɛtıtıv/ *adj* **1** ‹person› يَمْلِكُ روحَ المُنافَسةِ \ التَنافُس; ‹environment› تَنافُسِيّ **2** ‹price, product› تَنافُسِيّ

competitiveness /kəm'pɛtıtıvnəs/ *n* **1** (of a company) قُدْرة تَنافُسيّة **2** (of a person) تَنافُسيّة

competitor /kəm'pɛtıtə/ *n* **1** (in contest) مُنافِس **2** (in commerce) مُنافِس

compilation /kɒmpı'leıʃ(ə)n/ *n* مُصَنَّف (مُصَنَّفات)

compilation album *n* أَلْبوم مُنَوَّعاتٍ \ تَجْميعٍ

compile /kəm'pʌıl/ *vt* **1** صَنَّفَ ‹a list, report› **2** جَمَّعَ ‹data, evidence›

complacency /kəm'pleıs(ə)nsi/ *n* اعْتِداد \ غُرور \ إعْجاب بالنَفْسِ; **there is no room for ~** لا مَجالَ للاعْتِدادِ بالنَفْسِ

complacent /kəm'pleıs(ə)nt/ *adj* مُعْتَدّ \ مَغْرور \ مُعْجَب بِنَفْسِهِ

complain /kəm'pleın/ **A** *vt* شَكا ,اشْتَكى (u; شَكْوى); **I ~ed that the water was cold** اشْتَكَيْتُ أنّ الماءَ كانَ بارِداً **B** *vi* **1** (to protest informally) «neighbours» تَذَمَّرَ ,اشْتَكى; (to protest officially) «customers» قَدَّمَ شَكْوى; **'how's life?' — 'oh, I can't ~'** كَيفَ الحَياةُ مَعَكَ؟ — كُلُّ شَيْءٍ على ما يُرامُ'; **turn the music down, the neighbours will ~** اخْفِضْ صَوْتَ الموسيقى، سَوْفَ يَشْتَكي الجيرانُ; **the neighbours ~ed to the police about the noise** اشْتَكى الجيرانُ للشُرْطةِ بِخُصوصِ الضَوْضاءِ **2** (to inform about) «patients» اشْتَكى; **he ~ed of chest pains** اشْتَكى من آلامٍ في الصَدْرِ

complainant /kəm'pleɪnənt/ *n* مُدَّعٍ

complaint /kəm'pleɪnt/ *n* **1** (official/unofficial protest) شَكْوى (f; شَكاوى); **I've no ~s** لَيسَ لَدَيَّ أَيُّ شَكاوى; **there have been ~s about the noise** كانَتْ هُناكَ شَكاوى حول الضَوْضاءِ; **to make** *or* **lodge a ~ against the management** قَدَّمَ شَكْوى ضدّ الإدارةِ; **to have grounds** *or* **cause for ~** كانَ لَدَيْهِ أَسْبابٌ للشكْوى **2** (ailment) مَرَض (أَمْراض), عِلّة (عِلَل)

complement **A** *n* /'kɒmplɪm(ə)nt/ **1** (accompaniment) تَتِمّة, تَكْمِلة; **to be a ~ to sth** كانَ تَكْملةً لِشَيْءٍ **2** (quota, number) عَدَد تامّ; **an orchestra with a full ~ of instruments** أورْكِسْترا بِمَجْموعةٍ كامِلةٍ من الآلاتِ

B *vt* /'kɒmplɪmɛnt/ كَمَّلَ ‹*information, food*›

complementary /kɒmplɪ'mɛnt(ə)ri/ *adj* ‹*colour, role*› مُكَمِّل, تَكْميليّ

complementary medicine *n* طِبّ تَكْميليّ

complete /kəm'pliːt/ **A** *adj* **1** (total) ‹*failure, freedom*› كامِل, تامّ; **I wouldn't tell a ~ stranger** لن أُخْبِرَ شَخْصاً غَريباً تَماماً; **it came as a ~ surprise** جاءَ كَمُفاجَأةٍ تامّةٍ; **that's ~ and utter nonsense** ذلك هو الهُراءُ بِعَيْنِهِ; **they showed a ~ lack of concern** أَظْهَروا عَدَمَ الاهْتِمامِ التامِّ **2** (finished) مُكْتَمِل; **the repairs are now ~** اكْتَمَلَت الإصْلاحاتُ الآنَ **3** (entire) ‹*set, works*› مُكْتَمِل, كامِل; **my life was ~** كانَتْ حَياتي كامِلةً \ مُكْتَمِلةً; **it comes ~ with batteries/instructions** يَأْتي كامِلاً مع البَطّاريّاتِ \ التَعْليماتِ; **he has a ~ collection** لَدَيْهِ مَجْموعةٌ كامِلةٌ

B *vt* **1** (to finish) أَتَمَّ, أَنْهى, أَكْمَلَ ‹*the work, a course, an investigation*›; **the work was ~d on time/late** تَمَّ إِنْجازُ العَمَلِ في مَوْعِدِهِ \ مُتَأَخِّراً **2** (to fill in) أَكْمَلَ, عَبَّأَ ‹*a form, questionnaire*› **3** (to make whole) أَكْمَلَ ‹*a collection*›

completely /kəm'pliːtli/ *adv* ‹*different, new*› تَماماً, كُلِّيًّا

completion /kəm'pliːʃ(ə)n/ *n* إِتْمام, إِكْمال

complex /'kɒmplɛks/ **A** *adj* ‹*system, problem*› مُعَقَّد

B *n* **1** (buildings) مُجَمَّع **2** (anxiety) عُقْدة (عُقَد)

complexion /kəm'plɛkʃ(ə)n/ *n* بَشَرة

complexity /kəm'plɛksəti/ *n* (*pl* **complexities**) تَعْقيد (تَعْقيدات)

compliance /kəm'plʌɪəns/ *n* امْتِثال, خُضوع, إِذْعان

compliant /kəm'plʌɪənt/ *adj* ‹*media, workforce*› خاضِع, مُذْعِن, راضِخ (خُضْعان, خُضَّع)

complicate /'kɒmplɪkeɪt/ *vt* صَعَّبَ, عَقَّدَ ‹*an issue, a situation*›

complicated /'kɒmplɪkeɪtɪd/ *adj* ‹*issue, process*› مُعَقَّد

complication /kɒmplɪ'keɪʃ(ə)n/ *n* **1** (problem) تَعْقيد (تَعْقيدات); **it's a good idea; but there are several ~s** هذه فِكْرةٌ جَيِّدةٌ، وَلَكِنْ هُناكَ عِدّةُ تَعْقيداتٍ **2** (in care) مُضاعَفة

compliment **A** *n* /'kɒmplɪm(ə)nt/ مَديح (مَدائِحُ), ثَناء (أَثْنِية); **to pay sb a ~** مَدَحَ \ امْتَدَحَ شَخْصاً

B **(compliments)** *n pl* تَحِيّات; **with ~s** مع أَطْيَبِ التَحِيّاتِ

C *vt* /'kɒmplɪmɛnt/ **to ~ sb on their work** هَنَّأَ شَخْصاً على عَمَلِهِ

complimentary /kɒmplɪ'mɛnt(ə)ri/ *adj* **1** (praising) ‹*remark*› مُجامِل **2** (free) ‹*copy, ticket*› مَجّانيّ

comply /kəm'plʌɪ/ *vi* (**complies, complying, complied**) «companies, governments» امْتَثَلَ (ل) ‹*the law, regulations*›; اسْتَجابَ (ل) ‹*sb's wishes*›; **to ~ with the requirements/the law** امْتَثَلَ للمُتَطَلَّباتِ \ للقانونِ

component /kəm'pəʊnənt/ *n* (of machines) عُنْصُر (عَناصِرُ), مُكَوِّن (مُكَوِّنات)

component part *n* جُزْء مُكَوِّن

compose /kəm'pəʊz/ *vt* **1** **to be ~d of sth** كانَ مُكَوَّناً \ مُتَكَوِّناً \ مُؤَلَّفاً من شَيْءٍ **2** أَلَّفَ ‹*music, a symphony*› **3** **to ~ oneself** تَمالَكَ نَفْسَهُ

composed /kəm'pəʊzd/ *adj* ‹*person*› رابِط الجَأْشِ; ‹*manner*› هادِئ, رَصين (رِصان)

composer /kəm'pəʊzə/ *n* مُلَحِّن

composite /'kɒmpəzɪt/ **A** *adj* ‹*material, score*› مُرَكَّب; **it's a ~ material designed to be stronger than ...** هي مادّةٌ مُرَكَّبةٌ مُصَمَّمةٌ لِتَكونَ أَقْوى من...; **~ scores are more reliable** الدَرَجاتُ المُرَكَّبةُ أَكْثَرُ مَوْثوقيّةً

B *n* **1** (substance) مُرَكَّب (مُرَكَّبات) **2** (AmE) (of a suspect) صورة مُرَكَّبة

composition /kɒmpə'zɪʃ(ə)n/ *n* **1** (make-up) تَرْكيب (تَرْكيبات, تَراكيبُ), بِنْية (بِنًى, بُنًى), تَكْوين **2** (piece of music) قِطْعة موسيقيّة **3** (essay) إِنْشاء (إِنْشاءات)

compost /ˈkɒmpɒst/ *n* سَماد عُضْويّ \ طَبيعيّ

composure /kəmˈpəʊʒə/ *n* رَصانة ,هُدوء ,رَباطة جَأْشٍ

compound /ˈkɒmpaʊnd/ *n* 1 (built enclosure) مُجَمَّع 2 (in prisons) فِناء (أَفْنِية) 3 (in chemistry) مُرَكَّب (مُرَكَّبات) 4 (word) مَنْحوت ,كَلِمة مُرَكَّبة

compound fracture *n* كَسْر مَفْتوح \ مُرَكَّب

compound interest *n* فائدة مُرَكَّبة

comprehend /kɒmprɪˈhɛnd/ *vt* فَهِمَ ,أَدْرَكَ (a; فَهْم ,فَهَم) <*a meaning, situation*>

comprehensible /kɒmprɪˈhɛnsɪb(ə)l/ *adj* <*account, words*> مَفْهوم

comprehension /kɒmprɪˈhɛnʃ(ə)n/ *n* 1 فَهْم (أَفْهام) ,إِدْراك 2 (also **comprehension test**) اخْتِبار الاسْتيعاب \ الفَهْم

comprehensive /kɒmprɪˈhɛnsɪv/ A *adj* <*review, knowledge*> شامِل; **a ~ insurance policy** بوليصة تَأْمينٍ شامِلٍ
B *n* (also **comprehensive school**) (BrE) مَدْرَسة شامِلة

compress A /kəmˈprɛs/ *vt* كَبَسَ (i; كَبْس) <*gas*>; ضَغَطَ (a; ضَغْط) <*a file*>
B /ˈkɒmprɛs/ *n* كِماد ,كِمادة

compression /kəmˈprɛʃ(ə)n/ *n* 1 (of gases) انْضِغاط ,ضَغْط, كَبْس 2 (of data) ضَغْط

comprise /kəmˈprʌɪz/ *vt* 1 (to include) ضَمَّ (u; ضَمّ) ,شَمَلَ (u; شُمول ,شَمْل) ,تَأَلَّفَ (مِن) <*representatives, components*>; **the panel is ~d of experts** تَتَأَلَّفُ اللَجْنةُ من خُبَراءَ 2 (to form) شَكَّلَ <*a percentage, majority*>

compromise /ˈkɒmprəmʌɪz/ A *n* تَسْوِية ,حَلّ وَسَط; **to come to/reach a ~** تَوَصَّلَ إلى حَلّ وَسَطٍ \ تَسْوِيةٍ
B *vt* فَضَحَ (a; فَضْح) ,عَرَّضَ للخَطَرِ <*a reputation, security*>
C *vi* «negotiators, customers» قَبِلَ بِحَلٍّ وَسَطٍ ,قَدَّمَ تَنازُلاتٍ; **to ~ over an issue** قَدَّمَ تَنازُلاتٍ بِخُصوصِ مَسْأَلةٍ

compromising /ˈkɒmprəmʌɪzɪŋ/ *adj* <*evidence, photograph*> [من شَأْنِهِ إثارةُ فَضيحةٍ \ تَعْريضُ سُمْعةِ شَخْصٍ للخَطَرِ]

compulsion /kəmˈpʌlʃ(ə)n/ *n* 1 (force) إِكْراه ,قَسْر 2 (urge) اضْطِرار ,حاجة \ رَغْبة مُلِحّة

compulsive /kəmˈpʌlsɪv/ *adj* 1 (inveterate) <*liar*> قَهْريّ; <*gambler*> اسْتِحْواذيّ 2 (compelling) <*viewing, account*> لا يُقاوَمُ

compulsory /kəmˈpʌls(ə)ri/ *adj* <*attendance, subject*> إجْباريّ, إلْزاميّ

computation /kɒmpjʊˈteɪʃ(ə)n/ *n* حِساب (حِسابات); **methods of ~** طُرُق الحِسابِ; **statistical ~s** حِسابات إِحْصائيّة

computational /kɒmpjuːˈteɪʃ(ə)n(ə)l/ *adj* <*analysis, linguistics*> حاسوبيّ

compute /kəmˈpjuːt/ *vt* حَسَبَ (u; حِساب) ,عَدَّ (u; عَدّ) ,أَحْصى <*the total, solution*>

computer /kəmˈpjuːtə/ *n* حاسوب (حَواسيبُ) ,كُمْبْيوتَر; **a personal/mainframe ~** كُمْبْيوتَر شَخْصيّ \ مَرْكَزيّ

computer-aided design /kəm,pjuːtəeɪdɪd dɪˈzʌɪn/ *n* تَصْميم بِمُساعَدة الحاسوبِ

computer-aided learning /kəm,pjuːtəeɪdɪd ˈləːnɪŋ/ *n* تَعَلُّم بِمُساعَدةِ الحاسوبِ

computer crime *n* جَريمة كُمْبْيوتَر \ حاسوبٍ

computer dating *n* التَعارُف عن طَريق الكُمْبْيوتَر

computer engineer *n* مُهَنْدِس كُمْبْيوتَر

computer game *n* لُعْبة كُمْبْيوتَر

computer graphics *n* رُسومات \ رُسوميّات الحاسوبِ

computer hacker *n* قُرْصان حاسوبٍ ,هاكَر

computerize, -ise (BrE) /kəmˈpjuːtərʌɪz/ *vt* حَوْسَبَ <*a system, records*>

computer-literate /kəm,pjuːtəˈlɪt(ə)rət/ *adj* <*worker, child*> مُتَمَرِّس على الحاسوبِ

computer program *n* بَرْنامَج كُمْبْيوتَر

computer programmer, computer programer (AmE) *n* مُبَرْمِج كُمْبْيوتَر

computer programming *n* بَرْمَجة الكُمْبْيوتَر

computer science *n* عُلوم الحاسوبِ \ الكُمْبْيوتَر

computer scientist *n* عالِم كُمْبْيوتَر

computer studies *n* دِراسات الحاسوبِ \ الكُمْبْيوتَر

computing /kəmˈpjuːtɪŋ/ *n* حَوْسَبة ,مَعْلوماتيّة

comrade /ˈkɒmreɪd/ *n* 1 (friend) صاحِب ,رِفاق ,رُفَقاءُ) رَفيق) 2 (Pol) رَفيق (رِفاق ,رُفَقاءُ) (صُحْبة ,صَحابة ,صُحْبان ,أَصْحاب)

comradeship /ˈkɒmreɪdʃɪp/ *n* رُفْقة ,رِفاق ,رِفَق ,رُفَق ,أَرْفاق), صُحْبة

con /kɒn/ **A** *vt* **(-nn-)** (infml) احْتالَ (على), خَدَعَ (a; خَدْع, خُدْعة, خديعة), نَصَبَ (u; نَصْب) (على)
B *n* **1** (infml) (fraud) احْتِيال (احْتِيالات), خُدْعة (خُدَع, خُدْعات), نَصْب **2** (objection) حُجّة مُضادّة; ▸ **pro 3** (infml) (prisoner) مَحْكوم عَلَيْهِ

con artist, con man *n* (infml) نَصّاب, مُحْتال

concave /ˈkɒnkeɪv/ *adj* ‹*lens, mirror*› مُقَعَّر

conceal /kənˈsiːl/ *vt* أَخْفى, خَبَّأَ ‹*a weapon, the evidence*›; **to ~ the truth from sb** أَخْفى \ كَتَمَ الحَقيقةَ عن شَخْصٍ

concede /kənˈsiːd/ **A** *vt* **1** (to admit) أَقَرَّ (ب), اعْتَرَفَ (ب), سَلَّمَ (ب); **to ~ that sth is true/false** أَقَرَّ بِصِحّةِ \ بِعدمِ صِحّةِ شَيْءٍ **2** (to give way over) خَوَّلَ, مَنَحَ (a; مَنْح) ‹*a right*›; سَمَحَ (a; سَماح) (ب) ‹*reform*› **3** (in elections) أَقَرَّ بِهَزيمةٍ \ بِخَسارةٍ في ‹*an election*›; **to ~ victory to the opposition** أَقَرَّ للمُعارَضةِ بالغَلَبةِ **4** (in competitions) مَنَحَ (a; مَنْح) ‹*a goal, the set*›
B *vi* «management, company» اسْتَسْلَمَ, أَذْعَنَ; **to ~ to sb's demands** أَذْعَنَ لِمَطالِبِ شَخْصٍ

conceit /kənˈsiːt/ *n* خُيَلاء (dipt), عُجْب, غُرور

conceited /kənˈsiːtɪd/ *adj* ‹*manner*› مُتَكَبِّر; ‹*movie star*› مُخْتال, مَغْرور

conceivable /kənˈsiːvəb(ə)l/ *adj* ‹*reason, circumstance*› يُمْكِن تَصَوُّرُهُ \ تَخَيُّلُهُ, مَعْقول

conceive /kənˈsiːv/ **A** *vt* **1** (to imagine) تَخَيَّلَ, تَصَوَّرَ ‹*a plan, an idea*› **2** (to become pregnant) حَبِلَ (a; حَبَل), حَمَلَ (i; حَمْل) (ب, في) ‹*a child*›
B *vi* **1** (to imagine) تَخَيَّلَ, تَصَوَّرَ **2** (to become pregnant) «women» حَبِلَ (a; حَبَل), حَمَلَ (i; حَمْل)

concentrate /ˈkɒns(ə)ntreɪt/ **A** *vt* **1** رَكَّزَ ‹*one's efforts, attention*› **2** حَشَدَ (i-u; حَشْد) ‹*forces*›
B *vi* رَكَّزَ, تَرَكَّزَ; **the company is concentrating on manufacturing** تُرَكِّزُ الشَرِكةُ على الصِناعةِ

concentrated /ˈkɒns(ə)ntreɪtɪd/ *adj* **1** ‹*solution, extract*› مُرَكَّز **2** ‹*effort, attack*› مُرَكَّز, مُكَثَّف

concentration /kɒns(ə)nˈtreɪʃ(ə)n/ *n* تَرْكيز

concentration camp *n* مُعَسْكَر اعْتِقالٍ

concept /ˈkɒnsept/ *n* مَفْهوم (مَفاهيمُ)

conception /kənˈsepʃ(ə)n/ *n* **1** (of a child) حَمْل, حَبَل **2** (understanding) إدْراك; (idea) فِكْرة (فِكَر); (perception) تَصَوُّر (تَصَوُّرات)

conceptual /kənˈseptjʊəl/ *adj* ‹*problem*› تَصَوُّرِيّ, مَفاهيمِيّ; ‹*approach*› نَظَرِيّ

concern /kənˈsəːn/ **A** *vt* **1** (to worry) أَقْلَقَ ‹*the public, well-wishers*› **2** (to affect) مَسَّ (u; مَسّ, مَسيس) ‹*an interested party*›; **the ruling ~s all the debtors/creditors** يَمَسُّ القَرارُ كُلَّ المُدينينَ \ الدائِنينَ; **to whom it may ~** إلى من يَعْنيه \ يَخُصُّهُ الأَمْرُ **3** (to be about) خَصَّ (u; خَصّ, خُصوص, خُصوصيّة) ‹*the method, problem*›
B *n* **1** [u] (preoccupation) قَلَق **2** (worry) انْشِغال (انْشِغالات) **3** (company) شَرِكة

concerned /kənˈsəːnd/ *adj* **1** (anxious) ‹*expression, letter*› قَلِق; **to be ~ about the plan** كان قَلِقاً بِشأْنِ الخُطّةِ **2** (involved) **all those ~** كُلّ الأَطْرافِ المَعْنيّةِ

concerning /kənˈsəːnɪŋ/ *prep* حَوْلَ, بِشَأْنِ, بِخُصوصِ

concert /ˈkɒnsət/ *n* حَفْلة موسيقيّة

concerted /kənˈsəːtɪd/ *adj* ‹*effort, campaign*› مُنَسَّق

concert hall *n* قاعة حَفَلاتٍ موسيقيّةٍ

concertina /ˌkɒnsəˈtiːnə/ **A** *n* [أَكورْديون صَغير]
B *vi* «train, bus» تَهَشَّمَ

concerto /kənˈtʃəːtəʊ, kənˈtʃɛːtəʊ/ *n* (*pl* **concertos**) كونْشِرْتو

concession /kənˈseʃ(ə)n/ *n* (in negotiation) تَنازُل (تَنازُلات)

conciliation /kənˌsɪlɪˈeɪʃ(ə)n/ *n* (in a dispute) تَوْفيق, مُصالَحة

conciliatory /kənˈsɪlɪət(ə)ri/ *adj* ‹*tone, gesture*› اسْتِرْضائيّ, صُلْحيّ

concise /kənˈsʌɪs/ *adj* ‹*summary, statement*› وَجيز, موجَز, مُقْتَضَب

conclude /kənˈkluːd/ **A** *vt* **1** (to end) خَتَمَ (i; خَتْم) ‹*a speech, meeting*› **2** (to settle) أَبْرَمَ, أَتَمَّ ‹*an agreement, a deal*› **3** (to deduce) اسْتَنْتَجَ
B *vi* «story, event» انْتَهى; «speaker» اخْتَتَمَ

concluding /kənˈkluːdɪŋ/ *adj* ‹*chapter, remarks*› خِتاميّ

conclusion /kən'klu:ʒ(ə)n/ *n* **1** (judgement) اسْتِنْتاج (اسْتِنْتاجات); **to draw a ~** اسْتَخْلَصَ نَتيجةً; **to come to** *or* **reach a ~** انْتَهى \ خَلَصَ إلى نَتيجةٍ; **you mustn't jump to ~s** يَجِبُ ألاّ تَتَسَرَّعَ في إصْدارِ الأَحْكامِ **2** (end) خاتِمة (خَواتِمُ), نِهاية (خَواتيمُ); **in ~** في الخِتامِ, خِتاماً

conclusive /kən'klu:sɪv/ *adj* ‹*evidence*› قاطِع; ‹*result*› نِهائيّ; ‹*victory*› حاسِم

concoct /kən'kɒkt/ *vt* **1** أَعَدَّ, حَضَّرَ ‹*a dish, drink*› **2** دَبَّرَ ‹*a plan*› **3** اخْتَلَقَ ‹*a story, an excuse*›

concourse /'kɒŋkɔ:s/ *n* (large interior area) باحة, صالة رُكّابٍ

concrete /'kɒŋkri:t/ **A** *adj* ‹*evidence, proposal*› مَلْموس **B** *n* خَرَسانة

concubine /'kɒŋkjʊbʌɪn/ *n* حَظِيّة (حَظايا), مَحْظِيّة, سُرِّيّة (سَرايا)

concur /kən'kə:/ *vi* **(-rr-)** (fml) «opinions, experts» تَوافَقَ

concurrent /kən'kʌr(ə)nt/ *adj* (simultaneous) ‹*prison sentences, events*› مُتَزامِن

concuss /kən'kʌs/ *vt* **to be ~ed** أُصيبَ بارْتِجاجٍ (في المُخِّ)

concussion /kən'kʌʃ(ə)n/ *n* ارْتِجاج (في المُخِّ)

condemn /kən'dɛm/ *vt* **1** أَدانَ ‹*an attack, atrocity*›; **ministers ~ed the attack/statement** أَدانَ الوُزَراءُ الهُجومَ \ البَيانَ **2** حَكَمَ (u; حُكْم; على) ‹*a prisoner, rebel*› **3** [أَصْدَرَ بَياناً بِعَدَمِ صَلاحِيَةِ] ‹*a building, food*›

condemnation /ˌkɒndəm'neɪʃ(ə)n/ *n* إدانة

condensation /kɒndɛn'seɪʃ(ə)n/ *n* **1** (of gases, vapours) تَكْثيف; **the ~ of steam into water** تَكْثيفُ البُخارِ إلى ماءٍ **2** (on a window) بُخار ماءٍ مُتَكاثِف

condense /kən'dɛns/ **A** *vt* **1** كَثَّفَ ‹*steam, vapour*› **2** لَخَّصَ, اخْتَصَرَ ‹*a story, novel*› **B** *vi* «steam, vapour» تَكَثَّفَ, تَكاثَفَ

condensed /kən'dɛnst/ *adj* **1** ‹*soup, liquid*› مُكَثَّف **2** ‹*version, form*› مُلَخَّص, مُخْتَصَر

condensed milk *n* حَليب مُرَكَّز \ مُكَثَّف

condescend /kɒndɪ'sɛnd/ *vt* **to ~ to do sth** تَكَرَّمَ بِفِعْلِ شَيْءٍ

condescending /kɒndɪ'sɛndɪŋ/ *adj* ‹*attitude, tone*› اسْتِعْلائيّ, مُسْتَعْلٍ

condiment /'kɒndɪm(ə)nt/ *n* **1** (seasoning) تابِل (تَوابِلُ) **2** (sauce) صَلْصة

condition /kən'dɪʃ(ə)n/ **A** *n* **1** [u] (state) حالة, وَضْع; **to be in good/poor ~** كانَ في حالةٍ جَيِّدةٍ \ سَيِّئةٍ; **the house is in good/poor ~** البَيْتُ في حالةٍ جَيِّدةٍ \ سَيِّئةٍ; **the patient is in a critical/stable ~** المَريضُ في حالةٍ حَرِجةٍ \ مُسْتَقِرّةٍ; **to be in no ~ to do sth** كانَ في حالةٍ لا تَسْمَحُ لَهُ بِفِعْلِ شَيْءٍ **2** (stipulation) شَرْط (شُروط); **on ~ that ...** بِشَرْطِ أنْ ...; **I agree, on one ~** أُوافِقُ, بِشَرْطٍ واحِدٍ; **it's a ~ of your contract** هذا شَرْطٌ في عَقْدِكَ; **applicants must meet** *or* **satisfy the following ~s** يَجِبُ على المُتَقَدِّمينَ أنْ يَسْتَوْفوا الشُروطَ التالِيَةَ **3** [u] (disease) مَرَض, حالة مَرَضيّة; **a heart/skin ~** حالة مَرَضيّة قَلْبيّة \ جِلْدِيّة **4** [u] (fitness) لِياقة بَدَنيّة; **to be out of ~** لم تَكُنْ لِياقَتُهُ البَدَنيّةُ جَيِّدةً **5** [u] (situation) وَضْع; **the human ~** الوَضْعُ البَشَريّ **B** **(conditions)** *n pl* أَوْضاع, ظُروف; **to improve working/living ~s** حَسَّنَ ظُروفَ العَمَلِ \ المَعيشةِ; **he was working under difficult ~s** كانَ يَعْمَلُ تحت ظُروفٍ صَعْبةٍ; **weather ~s** الأَحْوال الجَوّيّة **C** *vt* **1** (to influence, determine) كَيَّفَ, هَيَّأَ ‹*a person, the mind*› **2** (to treat) وَضَعَ مُنَعِّماً \ بَلْسَماً على ‹*hair*›

conditional /kən'dɪʃ(ə)n(ə)l/ *adj* **1** ‹*agreement, offer*› مَشْروط **2** ‹*clause, phrase*› شَرْطيّ

conditioner /kən'dɪʃ(ə)nə/ *n* **1** (for hair) مُنَعِّم للشَعْرِ **2** (for fabric) مُنَعِّم للمَلابِسِ

conditioning /kən'dɪʃ(ə)nɪŋ/ *n* **1** (Psych) تَكْييف, إشْراط **2** (Sport) [تَمارين اللِياقةِ البَدَنيّةِ]

condo /'kɒndəʊ/ *n* (AmE infml) ▸ **condominium**

condolence /kən'dəʊl(ə)ns/ **A** *n* (fml) **a letter of ~** رِسالة تَعْزِيَةٍ **B** **(condolences)** *n pl* تَعازٍ

condom /'kɒndəm/ *n* واقٍ ذَكَرِيّ

condominium /ˌkɒndə'mɪnɪəm/ *n* (AmE) **1** (building) عِمارة **2** (apartment) شِقّة (شِقَق)

condone /kən'dəʊn/ *vt* تَسامَحَ (مع) ‹*violence, criminal behaviour*›

condor /'kɒndɔ:/ *n* نَسْر الكُنْدور

conducive /kən'dju:sɪv/ *adj* **to be ~ to sth** كانَ مُؤَدِّياً \ مُفْضِياً إلى شَيْءٍ

conduct **A** /'kɒndʌkt/ *n* تَصَرُّف ,سُلوك (تَصَرُّفات)

B /kən'dʌkt/ *vt* **1** أَدارَ ,(مَقادة ,قِيادة ,قِياد ,قَوْد ;u) قادَ ‹*a business, campaign*› **2** (Mus) قادَ (u; قَوْد ,قِياد ,قِيادة ,مَقادة) ‹*an orchestra*› **3** أَوْصَلَ ,(نَقْل ;u) نَقَلَ ‹*electricity, heat*›

conductor /kən'dʌktə/ *n* **1** (Mus) قائِد فِرْقةٍ موسيقيّةٍ **2** (on bus, train) قاطِع التَذاكِرِ ,مُحَصِّل **3** (of electricity, heat) مُوَصِّل ,ناقِل

cone /kəʊn/ *n* **1** (shape) مَخْروط (مَخاريطُ ,مَخْروطات) **2** (also **ice-cream cone**) قَرْن بوظةٍ **3** (for traffic) مَخْروط مُروريّ

confectioner /kən'fɛkʃ(ə)nə/ *n* حَلْوانيّ

confectionery /kən'fɛkʃ(ə)n(ə)ri/ *n* حَلْوَيات

confederate **A** *adj* (**Confederate**) ‹*states, flag*› كونْفِدِراليّ

B /kən'fɛd(ə)rət/ *n* **1** (ally) حَليف (حُلَفاءُ) **2** (**Confederate**) (in US history) مُؤَيِّد للكونْفِدِراليّة

confederation /kənfɛdə'reɪʃ(ə)n/ *n* (of countries) كونْفِدراليّة, (of organizations) اتِّحاد (اتِّحادات); اتِّحاد كونْفِدِراليّ

confer /kən'fəː/ **A** *vt* (**-rr-**) مَنَحَ (a; مَنْح) ‹*power, a right, degree*›; **to ~ sth on sb** مَنَحَ شَخْصاً شَيْئاً

B *vi* (**-rr-**) «jury, contestants» تَشاوَرَ ,تَباحَثَ

conference /'kɒnf(ə)r(ə)ns/ *n* **1** (congress) مُؤْتَمَر (مُؤْتَمَرات) **2** (meeting) اجْتِماع (اجْتِماعات)

conference call *n* مُؤْتَمَر عَبْرَ الهاتِفِ

conference centre, **conference center** (AmE) *n* مَرْكَز مُؤْتَمَراتٍ

conference room *n* غُرْفة مُؤْتَمَراتٍ

confess /kən'fɛs/ **A** *vt* **1** أَقَرَّ (ب) ,اعْتَرَفَ (ب) ‹*a crime, one's guilt*› **2** (Relig) اعْتَرَفَ (ب) ‹*one's sins*›

B *vi* **1** اعْتَرَفَ (ب) ,أَقَرَّ (ب); **to ~ to a crime** اعْتَرَفَ بِجَريمةٍ; **he ~ed to the murder** اعْتَرَفَ بالقَتْلِ **2** (Relig) «sinners» اسْتَغْفَرَ

confession /kən'fɛʃ(ə)n/ *n* **1** (of guilt) اعْتِراف **2** (in religion) اعْتِراف

confetti /kən'fɛti/ *n* نِثار

confidant /'kɒnfɪdant, ˌkɒnfɪ'dant/ *n* (*feminine form* **confidante**) نَجيّ (أَنْجِية) ,مُقَرَّب ,نَديم (نُدَماءُ ,نِدام)

confide /kən'fʌɪd/ **A** *vi* **to ~ in sb** اسْتَأْمَنَ شَخْصاً

B *vt* **to ~ a secret to sb** ائْتَمَنَ شَخْصاً على سِرٍّ

confidence /'kɒnfɪd(ə)ns/ *n* **1** (faith) إيمان ,ثِقة; **I have every ~ in him** لي كُلُّ الثِقةِ بِهِ **2** (self-assurance) ثِقة **3** (confidentiality) **in ~** في \ بِسِرّيّةٍ; **all calls will be treated in the strictest ~** سَتَتِمُّ مُعامَلةُ جَميعِ المُكالَماتِ بِسِرّيّةٍ تامّةٍ

confidence trick, **confidence game** (AmE) *n* خِدْعة احْتِيال ,ثِقةٍ

confident /'kɒnfɪd(ə)nt/ *adj* **1** (sure) ‹*prediction, assertion*› أَكيد, ‹*person*› واثِق; يَنِمُّ عن ثِقةٍ; **to be ~ of sth** كانَ واثِقاً من شَيْءٍ **2** (self-assured) ‹*person*› مُطْمَئِنّ ,واثِق من نَفْسِهِ; **he was in a ~ mood** كانَ واثِقاً من نَفْسِهِ \ مُطْمَئِنّاً

confidential /kɒnfɪ'dɛnʃ(ə)l/ *adj* ‹*information, document*› سِرّيّ

confidentiality /kɒnfɪdɛnʃɪ'alɪti/ *n* سِرّيّة

confidently /'kɒnfɪd(ə)ntli/ *adv* ‹*to speak, behave*› بِثِقةٍ; **she ~ expects a win** تَتَوَقَّعُ الفَوْزَ بِثِقةٍ

configuration /kənˌfɪgə'reɪʃ(ə)n/ *n* **1** (arrangement) هَيْئة, تَهْيِئة ,تَكْوين **2** (of hardware) تَرْتيب (تَرْتيبات) ,تَشْكيل

configure /kən'fɪgə/ *vt* هَيَّأَ ‹*a system, computer*›

confine /kən'fʌɪn/ *vt* **1** (to limit) حَصَرَ (i-u; حَصْر) ,قَصَرَ (u; قَصْر) ‹*activities, comments*›; **this problem is not ~d to young people** هذه المُشْكِلةُ لَيْسَتْ مَحْصورةً في الشَبابِ; **please ~ your comments to the matter in hand** الرَجاءُ أَنْ تَقْصِرَ تَعْليقاتِكَ على المَسْأَلةِ الّتي بين أَيْدينا **2** (to shut in) حَبَسَ (i; حَبْس) ‹*a person, an animal*›

confined /kən'fʌɪnd/ *adj* ‹*space*› ضَيِّق

confines /'kɒnfʌɪnz/ *n pl* تُخوم ,حُدود

confirm /kən'fəːm/ *vt* **1** (to make definite) أَكَّدَ ‹*a reservation, an appointment*› **2** (to substantiate) أَثْبَتَ ‹*a report, theory*› **3** (Rel_Chr) مَنَحَ سِرَّ التَثْبيتِ \ المَيْرون

confirmation /kɒnfə'meɪʃ(ə)n/ *n* **1** (ratification) تَثْبيت (تَثْبيتات) **2** (of news, rumour) تَأْكيد (تَأْكيدات) **3** (Rel_Chr) تَثْبيت

confirmed /kən'fəːmd/ *adj* ‹*smoker, liar*› مُزْمِن

confiscate /ˈkɒnfɪskeɪt/ *vt* صادَرَ ‹*the medicine, weapon*›

conflict **A** /ˈkɒnflɪkt/ *n* نِزاع (نِزاعات), خِلاف (خِلافات), صِراع (صِراعات); **it brought her into ~ with her neighbours** أَوْصَلَها الأَمْرُ إلى نِزاعٍ مع جيرانِها **B** /kənˈflɪkt/ *vi* «results, interests» تَناقَضَ, تَضارَبَ, تَعارَضَ

conflicting /kənˈflɪktɪŋ/ *adj* ‹*interests, evidence*› مُتَضارِب, مُتَعارِض, مُتَناقِض

conform /kənˈfɔːm/ *vi* **1** «equipment, toys» اِسْتَوْفى الشُّروطَ \ المَعاييرَ; **to ~ to the regulations** اِسْتَوْفى الشُّروطَ القانونيّةَ **2** «teenagers, members» تَكَيَّفَ (مع العاداتِ \ التَقاليدِ \ البيئةِ الاجْتِماعيّةِ)

conformist /kənˈfɔːmɪst/ *n, adj* مُمْتَثِل

conformity /kənˈfɔːmɪti/ *n* (fml) **in ~ with the regulations** وَفْقاً للقَوانينِ

confound /kənˈfaʊnd/ *vt* **1** (to perplex) حَيَّرَ, أَرْبَكَ ‹*an audience, enemy*› **2** (to prove wrong) أَدْحَضَ, فَنَّدَ, أَطاحَ (ب) ‹*expectations*›; أَفْحَمَ ‹*critics, experts*›

confront /kənˈfrʌnt/ *vt* **1** (to face) تَصَدّى (ل), جابَهَ, واجَهَ ‹*an enemy, danger*› **2** (to face up to) واجَهَ ‹*a challenge, reality*›

confrontation /ˌkɒnfrʌnˈteɪʃ(ə)n/ *n* مُواجَهة, مُجابَهة

confrontational /ˌkɒnfrənˈteɪʃ(ə)n(ə)l/ *adj* ‹*manner, interviewer*› عُدْوانيّ

confuse /kənˈfjuːz/ *vt* **1** (to bewilder) حَيَّرَ, أَرْبَكَ ‹*a consumer, reader*› **2** (to mix up) خَلَطَ (i; خَلْط; بين); **I ~ her with her sister** أَخْلطُ بَيْنَها وبَيْنَ أُخْتِها **3** (to complicate) عَقَّدَ, جَعَلَ مُبْهَماً ‹*the issue*›

confused /kənˈfjuːzd/ *adj* **1** (bewildered) ‹*person*› مُشَوَّش الفِكْرِ \ الذِهْن, حائر, مُتَحَيِّر, مُرْتَبِك; ‹*thoughts*› مُشَوَّش, مُضْطَرِب; **to get ~** تَشَوَّشَ, اِرْتَبَكَ **2** (unclear) ‹*account, instructions*› مُبْهَم

confusing /kənˈfjuːzɪŋ/ *adj* ‹*instructions, experience*› مُحَيِّر, مُرْبِك

confusion /kənˈfjuːʒ(ə)n/ *n* **1** (uncertainty) حَيْرة **2** (disorder) اِرْتِباك (اِرْتِباكات), تَشَوُّش

conga /ˈkɒŋgə/ *n* **1** (dance) رَقْصة الكونْجا **2** (also **conga drum**) طَبْلة الكونْجا

congeal /kənˈdʒiːl/ *vi* «fat, blood» خَثَرَ (u; خُثور, خُثورة), تَخَثَّرَ

congenial /kənˈdʒiːnɪəl/ *adj* ‹*companion, surroundings*› مُلائِم, مُناسِب

congenital /kənˈdʒɛnɪt(ə)l/ *adj* ‹*abnormality, disease*› خِلْقيّ

conger /ˈkɒŋgə/ *n* (also **conger eel**) قُنْجَر (نَوْع من ثَعابينِ البَحْرِ)

congested /kənˈdʒɛstɪd/ *adj* **1** (with traffic) ‹*road, motorway*› مُزْدَحِم; (with people) ‹*district*› مُكْتَظّ **2** (with blood or mucus) ‹*lungs, nose*› مُحْتَقِن

congestion /kənˈdʒɛstʃ(ə)n/ *n* **1** (with traffic) اِزْدِحام; (with people) اكْتِظاظ **2** (of lungs, nose) احْتِقان

congestion charge *n* رَسْم ازْدِحامٍ

conglomerate /kənˈglɒm(ə)rət/ *n* تَجَمُّع شَرِكاتٍ

Congo /ˈkɒŋgəʊ/ *pr n* **1** (**the (Democratic Republic of the) Congo**) جُمْهوريّة الكونْغو الديموقْراطيّة **2** (river) (**the Congo**) نَهْر الكونْغو

congratulate /kənˈgratjʊleɪt/ *vt* هَنَّأَ ‹*the winner, bridegroom*›; **to ~ sb on their success** هَنَّأَ شَخْصاً بِنَجاحِهِ

congratulation /kəngratjʊˈleɪʃ(ə)n/ **A** *n* تَهْنِئة (تَهانِئُ), مُبارَكة **B** (**congratulations**) *n pl* تَهانِئ; **~s!** أَلْف مَبْروكٍ!

congregate /ˈkɒŋgrɪgeɪt/ *vi* «a crowd, students» تَجَمَّعَ, احْتَشَدَ

congregation /kɒŋgrɪˈgeɪʃ(ə)n/ *n* طائِفة (طَوائِفُ)

congress /ˈkɒŋgrɛs/ *n* **1** (conference) مُؤْتَمَر (مُؤْتَمَرات) **2** (in US government) **C~** مَجْلِس النوّابِ الأَمْريكيّ

congressman /ˈkɒŋgrɛsmən/ *n* (*pl* **-men** AmE) عُضْو مَجْلِسِ النوّابِ الأَمْريكيِّ

congresswoman /ˈkɒŋgrɛswʊmən/ *n* (*pl* **-women**) (AmE) عُضْوة مَجْلِسِ النوّابِ الأَمْريكيِّ

conifer /ˈkɒnɪfə, ˈkəʊnɪfə/ *n* صَنَوْبَريّة

conjecture /kənˈdʒɛktʃə/ **A** *n* **1** (opinion) افْتِراض (افْتِراضات), تَخْمين (تَخْمينات) **2** (surmise) تَخْمين, حَزْر, حَدْس; **that is a matter for ~** تِلْكَ مَسْأَلَةٌ مَبْنيّةٌ على تَخْمينٍ **B** *vt* خَمَّنَ, حَزَرَ (i-u; حَزْر, مَحْزَرة), حَدَسَ (i-u; حَدْس) **C** *vi* «scientists, scholars» خَمَّنَ, حَزَرَ (i-u; حَزْر, مَحْزَرة), حَدَسَ (i-u; حَدْس)

conjugal /ˈkɒndʒʊɡ(ə)l/ *adj* ‹*bliss, rights*› زَوْجِيّ

conjugate /ˈkɒndʒʊɡeɪt/ **A** *vt* صَرَّفَ (صَرْف, i;) ‹*a verb*› صَرَّفَ

B *vi* «verbs» صُرِّفَ

conjugation /kɒndʒʊˈɡeɪʃ(ə)n/ *n* تَصْرِيف (الأَفْعالِ)

conjunction /kənˈdʒʌŋ(k)ʃ(ə)n/ *n* أداة \ حَرْف عَطْفٍ

conjunctivitis /kənˌdʒʌŋ(k)tɪˈvʌɪtɪs/ *n* الْتِهاب المُلْتَحِمةِ

conjure /ˈkʌndʒə/ *vi* «entertainers, magicians» مارَسَ السِحْرَ, شَعْوَذَ (شَعْوَذة ;i)

(Phrasal verb) **conjure up**: **~ up [sth]** اسْتَحْضَرَ [شَيْئاً] ‹*an image*›; أَعَدَّ [شَيْئاً] على نَحْوٍ سَرِيعٍ ‹*a meal*›

conjuror, **conjurer** /ˈkʌndʒ(ə)rə/ *n* ساحِر (سَحَرة)

conman /ˈkɒnman/ *n* (*pl* **men**) (infml) مُحْتال, نَصّاب

connect /kəˈnɛkt/ **A** *vt* **1** (to attach) وَصَّلَ ‹*a cable, an appliance*›; **~ the cable to the monitor** وَصِّل الكابِل بالشاشةِ **2** (to link) رَبَطَ (رَبْط ;i-u), وَصَّلَ ‹*a building, town*›; **to ~ sth to** *or* **with sth** وَصَّلَ شَيْئاً بِشَيْءٍ آخَر **3** وَصَّلَ ‹*the telephone, electricity, water supply*›; **the house is not ~ed to the water supply** البَيْتُ غَيْرُ مُتَّصِلٍ بِإمْداداتِ المِياهِ **4** (to associate) رَبَطَ (رَبْط ;i-u) ‹*an incident, a person*›; **there is no evidence to ~ him with the murder** لَيْسَ هُناكَ دَليلٌ يَرْبِطُهُ بِجَرِيمةِ القَتْلِ **5** (by telephone) وَصَّلَ ‹*a caller*›

B *vi* **1** «rooms» اتَّصَلَ, ارْتَبَطَ **2** «service, train» رَبَطَ (بين مَحَطَّتَيْنِ \ مَدينَتَيْنِ) **3** (to relate) «person» تَقارَبَ; **he seems unable to ~ with other people** يَبْدو غَيْرَ قادِرٍ على التَقارُبِ مع الآخَرِينَ

(Phrasal verb) **connect up**: **~ up [sth]**, **~ [sth] up** وَصَّلَ [شَيْئاً] ‹*a cable, computer*›; **to ~ the router up to the computer** وَصَّلَ جِهازَ التَوْجِيهِ بالكُمْبيوتَر

connected /kəˈnɛktɪd/ *adj* **1** ‹*ideas, events*› مُتَرابِط; **I like everything ~ with jazz** أُحِبُّ كُلَّ ما يَتَعَلَّقُ بِموسيقى الجاز **2** (related) ذو قَرابةٍ; **they are ~ by marriage** تَرْبِطُهُمْ عَلاقةُ زَواجٍ

Connecticut /kəˈnɛtɪkət/ *pr n* كونيتيكَت (f)

connecting /kəˈnɛktɪŋ/ *adj* **1** ‹*flight*› رَبْطٍ; ‹*train*› رابِط **2** ‹*room*› مُتَّصِل

connection /kəˈnɛkʃ(ə)n/ **A** *n* **1** (link) عَلاقة (عَلاقات), صِلة; **to have no ~ with sth** لَيْسَ لَهُ عَلاقةٌ بِشَيْءٍ; **to make the ~ between sth and sth** رَبَطَ العَلاقةَ بين شَيْءٍ وَشَيْءٍ; **in ~ with** على صِلةٍ ب; **in this ~ …** في هذا الخُصوصِ … **2** (relationship) عَلاقة (عَلاقات), ارْتِباط (ارْتِباطات) **3** (joining together) تَوْصِيل; (link between components) تَوْصِيلة, وُصْلة **4** (to the Internet) تَوْصِيلة, وُصْلة; **you will need an Internet ~** سَوْفَ تَحْتاجُ إلى وُصْلةِ إنْتَرْنِت **5** (by telephone) اتِّصال (اتِّصالات), وُصْلة (وُصْلات); **a bad ~** اتِّصال هاتِفيّ رَدِيء **6** (in travel) رِحْلة رَبْطٍ; **to miss one's ~** فاتَتْهُ رِحْلةُ الرَبْطِ

B (**connections**) *n pl* **1** (contacts) مَعارِف, عَلاقات; **to have useful ~s** كانَ لَهُ عَلاقاتٌ مُفيدةٌ **2** (relatives) أَقرِباء, أَقارِب; **she has family ~s in Italy** لَها أَقارِبُ في إيطاليا

connectivity /kɒnɛkˈtɪvɪti/ *n* رَبْط, اتِّصال

connive /kəˈnʌɪv/ *vi* **1** «plotters, hackers» تَآمَرَ (مع), تَواطَأَ (مع); **to ~ with sb to commit a fraud** تَآمَرَ \ تَواطَأَ مع شَخْصٍ لارْتِكابِ غِشٍّ **2** **to ~ in the fraud** تَواطَأَ في الاحْتِيالِ

connoisseur /ˌkɒnəˈsəː/ *n* ذَوّاق, خَبِير (خُبَراءُ)

connotation /kɒnəˈteɪʃ(ə)n/ *n* مَعْنًى إضافِيّ \ ضِمْنِيّ

conquer /ˈkɒŋkə/ *vt* (defeat) غَلَبَ (غَلْب, غَلَبة ;i), قَهَرَ (قَهْر ;a) ‹*a people*›; (invade) فَتَحَ (فَتْح ;a), اسْتَوْلى (على), انْتَصَرَ (على), غَزا (غَزْو ;u) ‹*a country*›; (overcome) تَغَلَّبَ (على), تَخَطّى ‹*one's shyness, addiction*›

conqueror /ˈkɒŋk(ə)rə/ *n* فاتِح, غازٍ (غُزاة)

conquest /ˈkɒŋkwest/ *n* فَتْح (فُتوح, فُتوحات), اسْتِيلاء, غَزْو

conscience /ˈkɒnʃ(ə)ns/ *n* ضَمِير (ضَمائِرُ), ذِمّة (ذِمَم); **to have a clear/guilty ~** كانَ مُرْتاحَ \ مُؤَنَّبَ الضَمِيرِ

conscientious /ˌkɒnʃɪˈɛnʃəs/ *adj* ‹*student, worker*› [قائِم بِعَمَلِهِ \ واجِبِهِ على أَكْمَلِ وَجْهٍ]

conscientious objector *n* مُسْتَنْكِف ضَمِيرِيّ (شَخْص يَرْفُضُ أداءَ الخِدْمةِ العَسْكَرِيّةِ لِأَسْبابٍ يُمْلِيها عَلَيْهِ ضَمِيرُهُ)

conscious /ˈkɒnʃəs/ *adj* **1** (awake, alert) ‹*patient*› واعٍ (واعونَ, وُعاة); ‹*moment*› إدْراكٍ, وَعْيٍ; **the patient was fully ~** كانَ المَرِيضُ في كامِلِ وَعْيِهِ **2** (aware) **to be ~ of sth** كانَ واعِياً \ مُدْرِكاً لِشَيْءٍ **3** (deliberate) ‹*decision, attempt*› واعٍ

consciously /ˈkɒnʃəsli/ *adv* 1 (deliberately) ‹*to act*› عَمْداً, عن وَعْيٍ; **she ~ failed to mention it** لم تَذْكُر الأَمْرَ عَمْداً 2 (in assertions) بِشَكْلٍ جازِمٍ, جازِماً; **she couldn't ~ say if it was him** لم تَتَمَكَّنْ من التَعَرُّفِ عَلَيْهِ بِشَكْلٍ جازِمٍ

consciousness /ˈkɒnʃəsnəs/ *n* 1 (alertness) وَعْي; **to lose/regain ~** فَقَدَ الوَعْيَ \ اسْتَرْجَعَ وَعْيَهُ 2 (awareness) وَعْي, إدْراك

consciousness-raising /ˈkɒnʃəsnəsˌreɪzɪŋ/ *n* رَفْع, تَوْعِية مُسْتَوى الوَعْيِ

conscript **A** /kənˈskrɪpt/ *vt* ‹*a citizen*› جَنَّدَ (تَجْنيداً إلْزامِيًّا) **B** /ˈkɒnskrɪpt/ *n* مُجَنَّد (تَجْنيداً إلْزامِيًّا)

conscription /kənˈskrɪpʃ(ə)n/ *n* خِدْمة إلْزامِيّة, تَجْنيد إلْزامِيّ

consecrate /ˈkɒnsɪkreɪt/ *vt* ‹*a church, ground*› قَدَّسَ

consecutive /kənˈsɛkjʊtɪv/ *adj* ‹*days, victories*› مُتَتالٍ, مُتَتابِع, مُتَعاقِب; **we won the title for three ~ years** فُزْنا باللَقَبِ لِثَلاثِ سَنواتٍ مُتَتالِيةٍ

consensus /kənˈsɛnsəs/ *n* إجْماع

consent /kənˈsɛnt/ **A** *n* قَبول, مُوافَقة; **age of ~** سِنّ القَبولِ **B** *vi* «participants, patients» وافَقَ (على); **to ~ to a proposal** وافَقَ على اقْتِراحٍ

consequence /ˈkɒnsɪkw(ə)ns/ *n* 1 (result) عاقِبة, تَبِعة (عَواقِبُ), نَتيجة (نَتائِجُ); **as a ~ of** نَتيجةً ل 2 (importance) أَهَمِّيّة

consequent /ˈkɒnsɪkw(ə)nt/ *adj* ‹*reduction, loss*› ناجِم, ناتِج, مُتَرَتِّب; **the price rises ~ on the devaluation** ارْتِفاع الأَسْعارِ النَاتِجُ عن تَخْفيضِ قيمة العُمْلةِ

consequently /ˈkɒnsɪkw(ə)ntli/ *adv* بِناءً, بالتالي, نَتيجةً لِذَلِكَ على هذا

conservation /kɒnsəˈveɪʃ(ə)n/ *n* حِماية, صَوْن, حِفْظ

conservation area *n* (BrE) مِنْطَقة مَحْمِيّة (لِأَهَمِّيَّتِها الطَبيعيّةِ \ الثَقافيّةِ)

conservationist /kɒnsəˈveɪʃ(ə)nɪst/ *n* ناشِط بيئيّ

conservatism /kənˈsəːvətiz(ə)m/ *n* 1 (in outlook) مُحافَظة 2 (in politics) رَجْعيّة, تَقْليديّة

conservative /kənˈsəːvətɪv/ **A** *adj* 1 (traditional) ‹*views, taste*› تَقْليديّ 2 (cautious) ‹*estimate, figure*› مُتَحَفِّظ 3 (Conservative) (in politics) ‹*candidate, MP*› مُحافِظ **B** *n* 1 (traditionalist) مُحافِظ, تَقْليديّ 2 (Conservative) مُحافِظ

Conservative Party *n* (**the Conservative Party**) حِزْب المُحافِظينَ

conservator /ˈkɒnsəˌveɪtə/ *n* (in a museum) حافِظ (حُفّاظ, حَفَظة)

conservatory /kənˈsəːvət(ə)ri/ *n* (*pl* **conservatories**) 1 (for plants) مُسْتَنْبَت (مُسْتَنْبَتات) 2 (school of music) مَعْهَد موسيقيّ

conserve /kənˈsəːv/ *vt* 1 ‹*a species, the environment*› حافَظَ (على) 2 ‹*energy, resources*› حافَظَ (على)

consider /kənˈsɪdə/ **A** *vt* 1 (to evaluate) دَرَسَ (u; دَرْس), نَظَرَ (u; نَظَر; في), فَكَّرَ (في) ‹*the issues, options, an offer*›; **each case is ~ed on its merits** يَتِمُّ النَظَرُ في كُلِّ حالةٍ وَفْقَ أُسُسٍ مَوْضوعيّةٍ; **the seller is ~ing the offer** يُفَكِّرُ البائِعُ في العَرْضِ; **to ~ whether** فَكَّرَ ما إذا; **they refused to ~ the possibility of changing the date** رَفَضوا النَظَرَ في إمْكانيّةِ تَغْيير المَوْعِدِ 2 (to deliberate over) دَرَسَ (u; دَرْس), نَظَرَ (u; نَظَر; في) ‹*a case, the evidence*›; **the jury is ~ing its verdict** تَدْرُسُ هَيْئةُ المُحَلَّفينَ حُكْمَها 3 (to take into account) راعى, وَضَعَ في الحُسْبانِ ‹*costs, risks*›; **you never once ~ed my feelings** لم تُراعِ مَشاعِري أَبَداً وَلَوْ مَرّةً واحِدةً; **I have a child to ~** لَدَيَّ طِفْلٌ يَجِبُ أنْ أَضَعَهُ في الحُسْبانِ; **all things ~ed** بالنَظَرِ إلى كُلِّ الاعْتِباراتِ 4 (to regard) اعْتَبَرَ; **to ~ that …** اعْتَبَرَ أنَّ; **he was ~ed to be an expert** كانَ يُعْتَبَرُ خَبيراً; **you should ~ yourself lucky** يَنْبَغي أنْ تَعْتَبِرَ نَفْسَكَ مَحْظوظاً **B** (**considered**) *adj* (fml) ‹*response, judgement*› مَدْروس; **in my ~ed opinion** في رَأْيِي الّذي فَكَّرْتُ فيه جَيِّداً

considerable /kənˈsɪd(ə)rəb(ə)l/ *adj* ‹*amount, number*› كَبير, ضَخْم; **a ~ sum of money** مَبْلَغ كَبير \ ضَخْم من المالِ

considerably /kənˈsɪd(ə)rəbli/ *adv* ‹*to vary, improve*› إلى حَدٍّ كَبيرٍ

considerate /kənˈsɪd(ə)rət/ *adj* ‹*driver, behaviour*› مُراعٍ لِمَشاعِرِ الآخَرينَ

consideration /kənsɪdəˈreɪʃ(ə)n/ *n* 1 [u] (of problems, issues) دِراسة, نَظَر, تَفْكير; **to give ~ to sth** نَظَرَ بِعَيْنِ الاعْتِبارِ إلى

شَيْءٍ; **the proposal deserves serious ~** يَسْتَحِقُّ الاقْتِراحُ دِراسةً جادّةً; **to take sth into ~** أَخَذَ شَيْئاً في الاعْتِبارِ; **after careful ~** بعد دِراسةٍ مُتَأَنِّيةٍ; **various options are under ~** يَجْري النَظَرُ في مُخْتَلَفِ الخِياراتِ **2** [u] (sensitivity) مُراعاة; **he shows a complete lack of ~ for others** لَيْسَ لَدَيْهِ أيُّ إحْساسٍ بِمَشاعِرِ الآخَرينَ; **out of ~ for sth/sb** مُراعاةً لِشَيْءٍ \ لِشَخْصٍ **3** (factor) عامِلٌ (عَوامِلُ); **cost is always a major ~** تُعْتَبَرُ التَكْلُفةُ دائِماً عامِلاً رَئيسيًّا **4** (fml) (fee) أُجْرة, مُقابِل; **for a ~** بِمُقابِلٍ

considering /kənˈsɪd(ə)rɪŋ/ **A** *prep* نَظَراً \ على \ باعْتِبارِ بالنَظَرِ إلى **B** *conj* نَظَراً \ بالنَظَرِ إلى أنّ, على \ باعْتِبارِ أنّ; **~ that she's never done it before, she made quite a good job of it** قَدَّمَتْ عَمَلاً جَيِّداً بالفِعْلِ، على اعْتِبارِ أنّها لم تَفْعَلْ ذلك من قَبْلُ

consign /kənˈsʌɪn/ *vt* (to dispose of) تَخَلَّصَ (من); **to ~ sth to the dustbin** أَلْقى شَيْئاً في صُنْدوقِ القُمامةِ

consignment /kənˈsʌɪnm(ə)nt/ *n* **1** (goods sent) بِضاعة **2** (sending) إرْسال (إرْسالات), مُرْسَلة

consist /kənˈsɪst/ *vi* **to ~ of sth** «group, work» تَأَلَّفَ من شَيْءٍ

consistency /kənˈsɪst(ə)nsi/ *n* (*pl* **consistencies**) **1** (regularity) اتِّساق, انْتِظام **2** (of a mixture) تَماسُك

consistent /kənˈsɪst(ə)nt/ *adj* **1** (unvarying) ‹*quality, performance*› ثابِت (ثُبوت) **2** (coherent) ‹*argument, policy*› مُتَماسِك, خالٍ من التَناقُضِ **3** (compatible) **to be ~ with sth** كانَ مُتَناسِباً \ مُتَوافِقاً مع شَيْءٍ

consistently /kənˈsɪst(ə)ntli/ *adv* **1** (unvaryingly) ‹*to perform, apply*› على نَحْوٍ ثابِتٍ **2** (continually) ‹*to fail, refuse*› باسْتِمْرارٍ, على الدَوامِ

consolation /ˌkɒnsəˈleɪʃ(ə)n/ *n* سَلْوى, عَزاء

consolation prize *n* جائِزة تَرْضِية

console¹ /kənˈsəʊl/ *vt* واسى ‹*a friend, victim*›

console² /ˈkɒnsəʊl/ *n* **1** (control panel) وَحْدة تَحَكُّمٍ **2** (for video games) مِنَصّة (مِنَصّات)

consolidate /kənˈsɒlɪdeɪt/ *vt* **1** عَزَّزَ, دَعَّمَ ‹*one's position, power*› **2** (Busn) دَمَجَ (u; دَمْج) ‹*operations, resources*›

consolidation /kənˌsɒlɪˈdeɪʃ(ə)n/ *n* **1** (of power) تَعْزيز, تَقْوِية (تَعْزيزات) **2** (of accounts, companies) دَمْج

consonant /ˈkɒns(ə)nənt/ *n* حَرْف ساكِن

consort /ˈkɒnsɔːt/ *n* قَرين (قُرَناءُ)

consortium /kənˈsɔːtɪəm/ *n* (*pl* **consortiums** or **consortia**) اتِّحاد (اتِّحادات)

conspicuous /kənˈspɪkjʊəs/ *adj* ‹*feature, position*› لافِت, بارِز, ظاهِر; **to be ~** كانَ بارِزاً; **to feel ~** أَحسَّ أَنَّهُ لافِتٌ \ مُلْفِتٌ للنَظَرِ; **to be ~ by one's/its absence** كانَ غِيابُهُ لافِتاً \ مُلْفِتاً للنَظَرِ

conspiracy /kənˈspɪrəsi/ *n* (*pl* **conspiracies**) مُؤامَرة

conspirator /kənˈspɪrətə/ *n* مُتَآمِر

conspire /kənˈspʌɪə/ *vi* تَآمَرَ (على); **to ~ to do sth** «conspirators» تَآمَرَ على فِعْلِ شَيْءٍ; **the circumstances ~d against him** كانَت الظُروفُ ضِدَّهُ \

constable /ˈkʌnstəb(ə)l/ *n* (BrE) شُرْطيّ

constant /ˈkɒnst(ə)nt/ *adj* (continual) ‹*pain, threat*› مُسْتَمِرّ; (unchanging) ‹*temperature, speed*› ثابِت (ثُبوت); (loyal) ‹*companion, servant*› وَفيّ, مُقيم على العَهْدِ

constantly /ˈkɒnst(ə)ntli/ *adv* ‹*to change, talk*› باسْتِمْرارٍ, على الدَوامِ

constellation /ˌkɒnstəˈleɪʃ(ə)n/ *n* كَوْكَبة

constipated /ˈkɒnstɪpeɪtɪd/ *adj* ‹*patient*› مُمْسِك, يُعاني من الإمْساكِ

constipation /kɒnstɪˈpeɪʃ(ə)n/ *n* إمْساك

constituency /kənˈstɪtjʊənsi/ *n* (*pl* **constituencies**) (district) دائِرة انْتِخابيّة; (voters) [ناخِبو دائِرةٍ انْتِخابيّةٍ]

constituent /kənˈstɪtjʊənt/ **A** *adj* ‹*part, element*› مُشَكِّل **B** *n* **1** ناخِب (مُقيم في دائِرةٍ انْتِخابيّةٍ) **2** (element) مُكَوِّن (مُكَوِّنات)

constitute /ˈkɒnstɪtjuːt/ *vt* شَكَّلَ ‹*a threat, an offence*›

constitution /kɒnstɪˈtjuːʃ(ə)n/ *n* **1** (of a country) دُسْتور (دَساتيرُ); (of a club) قانون (قَوانينُ) **2** (sb's physical state) بِنْية الجِسْمِ

constitutional /kɒnstɪˈtjuːʃ(ə)n(ə)l/ *adj* ‹*right, reform*› دُسْتوريّ

constrain /kən'streɪn/ (fml) *vt* 1 (to compel) أَلْزَمَ (على), أَرْغَمَ ‹*a person*› 2 (to limit) قَيَّدَ ‹*growth, movement*›

constraint /kən'streɪnt/ *n* قَيْد (قيود)

constrict /kən'strɪkt/ *vt* 1 (to make narrower) قَلَّصَ ‹*blood vessels, the throat*› 2 (to restrict) سَدَّ (u; سَدّ) ‹*the flow, breathing*›

construct /kən'strʌkt/ *vt* شَيَّدَ, بَنَى (i; بِناء, بُنْيان) ‹*a building, pipeline*›

construction /kən'strʌkʃ(ə)n/ *n* 1 [u] (the process) بِناء, تَشْيِيد 2 (a building) مَبْنًى (مَبانٍ) 3 (Ling) تَرْكِيب (تَراكِيبُ); **a genitive ~** إِضافة

construction engineer *n* مُهَنْدِس إِنْشاءاتٍ \ بِناءٍ

construction site *n* مَوْقِع بِناءٍ

construction worker *n* عامِل بِناءٍ

constructive /kən'strʌktɪv/ *adj* ‹*criticism, suggestion*› بَنّاء

construct state *n* إِضافة

construe /kən'stru:/ *vt* (fml) أَوَّلَ, فَسَّرَ ‹*a remark, reaction*›

consul /'kɒns(ə)l/ *n* قُنْصُل (قَناصِلُ)

consulate /'kɒnsjʊlət/ *n* قُنْصُلِيّة

consult /kən'sʌlt/ A *vt* اِسْتَشارَ ‹*an expert, a lawyer*›; راجَعَ ‹*a dictionary*›
B *vi* «colleagues, teams» تَشاوَرَ; **to ~ with sb** تَشاوَرَ مع شَخْصٍ

consultancy /kən'sʌlt(ə)nsi/ *n* (*pl* **consultancies**) (also **consultancy firm**) شركة اسْتِشارِيّة

consultant /kən'sʌlt(ə)nt/ *n* 1 (expert) مُسْتَشار, خَبِير (خُبَراءُ) 2 (BrE) (specialist doctor) طَبِيب أَخِصّائِيّ \ اسْتِشارِيّ

consultation /kɒnsəl'teɪʃ(ə)n/ *n* (medical) اِسْتِشارة (طِبِّيّة); (discussion) مُشاوَرة

consulting engineer /kən,sʌltɪŋ ɛndʒɪn'ɪə/ *n* مُهَنْدِس اسْتِشارِيّ

consulting room /kən'sʌltɪŋ ,ru:m/ *n* غُرْفة الاسْتِشارة الطِّبِّيّة

consumables /kən'sju:məb(ə)lz/ *n pl* مَوادّ اسْتِهْلاكِيّة

consume /kən'sju:m/ *vt* 1 (to eat or drink) أَكَلَ (u; أَكْل) ‹*food*›; شَرِبَ (a; شُرْب, مَشْرَب) ‹*drink*›; (to burn up) اسْتَهْلَكَ ‹*fuel*› 2 **to be ~d by guilt/jealousy** انْتابَهُ شُعورٌ فَظِيعٌ بالذَّنْبِ \ بالغَيْرةِ

consumer /kən'sju:mə/ *n* مُسْتَهْلِك

consumer goods *n* سِلَع اسْتِهْلاكِيّة

consumer price index *n* (also **CPI**) مُؤَشِّر أَسْعارِ المُسْتَهْلِكِ

consumer protection *n* حِماية المُسْتَهْلِكِ

consumer society *n* مُجْتَمَع اسْتِهْلاكِيّ

consummate /'kɒns(j)ʊmeɪt/ *vt* تَمَّمَ بالجِماعِ ‹*a marriage, love*›

consumption /kən'sʌm(p)ʃ(ə)n/ *n* اسْتِهْلاك

contact A /'kɒntakt/ *n* 1 (physical) مُلامَسة; **to come into ~ with sth** لامَسَ شَيْئاً 2 (communication) اتِّصال (اتِّصالات); **to be in ~ with sb** كانَ على اتِّصالٍ بِشَخْصٍ
B /kən'takt, 'kɒntakt/ *vt* ‹*a friend, the police*› اتَّصَلَ (ب)

contact lens *n* عَدَسة لاصِقة

contactless /'kɒntaktləs/ *adj* ‹*card, payment*› لا تَلامُسِيّ

contagious /kən'teɪdʒəs/ *adj* ‹*disease, virus*› مُعْدٍ

contain /kən'teɪn/ *vt* 1 (to hold) احْتَوَى ‹*a trace, additive*›; تَضَمَّنَ ‹*a mistake, information*› 2 (to control) احْتَوَى ‹*a blaze, flood, epidemic*›; كَبَحَ (a; كَبْح) ‹*a cost, problem*›; **to ~ one's emotions** كَبَتَ مَشاعِرَهُ; **she was so happy she could hardly ~ herself** كانَتْ سَعِيدةً جِدًّا لِدَرَجةِ أَنَّها لم تَتَمالَكْ نَفْسَها

container /kən'teɪnə/ *n* 1 (receptacle) وِعاء (أَواعٍ), عُلْبة (عُلَب) 2 (for transporting goods) حاوِية

container ship *n* سَفِينة حاوِياتٍ

contaminate /kən'tamɪneɪt/ *vt* لَوَّثَ ‹*water, soil, supply*›

contamination /kən,tamɪ'neɪʃ(ə)n/ *n* تَلَوُّث

contd *abbr* = **continued** تابِع

contemplate /'kɒntəmpleɪt/ *vt* 1 (to consider) فَكَّرَ مَلِيًّا في ‹*a fact, the future*›; **to ~ divorce** فَكَّرَ مَلِيًّا في الطَّلاقِ 2 (to look at) تَأَمَّلَ ‹*a landscape, painting*›

contemplation /,kɒntem'pleɪʃ(ə)n/ *n* (fml) [u] تَأَمُّل; **to be lost in ~** كانَ غارِقاً في التَّفْكِيرِ

contemporary /kən'tɛmp(ə)r(ər)i/ A *adj* 1 (of same period) ‹*account, witness*› مُعاصِر 2 (present-day) ‹*art, style*› مُعاصِر, حَدِيث

B *n* (*pl* **contemporaries**) مُعاصِر; **we were contemporaries at school** كُنّا مُتَعاصِرينَ في المَدْرَسةِ

contempt /kən'tɛm(p)t/ *n* اِزْدِراء ,احْتِقار; **~ of court** عِصْيان المَحْكَمةِ

contemptible /kən'tɛm(p)tɪb(ə)l/ *adj* ‹*behaviour, amount*› وَضيع ,خَسيس

contemptuous /kən'tɛm(p)tjʊəs/ *adj* ‹*attitude, remark*› مُحْتَقِر ,مُزْدَرٍ

contend /kən'tɛnd/ **A** *vt* صَرَّح ,جادَلَ (رَغْمَ مُعارَضةِ الآخَرينَ)

B *vi* **1** (to deal with) **to ~ with poverty/dementia** صارَعَ الفَقْرَ \ الخَرَفَ **2** (to compete) **to ~ with sb for sth** تَنافَسَ مع شَخْصٍ على شَيْءٍ; **three clubs are ~ing for promotion** تَتَنافَسُ ثَلاثةُ أَنْدِيةٍ من أَجْلِ التَّرْفيعِ

contender /kən'tɛndə/ *n* مُنافِس

content¹ /kən'tɛnt/ **A** *adj* مُكْتَفٍ

B *v refl* **to ~ yourself with the situation** رَضِيَ بالوَضْعِ

content² /'kɒntɛnt/ *n* **1** [u] (of food) كَمّيّة ,نِسْبة **2** [u] (of a play, programme) مَضْمون **3** (**contents** *n pl*) (of a bottle, building, attic) مُحْتَوَيات; (list in a book) فِهْرِس (فَهارِسُ)

contented /kən'tɛntɪd/ *adj* ‹*baby, workforce*› راضٍ ,مَبْسوط

contention /kən'tɛnʃ(ə)n/ *n* **1** (assertion) جِدال (قَوِيّ) **2** [u] (competition) مُنافَسة; **to be in/out of ~ for a prize** كانَ ضِمْنَ \ خارِجَ المُنافَسةِ لِنَيْلِ جائِزةٍ

contentious /kən'tɛnʃəs/ *adj* ‹*issue, decision*› مُثير للجَدَلِ

contentment /kən'tɛntm(ə)nt/ *n* قَناعة ,رِضًى

contest **A** /'kɒntɛst/ *n* **1** (competition) مُنافَسة ,مُسابَقة; **a beauty ~** مُسابَقة جَمالٍ **2** (struggle) نِزاع ,(صِراعات) صِراع (نِزاعات)

B /kən'tɛst/ *vt* **1** (to dispute) عارَضَ ‹*a decision, will*› **2** (to compete for) نافَسَ ‹*an election, primary*›

contestant /kən'tɛst(ə)nt/ *n* (in a competition) مُتَبارٍ; (in a game show) مُتَسابِق

context /'kɒntɛkst/ *n* سِياق; **in/out of ~** في \ خارِجَ السِياقِ

continent /'kɒntɪnənt/ *n* قارّة; (BrE), **the Continent** أوروبّا (باسْتِثْناءِ الجُزُرِ البَريطانيّةِ)

continental /kɒntɪ'nɛnt(ə)l/ *adj* **1** (relating to a continent) قارّيّ **2** (also **Continental**) (BrE) (in mainland Europe) أوروبّيّ (باسْتِثْناءِ الجُزُرِ البَريطانيّةِ)

continental breakfast *n* إفْطار كونْتينِنْتال \ أوروبّيّ

contingency /kən'tɪndʒ(ə)nsi/ *n* (*pl* **contingencies**) حَدَث طارِئ

contingency plan *n* خُطّة طَوارِئَ

contingent /kən'tɪndʒ(ə)nt/ *n* فِرْقة (فِرَق)

continual /kən'tɪnjʊəl/ *adj* **1** (uninterrupted) ‹*improvement, process*› مُسْتَمِرّ ,مُتَواصِل **2** (repeated) ‹*reminders, references*› مُتَكَرِّر; **~ reminders to do it had no effect** لم يَكُنْ هُناكَ أَثَرٌ للتَذْكيراتِ المُتَكَرِّرةِ بِفِعْلِهِ

continually /kən'tɪnjʊəli/ *adv* ‹*to update, change*› باسْتِمْرارٍ, على نَحْوٍ مُتَواصِلٍ

continuation /kəntɪnjʊ'eɪʃ(ə)n/ *n* **1** (of a trend, process) اسْتِمْرار **2** (resumption) مُتابَعة ,اسْتِئْناف (اسْتِئْنافات) **3** (extension) امْتِداد (امْتِدادات)

continue /kən'tɪnju:/ **A** *vt* **1** (to carry on with) اسْتَمَرَّ (في), تابَعَ ,واصَلَ ‹*one's work, studies, efforts*›; **demand ~s to grow** اِسْتَمَرَّ الطَلَبُ في الزِيادة; **he ~d his research up till he died** اسْتَمَرَّ في أَبْحاثِهِ حتّى وَفاتِهِ **2** (to resume) اسْتَأْنَفَ ‹*a conversation, journey*›; **'to be ~d'** 'البَقيّةُ تَتْبَعُ'; **'~d overleaf'** 'البَقيّةُ في الصَفْحةِ التالِيةِ'; **'what's more,' she ~d** 'عِلاوةً على ذلك,' اسْتَطْرَدَتْ قائِلةً **3** (to preserve) حافَظَ (على), أَبْقى (على) ‹*a tradition, practice*›

B *vi* **1** (to carry on) «trend, work, investigation» اسْتَمَرَّ; **he ~d on his way** واصَلَ طَريقَهُ **2** (to resume) «game, negotiations» اسْتُؤْنِفَ; **to ~ with sth** اسْتَأْنَفَ شَيْئاً **3** (to remain) بَقِيَ (بَقاء; a), اسْتَمَرَّ; **to ~ in office/in one's role** بَقِيَ في مَنْصِبِهِ; **she will ~ as minister** سَتَسْتَمِرُّ في مَنْصِبِها كَوَزيرةٍ **4** «road, path» اسْتَمَرَّ

C (**continuing**) *adj* ‹*threat, debate*› مُسْتَمِرّ ,مُتَواصِل

continuity /,kɒntɪ'nju:ɪti/ *n* اسْتِمْراريّة

continuous /kən'tɪnjʊəs/ *adj* ‹*improvement, process*› مُسْتَمِرّ; ‹*line*› مُتَواصِل

continuous assessment *n* (BrE Educ) تَقْويم \ تَقْييم مُسْتَمِرّ

continuously /kən'tɪnjʊəsli/ *adv* <*to monitor, operate*> باسْتِمْرارٍ, بِشَكْلٍ مُسْتَمِرٍّ

continuum /kən'tɪnjʊəm/ *n* (*pl* **continua**) (fml) مَجْموعة مُتَّصِلة

contort /kən'tɔːt/ **A** *vt* <*one's face, body*> لَوّى
B *vi* «face, body» الْتَوى

contortion /kən'tɔːʃ(ə)n/ *n* (الْتِواءات) الْتِواء

contour /'kɒntʊə/ *n* (خطّ مُحيط بالشَيْءِ) مَعْلَم ,خَطّ كِفافيّ

contour line *n* خَطّ الكُنْتور \ المَنْسوب

contraband /'kɒntrəband/ *n* مُهَرَّبات ,سِلَع مُهَرَّبة

contraception /kɒntrə'sɛpʃ(ə)n/ *n* مَنْع الحَمْلِ

contraceptive /kɒntrə'sɛptɪv/ *n* وَسيلة مَنْع الحَمْلِ

contract **A** /'kɒntrakt/ *n* (legal agreement) (عُقود) عَقْد; **a fixed-term ~** عَقْد مُحَدَّد المُدّةِ; **to draw up a ~** وَضَع عَقْداً
B /kən'trakt/ *vt* **1** تَعاقَدَ <*a firm, supplier*> **2** الْتَقَطَ <*a disease, virus*> **3** وَقَعَ (a; وُقوع) (تحت) <*a debt, loan*>
C /kən'trakt/ *vi* «muscles» انْقَبَضَ ,تَقَلَّصَ; «wood» انْكَمَشَ

Phrasal verb **contract out**: **~ out [sth], ~ [sth] out** أَبْرَمَ عَقْدَ [شَيْءٍ] من الباطِنِ <*the work, maintenance*>

contraction /kən'trakʃ(ə)n/ *n* **1** (of metal, wood) انْكِماش, (تَقَلُّصات) تَقَلُّص **2** (of industry) انْكِماش **3** (of a muscle) انْقِباض ,(تَقَلُّصات) تَقَلُّص

contractor /kən'traktə/ *n* مُتَعَهِّد ,مُقاوِل

contractual /kən'traktʃʊəl/ *adj* <*obligation, dispute*> تَعاقُديّ

contradict /kɒntrə'dɪkt/ *vt* (مع) تَعارَضَ ,ناقَضَ <*a statement, speaker*>

contradiction /kɒntrə'dɪkʃ(ə)n/ *n* (تَناقُضات) تَناقُض; **a ~ in terms** تَناقُض في المُصْطَلَحاتِ

contradictory /kɒntrə'dɪkt(ə)ri/ *adj* <*statements, evidence*> مُتَناقِض

contraflow /'kɒntrəfləʊ/ *n* **1** (BrE) (in road repairs) [حَرَكة مُرورٍ مُؤَقَّتة في الاتِّجاهِ العَكْسيِّ] **2** (AmE) (in emergencies) [تَدَفُّق مُروريّ مُؤَقَّت في اتِّجاهٍ واحِدٍ]

contraindication /ˌkɒntrəɪndɪ'keɪʃ(ə)n/ *n* مانِع اسْتِعْمالٍ

contralto /kən'traltəʊ/ *n* [مُغَنِّية ذات صَوْتٍ رَنّانٍ (أَوْطأ صَوْتٍ نِسائيٍّ)]

contraption /kən'trapʃ(ə)n/ *n* (infml) [أَداة \ آلة غَريبة الشَكْلِ]

contrary **A** *adj* **1** /'kɒntrəri/ <*view, evidence*> مُعاكِس ,مُضادّ
2 /kən'trɛːri/ <*person*> مولَع بالمُعارَضةِ ,عَنيد
B *n* /'kɒntrəri/ (*pl* **contraries**) **the ~** العَكْس; **on the ~** على \ بالعَكْسِ
C (**contrary to**) *prep phr* خِلافاً ل ,على عَكْسِ

contrast **A** /'kɒntrɑːst/ *n* **1** (difference) (تَبايُنات) تَبايُن ,(تَغايُرات) تَغايُر ,(اخْتِلافات) اخْتِلاف; **to be a ~ to sth** كانَ مُتَبايِناً مع شَيْءٍ; **in** *or* **by ~ with sth** مُقارَنةً بِشَيْءٍ; **in** *or* **by ~, he was well prepared** في المُقابِلِ، كانَ هو مُسْتَعِدًّا بِشَكْلٍ جَيِّدٍ **2** [u] (in images) تَبايُن
B /kən'trɑːst/ *vt* **to ~ sth with sth** قارَنَ شَيْئاً بِشَيْءٍ
C *vi* «approaches, styles» تَبايَنَ; **his views ~ sharply with hers** تَتَبايَنُ آراؤُهُ بِحِدّةٍ مع آرائِها

contrasting /kən'trɑːstɪŋ/ *adj* <*colours, styles, opinions*> مُتَبايِن, مُغايِر

contravene /ˌkɒntrə'viːn/ *vt* (fml) انْتَهَكَ ,خالَفَ <*a law, ban*>

contribute /kən'trɪbjuːt/ **A** *vt* **1** ساهَمَ; (ب) تَبَرَّعَ <*money, time*> **2** قَدَّمَ للنَشْرِ <*an article, a poem*> (ب) <*ideas, information*>
B *vi* **1** **to ~ to sth** (to help to cause) أَسْهَمَ في شَيْءٍ **2** (to give money) تَبَرَّعَ ,أَسْهَمَ; **the council will ~ towards the cost** سَيُسْهِمُ المَجْلِسُ في تَغْطِيةِ التَكاليفِ **3** **to ~ (to a debate/discussion)** (to participate) شارَكَ (في نِقاشٍ \ مُناقَشةٍ) **4** **to ~ to sth** (to a publication) اشْتَرَكَ \ ساهَمَ في شَيْءٍ

contribution /kɒntrɪ'bjuːʃ(ə)n/ *n* **1** (role played, participation) مُساهَمة **2** (donation) (تَبَرُّعات) تَبَرُّع; (to a pension scheme) مُساهَمة

contributor /kən'trɪbjʊtə/ *n* **1** (donor) مُتَبَرِّع **2** (writer) كاتِب مَقالٍ

con trick *n* (infml) احْتِيال ,خِدْعة ثِقةٍ

contrive /kən'trʌɪv/ *vt* **1** (to manage) **to ~ to do sth** وَجَدَ وَسيلةً لِعَمَلِ شَيْءٍ **2** (to create) ابْتَدَعَ ,ابْتَكَرَ <*a plan, system*>

contrived /kən'trʌɪvd/ *adj* <*plot, situation*> مُبْتَدَع ,مُدَبَّر

control /kən'trəʊl/ **A** *n* **1** [u] (command) تَحَكُّم ,سَيْطَرة; **to be in ~ of sth** (to have charge of) كانَ مَسْؤولاً عن شَيْءٍ; **she is in ~ of the situation** هي مُسَيْطِرةٌ على الوَضْعِ; **to**

have ~ over sth كانَ لَدَيْهِ سَيْطَرةٌ على شَيْءٍ; **to take ~ of sth** سَيْطَرَ على شَيْءٍ; **everything's under ~** كُلّ شَيْءٍ تحت السَّيْطَرةِ; **to be under government/military ~** كانَ تحت سَيْطَرةِ الحُكومةِ \ الجَيْشِ; **to bring/keep sth under ~** وَضَعَ \ أَبْقى شَيْئاً تحت السَيْطَرة; **the fire was brought under ~** تَمَّت السَيْطَرةُ على النارِ; **inflation was going out of ~** بَدَأَ التَضَخُّمُ يَخْرُجُ عن السَيْطَرةِ; **to gain/lose ~ of sth** فَرَضَ \ فَقَدَ السَيْطَرةَ على شَيْءٍ; **to lose ~, to lose ~ of oneself** فَقَدَ السَيْطَرةَ على نَفْسِهِ; **due to circumstances beyond our ~** نَظراً لِظُروفٍ خارِجةٍ عن إرادَتِنا **2** [u] (of a machine, car, horse) سَيْطَرة, تَحَكُّم; **he has superb ball ~** لَدَيْهِ قُدْرةٌ فائِقةٌ على التَحَكُّمِ في الكُرة; **to take ~ of an aircraft** تَوَلّى قِيادةَ طائِرةٍ; **to take ~ of a computer** تَحَكَّمَ في كُمْبيوتر; **the car skidded out of ~** انْزَلَقَت السَيّارةُ وَخَرَجَتْ عن السَيْطَرة; **he lost ~ of his motorbike** فَقَدَ السَيْطَرةَ على دَرّاجَتِهِ النارِيّة **3** (lever, switch) زِرّ \ أداة تَحَكُّمٍ; **to be at the ~s** أدارَ لَوْحةِ التَحَكُّمِ **4** (regulation) ضابِط (ضَوابِطُ), قاعِدة (قَواعِدُ); **to impose/relax ~s on imports** فَرَضَ ضَوابِطَ \ خَفَّفَ الضَوابِطَ على الوارِداتِ **5** (in experiments) عَيِّنة ضابِطة **6** (control key) مِفْتاح \ زِرّ تَحَكُّمٍ

B *vt* (-ll-) **1** (to exert power over) سَيْطَرَ (i; سَيْطَرة; على), تَحَكَّمَ (في) ‹*an area, a market, company*›; **enemy forces ~led the air/the port** سَيْطَرَتْ قوّاتُ العَدوِّ على الجَوِّ \ الميناءِ; **the family owns and ~s several companies** تَمْتَلِكُ الأُسْرةُ وَتُديرُ عِدّةَ شَرِكاتٍ; **the major oil companies ~ the market** تُسَيْطِرُ شَرِكاتُ النَفْطِ الكُبْرى على السوقِ **2** (to restrain) سَيْطَرَ (i; سَيْطَرة; على) ‹*an animal, a child, crowd*›; **the police used dogs to ~ the demonstrators** اسْتَخْدَمَت الشُرْطةُ الكِلابَ للسَيْطَرةِ على المُتَظاهِرينَ; **she fought to ~ her emotions** جاهَدَتْ لِكَيْ تُسَيْطِرَ على مَشاعِرِها **3** (to check) سَيْطَرَ (i; سَيْطَرة; على) ‹*a disease, inflation, a fire*› **4** (to operate) تَحَكَّمَ (في) ‹*a vehicle, boat*› **5** (to regulate) تَحَكَّمَ (في) ‹*the temperature, flow, pressure*›; نَظَّمَ ‹*imports, exports, immigration*› **6** (to monitor) راقَبَ ‹*quality*›

C *v refl* (-ll-) **to ~ oneself** سَيْطَرَ على نَفْسِهِ

control freak *n* (infml) مَهْووس بالسَيْطَرةِ

controlled /kən'trəʊld/ *adj* **1** ‹*environment, experiment*› مُتَحَكَّم فيهِ, خاضِع للرَقابةِ **2** (restrained) ‹*voice, manner*› تحت السَيْطَرةِ, مَكْبوح

controller /kən'trəʊlə/ *n* **1** (manager) مُشْرِف, مُراقِب **2** (device) جِهاز تَحَكُّمٍ

control panel *n* لَوْحة تَحَكُّمٍ

control room *n* غُرْفة تَحَكُّمٍ

control tower *n* بُرْج مُراقَبةٍ

controversial /kɒntrə'vɜːʃ(ə)l/ *adj* ‹*issue, plan*› مُثير للجَدَلِ

controversy /'kɒntrəvɜːsi, kən'trɒvəsi/ *n* (*pl* **controversies**) جَدَل, خِلاف (خِلافات)

contusion /kən'tjuːʒ(ə)n/ *n* كَدْمة (كَدَمات)

conundrum /kə'nʌndrəm/ *n* لُغْز (أَلْغاز), أُحْجِيّة (أَحاجٍ, أَحاجيّ)

conurbation /ˌkɒnə'beɪʃ(ə)n/ *n* مُجْتَمَع حَضَريّ

convalesce /ˌkɒnvə'lɛs/ *vi* «patients, players» تَماثَلَ للشِفاءِ, تَعافى

convalescence /ˌkɒnvə'lɛs(ə)ns/ *n* فَتْرة نَقاهةٍ

convalescent /kɒnvə'lɛs(ə)nt/ **A** *adj* ‹*phase, hospital*› نَقاهيّ **B** *n* مَريض في فَتْرةِ النَقاهةِ

convalescent home *n* دار نَقاهةٍ

convene /kən'viːn/ **A** *vt* دَعا (إلى) ‹*a meeting*› **B** *vi* «committee» اجْتَمَعَ; «parliament» انْعَقَدَ

convenience /kən'viːnɪəns/ *n* **1** [u] (advantage) مُلاءَمة; **at your ~** على راحَتِكَ **2** (practical feature, device) وَسيلة راحةٍ; **with every modern ~** بِكُلِّ وَسائِلِ الراحةِ الحَديثةِ

convenience food *n* وَجَبات, مَأْكولات سَريعة التَحْضيرِ, جاهِزة

convenient /kən'viːnɪənt/ *adj* **1** ‹*place, date*› مُلائِم, مُناسِب **2** ‹*gadget, method*› عَمَليّ **3** ‹*shop, school*› قَريب

conveniently /kən'viːnɪəntli/ *adv* **1** (handily) بِشَكْلٍ مُناسِبٍ; **the apartment is very ~ located** تَقَعُ الشَقّةُ في مَوْقِعٍ مُناسِبٍ **2** (expediently) بالشَكْلِ المُناسِبِ; **the regulations are often ~ ignored** كَثيراً ما يَتِمُّ تَجاهُلُ القَوانينِ بالشَكْلِ المُناسِبِ

convent /'kɒnv(ə)nt/ *n* دَيْر (للراهِباتِ)

convention /kən'venʃ(ə)n/ *n* 1 (social norm) [u] عُرْف 2 (rule) (تقاليدُ) تَقْليد 3 (treaty) اتِّفاقيّة 4 (conference) (اجْتِماعات) اجْتِماع ,(مُؤْتَمرات) مُؤْتَمَر

conventional /kən'venʃ(ə)n(ə)l/ *adj* ‹*idea, medicine*› تَقْليديّ

converge /kən'vəːdʒ/ *vi* «paths, rivers» تلاقى

convergence /kən'vəːdʒ(ə)ns/ *n* الْتِقاء

conversant /kən'vəːs(ə)nt/ *adj* **to be ~ with sth** كانَ مُطَّلِعاً على شَيْءٍ

conversation /kɒnvə'seɪʃ(ə)n/ *n* 1 (a talk) حَديث 2 [u] (talking) مُحادَثة

conversational /kɒnvə'seɪʃ(ə)n(ə)l/ *adj* ‹*style, tone*› تَحادُثيّ

converse /kən'vəːs/ *vi* «guests, students» (fml) تَحادَثَ

conversely /'kɒnvəːsli/ *adv* على العَكْسِ, بالمَقْلوبِ

conversion /kən'vəːʃ(ə)n/ *n* 1 (transformation) تَحْويل 2 (of building) (تَغْييرات) تَغْيير 3 (to new beliefs) اعْتِناق 4 (in rugby) تَحْويلة

conversion rate *n* سِعْر تَحْويلِ العُمْلةِ

convert A /kən'vəːt/ *vt* 1 (to change use of) غَيَّرَ ‹*a cooker*›; (to adapt) حَوَّلَ ‹*a barn, garage*›; **to ~ a barn into a house** حَوَّلَ حَظيرةً إلى مَنْزِلٍ 2 حَوَّلَ ‹*a currency, dollar*› 3 (in religion) هَدى (i; هَدْي) (إلى) ‹*a heathen, socialist*› 4 (in football) [غَيَّرَ مُحاوَلةً إلى] [سَجَّلَ هَدَفَ الجَزاءِ] ‹*penalty*›; (in rugby) [تَحْويلةٍ] ‹*a try*›

B /kən'vəːt/ *vi* اعْتَنَقَ (ديناً غَيْرَ دينِهِ)

C /'kɒnvəːt/ *n* مُهْتَدٍ (إلى دينٍ جَديدٍ)

convertible /kən'vəːtɪb(ə)l/ A *adj* ‹*currency, bond*› قابِل للتَحْويلِ

B *n* سَيّارة مَكْشوفة

convex /'kɒnveks/ *adj* ‹*lens, mirror*› مُحَدَّب

convey /kən'veɪ/ *vt* 1 (to transport) نَقَلَ (u; نَقْل) ‹*a load, baggage*› 2 (to express) عَبَّرَ (عن) ‹*a mood, an impression*› 3 (to communicate) بَلَّغَ ‹*a message, ones' thanks*›

conveyance /kən'veɪəns/ *n* 1 (of goods, passengers) نَقْل 2 (transfer of property, title) تَحْويل ,نَقْل 3 (also **conveyance deed**) وَثيقة نَقْلِ المِلْكيّةِ

conveyancer /kən'veɪənsə/ *n* [مُحَرِّر وَثيقةِ نَقْلِ المِلْكيّةِ]

conveyancing /kən'veɪənsɪŋ/ *n* قانون نَقْلِ المِلْكيّةِ

conveyor belt /kən'veɪə ˌbelt/ *n* حِزام ناقِل

convict A /kən'vɪkt/ *vt* أَدانَ ‹*a criminal, defendant*›; **to be ~ed of speeding/murder** كانَ مُداناً بِتُهْمةِ السُّرْعةِ المُفْرِطةِ \ القَتْلِ

B /'kɒnvɪkt/ *n* مُدان ,مَحْكوم عَلَيْهِ

conviction /kən'vɪkʃ(ə)n/ *n* 1 (for crime) إدانة 2 (fml) (belief) قَناعة ,إيمان راسِخ

convince /kən'vɪns/ *vt* (to persuade) أَقْنَعَ ‹*a judge, a voter*›; **she ~d him to increase her pay** أَقْنَعَتْهُ بِزيادةِ راتِبِها

convinced /kən'vɪnst/ *adj* مُقْتَنِع; **to be ~ of sth** كانَ مُقْتَنِعاً بِشَيْءٍ

convincing /kən'vɪnsɪŋ/ *adj* 1 ‹*evidence, account*› مُقْنِع 2 ‹*victory, lead*› ساحِق

convincingly /kən'vɪnsɪŋli/ *adv* ‹*to argue, claim*› بِصورةٍ مُقْنِعةٍ; **the Bulls won ~** فازَ فَريقُ البولْز فَوْزاً ساحِقاً

convivial /kən'vɪvɪəl/ *adj* ‹*atmosphere, evening*› بَهيج ,وِدّيّ

convoy /'kɒnvɔɪ/ *n* قافِلة (قَوافِل)

convulse /kən'vʌls/ *vt* 1 جَعَلَ يَتَشَنَّجُ ‹*a person, body*›; **he was ~d with pain/agony/laughter** انْتَفَضَ من الألَمِ \ العَذابِ \ الضَحِكِ 2 هَزَّ (u; هَزّ) ‹*a country, region*›

convulsion /kən'vʌlʃ(ə)n/ *n* تَشَنُّج (تَشَنُّجات)

coo /kuː/ *vi* (**coos, cooing, cooed**) «pigeons» هَدَلَ (i; هَديل)

cook /kʊk/ A *vt* طَها (a-u; طَهْو ,طَهْي), طَبَخَ (a-u; طَبْخ) ‹*a meal, the vegetables, meat, food*›

B *vi* 1 «person» طَها (a-u; طَهْو ,طَهْي), طَبَخَ (a-u; طَبْخ) 2 «food, pasta, dinner» طُبِخَ ,طُهِيَ

C (**cooked**) *adj* ‹*food, meal*› مَطْبوخ ,مَطْهوّ; **to be well ~ed** كانَ مَطْهوًّا بِشَكْلٍ جَيِّدٍ

D *n* طُهاة) طاهٍ), طَبّاخ; **he's a good ~** هو طاهٍ جَيِّدٌ

(Idioms) **to cook the books** (infml) تَلاعَبَ في الدَفاتِرِ; **what's cooking?** (infml) ما الّذي يَتِمُّ تَدْبيرُهُ؟

(Phrasal verb) **cook up** (infml): **~ up [sth]** 1 طَها [شَيْئاً] ‹*a meal, dish*› 2 اخْتَرَعَ \ ابْتَدَعَ [شَيْئاً] ‹*a plan, story*›

cookbook /'kʊkbʊk/ *n* كِتاب طَبْخ

cook-chill foods /kʊktʃɪl 'fu:dz/ *n pl* (BrE) [أَغْذِيَة مُجَمَّدَة جاهِزة للأَكْلِ]

cooker /'kʊkə/ *n* (BrE) فُرْن طَبْخٍ

cookery /'kʊk(ə)ri/ *n* فَنّ الطَّبْخ

cookery book *n* (BrE) كِتاب طَبْخٍ

cookie /'kʊki/ *n* **1** (biscuit) بَسْكوت **2** (Comput) (data file) مِلَفّ الكوكي ,مِلَفّ تَعْريفِ الارْتِباطِ ,سِجِلّ المُتَصَفِّحِ

cooking /'kʊkɪŋ/ *n* طَهْي ,طَبْخ; **to do the ~** قامَ بالطَّهْي; **French ~** فَنّ الطَّبْخ الفَرَنْسيّ

cooking apple *n* تُفّاحة للطَّبْخِ

cooking chocolate *n* شوكولاتة للطَّبْخِ

cool /ku:l/ **A** *adj* **1** ‹*water, breeze, day*› مُعْتَدِل البُرودة; **it's nice and ~ out here** الطَّقْسُ لَطيفٌ وَمُعْتَدِلُ البُرودة هُنا; **we'll go when the weather is ~er** سَوْفَ نَذْهَبُ عِنْدَما يَكونُ الطَّقْسُ أَكْثَرَ اعْتِدالاً **2** ‹*clothing*› يُعْطي شُعوراً بالبُرودة ,بارِد **3** ‹*colour*› بارِد **4** (calm) ‹*approach, appraisal*› رَصين ,هادِئ; **to stay *or* keep ~** احْتَفَظَ بِهُدوءِهِ; **to keep a ~ head** احْتَفَظَ بِهُدوءِهِ; **he's a ~ customer** هو رابِطُ الجَأْشِ **5** (unfriendly) ‹*response, reception*› فاتِر; **to be ~ towards sb** كانَ فاتِراً تُجاهَ شَخْصٍ **6** (infml) (for emphasis) **a ~ million dollars** ≈ مِلْيون دولارٍ بالتَّمامِ والكَمالِ **7** (infml) (impressive) ‹*person, music, idea*› باهِر ,رائِع; **those sunglasses are really ~** هذه نَظّارةُ الشَّمْسِ رائِعةٌ حَقّاً; **he thinks it's ~ to smoke** يَعْتَقِدُ أَنَّ التَّدْخينَ شَيْءٌ مُثيرٌ للإعْجابِ; **that's a ~ idea** هذه فِكْرةٌ لَطيفةٌ **8** (infml) (accepting) غَيْر مُمانِعٍ ,مُتَقَبِّل ,مُوافِق; **I'm ~ with that** لَيْسَ لَدَيَّ مانِعٌ في ذلك

B *n* **1** (coldness) اعْتِدالُ الحَرارةِ ,بُرودة مُعْتَدِلة; **in the ~ of the evening** في جَوِّ المَساءِ المُعْتَدِلِ **2** (calm) هُدوء; **to keep/lose one's ~** احْتَفَظَ بِهُدوءِهِ \ فَقَدَ هُدوءَهُ

C *vt* **1** بَرَّدَ ‹*food, drink, an engine*›; **the A/C system ~s the whole building** يُبَرِّدُ جِهازُ التَّكْييفِ المَبْنى كُلَّهُ **2** (to calm) هَدَّأَ ‹*sb's enthusiasm, temper*›

D *vi* **1** «food, drink, engine» بَرَدَ (a; بُرود) ,بَرُدَ (u; بُرود ,بَرْد) **2** «air, weather» بَرَدَ (a; بُرود ,بَرْد) ,بَرُدَ (u; بُرود) «temperature» انْخَفَضَ **3** «friendship, passion» فَتَرَ (u; فُتور); **wait until tempers ~** انْتَظِرْ حتّى تَهْدَأَ الأَعْصابُ

E *excl* (infml) **1** (excellent) مُمْتاز **2** (in agreement) اتَّفَقْنا, حَسَناً

(Phrasal verbs) **cool down** **A** **1** «weather, engine» بَرَدَ (a; بُرود ,بَرْد) ,بَرُدَ (u; بُرود) «temperature» انْخَفَضَ **2** «tempers, person» هَدَأَ (a; هُدوء) **B** **~ [sth] down** بَرَّدَ [شَيْئاً] ‹*food, an engine*›

• **cool off** **1** (to become cooler) «person, animal» بَرَّدَ جَسَدَهُ **2** (to calm down) هَدَأَ (a; هُدوء)

coolant /'ku:l(ə)nt/ *n* مادّة مُبَرِّدة

cool bag *n* حَقيبة تَبْريدٍ

cool box *n* صُنْدوق تَبْريد

cooler /'ku:lə/ *n* **1** (for drinks, food) مُبَرِّد **2** (for water) مُبَرِّد مِياهٍ

cooling /'ku:lɪŋ/ **A** *n* تَبْريد **B** *adj* ‹*drink, swim*› مُنْعِش; ‹*breeze*› عَليل; ‹*agent*› مُبَرِّد

cooling-off period /ˌku:lɪŋ'ɒf ˌpɪ:rɪəd/ *n* **1** (in contract) مُهْلة للتَّفْكيرِ **2** (in industrial relations) هُدْنة مُصالَحةٍ

coolly /'ku:lli/ *adv* **1** (calmly) ‹*to reply, observe*› بِبُرودة أَعْصابٍ **2** (coldly, without enthusiasm) ‹*to react, greet*› بِبُرودةٍ **3** (boldly) ‹*to announce, demand*› بِجُرْأةٍ

coolness /'ku:lnəs/ *n* **1** (in temperature) بُرودة مُعْتَدِلة, اعْتِدال الحَرارة **2** (of response, welcome) فُتور **3** (calm) رِباطة جَأْشٍ ,هُدوء

coon /ku:n/ *n* (AmE infml) = **raccoon** راكون

coop /ku:p/ *n* خُمّ (خِمَمة)

(Phrasal verb) **coop up: ~ [sb/sth] up** حَبَسَ [شَخْصاً \ شَيْئاً]

co-op /'kəʊɒp/ *n* (infml) = **cooperative** تَعاوُنيّة

cooperate /kəʊ'ɒpəreɪt/ *vi* (to work together) «employees, countries» تَعاوَنَ

cooperation /kəʊˌɒpə'reɪʃ(ə)n/ *n* تَعاوُن

cooperative /kəʊ'ɒp(ə)rətɪv/ **A** *adj* **1** ‹*attitude, manner*› مُتَعاوِن **2** ‹*effort, exercise*› تَعاوُنيّ **B** *n* (جَمْعيّة) تَعاوُنيّة

co-opt /ˌkəʊ'ɒpt/ *vt* [عَيَّنَ (أَعْضاءٌ حاليّونَ في لَجْنةٍ) عُضْواً جَديداً]; **to ~ sb onto a committee** عَيَّنَ شَخْصاً لِعُضْوِيّةِ لَجْنةٍ

coordinate **A** /kəʊ'ɔːdɪneɪt/ *vt* نَسَّقَ *<efforts, activities>*

B /kəʊ'ɔːdɪnət/ *n* **1** (on a map, graph) إِحْداثِيّات

2 **(coordinates)** (matching clothing) [أَلْبِسة نِسائيّة مُتَناسِقة]

coordinated /ˌkəʊ'ɔːdɪneɪtɪd/ *adj* *<response, policy>* مُتَناسِق; **her outfit is very well/badly ~** ثَوْبُها مُتَناسِقٌ \ غَيْرُ مُتَناسِقٍ للغايةِ

coordination /kəʊˌɔːdɪ'neɪʃ(ə)n/ *n* **1** (organization) تَنْسيق

2 (of senses, movements) (تَناسُقات) تَناسُق

coordinator /ˌkəʊ'ɔːdɪneɪtə/ *n* مُنَسِّق

co-owner /kəʊ'əʊnə/ *n* مالِك مُشْتَرَك

cop /kɒp/ *n* (infml) شُرْطيّ

cope /kəʊp/ *vi* «parents, infrastructure» دَبَّرَ \ تَدَبَّرَ أُمورَهُ; **can she ~?** هل يُمْكِنُها أَنْ تُدَبِّرَ أُمورَها؟; **they ~d well with the work** تَعامَلوا مع العَمَلِ بِشَكْلٍ جَيِّدٍ

Copenhagen /ˌkəʊp(ə)n'heɪg(ə)n/ *pr n* كوبِنْهاجَن (f)

copious /'kəʊpɪəs/ *adj* (plentiful) *<amount, supply>* وافِر

cop-out /'kɒpaʊt/ *n* (infml) [تَجَنُّب لِتَحَمُّلِ المَسْؤوليّة]

copper /'kɒpə/ *n* **1** [u] (metal) نُحاس **2** **(coppers)** (BrE) (coins) [قِطَع نَقْديّة نُحاسيّة] **3** [u] (colour) لَوْن نُحاسيّ

4 (BrE infml) (police officer) شُرْطيّ

Copt /kɒpt/ *n* (أَقْباط ,قِبْط) قِبْطيّ

Coptic /'kɒptɪk/ *adj* *<church, rite>* (أَقْباط ,قِبْط) قِبْطيّ

copy /'kɒpi/ **A** *n* (*pl* **copies**) **1** (duplicate) (نُسَخ) نُسْخة **2** (of book, newspaper) (نُسَخ) نُسْخة **3** (text) نَصّ دِعائيّ \ تَرْويجيّ

B *vt* **(copies, copying, copied)** **1** (to reproduce) نَسَخَ (a; نَسْخ) *<a letter, file>* **2** (to imitate) قَلَّدَ, حاكَى *<your brother, behaviour>*

C *vi* «students, exam candidates» نَقَلَ (u; نَقْل)

copycat /'kɒpɪkat/ *n* (infml pej) مُقَلِّد

copyright /'kɒpɪrʌɪt/ *n* مِلْكيّة أَدَبيّة ,حُقوق التَأْليفِ والنَشْرِ

copywriter /'kɒpɪrʌɪtə/ *n* كاتِب إِعْلاناتٍ

coquettish /kə'ketɪʃ/ *adj* لَعوب (f; لَعائِبُ) ,غَنِج

coral /'kɒr(ə)l/ *n* مَرْجان (n coll)

coral reef *n* شِعْب مَرْجانيّ

cord /kɔːd/ *n* **1** (string) حَبْل (أَحْبال ,حِبال) **2** (AmE) (cable) كابِل (أَسْلاك) ,سِلْك

cordial /'kɔːdɪəl/ **A** *adj* *<relations>* وِدّيّ; *<welcome>* حارّ

B *n* [مَشْروب مُحَلًّى بِنَكْهةِ الفَواكِهِ]

cordless /'kɔːdləs/ *adj* *<telephone, kettle>* لاسِلْكيّ

cordon /'kɔːd(ə)n/ *n* شَريط \ كُرْدون أَمْنيّ

(Phrasal verb) **cordon off**: **~ off [sth]**, **~ [sth] off** طَوَّقَ \ حاصَرَ [شَيْئاً] *<an area, street>*

corduroy /'kɔːdərɔɪ/ *n* كورْدْروي (قُماش قُطْنيّ مَتين مُخْمَليّ)

core /kɔː/ *n* **1** (of an apple, a pear) قَلْب (قُلوب) ,لُبّ (أَلْباب)

2 (essence, central part) لُبّ ,صَميم ,جَوْهَر **3** (group of people) مَجْموعة أَساسيّة **4** (of a planet) نَواة (نَوَيات ,نَوًى)

5 (of a nuclear reactor) قَلْب

co-respondent /kəʊrɪ'spɒnd(ə)nt/ *n* شَريك في الزِناءِ (في قَضيّةِ طَلاقٍ)

Corfu /kɔː'f(j)uː/ *pr n* كورْفو (f)

coriander /ˌkɒrɪ'andə/ *n* كُزْبَرة

cork /kɔːk/ *n* **1** (substance) فِلّين **2** (stopper) سِدادة فِلّينيّة ,فِلّينة

corkscrew /'kɔːkskruː/ *n* بِزال

cormorant /'kɔːm(ə)r(ə)nt/ *n* غاق (n coll)

corn /kɔːn/ *n* **1** (BrE) (wheat) قَمْح (قُموح) ,حِنْطة (حِنَط)

2 (AmE) (maize) ذُرة; **the C~ Belt** نِطاق الذُرةِ **3** (on foot) مِسْمار القَدَمِ

cornea /'kɔːnɪə/ *n* (*pl* **corneas** or **corneae**) قَرْنيّة

corner /'kɔːnə/ **A** *n* **1** (inside angle of a room, page, field) زاوية (زَوايا) ,رُكْن (أَرْكان) **2** (outside angle of a street) ناصِية (نَواصٍ); (of a table, building) زاوية (زَوايا); **the house on the ~** البَيْت على الناصِيةِ; **at** *or* **on the ~ of the street** عند ناصِيةِ \ رَأْسِ الشارِعِ; **to turn the ~** انْعَطَفَ عند الناصِيةِ; **just around the ~** قَريب جِدًّا; **spring is just around the ~** الرَبيعُ على الأَبْوابِ **3** (bend) مُنْعَطَف (مُنْعَطَفات); **she took the ~ too fast** أَخَذَتِ المُنْعَطَفَ بِسُرْعةٍ زائِدةٍ **4** (of one's eye, mouth) طَرَف (أَطْراف) ,جانِب (جَوانِبُ); **out of the ~ of one's eye** بِطَرَفِ عَيْنِهِ **5** (place) مِنْطَقة (مَناطِقُ) ,مَكان (أَماكِنُ ,أَمْكِنة); **a remote ~ of India** مِنْطَقة نائِية في الهِنْدِ; **I searched every ~ of the house** بَحَثْتُ في كُلِّ رُكْنٍ في البَيْتِ **6** (difficult situation) مَأْزِق (مَآزِقُ); **to be in a tight ~** كانَ في وَضْعٍ حَرِجٍ

[7] (in football, hockey) ضَرْبة رُكْنيّة; **to take the ~** نَفَّذَ الضَرْبةَ الرُكْنيّةَ [8] (in boxing) رُكْن (أَرْكان)

[B] *vt* [1] (to trap) حَصَرَ في الزاوِيةِ ‹*an animal, a suspect*›

[2] (to detain) حَصَرَ في الزاوِيةِ [3] (to monopolize) احْتَكَرَ ‹*the market*›

[C] *vi* «car» انْعَطَفَ

corner shop *n* بِقالة

cornerstone /ˈkɔːnəstəʊn/ *n* حَجَر الزاوِيةِ

cornet /ˈkɔːnɪt/ *n* [1] (musical instrument) بوق (أَبْواق, بوقات)

[2] (BrE) (for ice cream) قَرْن (قُرون), قِمْع (أَقْماع)

cornflakes /ˈkɔːnfleɪks/ *n pl* كورْن فْلِكْس, رَقائِق الذُرة

cornflour /ˈkɔːnflaʊə/ *n* (BrE) نَشاء الذُرة

cornflower /ˈkɔːnflaʊə/ *n* قَنْطَريون عَنْبَريّ

Cornish /ˈkɔːnɪʃ/ *adj* ‹*coast, village*› كورْنيشيّ (من كورْنْوال)

corn on the cob *n* كوز ذُرةٍ

cornstarch /ˈkɔːnstɑːtʃ/ *n* (AmE) نَشاء الذُرةِ

Cornwall /ˈkɔːnwəl/ *pr n* (Geog) كورْنْوال (f)

corny /ˈkɔːni/ *adj* (**cornier**, **corniest**) (infml) ‹*song, plot, joke*› سَخيف (سِخاف), مُبْتَذَل

coronary /ˈkɒr(ə)n(ə)ri/ [A] *adj* ‹*heart disease, artery*› تاجيّ

[B] *n* (*pl* **coronaries**) جُلْطة القَلْبِ

coronation /kɒrəˈneɪʃ(ə)n/ *n* تَتْويج

coroner /ˈkɒr(ə)nə/ *n* مُحَقِّق وَفَياتٍ

corporal /ˈkɔːp(ə)r(ə)l/ *n* عَريف (عُرَفاءُ)

corporal punishment *n* عُقوبة بَدَنيّة

corporate /ˈkɔːp(ə)rət/ *adj* [1] ‹*accounts, clients*› شَرِكةٍ

[2] ‹*decision, responsibility*› مُشْتَرَك, جَماعيّ

corporate identity, **corporate image** *n* هُويّة شَرِكةٍ

corporate raider *n* غازي \ صائد الشَرِكاتِ (مُمَوِّل يَشْتَري حِصَصاً كَثيرةً في شَرِكةٍ بِهَدَفِ السَيْطَرةِ عَلَيْها \ بَيْعِها من أَجْلِ الرِبْحِ)

corporate state *n* دَوْلة نِقابَويّة (دَوْلة تَقَعُ تحت سَيْطَرةِ مَجْموعاتٍ ذاتِ مَصالِحَ خاصّةٍ)

corporation /kɔːpəˈreɪʃ(ə)n/ *n* (commercial) شَرِكة; (non-commercial) هَيْئة

corporation tax *n* ضَريبة على أَرْباحِ الشَرِكاتِ

corps /kɔː/ *n* (*pl* **corps** /kɔːz/; *+ v sing or v pl*) (fighting) فَيْلَق (فَيالِقُ); (technical) سِلْك (أَسْلاك)

corpse /kɔːps/ *n* جُثّة (جُثَث), جُثْمان

corpulent /ˈkɔːpjʊl(ə)nt/ *adj* ‹*person*› سَمين (سِمان), بَدين (بُدُن), لَحيم

corpuscle /ˈkɔːpʌs(ə)l/ *n* كُرَيّة (دَمٍ)

corral /kəˈrɑːl/ *n* (AmE) حَظيرة (حَظائِرُ), زَريبة (زَرائِبُ)

correct /kəˈrɛkt/ [A] *adj* [1] (right) ‹*answer, number, decision*› صَحيح, صائِب; **that is ~** ذلك صَحيحٌ; **the ~ time** الوَقْتُ الصَحيح; **you are quite ~** أَنْتَ على صَوابٍ تَماماً; **his prediction proved ~** ثَبَتَتْ صِحّةُ تَوَقُّعِهِ [2] (proper) ‹*behaviour, person*› سَويّ, قَويم

[B] *vt* [1] (to put right) صَوَّبَ, صَحَّحَ ‹*a problem, an error, sb's grammar*›; صَحَّحَ (ل) ‹*a person*›; (fml) **~ me if I'm wrong** صَحِّحْني إذا أَخْطَأْتُ; (fml) **I stand ~ed** أَعْتَرِفُ بِخَطَئي

[2] صَحَّحَ ‹*a text, proofs, exam papers*›

[C] *v refl* **to ~ oneself** صَحَّحَ نَفْسَهُ

correction /kəˈrɛkʃ(ə)n/ *n* تَصْحيح (تَصْحيحات)

correction fluid *n* سائِل تَصْحيحٍ

correctly /kəˈrɛk(t)li/ *adv* ‹*to identify, answer*› على نَحْوٍ صَحيحٍ, بِطَريقةٍ صَحيحةٍ

correctness /kəˈrɛktnəs/ *n* صِحّة, صَواب

correlate /ˈkɒrəleɪt/ [A] *vt* رَبَطَ (i-u; رَبْط) (بين) ‹*data, findings*›

[B] *vi* «data, findings» ارْتَبَطَ بِعَلاقةٍ مُتَبادَلةٍ; **to ~ with sth** ارْتَبَطَ بِعَلاقةٍ مُتَبادَلةٍ بِشَيْءٍ

correlation /kɒrəˈleɪʃ(ə)n/ *n* عَلاقة طَرْديّة, ارْتِباط (ارْتِباطات)

correspond /kɒrɪˈspɒnd/ *vi* [1] (to match) **to ~ (with sth)** «numbers, evidence» تَطابَقَ \ تَوافَقَ (مع شَيْءٍ) [2] (to be equivalent) **to ~ (to sth)** «areas, systems» وازى \ قابَلَ (شَيْئاً)

[3] (to exchange letters) تَكاتَبَ, تَراسَلَ

correspondence /kɒrɪˈspɒnd(ə)ns/ *n* [1] (communication by letter) مُراسَلة, تَراسُل [2] (similarity) تَطابُق (تَطابُقات), تَوافُق

correspondence course *n* دَوْرة دِراسيّة بالمُراسَلةِ

correspondent /kɒrɪ'spɒnd(ə)nt/ *n* **1** (journalist) مُراسِل صُحُفيّ **2** (letter writer) مُراسِل

corresponding /ˌkɒrɪ'spɒndɪŋ/ *adj* (equivalent) ‹*period, increase*› مُوافِق, مُطابِق

corridor /'kɒrɪdɔː/ *n* مَجاز (بين الغُرَفِ)

corroborate /kə'rɒbəreɪt/ *vt* دَعَّمَ, عَزَّزَ ‹*findings, a theory*›

corrode /kə'rəʊd/ **A** *vt* حَتَّ (u; حَتٌّ), أَكَلَ (u; أَكْل), أَصْدَأَ ‹*the metal, bodywork*›

B *vi* «metals, pipes» صَدِئَ (a; صَداءة), تَأَكَّلَ, تَأَكْسَدَ

corrosion /kə'rəʊʒ(ə)n/ *n* تَحاتّ, تَأَكُّل

corrosive /kə'rəʊsɪv/ *adj* ‹*effect, substance*› أَكّال, مُسَبِّب للتآكُل

corrugated /'kɒrəgeɪtɪd/ *adj* ‹*roof, metal*› مُمَوَّج

corrugated iron *n* حَديد مُمَوَّج

corrupt /kə'rʌpt/ **A** *adj* **1** (dishonest) ‹*society, official*› مُرْتَشٍ, فاسِد (فاسِدونَ, فَسْدى) **2** (damaged) ‹*data, file*› تالِف

B *vt* **1** (to bribe) قَدَّمَ رَشْوةً ل, رَشا (u; رَشْو) ‹*a politician, official*› **2** (to deprave) أَفْسَدَ الأَخْلاقَ ‹*a child, society*›

3 (to damage) أَتْلَفَ ‹*data, a file*›

corruption /kə'rʌpʃ(ə)n/ *n* **1** [u] (of society) فَساد; **the civil service is riddled with ~** الخِدْمةُ المَدَنيّةُ مَليئةٌ بالفَسادِ

2 (of youth) إفْساد (خُلُقيّ)

corset /'kɔːsɪt/ *n* كورْسيه (كورْسيهات), مِشَدّ للبَطْنِ \ للخَصْرِ

Corsica /'kɔːsɪkə/ *pr n* كورْسيكا

cortex /'kɔːtɛks/ *n* (*pl* **cortices**) قِشْرة (قِشْر)

cos /kɒz/ *n* = **cosine** جَتا (جَيْب التمام)

cosh /kɒʃ/ *n* (BrE) هِراوة (هَراوى)

cosmetic /kɒz'metɪk/ **A** *adj* **1** (beautifying) ‹*powder, solution*› تَجْميليّ **2** (superficial) ‹*reform, change*› شَكْليّ

B *n pl* **(cosmetics)** مُسْتَحْضَرات التَجْميل

cosmetic surgery *n* جراحة تَجْميل \ تَجْميليّة

cosmic /'kɒzmɪk/ *adj* ‹*rays, force*› كَوْنيّ

cosmonaut /'kɒzmənɔːt/ *n* رائِد فَضاءٍ

cosmopolitan /ˌkɒzmə'pɒlɪt(ə)n/ *adj* ‹*city, outlook*› كوزْموبوليتانيّ (مُتَعَدِّد الأَجْناسِ والثَقافاتِ)

cosmos /'kɒzmɒs/ *n* كَوْن

cost /kɒst/ **A** *vt* **1** (*past tense, past participle* **cost** or **costed**) (to be priced at) «product, service» كانَ ثَمَنُهُ, كَلَّفَ; **how much does it ~?** ما ثَمَنُهُ؟; **tickets ~ £20** ثَمَنُ التَذاكِرِ £20; **it will ~ you $500** سَيُكَلِّفُكَ $500 **2** (*past tense, past participle* **cost**) (in losses) كَلَّفَ; **that decision cost him his job** كَلَّفَهُ ذلك القَرارُ وَظيفَتَهُ; **good manners ~ nothing** حُسْنُ الخُلُقِ لا يُكَلِّفُ شَيْئاً **3** (*past tense, past participle* **costed**) (in estimates) قَدَّرَ التَكاليفَ ‹*a project, work*›

B *n* **1** (price) سِعْر (أَسْعار), ثَمَن (أَثْمان), تَكْلِفة (تَكاليفُ); **at a ~ of £100** بِسِعْرِ £100; **labour ~s are high** تَكاليفُ العِمالةِ مُرْتَفِعةٌ; **at ~** بِسِعْرِ التَكْلِفةِ; **you must bear the ~ of any repairs** يَجِبُ عَلَيْكَ أَنْ تَتَحَمَّلَ تَكاليفَ أَيِّ إِصْلاحاتٍ; **at no extra ~** بِدونِ أَيِّ تَكْلِفةٍ إِضافيّةٍ; **to reduce** *or* **cut ~s** خَفَّضَ التَكاليفَ **2** (sacrifice) تَضْحِية; **at great personal ~** بِتَضْحِيةٍ شَخْصيّةٍ كَبيرةٍ; **at all ~s** بِأَيِّ ثَمَنٍ; **whatever the ~** مَهْما كانَ الثَمَنُ; **as he found to his ~** كَما تَعَلَّمَ بَعْدَما دَفَعَ الثَمَنَ

C **(costs)** *n pl* (Law) مَصاريف الدَعْوى; **the judge awarded ~s to the plaintiff** حَمَّلَ القاضي المُدَّعي مَصاريفَ الدَعْوى

co-star /'kəʊstɑː/ **A** *n* نَجْم يُشارِكُ نَجْماً آخَرَ البُطولةَ

B *vt* (-rr-) **a film ~ring Liz Taylor and Richard Burton** فيلْم يُشارِكُ في بُطولَتِهِ ليز تايْلور إلى جانِبِ ريتْشارْد بورْتُن

C *vi* (-rr-) «actors, artists» ظَهَرَ كَنَجْمٍ مُشارِكٍ

Costa Rica /ˌkɒstə 'riːkə/ *pr n* كوسْتاريكا

Costa Rican /ˌkɒstə' riːk(ə)n/ *n, adj* كوسْتَريكيّ

cost-benefit analysis /ˌkɒstˌbɛnəfɪt ə'naləsɪs/ *n* تَحْليل التَكْلِفةِ والعائِدِ

cost-cutting /'kɒstkʌtɪŋ/ *n* خَفْض التَكاليفِ

cost-effective /kɒstɪ'fɛktɪv/ *adj* ‹*operation, method*› ذو تَكْلِفةٍ اقْتِصاديّ, فَعّالة

costly /'kɒs(t)li/ *adj* (**costlier, costliest**) **1** ‹*exercise, habit*› مُكَلِّف **2** ‹*mistake, delay*› غالٍ, مُكَلِّف

cost of living *n* تكاليف المَعيشة

cost price *n* سِعْر التَكْلِفةِ

costume /'kɒstjuːm/ *n* (clothes) زِيّ (أَزْياء), بِذْلة (بِذَل)

costume jewellery, **costume jewelry** (AmE) *n* مُجَوْهَرات للأَزْياءِ (مُجَوْهَرات تَقْليدٍ رَخيصة تُسْتَخْدَمُ في المَسْرَحِ والسينَما)

cosy (BrE), **cozy** (AmE) /ˈkəʊzi/ *adj* (**cosier**, **cosiest**)
1▸ (comfortable) ‹*atmosphere, room*› [دافِئ ومُريح]
2▸ (intimate) ‹*chat, meal*› حَميم

cot /kɒt/ *n* 1▸ (BrE) (for baby) مَهْد (مُهود) 2▸ (AmE) (camp bed) [سَرير مُتَنَقِّل للتَخْييم]

cot death *n* مَوْت المَهْدِ, مَوْت الرُضَّع المُفاجِئ

Côte d'Ivoire /ˌkəʊt diːˈvwɑː/ *pr n* كوت ديفوار (f)

cottage /ˈkɒtɪdʒ/ *n* كوخ (أَكْواخ), بَيْت ريفيّ

cottage cheese *n* جُبْن قَريش

cotton /ˈkɒt(ə)n/ *n* 1▸ (plant, material) قُطْن (أَقْطان) 2▸ (cloth) قُماش قُطْنيّ 3▸ (BrE) (thread) [خَيْط غَزْلٍ قُطْنيٍّ]

cotton bud *n* (BrE) بُرْعُم القُطْنِ, قُطْن الأُذُنِ

cotton wool *n* قُطْن طِبّيّ

couch /kaʊtʃ/ *n* 1▸ (sofa) أَريكة (أَرائِكُ) 2▸ (psychoanalyst's) سَرير (أَسِرّة)

couch potato *n* [شَخْص كَسول يَقْضي وَقْتَهُ في مُشاهَدةِ بَرامِجِ التِلِفِزْيون]

cougar /ˈkuːɡə/ *n* (AmE) كوغَر, بوما

cough /kɒf/ **A** *vi* سَعَل (u; سُعال, سُعْلة)
B *n* سُعال; **to have a ~** كانَ لَدَيْهِ سُعالٌ

(Phrasal verb) **cough up**: **~ up [sth]** 1▸ نَفَث [شَيْئاً] ‹*blood*›
2▸ (infml) (to pay) دفَع [شَيْئاً]

cough mixture *n* شَراب السُعالِ

could /kʊd, kəd/ ▸ **can¹**

couldn't /ˈkʊd(ə)nt/ *abbr* = **could not** ▸ **can¹**

council /ˈkaʊns(ə)l/ *n* 1▸ (advisory body) مَجْلِس (مَجالِسُ); **the Council of Europe** مَجْلِس أوروبّا 2▸ (local government) مَجْلِس بَلَديّ

council estate *n* [مِنْطَقة سَكَنيّة مَمْلوكة للمَجْلِسِ البَلَديِّ]

council house *n* مَسْكَن حُكوميّ ≈ (بَيْت مَمْلوك للمَجْلِسِ البَلَديِّ)

council housing *n* إسْكان حُكوميّ ≈ (إسْكان يُوَفِّرُهُ المَجْلِس البَلَديُّ)

councillor, **councilor** (AmE) /ˈkaʊns(ə)lə/ *n* عُضْو مَجْلِسٍ

councilman /ˈkaʊns(ə)lmən/ *n* (*pl* **-men**) (AmE) عُضْو مَجْلِسٍ بَلَديٍّ

council scheme *n* (Scot) [مِنْطَقة سَكَنيّة مَمْلوكة للمَجْلِسِ البَلَديِّ]

council tax *n* (BrE) ضَريبة بَلَديّة

counsel /ˈkaʊns(ə)l/ **A** *n no art* (**counsel**, *pl*) (lawyer) مُحامٍ (مُحامونَ); **the judge called the ~ for the defence** دَعا القاضي المُحامِيَ للمُرافَعةِ
B *vt* (**-ll-** BrE, **-l-** AmE) 1▸ نَصَحَ (a; نُصْح, نَصْح, نَصاحة, نَصيحة), أَوْصى (ب) ‹*caution, prudence*›; **he ~ed caution/prudence when investing for retirement** نَصَحَ بِتَوَخّي الحيطةِ \ الحَذَرِ عند الاسْتِثْمارِ للتَقاعُدِ 2▸ أَشار (على), أَرْشَد ‹*a victim, patient*›

counselling (BrE), **counseling** (AmE) /ˈkaʊns(ə)lɪŋ/ *n* إرْشاد نَفْسيّ

counsellor (BrE), **counselor** (AmE) /ˈkaʊns(ə)lə/ *n*
1▸ (adviser) مُسْتَشار 2▸ (lawyer) مُحامٍ (مُحامونَ)

count /kaʊnt/ **A** *vt* 1▸ (to add up) عَدَّ (u; عَدّ), أَحْصى ‹*money, people, points*›; **all the votes have been ~ed** تَمَّ عَدُّ كُلِّ الأَصْواتِ 2▸ (to include) أَدْخَل في الحِسابِ, ضَمَّنَ; **~ing the children, there were 24 of us** إذا أَضَفْنا الأَطْفالَ، فَإنَّ عَدَدَنا كانَ 24; **five rooms, not ~ing the kitchen** خَمْس غُرَفٍ، لَيْسَ من ضِمْنِها المَطْبَخُ 3▸ (to consider) اعْتَبَرَ, اعْتَدَّ; **we ~ him as part of the family** نَعْتَبِرُهُ أَحَدَ أَفْرادِ العائِلةِ; **~ yourself lucky you weren't there** اعْتَبِرْ نَفْسَكَ مَحْظوظاً أَنَّكَ لم تَكُنْ هُناكَ
B *vi* 1▸ (to recite numbers) عَدَّ (u; عَدّ); **to ~ (up) to 50** عَدَّ إلى ال50 2▸ (to be of importance) «experience, opinions» أَثَّرَ, أَهَمَّ, اعْتُدَّ بِهِ; **every second ~s** كُلُّ ثانِيةٍ يُعْتَدُّ بِها; **all my work ~ed for nothing** لم يُحْسَبْ لِكُلِّ أَعْمالي أَيُّ حِسابٍ 3▸ (to be included) حُسِبَ, احْتُسِبَ; **this ~s towards your final mark** يُحْتَسَبُ هذا في دَرَجَتِكَ \ عَلامَتِكَ النِهائيّةِ 4▸ (to be considered) اعْتُبِرَ
C *n* 1▸ (to determine totals) عَدّ, إحْصاء (إحْصاءات); **she had nine horses at the last ~** كانَ لَدَيْها تِسْعةُ خُيولٍ طِبْقاً لِآخِرِ إحْصاءٍ; **to keep/lose ~ of sth** أَحْصى عَدَدَ \ أَخْفَقَ في عَدٍّ

شَيْءٍ; **I've lost ~ of the number of times I've phoned** لم أَعُدْ أَتَذَكَّرُ عَدَدَ المَرّاتِ الّتي اتَّصَلْتُ فيها ❷ (total) إحْصاء (إحْصاءات) ❸ (index) مُعَدَّل (مُعَدَّلات) ❹ (in debates) مَسْأَلة (مَسائِل), مَوْضوع; **he was wrong on both ~s** كانَ مُخْطِئاً في كِلْتا المَسْأَلَتَيْنِ ❺ (Law) (charge) تُهْمة (تُهَم); **she was found guilty/acquitted on all ~s** حُكِمَ عَلَيْها بالإدانةِ \ بالبَراءةِ عن كُلِّ التُهَم ❻ (in boxing) عَدّ; **to be out for the ~** (in boxing) خَسِرَ بالضَرْبةِ القاضِيةِ; (infml) (unconscious) كانَ فاقِداً للوَعْيِ ❼ (nobleman) كونْت

(Idioms) **to count one's blessings** أَحْصى نِعَمَ اللهِ عَلَيْهِ; **to count the cost of sth** عانى من تَبِعاتِ شَيْءٍ

(Phrasal verbs) **count against**: **~ against [sb]** «age, lack of experience, evidence» حُسِبَ \ احْتُسِبَ ضِدَّ [شَخْصٍ]
• **count in**: **~ [sb] in**: (to include) **~ me in!** اعْتَبِرْني مُشارِكاً!
• **count on**: **~ on [sb/sth]** اعْتَمَدَ على [شَخْصٍ \ شَيْءٍ] *‹sb's support, vote›*; **don't ~ on it!** لا تُعَوِّلْ عَلَيْهِ!
• **count out** A **~ out [sth]** عَدَّ [شَيْئاً] واحِداً واحِداً *‹money, coins›* B **~ [sb] out** ❶ (to exclude) **you can ~ me out** يُمْكِنُكَ أنْ تُخْرِجَني من حِساباتِكَ ❷ (in boxing) عَدَّ ل [شَخْصٍ] *‹a boxer›*
• **count up**: **~ up [sth]** حَسَبَ حاصِلَ \ إجْماليَّ [شَيْءٍ] *‹money, points›*

countdown /ˈkaʊntdaʊn/ *n* عَدّ تَنازُليّ \ عَكْسيّ

countenance /ˈkaʊnt(ə)nəns/ A *n* مُحَيًّا B *vt* قَبِلَ (a; قُبول, قَبول), وافَقَ (على), ارْتَضى (ب)

counter /ˈkaʊntə/ A *n* ❶ (shop checkout area) صُنْدوق الدَفْع; (shop display area) مِنْضَدة البَيْع; (in bank) شُبّاك (شَبابيكُ); (in a kitchen) مِنْضَدة (مَناضِدُ); (in bar) طاوِلة خِدْمةِ البار ❷ (in games) قُشاط B *vt* رَدَّ (u; رَدّ; على) *‹a threat, trend›* C *vi* «opponents, organizations» رَدَّ (u; رَدّ), شَنَّ هُجوماً مُضادًّا D **(counter to)** *phr ‹to behave, go›* عَكْسَ

counteract /kaʊntərˈakt/ *vt* (to oppose) ضادَّ *‹a tendency›*; (to neutralize) أَبْطَلَ *‹an effect›*

counter-attack /ˈkaʊntərətak/ *n* هُجوم مُضادّ

counterbalance /ˌkaʊntəˈbal(ə)ns/ *vt* أَبْطَلَ *‹an effect›*; وازَنَ *‹a loss›*

counter clerk *n* (AmE) مُوَظَّف شُبّاكٍ

counterclockwise /kaʊntəˈklɒkwʌɪz/ *adj, adv* (AmE) عَكْسَ اتِّجاهِ عَقارِبِ الساعةِ

counterfeit /ˈkaʊntəfɪt/ A *adj ‹signature, coin›* مُزَيَّف, مُزَوَّر, زائِف B *n* تَزْييف, تَزْوير C *vt* زَيَّفَ, زَوَّرَ *‹a banknote, goods›*

counterfoil /ˈkaʊntəfɔɪl/ *n* (BrE) أُرومة

counter-insurgency /ˌkaʊntərɪnˈsəːdʒ(ə)nsi/ *n* قَمْع التَمَرُّدِ

counteroffensive /ˈkaʊntərəfɛnsɪv/ *n* هُجوم مُضادّ

counterpart /ˈkaʊntəpɑːt/ *n* (of a person, thing) نَظير (نُظَراءُ; f pl نَظائِرُ)

counterpoint /ˈkaʊntəpɔɪnt/ *n* طِباق موسيقيّ

counterproductive /ˌkaʊntəprəˈdʌktɪv/ *adj ‹measure, policy›* ذو نَتيجةٍ عَكْسيّةٍ

countersign /ˈkaʊntəsʌɪn/ *vt* صَدَّقَ على إمْضاءٍ في *‹a letter, cheque›*

counterterrorism /kaʊntəˈtɛrərɪz(ə)m/ *n* مُكافَحة الإرْهابِ

countertop /ˈkaʊntətɒp/ *n* (AmE) سَطْح العَمَلِ (في المَطْبَخ)

countess /ˈkaʊntɪs/ *n* كونْتيسة (زَوْجة \ أَرْمَلة الكونْت)

countless /ˈkaʊntləs/ *adj ‹hours, times›* لا يُعَدُّ وَلا يُحْصى, لا حَصْرَ لَهُ

country /ˈkʌntri/ *n* (*pl* **countries**) ❶ (nation) دَوْلة (دُوَل), بَلَد (بُلْدان, بِلاد); (people) شَعْب (n coll, no singul n; شُعوب); **~ of origin** بَلَد المَنْشَأ ❷ [u] (countryside) ريف; **to live in the ~** عاشَ في الريفِ

country and western *n* موسيقى الريفِ (موسيقى شَعْبيّة أَمْريكيّة)

country club *n* نادٍ ريفيّ

country dancing *n* رَقْص شَعْبيّ

country house *n* مَنْزِل ريفيّ فَخْم

countryman /ˈkʌntrɪmən/ *n* (*pl* **-men**) مُواطِن

country music *n* موسيقى الريفِ

countryside /ˈkʌntrɪsaɪd/ *n* ريف (أَرْياف)

countrywide /kʌntriˈwaɪd/ *adj* ‹*strike, tour*› في جَميعِ أَنْحاءِ البَلَدِ

county /ˈkaʊnti/ *n* (*pl* **counties**) مُقاطَعة

county council *n* (BrE) مَجْلِس مُقاطَعةٍ

county court *n* مَحْكَمة مُقاطَعةٍ (مَحْكَمة مَحَلِّيّة)

coup /kuː/ *n* 1 (also **coup d'état**) انْقِلاب (انْقِلابات); **to carry out a ~** قامَ بانْقِلابٍ 2 **to pull off a ~** ضَرَبَ ضَرْبَتَهُ

coupé /ˈkuːpeɪ/ *n* سَيّارة كوبيه

couple /ˈkʌp(ə)l/ **A** *n* 1 (two or a small number) زَوْج (mf; أَزْواج); **a ~ of minutes/times** دَقيقَتانِ \ مَرَّتانِ 2 (romantic) زَوْج (mf; أَزْواج); **a married ~** زَوْجانِ

B *vt* 1 (to link) أَقْرَنَ; **this, ~d with a fall in demand, has affected profits** هذا، مَقْروناً بانْخِفاضٍ في الطَّلَبِ، أَثَّرَ على الأَرْباحِ 2 (to attach) رَبَطَ (i-u; رَبْط) ‹*a railway carriage, engine*›

couplet /ˈkʌplɪt/ *n* بَيْت (أَبْيات)

coupon /ˈkuːpɒn/ *n* 1 (discount voucher) كوبون (كوبونات) 2 (form) قَسيمة اشْتِراكٍ

courage /ˈkʌrɪdʒ/ *n* جُرْأة, شَجاعة

courageous /kəˈreɪdʒəs/ *adj* ‹*person, decision*› شُجاع (شُجْعان), جَريء

courgette /kʊəˈʒet/ *n* كوسة

courier /ˈkʊrɪə/ *n* 1 (for parcels, messages, etc) ساعٍ (ساعون, سُعاة) 2 (carrier) مُهَرِّب مُخَدِّراتٍ 3 (travel guide) مُرْشِد سِياحيّ

course /kɔːs/ **A** *n* 1 (route of a river) مَجْرًى (مَجارٍ); (of a ship, an aircraft) مَسار (مَسارات); **to be on ~** «ship» كانَ يَبْدو أَنَّهُمْ على المَسارِ الصَحيحِ; **they look on ~ for victory** في طَريقِهِمْ إلى الفَوْزِ; **to change ~** غَيَّرَ المَسارَ; **we were blown off ~** انْحَرَفْنا عن مَسارِنا الصَحيحِ بِسَبَبِ الريحِ 2 [u] (progress) مَجْرًى, سِياق; **in the ~ of my work** في سِياقِ عَمَلي; **in *or* over the ~ of time** بِمُرورِ الزَمَنِ; **in the normal ~ of events** في المَجْرى الطَبيعيِّ للأَحْداثِ; **to run *or* take its ~** أَخَذَ مَجْراهُ 3 (in proceeding) إجْراء (إجْراءات); **it is the only ~ open to him** هذا هو الإجْراءُ الوَحيدُ المُتاحُ أَمامَهُ; **~ of action** إجْراء (إجْراءات) 4 (of lectures, lessons) دَوْرة, بَرْنامَج دِراسيّ; **to take *or* do a ~ in sth** أَخَذَ \ أَجْرى دَوْرةً في بَرْنامَج دِراسيّ] شَيْءٍ; **to go on a ~** الْتَحَقَ بِدَوْرةٍ; **a degree ~** بَرْنامَج دِراسيّ [دَوْرة دِراسيّة, **a ~ of study** يُؤَهِّلُ الدارِسَ لِنَيْلِ دَرَجةٍ عِلْميّةٍ] 5 (of a meal) طَبَق (أَطْباق); **the first/main ~** وَجْبة من ثَلاثةِ أَطْباقٍ; **a three-~ meal** الطَبَق الأَوَّل \ الرَئيسيّ 6 (of medication) مَجْموعة جُرُعاتٍ; **a ~ of treatment** دَوْرة عِلاجيّة 7 (in golf, athletics) مَلْعَب (مَلاعِبُ); (in racing) مِضْمار (مَضاميرُ)

B *vi* (to flow) جَرى (i; جَرَيان)

C (**of course**) *adv phr* بالطَبْعِ, طَبْعاً, بِطَبيعةِ الحالِ; **of ~ not!** بالطَبْعِ لا!; **'did you lock the door?' — 'of ~ I did!'** 'هل أَغْلَقْتَ البابَ؟' — 'بالطَبْعِ فَعَلْتُ ذلك!'; **'can I come too?' — 'of ~ you can!'** 'هل يُمْكِنُني أنْ آتيَ أنا أَيْضاً؟' — 'بالطَبْعِ يُمْكِنُكَ ذلك!'; **of ~, I could be wrong** بالطَبْعِ، قد أَكونُ مُخْطِئاً

coursebook /ˈkɔːsbʊk/ *n* مُقَرَّر (مُقَرَّرات)

coursework /ˈkɔːswəːk/ *n* [أَعْمال المُقَرَّرِ]

court /kɔːt/ **A** *n* 1 (Law) مَحْكَمة (مَحاكِمُ); **to take sb to ~** رَفَعَ دَعْوى ضِدّ شَخْصٍ أمامَ المَحْكَمةِ 2 (for tennis, basketball) مَلْعَب (مَلاعِبُ), ساحة (ساح, ساحات) 3 (of sovereign) بَلاط; **the ~ of St. James's** [البَلاط المَلَكيّ البَريطانيّ]

B *vt* تَقَرَّبَ (إلى) ‹*a woman, voters*›

court case *n* دَعْوى (f; دَعاوٍ, دَعاوى), قَضيّة (قَضايا)

courteous /ˈkəːtjəs/ *adj* ‹*manner, staff*› كَيِّس (أَكْياس)

courtesy /ˈkəːtɪsi/ *n* كِياسة

courthouse /ˈkɔːthaʊs/ *n* 1 (for trials) مَحْكَمة (مَحاكِمُ) 2 (of US county) [مَبْنًى إداريّ لِمُقاطَعةٍ]

courtier /ˈkɔːtɪə/ *n* [أَحَد أَفْرادِ البَلاطِ]

court martial **A** *n* (*pl* **courts-martial**) مَحْكَمة عَسْكَريّة

B **court-martial** *vt* (-ll- BrE, -l- AmE) حاكَمَ عَسْكَريًّا ‹*an officer, soldier*›

court of first instance *n* مَحْكَمة الدَرَجةِ الأولى, مَحْكَمة ابْتِدائيّة

court order *n* أَمْر قَضائيّ

courtroom /ˈkɔːtruːm/ *n* قاعة مَحْكَمةٍ

court shoe *n* [حِذاء نِسائيّ كْلاسيكيّ بِدونِ رِباطٍ]

courtyard /ˈkɔːtjɑːd/ ***n*** فِناء (أَفْنِية) حَوْش (أَحْواش, حيشان)

cousin /ˈkʌz(ə)n/ ***n*** (son of father's brother) ابْن عَمٍّ; (son of father's sister) ابْن عَمَّةٍ; (son of mother's brother) ابْن خالٍ; (son of mother's sister) ابْن خالةٍ; (daughter of father's brother) بِنْت عمٍّ; (daughter of father's sister) بِنْت عَمَّةٍ; (daughter of mother's brother) بِنْت خالٍ; (daughter of mother's sister) بِنْت خالةٍ

cove /kəʊv/ ***n*** خَليج صَغير (شُروم) شَرْم

covenant /ˈkʌv(ə)nənt/ ***n*** **1** (clause in a contract) بَنْد (بُنود) **2** (payment agreement) تَعَهُّد بِدَفْعِ مَبْلَغٍ من المالِ لِمُؤَسَّسةٍ \ جَمْعِيَّةٍ خَيْرِيَّةٍ]

cover /ˈkʌvə/ **A** ***vt*** **1** (to protect, conceal) غَطّى *<a body, an object, sofa, food>*; **to ~ one's face/eyes** غَطّى وَجْهَهُ \ عَيْنَيْهِ; **she ~ed her head with a scarf** غَطَّتْ رَأْسَها بِوِشاحٍ **2** (to lie on) غَطّى *<the floor, ground, wall>*; **he was ~ed in blood/ spots** كانَ مُغَطًّى بالدِماءِ \ بالبُقَعِ; **the floor was ~ed with sand** كانَتِ الأَرْضِيَّةُ مُغَطّاةً بالرِمالِ; **a blanket ~ed the body** كانَتِ الجُثَّةُ مُغَطّاةً بِبَطّانِيَّةٍ **3** (in measurements) غَطّى *<an area>*; **our sales team ~ the whole country** يُغَطّي فَريقُ المَبيعاتِ لَدَيْنا الدَوْلَةَ كُلَّها **4** (with distances) قَطَعَ (a; قَطْع) *<a distance>*; **we ~ed 30 miles a day** قَطَعْنا 30 ميلاً في اليَوْمِ **5** (to deal with) غَطّى *<a subject, period, syllabus>* **6** (to apply to) «regulations, agreement» انْطَبَقَ (على), شَمَلَ (u; شُمول) **7** (to report on) غَطّى *<a story, an event>*; **it was extensively ~ed by the media** غَطَّتْهُ وَسائِلُ الإعلامِ بِشَكْلٍ واسِعٍ **8** (to pay for) غَطّى *<costs, losses>*; **£40 should ~ it** £40 كافِيَةٌ لِتَغْطِيَتِهِ; **to ~ one's costs** غَطّى نَفَقاتِهِ **9** (to insure) غَطّى *<a person, possession>*; **to be ~ed for/against sth** كانَ مُؤَمَّناً ضِدَّ شَيْءٍ **10** (to protect) حَمى, غَطّى (بِإطْلاقِ النارِ على العَدُوِّ); (to aim at) صَوَّبَ سِلاحاً نحو; **I've got you ~ed!** أَنْتَ في مَرْمى سِلاحي! **11** (to disguise) أَخْفى, غَطّى *<one's embarrassment, the smell>*

B ***n*** **1** (for a cushion, sofa, duvet) غِطاء (أَغْطِيَة) **2** (lid) غِطاء (أَغْطِيَة) **3** (for books, magazines) غِلاف (أَغْلِفَة); **the front/ back ~** الغِلافُ الأَماميّ \ الخَلْفِيّ; **to read a book from ~ to ~** قَرَأَ كِتاباً من الغِلافِ إلى الغِلافِ **4** (**covers *n pl***) (bedclothes) **the ~s** أَغْطِيَةُ السَريرِ **5** [u] (shelter) ساتِر; **to run for ~** جَرى بَحْثاً عن ساتِرٍ; **under ~** تحت غِطاءٍ; **under ~ of darkness** في جِنْحِ الظَلامِ; **take ~!** اتَّخِذْ لِنَفْسِكَ ساتِراً مَأْموناً! **6** [u] (military support) حِماية, غِطاء; **to provide air ~** وَفَّرَ غِطاءً جَوِّيًّا **7** [u] (facade) غِطاء; (fake identity) هُوِيّة سِرِّيّة; **to blow sb's ~** (infml) كَشَفَ هُوِيَّتَهُ الحَقيقِيَّةَ **8** [u] (for absentees) تَغْطِية; **to provide emergency ~** وَفَّرَ تَغْطِيَةً **9** [u] (BrE) (in insurance) غِطاء, تَغْطِية; في حالاتِ الطَوارِئ; **the policy provides ~ against theft** تُقَدِّمُ بوليصةُ التَأْمينِ تَغْطِيَةً ضدَّ السَرِقةِ **10** (song) أُغْنِيّة مُعاد تَسْجيلُها]

C ***v refl*** **to ~ oneself** وَقى نَفْسَهُ

D (**covered**); *suff* **snow-~ed** مُغَطًّى بالثَلْجِ; **chocolate-~ed** مُغَطًّى بالشوكولاتةِ

E (**covered**) ***adj*** *<market, walkway>* مَسْقوف

Idiom **to cover oneself with** *or* **in glory** حَقَّقَ نَجاحاً باهِراً

Phrasal verbs **cover for**: **~ for [sb]** (to replace) حَلَّ مَحَلَّ [شَخْصٍ] أثناء غِيابِهِ *<a colleague>*

• **cover up** **A** **1** (with clothes) [ارْتَدى الكَثيرَ من المَلابِسِ] **2** (to conceal the truth) **to ~ up for sb/sth** تَسَتَّرَ على شَخْصٍ \ شَيْءٍ **B** **~ up [sth], ~ [sth] up** **1** غَطّى [شَيْئاً] *<a body, cracks>* **2** (to conceal) أَخْفى \ طَمَسَ [شَيْئاً] *<the truth, evidence, crime>*

coverage /ˈkʌv(ə)rɪdʒ/ ***n*** **1** (Media) تَغْطِية **2** (Tel) تَغْطِية

coveralls /ˈkʌvərɔːlz/ ***n pl*** (AmE) بَدْلة الشُغْلِ

cover charge ***n*** رَسْم دُخولٍ

cover design ***n*** تَصْميم غِلافٍ

covering /ˈkʌv(ə)rɪŋ/ ***n*** **1** (for walls, floors) غِطاء (أَغْطِيَة); (protective) غِطاء (أَغْطِيَة) **2** (of snow, dust) غِطاء

covering letter ***n*** رِسالة تَغْطِيةٍ, خطاب تَقْديمٍ

cover note ***n*** إشْعار تَغْطِيةٍ

cover story ***n*** قِصّة غِلافٍ

covert /ˈkʌvət, ˈkəʊvəːt/ ***adj*** *<operation, agent>* سِرِّيّ

cover-up /ˈkʌvərʌp/ ***n*** تَغْطِية, إخْفاء, طَمْس

cover version ***n*** [نُسْخة جَديدة لِأُغْنِيّةٍ]

covet /ˈkʌvɪt/ ***vt*** طَمِعَ (a; طَمَع) (في), اشْتَهى *<wealth, possessions>*

covetous /ˈkʌvɪtəs/ ***adj*** (fml) *<glance, nature>* طامِع

cow /kaʊ/ *n* بَقَرة

coward /ˈkaʊəd/ *n* جَبان

cowardice /ˈkaʊədɪs/ *n* جُبْن

cowardly /ˈkaʊədli/ *adj* ‹*attack, behaviour*› جَبان

cowboy /ˈkaʊbɔɪ/ *n* **1** (on ranch) راعي بَقَرٍ **2** (BrE infml) (dishonest worker) نَصّاب

cower /ˈkaʊə/ *vi* «animal, person» تَكَمَّش ,انكَمَش

cowgirl /ˈkaʊgəːl/ *n* راعِية بَقَرٍ

cowhand /ˈkaʊhand/ *n* راعي بَقَرٍ

co-worker /kəʊˈwəːkə/ *n* زَميل (زُمَلاءُ)

cowpea /ˈkaʊpiː/ *n* لوبيا ظُفْرِيّة

cowshed /ˈkaʊʃɛd/ *n* إسْطَبْل بَقَرٍ

cox /kɒks/ *n* رُبّان (رَبابِنة ,رَبابينُ)

coy /kɔɪ/ *adj* **1** (shy) ‹*smile, glance*› خَجول **2** (reticent) ‹*person*› مُتَحَفِّظ

coyote /kɔɪˈəʊti/ *n* (*pl* **coyotes** or **coyote**) ذِئْب البَراري ,قَيّوط

coypu /ˈkɔɪpuː/ *n* (*pl* **coypus** or **coypu**) الكَيْب (نَوْع من القَوارِضِ)

cozy (AmE) *adj* ▸ **cosy**

CPA /siːpiːˈeɪ/ *n* (AmE) = **Certified Public Accountant** مُحاسِب قانونيّ مُعْتَمَد

crab /krab/ *n* سَرَطان البَحْرِ

crack /krak/ **A** *n* **1** (break) صَدْع (صُدوع) ,شَرْخ **2** (gap in the door, rock) فَلْق (فُلوق); (in the curtains) شَقّ (شُقوق); **leave the door open a ~** اُتْرُك البابَ مَفْتوحاً فَتْحةً صَغيرةً **3** (noise of breaking wood) طَقْطَقة; (of pistol shot, thunder) دَويّ **4** [u] (also **crack cocaine**) (infml) (drug) كوكايين الكْراك **5** [u] (daybreak) **at the ~ of dawn** عند بُزوغِ الفَجْرِ **6** (infml) (attempt) جَرَّب; **to have** *or* **take a ~ at sth** جَرَّب شَيْئاً; **she wants to have a ~ at the title** تُريدُ أنْ تُجَرِّبَ الحُصولَ على لَقَبِ البُطولةِ **7** (infml) (jibe) نُكْتة ساخِرة

B *vt* **1** شَرَخ (u; شَرْخ) ,صَدَعَ (a; صَدْع) ‹*the glass, china, plate*›; **he ~ed a rib** أُصيبَ بِشَرْخٍ في أَحَدِ ضُلوعِهِ **2** (to break) كَسَرَ (i; كَسْر) ‹*a nut, an egg*›; **to ~ a safe** كَسَرَ خَزْنةً; **to ~ one's head on sth** اصْطَدَمَ رَأْسُهُ بِشَيْءٍ **3** (infml) (to solve) حَلَّ (u; حَلّ) ‹*a case, problem*›; فَكَّ ‹*a code*›; **I think I've ~ed it** أَعْتَقِدُ أَنَّني تَوَصَّلْتُ إلى حَلٍّ; **hackers ~ed the bank's security codes** فَكَّ قَراصِنةُ الكُمْبيوتَر شَفَراتِ النِظامِ الأَمْنيِّ لِلبَنْكِ **4** (making a sound) فَرْقَعَ (i; فَرْقَعة) ‹*a whip*›; طَقْطَقَ (i; طَقْطَقة) ‹*one's knuckles*› **5** (infml) حَكى (i; حِكاية) ‹*a joke*› **6** (to overcome) حَطَّمَ ,كَسَرَ (i; كَسْر) ‹*sb's defences*›

C *vi* **1** «glass, cup, ice, paint» تَشَقَّقَ ,انْشَرَخَ ,انْصَدَعَ; **her heels ~ed with the dry cold** تَشَقَّقَ كَعْبا قَدَمَيْها بِسَبَبِ الطَقْسِ البارِدِ الجافِّ **2** (under pressure) «person» انْهارَ; **he ~ed under torture** انْهارَ تحت التَعْذيبِ **3** (making a sound) «twig» طَقْطَقَ (i; طَقْطَقة); «whip» فَرْقَعَ (i; فَرْقَعة) **4** (with emotion) «voice» تَهَدَّجَ

D *adj* ‹*troops, shot, team*› خاصّ

(Idioms) **not all it's cracked up to be** (infml) لَيْسَ بِنَفْسِ الرَوْعةِ [الّتي تُشاعُ عَنْهُ]; **to get cracking** (infml) شَرَعَ في العَمَلِ دون إبْطاءٍ; **come on, let's get ~ing!** هَيّا، لِنَشْرَعْ في العَمَلِ!

(Phrasal verbs) **crack down** «government, police» اتَّخَذَ إجْراءاتٍ صارِمةً; **to ~ down on sth/sb** اتَّخَذَ إجْراءاتٍ صارِمةً ضِدَّ شَيْءٍ \ شَخْصٍ

• **crack up** (infml) **A** **1** (to have a breakdown) انْهارَ **2** (to laugh) انْفَجَرَ ضاحِكاً **B** ~ **[sb] up** أَضْحَكَ [شَخْصاً] كَثيراً **C** ~ **[sth] up** دَمَّرَ [شَيْئاً]

crackdown /ˈkrakdaʊn/ *n* قَمْع

cracked /krakt/ *adj* **1** ‹*mirror, cup, wall*› مَكْسور ,مُتَصَدِّع; ‹*rib*› مُتَشَقِّق ‹*skin, lips*› **2** (infml) (crazy) ‹*person*› مَعْتوه (مَعاتيهُ)

cracker /ˈkrakə/ *n* **1** (biscuit) [بَسْكوت ناشِف رَقيق] **2** (for Christmas) [هَدِيّة صَغيرة داخلَ غلافٍ مُفَرْقِعٍ (في بَريطانِيا في أَعْيادِ الميلادِ)] **3** (cybercriminal) قُرْصان الحاسوبِ **4** (in oil refining) وَحْدة تَكْسيرٍ

crackle /ˈkrak(ə)l/ **A** *vi* «twigs, paper, radio» خَشْخَشَ (i; خَشْخَشة); «fire» قَرْقَعَ

B *n* (of twigs, paper, radio) خَشْخَشة; (of a fire) قَرْقَعة

cradle /ˈkreɪd(ə)l/ **A** *n* مَهْد (مُهود)

B *vt* هَدْهَدَ (i; هَدْهَدة) ‹*a baby*›; حَضَنَ في يَدَيْهِ ‹*a cup*›; أَمْسَكَ (ب) ‹*gun*›

craft /krɑːft/ *n* 1 (activity) حِرْفة ,صَنْعة (حِرَف) 2 (skill) مَهارة 3 (**crafts**, *pl*) (craftwork) عَمَل حِرَفيّ \ يَدَويّ 4 (*pl* **craft**) (boat) قارِبُ (قَوارِبُ)

craftsman /ˈkrɑːf(t)smən/ *n* (*pl* **-men** /-mən/) حِرَفيّ

crafty /ˈkrɑːfti/ *adj* (**craftier**, **craftiest**) <*person*> داهٍ (دُهاة); <*tactic*> ماكِر

crag /krag/ *n* جُرُف صَخْريّ

craggy /ˈkragi/ *adj* (**craggier**, **craggiest**) 1 <*mountain, coastline*> صَخْريّ 2 <*face*> خَشِن

cram /kram/ **A** *vt* (**-mm-**) 1 (to force) حَشَرَ (i-u; حَشْر) <*clothes, people*>; **I ~med everything into one case** حَشَرْتُ كُلَّ شَيْءٍ في حَقيبةٍ واحِدةٍ; **we ~med a lot into three days** حَشَرْنا الكَثيرَ في ثَلاثةِ أيّامٍ 2 (to fill) حَشا (u; حَشْو) <*a room, one's mouth*>; **~med full** مُكْتَظّ
B *vi* (**-mm-**) **to ~ into sth** انْحَشَرَ في شَيْءٍ

cramp /kramp/ **A** *n* شَدّ \ تَقَلُّص عَضَليّ; **to have/get ~** (BrE) *or* **a ~** (AmE) عانى من \ أُصيبَ بِشَدٍّ عَضَليٍّ
B *vt* أعاقَ (إعاقة) عَرْقَلَ (عَرْقَلة) <*one's progress*>; **we're ~ed for space** المَكانُ ضَيِّقٌ عَلَيْنا

(Idiom) **to cramp sb's style** أعاقَ حُرّيّةَ شَخْصٍ

cramped /krampt/ *adj* 1 <*conditions*> خانِق; <*space*> ضَيِّق, مَحْصور; **they live in ~ conditions** يَعيشونَ في ظُروفٍ خانِقةٍ
2 <*handwriting*> صَعْب القِراءة

cranberry /ˈkranb(ə)ri/ *n* (*pl* **cranberries**) آس بَرّيّ

crane /kreɪn/ *n* 1 (for lifting) رافِعة (رَوافِعُ) 2 (bird) كُرْكيّ (كَراكيّ), غُرْنوق (غَرانيقُ)

cranial /ˈkreɪnɪəl/ *adj* <*nerve, injury*> جُمْجُميّ

cranium /ˈkreɪnɪəm/ *n* (*pl* **craniums** or **crania**) جُمْجُمة (جَماجِمُ)

crank /kraŋk/ *n* 1 (infml) (eccentric) شَخْص غَريب الأطْوارِ 2 (gear mechanism) ذِراع تَدْويرٍ \ تَشْغيلٍ 3 (handle) ذِراع تَدْوير \ تَشْغيلٍ

cranny /ˈkrani/ *n* (*pl* **crannies**) شَقّ (شُقوق) فَجْوة (فَجَوات, فِجاء); ▸**nook**

crap /krap/ *n* (vulg) 1 (excrement) خَراء 2 (rubbish) تَفاهة 3 (nonsense) هُراء, كَلام فارِغ

crash /kraʃ/ **A** *n* 1 (noise) صَوْت اصْطِدامٍ \ تَحَطُّم 2 (accident) حادِث اصْطِدامٍ \ تَحَطُّم; **a car ~** حادِث اصْطِدامِ سَيّارةٍ; **a plane/train ~** حادِث تَحَطُّمِ طائِرةٍ \ قِطارٍ; **to have a ~** تَعَرَّضَ لِحادِثِ اصْطِدامٍ 3 (financial failure) انْهيار (انْهيارات) 4 (in computing) عُطْل (أعْطال)
B *vt* 1 (in accidents) تَعَرَّضَ لِحادِثِ اصْطِدامٍ <*a car*>; تَعَرَّضَ لِحادِثِ تَحَطُّمٍ <*a plane*>; **he ~ed his car** اصْطَدَمَ بِسَيّارَتِهِ; **she ~ed the car into a tree** اصْطَدَمَتْ في شَجَرةٍ بِسَيّارَتِها 2 (infml) (to gatecrash) **to ~ a party** تَطَفَّلَ على حَفْلٍ
C *vi* 1 (in accidents) «car, train» اصْطَدَمَ; «plane» تَحَطَّمَ; **the car ~ed into the wall** اصْطَدَمَت السَيّارةُ بالحائِطِ
2 (making loud noises) «waves, thunder» هَدَرَ (i; هَدْر, هَدير) 3 (to fall) **to ~ to the ground** «person, plate, tree» وَقَعَ \ سَقَطَ على الأرْضِ 4 (to lose value) «stock market, valuations, market» انْهارَ 5 (to fail) «computer, website» تَعَطَّلَ 6 (infml) (to sleep overnight) «person» باتَ (i; مَبيت)

(Phrasal verb) **crash out** (infml) 1 (to go to sleep) ≈ نامَ (a; نَوْم, نيام) 2 (in competitions) خَرَجَ بِهَزيمةٍ ثَقيلةٍ

crash barrier *n* حاجِز سَلامةٍ

crash course *n* دَوْرة مُكَثَّفة

crash diet *n* رِجيم قاسٍ

crash helmet *n* خوذة الأمانِ \ السَلامةِ

crash landing *n* هُبوط اضْطِراريّ

crass /kras/ *adj* (**crasser**, **crassest**) <*commercialism, stupidity*> فَظيع

crate /kreɪt/ *n* 1 (for general merchandise) صُنْدوق (صَناديقُ) 2 (for bottles) صُنْدوق (صَناديقُ)

crater /ˈkreɪtə/ *n* 1 (of a volcano) فوَّهة بُرْكانيّة 2 (result of an impact) فوَّهة صَدْميّة

cravat /krəˈvat/ *n* رَبْطة عُنُقٍ

crave /kreɪv/ *vt* تَعَطَّشَ (إلى) <*attention, affection, power*>; تاقَ (u; تَوْق, تَوَقان) (إلى) <*food*>

craving /ˈkreɪvɪŋ/ *n* تَوْق; **to have a ~ for sth** تاقَ إلى شَيْءٍ

crawfish /ˈkrɔːfɪʃ/ *n* (*pl* **crawfish**) ▸**crayfish**

crawl /krɔːl/ [A] *vi* [1] «person, baby, insect» زَحَفَ (a; زَحْف) [2] «traffic, vehicle» تَقَدَّمَ بِبُطْءٍ [3] (to teem) **to be ~ing with maggots/tourists** عَجَّ بالديدانِ \ بالسُيّاحِ [4] (infml) (to be obsequious) تَذَلَّلَ
[B] *n* [1] (swimming stroke) سِباحة الصَدْرِ [2] (slow pace) سُرْعة بَطيئة; **to go at a ~** سارَ بِسُرْعةٍ بَطيئةٍ

crawler lane /ˈkrɔːlə ˌleɪn/ *n* (BrE) [مَسار على تَلٍّ مُخَصَّص للمَرْكَباتِ الثَقيلةِ]

crayfish /ˈkreɪfɪʃ/ *n* (*pl* **crayfish** or **crayfishes**) [1] (freshwater) جَراد النَهْرِ \ سَرَطان [2] (marine) جَراد البَحْرِ

crayon /ˈkreɪən/ *n* (wax) قَلَم شَمْعٍ; (pencil) قَلَم مُلَوَّن

craze /kreɪz/ *n* صَرْعة (صَرَعات)

crazy /ˈkreɪzi/ *adj* (**crazier, craziest**) (infml) [1] (mad) ‹*person*› مَجْنون (مَجانينُ), مَخْبول (مَخْبولونَ, مَخابيلُ); **to go ~** جُنَّ [2] (foolish) ‹*idea*› مَجْنون [3] (very keen) **to be ~ about sth/sb** جُنَّ بِشَيْءٍ \ بِشَخْصٍ

creak /kriːk/ *vi* «door, floorboards» صَرَّ (i; صَرّ, صَرير)

cream /kriːm/ [A] *n* [1] (on milk) قِشْدة, كْريمة; **~ of mushroom soup** حَساء فُطْرٍ دَسِم [2] (lotion) كْريم
[B] *adj* ‹*colour, suit*› قِشْديّ

(Phrasal verb) **cream off**: **~ off [sth], ~ [sth] off** اسْتَحْوَذَ على [شَيْءٍ] (الأَفْضَلِ من شَيْءٍ) ‹*the best, profits*›

cream bun *n* كَعْكة الكْريمةِ

cream cake *n* كيكة الكْريمةِ

cream cheese *n* جُبْن كْريمةٍ

creamer /ˈkriːmə/ *n* [1] (milk substitute) [سائِل \ مَسْحوق يُسْتَخْدَمُ كَبَديلٍ للحَليبِ \ للقِشْدةِ (في الشايِ \ القَهْوةِ)] [2] (AmE) (jug) [دَوْرَق الكْريمةِ]

cream soda *n* كْريم صودا (مَشْروب غازيّ بِنَكْهةِ الفانيلا)

creamy /ˈkriːmi/ *adj* (**creamier, creamiest**) [1] (containing cream) ‹*sauce, milk*› دَسِم [2] (like cream) ‹*consistency, taste*› دَسِم; ‹*complexion, skin*› قِشْديّ

crease /kriːs/ [A] *n* [1] (ironed) طَيّ (أَطْواء) [2] (wrinkle) تَجَعُّد (تَجَعُّدات)
[B] *vt* ‹*the suit, blouse*› جَعَّدَ
[C] *vi* «cloth» تَجَعَّدَ

create /kriːˈeɪt/ *vt* خَلَقَ (u; خَلْق) ‹*jobs, an impression, a problem*›

creation /kriːˈeɪʃ(ə)n/ *n* خَلْق

creationism /kriːˈeɪʃ(ə)nɪz(ə)m/ *n* نَظَرِيّة الخَلْقِ (الاعْتِقاد بِأَنَّ اللهَ خَلَقَ العالَمَ كَما جاءَ في الكُتُبِ السَماوِيّةِ)

creationist /ˌkriːˈeɪʃnɪst/ *n* [شَخْص يُؤْمِنُ بِخَلْقِ اللهِ للكَوْنِ]

creative /kriːˈeɪtɪv/ *adj* [1] ‹*process, thinking*› إِبْداعيّ, خَلّاق [2] ‹*person, team*› مُبْدِع, خلّاق

creativity /ˌkriːeɪˈtɪvɪti/ *n* إِبْداع (إِبْداعات)

creator /kriːˈeɪtə/ *n* خالِق

creature /ˈkriːtʃə/ *n* [1] (living being) مَخْلوق (مَخاليقُ), كائِن (كائِنات) [2] (animal) مَخْلوق (مَخاليقُ), كائِن (كائِنات); **sea ~s** مَخْلوقات \ كائِنات مائِيّة

(Idiom) **a creature of habit** مَخْلوق تَحْكُمُهُ العادةُ

crèche /krɛʃ/ *n* (BrE) (for babies) حَضانة; (for toddlers) رَوْضة (رَوْض, رَوْضات, رِياض, رِيضان)

credentials /krɪˈdɛnʃ(ə)lz/ *n pl* [1] (qualifications) مُؤَهِّلات [2] (identity document) وَثيقة إِثْباتِ الهُوِيّةِ [3] (of an ambassador) أَوْراق اعْتِمادٍ

credibility /krɛdɪˈbɪlɪti/ *n* مِصْداقيّة

credible /ˈkrɛdɪb(ə)l/ *adj* ‹*evidence, explanation*› مَعْقول, يُمْكِنُ تَصْديقُهُ

credit /ˈkrɛdɪt/ [A] *n* [1] [u] (recognition) تَقْدير, اعْتِراف بالفَضْلِ; **to take the ~ for sth/doing sth** نَسَبَ الفَضْلَ إِلى نَفْسِهِ في شَيْءٍ \ فِعْلِ شَيْءٍ; **he is more intelligent than he is given ~ for** هو أَكْثَرُ ذَكاءً مِمّا يُشْهَدُ لَهُ بِهِ [2] (in estimations) مَفْخَرة, مَوْضِع فَخْرٍ; **you are a ~ to your family/the team** أَنْتَ مَوْضِعُ فَخْرٍ لِأُسْرَتِكَ \ للفَريقِ; **it does you ~** هو مَدْعاةُ فَخْرٍ لك; **she has two medals to her ~** لَدَيْها ميدالِيَتانِ في رَصيدِها [3] [u] (credence) مِصْداقِيّة [4] [u] (for loans) اِئْتِمان; **the bank refused to extend further ~** رَفَضَ البَنْكُ مَنْحَ المَزيدِ من التَسْهيلاتِ الائْتِمانيّةِ; **her ~ is good/bad** وَضْعُها الائْتِمانيُّ جَيِّدٌ \ سَيِّءٌ; **to buy/sell sth on ~** اشْتَرى \ باعَ بالدَيْنِ [5] (in accounts) رَصيد دائِن; **the account is in ~** الحِسابُ فيهِ رَصيدٌ [6] (for degrees, diplomas) وَحْدة دِراسيّة مُعْتَمَدة
[B] (**credits**) *n pl* (in cinema, TV) [قائِمة بِأَسْماءِ المُشارِكينَ في

فيلْم \ بَرْنامَج تِلِفِزْيونيّ]

C *vt* **1** (to ascribe) **to ~ sb with a discovery/invention** نَسَبَ أَوْدَعَ الفَضْلَ لِشَخْصٍ في اكْتِشافٍ \ اخْتِراعٍ **2** (in accounts) ‹*money*›; **to ~ £250 to an account, to ~ an account with £250** أَوْدَعَ £250 في حِسابٍ **3** (to believe) صَدَّقَ; **would you ~ it!** هل تُصَدِّقُ هذا!

Idiom **to give credit where credit is due** نَسَبَ الفَضْلَ لِأَصْحابِهِ

credit account *n* حِساب ائْتِمانٍ

credit card *n* بِطاقة ائْتِمانٍ

credit crunch *n* أَزْمة القُروضِ الائْتِمانيّةِ

credit derivative *n* مُشْتَقّ الائْتِمانِ

credit limit *n* حَدّ \ سَقْف ائْتِمانيّ

credit note *n* [إيصال \ إِشْعار اسْتِبْدالِ مُشْتَرَياتٍ \ بِضاعةٍ]

creditor /ˈkrɛdɪtə/ *n* دائِن

credit rating *n* تَصْنيف ائْتِمانيّ

credit reference agency *n* وَكالة تَصْنيفٍ ائْتِمانيٍّ

credit transfer *n* حَوالة مَصْرِفيّة

creditworthiness /ˈkrɛdɪtwəːðɪnəs/ *n* جَدارة ائْتِمانيّة

creditworthy /ˈkrɛdɪtwəːði/ *adj* ‹*borrower, company*› ذو جَدارةٍ ائْتِمانيّةٍ

credulous /ˈkrɛdjʊləs/ *adj* ‹*tourist, customer*› ساذَج (سُذَّج)

creed /kriːd/ *n* (religious faith) عَقيدة (عَقائِدُ); (set of beliefs) مُعْتَقَد (مُعْتَقَدات)

creek /kriːk/ *n* **1** (BrE) (inlet) شَرْم (شُروم), خَليج صَغير **2** (AmE) (stream) جَدْوَل (جَداوِلُ), نُهَير (نُهَيْرات)

creep /kriːp/ **A** *vi* (*past tense, past participle* **crept**) **1** (to move stealthily) **to ~ in/out** تَسَلَّلَ إلى الداخِلِ \ الخارِجِ; **don't ~ up on me like that!** لا تَتَسَلَّ من خَلْفي هكذا!; **a few errors have crept in** تَسَلَّلَتْ بَعْضُ الأَخْطاءِ فيهِ **2** (to move slowly) «shadows, vehicles» تَحَرَّكَ بِبُطْءٍ

B *n* (infml) **1** (wretch) بائِس (بُؤَساءُ) **2** (flatterer) مُتَذَلِّل, مُقْرِف

Idiom **to give sb the creeps** (infml) (induce fear) اقْشَعَرَّ لَهُ بَدَنُ شَخْصٍ; (induce revulsion) أَثارَ اشْمِئْزازَ شَخْصٍ

creeper /ˈkriːpə/ *n* نَبات مُتَسَلِّق

creepy /ˈkriːpi/ *adj* (**creepier**, **creepiest**) (infml) ‹*feeling, story*› مُخيف

creepy-crawly /kriːpiˈkrɔːli/ *n* (*pl* **creepy-crawlies**) (infml) [كائِن زاحِف صَغير]

cremate /krɪˈmeɪt/ *vt* أَحْرَقَ, رَمَّدَ ‹*a body, remains*›

cremation /krɪˈmeɪʃ(ə)n/ *n* تَرْميد \ إِحْراق جُثّةٍ

crematorium /ˌkrɛməˈtɔːrɪəm/ *n* (*pl* **crematoriums** or **crematoria**) مَحْرَقة جُثَثٍ

crêpe, crepe /kreɪp/ *n* **1** (pancake) [فَطيرة رَقيقة] **2** (fabric) قُماش الكْريب المُجَعَّد

crêpe paper *n* وَرَق كْريب (وَرَق مُجَعَّد يُسْتَخْدَمُ عادةً في الزينة)

crept /krɛpt/ *past tense, past participle* ▸ **creep**

crescendo /krɪˈʃɛndəʊ/ *n* (*pl* **crescendos**) (Mus) [تَصاعُد في جَهارةِ الصَوْتِ]; (climax) ذُرْوة (ذُرًى)

crescent /ˈkrɛs(ə)nt/ *n* **1** (of the moon) هِلال (أَهِلّة, أَهاليلُ) **2** ((as a symbol) **the Crescent**) الهِلال **3** (of houses) [مَنازِل مَصْفوفة على شَكْلِ هِلالٍ]

crescent moon *n* هِلال (أَهِلّة)

cress /krɛs/ *n* رَشاد

crest /krɛst/ *n* **1** (of a bird) تاج (تيجان), عُرْف (أَعْراف) **2** (of a wave) ذُرْوة (ذُرًى) **3** (of a hill) قِمّة (قِمَم) **4** (coat of arms) شِعار (شُعُر, أَشْعِرة, شِعارات)

crestfallen /ˈkrɛstfɔːlən/ *adj* ‹*expression, person*› مُكْتَئِب

Crete /kriːt/ *pr n* كْريت (f)

Creutzfeldt-Jakob disease /ˌkrɔɪtsfɛltˈjakɒb dɪˌziːz/ *n* مَرَض كْروتْزْفيلْد جاكوب

crevice /ˈkrɛvɪs/ *n* صَدْع (صُدوع), شَقّ (شُقوق)

crew /kruː/ *n* **1** (on a ship, plane) طاقِم (طَواقِمُ); (in rowing, yachting) طاقِم (طَواقِمُ) **2** (in film production) طاقِم (طَواقِمُ)

crew cut *n* حِلاقة عَسْكَريّة (قَصّة شَعْرٍ قَصيرة جِدًّا)

crew neck *n* ياقة عالية

crew neck sweater *n* [كَنْزة بِياقةٍ مُسْتَديرةٍ ضَيِّقةٍ]

crib /krɪb/ *n* **1** (AmE) (cot) مَهْد (مُهود) **2** (BrE) (nativity scene) مَشْهَد المَهْدِ **3** (infml) (plagiarism) سَرِقة فِكْرِيّة

crib death *n* (AmE) ▸ **cot death**

crick /krɪk/ *n* **to have/get a ~ in one's neck** عانى من \ أُصيبَ بِتَصَلُّبٍ في عُنُقِه

cricket /ˈkrɪkɪt/ *n* 1 (insect) صَرّار 2 [u] (game) كْرِيكِت

cricketer /ˈkrɪkɪtə/ *n* لاعِب الكْرِيكِت

crime /krʌɪm/ *n* 1 (offence) جَريمة (جَرائِمُ), جِناية 2 (criminal activity) جَريمة (جَرائِمُ)

criminal /ˈkrɪmɪn(ə)l/ *n* مُجْرِم

criminal law *n* القانون الجِنائيّ

criminal record *n* سِجِلّ جِنائيّ, صَحيفة السَوابِق

criminologist /ˌkrɪmɪˈnɒlədʒɪst/ *n* باحِث \ خَبير في عِلْمِ الإجْرام

crimson /ˈkrɪmz(ə)n/ A *adj* ‹velvet, flower› قِرْمِزيّ

B *n* قِرْمِز

cringe /krɪn(d)ʒ/ *vi* 1 (in fear) انْكَمَشَ 2 (with embarrassment) انْكَمَشَ; (in disgust) انْكَمَشَ

cripple /ˈkrɪp(ə)l/ A *vt* 1 ‹a person› شَلَّ (شَلَل) 2 ‹the economy, an industry› شَلَّ (شَلَل)

B *n* (old use or offensive) أَعْرَج (dipt; عُرْج)

crippling /ˈkrɪplɪŋ/ *adj* 1 ‹disease, injury› مُقْعِد 2 ‹debt› ثَقيل; ‹strike, blow› شَديد الوَطْأة

crisis /ˈkrʌɪsɪs/ *n* (*pl* **crises**) أَزْمة (أَزَمات)

crisp /krɪsp/ A *adj* 1 ‹banknotes, sheets› غَيْر مُجَعَّد, مَفْرود 2 ‹biscuits, bacon› مُقَرْمِش (colloq) 3 ‹lettuce, apple› غَضّ 4 ‹air, day› مُنْعِش 5 ‹voice, style› حازِم

B *n* (BrE) (also **potato crisp**) رَقيقة بَطاطا مَقْلِيّة

crispbread /ˈkrɪspbred/ *n* خُبْز مُقَرْمِش

criss-cross /ˈkrɪskrɒs/ A *adj* ‹pattern› ذو خُطوطٍ مُتَقاطِعة

B *vt* ‹the country, state› قَطَعَ طولاً وَعَرْضاً

criterion /krʌɪˈtɪərɪən/ *n* (*pl* **criteria**) مِعْيار (مَعاييرُ)

critic /ˈkrɪtɪk/ *n* 1 (reviewer) ناقِد (ناقِدونَ, نُقّاد, نَقَدة); **art/music ~** ناقِد فَنّيّ \ موسيقيّ; **the ~s loved it** أَحَبَّهُ النُقّادُ

2 (opponent) مُنْتَقِد

critical /ˈkrɪtɪk(ə)l/ *adj* 1 ‹point, stage› حَرِج; **the negotiations have reached a ~ stage** وَصَلَت المُفاوَضاتُ إلى نُقْطةٍ حَرِجةٍ 2 ‹condition› حَرِج; **his condition is ~** حالَتُهُ حَرِجةٌ

3 ‹comment, remark› ناقِد; **to be ~ of sb's behaviour** انْتَقَدَ سُلوكَ شَخْصٍ 4 ‹analysis, reflection› نَقْديّ

critically /ˈkrɪtɪkli/ *adv* 1 (using judgement) ‹to think, examine› بِشَكْلٍ نَقْديٍّ 2 (disapprovingly) ‹to speak› بِشَكْلٍ مُنْتَقِداً 3 (extremely) ‹ill› بِشِدّةٍ; ‹important› جِدًّا

criticism /ˈkrɪtɪsɪz(ə)m/ *n* 1 (disapproval) نَقْد, انْتِقاد (انْتِقادات) 2 [u] (Literat, Art) نَقْد

criticize, **-ise** (BrE) /ˈkrɪtɪsʌɪz/ *vt, vi* ‹a decision, policy› انْتَقَدَ

critique /krɪˈtiːk/ A *n* نَقْد; **a detailed ~ of her work** نَقْد تَفْصيليّ لِعَمَلِها

B *vt* (AmE) (analyse) نَقَدَ (u; نَقْد)

croak /krəʊk/ A *n* (of a frog) نَقيق; (of a raven) نَعيق; (of a person) بُحّة, جُشّة

B *vi* «frogs» نَقَّ (i; نَقيق); «ravens» نَعَقَ (a-i; نَعْق, نَعيق); «person» بَحَّ, جَشَّ (a; بَحّ, بَحاح, بُحاح)

C *vt* قالَ بِصَوْتٍ مَبْحوحٍ \ أَجَشّ

Croat /ˈkrəʊat/ *n* كْرُواتيّ

Croatia /krəʊˈeɪʃə/ *pr n* كْرُواتِيا

Croatian /krəʊˈeɪʃ(ə)n/ A *n* 1 (citizen) كْرُواتيّ 2 (language) (اللُغة) الكْرُواتيّة

B *adj* كْرُواتيّ

crochet /ˈkrəʊʃeɪ/ A *n* كْروشيه

B *vt* ‹a blanket, shawl› حَبَكَ بِإِبْرةٍ مَعْقوفةٍ

crockery /ˈkrɒk(ə)ri/ *n* فَخّار

crocodile /ˈkrɒkədʌɪl/ *n* تِمْساح (تَماسيحُ)

crocodile tears *n* دُموع التَماسيح

crocus /ˈkrəʊkəs/ *n* زَعْفَران

croissant /ˈkrwasɒ̃/ *n* كْرُواسون

crony /ˈkrəʊni/ *n* (*pl* **cronies**) (pej) رَفيق سوءٍ

crook /krʊk/ *n* (infml) مُحْتال, نَصّاب

crooked /ˈkrʊkɪd/ *adj* 1 ‹line› أَعْوَج (dipt; عوج); ‹path, street› مُتَعَرِّج; ‹teeth› مُلْتَوٍ; ‹smile› مائِل 2 (infml) (dishonest) ‹politician, businessman, deal› غَيْر نَزيهٍ

crop /krɒp/ A *n* 1 (of grain, coffee, etc) مَحْصول (مَحاصيلُ); **a cereal ~** مَحْصول الحُبوبِ; **the ~s failed** فَشِلَت المَحاصيلُ

2 (harvest) حَصاد; **a bumper potato ~** مَحْصول وَفير من البَطاطِسِ **3** (infml) (of students, movies, players) حَصيلة (حَصائِل); **this year's ~ of graduates** حَصيلة الخِرّيجينَ لِهَذا العامِ **4** (hairstyle) [قَصّة شَعْرٍ قَصيرة جِدًّا] **5** (whip) سَوْط (سِياط)

B *vt* **(-pp-)** **1** (to cut short) قَصَّ قَصيراً *<hair, a tail>* **2** «horses, sheep» قَضَمَ (a-i; قَضْم), رَعى (a; رَعْي, رِعاية) *<grass>* (مَرْعًى) **3** قَصَّ الأَطْرافَ *<an image, a photograph>*

(Phrasal verb) **crop up** (infml) **1** (to arise) «problem, question» ظَهَرَ فَجْأةً **2** (to be mentioned) «name, subject» وَرَدَ (i; وُرود), ذُكِرَ

crop top *n* [قَميص قَصير يَكْشِفُ عن البَطْنِ]

croquet /ˈkrəʊkeɪ/ *n* كْروكيه (لُعْبة بِكُراتٍ خَشَبيّة)

croquette /krə(ʊ)ˈket/ *n* كْروكيت

cross /krɒs/ **A** *n* **1** (mark, shape) [علامة تَقاطُعٍ على شَكْلِ x حَرْفِ]; **put a ~ in the appropriate box** ضَعْ علامة تَقاطُعٍ في المُرَبَّعِ المُناسِبِ **2** (Christian symbol) صَليب (صُلْبان); **the C~** الصَّليب **3** (hybrid) هَجين (هُجُن, هُجَناءُ) **4** (in football) تَمْريرة عَرْضيّة

B *vt* **1** (to the other side) عَبَرَ (u; عُبور, عَبْر), قَطَعَ (a; قَطْع) *<a road, border, line>*; **it ~ed his mind that ...** خَطَرَ لَهُ \ في بالِهِ أنّ ...; **a smile ~ed her face** ارْتَسَمَتْ بَسْمةٌ على وَجْهِها; **it ~es the line between satire and bad taste** يَتَجاوَزُ الخَطَّ الفاصِلَ بين الهِجاءِ وَقِلّةِ الذَوْقِ **2** (to span) «bridges, roads» امْتَدَّ عَبْرَ \ على طولِ *<a river>* **3** (with arms) **to ~ one's arms** تَكَتَّفَ, شَبَّكَ ذِراعَيْهِ على صَدْرِهِ; (with legs) **to ~ one's legs** وَضَعَ ساقاً على ساقٍ **4** (to intersect with) تَقاطَعَ (مع) *<a line, an axis>* **5** (in writing) [وَضَعَ شَرْطةً في مُنْتَصَفِ حَرْفٍ]; **to ~ a 't'** [وَضَعَ الشَرْطةَ في مُنْتَصَفِ حَرْفِ ال 't' / رَقْمِ] **6** هَجَّنَ *<breeds, plants>*; **to ~ one species with another** هَجَّنَ سُلالةً بِسُلالةٍ أُخْرى **7** (in football) مَرَّرَ عَرْضِيًّا *<the ball>* **8** (to go against) أَغْضَبَ, أَزْعَجَ *<a person>*

C *vi* **1** (also **cross over**) (to the other side) «pedestrians, animals» عَبَرَ (u; عُبور); **don't ~ when the lights are red** لا تَعْبُرْ عِنْدَما يَكونُ الضَوْءُ أَحْمَرَ; **to ~ into Italy** عَبَرَ الحُدودَ إلى إيطاليا **2** (to intersect) «roads, paths» تَقاطَعَ; **I'm sure our paths will ~ again** أنا واثِقٌ أنّ دُروبَنا سَتَتَقاطَعُ مَرّةً أُخْرى; **our letters must have ~ed** لا بُدَّ أنّ رَسائِلَنا قد أُرْسِلَتْ في نَفْسِ الوَقْتِ

D *v refl* **to ~ oneself** رَسَمَ إشارةَ الصَليبِ

E *adj* *<look, expression>* غَضْبان, غَضِبٌ, انْزِعاجٍ; **to be ~ with sb** كانَ مُنْزَعِجاً من شَخْصٍ; **to be ~ about sth** كانَ مُنْزَعِجاً من شَيْءٍ; **to get ~** غَضِبَ (a; غَضَب)

(Idioms) **cross my heart** أُقْسِمُ باللهِ أنّي صادِقٌ; **to cross one's fingers** تَمَنّى التَوْفيقَ \ حَظًّا حَسَناً

(Phrasal verbs) **cross off**: **~ [sth/sb] off, ~ off [sth/sb]** شَطَبَ [شَيْئاً \ شَخْصاً] *<a name, an item>*

• **cross out**: **~ out** [sth], **~** [sth] **out** شَطَبَ [شَيْئاً] *<a word, number>*

crossbar /ˈkrɒsbɑː/ *n* **1** (of a bicycle) قَضيب (قُضْبان) **2** (in football, rugby) عارِضة (عارِضات)

cross-border /ˌkrɒsˈbɔːdə/ *adj* *<raid, trade>* عابِر ل \ عَبْرَ الحُدودِ

crossbow /ˈkrɒsbəʊ/ *n* بِرْقيل (بَراقيلُ)

cross-breed /ˈkrɒsbriːd/ *n* هَجين (هُجُن, هُجَناءُ)

cross-Channel /ˌkrɒsˈtʃan(ə)l/ *adj* *<ferry, trip>* عابِر للقَنالِ الإنْجليزيِّ

cross-check /ˌkrɒsˈtʃek/ *vt* دَقَّقَ (في) *<information>*

cross-country /ˌkrɒsˈkʌntri/ *adj* *<skiing, running, trip>* عَبْرَ الحُقولِ \ الريفِ

cross-cultural /ˌkrɒsˈkʌltʃ(ə)r(ə)l/ *adj* *<study, exchange>* عابِر للثَقافاتِ

cross-examination /ˌkrɒsɪɡˌzamɪˈneɪʃ(ə)n/ *n* اسْتِجْواب (اسْتِجْوابات)

cross-examine /ˌkrɒsɪɡˈzamɪn/ *vt* اسْتَجْوَبَ *<the defendant, witness>*

cross-eyed /ˈkrɒsʌɪd/ *adj* **to be ~** كانَ أَحْوَلَ العَيْنَيْنِ

crossfire /ˈkrɒsfʌɪə/ *n* مَرْمى نيرانٍ; **to get caught in the ~** وَقَعَ في مَرْمى النيرانِ

crossing /ˈkrɒsɪŋ/ *n* **1** (sea journey) رِحْلة بَحْرِيّة **2** (for pedestrians) مَعْبَر (مَعابِرُ), مَمَرّ (مَمَرّات)

cross-legged /krɒsˈlɛgɪd, krɒsˈlɛgd/ *adv* ‹*to sit*› رِجْلاً على رِجْلٍ

crossover /ˈkrɒsəʊvə/ *n* [تَغْيير النَمَطِ الموسيقيِّ لِزِيادةِ الشَعْبِيَّةِ]

cross-party /ˈkrɒs,pɑːti/ *adj* ‹*amendment, support*› عابِر للأَحْزابِ

cross-purposes /ˌkrɒsˈpəːpəsɪz/ *n pl* **to be talking at ~** أَساءا فَهْمَ بَعْضِهِما البَعْض

cross-question /ˌkrɒsˈkwɛstʃ(ə)n/ *vt* Law اسْتَنْطَقَ, اسْتَجْوَبَ ‹*interviewees, witnesses*›

cross reference *n* إحالة مُزْدَوِجة

crossroads /ˈkrɒsrəʊdz/ *n* (*pl* **crossroads**) تَقاطُع \ مُلْتَقى طُرُقٍ; **to reach a ~ in the negotiations** وَصَلَت المُفاوَضاتُ إلى مُفْتَرَقِ طُرُقٍ

cross section *n* 1 (cut, diagram) مَقْطَع عَرْضيّ 2 (sample) عَيِّنة

crosswalk /ˈkrɒswɔːk/ *n* (AmE) مَعْبَر المُشاةِ

crossword /ˈkrɒswəːd/ *n* (also **crossword puzzle**) كَلِمات مُتَقاطِعة

crotch /krɒtʃ/ *n* [مِنْطَقة ما بين الفَخِذَيْنِ]

crouch /kraʊtʃ/ *vi* (also **crouch down**) «person» قَرْفَص (i; قَرْفَصة); «animal» رَبَضَ (i; رَبْض, رُبوض)

croup /kruːp/ *n* (in children) خانوق (خَوانِقُ, خَوانيقُ)

croupier /ˈkruːpɪə/ *n* [مُدير مائِدةِ قِمارٍ]

crow /krəʊ/ A *n* غُراب (غِرْبان)

B *vi* 1 (*past tense* **crowed** or **crew**; *past participle* **crowed**) «cockerel» صاحَ (i; صَيْح, صِياح) 2 (to exult) صاحَ مُنْتَشِياً

(Idiom) **as the crow flies** على خطٍّ مُسْتَقيمٍ

crowbar /ˈkrəʊbɑː/ *n* عَتَلة

crowd /kraʊd/ A *n* 1 (of people) حَشْد (حُشود); **there were ~s of people** كانَتْ هُناكَ حُشودٌ من الناسِ; **a ~ gathered at the scene** تَجَمَّعَ حَشْدٌ عند مَوْقِعِ الحَدَثِ 2 (in stadiums, exhibitions) جُمْهور (n coll, no singul n; جَماهيرُ); **a ~ of 40,000 watched the game** شاهَدَ اللُعْبةَ جُمْهورٌ من 40,000; **the exhibition has drawn huge ~s** جَذَبَ المَعْرِضُ جَماهيرَ حاشِدةً 3 (infml) (group) مَجْموعة (مَجْموعات, مُتَفرِّجٍ; مَجاميعُ); **'who's coming?' — 'the usual ~'** 'مَنْ سَيأْتي ؟' — 'المَجْموعةُ المُعْتادةُ'

B *vt* 1 (to fill) مَلأَ (a; مَلْء) ‹*the streets, platform, beach*›; **thousands of protesters ~ed the square** مَلأَ آلافُ المُحْتَجّينَ المَيْدانَ 2 (to cram) كَدَّسَ ‹*people, objects*›; **four families were ~ed into one apartment** تَكَدَّسَتْ أَرْبَعُ أُسَرٍ في شَقّةٍ واحِدةٍ 3 (infml) (to jostle) زاحَمَ, زَحَمَ (a; زَحْم)

C *vi* **to ~ into a room/lift** تَكَدَّسَ في غُرْفةٍ \ مِصْعَدٍ; **to ~ onto a bus/train** تَكَدَّسَ في حافِلةٍ \ قِطارٍ

(Phrasal verbs) **crowd around, crowd round** (BrE) 1 احْتَشَدَ 2 **~ around [sth/sb]** الْتَفَّ حول [شَيْءٍ \ شَخْصٍ]

• **crowd out: ~ [sth/sb] out** زاحَمَ [شَيْئاً \ شَخْصاً] ‹*plants, businesses*›

crowded /ˈkraʊdɪd/ *adj* ‹*street, room, train*› مُزْدَحِم; **it's too ~ in here** الازْدِحامُ شَديدٌ هُنا

crowd-puller /ˈkraʊdpʊlə/ *n* مَعْشوق, نَجْم شُبّاكِ التَذاكِرِ الجَماهيرِ

crown /kraʊn/ A *n* 1 (headgear) تاج (تيجان) 2 (of hill) قِمّة (قِمَم); (of head) هامة (هام, هامات) 3 (in dentistry) وَضْع \ تَرْكيب تاجٍ

B *vt* 1 ‹*the monarch*› تَوَّجَ 2 ‹*a tooth*› وَضَعَ \ رَكَّبَ تاجاً على

Crown Court *n* (BrE) مَحْكَمة التاجِ (مَحْكَمة جِنائيّة في إنْجِلْترا ووَيْلْز)

crowning /ˈkraʊnɪŋ/ *adj* ‹*achievement, moment*› مُتَوِّج

Crown Jewels *n* (in UK) مُجَوْهَرات التاجِ

crown prince *n* وَليّ عَهْدٍ

crown princess *n* وَلِيّة عَهْدٍ

crow's feet *n pl* تَجاعيد حول العَيْنَيْنِ

crow's nest *n* مِنَصّة مُراقَبة (في سَفينة)

crucial /ˈkruːʃ(ə)l/ *adj* ‹*role, issue*› حاسِم

crucially /ˈkruːʃ(ə)li/ *adv* بِشَكْلٍ حاسِمٍ; **~, he was there** وُجودُهُ هُناكَ كانَ حاسِماً

crucifix /ˈkruːsɪfɪks/ *n* صَليب (صُلُب, صُلْبان)

crucifixion /kruːsɪˈfɪkʃ(ə)n/ *n* صَلْب, تَصْليب

crucify /ˈkruːsɪfʌɪ/ *vt* (**crucifies, crucifying, crucified**) صَلَبَ (i; صَلْب)

crude /kru:d/ *adj* (**cruder**, **crudest**) 1 (unsophisticated) ‹*attempt, method*› بُدائيّ 2 (rudimentary) ‹*weapon, forgery*› بُدائيّ 3 (vulg) (rude) ‹*joke, remark*› فَظّ ,مُبْتَذَل (أَفْظاظ) 4 (unprocessed) ‹*oil, data*› خام

crude oil *n* نَفْط خام

cruel /krʊəl/ *adj* (**crueller**, **cruellest**) ‹*treatment, guard*› وَحْشيّ, قاسٍ (قُساة)

cruelty /ˈkrʊəlti/ *n* قَساوة ,وَحْشيّة

cruet /ˈkru:ɪt/ *n* [زُجاجة صَغيرة \ مَجْموعة زُجاجاتٍ صَغيرةٍ للمِلْحِ إلخ]

cruise /kru:z/ A *vi* 1 «plane, car» [سارَ بِسُرْعةٍ اقْتِصاديّةٍ ثابِتةٍ] 2 «ship» أَبْحَرَ

B *n* رِحْلة بَحْريّة

cruiser /ˈkru:zə/ *n* 1 (cabin cruiser) باخِرة سِياحيّة 2 (warship) طَرّاد 3 (AmE) (police car) سَيّارة الدَوْريّةِ

cruising speed /ˈkru:zɪŋ spi:d/ *n* سُرْعة تَطْوافيّة

crumb /krʌm/ *n* فُتات (mf; فَتائِتُ)

crumble /ˈkrʌmb(ə)l/ A *vi* 1 «buildings, walls» تَداعى; «plaster» تَفَتَّتَ 2 «relationship, economy» تَرَدّى

B *vt* فَتَّتَ ‹*cheese, bread*›

crummy /ˈkrʌmi/ *adj* (**crummier**, **crummiest**) (infml) ‹*job, hotel*› حَقير

crumpet /ˈkrʌmpɪt/ *n* [كَعْكة مُسْتَديرة لَيِّنة تُؤْكَلُ مُحَمَّصةً مع الزُبْدةِ]

crumple /ˈkrʌmp(ə)l/ A *vt* هَشَّمَ ,جَعَّدَ ,غَضَّنَ ‹*paper, clothes*›; ‹*metal*›; **she ~d the letter into a ball** غَضَّنَت \ طَوَت الرِسالةَ على شَكْلِ كُرةٍ

B *vi* «face» تَغَضَّنَ

crunch /krʌn(t)ʃ/ A *vt* 1 قَرْقَشَ ‹*a bone, an apple*› 2 «tyres, boots» أَصْدَرَ صَريراً على \ فوق ‹*gravel, snow*›

B *vi* «gravel, snow» أَصْدَرَ صَريراً

C *n* (of gravel, snow) صَرير

(Idiom) **when it comes to the crunch** عِنْدَما تَحينُ ساعةُ الحَقيقةِ

crunchy /ˈkrʌntʃi/ *adj* (**crunchier**, **crunchiest**) ‹*texture, apple*› مُقَرْقِش (colloq)

crusade /kru:ˈseɪd/ *n* 1 (also **Crusade**) (Hist) حَمْلة صَليبيّة; **the c~s** الحَمَلات الصَليبيّة 2 (campaign) حَمْلة (حَمَلات)

crusader /kru:ˈseɪdə/ *n* 1 (activist) ناشِط 2 (Hist) (**Crusader**) صَليبيّ

crush /krʌʃ/ A *vt* 1 (to put down) سَحَقَ (a; سَحْق), قَضى (i; قَضاء) (على) ‹*the rebellion, resistance, opposition*› 2 (to annihilate) حَطَّمَ ‹*sb's spirit, hopes*›; **he felt ~ed by her rejection** شَعَرَ أنّهُ مُحطَّمٌ بِسَبَبِ رَفْضِها لَهُ 3 (to squash) سَحَقَ (a; سَحْق), هَرَسَ (u; هَرْس) ‹*one's fingers, the fruit, rubbish*›; **to be ~ed to death** ماتَ سَحْقاً 4 (to crease) جَعَّدَ ‹*fabric, a garment*›

B *n* 1 [u] (crowd) زِحام 2 (infml) (infatuation) وَلَع ,غَرام; **to have a ~ on sb** أُغْرِمَ بِشَخْصٍ

crush barrier *n* حاجِز جُمْهورٍ

crushing /ˈkrʌʃɪŋ/ *adj* ‹*blow, defeat*› ماحِق ,ساحِق ,مُدَمِّر

crust /krʌst/ *n* 1 (on bread) قِشْر (قُشور) 2 (outer layer) **the earth's ~** القِشْرة الأَرْضيّة

crustacean /krʌˈsteɪʃ(ə)n/ *n* قِشْريّات

crusty /ˈkrʌsti/ *adj* (**crustier**, **crustiest**) 1 ‹*bread*› مُقَرْمِش 2 (surly) ‹*old man, exterior*› مُتَجَهِّم

crutch /krʌtʃ/ *n* عُكّاز (عَكاكيزُ)

crux /krʌks/ *n* **the ~ of the matter/problem** لُبّ المَوْضوعِ \ المُشْكِلة

cry /kraɪ/ A *vt* (**cries**, **crying**, **cried**) 1 (to shout) صَرَخَ (u; صَريخ ,صُراخ); **'look out!' he cried** صَرَخَ قائِلاً 'انْتَبِهْ!' 2 (to shed) ذَرَفَ (i; ذَرْف) ‹*tears*›

B *vi* (**cries**, **crying**, **cried**) 1 (to weep) «child, baby» بَكى (i; بُكاء); **there's no use ~ing about it** لا فائِدةَ من البُكاءِ عَلَيْهِ; **to ~ with laughter** بَكى من كَثْرةِ الضَحِكِ 2 (to shout, call) صاحَ (i; صِياح) ,صَرَخَ (u; صَريخ ,صُراخ); **to ~ for help** صاحَ طَلَباً للمُساعَدةِ 3 «bird, animal» صاحَ (i; صِياح)

C *n* (*pl* **cries**) 1 (shout, yell) صَرْخة ,صَيْحة (صَرَخات); **nobody heard his cries for help** لم يَسْمَعْ أَحَدٌ اسْتِغاثاتِهِ 2 (of birds, animals) صَيْحة 3 (weeping) بُكاء; **to have a ~** بَكى (i; بُكاء)

Idioms **to cry one's eyes** *or* **heart out** بَكى بِمَرارةٍ; **to be a far cry from sth** كانَ مُخْتَلِفاً كُلَّ الاخْتِلافِ عن شَيْءٍ; **it's no use crying over spilt** *or* (AmE) **spilled milk** لا فائِدةَ من البُكاءِ على اللَّبَنِ المَسْكوبِ

Phrasal verbs **cry off** (BrE) «guests, players» تَراجَعَ

• **cry out** 1 (to shout) صَرَخَ (u; صَريخ, صُراخ); **to ~ out in pain/alarm** صَرَخَ أَلَماً \ خَوْفاً 2 (to need) **to be ~ing out for sth** كانَ في أَمَسِّ الحاجةِ لِشَيْءٍ; **the system is ~ing out for reform** يَحْتاجُ النِظامُ إلى الإصْلاحِ بِشَكْلٍ مُلِحٍّ

cryogenics /ˌkrʌɪə(ʊ)ˈdʒɛnɪks/ *n sing* فيزياء, عِلْم التَبْريدِ دَرَجاتِ الحَرارةِ المُنْخَفِضةِ

cryotherapy /ˌkrʌɪə(ʊ)ˈθɛrəpi/ *n* عِلاج بالتَبْريدِ

crypt /krɪpt/ *n* ديماس (دَياميسُ)

cryptic /ˈkrɪptɪk/ *adj* ‹message, clue› مُلْغِز

crystal /ˈkrɪst(ə)l/ *n* بِلَّوْر (بِلَّوْرات)

crystal ball *n* كُرة بِلَّوْريّة يَسْتَخْدِمُها العَرّافونَ في قِراءةِ الطالِعِ

crystal clear *adj* (*before n* **crystal-clear**) 1 ‹water› صافٍ 2 ‹explanation, meaning› واضِح

crystallize, -ise (BrE) /ˈkrɪst(ə)lʌɪz/ A *vt* 1 (chemically) بَلْوَرَ (i; بَلْوَرة) ‹minerals, salt› 2 (to make clear) بَلْوَرَ (i; بَلْوَرة) ‹ideas, thoughts›

B (**crystallized**) *adj* ‹fruit, ginger› مُسَكَّر

C-section *n* ▸ **caesarean**

CS gas /ˌsiːɛs ˈɡas/ *n* غاز سي إس (مُسيل للدُموعِ)

CST /siːɛsˈtiː/ *n* (AmE) = **Central Standard Time** تَوْقيت وَسَط أَمْريكا

CT /siːˈtiː/ A *n* = **computerized tomography** تَصْوير مَقْطَعِيّ أَشِعّة مَقْطَعِيّة, مُحَوْسَب

B *abbr* = **Connecticut**

cub /kʌb/ *n* 1 (of a fox) هِجْرِس (هَجارِسُ); (of a lion) شِبْل (أَشْبال); (of a tiger) فِزْر; (of a bear) دَيْسَم; (of a wolf) دَغْفَل 2 (**Cub (Scout)**) جُرْموز (جَراميزُ), شِبْل في الكَشّافةِ; **the C~s** مَرْحَلة \ فَرْع الأَشْبالِ في الكَشّافةِ

Cuba /ˈkjuːbə/ *pr n* كوبا

Cuban /ˈkjuːb(ə)n/ *n, adj* كوبِيّ

cubbyhole /ˈkʌbihəʊl/ *n* [مَكان ضَيِّق مُقْفَل]

cube /kjuːb/ *n* 1 (shape) مُكَعَّب (مُكَعَّبات) 2 (of cheese, sugar) مُكَعَّب (مُكَعَّبات); **an ice ~** مُكَعَّب ثَلْجٍ

cubic /ˈkjuːbɪk/ *adj* ‹metre, yard› تَكْعيبِيّ, مُكَعَّب

cubicle /ˈkjuːbɪk(ə)l/ *n* كَبينة [مساحة مُغْلَقة جُزْئِيًّا \ كُلِّيًّا بِفاصِلٍ]

cuckoo /ˈkʊkuː/ *n* (*pl* **cuckoos**) وَقْوَق

cuckoo clock *n* ساعة الوَقْواقِ

cucumber /ˈkjuːkʌmbə/ *n* خِيار

cud /kʌd/ *n* **to chew the ~** اجْتَرَّ

cuddle /ˈkʌd(ə)l/ A *vt* حَضَنَ (u; حَضْن, حِضانة), احْتَضَنَ ‹a baby, kitten›

B *vi* «lovers» تَعانَقَ

C *n* عِناق, حَضْن

cuddly /ˈkʌdli/ *adj* (**cuddlier**, **cuddliest**) ‹teddy bear, dog› [ناعِم وَيُشْعِرُكَ بالرَغْبةِ في احْتِضانِهِ]

cuddly toy *n* (BrE) [دُمْية لَيِّنة]

cue /kjuː/ *n* 1 (for an actor, musician) إشارة; **right on ~** في اللَحْظةِ المُناسِبةِ بالضَبْطِ 2 (hint) إشارة 3 (in billiards, snooker) عَصا لُعْبةِ البِلْيارْدِ

cuff /kʌf/ *n* 1 (on shirt) كُمّ (أَكْمام, كِمَمة) 2 (AmE) (on trouser leg) ثَنْية (ثَنَيات)

cufflink /ˈkʌflɪŋk/ *n* زِرّ الكُمِّ

cuisine /kwɪˈziːn/ *n* مَطْبَخ (أُسْلوب طَبْخٍ)

cul-de-sac /ˈkʌldəˌsak/ *n* (*pl* **cul-de-sacs**) طَريق مَسْدود

culinary /ˈkʌlɪn(ə)ri/ *adj* ‹skill, herb› الطَبْخِ

cull /kʌl/ A *vt* [قَتَل بِشَكْلٍ انْتِقائِيٍّ] ‹seals, badgers›

B *n* [قَتْل صِنفٍ من الحَيَواناتِ بِشَكْلٍ انْتِقائِيٍّ]

culminate /ˈkʌlmɪneɪt/ *vi* **to ~ in sth** بَلَغَ أَوْجَ \ ذُرْوةَ شَيْءٍ

culmination /kʌlmɪˈneɪʃ(ə)n/ *n* (fml) ذُرْوة, أَوْج (ذُرًى)

culottes /kjuːˈlɒt(s)/ *n pl* [بَنْطَلون نِسائيّ عَريض يَصِلُ إلى الرُكْبةِ]

culprit /ˈkʌlprɪt/ *n* جانٍ (جُناة), مُذْنِب

cult /kʌlt/ *n* 1 (worship, belief) عِبادة 2 (sect) طائِفة (طَوائِفُ)

cult figure *n* [شَخْصيّة بارِزة في مَجالٍ مُعَيَّنٍ]

cultivate /ˈkʌltɪveɪt/ *vt* **1** زَرَعَ (a; زَرْع) ‹*land, crops*› **2** نَمّى ‹*a relationship, an image*›

cultivation /kʌltɪˈveɪʃ(ə)n/ *n* (Agric) زِراعة, فِلاحة, حِراثة; **under ~** تحت الزِراعةِ

cultivator /ˈkʌltɪveɪtə/ *n* **1** (machine) مِحْراث (مَحاريثُ) **2** (person) مُزارِع, زارِع (زُرّاع, زارِعونَ)

cultural /ˈkʌltʃ(ə)r(ə)l/ *adj* ‹*heritage, diversity*› ثَقافيّ

culturally /ˈkʌltʃ(ə)rəli/ *adv* ‹*similar, different*› ثَقافيًّا

culture /ˈkʌltʃə/ *n* **1** (artistic activity) ثَقافة **2** (civilization) حَضارة, ثَقافة **3** (Bio) (cultivation of bacteria, cells) اِسْتِزْراع, اِسْتِنْبات; (cultivated bacteria, cells) مَزْرَعة (مَزارِعُ)

cultured /ˈkʌltʃəd/ *adj* ‹*person*› مُثَقَّف; ‹*tastes, voice*› رَفيع

culture shock *n* صَدْمة ثَقافيّة

cumbersome /ˈkʌmbəs(ə)m/ *adj* **1** ‹*equipment, clothing*› ثَقيل **2** ‹*process, system*› مُعَقَّد

cumin /ˈkʌmɪn/ *n* كَمّون

cumulative /ˈkjuːmjʊlətɪv/ *adj* ‹*effect, total*› تَراكُميّ

cuneiform /ˈkjuːnɪfɔːm, kjuːˈneɪɪfɔːm/ **A** *adj* مِسْماريّ **B** *n* كِتابة مِسْمارِيّة

cunning /ˈkʌnɪŋ/ **A** *adj* **1** ‹*opponent, thief*› ماكِر (مَكَرة), مُخادِع **2** ‹*plan, trick*› بارِع; ‹*device*› مُبْتَكَر **B** *n* مَكْر, خِداع

cup /kʌp/ **A** *n* **1** (for tea, coffee) فِنْجان (فَناجينُ), كوب (أكْواب) **2** (trophy) كَأْس (mf; كُؤوس); **the Davis ~** كَأْس ديفيس **3** (of bra) حَجْم تَكَوُّرِ الصَدْريّة **B** *vt* (**-pp-**) ‹*hands*› [جَعَلَ على شَكْلِ فِنْجانٍ \ كوبٍ]

cupboard /ˈkʌbəd/ *n* صِوان (أَصْونة), خِزانة (خِزانات, خَزائِنُ)

curable /ˈkjʊərəb(ə)l/ *adj* ‹*disease, addiction*› قابِل للعِلاجِ \ للشِفاءِ

curate /ˈkjʊərət/ *n* كاهِن مُعاوِن

curator /kjʊ(ə)ˈreɪtə, AmE *n* قَيِّم مَتْحَفٍ

curb /kəːb/ **A** *n* **1** (restraint) رادِع (رَوادِعُ), كابِح (كَوابِحُ) **2** (AmE) (pavement edge) حافّة رَصيفٍ **B** *vt* كَبَحَ (a; كَبْح), لَجَمَ (u; لَجْم) ‹*violence*›; حَدَّ (u; حَدّ; من) ‹*spending*›

curd /kəːd/ *n* (also **curds**) رَوْبة, خُثارة لَبَنٍ

curdle /ˈkəːd(ə)l/ **A** *vi* «milk» رابَ (u; رَوْب, رُؤوب); «sauce» تَخَثَّرَ **B** *vt* ‹*the milk*› رَوَّبَ; ‹*a sauce*› خَثَّرَ

cure /kjʊə/ **A** *vt* **1** ‹*a disease*› عالَجَ; شَفى (i; شِفاء), أبْرَأَ ‹*a patient*› **2** (with salt) مَلَّحَ; (with smoke) دَخَّنَ **B** *n* عِلاج; **a ~ for diabetes** عِلاج لِمَرَضِ السُكَّريِّ

cure-all /ˈkjʊərɔːl/ *n* دَواء لِكُلِّ داءٍ

curfew /ˈkəːfjuː/ *n* حَظْر تَجَوُّلٍ

curio /ˈkjʊərɪəʊ/ *n* تُحْفة (تُحَف), طُرْفة (طُرَف)

curiosity /kjʊərɪˈɒsɪti/ *n* (*pl* **curiosities**) **1** (inquisitiveness) فُضول, حُبّ اسْتِطْلاعٍ **2** (object) تُحْفة (تُحَف), طُرْفة (طُرَف)

curious /ˈkjʊərɪəs/ *adj* **1** (inquisitive) ‹*onlooker, child*› فُضوليّ, مُحِبّ للاسْتِطْلاعِ \ للمَعْرِفةِ **2** (strange) ‹*fact, choice*› غَريب, غَيْر مَأْلوفٍ

curiously /ˈkjʊərɪəsli/ *adv* **1** ‹*to ask, look*› بِشَكْلٍ فُضوليٍّ **2** (unusually) ‹*silent, old-fashioned*› بِصورةٍ غَيْرِ مَأْلوفةٍ **3** (strangely) بِغَرابةٍ, بِصورةٍ غَريبةٍ; **~ (enough), we had never met before** من الغَريبِ أنّنا لم نَلْتَقِ أبَداً من قَبْلُ

curl /kəːl/ **A** *vt* **1** ‹*one's hair*› جَعَّدَ **2** (to twist) **to ~ one's fingers around sth** لَفَّ أصابِعَهُ حول شَيْءٍ; **he ~ed the shot into the top of the net** أرْسَلَ كُرةً قَوْسيّةً إلى أعْلى الشَبَكةِ; **to ~ one's lip** لَوى شَفَتَهُ **B** *vi* **1** «hair» تَجَعَّدَ **2** «paper, leaves» اِلْتَفَّ, اِلْتَوى; **smoke ~ed upwards** تَمَوَّجَ الدُخانُ إلى الأعْلى **C** *n* **1** (of hair) خُصْلة شَعْرٍ مُجَعَّدة **2** (of smoke) حَلْقة (حَلَق, حَلَقات); **with a ~ of one's lip** لاوِياً شَفَتَهُ

(Phrasal verb) **curl up** **1** «person, cat» [جَلَسَ \ رَقَدَ مع ثَنْيِ الرُكْبَتَيْنِ]; **to ~ up in bed** رَقَدَ على السَريرِ ثانياً رُكْبَتَيْهِ; **to ~ up into a ball** تَكَوَّرَ **2** «paper, leaves» اِلْتَفَّ

curler /ˈkəːlə/ *n* مِعْقَص (مَعاقِصُ)

curlew /ˈkəːl(j)uː/ *n* كَرَوان (كِرْوان, كَراوينُ)

curling /ˈkəːlɪŋ/ *n* الكيرْلِنْغ (رِياضة جَماعيّة يَقومُ خِلالَها كُلُّ فَريقٍ بِدَفْعِ أقْراصٍ من الجَرانيت على الجَليدِ)

curly /ˈkəːli/ *adj* (**curlier**, **curliest**) ‹*hair*› مُجَعَّد; ‹*tail*› مَعْقوف

currant /ˈkʌr(ə)nt/ *n* زَبِيب (n coll), كِشْمِش

currency /ˈkʌr(ə)nsi/ *n* (*pl* **currencies**) عُمْلة (عُمْلات), ; **to trade in foreign ~** تاجَرَ في العُمُلاتِ الأَجْنَبِيّةِ

current /ˈkʌr(ə)nt/ **A** *adj* **1** (present) ‹*system, year, research*› حاليّ; **in the ~ tax year revenue is expected to increase/ decrease** من المُتَوَقَّعِ أنْ يَنْخَفِضَ \ يَرْتَفِعَ العائِدُ في العامِ الضريبيِّ الحاليِّ **2** (in common use) ‹*term, word*› شائِع, دارِج; **an expression in ~ use** تَعْبِير دارِج **3** (valid) ‹*licence*› سارٍ; ‹*address*› حاليّ

B *n* **1** (of water, air) تَيّار (تَيّارات) **2** (of electricity) تَيّار (تَيّارات), تَوَجُّه **3** (of opinion) تَيّار (تَيّارات)

current account *n* (BrE) حِساب جارٍ

current affairs *n* أَحْداث جارية

currently /ˈkʌrəntli/ *adv* ‹*to work, live*› حالِيًّا, في الوَقْتِ الحاضِرِ

curriculum /kʌˈrɪkjʊləm/ *n* (*pl* **curriculums** or **curricula**) مَنْهَج \ مُقَرَّر دِراسيّ

curriculum vitae *n* (*pl* **curricula vitae**) سيرة ذاتيّة

curry /ˈkʌri/ **A** *n* (*pl* **curries**) كاري

B *vt* (**curries**, **currying**, **curried**)

Idiom **to curry favour** تَزَلَّفَ (إلى)

curse /kəːs/ **A** *n* **1** (evil spell) لَعْنة (لَعْنات) **2** (oath) سِباب, لَعْنة (لَعْنات) **3** (scourge) بَلْوى, لَعْنة (لَعْنات)

B *vt* **1** لَعَنَ (a; لَعْن) ‹*one's luck, enemy*› **2** **to be ~d with sth** لُعِنَ \ أُبْتُلِيَ بِشَيْءٍ

C *vi* سَبَّ (u; سَبّ), شَتَمَ (i-u; شَتْم)

cursor /ˈkəːsə/ *n* مُؤَشِّر (الحاسوبِ)

cursory /ˈkəːs(ə)ri/ *adj* ‹*glance, inspection*› خاطِف

curt /kəːt/ *adj* ‹*reply*› مُقْتَضَب; ‹*nod*› جافّ

curtail /kəːˈteɪl/ *vt* **1** (to cut short) قَطَعَ (a; قَطْع) ‹*visit*›; أَنْهى ‹*a career*› قبل الأوانِ **2** (to restrict) قَيَّدَ ‹*rights, freedom*› **3** (to reduce) خَفَّضَ, قَلَّصَ ‹*spending, services*›

curtain /ˈkəːt(ə)n/ *n* **1** (at a window) سِتارة (سَتائِرُ) **2** (Theat) سِتار (سُتُر)

curtain call *n* [الهُتاف والتحيّة للفنّانينَ في نِهايةِ العَرْضِ على المَسْرَحِ]

curtsy, **curtsey** /ˈkəːtsi/ **A** *n* (*pl* **curtseys** or **curtsies**) انْحِناءة احْتِرامٍ (تُؤَدّيها النِساءُ بِثَني الرُكْبَتَيْنِ)

B *vi* (*past tense, past participle* **curtseyed** or **curtsied**) انْحَنى احْتِراماً

curve /kəːv/ **A** *n* مُنْحَنًى (مُنْحَنيات), مُنْعَطَف (مُنْعَطَفات)

B *vi* «surface, wall» تَقَوَّسَ; «road, river» انْحَنى, انْعَطَفَ

curved /kəːvd/ *adj* ‹*surface, line*› مُنْحَنٍ; ‹*wall, ceiling*› مُقَوَّس

cushion /ˈkʊʃ(ə)n/ **A** *n* **1** (for a chair) وِسادة (وِسادات, وَسائِدُ), مِخَدّة (مَخادُّ) **2** (reserve) احْتِياط

B *vt* خَفَّفَ من وَطْأةِ ‹*a blow, an impact*›; **to ~ sb against a threat** خَفَّفَ من وَطْأةِ التَهْديدِ على شَخْصٍ

cushy /ˈkʊʃi/ *adj* (**cushier**, **cushiest**) (infml) ‹*job, life*› سَهْل, هَيِّن

custard /ˈkʌstəd/ *n* (BrE) (creamy) مُهَلَّبِيّة

custodial sentence /kəˌstəʊdiəl ˈsent(ə)ns/ *n* حُكْم بالحَبْسِ

custodian /kʌˈstəʊdɪən/ *n* **1** (in a museum) أمين (أُمَناءُ), قَيِّم **2** (of morals) وَصيّ (أَوْصِياءُ), قَيِّم

custody /ˈkʌstədi/ *n* **1** (of the accused) حَبْس, احْتِجاز **2** (of a child) رِعاية, وِصاية

custom /ˈkʌstəm/ *n* **1** (tradition) عُرْف (أَعْراف), عادة (عادات), عَوائِدُ **2** (patronage) [u] زِبانة

customary /ˈkʌstəm(ə)ri/ *adj* **1** (traditional) ‹*practice, usage*› تَقْليديّ, مُتَعارَف عَلَيْه; **it is ~ to shake hands/bring a gift** المُصافَحةُ \ إحْضارُ هَديّةٍ أَمْرٌ مُتَعارَفٌ عَلَيْه **2** (habitual) ‹*good humour, greeting*› مُعْتاد

custom-built /ˌkʌstəmˈbɪlt/ *adj* ‹*vehicle, computer*› مَصْنوع \ مُصَمَّم حَسَبَ الطَلَبِ; **this bicycle is ~** هذه الدرّاجةُ مُصَمَّمةٌ حَسَبَ الطَلَبِ

customer /ˈkʌstəmə/ *n* زَبون (زَبائِنُ)

customer services *n* خِدْمة العُمَلاءِ

customize, -ise (BrE) /ˈkʌstəmʌɪz/ *vt* عَدَّلَ (وَفْقاً لِمُتَطَلَّباتِ الزَبونِ) ‹*a computer, car*›

custom-made /ˌkʌstəmˈmeɪd/ *adj* ‹*suit, furniture*› مَصْنوع حَسَبَ الطَلَبِ

customs /ˈkʌstəmz/ *n* جُمْرُك (جَمارِكُ); **to go through ~** مَرَّ بالجَمارِكِ

customs duties *n* رُسوم جُمْرُكيّة

customs hall *n* صالة جَمارِكَ (في المَطارِ)

customs officer *n* ضابِط \ مُوَظَّف جَمارِكَ

customs union *n* اتِّحاد جُمْرُكيّ

cut /kʌt/ **A** *vt* (*present participle* **-tt-**; *past tense, past participle* **cut**) **1** (with a knife) قَطَعَ (a; قَطْع) ‹*wood*›; (with scissors) قَصَّ (u; قَصّ) ‹*paper, fabric*›; **to ~ sth out of a magazine** قَصَّ شَيْئاً من مَجَلّةٍ; **to ~ sth in half** *or* **in two** قَطَعَ شَيْئاً نِصْفَيْنِ; **I ~ the bag open** فَتَحْتُ الحَقيبةَ بِأَداةٍ حادّةٍ; **firemen had to ~ him free** اضْطُرَّ رِجالُ الإطْفاءِ إلى إخْراجِهِ من تحت الحُطامِ **2** (to draw blood) قَطَعَ (a; قَطْع)، جَرَحَ (a; جَرْح) ‹*one's hand*›; **to ~ sb's throat** قَطَعَ عُنُقَ شَخْصٍ **3** (to trim) قَصَّ (u; قَصّ) ‹*sb's hair, the grass*›; **to have one's hair cut** قَصَّ شَعْرَهُ **4** (to carve out) شَقَّ (u; شَقّ)، حَفَرَ (i; حَفْر) ‹*a path, tunnel*› **5** (to shape, fashion) قَطَعَ (a; قَطْع) ‹*gems, stone*›; **to have a key ~** عَمِلَ نُسْخةً لِمِفْتاحٍ **6** (to reduce) خَفَضَ (i; خَفْض)، خَفَّضَ ‹*costs, taxes, prices*›; **the company is to ~ 2,000 jobs** سَوْفَ تَسْتَغْني الشَرِكةُ عن 2000 مَنْصِبٍ; **it cut 20 minutes off the journey** قَصَّرَ هذا مُدّةَ الرِحْلةِ ب 20 دَقيقةٍ; **I had to ~ my visit short** اضْطُرِرْتُ إلى أنْ أَخْتَصِرَ زِيارَتي **7** (to edit by shortening) قَصَّرَ ‹*a film, an article*›; (by deleting) حَذَفَ (i; حَذْف) ‹*a scene*› **8** (to grow) ظَهَرَ لَهُ ‹*a tooth*› **9** (to record) سَجَّلَ ‹*an album, a disc*› **10** (in computing) قَصَّ (u; قَصّ) ‹*text, a paragraph*›; **to ~ and paste sth** قَصَّ وَلَصَقَ [قَسَمَ إلى جُزْأَيْنِ بِسَحْبِ جُزْءٍ من الأَعْلى] **11** (in cards) شَيْئاً ‹*the cards, pack*› **12** (to intersect) «*lines*» قَطَعَ (a; قَطْع)، تَقاطَعَ (مع) ‹*a circle*› **13** (infml) (to stop) **~ the chatter!** كَفى ثَرْثَرةً! **14** (infml) (to fail to attend) **to ~ class/school** تَغَيَّبَ عن الدَرْسِ \ المَدْرَسةِ

B *vi* (*present participle* **-tt-**; *past tense, past participle* **cut**) **1** «knife, blade» قَطَعَ (a; قَطْع); **the chains ~ into his flesh** قَطَعَت السَلاسِلُ لَحْمَهُ **2** (in cinema) **~!** [أَوْقِفِ التَصْوير!]; **the camera ~s from the street to the courtroom** تَنْتَقِلُ الكاميرا من الشارِعِ إلى قاعةِ المَحْكَمةِ **3** (in cards) [قَسَمَ الوَرَقَ إلى جُزْأَيْنِ بِسَحْبِ جُزْءٍ من الأَعْلى]

C *v refl* (*present participle* **-tt-**; *past tense, past participle* **cut**) **to ~ oneself** جَرَحَ نَفْسَهُ

D *n* **1** (incision) شَقّ (شُقوق) **2** (wound) جُرْح (جِراح، جُروح) **3** (in funding, staff) خَفْض، تَخْفيض (تَخْفيضات); **a ~ in interest rates** خَفْض مُعَدَّلاتِ الفائِدةِ; **to make job ~s** قامَ بِخَفْضِ الوَظائِفِ; **he agreed to take a ~ in pay** وافَقَ على خَفْضِ أَجْرِهِ **4** (infml) (share) حِصّة (حِصَص) **5** (trim) قَصّ; **a ~ and blow-dry** قَصّة وَتَصْفيفة **6** (style of hair) قَصّة; (of a garment) تَفْصيلة **7** (of meat) قِطْعة (قِطَع) **8** (deletion) حَذْف **9** (version) نُسْخة (نُسَخ) **10** (transition shot) [انْتِقال من مَشْهَدٍ إلى آخَرَ]

E (**cut**) *adj* ‹*flowers*› مَقْطوف; ‹*grass*› مَقْصوص، مَجْزوز

(Idioms) **to be a cut above sth/sb** (infml) كانَ أَفْضَلَ من شَيْءٍ \ شَخْصٍ بِشَكْلٍ مَلْحوظٍ; **to be cut out for sth/to be sth** (infml) امْتَلَكَ المُواصَفاتِ الّتي تُؤَهِّلُهُ لِشَيْءٍ \ لِأَنْ يَكونَ شَيْئاً; **he's not really ~ out to be a policeman** هو حَقّاً لا يَمْتَلِكُ المُواصَفاتِ الّتي تُؤَهِّلُهُ لِأَنْ يَكونَ شُرْطيّاً; **to cut a long story short** (infml) باخْتِصارٍ; **to cut and run** (infml) هَرَبَ من المَسْؤوليّةِ; **to cut both ways** كانَ سِلاحاً ذا حَدَّيْنِ; **to cut corners** اخْتَصَرَ الطَريقَ; **to cut it fine** لَم يَتْرُكْ وَقْتاً كافِياً; **to cut sb dead** (infml) تَنَكَّرَ لِشَخْصٍ; **to cut sb down to size** (infml) عَرَّفَ شَخْصاً حَجْمَهُ

(Phrasal verbs) **cut across**: **~ across [sth]** **1** (to take a short cut) سَلَكَ طَريقاً مُخْتَصَراً عَبْرَ [شَيْءٍ] ‹*a field*› **2** (to transcend) تَجاوَزَ [شَيْئاً] ‹*party lines, boundaries*›

• **cut back**: **A** **to ~ back on sth** خَفَّضَ شَيْئاً **B** **~ back [sth], ~ [sth] back** **1** (to reduce) خَفَّضَ [شَيْئاً] ‹*spending, working hours*› **2** (to prune) هَذَّبَ \ قَلَّمَ [شَيْئاً] ‹*a tree, bush*›

• **cut down**: **A** **to ~ down on smoking/alcohol** قَلَّلَ من التَدْخينِ \ تَناوُلِ الكُحولِ; **'cigarette?' — 'no, I'm trying to ~ down'** 'سيجارة؟' — 'لا، فَأَنا أُحاوِلُ أَنْ أُقَلِّلَ من التَدْخينِ' **B** **~ down [sth], ~ [sth] down** **1** (to chop down) قَطَعَ [شَيْئاً] ‹*a tree, forest*› **2** (to reduce) قَلَّلَ [شَيْئاً] ‹*the number, time, costs*› **3** (to make shorter) قَصَّرَ [شَيْئاً] ‹*an article, a speech*›

• **cut in** **1** (to interrupt) قاطَعَ; **to ~ in on sb/a conversation** قاطَعَ شَخْصاً \ مُحادَثةً **2** (in driving) [انْحَرَفَ \ انْعَطَفَ فَجْأةً باتِّجاهِ مَرْكَبةٍ أُخْرى]

• **cut into**: ~ **into [sth]** (to impinge on) اسْتَقْطَعَ من [شَيْءٍ] ‹*the time, profits*›

• **cut off** **A** ~ **off [sth]**, ~ **[sth] off** **1** (to remove) قَطَعَ [شَيْئاً] ‹*sb's hand*›; قَصَّ [شَيْئاً] ‹*hair*›; **to ~ off sb's head** قَطَعَ رَأْسَ شَخْصٍ; **she had all her hair ~ off** قَصَّتْ شَعْرَها كُلَّهُ **2** (to disconnect) قَطَعَ [شَيْئاً] ‹*the gas, electricity, telephone*› **B** ~ **off [sth]** **1** (to suspend temporarily) عَلَّقَ [شَيْئاً]; (to stop) أَوْقَفَ [شَيْئاً] ‹*funding, aid*› **2** (to block) اعْتَرَضَ [شَيْئاً] ‹*sb's escape route, retreat*› **C** ~ **[sb] off** **1** (to disconnect) قَطَعَ مُكالَمةَ [شَخْصٍ] ‹*a caller*›; **we've been ~ off** (from gas, electricity, etc) تَمَّ قَطْعُ الإِمْداداتِ عَنّا **2** (to interrupt) قاطَعَ [شَخْصاً] ‹*a speaker*› **3** (to disinherit) حَرَمَ [شَخْصاً] من الميراث; **he cut me off without a penny** لم يورِثْني مِلّيماً واحداً **D** ~ **[sth/sb] off** (to isolate) عَزَلَ [شَيْئاً \ شَخْصاً] ‹*a person, an area*›; **to feel cut off** شَعَرَ بالعُزْلة; **to ~ oneself off from friends/family** عَزَلَ نَفْسَهُ عن الأَصْدِقاءِ \ الأُسْرة

• **cut out** **A** «engines» تَعَطَّلَ **B** ~ **out [sth]** ابْتَعَدَ \ امْتَنَعَ عن [شَيْءٍ] ‹*fatty food, alcohol*› **C** ~ **[sth] out**, ~ **out [sth]** **1** قَصَّ [شَيْئاً] ‹*a piece, picture*› **2** اسْتَأْصَلَ [شَيْئاً] ‹*a tumour*› **3** (to delete) حَذَفَ [شَيْئاً] ‹*a scene, paragraph*› **4** (to block out) عَزَلَ [شَيْئاً] ‹*the light, noise*› **5** (infml) (to stop) **~ it out!** كُفَّ عن هذا!

• **cut up** **A** ~ **[sth] up**, ~ **up [sth]** **1** قَصْقَصَ [شَيْئاً] ‹*a magazine, picture*› **2** قَطَّعَ [شَيْئاً] ‹*vegetables, meat*› **B** **to be very cut up about sth** تَقَطَّعَ غَيْظاً من شَيْءٍ

cut and paste *n* قَصّ ولَصْق

cutback /ˈkʌtbak/ *n* تَخْفيض (تَخْفيضات), تَقَشُّف

cute /kjuːt/ *adj* (**cuter**, **cutest**) (infml) **1** (sweet) ‹*baby, puppy*› ظَرِيف (ظُرَفاءُ) **2** (attractive) جَذّاب

cut glass *n* زُجاج مُزَخْرَف

cuticle /ˈkjuːtɪk(ə)l/ *n* إهاب (الظُفْر)

cutlery /ˈkʌtləri/ *n* أَدَوات الطَعامِ (سَكاكين وشُوَك ومَلاعِق)

cutlet /ˈkʌtlɪt/ *n* كُسْتَليتة

cut-off, **cut-off point** /ˈkʌtɒf/ *n* حَدّ (حُدود); **April 30th is the ~ for applications** آخِرُ مَوْعِدٍ \ أَجَلٍ لِتَقْديمِ الطَلَباتِ هو 30 أَبْريل \ نيسان

cut-price (BrE) /ˌkʌtˈprʌɪs/, **cut-rate** (AmE) /ˌkʌtˈreɪt/ *adj* ‹*ticket, holiday*› مُخَفَّض السِعْرِ

cut-throat /ˈkʌtθrəʊt/ *adj* ‹*competition*› حادّ

cutting /ˈkʌtɪŋ/ **A** *n* **1** (from a plant) شَتْلة (شَتائِلُ, شُتول), فَسيلة (فَسائِلُ), عُقْلة (عُقَل) **2** (BrE) (from a newspaper) قُصاصة

B *adj* **1** ‹*remark, comment*› لاذِع (لَواذِعُ) **2** ‹*wind, breeze*› قارِص

cutting edge **A** *n* طَليعة, أَحْدَث ما تَمَّ التَوَصُّلُ إلَيْه; **to be at/on the cutting of technological development** كانَ في طَليعةِ التَطَوُّرِ التِكْنولوجيِّ;

B (**cutting-edge**) *adj before n* ‹*technology, research*› الأَحْدَث, الأَكْثَر تَقَدُّماً

CV, **cv** /siːˈviː/ *n* = **curriculum vitae** سيرة ذاتيّة

cwt *abbr* = **hundredweight**

cyanide /ˈsʌɪənʌɪd/ *n* سِيانيد

cyberattack /ˈsʌɪbərətak/ *n* هُجوم إِلِكْترونيّ

cybercafe /ˈsʌɪbəkafeɪ/ *n* مَقْهى إِنْتَرْنِت

cyberculture /ˈsʌɪbəˌkʌltʃə/ *n* ثَقافة الإِنْتَرْنِت

cyberspace /ˈsʌɪbəspeɪs/ *n* فَضاء إِلِكْترونيّ

cycle /ˈsʌɪk(ə)l/ **A** *n* **1** (of events) دَوْرة; **the life ~ of a caterpillar** دَوْرة حَياةِ يَرَقةٍ **2** (Mus, Literat) (series) سِلْسِلة (سَلاسِلُ) **3** (bicycle) دَرّاجة **4** (Elec) دَوْرة, لَفّة

B *vt* قَطَعَ بالدَرّاجةِ ‹*a distance, route*›

C *vi* رَكِبَ دَرّاجةً

cycle lane *n* مَسار دَرّاجاتٍ (على جانِبِ الطَريق)

cycle race *n* سِباق دَرّاجاتٍ

cycling /ˈsʌɪklɪŋ/ *n* رُكوب الدَرّاجةِ

cycling shorts /ˈsʌɪklɪŋ ʃɔːts/ *n pl* شورْت رُكوبِ الدَرّاجات

cyclist /ˈsʌɪklɪst/ *n* دَرّاج, راكِب دَرّاجةٍ

cyclone /ˈsʌɪkləʊn/ *n* إِعْصار (أَعاصيرُ), زَوْبَعة (زَوابِعُ)

cygnet /ˈsɪgnɪt/ *n* (Zool) فَرْخ الإِوَزِّ العِراقيِّ \ التِمِّ

cylinder /ˈsɪlɪndə/ *n* **1** (shape) أُسْطُوانة **2** (of an engine) أُسْطُوانة **3** (of gas) أُسْطُوانة

cymbals /ˈsɪmb(ə)lz/ *n* صَنْج (صُنوج)

cynic /'sɪnɪk/ *n* شَكّاك (شَكّاكونَ)

cynical /'sɪnɪk(ə)l/ *adj* **1** (sceptical) ‹*person*› شَكّاك (شَكّاكونَ)، ‹*view*› مُرْتاب؛ **2** (unscrupulous) ‹*attempt, exploitation*› مَليء بالشُكوكِ يَنِمُّ عن انْعِدامِ الضَميرِ

cynicism /'sɪnɪsɪz(ə)m/ *n* شُكوك

cypher *n* ▸ **cipher**

cypress /'sʌɪprəs/ *n* سَرْو

Cypriot /'sɪpriət/ **A** *n* قُبْرُصيّ (قَبارِصة); **a Greek/Turkish ~** قُبْرُصيّ يونانيّ \ تُرْكيّ

B *adj* ‹*culture, history*› قُبْرُصيّ

Cyprus /'sʌɪprəs/ *pr n* قُبْرُص (f)

cyst /sɪst/ *n* كيس (أَكْياس)

cystic fibrosis /,sɪstɪk fʌɪ'brəʊsɪs/ *n* تَلَيُّف كيسيّ

cystitis /sɪ'stʌɪtɪs/ *n* الْتِهاب المَثانةِ

czar /zɑː/ *n* ▸ **tsar**

Czech /tʃɛk/ **A** *n* **1** (person) تْشيكيّ **2** (language) (اللُغة) التْشيكيّة

B *adj* ‹*language, people*› تْشيكيّ

Czechoslovak /tʃɛkəʊ'sləʊvak/, **Czechoslovakian** /,tʃɛkəslə'vakɪən/ *n, adj* (Hist) تْشيكوسْلوفاكيّ

Czechoslovakia /,tʃɛkə(ʊ)slə'vakɪə/ *pr n* (Hist) تْشيكوسْلوفاكِيا

Czech Republic *pr n* (**the Czech Republic**) التْشيك (f)

Dd

D, **d** /diː/ **A** *n* **1** (letter) دال ≈ (الحَرْف الرابع من الأَبْجَدِيّة الإنْكليزِيّة) **2** (**D**) (Mus) ري ≈ (نَغْمة من نَغَمات السُلَّم الموسيقيّ)

B *abbr* (**d**) = **died** [سَنة الوَفاةِ]

DA /diːˈeɪ/ *n* (AmE) = **district attorney** مُدَّع عامّ (على الصَعيدِ المَحَلّيّ)

dab /dab/ **A** *vt* (**-bb-**) <*a stain*> مَسَحَ (a; مَسْح); <*antiseptic*> وَضَعَ (a; وَضْع); **to ~ one's eyes** مَسَحَ عَيْنَيْه

B *n* **1** (of paint, cream) [مِقْدار ضَئيل] **2** (fish) داب

DAB /diːeɪˈbiː/ *abbr* = **digital audio broadcasting** بَثّ صَوْتيّ رَقْميّ

dabble in /ˈdab(ə)l/ *vt* **to ~ sth** <*painting, poetry*> شَغَلَ نَفْسَهُ بِشَيْءٍ

DAB radio *n* رادِيو رَقْميّ

dace /deɪs/ *n* (*pl* **dace**) داس (سَمَك نَهْريّ من الشَبّوطيّاتِ)

dachshund /ˈdakshʊnd/ *n* دَشْهُنْد (نَوْع من الكِلابِ)

dad, **Dad** /dad/ *n* (infml) (father) أَب (آباء)، والِد; (form of address) بابا

daddy, **Daddy** /ˈdadi/ *n* (infml) (father) أَب (آباء)، والِد; (form of address) بابا

daddy-long-legs /ˌdadɪˈlɒŋlɛgz/ *n* (*pl* **daddy-long-legs**) (infml) (BrE) طَيْثار; (AmE) [نَوْع من العَناكِبِ]

daffodil /ˈdafədɪl/ *n* نَرْجِس

daft /dɑːft/ *adj* (**dafter**, **daftest**) (BrE infml) <*idea, grin*> أَهْبَل (dipt; هُبْل)، مَجْنون (مَجانينُ)

Dagestan /ˌdagɪˈstɑːn/ *pr n* داغِسْتان

dagger /ˈdagə/ *n* خَنْجَر (خَناجِرُ)

dahlia /ˈdeɪlɪə/ *n* داليا (زَهْرة)

daily /ˈdeɪli/ **A** *adj* **1** <*life, flight*> يَوْميّ; **on a ~ basis** يَوْميًّا، بِشَكْلٍ يَوْميٍّ **2** <*wage, rate*> يَوْميّ

B *adv* <*to deliver, exercise*> كُلَّ يَوْم، يَوْميًّا; **twice ~** مَرَّتَيْنِ في اليَوْمِ; **the museum is open ~** المَتْحَفُ مَفْتوحٌ يَوْميًّا

C *n* (*pl* **dailies**) (newspaper) صَحيفة يَوْميّة

dainty /ˈdeɪnti/ *adj* (**daintier**, **daintiest**) <*flower, vase*> رَقيق (رِقاق، أَرِقّاءُ)، أَنيق; <*movement*> رَشيق

dairy /ˈdɛːri/ **A** *n* (*pl* **dairies**) **1** [u] (products) أَلْبان، مُشْتَقّات الحَليبِ **2** (on a farm) مَعْمَل أَلْبانٍ; (shop) مَحَلّ أَلْبانٍ **3** (company) مَلْبَنة (مَلابِنُ)

B *adj* <*cow, product*> حَليب

daisy /ˈdeɪzi/ *n* (*pl* **daisies**) أُقْحُوان

dally /ˈdali/ *vi* (**dallies**, **dallying**, **dallied**) (to linger) تَباطَأَ

dam /dam/ **A** *n* سَدّ (سُدود); **the Aswan High Dam** سَدّ أَسْوان العالي

B *vt* (**-mm-**) <*a river, stream*> بَنى سَدًّا على

damage /ˈdamɪdʒ/ **A** *n* **1** (to buildings, cars, the environment) ضَرَر (أَضْرار)، تَلَف; **storm/water ~** أَضْرار العاصِفةِ \ الماءِ; **£300-worth of ~** أَضْرار بِقيمةِ £300; **it caused a lot of ~ to buildings** أَلْحَقَ أَضْراراً كَبيرةً في المَباني **2** (to sb's health, an organ) ضَرَر (أَضْرار)، تَلَف; **it can cause brain ~** يُمْكِنُ أَنْ يُسَبِّبَ تَلَفاً في المُخِّ **3** (to reputations, business, etc) ضَرَر (أَضْرار); **the scandal did a lot of ~ to his reputation** أَلْحَقَت الفَضيحةُ ضَرَراً كَبيراً بِسُمْعَتِهِ; **it's too late, the ~ is done** فاتَ الأَوانُ، لَقَدْ وَقَعَ الضَرَرُ بالفِعْلِ

B (**damages**) *n pl* تَعْويضات; **to be liable for ~s** كانَ مُطالَباً بِدَفْعِ تَعْويضاتٍ; **to claim for ~s** طالَبَ بِتَعْويضاتٍ

C *vt* **1** <*a building, vehicle, crop*> أَتْلَفَ، أَلْحَقَ ضَرَراً بِ **2** <*sb's health, liver*> ضَرَّ (u; ضَرّ)، أَضَرَّ (بِ) **3** <*sb's reputation, career*> أَضَرَّ (بِ)

damaging /ˈdamɪdʒɪŋ/ *adj* <*effect, criticism*> مُضِرّ، ضارّ

Damascus /də'maskəs/ *pr n* دِمَشْق (dipt f)

dame /deɪm/ *n* 1 (**Dame** BrE (title)) سَيِّدة ≈ (لَقَب شَرَفٍ بَريطانيّ) 2 (AmE infml) (woman) امْرَأة (نساء)

damn /dam/ A *vt* 1 (infml) (in swearing) **~ you!** عَلَيْكَ اللَعْنَةُ!; **~ it!** تَبًّا! ,اللَعْنَة!; **well I'll be ~ed!** يا لَلْمُفاجَأةِ!; **and ~ the expense!** وَلا أُبالي بالتَكْلِفةِ! 2 (Relig) لَعَنَ (a; لَعْن) ‹*a heretic, sinner*› 3 (to condemn) أدانَ ‹*sb's behaviour, actions*›; **we're ~ed if we do and ~ed if we don't** سَواءً فَعَلْناهُ أم لم نَفْعَلْهُ لن يَرْضى عَنّا أَحَدٌ

B *n* (infml) **not to give a ~ about sb/sth** لم يُبالِ إطْلاقاً بِشَخْصٍ \ بِشَيْءٍ; **he doesn't give a ~ about us** لا يُبالي بِنا إطْلاقاً

C *excl* (infml) اللَعْنَة; **~! I've forgotten my keys!** اللَعْنَة! لَقَدْ نَسيتُ مَفاتيحي!

D *adj* (infml) **I can't see a ~ thing** تَبًّا، لا أَسْتَطيعُ أنْ أَرى شَيْئاً; **your ~ husband** زَوْجُكِ البَغيض

E *adv* (infml) (very) **that was a ~ good meal** تِلْكَ كانَتْ وَجْبةً جَيِّدةً جِدًّا; **I should ~ well hope so!** آمُلُ ذلك كَثيراً!

damnation /dam'neɪʃ(ə)n/ *n* هَلاك

damned /damd/ A *adj* (infml) ▸ **damn** D

B *n* (**the damned**) المَلْعونونَ

damning /'damɪŋ/ *adj* ‹*report, indictment*› لاذِع

damp /damp/ A *adj* (**damper**, **dampest**) ‹*atmosphere, clothes, skin*› رَطْب; **the house smells ~** رائِحةُ البَيْتِ رَطْبةٌ

B *n* رُطوبة

C *vt* **~ down [sth]**, **~ [sth] down** أَخْمَدَ [شَيْئاً] ‹*a fire, blaze*›

damp course, **damp-proof course** *n* (BrE) [طَبَقة مُقاوِمة لِلرُّطوبةِ]

dampen /'damp(ə)n/ *vt* 1 (to moisten) بَلَّلَ ,رَطَّبَ ‹*a cloth, sponge*› 2 (to discourage) كَبَحَ (a; كَبْح) ‹*one's hopes, enthusiasm*›

damper /'dampə/ *n*

(Idiom) **to put a damper on sth** (infml) كَدَّرَ شَيْئاً; **his arrival put a ~ on the cheerful mood** كَدَّرَ وُصولُهُ جَوَّ المَرَحِ

damson /'damz(ə)n/ *n* دامْسون (نَوْع من البَرْقوق)

dance /dɑːns/ A *vt* رَقَصَ (a-u; رَقْص) ‹*a waltz, duet*›

B *vi* 1 (to music) «*dancers, soloists*» رَقَصَ (a-u; رَقْص) 2 «*flames, flowers*» رَقَصَ (a-u; رَقْص)

C *n* 1 [u] (art form) رَقْص (n coll) 2 (act) رَقْصة (رَقَصات) 3 (social gathering) حَفْلة رَقْصٍ 4 (set of steps) رَقْصة (رَقَصات)

dance floor *n* حَلْبة \ ساحة رَقْصٍ

dance hall *n* صالة رَقْصٍ

dancer /'dɑːnsə/ *n* رَقّاص ,راقِص

dancing /'dɑːnsɪŋ/ *n* رَقْص (n coll)

D and C *n* = **dilatation and curettage** عَمَليّة تَوْسيعٍ وَكَحْتٍ

dandelion /'dandɪlʌɪən/ *n* طَرَخْشَقون

dandruff /'dandrʌf/ *n* قِشْرة الرَأْسِ; **anti-~ shampoo** شامْبو قِشْرةِ الرَأْسِ

Dane /deɪn/ *n* دانْمارْكيّ

danger /'deɪndʒə/ *n* خَطَر (أَخْطار); **in ~** في خَطَرٍ; **to be in ~ of being hurt** كانَ هُناكَ خَطَرٌ عَلَيْهِ من أنْ يَتَأَذّى

danger list *n* (BrE) **to be on the danger list** كانَ على قائِمةِ الحالاتِ الحَرِجةِ

dangerous /'deɪndʒ(ə)rəs/ *adj* ‹*driving, place*› خَطِر; ‹*accusation, liaison*› خَطير

dangerously /'deɪndʒ(ə)rəsli/ *adv* ‹*close, ill*› بِشَكْلٍ خَطيرٍ

danger signal *n* إشارة إنْذارٍ

dangle /'daŋg(ə)l/ A *vt* ‹*the keys, a weight*› دَلّى

B *vi* «*earrings, arms*» تَدَلّى

Danish /'deɪnɪʃ/ A *adj* ‹*ambassador, food, lesson*› دانْماركيّ

B *n* (language) (اللُغة) الدانْماركيّة

Danish pastry *n* فَطيرة دانْماركيّة (نَوْع من المُعَجَّناتِ المُنْتَفِخةِ)

dank /daŋk/ *adj* ‹*basement, air*› [شَديد الرُطوبةِ وَفاسِد الهَواءِ]

Danube /'danjuːb/ *pr n* (**the Danube**) نَهْر الدانوب

dapper /'dapə/ *adj* ‹*man, suit*› مُهَنْدَم ,أنيق

dare /dɛː/ A *modal aux* 1 (to have the courage to) جَرُؤَ (u; جَراءة ,جُرْأة) ,أَقْدَمَ (على); **to ~ to do sth** جَرُؤَ على فِعْلِ شَيْءٍ; **nobody ~d ask, nobody ~d to ask** لم يَجْرُؤْ أحَدٌ على السُؤالِ; **they don't ~** *or* **they ~n't take the risk** لا يَجْرُؤونَ على المُجازَفةِ; **I ~ say it** دَعْني أَتَجَرَّأْ وَأَقولُهُ; **I ~ say** على ما أَظُنُّ 2 (expressing anger, indignation) جَرُؤَ (u; جُرْأة ,جَراءة;

(على); **don't you ~!** إيّاكَ أنْ تَفْعَلَ ذلك! ; **don't you ~ speak to me like that!** إيّاكَ أنْ تَتَحَدَّثَ مَعي بِهَذا الشَكْلِ! ; **how ~ you suggest that?** كيف تَجْرُؤُ على أنْ تَقْتَرِحَ ذلك؟

B *vt* تَحَدّى; **to ~ sb to do sth** تَحَدّى شَخْصاً أنْ يَفْعَلَ شَيْئاً; **go on, I ~ you to jump!** هَيّا، أَتَحَدّاكَ أنْ تَقْفِزَ!

C *n* تَحَدٍّ (تَحَدِّيات); **to do sth for a ~** فَعَلَ شَيْئاً بِهَدَفِ التَحَدّي

daredevil /ˈdɛːdɛv(ə)l/ **A** *n* مُتَهَوِّر

B *adj* ‹exploit, stunt› مُتَهَوِّر, مُجازِف

dargah /ˈdɑːgɑː/ *n* دَرْكاه

daring /ˈdɛːrɪŋ/ **A** *adj* ‹pilot, suggestion› جَريء (أَجْرِياءُ)

B *n* (courage) جُرْأة

dark /dɑːk/ **A** *adj* **1** (lacking in light) ‹room, sky› مُظْلِم; **it is getting ~** بَدَأَ الظَلامُ يَحُلُّ; **it's very ~ in here** المَكانُ مُظْلِمٌ جِدّاً هُنا **2** (in colour) ‹clothes, colour› داكِن, غامِق **3** ‹hair, skin› داكِن; **her beautiful ~ eyes** عَيْناها الداكِنَتانِ الجَميلَتانِ **4** (gloomy) ‹period› مُظْلِم; ‹mood› كَئيب, مُكْتَئِب **5** (sinister) ‹thought› مُظْلِم; ‹secret› خَطير; **she had a ~ side** كانَ لَدَيْها جانِبٌ مُظْلِمٌ; **~ forces are at work here** قُوى الظَلامِ \ الشَرِّ تَعْمَلُ هُنا **6** (disapproving) ‹look› اسْتِهْجانِيّ; **I got ~ looks when I walked in late** لَقيتُ نَظَراتِ اسْتِهْجانٍ عِنْدَما دَخَلْتُ مُتَأَخِّراً

B *n* **the ~** الظَلام; **to sit in the ~** جَلَسَ في الظَلامِ; **before/until ~** قبل \ حتّى حُلولِ الظَلامِ; **after ~** بعد حُلولِ الظَلامِ

(Idioms) **to be in the dark about sth** كانَ على غَيْرِ درايةٍ بِشَيْءٍ; **to keep sb in the dark about sth** أَخْفى شَيْئاً عن شَخْصٍ

Dark Ages *n* (**the Dark Ages**) العُصور المُظْلِمة

darken /ˈdɑːk(ə)n/ **A** *vt* عَتَّمَ ‹the sky›; أَظْلَمَ, أَطْفَأَ الأنْوارَ \ عَتَّمَ ‹the room›

B *vi* **1** «clouds, sky» دَجا (u; دُجوّ), أَظْلَمَ, اكْفَهَرَّ **2** «one's face» اكْفَهَرَّ

dark glasses *n* نَظّارات قاتِمة

darkness /ˈdɑːknəs/ *n* (absence of light) ظَلام; (of a colour) قَتامة

darkroom /ˈdɑːkruːm/ *n* غُرْفة تَحْميضٍ

dark-skinned /dɑːkˈskɪnd/ *adj* ‹person› داكِن البَشْرة, أَسْمَر (dipt; سُمْر), أَسْوَد (dipt; سود)

darling /ˈdɑːlɪŋ/ **A** *n* حَبيبي

B *adj* ‹baby, kitten› حَبيب (أَحِبّاءُ), عَزيز (أَعِزّاءُ)

darn /dɑːn/ *vt* رَفَأَ (a; رَفْء), رَتَقَ (i-u; رَتْق) ‹a sock, sweater›

dart /dɑːt/ **A** *n* سَهْم (أَسْهُم, سِهام), نَبْل (n coll; نِبال); **to play ~s** لَعِبَ لُعْبةَ السِهامِ المُرَيَّشةِ \ رَمْيِ النِبالِ

B *vi* «mouse, children» انْطَلَقَ كالسَهْمِ; **to ~ in/out** انْدَفَعَ إلى الداخِلِ \ الخارِجِ

dartboard /ˈdɑːtbɔːd/ *n* لَوْحة السِهامِ المُرَيَّشة

dash /daʃ/ **A** *vt* **1** (to smash) **to ~ sb/sth against a wall/the rocks** حَطَّمَ شَخْصاً \ شَيْئاً على الحائِطِ \ الصُخورِ; **she ~ed the plate/his camera to the ground** حَطَّمَت الطَبَقَ \ كاميرتَهُ على الأَرْضِ **2** (to destroy) حَطَّمَ, قَوَّضَ ‹sb's hopes, dreams›

B *vi* (infml) (to hurry) «person» انْدَفَعَ, هَرْوَلَ (i; هَرْوَلة); «vehicles» أَسْرَعَ; **to ~ out of/into the shop** خَرَجَ مُسْرِعاً من \ هَرَعَ إلى المَتْجَرِ; **I must ~!** لا بُدَّ أنْ أُسْرِعَ!

C *n* **1** (infml) (rush) إسْراع, هَرْوَلة, انْدِفاع; **a last-minute ~ to the hospital** هَرْوَلة في آخِرِ لَحْظةٍ إلى المُسْتَشْفى; **to make a ~ for it** هَرَبَ (u; هُروب); **to make a ~ for the train** هَرْوَلَ إلى القِطارِ **2** (small amount of a liquid) مِقْدار قَليل; (of pepper, salt) رَشّة, ذَرّة; (of colour) لَمْسة **3** [u] (flair) حَماسة وَتَأَنُّق **4** (in punctuation) شَرْطة (شُرَط)

(Phrasal verb) **dash off** **1** خَرَجَ مُسْرِعاً **2** **~ off [sth], ~ [sth] off** خَطَّ [شَيْئاً] بِسُرْعةٍ ‹a letter, sketch, an essay›

dashboard /ˈdaʃbɔːd/ *n* لَوْحة قِيادةٍ \ عَدّاداتٍ

data /ˈdeɪtə/ *n pl* **1** (facts, information) مَعْلومات, حَقائِق **2** (on a computer) بَيانات

database /ˈdeɪtəbeɪs/ *n* قاعِدة بَياناتٍ

data entry *n* إدْخال بَياناتٍ

data highway *n* طَريق البَياناتِ السَريع

data processing *n* مُعالَجة مَعْلوماتٍ

data protection *n* حِماية بَياناتٍ

data security *n* أَمْن بَياناتٍ

data storage device *n* جِهاز تَخْزينِ بَياناتٍ

date /deɪt/ **A** *n* **1** (specific day and month) تاريخ (تَواريخُ); **what ~ is it today?, what's the ~ today?** ما (هو) تاريخُ اليَوْمِ؟; **~ of birth** تاريخ الميلادِ; **there's no ~ on the**

letter لَيْسَ هُناكَ تاريخٌ على الرِسالةِ; to fix *or* set a ~ حَدَّدَ تاريخاً; at a later ~ في تاريخٍ لاحِقٍ ② (year) (تواريخُ) تاريخ ③ (meeting) (مَواعِدُ) مَوْعِد; we have a lunch ~ on Friday لَدَيْنا مَوْعِدُ غَداءٍ يَوْمَ الجُمْعَةِ; he went on a ~ with my sister خَرَجَ في مَوْعِدٍ مع أُخْتي; to make a ~ for Monday حَدَّدَ \ ضَرَبَ مَوْعِداً لِيَوْمِ الاثْنَيْنِ ④ (companion) (رفاق ,رُفَقاءُ) رَفيق; who's your ~ for the prom? مَنْ رَفيقَتُكَ في الحَفْلَةِ الراقِصةِ؟ ⑤ (fruit) (n coll; تُمور) تَمْر ⑥ (Bot) (tree) ▸ **date palm**

B (**to date**) *adv phr* حتّى تاريخِهِ \ الآنَ

C *vt* ① (to mark with a date) أَرَّخَ ‹*an invoice, a letter*›; **a cheque/letter ~d 21 June 2013** شيك \ خِطاب مُؤَرَّخ بِتاريخِ 21 يونيو 2013 ② (in determinations) قَدَّرَ العُمْرَ ‹*a skeleton, building*› ③ (to tell the age of) كَشَفَ عن العُمْرِ ‹*a novel, film*›; **that really ~s you!** هذا حَقًّا يَكْشِفُ عن عُمْرِكَ! ④ (to go out with) واعَدَ; **I ~d him for a couple of months** واعَدْتُهُ لِبِضْعِ شُهورٍ

D *vi* ① (to originate) **to ~ from Roman times, to ~ back to Roman times** «manuscripts, building, customs» رَجَعَ تاريخُهُ إلى العُصورِ الرومانيّةِ ② (to go out of fashion) «clothes, slang» انْتَهَتْ موضَتُهُ ▸ **out of date, up to date**

dated /ˈdeɪtɪd/ *adj* ‹*clothes, style*› غَيْر مُعاصِرٍ; ‹*expression, language*› مَهْجور ,بالٍ

date palm *n* (n coll; نَخيل) نَخْل

date rape *n* اغْتِصاب (بِاسْتِخْدامِ حُبوبِ الاغْتِصابِ)

dating /ˈdeɪtɪŋ/ *n* مُواعَدة

dating agency *n* وَكالة \ مَكْتَب مُواعَدةٍ

dating site *n* مَوْقِع مُواعَدةٍ

daub /dɔːb/ *vt* **to ~ sth with sth** لَطَّخَ شَيْئاً بِشَيْءٍ

daughter /ˈdɔːtə/ *n* (بَنات) بِنْت ,(بَنات) ابْنة (f; بَنات)

daughter-in-law /ˈdɔːtərɪnlɔː/ *n* (*pl* **daughters-in-law**) كَنّة (كَنائِنُ), زَوْجة ابْنٍ

daunt /dɔːnt/ *vt* أَخافَ

daunting /ˈdɔːntɪŋ/ *adj* ‹*prospect, task*› مُخيف

dawdle /ˈdɔːd(ə)l/ *vi* مَهَلَ (a; مَهْل ,مُهْلة)

dawn /dɔːn/ **A** *n* ① فَجْر; **at ~** عند الفَجْرِ; **before ~** قبل الفَجْرِ; **at the crack of ~** عند بُزوغِ الفَجْرِ; **when ~ broke** عِنْدَما بَزَغَ الفَجْرُ; **to work from ~ to *or* till dusk** عَمِلَ من الصَباحِ حتّى المَساءِ ② (of a civilization, an era) (مَطالِعُ) مَطْلَع; **at the ~ of the 21st century** في مَطْلَعِ القَرْنِ الحادي والعِشْرينَ

B *vi* ① (to become light) طَلَعَ (u; طُلوع ,مَطْلَع), بَزَغَ (u; بُزوغ); **the day ~ed sunny and warm** طَلَعَ النَهارُ مُشْرِقاً وَدافِئاً ② (to become apparent) **to ~ on sb** اتَّضَحَ لِشَخْصٍ; **it ~ed on me why they needed the flight number** اتَّضَحَ لي لِماذا احْتاجوا رَقْمَ الرِحْلةِ

dawn chorus *n* زَقْزَقة العَصافير عند الفَجْرِ

dawn raid *n* مُداهَمة عند الفَجْرِ

day /deɪ/ *n* ① (twenty-four hours) (أَيّام) يَوْم; **what ~ is it today?** أَيُّ الأَيّامِ اليَوْمُ؟; **every ~** كُلّ يَوْمٍ; **every other ~** كُلّ يَوْمَيْنِ; **one ~, some ~** يَوْماً ما; **any ~ now** عَمّا قَريبٍ; **the ~ after** اليَوْم التالي; **the ~ before** اليَوْم السابق; **the ~ before yesterday** أَوَّل أَمْسِ; **the ~ after tomorrow** بعد غَدٍ; **the ~ before/after the wedding** اليَوْم السابِق \ التالي لِيَوْمِ الزِفافِ; **from that ~ onwards** ابْتِداءً من هذا اليَوْمِ; **from one ~ to the next** من يَوْمٍ لآخَرَ; **one fine ~** في يَوْمٍ من الأَيّامِ; **it's 15 years to the ~ since he died** مَضى 15 عاماً منذ يَوْمِ وَفاتِهِ ② (time spent on an activity) (أَيّام) يَوْم, نَهار; **the working ~** يَوْم العَمَلِ; **a busy ~** يَوْم حافِل; **an enjoyable ~'s tennis** يَوْم تِنِس مُمْتِع; **we spent all ~ working/at the beach** قَضَيْنا اليَوْمَ كُلَّهُ في العَمَلِ \ على الشاطِئِ; **all that ~** طوال ذلك اليَوْمِ; **during the ~** أَثْناء النَهارِ; **for the ~** لِيَوْمٍ كامِلٍ; **to be paid by the ~** تَقاضى أَجْرَهُ باليَوْمِ; **have a nice ~!** أَتَمَنّى لَكَ نَهاراً سَعيداً! ③ (as opposed to night) نَهار; **the ~s are getting colder/hotter** بَدَأَت الأَيّامُ تُصْبِحُ أَشَدَّ بُرودةً \ حَرارةً; **to work ~s** عَمِلَ بالنَهارِ; **we rested by ~** اسْتَرَحْنا خلال النَهارِ ④ (a particular day) يَوْم; **to her dying ~** إلى يَوْمِ مَماتِها ⑤ (time past) زَمَن (أَزْمان); **in my ~ *or* ~s** في زَمَني; **in those ~s** في تِلْكَ الأَيّامِ; **these ~s** في أَيّامِنا هذه ,في هذه الأَيّامِ; **in the ~s of the Pharaohs** في أَيّامِ الفَراعِنةِ ▸ **week**

(Idioms) **day after day** يَوْماً بعد يَوْمٍ; **day in day out** يَوْماً بعد يَوْمٍ; **the Day of Judgement** يَوْم الحِسابِ; **it's all in a day's work** الأَمْرُ كُلُّهُ جُزْءٌ من روتين العَمَلِ; **it's early days yet** (BrE) ما زالَ الوَقْتُ مُبَكِّراً; **it's one of those days!** يَوْم مَشْؤوم \ أَسْوَد!; **to call it a day** اكْتَفى بِما فَعَلَهُ اليَوْمَ; **to have had its** day كانَ أَحْسَنَ وَلَّتْ \ أَدْبَرَتْ أَيّامُهُ; **to have seen better days** أَنْقَذَ المَوْقِفَ; **to save the day** حالاً مِمّا هو عَلَيْهِ اليَوْمَ; **a goal from Benson saved the ~ for United** أَنْقَذَ هَدَفُ بِنْسون مَوْقِفَ يونايْتِد; **to carry** *or* **win the day** أَحْرَزَ فَوْزاً

daybreak /ˈdeɪbreɪk/ *n* فَجْر

day care *n* رِعاية نَهارِيّة

daydream /ˈdeɪdriːm/ **A** *n* حُلْم اليَقَظةِ
B *vi* حَلَمَ حُلْمَ اليَقَظةِ

daylight /ˈdeɪlʌɪt/ *n* ضَوْء النَهارِ; **in ~** في وَضَحِ النَهارِ; ▸ **broad**

day nurse *n* [مُمَرِّضة تَعْمَلُ في النَهارِ]

day nursery *n* حضانة نَهارِيّة

day release *n* [إجازة لِيَوْمٍ واحِدٍ لِأَغْراضٍ تَعْليميّة]

day return *n* (BrE) تَذْكِرة ذَهابٍ وإِيابٍ (في نَفْسِ اليَوْمِ)

day room *n* صالة جُلوسٍ

day school *n* مَدْرَسة نَهارِيّة

day surgery *n* جِراحة اليَوْمِ الواحِدِ

daytime /ˈdeɪtʌɪm/ *n* نَهار (أَنْهُر); **in** *or* **during the ~** في النَهارِ

day-to-day /deɪtəˈdeɪ/ *adj* **1** ‹*life, responsibilities*› يَوْمِيّ
2 ‹*running, operation*› يَوْمِيّ

day trip *n* رِحْلة لِيَوم واحِدٍ

day tripper *n* [شَخْص في رِحْلةٍ لِيَوم واحِدٍ]

daze /deɪz/ *n* **in a ~** في حالةِ ذُهولٍ, مُشَوَّشاً

dazed /deɪzd/ *adj* ‹*look, survivor*› مُشَوَّش, ذاهِل

dazzle /ˈdaz(ə)l/ *vt* **1** «light, sun» أَبْهَرَ البَصَرَ, أَعْمى
2 «beauty» أَبْهَرَ; «skill» أَدْهَشَ

dazzling /ˈdazlɪŋ/ *adj* **1** ‹*light, sun*› مُبْهِر **2** ‹*display, performance*› مُبْهِر

DC /diːˈsiː/ *abbr* **1** = **direct current** تَيّار مُسْتَمِرّ **2** = **District of Columbia**

D-Day /ˈdiːdeɪ/ *n* (in World War II) [يَوْم إِنْزالِ نورْماندي]

DE *abbr* ▸ **Delaware**

DEA /diːiːˈeɪ/ *n* (AmE) = **Drug Enforcement Administration** [إدارة مُكافَحةِ المُخَدِّراتِ]

deacon /ˈdiːk(ə)n/ *n* شَمّاس (شَمامِسة)

deaconess /ˌdiːkəˈnɛs/ *n* شَمّاسة

dead /dɛd/ **A** *n* **1** (**the dead** *n pl*) المَوْتى **2** (state of being dead) **to rise/be raised from the ~** عادَ إلى, بُعِثَ بعد المَوْتِ الحَياةِ **3** (extreme point) **at ~ of night, in the ~ of night** في جَوْفِ \ مُنْتَصَفِ اللَيْلِ; **in the ~ of winter** في عِزِّ الشِتاءِ
B *adj* **1** (no longer living) ‹*tree, patient*› مَيِّت (مَوْتى, أَمْوات); **the ~ man/woman** الرَجُل المَيِّت \ المَرْأة المَيِّتة; **a ~ body** جُثّة مَيِّتة; **to drop down ~** سَقَطَ مَيِّتاً; **to shoot sb ~** قَتَلَ شَخْصاً رَمْياً بالرَصاصِ; **to give sb up for ~** اعْتَبَرَ شَخْصاً في عِداد المَوْتى **2** (no longer current) ‹*language*› بائِد, مَيِّت; ‹*relationship*› مَقْطوع **3** (infml) (exhausted) **to be ~** كانَ مُنْهَكاً; **to be ~ on one's feet** كانَ لا يَكادُ يَقِفُ على قَدَمَيْهِ من كَثْرةِ الإعْياءِ **4** (boring) **to be ~** «party, resort» كانَ مُمِلاًّ **5** (not functioning) ‹*battery, wire*› مُتَوَقِّف عن العَمَلِ; **the phone went ~** تَوَقَّفَ الهاتِفُ عن العَمَلِ **6** (numb) ‹*arm, finger*› يُعاني من خَدَرٍ \ خَدَلانٍ **7** (absolute) ‹*silence, calm*› مُطْلَق, كامِل, تامّ; **to come to a ~ stop** تَوَقَّفَ فَجْأةً \ تَماماً
C *adv* (absolutely) مُطْلَقاً, تَماماً; **you're ~ right!** أَنْتَ مُحِقٌّ تَماماً!; **he's ~ certain about it** هو على يَقينٍ تامٍّ بِهَذا; **to be ~ on time** كانَ في المَوْعِدِ تَماماً; **he was sitting ~ still** كانَ جالِساً لا يُحَرِّكُ ساكِناً

deaden /ˈdɛd(ə)n/ *vt* خَفَّفَ من الحِدّةِ ‹*pain, sound*›

dead end **A** *n* طَريق مَسْدود
B (**dead-end**) *adj* ‹*job*› [بِلا مُسْتَقْبَلٍ]

dead heat *n* [تَعادُل في سِباقٍ]

deadline /ˈdɛdlʌɪn/ *n* آخِر مَوْعِدٍ

deadlock /ˈdɛdlɒk/ *n* مَأْزِق (مَآزِق), طَريق مَسْدود; **the negotiations have reached (a) ~** وَصَلَت المُفاوَضاتُ إلى طَريقٍ مَسْدودٍ

dead loss *n* (infml) **to be a ~** [كانَ عَديمَ النَفْعِ]

deadly /ˈdɛdli/ **A** *adj* (**deadlier, deadliest**) **1** (lethal) ‹*disease*› مُميت; ‹*weapon*› قاتِل; ‹*poison*› فَتّاك **2** (hated) ‹*enemy*› لَدود (أَلِدّاءُ)
B *adv* (extremely) ‹*dull, boring*› [لِلغاية]

deadpan /ˈdɛdpan/ *adj* ‹*humour*› [دون أَيِّ تَعابيرَ على الوَجْهِ]; ‹*expression*› جافّ

Dead Sea *pr n* (**the Dead Sea**) البَحْر المَيِّت

deaf /dɛf/ **A** *n* (**the deaf** *n pl*) الصُمّ

B *adj* ‹*child, student*› أَصَمّ (dipt; صُمّ), أَطْرَش (dipt; طُرْش); **to go ~** أَصابَهُ الصَمَمُ; **~ and dumb** أَصَمّ وَأَبْكَم

(Idiom) **to turn a deaf ear to sth** صَمَّ أُذُنَهُ عن شَيْءٍ

deaf aid *n* سَمّاعات الأُذُنِ

deafen /ˈdɛf(ə)n/ *vt* أَصَمَّ

deafening /ˈdɛfnɪŋ/ *adj* ‹*roar, noise*› يُصِمُّ الآذانَ

deaf mute *n* (old use or offensive) أَصَمّ وَأَبْكَم

deafness /ˈdɛfnəs/ *n* طَرَش, صَمَم

deal /diːl/ **A** *vt* (*past tense, past participle* **dealt**) **1** (to deliver) **to ~ a blow to sb/sth, to ~ sb/sth a blow** وَجَّهَ ضَرْبَةً لِشَخْصٍ \ لِشَيْءٍ **2** وَزَّعَ ‹*cards, a hand*›

B *vi* (*past tense, past participle* **dealt**) **1** (to do business) «businessmen, firms» تاجَرَ; **to ~ in electrical goods/used cars** تاجَرَ في الأَجْهِزةِ الكَهْرَبائِيّةِ \ السَيّاراتِ المُسْتَعْمَلةِ **2** (on an exchange) «brokers, dealers» تاجَرَ; **to ~ in oil futures/shares** تاجَرَ في العُقودِ الآجِلةِ لِلنَفْطِ \ الأَسْهُمِ

C *n* **1** (in business, finance) صَفْقة (صَفَقات); (with a friend, criminal, terrorist) اتِّفاق (اتِّفاقات); **to make** *or* **do a ~ with sb** عَقَدَ صَفْقةً مع شَخْصٍ; **a pay ~** اتِّفاق على الأَجْرِ; **a property/an arms ~** صَفْقة عَقارِيّة \ أَسْلِحةٍ; **it's a ~!** اتَّفَقْنا!; **the ~'s off** الاتِّفاقُ لاغٍ; **to be in on the ~** (infml) شارَكَ في المُخَطَّطِ **2** (offer, bargain) **the best ~s in** *or* **on electrical goods** أَفْضَل العُروضِ على الأَجْهِزةِ الكَهْرَبائِيّةِ **3** (amount) **a great** *or* **good ~** قَدْر كَبِير; **he's a good ~ older than me** هو أَكْبَرُ مِنّي بِكَثِيرٍ; **they have a great ~ in common** لَدَيْهِم الكَثِيرُ من القَواسِمِ المُشْتَرَكةِ; **this project means a great ~ to me** هذا المَشْروعُ يَعْني الكَثِيرَ بالنِسْبةِ لي **4** (infml) (treatment) مُعامَلة; **to give sb a fair ~** عامَلَ شَخْصاً مُعامَلةً عادِلةً; **he got a raw ~** عومِلَ مُعامَلةً مُجْحِفةً **5** (in cards) تَوْزيع الوَرَقِ; **it's my ~** هذا دَوْري لِتَوْزيعِ الوَرَقِ

(Idioms) **big deal!** (infml) لَيْسَ بالأَمْرِ الجَلَلِ!; **to make a big deal out of sth** هَوَّلَ شَيْئاً

(Phrasal verbs) **deal out**: **~ out [sth], ~ [sth] out** فَرَضَ [شَيْئاً] ‹*a punishment, fine*›

• **deal with** **A** **~ with [sth]** (to tackle) عالَجَ [شَيْئاً] ‹*a complaint, problem, an emergency*› **B** **~ with [sb]** **1** (to attend to) تعامَلَ مع [شَخْصٍ] ‹*a client, the public*› **2** (to do business with) تعامَلَ مع [شَخْصٍ] ‹*a supplier, company*›

dealer /ˈdiːlə/ *n* **1** (in car parts, appliances) تاجِر (تُجّار); (in drugs) (infml) تاجِر مُخَدِّراتٍ **2** (on the stock exchange) مُضارِب **3** (in cards) مُوَزِّع

dealing /ˈdiːlɪŋ/ **A** *n* تِجارة; **~ on the Stock Exchange** التِجارة في البورْصةِ; **~ in drugs** تِجارة المُخَدِّراتِ

B (**dealings**) *n pl* تَعامُلات; **to have ~s with sb** كانَتْ لَدَيْهِ تَعامُلاتٌ مع شَخْصٍ

dealt /dɛlt/ *past tense, past participle* ▸ **deal**

dean /diːn/ *n* **1** (Rel_Chr) [كاهِن ذو رُتْبةٍ عالِيةٍ في الكَنيسةِ] **2** (at a university) عَميد (عُمَداءُ)

dear /dɪə/ **A** *adj* **1** (loved) ‹*friend*› مَحْبوب, عَزِيز (أَعِزّاءُ) **2** (in letters) عَزِيزي; **Dear Sir/Madam** سَيِّدي \ سَيِّدتي الفاضِل(ة) \ المُحْتَرَم(ة); **Dear Mr and Mrs Jones** [السَيِّد والسَيِّدة جونْز المُحْتَرَمَيْن]; **Dear Anne** عَزيزَتي آن **3** (lovable) ‹*puppy, baby*› لَذيذ (لِذاذ) **4** (expensive) غالٍ

B *n* **1** (as a form of address) عَزيزي, حَبيبي **2** (lovable person) [شَخْص مَحْبوب]; **you poor ~!** يا عَزيزي المِسْكين!

C *excl* **oh ~!** يا إِلَهي!

dearly /ˈdɪəli/ *adv* **1** (very much) ‹*to love, miss*› [كَثيراً]; **I would ~ love to see him again** أَتَمَنّى من كُلِّ قَلْبي أَنْ أَراهُ مَرّةً أُخْرى **2** (at great cost) ‹*to pay*› غالِياً

death /dɛθ/ *n* (of persons, animals, civilization) مَوْت; (of dreams, hopes) تَحَطُّم; (of plans) فَشَل; **at the time of his ~** وَقْتَ مَوْتِهِ; **a ~ in the family** حالة وَفاةٍ في العائِلةِ; **~ by drowning** المَوْت غَرَقاً; **the number of ~s caused by …** عَدَد الوَفَياتِ الناجِمةِ عن …; **to put sb to ~** أَعْدَمَ \ قَتَلَ شَخْصاً; **a fight to the ~** قِتال حَتّى المَوْتِ; **to work oneself to ~** أَنْهَكَ \ أَرْهَقَ نَفْسَهُ في العَمَلِ; **she fell to her ~** سَقَطَتْ مَيِّتةً; **to die a violent ~** ماتَ مِيتةً عَنيفةً

(Idioms) **to be at death's door** كانَ على حافّةِ المَوْتِ; **to be bored/worried to death** شَعَرَ بالمَلَلِ \ بالقَلَقِ الشَديدِ; **to be the death of sb** كانَ مَصْدَرَ إِزْعاجٍ \ قَلَقٍ شَديدٍ لِشَخْصٍ; **to frighten** *or* **scare sb to death** (infml) أَفْزَعَ \ أَرْعَبَ شَخْصاً بِشِدّةٍ

deathbed /ˈdɛθbɛd/ *n* فِراش المَوْتِ

death camp *n* مُعَسْكَر مَوْتٍ

death certificate *n* شَهادة وَفاةٍ

death penalty *n* عُقوبة إعْدامٍ

death row *n* جِناح المَحْكومِ عَلَيْهِم بالإِعْدامِ

death sentence *n* عُقوبة الإِعْدامِ

death squad *n* فِرْقة مَوْتٍ (جَماعة مُكَلَّفة بالقَضاءِ على خُصومٍ سِياسيّينَ)

death threat *n* تَهْديد بالقَتْلِ

death toll *n* حَصيلة القَتْلى

deathtrap /ˈdɛθtrap/ *n* [مَصْدَر هَلاكٍ]

death warrant *n* **1** (official document) أَمْر إِعْدامٍ **2** (cause of destruction, failure) ضَرْبة قاضِية

deathwatch beetle /ˌdɛθwɒtʃ ˈbiːt(ə)l/ *n* خُنْفُساء المَوْتِ

death wish *n* رَغْبة في المَوْتِ

debacle /deɪˈbɑːk(ə)l/ *n* فَشَل

debar /dɪˈbɑː/ *vt* **(-rr-)** مَنَعَ ,اسْتَثْنى (a; مَنْع) ‹a voter, claimant›

debase /dɪˈbeɪs/ *vt* **1** (to devalue) حَطَّ من الشَأْنِ ‹an ideal, a language› **2** (to demean) جَرَّدَ من آدَمِيّة ‹a person›

debatable /dɪˈbeɪtəb(ə)l/ *adj* ‹issue, question› قابِل ,جَدَلِيّ لِلمُناقَشةِ

debate /dɪˈbeɪt/ **A** *n* (in legislature) مُناقَشة; (discussion) مُناظَرة **B** *vt* (to discuss formally) ناقَشَ ‹a proposal, motion›; (to weigh up) فَكَّرَ (في) ‹an idea, a possibility›

debauchery /dɪˈbɔːtʃ(ə)ri/ *n* فُجور ,إِباحِيّة

debenture /dɪˈbɛntʃə/ *n* سَنَد (أَسْناد ,سَنَدات)

debilitating /dɪˈbɪlɪteɪtɪŋ/ *adj* ‹disease, pain› موهِن

debit /ˈdɛbɪt/ **A** *n* **1** (amount) قَيْد ,مَبْلَغ مَسْحوب ,سَحْب **2** (entry in an account) (خانة) مَدين سَحْبٍ **B** *vt* خَصَمَ (i; خَصْم) ‹an account, a payment›

debit card *n* بِطاقة الدَفْعِ

debonair /ˌdɛbəˈnɛː/ *adj* ‹charm› [مُتَأَنِّق في مَظْهَرِهِ وَتَصَرُّفاتِهِ]

debrief /diːˈbriːf/ *vt* اسْتَجْوَبَ ‹an agent, a defector›

debriefing /diːˈbriːfɪŋ/ *n* مُساءَلة ,(اسْتِجْوابات) اسْتِجْواب

debris /ˈdɛbriː/ *n* **1** (rubble) أَنْقاض **2** (of a plane, etc) حُطام, شَظايا **3** (rock fragments) شَظايا

debt /dɛt/ *n* **1** [u] (indebtedness) دَيْن (دُيون); **to be in ~ to sb** كانَ مَدْيوناً \ مَديناً لِشَخْصٍ; **I am $500 in ~** أنا مَدْيونٌ بِمَبْلَغِ 500 دولار; **to get into ~** أَصْبَحَ مَدْيوناً **2** (money owing) دَيْن (دُيون); **bad ~s** دُيون فاسِدة

debt collector *n* مُحَصِّل دُيونٍ

debtor /ˈdɛtə/ *n* مَدين ,مَدْيون

debt-ridden *adj* ‹country, economy› [مُثْقَل بالدُيونِ]

debug /diːˈbʌg/ *vt* **(-gg-)** [صَحَّحَ الخَطَأَ في] ‹a computer, system›

debunk /diːˈbʌŋk/ *vt* كَشَفَ \ فَضَحَ الزَيْفَ ‹a theory, an idea›; فَنَّدَ ‹a myth›

debut /ˈdeɪbjuː/ *n* (*pl* **debuts** /-bjuːz/) [الظُهور أو العَرْض الأَوَّل]

decade /ˈdɛkeɪd, dɪˈkeɪd/ *n* عَقْد (عُقود)

decadence /ˈdɛkəd(ə)ns/ *n* تَفَسُّخ ,انْحِطاط ,تَدَهْوُر أَخْلاقِيّ

decadent /ˈdɛkəd(ə)nt/ *adj* ‹lifestyle› مُنْحَطّ; ‹civilization› مُتَدَهْوِر ,مُتَفَسِّخ

decaffeinated /diːˈkafɪneɪtɪd/ *adj* ‹coffee, tea› مَنْزوع الكافِيين

decanter /dɪˈkantə/ *n* دَوْرَق ,غَرّافة (دَوارِق)

decapitate /dɪˈkapɪteɪt/ *vt* قَطَعَ الرَأْسَ

decathlon /dɪˈkaθlɒn/ *n* عُشارِيّ

decay /dɪˈkeɪ/ **A** *vi* «vegetation, corpses» تَحَلَّلَ ,تَعَفَّنَ; «society» انْحَلَّ; «buildings» تَهَدَّمَ ,تَهَرَّأَ; «teeth» تَسَوَّسَ **B** *n* (of organic matter) تَحَلُّل ,تَعَفُّن; (of a building) تَهَدُّم ,هَرْء; (of society) انْحِلال

deceased /dɪˈsiːst/ **A** *n* (*pl* **deceased**) **(the deceased)** (fml) الفَقيد ,المُتَوَفّى **B** *adj* (fml) ‹relative, spouse› مُتَوَفًّى

deceit /dɪˈsiːt/ *n* خِداع

deceitful /dɪˈsiːtfʊl/ *adj* ‹act, tactic› مُضَلِّل ,(مَكَرة) ماكِر

deceive /dɪˈsiːv/ *vt* خَدَعَ (a; خَدْع) ‹a friend, voter›

decelerate /diːˈsɛləreɪt/ *vi* خَفَّضَ السُرْعة ,أَبْطَأَ

December /dɪˈsɛmbə/ *n* ديسَمْبِر (NA, Gulf), كانون الأَوَّل (Levant, Iraq), دُجَنْبِر (Mor) ▸ **March**

decency /ˈdiːs(ə)nsi/ *n* **1** (good manners) أَدَب **2** (propriety) حِشْمة ,لِياقة

decent /ˈdiːs(ə)nt/ *adj* 1 (respectable) ‹*family, man*› مُحْتَرَم, مُهَذَّب; **no ~ person would do a thing like that** لا يُمْكِنُ لِإنْسانٍ مُحْتَرَمٍ أنْ يَفْعَلَ شَيْئاً كَهَذا; **to give sb a ~ burial** أقامَ مَراسِمَ دَفْنٍ لائِقَةً لِشَخْصٍ; **he did the ~ thing and resigned** فَعَلَ الشَّيْءَ المُناسِبَ وَاسْتَقالَ; **after a ~ interval, he remarried** بعد فاصِلٍ زَمَنِيٍّ مَقْبولٍ، تَزَوَّجَ مَرَّةً ثانِيةً 2 (infml) (good, kind) ‹*people, fellow*› لَطيف (لُطَفاءُ ,لِطاف), كَريم (كِرام ,كُرَماءُ); **it's ~ of him to help** هذا لُطْفٌ مِنْهُ أنْ يَتَقَدَّمَ بالمُساعَدةِ 3 (adequate) ‹*housing, wage, standards*› مَقْبول ,لائِق; **they have a ~ chance of winning** لَدَيْهِمْ فُرْصةٌ جَيِّدَةٌ للفَوْزِ; **to make a ~ living** حَقَّقَ دَخْلاً جَيِّداً 4 (infml) (fit to be seen) ‹*clothes*› لائِق ,مُحْتَشِم; **I have nothing ~ to wear** لَيْسَ لَدَيَّ مَلابِسُ لائِقةٌ لِأَرْتَدِيها

decently /ˈdiːs(ə)ntli/ *adv* 1 (fairly) ‹*to pay, treat*› بِاحْتِرامٍ 2 (reasonably) ‹*to perform, play*› بِشَكْلٍ مَعْقولٍ; بِشَكْلٍ لائِقٍ; **it's a ~ sized hotel** هو فُنْدُقٌ ذو مِساحةٍ كَبيرةٍ 3 (in a morally acceptable way) ‹*to behave, dress*› بِاحْتِشامٍ, بِشَكْلٍ لائِقٍ 4 (politely) بِأَدَبٍ, بِشَكْلٍ لائِقٍ \ مُهَذَّبٍ; **we left as soon as we ~ could** غادَرْنا حالَما تَمَكَّنّا من الانْصِرافِ بِلُطْفٍ

decentralize, **-ise** (BrE) /diːˈsɛntrəlʌɪz/ *vt* طَبَّقَ اللامَرْكَزِيَّةَ ‹*authority, power*›

deception /dɪˈsɛpʃ(ə)n/ *n* 1 (deceiving) [u] خِداع ,تَضْليل, 2 (a trick) حيلة (حِيَل), خُدْعة (خُدَع), مُراوَغة

deceptive /dɪˈsɛptɪv/ *adj* ‹*impression, appearance*› خَدّاع ,مُضَلِّل

decibel /ˈdɛsɪbɛl/ *n* ديسيبَل

decide /dɪˈsʌɪd/ **A** *vt* 1 (to reach a decision) **to ~ to do sth** قَرَّرَ أنْ يَفْعَلَ شَيْئاً; **I ~d to accept** قَرَّرْتُ أنْ أَقْبَلَ; **I ~d that I would resign** قَرَّرْتُ أنَّني سَأَسْتَقيلُ; **he hasn't ~d whether to stay** لم يُقَرِّرْ ما إذا كانَ سَيَبْقَى 2 (to settle) حَسَمَ (i; حَسْم) ‹*a result, dispute, matter*›; **the game was ~d in the last minute** حُسِمَتِ المُباراةُ في اللَّحْظةِ الأَخيرةِ 3 (to persuade) **to ~ sb to do sth** حَمَلَ شَخْصاً على فِعْلِ شَيْءٍ; **what finally ~d you to buy it?** ما الّذي حَمَلَكَ في النِهايةِ على شِرائِهِ؟
B *vi* 1 (to make up one's mind) قَرَّرَ ,وَصَلَ إلى قرارٍ; **let her ~ for herself** دَعْها تُقَرِّرُ بِنَفْسِها; **I like them both; I can't ~** يُعْجِبُني كِلاهُما؛ لا أَسْتَطيعُ أنْ أُقَرِّرَ; **to ~ in favour of/against doing sth** تَوَصَّلَ إلى قَرارٍ بِفِعْلِ \ بالامْتِناعِ عن فِعْلِ شَيْءٍ 2 (to come to a decision) «judges, panel» حَكَمَ (u; حُكْم), أَصْدَرَ حُكْماً; **they ~d in our favour/against us** حَكَموا في صالِحِنا \ ضِدَّنا; **to ~ between two applicants/options** اخْتارَ بين مُتَقَدِّمَيْنِ \ خِيارَيْنِ

Phrasal verb **decide on** **A** **~ on [sth]** 1 (to choose) اخْتارَ [شَيْئاً] ‹*a book, strategy*›; **she ~d on a career in law** اخْتارَتْ مِهْنَةً في القانونِ 2 (to come to a decision on) وَصَلَ إلى قَرارٍ, قَرَّرَ بِخُصوصِ [شَيْءٍ] ‹*a policy, course of action*› **B** **~ on [sb]** اخْتِيارَ [شَخْصٍ] ‹*an applicant, a team*›

decided /dɪˈsʌɪdɪd/ *adj* 1 (definite) ‹*advantage, lack*› جَلِيّ 2 (determined) ‹*manner, tone, opinions*› حاسِم ,قاطِع

decidedly /dɪˈsʌɪdɪdli/ *adv* ‹*odd, uncomfortable*› قَطْعاً ,حَتْماً

decider /dɪˈsʌɪdə/ *n* 1 (game) مُباراة حَسْمٍ; (race) سِباق حَسْمٍ 2 (goal) هَدَف حَسْمٍ; (point) نُقْطة حَسْمٍ

deciduous /dɪˈsɪdjʊəs/ *adj* ‹*tree, shrub*› نَفْضِيّ

decimal /ˈdɛsɪm(ə)l/ **A** *adj* ‹*system, currency*› عُشْرِيّ **B** *n* كَسْر عُشْرِيّ

decimalization, **-isation** (BrE) /dɛsɪməlʌɪˈzeɪʃ(ə)n/ *n* [تَحَوُّل إلى النِظامِ العُشْرِيِّ]

decimal point *n* نُقْطة عُشْرِيّة

decimate /ˈdɛsɪmeɪt/ *vt* [قَلَّصَ العَدَدَ بِشَكْلٍ كَبيرٍ] ‹*a population, an industry*›

decipher /dɪˈsʌɪfə/ *vt* فَكَّ (u; فَكّ), حَلَّ (u; حَلّ) ‹*a code*›; فَكَّ الرُموزَ ‹*a message*›

decision /dɪˈsɪʒ(ə)n/ *n* قَرار (قَرارات); **the right/wrong ~** القَرارُ الصائِبُ \ الخاطِئُ; **it was a rash/wise ~** كانَ قراراً مُتَسَرِّعاً \ حَكيماً; **the judges' ~ is final** قَرارُ الحُكّامِ نِهائِيٌّ; **to make** *or* **take a ~** اتَّخَذَ قَراراً; **to come to** *or* **reach a ~** تَوَصَّلَ إلى قَرارٍ

decision-maker /dəˈsɪʒ(ə)n,meɪkə/ *n* صانِع قَرارٍ

decision-making /dəˈsɪʒ(ə)n,meɪkɪŋ/ *n* صِناعة قَرارٍ \ اتِّخاذ

decisive /dɪˈsʌɪsɪv/ *adj* 1 (conclusive) ‹*battle, factor*› حاسِم 2 (purposeful) ‹*manner, answer*› حازِم (حَزَمة)

deck /dɛk/ *n* 1 (on a ship) ظَهْر (ظُهور ,أَظْهُر), سَطْح (سُطوح) 2 (BrE) (on a bus) طَبَقة 3 (AmE) (terrace) تِراس 4 (AmE) (of cards) شَدّة (وَرَق لَعِبٍ)

deckchair /ˈdɛktʃɛː/ *n* كُرْسيّ شاطِئٍ

declaration /dɛkləˈreɪʃ(ə)n/ *n* إعْلان (إعْلانات)

declare /dɪˈklɛː/ *vt* **1** (to state) أَعْلَنَ, صَرَّحَ (ب) ‹*one's intention, support*› **2** (to proclaim) أَعْلَنَ ‹*war, independence*› **3** صَرَّحَ (ب) ‹*income, goods*›

declassify /diːˈklasɪfʌɪ/ *vt* (**declassifies**, **declassifying**, **declassified**) أَفْرَجَ (عن), رَفَعَ السِّرِّيَّةَ (عن) ‹*a document*› رَفَعَ السِّرِّيَّةَ (عن) ‹*information*›

declension /dɪˈklɛnʃ(ə)n/ *n* إعْراب

decline /dɪˈklʌɪn/ **A** *vt* **1** (fml) (to refuse) رَفَضَ (i-u; رَفْض) ‹*an offer, invitation*› **2** (Ling) صَرَّفَ ‹*a noun*›
B *vi* **1** (to wane) «sb's influence, empire, career» تَرَدَّى, ضَعُفَ (u; ضَعْف) **2** (to fall) «sales, production, trade» انْخَفَضَ; **orders are declining** انْخَفَضَت الطَّلَباتُ **3** «sb's health, morale» تَدَهْوَرَ, تَراجَعَ **4** (fml) (to refuse) رَفَضَ (i-u; رَفْض) **5** (Ling) «noun, pronoun» صُرِّفَ; **how does this noun ~?** ما هي تَصْريفاتُ هذا الاسْمِ؟
C (**declining**) *adj* **1** (becoming less important) ‹*empire, influence*› مُتَرَدٍّ, مُتَراجِع **2** (falling) ‹*sales, rate*› آخِذ في الانْخِفاضِ; **declining oil production** إنْتاج البِتْرولِ الآخِذ في الانْخِفاضِ
D *n* **1** (of a civilization, sb's popularity) تَرَدٍّ, تَدَهْوُر, تَراجُع; **the empire was in ~** كانَت الإمْبَراطوريّةُ آخِذةً في التَدَهْوُرِ; **there has been a ~ in his support** كانَ هُناكَ تَراجُعٌ في تَأْيِيدِهِ **2** (in trade, demand) انْخِفاض (انْخِفاضات); **a 5% ~ in exports** انْخِفاض في الصادِراتِ بِنِسْبة ‎5٪‎; **to go into ~** بَدَأَ في الانْخِفاضِ **3** (in health) تَدَهْوُر

decode /diːˈkəʊd/ *vt* فَكَّ \ حَلَّ رُموزَ الشِفْرةِ ‹*a message, signal*›

decolonize, -ise (BrE) /diːˈkɒlənʌɪz/ *vt* أَنْهى الاسْتِعْمارَ ‹*a territory*›

decompose /diːkəmˈpəʊz/ *vi* «body» تَحَلَّلَ; «matter» فَسَدَ (i-u; فَساد)

decompress /ˌdiːkəmˈprɛs/ *vt* فَكَّ الضَغْطَ ‹*a file, an archive*›

decontrol /ˌdiːk(ə)nˈtrəʊl/ *vt* (**-ll-**) أَلْغى الرَقابةَ, حَرَّرَ ‹*prices, a commodity, trade*›

decor /ˈdeɪkɔː/ *n* ديكور (ديكورات), زَخْرَفة

decorate /ˈdɛkəreɪt/ **A** *vt* **1** زَيَّنَ, حَلّى ‹*a cake, tree*› **2** (with paint) صَبَغَ (a-i-u; صَبْغ) ‹*a room, interior*›
B *vi* [صَبَغَ الجُدْرانَ \ عَلَّقَ وَرَقَ الجُدْرانِ]

decoration /dɛkəˈreɪʃ(ə)n/ *n* **1** (object) زينة **2** (action) تَزْيين, **3** (Mil) وِسام (أَوْسِمة), نيشان (نَياشينُ) زَخْرَفة

decorative /ˈdɛk(ə)rətɪv/ *adj* ‹*object, art*› زُخْرُفيّ, تَزْيينيّ

decorator /ˈdɛkəreɪtə/ *n* مُزَخْرِف, عامِل ديكور

decorous /ˈdɛk(ə)rəs/ *adj* ‹*behaviour, manner*› لائِق

decorum /dɪˈkɔːrəm/ *n* لِياقة

decoy /ˈdiːkɔɪ/ *n* طُعْم (طُعوم)

decrease **A** *vi* /dɪˈkriːs/ «prices, temperatures» انْخَفَضَ; «population» تَناقَصَ
B *vt* /dɪˈkriːs/ خَفَّضَ ‹*a risk, an amount*›
C *n* /ˈdiːkriːs/ تَناقُص (تَناقُصات), انْخِفاض (انْخِفاضات), تَضاؤُل

decreasing /dɪˈkriːsɪŋ/ *adj* ‹*number, rate*› مُتَضاءِل

decree /dɪˈkriː/ **A** *n* **1** (edict) مَرْسوم (مَراسيمُ) **2** (court judgment) قَرار (قَرارات)
B *vt* أَصْدَرَ مَرْسوماً ‹*a ban*›

decree absolute *n* [حُكْم نِهائيّ بالطَلاقِ (طِبْقاً للقانونِ البَريطانيِّ)]

decree nisi *n* [حُكْم ابْتِدائيّ بالطَلاقِ (طِبْقاً للقانونِ البَريطانيِّ)]

decrepit /dɪˈkrɛpɪt/ *adj* **1** ‹*furniture*› بالٍ, رَثّ; ‹*building*› مُتَداعٍ **2** ‹*old person*› عاجِز (عَجَزة)

decriminalize, -ise (BrE) /diːˈkrɪmɪnəlʌɪz/ *vt* رَفَعَ الحَظْرَ عن ‹*drugs, prostitution*›

dedicate /ˈdɛdɪkeɪt/ *vt* **1** كَرَّسَ, قَدَّمَ ‹*one's life, time*›; **I ~d ten years of my life to the project** كَرَّسْتُ عَشْرَ سَنَواتٍ من عُمْري للمَشْروعِ **2** أَهْدى ‹*a book, composition*›

dedicated /ˈdɛdɪkeɪtɪd/ *adj* **1** ‹*staff, fans*› مُلْتَزِم, مُتَفانٍ **2** ‹*server, telephone line*› مُخَصَّص

dedication /dɛdɪˈkeɪʃ(ə)n/ *n* **1** (devotion) إخْلاص, تَكْريس **2** (message) إهْداء (إهْداءات)

deduce /dɪˈdjuːs/ *vt* اسْتَخْلَصَ, اسْتَدَلَّ, اسْتَنْبَطَ ‹*a conclusion, meaning*›

deduct /dɪˈdʌkt/ *vt* خَصَمَ (i; خَصْم), طَرَحَ (a; طَرْح), اقْتَطَعَ ‹*tax, expenses*›

deduction /dɪˈdʌkʃ(ə)n/ *n* **1** (subtraction) طَرْح; (amount) مُسْتَقْطَع **2** (conclusion) اسْتِنْتاج (اسْتِنْتاجات), اسْتِنْباط (اسْتِنْباطات), اسْتِدْلال (اسْتِدْلالات)

deed /diːd/ *n* **1** (action) فِعْل (أَفْعال) **2** (for property) عَقْد (عُقود)

Idiom **in word and deed** قَوْلاً وفِعْلاً

deed poll *n* (*pl* **deeds poll**) [وَثيقة قانونيّة تُسْتَخْدَمُ لِتَغْيير اسْم]

deem /diːm/ *vt* (fml) رَأى (a; رُؤْيَة, رَأْي), اعْتَبَرَ

deep /diːp/ **A** *adj* **1** (vertically) ‹*hole, water, wound, snow*› عَميق; **how ~ is the river/the water?** ما عُمْقُ النَّهْرِ \ الماءِ؟; **the lake is 13 m ~** يَبْلُغُ عُمْقُ البُحَيْرَةِ 13 م; **a hole 5 cm ~** ثُقْب بعُمْق 5 سم **2** (horizontally) ‹*cupboard, strip, band*› عميق; **the shelf is 30 cm ~** يَبْلُغُ عُمْقُ الرَفِّ 30 سم **3** (with colours, hues) ‹*blue, suntan*› قاتِم, داكِن; **her ~ green eyes** عَيْناها الخضراوانِ الداكِنَتانِ **4** (intense) ‹*admiration, love, regret*› شَديد; **to be in ~ trouble** كانَ في وَرْطَةٍ كَبيرَةٍ; **we heard a ~ sigh** سَمِعْنا تَنَهُّداً عَميقاً **5** (profound) ‹*coma, sleep*› عَميق; **she's in a ~ coma** هي في غَيْبوبَةٍ عَميقَةٍ **6** (impenetrable) ‹*jungle*› كَثيف; ‹*darkness*› دامِس, حالِك; **they live in ~est Wales** (hum) يَعيشونَ في مِنْطَقَةٍ نائِيَةٍ جِدًّا في ويلز **7** (learned) ‹*thinker*› مُتَعَمِّق; ‹*meaning, discussion*› عَميق; **at a ~er level** على مُسْتَوًى أَعْمَقَ **8** (low) ‹*note, voice*› عَميق **9** (absorbed) **to be ~ in thought/conversation** كانَ مُسْتَغْرِقاً في التَفْكيرِ \ الحَديثِ; **he was ~ in his work** كانَ مُسْتَغْرِقاً في عَمَلِهِ

B *n* (liter) (sea) **the ~** البَحْر

C *adv* **1** (far down) ‹*to dig, bury*› عَميقاً; **~ beneath the earth's surface** عَميقاً تحت سَطْحِ الأَرْضِ; **to dive ~** غاصَ في الأَعْماقِ; **to dig ~er into an affair** بَحَثَ مَسْأَلَةً بِاسْتِفاضَةٍ; **to sink ~er into debt** غَرِقَ في الدُيونِ أَكْثَرَ **2** (a long way in) ‹*to venture, go*› عَميقاً; **they penetrated ~ into enemy territory/the forest** تَوَغَّلوا عَميقاً داخِلَ أَراضي العَدُوِّ \ الغابَةِ; **to talk ~ into the night** تَحَدَّثَ حتّى وَقْتٍ مُتَأَخِّرٍ من اللَيْلِ **3** (emotionally) **~ down** *or* **inside** في الأَعْماقِ; **her faith/loyalty runs ~** يَجْري إيمانُها \ وَلاؤُها في أَعْماقِها

deepen /ˈdiːp(ə)n/ **A** *vt* **1** (vertically) عَمَّقَ ‹*a well, channel*› **2** (horizontally) وَسَّعَ ‹*a cupboard, shelf*› **3** (to intensify) زادَ (i; زِيادة), عَمَّقَ (من) ‹*sb's concern, awareness, love*›; **the news ~ed their concern** زادَتِ الأَخْبارُ من قَلَقِهِمْ; **the visit ~ed our understanding of the problem** عَمَّقَت الزِيارةُ فَهْمَنا للمُشْكِلَةِ **4** (to make darker) غَمَّقَ ‹*a colour, one's tan*› **5** (to make lower) عَمَّقَ ‹*one's voice, the pitch*›

B *vi* **1** «water, river, snow» عَمُقَ (u; عُمْق), ازْدادَ عُمْقاً **2** (to intensify) «sb's admiration, love, regret» زادَ (i; زِيادة), اشْتَدَّ **3** (to worsen) «crisis, rift, coma» ازْدادَ سوءاً; **her coma is ~ing** تَزْدادُ غَيْبوبَتُها سوءاً; **as the crisis ~s, you find out who your friends are** عِنْدَما تَزْدادُ الأَزْمةُ سوءاً، تَعْرِفُ مَنْ هُمْ أَصْدِقاؤُكَ **4** (to grow darker) «colour, hues» أَصْبَحَ داكِناً \ غامِقاً **5** (to grow lower) «voice, pitch» عَمُقَ (u; عُمْق)

C (**deepening**) *adj* **1** ‹*water, river, snow*› مُتَزايِد العُمْقِ **2** (intensifying) ‹*rift, crisis, mystery*› مُتَزايِد

deep end *n* [أَعْمَق جُزْء في المَسْبَحِ]

Idiom **to be thrown in at the deep end** (infml) [وُضِعَ في مُواجَهةٍ صَعْبَةٍ]

deep-fat fryer /ˌdiːpfat ˈfrʌɪə/ *n* قَلّاية

deep freeze *n* فِريزر, مُجَمِّدة

deep-fry /ˌdiːpˈfrʌɪ/ *vt* (**-fries, -frying, -fried**) قَلى قَلْياً عَميقاً ‹*French fries, vegetables*›

deeply /ˈdiːpli/ *adv* **1** ‹*to breathe, sigh*› بِعُمْقٍ **2** ‹*to think*› بِعُمْقٍ; ‹*to care, feel*› بِشِدّةٍ; ‹*concerned, involved*› بِشِدّةٍ

deep-rooted /ˌdiːpˈruːtɪd/ *adj* ‹*problem, fear*› مُتَأَصِّل, راسِخ

deep-sea /ˌdiːpˈsiː/ *adj* ‹*fishing, diver*› في أَعْماقِ البَحْرِ

deep-seated /diːpˈsiːtɪd/ *adj* ▸**deep-rooted**

deep-set /ˌdiːpˈsɛt/ *adj* ‹*eyes*› غائِر

deep-vein thrombosis /ˌdiːpˌveɪn θrɒmˈbəʊsɪs/ *n* تَجَلُّط وَريديّ عَميق

deer /dɪə/ *n* (*pl* **deer**) أَيِّل (أَيائِل)

de-escalate /diːˈɛskəleɪt/ *vt* خَفَّفَ من, نَزَعَ الفَتيلَ من ‹*tension, a situation*›

deface /dɪˈfeɪs/ *vt* شَوَّهَ ‹*a wall, portrait, monument, a book*›

de facto /deɪ ˈfaktəʊ/ *adj* <*ruler, government*> فِعْليّ

defamation /ˌdɛfəˈmeɪʃ(ə)n/ *n* افْتِراء, تَجْريح, تَشْهير

defame /dɪˈfeɪm/ *vt* شَهَّرَ (ب), افْتَرى (على) <*a doctor, sb's family*>

default /dɪˈfɔːlt/ **A** *n* **1** (on a loan) عجز عن السّدادِ **2** (Comput) قيمة مَبْدئيّة, وَضْع افْتِراضيّ **3** (**by default**) غِيابيًّا; **to win by ~** فازَ غِيابيًّا

B *vi* **1** «borrowers» قَصَّرَ **2** (Comput) عادَ (للوَضْعِ الافْتِراضيِّ)

default option, **default setting** *n* خِيار افْتِراضيّ

defeat /dɪˈfiːt/ **A** *vt* **1** (to beat) غَلَبَ (i; غَلَبة), هَزَمَ (i; هَزْم) <*the enemy, a rival, the government*> **2** (to reject) رَفَضَ (i-u; رَفْض) <*a bill, proposal*> **3** (to frustrate) أَفْشَلَ, أَحْبَطَ <*an attempt, a takeover*>; **that ~s the whole purpose** لا يُحَقِّقُ ذلك الغَرَضَ المَقْصودَ **4** (to baffle) أَرْبَكَ, حَيَّرَ; **the third question ~ed me** أَرْبَكَني السُّؤالُ الثالِثُ

B *n* **1** (in battles, elections, contests) هزيمة (هَزائِمُ), خَسارة (خَسائِرُ); **to suffer a ~** عانى من هَزيمةٍ; **the finalist's 3–2 ~ by Italy** هَزيمة 3–2 في الدَوْرِ النِهائيِّ أمام إيطاليا; **to admit ~** أَقَرَّ بالهَزيمةِ **2** (of a proposal, bill) رَفْض

defeatist /dɪˈfiːtɪst/ **A** *n* مُنْبَطِح

B *adj* <*attitude, person*> انْهِزاميّ

defect¹ /ˈdiːfɛkt/ *n* **1** (flaw) عَيْب (عُيوب), خَلَل (خِلال), نَقْص **2** (disability) خَلَل (خِلال), عاهة, عَيْب (عُيوب); **a speech ~** خَلَل في النُطْقِ

defect² /dɪˈfɛkt/ *vi* (one's country) هَرَبَ (u; هُروب); (one's religion) ارْتَدَّ (عن); (one's party) انْشَقَّ (عن); (one's cause) خانَ (u; خَوْن, خِيانة), تَخَلّى (عن)

defective /dɪˈfɛktɪv/ *adj* <*product, part*> بِهِ عَيْبٌ, مَعيب, مَعْطوب; <*workmanship*> ناقِص

defector /dɪˈfɛktə/ *n* (from one's country, party) مُنْشَقّ; (one's cause) خائِن (خوّان); (one's religion) مُرْتَدّ

defence (BrE), **defense** (AmE) /dɪˈfɛns/ **A** *n* **1** (of a nation, principle) دِفاع; **to put up a spirited ~** دافَعَ دِفاعاً مُسْتَميتاً; **to fight in the ~ of freedom** حارَبَ دِفاعاً عن الحُرّيّةِ **2** (means of protection) وَسائِل دِفاعٍ \ حِمايةٍ, دِفاعات; **they had no ~ against modern weapons** لم تَكُنْ لَدَيْهِمْ وَسائِلُ للحِمايةِ ضدّ الأَسْلحةِ الحَديثةِ **3** (support) دِفاع, تَبْرير (تَبْريرات); **in my own ~ I must say that ...** دِفاعاً عن نَفْسي يَجِبُ أنْ أَقولَ إنّ ...; **in ~ of the right to strike** دِفاعاً عن حَقِّ الإضْرابِ **4** (in trials) دِفاع; **the case for the ~** الدُفوع; **the ~** الدِفاع **5** (defending players) دِفاع, لاعِبو دِفاعٍ; **to play in (the) ~** لَعِبَ في الدِفاعِ

B (**defences**) *n pl* **1** (in war) دِفاعات, وَسائِل دِفاعٍ; **air ~s** دِفاعات جَوّيّة **2** (of organisms) دِفاعات

defence budget (BrE), **defense budget** (AmE) *n* ميزانيّة دِفاعٍ

defence industry (BrE), **defense industry** (AmE) *n* تَصْنيع حَرْبيّ \ عَسْكَريّ

defence lawyer (BrE), **defense lawyer** (AmE) *n* مُحامي دِفاعٍ

defenceless (BrE), **defenseless** (AmE) /dɪˈfɛnsləs/ *adj* <*animal, child*> مَغْلوب على أَمْرِهِ

defence witness (BrE), **defense witness** (AmE) *n* شاهِد دِفاعٍ

defend /dɪˈfɛnd/ **A** *vt* **1** (against attack) دافَعَ (عن) <*a fort, city*>; **to ~ the rights of a minority** دافَعَ عن حُقوقِ أَقَلِّيّةٍ; **to ~ the right to freedom of worship** دافَعَ عن حَقِّ حُرِّيّةِ العِبادةِ **2** (Law) دافَعَ (عن), تَوَلّى الدِفاعَ عن <*the accused, a client*> **3** (to justify) دافَعَ (عن), بَرَّرَ <*sb's actions, a decision*> **4** «title-holder» دافَعَ (عن) <*a title, record*>

B *vi* «team» دافَعَ

C *v refl* **to ~ oneself** دافَعَ عن نَفْسِهِ

D (**defending**) *adj* **1** (Sport) <*champion*> مُدافِع عن اللَقَبِ \ الكَأْسِ **2** (Law) <*counsel*> دِفاع

defendant /dɪˈfɛnd(ə)nt/ *n* مُدَّعًى عَلَيْهِ

defender /dɪˈfɛndə/ *n* **1** (of policies, rights, etc) مُدافِع, حامٍ (حُماة) **2** (in sport) مُدافِع

defense (AmE) *n* ▸ **defence**

defenseless (AmE) *adj* ▸ **defenceless**

defensive /dɪˈfɛnsɪv/ **A** *adj* <*walls, reaction*> دِفاعيّ; **to be ~ about sth** اتَّخَذَ مَوْقِفاً دِفاعيًّا حول شَيْءٍ

B *n* **to put sb/to be on the ~** وَضَعَ شَخْصاً في مَوْقِفٍ دِفاعيٍّ \ اتَّخَذَ وَضْعاً دِفاعيًّا

defer /dɪˈfəː/ **A** *vt* **(-rr-)** أَجَّلَ <*a decision, payment*> **B** *vi* **(-rr-)** (fml) **to ~ to sb/sb's judgement** انْصاعَ لِرَأْيِ شَخْصٍ

deference /ˈdɛf(ə)rəns/ *n* مُراعاة, احْتِرام

deferential /dɛfəˈrɛnʃ(ə)l/ *adj* <*attitude, tone*> مُراعٍ, مُجامِل

deferment /dɪˈfəːmənt/, **deferral** /dɪˈfəːr(ə)l/ *n* **1** (of a payment) تَأْجيل; (of a decision) تَأْجيل, تَعْليق **2** (AmE) (of military service) تَأْجيل

defiance /dɪˈfʌɪəns/ *n* تَحَدٍّ (تَحَدِّيات); **in ~ of the law/my wishes** تَحَدِّيًا للقانونِ \ لِرَغْبَتي

defiant /dɪˈfʌɪənt/ *adj* <*child, protester, attitude, behaviour*> مُتَحَدٍّ (مُتَحَدِّيون), جَريء (جُرَآءُ, أَجْرِياءُ)

defibrillator /diːˈfɪbrɪleɪtə/ *n* جِهاز الصَّدَماتِ الكَهْرَبائيّة

deficiency /dɪˈfɪʃ(ə)nsi/ *n* (*pl* **deficiencies**) **1** (of funds, vitamins) نَقْص **2** (weakness) عَيْب (عُيوب)

deficient /dɪˈfɪʃ(ə)nt/ *adj* **1** <*nutrient, rainfall*> غَيْر كافٍ, ناقِص; **a diet ~ in protein** نِظام غِذائيّ مُنْخَفِض البْروتين **2** <*service, system*> ناقِص, قاصِر, ضَعيف

deficit /ˈdɛfɪsɪt/ *n* عَجْز

define /dɪˈfʌɪn/ *vt* **1** (to give a definition of) عَرَّفَ <*a word, phrase*> **2** (to specify) حَدَّدَ, تَخَمَ (i; تَخْم) <*a limit, duty*> **3** (to characterize) مَيَّزَ <*an identity, image*>

definite /ˈdɛfɪnɪt/ *adj* (categorical) <*answer, manner*> قاطِع, مُؤَكَّد, حاسِم; (final) <*price, date*> نِهائيّ; (clear) <*advantage, possibility*> أَكيد

definite article *n* أداة تَعْريفٍ

definitely /ˈdɛfɪnɪtli/ *adv* **1** (certainly) قَطْعاً, بالتَّأْكيدِ; **Are you coming? — ~!** هل أَنْتَ آتٍ؟ – قَطْعاً!; **he's ~ wrong** هو مُخْطِئٌ بالتَّأْكيدِ **2** (definitively) <*to answer, commit*> بِشَكْلٍ قَطْعيٍّ

definition /dɛfɪˈnɪʃ(ə)n/ *n* **1** (of a word) تَعْريف **2** (of the nature of sth) تَعْريف

definitive /dɪˈfɪnɪtɪv/ *adj* **1** (conclusive) <*answer, decision*> نِهائيّ **2** (authoritative) <*study, biography*> [أَفْضَل]

deflate /dɪˈfleɪt/ *vt* **1** فَرَّغَ من الهَواءِ <*a balloon, tyre*> **2** ثَبَّطَ, قَوَّضَ <*sb's confidence, hopes*>

deflation /dɪˈfleɪʃ(ə)n/ *n* انْكِماش

deflationary /diːˈfleɪʃ(ə)nri/ *adj* <*policy, measure*> انْكِماشيّ

deflect /dɪˈflɛkt/ *vt* حَرَّفَ <*a shot, missile*>; صَدَّ (u; صَدّ, صُدود) <*criticism*>; تَفادى, تَحاشى <*attention*>

defoliant /diːˈfəʊliənt/ *n* [مادّة كيمْيائيّة لِتَجْريدِ الأَشْجارِ من الوَرَقِ]

deforest /diːˈfɒrɪst/ *vt* أَزالَ الأَشْجارَ \ الغاباتِ في <*an area, a region*>

deforestation /diːfɒrɪˈsteɪʃ(ə)n/ *n* إزالة الأَشْجارِ \ الغاباتِ

deformation /ˌdiːfɔːˈmeɪʃ(ə)n/ *n* تشويه (تَشْويهات)

deformed /dɪˈfɔːmd/ *adj* <*limb, spine*> مُشَوَّه

deformity /dɪˈfɔːmɪti/ *n* (*pl* **deformities**) تَشَوُّه

defragment /ˌdiːfragˈmɛnt/ *vt* أَلْغى التَجْزِئَةَ <*a hard disk*>

defraud /dɪˈfrɔːd/ *vt* غَشَّ (u; غِشّ), نَصَبَ (u; نَصْب) (على) <*a bank, an investor*>

defray /dɪˈfreɪ/ *vt* (fml) سَدَّدَ, غَطّى <*costs, expenses*>

defrost /diːˈfrɒst/ **A** *vt* **1** أَذابَ <*a chicken, prawns*> **2** أَذابَ الثَّلْجَ <*a refrigerator, freezer*> **B** *vi* «refrigerators, frozen food» ذابَ (u; ذَوَبان)

defroster /diːˈfrɒstə/ *n* (AmE) مُزيل صَقيعٍ

deft /dɛft/ *adj* (**defter, deftest**) <*movement, pass*> ماهِر (مَهَرة), بارِع

deftly /ˈdɛftli/ *adv* بِبَراعةٍ

defunct /dɪˈfʌŋkt/ *adj* <*theory*> بالٍ; <*institution*> [تَوَقَّفَ نَشاطُهُ]

defuse /diːˈfjuːz/ *vt* **1** فَكَّكَ <*a device, bomb*> **2** نَزَعَ الفَتيلَ <*a situation, crisis*>

defy /dɪˈfʌɪ/ *vt* (**defies, defying, defied**) **1** (to disobey) تَحَدّى, ازْدَرى <*an order, the odds*> **2** (to challenge) فاقَ الحَدَّ <*belief*>; **his actions ~ explanation** يَصْعُبُ تَفْسيرُ تَصَرُّفاتِهِ

degenerate **A** /dɪˈdʒɛn(ə)rət/ *adj* <*society, life*> مُنْحَطّ, مُنْحَلّ **B** /dɪˈdʒɛnəreɪt/ *vi* «health, morals» تَدَهْوَرَ; «discussions» تَهاوى

degeneration /dɪˌdʒɛnəˈreɪʃ(ə)n/ *n* **1** انْتِكاس, تَنَكُّس **2** (of quality) انْحِدار (انْحِدارات), تَدَهْوُر, انْحِطاط

degenerative /dɪˈdʒɛn(ə)rətɪv/ *adj* <*disease, process*> [يُؤَدّي إلى الانْتِكاسِ]

degradation /ˌdɛɡrəˈdeɪʃ(ə)n/ *n* هَوان

degrade /dɪˈɡreɪd/ *vt* 1 أَذَلَّ, أَهانَ, حَطَّ من القَدْرِ *‹a woman, human being›* 2 أَضَرَّ (ب) *‹a habitat, effectiveness›*

degrading /dɪˈɡreɪdɪŋ/ *adj* *‹conditions, portrayal›* مُهين

degree /dɪˈɡriː/ *n* 1 (in angles, navigation) دَرَجة; **at an angle of 40 ~s** على زاوِيةٍ مِقْدارُها 40 دَرَجةً; **turn the lever 180 ~s** لُفَّ الذِراعَ 180 دَرَجةً; **at 20 ~s south of the equator** عند دائرة عَرْضٍ 20 دَرَجةً جَنوبَ خَطِّ الاسْتِواءِ 2 (in temperatures) دَرَجة; **20 ~s Celsius** *or* **centigrade** 20 دَرَجةً مِئَوِيّةً; **it was 40 ~s in the shade** كانَتْ دَرَجةُ الحَرارة 40 دَرَجةً في \ تحت الظِلِّ; **he had a temperature of 104 ~s** كانَتْ دَرَجةُ حَرارَتِهِ 104 دَرَجاتٍ (فَهْرنْهايْتِيّة) 3 (qualification) شَهادة, دَرَجة (عِلْمِيّة); **a first** *or* **bachelor's ~** (شَهادة) بَكالورِيوس; **to get a ~ in Chemistry** حَصَلَ على بَكالورِيوس في الكيمِياءِ; **to study for a higher ~** دَرَس دِراساتٍ عُلْيا 4 (level) دَرَجة, مُسْتَوًى (مُسْتَوَيات); **an alarming ~ of ignorance** دَرَجة مُقْلِقة من الجَهْلِ; **a high ~ of readiness** دَرَجة عالِية من الاسْتِعْدادِ; **with varying ~s of success** بِدَرَجاتٍ مُخْتَلِفةٍ من النَجاحِ; **to some ~** إلى حَدٍّ ما; **to a greater/lesser ~** بِدَرَجةٍ أَكْبَرَ \ أَقَلَّ 5 (in classifications) **third ~ burns** حُروق من الدَرَجةِ الثالِثةِ; **a charge of first ~ murder** (AmE) اتِّهام بِجَرِيمةِ قَتْلٍ من الدَرَجةِ الأُولى

dehydrated /diːˈhʌɪdreɪtɪd/ *adj* 1 (dried, powdered) *‹soup, vegetables›* مُجَفَّف 2 (lacking fluids) *‹infant, patient›* يُعاني من [الجَفافِ]; **to become ~** أَصْبَحَ يُعاني من الجَفافِ

dehydration /diːhʌɪˈdreɪʃ(ə)n/ *n* جَفاف (فَقْد الجِسْمِ لِكَمِّيّةٍ كَبيرةٍ من الماءِ)

de-icer /diːˈʌɪsə/ *n* مُزيل \ مُذيب الجَليدِ

deign /deɪn/ *vt* (fml) **to ~ to do sth** تَفَضَّلَ \ تكرَّمَ بِفعْلِ شَيْءٍ

deity /ˈdeɪɪti/ *n* (*pl* **deities**) إلَه (آلِهة)

dejected /dɪˈdʒɛktɪd/ *adj* *‹look, expression›* كَئيب

de jure /deɪ ˈjʊəreɪ/ *adj* *‹ruler, government›* قانونيّ, شَرْعيّ

Delaware /ˈdɛləwɛː/ *pr n* ديلاوير (وِلاية أَمْريكيّة)

Delawarean /ˈdɛləwɛːrɪən/ *pr n, adj* [(شَخْص) من ديلاوير]

delay /dɪˈleɪ/ **A** *vt* 1 (to put back) أَجَّلَ *‹a decision, publication›*; **to ~ doing sth** أَجَّلَ فِعْلَ شَيْءٍ 2 (to cause to be late) أَخَّرَ *‹a train, sb's arrival, sb's departure›*; **the flights were ~ed by 12 hours** تَأَخَّرَت الرِحْلاتُ الجَوِّيّةُ 12 ساعةً; **the strike ~ed publication by a week** أَدّى الإضْرابُ إلى تَأَخُّرِ النَشْرِ لِمُدّةِ أُسْبوعٍ **B** (**delaying**) *adj* *‹action, tactics›* مُعَطِّل, مُؤَخِّر; **the strikers' ~ing tactics were successful/unsuccessful** كانَتْ تَكْتيكاتُ التَأْخيرِ الّتي اتَّبَعَها المُضْرِبونَ ناجِحةً \ فاشِلةً **C** *n* 1 (to flights, trains) تَأْخير, تَأَخُّر; **~s are expected on all major roads leaving the city** التَأْخيراتُ مُتَوَقَّعةٌ على جَميعِ الطُرُقِ الرَئيسيّةِ المُؤَدِّيةِ إلى خارِجِ المَدينةِ 2 (time lapse) تَأْخير, تَأَخُّر; **there will be a few minutes' ~** سَوْفَ يَكونُ هُناكَ تَأَخُّرٌ لِبِضْعِ دَقائِقَ 3 (slowness) **without ~** دون إبْطاءٍ; **I hope we can start without ~** أَتَمَنّى أنْ نَسْتَطيعَ البَدْءَ دون تَأْخيرٍ

delayed /dɪˈleɪd/ *adj* *‹reaction, action›* مُؤَجَّل, مُؤَخَّر

delayed-action /dəˌleɪdˈakʃ(ə)n/ *adj* *‹bomb›* مُوْقوت; *‹shutter release›* [ذو خاصّيّةِ المُوقِّتِ الذاتيّ \ التنازُليّ]

delectable /dɪˈlɛktəb(ə)l/ *adj* *‹dish, food›* لَذيذ; **a ~ mixture of wine, fruit, and cream** خليط لَذيذ من الخَمْرِ والفاكِهةِ والقِشْدةِ

delegate **A** /ˈdɛlɪɡət/ *n* 1 مُمَثِّل, مُفَوَّض, مَنْدوب 2 (in US politics) نائب (نُوّاب) **B** /ˈdɛlɪɡeɪt/ *vt* فَوَّضَ *‹responsibility, a task›*

delegation /dɛlɪˈɡeɪʃ(ə)n/ *n* 1 [u] (action of delegating) تَفْويض 2 (deputation) وَفْد (وُفود), بَعْثة (بَعَثات)

delete /dɪˈliːt/ *vt* 1 (to cross out) حَذَفَ (i; حَذْف), شَطَبَ (u; شَطْب) *‹a word, character›* 2 (on a computer) حَذَفَ (i; حَذْف) *‹a file, an email›*

deleterious /ˌdɛlɪˈtɪərɪəs/ *adj* (fml) *‹effect, consequences›* ضارّ, مُؤْذٍ

deletion /dɪˈliːʃ(ə)n/ *n* (the act) شَطْب, حَذْف; (the thing deleted) **~s** مَحْذوفات

deliberate **A** /dɪˈlɪb(ə)rət/ *adj* 1 (intentional) *‹provocation, mistake›* عَمْديّ, مُتَعَمَّد 2 (measured) *‹decision, approach›* مَدْروس **B** /dɪˈlɪbəreɪt/ *vi* (fml) «jurors, delegates» تَشاوَرَ, تَداوَلَ **C** /dɪˈlɪbəreɪt/ *vt* (fml) تَدارَسَ *‹a bill, an amendment›*

deliberately /dɪˈlɪb(ə)rətli/ *adv* **1** (intentionally) ‹*to do sth, say sth*› عَمْداً, بِتَعَمُّدٍ **2** (unhurriedly) ‹*to advance, walk*› بِتَرَوٍّ, بِتَأَنٍّ

deliberation /dɪˌlɪbəˈreɪʃ(ə)n/ *n* **1** (reflection) تَفْكير مُتَأَنٍّ **2** (**deliberations** *n pl*) (discussion) مُشاوَرة, مُداوَلة

delicacy /ˈdɛlɪkəsi/ *n* (*pl* **delicacies**) **1** [u] (of porcelain, carving) رِقّة; (of the situation) هَشاشة; (tact) كِياسة **2** (item of food) من أَطايِبِ الطَعامِ; **a local ~** من أَطايِبِ الطَعامِ المَحَلّيِّ

delicate /ˈdɛlɪkət/ *adj* **1** (fine, intricate) ‹*lace, features*› رَقيق **2** (fragile, needing care) ‹*china*› هَشّ, رَقيق; ‹*health*› ناعِم **3** (needing skill, tact) ‹*situation, subject*› دَقيق **4** (subtle) ‹*shade*› ناعِم; ‹*taste*› رَفيع سَقيم

delicately /ˈdɛlɪkətli/ *adv* **1** (intricately) ‹*carved, painted*› بِشَكْلٍ دَقيقٍ, بِدِقّةٍ **2** (subtly) ‹*scented, flavoured*› بِشَكْلٍ مُتَمَيِّزٍ **3** (sensitively) ‹*to handle*› بِرِفْقٍ; ‹*to phrase*› بِعِنايةٍ

delicatessen /ˌdɛlɪkəˈtɛs(ə)n/ *n* [مَحَلّ يَبيعُ أَطْعِمةً فاخِرةً]

delicious /dɪˈlɪʃəs/ *adj* ‹*meal, flavour*› لَذيذ, شَهِيّ

delight /dɪˈlʌɪt/ **A** *vt* أَسَرَّ, أَبْهَجَ ‹*audiences, fans*›
B *vi* **to ~ in (doing) sth** اِسْتَمْتَعَ ب (فِعْلِ) شَيْءٍ
C *n* **1** (joy) سُرور شَديد, بَهْجة; **to take ~ in doing sth** اِسْتَمْتَعَ بِفِعْلِ شَيْءٍ **2** (source of joy) مَبْهَجة (dipt; مَباهِجُ)

delighted /dɪˈlʌɪtɪd/ *adj* ‹*smile*› بَهْجِة; ‹*parents, customers*› مُبْتَهِج, مَسْرور جِدًّا; **Tom was ~ to see them** كانَ توم مُبْتَهِجاً لِرُؤْيَتِهِمْ; **we're ~ with the results** نَحْنُ مَسْرورونَ جِدًّا بالنَتائِجِ

delightful /dɪˈlʌɪtfʊl/ *adj* ‹*surprise*› سارّ; ‹*person, place*› ساحِر; ‹*evening*› بَهيج

delineate /dɪˈlɪnieɪt/ *vt* (fml) **1** (to describe) وَصَفَ \ صَوَّرَ بِدِقّةٍ ‹*sb's role, a character*› **2** (to indicate) حَدَّدَ ‹*a boundary, an area*›

delinquency /dɪˈlɪŋkwənsi/ *n* \ جُنْحة (يَرْتَكِبُها القاصِرونَ الأَحْداثُ)

delinquent /dɪˈlɪŋkwənt/ **A** *adj* ‹*behaviour, act*› جانِح
B *n* جانِح

delirious /dɪˈlɪrɪəs/ *adj* **1** (semi-conscious) ‹*condition*› هَذَيانِ; ‹*patient*› مُصاب بِهَذَيانٍ **2** (very happy) ‹*excitement, fan*› هيسْتيرِيّ

delirium /dɪˈlɪrɪəm/ *n* (confusion) هَذَيان; (excitement, joy) هيسْتيرِيا

delirium tremens *n* هَذَيان ارْتِعاشِيّ

deliver /dɪˈlɪvə/ **A** *vt* **1** (to an address) وَصَّلَ ‹*the goods, milk, mail*› **2** «midwife» ساعَدَ في عَمَلِيّةِ الوِلادةِ ‹*a baby*› **3** (fml) (to give) أَلْقى ‹*a speech, lecture*› **4** (fml) (to hand down) نَطَقَ (u; ب) نُطْق ‹*a verdict*›
B *vi* «tradesmen, couriers» قَدَّمَ خِدْمةَ التَوْصيلِ
(Idiom) **to deliver the goods** (infml) أَوْفى بِالْتِزاماتِهِ

delivery /dɪˈlɪv(ə)ri/ *n* (*pl* **deliveries**) **1** (of goods, milk, mail) تَوْصيل, تَسْليم; **there is no ~ on Sundays** لا توجَدُ خَدَماتُ تَوْصيلٍ أَيّامَ الأَحَدِ **2** (item delivered) طَرْد (طُرود) **3** (of a baby) إِنْجاب, وِلادة **4** (way of speaking) إِلْقاء

delivery man *n* مُوَصِّل طَلَبات, رَجُل تَوْصيل

delivery service *n* خِدْمة تَوْصيلٍ

delivery truck, **delivery van** (BrE) *n* شاحِنة نَقْل

delta /ˈdɛltə/ *n* **1** (Greek letter) [الحَرْف الرابع من الأَبْجَدِيّة اليونانِيّةِ] **2** (of a river) دِلْتا; **the Nile D~** دِلْتا النيل

delude /dɪˈljuːd/ *vt* خَدَعَ, ضَلَّلَ (a; خَدْع, خُدْعة, خَديعة) ‹*the public, followers*›

deluge /ˈdɛljuːdʒ/ *n* **1** (downpour) مَطَر غَزير **2** (flood) طوفان **3** (of calls, complaints) كَمّ كَبير

delusion /dɪˈljuːʒ(ə)n/ *n* **1** (mistaken idea) وَهْم (أَوْهام) **2** (vain hope) وَهْم (أَوْهام)

deluxe /dɪˈlʌks/ *adj* ‹*edition, room*› فاخِر

delve /dɛlv/ *vi* **to ~ into a subject** تَقَصّى في مَوْضوعٍ; **to ~ into the past** نَبَشَ \ نَقَّبَ في الماضي

demagogue /ˈdɛməgɒg/ *n* ديماغوجِيّ

demand /dɪˈmɑːnd/ **A** *n* **1** (insistent request) طَلَب (طَلَبات), مَطْلَب (مَطالِبُ); **payable on ~** مُسْتَحَقّ الدَفْعِ عند الطَلَبِ **2** [u] (in business) طَلَب; **to be in ~** كانَ مَطْلوباً **3** (**demands** *n pl*) (pressure) مُتَطَلَّبات; **the ~s of the job have made him ill** أَمْرَضَتْهُ أَعْباءُ العَمَلِ
B *vt* **1** (to request) طالَبَ (ب) ‹*a ransom, an inquiry*› **2** (to require) اِقْتَضى, تَطَلَّبَ ‹*skill, patience*›

demanding /dɪˈmɑːndɪŋ/ *adj* **1** ‹*job, task*› مُرْهِق **2** ‹*person*› صَعْب الإِرْضاءِ

demarcation /diːmɑːˈkeɪʃ(ə)n/ *n* حَدّ \ خَطّ فاصِل

demarcation line *n* خَطّ حُدودٍ

demean /dɪˈmiːn/ *vt* قَلَّل من الشَأْنِ, حَطَّ من القَدْرِ <*sb's work, status*>; **to ~ oneself** حَطَّ من قَدْرِ نَفْسِهِ

demeaning /dɪˈmiːnɪŋ/ *adj* <*stereotype, comment*> مُذِلّ, مُهين

demeanour (BrE), **demeanor** (AmE) /dɪˈmiːnə/ *n* سُلوك, تَصَرُّف

demented /dɪˈmɛntɪd/ *adj* 1▸ (with worry, anger) <*child*> مُخَبَّل; **~ with worry, she roamed the town looking for her lost child** أَفْقَدها القَلَقُ صَوابَها، فجابَت المَدينة بَحْثاً عن ابْنِها المَفْقودِ 2▸ (suffering from dementia) <*patient, relative*> خَرِف

dementia /dɪˈmɛnʃə/ *n* خرف

demerara sugar, **demerara** /dɛməˌrɛːrə ˈʃʊgə/ *n* سُكَّر أَسْمَر \ بُنِّيّ

demerit /diːˈmɛrɪt/ *n* 1▸ (disadvantage) عَيْب (عُيوب), مَساءة 2▸ (AmE) (for wrongdoing) عَلامة سَيِّئة (تُمْنَحُ بِسَبَبِ إساءةِ التَصَرُّفِ \ مُخالَفةِ القَوانينِ) (مَساوِئُ)

demilitarize, **-ise** (BrE) /diːˈmɪlɪtərʌɪz/ *vt* جَرَّدَ من الصِفةِ العَسْكَرِيّةِ \ السِلاحِ <*an area, country*>; **a ~d zone** مِنْطَقة مُجَرَّدة من \ مَنْزوعة السِلاحِ

demise /dɪˈmʌɪz/ (fml) *n* 1▸ (of a system, an institution) فَشَل, زَوال 2▸ (death) وَفاة (وَفَيات)

demist /diːˈmɪst/ *vt* (BrE) أَزالَ الصَقيعَ من <*a rear window, windscreen*>

demister /diːˈmɪstə/ *n* (BrE) مُزيل صَقيعٍ

demo /ˈdɛməʊ/ *n* (infml) 1▸ (protest) مُظاهَرة 2▸ (of music, software) عَرْض تَقْديميّ

demobilize, **-ise** (BrE) /diːˈməʊbɪlʌɪz/ *vt* سَرَّحَ <*a serviceman, the reserves*>

democracy /dɪˈmɒkrəsi/ *n* (*pl* **democracies**) ديموقْراطِيّة

democrat /ˈdɛməkrat/ *n* 1▸ (supporter of democracy) ديموقْراطيّ 2▸ (**Democrat**) (in US politics) عُضْو ديموقْراطيّ في الحِزْبِ الديموقْراطيِّ الأَمْريكيِّ

democratic /dɛməˈkratɪk/ *adj* <*election, system*> ديموقْراطيّ; **a ~ country/government** بَلَد ديموقْراطيّ \ حُكومة ديموقْراطِيّة

Democratic Party *n* (in US politics) الحِزْب الديموقْراطيّ (الأَمْريكيّ)

demographic /ˌdɛməˈgrafɪk/ *adj* <*change, study*> ديموغْرافيّ

demography /dɪˈmɒgrəfi/ *n* عِلْم السُكّانِ, ديموغْرافِيا

demolish /dɪˈmɒlɪʃ/ *vt* 1▸ هَدَّمَ, دَمَّرَ <*a building, house*> 2▸ دَحَضَ (a; دُحوض, دَحْض) <*an argument, a myth*>

demolition /dɛməˈlɪʃ(ə)n/ *n* هَدْم, تَدْمير

demon /ˈdiːmən/ *n* شَيْطان (شَياطينُ)

demonstrate /ˈdɛmənstreɪt/ **A** *vt* 1▸ بَرْهَنَ (i; بَرْهَنة) <*a theory, fact*> 2▸ أَظْهَرَ <*an ability, a skill*> 3▸ شَرَحَ (a; شَرْح), عَرَضَ (i; عَرْض) <*a machine, product*>
B *vi* «workers, students» تَظاهَرَ

demonstration /dɛmənˈstreɪʃ(ə)n/ *n* 1▸ (march) مُظاهَرة, مَسيرة 2▸ (of feelings, quality) إِظْهار 3▸ (of a theory) بَرْهَنة, إِثْبات (إِثْباتات) 4▸ (of a machine) عَرْض (عُروض)

demonstrative /dɪˈmɒnstrətɪv/ *adj* <*person, gesture*> مُعَبِّر

demonstrator /ˈdɛmənstreɪtə/ *n* 1▸ (in protest) مُتَظاهِر 2▸ (of equipment, a skill) عارِض

demoralize, **-ise** (BrE) /dɪˈmɒrəlʌɪz/ *vt* ثَبَّطَ العَزيمةَ \ الهِمّةَ, أَضْعَفَ الروحَ المَعْنَوِيّةَ <*troops, staff*>

demoralizing, **-ising** (BrE) /dɪˈmɒrəlʌɪzɪŋ/ *adj* <*effect, defeat*> يُضْعِفُ الروحَ المَعْنَوِيّةَ, مُثَبِّط

demote /diːˈməʊt/ *vt* أَنْزَلَ الرُتْبةَ \ الدَرَجةَ <*an employee, a sergeant*>

demotion /diːˈməʊʃ(ə)n/ *n* (of a person) تَجْريد \ إِنْزال من رُتْبةٍ; (of a football team) إِنْزال إلى قِسْمٍ أَدْنى

demur /dɪˈməː/ **A** *vi* (-rr-) (fml) اِعْتَرَضَ, اِحْتَجَّ
B *n* (fml) اِعْتِراض (اِعْتِراضات), اِحْتِجاج (اِحْتِجاجات); **to do sth without ~** قامَ بِشَيْءٍ دون اعْتِراضٍ

demure /dɪˈmjʊə/ *adj* <*smile, young lady*> مُحْتَشِم

demurrage /dɪˈmʌrɪdʒ/ *n* (delay) [تَأَخُّر \ تَقاعُس عن الشَحْنِ أو التَفْريغ]; (financial compensation) [غَرامة تَأْخيرٍ \ تَقاعُسٍ عن الشَحْنِ أو التَفْريغ]

den /dɛn/ *n* 1▸ (of a lion) عَرين (عُرُن); (of a fox) جُحْر (جُحور) 2▸ (haunt) وَكْر (وُكور, أَوْكار) 3▸ (room) خَلْوة

denationalize, **-ise** (BrE) /diːˈnaʃ(ə)nəlʌɪz/ *vt* أَلْغَى التَأْمِيمَ, خَصْخَصَ (i; خَصْخَصة) *‹a public utility, an industry›*; **the government has plans to ~ the railways** تُخَطِّطُ الحُكُومةُ لِخَصْخَصةِ السِكَكِ الحَدِيدِيّةِ

denial /dɪˈnʌɪəl/ *n* ① (of an accusation, a rumour) إِنْكار ② (of a request, claim) رَفْض; (of sb's rights, freedom) إِنْكار

denier /ˈdɛnɪə/ *n* [وَحْدة وَزْنٍ لِتَعْيِينِ نَفاسةِ الحَرِيرِ أو النَيْلون]

denigrate /ˈdɛnɪɡreɪt/ *vt* (من) اِنْتَقَصَ *‹sb's efforts, achievements›*; حَطَّ \ اِنْتَقَصَ من القَدْرِ *‹a person›*

denim /ˈdɛnɪm/ **A** *n* دِنِيم (قُماش قُطْنِيّ مَتِين) **B** *adj ‹jacket, jeans›* مَصْنُوع من الدِنِيم

Denmark /ˈdɛnmɑːk/ *pr n* الدانْمارْك (f)

denomination /dɪˌnɒmɪˈneɪʃ(ə)n/ *n* ① (Rel_Chr) طائِفة (طَوائِفُ) ② (Fin) قِيمة اسْمِيّة

denominator /dɪˈnɒmɪneɪtə/ *n* مَقام (مَقامات); **the lowest common ~** المَقام المُشْتَرَك الأَصْغَر

denote /dɪˈnəʊt/ *vt* دَلَّ (u; دَلالة على), أَشارَ (إلى) *‹a location, meaning›*

denouement /deɪˈnuːmɒ̃/ *n* حَلّ العُقْدةِ (في مَسْرَحِيّةٍ \ فِيلْمٍ \ قِصّةٍ)

denounce /dɪˈnaʊns/ *vt* ① (to inform against) بَلَّغَ (عن) *‹a wrongdoer›*; **to ~ sb to sb** بَلَّغَ عن شَخْصٍ لِشَخْصٍ ② (to condemn) أَدانَ *‹a government›*; شَجَبَ (u; شَجْب), اِسْتَنْكَرَ *‹an attack›*

dense /dɛns/ *adj* (**denser**, **densest**) ① (closely spaced) *‹forest, vegetation›* كَثِيف; **the population is most ~ on the coast** تَبْلُغُ الكَثافةُ السُكّانِيّةُ أَعْلاها في الساحِلِ ② (thick) *‹fog, cloud›* كَثِيف ③ (stupid) غَبِيّ (أَغْبِياءُ), أَبْلَه (dipt) ④ (Phys) *‹substance, rock›* كَثِيف

densely /ˈdɛnsli/ *adv ‹populated, forested, packed›* بِكَثافةٍ, بِشَكْلٍ كَثِيفٍ

density /ˈdɛnsɪti/ *n* (*pl* **densities**) ① (of population, traffic, fog) كَثافة ② (of solids, gases) كَثافة

dent /dɛnt/ **A** *n* (in metal) بَعْج; (in wood) نُقْرة (نُقَر) **B** *vt* ① بَعَجَ (a; بَعْج) *‹a car, surface›* ② زَعْزَعَ (i; زَعْزَعة), قَلَّلَ *‹sb's confidence, pride›*; أَثَّرَ سَلْباً على *‹sb's reputation›*

dental /ˈdɛnt(ə)l/ *adj* ① *‹hygiene, decay›* الأَسْنانِ ② *‹school, student›* طِبِّ الأَسْنانِ

dental floss *n* خَيْط الأَسْنانِ

dental hygienist *n* اخْتِصاصِيّ صِحّةِ الأَسْنانِ

dental nurse *n* مُمَرِّض طَبِيبِ الأَسْنانِ

dental surgeon *n* جَرّاح الأَسْنانِ

dental surgery *n* (BrE) ① (place) عِيادة طَبِيبِ الأَسْنانِ ② (activity) جِراحة الأَسْنانِ

dentist /ˈdɛntɪst/ *n* طَبِيب الأَسْنانِ

dentistry /ˈdɛntɪstri/ *n* طِبّ الأَسْنانِ

dentist's office *n* (AmE) عِيادة طَبِيبِ الأَسْنانِ

dentures /ˈdɛntʃəz/ *n pl* طَقْم أَسْنانٍ

deny /dɪˈnʌɪ/ *vt* (**denies**, **denying**, **denied**) ① أَنْكَرَ *‹a charge, an allegation, a rumour›*; **she denied having seen him** أَنْكَرَتْ أَنَّها رَأَتْهُ ② رَفَضَ (i-u; رَفْض) *‹a request›*; أَنْكَرَ *‹right›*; **to ~ sb sth** رَفَضَ أَنْ يَمْنَحَ شَخْصاً شَيْئاً

deodorant /diˈəʊd(ə)rənt/ *n* مُزِيل رائِحةِ العَرَقِ \ الرَوائِحِ الكَرِيهةِ

depart /dɪˈpɑːt/ *vi* ① (to leave) «guests, flight» غادَرَ ② (to deviate) **to ~ from the truth/script** حادَ عن الحَقِيقةِ \ النَصِّ

department /dɪˈpɑːtmənt/ *n* ① (of a company, university) قِسْم (أَقْسام) ② (of a store) قِسْم (أَقْسام) ③ (of government) مَصْلَحة (مَصالِحُ), إِدارة

departmental /diːpɑːtˈment(ə)l/ *adj ‹budget, head›* قِسْمٍ, مَصْلَحةٍ

department store *n* [مَتْجَر كَبِير مُتَعَدِّد الأَقْسامِ]

departure /dɪˈpɑːtʃə/ *n* ① (of a person, train) مُغادَرة, اِنْطِلاق ② (from the rules, a tradition) اِنْحِراف (اِنْحِرافات)

departure gate *n* بَوّابة مُغادَرةٍ

departure lounge *n* صالة مُغادَرةٍ

departures board *n* لَوْحة الرِحْلاتِ المُغادِرةِ

departure time *n* وَقْت مُغادَرةٍ

depend /dɪˈpɛnd/ *vi* **that ~s** *or* **it all ~s** يَتَوَقَّفُ ذلك على أُمُورٍ أُخرى

Phrasal verb **depend on**: **~ on [sb/sth]** (to be determined by) «success, survival» تَوَقَّفَ \ اِعْتَمَدَ على [شَخْصٍ \ شَيْءٍ]; (to rely on) «families, colleagues» اِتَّكَلَ \ اِعْتَمَدَ على [شَخْصٍ \ شَيْءٍ]

dependable /dɪˈpɛndəb(ə)l/ *adj* ‹*source, worker*› مَوْثوق بِهِ

dependant /dɪˈpɛnd(ə)nt/ *n* (BrE) ▸ **dependent**

dependence /dɪˈpɛnd(ə)ns/ *n* تَبَعِيّة, اعْتِماد, اتِّكال; **our ~ on oil** اعْتِمادُنا على النَفْطِ; **emotional ~** تَبَعِيّة عاطِفِيّة

dependency /dɪˈpɛnd(ə)nsi/ *n* (*pl* **dependencies**) 1 [u] (reliance) إدْمان; **alcohol/drug ~** إدْمان الكُحولِ \ المُخَدِّراتِ 2 (territory) تَبَعِيّة; **Christmas Island is an Australian ~** جَزيرةُ كْريسْماس تابِعةٌ لِأُسْتُراليا

dependent /dɪˈpɛnd(ə)nt/ A *adj* (reliant) ‹*relative, child*› مُعْتَمِد; **to be ~ on one's parents** كانَ عالةً على والِدَيْهِ; **to be ~ on welfare/drugs** اعْتَمَدَ على الخَدَماتِ الاجْتِماعِيّةِ \ الأَدْوِيةِ

B *n* مُعال

depict /dɪˈpɪkt/ *vt* 1 (visually) صَوَّرَ, رَسَمَ (u; رَسْم) ‹*a scene, figure*› 2 (in writing) صَوَّرَ, وَصَفَ (i; وَصْف) ‹*characters, events*›

depiction /dɪˈpɪkʃ(ə)n/ *n* 1 (picture) رَسْم (رُسوم, رُسومات), تَصْوير (تَصاوير) 2 (description) وَصْف

depilatory /dɪˈpɪlət(ə)ri/ A *adj* ‹*cream, product*› مُزيل لِلشَعْرِ

B *n* (*pl* **depilatories**) مُسْتَحْضَر لِإزالةِ الشَعْرِ

deplete /dɪˈpliːt/ *vt* اسْتَنْفَدَ, اسْتَنْزَفَ ‹*resources, reserves*›

depletion /dɪˈpliːʃ(ə)n/ *n* نُضوب

deplorable /dɪˈplɔːrəb(ə)l/ *adj* ‹*condition, behaviour*› يُرْثى لَهُ, يَبْعَثُ على الأَسى

deplore /dɪˈplɔː/ *vt* «critics» اسْتَنْكَرَ, اسْتَهْجَنَ ‹*violence, actions*›

deploy /dɪˈplɔɪ/ *vt* 1 نَشَرَ (u; نَشْر) ‹*weaponry, men*› 2 وَضَعَ مَوْضِعَ التَنْفيذِ ‹*technology, resources*›

deployment /dɪˈplɔɪmənt/ *n* نَشْر (القوّاتِ \ المُعَدّاتِ العَسْكَرِيّةِ); **the ~ of an additional 26,000 troops to the area** نَشْر 26,000 جُنْدِيًّا إضافِيًّا في المِنْطَقةِ

depopulation /diːpɒpjʊˈleɪʃ(ə)n/ *n* تَناقُص عَدَدِ السُكّانِ

deport /dɪˈpɔːt/ *vt* رَحَّلَ ‹*an immigrant, alien*›

deportation /diːpɔːˈteɪʃ(ə)n/ *n* تَرْحيل (تَراحيل), إبْعاد

deportment /dɪˈpɔːtmənt/ *n* 1 (BrE) (way of standing and walking) [الوَقْفة والمِشْية] 2 (behaviour) سُلوك, تَصَرُّف (تَصَرُّفات)

depose /dɪˈpəʊz/ *vt* أَطاحَ (ب), خَلَعَ (a; خَلْع) ‹*a leader, king, dictator*›

deposit /dɪˈpɒzɪt/ A *n* 1 (to a bank account) وَديعة (وَدائِعُ); **on ~** كَوَديعةٍ 2 (on a house) عُرْبون (عَرابينُ), مُقَدَّم; (on a holiday, goods) دُفْعة أولى 3 (against damage, breakages) إيداع ضَمانٍ 4 (of silt, mud, fat) راسِب (رَواسِبُ); (of coal, a mineral) قَرارة

B *vt* 1 وَضَعَ (a; وَضْع) ‹*rubbish, luggage*›; **to ~ sth with sb** وَضَعَ \ تَرَكَ شَيْئاً عند شَخْصٍ 2 أَوْدَعَ ‹*money, valuables, a cheque*›

deposit account *n* (BrE) حِساب إيداعٍ \ وَديعةٍ

deposition /ˌdɛpəˈzɪʃ(ə)n/ *n* (fml) إفادة

depositor /dɪˈpɒzɪtə/ *n* مودِع

depot /ˈdɛpəʊ/ *n* 1 (for storage) مَخْزَن (مَخازِنُ), مُسْتَوْدَع (مُسْتَوْدَعات) 2 (BrE) (for vehicle storage) مُسْتَوْدَع (مَرْكَباتٍ) 3 (AmE) (bus/railway station) مَحَطّة (حافِلاتٍ \ قِطاراتٍ)

depraved /dɪˈpreɪvd/ *adj* ‹*act, mind*› لَئيم, سافِل

depravity /dɪˈpravɪti/ *n* انْحِلال \ فَساد أَخْلاقِيّ

deprecating /ˈdɛprɪkeɪtɪŋ/ *adj* ‹*remark, manner*› مُسْتَنْكِر

depreciate /dɪˈpriːʃɪeɪt/ *vi* «currency, assets» انْخَفَضَتْ قيمَتُهُ

depreciation /dɪˌpriːʃɪˈeɪʃ(ə)n/ *n* 1 (of a currency) انْخِفاض القيمةِ 2 (of an asset) اهْتِلاك, إهْلاك

depress /dɪˈprɛs/ *vt* 1 (to sadden) أَحْزَنَ 2 خَفَضَ (i; خَفْض) ‹*prices*›; أَصابَ بالكَسادِ ‹*markets*› 3 ضَغَطَ (a; ضَغْط على) ‹*a button, key*› 4 ضَغَطَ (a; ضَغْط على) ‹*the clutch*›

depressed /dɪˈprɛst/ *adj* 1 (unhappy) ‹*teenager*› حَزين, مُكْتَئِب; **I'm ~ about my job** أنا مُكْتَئِبٌ بِسَبَبِ وَظيفَتي 2 (Psych) ‹*patient*› مُكْتَئِب 3 ‹*region, industry*› يُعاني من الكَسادِ \ البِطالةِ

depressing /dɪˈprɛsɪŋ/ *adj* ‹*news, thought*› مُحْزِن, كَئيب

depression /dɪˈprɛʃ(ə)n/ *n* 1 (mental condition) اكْتِئاب, كَآبة (اكْتِئابات) 2 (economic) كَساد

depressive /dɪˈprɛsɪv/ A *adj* 1 ‹*state, illness*› اكْتِئابٍ 2 ‹*effect, policy*› ذو تَأْثيرٍ سَلْبِيٍّ

B *n* [شَخْص يُعاني من اكْتِئابٍ]

deprivation /dɛprɪˈveɪʃ(ə)n/ *n* 1 (hardship) حِرْمان 2 (lack) حِرْمان

deprive /dɪˈprʌɪv/ *vt* **to ~ sb of sth** حَرَمَ شَخْصاً من شَيْءٍ

deprived /dɪˈprʌɪvd/ *adj* ‹*area, community, child*› مَحْروم

Dept *abbr* = **Department** قِسْم (أَقْسام)

depth /dɛpθ/ **A** *n* 1 (of a hole, lake, mine) عُمْق (أَعْماق); **the well has a ~ of 120 metres** يَبْلُغُ عُمْقُ البِئْرِ 120 مِتْراً; **to be out of one's ~** (in water) [لَم تُلامِسْ قَدَماهُ قَعْرَ المِياهِ لِعُمْقِها]; (in a situation) كانَ أمامَ مَوْقِفٍ يَتَجاوَزُ قُدُراتِهِ 2 (of a shelf, cupboard) عُمْق (أَعْماق) 3 (of knowledge) عُمْق; **to examine sth in ~** تَعَمَّقَ في فَحْصِ شَيْءٍ 4 (of feeling) عُمْق

B (**depths**) *n pl* **the ~s** (of the ocean) أَعْماق; **in the ~s of winter** في ذُرْوَةِ الشِتاءِ; **to be in the ~s of despair** كانَ في قِمَّةِ اليَأْسِ

deputation /dɛpjʊˈteɪʃ(ə)n/ *n* وَفْد (وُفود)

deputize, **-ise** (BrE) /ˈdɛpjʊtʌɪz/ *vi* **to ~ for sb** «players, employees» نابَ عن شَخْصٍ

deputy /ˈdɛpjʊti/ *n* (*pl* **deputies**) 1 (replacement) نائِب (نُوّاب) 2 (politician) نائِب (نُوّاب)

deputy chairman *n* نائِب رَئيسِ مَجْلِسٍ

deputy president *n* نائِب رَئيسٍ

derail /dɪˈreɪl/ *vt* 1 أَخْرَجَ عن خَطِّ سَيْرِهِ ‹*a train*› 2 عَرْقَلَ (i; عَرْقَلة) ‹*a process, plan*›

deranged /dɪˈreɪndʒd/ *adj* ‹*killer, mind*› مُخْتَلّ

derby /ˈdɑːbi/ *n* (*pl* **derbies**) 1 (BrE) (sports competition) دِرْبي (مَحَلّيّ); **the Derby** (horse race) [دِرْبي \ سِباق إبْسوم للخُيولِ] 2 (AmE) (hat) [قُبَّعة سَوْداء كُرَوِيّة]

deregulate /diːˈrɛgjʊleɪt/ *vt* رَفَعَ القُيودَ الحُكومِيّةَ عن ‹*prices, air travel*›

deregulation /diːrɛgjəˈleɪʃ(ə)n/ *n* تَحْرير الاقْتِصادِ \ التِجارةِ

derelict /ˈdɛrəlɪkt/ *adj* ‹*building, site*› مُهْمَل, مَهْجور

deride /dɪˈrʌɪd/ *vt* سَخِرَ (a; سُخْرِيّة ,من) هَزَأَ (a; هَزْء ,هُزْء ,من) ‹*an idea, sb's work*›

derision /dɪˈrɪʒ(ə)n/ *n* سُخْرِيّة ,اسْتِهْزاء (اسْتِهْزاءات)

derisive /dɪˈrʌɪsɪv/ *adj* ‹*laughter, comment*› مُسْتَهْزِئ ,ساخِر

derisory /dɪˈrʌɪs(ə)ri/ *adj* ‹*offer, sum*› يَبْعَثُ على السُخْرِيّةِ

derivative /dɪˈrɪvətɪv/ **A** *adj* ‹*word*› مُشْتَقّ; **his work is very ~** [يَعْتَمِدُ عَمَلُهُ بِشَكْلٍ كَبيرٍ على نَقْلِ ما وَرَدَ في أَعْمالٍ سابِقةٍ]

B *n* 1 (substance) مُشْتَقّ (مُشْتَقّات) 2 (word) مُشْتَقّ (مُشْتَقّات) 3 (**derivatives** *n pl*) (financial product) مُشْتَقّات مالِيّة

derive /dɪˈrʌɪv/ **A** *vt* حَصَلَ (u; حُصول ;على) ‹*benefit, income*›; اسْتَمَدَّ ‹*pleasure, satisfaction*›; **I ~ great pleasure from singing** أَسْتَمِدُّ سَعادةً بالِغةً من الغِناءِ; **its name is ~d from the Greek** اسْمُهُ مُشْتَقٌّ من اللُغةِ اليونانِيّةِ

B *vi* **to ~ from sth** «words, names» اُشْتُقَّ من شَيْءٍ

dermatitis /ˌdəːməˈtʌɪtɪs/ *n* الْتِهاب جِلْدِيّ

dermatologist /dəːməˈtɒlədʒɪst/ *n* أَخِصّائِيّ أَمْراضٍ جِلْدِيّةٍ

dermatology /ˌdəːməˈtɒlədʒi/ *n* طِبّ أَمْراضٍ جِلْدِيّةٍ

derogatory /dɪˈrɒgət(ə)ri/ *adj* ‹*term, comment*› تَحْقيرِيّ ,ازْدِرائِيّ

derrick /ˈdɛrɪk/ *n* 1 (on ships) رافِعة (رَوافِعُ) ,مِرْفاع (مَرافيعُ) 2 (also **oil derrick**) حَفّارة نَفْطٍ

derv /dəːv/ *n* (BrE) ديزِل

dervish /ˈdəːvɪʃ/ *n* دَرْويش (دَراويشُ)

descend /dɪˈsɛnd/ **A** *vt* 1 نَزَلَ (i; نُزول ,من) هَبَطَ (i-u; هُبوط; تَحَدَّرَ \ انْحَدَرَ (من) ‹*stairs, a mountain*› 2 **to be ~ed from sb** انْحَدَرَ من شَخْصٍ

B *vi* 1 (to move downwards) «climber, plane» نَزَلَ (i; نُزول); «road, path» انْحَدَرَ; «darkness, mist» هَبَطَ (i-u; هُبوط); **silence ~ed on the room** خَيَّمَ الصَمْتُ على الغُرْفةِ; **in ~ing order of priority** تَرْتيباً تَنازُلِيًّا حَسْبَ الأَوْلَوِيّةِ 2 (to arrive in force) **to ~ on sth** تَوافَدَ على شَيْءٍ; **to ~ on sb** نَزَلَ \ حَلَّ (ضَيْفاً) على شَخْصٍ

descendant /dɪˈsɛnd(ə)nt/ *n* سَليل

descent /dɪˈsɛnt/ *n* 1 (by climbers, a plane) هُبوط ,نُزول; (in terrain) انْحِدار (انْحِدارات) 2 (decline) وُقوع; **her ~ into depression** إصابَتُها بالاكْتِئابِ 3 (origin, background) أَصْل (أُصول)

describe /dɪˈskrʌɪb/ *vt* وَصَفَ (i; وَصْف) ‹*an event, a house*›; **he ~s himself as a progressive** يَصِفُ نَفْسَهُ بالتَقَدُّمِيِّ

description /dɪˈskrɪpʃ(ə)n/ *n* وَصْف (أَوْصاف); **to give a detailed ~ of sth** أَعْطى وَصْفاً دَقيقاً لِشَيْءٍ

descriptive /dɪˈskrɪptɪv/ *adj* ‹*word, passage*› وَصْفيّ; **a ~ grammar of English** قَواعِد وَصْفيّة لِلُّغةِ الإنْجْليزيّةِ

desecrate /ˈdesɪkreɪt/ *vt* انْتَهكَ القُدْسيّةَ \ الحُرْمة ,دَنَّس ‹*a grave, temple*›

desert¹ /dɪˈzəːt/ **A** *vt* **1** (to abandon) هَجَر (u; هَجْر), تَخلّى (عن) ‹*your wife, post*› **2** (to fail) خَذَلَ (u; خَذْل) ‹*a performer, student*›

B *vi* «soldier» فَرّ من الجُنْديّةِ

desert² /ˈdezət/ *n* صَحْراء (dipt f; صَحارى ,صَحارٍ); **suitable for ~ climates** مُناسِب لِلمَناخِ الصَحْراويّ

deserted /dɪˈzəːtɪd/ *adj* ‹*beach, street*› مَهْجور

deserter /dɪˈzəːtə/ *n* [شَخص فارّ \ هارِب من الجُنْديّةِ]; **they were shot as ~s** قُتِلوا رَمْيا بالرَصاصِ لِفِرارِهِمْ من الجُنْديّةِ; **a ~ from the cause** شَخص تَخلّى عن القَضيّةِ

desertification /deˌzəːtɪfɪˈkeɪʃ(ə)n/ *n* تَصَحُّر

desertion /dɪˈzəːʃ(ə)n/ *n* **1** (from the armed forces) فِرار من الجُنْديّةِ **2** (of a spouse) هَجْر

deserts /dɪˈzəːts/ *n pl* **he got his just ~** لَقِيَ جَزاءَهُ العادِلَ

deserve /dɪˈzəːv/ *vt* اسْتَحَقَّ ‹*attention, an award*›; **they ~ to win** يَسْتَحِقّونَ الفَوْزَ

deserving /dɪˈzəːvɪŋ/ *adj* ‹*winner, cause*› مُسْتَحِقّ

desiccated /ˈdesɪkeɪtɪd/ *adj* ‹*leaves, landscape*› مُجَفَّف

desiccated coconut *n* جَوْز هِنْديّ مُجَفَّف

design /dɪˈzaɪn/ **A** *n* **1** (plan) تَصْميم (تَصاميم ,تَصْميمات); **a revolutionary new ~** تَصْميم ثَوْريّ جَديد **2** (drawing of a car, building, an appliance) تَصْميم (تَصاميمُ ,تَصْميمات); **to unveil new ~s** كَشَفَ النِقابَ عن تَصاميمَ جَديدةٍ **3** (prototype of a car, an appliance) نَموذَج (نَموذَجات ,نَماذِجُ), موديل (موديلات); (of a clothing item) تَصْميم (تَصاميمُ ,تَصْميمات) **4** [u] (art of designing) تَصْميم; **to study industrial/web ~** دَرَسَ التَصْميمَ الصِناعيَّ \ تَصْميمَ مَواقِعِ الإنْتَرْنِت **5** (on cloth) تَصْميم ,زَخْرَفة (تَصاميمُ ,تَصْميمات); **a bold leaf ~** زَخْرَفة نَباتيّة ظاهِرة **6** (intention) نيّة ,قَصْد (نَوايا ,نيّات); **more by accident than by ~** بِمَحْضِ الصُدْفةِ; **to have ~s on sb's job** رَغِبَ في وَظيفةِ شَخْصٍ

B *vt* صَمَّمَ ‹*a car, bridge, machine, dress*›; **it's well/badly ~ed** هو مُصَمَّمٌ بِطَريقةٍ جَيِّدةٍ \ سَيِّئةٍ; **a course ~ed for secondary students** دَوْرة دِراسيّة مُصَمَّمة لِطُلّابِ المَرْحَلةِ الثانَويّةِ

designate **A** /ˈdezɪgneɪt/ *vt* **1** خَصَّصَ ‹*land, a road*›; **he ~d his son as his heir** اخْتارَ ابْنَهُ وَريثاً لَهُ; **a law to ~ the land as a nature reserve** قانون لِتَخْصيصِ الأَرْضِ كَمَحْميّةٍ طَبيعيّةٍ

2 عَيَّنَ ‹*a successor, beneficiary*›

B *adj after n* /ˈdezɪgnət/ ‹*governor, president*› مُعَيَّن (لم يَتَقَلَّدْ بَعْدُ مَهامَّهُ رَسْميًّا)

designated driver /ˌdesɪgneɪtɪd ˈdraɪvə/ *n* [شَخْص يَمْتَنِعُ عن شُرْبِ الكُحولِ في حَفْلةٍ لِيُوَصِّلَ الآخَرينَ إلى بُيوتِهِمْ]

designation /dezɪgˈneɪʃ(ə)n/ *n* (of a person) تَعْيين (تَعْيينات), تَسْمِية; (of a place) تَخْصيص; **the ~ of the area as a protected site** تَخْصيص المِنْطَقةِ كَمَحْميّةٍ

designer /dɪˈzaɪnə/ *n* مُصَمِّم

designer clothes *n* [مَلابِس تَحْمِلُ اسْمَ مُصَمِّمِ أَزْياءٍ مَشْهورٍ]

designer label *n* عَلامة مارْكةٍ مَشْهورةٍ لِلمَلابِسِ

design fault *n* عَيْب في التَصْميمِ

desirable /dɪˈzaɪərəb(ə)l/ *adj* **1** ‹*outcome, area*› مَرْغوب فيه

2 (sexually) ‹*woman, mate*› جَذّاب

desire /dɪˈzaɪə/ **A** *n* (wish) رَغْبة (رَغَبات), تَوْق; **a universal ~ for peace** رَغْبة عالَميّة في السَلامِ; (sexual) شَهْوة (شَهَوات)

B *vt* (to wish for) رَغِبَ (a; رَغْبة ,رَغَب; في), تَمَنّى ‹*happiness, peace*›; **it leaves a lot to be ~d** هو غَيْرُ مُرْضٍ على الإطْلاقِ; (sexually) رَغِبَ (a; رَغْبة ,رَغَب; في), اشْتَهى ‹*a woman, man*›

desirous /dɪˈzaɪərəs/ *adj* (fml) راغِب ,تَوّاق

desist /dɪˈzɪst/ *vi* (fml) كَفَّ (u; كَفّ ;عن), انْتَهى (عن); **to ~ from violence/crime** كَفَّ عن العُنْفِ \ الإجْرامِ

desk /desk/ *n* **1** (in office) مَكْتَب (مَكاتِبُ); (in classroom) مَكْتَب, طاوِلة (مَناضِدُ ,مِنْضَدات), مِنْضَدة **2** (in hotel, airport) مَكْتَب اسْتِعْلاماتٍ **3** (Media) (in news office) مَكْتَب إعْلاميّ

desktop /ˈdesktɒp/ *n* سَطْح المَكْتَبِ

desktop computer *n* حاسوب مَكْتَبيّ

desktop publishing *n* نَشْر مَكْتَبيّ

desolate /ˈdesələt/ *adj* ‹*landscape, wasteland*› مَهْجور ,مُقْفِر

despair /dɪˈspɛː/ **A** *n* قُنوط ,يَأْس; **in ~** في حالةِ يَأْسٍ

B *vi* «nations, crowds» يَئِسَ (a-i; يَأْس) ,فَقَدَ الأَمَلَ; **don't ~!** لا تَيْأَسْ!; **he ~s of ever seeing them again** لَيْسَ لَدَيْهِ أَمَلٌ في رُؤْيَتِهِمْ مُجَدَّداً

despairing /dɪˈspɛːrɪŋ/ *adj* ‹*cry, mood*› يائِس

despatch /dɪˈspatʃ/ *vt, n* ▸ **dispatch**

desperate /ˈdɛsp(ə)rət/ *adj* ‹*plea, attempt*› يائِس; ‹*need*› ماسّ, ‹*situation*› مَيْؤوس مِنْهُ ,مُلِحّ; **the children are ~ for affection** الأَطْفالُ بِحاجةٍ ماسّةٍ إلى الحَنانِ

desperately /ˈdɛsp(ə)rətli/ *adv* **1** ‹*try*› بِاسْتِماتةٍ; ‹*plead*› بِإلْحاحٍ; **the children ~ need help** الأَطْفالُ بِحاجةٍ ماسّةٍ إلى المُساعَدةِ **2** ‹*poor*› بِشَكْلٍ مُدْقِعٍ; ‹*ill*› بِشِدّةٍ; **the kitten was ~ weak** كانَتِ القِطّةُ الصَغيرةُ ضَعيفةً جِدًّا

desperation /dɛspəˈreɪʃ(ə)n/ *n* يَأْس

despicable /dɪˈspɪkəb(ə)l, ˈdɛspɪkəb(ə)l/ *adj* ‹*act, coward*› حَقير (حُقَراءُ), خَسيس (أَخِسّاءُ), سافِل (سَفَلة)

despise /dɪˈspʌɪz/ *vt* اِحْتَقَرَ ,اِزْدَرى ‹*hypocrisy, an opponent*›

despite /dɪˈspʌɪt/ *prep* بالرَغْمِ من ,على الرَغْمِ من; **~ the fact that ...** بالرَغْمِ من حَقيقةِ أَنّ ... ; **~ the negative feedback, we decided to buy it** بالرَغْمِ من التَعْليقاتِ السَلْبيّةِ، قَرَّرْنا أَنْ نَشْتَرِيَهُ; **~ the fact that we are related, he refused to help us** بالرَغْمِ من أَنّنا أَقْرِباءُ، إلاّ أَنّهُ رَفَضَ أَنْ يُساعِدَنا

despondent /dɪˈspɒnd(ə)nt/ *adj* قانِط ,يائِس

despot /ˈdɛspɒt/ *n* طاغِية (m), مُسْتَبِدّ

despotic /dɪˈspɒtɪk/ *adj* اِسْتِبْداديّ ,طُغْيانيّ ,تَعَسُّفيّ

dessert /dɪˈzəːt/ *n* تَحْلية (حَلَوِيّات \ فَواكِه تُقَدَّمُ في آخِرِ الطَعامِ)

dessertspoon /dɪˈzəːtspuːn/ *n* **1** (utensil) مِلْعَقة مُتَوَسِّطة [الحَجْمِ تُسْتَعْمَلُ لِأَكْلِ التَحْلِية] **2** (also **dessertspoonful**) مِلْعَقة مُتَوَسِّطة الحَجْمِ

dessert wine *n* خَمْر حُلْو يُقَدَّمُ بعد الطَعامِ]

destabilize, -ise (BrE) /diːˈsteɪbəlʌɪz/ *vt* زَعْزَعَ (i; زَعْزَعة) ‹*the economy, a regime*›

destination /ˌdɛstɪˈneɪʃ(ə)n/ *n* وِجْهة

destined /ˈdɛstɪnd/ *adj* **1** (fated) **to be ~ for great things/ oblivion** كانَ مُقَدَّراً لَهُ أَنْ يَعيشَ عَظيماً \ يَطْوِيَهُ النِسْيانُ **2** (bound for) قاصِد ,مُتَّجِه; **a ship ~ for Port Said** سَفينة مُتَّجِهة إلى بور سَعيد

destiny /ˈdɛstɪni/ *n* (*pl* **destinies**) **1** (fate) قَدَر (أَقْدار) **2** (future events) قَدَر (أَقْدار)

destitute /ˈdɛstɪtjuːt/ *adj* ‹*woman, child*› مُعْوِز ,مُعْدِم

destroy /dɪˈstrɔɪ/ *vt* **1** (to ruin) دَمَّرَ ,خَرَّبَ ‹*a building, city*› **2** (to kill) قَتَلَ (u; قَتْل) ‹*an animal, a herd*› **3** (to end) دَمَّرَ ‹*sb's reputation*›; قَضى (i; قَضاء على) ‹*the evidence*›

destroyer /dɪˈstrɔɪə/ *n* **1** (warship) مُدَمِّرة **2** (person, object) مُدَمِّر ,مُخَرِّب

destruction /dɪˈstrʌkʃ(ə)n/ *n* **1** (of a city) تَدْمير; **to cause ~** سَبَّبَ دَماراً **2** (of hopes, reputation) تَدْمير

destructive /dɪˈstrʌktɪv/ *adj* ‹*child*› مُخَرِّب; ‹*weapon*› مُدَمِّر

desultory /ˈdɛsəlt(ə)ri/ *adj* ‹*conversation*› غَيْر مُتَرابِطٍ; ‹*attempt*› عَشْوائيّ

detach /dɪˈtatʃ/ *vt* فَصَلَ (i; فَصْل) ‹*a trailer, yourself*›; **to ~ the trailer from the van** فَصَلَ المَقْطورةَ عن العَرَبةِ

detachable /dɪˈtatʃəb(ə)l/ *adj* ‹*coupon, hood*› قابِل للفَصْلِ

detached /dɪˈtatʃt/ *adj* **1** ‹*building, outhouse*› مُنْفَصِل ,مُسْتَقِلّ **2** ‹*manner, individual*› غَيْر مُتَحَيِّزٍ

detached house *n* بَيْت مُنْفَصِل

detached retina *n* شَبَكيّة مُنْفَصِلة

detachment /dɪˈtatʃmənt/ *n* **1** (separation) اِنْفِصال (اِنْفِصالات) **2** (in manner) لامُبالاة ,عَدَم اِهْتِمامٍ **3** (military group) مَفْرَزة عَسْكَرِيّة

detail /ˈdiːteɪl/ **A** *n* تَفْصيل (تَفاصيلُ ,تَفْصيلات); **to describe sth in ~** وَصَفَ شَيْئاً بالتَفْصيلِ; **to go into ~s** دَخَلَ \ خاضَ في التَفاصيلِ

B *vt* **1** (to give details) أَعْطى التَفاصيلَ ‹*the findings, facts*› **2** (to assign) كَلَّفَ بِمُهِمّةٍ ‹*a battalion, soldier*›

detailed /ˈdiːteɪld/ *adj* ‹*information, analysis*› مُفَصَّل

detain /dɪˈteɪn/ *vt* **1** (to delay) أَخَّرَ ‹*a colleague, guest*› **2** (in custody) اِحْتَجَزَ ,سَجَنَ (u; سَجْن) ‹*a suspect, an immigrant, a prisoner*›

detainee /ˌdiːteɪˈniː/ *n* مُعْتَقَل

detect /dɪˈtɛkt/ *vt* اِكْتَشَفَ ,وَجَدَ (i; وُجود) ‹*a fault, trace*›

detectable /dɪˈtɛktəb(ə)l/ *adj* ‹*signal, defect*› قابِل للكَشْفِ, يُمْكِنُ اكْتِشافُهُ

detection /dɪˈtɛkʃ(ə)n/ *n* (of an error, crime) كَشْف; (of a substance) اكْتِشاف; **to escape ~** لم يُكْتَشَفْ

detective /dɪˈtɛktɪv/ *n* رَجُل التَحَرّي \ المَباحِث

detective story *n* قِصّة بوليسيّة

detector /dɪˈtɛktə/ *n* كاشِف

detente /deɪˈtɑːnt/ *n* (Pol) انْفِراج

detention /dɪˈtɛnʃ(ə)n/ *n* [1] (custody of offenders, immigrants) احْتِجاز [2] (in school) [احْتِجاز تِلْميذٍ في المَدْرَسةِ (كَعُقوبةٍ)]; **to be in ~** [احْتُجِز في المَدْرَسةِ كَعُقوبةٍ]

detention centre (BrE), **detention center** (AmE) *n* [1] (for young offenders) مَرْكَز احْتِجازٍ [2] (for illegal immigrants) مَرْكَز احْتِجازٍ

deter /dɪˈtəː/ *vt* (**-rr-**) [1] (to discourage) رَدَعَ (a; رَدْع) ‹*a criminal, thief*›; **to ~ sb from doing sth** رَدَعَ شَخْصاً عن فِعْلِ شَيْءٍ [2] (to prevent) رَدَعَ (a; رَدْع), مَنَعَ (a; مَنْع) ‹*vandalism, crime*›

detergent /dɪˈtəːdʒ(ə)nt/ *n* مُنَظِّف (مُنَظِّفات)

deteriorate /dɪˈtɪərɪəreɪt/ *vi* «health, condition» ساءَ, تَدَهْوَرَ (u; سوء), تَرَدّى

deterioration /dɪˌtɪərɪəˈreɪʃ(ə)n/ *n* (in the weather, sb's health, condition) تَرَدٍّ, سوء, تَدَهْوُر

determinant /dɪˈtəːmɪnənt/ *n* (fml) عامِل مُحَدِّد

determination /dɪˌtəːmɪˈneɪʃ(ə)n/ *n* تَصْميم, عَزْم

determine /dɪˈtəːmɪn/ *vt* [1] (to ascertain) حَدَّدَ ‹*the cause, cost*› [2] (to decide) حَسَمَ (i; حَسْم), حَدَّدَ ‹*the outcome, result*›

determined /dɪˈtəːmɪnd/ *adj* مُصَمِّم, عازِم; **to be ~ to succeed** كانَ عازِماً على النَجاحِ

deterrent /dɪˈtɛrənt/ *n* [1] (to discourage crime) رادِع (رَوادِعُ); **to serve as** *or* **act as a ~** كانَ دَوْرُهُ رَدْعِيًّا [2] (military) سِلاح رادِع; **the nuclear ~** الرادِع النَوَوِيّ

detest /dɪˈtɛst/ *vt* مَقَتَ (u; مَقْت), كَرِهَ بِشِدّةٍ ‹*violence, a neighbour, dancing*›

dethrone /diːˈθrəʊn/ *vt* خَلَعَ (a; خَلْع) ‹*a king, queen*›

detonate /ˈdɛt(ə)neɪt/ *vt* فَجَّرَ ‹*a bomb, device*›

detour /ˈdiːtʊə/ *n* طَرِيق جانِبِيّ; تَحْويلة (تَحاوِيلُ); **to make/take a ~** سَلَكَ تَحْويلةً \ طَرِيقاً جانِبِيًّا; **D~** (in traffic management) تَحْويلة (تَحاوِيلُ)

detox /diːˈtɒks/ *n* تَطْهير الجِسْمِ من السُمومِ, إزالة السُمومِ من الجِسْمِ (في عِلاجِ الإدْمانِ); **to be in ~** كانَ في مَرْحَلةِ إزالةِ السُمومِ من الجِسْمِ

detox clinic *n* مَصَحّة لِمُعالَجةِ الإدْمانِ

detoxification /diːˌtɒksɪfɪˈkeɪʃ(ə)n/, **detoxication** /diːˌtɒksɪˈkeɪʃ(ə)n/ *n* تَطْهير الجِسْمِ من السُموم, إزالة السُمومِ من الجِسْمِ (في عِلاجِ الإدْمانِ)

detoxify /diːˈtɒksɪfʌɪ/ *vt* (**detoxifies, detoxifying, detoxified**) [1] أَزالَ المَوادَّ السامّةَ من ‹*the soil, foodstuffs*› [2] عالَجَ من الإدْمانِ ‹*a drug addict, an alcoholic*›

detract /dɪˈtrakt/ *vi* **to ~ from the victory/success** انْتَقَصَ \ قَلَّلَ من قيمةِ الفَوْزِ \ النَجاحِ

detractor /dɪˈtraktə/ *n* [شَخْص يَسْتَخِفُّ \ يَسْتَهينُ بالآخَرينَ]

detriment /ˈdɛtrɪmənt/ *n* أَذًى, ضَرَر (أَضْرار); **to the ~ of one's health** على حِسابِ صِحَّتِهِ

detrimental /ˌdɛtrɪˈmɛnt(ə)l/ *adj* ‹*effect, influence*› مُضِرّ, ضارّ, مُؤْذٍ

deuce /djuːs/ *n* [تَعادُل في مُباراةِ تِنِس]

devaluation /diːvaljʊˈeɪʃ(ə)n/ *n* [1] (of a currency) انْخِفاض القيمةِ [2] (of values) تَقْليل من القيمةِ \ الشَأْنِ

devalue /diːˈvaljuː/ [A] *vt* [1] خَفَّضَ القيمةَ ‹*a currency*› [2] (to underestimate) قَلَّلَ من القيمةِ \ الشَأْنِ ‹*an employee, an achievement*›

[B] *vi* «currency» انْخَفَضَتْ قيمَتُهُ; «property, shares» انْخَفَضَ سِعْرُهُ

devastate /ˈdɛvəsteɪt/ [A] *vt* [1] (to lay waste) اجْتاحَ, دَمَّرَ ‹*an area, a country*› [2] (to overwhelm) صَدَمَ بِشِدّةٍ, أَفْجَعَ ‹*families, communities*›

[B] (**devastated**) *adj* مَصْدوم بِشِدّةٍ, مَفْجوع; **he was ~d by Sara's death** كانَ مَفْجوعاً بِمَوْتِ سارة

devastated /ˈdɛvəsteɪtɪd/ *adj* [1] (destroyed) ‹*area, city*› مُدَمَّر بالكامِلِ [2] (shocked) ‹*parents, family*› مَصْدوم بِشِدّةٍ, مَفْجوع

devastating /ˈdɛvəsteɪtɪŋ/ *adj* [1] ‹*attack, earthquake*› مُدَمِّر [2] ‹*blow, loss*› مُفْجِع

devastation /ˌdɛvəˈsteɪʃ(ə)n/ *n* خَراب, دَمار

develop /dɪˈvɛləp/ **A** *vt* 1 (to acquire) طَوَّرَ, نَمَّى ‹*a skill, knowledge*›; **to ~ an awareness of sth** نَمَّى وَعْيَهُ بِشَيْءٍ; **she's ~ing her nursing skills** تُنَمِّي مَهاراتِها في التَّمْريضِ 2 (to acquire) أُصيبَ بِ ‹*an illness, infection*›; **to ~ cancer** أُصيبَ بالسَّرَطانِ 3 (to refine) حَسَّنَ, طَوَّرَ ‹*a plan, technique, theory*› 4 (in marketing) طَوَّرَ ‹*a market*›; وَسَّعَ ‹*contacts*› 5 (to urbanize) أَنْشَأَ مَبانٍ على ‹*land, a site*› 6 (Phot) ظَهَّرَ, حَمَّضَ ‹*a negative, film*›
B *vi* 1 (to grow) «children, embryos, plants» نَما (u; نُموّ); **the country is ~ing at a high/low rate** تَنْمو الدَّوْلَةُ بِمُعَدَّلٍ سَريعٍ \ بَطيءٍ 2 (to change) «friendships, relationships, illnesses» تَطَوَّرَ; **their friendship is ~ing into sth else** تَتَطَوَّرُ صَداقَتُهُما إلى شَيْءٍ آخَرَ; **the cough ~ed into pneumonia** تَطَوَّرَ السُّعالُ إلى الْتِهابٍ رِئَويٍّ 3 (economically) «city, business» تَطَوَّرَ 4 (to progress, advance) «crisis, story» تَطَوَّرَ

developer /dɪˈvɛləpə/ *n* 1 (of products) مُطَوِّر 2 (also **property developer**) مُطَوِّر عَقاريّ

developing /dɪˈvɛləpɪŋ/ *adj* ‹*country*› نامٍ; ‹*relationship*› مُتَنامٍ

developing country *n* دَوْلَة نامِية

development /dɪˈvɛləpmənt/ *n* 1 [u] (of a person, idea) تَطَوُّر 2 [u] (of a product) تَطْوير, تَنْمِية 3 [u] (of land, a site, city centre) تَطْوير 4 (housing) مَشْروع انْشائيّ 5 (innovation) تَطَوُّر (تَطَوُّرات); **recent ~s in cancer treatment** تَطَوُّرات حَديثة في عِلاجِ السَّرَطانِ 6 (event) تَطَوُّر (تَطَوُّرات); **a surprise ~ in the negotiations** تَطَوُّر مُفاجِئ في المُفاوَضاتِ

developmental /dɪˌvɛləpˈmɛnt(ə)l/ *adj* ‹*stage, disability*› تَنْمَويّ

deviant /ˈdiːvɪənt/ **A** *adj* ‹*behaviour, act*› مُنْحَرِف
B *n* مُنْحَرِف

deviate /ˈdiːvɪeɪt/ *vi* 1 (from a course) «planes, storms» خَرَجَ (u; خُروج; عن); **to ~ from a course of action** خَرَجَ عن مَسارِ العَمَلِ 2 (from a norm) «behaviour, inflation» خَرَجَ (u; خُروج; عن)

deviation /ˌdiːvɪˈeɪʃ(ə)n/ *n* خُروج; **a ~ from the norm** خُروج عن المُعْتادِ

device /dɪˈvaɪs/ *n* 1 (tool, gadget) جِهاز (أَجْهِزة), أَداة (أَدَوات) 2 (also **explosive device, incendiary device**) قُنْبُلة (قَنابِل), عُبْوّة ناسِفة 3 (stratagem) وَسيلة (وَسائِل)
Idiom **to leave sb to their own devices** تَرَكَ شَخْصاً وَشَأْنَهُ

devil /ˈdɛv(ə)l/ *n* 1 (**the Devil**) (Satan) إبْليس, الشَّيْطان (dipt) 2 (infml) (naughty child) طِفْل مُشاغِب, شَيْطان (شَياطينُ); **her son is a little ~** ابْنُها شَيْطانٌ صَغيرٌ 3 (infml) (for emphasis) **what the ~ do you mean?** ماذا تَعْني بِحَقِّ الجَحيمِ؟ 4 (infml) (expressing admiration, sympathy) **he's a lucky ~** كم هو مَحْظوظٌ; **you poor ~** أَيُّها البائِسُ \ التَعيسُ
Idioms **better the devil you know** شَيْطانٌ تَعْرِفُهُ خَيْرٌ من شَيْطانٍ تَجْهَلُهُ; **talk of the devil!** كُنّا نَتَحَدَّثُ عَنْهُ للتَوِّ!; **the devil finds work for idle hands** ≈ الفَراغُ مَفْسَدةٌ

devil's advocate *n* مُحامي الشَّيْطانِ (مَنْ يُعَبِّرُ عن الرَّأْيِ الآخَرِ لِمُجَرَّدِ الجِدالِ)

devious /ˈdiːvɪəs/ *adj* ‹*plot, grin*› مُراوِغ

devise /dɪˈvaɪz/ *vt* اخْتَرَعَ, ابْتَكَرَ ‹*a plan, system*›

devoid /dɪˈvɔɪd/ *adj* **to be ~ of sth** ‹*of talent, meaning*› كانَ خالِياً \ مُجَرَّداً من شَيْءٍ

devolution /ˌdiːvəˈluːʃ(ə)n/ *n* (of powers) لامَرْكَزِيّة

devolve /dɪˈvɒlv/ *vt* نَقَلَ (u; نَقْل) ‹*power, responsibilities*›

devote /dɪˈvəʊt/ *vt* **to ~ sth to sth** كَرَّسَ \ خَصَّصَ شَيْئاً لِشَيْءٍ ‹*one's time, energy*›

devoted /dɪˈvəʊtɪd/ *adj* ‹*family, fan*› مُخْلِص

devotee /ˌdɛvəʊˈtiː/ *n* هاوٍ (هُواة)

devotion /dɪˈvəʊʃ(ə)n/ *n* إخْلاص

devour /dɪˈvaʊə/ *vt* الْتَهَمَ ‹*food, a book*›

devout /dɪˈvaʊt/ *adj* ‹*Catholic*› مُتَدَيِّن, تَقيّ (أَتْقِياءُ); ‹*prayer*› خاشِع; ‹*supporter, follower*› مُخْلِص

dew /ˈdjuː/ *n* نَدًى (أَنْداء, أَنْدِية)

dexterity /dɛkˈstɛrɪti/ *n* مَهارة, حِذْق

Dhaka, Dacca /ˈdaka/ *pr n* دَكّا

dhikr /ˈðɪk(ə)/ *n* 1 [u] (worship) ذِكْر 2 (ceremony) مَجْلِس ذِكْرٍ

dhow /daʊ/ *n* داو

Dhu al-Hijja /ðuːl ˈhɪdʒa/ *n* ذو الحِجّة

Dhu al-Qaada /ðuːl 'kadɑ/ *n* ذو القَعْدةِ

diabetes /ˌdʌɪə'biːtiːz/ *n* مَرَض السُكَّرِيّ

diabetic /dʌɪə'bɛtɪk/ **A** *adj* ‹diet, chocolate› سُكَّرِيّ (مُتَعَلِّق بِمَرَضِ السُكَّرِيِّ)

B *n* مَرِيض السُكَّرِيِّ

diabolical /dʌɪə'bɒlɪk(ə)l/ *adj* **1** (BrE infml) (terrible) ‹weather, food› فَظيع, جَهَنَّمِيّ **2** (evil) ‹plan, crime› شَيْطانِيّ

diagnose /'dʌɪəgnəʊz/ *vt* شَخَّصَ ‹an illness, a disorder›; تَعَرَّفَ (على) ‹a fault, problem›

diagnosis /ˌdʌɪəg'nəʊsɪs/ *n* (*pl* **diagnoses**) تَشْخيص

diagnostic /dʌɪəg'nɒstɪk/ **A** *adj* ‹test, evaluation› تَشْخيصِيّ

B (**diagnostics**) *n pl* (Med) أُسْلوب \ فَنّ التَشْخيص; (Comput) بَرْنامَج \ أَساليب تَشْخيصٍ

diagonal /dʌɪ'ag(ə)n(ə)l/ *adj* ‹pattern, stripe› مائِل, قُطْرِيّ

diagonally /dʌɪ'ag(ə)n(ə)li/ *adv* ‹to move, swim› بِشَكْلٍ قُطْرِيٍّ

diagram /'dʌɪəgram/ *n* رَسْم بَيانِيّ

dial /dʌɪəl/ **A** *n* **1** (on a clock, watch) وَجْه **2** (on a gauge) مُؤَشِّر (مُؤَشِّرات) **3** (selector) لَوْحة (أَلْواح, لَوْحات) **4** (on a telephone) قُرْص (أَقْراص)

B *vt* (-ll- BrE, -l- AmE) طَلَبَ (u; طَلَب, مَطْلَب) ‹a number›

dialect /'dʌɪəlɛkt/ *n* لَهْجة (لَهَجات)

dialling code /'dʌɪəlɪŋ ˌkəʊd/ *n* (BrE) رَمْز الاتِّصالِ الهاتِفِيِّ, كود البَلَدِ

dialog box (also **dialogue box** BrE) *n* صُنْدوق \ مُرَبَّع الحِوارِ

dialogue (BrE), **dialog** (AmE) /'dʌɪəlɒg/ *n* حِوار (حِوارات)

dial tone, **dialling tone** *n* نَغْمة الاتِّصالِ, طَنين

dialysis /dʌɪ'alɪsɪs/ *n* (*pl* **dialyses**) غَسيل الكُلى

diameter /dʌɪ'amɪtə/ *n* قُطْر (أَقْطار)

diamond /'dʌɪəmənd/ *n* **1** (gem) ماس **2** (shape) مُعَيَّن **3** (**diamonds** *n pl*) (in cards) ديناريّ

diaper /'dʌɪəpə/ *n* حِفاظة

diaphragm /'dʌɪəfram/ *n* **1** (in the chest) حِجاب حاجِز **2** (membrane) غِشاء (أَغْشِية), دَيافْرام **3** (vibrating disc, cone) دَيافْرام, غِشاء الاهْتِزازِ **4** (contraceptive) واقٍ أُنْثَوِيّ

diarrhoea (BrE), **diarrhea** (AmE) /ˌdʌɪə'rɪə/ *n* إِسْهال

diary /'dʌɪəri/ *n* (*pl* **diaries**) **1** (for appointments) مُفَكِّرة \ مُذَكِّرة يَوْمِيّة **2** (journal) يَوْمِيّات

dice /dʌɪs/ **A** *n* (*pl* **dice**) زَهْر النَرْدِ

B *vt* قَطَّعَ إِلى مُكَعَّباتٍ ‹the meat, vegetables›

dick /dɪk/ *n* (vulg) قَضيب الرَجُلِ

dictate /dɪk'teɪt/ *vt* **1** (to read out) أَمْلى ‹a letter, text› **2** (to prescribe, lay down) فَرَضَ (i; فَرْض), أَمْلى ‹a law, policy›

dictation /dɪk'teɪʃ(ə)n/ *n* إِمْلاء (أَمالٍ, أَمالِيّ)

dictator /dɪk'teɪtə/ *n* دِكْتاتور, حاكِم مُطْلَق

dictatorial /dɪktə'tɔːrɪəl/ *adj* ‹regime, powers› دِكْتاتورِيّ, مُسْتَبِدّ

dictatorship /dɪk'teɪtəʃɪp/ *n* دِكْتاتورية, حُكْم مُطْلَق

diction /'dɪkʃ(ə)n/ *n* إِلْقاء, أُسْلوب (أَساليبُ)

dictionary /'dɪkʃ(ə)n(ə)ri/ *n* (*pl* **dictionaries**) قاموس (قواميسُ), مُعْجَم (مَعاجِمُ)

did /dɪd/ *past tense* ▸ **do**

didactic /dʌɪ'daktɪk, dɪ'daktɪk/ *adj* ‹purpose, literature› تَعْليمِيّ, تَوْجيهِيّ

diddle /'dɪd(ə)l/ *vt* (infml) غَشَّ (u; غِشّ, غَشّ), خَدَعَ (a; خَدْع, خِدْع, خُدْعة, خَديعة) ‹a customer, company›

didn't /'dɪd(ə)nt/ *abbr* = **did not** ▸ **do** A, C

die /dʌɪ/ **A** *n* (*pl* **dice**) زَهْر النَرْدِ

B *vt* (3rd person present sing **dies**, present participle **dying**, past tense, past participle **died**) **to ~ a natural/violent death** ماتَ ميتةً طَبيعيّةً \ عَنيفةً; **to ~ a hero's/martyr's death** ماتَ ميتةَ الأَبطالِ \ الشُهَداءِ

C *vi* (3rd person present sing **dies**, present participle **dying**, past tense, past participle **died**) **1** (to reach the end of one's life) ماتَ (u; مَوْت), تُوُفِّيَ; **she ~d a year ago** تُوُفِّيَت العامَ الماضِيَ; **I am dying** أَنا أَحْتَضِرُ; **to ~ in one's sleep/bed** ماتَ أَثْناء نَوْمِهِ \ في سَريرِهِ; **to ~ of** *or* **from starvation** ماتَ جوعاً; **to ~ of natural causes** ماتَ من أَسْبابٍ طَبيعيّةٍ **2** (to lose one's life) ماتَ (u; مَوْت); **to ~ in action** ماتَ في القِتالِ; **to ~ for one's beliefs/country** ماتَ من أَجْلِ مُعْتَقَداتِهِ \ وَطَنِهِ **3** «plants, crops» هَلَكَ (i; هَلاك), ماتَ (u; مَوْت) **4** (of boredom, shame, fright) ماتَ (u; مَوْت); **we nearly ~d with embarrassment!** كِدْنا نَموتُ خَجَلاً!; **I nearly ~d laughing**

كِدْتُ أَموتُ من (كَثْرَةِ) الضَحِكِ 5 (infml) (to long for) **to be dying to do sth** كانَ يَتوقُ \ يَتَشَوَّقُ إلى فِعْلِ شَيْءٍ; **we were dying to leave** كُنّا نَتَحَرَّقُ شَوْقاً لِأَنْ نُغادِرَ; **to be dying for sth** كانَ يَتوقُ إلى شَيْءٍ; **we're all dying for a drink/holiday** نَحْنُ جَميعاً نَتوقُ إلى شَرابٍ \ إجازةٍ; **to be dying for sb/sth to do sth** تَمَنّى بِشِدّةٍ لِشَخْصٍ \ لِشَيْءٍ أَنْ يَفْعَلَ شَيْئاً; **I was dying for him to fail** كُنْتُ أَتَمَنّى بِشِدّةٍ أَنْ يَفْشَلَ; **clothes to ~ for** مَلابِس في غايةِ الرَوْعةِ 6 (to go out) «lights, flames» خَمَدَ (u; خُمود), انْطَفَأَ, خَبا (u; خَبْو, خُبوّ) 7 (to fade) «love, enthusiasm» ماتَ (u; مَوْت), تَلاشى, خَبا (u; خَبْو, خُبوّ) 8 (to stop) «machines, engines» تَعَطَّلَ, تَوَقَّفَ عن العَمَلِ

Idiom **never say die!** لا تَيْأَسْ أَبَداً!

Phrasal verbs **die away** «applause, sound» خَفَتَ (u; خُفوت), خَبا (u; خَبْو, خُبوّ)

- **die back** «plants, flower» ذَبَلَ (u; ذَبْل, ذُبول), ذَوى (i; ذَوِيّ)
- **die down** 1 (in intensity) «flames, wind» خَمَدَ (u; خُمود); **when all the fuss ~s down** عِنْدَما يَسْكُنُ الهَرَجُ والمَرَجُ; **the fighting ~d down when it got light** خَمَدَ القِتالُ مع طُلوعِ النَهارِ 2 (in volume) «applause, laughter» خَفَتَ (u; خُفوت)
- **die off** «species, plants» انْقَرَضَ, انْدَثَرَ; «veterans» فَنِيَ (a; فَناء)
- **die out** 1 «traditions, languages» انْدَثَرَ, تَلاشى 2 «species» انْقَرَضَ, انْدَثَرَ; «settlers» فَنِيَ (a; فَناء) 3 «showers, rain» انْعَدَمَ, تَلاشى; **the showers will ~ out from the west** سَوْفَ تَنْعَدِمُ الأَمْطارُ في الغَرْبِ

diehard /ˈdʌɪhɑːd/ A *n* مُتَعَصِّب, عَنيد (عُنُد) B *adj* ‹*fan, opponent*› مُتَعَصِّب

diesel /ˈdiːz(ə)l/ A *n* (also **diesel fuel, diesel oil**) [u] (fuel) ديزِل B *adj* ‹*engine, locomotive*› ديزِل

diet /ˈdʌɪət/ A *n* 1 (food intake) غِذاء (أَغْذِية) 2 (for losing weight) نِظام \ بَرْنامَج \ حِمْية غِذائيّ(ة), رِجيم; **to go on a ~** بَدَأَ رِجيماً \ نِظاماً غِذائيّاً B *vi* عَمِلَ رِجيماً \ حِمْيةً غِذائيّةً

dietary /ˈdʌɪət(ə)ri/ *adj* ‹*problem, habit*› غِذائيّ

diet cola *n* كولا دايِت \ لايْت

dietetic /ˌdʌɪəˈtɛtɪk/ A *adj* ‹*information, advice*› غِذائيّ B (**dietetics**) *n pl + v sg* عِلْم الغِذاءِ والتَغْذِيةِ

dietitian, dietician /dʌɪəˈtɪʃ(ə)n/ *n* أَخِصّائيّ تَغْذِيةٍ

differ /ˈdɪfə/ *vi* 1 (to be different) «individuals, tastes» اخْتَلَفَ; **how do they ~?** ما وَجْهُ الاخْتِلافِ بَيْنَهُمْ؟; **to ~ from sb/sth** اخْتَلَفَ عن شَخْصٍ \ شَيْءٍ 2 (to disagree) «experts, opinions» اخْتَلَفَ

difference /ˈdɪf(ə)rəns/ *n* 1 (dissimilarity) اخْتِلاف (اخْتِلافات), فَرْق (فُروق); **to tell the ~** فَرَّقَ \ مَيَّزَ بَيْنَهُما; **it will make a ~ to the outcome** سَتُحْدِثُ فَرْقاً في النَتيجةِ; **it makes no ~ to me** لا تَفْرِقُ مَعي 2 (disagreement) خِلاف (خِلافات)

different /ˈdɪf(ə)rənt/ *adj* 1 (not the same) ‹*types, ways*› مُخْتَلِف; **~ from, to** *or* (AmE) **than** مُخْتَلِف عن 2 (unusual) ‹*angles, styles*› مُخْتَلِف, غَيْر مُعْتادٍ

differential /ˌdɪfəˈrɛnʃ(ə)l/ A *adj* ‹*treatment*› مُتَفاوِت, تَفاضُليّ B *n* تَبايُن (تَبايُنات)

differentiate /ˌdɪfəˈrɛnʃɪeɪt/ A *vt* ‹*a species, product*› فَرَّقَ, مَيَّزَ; **to ~ sth (from sth)** مَيَّزَ شَيْئاً (عن شَيْءٍ) B *vi* فَرَّقَ, مَيَّزَ

differentiation /ˌdɪfərɛnʃɪˈeɪʃ(ə)n/ *n* تَفْرِقة, تَمْييز (تَمْييزات)

differently /ˈdɪfrəntli/ *adv* ‹*to think, to see sth*› بِطَريقةٍ مُخْتَلِفةٍ, بِشَكْلٍ مُخْتَلِفٍ; **they think ~** يُفَكِّرونَ بِطَريقةٍ مُخْتَلِفةٍ; **I view things ~** أَرى الأُمورَ بِشَكْلٍ مُخْتَلِفٍ

difficult /ˈdɪfɪk(ə)lt/ *adj* ‹*exam, decision*› صَعْب (صِعاب); **he is finding it ~ to give up smoking** يَجِدُ صُعوبةً في الإقْلاعِ عن التَدْخينِ

difficulty /ˈdɪfɪk(ə)lti/ *n* (*pl* **difficulties**) 1 [u] (of situation, task) صُعوبة; **she had great ~ walking** كانَتْ تَجِدُ صُعوبةً كَبيرةً في المَشْيِ 2 (problem) صُعوبة; **to get into difficulties** وَجَدَ \ واجَهَ صُعوباتٍ

diffident /ˈdɪfɪd(ə)nt/ *adj* ‹*child, manner, smile*› خَجول

diffuse A /dɪˈfjuːz/ *vt* نَشَرَ (u; نَشْر) ‹*the light, heat*› B /dɪˈfjuːs/ *adj* ‹*light, population*› مُنْتَشِر

diffusion /dɪˈfjuːʒ(ə)n/ *n* نَشْر

dig /dɪg/ A *vt* (*present participle* **-gg-**; *past participle* **dug**) 1 (to make) حَفَرَ (i; حَفْر) ‹*a hole, tunnel*› 2 (in gardening) قَلَّبَ ‹*the garden, soil*› 3 (to extract) قَلَعَ (a; قَلْع) ‹*potatoes*› 4 (to thrust) غَرَسَ (i; غَرْس) ‹*hands, one's nails*›

B *vi* (*present participle* **-gg-**; *past participle* **dug**) **1** (in the ground, rubble) «person, dog» حَفَرَ (i; حَفْر) **2** (in archaeology) نَقَّبَ; **to ~ for gold/treasure** نَقَّبَ عن الذَهَبِ \ الكَنْزِ **3** (to search) بَحَثَ, فَتَّشَ (a; بَحْث); **I dug in** *or* **into my pocket for the ticket** فَتَّشْتُ في جَيْبي عن التَذْكِرةِ **4** (to jab) **to ~ into sb** «fingernails, claws» وَخَزَ شَخْصاً

C *n* **1** (poke) نَكْزة, نَقْرة; **to give sb a ~ in the ribs** نَقَرَ \ نَكَزَ شَخْصاً على ظَهْرِهِ **2** (infml) (jibe) اسْتِهْزاء (اسْتِهْزاءات), سُخْرِيّة; **to take** *or* **have a ~ at sb** سَخِرَ من شَخْصٍ **3** (excavation) حَفْر, تَنْقيب (تَنْقيبات)

D (**digs**) *n pl* **1** (BrE infml) (lodgings) [غُرْفة \ غُرَف مُسْتَأْجَرة] **2** (AmE infml) (dwelling) مَسْكَن, سَكَن (مَساكِنُ)

(Phrasal verbs) **dig in A 1** «troops, armies» حَفَرَ خَنْدَقاً **2** (infml) (to eat) شَرَعَ في الأَكْلِ; **~ in everybody!** هَيّا جميعاً اشْرَعوا في الأَكْلِ! **B ~ in [sth], ~ [sth] in** خَلَطَ [شَيْئاً] بالتُرْبة ‹*compost*›

• **dig out**: **~ out [sth], ~ [sth] out 1** اسْتَخْرَجَ [شَيْئاً] ‹*the victims, a splinter, car*› **2** (infml) (to bring out) عَثَرَ على [شَيْءٍ] ‹*a copy, old photos*›

• **dig up**: **~ up [sth], ~ [sth] up 1** (to unearth) اسْتَخْرَجَ [شَيْئاً] من الأَرْضِ ‹*a body, the treasure, plants*› **2** (to excavate) حَفَرَ [شَيْئاً] ‹*a road, grave*› **3** (infml) (to discover) اكْتَشَفَ [شَيْئاً] ‹*information, facts*›

digest /dʌɪˈdʒɛst, dɪˈdʒɛst/ *vt* **1** (Anat) هَضَمَ (i; هَضْم) ‹*food, a meal*› **2** (understand) اسْتَوْعَبَ ‹*facts, implications*›

digestible /dʌɪˈdʒɛstəb(ə)l/ *adj* **1** (of food) قابِلٌ للهَضْمِ **2** (comprehensible) مَفْهوم

digestion /dʌɪˈdʒɛstʃ(ə)n, dɪˈdʒɛstʃ(ə)n/ *n* هَضْم

digestive /dʌɪˈdʒɛstɪv, dɪˈdʒɛstɪv/ *adj* ‹*system, tract*› هَضْميّ

digger /ˈdɪɡə/ *n* **1** (machine) حَفّارة, حَفّار (ميكانيكيّ \ آليّ) **2** (worker) حَفّار

digit /ˈdɪdʒɪt/ *n* **1** (number) رَقْم (أَرْقام) **2** (finger, toe) إِصْبَع (mf; أَصابِعُ)

digital /ˈdɪdʒɪt(ə)l/ *adj* ‹*watch, display*› رَقْميّ

digital camera *n* كاميرا \ آلة تَصْوير رَقْميّة

digital divide *n* فَجْوة رَقْميّة

digital signature *n* تَوْقيع رَقْميّ

digital television, digital TV *n* تِلِفِزْيون رَقْميّ

digitize, -ise (BrE) /ˈdɪdʒɪtʌɪz/ *vt* رَقْمَنَ (i; رَقْمَنة) ‹*a collection, signal*›

diglossia /dʌɪˈɡlɒsɪə/ *n pl* ازْدِواج لُغَويّ \ اللُغة, ازْدِواجيّة لُغَويّة

dignified /ˈdɪɡnɪfʌɪd/ *adj* مَهيب, وَقور (وُقُر)

dignity /ˈdɪɡnɪti/ *n* وَقار, هَيْبة, كَرامة

digress /dʌɪˈɡrɛs/ *vi* «a speech, speaker» خَرَجَ عن, اسْتَطْرَدَ; **but I ~** لَكِنّي اسْتَطْرَدْتُ \ خَرَجْتُ عن المَوْضوعِ; **to ~ from a topic** خَرَجَ عن مَوْضوعٍ

digression /dʌɪˈɡrɛʃ(ə)n/ *n* خُروج عن المَوْضوعِ, اسْتِطراد

dike /dʌɪk/ *n* ▸ **dyke**

diktat /ˈdɪktat/ *n* أَمْر (أَوامِرُ), مَرْسوم (مَراسيمُ)

dilapidated /dɪˈlapɪdeɪtɪd/ *adj* ‹*building, shack*› مُتَهَدِّم

dilate /dʌɪˈleɪt/ **A** *vt* ‹*a blood vessel, nostrils*› وَسَّعَ **B** *vi* «pupils, cervix» اتَّسَعَ

dilation /dʌɪˈleɪʃ(ə)n/ *n* اتِّساع (اتِّساعات)

dilemma /dʌɪˈlɛmə, dɪˈlɛmə/ *n* مُعْضِلة (مُعْضِلات, مَعاضِلُ), وَرْطة (وَرَطات, وِراط), مَأْزِق (مَآزِقُ)

diligence /ˈdɪlɪdʒ(ə)ns/ *n* (persistence) اجْتِهاد, مُثابَرة; (care) اهْتِمام (اهْتِمامات)

diligent /ˈdɪlɪdʒ(ə)nt/ *adj* ‹*campaigner, worker*› مُجْتَهِد; ‹*effort, work*› مُثابِر

dilute /dʌɪˈljuːt/ *vt* خَفَّفَ ‹*the wine, weedkiller*›; **~d sulphuric acid** حَمْض الكِبْريتِ المُخَفَّف

dilution /dʌɪˈluːʃ(ə)n/ *n* تَخْفيف

dim /dɪm/ **A** *adj* (**-mm-**) **1** ‹*room, stage*› مُظْلِم, مُعْتِم **2** ‹*light*› ضَعيف, خافت; **to grow ~** خَفَتَ (u; خُفوت) **3** ‹*outline, shape*› مُبْهَم, مُعْتِم **4** ‹*memory, idea*› مُبْهَم **5** (infml) (stupid) ‹*pupil, remark*› بَليد **B** *vt* (**-mm-**) أَخْفَتَ ‹*a light, headlights*›

(Idiom) **to take a dim view of sth** (infml) اسْتَنْكَرَ شَيْئاً

dime /dʌɪm/ (AmE) *n* دايم (عَشَرة سِنْتاتٍ أَمْريكيّةٍ أو كَنَديّةٍ)

(Idiom) **they're a dime a dozen** [هُمْ كُثْرٌ وَلَكِنَّهُمْ بِلا قيمةٍ]

dimension /dɪˈmɛnʃ(ə)n/ *n* بُعْد (أَبْعاد); **to take the ~s of a room** قاسَ أَبْعادَ غُرْفةٍ

-dimensional /dɪˈmenʃ(ə)n(ə)l/ *combining form* الأَبْعادِ; **three~** ثُلاثيّ الأَبْعادِ

dime store *n* [مَتْجَر سِلَعٍ رَخيصةٍ]

diminish /dɪˈmɪnɪʃ/ **A** *vt* ‹*the value, supply*› قَلَّلَ **B** *vi* «costs, threats» قَلَّ (قِلّة, قُلّ, قِلّ)

diminutive /dɪˈmɪnjʊtɪv/ **A** *adj* ‹*size, figure*› صَغير جِدًّا **B** *n* (Ling) تَصْغير

dimly /ˈdɪmli/ *adv* **1** ‹*lit*› بِشَكْلٍ خافِتٍ **2** ‹*to remember, perceive*› بِشَكْلٍ غامِضٍ \ غَيْر واضِحٍ

dimmer /ˈdɪmə/ *n* (also **dimmer switch**) خافت الإضاءة

dimple /ˈdɪmp(ə)l/ *n* ‹*cheek*› غَمّازة; ‹*chin*› (نُقَر) نُقْرة ,نونة

dimwit /ˈdɪmwɪt/ *n* (infml) مُغَفَّل

din /dɪn/ *n* ضَجيج

dinar /ˈdiːnɑː/ *n* (دَنانيرُ) دينار

dine /dʌɪn/ *vi* تَعَشّى

diner /ˈdʌɪnə/ *n* **1** (person) مُتَناوِل العَشاءِ **2** (AmE) (restaurant) [مَطْعَم صَغير وَرَخيص على الطَريقِ السَريعِ]

dinghy /ˈdɪŋgi/ *n* **1** (also **sailing dinghy**) زَوْرَق \ قارِب صَغير **2** (inflatable) زَوْرَق \ طَوْف مَطّاطِيّ

dingy /ˈdɪndʒi/ *adj* (**dingier**, **dingiest**) ‹*grey, brown*› داكِن; ‹*apartment, pub*› قَذِر

dining car *n* عَرَبة مَطْعَمٍ (في قِطارٍ)

dining room *n* (in a house) غُرْفة طَعام; (in a hotel) قاعة طَعام

dining table *n* مائدة طَعام

dinner /ˈdɪnə/ *n* **1** (evening meal) عَشاء (أَعْشِية); **to have ~** تَناوَلَ العَشاءَ **2** (banquet) مَأْدُبة (مَآدِبُ)

dinner dance *n* [حَفْلة عَشاءٍ يَتْبَعُها الرَقْصُ]

dinner jacket *n* بَدْلة السَهْرةِ

dinner party *n* حَفْلة عَشاءٍ

dinner service, **dinner set** *n* طَقْم السُفْرةِ

dinner table *n* سُفْرة ,مائِدة الطَعامِ (Egypt)

dinner time *n* وَقْت \ مَوْعِد العَشاءِ

dinosaur /ˈdʌɪnəsɔː/ *n* (دَيْناصورات) دَيْناصور

dint /dɪnt/ (**by dint of**) *prep phr* بِفَضْلِ

diocese /ˈdʌɪəsɪs/ *n* أَبْرَشِيّة

dioxide /dʌɪˈɒksʌɪd/ *n* ثاني أُكْسيد

dioxin /dʌɪˈɒksɪn/ *n* دِيوكْسين

dip /dɪp/ **A** *vt* (**-pp-**) **1** (to insert) غَمَسَ (i; غَمْس) ‹*one's finger, a paintbrush*›; **~ the fish in the batter** اغْمِس السَمَكَ في الخَليطِ; **he ~ped his hand into the jar** أَدْخَلَ يَدَهُ في الجَرّةِ **2** (BrE) **to ~ one's headlights** خَفَضَ ضَوْءَ مَصابيحِهِ الأَماميّةِ

B *vi* (**-pp-**) **1** (to slope down) «land, road» انْحَدَرَ; **the fields ~ down to the river** تَنْحَدِرُ الحُقولُ نحو النَهْرِ **2** (to move downwards) «birds, planes» هَبَطَ (i-u; هُبوط) **3** (to decrease) «prices, demand» انْخَفَضَ ,تراجَعَ; **the temperature ~ped below freezing** انْخَفَضَت الحَرارةُ تحت دَرَجةِ التَجَمُّدِ

C *n* **1** (swim) غَطْسة; **to take a ~** غَطَسَ غَطْسةً **2** (in the ground) مُنْحَدَر صَغير **3** (in sales, demand, etc) تَراجُع قَصير **4** (Culin) غَموس **5** (also **sheep dip**) [غَسول للخِرْفانِ ضِدّ الطُفَيْليّات]

(Phrasal verb) **dip into**: **~ into [sth]** **1** (to read) قَرَأَ مُقْتَطفاتٍ من [شَيْءٍ] ‹*a book, magazine*› **2** (to make use of) اسْتَهْلَكَ [شَيْئًا] ‹*one's savings, reserves*›

diphtheria /dɪfˈθɪərɪə/ *n* خُناق ,دِفْتيريا

diphthong /ˈdɪfθɒŋ/ *n* [حَرْفا عِلّةٍ مُتَّصِلانِ]

diploid /ˈdɪplɔɪd/ *adj* ‹*nucleus*› ثُنائيّ الصِبْغيّة; ‹*organism*› ضِعْفانيّ

diploma /dɪˈpləʊmə/ *n* (دِبْلومات) دِبْلوم

diplomacy /dɪˈpləʊməsi/ *n* دِبْلوماسيّة

diplomat /ˈdɪpləmat/ *n* (مُوَظَّف) دِبْلوماسيّ

diplomatic /dɪpləˈmatɪk/ *adj* **1** (tactful) ‹*suggestion, teacher*› دِبْلوماسيّ **2** (Pol) ‹*relations, efforts*› دِبْلوماسيّ

diplomatic bag (BrE), **diplomatic pouch** (AmE) *n* حَقيبة دِبْلوماسيّة

diplomatic corps *n* هَيْئة دِبْلوماسيّة

diplomatic immunity *n* حَصانة دِبْلوماسيّة

dipsomania /ˌdɪpsəʊˈmeɪnɪə/ *n* إدْمان كُحوليّ

dipsomaniac /dɪpsəˈmeɪnɪak/ *n* مُدْمِن كُحولٍ

dipstick /ˈdɪpstɪk/ *n* عَصا قِياسِ مُسْتَوى الزَيْتِ

diptote /ˈdɪptəʊt/ *n* مَمْنوع من الصَرْفِ

diptotic /dɪp'tɒtɪk/ *adj* ‹*noun*› غَيْر مُنْصَرِفٍ, مَمْنوع من الصَرْفِ

dire /'dʌɪə/ *adj* **1** (very serious) ‹*consequences*› وَخيم; ‹*situation*› عَصيب, رَهيب; ‹*poverty*› مُدْقِع; **the system is in ~ need of reform** النِظامُ بِحاجةٍ ماسّةٍ للإصْلاحِ; **to be in ~ straits** كانَ في حالةٍ عَصيبةٍ **2** (ominous) ‹*warning*› شَديد; ‹*prediction*› سَيِّئ جِدًّا, (فُظَعاءُ) فَظيع **3** (BrE infml) (very bad) مُتَشائِم

direct /dʌɪ'rɛkt, dɪ'rɛkt/ **A** *adj* **1** (without intermediaries) ‹*result, link, contact*› مُباشِر; **keep the plants away from ~ sunlight** احْتَفِظْ بالنَباتاتِ بَعيداً عن ضَوْءِ الشَمْسِ المُباشِرِ; **to be a ~ descendant of sb** كانَ سَليلاً مُباشِراً لِشَخْصٍ; **a ~ quotation from ...** اقْتِباس مُباشِر من ... **2** (without detours) ‹*flight, route*› مُباشِر **3** (exact) ‹*comparison, contrast*› مُباشِر; **the ~ opposite** النَقيض المُباشِر **4** (straightforward) ‹*approach, answer*› مُباشِر; **to be ~ with sb** كانَ صَريحاً مع شَخْصٍ

B *adv* **1** (without intermediaries) ‹*to sell, deal*› بِشَكْلٍ مُباشَرةً **2** (without detours) ‹*to fly, go*› مُباشَرةً, بدونِ تَوَقُّفٍ; **the concert was broadcast ~ from Vienna** أُذيعَ الحَفْلُ مُباشَرةً من فِيينا

C *vt* **1** (to aim) ‹*a question, criticism, comment*› وَجَّهَ **2** (to focus) ‹*one's efforts, energy*› رَكَّزَ, وَجَّهَ; **to ~ sb's attention to sth** وَجَّهَ انْتِباهَ شَخْصٍ إلى شَيْءٍ **3** (in film, theatre) ‹*a film, play*› أَخْرَجَ **4** (to manage) ‹*operations, a project*› قادَ, أدارَ (u; قِيادة) **5** (fml) (to instruct) **to ~ sb to do sth** أَمَرَ شَخْصاً بِفِعْلِ شَيْءٍ **6** (fml) (to show the way to) أَرْشَدَ, دَلَّ (u; دَلالة); **can you ~ me to the station?** هل يُمْكِنُكَ أنْ تَدُلَّني على المَحَطّةِ؟

D *vi* (in film, theatre) قامَ بالإخْراجِ

direct action *n* ضَغْط مُباشِر

direct current *n* تَيّار مُباشِر \ مُسْتَمِرّ

direct debit *n* خَصْم مُباشِر

direct hit *n* إصابة \ ضَرْب \ قَصْف مُباشِر(ة)

direction /dʌɪ'rɛkʃ(ə)n, dɪ'rɛkʃ(ə)n/ **A** *n* **1** (course) اتِّجاه (اتِّجاهات); **sense of ~** إدْراك الاتِّجاهاتِ **2** (purpose) [u] تَوْجيه; **he lacks ~** يَنْقُصُهُ التَوْجيهُ **3** (supervision) [u] إدارة, إشْراف, قِيادة

B (**directions**) *n pl* **1** (for a route) إرْشادات **2** (for use) تَعْليمات \ إرْشادات, تَوْجيهات, تَعْليمات; **~s for use** تَوْجيهات \ إرْشادات الاسْتِخْدامِ

directive /dʌɪ'rɛktɪv, dɪ'rɛktɪv/ *n* تَوْجيه (تَوْجيهات)

directly /dʌɪ'rɛktli, dɪ'rɛktli/ *adv* **1** (straight) ‹*above, drive, report*› مُباشَرةً **2** (at once) حالاً, فَوْراً, مُباشَرةً **3** (very soon) حالاً, فَوْراً **4** (frankly) ‹*speak*› بِصَراحةٍ, بلا حَرَجٍ

direct mail *n* بَريد مُباشِر

direct marketing *n* تَسْويق مُباشِر

director /dʌɪ'rɛktə, dɪ'rɛktə/ *n* **1** (of a company, department, project) مُدير **2** (of a play, film) مُخْرِج; (of a choir) مُدَرِّب; (of an orchestra) قائِد (قادة, قوّاد)

directory /dʌɪ'rɛkt(ə)ri, dɪ'rɛkt(ə)ri/ *n* **1** (also **telephone directory**) (phone book) دَليل (أدِلّة, دَلائِلُ) **2** (index, yearbook) دَليل (أدِلّة, دَلائِلُ) **3** (computer file) دَليل (أدِلّة, دَلائِلُ)

directory enquiries (BrE), **directory assistance** (AmE) *n* دَليل الهاتِفِ

direct rule *n* حُكْم مُباشِر

direct speech *n* خِطاب مُباشِر

dirge /də:dʒ/ *n* أُغْنِيّة حَزينة \ حِداديّة

dirham /'dɪərəm/ *n* دِرْهَم (دَراهِمُ)

dirt /də:t/ *n* تُراب (أَتْرِبة)

dirt track *n* **1** (lane) طَريق تُرابيّ **2** (for racing) حَلْبة سِباقٍ رَمْليّة

dirty /'də:ti/ **A** *adj* (**dirtier, dirtiest**) **1** (not clean) ‹*clothes, hands, dishes*› قَذِر, مُتَّسِخ; **to get ~** اتَّسَخَ; **don't get your clothes ~** لا تُوَسِّخْ مَلابِسَكَ; **the work is arduous and ~** العَمَلُ مُجْهِدٌ وَقَذِرٌ **2** (not sterile) ‹*needle*› مُلَوَّث, غَيْر مُعَقَّم **3** (infml) (obscene) ‹*joke, story, mind*› قَذِر; **he said a ~ word** قالَ كَلِمةً بَذيئةً **4** (infml) (unscrupulous) ‹*fight, election, player*› قَذِر; **that was a ~ trick!** كانَتْ تِلْكَ خُدْعةً دَنيئةً!; **politics is a ~ business** السِياسةُ عَمَلٌ قَذِرٌ **5** ‹*colour*› باهِت

B *adv* (infml) **1** (dishonestly) **to play** *or* **fight ~** لَعِبَ \ قاتَلَ بِقَذارةٍ **2** (obscenely) **to talk ~** تَلَفَّظَ بِكَلامٍ فاحِشٍ

C *vt* (**dirties, dirtying, dirtied**) ‹*one's clothes, the floor*› وَسَّخَ

Idioms **to do sb's dirty work** قامَ بالأعْمالِ القَذِرةِ لِحِسابِ شَخْصٍ; **to give sb a dirty look** (infml) نَظَرَ شَزْراً إلى شَخْصٍ

dirty tricks *n pl* ألاعيب \ حِيَل \ أَعْمال قَذِرة

disability /dɪsəˈbɪlɪti/ *n* (*pl* **disabilities**) إعاقة, عَجْز

disability allowance *n* بَدَل إعاقةٍ \ عَجْزٍ

disability pension *n* مَعاش إعاقةٍ \ عَجْزٍ

disable /dɪsˈeɪb(ə)l/ *vt* **1▸** (to harm) أصابَ بالعَجْزِ ‹*a patient, victim*› **2▸** (to render useless) عَطَّلَ ‹*a machine, weapon*›

disabled /dɪsˈeɪb(ə)ld/ **A** (**the disabled** *n pl*) المُعاقونَ, المُعَوَّقونَ **B** *adj* ‹*people, children*› مُعاق, مُعَوَّق; **to be severely ~** كانَ شَديدَ الإعاقةِ

disabled access *n* مَدْخَل للمُعاقينَ

disabled toilet *n* حَمّام المُعاقينَ

disabuse /ˌdɪsəˈbjuːz/ *vt* (fml) حَرَّرَ من الوَهْمِ ‹*the public, readers*›

disadvantage /dɪsədˈvɑːntɪdʒ/ *n* عَيْب (عُيوب); **to be at a ~ to sb** عانى من نَقْصٍ مُقارَنةً بِشَخْصٍ آخَرَ; **to weigh up the advantages and the ~s of an offer** وَزَنَ مَزايا وَعُيوبَ عَرْضٍ; **her lack of a degree was a ~ to her** شَكَّلَ عَدَمُ حُصولِها على شَهادةٍ عائِقاً لَها

disadvantaged /dɪsədˈvɑːntɪdʒd/ *adj* ‹*community, minority*› مَحْروم, أَقَلّ حَظًّا

disadvantageous /ˌdɪsadv(ə)nˈteɪdʒəs/ *adj* ‹*terms, position*› مُضِرّ

disaffected /dɪsəˈfɛktɪd/ *adj* ‹*voters, members*› مُسْتاء

disagree /dɪsəˈgriː/ *vi* **1▸** (to fail to agree) كانَ غَيْرَ مُتَّفِقٍ; **I ~ with you** أُخالِفُكَ الرَّأْيَ **2▸** «facts, accounts» اخْتَلَفَ; **the government statistics ~ with the NGO's** تَخْتَلِفُ إحْصائيّاتُ الحُكومةِ عن إحْصائيّاتِ المُنَظَّمةِ غَيْرِ الحُكوميّةِ **3▸ to ~ with sb** «food» سَبَّبَ لِشَخْصٍ المَرَضَ

disagreeable /dɪsəˈgriːəb(ə)l/ *adj* ‹*smell*› كَريه; ‹*task*› مُزْعِج

disagreement /dɪsəˈgriːmənt/ *n* **1▸** (difference of opinion) خِلاف (خِلافات) **2▸** (quarrel) خِلاف (خِلافات), نِزاع (نِزاعات) **3▸** (disparity) اخْتِلاف (اخْتِلافات), تَعارُض

disallow /dɪsəˈlaʊ/ *vt* رَفَضَ (i-u; رَفْض), مَنَعَ (a; مَنْع) ‹*a claim, a goal*›

disappear /dɪsəˈpɪə/ *vi* **1▸** (to vanish) «figures, clouds» اخْتَفى **2▸** (to go away) «symptoms, worries» زالَ (a; زَوال)

disappearance /dɪsəˈpɪərəns/ *n* اخْتِفاء (اخْتِفاءات)

disappoint /dɪsəˈpɔɪnt/ *vt* (to let down) خَذَلَ (u; خَذْل) ‹*a candidate, one's family*›; (to upset) خَيَّبَ ‹*sb's hopes, a desire*›

disappointed /dɪsəˈpɔɪntɪd/ *adj* ‹*supporters, investors*› مَخْذول (مَخاذيلُ), خائِب الأَمَلِ, غَيْر سَعيدٍ; **to be ~** كانَ مَخْذولاً \ خائِبَ الأَمَلِ; **I am ~ with the results** لَسْتُ سَعيداً بالنَتائِجِ

disappointing /dɪsəˈpɔɪntɪŋ/ *adj* ‹*record, result*› مُخَيِّب للأَمَلِ

disappointment /dɪsəˈpɔɪntmənt/ *n* **1▸** [u] (feeling of sadness) خَيْبة أَمَلٍ **2▸** (letdown) خَيْبة أَمَلٍ

disapproval /dɪsəˈpruːv(ə)l/ *n* اسْتِنْكار (اسْتِنْكارات)

disapprove /dɪsəˈpruːv/ *vi* «parents, voters» اِسْتَنْكَرَ; **he ~s of smoking** يَسْتَنْكِرُ التَدْخينَ

disapproving /ˌdɪsəˈpruːvɪŋ/ *adj* ‹*tone, look*› مُسْتَنْكِر

disarm /dɪsˈɑːm/ **A** *vt* **1▸** (to take weapons from) نَزَعَ السِلاحَ عن ‹*a burglar, an opponent*› **2▸** (to charm) جَعَلَ يَلينُ ‹*your boss, critics*› **B** *vi* «soldiers, country» نَزَعَ السِلاحَ

disarmament /dɪsˈɑːməmənt/ *n* نَزْع السِلاحِ

disarming /dɪsˈɑːmɪŋ/ *adj* ‹*smile*› خَلّاب, ساحِر, فاتِن (فَواتِنُ); ‹*honesty*› يَجْعَلُهُ يَلينُ

disarray /dɪsəˈreɪ/ *n* فَوْضى (f), عَدَم النِظامِ \ التَرْتيبِ; **in ~** في حالةٍ من الفَوْضى \ عَدَمِ النِظامِ

disassociate /dɪsəˈsəʊʃieɪt/ *vt, vi* ▸**dissociate**

disaster /dɪˈzɑːstə/ *n* **1▸** (catastrophe) كارِثة (كَوارِثُ); **an environmental/financial ~** كارِثة بيئيّة \ ماليّة **2▸** (infml) (fiasco) فَشَل **3▸** (infml) (hopeless person) مَيْؤوس منْهُ; **she is a complete ~** هي مَيْؤوسٌ مِنْها تَماماً **4▸** (misfortune) مُصيبة (مَصائِبُ, مُصيبات); [u] **~ struck** وقَعَتْ مُصيبةٌ

disaster area *n* مِنْطَقة كَوارِثَ

disaster fund *n* صُنْدوق كَوارِثَ

disaster movie *n* فيلْم كارِثةٍ

disastrous /dɪˈzɑːstrəs/ *adj* **1▸** ‹*consequence, fire*› كارِثيّ, فادِح **2▸** ‹*defeat, event*› فادِح

disband /dɪsˈband/ **A** *vt* حَلَّ (u; حَلّ) ‹*an organization, an army*› **B** *vi* «organizations, armies» انْحَلَّ

disbelief /dɪsbɪˈliːf/ *n* تَكْذيب, عَدَم التَصْديقِ

disbelieve /dɪsbɪ'liːv/ *vt* (fml) لم يُصَدِّقْ ‹*a story, witness*›

disc (BrE), **disk** (AmE) /dɪsk/ *n* 1 (round, flat object) قُرْص (أقْراص) 2 (between vertebrae) غُضْروف (غَضاريفُ); **a slipped ~** غُضْروف مُنْزَلِق 3 (CD) قُرْص مُدَمَّج

discard /dɪ'skɑːd/ *vt* (to dispose of) أَلْقى, رَمى (i; رَمْي, رِماية) ‹*a possession, wrapper*›; (to reject) رَفَضَ (i-u; رَفْض) ‹*an idea, a plan*›; (to take off) خَلَعَ (a; خَلْع), نَزَعَ (i; نَزْع) ‹*a garment*›

discern /dɪ'sɜːn/ *vt* (fml) 1 (to detect) لاحَظَ ‹*a difference*›; اكْتَشَفَ ‹*the truth*› 2 (to see) مَيَّزَ ‹*an outline, a shape*›

discerning /dɪ'sɜːnɪŋ/ *adj* ‹*reader, public*› مُمَيِّز, بَصير (بُصَراءُ)

discharge A /dɪs'tʃɑːdʒ/ *vt* 1 (from hospital) سَمَحَ بالخُروجِ ‹*a patient*›; **to be ~d from hospital** سُمِحَ لَهُ بالخُروجِ من المُسْتَشْفى 2 (from armed forces) صَرَفَ من الخِدْمةِ ‹*a soldier, an officer*›; **to be ~d from the army/navy** صُرِفَ من الخِدْمةِ في الجَيْشِ \ القوّاتِ البَحْرِيّةِ 3 (to release from service) أعْفى ‹*a jury*›; (from liability) بَرَّأَ الذِمّةَ ‹*a bankrupt*› 4 (to emit) فَرَّغَ, صَرَّفَ ‹*sewage, waste*› 5 «wounds» أفْرَزَ ‹*pus*› 6 «batteries» أفْرَغَ, فَرَّغَ ‹*electricity*› 7 (fml) (to carry out) أنْجَزَ, أكْمَلَ ‹*a duty, responsibility*› 8 (fml) (to fire) أطْلَقَ النارَ من ‹*a gun*› 9 (to settle) سَدَّدَ ‹*a debt*›

B /dɪs'tʃɑːdʒ/ *vi* «batteries» فَرَغَ (a; فُروغ, فَراغ)

C /'dɪstʃɑːdʒ/ *n* 1 (release of a patient) سَماح بالخُروجِ; (of a soldier) تَسْريح, صَرْف من الخِدْمةِ; (of a defendant) إطْلاق سَراحٍ, إخْلاء سَبيلٍ 2 (of waste, gas) تَفْريغ, تَصْريف 3 (of pus, fluid) إفْراز 4 (of electricity) تَفْريغ 5 (of one's duty, responsibility) إنْجاز 6 (of a firearm) إطْلاق النارِ 7 (of a debt) سَداد

disciple /dɪ'sʌɪp(ə)l/ *n* 1 (Rel_Chr) حَواريّ 2 (follower) تِلْميذ (تَلاميذُ, تَلامِذة), تابِع (أتْباع)

disciplinary /'dɪsɪplɪn(ə)ri/ *adj* ‹*action, hearing*› تَأْديبيّ

discipline /'dɪsɪplɪn/ A *n* 1 (in behaviour) انْضِباط, تَأْديب 2 (subject) عِلْم (عُلوم)

B *vt* 1 (to control) أدَّبَ ‹*a pupil*› 2 (to punish) أوْقَعَ عُقوبةً تَأْديبيّةً على ‹*an employee, pupil*›

disciplined /'dɪsəplɪnd/ *adj* ‹*manner, behaviour*› مُنْضَبِط

disc jockey *n* دي جَيْ

disclaim /dɪs'kleɪm/ *vt* تَنَصَّلَ (من), أنْكَرَ ‹*involvement, responsibility*›; **she ~ed all knowledge of his whereabouts** أنْكَرَتْ أيّةَ مَعْرِفةٍ بِمَكانِهِ; **he ~ed any connection with him** أنْكَرَ أيّةَ صِلةٍ بِهِ

disclaimer /dɪs'kleɪmə/ *n* تَنَصُّل من المَسْؤوليّةِ

disclose /dɪs'kləʊz/ *vt* أفْشى, كَشَفَ (i; كَشْف) ‹*a name, information*›

disclosure /dɪs'kləʊʒə/ *n* إفْشاء

disco /'dɪskəʊ/ *n* (*pl* **discos**) (place) نادي رَقْصٍ, ديسْكو; (event) حَفْلة رَقْصٍ \ ديسْكو

discolour (BrE), **discolor** (AmE) /dɪs'kʌlə/ A *vt* غَيَّرَ اللَوْنَ ‹*the fabric, paper*›; **smoking ~s your teeth** يُغَيِّرُ التَدْخينُ لَوْنَ الأسْنانِ

B *vi* «fabric, paper» تَغَيَّرَ لَوْنُهُ

discomfort /dɪs'kʌmfət/ *n* 1 (physical) ألَم بَسيط \ خَفيف 2 (embarrassment) انْزِعاج, حَرَج

disconcert /ˌdɪskən'sɜːt/ *vt* أزْعَجَ ‹*viewers*›; أرْبَكَ ‹*newcomers*›

disconcerting /ˌdɪskən'sɜːtɪŋ/ *adj* ‹*experience, habit*› مُرْبِك, مُقْلِق

disconnect /dɪskə'nɛkt/ *vt* فَصَلَ (i; فَصْل) ‹*a phone, cable*›; **if you don't pay the gas bill we'll be ~ed** إذا لم تَدْفَعْ فاتورةَ الغازِ سَتُفْصَلُ عَنّا الخِدْمةُ

discontent /dɪskən'tɛnt/ *n* تَذَمُّر (تَذَمُّرات), اسْتِياء (اسْتِياءات)

discontented /dɪskən'tɛntɪd/ *adj* مُسْتاء, مُتَذَمِّر

discontinue /dɪskən'tɪnjuː/ *vt* أوْقَفَ ‹*a service, model, production*›; وَقَفَ (i; وَقْف, وُقوف) ‹*treatment*›; (Law) أوْقَفَ, وَقَّفَ ‹*a case, proceedings*›

discord /'dɪskɔːd/ *n* 1 (conflict) خِلاف (خِلافات) 2 (Mus) تَنافُر (تَنافُرات)

discotheque /'dɪskətɛk/ *n* (place) نادي رَقْصٍ, ديسْكو; (event) حَفْلة رَقْصٍ \ ديسْكو

discount A /'dɪskaʊnt/ *n* تَخْفيض (تَخْفيضات), خَصْم (خُصوم, أخْصام); **to give sb a ~** أعْطى شَخْصاً تَخْفيضاً \ خَصْماً; **to sell sth at a ~** باعَ شَيْئاً بِتَخْفيضٍ \ بِخَصْمٍ

B /dɪs'kaʊnt/ *vt* 1 (to reduce the price of) خَفَّضَ ‹*prices, goods*› 2 (to rule out) اسْتَبْعَدَ ‹*a possibility, report*›

discount store *n* مَحَلّ تَخْفيضاتٍ

discourage /dɪs'kʌrɪdʒ/ *vt* **1** (depress) ثَبَّطَ, أَحْبَطَ ‹*a student, teacher*› **2** (deter) حاوَلَ المَنْعَ \ الإعاقةَ ‹*a crime, investment*›; **to ~ sb from taking part** حاوَلَ مَنْعَ شَخْصٍ من الاشْتِراكِ

discouraging /dɪ'skʌrɪdʒɪŋ/ *adj* ‹*news, result*› مُحْبِط, مُثَبِّط

discourse /'dɪskɔːs/ *n* (fml) حَديث, خِطاب (خِطابات, أَخْطِبَة)

discourteous /dɪs'kɜːtjəs/ *adj* ‹*behaviour, person*› فَظّ (أَفْظاظ), غَيْر مُهَذَّبٍ

discover /dɪ'skʌvə/ *vt* اكْتَشَفَ ‹*the truth, treasure*›; **she ~ed that he had been lying to her** اكْتَشَفَتْ أنَّهُ كانَ يَكْذِبُ عَلَيْها

discoverer /dɪ'skʌv(ə)rə/ *n* **1** (of a process, phenomenon) مُكْتَشِف **2** (explorer) مُكْتَشِف

discovery /dɪ'skʌv(ə)ri/ *n* (*pl* **discoveries**) اكْتِشاف (اكْتِشافات)

discredit /dɪs'kredɪt/ *vt* شَوَّهَ السُّمْعَةَ ‹*an opponent, organization*›; أَفْقَدَ مِصْداقِيَّتَهُ ‹*a report, theory*›

discreet /dɪ'skriːt/ *adj* ‹*inquiry*› سِرِّيّ; ‹*secretary*› كَتوم (كُتُم), حَذِر

discreetly /dɪ'skriːtli/ *adv* ‹*to act, place*› بِتَكَتُّم, بِحَذَر

discrepancy /dɪs'krep(ə)nsi/ *n* (*pl* **discrepancies**) تَناقُض (تَناقُضات), تَفاوُت (تَفاوُتات)

discrete /dɪ'skriːt/ *adj* ‹*category, entity*› مُنْفَصِل, مُمَيَّز

discretion /dɪ'skreʃ(ə)n/ *n* **1** (tact) تَكَتُّم (تَكَتُّمات), حَذَر **2** (judgement) حُرِّيّة تَصَرُّفٍ \ اخْتِيارٍ

discretionary /dɪ'skreʃ(ə)n(ə)ri/ *adj* ‹*powers, grant*› تَقْديرِيّ

discriminate /dɪ'skrɪmɪneɪt/ *vi* **1** (act with bias) «laws, employers» مَيَّزَ, انْحازَ; **to ~ against sb** انْحازَ ضِدّ شَخْصٍ **2** (distinguish); **to ~ between right and wrong** مَيَّزَ بين الحَقِّ والباطِلِ

discriminating /dɪ'skrɪmɪneɪtɪŋ/ *adj* ‹*taste, reader*› ذَوّاق

discrimination /dɪˌskrɪmɪ'neɪʃ(ə)n/ *n* **1** (prejudice) تَمْييز (تَمْييزات) **2** (discernment) تَمْييز (تَمْييزات)

discriminatory /dɪ'skrɪmɪnɪˌt(ə)ri/ *adj* ‹*practices, treatment*› تَمْييزِيّ

discus /'dɪskəs/ *n* (*pl* **discuses**) قُرْص (أَقْراص)

discuss /dɪ'skʌs/ *vt* ناقَشَ ‹*an issue, a topic*›

discussion /dɪ'skʌʃ(ə)n/ *n* نِقاش (نقاشات), مُناقَشة

disdain /dɪs'deɪn/ **A** *n* ازْدِراء, احْتِقار **B** *vt* ازْدَرى ‹*an offer, idea*›

disdainful /dɪs'deɪnfʊl/ *adj* ‹*look, attitude*› مُزْدَرٍ

disease /dɪ'ziːz/ *n* مَرَض (أَمْراض), داء (أَدْواء)

diseased /dɪ'ziːzd/ *adj* ‹*tissue, cell, animal, plant*› مَريض (مَرْضى, مَراضى)

disembark /dɪsɪm'bɑːk/ **A** *vt* نَزَّلَ, أَنْزَلَ ‹*the cargo, passengers*› **B** *vi* «passengers, crew» نَزَلَ (i; نُزول)

disembodied /dɪsɪm'bɒdid/ *adj* ‹*head, spirit*› مُنْفَصِل عن \ دونَ جَسَدٍ; ‹*voice, sound*› بِلا مَصْدَرٍ \ جَسَدٍ

disembowel /ˌdɪsɪm'baʊəl/ *vt* (**-ll-** BrE, **-l-** AmE) نَزَعَ \ أَخْرَجَ الأَحْشاءَ من ‹*one's victim, prey*›

disenchanted /dɪsɪn'tʃɑːntɪd/ *adj* ‹*voter, fan*› خائِب الظَّنِّ \ الأَمَلِ; **to be ~ with sth/sb** خابَ أَمَلُهُ في شَيْءٍ \ شَخْصٍ

disenfranchise /ˌdɪsɪn'frantʃʌɪz/ *vt* **to ~ sb** حَرَمَ شَخْصاً من التَّصْويتِ

disengage /ˌdɪsɪn'geɪdʒ/ *vt* حَرَّرَ ‹*one's arm*›; رَفَعَ قَدَمَهُ عن ‹*the clutch*›

disentangle /dɪsɪn'taŋg(ə)l/ *vt* **1** (to unravel) فَكَّ (u; فَكّ) ‹*a knot, hair*› **2** (to free) حَرَّرَ ‹*oneself, one's fingers*›

disfavour (BrE), **disfavor** (AmE) /dɪs'feɪvə/ *n* (fml) ازْدِراء, اسْتِياء

disfigure /dɪs'fɪgə/ *vt* شَوَّهَ ‹*a face, town*›

disgrace /dɪs'greɪs/ **A** *n* عار, خِزْي; **to be in ~** كانَ في حالَةٍ من الخِزْيِ \ العارِ **B** *vt* جَلَبَ العارَ إلى \ سَبَّبَ ‹*a team, school*›

disgraceful /dɪs'greɪsfʊl/ *adj* ‹*conduct, neglect*› مُخْزٍ, فاضِح

disgruntled /dɪs'grʌntəld/ *adj* ‹*employee, customer*› مُتَذَمِّر, ساخِط

disguise /dɪs'gʌɪz/ **A** *vt* **1** (change the appearance) نَكَّرَ ‹*an identity*›; غَيَّرَ ‹*a voice*› **2** (conceal) أَخْفى, سَتَرَ (i-u; سَتْر) ‹*contempt, truth*› **B** *n* تَنَكُّر (تَنَكُّرات); **in ~** مُتَنَكِّر

disgust /dɪs'gʌst/ **A** *n* تَقَزُّز, اشْمِئْزاز, قَرَف **B** *vt* قَرَّفَ, نَفَّرَ

disgusting /dɪs'gʌstɪŋ/ *adj* مُثير للاشمِئزازِ, مُقرِف, مُقزِّز

dish /dɪʃ/ *n* **1** (bowl) طَبَق (أطْباق), صَحْن (صُحون); **to do/wash the ~es** غَسَلَ الأطْباقَ \ الصُحونَ **2** (food) طَبَق (أطْباق) **3** (also **satellite dish**) دِش (دِشات), صَحْن هَوائيّ, طَبَق القَمَرِ الصِناعيّ

Phrasal verbs **dish out**: **1** ~ **out** [**sth**] غَرَفَ [شَيْئاً] ‹*pasta, a dessert*› **2** ~ **out** [**sth**] أعْطى \ قَدَّمَ [شَيْئاً] ‹*advice*›; أغْدَقَ [شَيْئاً] ‹*money*›

• **dish up**: ~ **up** [**sth**] قَدَّمَ [شَيْئاً] ‹*a meal, dinner*›

dishcloth /'dɪʃklɒθ/ *n* (for washing) فوطة غَسيلِ أطْباقٍ; (for drying) فوطة تَنْشيفٍ \ مَطْبَخٍ

disheartening /dɪs'hɑ:tnɪŋ/ *adj* ‹*experience, results*› مُثَبِّط للعَزيمةِ

dishevelled (BrE), **disheveled** (AmE) /dɪ'ʃevəld/ *adj* ‹*hair*› أشْعَث (دِيت); ‹*clothes, appearance*› غَيْر مُرَتَّب

dishonest /dɪs'ɒnɪst/ *adj* ‹*businessman, answer, tactics*› خادِع, غَيْر أمينٍ

dishonesty /dɪs'ɒnɪsti/ *n* عَدَم أمانةٍ, خِداع

dishonour (BrE), **dishonor** (AmE) /dɪs'ɒnə/ *n* عار, خِزْي

dishonourable (BrE), **dishonorable** (AmE) /dɪs'ɒn(ə)rəb(ə)l/ *adj* ‹*conduct*› شائِن, جالِب للعارِ, مُخْزٍ; ‹*intentions*› غَيْر شَريفٍ

dishrag /'dɪʃrag/ *n* (AmE) ▸ **dishcloth**

dish towel *n* فوطة مَطْبَخٍ

dishwasher /'dɪʃwɒʃə/ *n* غَسّالة أطْباقٍ \ صُحونٍ

dishwater /'dɪʃwɔ:tə/ *n* ماء غَسيلِ الأطْباقِ \ الصُحونِ

disillusion /ˌdɪsɪ'lju:ʒ(ə)n/ **A** *n* خَيْبة أمَلٍ **B** *vt* خَيَّبَ الأمَلَ ‹*supporters, young people*›

disillusioned /dɪsɪ'lu:ʒ(ə)nd/ *adj* ‹*voter, fan*› خائِب الأمَلِ

disillusionment /dɪsɪ'lu:ʒ(ə)nmənt/ *n* خَيْبة الأمَلِ

disinfect /dɪsɪn'fekt/ *vt* عَقَّمَ, طَهَّرَ ‹*a wound, ward*›

disinfectant /dɪsɪn'fekt(ə)nt/ *n* مُطَهِّر

disinformation /ˌdɪsɪnfə'meɪʃ(ə)n/ *n* مَعْلومات زائِفة

disingenuous /ˌdɪsɪn'dʒenjʊəs/ *adj* ‹*explanation, proposal*› مُراوِغ, مُخادِع

disinherit /dɪsɪn'herɪt/ *vt* حَرَمَ من الميراثِ ‹*a son, an heir*›

disintegrate /dɪs'ɪntɪgreɪt/ *vi* (as the result of impact) تَفَكَّكَ, تَحَطَّمَ; (as the result of decay) تَحَلَّلَ, تَفَتَّتَ

disintegration /dɪsˌɪntɪ'greɪʃ(ə)n/ *n* (of a family, society) تَفَتُّت, تَفَكُّك

disinterested /dɪs'ɪntərɪstɪd/ *adj* (impartial) ‹*observer, position*› مُحايِد; (uninterested) ‹*manner, reply*› غَيْر مُهْتَمٍّ

disjointed /dɪs'dʒɔɪntɪd/ *adj* ‹*conversation, speech*› غَيْر مُفَكَّك, مُتَرابِطٍ

disk /dɪsk/ *n* **1** (Comput) قُرْص (أقْراص) **2** (AmE) ▸ **disc**

disk drive, disk drive unit *n* مُحَرِّك أقْراص

diskette /dɪ'sket/ *n* قُرْص مَرِن \ لَيِّن

dislike /dɪs'laɪk/ **A** *vt* نَفَرَ (i-u; مِن نَفْر), كَرِهَ (a; كُرْه, كَراهيّة) ‹*an idea, a fact*›; **I ~ dogs** لا أُحِبُّ الكِلابَ; **he ~s wearing a tie** لا يُحِبُّ ارتداءَ رِباطِ العُنُقِ **B** *n* (emotion) كَراهِية, عَدَم مَحَبّةٍ, نُفور; (sth disliked) [شَيْء] غَيْر مَحْبوبٍ; **I have a strong ~ of dogs** لا أُحِبُّ الكِلابَ; **to take a ~ to sb** شَعَرَ بالنُفورِ من شَخْصٍ على الإطْلاقِ; **I know all his likes and ~s** أعْرِفُ كُلَّ ما يُحِبُّهُ وما لا يُحِبُّهُ

dislocate /'dɪsləkeɪt/ *vt* خَلَعَ (a; خَلْع) ‹*a hip, shoulder*›; **to ~ one's shoulder** خَلَعَ كِتْفَهُ

dislocation /ˌdɪsləʊ'keɪʃ(ə)n/ *n* **1** (of a hip, knee) خَلْع **2** (fml) (disruption) تَعْطيل

dislodge /dɪs'lɒdʒ/ *vt* حَرَّكَ من مَوْضِعِهِ ‹*a rock, an obstacle*›

disloyal /dɪs'lɔɪəl/ *adj* ‹*act, remark*› خائِن (خَوّان), غَيْر مُخْلِصٍ

dismal /'dɪzm(ə)l/ *adj* (gloomy) ‹*weather*› كَئيب; ‹*sight*› تَعِس; (infml) (very bad) ‹*failure, attempt*› [رَديء جِدّاً]

dismantle /dɪs'mant(ə)l/ *vt* (to take apart) فَكَّكَ ‹*a construction, settlement*›; (to phase out) حَلَّ (u; حَلّ) ‹*an organization, a service*›

dismay /dɪs'meɪ/ **A** *n* دَهْشة, هَلَع, فَزَع; **they looked at him in** *or* **with ~** نَظَروا إليه بِدَهْشةٍ; **much to my ~** [ما فَزَعَني \ دَهَشَني] **B** *vt* خَيَّبَ الأمَلَ ‹*a supporter, fan*›

dismember /dɪs'membə/ *vt* **1** مَزَّقَ, قَطَّعَ \ بَتَرَ الأطْرافَ ‹*a body, prey*› **2** قَسَّمَ ‹*a country, an organization*›

dismiss /dɪs'mɪs/ *vt* **1** (to send away) صَرَفَ ‹*a class, witness*› **2** (to fire) طَرَدَ (u; طَرْد), أقالَ ‹*an employee, a minister*›

[3] (to disregard) صَرَفَ النَظَرَ ,نَبَذَ (i; نَبْذ) ‹*a thought, worries*›

[4] (to reject) رَدَّ (u; رَدّ) ‹*the charges, an appeal*›

dismissal /dɪsˈmɪs(ə)l/ *n* [1] (of an employee, minister) طَرْد, نَبْذ ,إبْعاد ,إقالة; (sending away) صَرْف [2] (of a theory, request) رَدّ (رُدود) (أنْباذ) [3] (of an appeal, claim)

dismissive /dɪsˈmɪsɪv/ *adj* ‹*gesture, attitude*› غَيْرُ مُبالٍ \ مُكْتَرِثٍ

dismount /dɪsˈmaʊnt/ *vi* نَزَلَ (i; نُزول) ,تَرَجَّلَ (تَرَجُّل); **she ~ed from her horse/bike** نَزَلَتْ من على حِصانها \ دَرّاجَتِها

disobedience /dɪsəˈbiːdiəns/ *n* عَدَم الطاعة ,عِصْيان

disobedient /dɪsəˈbiːdɪənt/ *adj* ‹*child, behaviour*› عاصٍ (عُصاة), عاقّ ,غَيْر مُطيع

disobey /dɪsəˈbeɪ/ [A] *vt* عَصى (i; عِصْيان) ‹*a parent, teacher*›; خالَفَ ,قاوَمَ ‹*an order, a command*›

[B] *vi* «children, pupils» خَرَجَ على الطاعةِ

disorder /dɪsˈɔːdə/ *n* [1] (disturbances) اضْطِراب (اضْطِرابات), شَغَب [2] (malfunction, disease) خَلَل (خِلال) ,اضْطِراب (اضْطِرابات) [3] (confusion) فَوْضى (f)

disorderly /dɪsˈɔːd(ə)li/ *adj* [1] (untidy) ‹*room*› غَيْر ,فَوْضَوِيّ مُنَظَّم ‹*queue*›; فَوْضَويّ ‹*person*› (disorganized) [2] غَيْر مُنَظَّمٍ [3] (unruly) ‹*crowd, meeting, behaviour*› فَوْضَويّ

disorganized /dɪsˈɔːɡ(ə)nʌɪzd/ *adj* ‹*campaign, plan*› غَيْر مُنَظَّمٍ

disorient /dɪsˈɔːrɪent/ *vt* ▸ **disorientate**

disorientate /dɪsˈɔːrɪenteɪt/ *vt* (to disorient) أَضَلَّ ,أَرْبَكَ ‹*a walker, driver*›; (to confuse) حَيَّرَ ‹*a viewer, patient*›

disown /dɪsˈəʊn/ *vt* تَبَرَّأَ (من) ‹*a child, article*›

disparaging /dɪˈsparɪdʒɪŋ/ *adj* ‹*remark, tone*› مُهين ,مُحْتَقِر

disparate /ˈdɪsp(ə)rət/ *adj* ‹*group, elements*› مُتَباين ,مُتَفاوِت

disparity /dɪˈsparɪti/ *n* (*pl* **disparities**) تَفاوُت (تَفاوُتات), تَبايُن (تَبايُنات)

dispassionate /dɪsˈpaʃ(ə)nət/ *adj* ‹*stance, comment*› مُتَجَرِّد, نَزيه (نُزَهاءُ ,نِزاه)

dispatch /dɪˈspatʃ/ [A] *vt* [1] (to send) أَوْفَدَ ‹*an envoy*›; أَرْسَلَ ‹*a letter*› [2] (fml) (to carry out) أَنْجَزَ بِسُرْعةٍ ‹*a task, duty*›; (to kill) قَتَلَ (u; قَتْل) ‹*a traitor, an enemy*›; (infml) (to consume) تَناوَلَ بِسُرْعةٍ ‹*a drink, meal*›

[B] *n* [1] (official report) تَقْرير رَسْميّ; (journalistic report) تَقْرير صُحُفيّ [2] (sending) إرْسال (إرْسالات)

dispel /dɪˈspɛl/ *vt* (**-ll-** BrE, **-l-** AmE) أَزالَ ,بَدَّدَ ‹*a doubt, fear*›

dispensary /dɪˈspens(ə)ri/ *n* (*pl* **dispensaries**) (BrE) (in a hospital) صَيْدَليّة; (in a school) مُسْتَوْصَف (مُسْتَوْصَفات)

dispensation /dɪspɛnˈseɪʃ(ə)n/ *n* [1] (exemption) إعْفاء (إعْفاءات) [2] (of justice) إقامة; (of drugs) تَوْزيع (تَوْزيعات); (of funds, aid) إمْداد (إمْدادات)

dispense /dɪˈspɛns/ *vt* [1] وَزَّعَ ‹*coffee, money*› [2] صَرَفَ (i; صَرْف) ‹*a medicine, prescription*› [3] وَضَعَ مَوْضِعَ التَنْفيذِ ‹*a law*›; أَقامَ ‹*justice*›

(Phrasal verb) **dispense with** [1] (to manage without) اسْتَغْنى (عن) ‹*a service, pleasantries*› [2] (to get rid of) تَخَلَّصَ (من) ‹*a policy, regulation*›

dispenser /dɪˈspɛnsə/ *n* مُوَزِّع آليّ; **a cash ~** صَرّاف آليّ; **a soap ~** مُوَزِّع آليّ للصابون

dispersal /dɪˈspəːs(ə)l/ *n* تَشْتيت ,تَبْديد

disperse /dɪˈspəːs/ [A] *vt* نَثَرَ (i-u; نَثْر ,نِثار) ‹*the seeds, leaflets*›; شَتَّتَ ‹*a crowd, gang*›; أَزالَ ‹*the gas, fumes*›

[B] *vi* [1] «crowds, spectators» تَفَرَّقَ ,تَشَتَّتَ [2] «fumes, pollution» تَبَدَّدَ

dispirited /dɪˈspɪrɪtɪd/ *adj* ‹*troops, voice*› كَئيب ,مُثَبَّط الهِمّةِ

displace /dɪsˈpleɪs/ *vt* [1] (to replace) حَلَّ المَحَلَّ ‹*a competitor, leader*› [2] (to expel) هَجَّرَ ,رَحَّلَ ‹*refugees, a family*› [3] (Naut, Phys) (to move) أَزاحَ ‹*tonnes, a volume*›

displaced person /ˌdɪspleɪst ˈpəːs(ə)n/ *n* مُهَجَّر ,مُرَحَّل

displacement /dɪsˈpleɪsmənt/ *n* تَرْحيل (تَراحيلُ), تَهْجير

display /dɪˈspleɪ/ [A] *vt* [1] (to put on show) عَرَضَ (i; عَرْض) ‹*goods for sale, a sign, exhibits*›; **all the items ~ed are for sale** الأشياءُ المَعْروضةُ كُلُّها للبَيْعِ [2] (on screen) عَرَضَ (i; عَرْض) ‹*information, images*› [3] (to reveal) أَبْدى ,أَظْهَرَ ‹*one's skill, talent, knowledge*›; **he really ~ed his ignorance by his question** أَظْهَرَ جَهْلَهُ حَقًّا بِهَذا السُؤالِ [4] (to flaunt) اسْتَعْرَضَ ‹*one's wealth*›

[B] *vi* «male bird, peacock» اسْتَعْرَضَ

[C] *n* [1] (of objects) مَعْروضات; **to be on ~** عُرِضَ; **to put sth on ~** عَرَضَ شَيْئاً [2] (show) عَرْض (عُروض); **a fireworks ~** عَرْض للألْعابِ الناريّةِ [3] (demonstration) إظْهار; **in a rare**

~ **of emotion** عَرْض في لَحْظَةِ صِدْقٍ نادِرةٍ **4** (on screen) **5** (Zool) (اسْتِعْراضات) اسْتِعْراض

display case *n* (also **display cabinet**) خزانة عَرْضٍ

displease /dɪsˈpliːz/ **A** *vt* ضايَقَ, أثارَ الاسْتِياءَ **B** (**displeased**) *adj* مُسْتاء; **to be ~d with sth/sb** كانَ مُسْتاءاً من شَيْءٍ \ شَخْصٍ

displeased /dɪsˈpliːzd/ *adj* ‹customer, boss› مُتَضايِق, مُسْتاء

displeasure /dɪsˈplɛʒə/ *n* تَضايُق, اسْتِياء

disposable /dɪˈspəʊzəb(ə)l/ *adj* **1** (throwaway) ‹cup, razor› [صالِح للاسْتِعْمالِ مَرّةً واحِدةً] **2** (available) ‹income, assets› مُتاح

disposal /dɪˈspəʊz(ə)l/ *n* **1** (removal, riddance) تَخَلُّص (تَخَلُّصات); **the problem of waste ~** مُشْكِلة التَخَلُّصِ من النُفايات; **arrangements were made for the ~ of the body** اُتُّخِذَتْ إجْراءاتٌ للتَخَلُّصِ من الجُثّةِ **2** (sale) بَيْع (بُيوعات ,بُيوع) **3** (power to use) حَقّ التَصَرُّفِ; **to have sth at his ~** كانَ عِنْدَهُ شَيْءٌ تحت تَصَرُّفِهِ; **to be at sb's ~** كانَ رَهْنَ إشارةِ شَخْصٍ

dispose of /dɪˈspəʊz/ *vt* **to ~ sth** (to get rid of) تَخَلَّصَ من شَيْءٍ ‹waste, a body›; (to deal with speedily) حَسَمَ \ سَوّى شَيْئاً ‹a problem, question›

disposition /dɪspəˈzɪʃ(ə)n/ *n* **1** (temperament) مِزاج (أمْزِجة) **2** (inclination) مَيْل (مُيول ,أمْيال), رَغْبة (رَغَبات); **she has a ~ to learn** عِنْدَها رَغْبةٌ للتَعَلُّمِ **3** (arrangement) تَرْتيب (تَرْتيبات)

dispossess /dɪspəˈzɛs/ *vt* **to ~ sb of their land** نَزَعَ الأَرْضَ من حِيازةِ شَخْصٍ

disproportionate /ˌdɪsprəˈpɔːʃ(ə)nət/ *adj* ‹number, size› غَيْر مُتَكافِئ

disprove /dɪsˈpruːv/ *vt* دَحَضَ (a; دَحْض ,دُحوض) ‹a belief, claim›

dispute /dɪˈspjuːt/ **A** *n* **1** [u] (controversy, clash) خِلاف, جِدال **2** (quarrel) نِزاع (نِزاعات), خُصومة **3** (conflict) مُنازَعة **B** *vt* **1** (to question the truth of) اعْتَرَضَ (على) ‹a claim, decision› **2** (to fight for) تَنازَعَ (على) ‹a border, territory›

disqualify /dɪsˈkwɒlɪfʌɪ/ *vt* (**disqualifies, disqualifying, disqualified**) **1** (to make ineligible) اسْتَبْعَدَ ‹a candidate, an applicant›; **your age disqualifies you from this post** لا يُؤَهِّلُكَ سِنُّكَ لِهَذا المَنْصِبِ **2** (to eliminate) أَبْعَدَ, اسْتَبْعَدَ, أَقْصى ‹a competitor, runner›

disquiet /dɪsˈkwʌɪət/ *n* (fml) جَزَع, هَلَع

disregard /dɪsrɪˈɡɑːd/ **A** *vt* تَجاهَلَ ‹evidence, sb's feelings, the law, instructions› **B** *n* تَجاهُل, لا مُبالاة; **he showed a complete ~ for the safety of others** أظْهَرَ لا مُبالاةً تامّةً إزاءَ سَلامةِ الآخَرينَ

disrepair /dɪsrɪˈpɛː/ *n* حاجة إلى تَرْميم; **the building had fallen into ~** أَصْبَحَ المَبْنى بِحاجةٍ إلى التَرْميم

disreputable /dɪsˈrɛpjʊtəb(ə)l/ *adj* ‹character, conduct› مُشين, سَيِّئ السُمْعةِ; ‹area› (not respectable) مُخْزٍ

disrepute /ˌdɪsrɪˈpjuːt/ *n* خِزْي; **to bring sth into ~** أساءَ لِسُمْعةِ شَيْءٍ

disrespect /dɪsrɪˈspɛkt/ *n* قِلّة احْتِرام; **to show ~ to sb/for sth** أظْهَرَ قِلّةَ احْتِرامٍ لِشَخْصٍ \ لِشَيْءٍ

disrespectful /dɪsrɪˈspɛktfʊl/ *adj* ‹person, behaviour, attitude› قَليل الاحْتِرامِ

disrupt /dɪsˈrʌpt/ *vt* أَحْدَثَ اضْطِراباً في ‹sb's life, routine›; قَطَعَ (a; قَطْع) ‹a service, supply›; عَطَّلَ ‹traffic, plans›; قاطَعَ ‹a meeting›

disruption /dɪsˈrʌpʃ(ə)n/ *n* (to sb's life) اضْطِراب (اضْطِرابات); (to a service, supply) انْقِطاع; (to traffic) تَعْطيل

disruptive /dɪsˈrʌptɪv/ *adj* ‹behaviour, effect› مُخِلّ بالنِظامِ; ‹pupil› مُشَوِّش

dissatisfaction /dɪssatɪsˈfakʃ(ə)n/ *n* اسْتِياء, عَدَم رِضًى (اسْتِياءات)

dissatisfied /dɪsˈsatɪsfʌɪd/ *adj* ‹customers, voters› غَيْر راضٍ, مُسْتاء

dissect /dɪˈsɛkt/ *vt* شَرَّحَ ‹a body, an animal›

disseminate /dɪˈsɛmɪneɪt/ *vt* نَشَرَ (u; نَشْر) ‹information, knowledge›

dissemination /dɪˌsɛmɪˈneɪʃ(ə)n/ *n* نَشْر; **the ~ of information** نَشْر المَعْلوماتِ

dissent /dɪˈsɛnt/ **A** *n* مُعارَضة **B** *vi* «scientists, members» خَرَجَ (u; خُروج ;عن ,على), خالَفَ; **to ~ from a theory** خَرَجَ على نَظَرِيّةٍ **C** (**dissenting**) *adj* ‹view, opinion› مُعارِض, مُخالِف

dissertation /ˌdɪsəˈteɪʃ(ə)n/ *n* (BrE) أُطْروحة

disservice /dɪsˈsɜːvɪs/ *n* (fml); **to do a ~ to sth/sb** أَلْحَقَ الأَذى بِشَيْءٍ \ بِشَخْصٍ

dissident /ˈdɪsɪd(ə)nt/ *n, adj* مُنْشَقّ

dissimilar /dɪˈsɪmɪlə/ *adj* ‹*backgrounds, circumstances*› غَيْر مُتَبايِن, مُتَشابِهٍ

dissipate /ˈdɪsɪpeɪt/ *vt* **1** (to dispel) بَدَّدَ ‹*tension, fear*› **2** بَدَّدَ ‹*energy, heat*› **3** (to waste) بَذَّرَ ‹*resources, one's fortune*›

dissociate /dɪˈsəʊʃɪeɪt/ *vt* **1** (to separate) فَصَلَ (i; فَصْل) ‹*a concept, an idea*› **2** (to distance) **to ~ oneself from sth/sb** نَأى بِنَفْسِهِ عن شَيْءٍ \ شَخْصٍ

dissolute /ˈdɪsəluːt/ *adj* ‹*life, behaviour*› فاجِر, (مَواجِنُ) ماجِن (فَجَرة, فُجّار)

dissolution /ˌdɪsəˈluːʃ(ə)n/ *n* **1** (of Parliament) حَلّ (حُلول); (of a partnership) تَصْفِية; (of marriage) فَسْخ **2** (of chemicals) تَذْويب

dissolve /dɪˈzɒlv/ **A** *vt* **1** أَذابَ, ذَوَّبَ ‹*a tablet, stock cube, grease*› **2** فَسَخَ (a; فَسْخ) ‹*a partnership*›; حَلَّ (u; حَلّ) ‹*parliament*›; فَضَّ (u; فَضّ) ‹*assembly*›
B *vi* «tablets, powder» ذاب, انْحَلَّ (u; ذَوَبان)

dissuade /dɪˈsweɪd/ *vt* أَقْنَعَ بالعُدول (عن), ثَنى (i; ثَنْي; عن) ‹*a person*›; **to ~ sb from doing sth** أَقْنَعَ شَخْصاً بالعُدولِ عن فِعْلِ شَيْءٍ

distance /ˈdɪst(ə)ns/ **A** *n* **1** (between two points) مَسافة; **at a ~ of 50 metres** على بُعْدِ 50 مِتْراً; **it's a short ~ away** هو على بُعْدِ مَسافةٍ قَصيرةٍ من هُنا; **we parked some ~ from the house** رَكَنّا سَيّارَتَنا على مَسافةٍ بَعيدةٍ من المَنْزِلِ; **at/from a safe ~** على \ من مَسافةٍ آمِنةٍ; **it's within walking ~** هو على بُعْدِ بِضْعِ دَقائِقَ مَشْياً \ سَيْراً على الأَقْدامِ; **to keep sb at a ~** وَضَعَ مَسافةً بَيْنَهُ وَبَيْنَ شَخْصٍ; **to keep one's ~** (to keep away) بَقِيَ بَعيداً; (to remain aloof) نَأى بِنَفْسِه **2** (far-off-point) مَسافة بَعيدة; **from a ~** من مَسافةٍ بَعيدةٍ; **in the ~** من بَعيدٍ
B *vt* (**distances, distancing, distanced**) أَبْعَدَ ‹*an organization, an audience*›
C *v refl* **to ~ oneself from sth/sb** (to dissociate oneself) نَأى بِنَفْسِهِ عن شَيْءٍ \ شَخْصٍ

Idiom **to go the full distance** أَكْمَلَ المِشْوارَ

distance learning *n* تَعَلُّم عن بُعْدٍ

distance race *n* سِباق المَسافاتِ الطَويلةِ

distant /ˈdɪst(ə)nt/ *adj* **1** (remote) ‹*land, galaxy*› بَعيد, ناءٍ; **the ~ sound of traffic** صَوْت حَرَكةِ المُرورِ البَعيد; **it's 40 kilometres ~** هو على بُعْدِ 40 كيلومِتْراً; **in the not too ~ future** في المُسْتَقْبَلِ غَيْرِ البَعيدِ; **in the ~ past** في الماضي البَعيدِ **2** (not close) ‹*relative, cousin*› [تَرْبِطُهُ صِلةُ قَرابةٍ غَيْرُ مُباشِرةٍ] **3** (faint) ‹*memory, possibility*› بَعيد **4** (unemotional) ‹*manner, person*› مُتَحَفِّظ; **he was ~, but polite** كانَ مُتَحَفِّظاً, وَلَكِنَّهُ كانَ مُهَذَّباً

distantly /ˈdɪst(ə)ntli/ *adv* **1** (remotely) ‹*to hear, glimpse*› من بَعيدٍ **2** ‹*to recall*› بِصورةٍ غَيْرِ مُحَدَّدةٍ \ دَقيقةٍ; **to be ~ related** [رَبَطَتْ بَيْنَهُمْ صِلةُ قَرابةٍ بَعيدةٍ] **3** (distractedly) ‹*to nod, smile*› لاهِياً, بِدونِ تَرْكيزٍ

distaste /dɪsˈteɪst/ *n* نُفور, كُرْه

distasteful /dɪsˈteɪstfʊl/ *adj* **1** (unpleasant) ‹*odour*› كَريه; ‹*task, subject*› مُزْعِج **2** (in bad taste) ‹*joke, remark*› غَيْر لائِقٍ, مُبْتَذَل

distend /dɪˈstɛnd/ **A** *vt* نَفَخَ (a; نَفْخ) ‹*the stomach, bladder*›
B *vi* «cheeks, veins» انْتَفَخَ

distil (BrE), **distill** (AmE) /dɪˈstɪl/ **A** *vt* (**-ll-**) (to purify) قَطَّرَ, اسْتَقْطَرَ ‹*a liquid, spirits*›; **~led water** ماء مُقَطَّر; **to ~ brandy from wine** قَطَّرَ شَرابَ البْرانْدي من النَبيذِ
B *vi* (**-ll-**) «liquids, alcohol» تَقَطَّرَ

distillation /ˌdɪstɪˈleɪʃ(ə)n/ *n* **1** (process) تَقْطير **2** (product) قُطارة **3** (essence) جَوْهَر (جَواهِرُ), خُلاصة

distillery /dɪˈstɪləri/ *n* (*pl* **distilleries**) مَعْمَل تَقْطيرٍ

distinct /dɪˈstɪŋkt/ *adj* **1** (different) ‹*group, type*› مُتَمَيِّز, مُخْتَلِف; **travellers, as ~ from tourists, tend to be more independent** يَتَمَيَّزُ المُسافِرونَ عن السُيّاحِ بِمَيْلِهِمْ إلى أنْ يَكونوا أَكْثَرَ اسْتِقْلالِيّةً **2** (clear) ‹*image, outline*› واضِح, جَلِيّ **3** (definite) ‹*possibility, advantage*› مُؤَكَّد; **I got the ~ impression he was lying** خَلَّفَ لَدَيَّ انْطِباعاً مُؤَكَّداً أَنَّهُ كانَ يَكْذِبُ

distinction /dɪˈstɪŋkʃ(ə)n/ *n* **1** (difference) تَمْييز (تَمْييزات), فَرْق (فُروق); **to make** *or* **draw a ~ between sth and sth**

لا أرى الفَرْقَ ~ **I don't see the**; قامَ بالتَمْييزِ بين شَيْءٍ وَشَيْءٍ **2** (merit, excellence) تَمَيُّز; **an artist of great ~** فَنّان يَتَّصِفُ بالتَمَيُّزِ **3** (specific honour) وِسام (أَوْسِمة) **4** (Educ) امْتِياز

distinctive /dɪ'stɪŋktɪv/ *adj* ‹*feature, voice*› مُمَيِّز

distinctly /dɪ'stɪŋktli/ *adv* **1** (clearly) ‹*to hear, speak*› بِوُضوحٍ; ‹*to remember*› دون رَيْبٍ **2** (decidedly) ‹*different, uncomfortable*› تماماً, قَطْعاً

distinguish /dɪ'stɪŋgwɪʃ/ **A** *vt* **1** (to differentiate) مَيَّزَ, فَرَّقَ ‹*types, species*›; **to ~ sth from sth** مَيَّزَ شَيْئاً عن شَيْءٍ **2** (to make out) مَيَّزَ, رَأى بِوُضوحٍ ‹*an object*› **B** *vi* مَيَّزَ, لاحَظَ الفَرْقَ; **to ~ between** مَيَّزَ بين

distinguished /dɪ'stɪŋgwɪʃt/ *adj* **1** (elegant) ‹*air, appearance*› مُتَأَنِّق **2** (successful) ‹*career, scholar*› مُبَجَّل, بارِز

distinguishing /dɪ'stɪŋgwɪʃɪŋ/ *adj* ‹*feature, mark*› فارِق, مُمَيِّز

distort /dɪ'stɔːt/ *vt* **1** (to deform) شَوَّهَ ‹*metal, an image*›; مَسَخَ (a; مَسْخ) ‹*sb's face, voice*› **2** (to misrepresent) حَرَّفَ ‹*facts, meaning*›

distortion /dɪ'stɔːʃ(ə)n/ *n* **1** (of the truth, facts) تَحْريف (تَحْريفات) **2** (of images, sound) تَشْويه (تَشْويهات), تَشَوُّه (تَشَوُّهات)

distract /dɪ'strakt/ *vt* **1** صَرَفَ (i; صَرْف), أَلْهى ‹*a driver, worker*›; **to ~ sb's attention** صَرَفَ انْتِباهَ شَخْصٍ **2** (to amuse) لَهّى, سَلّى ‹*a child*›

distracting /dɪ'straktɪŋ/ *adj* ‹*noise, movement*› مُشَتِّت للانْتِباهِ, مُلْهٍ

distraction /dɪ'strakʃ(ə)n/ *n* **1** (interruption) تَشْتيت, إِلْهاء الانْتِباهِ **2** (entertainment) تَسْلِية (تَسالٍ, تَسْلِيات), تَرْفيه **3** (madness) **to drive sb to ~** أَخْرَجَ شَخْصاً عن صَوابِه

distraught /dɪ'strɔːt/ *adj* ‹*mother, parent*› مُضْطَرِب, مُهْتاج

distress /dɪ'stres/ **A** *n* **1** (emotional) كَرْب (كُروب), كَدَر (أَكْدار); **to cause sb ~** سَبَّبَ الكَرْبَ لِشَخْصٍ **2** (physical) أَلَم (آلام) **3** (of a ship, aircraft) **in ~** في خَطَرٍ **B** *vt* (to cause worry) أَقْلَقَ; (to cause sorrow) أَحْزَنَ ‹*viewers, residents*›

distressed /dɪ'strest/ *adj* ‹*mother, victim*› مَحْزون, مَكْروب

distressing /dɪ'stresɪŋ/ *adj* ‹*news, experience*› مُؤْلِم, مُحْزِن; **I found it all deeply ~** وَجَدْتُ الأَمْرَ كُلَّهُ مُحْزِناً للغايةِ

distribute /dɪ'strɪbjuːt/ *vt* **1** (to hand or share out) فَرَّقَ, وَزَّعَ ‹*leaflets, money*› **2** (to spread) حَصَّصَ, وَزَّعَ ‹*a load, burden*› **3** (Busn) سَوَّقَ, وَزَّعَ ‹*a product, film*›

distribution /dɪstrɪ'bjuːʃ(ə)n/ *n* **1** (of resources, newspapers) تَوْزيع **2** (of a population, wildlife, etc) تَوَزُّع, تَوْزيع

distributor /dɪ'strɪbjʊtə/ *n* **1** (in commerce) مَنْدوب \ وَكيل تَوْزيعٍ **2** (in an engine) مُوَزِّع

district /'dɪstrɪkt/ *n* (of a country) مِنْطَقة (مَناطِقُ); (of a city) دائِرة (دَوائِرُ); (administrative) مُقاطَعة

district attorney *n* (AmE) [مُدَّعٍ عامّ في مُقاطَعةٍ]

district council *n* (BrE) مَجْلِس مُقاطَعةٍ

district court *n* (AmE) مَحْكَمة فيدراليّة

District of Columbia *n* قِطاع كولومْبيا

distrust /dɪs'trʌst/ **A** *n* عَدَم ثِقةٍ, ارْتِياب **B** *vt* لم يَثِقْ (ب, في), ارْتابَ ‹*politicians, the media*›

distrustful /dɪs'trʌstfʊl/ *adj* مُرْتاب; **to be ~ of sth/sb** كانَ مُرْتاباً من شَيْءٍ \ شَخْصٍ

disturb /dɪ'stəːb/ *vt* **1** (to interrupt) قاطَعَ ‹*a person, the silence, one's sleep*›; **sorry to ~ you** آسِف لِمُقاطَعَتِكَ **2** (to worry) أَقْلَقَ, ضايَقَ «*news, thoughts*» **3** (to disarrange) بَعْثَرَ (i; بَعْثَرة) ‹*the papers*›; أَخَلَّ ‹*the balance, the status quo*›

disturbance /dɪ'stəːb(ə)ns/ *n* **1** (inconvenience) إِزْعاج, تَشْويش **2** (disorder) فَوْضى (f), شَغَب; **to cause a ~** سَبَّبَ فَوْضى

disturbed /dɪ'stəːbd/ *adj* **1** ‹*mind, child*› مُخْتَلّ **2** ‹*sleep, night*› مُضْطَرِب

disturbing /dɪ'stəːbɪŋ/ *adj* (worrying) ‹*trend, report*› مُقْلِق; (upsetting) ‹*images, scenes*› مُرْبِك

disuse /dɪs'juːs/ *n* عَدَم اسْتِعْمالٍ; **it's an expression that has fallen into ~** هو مُصْطَلَحٌ لم يَعُدْ مُتَداوَلاً

disused /dɪs'juːzd/ *adj* ‹*railway, quarry*› غَيْر مُسْتَعْمَلٍ

ditch /dɪtʃ/ **A** *n* (by a field, road) مَصْرِف (مَصارِفُ) **B** *vt* **1** (infml) تَخَلّى (عن) ‹*a plan*› **2** (infml) تَرَكَ (u; تَرْك), هَجَرَ (u; هَجْر) ‹*a boyfriend, girlfriend*› **3** [حَطَّ على الماءِ في حالةِ اضْطِرارٍ] ‹*a plane*›

dither /'dɪðə/ *vi* «*governments, officials*» تَرَدَّدَ

ditto /ˈdɪtəʊ/ *adv* كَذَلِكَ; **'I can't stand him' — '~'** 'لا أُطيقُهُ' — 'وَأَنا كَذَلِكَ'

diuretic /ˌdʌɪjʊəˈrɛtɪk/ **A** *adj* ‹*drug*› مُدِرّ للبَوْلِ **B** *n* مُدِرّ البَوْلِ

diva /ˈdiːvə/ *n* ديفا (مُغَنِّية من الطِرازِ الأَوَّلِ)

divan /dɪˈvan/ *n* **1** [أَريكة بِدونِ مِسْنَدٍ أو ذِراعَيْنِ] **2** (also **divan bed**) (BrE) [سَرير بِدونِ مِسْنَدٍ للرَأْسِ أو للقَدَمَيْنِ]

dive /dʌɪv/ **A** *vi* (*past tense* **dived**, **dove** AmE) **1** (into water) «swimmers, divers» غَطَسَ (i; غَطْس) **2** (under water) «scuba divers, deep-sea divers» غاصَ (u; غَوْص) **3** (to go underwater) «submarine, whale» غاصَ (u; غَوْص) **4** «bird, plane» انْقَضَّ **5** (to lunge) **to ~ into the bushes/under the bed** انْدَفَعَ على الشُجَيْراتِ \ تحت السَريرِ; **to ~ for cover** ارْتَمى انْبَطَحَ أَرْضاً للاحْتِماءِ; **the goalkeeper ~d to the right** ارْتَمى حارِسُ المَرْمى على اليَمينِ

B *n* **1** (into the water) غَطْسة **2** (in deep-sea diving) غَطْسة **3** (of planes, birds) هُبوط عَموديّ **4** (by goalkeeper) **he made a ~ for the ball** ارْتَمى على الكُرة **5** (infml pej) (bar, club) [بار \ نادٍ لَيْليّ مَشْبوه \ سَيِّئ السُمْعةِ]

(Idiom) **take a dive** تَراجَعَ بِحِدّةٍ; **profits have taken a ~** هَبَطَت الأَرْباح هُبوطاً حادًّا \ مُفاجِئاً

(Phrasal verb) **dive in** **1** (into water) غَطَسَ (i; غَطْس) **2** (to start) تَعَجَّلَ ,انْدَفَعَ

dive-bomb /ˈdʌɪvbɒm/ *vt* [قَذَفَ بالقَنابِلِ بِطَريقةِ الانْقِضاضِ] ‹*a target, building*›

diver /ˈdʌɪvə/ *n* غَوّاص ,غَطّاس

diverge /dʌɪˈvəːdʒ/ *vi* **1** «paths, lines» افْتَرَقَ **2** «opinions, views» اخْتَلَفَ

divergence /dʌɪˈvəːdʒ(ə)ns/ *n* انْعِطاف (انْحِرافات) انْحِراف, (انْعِطافات) (اخْتِلافات) اخْتِلاف

divergent /dʌɪˈvəːdʒ(ə)nt/ *adj* ‹*views, paths*› مُتَبايِن

diverse /dʌɪˈvəːs/ *adj* **1** (varied) ‹*group, range*› مُتَنَوِّع **2** (different) ‹*opinions, needs*› مُخْتَلِف

diversification /dʌɪˌvəːsɪfɪˈkeɪʃ(ə)n/ *n* (تَنْويعات) تَنْويع

diversify /dʌɪˈvəːsɪfʌɪ/ **A** *vt* (**diversifies**, **diversifying**, **diversified**) نَوَّعَ ‹*an economy, investments*› **B** *vi* «companies, economies» نَوَّعَ

diversion /dʌɪˈvəːʃ(ə)n/ *n* **1** (of a river) [تَحْويل مَجْرًى \ مَسارٍ]; (of money, resources) تَحْويلة (تَحْويلات) تَحْويل **2** (of traffic) تَحْويلة **3** (entertainment) تَسْلِية (تَسالٍ ,تَسْليات) **4** (in battle) تَضْليل

diversity /dʌɪˈvəːsɪti/ *n* تَنَوُّع (تَنَوُّعات)

divert /dʌɪˈvəːt/ *vt* **1** (to redirect) حَوَّلَ ‹*a river, resources, traffic, a plane*› **2** (to distract) صَرَفَ (i; صَرْف) ,أَلْهى; **to ~ attention from sth** حَوَّلَ الانْتِباهَ عن شَيْءٍ

divest /dʌɪˈvest/ *vt* (fml) **to ~ sb of sth** (of power, assets etc.) جَرَّدَ شَخْصاً من شَيْءٍ

divide /dɪˈvʌɪd/ **A** *vt* **1** (to split into parts) قَسَّمَ ‹*land, a house*›; **students were ~d into four groups** قُسِّمَ الطُلّابُ إلى أَرْبَعِ مَجاميعَ **2** (to share) قَسَّمَ ‹*the money, food*›; **he ~s his time between London and New York** يُقَسِّمُ وَقْتَهُ بين لُنْدُن وَنيويورْك **3** (to separate) فَصَلَ (i; فَصْل) ‹*an area, a room, country*› **4** (in disagreements) قَسَّمَ ‹*a country, party, community*› **5** (Maths) قَسَمَ (i; قَسْم) ‹*a number*›; **to ~ 14 by 2** قَسَمَ 14 على 2

B *vi* **1** «road, river, cell» انْقَسَمَ **2** (Math) «number» انْقَسَمَ

C *n* **1** (split) فَجْوة (فَجَوات) ,انْقِسام (انْقِسامات); **the North-South ~** الفَجْوة بين الشَمالِ والجَنوبِ **2** (AmE) (watershed) مَقْسِم الماءِ

(Phrasal verb) **divide up**: **~ [sth] up**, **~ up [sth]** **1** (into parts) قَسَّمَ [شَيْئاً] ‹*land, an area*› **2** (to share) قَسَّمَ [شَيْئاً] ‹*tasks, money*›

divided highway *n* (AmE) طَريق سَريع مُقَسَّم \ مُزْدَوِج

dividend /ˈdɪvɪdɛnd/ *n* حِصّة أَرْباحٍ

divider /dɪˈvʌɪdə/ *n* **1** (also **room divider**) بَرافان (فاصِل غُرَفٍ) **2** (in a file) فاصِل

dividing line *n* خَطّ فاصِل

divine /dɪˈvʌɪn/ **A** *adj* **1** ‹*inspiration, intervention*› رَبّانيّ ,إلَهيّ **2** (infml) (wonderful) رائِع; **you look ~, darling!** حَبيبَتي، تَبْدينَ رائِعةً!

B *vt* **1** (to intuit) حَزَرَ (i-u; حَزْر ,مَحْزَرة) ,حَدَسَ (i-u; حَدْس) ‹*sb's thoughts, intentions*›; تَكَهَّنَ (ب) ‹*course of events*› **2** (to find) [اكْتَشَفَ عن طَريقِ الاسْتِنْباءِ \ الاسْتِطْلاعِ] ‹*water, minerals*›

diving /ˈdaɪvɪŋ/ *n* (as a sport) غَطْس; (in the sea) غَوْص

diving board *n* مِنَصّة قَفْزٍ

diving suit *n* بَدْلة غَوْصٍ

divinity /dɪˈvɪnɪti/ *n* (*pl* **divinities**) **1** [u] (divine nature) أُلوهيّة **2** (deity) إلَه (آلِهة) **3** [u] (theology) عِلْم اللاهوتِ

division /dɪˈvɪʒ(ə)n/ *n* **1** (in arithmetic) قِسْمة; (creation of shares) تَقْسيم (تَقْسيمات) **2** (in army) فِرْقة (فِرَق)

divisive /dɪˈvaɪsɪv/ *adj* ‹issue, policy› مُسَبِّب للانْقِسامِ \ للشِقاقِ

divorce /dɪˈvɔːs/ **A** *n* طَلاق; **he/she has asked me for a ~** طَلَبَ \ طَلَبَتْ مِنّي الطَلاق; **to file for ~** رَفَعَ دَعْوى طَلاقٍ **B** *vt* **1** ‹one's spouse› طَلَّقَ; **to ~ him/her** طَلَّقَتْهُ \ طَلَّقَها; **to get ~d** انْفَصَلَ, تَطَلَّقَ **2** (to separate) ‹two concepts› فَصَلَ (i; فَصْل); **the constitution attempts to ~ religion and politics** يُحاوِلُ الدُسْتورُ أنْ يَفْصِلَ الدينَ عن السِياسةِ **C** *vi* انْفَصَلَ

divorce decree *n* (AmE) مَرْسوم الطَلاقِ

divorcee /ˌdɪvɔːˈsiː/ *n* مُطَلَّق

divulge /daɪˈvʌldʒ/ *vt* ‹information, details› أَفْشَى

diwan /dɪˈwɑːn/ *n* ديوان (دَواوينُ)

DIY /diːaɪˈwaɪ/ *n* (BrE) = **do-it-yourself** افْعَلْها بِنَفْسِكَ

dizzy /ˈdɪzi/ *adj* (**dizzier, dizziest**) **1** (giddy) مُصاب ,دائخ; **to feel ~** أَحَسَّ بِدُوارٍ \ دَوْخةٍ **2** (causing dizziness) ‹height, speed› يُسَبِّبُ دُواراً \ دَوْخةً ;بِدُوارٍ

DJ /ˈdiːdʒeɪ/ *n* = **disc jockey** دي جَيْ

Djibouti /dʒɪˈbuːti/ *pr n* جيبوتي (f)

djinn /dʒɪn/ *n* ▸ **jinn**

DNA /diːenˈeɪ/ **A** *n* = **deoxyribonucleic acid** حَمْض نَوَويّ **B** *adj before n* ‹test, profile› الحَمْضِ النَوَويِّ

do /duː, də/ **A** *vt* (*3rd person present sing* **does**, *past tense* **did**, *past participle* **done**) **1** (to carry out) فَعَلَ (a; فِعْل), عَمِلَ (a; عَمَل) ‹a job, work›; **I'm ~ing the ironing** أَقومُ بالكَيِّ; **will you ~ it for me?** هل يُمْكِنُكَ أنْ تَفْعَلَ ذلك من أَجْلي؟; **are you ~ing anything tonight?** هل تَعْتَزِمُ فِعْلَ شَيْءٍ هذا المَساءَ؟; **what can I ~ for you?** ماذا يُمْكِنُني أنْ أَفْعَلَ لَكَ؟ **2** (to tidy, clean) **to ~ one's hair** سَوّى شَعْرَهُ; **to ~ one's nails** سَوّى أَظافِرَهُ; **to ~ the dishes** غَسَلَ الصُحونَ **3** (to have an effect on) فَعَلَ (a; فِعْل), صَنَعَ (a; صِناعة); **I must have ~ne something to my back** لا بُدَّ أنّني آذَيْتُ ظَهْري; **what have you ~ne to her?** ماذا فَعَلْتَ بِها؟; **that hat ~es nothing for her** تِلْكَ القُبَّعةُ لا تُناسِبُها **4** (to spend) «prisoners» قَضى في السِجْنِ; «soldiers etc.» أَتَمَّ ‹a period of time›; **he did three years for robbery** قَضى فَتْرةَ ثَلاثِ سَنَواتٍ في السِجْنِ لِقِيامِهِ بالسَرِقةِ **5** (to study) دَرَسَ (u; دَرْس) ‹physics, Arabic›; **I did Russian at university** دَرَسْتُ الروسيّةَ في الجامِعةِ **6** (to work at) عَمِلَ (a; عَمَل); **what ~es she do for a living?** ماذا تَعْمَلُ لِكَسْبِ رِزْقِها؟ **7** (to cook) طَبَخَ (a-u; طَبْخ), طَهَا (a-u; طَهْي, طَهْو) ‹an omelette, bacon›; (to prepare) حَضَّرَ, أَعَدَّ ‹the vegetables, salad›; **I'd like the steak well ~ne** أُحِبُّ شَريحةَ اللَحْمِ ناضِجةً **8** (to provide) قَدَّمَ; **they ~n't ~ travellers' cheques** لا يُصْدِرونَ شيكاتِ المُسافِرينَ; **they ~ an excellent fish soup** يُقَدِّمونَ حَساءَ سَمَكٍ مُمْتازاً **9** (to put on) عَرَضَ (i; عَرْض) ‹a play› **10** (infml) (to imitate) قَلَّدَ ‹a celebrity, sb's voice›; **he ~es Tony Blair very well** يُقَلِّدُ توني بلير بِشَكْلٍ مُمْتازٍ **11** (to travel) قَطَعَ (a; قَطْع); **we've ~ne 300 miles today** قَطَعْنا 300 ميلٍ اليَوْمَ **12** (to travel at) ساقَ (u; سِياقة); **I was ~ing 70 miles an hour** كُنْتُ أَقودُ السَيّارةَ بِسُرْعةِ 70 ميلاً في الساعةِ **13** (infml) (to visit as a tourist) زارَ (u; زِيارة) **14** (infml) (to take) **to ~ drugs** تَعاطى المُخَدِّراتِ **15** (BrE) (infml) (to cheat) **we've been ~ne!** لَقَدْ أُحْتيلَ عَلَيْنا! **16** (BrE) (infml) (to prosecute, convict) **I got ~ne for speeding** لَقَدْ حوكِمْتُ بِتُهْمةِ تَجاوُزِ السُرْعةِ **B** *vi* (*3rd person present sing* **does**, *past tense* **did**, *past participle* **done**) **1** (to behave) فَعَلَ (a; فِعْل); **~ as you're told!** اِفْعَلْ كَما يُقالُ لَكَ!; **well ~ne!** أَحْسَنْتَ! **2** (to get on) **how did you ~ in your exams?** كيف كانَت امْتِحاناتُكَ؟; **how are we ~ing for time?** كم بَقِيَ من الوَقْتِ؟; **the patient is ~ing well** يَتَحَسَّنُ المَريضُ بِشَكْلٍ مُسْتَمِرٍّ; **she's ~ne well for herself** أَحْسَنَتْ صُنْعاً بِنَفْسِها **3** (to be suitable, acceptable) ناسَبَ; **that box will ~** ذلك الصُنْدوقُ يَفي بالغَرَضِ; **this really won't ~!** هذا غَيْرُ مَقْبولٍ! **4** (to suffice) كَفى (i; كِفاية); **£20 will ~** 20 جُنَيْهاً سَتَكْفي; **that will ~!** هذا يَكْفي! **5** (infml) (to finish) انْتَهى; **are you ~ne?** هل انْتَهَيْتَ؟; **just tell her and**

have *or* be ~ne with it اعْتَرِفْ لَها وَانْتَهِ من ذلك

C *v aux* (*3rd person present sing* **does**, *past tense* **did**, *past participle* **done**) **1** (in questions, negatives) **did you speak to him?** هل تَكَلَّمْتَ مَعَهُ؟; **I didn't speak to him** لم أَتَكَلَّمْ مَعَهُ; **~esn't she look beautiful?** أَلَيْسَتْ تَبْدو جَميلةً؟; **what did she say?** ماذا قالَتْ؟; **~n't you like it?** أَلا تُحِبُّهُ؟ **2** (in place of a main verb) **you play better than I ~** تَلْعَبُ بِشَكْلٍ أَفْضَلَ مِنّي; **he likes the house and so ~ I** يُعْجِبُهُ البَيْتُ كَما يُعْجِبُني; **'who wrote it?' — 'I did'** 'مَنْ كَتَبَهُ؟' – 'أَنا'; **'I know who did it' — '~ you?'** 'أَنا أَعْرِفُ مَنْ فَعَلَها' – 'فِعْلاً؟'; **he wanted to live there, but she didn't** أَرادَ أَنْ يَعيشَ هُناكَ، وَلَكِنَّها لم تُرِدْ ذلك **3** (for emphasis) **~ sit down** تَفَضَّلِ اجْلِسْ; **~ shut up!** اُسْكُتْ!; **I ~ wish you'd let me help you** وَدِدْتُ لو سَمَحْتَ لي بِأَنْ أُساعِدَكَ!; **you must admit, she did look ill** يَجِبُ أَنْ تَعْتَرِفَ، لَقَدْ بَدَتْ مَريضةً بالفِعْلِ **4** (in tag questions) **he lives in Tripoli, ~esn't he?** يَعيشُ في طَرابُلُسَ، أَلَيْسَ كَذَلِكَ؟; **you didn't believe him, did you?** لم تُصَدِّقْهُ، أَلَيْسَ كَذَلِكَ؟

D *n* (*pl* **dos**) (BrE infml) حَفْلة (حَفَلات); **his leaving ~ is tomorrow** حَفْلةُ وَداعِهِ غَداً

(Idioms) **dos and don'ts** أَوامِر وَنَواهٍ, قَواعِد وَأَحْكام; **that does it!** (infml) طَفَحَ الكَيْلُ!; **that's done it!** (infml) ها هو ذا قد فَسَدَ الأَمْرُ!

(Phrasal verbs) **do away with**: **~ away with [sth]** تَخَلَّصَ من [شَيْءٍ] ‹*a system, an organization*›; اسْتَغْنى عن [شَيْءٍ] ‹*the need for sth*›

• **do in** (infml): **~ [sb] in** **1** (to kill) تَخَلَّصَ, قَضى على [شَخْصٍ], قَتَلَ [شَخصاً], من [شَخْصٍ] **2** (to tire out) **by the end of it I was ~ne in** كُنْتُ مُرْهَقاً بِنِهايةِ ذلك

• **do out of** (infml): **to do ~ sb out of sth** جَرَّدَ شَخْصاً من شَيْءٍ

• **do up** **A** «dress, coat» زُرِّرَ **B** **~ [sth] up, ~ up [sth]** **1** زَرَّرَ, أَقْفَلَ [شَيْئاً] ‹*coat*›; رَبَطَ [شَيْئاً] ‹*a necklace, one's shoelaces*›; [شَيْئاً] ‹*a zip*› **2** (to wrap) لَفَّ [شَيْئاً] ‹*a parcel*› **3** (BrE infml) (to renovate) رَمَّمَ [شَيْئاً] ‹*a house, room*› **C** **~ [sb] up** (infml) **she was all ~ne up and ready to go out** كانَتْ مُهَنْدَمةً وَجاهِزةً للخُروجِ

• **do with**: **~ with [sth/sb]** **1** (expressing connection) كانَ لَهُ عَلاقةٌ ب [شَيْءٍ \ شَخْصٍ]; **I'm sure he had something to ~ with it** أنا مُتَأَكِّدٌ أنّ لَهُ عَلاقةٌ بِهَذا الأَمْرِ; **what's that got to ~ with it?** ما عَلاقةُ ذلك بِما نَحْنُ فيهِ؟; **what's it got to ~ with you?** ما عَلاقَتُكَ بالأَمْرِ؟ **2** (to benefit from) ≈ احْتاجَ إلى [شَيْءٍ \ شَخْصٍ]; **I could ~ with a drink/a holiday** ≈ أَحْتاجُ إلى مَشْروبٍ \ عُطْلةٍ **3** (BrE infml) (to tolerate) **I can't be ~ing with all this new technology** لا يُمْكِنُني تَحَمُّلُ كُلّ هذه التِكْنولوجِيا الحَديثةِ

• **do without**: **~ without [sb/sth]** دَبَّرَ أَمْرَهُ بدونِ [شَخصٍ \ شَيْءٍ] ‹*luxuries, sb's help*›

docile /ˈdəʊsʌɪl/ *adj* ‹*animal, nature*› وَديع (وُدَعاءُ), طَيِّع

dock /dɒk/ **A** *n* **1** (for loading, unloading ships) حَوْض جافّ (رَصيف شَحْنٍ وَتَفْريغٍ); (for repair of ships) حَوْض **2** (AmE) (wharf) رَصيف (أَرْصِفة) **3** (**docks**, *pl*) رَصيف ميناءٍ **4** (BrE) (in a court) قَفَص الاتِّهام **5** (Bot) حُمّاض

B *vt* **1** خَصَمَ (i; خَصْم), حَسَمَ (i; حَسْم) ‹*points, sb's wages*› **2** بَتَرَ (u; بَتْر) ‹*a tail*› **3** قادَ إلى حَوْضٍ \ رَصيفٍ ‹*a ship*›

C *vi* رَسا (u; رَسْو)

docker /ˈdɒkə/ *n* عامِل شَحْنٍ وَتَفريغٍ بالسُفُنِ

dockworker /ˈdɒkwəːkə/ *n* عامِل شَحْنٍ وَتَفْريغٍ بالسُفُنِ

dockyard /ˈdɒkjɑːd/ *n* تَرْسانة بَحْرِيّة

doctor /ˈdɒktə/ **A** *n* **1** (of medicine) دُكْتور, طَبيب (أَطِبّة, أَطِبّاءُ) (دَكاتِرة); **D~ Jones** دُكْتور جونْز **2** (with a higher degree) دُكْتور (دَكاتِرة); **he and his wife are both ~s of physics** هو وَزَوْجَتُهُ كِلاهُما دُكْتورانِ في الفيزِياءِ

B *vt* **1** زَيَّفَ; تَلاعَبَ (ب) ‹*the figures, text*› **2** سَمَّمَ ‹*the food, wine*›

(Idiom) **that's just what the doctor ordered!** هذا هو المَطْلوبُ بالضَبْطِ!

doctoral /ˈdɒkt(ə)r(ə)l/ *adj* ‹*student, dissertation*› دُكْتوراهٍ

doctorate /ˈdɒkt(ə)rət/ *n* دُكْتوراه

doctor's office *n* (AmE) عِيادة طَبيبٍ

doctrine /ˈdɒktrɪn/ *n* مَذْهَب (مَذاهِبُ)

docudrama /ˈdɒkjʊˌdrɑːmə/ *n* دراما وَثائِقيّة, ديكودْراما

document /ˈdɒkjʊmənt/ **A** *n* وَثيقة (وَثائِقُ), مُسْتَنَد (مُسْتَنَدات)

B /ˈdɒkjʊmɛnt/ *vt* سَجَّلَ, وَثَّقَ ‹*life, history*›

documentary /dɒkjʊ'mɛnt(ə)ri/ **A** *n* (*pl* **documentaries**) فيلْم \ بَرْنامَج وَثائِقِيّ

B *adj* ‹*evidence*› وَثائِقِيّ

documentation /ˌdɒkjʊmɛn'teɪʃ(ə)n/ *n* مُسْتَنَدات, وَثائِق

dodge /dɒdʒ/ **A** *vt* **1** تَفادى ‹*bullets*›; تَجَنَّبَ ‹*a blow*›; تَمَلَّص (من), راغَ (u; رَوْغ) ‹*one's pursuers*› **2** تَمَلَّص (من) ‹*a question, responsibility*›; تَهَرَّبَ (من) ‹*taxes*›

B *vi* راغَ (u; رَوْغ), انْسَلَّ

dodgem /'dɒdʒəm/, **dodgem car** *n* (BrE) سَيّارة مَلاهٍ

dodger /'dɒdʒə/ *n* (infml) مُتَمَلِّص, مُتَهَرِّب; **a tax ~** مُتَهَرِّب من الضَرائِب; **a fare ~** [مُتَهَرِّب من دَفع الأُجْرة]

dodgy /'dɒdʒi/ *adj* (**dodgier**, **dodgiest**) (infml) **1** (dishonest) ‹*character, deal*› نَصّاب, مُحْتال **2** (unreliable) ‹*brakes*› غَيْر آمِن; ‹*knee*› غَيْر مُسْتَقِرّ

doe /dəʊ/ *n* (female deer) أَيِّلة; (female rabbit, hare) أَرْنَبة

does /dʌz, dəz/ *3rd pers sing pres* ▸**do**

doesn't /'dʌz(ə)nt/ = **does not** ▸**do** C

dog /dɒg/ **A** *n* **1** (canine) كَلْب (كِلاب) **2** (male fox) ثَعْلَب (ثَعالِبُ); (male wolf) ذِئْب (ذِئاب) **3** (infml) (person) مَلْعون (مَلاعينُ); **you lucky ~!** يا لَكَ من مَحْظوظٍ! **4** (infml) (sth worthless) [شَيْء لا قيمةَ لَهُ]

B (**the dogs**) *n pl* (BrE infml) سِباق الكِلابِ السَلوقيّة

C *vt* (**-gg-**) **1** (to follow) **to ~ sb's footsteps** تَبِعَ \ تَتَبَّعَ خَطَواتِ شَخْصٍ **2** (to plague) لاحَقَ; **the project has been ~ged by problems/controversy** لاحَقَت المَشاكِلُ \ لاحَقَ الجَدَلُ المَشْروعَ

Idioms **a dog's dinner** *or* **breakfast** (BrE infml) [شَيْء رَديء للغاية]; **it's dog eat dog** المُنافَسةُ شَرِسةٌ \ لا تَعْرِفُ الرَحْمة; **to go to the dogs** (infml) آلَ إلى الانْهِيار

dog collar *n* **1** (for a dog) طَوْق (أَطْواق) **2** (for a cleric) قَبّة إكْليرِكيّة

dog-eared /'dɒgɪəd/ *adj* ‹*book, page*› [ذو صَفَحاتٍ بالِيةٍ \ مَطْوِيّةِ الزَوايا]

dogfight /'dɒgfʌɪt/ *n* **1** (between dogs) مَعْرَكة بين الكِلابِ **2** (between planes) قِتال جَوّيّ تَلاحُمِيّ

dogfish /'dɒgfɪʃ/ *n* (*pl* **dogfish**) كَلْب البَحْرِ

dog food *n* طَعام الكِلابِ

dogged /'dɒgɪd/ *adj* ‹*determination, pursuit*› دَؤوب, مُواظِب

doggedly /'dɒgɪdli/ *adv* ‹*to pursue*› بِمُثابَرة, بِشَكْلٍ مُواظِبٍ; ‹*to refuse*› بِحَزْمٍ, بِعِنادٍ

doggerel /'dɒg(ə)rəl/ *n* [شِعْر رَكيك (شِعْر هَزْلِيّ مُحَطَّم الأَوْزانِ)]

doggy-paddle /'dɒgi,pad(ə)l/ (BrE), **dog-paddle** (AmE) *n* ضَرْبة التَجْديفِ الكِلابِيّ

dog handler *n* [سائِس \ مُرَوِّض كِلابٍ مُحْتَرِف]

doghouse /'dɒghaʊs/ *n* (AmE) بَيْت كَلْبٍ

Idiom **to be in the doghouse** [كانَ في مَوْقِفٍ مَعيب وَمُخْزٍ]

dogma /'dɒgmə/ *n* عَقيدة (عَقائِدُ)

dogmatic /dɒg'matɪk/ *adj* ‹*belief, approach*› عَقائِدِيّ, دوغْماتِيّ, مُتَعَصِّب

do-gooder /duː'gʊdə/ *n* (infml pej) [فاعِل خَيْرٍ مُتَطَفِّل (بالرَغْمِ من حُسْنِ نِيَّتِهِ)]

dogsbody /'dɒgzbɒdi/ *n* (*pl* **dogsbodies**) (BrE) صَبِيّ (صِبْية, صِبْيان), غُلام (غِلْمة, غِلْمان)

dog tag *n* **1** (used by armed forces) [بِطاقة تَعْريفٍ عَسْكَرِيّة من المَعْدِنِ (تُعَلَّقُ حول الرَقَبة)] **2** (on a dog's collar) [لَوْحة تَعْريفٍ مَعْدِنية لِكَلْبٍ]

dog track *n* مِضْمار لِسِباقِ الكِلابِ

doh /dəʊ/ *n* دو (نَغْمة من نَغَماتِ السُلَّمِ الموسيقيّ)

Doha /'dəʊhɑː/ *pr n* الدَوْحة

doily /'dɔɪli/ *n* (*pl* **doilies**) مِفْرَش (للصُحونِ)

doing /'duːɪŋ/ **A** *n* (work) **this is your ~!** هذا من صَنيعِكَ!; **it takes some ~** يَقْتَضي الأَمْرُ بَذْلَ جُهْدٍ كَبيرٍ

B (**doings**) *n pl* (activities) أَعْمال, أَنْشِطة

do-it-yourself /ˌduːɪtjɔː'sɛlf/ *n* افْعَلْها بِنَفْسِكَ

doldrums /'dɒldrəmz/ *n pl*

Idiom **to be in the doldrums** «person» كانَ في حالةِ اكْتِئابٍ \ فُتورٍ; «economy, market» كانَ في حالةِ كَسادٍ \ رُكودٍ \ جُمودٍ

dole /dəʊl/ *n* (BrE) إعانة حُكوميّة (للعاطِلينَ عن العَمَلِ); **to be on the ~** [اسْتَفادَ من إعانةٍ حُكوميّةٍ للعاطِلينَ عن العَمَلِ]

Phrasal verb **dole out**: **~ out** [sth], **~** [sth] **out** وَزَّعَ [شَيْئاً] <*money, advice*>

doleful /ˈdəʊlfʊl/ *adj* <*expression, voice*> حُزْناءُ حَزين, كَئيب, (حَزانى)

doll /dɒl/ *n* دُمْية (دُمًى)

Phrasal verb **doll up** (infml): **to get all ~ed up** [تَزَيَّنَ بِأَحْلى حُلَّةٍ]

dollar /ˈdɒlə/ *n* دولار (دولارات); **the Hong Kong ~** دولار هونغ كونغ

Idiom **the sixty-four thousand dollar question** السُؤال الجَوْهَرِيّ

dollar bill *n* [وَرَقة نَقْديّة بِقيمةِ دولار واحِدٍ]

dollop /ˈdɒləp/ *n* (infml) [قَدْر من سائِلٍ كَثيفٍ]

doll's house (BrE), **dollhouse** (AmE) /ˈdɔːlhaʊs/ *n* بَيْت أَلْعابٍ

dolly /ˈdɒli/ *n* (*pl* **dollies**) (infml) دُمْية (دُمًى)

dolphin /ˈdɒlfɪn/ *n* (*pl* **dolphins** or **dolphin**) دُلْفين (دَلافينُ)

domain /dəʊˈmeɪn/ *n* **1** (sphere) نِطاق (نُطُق), مَجال (مَجالات), مَيْدان (مَيادينُ); **in the public ~** في \ ضِمْنَ نِطاقِ المِلْكيّةِ العامّةِ **2** (on the Internet) نِطاق (نُطُق)

domain name *n* اسْم نِطاقٍ

dome /dəʊm/ *n* قُبّة (قِباب, قُبَب); **the D~ of the Rock** مَسْجِد قُبّةِ الصَخْرةِ

domestic /dəˈmɛstɪk/ *adj* **1** (of the home) <*life*> عائِلِيّ; <*dispute*> أَهْلِيّ **2** (not foreign) <*market, policy*> مَحَلِّيّ; <*flight, economy*> داخِلِيّ **3** (not wild) <*animal, pet*> داجِن, أَليف

domestic appliance *n* جِهاز مَنْزِلِيّ

domesticated /dəˈmɛstɪkeɪtɪd/ *adj* <*animal, species*> مُرَوَّض, مُدَجَّن

domesticity /ˌdɒmɛˈstɪsɪti, ˌdəʊmɛˈstɪsɪti/ *n* [حَياة مَنْزِليّة \ عائِليّة]

domestic violence *n* عُنْف مَنْزِلِيّ

domicile /ˈdɒmɪsʌɪl/ *n* مَحَلّ إِقامةٍ

dominance /ˈdɒmɪnəns/ *n* هَيْمَنة, سَيْطَرة

dominant /ˈdɒmɪnənt/ *adj* **1** <*nation, influence*> مُهَيْمِن, مُسَيْطِر **2** <*taste, quality*> سائِد, غالِب **3** <*gene*> سائِد

dominate /ˈdɒmɪneɪt/ *vt* سَيْطَرَ (i; سَيْطَرة), هَيْمَنَ (i; هَيْمَنة) <*an industry, a country*>

domination /dɒmɪˈneɪʃ(ə)n/ *n* هَيْمَنة, سَيْطَرة

domineering /dɒmɪˈnɪərɪŋ/ *adj* <*mother, husband*> مُسْتَبِدّ

Dominica /dɒmɪˈnikə/ *pr n* دومينيكا

Dominican Republic /dəˌmɪnɪk(ə)n rɪˈpʌblɪk/ *pr n* (**the Dominican Republic**) جُمْهوريّة الدومِنيكان

dominion /dəˈmɪnjən/ *n* **1** (liter) (authority) سُلْطان, سِيادة **2** (territory) مُسْتَوْطَنة

domino /ˈdɒmɪnəʊ/ **A** *n* (*pl* **dominoes**) دومينو **B** (**dominoes**) *n sing* الدومينو

don /dɒn/ **A** *n* (BrE Educ) [أُسْتاذ جامِعِيّ \ رَئيس كُلِّيّةٍ (خُصوصاً في أُكْسْفورْد أو كامْبْرِيدْج)] **B** *vt* (**-nn-**) (liter) لَبِسَ, ارْتَدى (a; لُبْس) <*a suit, mask*>

donate /dəʊˈneɪt/ *vt* تَبَرَّعَ <*money, blood*>

donation /dəʊˈneɪʃ(ə)n/ *n* **1** (gift) عَطيّة, هِبة, تَبَرُّع (تَبَرُّعات) (عَطايا) **2** [u] (action) مَنْح هِبةٍ \ عَطيّةٍ, تَبَرُّع

done /dʌn/ **A** *past participle* ▸ **do** **B** *adj* **1** (finished) مُنْجَز, مُنْتَهٍ; **are you ~ yet?** هل انْتَهَيْتَ بَعْدُ؟ **2** (cooked) مُسْتَوٍ, مَطْهوّ **3** (acceptable) [يَتَناسَبُ مع العُرْفِ والعادةِ \ الذَوْقِ العامِّ]; **it's just not ~** [هو فَقَطْ لا يَتَناسَبُ مع العُرْفِ والعادةِ]

dongle /ˈdɒŋg(ə)l/ *n* دُنْغْل

donkey /ˈdɒŋki/ *n* حِمار (حُمُر, حَمير)

donor /ˈdəʊnə/ *n* **1** (of an organ) مُتَبَرِّع **2** (of money) مُتَبَرِّع

donor card *n* بِطاقة تَبَرُّعٍ بالأَعْضاء

don't /dəʊnt/ *abbr* = **do not** ▸ **do** C

doodle /duːd(ə)l/ *vi* خَرْبَشَ (i; خَرْبَشة)

doom /duːm/ **A** *n* (grim fate) مَصير مَشْؤوم; (death) أَجَل, مَوْت مَحْتوم **B** *vt* حَكَمَ على (بالفَشَلِ \ بالإِخْفاقِ \ بالهَلاكِ) <*sb's efforts, relationship*>; **a plan that was ~ed to fail** خُطّة كانَتْ مَحْكوماً عَلَيْها بالفَشَلِ

doomed /duːmd/ *adj* <*efforts, relationship*> [مَحْكوم عَلَيْهِ بالفَشَلِ \ بالإِخْفاقِ \ بالهَلاكِ]

doomsday /ˈduːmzdeɪ/ *n* يَوْم الحِسابِ \ القِيامةِ \ الحَشْرِ, دَيْنونة

door /dɔː/ *n* **1** (of a building, room, vehicle) باب (mf; أَبواب, بيبان); **the front/back door** الباب الأماميّ \ الخَلْفيّ; **there's someone at the ~** هُناكَ شَخْصٌ عند \ على \ لدى البابِ; **out of ~s** في الهَواءِ الطَلْقِ; **they live two ~s down** يُقيمونَ على بُعْد مَنْزِلَيْن (من مَنْزِلنا) **2** (doorway) مَدْخَل (مَداخِلُ)

Idiom **to open the door to sth** فَتَحَ البابَ لِشَيْءٍ

doorbell /ˈdɔːbɛl/ *n* جَرَس (أَجْراس)

doorknob /ˈdɔːnɒb/ *n* مِقْبَض بابٍ

doorman /ˈdɔːmən/ *n* (*pl* **-men**) بَوّاب

doormat /ˈdɔːmat/ *n* مِمْسَحة أَقْدامٍ

doorstep /ˈdɔːstɛp/ *n* عَتَبة (عَتَبات, أَعْتاب)

doorstop /ˈdɔːstɒp/ *n* حاجِز بابٍ

door-to-door /dɔːtəˈdɔː/ *adj* ‹*salesman, campaign*› مُتَنَقِّل, مُتَجَوِّل

doorway /ˈdɔːweɪ/ *n* مَدْخَل (مَداخِلُ)

dope /dəʊp/ **A** *n* **1** (infml) (drugs) مُخَدِّرات; (infml) (cannabis) حَشيش (حَشائِشُ) **2** (infml) (fool) غَبِيّ (أَغْبِياءُ), مُغَفَّل **B** *vt* ‹*a horse, an athlete*› خَدَّرَ (بِواسِطةِ مادّةٍ مُنَشِّطةٍ لِرَفْعِ مُسْتَوى الأَداءِ)

dope test *n* اخْتِبار كَشْفِ المُنَشِّطاتِ

dopey, **dopy** /ˈdəʊpi/ *adj* (**dopier**, **dopiest**) (infml) **1** (stupid) ‹*grin, comedy*› سَخيف, غَبِيّ; ‹*kid*› بَليد **2** (befuddled) مُخَدَّر

dormant /ˈdɔːmənt/ *adj* **1** ‹*talent, emotion*› كامِن **2** ‹*volcano*› خامِد

dormitory /ˈdɔːmɪt(ə)ri/ *n* (*pl* **dormitories**) **1** (BrE) (room) عَنْبَر نَوْمٍ (غُرْفة مُتَعَدِّدة الأَسِرّةِ) **2** (AmE) (student residence) سَكَن جامِعِيّ

dormitory town *n* بَلْدة مُسافِرينَ

dormouse /ˈdɔːmaʊs/ *n* (*pl* **dormice**) زُغْبة

dorsal /ˈdɔːs(ə)l/ *adj* ‹*fin, spine*› ظَهْرِيّ

dory /ˈdɔːri/ *n* سَمَك دوري

DOS /dɒs/ *n* = **disk operating system** دوس

dosage /ˈdəʊsɪdʒ/ *n* جُرْعة (جُرَع, جُرْعات); **do not exceed the stated ~** لا تَتَجاوَز الجُرْعةَ المُحَدَّدةَ

dose /dəʊs/ **A** *n* جُرْعة (جُرَع, جُرْعات); **to administer the correct ~** أَعْطى الجُرْعةَ الصَحيحةَ **B** *vt* ‹*a patient, sheep*› جَرَّعَ (أَعْطى جُرْعةً من دَواءٍ)

Idiom **to give sb a dose of their own medicine** سَقى \ أَذاقَ شَخْصاً جُرْعةً من نَفْسِ الكَأْسِ

dossier /ˈdɒsɪə, ˈdɒsɪeɪ/ *n* مِلَفّ (مِلَفّات), إِضْبارة (إِضْبارات, أَضابيرُ)

dot /dɒt/ **A** *n* (point) نُقْطة (نُقَط, نِقاط); (on fabric) بُقْعة (بُقَع) **B** *vt* (in writing) ‹*your i's*› نَقَطَ (u; نَقْط), نَقَّطَ; **sign on the ~ted line** وَقِّعْ فوق الخَطِّ المُنَقَّطِ

Idiom **on the dot** تَماماً, بالضَبْطِ

dot-com /dɒtˈkɒm/, **dot-com company** *n* شَرِكة دوت كوم

dote /dəʊt/ *vi* **to ~ on sb** شَغِفَ \ انْشَغَفَ بِشَخْصٍ, شَغَفَهُ حُبُّ شَخْصٍ

doting /ˈdəʊtɪŋ/ *adj* ‹*parents, wife*› مَشْغوف (بِ), شَغوف (بِ); **her ~ parents** والِداها المَشْغوفانِ بِحُبِّها

dotty /ˈdɒti/ *adj* (**dottier**, **dottiest**) (BrE infml) ‹*old lady*› غَريب الأَطْوارِ, خَرِف; ‹*idea*› سَخيف

double /ˈdʌb(ə)l/ **A** *adj* **1** (twice as much) ‹*portion, dose*› ضِعْف (أَضْعاف) **2** (when spelling, giving numbers) مُكَرَّر; **Anne is spelled with a ~ 'n'** تُكْتَبُ آنْ بِحَرْفِ 'n' مُكَرَّرٍ; **two ~ four (244)** اثْنانِ أَرْبَعة أَرْبَعة; **inflation reached ~ figures** بَلَغَ التَضَخُّمُ أَرْقاماً من خانَتَيْنِ **3** (dual) ‹*purpose, advantage*› مُزْدَوِج; **to lead a ~ life** عاشَ حَياةً مُزْدَوِجةً **4** (for two people) ‹*bedroom, sheet*› مُزْدَوِج (لِشَخْصَيْنِ)

B *adv* **1** (twice as much) ‹*to pay, charge, cost*› الضِّعْفَ **2** (in two) ‹*to fold*› بِشَكْلٍ مُزْدَوِجٍ; **he was bent ~ with laughter** تَمايَلَ من شِدّةِ الضَحِكِ; **to see ~** رَأى الأَشْياءَ مُزْدَوِجةً

C *n* **1** (also **double room**) غُرْفة مُزْدَوِجة **2** (drink) [مَشْروب كُحوليّ بِجُرْعَتَيْنِ] **3** (lookalike) شَبيه (أَشْباه) **4** (of actor, actress) دوبْلير (مُمَثِّل بَديل) **5** (two victories, titles) فَوْز مُزْدَوِج

D (**doubles**) *n pl* (in tennis) زَوْجِيّ; **the mixed/ladies' ~s** الزَوْجِيّ المُخْتَلَط \ زَوْجِيّ السَيِّداتِ

E *vt* **1** (to increase by two) ‹*the number, size, amount*› ضاعَفَ

2 (to fold) طَوى (i; طَيّ) ‹a blanket, fabric›

F vi 1 (to increase by two) «population, prices» تَضاعَفَ

2 (in films) **to ~ for sb** قامَ بِدَوْرِ الدوبْلير لِشَخْصٍ 3 (to have two roles) [أُسْتُخْدِمَ لِغَرَضٍ آخَرَ]; **her bedroom ~s as an office** تُسْتَخْدَمُ غُرْفةُ نَوْمِها كَمَكْتَبٍ أَيْضاً

(Phrasal verbs) **double back** «walkers, vehicle» عادَ أَدْراجَهُ; **the river ~s back on itself** [يَعودُ النَهْرُ إلى مَسارِهِ الأَصْليّ في حَرَكةٍ دائِرِيّةٍ]

• **double up** 1 (to bend one's body) تَقَوَّسَ; **to ~ up in pain/ with laughter** تَقَوَّسَ من الأَلَمِ \ الضَحِكِ 2 (in hotels) تَقاسَمَ غُرْفةً

double act *n* عَرْض ثُنائيّ

double-barrelled (BrE), **double-barreled** (AmE) /ˌdʌb(ə)lˈbarəld/ *adj* 1 ‹shotgun› مُزْدَوِج الماسورة 2 (BrE) ‹surname› ثُنائيّ (يَتأَلَّفُ من اسْمَيْنِ يَفْصِلُهُما خَطُّ وَصْلٍ)

double bass *n* كَمان أَجْهَر

double bed *n* سَرير مُزْدَوِج

double-book /dʌbəlˈbʊk/ *vt* **to ~ a room/seat** حَجَزَ غُرْفةً \ مَقْعَداً حَجْزاً مُزْدَوِجاً

double-breasted /ˌdʌb(ə)lˈbrɛstɪd/ *adj* ‹suit, blazer› مُزْدَوِج الصَدْرِ (ذو صَفَّيْنِ من الأَزْرارِ)

double-check /ˌdʌb(ə)lˈtʃɛk/ *vt* أَعادَ النَظَرَ \ التَحْقيقَ في ‹spelling, calculations›

double chin *n* لُغْد (لَغاديدُ, لُغْدود, أَلْغاد)

double-click /ˌdʌb(ə)lˈklɪk/ *vt, vi* **to (on) sth** نَقَرَ مَرَّتَيْنِ على شَيْءٍ ‹an icon, a file›

double cream *n* (BrE) [قِشْطة مُكَثَّفة مع مُحْتَوًى عالٍ من الدُهونِ]

double-cross /ˌdʌb(ə)lˈkrɒs/ *vt* خانَ (u; خَوْن, خِيانة), خَدَعَ (a; خَدْع) ‹an associate›

double-decker /ˌdʌb(ə)lˈdɛkə/ *n* (BrE) 1 (also **double-decker bus**) حافِلة ذات طابِقَيْنِ 2 (also **double-decker sandwich**) [ساندْوِتْش بِثَلاثِ شَرائِحِ خُبْزٍ]

double door *n* باب ذو دَفَّتَيْنِ

double Dutch *n* (infml) رَطانة

double-edged /dʌbəlˈɛdʒd/ *adj* ‹blade, knife› ذو حَدَّيْنِ

(Idiom) **to be a double-edged sword** كانَ سَيْفاً ذا حَدَّيْنِ

double glazing *n* زُجاج مُزْدَوِج

double-jointed /dʌbəlˈdʒɔɪntɪd/ *adj* ‹elbows, thumbs› مُزْدَوِج المَفْصَلِ; **to be ~** كانَ مُزْدَوِجَ المَفْصَلِ

double-park /ˌdʌb(ə)lˈpɑːk/ A *vt* رَكَنَ, أَوْقَفَ وُقوفاً مُزْدَوِجاً في صَفٍّ ثانٍ ‹a car›

B *vi* «drivers» أَوْقَفَ السَيّارةَ وُقوفاً مُزْدَوِجاً

double pneumonia *n* الْتِهاب رِئَويّ مُزْدَوِج

double room *n* غُرْفة مُزْدَوِجة \ لِاثْنَيْنِ

double standard *n* مِعْيار مُزْدَوِج, ازْدِواجيّة المَعاييرِ; **to have double standards** طَبَّقَ مَعاييرَ مُزْدَوِجةً

double take *n* **to do a double take** [تَفاجَأَ بِشَيْءٍ]

double vision *n* رُؤْية مُزْدَوِجة

double yellow lines *n* (BrE) خُطوط صَفْراء مُزْدَوِجة (لِمَنْعِ وُقوفِ السَيّاراتِ)

doubly /ˈdʌbli/ *adv* ‹disappointing, difficult› مُضاعَفاً

doubt /daʊt/ A *n* شَكّ (شُكوك); **there is little/no ~ that ...** لَيْسَ هُناكَ شَكٌّ أَنَّ ...; **I have no ~ that she is right** لَيْسَ لَدَيَّ شَكٌّ بِأَنَّها على حَقٍّ; **to have ~s about sth** كانَتْ لَدَيْهِ شُكوكٌ حول شَيْءٍ; **we were left in no ~ about his intentions** لم يَعُدْ لَدَيْنا أَيُّ شَكٍّ في نَواياهُ; **there is some ~ about its authenticity** هُناكَ بَعْضُ الشَكِّ في أَصالَتِهِ; **no ~ you already know** لا شَكَّ أَنَّكَ تَعْرِفُ مُسْبَقاً; **to be in ~** «sb's future» كانَ مَشْكوكاً فيهِ; «person» شَكَّ (u; شَكّ) \ غَيْرَ أَكيدٍ; **if/when in ~** في حالةِ الشَكِّ; **without ~** بِدونِ شَكٍّ; **to prove sth beyond ~** أَثْبَتَ شَيْئاً بِما لا يَدَعُ مَجالاً للشَكِّ

B *vt* 1 (to consider unlikely) شَكَّ (u; شَكّ) (في); **I ~ it!** أَشُكُّ في هذا!; **to ~ if** *or* **whether ...** شَكَّ في أَنّ ...; **I ~ that she'll come** أَشُكُّ أَنَّها سَتَأْتي 2 (to mistrust) شَكَّ (u; شَكّ) (في) ‹sb's ability, sincerity, honesty›

doubtful /ˈdaʊtfʊl/ *adj* 1 (uncertain) ‹look› شاكّ; **I am ~ about his chances of success** أنا مُتَشَكِّكٌ بِشَأْنِ فُرَصِ نَجاحِهِ 2 (improbable) غَيْر مُحْتَمَلٍ; **it is ~ that she'll agree** من المَشْكوكِ فيه أَنَّها سَتُوافِقُ 3 (questionable) ‹value, character› مُرْتاب فيه \ بِهِ

doubtfully /ˈdaʊtf(ə)li/ *adv* ‹*to ask, stare*› (with disbelief) بِارْتِيابٍ; (hesitantly) بِتَرَدُّدٍ; (unconvincingly) بِطَرِيقَةٍ غَيْرِ مُقْنِعَةٍ

doubtless /ˈdaʊtləs/ *adv* ‹*to inspire, contribute*› بِلا ,دون شَكٍّ دون رَيْبٍ; **the police will ~ want to speak to you** دون شَكٍّ سَوْفَ تُرِيدُ الشُّرْطةُ أنْ تَتَحَدَّثَ إلَيْكُمْ

douche /duːʃ/ **A** *n* (device, process) دوش; (liquid) [سائِل لِتَنْظِيفِ الجِسْمِ]

B *vt* (**douches**, **douching**, **douched**) نَظَّفَ بِدوش ‹*part of the body*›

C *v refl* **to ~ oneself** تَنَظَّفَ بِدوش

dough /dəʊ/ *n* **1** (Culin) عَجِين **2** (infml) (money) مال (أَمْوال), فُلوس

doughnut, **donut** /ˈdəʊnʌt/ *n* فَطِيرة (مَقْلِيّة على شَكْلِ دائِرةٍ)

dour /ˈdaʊə/ *adj* ‹*expression, mood*› قاسٍ, كَئِيب; ‹*affair, struggle*› صارِم, مُكْفَهِرّ

douse, **dowse** /daʊs/ *vt* **1** أَطْفَأَ ‹*flames, a fire*› **2** غَمَرَ (u; غَمْر) ‹*a vehicle, body*›; **to ~ sth/sb in** *or* **with sth** غَمَرَ شَيْئاً \ شَخْصاً بِشَيْءٍ

dove¹ /dʌv/ *n* حَمام (n coll; حَمامات)

dove² /dəʊv/ (AmE) *past tense* ▸ **dive**

Dover /ˈdəʊvə/ *pr n* دوفِر (ميناء في جَنوبِ إنْجِلْتِرا)

Dover sole *n* سَمَك موسى

dovetail /ˈdʌvteɪl/ **A** *n* تَعْشِيقة (تَعْشِيق الخَشَبِ); **a ~ joint** رِباط (رُبُط), تَعْشِيقة (أَرْبِطة)

B *vt* لاءَمَ ‹*plans, arguments*›

C *vi* (also **dovetail together**) «nicely, well» تَناسَبَ

dowager /ˈdaʊədʒə/ *n* [أَرْمَلة من الأَشْرافِ \ النُّبَلاءِ]

dowdy /ˈdaʊdi/ *adj* (**dowdier**, **dowdiest**) ‹*housewife, spinster*› بالٍ, رَثّ; ‹*clothes*› قَلِيل الأَناقةِ

down¹ /daʊn/ **A** *adv* **1** (in a downward direction) إلى الأَسْفَلِ; **to go/come ~** نَزَلَ (i; نُزول); **from the waist ~** من الخَصْرِ إلى الأَسْفَلِ; **face ~** جاثِماً; **~ with tyrants!** فَلْيَسْقُطِ الطُّغاةُ!

2 (with position) تَحْتُ; **~ here/there** هُنا \ هُناكَ تَحْتُ; **the second drawer ~** الدُّرْج الثاني إلى الأَسْفَلِ; **two floors ~** طابِقَيْنِ إلى الأَسْفَلِ; **~ below** تَحْتُ; **~ at the bottom of the hill/page** في أَسْفَلِ التَّلِّ \ الصَّفْحةِ **3** (downstairs) في الدَّوْرِ الأَسْفَلِ; **is Val ~ yet?** هل نَزَلَتْ فال تَحْتُ بَعْدُ؟; **I'll be ~ in a minute** سَأَكونُ تَحْتُ في لَحْظةٍ **4** (movement or position towards the south) نَحْوَ الجَنوبِ; (in the south) في الجَنوبِ; **I drove ~ to London** قُدْتُ سَيّارَتي جَنوباً إلى لُنْدُن; **she lives ~ south** تَسْكُنُ في الجَنوبِ **5** (reduced) مُنْخَفِض; **profits are well ~ on last year's** الأَرْباحُ مُنْخَفِضةٌ جِدًّا عَمّا كانَتْ عَلَيْهِ في العامِ الماضي; **to get one's weight ~** خَفَّضَ \ نَزَّلَ وَزْنَهُ; **I'm ~ to my last cigarette** أنا على آخِرِ سيجارةٍ لَدَيَّ **6** (in writing) مُسَجَّلاً, مُدَوَّناً; **I've got you ~ for Friday** سَجَّلْتُ اسْمَكَ في القائِمةِ لِيَوْمِ الجُمْعةِ; **get it ~ in writing** *or* **on paper** دَوِّنْهُ **7** (behind) مُتَخَلِّفاً; **we were two goals ~** كُنّا مُتَخَلِّفِينَ بِهَدَفَيْنِ

B *prep* **1** (from top to bottom of) [من القِمّة إلى \ حتّى الأَسْفَلِ]; **we ran ~ the hill** رَكَضْنا إلى أَسْفَلِ التَّلِّ; **it fell ~ a hole** سَقَطَ في حُفْرةٍ; **halfway ~ the page** في مُنْتَصَفِ الصَّفْحةِ **2** (along); **they live ~ the road** يَسْكُنونَ باتِّجاهِ هذا الطَّرِيقِ; **her office is just ~ the corridor** [مَكْتَبُها إلى أَسْفَلِ المَمَرِّ فَقَطْ]

C *adj* **1** (infml) (depressed) مُكْتَئِب, كَئِيب; **to feel ~** شَعَرَ بالكَآبةِ **2** (out of action) مُعَطَّل; **the computers/telephone lines are ~** الكُمْبيوترات \ خُطوطُ الهاتِفِ مُعَطَّلةٌ **3** (going downwards) ‹*escalator*› مُنْحَدِر

D *vt* **1** عَبَّ (u; عَبّ) ‹*a drink, bottle*› **2** أَسْقَطَ ‹*a plane, an opponent*›

down² /daʊn/ *n* زَغَب, رِيش ناعِم

down and out **A** *n* شَخْص فاشِل

B *adj* (*before n* **down-and-out**) **to be down and out** كانَ فاشِلاً

downbeat /ˈdaʊnbiːt/ *adj* ‹*assessment, mood*› مُتَشائِم

downcast /ˈdaʊnkɑːst/ *adj* **1** (directed downwards) ‹*eyes, look*› مُسْبَل, مُسْدَل **2** (dejected) ‹*face, mood*› مُكْتَئِب

downfall /ˈdaʊnfɔːl/ *n* سُقوط, انْهِيار (انْهِيارات); **drink/pride will be his ~** الشُّرْبُ \ الكِبْرِياءُ سَيَكونُ سَبَبَ هَلاكِهِ

downgrade /ˈdaʊngreɪd/ *vt* خَفَّضَ المَنْزِلةَ ‹*an employee, a hotel*›; **the hotel has been ~d from three to two stars** خُفِّضَتْ فِئةُ الفُنْدُقِ من ثَلاثِ نُجومٍ إلى نَجْمَتَيْنِ

downhearted /daʊnˈhɑːtɪd/ *adj* مُكْتَئِب, مُنْقَبِض

downhill /daʊn'hɪl/ *adv ‹to roll, flow›* مُنْحَدِراً

Idiom **to go downhill** تَدَهْوَرَ

Downing Street /'daʊnɪŋ stri:t/ *n* (BrE) (بَيْت داوْنينْج سْتْريت أَصْدَرَ رَئيسِ وُزَراءِ بَريطانِيا) ‎**~ issued a statement saying ...**; رَئيس وُزَراءِ بَريطانِيا بَياناً جاءَ فيهِ ...

download /'daʊnləʊd/ **A** *vt* /daʊn'ləʊd/ نَزَّلَ *‹an update, a file›*

B *n* **1** (data) مِلَفّ مُنَزَّل **2** (process) تَنْزيل

downmarket /daʊn'mɑ:kɪt/ **A** *adj ‹district, store›* مُتَدَنٍّ, رَخيص

B *adv ‹to go›* مُتَدَنِّياً

down payment *n* دُفْعة تحت الحِسابِ \ أُولى \ مَبْدَئيّة, عَرَبون

downplay /daʊn'pleɪ/ *vt* [قَلَّلَ من القيمةِ \ الأَهَمِّيّةِ] *‹a threat, an incident›*

downpour /'daʊnpɔ:/ *n* مَطَر غَزير

downright /'daʊnrʌɪt/ **A** *adj ‹lie›* صَريح, مَحْض; *‹dishonesty, stupidity›* صِرْف

B *adv ‹dangerous, rude›* تَماماً, كُلِّيًّا

downriver /daʊn'rɪvə/ *adv ‹to float, swim›* في اتِّجاه مَجْرى النَّهرِ; **the bridge is ~ from Windsor** الجِسْرُ في اتِّجاهِ مَجْرى النَّهْرِ من وِنْدْسور

downshift /'daʊnʃɪft/ *vi* (AmE) «drivers» [نَقَلَ ناقِلَ الحَرَكةِ إلى سُرْعةٍ أَقَلَّ]

downside /'daʊnsʌɪd/ *n* جانِب سَلْبيّ

downsize /'daʊnsʌɪz/ **A** *vt* خَفَّضَ, قَلَّصَ *‹operations, a workforce›*

B *vi* «companies» تَقَلَّصَ

Down's syndrome /daʊnz ˌsɪndrəʊm/ *n* مُتَلازِمة داوْن

downstairs /daʊn'stɛ:z/ **A** *adv* **1** *‹to go›* إلى الطابَقِ الأَسْفَلِ; **I went ~ to the kitchen** نَزَلْتُ إلى المَطْبَخِ في الطابَقِ الأَسْفَلِ

2 *‹to be›* في الطابَقِ الأَسْفَلِ; **to live ~** كانَ ساكِناً في الطابَقِ الأَسْفَلِ

B *adj ‹room, neighbour›* في الطابَقِ السُفْلِيِّ; **a ~ apartment** *or* (BrE) **flat** شِقّة في الطابَقِ السُفْلِيِّ

C *n* **(the downstairs)** الطابَق الأَسْفَل

downstream /'daʊnstri:m/ *adv ‹to float, flow›* في اتِّجاهِ مَجْرى النَّهرِ

down to earth *adj* (before *n* **down-to-earth**) *‹person, approach›* مُتَواضِع

downtown /'daʊntaʊn/ (AmE) **A** *adj ‹store, hotel›* [في مَرْكَزِ المَدينةِ التِجاريِّ]; **~ Chicago** وَسَط مَدينةِ شيكاغو

B *adv ‹to go›* نَحو مَرْكَزِ المَدينةِ; *‹live›* في مَرْكَزِ المَدينةِ

downtrodden /'daʊntrɒd(ə)n/ *adj ‹workers, minorities›* مُضْطَهَد

downturn /'daʊntə:n/ *n* (Econ) انْكِماش, كَساد

down under /ˌdaʊn 'ʌndə/ *adv* (infml) [في \ نحو أُسْتْرالِيا أو نيوزيلانْدا]

downward /'daʊnwəd/ **A** *adv* (also **downwards**) *‹to move, point›* إلى تَحْتٍ \ الأَسْفَلِ

B *adj ‹slope, trend›* مُنْحَدِر

downwind /daʊn'wɪnd/ *adv ‹to live, sail›* بِاتِّجاهِ الريحِ; **to be ~ of/from the industrial plant** كانَ بِاتِّجاهِ الريحِ من المَصْنَعِ

dowry /'daʊəri/ *n* (*pl* **dowries**) مَهْر (مُهور)

doze /dəʊz/ *vi* «people, animals» غَفا, نامَ نَوْماً خَفيفاً (u; غَفْو, غُفُوّ)

Phrasal verb **doze off** غَفا (u; غَفْو, غُفُوّ)

dozen /'dʌz(ə)n/ *n* (*pl* **dozen** or **dozens**) دَسْتة, دَزّينة; **a ~ eggs** دَزّينة بَيْض; **they're £1 a ~** اثْنَتا عَشْرةَ بَيْضةً, الدَزّينةُ بِجُنَيْهٍ إِسْتَرْلينيٍّ; **I took ~s of photos** أَخَذْتُ العَديدَ \ العَشَرات من الصُوَر

dozy /'dəʊzi/ *adj* (**dozier, doziest**) *‹to feel, look›* نَعْسان (dipt; f نَعْسى); نَعاس

Dr /'dɒktə/ *abbr* **1** = **doctor** (in titles) د (دُكْتور) **2** = **drive** (in addresses) ش (شارِع)

drab /drab/ *adj ‹colour›* باهِت; *‹building›* مُمِلّ; *‹existence›* رَتيب, غَيْر مُشَوِّق

draft /drɑ:ft/ **A** *n* **1** (of a letter, speech) مُخَطَّط, مُسَوَّدة تَمْهيديّ **2** (on a bank) حِوالة مَصْرِفيّة **3** (AmE) (conscription) تَجْنيد **4** (AmE) ▸**draught**

B *vt* **1** أَعَدَّ *‹a letter, contract›* **2** (AmE) (to conscript) جَنَّدَ *‹students, labourers›*; **to be ~ed into the army** تَجَنَّدَ في الجَيْشِ

Phrasal verb **draft in** (BrE): **~ in [sb]**, **~ [sb] in** جَنَّدَ \ عَبَّأَ [شَخْصاً] *‹reinforcements, the police›*

draft dodger *n* (AmE) مُتَهَرِّب من الخِدْمةِ العَسْكَرِيَّة

draftee /drɑːfˈtiː/ *n* (AmE) مُجَنَّد

draftproof (AmE) *adj, vt* ▸ **draughtproof**

draftsman (AmE) *n* (*pl* **-men**) ▸ **draughtsman**

draftswoman (AmE) *n* (*pl* **-women**) ▸ **draughtswoman**

drafty (AmE) *adj* ▸ **draughty**

drag /drag/ **A** *vt* **(-gg-)** **1** (to pull) جَرَّ (u; جَرّ) ‹*a body, child*›; **to ~ sth/sb along the ground** جَرَّ شَيْئاً \ شَخصاً على الأَرْضِ; **don't ~ my mother into this** لا تُقْحِمْ أُمّي في هذا; **I managed to ~ the truth out of her** اِسْتَطَعْتُ أنْ أَنْتزِعَ مِنها الحَقيقةَ; **can you bear to ~ yourself away from the pool?** هل يُمْكِنُكَ أنْ تَتحَمَّلَ مُغادَرةَ المَسْبَحِ ؟ **2** (to search) مَشَّطَ ‹*a river, lake*› **3** (in computing) سَحَبَ (a; سَحْب) ‹*a file, an icon*› **4** (in walking) جَرْجَرَ (i; جَرْجَرة) ‹*a wounded limb, coat*›; **to ~ one's feet** جَرْجَرَ خُطاهُ

B *vi* **(-gg-)** **1** (to trail) «feet, coat» اِنْجَرَّ (على الأَرْضِ); **to ~ in the mud** تَمَرَّغَ في الوَحَلِ **2** (infml) (to pass slowly) «time, day, movie» مَرَّ بِبُطْءٍ

C *n* **1** (infml) (tiresome thing) [شَيْء مُمِلّ \ مُزْعِج]; (tiresome person) [شَخص مُمِلّ \ مُزْعِج]; **what a ~!** تَعْساً لَهُ!; **he's such a ~!** يا لَهُ من شَخْصٍ مُمِلٍّ! **2** [u] (resistant force) قوّة مُقاوَمةِ المائِعِ **3** [u] (infml) (women's clothes) [مَلابِس نِسائيّة يَرْتَديها رَجُلٌ]; **to be in ~** كانَ يَرْتَدي مَلابِسَ نِسائيَّةً **4** (infml) (on a cigarette) نَفَس (أَنْفاس)

(Phrasal verbs) **drag on** (infml) «war, trial, process» طالَ (u; طول)

• **drag out** (infml): **~ [sth] out** أطالَ [شَيْئاً] ‹*a meeting, scene, class*›

• **drag up** (infml): **~ [sth] up, ~ up [sth]** أعادَ [شَيْئاً] إلى الذاكِرةِ ‹*a memory, the past*›

drag and drop *n* سَحْب وإسْقاط \ إفْلات

dragon /ˈdrag(ə)n/ *n* (creature) تِنّين (تَنانينُ); (fierce woman) (pej hum) [امْرَأة صارِمة \ عَنيفة]

dragonfly /ˈdrag(ə)nflʌɪ/ *n* (*pl* **dragonflies**) يَعْسوب (يَعاسيبُ)

drag racing *n* سِباق جَرٍّ, دْراج ريس

drain /dreɪn/ **A** *vt* **1** (to take water from) جَفَّفَ ‹*a field*›; أَفْرَغَ ‹*a swimming pool*› **2** (to empty) اِشْتَفَّ ‹*a glass*› **3** (food) صَفّى ‹*pasta, vegetables*› **4** (fluid) فَرَّغَ, صَرَّفَ ‹*a wound, lungs, abscess*› **5** (to use up) اسْتَهْلَكَ, اسْتَنْفَدَ ‹*resources, funds*› **6** (to exhaust) أَنْهَكَ ‹*a worker*›; **I feel completely ~ed!** أَشْعُرُ أَنَّني مُنْهَكٌ تماماً!

B *vi* **1** «liquids» تَسَرَّبَ; «rivers, pipes» صَبَّ (u; صَبّ) **2** «dishes, food» جَفَّ (i; جُفوف, جَفاف)

C *n* **1** (pipe in a street) أُنْبوب (أَنابيبُ), ماسورة (مَواسيرُ); (in a building) مَصْرِف (مَصارِفُ), بالوعة (بالوعات, بَواليعُ); (channel, ditch) مَجْرًى (مَجارٍ), قَناة صَرْفٍ **2** (of people, skills, money) عِبْء (أَعْباء); **to be a ~ on sb's resources** كانَ عِبْئاً على مَوارِدِ شَخْصٍ **3** (tube) دَرْنَقة

(Idiom) **to go down the drain** ذَهَبَ سُدًّى \ هَباءً

drainage /ˈdreɪnɪdʒ/ *n* **1** (of land, soil) تَصْريف المِياهِ **2** (system of drains) شَبَكة صَرْفٍ

draining board (BrE) /ˈdreɪnɪŋ bɔːd/, **drainboard** (AmE) /ˈdreɪnbɔːd/ *n* [لَوْحة لِتَصْريفِ الماءِ عن آنِيةِ الطَعامِ بعد غَسْلِها]

drainpipe /ˈdreɪnpʌɪp/ *n* أُنْبوب \ ماسورة تَصْريفٍ

drake /dreɪk/ *n* ذَكَر البَطِّ

drama /ˈdrɑːmə/ *n* **1** [u] (genre) الفَنّ \ الأَدَب المَسْرَحِيّ **2** (play) تَمْثيليّة, مَسْرَحيّة **3** [u] (excitement) [حَدَث مُثير]

dramatic /drəˈmatɪk/ *adj* **1** ‹*art, production*› تَمْثيلِيّ, مَسْرَحِيّ **2** (striking) ‹*change, increase*› هائِل (هَوائِلُ), فادِح **3** (exciting) ‹*events, scenes*› مُذْهِل, مُثير

dramatically /drəˈmatɪkli/ *adv* **1** (radically) ‹*to increase, change*› بِشَكْلٍ هائِلٍ; **the chances of a settlement improved ~** تَحَسَّنَتْ فُرَصُ التَسْوِيةِ تَحَسُّناً هائلاً **2** (in a theatrical way) ‹*to pause, sigh*› مَسْرَحيًّا, بِشَكْلٍ مَسْرَحيٍّ

dramatics /drəˈmatɪks/ *n pl* فَنّ التَمْثيلِ \ مَسْرَحِيّ

dramatist /ˈdramətɪst/ *n* كاتِب مَسْرَحِيّ

dramatize, -ise (BrE) /ˈdramətʌɪz/ *vt* **1** ‹*a novel, story*› (for the stage, TV, radio) [حَوَّلَ للمَسْرَحِ \ للتلِفِزْيون \ للإذاعةِ] **2** (to exaggerate) ‹*a situation*› هَوَّلَ (من), بالَغَ (في)

drank /draŋk/ *past tense* ▸ **drink**

drape /dreɪp/ *vt* **1** (to arrange) جَلَّلَ (ب) ‹*a flag, towel*›; **she ~d the towel over the chair** جَلَّلَت الكُرْسيَّ بالمِنْشَفةِ **2** (to cover) لَفَّ (u; لَفّ), غَطّى ‹*a coffin, body*›; **the coffin was ~d with *or* in a flag** كانَ النَعْشُ مَلْفوفاً بِعَلَمٍ

drapes /dreɪps/ *n pl* (AmE) سَتائِر

drastic /ˈdrastɪk/ *adj* ‹*change, measures*› شديد (شِداد ,أَشِدّاءُ)، صارِم (صَوارِمُ)

drastically /ˈdrastɪkli/ *adv* ‹*to reduce, change*› بِصورةٍ شَديدةٍ \ صارِمةٍ

draught (BrE), **draft** (AmE) /drɑːft/ **A** *n* **1** (cold air) مَجْرًى \ تَيّار هوائيّ **2** (of drink) شُرْبة (شُرَب)، جُرْعة (جُرَع ,جُرَعات)؛ (of breath) اسْتِنْشاق **3** (from a barrel) **on ~** [في براميل] **B** *adj* ‹*beer, cider*› مَسْحوب (جاهِز لِيُسْحَبَ من بَرْميل)

draughtproof (BrE), **draftproof** (AmE) /ˈdrɑːftpruːf/ **A** *adj* ‹*window, door*› [مُقاوِم للتَيّارِ الهَوائيِّ] **B** *vt* ‹*a room, window*› [جَعَلَ غَيْرَ مُنْفِذٍ للتَيّارِ الهَوائيِّ]

draughts /drɑːfts/ *n sing* (BrE) لُعْبة الداما

draughtsman (BrE), **draftsman** (AmE) /ˈdrɑːftsmən/ *n* (*pl* **-men**) مُصَمِّم ,رَسّام هَنْدَسيّ

draughtswoman (BrE), **draftswoman** (AmE) *n* (*pl* **-women**) رَسّامة هَنْدَسيّة

draughty (BrE), **drafty** (AmE) /ˈdrɑːfti/ *adj* (**draughtier**, **draughtiest**) ‹*room, corridor*› [مُعَرَّض للتَيّاراتِ الهَوائيّةِ]

draw /drɔː/ **A** *vt* (*past tense* **drew**; *past participle* **drawn**) **1** (with pen, pencil) رَسَمَ (u; رَسْم) ‹*map, line, portrait*›; **to ~ a picture/diagram of the port** رَسَمَ صورةً \ مُخَطَّطاً للميناءِ **2** (to pull) سَحَبَ (a; سَحْب)، جَرَّ (u; جَرّ) ‹*a cart, plough*›; **he drew her towards him** سَحَبَها إلَيْهِ; **he drew his finger along the shelf** مَرَّرَ إصْبَعَهُ على طولِ الرَفِّ; **to ~ the curtains** (open) سَحَبَ السَتائِرَ؛ (shut) أَغْلَقَ السَتائِرَ; **to ~ blood** أَسالَ الدَمَ; **to ~ breath** أَخَذَ نَفَساً **3** (to pull out) سَحَبَ (a; سَحْب)، أَشْهَرَ ‹*a gun, knife*›; **he drew the cork carefully** سَحَبَ السِدادَ بِحَذَرٍ **4** (to derive) اِسْتَمَدَّ ‹*inspiration, satisfaction*›; **I drew comfort from the fact that I wasn't alone** اِسْتَمْدَدْتُ راحَتي من كَوْني لم أَكُنْ وَحيداً; **our readers are ~n from all walks of life** نَسْتَقْطِبُ قُرّاءً من جَميعِ شَرائِحِ المُجْتَمَعِ **5** (to attract) جَذَبَ (i; جَذْب) ‹*a crowd, an audience*›; **to ~ sb's attention to sth** جَذَبَ انْتِباهَ شَخْصٍ لِشَيْءٍ; **to ~ sb into a conversation/an argument** جَذَبَ شَخْصاً إلى حَديثٍ \ جِدالٍ; **they were ~n together by their love of animals** انْجَذَبوا لِبَعْضِهِمْ بِسَبَبِ حُبِّهِمْ للحَيَواناتِ **6** (to elicit) جَلَبَ (i-u; جَلْب)، أَثارَ ‹*criticism, a response, praise*› **7** (to identify) بَيَّنَ ‹*a distinction, parallel, comparison*›; **to ~ a conclusion** وَصَلَ إلى نَتيجةٍ ,اسْتَنْتَجَ **8** (in revelations) **to be ~n** جُرَّ \ انْجَرَّ في الكَلامِ; **the minister refused to be ~n** رَفَضَ الوَزيرُ أنْ يُسْتَدْرَجَ في الكَلامِ **9** (to choose) سَحَبَ (a; سَحْب) ‹*a number, name, a card*› **10** (Fin) (to withdraw) سَحَبَ (a; سَحْب) ‹*money*›; (to write out) حَرَّرَ ‹*a cheque*›; (to take) تَلَقّى ‹*a pension, salary*› **11** (in scoring) **to ~ a game/match** تَعادَلَ في لُعْبةٍ \ مُباراةٍ

B *vi* (*past tense* **drew**; *past participle* **drawn**) **1** (to make a picture) رَسَمَ (u; رَسْم) **2** (to move) **to ~ near** دَنا (u; دُنُوّ, دَناوة); **to ~ ahead of sb/sth** سَبَقَ شَخْصاً \ شَيْئاً; **the police car/boat drew alongside** اقْتَرَبَتْ سَيّارةُ الشُرْطةِ \ السَفينةُ; **the train drew into the station** دَخَلَ القِطارُ المَحَطّةَ; **to ~ level with sb** تَساوى مع شَخْصٍ; **to ~ to a close** *or* **an end** شارَفَ على الانْتِهاءِ; **to ~ near** *or* **close** «time, day» اقْتَرَبَ **3** (in scoring) «teams» تَعادَلَ; **they drew 1-1** تَعادَلوا بِنَتيجةِ 1–1

C *n* **1** (for a lottery, sports competition) سَحْب القُرْعةِ; **the ~ for the European Cup** سَحْب القُرْعةِ لِكَأْسِ أوروبّا **2** (in scores) تَعادُل (تَعادُلات); **the game ended in a ~** انْتَهَت اللُعْبةُ بِتَعادُلٍ **3** (attraction) عُنْصُر جَذْبٍ

Idioms **to ~ a blank** فَشِلَ (a; فَشَل); **to ~ the line at sth/doing sth** رَفَضَ تَجاوُزَ الخَطِّ الأَحْمَرِ في شَيْءٍ \ فِعْلِ شَيْءٍ

Phrasal verbs **draw aside**: **1** ~ [**sth**] **aside** سَحَبَ [شَيْئاً] جانِباً ‹*a curtain, veil*› **2** ~ [**sb**] **aside** أَخَذَ [شَخْصاً] جانِباً

• **draw away** **A** **1** (to move off) «vehicle, person» غادَرَ **2** (to move ahead) تَقَدَّمَ (على بَقيّةِ المُتَسابِقينَ) **B** ~ [**sth**] **away**, ~ **away** [**sth**] سَحَبَ [شَيْئاً] ‹*one's hand, arm*›

• **draw back** **A** «person, animal» تَراجَعَ إلى الخَلْفِ **B** ~ [**sth**] **back**, ~ **back** [**sth**] (to pull back) سَحَبَ [شَيْئاً] ‹*the curtains, one's hand*›

• **draw down**: ~ [**sth**] **down**, ~ **down** [**sth**] **1** (to pull down) سَحَبَ [شَيْئاً] أَنْزَلَ [شَيْئاً] ‹*the blinds, covers*› **2** (to withdraw) سَحَبَ [شَيْئاً] ‹*funds, income*› **3** (to pull out) سَحَبَ [شَيْئاً] ‹*forces, troops*›

• **draw in** **A** **1** «days, nights» قَصُرَ (u; قِصَر) **2** (to arrive) «train, bus» وَصَلَ (i; وُصول) **B ~ [sth] in, ~ in [sth] 1** (in pictures) [شَيْئاً] أَدْمَجَ ‹*the details, background*› **2** (to suck in) [شَيْئاً] شَفَطَ ‹*air, fumes*› **3** (to retract) [شَيْئاً] سَحَبَ ‹*claws*› **4** (to attract) [شَيْئاً] جَذَبَ ‹*a crowd, an audience*›

• **draw off**: **~ [sth] off, ~ off [sth]** [شَيْئاً] صَرَّفَ \ أَزالَ ‹*liquid, fluid*›

• **draw on A** «the night, day» شارَفَ على الانْتِهاءِ \ الانْقِضاءِ **B ~ on [sth]** «person» اسْتَعانَ ب [شَيْءٍ] ‹*sb's work, knowledge*›; **to ~ on one's experience** اسْتَعانَ بِتَجْرِبَتِهِ الخاصّةِ

• **draw out A 1** (to depart) «train, bus» خَرَجَ (u; خُروج), تَحَرَّكَ خارِجاً; **the train drew out of the station** تَحَرَّكَ القِطارُ إلى خارِجِ المَحَطّةِ; **a car drew out in front of me** قَطَعَتْ سَيّارةٌ طَريقي **2** (to become longer) «days» طالَ (u; طول)

B ~ [sth] out, ~ out [sth] 1 (to extract) سَحَبَ \ أَخْرَجَ [شَيْئاً] ‹*a knife, needle*› **2** (to withdraw) [شَيْئاً] سَحَبَ ‹*money, cash*› **3** (to prolong) [شَيْئاً] أَطالَ \ مَدَّدَ ‹*a process, negotiations*›; **it's a long ~n out process** إنَّها عَمَلِيّةٌ طَويلةٌ جِدًّا

C ~ [sb] out أَخْرَجَ [شَخْصاً] من صَمْتِهِ

• **draw up A** «car, taxi» تَوَقَّفَ **B ~ up [sth], ~ [sth] up 1** (to prepare) [شَيْئاً] حَضَّرَ ‹*a plan, proposal, inventory*› **2** (to draft) [شَيْئاً] حَرَّرَ ‹*a will, contract*› **3** (to bring near) [شَيْئاً] سَحَبَ ‹*a chair*› **C ~ oneself up** اسْتَقامَ

drawback /ˈdrɔːbak/ *n* عائِق (عَوائِق)

drawbridge /ˈdrɔːbrɪdʒ/ *n* جِسْر مُتَحَرِّك

drawer /drɔː/ *n* دُرْج (أَدْراج), جارور (جَوارير)

drawing /ˈdrɔːrɪŋ/ *n* رَسْم (رُسوم), صورة (صُوَر)

drawing board *n* لَوْح الرَسْمِ

drawing pin *n* (BrE) دَبّوس (دَبابيسُ)

drawing room *n* غُرْفة الجُلوسِ, صالة الاسْتِقْبالِ

drawl /drɔːl/ *n* [مَطّ \ تَشَدُّق في الحَديثِ \ الكَلامِ]

drawn /drɔːn/ **A** *past participle* ▸ **draw**

B *adj* ‹*face, features*› مُرْهَق

drawstring /ˈdrɔːstrɪŋ/ *n* رِباط (لِكيسٍ أو ثِيابٍ)

drawstring bag *n* [كيس يُفْتَحُ ويُغْلَقُ بِرِباطٍ]

drawstring waist *n* [خَصْر بِرِباطٍ]

dread /drɛd/ **A** *vt* هابَ (a; هَيْبة), تَوَجَّسَ ‹*a prospect, possibility*›

B *n* رَهْبة, تَوَجُّس (تَوَجُّسات), فَزَع (أَفْزاع)

dreadful /ˈdrɛdfʊl/ *adj* **1** (terrifying) ‹*news, disease*› فَظيع (فُظَعاءُ), رَهيب; ‹*nightmare*› مُرْعِب **2** (very bad) ‹*conditions, weather*› فَظيع, رَهيب; **I feel ~** أنا في حالةٍ يُرْثى لَها

dreadfully /ˈdrɛdf(ə)li/ *adv* ‹*disappointed, tired*› إلى حَدٍّ بِشِدّةٍ, كَبيرٍ جِدًّا

dream /driːm/ **A** *n* **1** (while asleep) حُلْم (أَحْلام); **I had a ~ about you/about dying** حَلَمْتُ بِكَ \ بالمَوْتِ **2** (reverie) حُلْم يَقَظةٍ; **to be in a ~** كانَ يَحْلُمُ **3** (aspiration, ideal) حُلْم (أَحْلام); **it was a ~ come true** كانَ حُلْماً وتَحَقَّقَ; **the family's ~s of a better future were shattered** تَناثَرَتْ أَحْلامُ العائِلةِ في مُسْتَقْبَلٍ أَفْضَلَ

B *modifier* ‹*job, house*› الأَحْلام

C *vt* (*past tense, past participle* **dreamt** or **dreamed**) **1** (while asleep) حَلَمَ (u; حُلْم) ‹*a dream, something*› **2** (to imagine) تَصَوَّرَ, تَوَقَّعَ; **I never ~ed that he'd agree!** لم أَتَوَقَّعْ قَطُّ أنَّهُ سَيُوافِقُ!

D *vi* (*past tense, past participle* **dreamt** or **dreamed**) **1** (while asleep) حَلَمَ (u; حُلْم); **to ~ about** *or* **of sth/sb** حَلَمَ بِشَيْءٍ \ بِشَخْصٍ **2** (in reverie) حَلَمَ (u; حُلْم) **3** (emphatic: to consider) فَكَّرَ; **I wouldn't ~ of going there** ما كُنْتُ لأُفَكِّرَ بالذَهابِ إلى هُناكَ

Idiom **like a dream** (infml) بِشَكْلٍ ناجحٍ \ جَيِّدٍ; **the plan worked like a ~** نَجَحَت الخُطّةُ نَجاحاً كَبيراً \ باهراً

Phrasal verb **dream up**: **~ up [sth]** (infml) جاءَ ب [شَيْءٍ] ‹*an idea, a plan*›

dreamer /ˈdriːmə/ *n* حالِم

dreamt /drɛmt/ *past tense, past participle* ▸ **dream**

dream ticket *n* [ثُنائيّ يُشَكِّل وَرَقةً رابِحةً لِحِزْبٍ سِياسيٍّ في الانْتِخاباتِ الرِئاسيّةِ]

dreamworld /ˈdriːmwəːld/ *n* عالَم خَيالٍ

dreamy /ˈdriːmi/ *adj* (**dreamier, dreamiest**) **1** (distracted) ‹*smile, sigh*› حالِم; ‹*person*› شارِد الذِهْنِ \ الفِكْرِ **2** (gentle) ‹*melody, ballad*› مُريح, هادِئ

dreary /ˈdrɪəri/ *adj* (**drearier, dreariest**) **1** ‹*weather, landscape*› كَئيب, موحِش **2** ‹*existence, routine*› رَتيب, مُمِلّ, مُضْجِر

dredge /drɛdʒ/ *vt* جَرَف (u; جَرْف) ‹*a river, harbour*›

Phrasal verb **dredge up**: **~ up [sth], ~ [sth] up** 1 أَخْرَجَ [شَيْئاً] من القاعِ, حفَرَ [شَيْئاً] ‹*sand, silt*› 2 أَحْيا [شَيْئاً] ‹*memories, the past*›

dredger /ˈdrɛdʒə/ *n* جَرّافة, كَرّاكة

dregs /drɛgz/ *n pl* 1 (sediment) راسِب (رَواسِبُ), ثُفْل, حُثالة 2 (worthless elements) حُثالة, ثُمالة (ثُمال); **the ~ of society** حُثالة المُجْتَمَع

drench /drɛntʃ/ *vt* نَقَع (a; نَقْع), غَمَر (u; غَمْر), بَلَّل ‹*sb's clothes, face*›

dress /drɛs/ **A** *vt* 1 أَلْبَسَ ‹*a child, an elderly person*›; **to get ~ed** لَبِسَ \ ارْتَدى مَلابِسَهُ; **to be ~ed in red/furs** لَبِسَ الأَحْمَرَ \ الفِراءَ 2 هَيَّأَ ‹*meat, a salad*›; نَظَّفَ ‹*fish*› 3 ضَمَّدَ ‹*a wound*›

B *vi* (to put on clothes) ارْتَدى مَلابِسَ; **she ~ed quickly** ارْتَدَتْ مَلابِسَها بِسُرْعةٍ; **he usually ~es in black** يَرْتَدي عادةً مَلابِسَ سَوْداءَ

C *n* 1 (garment) فُسْتان (فَساتينُ), ثَوْب (ثِياب) 2 (style of dressing) لِباس (أَلْبِسة), زِيّ (أَزْياء); **formal ~ should be worn** يَنْبَغي ارْتِداءُ المَلابِسِ الرَسْمِيّةِ

Phrasal verbs **dress down**: 1 لَبِسَ مَلابِسَ عادِيّةً 2 **~ [sb] down, ~ down [sb]** أَنَّبَ [شَخْصاً] ‹*a student, soldier*›

• **dress up A ~ up** 1 (infml) (smartly) لَبِسَ مَلابِسَ رَسْمِيّةً \ أَنيقةً 2 (in fancy dress) لَبِسَ مَلابِسَ تَنَكُّرِيّةً **B ~ [sb] up, ~ up [sb]** (to disguise) أَلْبَسَ [شَخْصاً] لِباساً تَنَكُّرِيًّا ‹*oneself, a person*›; **he ~ed himself up as a judge** تَنَكَّرَ في لِباسِ قاضٍ **C ~ [sth] up, ~ up [sth]** (to improve) جَعَلَ [شَيْئاً] مُسْتَساغاً ‹*the facts, a policy*›

dressage /ˈdrɛsɑːdʒ/ *n* تَرْويض (الخَيْل), تَدْريب (تَدْريبات)

dress circle *n* شُرْفة (شُرَف)

dresser /ˈdrɛsə/ *n* 1 (person) **he's a snappy** *or* **stylish ~** هو حَسَنُ \ أَنيقُ الهِنْدامِ 2 (for dishes) خِزانة ذات رُفوفٍ [لِلأَطْباقِ] 3 (AmE) (for clothes) كومودينو (خِزانة ذات أَدْراجٍ)

dressing /ˈdrɛsɪŋ/ *n* 1 (bandage) ضِمادة (ضَمائِدُ) 2 (sauce) خَلْطة السَلَطةِ 3 (AmE) (stuffing) حَشْو

dressing gown *n* (BrE) روب (أَرْواب), مِبْذَل (مَباذِلُ)

dressing room *n* غُرْفة تَبْديلِ المَلابِسِ

dressing table *n* طاوِلة الزينةِ \ مِنْضَدة (في غُرْفةِ النَوْمِ)

dressmaker /ˈdrɛsmeɪkə/ *n* خَيّاط (لِلسَّيِّداتِ)

dress rehearsal *n* بْروفة أَخيرة

dress sense *n* ذَوْق سَليم في المَلابِسِ; **he has good/no dress sense** لَدَيْهِ ذَوْقٌ سَليمٌ \ غَيْرُ سَليمٍ في المَلابِسِ

dress suit *n* لِبْس رَسْمِيّ

dress uniform *n* بِزّة مَراسِمَ

dressy /ˈdrɛsi/ *adj* (**dressier, dressiest**) (infml) ‹*clothes*› أَنيق, مُتَأَنِّق, مُهَنْدَم; ‹*occasion*› رَسْمِيّ

drew /druː/ *past tense* ▸ **draw**

dribble /ˈdrɪb(ə)l/ **A** *vi* 1 «liquid» قَطَرَ (u; قَطْر), نَقَّطَ, نَضَّ (i; نَضّ); «patients, babies» رَيَّلَ 2 (in football, hockey) دَحْرَجَ الكُرةَ

B *n* (stream of liquid) قَطْر; (of saliva) رِيالة

dribs and drabs *adv phr* (**in dribs and drabs** (infml)) ‹*to arrive, pay sb*› شَيْئاً فَشَيْئاً

dried /drʌɪd/ *adj* ‹*fruit, flower, milk*› مُجَفَّف

drier /ˈdrʌɪə/ *n* ▸ **dryer**

drift /drɪft/ **A** *vi* 1 (to be carried by the current) «boat» انْجَرَفَ \ انْساقَ مع التَيّارِ; (by the wind) «smoke» تَطايَرَ; «clouds» ساقَتْهُ الريحُ 2 (to pile up) «snow» تَراكَمَ, تَجَمَّعَ 3 (to move aimlessly) «one's mind, thoughts» شَرَدَ (u; شُرود); **the guests began to ~ away** بَدَأَ الضُيوفُ بالمُغادَرةِ; **to ~ from job to job** انْتَقَلَ من وَظيفةٍ إلى أُخْرى

B *n* 1 (of snow) كَوْم (أَكْوام) 2 (infml) (general meaning) فَحْوى (f; فَحاوٍ, فَحاوى); **I got the ~ of what he said** فَهِمْتُ فَحْوى ما قالَهُ 3 (flow of the current) تَدافُع; (of events) تَعاقُب (تَعاقُبات); **the ~ from the land** النُزوح من الريفِ; **the ~ towards chaos/anarchy** الجُنوح إلى الفَوْضى

Phrasal verbs **drift apart** «couples, friends» افْتَرَقَ

• **drift off** غَفا (u; غَفْو, غُفُوّ)

driftwood /ˈdrɪftwʊd/ *n* خَشَب طافٍ [على سَطْحِ المِياهِ]

drill /drɪl/ **A** *n* 1 (for drilling holes) مِثْقَب; (for oil or mines) حَفّار (حَفّارات); **a power ~** مِثْقاب آلِيّ 2 [u] (military instruction) تَدْريب عَسْكَرِيّ 3 (exercise) تَمْرين (تَمْرينات, تَمارينُ) 4 (procedure) إِجْراء واجِب اتِّباعُهُ [في حالاتِ الطَوارِئِ]; **make yourself familiar with the evacuation ~**

تَعَرَّفْ على الإِجْراءاتِ الواجِبِ اتِّباعُها في عَمَلِيَّةِ الإِخْلاءِ

B *vt* **1** حَفَرَ (i; حَفْر) *<an oil well, borehole, tunnel>* **2** ثَقَبَ (u; ثَقْب) *<wood, masonry>*; **to ~ a hole in the wall** صَنَعَ ثُقْباً في الجِدارِ **3** حَفَرَ (i; حَفْر) *<a tooth>* **4** (Mil) أَخْضَعَ لِتَدْرِيباتٍ عَسْكَرِيَّةٍ *<soldiers>* **5** (to instruct) **to ~ sb in sth** مَرَّنَ شَخْصاً على شَيْءٍ **6** (in learning) **to ~ sth into sb** حَشا رَأْس شَخْصٍ بِشَيْءٍ

C *vi* **1** «oil companies, crews» نَقَّبَ; **to ~ for oil** نَقَّبَ عن النِّفْطِ **2** (in wood, masonry) ثَقَبَ (u; ثَقْب) **3** (Mil) «soldiers» تَدَرَّبَ

drilling /ˈdrɪlɪŋ/ *n* نَقْب, حَفْر

drily /ˈdrʌɪli/ *adv* (with dry humour) *<to remark, observe>* بِسُخْرِيَّةٍ; (coldly) *<to note, reply>* بِجَفافٍ

drink /drɪŋk/ **A** *vt* (*past tense* **drank**; *past participle* **drunk**) شَرِبَ (a; مَشْرَب, شُرْب) *<water, beer>*; **is the water safe to ~?** هل الماءُ صالِحٌ للشُّرْبِ؟

B *vi* (*past tense* **drank**; *past participle* **drunk**) **1** (to consume liquid) شَرِبَ (a; مَشْرَب, شُرْب); **to ~ from *or* out of a cup** شَرِبَ من قَدَحٍ **2** (to consume alcohol) شَرِبَ الكُحولَ; **don't ~ and drive** لا تَقُدْ وَأَنْتَ تحت تَأْثِيرِ الكُحولِ **3** (as a toast) **to ~ to sb/sth** شَرِبَ نَخْبَ شَخْصٍ \ شَيْءٍ

C *n* **1** (non-alcoholic) مَشْروب (مَشْروبات), شَراب (أَشْرِبة); **we have a wide range of hot and cold ~s** لَدَيْنا تَشْكيلةٌ واسِعةٌ من المَشْروباتِ الساخِنةِ والبارِدةِ **2** (alcoholic) كَأْس (mf; كُؤوس); **to go for a ~** ذَهَبَ لِتَناوُلِ كَأْسٍ **3** (act of drinking) جُرْعة (جُرُعات, جُرَع); **have a ~ of water** اشْرَبْ جُرْعَةَ ماءٍ **4** [u] (alcoholic) مَشْروبات كُحولِيّة; **there was plenty of food and ~** كانَتْ هُناكَ وَفْرةٌ في الأَطْعِمةِ والمَشْروباتِ; **to have a ~ problem** كانَتْ لَدَيْهِ مُشْكِلةُ إِدْمانِ الكُحولِ

(Phrasal verbs) **drink in**: **~ in [sth]** غَرِقَ في [شَيْءٍ] *<the atmosphere, sb's words>*

• **drink up** **1** اشْتَفَّ الشَرابَ بِسُرْعةٍ **2** **~ up [sth]**, **~ [sth] up** اشْتَفَّ [شَيْئاً] *<one's milk, beer>*

drinkable /ˈdrɪŋkəb(ə)l/ *adj* **1** (safe) *<water, milk>* صالِح للشُّرْبِ **2** (palatable) *<wine, coffee>* شَهِيّ, لَذِيذ

drink-driving /ˌdrɪŋkˈdrʌɪvɪŋ/ (BrE) *n* (BrE) القِيادة تحت تَأْثِيرِ الكُحولِ

drinker /ˈdrɪŋkə/ *n* (a person who drinks) شارِب; (a person who drinks alcohol) شِرِّيب, سِكِّير, شارِب كُحولٍ; **coffee/beer ~s** شارِبو القَهْوةِ \ البِيرةِ

drinking /ˈdrɪŋkɪŋ/ *n* (of alcohol) شُرْب كُحولٍ \ خَمْرٍ; (of liquid) شُرْب; **the dangers of ~ and driving** مَخاطِر الشُّرْبِ والقِيادةِ

drinking chocolate *n* مَشْروب الشوكولاتةِ \ الكاكاو

drinking laws *n* قَوانِين الكُحولِ \ الخُمور

drinking water *n* ماء الشُّرْبِ

drip /drɪp/ **A** *vi* **(-pp-)** **1** «water, liquids» قَطَرَ; **water ~ped from *or* off the branches** قَطَرَ الماءُ من الفُروعِ **2** «taps» نَقَّطَ, تَقَطَّرَ

B *n* **1** (drop) قَطْرة (قَطَرات), نُقْطة (نُقَط, نِقاط) **2** (sound) **3** (medical apparatus) [جِهاز حَقْنِ السَوائِلِ عن طَرِيقِ الوَرِيدِ]; **to be on a ~** أُعْطِيَ دَواءً \ مَحالِيلَ التَغْذِيةِ عن طَرِيقِ الوَرِيدِ) **4** (infml) (nonentity) شَخْص ساذِج \ تافِه

drip-dry /ˌdrɪpˈdrʌɪ/ *adj* *<clothes, fabric>* يَجِفُّ بِسُرْعةٍ \ دون تَغَضُّنٍ

drip-feed /drɪpˈfiːd/ *vt* **1** [أَعْطى دَواءً \ مَحالِيلَ التَغْذِيةِ عن طَرِيقِ الوَرِيدِ] *<a patient>* **2** [أَعْطى \ قَدَّمَ تَدْرِيجِيًّا] *<information>*

dripping /ˈdrɪpɪŋ/ *adj* *<tap, tree>* مُنَقِّط; *<clothes, washing>* [مَبْلول جِدًّا]; **my clothes are ~ wet** ثِيابِي مَبْلولةٌ جِدًّا; **he was ~ with sweat** كانَ مُتَصَبِّباً عَرَقاً

drive /drʌɪv/ **A** *vt* (*past tense* **drove**; *past participle* **driven**) **1** قادَ (u; قِيادة), ساقَ (u; سِياقة) *<a car, truck, bus>*; **she drove me home** وَصَّلَتْنِي للمَنْزِلِ بِسَيّارَتِها; **I ~ 50 miles every day** أَقْطَعُ 50 مِيلاً بِسَيّارَتِي يَوْمِيًّا; **what car do you ~?** ما نَوْعُ سَيّارَتِكَ؟; **he drove the car into the garage/a wall** دَخَلَ بالسَيّارةِ إلى المَرْأَبِ \ في حائِطٍ **2** (to force) «fear, need» دَفَعَ (a; دَفْع); **fear drove them to sell their assets and leave** دَفَعَهُم الخَوْفُ لِأَنْ يَبِيعوا مُمْتَلَكاتِهِمْ وَيُغادِروا; **small shops are being ~n out of business** تُضْطَرُّ المَتاجِرُ الصَغِيرةُ إلى الإِغْلاقِ; **he was driven to despair/suicide** دُفِعَ بِهِ إلى اليَأْسِ \ الانْتِحارِ **3** (to herd) ساقَ (u; سِياقة) *<cattle, people>*; **thousands were ~n out**

of their homes أُضْطُرَّ الآلافُ إلى مُغادَرةِ بُيوتِهِمْ **4** (to hit) دَقَّ (u; دَقّ) ‹*a nail, stake*› **5** (to power) سَيَّرَ, شَغَّلَ ‹*an engine, a pump*›; **the generator is ~n by steam** يَعْمَلُ المُوَلِّدُ بالبُخارِ **6** **to ~ the ball** (in football, tennis) ضَرَبَ الكُرةَ بِقوّةٍ; (in golf) ضَرَبَ الكُرةَ من نُقْطةِ الانْطِلاقِ

B *vi* (*past tense* **drove**; *past participle* **driven**) (in vehicles) قادَ (u; قِيادة), ساقَ (u; سِياقة); **to ~ to work/into town** قادَ سَيّارَتَهُ إلى العَمَلِ \ المَدينةِ; **she was driving at 90 mph** كانَتْ تَقودُ بِسُرْعةِ 90 ميلاً في الساعةِ; **he waved as he drove past** لَوَّحَ لَنا عِنْدَما مَرَّ أمامَنا بِسَيّارَتِهِ

C *n* **1** (car journey) جَوْلة بالسَّيّارة; **to go for a ~** ذَهَبَ في جَوْلةٍ بالسَّيّارة; **it's only five minutes ~ from here** يَقَعُ على بُعْدِ خَمْسِ دَقائِقَ بالسَّيّارةِ من هُنا **2** (organized effort) حَمْلة (حَمَلات); **the government's ~ to raise educational standards** الحَمْلة الحُكوميّة لِرَفْعِ المَعاييرِ التَّعْليميّةِ **3** [u] (motivation) حافِز, دافِع; **she has the ~ to succeed** لَدَيْها حافِزٌ للنَجاحِ **4** (to a house, building) طَريق مُؤَدٍّ إلى بَيْتٍ \ مَبْنًى] **5** (of a computer) مُشَغِّل \ مُحَرِّك أَقْراصٍ **6** (stroke in tennis) ضَرْبة (ضَرَبات); (shot in golf) ضَرْبة من نُقْطةِ الانْطِلاقِ **7** [u] (propulsion system) دَفْع

(Idiom) **to drive sb to drink** دَفَعَ شَخْصاً للشُرْبِ

(Phrasal verbs) **drive at: what are you driving at?** ماذا تَقْصِدُ بالضَبْطِ؟

• **drive away** **A** «driver, vehicle» انْطَلَقَ, غادَرَ **B** **~ [sth] away** ب [شَيْءٍ] ‹*a vehicle*› **C** **~ away [sth/sb], ~ [sth/sb] away** **1** (to repel) طَرَدَ [شَيْئاً \ شَخْصاً] ‹*insects, evil spirits*› **2** (to put off) أَبْعَدَ [شَيْئاً \ شَخْصاً] ‹*customers, tourists*›

• **drive back: ~ back [sth/sb], ~ [sth/sb] back** تَصَدّى ل [شَيْءٍ \ شَخْصٍ] ‹*the enemy, crowd*›

• **drive off** «driver, vehicle» غادَرَ

• **drive on** **A** «driver, vehicle» اسْتَمَرَّ في السَيْرِ **B** **~ [sb] on** دَفَعَ [شَخْصاً] للاسْتِمْرارِ

• **drive out: ~ out [sth/sb], ~ [sth/sb] out** طَرَدَ [شَيْئاً \ شَخْصاً] ‹*inhabitants, invaders*›

drive-by shooting /ˌdrʌɪvbʌɪ ˈʃuːtɪn/ *n* إطْلاق نارٍ من مَرْكَبةٍ مُتَحَرِّكةٍ]

drive-in /ˈdrʌɪvɪn/ *n* **1** (a cinema) سينما سَيّاراتٍ (مَكان مُشاهَدةِ أَفْلامٍ من السَيّاراتِ الواقِفةِ] **2** (a restaurant) مَطْعَم يَخْدِمُ الناسَ وَهُمْ في سَيّاراتِهِمْ]

drivel /ˈdrɪv(ə)l/ (infml) *n* [u] لَغْو, هُراء, كَلام فارِغ \ بِلا مَعْنًى; **to talk ~** تَكَلَّمَ كَلاماً فارِغاً

driven /ˈdrɪv(ə)n/ **A** *past participle* ▸ **drive**

B *adj* ‹*man, personality*› مُنْدَفِع

C (**-driven**); *in combination* **petrol-/steam-~** يَعْمَلُ بالبَنْزين \ بالبُخارِ; **a market-~ economy** اقْتِصاد السوقِ

driver /ˈdrʌɪvə/ *n* **1** (of a car, bus, taxi, etc) سائِق (سوّاق); **a truck ~** سائِق شاحِنةٍ; **she's a good/bad ~** هي سائِقةٌ جَيِّدةٌ \ سَيِّئةٌ **2** (of a racing car) سائِق (سَيّارة سِباقٍ) **3** (in golf) مِضْرَب خاصّ في لُعْبة الجولف]

driveway /ˈdrʌɪvweɪ/ *n* ▸ **drive** C4

driving /ˈdrʌɪvɪŋ/ **A** *adj* **1** ‹*rain, hail*› غَزير; ‹*wind*› قَوِيّ **2** ‹*force, ambition*› مُحَرِّك, دافِع

B *n* سِواقة, سِياقة, قِيادة; **rally ~** سِياقة الرالي

driving force *n* قوّة دافِعة

driving instructor *n* مُدَرِّب سِياقةٍ \ قِيادةِ سَيّاراتٍ

driving lesson *n* دَرْس قِيادةٍ

driving licence (BrE), **driver's license** (AmE) *n* رُخْصة سِياقةٍ \ قِيادةٍ

driving school *n* مَدْرَسة سِياقةٍ \ قِيادةِ سَيّاراتٍ

driving seat *n* مَقْعَد السائِقِ;

(Idiom) **to be in the driving seat** كانَ في مَقْعَدِ القِيادة

driving test *n* اخْتِبار قِيادة

drizzle /ˈdrɪz(ə)l/ **A** *n* رَذاذ, مَطَر خَفيف, رَشاش

B *vi* تَساقَطَ الرَذاذُ

droll /drəʊl/ *adj* **1** (amusing) ‹*comedy, manner*› مُضْحِك, مُهَرِّج, هَزْلِيّ **2** (liter) (odd) ‹*sense of humour, delivery*› غَريب

drone /drəʊn/ **A** *vi* «bees, planes» طَنَّ (i; طَنين), دَنْدَنَ (i; دَنْدَنة); **she's always droning (on) about how bad the traffic is** تُسْهِبُ دائِماً عن مَدى سوءِ حَرَكةِ السَيْرِ

B *n* **1** (sound of an engine, a plane) دَنين, دَنْدَنة, هَمْهَمة (هَماهِمُ); (of insects) طَنين, طَنْطَنة; (of sb's voice) هَمْهَمة

صَوْت رَتيب (هَماهِمُ), 2 (bee) ذَكَر النَّحْلَةِ 3 (aircraft) طائِرة بلا طَيّارٍ

drool /dru:l/ *vi* 1 «dogs, babies» رَيَّلَ, سالَ لُعابُهُ 2 (to desire) نَظَرَ باشْتِهاءٍ; **to ~ over sth/sb** نَظَرَ إلى شَيْءٍ \ شَخْصٍ باشْتِهاءٍ

droop /dru:p/ *vi* 1 «flower, dog's tail» ارْتَخى, تَدَلّى 2 «head, eyelids» انْحَنى

drop /drɒp/ A *vt* (-pp-) 1 (to allow to fall by accident) أَوْقَعَ ‹a ball, glass›; (on purpose) أَسْقَطَ ‹one's bags, litter, a bomb› 2 (by parachute) أَنْزَلَ (بالمِظَلاّتِ) ‹supplies, troops› 3 (also **drop off**) (to set down, leave) أَنْزَلَ ‹a passenger, package› 4 (to lower) خَفَّضَ ‹prices›; **to ~ one's eyes/voice** نَظَرَ إلى الأَسْفَلِ \ خَفَّضَ صَوْتَهُ 5 (infml) (to send) بَعَثَ (a; بَعْث) ‹a note, card›; **~ us a line** ابْعَثْ \ اُكْتُبْ لَنا رِسالةً قَصيرةً 6 (to abandon) أَسْقَطَ ‹the charges, case›; تَرَكَ (u; تَرْك), تَخَلّى (عن) ‹a plan›; **to ~ everything** تَرَكَ كُلَّ ما في يَدِهِ; **can we ~ that subject, please?** هَلاّ غَيَّرْنا هذا المَوْضوعَ، رَجاءً؟ 7 تَرَكَ (u; تَرْك) ‹a subject› 8 (to exclude socially) تَخَلّى (عن), تَرَكَ (u; تَرْك) ‹a friend, boyfriend›; (from team) اسْتَبْعَدَ ‹a player›; **they ~ped us when they moved to Knightsbridge** تَجاهَلونا عِنْدَما انْتَقَلوا إلى نايْتسْبْريدْج; **he has been ~ped from the team** اُسْتُبْعِدَ من الفَريقِ 9 (to omit) حَذَفَ (i; حَذْف) ‹a word, paragraph› 10 (to lose) خَسِرَ (a; خُسْر) ‹a point, game›

B *vi* (-pp-) 1 (to fall) «curtain, leaves» سَقَطَ (u; سُقوط, مَسْقَط); **her jaw ~ped in surprise** اسْتَغْرَبْتُ كَثيراً; **she was so tired she just ~ped into the chair** كانَتْ مُتْعَبةً إلى دَرَجةِ أَنَّها انْهارَتْ على الكُرْسيِّ; **they ~ped to the ground** ارْتَمَوْا على الأَرْضِ; **the plane ~ped to 1,000 metres** نَزَلَت الطائِرةُ إلى ارْتِفاعِ أَلْفِ مِتْرٍ 2 (to slope) «ground, road» انْحَدَرَ; **the road ~s steeply/gently down the mountainside** يَنْحَدِرُ الطَريقُ بِشَكْلٍ حادٍّ \ قَليلاً أَسْفَلَ الجَبَلِ 3 (to decrease) «prices, rate, level» نَزَلَ (i; نُزول), هَبَطَ (i-u; هُبوط); **her weight ~ped from 70 to 55 kilos** نَزَلَ وَزْنُها من 70 إلى 55 كيلو; **the temperature has ~ped by seven degrees** نَزَلَتْ \ هَبَطَتْ دَرَجةُ الحَرارة سَبْعَ دَرَجاتٍ; **the wind ~s in the evening** تَقِلُّ شِدّةُ الرِياحِ في المَساءِ

C *n* 1 (of liquid) قَطْرة (قَطَرات); **we could do with a ~ of rain** نَحْتاجُ إلى قَطَراتٍ من المَطَرِ; **'milk?' — 'just a ~'** 'حَليب؟' — 'نُقْطة واحِدة فَقَطْ' 2 (decrease) انْخِفاض (انْخِفاضات); **a 20% ~ in demand/property values** انْخِفاض بِنِسْبة 20٪ في الطَلَبِ \ قِيَمِ العَقاراتِ 3 (vertical distance) انْخِفاض, هُبوط (انْخِفاضات); **there is a ~ of 200 metres to the bottom** هُناكَ هُبوطٌ بِمِقْدارِ 200 مِتْرٍ إلى الأَسْفَلِ; **there was a steep ~ on either side** كانَ هُناكَ انْخِفاضٌ حادٌّ على كِلا الجانِبَيْنِ 4 (sweet) حَلْوى (f; حَلاوى) 5 (of supplies, troops) إنْزال مِظَلّيّ \ جَوّيّ 6 (infml) (delivery) تَوْصيل 7 (**drops** *n pl*) قَطَرات; **eye/nose ~s** قَطَرات العَيْنِ \ الأَنْفِ

Idiom **a drop in the ocean** *or* **bucket** نُقْطة في بَحْرٍ

Phrasal verbs **drop away** 1 (to decrease) «attendances, interest» قَلَّ (i; قِلّة) 2 (to go down) «ground, road» انْحَدَرَ

• **drop back** (deliberately) رَجَعَ إلى الخَلْفِ; (being left behind) تَراجَعَ

• **drop by** «friends» مَرَّ (u; مُرور, مَمَرّ)

• **drop in** «friends» مَرَّ (u; مُرور); **to ~ in on sb** مَرَّ على شَخْصٍ

• **drop off** A 1 (to fall off) «handle, flowers» سَقَطَ (u; سُقوط, مَسْقَط) 2 (infml) (to fall asleep) غَفا (u; غَفْو, غُفُوّ) 3 (to decrease) «sales, attendance» انْخَفَضَ B **~ [sth/sb] off, ~ off [sth/sb]** ▸ **drop** A3

• **drop out** (to withdraw from a contest, race, project) انْسَحَبَ; (from school, university) تَوَقَّفَ عن الدِراسة; (from society) تَخَلّى عن نَمَطِ الحَياةِ التَقْليديِّ

• **drop round** A «friends» مَرَّ (u; مُرور) B **~ [sth] round** وَصَّلَ \ أَخَذَ [شَيْئاً] إلى بَيْتِ شَخْصٍ في طَريقِهِ

drop-dead /ˌdrɒpˈdɛd/ *adv* (infml) **~ gorgeous** في مُنْتَهى الجَمالِ

drop-down menu /ˌdrɒpdaʊn ˈmɛnju:/ *n* قائِمة مُنْسَدِلة

droplet /ˈdrɒplət/ *n* قُطَيْرة

dropout /ˈdrɒpaʊt/ *n* 1 (from society) هاجِر \ تارِك المُجْتَمَع; (from school, university, etc) مُتَسَرِّب من التَعْليم 2 (in rugby) ضَرْبة إسْقاطٍ

dropper /ˈdrɒpə/ *n* قَطّارة

droppings /ˈdrɒpɪŋz/ *n pl* بَعْر، (أَرْواث) رَوْث

drop shot *n* [ضَرْبة خفيفة تَقَع بالقُرْب من الشَبَكةِ بِحَيْثُ أنَّهُ يَصْعَبُ على المُنافِسِ إدْراكُها]

dross /drɒs/ *n* [u] 1 (a worthless thing) دَبَش، خَبَث; **the magazine was complete ~** [كانَت المَجَلّةُ قِمّةَ التَفاهةِ] 2 (metallurgy) رَغْوة مَعادِنَ

drought /draʊt/ *n* مَحْل، قَحْط، جَفاف

drove /drəʊv/ A *past tense* ▸ **drive**

B *n* 1 (of animals) (قُطْعان) قَطيع، (أَسْراب) سِرْب، (فِرَق) فِرْق; **a ~ of cattle** قَطيع من الماشِية 2 (**droves** *n pl*) (of people) حَشْد (حُشود)، فِرْق، (أَسْراب) سِرْب; **~s of people** حَشْد من الناسِ; **people are leaving the city in ~s** يُغادِرُ الناسُ المَدينةَ في جَماعاتٍ حاشِدةٍ

drown /draʊn/ A *vt* 1 أَغْرَق، غَرَّق ‹*a person, an animal*› 2 (also **drown out**) طَغَى على ‹*sb's voice, a sound*›

B *vi* «people, animals» غَرِق (a; غَرَق)

drowning /ˈdraʊnɪŋ/ *n* غَرَق

drowsy /ˈdraʊzi/ *adj* (**drowsier**, **drowsiest**) ‹*patients, drivers*› نَعْسان (dipt; نَعْسى f) نِعاس، وَسِن; **the heat made me feel ~** جَعَلَتْني الحَرارةُ أَشْعُرُ بالنُعاسِ

drudge /drʌdʒ/ *n* (a person) شَخْص كادِح; [u] (work) [عَمَل مُضْنٍ]

drudgery /ˈdrʌdʒ(ə)ri/ *n* [u] كَدْح; **it's sheer ~** [العَمَلُ مُجَرَّدُ كَدْحٍ]

drug /drʌɡ/ A *n* 1 (medication) (عَقاقيرُ) عَقّار، (أَدْوِية) دَواء 2 (narcotic) (مُخَدِّرات) مُخَدِّر; **to be on ~s** تَعاطَى المُخَدِّراتِ

B *vt* (**-gg-**) خَدَّرَ ‹*a victim*›

drug abuse *n* تَعاطي \ اسْتِهْلاك مُخَدِّراتٍ

drug abuser *n* مُتَعاطي مُخَدِّراتٍ

drug addict *n* مُدْمِن مُخَدِّراتٍ

drug addiction *n* إدْمان (على) مُخَدِّراتٍ

drug dealer *n* تاجِر \ مُرَوِّج مُخَدِّرات

drugged /drʌɡd/ *adj* ‹*person*› مُخَدَّر; ‹*drink, food*› فيه مُخَدِّرٌ

druggist /ˈdrʌɡɪst/ *n* (AmE) (صَيادلة) صَيْدَليّ

drug mule *n* مُهَرِّب مُخَدِّراتٍ

drugstore /ˈdrʌɡstɔː/ *n* (AmE) صَيْدَليّة

drug-taking /ˈdrʌɡteɪkɪŋ/ *n* تَناوُل \ تَعاطي مُخَدِّراتٍ

drug user *n* مُتَعاطي مُخَدِّراتٍ

drum /drʌm/ A *n* 1 (musical instrument) (أَطْبال، طُبول) طَبْل; **Ed Begley is on ~s** إيد بيجْلي على الدرامْز 2 (for oil) (بَراميلُ) بِرْميل 3 (of a washing machine) أُسْطُوانة

B *vt* (**-mm-**) نَقَّرَ (ب) ‹*feet, fingers*›; **to ~ sth into sb** (infml) [عَلَّمَ شَخْصاً شَيْئاً بالتَكْرارِ]

C *vi* (**-mm-**) 1 «rain, hooves» نَقَر (u; نَقْر)، دَقّ (u; دَقّ) 2 «drummers» قَرَعَ الطَبْلَ، عَزَفَ على الدرامْز

Phrasal verb **drum up**: **~ up [sth]** [جَمَعَ \ حَشَدَ [شَيْئاً]] ‹*business, support*›

drumbeat /ˈdrʌmbiːt/ *n* قَرْع الطَبْلِ

drum kit *n* آلة درامْز

drummer /ˈdrʌmə/ *n* عازِف درامْز، طَبّال

drumstick /ˈdrʌmstɪk/ *n* 1 (for drumming) عَصا الطَبْلِ \ الدرامْز 2 (of chicken, turkey) كاحِل الدَجاجِ

drunk /drʌŋk/ A *past participle* ▸ **drink**

B *adj* سَكْران (dipt; سُكارى، سَكارى)، ثَمِل، مَخْمور; **to get ~ (on sth)** أَسْكَرَهُ (شَيْءٌ)، ثَمِلَ (نَتيجةَ شُرْبِ شَيْءٍ); **~ and disorderly** سَكْران وَمُخالِف للنِظامِ

C *n* سِكّير

drunkard /ˈdrʌŋkəd/ *n* خِمّير، شِرّيب، سِكّير

drunk driver *n* سائِق سَكْران

drunk driving *n* القِيادة تحت تَأْثيرِ الكُحولِ \ السُكْرِ

drunken /ˈdrʌŋk(ə)n/ *adj* 1 ‹*man, woman*› سَكْران (dipt; سُكارى، سَكارى)، ثَمِل 2 ‹*brawl, party*› [في حالةِ سُكْرٍ]

drunkenness /ˈdrʌŋk(ə)nˌnəs/ *n* (state) ثَمْلة، سُكْر; (habit) إدْمان على الكُحولِ

Druze /druːz/ *n* (*pl* **Druze, Druzes**) (دُروز) دُرْزيّ

dry /draɪ/ A *adj* (**drier**, **driest**) 1 (not wet) ‹*soil, skin*› جافّ، ناشِف; **the tank has run ~** جَفَّ الخَزّانُ; **her mouth/throat was ~** كانَ فَمُها \ حَلْقُها جافًّا; **on ~ land** على اليابِسةِ; **'keep in a cool ~ place'** 'يُحْفَظُ في مَكانٍ بارِدٍ وَجافٍّ' 2 (not rainy) ‹*climate, weather, conditions*› جافّ، غَيْر مُمْطِرٍ; **it will be ~ tomorrow** سَيَكونُ الجَوُّ جافًّا غَداً; **the ~ season lasts**

from October to March يَسْتَمِرُّ المَوْسِمُ الجافُّ من أُكْتوبِر إلى مارِس **3** ‹wine, sherry› جافّ **4** ‹humour, wit› غَيْر حُلْوٍ **5** (dull) ‹subject matter, style› جافّ **6** (forbidding alcohol) ‹state, country› [يَمْنَعُ اسْتِهْلاكَ \ بَيْعَ المَشْروباتِ الكُحوليّة]

B *vt* (**dries**, **drying**, **dried**) جَفَّفَ ‹clothes, the dishes, fruit›; **to ~ one's hair/hands** جَفَّفَ شَعْرَهُ \ يَدَيْهِ; **to ~ one's eyes/tears** مَسَحَ عَيْنَيْهِ \ دُموعَهُ

C *vi* (**dries**, **drying**, **dried**) **1** «paint, clothes» جَفَّ (i; جَفاف, جُفوف) **2** (also **dry up**) (BrE) (to dry the dishes) نَشَّفَ الأَواني

D *v refl* (**dries**, **drying**, **dried**) **to ~ oneself** نَشَّفَ نَفْسَهُ

(Phrasal verbs) **dry off** **1** «person, clothes» جَفَّ (i; جَفاف, جُفوف) **2** **~ off [sb/sth]**, **~ [sb/sth] off** جَفَّفَ \ نَشَّفَ [شَخْصاً \ شَيْئاً] ‹a child, clothes›

• **dry out** **1** «soil, wood» جَفَّ (i; جَفاف, جُفوف) **2** (infml) «alcoholics» تَخَلَّصَ من الإِدْمانِ على الكُحولِ

• **dry up** **A** **1** «river, well» جَفَّ (i; جَفاف, جُفوف) **2** (infml) «speaker, interviewee» تَعَقَّدَ \ انْعَقَدَ لِسانُهُ **3** (to run out) «money, source» نَفِدَ (a; نَفاد, نَفْد) **4** (BrE) (to dry the dishes) ▸ **dry** C2 **B** **~ up [sth]**, **~ [sth] up** **1** جَفَّفَ [شَيْئاً] ‹a puddle, river› **2** نَشَّفَ [شَيْئاً] ‹dishes, plates›

dry-clean /ˌdrʌɪˈkliːn/ *vt* نَظَّفَ تَنْظيفاً جافًّا ‹clothes, a dress›

dry-cleaner's /drʌɪˈkliːnəz/ *n* مَحَلّ تَنْظيفٍ جافٍّ

dry dock *n* حَوْض جافّ

dryer /ˈdrʌɪə/ *n* **1** (machine for drying clothes) نَشّافة; (rack for drying clothes) مُجَفِّف **2** (for hair) مُجَفِّف شَعْرٍ

dry goods *n* (AmE old use) بَضائِع جافّة (مَوادّ غِذائيّة)

dry ice *n* جَليد جافّ, ثاني أُكْسيد الكَرْبون المُجَمَّد

dryly /ˈdrʌɪli/ *adv* ▸ **drily**

dryness /ˈdrʌɪnəs/ *n* **1** (of the skin, weather, soil) جَفاف **2** (of sb's manner) بُرودة, جُمود **3** (of a wine) [خُلوّ الخَمْرِ من الحُلْوِ]

dry rot *n* نَخْر الخَشَبِ (تُسَبِّبُهُ الفُطْريّاتُ)

DTP /diːtiːˈpiː/ *n* = **desktop publishing** نَشْر مَكْتَبيّ

dual /ˈdjuːəl/ **A** *adj* ‹role, purpose› مُزْدَوِج, ثُنائيّ

B *n* مُثَنًّى

dual carriageway *n* (BrE) طَريق مُزْدَوِج

dual control *adj* ‹car, trainer› مُزْدَوِج التَحَكُّمِ

dual nationality *n* ازْدِواج الجِنْسيّةِ

dual-purpose /ˌdjuːlˈpəːpəs/ *adj* ‹device, furniture› مُزْدَوِج, ثُنائيّ الغَرَضِ, الهَدَفِ

dub /dʌb/ *vt* (**-bb-**) **1** (Cin) دَبْلَجَ ‹a film› **2** (to nickname) سَمّى, لَقَّبَ ‹the event, performer›

Dubai /djuːˈbʌɪ/ *pr n* دُبَيّ (f)

dubious /ˈdjuːbɪəs/ *adj* **1** (doubtful) ‹person› مُتَرَدِّد, شاكّ; **to be ~ about sth** شَكَّ في شَيْءٍ **2** (questionable) ‹distinction, honour› مُلْتَبِس; ‹claim, reputation› مَشْكوك فيه; ‹past› مُريب

Dublin /ˈdʌblɪn/ *pr n* دَبْلِن (f)

duchess /ˈdʌtʃɪs/ *n* دوقة

duchy /ˈdʌtʃi/ *n* (*pl* **duchies**) دوقيّة

duck /dʌk/ **A** *n* (generic) بَطّ (n coll); (female) بَطّة

B *vt* **1** (to lower) **to ~ one's head** خَفَضَ رَأْسَهُ بِسُرْعةٍ **2** (to avoid) تَمَلَّصَ (من) (لِيَتَفادى شَيْئاً) ‹a question, one's responsibilities› **3** (infml) (in the water) غَطَّسَ ‹a swimmer›

C *vi* «spectators, boxers» خَفَضَ رَأْسَهُ بِسُرْعةٍ

(Idioms) **like water off a duck's back** لم يَتْرُكْ أَثَراً; **to take to sth like a duck to water** تَعَلَّمَ شَيْئاً بِسُهولةٍ بالِغةٍ

duckling /ˈdʌklɪŋ/ *n* فَرْخ بَطٍّ

duct /dʌkt/ *n* **1** (for cables, air, etc) أُنْبوب (أَنابيبُ), ماسورة (مَواسيرُ), قَناة (قَنَوات) **2** (in the body) قَناة (قَنَوات), مَجْرًى (مَجارٍ)

dud /dʌd/ (infml) **A** *n* إِخْفاق (شَيْء بِهِ خَلَلٌ أو نَقْصٌ)

B *adj* **1** ‹banknote, coin› زائِف; ‹cheque› بِلا رَصيدٍ **2** ‹bullet, shell› غَيْر مُنْفَجِرٍ; ‹battery› مُعَطَّل

dude /djuːd/ (infml) *n* رَجُل (رِجال)

dudgeon /ˈdʌdʒ(ə)n/ *n*

(Idiom) **to be in high dudgeon** [كانَ غاضِباً جِدًّا]

due /djuː/ **A** *adj* **1** (payable) مُسْتَحَقّ; **to be ~** كانَ مُسْتَحَقَّ الدَفْعِ; **the rent is ~ on the 6th of each month** يَتَوَجَّبُ دَفْعُ الإِيجارِ في السادِسِ من كُلِّ شَهْرٍ **2** (expected) مُتَوَقَّع; **the bus is ~ in five minutes** من المُتَوَقَّعِ أَنْ تَصِلَ الحافِلةُ خِلال خَمْسِ دَقائِقَ; **building work is ~ to start in May** من

المُقَرَّر بَدْءُ أَعْمالِ البِناءِ في مايو; **I'm ~ at a lecture at 2 pm** يُفْتَرَضُ أنْ أَحْضُرَ مُحاضَرةً الساعة 2 بعد الظُهْرِ; **when's the baby ~?** مَتى مَوْعِدُ الوِلادةِ؟ **3** (entitled to) مُسْتَحِقّ; **to be ~ a month's back pay** كانَ لَدَيْهِ راتِبُ شَهْرٍ مُسْتَحَقٌّ **4** (owed) مُسْتَحَقّ; **thanks are ~ to the hospital staff** لا بُدَّ من تَقْديمِ الشُكْرِ للعامِلينَ في المُسْتَشْفى; **to give/pay sb what is ~ to him** أَعْطى شَخْصاً \ دَفَعَ لِشَخْصٍ ما هو مُسْتَحَقٌّ لَهُ; **he never received the recognition he was ~** لم يَحْصُلْ أَبَداً على التَقْديرِ الّذي يَسْتَحِقُّهُ **5** (fml) (appropriate) *‹regard, care›* مُناسِب; **after ~ consideration** بعد تَفْكيرٍ عَميقٍ; **with all ~ respect** مع احْتِرامي الفائِقِ; **we will write to you in ~ course** سَنَتَّصِلُ بِكَ في الوَقْتِ المُناسِبِ

B *n* حَقّ (حُقوق); **to give sb their ~** كانَ مُنْصِفاً مع شَخْصٍ

C **(dues)** *n pl* مُسْتَحَقّات

D *adv* (in navigation) **to face ~ north/south** كانَ مُواجِهاً لِلشَمالِ \ للجَنوبِ مُباشَرةً; **the airport is ~ west of the capital** يَقعُ المَطارُ غَرْبَ العاصِمةِ بالضَبْطِ

E **(due to)** *prep phr* بِسَبَبِ; **~ to unforeseen circumstances** نَظَراً لِظُروفٍ غَيْرِ مُتَوَقَّعةٍ; **its success is largely ~ to her** يَعودُ الفَضْلُ في نَجاحِهِ بِشَكْلٍ كَبيرٍ إِلَيْها; **the death was ~ to natural causes** كانَ المَوْتُ ناتِجاً عن أَسْبابٍ طَبيعيّةٍ

duel /'djuːəl/ *n* مُبارَزة

duet /djuː'ɛt/ *n* ثُنائِيّ

duffel bag, **duffle bag** *n* كيس العُدّةِ

duffel coat, **duffle coat** *n* [نَوْع من المَعاطِفِ]

dug /dʌg/ *past tense, past participle* ▸ **dig**

dugout /'dʌgaʊt/ *n* **1** (a boat) [زَوْرَق من جُذْعِ شَجَرةٍ] **2** (in sport) مَقْصورة (مَقاصيرُ) **3** (a soldier's shelter) مَخْبَأ (مَخابِئُ)

duke /djuːk/ *n* دوق

dull /dʌl/ **A** *adj* **1** (boring) *‹film, life›* مُمِلّ **2** (overcast) *‹weather, sky›* مُعْتِم **3** (not bright or clear) *‹colour›* باهِت; *‹eyes, complexion›* شاحِب; *‹light, thud›* خافِت **4** *‹pain, ache›* بَسيط, طَفيف **5** *‹blade, knife›* مَفْلول, كَليل

B *vt* **1** [جَعَلَ باهِتاً \ خافِتاً] *‹a colour, surface, the shine of sth›* **2** *‹pain›* خَفَّفَ; *‹the senses›* أَضْعَفَ **3** (AmE) ثَلَمَ (i; ثَلْم) فَلَّ (u; فَلّ) *‹a blade, knife›*

dully /'dʌl,li/ *adv* **1** (boringly) *‹to reply, stare›* بِفُتورٍ **2** (dimly) *‹to gleam, shine›* [بِشَكْلٍ باهِتٍ]

duly /'djuːli/ *adv* **1** (properly) *‹elected, noted›* [قانونيًّا \ رَسْميًّا] **2** (as expected) *‹to arrive, deliver›* في ميعادِهِ, كَما يَنْبَغي

dumb /dʌm/ *adj* **1** (silent) صامِت, صُموت (صَوامِتُ) **2** (old use or offensive) (unable to speak) أَخْرَس (dipt; خُرْس, خُرْسان), أَبْكَم (dipt; بُكْم); **to be struck ~** أُصيبَ بالبُكْمِ **3** (infml) (stupid) *‹person›* أَحْمَق (dipt; حُمْق; f حَمْقى); *‹question, idea›* سَخيف, تافِه

(Phrasal verb) **dumb down**: **~ [sth] down, ~ down [sth]** بَسَّطَ [شَيْئاً] *‹a course, TV programme›*

dumb-bell /'dʌmbɛl/ *n* **1** (in weight training) دَمْبِل (ثِقْل حَديديّ) **2** (AmE infml) (fool) أَحْمَق (dipt; حُمْق; f حَمْقى), غَبِيّ (أَغْبِياءُ)

dumbfound /dʌm'faʊnd/ *vt* صَعَقَ (a; صَعْق), شَدَهَ (a; شَدْه) *‹spectators, everybody›*

dumbstruck /'dʌmstrʌk/ *adj* *‹silence, fool›* مَشْدوه, مَصْعوق

dumb waiter *n* [مِصْعَد نَقْل المَؤْكولاتِ في مَطْعَمٍ]

dummy /'dʌmi/ **A** *n* **1** (model) دُمْية (لِعَرْضِ المَلابسِ) **2** (BrE) (for a baby) مَصّاصة **3** (AmE infml) (stupid person) غَبِيّ (أَغْبِياءُ), جاهِل (جَهَلة)

B *adj* *‹drawer, book›* زائِف

dummy run *n* تَجْرِبة (تَجارِبُ), تَمْرين (تَمْرينات)

dump /dʌmp/ **A** *n* **1** (site for waste) مَزْبَلة (مَزابِلُ), مَقْلَب (مَقالِبُ), مَوْقِع رَدْمِ النُفاياتِ **2** (Mil) (store) [مُسْتَوْدَع عَسْكَرِيّ] **3** (infml) (unpleasant place) [مَكان كَئيب]

B *vt* **1** (to dispose of) رَمى (i; رِماية), رَدَمَ (i-u; رَدْم) *‹refuse, waste›*; *‹sewage›* صَرَّفَ; تَخَلَّصَ (من) *‹nuclear waste›* **2** (to put down) طَرَحَ (a; طَرْح) *‹bags, a load›* **3** (infml) (to abandon) هَجَرَ (u; هَجْر), نَبَذَ (i; نَبْذ) *‹a boyfriend, girlfriend›*

(Idiom) **to be down in the dumps** (infml) كانَ مُغْتَمًّا \ مَهْموماً

dumper, **dumper truck** (BrE), **dump truck** (AmE) /'dʌmpə/ *n* شاحِنة قَلّابة

dumper truck (BrE), **dump truck** (AmE) *n* شاحِنة قَلّابة

dumping /'dʌmpɪŋ/ *n* **1** (Ecol) رَدْم (النُفاياتِ) **2** (Econ) إِغْراق الأَسْواقِ (بَيْع السِلَعِ بِأَسْعارٍ مُنْخَفِضةٍ)

dumpling /'dʌmplɪŋ/ *n* [عَجينة كُرَوِيّة مَسْلوقة]

dumpster /ˈdʌmpstə/ *n* حاوِية قُمامةٍ

dump truck *n* ▸**dumper truck**

dumpy /ˈdʌmpi/ *adj* (**dumpier, dumpiest**) *<housewife, boy>* [بَدين وَقَصير]

dunce /dʌns/ *n* مُغَفَّل, بَليد

dune /djuːn/ *n* (تِلال) تَلّ, (أَكْثِبة) كَثيب

dung /dʌŋ/ *n* **1** (excrement) (الحَيَوانِ) رَوْث **2** (manure) (أَسْمِدة) سَماد

dungarees /dʌŋɡəˈriːz/ *n pl* (BrE) [سِرْوال بِحَمّالَتَيْنِ]

dungeon /ˈdʌndʒ(ə)n/ *n* زِنْزانة (تحت الأَرْضِ)

duo /ˈdjuːəʊ/ *n* ثُنائيّ

dupe /djuːp/ **A** *vt* خدعَ (a; خدع) *<a customer, the public>*; **to be ~d** خُدِعَ

B *n* (سُذَّج) ساذَج

duplex /ˈdjuːplɛks/ *n* (AmE) (an apartment) [شِقّة مُؤَلَّفة من طابِقَيْنِ]; (a house) [بَيْت ذو سَقفٍ مُشْتَرَكٍ مع بَيْتٍ آخَرَ]

duplicate /ˈdjuːplɪkət/ **A** *adj* *<file, record>* مُسْتَنْسَخ; **a ~ key** مِفتاح مُسْتَنْسَخ; **a ~ copy** نُسْخة طِبْقَ الأَصْلِ

B *n* (صُوَر) صورة, (نُسَخ) نُسْخة; **in ~** من نُسْخَتَيْنِ

C *vt* /ˈdjuːplɪkeɪt/ **1** (to copy) صَوَّرَ, اسْتَنْسَخَ *<a document>*

2 (to repeat) اسْتَنْسَخَ *<sb's work, success>*

duplication /djuːplɪˈkeɪʃ(ə)n/ *n* تَكْرار

durable /ˈdjʊərəb(ə)l/ *adj* *<material, peace>* مَتين

duration /djʊˈreɪʃ(ə)n/ *n* (امْتِدادات) امْتِداد

duress /djʊəˈrɛs/ *n* **under ~** تحت الإكْراهِ

during /ˈdjʊərɪŋ/ *prep* خِلالَ

dusk /dʌsk/ *n* غَسَق; **at ~** عند الغَسَقِ

dust /dʌst/ **A** *n* (أَغْبِرة) غُبار

B *vt* **1** (to remove dust from) أَزالَ الغُبارَ عن *<furniture, surfaces>* **2** (to sprinkle) **to ~ sth with sth** نَثَرَ شَيْئاً على شَيْءٍ *<a cake>*

dustbin /ˈdʌstbɪn/ *n* (BrE) صُنْدوق قُمامةٍ

dustcart /ˈdʌstkɑːt/ *n* (BrE) سَيّارة قُمامةٍ

duster /ˈdʌstə/ *n* **1** (for furniture) (مَنافِض) مِنْفَضة **2** (for a blackboard) مَسّاحة

dust jacket *n* غِلاف خارِجيّ

dustman /ˈdʌstmən/ *n* (*pl* **-men** BrE) جامِع قُمامةٍ, عامِل نَظافةٍ, زَبّال

dustpan /ˈdʌstpan/ *n* (جَواريف) جاروف

dusty /ˈdʌsti/ *adj* (**dustier, dustiest**) **1** *<furniture, room>* مُغَبَّر

2 *<road, town>* مُغَبَّر, مُتْرِب

Dutch /dʌtʃ/ **A** *adj* *<ambassador, food, lesson>* هولَنْديّ

B *n* **1** (people) (**the Dutch**) الهولَنْدِيّون **2** (language) (اللُّغة) الهولَنْدِيّة

Dutchman /ˈdʌtʃmən/ *n* (*pl* **-men**) هولَنديّ

Dutchwoman /ˈdʌtʃwʊmən/ *n* (*pl* **-women**) هولَنْديّة

dutiable /ˈdjuːtɪəb(ə)l/ *adj* *<item, goods>* خاضِع للضَريبة

dutiful /ˈdjuːtɪfʊl/ *adj* *<daughter, citizen>* مُطيع

duty /ˈdjuːti/ *n* (*pl* **duties**) **1** (obligation) (واجِبات) واجِب; **to have a ~ to do sth** وَجَبَ عَلَيْهِ أَنْ يَفْعَلَ شَيْئاً; **to do one's ~** قامَ بِواجِبِهِ; **to feel ~ bound to help** شَعَرَ بِوُجوبِ المُساعَدةِ

2 (task) (واجِبات) واجِب; **to take up one's duties** اسْتَلَمَ مَنْصِبَهُ \ مَهامَّهُ; **to carry out one's duties** مارَسَ مَهامَّهُ **3** (service) **to be on/off ~** «police officer» كانَ \ لم يَكُنْ في فَتْرةِ الخِدْمةِ; «doctor» كانَ مُناوِباً \ غَيْرَ مُناوِبٍ; **to go on ~** باشَرَ عَمَلَهُ **4** (tax) رُسوم; **to pay customs duties** دَفَعَ رُسومَ الجَمارِكِ

duty-free /ˌdjuːtɪˈfriː/ **A** *adj* *<goods, imports>* مُعْفًى من الضَرائِبِ \ الرُسومِ

B *adv* *<to shop, buy>* بِدونِ دَفْعِ الضَرائِبِ \ الرُسومِ

duty-free shop *n* مَتْجَر سوقٍ حُرّةٍ

duvet /ˈdjuːveɪ/ (BrE) *n* (لُحُف) لِحاف

duvet cover *n* غِطاء لِحافٍ

DVD /diːviːˈdiː/ *n* = **digital versatile disc** أُسْطُوانة دي في دي, فيديو

DVD burner, DVD writer *n* مُسَجِّل دي في دي

DVD player *n* مُشَغِّل دي في دي

DVD recorder *n* مُسَجِّل دي في دي

DVT /diːviːˈtiː/ *n* = **deep-vein thrombosis** التَجَلُّط الوَريديّ العَميق

dwarf /dwɔːf/ **A** *n* (*pl* **dwarfs** or **dwarves** /dwɔːvz/) **1** (Mythol) قَزَم (أَقْزام) **2** (offensive) (very small person) قَزَم (أَقْزام)

B *adj* ‹*tree, shrub*› قَزَميّ

C *vt* جَعَلَ يَبْدو صَغيراً ‹*a building*›

dwell /dwɛl/ *vi* (*past tense, past participle* **dwelled** or **dwelt**) (liter) سَكَنَ (u; سُكْنى, سَكَن)

(Phrasal verb) **dwell on**: **~ on [sth]** **1** (to think about) خاضَ في [شَيْءٍ]; **let's not ~ on the past** دَعْنا لا نَخوضُ في الماضي **2** (to talk about) خاضَ في [شَيْءٍ]; **he ~ed at some length on this topic** خاضَ في المَوْضوعِ بِإسْهابٍ

dwelling /ˈdwɛlɪŋ/ *n* (liter) مَسْكَن (مَساكِنُ)

dwelt /dwɛlt/ *past tense, past participle* ▸ **dwell**

dwindle /ˈdwɪnd(ə)l/ *vi* «numbers, population» تَناقَصَ

dwindling /ˈdwɪndlɪŋ/ *adj* ‹*numbers, supplies*› مُتَضائِل, مُتَقَلِّص, مُتَناقِص

dye /dʌɪ/ **A** *n* صِبْغة

B *vt* (**dyes, dyeing, dyed**) صَبَغَ (a-i-u; صَبْغ, صِبَغ) ‹*hair, fabric*›

dying /ˈdʌɪɪŋ/ **A** *present participle* ▸ **die**

B *adj* **1** (near death) ‹*person, animal*› مُحْتَضِر **2** (vanishing) ‹*breed, art*› آيِل للزَوالِ **3** (final) ‹*moments, wishes*› أَخير

dyke, dike /dʌɪk/ *n* **1** (to prevent flooding) سَدّ, حاجِز للماءِ (أَسْداد, سُدود) **2** (BrE) (ditch) قَناة

dynamic /dʌɪˈnamɪk/ *adj, n* ديناميكيّ, حَرَكيّ

dynamism /ˈdʌɪnəmiz(ə)m/ *n* (all contexts) حَرَكيّة, ديناميّة, قوّة دافِعة

dynamite /ˈdʌɪnəmʌɪt/ *n* ديناميت

dynamo /ˈdʌɪnəməʊ/ *n* (*pl* **dynamos**) دينامو, مُوَلِّد كَهْرَبائيّ

dynasty /ˈdɪnəsti/ *n* (*pl* **dynasties**) سُلالة \ أُسْرة حاكِمة; **the Habsburg ~** أُسْرة هابْسْبورْغ; **the tenth ~ of Egypt** الأُسْرة المِصْريّة العاشِرة

dysentery /ˈdɪs(ə)nt(ə)ri/ *n* دوسَنْطارِيا

dysfunction /dɪsˈfʌŋkʃ(ə)n/ *n* خَلَل (خِلال)

dysfunctional /dɪsˈfʌŋkʃ(ə)n(ə)l/ *adj* مُخْتَلّ

dyslexia /dɪsˈlɛksɪə/ *n* عُسْر القِراءةِ, عَمى الكَلِماتِ

dyslexic /dɪsˈlɛksɪk/ **A** *adj* ‹*student, child*› مُعانٍ من عُسْرِ القِراءةِ

B *n* [شَخْص يُعاني من عُسْرِ القِراءةِ]

dyspepsia /dɪsˈpɛpsɪə/ *n* عُسْر هَضْمٍ

dyspraxia /dɪsˈpraksɪə/ *n* [خَلَل في الأَداءِ]

Ee

E, e /iː/ **A** *n* **1** (letter) [الحَرْف الخامس من الأَبْجَدِيّة الإِنْكْليزِيّة]
2 (E) (Mus) (نَغْمة من نَغَمات السُلَّم الموسيقِيّ) ≈ مي
B *abbr* (E) **1** = **East** شَرْق **2** = **Ecstasy** (infml) (drug) حُبوب النَشْوة

each /iːtʃ/ **A** *determiner* ‹*member, month, nail*› كُلّ; **~ member is entitled to ...** ... يَحِقُّ لِكُلِّ عُضْوٍ أَنْ; **~ time you shop ...** ... كُلّ مَرّةٍ تَتَسَوَّقُ فيها; **~ item undergoes stringent tests** تَخْضَعُ كُلّ قِطْعةٍ لِاخْتِباراتٍ صارِمةٍ; **~ and every customer** كُلّ (واحِدٍ من) الزَبائِنِ
B *pron* كُلّ واحِدٍ; **~ will receive ...** ... كُلُّ واحِدٍ سَيَسْتَلِمُ; **~ of you/of them will be rewarded** سَيُكافَأُ كُلُّ واحِدٍ مِنْكُمْ \ مِنْهُمْ; **the children ~ asked for one** طَلَبَ كُلُّ واحِدٍ من الأَطْفالِ واحِداً; **three bundles of ten notes ~** ثَلاث حُزَمٍ كُلّ حُزْمةٍ فيها عَشْرُ أَوْراقٍ نَقْدِيّةٍ; **~ is equally desirable** (of two) كُلٌّ مِنْهُما مَرْغوبٌ فيه بِنَفْسِ الدَرَجةِ; (of several) كُلٌّ مِنْهُمْ مَرْغوبٌ فيهِ بِنَفْسِ الدَرَجةِ; **I'll try a little of ~** سَأُجَرِّبُ القَليلَ من كُلٍّ واحِدٍ; **oranges at 50p ~** 50 بِنْساً للبُرْتُقالةِ الواحِدةِ

each other *pron* (also **one another**) **they know each other** يَعْرِفُ بَعْضُهُما \ بَعْضُهُمْ بَعْضاً; **you help each other** يُساعِدُ بَعْضُكُما \ بَعْضُكُمْ بَعْضاً; **they hate each other** يَكْرَهُ بَعْضُهُما \ بَعْضُهُمْ بَعْضاً; **they're fond of each other** هُما مولَعانِ بِبَعْضِهِما \ هُمْ مولَعونَ بِبَعْضِهِمْ

eager /ˈiːɡə/ *adj* ‹*anticipation, student, face*› مُتَلَهِّف; **he is ~ to please** هو مُتَلَهِّفٌ لِإِسْعادِ الآخَرينَ; **voters are ~ for change** الناخِبونَ مُتَلَهِّفونَ للتَغْيير

eagerly /ˈiːɡəli/ *adv* ‹*to accept, wait*› بِشَغَفٍ, بِتَلَهُّفٍ; **the band's ~ awaited CD** أُسْطُوانة الفِرْقةِ الّتي يَنْتَظِرُها الناسُ بِشَغَفٍ

eagle /ˈiːɡ(ə)l/ *n* نَسْر (نُسور)

ear /ɪə/ *n* **1** (organ) أُذُن (f; آذان) **2** [u] (hearing) مَوْهِبة; **to play music by ~** عَزَفَ قِطْعةً موسيقيّةً مُعْتَمِداً على أُذُنِهِ \ دون قِراءة [النوتاتِ]; **to have an ~ for languages** كانَ عِنْدَهُ قُدْرةٌ على تَعَلُّمِ اللُغاتِ; **to have an ~ for music** كانَ عِنْدَهُ أُذُنٌ موسيقيّةٌ
3 (of wheat, corn) سُنْبُل (n coll; سَنابِل, سُنْبُلات)

Idioms **to be all ears** كانَ كُلُّهُ آذاناً صاغِيةً; **to be out on one's ear** طُرِدَ شَرَّ طَرْدةٍ; **to have sb's ear** كانَ ذا حُظْوةٍ عند شَخْصٍ; **to play it by ear** تَرَكَ الأُمورَ تَأْخُذُ مَجْراها الطَبيعيَّ

earache /ˈɪəreɪk/ *n* أَلَم في الأُذُنِ

eardrum /ˈɪədrʌm/ *n* طَبْلة الأُذُنِ

ear infection *n* الْتِهاب الأُذُنِ

earl /əːl/ *n* إيرْل (لَقَب نَبيل)

earlobe /ˈɪələʊb/ *n* شَحْمة الأُذُنِ

early /ˈəːli/ **A** *adj* (**earlier**, **earliest**) **1** (not late) ‹*evening, morning*› مُبَكِّر, باكِر; **I'm a bit ~** وَصَلْتُ مُبَكِّراً قَليلاً; **at an ~ age** في عُمْرٍ مُبَكِّرٍ; **to be in one's ~ thirties** كانَ في بِدايةِ الثَلاثيناتِ من عُمْرِه; **to make an ~ start** بَدَأَ باكِراً; **at the earliest** على أَقَلّ تَقْديرٍ; **in the ~ hours** في الساعاتِ الباكِرةِ; **in ~ spring** في بِدايةِ الرَبيعِ **2** (one of the first) ‹*attempt, version, work*› أَوَّل (dipt; أَوائِل; f أُولى); **~ man** إِنْسان بُدائيّ; **an ~ train** قِطار الصَباحِ الباكِرِ; **in the ~ years** في السَنَواتِ الأُولى **3** (sooner than expected) ‹*detection, settlement, death*› مُبَكِّر; **to have an ~ lunch/night** تناوَلَ غَداءً \ ذَهَبَ للنَوْمِ مُبَكِّراً; **to take ~ retirement** حَصَلَ على تَقاعُدٍ مُبَكِّرٍ; **I caught an earlier train** أَدْرَكْتُ قِطاراً في وَقْتٍ سابِقٍ; **at the earliest possible opportunity** في أَقْرَبِ فُرْصةٍ مُمْكِنةٍ **4** (Agric) **~ potatoes/crops** باكورة البَطاطِسِ \ المَحاصيلِ
B *adv* (**earlier**, **earliest**) **1** (sooner) ‹*to arrive, leave*› باكِراً; **we finished two days/three weeks ~** انْتَهَيْنا قبل المَوْعِدِ

(not late) ② تقاعَدَ مُبَكِّراً ~ **to retire** ;بِيَوْمَيْنِ \ بِثَلاثةِ أسابيعَ ‹to start, get up› باكِراً; **it's too ~ to say** هذا كَلامٌ سابِقٌ لِأَوانِهِ; **can you make it earlier?** هل تَسْتَطيعُ أنْ تَصِلَ باكِراً؟; **as I said earlier** كَما قُلْتُ سابِقاً; **as ~ as 2009** بَدْءاً من 2009; **~ next year** في أوائِلِ السَنةِ القادِمةِ; **to arrive ~ in the afternoon** وَصَلَ باكِراً في المَساءِ; **it was agreed very ~ on** تَمَّ الاتِّفاقُ بِشَكْلٍ مُبَكِّرٍ جِدًّا

earmark /ˈɪəmɑːk/ *vt* رَصَدَ (u; رَصْد) ‹money›; خَصَّصَ ‹a site›

earmuffs /ˈɪəmʌfs/ *n pl* واقي أُذُنٍ

earn /ɜːn/ *vt* ① كَسَبَ (i; كَسْب), جَنى (i; جَنْي) ‹money, interest›; **to ~ a living** كَسَبَ القوتَ \ لُقمةَ العَيْشِ ② كَسَبَ (i; كَسْب) ‹a reputation, respect›

earner /ˈɜːnə/ *n* كاسِب

earnest /ˈɜːnɪst/ **A** *n* **in ~** (more intensely) بِشِدّةٍ; (seriously) بِجِدّيّةٍ

B *adj* جِدّيّ

earning power /ˈɜːnɪŋ ˌpaʊə/ *n* قُدْرة على الكَسْبِ

earnings /ˈɜːnɪŋz/ *n pl* (of a worker) مَكْسَب (مَكاسِبُ), دَخْل; (of a company) رِبْح (أَرْباح)

ear, nose, and throat specialist *n* أخِصّائيّ (أَمْراضِ) الأُذُنِ والأَنْفِ والحَنْجَرة

earphones /ˈɪəfəʊnz/ *n pl* سَمّاعات أُذُنٍ

earplug /ˈɪəplʌɡ/ *n* سَدّادة أُذُنٍ

earring /ˈɪərɪŋ/ *n* قُرْط (أَقْراط, قِراط)

earshot /ˈɪəʃɒt/ *n* مَدى \ مَرْمى السَمْعِ; **to be out of/within ~ of sb** لم يَكُنْ \ كانَ على مَسْمَعٍ من شَخْصٍ

earth /ɜːθ/ **A** *n* ① (also **Earth**) (planet) أَرْض (f; أَراضٍ) ② (soil) تُراب (أَتْربة) ③ (infml) (as an intensifier) **how on ~ did you know?** كيف باللهِ عَلَيْكَ \ بِحَقِّ السَماءِ عَرَفْتَ؟; **what on ~ did he mean?** ماذا بِحَقِّ السَماءِ قَصَدَ؟ ④ (BrE Elec) سِلْك تَأْريضٍ

B *vt* (BrE Elec) أَوْصَلَ بالأَرْضِ ‹an oven, a circuit›

(Idioms) **to bring sb down to earth** أَعادَ شَخْصاً إلى أَرْضِ الواقِعِ; **to cost the earth** كَلَّفَ الغالِيَ والنَفيسَ; **to come down to earth** عادَ إلى أَرْضِ الواقِعِ

earthenware /ˈɜːθ(ə)nweː/ *n* ① (material) خَزَف ② (pots, dishes) خَزَفيّات

earth mover *n* حَفّارة

earthquake /ˈɜːθkweɪk/ *n* زِلْزال (زَلازِلُ)

earth tremor *n* هَزّة أَرْضيّة خَفيفة

earthworm /ˈɜːθwɜːm/ *n* دودة أَرْضٍ

earwig /ˈɪəwɪɡ/ *n* أبو مِقَصٍّ

ease /iːz/ **A** *n* ① (lack of difficulty) سُهولة; **for ~ of use/reference** لِتَسْهيلِ الاسْتِعْمالِ \ العُثورِ على المَرْجِعِ ② (freedom from anxiety) طُمَأْنينة; **to feel at ~** شَعَرَ بالطُمَأْنينةِ; **at ~!** اسْتَرِحْ!; **to put sb at ~** *or* **at their ~** جَعَلَ شَخْصاً يَشْعُرُ بالراحةِ ③ (affluence) بُحْبوحة, سَعة العَيْشِ

B *vt* (**eases, easing, eased**) ① (to lessen) خَفَّفَ ‹the pain, tension, a shortage›; **to ~ sb's burden** خَفَّفَ العِبْءَ عن كاهِلِ شَخْصٍ ② (to make easier) سَهَّلَ ‹communications, a situation› ③ (to move carefully) **to ~ sth into sth** وَضَعَ شَيْئاً في شَيْءٍ بِهُدوءٍ; **to ~ sth out of sth** أَخْرَجَ شَيْئاً من شَيْءٍ بِهُدوءٍ

C *vi* (**eases, easing, eased**) ① (to lessen) «tension, pain, traffic» خَفَّ (i; خَفّ) ② «prices, interest rates» انْخَفَضَ

(Phrasal verbs) **ease off A** (to lessen) «demand, rain» خَفَّ (i; خَفّ) **B ~ [sth] off, ~ off [sth]** (to remove gently) نَزَعَ [شَيْئاً] بِلُطْفٍ ‹a lid, one's boot›; **he was able to ~ the lid off without spilling the contents** اسْتَطاعَ أنْ يَنْزَعَ الغِطاءَ بِلُطْفٍ دون أنْ يُريقَ المُحْتَوَياتِ

• **ease up** ① (to lessen) «traffic, storm» هَدَأَ (a; هُدوء), خَفَّ (i; خَفّ) ② (to relax) «team, workers» اسْتَراحَ

easel /ˈiːz(ə)l/ *n* مِسْنَد \ حامِل لَوْحةِ رَسّامٍ

easily /ˈiːzɪli/ *adv* ① (without difficulty) ‹to open, win› بِسُهولةٍ, بِيُسْرٍ; **he lifted it ~** حَمَلَهُ بِسُهولةٍ; **it is ~ obtainable** من السَهْلِ الحُصولُ عَلَيْهِ ② (readily) ‹to laugh, cry› بِسُهولةٍ; **to get bored ~** أُصيبَ بالمَلَلِ بِسُهولةٍ; **to be ~ forgotten** نُسِيَ بِسُهولةٍ ③ (without worries) ‹to sleep, talk› بِسُهولةٍ; **we can breathe ~** نَسْتَطيعُ أنْ نَتَنَفَّسَ بِسُهولةٍ ④ (without doubt) بِدونِ أَدْنى شَكٍّ; **~ the funniest novel of the year** الرِواية الأَكْثَر طَرافةً لِهَذا العامِ بِدونِ أَدْنى شَكٍّ ⑤ (very probably) **he could ~ die** من المُحْتَمَلِ جِدًّا أنْ يَموتَ

easiness /ˈiːzinəs/ *n* ① (of an exam, a climb) سُهولة ② (of life, conditions) سُهولة

east /iːst/ **A** *n* **1** (compass direction) شَرْق **2** (**the East**) الشَرْق

B *adj* ‹*coast, side, wind*› شَرْقيّ

C *adv* ‹*to face, move*› شَرْقاً

eastbound /ˈiːstbaʊnd/ *adj* ‹*lane, train*› مُتَّجِه شَرْقاً

East End *pr n* (**the East End**) إيسْت إينْد (حَيّ في لَنْدَن)

Easter /ˈiːstə/ *n* عيد الفِصْح

Easter Day, **Easter Sunday** *n* عيد الفِصْح

Easter egg *n* بَيْضة عيدِ الفِصْح

easterly /ˈiːst(ə)li/ **A** *adj* ‹*direction, route, wind*› شَرْقيّ

B *n* (*pl* **easterlies**) ريح شَرْقيّة

Easter Monday *n* اليَوْم الثاني لعيدِ الفِصْح

eastern /ˈiːst(ə)n/ *adj* **1** ‹*side, region*› شَرْقيّ; **in the ~ Mediterranean** في الجانِبِ الشَرْقيِّ للبَحْرِ المُتَوسِّطِ **2** (also **Eastern**) (oriental) ‹*religion, philosophy*› شَرْقيّ

east-facing /ˈiːstfeɪsɪŋ/ *adj* ‹*window, balcony, room*› ذو واجِهةٍ شَرْقيّةٍ ,شَرْقيّ

East Timor *pr n* تَيْمور الشَرْقيّة

eastward /ˈiːstwəd/ **A** *adj* ‹*expansion, migration*› مُتَّجِه شَرْقاً

B *adv* (also **eastwards** BrE) ‹*to travel, move*› شَرْقاً

easy /ˈiːzi/ **A** *adj* (**easier, easiest**) **1** (not difficult) ‹*exam, question*› سَهْل; **that's ~ to repair** من السَهْلِ إصْلاحُ ذلك; **to be an ~ winner** رَبِحَ \ انْتَصَرَ بِسُهولةٍ; **it's within ~ reach of the station** من السَهْلِ الوُصولُ إلَيْهِ من المَحَطّةِ; **he took the ~ way out** اخْتارَ الحَلَّ السَهْلَ; **they live an ~ life** يَعيشونَ حَياةً سَهْلةً; **that's easier said than done** الحَديثُ عن ذلك أَسْهَلُ من القِيامِ بِهِ; **she makes it look ~** تَجْعَلُهُ يَبْدو سَهْلاً **2** (untroubled) ‹*smile*› رائق; ‹*elegance*› مُريح; **he has a very ~ manner** لَدَيْهِ طَريقةٌ سَهْلةٌ في التَعامُلِ **3** (infml) (having no preference) **'which one would you like?' — 'I'm ~'** 'أَيُّ واحِدٍ تُريدُ؟' — 'لا فَرْقَ عِنْدي' **4** (undemanding) ‹*credit, terms*› مُيَسَّر

B *adv* (**easier, easiest**) **1** (in a relaxed way) **to take it** *or* **things ~** أَخَذَ الأُمورَ بِسُهولةٍ **2** (infml) (sparingly) **to go ~ on** *or* **with the cream/salt** خَفَّفَ من الكْريمةِ \ المِلْحِ; **~ does it!** تَمَهَّلْ قَليلاً!

(Idioms) **easy come, easy go** ما يَأْتي بِسُهولةٍ يَذْهَبُ بِسُهولةٍ; **to be easy on the eye/ear** راقَ للعَيْنِ \ للأُذُنِ

easy chair *n* أَريكة مُريحة

easy-going /iːzɪˈɡəʊɪŋ/ *adj* ‹*nature, manner, person*› سَلِس

easy terms *n* شُروط مُيَسَّرة

eat /iːt/ **A** *vt* (*past tense* **ate**, *past participle* **eaten**) أَكَلَ (u; أَكْل), تناوَلَ ‹*food, a cake, meal*›; **to ~ one's breakfast/lunch/dinner** تَناوَلَ فُطورَهُ \ غَداءَهُ \ عَشاءَهُ; **to ~ sth for lunch/dinner** تَناوَلَ شَيْئاً في الغَداءِ \ العَشاءِ; **to ~ sb/sth alive** أَكَلَ شَخْصاً \ شَيْئاً حَيّاً

B *vi* (*past tense* **ate**; *past participle* **eaten**) **1** (to consume food) أَكَلَ (u; أَكْل); **he was too ill to ~** لم يَأْكُلْ لِأَنَّهُ كانَ مَريضاً جِدًّا **2** (to have a meal) أَكَلَ (u; أَكْل), تَناوَلَ الطَعامَ; **we normally ~ at six** نَأْكُلُ عادةً في السادِسةِ

(Phrasal verbs) **eat away**: **1** **~ [sth] away, ~ away [sth]** (to erode) «water, wind» عَرّى [شَيْئاً] ‹*a cliff, rock*›; «acid, rust» أَكَلَ [شَيْئاً] ‹*metal, a surface*›; **the wind and rain have ~en away the cliffs** عَرَّت الرياحُ والأَمْطارُ الأَجْرافَ **2** **~ away at [sth]** (to undermine) «criticisms» قَوَّضَ [شَيْئاً] ‹*one's confidence, composure*›

• **eat into**: **~ into [sth]** **1** (to erode) «acid, rust» أَكَلَ [شَيْئاً] ‹*metal, paint*› **2** (to encroach on) «interruptions, one's duties» طَغى على [شَيْءٍ] ‹*one's day, leisure time*› **3** (to use up) «bills, costs» اسْتَنْزَفَ [شَيْئاً] ‹*one's savings, profits*›

• **eat out** تَناوَلَ الطَعامَ \ أَكَلَ في مَطْعَمٍ

• **eat up** **A** **come on, ~ up!** هَيّا، كُلْ كُلَّ طَعامِكَ! **B** **~ [sth] up, ~ up [sth]** **1** (to finish) أَكَلَ [شَيْئاً] بالكامِلِ ‹*one's food, vegetables*› **2** (to consume in quantity) اسْتَهْلَكَ [شَيْئاً] بِكَمّيّاتٍ كَبيرةٍ ‹*fuel, petrol*› **3** (to use up) «expenses, costs» اسْتَنْزَفَ [شَيْئاً] ‹*one's savings, profits*› **4** (to be obsessed) **to be ~en up with worry/curiosity/guilt** مَلَأَهُ القَلَقُ \ الفُضولُ \ الشُعورُ بالذَنْبِ

eaten /ˈiːt(ə)n/ *past participle* ▸ **eat**

eater /ˈiːtə/ *n* آكِل (أَكَلة, آكِلونَ); **a big ~** أَكول; **I'm a vegetarian but my husband is a meat ~** أنا نَباتيّةٌ وَلَكِنَّ زَوْجي يَأْكُلُ اللُحومَ

eating /ˈiːtɪŋ/ *n* أكْلُ; **healthy ~ is essential** الأكْلُ الصِحّيُّ ضَروريٌّ

eating disorder *n* اضْطِراب الأكْلِ \ الشَهيّةِ

eating habits *n* عادات الأكْلِ

eaves /iːvz/ *n pl* حافة \ حَرْف سَقْفٍ

eavesdrop /ˈiːvzdrɒp/ *vi* **(-pp-) to ~ on sth/sb** تَنَصَّتَ على شَيْءٍ \ شَخْصٍ

e-banking /ˈiːbaŋkɪŋ/ *n* الخِدْمات المَصْرِفيّة عَبْرَ الإنْتَرْنِت

ebb /ɛb/ **A** *n* جَزْر

B *vi* **1** «tide» جَزَرَ (u; جَزْر) **2** «confidence, enthusiasm» تَناقَصَ

(Idioms) **the ebb and flow of sth** المَدّ والجَزْر في شَيْءٍ; **to be at a low ebb** كانَ في حالةٍ سَيِّئةٍ

(Phrasal verb) **ebb away** «strength, support» تَناقَصَ; **her life was ~ing away** كانَتْ حَياتُها في تَدَهْوُرٍ

ebony /ˈɛb(ə)ni/ *n* **1** (wood) أبْنوس **2** (colour) أسْوَد بُنّيّ غامِق

e-book /ˈiːbʊk/ *n* كِتاب إلِكْتْرونيّ

EC /iːˈsiː/ *abbr* **(the EC) 1** = **European Commission** المُفَوَّضيّة الأوروبّيّة **2** (Hist) = **European Community** الاتِّحاد الأوروبّيّ

e-card /ˈiːkɑːd/ *n* بِطاقة تَهْنِئةٍ إلِكْتْرونيّة

e-cash /ˈiːkaʃ/ *n* نَقْد إلِكْتْرونيّ

eccentric /ɪkˈsɛntrɪk/ **A** *adj* ‹behaviour, person› غَريب الأطْوار, شاذّ (شَواذٌّ ,شُذّاذ)

B *n* شَخْص شاذّ \ غَريب الأطْوارِ

eccentricity /ˌɛksɛnˈtrɪsɪti/ *n* (*pl* **eccentricities**) (condition) شُذوذ ,غَرابة; (characteristic) سُلوك \ عادة غَريبة

ecclesiastical /ɪˌkliːzɪˈastɪk(ə)l/ *adj* ‹court, vestments› كَنَسيّ

ECG /iːsiːˈdʒiː/ *n* = **electrocardiogram, electrocardiograph** تَخْطيط \ رَسْم القَلْبِ

echo /ˈɛkəʊ/ **A** *n* (*pl* **echoes**) صَدًى

B *vt* **(echoes, echoing, echoed)** رَدَّدَ ‹views, concerns›

C *vi* «voices, footsteps» تَرَدَّدَ صَداهُ ,أصْدى

e-cigarette *n* ▸ **electronic cigarette**

eclampsia /ɪˈklampsɪə/ *n* تَشَنُّج أثْناء الحَمْلِ ,تَسَمُّم الحَمْلِ

eclectic /ɪˈklɛktɪk/ **A** *adj* ‹mix, tastes› مُتَنَوِّع (مُنْتَقًى من مَصادِرَ شَتّى)

B *n* شَخْص انْتِقائيّ (يَسْتَمِدُّ أفْكارَهُ \ ذَوْقَهُ من مَجْموعةٍ مُنْتَقاةٍ من المَصادِرِ)

eclipse /ɪˈklɪps/ **A** *n* (solar) كُسوف; (lunar) خُسوف

B *vt* **1** (Astron) كَسَفَ (i; كُسوف) ‹the sun› **2** غَطّى (على), تَفَوَّقَ (على) ‹a record, an achievement›

eco-friendly /iːkəʊˈfrɛndli/ *adj* ‹product, design› صَديق للبيئةِ, غَيْر مُضِرٍّ بالبيئةِ

ecological /iːkəˈlɒdʒɪk(ə)l/ *adj* ‹system, disaster› إيكولوجيّ ,بيئيّ

ecologist /iːˈkɒlədʒɪst/ *n* عالِم البيئةِ

ecology /ɪˈkɒlədʒi/ *n* عِلْم البيئةِ, إيكولوجيا

e-commerce /ˈiːkɒməːs/ *n* تِجارة إلِكْتْرونيّة

econometrician /ɪkɒnəməˈtrɪʃ(ə)n/ *n* مُخْتَصّ بالاقْتِصادِ القِياسيِّ

economic /iːkəˈnɒmɪk, ɛkəˈnɒmɪk/ *adj* **1** (financial) ‹forecast, crisis› اقْتِصاديّ **2** (profitable) ‹proposition, business› مُرْبِح

economical /iːkəˈnɒmɪk(ə)l, ɛkəˈnɒmɪk(ə)l/ *adj* ‹method, car› اقْتِصاديّ

economically /iːkəˈnɒmɪkli, ɛkəˈnɒmɪkli/ *adv* **1** ‹strong, viable› اقْتِصاديًّا **2** ‹to operate, run› بِطَريقةٍ اقْتِصاديّةٍ

economic migrant *n* مُهاجِر لأسْبابٍ اقْتِصاديّةٍ

economic refugee *n* لاجِئ لأسْبابٍ اقْتِصاديّةٍ

economics /iːkəˈnɒmɪks, ɛkəˈnɒmɪks/ **A** *n sing* عِلْم الاقْتِصادِ

B *n pl* (financial aspects) الجانِب الاقْتِصاديّ

economist /ɪˈkɒnəmɪst/ *n* خَبير اقْتِصاديّ

economize, -ise (BrE) /ɪˈkɒnəmʌɪz/ *vi* اقْتَصَدَ; **to ~ on fuel/labour costs** اقْتَصَدَ في نَفَقاتِ الوَقودِ \ العِمالةِ

economy /ɪˈkɒnəmi/ *n* (*pl* **economies**) **1** (system) اقْتِصاد; **the ~ grew by one per cent** نَما الاقْتِصادُ بِواحِدٍ في المائةِ; **the western economies are in crisis/very healthy** الاقْتِصاديّاتُ الغَرْبيّةُ في أزْمةٍ \ وَضْعٍ جَيِّدٍ جِدًّا

2 (**economies**, *pl*) (saving) **to make economies** وَفَّرَ **3** [u] (thrift) اقْتِصاد

economy class *n* دَرَجة اقْتِصاديّة

economy-class syndrome /iːˈkɒnəmiklas ˌsɪndrəʊm/ *n* تَجَلُّط وَريديّ عَميق بالقَدَمَيْنِ (ناتِج عن الجُلوسِ لِفَتَراتٍ طَويلةٍ خلال الرِحْلاتِ الجَوّيّةِ)

economy size *n* عُبوّة اقْتِصاديّة

ecosystem /ˈiːkəʊsɪstəm/ *n* نِظام بيئيّ

eco-warrior /ˈiːkəʊwɒrɪə/ *n* ناشِط بيئيّ

ecstasy /ˈɛkstəsi/ *n* (*pl* **ecstasies**) ❶ (emotional state) نَشْوة ❷ [u] (drug) [حُبوب النَشْوةِ]

ecstatic /ɪkˈstatɪk/ *adj* ‹*applause*› حارّ; ‹*smile*› مُنْتَشٍ; **the team was ~ about the victory** كانَ الفَريقُ مُنْتَشِياً بالنَصْرِ

ECT /iːsiːˈtiː/ *n* = **electroconvulsive therapy** عِلاج بالصَدَماتِ الكَهْرَبائيّةِ

Ecuador /ˈɛkwədɔː/ *pr n* إكْوادور (f)

Ecuadorian /ˌɛkwəˈdɔːrɪən/ *n, adj* إكْوادوريّ

ecumenical /ˌiːkjʊˈmɛnɪk(ə)l, ɛkjʊˈmɛnɪk(ə)l/ *adj* ‹*movement, council*› [يُمَثِّلُ مُخْتَلِفَ الطَوائِفِ المَسيحيّةِ]

eczema /ˈɛksɪmə/ *n* إكْزيما

eddy /ˈɛdi/ **A** *n* (*pl* **eddies**) حَلَزون (حَلَزونات)

B *vi* (**eddies**, **eddying**, **eddied**) «water, smoke» تَحَرَّكَ بِشَكْلٍ حَلَزونيٍّ

Eden /ˈiːd(ə)n/ *pr n* جَنّةُ عَدْنٍ

edge /ɛdʒ/ **A** *n* ❶ (of a table, road, lake, coin) حافة (حافات, حَوافٍ); (of a wood, clearing, field) طَرَف (أطْراف); **the film had us on the ~ of our seats** جَعَلَنا الفيلمُ نَجْلِسُ مُتَسَمِّرينَ ❷ (of a plank) حاشِية (حَواشٍ), حافة (حافات, حَوافٍ) ❸ (of a blade, knife) شَفْرة (شَفَرات), حَدّ (حُدود), حافة (حافات, حَوافٍ) ❹ (advantage) **to have the ~ over a competitor/rival** تَفَوّقَ على مُنافِسٍ; **it gives them the ~ over the competition** هذا يَجْعَلُهُمْ يَتَفَوّقونَ في المُنافَسةِ ❺ (showing nervousness) **to be on ~** كانَ حادَّ المِزاجِ; **that sound sets my teeth on ~** ذلك الصَوْتُ يُوَتِّرُ أعْصابي ❻ ((infml) (extreme situation) **the edge**) حافة الانْهِيار; **to live on the ~** عاشَ على حافةِ الخَطَرِ; **to push sb over the ~** دَفَعَ شَخْصاً إلى حافةِ الانْهِيارِ

B *vt* ❶ (to move slowly) **to ~ sth towards sb/sth** دَفَعَ شَيْئاً نحو شَخْصٍ \ شَيْءٍ تَدْريجيّاً; **to ~ one's way to safety** وَجَدَ طَريقَهُ إلى بَرِّ الأمانِ ❷ (to trim) كَفَّ (u; كَفّ) ‹*a collar, handkerchief*›

C *vi* (to advance) **to ~ forward** تَقَدَّمَ إلى الأمامِ; **to ~ towards a settlement** تَقَدَّمَ نحو إحْرازِ تَسْوِيةٍ

(Idioms) **to give an edge to sth** أضْفى حَيَوِيّةً على شَيْءٍ; **to take the edge off sth** سَرَقَ البَريقَ من شَيْءٍ; **to lose one's edge** فَقَدَ بَوْصَلَتَهُ

(Phrasal verbs) **edge out** **A** «cars, drivers» انْحَرَفَ إلى الخارِجِ

B **~ [sb] out, ~ out [sb]** زَحْزَحَ [شَخْصاً]; **to ~ sb out of the market/their job** زَحْزَحَ شَخْصاً من السوقِ \ عَمَلِهِ

• **edge up** ❶ (to increase) «prices, figures, total» ازْدادَ بِشَكْلٍ تَدْريجيٍّ ❷ (to approach) **to ~ up to sb/sth** اقْتَرَبَ من شَخْصٍ \ شَيْءٍ بِحَذَرٍ

edgeways /ˈɛdʒweɪz/, **edgewise** /ˈɛdʒwʌɪz/ *adv*

(Idiom) **to find it hard to get a word in edgeways** لاقى صُعوبةً في الإدْلاءِ بِرَأْيِه (لأنَّ الطَرَفَ الآخَرَ يَتَحَدَّثُ بِاسْتِمْرارٍ)

edging /ˈɛdʒɪŋ/ *n* (in the garden) حَدّ (حُدود); (on fabric) حاشِية (حَواشٍ)

edgy /ˈɛdʒi/ *adj* (**edgier**, **edgiest**) ‹*to feel, seem*› مُتَوَتِّر

edible /ˈɛdɪb(ə)l/ *adj* ‹*fungus, food*› صالِح للأكْلِ

edifice /ˈɛdɪfɪs/ *n* صَرْح (صُروح), مَبْنًى كَبير, عِمارة (عِمارات, عَمائِرُ)

edifying /ˈɛdɪfʌɪɪŋ/ *adj* ‹*spectacle, tale*› مُثَقِّف

Edinburgh /ˈɛdɪnb(ə)rə/ *pr n* أدِنْبَرة

edit /ˈɛdɪt/ *vt* ❶ (in publishing) أعَدَّ للنَشْرِ ‹*a collection, an anthology*› ❷ (to cut down) نَقَّحَ ‹*a text, document*› ❸ قامَ بِمونْتاج ‹*a film, programme*› ❹ (to manage) حَرَّرَ ‹*a newspaper, magazine*›

editing /ˈɛdɪtɪŋ/ *n* ❶ (of written text) تَصْحيح (تَصْحيحات), تَنْقيح (تَنْقيحات) ❷ (of films, recordings) مونْتاج ❸ (of essays, letters) إعْداد للنَشْرِ, تَحْرير ❹ (of electronic data) تَصْحيح (تَصْحيحات)

edition /ɪˈdɪʃ(ə)n/ *n* طَبْعة

editor /ˈɛdɪtə/ *n* ❶ (of a newspaper, magazine) مُحَرِّر ❷ (of a text) مُصَحِّح ❸ (of an anthology, a series) مُحَرِّر ❹ (of a film, TV or radio programme) مَسْؤول مونْتاج ❺ (of electronic data) مُحَرِّر

editorial /ɛdɪ'tɔːrɪəl/ **A** *adj* ‹*staff, board, policy*› تَحْريريّ
B *n* افْتِتاحيّة

EDT /iːdiː'tiː/ *n* (AmE) = **Eastern Daylight Time** تَوْقيت الساحِلِ الشَرْقيِّ

educate /'ɛdjʊkeɪt/ *vt* **1** (to teach) عَلَّمَ ‹*children, students*›
2 (to inform) ثَقَّفَ ‹*the public, consumers*›

educated /'ɛdjʊkeɪtɪd/ *adj* ‹*person*› مُثَقَّف ,مُتَعَلِّم

(Idiom) **an educated guess** [تَخْمين مَبْنيّ على أَساسٍ عَقْلانيٍّ]

education /ɛdjʊ'keɪʃ(ə)n/ *n* (تَعاليم, تَعْليمات) تَعْليم; **primary/ secondary ~** التَعْليم الابْتِدائيّ \ الثانَويّ; **a university ~** تَعْليم جامِعيّ; **he will get a better ~ at this school** سَيَحْصُلُ على تَعْليمٍ أَفْضَلَ في هذه المَدْرَسةِ

educational /ɛdʒuː'keɪʃ(ə)n(ə)l/ *adj* **1** ‹*establishment, system, needs*› تَرْبَويّ ,تَعْليميّ **2** (instructive) ‹*toy, experience*› تَعْليميّ, تَرْبَويّ

education authority *n* سُلْطة تَرْبَويّة \ تَعْليميّة

education system *n* نِظام تَرْبَويّ \ تَعْليميّ

educator /'ɛdʒʊkeɪtə/ *n* (مُرَبّونَ) مُرَبٍّ

Edwardian /ɛd'wɔːdɪən/ *n, adj* إدْوارْديّ

EEA /iːiː'eɪ/ *n* **1** = **European Economic Area** المِنْطَقة الاقْتِصاديّة الأوروبّيّة **2** = **European Environment Agency** الوَكالة الأوروبّيّة للبيئةِ

EEC /iːiː'siː/ *n* (Hist) (**the EEC**) = **European Economic Community** السوق الأوروبّيّة المُشْتَرَكة

eel /iːl/ *n* أَنْقَليس ,حَنْكَليس

e'er /ɛː/ *adv* (old use) ▸ **ever**

eerie /'ɪəri/ *adj* (**eerier**, **eeriest**) ‹*silence, sound, place*› مُخيف

efface /ɪ'feɪs/ *vt* (fml) مَحى (i; مَحْي) ‹*a memory, an inscription*›

effect /ɪ'fɛkt/ **A** *n* **1** (result) (آثار) أَثَر ,(نَتائِجُ) نَتيجة; **the ~s were immediate** كانَت النَتائِجُ فَوْريّةً; **the ~s of the test were catastrophic** كانَتْ نَتائِجُ الامْتِحانِ كارِثيّةً; **to use sth to good ~** أَحْسَنَ اسْتِعْمالَ شَيْءٍ **2** [u] (efficacy, validity) **it was to little/no ~** كانَ لَهُ تَأْثيرٌ ضَعيفٌ \ مَعْدومٌ; **the measures were of no ~** لم يَكُنْ للإجْراءاتِ أَيُّ تَأْثيرٍ; **to take ~** قامَ بِمَفْعولِهِ; **the price increases come into ~ today** أَصْبَحَتْ زِياداتُ الأَسْعارِ سارية المَفْعولِ اليَوْمَ ساري; **with ~ from 1 January** المَفْعولِ اعْتِباراً من 1 يَنايِر; **to resign with immediate ~** قَدَّمَ اسْتِقالةً سارِيةَ المَفْعولِ فَوْراً **3** (pointing out meaning) **she left a note to the ~ that ...** تَرَكَتْ رِسالةً موجَزةً مَفادُها أَنّ ...; **or words to that ~** أو كَلِمات تَحْمِلُ نَفْسَ المَعْنى **4** (impression) تَأْثير; **he paused for ~** صَمَتَ بُرْهةً لِيَتْرُكَ وَقْعاً; **she dresses like that for ~** تَرْتَدي تِلْكَ المَلابِسَ في النُفوسِ لإثارة الإعْجابِ **5** (Sci) (attested outcome) (ظَواهِرُ) ظاهِرة; **the Doppler/placebo ~** تَأْثير دوبْلَر \ بْلاسيبو (آثار) أَثَر ,تَأْثير
B (**effects**) *n pl* (belongings) مُمْتَلَكات
C (**in effect**) *adv phr* في الواقِعِ \ الحَقيقةِ
D *vt* (fml) أَدّى (إلى) ‹*a repair, sale, an improvement*›

effective /ɪ'fɛktɪv/ *adj* **1** (successful) ‹*method, treatment*› فَعّال; **discounts are an ~ way of attracting customers** التَخْفيضاتُ طَريقةٌ فَعّالةٌ لِجَذْبِ الزَبائِنِ **2** (real) ‹*control*› فِعْليّ **3** (operative) **to become ~** «law, policy» دَخَلَ حَيِّزَ التَنْفيذِ

effectively /ɪ'fɛktɪvli/ *adv* **1** (successfully) ‹*to work, communicate*› بِفَعّاليّةٍ ,بِشَكْلٍ فَعّالٍ **2** (in reality) ‹*to end, control*› على أَرْضِ الواقِعِ

effectiveness /ɪ'fɛktɪvnəs/ *n* فَعّاليّة

effeminate /ɪ'fɛmɪnət/ *adj* ‹*man, behaviour*› مُخَنَّث

effervescent /ɛfə'vɛs(ə)nt/ *adj* **1** ‹*personality, presence*› طافِح بالحَيَويّةِ **2** ‹*drink, tablet*› فَوّار

efficacy /'ɛfɪkəsi/ *n* فَعّاليّة

efficiency /ɪ'fɪʃ(ə)nsi/ *n* (of a worker) كَفاءة; (of a machine, system) فاعِليّة

efficient /ɪ'fɪʃ(ə)nt/ *adj* ‹*worker, system, machine*› فَعّال

efficiently /ɪ'fɪʃ(ə)ntli/ *adv* ‹*to work, operate*› بِكَفاءةٍ ,بِفَعّاليّةٍ

effigy /'ɛfɪdʒi/ *n* (*pl* **effigies**) (تماثيل) تِمْثال

effluent /'ɛflʊənt/ *n* (sewage) مِياه المَجاري \ الصَرْفِ الصِحّيِّ; (factory waste) مُخَلَّفات صِناعيّة

effort /'ɛfət/ *n* **1** (energy) (مَجْهودات) مَجْهود ,جُهْد; **to put a lot of ~ into sth/into doing sth** وَضَعَ الكَثيرَ من الجُهْدِ في شَيْءٍ \ فِعْلِ شَيْءٍ; **it was a waste of ~** كانَ مَضْيَعةً للجُهْدِ; **it's worth the ~** يَسْتَحِقُّ المَجْهودَ **2** (difficulty) أَمْر مُجْهِد; **it's an ~ to stand up** الوُقوفُ مُجْهِدٌ **3** (attempt) جُهْد, (مَجْهودات) مَجْهود ,مُحاوَلة; **at least he made the ~** على

لم يَبْذُلْ الأَقَلَّ حاوَلَ جُهْدَهُ; **he made no ~ to apologize** هذه مُحاوَلَتي ~ **this is my latest/first**; أَيَّ جُهْدٍ لِيَعْتَذِرَ تِلْكَ لَيْسَتْ مُحاوَلةً ~ **that's not a bad**; الأخيرةُ \ الأولى المَجْهود ~ **the war**; (مَجْهودات) مَجْهود (initiative) **4** سَيِّئةً كانَ مَجْهوداً مُشْتَرَكاً ~ **it was a joint**; الحَرْبيّ

effortless /ˈɛfətləs/ *adj* **1** (easy) *‹ease, mastery›* لا يَتَطَلَّبُ جُهْداً **2** (innate) *‹grace, superiority›* تِلْقائيّ

effusion /ɪˈfjuːʒ(ə)n/ *n* **1** (of emotions) تَدَفُّق (تَدَفُّقات) **2** (of blood, pus) تَدَفُّق (تَدَفُّقات)

EFL /iːɛfɛl/ *n* = **English as a Foreign Language** الإِنْجليزيّة كَلُغةٍ أَجْنَبِيّة

e.g. /iːˈdʒiː/ *abbr* (Latin) = **exempli gratia** (for example) على مثلاً, مِثْلَ, سَبيلِ المِثالِ

egalitarian /ɪ,galɪˈtɛːrɪən/ *adj* *‹society, principles›* قائِم على المُساواةِ

egg /ɛg/ *n* بَيْض (n coll; بُيوض)

(Idiom) **don't put all your eggs in one basket** لا تَضَعْ كُلَّ البَيْضِ في سَلّةٍ واحِدةٍ

(Phrasal verb) **egg on: ~ [sb] on** حَرَّضَ [شَخْصاً]

egg cup *n* [كوب لِحَمْلِ بَيْضةٍ مَسْلوقةٍ]

eggplant /ˈɛgplɑːnt/ *n* (AmE) باذِنْجان (باذِنْجانات)

eggshell /ˈɛgʃɛl/ *n* قِشْر بَيْضٍ

egg white *n* بَياض بَيْضٍ

egg yolk *n* صَفار بَيْضٍ, مُحّ (أَمْحاح)

ego /ˈiːgəʊ, ˈɛgəʊ/ *n* (*pl* **egos**) الأَنا; **to boost/deflate sb's ~** رَفَعَ \ ثَبَّطَ من مَعْنَويّاتِ شَخْصٍ

egoism /ˈɛgəʊɪz(ə)m, ˈiːgəʊɪz(ə)m/ *n* حُبّ الذات, أَثَرة, أَنانيّة

egoist /ˈɛgəʊɪst, ˈiːgəʊɪst/ *n* أَنانيّ

egotist /ˈɛgətɪst, ˈiːgətɪst/ *n* أَنانيّ

Egypt /ˈiːdʒɪpt/ *pr n* مِصْر (dipt f); **Upper ~** مِصْر العُلْيا; **Lower ~** مِصْر السُفْلى

Egyptian /ɪˈdʒɪpʃ(ə)n/ **A** *adj* *‹culture, history›* مِصْريّ **B** *n* **1** (citizen) مِصْريّ; **the Ancient ~s** المِصْريّونَ القُدَماء **2** (language) الهيروغْليفيّة, المِصْريّة القَديمة

Egyptologist /iːdʒɪpˈtɒlədʒɪst/ *n* عالِم مِصْريّاتٍ

eh /eɪ/ *excl* (infml) (as enquiry) صَحيح, نَعَمْ; (indicating surprise) آه; (eliciting agreement) أَلَيْسَ كَذَلِكَ; **simple, ~?** بَسيط, أَلَيْسَ كَذَلِكَ؟

EHIC /iːhɪk/ *n* = **European Health Insurance Card** بِطاقة التَّأمين الصِحّيّ الأوروبّيّة

Eid al-Adha /iːd alˈɑːdhɑː/ *n* عيد الأَضْحى

Eid al-Fitr /iːd alˈfɪtrə/ *n* عيد الفِطْرِ

eiderdown /ˈʌɪdədaʊn/ *n* [لِحاف مَحْشوّ بالريشِ الناعِمِ]

eight /eɪt/ *n, adj* ثَمانِية ▸ see also **five**

eighteen /eɪˈtiːn/ *n, adj* ثَمانِيَةَ عَشَرَ

eighteenth /eɪˈtiːnθ/ **A** *n* **1** (in a series) ثامِنَ عَشَرَ **2** (fraction) جُزْء من ثَمانِيَةَ عَشَرَ **3** (**the eighteenth**) (of a month) الثامِنَ عَشَرَ **B** *adj* ثامِنَ عَشَرَ **C** *adv* في المَرْكَزِ الثامِنَ عَشَرَ

eighth /eɪtθ/ **A** *n* **1** (in a series) ثامِن **2** (fraction) ثُمْن (أَثْمان) **3** (**the eighth**) (of a month) الثامِن **B** *adj* *‹day, place›* ثامِن **C** *adv* في المَرْكَزِ الثامِنِ

eighth note *n* (AmE) نوتة ثامِنة

eighties /ˈeɪtiz/ *n pl* **1** (decade) (**the eighties**) الثَمانينات **2** (age) **to be in one's ~** كانَ في الثَمانيناتِ (من عُمْرِهِ)

eightieth /ˈeɪtɪəθ/ **A** *n* **1** (**the eightieth**) (in a series) الثَمانونَ **2** (fraction) جُزْء من ثَمانينَ **B** *adj* *‹birthday, anniversary›* الثَمانونَ **C** *adv* في المَرْكَزِ الثَمانينَ

eighty /ˈeɪti/ *n, adj* ثَمانونَ

Éire /ɛːrə/ *pr n* [إيرْلَنْدا باللُغةِ الغيلِيّةِ]

either /ˈʌɪðə/ **A** *conj* **1** (as alternatives) **I was expecting him ~ on Tuesday or Wednesday** كُنْتُ أَتَوَقَّعُ قُدومَهُ إمّا الثُلاثاءَ أو الأَرْبِعاءَ; **it's available in ~ pink or blue** هو مُتَوَفِّرٌ إمّا باللَوْنِ الوَرْديِّ وإمّا الأَزْرَقِ; **you'll ~ love it or hate it** إمّا أَنَّكَ سَتُحِبُّهُ أو تَكْرَهُهُ; **it's ~ him or me** إمّا هو وَإمّا أنا **2** (in the negative) **I wouldn't reward ~ Patrick or Amy** لا أَرْغَبُ في مُكافَأةِ أَيٍّ من باتْريك أو إيمي; **you're not being ~ truthful or fair** أَنْتَ

لا تَتَصَرَّفُ بِصِدْقٍ وَلا بِعَدْلٍ **3** (as an ultimatum) ~ **you stop gambling, or I'm leaving you** إِمّا أَنْ تَتَوَقَّفَ عن القِمارِ، وَإِمّا سَأَتْرُكُكَ

B *adv* أَيْضاً; **I can't do it ~** أَنا أَيْضاً لا يُمْكِنُني أَنْ أَفْعَلَهُ; **not only was it expensive, but it didn't work ~** لم يَكُنْ غالِياً فَحَسْبُ، بَلْ إِنَّهُ أَيْضاً لم يَعْمَلْ; **'I can't sleep' — 'I can't, ~'** 'لا أَسْتَطيعُ النَوْمَ' — 'وَلا أنا أَيْضاً'; **I don't like cheats, and I don't like liars, ~** لا أُحِبُّ الغَشّاشينَ، وَلا الكَذّابينَ كَذٰلِكَ

C *determiner* **1** (one or the other) أَيّ; **you can take ~ road** يُمْكِنُكَ أَنْ تَأْخُذَ أَيَّ الطَريقَيْنِ; **~ one will do** أَيٌّ مِنْهُما سَيَفي; (in the negative) **I can't see ~ child** لا يُمْكِنُني أَنْ أَرى أَيًّا من الطِفْلَيْنِ **2** (both) **~ proposal is acceptable, ~ one of the proposals is acceptable** كِلا العَرْضَيْنِ مَقْبولٌ; **he had a bag in ~ hand** كانَ يَحْمِلُ حَقيبةً في كِلْتا يَدَيْهِ; **at ~ side of the street** في كِلا جانِبَي الطَريقِ; **~ way, it will be difficult** في كِلْتا الحالَتَيْنِ، سَيَكونُ هذا صَعْباً; **I don't mind ~ way** لا أُمانِعُ أَيًّا كانَت الطَريقةُ; **~ way, please confirm it** في كِلا الحالَيْنِ، أَكِّدْهُ من فَضْلِكَ

D *pron* **1** (one or other) أَيّ; **I don't believe ~ of you** لا أُصَدِّقُ أَيًّا مِنْكُما; **you can take ~ (of them)** يُمْكِنُكَ أَنْ تَأْخُذَ أَيًّا مِنْهُما; **I don't like ~ (of them)** لا يُعْجِبُني أَيٌّ مِنْهُما; **there was no sound from ~ of the rooms** لم يَصْدُرْ صَوْتٌ من أَيٍّ من الغُرْفَتَيْنِ; **I might marry ~ (of them)** قد أَتَزَوَّجُ أَيًّا مِنْهُما **2** (both) **~ of the two is possible** كِلاهُما مُمْكِنٌ; **~ of us could win** يُمْكِنُ لِكِلَيْنا أَنْ يَفوزَ; **~ would be difficult to repair** سَيَكونُ من الصَعْبِ إِصْلاحُ كِلَيْهِما

ejaculate /ɪ'dʒakjʊleɪt/ *vi* قَذَفَ المَنيّ ,أَمْنى ‹*prematurely, involuntarily*›

eject /ɪ'dʒɛkt/ **A** *vt* **1** قَذَفَ (i; قَذْف) ‹*lava, debris*› **2** أَخْرَجَ ‹*a CD, cassette*› **3** طَرَدَ (u; طَرْد) ‹*troublemakers, protesters*›

B *vi* «pilots» قَفَزَ من الطائِرةِ

eke out /iːk/ *vt* **1** (to make last) **to ~ sth, to eke sth out** اِقْتَصَدَ في شَيْءٍ ‹*one's income, supplies*› **2** (to manage to make) **to ~ a living** *or* **an existence** كَدَحَ لِيُوَفِّرَ لُقْمةَ العَيْشِ

elaborate **A** /ɪ'lab(ə)rət/ *adj* ‹*plan*› مُفَصَّل; ‹*design, system*› مُتْقَن; ‹*costume, decoration*› دَقيق

B /ɪ'labəreɪt/ *vt* فَصَّلَ ‹*a theory, a point, an idea*›

C *vi* «authors, speakers» فَصَّلَ; **to ~ on sth** فَصَّلَ في شَيْءٍ

elapse /ɪ'laps/ *vi* «time, years» مَضى (i; مُضِيّ), انْقَضى

elastic /ɪ'lastɪk/ **A** *adj* ‹*material, waistband*› مَرِن, مَطّاطِيّ

B *n* مَطّاط

elasticated /ɪ'lastɪkeɪtɪd/ *adj* ‹*waistband, strap*› مُتَمَغِّط, مَطّاطِيّ

elastic band *n* (BrE) رِباط \ شَريط مَطّاطِيّ

elated /ɪ'leɪtɪd/ *adj* ‹*mood, fans*› سَعيد جِدًّا

elbow /'ɛlbəʊ/ **A** *n* كوع (أَكْواع, كيعان) مِرْفَق (مَرافِقُ)

B *vt* ضَرَبَ \ دَفَعَ بالكوعِ

elbow grease *n* (infml) [جُهْد بَدَنِيّ]

elbow room *n* مَجال للحَرَكةِ

elder /'ɛldə/ **A** *adj* ‹*brother*› أَكْبَر; ‹*daughter*› كُبْرى

B *n* **1** (older person) أَكْبَر سِنًّا; **we should respect our ~s** يَنْبَغي أَنْ نَحْتَرِمَ كِبارَنا **2** (of a tribe, group) كَبير (كِبار, كُبَراءُ)

3 (tree) خَمان

elderberry /'ɛldəbɛri/ *n* (*pl* **elderberries**) ثَمَر الخَمانِ

elderly /'ɛld(ə)li/ **A** *adj* ‹*woman, man*› مُسِنّ, كَبير في السِنِّ

B *n pl* **the ~** المُسِنّونَ

eldest /'ɛldɪst/ **A** *adj* ‹*brother, daughter*› الأَكْبَر

B *pron* **the ~** الأَكْبَر

e-learning /'iːləːnɪn/, /'iːləːnɪŋ/ *n* تَعْليم إِلِكْترونِيّ

elect /ɪ'lɛkt/ *vt* **1** (by vote) انْتَخَبَ ‹*a president, government*›

2 (to choose) **to ~ to do sth** اخْتارَ القِيامَ بِشَيْءٍ

election /ɪ'lɛkʃ(ə)n/ *n* **1** (event) انْتِخاب (انْتِخابات); **~s are held every five years** تُعْقَدُ الانْتِخاباتُ كُلَّ خَمْسةِ أَعْوامٍ

2 (action) انْتِخاب (انْتِخابات); **to stand for ~** رَشَّحَ نَفْسَهُ للانْتِخاباتِ

election campaign *n* حَمْلة انْتِخابِيّة

elective /ɪ'lɛktɪv/ **A** *adj* **1** (elected) ‹*office, committee*› انْتِخابِيّ

2 ‹*course, year*› اخْتِيارِيّ

B *n* (AmE) (optional course) مادّة اخْتِيارِيّة

elector /ɪ'lɛktə/ *n* ناخِب

electoral /ɪ'lɛkt(ə)rəl/ *adj* ‹*system, reform*› انْتِخابِيّ

electoral register, **electoral roll** *n* سِجِلّ الناخِبينَ

electorate /ɪ'lɛkt(ə)rət/ *n* هَيْئَة ناخِبة

electric /ɪ'lɛktrɪk/ *adj* **1** ‹*drill, motor*› كَهْرَبائِيّ **2** (thrilling) ‹*atmosphere, moment*› مُثِير

electrical /ɪ'lɛktrɪk(ə)l/ *adj* ‹*equipment, circuit*› كَهْرَبائِيّ; **~ engineering** هَنْدَسة كَهْرَبائِيّة

electrical engineer *n* مُهَنْدِس كَهْرَبائِيّ

electric blanket *n* بَطّانِيّة كَهْرَبائِيّة

electric chair *n* كُرْسِيّ كَهْرَبائِيّ

electric eel *n* أَنْقَلِيس رَعّاد

electrician /ˌɪlɛk'trɪʃ(ə)n/ *n* كَهْرَبائِيّ

electricity /ˌɪlɛk'trɪsɪti/ *n* كَهْرَباء (f)

electrics (BrE) /ɪ'lɛktrɪks/ *n* (infml) كَهْرَباء (f)

electric shock *n* صَدْمة كَهْرَبائِيّة

electrify /ɪ'lɛktrɪfʌɪ/ *vt* (**electrifies, electrifying, electrified**) **1** كَهْرَبَ (i; كَهْرَبة) ‹*a fence, the rail system*› **2** (to thrill) أَثارَ, هَيَّجَ ‹*an audience, a crowd*›

electrocardiogram /ɪˌlɛktrəʊ'kɑːdɪəgram/ *n* تَخْطِيط \ رَسْم القَلْب

electrocardiograph /ɪˌlɛktrəʊ'kɑːdɪəgrɑːf/ *n* جِهاز تَخْطِيطِ \ رَسْمِ القَلْب

electrocute /ɪ'lɛktrəkjuːt/ *vt* صَعَقَ بالكَهْرَباءِ ‹*a criminal, an animal*›

electrode /ɪ'lɛktrəʊd/ *n* إِلِكْتْرود, قُطْب كَهْرَبائِيّ

electroencephalogram /ɪˌlɛktrəʊɪn'sɛfələgram/ *n* تَخْطِيط \ رَسْم المُخّ الكَهْرَبائِيّ

electroencephalograph /ɪˌlɛktrəʊɪn'sɛfələgrɑːf/ *n* جِهاز التَخْطِيطِ \ الرَسْمِ الكَهْرَبائِيّ للمُخّ

electrolysis /ˌɪlɛk'trɒlɪsɪs/ *n* **1** تَحْلِيل كَهْرَبائِيّ **2** (hair removal) إزالة الشَعْرِ بالكَهْرَباءِ

electron /ɪ'lɛktrɒn/ *n* إِلِكْتْرُون

electronic /ɪlɛk'trɒnɪk/ *adj* **1** ‹*calculator, equipment*› إِلِكْتْرُونِيّ **2** ‹*banking, voting*› إِلِكْتْرُونِيّ

electronically /ɪlɛk'trɒnɪkli/ *adv* ‹*to monitor, transmit*› إِلِكْتْرُونِيًّا

electronic cigarette *n* سِيجارة إِلِكْتْرُونِيّة

electronic engineer *n* مُهَنْدِس إِلِكْتْرُونِيّاتٍ

electronic publishing *n* نَشْر إِلِكْتْرُونِيّ

electronics /ɪlɛk'trɒnɪks/ *n* هَنْدَسة إِلِكْتْرُونِيّة

electronic signature *n* تَوْقِيع إِلِكْتْرُونِيّ

elegance /'ɛlɪg(ə)ns/ *n* أَناقة

elegant /'ɛlɪg(ə)nt/ *adj* ‹*woman, resort*› أَنِيق

element /'ɛlɪmənt/ *n* **1** (part, aspect) عُنْصُر (عَناصِرُ); **the criminal ~s of society** العَناصِر الإجرامِيّة في المُجْتَمَع; **an ~ of luck** عامِل الحَظِّ **2** (**elements** *n pl*) (rudiments) أُصول, مَبادِئ; **the ~s of painting/geometry** أُصول الرَسْم \ الهَنْدَسةِ **3** (**the elements** *n pl*) (weather) العَوارِض الجَوِّيّة **4** (Chem) عُنْصُر (عَناصِرُ) **5** (in a kettle, heater) عُنْصُر تَسْخِينٍ

Idiom **to be in one's element** كان على سَجِيَّتِه

elementary /ɛlɪ'mɛnt(ə)ri/ *adj* ‹*principles*› أَساسِيّ; ‹*level*› أَوَّلِيّ

elementary school *n* (AmE) مَدْرَسة اِبْتِدائِيّة

elephant /'ɛlɪf(ə)nt/ *n* فِيل (فِيَلة)

Idiom **the elephant in the room** [مُشْكِلة كَبِيرة يَتَجاهَلُها النَاسُ]

elephantiasis /ˌɛlɪf(ə)n'tʌɪəsɪs/ *n* داء الفِيل

elevate /'ɛlɪveɪt/ *vt* **1** (to lift up) رَفَعَ (a; رَفْع) ‹*a platform, building*› **2** (to increase) رَفَعَ (a; رَفْع) ‹*pressure, temperature*› **3** (to promote) رَقَّى; **he was ~d to the nobility** رُقِّي إلى طَبَقة النُبَلاء; **the film was ~d to cult status** [أَصْبَحَ للفِيلْمِ مَجْمُوعةٌ من المُعْجَبِينَ المَهْوُوسِينَ]

elevated railroad /ˌɛlɪveɪtɪd 'reɪlrəʊd/ *n* (AmE) سِكّة حَدِيدٍ مُرْتَفِعة

elevation /ˌɛlɪ'veɪʃ(ə)n/ *n* **1** (angle) زاوِية اِرْتِفاع **2** (altitude) اِرْتِفاع **3** (fml) (promotion) تَرْقِية

elevator /'ɛlɪveɪtə/ *n* (AmE) مِصْعَد (مَصاعِدُ)

eleven /ɪ'lɛv(ə)n/ **A** *n* **1** (number, quantity) أَحَدَ عَشَرَ **2** (sports team) فَرِيق من أَحَدَ عَشَرَ لاعِبًا **B** *adj* أَحَدَ عَشَرَ

eleventh /ɪ'lɛv(ə)nθ/ **A** *n* **1** (in a series) حادِيَ عَشَرَ **2** (fraction) جُزْء من أَحَدَ عَشَرَ **3** (**the eleventh**) (of a month) الحادِيَ عَشَرَ **B** *adj* ‹*century, day*› حادِيَ عَشَرَ **C** *adv* في المَرْكَزِ الحادِيَ عَشَرَ

elf /ɛlf/ *n* (*pl* **elves**) جِنّيّ صَغير (مَخْلوق أُسْطوريّ خارِق على هَيْئَةِ إنْسانٍ بِأُذُنَين مُدَبَّبَتَيْن)

elicit /ɪ'lɪsɪt/ *vt* انْتَزَعَ ‹*a reaction, smile*›

eligibility /ˌɛlɪdʒə'bɪlɪti/ *n* اسْتِحْقاق, أَهْلِيّة

eligible /'ɛlɪdʒɪb(ə)l/ *adj* **1** (entitled) ‹*voter*› مُؤَهَّل; ‹*applicant*› مُسْتَحِقّ; **to be ~ for sth** اسْتَحَقَّ شَيْئاً; **to be ~ to do sth** كانَ مُؤَهَّلاً لِفِعْلِ شَيْءٍ **2** (marriageable) ‹*bachelor*› مَرْغوب فيهِ كَزَوْجٍ

eliminate /ɪ'lɪmɪneɪt/ *vt* **1** (to remove) قَضى (i; قَضاء; على) ‹*a problem, risk, poverty*› **2** (to rule out) اسْتَبْعَدَ ‹*a suspect, candidate*›

elimination /ɪlɪmɪ'neɪʃ(ə)n/ *n* **1** (removal) إزالة, قَضاء **2** (ruling out) اسْتِبْعاد; **he had to find the correct answer by a process of ~** كانَ عَلَيْهِ أَنْ يَجِدَ الإجابةَ الصَحيحةَ من خِلالِ عَمَلِيّةِ حَذْفٍ \ اسْتِبْعادٍ (للإجاباتِ الأُخْرى)

elite /eɪ'liːt/ **A** *n* نُخْبة (نُخَب) **B** *adj* ‹*group, school*› النُخْبة

elixir /ɪ'lɪksɪə/ *n* إكْسير

elk /ɛlk/ *n* (*pl* **elks** or **elk**) **1** (European, Asian) إلْكة **2** (AmE) (wapiti) إلْكة

elm, **elm tree** /ɛlm/ *n* شَجَرة البَقِّ

elocution /ˌɛlə'kjuːʃ(ə)n/ *n* فَصاحة

elongated /'iːlɒŋgeɪtɪd/ *adj* ‹*shape, leaf*› مُمَدَّد, مَمْدود

elongation /iːlɒŋ'geɪʃ(ə)n/ *n* اسْتِطالة

elope /ɪ'ləʊp/ *vi* «women, men, couples» [فَرَّ بِقَصْدِ الزَواجِ]

eloquent /'ɛləkwənt/ *adj* ‹*speech, speaker*› فَصيح (فُصَحاءُ, فُصُح, فِصاح)

El Salvador /ɛl 'salvədɔː/ *pr n* السَلْفادور (f)

else /ɛls/ **A** *adv* آخَر; **somebody ~ must have it** لا بُدَّ أَنَّهُ لَدى شَخْصٍ آخَرَ; **nobody ~ knows** لا أَحَدَ آخَرَ يَعْلَمُ; **nothing ~ will do** لَن يُجْدِيَ أَيُّ شَيْءٍ آخَرَ; **something ~ is needed** هُناكَ حاجةٌ إلى شَيْءٍ آخَرَ; **somewhere** *or* **someplace** (AmE) **~** مَكان آخَر; **where ~ can it be?** في أَيِّ مَكانٍ آخَرَ يُمْكِنُ أَنْ يَكونَ؟; **who ~ is coming?** مَنْ سَيَأْتي أَيْضاً؟; **how ~ can we do it/ explain it?** كيفَ لَنا أَنْ نَفْعَلَهُ \ نَشْرَحَهُ بِشَكْلٍ مُخْتَلِفٍ؟; **what ~ would you like?** ما الّذي تُريدُهُ غَيْرَ ذلكَ؟; **there's little** *or* **not much ~ to say** لَيْسَ هُناكَ ما يُقالُ أَكْثَرَ من ذلكَ; **he talks of little ~** لا يَتَحَدَّثُ تَقْريباً إلاّ عن هذا; **everyone ~ but me went to the beach** ذَهَبَ الجَميعُ إلى الشاطِئِ إلاّ أنا; **was anyone ~ there?** هل كانَ هُناكَ أَيُّ شَخْصٍ آخَرَ؟; **anyone ~ but you would get up early** أَيُّ شَخْصٍ سِواكَ كانَ سَيَسْتَيْقِظُ مُبَكِّراً; **anywhere ~ it wouldn't matter** لن يَكونَ هذا مُهِمّاً في أَيِّ مَكانٍ آخَرَ; **he didn't see anybody ~** لم يَرَ أَيَّ شَخْصٍ آخَرَ; **she didn't say anything ~** لم تَقُلْ أَيَّ شَيْءٍ غَيْرَ ذلك; **nothing ~ but a change of government can save the economy** لا يُمْكِنُ أَنْ يُنْقِذَ الاقْتِصادَ سِوى تَغْيير الحُكومةِ; **if nothing ~ he's polite** هو على الأَقَلِّ مُؤَدَّبٌ جِدّاً; **whatever ~ he might be he's not a liar** قد تَكونُ فيهِ كُلُّ الصِفاتِ السَيِّئةِ وَلكِنَّهُ لَيْسَ كَذّاباً **B** (**or else**) *conj phr* (before consequence) وَإلاّ; (before alternative) أَوْ; **eat this or ~ you'll be hungry later** كُلْ هذا وَإلاّ سَتَجوعُ لاحِقاً; **either he's already left or ~ he can't hear the phone** إمّا أَنَّهُ قد غادَرَ أو أَنَّهُ لا يَسْتَطيعُ سَماعَ الهاتِفِ

elsewhere /ɛls'wɛː/ *adv* في \ إلى مَكانٍ آخَرَ; **from ~** من أَماكِنَ أُخْرى; **she is seeking employment ~** تَبْحَثُ عن عَمَلٍ في مَكانٍ آخَرَ

ELT /iːɛl'tiː/ *n* = **English Language Teaching** تَدْريس اللُغةِ الإنْجليزيّةِ

elucidate /ɪ'luːsɪdeɪt/ *vt* وَضَّحَ

elude /ɪ'ljuːd/ *vt* (to escape) أَفْلَتَ (من) ‹*a pursuer, danger*›; **her name ~s me** لا أَسْتَطيعُ أَنْ أَتَذَكَّرَ اسْمَها

elusive /ɪ'luːsɪv/ *adj* **1** ‹*enemy, animal*› يَصْعُبُ إيجادُهُ \ الإمْساكُ بِهِ **2** ‹*goal, victory*› صَعْب المَنالِ

elves /ɛlvz/ *n pl* ▸ **elf**

emaciated /ɪ'meɪʃɪeɪtɪd/ *adj* ‹*body, face, animal*› نَحيل (نَحْلى, نُحَّل), هَزيل (هَزْلى)

email, **e-mail** /'iːmeɪl/ **A** *n* **1** (system) بَريد إلِكْتْرونيّ; **to have ~** كانَ لَدَيْهِ بَريدٌ إلِكْتْرونيٌّ **2** (message) رِسالة إلِكْتْرونيّة; **to send sb an ~** أَرْسَلَ رِسالةً إلِكْتْرونيّةً لِشَخْصٍ **B** *vt* **1** ‹*a person, the winner*› أَرْسَلَ رِسالةً إلِكْتْرونيّةً ل; **I'll ~ you to let you know I've arrived safely** سَأُرْسِلُ لَكَ رِسالةً إلِكْتْرونيّةً أُعْلِمُكَ فيها أَنّني وَصَلْتُ بِسَلامٍ **2** أَرْسَلَ بالبَريدِ

الإلِكْتْرونيِّ ‹*a contract, photograph*›; **to ~ the files to sb** أَرْسَلَ المِلَفّاتِ لِشَخْصٍ بالبَريدِ الإلِكْتْرونيِّ; **I'll ~ the information to you** سَأُرْسِلُ لَكَ المَعْلوماتِ بالبَريدِ الإلِكْتْرونيِّ

email address *n* عُنْوان بَريدٍ إلِكْتْرونيٍّ

email message *n* رِسالة بالبَريدِ الإلِكْتْرونيِّ

emanate /ˈɛməneɪt/ *vi* «gas, light» اِنْبَعَثَ; **the rumours ~d from a government source** نَبَعَت الإشاعاتُ من مَصْدَرٍ حُكوميٍّ

emancipate /ɪˈmansɪpeɪt/ *vt* حَرَّرَ ‹*slaves, women*›

emancipated /ɪˈmansɪpeɪtɪd/ *adj* ‹*woman, views*› مُتَحَرِّر

emancipation /ɪˌmansɪˈpeɪʃ(ə)n/ *n* تَحْرير

embalm /ɪmˈbɑːm/ *vt* حَنَّطَ ‹*a body, corpse*›

embankment /ɪmˈbaŋkmənt/ *n* **1** (for a railway, road) سَدّ [مُرْتَفَع يُبْنَى لِإِنْشاءِ طَريق \ سِكَّةِ حَديد] **2** (by a river) (أَسْداد, سُدود)

embargo /ɪmˈbɑːɡəʊ/ *n* (*pl* **embargoes**) حِصار (حُصُر), حَظْر; **to impose/lift an ~ on sth** فَرَضَ \ رَفَعَ حِصاراً \ حَظْراً على شَيْءٍ

embark /ɪmˈbɑːk/ *vi* **1** (on a ship, an aircraft) صَعِدَ (على مَتْنِ) **2** **to ~ on a campaign** شَرَعَ في حَمْلَةٍ

embarkation /ɛmbɑːˈkeɪʃ(ə)n/ *n* (of passengers) صُعود, رُكوب; (of goods) شَحْن

embarrass /ɪmˈbarəs/ *vt* أَحْرَجَ ‹*a person, government*›

embarrassed /ɪmˈbarəst/ *adj* ‹*silence, smile*› مُحْرَج, خَجْلان (خَجْلى)

embarrassing /ɪmˈbarəsɪŋ/ *adj* ‹*moment, situation*› مُحْرِج; **it was so ~!** كانَ الأَمْرُ مُحْرِجاً للغاية!

embarrassment /ɪmˈbarəsmənt/ *n* **1** (feeling) إِحْراج **2** (cause of embarrassment) مَبْعَث إِحْراجٍ; **the situation has become an ~ to the government** أَصْبَحَ الوَضْعُ مَبْعَثَ إِحْراجٍ للحُكومةِ

embassy /ˈɛmbəsi/ *n* (*pl* **embassies**) سِفارة

embed /ɪmˈbɛd/ *vt* (**-dd-**) **to be ~ded in sth** كانَ مَغْروزاً في شَيْءٍ ‹*a bullet, stake*›; **a journalist ~ded with the coalition forces** صَحَفيٌّ مُرافِق لِقوّاتِ التَحالُفِ

embedded /ɪmˈbɛdɪd/ *adj* **1** ‹*system, software*› مُضَمَّن **2** ‹*reporter, journalist*› مُرافِق

embellish /ɪmˈbɛlɪʃ/ *vt* زَيَّنَ, جَمَّلَ, نَمَّقَ ‹*a statement, story*›

embers /ˈɛmbəz/ *n pl* جَمْر

embezzle /ɪmˈbɛz(ə)l/ *vt* اخْتَلَسَ ‹*funds, money*›

embittered /ɪmˈbɪtəd/ *adj* ‹*rival*› لَدود (أَلِدّاءُ); ‹*fighting*› مَرير

emblem /ˈɛmbləm/ *n* شِعار (شِعارات)

embodiment /ɪmˈbɒdimənt/ *n* تَجْسيد

embody /ɪmˈbɒdi/ *vt* (**embodies, embodying, embodied**) جَسَّدَ ‹*principles, values*›

embolism /ˈɛmbəliz(ə)m/ *n* انْسِداد وَريديّ

emboss /ɪmˈbɒs/ *vt* دَمَغَ (a; دَمْغ) ‹*leather, metal*›

embrace /ɪmˈbreɪs/ **A** *vt* **1** (to hug) حَضَنَ (u; حَضْن, حِضانة), احْتَضَنَ **2** (to accept) احْتَضَنَ ‹*an idea, change*› **B** *vi* «couples, friends» تَعانَقَ **C** *n* حَضْن, احْتِضان

embrocation /ˌɛmbrəˈkeɪʃ(ə)n/ *n* مَرْهَم مُسَكِّن للأَلَمِ

embroider /ɪmˈbrɔɪdə/ **A** *vt* **1** طَرَّزَ, وَشى (i; وَشْي), وَشَّى, زَخْرَفَ (i; زَخْرَفة) ‹*a garment, cloth*› **2** بالَغَ (في) ‹*a story, the truth*› **B** *vi* طَرَّزَ

embroidery /ɪmˈbrɔɪd(ə)ri/ *n* (*pl* **embroideries**) تَطْريز

embroil /ɪmˈbrɔɪl/ *vt* **to be/become ~ed in sth** تَوَرَّطَ في شَيْءٍ ‹*a dispute, controversy*›

embryo /ˈɛmbrɪəʊ/ *n* جَنين (أَجِنّة, أَجْنُن)

embryonic /ˌɛmbrɪˈɒnɪk/ *adj* **1** ‹*tissue, research*› جَنينيّ **2** ‹*idea, organization*› بُدائيّ

emend /ɪˈmɛnd/ *vt* (fml) نَقَّحَ ‹*a document, proof*›

emerald /ˈɛm(ə)rəld/ **A** *n* **1** (gem) زُمُرُّد (n coll) **2** (also **emerald green**) (colour) لَوْن أَخْضَر زُمُرُّديّ **B** *adj* ‹*suit*› زُمُرُّديّ; **the E~ Isle** الجَزيرة الزُمُرُّديّة

emerge /ɪˈməːdʒ/ *vi* **1** (to come out) بَرَزَ (u; بُروز) **2** (to become apparent) «problem, pattern, truth» ظَهَرَ (a; ظُهور)

emergence /ɪˈməːdʒ(ə)ns/ *n* (of the truth) ظُهور, تَجَلٍّ; (of a problem) نُشوء, بُروز; (of a religion, literary genre) بُزوغ, انْبِثاق

emergency /ɪˈmə:dʒ(ə)nsi/ **A** *n* (*pl* **emergencies**) (situation) طارِئ; **in an ~, in case of ~** للضَرورةِ, في حالةِ الطَوارِئِ المُلِحّةِ; **in times of national ~** في أَوْقاتِ الطَوارِئِ والأَزَماتِ الوَطَنيّةِ

B *adj before n* ‹*surgery, session*› عاجِل, طارِئ

emergency exit *n* مَخْرَج طَوارِئ

emergency landing *n* هُبوط اضْطِراريّ \ طارِئ

emergency room *n* (AmE) غُرْفة طَوارِئ \ اسْتِعْجالات

emergency services *n* الخِدْمات \ مَصالِح الطَوارِئِ

emergency stop *n* تَوَقُّف طارِئ \ فَوْريّ

emery paper /ˈɛm(ə)ri ˌpeɪpə/ *n* وَرَق صَنْفَرة \ زُجاج

emetic /ɪˈmɛtɪk/ **A** *adj* ‹*drug, effect*› مُسَبِّب للقَيْءِ, مُقَيِّئ

B *n* مُقَيِّئ (مُقَيِّئات)

emigrant /ˈɛmɪɡrənt/ *n* مُهاجِر, مُغْتَرِب, نازِح; **Jewish/Irish ~s to the USA** المُهاجِرون اليَهود \ الإيرْلَنْديّون إلى الوِلاياتِ المُتَّحِدةِ الأَمْريكيّةِ

emigrate /ˈɛmɪɡreɪt/ *vi* «families, workers» هاجَرَ, اغْتَرَبَ, نَزَحَ (a-i; نَزْح, نُزوح)

emigration /ˌɛmɪˈɡreɪʃ(ə)n/ *n* هِجْرة, اغْتِراب, نُزوح

émigré /ˈɛmɪɡreɪ/ *n* لاجِئ

eminent /ˈɛmɪnənt/ *adj* ‹*scientist, career*› مَرْموق, بارِز

emir /ɛˈmiːə/ *n* أَمير (أُمَراءُ)

emission /ɪˈmɪʃ(ə)n/ *n* انْبِعاث (انْبِعاثات)

emit /ɪˈmɪt/ *vt* (**-tt-**) (to discharge) أَطْلَقَ ‹*steam, gas*›; أَصْدَرَ ‹*light*›

emoticon /ɪˈməʊtɪkɒn, ɪˈmɒtɪkɒn/ *n* رَمْز تَعْبيريّ (يُسْتَخْدَمُ للتَعْبيرِ عن المَشاعِرِ في مَواقِعِ الدَرْدَشةِ)

emotion /ɪˈməʊʃ(ə)n/ *n* **1** [u] (strength of feeling) شُعور **2** (feeling) عاطِفة (عَواطِفُ), إحْساس (إحْساسات, أَحاسيسُ)

emotional /ɪˈməʊʃ(ə)n(ə)l/ *adj* (relating to feelings) ‹*support, well-being*› عاطِفيّ; (sensitive) ‹*reaction, nature*› حَسّاس (moving) ‹*speech, experience*› مُؤَثِّر

emotionally /ɪˈməʊʃ(ə)n(ə)li/ *adv* **1** (with emotion) ‹*to speak, react*› بِشَكْلٍ عاطِفيٍّ **2** (from an emotional standpoint) ‹*deprived, involved*› عاطِفيًّا

emotive /ɪˈməʊtɪv/ *adj* ‹*issue, language*› مُثير للعَواطِفِ, انْفِعاليّ

empathize, -ise (BrE) /ˈɛmpəθʌɪz/ *vi* **to ~ with one's audience** تَعاطَفَ مع جُمْهورِهِ

empathy /ˈɛmpəθi/ *n* تَعاطُف, تَقَمُّص عاطِفيّ

emperor /ˈɛmp(ə)rə/ *n* إمْبَراطور (أَباطِرة)

emphasis /ˈɛmfəsɪs/ *n* (*pl* **emphases**) تَشْديد, تَأْكيد (تَأْكيدات); **to put the ~ on efficiency** قامَ بالتَشْديدِ على الفَعّاليّةِ

emphasize, -ise (BrE) /ˈɛmfəsʌɪz/ *vt* **1** (to give importance to) أَكَّدَ, شَدَّدَ (على) ‹*a policy, need*› **2** (to highlight) أَظْهَرَ, أَبْرَزَ ‹*a shape, feature*› **3** (to stress vocally) نَبَرَ, شَدَّدَ (i; نَبْر) ‹*a word, syllable*›

emphatic /ɪmˈfatɪk/ *adj* **1** (insistent, firm) ‹*statement, refusal*› تَأْكيديّ; (clear) ‹*win, defeat*› أَكيد, مُؤَكَّد **2** (Ling) ‹*consonant, sound*› مُفَخَّم

emphysema /ˌɛmfɪˈsiːmə/ *n* نُفاخ رِئَويّ

empire /ˈɛmpʌɪə/ *n* إمْبَراطوريّة

empirical /ɛmˈpɪrɪk(ə)l/ *adj* ‹*study, evidence*› تَجْريبيّ

employ /ɪmˈplɔɪ/ *vt* **1** (to give work to) شَغَّلَ, وَظَّفَ ‹*a worker, contractor*› **2** (to use) اسْتَخْدَمَ ‹*a technique, tool*›

employable /ɪmˈplɔɪəb(ə)l/ *adj* ‹*candidate, graduate*› (qualified) لَدَيْهِ المُؤَهِّلاتُ المَطْلوبةُ; (capable of working) قادِر على العَمَلِ

employee /ɪmˈplɔɪiː, ɛmplɔɪˈiː/ *n* أَجير (أُجَراءُ), مُسْتَخْدَم

employer /ɪmˈplɔɪə/ *n* مُسْتَخْدِم, رَبّ العَمَلِ \ صاحِب

employment /ɪmˈplɔɪm(ə)nt/ *n* **1** (work) عَمَل (أَعْمال), شُغْل (أَشْغال, شُغول), وَظيفة (وَظائِفُ); **to be in ~** كانَ لَدَيْهِ وَظيفةٌ **2** (act of employing) تَشْغيل, تَوْظيف (تَوْظيفات)

employment agency *n* وِكالة تَوْظيفٍ \ تَشْغيلٍ

empower /ɪmˈpaʊə/ *vt* خَوَّلَ, فَوَّضَ ‹*a consumer, citizen*›

empress /ˈɛmprɪs/ *n* إمْبَراطورة

emptiness /ˈɛmptinəs/ *n* (of a vehicle, building, life) فَراغ (فَراغات), خَلاء; (in your stomach) خَواء; (of a promise, threat) عَدَم جِدّيّة

empty /ˈɛmpti/ **A** *adj* (**emptier**, **emptiest**) **1** ‹*container, space*› فارِغ, خالٍ, خاوٍ **2** ‹*promise, threat*› فارِغ

B *vt* (**empties**, **emptying**, **emptied**) أَفْرَغَ ‹*a container, one's pockets*›; **she emptied the contents of her bag onto the table**

أَفْرَغَتْ مُحْتَوِيَاتِ حَقِيبَتِها فوق الطاوِلَةِ

C *vi* **1** «streets, rooms» خَلا (u; خُلُوّ) **2** **to ~ into sth** «river, stream» صَبَّ في شَيْءٍ

(Phrasal verb) **empty out**: **~ [sth] out, ~ out [sth]** أَفْرَغَ [شَيْئاً] ‹*a cupboard, one's pockets*›

empty-handed /ˌɛmptɪˈhandɪd/ *adj* ‹*to arrive, leave*› فارِغ \ خائِب ,صِفْر اليَدَيْنِ

emu /ˈiːmjuː/ *n* إيمو

emulate /ˈɛmjʊleɪt/ *vt* (fml) ضاهى ,حاكى ‹*a style, mannerism*›

emulsify /ɪˈmʌlsɪfʌɪ/ **A** *vt* (**emulsifies, emulsifying, emulsified**) اسْتَحْلَبَ ‹*a starch, an oil*›
B *vi* «starch, oils» تَحَوَّلَ إلى مُسْتَحْلَبٍ

emulsion /ɪˈmʌlʃ(ə)n/ *n* **1** (of liquids) مُسْتَحْلَب (مُسْتَحْلَبات) **2** (BrE) (also **emulsion paint**) دِهان \ طِلاء مائِيّ مُسْتَحْلَب [للجُدْرانِ]

enable /ɪˈneɪb(ə)l/ *vt* **1** **to ~ sb to study in America** (to provide means for) مَكَّنَ شَخْصاً من الدِراسةِ في أَمْرِيكا **2** (to make possible) سَمَحَ ,مَكَّنَ (a; سَماح ;ب) ‹*growth, learning*›

enact /ɪˈnakt/ *vt* **1** (to pass) سَنَّ ,شَرَّعَ (u; سَنّ) ‹*a law, bill*›
2 (to perform) عَرَضَ (i; عَرْض) ‹*a scene, fantasy*›

enamel /ɪˈnam(ə)l/ *n* (on metal, wood, teeth) ميناء ,مينا

enamoured (BrE), **enamored** (AmE) /ɪˈnaməd/ *adj* **to be ~ of sb/sth** (fml) وَلِعَ بِشَخْصٍ \ شَيْءٍ ‹*a partner, an activity*›; **I'm not very ~ of the idea** لَسْتُ مولَعاً جدًّا بالفِكْرةِ

enc. *abbr* = **enclosed** مُرْفَق

encampment /ɪnˈkampmənt/ *n* مُخَيَّم (مُخَيَّمات)

encapsulate /ɪnˈkapsjʊleɪt/ *vt* **1** (to summarize) أَوْجَزَ, لَخَّصَ ‹*a period of history, opinions*› **2** (to include, incorporate) تَضَمَّنَ (على نَحْوٍ موجَزٍ) ‹*information, a scene*›

encase /ɪnˈkeɪs/ *vt* لَفَّ (u; لَفّ), غَلَّفَ ‹*a frame, filling*›; **to be ~d in sth** كانَ مَلْفوفاً في شَيْءٍ ‹*plastic, plaster*›

enchant /ɪnˈtʃɑːnt/ *vt* **1** (to charm) سَحَرَ (a; سِحْر), سَلَبَ العَقْلَ **2** (to cast a spell on) عَمِلَ سِحْراً ل ‹*a castle, kingdom*›

enchanting /ɪnˈtʃɑːntɪŋ/ *adj* ‹*smile, scene*› خَلاّب ,ساحِر

encircle /ɪnˈsəːk(ə)l/ *vt* أَحاطَ (ب), طَوَّقَ ‹*a building, fort*›

enclave /ˈɛnkleɪv/ *n* مُكْتَنَف ,جَيْب داخِلِيّ

enclose /ɪnˈkləʊz/ *vt* **1** (in a letter) أَرْفَقَ ‹*a copy, document*›
2 (to fence in) سَيَّجَ ‹*a building, property*›

enclosure /ɪnˈkləʊʒə/ *n* **1** (area) مِنْطَقة مُسَيَّجة **2** (with a letter) مُرْفَق (مُرْفَقات)

encode /ɪnˈkəʊd/ *vt, vi* **1** حَوَّلَ إلى رُموزٍ ‹*a message, signal*›
2 شَفَّرَ (بِاسْتِخْدامِ نِظامِ تَرْميزٍ \ تَشْفيرٍ) ‹*an instruction, a file*›

encompass /ɪnˈkʌmpəs/ *vt* (fml) شَمِلَ ,حَمَلَ في \ بين طَيّاتِهِ (a; شَمْل) ‹*a subject, range*›

encore /ˈɒŋkɔː/ **A** *n* إعادة أَداءِ مَقْطَعٍ غِنائِيٍّ (عند نِهاية حَفْلٍ فَنِّيٍّ بِطَلَبٍ من الجُمْهورِ)
B *excl* **~!** مَرَّةً ثانِيةً \ أُخْرى!

encounter /ɪnˈkaʊntə/ **A** *vt* **1** (to meet) صادَفَ ,لاقى, اصْطَدَمَ (ب) ‹*a danger, difficulty*› **2** (to come across) صادَفَ, الْتَقى (ب) ‹*a friend, stranger*›
B *n* لِقاء (لِقاءات)

encourage /ɪnˈkʌrɪdʒ/ *vt* **1** (to support) حَثَّ ,شَجَّعَ (u; حَثّ; على) ‹*a pupil, child*›; **she/it ~d me to carry on** شَجَّعَتْني \ شَجَّعَني الأَمْرُ على المُواصَلةِ **2** (to foster) شَجَّعَ ‹*industry, competition*›

encouragement /ɪnˈkʌrɪdʒmənt/ *n* تَشْجيع (تَشْجيعات)

encouraging /ɛŋˈkʌrɪdʒɪŋ/ *adj* ‹*start, sign*› مُشَجِّع

encroach /ɪnˈkrəʊtʃ/ *vi* **to ~ on sb's land** اسْتَوْلى \ تَعَدّى على أَرْضِ شَخْصٍ

encrypt /ɛnˈkrɪpt/ *vt* شَفَّرَ

encryption /ɛnˈkrɪpʃ(ə)n/ *n* تَشْفير

encumber /ɪnˈkʌmbə/ *vt* عاقَ (u; عَوْق), عَرْقَلَ (i; عَرْقَلة) ‹*a motorist, hiker*›

encyclopedia, encyclopaedia /ɪnˌsʌɪkləˈpiːdɪə/ *n* دائِرة مَعارِفَ ,مَوْسوعة

end /ɛnd/ **A** *n* **1** (of the week, a holiday, journey) نِهاية; **at the ~ of the year/story** في نِهايةِ السَنةِ \ القِصّةِ; **at the ~ of May** في نِهايةِ مايو; **by the ~ of the month/game** عند نِهايةِ الشَهْرِ \ المُباراةِ; **for days on ~** لِأَيّامٍ عَديدةٍ; **'The End'** 'النِهاية'; **to put an ~ to corruption/the conflict** وَضَعَ حَدًّا للفَسادِ \ للصِراعِ; **to come to an ~** وَصَلَ إلى النِهايةِ; **in the ~ I went home**

[2] (of a road, branch, queue) نِهاية; في النِهايةِ ذَهَبْتُ إلى البَيْتِ **at the ~ of the street** في نِهايةِ الشارِعِ; **from one ~ of the house to the other** في جَميعِ أَنْحاءِ البَيْتِ; **to lay the posts ~ to ~** وَضَعَ القُضْبانَ على الأَرْضِ مُتَّصِلاً بَعْضُها بِبَعْضٍ; **the third from the ~** الثالِثُ من النِهايةِ; **to stand sth on its ~ *or* on ~** أَوْقَفَ شَيْئاً على حافَتِهِ [3] (of a scale, spectrum) طَرَف (أَطْراف); **at the lower ~ of the scale** في أَسْفَلِ السُلَّمِ [4] (fml) (aim) غاية; حَدّ (حُدود); **it is a means to an ~** هِيَ وَسيلةٌ للوُصولِ إلى غايةٍ; **to this ~** لِهَذِهِ الغايةِ, لِهَذا السَبَبِ; **for one's own ~s** لِمَصْلَحَتِهِ الخاصّةِ [5] (in games) أَحَد نِصْفَي المَلْعَبِ; **to change ~s** قامَ بِتَغْييرِ نِصْفَي المَلْعَبِ [6] (death) نِهاية, خاتِمة, خَواتِمُ (خَواتيمُ); **to meet one's ~** لَقِيَ حَتْفَهُ; **to be nearing one's ~** اقْتَرَبَتْ نِهايَتُهُ \ خاتِمَتُهُ; **to come to a bad ~** ماتَ ميتةً مُحْزِنةً

[B] *vt* أَنْهى ‹*a strike, war, marriage*›; **he ~ed the fight with a knockout** أَنْهى المُباراةَ بِضَرْبةٍ قاضِيةٍ; **he ~ed his days in hospital** قَضى أَيّامَهُ الأَخيرةَ في المُسْتَشْفى; **to ~ it all, to ~ one's life** وَضَعَ حَدًّا لِحَياتِهِ

[C] *vi* [1] «week, career, marriage» اِنْتَهى; **to ~ in failure/divorce** اِنْتَهى بالفَشَلِ \ بالطَلاقِ; **the story ~s happily/tragically** تَنْتَهي القِصّةُ نِهايةً سَعيدةً \ مَأْساوِيّةً; **where will it all ~?** إلى أَيْنَ سَتَؤولُ الأُمورُ؟ [2] «paths, roads» اِنْتَهى

(Idioms) **all's well that ends well** الأُمورُ بِخَواتيمِها; **to make ends meet** عاشَ على الكَفافِ; **to tie up the loose ends** حَلَّ القَضايا الجانِبيّةَ \ العالِقةَ

(Phrasal verb) **end up**: **to ~ up as president/an alcoholic** اِنْتَهى بِهِ المَطافُ رَئيساً \ مُدْمِناً على الكُحولِ; **to ~ up in hospital/Damascus** اِنْتَهى بِهِ المَطافُ في المُسْتَشْفى \ دِمَشْقَ

endanger /ɪnˈdeɪndʒə/ *vt* عَرَّضَ للخَطَرِ ‹*one's health, reputation*›; هَدَّدَ بالانْقِراضِ ‹*a species*›

endangered species /ɪnˈdeɪndʒəd ˌspiːʃiːz/ *n* أَنْواع مُهَدَّدة بالانْقِراضِ

endear /ɪnˈdɪə/ *vt* **to ~ oneself to sb** حَبَّبَ نَفْسَهُ إلى شَخْصٍ ‹*the public, audience*›

endearing /ɪnˈdɪərɪŋ/ *adj* ‹*quality, smile*› مُحَبَّب (إلى القَلْبِ)

endearment /ɪnˈdɪəmənt/ *n* [1] [u] (affection) مَوَدّة, حَنان [2] (words of affection) عِبارة حُبٍّ \ حَنانٍ

endeavour, **endeavor** (AmE) /ɪnˈdɛvə/ [A] *vt* **to ~ to do sth** سَعى للقِيامِ بِشَيْءٍ

[B] *n* (attempt) مُحاوَلة, مَسْعًى (مَساعٍ); [u] (industriousness) كَدّ, اجْتِهاد

endemic /ɛnˈdɛmɪk/ *adj* ‹*disease, corruption, species*› مُسْتَوْطِن; **malaria is ~ in many tropical countries** المَلارِيا مُسْتَوْطِنةٌ في العَديدِ من البُلْدانِ الاسْتِوائيّةِ

end house *n* [أَبْعَد بَيْتٍ في سِلْسِلةِ بُيوتٍ]

ending /ˈɛndɪŋ/ *n* [1] (conclusion) نِهاية, خاتِمة, خَواتِمُ (خَواتيمُ) [2] (of a word) لاحِقة (لَواحِقُ)

endive /ˈɛndɪv/ *n* [1] (BrE) (lettuce) هِنْدِباء أَنْديفيّة [2] (AmE) (chicory) هِنْدِباء بَرّيّة

endless /ˈɛndləs/ *adj* [1] ‹*patience, supply*› لا نِهايةَ لَهُ [2] ‹*permutations, ideas*› لا يُحْصى, لا حَصْرَ لَهُ; **the possibilities are ~** الاحْتِمالاتُ لا يُمْكِنُ حَصْرُها

endlessly /ˈɛndlɪsli/ *adv* [1] (with no limits) ‹*tolerant, kind*› بِلا حُدودٍ [2] (without stopping) ‹*to talk, argue*› بِلا نِهايةٍ; ‹*to search, play*› دون تَوَقُّفٍ [3] (with no apparent end) ‹*to stretch, extend*› إلى ما لا نِهاية

endogenous /ɛnˈdɒdʒɪnəs/ *adj* ‹*retrovirus, depression*› داخِليّ المَنْشَأِ

endometriosis /ˌɛndəʊmiːtrɪˈəʊsɪs/ *n* البِطانة الرَحِميّة الهاجِرة

endorse /ɪnˈdɔːs/ *vt* [1] أَيَّدَ, أَقَرَّ ‹*a point of view, a decision*› [2] ‹*a candidate*› زَكّى [3] وَصّى ب (عن طَريقِ الإعْلاناتِ التِجاريّةِ) ‹*a product*› [4] ظَهَّرَ ‹*a cheque*›

endorsement /ɪnˈdɔːsmənt/ *n* [1] [u] (approval) مُوافَقة, مُصادَقة; (political backing) تَزْكية [2] [u] (recommendation) تَوْصِية (ضِمْنَ إعْلانٍ تِجاريٍّ يُقَدِّمُهُ نَجْمٌ) [3] (on a driving licence) مُلاحَظة جَزائيّة (وَفْقَ نِظامِ النِقاطِ)

endow /ɪnˈdaʊ/ *vt* [1] (to enjoy) **to be ~ed with beauty/intelligence** تَمَتَّعَ بالجَمالِ \ الذَكاءِ [2] (to fund) مَوَّلَ ‹*a charity, college*›

endowment /ɪnˈdaʊmənt/ *n* [1] [u] (of an institution) دَعْم مادّيّ, تَمْويل; (of a prize, academic post) تَبَرُّع (تَبَرُّعات) [2] (money given) مِنْحة (مِنَح)

end product *n* مُنْتَج نِهائِيّ

end result *n* نَتِيجة نِهائِيّة

endurance /ɪnˈdjʊərəns/ *n* تَكَبُّد, تَحَمُّل

endurance test *n* اخْتِبار القُدْرة على التَحَمُّل

endure /ɪnˈdjʊə/ **A** *vt* تَكَبَّدَ, تَحَمَّلَ ‹*hardship, humiliation*›

B *vi* «traditions, relationships» اسْتَمَرَّ, بَقِيَ (a; بَقاء)

end user *n* مُسْتَعْمِل \ مُسْتَخْدِم نِهائِيّ

enema /ˈɛnɪmə/ *n* حُقْنة شَرَجِيّة

enemy /ˈɛnəmi/ **A** *n* (*pl* **enemies**) عَدُوّ (أَعْداء)

B *adj* ‹*forces, aircraft, territory*› العَدُوّ

energetic /ˌɛnəˈdʒɛtɪk/ *adj* ‹*exercise, campaigner*› نَشِيط (نشاط)

energize, -ise (BrE) /ˈɛnədʒʌɪz/ *vt* نَشَّطَ (أَعْطى طاقةً وَحَيَوِيّةً) ‹*the campaign, voters*›

energy /ˈɛnədʒi/ *n* **1** (power) طاقة **2** [u] (vitality) نَشاط, حَيَوِيّة **3** (effort) قُدْرة (قُدُرات) **4** [u] (Phys) طاقة

energy drink *n* مَشْروب طاقة

energy-saving /ˈɛnədʒiˌseɪvɪŋ/ *adj* ‹*device, feature*› تَوْفير \ مُوَفِّر للطاقةِ, ادِّخار الطاقةِ

enforce /ɪnˈfɔːs/ *vt* فَرَضَ (i; فَرْض) ‹*the law, discipline*›

enforcement /ɛnˈfɔːsmənt/ *n* (of a law, regulation) فَرْض

engage /ɪnˈgeɪdʒ/ **A** *vt* **1** (fml) (to occupy) شَغَلَ (a; شَغْل, شُغْل), اسْتَحْوَذَ (على); (to attract) شَدَّ (i-u; شَدّ), جَذَبَ (i; جَذْب) ‹*sb's attention, interest*› **2** (fml) (to employ) اسْتَخْدَمَ, اسْتَأْجَرَ ‹*staff, a performer*› **3** عَشَّقَ ‹*a gear, the clutch*›

B *vi* (fml) (to take part in) **to ~ in sport/politics** زاوَلَ الرِياضةَ \ السِياسةَ; **to ~ in conversation/discussion** تَجاذَبَ أَطْرافَ الحَدِيثِ \ النِقاشِ

engaged /ɪnˈgeɪdʒd/ *adj* **1** (before marriage) **to be ~ to sb** كانَ مَخْطوبًا لِ \ مُرْتَبِطًا بِشَخْصٍ; **to get ~** (man) خَطَبَ (u; خِطْبة, خَطْب); (woman) خُطِبَتْ **2** (fml) (busy) مَشْغول, مُنْهَمِك, مُنْشَغِل; **I am otherwise ~** أَنا مَشْغولٌ \ مُنْشَغِلٌ بِشَيْءٍ آخَرَ; **they are ~ in a new business venture** هُمْ مُنْهَمِكونَ في مُغامَرةٍ تِجارِيّةٍ جَدِيدةٍ **3** (BrE) (in use) ‹*telephone line, WC*› مَشْغول, قَيْدَ الاسْتِخْدامِ; **the line's ~** الخَطُّ مَشْغولٌ \ قَيْدَ الاسْتِخْدامِ

engaged tone *n* (BrE) إِشارة مَشْغولٍ (على الهاتِفِ)

engagement /ɪnˈgeɪdʒmənt/ *n* **1** (agreement before marriage) خِطْبة; (period before marriage) خُطوبة **2** (appointment) مَوْعِد (مَواعِدُ); (commitment) الْتِزام (الْتِزامات), تَعَهُّد (تَعَهُّدات)

engagement ring *n* خاتَم خُطوبةٍ

engaging /ɪnˈgeɪdʒɪŋ/ *adj* ‹*shyness, laugh, smile*› خَلّاب, ساحِر; ‹*person, character*› مُحَبَّب, جَذّاب; ‹*performance, tale*› مُشَوِّق

engender /ɪnˈdʒɛndə/ *vt* وَلَّدَ ‹*loyalty, feelings*›; تَسَبَّبَ, أَحْدَثَ (في) ‹*a phenomenon, situation*›

engine /ˈɛndʒɪn/ *n* **1** (of a car, plane, ship) مُحَرِّك (مُحَرِّكات) **2** (locomotive) قاطِرة **3** (driving force) قُوّة دافِعة

engine driver *n* (BrE) سائِق قِطارٍ

engineer /ɛndʒɪˈnɪə/ **A** *n* **1** مُهَنْدِس **2** (AmE) (train driver) سائِق قِطارٍ

B *vt* **1** (to bring about) دَبَّرَ ‹*a coup, a situation*›; خَطَّطَ (لِ) ‹*sb's downfall*› **2** (to build) هَنْدَسَ (i; هَنْدَسة), صَمَّمَ ‹*a system, structure*›

engineering /ɛndʒɪˈnɪərɪŋ/ *n* هَنْدَسة

engine oil *n* زَيْت المُحَرِّكِ \ التَزْيِيتِ

England /ˈɪŋglənd/ *pr n* إِنْكِلْتِرا

English /ˈɪŋglɪʃ/ **A** *adj* ‹*language, law, literature*› إِنْجْلِيزِيّ

B *n* **1** (language) (اللُغة) الإِنْجْلِيزِيّة **2** (people) (**the English**) الإِنْجْلِيز

English Channel /ˌɪŋglɪʃ ˈtʃan(ə)l/ *pr n* (**the English Channel**) القَنال الإِنْجْلِيزِيّ

Englishman /ˈɪŋglɪʃmən/ *n* (*pl* **-men**) إِنْجْلِيزِيّ (إِنْجْلِيز)

English-speaking /ˈɪŋglɪʃˌspiːkɪŋ/ *adj* ‹*country, community*› ناطِق \ مُتَحَدِّث بالإِنْجْلِيزِيّة

Englishwoman /ˈɪŋglɪʃwʊmən/ *n* (*pl* **-women**) إِنْجْلِيزِيّة

engrave /ɪnˈgreɪv/ *vt* نَقَشَ (u; نَقْش), حَفَرَ (i; حَفْر) ‹*an inscription, a design*›

engraver /ɪnˈgreɪvə/ *n* نَقّاش

engraving /ɪnˈgreɪvɪŋ/ *n* (picture) صورة للَوْحةٍ مَعْدِنِيّةٍ مَنْقوشةٍ; [u] (process of engraving) حَفْر, نَقْش

engross /ɪnˈgrəʊs/ *vt* **1** شَدَّ الانْتِباهَ, اسْتَحْوَذَ (على) ‹*an audience, a reader*›; **to be ~ed in a book/a game** كانَ مُسْتَغْرِقًا في قِراءةِ كِتابٍ \ لَعِبِ لُعْبةٍ **2** بَيَّضَ ‹*a will, deed*›

engulf /ɪn'gʌlf/ *vt* (to sweep over) غَمَرَ (u; غَمْر), اجْتاحَ, اكْتَسَحَ ‹*a building, boat*›; **grief ~ed the whole population** غَمَرَ \ اجْتاحَ \ اكْتَسَحَ الحُزْنُ قُلوبَ السُكّانِ بِرُمَّتِهِمْ

enhance /ɪn'hɑːns/ *vt* (to improve) حَسَّنَ, نَمّى ‹*the performance, quality*›

enhancement /ɪn'hɑːnsmənt/ *n* تَحْسين (تَحْسينات)

enigma /ɪ'nɪgmə/ *n* (*pl* **enigmas**) لُغز (أَلْغاز)

enigmatic /ˌɛnɪg'matɪk/ *adj* ‹*expression, statement*› غامِض (غَوامِض), مُبْهَم

enjoy /ɪn'dʒɔɪ/ **A** *vt* **1** (to like) اسْتَمْتَعَ (ب) ‹*an experience, a meal*›; **I ~ travelling/music** أُحِبُّ السَفَرَ \ الموسيقى; **we ~ed the party** اسْتَمْتَعْنا بالحَفْلَةِ **2** (to benefit from) تَمَتَّعَ (ب), حَظِيَ (a; حُظْوة; ب) ‹*popularity, a privilege*›
B *vi* (infml) **~!** تَمَتَّعْ !
C *v refl* **to ~ oneself** اسْتَمْتَعَ \ تَمَتَّعَ بِوَقْتِهِ; **~ yourselves!** اسْتَمْتِعوا!

enjoyable /ɪn'dʒɔɪəb(ə)l/ *adj* ‹*occasion, activity*› مُمْتِع

enjoyment /ɪn'dʒɔɪmənt/ *n* لَذّة ,مُتْعة

enlarge /ɪn'lɑːdʒ/ *vt* **1** كَبَّرَ ‹*a photograph, document*› **2** وَسَّعَ ‹*a cavity, one's vocabulary*›

enlargement /ɪn'lɑːdʒmənt/ *n* **1** (of a carpark, airport) [u] تَوْسيع **2** [u] (of an organization) تَوْسيع **3** (of a photo) تَكْبير (تَكْبيرات)

enlighten /ɪn'lʌɪt(ə)n/ *vt* نَوَّرَ (العَقْل) ‹*a population, reader*›

enlightened /ɪn'lʌɪt(ə)nd/ *adj* ‹*attitude, mind*› مُسْتَنير

enlightening /ɪn'lʌɪtnɪŋ/ *adj* ‹*book, experience*› تَثْقيفيّ

enlightenment /ɪn'lʌɪt(ə)nmənt/ **A** *n* اسْتِنارة (العَقْل)
B **(the Enlightenment)** *pr n* التَنْوير

enlist /ɪn'lɪst/ **A** *vt* **1** طَوَّعَ ,جَنَّدَ ‹*a sailor, soldier*› **2** حَشَدَ (i-u; حَشْد) ‹*the support, help*›
B *vi* «recruits, soldiers» تَطَوَّعَ ,تَجَنَّدَ

enlisted man /ɪn'lɪstɪd man/ *n* (AmE) مُجَنَّد (دون رُتْبة ضابِط)

enmity /'ɛnmɪti/ *n* (*pl* **enmities**) (fml) عَداوة

enormity /ɪ'nɔːmɪti/ *n* (*pl* **enormities**) شَناعة ,فَظاعة ,جَسامة

enormous /ɪ'nɔːməs/ *adj* ‹*amount, pressure*› هائِل ,ضِخام) ضَخْم

enormously /ɪ'nɔːməsli/ *adv* ‹*to change, benefit*› بِشَكْلٍ ,جِدّاً كَبيرٍ \ هائِلٍ; **he has been ~ successful** حَقَّقَ نَجاحاً هائِلاً

enough /ɪ'nʌf/ **A** *determiner* كافٍ (إلى حَدٍّ); **there is ~ money** هُناكَ ما يَكْفي من المالِ; **there are ~ seats** هُناكَ ما يَكْفي من المَقاعِدِ; **they have more than ~ time** لَدَيْهِمْ أَكْثَرُ مِمّا يَكْفي من الوَقْتِ
B *pron* ما يَكْفي; **is there ~?** هل هُناكَ ما يَكْفي ؟; **there's more than ~ for everybody** هُناكَ أَكْثَرُ مِمّا يَكْفي الجَميعَ; **I've got ~ to worry about** لَدَيَّ ما يَكْفيني من الهُمومِ; **I've had ~ of him** طَفَحَ الكَيْلُ مِنْهُ; **I think you have said ~** أَظُنُّكَ قُلْتَ ما فيه الكِفايةُ; **~ said!** لا حاجةَ لِقَوْلِ المَزيد!
C *adv* بِما يَكْفي ,إلى حَدٍّ كافٍ; **it's quite big ~** هو كَبيرٌ جِدّاً; **it's big ~ for us** هو كَبيرٌ كِفايةً بالنِسْبةِ لَنا; **big ~ to hold 50 people** كَبير بِما يَكْفي لِيَسَعَ 50 شَخْصاً; **is he old ~ to vote?** هل بَلَغَ سِنَّ التَصْويتِ؟; **you're not trying hard ~** أَنْتَ لا تُحاوِلُ بِجُهْدٍ كافٍ; **curiously ~, I like her** قد يَبْدو الأَمْرُ غَريباً، وَلَكِنَّها تُعْجِبُني

enquire /ɪn'kwʌɪə/ **A** *vt* سَأَلَ (a; سُؤال)
B *vi* **to ~ about the price/availability of sth** اسْتَفْسَرَ \ اسْتَعْلَمَ عن سِعْرِ \ تَوَفُّرِ شَيْءٍ; **to ~ after the patient** اسْتَعْلَمَ \ اسْتَخْبَرَ عن صِحّةِ المَريضِ

enquiring /ɪn'kwʌɪərɪŋ/ *adj* ‹*mind, spirit*› مُحِبّ للاسْتِطْلاع; ‹*look, glance*› تَساؤُلِ ,اسْتِفْسارِ

enquiry, inquiry /ɪn'kwʌɪri/ *n* (*pl* **enquiries**) **1** (request for information) اسْتِفْسار (اسْتِفْسارات), اسْتِعْلام (اسْتِعْلامات); **to make enquiries about sth** قامَ بالاسْتِفْسارِ عن شَيْءٍ; **all enquiries to....** لِجَميعِ الاسْتِفْساراتِ **2** (investigation) تَحْقيق (تَحْقيقات); **an official ~ into the accident** تَحْقيق رَسْميّ في الحادِث

enrage /ɪn'reɪdʒ/ *vt* أَسْخَطَ ,أَغاظَ ‹*a campaigner, motorist*›

enrich /ɪn'rɪtʃ/ *vt* **1** أَغْنى ,أَثْرى ‹*the mind, soil*› **2** أَغْنى ,أَثْرى ‹*a capitalist, stockholder*›

enrichment /ɪn'rɪtʃmənt/ *n* إغْناء ,إثْراء

enrol, enroll (AmE) /ɪn'rəʊl/ **A** *vt* (-ll-) قَيَّدَ الاسْمَ ,سَجَّلَ ‹*a student, member*›

B *vi* (-ll-) «participants, students» قَيَّدَ اسْمَهُ, سَجَّلَ نَفْسَهُ

enrolment, **enrollment** (AmE) /ɪnˈrəʊlmənt/ *n* تَسْجِيل (تَسْجِيلات)

en route /ɒn ˈruːt/ *adv* ‹*to stop off, visit sth/sb*› في الطَّرِيق

ensemble /ɒnˈsɒmb(ə)l/ *n* 1 (group of performers) طاقِم (طَواقِم), فِرْقة (فِرَق); (passage) [أداء موسيقيّ مُوَحَّد] 2 (set of clothes) [طَقْم مُتَناسِق]

enshrine /ɪnˈʃraɪn/ *vt* حَفِظَ (a; حِفْظ), صانَ (u; صَوْن, صِيانة) ‹*a principle, right*›

enslave /ɪnˈsleɪv/ *vt* اسْتَعْبَدَ ‹*a captive*›

ensue /ɪnˈsjuː/ *vi* (afterwards) «chaos, events» تَلا (u; تُلُوّ), أَعْقَبَ; (as a result) نَجَمَ, تَرَتَّبَ (u; نُجوم); **in the ensuing fight** في المَعْرَكةِ الّتي تَلَتْ \ أَعْقَبَتْ ذلك

ensuing /ɪnˈsjuːɪŋ/ *adj* ‹*battle, chaos*› لاحِق, آتٍ, تالٍ; **in the ~ fight** في المَعْرَكةِ اللاحِقة

en suite /ɒ̃ ˈswiːt/ *adj* بِحَمّام خاصّ

ensure /ɪnˈʃɔː/ *vt* كَفَلَ (a-u; كَفالة, كُفول, كَفْل), ضَمِنَ (a; ضَمان) ‹*success, cooperation*›

ENT /iːenˈtiː/ *n* = **ear, nose, and throat** الأَنف والأُذُن والحَنْجَرة

entail /ɪnˈteɪl/ *vt* اقْتَضَى, اسْتَوْجَبَ, اسْتَلْزَمَ ‹*travel, expense*›

entangle /ɪnˈtaŋg(ə)l/ *vt* 1 (to cause to become twisted) شَبَّكَ, شَبَكَ (i; شَبْك) ‹*a wire, leg*› 2 (to involve) وَرَّطَ ‹*a colleague, friend*›

enter /ˈɛntə/ **A** *vt* 1 (to go into) دَخَلَ (u; دُخول) ‹*a room, building*› 2 (to penetrate) «bullets, arrows» دَخَلَ (u; دُخول) ‹*one's heart, body*› 3 (to begin) دَخَلَ (u; دُخول) ‹*a phase, period*›; **the country is ~ing a recession** تَدْخُلُ البِلادُ مَرْحَلةَ رُكودٍ اقْتِصاديٍّ 4 (to join) الْتَحَقَ (ب) ‹*a profession, company*›; **to ~ the war** دَخَلَ الحَرْبَ; **to ~ the Church** دَخَلَ الكَنِيسةَ 5 (competitively) دَخَلَ (u; دُخول) ‹*a race, competition*›; **to ~ a competitor/horse for a race** سَجَّلَ مُنافِساً \ حِصاناً في سِباقٍ; **to ~ a poem for the competition** قَدَّمَ قَصِيدةً لِلمُسابَقة 6 (on a form) أَدْخَلَ ‹*a detail, figure, number*›; **to ~ an item in the ledger** سَجَّلَ, أَدْخَلَ, قَيَّدَ شَيْئاً في دَفْتَرِ الحِساباتِ 7 (to key in) أَدْخَلَ ‹*data, details*› 8 **to ~ sb's head** خَطَرَ على بالِ شَخْصٍ

B *vi* 1 (to go in, come in) دَخَلَ (u; دُخول); **to ~ through the window/by the back door** دَخَلَ عَبْرَ النافِذة \ من البابِ الخَلْفيِّ 2 (for a competition) دَخَلَ مُسابَقةً; **to ~ for an exam/a race** تَرَشَّحَ لامْتِحانٍ \ لِسِباقٍ

Phrasal verbs **enter into**: **~ into [sth]** 1 (to become involved in) دَخَلَ في [شَيْءٍ] ‹*negotiations, a debate*› 2 (to commit to) دَخَلَ في [شَيْءٍ] ‹*an agreement, a contract*› 3 (to be part of) **to ~ into one's calculations/plans** كانَ جُزْءاً من حِساباتِهِ \ مُخَطَّطاتِهِ; **that doesn't ~ into it** لَيْسَ لِذلِكَ دَخْلٌ \ عَلاقةٌ بِهِ

• **enter on**: **~ on [sth]** (fml) دَخَلَ [شَيْئاً] ‹*a career, marriage*›

• **enter up**: **~ up [sth]**, **~ [sth] up** دَوَّنَ \ سَجَّلَ [شَيْئاً] ‹*a figure, total*›

• **enter upon** (fml) ▸ **enter on**

enteric /ɛnˈtɛrɪk/ *adj* ‹*virus, disorder*› مِعَوِيّ

enteritis /ˌɛntəˈraɪtɪs/ *n* الْتِهاب مِعَوِيّ

enterprise /ˈɛntəpraɪz/ *n* 1 (project) مَشْروع (مَشْروعات, مَشاريعُ); [u] (initiative) إقْدام, مُبادَرة 2 (company) مُؤَسَّسة, شَرِكة تِجارِيّة, تِجارِيّة; [u] (business activity) نَشاط تِجاريّ

enterprising /ˈɛntəpraɪzɪŋ/ *adj* ‹*plan, businessman*› مُبادِر (يَتَمَيَّز بالإقْدام)

entertain /ɛntəˈteɪn/ **A** *vt* 1 (to keep amused, make laugh) سَلَّى, رَفَّهَ (عن) ‹*an audience, a crowd*› 2 (to play host to) اسْتَضافَ ‹*a guest, visitor*› 3 (to have in the mind) فَكَّرَ (في) ‹*a possibility, a suggestion*›; كانَ عِنْدَهُ \ لَدَيْهِ ‹*doubt, ambition, idea*›

B *vi* (to have guests) «hosts, friends» اسْتَقْبَلَ ضُيوفاً

entertainer /ɛntəˈteɪnə/ *n* فَنّان (مُمَثِّل \ مُغَنٍّ \ مُقَدِّم بَرامِج...إلخ)

entertaining /ɛntəˈteɪnɪŋ/ *adj* ‹*movie, performer*› مُمْتِع, مُسَلٍّ

entertainment /ɛntəˈteɪnmənt/ *n* 1 [u] (amusement) تَسْلِية, تَرْفيه 2 (event) [حَفْل تَرْفيهيّ]

entertainment industry *n* صِناعة التَّرْفِيهِ والتَّسْلِيةِ

enthral, **enthrall** (AmE) /ɪnˈθrɔːl/ *vt* (-ll-) فَتَنَ (i; فَتْن, فُتون), أَسَرَ (i; أَسْر) ‹*an audience, a crowd*›

enthusiasm /ɪnˈθjuːziazəm/ *n* حَماس, تَحَمُّس

enthusiast /ɪnˈθjuːziast/ *n* مُتَحَمِّس

enthusiastic /ɪnˌθjuːzɪˈastɪk/ *adj* ‹*crowd, response*› حَماسيّ, مُفْعَم بالحَماسِ

enthusiastically /ɪnθjuːzɪ'astɪkli/ *adv* *<to greet, sing>* بِتَحَمُّسٍ, بِحَماسٍ

entice /ɪn'tʌɪs/ *vt* أَغْوى ,أَغْرى *<a customer, user>*

entire /ɪn'tʌɪə/ *adj* *<life, world>* كُلّ, كامِل (كَمَلة)

entirely /ɪn'tʌɪəli/ *adv* *<destroy, different>* بالكامِلِ, كُلِّيًّا, تَماماً

entirety /ɪn'tʌɪərəti/ *n* كافّة, كامِل, كُلّ; **in its ~** بِرُمَّتِهِ, بِمُجْمَلِهِ, كُلِّيَّةً

entitle /ɪn'tʌɪt(ə)l/ *vt* 1 **to ~ sb to sth** (to authorize) خَوَّلَ \ فَوَّضَ إلى شَخْصٍ شَيْئاً *<a claimant, citizen>*; **to be ~d to sth** اسْتَحَقَّ شَيْئاً, حَقَّ لَهُ شَيْءٌ 2 (fml) (to call) عَنْوَنَ (i; عَنْوَنة) *<a text, book>*

entitlement /ɪn'tʌɪtəlmənt/ *n* اسْتِحْقاق, حَقّ

entity /'ɛntɪti/ *n* (*pl* **entities**) كِيان (كِيانات), كَيْنونة

entourage /'ɒntʊrɑːʒ/ *n* حاشِية (حَواشٍ), خاصّة (خَواصُّ), (إلى) مُقَرَّبون

entrails /'ɛntreɪlz/ *n pl* أَحْشاء

entrance¹ /'ɛntrəns/ *n* 1 (way in) مَدْخَل (مَداخِلُ) 2 (act of entering) دُخول; (Theat) [دُخول إلى الخَشَبة]; **to make a/one's ~** [دَخَلَ بِطَريقةٍ مُلْفِتةٍ لِلنَظَرِ \ مُثيرةٍ لِلانْتِباه] 3 (admission to an event, a museum) حَقّ الدُخول; (to a university) قَبول

entrance² /ɪn'trɑːns/ *vt* فَتَنَ (i; فُتون, فَتْن) *<audiences, visitors>*

entrance fee *n* (for an event, a museum) رَسْم دُخولٍ

entrance hall *n* 1 (in a house) رَدْهة (رَدَهات) 2 (in a public building) رَدْهة مَدْخَلٍ

entrant /'ɛntrənt/ *n* (in a competition) مُشارِك; (for an exam) داخِل

entreat /ɪn'triːt/ *vt* (liter) تَوَسَّلَ (إلى), تَضَرَّعَ (إلى) *<God, a king>*

entreaty /ɪn'triːti/ *n* (*pl* **entreaties**) (liter) تَوَسُّل (تَوَسُّلات), تَضَرُّع (تَضَرُّعات)

entrench /ɪn'trɛntʃ/ *vt* ثَبَّتَ, رَسَّخَ *<a habit, belief>*; **the group's ~ed attitude to change** مَوْقِف الجَماعةِ الراسِخ \ الثابِت تُجاهَ التَغْيير

entrepreneur /ˌɒntrəprə'nəː/ *n* رَجُل أَعْمالٍ, مُقاوِل

entrepreneurial /ˌɒntrəprə'nəːrɪəl/ *adj* *<initiative, skills>* [في إدارةِ المَشاريعِ \ الأَعْمالِ التِجاريّةِ]

entrust /ɪn'trʌst/ *vt* عَهِدَ (a; عَهْد), كَلَّفَ *<a task>*; ائْتَمَنَ, أَوْدَعَ *<money>*; **to ~ a task to sb** عَهِدَ إلى شَخْصٍ بِمَهَمّةٍ (على); **to ~ sb with the money** ائْتَمَنَ شَخْصاً على المالِ; **to ~ the documents to sb** أَوْدَعَ المِلَفّاتِ عند شَخْصٍ; **I ~ the children to your care** أَضَعُ \ أَتْرُكُ الأَطْفالَ في عُهْدَتِك

entry /'ɛntri/ *n* 1 (act of entering) دُخول; **to gain ~ to a building** سُمِحَ لَهُ بالدُخولِ إلى بِنايةٍ; **'no ~'** 'مَمْنوعُ الدُخولُ' 2 (admission to a bar, museum, park, country) دُخول; (to a club, university) انْضِمام, الْتِحاق 3 (door, gate) مَدْخَل (مَداخِلُ) 4 (item in a reference book) مَدْخَل (مَداخِلُ); (in a register, log) مُلاحَظة; (in a ledger) بَنْد مَصاريفَ; **to write an ~ in one's diary** كَتَبَ مُدَوَّنةً في مُذَكِّراتِهِ 5 (application for competition) طَلَب مُشارَكةٍ في مُسابَقةٍ; (item in competition) [عَمَل مُشارِك \ للدُخولِ في مُسابَقةٍ]

entry form *n* اسْتِمارة طَلَبٍ \ قَبولٍ

entry permit *n* تَصْريح دُخولٍ

entryphone® /'ɛntrɪfəʊn/ *n* (BrE) [هاتِف داخِلِيّ (عند مَدْخَلِ مَبْنًى)]

entwine /ɪn'twʌɪn/ *vt* 1 (to twist together) ضَفَرَ (i; ضَفْر), جَدَلَ (i-u; جَدْل) *<ribbon, stems>* 2 (liter) (to be interrelated) **to be ~d** تَشابَكَ; **their lives were inextricably ~d** تَشابَكَت خُيوطُ حَياتِهِمْ بِشَكْلٍ مُعَقَّدٍ \ وَثيقٍ

E-number /'iːnʌmbə/ *n* [رَقْم يَدُلُّ على إضافاتٍ غِذائيّةٍ]

envelop /ɪn'vɛləp/ *vt* لَفَّ (u; لَفّ) *<a body, city>*

envelope /'ɛnvələʊp, 'ɒnvələʊp/ *n* ظَرْف (ظُروف); **to put the money in an ~** وَضَعَ المالَ في ظَرْفٍ

(Idiom) **to push the envelope** [تَخَطّى الحُدودَ والإمْكاناتِ]

enviable /'ɛnvɪəb(ə)l/ *adj* *<beauty, reputation>* مُثير يُحْسَدُ عَلَيْهِ لِلحَسَدِ

envious /'ɛnvɪəs/ *adj* *<tone, glances>* حَسود (حُسود); **to be ~ of sb/sth** غارَ من شَخْصٍ \ شَيْءٍ

environment /ɪn'vʌɪrənmənt/ *n* 1 (surroundings) مُحيط, بيئة; **a safe ~ in which to bring up children** بيئة آمِنة \ مُحيط آمِن حَيْثُ يُنَشَّأُ الأَطْفالُ 2 (Ecol) **the ~** البيئة

environmental /ɪnvʌɪrən'mɛnt(ə)l/ *adj* بيئِيّ

environmental group *n* مُنَظَّمة بيئيّة

environmental health *n* صِحّة بيئيّة

environmentalist /ɪn,vʌɪrən'mɛntəlɪst/ *n* [مُناصِر لِحِماية البيئة]

environmentally /ɪn,vʌɪrən'mɛnt(ə)li/ *adv* <*sound, damaging*> بيئيًّا; **an ~ friendly product** مُنتَج صَديق للبيئة \ غَيْر ضارّ بيئيًّا

environmental studies *n* (BrE) دِراسات بيئيّة

environment-friendly /ɪnvʌɪərənmənt'frɛndli/ *adj* صَديق للبيئة

environs /ɪn'vʌɪrənz/ *n pl* أرْباض ,نَواحٍ ,ضَواحٍ

envisage /ɪn'vɪzɪdʒ/ *vt* **1** (to foresee) (ب) تَنَبَّأ ,تَوَقَّع <*a possibility, success*>; **he ~d great success for his project** تَوَقَّع نَجاحاً كَبيراً لِمَشروعِه **2** (to visualize) تَخَيَّل ,تَصَوَّر <*a scenario, circumstances*>

envision /ɛn'vɪʒ(ə)n/ *vt* (AmE) (ب) تَنَبَّأ ,تَوَقَّع <*a possibility, success*>

envoy /'ɛnvɔɪ/ *n* موفَد ,مَنْدوب ,مَبْعوث

envy /'ɛnvi/ **A** *n* حَسَد (حُسود); **his win caused considerable ~ among his colleagues** أثار فَوْزُه حَسَداً كَبيراً وَسْطَ زُمَلائِه

B *vt* (**envies, envying, envied**) حَسَد (u; حَسَد) <*a friend, colleague*>; غار (a; غَيْرة (من)) <*sb's success, abilities*>; **it's unfair to ~ him his good fortune** لَيسَ من العَدْلِ أنْ تَحْسُدَهُ على حَظِّهِ الجَيِّد

(Idiom) **to be green with envy** أكَلَ الحَسَدُ قَلْبَهُ

enzyme /'ɛnzʌɪm/ *n* أنْزيم (أنْزيمات)

epic /'ɛpɪk/ **A** *n* (poem) مَلْحَمة شِعْرِيّة; (film) مَلْحَمة سينَمائِيّة; (novel) مَلْحَمة

B *adj* **1** <*journey, battle*> بُطوليّ **2** <*poem, tale*> مَلْحَميّ

epidemic /ɛpɪ'dɛmɪk/ *n* وَباء (أوْبِئة)

epidural /,ɛpɪ'djʊ(ə)rəl/ *n* [تَخْدير فوق الجافِيَة]

epiglottis /,ɛpɪ'glɒtɪs/ *n* لَهاة (لَهَوات ,لَهَيات ,لَهاً ,لُهيّ), لِسان المِزْمار ,غَلْصَمة (غَلاصِمُ)

epigram /'ɛpɪgram/ *n* **1** (saying) حِكْمة (حِكَم), مَثَل (أمْثال) **2** (poem) قَصيدة الإبيجْراما

epilepsy /'ɛpɪlɛpsi/ *n* صَرْع

epileptic /,ɛpɪ'lɛptɪk/ **A** *adj* <*fit*> صَرْعيّ; <*patient*> بالصَرْعِ

B *n* [مُصاب بالصَرْعِ]

epilogue /'ɛpɪlɒg/ *n* خاتِمة (خَواتيمُ ,خَواتِمُ)

epiphany /ɪ'pɪf(ə)ni/ *n* **1** (revelation) لَحْظة وَحْي \ إلْهام **2** (**Epiphany**) (Chr) عيد الغِطاسِ

episode /'ɛpɪsəʊd/ *n* **1** (event) حَدَث (أحْداث), حادِثة (حَوادِثُ); **I'd like to forget the whole ~** أوَدُّ أنْ أنْسى الحادِثةَ بأكْمَلِها **2** (in series) حَلْقة (حَلَقات)

epistle /ɪ'pɪs(ə)l/ *n* **1** (fml hum) رِسالة (رَسائِلُ ,رِسالات), مَكْتوب (مَكاتيبُ) **2** (**the Epistle**) الرِسالة (في الإنْجيل)

epitaph /'ɛpɪtɑːf/ *n* [نَقْش على ضَريحٍ \ قَبْرٍ (تَكْريماً للمَيِّت)]

epitome /ɪ'pɪtəmi/ *n* (fml) رَمْز ,مِثال

epitomize, -ise (BrE) /ɪ'pɪtəmʌɪz/ *vt* جَسَّدَ ,مَثَّل <*an attitude, generosity*>

epoch /'iːpɒk/ *n* عَهْد (عُهود) عَصْر (عُصور ,أعْصُر); **the end of an ~** نِهاية عَهْدٍ \ عَصْرٍ

equal /'iːkwəl/ **A** *adj* **1** (same) <*number, amounts, part*> مُتَساوٍ; **a sum ~ to one month's salary** مَبْلَغ مُساوٍ لِراتِبِ شَهْر; **'~ work for ~ pay'** 'أجْرٌ مُتَساوٍ لِعَمَلٍ مُتَساوٍ'; **divide it into ~ shares** قَسِّمْهُ إلى حِصَصٍ مُتَساوِيةٍ **2** <*rights, opportunities*> مُتَساوٍ; **everyone is ~ before the law** كُلُّ الناسِ مُتَساوونَ أمامَ القانونِ; **they're competing on ~ terms** يَتَنافَسونَ على قَدَمِ المُساواةِ **3** (capable) **to be ~ to the task** كانَ في مُسْتَوى المُهِمّة

B *adv* مُناصَفةً; **to come ~ third** احْتَلَّ المَرْتَبةَ الثالِثةَ مُناصَفةً

C *n* نَظير (نُظَراءُ; f pl نَظائِرُ), مَثيل (أمْثال); **to treat sb as an ~** عامَلَ شَخْصاً كَنَظيرٍ

D *vt* **1** (to add up to) ساوى **2** (to match) عادَلَ <*a record, time*>; **to ~ the world record** عادَلَ الرَقْمَ القِياسيَّ العالَميَّ

(Idiom) **all things being equal** إذا سارَت الأُمورُ على ما يُرامُ

equality /ɪ'kwɒlɪti/ *n* تَكافُؤ ,تَساوٍ ,مُساواة; **we support ~ of opportunity for all** نَحْنُ نُؤَيِّدُ تَكافُؤَ الفُرَصِ للجَميع

equalize, -ise (BrE) /'iːkwəlʌɪz/ **A** *vt* عادَلَ ,ساوى <*opportunities*>; وازَنَ <*prices*>

B *vi* (Sport) [عَدَّلَ (النَتيجة)]

equalizer, -iser (BrE) /'iːkwəlʌɪzə/ *n* (BrE) [هَدَف التَعادُلِ]

equally /'iːkwəli/ *adv* **1** (in equal parts) <*to divide, share*> بالتَساوي ,على السَواءِ; **the inheritance was divided ~**

between the three children تَمَّ تَقْسيمُ الميراثِ بالتَساوي بين الأَوْلادِ الثَلاثةِ **2** (to the same degree) ‹*to treat, apply*› على قَدَمِ المُساواةِ, حَدٍّ سَواءٍ; **they are ~ important/difficult** هُمْ في نَفْسِ الدَرَجةِ من الأَهَمِّيّةِ \ الصُعوبةِ; **we treat all the children ~** نُعامِلُ الأَوْلادَ جَميعاً على قَدَمِ المُساواةِ **3** (at the same time) في الوَقْتِ نَفْسِه, في نَفْسِ الوَقْتِ; **~, you could argue that ...** وَفي نَفْسِ الوَقْتِ، يُمْكِنُكَ القَوْلُ إنّ ...

equate /ɪˈkweɪt/ *vt* **to ~ wealth with happiness** ساوى الغِنى بالسَعادةِ; **how can you ~ these two things?** كيف يُمْكِنُكَ أنْ تُساوِيَ بين هَذَيْنِ الشَيْئَيْنِ؟

equation /ɪˈkweɪʒ(ə)n/ *n* مُعادَلة

equator /ɪˈkweɪtə/ *n* خطّ الاسْتِواءِ

equilibrium /ˌiːkwɪˈlɪbrɪəm/ *n* توازُن

equinox /ˈiːkwɪnɒks, ˈɛkwɪnɒks/ *n* اعْتِدال

equip /ɪˈkwɪp/ *vt* **(-pp-)** **1** (to supply) زَوَّدَ, جَهَّزَ ‹*an army, a kitchen*›; **to ~ the office with the latest technology** جَهَّزَ المَكْتَبَ بِأَحْدَثِ التِكْنولوجِيا; **a well/fully ~ped kitchen** مَطْبَخ مُجَهَّز بشكْلٍ جيِّدٍ \ بالكامِلِ **2** (to provide skills) أَعَدَّ, هَيَّأَ ‹*a teacher, student*›; **to ~ trainees for their future career** أَعَدَّ \ هَيَّأَ المُتَمَرِّنينَ لِمُسْتَقْبَلِهِم المِهْنيِّ

equipment /ɪˈkwɪpmənt/ *n* مُعَدّات, تَجْهيزات; **electrical/photographic ~** مُعَدّات كَهْرَبائيّة \ تَصْويريّة; **a piece/an item of ~** جُزْء \ قِطْعة من المُعَدّاتِ

equitable /ˈɛkwɪtəb(ə)l/ *adj* ‹*share, solution*› مُنْصِف, عادِل

equity /ˈɛkwɪti/ **A** *n* **1** (fairness) إنْصاف, عَدْل **2** (investment) حِصّة (حِصَص)

B **(equities)** *n pl* حُقوق المُساهِمينَ

equivalent /ɪˈkwɪvələnt/ **A** *adj* ‹*qualification, rank*› مُتَكافِئ; ‹*amount, dose*› مُتَساوٍ; ‹*meaning*› مُرادِف

B *n* نَظير (نُظَراءُ; f pl نَظائِرُ); **Kabutocho, Japan's ~ of Wall Street** (بورْصة) كابوتوشو، نَظيرة وول سْتْريت في اليابان

ER /iːˈɑː/ *abbr* = **emergency room** غُرْفة طَوارِئَ

era /ˈɪərə/ *n* عَهْد (عُهود), عَصْر (أَعْصُر, عُصور); **the rock and roll ~** عَصْر الروك آنْد رول

eradicate /ɪˈradɪkeɪt/ *vt* قَضى (i; قَضاء; على), اسْتَأْصَلَ ‹*poverty, disease*›

erase /ɪˈreɪz/ *vt* مَحا (u; مَحْو) ‹*writing, a memory*›; **he tried to ~ the memory of that difficult time** حاوَلَ مَحْوَ ذِكْرى ذلك الوَقْتِ العَصيبِ

eraser /ɪˈreɪzə/ *n* مِمْحاة (مَماحٍ)

e-reader /ˈiːriːdə/ *n* قارِئ إلِكْتْرونيّ

erect /ɪˈrɛkt/ **A** *adj* ‹*posture, ears, penis*› مُنْتَصِب; **with head ~** بِرَأْسٍ مُنْتَصِبٍ

B *vt* بَنى (i; بِناء, بُنْيان), شَيَّدَ ‹*a building, dwelling*›; نَصَبَ (u; نَصْب) ‹*scaffolding, a tent*›; أَقامَ ‹*a barricade, a monument*›

erectile /ɪˈrɛktʌɪl/ *adj* ‹*tissue, dysfunction*› الانْتِصابِ

erection /ɪˈrɛkʃ(ə)n/ *n* **1** (of penis) انْتِصاب (انْتِصابات) **2** (fml) [u] (of a building, fence, etc) إقامة, تَشْييد; (a building) مَبْنًى (مَبانٍ); **the ~ of the new bridge/hospital** تَشْييد الجِسْرِ \ المُسْتَشْفى الجَديدِ

Eritrea /ˌɛrɪˈtreɪə/ *pr n* إريتْريا

ermine /ˈəːmɪn/ *n* (animal) قاقُم; [u] (fur) فَرْو القاقُمِ

erode /ɪˈrəʊd/ *vt* **1** «water, wind» حَتَّ (u; حَتّ), آكَلَ (Form IV; imperf يُؤْكِلُ) ‹*the shore, rock, soil*› **2** نَقَصَ ‹*confidence, rights*›

erosion /ɪˈrəʊʒ(ə)n/ *n* **1** (by water, wind, sea) تَآكُل, تَأَكُّل, تَحاتّ **2** (of rights, support) تَدَهْوُر, تَلاشٍ

erotic /ɪˈrɒtɪk/ *adj* ‹*fiction, pleasure*› إيروتيكيّ, إباحيّ, جِنْسيّ

err /əː/ *vi* (fml) «judges, experts» أَخْطأَ

Idiom **to err on the side of caution** لَزِمَ جانِبَ الحَذَرِ

errand /ˈɛrənd/ *n* [مُهِمّة]; **to run an ~ for sb** قامَ بِمُهِمّةٍ لِشَخْصٍ

erratic /ɪˈratɪk/ *adj* ‹*behaviour, driver*› مُتَقَلِّب, غَيْر مُسْتَقِرٍّ; **her behaviour is ~ to say the least** أَقَلُّ ما نَسْتَطيعُ قَوْلَهُ هو أنّ سُلوكَها غَيْرُ مُسْتَقِرٍّ

erroneous /ɪˈrəʊnɪəs/ *adj* ‹*statement, conclusion*› خاطِئ

error /ˈɛrə/ *n* خَطَأ (أَخْطاء), غَلَط (أَغْلاط); **to make an ~** قامَ بِخَطَأٍ

Idiom **to see the error of one's ways** أَدْرَكَ خَطَأَهُ

erstwhile /ˈəːstwʌɪl/ (liter) *adj* (liter) ‹*assistant, friend*› سابِق (سُبّاق, سابِقونَ)

erudite /ˈɛrʊdʌɪt/ *adj* (fml) ‹*scholar*› مُتَبَحِّر, واسِع المَعْرِفةِ; ‹*discussion*› [عِلْميّ دالّ على سِعةِ الاطِّلاعِ

erupt /ɪ'rʌpt/ *vi* **1** «volcanoes» ثار (u; ثَوْرة, ثَوَران), اِنْفَجَرَ; «lava» خَرَجَ (u; خُروج) **2** «fighting, scandals» اِنْدَلَعَ

eruption /ɪ'rʌpʃ(ə)n/ *n* **1** (of a volcano) ثَوَران; **a volcanic ~** ثَوَران \ اِنفِجار بُرْكانيّ **2** (of violence, anger, etc) تَفَجُّر, اِنْدِلاع

escalate /'ɛskəleɪt/ **A** *vi* **1** «conflicts, tensions» تَصاعَدَ **2** «prices, unemployment» تَزايَدَ

B *vt* صَعَّدَ ‹*a war, dispute*›

escalation /ɛskə'leɪʃ(ə)n/ *n* **1** (rapid increase) تَصاعُد; **cost ~s** تَصاعُد \ اِرْتِفاع التَكاليفِ **2** (intensification) تَصْعيد, اِسْتِفْحال; **an ~ of violence** اِسْتِفْحال عُنْفٍ

escalator /'ɛskəleɪtə/ *n* سُلَّم مُتَحَرِّك

escapade /'ɛskəpeɪd, ˌɛskə'peɪd/ *n* مُغامَرة, فِعْل طائِش

escape /ɪ'skeɪp/ **A** *vt* **1** هَرَبَ (u; هُروب; من), فَرَّ (i; فَرّ, فِرار, مَفَرّ; من) ‹*capture, the police*›; **he was lucky to ~ jail** كانَ مَحْظوظاً أنْ يَهْرُبَ من السِجْنِ **2** تَجَنَّبَ ‹*sb's notice, detection*›; **it hasn't ~d my attention that you arrived late** لم يَغِبْ عَنّي حُضورُكَ المُتَأَخِّرُ

B *vi* **1** (to get away) «prisoners, thieves» هَرَبَ (u; هُروب), فَرَّ (i; فَرّ, فِرار, مَفَرّ); **he ~d from prison twice** هَرَبَ من السِجْنِ مَرَّتَيْنِ **2** «liquid, air» تَسَرَّبَ; **air is escaping from the tyre** يَتَسَرَّبُ الهَواءُ من العَجَلةِ

C *n* **1** (from prison, captivity) هُروب, فِرار **2** (from danger) نَجاة; **to have a narrow/lucky ~** نَجا بالكادِ **3** (of gas, air) تَسَرُّب (تَسَرُّبات) **4** (computer key) مِفْتاح الهُروب; **press ~ to get back to the menu** اِضْغَطْ على مِفْتاحِ الهُروبِ للعَوْدةِ إلى القائِمةِ

escape clause *n* شَرْط التَخَلُّصِ

escape key *n* مِفْتاح الهُروبِ

escape route *n* طَريق الفِرارِ \ الهُروبِ

escapism /ɪ'skeɪpɪz(ə)m/ *n* الهُروب من الواقِعِ

escapist /ɪ'skeɪpɪst/ *adj* ‹*literature, entertainment*› [مُساعِد على الهُروبِ من الواقِعِ]

eschew /ɪs'tʃuː/ *vt* (fml) تَحاشَى, تَجَنَّبَ ‹*discussion, temptation, violence*›

escort **A** /'ɛskɔːt/ *n* **1** (for security) مُواكَبة **2** (companion) مُرافِق **3** (prostitute) بائِعة هَوًى

B /ɪ'skɔːt/ *vt* **1** (for security) واكَبَ, رافَقَ ‹*a convoy, journalist*› **2** (to lead) أَدَّى, قادَ ‹*a prisoner, group*› **3** (to a function) رافَقَ

escrow /'ɛskrəʊ/ *n* سَنَد مُعَلَّق التَسْليمِ

Eskimo /'ɛskɪməʊ/ *n* (*pl* **Eskimos**) **1** (native) إِسْكيمو **2** (language) لُغة الإِسْكيمو

ESL /iːɛs'ɛl/ *n* = **English as a Second Language** الإِنْجْليزيّة كَلُغةٍ ثانيةٍ

ESOL /'iːsɒl/ *n* = **English for Speakers of Other Languages** اللُغة الإِنْجْليزيّة للناطِقينَ بِغَيْرِها

esophagus (AmE) *n* ▸ **oesophagus**

esoteric /ˌiːsə'tɛrɪk, ˌɛsə'tɛrɪk/ *adj* ‹*knowledge*› باطِنيّ; ‹*language*› [مَقْصور على فِئةٍ مُعَيَّنةٍ]

especially /ɪ'spɛʃ(ə)li/ *adv* **1** (above all) ‹*to like, focus*› بِصورةٍ \ بِشَكْلٍ خاصٍّ; **I like him ~** أُحِبُّهُ بِشَكْلٍ خاصٍّ **2** (on purpose) ‹*to design, write*› خِصّيصاً, خُصوصاً; **I made it ~ for you** صَنَعْتُهُ خِصّيصاً لَكَ **3** (particularly) ‹*important, true*› خاصّةً, مَخْصوصاً, بالخُصوصِ; **the website will be ~ useful as a teaching tool** سَيَكونُ المَوْقِعُ مُفيداً خاصّةً كَأَداةِ تَعْليمٍ

Esperanto /ˌɛspə'rantəʊ/ *n* الإِسْبِرانْتو

espionage /'ɛspɪənɑːʒ/ *n* تَجَسُّس

espouse /ɪ'spaʊz/ *vt* (fml) (to embrace) اِعْتَنَقَ ‹*a belief*›; (to support) أَيَّدَ, ناصَرَ ‹*a cause*›

espresso /ɛ'sprɛsəʊ/ *n* (*pl* **espressos**) إِسْبْريسو

essay /'ɛseɪ/ *n* **1** (academic) مَوْضوع إِنْشائيّ; **an ~ on/about energy conservation** مَوْضوع إِنْشائيّ حول المُحافَظةِ على الطاقةِ **2** (literary) مَقال

essence /'ɛs(ə)ns/ *n* **1** (important quality) جَوْهَر (جَواهِرُ), لُبّ (لُبوب), ماهيّة; **the ~ of the problem is that he cannot be trusted** جَوْهَرُ المُشْكِلةِ هو أَنَّهُ غَيْرُ مَوْثوقٍ فيهِ **2** (extract) روح (mf; أَرْواح), خُلاصة; **vanilla ~** روح الفانيلْيا

essential /ɪ'sɛnʃ(ə)l/ **A** *adj* (necessary) ‹*supplies, service*› أَساسيّ, ضَروريّ, لا يَسْتَغْنى عَنْهُ; (intrinsic) ‹*difference, characteristic*› جَوْهَريّ; **it is ~ that we agree** مِن الضَروريِّ أنْ نَتَّفِقَ; **the ~ difference between them is in their attitude** الفَرْقُ الجَوْهَريُّ بَيْنَهُما يَكْمُنُ في سُلوكِهِما

B *n* **1** (vital component) شَيْء أَساسيّ, ضَرورة; **a car is not an ~** السَّيّارةُ لَيْسَتْ بِضَرورةٍ **2** (important element) عُنْصُر أَساسيّ; **the ~s of English grammar** أَساسيّات قَواعِدِ اللغةِ الإنْجليزيّةِ

essentially /ɪˈsenʃ(ə)li/ *adv* (basically) أَساسيًّا; (intrinsically) ‹*unchanged, correct*› في الأَساسِ, أَصْلاً; **that, ~, is the difference between them** هٰذا هو أَساسيًّا الفَرْقُ بَيْنَهُما; **their accounts are ~ identical** أَقْوالُهُما مُتَطابِقةٌ في الأَساسِ

essential oil *n* زَيْت عِطْريّ

EST /iːesˈtiː/ *abbr* (AmE) = **Eastern Standard Time** التَوْقيت الشَرْقيّ

establish /ɪˈstablɪʃ/ *vt* **1** (to set up) شَيَّد, أَنْشَأ, أَسَّس ‹*a company, committee*›; أَقامَ ‹*a relationship, rule*›; **the company has ~ed a reputation for quality** اكْتَسَبَت الشركةُ سُمْعةً جَيِّدةً لِجَوْدَتِها **2** (to prove) أَثْبَتَ ‹*a motive, sb's innocence*›; **they have ~ed that the horse was drugged** أَثْبَتوا أنّ الحِصانَ كانَ مُخَدَّراً **3** (to succeed) أَثْبَتَ ‹*yourself, himself*›; **the company quickly ~ed itself as a market leader** أَثْبَتَت الشَرِكةُ مَكانَتَها بِسُرعةٍ كَرائِدٍ في السوقِ

established /ɪˈstablɪʃt/ *adj* **1** ‹*institution*› قائِم, ثابِت, راسِخ; ‹*artist*› مُعْتَرَف بِهِ **2** ‹*church, religion*› رَسْميّ

establishment /ɪˈstablɪʃmənt/ *n* **1** (fml) (a shop, business) مُؤَسَّسة; **an educational/a commercial ~** مُؤَسَّسة تَعْليميّة \ تِجاريّة **2** (**the Establishment**) الطَبَقة الحاكِمة; **the military ~** الكَوادِر العَسْكَريّة **3** [u] (of links, bonds) تَأْسيس, إقامة; **the ~ of diplomatic relations** إقامة العَلاقاتِ الدبْلوماسيّة

estate /ɪˈsteɪt/ *n* **1** (land) ضَيْعة (ضِياع), عِزْبة **2** (BrE) (residential) مِنْطَقة عَقاريّة \ سَكَنيّة; (industrial) مِنْطَقة صِناعيّة **3** (assets) تَرِكة **4** (also **estate car**) (BrE) سَيّارة صالون عائِليّة, سَيّارة سْتيشَن واجَن

estate agency *n* (BrE) وِكالة عَقاريّة

estate agent *n* (BrE) سِمْسار, وَكيل عَقاريّ (سَماسِرة)

esteem /ɪˈstiːm/ *n* (fml) احْتِرام, تَقْدير (تَقاديرُ, تَقْديرات) (احْتِرامات); **I hold him in high ~** أُقَدِّرُهُ تَقْديراً كَبيراً

esthetic (AmE) *adj* ▸ **aesthetic**

estimate **A** /ˈestɪmeɪt/ *vt* قَدَّرَ, قَيَّمَ ‹*the cost, number*›
B /ˈestɪmət/ *n* **1** (calculation) تَخْمين (تَقْييمات), تَقْييم (تَثْمينات) تَثْمين, (تَقْديرات) تَقْدير **2** (of costs) (تَخْمينات)

estimation /estɪˈmeɪʃ(ə)n/ *n* **1** (esteem) احْتِرام (احْتِرامات), اعْتِبار (اعْتِبارات); **to go up/down in sb's ~** زادَ \ نَقَصَ في احْتِرامِ شَخْصٍ لَهُ **2** (judgement, opinion) اعْتِبار (اعْتِبارات), تَقْدير (تَقْديرات)

Estonia /ɪˈstəʊnɪə/ *pr n* إسْتونيا

Estonian /ɪˈstəʊnɪən/ **A** *adj* ‹*ambassador, food, lesson*› إسْتونيّ
B *n* **1** (citizen) إسْتونيّ **2** (language) (اللُغة) الإسْتونيّة

estrange /ɪˈstreɪndʒ/ **A** *vt* نَفَّرَ; **to be ~d from sb** كانَ مُنْفَصِلاً عن شَخْصٍ
B (**estranged**) *adj* **his ~d wife** زَوْجَتُهُ المُنْفَصِلة عَنْهُ

estrogen (AmE) *n* ▸ **oestrogen**

estuary /ˈestjʊəri/ *n* (*pl* **estuaries**) مَصَبّ نَهْرٍ

ETA /iːtiːˈeɪ/ *n* = **estimated time of arrival** مَوْعِد الوُصولِ المُتَوَقَّع

etc. /et ˈset(ə)rə/ *abbr* (Latin) = **et cetera: and others** إلخ, إلى آخِرِهِ

et cetera, **etcetera** /etˈ set(ə)rə/ *adv* إلى آخِرِهِ, وَهَلُمَّ جَرًّا

etch /etʃ/ *vt* (to engrave) حَفَرَ (i; حَفْر), نَقَشَ (u; نَقْش) ‹*initials, a name*›

etching /ˈetʃɪŋ/ *n* (picture) صورة مَطْبوعة من لَوْحٍ مَعْدِنيٍّ [مَحْفور]; [u] (technique) الحَفْر, فَنّ الحَفْرِ على المَعْدِنِ, تَنْميش, الحَمْضيّ

ETD /iːtiːˈdiː/ *n* = **estimated time of departure** مَوْعِد المُغادَرة المُتَوَقَّع

eternal /ɪˈtəːn(ə)l/ *adj* ‹*life*› أَبَديّ; ‹*optimist*› دائِم; ‹*arguments*› دون تَوَقُّفٍ, لا نِهائيّ

eternity /ɪˈtəːnɪti/ *n* (*pl* **eternities**) **1** [u] (unlimited time) أَبَد (أُبود, آباد), خُلود, أَبَديّة **2** (infml) (a long time) أَبَد (أُبود, آباد)

ethanol /ˈeθənɒl/ *n* إيثانول

ethereal /ɪˈθɪərɪəl/ *adj* (liter) ‹*voice, beauty*› سَماويّ, أَثيريّ

ethic /ˈeθɪk/ **1** *n sing* (principle) أَخْلاق **2** (**ethics** *n pl*) (moral principles) آداب, أَخْلاق; (philosophy) عِلْم الأَخْلاقِ

ethical /ˈɛθɪk(ə)l/ *adj* **1** ‹*issue, dilemma, code*› أَخْلاقيّ **2** ‹*investment, product*› أَخْلاقيّ

Ethiopia /ˌiːθɪˈəʊpɪə/ *pr n* أَثْيوبِيا

Ethiopian /iːθɪˈəʊpɪən/ **A** *n* **1** (citizen) أَثْيوبيّ **2** (language) (اللُغة) الأَثْيوبيّة **B** *adj* ‹*custom, culture*› أَثْيوبيّ

ethnic /ˈɛθnɪk/ *adj* ‹*group, conflict*› عِرْقيّ, إِثْنيّ; **leaders of ~ communities** زُعَماء مَجْموعاتٍ إِثْنيّةٍ

ethnic cleansing *n* التَطْهير العِرْقيّ

ethnicity /ɛθˈnɪsɪti/ *n* (*pl* **ethnicities**) انْتِماء عِرْقيّ, إِثْنيّة

ethnic minority *n* أَقَلّيّة عِرْقيّة

ethos /ˈiːθɒs/ *n* أَخْلاقيّات

e-ticket /ˈiːtɪkɪt/ *n* تَذْكَرة إِلِكْترونيّة

etiquette /ˈɛtɪkɛt, ˈɛtɪkət/ *n* إِتيكيت, آداب السُلوك

etymology /ˌɛtɪˈmɒlədʒi/ *n* (*pl* **etymologies**) **1** [u] (study of the origins of words) عِلْم الاشْتِقاقِ **2** (origin of a word) تَأْثيل, اشْتِقاق

EU /iːˈjuː/ *abbr* = **European Union** الاتِّحاد الأوروبّيّ

eucalyptus /juːkəˈlɪptəs/ *n* (*pl* **eucalyptuses**) أوكالِبْتوس

Eucharist /ˈjuːkərɪst/ *n* (**the Eucharist**) (ceremony) قُدّاس; (bread and wine) القُرْبان المُقَدَّس

eulogy /ˈjuːlədʒi/ *n* (*pl* **eulogies**) (liter) (praise) مَديح (مَدائِحُ); (after sb's death) تَأْبين

eunuch /ˈjuːnək/ *n* **1** (castrated man) خِصْيان) خَصيّ, مَخْصيّ, **2** (weak person) مَخْصيّ (خِصْية)

euphemism /ˈjuːfəmɪz(ə)m/ *n* تَعْبير مُلَطِّف \ كِنائيّ

euphemistic /juːfɪˈmɪstɪk/ *adj* ‹*term, phrase*› كِنائيّ, مُلَطِّف

euphoria /juːˈfɔːrɪə/ *n* غِبْطة, نَشْوة

euphoric /juːˈfɒrɪk/ *adj* ‹*celebration, crowd*› نَشْوان, مُنْتَشٍ (نَشْوى f ;نَشاوى)

Euphrates /juːˈfreɪtiːz/ *pr n* (**the Euphrates**) الفُرات

euro /ˈjʊərəʊ/ *n* (*pl* **euros** or **euro**) يورو (ME), أورو (NA); **a fifty-~ note** وَرَقة نَقْديّة من فِئةِ خَمْسين يورو

Euro- /jʊərəʊ/ *prefix* أوروبّيّ; **~ elections** انْتِخابات أوروبّيّة

Eurocrat /ˈjʊərəʊkrat/ *n* بيروقْراطيّ في الاتِّحادِ الأوروبّيِّ]

Euro-MP /ˈjʊərəʊempiː/ *n* نائِب في البَرْلَمانِ الأوروبّيِّ

Europe /ˈjʊərəp/ *pr n* **1** (continent) أوروبّا **2** (the EU) الاتِّحاد الأوروبّيّ

European /jʊərəˈpiːən/ *n, adj* أوروبّيّ

European Commission *pr n* المُفَوَّضيّة الأوروبّيّة

European Economic Area *pr n* المِنْطَقة الاقْتِصاديّة الأوروبّيّة

European Parliament *n* البَرْلَمان الأوروبّيّ

European Union *n* الاتِّحاد الأوروبّيّ

Eurosceptic /ˈjɔːrəʊˌskeptɪk/ *n* (BrE) [مُعارِض للاتِّحادِ الأوروبّيِّ

eurozone /ˈjʊərəʊzəʊn/ *n* مِنْطَقة اليورو

euthanasia /juːθəˈneɪzɪə/ *n* قَتْل رَحيم

evacuate /ɪˈvakjʊeɪt/ *vt* **1** رَحَّلَ, أَجْلى ‹*civilians, children*› **2** أَخْلى ‹*a building, an area*›

evacuation /ɪˌvakjʊˈeɪʃ(ə)n/ *n* (of inhabitants) تَرْحيل, إِجْلاء (تَراحيلُ); (of a town) إِخْلاء

evacuee /ɪˌvakjuːˈiː/ *n* مُرَحَّل

evade /ɪˈveɪd/ *vt* **1** (من) تَهَرَّبَ ,(من) فَلَتَ, تَفادى (i; فَلْت) ‹*one's pursuer*›; (من) تَمَلَّصَ ‹*one's responsibility*›; **to ~ capture/ detection** تَفادى القَبْضَ عَلَيْهِ \ الاكْتِشافَ **2** تَجَنَّبَ ‹*a question, an issue*› **3** (من) تَهَرَّبَ ‹*tax*›

evaluate /ɪˈvaljʊeɪt/ *vt* قَيَّمَ ‹*sth's effectiveness, a patient*›; (AmE) قَدَّرَ ‹*property, sth's worth*›; **pupils will be ~d by their teachers** سَيُقَيِّمُ المُدَرِّسون تَلاميذَهُم

evaluation /ɪˌvaljʊˈeɪʃ(ə)n/ *n* تَقْييم (تَقْييمات), تَقْدير (تَقْديرات, تَقاديرُ)

evangelical /iːvanˈdʒɛlɪk(ə)l/ *adj* **1** ‹*Protestant, missionary*› إِنْجيليّ **2** ‹*zeal*› [كَبير]

evangelize, -ise (BrE) /ɪˈvandʒəlʌɪz/ **A** *vt* نَصَّرَ ‹*the continent, community*› **B** *vi* «missionaries» بَشَّرَ بالإِنْجيلِ

evaporate /ɪˈvapəreɪt/ *vi* **1** (to change to vapour) «water, sweat» تَبَخَّرَ; **the water soon ~d in the sunshine** سُرْعان ما تَبَخَّرَ الماءُ في الشَمْسِ **2** (to disappear) «confidence, support» زالَ (a; زَوال), تَلاشى; **all hope of saving his life has ~d** تَلاشَتْ كُلُّ الآمالِ لإِنْقاذِ حَياتِهِ

evaporated milk /ɪˌvapəreɪtɪd ˈmɪlk/ *n* حليب مُكَثَّف

evaporation /ɪvapəˈreɪʃ(ə)n/ *n* تَبَخُّر

evasion /ɪˈveɪʒ(ə)n/ *n* **1** (avoiding doing sth) تَمَلُّص, تَهَرُّب, تَجَنُّب; **the ~ of your responsibilities** التَمَلُّص من مَسْؤولِيّاتِك **2** (avoiding talking) [كَلام \ رَدّ مَرْماهُ التَمَلُّص من مَوْضوع]

evasive /ɪˈveɪsɪv/ *adj* ‹answer, behaviour› غامِض (غَوامِض), مُراوِغ, مُتَجَنِّب; **he was ~ about his phone number** كانَ غامِضًا بِشأْنِ رَقْمِ هاتِفِه

(Idiom) **to take evasive action** قامَ بِحَرَكَةٍ مُراوِغَةٍ

eve /iːv/ *n* عَشِيَّة (عَشايا, عَشِيّات); **on the ~ of the election** عَشِيَّةَ الانْتِخاباتِ

even¹ /ˈiːv(ə)n/ **A** *adv* **1** (for emphasis) حَتّى; **don't tell anyone, not ~ Bob** لا تُخْبِرْ أَيَّ أَحَدٍ, وَلا حتّى بوب; **~ when he knew, he didn't do anything** حتّى عِنْدما عَلِم, لم يَفْعَلْ أيَّ شَيْءٍ; **I can't ~ swim, never mind dive** لا يُمْكِنُني حتّى أنْ أَعوم, فما بالُك بالغَوصِ; **~ if I could, I wouldn't go** حتّى لو اسْتَطَعْتُ, فلَنْ أَذْهَب **2** (with comparatives) [أَكْثَر]; **it's ~ colder today** الجَوُّ اليومَ أَبْرَدُ; **~ more carefully** أَكْثَر \ بِحِرْصٍ أَكْبَر **3** (showing surprise) حَتّى; **he didn't ~ try** هو حتّى لم يُحاوِل; **he left without ~ apologizing** غادَرَ بِدونِ حتّى أنْ يَعْتَذِرَ **4** (simultaneously) **they are working on it, ~ as we speak** هُمْ يَعْمَلونَ عَلَيْه, في نَفْسِ اللَحْظَةِ الّتي نَتَكَلَّمُ فيها

B (**even so**) *adv phr* مع ذلِكَ, بالرَغْمِ من ذلك; **it was interesting ~ so, ~ so it was interesting** كانَ مُثيراً للاهْتِمامِ بالرَغْمِ من ذلك

C (**even then**) *adv phr* (at that time) وَقْتَها

D (**even though**) *conj phr* بالرَغْمِ من أنّ; **~ though he was a doctor, he failed to spot the problem** بالرَغْمِ من أنّهُ كانَ طَبيباً, إلاّ أنَّهُ فَشِلَ في اكْتِشافِ المُشْكِلةِ

even² /ˈiːv(ə)n/ *adj* **1** (level) ‹ground, surface› مُسْتَوٍ **2** (uniform) ‹temperature, speed› مُنْتَظِم **3** (calm) ‹voice, tone› هادِئ **4** (equal) ‹contest› مُتَعادِل **5** (owing nothing) **now we're ~** أَصْبَحْنا الآنَ مُتَعادِلَيْن; **to get ~ with sb** انْتَقَمَ من شَخْصٍ **6** (fair) ‹distribution› مُتَكافِئ, مُتَساوٍ **7** (not odd) ‹number› زَوْجِيّ

(Phrasal verbs) **even out** **1** «differences, imbalance» تَساوى **2** **~ [sth] out, ~ out [sth]** قَضى على [شَيْءٍ] ‹an inequality›; عَدَلَ في تَوْزيعِ [شَيْءٍ], وَزَّعَ [شَيْئاً] بِشَكْلٍ مُتَساوٍ ‹a burden›

• **even up**: **~ [sth] up, ~ up [sth]** **1** سَوّى [شَيْئاً] ‹ground, a surface› **2** عَدَّلَ [شَيْئاً] ‹a contest, situation›

evening /ˈiːv(ə)nɪŋ/ **A** *n* **1** (part of the day) مَساء (مَساءات, أَمْساء); **in the ~** في المَساءِ; **on Friday ~** يَوْمَ الجُمْعةِ مَساءً; **on Friday ~s** في مَساءاتِ الجُمْعةِ; **every ~** كُلَّ مَساءٍ; **I'll be in all ~** سَأَكونُ في البَيْتِ طوالَ المَساءِ; **tomorrow/yesterday ~** غَداً \ أَمْسِ مَساءً; **I'll see you this ~** أَراكَ هذا المَساءَ **2** (event) **a musical/theatrical ~** أُمْسِيّة موسيقيّة \ مَسْرَحيّة

B *excl* (**good evening** also (infml) **evening**) مَساءَ الخَيْر; **good ~, sir. Can I help you?** مَساءَ الخَيْرِ يا سَيِّدي. هل أَسْتَطيعُ مُساعَدَتَك؟; **~, John!** مَساءَ الخَيْرِ يا جون!

evening bag *n* حَقيبة سَهْرة

evening class *n* دَرْس مَسائيّ

evening dress *n* **1** (for a woman) ثَوْب سَهْرة **2** (dress code) لِباس سَهْرة

evening meal *n* وَجْبة العَشاءِ

evening paper *n* جَريدة مَسائيّة

evenly /ˈiːvnli/ *adv* **1** (equally) ‹to spread, divide› بالتَساوي **2** (placidly) ‹to say, breathe› بِهُدوءٍ

event /ɪˈvɛnt/ *n* **1** (a happening) حَدَث (أَحْداث), حادِث (حَوادِث), حادِثة (حادِثات, حَوادِث); **a social ~** حَفْلة (حَفَلات); **the show was a success despite recent ~s** كانَ العَرْضُ ناجِحاً بالرَغْمِ من الأَحْداثِ الأَخيرةِ **2** (in sport) مُنافَسة; **a sporting ~** مُنافَسة رِياضيّة; **a track ~** مُنافَسة سِباقٍ **3** [u] (a situation) حال (mf), حالة; **call this number in the ~ of a fire/an accident** اتَّصِلْ بِهَذا الرَقْمِ في حالةِ حَريقٍ \ حادِثٍ; **in the ~ of my death** في حالِ مَوْتي

(Idioms) **after the event** بعدَ حُدوثِ الشَيْءِ; **it's easy to be wise after the ~** من السَهْلِ أنْ تَكونَ حَكيماً بعدَ حُدوثِ الشَيْءِ; **in any event/at all events** مَهْما كانَ, على أَيّةِ حالٍ

eventful /ɪˈvɛntfʊl/ *adj* ‹day, career› زاخِر بالأَحْداثِ; **he has had an ~ life** كانَتْ حَياتُهُ زاخِرةً بالأَحْداثِ

eventing /ɪˈvɛntɪŋ/ *n* (BrE) مُباراة فُروسيّة

eventual /ɪ'vɛntʃʊəl/ *adj* ‹*aim, result*› نهائيّ, في النِهايةِ

eventuality /ɪˌvɛntʃʊ'ælɪti/ *n* (*pl* **eventualities**) اِحْتِمال (اِحْتِمالات)

eventually /ɪ'vɛntʃuːəli/ *adv* ‹*become, win*› في آخِرِ الأَمْرِ, في نِهايةِ المَطافِ, مع الوَقْتِ

ever /'ɛvə/ *adv* 1 (absolutely) على الإطْلاقِ; **it's the best film I've ~ seen** إنَّهُ أَفْضَلُ فيلْم رَأَيْتُهُ على الإطْلاقِ; (with negation) أَبَداً, قَطُّ; **nobody will ~ forget her** لن يَنْساها أَحَدٌ أَبَداً; **hardly ~** نادِراً; (in one's life) على الإطْلاقِ; **have you ~ lived abroad?** هل عِشْتَ في الخارِجِ من قَبْلُ؟ 2 (with comparatives, superlatives) [في أيِّ وَقْتٍ]; **he's working harder than ~** يَعْمَلُ بِجُهْدٍ أَكْثَر من أيِّ وَقْتٍ مَضى; **it was the team's worst ~ defeat** كانَتْ أَسْوَأَ هَزيمةٍ في تاريخِ النادي 3 (always) دائِماً, في كُلِّ وَقْتٍ; **she's as cheerful as ~** هي مُبْتَهِجةٌ كَما هي دائِماً; **the danger is ~ present** الخَطَرُ مُتَواجِدٌ في كُلِّ وَقْتٍ; **they lived happily ~ after** عاشا عيشةً سَعيدةً إلى الأَبَدِ 4 (as intensifier) **when will you ~ learn?** متى سَتَتَعَلَّمُ؟; **don't you ~ do that again!** لا تَفْعَلْ ذلك مَرَّةً أُخْرى أَبَداً!; **thanks ~ so much** (BrE infml) شُكْراً جَزيلاً 5 **(ever since) ~ since we arrived** منذ أَنْ وَصَلْنا; **we've been friends ~ since** أَصْبَحْنا أَصْدِقاءَ منذ ذلك الحينِ

evergreen /'ɛvəgriːn/ *n* شَجَرة دائِمة الخُضْرةِ

everlasting /ɛvə'lɑːstɪŋ/ *adj* ‹*life, happiness*› دائِم, خالِد, أَبَديّ

every /'ɛvri/ **A** *determiner* 1 (each) **~ house in the street** كُلّ بَيْتٍ في الشارِعِ; **~ time I go there** كُلّ مَرّةٍ أَذْهَبُ هُناكَ; **from ~ side** من كُلِّ جانِبٍ; **I've read ~ one of her books** قَرَأْتُ كُلَّ كِتابٍ من كُتُبِها; **~ one of us is implicated** كُلُّ واحِدٍ مِنّا مُتَوَرِّطٌ; **I enjoyed ~ minute of it** اسْتَمْتَعْتُ بِكُلِّ دَقيقةٍ فيهِ; **five out of ~ ten** خَمْسة من كُلِّ عَشَرةٍ; **there are three women for ~ ten men** هُناكَ ثَلاثُ نِساءٍ لِكُلِّ عَشَرةِ رِجالٍ; **it was a success/failure in ~ way** كانَ نَجاحاً \ فَشَلاً بِكُلِّ المَقاييسِ 2 (with emphasis) **her ~ word/action** كُلّ كَلِمةٍ \ تَصَرُّفٍ لَها; **your ~ wish** كُلّ رَغْبةٍ لَكَ; **I have ~ confidence in you** كُلّي ثِقةٌ فيكَ; **they have ~ right to complain** لَدَيْهِمْ كُلُّ الحَقِّ في الشَكْوى; **I wish you ~ success** أَتَمَنّى لَكَ كُلَّ النَجاحِ; **not ~ family is so lucky** لَيْسَتْ كُلُّ أُسْرةٍ مَحْظوظةً بِهذا الشَكْلِ; **he is ~ bit as handsome as his father** هو وَسيمٌ مِثْلَ أَبيهِ تَماماً; **she answered ~ single question** أَجابَتْ على كُلِّ الأَسْئِلةِ سُؤالاً سُؤالاً; **she ate ~ last crumb of the cake** أَكَلَت الكَعْكةَ حتّى آخِرَ قِطْعةٍ 3 (showing frequency) **~ day/Thursday** كُلّ يَوْمٍ \ خَميسٍ; **~ month/week/year** كُلَّ شَهْرٍ \ أُسْبوعٍ \ سَنةٍ; **~ second day/third week** كُلّ يَوْمَيْنِ \ ثَلاثةِ أَسابيعَ; **once ~ few days** مَرّة كُلَّ بِضْعةِ أَيّامٍ; **~ 10 kilometres** كُلَّ 10 كيلومِتْراتٍ

B **(every other)** *adj phr* (alternate) **~ other day** يَوْماً بعد يَوْمٍ; **~ other Sunday** يَوْمَ الأَحَدِ كُلَّ أُسْبوعَيْنِ; **~ other page** كُلَّ صَفْحَتَيْنِ

Idioms **every man for himself!** ≈ اللّهُمَّ نَفْسي!; **every now and again, every now and then** بين الحينِ والآخَرِ; **every once in a while** من وَقْتٍ لآخَرَ

everybody /'ɛvrɪbɒdi/ *pron* كُلّ شَخْصٍ; **~ except me** الجَميع ما عَدايَ; **~ else knew about it, but no one had told me** عَلِمَ الجَميعُ بِهِ, وَلَكِنْ لم يُخْبِرْني أَحَدٌ; **you can't please ~** لا يُمْكِنُكَ أَنْ تُرْضيَ جَميعَ الناسِ; **he's mad, ~ knows that** هو مَجْنونٌ, كُلُّ الناسِ يَعْرِفونَ ذلك; **~ who is anybody** شَخْصيّاتُ المُجْتَمَعِ; **is ~ agreed?** هل كُلُّنا مُتَّفِقونَ؟; **~ knows ~ else around here** كُلُّ الناسِ يَعْرِفونَ بَعْضَهُمْ بَعْضاً في هذه المِنْطَقةِ

everyday /'ɛvrɪdeɪ/ *adj* ‹*life, occurrence*› يَوْميّ; ‹*clothes, objects*› عاديّ; **the Internet has become part of ~ life** أَصْبَحَ الإنْتَرْنت جُزْءاً من الحَياةِ اليَوْميّةِ; **clothes for ~ wear** مَلابِس للأَيّامِ العادِيّةِ

everyone /'ɛvrɪwʌn/ *pron* ▸ **everybody**

everything /'ɛvrɪθɪŋ/ *pron* كُلّ شَيْءٍ; **you mustn't believe ~ (that) you hear** لا تُصَدِّقْ كُلَّ ما تَسْمَعُهُ; **money isn't ~** لَيْسَ المالُ كُلَّ شَيْءٍ; **is ~ alright?** هل كُلُّ شَيْءٍ على ما يُرامُ؟

everywhere /'ɛvrɪwɛː/ *adv* ‹*go, search*› في كُلِّ مَكانٍ; **I've looked ~ for it** بَحَثْتُ عَنْهُ في كُلِّ مَكانٍ

evict /ɪ'vɪkt/ *vt* طَرَدَ (u; طَرْد) ‹*a tenant, squatter*›

eviction /ɪ'vɪkʃ(ə)n/ *n* طَرْد, إخْلاء قَسْريّ

evidence /'ɛvɪd(ə)ns/ *n* 1 (facts, information) بُرْهان (بَراهينُ); (proof) دَليل (دَلائِلُ, أَدِلّة), بَيِّنة; **a piece of ~** دَليل (دَلائِلُ, أَدِلّة

2 (testimony) شَهادة; **to give ~** أَدْلى بِشَهادَتِهِ **3** (indication) دَليل (آثار) أَثَر ,(أَدِلّة ,دَلائِل)

evident /ˈɛvɪd(ə)nt/ *adj* ‹*pleasure, intention*› بَيِّن ,جَليّ ,واضِح

evidently /ˈɛvɪd(ə)ntli/ *adv* **1** (apparently) كَما يَبْدو; **~, he has no intention of helping** كَما يَبْدو لَيْسَ في نِيَّتِهِ أَنْ يُساعِدَ **2** (clearly) ‹*unaware, false*› مِن الواضِح; **they are ~ unaware of the truth** مِن الواضِح أَنَّهُم لا يَعْرِفونَ الحَقيقةَ

evil /ˈiːv(ə)l/ **A** *adj* ‹*criminal, monster, act*› شِرّير (أَشْرار); **an ~ spirit** روح شِرّيرة; **she has an ~ temper** لَها مِزاجٌ حادٌّ **B** *n* **1** [u] (wickedness) شَرّ; **the forces of ~** قُوى الشَرِّ; **to speak ~ of sb** تَكَلَّمَ بِسوءٍ عن شَخْصٍ **2** (negative aspect) (أَضْرار); **the ~s of drink/drugs** أَضْرار الكُحولِ \ ضَرَر المُخَدِّراتِ

Idiom **the lesser of two evils** أَهْوَن الشَرَّيْنِ

evildoer /ˈiːvəlduːə/ *n* (liter) شِرّير ,مُذْنِب (أَشْرار ,أَشِرّاءُ)

evocative /ɪˈvɒkətɪv/ *adj* ‹*picture, description*› (of emotions) مُثير لِلعَواطِفِ \ لِلشُجونِ; (of memories) [مُعيد إلى الذاكِرة]

evoke /ɪˈvəʊk/ *vt* **1** (to bring to mind) اسْتَحْضَرَ ‹*a memory*›; حَرَّكَ ‹*a feeling*› **2** (to elicit) أَثارَ ‹*a response, an interest*›

evolution /ˌiːvəˈluːʃ(ə)n/ *n* **1** (biological process) تَطَوُّر ,نُشوء ,(تَطَوُّرات); **the ~ of the human species** تَطَوُّر الجِنْسِ البَشَرِيِّ; **Darwin's theory of ~** نَظَرِيّة داروين لِلتَطَوُّرِ **2** (gradual development) نُمُوّ ,تَطَوُّر; **the ~ of language** تَطَوُّر اللُغةِ

evolutionary /iːvəˈluːʃ(ə)n(ə)ri/ *adj* ‹*development, theory*› تَطَوُّري

evolve /ɪˈvɒlv/ *vi* **1** (to develop biologically) «species, humans» تَطَوَّرَ **2** (to grow) «ideas, companies» نَما ,تَطَوَّرَ (u; نُمُوّ)

ewe /juː/ *n* (Zool) نَعْجة (نِعاج ,نَعَجات) ,شاة (n coll; singul n شاة; شِياه ,شِياء ,شِواه)

ex /ɛks/ *n* (*pl* **exes**) (former partner) (infml) زَوْج \ صَديق سابِق, زَوْجة \ صَديقة سابِقة

ex- /ɛks/ *prefix* سابِق; **his ~wife** زَوْجَتُهُ السابِقة; **her ~husband** زَوْجُها السابِق

exacerbate /ɪgˈzasəbeɪt/ *vt* فاقَمَ ‹*pain, a disease*›; أَزَّمَ ,صَعَّدَ ‹*a situation*›

exact /ɪgˈzakt/ *adj* ‹*date, science*› مَضْبوط ,دَقيق; **what were his ~ words?** ماذا قالَ بالضَبْطِ؟; **there were 54 people at the party, to be (more) ~** حَضَرَ الحَفْلةَ 54 شَخْصاً على وَجْهِ التَحْديدِ

exacting /ɪgˈzaktɪŋ/ *adj* ‹*task, employer*› مُتَطَلِّب

exactly /ɪgˈzaktli/ *adv* ‹*know, match*› بِالضَبْطِ ,تَماماً; **your answer is ~ right** إِجابَتُكَ صَحيحةٌ تَماماً; **I understand ~ how you feel** أَفْهَمُ شُعورَكَ تَماماً

exaggerate /ɪgˈzadʒəreɪt/ *vt, vi* (في) غالى ,ضَخَّمَ ,(في) بالَغَ ‹*the importance, a claim*›; **you are exaggerating the difficulties** تُضَخِّمُ الصُعوباتِ

exaggeration /ɪgˌzadʒəˈreɪʃ(ə)n/ *n* مُبالَغة

exalt /ɪgˈzɔːlt/ (fml) *vt* **1** (to glorify) مَجَّدَ ‹*an act, a virtue*› **2** (to raise in rank, power) رَفَعَ ,رَقّى ‹*a peasant, worker*›

exam /ɪgˈzam/ *n* امْتِحان (امْتِحانات); **to take** *or* (BrE) **sit an ~** أَدّى امْتِحاناً

examination /ɪgˌzamɪˈneɪʃ(ə)n/ *n* **1** (inspection) تَفَقُّد (تَفَقُّدات) ,(تَحَرِّيات) تَحَرٍّ ,(study) فَحْص (فُحوص) ,بَحْث (بُحوث); **on closer ~** عند إِمْعانِ النظرِ **2** (Educ fml) امْتِحان (امْتِحانات) **3** (of a patient) فَحْص (فُحوص) ,كَشْف (كُشوف)

examination paper *n* وَرَقة امْتِحانٍ

examine /ɪgˈzamɪn/ *vt* **1** (to inspect) فَحَصَ (a; فَحْص) ,فَتَّشَ ‹*a passport, the baggage*› **2** (to study, analyse) دَرَسَ (u; دَرْس), بَحَثَ (a; بَحْث) ,فَحَصَ ‹*an issue, evidence*› **3** فَحَصَ (a; فَحْص) ,كَشَفَ (i; كَشْف; على) ‹*a patient*› **4** (Educ) امْتَحَنَ ‹*a student, candidate*›

examiner /ɪgˈzamɪnə/ *n* مُمْتَحِن

exam paper *n* وَرَقة امْتِحانٍ

example /ɪgˈzɑːmp(ə)l/ *n* **1** (specimen, illustration) مِثال (أَمْثِلة) ,مَثَل (أَمْثال); **for ~** مَثَلاً ,على سَبيلِ المِثالِ **2** (model) قُدْوة ,مِثال (أَمْثِلة) **3** (as a warning) **to make an ~ of sb** جَعَلَ شَخْصاً عِبْرةً لِلآخَرينَ

exasperated /ɪgˈzaspəreɪtɪd/ *adj* ‹*voice, sigh*› ساخِط ,غاضِب, مُسْتاء

exasperating /ɪgˈzɑːspəreɪtɪŋ/ *adj* ‹*day, situation*› مُزْعِج

exasperation /ɪgˌzɑːspəˈreɪʃ(ə)n/ *n* انْزِعاج ,غَضَب ,سُخْط

excavate /ˈɛkskəveɪt/ **A** *vt* حَفَرَ (i; حفر) ‹*a site, tunnel*›; اسْتَخْرَجَ ‹*objects*›; كَشَفَ (i; كَشْف) (عن) ‹*ruins*› **B** *vi* نَقَّبَ عن آثارٍ

excavation /ɛkskəˈveɪʃ(ə)n/ *n* [u] (action of excavating) حَفْر; (site) مَوْقِع حَفْرِيّاتٍ

excavator /ˈɛkskəveɪtə/ *n* **1** (person) مُنَقِّب **2** (machine) جَرّافة

exceed /ɪkˈsiːd/ *vt* **1** (to be more than) زادَ (i; زِيادة) (عن) ‹*a number, value*› **2** (to go beyond) تَعَدّى, تَجاوَزَ ‹*a limit, maximum*›; فاقَ (u; فَواق) ‹*expectations*›

exceedingly /ɪkˈsiːdɪŋli/ *adv* (fml) ‹*popular, dangerous*› للغايةِ, إلى أبْعَدِ حَدٍّ

excel /ɪkˈsɛl/ *vi* (-ll-) «athletes, students» بَرَعَ (a-u; بَراعة) (في), تَفَوَّقَ (في); **to ~ in/at sports/physics** تَفَوَّقَ في الرياضةِ \ الفيزْياءِ

excellence /ˈɛksələns/ *n* امْتِياز, تَفَوُّق

excellent /ˈɛksələnt/ *adj* ‹*job, performance*› مُمْتاز

except /ɪkˈsɛpt/ **A** *prep* **everybody ~ Lisa** الجَميع ما عَدا ليزا; **nothing ~ a refund would be acceptable** لا شَيْءَ سَيَكونُ مَقبولاً سِوى اسْتِرْدادِ المالِ; **nobody ~ Hassan understood** ما فَهِمَ أحَدٌ سِوى حَسَنٍ; **~ when conditions are very good ...** إلاّ عِنْدَما تَكونُ الظُروفُ مُواتيةً جِدًّا ...; **we agree ~ that ...** نَحْنُ مُوافِقونَ إلاّ أنّ ...; **who could have done it ~ him?** مَنْ من المُمْكِنِ أنْ يَكونَ قد فعَلَ هذا سِواهُ؟ **B** (**except for**) *prep phr* ما عَدا, بِاسْتِثْناءِ **C** *vt* اسْتَثْنى; **not ~ing ...** دون اسْتِثْناءِ ...; **present company ~ed** بِاسْتِثْناءِ الحُضورِ

exception /ɪkˈsɛpʃ(ə)n/ *n* **1** (special case) اسْتِثْناء (اسْتِثْناءات); **with the ~ of** ما عَدا, بِاسْتِثْناءِ; **to make an ~ for sb** اسْتَثْنى شَخْصاً **2** **to take ~ to sth** (to object) اعْتَرَضَ على شَيْءٍ, احْتَجَّ على شَيْءٍ

exceptional /ɪkˈsɛpʃ(ə)n(ə)l/ *adj* **1** (not typical) ‹*circumstances, case*› اسْتِثْنائيّ **2** (outstanding) ‹*talent, quality*› خارِق (خَوارِقُ)

exceptionally /ɪkˈsɛpʃ(ə)n(ə)li/ *adv* ‹*quick, difficult*› بِشَكْلٍ اسْتِثْنائيٍّ

excerpt /ˈɛksəːpt/ *n* مَقْطَع (مَقاطِعُ), فِقْرة (فِقْرات)

excess /ɪkˈsɛs/ **A** *n* **1** (surfeit) كَمِّيّة مُفْرِطة; (immoderation) إفْراط **2** (surplus) زِيادة; **in ~ of** يَزيدُ عن **B** *adj* **~ weight/baggage** وَزْن \ أَمْتِعة زائِد(ة)

excessive /ɪkˈsɛsɪv/ *adj* ‹*force, amount*› مُفْرِط, زائِد

excessively /ɛkˈsɛsɪvli/ *adv* **1** (more than necessary) ‹*to drink, spend*› بِإفْراطٍ **2** (very) ‹*harsh, long*› للغايةِ, جِدًّا

exchange /ɪksˈtʃeɪndʒ/ **A** *n* **1** (of ideas, gunfire, prisoners) تَبادُل (تَبادُلات); **in ~ for sth** عِوَضاً عن \ من, مُقابِلَ شَيْءٍ **2** (of goods) اسْتِبْدال (اسْتِبْدالات) **3** [u] (of currency) صَرْف **4** (dialogue) مُحاوَرة **5** (also **telephone exchange**) بَدّالة, مَرْكَز \ سَنْتْرال الهاتِفِ **B** *vt* **1** تَبادَلَ ‹*information, views*›; **to ~ sth with sb** تَبادَلَ شَيْئاً مع شَخْصٍ **2** اسْتَبْدَلَ ‹*a purchase, voucher*›; **to ~ sth for sth** اسْتَبْدَلَ شَيْئاً بِشَيْءٍ

exchange control *n* رِقابة على الصَرْفِ

exchange rate *n* سِعْر الصَرْفِ

exchange visit *n* زيارة تَبادُليّة

exchequer /ɪksˈtʃɛkə/ *pr n* **the E~** (BrE) وِزارة الماليّةِ (في بريطانيا)

excise /ˈɛksʌɪz/ *n* (also **excise duty**) ضَريبة المُكوسِ

excitable /ɪkˈsʌɪtəb(ə)l/ *adj* ‹*crowd, disposition*› سَريع الانْفِعالِ

excite /ɪkˈsʌɪt/ *vt* **1** هَيَّجَ, حَمَّسَ ‹*children, crowds*› **2** أثارَ ‹*interest, curiosity, admiration*›

excited /ɪkˈsʌɪtɪd/ *adj* ‹*children, crowd*› مُتَحَمِّس; **to get ~** تَحَمَّسَ

excitement /ɪkˈsʌɪtmənt/ *n* تَحَمُّس

exciting /ɪkˈsʌɪtɪŋ/ *adj* ‹*news, prospect*› مُثير

exclaim /ɪkˈskleɪm/ *vt, vi* صاحَ (i; صِياح), صَرَخَ (u; صُراخ)

exclamation /ɛkskləˈmeɪʃ(ə)n/ *n* صَرْخة (صَرَخات), صَيْحة, هُتاف

exclamation mark (BrE), **exclamation point** (AmE) *n* عَلامة تَعَجُّبٍ

exclude /ɪkˈskluːd/ *vt* **1** (to debar) مَنَعَ (a; مَنْع) ‹*a group, member*›; **to ~ sb from sth** مَنَعَ شَخْصاً من شَيْءٍ **2** (to rule out) اسْتَبْعَدَ ‹*a possibility*›

excluding /ɪk'sklu:dɪŋ/ *prep* بِدونِ; **the cost is €320 ~ VAT** السِعْرُ 320 يورو بِدونِ ضَريبةِ القيمةِ المُضافةِ

exclusion /ɪk'sklu:ʒ(ə)n/ *n* **1** (of minorities, groups) إقْصاء **2** (of pupils) إقْصاء

exclusion zone *n* مِنْطَقة مَحْظورة

exclusive /ɪk'sklu:sɪv/ *adj* **1** (select) ‹*club, school*› حَصْريّ **2** ‹*interview, rights*› حَصْريّ **3** (not including) **~ of sth** دون اعْتِبارِ شَيْءٍ

exclusively /ɪk'sklu:sɪvli/ *adv* ‹*available, male*› حَصْريًّا

excommunicate /,ɛkskə'mju:nɪkeɪt/ *vt* حَرَمَ كَنَسيًّا ‹*a priest, king*›

excrement /'ɛkskrɪmənt/ *n* بِراز

excruciating /ɪk'skru:ʃieɪtɪŋ/ *adj* **1** ‹*pain*› لا يُطاق; ‹*death*› مُضْجِر **2** (very unpleasant) ‹*experience*› مُؤْلِم; ‹*detail*› مُؤْلِم

excursion /ɪk'skə:ʃ(ə)n/ *n* نُزْهة (نُزَه ,نُزْهات)

excuse **A** /ɪk'skju:z/ *vt* **1** (to forgive) غَفَرَ (i; غُفْران) ‹*sb's error, rudeness*›; **to ~ sb for sth/for doing sth** عَذَرَ شَخْصاً على شَيْءٍ \ فِعْلِ شَيْءٍ; **~ me!** (bumping into sb) سامِحْني!; (in enquiries) مَعْذِرةً!; (not having heard properly) عَفواً! **2** (to justify) عَذَرَ (i; عُذْر ,مَعْذِرة) ‹*sb's behaviour, actions*› **3** (to exempt) أَعْفى; **to ~ sb from sth/from doing sth** أَعْفى شَخْصاً من شَيْءٍ \ فِعْلِ شَيْءٍ

B /ɪk'skju:s/ *n* **1** (pretext) عُذْر (أَعْذار) ,ذَريعة (ذَرائِعُ); **it was just an ~ to get out for a while** كانَتْ فَقَطْ ذَريعةً للخُروجِ لِبُرْهةٍ; **this gave me an ~ to leave early** أعْطاني هذا ذَريعةً للمُغادَرةِ مُبَكِّراً; **you're always making ~s!** أَنْتَ دائِماً تَتَصَنَّعُ \ تَخْتَلِقُ الأَعْذارَ!; **any ~ will do!** أيُّ عُذْرٍ سَيَفي بالغَرَضِ! **2** (for an indulgence) حُجّة (حُجَج) ,مُبَرِّر (مُبَرِّرات); **it's a great ~ for a celebration** إنَّهُ مُبَرِّرٌ رائِعٌ للاحْتِفالِ; **it was a good ~ for going out** كانَتْ حُجّةً جَيِّدةً للخُروجِ

ex-directory /,ɛksdʌɪ'rɛkt(ə)ri, ,ɛksdɪ'rɛkt(ə)ri/ *adj* ‹*number, subscriber*› [غَيْر مُسَجَّلٍ في دَليلِ الهاتِفِ]

exec /ɪg'zɛk/ *n* (infml) = **executive** مَسْؤول تَنْفيذيّ

execute /'ɛksɪkju:t/ *vt* **1** (to carry out, perform) نَفَّذَ ‹*a plan, mission*›; أَدّى ‹*one's duty*› **2** (to put to death) أَعْدَمَ ‹*a prisoner, murderer*›

execution /,ɛksɪ'kju:ʃ(ə)n/ *n* **1** (killing) إعْدام (إعْدامات) **2** (of a plan, an order) تَنْفيذ; (of one's duty) تَأْدِية

executioner /ɛksɪ'kju:ʃ(ə)nə/ *n* جَلّاد

executive /ɪg'zɛkjʊtɪv/ **A** *adj* **1** ‹*power, position*› تَنْفيذيّ **2** ‹*suite, car*› تَنْفيذيّ (فاخِر)

B *n* **1** (manager) مَسْؤول تَنْفيذيّ **2** (committee) هَيْئة تَنْفيذيّة **3** (branch of government) **the ~** السُلْطة التَنْفيذيّة

executive director *n* مُدير تَنْفيذيّ

executor /ɪg'zɛkjʊtə/ *n* (Law) مُنَفِّذ وَصيّةٍ ,وَصيّ (أَوْصِياءُ)

exemplary /ɪg'zɛmpləri/ *adj* ‹*record, student*› نَموذَجيّ ,مِثاليّ

exemplify /ɪg'zɛmplɪfʌɪ/ *vt* (**exemplifies**, **exemplifying**, **exemplified**) **1** (to be an example of) مَثَّلَ ‹*a quality, style*›; **his career exemplified the spirit of sportsmanship** مَثَّلَتْ مَسيرَتُهُ المِهْنيّةُ الروحَ الرياضيّةَ **2** (to demonstrate) وَضَّحَ ‹*a point*›

exempt /ɪg'zɛmpt/ **A** *adj* ‹*income, goods*› مُعْفًى; **to be ~ from sth** كانَ مُعْفًى من شَيْءٍ

B *vt* أَعْفى (من) ‹*a company, citizen*›; **to ~ sth/sb from sth** أَعْفى شَيْئاً \ شَخْصاً من شَيْءٍ

exemption /ɪg'zɛmpʃ(ə)n/ *n* إعْفاء (إعْفاءات); **~ from sth** إعْفاء من شَيْءٍ

exercise /'ɛksəsʌɪz/ **A** *n* **1** [u] (exertion) تَمارين; **to take (physical) ~** قامَ بِتَمارينَ رياضيّةٍ; **older people need mental ~** يَحْتاجُ كِبارُ السِنِّ إلى (مُمارَسةِ) التَمارينِ الذِهْنيّةِ **2** (training task) تَمْرين (تَمارينُ ,تَمْرينات); **a maths ~** تَمْرين رِياضيّاتٍ; **stretching ~s** تَمارين تَمَدُّدِ العَضَلاتِ **3** (operation) عَمَليّة; **an ~ in diplomacy** عَمَليّة ديبْلوماسيّة; **it was an academic ~** كانَتْ مُمارَسةً أكاديميّةً; **a public relations ~** مُناوَرة في العَلاقاتِ العامّةِ **4** [u] (of one's power, rights) مُمارَسة **5** (Mil) مُناوَرة; **to go on an ~** قامَ بِمُناوَرةٍ

B *vt* **1** (to enforce) مارَسَ ‹*a right, one's authority*›; **to ~ care/caution** تَوَخّى الحِرْصَ \ الحَذَرَ; **to ~ patience/tolerance** أَبْدى صَبْراً \ تَسامُحاً **2** (physically) دَرَّبَ ,مَرَّنَ ‹*one's body, mind*›; **to ~ a dog/horse** مَرَّنَ كَلْباً \ حِصاناً **3** (to worry) **to ~ sb's mind** شَغَلَ عَقْلَ شَخْصٍ

C *vi* «person, player» مارَسَ الرِياضةَ

exercise bike *n* درّاجة تَدْريبٍ

exercise book *n* كُرّاسة (كُرّاسات ,كَراريسُ)

exert /ɪgˈzəːt/ **A** *vt* مارَسَ ‹*influence, pressure*›; **he ~ed a strong influence on other artists** مارَسَ تَأْثيراً قَويًّا على الفَنّانينَ الآخَرين

B *v refl* **to ~ oneself** أَجْهَدَ نَفْسَهُ

exertion /ɪgˈzəːʃ(ə)n/ *n* **1** (physical effort) مَجْهود (مَجْهودات) **2** (application) مُمارَسة

exfoliator /ɛksˈfəʊlieɪtə/ *n* مُقَشِّر للجِلْدِ

exhale /ɛksˈheɪl/ **A** *vi* زَفَرَ (i; زَفير)

B *vt* زَفَرَ (i; زَفير) ‹*breath*›; نَفَثَ (i-u; نَفْث) ‹*smoke*›

exhaust /ɪgˈzɔːst/ **A** *vt* **1** (to tire) أَنْهَكَ **2** (to use up) اسْتَنْزَفَ ‹*resources, supplies*›; اسْتَنْفَدَ ‹*possibilities, patience*›

B *n* **1** (also **exhaust pipe**) أُنْبوب العادِمِ **2** [u] (also **exhaust fumes**) عادِم

exhausting /ɪgˈzɔːstɪŋ/ *adj* ‹*journey, schedule*› مُرْهِق

exhaustion /ɪgˈzɔːstʃ(ə)n/ *n* إنْهاك

exhaustive /ɪgˈzɔːstɪv/ *adj* ‹*report, list*› شامِل

exhibit /ɪgˈzɪbɪt/ **A** *vt* **1** عَرَضَ (i; عَرْض) ‹*paintings, products*› **2** (fml) (to manifest) أَظْهَرَ ‹*behaviour, symptoms*›

B *n* **1** (in museums, art galleries etc) مَعْروض (مَعْروضات) **2** (in a court of law) عَرْض (عُروض) **3** (AmE) (exhibition) مَعْرِض (مَعارِضُ)

exhibition /ɛksɪˈbɪʃ(ə)n/ *n* **1** (of art, goods) مَعْرِض (مَعارِضُ) **2** (spectacle) **to make an ~ of oneself** جَعَلَ نَفْسَهُ فُرْجةً

exhibition centre (BrE), **exhibition center** (AmE) *n* مَرْكَز مَعارِضَ

exhibitionism /ɛksɪˈbɪʃ(ə)niz(ə)m/ *n* **1** (attention seeking) هَوَس التَعَرّي; **2** (urge to expose oneself) اسْتِعْراضيّة (offence) اسْتِعْراء

exhibitionist /ˌɛksɪˈbɪʃ(ə)nɪst/ **A** *n* افْتِضاحيّ

B *adj* ‹*behaviour, tendencies*› اسْتِعْراضيّ

exhilarate /ɪgˈzɪləreɪt/ *vt* أَبْهَجَ ‹*a crowd, participant*›

exhilarating /ɪgˈzɪləreɪtɪŋ/ *adj* ‹*experience, feeling*› مُبْهِج

exile /ˈɛksʌɪl/ **A** *n* **1** (voluntary) مُغْتَرِب; (forced) مَنْفيّ **2** [u] (expulsion) نَفْي

B *vt* نَفى (i; نَفْي) ‹*a dissident, an opponent*›

exist /ɪgˈzɪst/ *vi* **1** (to be in existence) «God, life» وُجِدَ; **does life ~ elsewhere in the universe?** هل توجَدُ حَياةٌ في مَكانٍ آخَرَ في الكَوْنِ؟ **2** (to survive) عاشَ (i; عَيْش ,عيشة ,مَعيشة); **to ~ on sth** عاشَ على شَيْءٍ

existence /ɪgˈzɪst(ə)ns/ *n* **1** [u] (being) وُجود; **there are only two copies in ~** هُناكَ نُسْخَتانِ فَقَطْ في حَيِّزِ الوُجودِ **2** (way of life) حَياة (حَيَوات)

existential /ˌɛgzɪˈstɛnʃ(ə)l/ *adj* ‹*crisis, despair*› وُجوديّ

existing /ɪgˈzɪstɪŋ/ *adj* ‹*system, law*› حاليّ ,راهِن

exit /ˈɛksɪt/ *n* **1** (from a building, motorway) مَخْرَج (مَخارِجُ), مَنْفَذ (مَنافِذُ) **2** (departure) خُروج; **she made a hasty ~** قامَتْ بالخُروجِ بِسُرْعةٍ

exodus /ˈɛksədəs/ *n* هِجْرة جَماعيّة

exorbitant /ɪgˈzɔːbɪt(ə)nt/ *adj* ‹*price, increase*› فادِح ,باهِظ

exorcise /ˈɛksɔːsʌɪz/ *vt* طَرَدَ (u; طَرْد) ‹*a demon, ghost*›

exotic /ɪgˈzɒtɪk/ *adj* ‹*species, place*› أَجْنَبيّ ,غَريب

expand /ɪkˈspand/ **A** *vt* وَسَّعَ ‹*business, one's horizons, chest, an essay*›

B *vi* «metal, company, economy, city» اتَّسَعَ

(Phrasal verb) **expand on: ~ on [sth]** تَناوَلَ [شَيْئاً] بالتَفْصيل

expanding /ɪkˈspandɪŋ/ *adj* ‹*population, market, economy*› نامٍ ,مُتَزايد ,مُتَوَسِّع

expanse /ɪkˈspans/ *n* رُقْعة مُمْتَدّة ,مُتَّسَع

expansion /ɪkˈspanʃ(ə)n/ *n* **1** (of power) تَوَسُّع (تَوَسُّعات); (of industry, services) اتِّساع (اتِّساعات) **2** (of a solid, gas) تَمَدُّد

expansive /ɪkˈspansɪv/ *adj* (effusive) ‹*gesture, mood*› [صَريح وَمُعَبِّر]

expatriate /ɪksˈpatrɪeɪt/ *n, adj* مُغْتَرِب

expect /ɪkˈspɛkt/ **A** *vt* **1** (to anticipate) تَوَقَّعَ ‹*trouble, a result*›; **to ~ the worst** تَوَقَّعَ الأَسْوَأَ; **what did you ~?** ماذا كُنْتَ تَتَوَقَّعُ؟; **you knew what to ~** عَرَفْتَ ما يُمْكِنُ تَوَقُّعُهُ; **it was better/worse than ~ed** كانَ أَحْسَنَ \ أَسْوَأَ مِمّا كانَ مُتَوَقَّعاً; **to ~ sb to do sth** تَوَقَّعَ من شَخْصٍ أَنْ يَفْعَلَ شَيْئاً; **we ~ed you to pass easily** كُنّا نَتَوَقَّعُ مِنْكَ أَنْ تَنْجَحَ بِسُهولةٍ **2** (to rely on)

تَوَقَّعَ *<sb's help, sympathy>* ③ (to await) انْتَظَرَ, تَرَقَّبَ *<company, a guest>*; **we have been ~ing you** كُنّا نَتَوَقَّعُ مَجيئَكَ; **they are ~ed to arrive at six** مِن المُتَوَقَّعِ أَنْ يَصِلوا على السادِسةِ; **to be ~ing twins/a baby** كانَ يَنْتَظِرُ تَوْأَماً \ مَوْلوداً ④ (to require) *<commitment, hard work>* تَوَقَّعَ; **I ~ you to be punctual** أَتَوَقَّعُ مِنْكَ أَنْ تَكونَ دَقيقاً في مَواعيدِكَ; **I can't be ~ed to know everything** لا يُفْتَرَضُ بي أَنْ أَعْرِفَ كُلَّ شَيْءٍ ⑤ (BrE) (to suppose) **I ~ so** أَتَوَقَّعُ ذلك; **I don't ~ so** لا أَتَوَقَّعُ ذلك; **I ~ you're tired** أَظُنُّكَ مُتْعَباً

B *vi* ① (to anticipate) **to ~ to do sth** تَوَقَّعَ أَنْ يَفْعَلَ شَيْئاً; **I was ~ing to do better** كُنْتُ أَتَوَقَّعُ أَنْ يَكونَ أَدائي أَحْسَنَ ② (to require) **to ~ to do sth** تَوَقَّعَ أَنْ يَفْعَلَ شَيْئاً; **I ~ to see you there** أَتَوَقَّعُ أَنْ أَراكَ هُناكَ ③ (to be pregnant) **to be ~ing** كانَتْ تَنْتَظِرُ مَوْلوداً; **she's ~ing for January** تَنْتَظِرُ مَوْلوداً في يَنايِر

expectancy /ɪk'spɛkt(ə)nsi/ *n* تَوَقُّع, تَرَقُّب (تَرَقُّبات)

expectant /ɪk'spɛkt(ə)nt/ *adj* ① *<crowd, face>* مُتَرَقِّب ② *<mother>* حامِل (f; حَوامِل); *<father>* يَتَرَقَّبُ \ يَنْتَظِرُ مَوْلوداً

expectation /ɛkspɛk'teɪʃ(ə)n/ *n* ① (assumption, prediction) تَوَقُّع (تَوَقُّعات), تَرَقُّب (تَرَقُّبات); **contrary to ~s** على عَكْسِ التَوَقُّعاتِ ② (hope) تَطَلُّع (تَطَلُّعات); **to live up to sb's ~s** ارْتَقى إلى (مُسْتَوى) تَطَلُّعاتِ شَخْصٍ

expedient /ɪk'spiːdiənt/ (fml) *adj* ① (appropriate) *<method, solution>* مُلائِم, مُناسِب ② (advantageous) *<alliance, policy>* نَفْعِيّ

expedition /ɛkspɪ'dɪʃ(ə)n/ *n* رِحْلة, بَعْثة (بَعَثات)

expel /ɪk'spɛl/ *vt* **(-ll-)** طَرَدَ (u; طَرْد) *<a member>*

expend /ɪk'spɛnd/ *vt* (fml) أَنْفَقَ *<one's effort, energy>*

expendable /ɪk'spɛndəb(ə)l/ *adj* *<commodity, luxury, worker>* يُمْكِنُ الاسْتِغْناءُ عَنْهُ

expenditure /ɪk'spɛndɪtʃə/ *n* ① (amount) نَفَقات ② (spending) إِنْفاق

expense /ɪk'spɛns/ *n* ① (cost) كُلْفة (كُلَف); **she published it at her own ~** نَشَرَتْهُ على نَفَقَتِها الخاصّةِ; **they had a good laugh at my ~** اتَّخَذوني مَوْضِعَ سُخْرِيّةٍ; **at the ~ of quality/accuracy** على حِسابِ الجَوْدةِ \ الدِقّةِ ② (**expenses** *n pl*) (Busn) نَفَقات

expense account *n* حِساب النَفَقاتِ \ المَصْروفاتِ

expensive /ɪk'spɛnsɪv/ *adj* *<car, restaurant>* غالٍ; **it was an ~ mistake** كانَ خَطأً فادِحاً

experience /ɪk'spɪəriəns/ **A** *n* ① [u] (know-how) خِبْرة; **in my ~** حَسْبَ خِبْرَتي; **~ in programming is essential** الخِبْرةُ في البَرْمَجةِ أساسيّةٌ; **to have ~ with acute patients** كانَ لَدَيْهِ خِبْرةٌ مع المَرْضى من ذَوي الحالاتِ الحادّةِ; **to know/learn from ~** عَرَفَ \ تَعَلَّمَ عن طَريقِ الخِبْرةِ ② (event) تَجْرِبة (تَجارِبُ); **a new ~** تَجْرِبة جَديدة; **visiting the Pyramids was a unique ~** كانَتْ زِيارةُ الأَهْراماتِ تَجْرِبةً فَريدةً

B *vt* (fml) جَرَّبَ *<a defeat, an emotion, change>*; **to ~ hunger at first hand** عاشَ تَجْرِبةَ الجوعِ بِشَكْلٍ مُباشِرٍ; **they have not yet ~d a home defeat** لم يُجَرِّبوا بَعْدُ الخَسارةَ على أَرْضِهِمْ

experienced /ɪk'spɪəriənst/ *adj* *<staff, player>* ذو خِبْرةٍ, مُحَنَّك

experiment /ɪk'spɛrɪmənt/ **A** *n* اخْتِبار (اخْتِبارات), تَجْرِبة (تَجارِبُ)

B *vi* ① (Sci) أَجْرى اخْتِباراً \ تَجْرِبةً; **to ~ on sth/sb** أَجْرى اخْتِباراً على شَيْءٍ \ شَخْصٍ ② (to try out new ideas) جَرَّبَ; **to ~ with sth** جَرَّبَ شَيْئاً

experimental /ɪkˌspɛrɪ'mɛnt(ə)l/ *adj* ① *<data, conditions>* اخْتِباريّ ② (untested) *<drug, treatment>* تَجْريبيّ

experimentation /ɪkˌspɛrɪmɛn'teɪʃ(ə)n/ *n* تَجْريب (تَجاريبُ)

expert /'ɛkspəːt/ **A** *n* خَبير (خُبَراءُ); **an ~ in/on sth** خَبير في شَيْءٍ

B *adj* *<advice, opinion>* خَبير

expertise /ˌɛkspəː'tiːz/ *n* خِبْرة

expiate /'ɛkspieɪt/ *vt* «person» كَفَّرَ (عن) *<a crime, sin>*

expiration /ˌɛkspɪ'reɪʃ(ə)n/ *n* ① (AmE) (of a contract, period of time) انْتِهاء; (of a deadline, mandate) انْقِضاء ② (of breath) زَفير; (of gas, vapour) انْبِعاث (انْبِعاثات)

expire /ɪk'spʌɪə/ *vi* «visa, license, lease» انْتَهَتْ مُدّةُ صَلاحيَّتِهِ; «term, period» انْتَهى

expiry /ɪk'spʌɪri/ *n* ① (BrE) (of a contract, period of time) انْتِهاء الأَجَلِ ② (BrE) (of a deadline, mandate) انْقِضاء المَوْعِدِ

expiry date *n* تاريخ انْتِهاءِ الصَلاحيّةِ

explain /ɪk'spleɪn/ **A** *vt* شَرَحَ (a; شَرْح), وَضَّحَ *<a situation, decision>*; **could you ~ how to use the photocopier?** هل يُمْكِنُكَ أَنْ تُوَضِّحَ كَيْفيّةَ اسْتِعْمالِ آلةِ النَسْخِ؟; **she ~ed**

that it was an accident أَوْضَحَتْ أَنَّهُ كانَ حادِثاً

B *v refl* **to ~ oneself** (provide further clarification) شَرَحَ \ وَضَّحَ رَأْيَهُ \ فِكْرَتَهُ; (justify oneself) بَرَّرَ مَوْقِفَهُ \ تَصَرُّفَهُ

explanation /ɛksplə'neɪʃ(ə)n/ *n* شَرْح (شُروح), تَوْضيح (تَوْضيحات); **he gave a brief ~ of the plan** أَعْطى شَرْحاً مُوجَزاً لِلخُطَّةِ

explanatory /ɪk'splanət(ə)ri/ *adj* ‹*note, statement*› تَفْسيرِيّ, إيضاحِيّ

explicit /ɪk'splɪsɪt/ *adj* ‹*reference, instructions*› واضِح, بَيِّن; **sexually ~ material** مادّة جِنْسيّة صَريحة

explicitly /ɪk'splɪsɪtli/ *adv* ‹*to state, forbid*› بِوُضوحٍ, بِصَراحةٍ

explode /ɪk'spləʊd/ **A** *vt* **1** فَجَّرَ ‹*a bomb, device*› **2** دَحَضَ (a; دَحْض, دُحوض), فَنَّدَ ‹*a myth, theory*›
B *vi* **1** «bomb, vehicle» اِنْفَجَرَ **2** (with rage) اِنْفَجَرَ
3 «population» اِنْفَجَرَ

exploit **A** /ɪk'splɔɪt/ *vt* **1** اِسْتَغَلَّ ‹*resources, opportunities*›
2 اِسْتَغَلَّ ‹*a weakness, situation, children*›
B /'ɛksplɔɪt/ *n* مَأْثُرة (مَآثِر)

exploitation /ɛksplɔɪ'teɪʃ(ə)n/ *n* اِسْتِغْلال

exploration /ɛksplə'reɪʃ(ə)n/ *n* **1** (Geog) اِسْتِكْشاف (اِسْتِكْشافات) **2** (of a subject) اِسْتِطْلاع (اِسْتِطْلاعات), اِسْتِقْصاء (اِسْتِقْصاءات)

exploratory /ɪk'splɒrət(ə)ri/ *adj* **1** ‹*study, analysis*› اِسْتِكْشافِيّ **2** ‹*talks*› اِسْتِطْلاعِيّ **3** ‹*surgery*› اِسْتِكْشافِيّ, اِسْتِقْصائِيّ

explore /ɪk'splɔː/ *vt* **1** اِسْتَكْشَفَ ‹*an area, a town*› **2** اِسْتَطْلَعَ ‹*possibilities, options*›; اِسْتَعْرَضَ, بَحَثَ (a; بَحْث) ‹*an issue, a theme*›

explorer /ɛk'splɔːrə/ *n* مُسْتَكْشِف

explosion /ɪk'spləʊʒ(ə)n/ *n* **1** (of a bomb) اِنْفِجار (اِنْفِجارات) **2** (of anger, violence) اِنْفِجار (اِنْفِجارات); **an ~ of interest in genealogy** زِيادة شَديدة في الاهْتِمام بِعِلْم الأَنْسابِ

explosive /ɪk'spləʊsɪv/ **A** *adj* ‹*device, charge*› مُتَفَجِّر
B *n* مُتَفَجِّر (مُتَفَجِّرات)

exponent /ɪk'spəʊnənt/ *n* **1** (of a theory) مُؤَيِّد **2** (of an art style, a sport) مُمَثِّل

export **A** /ɪk'spɔːt/ *vt* **1** صَدَّرَ ‹*manufactures, technology*›
2 صَدَّرَ ‹*data, a file*›
B /'ɛkspɔːt/ *n* **1** (item exported) صادِر (صادِرات); **cotton is the country's main ~** القُطْنُ هو الصادِرُ الأَساسِيُّ لِلبَلَدِ **2** [u] (process) تَصْدير

exporter /ɪk'spɔːtə/ *n* مُصَدِّر

expose /ɪk'spəʊz/ *vt* **1** كَشَفَ (i; كَشْف) ‹*skin, a wire*›; **to ~ sb to sth** عَرَّضَ شَخْصاً لِشَيْءٍ **2** (to disclose) كَشَفَ (i; كَشْف) ‹*a scandal, corruption*›; فَضَحَ (a; فَضْح) ‹*a wrongdoer*› **3** (Phot) عَرَّضَ لِلضَوْءِ ‹*a photo, film*›

exposition /ɛkspə'zɪʃ(ə)n/ *n* (of theory, principles) عَرْض (عُروض), شَرْح (شُروح)

exposure /ɪk'spəʊʒə/ *n* **1** (to radiation, light, risk) تَعَرُّض **2** (publicity) دِعاية, تَرْويج **3** (unmasking) فَضْح **4** (to the elements) [تَعَرُّض لِعَوامِلِ الجَوِّ; **to be suffering from ~** عانى مِن التَعَرُّضِ لِقَسوةِ الجَوِّ **5** (Phot) (time) تَعْريض (لِلضَوْءِ); (picture) صورة (صُوَر)

expound /ɪk'spaʊnd/ **A** *vt* فَسَّرَ \ شَرَحَ بِالتَفْصيل ‹*a theory, view*›
B *vi* **~ on sth** شَرَحَ شَيْئاً بِالتَفْصيل

express /ɪk'sprɛs/ **A** *n* قِطار سَريع; **the Trans-Siberian Express** القِطار السَريع العابِر لِسيبيريا
B *adj before n* **1** (rapid) ‹*letter, train*› سَريع; **an ~ delivery service** خِدْمة تَوْصيلٍ سَريعٍ **2** (fml) (explicit) ‹*instruction, undertaking*› صَريح; **it's an ~ condition of the agreement** هو شَرْطٌ صَريحٌ في العَقْدِ
C *adv* **to send a letter ~** أَرْسَلَ رِسالةً بالبَريدِ السَريعِ
D *vt* **1** (fml) (to make known) عَبَّرَ (عن) ‹*a wish, one's thanks, fears*›; **to ~ interest in a product** أَعْرَبَ عن اهْتِمامِهِ بِمَنْتَجٍ; **words can't ~ how I feel** لا تَسْتَطيعُ الكَلِماتُ أَنْ تُعَبِّرَ عَمّا أَشْعُرُ بِهِ **2** (to state) عَبَّرَ (عن) ‹*a figure, quantity*›; **the figures are ~ed as percentages** يَتِمُّ التَعْبيرُ عن الأَرْقامِ بالنِسَبِ المِئَوِيّةِ **3** (to squeeze out) عَصَرَ (i; عَصْر) ‹*juice*›; حَلَبَ (i-u; حَلْب) ‹*milk*› **4** (to send) أَرْسَلَ بالبَريدِ السَريعِ ‹*a package, document*›
E *v refl* **to ~ oneself** عَبَّرَ عن نَفْسِهِ; **she ~es herself well** تُعَبِّرُ عن نَفْسِها بِشَكْلٍ جَيِّدٍ

expression /ɪk'sprɛʃ(ə)n/ *n* **1** (assertion) تَعْبير (تَعابيرُ); **an ~ of support/gratitude** تَعْبير عن الدَعْمِ \ العِرْفانِ بالجَميلِ **2** (look) تَعْبيرات الوَجْهِ, سيماء (سِيَم) **3** (phrase) تَعْبير (تَعْبيرات)

expressive /ɪk'sprɛsɪv/ *adj* ‹*face, language*› مُعَبِّر

expressly /ɪk'sprɛsli/ *adv* 1 (explicitly) ‹*to state, forbid*› بِوُضوحٍ, صَراحةً 2 (specifically) ‹*designed, written*› خِصّيصاً

expressway /ɪk'sprɛsweɪ/ *n* (AmE) طَريق سَريع

expropriate /ɛks'prəʊprɪeɪt/ *vt* نَزَعَ المِلْكيّةَ ‹*assets, property*›

expulsion /ɪk'spʌlʃ(ə)n/ *n* (of a pupil, member) طَرْد

exquisite /'ɛkskwɪzɪt, ɪk'skwɪzɪt/ *adj* 1 ‹*beauty, taste*› رائِع; ‹*work, craftsmanship*› مُتْقَن 2 ‹*pleasure, pain*› شَديد

ex-serviceman /ɛks'sə:vɪsmən/ *n* (*pl* **-men**) جُنْديّ سابِق

extant /ɛk'stant/ *adj* ‹*copy, document*› مَوْجود

extend /ɪk'stɛnd/ **A** *vt* 1 (to enlarge) وَسَّعَ ‹*a house, factory, runway*›; **to ~ one's vocabulary** أَثْرى مُفْرَداتِهِ 2 (to prolong) مَدَّدَ ‹*a visit, visa, loan*›; **the deadline was ~ed by a month** تَمَّ تَمْديدُ المَوْعِدِ النِهائيِّ شَهْراً 3 (to stretch out) مَدَّ (u; مَدّ) ‹*an arm, a wing*›; **to ~ one's hand** مَدَّ يَدَهُ 4 (fml) (to offer) قَدَّمَ ‹*an invitation, one's congratulations*›; **to ~ an invitation to sb** دَعا شَخْصاً

B *vi* 1 (over an area) «desert, network, carpet» امْتَدَّ; **the weather front ~s over the whole of the area** تَمْتَدُّ الجَبْهةُ الهَوائيّةُ على كُلِّ المِنْطَقةِ; **the cultivated area ~s from the river to the foothills** تَمْتَدُّ المِنْطَقةُ المَزْروعةُ من النَهْرِ حتّى التِلالِ السَفْحيّةِ 2 (to last) امْتَدَّ; **the drought ~ed into September** امْتَدَّ الجَفافُ حتّى شَهْرِ سِبْتَمْبَر 3 (to reach) «generosity, interest» **to ~ beyond sth** امْتَدَّ إلى ما وراء شَيْءٍ; **the court's jurisdiction can ~ beyond national borders** يُمْكِنُ لِاخْتِصاصِ المَحْكَمةِ أنْ يَمْتَدَّ إلى ما وراء الحُدودِ الوَطَنيّةِ

C (**extended**) *adj* 1 (in time) ‹*stay, warranty*› مُمْتَدّ 2 (in space) ‹*area*› مُمْتَدّ 3 (in relationships) ‹*family*› مُمْتَدّ

extension /ɪk'stɛnʃ(ə)n/ *n* 1 (of powers, services) تَوْسيع (تَوْسيعات) 2 (prolongation of a visa, contract, deadline) تَمْديد (تَمْديدات) 3 (to a building) مُلْحَق (مَلاحِقُ, مُلْحَقات) 4 (extra section of a road, railway, table) وُصْلة تَمْديدٍ 5 (Elec) (also **extension lead** BrE, **extension cord** AmE) وُصْلة (وُصَل, وُصْلات) 6 (Tel) (telephone) تَحْويلة (تَحاويلُ), بَدّالة; (line) خَطّ داخِليّ

extensive /ɪk'stɛnsɪv/ *adj* 1 ‹*area, experience, research, use*› شاسِع, واسِع 2 ‹*damage, repairs*› واسِع

extensively /ɪk'stɛnsɪvli/ *adv* 1 (widely) ‹*to travel, to use*› على نِطاقٍ واسِعٍ; **she has travelled ~ in South America** سافَرَتْ على نِطاقٍ واسِعٍ في أَمْريكا الجَنوبيّةِ 2 (comprehensively) ‹*to study*› على نِطاقٍ واسِعٍ; ‹*to write, read*› بِإسْهابٍ

extent /ɪk'stɛnt/ *n* 1 (of an area) امْتِداد (امْتِدادات) 2 (of damage, a problem, sb's knowledge) مَدًى 3 (degree) دَرَجة, حَدّ (حُدود); **to a certain/great ~** إلى حَدٍّ مُعَيَّنٍ \ كَبيرٍ; **to some ~** إلى حَدٍّ ما

extenuating /ɪk'stɛnjʊeɪtɪŋ/ *adj* **~ circumstances** ظُروف مُخَفِّفة

exterior /ɪk'stɪərɪə/ **A** *adj* ‹*wall, surface*› خارِجيّ

B *n* 1 (of a building, vehicle) خارج 2 (demeanour) مَظْهَر (مَظاهِرُ)

exterminate /ɪk'stə:mɪneɪt/ *vt* ‹*a population, species*› أَبادَ, أَفْنى

extern /ɛk'stə:n/ *n* (AmE) طَبيب غَيْر مُقيم

external /ɪk'stə:n(ə)l/ *adj* 1 (outside) ‹*surface, walls, factor*› خارِجيّ 2 (foreign) ‹*affairs, debt*› خارِجيّ 3 (on the surface) ‹*wound, examination*› خارِجيّ; **'for ~ use only'** 'للاسْتِعْمالِ الخارِجيِّ فَقَطْ'

externally /ɛks'tə:n(ə)li/ *adv* 1 (on the outside) ‹*to treat, be damaged*› خارِجيًّا; **'apply ~'** 'للاسْتِعْمالِ الخارِجيِّ' 2 (in organizations) ‹*to advertise, assess*› خارِجيًّا

extinct /ɪk'stɪŋkt/ *adj* 1 ‹*species, animal*› مُنْقَرِض; **to become ~** أَصْبَحَ مُنْقَرِضاً 2 ‹*volcano*› هامِد, خامِد

extinction /ɪk'stɪŋkʃ(ə)n/ *n* انْقِراض

extinguish /ɪk'stɪŋgwɪʃ/ *vt* 1 ‹*a fire*› أَخْمَدَ; ‹*a cigarette, light*› أَطْفَأَ 2 ‹*a threat, life*› قَضى (i; قَضاء) (على)

extinguisher /ɪk'stɪŋgwɪʃə/ *n* مِطْفَأة (مَطافِئُ)

extortion /ɪk'stɔ:ʃ(ə)n/ *n* ابْتِزاز

extortionate /ɪk'stɔ:ʃ(ə)nət/ *adj* ‹*price, rate*› ابْتِزازيّ; ‹*demands*› مُفْرِط

extra /'ɛkstrə/ **A** *adj* 1 (additional) ‹*time, money*› إضافيّ, زائِد; **at no ~ charge** بِدونِ أَجْرٍ إضافيٍّ; **take ~ care on icy roads** خُذ المَزيدَ من الحيطةِ على الطُرُقاتِ الجَليديّةِ; **they put on ~**

buses أضافوا حافِلاتٍ **2** (spare) إضافيّ

B *adv* **1** (extremely) للغايةِ; **we worked ~ hard** عَمِلْنا بِجُهْدٍ

أكْثَر من المُعْتادِ **2** (in addition) مَزيداً; **you have to pay ~ for that** يَجِبُ أنْ تَدْفَعَ المَزيدَ لِذَلِكَ

C *n* **1** (additional item) شَيْء إضافيّ; **optional ~s** زَوائِد

2 (actor) كومْبارْس

extract **A** /ɪk'strakt/ *vt* **1** نَزَعَ (i; نَزْع), اقْتَلَعَ ‹*a tooth, bullet*›; اسْتَخْرَجَ ‹*minerals, oil*› **2** انْتَزَعَ ‹*information, a confession*›

B /'ɛkstrakt/ *n* **1** (excerpt) مُقْتَطَف **2** (concentrate) مُسْتَخْلَص (مُسْتَخْلَصات)

extraction /ɪk'strakʃ(ə)n/ *n* **1** (of a tooth) خَلْع, اقْتِلاع **2** (of minerals) اسْتِخْراج (اسْتِخْراجات) **3** (origin) أَصْل (أُصول); **of French ~** من أَصْلٍ فَرَنْسيٍّ

extracurricular /ɛkstrəkə'rɪkjʊlə/ *adj* ‹*activities, studies*› خارِجَ المَنْهَجِ الدِراسيِّ

extradite /'ɛkstrədʌɪt/ *vt* سَلَّمَ, رَحَّلَ (إلى الدولَةِ الّتي وقع الجُرْمُ على أراضيها) ‹*a terrorist, defendant*›

extradition /ɛkstrə'dɪʃ(ə)n/ *n* تَسْليم, تَرْحيل (إلى الدَوْلةِ الّتي وقعَ الجُرْمُ على أراضيها)

extraordinarily /ɪk'strɔːd(ə)nrəli/ *adv* ‹*gifted, kind*› بِشَكْلٍ خارِقٍ للعادةِ \ اسْتِثْنائيٍّ; ‹*large, difficult*› بِشَكْلٍ مَلْحوظٍ

extraordinary /ɪk'strɔːd(ə)n(ə)ri/ *adj* **1** (remarkable) ‹*story, life*› غَيْر عاديٍّ **2** (unusually great) ‹*success, effort*› مُذْهِش, فوق العادةِ **3** (special) ‹*meeting, powers*› خارق للعادةِ

extrapolate /ɪk'strapəleɪt/ *vt* عَمَّمَ ‹*results, data*›

extrasensory perception /ɛkstrə,sɛns(ə)ri pə'sɛpʃ(ə)n/ *n* إدْراك فائِق للحَواسِّ

extraterrestrial /,ɛkstrətə'rɛstrɪəl/ *adj* ‹*life*› خارِجَ الأَرْضِ; ‹*being*› فَضائيّ

extra time *n* (in soccer) وَقْت إضافيّ

extravagance /ɪk'stravəg(ə)ns/ *n* **1** [u] (prodigality) بَذْخ, إسْراف **2** (luxury item) [شَيْء مُتْرَف \ كَماليّ]

extravagant /ɪk'stravəg(ə)nt/ *adj* **1** (lavish) ‹*lifestyle, party*› باذِخ; ‹*person*› مُبَذِّر, مُسْرِف **2** (exaggerated) ‹*claim, gesture*› مُبالَغ فيه

extravaganza /ɪk,stravə'ganzə/ *n* [عَرْض \ اسْتِعْراض تَرْفيهيّ ضَخْم]

extreme /ɪk'striːm/ **A** *adj* (furthest in range) ‹*case, views, heat*› أَقْصى (f قُصْوى); **to be on the ~ right/left** كانَ في أَقْصى اليَمينِ \ اليَسارِ; **to go to ~ lengths** *or* **measures** اتَّخَذَ أَقْصى الإجْراءاتِ; **to live in ~ poverty** عاشَ في فَقْرٍ مُدْقِعٍ

B *n* حَدّ أَقْصى; **~s of temperature** دَرَجات الحَرارةِ القُصْوى; **to go from one ~ to the other** انْتَقَلَ من النَقيضِ إلى النَقيضِ; **to take/carry sth to ~s** ذَهَبَ بِشَيْءٍ إلى أَبْعَدِ الحُدودِ, أَفْرَطَ في شَيْءٍ; **to go to any ~** بَذَلَ كُلَّ ما في وُسْعِهِ; **to be cautious in the ~** كانَ حَذِراً إلى أَقْصى حَدٍّ

extremely /ɪk'striːmli/ *adv* ‹*difficult, important*› إلى أَقْصى حَدٍّ, للغايةِ; **the film did ~ well** حَقَّقَ الفيلْم نَجاحاً كَبيراً للغايةِ

extreme sports *n* [رياضات خَطيرة \ مُثيرة]

extremism /ɪk'striːmiz(ə)m/ *n* تَطَرُّف

extremist /ɪk'striːmɪst/ *n, adj* مُتَطَرِّف

extremity /ɪk'strɛmɪti/ *n* (*pl* **extremities**) **1** (furthest point) طَرَف (أَطْراف) **2** (**extremities** *n pl*) (of the body) أَطْراف

extricate /'ɛkstrɪkeɪt/ *vt* انْتَشَلَ ‹*a victim, vehicle*›

extrovert /'ɛkstrəvəːt/ **A** *n* شَخْص مُنْبَسِط

B *adj* ‹*person, personality*› انْبِساطيّ

exude /ɪg'zjuːd/ *vt* **1** نَزَّ (i; نَزيز, نَزّ), نَتَعَ (i-u; نُتوع) ‹*sap, resin*›

2 أَشَعَّ ‹*confidence, charm*›

exult /ɪg'zʌlt/ *vi* **to ~ in sth** ابْتَهَجَ لِشَيْءٍ

exultation /,ɛgzʌl'teɪʃ(ə)n/ *n* ابْتِهاج (ابْتِهاجات)

eye /ʌɪ/ **A** *n* **1** (Anat) عَيْن (f; عُيون, أَعْيُن); **in front of** *or* **before my very ~s** أمامَ عَيْنَيَّ; **keep your ~s on the road!** أَبْقِ عَيْنَيْكَ على الطَريقِ!; **I could do it with my ~s closed** أَسْتَطيعُ أنْ أَفْعَلَهُ بِعَيْنَيْنِ مُغْمَضَتَيْنِ; **to keep an ~ on sb/sth** راقَبَ شَخْصاً \ شَيْئاً; **to have one's ~ on sth** (to want) وَضَعَ عَيْنَهُ على شَيْءٍ ‹*a house, car*›; (to aim for) وَضَعَ شَيْئاً نُصْبَ عَيْنَيْهِ ‹*a job, title*›; **to cast** *or* **run one's ~ over sth** أَلْقى نَظْرَةً على شَيْءٍ; **to catch sb's ~** لَفَتَ انْتِباهَ شَخْصٍ; **she couldn't take her ~s off him** لم تَسْتَطِعْ أنْ تَرْفَعَ عَيْنَيْها عَنْهُ; **to open/close one's ~s** فَتَحَ \ أَغْلَقَ عَيْنَيْهِ; **to close one's ~s to sth** تَغاضى عن شَيْءٍ; **to open sb's ~s to sth** لَفَتَ انْتِباهَ شَخْصٍ إلى شَيْءٍ;

to keep one's ~s open for sb/sth أبقى عَيْنَيْهِ مفْتوحَتَيْنِ على شَخْصٍ \ شَيْءٍ; to keep one's ~s peeled *or* skinned بَقِيَ على أبقى عَيْنَيْهِ مَفْتوحَتَيْنِ ,مُتَيَقِّظاً; as far as the ~ can see مَرْمى \ مَدى البَصَرِ **2** (opinion) in the ~s of the church/law في نَظَرِ الكَنيسةِ \ القانونِ; in my father's ~s في نَظَرِ والِدي **3** (judgement) to have a good ~ for sth كانَ لَهُ عَيْنٌ ثاقِبَةٌ لِشَيْءٍ; to have a good ~ for detail/a bargain كانَ لَهُ عَيْنٌ ثاقِبَةٌ للتَفاصيلِ \ للصفَقاتِ **4** (of a hurricane, tornado, storm) عَيْن (f; أَعْيُن ,عُيون) **5** (of a needle) ثُقْب (أَثْقاب ,ثُقوب); (fastener) عَيْن (لِإغْلاقِ فُتْحاتِ المَلابِسِ) **6** (of a potato) عَيْن (f; عُيون)

B (-eyed); *in combination* blue-/brown-~d أَزْرَق \ بُنّيّ العَيْنَيْنِ

C *vt* **1** (to look at) حَدَّقَ (في) ‹*a stranger, car*›; to ~ sth/sb with suspicion/envy نَظَرَ إلى شَيْءٍ \ شَخْصٍ بِعَيْنِ الريبةِ \ الحَسَدِ **2** (infml) (ogle) ▸ eye up

(Idioms) an eye for an eye, a tooth for a tooth العَيْنُ بالعَيْنِ والسِنُّ بالسِنِّ; to be all eyes نَظَرَ بِشَغَفٍ \ باهْتِمامٍ كبيرٍ; to be up to one's eyes in work كانَ غارِقاً حتّى أُذُنَيْهِ في العَمَلِ; to see eye to eye over sth نَظَرَ إلى شَيْءٍ بِنَفْسِ المِنْظارِ; to turn a blind eye to sth غَضّ الطَرْفَ عن شَيْءٍ

(Phrasal verbs) eye up: ~ [sb] up, ~ up [sb] (infml) نَظَرَ إلى [شَخْصٍ] بِعَيْنِ الشَهْوةِ ‹*a boy, woman*›

• eye up and down: ~ [sb] up and down (with suspicion) نَظَرَ إلى [شَخْصٍ] بعَيْنِ الريبةِ; (in admiration) نَظَرَ إلى [شَخْصٍ] بعَيْنِ الإعْجابِ

eyeball /ˈʌɪbɔːl/ *n* مُقْلة العَيْنِ

eyebrow /ˈʌɪbraʊ/ *n* حاجِبُ (حَواجِبُ); to raise one's ~s at sth أبْدى اسْتِغْرابَهُ \ دَهْشَتَهُ من شَيْءٍ

eyebrow pencil *n* قَلَم الحَواجِبِ

eye-catching /ˈʌɪˌkatʃɪŋ/ *adj* ‹*design, display*› لافِت للنَظَرِ

eye drops /ˈʌɪ drɒps/ *n pl* قَطَرات العَيْنِ

eyeglasses /ˈʌɪglɑːsɪz/ *n pl* (AmE) نَظّارة

eyelash /ˈʌɪlaʃ/ *n* هُدْب (أَهْداب)

eyelet /ˈʌɪlɪt/ *n* ثُقْب صَغير في القُماشِ \ الجِلْدِ لِإدْخالِ خُيوطٍ [إضافيّةٍ]

eyelid /ˈʌɪlɪd/ *n* جَفْن (أَجْفان ,جُفون)

eyeliner /ˈʌɪlʌɪnə/ *n* مُحَدِّد العُيونِ

eye-opener /ˈʌɪˌəʊp(ə)nə/ *n* مَوْقِف \ حَدَث يُنيرُ البَصيرةَ]

eyeshadow /ˈʌɪʃadəʊ/ *n* ظِلّ العُيونِ

eyesight /ˈʌɪsʌɪt/ *n* نَظَر (أَنْظار), بَصَر (أَبْصار); to have good/poor ~ كانَ بَصَرُهُ جَيِّداً \ ضَعيفاً

eye socket *n* نُقْرة العَيْنِ (مَحاجِرُ) مِحْجَر

eyesore /ˈʌɪsɔː/ *n* [شَيْء قَبيح المَنْظَرِ]

eye strain *n* إجْهاد العَيْنِ

eye test *n* اخْتِبار \ فَحْص البَصَرِ

eye tooth *n* ناب (في الفَكِّ العُلْويِّ)

eyewash /ˈʌɪwɒʃ/ *n* غَسول للعَيْنِ

eye-watering /ˈʌɪˌwɔːtərɪŋ/ *adj* **1** (bringing tears to the eyes) مُسيل للدُموعِ **2** (of figure, amount) [عالٍ \ كَبير جدًّا]

eyewitness /ˈʌɪwɪtnəs/ *n* شاهِد عِيانٍ

e-zine /ˈiːziːn/ *n* مَجلّة إلِكْترونيّة

Ff

F, **f** /ɛf/ **A** *n* **1** (letter) فاء ≈ الحَرْف السادِس من الأَبْجَدِيّة فا ≈ نَغْمة من نَغَماتِ السُلَّم الموسيقيّ) الإنْكليزيّة) **2** (**F**) (Mus) **B** *abbr* **1** (**f**) = **female** أُنْثى (f; أُناثى, إناث) **2** (**F**) = **Fahrenheit** فَهْرِنهايْت

fa /fɑː/ *n* ▸**fah**

FA /ɛfˈeɪ/ *n* (BrE) **1** = **Football Association**; **the ~** [اتِّحاد كُرةِ القَدَم في إنْكِلْترا] **2** (vulg) = **fuck all**; **sweet ~** لا شَيْءَ على الإطْلاقِ

fable /ˈfeɪb(ə)l/ *n* [قِصّة ذات مَغْزًى أَخْلاقيٍّ]

fabric /ˈfabrɪk/ *n* **1** (cloth) نَسيج (أَنْسِجة, نُسُج) **2** (of building) بِنْية (بُنًى, بِنًى); **the ~ of society** بِنْية \ نَسيج المُجْتَمَع

fabricate /ˈfabrɪkeɪt/ *vt* اخْتَلَقَ, لَفَّقَ ‹*a story, the evidence*›

fabrication /fabrɪˈkeɪʃ(ə)n/ *n* **1** (lie) اخْتِلاق, تَلْفيق **2** (of an object) صِناعة

fabric conditioner, **fabric softener** *n* مُنَعِّم المَلابِس

fabulous /ˈfabjʊləs/ *adj* **1** ‹*wealth, palace, event*› خُرافيّ, أُسْطوريّ **2** (infml) (wonderful) ‹*feeling, performance, party*› رائِع

facade, **façade** /fəˈsɑːd/ *n* واجِهة

face /feɪs/ **A** *n* **1** (of a person, animal) وَجْه (وُجوه); **to be lying ~ up/down** كانَ يَرْقُدُ على ظَهْرِهِ \ بَطْنِهِ; **to slam the door in sb's ~** صَفَقَ البابَ في وَجْهِ شَخْصٍ; **to laugh in sb's ~** ضَحِكَ بِاسْتِهْزاءٍ \ بِوَقاحةٍ في وَجْهِ شَخْصٍ; **I said it to his ~** قُلْتُ لَهُ هذا في وَجْهِهِ **2** (expression) تَعْبير الوَجْهِ; **to pull** *or* **make a ~** قَطَّبَ وَجْهَهُ **3** (aspect) **to change the ~ of the countryside** غَيَّرَ وَجْهَ الريفِ; **the changing ~ of Europe** الوَجْه المُتَغَيِّر لِأوروبّا; **the acceptable ~ of capitalism** الوَجْه المَقْبول للرَأْسماليّة; **on the ~ of it** في ظاهِرِهِ **4** [u] (dignity) **to lose ~** فَقَدَ ماءَ وَجْهِهِ; **to save ~** حَفِظَ ماءَ وَجْهِهِ **5** (of a clock, dial) وَجْه (وُجوه, أَوْجُه), ميناء (f; مَوانٍ, مَوانِئُ) **6** (of a coin) وَجْه (وُجوه, أَوْجُه); **to disappear off the ~ of the earth** اخْتَفى من على وَجْهِ الأَرْضِ **7** (of a mountain, cliff) سَطْح (سُطوح, أَسْطُح), وَجْه (وُجوه, أَوْجُه) **8** (of a card, document) وَجْه (وُجوه, أَوْجُه)

B (**in the face of**) *prep phr* (despite) بالرَغْمِ من

C *vt* **1** (to look towards) واجَهَ ‹*the audience, road, sea*›; **to ~ north/south** كانَ مُواجِهاً للشَمالِ \ للجَنوبِ; **we stood facing the school** وَقَفْنا مُقابِلَ المَدْرَسةِ **2** (to confront) واجَهَ, جابَهَ ‹*a challenge, crisis, ruin*›; **to be ~d with many problems** نُواجِهُ فَريقاً مَشاكِلَ عَديدةً; **we're facing a very strong team** قَوِيًّا جِدًّا **3** (to acknowledge) **~ the facts!** واجِه الحَقائِقَ!; **let's ~ it, nobody's perfect** دَعْنا نُواجِهُ الحَقيقةَ، لا أَحَدَ كامِلٌ **4** (to tolerate the prospect of) **he couldn't ~ the thought of losing her** لم يَتَقَبَّلْ فِكْرةَ الابْتِعادِ عَنْها **5** (with risk, possibility) واجَهَ ‹*a fine, suspension*› **6** (Constr) كَسا (u; كَسْو), غَطّى ‹*a façade, wall*›

D *vi* **1** **to ~ towards the camera/audience** واجَهَ الكاميرا \ الجُمْهورَ; **the building ~d towards the park/mountains** واجَهَ \ قابَلَ المَبْنى المُنْتَزَهَ \ الجِبالَ; **to ~ backwards/forwards** كانَ مُقابِلاً للجِهةِ الخَلْفيّةِ \ الأَماميّةِ; **to be facing up/down** «cards, documents» كانَ مَوْضوعاً على وَجْهِهِ **2** (Mil) **about ~!** للخَلْفِ دُرْ!; **left ~!** للأَماميِّ \ الخَلْفيِّ للشَمالِ دُرْ!

(Idioms) **to be in your face** (infml) كانَ مُتَبَجِّحاً; **to feed** *or* **stuff one's face** (infml) أَكَلَ بِشَراهةٍ; **to fly in the face of sth** تَعارَضَ مع شَيْءٍ

(Phrasal verb) **face up**: **1** **~ up to [sth]** واجَهَ [شَيْئاً] ‹*a problem, one's responsibilities*› **2** **~ up to [sb]** وَقَفَ في وَجْهِ [شَخْصٍ] ‹*the enemy, a rival*›

Facebook® /ˈfeɪsbʊk/ **A** *n* فَيْس بوك

B *vi* [قَضى وَقْتاً على الفَيْس بوك]

C *vt* [اِتَّصَلَ ب \ نَشَرَ على الفَيْس بوك]

facecloth /ˈfeɪsklɒθ/ *n* (BrE) مِنْشَفة وَجْهٍ

faceless /ˈfeɪsləs/ *adj* ‹*bureaucrat, corporation*› مَجْهول

facelift /ˈfeɪslɪft/ *n* **1** (operation) عَمَلِيّة شَدِّ الوَجْهِ; **to have a ~** أَجْرى عَمَلِيّة شَدِّ الوَجْهِ **2** (improvement) تَحْسين المَظْهَرِ الجَماليِّ; **to give sth a ~** قامَ بِتَحْسينِ المَظْهَرِ الجَماليِّ لِشَيْءٍ

face mask *n* **1** (for protection) كِمامة (كَمائِمُ, كِمامات) **2** (cosmetic) قِناع للوَجْهِ

face pack *n* [مُسْتَحْضَر تَجْميليّ يوضَعُ على شَكْلِ قِناعٍ للعِنايةِ بالوَجْهِ]

facet /ˈfasɪt/ *n* **1** (of a problem) جانِب (جَوانِبُ) **2** (of a gem) سُطَيْح

facetious /fəˈsiːʃəs/ *adj* ‹*remark, suggestion*› ساخِر

face-to-face /ˌfeɪstəˈfeɪs/ **A** *adj before n* ‹*meeting, interview*› شَخْصيّ

B (**face to face**) *adv* ‹*to meet, talk*› وَجْهاً لِوَجْهٍ

face value *n* قيمة اِسْمِيّة; **to take sb/sth at face value** صَدَّقَ شَخْصاً \ شَيْئاً دون تَمْحيصٍ

facial /ˈfeɪʃ(ə)l/ **A** *adj* ‹*expression*› وَجْهيّ; ‹*hair*› الوَجْهِ

B *n* مُسْتَحْضَر للعِنايةِ بالوَجْهِ

facile /ˈfasʌɪl/ *adj* ‹*explanation, comparison*› سَطْحيّ

facilitate /fəˈsɪlɪteɪt/ *vt* يَسَّرَ, سَهَّلَ ‹*communication, access*›

facility /fəˈsɪlɪti/ **A** *n* (*pl* **facilities**) **1** (installation) مِرْفَق (مَرافِقُ), مُنْشَأة; **a manufacturing ~** مَصْنَع (مَصانِعُ) **2** (ability) مَقْدِرة; **to have a ~ for languages** كانَ لَدَيْهِ مَقْدِرةٌ على تَعَلُّمِ اللُغاتِ **3** [u] (fml) (ease) سُهولة **4** (feature) خاصّيّة (خاصّيّات, خَصائِصُ), ميزة; **a pause ~** خاصّيّة الإيقافِ المُؤَقَّتِ **5** (Busn) **credit/overdraft ~** تَسْهيلات الاِئْتِمانِ \ السَّحْبِ على المَكْشوفِ

B (**facilities**); *npl* **1** (enhancement) مَرافِق; **facilities for the disabled** مَرافِق للمُعاقين; **to have cooking facilities** كانَ بِهِ مَرافِقُ للطَهْيِ **2** (infrastructure) مِرْفَق (مَرافِقُ); **sporting/changing facilities** مَرافِق رِياضيّة \ لِتَغْييرِ المَلابِسِ; **parking facilities** أَماكِن لِرَكْنِ السَّيّاراتِ

facing /ˈfeɪsɪŋ/ *n* **1** (Archit, Constr) تَلْبيس **2** (inside garment) سِجاف (سُجُف) **3** (outside garment) ظِهارة (ثَوْبٍ)

facsimile /fakˈsɪmɪli/ *n* صورة طِبْقَ الأَصْلِ

fact /fakt/ **A** *n* **1** (verifiable event, piece of information) حَقيقة (حَقائِقُ); **~s and figures** حَقائِق وَأَرْقام; **to know sth for a ~** كانَ على يَقينٍ أَنَّهُ صَحيحٌ; **owing to the ~ that he was a minor** نَظَراً إلى أَنَّهُ كانَ قاصِراً; **the ~ of the matter is ...** حَقيقةُ الأَمْرِ هي ...; **the ~ remains that he is not here** تَبْقى الحَقيقةُ أَنَّهُ لَيْسَ هُنا; **space travel is now a ~** السَفَرُ في الفَضاءِ حَقيقةٌ الآنَ **2** [u] (truth) حَقيقة, واقِع; **to be based on ~** كانَ مَبْنِيًّا على أَحْداثٍ \ وَقائِعَ حَقيقيّةٍ

B (**in fact, as a matter of fact**) *adv phr* في حَقيقةِ الأَمْرِ, في الواقِعِ

Idiom **the facts of life** الحَقائِق الجِنْسيّة

fact-finding /ˈfaktfʌɪndɪŋ/ *adj* ‹*mission, tour*› اِسْتِقْصائيّ

faction /ˈfakʃ(ə)n/ *n* فِئة مُنْشَقّة

factor /ˈfaktə/ *n* **1** (consideration) عامِل (عَوامِلُ); **a common ~ in all the cases** عامِل مُشْتَرَك في كُلِّ الحالاتِ **2** (number) عامِل (عَوامِلُ); **the highest common ~** العامِل المُشْتَرَك الأَكْبَر

factory /ˈfakt(ə)ri/ *n* (*pl* **factories**) مَصْنَع (مَصانِعُ), مَعْمَل (مَعامِلُ)

factory farming *n* تَرْبية صِناعيّة

factory floor *n* **1** (place) مَشْغَل التَصْنيعِ **2** (workers) عِمالة

factory ship *n* [سَفينة صَيْدٍ تَقومُ بِتَجْهيزِ الأَسْماكِ]

factory shop *n* [مَتْجَر لِبَيْعِ مُنْتَجاتِ مَصْنَعٍ مُباشَرةً دون وُسَطاءَ]

factory worker *n* عامِل مَصْنَعٍ

fact sheet *n* نَشْرة \ وَرَقة مَعْلوماتٍ

factual /ˈfaktʃʊəl/ *adj* ‹*account, basis*› واقِعيّ

faculty /ˈfakəlti/ *n* (*pl* **faculties**) **1** (ability) قُدْرة, مَقْدِرة (قُدُرات); **she's in full possession of her faculties** هي في كامِلِ قُدُراتِها **2** (of a university) كُلّيّة; **the law/arts ~** كُلّيّة القانونِ \ الفُنونِ **3** (AmE) (university staff) [أَعْضاء هَيْئةِ التَدْريسِ والبَحْثِ في كُلّيّةٍ]

fad /fad/ *n* **1** (craze) موضة عابِرة; **it's just a passing ~** هي مُجَرَّدُ موضةٍ عابِرةٍ **2** (whim) نَزْوة (نَزَوات)

fade /feɪd/ **A** *vt* جَعَلَ لَوْنَهُ باهِتاً ‹*a fabric, one's jeans*›

B *vi* **1** (to lose colour) «fabrics, colours» بَهِتَ (a; بَهْت), نَصَلَ (a-u; نُصول) **2** (to disappear) «hopes, memories» تَلاشى

(Phrasal verbs) **fade away** «sounds» خَفَتَ (u; خُفوت), خبا (u; خُبوّ, خَبْو)

• **fade out** (Cin) «shot» تَلاشى

faded /feɪdɪd/ *adj* ‹*curtains, colours*› باهِت

faeces (BrE), **feces** (AmE) /ˈfiːsiːz/ *n pl* غائِط, بِراز

fag¹ /fag/ *n* (BrE infml) سيجارة (سيجارات, سَجايِرُ, سَجائِرُ)

fag² /fag/ *n* (AmE offensive) لوطيّ

fah, fa /fɑː/ *n* فا (نوتة موسيقيّة)

Fahrenheit /ˈfarənhʌɪt/ *adj* ‹*scale, thermometer*› فَهْرِنْهايْتيّ (مِقْياس دَرَجَةِ حَرارةٍ)

fail /feɪl/ **A** *vt* **1** (not to pass) رَسَبَ (u; رُسوب) (في), أَخْفَقَ (في) ‹*an exam, a driving test*› **2** (to disallow) أَعْطى دَرَجَةَ رُسوبٍ ‹*a candidate, student*› **3** (fml) (not fulfil) **to ~ to do sth** تَخَلَّفَ عن فِعْلِ شَيْءٍ; **to ~ to keep one's word** أَخْلَفَ وَعْدَهُ; **she ~ed to mention that!** فاتَها أَنْ تَذْكُرَ ذلك! **4** (to let down) خَذَلَ (u; خَذْل) ‹*one's family, a friend*›; **my memory is ~ing me** تَخْذُلُني ذاكِرَتي; **words ~ me!** لا أَجِدُ الكَلِماتِ المُناسِبةَ!

B *vi* **1** (in exams) «students» رَسَبَ (u; رُسوب), أَخْفَقَ; **he ~ed in biology** رَسَبَ في مادّةِ عِلْمِ الأَحْياءِ **2** (to be unsuccessful) «plans, marriages» فَشِلَ (a; فَشَل); **if all else ~s, try …** في حالِ فَشَلِ كُلِّ المُحاوَلاتِ السابِقةِ, حاوِلْ …; **this treatment rarely ~s** نادِراً ما يَفْشَلُ هذا العِلاجُ **3** (to decline) «eyesight, health» ضَعُفَ (u; ضَعْف, ضُعْف) **4** (to stop functioning) «heart, immune system» تَوَقَّفَ **5** (to malfunction) «brakes, engine» تَعَطَّلَ عن أداءِ مُهِمَّتِهِ **6** «crops, harvest» فَشِلَ (a; فَشَل) **7** (to go bankrupt) «banks, companies» أَفْلَسَ

C (**failed**) *adj* ‹*writer, state*› فاشِل

D *n* (Educ) دَرَجة رُسوبٍ; **a ~ in chemistry** دَرَجة رُسوبٍ في الكيمِياءِ

E (**without fail**) *adv phr* ‹*to arrive, deliver*› بِلا شَكٍّ, بالتَأْكيدِ

failing /ˈfeɪlɪŋ/ **A** *n* نُقْطة ضَعْفٍ

B *prep* **~ that** في حالةِ فَشَلِ ذلك; **~ all else, go to the police** في حالِ فَشَلِ كُلِّ المُحاوَلاتِ الأُخْرى, اذْهَبْ إلى الشُرْطةِ

fail-safe /ˈfeɪlseɪf/ *adj* ‹*device, mechanism*› آمِن من التَعَطُّلِ

failure /ˈfeɪljə/ *n* **1** [u] (lack of success) إِخْفاق, فَشَل; **his ~ to understand the problem** فَشَلُهُ في فَهْمِ المُشْكِلةِ; **to end in ~** انْتَهى \ باءَ بالفَشَلِ **2** (unsuccessful person) (شَخْص) فاشِل; (action, event) [شَيْء فاشِل]; **he was a ~ as a teacher** فَشِلَ كَمُدَرِّسٍ **3** (of organs) قُصور, فَشَل **4** (of engines, brakes) تَوَقُّف, تَعَطُّل; **a power ~** انْقِطاع الكَهْرَباءِ **5** (of crops, harvests) فَشَل **6** (non-fulfilment) **~ to pay** عَجْز عن السَدادِ; **his ~ to keep his promise** إِخْفاقُهُ في تَنْفيذِ وَعْدِهِ

faint /feɪnt/ **A** *adj* (**fainter, faintest**) **1** ‹*line*› غَيْر واضِحٍ; ‹*smell, hope*› ضَعيف; ‹*sound*› خافِت; ‹*smile*› باهِت; **I haven't the ~est idea** لَيْسَ لَدَيَّ أَدْنى فِكْرةٍ **2** **to feel ~** (Med) أَحَسَّ بِأَنَّهُ سَيُغْمى عَلَيْهِ

B *vi* أُغْمِيَ عَلَيْهِ

faint-hearted /ˌfeɪntˈhɑːtɪd/ *n* **the ~** ذوو القُلوبِ الضَعيفةِ

faintly /ˈfeɪntli/ *adv* **1** (barely perceptibly) ‹*to see, hear, smile*› بَعْضَ الشَيْءِ **2** (slightly) ‹*ridiculous, reminiscent, tinged*› بالكادِ

fair /fɛː/ **A** *adj* **1** (just, reasonable) ‹*trial, wage, share*› عادِل, مُنْصِف; **it's not ~!** لَيْسَ هذا عَدْلاً!; **this deal is ~ to everyone** هذا الاتِّفاقُ عادِلٌ لِكُلِّ الأَطْرافِ; **it's only ~ that she should get half** مِن العَدْلِ أَنْ تَحْصُلَ هي على النِصْفِ; **that's a ~ comment/question** هذا تَعْليقٌ \ سُؤالٌ وَجيهٌ; **to be ~, he did try to pay** لِكَيْ أَكونَ مُنْصِفاً, فَقَدْ حاوَلَ فِعْلاً أَنْ يَدْفَعَ; **~ enough!** مَفْهوم! **2** (moderately good) ‹*performance, prospect*› مُتَوَسِّط; **his condition is ~** حالَتُهُ مُتَوَسِّطةٌ **3** (Educ) (in assessment) مَقْبول **4** (quite large) ‹*number, amount*› كَبير; **at a ~ speed** بِسُرْعةٍ كَبيرةٍ; **the house is a ~ size** البَيْتُ مِساحَتُهُ كَبيرةٌ; **it caused a ~ amount of damage** تَسَبَّبَ في قَدْرٍ كَبيرٍ من الضَرَرِ; **to be a ~ way off** كانَ بَعيداً بِدَرَجةٍ كَبيرةٍ **5** ‹*weather, wind*› مُعْتَدِل **6** (light-coloured) ‹*complexion, skin*› فاتِح; ‹*hair*› أَشْقَر (dipt) **7** (liter) (beautiful) ‹*maid, city*› جَميل, جَذّاب; **the ~ sex** الجِنْس اللَطيف

B *adv* ‹*to play*› بِشَكْلٍ شَريفٍ \ نَظيفٍ

C *n* **1** (funfair) مَهْرَجان تَرْفيهيّ **2** (exhibition) مَعْرِض (مَعارِض); **the Cairo International Book F~** مَعْرِض القاهِرةِ الدُوَليّ للكِتابِ

(Idiom) **to win fair and square** فازَ عن جَدارةٍ

fairground /ˈfeːgraʊnd/ *n* أَرْض \ مَدينة المَعارِضِ

fair-haired /feːˈheːd/ *adj* ‹*boy*› أَشْقَر (dipt; شُقْر)

fairly /ˈfeːli/ *adv* **1** (quite, rather) إِلى حَدٍّ ما ,نَوْعاً ما; **a ~ large area** مِنْطَقة كَبيرة نَوْعاً ما; **I'm ~ sure of the facts** أنا مُتَأَكِّدٌ نَوْعاً ما من الحَقائِقِ **2** (lawfully) ‹*to win, obtain*› بِطَريقةٍ شَرْعيّةٍ; **they won ~ and squarely** حَقَّقوا فَوْزاً حاسِماً

fair-minded /feːˈmʌɪndɪd/ *adj* ‹*approach, observer*› عادِل, غَيْر مُتَحَيِّزٍ ,مُنْصِف

fairness /ˈfeːnəs/ *n* **1** (of a person, judgement) إِنْصاف; **in all ~** للأَمانةِ ,بِكُلِّ إِنْصافٍ **2** (of complexion) بَياض; (of hair) شُقْرة

fair play *n* (Sport) لَعِب نَظيف; (in general) عَدْل ومُساواة

fair-sized /ˌfeːˈsʌɪzd/ *adj* ‹*crowd, house*› كَبير نَوْعاً ما

fair trade *n* تِجارة عادِلة

fairy /ˈfeːri/ *n* (*pl* **fairies**) جِنِّيّة

fairy godmother *n* جِنِّيّة طَيِّبة

fairyland /ˈfeːrɪland/ *n* عالَم الخَيالِ

fairy story, **fairy tale** *n* قِصّة خُرافيّة

faith /feɪθ/ *n* **1** (confidence) ثِقة; **to have ~ in sb's ability** كانَ عِنْدَهُ ثِقةٌ بِقُدْرةِ شَخْصٍ; **to act in good/bad ~** تَصَرَّفَ بِحُسْنِ \ بِسوءِ نيّةٍ **2** (belief) إيمان; **to have a strong ~** كانَ إيمانُهُ قَوِيًّا; **to lose one's ~** فَقَدَ إيمانَهُ

faithful /ˈfeɪθfʊl/ **A** *adj* **1** (loyal) ‹*companion, servant*› وَفِيّ (أَوْفِياءُ) **2** (sexually) ‹*partner, husband*› مُخْلِص

B *n* (**the faithful**) المُؤْمِنونَ

faithfully /ˈfeɪθf(ə)li/ *adv* **1** ‹*to serve, follow*› بِإِخْلاصٍ ,بِوَفاءٍ **2** ‹*to translate, record*› بِأَمانةٍ **3** (as letter ending) **yours ~** مع خالِصِ تَحيّاتي

faith healer *n* مُعالِج عن طَريقِ الإيمانِ والصَلاةِ

faith healing *n* عِلاج عن طَريقِ الإيمانِ والصَلاةِ

fake /feɪk/ **A** *adj* ‹*passport, diamond*› مُزَيَّف

B *n* **1** (forgery) تَزْوير ,تَزْييف **2** (impersonator) مُنْتَحِل دَجّال ,شَخْصيّةٍ \ صِفةٍ

C *vt* **1** ‹*a signature, document*› زَوَّرَ ,زَيَّفَ **2** ‹*an illness, orgasm*› تَظاهَرَ ,ادَّعى (ب)

D *vi* «mourners, patients» تَظاهَرَ

fakir /ˈfeɪkɪə/ *n* دَرْويش (دَراويش)

falafel /fəˈlaf(ə)l/ *n* فَلافِل

falcon /ˈfɔːlk(ə)n/ *n* صَقْر (صُقور)

Falkland Islands /ˈfɔːlklənd ˌʌɪləndz/, **Falklands** /ˈfɔːlkləndz/ *pr n pl* جُزُر فولْكْلانْد

fall /fɔːl/ **A** *vi* (*past tense* **fell**; *past participle* **fallen**) **1** (from a height) سَقَطَ (u; سُقوط) ,وَقَعَ (a; وُقوع); **to ~ 10 metres** سَقَطَ من ارْتِفاعِ 10 أَمْتارٍ; **to ~ out of a drawer/sb's hands** وَقَعَ من دُرْجٍ \ يَدَيْ شَخْصٍ; **to ~ off a table/wall** وَقَعَ من على طاوِلةٍ \ حائِطٍ; **the bag fell on my head** سَقَطَت الحَقيبةُ على رَأْسي; **to ~ on** *or* **to the ground** وَقَعَ على الأَرْضِ; **to ~ in** *or* **into the river** سَقَطَ في النَهْرِ; **to ~ down a hole/the stairs** وَقَعَ في حُفْرةٍ \ على الدَرَجِ **2** (to drop) «speed, volume, quality» انْخَفَضَ; **the price fell by £500/more than 15%** انْخَفَضَ السِعْرُ 500 جُنَيْهٍ \ أَكْثَر من 15٪; **to ~ below zero/5%** انْخَفَضَ تحت الصِفْرِ \ 5٪ **3** (in defeats) «leaders, regimes, towns» سَقَطَ (u; سُقوط); **to ~ from power** سَقَطَ من السُلْطةِ **4** (to die) ماتَ (u; مَوْت) ,قُتِلَ **5** (to close in) «darkness, night, shadow» حَلّ (حُلول) ,خَيَّمَ **6** (to occur) «events, birthdays» صادَفَ \ وافَقَ تاريخاً; **Christmas ~s on a Monday** يُوافِقُ عيدُ الميلادِ المَجيدِ يَوْمَ الاثْنَيْنِ; **to ~ into a category** انْدَرَجَ تحت فِئةٍ **7** (fml) (to be incumbent on) **to ~ to sb to do sth** وَقَعَ على عاتِقِ شَخْصٍ فِعْلُ شَيْءٍ

B *n* **1** (by a person, horse) وُقوع ,سُقوط; (of snow) تَساقُط; **to have** *or* **take a ~** وَقَعَ (a; وُقوع) ,سَقَطَ (u; سُقوط) **2** (decrease) انْخِفاض (انْخِفاضات); **a ~ in value** انْخِفاض في القيمةِ **3** (of a leader, regime, town) سُقوط; **the president's ~ from power** سُقوط الرَئيسِ من السُلْطةِ; **the ~ of the town came within days** سَقَطَت المَدينةُ في غُضونِ أَيّامٍ **4** (**the Fall**) سُقوط الإِنْسانِ **5** (AmE) (season) خَريف; **in the ~ of 2013** في خَريفِ 2013; ▸**summer 6** (in pitch, intonation) انْخِفاض **7** (in wrestling) تَثْبيت (تَثْبيتات)

C **(falls)** *n pl* (waterfall) شَلّالات

(Idiom) **to stand or fall on sth** تَوَقَّفَ على شَيْءٍ; **the evidence stands or ~s on the reliability of the witness** يَتوَقَّفُ الدَّليلُ على مِصْداقيّةِ الشاهِدِ

(Phrasal verbs) **fall about** (BrE infml): **to ~ about laughing** *or* **with laughter** انْفَجَرَ ضاحِكاً \ من الضَحِكِ

• **fall apart** **1** «house» وَقَعَ (a; وُقوع), انْهارَ; «bus» تَحَطَّمَ; «shoes» تمَزَّقَ **2** (infml) «sb's marriage, the country» انْهارَ

• **fall away** **1** (to drop) «ground» انْحَدَرَ **2** (to decline) «demand, support» انْخَفَضَ

• **fall back** (Mil) تَراجَعَ

• **fall back on**: **~ back on [sth]** لَجَأَ إلى [شَيْءٍ] ‹*one's savings, experience*›

• **fall behind** **A** **1** (in schedules) «workers, students» تَأَخَّرَ, تَخَلَّفَ; **to ~ behind with rent** تَأَخَّرَ في دَفْعِ الإيجارِ **2** (in progress) «countries, students» تَخَلَّفَ; **the country is ~ing behind its economic rivals** تَتَخَلَّفُ الدَوْلَةُ عن مُواكَبَةِ مُنافِسيها الاقْتِصاديّينَ **B** **~ behind [sth/sb]** تَأَخَّرَ وراء [شَيْءٍ \ شَخْصٍ] ‹*a competitor*›

• **fall down** **1** «children, runners» سَقَطَ \ وَقَعَ على الأَرْضِ **2** «houses, scaffolding» انْهارَ; «trees» سَقَطَ (u; سُقوط)

• **fall for**: **1** **~ for [sth]** انْطلى عَلَيْهِ [شَيْءٌ] ‹*a trick, story*› **2** **~ for [sb]** وَقَعَ في حُبِّ [شَخْصٍ] ‹*a man, stranger*›

• **fall in** **1** «roof, sides» سَقَطَ (u; سُقوط), تَهاوى **2** (Mil) اصْطَفَّ

• **fall in with**: **~ in with [sth/sb]** **1** (to get involved with) تَوَرَّطَ في [شَيْءٍ] \ مع [شَخْصٍ] ‹*a gang, undesirables*› **2** (to go along with) تَقَبَّلَ [شَيْئاً \ شَخْصاً] ‹*a proposal, sb's plans*›

• **fall off** **1** «rider» سَقَطَ (u; سُقوط) **2** «labels» انْفَصَلَ, انْخَلَعَ; «leaves» سَقَطَ (u; سُقوط) **3** «sales, attendance, interest» تَقَلَّصَ

• **fall on** **A** **~ on [sb]** **1** (to attach to) «suspicion, blame» وَقَعَ على [شَخْصٍ] **2** (to attack) هاجَمَ [شَخْصاً] ‹*a passer-by, victim*› **B** **~ on [sth]** انْقَضَّ على [شَيْءٍ] ‹*the food, treasure*›

• **fall open** «books, robes» انْفَتَحَ

• **fall out** **1** «pages» انْفَصَلَ; «hair» سَقَطَ (u; سُقوط) **2** «soldiers» انْصَرَفَ **3** **to ~ out with [sb]** (to quarrel) تَشاجَرَ مع [شَخْصٍ]

• **fall over** **A** «lamp, children, bottle, chairs» وَقَعَ (a; وُقوع) **B** **~ over [sth/sb]** تَعَثَّرَ ب[شَيْءٍ \ شَخْصٍ] ‹*a toy, the cat*›

• **fall through** «plans, deals» أَخْفَقَ

• **fall upon** ▸**fall on**

fallacy /ˈfaləsi/ *n* (*pl* **fallacies**) مُغالَطة

fallen /ˈfɔːlən/ **A** *past participle* ▸**fall** **B** **(the fallen** *n pl***)** القَتْلى **C** *adj* **1** ‹*leaf, tree*› ساقِط **2** ‹*soldier, comrade*› قَتيل (قَتْلى)

fallible /ˈfalɪb(ə)l/ *adj* ‹*being*› غَيْر مَعْصوم (من الخَطَأ)

falling-off /fɔːlɪŋˈɒf/ *n* (also **falloff**) انْخِفاض, هُبوط (انْخِفاضات)

falling-out /ˌfɔːlɪŋˈaʊt/ *n* خِلاف (خِلافات), شِجار; **to have a ~ with sb** كانَ على خِلافٍ مع شَخْصٍ

fallopian tube /fəˌləʊpɪən ˈtjuːb/ *n* قَناة فالوب

fallout /ˈfɔːlaʊt/ *n* [u] سَقْط

fallow /ˈfaləʊ/ *adj* بور (mf); **to lie ~** ‹*land*› بارَ (u; بَوار, بَوْر); ‹*idea*› [لم تُطَوَّرْ \ تُسْتَخْدَمْ]; **a ~ period** فَتْرة رُكودٍ

false /fɔːls/ *adj* **1** (untrue) ‹*allegation, rumour*› كاذِب, زائِف, غَيْر حَقيقيٍّ; **the rumours proved to be ~** ثَبَتَ أنّ الإشاعاتِ كاذِبةٌ **2** (fraudulent) ‹*banknotes, passport*› مُزَيَّف, مُزَوَّر **3** (mistaken) ‹*impression, idea*› خاطِئ; **a ~ sense of security** إحْساس خاطِئ بالأَمانِ **4** (artificial) ‹*eyelashes, ceiling*› صِناعيّ

false alarm *n* إنْذار كاذِب

false economy *n* تَوْفير وَهْميّ (إجْراءات تَوْفيريّة تُؤَدّي في الواقِعِ إلى زِيادةِ النَفَقاتِ)

falsehood /ˈfɔːlshʊd/ *n* **1** [u] (dishonesty) كِذْب **2** (lie) كِذْب

falsely /ˈfɔːlsli/ *adv* **1** (untruthfully) ‹*to claim, advertise*› كَذِباً **2** (fraudulently) ‹*to accuse, imprison*› زوراً, بُهْتاناً

false pretences /ˌfɔːls prɪˈtɛnsɪz/ (BrE), **false pretenses** (AmE) *n pl* **under ~** تحت ذَرائِعَ \ مَزاعِمَ واهِيةٍ

false start *n* انْطِلاقة خاطِئة

false teeth *n* طَقْم أَسْنانٍ

falsify /ˈfɔːlsɪfʌɪ/ *vt* (**falsifies, falsifying, falsified**) زَوَّرَ ‹*a record, document*›

falsity /ˈfɔːlsɪti/ *n* عَدَم صِحّةٍ, بُطْلان

falter /ˈfɔːltə/ *vi* 1 (when speaking) «voice, speaker» تَلَعْثَمَ, تَلَجْلَجَ 2 (to weaken) «enthusiasm, interest» ضَعُفَ (u; ضَعْف, ضُعْف)

faltering /ˈfɔːltərɪŋ/ *adj* ‹*economy, demand*› مُتَعَثِّر; ‹*voice*› مُتَلَعْثِم

fame /feɪm/ *n* صيت, شُهْرة; **her ~ faded/remains undiminished** تَلاشَتْ \ لم تَتَراجَعْ شُهْرَتُها

famed /feɪmd/ *adj* ‹*place, person*› شَهير, مَشْهور; **a city ~ for its fine architecture** مَدينة مَشْهورة بِفَنِّها المِعْماريِّ الفاخِرِ

familiar /fəˈmɪlɪə/ *adj* ‹*face, name*› مَأْلوف; **the name sounds ~** يَبْدو الاسْمُ مَأْلوفاً; **to be ~ with the Reid family** كانَ يَعْرِفُ عائِلَةَ ريد مَعْرِفَةً جَيِّدةً

familiarity /fəmɪlɪˈarɪti/ *n* 1 (knowledge) (إلْمامات) إلْمام, الإلْمامُ بِلُغَةِ البَرْمَجةِ; **~ with C is essential** (مَعارِف) مَعْرِفة 'سي' أَساسيٌّ 2 (being well-known) أُلْفة; **~ breeds contempt** الأُلْفةُ تُوَلِّدُ الازْدِراءَ

familiarize, -ise (BrE) /fəˈmɪlɪərʌɪz/ **A** *vt* **to ~ a student/the public with sth** أَحاطَ طالِباً \ الجُمْهورَ عِلْماً بِشَيْءٍ

B *v refl* **to ~ yourself with a system/the rules** أَحاطَ عِلْماً \ أَلَمَّ بِنِظامٍ \ بالقَوانينِ

family /ˈfam(ə)li/ *n* (*pl* **families**) (أُسَر) أُسْرة, (عائِلات) عائِلة, (عَوائِل) عائِلة; **the nuclear ~** الأُسْرة النَوَوِيّة; **the Smith ~** عائِلة سْميث; **she has an extensive extended ~** لَدَيْها عائِلةٌ مُمْتَدّةٌ كَبيرةٌ

family name *n* اسْم العائِلةِ

family planning *n* تَنْظيم الأُسْرةِ

family tree *n* شَجَرة عائِلةٍ

family unit *n* وَحْدة الأُسْرةِ (الأُسْرة كَوَحْدةٍ اجْتِماعيّةٍ)

famine /ˈfamɪn/ *n* مَجاعة

famished /ˈfamɪʃt/ *adj* (infml) جائِع جِدًّا ‹*survivors, cattle*›; **I'm ~!** أنا جائِعٌ جِدًّا!

famous /ˈfeɪməs/ *adj* ‹*name, landmark*› مَشْهور; **to be ~ for sth** كانَ مَشْهوراً بِشَيْءٍ

famously /ˈfeɪməsli/ *adv* 1 ‹*to remark*› بِشَكْلٍ مَعْروفٍ 2 (wonderfully) بِشَكْلٍ رائِعٍ \ مُمْتازٍ; **we got on ~** انْسَجَمْنا مع بَعْضِنا البَعْضَ بِشَكْلٍ مُمْتازٍ

fan /fan/ **A** *n* 1 (of a star) مُعْجَب 2 (supporter) مُشَجِّع 3 (mechanical device for cooling) (مَراوِحُ) مِرْوَحة; (hand-held device for cooling) مِرْوَحة يَدٍ

B *vt* (**-nn-**) 1 رَوَّحَ (على) ‹*one's face*› 2 زادَهُ اشْتِعالاً, هَوّى ‹*the flames, resentment*›

Phrasal verb **fan out** «searchers» انْتَشَرَ

fanatic /fəˈnatɪk/ *n* مُتَعَصِّب

fanatical /fəˈnatɪk(ə)l/ *adj* ‹*supporter, follower*› مُتَعَصِّب; ‹*devotion, hatred*› مُفْرِط; **to be ~ about jazz** كانَ مَهْووساً بِموسيقى الجاز

fanaticism /fəˈnatɪsɪz(ə)m/ *n* تَعَصُّب

fan belt *n* سَيْر مِرْوَحةٍ

fanciful /ˈfansɪfʊl/ *adj* ‹*child*› واسِع الخَيالِ; ‹*notion*› وَهْميّ; ‹*decoration, design*› مُبْتَكَر

fan club *n* نادي المُعْجَبينَ

fancy /ˈfansi/ **A** *vt* (*3rd person present sing* **fancies**, *present participle* **fancying**, *past tense, past participle* **fancied**) 1 (infml) (to want) رَغِبَ (a; رَغْبة ,رَغَب) (في), أَحَبَّ ‹*food, a drink*›; **what do you ~ for lunch?** ماذا تُحِبُّ في الغَداءِ؟; **do you ~ going to the cinema?** هل تَرْغَبُ في الذَهابِ إلى السينَما؟; **I don't ~ the idea of sharing a flat** لا أُحِبُّ فِكْرَةَ الاشْتِراكِ في شَقّةٍ 2 (BrE) (infml) (to feel attracted to) **I ~ her** أَميلُ إلَيْها 3 (infml) (expressing surprise) **well, ~ that!** حَسَناً, تَصَوَّرْ هذا!; **~ seeing you here!** تَصَوَّرْ أَنْ أَراكَ هُنا! 4 (Sport) [رَشَّحَ للفَوْزِ] ‹*an athlete, a horse*›

B *v refl* (*3rd person present sing* **fancies**, *present participle* **fancying**, *past tense, past participle* **fancied**) 1 (pej) (to be conceited) **to ~ oneself** اغْتَرَّ بِنَفْسِهِ 2 (infml) (to wrongly imagine) **to ~ oneself as a racing driver/film star** تَخَيَّلَ نَفْسَهُ كَسائِقِ سَيّاراتِ السِباقِ \ كَنَجْمٍ سينَمائيٍّ

C (**fancied**) *past participle, adj* (Sport) ‹*competitor, horse*› [مُرَشَّح للفَوْزِ]

D *adj* (**fancier, fanciest**) 1 (decorative) ‹*design, paper*› مُزَخْرَف 2 (not plain) ‹*food*› غَيْر عاديٍّ, فاخِر 3 (pej) (pretentious) ‹*hotel, address*› فاخِر, مُتْرَف; **they must have paid a ~ price for it** لا بُدَّ أَنَّهُمْ دَفَعوا مَبْلَغاً خُرافيًّا مُقابِلَ هذا

E *n* (*pl* **fancies**) **1** (infml) (liking) **to catch** *or* **take sb's ~** «a car, woman» خَطَفَ قَلْبَ شَخْصٍ **2** (whim) نَزْوة (نَزَوات); **it's just a passing ~** ما هي إلّا نَزْوةٌ عارِضةٌ

fancy dress *n* (BrE) لِباس تَنَكُّرِيّ

fancy dress party *n* (BrE) حَفْلة تَنَكُّرِيّة

fancy goods *n* (BrE) خُرْدة (خُرْدَوات)

fanfare /ˈfanfɛː/ *n* (piece of music) لَحْن بوقيّ \ جَوْقيّ (لَحْن بَهْرَجة; (for publicity) قَصير عند تَقْديم \ إدْخال شَخْصٍ مُهِمٍّ)

fang /faŋ/ *n* (of a dog, wolf, snake) ناب (أَنْياب)

fan heater *n* مِدْفَأة مِرْوَحيّة

fan mail *n* رَسائِل المُعْجَبين

fanny /ˈfani/ *n* (*pl* **fannies**) **1** (BrE vulg) (vagina) مَهْبِل (مَهابِلُ) **2** (AmE infml) (buttocks) مَقْعَدة

fantasize, -ise (BrE) /ˈfantəsʌɪz/ *vi* «teenagers» اسْتَغْرَقَ في أَحْلامِ اليَقَظةِ; **to ~ about sth** اسْتَغْرَقَ في تَخَيُّلِ شَيْءٍ

fantastic /fanˈtastɪk/ *adj* **1** (wonderful) ‹*job, meal*› رائع **2** (unrealistic) ‹*story, idea*› غَيْر واقِعِيٍّ \ مَعْقولٍ **3** (huge) ‹*amount, salary*› ضَخْم

fantasy /ˈfantəsi/ *n* (*pl* **fantasies**) **1** (in psychology) وَهْم (أَوْهام), تَوَهُّم **2** (fiction) قِصّة خَياليّة

fanzine /ˈfanziːn/ *n* مَجَلّة هُواةٍ

FAQ /ɛfeɪˈkjuː/ *n* = **frequently asked questions** \ أَسْئِلة شائِعة مُتَداوَلة \ مُتَكَرِّرة

far /fɑː/ **A** *adv* (*comparative* **further** or **farther**; *superlative* **furthest** or **farthest**) **1** (to, at, from a long distance) بَعيداً, من بَعيد; **~ off, ~ away** بَعيداً; **have you come ~?** هَل جِئْتَ من بَعيدٍ؟; **is it ~ to Milton?** هل المَسافةُ بَعيدةٌ إلى ميلْتون؟; **to be ~ from home** كانَ بَعيداً عن المَنْزِلِ \ الوَطَنِ; **~ beyond the city** بَعيداً خارِجَ حُدودِ المَدينةِ; **how ~ is it to Leeds?** كم تَبْلُغُ المَسافةُ إلى ليدْز؟; **how ~ is New York from Boston?** كم تَبْلُغُ المَسافةُ من بوسْطِن إلى نْيويورْك؟ **2** (a long time) **~ back in the past** منذ زَمَنٍ بَعيدٍ في الماضي; **as ~ back as 1985** منذ زَمَنٍ يَرْجِعُ تاريخُهُ إلى 1985; **the holidays are not ~ off** لَيْسَ وَقْتُ الإجازاتِ بَعيداً; **he's not ~ off 70** سِنُّهُ لَيْس بَعيداً عن ال 70 **3** (as an intensifier) بِكَثيرٍ; **~ better** أَفْضَل كَثيراً; **~ too fast** سَريع جِدًّا; **~ too much money** مال وَفير جِدًّا; **~ more** أَكْثَر بِكَثيرٍ; **~ above the average** أَعْلى بِكَثيرٍ من المُتَوَسِّطِ **4** (to the extent that) **how ~ have they got with their investigation?** إلى أَيْنَ وَصَلوا في تَحْقيقاتِهِمْ؟; **how ~ are you prepared to take this matter?** إلى أَيِّ حَدٍّ أَنْتَ مُسْتَعِدٌّ لِتَوَلّي هذا الأَمْرِ؟; **as** *or* **so ~ as possible** إلى أَقْصى حَدٍّ مُمْكِنٍ; **as** *or* **so ~ as we know** على حَدِّ عِلْمِنا; **to go too ~** تَجاوَزَ الحَدَّ المَقْبولَ; **she took** *or* **carried the joke too ~** تَمادَتْ في المِزاحِ عن الحَدِّ المَقْبولِ

B (**by far**) *adv phr* بِدَرَجةٍ كَبيرةٍ, إلى حَدٍّ بَعيد; **it's by ~ the best, it's the best by ~** هو الأَفْضَلُ بِمَراحِلَ

C (**far and away**) *adv phr* إلى حَدٍّ كَبيرٍ, بِمَراحِلَ

D (**far from**) *prep phr* على النَّقيضِ من; **I am ~ from satisfied** أنا لَسْتُ راضِياً على الإطلاق

E (**so far**) *adv phr* **1** (up till now) حتّى الآنِ; **so ~, so good** حتّى الآنَ, كُلُّ شَيْءٍ على ما يُرامُ **2** (up to a point) إلى حَدٍّ ما; **you can only trust him so ~** يُمْكِنُكَ أَنْ تَثِقَ بِهِ وَلَكِنْ إلى حَدٍّ ما

F *adj* (*comparative* **further** or **farther**; *superlative* **furthest** or **farthest**) **1** (distant) ‹*horizon*› بَعيد (بُعَداءُ); ‹*east, left*› أَقْصى (f قُصْوى); **in the ~ north/south** في أَقْصى الشَّمالِ \ الجَنوبِ; **in the ~ distance** من مَسافةٍ بَعيدةٍ **2** (more distant, other) ‹*corner, end*› أَبْعَد (أَباعِدُ) (dipt), أَقْصى (f قُصْوى); **at the ~ end of the room** في الطَّرَفِ الأَقْصى لِلحُجْرةِ; **on the ~ side of the road** في الجانِبِ الأَقْصى لِلطَّريقِ **3** (Pol) **the ~ right/left** أَقْصى اليَمينِ \ الشِّمالِ

Idioms **far and wide** في كُلِّ مَكانٍ, في كُلِّ حَدَبٍ وَصَوْبٍ; **to go far** حَقَّقَ نَجاحاً كَبيراً

faraway /ˈfɑːrəweɪ, fɑːrəˈweɪ/ *adj* ‹*place, land*› قَصِيّ, بَعيد; ‹*look*› شارِد, هائِم

farce /fɑːs/ *n* مَسْرَحيّة هَزْلِيّة

farcical /ˈfɑːsɪk(ə)l/ *adj* ‹*situation, comedy, idea*› مُضْحِك, هَزْلِيّ

fare /fɛː/ **A** *n* **1** (on a bus, train) أُجْرة رُكوبٍ; (on a plane) سِعْر التَّذْكِرة; **train ~s are going up** أُجْرةُ رُكوبِ القِطارِ في تَصاعُدٍ **2** [u] (food) [مَجْموعة من الأَطْعِمة]

B *vi* **to ~ well** أَبْلى بَلاءً حَسَناً; **to ~ badly** أَخْفَقَ; **the team ~d well/poorly in the championship** لَعِبَ \ لم يَلْعَب الفَريقُ بِشَكْلٍ جَيِّدٍ في البُطولةِ

Far East *pr n* **(the Far East)** الشَّرْق الأَقْصى

farewell /fɛːˈwɛl/ **A** *excl* (liter) وَداعاً

B *n* وَداع

far-fetched /ˌfɑːˈfɛtʃt/ *adj* ‹*idea, story*› بَعيد الاحْتِمالِ

farm /fɑːm/ **A** *n* مَزْرَعة (مَزارِعُ)

B *vt* زَرَعَ (a; زَرْع) ‹*land*›

C *vi* قامَ بِأَعْمالٍ زِراعيّةٍ

(Phrasal verb) **farm out** **A** **~ out [sth]** عَهِدَ ب [شَيْءٍ] ‹*work*› **B** **~ [sb] out** [عَهِدَ بِضيافةِ [شَخْصٍ] ‹*guest*›

farmer /ˈfɑːmə/ *n* مُزارِع

farmers' market *n* سوق المُزارِعين

farmhand, **farmworker** *n* فَلّاح أَجير, عامِل زِراعيّ

farmhouse /ˈfɑːmhaʊs/ *n* بَيْت مُزارِعٍ

farming /ˈfɑːmɪŋ/ *n* زِراعة; **sheep/dairy ~** تَرْبِية الأَغْنامِ \ صِناعة الأَلْبانِ

farmland /ˈfɑːmland/ *n* أَرْض زِراعيّة

farmyard /ˈfɑːmjɑːd/ *n* فِناء \ حَوْش مَزْرَعةٍ

far-off /ˌfɑːˈrɒf/ *adj* **1** ‹*land, place*› ناءٍ, بَعيد **2** ‹*days*› خالٍ; ‹*future*› بَعيد

far-reaching /ˌfɑːˈriːtʃɪŋ/ *adj* ‹*implications, consequences*› بَعيد المَدى

Farsi /ˈfɑːsiː/ *n* (اللُغة) الفارِسيّة

far-sighted /ˌfɑːˈsʌɪtɪd/ *adj* **1** (showing foresight) ‹*decision, view*› يَنِمُّ عن بُعْدِ نَظَرٍ; ‹*leader*› بَعيد النَظَرِ **2** (AmE) (long-sighted) طَويل النَظَرِ

fart /fɑːt/ (vulg) **A** *vi* ضَرَطَ (i; ضَرْط, ضُراط), فَسا (u; فَسْو, فُساء)

B *n* **1** (wind) ضُراط, فُساء **2** (a stupid person) أَحْمَق (dipt; f حَمْقى; حُمْق)

(Phrasal verb) **fart about**, **fart around** (vulg) ضَيَّعَ \ أَهْدَرَ الوَقْتَ

farther /ˈfɑːðə/ **A** *adv* (*comparative of* ▸**far**) ▸**further** A

B *adj* (*comparative* ▸**far**) ▸**further** C

farthest /ˈfɑːðɪst/ **A** *adj* (*superlative of* ▸**far**) ▸**furthest** A

B *adv* (*superlative* ▸**far**) ▸**furthest** B

fascinate /ˈfasɪneɪt/ *vt* فَتَنَ (i; فُتون, فَتْن), سَحَرَ (a; سِحْر) ‹*children, readers*›

fascinated /ˈfasɪneɪtɪd/ *adj* ‹*viewer, children*› مَفْتون; **she was ~ by the supernatural** كانَتْ مَفْتونةً بالقُوى الخارِقةِ للطَبيعةِ

fascinating /ˈfasɪneɪtɪŋ/ *adj* ‹*story, insight*› مُثير, مُشَوِّق للاهْتِمامِ

fascination /ˌfasɪˈneɪʃ(ə)n/ *n* وَلَع, افْتِتان

fascism /ˈfaʃɪz(ə)m/ *n* فاشيّة

fascist /ˈfaʃɪst/ *n, adj* فاشِسْتيّ, فاشيّ

fashion /ˈfaʃ(ə)n/ **A** *n* **1** موضة; **to be in ~** كانَ على الموضةِ; **to go out of ~** لم يَعُدْ على الموضةِ **2** (manner) مِنْوال; **in a similar ~** على نَفْسِ المِنْوالِ; **after a ~** إلى حَدٍّ ما

B *vt* شَكَّلَ ‹*wood, clay*›; صاغَ (u; صَوْغ, صِياغة) ‹*an artwork, a sculpture*›

fashionable /ˈfaʃ(ə)nəb(ə)l/ *adj* ‹*clothing, style, person*› يُسايِرُ الموضةَ; ‹*restaurant, area*› ذو شَعْبيّة

fashionably /ˈfaʃnəbli/ *adv* ‹*dressed, long*› بِشَكْلٍ مُسايِرٍ للموضةِ

fashion designer *n* مُصَمِّم أَزْياءٍ

fashion show *n* عَرْض أَزْياءٍ

fast /fɑːst/ **A** *n* صَوْم; **to go on a ~** صامَ (u; صَوْم); **to break one's ~** أَفْطَرَ

B *adj* **(faster, fastest)** **1** (rapid, speedy) ‹*car, train, lane*› سَريع (سِراع); **to be a ~ reader/worker** كانَ قارِئاً \ عامِلاً سَريعاً **2** (ahead of time) ‹*watch, clock*› مُتَقَدِّم; **you're five minutes ~** ساعَتُكَ مُتَقَدِّمةٌ بِخَمْسِ دَقائِقَ **3** (permanent) ‹*colour, dye*› ثابِت **4** (secure) **to make the hatch/door ~** جَعَلَ الفُتْحةَ مُغْلَقةً \ البابَ مُغْلَقاً بِإِحْكامٍ

C *adv* **1** (quickly) ‹*to walk, speak*› بِسُرْعةٍ **2** (firmly) ‹*to hold, to be stuck*› بِشِدّةٍ; ‹*to be shut*› بِإِحْكامٍ; **to be ~ asleep** غَرِقَ في النَوْمِ

D *vi* صامَ (u; صَوْم); **to ~ from dawn to dusk** صامَ من الفَجْرِ إلى المَغْرِبِ

(Idiom) **to play fast and loose with sth/sb** تَلاعَبَ \ عَبِثَ بِشَيْءٍ \ بِشَخْصٍ

fasten /ˈfɑːs(ə)n/ **A** *vt* **1** (to do up) شَدَّ (i-u; شَدّ) ‹*a seat belt, buttons*›; (to close) أَغْلَقَ ‹*a lid, door*› **2** (to attach) ثَبَّتَ ‹*a rope, chain*›; **the chairs were ~ed to the floor** كانَتْ الكَراسيُّ مُثَبَّتةً

على الأَرْضِ; **I ~ed the rope around my waist** شَدَدْتُ الحَبْلَ حول خَصْري

B *vi* «door, necklace» انْغَلَقَ

fastener /ˈfɑːsnə/ *n* **1** (for garments) سَحّاب **2** (for machinery, furniture) مِشْبَك (مَشابِكُ), قُفْل (أَقْفال, قُفول)

fast food *n* وَجْبة سَريعة

fast food restaurant *n* مَطْعَم للوَجَباتِ السَريعةِ

fast forward **A** *n* (also **fast forward button**) زِرّ التَقْديمِ السَريعِ

B (**fast-forward**) *vt* ‹*a tape, cassette*› قَدَّمَ بِسُرْعةٍ

C *vi* قَدَّمَ بِسُرْعةٍ

fast-growing /ˌfɑːstˈgrəʊɪŋ/ *adj* ‹*company, economy*› سَريع النُموِّ

fastidious /faˈstɪdɪəs/ *adj* **1** (extremely careful) ‹*attention*› دَقيق جِدًّا **2** (easily disgusted) ‹*eater*› صَعْب الإِرْضاءِ; ‹*homeowner*› [شَديد الاهْتِمامِ بالنَظافةِ]

fast lane *n* الحارة السَريعة (على الطَريقِ)

fast track **A** *n* مَسار سَريع

B (**fast-track**) *vt* سَرَّعَ ‹*an application, legislation*›

fat /fat/ **A** *n* **1** [u] (in the body) دُهْن (دُهون); **body ~** دُهون الجِسْمِ **2** (in one's diet) دُهْن (دُهون), دَسَم **3** [u] (on meat) شَحْم (شُحوم), دُهْن (دُهون) **4** (used for cooking) سَمْن (سُمون), دُهْن (دُهون)

B *adj* (**-tt-**) **1** (overweight) ‹*boxer, child*› بَدين (بُدُن, بُدْن), سَمين (سِمان); ‹*cheek, arm*› مُمْتَلِئ; **to get ~** سَمِنَ (a; سِمَن, سَمانة), بَدُنَ (u; بَدانة) **2** (full) ‹*wallet, envelope*› مُمْتَلِئ; (large) ‹*book*› ضَخْم **3** (infml) (large) ‹*profit, fee*› كَبير; **to make a ~ profit** حَقَّقَ رِبْحاً كَبيراً **4** (infml) (very little) **that's a ~ lot of good!** هذا لا فائِدةَ مِنْهُ!; **a ~ lot you know about it!** أَنْتَ لا تَعْلَمُ عَنْهُ شَيْئاً!

Fatah /ˈfatə/ *n* حَرَكة فَتْح

fatal /ˈfeɪt(ə)l/ *adj* **1** ‹*accident, disease*› قاتِل, مُميت **2** ‹*flaw, mistake*› مُهْلِك

fatalist /ˈfeɪtəlɪst/ *n* جَبْرِيّ

fatalistic /feɪtəˈlɪstɪk/ *adj* ‹*attitude, outlook*› قَدَرِيّ

fatality /fəˈtalɪti/ *n* (*pl* **fatalities**) وَفاة (وَفَيات)

fatally /ˈfeɪt(ə)li/ *adv* **1** ‹*wounded, ill*› على نَحْوٍ مُهْلِكٍ **2** ‹*flawed*› بِشَكْلٍ فادِحٍ

fate /feɪt/ *n* **1** [u] (destiny) قَدَر **2** (end, outcome) مَصير (مَصايِرُ)

fated /ˈfeɪtɪd/ *adj* **1** (destined) مَحْتوم, مَكْتوب, مُقَدَّر; **we were ~ to meet** كانَ مُقَدَّراً لَنا أَنْ نَلْتَقِيَ **2** (doomed) ‹*flight, love*› مَشْؤوم

fateful /ˈfeɪtfʊl/ *adj* ‹*day, decision*› مَشْؤوم

fat-free /fatˈfriː/ *adj* ‹*foods, diet*› خالٍ من الدُهونِ

father /ˈfɑːðə/ **A** *n* أَب (آباء), والِد; **Einstein, the ~ of the theory of relativity** آينِشْتاين، أَبو النَظَرِيّةِ النِسْبِيّةِ

B *vt* كانَ الأَبَ في ‹*a child*›; كانَ الوالِدَ ‹*a family*›

Father Christmas *n* بابا نُويل

fatherhood /ˈfɑːðəhʊd/ *n* أُبوّة

father-in-law /ˈfɑːðərɪnlɔː/ *n* (*pl* **fathers-in-law**) حَم

fatherland /ˈfɑːðəland/ *n* وَطَن (أَوْطان)

fatherly /ˈfɑːðəli/ *adj* ‹*advice, affection*› أَبَوِيّ

Father's Day *n* عيد الأَبِ

fathom /ˈfaðəm/ **A** *n* 6 قامة (وَحْدة قِياسِ عُمْقِ المِياهِ تُعادِلُ أَقْدام)

B *vt* (also **fathom out** BrE) سَبَرَ الغَوْرَ ‹*a mystery*›; فَهِمَ (a; فَهْم) ‹*meaning*›

fatigue /fəˈtiːg/ *n* **1** إِعْياء, تَعَب **2** (**fatigues** *n pl*) (AmE) زِيّ عَسْكَرِيّ

Fatiha /ˈfɑːtɪə/ *n* الفاتِحة

Fatimid /ˈfatɪmɪd/ *n* فاطِمِيّ

fatten /ˈfat(ə)n/ *vt* (also **fatten up**) سَمَّنَ ‹*pigs, cattle*›

fattening /ˈfat(ə)nɪŋ/ *adj* ‹*food, meal*› مُسَمِّن

fatty /ˈfati/ *adj* (**fattier**, **fattiest**) ‹*food, fish*› دَسِم; ‹*tissue, deposit*› دُهْنِيّ

fatuous /ˈfatjʊəs/ *adj* (fml) ‹*remark, claim*› سَخيف, تافِه

fatwa /ˈfatwɑː/ *n* فَتْوى (f; فَتاوٍ, فَتاوى)

faucet /ˈfɔːsɪt/ *n* (AmE) حَنَفِيّة, صُنْبور (صَنابيرُ); **to turn the ~ on/off** فَتَحَ \ أَغْلَقَ الحَنَفِيّةَ

fault /fɔːlt/ **A** *n* **1** (cause of a problem) عَيْب (عُيوب), خَلَل (خِلال); **a structural/design ~** عَيْب بِنائِيّ \ في التَصْميمِ;

to find ~ with sb/sth عابَ \ انْتَقَدَ شَخْصاً \ شَيْئاً 2 (in sb's character) عَيْب (عُيوب), نَقيصة (نَقائِص) 3 [u] (responsibility) خَطَأ, ذَنْب; whose ~ is it? خَطأُ مَنْ هذا؟; it's my/your ~ that we lost هذا خَطَئي \ خَطَؤُكَ أَنَّنا خَسِرْنا; it's your own ~ خَطَؤُكَ أَنْتَ; to be at ~ كانَ مُخْطِئاً 4 (in tennis) خَطأ (أَخْطاء) 5 (Geol) صَدْع (صُدوع); the San Andreas ~ صَدْع سان أَنْدرْياس

B vt عابَ (i; عَيْب), انْتَقَدَ ‹an argument, a performance›; you can't ~ her logic لا يُمْكِنُكَ أَنْ تَجِدَ خَطَأً في مَنْطِقِها

faultless /ˈfɔːltləs/ adj ‹performance, logic› لا غُبارَ عَلَيْه, خالٍ من العُيوبِ

faulty /ˈfɔːlti/ adj (faultier, faultiest) ‹equipment, goods› مَعيب; ‹memory, logic› ناقِص

fauna /ˈfɔːnə/ n (pl faunas or faunae) حَيَوانات (في مِنْطَقةٍ \ حِقْبةٍ)

faux pas /fəʊ ˈpɑː/ n (pl faux pas) زَلّة, هَفْوة (هَفَوات)

favour (BrE), **favor** (AmE) /ˈfeɪvə/ **A** n 1 (kindness) فَضْل (أَفْضال, فُضول), مَعْروف, جَميل; to do sb a ~ صَنَعَ مَعْروفاً لِشَخْصٍ; I did it as a ~ فَعَلْتُ هذا كَخِدْمةٍ; to ask a ~ of sb طَلَبَ خِدْمةً من شَخْصٍ; to owe sb a ~ دانَ لِشَخْصٍ بِمَعْروفٍ; to return the ~ رَدَّ الجَميلَ; to call in a ~ طَلَبَ رَدَّ الجَميلِ 2 [u] to look on or regard sb/sth with ~ (approval) نَظَرَ إلى شَخْصٍ \ شَيْءٍ بِاسْتِحْسانٍ; to win/lose ~ with sb حَظِيَ بِاسْتِحْسانِ شَخْصٍ \ لم يَعُدْ يَلْقى قُبولاً من شَخْصٍ; to find ~ with sb لَقِيَ اسْتِحْساناً من شَخْصٍ; to be out of ~ with sb لم يَحْظَ بِاسْتِحْسانِ شَخْصٍ; to fall or go out of ~ لم يَعُدْ يَلْقى الاسْتِحْسانَ 3 [u] (advantage) to be in sb's ~ «winds, circumstances» كانَ في صالِحِ شَخْصٍ; the wind is in our ~ الرِيحُ في صالِحِنا; the plan has a lot in its ~ في الخُطّةِ الكَثيرُ من الميزاتِ; in his ~, he has a very good degree أَحَدُ النِقاطِ في صالِحِهِ أَنَّهُ حاصِلٌ على دَرَجةٍ عِلْميّةٍ جَيِّدةٍ جِدّاً

B (in favour of) prep phr 1 (on the side of) مُؤَيِّد لـ; to be in ~ of sb/sth كانَ مُؤَيِّداً لِشَخْصٍ \ لِشَيْءٍ; to speak in ~ of a candidate/an idea تَحَدَّثَ مُؤَيِّداً لِمُرَشَّحٍ \ لِفِكْرةٍ 2 (to the advantage of) to work/decide in ~ of sb كانَ لَهُ أَثَرٌ \ أَصْدَرَ قَراراً لِصالِحِ شَخْصٍ

C vt 1 (to prefer) آثَرَ, فَضَّلَ (imperf يُؤْثِرُ) ‹a policy, solution, candidate›; which of the two alternatives do you ~? أَيَّ الخِيارَيْنِ تُفَضِّلُ؟ 2 (to benefit) «plan, circumstances» أَفادَ ‹a party, small businesses›

D (favoured) adj 1 (preferred) ‹destination, tactic› مُفَضَّل 2 (most likely) ‹date› مُرَجَّح

favourable (BrE), **favorable** (AmE) /ˈfeɪv(ə)rəb(ə)l/ adj ‹conditions› مُواتٍ; ‹weather› مُناسِب; ‹impression, reaction› جَيِّد; ‹report, result, sign› إيجابيّ; to get a ~ reception اُسْتُقْبِلَ اسْتِقْبالاً جَيِّداً \ طَيِّباً

favourably (BrE), **favorably** (AmE) /ˈfeɪv(ə)rəbli/ adv ‹to speak, write› بِاسْتِحْسانٍ; ‹to look on, consider› بِعَيْنِ الرِضا; to compare ~ with sth كانَتِ المُقارَنةُ بِشَيْءٍ لِصالِحِهِ

favourite (BrE), **favorite** (AmE) /ˈfeɪvərɪt/ **A** adj ‹band, sport, food› مُفَضَّل, مَحْبوب

B n 1 (preferred book, band, child, etc) مُفَضَّل (شَيْء); to be a great ~ with sb كانَ الشَيْءَ \ الشَخْصَ المُفَضَّلَ جِدًّا عند شَخْصٍ 2 (in sports) مُفَضَّل (شَيْء \ شَخْص)

C (favorites) n pl (Comput) مُفَضَّلات

favouritism (BrE), **favoritism** (AmE) /ˈfeɪvərɪtɪz(ə)m/ n مُحاباة

fawn /fɔːn/ **A** n 1 خُشْف 2 بُنّيّ فاتِح

B adj بُنّيّ فاتِح

C vi to ~ on or over sb تَمَلَّقَ شَخْصاً, تَزَلَّفَ إلى شَخْصٍ

fax /faks/ **A** n فاكْس

B vt ‹a document, letter› أَرْسَلَ بالفاكْس

fax machine n جِهاز فاكْس

faze /feɪz/ vt (infml) «prospect, criticism» أَرْبَكَ

FBI /ɛfbiːˈʌɪ/ n (AmE) = Federal Bureau of Investigation; the ~ مَكْتَب التَحْقيقاتِ الفيدراليّ

FDA /ɛfdiːˈeɪ/ n (AmE) = Food and Drug Administration; the ~ إدارة الأَغْذِيةِ والعَقاقيرِ

FE /ɛfˈiː/ n (BrE) = further education التَعْليم المُسْتَمِرّ \ المُتَواصِل

fear /fɪə/ **A** n 1 [u] (fright) خَوْف, خَشْية; he did it out of ~ فَعَلَهُ بِدافِعِ الخَوْفِ; to live in ~ of one's life كانَ يَعيشُ خائِفاً على حَياتِهِ 2 (apprehension) خَوْف; my ~s for his

safety proved groundless ثَبَتَ أَنَّ خَوْفي على سَلامَتِهِ لم يَكُنْ لَهُ أَساسٌ; **the operation holds no ~s for her** لا تَنْطَوي العَمَليَّةُ على أَيِّ مَخاوِفَ بالنِسْبَةِ لَها **3** (possibility) احْتِمال (احْتِمالات); **there's no ~ of him being late** لَيْسَ هُناكَ احْتِمالٌ أنْ يَتأَخَّرَ; **I left quietly for ~ of waking them** غادَرْتُ بِهُدوءٍ خَشْيَةَ أنْ أوقِظَهُمْ

B *vt* (to be afraid of) خافَ (a; خَوْف, مَخافة, خيفة; من), خَشِيَ (a; خَشْية) ‹*death, an illness, a criminal*›; **a ruler who was greatly ~ed** حاكِم كانَ الناسُ يَخافونَ مِنْهُ بِشِدّةٍ; **a woman to be ~ed** امْرَأة يَنْبَغي الخَوْفُ مِنْها; **I ~ that she may be dead** أَخْشى أَنَّها رُبَّما تَكونُ قد ماتَتْ; **it is ~ed that the storm may get worse** ما يُخْشى مِنْهُ هو أنْ تَزْدادَ العاصِفةُ سوءاً; **to ~ the worst** خَشِيَ وُقوعَ أَسْوَأِ التَقْديراتِ; **20 people are ~ed to have died** *or* **are ~ed dead in the accident** يُخْشى أنّ 20 شَخْصاً قد ماتوا في الحادِثِ

C *vi* **to ~ for sth/sb** خَشِيَ على شَيْءٍ \ شَخْصٍ; **I ~ for her safety/for her** أَخْشى على سَلامَتِها \ عَلَيْها

fearful /ˈfɪəfʊl/ *adj* **1** (afraid) ‹*expression*› خائِف **2** (dreadful) ‹*noise, sight*› مُرْعِب; ‹*rage, heat*› رَهيب

fearless /ˈfɪələs/ *adj* ‹*leader, warrior*› جَسور (جُسُر), مِقْدام (مَقاديمُ)

fearsome /ˈfɪəs(ə)m/ *adj* **1** (frightening) ‹*monster, claws*› مُرْعِب, مُخيف **2** (frightful) ‹*task*› مُزْعِج **3** (formidable) ‹*reputation, intellect*› هائِل

feasibility /fiːzɪˈbɪlɪti/ *n* قابِليّة التَنْفيذ; **the economic ~ of the project** الجَدْوى الاقْتِصاديّة للمَشْروع

feasible /ˈfiːzɪb(ə)l/ *adj* **1** (practicable) ‹*option, solution*› قابِل للتَنْفيذ, عَمَليّ **2** (believable) ‹*explanation, excuse*› مَعْقول

feast /fiːst/ **A** *n* **1** (meal) وَليمة (وَلائِمُ), مَأْدُبة (مَآدِبُ) **2** (religious) عيد (أَعْياد)

B *vi* «guests» تَناوَلَ مَطايِبَ الطَعامِ والشَرابِ

feat /fiːt/ *n* مَأْثُرة (مَآثِرُ)

feather /ˈfɛðə/ *n* ريشة

feather duster *n* مِنْفَضة ريشٍ

feature /ˈfiːtʃə/ **A** *n* **1** (characteristic, aspect) سِمة **2** (of the face) مَلْمَح (مَلامِحُ) **3** (additional element) ميزة **4** (report in a newspaper) مَقال; (on TV, radio) بَرْنامَج (بَرامِجُ) **5** (film) فيلْم طَويل

B *vt* **1** (to present) أَبْرَزَ ‹*work, images*› **2** (Cin, Theat) أَظْهَرَ ‹*an actor, a performer*› كَضَيْفِ شَرَفٍ; **featuring Annette Bening as Sarah Turner** مُظْهِراً أَنيت بِنينغ كَضَيْفةِ شَرَفٍ في دَوْرِ سارة تُرْنِر

C *vi* «dish, name» ظَهَرَ (a; ظُهور); **fish ~s prominently on the menu** يَظْهَرُ السَمَكُ بِصورةٍ بارِزةٍ في قائِمةِ الطَعامِ

feature film *n* فيلْم طَويل

February /ˈfɛbrʊəri/ *n* فِبْراير (Mor, Egypt, Gulf), شُباط (dipt; Levant, Iraq), فيفْريّ (Algeria, Tunisia) ▸ **March**

feces (AmE) *n pl* ▸ **faeces**

fed /fɛd/ *past tense, past participle* ▸ **feed**

federal /ˈfɛd(ə)rəl/ *adj* ‹*government, court*› اتِّحاديّ, فيدِراليّ

Federal Republic of Germany *pr n* (**the Federal Republic of Germany**) جُمْهوريّة أَلْمانيا الاتِّحاديّة

Federal Reserve Board *n* (AmE) مَجْلِس الاحْتياطيّ الاتِّحاديّ

federation /fɛdəˈreɪʃ(ə)n/ *n* اتِّحاد (اتِّحادات)

fed up *adj* (infml) مُتَضايِق, مُنْزَعِج; **to be fed up with sth/sb** ضاقَ ذَرْعاً بِشَيْءٍ \ بِشخصٍ

fee /fiː/ *n* **1** (for a service) أَجْر (أُجور) **2** (for admission, membership) رَسْم (رُسوم, أَرْسُم)

feeble /ˈfiːb(ə)l/ *adj* (**feebler, feeblest**) **1** (weak) واهِن (وُهُن), ضَعيف (ضِعاف, ضُعَفاءُ) **2** (unconvincing) ‹*attempt, excuse*› واهٍ; ‹*joke*› بائِخ

feed /fiːd/ **A** *vt* (*past tense, past participle* **fed**) **1** (to give food to) أَطْعَمَ, غَذّى ‹*an animal, a family, plant*›; **to ~ a baby** (on the breast) أَرْضَعَ طِفْلاً; (with a bottle) أَعْطى طِفْلاً رَضْعةً (صِناعيّةً); **we had ten people to ~** كانَ عَلَيْنا إِطْعامُ عَشَرةِ أَشْخاصٍ **2** (to provide material to) غَذّى ‹*a lake, river*›; **to ~ information/secrets to sb, to ~ sb with information/secrets** أَمَدَّ شَخْصاً بِمَعْلوماتٍ \ بِأَسْرارٍ **3** (to fuel) شَجَّعَ ‹*sb's ambition, prejudice, desire*› **4** (to pass) مَرَّرَ ‹*the ball*› **5** لَقَّنَ ‹*a comedian*›

B *vi* (*past tense, past participle* **fed**) (to eat) «people, babies, animals» أَكَل (u; أَكْل), تَغَذَّى; **to ~ on sth** أَكَل شَيْئاً

C *v refl* (*past tense, past participle* **fed**) **to ~ oneself** «children, invalids» تناوَلَ الطَّعامَ بِنَفْسِهِ

D *n* (BrE) **1** (meal for an animal) وَجْبة (وَجَبات); (for a baby) بَتّ **2** [u] (Agric) عَلَف (أَعْلاف) **3** (in broadcasting) رَضْعة **4** (data stream) تَغْذِية, موجَز **5** (mechanism) مُغَذٍّ

(Phrasal verb) **feed up** (BrE): ~ **[sth/sb] up** غَذّى [شَيْئاً \ شَخصاً] *<a child, an invalid>* تَغْذِية جَيِّدةً

feedback /ˈfiːdbak/ *n* تَغْذِية راجِعة \ اسْتِرْجاعيّة

feeder /ˈfiːdə/ *n* **1** (for birds, animals) مِعْلَف (مَعالِفُ) **2** (also **feeder road**) طَريق فَرْعِيّ **3** (BrE) (also **feeder bib**) مَرْيَلة **4** (BrE) (also **feeder bottle**) زُجاجة رَضاعةٍ, طِفْلٍ صَدْرِيّة **5** (for a printer, photocopier) مُغَذٍّ, مُلَقِّم

feeding bottle /ˈfiːdɪŋ ˌbɒt(ə)l/ *n* زُجاجة رَضاعةٍ

feel /fiːl/ **A** *vt* (*past tense, past participle* **felt**) **1** (to experience) شَعَرَ (u; شُعور; بـ) *<affection, pride, a desire>*; **she felt a sense of isolation** شَعَرَتْ بالعُزْلةِ; **I no longer ~ anything for her** لم أَعُدْ أَشْعُرُ تُجاهَها بِأَيِّ شَيْءٍ; **he's ~ing the effects of the journey** بَدَأَ يَشْعُرُ بآثارِ الرِحْلةِ; **the consequences will be felt for years** سَيَسْتَمِرُّ أَثَرُ التَبِعاتِ لِسِنينَ; **to ~ sb's loss very deeply** تَأَثَّر بِفِراقِ شَخْصٍ تَأَثُّراً بالِغاً **2** (to think) **I ~ that I should warn you** أَشْعُرُ أَنَّهُ يَنْبَغي عَلَيَّ أَنْ أُحَذِّرَكَ; **I ~ he's hiding something** أَشْعُرُ أَنَّهُ يُخْفي شَيْئاً **3** (physically) شَعَرَ (u; شُعور; بـ), أَحَسَّ (بـ) *<the pressure, pain>*; **she doesn't ~ the cold** لا تَشْعُرُ بالبَرْدِ; **I felt a knife against my throat/an arm around my shoulder** شَعَرْتُ بِسِكّينٍ على عُنُقي \ بِذِراعٍ حول كَتِفي **4** (to touch) لَمَسَ (i-u; لَمْس), تَلَمَّسَ, تَحَسَّسَ *<the texture, thickness, a carving>*; **~ how cold/soft it is** الْمِسْهُ لِتَتَعرَّفَ كم هو بارِدٌ \ ناعِمٌ; **to ~ the weight of the parcel** تَحَسَّسَ ثِقَلَ الطَرْدِ; **to ~ one's breasts for lumps** تَحَسَّسَتْ ثَدْيَيْها بَحْثاً عن كُتَلٍ; **to ~ one's way** تَحَسَّسَ طَريقَهُ **5** (to be aware of) شَعَرَ (u; شُعور; بـ), أَدْرَكَ *<the tension, importance, sb's presence>*; **I could ~ her frustration** شَعَرْتُ بِإِحْباطِها

B *vi* (*past tense, past participle* **felt**) **1** (emotionally) شَعَرَ (u; شُعور), أَحَسَّ; **to ~ afraid** شَعَرَ بالخَوْفِ; **she felt as if** *or* **as though she had been tricked** أَحَسَّتْ كَأَنَّها قد خُدِعَتْ; **how do you ~?** بِماذا تَشْعُرُ؟; **how do you ~ about marriage?** ما رَأْيُكَ في الزَواجِ؟; **how does it ~** *or* **what does it ~ like to be a dad?** كيف يَكونُ شُعورُ الشَخْصِ عِنْدَما يُصْبِحُ أَباً؟; **2** (physically) شَعَرَ (u; شُعور), أَحَسَّ; **to ~ hot/tired** شَعَرَ بارْتِفاعِ دَرَجةِ الحَرارةِ \ بالإِرْهاقِ; **to ~ hungry/thirsty** شَعَرَ بالجوعِ \ بالعَطَشِ; **to ~ sick** شَعَرَ بالمَرَضِ; **it felt as if I was floating** شَعَرْتُ كَأَنَّني أَطْفو; **she isn't ~ing herself today** تَشْعُرُ اليَوْمَ أَنَّها لَيْسَتْ على ما يُرامُ **3** (with sensations) **to ~ warm/soft/smooth** «stones, surfaces, sb's skin» كانَ مَلْمَسُهُ دافِئاً \ لَيِّناً \ ناعِماً; **her skin felt soft** كانَ جِلْدُها ناعِماً; **it ~s like leather** يَبْدو مَلْمَسُهُ يَبْدو كالجِلْدِ; **the house ~s empty** البَيْتُ فارِغاً يَبْدو; **it ~s strange living alone** تَشْعُرُ بِإِحْساسٍ غَريبٍ عِنْدَما تَعيشُ وَحْدَكَ; **something doesn't ~ right** هُناكَ شَيْءٌ لا يَبْدو سَليماً; **the bone ~s as if it's broken** يَبْدو العَظْمُ كَأَنَّهُ مَكْسورٌ **4** (to want) **to ~ like sth/like doing sth** شَعَرَ بالرَغْبةِ في شَيْءٍ \ فِعْلِ شَيْءٍ; **do you ~ like a drink?** هل تَشْعُرُ بالرَغْبةِ في شَرابٍ؟; **I don't ~ like it** لا أَشْعُرُ بالرَغْبةِ فيهِ; **I felt like crying** أَحْسَسْتُ بالرَغْبةِ في البُكاءِ **5** (to grope) **to ~ in one's bag/a drawer** تَحَسَّسَ بِيَدَيْهِ في حَقيبَتِهِ \ دُرْجٍ; **to ~ along the edge/wall** تَحَسَّسَ طَريقَهُ بِجِوارِ الحافّةِ \ الحائطِ

C *v refl* (*past tense, past participle* **felt**) **to ~ oneself doing sth** شَعَرَ بِنَفْسِهِ يَفْعَلُ شَيْئاً; **she felt herself losing her temper** شَعَرَتْ بِنَفْسِها تَفْقِدُ أَعْصابَها

D *n* **1** (atmosphere) جَوّ (أَجْواء); **it has the ~ of a country village** فيهِ جَوُّ الريفِ; **there was a relaxed ~ about the place** كانَ المَكانُ بِهِ جَوٌّ يَبْعَثُ على الاسْتِرْخاءِ **2** (sensation to the touch) مَلْمَس (مَلامِسُ); **to have an oily/silky ~** كانَ مَلْمَسُهُ دُهْنِيًّا \ حَريرِيًّا; **I like the ~ of leather** أُحِبُّ مَلْمَسَ الجِلْدِ **3** (understanding) **to get the ~ of the controls/the system** تَعَرَّفَ على أَزْرارِ التَحَكُّمِ \ النِظامِ; **to get the ~ of doing sth** تَعَرَّفَ على كَيْفيّةِ عَمَلِ شَيْءٍ **4** (flair) مَوْهِبة (مَواهِبُ); **to have a ~ for languages** لَدَيْهِ مَوْهِبةٌ في تَعَلُّمِ اللُغاتِ

(Phrasal verbs) **feel around, feel about** تَحَسَّسَ; **I started to ~ around in my bag/the drawer** بَدَأْتُ أَتَحَسَّسُ بِيَدَيَّ في

تَحَسَّسْتُ بِيَدَيْها حَقيبَتي \ الدُرْجَ; **she felt around for her keys** بَحْثاً عن مَفاتيحِها

• **feel for**: 1 ~ **for** [sth] تَحَسَّسَ بِيَدَيْهِ بَحْثاً عن [شَيْءٍ] 2 ~ **for** [sb] تَعاطَفَ مع [شَخْصٍ]

• **feel out**: ~ **out** [sb], ~ [sb] **out** اِسْتَشْعَرَ رَأْيَ [شَخْصٍ]

• **feel up to**: ~ **up to** [sth] شَعَرَ بالقُدْرةِ على [شَيْءٍ]; **do you ~ up to talking to her/going for a walk?** هل تَشْعُرُ بالقُدْرةِ على التَحَدُّثِ مَعَها \ الذَهابِ في تَمْشِيةٍ

feeler /ˈfiːlə/ *n* 1 (Zool) قَرْن اسْتِشْعارٍ, مَجَسّ (مَجاسُّ, مِجَسّات) 2 (tentative enquiry) **to put out ~s** جَسَّ النَبْضَ

feel-good /ˈfiːlɡʊd/ *adj* ‹*story, movie*› يُشْعِرُ بالارْتِياحِ \ بالسَعادةِ; **the ~ factor** [شَيْء يَبْعَثُ على الشُعورِ بالارْتِياحِ]

feeling /ˈfiːlɪŋ/ **A** *n* 1 (emotion) شُعور; **it is a strange ~ to be on my own** شُعورٌ غَريبٌ أنْ أكونَ وَحْدي; **to hurt sb's ~s** جَرَحَ مَشاعِرَ شَخْصٍ; **to spare sb's ~s** حافَظ على مَشاعِرِ شَخْصٍ 2 (opinion, belief) رَأْي (آراء); **to have strong ~s about sth** كانَتْ لَدَيْهِ آراءٌ مُتَشَدِّدةٌ بِخُصوصِ شَيْءٍ; **I have very mixed ~s about it** لَدَيَّ مَشاعِرُ مُتَضارِبةٌ بِخُصوصِهِ; **~s were running high** كانَت المَشاعِرُ مُلْتَهِبةً 3 [u] (sensitivity) إحْساس; **to speak with ~** تَحَدَّثَ بِإحْساسٍ 4 (impression) إحْساس (إحْساسات, أَحاسيسُ), شُعور; **I had a ~ you'd say that** كُنْتُ أَشْعُرُ أَنَّكَ سَتَقولُ هذا; **I have a bad ~ about this** لا أَشْعُرُ بالارْتِياحِ بِخُصوصِ هذا; **I have a bad ~ about her** لا أَشْعُرُ بالارْتِياحِ نَحْوَها 5 [u] (physical sensation) شُعور, إحْساس; **a dizzy/nauseous ~** شُعور بالدَوارِ \ بالغَثَيانِ; **I have no ~ in my feet** لا أَشْعُرُ بِقَدَمَيَّ 6 (atmosphere) جَوّ (أَجْواء); **there was a ~ of tension** كانَ هُناكَ جَوٌّ من التَوَتُّرِ

B *adj* ‹*person*› عاطِفيّ

fee-paying /ˈfiːpeɪɪŋ/ *adj* ‹*school*› ذو رُسومٍ; ‹*student*› دافِعُ الرُسومِ

feet /fiːt/ *n pl* ▸ **foot**

feign /feɪn/ *vt* ‹*interest, illness*› تَظاهَرَ, ادَّعى (ب)

feline /ˈfiːlaɪn/ **A** *adj* ‹*companion, virus*› سِنَّوْريّ; ‹*grace*› مِثْلُ الغَزالِ

B *n* سِنَّوْر (سَنانيرُ)

fell /fɛl/ **A** *past tense* ▸ **fall**

B *vt* قَطَعَ (a; قَطْع) ‹*a tree*›; أَسْقَطَ ‹*an opponent, a victim*›

fellow /ˈfɛləʊ/ **A** *n* 1 (infml) (man) رَجُل (رِجال) 2 (of a learned society) عُضْو في جَمْعيّةٍ عِلْميّةٍ 3 (BrE) (of a university college) أُسْتاذ (أَساتِذة)

B *adj* [قَرين]; **~ members/citizens** زُمَلاء \ أَبْناء بَلَدٍ واحِدٍ; **he tried to help his ~ men** حاوَلَ مُساعَدةَ قُرَنائِهِ; **her ~ Americans** قُرَناؤُها الأَمْريكيّونَ

fellow feeling *n* [تَعاطُف وَإحْساس بالآخَرينَ]

fellowship /ˈfɛləʊʃɪp/ *n* 1 [u] (companionship) صُحْبة, رُفْقة 2 (association) زَمالة 3 (of a university college) أُسْتاذيّة 4 (research grant) مِنْحة (مِنَح)

felon /ˈfɛlən/ *n* مُجْرِم

felony /ˈfɛləni/ *n* (*pl* **felonies**) جِناية

felt /fɛlt/ **A** *past tense, past participle* ▸ **feel**

B *n* لِبْد (لُبود, أَلْباد)

felt-tip pen, felt-tip /ˌfɛltˌtɪp ˈpɛn/ *n* قَلَم لُبّادٍ

felucca /fɛˈlʌkə/ *n* فَلوكة (فَلائكُ)

female /ˈfiːmeɪl/ **A** *adj* 1 ‹*animal, plant*› أُنْثى (f) 2 ‹*sex*› مُؤَنَّث; ‹*figure, voice*› نِسائيّ; **the audience was mostly ~** كانَ مُعْظَمُ الجُمْهورِ من الإناثِ; **a ~ student** طالِبة

B *n* 1 (animal, plant) أُنْثى (f; إناث) 2 (woman, girl) أُنْثى (f; إناث)

feminine /ˈfɛmɪnɪn/ *adj* 1 ‹*voice, beauty*› أُنْثَويّ 2 ‹*ending, noun*› مُؤَنَّث

femininity /ˌfɛmɪˈnɪnɪti/ *n* أُنوثة

feminism /ˈfɛmɪnɪz(ə)m/ *n* نِسْويّة (حَرَكة نِسائيّة تُنادي بالمُساواةِ بين الجِنْسَيْنِ)

feminist /ˈfɛmənɪst/ **A** *n* مُناصِر للنِسْويّةِ \ للمُساواةِ بين الجِنْسَيْنِ

B *adj* ‹*movement, theory*› نِسْويّ

fen /fɛn/ **A** *n* مُسْتَنْقَع (مُسْتَنْقَعات)

B (**the Fens**) *n pl* [أَراضٍ رَطْبة مُنْخَفِضة شَرْقَ إنْجِلْترا]

fence /fɛns/ **A** *n* 1 (in gardens, parks) سور (أَسْوار), سِياج (سِياجات) 2 (for horse jumps) حاجِز (حَواجِزُ)

B *vt* سَيَّجَ, سَوَّرَ ‹*an area*›; **it would look better if we ~d that**

section سَيكونُ المَظهَرُ أفضَلَ لو سَيَّجْنا ذلك الجُزْءَ

C *vi* «fencers, competitors» بارَزَ

(Idiom) **to sit on the fence** الْتَزَمَ الحِيادَ

(Phrasal verbs) **fence in**: ~ **[sth] in**, ~ **in [sth]** سَوَّرَ [شَيْئاً] <an area>

• **fence off**: ~ **[sth] off**, ~ **off [sth]** سَيَّجَ \ سَوَّرَ [شَيْئاً] <an area>

fencer /ˈfɛnsə/ *n* (Sport) لاعِب الشيشِ

fencing /ˈfɛnsɪŋ/ *n* **1** (Sport) مُبارَزة \ لُعْبة الشيش **2** (barrier) أَدَوات تَسْييجٍ (material); سِياجات

fend /fɛnd/ *vi* **to** ~ **for oneself** عالَ نَفْسَهُ

(Phrasal verb) **fend off**: **1** ~ **off [sb/sth]**, ~ **[sb/sth] off** \ تَوَقَّى صَدَّ [شَخْصاً / شَيْئاً] <an attack, attacker, a blow> **2** ~ **off [sth]** تَفادى [شَيْئاً] <criticism, questions>

fender /ˈfɛndə/ *n* **1** (AmE) (of a car) رَفْرَف (رَفارِفُ) **2** (for a fire) مَصَدّ (مَصَدّات)

fender bender *n* (AmE infml) حادِث سَيّارةٍ بسيط

fennel /ˈfɛn(ə)l/ *n* شمار

ferment A /fəˈmɛnt/ *vt* **1** (chemically) خَمَّرَ <wine, sugar> **2** (to stir up) أَثارَ <trouble, unrest>

B /fəˈmɛnt/ *vi* «wine, fruit» تَخَمَّرَ

C /ˈfəːmɛnt/ *n* هَيَجان

fern /fəːn/ *n* خُنْشار

ferocious /fəˈrəʊʃəs/ *adj* <attack, beast> مُتَوَحِّش

ferocity /fəˈrɒsɪti/ *n* شَراسة

ferret /ˈfɛrɪt/ *n* ابْن مِقْرَض

(Phrasal verbs) **ferret about/around** فَتَّشَ

• **ferret out** (infml): **1** ~ **[sb/sth] out**, ~ **out [sb/sth]** فَتَّشَ عن [شَخْصٍ \ شَيْءٍ] <a bargain> **2** ~ **[sb/sth] out**, ~ **out [sb/sth]** اكْتَشَفَ [شَيْئاً \ شَخْصاً] <the truth, information>

ferry /ˈfɛri/ **A** *n* (*pl* **ferries**) (ship) عَبّارة; (boat) مُعَدِّية

B *vt* (**ferries, ferrying, ferried**) نَقَلَ (u; نَقْل) <the passengers, supplies>

fertile /ˈfəːtʌɪl/ *adj* **1** <soil, land> خِصْب **2** <human, animal, egg> خِصْب **3** <imagination> خِصْب

Fertile Crescent *n* (**the Fertile Crescent**) الهِلال الخَصيب

fertility /fəˈtɪlɪti/ *n* **1** (of land) خُصوبة **2** (of humans, animals) خُصوبة **3** (inventiveness) خُصوبة

fertility clinic *n* عِيادة خُصوبةٍ

fertility treatment *n* عِلاج خُصوبةٍ

fertilize, -ise (BrE) /ˈfəːtɪlʌɪz/ *vt* **1** لَقَّحَ <an egg, a female> **2** خَصَّبَ, سَمَّدَ <the soil, crops>

fertilizer, -iser (BrE) /ˈfəːtɪlʌɪzə/ *n* سَماد (أَسْمِدة)

fervent /ˈfəːv(ə)nt/ *adj* <supporter> مُتَحَمِّس; <hope> قَوِيّ

fervour (BrE), **fervor** (AmE) /ˈfəːvə/ *n* تَحَمُّس

fester /ˈfɛstə/ *vi* «wounds» تَقَرَّحَ; «disputes» احْتَدَّ

festival /ˈfɛstɪv(ə)l/ *n* **1** (religious) عيد (أَعْياد) **2** (arts event) مَهْرَجان (مَهْرَجانات); **the Cannes film** ~ مَهْرَجان كان السينمائيّ

festive /ˈfɛstɪv/ *adj* <occasion, atmosphere> احْتِفاليّ; **the** ~ **season** المَوْسِم الاحْتِفاليّ

festivity /fɛˈstɪvɪti/ *n* **1** [u] احْتِفال **2** (**festivities** *n pl*) احْتِفالات

festoon /fɛˈstuːn/ **A** *n* [شَريط من الوَرَق أو الأَزْهار للزينة]

B *vt* [زَيَّنَ بالأَشْرِطة المُلَوَّنة إلخ] <a wall, tree>

feta, feta cheese /ˈfɛtə/ *n* جُبْنة فيتا

fetal (AmE) *adj* ▸**foetal**

fetch /fɛtʃ/ **A** *vt* **1** جَلَبَ (i-u; جَلْب) <an object>; أَتى (i; إتْيان) (ب) <a person>; **could you** ~ **me my glasses?** هل تَسْتَطيعُ أَنْ تَجْلِبَ لي نَظّارَتي؟; **I'll** ~ **you from the airport** سَآتي بِكَ من المَطارِ **2** جَلَبَ (i-u; جَلْب) <a price, sum>

(Idiom) **to fetch and carry for sb** [قامَ بأَعْمالٍ وَضيعةٍ لِشَخْصٍ وكَأَنَّهُ خادِمٌ]

fetching /ˈfɛtʃɪŋ/ *adj* <outfit, young lady> جَذّاب

fete /feɪt/ **A** *n* حَفْلة (حَفَلات), مَهْرَجان (مَهْرَجانات)

B *vt* احْتَفى (ب) <a writer, an actor>

fetish /ˈfɛtɪʃ/ *n* هَوَس

fetter /ˈfɛtə/ **A** (**fetters**) *n pl* قُيود, أَغْلال

B *vt* غَلَّ, قَيَّدَ (u; غَلّ) <a prisoner, slave>

fettle /ˈfɛt(ə)l/ *n*

(Idiom) **in fine** *or* **good fettle** في حالةٍ جَيِّدةٍ

fetus (AmE) ▸**foetus**

feud /fjuːd/ **A** *n* نِزاع (نِزاعات)

B *vi* «families, groups» تَنازَعَ (على)

feudal /ˈfjuːd(ə)l/ *adj* ‹*lord, system*› إقْطاعيّ; **living conditions under the ~ system** ظُروف المَعيشةِ تحت النِظام الإقْطاعيِّ

feudalism /ˈfjuːdəlɪz(ə)m/ *n* إقْطاعيّة

fever /ˈfiːvə/ *n* حُمّى (f; حُمِّيات)

feverish /ˈfiːvərɪʃ/ *adj* **1** (Med) ‹*patient, dreams*› مَحْموم

2 (excited) ‹*speculation, activity*› مَحْموم

fever pitch *n* حُمّى المَلاعِب

few /fjuː/ **A** *determiner* **1** (not many) قَليل (قَلائِلُ ,أَقِلّاءُ); **we get very ~ visitors** قَليلٌ جِدًّا من الناسِ مَنْ يَأْتون لِزِيارَتِنا **2** (couple of) **every ~ days** كُلَّ بِضْعةِ أيّامٍ; **the first ~ weeks were the hardest** كانَت الأَسابيعُ القَليلةُ الأولى الأَصْعَبَ

B *pron* (**fewer, fewest**); **~ of us succeeded** نَجَحَ قَليلٌ مِنّا; **~er than 10% of people** أَقَلّ من 10٪ من الناسِ

C (**a few**) *determiner, pron* **1** (as determiner) بَعْض; **a ~ people** بَعْضُ الناسِ; **a ~ of us** بَعْضٌ مِنّا; **quite a ~ people** عَدَد لا بَأْسَ بِهِ من الناسِ **2** (as pronoun) قَليل; **I only need a ~** أَحْتاجُ إلى القَليلِ فَقَطْ; **I would like a ~ more** أَوَدُّ الحُصولَ على بَعْضِ المَزيدِ

(Idiom) **to be few and far between** كانَ نادِرَ الوُجودِ

fewer /ˈfjuːə/ **A** *determiner* (*comparative of* ▸**few**) عَدَد أَقَلّ من

B *pron* (*comparative of* ▸**few**) أَقَلّ (dipt)

fewest /ˈfjuːɪst/ *determiner* (*superlative of* ▸**few**) أَقَلّ عَدَدٍ من

fez /fɛz/ *n* (*pl* **fezzes**) طَرْبوش (طَرابِيشُ)

fiancé /fɪˈɒnseɪ/ *n* خَطيب (خُطَباءُ)

fiancée /fɪˈɒnseɪ/ *n* خَطيبة

fiasco /fɪˈaskəʊ/ *n* (*pl* **fiascos**) فَشَل ,إخْفاق

fib /fɪb/ (infml) **A** *n* أُكْذوبة (أَكاذيبُ); **to tell ~s** قالَ أَكاذيبَ

B *vi* (**-bb-**) «children» كَذَبَ (i; كِذْب ,كَذِب)

fibre (BrE), **fiber** (AmE) /ˈfʌɪbə/ *n* **1** (thread) ليف (أَلْياف)

2 (in diet) ليف (أَلْياف)

fibreglass (BrE), **fiberglass** (AmE) /ˈfʌɪbəɡlɑːs/ *n* أَلْياف زُجاجيّة

fibre-optic (BrE), **fiber optic** (AmE) /ˌfʌɪbəˈrɒptɪk/ *adj* ‹*cable, network*› الأَلْياف البَصَريّة

fibrosis /fʌɪˈbrəʊsɪs/ *n* تَلَيُّف

fibrositis /ˌfʌɪbrəˈsʌɪtɪs/ *n* الْتِهاب ليفيّ

fickle /ˈfɪk(ə)l/ *adj* ‹*consumers, weather*› مُتَقَلِّب

fiction /ˈfɪkʃ(ə)n/ *n* أَدَب قَصَصيّ

fictional /ˈfɪkʃ(ə)n(ə)l/ *adj* ‹*character, world*› خَياليّ

fictionalize, -ise (BrE) /ˈfɪkʃ(ə)nəlʌɪz/ *vt* [رَوى شَيْئاً حَقيقيًّا في قالِبٍ خَياليٍّ] ‹*a story, character*›

fictitious /fɪkˈtɪʃəs/ *adj* **1** (false) ‹*name, company*› مُزَيَّف

2 (fictional) ‹*character, place*› خَياليّ

fiddle /ˈfɪd(ə)l/ **A** *n* (infml) **1** كَمَنْجة ,كَمان **2** (BrE) (fraud) خُدْعة (خُدَع); **I'm sure he's on the ~** أنا مُتَأَكِّدٌ أَنَّهُ مُخادِعٌ

B *vt* تَلاعَبَ (بِ) ‹*a tax return, figures*›

C *vi* **1** (fidget) **to ~ with sth** ‹*hair, a necklace*› عَبِثَ بِشَيْءٍ

2 (adjust) **to ~ with sth** ضَبَطَ شَيْئاً ‹*a knob, controls*›

(Idiom) **to play second fiddle to sb** قامَ بِدَوْرٍ أَقَلَّ أَهَمِّيّةً من شَخْصٍ

fiddler /ˈfɪdlə/ *n* عازِف الكَمانِ

fidelity /fɪˈdɛlɪti/ *n* إخْلاص

fidget /ˈfɪdʒɪt/ *vi* «children» تَمَلْمَلَ

field /fiːld/ **A** *n* **1** (in farming) حَقْل (حُقول) **2** مَلْعَب (مَلاعِبُ); **a football ~** مَلْعَب كُرةِ قَدَمٍ; **to take to the ~** نَزَلَ إلى المَلْعَبِ **3** (competitors) لاعِبونَ; **to be ahead of the ~** كانَ مُتَقَدِّماً على اللاعِبينَ **4** (of knowledge) مَجال (مَجالات) **5** (for oil, gas) حَقْل (حُقول) **6** (real environment) **to test sth in the ~** اخْتَبَرَ شَيْئاً خارِجَ المَعْمَلِ **7** (Mil) **the ~ of battle** مَيْدان المَعْرَكةِ **8** (range) مَجال; **a magnetic/gravitational ~** مَجال مَغْنَطيسيّ \ جاذِبيّةٍ; **~ of vision** مَجال الرُؤْيةِ; **~ of fire** مَرْمى النارِ **9** (for data) حَقْل (حُقول)

B *vt* **1** الْتَقَطَ \ أَوْقَفَ ‹*the ball*› **2** (to mobilize) اخْتارَ ‹*a team, a candidate, player*› **3** (to deal with) أَجابَ (عن) ‹*a question*›

C *vi* (Sport) [نَزَلَ إلى المَلْعَبِ]

Idiom **to play the field** (infml) [أقامَ علاقاتٍ غراميّةً مع أكْثَرَ من شَخْصٍ]

field day *n* (AmE) يَوْم رِياضيّ;

Idiom **to have a field day** كانَ لَهُ يَوْمٌ مَشْهودٌ

fielder /ˈfiːldə/ *n* [مُتَلَقّي الضَرَباتِ في البيسْبول]

field event *n* [ألْعاب القُوى ما عَدا العَدْوِ]

field glasses *n* مِنْظار (مَناظيرُ)

field hockey *n* (AmE) هوكي الحَقْلِ

field hospital *n* مُسْتَشْفًى مَيْدانيّ

field marshal *n* مُشير

field sports *n* [رِياضة الصَيْدِ والقَنْصِ]

field study *n* دِراسة مَيْدانيّة

field test *n* اخْتِبار مَيْدانيّ

field trip *n* رِحْلة مَيْدانيّة

fieldwork /ˈfiːldwɜːk/ *n* عَمَل مَيْدانيّ

fieldworker /ˈfiːəldwɜːkə/ *n* **1** (in research) باحِث مَيْدانيّ **2** (for a social organization) عامِل مَيْدانيّ

fiend /fiːnd/ *n* **1** (evil spirit) عِفْريت (عَفاريتُ) **2** (cruel person) شِرّير (أشْرار) **3** (infml) (fanatic) مُدْمِن

fiendish /ˈfiːndɪʃ/ *adj* **1** (cruel) ‹*tyrant, cruelty*› مُتَوَحِّش, وَحْشيّ; ‹*grin*› شَيْطانيّ **2** (ingenious) ‹*plot, gadget*› شَيْطانيّ **3** (infml) (difficult) ‹*trap, puzzle*› عَويص (عِواص)

fierce /fɪəs/ *adj* **1** (aggressive) ‹*animal, battle*› شَرِس **2** (intense) ‹*competition, heat, wind*› شَديد

fiercely /ˈfɪəsli/ *adv* **1** (aggressively) ‹*to fight*› بِشَراسةٍ; ‹*to glare, quarrel*› بِغَضَبٍ شَديدٍ **2** (intensely) ‹*to compete, oppose*› بِشَراسةٍ; ‹*to burn*› بِضَراوةٍ; ‹*competitive, loyal*› بِشِدّةٍ

fiery /ˈfʌɪəri/ *adj* (**fierier**, **fieriest**) ‹*orator, temper*› ناريّ; ‹*sunset, sky*› أحْمَر (dipt); ‹*chilli*› حارّ; ‹*furnace, volcano*› مُلْتَهِب

FIFA /ˈfiːfə/ *n* = **Fédération internationale de football association** الفيفا (الاتِّحاد الدُوَليّ لِكُرةِ القَدَمِ)

fife /fʌɪf/ *n* [آلة موسيقيّة تُشْبِهُ النايَ]

fifteen /fɪfˈtiːn/ **A** *n* **1** (number, quantity) خَمْسةَ عَشَرَ; **~ of the children (came)** (جاءَ) خَمْسةَ عَشَرَ من الأطْفالِ **2** (rugby team) [فَريق رُكْبي]; **the Welsh ~** [فَريق الرُكْبي الويلْزيّ]

B *adj* خَمْسةَ عَشَرَ

fifteenth /fɪfˈtiːnθ/ **A** *n* **1** (in a series) خامِسَ عَشَرَ **2** (fraction) جُزْء من خَمْسةَ عَشَرَ **3** (**the fifteenth**) (of a month) الخامِسَ عَشَرَ

B *adj* ‹*century, day*› خامِسَ عَشَرَ

C *adv* في المَرْكَزِ الخامِسَ عَشَرَ

fifth /fɪfθ/ **A** *n* **1** (in a series) خامِس; **she was the ~ to arrive** وَصَلَتْ كَخامِسةٍ **2** (fraction) خُمْس; **a ~ of the school population** خُمْس عَدَدِ طُلّابِ المَدْرَسةِ **3** (**the fifth**) (of a month) الخامِس

B *adj* (in order) ‹*time, attempt*› خامِس; **he was ~** أحْرَزَ المَرْتَبةَ الخامِسةَ

fifties /ˈfɪftiz/ *n pl* **1** (decade) (**the fifties**) الخَمْسينات **2** (age) **to be in one's ~** كانَ في الخَمْسيناتِ (من عُمْرِهِ)

fiftieth /ˈfɪftɪəθ/ **A** *n* **1** (**the fiftieth**) (in a series) الخَمْسونَ **2** (fraction) جُزْء من خَمْسينَ

B *adj* ‹*anniversary, time*› الخَمْسونَ

C *adv* في المَرْكَزِ الخَمْسينَ

fifty /ˈfɪfti/ *n, adj* خَمْسونَ

fifty-fifty /ˌfɪftiˈfɪfti/ **A** *adj* **to have a ~ chance of doing sth** [كانَتْ فُرَصُ النَجاحِ والفَشَلِ في فِعْلِ شَيْءٍ مُتَساوِيةً]

B *adv* مُناصَفةً, بالتَساوي

fig /fɪɡ/ *n* **1** تين **2** (also **fig tree**) شَجَرة تينٍ

fig. /fɪɡ/ *abbr* = **figure** شَكْل (أشْكال)

fight /fʌɪt/ **A** *vt* (*past tense, past participle* **fought**) **1** (violently) ‹*an opponent*› تَعارَكَ (مع); ‹*an enemy*› حارَبَ; ‹*a boxer*› واجَهَ; **he fought the champion three times** واجَهَ حائِزَ اللَقَبِ ثَلاثَ مَرّاتٍ **2** (to struggle against) ‹*disease, evil, a fire*› كافَحَ; **to ~ one's way through a crowd** شَقَّ طَريقَهُ بِصُعوبةٍ وَسْطَ الزِحامِ **3** (to take part in) ‹*a campaign, war, battle*› خاضَ (u; خَوْض) **4** «candidates» ‹*a campaign, an election*› خاضَ (u; خَوْض) **5** (legally) ‹*a case*› خاضَ (u; خَوْض)

B *vi* (*past tense, past participle* **fought**) **1** (violently) «countries» حارَبَ; «children, animals» تَعارَكَ, تَقاتَلَ; **to ~ for one's country** حارَبَ من أجْلِ بَلَدِهِ; **to ~ for one's life** صارَعَ المَوْتَ **2** (in boxing) لاكَمَ **3** (to struggle) «organizations, volunteers» ناضَلَ, كافَحَ; **to ~ for our**

rights كافَحَ من أَجْلِ حُقوقِنا; **to ~ against tyranny** كافَحَ ضدّ الطُغْيانِ **4** (infml) (to argue) تَشاجَرَ

C *n* **1** (between people, animals) شِجار, قِتال, عِراك; **to have a ~ with sb** تَعارَكَ مع شَخْصٍ; **to get into a ~** دَخَلَ في عِراكٍ **2** (in boxing) مُباراة (مُبارَيات) **3** (struggle) كِفاح (كِفاحات); **the ~ for equality/against crime** الكِفاح من أَجْلِ المُساواةِ \ ضدّ الجَريمةِ; **he lost his ~ against cancer** تُوُفِّيَ بعد صِراعٍ مع السَرَطانِ; **to put up a ~** كافَحَ **4** (infml) (argument) شِجار, خِلاف (خِلافات); **to have a ~ with sb** تَشاجَرَ مع شَخْصٍ **5** [u] (combative spirit) صُمود

Phrasal verbs **fight back** **1** (physically, tactically) قاوَمَ **2** **~ back [sth]** كَتَمَ [شَيْئاً] ‹*tears*›

• **fight off**: **1** **~ off [sb], ~ [sb] off** صَدَّ هُجومَ [شَخْصٍ] ‹*an attacker, the enemy*› **2** **~ off [sth], ~ [sth] off** «company» قاوَمَ [شَيْئاً] ‹*a takeover bid, challenge*›; «patient» قاوَمَ [شَيْئاً] ‹*a cold, cough*›

• **fight on** واصَلَ الكِفاحَ

fighter /ˈfʌɪtə/ *n* **1** (Sport) مُلاكِم **2** (determined person) مُكافِح **3** (also **fighter plane**) طائِرة مُقاتِلة

fighter pilot *n* طَيّار مُقاتِل

fighting /ˈfʌɪtɪŋ/ **A** *n* مَعْرَكة, قِتال

B *adj* **1** ‹*spirit, force*› مُقاتِل **2** **~ talk** لُغة عُدْوانيّة

figment /ˈfɪgmənt/ *n* (fml) **a ~ of your imagination** من نَسْجِ خَيالِكَ

figurative /ˈfɪg(ə)rətɪv/ *adj* ‹*language, translation*› مَجازيّ

figure /ˈfɪgə/ **A** *n* **1** (number) رَقْم (أَرْقام); (amount) مَبْلَغ (مَبالِغ); **a six-~ sum** مَبْلَغ مُكَوَّن من سِتّةِ أَرْقامٍ; **inflation is in double ~s** يَصِلُ التَضَخُّمُ إلى مُعَدَّلٍ ثُنائيِّ الأَرْقامِ; **to have a head for ~s, to be good with ~s** كانَ ماهِراً في الحِسابِ **2** (personality) شَخْصيّة, شَخْص (mf; شُخوص, أَشْخاص); **a well-known ~ in the horse-racing world** شَخْصيّة مَعْروفة في عالَمِ سِباقاتِ الخَيْلِ **3** (in painting, sculpture) شَخْص (mf; شُخوص, أَشْخاص) **4** (archetype) **a father ~** رَمْز الأُبُوّةِ; **an authority ~** رَمْز السُلْطةِ **5** (body shape) قَدّ, قَوام (قُدود); **she has a good ~** لَدَيْها قَوامٌ جَميلٌ; **to keep one's ~** حافَظَ على قَوامِهِ **6** (geometric or other shape) (geometric shape) شَكْل (أَشْكال) **7** (in text) شَكْل (أَشْكال); **see ~ 4** اُنْظُر الشَكْلَ رَقْم 4

B *vt* (infml) (to suppose) ظَنَّ (u; ظَنّ), تَصَوَّرَ; **I ~d that it was time to go** ظَنَنْتُ أَنَّهُ حانَ الوَقْتُ للذَهابِ

C *vi* **1** (to feature, appear) **to ~ in a film/an advertisement** «names, characters» ظَهَرَ في فيلْمٍ \ إعْلانٍ **2** (infml) (to make sense) [كانَ مَنْطِقيًّا]

Phrasal verb **figure out**: **A** **~ out [sth], ~ [sth] out** فَهِمَ [شَيْئاً] ‹*reason*›; اكْتَشَفَ [شَيْئاً] ‹*the answer*›; **to ~ out who/why/how etc** اكْتَشَفَ مَنْ \ لِماذا \ كيف \ إلخ **B** **~ out [sb], ~ [sb] out** فَهِمَ طَبيعةَ [شَخْصٍ]

figurehead /ˈfɪgəhɛd/ *n* (symbolic leader) رَئيس صوريّ; (of a ship) [تِمْثال في مُقَدِّمةِ سَفينةٍ]; **he was just a ~** كانَ مُجَرَّدَ رَئيسٍ صوريٍّ

figure of speech *n* تَعْبير مَجازيّ

figure skating *n* التَزَلُّج الفَنّيّ على الجَليدِ

Fiji /ˈfiːdʒi/ *pr n* (or **the Republic of Fiji**) فيجي (f)

filament /ˈfɪləmənt/ *n* **1** (Elec) فَتيلة (فَتيلات, فَتائِلُ) **2** (of fibre) شُعَيْرة, سِلْك (أَسْلاك), خَيْط (خُيوط, خيطان)

filch /fɪltʃ/ *vt* (infml) سَرَقَ (i; سَرِقة), اخْتَلَسَ ‹*money, sweets*›

file /fʌɪl/ **A** *n* **1** (for papers) مِلَفّ (مِلَفّات) **2** (record) مِلَفّ (مِلَفّات) **3** (Comput) مِلَفّ (مِلَفّات) **4** (tool) مِبْرَد (مَبارِدُ) **5** **in single ~** في صَفٍّ واحِدٍ

B *vt* **1** أَوْدَعَ ‹*a document, letter*› **2** (Law) رَفَعَ (a; رَفْع) ‹*a suit, complaint*›; قَدَّمَ ‹*an application*› **3** بَرَدَ (a; بَرْد, بُرود) ‹*wood, metal*›; **to ~ one's nails** بَرَدَ أَظافِرَهُ

C *vi* **1** «prisoners, children, people» تَحَرَّكَ في طابورٍ **2** **to ~ for divorce/bankruptcy** (Law) رَفَعَ قَضيّةَ طَلاقٍ \ إفْلاسٍ

file cabinet *n* (AmE) خِزانة مِلَفّاتٍ

file card *n* (AmE) [بِطاقة صَغيرة لِتَوْثيقِ المَعْلوماتِ]

file clerk *n* (AmE) مُوَظَّف السِجِلّاتِ

file-sharing *n* مُشارَكة المِلَفّاتِ

filing /ˈfʌɪlɪŋ/ *n* **1** (office work) تَرْتيب \ حِفْظ \ إيداع مِلَفّاتٍ **2** (of metal) بُرادة

filing cabinet *n* (BrE) خِزانة مِلَفّاتٍ

filing clerk *n* (BrE) مُوَظَّف السِجِلاّتِ

Filipino /ˌfɪlɪˈpiːnəʊ/ *n, adj* (*n pl* **Filipinos**) فيليبّينيّ

fill /fɪl/ **A** *vt* **1** مَلأَ (a; مَلْء) ‹*a basket, box, bottle*›; **to ~ a sack with sand** مَلأَ كيساً رَمْلاً; **tears ~ed his eyes** مَلأَت الدُموعُ عَيْنَيْهِ; **the rain has begun to ~ the reservoirs** بَدَأ المَطَرُ يَمْلأُ الخَزّاناتِ **2** «crowds, smoke» مَلأَ (a; مَلْء) ‹*the streets, a building, room*› **3** (to plug) رَدَمَ (i-u; رَدْم), سَدَّ (u; سَدّ) ‹*a crack, hole*›; **to ~ a hole with earth/cement** رَدَمَ حُفْرةً بالتُرابِ \ بالإسْمَنْت **4** «dentist» حَشا (u; حَشْو) ‹*a tooth, cavity*› **5** (to fulfil) **to ~ a need in the market/community** سَدَّ حاجةً في السوقِ \ المُجْتَمَعِ; **to ~ a vacuum/void** مَلأَ فَراغاً **6** (to occupy space) مَلأَ (a; مَلْء) ‹*a page, DVD, disk*›; (time) مَلأَ (a; مَلْء), شَغَلَ (a; شُغْل) ‹*one's time, a day, the hours*› **7** «companies, universities» عَيَّنَ شَخْصاً في ‹*a post, vacancy*›; «applicants» شَغَلَ (a; شُغْل) ‹*a post*› **8** (to make full) حَشا (u; حَشْو) ‹*pie, a cushion*› **9** «wind» نَفَخَ (a; نَفْخ) ‹*a sail*›

B *vi* **1** «buckets, eyes, streets» اِمْتَلأَ; **her eyes ~ed with tears** اِمْتَلأَتْ عَيْناها بالدُموعِ; **the reservoirs ~ed with water** اِمْتَلأَت الخَزّاناتُ بالمِياهِ; **the streets were ~ing with people** كانَت الشَوارِعُ تَكْتَظُّ بالناسِ **2** «sails» اِنْتَفَخَ

C (**-filled**); *in combination* **a smoke-~ed room** غُرْفة مُمْتَلِئة بالدُخانِ

D *n* **to eat/drink one's ~** أكَلَ \ شَرِبَ مِلْءَ بَطْنِهِ

(Idiom) **to have had one's fill** أخَذَ كِفايَتَهُ

(Phrasal verbs) **fill in A to ~ in for sb** حَلَّ مَحَلَّ شَخْصٍ **B ~ in [sth]** (to occupy) شَغَلَ [شَيْئاً] ‹*time, an hour, a day*› **C ~ in [sth], ~ [sth] in 1** (to complete) مَلأَ [شَيْئاً] ‹*a form, the date*›; **remember to sign the form when you have ~ed it in** تَذَكَّرْ أنْ تُوَقِّعَ النَموذَجَ بعد أنْ تَمْلأَهُ **2** (to plug) سَدَّ [شَيْئاً] ‹*a hole, crack*›; **they need to ~ in all the holes in the existing roads before planning new ones** يَنْبَغي أنْ يَرْدِموا كُلَّ الحُفَرِ في الطُرُقِ الحالِيّةِ قبل التَخْطيطِ لِطُرُقٍ جَديدةٍ **D ~ in [sb], ~ [sb] in** (to inform) أطْلَعَ [شَخْصاً]

• **fill out 1** «people» زادَ وَزْنُهُ; «sb's face, cheeks» اِمْتَلأَ **2 ~ out [sth], ~ [sth] out** مَلأَ [شَيْئاً] ‹*a form, an application*›; **remember to sign your application when you have ~ed it out** تَذَكَّرْ أنْ تُوَقِّعَ الطَلَبَ بعد أنْ تَمْلأَهُ

• **fill up 1** (to become full) «the theatre, bath, bus» اِمْتَلأَ **2** (by eating) **to ~ up on bread/sweets** مَلأَ بَطْنَهُ بالخُبْزِ \ بالحَلْوى **3 ~ up [sth], ~ [sth] up** مَلأَ [شَيْئاً] ‹*a bucket, box, room*› **4 ~ up [sb], ~ [sb] up** (infml) أشْبَعَ [شَخْصاً]

filler /ˈfɪlə/ *n* حَشْوة

fillet /ˈfɪlɪt/ **A** *n* شَريحة (شَرائِح); **~ steak** شَريحة من لَحْمِ البَقَرِ

B *vt* شَفّى, شَرَّحَ ‹*fish, steak*›

filling /ˈfɪlɪŋ/ **A** *n* **1** (for sandwiches, pies) حَشْوة **2** (for a tooth) حَشْوة; **to have a ~** حَشا ضِرْساً

B *adj* (infml) ‹*food, dish*› مُشْبِع; **pulses are very ~** البُقولُ مُشْبِعةٌ جِدًّا

filling station *n* مَحَطّة بَنْزين

filly /ˈfɪli/ *n* (*pl* **fillies**) مُهْرة (مُهَر)

film /fɪlm/ **A** *n* **1** (motion picture) فيلْم (أفْلام); **to go to see a ~** ذَهَبَ لِيُشاهِدَ فيلْماً **2** (for a camera) فيلْم (أفْلام) **3** (layer) طَبَقة رَقيقة

B *vt* صَوَّرَ ‹*a race, game*›

C *vi* «cameramen, crew» صَوَّرَ فيلْماً

film critic *n* ناقِد سينَمائيّ

film director *n* مُخْرِج سينَمائيّ

film festival *n* مَهْرَجان سينَمائيّ

film industry *n* صِناعة الأفْلامِ

filming /ˈfɪlmɪŋ/ *n* تَصْوير

film producer *n* مُنْتِج سينَمائيّ \ أفْلامٍ

filmset /ˈfɪlmsɛt/ *n* مَوْقِع تَصْويرٍ سينَمائيٍّ

film star *n* نَجْم سينَمائيّ

film studio *n* اسْتوديو أفْلامٍ

filter /ˈfɪltə/ **A** *n* مِصْفاة (مَصافٍ), فِلْتِر; **an oil ~** فِلْتِر زَيْتٍ; **a water ~** فِلْتِر ماءٍ

B *vt* صَفّى ‹*air, coffee*›

C *vi* «light, sound» تَسَرَّبَ

filter paper *n* وَرَق تَرْشيحٍ

filter-tipped /ˌfɪltəˈtɪpt/ *adj* ‹*cigarette*› بِفِلْتِر

filth /fɪlθ/ *n* قَذارة

filthy /ˈfɪlθi/ *adj* (**filthier**, **filthiest**) 1 ‹*floor, toilet*› قَذِر 2 ‹*language, mind*› قَذِر 3 (BrE infml) ‹*weather*› سَيِّئ (بارِد وماطِر)

fin /fɪn/ *n* زَعْنِفة (زَعانِفُ)

final /ˈfaɪn(ə)l/ A *adj* 1 (last) ‹*meeting, day*› أخير 2 (unalterable) ‹*decision, offer*› نِهائيّ
B *n* 1 (also **finals**) (Sport) دَوْر نِهائيّ 2 (**finals** *n pl*) (Educ) امْتِحانات نِهائيّة

finale /fɪˈnɑːli/ *n* خاتِمة (رائِعة)

finalist /ˈfaɪnəlɪst/ *n* مُتأهِّل ل \ مُشْتَرِك في الدَوْرِ النِهائيِّ

finalize, -ise (BrE) /ˈfaɪnəlaɪz/ *vt* وَضَعَ اللَمَساتِ الأَخيرةَ على, أَنْجَزَ ‹*a deal, schedule*›

finally /ˈfaɪn(ə)li/ *adv* 1 (eventually) ‹*to arrive, decide*› أخيراً 2 (lastly) أخيراً; **~, I would like to thank my wife ...** أَوَدُّ أخيراً أنْ أَشْكُرَ زَوْجَتي ...

finance /ˈfaɪnans, fɪˈnans/ A *n* 1 (in banking, business) أَمْوال, مالِيّة 2 (funds) تَمْويل 3 (**finances** *n pl*) مَوارِد مالِيّة; **he's very good at managing his ~s** يَتَصَرَّفُ في مَوارِدِهِ المالِيَّةِ بِشَكْلٍ جَيِّدٍ
B *vt* ‹*a project, purchase*› مَوَّلَ

finance company *n* شَرِكة مالِيّة

financial /faɪˈnanʃ(ə)l, fɪˈnanʃ(ə)l/ *adj* ‹*services, crisis, support*› ماليّ

financial adviser *n* مُسْتَشار ماليّ

financially /faɪˈnanʃ(ə)li, fɪˈnanʃ(ə)li/ *adv* ‹*to support*› ماليًّا

financial year *n* (BrE) سَنة مالِيّة

financier /faɪˈnansɪə/ *n* خَبير ماليّ

financing /ˈfaɪnansɪŋ, fɪˈnansɪŋ/ *n* تَمْويل

finch /fɪntʃ/ *n* حَسّون (حَساسينُ)

find /faɪnd/ A *vt* (*past tense, past participle* **found**) 1 (by chance) ‹*some money, a body, credit card*› وَجَدَ (i; وَجْد), عَثَرَ (u; عُثور; على), لَقِيَ (a; لُقْية); **to leave sth as one found it** تَرَكَ شَيْئاً كَما وَجَدَهُ 2 (by searching) ‹*one's keys, ticket, a lost child*› وَجَدَ (i; وَجْد), عَثَرَ (u; عُثور; على); **to ~ sth on a map** وَجَدَ شَيْئاً على الخَريطةِ; **to ~ one's way out of a building/city** وَجَدَ طَريقَهُ خارِجَ المَبْنى \ المَدينةِ; **we found that the box was empty** وَجَدْنا أنّ الصُنْدوقَ كانَ فارِغاً 3 (with needs) ‹*a job, seat, solution*› وَجَدَ (i; وَجْد); **to ~ the time/money for sth** وَجَدَ الوَقْتَ \ المالَ لِشَيْءٍ; **to ~ sth for sb, to ~ sb sth** وَجَدَ شَيْئاً لِشَخْصٍ 4 (fml) (to be) **to be found** «species, painting» كانَ يوجَدُ; **it is to be found in the Museum of Antiquities** يوجَدُ في مَتْحَفِ الآثارِ 5 (to consider) وَجَدَ (i; وَجْد), اعْتَبَرَ; **I ~ him a bore** أَجِدُهُ مُمِلاًّ; **I ~ it hard to concentrate** أَجِدُ أَنَّهُ من الصَعْبِ أنْ أُرَكِّزَ 6 (to experience) ‹*satisfaction, pleasure*› وَجَدَ (i; وَجْد) 7 (to reach) **to ~ its mark/target** «missile, bullet» وَصَلَ إلى هَدَفِهِ; **how did it ~ its way into your pocket?** كيف وَجَدَ طَريقَهُ إلى جَيْبِكَ؟ 8 (in sentencing) **to ~ the accused innocent/guilty** قَرَّرَ أنّ المُتَّهَم بَريءٌ \ مُذْنِبٌ; **the court ~s that ...** قَرَّرَت المَحْكَمةُ أنّ ... 9 (to arrive to discover) وَجَدَ (i; وَجْد); **I found them working in the garden** وَجَدْتُهُمْ يَعْمَلونَ في الحَديقةِ; **she then found that the train had left** ثُمَّ وَجَدَتْ أنّ القِطارَ قد غادَرَ 10 (Comput) بَحَثَ (a; بَحْث; عن)
B *vi* (*past tense, past participle* **found**) (Law) **to ~ for/against sb** «judge, jury» أَصْدَرَ حُكْماً لِصالِحِ \ ضدّ شَخْصٍ
C *v refl* (*past tense, past participle* **found**) **to ~ oneself** 1 (to discover) وَجَدَ نَفْسَهُ; **I found myself in Amman/working in Beirut** وَجَدْتُ نَفْسي في عَمّانَ \ أَعْمَلُ في بَيْروتَ; **to ~ oneself unable to do sth** وَجَدَ نَفْسَهُ غَيْرَ قادِرٍ على فِعْلِ شَيْءٍ 2 (with vocations) وَجَدَ نَفْسَهُ
D *n* (discovery) اكْتِشاف (اكْتِشافات)

Phrasal verb **find out** A عَلِمَ (a; عِلْم), اكْتَشَفَ; **I hope nobody ~s out** آمُلُ ألاّ يَعْلَمَ أَحَدٌ بالأَمْرِ B **~ out [sth], ~ [sth] out** ‹*the answer, truth, sb's name*› اكْتَشَفَ [شَيْئاً]; **to ~ out that ...** اكْتَشَفَ أنّ ... C **~ [sb] out** كَشَفَ أَمْرَ [شَخْصٍ]; **they were soon found out** انْكَشَفَ أَمْرُهُمْ بعد فَتْرةٍ وَجيزةٍ D **~ out about [sb/sth]** ‹*the requirements, a plan, an affair*› اكْتَشَفَ الحَقيقةَ عن [شَخْصٍ \ شَيْءٍ]

findings /ˈfaɪndɪŋz/ *n pl* نَتائِج بَحْثٍ

fine /faɪn/ A *adj* 1 (very good) ‹*performance, writer, example*› رائِع, عَظيم 2 (satisfactory) ‹*the meal, arrangements, holiday*›

جَيِّد ,حَسَن; **OK, that's ~** حَسَناً, هذا جَيِّدٌ; **I'm ~, thanks** أنا بِخَيْرٍ, شُكْراً; **that's ~ by** *or* **with me** هذا مُناسِبٌ بالنِسْبة لي **3** (expressing irony) **a ~ friend you are!** يا لَكَ من صَديقٍ غَيْرِ مُخْلِصٍ!; **he's a ~ one to talk!** هو آخِرُ مَنْ يَتَحَدَّثُ في هذا الأَمْرِ! **4** (dry and clear) ‹*morning, the weather*› صافٍ ,صَحْو; **it's** *or* **the weather's ~** الطَقْسُ لَطيفٌ **5** (delicate, narrow) ‹*hair, fabric, layer*› رَقيق ,دَقيق **6** (of small particles) ‹*powder, spray, soil*› ناعِم **7** (subtle) ‹*distinction, adjustment*› دَقيق **8** (of high quality) ‹*crystal, wine*› راقٍ ,فاخِر **9** (pure) ‹*gold, silver*› نَقيّ **10** (commendable) ‹*woman, husband*› لَطيف (لُطَفاءُ ,لِطاف) **11** (refined, grand) ‹*manners*› عالٍ ,حَميد; ‹*clothes*› أَنيق

B *n* (punishment) غَرامة

C *adv* (infml) ‹*to get along, come along*› بِشَكْلٍ حَسَنٍ \ رائِعٍ; **you're doing ~** أَنْتَ تُؤَدّي أداءً حَسَناً

D *vt* ‹*an offender, a company*› غَرَّمَ; **to be ~d for speeding** أُعْطِيَ غرامةً لِتَجاوُزِ السُرْعةِ

fine art *n* فُنون جَميلة

finely /ˈfʌɪnli/ *adv* **1** (not coarsely) ‹*chopped, grated*› بِشَكْلٍ ناعِمٍ \ دَقيقٍ **2** (carefully) ‹*balanced, judged*› بِعِنايةٍ **3** (to a high standard) ‹*written, painted*› بِشَكْلٍ مُتَميِّزٍ \ رائِعٍ

fine print *n* حُروف صَغيرة (الشُروط التَفْصيليّة في أَسْفَلِ عَقْدٍ)

finery /ˈfʌɪn(ə)ri/ *n* [أَفْخَر المَلابِسِ والحُلِيِّ]

finesse /fɪˈnɛs/ *n* بَراعة

fine-tune /ˈfʌɪntjuːn/ *vt* ‹*a strategy, the economy*› عَدَّلَ

finger /ˈfɪŋɡə/ **A** *n* **1** (of the hand) إِصْبَع (mf; أَصابِعُ); **first/index ~** إِصْبَع السَبّابةِ; **to point one's ~ at sb/sth** أَشارَ بِإِصْبَعِهِ نحو شَخْصٍ \ شَيْءٍ; **he didn't lift a ~ to help** لم يُحَرِّكْ ساكِناً للمُساعَدةِ **2** (of a glove) إِصْبَع (mf; أَصابِعُ)

B *vt* ‹*the beads, the fruit*› تَحَسَّسَ بأَصابِعِهِ

(Idioms) **to keep your fingers crossed** تَمَسَّكَ \ تَشَبَّثَ بالأَمَلِ; **to point the finger at sb** أَشارَ بِإِصْبَعِ الاتِّهامِ إلى شَخْصٍ; **to slip through your fingers** أَفْلَتَ من يَدِكَ

fingernail /ˈfɪŋɡəneɪl/ *n* ظُفْر (أَظافِرُ ,أَظْفار)

fingerprint /ˈfɪŋɡəprɪnt/ *n* بَصْمة (بَصَمات)

fingertip /ˈfɪŋɡətɪp/ *n* بَنان (n coll)

(Idiom) **to have sth at one's fingertips** كانَ عِنْدَهُ شَيْءٌ في مُتَناوَلِ يَدِهِ

finicky /ˈfɪnɪki/ *adj* **1** ‹*eater, habits*› نَيِّق; **he's ~ about his diet** هو نَيِّقٌ في حِمْيَتِهِ **2** ‹*job, gadget*› مُعَقَّد; **it's a very ~ mechanism** هي آليّةٌ مُعَقَّدةٌ جِدًّا

finish /ˈfɪnɪʃ/ **A** *vt* **1** (to complete) أَتَمَّ ,أَنْهى ,أَكْمَلَ ‹*a task, building, novel*›; **to ~ doing sth** انْتَهى من فِعْلِ شَيْءٍ **2** (to leave) أَنْهى; **to ~ school/work** أَنْهى دِراسَتَهُ \ عَمَلَهُ **3** (to consume) أَنْهى ‹*one's drink, meal*› **4** (to ruin) قَضى (i; قَضاء) (على) ‹*a person, sb's career*› **5** (infml) (to exhaust, demoralize) أَضْنى ,أَنْهَكَ ‹*a person*›; **the walk has ~ed me!** أَنْهَكَني المَشْيُ

B *vi* **1** (to end) «holidays, meetings» انْتَهى; **the course ~es on Thursday** تَنْتَهي الدَوْرةُ يَوْمَ الخَميسِ **2** (in races) أَنْهى السِباقَ; **he ~ed third** أَنْهى السِباقَ في المَرْكَزِ الثالِثِ **3** (in conversations) أَنْهى حَديثَهُ

C (**finished**) *adj* **beautifully/poorly ~ed** ‹*furniture, interior*› تَشْطيبُهُ رائِعٌ \ رَديءٌ; **the ~ed product** المُنْتَج النِهائيّ

D *n* **1** (end) نِهاية; **from start to ~** من البِداية إلى النِهايةِ; **it will be a fight to the ~** سَتكونُ حَرْباً حتّى النِهايةِ **2** (in races) نِهاية; **it was a close ~** كانَت النَتائِجُ مُتَقارِبةً عند النِهايةِ **3** (in workmanship) تَشْطيب

(Phrasal verbs) **finish off** **A** **~ [sth] off, ~ off [sth]** **1** (to complete) أَكْمَلَ \ أَنْهى [شَيْئاً] ‹*a letter, task*› **2** (to round off) خَتَمَ [شَيْئاً] ‹*a meal*› **B** **~ [sb] off** (infml) **1** (to exhaust, demoralize) أَنْهَكَ [شَخْصاً] ‹*a person*› **2** (to kill) أَجْهَزَ على [شَخْصٍ] ‹*a person, an animal*›

• **finish up** **1** (in a place, situation) انْتَهى بِهِ الأَمْرُ (إلى) **2** **~ [sth] up, ~ up [sth]** لم يُبْقِ من [شَيْءٍ] شَيْئاً ‹*the milk, paint*›

• **finish with** **A** **~ with [sth]** فَرَغَ من [شَيْءٍ] ‹*a book*›; لم يَعُدْ بِحاجةٍ إلى [شَيْءٍ] ‹*tool*› **B** **~ with [sb]** (infml) (to split up) قَطَعَ صِلَتَهُ ب [شَخْصٍ] ‹*one's girlfriend, partner*›

finishing line (BrE) /ˈfɪnɪʃɪŋ ˌlʌɪn/, **finish line** (AmE) /ˈfɪnɪʃ lʌɪn/ *n* خطّ النِهايةِ

finishing school /ˈfɪnɪʃɪŋ skuːl/ *n* [مَدْرَسة خاصّة بِبَناتِ الطَبَقةِ الغَنيّةِ]

finishing touch /ˌfɪnɪʃɪŋ ˈtʌtʃ/ *n* لَمَسات أَخيرة; **to put the ~ to sth** وَضَعَ اللَمَساتِ الأَخيرةَ على شَيْءٍ

finish line *n* (AmE) ▸**finishing line**

finite /ˈfʌɪnʌɪt/ *adj* ‹*resources, amount*› مَحْدود

Finland /ˈfɪnlənd/ *pr n* فِنْلَنْدا

Finn /fɪn/ *n* فِنْلَنْديّ

Finnish /ˈfɪnɪʃ/ **A** *adj* ‹*ambassador, food*› فِنْلَنْديّ
B *n* (اللُغة) الفِنْلَنْديّة

fiord *n* ▸**fjord**

fiqh /fiːk/ *n* فِقْه

fir /fəː/ *n* (also **fir tree**) شوح

fire /ˈfʌɪə/ **A** *n* **1** [u] (burning) نار (f; نيران); **to set ~ to sth, to set sth on ~** أَشْعَلَ \ أَضْرَمَ النارَ في شَيْءٍ; **to be on ~** كانَ يَحْتَرِقُ; **to catch ~** اشْتَعَلَتْ فيهِ النارُ **2** (blaze) حريق (حَرائِقُ); **to start a ~** أَشْعَلَ حَريقاً **3** (for warmth) نار (f; نيران) **4** [u] (shots) نار (f; نيران); **to open ~ on sb** أَطْلَقَ النارَ على شَخْصٍ; **the police came under ~** تَعَرَّضَت الشُرْطةُ لِطَلَقاتِ الرَصاصِ; **to return sb's ~** رَدَّ على الرَصاصِ الّذي أَطْلَقَهُ شَخْصٌ; **to be under ~** (from gun) أُطْلِقَ عَلَيْهِ الرَصاصُ; (to be criticized) تَعَرَّضَ لِانْتِقادٍ حادٍّ **5** [u] (passion) حَماسة
B *excl* **1** (raising the alarm) حَريق **2** (order to shoot) اضْرِبْ
C *vt* **1** (Mil) أَطْلَقَ النارَ من ‹*a gun, weapon*›; أَطْلَقَ ‹*missile*›; **to ~ a shot at sb** أَطْلَقَ طَلْقةً على شَخْصٍ; **to ~ questions at sb** أَمْطَرَ شَخْصاً بِوابِلٍ من الأَسْئِلة **2** (to inspire) **to be ~d with enthusiasm** امْتَلأَ بالحَماسِ; **to ~ sb's imagination** أَلْهَبَ خَيالَ شَخْصٍ **3** (infml) (from a job) فَصَلَ (i; فَصْل), أَقالَ, عَزَلَ (i; عَزْل) ‹*an employee, a worker*›; **you're ~d!** أَنْتَ مَفْصولٌ! **4** (Tech) حَرَقَ (i; حَرْق) ‹*ceramics, a pot*›
D *vi* **1** (Mil) أَطْلَقَ النارَ \ الرَصاصَ **2** (Aut) «the engine» اشْتَغَلَ, دارَ (u; دَوْر, دَوَران)

(Idiom) **to play with fire** لَعِبَ بالنارِ

(Phrasal verb) **fire up**: **~ [sb] up, ~ up [sb]** أَلْهَبَ حَماسَ [شَخْصٍ]

fire alarm *n* جِهاز إِنْذارِ الحَريقِ

firearm /ˈfʌɪərɑːm/ *n* سِلاح ناريّ

firebomb /ˈfʌɪəbɒm/ **A** *n* قُنْبُلة حارِقة
B *vt* أَلْقى قُنْبُلةً حارِقةً على ‹*a house, truck*›

fire brigade (BrE), **fire department** (AmE) *n* إِطْفائيّة, حِماية مَدَنيّة (NA), مَطافِئ

fire door *n* مَخْرَج طَوارِئَ

fire drill *n* تَدْريبات للوِقايةِ من الحَريقِ

fire engine *n* سَيّارة مَطافِئَ, سَيّارة إِطْفاءٍ, سَيّارة حِمايةٍ مَدَنيّةٍ (NA)

fire escape *n* (exit) مَخْرَج طَوارِئَ; (stairs) سُلَّم نَجاةٍ

fire exit *n* مَخْرَج طَوارِئَ

fire extinguisher *n* جِهاز إِطْفاءِ حَرائِقَ, طَفّاية حَريقٍ

firefight /ˈfʌɪəfʌɪt/ *n* اشْتِباك (مُسَلَّح)

firefighter /ˈfʌɪəfʌɪtə/ *n* إِطْفائيّ, رَجُل إِطْفاءٍ, عَوْن حِمايةٍ مَدَنيّةٍ (NA)

firefly /ˈfʌɪəflʌɪ/ *n* ذُبابة النارِ

fireguard /ˈfʌɪəgɑːd/ *n* [حاجِز للوِقايةِ من نارِ المِدْفَأةِ]

firelighter /ˈfʌɪəlʌɪtə/ *n* مُكَعَّب إِشْعالِ النارِ

fireman /ˈfʌɪəmən/ *n* (*pl* **-men**) إِطْفائيّ, رَجُل إِطْفاءٍ

fireplace /ˈfʌɪəpleɪs/ *n* مِدْفَأة (مَدافِئُ)

firepower /ˈfʌɪəpaʊə/ *n* قوّة ناريّة

fireproof /ˈfʌɪəpruːf/ *adj* ‹*building, suit*› مُقاوِم للنارِ

fire sale *n* [بَيْع تَصْفيةٍ لِبِضاعةِ مَحَلٍّ تَعَرَّضَ لِحَريقٍ]

fire service *n* إِطْفائيّة, مَطافِئ

fireside /ˈfʌɪəsʌɪd/ *n* [مِساحة بالقُرْبِ من مِدْفَأةِ المَنْزِلِ]

fire station *n* إِطْفائيّة

fire truck *n* (AmE) سَيّارة إِطْفاءٍ

firewall /ˈfʌɪəwɔːl/ *n* **1** (in a building) جِدار مُقاوِم للحَريقِ **2** (in computing) جِدار ناريّ

fire warden *n* إِطْفائيّ حَرائِقِ الغاباتِ

firewood /ˈfʌɪəwʊd/ *n* حَطَب (أَحْطاب)

firework /ˈfʌɪəwəːk/ *n* أَلْعاب ناريّة; **a ~s display** عَرْض أَلْعابٍ ناريّةٍ

firing /ˈfʌɪərɪŋ/ *n* إِطْلاق نارٍ

firing line *n* خَطّ نارٍ

firing squad *n* كَتيبة الإِعْدامِ (تُنَفِّذُ الحُكْمَ رَمْياً بالرَصاصِ)

firm /fəːm/ **A** *n* (business) شَرِكة; **a ~ of architects** شَرِكة هَنْدَسةٍ مِعْمارِيّةٍ

B *adj* **1** (hard) ‹*fruit*› صُلْب ,مُكْتَنِز; ‹*mattress*› ثابِت ,وَطيد; ‹*handshake*› قَوِيّ; **to give sth a ~ tap/tug** دَفَعَ \ شَدَّ شَيْئاً بِقُوّةٍ **2** (steady) ‹*table, ladder*› ثابِت **3** (strong) ‹*basis, foundation*› مَتين ,راسِخ ,قَوِيّ; ‹*favourite*› دائِم; **it is my ~ belief that ...** أنا على يَقينٍ راسِخٍ أنّ ... ; **to be/remain ~ friends** دامَتْ بَيْنَهُمْ صَداقةٌ مَتينةٌ \ جَمَعَتْهُمْ **4** (definite) ‹*offer, intention, date*› مُؤَكَّد **5** (resolute) ‹*leadership, voice, stand*› صارِم; **to be ~ with sb** كانَ صارِماً مع شَخْصٍ **6** (stable) ‹*currency, market*› مُسْتَقِرّ ,ثابِت

C *adv* (against attack) **to stand ~** وَقَفَ صامِداً

firmly /ˈfəːmli/ *adv* **1** ‹*to answer, deny*› بِحَزْمٍ; **I ~ believe that we should ...** أُؤْمِنُ بِشِدّةٍ أَنَّهُ عَلَيْنا ... **2** ‹*to grip, press*› بِقُوّةٍ

first /fəːst/ **A** *pron* **1** (of a series, group) أَوَّل (dipt; أَوَّلونَ, أَوائِل; f أُولى; f pl أُولَيات) **2** (**the first**) (of a month) **the ~ of May** أَوَّل مايو; **we will meet again on the ~** سَوْفَ نَلْتَقي مَرّةً أُخْرى في أَوَّلِ الشَّهْرِ **3** (**First**) (in titles) **Elizabeth the First** إليزابيث الأولى **4** (initial moment) أَوَّل (dipt), بِداية; **the ~ I knew about his death was a call from his wife** كانَ أَوَّلُ مَعْرِفَتي بِمَوْتِهِ من مُكالَمةٍ من زَوْجَتِهِ **5** (beginning) بِداية; **from the very ~** من البِدايةِ الأولى **6** (new experience) **to be a ~ for sb** كانَتِ التَجْرُبةَ الأولى لِشَخْصٍ **7** (Aut) (gear) دَرَجة; **to be in ~** كانَ على السُّرْعةِ الأولى; ▸**gear 8** (BrE Educ) نِهائيّة; **to get a ~ in chemistry** حَصَلَ على الدَرَجةِ النِهائيّةِ في الكيمْياءِ

B *adj* **1** (of a series, group) ‹*episode, part, instalment*› أَوَّل (dipt; أَوَّلونَ, أَوائِل; f أُولى; f pl أُولَيات); **the ~ three pages** الصَّفَحات الثَلاثِ الأولى **2** (in phrases) **at ~ glance** *or* **sight** من أَوَّلِ نَظْرةٍ; **I'll call ~ thing tomorrow** سَوْفَ أُهاتِفُكَ أَوَّلَ شَيْءٍ في الصَّباحِ; **he doesn't know the ~ thing about politics** لا يَعْرِفُ أَلِفَ باءِ السِياسةِ

C *adv* **1** (before others) ‹*to arrive, leave, finish*› أَوَّلاً; **you go ~!** تَقَدَّمْ أَنْتَ أَوَّلاً!; **women and children ~** النِساءُ والأَطْفالُ أَوَّلاً; **to come ~/last** جاءَ في المَرْكَزِ الأَوَّلِ \ الأَخيرِ **2** (in importance) **to put one's family/work ~** وَضَعَ أُسْرَتَهُ \ عَمَلَهُ أَوَّلاً; **his career always comes ~** دائِماً ما يَضَعُ مِهْنَتَهُ قبل أيِّ شَيْءٍ آخَرَ **3** (to begin with) أَوَّلاً ,بِدايةً; **at ~** في البِدايةِ; **there are two reasons: ~ ...** هُناكَ سَبَبانِ: أَوَّلاً ... ; **~ of all, I'd like to mention ...** بِدايةً وَقَبْلَ أيِّ شَيْءٍ، أَوَدُّ أنْ أَذْكُرَ أنّ ... ; **when we were ~ married** في بِدايةِ زَواجِنا **4** (for the first time) ‹*to meet, visit, see*› أَوَّلَ مَرّةٍ; **I ~ met him in Paris** قابَلْتُهُ أَوَّلَ مَرّةٍ في باريس

(Idiom) **first come first served** مَنْ ,الأَوْلَويّةُ بِأَسْبَقيّةِ الحُضورِ يَأْتِ أَوَّلاً يُخْدَمْ أَوَّلاً

first aid *n* إسْعافات أَوَّليّة; **to give sb first aid** قَدَّمَ إسْعافاتٍ أَوَّليّةً لِشَخْصٍ

first aid kit *n* عُدّة إسْعافاتٍ أَوَّليّةٍ

first class **A** *adj* (*before n* **first-class**) **1** (excellent) ‹*hotel, writer*› من الدَرَجةِ الأولى; **it's in first-class condition, its condition is first class** حالَتُهُ من الدَرَجةِ الأولى **2** (transport) ‹*ticket, passenger*› الدَرَجةِ الأولى **3** (BrE) (for letters) ‹*stamp, mail*› الدَرَجةِ الأولى **4** (BrE) (university degree) ‹*degree*› بِتَقْديرِ امْتِيازٍ; ‹*honours*› بِمَرْتَبةِ الشَرَفِ الأولى; **she has a first-class degree in Oriental Languages** لَدَيْها شَهادةٌ في اللُغاتِ الشَرْقيّةِ بِتَقْديرِ امْتِيازٍ; **he graduated with first-class honours in chemistry** تَخَرَّجَ بِشَهادةٍ في الكيمْياءِ بِمَرْتَبةِ الشَرَفِ الأولى;

B *adv* ‹*to travel, fly*› في الدَرَجةِ الأولى; ‹*to send*› بِبَريدِ الدَرَجةِ الأولى

first cousin *n* (son of father's brother) اِبْن عَمٍّ; (son of father's sister) اِبْن عَمّةٍ; (son of mother's brother) اِبْن خالٍ; (son of mother's sister) اِبْن خالةٍ; (daughter of father's brother) بِنْت عَمٍّ; (daughter of father's sister) بِنْت عَمّةٍ; (daughter of mother's brother) بِنْت خالٍ; (daughter of mother's sister) بِنْت خالةٍ

first-degree /ˌfəːstdɪˈgriː/ *adj* **1** ‹*burn*› من الدَرَجةِ الأولى **2** (AmE) ‹*murder, manslaughter*› مع سَبْقِ الإصْرارِ والتَرَصُّدِ

first floor *n* **1** (BrE) (one above street level) طابَق أَوَّل **2** (AmE) (at street level) طابَق أَرْضيّ

first form *n* (BrE) الصَفّ الأَوَّل (في التَعْليمِ الثانَويِّ)

first grade *n* (AmE Educ) الصَفّ الأَوَّل (في التَعْليمِ الابْتِدائيِّ)

first-hand /ˌfɜːstˈhand/ **A** *adj* ‹*report, news*› [مُسْتَقًى من مَصْدَرٍ أَصْليٍّ \ أَوَّليٍّ]

B *adv* (directly) ‹*to find out*› مُباشَرةً

firstly /ˈfɜːstli/ *adv* أَوَّلاً; **there are two reasons: ~ ...** هُناكَ سَبَبانِ: أَوَّلاً ...

first name *n* الاسْم الأَوَّل \ الشَّخْصيّ

first night *n* عَرْض أَوَّل

first-rate *adj* ‹*cast, journalism*› من الطِرازِ الأَوَّلِ

first-time buyer /ˌfɜːsttʌɪm ˈbʌɪə/ *n* [شَخْص يَشْتَري بَيْتاً للمَرّةِ الأولى]

fiscal /ˈfɪsk(ə)l/ *adj* ‹*control, policy*› ماليّ

fiscal year *n* سَنة ماليّة

fish /fɪʃ/ **A** *n* (*pl* **fish, fishes**) **1** (Zool) سَمَك (n coll; سِماك, أَسْماك) **2** (Culin) [u] سَمَك (n coll)

B *vi* **1** (in fishing) اِصْطادَ; **to ~ for trout/cod** كانَ يَصْطادُ سَمَكَ السَلْمون المُرَقَّطِ \ القَد **2** (for a response) بَحَثَ (a; بَحْث); **to ~ for information** بَحَثَ عن مَعْلوماتٍ; **to ~ for compliments** بَحَثَ عن المُجامَلاتِ

(Phrasal verbs) **fish around** (infml) (to search) فَتَّشَ

• **fish out**: **~ out [sth], ~ [sth] out** (infml) **1** (from pockets, etc) [أَخْرَجَ [شَيْئاً] ‹*a coin, list*› **2** (from river, etc) [اِنْتَشَلَ [شَيْئاً] ‹*a body, bicycle*›

fish and chips *n* [سَمَك وبَطاطِس مَقْليّة]

fish and chip shop *n* [مَحَلّ السَمَكِ والبَطاطِسِ المَقْليّةِ]

fishbowl /ˈfɪʃbəʊl/ *n* حَوْض سَمَكٍ

fishcake /ˈfɪʃkeɪk/ *n* كَعْك \ فَطيرة سَمَكٍ

fisherman /ˈfɪʃəmən/ *n* (*pl* **-men**) صَيّاد سَمَكٍ

fishery /ˈfɪʃ(ə)ri/ *n* (*pl* **fisheries**) **1** (fish farm) مَزْرَعة أَسْماكٍ **2** (fishing ground) مَصْيَدة أَسْماكٍ

fish farm *n* مَزْرَعة أَسْماكٍ

fish finger (BrE), **fish stick** (AmE) *n* إِصْبَع السَمَكِ

fish hook *n* شِصّ (شُصوص)

fishing /ˈfɪʃɪŋ/ *n* صَيْد السَمَكِ; **to go ~** ذَهَبَ لِصَيْدِ السَمَكِ

fishing boat *n* سَفينة صَيْدِ سَمَكٍ

fishing net *n* شَبَكة صَيْدٍ

fishing rod *n* قَصَبة صَيْدٍ

fish market *n* سوق سَمَكٍ

fishmonger /ˈfɪʃmʌŋɡə/ *n* (BrE) بائِع سَمَكٍ, سَمّاك; **~'s** مَسْمَكة (مَسامِكُ)

fishnet /ˈfɪʃnɛt/ *adj* [قُماش شَبَكيّ رَقيق]

fishnet stockings /ˌfɪʃnɛt ˈstɒkɪŋz/ *n pl* جَوارِب شَبَكيّة

fish shop (BrE), **fish store** (AmE) *n* مَسْمَكة (مَسامِكُ)

fish slice *n* [مِلْوَق مَثْقوب]

fish stick *n* (AmE) ▸ **fish finger**

fish tank *n* حَوْض سَمَكٍ

fishy /ˈfɪʃi/ *adj* (**fishier, fishiest**) **1** (like fish) ‹*smell, taste*› السَمَكِ **2** (infml) (suspicious) ‹*to sound, seem*› مَشْكوك فيهِ, مَشْبوه

fission /ˈfɪʃ(ə)n/ *n* **1** (also **nuclear fission**) انْشِطار نَوَويّ **2** (reproduction) انْقِسام الخَلايا

fist /fɪst/ *n* قَبْضة (قَبَضات)

(Idiom) **to make a good/poor fist of sth/doing sth** (BrE infml) [أَجادَ \ أَساءَ شَيْئاً \ فعْلَ شَيْءٍ]

fist fight *n* عِراك بالأَيْدي

fit /fɪt/ **A** *adj* **1** (in good physical shape) لائِق; (in good health) صَحيح (صِحاح), مُعافًى; **he's ~ enough to play** هو لائِقٌ بِما يَكْفي للَّعِبِ; **to keep ~** احْتَفَظَ بِلِياقَتِهِ; **he's ~ and well now** هو بِصِحّةٍ وعافِيةٍ الآنَ **2** (suitable for) **to be ~ for sb** ‹*a hero, king*› كانَ مُناسِباً لِشَخْصٍ; **this apartment is ~ for a king** هذه الشَقّةُ تُناسِبُ مَلِكاً; **is the water ~ to drink?** هل الماءُ صالِحٌ للشُرْبِ؟; **the food was not ~ for human consumption** كانَ الطَعامُ غَيْرَ صالِحٍ للاسْتِهْلاكِ الآدَميِّ; **to see ~ to do sth** رَأى أَنَّهُ من المُناسِبِ أَنْ يَفْعَلَ شَيْئاً **3** (capable) **to be ~ to do sth** كانَ قادِراً على فِعْلِ شَيْءٍ; **he's not ~ to drive** لَيْسَ قادِراً على القِيادةِ; **to be in no ~ state to do sth** كانَ في حالةٍ لا تُؤَهِّلُهُ لِفِعْلِ شَيْءٍ **4** (infml) (attractive) **to be ~** «girl, singer, actor» كانَ مُثيراً \ جَذّاباً **5** (infml) (ready) **are you ~?** هل أَنْتَ جاهِزٌ؟; **to be ~ to drop/burst** كانَ على وَشْكِ الوُقوعِ من التَعَبِ \ الانْفِجارِ من كَثْرةِ الأَكْلِ

B *vt* (*past tense* **fitted, fit** AmE; *past participle* **fitted**) **1** (in sizing) «trousers, shoes, shirts» ناسَبَ ‹*a person*›; **to ~ size**

6 to 9 ناسَبَ المَقاساتِ من 6 إلى 9; **to ~ ages 3 to 5** ناسَبَ الأَعْمارَ من 3 إلى 5 سَنَواتٍ [2] (to find room for) **to ~ sth in** *or* **into a room/house/car** وَجَدَ مَكاناً لِشَيْءٍ في حُجْرةٍ \ بَيْتٍ \ سَيّارةٍ [3] (to correspond to) «key» تَوافَقَ (مع) ‹*a lock*› [4] (to install) رَكَّبَ, ثَبَّتَ ‹*a lock, window, shower*›; **to ~ an alarm in the house** رَكَّبَ جِهازَ إنْذارٍ في البَيْتِ; **to ~ the door with a lock** رَكَّبَ قُفْلاً على البابِ [5] (for clothes, equipment) **to ~ sb for a suit/hearing aid** قاسَ بَدْلَةً \ أداةً سَمْعِيّةً على شَخْصٍ [6] (to be compatible with) ناسَبَ, تَوافَقَ (مع) ‹*a description, the requirements*›; **the suspect ~s the description of the wanted man** تَتَوافَقُ مُواصَفاتُ المُتَّهَمِ مع مُواصَفاتِ الرَجُلِ المَطْلوبِ; **the punishment should ~ the crime** لا بُدَّ أنْ يَتَناسَبَ العِقابُ مع الجَريمةِ; ▸**bill**

[C] *vi* (*past tense* **fitted**, **fit** AmE; *past participle* **fitted**) [1] (in sizing) «trousers, shoes, lid» كانَ مَقاسُهُ مُناسِباً [2] (to have enough room) «toys, luggage, clothes» وُجِدَ مَكانٌ لَهُ [3] (to correspond) تَوافَقَ, تَناسَبَ; **to ~ into a lock/socket** «keys, plugs» تَوافَقَ مع قُفْلٍ \ مِقْبَسٍ; **his story doesn't ~ with the facts** قِصَّتُهُ لا تَتَوافَقُ مع الحَقائِقِ

[D] *n* [1] (of coughing) نَوْبة (نَوْبات); **to have an epileptic ~** أُصيبَ بِنَوْبةِ صَرَعٍ [2] (of rage, panic) نَوْبة (نَوْبات); **to have a ~** اِشْتاطَ غَضَباً; **to have sb in ~s** جَعَلَ شَخْصاً يَنْفَجِرُ من الضَحِكِ [3] (of trousers, dress) **to be a good/poor ~** كانَ مَقاسُهُ مُناسِباً \ غَيْرَ مُناسِبٍ

Idiom **in fits and starts** بِشَكْلٍ مُتَقَطِّعٍ وَغَيْرِ مُنْتَظِمٍ

Phrasal verbs **fit in** [A] [1] «passengers, luggage» وَجَدَ مَكاناً; **will you all ~ in?** هل سَتَجِدونَ مَكاناً لَكُمْ جَميعاً؟ [2] (in human interaction) انْسَجَمَ, تَآلَفَ, تَناغَمَ; **he doesn't ~ in with the rest of the team** لا يَنْسَجِمُ مع بَقِيّةِ الفَريقِ; **I'll ~ in with your plans** سَوْفَ أُكَيِّفُ نَفْسي مع خِطَطِكَ [B] **~ [sth] in, ~ in [sth]** [1] (to find room for) وَجَدَ مَكاناً لِ [شَيْءٍ] ‹*books, furniture, clothes*› [2] (to find time for) وَجَدَ وَقْتاً لِ [شَيْءٍ] ‹*a game, meeting*› [C] **~ in [sb], ~ [sb] in** رَتَّبَ مَوْعِداً لِ [شَخْصٍ] ‹*a patient, client*›

• **fit out**: [A] **~ [sth] out, ~ out [sth]** جَهَّزَ [شَيْئاً] ‹*an office, an apartment*› [B] **~ [sb] out, ~ out [sb]** زَوَّدَ \ أَمَدَّ [شَخْصاً]; **to ~ sb out with clothing** زَوَّدَ شَخْصاً بالمَلْبَسِ

fitful /ˈfɪtfʊl/ *adj* ‹*sleep, progress*› مُتَقَطِّع

fitfully /ˈfɪtf(ə)li/ *adv* ‹*to sleep, rain*› بِشَكْلٍ مُتَقَطِّعٍ

fitna /ˈfɪtnə/ *n* فِتْنة (فِتَن)

fitness /ˈfɪtnəs/ *n* [1] (healthiness) لِياقة بَدَنِيّة; **how to improve your physical ~** كيف تُحَسِّنُ لِياقَتَكَ البَدَنِيّةَ [2] (suitability) كَفاءة; **he convinced us of his ~ for the job** أَقْنَعَنا بِكَفاءَتِهِ لِلحُصولِ على الوَظيفةِ

fitted /ˈfɪtɪd/ *adj* [1] (furniture) ‹*wardrobe, cupboard*› مُثَبَّت في الحائِطِ; ‹*kitchen, bedroom*› مُجَهَّز (ب) [2] (clothing, bedding) ‹*jacket, sheet*› [مُناسِب] (ل), [مُلائِم] (ل)

fitted carpet *n* موكيت

fitter /ˈfɪtə/ *n* [1] (of machines, electrical equipment) فَنّيّ تَرْكيبِ مُعَدّاتٍ [2] (of a carpet) فَنّيّ تَرْكيبِ موكيت [3] (of a garment) فَنّيّ أَخْذِ قِياساتٍ

fitting /ˈfɪtɪŋ/ [A] *n* [1] (**fittings**) (in a room) لَوازِم; **electrical/bathroom ~s** لَوازِم كَهْرَبائِيّة \ الحَمّامِ [2] (**fittings**) (in a house) تَجْهيزات [3] (for clothes) تَجْريب

[B] *adj* ‹*conclusion, tribute*› مُلائِم

fitting room *n* غُرْفة قِياسٍ \ تَجْريبِ المَلابِسِ

five /faɪv/ *n, adj* [1] (amounting to five) ‹*boys*› خَمْسة; ‹*girls*› خَمْس; **give me ~ nails** أَعْطِني خَمْسةَ مَسامير; **~ kilos of flour, please** خَمْسة كيلوجْرام من الدَقيقِ، من فَضْلِكَ; **'how many children were there?' — 'there were ~'** 'كم طِفْلاً كانَ هُناكَ؟' — 'كانَ هُناكَ خَمْسةٌ' [2] (fifth in a series) ‹*page, number, year*› خامِس; **look at page ~** أُنْظُرْ إلى الصَفْحةِ الخامِسةِ [3] (five years old) خَمْس سَنَواتٍ; **'how old is she?' — 'she's ~'** 'كم عُمْرُها؟' — 'خَمْسُ سَنَواتٍ'

five-a-side /ˌfaɪvəˈsaɪd/ *n* (also **five-a-side football**) كُرة القَدَمِ الخُماسِيّة

fiver /ˈfaɪvə/ *n* (infml) [1] (BrE) وَرَقة نَقْدِيّة بِخَمْسةِ جُنَيْهاتٍ [اسْتِرْلينِيّةٍ] [2] (AmE) وَرَقة نَقْدِيّة بِخَمْسةِ دولاراتٍ

five-year plan /faɪvjəː ˈplan/ *n* خُطّة خَمْسِيّة, مُخَطَّط خُماسِيّ

fix /fɪks/ [A] *vt* [1] (to set) حَدَّدَ ‹*a date, price, limit*› [2] (to repair) أَصْلَحَ ‹*a television, puncture*›; **to ~ one's hair** أَصْلَحَ

تَسْريحة شَعْرِهِ **3** (to attach) ثَبَّتَ ‹*a handle, shelf, notice*›; **to ~ the mirror to the wall** ثَبَّتَ المِرْآةَ على الحائِطِ **4** (infml) (to organize) رَتَّبَ ‹*a meeting, visit*›; **how are you ~ed for time/money?** ما هي ظُروفُكَ بالنِسْبَةِ للوَقْتِ \ للمالِ؟ **5** (infml) (to prepare) أَعَدَّ ‹*a drink, meal*›; **let me ~ you a drink** دَعْني أُعِدُّ لَكَ شَراباً; **she ~ed us a meal** أَعَدَّتْ لَنا وَجْبَةً **6** (fml) (to look at) **to ~ one's eyes** *or* **gaze on sb** ثَبَّتَ نَظَرَهُ على شَخْصٍ **7** (infml) (to rig) تَلاعَبَ في النَتيجةِ ‹*a race, match, an election*› **8** (chemically) ثَبَّتَ ‹*a plate, dye*›

B (**fixed**) *adj* **1** ‹*price, menu*› ثابت, مُحَدَّد ‹*order*›; **of no ~ed address** بِدونِ عُنْوانٍ مُحَدَّدٍ **2** ‹*smile, expression*› ثابت

C *n* **1** (infml) (to have a problem) **to be in a ~** كانَ في مَأْزِق **2** (infml) (of drugs) جُرْعة (جُرَع, جُرْعات) **3** (infml) (solution) حَلّ (حُلول), إصْلاح (إصْلاحات) **4** (in navigation) **to take a ~ on sth** حَدَّدَ مَوْقِعَهُ بِناءً على شَيْءٍ **5** (infml) (rigged game, race) **it was a ~** كانَ بِهِ تَلاعُبٌ

Phrasal verbs **fix on**: **~ on** [**sth**] قَرَّرَ [شَيْئاً] ‹*a date, price, venue*›

• **fix up** **A** **~ up** [**sth**], **~** [**sth**] **up** (infml) **1** (to organize) نَظَّمَ [شَيْئاً] ‹*a holiday, meeting*› **2** (to repair) أَصْلَحَ [شَيْئاً] ‹*a room, house*› **B** **~ sb up with sth** أَعَدَّ شَيْئاً لِشَخْصٍ ‹*accommodation, a drink, vehicle*›

fixation /fɪk'seɪʃ(ə)n/ *n* تَعَلُّق مَرَضيّ

fixed assets /fɪkst 'asets/ *n pl* أُصول ثابِتة

fixed costs /fɪkst 'kɒsts/ *n pl* تَكاليف ثابِتة

fixed-rate /ˌfɪkst'reɪt/ *adj* ‹*mortgage, loan*› ذو سِعْرِ فائِدةٍ ثابِتٍ

fixture /'fɪkstʃə/ *n* **1** (in sport) مَوْعِد رِياضيّ **2** (**fixtures**) *n pl* (fixed objects) تَجْهيزات ثابِتة; **the ~s and fittings are included in the price** يَشْمَلُ السِعْرُ كُلَّ تَجْهيزاتِ المَنْزِلِ

fizz /fɪz/ *vi* «drinks, champagne» فارَ (u; فَوْر, فَوَران)

fizzle out /'fɪz(ə)l/ *vi* «fire» اِنْطَفَأَ; «protest» فَشِلَ (a; فَشَل)

fizzy /'fɪzi/ *adj* (**fizzier, fizziest**) ‹*drink, water*› غازيّ

fjord /'fiːɔːrd/ *n* مَضيق (مَضائِق, مَضايِق), مَمَرّ مائيّ

FL *abbr* ▸**Florida**

flabby /'flabi/ *adj* (**flabbier, flabbiest**) ‹*arms, muscles*› مُتَرَهِّل

flag /flag/ **A** *n* **1** (of a country) عَلَم (أَعْلام), راية; **to sail under the Panamanian ~** أَبْحَرَ تحت العَلَمِ البَنَميِّ **2** (as a signal) عَلَم (أَعْلام), راية **3** (*also* **flagstone**) بَلاطة (بَلاطات, أَبْلِطة)

B *vt* (**-gg-**) (to highlight) وَضَعَ عَلامةً (على) ‹*a paragraph, an article*›; نَبَّهَ (إلى) ‹*a problem, threat*›

C *vi* (**-gg-**) **1** (to wane) «interest» تَراجَعَ; «conversation» فَتَرَ (u; فُتور) **2** (to tire) «athletes, campaigners» تَعِبَ (a; تَعَب)

Idiom **to fly the flag** رَفَعَ العَلَمَ

Phrasal verb **flag down**: **~** [**sth**] **down**, **~ down** [**sth**] أَوْقَفَ [شَيْئاً] ‹*a car, train, taxi*›

Phrasal verb **flag up**: **~** [**sth**] **up**, **~ up** [**sth**] أَشارَ إلى [شَيْءٍ] ‹*a problem, shortage*›

flagpole /'flagpəʊl/ *n* سارِية عَلَمٍ

flagrant /'fleɪgrənt/ *adj* ‹*violation, disregard*› صارِخ

flagship /'flagʃɪp/ *n* **1** (ship) بارِجة الأَميرال **2** (showpiece) ميزة

flagship enterprise *n* مَشْروع رائِد

flagship store *n* مَتْجَر رائِد

flagstone /'flagstəʊn/ *n* بَلاطة (بَلاطات, أَبْلِطة)

flair /flɛː/ *n* **1** (talent) مَلَكة; **to have a ~ for languages** كانَ لَدَيْهِ مَلَكة تَعَلُّمِ اللُغاتِ **2** (style) ذَوْق (أَذْواق)

flak, flack /flak/ *n* [u] **1** (Mil) نيران مُضادّة للطائِراتِ **2** (infml) (criticism) نَقْد لاذِع; **to get** *or* **take a lot of ~** تَعَرَّضَ إلى الكَثيرِ من الانْتِقاداتِ اللاذِعةِ

flake /fleɪk/ **A** *n* **1** (also **snow flake**) نُدْفة (نُدَف), رُقاقة **2** (of cereal) رَقيقة (رَقائِق); **a bowl of oat/corn ~s** زُبْدِيّة من رَقائِق الشوفانِ \ الذُرةِ **3** (of paint, skin) قِشْرة (قِشَر)

B *vi* (also **flake off**) «paint, skin» تَقَشَّرَ

flak jacket, flak vest *n* سُتْرة واقِية من الرَصاص

flaky /'fleɪki/ *adj* (**flakier, flakiest**) **1** (breaking into flakes) ‹*piecrust, biscuit*› [مُكَوَّن من رَقائِق]; ‹*plaster, paint*› مُتَقَشِّر, قابِل للتَقَشُّرِ **2** (infml) (eccentric) ‹*idea, comment*› غَريب

flaky pastry *n* مُعَجَّنات مُكَوَّنة من رَقائِق

flamboyant /flamˈbɔɪənt/ *adj* 1 ‹*gesture, personality*› مُلْفِت للانْتِباهِ 2 ‹*colour*› صارِخ؛ ‹*hat*› مُبَهْرَج

flame /fleɪm/ *n* لَهَب؛ **the building was in ~s** الْتَهَمَ اللَهَبُ البِناية؛ **to go up in ~s** أَتَتْ عَلَيْهِ أَلْسِنةُ اللَهَبِ؛ **to burst into ~s** الْتَهَبَتْ فيهِ النارُ

(Idiom) **an old flame** حَبيب قَديم

flameproof /ˈfleɪmpruːf/ *adj* 1 (inflammable) ‹*fabric, furniture*› غَيْر قابِلٍ \ مُضادّ للاشْتِعالِ 2 (ovenproof) ‹*dish, cookware*› صالِح للفُرْنِ

flamer /ˈfleɪmə/ *n* [شَخْص يُرْسِل رَسائِلَ إِلِكْترونيّةً مُسْتَفِزّةً \ مُهينةً]

flamethrower /ˈfleɪmθrəʊə/ *n* قاذِفة اللَهَبِ

flaming /ˈfleɪmɪŋ/ **A** *n* [إِرْسال الرَسائِلِ الإِلِكْترونيّةِ المُسْتَفِزّة \ المُهينةِ]

B *adj* 1 (burning) ‹*wreckage, torch*› مُلْتَهِب 2 (violent) ‹*row, temper*› مُلْتَهِب

flamingo /fləˈmɪŋgəʊ/ *n* (*pl* **flamingos** or **flamingoes**) نُحام, بَشَروش, فلامِنْجو (ME)

flammable /ˈflaməb(ə)l/ *adj* ‹*gas, liquid*› لَهوب, قابِل للاشْتِعالِ

flan /flan/ *n* فْلان (فَطيرة مَحْشوّة بالفَواكِهِ, بالجُبْنِ إلخ ...)

Flanders /ˈflɑːndəz/ *n* فلانْدَرْز (f)

flank /flaŋk/ **A** *n* 1 (Anat) خاصِرة (خَواصِرُ) 2 (Mil) جَناح (أَجْنِحة)

B *vt* **to be ~ed by sb/sth** كانَ مُحاطاً بِشَخْصٍ \ بِشَيْءٍ

flannel /ˈflan(ə)l/ *n* 1 [u] فانِلّة; **a grey ~ suit** بَدْلة رَماديّة من الفانِلّا؛ **~ pyjamas** بيجامة من الفانِلّا؛ **a ~ shirt** فانِلّة 2 (also **face flannel**) (BrE) مِنْشَفة وَجْهٍ

flap /flap/ **A** *vt* (**-pp-**) ‹*arms, wings*› رَفْرَفَ (i; رَفْرَفة)

B *vi* (**-pp-**) «wings, flags, hair» خَفَقَ (i-u; خَفْق, خَفَقان, خُفوق)

C *n* 1 (on a pocket) غِطاء؛ (on an envelope) حاشِية؛ (on a tent) باب؛ (on a table) مِصْراع (جُزْء من الطاوِلةِ يُمْكِنُ طَيُّهُ أو مَدُّهُ) 2 (of a plane) قَلّاب (حافّة جَناحِ طائِرةٍ) 3 (of wings, sails) رَفْرَفة 4 (infml) (confusion) ذُعْر؛ **to get into a ~ over/about sth** أَصابَهُ الذُعْرُ بِسَبَبِ \ حول شَيْءٍ

flapjack /ˈflapdʒak/ *n* 1 (BrE) (cookie) فَطيرة (من الشوفانِ) 2 (AmE) (pancake) فَطيرة (من الدَقيقِ والبَيْضِ والحَليبِ)

flare /fleː/ **A** *n* 1 إِشارة ضَوْئيّة 2 (of a flame) تَوَقُّد 3 (of a skirt) [جُزْء سُفْليّ واسِع]

B *vi* 1 (to burn) «fireworks, matches» اشْتَعَلَ 2 (Clothing) «skirts, trousers» اتَّسَعَ (في الجُزْءِ السُفْليِّ)

(Phrasal verb) **flare up** 1 (to burn brightly) «fires» اتَّقَدَ 2 (to erupt) «trouble, violence» احْتَدَمَ؛ «tempers, anger» اضْطَرَمَ؛ «epidemics, revolutions» انْدَلَعَ 3 (to recur) «illness, symptoms» عاوَدَ

flares /fleːz/ *n pl* بَنْطَلون واسِع الأَطْرافِ؛ **a pair of ~** بَنْطَلون واسِع الأَطْرافِ

flare-up /ˈfleːrʌp/ *n* تَوَتُّر (تَوَتُّرات)

flash /flaʃ/ **A** *vt* 1 (infml) (to display) أَظْهَرَ ‹*money, an ID card*›; **they ~ed their badges at the guard** أَظْهَروا بِطاقاتِهِمْ \ شاراتِهِمْ للحارِسِ 2 (to shine) أَوْمَضَ ‹*your headlights, a torch*› 3 ‹*look*› أَلْقَى؛ **to ~ a smile** ابْتَسَمَ ابْتِسامةً خاطِفةً 4 (to transmit) بَثَّ (i-u; بَثّ) ‹*a picture, message*›

B *vi* 1 (to shine) «torches, warning lights» شَعَّ (i; شَعّ, شِعاع); **to ~ on and off** وَمَضَ وخَبا 2 (to appear suddenly) «thoughts» خَطَرَ (i; خُطور); «images» لاحَ (u; لَوْح); **the thought ~ed through my mind** خَطَرَت الفِكْرةُ على بالي 3 (infml) (to expose oneself) تَعَرّى

C *n* 1 (of light) وَمْضة؛ (of jewels) بَريق؛ **a ~ of lightning** وَميض بَرْقٍ 2 (instant) **it was all over in a ~** انْتَهى كُلّ شَيْءٍ في وَمْضةِ عَيْنٍ؛ **a ~ of inspiration/genius** لَحْظة إِلْهام \ عَبْقريّةٍ 3 (Phot) فلاش 4 (Comput) (**Flash**®) فْلاش 5 (news item) خَبَر (أَخْبار) 6 (stripe on uniform) شارة عَسْكَريّة؛ (on a car) شَريط (أَشْرِطة, شَرائِطُ)

D *adj* (infml) ‹*suit, hotel*› فَخْم

(Idioms) **quick as a flash** سَريع كالبَرْقِ؛ **to be a flash in the pan** مَرَّ كَلَمْحِ البَصَرِ

(Phrasal verbs) **flash by, flash past** «birds, runners, landscape» مَرَّ كالبَرْقِ

• **flash up** «messages, results» ظَهَرَ (فَجْأةً)

flashback /ˈflaʃbak/ *n* فْلاش باك, مَشْهَد \ مَقْطَع اسْتِرْجاعيّ

flashbulb /ˈflaʃbʌlb/ *n* مِصْباح فْلاش

flashcube /ˈflaʃkjuːb/ *n* [فْلاش مُكَعَّب يَحْتَوي على أَرْبَعةِ مَصابيحَ]

flash drive *n* (Comput) مُحَرِّك أَقْراصٍ مَحْمول

flashgun /ˈflaʃɡʌn/ *n* كَشّاف ضَوْئيّ, فْلاش

flashing /ˈflaʃɪŋ/ **A** *n* [u] [حَشْوة مَعْدِنيّة لِمَنْع التَسَرُّبِ] **B** *adj* ‹*light, sign*› وامِض

flashlight /ˈflaʃlʌɪt/ *n* **1** (electric torch) كَشّاف ضَوْئيّ \ كَهْرَبائيّ **2** (flashgun) فِلاش

flashy /ˈflaʃi/ *adj* (**flashier**, **flashiest**) (infml) ‹*car, jewellery*› مُبَهْرَج

flask /flɑːsk/ *n* **1** (for chemicals) دَوْرَق (دَوارِقُ) **2** (for oil, wine) قارورة (قَواريرُ) **3** (for hot drinks) تُرْمُس (تَرامِس)

flat /flat/ **A** *adj* **1** (level) ‹*surface, road, roof*› مُسَطَّح; **to be squashed ~** كان مُسَطَّحاً **2** (deflated) ‹*tyre, ball*› فارغ مِن الهَواءِ; **to have a ~ tyre** كانَ عِنْدَهُ إطارٌ فارِغٌ \ مَثْقوبٌ **3** (pressed close) **her feet were ~ on the floor** كانَتْ قَدَماها مُفْلَطَحَتَيْن على الأَرْضيّة **4** (low) ‹*shoes, heels*› مُسطَّح **5** (emphatic) ‹*refusal, denial*› قاطِع **6** (unvarying) ‹*fare, fee, rate*› ثابِت **7** (monotonous) ‹*voice, tone*› رَتيب **8** (not fizzy) ‹*beer, lemonade*› باسِل **9** (depressed) **to feel ~** كانَ مُحْبَطاً **10** (BrE) (discharged) ‹*battery*› فارِغ **11** (lacking demand) ‹*market, trade, profits*› كاسِد **12** (Mus) ‹*note*› خَفْض; **her singing is ~** غناؤُها ناشِزٌ

B *adv* **1** (horizontally) ‹*to place, lie*› أُفُقيًّا; **to lie ~ on one's back** تَمَدَّدَ على ظَهْرِه; **to fall ~ on one's face** سَقَطَ على وَجْهِهِ **2** (in close contact) [بِشَكْلٍ قَريبٍ جِدًّا]; **she pressed her nose ~ against the window** ضَغَطَتْ أَنْفَها بِشِدّةٍ على النافِذةِ **3** (exactly) بالضَبْطِ; **in 10 minutes ~** في 10 دَقائقَ بالضَبْط **4** (infml) (emphatically) بِشَكْلٍ قاطِع; **to turn sb/sth down ~** رَفَضَ شَخْصاً \ شَيْئاً بِشَكْلٍ قاطِعٍ **5** (Mus) ‹*to sing, play*› بِصَوْتٍ خافِتٍ

C *n* **1** (BrE) (apartment) شِقّة (شِقَق); **one-bedroom ~** شِقّة ذات غُرْفةِ نَوْمٍ واحِدةٍ **2** (level part) **the ~ of your hand/sword** كَفّ يَدِك \ سَطْح السَيْفِ **3** (infml) (on cars, bikes) إطار فارِغ مِن الهَواء \ مَثْقوب **4** (Mus) (note, sign) عَلامة الخَفْضِ في الموسيقى

D (**flats**) *n pl* **1** (AmE) (infml) (shoes) حِذاء بِدونِ كَعْبٍ **2** (land) سَهْل (سُهول)

(Idiom) **to fall flat** «jokes» كانَ فاشِلاً; «suggestions» كانَ سَخيفاً

flatly /ˈflatli/ *adv* **1** (absolutely) ‹*to refuse, deny*› بِشَكْلٍ قاطِعٍ **2** (unemotionally) ‹*to reply, answer*› دون اهْتِمامٍ

flatmate /ˈflatmeɪt/ *n* (BrE) زَميل سَكَنٍ

flatness /ˈflatnəs/ *n* **1** (of the landscape) اسْتِواء **2** (dullness) فُتور

flat out **A** *adj* (infml) ‹*to be, to lie*› طَريح (طَرْحى); **B** *adv* (infml) ‹*to work*› بِأَقْصى جُهْدٍ مُمْكِنٍ; ‹*to drive*› بِأَقْصى سُرْعةٍ مُمْكِنةٍ

flat rate **A** *n* (BrE) سِعْر مُوَحَّد; **B** (**flat-rate**) *adj* (BrE) ‹*fee, tax*› مُوَحَّد القيمة

flatten /ˈflat(ə)n/ **A** *vt* **1** (to level) سَوّى (بالأَرْض) ‹*a tree, crop, fence*› **2** (to smooth out) مَهَّدَ ‹*the ground, a surface*› **3** (to make flat) سَوّى ‹*metal*› **4** (infml) (to defeat) سَحَقَ (a; سَحْق) ‹*an opponent*›; **she ~ed her opponent in the final** سَحَقَتْ خَصْمَها في الدَوْرِ النِهائيِّ

B *vi* ▸ **flatten out**

C *v refl* **to ~ oneself against a wall/the door** الْتَصَقَ بالحائِطِ \ البابِ; **they had to ~ themselves against the wall to let the truck pass** كانَ عَلَيْهِمْ أنْ يَلْتَصِقوا بالحائطِ لِيَدَعوا الشاحِنةَ تَمُرُّ

(Phrasal verb) **flatten out** **1** (to become level) «roads, ground» تَمَهَّدَ **2** (to stop rising/falling) «growth, production» اسْتَقَرَّ **3** **~ out** [sth], **~** [sth] **out** فَتَحَ [شَيْئاً] ‹*a map, roll of paper*›

flatter /ˈflatə/ *vt* **1** (to please somebody) جامَلَ; (to get something in return) داهَنَ, تَمَلَّقَ ‹*an audience, a superior*› **2** أَبْرَزَ الجَمالَ ‹*the wearer, your figure*›; **that skirt ~s your figure** تِلْكَ التَنّورةُ تُبْرِزُ جَمالَ قَوامِكِ

flattering /ˈflatərɪŋ/ *adj* **1** ‹*remarks, compliments*› مُجامِل, مُداهِن **2** ‹*portrait, jeans*› مُبْرِز للجَمالِ

flattery /ˈflat(ə)ri/ *n* تَمَلُّق (تَمَلُّقات), مُداهَنة; **with a little ~, he soon won her round** حَصَلَ على مُوافَقَتِها بِسُرْعةٍ بِشَيْءٍ من التَمَلُّقِ

flatulence /ˈflatjʊləns/ *n* تَطَبُّل البَطْنِ بِسَبَبِ تَجَمُّعِ الغازاتِ

flaunt /flɔːnt/ *vt* تَباهى (بـ) ‹*your wealth, jewels*›

flautist /ˈflɔːtɪst/ *n* زَمّار

flavour (BrE), **flavor** (AmE) /ˈfleɪvə/ **A** *n* نَكْهة

B *vt* نَكَّهَ ‹*a sauce, drink*›

(Idiom) **to be flavour of the month** (infml) [نالَ حُظْوةً كَبيرةً لِوَقْتٍ مُعَيَّنٍ]

flavouring (BrE), **flavoring** (AmE) /ˈfleɪvərɪŋ/ *n* نَكْهة

flaw /flɔː/ *n* (in an object, a character) عَيْب (عُيوب); (in reasoning) خَطأ (أَخْطاء)

flawed /flɔːd/ *adj* ‹*system, logic*› ذو عَيْبٍ \ نَقيصة

flawless /ˈflɔːləs/ *adj* ‹*complexion, gem, performance*› خالٍ من العُيوب

flax /flæks/ *n* **1** (plant) كَتّان **2** (textile) أَلْياف الكَتّانِ

flay /fleɪ/ *vt* سَلَخَ (a-u; سَلْخ) ‹*a corpse, carcass, the skin*›

flea /fliː/ *n* بُرْغوث (بَراغيث)

flea market *n* سوق السِلَعِ المُسْتَعْمَلةِ

flea-ridden *adj* (infml) ‹*hotel, taxi*› رَديء (أَرْدِياءُ)

fleck /flek/ **A** *n* (of blood, mud) نُقْطة (نُقَط, نِقاط); (of dust) ذَرّة; (of colour) بُقْعة (بُقَع); (light) وَمْضة

B *vt* **her shoes were ~ed with mud** اتَّسَخَ حِذاؤُها بالطينِ

fled /fled/ *past tense, past participle* ▸ **flee**

fledgling, **fledgeling** /ˈfledʒlɪŋ/ *n* (bird) فَرْخ (أَفْراخ, فِراخ)

flee /fliː/ **A** *vt* (*past tense, past participle* **fled**) هَرَبَ (u; هُروب من) ‹*a place, persecution*›

B *vi* (*past tense, past participle* **fled**) «refugees, prisoners» هَرَبَ (u; هُروب)

fleece /fliːs/ *n* **1** (on a sheep) صوف; (from a sheep) جِزّة (جِزَز, جَزائِزُ) **2** (fabric) فَرْو (n coll; فِراء)

fleet /fliːt/ *n* **1** (of ships, small boats) أُسْطول (أَساطيلُ) **2** (of road vehicles) أُسْطول (أَساطيلُ)

fleeting /ˈfliːtɪŋ/ *adj* ‹*moment, visit*› عابِر, خاطِف

Flemish /ˈflemɪʃ/ **A** *adj* ‹*food, lesson*› فْلامَنْكيّ

B *n* **1** (**the Flemish**) (people) الفْلامَنْك **2** (language) (اللُغة) الفْلامَنْكيّة

flesh /fleʃ/ *n* **1** (body tissue) لَحْم (n coll; لُحوم, لِحام); **in the ~** بِشَحْمِهِ وَلَحْمِهِ; **they are your own ~ and blood** هُمْ من لَحْمِكَ وَدَمِكَ **2** (of a fruit, vegetable) لُبّ (لُبوب)

fleshy /ˈfleʃi/ *adj* (**fleshier**, **fleshiest**) ‹*legs, arms*› سَمين (سِمان); ‹*fruit*› غَضّ

flew /fluː/ *past tense* ▸ **fly**

flex /fleks/ **A** *n* (BrE) كابِل مَرِن

B *vt* ثَنى (i; ثَنْي) ‹*one's arms, joint*›; **to ~ one's muscles** اسْتَعْرَضَ عَضَلاتِهِ

flexibility /ˌfleksɪˈbɪlɪti/ *n* **1** (ability to bend) مُرونة **2** (adaptability) مُرونة

flexible /ˈfleksɪb(ə)l/ *adj* **1** ‹*wire, tube*› مَرِن **2** ‹*arrangement, plan*› مَرِن **3** ‹*worker, actor*› مَرِن

flexitime (BrE) /ˈfleksɪtaɪm/, **flextime** (AmE) /ˈflekstaɪm/ *n* [نظام ساعاتِ عَمَلٍ مَرِنةٍ]; **we are on ~** [نَعْمَلُ وَفْقَ نِظامِ ساعاتِ عَمَلٍ مَرِنةٍ]

flick /flɪk/ **A** *vt* **1** (with a whip) ضَرَبَ (بالسَوْطِ) **2** (to move) حَرَّكَ ‹*a switch, lever*›; **he ~ed his ash onto the floor** نَفَضَ رَمادَهُ على الأَرْضيةِ; **the cow ~ed its tail** حَرَّكَت البَقَرةُ ذَيْلَها; **she ~ed her hair out of her eyes** أَبْعَدَتْ شَعْرَها عن عَيْنَيْها بِحَرَكةٍ خَفيفةٍ من يَدِها **3** (Sport) سَدَّدَ ‹*the ball, a shot*›

B *n* (sharp movement with fingers) نَقْرة (إِصْبَع); (with a tail, whip, duster) ضَرْبة; **at the ~ of a switch** في رَمْشةِ عَيْنٍ

C (**flicks**) *n pl* (old use) سينَما

(Phrasal verbs) **flick off**: **~ [sth] off**, **~ off [sth]** **1** نَفَضَ [شَيْئاً] ‹*crumbs, cigarette ash*› **2** **~ [sth] off**, **~ off [sth]** أَغْلَقَ [شَيْئاً] ‹*radio, switch*›

• **flick on**: **~ [sth] on**, **~ on [sth]** فَتَحَ [شَيْئاً] ‹*switch, radio*›

• **flick over**: **~ [sth] over**, **~ over [sth]** تَصَفَّحَ [شَيْئاً] ‹*the pages*›

• **flick through**: **~ through [sth]** تَصَفَّحَ [شَيْئاً] ‹*a magazine, report*›

flicker /ˈflɪkə/ **A** *vi* **1** (of light, flames) «fire, lights» تَلَعْلَعَ **2** «eyes, indicators» رَفَّ (i-u; رَفّ, رَفيف)

B *n* **1** (of a flame) تَلَعْلُع **2** (of the eyelids) رَفيف

flick knife *n* (BrE) سِكّين زُنْبُركيّة (تَخْرُجُ من المِقْبَضِ عند الضَغْطِ على زِرّ)

flier /ˈflʌɪə/ *n* ▸ **flyer**

flies /flʌɪ/ **A** *3rd pers pres sing* ▸ **fly** A, ▸ **fly** B

B *pl* ▸ **fly** D

flight /flʌɪt/ *n* **1** (journey) رِحْلة (رِحْلات); **the ~ from Riyadh to London** الرِحْلة من الرِياضِ إلى لُنْدُن; **a scheduled/charter ~** رِحْلة مُحَدَّدة المَوْعِد \ في طائرةٍ مُسْتَأْجَرةٍ **2** (course of a bird, insect) رِحْلة (رِحْلات); (of a ball) مَسار الطَيَرانِ **3** [u] (ability to fly) تَحْليق; **an eagle in full ~** نِسْر أثناء الطَيَرانِ **4** (of birds) سِرْب (أَسْراب) **5** (of planes, helicopters) سِرْب (أَسْراب) **6** [u] (escape) فِرار, هُروب; **to take ~** لاذَ بالفِرارِ; **the ~ from the land began in ...** النُزوحُ بَدَأَ في ... **7** (of steps, stairs) سُلَّم (سَلالِمُ); **we live four ~s up** نَسْكُنُ في الطابِقِ الرابِعِ **8** (of imagination) **a ~ of fancy** شَطْحة خَيالٍ

(Idiom) **to be in the top flight** كانَ في القِمّةِ

flight attendant *n* مُضيف طَيَرانٍ

flight bag *n* [حَقيبة يُسْمَحُ بِأَخْذِها إلى مَقْصورة الطائرةِ]

flight deck *n* **1** (on planes) قَمْرة \ مَقْصورة القِيادةِ **2** (on aircraft carriers) سَطْح الطَيَرانِ

flight engineer *n* مُهَنْدِس طَيَرانٍ

flight information *n* مَعْلومات عن الرِحْلاتِ الجَوّيّة

flight number *n* رَقْم رِحْلةٍ

flight path *n* مَسار رِحْلةِ طَيَرانٍ

flimsy /ˈflɪmzi/ *adj* (**flimsier, flimsiest**) **1** ‹*fabric, garment*› خَفيف **2** ‹*structure, door*› مُهَلْهَل **3** ‹*argument, evidence*› واهٍ

flinch /flɪntʃ/ *vi* انْكَمَشَ; **to ~ from doing one's duty** أَحْجَمَ \ نَكَصَ عن أداءِ واجِبِه

fling /flɪŋ/ **A** *vt* (*past tense, past participle* **flung**) (to hurl) قَذَفَ (i; قَذْف) ‹*a ball, stone*›; **she flung the plate at him** قَذَفَت الصَحْنَ عَلَيْهِ; **he flung the accusation back at her** رَدَّ التُهْمَةَ عَلَيْها; **she flung her arms around his neck** وَضَعَتْ ذِراعَيْها حول رَقَبَتِهِ

B *v refl* (*past tense, past participle* **flung**) **to ~ oneself** رَمى نَفْسَهُ; **to ~ oneself off a bridge/to the ground** رَمى نَفْسَهُ من على جِسْرٍ \ على الأَرْضِ

C *n* **1** (infml) (spree) [انْغِماس في المَلَذّاتِ] **2** (infml) (affair) **to have a ~** عاشَ نَزْوةً

(Phrasal verbs) **fling about, ~ around: ~ [sth] about** (infml) بَعْثَرَ (i; بَعْثَرة) ‹*money*›

• **fling back: ~ [sth] back, ~ back [sth] 1** رَدَّ [شَيْئاً] ‹*a ball, stone*› **2** أَزاحَ [شَيْئاً] ‹*a blanket, cover*›

• **fling down: ~ [sth] down, ~ down [sth]** رَمى [شَيْئاً] على الأَرْضِ ‹*a racket, bike*›

• **fling on: ~ on [sth], ~ [sth] on** (infml) لَبِسَ [شَيْئاً] على عَجَلٍ ‹*a dress, coat*›

• **fling open: ~ [sth] open, ~ open [sth]** فَتَحَ [شَيْئاً] بِقوّةٍ ‹*a door, window*›

flint /flɪnt/ *n* **1** [u] (piece of stone) صَوّان **2** (for a lighter) حَجَر القَدّاحةِ

flip /flɪp/ **A** *vt* (**-pp-**) رَمى في الهَواءِ (بِحَيْثُ يَنْقَلِبُ) ‹*a pancake*›; **we'll ~ a coin to decide** سَنَرْمي قِطْعةً مَعْدِنيّةً في الهَواءِ لِنُقَرِّرَ

B *vi* (**-pp-**) (infml) فَقَدَ أَعْصابَهُ

flip chart *n* سَبّورة وَرَقيّة (قَلّابة)

flip-flop /ˈflɪpflɒp/ *n* (BrE) بابوج (بَوابيجُ)

flippant /ˈflɪp(ə)nt/ *adj* ‹*remark, attitude*› وَقِح

flipper /ˈflɪpə/ *n* **1** (of a sea animal) زَعْنِفة (زَعانِفُ) **2** (for a swimmer) زَعْنِفة سِباحةٍ

flip side *n* **1** (reverse side) جِهة خَلْفيّة **2** (infml) (different aspect) وَجْه آخَر

flirt /flɜːt/ **A** *vi* تَغَنَّجَ

B *n* [شَخْص لَعوب \ مِغْناج]; **she is a terrible ~** [هِيَ فَتاةٌ لَعوبٌ بِشَكْلٍ فَظيعٍ]

flirtation /flɜːˈteɪʃ(ə)n/ *n* **1** (relationship) عَلاقة غَراميّة عابِرة; [u] (coquetry) مُغازَلة **2** (interest) اسْتِهْواء

flirtatious /flɜːˈteɪʃəs/ *adj* ‹*smile, remark*› غَزَليّ

flit /flɪt/ *vi* (**-tt-**) (also **flit about**) «birds, butterflies» هَفا (u; هَفْو)

float /fləʊt/ **A** *vi* **1** (on a liquid) «swimmers, boats» طَفا (u; طَفْو); (in the air) «balloons» حَلَّقَ; **to ~ on one's back**

طَفا على ظَهْرِهِ; **the boat was ~ing out to sea** كانَ المَرْكَبُ يَطْفو في البَحْرِ; **the balloons ~ed up in the air** حَلَّقَت البالوناتُ عالِياً في الهَواءِ **2** «currencies» اسْتَقَرَّ

B *vt* **1** عَوَّمَ ‹*a boat, log*› **2** (Fin) قامَ بالتَعْويمِ ‹*shares, a company*› **3** (to propose) اقْتَرَحَ ‹*an idea, a suggestion*›

C *n* **1** (on a fishing line) فِلّينة صِنّارةِ صَيْدٍ; (on a fishing net) عَوّامة من فِلّينٍ **2** (in a cistern) عَوّامة **3** (for swimming) أداة طَفْوٍ **4** (AmE) (life jacket) سُتْرة نَجاةٍ **5** (in parades) [عَرَبة ذات مِنَصّة اسْتِعْراضٍ] **6** (petty cash) مَبْلَغ صَغير **7** (AmE) (drink) [مَشْروب غازيّ بالبوظةِ]

(Phrasal verbs) **float about**, **float around** **1** (to circulate) «ideas, rumours» انْتَشَرَ **2** (infml) (to be at hand) كانَ هُنا في مَكانٍ ما

• **float away ▸ float off**

• **float off** **1** (to move away) «lifeboats» طَفا (u; طَفْو); «balloons» حَلَّقَ **2** (to refloat) «yacht, tanker» عَوَّمَ

floating /ˈfləʊtɪŋ/ *adj* **1** ‹*bridge, restaurant*› عائِم **2** ‹*currency*› عائِم; ‹*population*› مُتَنَقِّل

floating voter *n* [ناخِب لم يُقَرِّرْ بَعْدُ لِمَنْ سَيُدْلي بِصَوْتِهِ]

flock /flɒk/ **A** *n* (group of sheep, goats) قَطيع (قُطْعان); (of birds) سِرْب (أَسْراب); (of people) حَشْد

B *vi* «fans, pilgrims» توافَدَ

floe /fləʊ/ *n* طَوْف جَليديّ

flog /flɒg/ *vt* **(-gg-)** **1** (to beat) ضَرَبَ ضَرْباً مُبَرِّحاً ‹*a prisoner, servant*› **2** (infml) (to sell) باعَ (i; مَبيع ,بَيْع) ‹*the kit, encyclopedias*›

flood /flʌd/ **A** *n* **1** (of water) فَيَضان; **the river was in ~** فاضَ النَهْرُ; **the F~** الطوفان **2** (large quantity) **a ~ of visitors/complaints** عَدَد هائِل من الزائِرينَ \ الشَكاوى; **to be in ~s of tears** بَكى بُكاءً مُرًّا

B *vt* **1** «river, rain» غَمَرَ (u; غَمْر) ‹*the area, house*› **2** (to fill) غَمَرَ (u; غَمْر) ‹*a room, sb's mind*› **3** (to over-supply) اكْتَسَحَ ‹*the market, shops*› **4** (Mech) أَشْبَعَ بالمَحْروقاتِ ‹*the engine, carburettor*›

C *vi* **1** «meadows, streets, houses» تَعَرَّضَ إلى الفَيَضانِ **2** «protesters, cars» تَدَفَّقَ; «light» انْهَمَرَ; **tears ~ed down his cheeks** انْهَمَرَت الدُموعُ على خَدَّيْهِ

(Phrasal verbs) **flood back** «memories» تَدَفَّقَ; «anger» انْفَجَرَ

• **flood in** «contributions, light, people» تَدَفَّقَ

• **flood out** **A** **~ out** «workers, travellers» خَرَجَ مُسْرِعاً

B **to be ~ed out** «people» [أُجْبِرَ على الخُروجِ بِسَبَبِ الفَيَضانِ]

floodgate /ˈflʌdgeɪt/ *n* بَوّابة سَدٍّ (للتَحَكُّم في مَنْسوبِ المِياهِ)

flooding /ˈflʌdɪŋ/ *n* فَيَضان; **this road is liable to ~** هذا الطَريقُ مُعَرَّضٌ للفَيَضانِ

floodlight /ˈflʌdlaɪt/ **A** *n* كَشّاف ضَوْئيّ

B *vt* (*past tense, past participle* **floodlit**) أَنارَ بِكَشّافاتٍ ضَوْئيّةٍ ‹*a building, stadium*›

flood tide *n* مَدّ (مُدود)

floor /flɔː/ **A** *n* **1** (of a room, house) أَرْضيّة; **we sat on the ~** جَلَسْنا على الأَرْضيّة; **to take the ~** «dancers» دَخَلَ حَلْبةَ الرَقْصِ **2** (of the sea, a valley) قاع (قيعان); **the forest ~** أَرْضيّة الغابة **3** (of a parliament, chamber) أَرْضيّة; **to take questions from the ~** تَلَقّى أَسْئِلةً من الحاضِرينَ **4** (level) طابَق (طَوابِقُ); **the first ~** (BrE) (one level up) الطابَق الأَوَّل; (AmE) (at ground level) الطابَق الأَرْضيّ; **the ground/bottom ~** الأَرْضيّة; **the top ~** الطابَق العُلْويّ **5** (for prices, charges) حَدّ أَدْنى

B *vt* **1** بَلَّطَ ‹*a room, garage*›; **an oak-~ed room** غُرْفة مُبَلَّطة بِخَشَبِ البَلّوط **2** «boxer» طَرَحَ (أَرْضاً) ‹*an opponent*› **3** (to silence) أَفْحَمَ ‹*a rival, critic, candidate*›

(Idiom) **to wipe the floor with sb** (infml) مَسَحَ بِشَخْصٍ الأَرْضَ

floorboard /ˈflɔːbɔːd/ *n* [لَوْح خَشَبيّ للأَرْضيّاتِ]

floorcloth /ˈflɔːklɒθ/ *n* مِمْسَحة (مَماسِحُ ,مِمْسَحات)

flooring /ˈflɔːrɪŋ/ *n* أَرْضيّة

floor show *n* عُروض كَباريه (تُقَدَّمُ على الأَرْضيّةِ بَدَلَ خَشَبةِ المَسْرَحِ)

flop /flɒp/ **A** *vi* **(-pp-)** **1** (when sitting, lying) ارْتَمى; **she ~ped into her chair** ارْتَمَتْ على كُرْسِيِّها **2** (infml) (to fail) «movies, projects» فَشِلَ فَشَلاً ذَريعاً

B *n* (infml) فَشَل ذَريع

floppy /ˈflɒpi/ *adj* (**floppier**, **floppiest**) ‹*ears, bag*› مُتَدَلٍّ

floppy disk *n* قُرْص مَرِن \ لَيِّن

flora /ˈflɔːrə/ *n* (*pl* **floras** or **florae**) نَباتات (في مِنْطَقةٍ \ حِقْبة)

floral /ˈflɔːrəl/ *adj* ‹*design, fabric*› مُزَخْرَف بالأَزْهارِ

floret /ˈflɒrɪt/ *n* زَهْرة صَغيرة

florid /ˈflɒrɪd/ *adj* **1** (ornate) ‹*language, decoration*› مُنَمَّق **2** (ruddy) ‹*face, complexion*› مُتَوَرِّد

Florida /ˈflɒrɪdə/ *pr n* فلوريدا

Floridian /flɒˈrɪdɪən/ *pr n, adj* [(شَخْص) من فلوريدا]

florist /ˈflɒrɪst/ *n* بائِع زُهورٍ, زَهّار; **the ~'s** مَحَلّ الزُهورِ

floss /flɒs/ *n* خَيْط تَنْظيفِ الأَسْنانِ

flotation /fləʊˈteɪʃ(ə)n/ *n* (of a company, shares) تَعْويم

flotsam /ˈflɒtsəm/ *n* ~ **and jetsam** خُرْدَوات

flounce /flaʊns/ **A** *vi* **to ~ in/out** دَخَلَ \ خَرَجَ مُغْتاظاً **B** *n* [حَرَكة مُفاجِئة تُعَبِّرُ عن اسْتِياءٍ \ ضَجَرٍ]

flounder /ˈflaʊndə/ **A** *n* (fish) سَمَك مُفَلْطَح **B** *vi* **1** (to falter) «students, speakers» تَخَبَّطَ **2** «negotiations, economy» تَعَثَّرَ **3** (to thrash about) «people, animals» تَخَبَّطَ

flour /ˈflaʊə/ *n* دَقيق, طَحين

flourish /ˈflʌrɪʃ/ **A** *vt* لَوَّحَ (ب) ‹*a ticket, letter*› **B** *vi* «trade, children» ازْدَهَرَ **C** *n* **1** (gesture) [إيماءة للتَرْحيبِ] **2** (in handwriting) زَخْرَفة, تَنْميق **3** (positive note) [نَجاح باهِر]

flourishing /ˈflʌrɪʃɪŋ/ *adj* ‹*business, town*› مُزْدَهِر

flout /flaʊt/ *vt* خالَفَ عَلَناً ‹*a law, ban*›

flow /fləʊ/ **A** *vi* **1** (to move) «water, gas, traffic» انْسابَ, تَدَفَّقَ; **the river ~s into the sea at ...** يَصُبُّ النَهْرُ في البَحْرِ عند ...; **the A/C system keeps the air ~ing** نِظامُ التَكْييفِ يُحافِظُ على تَدَفُّقِ الهَواءِ; **applications keep ~ing in** ما زالَت الاسْتِماراتُ تَتَدَفَّقُ بِأَعْدادٍ كَبيرةٍ **2** (to be continuous) «conversation, words» انْسابَ, تَدَفَّقَ **3** (infml) «wine, beer» تَوَفَّرَ **4** (to hang gracefully) «hair, dress» تَدَلّى **B** *n* تَدَفُّق (تَدَفُّقات); **the river is in full ~** ارْتَفَعَ مَنْسوبُ مِياهِ النَهْرِ إلى الذُرْوةِ; **to improve the traffic ~** حَسَّنَ حَرَكةَ السَيْرِ

flow chart, **flow diagram**, **flow sheet** *n* خَريطة تَدَفُّقٍ

flower /ˈflaʊə/ **A** *n* زَهْر (n coll; زُهور) **B** *vi* «plants, trees» أَزْهَرَ

flower arranging *n* تَنْسيق الزُهورِ

flower bed *n* حَوْض زُهورٍ

flowering /ˈflaʊərɪŋ/ **A** *n* **1** (blooming) إزْهار **2** (of ideas) ازْدِهار (ازْدِهارات) **B** *adj* (producing blooms) ‹*shrub, plant*› مُزْهِر

flowerpot /ˈflaʊəpɒt/ *n* أَصيص (أُصُص)

flower seller *n* بائِع زُهورٍ

flower shop *n* مَحَلّ زُهورٍ

flowery /ˈflaʊəri/ *adj* **1** ‹*design, pattern*› زَهْرِيّ, مُشَجَّر **2** ‹*language, style*› مُنَمَّق

flowing /ˈfləʊɪŋ/ *adj* ‹*beard, robe*› مُنْسَدِل, مُسْتَرْسِل; ‹*handwriting, movement*› انْسِيابِيّ

flown /fləʊn/ *past participle* ▸ **fly**

flu /fluː/ *n* إنْفِلْوَنْزا

fluctuate /ˈflʌktjʊeɪt/ *vi* «levels, rates» تَقَلَّبَ

fluctuation /ˌflʌktʃʊˈeɪʃ(ə)n/ *n* [u] تَقَلُّب (تَقَلُّبات)

flue /fluː/ *n* (of a chimney, stove) مِدْخَنة (مَداخِنُ)

fluency /ˈfluːənsi/ *n* طَلاقة

fluent /ˈfluːənt/ *adj* **1** **to be ~ in Italian** كانَ يَتَكَلَّمُ اللُغةَ الإيطاليّةَ بِطَلاقةٍ **2** ‹*account, speaker*› فَصيح (فُصَحاءُ, فِصاح, فُصُح)

fluently /ˈfluːəntli/ *adv* ‹*to speak*› بِطَلاقةٍ; ‹*to read*› بِسَلاسةٍ

fluff /flʌf/ *n* زَغَب

fluffy /ˈflʌfi/ *adj* (**fluffier**, **fluffiest**) ‹*toy, garment*› مَنْفوش

fluid /ˈfluːɪd/ **A** *n* سائِل (سَوائِلُ); **a bottle of cleaning ~** قِنّينة من سائِلٍ مُنَظِّفٍ **B** *adj* **1** ‹*form*› مائِع, سائِل **2** ‹*situation*› غَيْر مُسْتَقِرٍّ

fluid ounce *n* آوْنْس سائِلِيّ, آوْنْصة سائِلة

fluke /fluːk/ *n* (infml) ضَرْبة حَظٍّ

flummox /ˈflʌməks/ *vt* (infml) جَعَلَ في حَيْرةٍ من أَمْرِهِ ,حَيَّرَ ‹*a user, voter*›

flung /flʌŋ/ *past tense, past participle* ▸ **fling**

fluorescence /flɔːˈrɛs(ə)ns/ *n* فَلْوَرة

fluorescent /flɔːˈrɛs(ə)nt/ *adj* ‹*dye, jacket*› فَلْوَرِيّ; **~ lighting** إضاءة فَلْوَرِيّة

fluoride /ˈflɔːrʌɪd/ *n* فُلوريد

fluorine /ˈflɔːriːn/ *n* فُلور

flurry /ˈflʌri/ *n* (*pl* **flurries**) [1] (of wind) هَبّة; (of snow) دُفْقة (دُفَقات ,دُفُقات) [2] (outburst) هَرْج; **a ~ of activity** هَرْج وَمَرْج

flush /flʌʃ/ **A** *vt* **to ~ the toilet** شَطَفَ المِرْحاض
B *vi* [1] (to blush) «cheeks, face» تَوَرَّدَ ,احْمَرَّ [2] «WCs» شُطِفَ
C *n* [1] (of shame) تَوَرُّد; (of anger, passion) احْمِرار [2] (in cards) [أَوْراق مُتَسَلْسِلة من نَفْسِ النَوْعِ]
D *adj* يَمْلِكُ مالاً وَفيراً

Phrasal verb **flush out**: **~ out [sb/sth]** أَخْرَجَ [شَخْصاً \ شَيْئاً] من مَخْبَئِهِ ‹*the rebels, a criminal*›

flushed /flʌʃt/ *adj* ‹*cheeks, face*› مُتَوَرِّد ,مُحْتَقِن; **~ with success** في غَمْرة النَجاح

fluster /ˈflʌstə/ **A** *vt* شَوَّشَ (على) ‹*a teacher, leader*›; **to get ~ed** تَشَوَّشَ فِكْرُهُ
B *n* تَشَوُّش

flute /fluːt/ *n* مِزْمار (مَزامِيرُ)

flutist /ˈfluːtɪst/ *n* (AmE) ▸ **flautist**

flutter /ˈflʌtə/ **A** *vt* [1] (to beat) **the bird ~ed its wings** رَفْرَفَ العُصْفورُ جَناحَيْه [2] (to wave) لَوَّحَ مُحَرِّكاً (بـ) ‹*a fan, handkerchief*›; **to ~ one's eyelashes at sb** رَفْرَفَ رُموشَ عَيْنَيْه لِشَخْصٍ
B *vi* [1] (to beat) «wings» رَفْرَفَ (i; رَفْرَفة) [2] (to fly) «birds, moths» طار (i; طَيَران) [3] (to move) «flags, curtains» رَفْرَفَ (i; رَفْرَفة) [4] (to beat irregularly) «heart» ارْتَجَفَ
C *n* [1] (of wings) خَفْقة ,رَفْرَفة (خَفَقات); (of lashes) رَمْشة; (of flags, bunting) رَفْرَفة [2] (stir) **a ~ of excitement/anticipation** حالة من الحَماسِ \ التَوَقُّعِ; **to be all in a ~** كانَ في حالةٍ من الهَيَجانِ [3] (BrE) (infml) (bet) **to have a ~ on the horses** وَضَعَ رِهاناً على الحِصانِ [4] (in the heart) سُرْعة في خَفَقانِ القَلْبِ [5] (in sound) خَلَل صَوْتِيّ

fluttering /ˈflʌtərɪŋ/ **A** *n* [1] (of birds, wings) رَفْرَفة [2] (of flags, clothes) رَفْرَفة [3] (of the heart) خَفَقان
B *adj* ‹*banner, flag*› مُرَفْرِف ,خافِق

flux /flʌks/ *n* **to be in (a state of) ~** كانَ في (حالةِ) تَغَيُّرٍ مُسْتَمِرٍّ

fly /flʌɪ/ **A** *vt* (*3rd person present sing* **flies**, *present participle* **flying**, *past tense* **flew**, *past participle* **flown**) [1] (to operate) قادَ (u; قِيادة) ‹*an aircraft*›; **the pilot flew the plane to Sharjah** قادَ الطَيّارُ الطائِرةَ إلى الشارِقةِ; **to ~ a kite** لَعِبَ بالطائِرةِ الوَرَقِيّةِ [2] (to transport) نَقَلَ جَوًّا ‹*supplies, the wounded*›; **to ~ supplies in/out of an area** نَقَلَ مَؤونةً إلى \ خارِجَ مِنْطَقةٍ [3] (to cross) عَبَرَ (u; عُبور) ,طارَ فوقَ ‹*the Atlantic, Indian Ocean*› [4] (with distances) طارَ (i; طَيَران) ‹*a distance*›; **I ~ at least 50,000 miles a year** (as a passenger) أُسافِرُ جَوًّا مَسافةَ 50000 ميلٍ كُلَّ سَنةٍ على الأَقَلِّ; (as a pilot) أُطيرُ مَسافةَ 50000 ميلٍ كُلَّ سَنةٍ على الأَقَلِّ [5] (to display) رَفَعَ (a; رَفْع) ‹*a flag*›
B *vi* (*3rd person present sing* **flies**, *present participle* **flying**, *past tense* **flew**, *past participle* **flown**) [1] (to be in the air) «birds, aircraft, rocket» طارَ (i; طَيَران); **to ~ over** *or* **across sth** حَلَّقَ عَبْرَ شَيْءٍ; **a bird flew past the window** طارَ طَيْرٌ أَمامَ النافِذةِ; **to ~ into the airport** وَصَلَ إلى المَطارِ [2] (to travel) «passengers, pilots» سافَرَ جَوًّا; **to ~ from Riyadh to Kuwait** سافَرَ جَوًّا من الرِياضِ إلى الكُوَيْتِ; **we ~ to Baghdad twice a week** نَقومُ بِرِحْلَتَيْنِ إلى بَغْدادَ أُسْبوعِيًّا [3] (to be propelled) «bullets, glass» انْطَلَقَ; **shards flew everywhere** تطايَرَت الشَظايا في كُلِّ مَكانٍ; **the door flew open** انفَتَحَ البابُ بِقُوّةٍ فَجْأةً; **he sent the tray ~ing** قَذَفَ بالصينِيّةِ في الهَواءِ [4] «insults, threats» انْتَشَرَ; **the rumours are ~ing** تَنْتَشِرُ الإشاعاتُ; **to ~ into a rage** انْفَجَرَ من الغَضَبِ [5] (infml) (to rush, hurry) «people, cars» انْطَلَقَ بِسُرْعةٍ; **I must ~!** يَجِبُ أَنْ أُغادِرَ الآنَ!; **to ~ past** مَرَّ بِسُرْعةٍ [6] (to pass quickly) «time, holidays» مَرَّ بِسُرْعةٍ; **how time flies!** لَقَدْ مَرَّ الوَقْتُ بِسُرْعةٍ! [7] (to wave) «flags» رَفْرَفَ (i; رَفْرَفة); «hair» تَمَوَّجَ; **to ~ in the wind** تَمَوَّجَ في الريحِ

C *n* (*pl* **flies**) (insect) ذُباب (n coll; ذِبّان)

D (**flies**) *n pl* (of trousers) [سِلْسِلة أو أزْرار]

E *adj* (BrE) (infml) (clever) شاطِر (شُطّار)

Idiom **to drop like flies** تَساقَطَ كالذُبابِ

Phrasal verbs **fly away** «birds, insects» طارَ بَعيداً

• **fly in** 1 «delegates, team» وَصَلَ عن طَريقِ الجَوّ 2 ~ **[sth/sb] in**, ~ **in [sth/sb]** حَمَلَ [شَيْئاً \ شَخْصاً] جَوًّا ‹*food, supplies, troops*›

fly-by-night /'flʌɪbʌɪnʌɪt/ *adj* ‹*dealer, firm*› غَيْر جَدير بالثِقة

flycatcher /'flʌɪkatʃə/ *n* خاطِف الذُبابِ

fly-drive /'flʌɪdrʌɪv/ *adj* ‹*holiday, package*› [يَتَضمَّنُ رِحْلةً جَوِّيّةً وَسَيّارةً مُؤَجَّرةً]

flyer /'flʌɪə/ *n* 1 (leaflet) مَنْشور إعْلانيّ 2 (pilot) طَيّار

flying /'flʌɪɪŋ/ **A** *adj* 1 (able to fly) ‹*insect, machine*› طائِر 2 (in the air) ‹*bullets, broken glass*› طائِش; **to take a ~ leap** قَفَزَ قَفْزةً عالِيةً

B *n* 1 (in a plane) **to be afraid of ~** كانَ خائفاً من الطَيَرانِ; **to take up ~** تَدَرَّبَ على الطَيَرانِ \ قِيادةِ الطائِراتِ 2 (by birds) طَيَران; **adapted for ~** مُهَيَّأً للطَيَرانِ

Idiom **to pay** *or* **make a flying visit** قامَ بِزيارةٍ خاطِفةٍ

flying buttress *n* (Archit) دِعامة طائِرة (بُروز خارِجيّ يُشَكِّلُ قَوْساً من الجِدار الّذي يَخْرُجُ مِنْهُ بغَرَضِ زيادة قُدْرة تَحَمُّلِه)

flying fish *n* سَمَك طائِر

flying instructor *n* مُعَلِّم طَيَران

flying jacket *n* سُتْرة طَيّار

flying saucer *n* طَبَق \ صَحْن طائِر

flying start *n* 1 (in a race) انْطِلاقة سَريعة 2 (good beginning) انْطِلاقة مُمْتازة; **to get off to a flying start** انْطَلَقَ انْطِلاقةً مُمْتازةً

flyleaf /'flʌɪli:f/ *n* (*pl* **flyleaves**) [صَفْحة بَيْضاء في أوَّلِ \ آخِرِ الكِتابِ]

fly-on-the-wall /flʌɪɒnðə'wɔ:l/ *adj* ‹*documentary, series*› واقِعيّ

flyover /'flʌɪəʊvə/ *n* 1 (BrE Transp) جِسْر عُلْويّ 2 (AmE Aviat) (aerial display) عَرْض جَوّيّ

fly-past /'flʌɪpɑ:st/ *n* (BrE) عَرْض جَوّيّ

fly spray *n* قاتِل الحَشَراتِ

fly swatter *n* مِنَشّة

flywheel /'flʌɪwi:l/ *n* حَذّافة (عَجَلة تَنْظيم السُرْعةِ)

FM /ɛf'ɛm/ *n* = **frequency modulation** إف إم

foal /fəʊl/ *n* مُهْر (أمْهار)

foam /fəʊm/ **A** *n* 1 (on sea, drinks) رَغْوة (رَغاوٍ) 2 (chemical) رَغْوة (رَغاوٍ)

B *vi* (also **foam up**) «waves, drinks» أرْغَى; **to ~ at the mouth** أرْغَى وَأزْبَدَ

foam bath *n* رَغْوة الاسْتِحْمام

foam rubber *n* مَطّاط رَغْويّ

fob /fɒb/ *n* (for watch) سِلْسِلة ساعةِ الجَيْبِ

Phrasal verb **fob off** (**-bb-**) **A** ~ **[sb] off**, ~ **off [sb]** (to palm off) [تَخَلَّصَ من [شَخْصٍ] عن طَريقِ اخْتِلاقِ الأعْذارِ] ‹*an enquirer, a customer*› **B** ~ **[sth] off**, ~ **off [sth]** (to get rid of) [تَخَلَّصَ من [شَيْءٍ] عن طَريقِ البَيْعِ بالغِشِّ] ‹*a product, the goods*›

fob watch *n* ساعة جَيْبٍ

focal /'fəʊk(ə)l/ *adj* 1 ‹*length, infection*› بُؤْريّ 2 ‹*issue, activity*› مَرْكَزيّ

focus /'fəʊkəs/ **A** *n* (*pl* **focuses, foci**) 1 (Phot) (focal point) بُؤْرة (بُؤَر); **in/out of ~** في \ خارِجَ البُؤْرةِ 2 (of attention, interest) مَرْكَز (مَراكِزُ), مِحْوَر (مَحاوِرُ)

B *vt* (**-s-** or **-ss-**) 1 (Phys) رَكَّزَ ‹*a ray, beam*› 2 (Phot) رَكَّزَ ‹*a lens, camera*›

C *vi* (**-s-** or **-ss-**) 1 «eyes, camera» تَرَكَّزَ 2 **to ~ on a subject** «reports, lecturers» رَكَّزَ على مَوْضوعٍ

focus group *n* مَجْموعة نِقاشٍ

fodder /'fɒdə/ *n* عَلَف (أعْلاف)

foe /fəʊ/ *n* (liter) عَدوّ (أعْداء)

foetal (BrE), **fetal** (AmE) /'fi:t(ə)l/ *adj* ‹*development, position*› جَنينيّ

foetus (BrE), **fetus** (AmE) /'fi:təs/ *n* جَنين (أجِنّة)

fog /fɒg/ *n* 1 (cloud) ضَباب 2 (confusion) ضَبابيّة

fogbound /'fɒgbaʊnd/ *adj* ‹*airport*› مَشْلول بِفِعْلِ الضَبابِ; ‹*passenger*› مُتأخِّر بِسَبَبِ الضَبابِ

foggy /ˈfɒgi/ *adj* (**foggier, foggiest**) [1] ‹*weather, day*› ضَبابيّ; **it's ~** الجَوُّ ضَبابيٌّ [2] ‹*idea, notion*› ضَبابيّ; **I haven't the foggiest idea** لَيْسَتْ لَدَيَّ أَيَّةُ فِكْرةٍ

foghorn /ˈfɒghɔːn/ *n* نَفير الضَّبابِ

fog lamp *n* ▸ **fog light**

fog light *n* مِصْباح \ كَشّاف الضَّبابِ

foible /ˈfɔɪb(ə)l/ *n* نُقْطة ضَعْفٍ

foil /fɔɪl/ [A] *vt* أَحْبَطَ ‹*a robbery, plan*›
[B] *n* سلوفان; **cooking/aluminium ~** ورَق أَلَمِنْيوم

foist /fɔɪst/ *vt* **to ~ sth (off) on** *or* **onto sb** فَرَضَ شَيْئًا على شَخْصٍ ‹*an opinion, idea*›

fold /fəʊld/ [A] *vt* [1] (to bend or bring together) طَوى (i; طَيّ) ‹*a towel, table*›; **~ it in half** اطْوِهِ إلى نِصفَيْنِ [2] (to intertwine) شَبَّكَ ‹*one's arms, hands*› [3] (to add) أَضافَ ‹*the flour, ingredients*›; **to ~ sth into sth** أَضافَ شَيْئًا إلى شَيْءٍ
[B] *vi* [1] «tables, deckchairs» طُوِيَ [2] (infml) (to fail) «companies, projects» فَشِلَ (a; فَشَل)
[C] *n* [1] (crease) طَيّ (أَطْواء) [2] (sheep pen) حَظيرة غَنَمٍ
[D] (**-fold**); *in combination* **his income increased five~** ازْدادَ دَخْلُهُ خَمْسةَ أَضْعافٍ; **the problem is three-~** للمُشْكِلةِ ثَلاثةُ أَوْجُهٍ

(Phrasal verbs) **fold away**: [1] **~ away** «bed, table» انْطَوى [2] **~ away [sth], ~ [sth] away** طَوى [شَيْئًا] ‹*a chair, bed*›
• **fold back**: [1] **~ back** «shutters, the door» انْفَتَحَ [2] **~ back [sth], ~ [sth] back** فَتَحَ [شَيْئًا] ‹*the shutters, blanket, one's collar*›
• **fold down**: [1] **~ down** «car seat, pram hood» طُوِيَ [2] **~ [sth] down, ~ down [sth]** أَطْبَقَ [شَيْئًا] ‹*the seat, hood*›; **to ~ down the corner of the page** أَطْبَقَ زاوِيةَ الصَّفْحةِ
• **fold in**: **~ in [sth], ~ [sth] in** «baker, cook» أَضافَ [شَيْئًا] ‹*the sugar, flour*›
• **fold out**: **~ out [sth], ~ [sth] out** فَتَحَ \ بَسَطَ [شَيْئًا] ‹*the map, newspaper*›
• **fold up**: [1] **~ up** «chairs, umbrellas» انْثَنى, انْطَوى; **it ~s up very compactly** يُمْكِنُ طَيُّهُ إلى حَجْمٍ صَغيرٍ جِدًّا [2] **~ [sth] up, ~ up [sth]** طَوى [شَيْئًا] ‹*a newspaper, an umbrella*›

folder /ˈfəʊldə/ *n* [1] (for papers) مِلَفّ (مِلَفّات) [2] (Comput) مُجَلَّد (مُجَلَّدات)

folding /ˈfəʊldɪŋ/ *adj* ‹*table, bed*› قابِل للطَّيِّ

foliage /ˈfəʊlɪɪdʒ/ *n* أَوْراق الشَّجَرِ

folio /ˈfəʊlɪəʊ/ *n* (*pl* **folios**) (paper) [وَرَقة مَطْوِيّة مَرّةً واحِدةً]; (book) [كِتاب كَبير الحَجْمِ (تُعْطي أَرْبَعَ صَفَحاتٍ)]

folk /fəʊk/ [A] *n* [1] (**also folks**) (infml) (people) أُناس [2] (**folks**) (AmE infml) (relatives) أَهْل; (parents) والِدانِ
[B] *adj* [1] (traditional) ‹*art, medicine*› شَعْبيّ; **a ~ song** أُغْنيّة فولْكْلوريّة \ شَعْبيّة [2] (common) ‹*hero, wisdom*› شَعْبيّ

folklore /ˈfəʊklɔː/ *n* فولْكْلور

folk music *n* موسيقى فولْكْلوريّة \ شَعْبيّة

folk song *n* أُغْنيّة فولْكْلوريّة \ شَعْبيّة

follow /ˈfɒləʊ/ [A] *vt* [1] (to come after) تَبِعَ (a; تَبَع) ‹*a person, car*›; **to ~ sb** تَبِعَ شَخْصًا; **they ~ed us on a later flight** لَحِقوا بِنا فيما بَعْدُ على مَتْنِ رِحْلةٍ جَوِّيّةٍ; **she ~ed her father into medicine/politics** سارَتْ على خُطى أَبيها في مَجالِ الطِّبِّ \ السِّياسةِ [2] (in time) تَلا (u; تُلُوّ), عَقَبَ (u; عَقْب) ‹*an event, a period, incident*› [3] (in lists) تَلا (u; تُلُوّ) ‹*sb's name, an item*› [4] (to go along) تَبِعَ (a; تَبَع) ‹*a path, river*› [5] (to be guided by) تَبِعَ (a; تَبَع) ‹*the instructions, clue*›; اسْتَعانَ (ب) ‹*map*› [6] (to be led by) اقْتَدى (ب) ‹*an example, sb's teachings, a religion*› [7] (to monitor) تابَعَ ‹*a sport, a trial, the stock market*› [8] (to understand) تَمَكَّنَ من المُتابَعةِ ‹*an explanation, sb's reasoning, the plot*›; **if you ~ me, if you ~ my meaning** إذا تَمَكَّنْتَ من مُتابَعتي [9] (to practise) امْتَهَنَ ‹*a career, profession*›
[B] *vi* [1] (to come after) «people, animals» لَحِقَ (a; لَحاق); **she ~ed in the car** لَحِقَتْ في السَّيّارةِ; **to ~ in sb's footsteps** سارَ على خُطى شَخْصٍ [2] (in time) **there ~ed a lengthy debate, a lengthy debate ~ed** تَلا ذلكَ مُناظَرةٌ طَويلةٌ; **there's ice cream to ~** تُوَزَّعُ البوظةُ لاحِقًا; **the results were as ~s** كانَتْ النَّتائِجُ كَما يَلي [3] (to be a consequence) تَرَتَّبَ; **it ~s that ...** يَتَرَتَّبُ على ذلكَ أَنَّ ...; **it doesn't necessarily ~ that ...** لَيْسَ بالضَّرورةِ أَنْ يَتَرَتَّبَ على ذلكَ أَنَّ ... [4] (to understand) «person» فَهِمَ (a; فَهْم); **I don't ~** لا أَفْهَمُ

(Phrasal verbs) **follow about, follow around**: **~ [sb] about** تَبِعَ [شَخْصاً] ‹*a tourist, one's brother*›

• **follow out**: **~ out [sth]** (AmE) اتَّبَعَ [شَيْئاً] ‹*advice, an order*›

• **follow through** **1** (Sport) «tennis players, golfers» أَكْمَلَ الضَّرْبةَ **2** **~ through [sth], ~ [sth] through** واصَلَ [شَيْئاً] إلى النِهايةِ ‹*an experiment, a threat, an idea*›

• **follow up**: **~ up [sth], ~ [sth] up** **1** (to confirm) عَزَّزَ [شَيْئاً] ‹*a victory, success*› **2** (to act upon) تابَعَ [شَيْئاً] ‹*a complaint, a suggestion, letter*›

follower /ˈfɒləʊə/ *n* **1** (adherent) تابِع (تابِعونَ ,أَتْباع) **2** (of a sport, series, trial) مُتابِع

following /ˈfɒləʊɪŋ/ **A** *prep* **1** (as a result of) إِثْرَ ‹*this incident, your request, the allegations*› **2** (after) بَعْدَ ‹*his arrival, her speech*›

B *n* **1** (of a religion) تابِع (أَتْباع); (of a leader) نَصير (أَنْصار); (of a series) مُتابِع; (of a team) مُشَجِّع **2** (**the following**) (before lists) التالي; **you will need the ~ items** سَتَحْتاجُ إلى المَوادِّ التالِيةِ; **the ~ is a guide to the subject** التالي هو دَليلٌ لِلمَوْضوعِ

C *adj* **1** (next) ‹*chapter, remarks*› تالٍ (تَوالٍ); **the ~ day/year** اليَوْمَ \ العامَ التالي **2** (from behind) **a ~ wind/breeze** ريح \ نَسيم آتٍ من خَلْفٍ

follow-up /ˈfɒləʊʌp/ *n* **1** (sequel) تَتِمّة **2** (further treatment) مُتابَعة

folly /ˈfɒli/ *n* [u] (foolishness) حَماقة ,غَباء

fond /fɒnd/ *adj* (**fonder, fondest**) **1** **to be ~ of sth/sb** كانَ مولَعاً \ مُغْرَماً بِشَيْءٍ \ بِشَخْصٍ; **she's very ~ of her uncle** تُحِبُّ عَمَّها \ خالَها كَثيراً; **he's ~ of chocolate** هو مولَعٌ بالشوكولاتةِ **2** ‹*look, gesture*› رَقيق ,حَنون

fondle /ˈfɒnd(ə)l/ *vt* داعَبَ ‹*a pet, lover*›

fondly /ˈfɒndli/ *adv* **1** (lovingly) ‹*to smile, remember*› بِحُبٍّ, بِحَنانٍ **2** (foolishly) ‹*to believe, expect*› بِسَذاجةٍ

fondness /ˈfɒndnəs/ *n* **1** (love for a person) وَلَع **2** (liking for a thing) وَلَع

font /fɒnt/ *n* **1** (for baptism) جُرْن (المَعْموديّة) **2** (in printing) خَطّ (خُطوط)

food /fuːd/ *n* **1** (for nutrition) أَكْل ,غِذاء (أَغْذِية) ,طَعام (أَطْعِمة); **~ is in plentiful/short supply** الأَكْلُ وافِرٌ \ قَليلٌ **2** (specific kind) طَعام (أَطْعِمة)

food aid *n* مَعونة \ مُساعَدة غِذائيّة

food chain *n* سِلْسِلة غِذائيّة

foodie /ˈfuːdi/ *n* (BrE infml) ذَوّاق

food poisoning *n* تَسَمُّم غِذائيّ

food processor *n* [جِهاز مُتَعَدِّد الوَظائِف لِتَحْضيرِ الطَعامِ]

food security *n* أَمْن غِذائيّ

foodstuff /ˈfuːdstʌf/ *n* مادّة غِذائيّة

fool /fuːl/ **A** *n* **1** (stupid person) أَحْمَق ,مُغَفَّل (dipt; حُمْق; f حَمْقى); **you ~!** أَنْتَ مُغَفَّلٌ !; **she's no ~** لَيْسَتْ مُغَفَّلةً; **to make sb look like a ~, to make a ~ of sb** جَعَلَ شَخْصاً يَبْدو أَحْمَقَ; **I was ~ enough to agree/to pay him** كُنْتُ أَحْمَقَ بِما يَكْفي لِأُوافِقَ \ لِأَدْفَعَ لَهُ; **any ~ can do that** أَيُّ غَبيٍّ يَسْتَطيعُ أَنْ يَفْعَلَ ذلك **2** (Hist) (jester) مُهَرِّج; **to act** *or* **play the ~** اسْتَعْبَطَ **3** (Culin) **a fruit ~** [حَلْوَيات بالفاكِهةِ]

B *vt* (to deceive) «promises, partner» خَدَعَ (a; خَدْع); **don't let that ~ you!** لا تَدَعْ ذلك يَخْدَعُكَ; **you don't ~ me for a minute** لا تَسْتَطيعُ أَنْ تَخْدَعَني وَلَوْ لِدَقيقةٍ; **they ~ed us into helping them** خَدَعونا لِنُساعِدَهُمْ

C *vi* (to joke) مَزَحَ (a; مَزْح); **don't listen to her, she's just ~ing** لا تُنْصِتْ إلَيْها، إنَّها فَقَطْ تَمْزَحُ

D *v refl* **to ~ oneself** خادَعَ نَفْسَهُ

E *adj* (AmE) (infml) ‹*politician*› سَخيف (سُخَفاءُ); **that's a damn ~ thing to do/say** إنَّهُ لَمِنَ الغَباءِ أَنْ تَقولَ \ تَفْعَلَ شَيْئاً مِثْلَ ذلك

(Phrasal verb) **fool about** (BrE infml) **fool around** (infml) **1** (to act stupidly) عَبِثَ (a; عَبَث); **stop ~ing around with that knife!** تَوَقَّفْ عن العَبَثِ بِتِلْكَ السِكّينِ **2** (to waste time) تَسَكَّعَ

foolhardy /ˈfuːlhɑːdi/ *adj* ‹*action, climber*› مُتَهَوِّر ,طائِش

foolish /ˈfuːlɪʃ/ *adj* **1** ‹*man, child*› أَحْمَق (dipt; حُمْق; f حَمْقى) **2** ‹*grin, expression*› أَحْمَق **3** ‹*decision, question*› أَحْمَق

foolproof /ˈfuːlpruːf/ *adj* **1** ‹*method, plan*› ناجِع **2** ‹*machine, system*› سَهْل الاسْتِعْمالِ

foolscap /ˈfuːlskap/ *n* (BrE) فولْسْكاب

foot /fʊt/ **A** *n* (*pl* **feet**) **1** (person's) قَدَم (f; أَقْدام); (animal's) رِجْل (f; أَرْجُل); (of a stocking, sock) [جُزْء من الجَوْرَبِ يُغَطّي القَدَمَ]; **I broke a bone in my ~** كَسَرْتُ عَظْماً في قَدَمي; **to arrive/travel on ~** وَصَلَ \ سافَرَ مَشْياً على الأَقْدام; **to set ~ in a place** وَضَعَ قَدَماً في مَكانٍ; **to help sb to their feet** ساعَدَ شَخْصاً لِيَقِفَ على قَدَمَيْه \ رِجْلَيْهِ; **to be on one's feet again** وَقَفَ على قَدَمَيْه \ رِجْلَيْهِ **2** (measurement) قَدَم (f; أَقْدام) (= 0.3048 m); **he is six ~ three (inches tall), he is six feet three (inches tall)** يَبْلُغُ طولُهُ سِتَّ أَقْدامٍ وَثَلاثَ بوصاتٍ **3** (bottom of a hill, mountain) سَفْح (سُفوح); (of a letter, page) أَسْفَل (dipt); (of the stairs) أَسْفَل (dipt); **at the ~ of his bed** عند مُؤَخِّرةِ سَريرِهِ

B *vt* **to ~ the bill for sth** تَحَمَّلَ مَصاريفَ شَيْءٍ

(Idioms) **my foot!** (infml) [لا أُصَدِّقُ!]; **to fall** *or* **land on one's feet** رُبَّ ضارَةٍ نافِعَةٌ; **to find one's feet** رَسَّخَ أَقْدامَهُ; **to get under sb's feet** عَطَّلَ شَخْصاً; **to keep one's feet on the ground** [حافَظَ على تَواضُعِهِ]; **to put one's feet up** (infml) مَدَّ رِجْلَيْهِ وَاسْتَراحَ; **to put one's foot down** تَصَرَّفَ بِحَزْمٍ; **to shoot oneself in the foot** (infml) وَضَعَ إِصْبَعَهُ في عَيْنِهِ; **to stand on one's own two feet** وَقَفَ على رِجْلَيْهِ; **to start off on the wrong/right foot** بَدَأَ بِدايَةً خاطِئَةً \ صَحيحَةً

footage /ˈfʊtɪdʒ/ *n* صُوَر ,لَقَطات

foot-and-mouth disease /ˌfʊt(ə)nˈmaʊθ dɪˌziːs/ (BrE), **hoof-and-mouth disease** (AmE) *n* حُمّى قُلاعِيّة

football /ˈfʊtbɔːl/ *n* **1** (BrE) [u] (soccer) كُرة القَدَم **2** (AmE) [u] (American football) كُرة القَدَمِ الأَمْرِيكيّة **3** (ball) كُرة (كُرات, كُرًى)

football coach *n* **1** (in soccer) مُدَرِّب كُرَوِيّ **2** (in American football) مُدَرِّب كُرَوِيّ

footballer /ˈfʊtbɔːlə/ *n* (BrE) لاعِب كُرةِ قَدَمٍ

football match *n* (BrE) مُباراة كُرةِ قَدَمٍ

football player *n* **1** (in soccer) لاعِب كُرةِ قَدَمٍ **2** (in American football) لاعِب كُرةِ القَدَمِ الأَمْرِيكيّةِ

football pools *n* (BrE) [مُراهَنات على نَتائِجِ مُبارَياتِ كُرةِ القَدَمِ]

footbrake /ˈfʊtbreɪk/ *n* فَرْمَلة \ مِكْبَح القَدَمِ

footbridge /ˈfʊtbrɪdʒ/ *n* جِسْر مُشاةٍ

footer /ˈfʊtə/ *n* تَذْييل الصَفْحةِ

foothills /ˈfʊthɪlz/ *n pl* تِلال سَفْحيّة

foothold /ˈfʊthəʊld/ *n* **1** (in climbing) مَوْطِئ قَدَمٍ **2** (in business, politics) مَوْطِئ قَدَمٍ

footing /ˈfʊtɪŋ/ *n* **1** (basis) أَساس (أَساسات, أُسُس), قاعِدة (قَواعِد); **to be on an equal ~ with sb** كانَ على قَدَمِ المُساواةِ مع شَخْصٍ **2** (grip for feet) **to lose one's ~** زَلَّتْ قَدَمُهُ

footlights /ˈfʊtlaɪts/ *n pl* [أَضْواء على مُقَدِّمةِ خَشَبةِ المَسْرَحِ]

footloose /ˈfʊtluːs/ *adj* <*traveller, youngster*> حُرّ

footman /ˈfʊtmən/ *n* (*pl* **-men**) خادِم (خَدَمة, خُدّام), وَصيف (وُصَفاء)

footnote /ˈfʊtnəʊt/ *n* تَعْليق (تَعْليقات, تَعاليق), حاشِية (حَواشٍ)

foot passenger *n* مُسافِر مُتَرَجِّل

footpath /ˈfʊtpɑːθ/ *n* (in countryside) مَمْشى (مَماشٍ); (in town) مَمَرّ الراجِلينَ

footprint /ˈfʊtprɪnt/ *n* أَثَر قَدَمٍ

foot soldier *n* جُنْديّ مُشاةٍ

footstep /ˈfʊtstɛp/ *n* خَطْوة (خَطَوات)

(Idiom) **to follow in sb's footsteps** سارَ على \ اتَّبَعَ خُطى شَخْصٍ

footstool /ˈfʊtstuːl/ *n* مِسْنَد قَدَمٍ

footwear /ˈfʊtwɛː/ *n* نَعْل (mf; نِعال, أَنْعُل)

for /fɔː, fə/ **A** *prep* **1** (intended for) لِ, لِأَجْلِ; **who are the flowers ~?** لِمَنْ هذه الزُهورُ؟; **a game ~ young people** لُعْبة لِلشَبابِ; **to buy sth ~ sb** اشْتَرى شَيْئاً لِشَخْصٍ; **he cooked dinner ~ us** طَهى عَشاءً لَنا **2** (indicating purpose) لِ, مِن أَجْلِ; **what's it ~?** ما الغَرَضُ مِنْهُ؟; **it's ~ removing stains** يُسْتَعْمَلُ لِإِزالةِ البُقَعِ; **'I need it'—'what ~?'** 'أَحْتاجُهُ'—'لِماذا؟'; **I need something ~ my cough** أَحْتاجُ شَيْئاً لِسُعالي; **what did you say that ~?** مِن أَجْلِ ماذا قُلْتَ ذلك؟; **to go ~ a swim** ذَهَبَ لِلسِباحةِ; **I sent it away ~ cleaning** أَرْسَلْتُهُ لِلتَنْظيفِ; **see our website ~ further information** زوروا مَوْقِعَنا على الإِنْتَرْنِت لِمَزيدٍ من المَعْلوماتِ **3** (in employment) في, لَدى; **to work ~ an oil company** عَمِلَ في

شَرِكة بِتْرول; **to play ~ Tunisia** لَعِبَ في تونِسَ **4** (indicating cause, reason) لِ; **my reason ~ calling** سَبَبَ اتِّصالي; **~ this reason** لِهَذا السَّبَبِ; **his grounds ~ divorce** أَسْبابُهُ للطَلاقِ; **to jump ~ joy** قَفَزَ من الفَرْحَةِ; **imprisoned ~ murder** حُبِسَ في جَريمةِ قَتْلٍ; **I buy it ~ its flavour** أَشْتَريهِ لنَكْهَتِهِ; **if it weren't ~ her, we wouldn't be here** لَوْلاها، لما كُنّا هُنا; **she is annoyed with me ~ contradicting her** هي مُتَضايِقةٌ مِنّي لِأَنّي عارَضْتُها **5** (indicating consequence) لِ; **there's no time ~ us to have a drink** لَيْسَ لَدَيْنا وَقْتٌ لِتَناوُلِ شَرابٍ; **they spoke too quickly ~ me to understand** تَحَدَّثوا بسُرْعةٍ كَبيرةٍ جِدًّا فَلَمْ أَفْهَمْ مِنْهُمْ شَيْئاً **6** (indicating attitude) لِ; **it's easy ~ you to say/do that** مِن السَّهْلِ عَلَيْكَ أَنْ تَقولَ \ تَفْعَلَ ذلِكَ; **it was too confusing ~ me** كانَ مُحَيِّراً جِدًّا بالنِسْبةِ لي; **living in London is not ~ me** الحَياةُ في لَنْدَن لا تُناسِبُني **7** (considering) بالنِسْبةِ لِ; **to be mature ~ one's age** كانَ ناضِجاً بالنِسْبةِ لِسِنِّهِ **8** (towards) نَحْوَ; **to have respect ~ sb** احْتَرَمَ شَخْصاً; **to feel sorry ~ sb** شَعَرَ بالأَسى نَحْوَ شَخْصٍ; **to feel contempt ~ sb** احْتَقَرَ شَخْصاً **9** (on behalf of) بالنِيابةِ \ نِيابةً عن; **to be pleased ~ sb** فَرِحَ لِشَخْصٍ; **say hello to Mike ~ me** بَلِّغْ سَلامي لِمايْك; **I speak ~ all the residents** أَتَحَدَّثُ نِيابةً عن كُلِّ السُكّانِ; **I'll repair it ~ you** سَأُصْلِحُها لَكَ **10** (as regards) بِخُصوصِ; **she's a great one ~ jokes** هي تُجيدُ إلْقاءَ النُكَتِ; **are you all right ~ money?** هل لَدَيْكَ من المالِ ما يَكْفيكَ؟ **11** (expressing passing time) لِمُدّةِ, مُنْذُ; **we've lived here ~ 12 years** نَعيشُ هُنا مُنْذُ 12 عاماً; **I was in Dubai ~ 2 weeks** مَكَثْتُ أُسْبوعَيْنِ في دُبَيِّ; **the best show I've seen ~ years** أَفْضَلُ عَرْضٍ رَأَيْتُهُ مُنْذُ سِنينَ; **the storm lasted ~ hours** اسْتَمَرَّت العاصِفةُ لِعِدّةِ ساعاتٍ; **will he be away ~ long?** هل سَيَبْقى بَعيداً لِفَتْرةٍ طَويلةٍ؟; **she'll be gone ~ a year** سَتُغادِرُ لِمُدّةِ عامٍ **12** (on the occasion of) بِمُناسَبةِ; **he got a bike ~ his birthday** حَصَلَ على دَرّاجةٍ بِمُناسَبةِ عيدِ ميلادِهِ **13** (indicating scheduled time) بِحُلولِ, في; **it will be ready ~ Saturday** سَيَكونُ جاهِزاً يَوْمَ السَبْتِ; **it won't be ready ~ a week** لن يَكونَ جاهِزاً قبل أُسْبوعٍ; **it is scheduled ~ next month** من المُقَرَّرِ إجْراؤُهُ الشَهْرَ القادِمَ; **it's time ~ bed** حانَ وَقْتُ النَوْمِ **14** (indicating distance) على مَسافةِ; **to drive ~ miles** قادَ لِعِدّةِ أَمْيالٍ; **the last shop ~ 30 miles** آخِر مَتْجَرٍ على مَسافةِ \ بُعْد 30 ميلاً **15** (indicating destination) إلى; **a ticket ~ Doha** تَذْكِرة إلى الدَوْحةِ; **to leave ~ work** غادَرَ إلى العَمَلِ; **to swim ~ the shore** سَبَحَ باتِّجاهِ الشاطِئِ **16** (indicating cost, value) بِ, مُقابِلَ; **it was sold ~ £200** بيعَ ب £200; **a cheque ~ €50** شيك ب 50 يورو; **I wouldn't do it ~ anything in the world!** لن أَفْعَلَ هذا مَهْما كانَ الثَمَنُ! **17** (in favour of) **to be ~ peace/reunification** كانَ مُؤَيِّداً لِلسَلامِ \ لِإعادةِ التَوْحيدِ; **to be all ~ it** كانَ مُؤَيِّداً لَهُ قَلْباً وَقالِباً; **who's ~ a game of football?** مَنْ يَرْغَبُ في مُباراةِ كُرةِ قَدَمٍ؟ **18** (stressing appropriateness) مُناسِب لِ; **she's the person ~ the job** هي الشَخْصُ المُناسِبُ لِلوَظيفةِ; **that's ~ us to decide** القَرارُ في ذلك يَعودُ لَنا **19** (in support of) لِصالِحِ; **the argument ~ recycling** الحُجّة الداعمة لِإعادةِ التَدْوير; **there's no evidence ~ that** لَيْسَ هُناكَ دَليلٌ على ذلك **20** (indicating availability) لِ; **~ sale** لِلبَيْعِ; **they had bicycles ~ hire** كانَتْ لَدَيْهِمْ دَرّاجاتٌ لِلإيجارِ **21** (in ratios) لِكُلِّ; **one teacher ~ five pupils** مُدَرِّس لِكُلِّ خَمْسةِ تَلاميذَ **22** (equivalent to) يَرْمُزُ إلى; **T ~ Tom** يَرْمُزُ حَرْفُ التاءِ إلى توم; **what's the Arabic ~ 'boot'?** ما مَعْنى كَلِمةِ boot في اللُغةِ العَرَبيّةِ؟; **the technical term ~ the condition** المُصْطَلَح الفَنّيّ لِلحالةِ **23** (in explanations); **I, ~ one, agree with her** أنا، من جانِبي، أَتَّفِقُ مَعَها; **~ one thing, it is too expensive** لِسَبَبٍ واحِد، وَهُوَ أَنَّهُ غالٍ جِدًّا

B *conj* (fml) لِأَنَّ

Idiom **to be for it** (infml) أَوْقَعَ نَفْسَهُ في وَرْطةٍ

forage /ˈfɒrɪdʒ/ *vi* «birds, animals» بَحَثَ عن الطَعامِ; **to ~ for food** بَحَثَ عن الطَعامِ

foray /ˈfɒreɪ/ *n* **1** (raid) غارة **2** (first venture) مُغامَرة

forbid /fəˈbɪd/ *vt* (*present participle* **-dd-**; *past tense* **forbad** or **forbade**; *past participle* **forbidden**) مَنَعَ (a; مَنْع); **to ~ sb to do sth** مَنَعَ شَخْصاً من القِيامِ بِشَيْءٍ

forbidden /fəˈbɪd(ə)n/ *adj* ‹*subject, product, place*› مَمْنوع, مَحْظور

forbidden fruit *n* فاكِهة مُحَرَّمة

forbidding /fəˈbɪdɪŋ/ *adj* ‹*landscape, expression*› مُخيف

force /fɔːs/ **A** **1** (Phys) قوّة (قُوًى, قوّات); **the ~ of gravity** قوّة الجاذِبِيّة *n* **2** [u] (strength of a blow, an explosion) قوّة (قوّات, قُوًى); **he was knocked over by the ~ of the blast** دَفَعَتْهُ قوّةُ الانْفِجارِ جانِباً **3** [u] (violent means) قوّة (قُوًى, قوّات); **by ~** بالقوّةِ; **the government is prepared to use ~** الحُكومةُ مُسْتعِدّةٌ لِاسْتِعْمالِ القوّة **4** [u] (of intellect, character) قوّة (قُوًى, قوّات); **from** *or* **out of ~ of habit** بِحُكْمِ العادةِ; **she dominates the party by ~ of personality** تُهَيْمِنُ على الحزْبِ بِقوّةِ شَخْصيّتِها **5** (power) قوّة (قُوًى, قوّات); **a ~ for good** قوّة للخَيْرِ; **to be a world ~** كانَ قوّةً عالَميّةً **6** (unit) قوّة (قوّات, **7** (Meteorol) قوّة الريح; **a ~ 8 gale** عاصِفة بقوّة 8 دَرَجاتٍ (قُوًى (على مِقْياسِ بوفورْت)

B (**forces**) *n pl* قوّات مُسلَّحة; **the armed ~s** القوّات المُسلَّحة

C (**in force**) *adv phr* **1** (in effect) **to be in ~** «laws, ban» كانَ سارِيَ المَفْعولِ **2** (in large numbers) بِأَعْدادٍ كَبيرةٍ

D *vt* (**forces, forcing, forced**) **1** (to compel) فَرَض (i; فَرْض) *<a change, cancellation>*; **to ~ sb to do sth** أَجْبَرَ شَخْصاً على عَمَلِ شَيْءٍ; **she ~d him to his knees** أَجْبَرَتْهُ على الرُكوعِ **2** (to push, thrust) **to ~ one's way through sth** شَقَّ طَريقَهُ بين شَيْءٍ *<a crowd, the jungle>* **3** (to break open) خلع (a; خَلْع), فَتَحَ عُنْوةً *<a door, lock, safe>*; **to ~ an entry into the building** دَخَلَ المَبْنى عُنْوةً **4** سَرَّعَ النُموَّ *<a plant>*

E *v refl* (to push oneself) **to ~ oneself to continue/to eat sth** أَجْبَرَ نَفْسَهُ على مُواصَلةِ \ أَكْلِ شَيْءٍ

(Idiom) **to force sb's hand** أَخَذ شَخْصاً على حينِ غِرّةٍ

(Phrasal verbs) **force back**: **~ [sth] back, ~ back [sth]** **1** أَجْبَرَ [شَيْئاً] على التراجُعِ *<a crowd, an army>* **2** كَبَحَ [شَيْئاً] *<one's tears, anger>*

• **force down**: **~ [sth] down, ~ down [sth]** **1** أَجْبَرَ [شَيْئاً] على الهُبوطِ *<an aircraft>*; **the fighters ~d down the airliner** أَجْبَر المُقاتِلونَ الطائِرةَ على الهُبوطِ **2** ابْتَلَعَ [شَيْئاً] بِصُعوبةٍ *<food, medicine>*; **to ~ sth down sb** أَجْبَرَ شَخْصاً على ابْتِلاعِ شَيْءٍ **3** (to reduce) قَلَّصَ [شَيْئاً] *<prices, wages, inflation>*

• **force on**: **~ [sth] on sb** فَرَضَ [شَيْئاً] على شَخْصٍ; **the decision was ~d on him** فُرِضَ القرارُ عَلَيْهِ

• **force open**: **~ [sth] open, ~ open [sth]** فَتَحَ, خَلَعَ [شَيْئاً] بالقوّةِ *<a door, box, safe>*

• **force out**: **~ [sb/sth] out, ~ out [sb/sth]** **1** أَجْبَرَ [شَخْصاً \ شَيْئاً] على الخُروجِ *<an enemy, a thief>*; **to ~ the information out of sb** أَرْغَمَ على [شَيْءٍ] **2** انْتَزَعَ اعْتِرافاً من شَخْصٍ *<a word, scream>*

• **force through**: **~ [sth] through, ~ through [sth]** مَرَّرَ [شَيْئاً] *<legislation, measures>*

• **force up**: **~ [sth] up, ~ up [sth]** أَجْبَرَ [شَيْئاً] على الارْتِفاعِ *<prices, demand, the exchange rate>*

forced /fɔːst/ *adj* **1** *<landing>* إِجْباريّ; *<marriage>* إِكْراهٍ **2** *<conversation, smile>* مُتَكَلَّف

force-feed /ˌfɔːsˈfiːd/ *vt* (*past tense, past participle* **-fed**) أَرْغَمَ \ أَجْبَرَ على الأَكْلِ *<an animal, a prisoner>*

forceful /ˈfɔːsfʊl/ *adj* *<personality, advocate>* قَويّ (أَقْوِياءُ)

forceps /ˈfɔːseps/ *n* (*pl* **forceps**) (also **a pair of forceps**) مِلْقَط جِراحةٍ

forcible /ˈfɔːsɪb(ə)l/ *adj* *<eviction, removal>* قَسْريّ, إِجْباريّ

forcibly /ˈfɔːsɪbli/ *adv* *<to restrain, remove>* بالقوّةِ

ford /fɔːd/ **A** *n* مَخاضة (مَخاضات, مَخاوِضُ)

B *vt* **to ~ a river/stream** خاضَ في نَهْرٍ \ جَدْوَلٍ

fore /fɔː/ *n* **to the ~** في الصَدارةِ

forearm /ˈfɔːrɑːm/ *n* زَنْد (زُنود), ساعِد (سَواعِدُ)

foreboding /fɔːˈbəʊdɪŋ/ *n* تَوَجُّس (من وُقوعِ مَكْروهٍ)

forecast /ˈfɔːkɑːst/ **A** *vt* (*past tense, past participle* **forecast** or **forecasted**) **1** تَنَبَّأَ (ب) *<rain, snow>* **2** تَنَبَّأَ (ب) *<a profit, an outcome>*

B *n* **1** (also **weather forecast**) تَنَبُّؤات جَوّيّة **2** (outlook) تَنَبُّؤ (تَنَبُّؤات)

forecaster /ˈfɔːkɑːstə/ *n* **1** (of trends) مُتَنَبِّئ **2** ▸ **weather forecaster**

foreclosure /fɔːˈkləʊʒə/ *n* (fml) غَلْق \ حَبْس الرَهْنِ

forecourt /ˈfɔːkɔːt/ *n* ساحة (ساحات)

forefathers /ˈfɔːfɑːðəz/ *n pl* أَسْلاف

forefinger /ˈfɔːfɪŋgə/ *n* سَبّابة

forefront /ˈfɔːfrʌnt/ *n* **at the ~ of research/a campaign** في صَدارةِ البَحْثِ \ حَمْلةٍ

forego /fɔːˈɡəʊ/ *vt* (*3rd person present sing* **foregoes**; *present participle* **foregoing**; *past tense* **forewent**; *past participle* **foregone**) ▸ **forgo**

foregone /fɔːˈɡɒn/ *adj* **it is a ~ conclusion** إنَّهُ تَحْصِيلُ حاصِلٍ, إنَّهُ اسْتِنْتاجٌ مَفروغٌ مِنْهُ

foreground /ˈfɔːɡraʊnd/ *n* صَدْر (صُدور)

forehand /ˈfɔːhand/ *n* ضَرْبة أَمامِيّة

forehead /ˈfɒrɪd, ˈfɔːhɛd/ *n* جَبين (جُبُن, أَجْبِنة, أَجْبُن)

foreign /ˈfɒrən/ *adj* 1 <*country, imports*> أَجْنَبيّ (أَجْنَبيّونَ, أَجانِبُ); **a ~ language** لُغة أَجْنَبيّة; **in ~ parts** خارِجَ البِلادِ 2 (alien) <*concept*> غَريب; **the idea was totally ~ to her** كانَت الفِكْرةُ غَريبةً عَلَيْها تَماماً

foreign affairs *n* شُؤون خارِجيّة

Foreign and Commonwealth Office *n* (BrE) وِزارة الخارِجيّة والكومَنْولْث

foreign body *n* جِسْم غَريب

foreign correspondent *n* مُراسِل في دَوْلةٍ أَجْنَبيّةٍ

foreigner /ˈfɒrɪnə/ *n* أَجْنَبيّ (أَجْنَبيّونَ, أَجانِبُ)

foreign exchange *n* نَقْد أَجْنَبيّ

foreign exchange dealer *n* تاجِر عُمْلاتٍ أَجْنَبيّةٍ

foreign exchange market *n* سوق تَداوُلِ العُمْلاتِ الأَجْنَبيّةِ

Foreign Legion *n* فَيْلَق أَجْنَبيّ

foreign minister *n* وَزير خارِجيّة

Foreign Office *n* (BrE) وِزارة الخارِجيّة

Foreign Secretary *n* (BrE) وَزير خارِجيّة

foreleg /ˈfɔːlɛɡ/ *n* رِجْل أَماميّة

forelock /ˈfɔːlɒk/ *n* [تَسْريحة يُرْفَعُ \ يُثَبَّتُ فيها الشَعْرُ عند مُقَدِّمةِ الرَأْسِ]

foreman /ˈfɔːmən/ *n* (*pl* **-men** /-mən/) 1 (in a workplace) مَسْؤول عُمّالٍ 2 (of a jury) مُتَحَدِّث بِاسْمِ هَيْئةِ المُحَلَّفينَ

foremost /ˈfɔːməʊst/ **A** *adj* <*expert, scholar*> بارِز **B** *adv* **first and ~** قبل كُلِّ شَيْءٍ

forename /ˈfɔːneɪm/ *n* اسْم شَخْصيّ

forensic /fəˈrɛnsɪk/ **A** *adj* <*evidence, expert*> جِنائيّ **B** (**forensics**) *n pl* 1 (tests, techniques) [أَساليب الكَشْفِ عن الأَدِلّةِ الجِنائيّةِ] 2 (laboratory, department) مَخْبَر الأَدِلّةِ الجِنائيّةِ

forensic medicine *n* طِبّ شَرْعيّ

forensic science *n* طِبّ شَرْعيّ \ عَدْليّ

forensic scientist *n* طَبيب شَرْعيّ \ عَدْليّ

forerunner /ˈfɔːrʌnə/ *n* سابق (سابِقونَ, سُبّاق)

foresee /fɔːˈsiː/ *vt* (*past tense* **foresaw**; *past participle* **foreseen**) تَنَبَّأَ (ب) <*a problem, an attack*>; **to ~ the future** تَنَبَّأَ بالمُسْتَقْبَلِ

foreseeable /fɔːˈsiːəb(ə)l/ *adj* <*consequences, risk*> مُرْتَقَب; **in the ~ future** في المُسْتَقْبَلِ المَنْظورِ

foreshadow /fɔːˈʃadəʊ/ *vt* أَنْبَأَ (ب) <*an event, a revolution*>

foreshore /ˈfɔːʃɔː/ *n* ساحِل (سَواحِلُ), شاطِئ (شَواطِئُ, شُطْآن)

foresight /ˈfɔːsʌɪt/ *n* بَصيرة (بَصائِرُ)

foreskin /ˈfɔːskɪn/ *n* قُلْفة (قُلَف), غُلْفة (غُلَف)

forest /ˈfɒrɪst/ *n* غابة (غابات, غاب)

forestall /fɔːˈstɔːl/ *vt* 1 (to prevent) تَجَنَّبَ (باتِّخاذِ إجْراءاتٍ مُسْبَقاً) <*an action, event*> 2 (to pre-empt) اسْتَبَقَ <*a misunderstanding, criticism*>

forester /ˈfɒrɪstə/ *n* حارِس غاباتٍ

forest fire *n* حَريق غابةٍ

forest ranger *n* حارِس غابةٍ

forestry /ˈfɒrɪstri/ *n* حِراجة

forestry worker *n* (BrE) عامِل غاباتٍ

foretaste /ˈfɔːteɪst/ *n* بادِرة

foretell /fɔːˈtɛl/ *vt* (*past tense, past participle* **foretold**) تَنَبَّأَ (ب) <*a death, an outcome*>; **to ~ the future** تَنَبَّأَ بالمُسْتَقْبَلِ

forever /fəˈrɛvə/ *adv* إلى الأَبَدِ; **I'll love you ~** سَأُحِبُّكَ إلى الأَبَدِ; **the desert seemed to go on ~** بَدَت الصَحْراءُ وَكَأَنَّها تَمْتَدُّ بِلا نِهايةٍ

forewarn /fɔːˈwɔːn/ *vt* حَذَّرَ مُسْبَقاً <*the police, public*>; **to ~ sb of sth** حَذَّرَ شَخْصاً من شَيْءٍ مُسْبَقاً

foreword /ˈfɔːwəːd/ *n* تَمْهيد (تَمْهيدات), مُقَدِّمة

forfeit /ˈfɔːfɪt/ **A** *vt* 1 تَنازَلَ (عن) <*a right, deposit*> 2 خَسِرَ تِلْقائيًّا <*a match*> **B** *n* 1 (of a right, an asset) مُصادَرة 2 (in games) [عُقوبة بَسيطة عند خَسارةِ جَوْلةٍ في بَعْضِ الأَلْعابِ]

forgave /fəˈgeɪv/ *past tense* ▸ **forgive**

forge /fɔːdʒ/ **A** *vt* **1** طَرَقَ (u; طَرْق) ‹*metal*› **2** زَيَّفَ ‹*a banknote, signature*› **3** شَكَّلَ, أَقامَ ‹*an alliance, a bond*› **B** *vi* **to ~ ahead** «drivers, cars» تَقَدَّمَ بِسُرْعةٍ; **to ~ ahead with a plan** أَحْرَزَ تَقَدُّماً كَبيراً في خُطَّةٍ **C** *n* **1** (workshop) وَرْشة حِدادةٍ **2** (furnace) كور (أَكْوار, كيران, أَكْوُر)

forger /ˈfɔːdʒə/ *n* مُزَوِّر

forgery /ˈfɔːdʒ(ə)ri/ *n* (*pl* **forgeries**) تَزْوير

forget /fəˈgɛt/ **A** *vt* (*present participle* **-tt-**; *past tense* **-got**; *past participle* **-gotten**) **1** نَسِيَ (a; نَسْي, نِسْيان) ‹*a name, word*› **2** نَسِيَ (a; نَسْي, نِسْيان) ‹*a book, an umbrella*› **B** *vi* (*present participle* **-tt-**; *past tense* **-got**; *past participle* **-gotten**) نَسِيَ (a; نَسْي, نِسْيان); **I'm sorry, I forgot** أنا آسِفٌ, لَقَدْ نَسيتُ **C** *v refl* (*present participle* **-tt-**; *past tense* **-got**; *past participle* **-gotten**) **to ~ oneself** نَسِيَ نَفْسَهُ

Phrasal verb **forget about**: **~ about [sth/sb]** نَسِيَ [شَيْئاً \ شَخْصاً] ‹*an appointment, a birthday*›

forgetful /fəˈgɛtfʊl/ *adj* كَثير النِّسْيانِ

forget-me-not /fəˈgɛtminɒt/ *n* أُذُن الفَأْرِ

forgive /fəˈgɪv/ *vt* (*past tense* **forgave**; *past participle* **forgiven**) غَفَرَ (i; غُفْران) ‹*a sin, mistake*›; **to ~ sb for sth/for doing sth** سامَحَ شَخْصاً على شَيْءٍ \ فِعْلِ شَيْءٍ

forgiveness /fəˈgɪvnəs/ *n* غُفْران, سَماح

forgo /fɔːˈgəʊ/ *vt* (*3rd person present sing* **forgoes**; *past tense* **forwent**; *past participle* **forgone**) تَنازَلَ (عن), اسْتَغْنى (عن) ‹*a pleasure, bonus*›

forgot /fəˈgɒt/ *past tense* ▸ **forget**

forgotten /fəˈgɒt(ə)n/ *past participle* ▸ **forget**

fork /fɔːk/ **A** *n* **1** (for eating) شَوْكة **2** (garden tool) شَوْكة **3** (road) تَفَرُّع (تَفَرُّعات) **B** *vi* انْعَطَفَ

Phrasal verb **fork out** (infml): **1** **to ~ out for sth** تَكَبَّدَ تكاليفَ باهِظةً في شَيْءٍ **2** **~ out [sth]** دفَعَ [شَيْئاً] ‹*money, a fortune*›

forked lightning /ˌfɔːkt ˈlʌɪtnɪŋ/ *n* بَرْق مُتَفَرِّع

forklift /ˈfɔːklɪft/ *n* (also **forklift truck**) رافِعة شَوْكيّة

forlorn /fəˈlɔːn/ *adj* **1** (sad) ‹*figure, appearance*› بائِس (بُؤَساءُ), يائِس **2** (desperate) ‹*attempt, hope*› مُهْمَل

form /fɔːm/ **A** *n* **1** (kind, type) شَكْل (أَشْكال); **some ~ of control/protest is needed** يُحْتاجُ إلى بَعْضِ أَنْواعِ السَّيْطَرةِ \ الاحْتِجاجِ; **in the ~ of crystals/a loan** في شَكْلِ بِلَّوراتٍ \ قَرْضٍ; **he won't touch alcohol in any ~** لن يَلْمَس الكُحولَ بِأَيِّ أَشْكالِهِ; **the help took the ~ of vouchers/advice** كانَت المُساعَدةُ في شَكْلِ قَسائِمَ \ نَصيحةٍ **2** (document) اسْتِمارة; **to fill in** *or* **complete a ~** مَلَأَ اسْتِمارةً **3** (shape) شَكْل (أَشْكال) **4** [u] (condition) حالة; **to study the horses' ~** دَرَسَ حالةَ الخُيولِ \ الأَحْصِنةِ; **to be on good ~** كانَ في حالةٍ جَيِّدةٍ; **to return to ~** اسْتَعادَ لِياقَتَهُ البَدَنِيّةَ; **true to ~, she was late** كانَتْ مُتَأَخِّرةً كَعادَتِها **5** (structure) شَكْل (أَشْكال); **the tension between ~ and content** التَوَتُّر بين الشَّكْلِ والمَضْمونِ **6** (BrE Educ) (class, group) صَفّ (صُفوف); (year) سَنة (سَنَوات) **7** [u] (etiquette) **it is bad ~** إنَّهُ سُلوكٌ سَيِّءٌ; **purely as a matter of ~** إنَّها قَطْعاً مَسْأَلةُ شَكْلِيّاتٍ **8** (prescribed set of words) نَوْعيّة **9** (in grammar) شَكْل (شُكول, أَشْكال); **a Form V verb** فِعْل من الوَزْنِ الخامِسِ **B** *vt* **1** (to create) شَكَّلَ, كَوَّنَ ‹*a club, queue, an alliance*›; **the band was ~ed in Birmingham** تَشَكَّلت الفِرْقةُ في بيرمينْغْهام **2** (to constitute) شَكَّلَ ‹*a jury, committee*›; **they ~ed a disaster committee** شَكَّلوا لَجْنةَ كَوارِثَ; **to ~ part of sth** شَكَّلَ جُزْءاً من شَيْءٍ; **to ~ the basis of sth** شَكَّلَ قاعِدةَ شَيْءٍ **3** (fml) (to conceive) كَوَّنَ ‹*an impression, opinion*› **4** (to mould) شَكَّلَ ‹*attitudes, sb's personality, ideas*› **C** *vi* «queue, puddles, residue» تَشَكَّلَ

Phrasal verb **form into**: **A** **~ into [sth]**: (to organize into) **to ~ into groups/teams** تَوَزَّعَ على مَجْموعاتٍ \ فِرَقٍ **B** **~ [sth] into [sth]**: (to give a shape to) **to ~ the dough into a loaves** شَكَّلَ العَجينَ إلى أَرْغِفةٍ

formal /ˈfɔːm(ə)l/ *adj* **1** (official) ‹*complaint, occasion*› رَسْميّ **2** (not casual) ‹*language, clothing*› شَكْليّ; **~ spoken Arabic** عامّيّة المُثَقَّفينَ **3** (Educ) ‹*training, qualification*› تَقْليديّ

formal dress *n* مَلابِس السَهْرةِ

formality /fɔːˈmalɪti/ *n* (*pl* **formalities**) **1** (legal or social convention) إجْراء شَكْليّ **2** [u] (of an occasion) شَكْلِيّة **3** [u] (of language, clothing) شَكْلانِيّة

formalize, -ise (BrE) /ˈfɔːməlʌɪz/ *vt* أَضْفى عَلَيْهِ صِفةً رَسْمِيّةً ‹*an arrangement, agreement*›

formally /ˈfɔːm(ə)li/ *adv* **1** (officially) ‹*to open, declare*› رَسْمِيًّا **2** (not casually) ‹*to dress, celebrate*› شَكْلِيًّا

format /ˈfɔːmat/ **A** *n* شَكْل **B** *vt* (**-tt-**) هَيَّأَ ‹*a document, disk*›

formation /fɔːˈmeɪʃ(ə)n/ *n* **1** (creation) تكْوين ,تَكَوُّن **2** (configuration) تَشْكيل (تَشْكيلات); **to fly in ~** حَلَّقَ في سِرْب; **will he play a 4-3-3 ~?** هل سَيَلْعَبُ بِتَشْكيلة 4–3–3؟

form captain *n* (BrE) [طالِب مُخْتار لقِيادةِ صَفٍّ \ قِسْمٍ]

former /ˈfɔːmə/ **A** *n* **the ~** (singular noun) الأَوَّل; (plural noun) السابِقونَ **B** *adj* **1** ‹*era, life*› سالِف; ‹*size, state*› سابِق **2** ‹*leader, husband*› سابِق **3** (first of two) ‹*course of action, alternative*› أَوَّل (dipt)

formerly /ˈfɔːm(ə)li/ *adv* سابِقاً ,فيما مَضى

formidable /ˈfɔːmɪdəb(ə)l, fɔːˈmɪdəb(ə)l/ *adj* ‹*challenge, opponent*› هائِل (هَوائِلُ)

formula /ˈfɔːmjʊlə/ *n* (*pl* **formulae** or **formulas**) **1** (method) صيغة ,تَرْكيبة (تَراكيبُ ,تَرْكيبات); **a ~ for success** صيغة للنَجاحِ **2** (baby milk) حَليب اصْطِناعيّ

formulate /ˈfɔːmjʊleɪt/ *vt* **1** (to develop) صاغَ (u; صَوْغ ,صِياغة), وَضَعَ (a; وَضْع) ‹*a plan, policy*› **2** (to express) أَدْلى (ب), عَبَّرَ ‹*an idea, argument*›

formulation /fɔːmjuːˈleɪʃ(ə)n/ *n* صِياغة

fornication /ˌfɔːnɪˈkeɪʃ(ə)n/ *n* (fml) زِنًى

forsake /fəˈseɪk/ *vt* (*past tense* **forsook**; *past participle* **forsaken**) **1** (to abandon) (liter) تَرَكَ (u; تَرْك), هَجَرَ (u; هَجْر) ‹*a friend, home*› **2** (fml) (to relinquish) تَخَلّى (عن) ‹*a habit, belief*›

fort /fɔːt/ *n* حِصْن (حُصون)

forte /ˈfɔːteɪ/ *n* **to be sb's ~** كانَ مَوْطِنَ قوّةِ شَخْصٍ

forth /fɔːθ/ *adv* **from this/that day ~** من هذا \ ذلك اليَوْمِ فَصاعِداً; ▸ **back**

forthcoming /fɔːθˈkʌmɪŋ/ *adj* **1** ‹*election, book*› مُقْبِل ,وَشيك **2** **to be ~ about sth** كانَ صَريحاً في شَيْءٍ

forthright /ˈfɔːθrʌɪt/ *adj* ‹*manner, opinion*› صَريح (صُرَحاءُ), مُباشِر

forthwith /fɔːθˈwɪθ/ *adv* (fml liter) ‹*to proceed, cease*› حالاً, على الفَوْرِ, تَوًّا

forties /ˈfɔːtiz/ *n pl* **1** (decade) (**the forties**) الأَرْبَعينات **2** (age) **to be in one's ~** كانَ في الأَرْبَعيناتِ (من عُمْرِهِ)

fortieth /ˈfɔːtɪəθ/ **A** *n* **1** (**the fortieth**) (in a series) الأَرْبَعونَ **2** (fraction) جُزْء من أَرْبَعينَ **B** *adj* الأَرْبَعونَ **C** *adv* في المَرْكَزِ الأَرْبَعينَ

fortification /ˌfɔːtɪfɪˈkeɪʃ(ə)n/ *n* (defensive wall) حِصْن (حُصون); [u] (action of fortifying) تَحْصين

fortify /ˈfɔːtɪfʌɪ/ *vt* (**fortifies**, **fortifying**, **fortified**) **1** (Mil) حَصَّنَ ‹*a position, person*› **2** (Culin) [زادَ من نِسْبةِ الكُحول في النَبيذِ أو الفيتامين أو المَعادِنِ في الطَعام] ‹*wine, cereal*›

fortnight /ˈfɔːtnʌɪt/ *n* (BrE) أُسْبوعانِ

fortnightly /ˈfɔːtnʌɪtli/ *adj, adv* كُلَّ أُسْبوعَيْنِ

fortress /ˈfɔːtrɪs/ *n* حِصْن (حُصون), قَلْعة (قِلاع ,قُلوع)

fortuitous /fɔːˈtjuːɪtəs/ *adj* (fml) ‹*event*› وَليد صُدْفةٍ; ‹*remark*› عَرَضيّ

fortunate /ˈfɔːtʃ(ə)nət/ *adj* ‹*position*› مَحْظوظ ,مَوْفور الحَظِّ; ‹*circumstances*› مَيْمون

fortunately /ˈfɔːtʃ(ə)nətli/ *adv* لِحُسْنِ الحَظِّ; **~, nobody was seriously hurt** لِحُسْنِ الحَظِّ لم يُصَبْ أَحَدٌ إصاباتٍ خَطيرة

fortune /ˈfɔːtʃuːn/ *n* **1** (large sum of money) ثَرْوة; **to make a ~** جَمَعَ ثَرْوةً ,اغْتَنى; **to cost a ~** كَلَّفَ مَبْلَغاً كَبيراً **2** [u] (luck) حَظّ ,نَصيب ,بَخْت **3** **to tell sb's ~** قَرَأَ لِشَخْصٍ البَخْتَ

fortune teller *n* قارئ بَخْتٍ ,عَرّاف

forty /ˈfɔːti/ *n, adj* أَرْبَعونَ

forum /ˈfɔːrəm/ *n* (*pl* **forums** or **fora**) **1** (public place) ساحة عامّة **2** (meeting) مُنْتَدًى (مُنْتَدَيات)

forward /ˈfɔːwəd/ **A** *adv* (also **forwards**) **1** (to the front) ‹*to step, move, fall*› إلى الأَمامِ; **to face ~** كانَ مُواجِهاً للجِهةِ

الأَمامِيّةِ; **the fans rushed ~** انْدَفَعَ المُعْجَبونَ إلى الأَمامِ; **the bus moved ~ three metres** تَحَرَّكَت الحافِلةُ ثَلاثةَ أَمْتارٍ; **to go ~** سارَ إلى الأَمامِ; **to go ~** إلى الأَمامِ **2** (in time) **to go ~ in time** مَضى قُدُماً \ إلى المُسْتَقْبَلِ; **from this day ~** من اليَوْمِ فَصاعِداً; **to bring the date of the meeting ~** قَدَّمَ مَوْعِدَ الاجْتِماعِ **3** (toward the end) **to wind a tape ~** سَرَّعَ شَريطاً إلى الأَمامِ

B *adj* **1** (bold) ‹*behaviour, child*› جَريء **2** (to the front) ‹*roll, gear*› أَماميّ; **the seat is too far ~** المَقْعَدُ مُتَقَدِّمٌ جِدًّا إلى الأَمامِ **3** (advanced) ‹*season, plant*› مُتَقَدِّم; **I'm no further ~ with the plans** لم أُحْرِزْ أَيَّ تَقَدُّمٍ في الخُطَطِ **4** ‹*rate, delivery*› آجِل

C *n* لاعِب هُجوم, مُهاجِم

D *vt* **1** (to send on) حَوَّلَ ‹*a letter, an email*› **2** (to dispatch) أَرْسَلَ ‹*a catalogue, parcel, the goods*›

forwarding address /ˈfɔːwədɪŋ əˌdrɛs/ *n* العُنْوان الجَديد (لِتَحْويلِ البَريدِ)

forward-looking /ˌfɔːwədˈlʊkɪŋ/ *adj* ‹*company, design*› تَقَدُّميّ

forward planning *n* تَخْطيط مُتَقَدِّم \ مُسْتَقْبَليّ

forwards /ˈfɔːwədz/ ▸ **forward** A

fossil /ˈfɒs(ə)l/ *n* أُحْفورة (أَحافيرُ)

fossil fuel *n* وَقود أُحْفوريّ

foster /ˈfɒstə/ **A** *adj* ‹*child, parent*› بالتَبَنّي

B *vt* **1** (to encourage) شَجَّعَ ‹*a talent, spirit*›; احْتَضَنَ, نَمّى ‹*growth, understanding*› **2** (to care for) [تَبَنّى لِوَقْتٍ مَحْدودٍ] ‹*a child*›

foster family *n* أُسْرة حاضِنة \ بالتَبَنّي

foster home *n* [بَيْت مُؤَقَّت لِطِفْلٍ]

fought /fɔːt/ **A** *past tense, past participle* ▸ **fight**

B (**-fought**); *in combination*

foul /faʊl/ **A** *adj* **1** (putrid) ‹*taste*› كَريه; ‹*slum*› وَسِخ; ‹*water*› آسِن **2** (very bad) ‹*weather, day*› سَيِّئ; **to have a ~ temper** كانَ لَهُ مِزاجٌ سَيِّئٌ **3** (offensive) ‹*language*› بَذيء; **to have a ~ mouth** كانَ لَهُ فَمٌ قَذِرٌ

B *n* مُخالَفة; **to commit a ~ on an opponent** قامَ بِمُخالَفةٍ على خَصْمٍ

C *adv* **to smell ~** كانَتْ رائِحَتُهُ كَريهةً

D *vt* **1** (to pollute) لَوَّثَ ‹*the beach, atmosphere, river*› **2** (with excrement) «dogs, pets» وَسَّخَ ‹*the pavement, park*› **3** (to entangle) «nets, weeds» تَشابَكَ ‹*the propeller*› **4** (to clog) «dirt, dust» سَدَّ (u; سَدّ) ‹*a mechanism, an instrument*› **5** (Sport) ارْتَكَبَ مُخالَفةً على ‹*an opponent*›

(Idiom) **to fall foul of sb/sth** سَقَطَ ضَحيّةَ شَخْصٍ \ شَيْءٍ

(Phrasal verb) **foul up** (infml) **A** (to make mistakes) خالَفَ **B** **~ up [sth], ~ [sth] up** أَفْسَدَ [شَيْئاً] ‹*a plan, system*›

foul-mouthed /ˌfaʊlˈmaʊθd/ *adj* ‹*language, child*› بَذيء اللِسانِ

foul play *n* **1** (dishonest behaviour, crime) عَمَل شائِن **2** (in sport) مُخالَفة

foul-up /ˈfaʊlʌp/ *n* (infml) عُطْل غَبيّ

found /faʊnd/ **A** *past tense, past participle* ▸ **find**

B *vt* **1** أَنْشَأَ, أَسَّسَ ‹*a school, company*› **2** **to ~ sth on sth** أَنْشَأَ شَيْئاً اسْتِناداً إلى شَيْءٍ

foundation /faʊnˈdeɪʃ(ə)n/ **A** *n* **1** (of a school, company) تَأْسيس **2** (charity) مُؤَسَّسة خَيْريّة **3** (also **foundation cream**) كْريم الأَساسِ

B (**foundations**) *n pl* أَساس (أُسُس, أَساسات)

foundation course *n* (BrE) دَوْرة تَأْسيسيّة

founder /ˈfaʊndə/ *n* مُنْشِئ, مُؤَسِّس

foundry /ˈfaʊndri/ *n* (*pl* **foundries**) مَسْبَك (مَسابِكُ), مَصْهَر (مَصاهِرُ)

fountain /ˈfaʊntɪn/ *n* **1** (ornamental) نافورة (نَوافيرُ) **2** (for drinking water) سَبيل (mf; أَسْبِلة)

fountain pen *n* قَلَم حِبْرٍ

four /fɔː/ *n, adj* أَرْبَعة ▸ see also **five**

four-by-four /ˌfɔːbʌɪˈfɔː/ *n* سَيّارة ذات دَفْعٍ رُباعيٍّ

four-letter word /ˌfɔːˌlɛtə ˈwəːd/ *n* [كَلِمة بَذيئة ذات أَرْبَعةِ أَحْرُفٍ]

four-poster bed /ˌfɔːˌpəʊstə ˈbɛd/, **four-poster** *n* [سَرير ذو أَرْبَعةِ أَعْمِدةٍ]

four-seater /ˌfɔːˈsiːtə/ *n* سَيّارة ذات أَرْبَعةِ مَقاعِدَ

foursome /ˈfɔːs(ə)m/ *n* (infml) رُباعيّ (مَجْموعة من أَرْبَعةِ أَشْخاصٍ)

four-star /fɔːstɑː/ *adj* ‹*hotel, restaurant*› أَرْبَعةِ نُجوم

fourteen /fɔːˈtiːn/ *n, adj* أَرْبَعةَ عَشَرَ

fourteenth /fɔːˈtiːnθ/ **A** *n* **1** (in a series) رابِعَ عَشَرَ **2** (fraction) جُزْء من أَرْبَعةَ عَشَرَ **3** (**the fourteenth**) (of a month) الرابِعَ عَشَرَ

B *adj* ‹*century, day*› رابِعَ عَشَرَ

C *adv* في المَرْكَزِ الرابعَ عَشَرَ

fourth /fɔːθ/ **A** *n* **1** (in a series) رابِع **2** (**the fourth**) (of a month) الرابِع **3** (also **fourth gear**) (Aut) التُرْس الرابِع

B *adj* ‹*century, day*› رابِع

C *adv* ‹*to come, finish*› في المَرْكَزِ الرابِع

fourthly /ˈfɔːθli/ *adv* رابعاً

four-wheel drive /ˌfɔːˌwiəl ˈdrʌɪv/ *n* **1** (transmission system) دَفْع رُباعيّ **2** (vehicle) سَيّارة رُباعيّة الدَفْع

fowl /faʊl/ *n* (*pl* **fowl** or **fowls**) داجِن (دَواجِنُ)

fox /fɒks/ *n* ثَعْلَب (ثَعالِبُ)

foxglove /ˈfɒksglʌv/ *n* كَفّ الثَعْلَب, قَمعيّة

foxhole /ˈfɒkshəʊl/ *n* خَنْدَق (خَنادِقُ)

foxhound /ˈfɒkshaʊnd/ *n* [كَلْب يُسْتَخْدَمُ في صَيْدِ الثَعالِبِ]

fox hunting *n* صَيْد الثَعالِب

foyer /ˈfɔɪeɪ/ *n* بَهْو (أَبْهاء)

fracas /ˈfrakɑː/ *n* جَلَبة (جَلَب), شِجار, صَخَب

fraction /ˈfrakʃ(ə)n/ *n* **1** (Math) كَسْر (كُسور) **2** (small part) جُزْء ضَئيل

fracture /ˈfraktʃə/ **A** *n* كَسْر (كُسور)

B *vt* كَسَرَ (i; كَسْر) ‹*a bone, rock*›

C *vi* «bones, rocks» اِنْكَسَرَ

fragile /ˈfradʒʌɪl/ *adj* **1** ‹*object, structure, peace*› هَشّ **2** ‹*person*› ضَعيف (ضِعاف, ضُعَفاءُ); ‹*health*› هَشّ

fragment /ˈfragmənt/ *n* (of bone, rock, metal) كِسْرة (كِسَر, كِسْرات); (of a text, conversation) قِطْعة (قِطَع)

fragmentation /fragmenˈteɪʃ(ə)n/ *n* (of an object, device, process) تَجْزِئة

fragrance /ˈfreɪgrəns/ *n* **1** (smell) رائِحة ذَكيّة, أَريج, شَذاً **2** (perfume) عِطْر (عُطور, عُطورات)

fragrant /ˈfreɪgrənt/ *adj* ‹*flowers, oils*› ذَكيّ الرائِحة, أَريجيّ, شَذيّ

frail /freɪl/ *adj* ‹*elderly person, body*› ضَعيف البِنْية, واهِن (وُهُن), (وُهاة) واهٍ; ‹*health*› ضَعيف

frame /freɪm/ **A** *n* **1** (of a building, bicycle, bed) هَيْكَل (هَياكِلُ) **2** (of a picture, window, door, racquet) إطار (إطارات, أُطُر)

B (**frames**) *n pl* (of spectacles) إطار نَظّارة

C *vt* **1** أَطَّرَ ‹*a picture, photograph*› **2** صاغَ (u; صَوْغ, صِياغة) ‹*a question, response*›; وَضَعَ (a; وَضْع) ‹*a policy*› **3** (infml) (to incriminate falsely) لَفَّقَ تُهْمةً ضِدّ

frame of mind *n* حالة نَفْسيّة

framework /ˈfreɪmwəːk/ *n* **1** (of a structure) بِنْية, هَيْكَل **2** (for discussion, cooperation) نِطاق; (of a system, novel) إطار

franc /fraŋk/ *n* فَرَنْك (فَرَنْكات)

France /frɑːns/ *pr n* فَرَنْسا

franchise /ˈfrantʃʌɪz/ *n* **1** [u] (right to vote) حَقّ الاِنْتِخاب **2** (commercial) اِمْتِياز (اِمْتِيازات)

frank /fraŋk/ *adj* ‹*discussion, admission*› صَريح

frankfurter /ˈfraŋkfəːtə/ *n* [سُجُقّ من لَحْم الخِنْزير والبَقَرِ]

frankincense /ˈfraŋkɪnsens/ *n* بَخور, لُبان

frankly /ˈfraŋkli/ *adv* ‹*to speak, admit*› بِصَراحةٍ

frantic /ˈfrantɪk/ *adj* **1** (distraught) هائِج **2** (frenetic) ‹*effort, search*› جُنونيّ, مَحْموم

frantically /ˈfrantɪkli/ *adv* ‹*to search, wave*› باهْتِياج

fraternal /frəˈtəːn(ə)l/ *adj* ‹*greetings, relations*› أَخَويّ

fraternal twin *n* تَوْأَم غَيْر مُتَطابِق

fraternity /frəˈtəːnɪti/ *n* (*pl* **fraternities**) **1** [u] (friendship) أُخُوّة **2** (group) رابِطة **3** (AmE) (in colleges) أَخَويّة

fraternize, -ise (BrE) /ˈfrat(ə)nʌɪz/ *vi* «staff, teachers» تَآخى

fraud /frɔːd/ *n* **1** [u] (deception) اِحْتِيال, نَصْب **2** (person) نَصّاب, مُحْتال

fraudster /ˈfrɔːdstə/ *n* نَصّاب, مُحْتال

fraudulent /ˈfrɔːdjʊlənt/ *adj* ‹*claim, activity*› اِحْتِياليّ

fraught /frɔːt/ *adj* **1** مَشْحون, مُفْعَم; **to be ~ with danger/ difficulties** كانَ مَحْفوفاً بالمَخاطِرِ \ بالمَصاعِبِ **2** (tense) ‹*relationship, atmosphere*› مُتَوَتِّر

fray /freɪ/ *vi* «material, rope» نَسَلَ (u; نَسْل ,نُسول)

frayed /freɪd/ *adj* 1 ‹nerves› مُرْهَق; **tempers were ~** كانَت الأَعْصابُ مُتَوَتِّرةً 2 ‹material, rope› مُهْتَرِئ

frazzle /ˈfraz(ə)l/ *n* (infml) 1 **to be burnt to a ~** كانَ مُحْتَرِقاً بالكامِلِ 2 **to be worn to a ~** كانَ مُنْهَكاً تَماماً

freak /friːk/ A *n* 1 (abnormal specimen) مَخْلوق غَريب 2 (unusual occurrence) [أَمْر خارِق للعادةِ
B *adj* ‹accident, storm› خارِق للعادةِ

Phrasal verb **freak out** (infml) A **~ out** فَقَدَ صَوابَهُ B **~ [sb] out** أَخافَ [شَخْصاً]

freckle /ˈfrɛk(ə)l/ *n* نَمَش

free /friː/ A *adj* 1 (unhindered, unrestricted) ‹person, press, election› حُرّ; ‹access, choice› مُطْلَق; **to be ~ of sb** كانَ غَيْرَ خاضِعٍ لِشَخْصٍ; **to be ~ to do sth** كانَ حُرًّا في فِعْلِ شَيْءٍ; **feel ~ to ask questions** لا تَتَرَدَّدْ في طَرْحِ الأَسْئِلةِ; **to break ~ of the restrictions/sb's influence** تَخَلَّصَ من القُيودِ \ تَأْثيرِ شَخْصٍ; **to set sb ~ from prison/an obligation** حَرَّرَ شَخْصاً من السِجْنِ \ واجِبٍ; **the children are allowed ~ expression** يُسْمَحُ للأَوْلادِ بِحُرِّيّةِ التَعْبيرِ; **the ~ movement of labour** حُرِّيّة تَنَقُّلِ اليَدِ العامِلةِ 2 (not captive or tied) ‹person, limb, animal, bird› طَليق (طُلَقاءُ); **one more tug and I was ~** شَدّة قَوِيّة أُخْرى وَأَصْبَحْتُ طَليقاً; **to set a prisoner/an eagle ~** أَطْلَقَ سَراحَ سَجينٍ \ نَسْرٍ; **to pull sb ~ from sth** أَنْقَذَ شَخْصاً من شَيْءٍ; **how did the dog get ~?** كيف أَفْلَتَ الكَلْبُ؟; **the prisoners/horses broke ~** فَرَّ السُجَناءُ \ فَرَّت الخُيولُ; **the boat broke ~ of *or* from its moorings** تَخَلَّصَ الزَوْرَقُ من مَراسيهِ; **they had to cut the driver ~ from the car** كانَ عَلَيْهِمْ تَخْليصُ السائِقِ من السَيّارةِ 3 (devoid) **to be ~ from *or* of sth** كانَ خالِياً من شَيْءٍ; **~ of litter/weeds** خالٍ من النُفاياتِ \ الأَعْشابِ الضارّةِ; **a day ~ from interruptions** يَوْم خالٍ من المُقاطَعاتِ; **to be ~ of debt** لم يَكُنْ لَدَيْهِ دُيونٌ; **to be ~ of pain** لم يَكُنْ يُعاني من الأَلَمِ; **this soup is ~ from artificial colourings** هذا الحَساءُ خالٍ من التَلْوينِ الاصْطِناعِيِّ 4 (costing nothing) ‹ticket, meal, delivery› مَجّانِيّ; **~ admission** دُخول مَجّاني 5 (not occupied) ‹morning› خالٍ من المَواعيد; ‹seat, room› شاغِر; **are you ~ for lunch on Monday?** إذا لم تَكُنْ مُرْتَبِطاً بِمَوْعِدٍ يَوْمَ الاثْنَيْنِ، دَعْنا نَتَناوَلُ الغَداءَ مَعاً؟; **is this seat ~?** هل هذا المَقْعَدُ شاغِرٌ؟; **I'm trying to keep Tuesday ~** أُحاوِلُ أنْ أُفَرِّغَ نَفْسي تَماماً يَوْمَ الثُلاثاءِ 6 (not literal) ‹translation› حُرّ, غَيْر حَرْفِيٍّ 7 (generous, lavish) **to be ~ with sth** ‹food, money, advice› كانَ سَخِيًّا بِشَيْءٍ 8 (familiar) ‹manner› غَيْر مُتَحَفِّظ 9 (Chem) ‹atom, nitrogen› حُرّ

B *n* (**the free** *n pl*) الأَحْرار; **land of the ~** بَلَد الأَحْرارِ

C *adv* 1 (at liberty) ‹to run, roam› بِحُرِّيّةٍ; **to go ~** «hostages, criminals» أُطْلِقَ سَراحُهُ 2 (without payment) ‹to eat, travel› مَجّاناً; **children are admitted ~** يَدْخُلُ الأَوْلادُ مَجّاناً; **buy one, get one ~** اشْتَرِ واحِداً، واحْصُلْ على واحِدٍ مَجّاناً

D *vt* (**frees, freeing, freed**) 1 (from prison, captivity) ‹a prisoner, bird› أَطْلَقَ السَراحَ; (from wreckage) ‹the driver› خَلَّصَ; **to ~ sb from a burden/from oppression** خَلَّصَ شَخْصاً من عِبْءٍ \ الاضْطِهادِ 2 (to make available) ‹money, resources› حَرَّرَ; **to ~ sb to do sth** أَفْسَحَ المَجالَ لِشَخْصٍ لِفِعْلِ شَيْءٍ

E *v refl* **to ~ oneself** (from chains, wreckage) تَحَرَّرَ; (from a burden, an obligation) تَخَلَّصَ (من)

F (*in combination* **-free**) **smoke/sugar-~** خالٍ من التَدْخينِ \ السُكَّرِ

Idioms **to give sb/to have a free hand** مَنَحَ شَخْصاً تَفْويضاً مُطْلَقاً \ كانَ عِنْدَهُ تَفْويضٌ مُطْلَقٌ; **for free** ‹to repair, work› مَجّاناً, بِدونِ أَجْرٍ

freebie, freebee /ˈfriːbi/ *n* (infml) [شَيْء مَجّانِيّ]

freedom /ˈfriːdəm/ *n* 1 (liberty) حُرِّيّة; **the ~ of the press** حُرِّيّة الصَحافةِ; **the ~ of movement of labour** حُرِّيّة الحَرَكةِ والعَمَلِ; **the ~ of information act** قانون حُرِّيّةِ المَعْلوماتِ 2 (to use sth) حُرِّيّة تَصَرُّفٍ; **she gave me the ~ of her house** أَعْطَتْني حُرِّيّةَ التَصَرُّفِ في بَيْتِها 3 **~ from hunger/discrimination** (lack of) تَحَرُّر من الجوعِ \ التَمْييزِ

freedom fighter *n* مُناضِل من أَجْلِ الحُرِّيّةِ

free enterprise *n* اقْتِصاد حُرّ

free fall *n* سُقوط حُرّ

free-for-all /ˈfriːfərɔːl/ *n* مُشاجَرة عامّة

free gift *n* هَدِيّة مَجّانِيّة

freehold /ˈfriːhəʊld/ *n* تَمَلُّك حُرّ

freehold property *n* مِلْكيّة عَقاريّة مُطْلَقة

free kick *n* ضَرْبة حُرّة

freelance /ˈfriːlɑːns/ **A** *adj* ‹*writer, work*› مُسْتَقِلّ

B *adv* ‹*to work*› بِشَكْلٍ مُسْتَقِلٍّ

C *n* (also **freelancer**) عامِل مُسْتَقِلّ \ حُرّ

freely /ˈfriːli/ *adv* **1** (without restriction) ‹*to act, travel, speak*› بِحُرّيّةٍ; **to spend ~** أَنْفَقَ بِدونِ حِسابٍ; **he's breathing ~ now** يَتَنَفَّسُ بِسُهولةٍ الآنَ; **the observers can move ~ around the country** يَسْتَطيعُ المُراقِبونَ أنْ يَتَحَرَّكوا بِحُرّيّةٍ; **food is ~ available** الطَعامُ مُتَوَفِّرٌ بِكَثْرةٍ **2** (willingly) ‹*to admit, confess*› طَواعيّةً **3** (not strictly) ‹*to translate, adapt*› بِتَصَرُّفٍ

free market, **free market economy** *n* اقْتِصاد السوقِ الحُرّ

Freemason /ˈfriːmeɪs(ə)n/ *n* ماسونيّ

free port *n* ميناء حُرّ

Freepost /ˈfriːpəʊst/ *n* (BrE) خِدْمة خالِصَ الأُجْرة

free radical *n* شِقّ حُرّ

free-range /ˌfriːˈreɪndʒ/ *adj* ‹*chicken, eggs*› الحَظائِرِ المَفْتوحةِ

free speech *n* حُرّيّة التَعْبير

freestyle /ˈfriːstʌɪl/ *n* سِباحة حُرّة

free throw *n* رَمْية حُرّة

free trade *n* تِجارة حُرّة

freeware /ˈfriːwɛː/ *n* بَرامِج مَجّانيّة

freeway /ˈfriːweɪ/ *n* (AmE) طَريق سَريع

freewheel /friːˈwiːl/ *vi* (on a bike) «cyclists, children» تَدَحْرَجَ (دون الضَغْطِ على الدَوّاسةِ); (in a car) «motorists, drivers» [تَحَرَّكَ دون تَشْغيلِ المُحَرِّكِ]

free will *n* حُرّيّة الإرادةِ

freeze /friːz/ **A** *vt* (*past tense* **froze**; *past participle* **frozen**) **1** (in temperature) جَمَّدَ ‹*food, water, organ*› **2** (to restrict) ثَبَّتَ, جَمَّدَ ‹*wages, a price, the interest rate*› **3** (to block) جَمَّدَ ‹*sb's assets, a bank account*› **4** (to stop) أَوْقَفَ ‹*a frame, recording*› **5** (to anaesthetize) بَنَّجَ, خَدَّرَ ‹*sb's gum*› **6** (to remove) [اسْتَأْصَلَ عن طَريقِ الجِراحةِ بالتَبْريدِ] ‹*a wart*› **7** (Comput) جَمَّدَ ‹*a computer, window*›

B *vi* (*past tense* **froze**; *past participle* **frozen**) **1** (in low temperatures) «water, rivers, food» تَجَمَّدَ; **the passengers froze to death** تَجَمَّدَ الرُكّابُ حتّى المَوْتِ **2** (infml) (to be cold) «person, room» بَرُدَ (u; بُرود); **wrap up or you'll ~ to death** تَغَطَّ وَإلاّ مُتَّ من البَرْدِ **3** (to become motionless) تَجَمَّدَ في مَكانِهِ; ~! مَكانَكَ!

C *v impers* (*past tense* **froze**; *past participle* **frozen**) (Meteorol) تَجَمَّدَ; **it's going to ~ tonight** سَتَنْخَفِضُ الحَرارةُ اللَيْلَةَ إلى دَرَجةِ التَجَمُّدِ

D *n* **1** (Meteorol) تَجَمُّد; **the big ~** التَجَمُّد الكَبير \ العَظيم **2** (on prices, wages) تَثْبيت (تَثْبيتات), تَجْميد

(Phrasal verbs) **freeze out**: **~ [sb/sth] out, ~ out [sb/sth]** **1** (socially) قاطَعَ [شَخْصاً \ شَيْئاً] ‹*a colleague, friend*› **2** (in business) أَقْصى [شَخْصاً \ شَيْئاً] ‹*a competitor, company*›

• **freeze over** «lakes, rivers» تَجَمَّدَ

freeze-dried /ˌfriːzˈdrʌɪd/ *adj* ‹*food, coffee*› مُجَفَّف بالتَجْميد, مُجَفَّد

freeze-frame /ˌfriːzˈfreɪm/ *n* تَجْميد صورةٍ

freezer /ˈfriːzə/ *n* مُجَمِّد

freezing /ˈfriːzɪŋ/ **A** *adj* ‹*temperatures*› ما دون الصِفرِ; ‹*weather, conditions*› شَديد البُرودة; **I'm ~!** أَنا مُتَجَمِّدٌ من البَرْدِ!; **he had to wait outside in the ~ cold** كانَ عَلَيْه أنْ يَنْتَظِرَ خارِجاً في البَرْدِ القارِسِ

B *n* دَرَجة تَجَمُّدٍ; **three degrees above/below ~** ثَلاث دَرَجاتٍ فوق \ تحت دَرَجةِ التَجَمُّدِ

freezing point *n* دَرَجة تَجَمُّدٍ

freight /freɪt/ *n* **1** (goods) حُمولة **2** (transport system) شَحْن; **to ship goods by air ~** شَحَنَ البَضائِعَ عن طَريقِ الجَوِّ

freight car *n* (AmE) عَرَبة نَقْلِ البَضائِعِ (في قِطارٍ)

freighter /ˈfreɪtə/ *n* **1** (ship) سَفينة شَحْنٍ **2** (plane) طائِرة شَحْنٍ

freight operator *n* شَرِكة شَحْنٍ

freight train *n* قِطار شَحْنٍ

French /frentʃ/ **A** *adj* ‹*ambassador, food, lesson*› فَرَنْسيّ

B *n* **1** (**the French**) (people) الفَرَنْسيّونَ **2** (language) (اللُغة) الفَرَنْسيّة

French bean *n* لوبيا

French doors *n* (AmE) [أَبواب زُجاجيّة تُفْتَح على شُرْفةٍ \ فِناءٍ]

French dressing *n* صَلْصة سَلَطةٍ فَرَنْسيّة

French fries *n* بَطاطِس مَقْليّة

French horn *n* بوق فَرَنْسيّ

Frenchman /ˈfrɛntʃmən/ *n* (*pl* **-men**) فَرَنْسيّ

French toast *n* (BrE) [خُبْز يُغَمَّس في البَيْضِ والحَليبِ لِيُقْلى]

French windows *n* [نَوافِذ زُجاجيّة كَبيرة تُفْتَحُ على شُرْفةٍ \ حَديقةٍ]

Frenchwoman /ˈfrɛntʃwʊmən/ *n* (*pl* **-women**) فَرَنْسيّة

frenetic /frəˈnɛtɪk/ *adj* ‹*pace, activity*› مَسْعور

frenzied /ˈfrɛnzid/ *adj* ‹*attack, speculation*› مَسْعور

frenzy /ˈfrɛnzi/ *n* هَيَجان

frequency /ˈfriːkwənsi/ *n* (*pl* **frequencies**) 1 (rate) مُعَدَّل تَكْرارٍ 2 (in broadcasting) (تَرَدُّدات) تَرَدُّد, ذَبْذَبة

frequency modulation *n* تَضْمين التَرَدُّدِ

frequent /ˈfriːkwənt/ *adj* 1 (common) ‹*expression, custom*› شائع 2 (happening often) ‹*journey, occurrence*› مُتَكَرِّر

frequently /ˈfriːkwəntli/ *adv* كَثيراً ما, في أَحْيانٍ كَثيرةٍ

fresco /ˈfrɛskəʊ/ *n* (*pl* **frescoes**) لَوْحة جِصّيّة جِداريّة

fresh /frɛʃ/ *adj* 1 (not old) ‹*bread, fish, milk*› طازَج; **it looks ~** يَبْدو طازَجاً; **there's ~ coffee in the pot** توجَدُ قَهْوةٌ طازَجةٌ في الإِبْريق 2 (not processed) ‹*herbs, pasta*› طَبيعيّ; **~ orange juice** عَصير بُرْتُقالٍ طَبيعيٍّ 3 (not salty) ‹*water*› عَذْب (عِذاب); **supplies of ~ water are low** مَخْزوناتُ المِياهِ العَذْبةِ مُنْخَفِضةٌ 4 (unused) ‹*clothes, bandages*› جَديد 5 (new) ‹*evidence, information, supplies*› جَديد (جُدُد); **~ evidence has come to light** ظَهَرَ دَليلٌ جَديدٌ 6 (recent) ‹*injury, blood*› جَديد; **it is still ~ in her memory** ما زالَ حَيًّا في ذاكِرَتِها 7 (original) ‹*approach, outlook*› جَديد; **a ~ approach to an old problem** مُقارَبة جَديدة لِمُشْكِلةٍ قَديمةٍ 8 (energetic, alert) **to feel** *or* **be ~** شَعَرَ بِحَيَويّةٍ 9 (cool) ‹*evening, weather*› مُنْعِش 10 (Meteorol) (quite strong) **a ~ breeze** نَسيم مُنْعِش 11 (infml) (over-familiar) وَقِح (وُقُح)

(Idioms) **to be fresh out of university** تَخَرَّجَ لِتَوِّهِ من الجامِعةِ; **to be fresh out of prison** خَرَجَ لِتَوِّهِ من السِجْنِ; **to be fresh out of water/time** (infml) نَفَدَ الماءُ \ الوَقْتُ منذ قَليلٍ

fresh air *n* هَواء نَقيّ; **to get some fresh air** اِسْتَنْشَقَ بَعْضَ الهَواءِ النَقيِّ

freshen /ˈfrɛʃ(ə)n/ *vi* 1 «wind» اِشْتَدَّ; **the wind will ~ from the east** سَتَشْتَدُّ سُرْعةُ الريحِ القادِمةِ من الشَرْقِ 2 «weather» بَرُدَ (u; بُرود)

(Phrasal verb) **freshen up** ≈ تَأَنَّقَ

fresher /ˈfrɛʃə/ *n* (BrE infml) طالِب في السَنةِ الأولى

freshly /ˈfrɛʃli/ *adv* ‹*brewed, cut, picked*› حَديثاً; **~ washed/ironed sheets** مَلاءات غُسِلَتْ \ كُوِيَتْ حَديثاً

freshman /ˈfrɛʃmən/ *n* (*pl* **-men**) 1 (AmE) (at college) طالِب في السَنةِ الأولى 2 (AmE) (in Congress, business) عُضْو جَديد

freshness /ˈfrɛʃnəs/ *n* 1 (of bread, vegetables, eggs, milk) طَزاجة 2 (originality) أَصالة 3 (of a the water, one's breath) نَقاء 4 (of the weather) بُرودة

freshwater /ˈfrɛʃwɔːtə/ *adj before n* ‹*fish, lake*› المِياهِ العَذْبةِ

freshwoman /ˈfrɛʃˌwʊmən/ *n* (*pl* **-women**) 1 (AmE) (at college) طالِبة في السَنة الأولى 2 (AmE) (in Congress, a firm) عُضْوة جَديدة

fret /frɛt/ *vi* (**-tt-**) قَلِقَ (a; قَلَق; على)

fretful /ˈfrɛtfʊl/ *adj* ‹*child, passenger*› قَلِق

Freudian slip /ˌfrɔɪdiən ˈslɪp/ *n* زَلّة (لِسانٍ) فْرويْديّة

friar /ˈfrʌɪə/ *n* راهِب (رُهْبان)

friction /ˈfrɪkʃ(ə)n/ *n* 1 (rubbing) اِحْتِكاك (اِحْتِكاكات) 2 (conflict) نِزاع (نِزاعات)

Friday /ˈfrʌɪdeɪ/ *n* (يَوْم) الجُمْعةِ; **on ~** يَوْمَ الجُمْعةِ; **to attend ~ prayers** حَضَرَ صَلاةَ الجُمْعةِ ▸ **Wednesday**

fridge /frɪdʒ/ *n* بَرّاد, ثَلّاجة

fridge-freezer /ˌfrɪdʒˈfriːzə/ *n* ثَلّاجة ذات مُجَمِّدٍ

fried /frʌɪd/ **A** *past participle* ▸ **fry** A
B *adj* مَقْليّ; **a ~ egg** بَيْضة مَقْليّة

friend /frɛnd/ *n* صَديق (أَصْدِقاءُ); **he's a ~ of mine/my friend** هو صَديقٌ لي \ صَديقي; **to make ~s with sb** صادَقَ شَخْصاً; **I'm ~s with them** أنا صَديقٌ لَهُمْ

friendliness /ˈfrɛndlinəs/ *n* مَوَدّة, لُطْف

friendly /ˈfrɛndli/ **A** *adj* (**friendlier**, **friendliest**) ‹*person, attitude*› لَطيف, وَدود; ‹*government, nation*› صَديق; **to be ~ with sb** كانَ لَطيفاً مع شَخْصٍ

B *n* (*pl* **friendlies**) مُباراة وِدّيّة

friendly fire *n* نيران صَديقة

friendship /ˈfrɛndʃɪp/ *n* صَداقة

fries /frʌɪz/ *n pl* بَطاطِس مَقْلِيّة

frieze /friːz/ *n* (on a building, wall) إفْريز (أَفاريزُ)

frigate /ˈfrɪgət/ *n* فَرْقاطة

fright /frʌɪt/ *n* **1** [u] (fear) ذُعْر, هَلَع; **to take ~** انْتابَهُ الخَوْفُ

2 (scare) فَزَع (أَفْزاع); **I got the ~ of my life** انْتابَني فَزَعٌ \ خَوْفٌ شَديدٌ

frighten /ˈfrʌɪt(ə)n/ *vt* أَفْزَعَ, أَخافَ ‹*a child, an animal*›

(Phrasal verb) **frighten away, frighten off**: **~ away [sb/sth], ~ [sb/sth] away** نَفَّرَ [شَخْصاً \ شَيْئاً] ‹*an animal, intruder*›

frightened /ˈfrʌɪt(ə)nd/ *adj* ‹*child, animal*› خائِف (خُوَّف); **to be ~ of flying/dogs** كانَ خائِفاً من الطَيَرانِ \ الكِلابِ

frightening /ˈfrʌɪtnɪŋ/ *adj* ‹*experience, prospect*› مُرْعِب, مُخيف

frightful /ˈfrʌɪtfʊl/ *adj* **1** (horrifying) ‹*dream, accident*› مُرَوِّع, فَظيع **2** (BrE infml) (terrible) ‹*mess, bore*› مُرْعِب

frigid /ˈfrɪdʒɪd/ *adj* **1** ‹*woman, wife*› بارِد جِنْسِيّاً **2** ‹*temperature*› مُنْخَفِض جِدّاً; ‹*weather*› قارِس

frill /frɪl/ **A** *n* كَشْكَش (كَشاكِشُ)

B (**frills**) *n pl* (extra features) زَرْكَشات, تَحاسين; **a simple wedding with no ~s** عُرْس بَسيط دون مَظاهِرِ التَرَفِ

frilly /ˈfrɪli/ *adj* (**frillier**, **frilliest**) ‹*garment, petticoat*› مُزَيَّن بِكَشاكِش

fringe /frɪndʒ/ **A** *n* **1** (decorative trim) هُدْب (أَهْداب) **2** (BrE) (of hair) قُصّة, ناصِية (نَواصٍ) **3** (periphery) هامِش (هَوامِشُ); **on the ~s of society** على هامِشِ المُجْتَمَعِ

B *adj* ‹*meeting, group*› فَرْعِيّ

fringe benefit *n* مَزيّة إضافيّة (عِلاوةً على الأَجْرِ)

frisk /frɪsk/ *vt* فَتَّشَ ‹*a passenger, suspect*›

frisky /ˈfrɪski/ *adj* (**friskier**, **friskiest**) **1** (playful, high-spirited) ‹*puppy, kitten*› مَرِح (مَرْحى) **2** (infml) (sexy) يَشْعُرُ بِرَغْبةٍ جِنْسِيّةٍ

fritter /ˈfrɪtə/ *n* [فَطيرة مَقْلِيّة]

(Phrasal verb) **fritter away**: **~ away [sth], ~ [sth] away** بَدَّدَ \ ضَيَّعَ [شَيْئاً] ‹*money, resources*›

frivolous /ˈfrɪvələs/ *adj* ‹*attitude, behaviour*› أَرْعَن, طائِش (dipt)

frizzy /ˈfrɪzi/ *adj* (**frizzier**, **frizziest**) ‹*hair, beard*› مُتَجَعِّد

frock /frɒk/ *n* فُسْتان (فَساتينُ)

frog /frɒg/ *n* ضِفْدَع (ضَفادِعُ)

(Idiom) **to have a frog in one's throat** بَحَّ صَوْتُهُ

frogman /ˈfrɒgmən/ *n* (*pl* **-men**) غَوّاص

frogs' legs *n* طَبَق أَرْجُلِ الضَفادِعِ

frogspawn /ˈfrɒgspɔːn/ *n* بَيْض الضَفادِعِ

frolic /ˈfrɒlɪk/ *vi* (**-ck-**) «children, puppies» مَرِحَ (a; مَرَح), لَها (u; لَهْو)

from /frɒm, frəm/ *prep* **1** (showing origin) مِنْ; **where is he ~?** مِنْ أَيْنَ هو؟; **she comes ~ Richmond** هِيَ مِنْ ريتْشْموند; **a flight ~ Baghdad** رِحْلة جَوّيّة مِنْ بَغْدادَ; **people ~ Syria** ناس مِنْ سوريا; **the road ~ Fez to Kenitra** الطَريق مِنْ فاس إلى القَنيطْرة; **noises ~ upstairs** أَصْوات مِن الطابَقِ العُلْوِيِّ; **to take sth ~ one's bag** أَخَذَ شَيْئاً مِنْ حَقيبَتِهِ; **to take sth ~ the shelf** أَخَذَ شَيْئاً مِنْ (على) الرَفِّ; **to grow vegetables ~ seeds** زَرَعَ خُضْرَواتٍ مِن البُذورِ **2** (expressing distance) مِنْ; **it's not far ~ here** لَيْسَ بَعيداً مِنْ هُنا; **10 km ~ the sea** 10 كم مِن البَحْرِ **3** (expressing time) مِنْ; **open ~ 9 a.m until 5 p.m.** مَفْتوح مِنْ 9 صَباحاً حَتّى 5 مَساءً; **the season lasts ~ June to September** يَمْتَدُّ المَوْسِمُ مِنْ شَهْرِ يونيو حَتّى شَهْرِ سِبْتَمْبِر; **15 years ~ now** 15 عاماً مِن الآنَ; **~ today** مِن اليَوْمِ; **one month ~ now** بعد شَهْرٍ مِن الآنَ; **deaf ~ birth** أَصَمّ منذ الوِلادةِ **4** (showing basis) عَنْ; **to speak ~ experience** تَحَدَّثَ عَنْ خِبْرةٍ **5** (employed by) مِنْ; **a salesman ~ Davies and Co** مُوَظَّف مَبيعاتٍ مِنْ شَرِكةِ ديفيز وشُرَكائِهِ **6** (among) مِن ضِمْنِ \ بَيْنِ; **the winner was selected ~ a shortlist of six** تَمَّ اخْتِيارُ الفائِزِ من بَيْنِ سِتّةِ أَشْخاصٍ في القائِمةِ المُخْتَصَرةِ **7** (showing extent) مِنْ; **perfume ~ £20 a bottle** عِطْر ابْتِداءً مِنْ £20 للزُجاجةِ الواحِدةِ; **children ~ the ages of 12 to 15** الأَطْفال مِنْ سِنِّ 12 حَتّى 15; **to increase ~ 10% to 17%** ارْتَفَعَ مِنْ 10٪ إلى 17٪; **everything ~ paperclips to wigs** [كُلّ ما قد

[~ start يَخْطُرُ على البالِ بَدْءاً من مَشابِكِ وَرَقٍ إلى باروكاتٍ to finish, ~ beginning to end مِن البِدايةِ إلى النِهايةِ 8 (in subtraction) مِنْ; take 10 ~ 27 اطْرَحْ 10 مِنْ 27 9 (because of, due to) مِنْ; I know ~ speaking to her that she won't accept أَعْرِفُ مِنْ كَلامي مَعَها أَنَّها لن تَقْبَلَ; he knows them ~ the golf club يَعْرِفُهُمْ مِنْ نادي الجولْف 10 (judging by) مِنْ ~ the way he talks you'd think he was an expert تَحْسَبُهُ خَبيراً مِن الطَريقةِ الّتي يَتَحَدَّثُ بِها

frond /frɒnd/ *n* سَعَف (سَعَفات)

front /frʌnt/ A *n* 1 (facade of a house, shop) واجِهة; (forward part of a cupboard) واجِهة; (of a car, boat) مُقَدِّمة; (of a book) غِلاف (أَغْلِفة); (of a jacket, sweater) جِهة أَماميّة; the dress buttons at the ~ تُوجَدُ أَزْرارُ الفُسْتانِ في الجِهةِ الأَماميّةِ; write the address on the ~ of the envelope اُكْتُبِ العُنْوانَ على وَجْهِ الظَرْفِ; the main entrance is at the ~ يَقَعُ المَدْخَلُ الرَئيسيُّ في الواجِهةِ الأَماميّةِ 2 (forward part of buses, a queue) مُقَدِّمة; (of an auditorium) صَفّ أَماميّ; to sit at the ~ of the class جَلَسَ في الصَفِّ الأَماميِّ للفَصْلِ; I sat in the ~ with the driver جَلَسْتُ في المَقْعَدِ الأَماميِّ بِجانِبِ السائِقِ 3 (Mil) (in a war zone) جَبْهة (جَبَهات); to be at the ~ كانَ في الجَبْهةِ 4 (of one's body) جِهة أَماميّة; to spill sth down one's ~ سَكَبَ شَيْئاً على نَفْسِهِ من الأَمامِ 5 (BrE) (at the seaside) واجِهة بَحْريّة 6 (Meteorol) جَبْهة (جَبَهات); a cold/warm ~ جَبْهة هَوائيّة بارِدة \ ساخِنة 7 (area of activity) جَبْهة (جَبَهات); changes on the domestic *or* home ~ تَغْييرات على الجَبْهةِ الداخِليّةِ 8 (public show) واجِهة; to present a united ~ قَدَّمَ جَبْهةً مُوَحَّدةً 9 (infml) (for illegal activity) واجِهة; to be a ~ for illegal activities كانَ واجِهةً لِأَنْشِطةٍ غَيْرِ قانونيّةٍ

B *adj* 1 (facing the street) ‹bedroom, window, wall› أَماميّ 2 (furthest forward) ‹tyre, wheel, seat› أَماميّ; ‹leg, tooth› أَماميّ; ‹carriage› أَماميّ 3 (first) ‹page› أَماميّ 4 (leading) ‹runner, horse› في الطَليعةِ \ المُقَدِّمةِ

C (in front) *adv phr* to be in ~ (ahead in races) كانَ في الطَليعةِ \ المُقَدِّمةِ; (on a walk, while driving, etc) كانَ في الأَمامِ; at half way, Smith is still in ~ ما زالَ سْميث عند مُنْتَصَفِ المَسافةِ في الطَليعةِ \ المُقَدِّمةِ

D (in front of) *prep phr* 1 (before, ahead of) أَمامَ; walk in ~ of me امْشِ أَمامي 2 (in the presence of) أَمامَ

E *vt* 1 (infml) (to lead) قادَ (u; قِيادة) ‹a band, party› 2 (to present) قَدَّمَ ‹a TV show›

F *vi* (to face) to ~ onto the road/beach «houses, gardens» أَطَلَّ على الشارِعِ \ الشاطِئِ

frontal /'frʌnt(ə)l/ *adj* 1 ‹attack, assault› مُباشِر 2 ‹lobe, cortex› جَبْهيّ 3 ‹view, nudity› أَماميّ

front bench *n* (BrE) [مَقاعِد أَماميّة في مَجْلِسِ العُمومِ]

frontbencher /frʌnt'bentʃə/ *n* (BrE) وَزير (وُزَراءُ)

front door *n* باب \ مَدْخَل رَئيسيّ

frontier /'frʌntɪə/ A *n* حَدّ (حُدود)

B *adj* ‹town, zone› حُدوديّ

frontispiece /'frʌntɪspi:s/ *n* صورة صَدْرِ كِتابٍ

front line A *n* 1 (Mil) جَبْهة (جِباه ,جَبَهات), خط مُواجَهةٍ 2 (exposed position) طَليعة (طَلائِعُ); to be in the front line كانَ في الطَليعة

B (front-line) *adj* (Mil) ‹troops, defences› خطِّ المُواجَهةِ

front page A *n* صَفْحة أُولى;

B (front-page) *adj* ‹story, news› يَظْهَرُ في الصَفْحةِ الأُولى

front-wheel drive /,frʌnt,wiəl 'draɪv/ *n* دَفْع أَماميّ

frost /frɒst/ *n* 1 (ice crystals) صَقيع; an air/ground ~ صَقيع هَوائيّ \ أَرْضيّ 2 (freezing weather) جَوّ صَقيعيّ

Phrasal verb frost over, frost up «windows, ground» تَغَطّى بالصَقيع

frostbite /'frɒstbaɪt/ *n* عَضّة صَقيع

frosted /'frɒstɪd/ *adj* 1 ‹glass, window› غَيْر مُصَنفَر ,مُغَبَّش 2 ‹lipstick, nail varnish› بَرّاق 3 (AmE) ‹cake› مُغَطًّى بالسُكَّرِ

frosting /'frɒstɪŋ/ *n* (AmE) [خَليط من السُكَّرِ وَبَياضِ البَيْضِ \ الزُبْدةِ لِتَزْيينِ الكَعْكِ]

frosty /'frɒsti/ *adj* (frostier, frostiest) 1 ‹morning, weather› صَقيعيّ 2 (unfriendly) ‹reception, relationship› بارِد

froth /frɒθ/ *n* زَبَد (أَزْباد), رَغْوة (رَغاوٍ)

frothy /'frɒθi/ *adj* (frothier, frothiest) ‹beer, coffee› مُزْبِد ,رَغْويّ

frown /fraʊn/ **A** *vi* قَطَبَ (i; قُطوب, قَطْب), عَبَسَ (i; عُبوس), تَجَهَّمَ; **to ~ at sb** عَبَسَ في وَجْهِ شَخْصٍ **B** *n* عُبوس

(Phrasal verb) **frown on, frown upon: ~ on** *or* **upon [sth]** اسْتَنْكَرَ [شَيْئاً]; **divorce was ~ed upon** كانَ الطَلاقُ مُسْتَنْكَراً

froze /frəʊz/ *past tense* ▸ **freeze**

frozen /'frəʊz(ə)n/ **A** *past participle* ▸ **freeze** **B** *adj* **1** ‹*food, yoghurt*› مُجَمَّد; ‹*lake, ground*› مُتَجَمِّد **2** (very cold) مُتَجَمِّد من البَرْدِ; **my feet are ~!** قَدَماي مُتَجَمِّدَتانِ من البَرْدِ! **3** (motionless) جامِد في مَكانِهِ; **I stood there ~ in fear/horror** وَقَفْتُ جامِداً في مَكاني من الخَوْفِ \ الرُعْبِ

frugal /'fru:g(ə)l/ *adj* ‹*shopper, traveller*› مُقْتَصِد; ‹*meal, lifestyle*› بَسيط

fruit /fru:t/ *n* (*pl* **fruit, fruits**) فاكِهة (فَواكِهُ); **dried ~** فاكِهة مُجَفَّفة

fruit cake *n* كَعْكة فَواكِهَ مُجَفَّفةٍ

fruit cocktail *n* كوكْتيل فَواكِهَ

fruit cup *n* **1** (BrE) (drink) [عَصير فَواكِهَ مَمْزوج بالكُحولِ] **2** (AmE) (dessert) سَلَطة فَواكِهَ

fruiterer /'fru:t(ə)rə/ *n* (fml) فاكِهانيّ

fruit fly *n* ذُبابة فاكِهةٍ

fruitful /'fru:tfʊl/ *adj* **1** ‹*tree, plant*› مُثْمِر **2** ‹*partnership, discussion*› مُثْمِر

fruition /frʊ'ɪʃ(ə)n/ *n* **to come to ~** نَجَزَ (u; نَجْز)

fruit juice *n* عَصير فَواكِهَ

fruitless /'fru:tləs/ *adj* **1** ‹*tree, crop*› غَيْر مُثْمِرٍ **2** ‹*attempt, trip*› غَيْر مُثْمِرٍ \ مُجْدٍ

fruit machine *n* ماكينة القِمارِ \ الحَظِّ

fruit salad *n* سَلَطة فَواكِهَ

fruit tree *n* شَجَرة فاكِهةٍ

fruity /'fru:ti/ *adj* (**fruitier, fruitiest**) ‹*flavour, wine*› قَويّ (النَكْهةِ)

frustrate /frʌ'streɪt/ *vt* أَحْبَطَ ‹*sb's plans, efforts*›

frustrated /frʌ'streɪtɪd/ *adj* **1** (irritated, dissatisfied) مُحْبَط; **to be/get ~** كانَ مُحْبَطاً **2** (thwarted) ‹*ambition, attempt*› فاشِل

frustrating /frʌ'streɪtɪŋ/ *adj* ‹*experience, delay*› مُحْبِط

frustration /frʌ'streɪʃ(ə)n/ *n* [u] إِحْباط

fry /frʌɪ/ **A** *vt* (**fries, frying, fried**) قَلى (i; قَلْي) **B** (**fried**) *adj* مَقْليّ

frying pan /'frʌɪɪŋ pan/, **frypan** /'frʌɪpan/ (AmE) *n* مِقْلاة (مَقالٍ)

ft *abbr* = **foot**, = **feet** قَدَم (f; أَقْدام)

FTP /ɛfti:'pi:/ *n* = **file transfer protocol** بُروتوكول نَقْلِ المِلَفّاتِ

fuchsia /'fju:ʃə/ *n* فوشْيا

fuck /fʌk/ **A** *vt* (vulg) ناكَ (i; نيك) ‹*a person*› **B** *vi* (vulg) «couples, partners» مارَسَ الجِنْسَ

(Phrasal verb) **fuck off** (vulg) انْصَرَفَ, انْخَلَعَ; **~ off!** انْخَلِعْ!

fucking /'fʌkɪŋ/ **A** *adj* (vulg) ‹*idiot, liar, mess*› مَلْعون; **~ hell!** ≈ اللَعْنة! **B** *adv* (vulg) ≈ جِدًّا

fudge /fʌdʒ/ **A** *n* **1** (soft sweet) حَلْوى الفَدْج **2** (AmE) (rich chocolate) صَلْصة \ حَشْوة شوكولاتةٍ **B** *vt* (infml) **1** (to evade) تَهَرَّبَ (من) ‹*an issue, a problem*› **2** (to falsify) زَوَّرَ ‹*the numbers, accounts*›

fuel /fjʊəl/ **A** *n* (for heating) مَحْروقات; (for car, plane) وَقود **B** *vt* (**-ll-** BrE, **-l-** AmE) **1** زَوَّدَ بالوَقودِ ‹*the power station, furnace*› **2** أَثارَ ‹*a debate, hope*›

fuel injection *n* حَقْن وَقودٍ

fuel oil *n* زَيْت وَقودٍ

fuel tank *n* خَزّان وَقودٍ

fugitive /'fju:dʒɪtɪv/ *n* هارِب, فارّ

fugue /fju:g/ *n* فوجا (قالَب موسيقيّ يَتَّسِمُ بِتَتابُعِ الأَصْواتِ \ بِتَكْرارِ اللَحْنِ الرَئيسيِّ)

fulfil (BrE), **fulfill** (AmE) /fʊl'fɪl/ **A** *vt* (**-ll-**) **1** (to realize) حَقَّقَ ‹*an ambition, a dream*› **2** (to carry out) أَنْجَزَ ‹*a duty, role*› **3** (to satisfy) اسْتَوْفى ‹*a requirement, need*› **4** (emotionally) أَسْعَدَ **B** *v refl* (**-ll-**) **to ~ oneself** حَقَّقَ ذاتَهُ

fulfilment (BrE), **fulfillment** (AmE) /fʊl'fɪlmənt/ *n* **1** (of a dream) تَحْقيق **2** (of requirements) اسْتيفاء **3** (personal satisfaction) رِضًى; **her family gave her a sense of ~** مَنَحَتْها أُسْرَتُها شُعوراً بالرِضى

full /fʊl/ **A** *adj* **1** (filled) ‹*box, glass, room, hotel*› مُمْتَلِئ; **a ~ tank of petrol** خَزّان بنْزين مُمْتَلِئ; **the hotel is ~ to overflowing** الفُنْدُقُ مُمْتَلِئٌ بِشَكْلٍ كامِلٍ; **I've got my hands ~** أنا مَشْغولٌ حتّى النُخاع; **she's ~ of energy/ideas** هي مُمْتَلِئةٌ بالطاقةِ \ بالأَفْكارِ; **to be ~ of one's own importance** كانَ مُعْجَباً بِنَفْسِهِ **2** (from eating) **to be ~** *or* **~ up** كانَ شَبْعانَ **3** (busy) ‹*day, week*› مُكْتَظّ; **she leads a very ~ life** تَعيشُ حَياةً مُمْتَلِئةً بالمَشاغِلِ **4** (complete) ‹*name, story, details*› كامِل; **the ~ extent of the damage** المَدى الكامِل للضَرَرِ; **he has our ~ support** لَهُ مِنّا كُلُّ الدَعْمِ; **she has a ~ set of teeth** أَسْنانُها كامِلةٌ; **to be in ~ view** كانَ على مَرْأًى من الجَميعِ **5** (in status) ‹*member, partner*› كامِل; **to be a ~ member** كانَ عُضْواً كامِلاً **6** (maximum) ‹*volume, power*› كامِل; **at ~ volume** بِأَعْلى الصَوْتِ; **at ~ speed** بِكامِلِ السُرْعةِ; **in ~ daylight** في وَضَحِ النَهارِ; **to be in ~ bloom** كانَ في كامِلِ إِزْهارِهِ; **to make ~ use of an opportunity** اسْتَفادَ اسْتِفادةً كامِلةً من فُرْصةٍ **7** (for emphasis) ‹*hour, kilo*› كامِل **8** (rounded) ‹*figure, face*› مُمْتَلِئ **9** (Astron) **a ~ moon** بَدْر (كامِل)

B *adv* **1** (directly) ‹*to hit, punch*› مُباشَرةً; **it hit me ~ in the face** ضَرَبَني مُباشَرةً في الوَجْهِ **2** (very) **to know ~ well that ...** عَرَفَ جَيِّداً أنّ ...

C (**in full**) *adv phr* ‹*to describe, pay, publish*› بِشَكْلٍ كامِلٍ; **write your name in ~** أُكْتُبِ اسْمَكَ كامِلاً

D (**to the full**) *adv phr* **to enjoy/live sth to the ~** اسْتَمْتَعَ بِشَيْءٍ بِشَكْلٍ كامِلٍ

full back *n* ظَهير (ظُهَراءُ, أَظْهار)

full beam *n* ضَوْء مُبْهِر

full-blown /ˌfʊlˈbləʊn/ *adj* **1** ‹*disease, epidemic*› مُكْتَمِل (النُمُوّ) **2** ‹*recession, war*› شامِل

full board *n* إقامة كامِلة

full-cream milk /fʊlkriːm ˈmɪlk/ *n* (BrE) حَليب كامِل الدَسَمِ

full-grown /fʊlˈgrəʊn/ *adj* ‹*adult, tree*› ناضِج, بالِغ

full house *n* **1** (in a theatre) قاعة مُمْتَلِئة **2** (in poker) [ثَلاث أَوْراقٍ تَحْمِلُ نَفْسَ الرَقْمِ وَوَرَقَتانِ مُتَشابِهَتانِ]

full-length /ˌfʊlˈlɛŋθ/ *adj* ‹*coat, mirror*› كامِل الطول

full moon *n* بَدْر (بُدور)

full name *n* اسْم كامِل

fullness /ˈfʊlnəs/ *n* **1** (of a sleeve, dress) اتِّساع (اتِّساعات) **2** (of sb's breasts, lips) امْتِلاء **3** (of tone) قوّة

Idiom **in the fullness of time** (fml) في النِهايةِ

full price A *adj* (*before n* **full-price**) ‹*item*› بِسِعْرِهِ الأَصْليِّ (دون تَخْفيضٍ);

B *adv* «to charge, to pay» دون تَخْفيضٍ في السِعْرِ

full-scale /ˌfʊlˈskeɪl/ *adj* **1** (actual size) ‹*drawing, plan*› بالحَجْمِ الأَصْليِّ \ الطَبيعيِّ **2** (thorough) ‹*reorganization, investigation*› شامِل, كُلّيّ

full-size /fʊlˈsʌɪz/, **full-sized** /fʊlˈsʌɪzd/ *adj* **1** (life-size) ‹*replica, picture*› بالحَجْمِ الأَصْليِّ **2** (adult-size) ‹*bed, bicycle*› كَبير الحَجْمِ

full stop *n* (BrE) نُقْطة (عند نِهايةِ جُمْلةٍ)

full time A *adj* (*before n* **full-time**) ‹*job*› بِدَوام كامِلٍ; ‹*student*› مُتَفَرِّغ;

B *adv* ‹*to work*› بِدَوام كامِلٍ; ‹*to study*› بِشَكْلٍ مُتَفَرِّغٍ

fully /ˈfʊli/ *adv* **1** (completely) ‹*equipped, furnished, dressed*› بِشَكْلٍ كامِلٍ \ تامٍّ; ‹*to understand, recover*› تَماماً; **to be ~ qualified** كانَ مُؤَهَّلاً بِشَكْلٍ كامِلٍ; **the hotel is ~ booked** الفُنْدُقُ مَحْجوزٌ بالكامِلِ; **I ~ intend to go** أَنْوي تَماماً الذَهابَ **2** (comprehensively) ‹*to examine, study*› بِشَكْلٍ شامِلٍ **3** (at least) على الأَقَلِّ

fully fledged *adj* (BrE) **1** (full-grown) ‹*bird*› مُكْتَمِل النُمُوّ **2** (qualified) ‹*lawyer, officer*› مُؤَهَّل

fulsome /ˈfʊls(ə)m/ *adj* (fml) ‹*praise, manner*› مُغالًى \ مُبالَغ فيه

fumble /ˈfʌmb(ə)l/ *vi* تَخَبَّطَ; **she ~d in her pockets** تَفَقَّدَتْ جُيوبَها بارْتِباكٍ; **he ~d for the right words** تَلَعْثَمَ بَحْثاً عن الكَلِماتِ المُناسِبةِ

fume /fjuːm/ *vi* **1** (infml) «passengers, critics» ثارَتْ ثائِرَتُهُ, اسْتَشاطَ غَضَباً; **she was absolutely fuming** ثارَتْ ثائِرَتُها بِكُلِّ مَعْنى الكَلِمةِ **2** «volcanos» أَطْلَقَ دُخاناً

fumes /fjuːmz/ *n pl* أَبْخِرة, أَدْخِنة

fumigate /ˈfjuːmɪgeɪt/ *vt* ‹*a building, ward*› بَخَّرَ (للتَطْهير)

fun /fʌn/ *n* مُتْعة, تَسْلِية; **to have ~** تَسَلّى; **he did it for ~** فَعَلَها للتَسْلِيةِ; **she is great ~ to be with** رِفْقَتُها مُمْتِعةٌ جِدّاً

Idioms **to have fun and games** وَجَدَ صُعوبةً; **to make fun of** *or* **poke fun at sb/sth** سَخِرَ من شَخْصٍ \ شَيْءٍ

function /ˈfʌŋkʃ(ə)n/ **A** *n* **1** (role) مُهِمّة (مُهِمّات), وَظيفة (وَظائِفُ); **to carry out/perform a ~** نَفَّذَ \ أَدّى وَظيفةً; **the bodily ~s** وَظائِف الجِسْمِ **2** (reception, party) حَفْلة (حَفَلات) **3** (computer operation) دالّة **4** (expression) وَظيفة (وَظائِفُ)

B *vi* (to work) «machines, organs» عَمِلَ (a; عَمَل), اِشْتَغَلَ; **her liver is ~ing normally** يَعْمَلُ كَبِدُها بِشَكْلٍ طَبيعيٍّ; **the hall also ~s as a classroom** تُسْتَخْدَمُ القاعةُ كَحُجْرةِ دَرْسٍ أَيْضاً

functional /ˈfʌŋkʃ(ə)n(ə)l/ *adj* **1** (operational) ‹*machine*› شَغّال; ‹*differences*› وَظيفيّ **2** (practical) ‹*furniture, design*› عَمَليّ

function key *n* (Comput) مِفْتاح وَظيفةٍ

fund /fʌnd/ **A** *n* صُنْدوق (صَناديقُ), اعتِماد ماليّ

B (**funds**) *n pl* أَمْوال

C *vt* مَوَّلَ ‹*a project, an organisation*›

fundamental /fʌndəˈmɛnt(ə)l/ *adj* **1** (basic) ‹*principle, issue*› جَوْهَريّ, أَساسيّ **2** (essential) ‹*skill, constituent*› جَوْهَريّ

fundamentalism /fʌndəˈmentəliz(ə)m/ *n* أُصوليّة

fundamentalist /fʌndəˈmentəlɪst/ *n, adj* أُصوليّ

fundamentally /fʌndəˈmɛnt(ə)li/ *adv* **1** (radically) ‹*different, opposed*› جَوْهَريًّا **2** (in essence) ‹*sound, correct*› في الأَساسِ

funding /ˈfʌndɪŋ/ *n* (act of providing resources) تَمْويل

fundraiser /ˈfʌndreɪzə/ *n* (person) جامِع تَبَرُّعاتٍ; (event) حَفْل جَمْع تَبَرُّعاتٍ

fundraising /ˈfʌndreɪzɪŋ/ *n* جَمْع تَبَرُّعاتٍ

funeral /ˈfjuːn(ə)rəl/ *n* جَنازة (جَنائِزُ, جَنازات)

funeral director *n* حانوتيّ (حانوتيّة)

funeral home, **funeral parlour** (AmE), **parlor** *n* [شَرِكة مُتَخَصِّصة في تَشْييعِ المَوْتى وَإِقامةِ المَآتِمِ]

funfair /ˈfʌnfɛː/ *n* مَدينة \ حَديقة مَلاهٍ

fungus /ˈfʌŋgəs/ *n* (*pl* **fungi**) (plant) فُطْر (n coll; singul n فُطْر; فُطور)

funk /fʌŋk/ *n* (Mus) فانْك

funky /ˈfʌŋki/ *adj* (**funkier**, **funkiest**) **1** (Mus) (infml) ‹*music, rhythm*› الفانْك **2** (infml) (modern, fashionable) ‹*shoes, restaurant*› غَيْر تَقْليديٍّ, عَصْريّ

fun-loving /ˈfʌnlʌvɪŋ/ *adj* ‹*child, personality*› مَرِح (مَراحى, مَرْحى)

funnel /ˈfʌn(ə)l/ *n* **1** (for liquids) قِمْع (أَقْماع) **2** (for smoke) مِدْخَنة (مَداخِنُ)

funnily /ˈfʌn(ə)li/ *adv* **1** ‹*to walk, behave*› بِغَرابةٍ **2** **~ enough, I was starting to like the idea** من الغَريبِ فِعْلاً أَنَّني بَدَأْتُ أُحِبُّ الفِكْرةَ

funny /ˈfʌni/ *adj* (**funnier**, **funniest**) **1** (amusing) ‹*incident, joke*› مُسَلٍّ, مُضْحِك **2** (strange) ‹*smell, noise*› غَريب; **it's ~ that she hasn't phoned** من الغَريبِ أَنَّها لم تَتَّصِلْ هاتِفيًّا; **to taste/smell ~** كانَ لَهُ طَعْمٌ غَريبٌ \ رائِحةٌ غَريبةٌ **3** (infml) (unwell) مُتَوَعِّك; **I feel a bit ~** أَشْعُرُ بِبَعْضِ التَوَعُّكِ

funny bone *n* (infml) عَظْمة الكوعِ (حَيْثُ يَمُرُّ العَصَبُ الزَنْديُّ)

fur /fəː/ **A** *n* **1** (of an animal) فَرْو (n coll; فِراء) **2** (garment) فَرْو (n coll; فِراء)

B *adj* ‹*collar, coat*› فَرْوٍ

furious /ˈfjʊərɪəs/ *adj* **1** (angry) ‹*campaigner, boss*› مُغْتاظ, حانِق; **I was ~ with her for coming** كُنْتُ غاضِباً جِدًّا عَلَيْها لِمَجيئِها **2** (violent, intense) ‹*debate, storm*› عَنيف

furiously /ˈfjʊərɪəsli/ *adv* **1** (angrily) ‹*to react, glare*› بِغَضَبٍ **2** (violently, intensely) ‹*to struggle, nod*› بِعُنْفٍ, بِاهْتِياجٍ شَديدٍ

furlong /ˈfəːlɒŋ/ *n* فيرْلونْج (وَحْدة قِياسٍ تُعادِلُ ثُمْنَ ميلٍ)

furlough /ˈfəːləʊ/ *n* إِجازة تَغَيُّبٍ; **on ~** في إِجازةٍ

furnace /ˈfəːnɪs/ *n* **1** (in industry) مَصْهَر (مَصاهِرُ) **2** (boiler) سَخّان (سَخّانات)

furnish /ˈfəːnɪʃ/ *vt* **1** (to put furniture in) أَثَّثَ ‹*a room, house*› **2** (to supply) زَوَّدَ (بـ) ‹*a document, information*›; **to ~ sb with sth** زَوَّدَ شَخْصاً بِشَيْءٍ

furnishings /ˈfəːnɪʃɪŋz/ *n pl* مَفْروشات

furniture /ˈfəːnɪtʃə/ *n* أَثاث; **a piece of ~** قِطْعة أَثاثٍ; **they came back with 11 pieces of ~** رَجَعوا بِإِحْدى عَشْرة قِطْعةً من الأَثاثِ

furrow /ˈfʌrəʊ/ *n* **1** (in earth) أُخْدود (أَخاديدُ) **2** (on sb's face) أُخْدود (أَخاديدُ)

furry /ˈfəːri/ *adj* (**furrier, furriest**) (covered with fur) ‹*kitten, rabbit*› مَكْسوّ بالفَرْوِ; (covered with sth like fur) ‹*toy, lining*› [ناعِم كالفَرْوِ]

further /ˈfəːðə/ **A** *adv* (*comparative of* **far**) **1** (also **farther**) (in space, distance) ‹*to travel, extend*› أَبْعَد; **how much ~ is it?** كم يَبْعُدُ من هُنا؟; **I can't go any ~** لا يُمْكِنُني أنْ أذْهبَ أَبْعَدَ; **it's a mile ~ on** هو على بُعْدِ ميلٍ من هُنا; **~ north** أَبْعَد إلى الشمالِ; **to get ~ and ~ away** ابْتَعَدَ أَكْثَرَ فأَكْثَرَ; **it's ~ away** *or* **off** هو على مَسافةٍ بَعيدةٍ من هُنا **2** (also **farther**) (in time) أَبْعَد; **~ back than 1964** قبل عام 1964; **we must look ~ ahead** عَلَيْنا أنْ نَنْظُرَ أَكْثَرَ إلى الأمامِ \ المُسْتَقْبَلِ; **I won't delay you any ~** لن أُؤَخِّرَكَ أَكْثَرَ من ذلك **3** (more, to a greater degree) **I'll go so far but no ~** سَأَبْلُغُ هذا الحَدَّ لا أَكْثَرَ; **I haven't read ~ than page twenty** لم أتَجاوَزِ الصَفْحةَ رَقْمَ عِشْرينَ; **prices fell ~** انْخَفَضَت الأَسْعارُ أَكْثَرَ; **nothing could be ~ from the truth** هذا أَبْعَدُ ما يَكونُ عن الحَقيقةِ; **she didn't get any ~ with him than I did** لم تَصِلْ مَعَهُ إلى أَبْعَدِ مِمّا وَصَلْتُ أنا **4** (fml) (in addition) بالإضافةِ إلى ذلك; **the tenant ~ agrees to ...** بالإضافةِ إلى ذلك يُوافِقُ المُسْتَأْجِرُ على ...; **she ~ argued that ...** زَعَمَتْ أَيْضاً أنّ ...

B (**further to**) (fml) إيماءً إلى; **~ to your recent letter** إيماءً إلى رِسالَتِكَ الأَخيرةِ

C *adj* (*comparative of* **far**) **1** (additional) ‹*increase, change*› إضافيّ; **a ~ 10%** إضافيّة 10٪; **a ~ 500 people** 500 شَخْصٍ إضافيٍّ; **~ allegations have been made against him** تَمَّ تَقْديمُ المَزيد من الادِّعاءاتِ ضِدَّهُ; **~ research is needed** هُناكَ حاجةٌ لِمَزيدٍ من الأَبْحاثِ; **there's nothing ~ to discuss** لَيْسَ هُناكَ شَيْءٌ آخَرُ لِمُناقَشَتِهِ; **to have no ~ use for sth** لم يَعُدْ بِحاجةٍ إلى شَيْءٍ **2** (also **farther**) (fml) (more distant) ‹*end, side*› أَبْعَد; **on the ~ bank** على الضِفّةِ الأُخْرى

D *vt* دَعَمَ (a; دَعْم) ‹*sb's chances, career, cause*›

further education *n* (BrE) التَعْليم المُسْتَمِرّ \ المُتَواصِل

furthermore /fəːðəˈmɔː/ *adv* (fml) بالإضافةِ إلى ذلك, عِلاوةً على ذلك; **~, no new cases have been reported** عِلاوةً على ذلك، لم يَتِمَّ الإبْلاغُ عن أيِّ حالاتٍ جَديدةٍ; **it's costly and, ~, the process is untried** العَمَليّةُ مُكَلِّفةٌ، إضافةً إلى ذلك، فإنَّها لم تُجَرَّبْ من قَبْلُ

furthest /ˈfəːðɪst/ **A** *adj* (*superlative of* **far**) (also **farthest**) ‹*place, point, star*› أَبْعَد (dipt), أَقْصى (f قُصْوى)

B (*superlative of* **far**) *adv* **1** (also **farthest**) (in distance) ‹*to travel, extend, see*› بَعيداً **2** (also **farthest**) (in time) أَقْصى (f قُصْوى); **the ~ back I can remember** أَقْدَمُ شَيْءٍ أَسْتَطيعُ أنْ أَتَذَكَّرَهُ; **the ~ ahead we can look** أَقْصى ما يُمْكِنُ أنْ نَتَوَقَّعَهُ **3** (to the greatest extent) إلى أَقْصى حَدٍّ; **this plan goes ~ towards solving the problem** تَسْعى هذه الخُطّةُ إلى أَبْعَدِ حَدٍّ نحوحَلِّ المُشْكِلةِ

furtive /ˈfəːtɪv/ *adj* **1** (stealthy) ‹*glance*› مُسْتَرَق; ‹*movement*› مُخْتَلَس **2** (suspicious, shifty) ‹*expression, manner*› مُريب

furtively /ˈfəːtɪvli/ *adv* ‹*to glance, act*› خُفْيةً

fury /ˈfjʊəri/ *n* (anger) [u] حَنَق

fuse, fuze (AmE) /fjuːz/ **A** *vt* **1** (BrE) **to ~ the lights/iron** (to short-circuit) [عَطَّلَ الأَنْوارَ \ المِكْواةَ بِسَبَبِ انْصِهارِ مِصْهَرٍ] **2** (to fit with a fuse) زَوَّدَ بِفْيوزٍ \ بِمِصْهَرٍ ‹*a circuit, an appliance*›; **a ~d plug** قابِس مُزَوَّد بِمِصْهَرٍ **3** (to melt together) صَهَرَ (a; صَهْر) ‹*the metals, materials*› **4** (to merge) أَدْمَجَ ‹*the images, ideas*›

B *n* **1** (for electrical circuits) فْيوز, مِصْهَر (مَصَاهِر), صُهَيرة (مِصْهَرات) **2** (for explosives) فَتيل (فَتائِل, فَتيلات)

fuse box *n* عُلْبة الفْيوزاتِ

fuselage /ˈfjuːzəlɑːʒ, ˈfjuːzəlɪdʒ/ *n* جِسْم \ جِذْع طائِرةٍ

fuse wire *n* سِلْك الفْيوز

fusion /ˈfjuːʒ(ə)n/ *n* **1** (also **nuclear fusion**) انْشِطار نَوَويّ **2** (of styles) دَمْج; **the painting is a rich ~ of several styles** اللَوْحةُ دَمْجٌ غَنيٌّ لِعِدّةِ أَنْماطٍ

fuss /fʌs/ **A** *n* (infml) **1** (agitation) اهْتِياج; **to make a ~ about sth** أَثارَ ضَجّةً حول شَيْءٍ; **she made a big ~ about nothing** أَثارَتْ حالةً من الهَرْجِ والمَرْجِ بدونِ سَبَبٍ **2** (angry scene) **to kick up a ~ about sth** افْتَعَلَ مُشْكِلةً حول شَيْءٍ **3** (display of attention) **to make a ~ of a person/an animal** بالَغَ \ أَفْرَطَ في الإطْراءِ على شَخْصٍ \ حَيَوانٍ; **she doesn't want any ~** لا تُحِبُّ أَيَّ إطْراءٍ

B *vi* (infml) **1** (to worry) قَلِقَ (a; قَلَق; على); **he's always ~ing over** *or* **about his appearance** يَقْلَقُ دائماً بِشأْنِ مَظْهَرِه **2** (to be agitated) اهْتاجَ **3** (to show affection) **to ~ over sb** أَطْرى على شَخْصٍ

fussbudget /ˈfʌsbʌdʒət/ *n* (AmE infml) [شَخْص نَيِّق \ صَعْب الإرْضاءِ]

fusspot /ˈfʌspɒt/ *n* (infml BrE) **1** (finicky person) [شَخْص نَيِّق \ صَعْب الإرْضاءِ] **2** (worrier) قَلِق وَسَريع الاهْتِياج

fussy /ˈfʌsi/ *adj* (**fussier**, **fussiest**) **1** (difficult to please) ‹*tastes, baby*› صَعْب الإرْضاءِ; **I'm a ~ eater** يَصْعُبُ إرْضائي في الأَكْلِ **2** (over-elaborate) ‹*design, pattern*› [مُزَرْكَش بِشَكْلٍ مُبالَغٍ فيهِ]

futile /ˈfjuːtaɪl/ *adj* **1** (vain) ‹*endeavour, effort*› عَديم الجَدْوى **2** (inane) ‹*intervention, remark*› سَخيف, تافِه

futility /fjuːˈtɪlɪti/ *n* عَدَم جَدْوى

future /ˈfjuːtʃə/ **A** *n* **1** (time to come) مُسْتَقْبَل; **in the ~** في المُسْتَقْبَلِ; **in the near** *or* **not too distant ~** في المُسْتَقْبَلِ القَريبِ; **the aircraft of the ~** طائِرة المُسْتَقْبَلِ; **to see into the ~** اسْتَقْرَأَ المُسْتَقْبَلَ; **in ~ please call for an appointment** اتَّصِلْ بِنا من فَضْلِكَ في المُسْتَقْبَلِ لِتُحَدِّدَ مَوْعِداً **2** (prospects) مُسْتَقْبَل; **to have a bright ~** لَهُ مُسْتَقْبَلٌ مُشْرِقٌ **3** (Ling) (also **future tense**) (زَمَن) المُسْتَقْبَلِ; **in the ~** في المُسْتَقْبَلِ

B (**futures**) *n pl* (Fin) عُقود آجِلة

C *adj* **1** ‹*generations, earnings, developments*› مُسْتَقْبَليّ; **at some ~ date** في وَقْتٍ ما في المُسْتَقْبَلِ **2** ‹*queen, president*› مُسْتَقْبَليّ

futures trader *n* تاجِر عُقودٍ مُسْتَقْبَلِيّة

futuristic /fjuːtʃəˈrɪstɪk/ *adj* ‹*furniture*› ذو تَصْميمٍ مُسْتَقْبَليٍّ; ‹*vision*› مُسْتَقْبَليّ

fuze (AmE) ▸**fuse**

fuzzy /ˈfʌzi/ *adj* (**fuzzier**, **fuzziest**) **1** (frizzy) ‹*hair, beard*› مُتَجَعِّد **2** (blurry) ‹*image, photo*› غَيْر واضِحٍ **3** (vague) ‹*idea, mind*› مُشَوَّش

Gg

G, g /dʒiː/ **A** *n* **1** (letter) جيم ≈ (الحَرْف السابع من الأَبْجَدِيّة الإِنْكْلِيزِيّة) **2** (G) (Mus) صول ≈ (نَغْمة من نَغَماتِ السُلَّم الموسيقيّ)
B *abbr* (g) = **gram(s)** غِرام (غِرامات)

GA *abbr* ▸ **Georgia**

gab /gab/ *n* (infml) ▸ **gift**

gabble /ˈgab(ə)l/ *vi* «friends, on-lookers» هَذَرَ (i-u; هَذْر ,هَذَر), تَمْتَمَ (i; تَمْتَمة)

gable /ˈgeɪb(ə)l/ *n* جَمَلون (جُزْء أَعْلى مُثَلَّث الزَوايا لِجِدارٍ مُكْتَنَفٍ بِسَطْحَيْنِ مُنْحَدِرَيْنِ)

Gabon /gəˈbɒn/ *pr n* الغابون (f)

Gabriel /ˈgeɪbrɪəl/ *pr n* جِبْرِيل (dipt)

gadget /ˈgadʒɪt/ *n* آلة ,(عُدَد) عُدّة

Gaelic /ˈgeɪlɪk, ˈgalɪk/ *n* (اللُغة) الغيلِيّة

gaffe /gaf/ *n* هَفْوة ,زَلّة (هَفَوات)

gag /gag/ **A** *n* **1** (on the mouth) كِمامة (كِمامات ,كَمائِمُ)
2 (infml) (joke) نُكْتة (نُكَت)
B (-gg-) *vt* **1** «burglars, kidnappers» كَمَّمَ ,كَعَمَ (a; كَعْم) ‹a victim, prisoner› **2** أَبْكَمَ ,أَخْرَسَ ‹the press, media›
C *vi* (to choke) اخْتَنَقَ; (to retch) كادَ يَتَقَيَّأُ

gage (AmE) *n, vt* ▸ **gauge**

gaggle /ˈgag(ə)l/ *n* **1** (of geese) سِرْب (أَسْراب) **2** (infml) (disorderly group) جَماعة (فَوْضَوِيّة)

gain /geɪn/ **A** *vt* **1** (to acquire) كَسَبَ (i; كَسْب), اكْتَسَبَ ‹experience, an advantage›; حَصَلَ (u; حُصول) (على) ‹support›; **to ~ popularity** اكْتَسَبَ شَعْبِيّةً; **we have nothing to ~ from this** لَيْسَ هُناكَ ما نَكْسِبُهُ من هذا; **to ~ control of sth** سَيْطَرَ على شَيْءٍ; **to ~ ground on sb** لَحِقَ بِشَخْصٍ **2** (to increase) اكْتَسَبَ ‹momentum›; ازْدادَ ‹height›; **to ~ speed** ازْدادَتْ سُرْعَتُهُ; **to ~ weight** زادَ وَزْنُهُ; **to ~ 4 kilos** زادَ وَزْنُهُ 4 كيلوغراماتٍ; **to ~ 3 minutes** تَقَدَّمَ بِفارِق 3 دَقائِقَ **3** (to win) كَسَبَ (i; كَسْب) ‹a place, state›; حَقَّقَ ‹victory›; **to ~ points** كَسَبَ نِقاطاً; **they ~ed four states from the Democrats** كَسَبوا أَرْبَعَ وِلاياتٍ من الديموقراطِيّينَ; **to ~ the upper hand** أَصْبَحَتْ لَهُ اليَدُ العُلْيا
B *vi* **1** (to increase in) **to ~ in prestige/popularity** «concerts, institutions, performers» زادَتْ مَكانَتُهُ \ شَعْبِيَّتُهُ; **to ~ in confidence** زادَتْ ثِقَتُهُ **2** (to profit) **she hasn't ~ed by it** لَمْ تَسْتَفِدْ مِنْهُ
C *n* **1** (increase) زِيادة; **a ~ in weight/value** زِيادة في وَزْنٍ \ قيمةٍ **2** (in money terms) رِبْح ,كَسْب ,زِيادة (أَرْباح); **financial ~** مَكْسَب \ كَسْب ماليّ; **to do sth for material ~** فعَلَ شَيْئاً من أَجْلِ الكَسْبِ المادِّيّ; **shares made ~s today** ازْدادَتْ قيمةُ الأَسْهُمِ اليَوْمَ **3** (advantage) مَكْسَب (مَكاسِبُ); **the Progressives have made ~s** حَقَّقَ التَقَدُّمِيّونَ بَعْضَ المَكاسِبِ
Phrasal verb **gain on**: **~ on [sb/sth]** لَحِقَ ب [شَيْءٍ \ شَخْصٍ] ‹a rival, vehicle›; **the opposition are ~ing on the government** المُعارَضةُ في طَريقِها إلى اللَحاقِ بالحُكومةِ; **Aziz is ~ing on Smith all the time** يُواصِلُ عَزيز اللَحاقَ بِسْميث طوال الوَقْتِ

gainful /ˈgeɪnfʊl/ *adj* ‹occupation, enterprise› مُكْسِب ,مُرْبِح

gait /geɪt/ *n* (of a person) مِشْية; (of an animal) [طَريقة العَدْو]

gal. *abbr* = **gallon(s)** غالون (مِقْياس للسَوائِل)

gala /ˈgɑːlə/ *n* **1** احْتِفال (احْتِفالات), مَهْرَجان (مَهْرَجانات) **2** جَمْع حَفْل (جُموع)

gala performance *n* حَفْل فَنِّيّ

galaxy /ˈgaləksi/ *n* (*pl* **galaxies**) مَجَرّة

gale /geɪl/ *n* عاصِفة (عَواصِفُ), رِياح قَوِيّة; **~-force winds** رِياح عاصِفة; **a force 9 ~** عاصِفة بِقوّة 9

Galilee /ˈɡalɪliː/ *pr n* الجَليل

Galilee, Sea of *n* بَحْر الجَليلِ ,بُحَيْرة طَبَرِيّا

gall /ɡɔːl/ *n* (*pl* **gall** or **galls**) جَسارة ,وَقاحة; **to have the ~ to do sth** جَرُؤَ على القِيامِ بِشَيْءٍ

gallant /ˈɡalənt/ *adj* 1 (liter) (courageous) ‹*soldier, effort*› شُجاع (شُجْعان ,شَجَعة) ,باسِل (بُسَلاءُ ,بَواسِلُ) 2 (old use) (courteous) ‹*man, manners*› شَهْم (شِهام) ,نَبيل (نُبَلاءُ)

gall bladder *n* مَرارة

galleon /ˈɡalɪən/ *n* غَلْيون (سَفينة إِسْبانيّة شِراعيّة ضخمة)

gallery /ˈɡaləri/ *n* (*pl* **galleries**) 1 (also **art gallery**) (for display) قاعة عَرْض; (for sale) [مَتْجَر لِبَيْعِ الأَعْمالِ الفَنّيّة] 2 (balcony) شُرْفة (شُرُفات ,شُرَف); (for the press, public) مُدَرَّج; **the ~** (in a theatre) [الشُرْفة العُلْيا في مَسْرَحٍ]

galley /ˈɡali/ *n* 1 (kitchen) مَطْبَخ سَفينةٍ \ طائرةٍ 2 (ship) [سَفينة كَبيرة ذات مَجاذيفَ]

Gallic /ˈɡalɪk/ *adj* ‹*shrug, wit*› فَرَنْسيّ (خاصّ بِبِلادِ الغالِ)

galling /ˈɡɔːlɪŋ/ *adj* ‹*defeat, reminder*› مُغيظ ,مُزْعِج

gallon /ˈɡalən/ *n* غالون (مِقْياس لِلسَوائِلِ)

gallop /ˈɡaləp/ A *n* عَدْو \ رَكْض الحِصانِ

B *vi* «rider, horse» عَدا (u; عَدْو)

gallows /ˈɡaləʊz/ *n* (*pl* **gallows**) مِشْنَقة (مَشانِقُ)

gallstone /ˈɡɔːlstəʊn/ *n* حَصْوة مَرارةٍ

galore /ɡəˈlɔː/ *adv* (infml) ‹*bargains, drinks*› بِغَزارةٍ ,بِوَفْرةٍ

galvanize, -ise (BrE) /ˈɡalvənʌɪz/ *vt* 1 (to rouse) أَثارَ ,دَفَعَ ,حَثَّ (a; دَفْع) ‹*a community, an audience*›; **to ~ sb into action** دَفَعَ شَخْصاً على القِيامِ بِعَمَلٍ 2 (**galvanized** *past participle*) ‹*iron, steel*› مَطْليّ بالزِنْك

Gambia /ˈɡambɪə/ *pr n* (or **the Gambia**) غامْبيا

gambit /ˈɡambɪt/ *n* 1 (stratagem) مُناوَرة 2 (in chess) حَرَكة [افْتِتاحيّة في الشِطْرَنْجِ]

gamble /ˈɡamb(ə)l/ A *vt* 1 (to bet) راهَنَ (ب) ‹*money*› 2 (to risk) غامَرَ (ب) ‹*one's future, reputation*›

B *vi* 1 (to bet) قامَرَ ,راهَنَ 2 (to take a risk) جازَفَ; **to ~ on sth** جازَفَ في شَيْءٍ

C *n* 1 (bet) رِهان 2 (risk) مُغامَرة; **to take a ~** خاضَ مُغامَرةً

gambler /ˈɡamblə/ *n* مُقامِر

gambling /ˈɡamblɪŋ/ *n* لُعْب قِمارٍ ,مُقامَرة

gambol /ˈɡamb(ə)l/ *vi* (**-ll-** BrE, **-l-** AmE) «children, lambs» قَفَزَ (مَرِحاً)

game /ɡeɪm/ A *n* 1 (activity) لُعْبة (لُعَب) 2 (session of chess, darts, etc.) دَوْر (أَدْوار); (of football, hockey, etc.) مُباراة (مُبارَيات); **let's have a ~ of cards/chess** هَيّا نَلْعَبُ دَوْراً من الوَرَقِ \ الشِطْرَنْجِ 3 (in tennis) شَوْط (أَشْواط) 4 (infml) (trick, scheme) خُدْعة (خُدَع ,خُدْعات) ,حيلة (حِيَل); **so that's his ~?** إذاً تِلْكَ هي لُعْبَتُهُ الدَنيئةُ؟ 5 (infml) (business, activity) عَمَل (أَعْمال) ,نَشاط (أَنْشِطة) ,مَجال (مَجالات); **how long have you been in the insurance ~?** منذ مَتى وَأَنْتَ في مَجالِ التَأْمينِ؟ 6 [u] (Culin) طَريدة (طَرائِدُ) ,فَريسة (فَرائِسُ)

B (**games**) *n pl* 1 (event) أَلْعاب 2 (Educ) (in UK) رِياضة

C *adj* 1 (infml) (willing to try) مُسْتَعِدّ ,جاهِز; **he's ~ for anything** هو مُسْتَعِدٌّ لِكُلِّ شَيْءٍ; **OK, I'm ~** حَسَناً، أنا جاهِزٌ 2 (brave) ‹*attempt, competitor*› شُجاع (شُجْعان) ,جَسور (جُسُر)

Idioms **to beat sb at his/their own game** [تَفَوَّقَ على شَخْصٍ في مَجالِهِ]; **to be fair game for sb** كانَ هَدَفاً مَشْروعاً لِشَخْصٍ; **to give the game away** أَفْشى السِرَّ; **to play games with sb** مارَسَ الأَلاعيبَ على شَخْصٍ; **to play the game** انْخَرَطَ في اللُعْبةِ

game bird *n* طَريدة (طائِر بَرّيّ يُصادُ لِلَحْمِهِ أو لِلرِياضةِ)

gamekeeper /ˈɡeɪmkiːpə/ *n* حارِس طَرائِدَ

game paté *n* [باتي لَحْمِ الطَرائِدِ]

game plan *n* خُطّة لُعْبةٍ

gamer /ˈɡeɪmə/ *n* [مُشارِك في أَلْعابِ الحاسوبِ \ تَمْثيلِ الأَدْوارِ]

game reserve *n* 1 (for protecting animals) مَحْميّة الحَيَواناتِ البَرّيّةِ 2 (for hunting animals) مَحْميّة لِلصَيْدِ

games console *n* نِظام لُعْبةِ فيديو ,مَنَصّة أَلْعابٍ

game show *n* بَرْنامَج مُسابَقاتٍ

games room *n* صالة أَلْعابٍ

games software *n* بَرامِج أَلْعابٍ

games teacher *n* مُدَرِّس رِياضةٍ

gaming /ˈɡeɪmɪŋ/ *n* لُعْب أَلْعابِ الحاسوبِ

gamma /ˈgamə/ *n* [غاما [الحَرْف الثالث في الأَبْجَديّةِ الإغْريقيّة

gamma globulin *n* غْلوبيولين غاما

gamma rays, **gamma radiation** *n* أَشِعّة غاما

gammon /ˈgamən/ *n* [لَحْم خَنْزيرٍ مُدَخَّن]

gamut /ˈgamət/ *n* سِلْسِلة كامِلة; **to run the (whole) ~ of sth** [مَرَّ على كافّةِ أَشْكالِ شَيْءٍ]

gander /ˈgandə/ *n* ذَكَر إِوَزٍّ

gang /gaŋ/ *n* ① (of criminals, youths) عِصابة (عِصابات), ② (infml) (of friends) زُمْرة (زُمَر), شِلّة (شِلَل) ③ (of workmen, etc) جَماعة (عَصائِبُ)

(Phrasal verb) **gang up**: **to ~ up on sb** تَحَزَّبَ ضدّ شَخْصٍ

gangland /ˈgaŋland/ *n* عالَم الجَريمةِ

gangmaster /ˈgaŋmɑːstə/ *n* (BrE) رَئيس عُمّالٍ

gangplank /ˈgaŋplaŋk/ *n* مَعْبَر (لَوْح خَشَبيّ يُسْتَخْدَمُ للعُبورِ إلى السَفينةِ)

gang rape *n* اغْتِصاب جَماعيّ

gangrene /ˈgaŋgriːn/ *n* غَرْغَرينا

gangster /ˈgaŋstə/ *n* مُجْرِم, قاطِع طَريقٍ, عُضْو في عِصابةٍ

gangway /ˈgaŋweɪ/ *n* ① (to a ship) [سُلَّم السَفينةِ المُتَحَرِّك] ② (BrE) (between seats) [مَمَرّ بين صُفوفِ المَقاعِدِ]

gaol *n*, *vt* (BrE) ▸**jail**

gap /gap/ *n* ① (space) فَجْوة (فَجَوات), فَراغ (فَراغات); **she filled in the ~s in the story** مَلأَت الفَراغاتِ المَوْجودةَ في القِصّةِ ② (in continuity) فَجْوة (فَجَوات), انْقِطاع \ فَتْرة تَوَقُّفٍ; **after a ~ of six years** بعد تَوَقُّفٍ دامَ سِتَّ سَنواتٍ ③ (in age, status) فارِق (فَوارِقُ), فَجْوة (فَجَوات); (between opinions) تَبايُن (تَبايُنات); **a 15-year age ~** فارِق في العُمْرِ 15 سَنةً; **to close the ~ between rich and poor** ضَيَّقَ الفَجْوةَ بينَ الأَغْنِياءِ والفُقَراءِ ④ (lack of sth) فَجْوة (فَجَوات, فِجاء); **the technology ~** الفَجْوة في التِكْنولوجِيا; **there's a ~ in my memory** هُناكَ فَجْوةٌ في ذاكِرَتي; **the trade ~** الفَجْوة التِجاريّة ⑤ (opportunity) فَجْوة (فَجَوات, فِجاء), فَراغ (فَراغات); **to fill a ~ in the market** سَدَّ فَراغاً في السوقِ

gape /geɪp/ *vi* ① (to stare) نَظَرَ \ حَدَّقَ فاغِرَ فاهُ; **to ~ at sth/sb** حَدَّقَ في شَيْءٍ \ شَخْصٍ مُنْدَهِشاً ② (to be open) ‹mouth, garment› انْفَتَحَ

gaping /ˈgeɪpɪŋ/ *adj* ‹hole› واسِع; ‹wound› مَفْتوح; ‹mouth› فاغِر

gap year *n* [سَنة انْقِطاعٍ عن الدِراسةِ]

garage /ˈgarɑːdʒ/ *n* ① (building) جَراج (كَراجات), كَراج ② (for fuel) مَحَطّة بَنْزين (جَراجات); (for repairs) وَرْشة سَيّاراتٍ, مَرْأَب (مَرائِبُ), كَراج (كَراجات)

garage mechanic *n* ميكانيكيّ سَيّاراتٍ

garb /gɑːb/ *n* (infml liter) لِباس (مَلابِسُ), مَلْبَس, رِداء (أَرْدِية), (أَلْبِسة)

garbage /ˈgɑːbɪdʒ/ *n* ① (AmE) (refuse) نُفاية, زُبالة, قُمامة ② (nonsense) كَلام تافِه, تَفاهة; **she was talking absolute ~** كانَتْ تَتَكَلَّمُ كَلاماً تافِهاً تَماماً

garbage bag *n* (AmE) كيس زُبالةٍ \ قُمامةٍ

garbage can *n* (AmE) بِرْميل \ صُنْدوق زُبالةٍ \ قُمامةٍ

garbage dump *n* (AmE) مَقْلَب قُمامةٍ

garbageman /ˈgɑːbɪdʒman/ *n* (*pl* **-men**) (AmE) زَبّال

garbage truck *n* (AmE) شاحِنة نُفاياتٍ

garbled /ˈgɑːb(ə)ld/ *adj* ‹message, account› مُشَوَّش

garden /ˈgɑːd(ə)n/ **A** *n* ① (with flowers) حَديقة (حَدائِقُ); (for vegetables) بُسْتان (بَساتينُ); **the back/front ~** (BrE) الحَديقة الخَلْفيّة \ الأَماميّة ② (**gardens** *n pl*) مُنْتَزَه (مُنْتَزَهات), حَديقة عامّة

B *vi* نَسَّقَ \ رَعى حَديقةً, عَمِلَ في حَديقةٍ

garden centre (BrE), **garden center** (AmE) *n* [مَتْجَر لِبَيْعِ مُسْتَلْزَماتِ الحَدائِقِ]

gardener /ˈgɑːdnə/ *n* بُسْتانيّ

gardening /ˈgɑːd(ə)nɪŋ/ *n* رِعاية حَديقةٍ, زِراعة نَباتاتٍ, بَسْتَنة; **who does the ~?** مَن الّذي يَقومُ بِرِعايةِ الحَديقةِ؟

gardening leave *n* [فَتْرة إِشْعارٍ يُدْفَعُ خِلالَها راتِبٌ للمُوَظَّفِ دون أنْ يَذْهَبَ للعَمَلِ]

garden-variety /ˈgɑːd(ə)nvərˌʌɪəti/ *adj* (AmE infml) ‹writer, film› مُعْتاد, عاديّ

gargle /ˈgɑːg(ə)l/ *vi* غَرْغَرَ (i; غَرْغَرة)

gargoyle /ˈgɑːgɔɪl/ *n* غَرْغول, كَرْغَل (ميزاب مَنْحوت من جانِبِ السَطْحِ على شَكْلِ إنْسانٍ أو حَيَوانٍ بَشِعِ الوَجْهِ)

garish /ˈgɛːrɪʃ/ *adj* ‹colour, makeup› صارِخ; ‹shirt› مُبَهْرَج

garland /ˈgɑːlənd/ *n* إكْليل \ طَوْق من الزُهورِ

garlic /ˈgɑːlɪk/ *n* ثوم

garment /ˈɡɑːmənt/ *n* ثَوْب (أَثْواب ثِياب), كِساء (أَكْسِية), لِباس (أَلْبِسة)

garner /ˈɡɑːnə/ *vt* (fml) جَمَّعَ, اسْتَجْمَعَ ‹*information*›; تَوَصَّلَ (إلى) ‹*a fact*›

garnet /ˈɡɑːnɪt/ *n* جارْنيت, عَقيق أَحْمَر

garnish /ˈɡɑːnɪʃ/ **A** *vt* زَيَّنَ, زَوَّقَ ‹*a dish, salad*› **B** *n* [شَيْء يُسْتَخْدَمُ لِتَزْيينِ الطَعامِ]

garret /ˈɡarət/ *n* عِلِّيّة (غُرْفة في أَعْلى البَيْتِ)

garrison /ˈɡarɪs(ə)n/ **A** *n* **1** (soldiers) حامِية **2** (place) ثُكْنة (مُعَسْكَرات) مُعَسْكَر, عَسْكَرِيّة **B** *vt* **1** (to station troops in) أَقامَ ثُكْنةً عَسْكَرِيّةً \ حامِيةً في ‹*a town*› **2** (to house) مَرْكَزَ ‹*troops*›

garrulous /ˈɡarjʊləs/ *adj* ‹*taxi driver, salesman*› مِهْذار, ثَرْثار (مَهاذيرُ)

garter /ˈɡɑːtə/ *n* **1** (for stockings) رَبْطة ساقٍ; (for socks) رِباط جَوْرَبٍ **2** (AmE) (suspender) حَمّالة جَوارِبَ

gas /ɡas/ **A** *n* (*pl* **gases** or **gasses**) **1** (Chem) غاز (غازات); **methane/natural ~** غاز المِيثان \ طَبيعِيّ; **~ central heating** [تَدْفِئة مَرْكَزِيّة تَعْمَلُ بالغازِ] **2** (AmE) (for cars) بَنْزين; **we stopped for ~** تَوَقَّفْنا للتَزَوُّدِ بالبَنْزين **3** (anaesthetic) غاز مُخَدِّر **B** *vt* (-ss-) (to kill) أَطْلَقَ غازاً سامًّا على ‹*the enemy, civilians*›

gas chamber *n* غُرْفة إعْدامٍ بالغازِ

gas cooker *n* مَوْقِد غازٍ

gaseous /ˈɡasɪəs, ˈɡeɪsɪəs/ *adj* ‹*substance, mixture*› غازِيّ

gas fire *n* مَوْقِد غازٍ

gas guzzler *n* (infml) [سَيّارة كَبيرة مُسْتَهْلِكة للوَقودِ]

gash /ɡaʃ/ **A** *n* جُرْح غائِر \ بَليغ **B** *vt* جَرَحَ جُرْحاً غائِراً ‹*one's leg, forehead*›

gasket /ˈɡaskɪt/ *n* حَشِيّة (حَشايا, حَشِيّات)

gaslight /ˈɡaslʌɪt/ *n* (lamp) مِصْباح غازٍ; [u] (illumination) ضَوْء مِصْباحِ غازٍ

gasman /ˈɡasman/ *n* (*pl* **-men**) عامِل في شَرِكةِ غازٍ

gas mask *n* قِناع غازٍ

gasoline /ˈɡasəliːn/ *n* (AmE) بَنْزين

gas oven *n* فُرْن غازٍ

gasp /ɡɑːsp/ **A** *vt* قالَ لاهِثاً **B** *vi* **1** (to inhale sharply) شَهِقَ (a; شَهيق) **2** (to pant) لَهَثَ (a; لُهاثة, لَهْث); **to ~ for breath/air** تَعَذَّرَ عَلَيْهِ التَنَفُّسُ **C** *n* نَهَج, لُهاث

gas pedal *n* (AmE) دَوّاسة وَقودٍ \ بَنْزين

gas pump *n* (AmE) مِضَخّة وَقودٍ \ بَنْزين

gas station *n* (AmE) مَحَطّة وَقودٍ \ بَنْزين

gas tank *n* (AmE) خَزّان وَقودٍ \ بَنْزين

gastric /ˈɡastrɪk/ *adj* ‹*juices, ulcer*› مَعِدِيّ

gastric flu *n* إِنْفِلْوَنْزا المَعِدةِ

gastritis /ɡaˈstrʌɪtɪs/ *n* اِلْتِهاب المَعِدةِ

gastroenteritis /ˌɡastrəʊɛntəˈrʌɪtɪs/ *n* اِلْتِهاب المَعِدةِ والأَمْعاءِ

gastrointestinal /ˌɡastrəʊɪnˈtɛstɪn(ə)l, ˌɡastrəʊɪntɛsˈtʌɪn(ə)l/ *adj* ‹*surgery, disease*› المَعِدةِ والأَمْعاءِ

gasworks /ˈɡaswəːks/ *n* (*pl* **gasworks**) مَصْنَع غازٍ

gate /ɡeɪt/ *n* **1** (entrance) بَوّابة **2** (in an airport) بَوّابة مُغادَرةٍ **3** (attendees) [عَدَد مُشاهِدي مُباراةٍ]

gatecrash /ˈɡeɪtkraʃ/ *vt* (infml) تَطَفَّلَ (على) ‹*a party, wedding*›

gatecrasher /ˈɡeɪtkraʃə/ *n* (infml) مُتَطَفِّل, طُفَيْلِيّ

gateway /ˈɡeɪtweɪ/ *n* (entrance) مَدْخَل (مَداخِلُ), مَنْفَذ (مَنافِذُ); (arch) قَوْس بَوّابةٍ, قَنْطَرة (قَناطِرُ)

gather /ˈɡaðə/ **A** *vt* **1** (to collect) جَمَعَ (a; جَمْع) ‹*the fruit, wood, evidence*›; **to ~ speed** ازْدادَتْ سُرْعَتُهُ, ازْدادَ سُرْعةً; **the movement is ~ing strength** تَزْدادُ الحَرَكةُ قُوّةً; **to ~ dust** تَراكَمَ الغُبارُ عَلَيْهِ **2** (to deduce) اِسْتَنْتَجَ; **I ~ he was here earlier** أَظُنُّ أَنَّهُ كانَ هُنا في وَقْتٍ سابِقٍ; **as you will have ~ed** كَما تُدْرِكُ الآنَ **3** (in sewing) زَمَّ (u; زَمّ) ‹*the fabric, skirt*›; **~ed at the waist** مَزْموم عند الخَصْرِ **B** *vi* **1** «people, the family» تَجَمَّعَ; **a crowd soon ~ed** سُرْعانَ ما تَجَمَّعَ حَشْدٌ **2** «clouds» تَجَمَّعَ

(Phrasal verbs) **gather around** ▸ **gather round**

• **gather in**: **~ [sth] in, ~ in [sth]** **1** جَمَعَ [شَيْئاً] ‹*the harvest*›; حَصَدَ [شَيْئاً] ‹*crops*› **2** جَمَعَ [شَيْئاً] ‹*the contributions, essays*›

• **gather round** **1** (to come together) تَجَمَّعَ; **~ round!** تَجَمَّعوا! **2** **~ round [sth]** (to meet around) تَجَمَّعَ حول

[شَيْءٍ] ‹*the table, campfire*› 3 ~ [sb] **round** (to bring together) [أَشْخاصاً] جَمَعَ ‹*children, students*›

• **gather together**: 1 ~ **[sth/sb] together**, ~ **together [sth/ sb]** (to bring together) [شَيْئاً \ أَشْخاصاً] جَمَعَ ‹*one's notes, belongings, the team*› 2 (to come together) «troops, protesters» تَجَمَّعَ

• **gather up**: ~ **[sth] up**, ~ **up [sth]** [شَيْئاً] جَمَعَ ‹*the toys, papers*›; **to ~ one's hair up in a bun** لَفَّتْ شَعْرَها على شَكْلِ كَعْكَةٍ

gathering /ˈgaðərɪŋ/ **A** *n* (meeting) (اجْتِماعات) اجْتِماع, (group of people) جَماعة; تَجَمُّع **B** *adj* ‹*storm*› يَسْتَجْمِعُ قُواهُ; ‹*darkness*› مُتَزايِد

gaudy /ˈgɔːdi/ *adj* (**gaudier, gaudiest**) ‹*colours, costumes*› مُبَهْرَج

gauge, gage (AmE) /geɪdʒ/ **A** *n* 1 (instrument) مِقْياس (مَقاييسُ) 2 (of metal, wire, a gun) (عِيارات) عِيار 3 (of railway tracks) [مَسافة بين قَضيبَيِ السِكَّةِ الحَديدِيّة] 4 (indicator) (مُؤَشِّرات) مُؤَشِّر **B** *vt* 1 (to estimate) قَدَّرَ ‹*a distance, size*› 2 (to judge) قَدَّرَ, قَيَّمَ ‹*sb's mood, public opinion*› 3 (to measure) قاسَ (i; قَيْس, قِياس) ‹*the temperature, depth*›

gaunt /gɔːnt/ *adj* ‹*face, figure*› هَزيل (هَزْلى), نَحيل (نَحْلى, نُحَّل)

gauntlet /ˈgɔːntlɪt/ *n* قُفّاز (قُفّازات, قَفافيزُ)

gauze /gɔːz/ *n* (fabric) شاش; (wire) شَبَكة مَعْدِنيّة; **a ~ dressing** ضِمادة من شاشٍ

gave /geɪv/ *past tense* ▸ **give**

gavel /ˈgav(ə)l/ *n* مِطْرَقة يَسْتَخْدِمُها قاضٍ أو رَئيسُ مَزادٍ

gay /geɪ/ **A** *adj* (**gayer, gayest**) 1 (homosexual) ‹*man, couple*› مِثْليّ; ‹*marriage, club*› المِثْلِيِّينَ 2 (happy) مَرِح (مَرْحى, مَراحى), مُبْتَهِج, سَعيد (سُعَداءُ) **B** *n* مِثْليّ, لوطيّ

Gaza /ˈgɑːzə/ *pr n* غَزّة (dipt)

Gaza Strip *pr n* (**the Gaza Strip**) قِطاع غَزّةَ

gaze /geɪz/ **A** *vi* حَدَّقَ, أَمْعَنَ النَظَرَ; **to ~ at sth/sb** حَدَّقَ في شَيْءٍ \ شَخْصٍ **B** *n* نَظْرة مُحَدِّقة

gazelle /gəˈzɛl/ *n* (*pl* **gazelles** or **gazelle**) غَزال (غِزْلان, غِزْلة), ظَبْي (ظِباء)

gazette /gəˈzɛt/ *n* 1 (newspaper title) جَريدة (جَرائِدُ), صَحيفة (صَحائِفُ, صُحُف) 2 (BrE) (official journal) جَريدة (جَرائِدُ)

gazetteer /ˌgazəˈtɪə/ *n* فِهْرِس \ مُعْجَم جُغْرافيّ

GB *abbr* ▸ **Great Britain**

GCSE /dʒiːsiːɛsˈiː/ *n* (in UK) = **General Certificate of Secondary Education** [امْتِحان التَعْليم الثانَويّ في بَريطانيا]

GDP /dʒiːdiːˈpiː/ *n* = **Gross Domestic Product** ناتِج مَحَلّيّ إجْماليّ

gear /gɪə/ **A** *n* 1 (equipment) عُدّة (عُدَد), مُعَدّات; **climbing/ camping ~** عُدّة التَسَلُّقِ \ التَخْييم 2 (infml) (possessions) أَمْتِعة 3 (infml) (clothes) مَلْبَس (مَلابِسُ); **football ~** مَلابِس كُرة القَدَمِ 4 (of engines) غِيار, تُرْس (أَتْراس, تُروس); **bottom** *or* **first ~** الغِيار \ التُرْس الأَوَّل; **to be in third ~** كانَ في الغِيارِ \ التُرْسِ الثالِثِ; **to change ~** نَقَلَ الغِيارَ; **to put a car in ~** عَشَّقَ سَيّارةً; **you're in the wrong ~** ناقِلُ السُرْعةِ لَدَيْكَ على التُرْس الخاطِئِ] 5 (wheel) تُرْس (أَتْراس, تُروس) **B** (**gears**) *n pl* تُروس **C** *vt* (to be tailored to) **to be ~ed to** *or* **towards sb/sth** كانَ مُصَمَّماً لِشَخْصٍ \ لِشَيْءٍ

Phrasal verb **gear up** 1 «climbers, athletes» تَحَضَّرَ, تَجَهَّزَ 2 ~ **[sb] up** أَعَدَّ [شَخْصاً]; **to be ~ed up for sth/to do sth** كانَ مُسْتَعِدّاً لِشَيْءٍ \ لِفِعْلِ شَيْءٍ

gearbox /ˈgɪəbɒks/ *n* صُنْدوق تُروسٍ

gear lever (BrE), **gear shift** (AmE) *n* ناقِل سُرْعةٍ

gearwheel /ˈgɪəwiːl/ *n* دولاب مُسَنَّن, عَجَلة مُسَنَّنة

gecko /ˈgɛkəʊ/ *n* (*pl* **geckos** or **geckoes**) أَبو بُرَيْصٍ, سامّ بُرْص, أَبْرَص, وَزَغ (n coll; أَوْزاغ)

gee /dʒiː/ *excl* (AmE infml) ياه (تَعْبير عن الدَهْشةِ أو الحَماسِ); ~, **it's nice to see you** ياه، أنا سَعيدٌ بِرُؤْيَتِكَ; ~, **thanks!** ياه، شُكْراً لَكَ!

geek /giːk/ *n* (infml) 1 (misfit) شَخْص غَريب الأَطْوارِ 2 (enthusiast) هاوٍ (هُواة)

geese /giːs/ *n pl* ▸ **goose**

gel /dʒɛl/ **A** *n* هُلام, جِلّ **B** *vi* (**-ll-**) 1 «liquids, substances» تَجَمَّدَ, تَصَلَّبَ 2 «plans, ideas» تَبَلْوَرَ

gelatin /ˈdʒɛlətɪn/, **gelatine** /ˈdʒɛlətiːn/ *n* جيلاتين, هُلام

gem /dʒɛm/ *n* **1** (precious stone) حَجَر كَريم, جَوْهَرة **2** (outstanding person or thing) جَوْهَرة

Gemini /ˈdʒɛmɪnʌɪ, ˈdʒɛmɪni/ *n* **1** (sign) بُرْج الجَوْزاءِ **2** (person) [مِن مَواليدِ بُرْجِ الجَوْزاءِ]

gender /ˈdʒɛndə/ *n* **1** (of a person, an animal) جِنْس (أَجْناس), **2** (of a word) جِنْس (أَجْناس) نَوْع (أَنْواع)

gene /dʒiːn/ *n* جين (n coll; جينات), مُوَرِّثة, وَحْدة وِراثيّة

genealogy /dʒiːnɪˈalədʒi/ *n* (line of descent) سِلْسِلة, سُلالة; (study) عِلْم الأَنْسابِ, النَسَبِ

general /ˈdʒɛn(ə)rəl/ **A** *adj* **1** (widespread) ‹*interest, reaction, opinion*› عامّ; **to be a ~ favourite** كانَ المُفَضَّلَ لدى الجُمْهورِ; **it's in ~ use** هو شائِعُ الاسْتِخْدامِ; **a ~ ban is in place** تَمّ فَرْضُ حَظْرٍ شامِلٍ **2** (overall) ‹*condition, impression, appearance*› عامّ; **do you get the ~ idea?** هل تَفْهَمُ الفِكْرةَ العامّةَ؟ **3** (usual) ‹*rule, principle, conclusion*› عامّ; **as a ~ rule** كَقاعِدةٍ عامّةٍ **4** (unspecific) ‹*description, assurance, information*› عامّ; **to talk in ~ terms** تَكَلَّمَ بِصِفةٍ عامّةٍ; **to give sb a ~ description of sth** أَعْطى شَخْصاً وَصْفاً عامًّا لِشَيْءٍ; **in that ~ direction** في ذلك الاتِّجاهِ العامِّ **5** (unspecialized) ‹*medicine*› عامّ; ‹*user, reader*› عادي; **~ office duties** الواجِبات المَكْتَبِيّة العامّة; **a manual for the ~ user** دَليل اسْتِعْمالٍ لِلقارِئِ العاديِّ; **~ assistant** مُساعِد عامّ **6** (standard) ‹*practice, method*› مُعْتاد; **the ~ method is to … .** الطَرِيقةُ المُعْتادةُ هي …

B (**in general**) *adv phr* **1** (non-specifically) بِشَكْلٍ عامٍّ **2** (overall) بِشَكْلٍ عامٍّ; **he is fed up with life in ~** تَعِبَ مِن الحَياةِ بِشَكْلٍ عامٍّ

C *n* (Mil) جِنِرال (جِنِرالات) (Levant), عَمَد (عَمَد) عِماد, فَرِيق أَوَّل

general delivery *n* (AmE) [بَرِيد مَحْفوظ لِحِينِ الطَلَبِ]

general election *n* انْتِخابات عامّة

generalization, **-isation** (BrE) /dʒɛn(ə)rəlʌɪˈzeɪʃ(ə)n/ *n* تَعْمِيم (تَعْمِيمات)

generalize, **-ise** (BrE) /ˈdʒɛn(ə)rəlʌɪz/ **A** *vt* عَمَّمَ ‹*results, findings*›

B *vi* «writers, speakers» عَمَّمَ

general knowledge *n* مَعْلومات عامّة

generally /ˈdʒɛn(ə)rəli/ *adv* **1** (widely) ‹*accepted, agreed*› بِشَكْلٍ عامٍّ, عُموماً; **it is ~ considered to be a fair settlement** يُعْتَبَرُ حَلاًّ عادِلاً بِشَكْلٍ عامٍّ **2** (usually) عادةً, في العُمومِ; **it's ~ best not to wait** مِن الأَفْضَلِ عَدَمُ الانْتِظارِ في العُمومِ; **I ~ go to the market on Tuesdays** عادةً أَذْهَبُ إلى السوقِ في أَيّامِ الثُلاثاءِ **3** (overall) بِشَكْلٍ عامٍّ; **to be ~ unwell** لم يَكُنْ على ما يُرامُ بِشَكْلٍ عامٍّ **4** (not in detail) ‹*to discuss, refer to*› بِشَكْلٍ عامٍّ; **to talk ~ about sth** تَحَدَّثَ عن شَيْءٍ بِشَكْلٍ عامٍّ

general manager *n* مُدير عامّ

general practitioner *n* طَبِيب \ مُمارِس عامّ

general public *n* (**the general public**) الجُمْهور العامّ, عامّة النّاسِ

general-purpose /dʒɛn(ə)r(ə)lˈpəːpəs/ *adj* ‹*tool, cleaning agent*› لِلأَغْراضِ العامّةِ

general store *n* مَتْجَر عامّ

general strike *n* إِضْراب عامّ \ شامِل

generate /ˈdʒɛnəreɪt/ *vt* **1** وَلَّدَ ‹*electricity, power*› **2** أَثارَ ‹*interest*›; حَقَّقَ, أَدَرَّ ‹*profits*›

generation /dʒɛnəˈreɪʃ(ə)n/ *n* **1** جيل (أَجْيال); **the younger/older ~** الجيل الجَدِيد \ القَدِيم **2** [u] (of electricity) تَوْلِيد, إِنْتاج; (of income) تَحْقِيق, إِدْرار

generation gap *n* فَجْوة بين الأَجْيالِ

generator /ˈdʒɛnəreɪtə/ *n* مُوَلِّد كَهْرَبائيّ

generic /dʒɪˈnɛrɪk/ *adj* **1** (general) ‹*name, fault*› عامّ **2** (not branded) ‹*drug, brand*› غَيْر مُسَجَّلٍ

generosity /dʒɛnəˈrɒsəti/ *n* كَرَم, سَخاء

generous /ˈdʒɛn(ə)rəs/ *adj* **1** (beneficent) ‹*person, gift*› كَرِيم (كِرام, كُرَماءُ), سَخيّ (أَسْخِياءُ) **2** (large) ‹*portion, amount*› كَبِير, وَفِير

generously /ˈdʒɛn(ə)rəsli/ *adv* **1** ‹*to sprinkle, grease*› بِوَفْرةٍ **2** ‹*to give, fund*› بِكَرَم, بِسَخاءٍ

genetic /dʒɪˈnɛtɪk/ *adj* ‹*variation, defect*› جينيّ, وِراثيّ

genetically /dʒɪˈnɛtɪkli/ *adv* ‹*engineered, linked*› وِراثيًّا

genetically modified /dʒəˌnɛtɪkli ˈmɒdɪfʌɪd/ *adj* مُعَدَّل وِراثيًّا

genetic engineering *n* الهَنْدَسة الوِراثيّة

genetics /dʒɪˈnɛtɪks/ *n sing* عِلْم الوِراثةِ \ الجيناتِ

Geneva /dʒɪˈniːvə/ *pr n* جِنيف (f)

Geneva Convention *n* (**the Geneva Convention**) اتِّفاقيّة جِنيف

genial /ˈdʒiːnɪəl/ *adj* ‹*person, manner*› لَطيف (لُطَفاءُ ,لِطاف), وَدود

genie /ˈdʒiːni/ *n* (*pl* **genii** or **genies**) جِنّ (n coll; sing n جِنّيّ), عِفْريت (عَفاريتُ), مارِد (مَرَدة)

genital /ˈdʒɛnɪt(ə)l/ *adj* ‹*organ, infection*› تَناسُليّ

genitalia /ˌdʒɛnɪˈteɪlɪə/ *n pl* أَعْضاء تَناسُليّة

genitals /ˈdʒɛnɪt(ə)lz/ *n pl* أَعْضاء تَناسُليّة

genitive /ˈdʒɛnɪtɪv/ **A** *adj* ‹*case, ending*› الجَرّ; **a ~ construction** إضافة

B *n* جَرّ

genito-urinary /ˌdʒɛnɪtəʊˈjʊərɪn(ə)ri/ *adj* ‹*infection, clinic*› مَسالِك بَوْليّة وتَناسُليّة

genius /ˈdʒiːnɪəs/ *n* **1** (gifted person) عَبْقَريّ (عَبْقَريّونَ ,عَباقِرة), نابغة (نَوابغُ) **2** [u] (brilliance) عَبْقَريّة, نُبوغ

genocide /ˈdʒɛnəsʌɪd/ *n* إبادة جَماعيّة

genome /ˈdʒiːnəʊm/ *n* جينوم, مَجْموعة الجيناتِ

genotype /ˈdʒɛnətʌɪp/ *n* نَمَط جينيّ

genre /ˈʒɒnrə/ *n* نَوْع (أَنْواع)

gent /dʒɛnt/ **A** *n* (BrE infml) (gentleman) سَيِّد (أَسْياد ,سادة), رَجُل (رِجال)

B (**the gents**) *sing* (BrE) (toilets) دَوْرة مِياهٍ للرجالِ; (on a sign) رجال

gentle /ˈdʒɛnt(ə)l/ *adj* **1** (tender, mild) ‹*person, nature*› لَطيف (لُطَفاءُ ,لِطاف), رَقيق (رِقاق ,أَرِقّاءُ); ‹*voice*› ناعِم **2** (not forceful) ‹*breeze, exercise, pressure*› خَفيف; ‹*hint, reminder*› وِدّيّ **3** (gradual) ‹*slope*› خَفيف

gentleman /ˈdʒɛntəlmən/ *n* (*pl* **-men**) **1** (man) سَيِّد (أَسْياد ,سادة), رَجُل (رِجال) **2** (well-bred man) رَجُل نَبيل \ مُهَذَّب

gently /ˈdʒɛntli/ *adv* **1** (without force) ‹*to pull, press*› بِلُطْفٍ, بِرِفْقٍ; ‹*to simmer*› على نارٍ هادِئةٍ ,بِبُطْءٍ **2** (tenderly) ‹*to say*› بِرِفْقٍ, بِلُطْفٍ; ‹*to smile*› بِرِقّةٍ ,بِحَنانٍ **3** (gradually) ‹*sloping*› تَدْريجيًّا ,رُوَيْداً رُوَيْداً

gentry /ˈdʒɛntri/ *n* طَبَقة عُلْيا \ راقية, طَبَقة الأَشْرافِ

genuine /ˈdʒɛnjʊɪn/ *adj* **1** (authentic) ‹*work of art, product*› حَقيقيّ ,أَصْليّ **2** (sincere) ‹*person*› مُخْلِص; ‹*concern, interest*› صادِق; ‹*attempt*› جادّ; ‹*mistake*› حَقيقيّ

genuinely /ˈdʒɛnjʊɪnli/ *adv* **1** (sincerely) ‹*to believe*› بِإخْلاصٍ; ‹*sorry, concerned*› بِصِدْقٍ **2** (truly) ‹*independent, happy*› حَقًّا

genus /ˈdʒiːnəs/ *n* (*pl* **genera**) جِنْس (أَجْناس)

geoengineering /ˌdʒiːəʊɛndʒɪˈnɪərɪŋ/ *n* الهَنْدَسة الجِيولوجيّة, هَنْدَسة الأَرْضِ

geographer /dʒɪˈɒɡrəfə/ *n* جُغْرافيّ, عالِم بالجُغْرافِيا

geographic /dʒɪəˈɡrafɪk/, **geographical** /dʒɪəˈɡrafɪk(ə)l/ *adj* ‹*location, research*› جُغْرافيّ

geographically /dʒɪəˈɡrafɪkli/ *adv* ‹*separated, distinct*› جُغْرافيًّا, من الناحِيةِ الجُغْرافيّةِ

geography /dʒɪˈɒɡrəfi/ *n* **1** (subject of study) جُغْرافِيا, عِلْم الجُغْرافِيا **2** (layout) مَعالِم

geological /dʒiːəˈlɒdʒɪk(ə)l/ *adj* ‹*period, formation*› جِيولوجيّ

geologist /dʒɪˈɒlədʒɪst/ *n* جِيولوجيّ, عالِم جِيولوجِيا

geology /dʒɪˈɒlədʒi/ *n* جِيولوجِيا, عِلْم طَبَقاتِ الأَرْضِ

geometric /ˌdʒɪəˈmɛtrɪk/, **geometrical** /dʒɪəʊˈmɛtrɪk(ə)l/ *adj* ‹*shape, pattern*› هَنْدَسيّ

geometry /dʒɪˈɒmɪtri/ *n* هَنْدَسة, عِلْم الهَنْدَسةِ

Georgia /ˈdʒɔːdʒə/ *pr n* **1** (US state) جورْجِيا **2** (in Caucasus) جورْجِيا

Georgian /ˈdʒɔːdʒ(ə)n/ **A** *n* **1** (citizen of the Republic) جورْجيّ; (of the US state) [شَخْص من ولايةِ جورْجِيا] **2** (language) (اللُغة) الجورْجِيّة

B *adj* **1** (of the Republic) ‹*border, dish*› جورْجيّ; (of the US state) ‹*county*› [من وِلاية جورْجِيا] **2** (in UK) ‹*architecture, period*› جورْجيّ [نِسْبةً إلى عَهْدِ المُلوكِ الأَرْبَعةِ جورْج الأَوَّل حتّى جورْج الرابِع]

gerbil /ˈdʒəːbɪl/ *n* يَرْبوع (يَرابيعُ)

geriatric /ˌdʒɛrɪˈatrɪk/ *adj* ‹*medicine*› شَيْخوخيّ (مُتَعَلِّق بِسِنِّ الشَيْخوخةِ); ‹*patient*› يُعاني من الشَيْخوخة

geriatrician /dʒɛrɪəˈtrɪʃ(ə)n/ *n* أَخِصّائيّ أَمْراضِ الشَيْخوخةِ

geriatrics /dʒerɪ'atrɪks/ *n sing* عِلْم الشَيْخوخةِ

germ /dʒɜːm/ *n* **1** (microorganism) جُرْثوم (جَراثيمُ) **2** (seed) بَذْرة (بَذرات)

German /'dʒɜːmən/ **A** *n* **1** (citizen) أَلْمانيّ (أَلْمان) **2** (the language) الأَلْمانيّة (اللغة); **to speak ~** تَكَلَّمَ الأَلْمانيّةَ **B** *adj* أَلْمانيّ (أَلْمان)

German measles *n* حَصْبة أَلْمانيّة

German shepherd *n* كَلْب الراعي الأَلْمانيِّ

Germany /'dʒɜːməni/ *pr n* أَلْمانِيا

germicide /'dʒɜːmɪsʌɪd/ *n* مُبيد للجَراثيمِ

germinate /'dʒɜːmɪneɪt/ **A** *vt* أَنْبَتَ ‹*the seeds, plants*› **B** *vi* «seeds, plants» نَبَتَ (u; نَبْت)

germination /dʒɜːmɪ'neɪʃ(ə)n/ *n* إِنْبات

germ warfare *n* حَرْب جُرْثوميّة

gerontologist /dʒerɒn'tɒlədʒɪst/ *n* أَخِصّائيّ أَمْراض الشَيْخوخةِ

gerontology /ˌdʒerən'tɒlədʒi/ *n* عِلْم الشَيْخوخةِ

gerund /'dʒerʌnd/ *n* صيغة المَصْدَرِ

gestation /dʒe'steɪʃ(ə)n/ *n* حَمْل

gesticulate /dʒe'stɪkjʊleɪt/ *vi* أَوْمَأَ (أَشارَ بِيَدَيْه)

gesture /'dʒestʃə/ **A** *n* **1** (body movement) إيماءة, إشارة **2** (token, expression) مُبادَرة, لَفْتة; **it was a nice ~** كانَتْ مُبادَرةً طَيِّبةً **B** *vi* أَوْمَأَ, أَشارَ

get /ɡet/ **A** *vt* (*present participle* **-tt-**, *past tense* **got**, *past participle* **got** or **gotten** AmE) **1** (to receive) اسْتَلَمَ ‹*a letter*›; حَصَلَ (u; حُصول; على) ‹*a salary, grant*›; اِلْتَقَطَ البَثَّ ‹*a TV channel*›; **our garden ~s a lot of sun** يَصِلُ حديقَتَنا الكَثيرُ من الشَمْسِ; **we ~ a lot of tourists here** يأتينا الكَثيرُ من السُيّاح; **you ~ what you pay for** يَأْخُذُ المَرْءُ بِقَدْرِ ما يَدْفَعُ **2** (to obtain by applying) حَصَلَ (u; حُصول; على) ‹*permission, a divorce, job*›; (by contacting) أَحْضَرَ ‹*a plumber, taxi*›; (by buying) اشْتَرى ‹*a laptop, ticket, suit*›; **to ~ sth for nothing/at a discount** حَصَلَ على شَيْءٍ مَجّاناً \ بِسِعْرٍ مُخَفَّضٍ; **I'll ~ sth to eat at the airport** سَأَشْتَري شَيْئاً آكُلُهُ في المَطارِ; **to ~ sb sth, to ~ sth for sb** اِشْتَرى شَيْئاً لِشَخْصٍ; **I got her a silver necklace** اشْتَرَيْتُ لَها قِلادةً فِضِّيّةً **3** **to ~ sth from sb** (to inherit) وَرِثَ شَيْئاً من شَخْصٍ ‹*money, a ring, one's red hair*› **4** (to acquire) اكْتَسَبَ ‹*a reputation*›; **to ~ a bad name** اكْتَسَبَ سُمْعةً سَيِّئةً **5** (to achieve) حَصَلَ (u; حُصول; على) ‹*a grade, mark, degree*›; **he got the answer/calculation right** كانَ جوابُهُ \ حِسابُهُ صَحيحاً **6** (to fetch) جَلَبَ, أَحْضَرَ (i-u; جَلْب) ‹*help, a person, ball*›; **~ a chair/your mother** أَحْضِرْ كُرْسِيًّا \ والِدَتَكَ; **to ~ sb sth, to ~ sth for sb** أَحْضَرَ شَيْئاً لِشَخْصٍ; **shall I ~ you your dessert?** هل آتيكَ بالحُلْوِ؟; **~ one from the cupboard** أَحْضِرْ واحِدةً من الخِزانةِ; **I got it from the table** جِئْتُ بِهِ من على الطاولة **7** **to ~ sb/sth to a place** (to move, manoeuvre) أَخَذَ شَخْصاً \ شَيْئاً إلى مَكانٍ; **to ~ the furniture upstairs/downstairs** نَقَلَ الأَثاثَ إلى الطابِقِ العُلْويِّ \ السُفْليِّ; **I'll ~ you there somehow** سَأوصِلُكَ إلى هُناكَ بِطَريقةٍ أو بِأُخْرى **8** **this is ~ting us nowhere** (to help progress) لن يوصِلَنا هذا إلى أَيْنَ سَيَصِلُ; **where will that ~ you?** إلى أَيِّ شَيْءٍ \ نَتيجةٍ سَيَصِلُ بِكَ هذا؟ **9** **can you ~ Harry on the phone?** (to contact) هل تَسْتَطيعُ الاتِّصالَ بِهاري؟ **10** **I'll ~ it!** (infml) أَتْرُكْهُ لي! **11** (to prepare) حَضَّرَ ‹*breakfast, lunch*› **12** (to take hold of) أَمْسَكَ (ب); **don't worry, I've got you** لا تَخَفْ، فَقَدْ أَمْسَكْتُ بِكَ **13** **to ~ money/the truth out of sb** (infml) انْتَزَعَ نُقوداً \ الحَقيقةَ من شَخْصٍ **14** (to catch) (infml) أَمْسَكَ (ب) ‹*a thief, sb's attacker*›; **they got him at the airport** أَمْسَكوا بِهِ في المَطارِ; **got you!** مَسَكْتُكَ! **15** (to defeat) (infml) هَزَمَ (i; هَزْم), تَغَلَّبَ (على); **now I've got you!** لا مَفَرَّ أَمامَكَ!; **you've got me there!** لا أَدْري ما أَقولُ! **16** (to understand) (infml) فَهِمَ (a; فَهْم) ‹*a joke, the point*›; **I didn't ~ the point/joke** لم أَفْهَمِ المَقْصودَ \ النُكْتةَ **17** (to contract) أُصيبَ ب ‹*a cold, disease*›; **he got the cough from his sister** انْتَقَلَتْ إلَيْهِ عَدْوى السُعالِ من أُخْتِهِ **18** (to use) اسْتَقَلَّ, أَخَذَ (u; أَخْذ) ‹*the bus, train*› **19** **to have got** (to have) كانَ لَدَيْه ‹*a new phone, some money, a lot of enemies*›; **I've got a headache** أُصِبْتُ بِصُداعٍ; **have you got any change?** هل لَدَيْكَ أَيّةُ فَكّةٍ؟; **I haven't got his e-mail address** لَيْسَ لَدَيَّ بَريدُهُ الإلِكْترونيُّ **20** (from sales) حَصَلَ (u; حُصول; على) ‹*£30, money*›; **what did you ~ for your car?** بِكَمْ بِعْتَ سَيّارَتَكَ؟; **we didn't ~ much for it** لم نَحْصُلْ على الكَثيرِ

من بَيْعِهِ [21] **to ~ a surprise** حَدَثَتْ لَهُ مُفاجَأةٌ; **to ~ a shock** أُصيبَ بِصَدْمةٍ; **to ~ a bang on the head** تَلَقّى ضَرْبَةً على رَأْسِهِ [22] (as punishment) عوقِبَ ب *‹five years in prison, twenty lashes, a fine›* [23] (to catch) سَمِعَ (a; سَمْع) *‹information, words›*; **I didn't ~ your name** لم أَسْمَع اسْمَكَ; **'where did you hear that?' - 'I got it from Paul'** 'أَيْنَ سَمِعْتَ بِذَلِكَ؟' - 'سَمِعْتُهُ من بول'; **~ this! he was arrested this morning** اسْمَعْ هذا! لَقَدْ أُلْقِيَ القَبْضُ عَلَيْهِ هذا الصَباحَ [24] **what ~s me is ...** (infml) ما يُضايِقُني هو ... [25] **to ~ to like sb** أَصْبَحَ يُحِبُّ شَخْصاً; **how did you ~ to hear of our organization?** كيف سَمِعْتَ بِمُنَظَّمَتِنا؟; **we got to know them last year** تَعَرَّفْنا عَلَيْهِم العامَ الماضِيَ [26] **to ~ to do sth** سَنَحَتْ لَهُ الفُرْصَةُ لِفِعْلِ شَيْءٍ [27] **to have got to do sth** (must) تَوَجَّبَ عَلَيْهِ القِيامُ بِشَيْءٍ; **it's got to be done** يَتَعَيَّنُ القِيامُ بِهِ; **we have got to warn her** يَجِبُ أَنْ نُحَذِّرَها; **I've got to call him** عَلَيَّ أَنْ أَتَّصِلَ بِهِ; **we have got to ~ going** عَلَيْنا المُغادَرةُ; **there has got to be a logical reason** لا بُدَّ أَنَّ هُناكَ سَبَباً مَنْطِقيًّا [28] **to ~ sb to pay/talk** (to persuade) جَعَلَ شَخْصاً يَدْفَعُ \ يَتَحَدَّثُ [29] **to ~ sth done** (to have sb do sth) [اِسْتَأْجَرَ شَخْصاً لِيَفْعَلَ لَهُ شَيْئاً]; **to ~ one's hair cut** قَصَّ شَعْرَهُ عند الحَلّاقِ; **I must ~ the car repaired** يَجِبُ أَنْ أَذْهَبَ للميكانيكيِّ لِيُصْلِحَ لي السَيّارةَ [30] (to cause sth to happen) **to ~ the car going** جَعَلَ السَيّارةَ تَعْمَلُ; **it is as hot as you can ~ it** تَمَّ تَسْخينُهُ بِأَقْصى دَرَجةٍ; **to ~ one's socks wet** ابْتَلَّتْ جَوارِبُهُ

B *vi* [1] (to become) أَصْبَحَ; **it's ~ting late** بَدَأَ الوَقْتُ يَتَأَخَّرُ; **how did he ~ like that?** كيف أَصْبَحَ هَكَذا؟; **to ~ ready** تَجَهَّزَ, اِسْتَعَدَّ; **to ~ rich/fat/old** أَصْبَحَ غَنيًّا \ سَميناً \ عَجوزاً [2] (in the passive) **to ~ hurt** جُرِحَ; **30 spectators got hurt/killed** جُرِحَ \ قُتِلَ 30 مُتَفَرِّجاً [3] (to become involved in) **to ~ into a sport/profession** بَدَأَ يُمارِسُ رِياضةً \ مِهْنَةً; **to ~ into a fight** دَخَلَ في شِجارٍ [4] (to arrive) **to ~ somewhere** وَصَلَ إلى مَكانٍ; **to ~ to the airport** وَصَلَ إلى المَطارِ; **we got here by bus** جِئْنا إلى هُنا بالحافِلةِ [5] (to progress) **it got to 7 o'clock** اِقْتَرَبَ الوَقْتُ من الساعةِ السابِعةِ; **where did you ~ to?** إلى أَيْنَ وَصَلْتَ؟; **we've got to page 5** وَصَلْنا إلى الصَفْحةِ 5; **I'm/we're getting there** أَقْتَرِبُ \ نَقْتَرِبُ من الوُصولِ إلى الهَدَفِ; **now we're ~ting somewhere!** وَأخيراً حَقَّقنا بَعْضَ التقدُّم!; **I'm ~ting nowhere with this essay** لم أُحْرِزْ أَيَّ تَقَدُّمٍ في هذه المَقالةِ

Idiom **what's got into you/her?** (infml) ماذا دَهاكَ \ دَهاها؟

Phrasal verbs **get about ▸ get around** A1

• **get across A** [1] (to the other side) «cars, runners» عَبَرَ (u; عَبْر, عُبور) [2] (to be understood) «messages» وَصَلَ (i; وَصْل, صِلة) **B ~ across [sth]** (to cross) عَبَرَ [شَيْئاً] *‹a river, road›* **C ~ [sth] across** [1] (to transport) نَقَلَ [شَيْئاً]; **how can we ~ it across?** كيف نَسْتَطيعُ نَقْلَهُ؟ [2] (to communicate) شَرَحَ [شَيْئاً] *‹a message, the meaning›*

• **get ahead** [1] (to make progress) تَقَدَّمَ; **to ~ ahead of a competitor/of an opponent** تَقَدَّمَ على مُنافِسٍ \ خَصْمٍ [2] **to ~ ahead of oneself** (in plans, projects) اسْتَبَقَ نَفْسَهُ

• **get along** [1] **how are you ~ting along?** (to be faring) كيف حالُكَ؟; (to be progressing) كيف تَسيرُ الأُمورُ مَعَكَ؟; **how's the project ~ting along?** كيف يَسيرُ المَشْروعُ؟ [2] (to be on friendly terms) تَفاهَمَ, تَصادَقَ; **we don't ~ along** لَسْنا على عَلاقةٍ طَيِّبةٍ [3] (infml) (to leave) غادَرَ; **we must be ~ting along now** يَجِبُ أَنْ نُغادِرَ الآنَ

• **get around A** [1] (to move about) تَحَرَّكَ, تَنَقَّلَ من مَكانٍ إلى مَكانٍ [2] (to travel) سافَرَ [3] **to ~ around to doing sth** اتَّسَعَ لَهُ الوَقْتُ لِفِعْلِ شَيْءٍ **B ~ around [sth]** (to avoid) تَحايَلَ \ الْتَفَّ على [شَيْءٍ] *‹a rule›*; تَفادى [شَيْئاً] *‹a problem›* **C ~ around [sb]** (BrE) (infml) (to persuade) أَقْنَعَ [شَخْصاً]

• **get at: ~ at [sb/sth]** (infml) [1] (to access) وَصَلَ إلى [شَخْصٍ \ شَيْءٍ] *‹a box, switch, one's emails›* [2] (to criticize) اِنْتَقَدَ [شَخْصاً] *‹a spouse, colleague›* [3] (to hint at) لَمَّحَ إلى [شَيْءٍ]; **what's he ~ting at?** إلى ماذا يُلَمِّحُ؟

• **get away** [1] (to leave) غادَرَ [2] (to escape) «fish, prisoners» هَرَبَ (u; هُروب) [3] (to escape unpunished) **to ~ away with a crime** أَفْلَتَ من العِقابِ في جَريمةٍ; **she ~s away with blue murder!** [لا أَحَدَ يُحاسِبُها على سوءِ تَصَرُّفاتِها]

• **get away from A ~ away from [sth]** [1] (to leave) اِبْتَعَدَ عن [شَيْءٍ] *‹a place, town›*; **'~ away from it all'** (in an advert) 'أُتْرُكْ كُلَّ شَيْءٍ خَلْفَكَ' [2] (to deny) أَنْكَرَ [شَيْئاً] *‹a fact›*; **there's no**

~ting away from it لا يُمْكِنُ نُكْرانُهُ **B** **~ away from [sb]** فَرَّ من [شَخْصٍ] ‹an attacker, the crowds›

• **get back** **A** 1 (to return) رَجَعَ (i; رُجوع); **we got back late/early** رَجَعْنا مُتَأَخِّرين \ باكِرينَ; **we got back behind the barrier** رَجَعْنا خَلْفَ الحاجِزِ 2 (to move backwards) رَجَعَ إلى الوَراءِ **B** **~ back to [sth]** 1 (to return to) عادَ \ رَجَعَ إلى [شَيْءٍ] ‹the house, city, the beach› 2 (to a previous state) عادَ \ رَجَعَ إلى [شَيْءٍ]; **to ~ back to sleep** عادَ إلى النَوْمِ; **to ~ back to normal** عادَ إلى حالَتِهِ الطَبيعيّةِ 3 (in discussions) عادَ \ رَجَعَ إلى [شَيْءٍ] ‹a topic, question›; **let's ~ back to the previous point** دَعْنا نَرْجِعُ إلى النُقْطةِ السابِقةِ **C** **~ back to [sb]** (on the phone) **I'll ~ back to you straight away** سَأَعودُ إِلَيْكَ حالاً **D** **~ [sb/sth] back** 1 (to regain) اسْتَعادَ [شَخْصاً \ شَيْئاً] ‹one's money, car, pet›; **she's ~ting her strength back** تَسْتَرِدُّ عافِيَتَها 2 (to return) أَرْجَعَ \ أَعادَ [شَخْصاً \ شَيْئاً] ‹a child, bag, pet›

• **get behind with**: **~ behind with [sth]** تَأَخَّرَ في [شَيْءٍ] ‹payments, work›

• **get by** 1 (to pass) مَرَّ (u; مُرور) 2 (to manage) تَدَبَّرَ أَمْرَهُ; **we ~ by on £30 a week** نُدَبِّرُ أُمورَنا بِثَلاثينَ جُنَيْهاً في الأُسْبوعِ; **I can ~ by in Italian** أَعْرِفُ بَعْضَ الإيطاليّةِ

• **get down** **A** 1 (to descend) نَزَلَ (i; نُزول) 2 (onto the floor) انْبَطَحَ; **to ~ down on one's hands and knees** انْبَطَحَ على يَدَيْهِ ورُكْبَتَيْهِ; **~ down!** انْبَطِحوا أَرْضاً! 3 (to apply oneself) **to ~ down to work/business** رَكَّزَ على العَمَلِ **B** **~ [sth] down, ~ down [sth]** 1 (from high up) أَنْزَلَ [شَيْئاً] ‹a book, jar› 2 (to swallow) بَلَعَ [شَيْئاً] ‹the medicine, tablets› 3 (in writing) كَتَبَ [شَيْئاً] ‹notes, a speech› **C** **~ [sb] down** 1 (from high up) أَنْزَلَ [شَخْصاً] 2 (to depress) أَحْبَطَ [شَخْصاً]

• **get in** **A** 1 (to enter a building) دَخَلَ (u; دُخول); (to step into a vehicle) رَكِبَ (a; رُكوب) 2 (to arrive) «trains, buses» وَصَلَ (i; وُصول) 3 (to participate) **to ~ in on a project/scheme** شارَكَ في مَشْروعٍ \ بَرْنامَجٍ 4 (to enter) «sunlight, water» دَخَلَ (u; دُخول) 5 (Pol) «candidates, political parties» فازَ في الانْتِخاباتِ 6 (to gain admission) «candidates, applicants» قُبِلَ 7 (to associate) **to ~ in with a bad crowd** اقْتَرَنَ بِصُحْبةٍ سَيِّئةٍ **B** **~ [sth] in, ~ in [sth]** 1 (to buy, order) اشْتَرى [شَيْئاً] ‹supplies, food› 2 (to harvest) حَصَدَ [شَيْئاً] ‹a crop› 3 (to plant) زَرَعَ [شَيْئاً] ‹bulbs, plants› 4 (to deliver) سَلَّمَ [شَيْئاً] ‹an essay, a competition entry› 5 (infml) (in schedules) ضَمَّنَ \ أَدْخَلَ [شَيْئاً] ‹some tennis, golf›

• **get into**: **~ into [sth]** 1 (to enter) دَخَلَ إلى [شَيْءٍ] ‹a building›; رَكِبَ [شَيْئاً] ‹a vehicle› 2 (to be accepted as a member) أَصْبَحَ عُضْواً في [شَيْءٍ]; (to be admitted as a student) قُبِلَ في [شَيْءٍ] 3 (to put on) لَبِسَ [شَيْئاً] ‹a pair of jeans, size 10› 4 (to become involved in) انْخَرَطَ في [شَيْءٍ] ‹work, diving›

• **get off** **A** 1 (from buses, trains) نَزَلَ (i; نُزول) 2 (to start a journey) انْطَلَقَ 3 (to leave work) غادَرَ 4 (infml) (to escape punishment) أَفْلَتَ من العِقابِ 5 (infml) (sexually) **to ~ off with sb** مارَسَ الجِنْسَ مع شَخْصٍ **B** **~ off [sth]** (to depart from) تَرَكَ [شَيْئاً] ‹the subject, point› **C** **~ [sb/sth] off** 1 (to dispatch) أَرْسَلَ [شَيْئاً] ‹a parcel, letter› 2 (infml) (to send to sleep) نَوَّمَ \ أَنامَ [شَخْصاً] ‹a baby›

• **get on** **A** 1 (to enter onto a bus, train) رَكِبَ (a; رُكوب) 2 (to be progressing generally) **how are you ~ting on?** كيف تَسيرُ الأُمورُ مَعَكَ؟; **how are you ~ting on at work?** كيف تَسيرُ الأُمورُ مَعَكَ في العَمَلِ؟ 3 (to be on friendly terms) تَفاهَمَ; **we don't ~ on** لَسْنا على عَلاقةٍ طَيِّبةٍ 4 (to grow old) كَبِرَ (a; كِبَر); **to be ~ting on a bit** تَقَدَّمَ في السِنِّ بَعْضَ الشَيْءِ 5 (to grow late) تَأَخَّرَ; **time's ~ting on** بَدَأَ الوَقْتُ يَتَأَخَّرُ **B** **~ on [sth]** (to board) اسْتَقَلَّ \ رَكِبَ [شَيْئاً] ‹a bus, train› **C** **~ [sth] on, ~ on [sth]** 1 (to put on) لَبِسَ [شَيْئاً] ‹one's boots, clothes› 2 (to put on) رَكَّبَ \ ثَبَّتَ [شَيْئاً] ‹a tyre, cover›

• **get on for**: **~ on for [sth]** (BrE) (to approach) اقْتَرَبَ من [شَيْءٍ]; **he's ~ting on for 40** يَقْتَرِبُ من الأَرْبَعينَ; **it's ~ting on for midnight** يَدْنو الوَقْتُ من مُنْتَصَفِ اللَيْلِ

• **get onto** **A** **~ onto [sth]** 1 (to board) صَعِدَ إلى [شَيْءٍ], اسْتَقَلَّ \ رَكِبَ [شَيْئاً] ‹a bus, train› 2 (in discussions) تَطَرَّقَ إلى [شَيْءٍ] ‹a topic, subject› 3 (in appointments) وَصَلَ إلى [شَيْءٍ] ‹a committee, board› **B** **~ onto [sb]** (BrE) (to contact) اتَّصَلَ ب [شَخْصٍ] ‹an organization, the manager›

• **get on with**: **A** **~ on with [sth]** (to continue with) **to ~ on**

with one's work/with preparing the meal واصَلَ عَمَلَهُ \ تَحْضيرَ الوَجْبَةِ; **let's ~ on with the job!** دَعْنا نُواصِلُ العَمَلَ! **B** **~ on with** [**sb**] (BrE) (to be on friendly terms with) كانَ على عَلاقةٍ طَيِّبةٍ مع [شَخْصٍ]

• **get out** **A** 1 (to exit) خَرَجَ (u; خُروج); **they all got out alive** خَرَجوا كُلُّهُمْ أَحياءً; **~ out!** أُخْرُجْ! 2 (socially) خَرَجَ (لِلتَّنَزُّهِ) 3 (of a town, company) رَحَلَ (a; رَحيل) 4 (from a vehicle) نَزَلَ (i; نُزول), خَرَجَ (u; خُروج) 5 (from prison, hospital) «prisoners, patients» خَرَجَ (u; خُروج) 6 (to be revealed) «secrets, news» انْكَشَفَ **B** **~** [**sth**] **out**, **~ out** [**sth**] 1 (to bring out) أَخْرَجَ [شَيْئاً] ‹*a handkerchief, an ID card*› 2 (to remove) أَزالَ [شَيْئاً] ‹*a stain*› 3 (to take on loan) اسْتَعارَ [شَيْئاً] ‹*a library book, DVD*› **C** **~ out of** [**sth**] 1 (to exit from) خَرَجَ من [شَيْءٍ] ‹*a building, meeting*›; **to ~ out of bed** نَهَضَ من السَريرِ; **she wants to ~ out of the sales department** تُريدُ تَرْكَ قِسْمِ المَبيعاتِ 2 (from vehicles) نَزَلَ من [شَيْءٍ] ‹*a car, bus*› 3 (to escape from) هَرَبَ من [شَيْءٍ] ‹*prison, a cage*› 4 (to avoid) تَجَنَّبَ [شَيْئاً] ‹*doing something, a meeting, trip*›; **how did you ~ out of washing the dishes?** كيف تَفادَيْتَ غَسْلَ الصُحونِ؟ 5 (to gain from) **to ~ sth out of a job/scheme** اسْتَفادَ شَيْئاً من وَظيفةٍ \ خُطّةٍ; **what did you ~ out of it?** ماذا اسْتَفَدْتَ مِنْهُ؟ **D** **~** [**sb**] **out** (to free) أَخْرَجَ [شَخْصاً] ‹*trapped person, hostage*›

• **get over** **A** (to cross) عَبَرَ (u; عُبور, عَبْر) **B** **~ over** [**sth**] 1 (from one side to the other) عَبَرَ [شَيْئاً] ‹*a stream*›; اجْتازَ [شَيْئاً] ‹*wall*› 2 (to recover from) تعافى من [شَيْءٍ] ‹*an operation, a bereavement*›; **I still can't ~ over it!** (expressing amazement) لا أَسْتَطيعُ أَنْ أُصَدِّقَهُ! **C** **~ over** [**sb**] (emotionally) تَخَلَّصَ من حُزْنِهِ على فِراقِ [شَخْصٍ]; **she never got over him** لم تَسْتَطِعْ أَبَداً أَنْ تَنْساهُ

• **get over with**: **~** [**sth**] **over with** (to get through) **to ~ a funeral/interview over with** وَضَعَ الجَنازةَ \ المُقابَلةَ خَلْفَهُ

• **get round** **A** (BrE) ▸**get around** A1 **B** **~ round** [**sth**] (BrE) ▸**get around** B **C** **~ round** [**sb**] ▸**get around** C

• **get through** **A** 1 (to pass) تَخَطّى 2 **to ~ through to sb** (to make sb understand) أَوْصَلَ فِكْرَتَهُ إلى شَخْصٍ 3 (to arrive) «supplies, mail, news» وَصَلَ (i; وُصول) 4 (to make it through) اجْتازَ **B** **~ through** [**sth**] 1 (to pass through) عَبَرَ \ اجْتازَ [شَيْئاً] ‹*a checkpoint, the mud, fence*› 2 (to reach the end of) أَنْهى [شَيْئاً] ‹*a task, book, one's revision*›; **I don't know how we got through the week** لا أَدْري كيف اجْتَزْنا هذا الأُسْبوعَ 3 (to succeed in) نَجَحَ في [شَيْءٍ] ‹*an exam, a round, heat*› 4 (Pol) **to ~ through Parliament/Congress** «bills, legislation» حَظِيَ بِمُوافَقةِ البَرْلَمانِ \ الكونْغْرِس 5 (to use up) اسْتَهْلَكَ [شَيْئاً] ‹*fuel, money, supplies*›; **we ~ through two loaves a day** نَسْتَهْلِكُ رَغيفَيْنِ في اليَوْمِ **C** **~** [**sb/sth**] **through** 1 **to ~ sb/sth through a checkpoint/the door** مَرَّ بِشَخْصٍ \ بِشَيْءٍ من خِلالِ نُقْطةِ تَفْتيشٍ \ البابِ 2 **to ~ sb through the day/an illness** أَعانَ شَخْصاً على تَحَمُّلِ اليَوْمِ \ مَرَضٍ 3 **to ~ a student through an exam** أَعانَ طالِباً في امْتِحانٍ 4 (in legislatures) مَرَّرَ [شَيْئاً] ‹*a bill, the legislation*›

• **get together** **A** (to assemble) «students, friends» اجْتَمَعَ, تَقابَلَ **B** **~** [**sb/sth**] **together**, **~ together** [**sb/sth**] 1 (to organize) جَمَّعَ [أَشْخاصاً \ شَيْئاً] ‹*interested parties, a group*› 2 (to accumulate) خَزَّنَ \ ادَّخَرَ [شَيْئاً] ‹*money, food*›

• **get up** **A** 1 (in the morning) صَحا, اسْتَيْقَظَ (u; صُحُوّ, صَحْو) 2 (from a chair, sofa) نَهَضَ (a; نُهوض), قامَ (u; قَوْمة, قِيام) 3 (to grow stronger) «storms, winds» اشْتَدَّ **B** **~** [**sth**] **up**, **~ up** [**sth**] (to organize) أَعَدَّ [شَيْئاً] ‹*a petition*›; نَظَّمَ [شَيْئاً] ‹*support, a group*› **C** **~ up to** [**sth**]: **to ~ up to mischief** تَشاقى; **to ~ up to a prank** عَمِلَ مَقْلَباً; **what did you ~ up to last night?** ماذا فَعَلْتَ اللَيْلَةَ الماضِيةَ؟

getaway /ˈgetəweɪ/ *n* فِرار, هُروب; **to make one's ~** لاذَ بالفِرارِ

get-together /ˈgettəgeðə/ *n* (infml) لِقاء (لِقاءات)

geyser /ˈgiːzə/ *n* 1 (hot spring) فَوّارة, حَمّة (نَبْع ماءٍ ساخِنٍ) 2 (BrE) (water heater) سَخّان ماءٍ

Ghana /ˈgɑːnə/ *pr n* غانا

Ghanaian /gɑːˈneɪən/ *n, adj* غانيّ

ghastly /ˈgɑːstli/ *adj* (**ghastlier**, **ghastliest**) 1 (horrific) ‹*sight, crime*› مُرْعِب, شَنيع, مُرَوِّع 2 (infml) (very bad) ‹*weather, food*› فَظيع

ghazi, **Ghazi** /ˈgɑːzi/ *n* (*pl* **ghazis**) غازٍ (غُزاة)

gherkin /'gəːkɪn/ *n* خِيار صَغير

ghetto /'gɛtəʊ/ *n* (*pl* **ghettos** or **ghettoes**) غيتو (غيتُوات)

ghost /gəʊst/ *n* شَبَح (أَشْباح)

Idiom **to give up the ghost** تَعَطَّلَ

ghostly /'gəʊstli/ *adj* (**ghostlier**, **ghostliest**) <*footsteps, sound*> شَبَحيّ

ghoul /guːl/ *n* **1** (evil spirit) روح شِرّيرة, غول (غيلان) **2** (person) غول (غيلان)

ghusl /'guːs(ə)l/ *n* غُسْل

GI /dʒiː'ʌɪ/ *n* (*pl* **GIs**) جُنْديّ (في جَيْشِ الوِلاياتِ المُتَّحِدة)

giant /'dʒʌɪənt/ **A** *n* عِمْلاق (عَمالِقة) **B** *adj* <*screen, wave*> ضَخْم (ضِخام), عِمْلاق (عَمالِقة)

gibber /'dʒɪbə/ *vi* بَرْبَرَ (i; بَرْبَرة), هَذَرَ (i-u; هَذَر, هَذْر), رَطَنَ (u; رَطانة)

gibberish /'dʒɪbərɪʃ/ *n* بَرْبَرة, كَلام غَيْر مَفْهومٍ, رَطانة; **to talk ~** رَطَنَ (u; رِطانة, رَطانة)

gibe ▸ **jibe**

giblets /'dʒɪblɪts/ *n pl* أَحْشاء (الطُيور)

Gibraltar /dʒɪ'brɔːltə/ *pr n* جَبَل طارِق

giddy /'gɪdi/ *adj* (**giddier**, **giddiest**) **1** (dizzy) <*person*> دائِخ, مُصاب بِدُوار; <*feeling*> بالدُوارِ, بالدَوْخةِ; **to feel ~** شَعَرَ بالدُوارِ \ بالدَوْخةِ **2** (exhilarating) **~ heights** مُرْتَفَعات رَهيبة \ مُثيرة

gift /gɪft/ *n* **1** (present) هَديّة (هَدايا), هِبة; **it was a ~** كانَ هَديّةً **2** (talent) مَوْهِبة (مَواهِبُ); **she has a ~ for languages** لَدَيْها مَوْهِبةُ تَعَلُّمِ اللُغاتِ

Idiom **to have the gift of the gab** (infml) كانَ طَلْقَ اللِسانِ

gift aid *n* اسْتِعادة المُؤَسَّساتِ الخَيْريّة لِضَريبةِ التَبَرُّعاتِ في المَمْلَكةِ المُتَّحِدة]

gifted /'gɪftɪd/ *adj* <*player, child*> مَوْهوب

gift shop *n* مَتْجَر هَدايا

gift token, **gift voucher**, **gift certificate** (AmE) *n* كوبون \ قَسيمة هَديّة

gig /gɪg/ *n* (infml) حَفْلة موسيقيّة

gigabyte /'gɪgəbʌɪt/ *n* جيجابايْت

gigantic /dʒʌɪ'gantɪk/ *adj* <*proportions, task*> ضَخْم (ضِخام), هائِل (هَوائِلُ)

giggle /'gɪg(ə)l/ **A** *vi* ضَحِكَ ضِحْكةً سَخيفةً **B** *n* ضِحْكة سَخيفة

gild /gɪld/ *vt* (*past tense, past participle* **gilded** or **gilt**) طَلى بالذَهَبِ <*a frame, statue*>

gill /gɪl/ *n* خَيْشوم (خَياشيمُ)

gilt /gɪlt/ *adj* <*frame, brooch*> مُذَهَّب, مَطْليّ بالذَهَبِ

gimmick /'gɪmɪk/ *n* خُدْعة (خُدَع, خُدْعات), حيلة (حِيَل)

gin /dʒɪn/ *n* جِنّ (شَراب مُسْكِر)

ginger /'dʒɪndʒə/ **A** *n* (plant) زَنْجَبيل **B** *adj* <*hair*> أَصْهَب (dipt; صُهْب); <*cat*> بُرْتُقاليّ

ginger ale *n* [شَراب غازيّ بِطَعْمِ الزَنْجَبيل]

ginger beer *n* جِعة الزَنْجَبيل

gingerbread /'dʒɪndʒəbrɛd/ *n* [u] (cake) كَعْك الزَنْجَبيلِ

gingerbread man /'dʒɪndʒəbrɛd ˌman/ *n* (biscuit) رَجُل كَعْكة الزَنْجَبيل (بَسْكويت بالزَنْجَبيل على شَكْلِ رَجُلٍ)

ginger-haired /ˌdʒɪndʒə'hɛːd/ *adj* <*boy, girl*> ذو شَعْرٍ أَصْهَب \ بُرْتُقاليّ

gingivitis /ˌdʒɪndʒɪ'vʌɪtɪs/ *n* الْتِهاب اللِثةِ

ginseng /'dʒɪnsɛŋ/ *n* جينْسِنْغ

gipsy *n* ▸ **gypsy**

giraffe /dʒɪ'rɑːf/ *n* (**giraffe** or **giraffes**) زَرافة

girder /'gəːdə/ *n* عارِضة (عَوارِضُ)

girdle /'gəːd(ə)l/ *n* **1** (corset) مِشَدّ (لِلبَطْنِ والأَوْراكِ) **2** (belt) حِزام (أَحْزِمة, حِزامات)

girl /gəːl/ *n* **1** (child) طِفْلة, بِنْت (بَنات); (young woman) فَتاة (فَتَيات), صَبيّة (صَبايا) **2** (daughter) اِبْنة (بَنات)

girlfriend /'gəːlfrɛnd/ *n* **1** (partner) صاحِبة, حَبيبة **2** (female friend) صَديقة, رَفيقة

Girl Guide *n* (BrE) فَتاة \ مُرْشِدة كَشّافة

girlish /'gəːlɪʃ/ *adj* <*behaviour, voice*> بَناتيّ

Girl Scout *n* فَتاة كَشّافة, مُرْشِدة

giro /'dʒʌɪrəʊ/ *n* (system) جيرو (مَدْفوعات بِطَريقةِ المُقاصّةِ بين البُنوكِ وَمَكاتِبِ البَريدِ)

girth /gɜːθ/ *n* 1 (of a person, tree, pillar) مُحيط 2 (belt for a horse) حِزام سَرْجٍ

gist /dʒɪst/ *n* لُبّ (لُبوب), فَحْوى (f; فَحاوٍ, فَحاوى), جَوْهَر (جَواهِرُ); **to get the ~ of sth** فَهِمَ فَحْوى شَيْءٍ

give /gɪv/ A *vt* (*past tense* **gave**; *past participle* **given**)

1 (changing ownership) أَعْطى ‹*a sum of money, present*›; **to ~ sb a present/drink** أَعْطى شَخْصاً هَدِيَّةً \ شَراباً; **to ~ sb a present for their birthday** أَعْطى شَخْصاً هَدِيَّةً بِمُناسَبة عِيدِ ميلادِهِ; **I'll ~ you £50 for it** سَأُعْطيك 50 جُنَيْهاً مُقابِلَهُ

2 (to hand over) أَعْطى ‹*a letter, key, glass of water*›; **~ this letter to your father** أَعْطِ هذه الرسالة إلى أبيك; **~ it to me!** أَعْطِني إيّاهُ!

3 (to transmit) **to ~ sb sth** أَعْدى شَخْصاً بشَيْءٍ ‹*a cold, virus*›; أَصابَ شَخْصاً بشَيْءٍ ‹*indigestion, a headache*›; **he's given me his cough** أَعْداني بِسُعالِهِ; **that noise ~s me a headache** تُصيبُني تِلْكَ الضَوْضاءُ بالصُداع; **the meal gave her indigestion/an upset stomach** أَصابَتْها الوَجْبةُ بِعُسْرٍ في الهَضْمِ \ بِاضْطِرابٍ في المَعِدةِ

4 (to provide, produce) أَعْطى ‹*milk, flavour, wool*›; **the herbs ~ the bread its special flavour** تُعْطي الأَعْشابُ الخُبْزَ نَكْهَتَهُ المُمَيَّزة; **~ me your answer as soon as possible** أَعْطِني جَوابَكَ بِأَسْرَعِ وَقْتٍ مُمْكِنٍ; **the study gave an unexpected result** أَظْهَرَت الدِراسةُ نَتيجةً غَيْرَ مُتَوَقَّعةٍ

5 (to communicate) أَعْطى ‹*information, the news*›; **they were unable to ~ any information** لم يَسْتَطيعوا إعْطاءَ أَيَّةِ مَعْلوماتٍ; **let me ~ you some advice** دَعْني أُعْطيكَ بَعْضَ النَصائِحِ

6 (to allow) **to ~ sb permission/authority to do sth** أَعْطى شَخْصاً الإذْنَ \ السُلْطةَ لِفِعْلِ شَيْءٍ; **to ~ sb time/two hours to do sth** أَعْطى شَخْصاً وَقْتاً \ ساعَتَيْنِ لِفِعْلِ شَيْءٍ; **to ~ sb enough room** أَفْسَحَ مَكاناً لِشَخْصٍ; **the polls ~ Labour a lead** تُظْهِرُ اسْتِطْلاعاتُ الرَأْيِ أنّ حِزْبَ العَمَلِ في الصَدارة; **how long do you ~ their marriage?** كم تَتَوَقَّعُ أنْ يَسْتَمِرَّ زَواجُهُما؟; **I was given to understand that ...** ما فَهِمْتُهُ هو أنّ ...

7 **to ~ sb a treatment for sth** أَعْطى شَخْصاً عِلاجاً لِشَيْءٍ; **they gave him a new heart/liver** زَرَعوا لَهُ قَلْباً \ كَبِداً جَديداً; **I was given antibiotics** أُعْطيتُ مُضاداتٍ حَيَوِيّةً

8 (Tel) وَصَّلَ (ب) ‹*an extension, a department*›; **~ me the sales department, please** وَصِّلْني بِقِسْمِ المَبيعاتِ، من فَضْلِكَ

B *vi* (*past tense* **gave**; *past participle* **given**) 1 (with donations) تَبَرَّعَ; **'please ~ generously'** 'يُرْجى التَبَرُّعُ بِسَخاءٍ' 2 (under pressure) «the mattress, sofa, shelves» تَمَطَّطَ 3 (to fall through) انْهارَ 4 (in negotiations) «negotiators, sides» قَدَّمَ تَنازُلاتٍ; **something has to ~** لا بُدَّ من تَنازُلاتٍ

C *n* (flexibility) مُرونة

Idiom **to give and take** أَخَذَ وَأَعْطى, قَدَّمَ تَنازُلاتٍ مُتَبادَلةً

Phrasal verbs **give away** A **~ away [sth], ~ [sth] away** 1 (as a gift) أَعْطى [شَيْئاً] مَجّاناً ‹*a sample, ticket, an item*›; **we're practically giving them away!** عَمَلِيًّا نَحْنُ نُوَزِّعُهُمْ مَجّاناً! 2 (to reveal) أَفْشى [شَيْئاً] ‹*a secret, the answer, ending*› 3 (to concede) وَهَبَ [شَيْئاً] ‹*a match, goal, the advantage*› B **~ [sb] away, ~ away [sb]** 1 (to betray) كَشَفَ [شَخْصاً]; **she gave herself away** كَشَفَتْ نَفْسَها 2 (in marriage) سَلَّمَ [شَخْصاً] (العَروس إلى عَريسها) ‹*the bride*›

• **give back**: **~ [sth] back, ~ back [sth]** (to return) أَعادَ [شَيْئاً] ‹*a book, key, sb's freedom*›; **if you can find it cheaper, we'll ~ you your money back** إنْ وَجَدْتَهُ بِسِعْرٍ أَرْخَصَ، سَنُعيدُ إلَيْكَ نُقودَكَ

• **give in** A (to yield) اِسْتَسْلَمَ; **whatever the setbacks, we will never ~ in!** أيًّا كانَت العَقَباتُ، لن نَسْتَسْلِمَ أَبَداً!; **to ~ in to sb/to temptation** اِسْتَسْلَمَ لِشَخْصٍ \ لِلمُغْرِياتِ B **~ in [sth], ~ [sth] in** (to hand in) سَلَّمَ [شَيْئاً] ‹*your homework, a ticket*›

• **give off**: **~ off [sth]** انْبَعَثَ مِنْهُ [شَيْءٌ] ‹*radiation, light, fumes*›

• **give onto**: **~ onto [sth]** أَطَلَّ على [شَيْءٍ] ‹*the street, garden*›

• **give out** A (to fail) «fuel, supplies» نَفَذَ (u; نُفوذ, نَفاذ), نَفِدَ (a; نَفْد, نَفاد); «the engine» تَعَطَّلَ; «sb's strength» خارَ (u; خُؤور) B **~ out [sth], ~ [sth] out** 1 (to distribute) وَزَّعَ [شَيْئاً] ‹*books, leaflets*› 2 (to emit) انْبَعَثَ مِنْهُ [شَيْءٌ] 3 (to make public) أَعْلَنَ عن [شَيْءٍ] ‹*the details, information*›

• **give over** A (infml) (to stop) تَوَقَّفَ B **~ over [sth], ~ [sth] over** 1 (to dedicate) خَصَّصَ [شَيْئاً] ‹*a room, some space*› 2 (to transfer) تنازَلَ عن [شَيْءٍ] ‹*a building, business*› C **~ oneself over to [sth]** (to devote oneself to) كَرَّسَ حَياتَهُ لِ [شَيْءٍ] ‹*good works, writing*›

• **give up** **A** (to stop trying) اِسْتَسْلَمَ; **we will never ~ up!** لن نَسْتَسْلِمَ أَبداً!; **I've given up on him** فَقَدْتُ أَمَلي فيه **B** **~ up [sth], ~ [sth] up** 1 (to renounce) تخلّى عن [شَيْءٍ] <*a title, right, claim*>; **he gave up his job to look after the children** تخلّى عن وَظيفتِهِ لِيَعْتَنِيَ بالأَطْفالِ 2 (to stop) توقَّفَ \ أَقْلَعَ عن [شَيْءٍ] <*smoking, drinking, a habit*>; **it was hard to ~ up smoking/the habit** كانَ صَعْباً الإقلاعُ عن التَدْخينِ \ العادةِ 3 (to abandon) تَخلّى عن [شَيْءٍ] <*a search, struggle*>; **we gave up hope of saving them** فَقَدْنا الأَمَلَ في إِنْقاذِهِمْ; **I gave up History** تَرَكْتُ مادّةَ التاريخ 4 (to surrender) سَلَّمَ [شَيْئاً] <*territory, one's passport*>; تَرَكَ [شَيْئاً] <*one's seat*> **C** **~ [sb] up** 1 (to hand over) سَلَّمَ [شَخْصاً]; **he gave himself up to the authorities/police** سَلَّمَ نَفْسَهُ للسُلُطاتِ \ للشُرْطةِ 2 (in relationships) تَخلّى عن [شَخْصٍ] <*one's friends*>

• **give way** 1 (to collapse) «bridges, chairs, barriers» تَحَطَّمَ; **his legs gave way** لم تَسْتَطِعْ رِجْلاهُ حَمْلَهُ; **the barriers gave way under the crush of the demonstrators** انْهارَت الحَواجِزُ بِسَبَبِ دَفْعِ المُتَظاهِرينَ 2 (BrE Aut) أَعْطى حَقَّ الأَوْلَوِيّة 3 (in negotiations) خَضَعَ (a; خُضوع); **to ~ way to sb's demands/to pressure** خَضَعَ لِمَطالِبِ شَخْصٍ \ للضَغْطِ 4 (to be replaced) **to ~ way to new ideas/technology** أَفْسَحَ المَجالَ لأَفكارٍ \ لِتِكْنولوجيا جَديدةٍ

giveaway /ˈɡɪvəweɪ/ *n* 1 (revelation) دَليل (دَلائِلُ, أَدِلّة), إشارة; **her face was a dead ~** كانَ وَجْهُها يَكْشِفُ بِوُضوحٍ عَمّا بِداخِلِها 2 (free gift) هَدِيّة (هَدايا), هِبة

given /ˈɡɪv(ə)n/ **A** *past participle* ▸ **give**

B *adj* 1 (specified) <*data*> مُحَدَّد, مُعَيَّن; **on the ~ date** في التاريخِ المُعَيَّنِ \ المُحَدَّدِ; **at any ~ moment** في أَيّةِ لَحْظةٍ 2 (fml) (prone to) **to be ~ to doing sth** كانَ عُرْضةً لِفِعْلِ شَيْءٍ; **she's ~ to losing her temper** هي عُرْضةٌ لأَنْ تَفْقِدَ أَعْصابَها

C *prep* 1 (with) مَعَ; **~ the right training, they would be very good** مَعَ التَدْريبِ الصَحيحِ، سَيَكونونَ جَيِّدينَ جِدّاً 2 (in view of the fact that) **~ that ...** نَظَراً إلى أنّ ...

D *n* مُسَلَّم بِهِ \ أَمْر مَفْروغ مِنْهُ; **it's a ~ in modern economic theory that ...** من مُسَلَّماتِ نَظَرِيّاتِ الاقْتِصادِ الحَديثةِ أنّ ...

given name *n* اسْم أَوَّل

Giza /ˈɡiːzə/ *pr n* الجيزة

glacé /ˈɡlaseɪ/ *adj* <*fruit*> مُغَطًّى \ مُغَلَّف بالسُكَّرِ

glacier /ˈɡlasɪə/ *n* مَثْلَجة (مَثالِجُ), كُتْلة جَليدِيّة, نَهْر جَليدِيّ

glad /ɡlad/ *adj* (**gladder**, **gladdest**) سَعيد (سُعَداءُ), مَسْرور, فَرِح; **to be ~ about sth** كانَ سَعيداً بِشَيْءٍ; **I'm so ~ you came** أنا مَسْرورٌ جِدّاً بِمَجيئِكَ; **he was only too ~ to help** كانَ سَعيداً جِدّاً بِأَنْ يُقَدِّمَ المُساعَدةَ

gladden /ˈɡlad(ə)n/ *vt* (liter) أَسَرَّ, أَسْعَدَ, أَفْرَحَ <*a heart, soul*>

gladly /ˈɡladli/ *adv* <*to pay, accept*> عن طيبِ خاطِرٍ, بِكُلِّ سُرورٍ

glamorize, -ise (BrE) /ˈɡlamərʌɪz/ *vt* عظَّمَ, أَظْهَرَ في مَظْهَرٍ جَذّابٍ <*violence, a lifestyle*>

glamorous /ˈɡlam(ə)rəs/ *adj* <*film star, lifestyle, job*> مَرْموق

glamour (BrE), **glamor** (AmE) /ˈɡlamə/ *n* رَوْنَق, بَهاء

glance /ɡlɑːns/ **A** *vi* **to ~ at sth** أَلْقى نَظْرةً سَريعةً على شَيْءٍ; **I ~d over at Mary** أَلْقَيْتُ نَظْرةً على ماري

B *n* لَمْحة (لَمَحات), نَظْرة خاطِفة \ سَريعة; **to take a ~ at sth** أَلْقى نَظْرةً على شَيْءٍ; **at first ~** لأَوَّلِ وَهْلةٍ

glancing /ˈɡlɑːnsɪŋ/ *adj* <*blow, header*> غَيْر مُباشِر, عَرَضِيّ

gland /ɡland/ *n* غُدّة (غُدَد); **to have swollen ~s** عانى من تَوَرُّمٍ في الغُدَدِ

glandular fever /ɡlɑːndjʊlə ˈfiːvə/ *n* حُمّى غُدِّيّة

glans /ɡlanz/ *n* حَشَفة (حَشَفات, حِشاف), رَأْس قَضيبٍ

glare /ɡlɛː/ **A** *vi* (to stare angrily) حَمْلَقَ (i; حَمْلَقة), حَدَّقَ; **to ~ at sb** حَدَّقَ في شَخْصٍ

B *n* 1 (angry stare) حَمْلَقة, نَظْرة ساخِطة \ غاضِبة 2 (strong light) ضَوْء باهِر \ ساطِع, بَريق

glaring /ˈɡlɛːrɪŋ/ *adj* 1 (obvious) <*omission, error*> واضِح, بَيِّن 2 (dazzling) <*light*> ساطِع, باهِر, صارِخ

glass /ɡlɑːs/ **A** *n* 1 [u] (material) زُجاج; **broken ~** زُجاج مَكْسور 2 (vessel) كَأْس (mf; كُؤوس), قَدَح (أَقْداح), كوب (أَكْواب); **a ~ of wine** كَأْس من النَبيذِ 3 (**glasses** *n pl*) (spectacles) نَظّارة; **I need a new pair of ~es** أَحْتاجُ إلى نَظّارةٍ جَديدةٍ 4 (magnifying glass) عَدَسة مُكَبِّرة

B *adj* <*door, bottle*> زُجاجِيّ

glass-blowing /ˈglɑːsˌbləʊɪŋ/ *n* نَفْخ الزُجاجِ

glassy /ˈglɑːsi/ *adj* (**glassier**, **glassiest**) **1** (of glass) ‹*substance, bead*› زُجاجيّ; (resembling glass) ‹*shine, water*› كالزُجاجِ **2** (dull, lifeless) ‹*stare, expression*› جامِد

glassy-eyed /ˌglɑːsiˈʌɪd/ *adj* ‹*stare, indifference*› [بِعُيونٍ فارِغةٍ \ بارِدةٍ]

glaucoma /glɔːˈkəʊmə/ *n* جْلَوْكوما ,مِياه زَرْقاء ,زَرَق

glaze /gleɪz/ **A** *vt* **1** (to fit with glass) زَجَّجَ **2** (to coat) (Art) صَقَلَ (u; صَقْل) ‹*pottery*›; (Culin) طَلَى (i; طَلْي) ‹*a cake, vegetables*› **B** *vi* (also **glaze over**) «eyes» شَرَدَ (u; شُرود) ,زاغَ (u; زَوْغ) **C** *n* **1** (on pottery) طِلاء زُجاجيّ **2** (Culin) [سائِل لِتَلْميعِ الأَطْعِمةِ]

glazed /gleɪzd/ *adj* **1** ‹*look, eyes*› شارِد **2** ‹*window, door*› مُزَجَّج **3** ‹*pottery*› مَصْقول

glazier /ˈgleɪzɪə/ *n* مُرَكِّب زُجاجٍ

gleam /gliːm/ **A** *vi* «surface, metal» لَمَعَ (a; لَمْع); «eyes» بَرَقَ (u; بَرْق) **B** *n* (of light) لُمْعة ,وَمْضة; (of metal) بَريق; **there was a mischievous ~ in her eyes** بَرَقَتْ في عَيْنَيْها لُمعةُ خُبْثٍ

gleaming /ˈgliːmɪŋ/ *adj* ‹*metal, surface*› لامِع

glean /gliːn/ *vt* جَمَعَ (a; جَمْع) ,اسْتَقى ‹*news, information*›

glee /gliː/ *n* (joy) بَهْجة ,فَرْحة; (spiteful pleasure) شَماتة

gleeful /ˈgliːfʊl/ *adj* ‹*laughter, smile*› مَرِح (مَرْحى) ,فَرْحان (dipt; فَرْحى)

glen /glɛn/ *n* [وادٍ ضَيِّق طَويل]

glib /glɪb/ *adj* (**-bb-**) (of words) ‹*remark, answer*› مُنَمَّق; (of a speaker) ‹*salesman, politician*› لَبِق

glide /glʌɪd/ *vi* **1** «boat, skater» انْسابَ ,انْزَلَقَ **2** «bird, plane» حَوَّمَ ,حَلَّقَ

glider /ˈglʌɪdə/ *n* طائِرة شِراعيّة

gliding /ˈglʌɪdɪŋ/ *n* طَيَران شِراعيّ

glimmer /ˈglɪmə/ **A** *vi* «torches, lamps» وَمَضَ (i; وَمْض) ,بَرَقَ (u; بَرْق) ,الْتَمَعَ **B** *n* **1** (faint light) ضَوْء ,وَميض (أَضْواء) **2** (trace) بَصيص, وَميض; **a ~ of hope** وَميض أَمَلٍ

glimpse /glɪmps/ **A** *n* **1** (view) لَمْحة ,نَظْرة خاطِفة (لَمَحات); **I caught a ~ of her face** أَخَذْتُ نَظْرةً خاطِفةً إلى وَجْهِها **2** (insight) نَظْرة (نَظَرات) **B** *vt* لَمَحَ (a; لَمْح) ,أَلْقى نَظْرةً خاطِفةً على ‹*a figure, face*›

glint /glɪnt/ **A** *vi* «eyes, coins» بَرَقَ (u; بَرْق) ,تَلَأْلَأَ **B** *n* **1** (of metal, light) بَريق **2** (in one's eye) وَمْضة

glisten /ˈglɪs(ə)n/ *vi* «eyes, skin» تَلَأْلَأَ

glitch /glɪtʃ/ *n* (infml) خَلَل (خِلال) ,تَعَطُّل

glitter /ˈglɪtə/ **A** *vi* «eyes, stars» لَمَعَ (a; لَمْع) ,تَأَلَّقَ ,بَرَقَ (u; بَرْق) **B** *n* **1** (sparkle) بَريق ,لَمَعان (بَرائِقُ) **2** (superficial attractiveness) بَهْرَجة **3** (decoration) [حُلًى صَغيرة مُتَأَلِّقة]

gloat /gləʊt/ *vi* (over one's success) تَباهى; (over another's defeat) شَمِتَ (a; شَمات); **he was ~ing over his victory** كانَ يَتَباهى بِفَوْزِه

global /ˈgləʊb(ə)l/ *adj* **1** (worldwide) ‹*economy, war*› عالَميّ **2** (comprehensive) ‹*analysis, solution*› إجْماليّ ,شُموليّ

globalization, **-isation** (BrE) /gləʊbəlʌɪˈzeɪʃ(ə)n/ *n* عَوْلَمة

globally /ˈgləʊb(ə)li/ *adv* **1** ‹*famous, influential*› بِشَكْلٍ عامٍّ **2** ‹*to compete, produce, sold, produced*› عالَميًّا

global warming *n* الاحْتِباس الحَراريّ ,الاحْتِرار العالَميّ

globe /gləʊb/ *n* **1** (world) (**the globe**) الكُرة الأَرْضيّة **2** (model) كُرة أَرْضيّة

globe artichoke *n* خُرْشوف (خَراشيفُ) ,أَرْضيّ شَوْكيّ

globetrotter /ˈgləʊbtrɒtə/ *n* مُسافِر حول العالَمِ ,رَحّال

globule /ˈglɒbjuːl/ *n* كُرَيّة

glockenspiel /ˈglɒk(ə)nʃpiːl/ *n* جْلوكِنْشْبيل (آلة موسيقيّة إيقاعيّة مؤلّفة من قُضْبانٍ حَديديّةٍ مُتَدَلّيةٍ تُضْرَبُ بِمِطْرَقَتَيْنِ)

gloom /gluːm/ *n* **1** (darkness) ظُلْمة ,ظَلام (ظُلُمات) **2** (despondency) غَمّ ,كَآبة (غُموم)

gloomily /ˈgluːmɪli/ *adv* ‹*to sigh, reply*› بِحُزْنٍ ,بِكَآبةٍ

gloomy /ˈgluːmi/ *adj* (**gloomier**, **gloomiest**) **1** (dark) ‹*place*› مُظْلِم; ‹*day, weather*› مَغْموم ,كَئيب **2** (dismal) ‹*face, voice*› مُحْزِن ,كَئيب; ‹*outlook, news*› حَزين ,مُغْتَمّ ,مُكْتَئِب

glorify /ˈglɔːrɪfʌɪ/ *vt* (**glorifies**, **glorifying**, **glorified**) **1** عَظَّمَ, مَجَّدَ ‹*God*› **2** مَجَّدَ ,عَظَّمَ ‹*violence, war*›

glorious /ˈglɔːrɪəs/ *adj* **1** (beautiful) ‹*day, weather*› بَهِيّ ,رائِع **2** (illustrious) ‹*past, victory*› عَظيم ,مَجيد

glory /ˈglɔːri/ **A** *n* (*pl* **glories**) **1** (honour) جَلال ,(أَمْجاد) مَجْد **2** (splendour) بَهاء ,تَأَلُّق

B *vi* (**glories**, **glorying**, **gloried**) **to ~ in one's freedom/in war** [بَهِجَ \ افْتَخَرَ بِحُرِّيَّتِهِ \ بالحَرْبِ]

gloss /glɒs/ *n* **1** (shine) بَريق ,لَمَعان **2** (also **gloss paint**) دِهان لَمّاع

(Phrasal verb) **gloss over**: **~ over** [**sth**] غَضَّ النَظَرَ عن شَيْءٍ ‹*an issue, a flaw*›

glossary /ˈglɒs(ə)ri/ *n* (*pl* **glossaries**) مُعْجَم \ قائِمة مُصْطَلَحاتٍ

glossy /ˈglɒsi/ *adj* (**glossier**, **glossiest**) ‹*hair, paper*› لامِع; ‹*brochure, photograph*› [مَطْبوع على وَرَقٍ لامِعٍ \ صَقيلٍ]

glossy magazine *n* [مَجَلّة ذات وَرَقٍ مَصْقولٍ]

glottal stop /ˌglɒtəl ˈstɒp/ *n* (هَمَزات) هَمْزة

glottis /ˈglɒtɪs/ *n* (*pl* **glottises**) مِزْمار الحَنْجَرةِ

glove /glʌv/ *n* (قُفّازات) قُفّاز; **to put on/wear/take off your ~s** [لَبِسَ \ ارْتَدى \ نَزَعَ قُفّازاتِهِ]; **a pair of ~s** زَوْج قُفّازاتٍ

(Idiom) **to be hand in glove with sb** [كان مُتَعاوِناً \ مُتَواطِئاً مع شَخْصٍ]

glove compartment *n* دُرْج السَيّارةِ

glow /gləʊ/ **A** *vi* **1** «light, fire» تَوَهَّجَ ,تَوَقَّدَ **2** «face, skin» تَوَرَّدَ ,احْمَرَّ; **her face ~ed with pleasure** أَشْرَقَ وَجْهُها بالبَهْجةِ; **his mother ~ed with pride** ارْتَسَمَتْ على مُحَيّا والِدَتِهِ عَلاماتُ الفَخْرِ

B *n* **1** (of heat) وَهَج ,حَرارة; (of light) ضَوْء **2** (of the complexion) تَوَرُّد **3** (feeling of contentment) [بَهْجة]; **I felt a warm ~ inside** [شَعَرْتُ بِبَهْجةٍ كَبيرةٍ بداخِلي]

glower /ˈglaʊə/ *vi* حَمْلَقَ; **she ~ed at her mother** حَمْلَقَتْ بِأُمِّها

glowing /ˈgləʊɪŋ/ *adj* (complimentary) ‹*report, tribute*› [مَليء بالمَديحِ \ بالإطْراءِ]

glow-worm /ˈgləʊwɜːm/ *n* حُباحِب (n coll)

glucose /ˈgluːkəʊs/ *n* **1** (Chem) غْلوكوز **2** (Culin) سُكَّرعِنَبٍ

glue /gluː/ **A** *n* لِصاق ,(صُموغ) صَمْغ ,غِراء

B *vt* (**glues**, **glueing** or **gluing**, **glued**) **1** صَمَّغَ ,أَلْصَقَ ,غَرّى ‹*paper, wood*›; **to ~ the broken parts together** غَرّى الأَجْزاءَ المُكَسَّرةَ بَعْضَها بِبَعْضٍ **2** (infml) (to be rooted) **to be ~d to the radio/TV** [لم يَتَحَرَّكْ من أَمامِ جِهازِ الراديو \ التِلْفازِ]

glue-sniffer /ˈgluːsnɪfə/ *n* [مُدْمِن اسْتِنْشاقِ الغِراءِ]

glue-sniffing /ˈgluːsnɪfɪŋ/ *n* شَمّ \ اسْتِنْشاق الغِراءِ

glum /glʌm/ *adj* (**-mm-**) ‹*expression, look*› حَزين ,مُكْتَئِب

glut /glʌt/ *n* كَثْرة ,وَفْرة

glutton /ˈglʌt(ə)n/ *n* أَكّال ,نَهِم

gluttony /ˈglʌt(ə)ni/ *n* نَهَم

glycerine (BrE), **glycerin** (AmE) /ˈglɪs(ə)riːn, ˈglɪsərɪn/ *n* غْليسَرين

GMO /dʒiːɛmˈəʊ/ *n* = **genetically modified organism** كائِن مُعَدَّل وِراثيًّا

GMT /dʒiːɛmˈtiː/ *n* = **Greenwich Mean Time** تَوْقيت غْرينيتْش

gnarled /nɑːld/ *adj* ‹*trunk, branch*› [فيهِ عُقَدٌ]

gnash /naʃ/ *vt* **to ~ one's teeth** صَرَّ بِأَسْنانِهِ

gnat /nat/ *n* بَعوض (n coll), (نَواميسُ) ناموس

gnaw /nɔː/ **A** *vt* قَرَضَ (i; قَرْض), قَضَمَ (a-i; قَضْم), عَضَّ (a; عَضّ) ‹*a bone, wood*›

B *vi* **to ~ at a bone/one's lip** عَضَّ \ قَضَمَ عَظْمةً \ شَفَتِهِ

gnome /nəʊm/ *n* (أَقْزام) قَزَم

GNP /dʒiːɛnˈpiː/ *n* = **gross national product** ناتِج قَوْمي إجْماليّ

gnu /gnuː/ *n* (*pl* **gnu** or **gnus**) ثَيْتَل أَفْريقيّ ,نو

GNVQ /dʒiːɛnviːˈkjuː/ *n* (BrE) = **General National Vocational Qualification** [شَهادة التَأْهيلِ الوَطَنيّة العامّة]

go /gəʊ/ **A** *vi* (*3rd person present sing* **goes**, *past tense* **went**, *past participle* **gone**) **1** (to move, travel) ذَهَبَ (a; ذَهاب); **to ~ to Baghdad/Algeria** ذَهَبَ إلى بَغْدادَ \ الجَزائِرِ; **to ~ to the museum** ذَهَبَ إلى المَتْحَفِ; **to ~ to town/to the country** ذَهَبَ إلى المَدينةِ \ الريفِ; **to ~ by bus/train** ذَهَبَ بالحافِلةِ \ بالقِطارِ; **they went home** ذَهَبوا إلى البَيْتِ; **to ~ fast/slowly** ذَهَبَ بِسُرْعةٍ \ بِبُطْءٍ; **I went into the room** دَخَلْتُ إلى الغُرْفةِ **2** (for activities) ذَهَبَ (a; ذَهاب); **to ~ shopping/riding/**

swimming ذَهَبَ للتَسَوُّقِ \ لِرُكوبِ الخَيْلِ \ للسِباحةِ ;**to ~ for a walk** ذَهَبَ في رِحْلةٍ ;**to ~ on a journey** خَرَجَ لِيَتَمَشّى **3** (to attend) ذَهَبَ (a; ذَهاب); **to ~ to school/work** ذَهَبَ إلى المَدْرَسةِ \ العَمَلِ ;**to ~ to the doctor's** ذَهَبَ إلى عِيادةِ الطَبيبِ **4** (with present participles) **she went running up the stairs** صَعِدَت الدَرَجَ راكِضةً **5** (to depart) «visitors, trains» ذَهَبَ (a; ذَهاب), غادَرَ, رَحَلَ (a; رَحيل); **I must ~, I must be going** عَلَيَّ أنْ أُغادِرَ **6** (euph) (to die) رَحَلَ (a; رَحيل), ماتَ (u; مَوْت); **when I am gone** بعد أنْ أَموتَ **7** (to disappear) ضاعَ (i; ضَياع); **all his income goes on food and rent** يُنْفَقُ كُلُّ دَخْلِهِ على الأكْلِ والإيجارِ ;**our food has all gone** نَفِدَ كُلُّ طَعامِنا ;**my bike has gone!** سُرِقَتْ دَرّاجَتي ! ;**there goes my chance of winning!** ها هو حَظّي في الفَوْزِ يَذْهَبُ أَدْراجَ الرِياحِ ! **8** (to be sent, transmitted) أُرْسِلَ ;**the letters went by post** أُرْسِلَت الخِطاباتُ عن طَريقِ البَريدِ ;**the proposals will ~ before parliament** سَتُقَدَّمُ المُقْتَرَحاتُ إلى البَرْلَمانِ **9** (to become) أَصْبَحَ ;**her hair has gone white** ابْيَضَّ \ شابَ شَعْرُها ;**he suddenly went white** شَحَبَ وَجْهُهُ فَجْأةً ;**the lights went red** تَحَوَّلَت الإشارةُ إلى الضَوْءِ الأَحْمَرِ ;**to ~ mad** جُنَّ, فَقَدَ صَوابَهُ, جُنونُهُ **10** (to become) صارَ, أَصْبَحَ (i; صَيْرورة, مَصير); (to remain) ظَلَّ (a; ظُلول; perf ظَلِلْتُ), بَقِيَ (a; بَقاء); **the people went hungry** جاعَ النّاسُ ;**we went for two days with no food** قَضَيْنا يَوْمَيْنِ بِدونِ طَعامٍ ;**the question went unanswered** بَقِيَ السُؤالُ دون جَوابٍ **11** (to fail) «one's memory, hearing» ضَعُفَ (u; ضَعْف, ضُعْف); «lights» انْطَفَأَ; «brakes» تَعَطَّلَ ;**his hard disk is going** يَتَعَطَّلُ قُرْصُهُ الصُلْبُ **12** (to break, collapse, etc) «beams, pillar» انْهارَ; «cables» انْقَطَعَ **13** (to pass) مَرَّ (u; مُرور), انْقَضى ;**our visit has gone very fast** انْقَضَتْ زِيارَتُنا بِسُرْعةٍ كَبيرةٍ ;**there are ten days to ~ before the inauguration** لا تَزالُ هُناكَ عَشَرةُ أَيّامٍ قبل حَفْلِ التَنْصيبِ **14** (to be disposed of) أُسْتُغْنِيَ عَنْهُ ;**the car will have to ~** يَجِبُ التَخَلُّصُ من السَيّارةِ ;**six days down and four to ~!** مَضَتْ سِتّةُ أَيّامٍ وَبَقِيَتْ أَرْبَعةٌ ! **15** (to function) «clocks, machines» عَمِلَ (a; عَمَل), اشْتَغَلَ ;**we set the pumps going** شَغَّلْنا المِضَخّاتِ ;**how is the car going?** كيف حالُ السَيّارةِ؟; **the alarm/bell goes at seven** يَنْطَلِقُ الجَرَسُ في السابِعةِ; **to keep going** «person, business, machine» واصَلَ, تابَعَ **16** (to start) **let's get going!** هَيّا نَبْدَأْ ! ;**to get the fire going** أَشْعَلَ النارَ **17** (to lead) «corridors, doors» أَدّى (إلى); **the road goes down to the sea** يُؤَدّي الطَريقُ إلى البَحْرِ **18** (to reach) **it's true as far as it goes** هذا صَحيحٌ إلى حَدٍّ ما ;**a hundred dollars doesn't ~ far these days** المِائةُ دولار لا تَفْعَلُ الكَثيرَ هذه الأَيّامَ ;**she'll ~ far!** أمامَها مُسْتَقْبَلٌ باهِرٌ ! **19** (infml) (to belong) وُضِعَ ;**where does the filing cabinet ~?** أَيْنَ سَتوضَعُ خِزانةُ المِلَفّاتِ؟ **20** (to fit) «the sofa, piano» ناسَبَ ;**it won't ~ into the box** لن يَدْخُلَ في الصُنْدوقِ **21** (to be expressed) «poems, songs» قالَ (u; قَوْل); **how does the song ~?** ما هي كَلِماتُ الأُغْنيةِ؟ ;**as the saying goes** كَما يَقولُ المَثَلُ **22** (to be accepted) كانَ مَقْبولاً \ مُسْتَساغاً ;**anything goes** كُلُّ شَيْءٍ مُباحٌ ;**it goes without saying that ...** غَنيٌّ عن القَوْلِ أنّ ... ;**what he says goes** ما يَقولُهُ يَجِبُ أنْ يُنَفَّذَ **23** (to be about to) **he is going to do sth** سَيَفْعَلُ شَيْئاً ;**it's going to snow** سَتَتَساقَطُ الثُلوجُ ;**I was just going to phone you** كُنْتُ على وَشْكِ الاتِّصالِ بِكَ **24** (infml) (to turn out) سارَ (i; سَيْر, مَسير, مَسيرة); **how are things going?, how's it going?** كيف تَسيرُ الأُمورُ؟ ;**the meeting went very well** سارَ الاجْتِماعُ بِشَكْلٍ طَيِّبٍ جِدًّا **25** (in comparisons) قِياساً (ب); **it's very quiet, as diesel engines ~** صَوْتُ المُحَرِّكِ هادِئٌ جِدًّا, قِياساً بِمُحَرِّكاتِ الديزِل الأُخْرى **26** (in sales) بيعَ ;**tickets for the match are going cheap** تُباعُ تَذاكِرُ المُباراةِ بِسِعْرٍ رَخيصٍ ;**the house went for £150,000** بيعَ البَيْتُ بِسِعْرِ 150,000 جُنَيْهٍ **27** (to be available) **to be going** كانَ مُتَوَفِّراً ;**there are plenty of jobs going** يوجَدُ الكَثيرُ من الوَظائِفِ المُتَوَفِّرةِ **28** (to contribute) أَسْهَمَ ;**the money will ~ towards a new roof** سَيُسْهِمُ المالُ في بِناءِ سَقْفٍ جَديدٍ ;**the qualities that ~ to make a good teacher** الصِفاتُ الّتي تُسْهِمُ في خَلْقِ مُعَلِّمٍ جَيِّدٍ **29** (to be given) «the award, prize, inheritance» ذَهَبَ (a; ذَهاب); **the award went to Hassan** ذَهَبَت الجائِزةُ إلى حَسَنٍ ;**the inheritance went to the five children** ذَهَبَ الميراثُ إلى الأَطْفالِ الخَمْسةِ **30** (infml) (emphatic use) **why did he ~ and spoil it?** لِماذا ذَهَبَ يُفْسِدُ الأَمْرَ؟ **31** (to take one's turn) «competitors, players» أَخَذَ دَوْرَهُ ;**they/you ~ first/next** هُمْ \ أَنْتَ أَوَّلاً \ تالياً **32** (to be in harmony) «colours, designs» تَناسَبَ, تَناسَقَ; **the curtains don't ~ with the carpet** السَتائِرُ غَيْرُ مُتَناسِقةٍ مع السَجّادةِ [33] **to ~** [للأَكْلِ خارِجَ المَطْعَمِ]

B *vt* (*3rd person present sing* **goes**, *past tense* **went**, *past participle* **gone**) (to travel) ذَهَبَ, سافَرَ (a; ذَهاب) ‹*a distance, 50 miles*›; **are you going my way?** هل أَنْتَ ذاهِبٌ في طَرِيقِي؟

C *n* (*pl* **goes**) [1] (attempt) مُحاوَلة; **to have a ~ at sth** حاوَلَ شَيْئاً; **he did it in one ~** فَعَلَهُ دَفْعةً واحِدةً; **to give sth another ~** حاوَلَ شَيْئاً مَرّةً أُخرى [2] [u] (infml) (energy) حَيَوِيّة, عُنْفُوان; **to be full of ~** كانَ في قِمّةِ الحَيَوِيّةِ \ العُنْفُوانِ [3] (BrE) (turn) دَوْر (أَدْوار); **whose ~ is it?** دَوْرُ مَنْ (الآنَ)؟

Idioms **from the word go** من البِدايةِ; **that's the way it goes!** هذا هو الطَبيعيُّ!; **there you go!** (infml) تَفَضَّلْ!; **to have a go at sb** (infml) اِنْتَقَدَ شَخْصاً; **to make a go of sth** جَعَلَ شَيْئاً يَنْجَحُ

Phrasal verbs **go about** **A** (to carry on) سارَ (i; سَيْر, مَسِير), تَجَوَّلَ; **she goes about barefoot** تَمْشي حافِيةَ القَدَمَيْنِ **B** **~ about [sth]** [1] (to undertake) قامَ ب [شَيْءٍ] ‹*a task*›; **I don't know how to ~ about it** لا أَعْرِفُ كيف أَقومُ بِهِ [2] (to be busy with) **to ~ about one's business** اِنْشَغَلَ بِعَمَلِهِ

• **go after**: **~ after [sth/sb]** [1] (to chase) لاحَقَ [شَيْئاً \ شَخْصاً] ‹*a thief, the stolen vehicle*› [2] (to try to get) بَحَثَ عن [شَيْءٍ \ شَخْصٍ] ‹*a job, promotion*›

• **go against** **A** **~ against [sb]** (to be unfavourable to) «the vote, verdict, decision» لم يَكُنْ في صالِحِ [شَخْصٍ]; **the war is going against them** تَسيرُ الحَرْبُ في غَيْرِ صالِحِهِمْ **B** **~ against [sth]** [1] (to conflict with) خالَفَ [شَيْئاً] ‹*a rule, sb's principles*›; **these figures ~ against the trend** تَأْتي هذه الأَرْقامُ ضِدَّ الاتِّجاهِ العامِّ [2] (to disregard) سارَ على خِلافِ [شَيْءٍ] ‹*sb's wishes, advice*›

• **go ahead** [1] (to go in front) سَبَقَ (i-u; سَبْق); **they went ahead and I followed minutes later** سبقوني وَأَنا تَبِعْتُهُمْ بَعْدَها بِدَقائِقَ [2] (to take the lead) «team, runner» تَقَدَّمَ [3] (to proceed) شَرَعَ (a; شَرْع, شُروع); **they have permission to ~ ahead with the project** لَدَيْهِمْ رُخْصةٌ للبَدْءِ في المَشْروعِ

• **go along** [1] (to travel) «people, cars» سارَ (i; سَيْر) [2] (to attend) حَضَرَ (u; حُضور)

• **go along with**: **~ along with [sb/sth]** [1] (to comply with) قَبِلَ ب [شَيْءٍ] ‹*a plan, an idea*›; **I can't ~ along with that idea** لا أَسْتَطيعُ قُبولَ تِلْكَ الفِكْرةِ [2] (to accompany) رافَقَ [شَخْصاً \ شَيْئاً] ‹*a friend, consignment*›

• **go around** **A** [1] (to pay a visit) «friend, neighbours» زارَ (u; زِيارة) [2] (in the course of events) تَنَقَّلَ, تَجَوَّلَ; **she ~es around on a bicycle** تَتَنَقَّلُ بِاسْتِخْدامِ دَرّاجةٍ [3] (to circulate) «rumours, illnesses» اِنْتَشَرَ [4] (to suffice) كَفَى (i; كِفاية); **there isn't enough food to ~ around** لَيْسَ هُناكَ ما يَكْفي من الطَعامِ **B** **~ around [sth]** [1] (to travel around) تَجَوَّلَ في [شَيْءٍ] ‹*a country, district*›; **they are ~ing around the district saying that ...** يَتَجَوَّلونَ في المِنْطَقةِ قائِلينَ إنّ .... [2] (to negotiate) دارَ \ اِلْتَفَّ حول [شَيْءٍ] ‹*a corner, bend*› [3] (to visit) تَجَوَّلَ في [شَيْءٍ] ‹*a house, museum, the shops*›

• **go at** **A** **~ at [sb]** (to attack) هَجَمَ على [شَخْصٍ] ‹*an intruder, opponent*› **B** **~ at [sth]** (to tackle) اِنْكَبَّ على [شَيْءٍ] ‹*a task, job*›

• **go away** (to leave) رَحَلَ (a; رَحيل), غادَرَ, اِنْصَرَفَ; **he's ~ing away for a few days** سَيَغيبُ بِضْعةَ أَيّامٍ; **~ away!** أُغْرُبْ عن وَجْهي!; **the smell has gone away** ذَهَبَت الرائِحةُ

• **go back** [1] (to a place) عادَ (u; عَوْد, عَوْدة), رَجَعَ (i; رُجوع); **let's ~ back home** هيّا نَعودُ إلى البَيْتِ; **to ~ back to work/school** عادَ إلى العَمَلِ \ المَدْرَسةِ [2] (to turn back) تَراجَعَ; **there's no ~ing back** لا عَوْدةَ للوَراءِ [3] (in time) عادَ (u; عَوْد, عَوْدة); **this tradition ~es back centuries** يَعودُ هذا التَقْليدُ إلى قُرونٍ مَضَتْ [4] (to a previous state) عادَ (إلى); **to ~ back to sleep** عادَ إلى النَوْمِ; **we have gone back to the old system** عُدْنا إلى النِظامِ القَديمِ

• **go back on**: **~ back on [sth]** رَجَعَ في \ تَراجَعَ عن [شَيْءٍ] ‹*a promise, decision*›

• **go before** **A** (in time) مَرَّ (u; مُرور), مَضَى (i; مُضِيّ) **B** **~ before [sb/sth]** عُرِضَ على [شَخْصٍ \ شَيْءٍ] ‹*a court, judge*›; **the bill went before Parliament** عُرِضَ مَشْروعُ القانونِ على البَرْلَمانِ

• **go by** **A** «trains, people, cars» مَرَّ (u; مُرور); **my time there went by very fast** مَضى وَقْتي هُناكَ سَريعاً جِدّاً **B** **~ by [sth]** [1] (to judge by) حَكَمَ بِناءً على [شَيْءٍ]; **don't ~ by first appearances** لا تَحْكُمْ بالمَظاهِرِ الأولى [2] (to act according to) [شَيْءٍ] سارَ حَسَبَ ‹*the rules, accepted procedure*›

• **go down** [A] [1] (to set) «the sun» غَرَبَ (u; غُرْب) [2] (to earth) «aircraft» سَقَطَ (u; مَسْقَط, سُقوط); **he went down in the penalty area** سَقَطَ في مِنْطَقةِ الجَزاءِ [3] (to sink) «the ship, yacht» غَرِقَ (a; غَرَق); **she went down with all hands** غَرِقَتْ وَمَعَها الطاقِمُ [4] (to make one's way to) **to go down to a place** ذَهَبَ إلى مَكانٍ; **we went down to the square** ذَهَبْنا إلى الساحةِ [5] (to be received) **to ~ down well/badly** «sb's behaviour, remarks» قوبِلَ بِاسْتِحْسانٍ \ بامْتِعاضٍ [6] (to decline) «water level, the tide» اِنْحَسَرَ; «the temperature, prices, standards» اِنْخَفَضَ [7] (to die down) «the wind, flames» هَدَأَ (a; هُدوء, هَدْء) [8] (to deflate) «tyre, balloon» فَرَغَ من الهَواءِ; «the swelling» تَقَلَّصَ [9] (to be defeated) اِنْهَزَمَ; (to be relegated) هَبَطَ (i-u; هُبوط) [10] (in memory) «the event, sb's name» ذُكِرَ; **he will ~ down as a great statesman** سَيُذْكَرُ كَرَجُلِ دَوْلةٍ عَظيمٍ [11] (to be recorded) **to ~ down on a list/on one's record** «facts» سُجِّلَ في قائِمةٍ \ دَفْتَرِهِ [12] (to fall ill) **to ~ down with flu/malaria** أُصيبَ بالإنْفِلْوَنْزا \ بالمَلارِيا [13] «computers, the network» تَعَطَّلَ [B] **~ down [sth]** [1] (to descend) نَزَلَ من على [شَيْءٍ] ‹*a hill*› [2] (to travel, walk along) سارَ في [شَيْءٍ] ‹*a road, path*›

• **go for** [A] **~ for [sb]** (to attack physically) هاجَمَ [شَخْصاً]; (verbally) اِنْتَقَدَ [شَخْصاً] بِشِدّةٍ [B] **~ for [sth]** (to try to achieve) حاوَلَ إحْرازَ [شَيْءٍ] ‹*a record, victory*›; **~ for it!** (infml) هَيّا لا تَتَرَدَّدْ! [C] **~ for [sb/sth]** [1] (infml) (to have a liking for) فَضَّلَ اِخْتِيارَ [شَخْصٍ \ شَيْءٍ] ‹*a colour, type*› [2] (to apply to) اِنْطَبَقَ على [شَخْصٍ \ شَيْءٍ]; **and the same ~es for you** ونَفْسُ الشَيْءِ يَنْطَبِقُ عَلَيْكَ [3] (to have in one's favour) **to have sth ~ing for one** كانَ هُناكَ شَيْءٌ لِصالِحِهِ

• **go forward** (to advance) مَضى قُدُماً, تَقَدَّمَ

• **go in** [1] (to enter) دَخَلَ (u; دُخول) [2] (to attack) «the police, troops» تَدَخَّلَ [3] (to disappear) «the sun» اِخْتَفى وراءَ الغَيْمِ \ السُحُبِ

• **go in for**: **~ in for [sth]** [1] (to be keen on) أَحَبَّ [شَيْئاً] ‹*a type of film, food*› [2] (to take up) دَخَلَ مَجالَ [شَيْءٍ]; **to ~ in for teaching/politics** دَخَلَ مَجالَ التَعْليمِ \ السِياسةِ [3] (to take part in) شارَكَ في [شَيْءٍ] ‹*an exam, a competition*›

• **go into**: **~ into [sth]** [1] (as a patient) دَخَلَ [شَيْئاً] ‹*hospital*› [2] (to take up) دَخَلَ [شَيْئاً] ‹*a trade, profession*›; **she has gone into politics/business** دَخَلَتْ عالَمَ السِياسةِ \ الأَعْمالِ [3] (to examine) تَطَرَّقَ إلى [شَيْءٍ] ‹*a problem, the circumstances, reason*›; **let's not ~ into that now** دَعْنا لا نَدْخُلُ في ذلك الآنَ [4] (to be expended) «effort, time» بُذِلَ من أَجْلِ [شَيْءٍ] ‹*a job, result*›; **a lot of work went into the proposal** بُذِلَ في هذا المُقْتَرَحِ الكَثيرُ من العَمَلِ

• **go off** [A] [1] (to explode) «bomb» اِنْفَجَرَ [2] (to fire) «gun» اِنْطَلَقَ [3] «the alarm clock, fire alarm» اِنْطَلَقَ [4] (to depart) غادَرَ; **he went off to work** غادَرَ إلى العَمَلِ [5] (BrE) (to go bad) «milk, fish» فَسَدَ (i-u; فَساد) [6] (to stop working) «the heating, lights» تَوَقَّفَ عن العَمَلِ, تَعَطَّلَ [7] (to take place) «the evening, party» جَرى (i; جَرْي); **the concert went off very well** جَرى الحَفْلُ على نَحْوٍ جَيِّدٍ جِدّاً [B] **~ off [sb/sth]** (BrE) (to stop liking) **to ~ off sb/an idea** لم يَعُدْ يَميلُ إلى شَخْصٍ \ فِكْرةٍ; **I've gone off coffee** أَصْبَحْتُ أَكْرَهُ القَهْوةَ

• **go off with** [A] **~ off with [sth]** (infml) هَرَبَ ب[شَيْءٍ] ‹*sb's money*› [B] **~ off with [sb]** هَرَبَ مع [شَخْصٍ] ‹*sb's husband, daughter*›

• **go on** [A] [1] (to take place) حَدَثَ (u; حُدوث); **how long has this been ~ing on?** منذ متى وَهَذا يَحْدُثُ؟; **there's a party ~ing on upstairs** هُناكَ حَفْلةٌ (مُقامةٌ) في الطابَقِ العُلْويِّ [2] (to continue) «speakers, trains» واصَلَ, اِسْتَمَرَّ; **she went on speaking** اِسْتَمَرَّت في حَديثِها; **the list ~es on** والقائِمةُ تَطولُ; **that's enough to be ~ing on with** يَكْفي هذا الآنَ [3] (to elapse) «time, the evening» مَرَّ (u; مُرور, مَرّ), مَضى (i; مُضِيّ); **as the day went on, he relaxed a bit** مع مُضِيِّ النَهارِ, اِسْتَرْخى قَليلاً [4] (infml) (to keep talking) **to ~ on about a topic/subject** مَضى يَتَحَدَّثُ في مَوْضوعٍ; **she always ~es on and on about her problems** هي دَوْماً تَتَحَدَّثُ بِاسْتِمْرارٍ عن مَشاكِلِها [5] (to start working) «the heating, lights» أوقِدَ [6] (to be close to) **to be going on for 50/for three o'clock** دَنا من الخَمْسينَ \ اِقْتَرَبَ الوَقْتُ من الثالِثةِ [7] (to fit) كانَ على

هذه الإطاراتُ لَيْسَتْ ناسَبَ المَقاسِ; **these tyres won't ~ on** أَسْتَنَدَ في الحُكْمِ على [شَيْءٍ] على المَقاسِ **B** **~ on** [sth] ‹*a piece of evidence, information*›; **that's all we have to ~ on** ذلك كُلُّ ما لَدَيْنا لِنَسْتَنِدَ عَلَيْهِ

• **go on at**: **~ on at** [sb] (infml) أَنَّبَ \ عَنَّفَ [شَخْصاً]

• **go out** **1** (to leave) خَرَجَ, غادَرَ (u; خُروج); **to ~ out walking** خَرَجَ لِيَتَمَشّى; **to ~ out for a drink** خَرَجَ لِيَشْرَبَ **2** (in relationships) **to ~ out with sb** أَقامَ عَلاقَةً مع شَيْئاً **3** (of fashion) «clothes, styles» أَصْبَحَ موضةً قديمةً شَخْصٍ **4** (to be extinguished) «the fire, lights» انْطَفَأَ **5** (to be sent) «invitations, letters» أُرْسِلَ **6** (in broadcasting) «programmes» عُرِضَ **7** (Sport) (to be eliminated) خَرَجَ (u; خُروج) **8** (expressing sympathy) «our sympathy, thoughts» كانَ مع; **my heart ~es out to them** قَلْبي مَعَهُمْ

• **go over** **A** **1** (to walk over) ذَهَبَ (a; ذَهاب); **I went over to see if I could help** ذَهَبْتُ لِكَيْ أَرى إنْ كُنْتُ أَسْتَطيعُ تَقْديمَ العَوْنِ **2** **to ~ over badly/well** (to be received) «speech, performance» قوبِلَ بِاسْتِياءٍ \ بِاسْتِحْسانٍ **3** (to switch) تَحَوَّلَ; **to ~ over to the rebels/to a different system** تَحَوَّلَ إلى المُتَمَرِّدينَ \ نِظامٍ مُخْتَلِفٍ **B** **~ over** [sth] **1** (to revise) راجَعَ [شَيْئاً] ‹*the accounts, details, article*›; **the police went over the house** فَتَّشَت الشُّرْطةُ البَيْتَ **2** (to clean) نَظَّفَ [شَيْئاً] ‹*the carpets, a house*›; **she went over the room with a duster** نَظَّفَت الغُرْفةَ بِمِنْفَضةِ الغُبارِ **3** (to exceed) تَجاوَزَ [شَيْئاً] ‹*an amount*›; **don't ~ over £40** لا تَتَجاوَزْ 40 جُنَيْهاً

• **go round** **A** (BrE) (to turn) «wheels, propellers» دارَ (u; دَوْرٍ, دَوَران) ▸**turn around** A2 **B** **~ round** [sth] (BrE) ▸**go around** B

• **go through** **A** **1** (to be approved) «agreement, amendment, divorce» تَمَّت المُوافَقةُ عَلَيْهِ **2** (to be completed) «deals, mergers» تَمَّ (i; تَمام) **B** **~ through** [sth] **1** (to pass through) اجْتازَ [شَيْئاً] ‹*a stage, phase*›; **as you ~ through life** وَأَنْتَ تَسيرُ في رِحْلَةِ الحَياةِ **2** (to undergo) مَرَّ ب [شَيْءٍ] ‹*an experience, ordeal*›; **she's gone through a lot** قاسَت الكَثيرَ; **to ~ through a crisis** مَرَّ بِأَزْمةٍ **3** (to check, examine) فَحَصَ [شَيْئاً] ‹*a document, file, list*› **4** (to search) فَتَّشَ [شَيْئاً] ‹*sb's luggage, a drawer*› **5** (to carry out) أَكْمَلَ \ أَنْهى [شَيْئاً] ‹*a procedure*›; **to ~ through the formalities** أَنْهى الإجْراءاتِ **6** (to use up) اسْتَهْلَكَ [شَيْئاً] ‹*one's savings, money*›

goad /gəʊd/ *vt* **1** (to prod) هَمَزَ (i-u; هَمْز) ‹*an animal, a beast*› **2** (to provoke) دَفَعَ, أَثارَ (a; دَفْع) ‹*an opponent, a rival*›

go-ahead /ˈgəʊəhɛd/ *n* (infml) **to give sb/a project the ~** أَعْطى شَخْصاً \ مَشْروعاً الإِذْنَ بالبَدْءِ \ الضَوْءَ الأَخْضَرَ

goal /gəʊl/ *n* **1** (in sport) (structure) مَرْمى (مَرام); (point scored) هَدَف (أَهْداف); **they won by three ~s to two** فازوا بِثَلاثَةِ أَهْدافٍ لِهَدَفَيْنِ; **who is in ~?** مَنْ حارِسُ المَرْمى ؟ **2** (aim, objective) هَدَف, غاية (أَهْداف); **to achieve/attain/reach your ~** حَقَّقَ هَدَفَهُ

goalkeeper /ˈgəʊlkiːpə/ *n* حارِس مَرْمًى

goal kick *n* ضَرْبة مَرْمًى

goalpost /ˈgəʊlpəʊst/ *n* عارِضة مَرْمًى

(Idiom) **to move/shift the goalposts** غَيَّرَ قَوانينَ اللُّعْبةِ

goat /gəʊt/ *n* مَعْز (n coll; أَمْعُز), ماعِز (مَواعِز), عنز (عُنوز)

goatherd /ˈgəʊthəːd/ *n* راعي ماعِزٍ

gobble /ˈgɒb(ə)l/ *vt* (also **gobble down**) الْتَهَمَ ‹*a meal, food*›

(Phrasal verb) **gobble up**: **~ [sth] up, ~ up [sth]** الْتَهَمَ \ ابْتَلَعَ [شَيْئاً]; **paying for it ~d up all our savings** اسْتَهْلَكَ شِراؤُهُ كُلَّ مُدَّخَراتِنا

gobbledegook, gobbledygook /ˈgɒbəldɪˌguːk/ *n* (infml) رَطانة, هُراء

go-between /ˈgəʊbɪtwiːn/ *n* وَسيط (وُسَطاءُ)

goblet /ˈgɒblɪt/ *n* كَأْس (mf; كُؤوس), قَدَح (أَقْداح)

goblin /ˈgɒblɪn/ *n* قَزَم (قَبيح المَنْظَرِ)

gobsmacked /ˈgɒbsmakt/ *adj* (BrE infml) مَصْدوم, مُنْدَهِش

God /gɒd/ **A** *n* **1** (supreme being) الرَبّ, الله; **G~ bless you** بارَكَ اللهُ فيكَ **2** (**god**) (deity) إلَه (آلِهة), رَبّ (أَرْباب), مَعْبود **B** *excl* **G~!** يا إلَهي !

godchild /ˈgɒdtʃʌɪld/ *n* (*pl* **-children**) ابْن \ ابْنة بالمَعْموديّةِ

god-daughter /ˈgɒddɔːtə/ *n* ابْنة بالمَعْموديّةِ

goddess /ˈgɒdɪs/ *n* إلاهة

godfather /ˈgɒdfɑːðə/ *n* أَب في العِمادِ, أَب روحيّ, عَرّاب

godmother /ˈgɒdmʌðə/ *n* أُمّ في العِمادِ, أُمّ روحيّة, عَرّابة

godparent /ˈɡɒdpɛːrənt/ *n* (man) أَب في العِمادِ ,عَرّاب; (woman) أُمّ في العِمادِ ,عَرّابة; **the ~s** الأَب والأُمّ في العِمادِ

godsend /ˈɡɒdsɛnd/ *n* هِبة من السَماءِ

godson /ˈɡɒdsʌn/ *n* ابْن بالمَعْموديّةِ

goes /ɡəʊz/ *3rd pers sing pres n pl* ▸ **go**

goggle /ˈɡɒɡ(ə)l/ *vi* (infml) «spectators, crowds» حَمْلَق (i; حَمْلَقة); **to ~ at sb/sth** حَمْلَقَ في شَخْصٍ \ شَيْءٍ

goggles /ˈɡɒɡ(ə)lz/ *n pl* (for protection) نَظّارة واقِية; (against the sun) نَظّارة شَمْسيّة; (for swimming) نَظّارة سِباحةٍ; (for diving) نَظّارة غَوْصٍ; **safety ~** نَظّارة واقِية

going /ˈɡəʊɪŋ/ **A** *n* **1** (progress); **I found the book heavy ~** وَجَدْتُ الكِتابَ صَعْبَ القِراءةِ; **she finds her new job hard ~** تَجِدُ صُعوبةً في عَمَلِها الجَديدِ **2** (conditions) أَوْضاع ,ظُروف; **when the ~ gets tough** عِنْدَما تُصْبِحُ الظُروفُ صَعْبةً; **they got out while the ~ was good** رَحَلوا عِنْدَما كانَت الظُروفُ ما زالَتْ جَيِّدةً **3** (departure) مُغادَرة

B *adj* **1** (current, accepted) **the ~ rate** السِعْر السائِد **2** (functioning) **a ~ concern** شَرِكة ناجِحة

goings-on /ˌɡəʊɪŋzˈɒn/ *n pl* (infml) (events) أَحْداث ,أَعْمال; (behaviour) تَصَرُّفات

go-kart /ˈɡəʊkɑːt/ *n* سَيّارة سِباقٍ صَغيرةٍ

Golan Heights /ˌɡəʊlan ˈhʌɪts/ *pr n* مُرْتَفَعات \ هَضْبة الجَوْلان

gold /ɡəʊld/ **A** *n* **1** (metal) ذَهَب; **a necklace made of ~** قِلادة مَصْنوعة من الذَهَبِ; **18-carat ~** ذَهَب عِيار 18 قيراطٍ **2** (also **gold medal**) ميداليّة ذَهَبيّة; **to win** *or* **take ~** *or* **a ~ medal** فازَ بِميداليّةٍ ذَهَبيّةٍ **3** (colour) صَفار ذَهَبيّ

B *adj* **1** (metal) ‹chain, coin› من الذَهَبِ ,ذَهَبيّ; **a ~ watch** ساعة ذَهَبيّة **2** ‹paint, writing› ذَهَبيّ اللَوْنِ

(Idioms) **to be worth your weight in gold** كانَ يُساوي ثِقْلَهُ ذَهَباً; **to have a heart of gold** كانَ ذا قَلْبٍ أَبْيَض

gold disc, **gold record** *n* أُسْطُوانة ذَهَبيّة

gold dust *n* مَسْحوق الذَهَبِ

golden /ˈɡəʊld(ə)n/ *adj* **1** (gold-coloured) ‹hair, sand› ذَهَبيّ **2** (made of gold) من الذَهَبِ ,ذَهَبيّ **3** (happy, prosperous) ‹years, days› ذَهَبيّ **4** (excellent) **a ~ opportunity** فُرْصة ذَهَبيّة

golden age *n* عَصْر ذَهَبيّ

golden rule *n* قاعِدة ذَهَبيّة

goldfish /ˈɡəʊldfɪʃ/ *n* (*pl* **goldfish**) سَمَك ذَهَبيّ

gold leaf *n* رُقاقة ذَهَبٍ

gold medal *n* ميداليّة ذَهَبيّة

gold mine *n* مَنْجَم ذَهَبٍ

gold-plated /ˌɡəʊldˈpleɪtɪd/ *adj* ‹jewellery, taps› مَطْليّ بالذَهَبِ

gold rush *n* حُمّى الذَهَبِ

goldsmith /ˈɡəʊldsmɪθ/ *n* صائِغ (صاغة)

golf /ɡɒlf/ *n* غولف ,جولْف; **to play ~** لَعِبَ الغولْف

golf ball *n* كُرة جولْف

golf club *n* **1** (stick) مِضْرَب جولْف ,مِجار (مَياجيرُ) \ عَصا **2** (society) نادي جولْف **3** (place) نادي جولْف

golf course *n* مَلْعَب جولْف

golfer /ˈɡɒlfə/ *n* لاعِب جولْف

gone /ɡɒn/ **A** *past participle* ▸ **go**

B *adj* **1** (not present); **when she went back her briefcase was ~** عِنْدَما عادَتْ كانَتْ حَقيبَتُها قد اخْتَفَتْ; **you were ~ a long time** كُنْتَ غائِباً لِمُدّةٍ طَويلةٍ **2** (used up) نافِد ,مُسْتَهْلَك; **the money was all ~** نَفِدَ كُلُّ المالِ **3** (dead) ‹person› مَيِّت; مُتَوَفًّى ,(مَوْتى ,أَمْوات); **after I am ~** بعد مَوْتي **4** (past) مُنْتَهٍ; **those days are ~ now** وَلّى عَهْدُ هذه الأَيّامِ الآنَ

C *prep* (BrE) بَعْدَ; **it's ~ six o'clock** إنَّها بعد الساعةِ السادِسةِ

gong /ɡɒŋ/ *n* جَرَس قُرْصيّ

gonna /ˈɡɒnə/ (infml) *abbr* = **going to**

gonorrhoea (BrE), **gonorrhea** (AmE) /ˌɡɒnəˈrɪə/ *n* سَيَلان

goo /ɡuː/ *n* (infml) [مادّة لَزِجة]

good /ɡʊd/ **A** *adj* (*comparative* **better**, *superlative* **best**) **1** (of high quality) ‹car, movie, school› جَيِّد (جِياد); **you need ~ qualifications to work here** تَحْتاجُ إلى مُؤَهِّلاتٍ جَيِّدةٍ لِكَيْ تَعْمَلَ هُنا; **the soil/water supply is ~** التُرْبةُ \ إمْداداتُ الماءِ جَيِّدةٌ; **that's a ~ question/point** هذا سُؤالٌ وَجيهٌ \ هذه نُقْطةٌ جَيِّدةٌ; **an example of ~ journalism** مِثال للصَحافةِ الجَيِّدةِ; **the quality of the materials is very ~** نَوْعيّةُ المَوادِّ جَيِّدةٌ جِدّاً; **it would be a ~ idea to ...** سَتكونُ فِكْرةً جَيِّدةً أَنْ . . .; **that's ~!** ذلك جَيِّدٌ! **2** (skilled) ‹accountant, hairdresser, teacher›

أَفْضَل الكُتّاب (جِياد) جَيِّد; **the best authors alive today** الأَحْياءِ اليَوْمَ; **she's a ~ swimmer** هي سَبّاحةٌ جَيِّدةٌ; **to be ~ at physics/football** كانَ ماهِراً في الفيزياءِ \ كُرةِ القَدَمِ; **to be no ~ at chess/tennis** لم يَكُنْ جَيِّداً في الشِطْرَنْجِ \ التِنِسِ; **to be ~ with numbers/children** كانَ ماهِراً في الحِسابِ \ التَعامُلِ مع الأَطْفالِ; **to be ~ with one's hands** كانَ ماهِراً في الأَعْمالِ اليَدَوِيّةِ; **her English is ~** لُغَتُها الإنْجليزيّةُ جَيِّدةٌ **3▸** (enjoyable, positive) ‹*news, holiday, reaction*› طَيِّب, جَيِّد; **the ~ weather** الطَقْس الجَيِّد; **to have a ~ time** اِسْتَمْتَعَ بِوَقْتِهِ; **have a ~ day!** أَتَمَنّى لَكَ يَوْماً سَعيداً!; **to have a ~ holiday** اِسْتَمْتَعَ بِعُطْلَتِهِ; **it was a ~ year for apples** كانَ عاماً جَيِّداً للتُفّاحِ; **it's ~ to see you again** تُسْعِدُني رُؤْيَتُكَ من جَديدٍ; **it's a ~ thing that he's going** هو شَيْءٌ طَيِّبٌ أَنَّهُ ذاهِبٌ; **'Let's eat out' —'What a ~ idea!'** 'هَيّا نَأْكُلُ في الخارِجِ' — 'يا لَها من فِكْرةٍ جَيِّدةٍ!'; **it's too ~ to be true** [الأَمْرُ مُريبٌ] **4▸** (happy) **to feel ~ about doing sth** شَعَرَ بالسَعادةِ لِفِعْلِ شَيْءٍ; **helping them makes me feel ~** مُساعَدَتُهُمْ تَجْعَلُني أَشْعُرُ بالسَعادةِ \ بالرِضا **5▸** (above average) ‹*eyesight, spelling, memory*› جَيِّد; **to have ~ hearing** كانَ سَمْعُهُ جَيِّداً **6▸** (infml) (well, healthy) **I don't feel too ~** لا أَشْعُرُ بِأَنَّني على ما يُرامُ; **you don't look too ~** لا يوحي شَكْلُكَ بِأَنَّكَ على ما يُرامُ; **'how are you?' — 'I'm ~!'** 'كيف حالُكَ؟' — 'أنا بِخَيْرٍ!' **7▸** (accurate) ‹*description, account*› دَقيق; **the clock keeps ~ time** الساعةُ دَقيقةٌ **8▸** (prestigious) ‹*family, marriage, address*› مُحْتَرَم; **he comes from a ~ family** هو من عائِلةٍ مُحْتَرَمةٍ; **I'm not ~ enough for her** لَسْتُ جَديراً بِها **9▸** (obedient) ‹*child, dog, behaviour*› مُطيع; **~ boy!** يا لَكَ من وَلَدٍ مُؤَدَّبٍ!; **have you been a ~ girl?** هل كُنْتِ مُؤَدَّبةً؟ **10▸** (favourable) ‹*opportunity, impression, sign*› جَيِّد; **it's the best opportunity you are likely to get** هذه أَفْضَلُ فُرْصةٍ يُمْكِنُكَ أَنْ تَحْصُلَ عَلَيْها; **New York is ~ for shopping** نْيويورْك جَيِّدةٌ للتَبَضُّعِ **11▸** (attractive) ‹*teeth, figure, legs*› جَميل; **she looks ~ in blue/in that dress** تَبْدو جَميلةً في اللَوْنِ الأَزْرَقِ \ ذلك الفُسْتانِ; **the new design looks really ~** التَصْميمُ الجَديدُ جَميلٌ بِحَقٍّ **12▸** (tasty) ‹*meal, food*› لَذيذ; **this soup is ~/tastes ~** هذا الحَساءُ لَذيذٌ \ مَذاقُهُ طَيِّبٌ **13▸** (not rotten) ‹*meat, cheese*› طازَج; **are the eggs still ~?** هل لا يَزالُ البَيْضُ طازَجاً؟ **14▸** (virtuous) ‹*man, woman*› طَيِّب, صالِح; **the ~ guys** الصالِحونَ; **your father was a ~ man** كانَ أَبوكَ رَجُلاً صالِحاً; **it won't look ~** لن يَبْدو بِشَكْلٍ جَيِّدٍ; **she's a ~ influence on the other children** تُؤَثِّرُ على الأَطْفالِ الآخَرينَ تَأْثيراً طَيِّباً **15▸** (kind) ‹*person*› طَيِّب, صالِح; **a ~ deed** عَمَل صالِح; **she was very ~ to me** كانَتْ طَيِّبةً جِدًّا مَعي; **to do sb a ~ turn** أَسْدى خِدْمةً لِشَخْصٍ; **they were very ~ about the whole thing** تَعامَلوا مع المَوْضوعِ بِرُمَّتِهِ بِشَكْلٍ جَيِّدٍ جِدًّا **16▸** (upbeat) ‹*mood, humour*› مَرِح; **he's always in a ~ mood** مِزاجُهُ دائِماً جَيِّدٌ **17▸** (infml) (reliable) **~ old Richard!** صَديقُنا ريتْشارد العَزيز!; **I use ~ old beeswax** أَسْتَعْمِلُ شَمْعَ العَسَلِ الأَصيلَ **18▸** (beneficial) **to be ~ for you** «fresh air, fruit» كانَ مُفيداً لَكَ; **exercise is ~ for you** التَمْرينُ مُفيدٌ لَكَ; **fresh fruit is ~ for you** *or* **your health** الفاكِهةُ الطازَجةُ مُفيدةٌ لَكَ \ لِصِحَّتِكَ; **to be ~ for morale** كانَ لَهُ أَثَرٌ جَيِّدٌ على الروحِ المَعْنَوِيّةِ **19▸** (effective) ‹*ointment, shampoo, method*› فَعّال, جَيِّد; **these tablets are ~ for headaches** هذه الأَقْراصُ جَيِّدةٌ لِعِلاجِ الصُداعِ; **vinegar is ~ for cleaning windows** الخَلُّ جَيِّدٌ في تَنْظيفِ الشَبابيكِ **20▸** (suitable) ‹*time, place*› جَيِّد, مُناسِب; **that's a ~ example of what I mean** ذلك مِثالٌ جَيِّدٌ لِما أَعْنيهِ **21▸** (close) ‹*friend, relationship*› حَميم; **my ~ friend Ahmed** صَديقي العَزيز أَحْمَد **22▸** (serviceable) **the car is ~ for another 10,000 km** سَتَتَحَمَّلُ السَيّارةُ عَشَرةَ آلافِ كيلومِتْرٍ أُخْرى **23▸** (substantial) ‹*salary, size, length*› كَبير; **he earns a ~ salary** يَكْسِبُ راتِباً كَبيراً; **a ~ twenty years ago** منذ ما لا يَقِلُّ عن عِشْرينَ سَنةً; **we waited a ~ hour** اِنْتَظَرْنا ما لا يَقِلُّ عن ساعةٍ **24▸** (thorough) ‹*clean, beating*› كامِل, تامّ; **we had a ~ laugh/look** ضَحِكْنا كَثيراً \ أَمْعَنّا النَظَرَ

B (**as good as**) *adv phr* (virtually) كَ, مِثْل; **it's as ~ as new** هو كالجَديدِ

C (**for good**) *adv phr* للأَبَدِ

D *excl* (expressing satisfaction) حَسَناً; **'I've finished' —'G~!'** 'اِنْتَهَيْتُ' — 'حَسَناً!'; **'I've found his wallet' —'G~ for you!'** 'وَجَدْتُ مَحْفَظَتَهُ' — 'أَحْسَنْتَ!'

E *n* **1▸** (virtue) خَيْر; **the conflict between ~ and evil** الصِراع بين الخَيْرِ والشَرِّ; **to be up to no ~** (infml) كانَ مُنْشَغِلاً \

مُنْهَمِكاً بِما لا خَيْرَ فيهِ; **to do ~** قامَ بِعَمَلِ الخَيْرِ ② (benefit) مَصْلَحة, مَنْفَعة (مَنافِعُ), (مَصالِحُ); **it's for your own ~** هذا في مَصْلَحَتِكَ \ صالِحِكَ أَنْتَ; **no ~ will come of waiting** لا خَيْرَ في الانْتِظارِ; **this will do you ~** هذا سَيُفيدُكَ ③ (use) **this drill is no ~** هذا المِثْقابُ عَديمُ الفائِدةِ; **it's no ~ crying** لا فائدةَ في البُكاءِ; **what ~ would it do me?** أَيُّ خَيْرٍ سَيَجْلِبُهُ لي؟ ④ (the **good** *n pl*) الطَّيِّبونَ, الخَيِّرونَ

F (**goods**) *n pl* ① (merchandise) بَضائِع, سِلَع; **manufactured ~s** سِلَع مُصَنَّعة; **electrical ~s** سِلَع كَهْرَبائيّة; **stolen ~s** سِلَع مَسْروقة ② (BrE) (freight) شَحْنة (شِحَن), شِحْنات ③ (property) **~s and chattels** أَمْلاك مَنْقولة

Idiom **to come up with the goods, to deliver the goods** أَدّى المَطْلوبَ مِنْهُ

goodbye /gʊd'baɪ/ **A** *excl* مع السَلامةِ, وَداعاً

B *n* وَداع; **to say ~ to sb** قالَ وَداعاً لِشَخْصٍ

good-for-nothing /gʊdfə'nʌθɪŋ/ **A** *adj before n* (infml) ‹*brother, secretary*› لا فائِدةَ مِنْهُ, عَديمُ القيمةِ

B *n* (infml) [شَخْص لا فائِدةَ مِنْهُ]

Good Friday *n* الجُمْعة الحَزينة \ العَظيمة

good-humoured (BrE), **good-humored** (AmE) /ˌgʊd'hjuːməd/ *adj* ‹*discussion, joke, smile*› وِدّيّ; **she wasn't her usual ~ self** لم تَكُنْ مُبْتَهِجةً كَعادَتِها

good-looking /ˌgʊd'lʊkɪŋ/ *adj* ‹*man, woman*› حَسَن المَظْهَرِ, جَميل, وَسيم (وِسام, وُسَماءُ)

good-natured /ˌgʊd'neɪtʃəd/ *adj* ‹*person*› طَيِّب (طَيِّبون), لَطيف (لِطاف), مُتَساهِل, القَلْبِ; ‹*teasing*› وِدّيّ; ‹*smile*› بَهيج

goodness /'gʊdnəs/ **A** *n* ① (moral worth) صَلاح, خَيْر, طيبة ② (nourishment) [مُكَوِّنات مُغَذِّية]

B *excl* أَعوذُ باللهِ!, يا إِلَهي!; **my ~!, ~ me!** يا إِلَهي ▸ see also **sake, thank**

goodnight, good night /gʊd'naɪt/ *excl* لَيْلة سَعيدة, تُصْبِحُ على خَيْرٍ

goods /gʊdz/ *n pl* ① (merchandise) سِلَع; **manufactured/household ~** سِلَع مَصْنوعة \ مَنْزِلِيّة ② (possessions) مُمْتَلَكات; **stolen ~** مَسْروقات ③ (BrE) (freight) بَضائِع

goods train *n* (BrE) قِطار بَضائِعَ \ شَحْنٍ

goodwill /gʊd'wɪl/ *n* ① (kindness) حُسْن النيّةِ, لَطافة, مَوَدّة ② (of business) شُهْرة تِجاريّة

goody /'gʊdi/ (infml) **A** *n* (*pl* **goodies**) (edible treat) [شَيْء لَذيذ المَذاقِ]; (gift item) [شَيْء مَجّانيّ]

B *excl* ياه! [صَوْت للتَعْبيرِ عن الفَرْحةِ أو الحَماسِ لِشَيْءٍ]

goofy /'guːfi/ *adj* (**goofier, goofiest**) ① (infml) ‹*charm, idea*› أَبْلَه (dipt), أَحْمَق (dipt; حُمْق f حَمْقى) ② (infml) ‹*grin, smile*› [بارِز الأَسْنانِ (الأَماميّةِ)]

Google® /'guːg(ə)l/ **A** *n* جوجَل

B *vt* (**google**) [بَحَثَ في جوجَل عن] ‹*a name, person*›

goose /guːs/ *n* (*pl* **geese**) إِوَزّ (n coll)

gooseberry /'gʊzb(ə)ri/ *n* (*pl* **gooseberries**) كِشْمِش

Idiom **to play gooseberry** (BrE infml) [تَطَفَّلَ على رَفيقَيْن]

goose pimples /'guːs ˌpɪmpəlz/, **gooseflesh** /'guːsfleʃ/, **goosebumps** (AmE) *n pl* (infml) قُشَعْريرة

gopher /'gəʊfə/ *n* غوفَر (نَوْع من القَوارِضِ الأَمْريكيّةِ)

gore /gɔː/ **A** *n* دَم مُتَخَثِّر

B *vt* نَطَحَ (بِقَرْنٍ أو بِنابٍ) ‹*an animal, a predator*›

gorge /gɔːdʒ/ **A** *n* [وادٍ عَميق وَضَيِّق]

B *v refl* (**gorges, gorging, gorged**) **to ~ oneself** [أَكَلَ بِنَهَمٍ \ أَفْرَطَ في الأَكْلِ]

gorgeous /'gɔːdʒəs/ *adj* ① (very attractive) ‹*woman, man*› رائِع, فائِق الجَمالِ, فاتِن (فَواتِنُ) ② (infml) (wonderful) ‹*day, view*› رائِع, بَهيّ ③ (sumptuous) ‹*colour, dress*› جَميل جِدًّا, رائِع

gorilla /gə'rɪlə/ *n* غوريلاّ (غوريلاّت)

gorse /gɔːs/ *n* جَوْلَق, وَزّال

gory /'gɔːri/ *adj* (**gorier, goriest**) ① ‹*film, images*› دامٍ, دَمَويّ ② (covered in blood) مُلَطَّخ بالدَمِ

gosh /gɒʃ/ *excl* (infml) يا إِلَهي, واللهِ

go-slow /ˌgəʊ'sləʊ/ *n* (BrE) [احْتِجاج عن طَريقِ التَباطُؤِ في العَمَلِ]

gospel /'gɒsp(ə)l/ *n* ① (Rel_Chr) إِنْجيل (أَناجيلُ) ② also **gospel music** [نَوْع من الموسيقى المَسيحيّةِ]

gossamer /'gɒsəmə/ *n* ① [u] (liter) (cobweb) خُيوط العَنْكَبوتِ ② (fabric) [قُماش رَقيق وَخَفيف]

gossip /ˈɡɒsɪp/ **A** *n* **1** (chat) ثَرْثَرة ,دَرْدَشة ,قيل وَقال **2** [u] (rumours, speculation) إشاعة ,نَميمة (نَمائِمُ); **a piece of ~** إشاعة **3** (pej) (busybody) [شَخْص يُحِبُّ القيلَ والقالَ \ نَشْرَ الإشاعاتِ]

B *vi* (**-p-**) **1** (to chat) ثَرْثَرَ (i; ثَرْثَرة) ,دَرْدَشَ (i; دَرْدَشة) **2** (to spread tales) [نَشَرَ إشاعاتٍ \ تَحَدَّثَ بالسوءِ]

gossip column *n* [عَمود أَخْبارِ المُجْتَمَعِ في مَجَلّةٍ أو جَريدةٍ]

got /ɡɒt/ **A** *past tense, past participle* ▸ **get**

B *phr* **1** (expressing possession) **we've ~ three children** عِنْدَنا ثَلاثةُ أَوْلادٍ **2** (expressing obligation, need) **I've ~ to go now** يَجِبُ عَلَيَّ أَنْ أَذْهَبَ الآنَ

Gothic /ˈɡɒθɪk/ *adj* **1** ‹*cathedral, architecture*› قوطيّ **2** ‹*gloom, horror*› قوطيّ

gotta /ˈɡɒtə/ (infml) *abbr* **1** = **have got to** **2** = **have got a**

gotten /ˈɡɒt(ə)n/ *past participle* (AmE) ▸ **get**

gouge /ɡaʊdʒ/ *vt* حَفَرَ (i; حَفْر) ,قَوَّرَ ‹*a hole, groove*›

Phrasal verb **gouge out**: **~ out [sth], ~ [sth] out** نَحَتَ \ نَقَشَ [شَيْئاً] ‹*a pattern, chunk*›; اِقْتَلَعَ \ خَلَعَ [شَيْئاً] ‹*an eye*›

gourd /ɡʊəd/ *n* **1** (container) [قَرْعة مُجَوَّفة مُجَفَّفة] **2** (vegetable) قَرْع (n coll), يَقْطين (n coll)

gourmet /ˈɡʊəmeɪ/ *n* غورْميه ,ذَوّاق (خَبير بالطعامِ والشرابِ)

gourmet meal *n* [وَجْبة فاخِرة]

gourmet restaurant *n* [مَطْعَم يُقَدِّمُ المَأْكولاتِ الشَهيّةَ والمَشْروباتِ الفاخِرةَ]

gout /ɡaʊt/ *n* داء المَفاصِلِ ,نِقْرِس

govern /ˈɡʌv(ə)n/ **A** *vt* **1** (to rule) حَكَمَ (u; حُكْم) ,سادَ (u; سِيادة) ‹*a country, state*› **2** (to determine) (في) تَحَكَّمَ ‹*behaviour, relationships*›; حَدَّدَ ,قَرَّرَ ‹*decisions, actions*›

B *vi* «parties, presidents» حَكَمَ (u; حُكْم) ,مارَسَ سُلْطةً

governance /ˈɡʌv(ə)nəns/ *n* (fml) حُكْم (أَحْكام)

governess /ˈɡʌv(ə)nəs/ *n* (*pl* **governesses**) [مُدَرِّسة خاصّة]

governing /ˈɡʌv(ə)nɪŋ/ *adj* ‹*party, class*› حاكِم; ‹*principle, philosophy*› مُتَحَكِّم ,مُسَيْطِر ,سائِد

governing body *n* مَجْلِس إدارةٍ

government /ˈɡʌv(ə)nˌmənt/ **A** *n* + *sing or pl verb* **1** (executive) حُكومة; **the inauguration of a new ~** تَنْصيب حُكومةٍ جَديدةٍ **2** [u] (system) نِظام حُكْمٍ ,حُكومة

B *adj before n* ‹*minister, funding*› حُكوميّ

governmental /ɡʌv(ə)nˈmɛnt(ə)l/ *adj* ‹*organization, authority*› تابِع للحُكومةِ ,حُكوميّ

government stock *n* سَنَدات حُكوميّة

governor /ˈɡʌv(ə)nə/ *n* (of a state, colony) مُحافِظ ,والٍ (وُلاة), حاكِم (حُكّام); (of a school) عُضْو مَجْلِسِ الإدارةِ; (BrE) (of a prison, bank) مُدير

governorate /ˈɡʌv(ə)nərət/ *n* مُحافَظة

gown /ɡaʊn/ *n* **1** (dress) ثَوْب (ثِياب) ,فُسْتان (فَساتينُ) **2** (of a judge, academic) عَباءة (عَباء ,أَعْبِئة) **3** (surgeon's) سَكْرابْز (لِباس \ ثَوْب الجَرّاحِ)

GP /dʒiːˈpiː/ *n* = **general practitioner** طَبيب \ مُمارِس عامّ; **I made an appointment to see my ~** أَخَذْتُ مَوْعِداً مع طَبيبي

GPS /dʒiːpiːˈɛs/ *n* = **Global Positioning System** جي بي أس, نِظام تَحْديد المَواقِعِ العالَميّ

gr *abbr* = **gram(s)**, = **gramme(s)** غْرام (غْرامات)

grab /ɡrab/ **A** *vt* (**-bb-**) **1** (to seize) أَمْسَكَ ‹*sb's arm, hand*›; اِنْتَزَعَ ,أَخَذَ (u; أَخْذ) ‹*one's bag, keys*›; اِنْتَهَزَ ‹*an opportunity*›; **he ~bed me by the arm** أَمْسَكَني من ذِراعي; **she ~bed the letter off me** اِنْتَزَعَت الرِسالةَ مِنّي **2** (to take quickly) أَخَذَ (بِسُرْعةٍ); **let's ~ something to eat first** دَعْنا نَأْكُلْ شَيْئاً أَوَّلاً **3** (to attract) لَفَتَ (i; لَفْت) ,جَذَبَ (i; جَذْب) ‹*sb's attention*›; **how does that ~ you?** ما رَأْيُكَ في ذلك؟

B *vi* (**-bb-**) **to ~ at sth/sb** [حاوَلَ مَسْكَ شَيْءٍ]

C *n* مَسْك ,قَبْض ,كَبْش; **she made a ~ for the knife** حاوَلَتْ أَنْ تَمْسِكَ السِكّينَ; **he made a ~ at my throat** [اِنْقَضَّ عَلَيَّ]

grace /ɡreɪs/ (fml) **A** *n* **1** (in movement) رَشاقة **2** (in behaviour) كِياسة; **to do sth with good/bad ~** فَعَلَ شَيْئاً بِكِياسةٍ \ بِفَظاظةٍ; **to have the ~ to do sth** كانَتْ لَدَيْهِ الكِياسةُ لِفِعْلِ شَيْءٍ; **the social ~s** الآداب الاجْتِماعيّة **3** [u] (time allowance) مُهْلة (مُهَل); **they were given a month's ~** مُنِحوا مُهْلةَ شَهْرٍ **4** [u] (spiritual state) فَضْل ,نَعْمة; **to fall from ~** وَقَعَ في الخَطيئةِ **5** (prayer) صَلاة المائِدةِ; **to say ~** تَلا صَلاةَ المائِدةِ **6** (quality) **sb's saving ~** الميزة الوَحيدة لِشَخْصٍ

B *vt* **1** (to adorn) زَيَّنَ ‹*the hall, room*› **2** (to honour) شَرَّفَ ‹*the event, gala*›

graceful /ˈgreɪsfʊl/ *adj* ‹*movement, dancer*› رَشيق; ‹*style*› أنيق

gracefully /ˈgreɪsf(ə)li/ *adv* **1** (elegantly) ‹*to move, slide*› بِأَدَبٍ ,بِلَباقةٍ **2** (graciously) ‹*admit, concede*› بِرِقّةٍ ,بِرَشاقةٍ بِلَطافةٍ

gracious /ˈgreɪʃəs/ **A** *adj* **1** (generous, dignified) ‹*host, acceptance*› لَبِق ,كَيِّس ,(لِطاف) لَطيف ,(كُرَماءُ) كَريم **2** (aristocratic) ‹*smile, living*› [أَرِسْتُقْراطِيّ] **3** (merciful) ‹*God, pardon*› (رَحوم) رَحيم

B (old use) *excl* **(good** *or* **goodness) ~!** يا إلَهي! ,يا سَلامُ!

graciously /ˈgreɪʃəsli/ *adv* ‹*to accept, concede*› [بِكَرَمٍ \ بِلُطْفٍ]

grade /greɪd/ **A** *n* **1** (quality) (مَراتِبُ) مَرْتَبة ,دَرَجة; **a high-/low-~ ore** خام ذو دَرَجةٍ عالِيةٍ \ مُنْخَفِضةٍ **2** (a mark) دَرَجة, (أَقْسام) قِسْم ,(صُفوف) صَفّ **3** (AmE) (class) (عَلامات) عَلامة (NA); **Pam is in (the) second ~** بام في الصَفِّ الثاني **4** (rank) رُتْبة **5** (AmE) (gradient) ▸**gradient**

B *vt* **1** (to arrange in order) (فَرْز ;i) فَرَزَ ,صَنَّفَ ‹*produce, accommodation, meat*› **2** (to assess) صَحَّحَ ,قَيَّمَ (بِمَنْحِ عَلامةٍ تَقْديريّة) ‹*a paper, an exam*›

Idiom **to make the grade** (infml) حَقَّقَ المُسْتَوى المَطْلوبَ

grade crossing *n* (AmE) مَمَرّ سِكّةٍ حَديديّةٍ

grader /ˈgreɪdə/ **A** *n* **1** (of produce) مُصَنِّف **2** (in road-making) آلة تَمْهيد الطُرُق

B (-grader); *suffix* (AmE) **eighth/ninth-~** تِلْميذ في الصَفِّ الثامِنِ \ التاسِعِ

grade school *n* (AmE) مَدْرَسة ابْتِدائيّة

gradient /ˈgreɪdɪənt/ *n* (انْحِدارات) انْحِدار ,(مُنْحَدَرات) مُنْحَدَر

gradual /ˈgradʒʊəl/ *adj* **1** ‹*change, process*› تَدْريجيّ **2** ‹*slope*› خَفيف

gradually /ˈgradʒʊli/ *adv* ‹*to increase, improve*› شَيْئاً ,تَدْريجيّاً فَشَيْئاً; ‹*to slope*› خَفيفاً ,بالتَدْريج

graduate A /ˈgradʒʊət/ *n* **1** (from university) حامِل لِشَهادةٍ **2** (AmE) (from high school) حامِل شَهادةٍ ثانَويّةٍ خِرّيج ,جامِعيّة

B /ˈgradjʊeɪt/ *vi* **1** (from university) «students» تَخَرَّجَ **2** (AmE) (from high school) «students, teenagers» [أَكْمَلَ المَرْحَلةَ الثانَويّةَ] **3** (to progress) «children, people» انْتَقَلَ تَدْريجيّاً

graduation /gradʒʊˈeɪʃ(ə)n/ *n* (Educ) تَخْريج

graffiti /grəˈfiːti/ *n* غْرافيتي

graft /grɑːft/ **A** *n* **1** (Bot) (an instance of grafting) تَطْعيم; (shoot or twig) (طُعوم) طُعْم ,(طُعوم) طُعْم **2** (Med) (piece of tissue) (surgery) تَطْعيم ,تَرْقيع **3** (BrE) (hard work) عَمَل مُضْنٍ \ شاقّ

B *vt* طَعَّمَ ‹*a tree, plant, skin, bone*›

grain /greɪn/ *n* **1** (of rice, wheat, sand, salt) بَذْرة ,(حَبّات) حَبّة (بَذَرات); **there is a ~ of truth in what you say** هُناكَ ذَرّةٌ من الصِحّةِ فيما تَقولُ **2** [u] (commodity) حَبّ (n coll; حُبوب), (قُموح) قَمْح **3** [u] (in wood) عُروق ,تَعَرُّق

Idiom **it goes against the grain** [هو مُخالِفٌ لِطَبيعة الأُمورِ]

gram, gramme /gram/ *n* (غْرامات) غْرام

grammar /ˈgramə/ *n* (عِلْم) النَحْوِ \ قَواعِدِ اللُغةِ

grammar school *n* (BrE) جْرامَر سْكول (مَدْرَسة مُتَوَسِّطة بَريطانيّة تَخْتَصُّ بِتَدْريسِ العُلومِ الإنْسانيّةِ)

grammatical /grəˈmatɪk(ə)l/ *adj* **1** (of grammar) ‹*error, rule*› نَحْويّ **2** (correct) ‹*sentence*› صَحيح نَحْويّاً

granary /ˈgran(ə)ri/ *n* (*pl* **granaries**) مَخْزَن قَمْح

granary bread *n* خُبْز كامِل الحُبوبِ ,خُبْز أَسْمَر

grand /grand/ *adj* **1** (magnificent) ‹*building*› عَظيم ,رائِع ,كَبير; ‹*reception, dinner*› رَفيع; ‹*opening*› فَخْم **2** (distinguished) ‹*personage*› ذو مَكانةٍ عالِيةٍ ,(أَجِلّاءُ) جَليل **3** (ambitious) ‹*scale, design*› ضَخْم ,(هَوائِلُ) هائِل **4** (ostentatious) ‹*gesture, entrance*› [مُلْفِت للانْتِباهِ] **5** (overall) ‹*final, prize*› إجْماليّ; **the ~ total** المَجْموع الكُلّيّ \ الإجْماليّ **6** (infml) (excellent) رائِع ,مُمْتاز

grandad /ˈgrandad/ *n* (infml) (أَجْداد) جَدّ

Grand Canyon *pr n pl* **(the Grand Canyon)** الأُخْدود العَظيم, جْراند كانْيون

grandchild /ˈgrantʃʌɪld/ *n* (*pl* **-children**) (boy) (أَحْفاد) حَفيد; (girl) حَفيدة

granddaughter /ˈgrandɔːtə/ *n* حَفيدة

grandeur /ˈgrandʒə/ *n* رَوْعة ,عَظَمة ,فَخامة

grandfather /ˈgranfɑːðə/ *n* (أَجْداد) جَدّ

grandfather clock *n* [ساعة دَقّاقة في إطارٍ خَشَبيٍّ]

grandiose /ˈgrandɪəʊs/ *adj* **1** ‹*style, room*› مُتَكَلَّف العَظَمَةِ, مُبالَغ فيه **2** ‹*plan, scheme*› فَخْم (فِخام)

grand jury *n* (AmE) هَيْئة المُحَلَّفِينَ الكُبْرى

grandma /ˈgranmɑː/ *n* (infml) جَدّة

grandmother /ˈgranmʌðə/ *n* جَدّة

grandpa /ˈgranpɑː/ *n* (infml) جَدّ (أَجْداد)

grandparent /ˈgranpɛːrənt/ *n* (male) جَدّ (أَجْداد); (female) جَدّة; **my ~s** جَدّي وَجَدَّتي

grand piano *n* بِيانو كَبير

Grand Prix *n* (سِباق) الجائِزة الكُبْرى

grand slam *n* **1** (in tennis, golf, etc) بُطولات كُبْرى **2** (in bridge) [نَوْع من الفَوْز في لُعْبَةِ البْرِيدْج]

grandson /ˈgransʌn/ *n* حَفيد (أَحْفاد)

grandstand /ˈgranstand/ *n* مُدَرَّج (مُدَرَّجات)

granite /ˈgranɪt/ *n* جَرانيت, صَوّان

granny /ˈgrani/ *n* (*pl* **grannies**) (infml) جَدّة

granny flat *n* (infml) [شَقّة مُخَصَّصة لِشَخْصٍ عَجوزٍ]

grant /grɑːnt/ **A** *vt* **1** (fml) (to allow) مَنَحَ (a; مَنْح) ‹*permission*›; لَبّى, أَعْطى المُوافَقةَ على ‹*a request*›; **they have been ~ed permission to visit the jail** مُنِحوا الإِذْنَ لِزِيارةِ السِجْنِ; **~ed that he has a point** أُقِرُّ أَنَّ لَهُ وُجْهةَ نَظَرٍ مَعْقولةً **2** (to give) **to ~ sb sth, to ~ sth to sb** مَنَحَ شَخْصاً شَيْئاً ‹*asylum, an interview, a licence*›

B *n* مِنْحة (مِنَح); **a research ~** مِنْحة بَحْثِيّة; **to apply for a ~ to improve the property** قَدَّمَ على مِنْحةٍ لِتَحْسِينِ العَقارِ

(Idiom) **to take sb for granted** لم يولِ شَخْصاً الاهْتِمامَ الكافِيَ; **to take sth for granted** اعْتَبَرَ شَيْئاً أَمْراً مُسَلَّماً بِهِ

granule /ˈgranjuːl/ *n* ذَرّة, حُبَيْبة

grape /greɪp/ *n* عِنَب (n coll; أَعْناب)

(Idiom) **sour grapes** العِنَب الحامِض (التَظاهُر بازْدِراءِ شَيْءٍ لا يُمْكِنُ الحُصولُ عَلَيْهِ)

grapefruit /ˈgreɪpfruːt/ *n* (*pl* **grapefruit** or **grapefruits**) لَيْمون هِنْديّ, لَيْمون الجَنّةِ, زِنْباع, كْرِيفون

grapeseed oil /ˈgreɪpsiːd ɔɪl/ *n* زَيْت بِذْرِ العِنَبِ

grapevine /ˈgreɪpvʌɪn/ *n* **1** (in a vineyard) كَرْم (كُروم) **2** (infml) (source of information) [مَصْدَر تَرْوِيج الإِشاعاتِ \ المَعْلوماتِ]; **I heard it on** *or* **through the ~** حَكَتْ لي العُصْفورةُ ≈ (بَلَغَني الخَبَرُ من مَصادِرَ غَيْرِ رَسْمِيّةٍ)

graph /grɑːf/ *n* رَسْم بَيانيّ; **I plotted a ~ of all the data** قُمْتُ بِرَسْمٍ بَيانيٍّ لِكُلِّ البَياناتِ

graphic /ˈgrafɪk/ *adj* **1** (Art) ‹*art*› جْرافيكيّ (مُتَعَلِّق بِفَنِّ الرَسْمِ \ الطِباعةِ \ الكِتابةِ \ النَقْشِ); ‹*representation*› تَشْكيليّ, تَخْطيطيّ, بَيانيّ **2** (vivid) ‹*description, account*› مُفَصَّل, حَيّ; **in ~ detail** بالتَفْصيلِ الحَيِّ

graphic design *n* التَصْميم الجْرافيكيّ, فَنّ الاتِّصالاتِ البَصَرِيّةِ

graphics /ˈgrafɪks/ *n pl* **1** (also **computer graphics**) رُسوميّات حاسوبيّة **2** (illustrations) رُسوم, رُسومات

graphics card *n* (Comput) بِطاقة عَرْضٍ مَرْئيٍّ, بِطاقة رُسوميّاتٍ, كَرْت شاشةٍ

graph paper *n* وَرَق للرَسْمِ البَيانيِّ

grapple /ˈgrap(ə)l/ *vi* **to ~ with sb/sth** (to wrestle) صارَعَ شَخْصاً \ شَيْئاً ‹*a robber, an attacker*›; (to deal with) تَعامَلَ مع شَيْءٍ ‹*an issue, a problem*›; **to ~ with one's conscience** كانَ في صِراعٍ مع النَفْسِ

grasp /grɑːsp/ **A** *vt* **1** (liter) مَسَكَ (i-u; مَسْك), أَمْسَكَ ‹*a rope, sb's hand*›; **to ~ hold of sb/sth** أَمْسَكَ بِشَخْصٍ \ بِشَيْءٍ; **to ~ an opportunity** اغْتَنَمَ \ انْتَهَزَ فُرْصةً **2** (to understand) فَهِمَ (a; فَهْم), أَدْرَكَ ‹*a concept, subject, the principles*›; **he immediately ~ed the significance of the announcement** أَدْرَكَ على الفَوْرِ أَهَمِّيّةَ الإِعْلانِ

B *vi* **to ~ at sb/sth** تَشَبَّثَ بِشَخْصٍ \ بِشَيْءٍ ‹*a rope, sb's hand*›

C *n* **1** (hold) مَسْك, إِمْساك; **to take a firm ~ of sth** مَسَكَ شَيْئاً بِقوّةٍ; **success is within their ~** النَجاحُ في مُتَناوِلِ أَيْديهِمْ **2** (understanding) فَهْم (أَفْهام); **to have a good ~ of the subject** فَهِمَ المَوْضوعَ بِشَكْلٍ جَيِّدٍ

grasping /ˈgrɑːspɪŋ/ *adj* ‹*landlords, capitalists*› جَشِع, طَمّاع

grass /grɑːs/ *n* **1** [u] (pasture) (lawn) عُشْب (n coll; أَعْشاب), حَشيش, نَجيل (نُجُل) **2** (plant) عُشْب (n coll; أَعْشاب) **3** [u] (infml) (marijuana) حَشيش

grass court *n* مَلْعَب عُشْبيّ

grasshopper /ˈgrɑːshɒpə/ *n* جَراد (n coll), جُنْدُب

grassland /ˈgrɑːsland/ *n* (also **grasslands**) مَرْج ,أَرْض عُشْبيّة (مُروج)

grass roots *n pl* (**the grass roots**) القاعِدة الشَعْبيّة

grassy /ˈgrɑːsi/ *adj* (**grassier**, **grassiest**) ‹*hill, field*› عُشْبيّ, مُعْشِب

grate /greɪt/ **A** *n* [مَشْبَك حَديديّ للمَوْقِد]
B *vt* بَشَرَ (u; بَشْر) ‹*cheese, carrot*›
C *vi* **1** (to annoy) وَتَّر ,ضايَق ,أَزْعَج; **her voice ~s on my nerves** يُوَتِّر صَوْتُها أَعْصابي **2** (to rasp) صَرَّ (i; صَرّ ,صَرير), قَعْقَعَ (i; قَعْقَعة)

grateful /ˈgreɪtfʊl/ *adj* ‹*smile, recipient*› شاكِر ,مَمْنون ,مُمْتَنّ; **I'm very ~ to them for their help** أنا مُمْتَنٌّ لَهُمْ كَثيراً لِمُساعَدَتِهِمْ

grater /ˈgreɪtə/ *n* مِبْشَرة (مَباشِر)

gratify /ˈgratɪfʌɪ/ *vt* (**gratifies**, **gratifying**, **gratified**) **1** (to please) أَرْضى ,أَسَرَّ ‹*a person*› **2** (to fulfil) أَشْبَعَ ‹*a desire, need*›

grating /ˈgreɪtɪŋ/ **A** *n* حاجِز مُشَبَّك
B *adj* ‹*sound, voice*› حادّ

gratitude /ˈgratɪtjuːd/ *n* شُكْر ,عِرْفان الجَميل ,امْتِنان

gratuitous /grəˈtjuːɪtəs/ *adj* ‹*violence, insult*› من دونِ داعٍ \ مُبَرِّر, لا داعِيَ لَهُ

gratuity /grəˈtjuːɪti/ *n* إكْراميّة

grave¹ /greɪv/ *n* (tomb) قَبْر (قُبور) ,لَحْد (لُحود); **to go to an early ~** ماتَ قبل أوانِهِ

Idioms **to dig one's own grave** حَفَرَ قَبْرَهُ بِيَدِه; **to turn in one's grave** تَقَلَّبَ في قَبْرِهِ

grave² /greɪv/ *adj* (**graver**, **gravest**) **1** (serious) ‹*risk, danger, illness*› خَطير **2** (solemn) ‹*expression, manner*› جِدّيّ ,وَقور (وُقُر)

grave³ /grɑːv/ *n* (also **grave accent**) [عَلامة ` توضَعُ فوق حُروفِ العِلّةِ في بَعْضِ اللُّغاتِ لتَوْضيحِ نُطْقِها]

gravedigger /ˈgreɪvdɪgə/ *n* حَفّار قُبورٍ

gravel /ˈgrav(ə)l/ *n* حَصْباء ,حَصًى (dipt f; n coll)

gravely /ˈgreɪvli/ *adv* **1** (extremely) ‹*ill, concerned*› بِشَكْلٍ بِشِدّةٍ **2** (solemnly) ‹*to reply, nod*› بِشَكْلٍ جِدّيٍّ \ رَسْميٍّ خَطيرٍ

gravestone /ˈgreɪvstəʊn/ *n* شاهِد قَبْرٍ

graveyard /ˈgreɪvjɑːd/ *n* مَقْبَرة (مَقابِرُ) ,مَدْفِن (مَدافِنُ)

gravitate /ˈgravɪteɪt/ *vi* **to ~ towards sth** انْجَذَبَ نحو شَيْءٍ, مالَ إلى شَيْءٍ

gravitation /gravɪˈteɪʃ(ə)n/ *n* جاذِبيّة (أَرْضيّة)

gravity /ˈgravɪti/ *n* **1** (Phys) جاذِبِيّة (أَرْضيّة) **2** (fml) (of a situation) أَهَمّيّة ,خُطورة

gravy /ˈgreɪvi/ *n* صَلْصة اللَحْمِ

gravy boat *n* [إناء توضَعُ فيهِ صَلْصةُ اللَحْمِ]

gray (AmE) *n*, *adj* ▸ **grey**

grayling /ˈgreɪlɪŋ/ *n* (*pl* **grayling** or **graylings**) تيمالوس

graze /greɪz/ **A** *n* خَدْش ,كَشْط (خُدوش)
B *vt* **1** (to break the skin) خَدَشَ (i; خَدْش) ‹*a knee, an arm*› **2** (to touch) مَسَّ بِشَكْلٍ عابِرٍ ‹*a wall, tree*›
C *vi* **1** «sheep, cow» رَعى (a; رَعْي) ,رَتَعَ (a; رَتْع) **2** «people» [أَكَلَ وَجَباتٍ صَغيرةً مُتَقَطِّعةً]

grease /griːs/ **A** *n* **1** (lubricant) شَحْم **2** (Culin) دُهْن
B *vt* **1** زَيَّتَ ,شَحَّمَ ‹*the bearings, machine parts*› **2** دَهَنَ (u; دَهْن) ‹*a cake tin, dish*›

greasepaint /ˈgriːspeɪnt/ *n* [مَكْياج مُمَثّلي المَسْرَحِ]

greaseproof paper /griːspruːf ˈpeɪpə/ *n* وَرَق زُبْدةٍ

greasy /ˈgriːsi/ *adj* (**greasier**, **greasiest**) **1** ‹*fingers, overalls*› مُزَيَّت ,مُدْهِن **2** ‹*hair, skin*› دُهْنيّ **3** ‹*food*› دَسِم

great /greɪt/ **A** *adj* **1** (large) ‹*height, width, speed*› كَبير; **a ~ number of people** عَدَد كَبير من الناسِ; **there has been a ~ improvement** كانَ هُناكَ تَحَسُّنٌ كَبيرٌ; **a pay rise of 10% or $1000, whichever is ~er** زِيادة في الراتِبِ بِمِقْدارِ 10٪ أو 1000 دولار، أيُّهما أَكْبَرُ **2** (as intensifier) ‹*success, danger*› هائِل ,عَظيم ,كَبير ‹*excitement, surprise, tragedy, heat*›; **to have ~ difficulty doing sth** لاقى صُعوبةً هائِلةً في فِعْلِ شَيْءٍ; **a ~ deal of money/effort** قَدْر كَبير من المالِ \ الجُهْدِ; **a ~ many people** عَدَد هائِل من الناسِ; **in ~ detail** بِأَدَقِّ التَفاصيلِ; **the map was a ~ help** كانَتْ الخَريطةُ مُفيدةً جِدًّا; **the dangers are ~ and so are the rewards** المَخاطِرُ عَظيمةٌ وَكَذَلِكَ المُكافَآتُ **3** (outstanding) ‹*writer, artist, painting*› عَظيم (عُظَماءُ ,عِظام); **the ~est economist of our time** أَعْظَم عُلَماءِ

الاقْتِصادِ في عَصْرِنا **4** (infml) (excellent) <*book, movie, weather*> رائِع; <*opportunity*> عَظيم; **it's ~ to be back** أنا سَعيدٌ جِدًّا بِعَوْدَتي; **to feel ~** شَعَرَ بِسَعادةٍ كَبيرةٍ; **you look ~!** تَبْدو رائِعاً!; **that dress looks ~ on you** يَبْدو ذلك الفُسْتانُ رائِعاً عَلَيْكِ; **to have a ~ time** أَمْضى وَقْتاً رائِعاً; **you're the ~est!** أَنْتَ الأَعْظَمُ! **5** (infml) (talented) <*singer, team*> ماهِر (مَهَرة); **to be ~ at tennis/football** كانَ ماهِراً في التِنِس \ كُرةِ القَدَم; **to be ~ with children/animals** كانَ ماهِراً في التَعامُلِ مع الأَطْفالِ \ الحَيَواناتِ **6** (infml) (enthusiastic) <*reader*> نَهِم; <*fan*> مُتَحَمِّس

B *n* (**the great** *n pl* (powerful people)) العُظَماءُ

C *adv* (infml) (well) بِشَكْلٍ رائِع; **it's going ~** يَسيرُ بِشَكْلٍ رائِعٍ; **I'm doing ~** أنا في حالةٍ مُمْتازةٍ

great-aunt /greɪt'ɑːnt/ *n* **1** (sister of your grandfather) عَمّة الأَبِ \ الأُمِّ; (sister of your grandmother) خالة الأَبِ \ الأُمِّ **2** (wife of your grandfather's brother) زَوْجة عَمِّ الأَبِ \ الأُمِّ; (wife of your grandmother's brother) زَوْجة خالِ الأَبِ \ الأُمِّ

great big *adj* (infml) ضَخْم \ كَبير جِدًّا; **a great big house** بَيْت كَبير جِدًّا

Great Britain *pr n* بَريطانِيا العُظْمى

Great Dane *n* كَلْب جْريت داين

great-grandchild /greɪt'grantʃʌɪld/ *n* (*pl* **-children**) **1** (male) ابْن الحَفيد(ة) **2** (female) ابْنة \ بِنْت الحَفيد(ة)

great-granddaughter /greɪt'grandɔːtə/ *n* ابْنة \ بِنْت الحَفيد(ة)

great-grandfather /greɪt'granfɑːðə/ *n* أبو جَدّ الأَبِ \ الأُمِّ, الجَدِّ \ الجَدّةِ

great-grandmother /greɪt'granmʌðə/ *n* أُمّ جَدّة الأَبِ \ الأُمِّ, الجَدِّ \ الجَدّةِ

great-grandparent /greɪt'granpɛːrənt/ *n* **1** (male) أبو الجَدِّ \ الجَدّةِ **2** (female) أُمّ الجَدِّ \ الجَدّةِ

great-grandson /greɪt'gransʌn/ *n* ابْن الحَفيد(ة)

Great Lakes *pr n pl* (**the Great Lakes**) البُحَيْرات العُظْمى (بِأَمْريكا الشَماليّةِ)

greatly /'greɪtli/ *adv* <*to admire, regret*> بِدَرَجةٍ كَبيرةٍ, بِشِدّةٍ; **he was ~ influenced by ...** كانَ ل ... تَأْثيرٌ كَبيرٌ عَلَيْه; **I ~ admire his work** أنا مُعْجَبٌ كَثيراً بِعَمَلِه; **the new model has been ~ improved** تَمَّ تَحْسينُ الموديل الجَديدِ بِشَكْلٍ كَبيرٍ

greatness /'greɪtnəs/ *n* (of a novel, painting) رَوْعة; (of a country, leader, artist) عَظَمة

great-uncle /greɪt'ʌŋk(ə)l/ *n* **1** (brother of your grandfather) عَمّ الأَبِ \ الأُمِّ; (brother of your grandmother) خال الأَبِ \ الأُمِّ **2** (husband of your grandfather's sister) زَوْج عَمّةِ الأَبِ \ الأُمِّ; (husband of your grandmother's sister) زَوْج خالةِ الأَبِ \ الأُمِّ

Greece /griːs/ *pr n* اليونان (f)

greed /griːd/ *n* جَشَع, طَمَع (أَطْماع)

greedy /'griːdi/ *adj* (**greedier**, **greediest**) جَشِع, طَمّاع; **to be ~ for power/knowledge** كانَ عِنْدَهُ نَهَمٌ لِلسُلْطةِ \ لِلمَعْرِفةِ

Greek /griːk/ **A** *adj* <*government, island*> (ancient) إِغْريقيّ (إِغْريق, أَغارِقة); (modern) يونانيّ (يونانيّونَ, يونان)

B *n* **1** (ancient person) إِغْريقيّ (إِغْريق, أَغارِقة); (modern person) يونانيّ (يونانيّونَ, يونان) **2** [u] (ancient language) (اللُغة) الإغْريقيّة; (modern language) (اللُغة) اليونانيّة

green /griːn/ **A** *adj* (**greener**, **greenest**) **1** (in colour) أَخْضَر (dipt; خُضْر); **she has ~ eyes** عَيْناها خَضْراوانِ; **a ~ dress** فُسْتان أَخْضَر; **to go** *or* **turn ~** تَغَيَّرَ \ تَحَوَّلَ ,اخْضَرَّ لَوْنُهُ إلى الأَخْضَرِ **2** (with vegetation) <*countryside, spaces*> أَخْضَر (dipt; خُضْر) **3** (not ready) <*fruit, wood*> غَيْر ناضِج **4** (inexperienced) <*recruit*> عَديم الخِبْرةِ **5** (ecologically sound) <*building, design*> صَديق للبيئةِ **6** (in politics) <*policies, candidate*> مُهْتَمّ بِحِمايةِ البيئةِ

B *n* **1** (colour) (اللَوْن) الأَخْضَر; **a dark/light ~** أَخْضَر غامِق \ فاتِح; **~ is his favourite colour** لَوْنُهُ المُفَضَّلُ هو الأَخْضَرُ **2** (grassy area) مِنْطَقة خَضْراء, خُضْرة (خُضَر) **3** (in golf) نَجيل حول حُفْرةِ الجولْف] **4** (in politics) شَخْص مُهْتَمّ [بِقَضايا البيئةِ]; **the G~s** حِزْب الخُضْرِ

C (**greens**) *n pl* (vegetables) خَضْراوات خَضْراء, خُضار أَخْضَر

(Idiom) **to give sb/sth the green light** أَعْطى شَخْصاً الضَوْءَ الأَخْضَرَ

greenback /'griːnbak/ *n* (AmE infml) دولار (دولارات)

green bean *n* فاصوليا خَضْراء

green belt *n* حِزام أَخْضَر

green card *n* **1** (BrE) (for driving insurance) بِطاقة خَضْراء (وَثيقة تَأْمينٍ دُوَليّةٍ لِسائِقي السَيّاراتِ) **2** (AmE) (for work &

residence) (بِطاقة خَضْراء (بِطاقة الإقامةِ الدائِمةِ الأَمْريكيّة

greenery /ˈɡriːn(ə)ri/ *n* (خُضَر) خُضْرة

greenfly /ˈɡriːnflʌɪ/ *n* (*pl* **greenflies** or **greenfly**) قَمْل نَباتٍ, مَنّ

greengrocer /ˈɡriːnɡrəʊsə/ *n* خُضَريّ; **the ~'s** مَحَلّ الخُضَريّ

greenhouse /ˈɡriːnhaʊs/ *n* صوبة, دَفيئة

greenhouse effect *n* ظاهِرة الاحْتِباسِ الحَراريّ

greenhouse gas *n* غاز دَفيئ

Greenland /ˈɡriːnlənd/ *pr n* جْرينْلانْد (f)

green onion *n* (AmE) بَصَل أَخْضَر

green pepper *n* فِلْفِل أَخْضَر

greenstick fracture /ˈɡriːnstɪk ˌfraktʃə/ *n* شَرْخ غُصْنٍ نَضير

Greenwich Mean Time /ɡrenɪtʃ ˈmiːn tʌɪm/ *n* تَوْقيت جْرينيتْش

greet /ɡriːt/ *vt* 1 (to welcome) (ب) رَحَّبَ ‹*visitors, guests*›; (to say hello to) (على) سَلَّمَ, حَيّا ‹*a friend*› 2 (to react to) اسْتَقْبَلَ ‹*news, an announcement*› 3 (to confront) (ل) تَبَدّى, ظَهَرَ (a; ل) ظُهور); **we were ~ed by an astonishing sight** ظَهَرَ لَنا مَنْظَراً عَجيباً

greeting /ˈɡriːtɪŋ/ *n* 1 (words, gesture) (تَحايا, تَحِيّات) تَحِيّة 2 (on a card) **birthday/Christmas ~s** تَهْنِئة بِمُناسَبةِ عيد ميلادٍ \ عيدِ الميلادِ المَجيد

greetings card (BrE), **greeting card** (AmE) *n* بِطاقة تَهْنِئةٍ

gregarious /ɡrɪˈɡɛːrɪəs/ *adj* 1 ‹*personality, fellow*› اجْتِماعيّ 2 ‹*species, instinct*› اجْتِماعيّ

Grenada /ɡrəˈneɪdə/ *pr n* جْرينادا

grenade /ɡrəˈneɪd/ *n* (قَنابِل) قُنْبُلة

grew /ɡruː/ *past tense* ▸**grow**

grey (BrE), **gray** (AmE) /ɡreɪ/ A *adj* (**greyer, greyest**) 1 (in colour) ‹*eyes, sky*› رَصاصيّ, رَماديّ; **a ~ hair** شَعْرة شائِبة \ بَيْضاء 2 (grey-haired) (شيب, شُيّاب) شائِب; **his hair was going ~** شابَ (شَعْرُهُ) 3 (dull) ‹*day, weather*› غائِم, رَماديّ
B *n* رَصاصيّ, رَماديّ

grey area *n* (unclear) أَمْر غَيْر واضِحٍ \ مُحَدَّدٍ; (transitional) ما بين شَيْئَيْنِ

grey-haired /ˈɡreɪhɛːd/ *adj* ‹*man, woman*› (شيب, شُيّاب) شائِب

greyhound /ˈɡreɪhaʊnd/ *n* سَلوقيّ (كَلْب صَيْدٍ)

greyhound racing *n* سِباق السَلوقيّ

grey squirrel *n* سِنْجاب رَماديّ

grid /ɡrɪd/ *n* 1 (of lines) شَبَكة 2 (of bars) (مَعْدِنيّة) شَبَكة 3 (of streets) شَبَكة 4 (BrE) (for electricity) شَبَكة كَهْرَباءٍ; **the national ~** شَبَكة الكَهْرَباءِ القَوْميّة 5 (in motor racing) خَطّ البِدايةِ

griddle /ˈɡrɪd(ə)l/ *n* (for meat) شَوّاية; (for pancakes, buns) صاج

gridiron /ˈɡrɪdʌɪən/ *n* 1 (cooking grill) شَبَكة شِواءٍ 2 (AmE) (football field) [مَلْعَب كُرةِ القَدَمِ الأَمْريكيّةِ]

gridlock /ˈɡrɪdlɒk/ *n* 1 (of traffic) تَوَقُّف حَرَكةِ المُرور, ازْدِحام \ تَكَدُّس مُروريّ 2 (deadlock) طَريق مَسْدود

grid reference *n* إحْداثيّات (في خَريطةٍ)

grief /ɡriːf/ *n* (أَحْزان) حُزْن, أَسًى

Idiom **to come to grief** (to fail) فَشِلَ (a; فَشَل); (to crash) اصْطَدَمَ

grief-stricken /ˈɡriːfstrɪk(ə)n/ *adj* ‹*relatives, family*› في حالةٍ من الأَسى الشَديدِ

grievance /ˈɡriːv(ə)ns/ *n* 1 (cause for complaint) شَكْوى (f; شَكاوى); **to air one's ~s** رَفَعَ شَكْواهُ, اشْتَكى 2 (official complaint) (تَظَلُّمات) تَظَلُّم

grieve /ɡriːv/ A *vt* 1 (to distress) حَزَّنَ, أَحْزَنَ ‹*a person*› 2 (to mourn) (على) حَدَّ (i; حِداد) ‹*a death, loss*›
B *vi* «mourners, the bereaved» (على) حَزِنَ (a; حُزْن); **he is grieving for his father** يَحْزَنُ على مَوْتِ أَبيهِ

grievous /ˈɡriːvəs/ *adj* (fml) ‹*loss, disappointment*› أَليم; ‹*mistake*› خَطير; ‹*damage*› بالِغ

grievous bodily harm *n* أَضْرار جَسَديّة بالِغة

grill /ɡrɪl/ A *n* شَوّاية
B *vt* 1 (BrE) (i; شَيّ) شَوى ‹*meat, fish*› 2 (infml) (to interrogate) اسْتَجْوَبَ ‹*a suspect, witness*›

grille /ɡrɪl/ *n* شَبَكة

grim /ɡrɪm/ *adj* (**-mm-**) 1 (depressing) ‹*news, reality*› مُحْبِط; **things were looking pretty ~** بَدَت الأُمورُ مُحْبِطةً 2 (forbidding) ‹*building, town*› مُحْبِط 3 (unsmiling) ‹*face*› (صَوارِمُ) صارِم 4 (unrelenting) ‹*determination*› صارِم

grimace /ˈgrɪməs/ **A** *n* تَكْشيرة

B *vi* كَشَّرَ

grime /grʌɪm/ *n* قَذارة

grimy /ˈgrʌɪmi/ *adj* (**grimier, grimiest**) ‹*window, hands*› مُتَّسِخ; ‹*city, streets*› قَذِر

grin /grɪn/ **A** *vi* (**-nn-**) اِبْتَسَمَ; **they ~ned at each other** اِبْتَسَما لِبَعْضِهِما اِبْتِسامةً عَريضةً

B *n* اِبْتِسامة عَريضة

Idiom **to grin and bear it** [تَحَمَّلَ الشِّدَّةَ دون شَكْوَى]

grind /grʌɪnd/ **A** *vt* (*past tense, past participle* **ground**) 1▸ (to crush) طَحَنَ (a; طَحْن) ‹*coffee beans, the pepper, corn*›; (AmE) فَرَمَ (i; فَرْم) ‹*meat*›; **to ~ sth to dust** طَحَنَ شَيْئاً طَحْناً ناعِماً; **to ~ one's teeth** صَرَّ أَسْنانَهُ 2▸ (to sharpen) شَحَذَ (a; شَحْذ) ‹*a knife*›; سَنَّ (u; سَنّ) ‹*blade*› 3▸ (to press) أَطْفَأَ, أَخْمَدَ ‹*a cigarette*›

B *vi* (*past tense, past participle* **ground**) 1▸ (to make harsh sound) «machines» [أَحْدَثَ صَوْتَ احْتِكاكٍ]; **to ~ to a halt** «trains, machines» تَوَقَّفَ عن الحَرَكةِ; **production ground to a halt as soon as the news came out** تَوَقَّفَ الانْتاجُ بِمُجَرَّدِ أَنْ ظَهَرَتِ الأَخْبارُ 2▸ (AmE infml) «students» ذاكَرَ بِجِدٍّ

C *n* 1▸ [u] (infml) (hard work) كَدْح; **the daily ~** أَعْباء الحَياةِ اليَوْمِيّة; **it'll be a hard ~** سَيَكونُ هذا عَمَلاً شاقّاً 2▸ (AmE infml) (hardworking student) [طالِب كادِح]

Phrasal verbs **grind down**: **~ [sb] down** «poverty, hardship» أَثْقَلَ كاهِلَ [شَخْصٍ]; **to be ground down by poverty/illness** طَحَنَهُ الفَقْرُ \ المَرَضُ

• **grind on** «speakers, negotiations, projects» اِسْتَمَرَّ بِصُعوبةٍ

• **grind out**: **~ out [sth]**, **~ [sth] out** 1▸ (to extinguish) أَخْمَدَ [شَيْئاً] ‹*a cigarette*› 2▸ (infml) (to produce) أَنْجَزَ [شَيْئاً] بِصُعوبةٍ ‹*a novel*›; حَقَّقَ [شَيْئاً] بِشِقِّ الأَنْفُسِ ‹*victory*›

• **grind up**: **~ up [sth]**, **~ [sth] up** (to crush) طَحَنَ [شَيْئاً] ‹*stone, corn*›

grinder /ˈgrʌɪndə/ *n* مِطْحَنة (مَطاحِنُ); **a coffee ~** مِطْحَنة بُنٍّ

grindstone /ˈgrʌɪndstəʊn/ *n* حَجَر الشَّحْذِ

Idiom **to keep one's nose to the grindstone** اِنْكَبَّ على العَمَلِ

grip /grɪp/ **A** *vt* (**-pp-**) 1▸ (to take hold of) قَبَضَ, أَمْسَكَ (i; قَبْض) 2▸ «panic, war» اِسْتَحْوَذَ (على) ‹*a country, city*› 3▸ (to enthral) جَذَبَ \ شَدَّ الانْتِباهَ ‹*an audience*›; **I was ~ped from the start** كُنْتُ مَشْدودَ الانْتِباهِ من البِدايةِ

B *n* 1▸ (hold) مَسْكة, قَبْضة (قَبَضات); **I kept a firm ~ on the rope** ظَلِلْتُ مُمْسِكاً الحَبْلَ بِقُوَّةٍ; **to tighten/loosen one's ~** قَوّى \ فَكَّ قَبْضَتَهُ 2▸ (way of holding) قَبْضة, مَسْكة (قَبَضات); **your ~ is wrong** مَسْكَتُكَ غَيْرُ صَحيحةٍ 3▸ (control) قَبْضة (قَبَضات); **the country is in the ~ of an economic crisis** البَلَدُ في قَبْضةِ أَزْمةٍ ماليّةٍ; **to come to ~s with a problem** تَعامَلَ مع مُشْكِلةٍ; **get a ~ on yourself!** سَيْطِرْ على نَفْسِكَ! 4▸ (of tyres) قَبْضة (قَبَضات)

gripe /grʌɪp/ **A** *vi* (infml) **to ~ about sth** تَذَمَّرَ من شَيْءٍ

B *n* (infml) (complaint) شَكْوى (f; شَكاوى)

gripping /ˈgrɪpɪŋ/ *adj* ‹*story, thriller*› مُثير

grisly /ˈgrɪzli/ *adj* (**grislier, grisliest**) ‹*murder, scene*› مُرَوِّع

gristle /ˈgrɪs(ə)l/ *n* غُضْروف (غَضاريفُ)

grit /grɪt/ **A** *n* 1▸ (stone) حَصًى (n coll); (sand) رَمْل (رِمال); (dust) تُراب (أَتْرِبة, تِرْبان) 2▸ (courage, resolve) شَجاعة, جُرْأة

B *vt* (**-tt-**) رَشَّ بالمِلْحِ ‹*a road*›

Idiom **to grit one's teeth** (to clench) صَرَّ على أَسْنانِهِ; (to be resolute) [صَمَدَ في وَجْهِ الصُّعوباتِ]

gritty /ˈgrɪti/ *adj* (**grittier, grittiest**) 1▸ (sandy) مُتْرِب, رَمْلِيّ; (gravelly) بِهِ حَصًى 2▸ (realistic, tough) ‹*personality*› صارِم (صَوارِمُ); ‹*novel, realism*› قاسٍ 3▸ (courageous) ‹*fighter, player*› شُجاع (شُجْعان)

grizzly /ˈgrɪzli/ *n* (*pl* **grizzlies**) (also **grizzly bear**) دُبّ أَشْهَب

groan /grəʊn/ **A** *vi* 1▸ أَنَّ, تَأَوَّهَ (i; أَنين, تَأْنان) 2▸ (to grumble) تَذَمَّرَ 3▸ (to creak) «timbers, metal» صَرَّ (i; صَرّ, صَرير)

B *n* 1▸ (of pain) أَنين; (of dismay) هَمْهَمة (هَمْهَمات, هَماهِمُ) 2▸ (complaint) تَذَمُّر (تَذَمُّرات)

grocer /ˈgrəʊsə/ *n* بَقّال (بَقّالونَ, بَقّالة); **the ~'s** (مَحَلّ) البِقالة

groceries /ˈgrəʊsərɪz/ *n pl* مُنْتَجات البِقالةِ

grocery /ˈgrəʊs(ə)ri/ *n* (also **grocery shop** BrE) (مَحَلّ) بِقالة

groggy /ˈgrɒgi/ *adj* (**groggier, groggiest**) (infml) ‹*person, voice*› دائِخ

groin /grɔɪn/ *n* مَغْبَن, أُرْبِيّة

grommet /ˈgrɒmɪt/ *n* 1 (eyelet) حَلْقة (حَلَقات, حَلَق) 2 (Med) أُنْبوب طَبْلَةِ الأُذُنِ

groom /gruːm/ A *vt* 1 (ب) اعْتَنى ‹*a horse, a dog*› 2 (to make neat) صَفَّفَ ‹*one's hair*› 3 (to prepare) دَرَّبَ, أَعَدَّ ‹*players, candidates*›; **he was ~ed for stardom from a young age** تَمَّ إعْدادُهُ للنُجوميّةِ من صِغَرِهِ
B *n* 1 (bridegroom) (**the groom**) العَريس 2 (for horses) سائِس (ساسة, سوّاس, سُيّاس)

groove /gruːv/ *n* أُخْدود (أَخاديدُ)

grope /grəʊp/ A *vt* 1 (to fumble for) تَلَمَّسَ; **he ~d his way to the door** تَلَمَّسَ طَريقَهُ إلى البابِ 2 (infml) (sexually) لامَسَ ‹*a woman*›
B *vi* تَحَسَّسَ; **to ~ for sth** تَحَسَّسَ بَحْثاً عن شَيْءٍ

gross /grəʊs/ A *adj* 1 ‹*income, profit*› إجْماليّ 2 ‹*injustice, exaggeration*› كَبير, عَظيم, فاضِح 3 ‹*behaviour, language*› فَظّ (أَفْظاظ) 4 (infml) (revolting) فَظيع (فُظَعاءُ) 5 (infml) (obese) ‹*creature, person*› بَدين (بُدُن, بُدْن), ضَخْم (ضِخام)
B *vt* «businesses, films» حَقَّقَ (رِبْحاً) إجْماليًّا
C *n* 1 (*pl* **gross**) (144) اثْنَتا عَشْرَةَ دَسْتةً \ دَزّينةً 2 (*pl* **grosses**) (amount) إجْماليّ (إجْماليّات)

gross domestic product *n* ناتِج مَحَلّيّ إجْماليّ

grossly /ˈgrəʊsli/ *adv* ‹*unfair, exaggerated*› بِدَرَجةٍ كَبيرةٍ; ‹*to underestimate, misrepresent*› بِشَكْلٍ فاضِحٍ

gross national product *n* ناتِج قَوْميّ إجْماليّ

grotesque /grəʊˈtɛsk/ *adj* ‹*caricature, figure*› مُشَوَّه

grotto /ˈgrɒtəʊ/ *n* (*pl* **grottos** or **grottoes**) مَغارة (مَغارات, مَغاوِرُ)

grotty /ˈgrɒti/ *adj* (**grottier**, **grottiest**) (infml) ‹*hotel, bedsit*› [ذو جَوْدةٍ مُنْخَفِضةٍ]

ground /graʊnd/ A *n* 1 [u] (earth's surface) أَرْض (f); **to throw sth on the ~** رَمى شَيْئاً على الأَرْضِ; **to sit on the ~** جَلَسَ على الأَرْضِ; **the plane got off the ~** أَقْلَعَت الطائِرةُ; **below ~** تحت الأَرْضِ; **to prepare the ~** مَهَّدَ, هَيَّأَ الأَرْضيّةَ 2 [u] (area) مساحة; **to cover a lot of ~** اجْتازَ مَسافةً كَبيرةً; **to meet on neutral ~** الْتَقوا على أَرْضٍ مُحايِدةٍ 3 [u] (subject) مَوْضوع; **to go over the same ~** تَحَدَّثَ عن نَفْسِ المَوْضوعِ; **to break fresh** *or* **new ~** فَتَحَ آفاقاً جَديدةً; **to be on dangerous ~** كانَ في وَضْعٍ حَسّاسٍ 4 (Sport) مَلْعَب (مَلاعِبُ), مَبْعَث (مَباعِثُ) 5 (reason) سَبَب (أَسْباب), داعٍ (دَواعٍ), ساحة 6 (in contests, discussions) **to gain ~ on sb** تَقَدَّمَ على شَخْصٍ; **to lose ~ to sb** مُنِيَ بِخَسارةٍ أمام شَخْصٍ; **to make up lost ~** عَوَّضَ خَسارةً; **to give ~ to sb** قَدَّمَ تَنازُلاتٍ لِشَخْصٍ; **to hold** *or* **stand one's ~** أَصَرَّ على مَوْقِفِهِ; **to shift one's ~** غَيَّرَ مَوْقِفَهُ 7 (AmE Elec) أَرَّضَ, وَصَّلَ بالأَرْضِ
B (**grounds**) *n pl* 1 (of a house, school, hospital) [الأَرْض أو الحَديقة المُحيطة بِبِنايةٍ] 2 (reasons) أُسُس, أَسْباب, دَواعٍ; **valid ~s for divorce** أُسُس سَليمة للطَلاقِ; **to have ~s for complaint** لَدَيْهِ دَواعٍ \ أَسْبابٌ للشَكْوى; **there are no ~s to believe it is true** لا يوجَدُ ما يَدْعو للاعْتِقادِ بِصِحَّتِهِ; **the plan was rejected on the ~s of cost** رُفِضَت الخُطّةُ بِسَبَبِ ارْتِفاعِ التَكاليفِ
C *past tense, past participle* ▸ **grind** A, B
D (**ground**) *adj* ‹*coffee, pepper*› مَطْحون
E *vt* 1 ‹*a flight, aircraft, pilot*› مَنَعَ من الإقْلاعِ 2 (Naut) أَبْحَرَ إلى الشاطِئِ ‹*a ship*›; **to be ~ed** عَلِقَ 3 (to base) **to ~ sth on** *or* **in sth** بَنى شَيْئاً على شَيْءٍ; **a well-~ed suspicion** شُبْهة مَبْنيّة على أُسُسٍ قَويّةٍ 4 (infml) (not let out) مَنَعَ من الخُروجِ ‹*a teenager, pupil*› 5 (AmE Elec) أَرَّضَ, وَصَّلَ بالأَرْضِ

(Idioms) **to be thin on the ground** كانَ نادِراً; **to go to ground** «foxes, suspects» اخْتَفى عن الأَنْظارِ; **to run sth into the ground** ‹*a car, an engine*› أَهْلَكَ شَيْئاً بِكَثْرةِ التَشْغيلِ; **to suit sb down to the ground** ناسَبَ شَخْصاً تَماماً

ground beef, **ground meat** *n* (AmE) لَحْم مَفْروم

ground cloth *n* (AmE) ▸ **groundsheet**

ground control *n* مَحَطّة التَحَكُّمِ الأَرْضيّة

ground floor *n* دَوْر أَرْضيّ

groundhog /ˈgraʊndhɒg/ *n* (AmE) جُرَذ الأَرْضِ

grounding /ˈgraʊndɪŋ/ *n* عِلْم أَساسيّ \ أَوَّليّ; **a ~ in maths is essential** من الضَروريّ مَعْرِفةُ أَساسيّاتِ الرِياضيّاتِ

groundless /ˈgraʊndləs/ *adj* ‹*accusation, fear*› لا أَساسَ لَهُ

ground level *n* مُسْتَوى الأَرْضِ

groundnut /ˈgraʊndnʌt/ *n* فول سودانيّ

groundnut oil *n* زَيْت الفولِ السودانيِّ

ground rules *n* قَواعِد أَساسيّة

groundsheet /ˈgraʊndʃiːt/ (BrE), **ground cloth** (AmE) *n* [أَرْضيّة خَيْمةٍ]

ground staff *n* (BrE) **1** (at sports grounds, parks, etc) [عُمّال مُوَظَّفو المَطارِ (at an airport) **2** يَعْتَنون بالمَلاعِبِ والحَدائِقِ]

ground-to-air /graʊndtuːˈɛː/ *adj before n* ‹*missile*› أَرْض جَوّ

ground troops *n* قوّات بَرّيّة

groundwork /ˈgraʊndwəːk/ *n* أَعْمال تَمْهيديّة \ تَحْضيريّة

ground zero *n* **1** (in nuclear explosions) أَرْض الصِفْرِ **2** (in New York) جْراوْنْد زيرو (مَوْقِع بُرْجَيْ مَرْكَزِ التِجارة العالَميِّ المُنْهارَيْنِ (في نيويورْك))

group /gruːp/ **A** *n* **1** مَجْموعة; **in ~s** في مَجْموعاتٍ; **a community/women's ~** مَجْموعة مُجْتَمَعٍ \ نِساءٍ **2** (Mus) (فِرَق) فِرْقة **3** (of companies) مَجْموعة

B *vt* (to gather) جَمَّعَ; (to categorize) صَنَّفَ ‹*students, buildings*›

C *vi* جَمَعَ (a; جَمْع); **to ~ together** جَمَعَ سَويّةً

group discussion *n* مُناقَشة جَماعيّة

grouper /ˈgruːpə/ *n* (**grouper** or **groupers**) هامور

grouping /ˈgruːpɪŋ/ *n* تَجَمُّع (تَجَمُّعات)

group work *n* عَمَل جَماعيّ

grouse /graʊs/ *n* (*pl* **grouse**) طَيْهوج

grout /graʊt/ **A** *n* مِلاط (مُلُط)

B *vt* [وَضَعَ المِلاطَ في] ‹*the tiles, joints*›

grove /grəʊv/ *n* [غابة صَغيرة]; **an olive ~** [غابة زَيْتونٍ صَغيرة]

grovel /ˈgrɒv(ə)l/ **A** *vi* (**-ll-** BrE, **-l-** AmE) **1** (to act obsequiously) تَذَلَّلَ **2** (to prostrate oneself) انْبَطَحَ

B (BrE, **grovelling** AmE, **groveling**) *adj* ‹*apology*› مُهين

grow /grəʊ/ **A** *vt* (*past tense* **grew**; *past participle* **grown**) **1** (to cultivate) زَرَعَ (a; زَرْع) ‹*vegetables, a crop*› **2** (to make larger/longer) أَطْلَقَ ‹*your hair, a beard, your nails*›; **the plants ~ 5 cm per day** تَنْمو النَباتاتُ 5 سَنْتِمِتْراتٍ في اليَوْمِ; **the economy has grown 2%** نَما الاقْتِصادُ 2٪ **3** (to develop) نَمّى ‹*the business, sales*›

B *vi* (*past tense* **grew**; *past participle* **grown**) **1** (to get larger) «children, plants, tumour» نَما (u; نُموّ); **to let one's hair/nails ~** تَرَكَ شَعْرَهُ يَنْمو \ أَظافِرَهُ تَنْمو; **it ~s to a height of 4 metres** يَنْمو إلى ارْتِفاعِ 4 أَمْتارٍ **2** (to increase) «population, spending, crime» ازْدادَ; **fears are ~ing that ...** تَزْدادُ المَخاوِفُ من أنّ ...; **unemployment has ~n to an all-time high** ازْدادَت البِطالةُ بِشَكْلٍ غَيْرِ مَسْبوقٍ; **to ~ in popularity** ازْدادَتْ \ نَمَتْ شَعْبيَّتُهُ **3** (to become) أَصْبَحَ ‹*hotter, more powerful, stronger*›; **to ~ old** كَبِرَ في العُمْرِ; **to ~ more and more impatient** فَقَدَ صَبْرَهُ أَكْثَرَ فَأَكْثَرَ **4** **to ~ to like sb/fear sth** أَصْبَحَ يُحِبُّ شَخْصاً \ يَخافُ من شَيْءٍ

(Phrasal verbs) **grow apart** (to become more distant) «family, friends» تَباعَدَ

• **grow into**: **~ into [sth]** **1** (to become) صارَ [شَيْئاً] ‹*a frog, an adult*› **2** (to fit into) كَبِرَ حتّى صارَ [شَيْءٌ] على مَقاسِهِ ‹*a suit, a pair of shoes*› **3** (to take on) صارَ جَديراً ب [شَيْءٍ] ‹*a role, position*›

• **grow out of**: **~ out of [sth]** **1** (to get too big for) كَبِرَ على [شَيْءٍ] ‹*a suit, pair of shoes*› **2** (to get too old for) كَبِرَ على [شَيْءٍ] ‹*one's toys*›

• **grow up** **1** (in childhood) «children» كَبِرَ (a; كِبَر), تَرَعْرَعَ; **when she ~s up, she wants to be a ...** عِنْدَما تَكْبُرُ، تُريدُ أنْ تُصْبِحَ ... **2** (to get bigger) «cities, industries» نَما (u; نُموّ), اتَّسَعَ

grower /ˈgrəʊə/ *n* مُزارِع

growing /ˈgrəʊɪŋ/ *adj* **1** ‹*child, economy*› نامٍ **2** (increasing) ‹*number, demand*› مُتَزايِد **3** (germinating) ‹*plant, stem*› نامٍ

growing pains *n* **1** (for a child) آلام النُموِّ **2** (for a business) آلام النُموِّ

growl /graʊl/ **A** *vi* «dog» هَرَّ (i; هَرير); «person» دَمْدَمَ (i; دَمْدَمة)

B *n* دَمْدَمة, هَرير

grown /grəʊn/ **A** *past participle* ▸ **grow**

B *adj* **he's a ~ man** هو رَجُلٌ بالِغٌ; **when the young are fully ~** عِنْدَما تَكْبُرُ الصِغارُ تَماماً

grown-up **A** /ˌgrəʊnˈʌp/ *adj* **1** (adult) ‹*son, daughter*› كَبير (كِبار), راشِد **2** (mature) ‹*conversation, discussion*› ناضِج

B /ˈgrəʊnʌp/ *n* كَبير (كِبار)

growth /grəʊθ/ *n* **1** (of humans, plants, animals) نُموّ **2** (in numbers) ازْدِياد (ازْدِيادات); **the ~ in the number of students**

ازْدِياد عَدَدِ الطُلاّبِ; **the rate of population ~** مُعَدَّل النُموِّ السُكّانيِّ 3 (economic) نُموّ; **the ~ of demand** نُموّ الطَلَبِ 4 (what has grown) نُموّ 5 (tumour) وَرَم (أَوْرام)

growth industry *n* صِناعة واعِدة

growth rate *n* مُعَدَّل النُموِّ

grub /grʌb/ *n* 1 (insect larva) يَرَقة 2 (infml) (food) طَعام (أَطْعِمة), أَكْل; **~'s up!** الأَكْلُ جاهِزٌ!

Phrasal verb **grub up**: ~ [sth] up, ~ up [sth] «bird» نَقَّبَ عن [شَيْءٍ] ‹a worm›; «machine» حَفَرَ [شَيْئاً] ‹a hedge›

grubby /'grʌbi/ *adj* (**grubbier**, **grubbiest**) ‹hands, clothes› مُتَّسِخ

grudge /grʌdʒ/ **A** *n* ضَغينة (ضَغائِنُ); **to bear sb a ~** حَمَلَ ضَغينةً لِشَخْصٍ

B *vt* 1 (to give unwillingly) اِسْتَخْسَرَ ‹money, time› 2 (to resent) حَسَدَ (u; حَسَد); **I don't ~ him his success** لا أَحْسُدُهُ على نَجاحِهِ

grudgingly /'grʌdʒɪŋli/ *adv* ‹to admit, agree› غَصْباً عَنْهُ

gruelling (BrE), **grueling** (AmE) /'grʊəlɪŋ/ *adj* ‹schedule, day› مُرْهِق

gruesome /'gru:s(ə)m/ *adj* ‹murder, discovery› شَنيع, بَشِع

gruff /grʌf/ *adj* (**gruffer**, **gruffest**) 1 ‹voice› أَجَشّ (dipt), غَليظ (غِلاظ) 2 ‹manner, reply› فَظّ (أَفْظاظ), غَليظ, خَشِن

grumble /'grʌmb(ə)l/ *vi* تَذَمَّرَ; **she's always grumbling about her job** دائِماً تَتَذَمَّرُ من عَمَلِها

grumpy /'grʌmpi/ *adj* (**grumpier**, **grumpiest**) ‹person› شَكِس (شُكْس); ‹face, voice› نَكِد (أَنْكاد), غاضِب

grunge /grʌndʒ/ *n* 1 (infml) (grime) وَساخة 2 (Mus) الجْرانْج (نَوْع من موسيقى الروك)

grunt /grʌnt/ **A** *vi* «pig» قَبَعَ (a; قُباع, قَبْع); «person» نَخَرَ (i-u; نَخير, نَخْر)

B *n* «animal» قُباع; «person» نَخير

GSM *abbr* = **Global System (or Standard) for Mobile** جي إس إم (النِظام العالَميّ للاتِّصالاتِ المُتَنَقِّلة)

G-string /'dʒi:strɪŋ/ *n* (garment) جي سْترينْج (سِرْوال داخِليّ رَفيع بِدونِ تَغْطِيةٍ خَلْفيّة)

guacamole /ˌgwakə'məʊleɪ, ˌgwakə'məʊli/ *n* جُواكامولي (سَلَطة بالأَفوكادو المَهْروسِ)

guarantee /garən'ti:/ **A** *n* 1 (for goods) ضَمان; **to be under ~** (BrE) كانَ مَشْمولاً بالضَمانِ; **all products have a two-year ~ against defective workmanship** هُناكَ ضَمانُ سَنَتَيْنِ على كُلِّ البَضائِعِ ضدّ عُيوبِ الصِناعةِ 2 (assurance) ضَمان; **a university education is no ~ of success in later life** لا يَضْمنُ التَعْليمُ الجامِعيُّ النَجاحَ في الحَياةِ فيما بَعْدُ 3 (for debts) (also **guaranty** /'gærənti/) كَفيل (كُفَلاءُ)

B *vt* 1 ضَمِنَ (a; ضَمان) ‹a product, the quality›; **it's ~d for five years** عَلَيْهِ ضَمانٌ لِمُدّةِ خَمْسِ سَنَواتٍ 2 (to assure) ضَمِنَ (a; ضَمان) ‹delivery, a result›; **to ~ to deliver sth** ضَمِنَ تَسْليمَ شَيْءٍ; **it's a ~d bestseller** من المَضْمونِ أنْ يَكونَ الأَكْثَرَ مَبيعاً 3 ضَمِنَ (a; ضَمان) ‹a loan, payment, debt›

guarantor /ˌgarən'tɔ:/ *n* ضامِن, كَفيل (كُفَلاءُ); **to stand ~ for sb/sth** ضَمِنَ شَخْصاً \ شَيْئاً

guaranty /'garənti/ *n* ▸ **guarantee** A3

guard /gɑ:d/ **A** *vt* 1 (to protect) حَرَسَ (u; حَرْس, حِراسة) ‹a place, a person› 2 (to prevent escape) حَرَسَ (u; حَرْس, حِراسة) ‹a hostage, prisoner› 3 (to keep secret) صانَ (u; صَوْن) ‹a secret›; حَمى (السِرِّيّة) ‹source›

B *n* 1 (for a place, an object, at prison) حارِس, حَرَس (حُرّاس); **to be on ~** تَوَلّى الحِراسةَ 2 (group) حَرَس (n coll; singul n حارِس) 3 (on machines) غِطاء واقٍ

Idiom **the old guard** (infml) الحَرَسُ القَديم

Phrasal verb **guard against**: ~ against [sth] اِحْتَرَسَ من [شَيْءٍ] ‹abuse, failure›

guard dog *n* كَلْب حِراسةٍ

guarded /'gɑ:dɪd/ *adj* ‹optimism› حَذِر; ‹response, welcome› مُتَحَفِّظ

guardian /'gɑ:dɪən/ *n* 1 (defender) حامٍ 2 (of a child) وَصيّ (أَوْصِياءُ)

guardian angel *n* مَلاك حارِس

guard of honour *n* حَرَس شَرَفٍ

guard rail *n* (of staircase) دَرابْزين (دَرابْزينات); (of road) حاجِز (حَواجِزُ)

guard's van *n* (BrE) [عَرَبة حارِسِ القِطارِ]

Guatemala /ˌgwɑːtəˈmɑːlə/ *pr n* غواتيمالا

Guatemalan /gwɑːtəˈmɑːlən/ *n, adj* غواتيماليّ

Guernsey /ˈgəːnzi/ *pr n* جيرْنْزي (f)

guerrilla /gəˈrɪlə/ *n* فِدائيّ ,مُقاتِل \ مُحارِب في حَرْبِ العِصاباتِ

guerrilla war *n* حَرْب عِصاباتٍ

guess /gɛs/ **A** *vt* **1** خَمَّنَ *<the answer, reason, sb's name>*; **see if you can ~ her age** أُنْظُرْ إنْ كُنْتَ تَسْتَطيعُ تَخْمينَ عُمْرِها; **you'll never ~ what has happened!** لن تُخَمِّنَ أبداً ما حَدَثَ!; **I ~ed as much!** هذا ما تَوَقَّعْتُهُ!; **~ what! I won first prize!** لن تُصَدِّقَ! رَبِحْتُ الجائِزَةَ الأولى! **2** (to suppose) ظَنَّ ,افْتَرَضَ (u; ظَنّ); تَصَوَّرَ; **I ~ you're tired** أَظُنُّ أنّكَ مُتْعَبٌ; **'is he right?' — 'I ~ so'** هل هو مُحِقٌّ؟' — 'أَظُنُّ ذلك'; **I ~ not** لا أَظُنُّ ذلك
B *vi* خَمَّنَ; **to ~ at their plans/the result** خَمَّنَ خِطَطَهُمْ \ النَتيجةَ; **you ~ed right/wrong** كانَ تَخْمينُكَ صَحيحاً \ خاطِئاً
C *n* تَخْمين (تَخْمينات); **to have** *or* **take a ~ at sth** خَمَّنَ شَيْئاً; **you can have three ~es!** لَكَ ثَلاثُ تَخْميناتٍ!; **that was a good ~!** كانَ ذلك تَخْميناً جَيِّداً!; **to make a wild ~** أَعْطى تَخْميناً عَشْوائِيًّا; **your ~ is as good as mine** لَيْسَ لَدَيَّ أَدْنى فِكْرةٍ; **it's anybody's ~!** لا أَحَدَ يَعْرِفُ!

guesswork /ˈgɛswəːk/ *n* تَخْمين (تَخْمينات)

guest /gɛst/ *n* **1** (in one's home) ضَيْف (ضُيوف); **we have ~s** لَدَيْنا ضُيوفٌ **2** (at a hotel) نَزيل (نُزَلاءُ) **3** (on a talk show) ضَيْف (ضُيوف)

(Idiom) **be my guest!** تَفَضَّلْ!

guest house /ˈgest haʊs/ *n* (BrE) بَيْت ضِيافةٍ

guest list *n* قائِمة ضُيوفٍ

guest room *n* غُرْفة ضُيوفٍ

guest speaker *n* ضَيْف مُتَحَدِّث

guest star *n* ضَيْف شَرَفٍ

guest worker *n* عامِل ضَيْف (عامِل مُؤَقَّت)

guffaw /gəˈfɔː/ **A** *n* قَهْقَهة
B *vi* قَهْقَهَ (i; قَهْقَهة)

Guiana /gʌɪˈanə/ *pr n* غِيانا

guidance /ˈgʌɪd(ə)ns/ *n* قِيادة, تَوْجيه ,إرْشاد; **under the ~ of an expert/a professional** تحت قِيادة خَبيرٍ \ مُحْتَرِفٍ

guide /gʌɪd/ **A** *n* **1** (on a tour) (visit) دَليل, مُرْشِد (أَدِلّاءُ); **our tour ~** مُرْشِد رِحْلَتِنا **2** (indication) مُؤَشِّر (مُؤَشِّرات), دَليل (دَلائِلُ); **as a rough ~** كَتَقْديرٍ تَقْريبيٍّ **3** (book) دَليل (أَدِلّة); **this week's TV ~** دَليل التِلِفِزْيونِ لِهَذا الأُسْبوعِ; **a ~ to Greece** دَليل سِياحيّ لليونان; **the user ~** دَليل المُسْتَخْدِمِ **4** (also **Girl Guide**) (BrE) ▸ **Girl Guide**
B *vt* **1** (to direct) أَرْشَدَ *<a person, vehicle>* **2** (to influence) وَجَّهَ *<a person, sb's actions>*; **I'll be ~d by you** أَنْتَ مَنْ سَيُوَجِّهُني **3** وَجَّهَ *<a rocket, missile>*

guidebook /ˈgʌɪdbʊk/ *n* دَليل (سِياحيّ)

guided missile /ˌgʌɪdɪd ˈmɪsʌɪl/ *n* صاروخ مُوَجَّه

guide dog *n* كَلْب مُرافَقةِ المَكْفوفينَ

guided tour /ˌgʌɪdɪd ˈtɔː/ *n* جَوْلة مع مُرْشِدٍ سِياحيٍّ

guideline /ˈgʌɪdlʌɪn/ *n* إرْشاد (إرْشادات)

guild /gɪld/ *n* نقابة

guile /gʌɪl/ *n* مَكْر

guillemot /ˈgɪlɪmɒt/ *n* غَلْموت

guillotine /ˈgɪlətiːn/ *n* مِقْصَلة ,مَقاصِلُ (مِقْصَلات)

guilt /gɪlt/ *n* **1** (for a crime) جُرْم ,أَجْرام (جُروم) **2** (feeling of blame) ذَنْب (ذُنوب)

guilt-ridden *adj* *<face, assistant>* شاعِر بالذَنْبِ

guilty /ˈgɪlti/ *adj* (**guiltier, guiltiest**) **1** (to blame) *<party, person>* مُذْنِب; **she was found ~ as charged** وَجَدَتْها المَحْكَمةُ مُذْنِبةً; **he's ~ of fraud** هو مُذْنِبٌ بالاحْتِيالِ **2** (ashamed) *<person>* شاعِر بالذَنْبِ **3** (shameful) *<secret, pleasure>* [يُسَبِّبُ الشُعورَ بالذَنْبِ]

guinea /ˈgɪni/ *n* (BrE) جُنَيْه (جُنَيْهات)

Guinea /ˈgɪni/ *pr n* غينيا

Guinea-Bissau /ˌgɪnɪbɪˈsaʊ/ *pr n* غينيا بيساو

guinea fowl, guinea hen *n* غِرْغِر ,دَجاج حَبَشيّ (n coll)

guinea pig *n* **1** (mammal) خِنْزير غينيا **2** (in an experiment) حَقْل تَجارِبَ; **to be a guinea pig** كانَ حَقْلَ تَجارِبَ

guise /gʌɪz/ *n* شَكْل ,مَظْهَر (أَشْكال ,مَظاهِرُ); **under the ~ of friendship** تحت قِناعِ الصَداقةِ; **in many different ~s** بِأَشْكالٍ مُخْتَلِفةٍ

guitar /gɪˈtɑː/ *n* قيثارة (قَياثيرُ), جيتار

guitarist /gɪˈtɑːrɪst/ *n* عازِف جيتار

gulch /gʌltʃ/ *n* (AmE) مَجْرى جَدْوَلٍ مائيٍّ, وَهْدة (وُهَد, وِهاد)

gulf /gʌlf/ *n* 1 (area of sea) خَليج (خُلْجان); **the Gulf** الخَليج
2 (difference) فَجْوة (فَجَوات, فِجاء)

Gulf States *pr n pl* (**the Gulf States**) دُوَل الخَليجِ

Gulf War *n* 1 (between Iraq and Iran) حَرْب الخَليجِ (الأولى)
2 (between Iraq and UN coalition: 1991) حَرْب الخَليجِ (الثانية) 3 (between Iraq and US-led coalition: 2003) حَرْب العِراقِ

gull /gʌl/ *n* نَوْرَس (نَوارِسُ)

gullet /ˈgʌlɪt/ *n* مَريء (أَمْرِئة, مُرُوء)

gullible /ˈgʌlɪb(ə)l/ *adj* ‹*tourists, customers*› ساذَج (سُذَّج)

gully /ˈgʌli/ *n* (*pl* **gullies**) 1 (ravine) وَهْدة (وُهَد, وِهاد)
2 (channel) مَصْرَف مِياهٍ

gulp /gʌlp/ **A** *vt* (also **gulp down**) اِزْدَرَدَ ‹*food, drink*›; اسْتَنْشَقَ بِسُرْعةٍ \ بِعُمْقٍ ‹*air*›
B *vi* ابْتَلَعَ ريقَهُ بِصُعوبةٍ
C *n* 1 (swallowing movement) بَلْع 2 (of liquid) جُرْعة (جُرَع, جُرُعات); (of air) نَفَس (أَنْفاس), رَشْفة; **in one ~** جُرْعةً واحِدةً

gum /gʌm/ *n* 1 (in the mouth) لِثة (لِثات, لِثًى) 2 (also **chewing gum**) لُبان, عِلْك (عُلوك, أَعْلاك) 3 (adhesive) صَمْغ (صُموغ) 4 (resin) صَمْغ (صُموغ), راتينَج

gumboil /ˈgʌmbɔɪl/ *n* خُرّاج لِثَويّ

gun /gʌn/ *n* 1 (pistol) مُسَدَّس (مُسَدَّسات), سِلاح ناريّ
2 (shotgun, rifle) بُنْدُقيّة (بَنادِقُ) 3 (cannon) مِدْفَع (مَدافِعُ)

Idiom **to jump the gun** (infml) اسْتَعْجَلَ

Phrasal verb **gun down**: **~ [sb] down, ~ down [sb]** أَطْلَقَ النارَ على [شَخْصٍ] ‹*civilians, bystanders*›

gun dog *n* كَلْب صَيْدٍ

gunfight /ˈgʌnfaɪt/ *n* مَعْرَكة بالرَصاصِ

gunfire /ˈgʌnfaɪə/ *n* إطْلاق النارِ

gunman /ˈgʌnmən/ *n* (*pl* **-men**) مُسَلَّح

gunner /ˈgʌnə/ *n* (BrE) مِدْفَعيّ

gunpoint /ˈgʌnpɔɪnt/ *n* **at ~** تحت تَهْديدِ السِلاحِ

gunpowder /ˈgʌnpaʊdə/ *n* بارود

gunrunning /ˈgʌnrʌnɪŋ/ *n* تَهْريب السِلاحِ

gunship /ˈgʌnʃɪp/ *n* مِرْوَحيّة حَرْبيّة

gunshot /ˈgʌnʃɒt/ *n* طَلْقة ناريّة

gunshot wound *n* جُرْح بِطَلْقٍ ناريٍّ

gunsmith /ˈgʌnsmɪθ/ *n* صانِع أَسْلِحةٍ (ناريّةٍ)

gurgle /ˈgəːg(ə)l/ **A** *vi* غَرْغَرَ (i; غَرْغَرة)
B *n* غَرْغَرة

guru /ˈgʊruː/ *n* (spiritual teacher) غورو; (expert) خَبير (خُبَراءُ)

gush /gʌʃ/ *vi* «blood, water» تَدَفَّقَ

gushing /ˈgʌʃɪŋ/, **gushy** /ˈgʌʃi/ *adj* (pej) ‹*letter, style*› مُتَدَفِّق الشُعورِ \ العاطِفةِ

gusset /ˈgʌsɪt/ *n* [وُصْلة قُماشٍ مُثَلَّثة لِتَوْسيعِ الثَوْبِ]

gust /gʌst/ *n* هَبّة

gusto /ˈgʌstəʊ/ *n* حَماس; **with ~** ‹*to play, sing*› بِحَماسٍ; ‹*to eat*› بِشَهيّة

gusty /ˈgʌsti/ *adj* (**gustier, gustiest**) ‹*day, conditions*› عاصِف

gut /gʌt/ **A** *n* مِعًى (أَمْعاء, أَمْعِية)
B *adj* ‹*feeling, reaction*› داخِليّ
C *vt* (**-tt-**) 1 أَخْرَجَ الأَحْشاءَ ‹*a fish*› 2 حَطَّمَ ‹*a building, room*›

Idiom **to hate sb's guts** (infml) كَرِهَ شَخْصاً بِشِدّةٍ

guts /gʌts/ **A** *n pl* (entrails) أَحْشاء
B *n sing* (infml) (courage) شَجاعة, جَراءة

gutsy /ˈgʌtsi/ *adj* (**gutsier, gutsiest**) (infml) ‹*performance*› شُجاع (شُجْعان, شَجَعة); ‹*effort*› جَريء (أَجْرِياءُ, جُرَآءُ)

gutter /ˈgʌtə/ *n* (on a roof) مِزْراب (مَزاريبُ); (in the street) مَجْرى صَرْفِ مِياهِ الأَمْطارِ

gutter press *n* (**the gutter press**) الصِحافة الصَفْراء

guttural /ˈgʌt(ə)rəl/ *adj* ‹*accent*› جافّ, صَعْب; ‹*sound*› حَلْقيّ, أَجَشّ (dipt)

guy /gaɪ/ *n* (infml) 1 رَجُل (رِجال), شَخْص (أَشْخاص; mf), شابّ (شَباب, شُبّان) 2 (**guys** *n pl*) شَباب; **I'll see you ~s tonight** أَراكُم اللَيْلةَ يا شَباب; **the good/bad ~s** (in films) الشَخْصيّات الطَيِّبة \ الشِرّيرة

Guyana /gaɪˈanə/ *pr n* غويانا

Guyanese /ˌgaɪəˈniːz/ *n, adj* غويانيّ

Guy Fawkes Night /gʌɪ 'fɔːks nʌɪt/ *n* (BrE) لَيْلَة جاي فوكْس

(احْتِفال سَنَويّ يَتِمُّ في الخامِسِ من نوفِمْبِر في المَمْلَكَةِ المُتَّحِدةِ احْتِفالاً بِفَشَلِ مُؤامَرة البارودِ في عامِ 1605 الّتي اشْتَرَكَ فيها جاي فوكْس لِتَدْمِيرِ المَلِكِ والبَرْلَمان)

guzzle /'gʌz(ə)l/ *vt* (infml) الْتَهَمَ, ازْدَرَدَ

gym /dʒɪm/ *n* 1 = **gymnasium** جِمْنازيوم, صالة رِياضةٍ

2 = **gymnastics** جُمْباز

gymkhana /dʒɪm'kɑːnə/ *n* مُنافَسة فُروسيّةٍ

gymnasium /dʒɪm'neɪzɪəm/ *n* (*pl* **gymnasiums** or **gymnasia**) جِمْنازيوم, صالة رِياضةٍ

gymnast /'dʒɪmnast/ *n* لاعِب جُمْبازٍ

gymnastics /dʒɪm'nastɪks/ *n pl* جُمْباز

gym shoe *n* حِذاء رِياضيّ

gynaecological (BrE), **gynecological** (AmE) /gʌinəkə'lɒdʒɪk(ə)l/ *adj* ‹procedure, disorder› أَمْراضِ النِساءِ

gynaecologist (BrE), **gynecologist** (AmE) /gʌɪnə'kɒlədʒɪst/ *n* طَبيب أَمْراضِ النِساءِ

gynaecology (BrE), **gynecology** (AmE) /ˌgʌɪnɪ'kɒlədʒi/ *n* عِلْم أَمْراضِ النِساءِ

gypsy /'dʒɪpsi/ *n* (*pl* **gypsies**) غَجَريّ (غَجَر)

gyrate /dʒʌɪ'rəɪt/ *vi* «dancers, kites» دارَ (u; دَوْر, دَوَران)

Hh

H, **h** /eɪtʃ/ *n* هاء ≈ (الحَرْف الثامِن من الأَبْجَدِيّةِ الإنْكْليزِيّةِ); **to drop one's '~'s** (BrE) [أَسْقَطَ حَرْفَ الهاءِ من لَفْظِهِ]

ha /hɑː/ **A** *abbr* = **hectare(s)** هِكْتار (هِكْتارات)

B *excl* **1** (to express triumph, scorn) أَها **2** '**~!~!**' (indicating laughter) 'ها ها!'

habeas corpus /ˌheɪbɪəs ˈkɔːpəs/ *n* [حَقّ المُثولِ أمام القَضاءِ (لِيُنْظَرَ في مَسْأَلَةِ الحَبْسِ)]

haberdashery /ˈhabədaʃ(ə)ri/ *n* (*pl* **haberdasheries**) **1** (BrE) (in a department store) مَحَلّ لَوازِمِ الخِياطَةِ **2** (BrE) (goods) لَوازِم الخِياطَةِ **3** (AmE) (clothes) مَلابِس رِجالِيّة

habit /ˈhabɪt/ *n* **1** (usual piece of behaviour) عادة (عادات، عَوائِدُ); **to get into the ~ of doing sth** تَعَوَّدَ على فِعْلِ شَيْءٍ; **to get out of the ~ of doing sth** تَخَلّى عن عادةِ فِعْلِ شَيْءٍ; **we shop there out of ~** نَتَسَوَّقُ هُناكَ بِحُكْمِ العادةِ **2** (addiction) إدْمان **3** (of a monk, nun) [رِداء الراهِبِ]

habitable /ˈhabɪtəb(ə)l/ *adj* ‹*room, accommodation*› صالِح لِلسَّكَنِ

habitat /ˈhabɪtat/ *n* بيئة طَبيعيّة، مَوْطِن (مَواطِنُ)

habitation /habɪˈteɪʃ(ə)n/ *n* (fml) سُكْنى، سَكَن (f); **unfit for human ~** غَيْر صالِحٍ لِسَكَنِ الإنْسانِ

habit-forming /ˈhabɪtfɔːmɪŋ/ *adj* ‹*drug, activity*› مُؤَدٍّ للإدْمانِ

habitual /həˈbɪtʃʊəl/ *adj* **1** (usual) ‹*behaviour, residence*› عاديّ، اعْتِياديّ **2** (persistent) ‹*liar, smoker*› مُزْمِن

habitual offender *n* مُجْرِم مُعْتاد

hack /hak/ **A** *vt* **1** (to chop) ‹*branches, a carcass*› قَطَّعَ بِضَرَباتٍ مُتَتالِيةٍ; **to ~ sth/sb to pieces** قَطَّعَ شَيْئاً \ شَخْصاً إِرْباً إِرْباً; **the victims were ~ed to death with machetes** تَلَقّى الضَحايا ضَرَباتٍ قاتِلةً بِسَكاكينَ طَوِيلةٍ; **to ~ one's way through the undergrowth** شَقَّ لِنَفْسِهِ طَريقاً بِقَطْعِ الشُجَيْراتِ **2** (to gain access to) ‹*a system, computer, voicemail*› اخْتَرَقَ **3** (infml) (to cope with) **he couldn't ~ it** لم يُحْسِن التَعامُلَ مع الوَضْعِ

B *vi* **1** **to ~ at sth/sb** ضَرَبَ شَيْئاً \ شَخْصاً ضَرَباتٍ مُتَتالِيةً **2** (to gain access) **to ~ into a system/computer** اخْتَرَقَ نِظاماً \ حاسوباً

C *n* (pej) **1** (journalist) [صَحَفيّ لا يوثَقُ بِهِ] **2** (writer) [كاتِب يَبْتَذِلُ في كِتاباتِهِ] **3** (also **party hack**) (politician) [سِياسيّ لا قيمةَ لَهُ في حِزْبِهِ]

Phrasal verbs **hack down**: **~ down [sth/sb]**, **~ [sth/sb] down** ‹*a tree, victim*› [وَجَّهَ ضَرَباتٍ مُتَتالِيةً لِ [شَيْءٍ \ شَخْصٍ] حتّى طَرَحَهُ أَرْضاً]

• **hack off**: **~ off [sth]**, **~ [sth] off** ‹*a branch, limb*› قَطَعَ [شَيْئاً] بِضَرَباتٍ مُتَتالِيةٍ

hacker /ˈhakə/ *n* (also **computer hacker**) قُرْصان حاسوبٍ

hacking /ˈhakɪŋ/ **A** *n* قَرْصَنة إلِكْتْرونيّة

B *adj* ‹*cough*› [مُتَقَطِّع وجافّ]

hackles /ˈhak(ə)lz/ *n pl* [شَعْر ظَهْرِ حَيَوانٍ (يَنْتَصِبُ عند الخَوْفِ \ الغَضَبِ)]; **to make sb's ~ rise** اسْتَفَزَّ شَخْصاً

hackney cab /hakni ˈkab/ *n* تاكْسي، سَيّارة أُجْرةٍ

hackneyed /ˈhaknɪd/ *adj* ‹*expression, idea*› مُبْتَذَل

hacksaw /ˈhaksɔː/ *n* مِنْشار مَعادِنَ، مِفْراص

had /had, həd/ *past tense, past participle* ▸ **have**

haddock /ˈhadək/ *n* (*pl* **haddocks** or **haddock**) حَدوق; **smoked ~** سَمَك حَدوق مُدَخَّن

Hadith /haˈdiːθ/ *n* حَديث (أَحاديثُ)

hadn't /ˈhad(ə)nt/ *abbr* = **had not** ▸ **have**

haematologist (BrE), **hematologist** (AmE) /hiːməˈtɒlədʒɪst/ *n* أَخِصّائيّ أَمْراضِ الدَمِ

haemoglobin (BrE), **hemoglobin** (AmE) /hiːməˈgləʊbɪn/ *n* خِضاب الدَمِ ,هيموجْلوبين

haemophilia (BrE), **hemophilia** (AmE) /ˌhiːməˈfɪlɪə/ *n* ناعور ,هيموفِيليا (نَواعيرُ)

haemophiliac (BrE), **hemophiliac** (AmE) /ˌhiːməˈfɪlɪak/ **A** *n* مَريض الهيموفيِليا

B *adj* <patient, sufferer> الهيموفيليا

haemorrhage (BrE), **hemorrhage** (AmE) /ˈhɛmərɪdʒ/ **A** *n* نَزيف

B *vi* نَزَفَ (i; نَزْف)

haemorrhoids (BrE), **hemorrhoids** (AmE) /ˈhɛmərɔɪdz/ *n pl* بَواسير

hafiz /ˈhɑːfɪz/ *n* حافظ (حَفَظَة ,حُفّاظ)

hag /hag/ *n* (pej) عَجوز شَمْطاء

haggard /ˈhagəd/ *adj* <face, appearance> مُنْهَك

haggis /ˈhagɪs/ *n* (*pl* **haggis** or **haggises**) هاغيس (طَبَق اسْكُتْلَنْديّ من أَحْشاءِ الخَروفِ)

haggle /ˈhag(ə)l/ *vi* ساوَمَ; **to ~ over the price** ساوَمَ على السِعرِ

Hague /heɪg/ *pr n* (**The Hague**) لاهاي (f)

Haifa /ˈhʌɪfə/ *pr n* حَيْفا

hail /heɪl/ **A** *n* **1** (frozen rain) [u] بَرَد (n coll) **2** (of bullets, insults) وابِل

B *v impers* تَساقَطَ البَرَدُ; **it's ~ing** السَماءُ تُمْطِرُ بَرَداً

C *vt* **1** (to call to) نادى <a friend>; (to signal) اسْتَوْقَفَ <a taxi>

2 (to acclaim) نَوَّهَ (ب) <a decision, leader>; **the press ~ed it as a major breakthrough** نَوَّهَتْ بِهِ الصِحافةُ كَتَقَدُّمٍ مُهِمٍّ

D *vi* **to ~ from somewhere** «parents, immigrants» انْحَدَرَ من مَكانٍ

Hail Mary *n* سَلام مَلائِكيّ \ مَرْيَميّ

hailstone /ˈheɪlstəʊn/ *n* حَبّة بَرَدٍ

hailstorm /ˈheɪlstɔːm/ *n* عاصِفة بَرَدِيّة

hair /hɛː/ **A** *n* **1** [u] (collective) شَعْر; **to have long/short ~** كانَ لَدَيْه شَعْرٌ طَويلٌ \ قَصيرٌ; **to brush/wash one's ~** مَشَطَ \ غَسَلَ شَعْرَهُ; **to get one's ~ cut** قَصَّ شَعْرَهُ; **to have one's ~ done** صَفَّفَ شَعْرَهُ **2** (single hair) شَعْرة; **two ~s** شَعْرَتانِ

B (**-haired**); *in combination* **a long/short-~ed youth** شاب ذو شَعْرٍ طَويلٍ \ قَصيرٍ

(Idioms) **to let one's hair down** أَطْلَقَ لِنَفْسِهِ العِنانَ; **to split hairs** خاضَ في التَفاصيلِ ,تَماحَكَ; **to tear one's hair out** قَلِقَ كَثيراً

hairband /ˈhɛːband/ *n* (for securing hair) طَوْق شَعْرٍ; (for tying hair back) رَبْطة شَعْرٍ

hairbrush /ˈhɛːbrʌʃ/ *n* فُرْشاة شَعْرٍ

hair clip *n* (BrE) مَسّاكة شَعْرٍ

haircut /ˈhɛːkʌt/ *n* **1** (act of cutting hair) حِلاقة **2** (hairstyle) تَسْريحة ,تَصْفيفة

hairdo /ˈhɛːduː/ *n* (infml) تَسْريحة ,تَصْفيفة

hairdresser /ˈhɛːdrɛsə/ *n* مُزَيِّن ,حَلّاق; **the ~'s** صالون الحِلاقةِ

hairdryer /ˈhɛːdrʌɪə/ *n* (hand-held) مُجَفِّف شَعْرٍ

hair gel *n* هُلام \ جِلّ شَعْرٍ

hairgrip /ˈhɛːgrɪp/ *n* (BrE) دَبّوس شَعْرٍ

hairline /ˈhɛːlʌɪn/ *n* خَطّ شَعْرٍ; **a receding ~** خَطّ شَعْرٍ مُتَراجِع

hairline fracture *n* كَسْر شَعْرِيّ

hairnet /ˈhɛːnɛt/ *n* شَبَكة شَعْرٍ

hairpiece /ˈhɛːpiːs/ *n* شَعْر مُسْتَعار

hairpin /ˈhɛːpɪn/ *n* دَبّوس شَعْرٍ

hairpin bend (BrE), **hairpin turn** (AmE) *n* مُنْعَطَف حادّ

hair-raising /ˈhɛːreɪzɪŋ/ *adj* <experience, adventure> يَقْشَعِرُّ لَهُ البَدَنُ

hair remover *n* مُزيل شَعْرٍ

hairslide /ˈhɛːslʌɪd/ *n* (BrE) مَسّاكة شَعْرٍ

hairspray /ˈhɛːspreɪ/ *n* مُثَبِّت شَعْرٍ

hair straighteners *n* جِهاز فَرْدِ الشَعْرِ ,مُمَلِّس شَعْرٍ

hairstyle /ˈhɛːstʌɪl/ *n* تَسْريحة شَعْرٍ

hairy /ˈhɛːri/ *adj* (**hairier**, **hairiest**) <legs, chest> أَشْعَر (dipt; شُعْر)

Haiti /ˈheɪti/ *pr n* هايتي (f)

Haitian /ˈheɪʃɪən/ *n, adj* هايتيّ

haji, hajji /ˈhadʒiː/ *n* (*pl* **hajis**) حاجّ (حَجيج ,حُجّاج)

hajj /hadʒ/ *n* حَجّ (حِجَج ,حَجّات); **to perform the ~** أَدّى مَناسِكَ الحَجِّ

hake /heɪk/ *n* (*pl* **hake** or **hakes**) نازِلِيّ

hakim /ha'kiːm/ *n* **1▸** (traditional physician) (حُكَماءُ) حَكيم **2▸** (judge, ruler) (حاكِمونَ ,حُكّام) حاكِم

halal /hə'lɑːl/ *adj* ‹*meat*› حَلال; **a ~ butcher** لَحّام \ جَزّار حَلالٍ

hale /heɪl/ *adj* **to be ~ and hearty** كانَ قَوِيًّا وَمُعافًى

half /hɑːf/ **A** *n* (*pl* **halves**) **1▸** (one of two parts) نِصْف (أَنْصاف); **the bottom/top ~ of the page** النِصْفُ السُفْلِيّ \ العُلْوِيّ من الصَفْحةِ; **to cut sth in ~** قَطَعَ شَيْئًا نِصْفَيْنِ **2▸** (fraction) نِصْف (أَنْصاف); **four and a ~** أَرْبَعة وَنِصْف; **an hour and a ~** ساعة وَنِصْف **3▸** (of a game, match) نِصْف (أَنْصاف), شَوْط (أَشْواط) **4▸** (of the playing area) نِصْف المَلْعَبِ **5▸** (BrE) (infml) (half pint) [نِصْف بايْنْت \ رُبْع لِتْرٍ من الجِعةِ]

B *pron* نِصْف; **only ~ of the students passed** نَجَحَ نِصْفُ الطَلَبةِ فَقَطْ; **to reduce sth by ~** أَنْقَصَ شَيْئًا إلى النِصْفِ; **~ past** *or* (AmE) **after two** الثانية والنِصْف; **~ two** (BrE infml) الثانية والنِصْف; **she's two and a ~** عُمْرُها سَنَتانِ وَنِصْفٌ; **it'll only take ~ a minute** لن يَأْخُذَ (الأَمْرُ) أَكْثَرَ من نِصْفِ دَقيقةٍ

C *adj* نِصْف; **a ~ circle** نِصْف دائِرةٍ; **in the last ~ century** في نِصْفِ القَرْنِ الأَخيرِ; **a ~-litre bottle** زُجاجة سِعَتُها نِصْف لِتْرٍ

D *adv* **1▸** (50%) بِنِسْبةِ ٪50; **the cinema was ~ full/empty** كانَت السينما نِصْف مُمْتَلِئةٍ \ فارِغةٍ; **it's ~ the price** إنَّهُ نِصْفُ السِعْرِ; **I could earn ~ as much again** يُمْكِنُني أنْ أَكْسِبَ نِصْفَ ما كَسِبْتُ مَرّةً أُخرى; **he's ~ Spanish ~ Irish** نِصْفُهُ إسْبانِيٌّ وَنِصْفُهُ الآخَرُ إيرْلَنْدِيٌّ **2▸** (partly) ‹*asleep, naked, drunk*› جُزْئِيًّا; **his eyes were ~ closed** كانَتْ عَيْناهُ نِصْف مُغْلَقَتَيْنِ; **it's not ~ as good/bad as they say** لا يَصِلُ إلى نَفْسِ مُسْتَوى الجَوْدةِ \ الرَداءةِ كَما يَقولونَ عَنْهُ; **I ~ expected it** تَوَقَّعْتُهُ جُزْئِيًّا **3▸** (BrE) (infml) **he was only ~ joking** كانَ فَقَطْ يَمْزَحُ إلى حَدٍّ ما (for emphasis) **it doesn't ~ stink!** لَيْسَ نَتِناً البَتّةَ!; **not ~ bad** لَيْسَ سَيِّئاً بَتاتاً; **'do you like whisky?' — 'not ~!'** 'هل تُحِبُّ الويسْكي؟' — 'البَتّةَ!'

Idioms **one's better** *or* **other half** (infml) نِصْفُهُ الثاني; **to go halves** تَقاسَمَ التَكاليفَ

half-and-half /ˌhɑːf(ə)n'hɑːf/ **A** *adv* ‹*to split, divide*› مُناصَفةً **B** *adj* ‹*mixture, split*› مُتَساوٍ

half back *n* لاعِب قَلْبِ الدِفاعِ

half board *n* نِصْف إقامةٍ (تَشْمَلُ الإفْطارَ والعَشاءَ)

half-brother /'hɑːfˌbrʌðə/ *n* أَخ غَيْر شَقيقٍ

half day *n* دَوام نِصْفِ يَوْمٍ

half fare *n* نِصْف أُجْرةِ سَفَرٍ

half-hearted /ˌhɑːf'hɑːtɪd/ *adj* ‹*attempt, smile, apology*› فاتِر

half-heartedly /ˌhɑːf'hɑːtɪdli/ *adv* ‹*to work, try*› بِشَكْلٍ فاتِرٍ \ يَفْتَقِرُ إلى الحَماسِ

half hour *n* نِصْف ساعةٍ

half-light /'hɑːflʌɪt/ *n* عَتَمة

half mast *n* **at half mast** مُنَكَّس

half-moon /ˌhɑːf'muːn/ *n* تَرْبيع القَمَرِ

half note *n* نِصْف نوتةٍ

halfpenny /'heɪpni/ *n* (BrE Hist) (*pl* **halfpennies**) (coin) نِصْف بِنسٍ

half-price /ˌhɑːf'prʌɪs/ *adj, adv* بِنِصْفِ السِعْرِ

half-sister /'hɑːfˌsɪstə/ *n* أُخت غَيْر شَقيقةٍ

half-staff *n* (AmE) ▸ **half mast**

half-term /ˌhɑːf'təːm/ *n* (BrE) عُطْلة مُنْتَصَفِ الفَصْلِ الدِراسيِّ

half-time /ˌhɑːf'tʌɪm/ *n* **1▸** (in sport) اسْتِراحة ما بين الشَوْطَيْنِ; **at ~** عند اسْتِراحة ما بين الشَوْطَيْنِ **2▸** (Busn) نِصْف دَوامٍ; **to work ~** عَمِلَ نِصْفَ دَوامٍ

half-time profits *n* أَرْباح نِصْف سَنَوِيّةٍ

half-time score *n* نَتيجة الشَوْطِ الأَوَّلِ

half-time whistle *n* صافِرة نِهايةِ الشَوْطِ الأَوَّلِ

half-time worker *n* عامِل نِصْفِ دَوامٍ

half-track /'hɑːftrak/ *n* عَرَبة نِصْف مُجَنْزَرةٍ

halfway /hɑːf'weɪ/ **A** *adv* (at or to the mid-point) عند مُنْتَصَفِ الطَريقِ; **we're ~ there** نَحْنُ في مُنْتَصَفِ الطَريقِ; **I left ~ through the film** غادَرْتُ في مُنْتَصَفِ الفيلْمِ; **it only goes ~ towards solving the problem** هذا يَحُلُّ المُشْكِلةَ جُزْئِيًّا فَقَطْ

B *adj* ‹*point, stage*› المُنْتَصَفِ; **the ~ mark** مُنْتَصَف

Idiom **to meet sb halfway** اتَّفَقَ مع شَخْصٍ على حَلٍّ وَسَطٍ

half-yearly /ˌhɑːf'jəːli/ *adj* ‹*meeting, profits*› نِصْف سَنَوِيّ

halibut /'halɪbət/ *n* (*pl* **halibut** or **halibuts**) هَلْبوت (سَمَك)

hall /hɔːl/ *n* **1** (entrance) رَدْهة (رَدَهات); (AmE) (corridor) رِواق (أَرْوِقة, أَرْوِقة) **2** (for gatherings) قاعة **3** (in a castle, mansion) بَهْو (أَبْهاء) **4** (BrE) (large country house) بَيْت ريفيّ

hallelujah, alleluia /ˌhalɪˈluːjə/ *excl* هَلِّلويا

hallmark /ˈhɔːlmɑːk/ *n* **1** (BrE) (on metal) دَمْغة **2** (characteristic) سِمة

hallo /həˈləʊ/ *excl* (BrE) ▸**hello**

hall of residence *n* (BrE) سَكَن جامِعِيّ

Halloween /haləʊˈiːn/ *n* هالووين (عَشيّة عيد جَميع القِدّيسينَ)

hallucinate /həˈluːsɪneɪt/ *vi* هَلْوَسَ (i; هَلْوَسة)

hallucination /həˌluːsɪˈneɪʃ(ə)n/ *n* هَلْوَسة (هَلاوِسُ)

hallway /ˈhɔːlweɪ/ *n* رَدْهة (رَدَهات)

halo /ˈheɪləʊ/ *n* (*pl* **halos** or **haloes**) **1** (around the head) هالة **2** (in astronomy) دارة, طُفاوة, هالة

halt /hɔːlt/ **A** *vt* وَقَّفَ, أَوْقَفَ ‹*a vehicle, process*›
B *vi* «vehicles, troops» تَوَقَّفَ
C *n* تَوَقُّف, وُقوف; **to come to a ~** تَوَقَّفَ

halter /ˈhɔːltə/ *n* **1** (for a horse) رَسَن (أَرْسان, أَرْسُن), مِقْوَد (مَقاوِدُ) **2** (also **halter top**) (AmE) [قَميص ذو حَمّالةٍ حول الرَقَبةِ]

halter-neck /ˈhɔːltənɛk/ **A** *adj* ‹*dress, top*› [بِحَمّالةٍ حول الرَقَبةِ]
B *n* [ثَوب (عاري الظَهْرِ والأَكْتافِ) بِحَمّالةٍ حول الرَقَبةِ]

halve /hɑːv/ **A** *vt* **1** (to reduce by half) نَصَّفَ ‹*a number, the rate*› **2** (to divide into halves) شَطَرَ (u; شَطْر) ‹*a cake, portion*›
B *vi* «prices, unemployment» انخفض إلى النِصْفِ

halves /hɑːvz/ *n pl* ▸**half**

ham /ham/ *n* [لَحْم فَخِذِ الخِنْزيرِ المُدَخَّنِ \ المُمَلَّحِ]

Hamas /haˈmas/ *n* حَماس

hamburger /ˈhambəːgə/ *n* [هَمْبَرْغَر [شُطيرة لَحْمٍ بَقَرٍ

hamlet /ˈhamlɪt/ *n* كَفْر (كُفور)

hammer /ˈhamə/ **A** *n* **1** (tool) مِطْرَقة (مَطارِقُ) **2** (auctioneer's) مِطْرَقة (مَطارِقُ); **to go under the ~** بيع في المَزادِ **3** (in field events) مِطْرَقة (مَطارِقُ); **to throw the ~** رمى المِطْرَقةَ
B *vt* **1** (to strike) طَرَقَ (u; طَرْق), دَقَّ (u; دَقّ) ‹*nails*› **2** (in metal work) طَرَّقَ ‹*a panel*›; **to ~ sth straight** *or* **flat** طَرَقَ \ دَقَّ طَرَّقَ شَيْئاً حتّى أَصْبَحَ مُسَطَّحاً **3** (to pound) بِقَبْضَتِهِ ‹*the door*› **4** (infml) (in teaching) **to ~ a subject into sb** طَبَعَ \ غَرَسَ مادّةً في ذِهْنِ شَخْصٍ; **we had grammar ~ed into us** طُبِعَتْ قَواعِدُ النَحْوِ والصَرْفِ في أَذْهانِنا **5** (infml) (to criticize) انْتَقَدَ بِشِدّةٍ ‹*the policy, book*›; **the critics ~ed his book** انْتَقَدَ النُقّادُ كِتابَهُ بِشِدّةٍ **6** (to hit) سَدَّدَ \ قَذَفَ بِقوّةٍ ‹*the shot, ball*›; **he ~ed the ball into the net** سَدَّدَ الكُرةَ في الشَبَكةِ
C *vi* **1** (to use a hammer) طَرَقَ \ دَقَّ بالمِطْرَقةِ **2** (to pound) «rain, hailstones» ضَرَبَ بِقوّةٍ شَديدةٍ; **hailstones ~ed against the windows** ضَرَبَتْ حَبّاتُ البَرَدِ على النَوافِذِ بِقوّةٍ

Phrasal verbs **hammer in**: **~ in [sth], ~ [sth] in** دَقَّ [شَيْئاً] بالمِطْرَقةِ ‹*the nail, tack*›

• **hammer out**: **1** **~ out [sth], ~ [sth] out** (to beat out) طَرَّقَ [شَيْئاً] ‹*the dents*› **2** (to work out) وَصَلَ إلى [شَيْءٍ] ‹*an agreement, a compromise*›

hammock /ˈhamək/ *n* أُرْجوحة شَبَكيّة

hamper /ˈhampə/ **A** *n* **1** (for a picnic) سَبَت (سَبَتات, أَسْبِتة) **2** (from a shop) [صُنْدوق هَدايا يَحْتَوي على أَطْعِمةٍ]
B *vt* عَرْقَلَ, أَعاقَ (i; عَرْقَلة) ‹*movement, education*›

hamster /ˈhamstə/ *n* هَمْسْتَر

hamstring /ˈhamstrɪŋ/ *n* وَتَر المَأْبِضِ

Hanafi /haˈnafi/ *adj* حَنَفيّ

Hanbali /ˈhanbali/ *adj* حَنْبَليّ (حَنابِلة)

hand /hand/ **A** *n* **1** (part of the body) يَد (f; أَيادٍ, أَيْدٍ); **she had a glass/gun in her ~** كانَ لَدَيْها كَأْسٌ \ مُسَدَّسٌ في يَدِها; **to get one's ~s on sth** وَضَعَ يَدَهُ على شَيْءٍ; **I'd like to get my ~s on the person who did this!** أَوَدُّ أَنْ أَضَعَ يَدي على الشَخْصِ الّذي فَعَلَ هذا!; **they were holding ~s** كانوا يُمْسِكونَ بِأَيْدي بَعْضِهِم البَعْض; **hold my ~ when we cross the road** أَمْسِكْ بِيَدي عِنْدَما نَقْطَعُ الطَريقَ; **~ in ~** يَداً بِيَدٍ; **wealth and power go ~ in ~** الثَراءُ والقوّةُ يَسيرانِ جَنْباً إلى جَنْبٍ; **on ~s and knees** على اليَدَيْنِ والرُكْبَتَيْنِ; **to do** *or* **make sth by ~** فَعَلَ شَيْئاً باليَدِ; **the letter was delivered by ~** سُلِّمَت الرِسالةُ باليَدِ; **~s off!** مَمْنوعٌ اللَمْسُ!; **~s up!** ارْفَعْ يَدَيْكَ! اسْتَسْلِمْ!; **she can turn her ~ to almost anything** بِمَقْدورِها أَنْ تُزاوِلَ

تقريباً أيَّ نشاطٍ مِهْنيٍّ مهما كان نَوْعُهُ ② (showing possession) **to be in sb's ~s** كانَ بين يَدَيْ شَخْصٍ; **to be in good** *or* **safe ~s** كانَ في أيادٍ أمينةٍ; **power is in the ~s of the provisional government** السُّلْطةُ في يَدِ الحُكومةِ المُؤَقَّتةِ; **to fall** *or* **get into the wrong ~s** وَقَعَ في الأَيادي الخاطِئةِ; **we have a serious problem on our ~s** لَدَيْنا مُشْكلةٌ خطيرةٌ بين أَيْدينا; **to take sb/sth off sb's ~s** أَخَذَ شَخْصاً \ شَيْئاً من بين يَدَيْ شَخْصٍ; **the matter is out of my ~s** الأَمْرُ خارجٌ عن نطاقِ سَيْطَرَتي; **his treatment at the ~s of his captors** المُعامَلَة الّتي لَقِيَها على يَد مُحْتَجزيه ③ (help) يَد المُساعَدة \ العَوْن; **to give sb a ~** مَدَّ يَدَ المُساعَدة لشَخْصٍ ④ (infml) (round of applause) **to give sb a big ~** صَفَّقَ لِشَخْصٍ تَصْفيقاً حارًّا ⑤ (of clock, watch) عَقْرَب (mf; عَقارِبُ) ⑥ (writing) خَطّ اليَد ⑦ (cards dealt) [وَرَق اللَعِب المُوَزَّع على لاعِبٍ]; (round in card game) جَوْلة [في لُعْبة الوَرَقِ] ⑧ (worker on a farm) مُزارِع; (in a factory) (on a ship) عامِل (عُمّال)

B **(in hand)** *adj phr* ① (current) حاليّ; **the job/matter in ~** المُهِمّة \ المَسْألة الحاليّة ② (in progress) جارٍ; **preparations are well in ~** التَحْضيراتُ جارِيةٌ على قَدَمٍ وَساقٍ ③ (under control) تحت السَيْطَرة; **the police have the situation in ~** تُبْقي الشُرْطةُ الوَضْعَ تحت السَيْطرةِ ④ (in reserve) جاهِز \ مُتَوفِّر (عند الحاجة); **we have plenty of supplies in ~** لَدَيْنا الكَثيرُ من المُؤَنِ الاحْتياطيّةِ; **they have a game in ~ over their nearest rivals** [لا تزالُ لَدَيهِم مُباراةٌ لم يَلْعَبوها وهِيَ فُرْصةٌ للفَوْزِ على أَقْرَبِ مُنافِسيهِمْ]

C **(on hand)** *adj phr* مَوْجود, حاضِر; **staff are always on ~ to help and advise** المُوَظَّفون دائِماً على اسْتِعْدادٍ للمُساعَدةِ والنُصْحِ

D **(out of hand)** *adv phr* ‹*to dismiss, reject*› دون تَمْحيصٍ

E **(to hand)** *adj phr* في مُتَناوَلِ اليَدِ; **use whatever you have to ~** اسْتَعْمِلْ أَيَّ شَيْءٍ في مُتَناوَلِ يَدِكَ; **I took the first coat that came to ~** أَخَذْتُ أَوَّلَ مِعْطَفٍ كانَ في مُتَناوَلِ يَدي

F *vt* **to ~ sb sth, to ~ sth to sb** ناوَلَ شَخْصاً شَيْئاً

(Idioms) **to get/keep one's hand in** أَصْبَحَ ماهِراً \ حافَظَ على مَهارَتِهِ في شَيْءٍ; **to get out of hand** «situation, party» خَرَجَ عن السَيْطَرةِ; **to have a hand in sth** كانَ لَهُ يَدٌ في شَيْءٍ; **to have one's hands full** كانَ غارِقاً في العَمَلِ حتّى أُذُنَيْهِ; **on the one hand ..., on the other hand ...** من جِهةٍ ...، وَمِنْ جِهةٍ أُخْرى ...; **to take sb/sth in hand** أَخَذَ زِمامَ أَمْرِ شَخْصٍ \ شَيْءٍ في يَدِهِ; **to win hands down** فازَ بِسُهولةٍ فائِقةٍ

(Phrasal verbs) **hand around** (AmE) ▸ **hand round**

• **hand back**: **~ [sth] back, ~ back [sth]** أَرْجَعَ [شَيْئاً] ‹*sb's passport, homework*›

• **hand down**: **~ [sth] down, ~ down [sth]** ① (to transmit) نَقَلَ [شَيْئاً] ‹*a tradition, story*› ② (to pass on after use) أَعْطى [شَيْئاً] لم يَعُدْ بِحاجةٍ إِلَيْهِ ‹*clothes, shoes*› ③ (to announce) أَعْلَنَ [شَيْئاً] على المَلأ ‹*a sentence, verdict*›

• **hand in**: **~ [sth] in, ~ in [sth]** سَلَّمَ [شَيْئاً] ‹*one's resignation, an assignment, a petition*›

• **hand out**: **~ [sth] out, ~ out [sth]** وَزَّعَ [شَيْئاً] ‹*leaflets, food*›

• **hand over** **A** **to ~ over to one's successor/deputy** سَلَّمَ زِمامَ \ أَحالَ الأُمور إلى خَليفَتِه \ نائِبِه **B** **~ [sth] over, ~ over [sth]** سَلَّمَ [شَيْئاً] ‹*the money, keys, power*› **C** ① **~ [sb] over, ~ over [sb]** سَلَّمَ [شَخْصاً] ‹*a criminal, prisoner*› ② **~ [sb] over** (in telephoning) وَصَّلَ [شَخْصاً] ‹*a person*›; **I'll ~ you over to my supervisor** سَأُوَصِّلُكَ بالمُشْرِف على عَمَلي

• **hand round**: **~ [sth] round, ~ round [sth]** دارَ ب [شَيْءٍ على الناس] ‹*a plate, drinks*›

handbag /ˈhandbag/ *n* حَقيبة يَد

hand baggage *n* أَمْتِعة يَد

handball /ˈhandbɔːl/ *n* [u] ① (in soccer) لَمْس الكُرة باليَدِ ② (game) كُرة اليَد

handbook /ˈhandbʊk/ *n* كُتَيِّب دَليل

handbrake /ˈhandbreɪk/ *n* فَرْمَلة \ مِكْبَح يَد

hand cream *n* كْريم تَرْطيبِ اليَد

handcuff /ˈhandkʌf/ *vt* صَفَّدَ ‹*a prisoner, suspect*›

handcuffs /ˈhandkʌfs/ *n pl* صَفَد (أَصْفاد)

handful /ˈhandfʊl/ *n* ① (amount) حَفْنة (حَفَنات), قَبْضة ② (small number) عَدَد قَليل ③ (infml) (troublemaker) مُشاغِب; **their child is a real ~** ابْنُهُمْ مُشاغِبٌ جِدًّا

hand grenade *n* قُنْبُلة يَدَويّة

handgun /ˈhandgʌn/ *n* مُسَدَّس (مُسَدَّسات)

handheld /ˈhandhɛld/ *adj* ‹*device, appliance*› يَدَوِيّ

handicap /ˈhandɪkap/ **A** *n* **1** (disadvantage) عَقَبة, عائِق **2** (old use or offensive) (mental) إعاقة **3** (old use or offensive) (physical) إعاقة **4** (disadvantage imposed in horseracing) [عِبْء إضافيّ يُفْرَضُ على الحِصانِ القَويّ (لِجَعْلِ فُرَصِ الفَوْزِ مُتَساوِيةً)]
B *vt* (-pp-) أَعاقَ ‹*a person, sb's chances*›; **lack of education has ~ped him throughout his life** أَعاقَهُ انْعِدامُ التَعْليمِ طوال حَياتِهِ; **to be ~ped by sth** أَعاقَهُ شَيْءٌ

handicapped /ˈhandɪkapt/ *adj* (old use or offensive) ‹*child, patient*› مُعاق; **mentally/physically ~** مُعاق عَقْلِيًّا \ جَسَدِيًّا

handicraft /ˈhandɪkrɑːft/ *n* **1** (skill, activity) حِرْفة يَدَوِيّة **2** (also **handicrafts** *n pl*) (objects) حِرَف \ أَشْغال يَدَوِيّة

handiwork /ˈhandɪwəːk/ *n* **1** (craftsmanship) صِناعة يَدَوِيّة **2** (product) **one's ~** عَمَل \ صُنْع يَدِهِ; **it looks like Laura's ~ to me** (pej) يَبْدو لي أنّهُ من صَنيعِ لورا القَبيحِ

handkerchief /ˈhaŋkətʃɪf, ˈhaŋkətʃiːf/ *n* (*pl* **handkerchieves** /-tʃiːvz/ or **handkerchiefs**) مِنْديل (مَناديلُ)

handle /ˈhand(ə)l/ **A** *vt* **1** (to touch) تَناوَلَ ‹*food, explosives, merchandise*›; **'~ with care'** 'احْمِلْ بِرِفْقٍ'; **to ~ the ball** لَمَسَ الكُرَةَ بِيَدِهِ; **the prisoners were roughly ~d** عومِلَ السُجَناءُ بِخُشونةٍ; **to ~ stolen goods** تَعامَلَ في السِلَعِ المَسْروقةِ
2 (to deal with) عالَجَ, تَعامَلَ (مع) ‹*a situation, problem, crisis*›; **he ~d the situation very well/badly** عالَجَ المَوْقِفَ بِطَريقةٍ جَيِّدةٍ \ سَيِّئةٍ جِدًّا; **the affair was badly ~d** تَمَّ التَعامُلُ مع القَضيّةِ بِشَكْلٍ سَيِّئٍ **3** (to be responsible for) تَعامَلَ (مع) تَوَلّى ‹*a case, sale, complaints*›; **she ~s the publicity for us** تَتَوَلّى الدِعايةَ لَنا; **the airport ~s 3,000 passengers a day** يَسْتَقْبِلُ المَطارُ 3,000 راكِبٍ في اليَوْمِ; **this processor ~s more data at faster speeds** يُعالِجُ هذا المُعالِجُ بَياناتٍ أَكْثَرَ بِسُرْعةٍ أَكْبَرَ
4 (to operate) قادَ (u; قِيادة) ‹*a car, boat*›; اسْتَخْدَمَ, اسْتَعْمَلَ ‹*a gun*›; **she ~s the horses beautifully** تَتَحَكَّمُ في الخَيْلِ بِطَريقةٍ جَميلةٍ; **can you ~ a shotgun?** هل تَسْتَطيعُ اسْتِعْمالَ بُنْدُقيّةٍ؟
B *vi* «car, boat, aircraft» عَمِلَ (a; عَمَل)
C *n* (of a door, suitcase, knife) مِقْبَض (مَقابِضُ); (of a racket, cup, pump) يَد (f; أَيْدٍ, أَيادٍ)

Idiom **to have/get a handle on sth** (to understand) فَهِمَ \ اسْتَوْعَبَ شَيْئًا; (to get used to) اعْتادَ على شَيْءٍ; (to master) سَيْطَرَ على شَيْءٍ

handlebars /ˈhand(ə)lbɑːz/ *n pl* مِقْوَد (مَقاوِدُ)

handler /ˈhandlə/ *n* **1** (of a dog) سائِس كِلابٍ **2** (worker) عامِل مُناوَلةٍ; **a baggage/cargo/food ~** عامِل مُناوَلةِ أَمْتِعةٍ \ شِحْناتٍ \ أَطْعِمةٍ

handling /ˈhandlɪŋ/ *n* **1** (of objects) تَناوُل; **old books require careful ~** يَتطلَّبُ حَمْلُ الكُتُبِ القَديمةِ إلى عِنايةٍ كَبيرةٍ
2 (management) تَعامُل, مُعالَجة; **he criticized the police's ~ of the case** انْتَقَدَ تَعامُلَ الشُرْطةِ مع القَضيّةِ; **the government's poor ~ of the financial crisis** سوء مُعالَجةِ الحُكومةِ لِلأَزْمةِ المالِيّةِ; **her sensitive ~ of the subject** حَسّاسِيّة تَعامُلِها مع المَوْضوعِ **3** (processing of data, information) مُعالَجة; (of baggage, cargo) مُناوَلة **4** (preparation and dispatch) رُسوم المُناوَلةِ **5** (of a car, boat, etc) عَمَل, أَداء

handling charge *n* **1** (for goods) رَسْم مُناوَلةٍ **2** (for administration) رَسْم إداريّ

hand luggage *n* أَمْتِعة يَدٍ

handmade /handˈmeɪd/ *adj* ‹*paper, clothes*› مَصْنوع يَدَوِيًّا

hand-me-down /ˈhandmiːdaʊn/ *n* (infml) [شَيْء مُسْتَعْمَل يَنْتَقِلُ من شَخْصٍ لِآخَرَ]

handout /ˈhandaʊt/ *n* **1** (of money, food) حَسَنة, صَدَقة **2** (for students) [وَرَقة تَحْمِلُ مَعْلوماتٍ عن الدَرْسِ (تُوَزَّعُ على الطُلّابِ)] **3** (leaflet) نَشْرة (نَشَرات)

hand-pick /handˈpɪk/ *vt* **1** (to gather by hand) انْتَقى بِيَدِهِ ‹*grapes, vegetables*› **2** (to select carefully) انْتَقى بِعِنايةٍ ‹*staff, a successor*›

handrail /ˈhandreɪl/ *n* (on stairs, balcony) دَرْبَزين (دَرْبَزينات)

handset /ˈhandsɛt/ *n* **1** (of a telephone) سَمّاعة **2** (mobile phone) هاتِف مَحْمول \ جَوّال

handshake /ˈhandʃeɪk/ *n* مُصافَحة

hand signal *n* إشارة يَدٍ

handsome /ˈhans(ə)m/ *adj* (**handsomer, handsomest**) **1** ‹*man, stranger*› وَسيم (وُسَماءُ, وِسام) **2** ‹*gift, offer*› سَخيّ

hands-on /handz'ɒn/ *adj* 1 ‹*experience, training*› عَمَلِيّ 2 ‹*manager*› مُلْتَزِم شَخْصِيًّا

handstand /'handstand/ *n* وُقوف على اليَدَيْنِ

hand-to-mouth /'handtəmaʊθ/ *adj* ‹*existence*› كَفافِ

handwriting /'handrʌɪtɪŋ/ *n* خَطّ يَدٍ

handwritten /hand'rɪt(ə)n/ *adj* ‹*message, letter*› مَكْتوب بِخَطِّ اليَدِ

handy /'handi/ *adj* (**handier**, **handiest**) 1 (readily accessible) ‹*location, shop*› يَسْهُلُ الوُصولُ إِلَيْهِ 2 (useful) ‹*book, pocket*› مُفيد; **to come in ~** كانَ مُفيداً 3 (skilful) ‹*player, assistant*› بارِع

handyman /'handɪman/ *n* (*pl* **-men**) [شَخْص يَقومُ بِمُخْتَلَفِ أَعْمالِ الإِصْلاحِ في المَنْزِلِ]

hang /haŋ/ A *vt* (*past tense, past participle* **hung**) 1 (to suspend) ‹*a coat, picture, one's hat*› عَلَّقَ; **~ your coat on that hook** عَلِّقْ مِعْطَفَكَ على ذلك الخَطّافِ; **to ~ the washing on the line** عَلَّقَ الغَسيلَ على الحَبْلِ; **they hung flags out of the windows** عَلَّقوا أَعْلاماً في النَوافِذِ 2 (to lower) **to ~ one's head in shame** طَأْطَأَ رَأْسَهُ خَجَلاً 3 (to adorn) **to be hung with pictures** كانَ مُزَيَّناً بالصُوَرِ 4 ‹*wallpaper*› رَكَّبَ 5 ‹*a door, gate*› رَكَّبَ 6 (*past tense, past participle* **hanged**) ‹*a criminal, traitor*› شَنَقَ (u; شَنْق)

B *vi* (*past tense, past participle* **hung**) 1 (to be suspended) «clothes, pictures, flag» كانَ مُعَلَّقاً; **her hair hung down her back** تَدَلّى شَعْرُها على ظَهْرِها; **the children were ~ing out of the window** كانَ الأَطْفالُ يَتَدَلَّوْنَ من النافِذةِ 2 (to fall) «fabric, garment» تَهَدَّلَ, تَدَلّى 3 (in the air) «clouds, smells» بَقِيَ (a; بَقاء), ظَلَّ (a; ظَلّ, ظُلول; perf ظَلِلْتُ) 4 (to be exhibited) «painting, portrait» عُرِضَ

C *v refl* (*past tense, past participle* **hanged**) **to ~ oneself** شَنَقَ نَفْسَهُ

D *n* 1 (of fabrics, garments) تَدَلٍّ, تَهَدُّل 2 (infml) (knack) **to get the ~ of sth/doing sth** اعْتادَ على طَريقةِ تَشْغيلِ \ عَمَلِ شَيْءٍ; **you'll soon get the ~ of it** قَريباً سَتَعْتادُ على طَريقةِ تَشْغيلِهِ \ عَمَلِهِ

Idioms **to let it all hang out** (infml) أَطْلَقَ لِنَفْسِهِ العِنانَ; **to hang up one's boots** (infml) اعْتَزَلَ اللَعِبَ

Phrasal verbs **hang around, hang about** (BrE infml) A 1 (to spend time idly) «youths, teenagers» تَسَكَّعَ 2 (to wait) «customers, vehicles» انْتَظَرَ 3 (to associate with) **to ~ around with sb** صاحَبَ شَخْصاً B **~ around [sth]** مَكَثَ في [شَيْءٍ] بلا هَدَفٍ ‹*the house, streets*›

• **hang back** 1 (to stay behind) بَقِيَ في الخَلْفِ 2 (with reluctance) أَحْجَمَ

• **hang on** A (infml) 1 (to hold tightly) تَشَبَّثَ, أَمْسَكَ بِشِدَّةٍ 2 (to wait) انْتَظَرَ 3 (to survive) صَمَدَ (u; صُمود); **~ on in there!** اُصْمُدْ! B **~ on [sth]** 1 (to depend on) تَوَقَّفَ \ اعْتَمَدَ على [شَيْءٍ] 2 (to listen attentively to) **to ~ on sb's words** *or* **sb's every word** أَنْصَتَ بِاهْتِمامٍ إلى كَلامِ شَخْصٍ

• **hang on to**: **~ on to [sth/sb]** 1 (to hold tightly to) تَشَبَّثَ ب [شَيْءٍ \ شَخْصٍ] ‹*sb's arm, a rope, person*› 2 (to retain) ‹*one's job, power*› تَشَبَّثَ \ تَمَسَّكَ \ تَعَلَّقَ ب [شَيْءٍ]

• **hang out** A 1 (to protrude) تَدَلّى; **his tongue/shirt was ~ing out** كانَ لِسانُهُ \ قَميصُهُ مُتَدَلِّياً 2 (infml) (to spend time) رَوَّحَ عن نَفْسِهِ B **~ out [sth], ~ [sth] out** عَلَّقَ [شَيْئاً] ‹*the washing, a flag*›

• **hang over**: **~ over [sb/sth]** «threat» حامَ حول [شَخْصٍ \ شَيْءٍ]; «possibility» كانَ مُواتِياً لِ [شَخْصٍ \ شَيْءٍ]; **a question mark ~s over the company's future** هُناكَ عَلامةُ اسْتِفْهامٍ حول مُسْتَقْبَلِ الشَرِكةِ

• **hang up** A (on the telephone) **to ~ up on sb** أَغْلَقَ الهاتِفَ في وَجْهِ شَخْصٍ B **~ up [sth], ~ [sth] up** عَلَّقَ [شَيْئاً] ‹*a coat, clothes*›

hangar /'haŋə/ *n* حَظيرة طائِراتٍ

hanger /'haŋə/ *n* (for clothes) مِعْلاق (مَعاليقُ)

hanger-on /ˌhaŋər'ɒn/ *n* (*pl* **hangers-on**) (infml) طُفَيْلِيّ

hang-glider /'haŋglʌɪdə/ *n* طائِرة شِراعيّة مُعَلَّقة

hang-gliding /'haŋglʌɪdɪŋ/ *n* طَيَران شِراعيّ مُعَلَّق

hanging /'haŋɪŋ/ *n* 1 [u] (execution) شَنْق, إِعْدام شَنْقاً 2 (on a wall) سَجّادة حائِط

hanging basket *n* سَلّة أَزْهارٍ مُعَلَّقة

hangman /'haŋmən/ *n* (*pl* **-men**) جَلّاد (مُنَفِّذ حُكْمِ الإِعْدامِ شَنْقاً)

hangover /'haŋəʊvə/ *n* **1** (infml) (from drink) خُمار; **to have a ~** أصابَهُ الخُمارُ **2** (survival) تَقْليد بالٍ

hang-up /'hɑːŋʌp/ *n* (infml) عُقْدة نَفْسِيّة

hanker /'haŋkə/ *vi* **to ~ after** *or* **for sth** تاقَ إلى شَيْءٍ

hanky, **hankie** (infml) /'haŋki/ *n* (*pl* **hankies**) (infml) مِنْديل (مَناديلُ)

Hanukkah /'hanʊkə/ *n* حانوكا (عيد الأنْوارِ \ الشُموعِ)

haphazard /hap'hazəd/ *adj* ‹*approach, plan*› عَشْوائيّ ,اعْتِباطيّ

hapless /'hapləs/ *adj* (liter) ‹*victim, attempt*› تَعيس (تُعَساءُ)

happen /'hap(ə)n/ *vi* **1** (to take place) «accident, event» حَدَثَ (u; حُدوث), حَصَلَ (u; حُصول), جَرى (i; جَرْي); **what's ~ing?** ماذا يَحْدُثُ؟; **how/when did it ~?** كيف \ مَتى حَصَلَ؟; **we must make sure this never ~s again** يَجِبُ أنْ نَتَأَكَّدَ أنّ هذا لن يَحْدُثَ مَرّةً أُخْرى; **a strange thing ~ed today** حَدَثَ شَيْءٌ غَريبٌ اليَوْمَ; **these things ~** هذه الأُمورُ تَحْدُثُ; **whatever ~s, don't answer** مَهْما حَدَثَ، لا تَرُدَّ; **she's the sort of person who makes things ~** هي من ذلك النَوْعِ من البَشَرِ الّذي يَسْتَطيعُ أنْ يَصْنَعَ النجاحَ **2** (to chance) **to ~ to do sth** فَعَلَ شَيْئاً صُدْفةً; **if you ~ to see her, say hello** إذا صادَفَ وَرَأَيْتَها، فَبَلِّغْها سَلامي; **it so ~s that he's my son** في الواقِعِ هو ابْني; **you wouldn't ~ to have a screwdriver, would you?** هل أَجِدُ مَعَكَ مِفَكًّا؟; **as it ~ed, the meeting ended early** في الواقِعِ انْتَهى الاجْتِماعُ مُبَكِّراً **3** (to befall) **to ~ to sb** حَدَثَ لِشَخْصٍ; **if anything ~s to her, I shall never forgive myself** إذا حَدَثَ لَها أيُّ شَيْءٍ، فَلَنْ أُسامِحَ نَفْسي أَبَداً **4** (to become of) حَدَثَ (u; حُدوث); **what will ~ to the children?** ماذا سَيَكونُ مَصيرُ الأَوْلادِ؟ **5** (fml) (emphatic use) **I ~ to know that it's true** أَعْلَمُ يَقيناً أَنَّهُ صَحيحٌ

Phrasal verb **happen on, happen upon**: **~ on [sth/sb]** وَجَدَ [شَيْئاً \ شخصاً] بِمَحْضِ الصُدْفةِ ‹*a website, restaurant*›

happening /'hap(ə)nɪŋ/ *n* حادِثة (حَوادِثُ), واقِعة

happily /'hapɪli/ *adv* **1** (positively, at ease) ‹*to laugh, chat, play*› بِسَعادةٍ; **to be ~ married** كانَ سَعيداً في زَواجِهِ; **they all lived ~ ever after** وَعاشوا في تَباتٍ وَنَباتٍ **2** (willingly) ‹*to accept, leave, give up*› عن طيبِ خاطِرٍ; **I'll ~ help if I can** سَأكونُ سَعيداً بِتَقْديمِ المُساعَدةِ إذا اسْتَطَعْتُ **3** (fml) (luckily) لِحُسْنِ الحَظِّ; **~, there was nobody in the house** لِحُسْنِ الحَظِّ، لم يَكُنْ هُناكَ أَحَدٌ في المَنْزِلِ

happiness /'hapinəs/ *n* سَعادة

happy /'hapi/ *adj* (**happier**, **happiest**) **1** (positively at ease) ‹*person, life, marriage*› سَعيد (سُعَداءُ); **I'm very ~ for you** أنا سَعيدٌ جِدًّا لَكَ; **to make sb ~** أَسْعَدَ شَخْصاً; **we're so ~ that he passed** نَحْنُ سُعَداءُ جِدًّا بِنَجاحِهِ; **the ~ couple** العَروسانِ **2** (pleased) سَعيد (سُعَداءُ), مَسْرور; **to be ~ with sth** كانَ مَسْروراً بِشَيْءٍ; **he's not ~ about it** هو غَيْرُ سَعيدٍ بِهِ; **to keep sb ~** حافَظَ على سَعادةِ شَخْصٍ **3** (willing) **to be ~ to do sth** كانَ مُسْتَعِدًّا لِأَنْ يَفْعَلَ شَيْئاً **4** (in greetings); **~ birthday!** عيد ميلادٍ سَعيد!; **~ Christmas!** عيد ميلادٍ سَعيد \ مَجيد!; **~ New Year!** سَنة جَديدة سَعيدة!, عام جَديد سَعيد! **5** (fml) (fortunate) ‹*coincidence, choice, situation*› سَعيد الحَظِّ, مَحْظوظ; **he's in the ~ position of not needing to work** هو سَعيدُ الحَظِّ لِأَنَّهُ لا يَحْتاجُ للعَمَلِ

happy ending *n* نِهاية سَعيدة

happy-go-lucky /ˌhapigəʊ'lʌki/ *adj* ‹*person, attitude*› خالي البالِ

happy medium *n* مَوْقِف وَسَط

haram /hɑː'rɑːm/ *adj* حَرام (mf; حُرُم)

harangue /hə'raŋ/ *vt* (*present participle* **haranguing**) وَجَّهَ كَلاماً شَديدَ اللَهْجةِ لِ ‹*an audience, the troops*›

harass /hə'ras/ **A** *vt* **1** (to pressurize) ضايَقَ ‹*an employee, a minority*› **2** (to attack) قامَ بِغاراتٍ مُتَكَرِّرةٍ على ‹*an enemy, army*›

B (**harassed**) *adj* مُتَضايِق

harassment /hə'rasmənt/ *n* مُضايَقة

harbour (BrE), **harbor** (AmE) /'hɑːbə/ **A** *n* **1** (for ships) مَرْفَأ (مَرافِئُ), ميناء (f; مَوانِئُ); **to enter/leave ~** دَخَلَ إلى \ خَرَجَ من الميناءِ **2** (refuge) مَأْوًى (مَآوٍ); **to give sb safe ~** وَفَّرَ لِشَخْصٍ مَأْوًى آمِناً

B *vt* **1** حَمَلَ (i; حَمْل) ‹*a disease, bacteria*› **2** أَضْمَرَ ‹*a grudge, suspicion*› **3** آوى ‹*a fugitive, criminal*›

harbour master (BrE), **harbor master** (AmE) *n* مُدير ميناءٍ

hard /hɑːd/ **A** *adj* (**harder**, **hardest**) **1** (firm, not yielding) ‹*ground, mattress*› صُلْب; **the melon is ~ to the touch** البَطّيخةُ

مَلْمَسُها صُلْبٌ; **the butter is too ~** الزُّبْدةُ صُلْبةٌ جِدًّا; **golf is played with a small, ~ ball** يُلْعَبُ الجولْف بِكُرةٍ صَغيرةٍ صُلْبةٍ **2** (finished) ‹*paint, glue*› جافّ; **is the cement ~ yet?** هل جَفَّ الإسْمَنْت بَعْدُ؟ **3** (not easy) ‹*problem, question, puzzle*› صَعْب, عَسير, عَويص; **to be ~ to open/find** كانَ من الصَّعْبِ فَتْحُهُ \ العُثورُ عَلَيْهِ; **it's a ~ poem to translate** هي قَصيدةٌ يَصْعُبُ تَرْجَمَتُها; **it was ~ not to laugh** كانَ من الصَّعْبِ عَدَمُ الضَحِكِ; **I've had a ~ day** كانَ يَوْمي صَعْباً; **she's ~ to please** من الصَّعْبِ إرْضاؤُها; **that's very ~ to believe** من الصَّعْبِ جِدًّا تَصْديقُ ذلك **4** (arduous) ‹*work, climb*› شاقّ; **the work is ~ and the hours long** العَمَلُ شاقٌّ والساعاتُ طَوِيلةٌ; **to be a ~ worker** كانَ عامِلاً مُجِدًّا \ مُجْتَهِداً **5** (intense) ‹*frost, winter*› قاسٍ; **the climate is very ~** المَناخُ قاسٍ جِدًّا **6** (uncomfortable) ‹*life, childhood, year*› صَعْب, قاسٍ; **it's a ~ world** هذا العالَمُ قاسٍ; **don't be so ~ on yourself!** لا تَكُنْ قاسِياً مع نَفْسِكَ!; **to give sb a ~ time** وَضَعَ الصِعابَ في طَريقِ شَخْصٍ; **this print is ~ on the eyes** من الصَّعْبِ قِراءةُ هذه الكِتابة; **to take a ~ line with sb** تَشَدَّدَ مع شَخْصٍ; **what ~ luck!** يا لَلْحَظِّ التَعِسِ \ العاثِرِ!; **to fall on ~ times** واجَهَ ظُروفاً عَصيبةً; **it's been a ~ year for farmers** كانَ عاماً صَعْباً للمُزارِعين **7** (unsentimental) ‹*mother, face, words*› صارِم, قاسٍ; **her father's a ~ man** أبوها رَجُلٌ صارِمٌ; **he plays the ~ man in police movies** يَلْعَبُ دَوْرَ الرَجُلِ القاسي في الأفْلامِ البوليسيّةِ **8** (forceful) ‹*push, shove, knock*› قَوِيّ; **give the door a ~ push** ادْفَع البابَ بِقوّةٍ **9** (unquestionable) ‹*evidence, facts*› واضِح, ثابِت; **the ~ facts are as follows...** الحَقائِقُ الثابِتةُ هي كَما يَلي ... **10** (harsh) ‹*light, colour*› غَيْر مُريحٍ, قاسٍ **11** (strong) ‹*drink, drug*› قَوِيّ **12** (Pol) **the ~ left/right** اليَسار \ اليَمين المُتَشَدِّد **13** ‹*water*› عَسِر **14** ‹*consonant*› صُلْب

B *adv* (**harder, hardest**) **1** (with force) ‹*to push, punch*› بِقوّةٍ; **to hit sb/sth ~** ضَرَبَ شَخْصاً \ شَيْئاً بِقوّةٍ; **to run as ~ as one can** جَرى بِأَقْصى سُرْعَتِهِ; **push ~!** ادْفَعْ بِقوّةٍ! **2** (with intensity) ‹*to work, study*› بِاجْتِهادٍ, بِجَدّ; ‹*look*› بِإمْعانٍ; **think/listen ~ before you answer** فَكِّرْ مَلِيًّا \ اسْتَمِعْ جَيِّداً قبل أنْ تُجيبَ; **try ~ to understand** حاوِلْ جاهِداً أنْ تَفْهَمَ; **she drives her students very ~** تَضْغَطُ على طُلّابِها بِقوّةٍ كَبيرةٍ; **to take the news very ~** تَلَقّى الأخْبارَ بِأَسًى شَديدٍ **3** (intensely) ‹*to rain, snow*› بِغَزارةٍ; **it rained/snowed ~ all day** تَساقَطَ المَطَرُ \ الثَلْجُ بِغَزارةٍ طوال اليَوْمِ **4** (with directions) ‹*to turn, veer*› بِشِدّةٍ; **turn ~ left/right at the traffic lights** اتَّجِهْ إلى أَقْصى اليَسارِ \ اليَمينِ عند إشارة المُرورِ

Idioms **to be hard put to do sth** وَجَدَ من الصَّعْبِ عَلَيْهِ فِعْلَ شَيْءٍ; **to feel hard done by** شَعَرَ بالظُلْمِ; **to play hard to get** تَمَنَّعَ, أَخْفى اهْتِمامَهُ, تَظاهَرَ بِعَدَمِ الاكْتِراثِ

hard and fast *adj* ‹*rule, distinction*› صارِم

hardback /ˈhɑːdbak/, **hardback book** *n* كِتاب مُجَلَّد \ ذو غِلافٍ مُقَوًّى

hardball /ˈhɑːdbɔːl/ *n* (AmE) [u] بِيسْبول; **to play ~ with sb** تَصَرَّفَ بِعُدْوانيّةٍ مع شَخْصٍ

hardboard /ˈhɑːdbɔːd/ *n* خَشَب مَضْغوط

hard-boiled /ˌhɑːdˈbɔɪld/ *adj* **1** ‹*egg*› مَسْلوق **2** (tough) ‹*detective, reporter*› صَعْب المِراسِ

hard copy *n* نُسْخة مَطْبوعة

hard core **A** *n* **1** (of a group, demonstrators) نَواة صُلْبة **2** (rubble) حَصًى (يُسْتَخْدَمُ كَأَساسٍ في البِناءِ) (n coll);
B (**hard-core**) *adj* **1** ‹*supporter, activist*› شَديد الوَلاءِ **2** ‹*pornography*› إباحيّ, خَلاعيّ

hard court *n* مَلْعَب صُلْب

hard disk *n* قُرْص صُلْب

hard-earned /ˈhɑːdəːnd/ *adj* ‹*cash, victory*› مُكْتَسَب بِشِقِّ الأَنْفُسِ

harden /ˈhɑːd(ə)n/ **A** *vt* **1** ‹*a surface, steel*› صَلَّبَ, قَسّى **2** ‹*a person, sb's resolve*› قَوّى; ‹*one's attitude*› صَلَّبَ, شَدَّدَ; **to ~ one's heart** قَسا قَلْبُهُ
B *vi* **1** «glue, paint» جَفَّ (i; جُفوف, جَفاف); «butter, wax» تَماسَكَ, تَصَلَّبَ **2** «public opinion, attitudes» تَشَدَّدَ **3** «face, expression» تَصَلَّبَ

hardened /ˈhɑːd(ə)nd/ *adj* **1** ‹*paint, wax*› مُتَيَبِّس **2** ‹*criminal*› مُتَأَصِّل; ‹*drinker*› مُدْمِن

hard hat *n* **1** (worn by factory and building workers) خوذة واقِية **2** (worn for riding) خوذة

hard-headed /ˌhɑːdˈhɛdɪd/ *adj* ‹*businessman, approach*› عَمَليّ

hard-hearted /ˌhɑːdˈhɑːtɪd/ *adj* ‹*attitude, parent*› قاسٍ (قُساة)

hard-hitting /ˌhɑːdˈhɪtɪŋ/ *adj* ‹*speech, criticism*› لاذِع

hard labour (BrE), **hard labor** (AmE) *n* أَعْمال شاقّة

hardliner /hɑːdˈlʌɪnə/ *n* مُتَشَدِّد

hardly /ˈhɑːdli/ *adv* 1 (scarcely) بالكادِ; **I ~ know her** لا أكادُ أَعرِفُها; **he ~ ever writes** لا يَكْتُبُ إلّا نادِراً; **there's ~ any left** لا يَكادُ يَتَبقّى شَيْءٌ مِنْهُ 2 (not at all) بَتاتاً; **it's ~ surprising** لَيْسَ من المُسْتَغْرَبِ بَتاتاً; **I could ~ leave her there on her own** لا أَسْتَطيعُ تَرْكَها هُناكَ وَحيدةً على الإطْلاقِ

hardness /ˈhɑːdnəs/ *n* صَلابة

hard of hearing *adj* ثَقيل السَمْعِ

hard-pressed /ˌhɑːdˈprɛst/ *adj* ‹*families, taxpayers*› تحت ضَغْطٍ شَديدٍ; **you'd be ~ to find a better person for the job** سَتَجِدُ أنَّه من الصَعْبِ عَلَيْكَ إيجادُ شَخْصٍ أَفْضَلَ للوَظيفةِ

hard sell *n* إسْتراتيجيّة بَيْعٍ تَعْتَمِدُ على أُسْلوبِ إقْناعٍ عَدائيٍّ \ تَهْديديٍّ

hardship /ˈhɑːdʃɪp/ *n* 1 [u] (suffering) مَشَقّة; **to suffer great ~** عانى من مَشَقّةٍ كَبيرةٍ 2 (cause of suffering) مَصاعِب; **the ~s of prison life** مَصاعِب حَياةِ السِجْنِ

hard shoulder *n* (BrE) كَتِف الطَريقِ (للتَوَقُّفِ في حالاتِ الطَوارِئِ)

hardtop /ˈhɑːdtɒp/ *n* 1 (car) سَيّارة ذات سَقْفٍ صُلْبٍ \ ثابِتٍ 2 (roof) سَقْف صُلْب \ ثابِت

hard up *adj* (infml) مُفْلِس; **to be hard up** كانَ مُفْلِساً

hardware /ˈhɑːdwɛː/ *n* 1 (tools, machinery) أَدَوات مَعْدِنيّة; **military ~** مُعَدّات عَسْكَريّة 2 (also **computer hardware**) عَتاد \ مُعَدّات الحاسوبِ

hardware shop (BrE), **hardware store** (AmE) *n* دُكّان خُرْدَواتٍ \ أَدَواتٍ مَعْدِنيّةٍ

hard-wearing /ˌhɑːdˈwɛːrɪŋ/ *adj* ‹*fabric, leather*› مَتين, شَديد التَحَمُّلِ

hard-working /ˌhɑːdˈwəːkɪŋ/ *adj* مُجْتَهِد, مُثابِر

hardy /ˈhɑːdi/ *adj* (**hardier**, **hardiest**) ‹*person, breed*› قَويّ (أَقْوِياءُ); ‹*plant*› مُقاوِم للبَرْدِ

hare /hɛː/ *n* أَرْنَب بَرّيّ

haricot /ˈharɪkəʊ/ *n* (BrE) (also **haricot bean**) (dried) فاصوليّة بَيْضاء; (fresh) فاصولِيّة خَضْراء

harm /hɑːm/ A *n* ضَرَر, أَذًى (أَضْرار); **to do sb ~** آذى شَخْصاً, أَلْحَقَ الضَرَرَ بِشَخْصٍ; **to do ~ to sth** سَبَّبَ ضَرَراً لِشَيْءٍ; **there's no ~ in asking** لا بَأْسَ في السُؤالِ; **no ~ done** [لا عَلَيْكَ, لم يَقَعْ أَيُّ ضَرَرٍ]; **he won't come to any ~** لن يُصيبَهُ أَيُّ أَذًى; **out of ~'s way** في مَأْمَنٍ; **to do more ~ than good** أَضَرَّ أَكْثَرَ مِمّا نَفَعَ B *vt* آذى (Form IV; imperf يُؤْذي) ‹*a person, an animal*›; أَضَرَّ (ب) ‹*the environment, sb's reputation*›

harmful /ˈhɑːmfʊl/ *adj* ‹*effect, substance, influence*› مُضِرّ, ضارّ, مُؤْذٍ

harmless /ˈhɑːmləs/ *adj* 1 ‹*substance*› غَيْر مُضِرٍّ; ‹*animal*› غَيْر مُؤْذٍ 2 (inoffensive) ‹*fun, joke*› غَيْر مُسيءٍ; ‹*person*› غَيْر مُؤْذٍ

harmonica /hɑːˈmɒnɪkə/ *n* هَرْمونيكا (آلة نَفْخٍ موسيقيّة)

harmonious /hɑːˈməʊnɪəs/ *adj* 1 ‹*relationship, society*› مُنْسَجِم 2 ‹*sound, melody*› مُتَناغِم

harmonize, -ise (BrE) /ˈhɑːmənʌɪz/ A *vt* نَسَّقَ ‹*laws, policies*› B *vi* 1 (Mus) «instruments, singers» تَناغَمَ 2 (to blend) «decor, buildings» انْسَجَمَ

harmony /ˈhɑːməni/ *n* (*pl* **harmonies**) 1 (Mus) تَوافُق 2 (agreement) انْسِجام; **in ~ with each other** في انْسِجامٍ مع بَعْضِهِما

harness /ˈhɑːnəs/ A *n* 1 (for a horse) طَقْم (أَطْقُم, طُقوم) 2 (for babies, parachutists) حِزام (أَحْزِمة, حِزامات); **to wear a safety ~** ارْتَدى حِزامَ أَمانٍ B *vt* 1 ‹*a horse*› جَهَّزَ بِطَقْمٍ 2 (to utilize) طَوَّعَ, سَخَّرَ ‹*power, technology*›

harp /hɑːp/ *n* هارْب, قيثارة (قَياثيرُ)

(Phrasal verb) **harp on** (infml): **~ on about [sth]** تَحَدَّثَ عن [شَيْءٍ] بِشَكْلٍ مُتَكَرِّرٍ وَمُمِلٍّ

harpist /ˈhɑːpɪst/ *n* عازِف قيثارةٍ

harpoon /hɑːˈpuːn/ A *n* حَرْبة (حِراب) B *vt* ‹*a whale, fish*› طَعَنَ بِحَرْبةٍ

harpsichord /ˈhɑːpsɪkɔːd/ *n* هارْبْسيكورْد, بِيان قيثاريّ

harpsichordist /ˈhɑːpsɪkɔːdɪst/ *n* عازِف هارْبْسيكورْد

harrowing /ˈharəʊɪŋ/ *adj* ‹*experience, ordeal*› مُؤْلِم جِدًّا; ‹*story, scene*› مُحْزِن جِدًّا

harry /ˈhari/ *vt* (**harries**, **harrying**, **harried**) 1 (to raid) شَنَّ غاراتٍ على ‹*the enemy*› 2 (to harass) ضايَقَ

harsh /hɑːʃ/ *adj* 1 (severe) ‹*punishment, treatment*› قاسٍ 2 (inhospitable) ‹*climate, conditions*› قاسٍ 3 (unpalatable) ‹*truth, reality*› مُرّ 4 (unkind) ‹*person, words*› قاسٍ 5 (jarring) ‹*voice*› أَجَشّ (dipt), غَليظ; ‹*light*› ساطِع; **the red is too ~** اللَوْنُ الأَحْمَرُ خَشِنٌ جِدًّا

harshly /ˈhɑːʃli/ *adv* ‹*to treat, speak, punish*› بِقَسْوةٍ

harvest /ˈhɑːvɪst/ **A** *n* 1 (of ripe fruit and crops) حَصاد; **farmers are extremely busy during the ~** المُزارِعونَ مَشْغولونَ للغاية خلال مَوْسِمِ الحَصادِ; **he is helping with the ~** يُساعِدُ في الحَصادِ 2 (yield) مَحْصول (مَحْصولات, مَحاصيلُ), غَلّة (غِلال, غَلاّت)

B *vt* 1 حَصَدَ (i-u; حَصاد), جَمَعَ (a; جَمْع) ‹*the crop, wheat, grapes*› 2 حَصَدَ (i-u; حَصاد) ‹*a field*› 3 حَصَّلَ ‹*stem cells, organs*›

harvester /ˈhɑːvɪstə/ *n* 1 (machine) حاصِدة (حاصِدات), حَصّادة (حَواصِدُ), آلة حَصادٍ 2 (worker) حَصّاد

harvest mite *n* سوس الحَصادِ

has /haz, həz, əz/ *3rd pers sing pres* ▸ **have**

has-been /ˈhazbiːn/ *n* (infml) [شَخْص أَفَلَ نَجْمُهُ]

hash /haʃ/ *n* 1 (Culin) [طَبَق من اللَحْمِ المَفْرومِ يُعادُ طَهْيُهُ مع البَطاطا] 2 (infml) (mess) **to make a ~ of sth** أَفْسَدَ شَيْئًا

hash browns *n* [طَبَق مَقْليّ من البَطاطا المَفْرومةِ والبَصَلِ]

Hashemite /ˈhaʃɪmʌɪt/ *adj* ‹*royal family*› هاشِميّ

hashish /ˈhaʃiːʃ/ *n* حَشيش

hashtag /ˈhaʃtag/ *n* عَلامة المُرَبَّعِ

hasn't /ˈhaz(ə)nt/ *abbr* = **has not** ▸ **have**

hassle /ˈhas(ə)l/ (infml) **A** *n* إِزْعاج

B *vt* ضايَقَ, أَزْعَجَ ‹*tourists, passers-by*›

haste /heɪst/ *n* عَجَلة, سُرْعة

hasten /ˈheɪs(ə)n/ **A** *vt* عَجَّلَ ‹*sb's death, departure*›; سَرَّعَ ‹*a process*›

B *vi* اسْتَعْجَلَ

hastily /ˈheɪstɪli/ *adv* 1 (quickly) ‹*arranged, assembled*› بِسُرْعةٍ, بِتَسَرُّعٍ 2 (rashly) ‹*to act, speak*› على وَجْهِ السُرْعةِ

hasty /ˈheɪsti/ *adj* (**hastier**, **hastiest**) 1 (quick) ‹*departure, marriage*› سَريع 2 (rash) ‹*decision, conclusion*› مُتَسَرِّع; **don't be too ~** لا تَكُنْ مُتَسَرِّعاً جِدًّا

hat /hat/ *n* قُبَّعة; **to put on/take off one's ~** لَبِسَ \ نَزَعَ قُبَّعَتَهُ

Idioms **at the drop of a hat** (infml) دون تَرَدُّدٍ; **old hat** (infml) [شَيْء قَديم الطِرازِ]; **to put one's hat into the ring** أَبْدى رَغْبَتَهُ في قُبولِ تَحَدٍّ; **to take one's hat off to sb** رَفَعَ قُبَّعَتَهُ إِكْبارًا \ إِجْلالاً لِشَخْصٍ

hatch /hatʃ/ **A** *n* 1 (in a floor, roof, wall) مَنْفَذ (مَنافِذُ) 2 (on an aircraft, a boat) [باب في طائِرةٍ \ سَفينةٍ \ غَوّاصةٍ]

B *vt* 1 حَضَنَ (u; حَضْن, حِضانة) ‹*the eggs*› 2 فَقَّصَ ‹*chicks*› 3 (to devise) حاكَ (u; حِياكة), دَبَّرَ ‹*a plan, plot*›

C *vi* 1 «eggs» فَقَسَ (i; فَقْس), فَرَّخَ 2 (also **hatch out**) «chicks, larvae» فَقَسَ (i; فَقْس)

hatchback /ˈhatʃbak/ *n* هاتْشْباك (سَيّارة بِخَمْسةِ أَبْوابٍ)

hatchet /ˈhatʃɪt/ *n* فَأْس صَغيرة, ساطور (سَواطيرُ)

Idiom **to bury the hatchet** دَفَنَ الأَحْقادَ, أَنْهى الخِلافَ

hate /heɪt/ **A** *n* 1 (hatred) كُرْه, بُغْض, مَقْت 2 (object of hatred) [شَيْء \ شَخْص مَكْروه]; ▸ **pet**

B *vt* 1 (to detest) كَرِهَ (a; كُرْه, كَراهِية), أَبْغَضَ ‹*a person, idea*›; **I ~ people telling me what to do** أَكْرَهُ الناسَ الَّذينَ يَقولونَ لي ماذا يَجِبُ أَنْ أَفْعَلَ 2 (to regret) أَسِفَ (a; أَسَف); **I ~ to say it, but it's true** آسِفٌ لِقَوْلِ هذا، وَلَكِنَّها الحَقيقةُ

hate crime *n* جَريمة حِقْدٍ \ كَراهِيةٍ

hateful /ˈheɪtfʊl/ *adj* حاقِد (حَقَدة), مُحْتَقِر

hate mail *n* رَسائل كَراهِيةٍ (من مَجْهولٍ)

hatred /ˈheɪtrɪd/ *n* كُرْه, بُغْض, حِقْد (أَحْقاد)

hat-trick /ˈhattrɪk/ *n* ثَلاثة انْتِصاراتٍ مُتَتالِيةٍ; **to score a ~** سَجَّلَ ثَلاثةَ أَهْدافٍ

haughty /ˈhɔːti/ *adj* (**haughtier**, **haughtiest**) ‹*manner, look*› مُتَكَبِّر, مُتَعَجْرِف, مُتَغَطْرِس

haul /hɔːl/ **A** *vt* (to pull) جَرَّ (u; جَرّ), سَحَبَ (a; سَحْب) ‹*a load, wagon*›; **they ~ed the boat out of the water** سَحَبوا القارِبَ إلى خارِجِ الماءِ

B *n* **1** (goods stolen) حَصيلة مَسْروقاتٍ **2** (goods found) حَصيلة **3** (of fish) حَصيلة صَيْدٍ **4** (of goals, medals etc) كَمّيّة (حَصائِلُ) **5** (arduous task) **it's a long ~ to Rome from here** الرِحْلةُ إلى روما من هُنا طَويلةٌ وَشاقّةٌ; **it will be a long ~ to recovery** سَيكونُ الطَريقُ إلى التَعافي طَويلاً وَشاقّاً **6** (in transportation) مَسافة; **a long-/short-~ flight** رِحْلة طَويلة \ قَصيرة المَدى

haulage /ˈhɔːlɪdʒ/ *n* **1** (transport) نَقْل البَضائِعِ بالشاحِناتِ **2** (charge) أُجْرة النَقْلِ

hauler *n* (AmE) ▸**haulier**

haulier (BrE) /ˈhɔːlɪə/, **hauler** (AmE) /ˈhɔːlə/ *n* **1** (firm) شَرِكة نَقْلٍ بَرّيٍّ للبَضائِعِ **2** (driver) سائِق شاحِنة نَقْلٍ

haunch /hɔːntʃ/ *n* **1** (of a person) وِرْك (f; أَوْراك); (of an animal) كَفَل (أَكْفال), عَجُز (أَعْجاز) **2** (as food) لَحْم الفَخِذ

haunt /hɔːnt/ **A** *vt* **1** «ghost» سَكَنَ (u; سَكَن) **2** «memory, image» لازَمَ

B *n* [مَكان يَتَرَدَّدُ عَلَيْهِ شَخْصٌ]; **I revisited all my old ~s** زُرْتُ ثانِيةً كُلَّ الأَماكِنِ القَديمةِ الّتي كُنْتُ أَتَرَدَّدُ عَلَيْها

haunted /ˈhɔːntɪd/ *adj* **1** ‹*house*› مَسْكون (بالأَرْواحِ) **2** ‹*look, eyes*› مَذْعور

haunting /ˈhɔːntɪŋ/ *adj* ‹*melody, image*› مُؤَثِّر, يَصْعُبُ نِسْيانُهُ

Havana /həˈvanə/ *pr n* هافانا

have /hav, həv/ **A** *vt* (*3rd person present sing* **has**, *present participle* **having**, *past tense, past participle* **had**) **1** (to possess) امْتَلَكَ, كانَ عِنْدَهُ \ لَدَيْهِ ‹*a car, business*›; **she has many friends** لَدَيْها العَديدُ من الأَصْدِقاءِ; **he has a business in Doha** لَدَيْهِ شَرِكةٌ تِجارِيّةٌ في الدوحةِ; **has he got a job?** هل لَدَيْهِ وَظيفةٌ؟; **the team has plenty of talent** الفَريقُ لَدَيْهِ مَوْهِبةٌ كَبيرةٌ; **he has fair/grey hair** لَدَيْهِ شَعْرٌ أَشْقَرُ \ رَماديٌّ; **she had the sense to refuse** كانَ لَدَيْها الحِسُّ السَليمُ بِأَنْ رَفَضَتْ **2** (to eat) تَناوَلَ ‹*a sandwich, dinner*›; **to ~ breakfast/lunch** تَناوَلَ الإفْطارَ \ الغَداءَ; **to ~ a meal** تَناوَلَ وَجْبةً **3** (to drink) تَناوَلَ ‹*a drink*›; شَرِبَ (a; شُرْب, مَشْرَب) ‹*lemonade*›; احْتَسى ‹*whisky*›; **to ~ a couple of coffees** تَناوَلَ كوبَيْنِ من القَهْوةِ **4** (to smoke) تَناوَلَ, دَخَّنَ, شَرِبَ (a; شُرْب, مَشْرَب) ‹*a cigarette, cigar*› **5** (to want) أَرادَ; **what will you ~?** ماذا تُريدُ؟; **I'll ~ a boiled egg/steak** أُريدُ بَيْضةً مَسْلوقةً \ شَريحةَ لَحْمٍ; **I wouldn't ~ it any other way** لا أُحِبُّهُ بِأَيِّ طَريقةٍ أُخْرى **6** (to allow) (*usu in neg*) **I won't ~ it!** لن أَقْبَلَ بِذَلِكَ; **she won't ~ him back** لا تُريدُ العَوْدةَ إلَيْهِ; **I offered her £25, but she wouldn't ~ it** عَرَضْتُ عَلَيْها 25 جُنَيْهاً، وَلَكِنَّها رَفَضَتْ **7** (to take possession of) «person» حَصَلَ (u; حُصول; على) ‹*a letter, parcel, information*›; **I must ~ the information/money soon** يَجِبُ أَنْ أَحْصُلَ على المَعْلوماتِ \ المالِ قَريباً; **we've had no news from him** لم تَصِلْنا أَيُّ مَعْلوماتٍ عَنْهُ **8** (to stage) أَقامَ ‹*a party*›; عَقَدَ (i; عَقْد) ‹*meeting*›; أَجْرى ‹*interview*›; **we're having people round on Saturday** سَنَسْتَقْبِلُ ضُيوفاً يَوْمَ السَبْتِ **9** (to exert) كانَ لَهُ ‹*an effect, influence*›; **his speech had an immediate effect** كانَ لِخِطابِهِ تَأْثيرٌ فَوْريٌّ; **she has influence in presidential circles** لَدَيْها نُفوذٌ في الدَوائِرِ الرِئاسيّةِ **10** (to be affected) **to ~ sth done to one** فُعِلَ بِهِ شَيْءٌ; **he had his car/watch stolen** سُرِقَتْ سَيّارَتُهُ \ ساعَتُهُ; **she has had her windows broken** كُسِرَتْ نَوافِذُها; **they like having stories read to them** يُحِبّونَ أَنْ تُقْرَأَ لَهُم القِصَصُ **11** (to spend) **~ a good day!** أَتَمَنّى لَكَ يَوْماً سَعيداً!; **did you ~ a good time?** هل اسْتَمْتَعْتَ بِوَقْتِكَ؟; **they had a hard *or* bad time** مَرّوا بِوَقْتٍ عَصيبٍ **12** (with illnesses) عانى (من), أُصيبَ ب; **to ~ toothache/a headache** عانى من أَلَمٍ بالأَسْنانِ \ صُداعٍ; **to ~ an accident/a heart attack** أُصيبَ في حادِثٍ \ بِنَوْبةٍ قَلْبيّةٍ; **to ~ a shock** تَعَرَّضَ لِصَدْمةٍ **13** (to cause to be) **he had his revolver/camera ready** جَهَّزَ كاميرَتَهُ \ مُسَدَّسَهُ; **we'll soon ~ everything ready/clean** سَنُعِدُّ \ سَنُنَظِّفُ كُلَّ شَيْءٍ عَمّا قَريبٍ; **we had it finished by 5 o'clock** أَنْهَيْناهُ بِحُلولِ الساعةِ 5 **14** (to cause sth to be done) **to ~ sth done** [ذَهَبَ إلى شَخْصٍ \ اسْتَدْعى شَخْصاً لِيَفْعَلَ لَهُ شَيْئاً]; **to ~ one's hair cut** قَصَّ شَعْرَهُ; **to ~ the house painted/the washing-machine repaired** طَلى المَنْزِلَ \ أَصْلَحَ الغَسّالةَ; **to ~ an injection/a dental check-up** أَخَذَ حُقْنةً \ أَجْرى فَحْصاً على أَسْنانِهِ **15** (to cause sb to do sth) **to ~ sb do sth** جَعَلَ شَخْصاً يَفْعَلُ شَيْئاً; **she had him close the door/wait in the corridor** جَعَلَتْهُ يُغْلِقُ البابَ \ يَنْتَظِرُ في الرِواقِ; **she had them digging the garden/writing poetry** جَعَلَتْهُم يُقَلِّبونَ الحَديقةَ \ يَكْتُبونَ

أَوَدُّ أَنْ أُعْلِمَكَ أَنَّ … ; **I would ~ you know that …** الشِّعْرَ حَمَلَ ⑯ (to hold) **he has us up all night** يوقِظُنا طوال اللَّيْلِ (i; حَمْل); **she had the glass in her hand** كانَتْ تَحْمِلُ الكَأْسَ; **he had his hand over his eyes** رَفَعَ يَدَهُ على عَيْنَيْهِ; في يَدِها; **she had her back to us** أَدارَتْ لَنا ظَهْرَها ⑰ (to give birth to) وَضَعَ (a; وَضْع), وَلَدَ (i; وِلادة, مَوْلِد) *<a baby, young>*; **she's having a baby in May** سَتَلِدُ في مايو ⑱ (to be: as impersonal verb) **to your right we ~ the Roman temple; to your left we have …** على اليَمينِ يوجَدُ المَعْبَدُ الروماني؛ وَعَلى اليَسارِ ... يوجَدُ ... ⑲ (also **have got**) (to puzzle) **you ~** *or* **you've got me there!** لَقَد اسْتَطَعْتَ أَنْ تُحَيِّرَني! ⑳ (also **have got**) (to have at one's mercy) **I've got you/him now!** لَقَدْ تَمَكَّنْتُ مِنْكَ \ مِنْهُ الآنَ! ㉑ (infml) (to have sex with) مارَسَ الجِنْسَ مع *<her, the maid>*

B *modal aux* (*3rd person present sing* **has**, *present participle* **having**, *past tense, past participle* **had**) ① (expressing obligation) **to ~ to do sth, to ~ got to do sth, I ~ (got) to pay within seven days** يَجِبُ عَلَيَّ أَنْ أَدْفَعَ خلال سَبْعَةِ أَيّامٍ; **we've (got) to check in now** عَلَيْنا أَنْ نُسَجِّلَ الدُخولَ الآنَ; **he has had to return home** كانَ عَلَيْهِ أَنْ يَعودَ إلى البَيْتِ ② (to need to) **you don't ~ to leave so early, you haven't got to leave so early** لَيْسَ عَلَيْكَ أَنْ تُغادِرَ في هذا الوَقْتِ المُبَكِّرِ; **something has (got) to be done** يَجِبُ فِعْلُ شَيْءٍ; **why did this ~ to happen to me?** لِماذا حَدَثَ هذا لي؟ ③ (for emphasis) **this has (got) to be the worst airline in the world** لا بُدَّ أَنَّ هذه هي أَسْوَأُ شَرِكةِ طَيَرانٍ في العالَمِ

C *v aux* (*3rd person present sing* **has**, *present participle* **having**, *past tense, past participle* **had**) ① (to form past tenses) **she has already left/arrived** قد غادَرَتْ \ وَصَلَتْ بالفِعْلِ; **he had shut the door before he realized that his keys were inside** أَغْلَقَ البابَ قبل أَنْ يُدْرِكَ أَنَّ مَفاتيحَهُ كانَتْ بالداخِلِ; **we haven't lost them** لم نَفْقِدْهُمْ; **~ you seen him?** هل رَأَيْتَهُ؟; **she has hurt herself** جُرِحَتْ ② (in tag questions etc) **you haven't seen my glasses, ~ you?** هل رَأَيْتَ نَظّارَتي؟; **you've met him before, haven't you?** لَقَدْ قابَلْتَهُ من قَبْلُ، أَلَيْسَ كَذلِكَ؟; **you haven't met him before, ~ you?** أَنْتَ لم تُقابِلْهُ من قَبْلُ، أَلَيْسَ كَذلِكَ؟ ③ (**having**) (in time clauses) **having finished the report, he went out** بعد أَنْ أَنْهى التَّقْريرَ، غادَرَ المَكانَ ④ (**having**) (because, since) **having already won twice, he's the favourite** لِأَنَّهُ فازَ مَرَّتَيْنِ، فَهُوَ النَجْمُ المُفَضَّلُ; **having lost money already, he is reluctant to commit more funds** لِأَنَّهُ خَسِرَ مالاً بالفِعْلِ، فَهُوَ لا يَرْغَبُ في إيداعِ المَزيدِ من الأَمْوالِ; **I was cautious, having been deceived before** كُنْتُ حَذِراً، لِأَنَّني خُدِعْتُ من قَبْلُ

(Idiom) **the haves and the have-nots** الأَغْنِياء والفُقَراء

(Phrasal verbs) **have around** (AmE) ▸ **have over**

• **have back**: ① **~ [sth] back, ~ back [sth]**: (to have returned) **when can I ~ my car/my money back?** متى يُمْكِنُني أَنْ أَسْتَرِدَّ سَيّارَتي \ مالي؟; **you can ~ it back tomorrow** تَسْتَطيعُ أَنْ تَسْتَرِدَّهُ غَداً ② **~ [sb] back**: (to allow to return) **she had him back on one condition** سَمَحَتْ لَهُ بالعَوْدةِ بِشَرْطٍ واحِدٍ

• **have in**: **~ [sb] in** اسْتَدْعى [شَخْصاً] *<the doctor, builders>*

• **have on**: ① **~ [sth] on, ~ on [sth]** (to be wearing) ارْتَدى [شَيْئاً] *<a coat, skirt>*; **to ~ nothing on** كانَ عارِياً ② **~ [sth] on** (to be busy) كانَ مَشْغولاً ب [شَيْءٍ]; **~ you got anything on this evening?** هل أَنْتَ مَشْغولٌ هذا المَساءَ؟ ③ **~ [sb] on** (infml) (to trick) خَدَعَ [شَخْصاً]; **he's trying to ~ you on** يُحاوِلُ أَنْ يَخْدَعَكَ ④ **~ sth on sb** (to have evidence about) كانَ لَدَيْهِ شَيْءٌ ضدّ شَخْصٍ

• **have over, have round**: **~ [sb] over** اسْتَضافَ [شَخْصاً] *<a neighbour>*; **to ~ sb over for the evening** اسْتَضافَ شَخْصاً لِيَقْضِيَ مَعَهُ المَساءَ

• **have up** (infml): **to be had up** مَثَلَ أمامَ المَحْكَمةِ; **he was had up for dangerous driving** مَثَلَ أمامَ المَحْكَمةِ بِتُهْمةِ القِيادةِ الخَطِرةِ

haven /ˈheɪv(ə)n/ *n* ① (safe place) مَلاذ, مَلْجَأ (مَلاجِئُ) ② (harbour) ميناء (f; مَوانِئُ), مَرْفَأ (مَرافِئُ)

haven't /ˈhav(ə)nt/ *abbr* = **have not** ▸ **have**

haversack /ˈhavəsak/ *n* حَقيبة ظَهْرٍ

havoc /ˈhavək/ *n* خَراب, دَمار; **the snow is causing ~ on the roads** يُسَبِّبُ الثَلْجُ فَوْضى عارِمةً في الطُرُقاتِ; **that food played ~ with my digestion** سَبَّبَ لي ذلك الطَعامُ

اضْطِراباتٍ في الجِهازِ الهَضْمِيِّ; **the kids ran around creating ~** رَكَضَ الأَوْلادُ في كُلِّ الاتِّجاهاتِ مُسَبِّبِينَ الفَوْضى ▸ see also **wreak**

Hawaii /həˈwʌɪi/ *pr n* هاواي (f)

Hawaiian /həˈwʌɪən/ *n, adj* هاوايي

hawk /hɔːk/ *n* 1 (bird) باز (بيزان) 2 (politician) سِياسِيٌّ يَتَبَنَّى سِياسةً عُدْوانيَّةً]

Idiom **to watch sb like a hawk** راقَبَ شَخْصاً عن كَثَبٍ

hawkish /ˈhɔːkɪʃ/ *adj ‹stance, adviser›* [يَتَبَنّى سِياسةً عُدْوانيَّةً]

hawthorn /ˈhɔːθɔːn/ *n* زُعْرور (زَعارير)

hay /heɪ/ *n* قَشّ, تِبْن (قُشوش)

hay fever *n* حُمّى القَشّ

hayseed /ˈheɪsiːd/ *n* (AmE infml) [شَخْص ريفيّ غَيْر مُتَحَضِّرٍ]

haystack /ˈheɪstak/ *n* كَوْمة تِبْنٍ

haywire /ˈheɪwʌɪə/ *adj* (infml) **to go ~** «plan» خابَ; «equipment» تَعَطَّلَ

hazard /ˈhazəd/ **A** *n* خطر (أخطار); **a safety ~** خطر على السَلامةِ

B *vt* حَزَرَ (i-u; حَزْر, مَحْزَرة) ‹*an opinion, estimate*›; **to ~ a guess** خمَنَ

hazard lights *n* أَضْواء الخطرِ

hazardous /ˈhazədəs/ *adj ‹waste, chemical›* خَطِر; ‹*journey, job*› مَحْفوف بالمَخاطِرِ

haze /heɪz/ *n* 1 (mist) سَديم (سُدُم), ضَباب رَقيق 2 (of smoke, dust) غَشاوة

hazel /ˈheɪz(ə)l/ **A** *n* 1 (tree, shrub) شَجَرة بُنْدُق 2 (wood) خَشب البُنْدُقِ

B *adj ‹eyes›* بُنْدُقيّ

hazelnut /ˈheɪzəlnʌt/ *n* بُنْدُق (n coll)

hazy /ˈheɪzi/ *adj* (**hazier, haziest**) 1 ‹*day, conditions*› ضَبابيّ 2 ‹*idea, memory*› غَيْر واضِحٍ

he /hiː/ *pron* هُوَ; **here ~ is** ها هُوَ ذا; **~'s a lawyer** هُوَ مُحامٍ; **~ didn't say that, I did** هُوَ لم يَقُلْ ذلك، أنا مَنْ قالَهُ; **his brother's poor, but ~'s rich** أخوهُ فَقيرٌ، لَكِنَّهُ غَنِيٌّ; **she's as tall as ~ is** هِي طَويلةٌ مِثْلَهُ; **~ and I go there often** أنا وَهُوَ نَذْهَبُ هُناكَ كَثيراً

head /hɛd/ **A** *n* 1 (of a person, animal) رَأْس (mf; رُؤُوس, أَرْؤُس); **the top of one's ~** أَعْلى رَأْسِهِ; **he had a hat on his ~** كانَ يَرْتَدي قُبَّعةً على رَأْسِهِ; **my ~ aches** رَأْسي يُؤْلِمُني; **to nod one's ~** أَوْمَأَ بِرَأْسِهِ; **he sat with his ~ in his hands** جَلَسَ واضِعاً رَأْسَهُ بين يَدَيْهِ; **he was drenched from ~ to foot** كانَ مُبْتَلّاً من رَأْسِهِ حتّى قَدَمَيْهِ; **she was promoted over the ~s of her colleagues** تَخَطَّتْ زُمَلاءَها في التَرْقِيةِ

2 (infml) (mind) رَأْس (mf; رُؤُوس, أَرْؤُس), ذِهْن (أَذْهان); **I can't get it into my ~ that ...** لا أَسْتَطيعُ أَنْ أَسْتَوْعِبَ أَنّ . . .; **his name has gone right out of my ~** سَقَطَ اسْمُهُ من ذاكِرَتي; **he has a good/bad ~ for figures** هو ماهِرٌ \ ضَعيفٌ في الحِسابِ; **to have a good/bad ~ for heights** لَدَيْهِ \ لَيْسَ لَدَيْهِ القُدْرةُ على تَحَمُّلِ الارْتِفاعاتِ; **her ~ was full of grand ideas** كانَ رَأْسُها مَليئاً بالأَفْكارِ العَظيمةِ; **he has taken it into his ~ to resign** اسْتَقَرَّ رَأْيُهُ على أنْ يَسْتَقيلَ; **whatever put that idea into her ~?** ما الّذي وَضَعَ تِلْكَ الفِكْرةَ في رَأْسِها؟; **I can't get that tune out of my ~** لا أَسْتَطيعُ أَنْ أُخْرِجَ هذا اللَحْنَ من رَأْسي; **to be** *or* **go above** *or* **over sb's ~** (too difficult) كانَ فوق مُسْتَوى تَفْكيرِ شَخْصٍ 3 (infml) (headache) صُداع; **to have a bad ~** كانَ لَدَيْهِ صُداعٌ سَيِّءٌ

4 (of a family, church, organization) رَئيس (رُؤَساءُ), زَعيم (زُعَماءُ); **a meeting of ~s of state** اجْتِماع لِرُؤَساءِ الدُوَلِ; **he's the ~ of the research team** هو رَئيسُ الفَريقِ البَحْثيِّ

5 (individual person, animal) **we paid £40 a ~** *or* **per ~** دَفَعْنا 40£ للفَرْدِ; **to count ~s** عَدَّ الرُؤُوسَ; **fifty ~ of cattle** خَمْسونَ رَأْساً من الماشِيةِ 6 (flattened part of a pin, axe) رَأْس (mf; رُؤُوس, أَرْؤُس) 7 (foremost part of a queue) مُقَدِّمة; (of a table) رَأْس (mf; رُؤُوس, أَرْؤُس); (of a staircase) أَعْلى **he was sitting at the ~ of the table** كانَ يَجْلِسُ على رَأْسِ الطاوِلةِ 8 (of cabbages, lettuces) رَأْس (mf; رُؤُوس, أَرْؤُس); **a cabbage with a firm ~** كُرُنْبة بِرَأْسٍ صُلْبٍ 9 (on beer) رَغْوة (رَغاوٍ) 10 (of a boil, pimple) رَأْس (mf; رُؤُوس, أَرْؤُس)

B (**heads**) *n pl* (in tossing coin) وَجْه, مَلِك (مُلوك, أَمْلاك)

(وُجوه ,أَوْجُه); **'~s or tails?'** 'مَلِك أم كِتابة؟'

C *vt* **1** (to be first in) تَقَدَّمَ, تَصَدَّرَ ‹*a procession, list, column*› **2** (to lead) رَأَسَ (a; رِئاسة), قادَ (u; قِيادة) ‹*a delegation, business, revolt*› **3** (to title) عَنْوَنَ (i; عَنْوَنة) ‹*an article, a chapter*›; **~ your letter with your address** ضَعْ عُنْوانَكَ أَعْلى الخِطابِ **4** (to steer) قادَ (u; قِيادة) ‹*the animals, boat*› **5** (in soccer) ضَرَبَ بِرَأْسِهِ; **to ~ the ball** ضَرَبَ الكُرةَ بِرَأْسِهِ

D *vi* «cars, boats» تَوَجَّهَ; **where was the train ~ing?** إلى أَيْنَ كانَ يَتَوَجَّهُ القِطارُ؟; **to ~ south/north** تَوَجَّهَ جَنوباً \ شَمالاً; **he ~ed back into town** تَوَجَّهَ عائِداً إلى المَدينةِ

E (*in combination* **-headed**) **a red-~ed boy** وَلَد شَعْرُهُ أَحْمَرُ; **a two-~ed monster** وَحْش بِرَأْسَيْنِ

(Idioms) **to come to a head** وَصَلَ إلى الذُّرْوةِ; **things came to a ~ when the redundancies were announced** وَصَلَت الأُمورُ إلى الذُّرْوةِ عِنْدما تَمَّ الإعْلانُ عن التخفيضاتِ في الوَظائِفِ; **off the top of one's head** ‹*to say, answer*› بِشَكْلٍ ارْتِجاليٍّ; **to go to sb's head** كَبُرَ في رَأْسِهِ; **to keep/lose one's head** تَحَمَّلَ \ فَقَدَ أَعْصابَهُ; **to keep one's head above water** تَماسَكَ في المَصاعِبِ; **to laugh/shout one's head off** (infml) ضَحِكَ \ صَرَخَ بِشِدّةٍ; **to be/go over one's head** فاقَ قُدْرَتَهُ على الفَهْمِ

(Phrasal verbs) **head for**: **~ for [sth]** تَوَجَّهَ إلى [شَيْءٍ]; **where were they ~ing for?** إلى أَيْنَ كانوا يَتَّجِهون؟; **they are ~ing for trouble** هُمْ مُقْبِلونَ على مَشاكِلَ

• **head off** **A** رَحَلَ (a; رَحيل); **it's time to ~ off** حانَ وَقْتُ الرَحيلِ **B** **~ off [sb/sth], ~ [sb/sth] off** (to divert) سَدَّ الطَريقَ على [شَخْصٍ \ شَيْءٍ] ‹*a question, complaint, quarrel*›

• **head up**: **~ up [sth]** تَرَأَّسَ [شَيْئاً] ‹*a team, department*›

headache /ˈhɛdeɪk/ *n* صُداع; **to have a ~** أَصابَهُ صُداعٌ

headband /ˈhɛdband/ *n* عِصابة رَأْسٍ

headboard /ˈhɛdbɔːd/ *n* [لَوْحة رَأْسيّة للسَرير]

headbutt /ˈhɛdbʌt/ *vt* نَطَحَ (a; نَطْح) ‹*an opponent, a player*›

head cold *n* زُكام

head cook *n* رَئيس طُهاةٍ

headdress /ˈhɛddrɛs/ *n* (of feathers) [غِطاء رَأْسٍ من الريشِ]; (of lace) [غِطاء رَأْسٍ من الدانْتيلاّ]

header /ˈhɛdə/ *n* **1** (infml) (dive) **to take a ~** وَقَعَ على رَأْسِهِ **2** (in soccer) ضَرْبة رَأْسٍ \ رَأْسيّة

head first *adv* **1** (with head foremost) بالرَأْسِ أَوَّلاً **2** (rashly) بِتَسَرُّعٍ بِدونِ رَوِيّةٍ

headhunt /ˈhɛdhʌnt/ *vt* [بَحَثَ عن شَخْصٍ مُؤَهَّلٍ لِشَغْلِ وَظيفةٍ مُعَيَّنةٍ] ‹*staff*›

headhunter /ˈhɛdhʌntə/ *n* [شَخْص يَخْتَصُّ باسْتِقْطابِ الكَفاءاتِ]

heading /ˈhɛdɪŋ/ *n* **1** (of a chapter, section) عُنْوان (عَناوينُ), رَأْسيّة **2** (letterhead) تَرْويسة **3** (topic) باب (mf; أَبْواب, بِيبان), قِسْم (أَقْسام)

head injury *n* إصابة الرَأْسِ

headland /ˈhɛdlənd/ *n* لِسان أَرْضِيّ

headlight /ˈhɛdlʌɪt/, **headlamp** /ˈhɛdlamp/ (BrE) *n* كَشّاف, مِصْباح أَماميّ; **dipped ~s** أَضْواء أَماميّة مُنْخَفِضة

headline /ˈhɛdlʌɪn/ *n* عُنْوان (في صَحيفةٍ أو مَجَلّةٍ); **the story made ~s around the world** تَصَدَّرَت القِصّةُ عَناوينَ الصُحُفِ حول العالَمِ; **here are the news ~s** إلَيْكُم عَناوينَ الأَخْبارِ

headlong /ˈhɛdlɒŋ/ *adv* **1** (with the head foremost) بالرَأْسِ أَوَّلاً **2** (rashly) بِطَيْشٍ, بِتَهَوُّرٍ

head louse *n* (*pl* **head lice**) قَمْل الرَأْسِ

headmaster /hɛdˈmɑːstə/ *n* ناظِر مَدْرَسةٍ

headmistress /hɛdˈmɪstrəs/ *n* ناظِرة مَدْرَسةٍ

head office *n* مَكْتَب رَئيسيّ

head-on /ˌhɛdˈɒn/ **A** *adj* ‹*collision, crash*› (في) الجُزْءِ الأَماميِّ **B** *adv* ‹*to collide, crash*› وَجْهاً لِوَجْهٍ

headphones /ˈhɛdfəʊnz/ *n pl* سَمّاعة رَأْسٍ

headquarters /hɛdˈkwɔːtəz/ *n pl* (Mil) مَقَرّ قِيادة; (of a company, political party) مَقَرّ رَئيسيّ

headrest /ˈhɛdrɛst/ *n* مِسْنَد رَأْسٍ

headroom /ˈhɛdruːm/ *n* **1** (inside car, room) حَيِّز الرَأْسِ **2** (at a bridge) ارْتِفاع

headscarf /ˈhɛdskɑːf/ *n* (*pl* **headscarves**) حِجاب (أَحْجِبة), مِنْديل رَأْسٍ, خِمار (أَخْمِرة, خُمُر)

headset /ˈhɛdsɛt/ *n* سَمّاعة رَأْسٍ

headstand /ˈhɛdstand/ *n* [وُقوف على الرَأْسِ]; **to do a ~** وَقَفَ على رَأْسِهِ

headstone /ˈhɛdstəʊn/ *n* (شَواهِدُ) شاهِد

headstrong /ˈhɛdstrɒŋ/ *adj* (عُنُد) عَنيد, مُصَمِّم

head teacher *n* ناظِر مَدْرَسةٍ

head waiter *n* نادِل رَئيسيّ

headway /ˈhɛdweɪ/ *n* تَقَدُّم; **to make ~** أَحْرَزَ تَقَدُّماً

heady /ˈhɛdi/ *adj* (**headier**, **headiest**) **1** (exciting) ‹*days, times*› مُثير **2** (potent) ‹*wine*› مُسْكِر; ‹*scent*› قَوِيّ

heal /hiːl/ **A** *vt* عالَجَ, داوى, (شِفاء ;i) شَفى ‹*a wound, sick person*› **B** *vi* «wound, cut» اِلْتَحَمَ, اِلْتَأَمَ, شُفِيَ

healer /ˈhiːlə/ *n* مُداوٍ, مُعالِج

healing /ˈhiːlɪŋ/ **A** *n* مُعافاة, شِفاء **B** *adj* ‹*process, powers*› الشِفاء; ‹*effect*› شافٍ

health /hɛlθ/ *n* عافِية, صِحّة; **to be in good/poor ~** كانَ في صِحّةٍ جَيِّدةٍ \ سَيِّئةٍ; **your good ~!** !بِ \ في صِحَّتِكَ! نَخْبُكَ

health care *n* رِعاية صِحّيّة

health centre (BrE), **health center** (AmE) *n* مَرْكَز صِحّيّ

health food *n* غِذاء صِحّيّ

healthily /ˈhɛlθɪli/ *adv* ‹*to eat, live*› بِطَريقةٍ صِحّيّةٍ, بِشَكْلٍ صِحّيٍّ

health insurance *n* تَأْمين صِحّيّ

health service *n* خِدْمة صِحّيّة

healthy /ˈhɛlθi/ *adj* (**healthier**, **healthiest**) **1** (in good health) ‹*adult, baby*› في صِحّةٍ جَيِّدةٍ, يَتَمَتَّع بِصِحّةٍ جَيِّدةٍ **2** (promoting good health) ‹*lifestyle, diet*› مُفيد لِلصِحّةِ, صِحّيّ; ‹*appetite*› ضَخْم; ‹*profit*› مُزْدَهِر; ‹*economy*› **3** [يَدُلُّ على صِحّةٍ جَيِّدةٍ]

heap /hiːp/ **A** *n* **1** (pile) كَوْم (أَكْوام, كيمان), رُكام; **the books were in a ~ on the floor** كانَت الكُتُبُ مُكَوَّمةً على الأَرْضِ **2** **~s** (BrE) *or* **a heap** (AmE) **of sth** (infml) (ال)كَثير من شَيْءٍ; **we've got ~s of time** لَدَيْنا الكَثيرُ من الوَقْتِ **B** *vt* **1** (to pile) كَوَّمَ, كَدَّسَ ‹*documents*› **2** (to load) مَلَأَ (مَلْء ;a); **they ~ed their plates with food** مَلَؤوا أَطْباقَهُمْ بالطَعامِ **3** (to bestow) **to ~ praise/scorn on sth** أَغْدَقَ على شَخْصٍ المَديحَ \ الاحْتِقارَ

heaped /hiːpt/ (BrE), **heaping** (AmE) /ˈhiːpɪŋ/ *adj* ‹*tablespoon, teaspoon*› مُكَدَّس, مُمْتَلِئ

hear /hɪə/ **A** *vt* (*past tense, past participle* **heard**) **1** (to perceive) سَمِعَ (a; سَمْع) ‹*a voice, sound, music*›; **I can ~ voices whispering** يُمْكِنُني أَنْ أَسْمَعَ أَصْواتاً تَتَهامَسُ; **I can't ~ you** لا أَسْتَطيعُ أَنْ أَسْمَعَكَ; **I had to shout to make myself heard** اُضْطُرِرْتُ لِأَنْ أَصْرُخَ حتّى يُسْمَعَ صَوْتي; **to ~ her talk, you'd think she was at death's door** إذا سَمِعْتَها وَهِيَ تَتَحَدَّثُ, سَتَظُنُّ أَنَّها على أَعْتابِ المَوْتِ; **we haven't heard the end** *or* **last of it** لم نَسْمَعْ نِهايةَ القِصّةِ **2** (to learn) سَمِعَ (a; سَمْع) ‹*the news, rumours*›; **I ~d that he'd left the country** سَمِعْتُ أَنَّهُ قد غادَرَ البَلَدَ; **I've ~d so much about you** لَقَدْ سَمِعْتُ الكَثيرَ عَنْكَ; **I've ~d it all before!** لَقَدْ سَمِعْتُ هذه القِصّةَ من قَبْلُ!; **have you ~d?** هل سَمِعْتَ بِما حَدَثَ؟; **I ~ you want to be a doctor** سَمِعْتُ أَنَّكَ تُريدُ أَنْ تَكونَ طَبيباً; **so I ~, so I've ~d** لَقَدْ سَمِعْتُ ذلك أنا أَيْضاً **3** (to listen to) سَمِعَ (a; سَمْع), اِسْتَمَعَ (إلى, ل) ‹*a story, speech*›; **to ~ what sb has to say** اِسْتَمَعَ لِما يُريدُ شَخْصٌ أَنْ يَقولَ; **to ~ Mass** سَمِعَ القُدّاسَ **4** نَظَرَ (u; نَظَر, مَنْظَر) (في ‹*a case*›; سَمِعَ (a; سَمْع) ‹*the evidence*› **B** *vi* (*past tense, past participle* **heard**) **1** (to perceive) سَمِعَ (a; سَمْع); **stop it! do you ~?** تَوَقَّفْ عن ذلك! هل سَمِعْتَ؟ **2** (to learn, be told) **to ~ about sth** سَمِعَ عن شَيْءٍ

(Phrasal verbs) **hear from**: **~ from [sb]** **1** (to be contacted by) تَلَقّى أَخْباراً من [شَخْصٍ] ‹*a friend, relative*›; **I'm waiting to ~ from the hospital** أنا في انْتِظارِ سَماعِ الأَخْبارِ من المُسْتَشْفى **2** (to listen to) سَمِعَ من [شَخْصٍ] ‹*readers, members*›

• **hear of**: **~ of [sb/sth]** **1** (to become aware of) سَمِعَ عن [شَخْصٍ \ شَيْءٍ]; **that's the first I've heard of it!** هذه هي أَوَّلُ مَرّةٍ أَسْمَعُ فيها عَنْهُ!; **I've never ~d of him** لم أَسْمَعْ عَنْهُ أَبَداً **2** (to consider) **I won't ~ of it!** لن أَسْمَحَ بِذلِكَ!

heard /hɜːd/ *past tense, past participle* ▸**hear**

hearing /ˈhɪərɪŋ/ *n* **1** [u] (sense) سَمْع; **his ~ is not very good** حاسّة السَمْعِ لَدَيْهِ لَيْسَتْ جَيِّدةً جِدّاً **2** [u] (earshot) مَدى السَمْعِ; **in/out of ~** ضِمْنَ \ خارِجَ مَدى السَمْعِ **3** (before a court) جَلْسة اسْتِماعٍ

hearing aid *n* سَمّاعة الأُذُنِ

hearing-impaired /ˌhɪərɪŋɪmˈpɛːd/ *adj* ضَعيف \ ثَقيل السَمْعِ

hearsay /ˈhɪəseɪ/ *n* أَقاويل

hearse /hɜːs/ *n* [سَيّارة نَقْل المَوْتى]

heart /hɑːt/ **A** *n* **1** (organ) قَلْب (قُلوب); **my ~ missed a beat** كادَ قَلْبي يَتَوَقَّفُ **2** (seat of the emotions) قَلْب (قُلوب); **to break sb's ~** كَسَرَ قَلْبَ شَخْصٍ; **to lose one's ~ to sb** تَعَلَّقَ قَلْبُهُ بِشَخْصٍ; **to open one's ~ to sb** فَتَحَ قَلْبَهُ لِشَخْصٍ; **to win sb's ~** فازَ بِقَلْبِ شَخْصٍ; **with a heavy/light ~** بِقَلْبٍ مَليءٍ بالحُزْنِ \ بالسَّعادةِ; **my ~ went out to him** تَعاطَفْتُ مَعَهُ بِشِدّة; **he spoke from the ~** تَحَدَّثَ من القَلْبِ; **from the bottom of one's ~** من أَعْماقِ قَلْبِهِ; **she wished with all her ~ that she hadn't done it** تَمَنَّتْ من كُلِّ قَلْبِها أَنَّها لم تَفْعَلْ ذلك; **in my ~ of ~s** في أَعْماقِ أَعْماقي; **the place was dear to his ~** كانَ المَكانُ عَزيزاً على قَلْبِهِ; **he's a child at ~** قَلْبُهُ قَلْبُ طِفْلٍ; **to have a change of ~** غَيَّرَ رَأْيَهُ; **my ~ sank** امْتَلَأَ قَلْبي حُزْناً **3** (courage, enthusiasm) شَجاعة; **to take/lose ~** تَشَجَّعَ \ وَهَنَتْ عَزيمَتُهُ; **we can take ~ from this news/decision** يُمْكِنُنا أَنْ نَتَشَجَّعَ بِهَذا الخَبَرِ \ القَرارِ; **I didn't have the ~ to refuse** لم تَكُنْ لَدَيَّ الشَّجاعةُ الكافِيةُ للرَّفْضِ; **my ~ isn't in it** لَسْتُ مُتَحَمِّساً لَهُ; **to be in good ~** كانَ مُنْشَرِحَ الصَّدْرِ **4** (cental part) قَلْب (قُلوب), لُبّ (أَلْباب), صُلْب \ لُبّ; **right in the ~ of the city** في قَلْبِ المَدينةِ تَماماً; **the ~ of the matter** جَوْهَر المَوْضوع **5** (**hearts** *n pl*) (in cards) قَلْب (قُلوب) **6** (of an artichoke, lettuce, etc) قَلْب (قُلوب)
B *modifier* <rate> القَلْب; <patient> بالقَلْب; <specialist> في أَمْراضِ القَلْبِ; **to have a ~ problem/condition** عانى من مُشْكِلةٍ بالقَلْبِ

Idioms **eat your heart out!** (infml) مُتْ غَيْظاً!; **to have one's heart set on sth/doing sth** عَقَدَ العَزْمَ على شَيْءٍ \ فِعْلِ شَيْءٍ; **to know/learn sth off by heart** حَفِظَ \ تَعَلَّمَ شَيْئاً عن ظَهْرِ قَلْبٍ; **to take sth to heart** تَأَثَّرَ بِشَيْءٍ تَأَثُّراً بالغاً

heartache /ˈhɑːteɪk/ *n* حُزْن, كَآبة (أَحْزان)

heart attack *n* نَوْبة قَلْبِيّة

heartbeat /ˈhɑːtbiːt/ *n* نَبْضة \ خَفْقة القَلْبِ

heartbreak /ˈhɑːtbreɪk/ *n* أَسًى, حَسْرة (حَسَرات)

heartbreaking /ˈhɑːtbreɪkɪŋ/ *adj* <story, loss> يُمَزِّقُ القَلْبَ, يُقَطِّعُ القَلْبَ

heartbroken /ˈhɑːtbrəʊk(ə)n/ *adj* <parents, family> مُنْكَسِر القَلْبِ; **I was ~ when I learned of her death** حَزِنْتُ حُزْناً بالِغاً عِنْدَما عَلِمْتُ بِوَفاتِها

heartburn /ˈhɑːtbɜːn/ *n* حُرْقة في المَعِدةِ

heart disease *n* مَرَض قَلْبٍ

heartening /ˈhɑːtnɪŋ/ *adj* <news, story> مُشَجِّع

heart failure *n* قُصور القَلْبِ

heartfelt /ˈhɑːtfelt/ *adj* <thanks, sympathy> خالِص, من القَلْبِ

hearth /hɑːθ/ *n* [أَرْضِيّة مَوْقِدٍ]

heartily /ˈhɑːtɪli/ *adv* **1** (warmly) <to welcome> بِحَرارةٍ **2** (with relish) <to laugh> من قَلْبِهِ; <to eat> بِشَهِيّةٍ **3** (wholeheartedly) <to recommend, agree> بِإخْلاصٍ, بِصِدْقٍ

heartless /ˈhɑːtləs/ *adj* <thief> عَديم العاطِفةِ, مُتَحَجِّر القَلْبِ; <act> خالٍ من العاطِفةِ

heart-lung machine /ˌhɑːtˈlʌŋ məʃiːn/ *n* جِهاز القَلْبِ والرِئةِ

heart-shaped /ˈhɑːtʃeɪpt/ *adj* <face, box> على شَكْلِ قَلْبٍ

heart surgeon *n* جَرّاح قَلْبٍ

heart surgery *n* جِراحة قَلْبٍ

heart-throb /ˈhɑːtθrɒb/ *n* (infml) [نَجْم تَهْفو لَهُ قُلوبُ المُعْجَباتِ]

heart-to-heart /ˌhɑːttəˈhɑːt/ *n* [حَديث من القَلْبِ إلى القَلْبِ]

heart transplant *n* زَرْع قَلْبٍ

hearty /ˈhɑːti/ *adj* (**heartier, heartiest**) **1** (jolly, warm) <person> مَرِح (مَراحى, مَرْحى); <welcome> حارّ; <laugh> من القَلْبِ **2** (substantial) <meal, breakfast> مُشْبِع, مُغَذٍّ **3** (healthy) <appetite> قَوِيّ

heat /hiːt/ **A** *n* **1** [u] (warmth) حَرّ, حَرارة; **the ~ of the summer** حَرارة الصَّيْفِ; **the ~ is exhausting** الحَرُّ مُرْهِقٌ; **in the ~ of the day** في حَرِّ النَّهارِ; **the plants wilted in the ~** ذَبُلَت النَباتاتُ بِسَبَبِ الحَرِّ **2** (in cooking) حَرارة; **cook at a low/moderate ~** اطْهِهِ على دَرَجةِ حَرارةٍ مُنْخَفِضةٍ \ مُتَوَسِّطةٍ; **turn up/turn down the ~** ارْفَعْ \ اخْفِضْ دَرَجةَ الحَرارةِ **3** (of a competition) دَوْر أَوَّلِيّ \ تَمْهيديّ **4** (of female animals) **to be on** (BrE) *or* **in** (AmE) **~** كانَتْ في فَتْرةِ الشَّبَقِ \ النَّزْوِ **5** (of an argument) احْتِدام; **in the ~ of the argument he swore** تَلَفَّظَ بالسِبابِ عند احْتِدامِ الجِدالِ; **in the ~ of the**

moment في لَحْظةِ الانْفِعالِ **6** (infml) (pressure) ضَغْط; **to turn the ~ up on the sales force to perform better** زادَ الضَغْطَ على فريقِ المَبيعاتِ لِتَحْسينِ أدائِهِمْ
B *vt* **1** دَفَّأَ ‹*a room, building*› **2** سَخَّنَ ‹*the food, soup*›
C *vi* «food, soup» سَخُنَ (u; سَخانة ,سُخونة)
(Phrasal verbs) **heat through 1** «food, drink» سَخُنَ (u; سُخونة ,سَخانة) **2** ~ [**sth**] **through** سَخَّنَ [شَيْئاً] ‹*the food*›
• **heat up 1** «food, engine» سَخُنَ (u; سَخانة ,سُخونة) **2** ~ [**sth**] **up**, ~ **up** [**sth**] (for the first time) سَخَّنَ [شَيْئاً] ‹*the oven*›; دَفَّأَ [شَيْئاً] ‹*a room*›; (to reheat) أعادَ تَسْخينَ [شَيْءٍ] ‹*food, soup*›

heated /ˈhiːtɪd/ *adj* **1** (warmed) ‹*rear window, pool*› مُدَفَّأ **2** (impassioned) ‹*debate, argument*› ساخِن ,مُحْتَدِم

heater /ˈhiːtə/ *n* (for air) مِدْفَأة (مَدافِئُ); (for water) مُسَخِّن

heath /hiːθ/ *n* بَراح ,أَرْض بور

heathen /ˈhiːð(ə)n/ *n, adj* وَثَنِيّ

heather /ˈheðə/ *n* خَلَنْج

heating /ˈhiːtɪŋ/ *n* تَسْخين ,تَدْفِئة

heat-resistant /ˈhiːtrəˌzɪst(ə)nt/ *adj* ‹*glass, tile*› مُقاوِم للحَرارة

heatstroke /ˈhiːtstrəʊk/ *n* لَفْحة حَرٍّ ,ضَرْبة حَرٍّ

heatwave /ˈhiːtweɪv/ *n* مَوْجة حَرٍّ

heave /hiːv/ **A** *vt* (*past tense, past participle* **heaved** or **hove**) **1** (to pull) جَرَّ (u; جَرّ) ,سَحَبَ (a; سَحْب); (to lift) رَفَعَ (a; رَفْع); **she ~d her suitcase up the stairs** جَرَّتْ \ سَحَبَتْ حَقيبَتَها إلى أَعْلى الدَرَجِ; **I ~d myself out of bed** سَحَبْتُ نَفْسي من الفِراشِ **2** (infml) (to throw) أَلْقى **3** (to utter) أَطْلَقَ; **to ~ a sigh** أَطْلَقَ تَنْهيدةً ,تَنَهَّدَ
B *vi* (*past tense, past participle* **heaved** or **hove**) **1** (to rise and fall) اهْتَزَّ; **his chest was heaving from the exertion** كانَ صَدْرُهُ يَهْتَزُّ من شِدّةِ الجُهْدِ **2** (to pull) جَرَّ (u; جَرّ)

heaven /ˈhev(ə)n/ *n* **1** (Relig) (also **Heaven**) السَماء; **the kingdom of ~** مَلَكوت السَماءِ; **to go to/be in ~** ذَهَبَ إلى الجَنّةِ **2** (in exclamations) **good ~s!** يا لَلْسَماءِ!; **~ forbid she should realize!** آهِ لو عَرَفَتْ لا سَمَحَ اللهُ!; **~ help us!** أَعِنّا يا اللهُ!; **thank ~** *or* **~s!** الحَمْدُ للهِ!; **what in ~'s name are you up to?** ما الّذي تُخَطِّطُ لَهُ بِحَقِّ السَماءِ؟ **3** (blissful state, place) نَعيم ,(جِنّات ,جَنّات) جَنّة; **the resort was ~** كانَ المُنْتَجَعُ جَنّةً **4** (fml) (sky) سَماء (f; سَماوات); **the ~s opened** هَطَلَتِ الأَمْطارُ بِغَزارةٍ
(Idiom) **to move heaven and earth** قَلَبَ السَماءَ على الأَرْضِ, فَعَلَ كُلَّ شَيْءٍ مُمْكِنٍ

heavenly /ˈhev(ə)nli/ *adj* **1** (Relig) ‹*being, kingdom*› سَماوِيّ **2** (infml) (wonderful) ‹*food, experience*› رائِع

heavenly body *n* (*pl* **heavenly bodies**) (Astron) جِرْم سَماوِيّ

heavily /ˈhevɪli/ *adv* **1** ‹*to lean, fall*› بِشِدّةٍ ,بِقوّةٍ; **~ laden carts** عَرَبات مُثْقَلة بالأَحْمالِ; **he fell ~ to the ground** وَقَعَ بِشِدّةٍ على الأَرْضِ **2** (noisily) ‹*to breathe*› بِصُعوبةٍ **3** (profoundly) ‹*to sleep, to sigh*› بِعُمْقٍ **4** (considerably) ‹*to rain, snow, to bleed*› بِشِدّةٍ; **to be ~ involved in sth** كانَ مُشارِكاً بِدَرَجةٍ كَبيرةٍ في شَيْءٍ; **~ subsidized** مُدَعَّم بِدَرَجةٍ كَبيرةٍ; **to lose ~** مُنِيَ بِخَسارةٍ ثَقيلةٍ; **she's always ~ made-up** هي دائِماً ما تَضَعُ الكَثيرَ من الماكِياج; **she was ~ pregnant** كانَتْ حامِلاً في شُهورِها الأَخيرة; **to be ~ dependent on sth** كانَ يَعْتَمِدُ بِشِدّةٍ على شَيْءٍ

heaviness /ˈhevinəs/ *n* **1** (of an object, a fabric) ثِقْل **2** (sluggishness) فُتور **3** (atmospheric) رُطوبة عالِية

heavy /ˈhevi/ **A** *adj* (**heavier, heaviest**) **1** (weighty) ‹*load, weight, bag*› ثَقيل; ‹*person*› بَدين; **how ~ are you?** ما وَزْنُكَ؟; **this case is too ~ for me to lift** هذه الحَقيبةُ ثَقيلةٌ جِدّاً لِدَرَجةِ أنّي لا أَسْتَطيعُ رَفْعَها; **he has a ~ build** هو ضَخْمُ البِنْيةِ **2** (durable) ‹*fabric, coat, shoes*› مَتين; **to wear ~ shoes** كانَ يَرْتَدي حِذاءً مَتيناً **3** (thick) ‹*type, line*› ثَقيل ,سَميك; **to wear ~ make-up** وَضَعَ مَكياج ثَقيلاً; **the sub-heading is printed in heavier type** العُنْوانُ الثانَوِيُّ مَكْتوبٌ بِخَطٍّ سَميكٍ **4** ‹*machinery*› ثَقيل; **'~ plant crossing'** 'مَعْبَر مَرْكَباتٍ ثُقيلةٍ' **5** ‹*artillery, machine gun*› ثَقيل **6** (intense) ‹*irony, humour*› شَديد; **with a ~ sigh** بِتَنْهيدةٍ عَميقةٍ; **to be a ~ sleeper** كانَ نَوْمُهُ ثَقيلاً; **with ~ irony** بِسُخْرِيّةٍ شَديدةٍ; **his eyelids began to get ~** بَدَأَتْ أَجْفانُهُ تَتَثاقَلُ; **with a ~ heart** بِقَلْبٍ مُثْقَلٍ بالهُمومِ; **a ~ blow** ضَرْبة موجِعة **7** (abundant) ‹*traffic*› مُزْدَحِم; ‹*gunfire*› كَثيف; ‹*bleeding*› شَديد; **trading was ~ on the stock market** كانَ التَعامُلُ كَثيفاً في سوقِ الأَوْراقِ المالِيّةِ; **to be a ~ smoker/drinker**

كانَ مُدَخِّناً شرِهاً \ كَثيرَ الشُّرْبِ; **to have a ~ workload** لَدَيْهِ عِبْءُ عَمَلٍ ثَقيلٌ **8** (severe) ‹*defeat, loss, fine*› ثَقيل; **they suffered ~ casualties/losses** مُنوا بِخَسائِرَ فادِحَةٍ; **there was ~ fighting all day** كانَ هُناكَ قِتالٌ كَثيفٌ طوال اليَوْمِ; **he has ~ debts** هو مُثْقَلٌ بالدُيونِ **9** (pronounced) ‹*accent, concentration*› شَديد; ‹*perfume*› ثَقيل **10** ‹*rain, cloud*› كَثيف; **the rain is getting heavier** يَزْدادُ المَطَرُ غزارةً; **it's very ~ today** اليَوْمُ شَديدُ الرُطوبةِ **11** (rich) ‹*meal, food, pastry*› ثَقيل; **they like ~ food** يُحِبّونَ الأَطْعِمةَ الثَقيلةَ; **they ordered a ~ Bordeaux** طَلَبوا زُجاجةَ بوردو عاليةِ التَرْكيز **12** (busy, packed) ‹*programme, schedule*› مُزْدَحِم; **March is always a ~ month** شَهْرُ مارس دائِماً مُزْدَحِمٌ **13** (difficult, serious) ‹*reading, book*› صَعْب **14** (with clay) ‹*soil*› ثَقيلُ القِوامِ **15** (loaded) **to be ~ with sth: the branches were ~ with fruit** كانَتِ الأَغْصانُ مَليئةً بالفاكِهةِ; **the air was ~ with the scent of orange blossom** كانَ الهَواءُ مُفْعَماً بِرائِحةِ زَهْرِ البُرْتُقالِ

B *n* (*pl* **heavies**) (infml) (bodyguard) [حارِس شَخْصيّ ضَخْم الجُثّةِ]; **the star emerged from his hotel surrounded by his heavies** خَرَجَ النَجْمُ من الفُنْدُقِ مُحاطاً بِحُرّاسِهِ الضِخام

C *adv* ‹*to weigh*› بِشَكْلٍ مُرْهِقٍ; **time hung ~ on her hands** مَرَّ الوَقْتُ ثَقيلاً عَلَيْها

heavy-duty /ˌhɛvɪˈdjuːti/ *adj* ‹*bag, clothing*› مَتين; ‹*vehicle, equipment*› خِدْمةٍ شاقّةٍ

heavy-handed /ˌhɛvɪˈhandɪd/ *adj* ‹*approach, treatment*› (clumsy) أَخْرَق (dipt; خُرْق); (overly forceful) شَديد الوَطْأةِ

heavy metal *n* **1** (metal) مَعْدِن ثَقيل **2** (rock music) هيفي ميتال

heavyweight /ˈhɛvɪweɪt/ **A** *n* **1** (boxer) [مُلاكِم من (فِئةِ) الوَزْنِ الثَقيلِ] **2** (important person or organization) [شَخْصيّة \ مُنَظَّمة من الوَزْنِ \ العِيارِ الثَقيلِ]; **a political ~** شَخْصية سِياسيّة من الوَزْنِ \ العِيارِ الثَقيل

B *adj* **1** (Sport) ‹*champion, boxing*› الوَزْنِ الثَقيلِ **2** ‹*fabric*› ثَقيل

Hebrew /ˈhiːbruː/ **A** *n* **1** (person) عِبْرِيّ, يَهودي (يَهود) **2** (language) (اللُغة) العِبْرِيّة

B *adj* ‹*language, history*› عِبْرِيّ

Hebrides /ˈhɛbrɪdiːz/ *pr n pl* (**the Hebrides**) جُزُر الهِبْريديس (جُزُر شَمالَ اسْكُتْلَنْدا)

Hebron /ˈhɛbrɒn/ *pr n* الخَليل (f)

heck /hɛk/ (infml) **A** *n* **what the ~ is going on?** ما الّذي يَجْري بِحَقِّ السَماءِ؟

B *excl* تَبّاً, يا لَلْهَوْل!

heckle /ˈhɛk(ə)l/ *vt* [قاطَعَ شَخْصاً الحَديثَ (بالأَسْئِلةِ والسُخْرِيّة)] ‹*a speaker, politician*›

heckler /ˈhɛklə/ *n* [شَخْص يُقاطِعُ حَديثاً (بالأَسْئِلةِ والسُخْرِيّةِ)]

hectare /ˈhɛktɛː/ *n* هِكْتار (هِكْتارات)

hectic /ˈhɛktɪk/ *adj* ‹*schedule, day*› حافِل; ‹*pace*› عالٍ; ‹*activity*› مُكَثَّف

he'd /hiːd/ *abbr* = **he had**, = **he would**

hedge /hɛdʒ/ **A** *n* [سِياج من شُجَيْراتٍ]

B *vi* (to equivocate) وارَبَ

Idiom **to hedge one's bets** (avoid committing oneself) احْتَفَظَ [تَحَوَّطَ وَلَمْ يُجازِفْ]; بِخَطِّ الرَجْعةِ (protect oneself against loss)

hedge fund *n* صُنْدوق تَحَوُّطٍ

hedgehog /ˈhɛdʒhɒg/ *n* قُنْفُذ (قَنافِذ)

hedgerow /ˈhɛdʒrəʊ/ *n* [سِياج طَويل من النَباتِ أو الشَجَرِ]

hedonism /ˈhiːd(ə)nɪz(ə)m/ *n* لَذِّيّة

hedonist /ˈhiːd(ə)nɪst/ *n* [شَخْص يَسْعى وراء اللَذّةِ أو المُتْعةِ في الحَياةِ]

heed /hiːd/ **A** *vt* انْتَبَهَ (إلى), الْتَفَتَ (إلى) ‹*a warning, advice*›

B *n* انْتِباه, الْتِفات; **to take ~ of** *or* **pay ~ to sth** انْتَبَهَ \ الْتَفَتَ إلى شَيْءٍ

heedless /ˈhiːdləs/ *adj*; **~ of the consequences/danger** غَيْر مُكْتَرِثٍ \ مُبالٍ بالعَواقِبِ \ الخَطَرِ

heel /hiːl/ **A** *n* **1** (of foot) كَعْب (كُعوب, كِعاب); **he's got blisters on his ~s** لَدَيْهِ بُثورٌ في كَعْبَيْهِ; **to turn on one's ~** اسْتَدارَ لِلخَلْفِ; **the dog was snapping at his ~s** كانَ الكَلْبُ يَعَضُّ على كَعْبَيْهِ **2** (of shoes, socks) كَعْب (كُعوب, كِعاب); **shoes with a low/high ~** حِذاء بِكَعْبٍ مُنْخَفِضٍ \ عالٍ

B (**heels**) *n pl* (also **high heels**) حِذاء بِكَعْبٍ عالٍ; **she's wearing ~s** تَرْتَدي حِذاءً بِكَعْبٍ عالٍ

C *vt* (to repair) أَصْلَحَ الكَعْبَ ‹*a shoe, boot*›

(Idioms) **to be hot on sb's heels** (in pursuit of) تَعَقَّبَ شَخْصاً (soon after) تَلا شَخْصاً مُباشَرةً بِشَكْلٍ حَثيثٍ; **to cool** *or* **kick one's heels** بَقِيَ مُنْتَظِراً لِوَقْتٍ طَويلٍ; **to bring sb to heel** وَضَعَ شَخْصاً تحت السَيْطَرةِ; **to dig in one's heels** تَشَبَّثَ بِمَوْقِفِهِ; **to drag one's heels** تَباطَأَ; **to fall head over heels** سَقَطَ رَأْساً على عَقِبٍ; **he's fallen head over ~s in love with her** وَقَعَ في حُبِّها من رَأْسِهِ حتّى قَدَمَيْهِ

(Phrasal verb) **heel over** «ships, yachts» مالَ على جانِبِهِ

heel bar *n* حانوت الإسْكافيِّ

hefty /ˈhɛfti/ *adj* (**heftier, heftiest**) (infml) **1** (large and heavy) ‹*person*› ضَخْم (ضِخام); ‹*suitcase, book*› ثَقيل **2** (powerful) ‹*blow*› قَوِيّ **3** (substantial) ‹*price, fine*› ضَخْم, باهِظ

hegemony /hɪˈdʒɛməni/ *n* هَيْمَنة, سَيْطَرة

Hegira /ˈhɛdʒɪrə/ *n* (**the Hegira**) الهِجْرة (النَبَوِيّة)

heifer /ˈhɛfə/ *n* بَقَرة صَغيرة

height /hʌɪt/ *n* **1** (tallness of a person) طول (أَطْوال); (of a building, tree, wall) اِرْتِفاع; **a woman of average** *or* **medium ~** اِمْرَأة مُتَوَسِّطة القامةِ; **what is your ~?, what ~ are you?** ما طولُكَ؟; **to be five metres in ~** كانَ ارتِفاعُهُ خَمْسةُ أَمْتارٍ **2** (of mountains, planes) اِرْتِفاع; **at a ~ of 10,000 metres** على ارْتِفاعِ 10000 مِتْرٍ; **to fall from a great ~** سَقَطَ من على اِرْتِفاعٍ شاهِقٍ; **to be scared of ~s** كانَ يَخافُ من الارْتِفاعاتِ **3** (in intensity) ذُرْوة (ذُرًى), أَوْج; **at the ~ of the season** في ذُرْوةِ المَوْسِمِ; **at the ~ of the storm/crisis** في ذُرْوةِ العاصِفةِ \ الأَزْمةِ; **to be at the ~ of one's popularity/powers** كانَ في ذُرْوة شَعْبِيَّتِهِ \ سُلْطَتِهِ; **the war was at its ~** كانَت الحَرْبُ في أَوْجِها; **to reach new ~s of popularity/success** وَصَلَ إلى آفاقٍ جَديدةٍ من الشَعْبِيّةِ \ النَجاحِ; **the ~ of luxury/stupidity** قِمّة الرَفاهِيةِ \ الغَباءِ; **to be the ~ of fashion** كانَ في أَعْلى دَرَجاتِ الموضة

heighten /ˈhʌɪt(ə)n/ *vt* [زادَ من حِدّةِ شَيْءٍ] ‹*tension, suspense*›; رَفَعَ (رَفْع a; ‹*awareness*›; أَبْرَزَ ‹*an effect*›

heinous /ˈheɪnəs/ *adj* (fml) ‹*crime, act*› فَظيع, شَنيع

heir /ɛː/ *n* وَريث (وُرَثاء), وارِث (وَرَثة, وُرّاث); **the ~ to the fortune** وَريث الثَرْوةِ

heiress /ɛːˈrɛs/ *n* وَريثة

heirloom /ˈɛːluːm/ *n* [شَيْء ثَمين تَتَوارَثُهُ عائِلةٌ جيلاً بعد جيلٍ]

heist /hʌɪst/ *n* (infml) سَرِقة, سَطْو

Hejaz, **Hijaz** /hɪˈdʒaz/ *pr n* الحِجاز (f)

held /hɛld/ *past tense, past participle* ▸ **hold**

helicopter /ˈhɛlɪkɒptə/ *n* طائِرة مِرْوَحِيّة \ حَوّامة, هِليكوبتِر عَموديّة

heliport /ˈhɛlɪpɔːt/ *n* [مَهْبِط طائِراتِ الهِليكوبْتِر]

helium /ˈhiːlɪəm/ *n* هِلْيوم; **a ~ balloon** بالون الهِلْيوم

helix /ˈhiːlɪks/ *n* (*pl* **helices**) لَوْلَب (لَوالِبُ)

hell /hɛl/ **A** *n* **1** (Relig) (also **Hell**) جَهَنَّم, النّار (dipt), الجَحيم; **to go to/be in ~** ذَهَبَ إلى \ كانَ في الجَحيمِ **2** (infml) (unpleasant experience) جَحيم; **his life was ~ on earth** كانَتْ حَياتُهُ جَحيماً على الأَرْضِ; **going through customs was sheer ~** كانَ المُرورُ من خِلالِ الجَمارِكِ جَحيماً مُطْبَقاً; **a neighbour from ~** جار من الجَحيمِ **3** (infml) (as intensifier) **it was a ~ of a shock** كانَ صَدْمةً كَبيرةً; **we had a ~ of a time** (bad) قَضَيْنا وَقْتاً تَعيسا جِدًّا; (good) قَضَيْنا وَقْتاً مُمْتِعاً جِدًّا; **it's a ~ of a lot worse/easier** هو أَسْوَأُ \ أَسْهَلُ بِكَثيرٍ جِدًّا; **she was as jealous as ~** كانَتْ شَديدةَ الغَيْرةِ; **to run/fight like ~** جَرى \ حارَبَ بِكُلِّ قُوَّتِهِ; **get the ~ out of here!** بِحَقِّ الجَحيمِ اخْرُجْ من هُنا!; **what the ~ are you doing?** بِحَقِّ الجَحيمِ ماذا تَفْعَلُ؟

B *excl* (infml) **oh ~! I've left the keys behind** آهٍ يا لَلْجَحيمِ! لَقَدْ تَرَكْتُ المَفاتيحَ هُناكَ

(Idioms) **come hell or high water** مَهْما كانَت الصِعابُ; **there was/will be hell to pay** (infml) سَتَنْفَتِحُ أَبْوابُ جَهَنَّمَ; **to raise (merry) hell** (infml) أَقامَ الدُنْيا وَأَقْعَدَها

he'll /hiːl/ *abbr* = **he will**

hello /həˈləʊ/ *excl* **1** (greeting) أَهْلاً; **she didn't even say ~** لم تَقُل حتّى أَهْلاً; **~! how are you?** أَهْلاً! كيف حالُكَ؟ **2** (used when answering a call) أَلو; (used when calling) أَلو

helm /hɛlm/ *n* دَفّة

helmet /ˈhɛlmɪt/ *n* خوذة (خُوَذ, خوذات)

helmsman /ˈhɛlmzmən/ *n* (*pl* **-men**) مُدير الدَفّةِ

help /hɛlp/ **A** *vt* **1** (to assist) أعانَ, عاوَنَ, ساعَدَ ‹*people, companies*›; **to ~ sb to do sth** ساعَدَ شَخصاً على أنْ يَفْعَلَ شَيْئاً; **can you ~ me with these bags?** هل يُمْكِنُكَ مُساعَدَتي في حَمْلِ هذه الحَقائِبِ؟; **can I ~ you?** (in a shop) هل يُمْكِنُني أنْ أُساعِدَكَ؟; **to ~ each other** ساعَدوا بَعْضَهُم البَعْضَ; **to ~ sb across the road** ساعَدَ شَخْصاً في عُبورِ الطَريقِ; **I ~ed him to his feet** ساعَدْتُهُ أنْ يَقِفَ على قَدَمَيْهِ; **he ~ed her on/off with her coat** ساعَدَها في ارْتِداءِ \ خَلْعِ مِعْطَفِها; **the injection will ~ to ease the pain** سَتُساعِدُ الحُقْنَةُ في تَخْفيفِ الأَلَمِ **2** (to improve) حَسَّنَ ‹*a situation, problem*›; **he didn't ~ matters by writing that letter** لم يُحَسِّنِ الأُمورَ بِكِتابَةِ ذلك الخِطابِ **3** (to avoid, prevent) **it can't be ~ed!** لا مَفَرَّ مِنْهُ!; **I can't ~ feeling guilty** لا يُمْكِنُني أنْ أَمْنَعَ نَفْسي من الشُعورِ بالذَنْبِ; **she can't ~ the way she was brought up** لا يُمْكِنُها أنْ تُغَيِّرَ الطَريقَةَ الَّتي تَرَبَّتْ عَلَيْها

B *vi* **1** (to assist) «people, information» ساعَدَ; **this map doesn't ~ much** هذه الخَريطةُ لا تُساعِدُ كَثيراً; **how can I ~?** كيفَ يُمْكِنُني أنْ أُساعِدَكَ؟; **he offered to ~ with the cost** عَرَضَ أنْ يُساعِدَ في تَحَمُّلِ التَكْلِفَةِ **2** (to be an improvement) **would it ~ if I turned the light off?** هل سَيَكونُ من الأَفْضَلِ أنْ أُطْفِئَ النورَ؟

C *v refl* **1** (to serve) **to ~ oneself** ساعَدَ نَفْسَهُ بِنَفْسِهِ; **~ yourself to coffee** ساعِدْ نَفْسَكَ بِنَفْسِكَ في الحُصولِ على القَهْوَةِ; **'can I use your phone?' — '~ yourself!'** 'هل يُمْكِنُني أنْ أَسْتَخْدِمَ تِلِفونَكَ؟' — 'تَفَضَّلْ!' **2** (infml) (to take) **to ~ oneself to sth** أَخَذَ شَيْئاً دون إذْنٍ

D *n* **1** [u] (assistance) مُعاوَنة, عَوْن, مُساعَدة; **do you need any ~ with that?** هل تَحْتاجُ إلى أيِّ مُساعَدَةٍ في ذلكَ؟; **he's going to die if we don't get ~** سَيَموتُ إذا لم نَجِدْ لَهُ مُساعَدَةً; **to be of ~ to sb** «person» كانَ عَوْناً لِشَخْصٍ; «information, book» كانَ مُجْدِياً لِشَخْصٍ; **it's a great ~ if you can speak the language** سَيَكونُ مُجْدِياً جِدًّا إذا اسْتَطَعْتَ التَحَدُّثَ بِنَفْسِ اللُغَةِ; **she needs professional ~** تَحْتاجُ إلى مُساعَدَةٍ من مُخْتَصٍّ **2** (cleaning woman) عامِلة نَظافَةٍ

E *excl* الغَوْثَ, النَجْدةَ

Phrasal verb **help out** **1** قَدَّمَ العَوْنَ **2** ~ **[sb] out** قَدَّمَ العَوْنَ لِ[شَخْصٍ]

help desk *n* مَكْتَب المُساعَدَةِ

helper /ˈhɛlpə/ *n* مُعين, مُعاوِن, مُساعِد

helpful /ˈhɛlpfʊl/ *adj* **1** (obliging) ‹*staff*› خَدوم **2** (useful) ‹*information, suggestion*› مُفيد, نافِع

helping /ˈhɛlpɪŋ/ *n* حِصّة [من طَعامٍ]

helpless /ˈhɛlpləs/ *adj* **1** (defenceless) ‹*victim, child*› مَغْلوب على أَمْرِهِ **2** (powerless) ‹*bystander, onlooker*› عاجِز, لا حيلةَ لَهُ; **I felt ~ to do anything about it** شَعَرْتُ أنَّني عاجِزٌ عن فِعْلِ أيِّ شَيْءٍ حِيالَ ذلك **3** ‹*rage*› لا يُمْكِنُ ضَبْطُهُ \ كَبْحُهُ \ كَبْتُهُ; ‹*laughter*› لا إراديّ

helplessly /ˈhɛlplɪsli/ *adv* ‹*to watch, stand by*› عاجِزاً; ‹*to struggle, try*› بِعَجْزٍ

helpline /ˈhɛlplʌɪn/ *n* خَطّ مُساعَدَةٍ

Helsinki /hɛlˈsɪŋki/ *pr n* هِلْسِنْكي (f)

helter-skelter /ˌhɛltəˈskɛltə/ **A** *adj* ‹*pace, rush*› فَوْضَويّ **B** *adv* شَذَر مَذَر, بِشَكْلٍ فَوْضَويٍّ

hem /hɛm/ *n* كُفّة (كُفَف)

Phrasal verb **hem in**: **~ [sb/sth] in, ~ in [sb/sth]** **1** (to surround) طَوَّقَ \ حاصَرَ [شَخْصاً \ شَيْئاً] **2** (to constrain) ضَيَّقَ الخِناقَ على [شَخْصٍ \ شَيْءٍ]

hematologist (AmE) *n* ▸ **haematologist**

hemisphere /ˈhɛmɪsfɪə/ *n* نِصْف الكُرة الأَرْضيّة

hemline /ˈhɛmlʌɪn/ *n* حاشِية \ حافة [ثَوْبٍ]

hemoglobin (AmE) *n* ▸ **haemoglobin**

hemophilia (AmE) *n* ▸ **haemophilia**

hemophiliac (AmE) *n* ▸ **haemophiliac**

hemorrhage (AmE) *n, vi* ▸ **haemorrhage**

hemorrhoids (AmE) *n pl* ▸ **haemorrhoids**

hemp /hɛmp/ *n* **1** (plant) قِنَّب **2** (fibre) أَلْياف القِنَّبِ **3** (drug) حَشيش

hen /hɛn/ *n* (chicken) دَجاجة; (female bird) أُنْثى [الطَيْرِ]

hence /hɛns/ *adv* **1** (for this reason) *before n* من ثَمَّ; *before adj* بالتالي, إذَنْ **2** (fml) (from now) من الآنِ

henceforth /hɛnsˈfɔːθ/, **henceforward** /hɛnsˈfɔːwəd/ *adv* (fml) بعد الآنِ ,من الآنِ فصاعِداً

henchman /ˈhɛntʃmən/ *n* (*pl* **-men**) (pej) تابِع (أَتْباع)

henhouse /ˈhɛnhaʊs/ *n* قُنّ (قِنان)

henna /ˈhɛnə/ *n* حِنّاء (n coll)

hen night *n* [حَفْل تَوْديعِ العُزوبِيّةِ للعَروسِ]

henpecked /ˈhɛnpɛkt/ *adj* **a ~ husband** زَوْج مُسْتَضْعَف \ مَقْهور \ خانِع (في عَلاقَتِهِ مع زَوْجَتِهِ)

hepatitis /ˌhɛpəˈtʌɪtɪs/ *n* اِلْتِهاب الكَبِدِ

hepatitis C *n* اِلْتِهاب الكَبِدِ الفَيْروسيّ (ج)

heptathlon /hɛpˈtaθlɒn/ *n* [مُسابَقة رِياضِيّة أولِمْبِيّة ذات سَبْعِ فَعّالِيّاتٍ]

her /həː, hə/ **A** *pron* **1** (direct object) ـها; **I saw ~** رَأَيْتُها; **call ~ now!** اتَّصِلْ بِها الآنَ! **2** (indirect obj, after prep) ـها; **I gave ~ the card** أَعْطَيْتُها البِطاقةَ; **I did it for ~** فَعَلْتُهُ من أَجْلِها; **give ~ my telephone number** أَعْطِها رَقْمَ تَلِيفوني **3** (emphatic) **it's ~!** هِيَ; إِنَّها هِيَ!

B *determiner* ـها; **she loves ~ job** تُحِبُّ عَمَلَها; **she broke ~ leg** كَسَرَتْ رِجْلَها

herald /ˈhɛrəld/ **A** *n* (Hist) (proclaimer, announcer) مُنادٍ; (messenger) مُرْسَل

B *vt* أَشارَ (إلى), دَلَّ (u; دَلالة; على)

heraldry /ˈhɛrəldri/ *n* [نِظام لِوَضْعِ وَتَصْنيفِ شِعاراتِ النَبالَةِ]

herb /həːb/ *n* تابِل (تَوابِلُ)

herbal /ˈhəːb(ə)l/ **A** *adj* ‹*supplement*› عُشْبيّ

B *n* كِتاب أَعْشابٍ

herbalist /ˈhəːbəlɪst/ *n* (shop) [مَحَلّ أَعْشابٍ]; (trader) [مُخْتَصّ في (بَيْعِ) الأَعْشابِ الطِبِّيّةِ]

herbal medicine *n* طِبّ (التَداوي ب) الأَعْشابِ

herbal tea *n* شاي عُشْبيّ

herbicide /ˈhəːbɪsʌɪd/ *n* مُبيد الأَعْشابِ

herb tea *n* شاي عُشْبيّ

herd /həːd/ **A** *n* (of animals) قَطيع (قُطْعان); (of people) طائِفة (طَوائِفُ), جَمْع غَفير, جَماعة مُحْتَشِدة

B *vt* رَعَى قَطيعاً, جَمَعَ شَمْلَ قَطيعٍ ‹*sheep, cattle*›; «police, the army» [قادَ \ ساقَ جَمْعاً غَفيراً من] ‹*protesters, hostages*›; **to ~ people into a room** قادَ جَمْعاً غَفيراً من الناسِ إلى غُرْفةٍ

here /hɪə/ *adv* **1** (indicating place) هُنا; **we get off ~** سَنَنْزِلُ هُنا; **put it ~** ضَعْهُ هُنا; **which one? this one ~ or that one?** أَيّ واحِدٍ؟ هذا أم ذاكَ؟; **far from/near ~** بَعيداً عن \ قَريباً من هُنا; **two kilometres from ~** على بُعْدِ كيلومِتْرَيْنِ من هُنا; **come over ~** تَعالَ هُنا; **up to ~, down to ~** إلى هُنا; **I'm up ~** أنا هُنا; **~ lies John Young** هُنا يَرْقُدُ جون يونْج; **~ comes the bus** ها هي الحافِلةُ قادِمةٌ; **~'s what you do** إِلَيْكَ ما يَنْبَغي أَنْ تَفْعَلَهُ; **~ you are** تَفَضَّلْ; **my colleague ~ will show you** سَيُبَيِّنُ لَكَ زَميلي هُنا; **~ and there** هُنا وَهُناكَ **2** (indicating presence) **she's not ~ right now** هي غَيْرُ مَوْجودةٍ الآنَ; **the train will be ~ any minute** سَيَأْتي القِطارُ هُنا في أَيِّ لَحْظةٍ; **'Matthew?'—'~, sir'** 'ماثيو؟' — 'حاضِرٌ يا سَيِّدي'; **now that summer's ~** الآنَ مع حُلولِ الصَيْفِ

Idioms **here goes!** (infml) فَلْنَبْدَأْ!; **here we go!** (infml) ها هو يَبْدَأُ!; **here's to ...** نَخْب ... ,في صِحّةِ ...; **here's to the happy couple!** نَخْبُ الزَوْجَيْنِ السَعيدَيْنِ!; **it's neither here nor there** لا يُفْرِقُ مَعَهُ

hereabouts /ˌhɪərəˈbaʊts/, **hereabout** (AmE) /ˈhɪərəbaʊt/ *adv* بالقُرْبِ من هُنا ,في الجِوارِ

hereafter /hɪərˈɑːftə/ *adv* (fml) **1** (from now on) من الآنِ فَصاعِداً **2** (in the future) مُسْتَقْبَلاً ,في المُسْتَقْبَلِ ,فيما بَعْدُ

here and now *n* (**the here and now**) الوَقْت الحاضِر \ الراهِن

hereby /hɪəˈbʌɪ/ *adv* (fml) بِموجِبِ هذا

hereditary /hɪˈrɛdɪt(ə)ri/ *adj* ‹*ruler, succession*› مُتَوارَث; ‹*deafness, predisposition*› وِراثيّ

heredity /hɪˈrɛdɪti/ *n* وِراثة

herein /hɪərˈɪn/ *adv* (fml) في \ ضِمْنَ هذا ,هُنا

heresy /ˈhɛrɪsi/ *n* (*pl* **heresies**) هَرْطَقة

heretic /ˈhɛrɪtɪk/ *n* هَرْطوقيّ (هَراطِقة)

heritage /ˈhɛrɪtɪdʒ/ *n* إِرْث ,ميراث (مَواريثُ)

hermetically /həːˈmɛtɪkli/ *adv*; **~ sealed** مُحْكَم الإغْلاقِ

hermit /ˈhəːmɪt/ *n* ناسِك (نُسّاك), زاهِد (زُهّاد)

hernia /ˈhəːnɪə/ *n* (*pl* **hernias** or **herniae**) فَتْق (فُتوق)

hero /ˈhɪərəʊ/ *n* (*pl* **heroes**) 1 (brave, admirable man; idol) بَطَل (أَبْطال) 2 (of a film, book) بَطَل (أَبْطال)، شَخْصيّة رَئيسيّة

heroic /hɪˈrəʊɪk/ *adj* بُطوليّ

heroin /ˈherəʊɪn/ *n* هيرُوين

heroin addict *n* مُدْمِن هيرُوين

heroine /ˈherəʊɪn/ *n* 1 (iconic woman) بَطَلة 2 (of a film, book) بَطَلة، شَخْصيّة رَئيسيّة

heroism /ˈherəʊɪz(ə)m/ *n* بُطولة، بَسالة

heron /ˈherən/ *n* مالِك الحَزين، بَلَشون

hero worship *n* [إِعْجاب مُفْرِط (بِشَخْص)]

herpes /ˈhɜːpiːz/ *n* هَرْبيس

herring /ˈherɪŋ/ *n* (*pl* **herrings** or **herring**) رِنْكة، رِنْجة

herring gull *n* نَوْرَس الرِنْجة

hers /hɜːz/ *pron* **my car is red but ~ is blue** سَيّارَتي حَمْراءُ لٰكِنَّ سَيّارَتَها زَرْقاءُ; **my results were good, but ~ were better** كانَتْ نَتائِجي جَيِّدَةً، لٰكِنَّ نَتائِجَها كانَتْ أَفْضَل; **the green hat is ~** القُبَّعةُ الخَضْراءُ لَها; **which house is ~?** أَيُّ بَيْتٍ بَيْتُها؟; **I'm a friend of ~** أَنا أَحَدُ أَصْدِقائِها; **it's not ~** لَيْسَ لَها; **the money wasn't ~ to give away** لم تَكُنِ الأَمْوالُ مِلْكَها حَتّى تَتَخَلّى عَنْها; **that cat of ~** (infml) قِطُّها اللَعينُ ذٰلِكَ; **~ was not an easy task** (fml) لم تَكُنْ مُهِمَّتُها مُهِمَّةً سَهْلَة

herself /hɜːˈself/ *pron* 1 (reflexive) نَفْسَها; **she's cut ~** جَرَحَتْ نَفْسَها; **she's talking to ~** تَتَكَلَّمُ مع نَفْسِها 2 (emphatic) (she herself) نَفْسُها; (by herself) بِنَفْسِها; **she ~ said that ...** هي نَفْسُها مَنْ قالَ إنّ ...; **she ~ didn't know** هي نَفْسُها لم تَعْرِفْ; **she made it ~** صَنَعَتْهُ بِنَفْسِها 3 (after prepositions) **she kept the money for ~** احْتَفَظَتْ بالأَمْوالِ لِنَفْسِها 4 (in expressions) **she's not ~ today** هي لَيْسَتْ على ما يُرامُ اليَوْمَ; **she's (all) by ~** هي بِمُفْرَدِها; **she had the house all to ~** كانَ البَيْتُ كُلُّهُ لَها

he's /hiːz/ *abbr* = **he is**, = **he has**

hesitant /ˈhezɪt(ə)nt/ *adj* ‹*smile, steps*› مُتَرَدِّد; **I was ~ about taking on the project** كُنْتُ مُتَرَدِّداً بِشَأْنِ تَوَلّي المَشْروعِ

hesitate /ˈhezɪteɪt/ *vi* 1 (to pause) تَرَدَّدَ 2 (to be reluctant) تَرَدَّدَ; **if you need anything, don't ~ to ask** إذا كُنْتَ بِحاجةٍ إلى أَيِّ شَيْءٍ، لا تَتَرَدَّدْ في أَنْ تَطْلُبَ مِنّي

hesitation /hezɪˈteɪʃ(ə)n/ *n* 1 (pause) تَرَدُّد; **he answered without ~** أَجابَ بِدونِ \ بلا \ من غَيْرِ تَرَدُّدٍ 2 (reluctance) تَرَدُّد

heterogeneous /ˌhet(ə)rəʊˈdʒiːnɪəs/ *adj* ‹*population, assortment*› مُتَغايِر

heterosexual /het(ə)rəʊˈsekʃʊəl/ **A** *adj* [يَشْتَهي الجِنْسَ الآخَرَ] **B** *n* [شَخْص يَشْتَهي الجِنْسَ الآخَرَ]

heterosexuality /het(ə)rəʊsekʃʊˈalɪti/ *n* اشْتِهاء الجِنْسِ الآخَرِ

hew /hjuː/ *vt* (*past participle* **hewed** or **hewn** /hjuːn/) 1 (to cut) قَطَعَ (بِفَأْسٍ أو أَداةٍ أُخْرى) ‹*wood, stone*›; (to extract) اسْتَخْرَجَ ‹*coal*› 2 (to make) حَفَرَ (حَفْر; i) ‹*a building*›; شَقَّ (شَقّ; u) ‹*road*›

hexagon /ˈheksəg(ə)n/ *n* مُسَدَّس (مُسَدَّسات)، شَكْل سُداسيّ

hey /heɪ/ *excl* (infml) 1 (calling attention) يا (فُلان) 2 (expressing surprise, protest) آه

heyday /ˈheɪdeɪ/ *n* أَوْج، ذُرْوة (ذُرًى); **in her ~** في أَوْجِ \ ذُرْوةِ مَجْدِها

Hezbollah /ˌhezbəˈlɑː/ *n* حِزْب اللهِ

HGV /eɪtʃdʒiːˈviː/ *n* (BrE) = **heavy goods vehicle** سَيّارة النَقْلِ الثَقيلِ

hi /hʌɪ/ *excl* (infml) مَرْحَباً، أَهْلاً

HI *abbr* ▸ **Hawaii**

hiatus /hʌɪˈeɪtəs/ *n* فَجْوة (فَجَوات)؛ انْقِطاع

hibernate /ˈhʌɪbəneɪt/ *vi* «animals, plants» دَخَلَ في (حالةِ) سُباتٍ شَتْويٍّ، أَسْبَتَ

hibernation /hʌɪbəˈneɪʃ(ə)n/ *n* إِسْبات، سُبات \ بَيات شَتْويّ; **to go into ~** دَخَلَ في سُباتٍ \ بَياتٍ شَتْويٍّ

hiccup, **hiccough** /ˈhɪkʌp/ **A** *n* 1 (a sound in the throat) فُواق، حازوقة; **to have (the) ~s** أُصيبَ بِفُواقٍ \ حازوقةٍ 2 (a setback) عَقَبة (عَقَبات، عِقاب)، عائِق (عَوائِق) **B** *vi* (**-pp-**, **-p-**) فاقَ (u; فُواق)

hick /hɪk/ *n* (AmE infml pej) ريفيّ

hid /hɪd/ *past tense* ▸ **hide**

hidden /ˈhɪd(ə)n/ **A** *past participle* ▸ **hide** **B** *adj* 1 ‹*camera, entrance*› مَخْفيّ 2 ‹*cost, meaning*› خَفيّ

hide /hʌɪd/ **A** *vt* (*past tense* **hid**; *past participle* **hidden**) **1** (to conceal) أَخْفى, خَبَّأَ; **I hid the letter from her** خَبَّأْتُ \ أَخْفَيْتُ الرِسالةَ عَنها; **to ~ oneself** اخْتَبَأَ **2** (to keep secret) كَتَمَ, أَخْفى (u; كِتْمان, كَتْم) ‹*one's feelings, a fact*› **3** (to mask, cover) أَخْفى **B** *vi* (*past tense* **hid**; *past participle* **hidden**) تَخَبَّأَ, اخْتَبَأَ; **he was hiding from the police** كانَ يَخْتَبِئُ من الشُرْطةِ **C** *n* (raw) جِلْد (أَجْلاد, جُلود); (tanned) جِلْد مَدْبوغ

(Phrasal verb) **hide away** **1** تَوارى, اخْتَبَأَ **2** **~ [sth] away, ~ away [sth]** أَخْفى \ خَبَّأَ [شَيْئاً]

hide-and-seek /hʌɪd(ə)n'siːk/ *n* غُمَّيْضة

hideaway /'hʌɪdəweɪ/ *n* (hiding place) مَخْبَأ (مَخابِئُ), مَلاذ; (retreat) مُعْتَزَل

hideous /'hɪdɪəs/ *adj* **1** (ugly) ‹*dress, building*› بَشِع **2** (horrific) ‹*monster, death*› بَشِع **3** (appalling) ‹*crime*› بَشِع

hideout /'hʌɪdaʊt/ *n* مَخْبَأ (مَخابِئُ)

hiding /'hʌɪdɪŋ/ *n* **1** (concealment); **to be in/go into ~** اخْتَبَأَ **2** (beating) ضَرْب مُبَرِّح

hiding place *n* مَخْبَأ (مَخابِئُ)

hierarchy /'hʌɪərɑːki/ *n* (*pl* **hierarchies**) تَسَلْسُل هَرَميّ, هَرَمِيّة

hieroglyph /'hʌɪərəglɪf/, **hieroglyphic** /hʌɪrə'glɪfɪk/ *n* حَرْف هيروغْليفيّ

hieroglyphics /hʌɪərə'glɪfɪks/ *n pl* كِتابة هيروغْليفيّة

hi-fi /'hʌɪfʌɪ/ *n* **1** (equipment) جِهاز هاي فاي (ذو دِقّةٍ عالِيةٍ في إِخْراجِ الصَوْتِ) **2** (reproduction) [u] = **high fidelity** هاي فاي (إِخْراج الصَوْتِ بِدِقّةٍ عالِيةٍ)

higgledy-piggledy /ˌhɪgəldɪ'pɪgəldi/ **A** *adv* ‹*to lie, be strewn*› بِشَكْلٍ فَوْضَويّ **B** *adj* ‹*fashion, assortment*› فَوْضَويّ

high /hʌɪ/ **A** *adj* **1** (tall) ‹*wall, mountain, building*› مُرْتَفِع, عالٍ; **it's fifty cm ~** ارْتِفاعُهُ خَمْسونَ سم; **how ~ is the cliff?** ما ارْتِفاعُ الجُرُفِ؟; **a five-metre ~ wall** جِدار ارْتِفاعُهُ خَمْسةُ أَمْتارٍ; **the water was waist-~** وَصَلَ الماءُ إلى مُسْتَوى الخَصْرِ **2** (far from the ground) ‹*shelf, cloud, ceiling*› مُرْتَفِع, عالٍ; **at ~ altitude** على ارْتِفاعٍ شاهِقٍ; **how ~ are we?** ما ارْتِفاعُنا؟ **3** (numerically large) (numerically large) ‹*ratio, price, frequency*› عالٍ, مُرْتَفِع; **at ~ speed** بِسُرْعةٍ عالِيةٍ; **to have a ~ temperature** كانَتْ دَرَجةُ حَرارَتِهِ مُرْتَفِعةً; **a food that is ~ in fat** طَعام نِسْبةُ الدُهونِ بِهِ مُرْتَفِعةٌ; **a number ~er than 20** رَقْم أَكْبَر من 20 **4** (great, intense) ‹*risk, fever*› شَديد; ‹*degree*› كَبير; **there is a ~ degree of risk** هُناكَ دَرَجةٌ كَبيرةٌ من المُخاطَرةِ; **our hopes/expectations are ~** لَدَيْنا آمالٌ \ تَوَقُّعاتٌ كَبيرةٌ; **a moment of ~ drama** لَحْظة مَليئة بالإثارةِ **5** (in importance) ‹*quality, status, standard*› مُرْتَفِع, عالٍ; **it has the ~est priority** كانَ لَهُ أَهَمِّيّةٌ قُصْوى; **to be ~ up in the organization** كانَ لَهُ مَنْصِبٌ كَبيرٌ في المُنَظَّمةِ; **to have friends in ~ places** كانَ لَهُ أَصْدِقاءُ في مَناصِبَ مُهِمّةٍ **6** (noble) ‹*ideal, principle*› نَبيل, سامٍ, مُرْتَفِع; **he has ~ ideals** لَدَيْهِ أَفْكارٌ نَبيلةٌ **7** (acute) ‹*note, voice*› عالٍ **8** (infml) (mature) ‹*fish, cheese*› فاسِد; **the cheese is pretty ~** هذا الجُبْنُ فاسِدٌ جِدًّا **9** (infml) (euphoric) غائِب عن الوَعْيِ; **to be ~ on drugs** كانَ تحت تَأْثيرِ المُخَدِّراتِ **B** *n* **1** (anticyclone) مِنْطَقة ضَغْطٍ جَوّيٍّ مُرْتَفِع **2** (on an index) مُسْتَوًى عالٍ; **the price of oil closed at a record ~** أَقْفَلَ سِعْرُ النَفْطِ على أَعْلى مُسْتَوًى لَهُ على الإِطْلاقِ; **turn the grill to ~** أَدِرِ الشَوّايةَ إلى الدَرَجةِ العالِيةِ; **morale is at an all-time ~** الروحُ المَعْنَويّةُ في أَعْلى دَرَجاتِها على الإِطْلاقِ **C** *adv* **1** (far upwards) ‹*to jump, climb, fly*› عالِياً; **the plane flew ~ over the city** طارَتِ الطائِرةُ عالِياً فوق المَدينةِ; **the desk was piled ~ with papers** كانَتْ على المَكْتَبِ كَوْمةٌ مُرْتَفِعةٌ من الأَوْراقِ; **interest rates may go as ~ as 12%** قد تَرْتَفِعُ مُعَدَّلاتُ الفائدةِ لِتَصِلَ إلى 12٪; **don't go any ~er than £5,000** لا تَتَخَطّى £5000 بِأَيِّ شَكْلٍ **2** (in intensity) أَدارَ التَدْفِئةَ إلى أَعْلى; عالِياً; **to turn the heating up ~** أَدارَ التَدْفِئةَ إلى أَعْلى; **the radio is too ~** صَوْتُ الراديو مُرْتَفِعٌ جِدًّا; **stocks are ~** المَخْزوناتُ مُتَوَفِّرةٌ بِكَثْرةٍ; **I rate their service pretty ~** تَقْييمي لِخِدْمَتِهِمْ مُرْتَفِعٌ جِدًّا **3** (of sounds) ‹*to sing, play*› بِصَوْتٍ عالٍ \ مُرْتَفِعٍ

(Idiom) **to hold one's head up high** رَفَعَ رَأْسَهُ عالِياً

high beam *n* (AmE) ضَوْء مُبْهِر

highbrow /'hʌɪbraʊ/ *adj* ‹*culture, art*› راقٍ, رَفيع

high chair *n* [كُرْسيّ أَكْلٍ عالٍ (للأَطْفالِ)]

high-class /ˌhʌɪ'klɑːs/ *adj* ‹*restaurant, hotel*› من الدَرَجةِ العالِيةِ, من الطِرازِ الرَفيعِ; ‹*area*› راقٍ; ‹*prostitute*› من طَبَقةٍ راقِيةٍ

high commission *n* مُفَوَّضِيّة عُلْيا

high commissioner *n* مُفَوَّض \ مَنْدوب سامٍ

high court *n* مَحْكَمة عُلْيا

High Court *n* **High Court of Justice**; المَحْكَمة العُلْيا

high court judge *n* قاضي القُضاةِ

high-definition TV /ˌhʌɪdefɪˌnɪʃ(ə)n tiːˈviː/ *n* تِلِفِزْيون عالي الوُضوحِ

high-dependency /hʌɪdɪˈpendənsi/ *adj* ‹*unit, care*› العِناية \ الرِعايةِ الخاصّةِ

high-end /hʌɪˈend/ *adj before n* ‹*product, boutique*› رَفيع ,راقٍ المُسْتَوى

higher education /ˌhʌɪə ɛdjuːˈkeɪʃ(ə)n/ *n* تَعْليم عالٍ

high fashion *n* [تَصْميم (وَخياطة) الأَزْياءِ الفاخِرةِ]

high finance *n* صَفَقات ماليّة كَبيرة

high-flown /ˌhʌɪˈfləʊn/ *adj* ‹*rhetoric, prose*› مُفخَّم ,طنّان

high-flyer, high-flier /ˌhʌɪˈflʌɪə/ *n* [شَخْص مُتَأَلِّق وَذَكيّ]

high-frequency /hʌɪˈfriːkwənsi/ *adj* ‹*radio, signal*› عالي التَرَدُّدِ

high-grade /ˈhʌɪgreɪd/ *adj* ‹*ore, paper*› ذو ,عالي \ فائِق الجَوْدةِ جَوْدةٍ عاليةٍ

high-handed /hʌɪˈhandɪd/ *adj* ‹*approach, attitude*› تَعَسُّفيّ, اسْتِبْداديّ

high-heeled /hʌɪˈhiːld/ *adj* ‹*shoe, boot*› عالي الكَعْبِ

high heels *n* كَعْب عالٍ

high jump *n* قَفْز عالٍ

highland /ˈhʌɪlənd/ **A** *n* (also **highlands**) مُرْتَفَع ;مِنْطَقة جَبَليّة (مُرْتَفَعات)

B *adj* ‹*area, community*› جَبَليّ

Highlands /ˈhʌɪləndz/ *pr n pl* (**the Highlands**) المُرْتَفَعات الإِسْكُتْلَنْديّة

high-level /ˌhʌɪˈlɛv(ə)l/ *adj* **1** ‹*meeting, talks*› على مُسْتَوى عالٍ \ رَفيع ;‹*official, executive*› رَفيع المُسْتَوى **2** (Comput) ‹*programming language*› عالي المُسْتَوى

highlight /ˈhʌɪlʌɪt/ **A** *n* **1** (most memorable part) أَبْرَز جُزْءٍ **2** (in a painting, photograph) بُقْعة مُضيئة \ مُنْعَكِسة

B (**highlights**) *n pl* **1** (of a sporting event) أَحْسَن اللَقَطاتِ **2** (in the hair) [خُصُلات شَعْرٍ مَصْبوغة (بِلَوْنٍ فاتِحٍ)]

C *vt* (*past tense, past participle* **highlighted**) **1** (to call attention to) أَلْقى \ سَلَّطَ الضَوْءَ على ‹*a need, problem*› **2** (with a pen) [أَبْرَزَ بِلَوْنٍ مُمَيِّزٍ (بِواسِطةِ قَلَمِ مارْكَر)] **3** (Comput) (shade) ظَلَّلَ; (select) حَدَّدَ ‹*text*›

highlighter /ˈhʌɪlʌɪtə/ *n* قَلَم مارْكَر \ تَأْشير (لِإِبْرازِ الكَلِماتِ أو الجُمَلِ المُهِمّةِ في نَصٍّ)

highly /ˈhʌɪli/ *adv* **1** ‹*dangerous, intelligent*› لِلغايةِ ,جِدًّا; **that is ~ unlikely** ذلك مُسْتَبْعَدٌ جِدًّا \ لِلغايةِ **2** **to speak/think ~ of sb** أَثْنى على شَخْصٍ \ قَدَّرَ شَخْصًا بِشَكْلٍ بالِغٍ

highly paid *adj* ‹*worker*› يَتَقاضى أَجْرًا مُرْتَفِعًا \ راتِبًا عالِيًا; ‹*job*› ذو أَجْرٍ مُرْتَفِعٍ \ راتِبٍ عالٍ

highly strung *adj* ‹*child, horse*› سَريع الانْفِعالِ ,عَصَبيّ المِزاجِ

highness /ˈhʌɪnəs/ *n* **His/ Her (Royal) H~** جَلالة المَلِكِ \ المَلِكة

high-pitched /hʌɪˈpɪtʃt/ *adj* ‹*voice, sound*› حادّ

high point *n* أَجْمَل \ أَرْوَع لَحَظاتِ شَيْءٍ

high-powered /ˌhʌɪˈpaʊəd/ *adj* **1** ‹*engine, microscope*› عالي القُدْرةِ **2** ‹*executive*› قَويّ النُفوذِ; ‹*job*› رَفيع

high profile *adj* ‹*politician, case*› [يَحْظى بِاهْتِمامٍ بالِغٍ \ بِدِعايةٍ كَبيرةٍ]

high-ranking /ˌhʌɪˈraŋkɪŋ/ *adj* ‹*position, official*› سامٍ (سُماة), ذو رُتْبةٍ عاليةٍ ,رَفيع المُسْتَوى

high-resolution /ˌhʌɪrɛzəˈluːʃ(ə)n/ *adj* ‹*photography, television*› عالي الدِقّةِ

high-rise /ˈhʌɪrʌɪz/ **A** *adj* ‹*building, block*› يَتَأَلَّفُ من ,شاهِق طَوابِقَ كَثيرةٍ; ‹*apartment, office*› [في الطابَقِ العُلْويّ لِمَبْنًى شاهِقٍ]

B *n* عِمارة \ بِناية شاهِقة

high-risk /ˌhʌɪˈrɪsk/ *adj* **1** (involving danger) ‹*occupation, strategy*› عالي \ شَديد الخُطورةِ **2** (at risk) ‹*group, patient*› مُعَرَّض \ عُرْضة لِخَطَرٍ شَديدٍ

high road *n* طَريق رَئيسيّ;

Idiom **to take the high road** [اِتَّخَذَ مَوْقِفًا إيجابِيًّا مُتَرَفِّعًا عن الصَغائِرِ]

high school *n* (AmE) (مَدْرَسة) ثانَويّة; (BrE) (مَدْرَسة) ثانَويّة (مُباشَرةً بعد المَرْحَلةِ الابْتِدائيّةِ)

high season *n* مَوْسِم الذُرْوةِ

high-speed /ˌhʌɪˈspiːd/ *adj* <*train, Internet connection*> فائِق \ عالي السُرْعةِ

high-spirited /ˌhʌɪˈspɪrɪtɪd/ *adj* <*youngster*> مَرِح, بَشوش (مَراحى, مَرْحى); <*behaviour*> بَهيج, مُفْعَم بالحَيَويّة

high street **A** *n* شارِع رَئيسيّ; **B** *adj before n* (**high-street**) **high-street spending** إنْفاق اِسْتِهْلاكيّ; **a high-street shop** [مَحَلّ من سِلْسِلة مَحَلاّتٍ تِجاريّةٍ كَبيرةٍ]

high-strung *adj* (AmE) ▸**highly strung**

high-tech /ˌhʌɪˈtɛk/ *adj* <*equipment, weapon*> عالي التِقْنيّة; **a ~ solution for a low-tech problem** حَلّ لِمُشْكِلةٍ بَسيطةٍ بالاسْتِعانة بِتِقْنيّةٍ عاليةٍ

high tide *n* حَرَكة \ فَتْرة المَدّ

high-up /ˈhʌɪʌp/ *adj* (infml) <*executive, job*> سام (سُماة)

highway /ˈhʌɪweɪ/ *n* **1** (AmE) (main road) طَريق رَئيسيّ; **a four-lane ~** طَريق رَئيسيّ بِأَرْبَعة مَمَرّاتٍ **2** (BrE fml) (roadway) الطَريق العامّ

Highway Code *n* (BrE) (**the Highway Code**) نِظام المُرورِ, قانون السَيْرِ

highwayman /ˈhʌɪweɪmən/ *n* (*pl* **-men**) قاطِع طَرِيقٍ

high wire *n* [حَبْل مَشْدود يُسْتَعْمَلُ في لُعْبةِ المَشْي على الحَبْلِ]

hijab /hɪˈdʒɑːb/ *n* حِجاب (أَحْجِبة, حُجُب); **to wear the ~** ارْتَدَت الحِجابَ

hijack /ˈhʌɪdʒak/ **A** *vt* اخْتَطَفَ <*a plane, ship*> **B** *n* اخْتِطاف (اخْتِطافات)

hijacker /ˈhʌɪdʒakə/ *n* خاطِف (خاطِفونَ, خُطّاف), مُخْتَطِف

hijacking /ˈhʌɪdʒakɪŋ/ *n* اخْتِطاف (اخْتِطافات)

hike /hʌɪk/ **A** *n* **1** (walk) نُزْهة طَوِيلة سَيْراً على الأَقْدامِ; **to go for a ~** ذَهَبَ في نُزْهةٍ طَويلةٍ سَيْراً على الأَقْدامِ **2** (in prices) ارْتِفاع; **a 5% ~ in fuel prices** ارْتِفاع أَسْعارِ الوَقودِ بِنِسْبة خَمْسةٍ في المِائةِ
B *vt* (also **hike up**) **1** رَفَعَ (a; رَفْع) <*a sock, one's trousers*> **2** رَفَعَ (a; رَفْع) <*the price, figures*>
Idiom **take a hike!** انْصَرِفْ!

hiker /ˈhʌɪkə/ *n* مُتَنَزِّه (سَيْراً على الأَقْدامِ لِمُدّةٍ طَويلةٍ)

hiking /ˈhʌɪkɪŋ/ *n* [التَنَزُّه سَيْراً على الأَقْدامِ (لِمَسافاتٍ طَويلةٍ)]

hilarious /hɪˈlɛːrɪəs/ *adj* <*story, comedy*> ظَريف \ مُضْحِك جِدًّا

hill /hɪl/ *n* **1** (low mountain) تَلّ (تِلال), هَضْبة (هِضاب) **2** (slope) تَلّة
Idiom **to be over the hill** [لم يَعُدْ في أَفْضَلِ حالاتِهِ (لِتَقَدُّمِهِ في السِنِّ)]

hillbilly /ˈhɪlbɪli/ *n* (*pl* **hillbillies**) (AmE pej) [شَخْص مُتَخَلِّف \ قَرَويّ]

hillside /ˈhɪlsʌɪd/ *n* جانِب \ مُنْحَدَر التَلّ

hilltop /ˈhɪltɒp/ *n* قِمّة التَلِّ

hilly /ˈhɪli/ *adj* (**hillier**, **hilliest**) <*country, landscape*> كَثير التِلالِ

hilt /hɪlt/ *n* (of a sword, dagger) مِقْبَض (السَيْفِ أو الخَنْجَرِ)
Idiom **up to the hilt** إلى أَقْصى حَدٍّ, كُلِّيّة, تَماماً; **to back sb to the ~** قَدَّمَ الدَعْمَ الكامِلَ لِشَخْصٍ; **we're up to the ~ in debt** نَحْنُ غارِقونَ في الدُيونِ

him /hɪm/ *pron* **1** (direct object) ـهُ; **call ~ now!** اتَّصِلْ بِهِ فَوْراً!; **I like ~** أُحِبُّهُ **2** (indirect obj, after prep) ـهُ; **I gave ~ the letter** أَعْطَيْتُهُ الرِسالةَ; **I sent it to ~** أَرْسَلْتُهُ لَهُ **3** (emphatic) هُوَ; **it's ~!** إنَّهُ هو!

Himalayas /ˌhɪməˈleɪəz/ *pr n pl* (**the Himalayas**) جِبال الهيمالايا

himself /hɪmˈsɛlf/ *pron* **1** (reflexive) نَفْسَهُ; **he's hurt ~** لَقَدْ أَذى نَفْسَهُ; **he was talking to ~** كانَ يُكَلِّمُ نَفْسَهُ **2** (emphatic) (he himself) نَفْسُهُ; (by himself) بِنَفْسِه; **he ~ said that ...** هو نَفْسُهُ مَنْ قالَ إنّ ...; **the doctor said so ~** الطَبيبُ نَفْسُهُ قالَ ذلك; **he made it ~** صَنَعَهُ بِنَفْسِهِ **3** (after prepositions) **he can care for ~** يَسْتَطيعُ أَنْ يَعْتَنِيَ بِنَفْسِهِ **4** (in expressions) **he's not ~ today** هو لَيْسَ على ما يُرامُ اليَوْمَ; **he's (all) by ~** هو بِمُفْرَدِهِ; **he had the office all to ~** كانَ المَكْتَبُ كُلُّهُ لَهُ

hind /hʌɪnd/ *adj* <*leg*> خَلْفيّ

hinder /ˈhɪndə/ *vt* عَرْقَلَ (i; عَرْقَلة), أَعاقَ

Hindi /ˈhɪndi/ *n* (اللُغة) الهِنْدِيّة

hindrance /ˈhɪndrəns/ *n* عائِق (عَوائِق), عَقَبة (عِقاب, عَقَبات)

hindsight /ˈhʌɪndsʌɪt/ *n* **with the benefit of ~** بعد, مُتَأَخِّراً فَواتِ الوَقْتِ

Hindu /hɪnˈduː/ **A** *n* هِنْدوسِيّ

B *adj* ‹*temple, gods*› هِنْدوسِيّ

Hinduism /ˈhɪnduɪz(ə)m/ *n* هِنْدوسيّة

hinge /hɪndʒ/ **A** *n* مُفَصَّلة

B *vi* (*present participle* **hingeing**) **to ~ on a decision** تَوَقَّفَ على قَرارٍ

hint /hɪnt/ **A** *n* **1** (allusion) تَلْميح (تَلاميحُ ,تَلْميحات) ,لَمْحة (لَمَحات) ,إشارة; **she didn't give any ~s about her future plans** لم تُعْطِ أَيَّ تَلْميحاتٍ حول خُطَطِها المُسْتَقْبَلِيّةِ; **to drop a ~** أَعْطى تَلْميحاً; **he was dropping ~s that he wanted a lift** كانَ يُعْطي تَلْميحاتٍ إلى أَنَّهُ يُريدُ تَوْصيلةً بالسَّيّارةِ; **to take a** *or* **the ~** فَهِمَ التَلْميحَ; **all right, I can take a ~!** حَسَناً، يُمْكِنُني أَنْ أَفْهَمَ التَلْميحَ! **2** (trace of garlic, spice) ذَرّة ,مِقْدار ضَئيل; (of colour, sarcasm) لَمْحة (لَمَحات); (of a smile) بادِرة (بَوادِرُ); **he disappears at the first ~ of trouble** يَخْتَفي عند ظُهورِ أَوَّلِ بادِرةٍ للمَتاعِبِ **3** (clue) عَلامة (عَلامات) ,إشارة **4** (piece of advice) تَلْميح (تَلاميحُ ,تَلْميحات) ,نَصيحة (نَصائِحُ); **here are some ~s on job seeking** هذه هي بَعْضُ النَصائِحِ \ التَلْميحاتِ حول البَحْثِ عن وَظيفةٍ

B *vt* لَمَّحَ (إلى) ,أَشارَ (إلى); **to ~ that ...** لَمَّحَ إلى أنّ ...

(Phrasal verb) **hint at**: **~ at [sth]** لَمَّحَ \ أَشارَ إلى [شَيْءٍ]

hip /hɪp/ **A** *n* وِرْك (f; أَوْراك); **to put one's hands on one's ~s** وَضَعَ يَدَيْهِ على وِرْكَيْهِ

B *excl* **~ ~ hooray!** مَرْحى!; **'three cheers for the bride and groom: ~, ~ ...' 'hooray!'** 'رَحِّبوا بالعَروسِ والعَريسِ ...' 'مَرْحى مَرْحى مَرْحى!'

(Idiom) **to shoot from the hip** [كانَتْ رَدّةُ فِعْلِهِ مُتَسَرِّعةً]

hip bone *n* عَظْم الوِرْكِ

hippo /ˈhɪpəʊ/ *n* (*pl* **hippos**) ▸ **hippopotamus**

Hippocratic oath /ˌhɪpəˌkratɪk ˈəʊθ/ *n* قَسَم أَبُقْراط

hippopotamus /ˌhɪpəˈpɒtəməs/ *n* (*pl* **hippopotamuses** or **hippopotami**) فَرَس النَهْرِ

hippy, **hippie** /ˈhɪpi/ *n* (*pl* **hippies**) هيبيّ (هيبيز)

hire /ˈhʌɪə/ **A** *vt* **1** ‹*a coach, hall*› اسْتَأْجَرَ **2** ‹*staff, a lawyer*› اسْتَخْدَمَ ,اسْتَأْجَرَ ,وَظَّفَ; **he has the power to ~ and fire** عِنْدَهُ سُلْطةُ التَوْظيفِ والفَصْلِ

B *n* (action) اسْتِخْدام ,اسْتِئْجار; (payment) أَجْر (أُجور); **boats/skis for ~** قَوارِبُ \ زَلّاجات للاسْتِئْجارِ; **the ~ of the car was £140 per week** كانَ إيجارُ السَيّارةِ مِائةً وَأَرْبَعينَ جُنَيْهاً في الأُسْبوعِ

(Phrasal verb) **hire out**: **~ [sth] out, ~ out [sth]** أَجَّرَ [شَيْئاً]

hire car *n* سَيّارة مُؤَجَّرة \ للتَأْجيرِ

hire purchase *n* شِراء بالتَقْسيطِ

his /hɪz/ **A** *determiner* ـهُ; **he's sold ~ car** باعَ سَيّارَتَهُ; **he broke ~ arm** كَسَرَ ذِراعَهُ

B *pron* **my car is green but ~ is blue** سَيّارَتي خَضْراءُ لَكِنَّ سَيّارَتَهُ زَرْقاءُ; **my results were good, but ~ were better** كانَتْ نَتائِجي جَيِّدةً، لَكِنَّ نَتائِجَهُ كانَتْ أَفْضَلَ; **the blue jacket is ~** الجاكيت الأَزْرَقُ لَهُ; **it's not ~** لَيْسَ لَهُ; **which house is ~?** أَيُّ بَيْتٍ بَيْتُهُ؟; **I'm a colleague of ~** أنا أَحَدُ زُمَلائِهِ; **the farm was not ~ to sell** لم تَكُنِ المَزْرَعةُ لَهُ حتّى يَبيعَها; **that dog of ~** (infml) كَلْبُهُ اللَعين ذلك; **~ was not an easy task** (fml) لم تَكُنْ مُهِمَّتُهُ مُهِمّةً سَهْلةً

Hispanic /hɪˈspanɪk/ **A** *adj* **1** (Spanish) ‹*culture, language*› [يَتَكَلَّمُ] إسْبانيّ (إسْبان) **2** (in the US) ‹*population, voters*› إسْبانيّ [الإسْبانيّةَ]

B *n* إسْبانيّ (إسْبان)

hiss /hɪs/ **A** *vi* «steam, snake» هَسْهَسَ (i; هَسْهَسة) ,فَحَّ (i-u; فَحّ, فَحيح)

B *n* هَسْهَسة

historian /hɪˈstɔːrɪən/ *n* مُؤَرِّخ

historic /hɪˈstɒrɪk/ *adj* **1** (important) ‹*moment, site*› تاريخيّ; **an event of ~ importance** حَدَثٌ لَهُ أَهَمّيّةٌ تاريخيّةٌ; **it was a ~ battle** كانَتْ مَعْرَكةً تاريخيّةً **2** (Ling) **the past ~** الماضي على سَبيلِ حِكايةِ الحالِ الماضيةِ; **in the ~ present** البَسيط

historical /hɪˈstɒrɪk(ə)l/ *adj* ‹*document, event*› تاريخيّ

historically /hɪˈstɒrɪkli/ *adv* **1** (relating to history) تاريخيًّا **2** (in the past) في الماضي

history /ˈhɪst(ə)ri/ *n* (*pl* **histories**) **1** (study of the past) تاريخ; **to make ~** صَنَعَ \ دَخَلَ التاريخَ **2** (record, experience) سِجِلّ (سِجِلّات); **to have a ~ of violence** كانَ لَدَيْهِ سِجِلُّ عُنْفٍ

(Idiom) **the rest is history** ما حَدَثَ فيما بَعْدُ مَعْروفٌ

hit /hɪt/ **A** *vt* (*present participle* **-tt-**; *past tense, past participle* **hit**) **1** (to strike) ضَرَبَ (i; ضَرْب) ‹*a person, table*›; **his father used to ~ him** اِعْتادَ أبوهُ أنْ يَضْرِبَهُ; **to ~ one's head on the door frame** ارْتَطَمَتْ رَأْسُهُ بِإطارِ البابِ **2** (to strike) ضَرَبَ (i; ضَرْب) ‹*a ball*›; **to ~ the ball hard** ضَرَبَ الكُرَةَ بِقوّةٍ **3** (as a target) أصابَ ‹*a target*›; **the school was ~ by a bomb** أُصيبَتِ المَدْرَسةُ بِقُنْبُلةٍ; **the stone ~ him in the face** أصابَهُ الحَجَرُ في وَجْهِهِ; **his shot ~ the goalpost** اصْطَدَمَتْ تَسْديدَتُهُ بالعارِضةِ **4** (to collide with) اصْطَدَمَ (ب) ‹*a vehicle, the ground*›; **she was ~ by a car** صَدَمَتْها سَيّارةٌ **5** (to affect adversely) «crisis, storm, earthquake» ضَرَبَ (i; ضَرْب) ‹*an area*›; **the areas hardest ~ by the recession** المَناطِقُ الأكْثَرُ تَضَرُّراً من الرُكودِ **6** (to reach) وَصَلَ (i; وُصول) (إلى) ‹*a level, point*› **7** (to meet with) تَعَرَّضَ (ل) ‹*a problem, traffic*› **8** (to become apparent to) **it suddenly ~ me that ...** خَطَرَ على بالي فَجْأةً أنّ ...

B *n* **1** (blow, stroke in sport) ضَرْبة (ضَرَبات) **2** (from a bomb, shell) ضَرْبة (ضَرَبات); **the ship took a direct ~** تَلَقَّت السَفينةُ ضَرْبةً مُباشِرةً **3** (infml) (success) [شَخْص أو شَيْء حَقَّقَ نَجاحاً وَشُهْرةً]; **the film was a huge ~ with audiences** حَقَّقَ الفيلْمُ نَجاحاً هائِلاً مع الجَماهيرِ; **she's made a big ~ with my son** ابْني مولَعٌ بِها بِدَرَجةٍ كَبيرةٍ **4** (at websites) زِيارة ,دُخول **5** (in searches) نَتيجة بَحْثٍ

(Idioms) **to hit it off** (infml) انْسَجَمَ; **to hit the road** (infml) غادَرَ; **to hit the roof** (infml) اشْتاطَ غَضَباً

(Phrasal verbs) **hit back** **1** رَدَّ الهُجومَ; **to ~ back at sb** رَدَّ على هُجوم شَخْصٍ **2** ~ **[sb] back** [شَخْصٍ] رَدَّ الضَرْبةَ ل **3** ~ **[sth] back** [شَيْئاً] أعادَ \ رَدَّ ‹*a ball*›

- **hit out**: **to ~ out at sth/sb** انْتَقَدَ شَيْئاً \ شَخْصاً بِشِدّةٍ
- **hit upon, hit on**: ~ **upon [sth]** [شَيْءٌ] خَطَرَ بِبالِهِ ‹*an idea, solution*›

hit and miss *adj* (*before n* **hit-and-miss**) ‹*approach, strategy*› عَشْوائيّ

hit-and-run /ˌhɪt(ə)nˈrʌn/ *adj* ‹*accident*› على طَريقةِ اضْرِبْ واهْرُبْ, بِأُسْلوبِ الكَرِّ والفَرِّ; **a ~ driver** سائِق صَدَمَ شَخْصاً وَهَرَبَ

hitch /hɪtʃ/ **A** *vt* **1** رَبَطَ (i-u; رَبْط) ‹*a trailer, horse*›; **to ~ a trailer to a truck** رَبَطَ مَقْطورةً بِشاحِنةٍ **2** (infml) **to ~ a ride** [حَصَلَ على تَوْصيلةٍ بالأوتوسْتوب]

B *vi* (infml) «hitchhikers, servicemen» [سافَرَ بالأوتوسْتوب]

C *n* **1** (problem) عَقَبة (عَقَبات), عائِق (عَوائِقُ); **a last-minute ~** عَقَبة آخِرِ لَحْظةٍ **2** (AmE) (limp) عَرَج

(Idiom) **to get hitched** (infml) تَزَوَّجَ

hitch-hike /ˈhɪtʃhʌɪk/ *vi* [حَصَلَ على تَوْصيلةٍ بِسَيّارةٍ أوْقَفَها على الطَريقِ]

hitch-hiker /ˈhɪtʃhʌɪkə/ *n* [شَخْص يَقِفُ على الطَريقِ للحُصولِ على تَوْصيلةٍ]

hitchhiking /ˈhɪtʃhʌɪkɪŋ/ *n* أوتوسْتوب (السَفَرِ بإيقافِ السَيّاراتِ على الطَريقِ)

hi-tech *adj* ▸ **high-tech**

hitherto /hɪðəˈtuː/ *adv* (fml) حتّى اليَوْمِ \ الآنِ

hit list *n* [قائِمة أشْخاصٍ يُرادُ قَتْلُهُمْ (لِأسْبابٍ إجْراميّةٍ \ سِياسيّةٍ)]

hitman /ˈhɪtman/ *n* (*pl* **-men**) (infml) قاتِل مأْجور

hit single *n* أُغْنيّة رائِجة

HIV /eɪtʃʌɪˈviː/ **A** *n* = **human immunodeficiency virus** مَرَض ضُعْفِ المَناعةِ المُكْتَسَبةِ; **to be infected with ~** كانَ مُصاباً بِمَرَضِ ضُعْفِ المَناعةِ المُكْتَسَبةِ

B *modifier* **~-positive** حامِل لِفَيْروس الإيدْز; **~-negative** غَيْر حامِلٍ لِفَيْروس الإيدْز

hive /hʌɪv/ **A** *n* (for bees) خَليّة نَحْلٍ; **to be a ~ of activity** عَجَّ بالنَشاطِ والحَرَكةِ

B (**hives**) *n pl* (Med) شَرًى (طَفْح جِلْديّ); **to come out in ~s** ظَهَرَ عَلَيْهِ الشَرى

HIV-negative /eɪtʃʌɪˌviːˈnɛɡətɪv/ *adj* غَيْر حامِلٍ لِفَيْروس الإيدْز

HIV-positive /eɪtʃʌɪˌviːˈpɒzətɪv/ *adj* حامِل لِفَيْروس الإيدْز

HMRC /eɪtʃɛmɑːˈsiː/ *n* = **Her (or His) Majesty's Revenue and Customs** [مَصْلَحة الضَرائِبِ البَريطانيّة]

HMS /eɪtʃɛmˈɛs/ *abbr* (BrE) = **Her/His Majesty's Ship** إيتْش إم إس (بادِئة تُمَيِّزُ سُفُنَ البَحْريّةِ البَريطانيّةِ)

hoard /hɔːd/ **A** *n* (of treasure, coins) كَنْز (كُنوز); (of food) مؤونة (مُؤَن)

B *vt* خَزَّنَ ‹*food*›, ادَّخَرَ, اكْتَنَزَ ‹*money*›

hoarding /ˈhɔːdɪŋ/ *n* (BrE) 1 (billboard) لَوْحة إعْلاناتٍ 2 (fence) (سِياجات) سِياج

hoarse /hɔːs/ *adj* ‹*voice, whisper*› أَبَحّ (dipt), أَجَشّ ,مَبْحوح (dipt); **to be ~** كانَ مَبْحوحاً

hoax /həʊks/ A *n* (خُدَع) خُدْعة ,(خُدْعات) خُدْعة (مَقالِبُ) مَقْلَب B *adj* ‹*call, bomb*› كاذِب (على سَبيلِ المُزاحِ \ الخِداعِ)

hob /hɒb/ *n* (BrE) صَفيحة تَسْخينٍ

hobble /ˈhɒb(ə)l/ *vi* عرج (a-u; عرج ,عَرَجان)

hobby /ˈhɒbi/ *n* (*pl* **hobbies**) هِواية

hobo /ˈhəʊbəʊ/ *n* (*pl* **hobos** *or* **hoboes**) (AmE) مُتَشَرِّد

hockey /ˈhɒki/ *n* 1 [u] (BrE) (played on grass) هوكي; **a ~ stick** عَصا الهوكي 2 [u] (AmE) (played on ice) هوكي الجَليدِ; ▸**ice hockey**

hod /hɒd/ *n* [آلة ذات يَدٍ خَشَبِيّةٍ ورَأسٍ على شَكْلِ V لِنَقْلِ الطوبِ / مَوادِّ البِناءِ]

hoe /həʊ/ A *n* مِعْزَق B *vt* (*present participle* **hoeing**) عَزَقَ (i; عَزْق) ‹*a garden, weeds*›

hog /hɒg/ A *n* (AmE) (خَنازيرُ) خِنْزير B *vt* (-gg-) اِسْتَأْثَرَ (ب) ‹*a sofa, sb's attention*›

Idiom **to go the whole hog** [قامَ بِشَيْءٍ على أَكْمَلِ وَجْهٍ مُمْكِنٍ]

Hogmanay /ˈhɒgmәneɪ/ *n* (Scot) [لَيْلة رَأسِ السَنة في اسْكُتْلَنْدا]

hoist /hɔɪst/ *vt* 1 رَفَعَ (a; رَفْع) ‹*heavy equipment*› 2 رَفَعَ (a; رَفْع) ‹*a flag, sail*›

hokum /ˈhəʊkəm/ *n* (infml) (nonsense) كَلام فارِغ ,هُراء

hold /həʊld/ A *vt* (*past tense, past participle* **held**) 1 (to grasp) قَبَضَ (i; قَبْض) (على), مَسَكَ (i-u; مَسْك) ‹*an object, sb's hand*›; **he was ~ing an envelope/a coin in his hand** كانَ يُمْسِكُ ظَرْفاً \ قِطْعةً نَقْدِيّةً في يَدِهِ; **can you ~ this for me?** هل تَسْتَطيعُ أنْ تُمْسِكَ لي بِهذا؟; **to ~ sth by the handle** أَمْسَكَ شَيْئاً من مِقْبَضِهِ 2 (to keep in position) أَمْسَكَ ‹*a ladder*›; **to ~ one's head still** أَبْقى رَأسَهُ ثابِتاً; **to ~ sth in place** *or* **position** ثَبَّتَ شَيْئاً في مَكانٍ أو وَضْعِيّةٍ 3 (to contain) اِتَّسَعَ احْتَوى ‹*an object, amount*› 4 (to have capacity for) اِتَّسَعَ ‹*350 people*›; **the tank ~s fifty litres** الخَزّانُ يَتَّسِعُ لِخَمْسينَ لِتْراً 5 (to support) تَحَمَّلَ ‹*a weight, person*› 6 (to organize) عَقَدَ (i; عَقْد) ‹*a meeting, talks, an election, event*›; **interviews will be held on 29th July** سَتُعْقَدُ المُقابَلاتُ يَوْمَ 29 يوليو; **the club ~s regular meetings** يَعْقِدُ النادي اجْتِماعاتٍ دَوْرِيّةً 7 (to possess) تَوَلّى ‹*a position, record*›; **he has held many positions of responsibility in government** تَوَلّى مَسْؤوليّاتٍ عَديدةً في الحُكومةِ 8 (to exercise) تَوَلّى ‹*power*› 9 (to own) مَلَكَ (i; مِلْك ,مُلْك) ‹*shares, a passport*› 10 (to store) اِحْتَفَظَ (ب) ‹*information, documents*› 11 (to restrain) سَيْطَرَ (على ;سَيْطَرة) ‹*a dog, thief*› 12 (to delay) أَخَّرَ ‹*a flight*›; وَضَعَ في الانْتِظارِ ‹*telephone call*›; **~ it!** (infml) انْتَظِرْ! 13 (to detain) اِحْتَجَزَ ‹*a person*›; **to ~ sb prisoner** أَسَرَ شَخْصاً; **to ~ sb hostage** اِحْتَجَزَ شَخْصاً رَهينةً 14 (to reserve) حَجَزَ (i-u; حَجْز) ‹*a booking, ticket*› 15 (to keep) «defenders» اِحْتَفَظَ (ب) ‹*a town, territory*› 16 (to assert) اِعْتَبَرَ ‹*a view, belief*›; **to ~ that ...** «person» اِعْتَقَدَ أنّ ... ;«law» نَصَّ على أنّ ...; **to ~ sb liable** *or* **responsible** حَمَّلَ شَخْصاً المَسْؤوليّةَ 17 (to retain) «speakers» شَدَّ (i-u; شَدّ) ‹*sb's attention, interest*› 18 (Tel) **please ~ the line** من فَضْلِكَ ابْقَ على الخَطِّ 19 (to maintain contact with) **to ~ the road well** تَشَبَّثَ بالطَريقِ جَيِّداً

B *vi* (*past tense, past participle* **held**) 1 (to remain intact) «shelf, dam» صَمَدَ (u; صُمود) ,قاوَمَ 2 (to continue) «weather» اِسْتَقَرَّ; «luck» اِسْتَمَرَّ 3 (to remain valid) «offer, theory» ما زالَتْ; **his ideas still ~ true** *or* **good today** ما زالَ صالِحاً أَفْكارُهُ صالِحةً لِليَوْمِ 4 (Tel) «caller» اِنْتَظَرَ; **will you ~?** هل تَسْتَطيعُ الانْتِظارَ

C *n* 1 (grasp) قَبْضة (قَبَضات); **she took** *or* **caught ~ of my hand** أَحْكَمَتْ قَبْضَتَها على يَدي; **to keep ~ of sth/sb** أَحْكَمَ قَبْضَتَهُ على شَيْءٍ \ شَخْصٍ; **to get ~ of sb** (to find) وَجَدَ شَخْصاً; (by telephone) تَحَصَّلَ على شَخْصٍ; **to get ~ of a copy/the information** تَحَصَّلَ على نُسْخةٍ \ المَعْلوماتِ; **the press got ~ of the story** اكْتَشَفَت الصَحافةُ القِصّةَ 2 (control) سَيْطَرة; **to have a ~ on** *or* **over sb** كانَتْ لَهُ سَيْطَرةٌ على شَخْصٍ; **to take ~** «flames» اِلْتَهَبَ; «ideas» تَرَسَّخَ; **he consolidated his ~ on power** عَزَّزَ إحْكامَ قَبْضَتِهِ على السُلْطةِ 3 (of a ship, plane) مَخْزَن (مَخازِنُ) 4 (in wrestling, judo) مَسْكة 5 (in climbing) نُتوء ,بُروز

D (**on hold**) *adv phr* 1 (Tel) مُنْتَظِراً على الهاتِفِ; **to put sb on ~** جَعَلَ شَخْصاً يَنْتَظِرُ على الهاتِفِ 2 **to put one's plans/a project on ~** أَجَّلَ بَرامِجَهُ \ مَشْروعَهُ

(Idiom) **to hold one's own** حافَظَ على رَباطَةِ جَأْشِهِ

(Phrasal verbs) **hold against**: **to ~ sth against sb** حَقَدَ على شَخْصٍ بِسَبَبِ شَيْءٍ; **to ~ it against sb that ...** حَمَلَ ضَغينةً لِشَخْصٍ بِسَبَبِ ...

• **hold back** **A** تَرَدَّدَ (في); **to ~ back from doing sth** تَرَدَّدَ في فِعْلِ شَيْءٍ **B** **~ [sb/sth] back**, **~ back [sb/sth]** 1 (to control) كَبَحَ [شَخْصاً \ شَيْئاً] ‹*the water, crowd, an animal*›; **to ~ back one's laughter/tears** كَبَحَ ضِحْكَتَهُ \ دُموعَهُ; **use this to ~ back your hair** اسْتَعْمِلْ هذا لِتَشُدَّ شَعْرَكَ 2 (to impede) مَنَعَ \ أَعاقَ [شَخْصاً \ شَيْئاً] ‹*progress, development, a student*› **C** **~ [sth] back**, **~ back [sth]** (to withhold) تَكَتَّمَ على [شَيْءٍ] ‹*information*›; حَجَزَ [شَيْئاً] ‹*payment*›

• **hold down** **A** **~ [sb/sth] down**, **~ down [sb/sth]** شَدَّ [شَخْصاً \ شَيْئاً] إلى الأَسْفَلِ ‹*a tent, piece of paper, carpet*›; **to ~ a patient/detainee down** شَلَّ حَرَكةَ مَريضٍ \ مُعْتَقَلٍ **B** **~ [sth] down**, **~ down [sth]** 1 (to press down) احْتَفَظَ بِ[شَيْءٍ] مَضْغوطاً ‹*a key, pedal*› 2 (to keep) احْتَفَظَ بِ [شَيْءٍ] ‹*a job*› 3 (to prevent from rising) «companies» حافَظَ على ثَباتِ [شَيْءٍ] ‹*costs, wages, prices*›

• **hold in**: **~ [sth] in**, **~ in [sth]** (to pull in) شَدَّ [شَيْئاً] ‹*one's stomach*›

• **hold off** **A** «creditors» أَجَّلَ; **I hope the rain ~s off** أَتَمَنّى أَلاّ تُمْطِرَ **B** **~ [sth/sb] off**, **~ off [sth/sb]** قاوَمَ [شَخْصاً \ شَيْئاً] ‹*the enemy, one's creditors*›; صَدَّ [شَخْصاً \ شَيْئاً] ‹*an attack*›; **to ~ off doing sth** امْتَنَعَ عن فِعْلِ شَيْءٍ

• **hold on** **A** 1 (infml) (to wait) انْتَظَرَ; **~ on, I'll just get him** انْتَظِرْ، سَآتي بِهِ 2 (to grip) مَسَكَ (i-u; مَسْك); **~ on tight!** امْسِكْ جَيِّداً! 3 (to last out) صَمَدَ (u; صُمود) **B** **~ [sth] on** «screws, glue» شَدَّ \ ثَبَّتَ [شَيْئاً]; **to be held on with** *or* **by sth** ثُبِّتَ بِشَيْءٍ

• **hold on to**: **~ on to [sb/sth]** 1 (to grip) أَمْسَكَ بِ [شَخْصٍ \ شَيْءٍ] ‹*an object, a person*› 2 (to retain) احْتَفَظَ بِ [شَخْصٍ \ شَيْءٍ] ‹*power, the lead, money*›

• **hold out** **A** 1 (to resist) صَمَدَ (u; صُمود); **to ~ out against an attack/the competition** صَمَدَ في وَجْهِ هُجومٍ \ المُنافَسةِ; **we are ~ing out for a better offer** سَنَنْتَظِرُ حتّى نَحْصُلَ على عَرْضٍ أَفْضَلَ 2 (to last) «supplies, stocks» دامَ (u; دَوام) **B** **~ [sth] out**, **~ out [sth]** مَدَّ [شَيْئاً] ‹*one's hand, a glass*› **C** **~ out [sth]** ‹*hope*› **I don't ~ out much hope** لا أُعَلِّقُ آمالاً كَبيرةً

• **hold over**: **~ [sth] over**, **~ over [sth]** أَجَّلَ [شَيْئاً] ‹*a meeting, an event*›

• **hold to**: 1 **~ to [sth]** تَشَبَّثَ بِ [شَيْءٍ] ‹*a belief, one's principles*› 2 **~ sb to [sth]** أَلْزَمَ شَخْصاً بِ [شَيْءٍ] ‹*a promise*›

• **hold together** **A** 1 (not to break) «structure» صَمَدَ (u; صُمود) 2 (to remain united) «coalition, family» تَماسَكَ **B** **~ [sth] together** 1 (to keep intact) ثَبَّتَ [شَيْئاً] ‹*a structure, chair*›; **to be held together with glue/tacks** شُدَّ \ ثُبِّتَ بالغِراءِ \ بالمَسامِيرِ 2 (in unions) حافَظَ على وِحْدةِ [شَيْءٍ] ‹*a family, party*›

• **hold up** **A** 1 (to remain valid) «theory, argument» صَمَدَ (u; صُمود) 2 (to remain strong) **to ~ up well** «profits, numbers» حافَظَ على قوَّتِهِ **B** **~ [sb/sth] up**, **~ up [sb/sth]** 1 (to support) دَعَمَ [شَخْصاً \ شَيْئاً] ‹*a shelf, picture, stockings*› 2 (to raise) رَفَعَ [شَخْصاً \ شَيْئاً] إلى أَعْلى ‹*an object*›; **to ~ one's hand up** رَفَعَ يَدَهُ إلى أَعْلى 3 (to delay) عَطَّلَ [شَخْصاً \ شَيْئاً] ‹*a person, flight, the traffic*› 4 (to present) **to be held up as an example** *or* **model of sth** اُعْتُبِرَ رَمْزاً \ مِثالاً لِشَيْءٍ; **to ~ sb up to ridicule** اسْتَهْزَأَ من شَخْصٍ 5 (to rob) سَطا على [شَيْءٍ] ‹*a bank*›; اعْتَدى على [شَخْصٍ] بالسَرِقةِ ‹*person*›

• **hold with** (to support) وافَقَ (على) ‹*a policy, trend*›

holdall /ˈhəʊldɔːl/ *n* (BrE) حَقيبة (للسَفَر)

holder /ˈhəʊldə/ *n* 1 (container for coins, a cup, candle) ماسِك، حامِل، حَمّالة 2 (owner of a passport, ticket, record) حامِل (حَمَلة); (of an account, policy) صاحِب (أَصْحاب)

holding /ˈhəʊldɪŋ/ *n* حِصّة (حِصَص)

holding company *n* شَرِكة قابِضة

hold-up /ˈhəʊldʌp/ *n* 1 (delay) تَعْويق 2 (traffic jam) ازْدِحام 3 (robbery) سَطْو

hole /həʊl/ *n* [1] (in the ground) حُفْرة (حُفَر); (in a wall, container) ثُقْب (ثُقوب, أَثْقاب) [2] (of foxes, rabbits) وَكْر (أَوْكار, وُكور)

hole in the wall *n* (infml) صَرّاف آلِيّ

holiday /ˈhɒlɪdeɪ/ *n* [1] (BrE) (vacation) إجازة, عُطْلة (عُطْلات, عُطَل); **to go on ~ in Portugal** ذَهَبَ في إجازةٍ إلى البُرْتُغال; **to get 20 days' paid ~** حَصَلَ على إجازةٍ مَدْفوعةِ الأَجْرِ لِعِشْرينَ يَوْماً; **the school ~(s)** عُطْلةُ المَدْرَسةِ [2] (time off work) عُطْلة (عُطُلات, عُطَل); **a national/public ~** عيد وَطَنِيّ \ عُطْلة رَسْمِيّة; **a religious ~** عُطْلة دينيّة [3] (incentive) [إعْفاء]; **a tax ~** إعْفاء ضَريبيّ مُؤَقَّت; [مُؤَقَّت من دَفْعٍ]

holiday camp *n* مُخَيَّم لِقَضاءِ العُطَل

holiday home *n* [مَنْزِل عائِليّ ثانٍ لِقَضاءِ العُطَل]

holiday job *n* [وَظيفة مُؤَقَّتة لِطالِبٍ خلال العُطْلةِ المَدْرَسيّة]

holidaymaker /ˈhɒlɪdeɪˌmeɪkə/ *n* (BrE) سائِح (في عُطْلةٍ)

holiday resort *n* مَصيف (مَصايِفُ), مُنْتَجَع لِقَضاءِ العُطْلاتِ

holistic /hɒˈlɪstɪk, həʊˈlɪstɪk/ *adj* ‹approach, medicine› شُموليّ

Holland /ˈhɒlənd/ *pr n* هولَنْدا

holler /ˈhɒlə/ (AmE infml) **A** *vt* هَتَفَ (i; هُتاف; ب) ‹instructions, encouragement›
B *vi* صاحَ (i; صِياح, صَيْح), صَرَخَ (u; صُراخ, صَريخ)

hollow /ˈhɒləʊ/ **A** *adj* [1] ‹tree, cylinder› أَجْوَف (dipt; جوف) [2] ‹eyes, cheeks› غائِر [3] ‹laugh, promise› أَجْوَف (dipt; جوف) [4] ‹victory› بِلا مَعْنًى
B *n* [1] (in the ground) تَجْويف (تَجاويفُ) [2] (in a surface, tree) تَجْويف (تَجاويفُ)

(Phrasal verb) **hollow out**: **~ [sth] out, ~ out [sth]** قَعَّرَ \ جَوَّفَ [شَيْئاً] ‹a log, tree›

holly /ˈhɒli/ *n* بَهْشِيّة

holocaust /ˈhɒləkɔːst/ *n* [1] (mass slaughter) مَحْرَقة [2] **the H~** (in World War II) مَحْرَقة اليَهودِ

hologram /ˈhɒləgram/ *n* هولوغْرام (صورة ثُلاثيّة الأَبْعادِ)

holster /ˈhəʊlstə/ *n* قِراب مُسَدَّسٍ

holy /ˈhəʊli/ *adj* (**holier, holiest**) ‹city, day› مُقَدَّس

Holy Bible *n* (**the Holy Bible**) الكِتاب المُقَدَّس

Holy Ghost *n* ▸ **Holy Spirit**

Holy Land *pr n* (**the Holy Land**) الأَرْض المُقَدَّسة

Holy Spirit, **Holy Ghost** *n* (**the Holy Spirit**) الروح القُدُس

Holy Week *n* أُسْبوع الآلامِ

homage /ˈhɒmɪdʒ/ *n* تَكْريم, إكْرام; **to pay ~ to sb** قَدَّمَ تَحيّةَ إجْلالٍ وَإكْبارٍ لِشَخْصٍ

home /həʊm/ **A** *n* [1] (dwelling place) بَيْت (بُيوت), مَنْزِل (مَنازِلُ), مَسْكَن (مَساكِنُ); **a ~ of one's own** بَيْتُهُ الخاصّ; **to work from ~** عَمِلَ من البَيْتِ; **to set up ~ in Beirut** اتَّخَذَ من بَيْروتَ بَيْتاً لَهُ; **to be far from ~** كانَ بَعيداً عن البَيْتِ [2] (family environment) بَيْت (بُيوت); **to leave ~** غادَرَ البَيْتَ; **we gave him a good ~** وَفَّرْنا لَهُ بَيْتاً طَيِّباً [3] (country, region) بَلَد (بِلاد, بُلْدان); **he regards Morocco as ~** يَعْتَبِرُ المَغْرِبَ بَلَدَهُ; **I've made my ~ in Syria now** اتَّخَذْتُ من سوريا بَلَداً لي; **the island is ~ to 3,000 people** تُؤْوي الجَزيرةُ 3000 نَسَمةٍ [4] (institution) دار (f; دور, دِيار); **a care ~** دار رِعايةٍ; **to put sb in a ~** وَضَعَ شَخْصاً في دارِ رِعايةٍ
B *adj* [1] (family) ‹life, comforts› عائِليّ [2] **~ country** بَلَد المَنْشَأ [3] (national) ‹affairs, market› وَطَنِيّ [4] (Sport) (at headquarters) ‹game, crowd› مَحَلِّيّ
C *adv* [1] إلى البَيْتِ; **to go/come ~** (to one's house) ذَهَبَ \ عادَ إلى البَيْتِ; (to one's country) ذَهَبَ \ عادَ إلى البَلَدِ; **on the way ~** في طَريقِ العَوْدةِ إلى البَيْتِ; **to take sb ~** أَخَذَ شَخْصاً إلى البَيْتِ; **what time did you get ~?** مَتى وَصَلْتَ إلى البَيْتِ؟ [2] (showing finality, purpose) **to hammer** *or* **drive a nail ~** دَقَّ مِسْماراً في المَوْقِعِ المُحَدَّدِ; **to drive the point/message ~** قامَ بِإيصالِ الرِسالةِ; **to bring sth ~ to sb** كَشَفَ شَيْئاً لِشَخْصٍ
D (**at home**) *adv phr* [1] (in one's house) ‹to stay, be educated› في البَيْتِ; **to live at ~** سَكَنَ في بَيْتِ العائِلةِ; **I called her but she wasn't at ~** اتَّصَلْتُ بِها وَلَكِنَّها لم تَكُنْ في البَيْتِ [2] (at ease) وَكَأَنَّهُ في بَيْتِهِ; **I feel at ~ here** أَشْعُرُ وَكَأَنّي في بَيْتي هُنا; **make yourself at ~** تَصَرَّفْ وَكَأَنَّكَ في بَيْتِكَ [3] (at a team's own ground) **to play/be at ~** لَعِبَ \ كانَ على أَرْضِهِ

(Idioms) **it's/he's nothing to write home about** (infml) لا يَسْتَحِقُّ الذِكْرَ; **there's no place like home** لا يوجَدُ مَكانٌ مِثْلَ الوَطَنِ; (BrE) **to be home and dry** بَلَغَ مُبْتَغاهُ

(Phrasal verb) **home in on**: **~ in on** [sth] ‹*a target*› صَوَّبَ نحو [شَيْءٍ]

home address *n* عُنْوان المَنْزِل

homeboy /ˈhəʊmbɔɪ/ *n* (AmE infml) مَعْرِفة (من نَفْسِ الحَيِّ \ المَدينةِ)

home brew *n* [مَشْروب كُحوليّ يُحضَّرُ في المَنْزِل]

homecoming /ˈhəʊmkʌmɪŋ/ *n* **1** (return home) عَوْدة \ رُجوع للوَطَن **2** (AmE) (school or college reunion) [حَفْل يَجْمَعُ شَمْلَ الطَلَبةِ السابِقين]

home computer *n* حاسوب مَنْزِليّ

home cooking *n* طَبْخ مَنْزِليّ

Home Counties *pr n pl* (**the Home Counties**) المُقاطَعات المُحيطة بِلُنْدُن

home economics *n* (BrE) تَدْبير مَنْزِليّ

home-grown /ˌhəʊmˈɡrəʊn/ *adj* **1** (from one's own garden) ‹*vegetables, produce*› مُنْتَج مَحلّيًّا **2** (not foreign) ‹*talent, player*› مَحَلّيّ

home help *n* (BrE) [شَخْص يُوَظَّفُ كَمُساعِدٍ في مَنْزِل]

homeland /ˈhəʊmland/ *n* وَطَن (أَوْطان)

homeland security *n* أَمْن وَطَنيّ

homeless /ˈhəʊmləs/ **A** *adj* ‹*people, teenagers*› مُشَرَّد, مُتَشَرِّد **B** *n pl* **the ~** المُشَرَّدونَ, المُتَشَرِّدونَ

homely /ˈhəʊmli/ *adj* (**homelier, homeliest**) **1** (BrE) (cosy, welcoming) ‹*hotel, room*› [يُعْطي شُعوراً بِحَميميّةِ وَدِفْءِ البَيْتِ] **2** (AmE) (plain) ‹*looks, girl*› غَيْر جَذّاب

home-made /ˌhəʊmˈmeɪd/ *adj* ‹*cake, bread*› مَصْنوع في المَنْزِل; ‹*bomb*› مَحَلّيّ الصُنْع

homemaker /ˈhəʊmmeɪkə/ *n* مُدَبِّرة مَنْزِل

home movie *n* [فيلْم هُواةٍ مَصْنوع في المَنْزِل]

Home Office *n* (**the Home Office**) وِزارة الداخِليّةِ (في بَريطانيا)

homeopathic /həʊmɪəˈpaθɪk/ *adj* ‹*method, remedy*› مِثْليّ

homeowner /ˈhəʊməʊnə/ *n* مالِك بَيْتٍ

home page *n* صَفْحة رَئيسيّة

home plate *n* (in baseball) صَحْن المَلْعَبِ (لَوْحة مَطّاطيّة يَقِفُ أَمامَها ضارِبُ الكُرةِ)

homeroom /ˈhəʊmruːm/ *n* (AmE Educ) [قاعة يَتَجَمَّعُ فيها طُلّابُ صَفٍّ واحِدٍ يَوْميًّا]

home rule *n* حُكْم ذاتيّ

home run *n* (in baseball) [ضَرْبة تَسْمَحُ لِضارِبِها القِيامَ بِدَوْرةٍ كامِلةٍ وَتَسْجيلَ نُقْطةٍ]

Home Secretary *n* (BrE) وَزير الداخليّةِ (في بَريطانيا)

home shopping *n* تَسَوُّق مَنْزِليّ

homesick /ˈhəʊmsɪk/ *adj* ‹*child*› مُشْتاق إلى البَيْتِ; ‹*worker*› مُشْتاق للعَوْدةِ إلى الوَطَنِ; **to be ~** كانَ عِنْدَهُ حَنينٌ إلى الوَطَنِ

homestead /ˈhəʊmstɛd/ *n* عِزْبة (عِزَب)

home team, **home side** *n* فَريق مُضيف

home town *n* مَسْقَط رَأْسٍ

home video *n* فيدِيو هُواةٍ

homeward /ˈhəʊmwəd/ **A** *adv* **1** (also **homewards**) ‹*to sail, travel*› نحو \ باتِّجاهِ أَرْضِ الوَطَنِ **2** **to be ~ bound** كانَ في طَريقِ العَوْدةِ إلى أَرْضِ الوَطَنِ **B** *adj* ‹*journey, flight*› العَوْدة إلى أَرْضِ الوَطَنِ

homework /ˈhəʊmwəːk/ *n* واجِب مَنْزِليّ \ مَدْرَسيّ; **you haven't done your ~!** لَم تُنْجِزْ واجِبَكَ المَدْرَسيَّ!; **we get lots of ~ at secondary school** لَدَيْنا الكَثيرُ من الواجِباتِ المَنْزِليّةِ في المَدْرَسةِ الثانَويّةِ

homeworker /ˈhəʊmwəːkə/ *n* [شَخْص يَعْمَلُ من مَنْزِلِه]

homeworking /ˈhəʊmwəːkɪŋ/ *n* عَمَل من المَنْزِل

homey /ˈhəʊmi/ *adj* (**homier, homiest**) (AmE) (cosy) ‹*atmosphere, restaurant*› مُريح

homicidal /hɒmɪˈsʌɪd(ə)l/ *adj* ‹*tendencies*› القَتْل; ‹*maniac*› ذو نَزْعةٍ للقَتْلِ

homicide /ˈhɒmɪsʌɪd/ *n* (crime) قَتْل

homing /ˈhəʊmɪŋ/ *adj* **1** ‹*instinct*› العَوْدةِ للوَطَنِ **2** ‹*missile, device*› مُوَجَّه

homing pigeon *n* حَمام زاجِل

homogeneous /ˌhɒməʊˈdʒiːnɪəs/ *adj* ‹*group, population*› مُتَجانِس

homologous /hɒˈmɒləɡəs/ *adj* ‹*cell, chromosome*› مُتَماثِل, مُتَشابِه

homosexual /ˌhəʊməʊˈsɛkʃʊəl/ *n, adj* لوطيّ, مِثْليّ

homosexuality /həʊməsɛkʃʊˈalɪti/ *n* لوطيّة, مِثْليّة

Hon. *abbr* (BrE) = **Honourable** مَعالٍ ,سَعادة ,فَخامة

Honduran /hɒn'djʊərən/ *n, adj* هُنْدوراسيّ

Honduras /hɒn'djʊərəs/ *pr n* هُنْدوراس (f)

hone /həʊn/ *vt* **1▸** (to perfect) شَحَذَ (a; شَحْذ) ,صَقَلَ (u; صَقْل) ‹*one's skills, talent*› **2▸** (to sharpen) سَنَّ (u; سَنّ) ,شَحَذَ (a; شَحْذ) ‹*a blade*›

honest /'ɒnɪst/ *adj* **1▸** (honourable, legitimate) ‹*businessman, politician*› أَشْراف ,شُرَفاءُ) شَريف) ,(أُمَناءُ) أَمين ,(نِزاه ,نُزَهاءُ) نَزيه **2▸** (sincere) ‹*opinion, belief, answer*› صادِق ,صَريح; **to be ~, I don't care** صَراحةً، لا أُبالي

honestly /'ɒnɪstli/ *adv* **1▸** (honourably, legitimately) ‹*to act, behave*› بِنَزاهةٍ ,بِأَمانةٍ **2▸** (truthfully, sincerely) ‹*to think, wish*› بِصِدْقٍ; ‹*to reply, say*› بِصَراحةٍ; **I ~ don't know, ~, I don't know** بِصَراحةٍ، لا أَدْري **3▸** (expressing impatience, annoyance) ≈ يا اللهُ; **~! you could have waited for me!** يا اللهُ! كانَ بِإِمْكانِكَ أَنْ تَنْتَظِرَني!

honesty /'ɒnɪsti/ *n* **1▸** (integrity) شَرَف ,إِخْلاص ,أَمانة **2▸** (sincerity) صِدْق; **in all ~** بِكُلِّ صِدْقٍ

honey /'hʌni/ *n* (*pl* **honeys**) **1▸** (sweet spread) عَسَل **2▸** (infml) (darling) حَبيبي

honeybee /'hʌnibiː/ *n* نَحْل (n coll)

honeycomb /'hʌnɪkəʊm/ *n* قُرْص عَسَلٍ; **a piece of ~** قِطْعة من قُرْصِ العَسَلِ

honeymoon /'hʌnɪmuːn/ *n* شَهْر عَسَلٍ

honeysuckle /'hʌnɪsʌk(ə)l/ *n* زَهْر العَسَلِ ,صَريمة الجَدْيِ

Hong Kong /hɒŋ 'kɒŋ/ *pr n* هونْغ كونْغ

honk /'hɒŋk/ **A** *vt* **to ~ one's horn** ضَغَطَ على بوقِ سَيّارَتِهِ **B** *vi* **1▸** «drivers» ضَغَطَ على البوقِ **2▸** «geese» قاقَ (u; قَوْق)

honor (AmE) ▸ **honour**

honorable (AmE) ▸ **honourable**

honorary /'ɒn(ə)rəri/ *adj* ‹*doctorate, position*› فَخْرِيّ

honour (BrE), **honor** (AmE) /'ɒnə/ **A** *n* **1▸** (reputation) سُمْعة; **a man of ~** رَجُل شَريف; **to give one's word of ~** أَعْطى كَلِمَتَهُ **2▸** (mark of esteem) شَرَف; **to consider sth a great ~** اِعْتَبَرَ شَيْئاً شَرَفاً عَظيماً; **the place of ~** المَقْعَد الشَرَفيّ; **a reception in ~ of the delegation** وَليمة على شَرَفِ الوَفْدِ; **to be buried with full military ~s** دُفِنَ بِكُلِّ التَشْريفاتِ العَسْكَرِيّةِ; **it is a great ~ for me to be here today** إِنَّهُ لَشَرَفٌ عَظيمٌ لي اليَوْمَ أَنْ أَكونَ هُنا **3▸** (to a judge) **Your Honour** *or* (AmE) **Honor** سِيادةَ \ جَنابَ \ حَضْرةَ القاضي **B** (**honours** AmE, **honors**) *n pl* (Educ) **to graduate with ~s** تَخَرَّجَ مع مَرْتَبةِ الشَرَفِ **C** *vt* **1▸** (to show respect for) اِحْتَرَمَ ,قَدَّرَ ‹*one's parents, the dead, flag*›; **to feel/be ~ed by your presence** شَرَّفَهُ حُضورُكَ; **you ~ us by the trust you show us** تُشَرِّفُنا بِثِقَتِكَ فينا; **welcome to our ~ed guests** مَرْحَباً بِضُيوفِنا الكِرام **2▸** (to be bound by) أَوْفى (ب) ‹*a debt, obligation, contract*›
(Idiom) **to do the honours** قامَ بِواجِبِ الضِيافة

honourable (BrE), **honorable** (AmE) /'ɒn(ə)rəb(ə)l/ *adj* **1▸** (honest, respectable) ‹*intention, action*› شَريف (شُرَفاءُ) **2▸** (creditable) ‹*defeat, settlement*› جَديرٌ بالاحْتِرامِ **3▸** (**Honourable**) (as a title) ‹*Gentleman, Lady*› سَعادة ,فَخامة, مَعالٍ

honour guard (BrE), **honor guard** (AmE) *n* حَرَس شَرَفٍ

honours degree (BrE), **honors degree** (AmE) *n* دَرَجة \ مَرْتَبة شَرَفٍ

hood /hʊd/ *n* **1▸** (of a coat) قَلَنْسُوة (قَلانِسُ ,قَلانيسُ) **2▸** (on a cooker) شَفّاط **3▸** (BrE) (on a car, pram) غِطاء حِمايةٍ **4▸** (AmE) (of a car) كَبّوت (كَبابيتُ) ,غِطاء مُحَرِّكٍ **5▸** (AmE) (criminal) مُجْرِم; ▸ **hoodlum**

hoodlum /'huːdləm/ *n* **1▸** (ruffian) شَخْص عُدْوانيّ \ مُثير لِلشَغَبِ **2▸** (criminal) مُجْرِم

hoodwink /'hʊdwɪŋk/ *vt* خَدَعَ (a; خَدْع) ,غَشَّ (u; غِشّ) ‹*the public, voters*›

hoof /huːf/ *n* (*pl* **hoofs** or **hooves**) حافِر (حَوافِرُ)

hoof-and-mouth disease *n* (AmE) ▸ **foot-and-mouth disease**

hook /hʊk/ **A** *n* **1▸** (for clothing, pictures) خُطّاف تَعْليقٍ **2▸** (in fishing) صِنّارة (صَنانيرُ) **3▸** (fastener) خُطّاف (خَطاطيفُ) **4▸** (Tel) حامِل سَمّاعةِ هاتِفٍ; **to leave the phone off the ~** وَضَعَ سَمّاعةَ الهاتِفِ جانِباً **5▸** (in boxing) لَكْمة خُطّافيّة; **a left/right ~ to the jaw** لَكْمة خُطّافيّة يُسْرى \ يُمْنى على الفَكِّ

B *vt* **1** (to attach) رَبَطَ (i-u; رَبْط) ‹*a trailer, lamp*›; **to ~ a caravan to/onto a car** رَبَطَ عَرَبةً بِسَيّارةٍ **2** (to bend around) ثَنى (i; ثَنْي) ‹*one's arm, finger*›; **I ~ed my arm in** *or* **through hers** شَبَّكْتُ ذِراعي في ذِراعِها **3** (infml) اصْطادَ بِصُنّارةٍ ‹*a fish*› **4** **to ~ the ball** (in soccer) سَدَّدَ الكُرةَ بِشَكْلٍ لَوْلَبِيٍّ; (in golf) [أَرْسَلَ الكُرةَ يَرْتَدُّ مَسارُها إلى اليَمينِ أو اليَسارِ]

(Idioms) **to get sb off the hook** أَنْقَذَ شَخْصاً من وَرْطةٍ; **he swallowed it hook, line and sinker** اِبْتَلَعَ الطُّعْمَ تماماً; **to let sb off the hook** [سَمَحَ لِشَخْصٍ بِأَنْ يَتَخَلَّصَ من وَرْطةٍ]

(Phrasal verb) **hook up** **A** **1** «garment» أُغْلِقَ **2** **to ~ up with sb** (to meet) تَقابَلَ مع شَخْصٍ; (to form a relationship) نامَ مع شَخْصٍ **3** (in broadcasting) «stations» [تَمَّ رَبْطُ المَحَطّاتِ التِلِفِزْيونيّةِ] **B** **~ up [sth/sb], ~ [sth/sb] up** **1** (to attach) وَصَلَ [شَيْئاً \ شَخْصاً] ‹*a trailer, caravan*› **2** (to fasten) أَغْلَقَ [شَيْئاً] ‹*a garment*› **3** وَصَلَ [شَيْئاً \ شَخْصاً] ‹*a device, patient*›

hooked /ˈhʊkt/ *adj* **1** (hook-shaped) ‹*nose, beak*› مَعْقوف **2** **to get ~ on drugs/computer games** (infml) (to become addicted) أَصْبَحَ مُدْمِناً على المُخَدِّراتِ \ أَلْعابِ الكُمْبيوتَر

hooker¹ /ˈhʊkə/ *n* [لاعِب وَسَطِ الصَفِّ الأَماميِّ لِلهُجومِ]

hooker² /ˈhʊkə/ *n* (infml) مومِس (مومِسات), عاهِرة (عاهِرات, عَواهِرُ)

hooky, **hookey** /ˈhʊki/ *n* (infml) **to play ~** تَغَيَّبَ عن المَدْرَسةِ دون إِذْنٍ

hooligan /ˈhuːlɪɡ(ə)n/ *n* مُخَرِّب, فَوْضَويّ

hoop /huːp/ *n* طارة, طَوْق (أَطْواق)

hooray /hʊˈreɪ/ *excl* مَرْحى

hoot /huːt/ **A** *n* **1** (of an owl) نَعيق **2** (of a car) صَوْت البوقِ; (of a ship) صَفير **3** (of laughter) قَهْقَهة

B *vi* **1** «owls» نَعَقَ (a-i; نَعيق, نَعْق) **2** «horns» صَوَّتَ; «sirens» صَفَّرَ

hooter /ˈhuːtə/ *n* (BrE) **1** (siren) صَفّارة إِنْذارٍ **2** (horn) بوق (سَيّارةٍ)

Hoover® /ˈhuːvə/ *n* (BrE) مِكْنَسة كَهْرَبائيّة

hooves /huːvz/ *n pl* ▸ **hoof**

hop /hɒp/ **A** *vi* (**-pp-**) **1** «children, patients» حَجَلَ (i-u; حَجْل, حَجَلان) **2** «rabbits, birds» نَطَّ (u; نَطّ) **3** (infml) «commuters, tourists» قَفَزَ (i; قَفْز); **to ~ on a bus** قَفَزَ على مَتْنِ حافِلةٍ; **I'll give you a lift, ~ in!** سَأُوَصِّلُكَ، هَيّا ارْكَبْ!

B *vt* (**-pp-**) (AmE infml) رَكِبَ (a; رُكوب) ‹*a train, plane*›

C *n* (of a person) حَجْلة; (of a rabbit, bird) نَطّ

D (**hops**) *n pl* حَشيشة الدينار

hope /həʊp/ **A** *n* **1** (expectation) أَمَل (آمال); **in the ~ of sth** على أَمَلِ شَيْءٍ; **to have high ~s of doing sth** كانَ عِنْدَهُ آمالٌ عَريضةٌ لِفِعْلِ شَيْءٍ; **we have great ~s for the future** عِنْدَنا آمالٌ عَظيمةٌ لِلمُسْتَقْبَلِ; **to give up** *or* **lose ~** فَقَدَ الأَمَلَ; **to raise sb's ~s** رَفَعَ سَقْفَ آمالِ شَخْصٍ; **to pin one's ~s on sth/sb** عَقَدَ آمالَهُ على شَيْءٍ \ شَخْصٍ **2** (chance) أَمَل (آمال); **to have no ~ of doing sth** ما كانَ عِنْدَهُ أَمَلٌ في فِعْلِ شَيْءٍ; **a plan with little ~ of success** خُطّة ذات أَمَلٍ ضَعيفٍ في النَجاحِ; **there is no ~ for them** لَيْسَ عِنْدَهُمْ أَمَلٌ; **there is no ~ of an improvement** لَيْسَ هُناكَ أَمَلٌ في التَحَسُّنِ; **you're my only/last ~** أَنْتَ أَمَلي الوَحيدُ \ الأَخيرُ; **he hasn't got a ~ in hell** (infml) لا أَمَلَ لَهُ البَتّةَ **3** (promising person) شَخْص واعِد

B *vt* أَمَلَ (u; أَمَل), تَمَنّى, رَجا (u; رَجاء, مَرْجاة); **to ~ to do sth** رَجا أَنْ يَفْعَلَ شَيْئاً; **we ~ that an agreement will be reached** نَتَمَنّى أَنْ يَتِمَّ الوُصولُ إلى اتِّفاقٍ; **it is to be ~d that ...** من المَأْمولِ أَنْ ...; **I ~ so** أَتَمَنّى ذلك; **I ~ not** لا أَتَمَنّى ذلك; **we cannot ~ to compete with big firms** لا أَمَلَ لَنا في مُنافَسةِ الشَرِكاتِ الكُبْرى; **I only** *or* **just ~ he remembers** أَتَمَنّى فَقَطْ أَنْ يَتَذَكَّرَ

C *vi* أَمَلَ (u; أَمَل); **to ~ for change/success** أَمَلَ في التَغْييرِ \ النَجاحِ; **I was hoping for news of them** كُنْتُ أَتَمَنّى خَبَراً مِنْهُمْ; **to ~ for the best** أَمَلَ في الأَفْضَلِ

(Idioms) **hope springs eternal** نَبْعُ الأَمَلِ لا يَنْضُبُ; **to hope against hope** راوَدَهُ أَمَلٌ يائِسٌ

hope chest *n* (AmE) **1** (chest) صُنْدوق جِهازِ العَروسِ **2** (contents) مُحْتَوَيات صُنْدوقِ جِهازِ العَروسِ

hopeful /ˈhəʊpfʊl/ **A** *adj* **1** (filled with hope) ‹*expression, attitude*› مُفْعَم بالأَمَلِ **2** (encouraging) ‹*development, news*› واعِد, باعِث لِلأَمَلِ

B *n* [شَخْص يَأْمُلُ في النَجاحِ]

hopefully /ˈhəʊpf(ə)li/ *adv* 1 (with luck) إنْ شاءَ اللهُ; **~, we'll get paid this week** نَأْمُلُ أنْ نَتَقاضى رَواتِبَنا هذا الأُسْبوعَ 2 (with hope) ‹*to say, wait*› آمِلاً, مُتَأَمِّلاً; **he looked ~ at his mother** نَظَرَ إلى والِدَتِهِ نَظْرَةً مُفْعَمةً بالأَمَلِ

hopeless /ˈhəʊpləs/ *adj* 1 (allowing no hope) ‹*attempt, case*› مَيْؤوس مِنْهُ; **it's ~!** الأَمْرُ مَيْئوسٌ مِنْهُ! 2 (infml) (incompetent) ‹*teacher, pupil*› غَيْر كُفْؤ; **you're ~!** لا أَمَلَ فيكَ! ; **the train service on this line is ~** خِدْمةُ القِطارِ على هذا الخَطِّ سَيِّئةٌ للغايةِ; **to be ~ at sport** لم يَكُنْ ماهِراً في الرِياضةِ

hopelessly /ˈhəʊpləsli/ *adv* 1 (irredeemably) ‹*inadequate, outdated*› بِشَكْلٍ مَيْؤوسٍ مِنْهُ; **they were ~ lost/in love** كانوا تائِهينَ \ وَقَعوا في الحُبِّ بِشَكْلٍ مَيْؤوسٍ مِنْهُ 2 (despairingly) ‹*to sigh, stare*› بِيأْسٍ

hopelessness /ˈhəʊplɪsnəs/ *n* 1 (despair) يَأس, قُنوط 2 (futility) عَبَثِيّة

hopscotch /ˈhɒpskɒtʃ/ *n* لُعْبة الحَجْلِة; **to play ~** لَعِبَ لُعْبةَ الحَجْلةِ

horde /hɔːd/ *n* حَشْد (حُشود); **~s of people** حُشود من الناسِ

horizon /həˈrʌɪz(ə)n/ *n* أُفُق (آفاق); **there's a ship on the ~** هُناكَ سَفينةٌ في الأُفُقِ

horizontal /hɒrɪˈzɒnt(ə)l/ *adj* ‹*plane, stripe*› أُفُقيّ

hormone /ˈhɔːməʊn/ *n* هُرْمون (هُرْمونات)

hormone replacement therapy *n* عِلاج بالهُرْموناتِ البَديلةِ

horn /hɔːn/ *n* 1 (of an animal) قَرْن (قُرون) 2 (wind instrument) بوق (أَبْواق, بوقات); (French horn) بوق فَرَنْسيّ 3 (of a car) بوق سَيّارةٍ 4 (of a ship) صافِرة, صَفّارة

hornbill /ˈhɔːnbɪl/ *n* أبو قَرْنٍ (طائِر)

hornet /ˈhɔːnɪt/ *n* دَبّور (دَبابيرُ), زُنْبور (زَنابيرُ)

Horn of Africa *n* (**the Horn of Africa**) القَرْن الأَفْريقيّ

horoscope /ˈhɒrəskəʊp/ *n* طالِع (طَوالِعُ), تَوَقُّعات الأَبْراجِ

horrendous /hɒˈrɛndəs/ *adj* 1 (horrifying) ‹*crime, account*› مُرَوِّع 2 (infml) (dreadful) ‹*mistake, cost*› مُريع

horrible /ˈhɒrɪb(ə)l/ *adj* 1 (unpleasant) ‹*place, clothes*› فَظيع 2 (shocking) ‹*death, crime*› رَهيب, شَنيع

horribly /ˈhɒrɪbli/ *adv* 1 (extremely) ‹*embarrassed, apt*› جِدّاً; **the plan went ~ wrong** سارَت الخُطّةُ بِشَكْلٍ سَيِّئٍ للغايةِ 2 (shockingly, dreadfully) ‹*burned, disfigured*› بِشَكْلٍ فَظيعٍ \ مُرَوِّعٍ

horrid /ˈhɒrɪd/ *adj* (BrE infml) ‹*weather, taste*› فَظيع

horrific /hɒˈrɪfɪk/ *adj* ‹*accident, account*› مُرَوِّع

horrify /ˈhɒrɪfʌɪ/ *vt* (**horrifies**, **horrifying**, **horrified**) رَوَّعَ, أَرْعَبَ ‹*the public, audience*›

horrifying /ˈhɒrɪfʌɪɪŋ/ *adj* ‹*experience, sight*› مُرْعِب, مُفْزِع

horror /ˈhɒrə/ *n* رُعْب, هَلَع; **the ~s of the prison camps** أَهْوال مُعَسْكَراتِ الاعْتِقالِ

horror film, **horror movie** *n* فيلْم رُعْبٍ

horror story *n* قِصّة رُعْبٍ

horse /hɔːs/ *n* 1 (animal) حِصان (أَحْصِنة), فَرَس (أَفْراس); **to eat like a ~** أَكَلَ بِشَراهةٍ 2 (also **vaulting horse**) (for gymnasts) حِصان قَفْزٍ \ مِنَصّة

Idiom **to flog/beat** (AmE) **a dead horse** ضَرَبَ في حَديدٍ بارِدٍ

Phrasal verb **horse about, horse around** عَبِثَ (a; عَبَث)

horseback /ˈhɔːsbak/ *n* **to go on ~** امْتَطى حِصاناً

horseback riding *n* رُكوب الحِصانِ

horsebox /ˈhɔːsbɒks/ *n* (BrE) عَرَبة نَقْلِ الخَيْلِ

horse breeder *n* مُرَبّي خَيْلٍ

horse chestnut *n* 1 (tree) كَسْتَناء الحِصانِ 2 (fruit) ثَمَر كَسْتَناءِ الحِصانِ

horse-drawn /ˈhɔːsdrɔːn/ *adj* ‹*carriage*› مَجْرور بِحِصانٍ \ بِأَحْصِنةٍ

horsefly /ˈhɔːsflʌɪ/ *n* (*pl* **horseflies**) نُعَرة (نُعَر, نُعَرات)

horseman /ˈhɔːsmən/ *n* (*pl* **-men**) فارِس (فُرْسان, فَوارِسُ), خَيّال (خَيّالة)

horsepower /ˈhɔːspaʊə/ *n* قُدْرة حِصانيّة

horse race *n* سِباق خَيْلٍ

horse racing *n* سِباق خُيولٍ

horseradish /ˈhɔːsradɪʃ/ *n* فُجْل الخَيْلِ

horseradish sauce *n* صَلْصة فُجْلِ الخَيْلِ

horse riding *n* (BrE) رُكوب الخَيْلِ

horseshoe /ˈhɔːʃuː/ *n* حَدْوة

horse show *n* سِباق فُروسيّةٍ

horse-trader /ˈhɔːstreɪdə/ *n* تاجِر خُيولٍ

horticulture /ˈhɔːtɪˌkʌltʃə/ *n* بَسْتَنة

horticulturist /hɔːrtɪˈkʌltʃərɪst/ *n* مُتَخَصِّص في البَسْتَنةِ

hose /həʊz/, **hosepipe** (BrE) /ˈhəʊzpʌɪp/ *n* 1 (for the garden, cleaning) خُرْطوم مِياهٍ; (fire hose) خُرْطوم إطْفاءِ \ حَريق 2 (tights) جَوارِب; (AmE) (pantyhose) جَوارِب نِسائيّة (من النَّيلون)

(Phrasal verb) **hose down**: **~ [sth] down, ~ down [sth]** غَسَلَ [شَيْئاً] بِخُرْطومٍ ‹*a floor, car*›

hosiery /ˈhəʊzɪəri/ *n* (fml) جَوارِب وَمَلابِس داخِليّة

hospice /ˈhɒspɪs/ *n* دار رِعاية طِبِّيّةٍ

hospitable /hɒˈspɪtəb(ə)l/ *adj* 1 (welcoming) ‹*host, atmosphere*› مِضْياف (mf) 2 (of environment) ‹*climate, conditions*› صالِح \ مُلائِم لِلحَياةِ

hospital /ˈhɒspɪt(ə)l/ *n* مُسْتَشْفًى (مُسْتَشْفَيات); **to be in** (BrE) **~, to be in the** (AmE) **~** كانَ في المُسْتَشْفى; **to be taken to** (BrE) **~, to be taken to the** (AmE) **~** نُقِلَ إلى المُسْتَشْفى

hospitality /hɒspɪˈtalɪti/ *n* حُسْن الوِفادةِ, كَرَم الضِيافةِ

hospitality industry *n* قِطاع الضِيافةِ

hospitalize, -ise (BrE) /ˈhɒspɪtəlʌɪz/ *vt* أَدْخَلَ إلى المُسْتَشْفى ‹*a patient, victim*›

hospital porter *n* (BrE) عامِل يَنْقُلُ المُعَدّاتِ \ المَرْضى في [المُسْتَشْفى]

host /həʊst/ **A** *n* 1 (of guests) مُضيف 2 (on radio, TV) مُضيف 3 (fml) (great number) كَمّ هائِل, عَدَد كَبير; **they had a whole ~ of questions** كانَ عِنْدَهُم كَمٌّ هائِلٌ من الأَسْئِلةِ; **there are a ~ of possibilities** هُناكَ عَدَدٌ كَبيرٌ من الاحْتِمالاتِ 4 (of a parasite) مُضيف (الطُفَيْليّاتِ) 5 (**the Host**) (in Eucharist) القُرْبان

B *vt* 1 اسْتَضافَ ‹*an event, a dinner*› 2 قَدَّمَ ‹*a show, programme*›

hostage /ˈhɒstɪdʒ/ *n* رَهينة (رَهائِنُ)

host country *n* بَلَد مُضيف

hostel /ˈhɒst(ə)l/ *n* 1 (youth hostel) نُزُل (أَنْزال), بَيْت شَبابٍ 2 (BrE) (for students) بَيْت طُلّابٍ; (for homeless people, refugees) [مَرْكَز لِإيواءِ المُشَرَّدينَ \ اللاجِئينَ]

hostess /ˈhəʊstɪs/ *n* 1 (to guests, visitors) مُضيفة 2 (BrE) (on a plane) مُضيفة جَوّيّة \ طَيَرانٍ; (on a train) مُضيفة قِطارٍ 3 (on a TV, radio show) مُضيفة

hostile /ˈhɒstʌɪl/ *adj* ‹*look, crowd, reaction*› مُعادٍ, عَدائيّ

hostility /hɒˈstɪlɪti/ *n* 1 [u] (antagonism) عَداء 2 (**hostilities** *n pl*) (warfare) عَمَليّات حَرْبيّة

hot /hɒt/ *adj* (**-tt-**) 1 (very warm) ‹*climate*› حارّ; ‹*shower, hands*› ساخِن; **to be** *or* **feel ~** شَعَرَ بالحَرارةِ; **it's ~ in the sun** الجَوُّ حارٌّ في الشَمْسِ; **the weather is ~ in July** الجَوُّ حارٌّ في يوليو; **serve the soup ~** قَدِّم الحَساءَ ساخِناً; **the engine is getting ~** تَرْتَفِعُ حَرارةُ المُحَرِّكِ; **the sun was at its ~test** كانَتْ أَشِعّةُ الشَمْسِ على أَشَدِّها; **digging is ~ work** الحَفْرُ عَمَلٌ شاقٌّ 2 (spicy) ‹*mustard, curry*› حِرّيف, حارّ 3 (latest) ‹*news*› ساخِن; **she has some ~ gossip** عِنْدَها بَعْضُ الأَخْبارِ الساخِنةِ 4 (infml) (newly arrived) **Dr Mayer arrived, ~ from New York** وَصَلَ الدُكْتورُ ماير لِلتَوِّ من نيويورْك; **it's ~ from** *or* **off the press** خَرَجَتْ لِلتَوِّ من المِطْبَعةِ 5 (fierce) ‹*competition, pace*› شَديد; **the competition's ~ in this business** المُنافسةُ شَديدةٌ في هذه المِهْنةِ 6 (infml) (angry) **to have a ~ temper** كانَ عِنْدَهُ مِزاجٌ حادٌّ; **to exchange ~ words** تَبادَلَ كَلِماتٍ قاسِيةً 7 (infml) (popular) **to be ~** «entertainer, show» كانَ مَشْهوراً; **this is the ~test club in town** هذا هو النادي الأَكْثَرُ شَعْبيّةً في المَدينةِ; **she's the ~test member of the group** هي أَكْثَرُ الأَعْضاءِ شَعْبيّةً في المَجْموعةِ 8 (infml) (assured) **a ~ tip** نَصيحة ثَمينة; **to be the ~ favourite** كانَ المُرَشَّحَ الأَوْفَرَ حَظًّا 9 (keen) **to be ~ on sports cars** كانَ مولَعاً بالسَيّاراتِ الرِياضيّةِ 10 (infml) (stolen) ‹*jewels, goods*› مَسْروق 11 (close) **you're getting ~** تَقْتَرِبُ من الجَوابِ; **to go in ~ pursuit of sb** انْطَلَقَ في مُلاحَقةٍ مَحْمومةٍ لِشَخْصٍ

(Idioms) **to be in/get into hot water** وَقَعَ في وَرْطةٍ; **to blow hot and cold** لا يَسْتَقِرُّ على حالٍ; **to be too hot to handle** [كانَ من الصَعْبِ تَحَمُّلُهُ]

(Phrasal verb) **hot up** (infml) (to become intense) «games, campaigns» أَصْبَحَ حامِياً; **things are ~ting up** الأَشْياءُ تُصْبِحُ حامِيةً

hot air *n* (infml) هُراء, كَلام فارِغ

hot-air balloon *n* مُنْطاد

hotbed /ˈhɒtbɛd/ *n* مَرْتَع (مَراتِعُ)

hot-blooded /ˌhɒtˈblʌdɪd/ *adj* <*male, lover*> مُتَحَمِّس

hot chocolate *n* مَشْروب الشوكولاتةِ \ الكاكاو الساخِن

hot dog *n* هوت دوغ (سَنْدويتْش سُجُقٍّ)

hotel /həʊˈtɛl/ *n* فُنْدُق (فَنادِقُ)

hotelier /həʊˈtɛlɪə/, **hotel keeper** *n* صاحِب \ مُدير فُنْدُقٍ

hotelkeeper /həʊˈtɛlkiːpə/ *n* (BrE) صاحِب \ مُدير فُنْدُقٍ

hot flush (BrE), **hot flash** (AmE) *n* [سُخونة ناتِجة عن انْقِطاع الطَمَثِ عند المَرْأةِ]

hot-headed /ˌhɒtˈhɛdɪd/ *adj* <*youngster*> أَهْوَج (dipt), مُتَهَوِّر; <*decision*> مُتَسَرِّع

hothouse /ˈhɒthaʊs/ *n* دَفيئة, بَيْت زُجاجيّ

hotline /ˈhɒtlʌɪn/ *n* 1 (for the public) خَطّ ساخِن 2 (between governments) خَطّ مُباشِر

hotly /ˈhɒtli/ *adv* <*contested, debated*> بِحَرارةٍ; <*to retort, protest*> بِحِدّةٍ

hotplate /ˈhɒtpleɪt/ *n* مَوْقِد, لَوْح تَسْخين (مَواقِدُ)

hot rod *n* سَيّارة مُعَدَّلة (لِزيادة سُرْعَتِها وَقُوَّتِها)

hotshot /ˈhɒtʃɒt/ *n* (infml) [شَخْص مُهِمّ \ ذو قُدُراتٍ عالِيةٍ]

hotspot *n* (infml) 1 (infml) (trouble spot) بُقْعة \ بُؤْرة ساخِنة 2 (infml) (fashionable place) [مَكان ذو شَعْبيّةٍ كَبيرةٍ] 3 (on a screen) نُقْطة اتِّصال

hot spring *n* يَنْبوع ساخِن, حَمّة (حَمّ, حِمام)

hot-tempered /ˌhɒtˈtɛmpəːd/ *adj* <*youngster, chef*> سَريع الانْفِعال

hot-water bottle /ˌhɒtˈwɔːtə ˌbɒt(ə)l/ *n* زُجاجة ماءٍ ساخِنٍ (لِتَدْفِئةِ السَريرِ \ جُزْءٍ من الجِسْمِ)

hound /haʊnd/ **A** *n* كَلْب (كِلاب)

B *vt* لاحَقَ, تَعَقَّبَ <*a celebrity, politician*>

hour /ˈaʊə/ **A** *n* 1 (sixty minutes) ساعة (ساعات); **after an ~** بعد ساعةٍ; **we waited for ~s** انْتَظَرْنا لِساعاتٍ; **it's an ~ (away) from central Beirut** هي على بُعْدِ ساعةٍ من وَسَطِ بَيْروتَ; **at 21.00 ~s** في التاسِعةِ مَساءً; **she earns $50 an** *or* **per ~** تَكْسِبُ خَمْسينَ دولارًا في الساعةِ; **to be paid by the ~** كانَ يَتَقاضى أَجْراً بالساعةِ 2 (time of day) ساعة (ساعات); **the bus leaves on the ~** يَنْطَلِقُ الباصُ على رَأْسِ الساعةِ; **we got home in the early ~s** وَصَلْنا إلى البَيْتِ في وَقْتٍ مُبَكِّرٍ; **he calls at all ~s of the day** يَتَّصِلُ أثناء كُلِّ ساعاتِ اليَوْمِ

3 (fml) (point in time) ساعة (ساعات); **it was the nation's finest/darkest ~** كانَتْ أَفْضَلَ \ أَحْلَكَ ساعةٍ في تاريخ الأُمّةِ; **he came in my ~ of need** جاءَ لَحْظةَ حاجَتي

B (**hours**) *n pl* ساعات; **business** *or* **opening ~s** ساعات العَمَلِ; **visiting ~s are 2.30 to 5.30 pm** ساعاتُ الزِيارة بين 2:30 و5:30 مَساءً; **after ~s** بعد ساعات العَمَلِ

hour hand *n* عَقْرَب الساعاتِ

houri /ˈhʊəri/ *n* (*pl* **houris**) حورِيّة (حورِيّات, حور)

hourly /ˈaʊəli/ **A** *adj* <*update*> في كُلِّ ساعةٍ; <*rate*> مُقَدَّر بالساعةِ; **there is an ~ bus/train service** هُناكَ خِدْمةُ حافِلةٍ \ قِطارٍ كُلَّ ساعةٍ

B *adv* <*to update*> كُلَّ ساعةٍ; <*to pay*> بالساعةِ; **trains run ~** تَسيرُ القِطاراتُ كُلَّ ساعةٍ

house **A** /haʊs/ *n* 1 (home) مَنْزِل (مَنازِلُ), بَيْت (بُيوت); **you can stay at my ~** تَسْتَطيعُ أنْ تَبْقى في بيتي; **she's at a friend's ~** هي في بيتِ صَديقٍ; **to go to sb's ~** ذَهَبَ إلى مَنْزِلِ شَخْصٍ

2 (also **House**) (Pol) بَرْلَمان; **the upper ~** الغُرْفة العُلْيا للبَرْلَمان 3 (firm) شَرِكة; **on the ~** على حِسابِ الشَرِكةِ 4 (auditorium) قاعة; **it played to a full ~** عُرِضَتْ لِقاعةٍ مَليئةٍ 5 (family line) بَيْت (بُيوت); **the H~ of Saud** بَيْت آلِ سَعودَ 6 (BrE) (division of a school) مَنْزِل (مَنازِلُ) 7 [u] (also **house music**) موسيقى الهاوس

B /haʊz/ *vt* 1 (to accommodate) آوى <*families, the homeless, prisoners*>; **to be badly** *or* **poorly ~d** تَمَّ إيواءُهُ في مَكانٍ غَيْرِ لائِقٍ 2 (to contain) احْتَوى <*a collection, library*>

Idioms **to bring the house down** أَثارَ عاصِفةً من التَصْفيقِ; **to put one's house in order** أَعادَ تَرْتيبَ البَيْتِ

house arrest *n* إقامة جَبْرِيّة

houseboat /ˈhaʊsbəʊt/ *n* عَوّامة

housebound /ˈhaʊsbaʊnd/ *adj* <*invalid, resident*> حَبيس المَنْزِلِ \ البَيْتِ; **she's completely ~** هي حَبيسةُ المَنْزِلِ كُلِّيًّا

housebroken *adj* (AmE) ▸ **house-trained**

house call *n* زِيارة طِبِّيّة مَنْزِلِيّة

housefly /ˈhaʊsflaɪ/ *n* (*pl* **houseflies**) ذُبابة مَنْزِلٍ

household /ˈhaʊshəʊld/ **A** *n* أُسْرة (أُسَر, أُسْرات); **~s with more than one wage earner** الأُسَر الَّتي تُحَصِّلُ أَكْثَرَ من دَخْلٍ واحِدٍ **B** *adj* ‹*expenses, bill*› مَنْزِليّ

household appliance *n* جِهاز كَهْرَبائيّ مَنْزِليّ

householder /ˈhaʊshəʊldə/ *n* صاحِب بَيْتٍ

household name *n* اسْم مَعْروف

house husband *n* [زَوْج ماكِث بالبَيْتِ يَهْتَمُّ بِشُؤونِ المَنْزِلِ]

housekeeper /ˈhaʊskiːpə/ *n* مُدَبِّرة مَنْزِلٍ

housekeeping /ˈhaʊskiːpɪŋ/ *n* **1** (management) تَدْبير مَنْزِليّ **2** (money) مَصْروف البَيْتِ

housemaid /ˈhaʊsmeɪd/ *n* خادِمة البَيْتِ

houseman /ˈhaʊsmən/ *n* (*pl* **-men**) (BrE) طَبيب تحت التَّمْرينِ

house martin *n* خُطّاف المَنْزِلِ

House of Commons *n* (**the House of Commons**) مَجْلِس العُمومِ (البَريطانيّ)

house officer *n* (BrE) طَبيب مُقيم

House of Lords *n* (**the House of Lords**) مَجْلِس اللورْداتِ

House of Representatives *n* (**the House of Representatives**) مَجْلِس النوّابِ (الأَمْريكيّ)

house physician *n* (BrE) طَبيب تحت التَّمْرينِ

houseplant /ˈhaʊsplɑːnt/ *n* نَبات مَنْزِليّ

house prices *n pl* أَسْعار المَنازِلِ

house-proud /ˈhaʊspraʊd/ *adj* ‹*homeowner, housewife*› فَخور بِمَنْزِلِهِ

Houses of Parliament *n* (**the Houses of Parliament**) غُرْفَتَي البَرْلَمان

house sparrow *n* عُصْفور دوريّ

house surgeon *n* (AmE) جَرّاح مُقيم

house-to-house /ˌhaʊstəˈhaʊs/ *adj* ‹*search, inquiries*› من بَيْتٍ إلى بَيْتٍ

house-trained /ˈhaʊstreɪnd/ *adj* (BrE) ‹*pet, puppy*› [مُدَرَّب على قَضاءِ حاجَتِهِ خارِجَ البَيْتِ]

house-warming party, house-warming /ˈhaʊswɔːmɪŋ pɑːti/ *n* [حَفْلة تُقامُ بِمُناسَبةِ الانْتِقالِ إلى بَيْتٍ جَديدٍ]

housewife /ˈhaʊswaɪf/ *n* (*pl* **-wives**) رَبّة مَنْزِلٍ

housework /ˈhaʊswɜːk/ *n* أَعْمال مَنْزِلِيّة

housing /ˈhaʊzɪŋ/ *n* **1** (dwellings) سَكَن **2** (provision of houses) إِسْكان; **the government's policy on ~** سِياسة الحُكومةِ بِشَأْنِ الإِسْكانِ

housing association *n* (BrE) جَمْعيّة سَكَنِيّة

housing development *n* عَقار سَكَنيّ

housing estate *n* (BrE) عَقار سَكَنيّ

housing project *n* (AmE) مَشْروع إِسْكانٍ

hovel /ˈhɒv(ə)l/ *n* [مَسْكَن حَقير]

hover /ˈhɒvə/ *vi* **1** (in the air) «helicopters, bees» حامَ, حَلَّقَ (u; حَوَمان, حَوْم) **2** (to linger) «waiters, students» حامَ (u; حَوَمان, حَوْم) **3** (on a scale) «ratings, unemployment» تَأَرْجَحَ; **the temperature ~s around 15 degrees** تَحومُ دَرَجةُ الحَرارةِ حول 15 دَرَجة

hovercraft /ˈhɒvəkrɑːft/ *n* (*pl* **hovercraft**) حَوّامة

how /haʊ/ **A** *adv, conj* **1** (in what way, by what means) كَيْفَ; **he knows ~ to fix it** يَعْرِفُ كَيْفَ يُصْلِحُهُ; **~ is it spelled?, ~ do you spell it?** كَيْفَ يُهَجّى هذا؟; **~ do you feel about it?** ما شُعورُكَ حِيالَهُ؟; **~ does the tune go?** كَيْفَ يُدَنْدَنُ اللَّحْنُ؟; **I wonder ~ it works** أَتساءَلُ كَيْفَ يَعْمَلُ; **I learned ~ to do it** تَعَلَّمْتُ كَيْفَ أَفْعَلُهُ **2** (enquiring about health, success etc) **~ are you?** كَيْفَ حالُكَ؟; **~'s your brother?** كَيْفَ حالُ أَخيكَ؟; **~'s your foot/head?** كَيْفَ حالُ قَدَمِكَ \ رَأْسِكَ؟; **~ was the exam?, ~ did the exam go?** كَيْفَ كانَ الامْتِحانُ؟; **~ was the film/book?** كَيْفَ كانَ الفيلْمُ \ الكِتابُ؟; **~ did you like the house?** ما رَأْيُكَ في البَيْتِ؟; **~ are things?, ~'s everything?** (infml) كَيْفَ تَسيرُ الأُمورُ؟; **~ do you do!** سَعِدْتُ بِلِقائِكَ! **3** (in questions of number, quantity etc) **~ much is this?, ~ much does this cost?** كم سِعْرُ هذا؟; **~ much does it weigh?** كم وَزْنُهُ؟; **~ often do you go there?** كم مَرّةً تَذْهَبُ إلى هُناكَ؟; **~ many times have you been to Tripoli?** كم مَرّةً ذَهَبْتَ إلى طَرابُلُس؟; **~ long have you lived here?** منذ مَتى وَأَنْتَ تَعيشُ هُنا؟; **~ much time/money is there left?** كم بَقِيَ من الوَقْتِ \ المالِ؟; **~ long will it take?** كم سَيَسْتَغْرِقُ من الوَقْتِ؟; **~ old is she?** كم عُمْرُها؟; **~ long is the rope?**

كم طولُ الحَبْلِ؟; ~ **far is it?** كم يَبْعُدُ؟; **I don't know ~ many people will come** لا أَعْلَمُ كم شَخصاً سَيأْتي; **tell me ~ old she is** أَخْبِرْني كم عُمْرُها **4** (in exclamations) ~ **wonderful/awful!** يا لَلْرَوْعةِ \ لَلْفَظاعةِ!; ~ **nice you look!** كم تَبْدو جَميلاً!; ~ **clever of you/him!** كم أَنْتَ \ هو ذَكيٌّ!; ~ **it rained!** كم كانَ يا لَلْغَزارةِ الّتي أَمْطَرَتْ بِها!; ~ **kind of you to help!** لُطْفاً مِنْكَ أنْ تُقدِّمَ المُساعَدةَ! **5** (expressing indignation) ~ **could you?** كَيْفَ يُمْكِنُهُ؟; ~ **can he say that?** كَيْفَ جَرُؤَتْ؟ أنْ يَقولَ ذلك؟ **6** (infml) (in whichever way) كَيْفَما, بِأَيِّ طَريقةٍ; **you can decorate it ~ you like** يُمْكِنُكَ أنْ تُزَيِّنَهُ كَيْفَما تَشاءُ **7** (introducing a fact) كَيْفَ; **he told me ~ he had found it on the bus** أَخْبَرَني كَيْفَ وَجَدَهُ في الحافِلةِ; **it's strange ~ he's never mentioned now** من الغَريبِ أَلاّ يَذْكُرَهُ أَحَدٌ الآنَ

B (**how come**) *adv phr* (infml) لِماذا; **'I don't like him'—'~ come?'** 'لا أُحِبُّهُ' — 'كَيْفَ هذا؟'; ~ **come you always get the best place/arrive first?** كَيْفَ تَحْصُلُ على أَفْضَلِ مَكانٍ \ تَصِلُ أَوَّلاً دائماً؟

C (**and how**) *adv phr* (infml) كَثيراً جِدًّا; **'Did you miss me?' - 'And ~!'** 'هل افْتَقَدْتَني؟' — 'كَثيراً جِدًّا!'; **'Did your mother tell you off?' - 'And ~!'** 'هل وَبَّخَتْكَ أُمُّكَ؟' — 'كَثيراً جِدًّا!'

D (**how's that**) *adv phr* (infml) (what do you think?) **I'll drive and you'll pay for the fuel: ~'s that?** سَوْفَ أَقودُ وَأَنْتَ تَدْفَعُ ثَمَنَ الوَقودِ: ما قَوْلُكَ في هذا؟

however /haʊˈɛvə/ **A** *conj* (nevertheless) وَلَكِنْ, وَمَعَ ذلك; ~, **the recession is not over yet** وَمَعَ ذلك، فالرُكودُ لم يَنْتَهِ بَعْدُ; **they can, ~, explain why** وَمَعَ ذلك، يُمْكِنُهُمْ أنْ يَشْرَحوا السَبَبَ; **if, ~, you choose not to accept the offer, we ...** وَلَكِنْ، إذا اخْتَرْتَ عَدَمَ قُبولِ العَرْضِ، فَنَحْنُ ...

B *adv* **1** (no matter how) ~ **hard I try, I can't** لا أَسْتَطيعُ، مَهْما حاوَلْتُ جاهِداً; ~ **poor she may be** مَهْما بَلَغَ بِها الفَقْرُ; **we'll do it ~ much it costs** سَنَفْعَلُهُ مَهْما تَكَلَّفَ; **do it ~ you like** افْعَلْهُ كَيْفَما يَحْلو لَكَ **2** (how on earth) كيف بِحَقِّ السَماءِ; ~ **did you guess?** كيف بِحَقِّ السَماءِ خَمَّنْتَ الأَمْرَ؟

howl /haʊl/ **A** *n* **1** (of a dog, wolf) عُواء **2** (of a person) صَيْحة

B *vi* **1** «wind» عَصَفَ (i; عَصْف, عُصوف); «wolves» عَوى (i; عُواء) **2** «patients, spectators» صاحَ (i; صَيْح, صِياح)

h.p. /eɪtʃˈpiː/ *abbr* = **horsepower** قُدْرة حِصانيّة

HQ /eɪtʃˈkjuː/ *n* = **headquarters** مَقَرّ \ مَرْكَز قِيادةٍ

hr *abbr* = **hour(s)** ساعة

HRH /eɪtʃɑːrˈeɪtʃ/ *n* (BrE) = **Her/His Royal Highness** صاحِبة \ صاحِب السُموِّ المَلَكيِّ

HRT /eɪtʃɑːˈtiː/ *n* = **hormone replacement therapy** عِلاج بالهُرْموناتِ البَديلةِ

HTML /eɪtʃtiːɛmˈɛl/ *n* = **Hypertext Markup Language** لُغة تَرْميزِ النَصِّ التَشَعُّبيِّ

hub /hʌb/ *n* **1** (of a wheel) قَبّ (أَقُبّ) **2** (focal point) مِحْوَر (مَحاوِرُ) **3** (in air travel) مَرْكَز (مَراكِزُ), مِحْوَر (مَحاوِرُ)

hubcap /ˈhʌbkap/ *n* غِطاء مِحْوَرِ العَجَلةِ

huddle /ˈhʌd(ə)l/ **A** *vi* **1** (to crowd together) «players, passengers» تَزاحَمَ **2** (to curl up) «survivors, animals» قَرْفَصَ (i; قَرْفَصة); **to ~ up** قَرْفَصَ (i; قَرْفَصة)

B *n* مَجْموعة (مَجاميعُ, مَجْموعات); **a ~ of huts** مَجْموعة أَكْواخٍ

hue /hjuː/ *n* لَوْن (أَلْوان)

hue and cry *n* لَجّة وَضَجّة

huff /hʌf/ *n* **to be in a ~** كانَ في نَوْبةِ غَضَبٍ

hug /hʌg/ **A** *vt* (-gg-) **1** (to embrace) ضَمَّ (u; ضَمّ), عانَقَ ‹a parent, lover› **2** (to keep close to) حاذى ‹the kerb, coastline›

B *n* ضَمّ, عِناق

huge /hjuːdʒ/ *adj* ‹amount, success› ضَخْم (ضِخام), هائِل (هَوائِلُ); **he's a ~ football fan** (infml) هو مُشَجِّعٌ مُتَحَمِّسٌ جِدًّا لِكُرةِ القَدَمِ

hugely /ˈhjuːdʒli/ *adv* ‹to increase, vary› على نَحْوٍ هائِلٍ

huh /hə/ *excl* (infml) (in surprise) ≈ وَيْ; (in inquiry) أَلَيْسَ كَذَلِكَ; (in derision, disgust) ≈ إيهٍ, ≈ أُفّ

hull /hʌl/ *n* (of a ship, plane) بَدَن (أَبْدان, أَبْدُن), هَيْكَل (هَياكِلُ)

hullo /hʌˈləʊ/ *excl* ▸ **hello**

hum /hʌm/ **A** *vt* (-mm-) دَنْدَنَ (i; دَنْدَنة) ‹a song, melody›

B *vi* (-mm-) **1** «machinery, bees» طَنَّ (i; طَنين) **2** «choristers, carol singers» دَنْدَنَ (i; دَنْدَنة)

C *n* طَنين, دَنْدَنة

human /ˈhjuːmən/ A *adj* <*behaviour, remains*> بَشَرِيّ, إنْسانيّ

B *n* إنْسان

human being *n* إنْسان, كائِن بَشَرِيّ

humane /hjʊˈmeɪn/ *adj* 1 <*treatment, approach*> إنْسانيّ

2 <*method, slaughter*> رَؤوف

human interest story *n* قِصّة إنْسانيّة

humanism /ˈhjuːmənɪz(ə)m/ *n* إنْسانيّة

humanist /ˈhjuːmənɪst/ *n* إنْسانيّ (يُؤْمِنُ بِمَذْهَبِ الإنْسانيّة)

humanitarian /hjʊˌmanɪˈtɛːrɪən/ *adj* <*aid, ideals*> إنْسانيّ

humanity /hjʊˈmanɪti/ *n* إنْسانيّة, جِنْس بَشَرِيّ; **he was charged with crimes against ~** اُتُّهِم بِجَرائِمَ ضِدّ الإنْسانيّة

human nature *n* طَبيعة بَشَريّة

human resources /hjuːmən rɪˈsɔːsɪz/ A *n pl* (employees) المَوارِد البَشَريّة

B *n sing* (department) إدارة المَوارِد البَشَرِيّة

human rights *n* حُقوق الإنْسان

human shield *n* دِرْع بَشَرِيّ

humble /ˈhʌmb(ə)l/ *adj* 1 <*man, account*> مُتَواضِع 2 (poor) **from ~ origins** من أُصولٍ فَقيرةٍ

humbly /ˈhʌmbli/ *adv* 1 <*to suggest, ask*> بِتَواضُعٍ 2 <*to live*> مُتَواضِعاً

humdrum /ˈhʌmdrʌm/ *adj* <*life, routine*> مُمِلّ, رَتيب

humid /ˈhjuːmɪd/ *adj* <*climate, air*> رَطْب

humidity /hjʊˈmɪdɪti/ *n* رُطوبة

humiliate /hjʊˈmɪlieɪt/ *vt* أَذَلَّ <*a colleague, an employee*>

humiliating /hjʊˈmɪlieɪtɪŋ/ *adj* <*failure, defeat*> مُذِلّ, مُخْزٍ

humiliation /ˌhjuːmɪlɪˈeɪʃ(ə)n/ *n* إذْلال, خِزْي

humility /hjʊˈmɪlɪti/ *n* تَواضُع

hummingbird /ˈhʌmɪŋbəːd/ *n* طَنّان

hummus /ˈhʊməs/ *n* حُمُّص بِطَحينة

humorless (AmE) *adj* ▸ **humourless**

humorous /ˈhjuːm(ə)rəs/ *adj* <*story, book*> طَريف, هَزْلِيّ

humour (BrE), **humor** (AmE) /ˈhjuːmə/ A *n* 1 (wit) فُكاهة, ظَرافة, دُعابة; **a good sense of ~** روح دُعابةٍ جَيِّدة 2 (mood) مِزاج (أَمْزِجة); **to be in good/bad ~** كانَ مِزاجُهُ جَيِّداً \ سَيِّئاً

B *vt* لاطَفَ, سايَرَ <*a client, child*>

humourless (BrE), **humorless** (AmE) /ˈhjuːmələs/ *adj* <*person, speech*> يَفْتَقِرُ إلى روحِ الدُعابةِ

hump /hʌmp/ *n* 1 (Anat) حَدَبة 2 (mound) رابِية (رَوابٍ), أَكَمة (آكام, أَكَمات)

(Idiom) **to be over the hump** نَجَح في تَخَطّي الأَصْعَبِ

hunch /hʌntʃ/ A *vt* **to ~ one's shoulders** حَنى \ ثَنى كَتِفَيْهِ

B *n* حَدْس, حِسّ داخِليّ

hunchback /ˈhʌntʃbak/ *n* 1 (old use or offensive) (person) أَحْدَب (dipt; حُدْب) 2 (hump) حَدَبة

hunched /hʌntʃt/ *adj* <*back, figure*> مُحَدَّب, مُنْحَنٍ

hundred /ˈhʌndrəd/ A *n* 1 (number) مِائة; **a** *or* **one ~ minus two equals ninety-eight** مِائةٌ ناقِص اثْنَيْنِ يُساوي ثَمانِيةً وَتِسْعين; **two ~** مِائَتانِ; **two ~ and one** مِائَتانِ وَواحِد; **a ~ thousand** مِائَة أَلْفٍ; **~s of times** مِئات المَرّاتِ; **we sell them by the ~** نَبيعُها مِائةً مِائةً; **in nineteen ~ and three** في سَنةِ أَلْفٍ وَتِسْعِمائةٍ وَثَلاثٍ; **in the nineteen ~s** في العَقْدِ الأَوَّلِ من القَرْنِ العِشْرينَ 2 (speed) **to do a ~** سارَ بِسُرْعةِ مِئةِ كيلومِتْرٍ بالساعةِ

B *adj* 1 (indicating quantity) مِائة; **two ~ euros** مِائَتا يورو; **two ~ and fifty houses** مِائَتانِ وَخَمْسون بَيْتاً; **about a ~ people** حَوالَيْ مِائةِ شَخْصٍ; **there are a ~** هُناكَ مِائةٌ; **I have nearly a ~** عِنْدي مِائةٌ تَقْريباً 2 (indicating age) **to be a ~ (years old)** كانَ عُمْرُهُ مِائةَ سَنةٍ

hundredfold /ˈhʌndrədfəʊld/ A *adj* <*increase, growth*> (إلى) مِائةِ ضِعْفٍ

B *adv* **a ~** <*to increase, multiply*> مِئةَ مَرّةٍ

hundredth /ˈhʌndrətθ/ A *n* 1 (**the hundredth**) (in a series) المِائة 2 (fraction) جُزْء من مِائةٍ; **three ~s of a second** ثَلاثة أَجْزاءٍ من مِائةٍ من الثانِيةِ

B *adj* <*day, client*> المِائة

C *adv* في المَرْكَزِ المِائةِ

hundredweight /ˈhʌndrədweɪt/ *n* (*pl* **hundredweight**) (BrE) [= 50.80 kg]; (AmE) [= 45.36 kg]; **six ~ of coal** سِتّة قَناطيرَ من الفَحْمِ

hung /hʌŋ/ *past tense, past participle* ▸ **hang**

Hungarian /hʌŋ'ɡeːrɪən/ **A** *adj* ‹*ambassador, food*› مَجَرِيّ (مَجَر)
B *n* **1** (citizen) مَجَرِيّ (مَجَر) **2** (language) (اللُغَة) المَجَرِيّة

Hungary /'hʌŋɡ(ə)ri/ *pr n* المَجَر (f)

hunger /'hʌŋɡə/ *n* **1** (need to eat) جوع; **to die of ~** ماتَ من الجوع **2** (strong desire) رَغْبة شَديدة, تَوْق

hunger strike *n* إضراب عن الطَعام

hung-over /hʌŋ'əʊvə/ *adj* مُعانٍ من خُمارٍ; **to be ~** عانى من خُمارٍ

hungrily /'hʌŋɡrɪli/ *adv* **1** ‹*to eat*› بِشَهْوةٍ, بِنَهَمٍ **2** ‹*to stare*› بِرَغْبةٍ شَديدةٍ, بِشَغَفٍ

hungry /'hʌŋɡri/ *adj* (**hungrier**, **hungriest**) **1** (for food) ‹*child, wolf*› جائع (جِياع); **to be ~** كانَ جائِعاً **2** (eager) تَوّاق; **to be ~ for justice/success** كانَ تَوّاقاً للعَدْلِ \ النَجاح

hunk /hʌŋk/ *n* (infml) **1** (of bread, cheese) قِطْعة (قِطَع) **2** (attractive man) رَجُل جَذّاب قَويّ البُنْيةِ

hunt /hʌnt/ **A** *vt* **1** (for sport or food) صادَ, اِصْطادَ (i; صَيْد) ‹*deer, foxes, whales*›; اِفْتَرَسَ ‹*prey*› **2** (to pursue) طارَدَ ‹*a killer, gang*›
B *vi* **1** (for prey) «animals» اِفْتَرَسَ **2** (for sport or food) **to go ~ing** ذَهَبَ إلى الصَيْدِ **3** (to search) **to ~ for clues/bargains** بَحَثَ عن أدِلّةٍ \ صَفَقاتٍ
C *n* **1** [u] (search) بَحْث; **the ~ is on for the killers** البَحْثُ جارٍ عن القَتَلةِ **2** (for animals) صَيْد; **a whale/lion ~** صَيْد حوتٍ \ أسَدٍ
Phrasal verbs **hunt down**: **1** **~ down** [**sb**], **~** [**sb**] **down** طارَدَ [شَخْصاً] ‹*a killer, criminal*› **2** **~ down** [**sth**], **~** [**sth**] **down** فَتَّشَ \ بَحَثَ عن [شَيْءٍ] ‹*a book, information*›
• **hunt out**, **hunt up**: **~ out** [**sth**], **~** [**sth**] **out** تَقَصّى عن [شَيْءٍ] ‹*a recipe, photo*›

hunter /'hʌntə/ *n* صَيّاد

hunting /'hʌntɪŋ/ *n* صَيْد

hunt saboteur *n* [شَخص يُحاوِلُ مَنْعَ \ عَرْقَلةَ عَمَلِيّاتِ صَيْدِ الحَيَواناتِ البَرِّيّةِ]

hurdle /'hɜːd(ə)l/ *n* **1** (Sport) (in race) حاجِز (حَواجِزُ) **2** (obstacle) عَقَبة (عِقاب, عَقَبات)

hurl /hɜːl/ *vt* **1** (to throw) قَذَفَ (i; قَذْف), رَشَقَ (u; رَشْق; ب) ‹*a stone, ball*› **2** (to shout) **to ~ insults/abuse at sb** قَذَفَ شَخْصاً بالشَتائِمِ

hurrah, hurray /hʊ'rɑː/ *n, excl* ▶ **hooray**

hurricane /'hʌrɪk(ə)n/ *n* إعْصار (أعاصيرُ)

hurry /'hʌri/ **A** *vt* (**hurries**, **hurrying**, **hurried**) **1** عَجَّلَ (في) ‹*a job, meal*› **2** اِسْتَعْجَلَ ‹*a person*›; **to ~ sb in/out** اِسْتَعْجَلَ شَخْصاً في الدُخولِ \ الخُروجِ
B *vi* أَسْرَعَ; **to ~ in/out** أَسْرَعَ في الدُخولِ \ الخُروجِ; **to ~ home** أَسْرَعَ إلى البَيْتِ
C *n* عَجَلة, عُجالة; **I'm in a ~** أنا مُسْتَعْجِلٌ \ على عَجَلةٍ من أَمْري; **to be in a ~ to do sth** كانَ مُسْتَعْجِلاً في فِعْلِ شَيْءٍ; **there's no ~** لا داعِيَ للعَجَلةِ; **what's the ~?** لِمَ العَجَلةُ؟; **to do sth in a ~** فَعَلَ شَيْئاً بِسُرْعةٍ
Phrasal verbs **hurry along** **1** (infml) أَسْرَعَ الخُطى **2** **~ along** [**sth**], **~** [**sth**] **along** عَجَّلَ في [شَيْءٍ] ‹*a process*›
• **hurry away** ▶ **hurry off**
• **hurry back** عَجَّلَ في العَوْدةِ
• **hurry off** غادَرَ بِسُرْعةٍ
• **hurry up** **A** (infml) أَسْرَعَ; **~ up!** أَسْرِعْ! **B** **1** **~** [**sb**] **up**, **~ up** [**sb**] اِسْتَعْجَلَ [شَخْصاً] **2** **~** [**sth**] **up** عَجَّلَ في [شَيْءٍ] ‹*a process*›

hurt /hɜːt/ **A** *vt* (*past tense, past participle* **hurt**) **1** (to injure) جَرَحَ (a; جَرْح); **to ~ one's hand/back** جَرَحَ يَدَهُ \ ظَهْرَهُ; **he wasn't ~** لم يُجْرَحْ; **someone could get ~** قد يُجْرَحُ شَخْصٌ ما **2** (to cause pain to) آلَمَ (Form IV; imperf يُؤْلِمُ), آذى (Form IV; imperf يُؤْذي); **you're ~ing my arm** تُؤْلِمُ ذِراعي; **it ~s him to walk** يُؤْلِمُهُ المَشْيُ **3** (emotionally) جَرَحَ (a; جَرْح); **to ~ sb's feelings** جَرَحَ مَشاعِرَ شَخْصٍ; **she's afraid of getting ~** هي خائِفةٌ من أنْ تَتَعرَّضَ للأذى **4** (to affect) أَضَرَّ ‹*business, sb's chances*›; **it wouldn't ~ her to apologize** لن يَضيرَها الاعْتِذارُ
B *vi* (*past tense, past participle* **hurt**) **1** (to cause pain) «head, back» آلَمَ, أَوْجَعَ (Form IV; imperf يُؤْلِمُ); **my throat ~s** حَلْقي يوجِعُني; **where does it ~?** أَيْنَ تُؤْلِمُكَ؟; **my shoes ~** حِذائي يوجِعُني \ يُؤْلِمُني **2** (emotionally) «words, actions» أَوْجَعَ,

آلَمَ (Form IV; imperf يُؤْلِمُ); **the truth often ~s** الحَقيقةُ كَثيراً ما تُؤْلِمُ **3** (to have adverse effects) أَضَرَّ; **it wouldn't ~ to try** لا ضَيرَ في المُحاوَلةِ

C *v refl* **to ~ oneself** آذى نَفْسَهُ

D *adj* **1** (physically) مَجْروح (مَجاريحُ); **are you ~?** هل جُرِحْتَ؟ **2** (emotionally) *<feelings, look>* جَريح (جَرْحى), مُتَأَلِّم; **to feel ~** تَأَلَّمَ; **she was ~ not to have been invited** تَأَلَّمَتْ لِعَدَمِ دَعْوَتِها

E *n* (emotional) أَلَم (آلام); **he doesn't care about the ~ he has caused us** لا يَهْتَمُّ \ يَحْفَلُ \ يَعْبَأُ بالأَلَمِ الّذي سَبَّبَهُ لَنا

hurtful /'hə:tfʊl/ *adj* *<criticism, remark>* موجِع, مُؤْلِم, مُؤْذٍ

hurtle /'hə:t(ə)l/ *vi* **to ~ down a hill/along a road** انْدَفَعَ بِقوّةٍ إلى أَسْفَلِ تَلٍّ \ على طولِ طَريقٍ

husband /'hʌzb(ə)nd/ *n* زَوْج (أَزْواج)

hush /hʌʃ/ **A** *n* سُكوت, صَمْت

B *excl* أُسْكُتْ, صَهْ

Phrasal verb **hush up**: **1** **~ up** صَمَتَ (u; صَمْت, صُموت), سَكَتَ (u; سُكوت) **2** **~ up [sth], ~ [sth] up** كَتَمَ \ أَخْفى [شَيْئاً] *<a scandal, an affair>* **3** **~ up [sb], ~ [sb] up** أَسْكَتَ [شَخْصاً] *<a witness, child>*

hushed /hʌʃt/ *adj* *<voice, room>* هادِئ; **in ~ tones** بِنَبْرةٍ هادِئةٍ

hush-hush /hʌʃ'hʌʃ/ *adj* (infml) سِرّيّ *<project, meeting>*

husk /hʌsk/ *n* قِشْرة (قِشْر)

husky /'hʌski/ **A** *n* (*pl* **huskies**) كَلْب الإِسْكيمو

B *adj* (**huskier, huskiest**) *<voice>* أَجَشّ (dipt), أَبَحّ (dipt)

hustings /'hʌstɪŋz/ *n* (**the hustings**) الحَمْلة الانْتِخابيّة

hustle /'hʌs(ə)l/ **A** *vt* **to ~ sb into/out of a building** دَفَعَ شَخْصاً بقوّةٍ داخِلَ \ خارجَ مَبْنًى *<a prisoner, celebrity>*

B *n* **1** (busy activity) **~ and bustle** مَعْمَعة, صَخَب وَضَجيج **2** (infml) (swindle) خِداع, احْتِيال (احْتِيالات)

hustler /'hʌslə/ *n* (AmE infml) **1** (swindler) مُحْتال, نَصّاب **2** (prostitute) بَغِيّ (f; بَغايا), عاهِرة (عاهِرات, عَواهِرُ)

hut /hʌt/ *n* كوخ (أَكْواخ)

hutch /hʌtʃ/ *n* قَفَص (أَقْفاص)

hyaena /hʌɪ'i:nə/ ▸**hyena**

hybrid /'hʌɪbrɪd/ **A** *n* **1** (Biol) هَجين (هُجُن) **2** (car) سَيّارة هَجينة

B *adj* *<species, cell, variety>* هَجين, مُوَلَّد

hybridization, -isation (BrE) /hʌɪbrɪdʌɪ'zeɪʃ(ə)n/ *n* تَهْجين

hydrant /'hʌɪdrənt/ *n* (also **fire hydrant**) صُنْبور حَريق

hydraulic /hʌɪ'drɔ:lɪk/ *adj* *<brake, fluid>* هَيْدْروليكيّ

hydrocarbon /ˌhʌɪdrəʊ'kɑ:b(ə)n/ *n* هيدْروكَرْبون

hydrocephalus /ˌhʌɪdrə'sɛfələs/ *n* اسْتِسْقاء دِماغيّ, مَوْه الرَّأْسِ

hydroelectric /hʌɪdrəʊɪ'lɛktrɪk/ *adj* *<power, dam>* كَهْرَمائيّ, هَيْدْروكَهْرَبائيّ

hydroelectricity /hʌɪdrəʊɪlɛk'trɪsɪti/ *n* الطاقة الكَهْرَمائيّة [الكَهْرَباء المُوَلَّدة عن طَريق القوّة المائيّة]

hydrofoil /'hʌɪdrəʊfɔɪl/ *n* قارِب مُحَلِّق

hydrogen /'hʌɪdrədʒ(ə)n/ *n* هيدْروجين

hydrophobic /hʌɪdrəʊ'fəʊbɪk/ *adj* **1** *<dog, patient>* مَسْعور (مَساعيرُ, مَسْعورونَ) **2** *<fats, alkanes>* كاره للماء

hyena, hyaena /hʌɪ'i:nə/ *n* ضَبْع (ضِباع, أَضْبُع)

hygiene /'hʌɪdʒi:n/ *n* نَظافة; **public ~** النَظافة العامّة

hygienic /hʌɪ'dʒi:nɪk/ *adj* *<conditions, utensil, kitchen>* صِحّيّ; **in/under ~ conditions** وَفْقاً للشُروطِ الصِحّيّةِ

hygienist /'hʌɪdʒi:nɪst/ *n* اخْتِصاصيّ صِحّةٍ

hymn /hɪm/ *n* تَرْتيلة

hype /hʌɪp/ *n* (infml) طَنّة وَرَنّة, دِعاية صاخِبة

Phrasal verb **hype up**: **~ up [sth], ~ [sth] up** رَوَّجَ [شَيْئاً] *<a movie, book>*

hyper /'hʌɪpə/ *adj* (infml) *<person>* فائِق النَشاطِ

hyperactive /hʌɪpər'aktɪv/ *adj* *<child, behaviour>* ناشِط على نَحْوٍ مُفْرِطٍ, فائِق النَشاطِ

hyperactivity /hʌɪpərak'tɪvɪti/ *n* نَشاط مُفْرِط

hyperglycaemia (BrE), **hyperglycemia** (AmE) /ˌhʌɪpəglʌɪ'si:mɪə/ *n* ارْتِفاع السُكَّرِ في الدَمِ

hyperlink /'hʌɪpəlɪŋk/ *n* وَصْلة \ رابِط تَشَعُّبيّ(ة)

hypermarket /'hʌɪpəmɑ:kɪt/ *n* (BrE) [سوق مَرْكَزيّ كَبير]

hypertension /hʌɪpə'tɛnʃ(ə)n/ *n* ارْتِفاع ضَغْطِ الدَمِ

hypertext /'hʌɪpətɛkst/ *n* نَصّ تَشَعُّبيّ

hyperventilate /hʌɪpəˈvɛntɪleɪt/ *vi* فَرطَ التَهْوِيَة \ التَنَفُّس

hyphen /ˈhʌɪf(ə)n/ *n* خطّ الوَصْلِ (خطّ قصير بين جُزْئَيْ كَلِمةٍ مُرَكَّبةٍ)

hypnosis /hɪpˈnəʊsɪs/ *n* تَنْوِيم مَغْناطيسيّ

hypnotherapy /ˌhɪpnəʊˈθɛrəpi/ *n* مُعالَجة بالتَنْوِيمِ المَغْناطيسيِّ

hypnotic /hɪpˈnɒtɪk/ *adj* 1 ‹*state, response*› [مُتَعلِّق بالتَنْويمِ] 2 ‹*stare, voice*› مُخدِّر, مُنَوِّم [المَغْناطيسيِّ]

hypnotism /ˈhɪpnətiz(ə)m/ *n* تَنْويم مَغْناطيسيّ

hypnotist /ˈhɪpnətɪst/ *n* مُنَوِّم مَغْناطيسيّ

hypnotize, **-ise** (BrE) /ˈhɪpnətʌɪz/ *vt* «hypnotist, doctor» ‹*subject, patient*› نَوَّمَ مَغْناطيسيًّا

hypoallergenic /ˌhʌɪpəʊaləˈdʒɛnɪk/ *adj* ‹*metals, textiles, cosmetics*› غَيْر مُسَبِّبٍ للحَسّاسيّةِ

hypochondria /ˌhʌɪpəˈkɒndrɪə/ *n* وَسْواس ,مَرَض المُراقِ المَرَضِ

hypochondriac /hʌɪpəʊˈkɒndrɪak/ *n* شخْص مُوَسْوَس بالمَرَضِ

hypocrisy /hɪˈpɒkrɪsi/ *n* (*pl* **hypocrisies**) نِفاق ,رِياء; **sheer ~** قِمّة في النِفاقِ

hypocrite /ˈhɪpəkrɪt/ *n* مُنافِق

hypocritical /ˌhɪpəˈkrɪtɪk(ə)l/ *adj* ‹*behaviour, statement*› مُنافِق; **it was ~ of her to say that** كانَ نِفاقاً مِنْها أنْ تَقولَ ذلك

hypodermic /hʌɪpəʊˈdəːmɪk/ *adj* ‹*needle, injection*› [مُعَدّ للاسْتِعْمالِ في الزَرْقِ تحت الجِلْدِ]

hypoglycaemia (BrE), **hypoglycemia** (AmE) /ˌhʌɪpəʊglʌɪˈsiːmɪə/ *n* نَقْص السُكَّرِ في الدَمِ

hypothermia /ˌhʌɪpəʊˈθəːmɪə/ *n* انْخِفاض في دَرَجةِ حَرارةِ الجِسْمِ

hypothesis /hʌɪˈpɒθɪsɪs/ *n* (*pl* **hypotheses**) فَرْضِيّة

hypothesize, **-ise** (BrE) /hʌɪˈpɒθɪsʌɪz/ *vi* وَضَعَ فَرْضِيّةً ,افْتَرَضَ

hypothetical /ˌhʌɪpəˈθɛtɪk(ə)l/ *adj* ‹*situation, question*› افْتِراضيّ

hysterectomy /ˌhɪstəˈrɛktəmi/ *n* (*pl* **hysterectomies**) اسْتِئْصال الرَحِمِ

hysteria /hɪˈstɪərɪə/ *n* هِسْتيرْيا

hysterical /hɪˈstɛrɪk(ə)l/ *adj* 1 (uncontrolled) ‹*laughter, fit*› هِسْتيريّ 2 (infml) (funny) ‹*event, joke*› هِسْتيريّ ,مُضْحِك للغاية

hysterics /hɪˈstɛrɪks/ *n* 1 (fit) هَرَع ,نَوْبة هِسْتيريّة; **to have ~** دَخَلَ في نَوْبةٍ هِسْتيريّةٍ 2 (laughter) **to be in ~** دَخَلَ في نَوْبةِ ضَحْكٍ هِسْتيريّةٍ

Ii

I[1], i /ʌɪ/ **A** *n* (letter) (الحَرْف التاسِع من الأَبْجَديّةِ الإنْكْليزيّةِ)

B *abbr* (**I**) = **Island** جَزيرة

(Idiom) **to dot the i's and cross the t's** تَأَكَّدَ من كُلِّ التَفاصيلِ

I[2] /ʌɪ/ *pron* أنا; **~ live in Milton** أَسْكُنُ في مِلْتون; **he and I share an apartment** أَنا وَهُوَ نَتَقاسَمُ شَقّةً; **he's a student but I'm not** هو طالِبٌ وَلَكِنَّني لَسْتُ كَذٰلِكَ

IA *abbr* ▸ **Iowa**

IBAN /ʌɪban/ *n* = **International Bank Account Number** الآيبان ,رَقم الحِسابِ المَصْرِفيِّ الدُوَليّ

Iberian /ʌɪˈbɪərɪən/ *n, adj* إيبيريّ

ibex /ˈʌɪbɛks/ *n* (*pl* **ibex** or **ibexes**) وَعْل (وُعول ,أَوْعال)

ice /ʌɪs/ **A** *n* [u] (frozen water) ثَلْج (ثُلوج); (on roads, canals) جَليد; **a coke with ~** كوب كولا بالثَلْج

B *vt* زَيَّنَ بالحَلْوى ‹*a cake*›

C (**iced**) *adj* ‹*water, tea*› مُثَلَّج

(Idioms) **to be skating on thin ice** عَرَّضَ نَفْسَهُ للوُقوعِ في مُشْكِلةٍ; **to break the ice** كَسَرَ حاجِزَ الرَهْبةِ; **to put sth on ice** أَجَّلَ شَيْئاً إلى أَجَلٍ غَيْرِ مُسَمًّى

(Phrasal verbs) **ice over** «roads, rivers» كَساهُ الثَلْجُ

• **ice up** «locks, wipers, roads» تَجَمَّدَ

ice age *n* عَصْر جَليديّ

iceberg /ˈʌɪsbəːg/ *n* جَبَل جَليدٍ \ جَليديّ

(Idiom) **the tip of the iceberg** ظاهِر المُشْكِلةِ ,سَطْح الأَزْمةِ

icebox /ˈʌɪsbɒks/ *n* **1** (BrE) (freezer compartment) فِريزِر ,مُجَمِّدة

2 (AmE) (fridge) بَرّاد ,ثَلّاجة

ice-cold /ˌʌɪsˈkəʊld/ *adj* ‹*lemonade, beer*› شَديد البُرودة

ice cream *n* آيس كْريم ,جيلاتي (Egypt)

ice cream soda *n* آيس كْريم بالصودا

ice cube *n* مُكَعَّب ثَلْجٍ

ice hockey *n* هوكي الجَليدِ

Iceland /ˈʌɪslənd/ *pr n* أَيْسْلَنْدا

Icelander /ˈʌɪsləndə/ *n* أَيْسْلَنْديّ

Icelandic /ʌɪsˈlandɪk/ **A** *adj* أَيْسْلَنْديّ

B *n* (اللُغة) الأَيْسْلَنْديّة

ice lolly *n* (BrE) [مَصّاصة حَلْوى مُثَلَّجةٍ]

ice pack *n* كيس ثَلْجٍ \ ثَلْجيّ

ice rink *n* مَيْدان تَزَلُّجٍ

ice skate **A** *n* حِذاء تَزَلُّجٍ

B *vi* (**ice-skate**) تَزَلَّجَ \ تَزَحْلَقَ على الجَليدِ

ice skating *n* تَزَلُّج \ تَزَحْلُق على الجَليدِ

icicle /ˈʌɪsɪk(ə)l/ *n* [كُتْلة ثَلْجيّة مُدَلّاة]

icing /ˈʌɪsɪŋ/ *n* طَبَقة زينةٍ

(Idiom) **to be the icing on the cake** [كانَ تَتْويجاً]

icing sugar *n* (BrE) سُكَّر مَطْحون

icon /ˈʌɪkɒn/ *n* **1** أَيْقونة **2** (image) أَيْقونة **3** (symbol) ,أَيْقونة (رُموز) رَمْز

iconize, -ise (BrE) /ˈʌɪk(ə)nʌɪz/ *vt* (Comp) حَوَّلَ إلى رَمْزٍ \ أَيْقونةٍ

ICU /ʌɪsiːˈjuː/ *n* = **intensive care unit** وَحْدة العِناية المُرَكَّزة

icy /ˈʌɪsi/ *adj* (**icier, iciest**) **1** ‹*road, pavement*› مُغَطًّى بالجَليدِ

2 ‹*water, wind*› شَديد البُرودة **3** ‹*stare, reception*› بارِد

id /ɪd/ *n* **the ~** الهُو ,اللاشُعور ,اللاوَعْي

ID **A** *n* /ʌɪˈdiː/ [u] = **identification** إثْبات شَخْصيّةٍ ,بِطاقة هُويّةٍ (NA), بِطاقة تَعْريفٍ (بالشَخْصيّةِ)

B *abbr* = **Idaho**

I'd /ʌɪd/ *abbr* = **I had**, = **I should**, = **I would**

Idaho /ˈʌɪdəhəʊ/ *pr n* أَيْداهو (f)

Idahoan /ˈʌɪdəhəʊən/ *pr n, adj* [(شَخْص) من أَيْداهو]

ID card *n* بِطاقةُ هُويّةٍ \ شَخْصيّة

idea /aɪˈdɪə/ *n* **1** (concept) فِكْرة (أَفْكار); **the ~ of studying abroad is very attractive** فِكْرةُ الدراسةِ بالخارِجِ هي فِكْرةٌ جَذّابةٌ جِدًّا; **I have no ~ what the reason is** لَيْسَ لَدَيَّ أيُّ فِكْرةٍ عن السَّبَبِ; **she has no ~!** لَيْسَ لَدَيْها أَيُّ فِكْرةٍ!; **whatever gave you that ~!** كيف طَرَأَتْ لكَ تِلْكَ الفِكْرةُ!; **if that's your ~ of a joke ...** لو كُنْتَ تَظُنُّ أنّ ذلك أُسْلوبٌ لائِقٌ للمِزاحِ ... **2** (plan, suggestion) فِكْرة (أَفْكار); **to be full of ~s** كانَ مَليئاً بالأَفْكارِ; **I have an ~!** لَدَيَّ فِكْرةٌ!; **he came up with the ~ of selling it** جاءَ بِفِكْرةِ بَيْعِهِ; **don't start getting ~s!** لا تُطْلِقْ لِأَفْكارِكَ العَنانَ! **3** (impression) انْطِباع (انْطِباعات); **I have an ~ that he might be lying** لَدَيَّ انْطِباعٌ بِأَنَّهُ قد يَكونُ كاذِباً **4** (aim) هَدَف (أَهْداف); **the ~ is to win all the cards** الهَدَفُ هو الفَوْزُ بِكُلِّ أَوْراقِ اللَعِبِ **5** (gist) **do you get the ~?** هل تَفْهَمُ المَضْمونَ؟ **6** (estimate) **to give sb an ~ of the cost/price** أَعْطى شَخْصاً فِكْرةً عن التَكْلِفةِ \ السِعْرِ

(Idiom) **what's the big idea?** (infml) ما الحِكْمةُ في هذا؟

ideal /aɪˈdiːəl/ **A** *adj* ‹conditions, place› مِثاليّ; **in an ~ world** في ظُروفٍ مِثاليّةٍ

B *n* مِثال أَعْلى

idealism /aɪˈdɪəlɪz(ə)m/ *n* (نَزْعة) مِثاليّة

idealist /aɪˈdɪəlɪst/ *n* ذو نَزْعةٍ مِثاليّةٍ, (شَخْص) مِثاليّ

idealistic /ˌaɪdɪəˈlɪstɪk/ *adj* ‹dream, idea› مِثاليّ

idealize, -ise (BrE) /aɪˈdɪəlaɪz/ *vt* صَوَّرَ في شَكْلٍ مِثاليٍّ ‹a hero, an image›

ideally /aɪˈdiːəlli/ *adv* **1** (perfectly) ‹situated, equipped› بِشَكْلٍ مِثاليٍّ **2** (by preference) **~, the tests should be free** من الناحِيةِ المِثاليّةِ, يَنْبَغي أنْ تَكونَ التَحاليلُ مَجّانيّةً

identical /aɪˈdentɪk(ə)l/ *adj* ‹sequence, pattern› مُتَطابِق

identical twin *n* تَوْأَم مُتَطابِق

identifiable /ˌaɪdentɪˈfaɪəb(ə)l/ *adj* ‹symptoms, style› يُمْكِنُ تَحْديدُهُ \ التَعَرُّفُ عَلَيْهِ; **it is ~ by its smell** يُمْكِنُ التَعَرُّفُ عَلَيْهِ من رائِحَتِهِ

identification /aɪˌdentɪfɪˈkeɪʃ(ə)n/ *n* **1** (of a body, suspect) تَعَرُّف **2** (proof of identity) إِثْبات الهُوِيّةِ

identification parade *n* (BrE) طابور عَرْضٍ (للتَعَرُّفِ على مُشْتَبَهٍ بِهِ)

identify /aɪˈdentɪfaɪ/ **A** *vt* (**identifies, identifying, identified**) ‹a problem, gene› حَدَّدَ; ‹a victim, body› تَعَرَّفَ (على)

B *vi* **to ~ with sb** تَعاطَفَ وُجْدانيًّا مع شَخْصٍ

identikit® /aɪˈdentɪkɪt/ *n* (also **identikit picture**) صورة مَرْسومة لِشَخْصٍ مُشْتَبَهٍ بِهِ

identity /aɪˈdentɪti/ *n* (*pl* **identities**) هُوِيّة; **to change/reveal one's ~** غَيَّرَ \ كَشَفَ هُوِيَّتَهُ

identity bracelet *n* سِوار للتَعْريفِ بِهُوِيّةِ شَخْصٍ

identity card *n* بِطاقة هُوِيّةٍ \ شَخْصيّة

identity parade *n* (BrE) طابور عَرْضٍ (للتَعَرُّفِ على مُشْتَبَهٍ بِهِ)

identity theft *n* سَرِقة الهُوِيّةِ

ideological /ˌaɪdiəˈlɒdʒɪk(ə)l/ *adj* ‹commitment, agenda› إيدْيولوجيّ

ideology /ˌaɪdɪˈɒlədʒi/ *n* (*pl* **ideologies**) إيدْيولوجِية

idiom /ˈɪdɪəm/ *n* عِبارة اصْطِلاحيّة, تَعْبير اصْطِلاحيّ

idiomatic /ˌɪdɪəˈmatɪk/ *adj* ‹expression, language› اصْطِلاحيّ

idiosyncrasy /ˌɪdɪəʊˈsɪŋkrəsi/ *n* (*pl* **idiosyncrasies**) خاصّيّة (خَصائِصُ, خاصّيّات)

idiosyncratic /ˌɪdɪəʊsɪŋˈkratɪk/ *adj* ‹style, interpretation› خاصّ, مُمَيَّز

idiot /ˈɪdɪət/ *n* مَعْتوه (مَعاتيهُ), أَبْلَه (dipt)

idiotic /ɪdɪˈɒtɪk/ *adj* ‹comment, behaviour› أَبْلَه (dipt), أَحْمَق (dipt; f حَمْقى; حُمْق)

idle /ˈaɪd(ə)l/ **A** *adj* (**idler, idlest**) **1** (lazy) ‹child, colleague› كَسول, خامِل **2** (without occupation) ‹worker› عاطِل; ‹day, moment› شاغِر **3** ‹factory, machinery› مُتَوَقِّف **4** (empty) ‹threat, chatter› فارِغ; **it's just ~ chatter** ما هذا إلّا حَديثٌ فارِغٌ

B *vi* **1** «workers, children» تَكاسَلَ **2** «engine, car» دارَ دون نَقْلِ الحَرَكةِ

(Phrasal verb) **idle away**: **~ away [sth], ~ [sth] away** أَضاعَ [شَيْئاً] ‹time, hours›

idleness /ˈaɪdlnəs/ *n* **1** (laziness) خُمول, كَسَل **2** (inaction) تَعَطُّل

idol /ˈʌɪd(ə)l/ *n* **1** (image) صَنَم (أَصْنام) **2** (person) مَعْبود (الجَماهيرِ)

idolize, -ise (BrE) /ˈʌɪdəlʌɪz/ *vt* وَقَّرَ, بَجَّلَ ‹*a singer*›

idyll /ˈɪdɪl/ *n* رَغَد العَيْشِ

idyllic /ɪˈdɪlɪk/ *adj* ‹*island, holiday*› وادِع

i.e. /ʌɪˈiː/ *abbr* (Latin) = **id est** (that is) أَيْ

IED /ʌɪiːˈdiː/ *n* = **improvised explosive device** عُبوّة ناسِفة بُدائيّة الصُنعِ

if /ɪf/ **A** *conj* **1** (in possibilities) إنْ, إذا; **~ you see smoke, turn it off** إذا رَأَيْتَ دُخاناً، أَوْقِفْهُ; **he'll do it ~ you pay him** سَيَفْعَلُهُ إذا دَفَعْتَ لَهُ; **I'll come with you ~ you like** سَأَذْهَبُ مَعَكَ إذا أَحْبَبْتَ; **~ so, take more cash** إذا كانَ الأَمْرُ كَذَلِك، خُذْ مَعَكَ المَزيدَ من النَقْدِ; **~ not, don't worry about it** إذا لم يَكُن الأَمْرُ كَذَلِك، فلا تَقْلَقْ بِخُصوصِهِ; **tomorrow, ~ not sooner** غداً، إذا لم يَكُنْ قبل ذلك; **~ I'm not mistaken** إذا لم أَكُنْ مُخْطِئاً **2** (in hypotheses) إنْ, لَوْ; **~ I were you, I would agree** لَوْ كُنْتُ مَكانَكَ، لَوافَقْتُ; **~ he resigns** *or* **~ he should resign, we'll be in serious difficulties** لو اسْتَقال، فَسَنُواجِهُ صُعوباتٍ خَطيرةً; **~ asked, I would say that ...** لَوْ سُئِلْتُ، لَأَجَبْتُ أَنّ ...; **~ it were to snow/snows** لَوْ تَساقَطَ الثَلْجُ; **~ she is to be believed** على حَدِّ قَوْلِها; **I don't care ~ he is married!** لا يُهِمُّني ما إذا كانَ مُتَزَوِّجاً! **3** (whether) ما إذا; **I wonder ~ they will come** أَتَساءَلُ ما إذا كانوا سَيَأْتونَ; **she asked ~ they had phoned** سَأَلَتْ عَمّا إذا كانوا قد اتَّصَلوا **4** (fml) (although) وَإنْ; **it's a good shop, ~ a little expensive** هو مَتْجَرٌ جَيِّدٌ وَإنْ كانَ غالياً بَعْضَ الشَيْءِ; **it was interesting, ~ nothing else** على الأَقَلِّ، كانَ مُثيراً للاهْتِمامِ; **we'll go even ~ it's dangerous** سَنَذْهَبُ حتّى وَإنْ كانَ في ذلك خَطَراً **5** (as polite formula) **~ you would follow me please** اتْبَعْني من فَضْلِكَ; **I'm sorry ~ you don't like it** يُؤْسِفُني أَنَّهُ لم يُعْجِبْكَ; **~ that's all right with you, I'll go now** إذا لم يَكُنْ عِنْدَكَ مانِعٌ، سَأَذْهَبُ الآنَ; **do you mind ~ I open the window?** هل تُمانِعُ في أَنْ أَفْتَحَ النافِذةَ؟ **6** (infml) (expressing surprise) **well, ~ it isn't Mr Qureshi!** يا لَلْمُفاجَأةِ، السَيِّدُ قُرَيْشيٌّ هُنا! **7** (used with *what*) **what ~ he died?** ماذا لَوْ ماتَ؟; **what ~ I say no?** ماذا لَوْ قُلْتُ لا؟

B (**if only**) *conj phr* **~ only I had known!** لَوْ أَنّي فَقَطْ كُنْتُ أَعْلَمُ!; **~ only we could go** أَتَمَنّى لَوْ كانَ بِوِسْعِنا أَنْ نَذْهَبَ

iffy /ˈɪfi/ *adj* (**iffier, iffiest**) (infml) ‹*proposition, deal*› (uncertain) غَيْر أَكيدٍ \ مُحَدَّدٍ; (doubtful) مَشْكوكٌ فيهِ

iftar /ˈɪftɑː/ *n* إفْطار

igloo /ˈɪgluː/ *n* بَيْت ثَلْجيّ

ignite /ɪgˈnʌɪt/ **A** *vt* أَشْعَلَ ‹*the fuel, wood*› **B** *vi* «fuel, gases» اشْتَعَلَ

ignition /ɪgˈnɪʃ(ə)n/ *n* **1** (system) إشْعال **2** (starting mechanism) (also **ignition switch**) مِفْتاح إشْعالٍ

ignition key *n* مِفْتاح إشْعالٍ

ignorance /ˈɪgn(ə)rəns/ *n* جَهْل

ignorant /ˈɪgn(ə)rənt/ *adj* جاهِل (جَهَلة); **to be ~ about a subject** كانَ جاهِلاً بِمَوْضوعٍ

ignore /ɪgˈnɔː/ *vt* **1** (to take no notice of) تَجاهَلَ ‹*a person, mistake*› **2** (to disobey) تَجاهَلَ ‹*advice, the rules*› **3** (to disregard) تَجاهَلَ ‹*a problem, fact*›

IL *abbr* ▸ **Illinois**

ilk /ɪlk/ *n* شاكِلة (شَواكِلُ), قَبيل, مَثيل (أَمْثال)

ill /ɪl/ **A** *adj* **1** (**iller, illest**) (unwell) مَريض (مَرْضى), عَليل (أَعِلّاءُ); **to feel ~** أَحَسَّ بالمَرَضِ; **she's too ~ to come** لا يُساعِدُها مَرَضُها على المَجيءِ **2** (bad) سَيِّئ; **~ effects** تَأْثيرات سَيِّئة

B *adv* (fml) **1** (badly) بِشَكْلٍ سَيِّئٍ; **to speak ~ of sb** تَكَلَّمَ بالسوءِ عن شَخْصٍ; **to think ~ of sb** أَساءَ الظَنَّ بِشَخْصٍ; **it all bodes ~ for the future** المُسْتَقْبَلُ لا يُبَشِّرُ بِخَيْرٍ **2** (scarcely); **it's a luxury we can ~ afford** هذا تَرَفٌ لا يُمْكِنُنا أَنْ نُوَفِّرَهُ

C *n* **1** (ailment) مَرَض (أَمْراض), عِلّة (عِلَل); **the ~s of society** عِلَل المُجْتَمَعِ **2** [u] (evil) شَرّ

I'll /ʌɪl/ *abbr* = **I shall**, = **I will**

ill-advised /ˌɪlədˈvʌɪzd/ *adj* ‹*attempt, decision*› غَيْر عَقْلانيٍّ; **you would be ~ to ignore the problem** لن يَكونَ من الحِكْمةِ أَنْ تَتَجاهَلَ المُشْكِلةَ

ill at ease *adj* غَيْر مُرْتاحٍ, مُتَضايِق

ill-bred /ˌɪlˈbrɛd/ *adj* ‹*person*› قَليل \ عَديم التَرْبية; ‹*behaviour*› سَيِّئ

illegal /ɪ'li:g(ə)l/ [A] *adj* <*immigrant, parking, drug*> غَيْر قانونيٍّ; **an amnesty for ~ immigrants** عَفْو عن المُهاجِرين غَيْرِ الشَّرْعيّين; **it's ~ to drive through a red light** تَجاوُزُ الإشارةِ الحَمْراءِ مُخالِفٌ للقانونِ
[B] *n* (AmE) مُهاجِر غَيْر شَرْعيٍّ

illegally /ɪ'li:g(ə)li/ *adv* <*imported, parked*> بِشَكْلٍ غَيْرِ قانونيٍّ

illegible /ɪ'lɛdʒɪb(ə)l/ *adj* <*writing, scribble*> غَيْر مَقْروءٍ

illegitimate /ˌɪlɪ'dʒɪtɪmət/ *adj* [1] <*child, son*> غَيْر شَرْعيّ [2] <*claim, regime*> غَيْر شَرْعيٍّ

ill-equipped /ɪlɪ'kwɪpt/ *adj* <*workers, team*> يفتقِرُ إلى التَّجْهيزاتِ

ill-fated /ˌɪl'feɪtɪd/ *adj* <*attempt, expedition*> مَحْكوم عَلَيْهِ بالفَشَل

ill feeling *n* ضَغينة (ضَغائِنُ)، عَداء (عَداءات)، كَراهِية

ill-fitting /ɪl'fɪtɪŋ/ *adj* <*dress, shoes*> ذو مَقاسٍ خاطِئٍ

ill-gotten /ˌɪl'gɒt(ə)n/ *adj*; **~ gains** مَكاسِب غَيْر مَشْروعةٍ

ill health *n* اعْتِلال الصِحّةِ

illicit /ɪ'lɪsɪt/ *adj* <*substance, activity*> غَيْر قانونيٍّ

ill-informed /ˌɪlɪn'fɔ:md/ *adj* <*comment, speculation*> مُسْتَنِد إلى أساسٍ ضَعيفٍ

Illinois /ˌɪlɪ'nɔɪ/ *pr n* إلينوي (f)

Illinoisan /ɪlə'nɔɪən/ *pr n, adj* [(شَخْص) من إلينوي]

illiteracy /ɪ'lɪt(ə)rəsi/ *n* أُمِّيّة

illiterate /ɪ'lɪt(ə)rət/ *adj* أُمِّيّ

illness /'ɪlnəs/ *n* مَرَض (أَمْراض)

illogical /ɪ'lɒdʒɪk(ə)l/ *adj* <*argument, fear*> غَيْر مَنْطقيٍّ

ill-treat /ˌɪl'tri:t/ *vt* أساءَ المُعامَلةَ <*a prisoner, woman*>

ill treatment *n* مُعامَلة سَيِّئة

illuminate /ɪ'lju:mɪneɪt/ *vt* [1] (to light up) أَضاءَ <*a building, street*> [2] (enlighten) بَصَّرَ <*a person*>; (elucidate) وَضَّحَ، بَيَّنَ <*a subject, theory*>

illuminated /ɪ'lu:mɪneɪtɪd/ *adj* [1] <*sign*> مُضاء، مُضيء [2] <*manuscript*> مُوَضَّح بالصُوَر

illumination /ɪˌlju:mɪ'neɪʃ(ə)n/ [A] *n* إضاءة [B] (**illuminations**) *n pl* أضْواء

illusion /ɪ'lju:ʒ(ə)n/ *n* وَهْم; **it gives the ~ of extra space** يوهِمُ بِوُجودِ مِساحةٍ أكْبَر

illustrate /'ɪləstreɪt/ *vt* [1] (with pictures) وَضَّحَ <*a text, book*> [2] (with examples, text) وَضَّحَ، أَوْضَحَ <*a point, theory*> [3] (to demonstrate) أَوْضَحَ، بَيَّنَ

illustration /ɪlə'streɪʃ(ə)n/ *n* [1] (picture) صورة (صُوَر)، رَسْم (رُسوم); **the ~s are in full colour** الصُوَرُ مَطْبوعةٌ بالألْوانِ [2] (example) مِثال تَوْضيحيّ

illustrator /'ɪləstreɪtə/ *n* رَسّام

illustrious /ɪ'lʌstrɪəs/ *adj* <*career*> جَذّاب; <*predecessor*> شَهير; <*history*> مُشَرِّف

ill will *n* ضَغينة (ضَغائِنُ)، حِقْد (أحْقاد، حُقود)

I'm /ʌɪm/ *abbr* = **I am**

image /'ɪmɪdʒ/ *n* [1] (visual reproduction) صورة (صُوَر) [2] (of companies, politicians) صورة (صُوَر)

image-conscious /'ɪmɪdʒkɒnʃəs/ *adj* <*politician, star*> مُهْتَمّ بِصورَتِهِ

imagery /'ɪmɪdʒ(ə)ri/ *n* تَصْوير (تَصاويرُ)

imaginable /ɪ'madʒɪnəb(ə)l/ *adj* يُمْكِنُ تَخَيُّلُهُ \ تَصَوُّرُهُ; **it's barely** *or* **scarcely ~** لا يُمْكِنُ تَصَوُّرُهُ; **the worst ~ situation** أَسْوأ مَوْقِفٍ يُمْكِنُ تَصَوُّرُهُ; **the funniest thing ~** أَطْرَف شَيْءٍ يُمْكِنُ تَخَيُّلُهُ

imaginary /ɪ'madʒɪn(ə)ri/ *adj* <*friend, scenario*> خَياليّ، وَهْميّ

imagination /ɪˌmadʒɪ'neɪʃ(ə)n/ *n* [1] (creative ability) خَيال (خَيالات، أَخْيِلة); **to show ~** أَظْهَرَ القُدْرةَ على التَخَيُّلِ; **not by any stretch of the ~** مَهْما أَطْلَقْنا لِخَيالِنا العَنانَ [2] (fanciful thoughts) تَخَيُّلات; **is it my ~, or ...?** هل هذا من نَسْجِ خَيالي، أم ...

imaginative /ɪ'madʒɪnətɪv/ *adj* <*child*> واسِع الخَيالِ; <*idea*> مُبْتَكَر; **they came up with a very ~ solution** جاؤوا بِحَلٍّ مُبْتَكَرٍ جِدًّا

imaginatively /ɪ'madʒɪnətɪvli/ *adv* <*written, designed*> بِشَكْلٍ مُبْتَكَرٍ; **the exhibits are presented very ~** يَتِمُّ تَقْديمُ المَعْروضاتِ بِطَريقةٍ مُبْتَكَرةٍ جِدًّا

imaginativeness /ɪ'madʒɪnətɪvnəs/ *n* إبْداع

imagine /ɪ'madʒɪn/ *vt* [1] (to visualize) تَخَيَّلَ، تَصَوَّرَ <*an object, a scene*>; **to ~ being rich/a famous footballer** تَخَيَّلَ أنْ يَكونَ غَنِيًّا \ لاعِبَ كُرةٍ مَشْهوراً; **I must have ~d it** لا بُدَّ أنّ ذلك

just ~ my surprise تخَيَّلْ ذلك!; **just ~!** كانَ من نَسْجِ خَيالي; **I can't ~ him travelling alone** فَقَطْ تَخَيَّلْ حَجْمَ مُفاجَأتي; **2** (to suppose) افْتَرَضَ, لا أَسْتَطيعُ أنْ أَتَخَيَّلَهُ يُسافِرُ بِمُفْرَدِهِ (u; ظَنَّ) ظَنَّ; **I ~ he's dead/still alive** أَظُنُّ أَنَّهُ مَيِّتٌ \ ما زالَ حَيًّا

imaging /ˈɪmɪdʒɪŋ/ *n* **1** (Med) تَصْوير **2** (Comput) تَصْوير

imam /ɪˈmɑːm/ *n* إمام (أَئِمّة)

imbalance /ɪmˈbaləns/ *n* اخْتِلال في التَوازُنِ

imbecile /ˈɪmbɪsiːl/ *n* أَبْلَه (مَعاتيهُ) مَعْتوه (dipt)

IMF /ʌɪɛmˈɛf/ *n* = **International Monetary Fund** صُنْدوق النَقْدِ الدُوَليّ

imitate /ˈɪmɪteɪt/ *vt* **1** قَلَّدَ, حاكى ‹*a sound, singer*› **2** قَلَّدَ ‹*a style, method*›

imitation /ɪmɪˈteɪʃ(ə)n/ **A** *n* **1** (of a sound, singer) تَقْليد (تَقاليدُ), **2** [u] (of a style, method) مُحاكاة, تَقْليد مُحاكاة **B** *adj* ‹*snow*› مُقَلَّد; **~ fur** فَرْو اصْطِناعيّ; **~ jewellery** جَواهِر مُقَلَّدة; **~ leather** جِلْد اصْطِناعيّ, مُقَلَّدة

immaculate /ɪˈmakjʊlət/ *adj* **1** ‹*clothes*› مُنَمَّق; ‹*gardens*› دَقيق; ‹*timing*› لا تَشوبُهُ شائِبةٌ; **2** ‹*performance*› مُنَسَّق بِعِنايةٍ تَماماً

immaterial /ɪməˈtɪərɪəl/ *adj* **1** ‹*argument, factor*› عَديم الأَهَمِّيّةِ **2** ‹*being, apparition*› غَيْر مادّيّ, روحيّ

immature /ɪməˈtjʊə/ *adj* **1** ‹*specimen, seed*› غَيْر كامِلِ التَطَوُّرِ **2** (childish) غَيْر ناضِجٍ

immaturity /ɪməˈtjʊərɪti/ *n* عَدَم نُضْجٍ

immediate /ɪˈmiːdɪət/ *adj* **1** ‹*effect, action*› فَوْريّ; **in the ~ future** في المُسْتَقْبَلِ القَريبِ **2** ‹*problem, concern*› عاجِل, آنيّ **3** ‹*relative, family*› مُباشِر; **in the ~ vicinity** في المَناطِقِ المُجاوِرةِ

immediately /ɪˈmiːdɪətli/ *adv* ‹*to leave, act*› فَوْراً, على الفَوْرِ; **~ after we spoke** فَوْراً بعد أنْ تَحَدَّثْنا; **he was ~ recognizable** أَمْكَنَ التَعَرُّفُ عَلَيْهِ على الفَوْرِ

immemorial /ɪmɪˈmɔːrɪəl/ *adj* ‹*tradition, antiquity*› مُمْعِن في القِدَمِ

immense /ɪˈmɛns/ *adj* ‹*height, building*› هائِل (هَوائِلُ)

immensely /ɪˈmɛnsli/ *adv* ‹*to help, enjoy*› لِلغايةِ, كَثيراً جدًّا; ‹*popular, proud*› بِدَرَجةٍ كَبيرةٍ

immerse /ɪˈməːs/ *vt* غَمَسَ, غَطَّسَ (i; غَمْس), غَمَرَ (u; غَمْر); **to ~ a cloth/one's hands in sth** غَمَسَ قُماشاً \ يَدَيْهِ في شَيْءٍ

immersion /ɪˈməːʃ(ə)n/ *n* **1** (in a liquid) غَمْس, غَمْر, تَغْطيس **2** (in a subject) تَعَرُّض; **language learning by total ~** تَعَلُّم اللُغةِ بالتَعَرُّضِ التامِّ لَها

immersion course *n* (BrE) دَوْرة انْغِماسٍ لُغَويٍّ (دَوْرة لُغَويّة يُعَرَّضُ فيها المَرْءُ إلى بيئةِ اللُغةِ المَعْنيّةِ حَصْريًّا)

immersion heater *n* سَخّان غَمْرٍ

immigrant /ˈɪmɪgrənt/ *n, adj* مُهاجِر

immigration /ɪmɪˈgreɪʃ(ə)n/ *n* **1** (process) هِجْرة **2** (also **immigration control**) مَكْتَب الهِجْرة (في مَداخِلِ بَلَدٍ)

imminent /ˈɪmɪnənt/ *adj* ‹*danger, threat*› وَشيك

immobile /ɪˈməʊbʌɪl/ *adj* ‹*vehicle, animal*› مُتَوَقِّف, ساكِن

immobilize, -ise (BrE) /ɪˈməʊbɪlʌɪz/ *vt* **1** أَوْقَفَ ‹*an engine*›; شَلَّ الحَرَكةَ ‹*a limb*› **2** عَطَّلَ عن العَمَلِ ‹*an organization*›; عَطَّلَ, أَوْقَفَ ‹*traffic*›

immobilizer, -iser (BrE) /ɪˈməʊbɪlʌɪzə/ *n* مانِع الحَرَكةِ (لِحِمايةِ السَيّارةِ من السرقةِ)

immoderate /ɪˈmɒd(ə)rət/ *adj* (fml) ‹*drinking, appetite*› مُفْرِط

immodest /ɪˈmɒdɪst/ *adj* **1** (indecent) فاحِش, غَيْر لائِقٍ \ **2** (boastful) مُحْتَشِمٍ غَيْر مُتَواضِعٍ

immoral /ɪˈmɒrəl/ *adj* ‹*behaviour, suggestion*› لا أَخْلاقيّ, مُنْحَلّ, فاسِد

immorality /ɪməˈralɪti/ *n* فُجور, فَساد

immortal /ɪˈmɔːt(ə)l/ *adj* ‹*memory, reputation*› خالِد

immortality /ɪmɔːˈtalɪti/ *n* خُلود

immortalize, -ise (BrE) /ɪˈmɔːtəlʌɪz/ *vt* خَلَّدَ ‹*an event, a place*›

immune /ɪˈmjuːn/ *adj* **1** ‹*patient*› (by inoculation) مُحَصَّن; (acquired resistance) دو مَناعةٍ; ‹*system*› مَناعيّ **2** (exempt) **to be ~ from attack/arrest** كانَ مُحَصَّناً ضِدَّ الهُجومِ \ إلْقاءِ القَبْضِ عَلَيْهِ **3** (oblivious) **to be ~ to flattery** كانَ لا يُجْدي مَعَهُ الإطْراءُ

immune system *n* جِهاز مَناعةٍ \ مَناعيّ

immunity /ɪˈmjuːnɪti/ *n* **1** (against disease, etc) مَناعة; **some people develop ~ to malaria** تَتَكَوَّنُ لدى بَعْضِ الناسِ مَناعةٌ ضِدَّ المَلاريا **2** (from arrest) حَصانة; (from tax) إعْفاء

immunization, -isation (BrE) /ɪmju:nʌɪ'zeɪʃ(ə)n/ *n* تَطْعيم, تَحْصين, تَلْقيح

immunize, -ise (BrE) /'ɪmjʊnʌɪz/ *vt* طَعَّمَ ,لَقَّحَ ,حَصَّنَ *<a child, an animal>*

immunodeficiency /ɪmju:nəʊdɪ'fɪʃ(ə)nsi/ *n* نَقْص \ فِقْدان المَناعةِ

imp /ɪmp/ *n* شَيْطان صَغير (طِفل مُشاغِب)

impact /'ɪmpakt/ *n* **1** (of a hammer, vehicle) اصْطِدام (اصْطِدامات) **2** (of an event) تَأْثير; **to make an ~** كانَ لَهُ تَأْثيرٌ

impacted /ɪm'paktɪd/ *adj* *<tooth, fractured bone>* عالِق

impair /ɪm'pɛ:/ *vt* أَضْعَفَ *<one's performance, ability>*; أَضَرَّ (ب) *<one's hearing, health>*

impaired /ɪm'pɛ:d/ *adj* *<hearing, vision>* ضَعيف, مُتَدَهْوِر

impairment /ɪm'pɛ:mənt/ *n* اعْتِلال, ضَعْف, تَدَهْوُر; **mental/ physical/visual ~** تَدَهْوُر عَقْليّ \ جِسْميّ \ بَصَريّ

impale /ɪm'peɪl/ *vt* طَعَنَ (a-u; طَعْن)

impart /ɪm'pɑ:t/ *vt* **1** كَشَفَ ,أَعْلَنَ (عن ;كَشْف ;i) *<knowledge, information>* **2** أَعْطى ,مَنَحَ (a; مَنْح) *<a feeling, an atmosphere>*

impartial /ɪm'pɑ:ʃ(ə)l/ *adj* *<advice, judge>* غَيْر مُتَحَيِّز, مُحايِد

impassable /ɪm'pɑ:səb(ə)l/ *adj* **1** *<road>* غَيْر سالِكٍ, وَعْر **2** *<barrier>* لا يُمْكِن عُبورُه

impasse /'ampɑ:s/ *n* طَريق مَسْدود

impassioned /ɪm'paʃ(ə)nd/ *adj* *<plea, speech>* مَشْحون بالعاطِفةِ

impassive /ɪm'pasɪv/ *adj* *<expression, features>* جامِد (جَوامِدُ)

impatience /ɪm'peɪʃ(ə)ns/ *n* **1** (eagerness) تَلَهُّف (تَلَهُّفات) **2** (irritation) ضيق الصَدْرِ, عَدَم الصَبْرِ

impatient /ɪm'peɪʃ(ə)nt/ *adj* **1** (eager) مُتَلَهِّف; **to be ~ for sth/ to do sth** تَلَهَّفَ لِشَيْءٍ لِفِعْلِ شَيْءٍ **2** (irritable) عَديم الصَبْرِ, ضَيِّق الصَدْرِ; **to get ~ with sb** فَقَدَ صَبْرَهُ مع شَخْصٍ

impatiently /ɪm'peɪʃ(ə)ntli/ *adv* *<to wait>* بِفارِغِ الصَبْرِ; *<to say, reply>* بِضيق صَدْرٍ

impeach /ɪm'pi:tʃ/ *vt* وَجَّهَ اتِّهاماً لِ بِغَرَضِ العَزْلِ من المَنْصِبِ *<a public official, president>*

impeachment /ɪm'pi:tʃmənt/ *n* اتِّهام (تَوْجيه اتِّهامٍ لِمَسْؤولٍ بِغَرَضِ عَزْلِهِ من مَنْصِبِهِ)

impeccable /ɪm'pɛkəb(ə)l/ *adj* *<behaviour, appearance>* لا تَشوبُهُ شائِبةٌ

impecunious /,ɪmpɪ'kju:nɪəs/ *adj* (fml) *<student, writer>* مُعْدِم, فَقير (فُقَراءُ)

impede /ɪm'pi:d/ *vt* عَرْقَلَ, أَعاقَ (عَرْقَلة ;i) *<progress, growth, movement>*; اعْتَرَضَ *<access>*

impediment /ɪm'pɛdɪmənt/ *n* **1** (hindrance) عائِق (عَوائِقُ), إِعاقة **2** (physical defect) عَقَبة

impel /ɪm'pɛl/ *vt* (**-ll-**) حَثَّ (u; حَثّ), دَفَعَ (a; دَفْع); **to feel ~led to do sth** شَعَرَ أَنَّهُ مُضْطَرٌّ لِفِعْلِ شَيْءٍ

impending /ɪm'pɛndɪŋ/ *adj* *<departure, crisis, announcement>* وَشيك

impenetrable /ɪm'pɛnɪtrəb(ə)l/ *adj* *<fortress, barrier>* غَيْر قابِلٍ للاخْتِراقِ, مَنيع

imperative /ɪm'pɛrətɪv/ **A** *adj* *<need, reason>* ضَروريّ, مُلِحّ
B *n* **1** (necessity) شَيْء ضَروريّ, ضَرورة **2** (Ling) صيغة الأَمْرِ

imperceptible /ɪmpə'sɛptɪb(ə)l/ *adj* *<movement>* غَيْر مَلْحوظٍ

imperfect /ɪm'pə:fɪkt/ **A** *adj* **1** *<product>* مَعْطوب, معيب, ناقِص **2** *<knowledge>*; بِهِ خَلَلٌ (Ling) **the ~ tense** (of English) الماضي المُسْتَمِرّ; (of Arabic) الفِعْل المُضارِع
B *n* (Ling) **the ~** (of English) الماضي المُسْتَمِرّ; (of Arabic) الفِعْل المُضارِع

imperfection /ɪmpə'fɛkʃ(ə)n/ *n* **1** (defect) عَيْب (عُيوب), خَلَل **2** [u] (imperfect state) نَقْص, قُصور (خِلال)

imperial /ɪm'pɪərɪəl/ *adj* **1** *<power, palace>* إِمْبَراطوريّ **2** (BrE) *<measurement, unit>* بَريطانيّ

imperialism /ɪm'pɪərɪəliz(ə)m/ *n* إِمْبِرياليّة

imperialist /ɪm'pɪərɪəlɪst/ *n, adj* إِمْبِرياليّ

imperil /ɪm'pɛrəl/ *vt* (**-ll-** BrE, **-l-** AmE) خاطَرَ, عَرَّضَ للخَطَرِ (ب) *<sb's life, one's future>*

imperious /ɪm'pɪərɪəs/ *adj* *<tone, manner>* مُتَعَجْرِف

impermeable /ɪm'pə:mɪəb(ə)l/ *adj* ‹*layer*› غَيْر نافِذٍ, كَتيم ‹*barrier*› مُحْكَم

impersonal /ɪm'pə:s(ə)n(ə)l/ *adj* ‹*style, organization*› غَيْر مُحايِد, شَخْصِيٍّ

impersonate /ɪm'pə:səneɪt/ *vt* **1** (to pretend to be) انْتَحَلَ الشَخْصِيّةَ ‹*a police officer, doctor*› **2** (to mimic) قَلَّدَ ‹*a character, singer*›

impersonator /ɪm'pə:səneɪtə/ *n* مُقَلِّد

impertinent /ɪm'pə:tɪnənt/ *adj* ‹*question, remark*› (وُقُح) وَقِح

impervious /ɪm'pə:vɪəs/ *adj* **1** ‹*layer, coating*› غَيْر نافِذٍ, كَتيم **2** (fml) (unaffected) **to be ~ to criticism/sb's charms** لا يُؤَثِّرُ الانْتِقادُ \ سِحْرُ شَخْصٍ عَلَيْهِ

impetigo /ˌɪmpɪ'tʌɪgəʊ/ *n* حَصَف (داء جِلْدِيّ)

impetuous /ɪm'petjʊəs/ *adj* ‹*person*› طائِش, مُنْدفِع, مُتَهَوِّر, أَهْوَج (dipt); ‹*decision*› مُتَسَرِّع; ‹*kiss*› خاطِف

impetus /'ɪmpɪtəs/ *n* (دَوافِعُ) دافِع, (حَوافِزُ) حافِز

impinge /ɪm'pɪndʒ/ *vi* **to ~ on sb's life/rights** أَثَّرَ سَلْباً على حَياةِ \ حُقوق شَخْصٍ

implacable /ɪm'plakəb(ə)l/ *adj* ‹*enemy*› (أَلِدّاءُ) لَدود; ‹*opposition*› لا يَعْرِفُ المُهادَنةِ, عَنيد

implant **A** /ɪm'plɑ:nt/ *vt* **1** زَرَعَ (a; زَرْع) ‹*a tissue, hormone, bone marrow*› **2** (to instill) غَرَسَ (i; غَرْس, غِراسة), رَسَّخَ ‹*a desire, an idea*›

B /'ɪmplɑ:nt/ *n* (عُضْو) مَزْروع

implausible /ɪm'plɔ:zɪb(ə)l/ *adj* ‹*claim, explanation*› غَيْر مَعْقولٍ \ غَيْر قابِلٍ لِلتَصْديق, مَنْطِقِيٍّ

implement **A** /'ɪmplɪmənt/ *n* (أَدَوات) أَداة

B /'ɪmplɪment/ *vt* **1** نَفَّذَ ‹*a policy, plan*› **2** طَبَّقَ ‹*a law*›

implementation /ɪmplɪmen'teɪʃ(ə)n/ *n* **1** (of a policy, plan) تَنْفيذ **2** (of a law) تَطْبيق

implicate /'ɪmplɪkeɪt/ *vt* (to show involvement of) وَرَّطَ; **he was ~d in the Enron scandal** كانَ مُتَوَرِّطًا في فَضيحةِ إِنْرون

implication /ɪmplɪ'keɪʃ(ə)n/ *n* **1** (possible consequence) (عَواقِبُ) عاقِبة, تَبِعة **2** (inference) (مَغازٍ) مَغْزًى **3** [u] (involvement) تَوَرُّط

implicit /ɪm'plɪsɪt/ *adj* **1** ‹*message, threat*› ضِمْنِيّ **2** ‹*faith, trust*› مُطْلَق

implicitly /ɪm'plɪsɪtli/ *adv* **1** (tacitly) ‹*to assume, to criticize*› على نَحْوٍ ضِمْنِيٍّ, بِشَكْلٍ ضِمْنِيٍّ **2** (absolutely) ‹*to trust, believe*› مُطْلَقٍ

implode /ɪm'pləʊd/ *vi* «star, light bulb» انْفَجَرَ داخِلِيًّا

implore /ɪm'plɔ:/ *vt* تَوَسَّلَ (إلى)

imply /ɪm'plʌɪ/ *vt* (**implies, implying, implied**) **1** (to insinuate) أَشارَ (إلى), أَلْمَحَ (إلى), عَنى (i; عَنْي) **2** (to involve) تَضَمَّنَ, انْطَوى (على)

impolite /ɪmpə'lʌɪt/ *adj* ‹*remark, gesture*› غَيْر مُهَذَّبٍ, فَظّ (أَفْظاظ)

import **A** /ɪm'pɔ:t/ *vt* **1** اسْتَوْرَدَ ‹*services, goods*› **2** اسْتَوْرَدَ ‹*a program, file*›

B /'ɪmpɔ:t/ *n* **1** (item imported) سِلْعة مُسْتَوْرَدة; **~s such as machine tools** الوارِداتُ مِثْلَ آلاتِ التَشْغيلِ **2** [u] (process) اسْتيراد

importance /ɪm'pɔ:t(ə)ns/ *n* أَهَمِّيّة

important /ɪm'pɔ:t(ə)nt/ *adj* ‹*role, contribution, decision*› مُهِمّ, هامّ; **his children are very ~ to him** أَوْلادُهُ مُهِمّونَ جِدًّا بِالنِسْبةِ لَهُ; **the ~ thing is not to lose your temper** المُهِمُّ هو أَنْ لا تَفْقِدَ أَعْصابَكَ

importantly /ɪm'pɔ:t(ə)ntli/ *adv* **1** (significantly) ‹*to differ, contribute*› على نَحْوٍ مُهِمٍّ; **more ~, he succeeded where she had failed** الأَهَمُّ من ذلك أَنَّهُ نَجَحَ حَيْثُ فَشِلَتْ هي **2** (pompously) ‹*to announce, strut*› بِتَعالٍ, بِزُهُوٍّ

importer /ɪm'pɔ:tə/ *n* مُسْتَوْرِد; **Britain is a major food ~** بَريطانيا مُسْتَوْرِدٌ رَئيسيٌّ لِلطَعامِ; **our firm purchases its materials direct from the ~** تَشْتَري شَرِكَتُنا مَوادَّها مُباشَرةً من المُسْتَوْرِدِ

impose /ɪm'pəʊz/ **A** *vt* فَرَضَ (i; فَرْض) ‹*sanctions, a sentence*›

B *vi* أَثْقَلَ; **to ~ on sb** أَثْقَلَ على شَخْصٍ

imposing /ɪm'pəʊzɪŋ/ *adj* ‹*person, building*› مَهيب, يَفْرِضُ الاحْتِرامَ

imposition /ɪmpə'zɪʃ(ə)n/ *n* **1** (unfair demand) عِبْء (أَعْباء) **2** [u] (of sanctions, a tax) فَرْض

impossibility /ɪmˌpɒsɪ'bɪlɪti/ *n* اسْتِحالة

impossible /ɪmˈpɒsɪb(ə)l/ **A** *n* **to attempt/achieve the ~** حاوَلَ \ حَقَّقَ المُسْتَحيلَ
B *adj* **1** ‹*task, dream*› مُسْتَحيل; **it's ~ for me to do what you ask** من المُسْتَحيلِ بالنِسْبةِ لي أنْ أفْعَلَ ما تَطْلُبُهُ; **the snow made it ~ for anyone to travel** جَعَلَت الثلوجُ من المُسْتَحيلِ على أيِّ شَخْصٍ أنْ يُسافِرَ **2** (very difficult) ‹*situation*› شَديد الصُعوبةِ **3** (infml) (intolerable) لا يُطاق; **you're ~!** أنْتَ لا تُطاقُ!

impostor /ɪmˈpɒstə/ *n* نَصّاب, دَجّال, مُحْتال

impotence /ˈɪmpət(ə)ns/ *n* **1** (powerlessness) عَجْز **2** (sexual) ضَعْف جِنْسيّ, عُنّة

impotent /ˈɪmpət(ə)nt/ *adj* **1** ‹*spectator*› عاجز (عَجَزة); **he felt ~ in the face of the threats** شَعَرَ بالعَجْزِ في وَجْهِ التَهْديداتِ **2** ‹*man*› عاجز جِنْسيًّا

impound /ɪmˈpaʊnd/ *vt* **1** احْتَجَزَ ‹*a vehicle, goods*› **2** احْتَجَزَ ‹*an animal*›

impoverish /ɪmˈpɒvərɪʃ/ *vt* أفْقَرَ ‹*society, soil*›

impoverished /ɪmˈpɒvərɪʃt/ *adj* ‹*country, family*› فَقير (فُقَراءُ)

impractical /ɪmˈpraktɪk(ə)l/ *adj* ‹*solution, suggestion*› غَيْر عَمَليٍّ

imprecise /ɪmprɪˈsʌɪs/ *adj* ‹*terms, concept*› غَيْر دَقيقٍ

impregnable /ɪmˈprɛɡnəb(ə)l/ *adj* ‹*fortress, defences*› مَنيع, حَصين

impregnate /ˈɪmprɛɡneɪt/ *vt* **1** (to saturate) شَبَّعَ ‹*a cloth, wood*› **2** (fml) (to fertilize) لَقَّحَ ‹*an egg*›; حَبَّلَ ‹*a female*›

impresario /ˌɪmprɪˈsɑːrɪəʊ/ *n* (*pl* **impresarios**) مُنَظِّم حَفَلاتٍ فَنّيّةٍ

impress /ˈɪmprɛs/ **A** *vt* **1** (to arouse respect in) بَهَرَ, أبْهَرَ (a; بَهْر) ‹*the panel, one's teacher, parents*›; **to be ~ed by** *or* **with the candidate/proposal** انْبَهَرَ بالمُرَشَّحِ \ بالاقْتِراحِ; **to be easily ~ed** كانَ يُمْكِنُ إقْناعُهُ بِسُهولةٍ **2** (to emphasize) **to ~ the importance of sth on sb** أكَّدَ على أهَمّيّةِ شَيْءٍ بالنِسْبةِ لِشَخْصٍ
B *vi* «players, quality, features» كانَ مُبْهِراً; **as a singer, she really ~es** كَمُطْرِبةٍ, هي مُبْهِرةٌ حَقًّا

impression /ɪmˈprɛʃ(ə)n/ *n* **1** (idea) انْطِباع (انْطِباعات); **to be under** *or* **have the ~ that ...** كانَ لَدَيْهِ انْطِباعٌ بِأنَّ ... **2** (impact) تَرَكَ انْطِباعاً انْطِباع (انْطِباعات); **to make a good/bad ~ on sb** كانَ مَثارَ الإعْجابِ حَسَناً \ سَيِّئاً لدى شَخْصٍ; **to make an ~** **3** (perception) انْطِباع (انْطِباعات); **first ~s are important** الانْطِباعاتُ الأولى مُهِمّةٌ; **to give an ~ of light/space** أعْطى إحْساساً بالضَوْءِ \ بالمِساحةِ **4** (imitation) تَقْليد **5** (imprint) طَبْعة; **to take an ~ of a key/fossil** أخَذَ طَبْعةَ المِفْتاحِ \ الأُحْفورةِ

impressionable /ɪmˈprɛʃ(ə)nəb(ə)l/ *adj* ‹*mind, age*› سَريع التَأَثُّرِ; **the young and ~ minds of our children** عُقول أوْلادِنا الصَغيرة والسَريعة التَأَثُّرِ

impressionist /ɪmˈprɛʃ(ə)nɪst/ *n* **1** (Impressionist) (Art) انْطِباعيّ **2** (mimic) مُقَلِّد

impressive /ɪmˈprɛsɪv/ *adj* ‹*performance, record*› مُثير للإعْجابِ

imprint **A** /ɪmˈprɪnt/ *vt* **1** (in the mind) طَبَعَ (a; طَبْع) **2** (on a surface) طَبَعَ (a; طَبْع)
B /ˈɪmprɪnt/ *n* **1** (mark) طَبْعة, أثَر (آثار) **2** (effect) أثَر (آثار)

imprison /ɪmˈprɪz(ə)n/ *vt* سَجَنَ (u; سَجْن), حَبَسَ (i; حَبْس) ‹*a criminal, dissident*›

imprisonment /ɪmˈprɪz(ə)nmənt/ *n* سَجْن, حَبْس

improbable /ɪmˈprɒbəb(ə)l/ *adj* **1** (unlikely to happen) ‹*event, outcome*› غَيْر مُحْتَمَلٍ, مُسْتَبْعَد **2** (implausible) ‹*story, coincidence*› غَيْر مَعْقولٍ, يَصْعُبُ تَصْديقُهُ

impromptu /ɪmˈprɒmptjuː/ *adj* ‹*performance, speech*› ارْتِجاليّ, مُرْتَجَل

improper /ɪmˈprɒpə/ *adj* **1** (inappropriate) غَيْر لائِقٍ **2** (dishonest) غَيْر شَريفٍ **3** (indecent) ‹*behaviour, suggestion*› غَيْر مُحْتَشِمٍ \ مُهَذَّبٍ **4** (incorrect) ‹*use, purpose*› غَيْر سَليمٍ, خاطِئ

improve /ɪmˈpruːv/ **A** *vt* **1** (in quality) حَسَّنَ ‹*conditions, one's diet, grammar*›; **to ~ one's German** حَسَّنَ مُسْتَواهُ في الألْمانيّةِ; **the aim is to ~ the quality of the water** الهَدَفُ هو تَحْسينُ جَوْدةِ الماءِ; **to ~ one's mind** ثَقَّفَ نَفْسَهُ **2** (in quantity) حَسَّنَ ‹*sb's wages, chances, productivity*›; **you need to ~ your score** تَحْتاجُ إلى تَحْسينِ دَرَجَتِكَ **3** (Agric) حَسَّنَ ‹*the soil, land*›
B *vi* **1** «relations, health, weather» تَحَسَّنَ; **working conditions have ~d greatly** تَحَسَّنَتْ ظُروفُ العَمَلِ بِشَكْلٍ

كَبير **2** to ~ on a score/an offer حَسَّنَ نَتيجةً \ عَرْضاً; **we ~d on last year's results** حَسَّنّا نَتائِجَنا مُقارَنةً بِنَتائِجِ العامِ الماضي **3** (to increase) «productivity, profits» تَحَسَّنَ **C** (**improved**) *adj* **1** (better) ‹*diet, efficiency, conditions*› أَفْضَل (dipt), مُحَسَّن **2** (increased) ‹*offer, benefits*› أَفْضَل (dipt)

improvement /ɪmˈpruːvmənt/ *n* **1** (positive change) تَحَسُّن; **an ~ on last year's performance** تَحَسُّن في الأَداءِ عن العامِ الماضي; **an ~ in working conditions/bilateral relations** تَحَسُّن في ظُروفِ العَمَلِ \ العَلاقاتِ الثُنائيّةِ; **they've made ~s to their scores** حَقَّقوا تَحَسُّناً في نَتائِجِهِمْ **2** [u] (in quality, procedures) تَحْسين; **there is still room for ~** ما زالَ هُناكَ مَجالٌ للتَحْسينِ **3** (alteration) تَحْسين (تَحْسينات); **home ~s** تَحْسينات مَنْزِليّة

improvise /ˈɪmprəvaɪz/ **A** *vt* ‹*dialogue, music*› ارْتَجَلَ **B** *vi* ارْتَجَلَ

imprudent /ɪmˈpruːd(ə)nt/ *adj* ‹*investment, remark*› غَيْر حَكيم

impudence /ˈɪmpjʊd(ə)ns/ *n* صَفاقة, وَقاحة

impudent /ˈɪmpjʊd(ə)nt/ *adj* ‹*remark, grin*› بَذيء, صَفيق, وَقِح

impulse /ˈɪmpʌls/ *n* نَزْوة (نَزَوات), دافِع عَفَوِيّ; **he often buys on ~** يَشْتَري في كَثيرٍ من الأَحْيانِ بِدافِعٍ عَفَوِيٍّ \ دون تَرَوٍّ

impulsive /ɪmˈpʌlsɪv/ *adj* ‹*decision, reaction*› مُنْدَفِع, مُتَهَوِّر, مُتَسَرِّع

impunity /ɪmˈpjuːnɪti/ *n* إفْلات من العُقوبةِ, حَصانة

impure /ɪmˈpjʊə/ *adj* **1** ‹*water, milk*› غَيْر نَقِيٍّ, مُلَوَّث **2** (liter) ‹*thoughts, motives*› نَجِس, فاسِد, دَنِس

impurity /ɪmˈpjʊərɪti/ *n* (*pl* **impurities**) **1** (contaminant) شائِبة (شَوائِبُ) **2** (adulteration) نَجاسة, تَلَوُّث

in /ɪn/ **A** *prep* **1** (inside) في; **~ the box** في الصُنْدوقِ; **~ the newspaper** في الجَريدةِ; **to be ~ school/town** كانَ في المَدْرَسةِ \ المَدينةِ; **to live ~ the city/country** عاشَ في المَدينةِ \ الريفِ; **~ the picture** في الصورةِ; **~ Rome/Libya** في روما \ ليبْيا **2** (showing occupation, activity) في; **to be ~ politics/insurance** كانَ يَعْمَلُ في مَجالِ السِياسةِ \ التَأْمينِ; **to be ~ the team** كانَ ضِمْنَ الفَريقِ **3** (present in) لَدى, عِنْدَ; **it's rare ~ people under fifty** هو نادِرٌ لَدى الأَشْخاصِ تحت سِنِّ الخَمْسينَ; **it's common ~ children** هو مُنْتَشِرٌ بين الأَطْفالِ **4** (showing manner, medium) في, بِ; **~ Greek** باللُغةِ اليونانيّةِ; **~ B flat** في الشَقّةِ 'ب'; **~ a skirt** مُرْتَدِيةً تَنّورةً; **dressed ~ black** مُرْتَدِياً مَلابِسَ سَوْداءَ; **~ pencil/ink** بِقَلَمِ رَصاصٍ \ حِبْرٍ; **to speak ~ a whisper** هَمَسَ, تَحَدَّثَ بِصَوْتٍ خافِتٍ; **~ a circle** على شَكْلِ دائِرةٍ; **put it ~ writing** أُكْتُبْهُ خَطِّيّاً; **to pay ~ cash** دَفَعَ نَقْداً **5** (as regards) **rich/poor ~ minerals** غَنِيّ ب \ يَفْتَقِرُ إلى المَوادِّ المَعْدِنيّةِ; **10 cm ~ length** 10 سم طولاً; **she is not lacking ~ courage** لا تَنْقُصُها الشَجاعةُ **6** (because of) في; **~ his haste, he left them behind** في عَجَلَتِهِ، تَرَكَهُمْ وَراءَهُ; **~ the confusion, he escaped** هَرَبَ وَسَطَ الاضْطِرابِ **7** (with present participle) بِ; **~ accepting, you agree to ...** بِقُبولِكَ، فَإنَّكَ تُوافِقُ ...; على ...; **~ doing so, she injured herself** إثْرَ قِيامِها بِذَلِكَ، جَرَحَتْ نَفْسَها **8** (with superlatives) في; **the tallest tower ~ the world** أَعْلى بُرْجٍ في العالَمِ **9** (in ratios) **a gradient of 1 ~ 4** دَرَجة مَيْلٍ \ انْحِدارٍ قَدْرُها 25٪; **a tax of 20 pence ~ the pound** ضَريبة بِقيمةِ 20 بِنْساً لِكُلِّ جُنَيْهٍ; **to have a one ~ five chance** كانَتْ نِسْبةُ نَجاحِهِ 1 على 5 **10** (with numbers) **she's ~ her twenties** هي في العِشْريناتِ من عُمْرِها; **to cut sth ~ three** قَطَعَ شَيْئاً إلى ثَلاثِ قِطَعٍ; **the temperature was ~ the thirties** كانَتْ دَرَجةُ الحَرارةِ في الثَلاثيناتِ **11** (during) في; **~ May** في (شَهْرِ) مايو; **~ 2013** في عام 2013; **~ summer** في فَصْلِ الصَيْفِ; **~ the night** في اللَيْلِ; **~ the mornings** في الصَباحاتِ; **at four ~ the morning** في الساعةِ الرابِعةِ صَباحاً; **~ the twenties** في العِشْريناتِ **12** (within) في; **~ ten minutes/an hour** في عَشْرِ دَقائِقَ \ ساعةٍ **13** (for) مُنْذُ; **it hasn't rained ~ weeks** لم تُمْطِرْ مُنْذُ أَسابيعَ; **it's been the coldest/wettest summer ~ thirty years** إنَّهُ الصَيْفُ الأَكْثَرُ بُرودةً \ مَطَراً مُنْذُ ثَلاثينَ عاماً **B** *adv* **1** (inside) **to come ~** دَخَلَ; **to ask** *or* **invite sb ~** دَعا شَخْصاً للدُخولِ **2** (at home) **to be ~** «person» كانَ في المَنْزِلِ; **to stay ~** بَقِيَ في المَنْزِلِ; **you're never ~** لا تَتَواجَدُ أَبَداً في المَنْزِلِ **3** (arrived) **to be ~** «ferry, bus, train» وَصَلَ (i; وُصول); **the ferry isn't ~ yet** لم تَصِلِ العَبّارةُ بَعْدُ **4** **the tide is ~** وَصَلَ المَدُّ إلى أَقْصاهِ **5** (Sport) **the shot/serve was ~** وَقَعَتِ الكُرةُ \ ضَرْبةُ الإرْسالِ داخِلَ المَلْعَبِ; **the ball was**

clearly ~ وَقَعَت الكُرةُ داخِلَ المَلْعَبِ بِشَكْلٍ واضِحٍ **6** (in stock) **we don't have any** ~ لَيْسَ مُتَوَفراً لَدَيْنا مِنْهُ أَيُّ شَيْءٍ; **to get some beer** ~ جَلَبَ بَعْضَ البيرة لِلبَيْعِ

C *adj* **to be** ~, **to be the** ~ **thing** كانَ على الموضةِ; **short skirts are** ~ **again** أَصْبَحَت التَنانيرُ القَصيرةُ على الموضةِ مُجَدَّداً

D (**in and out**) *phr* **to come** ~ **and out** جاءَ وَراحَ; **to weave** ~ **and out of the traffic** تَمايَلَ \ تَغَلْغَلَ وَسَطَ حَرَكَةِ المُرورِ

Idiom **to be in for a shock/surprise** كانَتْ في انْتِظارِه صَدْمةٌ \ مُفاجَأةٌ

IN *abbr* ▸ **Indiana**

in. *abbr* = **inch** بوصة

inability /ɪnəˈbɪlɪti/ *n* عَدَم قُدْرةٍ, عَجْز; **he was frustrated by his** ~ **to help** كانَ مُحْبَطاً لِعَدَمِ قُدْرَتِهِ على المُساعَدةِ

inaccessible /ɪnəkˈsɛsɪb(ə)l/ *adj* **1** (out of reach) ‹*area, village*› لا يُمْكِنُ الوُصولُ إِلَيْهِ, يَتَعَذَّرُ بُلوغُهُ **2** (difficult to understand) ‹*language, style*› صَعْبُ الفَهْمِ

inaccuracy /ɪnˈakjʊrəsi/ *n* (*pl* **inaccuracies**) خَطَأ, عَدَم دِقَّةٍ (أَخْطاء)

inaccurate /ɪnˈakjʊrət/ *adj* ‹*information, statement*› غَيْر دَقيقٍ, خاطِئ

inactive /ɪnˈaktɪv/ *adj* ‹*lifestyle, person*› كَسْلان, غَيْر نَشيطٍ, خامِل (dipt; كَسْلى, كُسالى, كَسالى)

inactivity /ˌɪnakˈtɪvɪti/ *n* كَسَل, خُمول

inadequacy /ɪnˈadɪkwəsi/ *n* (*pl* **inadequacies**) **1** (insufficiency) نَقْص, قُصور; **our failure was due to the** ~ **of our resources/the system/our preparation/the facilities** كانَ فَشَلُنا بِسَبَبِ قُصورٍ في مَوارِدِنا \ النِظامِ \ إِعْدادِنا \ المَرافِقِ **2** (defect) خَلَل (خِلال), نَقْص

inadequate /ɪnˈadɪkwət/ *adj* **1** (insufficient) ‹*funding, knowledge*› غَيْر كافٍ, ناقِص **2** (incompetent) عاجِز, غَيْر كُفْءٍ (عَجَزة)

inadvertently /ˌɪnədˈvəːt(ə)ntli/ *adv* بِدونِ قَصْدٍ

inadvisable /ɪnədˈvʌɪzəb(ə)l/ *adj* غَيْر مُسْتَحْسَنٍ \ مُسْتَصْوَبٍ

inane /ɪˈneɪn/ *adj* ‹*question, comment*› سَخيف, تافِه

inanimate /ɪnˈanɪmət/ *adj* ‹*object*› غَيْر حَيٍّ, جامِد

inapplicable /ɪnˈaplɪkəb(ə)l, ɪnəˈplɪkəb(ə)l/ *adj* ‹*regulation, principle*› غَيْر قابِلٍ لِلتَطْبيقِ

inappropriate /ɪnəˈprəʊprɪət/ *adj* ‹*behaviour, comment, time*› غَيْر مُناسِبٍ \ مُلائِمٍ

inarticulate /ˌɪnɑːˈtɪkjʊlət/ *adj* **1** ‹*person*› لا يَسْتَطيعُ التَعْبيرَ عَن نَفْسِهِ, غَيْر فَصيحٍ; **to be** ~ كانَ لا يَسْتَطيعُ التَعْبيرَ عن نَفْسِهِ **2** ‹*sound, cry*› غَيْر واضِحٍ

inasmuch as /ɪnəzˈmʌtʃ əz/ *phr* **1** (insofar as) بِقَدْرِ ما **2** (seeing that) نَظَراً لِأَنَّ

inattentive /ɪnəˈtɛntɪv/ *adj* ‹*pupil, driver*› شارِد الذِهْنِ, غافِل, غَيْر مُنْتَبِهٍ

inaudible /ɪnˈɔːdɪb(ə)l/ *adj* ‹*voice, whisper*› غَيْر مَسْموعٍ

inaugural /ɪˈnɔːgjʊrəl/ *adj* افْتِتاحِيّ

inaugurate /ɪˈnɔːgjʊreɪt/ *vt* **1** ‹*an exhibition, a service*› دَشَّنَ, افْتَتَحَ **2** ‹*a president*› نَصَّبَ

inauguration /ɪˌnɔːgjʊˈreɪʃ(ə)n/ *n* **1** (opening) تَدْشين, افْتِتاح **2** (investiture) تَنْصيب

inbreeding /ɪnˈbriːdɪŋ/ *n* (of people) زَواج الأَقارِبِ; (of animals) تَزاوُج داخِلِيّ

inbuilt /ˈɪnbɪlt/ *adj* ‹*mechanism*› مُدْمَج; ‹*bias*› مُتَأَصِّل

Inc /ɪŋk/ *abbr* (AmE) ▸ **Incorporated**

incapable /ɪnˈkeɪpəb(ə)l/ *adj* **1** (not able) غَيْر قادِرٍ, عاجِز; **to be** ~ **of doing sth** كانَ عاجِزاً عن فِعْلِ شَيْءٍ **2** (helpless) عاجِز

incapacitate /ˌɪnkəˈpasɪteɪt/ *vt* «illness, accident» أَقْعَدَ, أَعْجَزَ; **he was permanently ~d as a result of the attack** أُصيبَ بِعَجْزٍ دائِمٍ نَتيجةَ الهُجومِ

incapacity /ɪnkəˈpasɪti/ *n* **1** (inability) عَدَم قُدْرةٍ, عَجْز **2** عَدَم أَهْلِيّةٍ

incarcerate /ɪnˈkɑːsəreɪt/ *vt* سَجَنَ (u; سَجْن), حَبَسَ (i; حَبْس)

incarnate /ɪnˈkɑːnət/ *adj* مُجَسَّم, مُجَسَّد

incarnation /ɪnkɑːˈneɪʃ(ə)n/ *n* تَجَسُّد

incendiary /ɪnˈsɛndiəri/ *adj* **1** ‹*bomb, device*› حارِق **2** ‹*comment, issue*› مُهَيِّج, تَحْريضِيّ; ‹*issue*› مُثير لِلخِلافِ, شائِك

incense¹ /ˈɪnsɛns/ *n* بَخور

incense² /ɪnˈsɛns/ *vt* أَثارَ السَخَطَ, أَغْضَبَ; **the residents are ~d at the proposal** أَثارَ الاقْتِراحُ سَخطَ السُكّانِ

incentive /ɪnˈsɛntɪv/ *n* حافِز (حَوافِزُ), دافِع (دَوافِعُ); **to give sb the ~ to do sth** أَعْطى شَخْصاً الحافِزَ لِفِعْلِ شَيْءٍ

incentive scheme *n* نِظام الحَوافِزِ

inception /ɪnˈsɛpʃ(ə)n/ *n* ابْتِداء, اسْتِهْلال, بِداية

incessant /ɪnˈsɛs(ə)nt/ *adj* ‹*rain, chatter*› مُتَواصِل, دائِم, غَيْر مُنْقَطِعٍ

incessantly /ɪnˈsɛs(ə)ntli/ *adv* ‹*talk, complain*› دون انْقِطاعٍ, بِلا انْقِطاعٍ, باسْتِمْرارٍ, تَوَقُّفٍ

incest /ˈɪnsɛst/ *n* سِفاح القُرْبى, زِنا \ غَشَيان المَحارِمِ

incestuous /ɪnˈsɛstjʊəs/ *adj* ‹*relationship, marriage*› خاصّ [بِسِفاحِ القُرْبى]

inch /ɪntʃ/ **A** *n* (*pl* **inches**) **1** (unit of length) (= 2.54 cm) بوصة **2** (small distance) **to win by an ~** فازَ بِفارِقٍ ضَئيلٍ **B** *vi* **to ~ forward** تَقَدَّمَ بِبُطْءٍ

incidence /ˈɪnsɪd(ə)ns/ *n* وُقوع, حُدوث; **the high ~ of crime/cancer** ارْتِفاع مُعَدَّلِ الجَريمةِ \ السَرَطانِ

incident /ˈɪnsɪd(ə)nt/ *n* حادِث (حَوادِثُ), حادِثة (حَوادِثُ), واقِعة; **without ~** دون حَوادِثَ

incidental /ɪnsɪˈdɛnt(ə)l/ *adj* **1** (accompanying) ‹*effect, benefit*› عارِض, عَرَضيّ **2** (minor) ‹*expense, observation*› ثانَويّ

incidentally /ɪnsɪˈdɛnt(ə)li/ *adv* بالمُناسَبةِ

incidental music *n* موسيقى تَصْويريّة

incinerate /ɪnˈsɪnəreɪt/ *vt* حَوَّلَ إلى رَمادٍ, أَحْرَقَ ‹*waste, documents*›

incinerator /ɪnˈsɪnəreɪtə/ *n* مَحْرَقة

incision /ɪnˈsɪʒ(ə)n/ *n* شَقّ, قَطْع

incisor /ɪnˈsʌɪzə/ *n* سِنّ قاطِعة

incite /ɪnˈsʌɪt/ *vt* حَرَّضَ (على), حَثَّ (u; حَثّ على) ‹*hatred, violence*›; **to ~ sb to violence/to strike** حَرَّضَ شَخْصاً على العُنْفِ \ الإضْرابِ

inclination /ɪnklɪˈneɪʃ(ə)n/ *n* مَيْل (مُيول), نَزْعة (نَزَعات)

incline **A** /ɪnˈklʌɪn/ *vt* (fml) حَنى (i; حَنْي) ‹*one's head*› **B** /ɪnˈklʌɪn/ *vi* **to ~ to** *or* **towards a view/interpretation** مالَ إلى وِجْهةِ نَظَرٍ \ تَفْسيرٍ «historians, voters»

include /ɪnˈkluːd/ *vt* **1** (to contain as part) احْتَوى, تَضَمَّنَ, شَمَلَ (u; شُمول) ‹*an item, a feature*›; **service isn't ~d** الخِدْمةُ غَيْرُ مَشْمولةٍ **2** (to put in) أَدْرَجَ, أَرْفَقَ ‹*a note, cheque*›

including /ɪnˈkluːdɪŋ/ *prep* بما في ذلك, مُشْتَمِلاً على; **up to and ~ last Wednesday** حتّى الأَرْبِعاءِ الماضي وَمُشْتَمِلاً عَلَيْهِ; **not ~ service** بِدونِ الخِدْمةِ

inclusion /ɪnˈkluːʒ(ə)n/ *n* إدْراج, تَضْمين

inclusive /ɪnˈkluːsɪv/ *adj* ‹*price, fee*› شامِل, مُتَضَمِّن; **to be ~ of sth** كانَ شامِلاً شَيْئاً

incognito /ˌɪnkɒɡˈniːtəʊ/ *adv* ‹*to travel, live*› مُتَسَتِّراً, مُتَنَكِّراً, مُتَخَفِّياً

incoherent /ɪnkəʊˈhɪərənt/ *adj* ‹*style, account*› غَيْر مُتَفَكِّك, مُتَماسِك \ مُتَرابِط

income /ˈɪnkʌm/ *n* دَخْل, إيراد (إيرادات); **it's their chief source of ~** هو مَصْدَرُ دَخْلِهِم الرَئيسيّ

income bracket *n* شَريحة دَخْلٍ

income support *n* (BrE) دَعْم الدَخْلِ

income tax *n* ضَريبة دَخْلٍ

incoming /ˈɪnkʌmɪŋ/ *adj* **1** (inbound) ‹*flight, call*› قادِم; **the airport has been closed to ~ flights** تَمَّ إغْلاقُ المَطارِ أمامَ الرِحْلاتِ القادِمةِ **2** (about to take office) ‹*government, president*› قادِم, مُقْبِل

incommunicado /ˌɪnkəmjuːnɪˈkɑːdəʊ/ *adj* مَعْزول, في مَعْزِلٍ عن العالَمِ الخارِجيِّ

incomparable /ɪnˈkɒmp(ə)rəb(ə)l/ *adj* **1** (liter) (matchless) ‹*beauty, talent*› لا مَثيلَ لَهُ **2** (totally different) ‹*style, concept*› لا يُضاهى \ يُقارَنُ

incompatibility /ɪnkəmpatəˈbɪləti/ *n* (*pl* **incompatibilities**) عَدَم تَوافُقٍ

incompatible /ɪnkəmˈpatɪb(ə)l/ *adj* ‹*personalities, aims*› غَيْر مُتَوافِقٍ, مُتَعارِض

incompetence /ɪnˈkɒmpɪt(ə)ns/ *n* (of a surgeon, government) عَدَم كَفاءةٍ; (of a performance, sb's work) قُصور, عَجْز

incompetent /ɪn'kɒmpɪt(ə)nt/ *adj* ‹*leader, surgeon*› غَيْر كُفْءٍ; ‹*performance, work*› غَيْر مُتْقَنٍ

incomplete /ɪnkəm'pli:t/ *adj* 1 (not entire) ‹*set, documentation*› غَيْر كامِلٍ, ناقِص 2 (unfinished) ‹*work, building*› غَيْر, ناقِص مُكْتَمِلٍ

incomprehensible /ˌɪnkɒmprɪ'hensɪb(ə)l/ *adj* ‹*reason, accent*› لا يُمْكِنُ فَهْمُهُ, غَيْر مفهومٍ

incomprehension /ˌɪnkɒmprɪ'hɛnʃ(ə)n/ *n* عَدَم فَهْمٍ

inconceivable /ɪnkən'si:vəb(ə)l/ *adj* ‹*vastness, speed*› لا يُمْكِنُ لا يَتَصَوَّرُهُ عَقْلٌ, تَصَوُّرُهُ

inconclusive /ɪnkən'klu:sɪv/ *adj* ‹*findings*› غَيْر قَطْعِيٍّ; ‹*result*› غَيْر حاسِمٍ

incongruous /ɪn'kɒŋgrʊəs/ *adj* ‹*sight, behaviour*› في غَيْرِ مَحَلِّهِ, غَيْر لائِقٍ

inconsequential /ˌɪnkɒnsɪ'kwenʃ(ə)l/ *adj* غَيْر ذي, لا أَهَمّيّةَ لَهُ مَغْزًى ‹*detail, matter*›

inconsiderate /ɪnkən'sɪd(ə)rət/ *adj* ‹*behaviour, comment*› أَرْعَن (dipt; رُعْن), لا يُراعي الآخَرين

inconsistency /ɪnkən'sɪstənsi/ *n* (*pl* **inconsistencies**) 1 (of an argument, a statement) تَناقُض, تَضارُب 2 (of work, behaviour) عَدَم ثَباتٍ, (تَقَلُّبات) تَقَلُّب

inconsistent /ɪnkən'sɪstənt/ *adj* 1 (changeable) ‹*attitude, performance*› غَيْر ثابِتٍ, مُتَقَلِّب 2 (contradictory) مُتَناقِض, مُتَعارِض, مُتَضارِب; **to be ~ with the facts** كانَ مُتَناقِضاً مع الحَقائِقِ

inconspicuous /ɪnkən'spɪkjʊəs/ *adj* ‹*object, gesture*› غَيْر مُلْفِتٍ لِلنَظَرِ, غَيْر مَلْحوظٍ

incontinence /ɪn'kɒntɪnəns/ *n* سَلَس (البَوْلِ أو البُرازِ)

incontinent /ɪn'kɒntɪnənt/ *adj* مُصاب بِسَلَسِ (البَوْلِ أو البُرازِ)

inconvenience /ɪnkən'vi:nɪəns/ **A** *n* 1 [u] (trouble) مُضايَقة, إِزْعاج 2 (drawback, nuisance) مَصْدَر إِزْعاجٍ **B** *vt* ضايَقَ, أَزْعَجَ ‹*a passenger, customer*›

inconvenient /ɪnkən'vi:nɪənt/ *adj* ‹*time, location*› غَيْر مُلائِمٍ, مُزْعِج

incorporate /ɪn'kɔ:pəreɪt/ *vt* 1 (to take in) أَدْخَلَ, أَدْمَجَ ‹*an idea, a plan*›; **to ~ the proposals into the plan** أَدْخَلَ المُقْتَرَحاتِ في الخُطَّةِ 2 (to make part of) ضَمَّ (u; ضَمّ) ‹*a country, department*›; **Overseas Sales will be ~d into General Marketing** سَيُدْمَجُ قِسْمُ المَبيعاتِ الأَجْنَبيّةِ في التَسْويقِ العامِّ 3 (to constitute legally) أَسَّسَ ‹*a company, city, an organization*›

Incorporated /ɪn'kɔ:pəreɪtɪd/ *adj* ‹*company*› [شَرِكة مُسَجَّلة]; **Smith & Brown ~** شَرِكة سْميث وَبْراوْن

incorporation /ɪnkɔ:pə'reɪʃ(ə)n/ *n* 1 (of ingredients, components) ضَمّ, دَمْج 2 (of a business) تَأْسيس

incorrect /ɪnkə'rɛkt/ *adj* (erroneous) ‹*spelling, conclusion*› خاطِئ, غَيْر صَحيحٍ

incorrectly /ɪnkə'rɛktli/ *adv* ‹*to translate, address*› بِشَكْلٍ غَيْرِ صَحيحٍ, خَطَأً; ‹*to assume, answer*› على نَحْوٍ خاطِئٍ

incorrigible /ɪn'kɒrɪdʒɪb(ə)l/ *adj* ‹*behaviour, liar*› غَيْر قابِلٍ لِلإِصْلاحِ, لا يُمْكِنُ تَقْويمُهُ

increase **A** /ɪn'kri:s/ *vt* زادَ (i; زِيادة) ‹*sales, one's chances, the risk*›; **to ~ the offer by 5%/to $150** زادَ العَرْضَ بِنِسْبةِ ٥٪ \ لِيَصِلَ إلى $150; **to ~ one's chances of doing sth** زادَ من فُرَصِهِ في فِعْلِ شَيْءٍ

B /ɪn'kri:s/ *vi* «sales, one's chances» زادَ (i; زِيادة), اِزْدادَ; **the price ~d by 6%** زادَ السِعْرُ بِنِسْبةِ ٦٪; **his workload is increasing all the time** يَزْدادُ عِبْءُ العَمَلِ لَدَيْهِ طوال الوَقْتِ

C /'ɪŋkri:s/ *n* 1 (in amount) زِيادة; **an ~ in the cost of living** زِيادة في تَكْلُفةِ المَعيشةِ; **an ~ of 5%, a 5% ~** زِيادة بِمِقْدارِ ٥٪ 2 (in degree) اِزْدِياد (اِزْدِيادات); **to be on the ~** كانَ في اِزْدِيادٍ

increased /ɪn'kri:st/ *adj* ‹*demand, choice, probability*› مُتَزايِد; **an ~d risk of cancer** زِيادة خَطَرِ الإصابةِ بالسَرَطانِ

increasing /ɪn'kri:sɪŋ/ *adj* ‹*prices, number*› مُتَزايِد; **with increasing frequency** بِوَتيرةٍ مُتَزايِدةٍ

increasingly /ɪn'kri:sɪŋli/ *adv* ‹*dangerous, popular, difficult*› بِشَكْلٍ مُتَزايِدٍ

incredible /ɪn'krɛdɪb(ə)l/ *adj* 1 (not believable, extraordinary) ‹*story, excuse*› غَيْر مَعْقولٍ, لا يُصَدَّقُ 2 (infml) (wonderful) ‹*performance, experience*› رائِع, مُذْهِل, مُدْهِش

incredibly /ɪn'krɛdɪbli/ *adv* 1 (amazingly) مِمّا يُثيرُ الدَهْشةَ; **~, he was still alive** المُدْهِشُ أَنَّهُ كانَ لا يَزالُ على قَيْدِ الحَياةِ 2 (infml) (extremely) ‹*large, difficult*› بِشَكْلٍ مُدْهِشٍ

incredulous /ɪnˈkrɛdjʊləs/ *adj* ‹*expression, stare*› يَنُمُّ ,مُتَشَكِّك عن الشَكِّ

increment /ˈɪŋkrɪmənt/ **A** *n* **1** (on a salary) زِيادة **2** (increase) زِيادة

B *vt* زادَ (i; زِيادة), ازْدادَ ‹*a value, number*›

incremental /ɪŋkrəˈmɛnt(ə)l/ *adj* ‹*benefits, costs*› تَزايُديّ, مُتَزايِد

incriminate /ɪnˈkrɪmɪneɪt/ **A** *vt* (**incriminates, incriminating, incriminated**) جَرَّمَ ,أَدانَ ‹*a colleague, suspect*›; **to ~ sb in a case** أَدانَ شَخْصاً في قَضِيَّةٍ

B *v refl* (**incriminates, incriminating, incriminated**) **to ~ oneself** أَدانَ نَفْسَهُ

incriminating /ɪnˈkrɪmɪneɪtɪŋ/ *adj* ‹*evidence, document*› يُثْبِتُ إدانةٍ ,الإدانةَ

incubate /ˈɪŋkjʊbeɪt/ **A** *vt* **1** «hen» حَضَنَ (u; حَضْن ,حَضانة), حَضَنَ (بالتَعْريضِ) ‹*an egg*› **2** (to grow) رَخَمَ (u; رَخامة) (للحَرارةِ في المُخْتَبَرِ) ‹*bacteria, a culture*› **3** (to develop) احْتَضَنَ ‹*a scheme, an idea*›

B *vi* **1** «eggs» حُضِّنَ ,حُضِنَ **2** «diseases» حُضِنَ; تَطَوَّرَ «embryos» نَما (u; نُموّ) ,تَطَوَّرَ **3** «schemes, revolts»

incubation /ɪŋkjʊˈbeɪʃ(ə)n/ *n* **1** (of eggs, bacteria) حَضانة; **~ takes twenty days** تَسْتَغْرِقُ حَضانةُ البَيْضِ عِشْرينَ يَوْماً

2 (of diseases) فَتْرة \ طَوْر الحَضانةِ (الفَتْرة بين الإصابةِ بالمَرَضِ وَظُهورِ أَعْراضِه); **the period of ~ varies** تَتفاوَتُ فَتْرةُ الحَضانةِ

incubator /ˈɪŋkjʊbeɪtə/ *n* (for a child, eggs) حاضِنة (حَواضِنُ)

inculcate /ˈɪnkʌlkeɪt/ *vt* **to ~ a belief/principle in sb** \ غَرَسَ رَسَّخَ \ طَبَعَ اعْتِقاداً \ مَبْدَأً في (ذِهْنِ) شَخْصٍ

incumbent /ɪnˈkʌmb(ə)nt/ **A** *adj* **1** **to be ~ on** *or* **upon sb to do** كانَ واجِباً \ لِزاماً على شَخْصٍ أنْ يَقومَ بِهِ **2** (in a post) ‹*minister, president*› حاليّ

B *n* (fml) صاحِب \ شاغِل مَنْصِبٍ

incur /ɪnˈkɜː/ *vt* (**-rr-**) (fml) جَلَبَ على نَفْسِهِ ‹*anger, wrath*›; تَكَبَّدَ ‹*an expense, a liability*›

incurable /ɪnˈkjʊərəb(ə)l/ *adj* **1** ‹*disease*› مُسْتَعْصٍ, عُضال, لا يُرْجى الشِفاءُ مِنْهُ **2** ‹*optimist, romantic*› حتّى النُخاعِ ,أَبَديّ

incursion /ɪnˈkɜːʃ(ə)n/ *n* هَجْمة (هَجَمات), غارة

indebted /ɪnˈdɛtɪd/ *adj* **1** (owing gratitude) **to be ~ to sb (for sth)** ‹*patient, student*› كانَ مَديناً لِشَخْصٍ (بِشَيْءٍ)

2 (owing money) ‹*nation, customer*› مَدْيون ,مَدين بِمالٍ

indecency /ɪnˈdiːs(ə)nsi/ *n* **1** [u] (of an image, a proposal) قِلّة الاحْتِشامِ \ لِياقةٍ **2** (offence) فِعْل بَذيء \ فاحِش

indecent /ɪnˈdiːs(ə)nt/ *adj* (improper) ‹*behaviour, act*› غَيْر لائِقٍ, بَذيء

indecent assault *n* هَتْك عِرْضٍ

indecent exposure *n* تَعَرٍّ فاضِح ,كَشْف \ إظْهار العَوْرةِ

indecipherable /ˌɪndɪˈsʌɪf(ə)rəb(ə)l/ *adj* ‹*handwriting*› لا يُمْكِنُ فَكُّ طَلاسِمِهِ; ‹*code*› لا يُمْكِنُ حَلُّ رُموزِهِ \ شِفْرَتِهِ

indecision /ɪndɪˈsɪʒ(ə)n/ *n* تَرَدُّد ,حَيْرة

indecisive /ɪndɪˈsʌɪsɪv/ *adj* **1** (hesitant) ‹*customer, leader*› حائِر ,مُتَرَدِّد **2** (inconclusive) ‹*election, battle*› غَيْر حاسِمٍ \ نِهائيّ

indeed /ɪnˈdiːd/ *adv* **1** (for emphasis) بالفِعْلِ ,فِعْلاً; **thank you very much ~** أَشْكُرُكَ شُكْراً جَزيلاً; **it was very hot ~** لَقَدْ كانَ ساخِناً جِدًّا; **I was very sorry ~ to hear that** لَقَدْ تَأَسَّفْتُ جِدًّا لِسَماعِ ذلك; **that's very good news ~** ذلك خَبَرٌ جَيِّدٌ جِدًّا **2** (fml) (certainly) بالتَأْكيدِ ,بالفِعْلِ; **'are you interested?'—'~ I am!'** *or* **'yes ~!'** 'هل أَنْتَ مُهْتَمٌّ؟' — 'أَجَلْ, بالتَأْكيدِ!' **3** (fml) (in fact) حَقًّا; **she is polite, ~ charming** هي مُهَذَّبةٌ, وَجَذّابةٌ حَقًّا; **if ~ that is what consumers want** إذا كانَ ذلك حَقًّا \ فِعْلاً ما يُريدُ المُسْتَهْلِكونَ **4** (fml) (expressing surprise) **'he knows you'—'does he ~?'** 'هو يَعْرِفُكَ' — 'حَقًّا؟'

indefensible /ɪndɪˈfɛnsɪb(ə)l/ *adj* **1** ‹*crime, behaviour*› غَيْر مُبَرَّرٍ, لا يُغْتَفَرُ **2** ‹*argument, opinion*› باطِل ,لا يُمْكِنُ الدِفاعُ عَنْهُ **3** (Mil) ‹*position, territory*› لا يُمْكِنُ الدِفاعُ عَنْهُ \ حِمايَتُهُ

indefinite /ɪnˈdɛfɪnɪt/ *adj* **1** (not fixed) ‹*period, number*› غَيْر مُحَدَّدٍ **2** **the ~ article** أَداة \ حَرْف التَنْكيرِ

indefinitely /ɪnˈdɛfɪnɪtli/ *adv* ‹*to continue, postpone*› إلى أَجَلٍ غَيْر مُسَمًّى

indelible /ɪnˈdɛlɪb(ə)l/ *adj* **1** (pen) ‹*ink, stain*› لا يُمْحى, لا يُمْكِنُ مَحْوُهُ \ إزالَتُهُ; **an ~ marker** قَلَم مارْكَر لا يُمْحى **2** (memory) ‹*impression, image*› لا يُمْحى \ يُنْسى

indelicate /ɪnˈdɛlɪkət/ *adj* ‹*action, remark*› فَظّ ,غَيْر لَبِقٍ

indemnify /ɪnˈdɛmnɪfʌɪ/ *vt* (**indemnifies, indemnifying, indemnified**) [1] (to compensate) عَوَّضَ ‹*an employee, victim*› [2] (to protect) أَمَّنَ

indemnity /ɪnˈdɛmnɪti/ *n* (*pl* **indemnities**) [1] (payment) ضمان تَعْويضٍ (تَعْويضات) تَعْويض [2] (protection) [3] (exemption) (إعْفاءات) إعْفاء

indent /ɪnˈdɛnt/ *vt* [1] (P&P) [تَرَكَ مَسافةً فارِغةً قبل] ‹*a line, word*› [2] (to make notches in) سَنَّنَ ,حَزَّزَ ‹*an edge*›

independence /ˌɪndɪˈpɛnd(ə)ns/ *n* [1] (of a person) اسْتِقْلاليّة; **I've always valued my ~** كُنْتُ دَوْماً أُقَدِّرُ قيمةَ اسْتِقْلاليَّتي [2] (of a country) اسْتِقلال

Independence Day *n* عيد الاسْتِقْلالِ

independent /ˌɪndɪˈpɛnd(ə)nt/ *adj* [1] (self-reliant) ‹*worker, child*› مُسْتَقِلّ [2] (separate and fair) ‹*enquiry, adviser*› مُسْتَقِلّ بِذاتِهِ

independently /ˌɪndɪˈpɛnd(ə)ntli/ *adv* [1] (without help) ‹*to act, live*› بِاسْتِقْلاليّةٍ; **she took the decision quite ~** اتَّخَذَت القَرارَ بِاسْتِقْلاليّةٍ تامّةٍ [2] (separately) ‹*to administer, negotiate*› بِشَكْلٍ مُسْتَقِلٍّ; **the two departments operate ~ of each other** يَعْمَلُ القِسْمانِ بِشَكْلٍ مُسْتَقِلٍّ عن بَعْضِهِما البَعْضَ

in-depth /ɪnˈdɛpθ/ *adj* ‹*analysis, knowledge*› مُعَمَّق

indescribable /ˌɪndɪˈskrʌɪbəb(ə)l/ *adj* ‹*pain, beauty*› لا يوصَفُ, يَفوقُ الوَصْفَ

indestructible /ˌɪndɪˈstrʌktɪb(ə)l/ *adj* ‹*bond*› لا يُمْكِنُ هَدْمُهُ \ غَيْر قابِلٍ للتلَفِ ‹*plastic*› لا يُمْكِنُ تَحْطيمُهُ ‹*machine*›; تَدْميرُهُ

indeterminate /ˌɪndɪˈtəːmɪnət/ *adj* ‹*age, period*› غَيْر مُحَدَّدٍ

index /ˈɪndɛks/ *n* (*pl* **indexes** or **indices**) [1] (of a book) فِهْرِس (فَهارِسُ); **look it up in the ~** ابْحَثْ عَنْهُ في الفِهْرِسِ [2] (of prices, etc) مُؤَشِّر (مُؤَشِّرات); **the retail price ~** مُؤَشِّر أَسْعارِ التَجْزِئةِ

index card *n* بِطاقة فَهْرَسةٍ

index finger *n* سَبّابة

index-linked /ˌɪndɛksˈlɪŋkt/ *adj* ‹*savings, pension*› مُرْتَبِط بِمُؤَشِّرٍ

India /ˈɪndɪə/ *pr n* الهِنْد

Indian /ˈɪndɪən/ [A] *adj* [1] (of India) ‹*religion, philosophy*› هِنْديّ [2] (Native American) ‹*village, tribe*› هِنْديّ (نِسْبةً إلى الهُنود الحُمْرِ)

[B] *n* [1] (native of India) هِنْديّ (هُنود) [2] (Native American) هِنْديّ أَحْمَر

Indiana /ˌɪndɪˈanə/ *pr n* إنْدِيانا

Indianan /ˌɪndɪˈan(ə)n/ *pr n, adj* [(شَخْص) من إنْدِيانا]

Indian Ocean *pr n* (**the Indian Ocean**) المُحيط الهِنْديّ

Indian summer *n* [طَقْس دافِئ \ مُعْتَدِل في أَواخِرِ الخَريفِ]

indicate /ˈɪndɪkeɪt/ [A] *vt* [1] (إلى) أَشارَ ‹*the exit, house*›; **he ~d the shop I was looking for** أَشارَ إلى المَتْجَرِ الّذي كُنْتُ أَبْحَثُ عَنْهُ [2] (إلى) أَشارَ, (على) دَلَّ (u; دَلالة) ‹*a change, one's preference*›; **high pressure ~s dry weather is to be expected** يُشيرُ الضَغْطُ الجَوّيُّ المُرْتَفِعُ إلى أَنَّهُ من المُتَوَقَّعِ أَنْ يَكونَ الطَقْسُ جافّاً [3] (إلى) أَشارَ ‹*right, left*›

[B] *vi* «drivers» [أَشارَ إلى تَغْييرِ اتِّجاهِ السَيْرِ]; «cyclists» [لَوَّحَ بِيَدِهِ]

indication /ˌɪndɪˈkeɪʃ(ə)n/ *n* إشارة, مُؤَشِّر (مُؤَشِّرات), دَليل (دَلائِلُ); **they gave no ~ of how the work should be done** لم يُعْطُوا أَيَّةَ إشارةٍ عن كَيْفيّةِ إنْجازِ العَمَلِ

indicative /ɪnˈdɪkətɪv/ [A] *adj* [1] **to be ~ of sth** كانَ دالّاً \ دَلَّ على شَيْءٍ; **fidgeting is often ~ of nervousness** كَثيراً ما يَدُلُّ التَمَلْمُلُ على العَصَبيّةِ [2] ‹*mood, form*› دَلاليّ

[B] *n* رَفْع الفِعْلِ

indicator /ˈɪndɪkeɪtə/ *n* [1] (pointer) مُؤَشِّر (مُؤَشِّرات); (meter) عَدّاد (عَدّادات); (gauge) مِقْياس (مَقاييسُ); **a pressure/fuel ~** مُؤَشِّر الضَغْطِ \ الوَقودِ [2] (on a car) غَمّاز (غَمّازات) [3] (for travel information) [لَوْحة إلِكْترونيّة عَلَيْها مَواعيدُ الرِحْلاتِ]; **an arrivals/departures ~** لَوْحة مَواعيدِ رِحْلاتِ الوُصولِ \ الذَهابِ [4] (sign) مُؤَشِّر (مُؤَشِّرات); **performance ~s in primary education** مُؤَشِّرات الأَداءِ في التَعْليمِ الابْتِدائيِّ

indices /ˈɪndɪsiːz/ *n pl* ▸ **index**

indict /ɪnˈdʌɪt/ *vt* ‹*a suspect, the accused*› وَجَّهَ تُهْمةً إلى, اتَّهَمَ

indictable /ɪnˈdʌɪtəb(ə)l/ *adj* ‹*act, crime*› يُعاقِبُ عَلَيْهِ القانونُ; ‹*offender*› مُعَرَّض للمُلاحَقةِ القانونيّةِ \ القَضائيّةِ

indictment /ɪnˈdʌɪtmənt/ *n* [1] (formal statement, charge) لائِحة \ قَرار اتِّهامٍ; **to bring an ~ against sb** قَدَّمَ \ وَجَّهَ لائِحةَ اتِّهامٍ ضدَّ شَخْصٍ [2] (criticism) انْتِقاد (انْتِقادات)

indie /ˈɪndi/ *adj* (infml) ‹*band, label*› مُسْتَقِلّ (عن شَرِكاتِ التَوْزيعِ الكَبيرةِ)

indifference /ɪnˈdɪf(ə)rəns/ *n* عَدَمُ اكْتِراثٍ \ اهْتِمامٍ, لامُبالاة; **he showed complete ~ to her feelings** أَظْهَرَ عَدَمَ اكْتِراثٍ تامٍّ بِمَشاعِرِها

indifferent /ɪnˈdɪf(ə)rənt/ *adj* **1** (uninterested) ‹*attitude, shrug*› غَيْرُ عابِئٍ \ مُبالٍ \ مُهْتَمٍّ \ مُكْتَرِثٍ; **this government is ~ to public opinion** هذه الحُكومةُ غَيْرُ عابِئةٍ بالرَّأْيِ العامِّ **2** (mediocre) ‹*performance, meal*› دون الوَسَطِ

indigenous /ɪnˈdɪdʒɪnəs/ *adj* ‹*people, culture*› أَصْلِيّ, مُسْتَوْطِن; **koalas are ~ to Australia** الكُوال حَيَوانٌ مُسْتَوْطِنٌ في أُسْتُرالِيا

indigestible /ɪndɪˈdʒɛstəb(ə)l/ *adj* **1** ‹*meal, food*› عَسير \ صَعْب الهَضْمِ **2** (difficult to understand) ‹*text, book*› صَعْب الفَهْمِ, يَصْعُبُ فَهْمُهُ

indigestion /ɪndɪˈdʒɛstʃ(ə)n/ *n* عُسْر \ سوء الهَضْمِ; **to suffer from ~** عانى من عُسْرِ \ سوءِ الهَضْمِ

indignant /ɪnˈdɪgnənt/ *adj* ‹*letter, tone*› ناقِم, ساخِط; **to be ~ at sb's rudeness** شَعَرَ بالسُخْطِ بِسَبَبِ وَقاحةِ شَخْصٍ; **he was ~ about the way he had been treated** كانَ ساخِطاً على الطَريقةِ التي عومِلَ بها

indignation /ɪndɪgˈneɪʃ(ə)n/ *n* سُخْط, نِقْمة (نِقَم, نِقَمات)

indignity /ɪnˈdɪgnɪti/ *n* (*pl* **indignities**) إهانة

indigo /ˈɪndɪgəʊ/ **A** *n* (اللَوْن) النيلِيّ **B** *adj* ‹*sky, dress*› نيلِيّ

indirect /ɪndɪˈrɛkt, ɪndʌɪˈrɛkt/ *adj* **1** (tangential) ‹*consequence, evidence*› غَيْر مُباشِرٍ **2** (not straight) ‹*sunlight, route*› غَيْر مُباشِرٍ \ مُسْتَقيمٍ **3** (not directly connected) ‹*tax, subsidy*› غَيْر مُباشِرٍ **4** (in grammar) ‹*question, discourse*› غَيْر مُباشِرٍ

indirectly /ˌɪndɪˈrɛktli, ˌɪndʌɪˈrɛktli/ *adv* ‹*to affect, contribute*› بِشَكْلٍ غَيْرِ مُباشِرٍ

indirect object *n* مَفْعول به غَيْر مُباشِر

indirect speech *n* كَلام غَيْر مُباشِرٍ

indiscreet /ɪndɪˈskriːt/ *adj* (not tactful) ‹*remark, gossip*› غَيْر حَذِرٍ \ مُتَحَفِّظٍ

indiscretion /ɪndɪˈskrɛʃ(ə)n/ *n* (lack of discretion) تَصَرُّف غَيْر حَذِرٍ \ مُتَحَفِّظٍ; (lack of good judgement) تَصَرُّف بِعَدَمِ تَعَقُّلٍ \ طَيْش, تَبَصُّر

indiscriminate /ˌɪndɪˈskrɪmɪnət/ *adj* ‹*killing, violence*› عَشْوائِيّ

indispensable /ɪndɪˈspɛnsəb(ə)l/ *adj* ‹*tool, role*› لا غِنى عَنْهُ, لا يُمْكِنُ الاسْتِغْناءُ عَنْهُ

indisposed /ɪndɪˈspəʊzd/ *adj* (fml) **1** (ill) **to be ~** كانَ مُتَوَعِّكاً \ مُصاباً بِوَعْكةٍ **2** (unwilling) لا يَرْغَبُ; **to be ~ to help/fight** لم يَرْغَبْ في المُساعَدةِ \ القِتالِ

indisputable /ɪndɪˈspjuːtəb(ə)l/ *adj* ‹*fact, talent*› لا يَقْبَلُ الجِدالَ ‹*champion, winner*› لا يَخْتَلِفُ فيهِ اثْنانِ, الجَدَلَ \ الجِدالَ من دونِ مُنازِعٍ; **it is ~ that the earth's atmosphere is getting warmer** لا جِدالَ في أنّ الغِلافَ الجَوِّيَّ للأَرْضِ يُصْبِحُ مع الوَقْتِ أَكْثَرَ دِفْئاً

indistinct /ɪndɪˈstɪŋkt/ *adj* ‹*shape, voice, memory*› غَيْر واضِحٍ, مُبْهَم

indistinguishable /ɪndɪˈstɪŋgwɪʃəb(ə)l/ *adj* ‹*fabrics, images*› لا يُمْكِنُ تَمْييزُهُ \ تَفْريقُهُ; **to be ~ from sb/sth** لا يُمْكِنُ تَمْييزُهُ \ تَفْريقُهُ عن شَخْصٍ \ شَيْءٍ

individual /ɪndɪˈvɪdjʊəl/ **A** *adj* **1** (for one person or animal) ‹*freedom, portion*› فَرْدِيّ **2** (separate) ‹*member, item*› مُفْرَد, مُنْفَرِد; **each ~ case will need to be dealt with differently** سَيَكونُ من الضَروريِّ التَعامُلُ مع كُلِّ حالةٍ بِشَكْلٍ مُخْتَلِفٍ **3** (typical) ‹*style, identity*› خاصّ, فَرْدِيّ **B** *n* فَرْد (أَفْراد, فُرادى); **a wealthy/talented ~** شَخْص غَنِيّ \ فَرْد مَوْهوب

individuality /ˌɪndɪvɪdjʊˈalɪti/ *n* فَرْدِيّة

individually /ɪndɪˈvɪdjʊəli/ *adv* ‹*to test, assess*› بِشَكْلٍ, على حِدةٍ بِمُفْرَدِهِ, فَرْدِيٍّ; **the manager will interview each one ~** سَيُجْري المُديرُ مُقابَلةً مع كُلِّ فَرْدٍ على حِدةٍ

indivisible /ɪndɪˈvɪzɪb(ə)l/ *adj* ‹*unit*› لا يَتَجَزَّأُ, غَيْر قابِلٍ للتَجْزِئة \ للانْقِسامِ; ‹*number*› غَيْر قابِلٍ لِلقِسْمةِ

indoctrinate /ɪnˈdɒktrɪneɪt/ *vt* ‹*a child, student*› لَقَّنَ, شَرَّبَ; **they ~ their children with racist views** يُلَقِّنونَ أَوْلادَهُمْ أَفْكاراً عُنْصُرِيّةً

indolent /ˈɪndələnt/ *adj* (fml) ‹*teenager, husband*› كَسول, خامِل

Indonesia /ˌɪndəˈniːʒə/ *pr n* إنْدونيسيا

Indonesian /ɪndəˈniːʒ(ə)n/ **A** *adj* ‹*ambassador, food*› إنْدونيسِيّ **B** *n* **1** (citizen) إنْدونيسِيّ **2** (language) (اللُغة) الإنْدونيسِيّة

indoor /ˈɪndɔː/ *adj before n* ‹*plant*› مَنْزِليّ ,داخِليّ; ‹*shoes*› [يُمارَسُ في الأماكِنِ ‹*sport*› ;للاسْتِعْمالِ الداخِليِّ \ المَنْزِليِّ المُغْلَقةِ]

indoors /ɪnˈdɔːz/ *adv* ‹*to stay*› في المَبْنى \ المَنْزِلِ; ‹*to go*› إلى المَبْنى \ المَنْزِلِ

induce /ɪnˈdjuːs/ *vt* **1** (to persuade) **to ~ sb to do sth** حَثّ \ حَمَلَ شَخْصاً على القِيامِ بِشَيْءٍ **2** (to bring about) حَفَّزَ ‹*sleep, inflammation*›; **they will give you drugs to ~ labour** سَيُعْطونَكَ أَدْوِيةً لِتَحْفيزِ الوِلادةِ

inducement /ɪnˈdjuːsmənt/ *n* (دَوافِعُ) دافِع ,(حَوافِزُ) حافِز

induction /ɪnˈdʌkʃ(ə)n/ *n* **1** حَثّ; **an ~ coil** مِلَفّ حَثٍّ **2** (of labour) تَحْفيز **3** (of an office-holder) تَنْصيب ,تَقْليد **4** (AmE) (of recruits) تَجْنيد

induction course *n* دَوْرة تَدْريبيّة \ تَعْريفيّة (للمُسْتَجِدّينَ)

induction loop *n* دارة الحَثّ

indulge /ɪnˈdʌldʒ/ **A** *vt* **1** أَشْبَعَ ‹*a whim, desire*› **2** دَلَّلَ ‹*a child, worker*›
B *vi* **to ~ in sth** «guests, critics» انْغَمَسَ \ أَسْرَفَ في شَيْءٍ

indulgence /ɪnˈdʌldʒ(ə)ns/ *n* **1** (extravagance) لَذّة; **an occasional cigar is my one ~** سيجار من حينٍ لِآخَرَ هو مُتْعَتي الوَحيدةُ **2** [u] (tolerance) تَسامُح ,تَساهُل **3** [u] (partaking) انْغِماس; **too much ~ in anything is bad** كَثْرةُ الانْغِماسِ في أيِّ شَيْءٍ أمْرٌ سَيِّئٌ

indulgent /ɪnˈdʌldʒ(ə)nt/ *adj* ‹*parent, attitude*› مُتَسامِح ,مُتَساهِل

industrial /ɪnˈdʌstriəl/ *adj* ‹*area, development*› صِناعيّ

industrial action *n* (BrE) [نَشاط احْتِجاجيّ للعُمّالِ]

industrial democracy *n* ديموقْراطيّة صِناعيّة

industrial dispute *n* خِلاف بينَ الإدارةِ والعُمّالِ

industrial estate, **industrial park** *n* مِنْطَقة صِناعيّة

industrialist /ɪnˈdʌstriəlɪst/ *n* صِناعيّ ,صاحِب مَصْنَعٍ

industrialize, -ise (BrE) /ɪnˈdʌstriəlaɪz/ *vt* صَنَّعَ ‹*a country, region*›

industrial relations *n* عَلاقات صِناعيّة

Industrial Revolution *n* (**the Industrial Revolution**) الثَّوْرة الصِناعيّة

industrial waste *n* مُخَلَّفات \ نُفايات \ فَضَلات صِناعيّة

industrious /ɪnˈdʌstriəs/ *adj* ‹*worker*› كادّ ,كادِح; ‹*student*› مُجْتَهِد ,مُثابِر

industry /ˈɪndəstri/ *n* (*pl* **industries**) صِناعة (صَنائِعُ ,صِناعات); **the steel ~** صِناعة الصُلْبِ; **the tourist ~** الصِناعة السِياحيّة

inedible /ɪnˈɛdɪb(ə)l/ *adj* **1** (impossible to eat) ‹*plant, berry*› لا يُؤْكَلُ, غَيْر صالِحٍ للأَكْلِ **2** (unpalatable) ‹*meal, slop*› لا يُؤْكَلُ, غَيْر مُسْتَساغٍ

ineffective /ɪnɪˈfɛktɪv/ *adj* ‹*measure, remedy*› غَيْر فَعّالٍ \ مُجْدٍ \ ناجِعٍ

ineffectual /ɪnɪˈfɛktʃʊəl/ *adj* **1** (of an action) ‹*action, policy*› غَيْر فَعّالٍ \ مُجْدٍ \ ناجِعٍ **2** (of a person) ‹*parent, leader*› عاجِز, غَيْر قَديرٍ

inefficiency /ɪnɪˈfɪʃ(ə)nt(ə)nsi/ *n* عَدَم فَعّاليّةٍ

inefficient /ɪnɪˈfɪʃ(ə)nt/ *adj* ‹*method, worker*› غَيْر فَعّالٍ

ineligible /ɪnˈɛlɪdʒɪb(ə)l/ *adj* ‹*voter, candidate*› غَيْر مُؤَهَّلٍ; **she was ~ to vote** كانَتْ لا يَحِقُّ لَها التَصْويتُ

inept /ɪˈnɛpt/ *adj* (incompetent) ‹*leader*› غَيْر كُفْءٍ; (clumsy) ‹*performance*› أَخْرَق (dipt); (inappropriate) ‹*remark*› في غَيْرِ مَحَلِّهِ, غَيْر مُناسِبٍ

inequality /ɪnɪˈkwɒlɪti/ *n* (*pl* **inequalities**) عَدَم مُساواةٍ \ تَكافُؤٍ

inert /ɪˈnəːt/ *adj* **1** ‹*gas, atoms*› خامِل **2** ‹*body, patient*› خامِل

inertia /ɪˈnəːʃə/ *n* قُصور ذاتيّ

inevitable /ɪnˈɛvɪtəb(ə)l/ **A** *adj* **1** (certain, unavoidable) ‹*consequence, result*› لا يُمْكِنُ تَفاديه ,حَتْميّ ,مَحْتوم **2** (predictable) ‹*routine, storyline*› مُتَوَقَّع
B *n* **the ~** المَحْتوم

inevitably /ɪnˈɛvɪtəbli/ *adv* ‹*to involve, end*› حَتْماً

inexact /ˌɪnɪɡˈzakt/ *adj* ‹*measurement, description*› غَيْر دَقيقٍ \ مَضْبوطٍ; **it is an ~ science** هو عِلْمٌ غَيْرُ دَقيقٍ

inexcusable /ɪnɪkˈskjuːzəb(ə)l/ *adj* ‹*behaviour, delay*› لا يُغْتَفَرُ, لا مُبَرِّرَ لَهُ

inexhaustible /ɪnɪɡˈzɔːstəb(ə)l/ *adj* ‹*supply, energy*› لا يَنْفَدُ \ يَنْضُبُ

inexpensive /ɪnɪkˈspɛnsɪv/ *adj* ‹*meal, alternative*› غَيْر مُكَلِّفٍ

inexperience /ɪnɪkˈspɪərɪəns/ *n* قِلّة خِبْرةٍ \ تَجْرِبةٍ

inexperienced /ɪnɪk'spɪərɪənst/ *adj* ‹*driver, newcomer*› قليل (أغرار) غِرّ, الخِبْرةِ \ التَجْرِبةِ

inexpert /ɪn'ɛkspəːt/ *adj* ‹*gardener*› غَيْر خَبيرٍ \ حاذِقٍ \ ماهِرٍ; ‹*repair*› دون خِبْرةٍ \ مَهارةٍ (سابِقةٍ)

inexplicable /ɪnɪk'splɪkəb(ə)l/ *adj* ‹*delay, phenomenon*› لا يُمْكِنُ تَفْسيرُهُ \ شَرْحُهُ \ تَعْليلُهُ

inextricably /ɪn'ɛkstrɪkəbli, ɪnɪk'strɪkəbli/ *adv* ‹*linked, entwined*› بِشَكْلٍ مُتَلازِمٍ \ مُلازِمٍ \ لا يَتَجَزَّأُ

infallibility /ɪn,falɪ'bɪlɪti/ *n* عِصْمة

infallible /ɪn'falɪb(ə)l/ *adj* ① (of a person) ‹*instinct, memory*› لا يَخيبُ, لا يُخْطِئُ; **no one is absolutely ~** لا أَحَدَ مَعْصومٌ (من الخَطَأِ) على الإطْلاقِ ② (of a thing) ‹*method, remedy*› ناجِع

infamous /'ɪnfəməs/ *adj* ① (notorious) ‹*character*› رَديء \ سَيِّئ السُمْعةِ; ‹*crime*› أَنْكَر (dipt) ② (shameful) ‹*deed, action*› مُخْزٍ, شائِن

infancy /'ɪnf(ə)nsi/ *n* ① (babyhood) طُفولة ② (early stages) مَرْحَلة مُبَكِّرة

infant /'ɪnf(ə)nt/ *n* ① (baby) طِفْل (أَطْفال), رَضيع (رُضَعاءُ, رَضائِعُ) ② (BrE) (schoolchild) طِفْل (بين سِنِّ الخامِسةِ والسابِعةِ)

infantile /'ɪnf(ə)ntʌɪl/ *adj* ① (childish) ‹*joke, behaviour*› طُفوليّ, صِبْيانيّ ② ‹*paralysis, colic*› الأَطْفالِ, الرُضَّعِ

infant mortality *n* وَفَيات الأَطْفالِ (الرُضَّعِ)

infantry /'ɪnf(ə)ntri/ *n* مُشاة

infantryman /'ɪnf(ə)ntrɪmən/ *n* (*pl* **-men**) ماشٍ (مُشاة)

infant school *n* مَدْرَسة أَطْفالٍ \ حَضانةٍ

infatuated /ɪn'fatʃuːeɪtɪd/ *adj* **to be ~ with sb** كان مولَعاً بِشَخْصٍ

infatuation /ɪnfatʃuː'eɪʃ(ə)n/ *n* حُبّ عابِر, افْتِتان; **it's just an ~** إنَّهُ مُجَرَّدُ حُبٍّ عابِرٍ

infect /ɪn'fɛkt/ *vt* أَعْدى ‹*a patient*›; لَوَّثَ ‹*wound*›; **the wound became ~ed** تَلَوَّثَ الجُرْحُ

infection /ɪn'fɛkʃ(ə)n/ *n* (a disease) عَدْوى (f), الْتِهاب (الْتِهابات); [u] (becoming ill) عَدْوى, إصابة (f); **an ear/throat ~** الْتِهاب الأُذُنِ \ الحَلْقِ; **to increase the risk of ~** زادَ من خَطَرِ الإصابةِ بالعَدْوى

infectious /ɪn'fɛkʃəs/ *adj* ① (contagious) ‹*disease, virus*› مُعْدٍ; **influenza is highly ~** الإنْفِلْوَنْزا مُعْدِيةٌ جِدًّا \ شَديدةُ العَدْوى ② (with feelings) ‹*laughter, enthusiasm*› مُعْدٍ

infer /ɪn'fəː/ *vt* (**-rr-**) (fml) اسْتَدَلَّ, اسْتَنْبَطَ, اسْتَنْتَجَ (على) ‹*a relationship, an intention*›; **to ~ sth from the facts/data** اسْتَنْتَجَ \ اسْتَنْبَطَ شَيْئاً من الحَقائِقِ \ المُعْطَياتِ

inference /'ɪnf(ə)rəns/ *n* ① (act, process) اسْتِدْلال, اسْتِنْتاج (اسْتِنْتاجات) ② (conclusion) اسْتِنْباط (اسْتِنْباطات), اسْتِدْلال (اسْتِدْلالات)

inferior /ɪn'fɪərɪə/ **A** *adj* ‹*quality, status*› أَقَلّ, أَدْنى (dipt); **his latest work is ~ to what he did before** تَدَنّي مُسْتَوى عَمَلِهِ الأَخيرِ مُقارَنةً بِأَعْمالِهِ السابِقةِ; **to make sb feel ~** جَعَلَ شَخْصاً يَشْعُرُ بالدونيّةِ

B *n* مَرْؤوس

inferiority /ɪn,fɪərɪ'ɒrɪti/ *n* ① (in quality) نَقْص; (in status) دونيّة ② (towards others) إحْساس بالنَقْصِ \ بالدونيّةِ

inferiority complex *n* عُقْدة \ مُرَكَّب النَقْصِ \ الدونيّةِ

inferno /ɪn'fəːnəʊ/ *n* (*pl* **infernos**) جَحيم, كُتْلة من النيرانِ

infertile /ɪn'fəːtʌɪl/ *adj* ① ‹*couple, woman, man*› عَقيم, عُقْم, عاقِر (mf; عُقَّر; f pl عَواقِرُ) ② ‹*land, soil*› قاحِل, مُجْدِب, عَقام (عِقام)

infertility /ɪnfə'tɪləti/ *n* ① (biological) عُقْر, عُقْم; **millions of couples suffer from ~** يُعاني مَلايينُ الأَزْواجِ من العُقْمِ ② (of land) جَدْب

infest /ɪn'fɛst/ *vt* غَزا (u; غَزْو), اجْتاحَ ‹*a house, clothing*›

infidelity /ɪnfɪ'dɛlɪti/ *n* (*pl* **infidelities**) خِيانة

infighting /'ɪnfʌɪtɪŋ/ *n* صِراع \ اقْتِتال \ تَنافُس داخِليّ

infiltrate /'ɪnfɪltreɪt/ *vt* انْدَسَّ (في) ‹*a gang, an organization*›

infiltration /ɪnfɪl'treɪʃ(ə)n/ *n* ① (of liquid, gas) تَسَرُّب (تَسَرُّبات) ② (of troops, propaganda) تَسَلُّل

infinite /'ɪnfɪnɪt/ *adj* ① (limitless) ‹*variety, wisdom*› غَيْر مَحْدودٍ, لا نِهايةَ لَهُ ② (in maths) ‹*series*› لا نِهائيّ, غَيْر مُتَناهٍ

infinitely /'ɪnfɪnətli/ *adv* ‹*superior, preferable*› إلى حَدٍّ بَعيدٍ, للغايةِ

infinitesimal /,ɪnfɪnɪ'tesɪm(ə)l/ *adj* ‹*amount*› مُتَناهٍ في الصِغَرِ \ الدِقّةِ; ‹*chance*› ضَئيل جِدًّا

infinitive /ɪn'fɪnɪtɪv/ *n* مَصْدَر (مَصادِرُ)

infinity /ɪnˈfɪnɪti/ *n* **1** (endless space) لانِهائيّة, لامَحْدوديّة **2** (an infinite point) لانِهاية; **the plains seem to stretch into ~** تَبْدو السُهولُ وَكأنَّها تَمْتَدُّ إلى ما لا نِهايةَ **3** (in maths) لانِهاية

infirm /ɪnˈfəːm/ **A** *n* **the ~** + *v pl* العَجَزة, المُقْعَدونَ; **support for the aged and ~** إعانة للمُسِنّينَ والعَجَزة

B *adj* **1** (weak) ‹*step, appearance, person*› واهِن (وُهُن); **he walked with ~ steps** سارَ بخُطًى واهِنةٍ; **~ and feeble** واهِن وَضَعيف **2** (old use) **~ of purpose** ضَعيف الإرادةِ

infirmary /ɪnˈfəːm(ə)ri/ *n* (*pl* **infirmaries**) **1** (hospital) مُسْتَشْفًى (مُسْتَشْفَيات), مُسْتَوْصَف (مُسْتَوْصَفات) **2** (in school, prison) غُرْفة \ قاعة تَمْريضٍ

infirmity /ɪnˈfəːməti/ *n* (*pl* **infirmities**) عِلّة (عِلَل, عِلّات), عاهة, وَهْن

inflame /ɪnˈfleɪm/ *vt* **1** (to fire up) أَجَّجَ, أَلْهَبَ ‹*passion, resentment*›; ‹*a crowd, audience*› هَيَّجَ **2** (to exacerbate) ‹*a situation, tension*› فاقَمَ **3** (Med) ‹*a sore, tendon*› سَبَّبَ الْتِهاباً

inflamed /ɪnˈfleɪmd/ *adj* ‹*joints, tissue*› مُلْتَهِب

inflammable /ɪnˈflaməb(ə)l/ *adj* ‹*gas, liquid*› قابِل للاشْتِعالِ

inflammation /ɪnfləˈmeɪʃ(ə)n/ *n* الْتِهاب (الْتِهابات)

inflammatory /ɪnˈflamət(ə)ri/ *adj* **1** ‹*speech, remarks*› مُهَيِّج, مُلْهِب (للمَشاعِرِ) **2** ‹*condition, disease*› الْتِهابيّ

inflatable /ɪnˈfleɪtəb(ə)l/ *adj* ‹*mattress, dinghy*› قابِل للنَفْخِ

inflate /ɪnˈfleɪt/ *vt* ‹*a tyre, balloon*› نَفَخَ (a; نَفْخ)

inflation /ɪnˈfleɪʃ(ə)n/ *n* تَضَخُّم (تَضَخُّمات)

inflationary /ɪnˈfleɪʃ(ə)nri/ *adj* (Econ) ‹*pressure, spiral*› تَضَخُّميّ

inflection /ɪnˈflɛkʃ(ə)n/ *n* تَصْريف

inflexible /ɪnˈflɛksɪb(ə)l/ *adj* **1** (regulations, personality) ‹*rule, attitude*› مُتَشَدِّد, مُتَعَنِّت, مُتَصَلِّب **2** (material) ‹*material, plastic*› مُتَصَلِّب, غَيْر مَرِنٍ

inflict /ɪnˈflɪkt/ *vt* ‹*pain, damage*› أَلْحَقَ

influence /ˈɪnflʊəns/ **A** *n* **1** (force, factor) تَأْثير; **to be** *or* **have an ~ on sb/sth** كانَ لَهُ تَأْثيرٌ على شَخْصٍ \ شَيْءٍ; **to be under sb's ~** كانَ واقِعاً تحت تَأْثيرِ شَخْصٍ; **to be under the ~ of drugs** كانَ واقِعاً تحت تَأْثيرِ المُخَدِّرِ **2** [u] (power) نُفوذ, سُلْطة, سَطْوة; **to have ~ with sb** كانَ لَهُ نُفوذٌ عند شَخْصٍ; **to use one's ~** اسْتَخْدَمَ نُفوذَهُ

B *vt* ‹*a child, voter, sb's decision*› أَثَّرَ (على); **don't let him ~ you!** لا تَدَعْهُ يُؤَثِّرُ عَلَيْكَ!; **to be ~d by sb/sth** تَأَثَّرَ بِشَخْصٍ \ بِشَيْءٍ

influential /ˌɪnflʊˈɛnʃ(ə)l/ *adj* ‹*figure*› مُؤَثِّر; ‹*politician*› ذو نُفوذٍ \ سَطْوةٍ; ‹*newspaper*› ذو تَأْثيرٍ \ أَهَمِّيّة

influenza /ɪnflʊˈɛnzə/ *n* إنْفلُوَنْزا

influx /ˈɪnflʌks/ *n* تَدَفُّق (تَدَفُّقات); **an ~ of immigrants/visitors** تَدَفُّق المُهاجِرينَ \ الزوّار

info /ˈɪnfəʊ/ *n* (infml) مَعْلومات

infographic /ˌɪnfə(ʊ)ˈgrafɪk/ *n* مُخَطَّط مَعْلومات بَيانيّ

infomercial /ˌɪnfəʊˈməːʃ(ə)l/ *n* بَرْنامَج دِعائيّ

inform /ɪnˈfɔːm/ **A** *vt* ‹*the police, the public*› أَخْبَرَ, أَعْلَمَ, أَبْلَغَ, أَطْلَعَ; **keep me ~ed of any developments** أَبْقِني على اطِّلاعٍ بأيّةِ تَطَوُّراتٍ

B *vi* **to ~ on sb** وَشى بِشَخْصٍ; **one of the criminals ~ed on the rest of the gang** وَشى أَحَدُ المُجْرِمينَ بِقيّةِ أَفْرادِ العِصابةِ; **the neighbours ~ed on him** بَلَّغَ \ أَبْلَغَ عَنْهُ الجيرانُ

informal /ɪnˈfɔːm(ə)l/ *adj* **1** (natural) ‹*manner, chat*› خالٍ من التَكَلُّفِ \ الرَسْميّاتِ \ الشَكْليّاتِ **2** (unofficial) ‹*meeting, discussion*› غَيْر رَسْميٍّ

informality /ˌɪnfɔːˈmalɪti/ *n* **1** (of a meeting, person) عدم تَكَلُّفٍ \ تَمَسُّكٍ بالرَسْميّاتِ **2** (of a word, phrase) عامّيّة

informally /ɪnˈfɔːm(ə)li/ *adv* **1** (without ceremony) ‹*to dress, chat*› بِشَكْلٍ غَيْرِ رَسْميٍّ **2** (unofficially) ‹*to meet, discuss*› بِشَكْلٍ غَيْرِ رَسْميٍّ

informant /ɪnˈfɔːmənt/ *n* **1** (Journ) مُخْبِر **2** (Law) مُخْبِر

information /ɪnfəˈmeɪʃ(ə)n/ *n* مَعْلومات; **a piece of ~** مَعْلومة; **have you got any ~ on/about the product?** هل لَدَيْكَ أيّةُ مَعْلوماتٍ عن المُنْتَجِ؟

information desk *n* مَكْتَب اسْتِعْلاماتٍ

information pack *n* حُزْمة مَعْلوماتٍ

information superhighway *n* طَريق سَريع للمَعْلوماتِ

information technology *n* تِكْنولوجِيا المَعْلوماتِ

informative /ɪnˈfɔːmətɪv/ *adj* ‹*article, lecture*› غَنيّ بالمَعْلوماتِ

informed /ɪnˈfɔːmd/ *adj* ‹*choice, decision*› مَدْروس; ‹*citizen, consumer*› مُطَّلِع

informer /ɪnˈfɔːmə/ *n* مُخْبِر

infrared /ɪnfrəˈred/ *adj* ‹*camera, radiation*› تحت \ دون الحَمْراءِ

infrastructure /ˈɪnfrəstrʌktʃə/ *n* بِنْية تَحْتِيّة

infrequent /ɪnˈfriːkwənt/ *adj* ‹*visitor, train*› نادِر

infringe /ɪnˈfrɪndʒ/ **A** *vt* خَرَقَ ,اِنْتَهَكَ (i-u; خَرْق) ‹*a law, rights*›

B *vi* **to ~ on sb's privacy** اِنْتَهَكَ خُصوصيّةَ شَخْصٍ

infringement /ɪnˈfrɪndʒmənt/ *n* اِنْتِهاك (اِنْتِهاكات)

infuriate /ɪnˈfjʊərieɪt/ *vt* أَغْضَبَ ,أَحْنَقَ ‹*a colleague, friend*›

infuriating /ɪnˈfjʊərieɪtɪŋ/ *adj* ‹*attitude, behaviour*› مُغْضِب

infuse /ɪnˈfjuːz/ *vt* نَقَعَ (a; نَقْع) ‹*tea, herbs*›

infusion /ɪnˈfjuːʒ(ə)n/ *n* **1** (of cash, aid) ضَخّ **2** (of tea, herbs) نَقيع (أَنْقِعة) **3** (of fluids, a drug) حَقْن (حُقون)

ingenious /ɪnˈdʒiːnɪəs/ *adj* **1** (of a machine, idea) ‹*solution, device*› مُبْدِع, مُبْتَكَر **2** (of a person) ‹*inventor, engineer*› عَبْقَرِيّ (عَباقِرة) عَبْقَرِيّ

ingenuity /ˌɪndʒɪˈnjuːɪti/ *n* إِبْداع

ingenuous /ɪnˈdʒenjʊəs/ *adj* ‹*look, action*› ساذَج (سُذَّج)

ingot /ˈɪŋgət/ *n* سَبيكة (سَبائِكُ)

ingrained /ɪnˈgreɪnd/ *adj* **1** (fixed) ‹*habit, belief*› مُتَجَذِّر

2 (immovable) ‹*dirt, stain*› مُسْتَعْصٍ

ingratiate /ɪnˈgreɪʃieɪt/ *v refl* **to ~ oneself with sb** حَبَّبَ نَفْسَهُ إلى شَخْصٍ

ingratitude /ɪnˈgrætɪtjuːd/ *n* نُكْران الجَميلِ ,جُحود

ingredient /ɪnˈgriːdiənt/ *n* مُكَوِّن (مُكَوِّنات)

inhabit /ɪnˈhæbɪt/ *vt* سَكَنَ (u; سُكْنى ,سَكَن) ‹*a house, town*›

inhabitant /ɪnˈhæbɪt(ə)nt/ *n* ساكِن (سُكّان)

inhale /ɪnˈheɪl/ **A** *vt* اِسْتَنْشَقَ ‹*smoke, fumes*›

B *vi* «smokers, patients» اِسْتَنْشَقَ

inhaler /ɪnˈheɪlə/ *n* جِهاز اِسْتِنْشاقٍ ,بَخّاخ

inherent /ɪnˈhɛrənt/ *adj* ‹*quality, fault*› مُتَأَصِّل; **to be ~ in the design** كانَ جُزْءاً جَوْهَريًّا من التَصْميمِ

inherently /ɪnˈhɪərəntli, ɪnˈhɛrəntli/ *adv* ‹*comic, evil*› بِطَبيعَتِهِ

inherit /ɪnˈhɛrɪt/ *vt* وَرِثَ (i; إِرْث ,وِراثة ,وِرْث ,تُراث) ‹*a fortune, traits*›; **to ~ money from one's grandmother** وَرِثَ مالاً من جَدَّتِهِ

inheritance /ɪnˈhɛrɪt(ə)ns/ *n* إِرْث (مَواريثُ) ميراث ,تَرِكة

inheritance tax *n* ضَريبة الإِرْثِ \ الميراثِ

inhibit /ɪnˈhɪbɪt/ *vt* **1** أَعاقَ ,مَنَعَ (a; مَنْع) ‹*a desire, reaction*›

2 كَبَحَ ,أَعاقَ (a; كَبْح) ‹*growth, development*›

inhibited /ɪnˈhɪbɪtɪd/ *adj* ‹*personality, youth*› مَكْبوت

inhibition /ˌɪnhɪˈbɪʃ(ə)n/ *n* كَبْت

inhibitor /ɪnˈhɪbɪtə/ *n* مُثَبِّط (مُثَبِّطات)

inhospitable /ˌɪnhɒˈspɪtəb(ə)l/ *adj* **1** (unwelcoming) ‹*host, atmosphere*› بارِد **2** (environmentally) ‹*climate, conditions*› مُقْفِر

in-house /ɪnˈhaʊs/ *adj* ‹*staff, training*› داخِلِيّ

inhuman /ɪnˈhjuːmən/ *adj* ‹*act, treatment*› غَيْر إِنْسانِيٍّ

inhumane /ˌɪnhjʊˈmeɪn/ *adj* ‹*treatment*› غَيْر إِنْسانِيٍّ

inhumanity /ˌɪnhjʊˈmanɪti/ *n* (*pl* **inhumanities**) لاإِنْسانِيّة

inimitable /ɪˈnɪmɪtəb(ə)l/ *adj* ‹*voice, style*› فَريد من نَوْعِهِ

initial /ɪˈnɪʃ(ə)l/ **A** *adj* ‹*reaction, reticence*› أَوَّلِيّ

B *n* [حَرْف أَوَّل من اسْمٍ \ كَلِمةٍ]

C *vt* (BrE, **-ll-** AmE, **-l-**) [وَقَّعَ بالأَحْرُفِ الأولى من اسْمِهِ] ‹*a contract, document*›

initially /ɪˈnɪʃ(ə)li/ *adv* في البِدايةِ ,أَوَّلَ الأَمْرِ ,في بادِئِ الأَمْرِ

initiate /ɪˈnɪʃieɪt/ *vt* **1** (to start) بَدَأَ (ب), باشَرَ (a; بَدْء) ‹*a plan, talks*›; **to ~ proceedings against sb** بَدَأَ الإِجْراءاتِ القَضائيّةَ ضِدَّ شَخْصٍ **2** (in rituals) [أَدْخَلَ إلى جَماعةٍ مُغْلَقةٍ من خِلالِ أَداءِ طُقوسٍ] ‹*a recruit, member*›

initiation /ɪˌnɪʃɪˈeɪʃ(ə)n/ *n* **1** (of a process, job) بَدْء (بُدوء ,أَبْداء) **2** (into a sect, group) [طُقوس الاحْتِفالِ بِقُبولِ شَخْصٍ في جَمْعِيّةٍ أو طائِفةٍ]

initiative /ɪˈnɪʃətɪv/ *n* **1** (strategy) تَحَرُّك ,مُبادَرة (تَحَرُّكات); **a multinational peace ~** مُبادَرة سَلامٍ دُوَلِيّة **2** (independent ability) مُبادَرة; **she did it on her own ~** فَعَلَتْهُ من تِلْقاءِ نَفْسِها; **you need to use your ~** عَلَيْكَ أَنْ تُبادِرَ \ تَأْخُذَ زِمامَ المُبادَرةِ; **to take the ~** أَخَذَ زِمامَ المُبادَرةِ بِنَفْسِكَ

inject /ɪnˈdʒɛkt/ *vt* حَقَنَ (i-u; حَقْن) ‹*a drug, a dose*›; **to ~ oneself with insulin** حَقَنَ نَفْسَهُ بالأَنسولين

injection /ɪnˈdʒɛkʃ(ə)n/ *n* حُقْنة (حُقَن); **to give sb an ~** أَعْطى شَخْصاً حُقْنةً

injunction /ɪnˈdʒʌŋkʃ(ə)n/ *n* (instruction, order) أَمْر قَضائيّ

injure /ˈɪndʒə/ *vt* **1** جَرَحَ (a; جَرْح) ‹*a soldier, passenger*›; **he ~d his arm** جَرَحَ ذِراعَهُ **2** جَرَحَ (a; جَرْح) ‹*feelings*›; أَساءَ (إلى) ‹*one's reputation*›

injured /ˈɪndʒəd/ **A** *n* (**the injured** *n pl*) الجَرْحى

B *adj* **1** (harmed) ‹*patient, knee*› مَجْروح **2** (offended) ‹*pride, feelings*› مَجْروح; **I am the ~ party** أنا الطَرَفُ المُتَضَرِّرُ

injurious /ɪnˈdʒʊərɪəs/ *adj* (fml) ضارّ ‹*effect, influence*›

injury /ˈɪndʒ(ə)ri/ *n* (*pl* **injuries**) جُرْح (جُروح, جِراح); **a head injury** جُرْح \ إصابة في الرَأْسِ

injury time *n* الوَقْت الضائِع

injustice /ɪnˈdʒʌstɪs/ *n* **1** [u] (lack of fairness) انْعِدام \ ظُلْم غِياب العَدالةِ **2** (an unfair act) ظُلْم, إجْحاف; **to do sb an ~** ظَلَمَ شَخْصاً

ink /ɪŋk/ *n* حِبْر

inkjet printer /ˌɪŋkdʒɛt ˈprɪntə/ *n* طابِعة نافِثة للحِبْرِ

inkling /ˈɪŋklɪŋ/ *n* (feeling) حَدْس; (suspicion) ظَنّ (ظُنون), اعْتِقاد (اعْتِقادات); (idea) فِكْرة (فِكَر); **I had an ~ that all was not well** كانَ حَدْسي يَقولُ إنّ الأُمورَ لم تَكُنْ على ما يُرامُ; **I had no ~ of what was happening** لم تَكُنْ لَدَيَّ أَدْنى فِكْرةٍ عَمّا كانَ يَجْري

inkwell /ˈɪŋkwɛl/ *n* مِحْبَرة (مَحابِرُ), دَواة (دَوَيات, دُوِيّ)

inlaid /ɪnˈleɪd/ **A** *past tense, past participle* ▸ **inlay**

B *adj* ‹*jewellery, box*› مُرَصَّع, مُطَعَّم

inland A /ˈɪnlənd/ *adj* ‹*town, waterway*› داخِليّ

B /ɪnˈland/ *adv* ‹*to travel*› إلى الداخِلِ; ‹*to lie*› في الداخِلِ

Inland Revenue *n* ▸ **HMRC**

in-laws /ˈɪnlɔːz/ *n pl* حَم وَحَماة

inlay A /ɪnˈleɪ/ *vt* (*past tense, past participle* **inlaid**) رَصَّعَ ‹*jewellery, a box*›

B /ˈɪnleɪ/ *n* رَصيعة (رَصائِعُ)

inlet /ˈɪnlɛt/ *n* **1** (of the sea, a river) شَرْم (شُروم) **2** (for fuel, air) مَنْفَذ (مَنافِذُ)

inmate /ˈɪnmeɪt/ *n* نَزيل (نُزَلاءُ)

inmost /ˈɪnməʊst/ *adj* ▸ **innermost**

inn /ɪn/ *n* نُزُل (أَنْزال)

innards /ˈɪnədz/ *n pl* أَحْشاء

innate /ɪˈneɪt/ *adj* ‹*quality, gift*› فِطْريّ

inner /ˈɪnə/ *adj* **1** (internal) ‹*room, layer*› داخِليّ **2** (private) ‹*workings, thoughts*› داخِليّ

inner city A *n* (**the inner city**) مَرْكَز \ وَسَط المَدينةِ;

B (**inner-city**) *adj before n* ‹*problems, school*› في مَرْكَزِ المَدينةِ

inner ear *n* أُذُن داخِلِيّة

innermost /ˈɪnəməʊst/ *adj* **1** (furthest in) ‹*part, chamber*› الأَعْمَق **2** (most private) ‹*fears, thoughts*› عَميق

inner tube *n* إطار داخِليّ

inning /ˈɪnɪŋ/ *n* (AmE) (in baseball) شَوْط (أَشْواط)

innings /ˈɪnɪŋz/ *n* (*pl* **innings**) (in cricket, baseball) شَوْط (أَشْواط)

Idiom **he has had a good innings** ≈ أَخَذَ نَصيبَهُ (في شَيْءٍ)

innkeeper /ˈɪnkiːpə/ *n* صاحِب نُزُلٍ

innocence /ˈɪnəs(ə)ns/ *n* **1** (lack of guilt) بَراءة **2** (guilelessness) بَراءة; **she made the remark in all ~** قالَت التَعْليقَ بِكُلِّ بَراءةٍ

innocent /ˈɪnəs(ə)nt/ *adj* ‹*civilian, man*› بَريء (أَبْرياءُ); **he was found ~ of the charges** ظَهَرَتْ بَراءَتُهُ من التُهَمِ

innocuous /ɪˈnɒkjʊəs/ *adj* **1** (inoffensive) ‹*remark, statement*› بَريء (أَبْرياءُ) **2** (harmless) ‹*substance*› غَيْر ضارٍّ

innovation /ˌɪnəˈveɪʃ(ə)n/ *n* **1** [u] (invention of new ideas) ابْتِكار **2** (new idea) ابْتِكار (ابْتِكارات)

innovative /ˈɪnəvətɪv/ *adj* ‹*approach, product*› مُبْتَكَر

innovator /ˈɪnəveɪtə/ *n* مُبْتَكِر

innuendo /ˌɪnjʊˈɛndəʊ/ *n* (*pl* **innuendos** or **innuendoes**) تَلْميح (تَلْميحات, تَلاميحُ)

innumerable /ɪˈnjuːm(ə)rəb(ə)l/ *adj* ‹*occasions, examples*› لا يُعَدُّ, لا يُحْصى

inoculate /ɪ'nɒkjʊleɪt/ *vt* طَعَّمَ, لَقَّحَ ‹*a patient, child*›; **to ~ sb against yellow fever** لَقَّحَ شَخْصاً ضدّ الحُمّى الصَفْراء

inoculation /ɪˌnɒkjʊ'leɪʃ(ə)n/ *n* تَلْقيح; **the ~ of children against polio** تَلْقيح الأَطْفالِ ضدّ شَلَلِ الأَطْفالِ

inoffensive /ɪnə'fɛnsɪv/ *adj* ‹*manner, appearance*› مَقْبول

inordinate /ɪ'nɔːdɪnət/ *adj* ‹*amount, delay*› فاحِش, مُفْرِط

inorganic /ɪnɔː'ganɪk/ *adj* ‹*fertiliser, compound*› لاعُضْويّ

inpatient /'ɪnpeɪʃ(ə)nt/ *n* مَريض راقِد

input /'ɪnpʊt/ **A** *n* **1** (contribution) مُساهَمة **2** (of data) إدْخال **3** (of electricity) مُدْخَل

B *vt* (*present participle* **-tt-**; *past tense, past participle* **input** or **inputted**) أَدْخَلَ ‹*the data, code*›

inquest /'ɪnkwɛst/ *n* تَحْقيق (تَحْقيقات); **they held an ~ into his death** أَجْروا تَحْقيقاً في مَوْتِهِ

inquire /ɪn'kwʌɪə/ ▸ **enquire**

inquiring /ɪn'kwʌɪrɪŋ/ *adj* ‹*look, voice*› فاحِص; **to have an ~ mind** كانَ مُحِبًّا للاسْتِطْلاعِ

inquiry /ɪn'kwʌɪri/ *n* (*pl* **inquiries**) ▸ **enquiry**

inquisition /ɪŋkwɪ'zɪʃ(ə)n/ **A** *n* (investigation) تَحْقيق (تَحْقيقات), اسْتِقْصاء

B (**the Inquisition**) *pr n* (Hist, Rel_Chr) مَحاكِم التَفْتيشِ

inquisitive /ɪn'kwɪzɪtɪv/ *adj* **1** (inquiring) ‹*mind, nature*› مُتَحَرٍّ **2** (prying) ‹*neighbour, colleague*› فُضوليّ

inroads /'ɪnrəʊdz/ *n pl* **to make ~ into a market** اسْتَحْوَذَ على جُزْءٍ من سوقٍ; **to make ~ into a task** حَقَّقَ تَقَدُّماً في مُهِمّةٍ

insane /ɪn'seɪn/ *adj* **1** (foolish) ‹*idea, desire*› مَجْنون **2** (mad) ‹*patient, murderer*› مَجْنون (مَجانينُ)

insanitary /ɪn'sanɪt(ə)ri/ *adj* ‹*conditions, lodgings*› غَيْر صِحّيّ, وَسِخ, قَذِر

insanity /ɪn'sanəti/ *n* جُنون

insatiable /ɪn'seɪʃəb(ə)l/ *adj* ‹*appetite, hunger*› لا يُشْبَعُ

inscribe /ɪn'skrʌɪb/ *vt* نَقَشَ (u; نَقْش), حَفَرَ (i; حَفْر); **to ~ sth with a name/verse** نَقَشَ اسْماً \ آيةً على شَيْءٍ; **to ~ sth on a tombstone/monument** نَقَشَ شَيْئاً على نَصْبٍ \ مَعْلَمٍ

inscription /ɪn'skrɪpʃ(ə)n/ *n* نَقْش (نُقوش), حَفْر

insect /'ɪnsɛkt/ *n* حَشَرة

insecticide /ɪn'sɛktɪsʌɪd/ *n* مُبيد حَشَراتٍ

insectivore /ɪn'sɛktɪvɔː/ *n* آكِل حَشَراتٍ

insect repellent *n* طارِد حَشَراتٍ

insecure /ˌɪnsɪ'kjʊə/ *adj* **1** (not confident) ‹*teenager, character*› غَيْر واثِقٍ بِنَفْسِهِ **2** (not firmly fixed) ‹*window*› غَيْر مُقْفَلٍ بِإحْكامٍ; ‹*network*› غَيْر مُؤَمَّنٍ **3** (not reliable) ‹*job*› غَيْر مُسْتَقِرٍّ

insecurity /ɪnsɪ'kjʊərəti/ *n* (*pl* **insecurities**) **1** (anxiety) عَدَم الثِقةِ بالنَفْسِ **2** (of a situation) عَدَم الاسْتِقْرارِ

inseminate /ɪn'sɛmɪneɪt/ *vt* (Med) لَقَّحَ ‹*a horse, woman*›

insemination /ɪnsɛmɪ'neɪʃ(ə)n/ *n* تَلْقيح, تَخْصيب

insensible /ɪn'sɛnsɪb(ə)l/ *adj* **1** (indifferent) **to be ~ to criticism** لم يَتَأَثَّرْ بالنَقْدِ **2** (unconscious) غائب عن الوَعْيِ

insensitive /ɪn'sɛnsɪtɪv/ *adj* **1** (tactless) ‹*remark, behaviour*› غَيْر مُبالٍ **2** (lacking sensation) ‹*skin, reaction*› عَديم \ فاقِد الإحْساسِ

insensitivity /ɪnsɛnsə'tɪvəti/ *n* قَسْوة, قِلّة الإحْساسِ

inseparable /ɪn'sɛp(ə)rəb(ə)l/ *adj* ‹*twins, friends*› لا يَتَفارَقانِ, لا يُمْكِنُ الفَصْلُ بَيْنَهُما

insert /ɪn'səːt/ *vt* **1** أَدْخَلَ ‹*a coin, credit card*›; **~ your card in the slot** أَدْخِلْ بِطاقَتَكَ في الفَتْحةِ **2** أَدْخَلَ ‹*a tube, needle*› **3** ضَمَّنَ, أَدْخَلَ ‹*a clause, a paragraph*›

insertion /ɪn'səːʃ(ə)n/ *n* **1** [u] (action) إدْخال **2** (flier, leaflet) مُلْحَق (مُلْحَقات, مَلاحِقُ)

inshallah /ɪn'ʃalə/ *excl* إنْ شاءَ اللهُ

inshore /ɪn'ʃɔː/ **A** *adj* ‹*fishing, exploration*› [قَريب من الساحِلِ]

B *adv* ‹*to swim, drift*› إلى الساحِلِ

inside **A** /'ɪnsʌɪd/ *n* **1** (interior) داخِل; **the ~ of the house is in good order** المَنْزِلُ في حالةٍ جَيِّدةٍ من الداخِلِ; **it's soft on the ~** إنَّهُ طَرِيٌّ من الداخِلِ; **you can only open the door from the ~** يُمْكِنُكَ فَتْحُ البابِ فَقَطْ من الداخِلِ **2** (Sport, Transp) **to be on the ~** «runner, horse» كانَ في الحارة الداخِلِيّةِ; «car, truck» كانَ في الحارة اليُمْنى; **to overtake on the ~** تَجاوَزَ من اليَمينِ **3** (infml) (prison) **life on the ~** الحَياة داخِلَ السِجْنِ

B (**insides**) /ɪn'sʌɪdz/ *n pl* (intestines) أَحْشاء

C /ˈɪnsʌɪd/ *adj before n* **1** (interior) ‹*angle, measurement, pocket*› داخِليّ; **is there an ~ toilet?** هل هُناكَ حَمّامٌ داخِليٌّ؟ **2** (first-hand) ‹*information*› مُسْتَقًى من مَصادِرَ مُقَرَّبةٍ \ مُطَّلِعةٍ; ‹*source*› مُطَّلِع ,مُقَرَّب; **the ~ story** القِصّة الحَقيقيّة **3** (within an organization) **an ~ job** عَمَليّة من الداخِلِ (جَريمة يَرْتَكِبُها شَخْصٌ من داخِلِ المُنَظَّمةِ) **4** **the ~ lane** (of a road) الحارة اليُمْنى; (of an athletics track) الحارة الداخِليّة \ الأولى

D /ɪnˈsʌɪd/ *prep* (also **inside of** AmE) **1** (in the interior of) داخِلَ; **~ the box/car** داخِلَ الصُنْدوقِ \ السَيّارةِ; **to be ~ the house/building** كانَ داخِلَ البَيْتِ \ المَبْنى **2** (within) داخِلَ ‹*a city, harbour, prison*›; **it's just ~ the town** هو داخِلَ المَدينة بالضَبْطِ; **you're not allowed ~ his office** لَيْسَ مَسْموحاً لكَ الدُخولُ إلى مَكْتَبِهِ **3** (under) **~ (of) an hour/a year** خلال ساعةٍ \ سَنةٍ; **to finish ~ the time limit** انْتَهى خلال الوَقْتِ المُحَدَّدِ; **to be ~ the world record** كَسَرَ الرَقْمَ القِياسيَّ

E /ɪnˈsʌɪd/ *adv* **1** (indoors) ‹*to wait, play*› بالداخِلِ; **she's ~** هي بالداخِلِ; **to look ~** نَظَرَ بالداخِلِ; **to go** *or* **come ~** دَخَلَ (u; دُخول); **to bring the chairs/shopping ~** أَدْخَلَ الكَراسيَّ \ المُشْتَرَياتِ **2** (BrE) (infml) (in prison) **to be ~** كانَ داخِلَ \ في السِجْنِ

F (**inside out**) /ˈɪnsʌɪd,aʊt/ *adv phr* **your sweater is ~ out** كَنْزَتُكَ مَقلوبةٌ; **to turn sth ~ out** (to reverse) قَلَبَ شَيْئاً ظَهْراً لِبَطْنٍ ‹*your bag, coat*›; (to ransack) قَلَبَ شَيْئاً رَأْساً على عَقِبٍ ‹*a room, house*›; **to know a subject ~ out** عَرَفَ كُلَّ صَغيرةٍ وكَبيرةٍ عن مَوْضوعٍ

inside leg *n* [طول السِرْوالِ من مِنْطَقةِ ما بين الفَخِذَيْنِ إلى الكاحِلِ]

insider /ɪnˈsʌɪdə/ *n* [شَخْص مُطَّلِع على بَواطِنِ الأُمور]

insider dealing, **insider trading** *n* التَداوُل بِناءً على مَعْلوماتٍ داخِليّةٍ

insidious /ɪnˈsɪdɪəs/ *adj* ‹*trend, disease*› غادِر

insight /ˈɪnsʌɪt/ *n* **1** [u] (intuition) فَهْم ,إدْراك ,بَصيرة **2** (glimpse, understanding) فَهْم (أَفْهام); **to gain an ~ into a problem** تَعَمَّقَ في فَهْمِ مُشْكِلةٍ

insightful /ˈɪnsʌɪtfʊl/ *adj* ‹*analysis*› دَقيق ,عَميق; ‹*thinker*› بَصير (بُصَراءُ), نافِذ البَصيرةِ

insignia /ɪnˈsɪgnɪə/ *n pl* شارة

insignificant /ɪnsɪgˈnɪfɪk(ə)nt/ *adj* ‹*cost, detail*› تافِه (تَوافِهُ)

insincere /ɪnsɪnˈsɪə/ *adj* ‹*smile, compliment*› غَيْر صادِقٍ

insincerity /ɪnsɪnˈserəti/ *n* عَدَم الصِدْقِ

insinuate /ɪnˈsɪnjʊeɪt/ *vt* لَمَّحَ (إلى); **he ~d that she was a liar/was lying** لَمَّحَ إلى أنّها تَكْذِبُ

insinuation /ɪnsɪnjʊˈeɪʃ(ə)n/ *n* تَلْميح (تَلْميحات ,تَلاميحُ)

insipid /ɪnˈsɪpɪd/ *adj* **1** ‹*food*› لا طَعْمَ لَهُ ,عَديم المَذاقِ; ‹*taste*› غَيْر طَيِّبٍ **2** ‹*novel*› مُمِلّ; ‹*colour*› باهِت

insist /ɪnˈsɪst/ **A** *vt* **1** (to demand) أَصَرَّ (على); **she ~ed that they call the manager** أَصَرَّتْ على أنْ يُنادوا المُديرَ **2** (to maintain) أَصَرَّ (على); **they ~ed that it was true** أَصَروا على أنَّهُ كانَ صَحيحاً

B *vi* أَصَرَّ (على); **to ~ on doing sth** أَصَرّ على فِعْلِ شَيْءٍ

insistence /ɪnˈsɪst(ə)ns/ *n* إصْرار

insistent /ɪnˈsɪst(ə)nt/ *adj* **1** (unyielding) ‹*tone, manner*› مُصِرّ; **he was ~ that we come** أَصَرَّ على أنْ نأتِيَ **2** (repetitive) ‹*noise, rhythm*› مُسْتَمِرّ ,بِلا انْقِطاعٍ

insofar /ɪnsəʊˈfɑː/ *phr* **~ as** على قَدْرِ ما

insole /ˈɪnsəʊl/ *n* نَعْل (mf; نِعال ,أَنْعُل)

insolence /ˈɪnsələns/ *n* وَقاحة

insolent /ˈɪnsələnt/ *adj* ‹*remark, manner*› وَقِح (وُقُح)

insoluble /ɪnˈsɒljʊb(ə)l/ *adj* **1** ‹*problem, conflict*› غَيْر قابِلٍ للحَلِّ **2** ‹*compound, chemical, fibre*› غَيْر قابِلٍ للذَوَبانِ

insolvent /ɪnˈsɒlv(ə)nt/ *adj* ‹*company, debtor*› مُفْلِس (مَفاليسُ)

insomnia /ɪnˈsɒmnɪə/ *n* أَرَق; **she suffers from ~** تُعاني من الأَرَقِ

insomniac /ɪnˈsɒmniak/ **A** *n* [شَخْص يُعاني من الأَرَقِ]

B *adj* ‹*patient*› مُؤَرَّق

inspect /ɪnˈspɛkt/ *vt* **1** (to look closely at) فَحَصَ (a; فَحْص) ‹*a car, camera*› **2** (to examine) فَحَصَ (a; فَحْص) ‹*a passport*›; تَفَقَّدَ ,فَتَّشَ ‹*a school*› **3** (to scrutinize officially) تَفَقَّدَ ‹*a soldier, parade*›

inspection /ɪnˈspɛkʃ(ə)n/ *n* **1** (scrutiny) فَحْص (فُحوص) **2** (official examination) فَحْص (فُحوص) **3** (of troops) تَفَقُّد

inspector /ɪnˈspɛktə/ *n* **1** (official) مُفَتِّش **2** (BrE) (on a bus, train) مُحَصِّل ,مُفَتِّش **3** (AmE) (of buildings) مُراقِب أَبْنِيةٍ, مُفَتِّش **4** (police officer) فاحِص ,مُعايِن

inspiration /ɪnspɪˈreɪʃ(ə)n/ *n* **1** (stimulation of the mind) إلْهام **2** (sb or sth that inspires) مَصْدَر إلْهامٍ ,مُلْهِم ,(إلْهامات) إلْهام

inspirational /ɪnspɪˈreɪʃ(ə)n(ə)l/ *adj* ‹*captain, speech*› مُلْهِم

inspire /ɪnˈspʌɪə/ *vt* **1** (to motivate) أَلْهَمَ ‹*an artist, a composer*›; **what ~d you to do that?** ما الّذي أوْحى إلَيْكَ \ أَلْهَمَكَ أنْ تَفْعَلَ ذلكَ؟ **2** (to instil) أَلْهَمَ ‹*confidence, courage*›

inspired /ɪnˈspʌɪəd/ *adj* ‹*idea, performance*› مُلْهَم

inspiring /ɪnˈspʌɪərɪŋ/ *adj* ‹*leader, speech*› مُلْهِم

instability /ɪnstəˈbɪlɪti/ *n* (*pl* **instabilities**) عَدَم استِقْرار

install, **instal** (BrE) /ɪnˈstɔːl/ *vt* (**-ll-**) **1** رَكَّبَ ‹*equipment*› **2** نَصَّبَ ‹*software*› **3** نَصَّبَ ‹*an MP, a governor*›

installation /ɪnstəˈleɪʃ(ə)n/ *n* **1** (of a device) تَرْكيب **2** (of software, officials) تَنْصيب

instalment (BrE), **installment** (AmE) /ɪnˈstɔːlmənt/ *n* **1** (part payment) (أقْساط) قِسْط; **to pay by ~s** دَفَعَ بالتَّقْسيط **2** (of a series) (حَلَقات ,حَلَق) حَلْقة

instance /ˈɪnst(ə)ns/ *n* **1** (example) (مُثُل ,أَمْثِلة) مِثال; **for ~** على سَبيلِ المِثالِ **2** (case) حالة; **in this ~** في هذه الحالةِ

instant /ˈɪnst(ə)nt/ **A** *adj* **1** (immediate) ‹*access, effect*› فَوْريّ **2** (prepared quickly) ‹*coffee, soup*› سَريع ,فَوريّ **B** *n* **1** (precise moment) (لَحَظات) لَحْظة **2** (short time) بُرْهة (بُرَه ,بُراهات) **3** (infml) (coffee) قَهْوة فَوْريّة

instantaneous /ɪnst(ə)nˈteɪnɪəs/ *adj* ‹*communication, response*› لَحْظيّ ,فَوْريّ

instant camera *n* كاميرا فَوْريّة

instantly /ˈɪnst(ə)ntli/ *adv* ‹*to die, respond*› على الفَوْرِ ,فَوْراً

instant replay *n* (AmE) إعادة (بالتَّصْويرِ البَطيءِ)

instead /ɪnˈstɛd/ **A** *adv* بَدَلاً عَنْهُ; **I couldn't go, so she went ~** لم أَسْتَطِعِ الذهابَ، فَذَهَبَتْ هي بَدَلاً عَنّي **B** (**instead of**) *phr* بَدَلاً من

instep /ˈɪnstɛp/ *n* مُشْط القَدَمِ

instigate /ˈɪnstɪgeɪt/ *vt* بادَرَ (ب) ‹*an attack, violence*›

instigation /ɪnstɪˈgeɪʃ(ə)n/ *n* **to do sth at sb's ~** فَعَلَ شَيْئاً بِتَحْريضِ شَخْصٍ

instil (BrE), **instill** (AmE) /ɪnˈstɪl/ *vt* (**-ll-**) غَرَسَ (i; غَرْس ,غِراسة), رَسَّخَ ‹*a habit, an attitude*›; **to ~ sth into sb** غَرَسَ شَيْئاً في شَخْصٍ

instinct /ˈɪnstɪŋkt/ *n* **1** (natural tendency) (غَرائِزُ) غَريزة **2** (natural ability) (غَرائِزُ) غَريزة

instinctive /ɪnˈstɪŋktɪv/ *adj* ‹*dislike, reaction*› غَريزيّ

institute /ˈɪnstɪtjuːt/ **A** *n* مُؤَسَّسة **B** *vt* (fml) فَتَحَ (a; فَتْح) ‹*an inquiry*›; اسْتَحْدَثَ ‹*a rule*›

institution /ɪnstɪˈtjuːʃ(ə)n/ *n* **1** (established practice) مُؤَسَّسة **2** (organization) مُؤَسَّسة **3** (hospital, asylum, home) مُؤَسَّسة

institutional /ɪnstɪˈtjuːʃ(ə)n(ə)l/ *adj* **1** ‹*structure, reform*› تَأْسيسيّ ,مُؤَسَّسيّ **2** ‹*food, life*› مُؤَسَّسيّ **3** (Comm) ‹*investor, buying*› مُؤَسَّسيّ

institutionalize, **-ise** (BrE) /ɪnstɪˈtjuːʃ(ə)nəlʌɪz/ *vt* **1** (to establish officially) أَضْفى الطابَعَ المُؤَسَّسيّ ,وَطَّدَ ,أَرْسى ‹*an event, a practice*› **2** (to place in care) وَضَعَ في مُؤَسَّسةِ [رِعايةٍ] ‹*a patient, prisoner*›

instruct /ɪnˈstrʌkt/ *vt* **1** (to command) أَمَرَ (u; أَمْر) ‹*an employee, a customer*›; **to ~ sb to do sth** أَمَرَ شَخْصاً بأنْ يَقومَ بِشَيْءٍ **2** (fml) (to teach) أَرْشَدَ ,عَلَّمَ ‹*a student, learner*›; **to ~ sb in sth** عَلَّمَ شَخْصاً شَيْئاً

instruction /ɪnˈstrʌkʃ(ə)n/ *n* **1** (order) (أَوامِرُ) أَمْر ,إرْشاد **2** [U] (تَوْجيهات) تَوْجيه; **~s for use** تَعْليمات للاسْتِخْدامِ **3** (education) تَدْريس ,تَعْليم

instructional /ɪnˈstrʌkʃ(ə)n(ə)l/ *adj* ‹*booklet, video*› تَعْليميّ

instruction book *n* كِتاب تَعْليماتٍ \ إرْشاداتٍ

instructive /ɪnˈstrʌktɪv/ *adj* ‹*conversation, example, book*› مُفيد, غَنيّ بالمَعْلوماتِ

instructor /ɪnˈstrʌktə/ *n* **1** (in sports, driving) مُدَرِّب ,مُعَلِّم; **a driving ~** مُدَرِّب قِيادةٍ **2** (AmE) (at college) مُعَلِّم (في جامِعةٍ أو كُلِّيّةٍ أَقَلّ رُتْبةً من أُسْتاذٍ مُساعِدٍ)

instrument /ˈɪnstrʊmənt/ *n* **1** (tool) (أَدَوات) أَداة ,آلة **2** (musical) آلة موسيقيّة; **to play an ~** عَزَفَ على آلةٍ موسيقيّةٍ

3 (measuring device) مِقْياس (مَقاييسُ), جِهاز قِياسٍ; **to fly on ~s** [قادَ الطائِرةَ مُسْتَعيناً بِأَجْهِزةِ قِياسٍ]

instrumental /ɪnstrʊˈmɛnt(ə)l/ *adj* 1 ‹*action, figure*› فَعّال, ذو أَثَرٍ; **to be ~ in sth** كانَ أَداةً فَعّالةً في شَيْءٍ 2 ‹*music, accompaniment*› آلِيّ

instrumentalist /ɪnstrəˈmɛntəlɪst/ *n* عازِف

instrument panel *n* لَوْحة أَجْهِزة القِياسِ

insubordination /ˌɪnsəˌbɔːdɪˈneɪʃ(ə)n/ *n* تَمَرُّد, عِصْيان

insubstantial /ɪnsəbˈstanʃ(ə)l/ *adj* 1 (small) ‹*amount*› قَليل, تافِه; ‹*meal*› صَغير 2 (flimsy) ‹*building, structure*› واهٍ (وُهاة), مُهَلْهَل 3 (weak) ‹*evidence, accusation*› ضَعيف, واهٍ

insufferable /ɪnˈsʌf(ə)rəb(ə)l/ *adj* 1 ‹*liar, child*› كَريه, ثَقيل الدَمِ \ الظِلِّ, مُسْخِط 2 ‹*heat, conditions*› غَيْر مُحْتَمَلٍ \ مُطاق

insufficient /ɪnsəˈfɪʃ(ə)nt/ *adj* ‹*evidence, resources*› غَيْر كافٍ

insular /ˈɪnsjʊlə/ *adj* ‹*outlook, lifestyle*› مَعْزول, مُنْفَصِل, ضَيِّق الأُفُقِ

insulate /ˈɪnsjʊleɪt/ *vt* عَزَلَ (i; عَزْل) ‹*a roof, room*›

insulation /ɪnsjʊˈleɪʃ(ə)n/ *n* 1 [u] (action of insulating) عَزْل 2 (insulating material) مادّة عازِلة

insulin /ˈɪnsjʊlɪn/ *n* إِنْسولين

insult A /ɪnˈsʌlt/ *vt* أَهانَ ‹*a stranger, memory*› B /ˈɪnsʌlt/ *n* إِهانة, شَتيمة (شَتائِمُ)

insulting /ɪnˈsʌltɪŋ/ *adj* ‹*remarks, language*› مُهين, مُذِلّ, جارِح

insurance /ɪnˈʃʊərəns/ *n* تَأْمين (تَأْمينات); **to take out ~ against loss of income** أَمَّنَ ضِدَّ فُقْدانِ الدَخْلِ

insurance agent *n* وَكيل تَأْمينٍ

insurance broker *n* سِمْسار تَأْمينٍ

insurance policy *n* وَثيقة \ بوليصة تَأْمينٍ

insure /ɪnˈʃɔː/ *vt* أَمَّنَ ‹*property, a loan*›; **the house is ~d against fire** البَيْتُ مُؤَمَّنٌ ضِدَّ الحَريق

insurer /ɪnˈʃʊərə/ *n* مُؤَمِّن, شَرِكة تَأْمينٍ

insurgent /ɪnˈsəːdʒ(ə)nt/ *n, adj* ثائِر (ثُوّار, ثائِرونَ), مُتَمَرِّد

insurmountable /ˌɪnsəˈmaʊntəb(ə)l/ *adj* ‹*obstacle, problem*› مَنيع, تَعْجيزِيّ, مُسْتَعْصٍ

insurrection /ˌɪnsəˈrɛkʃ(ə)n/ *n* اِنْتِفاضة, فِتْنة (فِتَن), تَمَرُّد

intact /ɪnˈtakt/ *adj* ‹*object, building*› سَليم, غَيْر مُصابٍ بِأَذًى

intake /ˈɪnteɪk/ *n* 1 (quantity taken in) مَأْخوذ 2 [u] (act of taking sth in) أَخْذ 3 (inlet) مَدْخَل (مَداخِلُ), مَنْفَذ (مَنافِذُ), مَسْرَب

intangible /ɪnˈtandʒɪb(ə)l/ *adj* 1 (unable to be touched) ‹*object, goods*› مَعْنَوِيّ, غَيْر مَحْسوسٍ \ مَلْموسٍ 2 (undefinable) ‹*concept, quality*› غامِض (غَوامِضُ), غَيْر مُدْرَكٍ \ مُحَدَّدٍ \ قابِلٍ للتَعْريف

integral /ˈɪntɪɡrəl/ *adj* 1 (intrinsic) ‹*member, part*› جَوْهَرِيّ, أَساسِيّ, حَيَوِيّ 2 (built-in) ‹*lock, fitting*› مُدْمَج, داخِلِيّ

integrate /ˈɪntɪɡreɪt/ A *vt* دَمَجَ (u; دَمْج), ضَمَّ (u; ضَمّ), وَحَّدَ ‹*systems, technology*› B *vi* «immigrants, newcomers» اِنْدَمَجَ

integrated /ˈɪntɪɡreɪtɪd/ *adj* 1 ‹*system, solution*› مُتَكامِل, مُنْدَمِج 2 ‹*education, school*› مُدْمَج, مُنْدَمِج, مُتَكامِل

integrated circuit *n* دائِرة مُتَكامِلة

integration /ɪntɪˈɡreɪʃ(ə)n/ *n* اِنْدماج, تَكامُل, تَوْحيد, دَمْج

integrity /ɪnˈtɛɡrɪti/ *n* نَزاهة, اِسْتِقامة, أَمانة

intellect /ˈɪntəlɛkt/ *n* عَقْل (عُقول), ذِهْن (أَذْهان), قُوّة \ قُدْرة عَقْلِيّة

intellectual /ˌɪntəˈlɛktʃʊəl/ A *adj* فِكْرِيّ, عَقْلِيّ B *n* مُثَقَّف, مُفَكِّر

intellectually /ɪntəˈlɛktʃʊəli/ *adv* ‹*to write, discuss*› عَقْلِيًّا, ذِهْنِيًّا

intelligence /ɪnˈtɛlɪdʒ(ə)ns/ *n* 1 (mental capacity) ذَكاء, فِطْنة (فِطَن), إِدْراك 2 (information) اِسْتِخْبارات, مُخابَرات; **secret ~** مُخابَرات سِرِّيّة \ اِسْتِخْبارات 3 (secret service) إدارة الاسْتِخْبارات \ المُخابَراتِ; **the US Central I~ Agency** وَكالة المُخابَراتِ المَرْكَزِيّةِ الأَمْرِيكيّة

intelligent /ɪnˈtɛlɪdʒ(ə)nt/ *adj* ‹*person, conversation*› ذَكِيّ (أَذْكِياءُ), نَبيه (نُبَهاءُ)

intelligentsia /ɪnˌtɛlɪˈdʒɛntsɪə/ *n* **the ~** أَهْل الفِكْرِ, النُخْبة, المُثَقَّفة, المُثَقَّفينَ \ طَبَقة المُتَعَلِّمين

intelligible /ɪnˈtɛlɪdʒɪb(ə)l/ *adj* ‹*language, speech*› واضِح, جَلِيّ, بَيِّن, مَفْهوم

intemperate /ɪnˈtɛmp(ə)rət/ *adj* **1** (fml) (unrestrained) ‹*remark, language*› غَيْر مُقَيَّد, مُفْرِط, مُسْرِف **2** (extreme) ‹*climate*› غَيْر مُعْتَدِل, صارِم

intend /ɪnˈtɛnd/ *vt* **1** قَصَدَ (i; قَصْد) ‹*offence, harm*›; **no offence ~ed** لم أَقْصِدْ أيَّ إهانةٍ; **it was ~ed as a compliment/joke** كانَ المَقْصودُ مِنْهُ المُجامَلةَ \ المِزاحَ; **the letter was ~ed for me** كُنْتُ أنا المَقْصودَ بالرِسالةِ; **sooner than I had ~ed** في وَقْتٍ أَقْرَبَ مِمّا كُنْتُ أَنْوي **2** **to ~ to do sth** نَوى أَنْ يَفْعَلَ شَيْئاً; **we ~ making/to make the announcement** نَنْوي إصْدارَ الإعْلانِ; **the curfew is ~ed to prevent looting** المَقْصودُ من حَظْرِ التَجْوالِ هو مَنْعُ عَمَليّاتِ النَهْبِ

intended /ɪnˈtɛndɪd/ *adj* ‹*meaning, target*› مُتَعَمَّد, مُراد, مَقْصود, مَعْنِيّ; **this is ~ for you** أَنْتَ المَقْصودُ بِهَذا

intense /ɪnˈtɛns/ *adj* ‹*pressure, competition*› شَديد (شِداد, أَشِدّاءُ), قَوِيّ (أَقْوِياءُ), حادّ, قاسٍ (قُساة)

intensely /ɪnˈtɛnsli/ *adv* ‹*competitive, personal*› بِشِدّةٍ, بِحِدّةٍ

intensify /ɪnˈtɛnsɪfʌɪ/ **A** *vt* (**intensifies, intensifying, intensified**) شَدَّدَ, كَثَّفَ ‹*efforts*›; قَوّى ‹*pressure, a search*› **B** *vi* «fighting» تَصاعَدَ; «pressure, competition» اشْتَدَّ

intensity /ɪnˈtɛnsɪti/ *n* (*pl* **intensities**) قُوّة (قُوَى, قُوّات), شِدّة, حِدّة

intensive /ɪnˈtɛnsɪv/ *adj* **1** (activity) ‹*training, negotiations*› مُكَثَّف, مُرَكَّز, مُتْعِب, مُشَدَّد; **an ~ language course** دَوْرة لُغةٍ مُكَثَّفة **2** (farming) ‹*agriculture, farming*› كَثيف

intensive care *n* عِناية طِبِّيّة مُكَثَّفة \ مُرَكَّزة

intensive care unit *n* وِحْدة عِنايةٍ مُرَكَّزةٍ

intent /ɪnˈtɛnt/ **A** *n* (fml) (intention) نِيّة (نِيّات, نَوايا), قَصْد; **a declaration of ~** إعْلان نَوايا; **to signal/announce one's ~ to do sth** أَعْلَنَ عن نِيَّتِهِ أَنْ يَفْعَلَ شَيْئاً **B** *adj* **1** **to be ~ on sth/on doing sth** كانَ عازِماً على شَيْءٍ \ فِعْلِ شَيْءٍ; **the team is ~ on victory/on winning** الفَريقُ مُصِرٌّ على الفَوْزِ **2** (absorbed) ‹*expression, silence*› يَدُلُّ على التَرْكيزِ

Idiom **to all intents and purposes** من حَيْثُ الشَكْلِ والمَضْمونِ

intention /ɪnˈtɛnʃ(ə)n/ *n* نِيّة (نِيّات, نَوايا), هَدَف (أَهْداف), غَرَض (أَغْراض), قَصْد; **I have no ~ of giving up now** لَيْسَ لَدَيَّ أَيّةُ نِيّةٍ للتَخَلّي الآنَ

intentional /ɪnˈtɛnʃ(ə)n(ə)l/ *adj* ‹*act, discrimination*› مُتَعَمَّد, مَقْصود

intentionally /ɪnˈtɛnʃ(ə)n(ə)li/ *adv* ‹*to mislead, destroy*› عَمْداً, تَعَمُّداً, قَصْداً, عن عَمْدٍ \ قَصْدٍ

intently /ɪnˈtɛntli/ *adv* ‹*to watch, listen*› بِاهْتِمام, بِانْتِباهٍ, بِتَرْكيزٍ

inter /ɪnˈtəː/ *vt* (**-rr-**) (fml) دَفَنَ (i; دَفْن), قَبَرَ (i-u; قَبْر, مَقْبَر) ‹*a body, victim*›

interact /ɪntərˈakt/ *vi* **1** «people» تَفاعَلَ; **to ~ with the public/police** تَفاعَلَ مع الجُمْهورِ \ الشُرْطةِ **2** «factors, substances» تَفاعَلَ

interaction /ɪntərˈakʃ(ə)n/ *n* تَفاعُل (تَفاعُلات)

interactive /ɪntərˈaktɪv/ *adj* **1** (affecting each other) ‹*ideas, teaching*› تَفاعُلِيّ, مُتَفاعِل **2** (computing) ‹*TV, display*› تَفاعُلِيّ

intercede /ˌɪntəˈsiːd/ *vi* تَوَسَّطَ, تَدَخَّلَ, تَشَفَّعَ

intercept /ˌɪntəˈsɛpt/ *vt* **1** تَصَدّى, اعْتَرَضَ ‹*the aircraft, missile*› **2** اعْتَرَضَ ‹*a communication, signal*› **3** اعْتَرَضَ ‹*the forward*›

interception /ɪntəˈsɛpʃ(ə)n/ *n* **1** (of missiles, planes) اعْتِراض (اعْتِراضات) **2** (of signals, messages) اعْتِراض (اعْتِراضات) **3** (of forwards, throw) مُقاطَعة

interchange **A** /ɪntəˈtʃeɪndʒ/ *vt* تَبادَلَ ‹*ideas, data*› **B** /ˈɪntətʃeɪndʒ/ *n* **1** (on roads) مُفْتَرَق طُرُقٍ \ تَقاطُع \ مُلْتَقًى (ذو عِدّة مُسْتَوَياتٍ) **2** (of ideas etc) تَبادُل (تَبادُلات)

interchangeable /ɪntəˈtʃeɪndʒəb(ə)l/ *adj* ‹*parts, terms*› قابِل للاسْتِبْدالِ, تَبادُلِيّ

intercity /ɪntəˈsɪti/ *adj* ‹*coach, train*› [(رابِط) بين المُدُنِ]

intercom /ˈɪntəkɒm/ *n* إنْتَرْكُم (نِظام اتِّصالٍ داخِلِيٌّ)

intercourse /ˈɪntəkɔːs/ *n* (sexual) جِماع, مُمارَسة الجِنْس, مُضاجَعة; **to have ~ with sb** ضاجَعَ شَخْصاً

interdisciplinary /ɪntəˈdɪsɪplɪn(ə)ri/ *adj* ‹*degree, course*› مُتَعَدِّد الاخْتِصاصاتِ \ التَخَصُّصاتِ

interest /ˈɪntrɪst/ **A** *n* **1** [u] (attraction) أَهَمِّيّة, قيمة; **to be of great/little ~ to sb** كانَ ذا أَهَمِّيّةٍ كَبيرةٍ \ غَيْرَ ذي بالٍ بالنِسْبةِ لِشَخْصٍ; **that is of no ~ to me** ذلك لا قيمةَ لَهُ بالنِسْبةِ لي; **as a matter of ~ ...** من بابِ حُبِّ المَعْرِفةِ; **to hold sb's ~** حازَ اهْتِمامَ شَخْصٍ **2** (hobby) اهْتِمام (اهْتِمامات), هِواية **3** [u] (on a loan, deposit) فائِدة; **the account pays 3.5% ~** يَتِمُّ دَفْعُ 3.5٪

فائدةٌ عن الحِسابِ [4] (benefit) مَصْلَحة (مَصالِحُ)؛ **in the ~ of transparency/freedom** حِرْصاً على الشَّفافيّةِ \ العَدالةِ؛ **it is in your own ~ to attend** مِن مَصْلَحَتِكَ أَنْتَ أَنْ تَحْضُرَ؛ **to have sb's best ~s at heart** راعى مَصالِحَ شَخْصٍ بِكُلِّ إخْلاصٍ [5] (fml) (stake) مَصْلَحة (مَصالِحُ)؛ **my business ~s** مَصالِحي التِجاريّة؛ **to have an ~ in the property** كانَ لَهُ مَصْلَحةٌ في العَقارِ؛ **to have a vested ~ in doing sth** كانَ لَهُ مَصْلَحةٌ ذاتِيّةٌ في فِعْلِ شَيْءٍ؛ **to declare an ~ in a project** أَعْلَنَ أنّ لَهُ مَصْلَحةً في مَشْروعٍ

B *vt* (to attract) «topic» أثارَ الاهْتِمامَ؛ **economics ~s him enormously/doesn't ~ him at all** الاقْتِصادُ يُثيرُ اهْتِمامَهُ بِدَرَجةٍ كَبيرةٍ \ لا يُثيرُ اهْتِمامَهُ على الإطْلاقِ؛ **to ~ sb in sth/in doing sth** رَغَّبَ شَخْصاً في شَيْءٍ \ في فِعْلِ شَيْءٍ

interested /ˈɪntərɪstɪd/ *adj* [1] ‹*onlooker*› مُهْتَمّ؛ ‹*expression*› يَنُمُّ عن الاهْتِمامِ؛ **to be ~ in a subject/an activity** كانَ مُهْتَمّاً بِمَوْضوعٍ \ بِنَشاطٍ؛ **I am ~ in renting the property** أنا مُهْتَمٌّ باسْتِئْجارِ العَقارِ؛ **to get sb ~ in a project/sport** جَعَلَ شَخْصاً يَهْتَمّ بِمَشْروعٍ \ بِرِياضةٍ [2] (fml) ‹*party*› مَعْنيّ؛ **the ~ parties** الأطْراف المَعْنيّة

interest-free /ˌɪntrɛstˈfriː/ *adj* ‹*loan, period*› بِدونِ فَوائِدَ

interesting /ˈɪntərɪstɪŋ/ *adj* ‹*book, story, speaker*› مُثير للاهْتِمامِ، مُشَوِّق

interestingly /ˈɪntrəstɪŋli/ *adv* [1] (with interest) ‹*to speak, write*› بِشَكْلٍ مُشَوِّقٍ [2] (curiously) مِن المُثير للاهْتِمامِ؛ **~, his wife isn't with him** مِن المُثير للاهْتِمامِ أنّ زَوْجَتَهُ لَيْسَتْ مَعَهُ؛ **~ enough ...** مِن الغَريبِ أنّ ...

interest rate *n* نِسْبة \ سِعْر الفائِدةِ

interface /ˈɪntəfeɪs/ *n* (Comput) واجِهة

interfere /ɪntəˈfɪə/ *vi* [1] (to get involved) تَدَخَّلَ؛ **to ~ in sth** تَدَخَّلَ في شَيْءٍ [2] (to disrupt) عَرْقَلَ (i; عَرْقَلة)، أعاقَ؛ **I don't let my job ~ with my family life** لا أَدَعُ وَظيفَتي تَتعارَضُ مع حَياتي العائِليّةِ [3] (to tamper) **to ~ with sth** عَبَثَ \ تَلاعَبَ بِشَيْءٍ

interference /ɪntəˈfɪərəns/ *n* [1] (interfering) تَدَخُّل، تَداخُل؛ **~ in the affairs of another country** تَدَخُّل في شُؤونِ بَلَدٍ آخَرَ [2] (on radio, TV) تَشْويش، تَداخُل (تَداخُلات)

interfering /ˌɪntəˈfɪərɪŋ/ *adj* مُتَدَخِّل، فُضوليّ

intergovernmental /ɪntəɡʌv(ə)nˈmɛnt(ə)l/ *adj* ‹*agreement, commission*› حُكوميّ دُوَليّ

interim /ˈɪntərɪm/ **A** *n* **in the ~** في أَثْناءِ \ غُضونِ ذلك، في خِلالِ ذلك الوَقْتِ

B *adj* ‹*government, report*› مُؤَقَّت

interior /ɪnˈtɪərɪə/ **A** *adj* [1] (inner) ‹*wall, lighting*› داخِليّ، باطِنيّ [2] (inland) ‹*areas, towns*› في المَناطِقِ الداخِليّةِ (بعيد عن الساحِلِ \ الشاطِئِ)

B *n* [1] (inside part) داخِل، باطِن (بَواطِنُ)، جَوْف (أَجْواف)؛ **the ~ of the building/car** داخِل المَبْنى \ السَيّارةِ [2] (the interior) (of a country, continent) المَناطِق الداخِليّة [3] (the interior) (political affairs) الشُؤون الداخِليّة؛ **the Ministry of the I~** الوِزارة الداخِليّة

interior decorator *n* مُصَمِّم ديكور

interior design *n* تَصميم داخِليّ

interior designer *n* مُصَمِّم داخِليّ، مُهَنْدِس ديكور داخِليّ

interjection /ɪntəˈdʒɛkʃ(ə)n/ *n* مُداخَلة

interlink /ɪntəˈlɪŋk/ *vt* **to be ~ed** تَرابَطَ

interlock /ɪntəˈlɒk/ *vi* «parts, fingers» تَشابَكَ

interloper /ˈɪntələʊpə/ *n* مُتَطَفِّل

interlude /ˈɪntəljuːd/ *n* [1] (period) فَتْرة فاصِلة، فاصِل من الوَقْتِ [2] (Mus) فاصِل [3] (Theat) فَتْرة اسْتِراحةٍ [فَصْل إضافيّ يَتَخَلَّلُ فُصولَ مَسْرَحيّةٍ]

intermediary /ˌɪntəˈmiːdiəri/ *n* (*pl* **intermediaries**) وَسيط (وُسَطاءُ)

intermediate /ˌɪntəˈmiːdɪət/ *adj* [1] ‹*stage, step*› وَسيط (وُسَطاءُ) [2] ‹*course, level*› مُتَوَسِّط

interminable /ɪnˈtəːmɪnəb(ə)l/ *adj* ‹*list, debate*› مُطَوَّل

intermission /ɪntəˈmɪʃ(ə)n/ *n* انْقِطاع \ فَتْرة اسْتِراحةٍ، فاصِل

intermittent /ɪntəˈmɪt(ə)nt/ *adj* ‹*noise, activity*› مُتَقَطِّع، غَيْر مُتَواصِلٍ

intern **A** /ˈɪntəːn/ *n* [1] (AmE) (doctor) طَبيب مُتَمَرِّن \ تحت التَمْرينِ [2] (unpaid worker) مُتَدَرِّب

B /ɪnˈtəːn/ *vt* ‹*an alien, a detainee*› اعْتَقَلَ

internal /ɪnˈtəːn(ə)l/ *adj* **1** (inside) ‹*walls, surface*› داخِليّ, باطِنيّ **2** (private) ‹*dispute, arrangement*› داخِليّ **3** (domestic) ‹*politics, affairs, trade*› داخِليّ; **she's responsible for ~ affairs** هي مَسْؤولةٌ عن الشُؤونِ الداخِليّةِ **4** (inside) ‹*bleeding, examination*› داخِليّ

internally /ɪnˈtəːn(ə)li/ *adv* **1** (on the inside) ‹*to bleed, be damaged, to function*› داخِليًّا; **'not to be taken ~'** 'لا يُؤْخَذُ عن طَريقِ الفَمِ' **2** (in organizations) ‹*to recruit, assess*› داخليًّا

Internal Revenue Service *n* (AmE) مَصْلَحة الضَرائِبِ

international /ɪntəˈnaʃ(ə)n(ə)l/ **A** *adj* ‹*trade, sport*› عالَميّ, دُوَليّ

B *n* (sporting fixture) مُباراة دُوَليّة; (player) لاعِب دُوَليّ

International Court of Justice *n* مَحْكَمة العَدْل الدُوَليّة

internationalism /ɪntəˈnaʃ(ə)nəliz(ə)m/ *n* أُمَمِيّة (سِياسة التَعاوُنِ بين الدُوَلِ)

internationally /ɪntəˈnaʃ(ə)n(ə)li/ *adv* ‹*recognized, renowned*› عالَميًّا, دُوَليًّا; **an ~ famous singer** مُغَنٍّ مَشهور عالَميًّا; **to compete ~ a company needs...** كَيْ تَنافِسَ عالَميًّا تَحْتاجُ الشَرِكةُ إلى ...

International Monetary Fund *n* صُنْدوق النَقْدِ الدُوَليّ

international waters /ˌɪntəˌnaʃnəl ˈwɔːtəz/ *n pl* مِياه دُوَليّة

internee /ˌɪntəːˈniː/ *n* مُعْتَقَل

Internet /ˈɪntənɛt/ *n* إِنْتَرْنِت; **to be on the I~** كانَ مُتَّصِلاً بِشَبَكةِ الإِنْتَرْنِت

internet access *n* الدُخول \ الوُصول إلى الإِنْتَرْنِت

Internet cafe *n* مَقْهى إِنْتَرْنِت

Internet service provider *n* مُزَوِّد \ مُقَدِّم \ مُوَفِّر خِدْمةِ الإِنْتَرْنِت

internment /ɪnˈtəːnmənt/ *n* اِعْتِقال (اِعْتِقالات)

internship /ˈɪntəːnʃɪp/ *n* **1** (in a company, university) فَتْرة تَدْريبٍ **2** (AmE) (in a hospital) تَدْريب طِبِّيّ

interpersonal /ɪntəˈpəːs(ə)n(ə)l/ *adj* ‹*skills, communication*› بين الناسِ

interplay /ˈɪntəpleɪ/ *n* تَفاعُل (تَفاعُلات), تَأْثير مُتَبادَل

interpret /ɪnˈtəːprɪt/ **A** *vt* ‹*data, a dream*› أَوَّلَ, فَسَّرَ

B *vi* تَرْجَمَ (شَفَويًّا)

interpretation /ɪntəːprɪˈteɪʃ(ə)n/ *n* تَفْسير (تَفاسيرُ), تَأْويل (تَأْويلات)

interpreter /ɪnˈtəːprɪtə/ *n* مُتَرْجِم (شَفَويّ)

interrogate /ɪnˈtɛrəgeɪt/ *vt* اسْتَنْطَقَ, اسْتَجْوَبَ ‹*a prisoner, suspect*›

interrogation /ɪnˌtɛrəˈgeɪʃ(ə)n/ *n* اسْتِجْواب (اسْتِجْوابات), اسْتِنْطاق (اسْتِنْطاقات), تَحْقيق (تَحْقيقات)

interrogative /ˌɪntəˈrɒgətɪv/ *adj* ‹*sentence, pronoun*› اسْتِفْهاميّ

interrupt /ɪntəˈrʌpt/ **A** *vt* **1** أَوْقَفَ ‹*a conversation, process*› **2** قاطَعَ ‹*a speaker*›

B *vi* قاطَعَ

interruption /ɪntəˈrʌpʃ(ə)n/ *n* انْقِطاع, مُقاطَعة

intersect /ɪntəˈsɛkt/ *vi* «lines, roads» تَقاطَعَ

intersection /ɪntəˈsɛkʃ(ə)n/ *n* **1** (of lines) نُقْطة تَقاطُعٍ **2** (in roads) تَقاطُع \ مُلْتَقى طُرُقٍ

intersperse /ɪntəˈspəːs/ *vt* **to be ~d with sth** «speeches, scenes» تَخَلَّلَهُ شَيْءٌ

interstate /ɪntəˈsteɪt/ *n* (AmE) (also **interstate highway**) طَريق سَريع بين الولاياتِ في الولاياتِ المُتَّحِدةِ]

intertwine /ɪntəˈtwʌɪn/ **A** *vt* **1** ‹*fingers*› جَدَّلَ, ضَفَّرَ; شَبَّكَ ‹*threads*› فَتَلَ (فَتْل i) **2** شَبَّكَ ‹*lives, themes*›; **their lives became inextricably ~d** أَصْبَحَتْ حَياتُهُمْ مُرْتَبِطةً ارْتِباطاً لا يَنْفَصِمُ

B *vi* «fingers, threads» تَشابَكَ

interval /ˈɪntəv(ə)l/ *n* **1** (in time) فَتْرة (فَتَرات), مُدّة (مُدَد); **at regular ~s** على فَتَراتٍ مُنْتَظِمةٍ **2** (BrE) (in theatre) اسْتِراحة **3** (in space) مَسافة, بُعْد (أَبْعاد); **at 100 metre ~s** كلّ 100 مِترٍ

intervene /ɪntəˈviːn/ *vi* «governments, police» تَدَخَّلَ; **to ~ in an argument** تَدَخَّلَ في جِدالٍ

intervening /ɪntəˈviːnɪŋ/ *adj* ‹*years, months*› فاصِل; **in the ~ period** في الفَتْرةِ الفاصِلةِ, في الفارِقِ الزَمَنيِّ

intervention /ɪntəˈvɛnʃ(ə)n/ *n* تَدَخُّل; **his ~ was decisive** كانَ تَدَخُّلُهُ حاسِماً

interview /ˈɪntəvjuː/ **A** *n* **1** (for a job) مُقابَلة **2** (in newspaper) مُقابَلة

B *vt* **1** قابَلَ ‹*a candidate*› **2** «journalist» قابَلَ ‹*a celebrity*›; «police» حَقَّقَ (مع) ‹*a witness*›; **the police ~ed all the witnesses** حَقَّقَت الشُرْطةُ مع جَميعِ الشُهودِ

interviewee /ɪntəvjuːˈiː/ *n* **1** (for a job) [طالِب وَظيفةٍ تُجْرى **2** (on TV, radio) ضَيْف (ضُيوف) مَعَهُ مُقابَلةٌ]

interviewer /ˈɪntəvjuːə/ *n* [الشَخْص الّذي يَجْري المُقابَلةَ]

interwar /ɪntəˈwɔː/ *adj*; **the ~ years** *or* **period** الفَتْرة ما بين الحَرْبَيْن (العالَمِيَّتَيْن)

interweave /ɪntəˈwiːv/ *vt* (*past tense* **interwove**; *past participle* **interwoven**) **1** شَبَكَ (شَبْك ;i) ‹*wool, threads*› **2** مَزَجَ (مَزْج ;u, مِزاج) ‹*themes, rhythms*›

intestate /ɪnˈtesteɪt/ *adj* ‹*parent, client*› غَيْر موصٍ, بلا وَصِيّة; **to die ~** ماتَ غَيْرَ موصٍ

intestinal /ɪnˈtɛstɪn(ə)l, ɪntɛˈstʌɪn(ə)l/ *adj* ‹*infection, problem*› مِعَوِيّ

intestine /ɪnˈtɛstɪn/ *n* مِعًى (أَمْعاء)

intifada /ˌɪntɪˈfɑːdə/ *n* انْتِفاضة

intimacy /ˈɪntɪməsi/ *n* مَوَدّة, أُلْفة

intimate /ˈɪntɪmət/ *adj* **1** (close) ‹*relationship, friend*› حَميم (أَحِمّاءُ); **to be on ~ terms with sb** كانَ على عَلاقةٍ حَميمةٍ مع **2** (cosy) ‹*atmosphere*› مُريح **3** (detailed) ‹*knowledge*› شَخْصِيّ **4** (private, personal) ‹*details, life*› شَخْصيّ, حَميم عَميق

intimately /ˈɪntɪmətli/ *adv* بِشَكْلٍ وَثيقٍ, بِعُمْقٍ; **the problems are ~ related** المَشاكِلُ مُرْتَبِطةٌ ارْتِباطاً وَثيقاً

intimation /ˌɪntɪˈmeɪʃ(ə)n/ *n* تَلْميح (تَلْميحات, تَلاميحُ)

intimidate /ɪnˈtɪmɪdeɪt/ *vt* أَرْهَبَ ‹*a witness, an opponent*›

intimidating /ɪnˈtɪmɪdeɪtɪŋ/ *adj* ‹*person, behaviour*› مُرْعِب, رَهيب

intimidation /ɪnˌtɪmɪˈdeɪʃ(ə)n/ *n* تَخْويف (تَخْويفات) تَهْويل (تَهاويل, تَهْويلات)

into /ˈɪntuː, ˈɪntə/ *prep* **1** (indicating motion, direction) في; **to go ~ town** ذَهَبَ إلى المَدينةِ; **let's go ~ the house** لِنَدْخُل البَيْتَ; **pour it ~ a bowl** صُبَّهُ في وِعاءٍ; **to get ~ a car** دَخَلَ في سَيّارةٍ; **I got ~ bed** دَخَلْتُ في الفِراشِ **2** (indicating contact) بِ; **the car crashed ~ a wall** اصْطَدَمَت السَيّارةُ بِجِدارٍ; **I almost bumped ~ him** كِدْتُ أَصْطَدِمُ بِهِ **3** (indicating a change of state) إلى; **to translate sth ~ French** تَرْجَمَ شَيْئاً إلى الفَرَنْسِيّة; **form the dough ~ balls** شَكِّل العَجينةَ إلى كُراتٍ; **we split ~ two groups** تَقَسَّمْنا إلى مَجْموعَتَيْنِ **4** (in time) في; **well ~ the afternoon** حَتّى وَقْتٍ مُتَأَخِّرٍ من بَعْدِ الظُهْرِ; **ten minutes ~ the game** عَشْر دَقائِقَ في المُباراةِ **5** (infml) (keen on) **they're ~ drugs** يَتَناوَلونَ المُخَدِّراتِ; **she's really ~ motorbikes** هي مولَعةٌ حَقًّا بالدَرّاجاتِ النارِيّةِ **6** (in division) **8 ~ 24 goes 3 times** *or* **is 3** 24 مَقْسوم على 8 يُساوي 3

intolerable /ɪnˈtɒlərəb(ə)l/ *adj* ‹*situation, pressure*› غَيْر مُحْتَمَلٍ \ مُطاقٍ

intolerance /ɪnˈtɒlərəns/ *n* عَدَم تَسامُحٍ, تَعَصُّب

intolerant /ɪnˈtɒlərənt/ *adj* ‹*attitude, views*› غَيْر مُتَسامِحٍ

intonation /ɪntəˈneɪʃ(ə)n/ *n* تَنْغيم

intone /ɪnˈtəʊn/ *vt* جَوَّدَ, نَغَّمَ, رَتَّلَ, رَنَّمَ ‹*a prayer, speech*›

intoxicate /ɪnˈtɒksɪkeɪt/ *vt* **1** (with drugs, alcohol, etc) أَسْكَرَ, أَثْمَلَ ‹*a drinker, partygoer*› **2** (with a performance, power) أَثْمَلَ, أَفْتَنَ, هَيَّجَ, أَثارَ ‹*audience, a leader*›; **to be ~d with power** كانَ مَفْتوناً بالسُلْطةِ \ بالقوّة

intoxicated /ɪnˈtɒksɪkeɪtɪd/ *adj* مَخْمور, سَكْران, ثَمِل

intoxicating /ɪnˈtɒksɪˌkeɪtɪŋ/ *adj* ‹*liquor, substance*› مُسْكِر

intractable /ɪnˈtraktəb(ə)l/ *adj* **1** ‹*problem, conflict*› مُسْتَعْصٍ, صَعْب, (عُنُد) عَنيد **2** ‹*personality*› غَيْر قابِلٍ للحَلِّ, عَسير المِراسِ

intramuscular /ˌɪntrəˈmʌskjʊlə/ *adj* ‹*injection*› عَضَلِيّ

intranet /ˈɪntrənɛt/ *n* شَبَكة داخِلِيّة, إنْتْرانت

intransigent /ɪnˈtransɪdʒ(ə)nt/ *adj* ‹*attitude, behaviour*› عَنيد (عُنُد), مُتَصَلِّب

intransitive /ɪnˈtransətɪv/ *adj* ‹*verb, use*› غَيْر مُتَعَدٍّ

intrauterine device /ˌɪntrəjuːtərʌɪn dɪˈvʌɪs/ *n* لَوْلَب (مانِع للحَمْلِ)

intravenous /ˌɪntrəˈviːnəs/ *adj* ‹*drip, injection*› داخِل, وَريديّ; **an ~ drug user** مُسْتَخْدِم المُخَدِّراتِ عن طَريقِ الأَوْرِدةِ الحَقْنِ الوَريديّ

in tray *n* **1** (for papers) [صُندوق الرَسائِلِ والوَثائِقِ الوارِدةِ **2** (in computing) صُنْدوق البَريد الوارِدِ

intrepid /ɪnˈtrepɪd/ *adj* ‹*explorer, reporter*› جَسور ,مِقْدام

intricacy **A** /ˈɪntrɪkəsi/ *n* (*pl* **intricacies**) (تَعْقيدات) تَعْقيد

B (**intricacies**) *n pl* (of a story, subject) تَعْقيدات

intricate /ˈɪntrɪkət/ *adj* ‹*pattern, system*› مُعَقَّد

intrigue **A** /ɪnˈtriːg/ *vt* «idea, story» فَتَنَ (i; فُتون ,فَتْن)

B /ˈɪntriːg/ *n* (مَكايِدُ) مَكيدة

intriguing /ɪnˈtriːgɪŋ/ *adj* ‹*question, possibility*› جَذّاب

intrinsic /ɪnˈtrɪnzɪk, ɪnˈtrɪnsɪk/ *adj* ‹*value, characteristic*› جَوْهَريّ

introduce /ɪntrəˈdjuːs/ **A** *vt* (**introduces**, **introducing**, **introduced**) [1] (socially) قَدَّمَ ‹*a friend, colleague*›; **my sister ~d us** عَرَّفَتْنا أُخْتي على بَعْضِنا البَعْض; **to ~ sb to another person** قَدَّمَ شَخْصاً إلى شَخْصٍ آخَرَ; **he ~d me to the Prince/his cousin** قَدَّمَني إلى الأَميرِ \ ابْنِ عَمِّهِ [2] (to an activity, interest) عَرَّفَ; **to ~ sb to motor racing/poetry/drugs** عَرَّفَ شَخْصاً على سِباقاتِ السَيّاراتِ \ الشِعْرِ \ المُخَدِّراتِ; **he ~d me to Mozart** عَرَّفَني على موسيقى موزارْت [3] (to bring in) أَدْخَلَ ‹*a species, disease, plant*›; **she tried to ~ the subject into the conversation** حاوَلَتْ أَنْ تُثيرَ المَوْضوعَ أثناء المُحادَثةِ [4] (to establish) أَدْخَلَ ‹*a law, system, product*› [5] (to preface) قَدَّمَ (ل) ,مَهَّدَ (ل) ‹*a talk, programme*› [6] (for debate) طَرَحَ (a; طَرْح) ‹*a bill, proposal*› [7] (fml) (to cause to enter) أَدْخَلَ ‹*a tube, needle*›

B *v refl* (**introduces**, **introducing**, **introduced**) **to ~ oneself** قَدَّمَ نَفْسَهُ

introduction /ɪntrəˈdʌkʃ(ə)n/ *n* [1] (to a friend, audience) تَقْديم (تَقْديمات); **a letter of ~** خِطاب تَعْريفٍ; **our next guest needs no ~** ضَيْفُنا التالي غَنيٌّ عن التَعْريفِ [2] (to an activity, interest) تَعْريف [3] (beginner's guide) مُقَدِّمة; **'An I~ to the History of the Arabic Language'** 'مُقَدِّمة إلى تاريخ اللُغةِ العَرَبيّةِ' [4] (of a topic, character, player) إدْخال ,إدْراج [5] (fml) (of a species, plant) إدْخال [6] (of a law, system) وَضْع ,فَرْض [7] (fml) (of a tube, needle) إدْخال [8] (to a book) تَمْهيد (تَمْهيدات) ,مُقَدِّمة [9] (to a piece of music) مُقَدِّمة [10] (of a bill) طَرْح

introductory /ɪntrəˈdʌkt(ə)ri/ *adj* [1] ‹*remarks, paragraph, course*› تَمْهيديّ [2] ‹*offer*› تَمْهيديّ (بِقَصْدِ تَشْجيعِ الناسِ على شِراءِ مُنْتَجٍ جَديدٍ)

introspective /ɪntrəˈspektɪv/ *adj* ‹*personality, student*› اسْتِبْطانيّ

introvert /ˈɪntrəvəːt/ *n* انْطِوائيّ

introverted /ˈɪntrəʊvəːtɪd/ *adj* ‹*child, personality*› مُنْطَوٍ ,انْطِوائيّ على نَفْسِهِ

intrude /ɪnˈtruːd/ *vi* [1] (to interfere) تَطَفَّلَ (على); **to ~ on sb's privacy** تَطَفَّلَ على خُصوصيّةِ شَخْصٍ [2] (to encroach) اقْتَحَمَ

intruder /ɪnˈtruːdə/ *n* مُتَسَلِّل ,مُقْتَحِم

intrusion /ɪnˈtruːʒ(ə)n/ *n* [1] (interruption) مُقاطَعة [2] (interference) تَدَخُّل

intrusive /ɪnˈtruːsɪv/ *adj* ‹*questions, noise*› تَطَفُّليّ

intuition /ɪntjʊˈɪʃ(ə)n/ *n* حَدْس

intuitive /ɪnˈtjuːɪtɪv/ *adj* ‹*understanding, response*› حَدْسيّ

Inuit /ˈɪnjuːɪt, ˈɪnʊɪt/ *n, adj* (*pl* **Inuit** or **Inuits**) إسْكيمو ,إنويت

inundate /ˈɪnʌndeɪt/ *vt* [1] (to overwhelm) أَغْرَقَ; **the helpline has been ~d with calls** أَغْرِقَ خَطُّ المُساعَدةِ بالمُكالَماتِ [2] (to flood) أَغْرَقَ

invade /ɪnˈveɪd/ *vt* غَزا (u; غَزْو) ,اجْتاحَ ‹*the territory, country*›; **the fans ~d the pitch** اجْتاحَ المُشَجِّعونَ المَلْعَبَ

invader /ɪnˈveɪdə/ *n* غازٍ (غُزاة)

invalid¹ /ˈɪnvəlɪd/ **A** *n* عاجِز (عَجَزة)

B *adj before n* ‹*parent, child*› عاجِز (عَجَزة)

invalid² /ɪnˈvalɪd/ *adj* ‹*claim, passport*› باطِل

invalidate /ɪnˈvalɪdeɪt/ *vt* دَحَضَ (a; دَحْض) ,فَنَّدَ ‹*an argument, a theory*›

invalidity /ɪnvəˈlɪdɪti/ *n* [1] (of an argument, theory) بُطْلان [2] (of a person) عَجْز

invaluable /ɪnˈvaljʊəb(ə)l/ *adj* ‹*resource, experience*› لا يُقَدَّرُ بِثَمَنٍ; **he has been ~ to us** كانَتْ مُساعَدَتُهُ لَنا لا تُقَدَّرُ بثَمَنٍ

invariable /ɪnˈveːrɪəb(ə)l/ *adj* ‹*amount, temperature*› ثابِت

invariably /ɪnˈveːrɪəbli/ *adv* **to be ~ right/late** كانَ دائِماً \ بِشَكْلٍ دائِمٍ على حَقٍّ \ مُتَأَخِّراً

invasion /ɪnˈveɪʒ(ə)n/ *n* اجْتِياح ,غَزْو

invasive /ɪnˈveɪsɪv/ *adj* ‹*procedure, surgery*› باضِع; ‹*cancer*› اجْتِياحيّ; ‹*plant*› مُجْتاح

invective /ɪnˈvektɪv/ *n* ذَمّ ,قَدْح

invent /ɪnˈvɛnt/ *vt* 1 اخْتَرَعَ ‹*a device, machine*› 2 اخْتَلَقَ, اخْتَرَعَ ‹*a story, an excuse*›

invention /ɪnˈvɛnʃ(ə)n/ *n* 1 (device, process) اخْتِراع (اخْتِراعات) 2 [u] (action of inventing) اخْتِراع; **necessity is the mother of ~** الحاجةُ أُمُّ الاخْتِراعِ 3 [u] (creativity) ابْتِكار

inventive /ɪnˈvɛntɪv/ *adj* ‹*use, genius*› خَلّاق, مُبْدِع

inventor /ɪnˈvɛntə/ *n* مُخْتَرِع

inventory /ˈɪnv(ə)nt(ə)ri/ *n* (*pl* **inventories**) 1 (list) قائمة الجَرْدِ 2 (stocks) جَرْد (جُرود)

inverse /ˈɪnvəːs, ɪnˈvəːs/ A *adj* ‹*proportion, relationship*› عَكْسيّ B *n* عَكْس

inversion /ɪnˈvəːʃ(ə)n/ *n* قَلْب

invert /ɪnˈvəːt/ *vt* 1 (to reverse) عَكَسَ (i; عَكْس), قَلَبَ (i; قَلْب) ‹*a sequence, polarity*› 2 (to turn upside down) قَلَبَ (i; قَلْب) ‹*a mould, glass*›

invertebrate /ɪnˈvəːtɪbrət/ *n* لافَقاريّ

inverted commas /ˌɪnvəːtɪd ˈkɒməz/ *n pl* (BrE) عَلامات اقْتِباسٍ \ تَنْصيصٍ

invest /ɪnˈvɛst/ A *vt* «government, company, person» اسْتَثْمَرَ ‹*money, one's savings, time*›; **we have ~ed a lot of energy/time into the plans** اسْتَثْمَرْنا كَثيراً من الطاقة \ الوَقْتِ في الخُطَطِ B *vi* اسْتَثْمَرَ في; **to ~ in shares/in a savings account** اسْتَثْمَرَ في أَسْهُمٍ \ حِسابِ ادِّخارٍ

investigate /ɪnˈvɛstɪgeɪt/ A *vt* 1 حَقَّقَ (في) ‹*a case, allegation*› 2 (to study) دَرَسَ (u; دَرْس), فَحَصَ (a; فَحْص) ‹*possibilities, effects*› B *vi* (to find out) تَحَرّى

investigation /ɪnˌvɛstɪˈgeɪʃ(ə)n/ *n* 1 (study, examination) تَحْقيق (تَحْقيقات), تَحَرٍّ (تَحَرِّيات) 2 (formal inquiry) تَحْقيق (تَحْقيقات)

investigative /ɪnˈvɛstɪgətɪv/ *adj* ‹*committee, journalism*› تَحْقيقيّ

investigator /ɪnˈvɛstɪgeɪtə/ *n* مُفَتِّش, مُحَقِّق, رَجُل مَباحِثٍ

investiture /ɪnˈvɛstɪtʃə/ *n* تَنْصيب, تَقْليد مَنْصِبٍ

investment /ɪnˈvɛstmənt/ *n* 1 [u] (process) اسْتِثْمار; **funds for regional ~** أَمْوال للاسْتِثْمارِ الإقْليميِّ 2 (sum) اسْتِثْمار (اسْتِثْمارات); **he lost/recovered all his ~s** أَضاعَ \ اسْتَعادَ كُلَّ اسْتِثْماراتِهِ

investment analyst *n* مُحَلِّل اسْتِثْماريّ

investment bank *n* بَنْك اسْتِثْماريّ

investment banker *n* مَصْرِفيّ اسْتِثْماريّ

investment manager *n* مُدير اسْتِثْماراتٍ

investor /ɪnˈvɛstə/ *n* مُسْتَثْمِر

inveterate /ɪnˈvɛt(ə)rət/ *adj* ‹*gambler, liar*› مُزْمِن

invigilate /ɪnˈvɪdʒɪleɪt/ *vt* راقَبَ ‹*an examination*›

invigorating /ɪnˈvɪgəreɪtɪŋ/ *adj* ‹*walk, breeze*› مُنَشِّط

invisible /ɪnˈvɪzɪb(ə)l/ *adj* لامَرْئيّ, خَفيّ

invitation /ˌɪnvɪˈteɪʃ(ə)n/ *n* دَعْوة, اسْتِدْعاء (اسْتِدْعاءات) (NA); **at the ~ of** بِدَعْوةٍ من; **admission is by ~ only** الدُخولُ بالدَعْواتِ فَقَطْ

invite /ɪnˈvʌɪt/ *vt* 1 دَعا (u; دَعْوة), اسْتَدْعى, وَجَّهَ دَعْوةً (إلى) ‹*a friend, guest*›; **to ~ sb in** دَعا شَخْصاً إلى الدُخولِ; **he's ~d me out to dinner** دَعاني إلى تَناوُلِ العَشاءِ مَعَهُ في مَطْعَمٍ; **I don't think he'll be ~d back** لا أَظُنُّ أَنَّهُ سَيُدْعى إلى هُنا مَرّةً أُخْرى 2 دَعا للتَقْديمِ ‹*applications, comments*› 3 (to induce) **to ~ comparison with** *or* **to sth** اسْتَدْعى المُقارَنَةَ مع \ ب شَيْءٍ

inviting /ɪnˈvʌɪtɪŋ/ *adj* ‹*place*› جَذّاب; ‹*prospect*› مُغْرٍ; ‹*eyes, smile*› وَدود

in vitro /ɪn ˈviːtrəʊ/ *adj, adv* في المُخْتَبَرِ

in vitro fertilization *n* تَلْقيح صِناعيّ, تَخْصيب في المُخْتَبَرِ

invoice /ˈɪnvɔɪs/ A *n* فاتورة (فَواتيرُ); **~s are paid twice a month** تُدْفَعُ الفَواتيرُ مَرَّتَيْنِ في الشَهْرِ B *vt* أَرْسَلَ فاتورةً ‹*a customer*›; **to ~ a customer for goods delivered** أَرْسَلَ فاتورةً لِعَميلٍ على بَضائعَ تَمَّ تَسْليمُها

invoke /ɪnˈvəʊk/ *vt* اسْتَنَدَ (إلى) ‹*the law, right*›

involuntary /ɪnˈvɒlənt(ə)ri/ *adj* ‹*shiver, movement*› لا إراديّ

involve /ɪnˈvɒlv/ A *vt* (**involves**, **involving**, **involved**) 1 (to entail) انْطَوى (على) ‹*danger, a risk*›; **the job ~s some programming** تَتَضَمَّنُ الوَظيفةُ بَعْضَ البَرْمَجةِ; **there is a lot of work ~d** يَتَطَلَّبُ ذلك الكَثيرَ من العَمَلِ; **it ~s some risk** يَنْطَوي على بَعْضِ المُخاطَرةِ 2 (to bring in) أَشْرَكَ; **to ~ sb**

in a project/scandal أَشْرَكَ شَخْصاً في مَشْروعٍ \ وَرَّطَ شَخْصاً في فَضيحةٍ; **it will ~ them in heavy expenditure** سَيُثْقِلُ كاهِلَهُمْ بالكَثيرِ من النَفَقاتِ; **to be/get ~d in the plan/the rescue** شارَكَ في الخُطَّةِ \ الإِنْقاذِ; **to be/get ~d in doing sth** شارَكَ في فِعْلِ شَيْءٍ **3** (to affect) «accident» أَثَّرَ (على) *<a person, an animal, a vehicle>*; **the safety of the workers is ~d** يَتِمُّ تَعْريضُ سَلامةِ العُمّالِ للخطَرِ **4** (to engross) حازَ الانْتِباهَ *<a reader, an audience>* **5** (emotionally) **to be/get ~d with sb** تَعاطَفَ مع شَخْصٍ; **you're too ~d to make a dispassionate judgement** أَنْتَ مُتَعاطِفٌ مع المَوْضوعِ جِدًّا لِدَرَجةٍ لا تُؤَهِّلُكَ للحُكْمِ بِشَكْلٍ نَزيهٍ

B *v refl* (**involves, involving, involved**) (to commit to) **to ~ oneself in** *or* **with sth** اشْتَرَكَ في شَيْءٍ *<a project, task>*; **they ~d themselves in charitable/relief work** اشْتَرَكوا في أَعْمالِ الخَيْرِ \ الإغاثةِ

involved /ɪnˈvɒlvd/ *adj* **1** (complex) *<explanation, problem>* مُعَقَّد **2** (committed) *<politically, ideologically>* مُشارِك

involvement /ɪnˈvɒlvmənt/ *n* **1** [u] (in an activity, a campaign) مُشارَكة; **my ~ in the movement** مُشارَكَتي في الحَرَكةِ **2** (emotional) ارْتِباط (ارْتِباطات); (romantic) عَلاقة (عَلائِقُ, عَلاقات) **3** [u] (in a book, story, etc) انْهِماك, اسْتِغْراق

inward /ˈɪnwəd/ **A** *adj* **1** *<curve, movement>* داخِلِيّ **2** *<sigh, peace>* باطِنِيّ

B *adv* (also **inwards** BrE) **1** (towards the inside) إلى الداخِلِ **2** (towards the mind) بِشَكْلٍ روحانِيٍّ; **his thoughts turned ~** أَصْبَحَ يُفَكِّرُ بِشَكْلٍ روحانِيٍّ

inward-looking /ˈɪnwədlʊkɪŋ/ *adj* *<society, community>* انْطِوائِيّ

inwards /ˈɪnwədz/ (BrE) ▸ **inward** B

in-your-face /ɪnjəˈfeɪs/ *adj* (infml) *<style, attitude>* فَظّ (أَفْظاظ)

iodine /ˈʌɪədiːn/ *n* يود

ion /ˈʌɪən/ *n* أَيون

iota /ʌɪˈəʊtə/ *n* ذَرّة; **there's not one ~ of truth in what he says** لَيْسَ هُناكَ ذَرّةٌ واحِدةٌ من الصِدْقِ في ما قالَ

IOU /ʌɪəʊˈjuː/ *n* = **I owe you** إقْرار بالدَيْنِ

Iowa /ˈʌɪəwə/ *pr n* آيوا

Iowan /ˈʌɪəw(ə)n/ *pr n, adj* (شَخْص) من آيوا

iPod® /ˈʌɪpɒd/ *n* آي بود

IQ /ʌɪˈkjuː/ *n* = **intelligence quotient** نِسْبة الذَكاءِ

IRA /ʌɪɑːˈreɪ/ *n* **1** (in Ireland) **Irish Republican Army** الجَيْش الجُمْهورِيّ الإيرْلَنْدِيّ

Iran /ɪˈrɑːn/ *pr n* إيران (f)

Iranian /ɪˈreɪnɪən/ *n, adj* إيرانِيّ

Iraq /ɪˈrɑːk/ *pr n* العِراق

Iraqi /ɪˈrɑːki/ *n, adj* عِراقِيّ

irascible /ɪˈrasɪb(ə)l/ *adj* (fml) غَضوب (mf), سَريع الغَضَبِ

irate /ʌɪˈreɪt/ *adj* *<customer, letter>* حانِق

ire /ˈʌɪə/ *n* (liter) غَضَب, سُخْط

Ireland /ˈʌɪələnd/ *pr n* إيرْلَنْدا

iris /ˈʌɪrɪs/ *n* (*pl* **irises**) **1** (of the eye) قُزَحِيّة **2** (flower) سَوْسَن

Irish /ˈʌɪrɪʃ/ **A** *adj* *<accent, ambassador>* إيرْلَنْدِيّ

B *n* **1** (people) (**the Irish**) الشَعْب الإيرْلَنْدِيّ **2** (language) (اللُغة) الإيرْلَنْدِيّة

Irishman /ˈʌɪrɪʃmən/ *n* (*pl* **-men**) (رَجُل) إيرْلَنْدِيّ

Irish Republic *pr n* (**the Irish Republic**) جُمهورِيّة إيرْلَنْدا

Irish Sea *pr n* (**the Irish Sea**) البَحْر الإيرْلَنْدِيّ

Irishwoman /ˈʌɪrɪʃwʊmən/ *n* (*pl* **-women**) (امْرَأة) إيرْلَنْدِيّة

irk /əːk/ *vt* (fml) ضايَقَ

iron /ˈʌɪən/ **A** *n* **1** (metal) حَديد (n coll; حَدائِدُ); **a spade made of ~/an ~ spade** مِجْرَفة مَصْنوعة من حَديدٍ \ مِجْرَفة حَديدِيّة **2** (for clothes) مِكْواة (مَكاوٍ)

B *vt* كَوى (i; كَيّ) *<the clothes>*

(Phrasal verb) **iron out: ~ out [sth], ~ [sth] out** سَوّى [شَيْئاً] *<a problem, difficulty>*

Iron Curtain *n* (**the Iron Curtain**) السِتار الحَديدِيّ

ironic /ʌɪˈrɒnɪk/, **ironical** /ʌɪˈrɒnɪk(ə)l/ *adj* *<humour, comment>* ساخِر

ironically /ʌɪˈrɒnɪkli/ *adv* *<to say, ask>* بِسُخْرِيّة, بِشَكْلٍ ساخِرٍ

ironing /ˈʌɪənɪŋ/ *n* كَيّ; **to do the ~** قامَ بِكَيِّ المَلابِسِ

ironing board *n* طاوِلة كَيٍّ

iron lung *n* رِئة حَديديّة

ironmonger /ˈʌɪənmʌŋgə/ *n* تاجِر المُعِدّاتِ والآلاتِ المَعْدِنيّةِ; **an ~'s (shop)** دُكّان تاجِرِ المُعِدّاتِ والآلاتِ المَعْدِنيّةِ

irony /ˈʌɪrəni/ *n* (*pl* **ironies**) سُخْرِيّة; **there was ~ in her voice** كانَتْ هُناكَ سُخْرِيّةٌ في صَوْتِها

irradiation /ɪˌreɪdɪˈeɪʃ(ə)n/ *n* 1▸ (of an object, person) تَشْعيع 2▸ (of fruit, vegetables) تَشْعيع

irrational /ɪˈraʃ(ə)n(ə)l/ *adj* ‹*fear, behaviour*› غَيْر مَنْطِقيٍّ, غَيْر عَقْلانيٍّ

irreconcilable /ɪrɛk(ə)nˈsʌɪləb(ə)l/ *adj* ‹*partners, ideas*› غَيْر مُتَوائِمٍ, غَيْر مُتَلائِمٍ

irrefutable /ɪrɪˈfjuːtəb(ə)l, ɪˈrɛfjətəb(ə)l/ *adj* ‹*evidence, proof*› لا يُدْحَض, غَيْر قابِلٍ للطَعْنِ, دامِغ

irregular /ɪˈrɛgjʊlə/ **A** *adj* 1▸ (unpredictable) ‹*rhythm, heart beat*› غَيْر مُنْتَظِمٍ 2▸ (AmE) ‹*sale item*› مَعيب **B** *n* (guerrilla) غَيْر نِظاميٍّ

irregularity /ɪˌrɛgjuːˈlarɪti/ *n* (*pl* **irregularities**) 1▸ (in shape, frequency) عَدَم انْتِظامٍ, (انْحِرافات) انْحِراف 2▸ (breach of rules) (خُروق) خَرْق

irrelevant /ɪˈrɛlɪv(ə)nt/ *adj* ‹*information, question*› غَيْر مُتَّصِلٍ; **to be ~ to sth** لا عَلاقةَ لَهُ بالمَوْضوعِ, كانَ غَيْرَ مُتَّصِلٍ بالمَوْضوعِ

irreligious /ɪrɪˈlɪdʒəs/ *adj* ‹*society, person*› غَيْر مُتَدَيِّنٍ

irreparable /ɪˈrɛp(ə)rəb(ə)l/ *adj* ‹*damage, loss*› غَيْر قابِلٍ للإِصْلاحِ

irreplaceable /ɪrɪˈpleɪsəb(ə)l/ *adj* ‹*resource, loss*› لا يُعَوَّض, غَيْر قابِلٍ للاسْتِبْدالِ

irrepressible /ɪrɪˈprɛsɪb(ə)l/ *adj* ‹*spirits, energy*› لا يُمْكِنُ كَبْحُهُ, لا يُمْكِنُ السَيْطَرةُ عَلَيْهِ

irresistible /ɪrɪˈzɪstɪb(ə)l/ *adj* ‹*impulse, urge*› لا يُقاوَمُ; **she was looking ~** كانَتْ تَبْدو جَميلةً بِشَكْلٍ لا يُقاوَمُ

irrespective /ɪrɪˈspɛktɪv/ *phr* (**irrespective of**) (fml) بِقَطْعِ \ بِصَرْفِ النَظَرِ عن ‹*age, class, race*›; **all qualified applicants will be considered ~ of age, sex, religion or nationality** سَيُؤْخَذُ كُلُّ المُتَقَدِّمينَ المُؤَهَّلينَ بِعَيْنِ الاعْتِبارِ بِغَضِّ النَظَرِ عن العُمْرِ، الجِنْسِ، الدينِ أو الجِنْسيّةِ

irresponsible /ɪrɪˈspɒnsɪb(ə)l/ *adj* ‹*behaviour, adult*› لا مَسْؤول, طائِش, مُسْتَهْتِر, غَيْر مَسْؤولٍ; **it's ~ to let him cross the road by himself** إِنَّهُ سُلوكٌ غَيْرُ مَسْؤولٍ أَنْ تَدَعَهُ يَعْبُرُ الطَريقَ بِمُفْرَدِهِ; **the child is completely ~** الطِفْلُ طائِشٌ تَماماً

irreverent /ɪˈrɛv(ə)rənt/ *adj* ‹*comment, comedian*› عَديم الاحْتِرامِ

irreversible /ɪrɪˈvəːsɪb(ə)l/ *adj* ‹*damage*› غَيْر قابِلٍ للإِصْلاحِ; ‹*decision, process*› لا رَجْعةَ فيهِ

irrevocable /ɪˈrɛvəkəb(ə)l/ *adj* لا رَجْعةَ فيهِ, مُبْرَم

irrigate /ˈɪrɪgeɪt/ *vt* 1▸ سَقى (i; سَقْي), رَوى (i; رَيّ, رَيّ) ‹*fields, land*› 2▸ غَسَلَ (i; غَسْل), رَوى (i; رَيّ, رَيّ) ‹*a wound, an eye*›

irrigation /ɪrɪˈgeɪʃ(ə)n/ *n* (Agric) سَقْي, رَيّ

irrigation canal *n* قَناة رَيٍّ

irritable /ˈɪrɪtəb(ə)l/ *adj* ‹*mood, behaviour*› نَزِق

irritable bowel syndrome *n* مُتَلازِمة الأَمْعاءِ المُتَهَيِّجةِ

irritant /ˈɪrɪt(ə)nt/ *n, adj* مُثير

irritate /ˈɪrɪteɪt/ *vt* 1▸ (make angry) أَثارَ, أَغْضَبَ 2▸ (make sore) أَهاجَ

irritating /ˈɪrɪteɪtɪŋ/ *adj* ‹*noise, manner, mistake*› مُثير, مُزْعِج للغَضَبِ

irritation /ɪrɪˈteɪʃ(ə)n/ *n* 1▸ (feeling of annoyance, anger) انْزِعاج, سُخْط; (annoying factor, occurrence) مُضايَقة 2▸ (discomfort, inflammation) (تَهَيُّجات) تَهَيُّج, (الْتِهابات) الْتِهاب

is /ɪz/ *3rd pers sing pres* ▸ **be**

ISBN /ʌɪɛsbiːˈɛn/ *n* = **International Standard Book Number** ردمك (الرَقْم الدَوْليّ المُوَحَّد للكِتابِ)

-ish /ɪʃ/ *suffix* 1▸ (with adjs, advs) **greenish** مائِل إلى الخُضْرةِ; **darkish** مُظْلِم إلى حَدٍّ ما; **earlyish** مُبَكِّراً إلى حَدٍّ ما 2▸ (with figures, numbers etc) **he's thirtyish** هو, عُمْرُهُ يُقارِبُ الثَلاثينَ في الثَلاثينَ من عُمْرِهِ تَقْريباً

Islam /ˈɪzlɑːm/ *n* إِسْلام

Islamabad /ɪzˈlɑːməbad/ *pr n* إِسْلام آباد (f)

Islamic /ɪzˈlamɪk/ *adj* ‹*world, theology*› إِسْلاميّ; **according to ~ law** طِبْقاً للقانونِ الإِسْلاميِّ

Islamic Jihad *n* الجِهاد الإِسْلاميّ

Islamism /ˈɪzlamiz(ə)m/ *n* إِسْلامَويّة, إِسْلاميّة

Islamist /ˈɪzləmɪst/ *n, adj* إسْلاموِيّ, إسْلامِيّ

Islamization, -isation (BrE) /ɪzlamʌɪˈzeɪʃ(ə)n/ *n* أَسْلَمة

island /ˈʌɪlənd/ *n* جزيرة (جُزُر, جَزائِرُ)

islander /ˈʌɪləndə/ *n* [أَحَد سُكّانِ جَزيرةٍ]

isle /ʌɪl/ *n* جزيرة (جُزُر, جَزائِرُ)

Isle of Man *pr n* (**the Isle of Man**) جزيرة مان (جزيرة في البَحْرِ الإيرْلَنْديّ)

Isle of Wight *pr n* (**the Isle of Wight**) جَزيرة وايْت (جزيرة إنْجليزيّة)

Ismaili /ˌɪsmʌɪˈiːli, ˌɪsmɑːˈiːli/ *n* (*pl* **Ismailis**) إسْماعيليّ

isn't /ˈɪz(ə)nt/ *abbr* = **is not** ▸**be**

isobar /ˈʌɪsəʊbɑː/ *n* أَيْسوبار (خَطّ تَساوي الضَغْطِ الجَوّيّ)

isolate /ˈʌɪsəleɪt/ *vt* 1▸ «the doctors» عَزَلَ (i; عَزْل) ‹*a patient, strain*›; **all the patients were ~d** تَمَّ عَزْلُ كُلِّ المَرْضى; **to ~ the latest flu strain** عَزَلَ أَحْدَثَ سُلالةِ إنْفِلْوَنْزا 2▸ «negotiators» عَزَلَ (i; عَزْل) ‹*a country*›

isolated /ˈʌɪsəleɪtɪd/ *adj* 1▸ ‹*village, house*› مَعْزول 2▸ ‹*occurrence, instance*› مَعْزول

isolation /ʌɪsəˈleɪʃ(ə)n/ *n* 1▸ (of patients) عَزْل 2▸ (political, cultural) عُزْلة

isolationism /ʌɪsəˈleɪʃ(ə)nɪz(ə)m/ *n* انْعِزاليّة

isolationist /ʌɪsəˈleɪʃ(ə)nɪst/ *adj, n* انْعِزاليّ

isotope /ˈʌɪsətəʊp/ *n* نَظير (نَظائِرُ)

ISP /ʌɪɛsˈpiː/ *n* = **Internet service provider** مُزَوِّد خِدْمةِ الإنْتَرْنِت

Israel /ˈɪzreɪəl/ *pr n* إسْرائيل (dipt f)

Israeli /ɪzˈreɪli/ *n, adj* إسْرائيليّ

Israfel /ˈɪzrəfɛl/ *pr n* إسْرافيل (dipt)

issue /ˈɪʃuː, ˈɪsjuː/ **A** *n* 1▸ (topic, subject) مَسْأَلة (مَسائِلُ), مَوْضوع (مَواضيعُ, مَوْضوعات), قَضيّة (قَضايا); **to discuss the ~s of the day** ناقَشَ قَضايا اليَوْمِ; **to force the ~** فَرَضَ المَوْضوعَ; **to make an ~ out of sth** أَعْطى شَيْئاً أَكْبَرَ من حَجْمِهِ; **her beliefs are not at ~** مُعْتَقَداتُها لَيْسَتْ هي القَضيّةَ 2▸ [u] (fml) (of blankets, food, uniforms) تَوْزيع; (of a passport, licence) إصْدار; **give the date of ~ of your credit card** اُذْكُرْ تاريخَ إصْدارِ بِطاقَتِكَ الائْتِمانيّةِ 3▸ (of a newspaper, magazine) عَدَد (أَعْداد), إصْدار (إصْدارات); **a back ~ of 'The Examiner'** عَدَد قَديم من مَجَلّةِ 'الفاحِص' 4▸ (of coins, shares) إصْدار (إصْدارات) 5▸ [u] (fml) (of pus, blood) خُروج 6▸ [u] (fml) (descendants) ذُرّيّة, نَسْل

B *vt* 1▸ (to allocate) وَزَّعَ ‹*books, food, uniforms*›; **to ~ sb with a passport/certificate, to ~ a passport/certificate to sb** أَصْدَرَ جَوازَ سَفَرٍ \ شَهادةً لِشَخْصٍ 2▸ (to make public) أَصْدَرَ ‹*a declaration, statement, an ultimatum*›; **he was ~d with a summons to appear before the court** صَدَرَ بِحَقِّهِ طَلَبُ اسْتِدْعاءٍ لِلمُثولِ أَمامَ المَحْكَمةِ 3▸ (to release) أَصْدَرَ ‹*stamps, coins, shares*› 4▸ (to publish) أَصْدَرَ ‹*a book, magazine*›

C *vi* (fml) (to flow out) **to ~ from sth** «water, gas» نَبَعَ من شَيْءٍ; «smoke» صَدَرَ من شَيْءٍ

Istanbul /ˌɪstanˈbʊl/ *pr n* إسْطَنْبول (f)

it /ɪt/ *pron* 1▸ هُوَ, هِيَ; **here ~ is** ها هو ذا; **~'s me** إنَّهُ أنا; **~'s raining, ~ is raining** إنَّها تُمْطِرُ; **~'s time to go** حانَ الوَقْتُ لِلمُغادَرةِ; **~'s going to be difficult** سَيَكونُ أَمْراً صَعْباً; **will ~ be enough?** هل سَيَكونُ كافِياً؟; **today ~'s the tenth anniversary of ...** اليَوْمُ هو الذِكْرى العاشِرةُ لِ ... 2▸ (in questions) **who is ~?** مَنْ هو؟; **where is ~?** أَيْنَ هو؟; **what is ~?** (asking about the nature or cause of sth) ما هو؟; (what is the matter?) ما هي المُشْكِلةُ؟; **how was ~?** كيف كانَ؟ 3▸ (in games) **you're ~!** [دَوْرُكَ!]

(Idioms) **that's it!** (that is the point, the end, the answer) هذا هو!; (that is enough) هذا يَكْفي!; **to be with it** (infml) كانَ على عِلْمٍ بِما يَجْري; **to have it in for sb** (infml) حَمَلَ \ كَنَّ الضَغينةَ لِشَخْصٍ; **to take it out of sb** أَرْهَقَ شَخْصاً; **overtime takes it out of you** تُرْهِقُكَ الساعاتُ الإضافيّةُ في العَمَلِ; **to take it upon oneself to do sth** أَخَذَ على عاتِقِهِ أنْ يَفْعَلَ شَيْئاً

IT /ʌɪˈtiː/ *n* = **information technology** تَقْنِية المَعْلوماتِ, تكنولوجيا المَعْلوماتِ

Italian /ɪˈtaljən/ **A** *adj* ‹*ambassador, food, lesson*› إيطاليّ (طَلْيان) **B** *n* 1▸ (citizen) إيطاليّ (طَلْيان) 2▸ (language) الإيطاليّة (اللُغة)

italic /ɪˈtalɪk/ **A** *adj* ‹*letter, text*› مائِل **B** (**Italics**) *n pl* خَطّ مائِل; **in ~** بِخَطٍّ مائِلٍ

Italy /ˈɪt(ə)li/ *pr n* إيطاليا

itch /ɪtʃ/ **A** *n* **1** (irritation) حِكَّة **2** (want) رَغْبة (رِغاب ,رَغَبات)
B *vi* «rash, bites» حَكَّ (u; حَكّ) ,شَعَرَ بِحَكَّةٍ; **I was ~ing all over** كُنْتُ أَشْعُرُ بِحَكّةٍ في كُلِّ جِسْمي

itchy /ˈɪtʃi/ *adj* (**itchier**, **itchiest**) (infml) ‹*rash, bite*› مُثير للحَكّةِ

it'd /ˈɪtəd/ *abbr* = **it had**, = **it would**

item /ˈʌɪtəm/ *n* **1** (article) قِطْعة (قِطَع); **an ~ of clothing** قِطْعة مَلابِسَ; **an ~ of furniture** قِطْعة أَثاثٍ; **luxury ~s** سِلَع كَماليّة **2** (mention in the news) خَبَر (أَخبار); **a news ~** خَبَر **3** (in agendas) بَنْد (بُنود)

(Idiom) **to be an item** (infml) [أَصْبَحَتْ تَرْبِطُ بَيْنَهُما عَلاقةٌ]

itemize, -ise (BrE) /ˈʌɪtəmʌɪz/ *vt* فَصَّل ‹*expenses, a bill*›

itinerant /ʌɪˈtɪn(ə)rənt/ **A** *adj* ‹*life, preacher*› مُتَجَوِّل; **~ teacher** (AmE) مُعَلِّم مُتَجَوِّل (لتَقْديم المُساعَدةِ للطُلّابِ المُعاقينَ)
B *n* رَحّال (رَحّالة ,رُحَّل ,رُحّال) ,مُتَجَوِّل

itinerary /ʌɪˈtɪn(ə)rəri/ *n* (*pl* **itineraries**) خطّ سَيْرِ الرِحْلةِ

it'll /ˈɪt(ə)l/ *abbr* = **it will**

its /ɪts/ *determiner* ـه ,ـها; **he put the sword in ~ sheath** وَضَعَ السَيْفَ في غِمْدِهِ; **they chose the neighbourhood for ~ schools** اِخْتاروا الحَيَّ لِأَجْلِ مَدارِسِهِ; **it's time to clean ~ cage** حانَ الوَقْتُ لِتَنْظيفِ قَفَصِهِ

it's /ɪts/ *abbr* = **it is**, = **it has**

itself /ɪtˈsɛlf/ *pron* **1** (reflexive) نَفْسُهُ \ نَفْسُها; **the cat was washing ~** كانَ القِطُّ يَغْسِلُ نَفْسَهُ; **it's hurt ~** آذى نَفْسَهُ **2** (emphatic) نَفْسُهُ \ نَفْسُها; **the house ~ was small** كانَ البَيْتُ نَفْسُهُ صَغيراً; **the library is not in the university ~** لَيْسَت المَكْتَبةُ في الجامِعةِ نَفْسِها \ ذاتِها; **he was kindness ~** كانَ الطيبةَ نَفْسَها **3** (after prepositions) **the heating comes on by ~** يَعْمَلُ نِظامُ التَدْفِئةِ بِشَكْلٍ تِلْقائيٍّ; **the house stands by ~** يَقِفُ البَيْتُ وَحيداً; **learning Italian is not difficult in ~** تَعَلُّمُ اللُغةِ الإيطاليّةِ لَيْسَ صَعْباً في حَدِّ ذاتِهِ

ITV /ʌɪtiːˈviː/ *abbr* (BrE) = **Independent Television** [شَبَكة تِلِفِزْيون بَريطانيّة مُسْتَقِلّة]

IUD /ʌɪjuːˈdiː/ *n* = **intrauterine device** لَوْلَب طِبّيّ ,واقٍ رَحِميّ

I've /ʌɪv/ *abbr* = **I have**

IVF /ʌɪviːˈɛf/ *n* = **in vitro fertilization** تَلْقيح صِناعيّ

ivory /ˈʌɪv(ə)ri/ **A** *n* (*pl* **ivories**) **1** (substance) عاج **2** (colour) عاجيّ
B *adj* ‹*skin, dress*› عاجيّ

Ivory Coast *pr n* ساحِل العاج ,كوتْ ديفْوار

ivy /ˈʌɪvi/ *n* لَبْلاب

Ivy League *n* رابِطة اللَبْلابِ (رابِطة تَضُمُّ مَجْموعةً من أَفْضَل الجامِعاتِ الأَمْريكيّةِ)

Jj

J, j /dʒeɪ/ *n* جيم ≈ (الحَرْف العاشِر من الأَبْجَدِيّةِ الإنْكْليزيّة)

jab /dʒab/ **A** *vt* (**-bb-**) ضَغَطَ (a; ضَغْط؛ على) ‹a button›; طَعَنَ (a-u; طَعْن ,ب), وَخَزَ (i; وَخْز ;ب) ‹your finger›; **he ~bed his finger at me** وَجَّهَ إِصْبَعَهُ في اتِّجاهي; **she ~bed her elbow into my ribs** لَكَزَتْني في أَضْلاعي بِكوعِها

B *n* **1** (a strong hit) (with a stick, an elbow) ضَرْبة (ضَرَبات) **2** (BrE infml) (a vaccination) حُقْنة (حُقَن) **3** (in boxing) لَكْمة (لَكَمات)

jabber /ˈdʒabə/ *vi* [تَكَلَّمَ بِلُغةٍ غَيْرِ مَفْهومةٍ]

jack /dʒak/ *n* **1** (for a car) رافِعة (رَوافِعُ) **2** (in cards) وَلَد (وُلْد ,أَوْلاد) **3** (socket) مِقْبَس

(Idiom) **to be a jack of all trades (and master of none)** سَبْعُ صَنائِعَ والبَخْتُ ضائِعٌ

(Phrasal verbs) **jack in** (BrE infml): **~ [sth] in, ~ in [sth]** تَرَكَ [شَيْئاً] ‹your job, a task›; **she hated her job, and decided to ~ it in** كانَتْ تَكْرَهُ وَظيفَتَها، وَقَرَّرَتْ تَرْكَها

• **jack up**: **~ up [sth], ~ [sth] up** رَفَعَ [شَيْئاً] ‹a car, truck›

jackal /ˈdʒakɔːl/ *n* ابْن آوى (بَنو آوى)

jackdaw /ˈdʒakdɔː/ *n* [زاغ صَغير]

jacket /ˈdʒakɪt/ *n* **1** (a garment) جاكيت (جاكيتات); **a sports ~** سُتْرة رِياضيّة **2** (also **dust jacket**) (of a book) غِلاف (خارِجيّ) (أَغْطِية ,غِطاء) **3** (AmE) (of a record) غِلاف (غُلُف) ضدّ الغُبارِ

jacket potato *n* [بَطاطا مُحَمَّصة بِقِشْرِها]

jackhammer /ˈdʒakhamə/ *n* مِطْرَقة هَوائيّة

jack-in-the-box /ˈdʒakɪnðəbɒks/ *n* [لُعْبة تَتَأَلَّفُ من دُمْيةٍ مُثَبَّتةٍ على نابِضٍ داخِلَ صُنْدوقٍ كَرْتونيٍّ]

jackknife /ˈdʒaknʌɪf/ *vi* «trucks, vehicles» [أَخَذَ شَكْلَ مِطْواةٍ أَثْناء حادِثٍ مُروريٍّ]

jackpot /ˈdʒakpɒt/ *n* جاكبوت

(Idiom) **to hit the jackpot** (in a lottery) رَبِحَ الجاكْبوت; (to be successful) حَقَّقَ نَجاحاً هائِلاً

jackrabbit /ˈdʒakrabɪt/ *n* [أَرْنَب بَرّيّ]

Jacuzzi® /dʒəˈkuːzi/ *n* جاكوزي (بانْيو بِدَوّامةِ الماءِ والفَقاقيعِ الهَوائيّة)

jade /dʒeɪd/ *n* **1** (stone) يَشْم **2** (also **jade green**) أَخْضَر فاتِح

jaded /ˈdʒeɪdɪd/ *adj* ‹palate, view› سَؤوم

jagged /ˈdʒagɪd/ *adj* ‹edge, line› مُسَنَّن; ‹rock, peak› حادّ النِهايةِ

jaguar /ˈdʒagjʊə/ *n* نِمْر أَمْريكيّ

jail /dʒeɪl/ **A** *n* سِجْن (سُجون); **to be in ~ for murder** سُجِنَ لارْتِكابِهِ جَريمةَ قَتْلٍ; **to be sent to ~** أُرْسِلَ إلى السِجْنِ

B *vt* سَجَنَ (u; سَجْن) ‹an offender, a criminal›

jailer /ˈdʒeɪlə/ *n* (old use) سَجّان

jail sentence *n* حُكْم بالسِجْنِ

jalopy /dʒəˈlɒpi/ *n* (*pl* **jalopies**) (infml) [سَيّارة مُتَهالِكة]

jam /dʒam/ **A** *vt* (**- mm-**) **1** (to press) **to ~ things into a case/drawer** حَشَرَ الأَشْياءَ في صُنْدوقٍ \ دُرْجٍ; **she ~med her clothes into the bag** حَشَرَتْ مَلابِسَها في الحَقيبةِ; **to ~ one's hat on** ضَغَطَ القُبَّعةَ على رَأْسِهِ; **to ~ the brake on** ضَغَطَ على المِكْبَحِ بِقوّةٍ **2** (to wedge) زَنَقَ (a-i; زَنْق) ‹the door, window›; **~ the window so that it doesn't rattle** أَزْنُقِ النافِذةَ بِحَيْثُ لا تَهْتَزُّ; **we were ~med together like sardines in a can** انْحَشَرْنا مَعاً مِثْلَ السَرْدين في عُلْبةٍ **3** (also **jam up**) (to fill up) زَحَمَ (a; زَحْم); **cars ~med (up) the roads** زَحَمَت السَيّاراتُ الشَوارِعَ; **people ~med the exits** زَحَمَ الناسُ المَخارِجَ; **to be ~med with people/things** كانَ مُزْدَحِماً بالناسِ \ بالأَشْياءِ **4** (also **jam up**) (to block) سَدَّ (u; سَدّ) ‹the lock, motor, system›

⑤ (in broadcasts) شَوَّش (على) ‹*a transmission, frequency*›

B *vi* (-mm-) (to become stuck) «locks, windows» تَعَطَّل; **the printer keeps jamming** تَتَعَطَّلُ الطابِعةُ بِاسْتِمْرارٍ

C *n* ① (condiment) مُرَبّى (مُرَبَّيات); **apricot ~** مُرَبّى المِشْمِشِ

② (congestion of people) زِحام; (of traffic) اخْتِناق (اخْتِناقات); **there was such a ~ I couldn't get a ticket** كانَ هُناكَ زِحامٌ شَديدٌ لِدَرَجةِ أَنَّني لم أَسْتَطِع الحُصولَ على تَذْكِرةٍ

③ (operational failure) انْحِشار; **there's a ~ in the paper feed** هُناكَ انْحِشارٌ في تَغْذِيةِ الوَرَق ④ (infml) (difficult situation) وَرْطة (وَرَطات, وِراط), مَأْزِق (مَآزِق); **we're in a real ~ now!** نَحْنُ في وَرْطةٍ حَقيقيّةٍ الآنَ!; **to help sb out of a ~** ساعَدَ شَخْصاً في الخُروجِ من مَأْزِقٍ

Phrasal verb **jam in** **A** **~ in** «people» دَخَلَ بِصُعوبةٍ **B** **~ [sth/sb] in** ① (to wedge) حَشَرَ [شَيْئاً] ‹*clothes, books*› ② (to pack in) حَشَرَ [شَخْصاً] ‹*passengers*›

Jamaica /dʒəˈmeɪkə/ *pr n* جامايْكا

Jamaican /dʒəˈmeɪk(ə)n/ *n, adj* جامايْكيّ

jamb /dʒam/ *n* عِضادة

jam jar *n* بَرْطَمان مُرَبّى

jam-packed /ˌdʒamˈpakt/ *adj* (infml) ‹*bus, stadium*› مُكْتَظّ

jam session *n* [عَزْف دون تَمْرينٍ مُسْبَق]

jam tart *n* فَطيرة مُرَبّى

Jane Doe /dʒeɪn ˈdəʊ/ *n* (AmE) فُلانة الفُلانيّة ≈ (اسْم افْتِراضيّ يُسْتَخْدَمُ لتَسْمِيةِ المَرْأةِ حينَ يكونُ اسْمُها مَجْهولاً)

jangle /ˈdʒaŋg(ə)l/ *vi* «keys, bangles» صَلْصَلَ (i; صَلْصَلة), جَلْجَلَ (i; جَلْجَلة)

janitor /ˈdʒanɪtə/ *n* (AmE, Scot) بَوّاب

January /ˈdʒanjʊəri/ *n* يَنايِر (Mor, Egypt, Gulf), كانون الثاني (Levant, Iraq), جانْفيّ (Algeria, Tunisia) ▸ **March**

Japan /dʒəˈpan/ *pr n* اليابان (f)

Japanese /dʒapəˈniːz/ **A** *adj* ‹*food, city*› يابانيّ

B *n* (*pl* **Japanese**) ① (citizen) يابانيّ ② (language) (اللُغة) اليابانيّة

jar /dʒɑː/ **A** *n* ① (container) إناء (آنِية, أَوانٍ), وِعاء (أَوْعِية, أَواعٍ), بَرْطَمان (بَرْطَمانات) ② (jolt) ضَرْبة (ضَرَبات)

B *vt* (-rr-) تَعَرَّض لِرَجّةٍ \ صَدْمةٍ في ‹*one's knee, shoulder*›

C *vi* (-rr-) ① (to make a harsh sound) صَرَّ (i; صَرّ, صَرير), جَرَش (u; جَرْش); **to ~ on sb's nerves** أَثارَ أَعْصابَ شَخْصٍ

② (to clash) «colours» تَنافَرَ; «opinions» تَصادَمَ

jargon /ˈdʒɑːg(ə)n/ *n* [مُصْطَلَحات خاصّة بِمَجالٍ مُعَيَّنٍ]

jarring /ˈdʒɑːrɪŋ/ *adj* ‹*sound, chord*› صَرير, جَرْش

jasmine /ˈdʒazmɪn/ *n* ياسَمين

jaundice /ˈdʒɔːndɪs/ *n* يَرَقان

jaundiced /ˈdʒɔːndɪst/ *adj* ① (yellow) ‹*skin, baby*› مُصاب باليَرَقانِ ② (cynical) ‹*view, observer*› حَسود (حُسود)

jaunt /dʒɔːnt/ *n* نُزْهة (نُزَه, نُزْهات); **to go for a ~** قامَ بِنُزْهةٍ

jaunty /ˈdʒɔːnti/ *adj usu before n* (**jauntier**, **jauntiest**) ‹*hat*› مَرِح (مَرْحى, مَراحى); ‹*tune*› طَروب

Java /ˈdʒɑːvə/ *pr n* ① (island) جافا ② ®(Comput) جافا

javelin /ˈdʒavəlɪn/ *n* رُمْح (رِماح, أَرْماح)

jaw /dʒɔː/ *n* فَكّ (فُكوك)

Idiom **his jaw dropped** انْدَهَشَ; **my ~ dropped when I saw that he'd got married** انْدَهَشْتُ بِشِدّةٍ عِنْدَما وَجَدْتُ أَنَّهُ قد تَزَوَّجَ

jawbone /ˈdʒɔːbəʊn/ *n* عَظْم الفَكِّ

jay /dʒeɪ/ *n* أَبو زُرَيْق

jaywalk /ˈdʒeɪwɔːk/ *vi* «pedestrians, children» [مَشى \ عَبَرَ بِرُعونةٍ]

jaywalker /ˈdʒeɪwɔːkə/ *n* [مَنْ يَمْشي \ يَعْبُرُ بِرُعونةٍ]

jazz /dʒaz/ **A** *n* جاز

B *adj* ‹*musician, singer*› الجازِ

Phrasal verb **jazz up** (infml): **~ up [sth], ~ [sth] up** ① (to liven up) أَضْفى لَمْسةً من الحَيَوِيّةِ \ الانْتِعاشِ على [شَيْءٍ] ‹*a dress, an outfit*›; زَيَّنَ [شَيْئاً] ‹*a room*›; أَضْفى حَيَوِيّةً على [شَيْءٍ] ‹*a party, the atmosphere*› ② (to play like jazz) زادَ من حَيَوِيّةِ [شَيْءٍ] ‹*a tune, the music*›

jazzy /ˈdʒazi/ *adj* (**jazzier**, **jazziest**) ① ‹*music, rhythm*› جازيّ ② ‹*colour, pattern*› فاقِع الأَلْوانِ

jealous /ˈdʒɛləs/ *adj* ① (possessive) ‹*husband, wife*› غَيور (غُيُر); **he gets very ~** يَغارُ جِدًّا ② (envious) حَسود (حُسود);

her colleagues were ~ of her success حَسَدَها زُمَلائُها على نَجاحِها

jealousy /ˈdʒɛləsi/ *n* (*pl* **jealousies**) 1 [u] (possessiveness) (حُسود) حَسَد (envy) 2 غَيْرة

jeans /dʒiːnz/ *n pl* بَنْطَلون جينْز; **a pair of ~** بَنْطَلون جينْز; **she wore ~ and a T-shirt** ارْتَدَتْ بَنْطَلون جينْز وَتي شيرْت

Jeddah /ˈdʒɛdə/, **Jiddah** /ˈdʒɪdə/ *pr n* جِدّة (dipt)

jeep® /dʒiːp/ *n* سَيّارة جيب

jeer /dʒɪə/ **A** *vt* أَطْلَقَ صَيْحاتِ الاسْتِهْجانِ على ‹*a speaker, politician*›

B *vi* «crowds, protesters» أَطْلَقَ صَيْحاتِ الاسْتِهْجانِ; **to ~ at sb** أَطْلَقَ صَيْحاتِ الاسْتِهْجانِ في وَجْهِ شَخْصٍ

C *n* صَيْحة اسْتِهْجانٍ

jeering /ˈdʒɪərɪŋ/ *n* إطْلاق صَيْحاتِ الاسْتِهْجانِ

Jehovah /dʒɪˈhəʊvə/ *pr n* يَهْوه

Jehovah's witness *n* شاهِد يَهْوه

jellied /ˈdʒɛlid/ *adj* ‹*fish, fruit*› بالجيلي

jello® /ˈdʒɛləʊ/ *n* (AmE) حَلْوى جيلي

jelly /ˈdʒɛli/ *n* (*pl* **jellies**) 1 (BrE) (dessert) جيلي (حَلْوى) 2 (AmE) (jam) (مُرَبَّيات) مُرَبّى 3 (gelatinous substance) هُلام

jellyfish /ˈdʒɛlɪfɪʃ/ *n* (*pl* **jellyfish**) قِنْديل بَحْرٍ

jeopardize, -ise (BrE) /ˈdʒɛpədʌɪz/ *vt* عَرَّضَ للخَطَرِ ‹*security, lives*›

jeopardy /ˈdʒɛpədi/ *n* **in ~** في خَطَرٍ

Jericho /ˈdʒɛrɪkəʊ/ *pr n* أَريحا

jerk /dʒəːk/ **A** *n* 1 (sudden movement) هَزّة; **with a ~ of his head** بِهَزّة من رَأْسِهِ 2 (AmE infml) (obnoxious man) شَخْص أَخْرَق \ أَحْمَق

B *vt* هَزَّ (u; هَزّ) ‹*one's head, a lever, the rope*›

C *vi* 1 (to jolt) **to ~ to a halt** «vehicles» ارْتَجَّ ثُمَّ تَوَقَّفَ

2 «legs, muscles» تَشَنَّجَ

jerky /ˈdʒəːki/ *adj* (**jerkier, jerkiest**) ‹*movement*› مُرْتَجِف, مُهْتَزّ, مُرْتَعِش

jerry-built /ˈdʒɛrɪbɪlt/ *adj* (pej) ‹*cottage, shack*› [مَبْنيّ بِدونِ إتْقانٍ]

jerrycan /ˈdʒɛrɪkan/ *n* [صَفيحة بَنْزين \ ماءٍ]

jersey /ˈdʒəːzi/ *n* (*pl* **jerseys**) 1 (BrE) (sweater) ≈ سُتْرة, جيرْسي 2 (for sports) قَميص رِياضيّ 3 [u] (fabric) جيرْسي (نَوْع من النَسيجِ)

Jersey /ˈdʒəːzi/ *pr n* جيرْسي (جَزيرة)

Jerusalem /dʒəˈruːsələm/ *pr n* أورُشَليم, القُدْس (f)

Jerusalem artichoke *n* دَوّار الشَمْسِ الدَرَنيّ

jest /dʒɛst/ *n* نُكْتة (نُكَت, نِكات), مَزْحة; **in ~** على سَبيلِ الدُعابةِ \ المُزاحِ

jester /ˈdʒɛstə/ *n* مُهَرِّج المَلِكِ (في بِلاطِ مُلوكِ العُصورِ الوُسْطى)

Jesuit /ˈdʒɛzjʊɪt/ *n, adj* يَسوعيّ

Jesus /ˈdʒiːzəs/ *pr n* يَسوع (dipt); عيسى

jet /dʒɛt/ **A** *n* 1 (aircraft) طائِرة نَفّاثة; **a fighter/passenger ~** طائِرة نَفّاثة مُقاتِلة \ لِنَقْلِ المُسافِرينَ 2 (of water) تَدَفُّق (تَدَفُّقات), دَفْق; (of flame) لِسان (أَلْسِنة) 3 (stone) كَهْرَمان أَسْوَد

B *vi* (-tt-) (infml) **to ~ off to Beirut/Australia** طارَ إلى بَيْروتَ \ أُسْتُراليا

jet black *adj* (*before n* **jet-black**) ‹*hair, skin*› أَسْوَد فاحِم

jet engine *n* مُحَرِّك نَفّاث

jetfoil /ˈdʒɛtfɔɪl/ *n* [عَبّارة سَريعة]

jet lag *n* اضْطِراب الرِحْلاتِ الجَوِّيّةِ الطَويلةِ

jet-lagged /ˈdʒɛtlagd/ *adj* ‹*traveller, passengers*› يُعاني من اضْطِرابِ الرِحْلاتِ الجَوِّيّةِ الطَويلةِ; **to be ~** عانى من اضْطِرابِ الرِحْلاتِ الجَوِّيّةِ الطَويلةِ

jetsam /ˈdʒɛtsəm/ *n* مَقْذوفات البَحْرِ ▸ **flotsam**

jet set *n* (infml) طَبَقة \ عالَم الأَثْرِياءِ

jet-setter /ˈdʒɛtˌsɛtə/ *n* (infml) [شَخْص ثَريّ كَثير السَفَرِ]

jet ski® *n* دَرّاجة مائيّة, قارِب نَفّاث, جيت سْكي

jet-skiing /ˈdʒɛtskiːɪŋ/ *n* رُكوب الدَرّاجاتِ المائيّةِ

jettison /ˈdʒɛtɪs(ə)n/ *vt* تخَلَّصَ من (بالإلْقاءِ من سَفينةٍ أو طائِرةٍ)

jetty /ˈdʒɛti/ *n* (*pl* **jetties**) 1 (for boats) رَصيف ميناءٍ 2 (for planes) خُرْطوم الطائِرةِ

Jew /dʒuː/ *n* يَهوديّ (يَهود)

jewel /ˈdʒuːəl/ *n* 1 (gem) جَوْهَرة, حَجَر كَريم 2 (**jewels**, *pl*) (jewellery) مُجَوْهَرات 3 (person, building, etc) [شَيْء أو شَخْص ثَمين]

jeweller (BrE), **jeweler** (AmE) /ˈdʒuːələ/ *n* (person) مُجَوْهَراتيّ; (shop) مَحَلّ مُجَوْهَراتٍ; **a ~'s (shop)** مَحَلّ مُجَوْهَراتٍ

jewellery (BrE), **jewelry** (AmE) /ˈdʒuːəlri/ *n* مُجَوْهَرات; **to wear ~** لَبِسَ مُجَوْهَراتٍ

jewellery box *n* صُنْدوق مُجَوْهَراتٍ

Jewish /ˈdʒuːɪʃ/ *adj* ‹*community, faith*› يَهوديّ (يَهود)

Jew's harp *n* قيثار اليَهودِ

jib /dʒɪb/ *n* 1 (sail) شِراع أَماميّ 2 (of a crane) ذِراع (f; أَذْرُع)

jibe /dʒaɪb/ *n* سُخْريّة, اسْتِهْزاء (اسْتِهْزاءات)

Jiddah /ˈdʒɪdə/ ▸ **Jeddah**

jiffy /ˈdʒɪfi/ *n* (infml) لَحْظة (لَحَظات), وَهْلة (وَهَلات)

Jiffy bag® *n* (BrE) ظَرْف مُبَطَّن

jig /dʒɪg/ *n* 1 (dance) رَقْص ريفيّ سَريع الإيقاعِ 2 (device) أَداة تَثْبيتٍ وَتَوْجيهٍ

jiggle /ˈdʒɪg(ə)l/ *vt* هَزَّ (u; هَزّ) ‹*keys, one's legs*›

jigsaw /ˈdʒɪgsɔː/ *n* 1 (also **jigsaw puzzle**) لُعْبة تَجْميع صُوَر مُفَكَّكةٍ 2 (saw) مِنشار مُنْحَنَياتٍ \ تَخريم

jihad /dʒɪˈhɑːd/ *n* جِهاد; **greater/lesser ~** الجِهاد الأَكْبَر \ الأَصْغَر

jihadi /dʒɪˈhɑːdi/ *n* (*pl* **jihadis**) جِهاديّ

jilbab /dʒɪlˈbab/ *n* جِلْباب (جَلابيبُ)

jilt /dʒɪlt/ *vt* هَجَرَ (u; هَجْر), تَخَلّى (عن) ‹*a lover*›

jingle /ˈdʒɪŋg(ə)l/ **A** *n* 1 (of bells) رَنين; (of keys, coins) صَلْصَلة 2 (tune) أُغْنية دِعائيّة \ إعْلانيّة
B *vt* جَلْجَلَ (i; جَلْجَلة), خَشْخَشَ (i; خَشْخَشة) ‹*keys, coins*›
C *vi* «bells» رَنَّ (i; رَنين); «keys» خَشْخَشَ (i; خَشْخَشة), صَلْصَلَ (i; صَلْصَلة)

jingoism /ˈdʒɪŋgəʊɪz(ə)m/ *n* (pej) تَعَصُّب قَوْميّ

jingoist /ˈdʒɪŋgəʊɪst/ *n* مُتَعَصِّب قَوْميًّا, مُغالٍ في الوَطَنيّةِ

jinn, **djinn** /dʒɪn/ *n* (*pl* **jinn**, **jinns**) جِنّ (n coll; singul n جِنّيّ)

jinx /dʒɪŋks/ *n* نَحْس (نُحوس); **I think there's a ~ on the team** أَعْتَقِدُ أنّ الفَريقَ مَنْحوسٌ

jitney /ˈdʒɪtni/ *n* (AmE) 1 (bus) ميكْروباص 2 (taxi) سَيّارة أُجْرةٍ غَيْر مُرَخَّصةٍ

jitters /ˈdʒɪtəz/ *n pl* (infml) عَصَبيّة, تَوَتُّر \ قَلَق شَديد; **I got the ~** أنا مُتَوَتِّرٌ جِدًّا

jittery /ˈdʒɪt(ə)ri/ *adj* ‹*investors, nerves*› مُتَوَتِّر, قَلِق

Jnr /ˈdʒuːnjə/ *abbr* = **junior** الابْن

job /dʒɒb/ *n* 1 (post) وَظيفة (وَظائِفُ); **she has a ~ as a secretary in the ministry** تَعْمَلُ كَسِكْرِتيرة في الوِزارةِ; **what's your ~?** ما وَظيفَتُكَ؟; **a teaching ~** وَظيفة تَدْريسٍ; **to look for/get a ~** بَحَثَ عن \ حَصَلَ على وَظيفةٍ; **to be out of a ~** كانَ عاطِلاً عن العَمَلِ 2 (infml) (role) دَوْر (أَدْوار), وَظيفة (وَظائِفُ); **it's my ~ to get the kids up in the morning** إيقاظُ الأَطْفالِ في الصَباحِ هو مَسْؤوليَّتي 3 (duty) واجِب (واجِبات), وَظيفة (وَظائِفُ); **she's only doing her ~** هي فَقَطْ تُؤَدّي واجِبَها 4 (task) مُهِمّة (مُهِمّات, مَهامّ), وَظيفة (وَظائِفُ); **to find a ~ for sb to do** وَجَدَ لِشَخْصٍ شَيْئًا يَفْعَلُهُ 5 (assignment) عَمَل (أَعْمال); **the dam project was a big ~ for the local construction company** كانَ مَشْروعُ السَدِّ عَمَلاً كَبيراً جِدًّا بالنِسْبةِ لِشَرِكةِ الإنْشاءاتِ المَحَلّيّةِ; **to make a good/bad ~ of sth** عَمِلَ شَيْئًا بِشَكْلٍ جَيِّدٍ \ رَديءٍ 6 (infml) (difficult activity) **a real ~, quite a ~** مُهِمّة صَعْبة 7 (Comput) مُهِمّة (مَهامّ); **cancel all the pending print ~s** الْغِ كُلَّ مَهامِّ الطِباعةِ

Idioms **it's a good job ...** (BrE) (infml) إنّهُ لَشَيْءٌ طَيِّبٌ ...; **to be on the job** (working) كانَ يَقومُ بِعَمَلِهِ; **to do the job** (BrE) (infml) أَدّى الغَرَضَ; **that'll do the ~ nicely** ذلك سَيُؤَدّي الغَرَضَ بِشَكْلٍ طَيِّبٍ; **to give sb/sth up as a bad job** (BrE) (infml) يَئِسَ من إمْكانيّةِ إصْلاحِ شَخْصٍ \ شَيْءٍ

jobcentre /ˈdʒɒbsentə/ *n* (BrE) مَكْتَب الوَظائِفِ

job creation scheme *n* (BrE) بَرْنامَج خَلْقِ فُرَصٍ لِلعَمَلِ

job description *n* وَصْف \ تَوْصيف وَظيفيّ

job-hunt /ˈdʒɒbˌhʌnt/ *vi* «the unemployed, students» بَحَثَ عن وَظيفةٍ

job-hunting /ˈdʒɒbhʌntɪŋ/ *n* بَحْث عن وَظيفةٍ

jobless /ˈdʒɒbləs/ *adj* ‹*workers, young people*› عاطِل عن العَمَلِ, بِدونِ وَظيفةٍ

job lot *n* (pej) شَرْوة (مَجْموعة من السِلَعِ تُباعُ كُلُّها مَعاً)

jobseeker *n* (BrE) باحِث عن عَمَلٍ

jobseeker's allowance /dʒɒbsiːkəz əˈlaʊəns/ *n* (BrE) بَدَل البَحْثِ عن عَمَلٍ

job-share /ˈdʒɒbʃɛː/ *n* [وَظيفة يُشارِكُ فيها شَخْصانِ]

job sharing *n* [مُشارَكة في وَظيفةٍ واحِدةٍ]

jockey /ˈdʒɒki/ *n* فارِس, خَيّال (في سِباقاتِ الخَيْلِ)

jockey shorts *n* (AmE) [سِرْوال داخِليّ ضَيِّق]

jockstrap /ˈdʒɒkstrap/ *n* حِزام وِقايةٍ (حِزام رِجاليّ لِحِمايةِ الأَعْضاءِ التَناسُلِيّة)

jocular /ˈdʒɒkjʊlə/ *adj* ‹*person*› كَثير المِزاح; ‹*mood*› مَرِح; ‹*manner, remark*› هَزْلِيّ

jodhpurs /ˈdʒɒdpəz/ *n pl* بَنْطَلون \ سِرْوال فُروسِيّةٍ; **a pair of ~** بَنْطَلون \ سِرْوال فُروسِيّةٍ

joe /dʒəʊ/ *n* (AmE infml) الرَجُل العاديّ, رَجُل الشارِع

Joe Bloggs *n* (BrE infml) الرَجُل العاديّ, رَجُل الشارِع

jog /dʒɒg/ **A** *vt* **(-gg-)** **1** (to knock) دَفَعَ (a; دَفْع) ‹*sb's elbow, the table*› **2** (to stimulate) نَشَّطَ, أَنْعَشَ ‹*sb's memory, brain*› **B** *vi* **(-gg-)** «joggers, children» هَرْوَلَ (i; هَرْوَلة), رَكَضَ (u; رَكْض); **to go ~ging** خَرَجَ لِيُمارِسَ الرَكْضَ \ الهَرْوَلةَ **C** *n* **1** (a run) هَرْوَلة, رَكْض; **to go for a ~** خَرَجَ لِيُمارِسَ الرَكْضَ \ الهَرْوَلةَ **2** (a knock) دَفْعة (دَفَعات)

jogger /ˈdʒɒgə/ *n* [شَخْص يُمارِسُ الرَكْضَ]

jogging /ˈdʒɒgɪŋ/ *n* هَرْوَلة, رَكْض

john /dʒɒn/ *n* (AmE infml) **the ~** المِرْحاض

John Doe *n* (AmE) فُلان الفُلانيّ (اسْم افْتِراضيّ)

join /dʒɔɪn/ **A** *vt* **1** (to meet up with) رافَقَ ‹*a colleague, your family*›; **may I ~ you?** هل يُمْكِنُني أَنْ أُرافِقَكَ؟ **2** (to become a member of) انْضَمَّ (إلى) ‹*an organization, a party, a club, expedition*›; **~ the club!** (infml) الحالُ من بَعْضِهِ! **3** (to become part of) انْضَمَّ (إلى) ‹*a queue, line, demonstration*›; **to ~ the protests/strike** انْضَمَّ إلى الاحْتِجاجاتِ \ الإضْرابِ; **we ~ed the rush for the door** انْطَلَقْنا مع مَنْ هَرَعوا إلى البابِ **4** (to become an employee of) انْضَمَّ (إلى) ‹*a firm, company*›; **to ~ the navy/the secret service** انْضَمَّ إلى البَحْرِيّةِ \ جِهازِ المُخابَراتِ **5** (to be in association with) انْضَمَّ (إلى); **to ~ forces with sb** وَقَفَ جَنْباً إلى جَنْبٍ مع شَخْصٍ **6** (to board) رَكِبَ (a; رُكوب) ‹*a train, ship*› **7** (to attach) وَصَّلَ ‹*the ends, parts*› **8** (to link) رَبَطَ (i-u; رَبْط) ‹*the towns*›; وَصَّلَ (بين) ‹*dots*›; **the road that ~s the two cities** الطَريق الّذي يَرْبِطُ المَدينَتَيْنِ; **the causeway that ~s Bahrain to Saudi Arabia** الجِسْر الّذي يَرْبِطُ البَحْرَيْنِ بالمَمْلَكةِ العَرَبيّةِ السَعوديّةِ **9** (to merge with) الْتَقى (ب) ‹*a road, river*›

B *vi* **1** (to become a member) انْضَمَّ **2** (to connect, meet) «pieces, cables, pipes» اتَّصَلَ

C *n* وُصْلة (وُصَل, وُصْلات)

Phrasal verbs **join in** **1** (to participate) «singers, bystanders» شارَكَ **2** **~ in [sth]** (to participate in) شارَكَ في شَيْءٍ ‹*the celebrations, protest, discussion*›; **to ~ in the fun** شارَكَ في المَرَح

• **join up** **A** **1** (Mil) (to enlist) الْتَحَقَ بالجَيْشِ **2** (to meet up) «friends» الْتَقى **B** **~ up [sth], ~ [sth] up** وَصَّلَ بين [شَيْءٍ] ‹*the dots*›

joiner /ˈdʒɔɪnə/ *n* نَجّار بابٍ وَشُبّاكٍ

joint /dʒɔɪnt/ **A** *n* **1** (Anat) مَفْصِل (مَفاصِلُ); **to have painful** *or* **aching ~s** كانَ لَدَيْهِ أَلَمٌ في المَفاصِلِ; **his shoulder was out of ~** أُصيبَ بِخَلْعٍ في مَفْصِلِ الكَتِفِ **2** (in carpentry, plumbing) وُصْلة (وُصَل, وُصْلات) **3** (of meat) قِطْعة لَحْمٍ **4** (infml) (bar, club, etc) [مَطْعَم, نادٍ]; **a pizza ~** مَطْعَم بيتْزا **5** (infml) (cannabis cigarette) سيجارة حَشيشٍ

B *adj* ‹*operation, initiative, winner*› مُشْتَرَك; **I was ~ third** كُنْتُ الثالِثَ مُكَرَّراً

joint account *n* حِساب مُشْتَرَك

joint effort *n* جُهْد مُشْتَرَك

joint honours (BrE), **joint honors** (AmE) *n* شَهادة مُزْدَوَجة مع مَرْتَبةِ الشَرَف

jointly /ˈdʒɔɪntli/ *adv* ‹*owned, organized*› بِشَكْلٍ مُشْتَرَكٍ

joint owner *n* شَريك في المِلْكيّةِ

joint replacement *n* اسْتِبْدال مَفْصِلٍ

joint-stock company /ˌdʒɔɪntˈstɒk ˌkʌmp(ə)ni/ *n* شَرِكة مُساهَمةٍ

joint venture *n* مَشْروع مُشْتَرَك

joist /dʒɔɪst/ *n* عارِضة (عَوارِضُ), رافِدة (رَوافِدُ); **a timber/steel ~** عارِضة من الخَشَبِ \ الحَديدِ الصُلْبِ

joke /dʒəʊk/ **A** *n* **1** (story) نُكْتَة (نكات, نُكَت); **to tell a ~** حَكى نُكْتَةً; **to get/see the ~** فَهِمَ مَغْزى النُكْتَةِ; **to have a ~ about sth** سَخِرَ من شَيْءٍ **2** (laughing matter) نُكْتَة (نكات, نُكَت); **being out of work is no ~** كَوْنُ المَرْءِ بدونِ عَمَلٍ لَيْسَ أَمْراً مُضْحِكاً; **this is beyond a ~** هذا خارِجُ حُدودِ المِزاحِ; **to turn sth into a ~** حَوَّلَ شَيْئاً إِلى نُكْتَةٍ **3** (prank) مَقْلَب (مَقالِبُ); **to play a ~ on sb** عَمِلَ مَقْلَباً في شَخْصٍ **4** (ridiculous person/thing) أُضْحوكة (أَضاحيكُ); **their proposals are a ~** مُقْتَرَحاتُهُمْ أُضْحوكةٌ

B *vi* «speakers, friends» مَزَحَ (a; مَزْح); **to ~ about sth** مَزَحَ بِخُصوصِ شَيْءٍ; **he was joking with the bystanders** كانَ يَمْزَحُ مع المارَّةِ; **you must be joking!** لا بُدَّ أَنَّكَ تَمْزَحُ!; **I'm not joking!** أنا لا أَمْزَحُ!

joker /ˈdʒəʊkə/ *n* **1** (prankster) مُهَرِّج, شَخْص كَثير المِزاحِ **2** (infml) (inept person) شَخْص عَديم الكَفاءةِ **3** (in cards) جوكَر

jokey /ˈdʒəʊki/ *adj* (**jokier, jokiest**) ‹*tone, reference*› هَزْلِيّ

jolly /ˈdʒɒli/ **A** *adj* (**jollier, jolliest**) ‹*tune, mood, person*› مَرِح (مَرْحى)

B *adv* (BrE infml) (as an intensifier) جِدًّا; **~ good!** حَسَن جِدًّا!; **you can ~ well do it yourself!** يُمْكِنُكَ كَذٰلِكَ أَنْ تَفْعَلَهُ بِنَفْسِكَ!

jolt /dʒəʊlt/ **A** *vt* رَجَّ (u; رَجّ) ‹*passengers*›; **I was ~ed out of my seat** قَذَفَتْني الرَجَّةُ من مَقْعَدي

B *vi* «train, lift» ارْتَجَّ

C *n* **1** (jerk) ارْتِجاج (ارْتِجاجات) **2** (shock) صَدْمة (صَدَمات)

Jordan /ˈdʒɔːd(ə)n/ *pr n* الأُرْدُن

Jordanian /dʒɔːˈdeɪniən/ *n, adj* أُرْدُنِيّ

jostle /ˈdʒɒs(ə)l/ **A** *vt* دَفَعَ (a; دَفْع)

B *vi* «crowds, passengers» تَدافَعَ; **photographers ~d for position** تَدافَعَ المُصَوِّرونَ للحُصولِ على مَكانٍ

jot /dʒɒt/ *n* ≈ مِثْقال ذَرَّةٍ

Phrasal verb **jot down**: **~ down [sth], ~ [sth] down** دَوَّنَ [شَيْئاً] بِاسْتِعْجالٍ ‹*notes, ideas*›

joule /dʒuːl/ *n* جول (وَحْدة قِياسِ الطاقةِ)

journal /ˈdʒɜːn(ə)l/ *n* **1** (periodical) مَجَلّة عِلْمِيّة; (newspaper) جَريدة (جَرائِدُ), صَحيفة (صَحائِفُ, صُحُف) **2** (diary) مُذَكِّرة, مُفَكِّرة

journalism /ˈdʒɜːnəlɪz(ə)m/ *n* صَحافة

journalist /ˈdʒɜːnəlɪst/ *n* صَحَفِيّ, صُحُفِيّ; **a radio/TV ~** صَحافيّ في الإذاعةِ \ التِلِفِزْيون; **a newspaper ~** صَحافيّ في جريدةٍ

journalistic /dʒɜːnəˈlɪstɪk/ *adj* ‹*career, style*› صُحُفِيّ

journey /ˈdʒɜːni/ *n* (*pl* **journeys**) رِحْلة (رِحَل); **to make a ~** قامَ بِرِحْلةٍ

joust /dʒaʊst/ *vi* «knights, gladiators» بارَزَ بِرُمْحٍ (في العُصورِ الوُسْطى)

jovial /ˈdʒəʊviəl/ *adj* ‹*mood, fellow*› مَرِح (مَرْحى)

jowls /dʒaʊlz/ *n pl* ≈ أَسْفَل الخَدَّيْنِ

joy /dʒɔɪ/ *n* **1** (great pleasure) سُرور, سَعادة, فَرَح (أَفْراح); **to jump for ~** قَفَزَ من الفَرَحِ **2** (source of joy) مَصْدَر ابْتِهاجٍ; **her dancing is a ~ to watch** يَبْعَثُ رَقْصُها على البَهْجةِ

joyful /ˈdʒɔɪfʊl/ *adj* ‹*celebration, mood*› مُبْتَهِج, مَسْرور; **we were ~ at/about the news of her release** ابْتَهَجْنا لِسَماعِ خَبَرِ إِطْلاقِ سَراحِها

joyless /ˈdʒɔɪləs/ *adj* ‹*affair, existence*› كَئيب, تَعيس (تُعَساءُ), خالٍ من السَعادةِ

joyous /ˈdʒɔɪəs/ *adj* ‹*occasion, welcome*› مُبْهِج \ يَبْعَثُ على الفَرَحِ السَعادةِ

joyrider /ˈdʒɔɪraɪdə/ *n* [سارِق سَيّارةٍ للاسْتِمْتاعِ بها فَقَطْ]

joyriding /ˈdʒɔɪraɪdɪŋ/ *n* [سَرِقة سَيّارةٍ للاسْتِمْتاعِ بها فَقَطْ]

joystick /ˈdʒɔɪstɪk/ *n* **1** (in a plane) عَصا تَحَكُّمٍ **2** (for gaming) عَصا تَحَكُّمٍ, عَصا أَلْعابٍ

Jr /ˈdʒuːnjə/ *abbr* = **junior** الابْن

Juba /ˈdʒuːbə/ *pr n* جوبا

jubilant /ˈdʒuːbɪlənt/ *adj* ‹*crowd*› مُبْتَهِج; **a ~ mood** حالة من الابْتِهاجِ

jubilee /ˈdʒuːbɪliː/ *n* يوبيل

Judaism /ˈdʒuːdeɪɪz(ə)m/ *n* يَهودِيّة

judge /dʒʌdʒ/ **A** *n* **1** (in a court) قاضٍ (قُضاة); **the ~ found him guilty** حَكَمَ القاضي بِأَنَّهُ مُذْنِبٌ **2** (in competitions, etc) حَكَم (حُكّام), مُحَكِّم; **the ~s' decision is final** قَرارُ الحَكَمِ نِهائيٌّ; **to be a good ~ of character** لَدَيْهِ قُدْرةٌ جَيِّدةٌ على الحُكْمِ على الشَّخْصيّةِ

B *vt* **1** (in court) حَكَمَ (u; حُكْم) (على) ‹*the accused, prisoner*›; **to ~ sb guilty** حَكَمَ على شَخْصٍ بِأَنَّهُ مُذْنِبٌ **2** (in competitions, etc) حَكَّمَ (بين) ‹*the competitors, entries*›; **she was asked to ~ the short story competition** طُلِبَ منْها التَّحْكيمُ في مُسابَقةِ القِصّةِ القَصيرةِ; **who are you to ~ others?** مَنْ تَكونُ أَنْتَ لِتَحْكُمَ على الآخَرينَ؟ **3** (to estimate) قَدَّرَ ‹*the distance, reaction*›; **it was hard to ~ the extent of the damage** كانَ من الصَعْبِ تَقْديرُ حَجْمِ الضَرَرِ **4** (to rate) قَيَّمَ ‹*ability, performance, quality*›; **the operation was ~d a great success** اُعْتُبِرَت العَمَليّةُ ناجِحةً نَجاحاً كَبيراً

C *vi* حَكَمَ (u; حُكْم); **I am in no position to ~** لَسْتُ في مَوْقِعٍ يُمَكِّنُني من الحُكْمِ; **as far as one can ~** بِقَدْرِ ما يُمْكِنُ لِلمَرْءِ أَنْ يرى

judgement, **judgment** /ˈdʒʌdʒmənt/ *n* **1** (opinion) رَأْي (آراء), حُكْم (أَحْكام); **in my ~** في رَأْيي; **to pass ~ on sth** انْتَقَدَ شَيْئاً, أَصْدَرَ أَحْكاماً على شَيْءٍ **2** (of a judge) حُكْم (أَحْكام); **to hand down a ~** أَصْدَرَ حُكْماً **3** [u] (discernment) تَقْدير; **an error of ~** خَطأٌ في التَّقْديرِ; **I lent him the car against my better ~** أَعَرْتُهُ السَيّارةَ على الرَغْمِ من عَدَمِ وُثوقي بِهِ

judgemental, **judgmental** /dʒʌdʒˈmɛnt(ə)l/ *adj* ‹*attitude, hypocrite*› كَثير الانْتِقادِ, سَريع في إِطْلاقِ الأَحْكام; **don't be so ~!** لا تُسْرِعْ في إِطْلاقِ الأَحْكامِ!

Judgement Day, **Judgment Day** *n* يَوْم الحِسابِ

judicial /dʒuːˈdɪʃ(ə)l/ *adj* ‹*system, appointment*› قَضائيّ

judiciary /dʒʊˈdɪʃ(ə)ri/ *n* **1** (arm of government) قَضاء **2** (judges) قُضاة

judicious /dʒʊˈdɪʃəs/ *adj* ‹*use, selection*› حكيم (حُكَماءُ)

judo /ˈdʒuːdəʊ/ *n* جودو

jug /dʒʌg/ *n* **1** (BrE) دَوْرَق (دَوارِقُ) **2** (AmE) (flagon) إِبْريق (أَباريقُ)

juggernaut /ˈdʒʌgənɔːt/ *n* **1** (force) قوّة ماحِقة \ ساحِقة **2** (BrE) (truck) شاحِنة ثَقيلة عارِمة

juggle /ˈdʒʌg(ə)l/ **A** *vt* [قَذَفَ في الهَواءِ بِطَريقةٍ بَهْلَوانيّةٍ] ‹*balls*› **B** *vi* [قَذَفَ الكُراتِ في الهَواءِ والْتَقَطَها بِطَريقةٍ بَهْلَوانيّةٍ]

juggler /ˈdʒʌglə/ *n* [شَخْص يَقْذِفُ الكُراتِ في الهَواءِ ويَلْتَقِطُها بِطَريقةٍ بَهْلَوانيّةٍ]

jugular /ˈdʒʌgjʊlə/ *n* وَريد وِداجيّ

juice /dʒuːs/ *n* **1** (from fruit) عَصير; **a carton of apple ~** عُلْبة عَصيرِ تُفّاحٍ; **add the ~ of two lemons** أَضِفْ عَصيرَ لَيْمونَتَيْنِ; **two orange ~s please** كوبانِ من عَصيرِ البُرْتُقالِ, من فَضْلِكَ **2** (from meat) ماء (أَمْواه, مِياه) **3** (in the stomach) عُصارة; **gastric ~s** عُصارات مَعِديّة

juicer /ˈdʒuːsə/ *n* عَصّارة

juicy /ˈdʒuːsi/ *adj* (**juicier**, **juiciest**) **1** ‹*fruit*› غَضّ; ‹*steak*› طَريّ **2** (infml) ‹*gossip, details*› مُثير

ju-jitsu /dʒuːˈdʒɪtsuː/ *n* جوجيتْسو (رِياضة قِتاليّة يابانيّة)

jukebox /ˈdʒuːkbɒks/ *n* [جِهاز لِتَشْغيلِ الموسيقى يَعْمَلُ بالقِطَعِ النَقْديّةِ]

July /dʒʊˈlʌɪ/ *n* يولِيو (Mor, Egypt, Gulf), تَمّوز (dipt) (Levant, Iraq), جُويلية (Algeria, Tunisia) ▸ **March**

Jumada al-Thaniya /dʒuːˌmɑːdə alˈθɑːnijə/ *n* جُمادى الثانية

Jumada al-Ula /dʒuːˌmɑːdə alˈuːlə/ *n* جُمادى الأولى

jumble /ˈdʒʌmb(ə)l/ **A** *n* فَوْضى, خَليط مُشَوَّش \ غَيْر مُتَجانِسٍ (f)

B *vt* (also **jumble up**) خَلَطَ بِشَكْلٍ غَيْرِ مُنَظَّمٍ ‹*words, objects*›

jumble sale *n* (BrE) [بَيْع أَشْياءَ مُسْتَعْمَلةٍ لِلأَغْراضِ الخَيْريّةِ]

jumbo /ˈdʒʌmbəʊ/ **A** *n* (also **jumbo jet**) طائِرة جامْبو

B *adj* (infml) ‹*pack, bag*› ضَخْم

jump /dʒʌmp/ **A** *vt* **1** (to leap over) قَفَزَ (i; قَفْز, قَفَزان) فوق ‹*an obstacle, a ditch*›; **he ~ed three metres** قَفَزَ ثَلاثةَ أَمْتارٍ **2** (to get ahead) **to ~ the lights** تَجاوَزَ الإِشارةَ الحَمْراءَ; **to ~ the queue** تَخَطّى دَوْرَهُ في الطابورِ **3** (to escape) **to ~ ship** فَرَّ من السَفينةِ **4** (to miss out) تَخَطّى ‹*a stage, generation*› **5** (infml) (to attack) هاجَمَ ‹*a victim, passer-by*›

B *vi* **1** (to leap) قَفَزَ (i; قَفْز, قَفَزان); **to ~ across** *or* **over**

a ditch/hole **قَفَزَ فوق خِنْدَقٍ \ حُفْرةٍ; to ~ up and down** لم يَتَمالَكْ أَعْصابَهُ; **the movie suddenly ~s from 1890 to 1920** يَقْفِزُ الفيلْم فَجْأَةً بالأَحْداثِ من 1890 إلى 1920
2 (in surprise) فَزِعَ (a; فَزَع); **you made me ~!** لَقَدْ أَفْزَعْتَني!
3 (to rise) «prices, profits, the birthrate» قَفَزَ (i; قَفْز, قَفَزان)
C *n* **1** (leap) قَفْزة (قَفَزات), وَثْبة (وَثَبات) **2** (in prices, profits, etc) قَفْزة (قَفَزات) **3** (in one's career) قَفْزة, طَفْرة (قَفَزات)

(Idiom) **to be one jump ahead of sb** كانَ مُتَقَدِّماً على شَخْصٍ بِشَكْلٍ واضِحٍ

(Phrasal verbs) **jump about, jump around** قَفَزَ (i; قَفْز, قَفَزان), تَنَطَّطَ
• **jump at**: **~ at [sth]** اقْتَنَصَ [شَيْئاً] ‹*an offer, a chance*›
• **jump back** «people, animals» تَراجَعَ للوَراءِ
• **jump down** قَفَزَ للأَسْفَلِ
• **jump on**: **~ on [sth]** (to mount) قَفَزَ إلى [شَيْءٍ] ‹*a bus, train*›; قَفَزَ على [شَيْءٍ] ‹*a bicycle, horse*›
• **jump out** (from a car, window, etc) قَفَزَ (i; قَفْز, قَفَزان); **to ~ out of a window/car** قَفَزَ من نافِذَةٍ \ سَيّارةٍ; **I ~ed out of bed** قَفَزْتُ من سَريري; **the deer ~ed out in front of the bus** قَفَزَ الغَزالُ فَجْأَةً أمامَ الحافِلةِ
• **jump up** نَهَضَ بِسُرْعةٍ; **he ~ed up and offered me his seat** نَهَضَ بِسُرْعةٍ وَعَرَضَ عَلَيَّ مَقْعَدَهُ

jumper /ˈdʒʌmpə/ *n* **1** (BrE) (sweater) كَنْزة, سُتْرة (سُتَر) **2** (AmE) (pinafore) ثَوْب بِدونِ أَكْمامٍ

jumper cables *n* (AmE) كابِل تَشْغيلِ, كابِل تَوْصيلِ البَطّارِيّةِ السَيّارةِ

jump leads *n* (BrE) كابِل تَشْغيلِ, كابِل تَوْصيلِ البَطّارِيّةِ السَيّارةِ

jump rope *n* (AmE) حَبْل قَفْزٍ \ نَطٍّ

jump-start /ˈdʒʌmpstɑːt/ *vt* بَدَأَ تَشْغيلَ سَيّارةٍ ذاتِ بَطّارِيّةٍ فارِغةٍ ‹*a car*›

jumpsuit /ˈdʒʌmpsuːt/ *n* أَفَرول (بِزّة من قِطْعةٍ واحِدةٍ)

jumpy /ˈdʒʌmpi/ *adj* (**jumpier, jumpiest**) (infml) ‹*person, animal*› سَريع الاهْتِياجِ \ الفَزَعِ, مُضْطَرِب, عَصَبيّ المِزاجِ

junction /ˈdʒʌŋkʃ(ə)n/ *n* **1** (of roads, railway lines) تَقاطُع **2** (Elec) نُقْطة وَصْلٍ

juncture /ˈdʒʌŋktʃə/ *n* مَرْحَلة (مَراحِلُ); **at this ~, I would like to say...** في هذه المَرْحَلةِ أَوَدُّ أنْ أَقولَ ...

June /dʒuːn/ *n* يونيو (Mor, Egypt, Gulf), حُزَيْران (dipt) (Levant, Iraq), جُوان (Algeria, Tunisia) ▸ **March**

June War *n* ▸ **Six Day War**

jungle /ˈdʒʌŋg(ə)l/ *n* غابة (غابات, غاب), أَدْغال

junior /ˈdʒuːnɪə/ **A** *adj* **1** (in rank) ‹*doctor, officer*› مُبْتَدِئ; **she has a ~ post at the ministry** تَعْمَلُ في مَنْصِبٍ صَغيرٍ في الوزارةِ **2** (in sport) ‹*championship, football*› للناشِئينَ, للأَشْبالِ
3 (in names) **Howard Jackson, J~** هَوارْد جاكْسون الابْن
B *n* **1** (younger person) شَخْص أَصْغَر عُمْراً \ أَحْدَث سِنّاً; **he is three years her ~** يَصْغُرُها بِثَلاثِ سَنَواتٍ **2** (person of low rank) مُوَظَّف مُبْتَدِئ **3** (BrE) (in junior school) تِلْميذ **4** (AmE) (in high school) اِبْتِدائيّ (طالِب في الصَفِّ قبلَ الأخيرِ); **she's a ~ at a state college** هي طالِبةٌ في الصَفِّ قبلَ الأَخيرِ في كُلِّيّةٍ حُكوميّةٍ **5** (AmE) (infml) (to a youngster) صَغير (صُغَراءُ, صِغار)

junior college *n* (AmE) مَعْهَد فوقَ المُتَوَسِّطِ

junior high school *n* (AmE) مَدْرَسة إعْدادِيّة

junior minister *n* نائِب وَزيرٍ

junior school *n* (BrE) ≈ مَدْرَسة اِبْتِدائِيّة

junk /dʒʌŋk/ *n* **1** (infml) (discarded items) مُهْمَلات **2** (infml) (worthless things) أَشْياء رَديئة **3** (boat) سَفينة شِراعِيّة

junk food *n* طَعام غَيْر صِحّيٍّ, وَجَبات سَريعة

junkie /ˈdʒʌŋki/ *n* (infml) مُدْمِن مُخَدِّراتٍ

junk mail *n* بَريد غَيْر مَرْغوبٍ فيهِ

junk shop *n* مَتْجَر بَضائِعَ مُسْتَعْمَلةٍ

junkyard /ˈdʒʌŋkjɑːd/ *n* ساحة الخُرْدةِ

junta /ˈdʒʌntə/ *n* حُكومة عَسْكَرِيّة \ اِنْقِلابِيّة

Jupiter /ˈdʒuːpɪtə/ *pr n* المُشْتَري

jurisdiction /ˌdʒʊərɪsˈdɪkʃ(ə)n/ *n* وِلاية, اِخْتِصاص قَضائيّ; **the ~ of the court** الاخْتِصاص القَضائيّ للمَحْكَمةِ; **the ~ over the crime** الاخْتِصاص القَضائيّ بِشَأْنِ الجَريمةِ

jurisprudence /ˌdʒʊərɪsˈpruːd(ə)ns/ *n* **1** (philosophy of law) فِقْه قانونيّ, عِلْم الحُقوقِ **2** (legal system) تَشْريع

juror /ˈdʒʊərə/ *n* عُضْو هَيْئةِ مُحَلَّفينَ

jury /ˈdʒʊəri/ *n* (*pl* **juries**) هَيْئَة مُحَلَّفين; **trial by ~** مُحاكَمة أمام هَيْئَة مُحَلَّفين

jury box *n* [مَقْصورة هَيْئَةِ المُحَلَّفين]

juryman /ˈdʒʊərɪmən/ *n* (*pl* **-men**) عُضْو في هَيْئَة مُحَلَّفين

jury service (BrE), **jury duty** (AmE) *n* الخِدْمة في هَيْئَةِ مُحَلَّفين

jussive /ˈdʒʌsɪv/ **A** *n* جَزْم

B *adj* ‹*mood, sense*› مَجْزوم

just¹ /dʒʌst/ **A** *adv* **1** (very recently) **to have ~ done sth** فَعَلَ شَيْئاً للتوِّ; **she's ~ arrived** وَصَلَتْ للتوِّ; **I've ~ finished it** أَنْهَيْتُهُ منذ بُرْهةٍ وَجيزةٍ **2** (specifically) بِقَليلٍ; **~ before we leave** قبل أنْ نُغادِرَ بِقليلٍ; **it's ~ after 10 am** الساعةُ الآنَ بعد 10 صَباحاً بِقليلٍ; **~ two days ago** منذ يَوْمَيْنِ فَقَطْ; **~ last week** الأُسْبوعَ الماضِيَ فَقَطْ **3** (with quantities, distances) بِقَليلٍ; **~ over/under 20 kg** فوق \ تحت 20 كجم بِقَليلٍ; **~ over/under 15 cm** فوق \ تحت 15 سم بِقَليلٍ; **~ after you pass the station** بِمُجَرَّدِ أنْ تَتَخطّى المَحَطّةَ **4** (only, merely) فَقَطْ; **~ a cup of tea** كوب من الشاي فقط; **~ for fun** فَقَطْ من أَجْلِ التَرْفيهِ; **he's ~ a child** ما هو إلاّ طِفْلٌ; **not ~ men** لَيْسَ الرِجالُ فقطْ **5** (purposely) فَقَطْ; **he did it ~ to annoy us** فعلَ هذا فَقَطْ لِكَيْ يُضايِقَنا **6** (barely) بالكادِ; **~ on time** بالكادِ في الميعادِ; **he's ~ 20** عُمْرُهُ بالكادِ 20 عاماً; **I ~ caught the train** لَحِقْتُ بالقِطارِ بالكادِ **7** (simply) فَقَطْ; **~ tell the truth** فَقَطْ قُل الحَقيقةَ; **she ~ doesn't listen** هي بِبَساطةٍ لا تَسْتَمِعُ; **~ a moment** لَحْظة من فَضْلِكَ; **'that show was just dreadful'—'wasn't it ~!'** 'كانَ ذلكَ العَرْضُ رَهيباً' — 'بالتَأْكيدِ!' **8** (precisely) بالضَبْطِ, تَماماً; **it's ~ right** هذا صَحيحٌ تَماماً; **she looks ~ like her father** تُشْبِهُ والِدَها تَماماً; **that's ~ what I suggested** هذا بالضَبْطِ ما اقْتَرَحْتُهُ; **he likes everything to be ~ so** يُحِبُّ أنْ يكونَ كُلُّ شَيْءٍ مُرَتَّباً وَمُنَظَّماً **9** (possibly) **it might** *or* **could ~ be true** قد يكونُ صَحيحاً **10** (on the point of) **to be ~ about to do sth** كانَ على وَشْكِ أنْ يَفْعَلَ شَيْئاً; **he was ~ about to give the speech, when ...** كانَ على وَشْكِ أنْ يُلْقِيَ الكَلِمةَ، عِنْدَما ...; **he's ~ leaving** هو على وَشْكِ أنْ يُغادِرَ **11** (totally) **that's ~ ridiculous** ذلك سَخيفٌ تماماً **12** (easily) **I can ~ imagine her as president** يُمْكِنُني بِسُهولةٍ أنْ أَتَخَيَّلَها رَئيسةً; **I can ~ smell the pine forests** يُمْكِنُني بِسُهولةٍ أنْ أَشُمَّ رائِحةَ غاباتِ الصَنَوْبَرِ **13** (with imperatives) فَقَطْ; **~ keep quiet!** فَقَطْ الْتَزِم الهُدوءَ!; **~ look at the time!** فَقَطْ انْظُرْ إلى الوَقْتِ! **14** (equally) **~ as big/well as ...** تَماماً بِنَفْسِ حَجْمِ \ جَوْدةِ ...; **she's ~ as clever as her sister** هي ذَكيّةٌ مِثْلَ أُخْتِها تَماماً; **I can ~ as easily walk** يُمْكِنُني أنْ أَمْشِيَ بِنَفْسِ السُهولةِ

B (**just about**) *adv phr* تَقْريباً; **it's ~ about cooked/finished** نَضُجَ \ انْتَهى تَقْريباً; **we have ~ about everything we need** لَدَيْنا كُلُّ ما نَحْتاجُ إلَيْهِ تقريباً

C (**just as**) *conj phr* بَيْنَما; **he arrived ~ as I was leaving** وَصَلَ بَيْنَما كُنْتُ مُغادِراً

D (**just now**) *adv phr* (a short time ago) **I saw him ~ now** رَأَيْتُهُ منذ بُرْهةٍ وَجيزةٍ; (at the moment) **he's with the manager ~ now** هو مع المُديرِ الآنَ

(Idioms) **to be just as well** كانَ من حُسْنِ الحَظِّ; **it's ~ as well you brought your keys** من حُسْنِ الحَظِّ أنَّكَ أَحْضَرْتَ مَفاتيحَكَ

just² /dʒʌst/ *adj* **1** ‹*society, solution, reward*› مُنْصِف, عادِل; **as is only ~** بالشَكْلِ المُنْصِفِ \ العادِلِ **2** (justifiable) ‹*cause, demand*› عادِل

justice /ˈdʒʌstɪs/ *n* **1** (the law) عَدالة; **to bring a criminal to ~** قَدَّمَ مُجْرِماً إلى العَدالةِ **2** (fairness) إِنْصاف, عَدْل; **the portrait didn't do her ~** اللَوْحةُ لم تُعْطِها حَقَّها; **I didn't do myself ~** بَخَسْتُ حَقَّ نَفْسي

Justice Department *n* (**the Justice Department**) (AmE) وِزارة العَدْلِ

Justice of the Peace *n* ≈ قاضٍ في مَحْكَمةٍ ابْتِدائيّةٍ

justifiable /ˈdʒʌstɪˌfaɪəb(ə)l/ *adj* ‹*reason, anger*› يُمْكِنُ تَبْريرُهُ, مُبَرَّر, لَهُ ما يُبَرِّرُهُ

justification /dʒʌstɪfɪˈkeɪʃ(ə)n/ *n* تَبْرير (تَبْريرات), مُبَرِّر (مُبَرِّرات), مُسَوِّغ (مُسَوِّغات)

justified /ˈdʒʌstɪfaɪd/ *adj* ‹*criticism, fear*› مُبَرَّر, لَهُ ما يُبَرِّرُهُ

justify /ˈdʒʌstɪfaɪ/ *vt* (**justifies**, **justifying**, **justified**) بَرَّرَ ‹*actions, decisions*›

jut /dʒʌt/ *vi* (**-tt-**) «rocks, balconies» بَرَزَ (u; بُروز)، نَتَأَ (a; نَتْء، نُتوء)

(Phrasal verb) **jut out** بَرَزَ للخارِجِ

jute /dʒuːt/ *n* خَيْش (نَوْع من الأَلْيافِ الخَشِنَةِ)

juvenile /ˈdʒuːv(ə)nʌɪl/ **A** *adj* **1** (in law) ‹*court, crime*› الأَحْداثِ

2 (childish) ‹*behaviour, humour*› صِبْيانِيّ

B *n* حَدَث (أَحْداث)، قاصِر

juvenile delinquency *n* جُنوح الأَحْداثِ

juvenile delinquent *n* حَدَث جانِح

juvenile offender *n* مُجْرِم حَدَث

juxtapose /ˌdʒʌkstəˈpəʊz/ *vt* وَضَعَ جَنْباً إلى جَنْبٍ ‹*images, styles*›

Kk

K, k /keɪ/ **A** *n* (letter) كاف ≈ (الحَرْف الحادِيَ عَشَرَ من الأَبْجَدِيّةِ الإنْكْليزِيّةِ)

B *abbr* (**K**) **1** = **kilo** كيلو **2** = **kilobyte** كيلوبايْت

3 = **thousand** (infml) أَلْف (mf; آلاف ,أُلوف)

Kaaba /ˈkɑːəbə/ *pr n* (**the Kaaba**) الكَعْبة

Kabul /ˈkɑːbʊl/ *pr n* كابول (f)

kafir /ˈkafɪə/ *n* كافِر (كَفَرة ,كُفّار)

kaftan /ˈkaftan/ *n* قُفْطان (قَفاطينُ)

kagoul /kəˈguːl/ *n* (BrE) ▸ **cagoule**

Kairouan /ˌkʌɪərʊˈɑːn/ *n* القَيْرَوان (f)

kale /keɪl/ *n* [نَوع من الكُرُنْبِ]

kaleidoscope /kəˈlʌɪdəskəʊp/ *n* مِشْكال

Kampuchea /ˌkampʊˈtʃiːə/ *pr n* كَمْبودِيا (لَفْظة قَديمة)

kangaroo /ˌkaŋgəˈruː/ *n* كَنْغَر

Kansan /ˈkanz(ə)n/ *pr n, adj* [(شَخص) من كانْساس]

Kansas /ˈkanzəs/ *pr n* كانْساس (f)

Karachi /kəˈrɑːtʃi/ *pr n* كَراتْشي (f)

karaoke /ˌkarɪˈəʊkeɪ, ˌkarɪˈəʊki/ *n* كاراوْكي (غِناء زَبائِنِ مَقْهًى على موسيقى أَغانٍ شَهيرةٍ)

karat (AmE) *n* ▸ **carat**

karate /kəˈrɑːti/ *n* كاراتيه

Karbala /ˈkɑːb(ə)lə/ *pr n* كَرْبَلاء (dipt f)

karma /ˈkɑːmə/ *n* (fate, luck) قَدَر (أَقْدار); (in reincarnation) كَرْما

Kashmir /kaʃˈmɪə/ *pr n* كَشْمير (f)

Kashmiri /kaʃˈmɪəri/ **A** *adj* ‹*people, culture*› كَشْميريّ

B *n* **1** (inhabitant) كَشْميريّ **2** (language) (اللُغة) الكَشْميريّة

kayak /ˈkʌɪak/ *n* كاياك (زَوْرَق لِشَخصٍ واحِدٍ)

Kazakhstan /kazəkˈstan, kazəkˈstɑːn/ *pr n* كازاخْسْتان (f)

kebab /kɪˈbab/ *n* (also **shish kebab**) كَباب

kedgeree /ˈkɛdʒ(ə)riː/ *n* (BrE) [وَجْبة رُزٍّ مع شَرائِحَ من السَمَكِ (عادةً مع بَيْضٍ مَسْلوقٍ)]

keel /kiːl/ *n* رافِدة القَصّ

(Phrasal verb) **keel over** **1** «ships, boats» انْقَلَبَ **2** «people, horses» وَقَعَ (a; وُقوع)، سَقَطَ (u; سُقوط ,مَسْقَط)

keen /kiːn/ *adj* **1** (enthusiastic) مُتَحَمِّس; **he's a ~ Manchester United supporter** هو مُشَجِّعٌ مُتَحَمِّسٌ لِفَريقِ مانْشِسْتَر يونايْتِد; **to be ~ on the idea/horse racing** كانَ مُتَحَمِّساً لِلفِكْرةِ \ مولَعاً بِسِباقاتِ الخَيْلِ; **he's ~ on my sister** هو مُغْرَمٌ بِأُخْتي; **we were ~ to meet him** كُنّا حَريصينَ على لِقائِهِ; **to be ~ for sb to do sth** كانَ حَريصاً على أنْ يَفْعَلَ شَخْصٌ شَيْئاً **2** (intense) ‹*interest, desire, appetite*› قَويّ **3** (acute) ‹*intelligence, insight, sense of smell*› حادّ; **to have a ~ eye for detail** كانَ لَدَيْهِ قُدْرةٌ على مُلاحَظةِ أَدَقِّ التَفاصيلِ **4** (sharp) ‹*wind*› قَويّ; ‹*wit*› ثاقِب, حادّ **5** (in sports, competitions) ‹*game, rivalry, tournament*› تَنافُسيّ **6** (competitive) ‹*price*› حامي الوَطيسِ

keenly /ˈkiːnli/ *adv* **1** (intensely) ‹*interested, aware, disappointed*› بِشِدّةٍ; **a ~ awaited moment** لَحْظة تَمَّ انْتِظارُها طَويلاً; **he felt her loss ~** حَزِنَ عَلَيْها حُزْناً شَديداً **2** (enthusiastically) ‹*to support, campaign, watch*› بِشَغَفٍ

keenness /ˈkiːnnəs/ *n* **1** (enthusiasm) حَماس **2** (of the senses) حِدّة **3** (of the wind, air) قوّة ,شِدّة

keep /kiːp/ **A** *vt* (*past tense, past participle* **kept**) **1** (to retain) احْتَفَظَ (ب) ‹*the receipt, a seat*› **2** (to store) احْتَفَظَ (ب) ‹*the plates, tools, money*›; **where do you ~ your papers?** أَيْنَ تَحْتَفِظُ بِأَوْراقِكَ؟ **3** (to maintain) حَفِظَ (a; حِفْظ) ‹*a secret*›; حافَظَ (على) ‹*an appointment*›; **to ~ sth clean** حافَظَ على نَظافةِ شَيْءٍ; **to ~ sth warm** حافَظَ على حَرارةِ شَيْءٍ; **to ~ sb talking** جَعَلَ

أبقى شَخْصاً يَسْتَمِرُّ في الحَديثِ; **to ~ the engine running** أبقى المُحَرِّكَ دائراً; **to ~ sth from sb** أَخْفى شَيْئاً عن شَخْصٍ; **to ~ sth to oneself** احْتَفَظَ بِشَيْءٍ لِنَفْسِهِ **4** (not to lose) احْتَفَظَ (ب) *<one's job, (parliamentary) seat>*; **cotton keeps its colour/shape** يَحْتَفِظُ القُطْنُ بِلَوْنِهِ \ بِشَكْلِهِ **5** (to detain) **to ~ sb waiting** تَرَكَ شَخْصاً يَنْتَظِرُ; **I won't ~ you** لن أُطيلَ عَلَيْكَ; **she was kept in hospital for observation** أَبْقوها في المُسْتَشْفى تحت المُلاحَظةِ **6** (to breed) رَبّى *<chickens, rabbits>* **7** (to manage) أدار *<a hotel, stall>* **8** (to sustain) **to ~ sth going** أَبْقى على شَيْءٍ *<a conversation, fire>*; **make me some sandwiches to ~ me going** حَضِّرْ لي بَعْضَ الشَطائِرِ لِتُعينَني على الاسْتِمْرارِ **9** (to support) عالَ, أَعالَ (عَوْل; u عِيالة) *<a mistress, family>* **10** (to prevent) **to ~ sb from doing sth** حالَ بين شَخْصٍ وبَيْنَ فِعْلِ شَيْءٍ **11** (with written records) احْتَفَظَ (ب) *<accounts, a diary>* **12** (to conceal) **to ~ a letter/document from sb** أَخْفى رِسالةً \ وَثيقةً عن شَخْصٍ **13** (Mus) **to ~ time** حافَظَ على الإيقاعِ

B *vi* **1** (to continue) **to ~ doing sth** اسْتَمَرَّ في فِعْلِ شَيْءٍ; **to ~ going** اسْتَمَرَّ **2** **to ~ warm** ظَلَّ \ بَقِيَ دافِئاً; **to ~ calm** ظَلَّ \ بَقِيَ هادِئاً; **to ~ silent** ظَلَّ \ بَقِيَ صامِتاً **3** (to remain edible) «vegetables, fruit, milk» ظَلَّ صالِحاً للاسْتِهْلاكِ **4** (infml) (regarding health) **how are you ~ing?** كيف حالُكَ؟; **she's ~ing well** هي بخَيْرٍ

C *v refl* **to ~ oneself warm** أَبْقى جِسْمَهُ دافِئاً; **to ~ oneself to oneself** انْطَوى على نَفْسِهِ

D *n* **1** (living expenses) تكاليفُ \ مَصاريفُ المَعيشةِ; **to pay for one's ~** دَفَعَ تكاليفَ \ مَصاريفَ مَعيشَتِه **2** (of a castle) حِصْن (حُصون), قَلْعة (قِلاع, قُلوع)

E *adv phr* **(for keeps)** للأَبَدِ, أَبَداً; **it's ours for ~s** هو لَنا \ مِلْكُنا للأَبَدِ

Phrasal verbs **keep away A** (not come near) بَقِيَ بَعيداً; **~ away from sb/sth** ابْتَعَدَ عن شَخْصٍ \ شَيْءٍ **B ~ [sb/sth] away** (for safety) أَبْقى [شَخْصاً \ شَيْئاً] بَعيداً *<the baby, iron>*

• **keep back A** (to stay back) بَقِيَ بَعيداً **B ~ [sb/sth] back, ~ back [sb/sth] 1** (to restrain) أَبْقى [شَخْصاً \ شَيْئاً] بَعيداً *<the crowd, demonstrators>* **2** (to detain) لم يَسْمَحْ ل [شَخْصٍ] بالمُغادَرةِ *<a person, visitor>* **3** (not reveal) أَخْفى [شَيْئاً] *<the facts, truth>* **4** (to retain) حَجَزَ [شَيْئاً] *<the money, sb's share>*

• **keep down: ~ [sth] down 1** (not allow to rise) أَبْقى [شَيْئاً] مُنْخَفِضاً *<inflation, speed, your voice>*; **try to ~ your weight down** احْرِصْ على عَدَمِ زِيادةِ وَزْنِكَ **2** (in one's stomach) احْتَفَظَ ب [شَيْءٍ] *<food>* **3** (to repress) أَخْضَعَ \ قَمَعَ [شَيْئاً] *<the people, dissent>*

• **keep in A** (by the roadside) «car, cyclist» سارَ قَريباً من الرَصيفِ **B ~ [sb/sth] in 1** (not allow to go) حَجَزَ [شَخْصاً \ شَيْئاً] *<a patient, an animal>*; **they're ~ing her in** يَحْجِزونَها في المُسْتَشْفى; **~ the cat in** أَبْقِ القِطّةَ في الداخِلِ **2** (not allow to come out) أَبْقى [شَيْئاً] في مَكانِهِ, احْتَفَظَ ب [شَيْءٍ] *<dentures, contact lenses>* **3** (to restrain) شَدَّ [شَيْئاً] *<your stomach>*; حافَظَ على [شَيْءٍ] مَشْدوداً إلى الداخِلِ *<elbows>* **4** (after classes) مَنَعَ [شَخْصاً] من الخُروجِ *<a pupil, class>*

• **keep off A ~ off [sth] 1** (to stay off) ابْتَعَدَ عن [شَيْءٍ] *<the grass, land>* **2** (to avoid) ابْتَعَدَ عن [شَيْءٍ], تَجَنَّبَ [شَيْئاً] *<alcohol, fats, sugar>* **3** (not mention) تَجَنَّبَ الحَديثَ عن [شَيْءٍ] *<the subject, politics, religion>* **B ~ [sth] off, ~ off [sth]** (to protect from) أَبْقى [شَيْئاً] بعيداً *<the rain, insects>*

• **keep on A** (to continue) اسْتَمَرَّ (في); **to ~ on about sth** اسْتَمَرَّ في الحَديثِ عن شَيْءٍ; **to ~ on at sb to do sth** أَلَحَّ على شَخْصٍ في فِعْلِ شَيْءٍ **B ~ [sth] on 1** بَقِيَ يَرْتَدي [شَيْئاً] *<one's hat, shoes>* **2** ظَلَّ في [شَيْءٍ] *<an apartment>* **C ~ [sb] on** (in employment) أَبْقى [شَخْصاً] في العَمَلِ

• **keep out** بَقِيَ \ ظَلَّ في الخارِجِ; **'~ out!'** 'مَمْنوعٌ الدُخولُ!'

• **keep out of 1** (to avoid) تَجَنَّبَ, ابْتَعَدَ (عن); **to ~ out of the rain** تَجَنَّبَ المَطَرَ **2** (to stand back) تَفادى, تَجَنَّبَ *<an argument>*; **to ~ out of sb's way** ابْتَعَدَ عن طَريقِ شَخْصٍ

• **keep to A ~ to [sth]** (not deviate from) بَقِيَ في \ ظَلَّ على [شَيْءٍ] *<the road>*; تَقَيَّدَ \ الْتَزَمَ ب [شَيْءٍ] *<the facts, law, plan>* **B ~ sb to [sth]** (with obligations) أَلْزَمَ شَخْصاً بالوَفاءِ ب [شَيْءٍ] *<a promise>* **C ~ [sth] to [sth]** (with restrictions) لم يَدَعْ [شَيْئاً] يَتَجاوَزُ [شَيْئاً] *<a number>*; **~ the number of guests to 50** لا تَدَعْ عَدَدَ الضُيوفِ يَتَجاوَزُ الخَمْسينَ; **~ this to yourself** أَبْقِ هذا سِرًّا

• **keep up** **A** **~ up** «cars, runners» حافَظَ على نَفْسِ السُّرْعةِ **B** **~ [sb] up** (at night) أَبْقى [شَخْصاً] ساهِراً **C** **~ [sth] up,** **~ up [sth]** (to support) أَبْقى [شَيْئاً] في مَكانِهِ ‹*one's trousers*›; دَعَمَ [شَيْئاً] ‹*the wall*› **D** **~ [sth] up** (to continue) اسْتَمَرَّ في [شَيْءٍ] ‹*your studies, a correspondence*›; أَبْقى على [شَيْءٍ] ‹*your membership*›; **~ up the pressure on them** اسْتَمَرَّ في الضَغْطِ عَلَيْهِمْ; **he ~s up his French by going to evening classes** يُحافظُ على مُسْتَواهُ في الفَرَنْسيّةِ بالذَهابِ إلى دُروسٍ مَسائيّةٍ

• **keep up with**: **~ up with [sb/sth]** **1** (in tempo) سايَرَ [شَخْصاً \ شَيْئاً] ‹*a car, the class, demand*› **2** (mentally) واكَبَ [شَخْصاً \ شَيْئاً] ‹*the fashions, developments*›

keeper /'ki:pə/ *n* **1** (of an archive, museum) ≈ أَمين (أُمَناءُ) **2** (in a zoo) حارِس (حُرّاس ,حَرَس) **3** (infml) (in sport) حارِس المَرْمى

keep-fit /ki:p'fɪt/ *n* [تَمارين رياضيّة للمُحافَظَة على اللِياقَةِ]

keeping /'ki:pɪŋ/ **A** *n* (custody) **to be in sb's ~** كانَ في رِعايةِ شَخْصٍ; **to leave sb/sth in sb's ~** تَرَكَ شَخْصاً \ شَيْئاً في عُهْدةِ شَخْصٍ

B **(in keeping with)** *prep phr* مُتَماشٍ مع ‹*one's status, the occasion, the rules*›; **the design is in ~ with the surroundings/ the village** التَصْميمُ مُتَماشٍ \ مُتَناسِقٌ مع البيئة المُحيطةِ \ القَرية

C **(out of keeping with)** *prep phr* غَيْر مُتَماشٍ مع ‹*one's status, the occasion, the rules*›; **it is out of ~ with the area/the architecture of the other buildings** هو غَيْرُ مُتَماشٍ \ مُتَناسِقٍ مع المِنْطَقةِ \ التَصْميمِ المِعْماريِّ للمَباني الأُخْرى

keepsake /'ki:pseɪk/ *n* تَذْكار (تَذْكارات)

keg /kɛg/ *n* بِرْميل (بَراميلُ)

kennel /'kɛn(ə)l/ *n* (BrE) **1** (for a dog) بَيْت \ وِجار كَلْبٍ **2** (also **kennels**) (establishment) مَرْبى كِلابٍ

Kentuckian /kɛn'tʌkiən/ *pr n, adj* [(شَخْص) من كِنْتاكي]

Kentucky /kɛn'tʌki/ *pr n* كِنْتاكي (f)

Kenya /'kɛnjə/ *pr n* كينيا

Kenyan /'kɛnjən/ *n, adj* كينيّ

kept /kɛpt/ *past tense, past participle* ▸**keep**

kerb /kə:b/ *n* (BrE) حافّة رَصيفٍ

kernel /'kə:n(ə)l/ *n* **1** (of a nut) لُبّ (لُبوب) **2** (of wheat) حَبّ (n coll; حُبوب)

kerosene (BrE), **kerosine** (AmE) /'kɛrəsi:n/ *n* (AmE) كيروسين

kestrel /'kɛstrəl/ *n* عاسوق

ketchup /'kɛtʃəp/ (BrE) *n* صَلْصة طَماطِمَ

kettle /'kɛt(ə)l/ *n* غَلّاية; **to put the ~ on** وَضَعَ الغَلّايَةَ على النارِ

(Idiom) **to be a different kettle of fish** كانَ مَوْضوعاً ثانياً; **that's a completely different ~ of fish** [هَذانِ شَيْئانِ مُخْتَلِفانِ تَماماً]

kettledrum /'kɛtəldrʌm/ *n* طَبْل (كَبير)

key /ki:/ **A** *n* **1** (to a door) مِفْتاح (مَفاتيحُ); **a front-door ~** مِفْتاح بابٍ أَماميٍّ; **a bunch of ~s** سِلْسِلة \ حُزْمة مَفاتيحَ; **under lock and ~** مُغْلَق بالضَبّةِ والمِفْتاحِ; **radiator ~** مِفْتاح مِشْعاعٍ **2** (on computers, musical instruments) مِفْتاح (مَفاتيحُ) **3** (vital clue) مِفْتاح (مَفاتيحُ) **4** (to a map) مِفْتاح (مَفاتيحُ); (to abbreviations, symbols, a code) مِفْتاح رُموزٍ **5** (to a test, riddle) حَلّ (حُلول) **6** (Mus) مَقام (مَقامات); **to sing in/off ~** تَبِعَ \ خالَفَ النوتةَ الموسيقيّةَ في غِنائِهِ

B *adj* ‹*worker, role*› رَئيسيّ; **cost is ~ to the project** التَكْلِفةُ هي عامِلٌ أَساسيٌّ في المَشْروعِ

C *vt* أَدْخَلَ ‹*the data, text*›

(Phrasal verb) **key in**: **~ [sth] in, ~ in [sth]** أَدْخَلَ [شَيْئاً] ‹*the text, data, figures*›

keyboard /'ki:bɔ:d/ **A** *n* (of a computer, piano, etc) لَوْحة مَفاتيحَ

B **(keyboards)** *n pl* (electronic instrument) أورْج

key card *n* بِطاقة مِفْتاحٍ (بِطاقة مُمَغْنَطة للدُخول)

keyed-up /ki:d'ʌp/ *adj* مُتَوَتِّر; **I was getting ~ about meeting him** كُنْتُ بَدَأْتُ أَتَوَتَّرُ بِشَأْنِ لِقاءِهِ

keyhole /'ki:həʊl/ *n* ثُقْب القُفْلِ

keyhole surgery *n* جِراحة المَناظيرِ

keynote /'ki:nəʊt/ *n* **1** (Mus) لازِمة موسيقيّة **2** (main theme) فِكْرة أَساسيّة

keynote speech *n* خِطاب رَئيسيّ

keypad /'ki:pad/ *n* لَوْحة مَفاتيحَ

key ring *n* حَلْقة مَفاتيحَ

key signature *n* [إشارة مَقامِ قِطْعةٍ موسيقيّةٍ]

keyword /ˈkiːwəːd/ *n* كَلِمة رَئيسيّة

kg *abbr* = **kilogram(s)** كغ

khaki /ˈkɑːki/ **A** *n* اللَّوْن الكاكيّ; **to be wearing ~** ارْتَدى مَلابِسَ كاكيّةً

B *adj* ‹*uniform, shorts*› كاكيّ

Khartoum /kɑːˈtuːm/ *pr n* الخَرْطوم

khimar /kɪˈmɑː/ *n* خِمار (أَخْمِرة, خُمُر)

khula /kuːˈlɑː/ *n* خُلْع

kibbutz /kɪˈbʊts/ *n* (*pl* **kibbutzes** or **kibbutzim**) كيبوتْز

kiblah /ˈkɪblə/ *n* ▸**qiblah**

kick /kɪk/ **A** *vt* رَكَلَ (u; رَكْل) ‹*a person, door, ball*›; «horses, cows» رَفَسَ (i-u; رَفْس) ‹*a person, gate*›; **he ~ed me in the leg** رَكَلَني في ساقي; **he ~ed the ball over the wall** رَكَلَ الكُرةَ فوق الجِدارِ

B *vi* **1** «children» رَكَلَ (u; رَكْل); «horses» رَفَسَ (i-u; رَفْس) **2** (to recoil) «guns» ارْتَدَّ

C *n* **1** (by a person) رَكْلة; (by a horse) رَفْسة (رَفَسات); **to give sb/sth a ~** رَكَلَ \ رَفَسَ شَخْصاً \ شَيْئاً; **to aim** *or* **take a ~ at sb/sth** وَجَّهَ رَكْلةً إلى شَخْصٍ \ شَيْءٍ; ▸**free kick**, ▸**penalty kick** **2** (in swimming) ضَرْبة \ دَفْعة رِجْلٍ **3** (infml) (thrill) **to get a ~ from doing sth** اسْتَمْتَعَ بِفِعْلِ شَيْءٍ **4** (of a firearm) ارْتِداد (ارْتِدادات) **5** (infml) (strength, zest) قُوّة; **the cocktail had a ~ to it** كانَ الكوكْتيل قَوِيًّا

(Idioms) **a kick in the teeth** لَطْمة على الوَجْهِ; **to kick sb when they're down** هاجَمَ شَخْصاً وَقْتَ ضَعْفِهِ; **to kick a habit** تَخَلّى عن عادةٍ; **to be alive and kicking** (infml) كانَ مُفْعَماً بالحَيَوِيّةِ والنَشاطِ

(Phrasal verbs) **kick about** ▸**kick around**

• **kick around** **A** (infml) «clothes, friends» ظَهَرَ (a; ظُهور); «idea» طَرَحَ نَفْسَهُ **B** **~ around [sth]** «friends, tools» تَنَقَّلَ في [شَيْءٍ] ‹*the house, town*›; **he's been ~ing around Europe for a year** ظَلَّ يَتَنَقَّلُ في أوروبّا لِمُدّةِ عامٍ **C** **~ [sth] around** **1** (to play with) لَعِبَ ب [شَيْءٍ] ‹*a ball*› **2** (infml) (to discuss) طَرَحَ [شَيْئاً] للنِقاشِ ‹*an idea, a design*›

• **kick against**: **~ against [sth]** (to resist) عارَضَ [شَيْئاً] ‹*an idea, a suggestion, the system*›

• **kick down**: **~ [sth] down, ~ down [sth]** كَسَرَ [شَيْئاً] رَكْلاً ‹*a door*›

• **kick in**: **~ [sth] in, ~ in [sth]** كَسَرَ [شَيْئاً] رَكْلاً ‹*a door*›

• **kick off** **A** **1** (in soccer, rugby, etc) بَدَأَ (a; بَدْء) **2** (infml) (to start) «concerts, the day, tour» بَدَأَ (a; بَدْء) **B** **~ off [sth], ~ [sth] off** **1** (to remove) نَتَرَ [شَيْئاً] من قَدَمَيْهِ ‹*your shoes*› **2** (infml) (to start) بَدَأَ \ اسْتَهَلَّ [شَيْئاً] ‹*a meeting, tour, concert*›

• **kick out** (infml): **A** **to ~ out at sb** ثارَ على شَخْصٍ; **to ~ out against injustice/the system** ثارَ على الظُلْمِ \ النِظامِ **B** **~ [sb] out, ~ out [sb]** **1** (to eject) طَرَدَ [شَخْصاً] ‹*a troublemaker, an intruder*› **2** (to fire) فَصَلَ [شَخْصاً] ‹*an employee*›

• **kick over**: **~ [sth] over, ~ over [sth]** أَسْقَطَ [شَيْئاً] بِقَدَمِهِ ‹*a chair, lamp*›

• **kick up**: **A** **~ [sth] up, ~ up [sth]** أَثارَ [شَيْئاً] ‹*sand, dust*› **B** **~ up [sth]** (infml) **to ~ up a fuss** *or* **stink** أَثارَ زَوْبَعةً

kicking /ˈkɪkɪŋ/ **A** *n* رَفْس, رَكْل

B *adj* (infml) ‹*music, party*› حَيَوِيّ, مُثير

kick-off /ˈkɪkɒf/ *n*; (start of a football match) ضَرْبة الانْطِلاقة; (resumption of a football match) اسْتِئْناف المُباراةِ

kick-start /ˈkɪkstɑːt/ **A** *vt* **1** شَغَّلَ المُحَرِّكَ (بِذراعٍ) ‹*a motorbike*› **2** دَفَعَ العَجَلةَ ‹*the economy, process*›

B *n* **1** (also **kick-starter**) (on motorcycles) ذِراع تَشْغيلٍ **2** (to a process) دَفْعة (دَفَعات) المُحَرِّكِ

kid /kɪd/ **A** *n* **1** (infml) (child, youth) طِفْل (أَطْفال) **2** (young goat) جَدْي (جِدْيان, جِداء) **3** (goatskin) جِلْد الماعِزِ

B *vt* (**-dd-**) (infml) مازَحَ ‹*a person*›

C *vi* (**-dd-**) (infml) «children, people» ضَحِكَ (a; ضَحْك, ضَحِك), مازَحَ; **no ~ding!** (affirming) حَقًّا!; (questioning) حَقًّا؟

D *v refl* **to ~ oneself** خَدَعَ نَفْسَهُ

kidnap /ˈkɪdnap/ *vt* (**-pp-**) خَطَفَ (i; خَطْف) ‹*a hostage, journalist*›

kidnapper /ˈkɪdnapə/ *n* مُخْتَطِف

kidnapping /ˈkɪdnapɪŋ/ *n* خَطْف (اخْتِطافات) اخْتِطاف

kidney /ˈkɪdni/ *n* (*pl* **kidneys**) كُلْية (كُلًى)

kidney bean *n* لوبيا

kidney machine *n* جِهاز غَسْلِ الكُلى

kidney stone *n* حَصاة كُلْوِيّة

kill /kɪl/ **A** *vt* **1** (to cause to die) «murderers, soldiers, diseases» قَتَلَ (u; قَتْل) ‹*a person, an animal*›; **he was ~ed by the rebels** قُتِلَ على يَدِ المُتَمَرِّدِينَ; **to be ~ed in action/in a car crash** قُتِلَ في المَعْرَكَةِ \ في حادِثِ تَصادُمِ سَيّارةٍ **2** (infml) (to hurt) **my feet are ~ing me** قَدَمايَ تُؤْلِمانِني **3** (to stop) قتَلَ (u; قَتْل), أَحْبَطَ, وَأَدَ (i; وَأْد) ‹*an idea, a proposal*›; **his remark ~ed the conversation** وَأَدَ تَعْليقُهُ الحَديثَ **4** سَكَّنَ ‹*the pain*› **5** (infml) (to turn off) أَوْقَفَ ‹*the engine, machine*›; أَطْفَأَ ‹*the lights, power*› **6** (to while away) **to ~ time/a couple of hours** مَضّى الوَقْتَ \ بِضْعَ ساعاتٍ
B *vi* «obesity, drinking, measles» قَتَلَ (u; قَتْل), أَدّى للوَفاةِ; **'smoking ~s'** 'التَدْخينُ يَقْتُلُ'
C *v refl* **to ~ oneself** (deliberately) قَتَلَ نَفْسَهُ, انْتَحَرَ; (accidentally) ماتَ (u; مَوْت); **he had tried to ~ himself before** حاوَلَ أَنْ يَنْتَحِرَ من قَبْلُ; **he fell of the roof and ~ed himself** وَقَعَ من على السَقْفِ وَماتَ; **to ~ oneself laughing** كادَ يَموتُ من كَثْرةِ الضَحِكِ
D *n* **1** (in bullfighting, hunting) قَتْل; **to be in at the ~** شارَكَ; **to move in for the ~** تَقَدَّمَ للإجْهازِ في الإجْهازِ على الفَريسةِ **2** (prey) فَريسة (فَرائِسُ) على الفَريسةِ

(Phrasal verb) **kill off**: **A ~ off [sth], ~ [sth] off** قَضى على [شَيْءٍ] ‹*the weeds, insects*› **B ~ off [sb], ~ [sb] off** (Mil, Pol) قَضى على [شَخْصٍ] ‹*one's opponents, enemies*›; (Cin, Literat) تَخَلَّصَ من [شَخْصٍ] ‹*a character*›

killer /ˈkɪlə/ *n* **1** (murderer) قاتِل (قَتَلة) **2** (illness, poison) قاتِل (قَتَلة); **heroin/cancer is a ~** الهيرُوين \ السَرَطانُ يَقْتُلُ **3** (infml) (exam, question) بالِغُ الصُعوبةِ

killer app *n* (infml) تَطْبيق قاتِل (تَطْبيق يُسَبِّبُ ظُهورُهُ ضَجّةً شَديدةً)

killer bee *n* نَحْل قاتِل

killer disease *n* مَرَض قاتِل

killer whale *n* حوت قاتِل \ سَفّاح

killing /ˈkɪlɪŋ/ *n* (of a person) قَتْل

(Idiom) **to make a killing** (infml) حَقَّقَ رِبْحاً طائِلاً

killjoy /ˈkɪldʒɔɪ/ *n* (infml) مُفْسِد للمُتْعةِ

kiln /kɪln/ *n* فُرْن (أَفْران)

kilo /ˈkiːləʊ/ *n* كيلو

kilobyte /ˈkɪləbaɪt/ *n* كيلوبايْت

kilogram, **kilogramme** /ˈkɪləgram/ *n* كيلوغْرام (كيلوغْرامات)

kilometre (BrE), **kilometer** (AmE) /kɪˈlɒmɪtə/ *n* كيلومِتْر (كيلومِتْرات)

kilowatt /ˈkɪləwɒt/ *n* كيلوواط

kilt /kɪlt/ *n* [تَنّورة يَلْبَسُها الاسْكُتْلَنْديّونَ]

kimono /kɪˈməʊnəʊ/ *n* (*pl* **kimonos**) كيمونو (ثَوْب يابانِيّ)

kin /kɪn/ *n* أَقارِب; **his next of ~ have been informed** أُبْلِغَ أَقارِبُهُ

kind /kaɪnd/ **A** *n* **1** (sort, type) نَوْع (أَنْواع), صِنْف (أَصْناف), ضُروب (صُنوف); **this ~ of book/person** هذا النَوْعُ من الكُتُبِ \ البَشَرِ كُلّ أَصْنافِ الأَشْخاصِ; **all ~s of people, people of all ~s** كُلّ أَصْنافِ الأَشْخاصِ; **what ~ of dog is it?** ما نَوْعُ \ صِنْفُ هذا الكَلْبِ؟; **what ~ of person would do a thing like that?** أَيُّ نَوْعٍ من البَشَرِ يَفْعَلُ فِعْلةً كَهَذِهِ؟; **a criminal of the worst ~** من أَعْتى المُجْرِمينَ; **she said nothing of the ~** لم تَقُلْ شَيْئاً من هذا القَبيلِ; **it is the only one of its ~, it is one of a ~** لا مَثيلَ لَهُ **2** (in vague descriptions) **a ~ of sth** نَوْع من شَيْءٍ; **a ~ of intuition** حَدْس من نَوْعٍ ما; **I heard a ~ of rattling noise** سَمِعْتُ صَوْتاً يُشْبِهُ الخَشْخَشةِ **3** (fml) (specific group) طينة, جِنْس (أَجْناس); **he was happier with his own ~** كانَ أَسْعَدَ مع مَنْ هُمْ من جِنْسِهِ
B (**in kind**) *adv phr* **1** (in goods) عَيْناً; **to pay in ~** دَفَعَ عَيْناً **2** (in the same way) **to repay sb in ~** (with sth positive) قابَلَ الحُسْنى بالحُسْنى; (with sth negative) رَدَّ الإساءةَ بالإساءةِ
C (**kind of**) *adv phr* (infml) **he's ~ of cute/forgetful** هو ظَريفٌ \ كَثيرُ النِسْيانِ نَوْعاً ما; **they were both ~ of frightened** كانَ الاثْنانِ خائِفَيْنِ بَعْضَ الشَيْءِ; **'was it good?'—'~ of'** 'هل أَعْجَبَكَ؟' — 'بَعْضَ الشَيْءِ'
D *adj* (considerate) ‹*person, act, gesture*› طَيِّب; **to be ~ to sb** كانَ طَيِّباً مع شَخْصٍ; **she was very ~ to us** كانَتْ طَيِّبةً جِدًّا مَعَنا; **that's very ~ of you** ذلك كَرَمٌ كَبيرٌ مِنْكَ; **thank you for all your ~ letters** أَشْكُرُكُمْ على كُلِّ رَسائِلِكُم الطَيِّبة; **would you be ~ enough** *or* **so ~ as to pass me the salt?** (fml) هَلاّ تَكَرَّمْتَ بِأَنْ تُناوِلَني المِلْحَ؟

kinda /ˈkaɪndə/ (infml) *abbr* = **kind of**

kindergarten /ˈkɪndəˌɡɑːt(ə)n/ *n* رَوْضة أَطْفالٍ

kind-hearted /kʌɪndˈhɑːtɪd/ *adj* <*warder, soul*> طَيِّب

kindle /ˈkɪnd(ə)l/ *vt* **1** ▸ أَوْقَدَ, أَشْعَلَ <*a fire*> **2** ▸ وَلَّدَ <*a desire*>; أَلْهَبَ <*passion*>

kindly /ˈkʌɪndli/ **A** *adv* **1** ▸ (in a kind way) <*to look, treat*> بِعَطْفٍ, بِطيبةٍ, بِمَوَدّةٍ **2** ▸ (adding polite emphasis) بِلُطْفٍ وَرَجاءٍ; **passengers are ~ requested to...** يُرْجى من الرُّكّابِ أنْ . . . **3** ▸ (favourably) <*to look, think*> باسْتِحْسانٍ; **they didn't take ~ to my suggestion** لم يَسْتَحْسِنوا اقْتِراحي; **she doesn't take ~ to being contradicted** لا تُحِبُّ أنْ يُعارِضَها أَحَدٌ

B *adj* (**kindlier, kindliest**) <*smile, voice*> طَيِّب

kindness /ˈkʌɪndnəs/ *n* **1** ▸ [u] (quality) طيبة; **they treated us with great ~** عامَلونا بمُنْتَهى الطيبة; **he did it out of ~** فَعَلَهُ بِدافِعِ الطيبةِ; **an act of ~** عَمَل يَنُمُّ عن الطيبةِ **2** ▸ (fml) (act) جَميل, مَعْروف (جَمائِلُ); **to do sb a ~** قَدَّمَ مَعْروفاً لِشَخْصٍ

kindred /ˈkɪndrɪd/ *adj* <*subject*> مُتَقارِب; <*evil*> مُماثِل

kindred spirit *n* رَفيق الروح

kinetic /kʌɪˈnɛtɪk/ *adj* <*energy, theory*> حَرَكِيّ

kinetics /kɪˈnɛtɪks/ *n* عِلْم الحَرَكة

king /kɪŋ/ *n* **1** ▸ (monarch) مَلِك (مُلوك), عاهِل (عَواهِلُ) **2** ▸ (in chess) مَلِك (مُلوك), شاه **3** ▸ (in draughts, checkers) مَلِك (مُلوك) **4** ▸ (in cards) مَلِك (مُلوك)

kingdom /ˈkɪŋdəm/ *n* **1** ▸ (monarchy) مَمْلَكة (مَمالِكُ) **2** ▸ (division) مَمْلَكة (مَمالِكُ), عالَم (عَوالِمُ); **the animal ~** مَمْلَكة الحَيَوانات

kingfisher /ˈkɪŋfɪʃə/ *n* قِرِلّى, رَفْراف, قاوَنْد

king-sized /ˈkɪŋsʌɪzd/, **king-size** /ˈkɪŋsʌɪz/ *adj* كينغ سايْز (حَجْم كَبير) <*bed, cigarettes*>

kink /kɪŋk/ *n* (in a rope, tube) اِلْتِواء (اِلْتِواءات); (in hair) تَمَوُّج (تَمَوُّجات)

kinky /ˈkɪŋki/ *adj* (**kinkier, kinkiest**) (infml) <*sex*> شاذّ (شُذّاذ, شَواذُّ); <*clothes*> خارِج عن (نِطاقِ) المَأْلوف

kinship /ˈkɪnʃɪp/ *n* قُرْبى (f)

kiosk /ˈkiːɒsk/ *n* **1** ▸ (stand) كُشْك (أَكْشاك) **2** ▸ (BrE) (phone box) كابينة هاتِفٍ

kipper /ˈkɪpə/ *n* سَمَك الرِنْجةِ المُدَخَّن والمالِح

Kirghizia /kɪəˈɡɪzɪə/ *pr n* ▸ **Kirghizstan**

Kirghizstan /ˈkəːɡɪstan/ *pr n* قِرْغيزِسْتان (f)

kiss /kɪs/ **A** *vt* قَبَّلَ <*a person*>; **to ~ sb on** قَبَّلَ شَخْصاً على <*sb's cheek, lips*>; **we ~ed each other** قَبَّلْنا بَعْضَنا; **you can ~ your money goodbye!** لن تَسْتَرْجِعَ نُقودَكَ أَبَداً!

B *vi* قَبَّلَ

C *n* قُبْلة (قُبُلات, قُبْلات, قُبَل); **to give sb a ~** أَعْطى شَخْصاً قُبْلةً

Idioms **kiss my ass!** (vulg) مُتْ غَيْظاً!; **to kiss and make up** تَصالَحَ; **to kiss and tell** أَشاعَ تَفاصيلَ عَلاقَتِه الغَرامِيّةِ بين الناسِ

kiss of life *n* (BrE) قُبْلة الحَياة

kit /kɪt/ *n* **1** ▸ (essential items) عُدّة (عُدَد); **first aid ~** عُدّة الإسْعافاتِ الأَوَّلِيّةِ **2** ▸ (for model, etc) عُدّة (عُدَد) **3** ▸ (BrE) (clothes) مَلابِس; **gym ~** مَلابِس الرياضةِ البَدَنِيّةِ **4** ▸ (soldier's equipment) عُدّة (عُدَد)

kitbag /ˈkɪtbaɡ/ *n* كيس العُدّةِ

kitchen /ˈkɪtʃɪn/ *n* مَطْبَخ (مَطابِخُ)

kitchen foil *n* وَرَق أَلومنيوم

kitchen garden *n* بُسْتان الخُضَرِ والفَواكِهِ

kitchen roll *n* لَفّة وَرَقِيّة تُسْتَعْمَلُ للتَنْشيفِ في المَطْبَخِ

kitchen sink *n* مَجْلى \ حَوْض المَطْبَخِ;

Idiom **everything but the kitchen sink** كُلّ غالٍ وَرَخيصٍ

kitchen unit *n* خِزانة مَطْبَخٍ

kite /kʌɪt/ *n* **1** ▸ (toy) طائِرة وَرَقِيّة **2** ▸ (bird) حِدَأة (حِداء)

kitten /ˈkɪt(ə)n/ *n* هُرَيْرة

kitty[1] /ˈkɪti/ *n* (*pl* **kitties**) صُنْدوق مُشْتَرَك تودَعُ فيه مُساهَماتُ المُشْتَرِكينَ أو الأَعْضاءِ

kitty[2] /ˈkɪti/ *n* (*pl* **kitties**) قِطّ (قِطَط)

kiwi /ˈkiːwiː/ **A** *n* (bird) كيوي

B (**Kiwi**) *n* (infml) (New Zealander) شَخْص نيوزِيلَنْدِيّ

kiwi fruit *n* كيوي

kleptomaniac /klɛptəˈmeɪnɪak/ *n* مُصاب بِهَوَسِ السَرِقة

klutz /klʌts/ *n* (AmE infml) أَخْرَق (خُرْق; dipt)

km *abbr* = **kilometre(s)** كم

knack /nak/ *n* مَهارة; **to get the ~** اِكْتَسَبَ مَهارةً; **to lose the ~** فَقَدَ مَهارةً

knapsack /ˈnapsak/ *n* حَقيبة ظَهْرٍ

knave /neɪv/ *n* **1** (in cards) وَلَد (أَوْلاد ,وُلْد) **2** (old use) (rogue) وَغْد (أَوْغاد ,وُغْدان)

knead /niːd/ *vt* عَجَنَ (i-u; عَجْن) ‹dough, clay›

knee /niː/ **A** *n* **1** (joint) رُكْبة (رُكَب ,رُكْبات) **2** (lap) حِجْر
B *vt* ضَرَبَ بِرُكْبَتِهِ ‹a person›

(Idioms) **to bring sb/sth to his/its knees** أَخْضَعَ شَخْصاً \ شَيْئاً; **to go down on one's knees** رَكَعَ (a; رُكوع)

kneecap /ˈniːkap/ *n* رَضْفة (رَضْف ,دَاغِصة) (دَواغِص)

knee-deep /niːˈdiːp/ *adj* بِعُمْقٍ \ بِعُلوِّ الرُّكْبةِ; **the water was ~** كانَ الماءُ بِعُلوِّ الرُّكْبةِ

knee-high /ˌniːˈhʌɪ/ *adj* ‹grass, boots› طَويل حتّى الرُّكْبة

knee-jerk /ˈnidʒəːk/ *adj* ‹reaction, response› تِلْقائيّ

kneel /niːl/ *vi* (also **kneel down**; *past tense, past participle* **kneeled, knelt**) «congregation, mourners» رَكَعَ (a; رُكوع)

knee-length /ˈniːlɛŋθ/ *adj* ‹skirt, boots› بِطولِ الرُّكْبةِ

knelt /nɛlt/ *past tense, past participle* ▸ **kneel**

knew /njuː/ *past tense* ▸ **know**

knickerbockers /ˈnɪkəbɒkəz/ *n pl* بِنْطال قَصير (يُرْبَطُ تحت الرُّكْبةِ)

knickers /ˈnɪkəz/ *n pl* (BrE) سِرْوال داخِليّ

knick-knack /ˈnɪknak/ *n* [نَوْع بَسيط من الزينة]

knife /nʌɪf/ **A** *n* (*pl* **knives**) سِكّين (f; سَكاكين)
B *vt* طَعَنَ (a-u; طَعْن) ‹a victim›

(Idiom) **to go under the knife** (infml) خَضَعَ لِعَمَلِيّةٍ

knife-edge /ˈnʌɪfɛdʒ/ *n* **on a ~** [في حالةٍ بالِغةِ التَوَتُّرِ]; **the election result is on a ~** نَتائِجُ الانْتِخاباتِ غَيْرُ قابِلةٍ للتَكَهُّنِ بِها بالمَرّةِ

knifepoint /ˈnʌɪfpɔɪnt/ *n* **at ~** تحت التَهْديدِ بِسِكّينٍ

knight /nʌɪt/ **A** *n* **1** (in chess) حِصان (حُصُن ,أَحْصِنة) **2** (UK social rank) فارِس (فُرْسان); **the K~s of the Round Table** فُرْسان الطاوِلةِ المُسْتَديرة
B *vt* (in UK) مَنَحَ لَقَبَ فارِسٍ ل ‹an actor, athlete›

knighthood /ˈnʌɪthʊd/ *n* فُروسيّة

knit /nɪt/ **A** *vt* (*present participle* **-tt-**; *past tense, past participle* **knitted** or **knit**) **1** ‹a sweater, hat› حاكَ (u; حَوْك ,حِياكة) ,نَسَجَ (i-u; نَسْج) **2** [عَمِلَ على نُشوءِ نَسيجٍ مُتَرابِطٍ في] ‹community›; **the community is closely ~** المُجْتَمَعُ مُتَرابِطُ النَسيجِ
B *vi* (*present participle* **-tt-**; *past tense, past participle* **knitted** or **knit**) **1** (to make) حاكَ (u; حَوْك ,حِياكة) ,نَسَجَ (i-u; نَسْج) **2** «broken bones» اِلْتَحَمَ

knitting /ˈnɪtɪŋ/ *n* **1** [u] (process) حِياكة ,نَسْج **2** (material) [نَسيج يُحاكُ بالإِبَرِ]

knitwear /ˈnɪtwɛː/ *n* مَلابِس مَنْسوجة

knives /nʌɪvz/ *n pl* ▸ **knife**

knob /nɒb/ *n* **1** (of a door) (on a banister) مِقْبَض (مَقابِض) **2** (control button) زِرّ (أَزْرار ,زُرور)

knobbly (BrE) /ˈnɒbli/, **knobby** /ˈnɒbi/ (AmE) *adj* (**knobblier, knobbliest, knobblier, knobbliest**) ‹knees› [ذات نُتوءاتٍ]

knock /nɒk/ **A** *vt* **1** (to strike) قَرَعَ (a; قَرْع) ,ضَرَبَ (i; ضَرْب) ‹a bottle, table, TV›; **to ~ sth off the table/shelf** أَسْقَطَ شَيْئاً من على الطاوِلةِ \ الرَفِّ; **the explosion ~ed me off my feet** أَوْقَعَني الانْفِجارُ على الأَرْضِ; **to ~ one's head on the door post** اِصْطَدَمَ بِرَأْسِهِ في عِضادةِ البابِ; **to ~ sb flat** ضَرَبَ شَخْصاً فَسَقَطَ مُمَدَّداً على الأَرْضِ; **to ~ sb unconscious** ضَرَبَ شَخْصاً فَأَفْقَدَهُ وَعْيَهُ **2** (infml) (to criticize) هاجَمَ ,اِنْتَقَدَ ‹a method, rival, an achievement› **3** (infml) (to beat) **to ~ the spirit out of sb** قَتَلَ الروحَ المَعْنَويّةَ لدى شَخْصٍ; **to ~ some sense into sb** لَقَّنَ شَخْصاً دَرْساً
B *vi* **1** (on a door) «visitor» طَرَقَ (u; طَرْق); **to ~ at** *or* **on the door** طَرَقَ على البابِ **2** (to make a sound) «engine, water pipes» دَقَّ (u; دَقّ) ,خَبَطَ (i; خَبْط) **3** (to collide) **to ~ into sb/sth** اِصْطَدَمَ بِشَخْصٍ \ بِشَيْءٍ
C *n* **1** (blow) ضَرْبة (ضَرَبات); **there was a ~ at the door** كانَتْ هُناكَ طَرْقةٌ على البابِ; **I'll give you a ~ at 7.30** سَأَطْرُقُ على بابِكَ الساعةَ 7.30; **I got a ~ on the head** تَلَقَّيْتُ ضَرْبةً على رَأْسي **2** (setback) إِخْفاق ,اِنْتِكاسة (إِخْفاقات); **you have to learn to take the ~s** عَلَيْكَ أَنْ تَتَعَلَّمَ كيف تَتَعامَلُ مع المِحَنِ

Idiom **to knock sth on the head** قَضى على شَيْءٍ بِرُمَّتِهِ

Phrasal verbs **knock about** (infml) ▸ **knock around**

• **knock around** **A** (infml) «friends» تَجَوَّلَ; «clothes» تَبَعْثَرَ; **to ~ around with sb** تَنَزَّهَ مع شَخْصٍ **B** **~ around [sth]** (infml) «friends» تَجَوَّلَ في [شَيْءٍ] ‹*the house, area*›; «clothes» تَناثَرَ في [شَيْءٍ]; **we had been ~ing around Morocco for a few months** كُنّا نَتَجَوَّلُ في المَغْرِبِ لِبِضْعةِ أَشْهُرٍ **C** **~ [sb] around** (infml) (to beat) ضَرَبَ [شَخْصاً] بِشَكْلٍ مُتَكَرِّرٍ

• **knock back** **A** **~ back [sth], ~ [sth] back** (infml) **1** (to swallow) ابْتَلَعَ [شَيْئاً] ‹*a drink*› **2** (to reject) رَفَضَ [شَيْئاً] ‹*an offer, invitation*› **B** **~ [sb] back** (to shock) «the news, sb's reply» صَدَمَ [شَخْصاً]

• **knock down**: **~ [sb/sth] down, ~ down [sb/sth]** **1** (in a road accident) صَدَمَ [شَخْصاً \ شَيْئاً] ‹*a pedestrian, child*› **2** (with punches) «attackers, boxer» لَكَمَ [شَخْصاً] فَطَرَحَهُ أَرْضاً ‹*a victim, an opponent*› **3** (to demolish) هَدَمَ \ حَطَّمَ [شَيْئاً] ‹*a building, door*›; **the firemen ~ed down the door to get in** حَطَّمَ رِجالُ الإطْفاءِ البابَ حتّى يَتَمَكَّنوا من الدُخولِ **4** (to reduce) «sellers» خَفَّضَ [شَيْئاً] ‹*the price*›; **I ~ed him down to £50** خَفَّضْتُ مَعَهُ السِعْرَ إلى £50

• **knock in**: **~ [sth] in, ~ in [sth]** دَقَّ [شَيْئاً] ‹*a nail, peg, post*›

• **knock off** **A** **~ off** (infml) «workers» تَوَقَّفَ عن العَمَلِ **B** **~ [sb/sth] off, ~ off [sb/sth]** **1** (to cause to fall) أَسْقَطَ [شَخْصاً \ شَيْئاً] ‹*a person, vase, picture*› **2** (infml) (to deduct) **I'll ~ off 15% for cash** سَأَخْصِمُ 15٪ عند الدَفْعِ النَقْدِيِّ **3** (infml) (to steal) سَرَقَ [شَيْئاً] ‹*a car, laptop*› **4** (infml) (to stop) **~ it off!** كُفَّ عن ذلك!

• **knock out** **A** **~ [sth] out, ~ out [sth]** **1** (to remove) خَلَعَ [شَيْئاً] ‹*a peg, sb's tooth*› **2** (to destroy) دَمَّرَ [شَيْئاً] ‹*a tank, factory, radar*› **3** أَصْلَحَ [شَيْئاً] ‹*a dent, the panel*› **B** **~ [sb] out, ~ out [sb]** **1** (to leave unconscious) «explosions, blows, boxers» أَفْقَدَ [شَخْصاً] وَعْيَهُ ‹*an opponent, soldier*›; **the anaesthetic ~ed me out immediately** أَفْقَدَني المُخَدِّرُ وَعْيي على الفَوْرِ **2** (to eliminate) أَخْرَجَ [شَخْصاً] من المُنافَسةِ ‹*an opponent, a team, competitor*› **3** (infml) (to overwhelm) بَهَرَ \ أَثارَ إعْجابَ [شَخْصٍ] ‹*a spectator, the audience*›

• **knock over**: **~ [sb/sth] over, ~ over [sb/sth]** **1** (to cause to fall) أَسْقَطَ [شَخْصاً \ شَيْئاً] ‹*an ornament, table, person*› **2** (in a road accident) صَدَمَ [شَخْصاً \ شَيْئاً] ‹*a pedestrian, child*›

• **knock together**: **~ [sth] together, ~ together [sth]** (infml) صَنَعَ [شَيْئاً] على عَجَلٍ ‹*a shelter, a meal, an outfit*›

• **knock up** **A** (in tennis) تَمَرَّنَ قبل مُباراةِ التِنِس **B** **~ [sth] up, ~ up [sth]** (infml) (to make) صَنَعَ [شَيْئاً] على عَجَلٍ ‹*a shelter, a meal, an outfit*› **C** **~ [sb] up, ~ up [sb]** **1** (BrE) (infml) (to wake up) أَيْقَظَ [شَخْصاً] **2** (AmE) (infml) (to make pregnant) أَحْبَلَ [شَخْصاً]

knockabout /ˈnɒkəbaʊt/ *n* (BrE) لُعْبة كُرةِ قَدَمٍ بين أَصْدِقاءَ

knock-down /ˈnɒkdaʊn/ *adj* ‹*price*› أَدْنى

knocker /ˈnɒkə/ *n* حَلْقة البابِ (للطَرْقِ عَلَيْهِ)

knocking /ˈnɒkɪŋ/ *n* **1** (at a door) طَرْق **2** (in engines) طَقْطَقة

knock-kneed /ˌnɒkˈniːd/ *adj* ‹*child, man*› مُصاب بِصَكَكِ الرُكْبَتَيْن

knock-on effect /ˌnɒkˈɒn ɪˌfɛkt/ *n* ≈ تَداعِيات; **the closure of the factory will have a ~ in the region** سَيَتْرُكُ إغْلاقُ المَصْنَعِ تَداعِياتٍ على المِنْطَقةِ

knockout /ˈnɒkaʊt/ **A** *n* **1** (in boxing) ضَرْبة قاضِية **2** (attractive person) شَخص جَذّاب **B** *adj* **1** ‹*competition, tournament*› إقْصائيّ **2** ‹*pills, drops*› مُنَوِّم

knoll /nəʊl/ *n* تَلّ صَغير

knot /nɒt/ **A** *n* **1** (of string, rope) عُقْدة (عُقَد) **2** (in wood) عُقْدة (عُقَد) **3** (in hair, wool) عُقْدة (عُقَد) **4** (group) جَمْهَرة **5** (unit of measurement) عُقْدة (عُقَد) **B** *vt* (-tt-) عَقَدَ (i; عَقْد) ‹*a scarf, shoelace*›

Idiom **to tie the knot** (infml) عَقَدَ قِرانَهُ

know /nəʊ/ **A** *vt* (*past tense* **knew**; *past participle* **known**) **1** (to have knowledge of) عَرَفَ (i; مَعْرِفة) ‹*a person, language, the answer*›; **he ~s everything** يَعْرِفُ كُلَّ شَيْءٍ; **to ~ sb by name/sight** عَرَفَ شَخْصاً بالاسْمِ \ بالشَكْلِ; **to ~ sth by heart** عَرَفَ شَيْئاً عن ظَهْرِ قَلْبٍ; **to ~ how to do sth** (ability) اسْتَطاعَ فِعْلَ شَيْءٍ; (method) عَرَفَ كيف يَفْعَلُ شَيْئاً; **he ~s all/nothing about it** يَعْرِفُ كُلَّ شَيْءٍ \ لا يَعْرِفُ شَيْئاً عن ذلك; **to ~ that ...**

عَرَفَ أنّ ...; **to ~ for certain** *or* **for sure that ...** عَرَفَ حَقَّ المَعْرِفةِ أنّ ...; **I wasn't to ~ that he was lying** لم أكُنْ لِأَعرِفَ أنَّهُ كانَ يَكْذِبُ; **to ~ what poverty is** عَرَفَ ما هو الفَقْرُ; **you ~ what children are like** تَعْرِفُ طَبيعةَ الأَطْفالِ; **Sally Duffy, known professionally as Sarah Dover** سالي دافي المَعْروفة بِاسْمِها الفَنّيِّ سارة دوفر; **to let it be known** *or* **to make it known that ...** أَعْلَنَ أنّ ...; **to have known sb/sth to do sth** كانَ يَعْرِفُ عن شَخْصٍ \ شَيْءٍ أنَّهُ يَفْعَلُ شَيْئاً; **it has been known to snow there** يَسْقُطُ الثَلْجُ هُناكَ أَحياناً; **if I ~ you/him** حَسَبَ مَعْرِفتي بكَ \ بِهِ; **he is known to the police** هو مَعْروفٌ لدى الشُرْطةِ; **I ~ all about redundancy!** أَعْرِفُ كُلَّ شَيْءٍ عن البِطالةِ!; **(do) you ~ something?, do you ~ what?** هل أُخْبِرُكَ بِشَيْءٍ؟ ≈; **there's no ~ing how it will end** لا أَحَدَ يَعْرِفُ كيف سَيَنْتَهي الأَمْرُ; **to ~ one's way home** عَرَفَ الطَريقَ إلى المَنْزِلِ; **to ~ one's way around a city** عَرَفَ الطُرُقَ في مَدينةٍ; **I ~ that for a fact** أَعْرِفُ ذلكَ حَقَّ المَعْرِفةِ; **I ~ what!** ≈ عِنْدي فِكْرةٌ! **2** (to feel certain) عَرَفَ (i; مَعْرِفة); **I knew it!** كُنْتُ أَعرِفُ ذلكَ!; **I don't really ~ that I want to go** لَسْتُ مُتَيَقِّناً أنّي أُريدُ الذَهابَ **3** (to realize) عَرَفَ (i; مَعْرِفة); **you don't ~ how pleased I am** لا تَعْرِفُ كم أنا سَعيدٌ; **don't I ~ it!** ≈ أَعرِفُ ذلكَ جَيِّداً! **4** (to recognize) عَرَفَ (i; مَعْرِفة), مَيَّزَ; **she ~s a bargain when she sees one** تَعرِفُ الصَفْقةَ الجَيِّدةَ عِنْدَما تَراها; **I don't ~ one from the other** لا أَسْتَطيعُ أنْ أُمَيِّزَ واحِداً من الآخَرِ **5** **to be known for sth** (to be recognized as) اشْتَهَرَ بِشَيْءٍ; **to be known for doing sth** كانَ مَشهوراً بِفِعْلِ شَيْءٍ
6 (to experience) جَرَّبَ ‹*joy, sadness, love*›

B *vi* (*past tense* **knew**; *past participle* **known**) **1** (to have knowledge) عَرَفَ (i; مَعْرِفة), عَلِمَ (a; عِلْم); **as you ~** كَما تَعْرِفُ; **as you well ~** كَما تَعْرِفُ جَيِّداً; **I wouldn't ~** لا أَدْري; **to ~ about sth** (to have information about) كانَ على عِلْمٍ بِشَيْءٍ ‹*an event*›; (to have skill with) فَهِمَ في شَيْءٍ ‹*computing, cars*›; **to ~ of sth** عَلِمَ عن شَيْءٍ; **not that I ~ of** لَيْسَ على حَدِّ عِلْمي; **to let sb ~ about sth** أَخْبَرَ شَخْصاً بِشَيْءٍ ‹*a plan, arrangement, job*›; **we'll let you ~** سَنُخْبِرُكَ بالقَرارِ; **if you must ~** إذا كُنْتَ مُصِرًّا على أنْ تَعرِفَ; **you ~ better than to argue with him** أَنْتَ أَذْكى من أنْ تُجادِلَ مَعَهُ; **you should/ought to have known better** كانَ يَجِبُ أنْ تَتَصَرَّفَ بِحِكْمةٍ أَكْثَرَ; **they don't ~ any better** لا يَعْرِفونَ السُلوكَ اللائِقَ **2** (in indirect affirmations) **'is it useful?'—'I don't ~ about useful, but it was cheap'** 'هل هو مُفيدٌ؟'—'لا أَعْرِفُ ما إذا كانَ مُفيداً، وَلَكِنَّهُ كانَ رَخيصاً'; **'he won't win'—'oh I don't ~'** 'لَن يَفوزَ'—'آه، أنا لا أَعْرِفُ حَقًّا'; **I don't ~ about you, but ...** لا أَعرِفُ رَأْيَكَ، لَكِنْ ...

Idioms **not to know whether one is coming or going** شَعَرَ بالحيرةِ / بالتَوَهانِ; **to be in the know** كانَ من المُطَّلِعينَ على الأَمْرِ

knowable /ˈnəʊəb(ə)l/ *adj* ‹*details, information*› يُمكِنُ مَعْرِفَتُهُ

know-all /ˈnəʊɔːl/ *n* (BrE) مُتَعالِم, مُتَحَذْلِق

know-how /ˈnəʊhaʊ/ *n* مَعْرِفة فَنّيّة

knowing /ˈnəʊɪŋ/ *adj* ‹*look, smile*› يَنُمُّ عن مَعْرِفةٍ سابِقةٍ

knowingly /ˈnəʊɪŋli/ *adv* **1** (consciously) ‹*to offend, mislead*› عن قَصْدٍ **2** (with understanding) ‹*to smile, look*› بِشَكْلٍ يَنُمُّ عن مَعْرِفةٍ سابِقةٍ

know-it-all /ˈnəʊɪtɔːl/ *n* (infml) ▸ **know-all**

knowledge /ˈnɒlɪdʒ/ *n* **1** (of a subject, history, science) مَعْرِفة; **an in-depth/superficial ~ of the law** مَعْرِفة عَميقة \ سَطْحيّة بالقانونِ **2** (fml) **his ~ of the Koran** مَعْرِفَتُهُ بالقُرْآنِ (awareness) عِلْم, مَعْرِفة, دِراية; **he has no ~ of what happened** لَيْسَ لَدَيْهِ عِلْمٌ بِما جَرى; **to do sth without sb's ~** قامَ بِشَيْءٍ دونَ عِلْمِ شَخْصٍ; **to the best of my ~** على حَدِّ عِلْمي; **it is common** *or* **public ~ that he he lied** من المَعْروفِ أنَّهُ كَذِبَ

knowledgeable /ˈnɒlɪdʒəb(ə)l/ *adj* ‹*friend, teacher*› عَليم (عُلَماءُ), واسِع الاطِّلاعِ

known /nəʊn/ **A** *past participle* ▸ **know**
B *adj* **1** ‹*source, quantity*› مَعْلوم, مَعْروف; **the most dangerous threat ~ to man** أَخْطَرَ تَهْديدٍ عَرَفَهُ الإنْسانُ; **he is a ~ authority on ...** هو خَبيرٌ مَشْهورٌ في ...; **list the ~ sources** أُكْتُبْ قائِمةً بالمَصادِرِ المَعْروفةِ **2** (to be recognized as) **to be known for sth** كانَ مَعْروفاً بِشَيْءٍ

knuckle /ˈnʌk(ə)l/ *n* **1** (finger joint) بُرْجُمة (بَراجِمُ), مَفْصِل الإصْبَعِ **2** (Culin) (of lamb, mutton, etc) [مَفْصِل الرُكْبةِ أو الكاحِلِ]

(Phrasal verbs) **knuckle down** (infml) شَمَّرَ عن ساعِدِهِ

• **knuckle under** (infml) رَضَخَ ,أَذْعَنَ (a-i; رُضوخ)

knuckleduster /ˈnʌkəldʌstə/ *n* قَبْضة حَديديّة (قِطْعة حَديديّة بِها ثُقوبٌ للأَصابِعِ تُسْتَخْدَمُ لِتَقْوِيةِ الضَرْبةِ)

koala /kəʊˈɑːlə/, **koala bear** *n* دُبّ الكُوالا

kohlrabi /kəʊlˈrɑːbi/ *n* (*pl* **kohlrabies**) كُرُنْب ساقِيّ

kooky /ˈkuːki/ *adj* (**kookier, kookiest**) (infml) ‹*idea, character*› مَجْنون (مَجانينُ), غَريب (غُرَباءُ)

Koran /kəˈrɑːn/ *n* (**the Koran**) القُرْآن

Korea /kəˈrɪə/ *pr n* كورِيا

Korean /kəˈriːən/ **A** *adj* ‹*government, peninsula*› كورِيّ

B *n* **1** (person) كورِيّ; **a North/South ~** مُواطِن من كورِيا الشَماليّةِ \ الجَنوبيّةِ **2** (language) (اللُغة) الكوريّة

korfball /ˈkɔːfbɔːl/ *n* [u] كُرة الكورْف (لُعْبة تُشْبِهُ كُرةَ السَلّةِ)

kosher /ˈkəʊʃə/ *adj* ‹*food, butcher*› كوشر (الطَعام المُباح عند اليَهودِ)

Kosovan /ˈkɒsəv(ə)n/ *n, adj* كوسوفِيّ

Kosovar /ˈkɒsəvɑː/ *n* كوسوفِيّ

Kosovo /ˈkɒsəvəʊ/ *pr n* كوسوفو (f)

kowtow /kaʊˈtaʊ/ *vi* «colleagues, workers» خَضَعَ (a; خُضوع); **to ~ to sb** تَزَلَّفَ إلى شَخْصٍ

kph /keɪpiːˈeɪtʃ/ *abbr* = **kilometres per hour** كم/ س (كيلومِتْر في الساعةِ)

KS *abbr* ▸ **Kansas**

kung fu /kʊŋ ˈfuː/ *n* كونْغ فو

Kurd /kəːd/ *n* كُرْديّ (كُرْد ,أَكْراد)

Kurdish /ˈkəːdɪʃ/ **A** *adj* ‹*people, region*› كُرْديّ (أَكْراد)

B *n* (اللُغة) الكُرْديّة

Kurdistan /ˌkəːdɪˈstɑːn/ *pr n* كُرْدِسْتان (f)

Kuwait /kʊˈweɪt/ *pr n* **1** (the country) الكُوَيْت (f) **2** (the capital) الكُوَيْت العاصِمة ,مَدينة الكُوَيْت

Kuwaiti /kʊˈweɪti/ *n, adj* كُوَيْتِيّ

kwashiorkor /kwɒʃiˈɔːkɔː/ *n* كُواشيورْكور (مَرَض يَنْشأُ بِسَبَبِ نَقْصِ البْروتين)

KY, Ky *abbr* ▸ **Kentucky**

Kyrgyzstan /kəːgɪˈstan/ *pr n* قِرْغيزِسْتان (f)

Ll

L /ɛl/, **l** **A** *n* (letter) لام ≈ [الحَرْف الثانِي عَشَرَ من الأَبْجَدِيّة الإنْكليزِيّة]

B *abbr* **1** (**l**) = **litre(s)** (BrE) = **liter(s)** (AmE) لِتْر (لِتْرات) **2** (**l**) = **left** يَسار **3** (**L**) = **Lake** بُحَيْرة **4** (**L**) (in clothing sizes) = **large** كَبير **5** (**L**) (BrE) = **Learner** مُتَعَلِّم قِيادة سَيّارةٍ

la /lɑː/ *n* ▸ **lah**

LA *abbr* **1** = **Los Angeles** **2** ▸ **Louisiana**

lab /lab/ *n* مُخْتَبَر (مُخْتَبَرات)

lab coat *n* مِعْطَف مُخْتَبَرٍ

label /ˈleɪb(ə)l/ **A** *n* **1** (on clothing) بطاقة (بطاقات, بَطائِقُ); (on a jar, case) مُلْصَق (مُلْصَقات), لاصِقة; (on a diagram) عُنْوان (عَناوِينُ) **2** (Busn) (also **record label**) شَركة إنْتاجٍ موسيقيٍّ (also **fashion label**) شَركة تَصْميمِ مَلابِسَ

B *vt* (**-ll-** BrE, **-l-** AmE) **1** (for identification) وَضَعَ بِطاقةً على ‹*clothing*›; وَضَعَ مُلْصَقاً على ‹*a jar, suitcase*›; عَنْوَنَ (i; عَنْوَنة) ‹*a diagram*› **2** (to categorize) صَنَّفَ ‹*a person, sb's work*›; **to be ~led as a progressive/ troublemaker** وُصِفَ بِأَنَّهُ تَقَدُّمِيٌّ \ مُثِيرٌ للمَشاكِلِ

labia /ˈleɪbɪə/ *n pl* شِفْرانِ

labor (AmE) ▸ **labour**

laboratory /ləˈbɒrətri/ *n* (*pl* **laboratories**) مُخْتَبَر (مُخْتَبَرات)

labored (AmE) *adj* ▸ **laboured**

laborer (AmE) *n* ▸ **labourer**

laborious /ləˈbɔːrɪəs/ *adj* **1** ‹*work, task*› مُجْهِد, مُرْهِق **2** ‹*style, read*› مُبالَغ فيه

labor-saving (AmE) *adj* ▸ **labour-saving**

labour (BrE), **labor** (AmE) /ˈleɪbə/ **A** *n* **1** (liter) (task) عَمَل (أَعْمال); **the fruits of one's ~s** ثِمار كَدِّهِ; **the ~s of Hercules** أَعْمال هِرَقْل **2** [u] (workforce) عِمالة, أَيْدٍ عامِلة; **skilled/ unskilled ~** عِمالة ماهِرة \ غَيْر ماهِرة **3** [u] (in estimates) أَيْد عامِلة, عِمالة; **materials and ~** مَوادّ وَأَيْد عامِلة **4** [u] (in childbirth) مَخاض; **to be in/go into ~** كانَت \ دَخَلَت في المَخاضِ **5** [u] (Pol) (**Labour**) (in the UK) حِزْب العُمّالِ; (in Australia) **Labor** حِزْب العُمّالِ

B *vi* **1** (to work, try hard) «workers» كَدَّ (u; كَدّ), كَدَحَ (a; كَدْح); **to be ~ing under an illusion** جَرى وراء الوَهْم **2** (to have difficulties) «engines, runners» تَقَدَّمَ بِصُعوبةٍ \ بِمَشَقّةٍ; **he ~ed up the hill** صَعَدَ التَلَّ بِمَشَقّةٍ

Idiom **a labour of love** ≈ عَمَل تَطَوُّعِيّ

labour costs (BrE), **labor costs** (AmE) *n* تَكاليف العَمَلِ, أُجور العُمّالِ

Labour Day *n* (AmE) [عيد يَحْتَفِلُ فيهِ العُمّالُ في أَمْريكا في شَهْرِ أَيْلولَ]

laboured (BrE), **labored** (AmE) /ˈleɪbəd/ *adj* **1** (difficult) ‹*movement, breathing*› ثَقيل, صَعْب, مُتَثاقِل; **his breathing is very ~** تَنَفُّسُهُ ثَقيلٌ جِدًّا **2** (showing effort) ‹*joke, humour*› مُتَكَلَّف; **the introductions were very ~** كانَت المُقَدِّماتُ كَثيرةَ التَكَلُّفِ

labourer (BrE), **laborer** (AmE) /ˈleɪb(ə)rə/ *n* عامِل (عُمّال)

Labour Party *n* (**the Labour Party**) حِزْب العُمّالِ (في بَريطانيا)

labour relations (BrE), **labor relations** (AmE) *n* عَلاقات العَمَلِ (العَلاقة بين الإدارة والعُمّالِ)

labour-saving (BrE), **labor-saving** (AmE) /ˈleɪbəseɪvɪŋ/ *adj* ‹*appliance, feature*› مُوَفِّر للعِمالةِ \ للجُهْدِ, لِتَخْفيفِ عَناءِ العَمَلِ

labour union (BrE), **labor union** (AmE) *n* نِقابة عُمّاليّة

Labrador /ˈlabrədɔː/ *n* [فَصيلة من كِلابِ الصَيْدِ والمَكْفوفينَ]

labyrinth /ˈlabərɪnθ/ *n* (maze) تيه, مَتاهة (أَتْياه)

lace /leɪs/ **A** *n* **1** (fabric) دانْتيل **2** (on a shoe) رِباط (أَرْبِطة ,رُبُط)
B *vt* **1** (to fasten) رَبَطَ (i-u; رَبْط) ‹*a shoe, dress*› **2** (to fortify) [أَضاف بَعْضَ الخَمْرِ إلى] ‹*a drink, dish*›

lacerate /ˈlasəreɪt/ *vt* مَزَّق ‹*skin, flesh*›

lace-up shoe, **lace-up** /leɪsʌp ˈʃuː/ *n* حِذاء بِرِباطٍ

lack /lak/ **A** *n* نُقْصان ,نَقْص ,انْعِدام ,فِقْدان; **a ~ of salt/funds** فِقْدان المِلْحِ \ التَمْويلِ
B *vt* افْتَقَر (إلى) ‹*confidence, courage*›; **the coffee ~s taste** تَفْتَقِرُ القَهْوةُ إلى النَكْهةِ

lacking /ˈlakɪŋ/ *adj* ‹*resources, concern*› ناقِص ,مَعْدوم; **to be ~ in taste/originality** كانَ يَنْقُصُهُ الذَوْقُ \ القُدْرةُ الإبْداعيّةُ

lacklustre (BrE), **lackluster** (AmE) /ˈlaklʌstə/ *adj* **1** (dull) ‹*eyes, hair*› شاحِب **2** (mediocre) ‹*campaign, candidate*› باهِت

laconic /ləˈkɒnɪk/ *adj* ‹*style, speaker*› قَليل الكَلامِ ,وَجيز, مُقْتَضَب

lacquer /ˈlakə/ *n* **1** (**hair lacquer**) [طِلاء لِتَثْبيتِ الشَعْرِ]
2 (varnish) وَرْنيش

lacrosse /ləˈkrɒs/ *n* لُعْبة لاكروس (لُعْبة كُرةٍ تُسْتَخْدَمُ فيها المَضارِبُ ذاتُ المَقابِضِ الطَويلةِ لِتَسْديدِ الأَهْدافِ)

lactate /lakˈteɪt/ *vi* «mothers, women» أَلْبَنَ

lactation /lakˈteɪʃ(ə)n/ *n* إلْبان ,دَرّ الحَليبِ

lactose /ˈlaktəʊs, ˈlaktəʊz/ *n* لاكْتوز ,سُكَّر الحَليبِ \ اللَبَنِ

lacy /ˈleɪsi/ *adj* ‹*fabric, underwear*› [مُزَيَّن بِدانْتيلاّ]

lad /lad/ *n* (infml) صَبيّ (صِبْيان)

ladder /ˈladə/ **A** *n* **1** (for climbing) سُلَّم (سَلالِمُ) **2** (BrE) (in tights) تَمَزُّق
B *vt* مَزَّق ‹*my tights, stockings*›
C *vi* «stockings» تَمَزَّقَ

laddish /ˈladɪʃ/ *adj* (infml) ‹*culture, behaviour*› [فيه اسْتِعْراضٌ لِلرُجولةِ بِشَكْلٍ مُبالَغٍ فيه]

laden /ˈleɪd(ə)n/ *adj* ‹*lorry, cart*› مُثْقَل ,مُحَمَّل; **tables ~ with fruit** طاوِلات مُحَمَّلة بالفَواكِهِ

ladies' room /ˈleɪdiz rʊm/ (AmE) *n* دَوْرة ,حُجْرة السَيِّداتِ المِياهِ لِلسَيِّداتِ

ladle /ˈleɪd(ə)l/ *n* مِغْرَفة (مَغارِفُ), كَبْشة (كَبَشات)

lady /ˈleɪdi/ **A** *n* (*pl* **ladies**) **1** (woman) سَيِّدة; **ladies and gentlemen** سَيِّداتي وَسادَتي; **she's a real ~** هي سَيِّدةٌ بِكُلِّ مَعْنى الكَلِمةِ; **ask the ~ in reception** اسْأَل السَيِّدةَ في مَكْتَبِ الاسْتِقْبالِ **2** (BrE) (in titles) سَيِّدة (لَقَب امْرَأةٍ من طَبَقةِ النُبَلاءِ); **L~ Crawley** السَيِّدة كْرولي
B (**ladies**) *n pl* (BrE) مِرْحاض النِساءِ

ladybird (BrE) /ˈleɪdɪbəːd/, **ladybug** (AmE) /ˈleɪdɪbʌg/ *n* دُعْسوقة

lady-in-waiting /ˌleɪdɪɪnˈweɪtɪŋ/ *n* (*pl* **ladies-in-waiting**) وَصيفة (وَصائِفُ)

ladylike /ˈleɪdɪlʌɪk/ *adj* ‹*manner, behaviour*› لائِق بِسَيِّدةٍ مُحْتَرَمةٍ

lag /lag/ **A** *vt* (**-gg-**) كَسا (u; كَسْو) ‹*pipes, a tank*›
B *n* (also **time lag**) فارِق زَمَنيّ; **a [time] ~ of half an hour** فارِق زَمَنيّ بِفَتْرةِ نِصْفِ ساعةٍ

Phrasal verb **lag behind**: **1** **~ behind** «growth, the children» تَأَخَّرَ عن الرَكْبِ ,تَباطَأَ ,تَخَلَّفَ ,تَلَكَّأَ **2** **~ behind [sb/sth]** تَخَلَّفَ عن [شَخْصٍ \ شَيْءٍ] ‹*one's competitors, the rest*›

lager /ˈlɑːgə/ *n* بيرة; **a pint of ~** نِصْف لِتْرٍ من البيرةِ

lager lout *n* (BrE) [شابّ ثَمِل مُشاغِب]

lagoon /ləˈguːn/ *n* هَوْر ,بُحَيْرة شاطِئيّة (أَهْوار)

lah /lɑː/ *n* لا (نَغْمة من نَغَماتِ السُلَّمِ الموسيقيِّ)

laid /leɪd/ *past tense, past participle* ▸ **lay**

laid-back /leɪdˈbak/ *adj* (infml) ‹*approach, atmosphere*› مُسْتَريح, مُسْتَرْخٍ

laid up *adj* **to be laid up** كانَ طَريحَ الفِراشِ

lain /leɪn/ *past participle* ▸ **lie**

lair /lɛː/ *n* عَرين (عُرُن)

lake /leɪk/ *n* بُحَيْرة; **~ Victoria** بُحَيْرة فيكْتوريا

lamb /lam/ *n* **1** (animal) حَمَل (أَحْمال ,حُمْلان) **2** (meat) لَحْم الحَمَلِ; **a leg of ~** رِجْل حَمَلٍ

lambing /ˈlamɪŋ/ *n* وِلادة الحُمْلانِ

lambswool *n* صوف الحَمَلِ

lame /leɪm/ *adj* **1** (in walking) ‹*beggar, horse*› أَعْرَج (dipt; عُرْج), كَسيح (كُسْحان); **to be ~** كانَ كَسيحاً **2** (weak) ‹*excuse, joke*› واهٍ (وُهاة)

lament /ləˈmɛnt/ **A** *n* نَحيب ,رِثاء

B *vt* **1** (to complain) شَكا (u; شَكْوى) ‹the fact, lack›
2 (to grieve) رَثا (i-u; رِثاء) نَدَبَ (u; نَدْب) ‹sb's death, loss›

lamentable /ˈlaməntəb(ə)l/ *adj* ‹state, failure› يُرْثى لَهُ, مُؤْسِف

laminated /ˈlamɪneɪtɪd/ *adj* ‹glass, sheets› رَقائِقيّ; ‹card› مُغَلَّف

lamp /lamp/ *n* مِصْباح (مَصابيحُ); **a bedside/table ~** مِصْباح سَريرٍ \ طاوِلةٍ

lampoon /lamˈpuːn/ *vt* هَجا (u; هِجاء, هَجْو), سَخِرَ (a; سُخْرِيّة) ‹politicians, sb's ignorance›

lamp post *n* مِصْباح الشارِعِ

lamprey /ˈlampri/ *n* (*pl* **lampreys**) جَلَكَى, شِلْق

lampshade /ˈlampʃeɪd/ *n* غِطاء مِصْباحٍ

LAN /lan/ *n* = **local area network** شَبَكة مَحَلِّيّة

lance /lɑːns/ **A** *n* رُمْح (رِماح)
B *vt* قَطَعَ بِمِشْرَطٍ ‹a boil, an abscess›

lance corporal *n* (BrE) [وَكيل عَريفٍ في الجَيْشِ الإنْجليزيِّ]

lancet /ˈlɑːnsɪt/ *n* مِشْرَط (مَشارِطُ), مِبْضَع (مَباضِعُ), مِفْصَد (مَفاصِدُ)

land /land/ **A** *n* **1** [u] (terrain) أَرْض, بَرّ, يابِسة; **to travel by ~** سافَرَ بَرًّا; **the lie** *or* (AmE) **lay of the ~** تَضاريس الأَرْضِ; **to reach ~** وَصَلَ إلى اليابِسةِ **2** (property) أَرْض (f; أَراضٍ); **private/public ~** أَرْض خاصّة \ عامّة; **get off my ~!** ابْتَعِدْ عن أَرْضي! **3** [u] (in farming) أَرْض; **arable ~** أَرْض صالحة لِلزراعةِ; **to work the ~** اسْتَزْرَعَ الأَرْضَ **4** (country) بَلَد (بِلاد, بُلْدان); **the Promised L~** الأَرْض المَوْعودة
B *adj before n* **1** ‹development, clearance› أَرْضٍ **2** ‹prices, sale› أَرْضٍ **3** ‹transport, battle› بَرّيّ
C *vt* **1** هَبَطَ (i-u; هُبوط بِ) ‹a plane, spacecraft› **2** اصْطادَ ‹a fish› **3** (infml) (to get) حَصَلَ (u; حُصول على) ‹a job, contract› **4** (infml) **to ~ sb with a task/problem** أَلْقى بِمُهِمّةٍ \ مُشْكِلةٍ على عاتِقِ شَخْصٍ; **now you've really ~ed her in it!** والآنَ قد أَوْقَعْتَها حَقًّا في مُشْكِلةٍ! **5** (to deliver) وَجَّهَ ‹a blow, punch›
D *vi* **1** «aircraft, passengers» هَبَطَ (i-u; هُبوط) **2** (from a ship) «passengers» نَزَلَ من السَفينةِ **3** «birds, insects» حَطَّ (u; حُطوط); «gymnasts» هَبَطَ (i-u; هُبوط); **the ball ~ed in their garden** سَقَطَت الكُرةُ في حَديقَتِهِمْ; **the paint ~ed on me** وَقَعَ الطِلاءُ عَلَيَّ
E *v refl* **to ~ oneself in a difficult situation** أَوْقَعَ نَفْسَهُ في مَوْقِفٍ صَعْبٍ; **to ~ oneself with a task/problem** وَرَّطَ نَفْسَهُ في مُهِمّةٍ \ مُشْكِلةٍ
Phrasal verb **land up** (infml) (to end up) انْتَهى بِهِ المَطافُ; **he ~ed up with the bill** في نِهايةِ المَطافِ كانَ عَلَيْهِ دَفْعُ الفاتورةِ; **the car ~ed up in the ditch** انْتَهى المَطافُ بالسَيّارةِ في الخَنْدَقِ

land agent *n* **1** (on an estate) [ناظِر شُؤونِ عِزْبةٍ] **2** (broker) سِمْسار أَراضٍ

landfill /ˈlandfɪl/ *n* (disposal) دَفْن نُفاياتٍ; (waste) نُفايات; **a ~ (site)** مَكَبّ \ مَقْلَب نُفاياتٍ

landing /ˈlandɪŋ/ *n* **1** (at the top of the stairs) بَسْطة السُلَّمِ **2** (by a plane) هُبوط; **an emergency/a safe ~** هُبوط اضْطِراريّ \ آمِن; **a successful ~ on Mars** هُبوط ناجِح على سَطْحِ المِرّيخ **3** (from boat) (of people) وُصول; (of a cargo) وُصول وَإنْزال

landing card *n* بِطاقة وُصولٍ

landing craft *n* زَوْرَق إنْزالٍ

landing gear *n* عَجَلات الهُبوطِ

landing strip *n* مَدْرَج هُبوطٍ \ مَهْبِط طائِراتٍ

landlady /ˈlandleɪdi/ *n* (*pl* **landladies**) (of rented property) صاحِبة مَنْزِلٍ; (of a small hotel) صاحِبة فُنْدُقٍ صَغيرٍ; (BrE) (of a pub) صاحِبة حانةٍ

landlocked /ˈlandlɒkt/ *adj* ‹country, lagoon› مُحاط باليابِسةِ (بِدونِ مَنْفَذٍ بَحْريٍّ)

landlord /ˈlandlɔːd/ *n* (of rented property) صاحِب مَنْزِلٍ; (of a small hotel) صاحِب فُنْدُقٍ صَغيرٍ; (BrE) (of a pub) صاحِب حانةٍ

landmark /ˈlandmɑːk/ *n* مَعْلَم (مَعالِمُ)

landmine /ˈlandmʌɪn/ *n* لُغْم أَرْضيّ

landowner /ˈlandəʊnə/ *n* صاحِب \ مالِك أَرْضٍ

Land Registry *n* مَصْلَحة الشَهْرِ العَقاريِّ

landscape /ˈlandskeɪp/ *n* **1** (scenery) مَنْظَر طَبيعيّ; **the beauty of the Scottish ~** جَمال المَناظِرِ الطَبيعيّةِ في اسْكُتْلَنْدا **2** (painting) رَسْم المَناظِرِ الطَبيعيّةِ; **he specializes in ~s** هو مُتَخَصِّص في رَسْمِ المَناظِرِ الطَبيعيّةِ

landscape architect *n* مُهَنْدِس المَناظِرِ الطَبيعيّةِ

landscape gardener *n* مُصَمِّم حَدائِقَ

landscaper /ˈlanskeɪpə/ *n* مُصَمِّم حَدائِق

landslide /ˈlandslʌɪd/ *n* **1** انهيار صَخْريّ \ أَرْضيّ **2** (also **landslide victory**) انْتِصار ساحِق

lane /leɪn/ *n* **1** (in the country) دَرْب (دِراب, دُروب); (in a town) طَريق (mf; طُرُقات, طُرُق) **2** (on a road) مَمَرّ (مَمَرّات); **a bus/ cycle ~** مَسار حافِلةٍ \ دَرّاجاتٍ **3** (for ships, aircraft) مَمَرّ (مَمَرّات) **4** (for runners, swimmers) مِضْمار (مَضاميرُ)

language /ˈlaŋgwɪdʒ/ *n* **1** (means of communication) لُغة; **the structure of ~** بِنْية اللُغةِ **2** (of a nation) لُغة; **to learn/ speak a foreign ~** تَعَلَّمَ \ تَكَلَّمَ لُغةً أَجْنَبيّةً **3** (style of speech or writing) لُغة **4** (in swearing) **bad ~** سِباب, لُغة شَتائِمَ; **mind your ~!** احْفَظْ لِسانَكَ! **5** (Comput) لُغة (بَرْمَجةٍ)

language laboratory, **language lab** *n* مُخْتَبَر \ مَعْمَل لُغاتٍ

languid /ˈlaŋgwɪd/ *adj* ‹*pace, music*› مُتَراخٍ, هامِد, خافِت

languish /ˈlaŋgwɪʃ/ *vi* **1** (to lose vitality) فَتَرَ (u; فُتور), ضَعُفَ (u; ضَعْف, ضُعْف), ذَبَلَ (u; ذُبول), وَهَنَ (i; وَهْن, وَهَن), هَزَلَ (i; هَزْل) **2** (to lie neglected) قَبَعَ (a; قُبوع); **to ~ in jail** قَبَعَ في السِجْنِ

lank /laŋk/ *adj* ‹*hair*› سَبْط (سِباط), مُتَهَدِّل

lanky /ˈlaŋki/ *adj* (**lankier**, **lankiest**) ‹*teenager, body*› [مُفْرِط في الطولِ والنَحافةِ]

lantern /ˈlant(ə)n/ *n* فانوس (فَوانيسُ)

Laos /laʊs/ *pr n* لاوُس (f)

lap /lap/ **A** *n* **1** (of the body) حِجْر; **to have sth in one's ~** كانَ يَضعُ شَيْئًا في حِجْرِهِ **2** (of a track, course) لَفّة; **a ten-~ race** سِباق من عَشْرِ لَفّاتٍ; **to be on the last ~** كانَ في آخِرِ لَفّةٍ **3** (stage) مَرْحَلة (مَراحِلُ)

B *vt* (**-pp-**) **1** (in races) سَبَقَ (i-u; سَبْق) ‹*a driver, runner, car*› **2** (to drink) لَعِقَ (a; لَعْق) ‹*water, milk*›

C *vi* (**-pp-**) (to splash) «water, waves» ارْتَطَمَ

(Idiom) **to fall into sb's lap** كانَ من نَصيبِ شَخْصٍ

(Phrasal verb) **lap up**: **~ [sth] up, ~ up [sth]** **1** (to drink) لَعِقَ (a; لَعْق) ‹*the milk, water*› **2** (to enjoy) اسْتَمْتَعَ (ب) ‹*the flattery, a compliment*›

laparoscopy /ˌlapəˈrɒskəpi/ *n* تَنْظير البَطْنِ

lap belt *n* حِزام أَمانٍ (يوضَعُ فوق حِجْرِ شَخْصٍ)

lapel /ləˈpɛl/ *n* ثَنْية (ثَنَيات)

Lapland /ˈlapland/ *pr n* لابْلانْدا

Lapp /lap/ *n, adj* [(شَخْص) من لابْلانْدا]

lapse /laps/ **A** *n* **1** (error) زَلّة, هَفْوة (هَفَوات), عَثْرة (عَثَرات) **2** (interval) فاصِل

B *vi* **1** (to expire) «membership, license, insurance» انْقَضى وَقْتُهُ, انْتَفى, انْتَهى سَرَيانُهُ **2** (to fall, slip); **to ~ into silence/a coma** دَخَلَ في حالة صَمْتٍ \ غَيْبوبة; **she soon ~d into her old habits** سُرْعانَ ما سَيْطَرَتْ عَلَيْها عاداتُها القَديمةُ

laptop /ˈlaptɒp/ *n* (also **laptop computer**) لاب توب, حاسوب مَحْمول

lapwing /ˈlapwɪŋ/ *n* زَقْزاق شاميّ

larceny /ˈlɑːs(ə)ni/ *n* سَرِقة, (اخْتِلاسات) اخْتِلاس

larch /lɑːtʃ/ *n* لاريكس, أَرْزِيّة

lard /lɑːd/ *n* شَحْم خِنْزيرٍ

larder /ˈlɑːdə/ *n* خِزانة أَطْعِمةٍ

large /lɑːdʒ/ **A** *adj* **1** (big) ‹*car, nose, opening*› كَبير, ضَخْم; **they served very ~ portions** قَدَّموا كَمّيّاتٍ كَبيرةً; **the jacket is too ~ for him** السُتْرةُ كَبيرةٌ جِدًّا عَلَيْهِ **2** (substantial) ‹*appetite, crowd, fortune*› كَبير; **a ~ proportion of them smoke** كانَتْ نِسْبةٌ كَبيرةٌ مِنْهُمْ تُدَخِّنُ; **they won by a ~ majority** فازوا بِأَغْلَبيّةٍ كَبيرةٍ; **he has a ~ family** لَدَيْهِ أُسْرةٌ كَبيرةٌ **3** (fat) ‹*person*› بَدين (بُدْن, بُدْن); **sizes come in small, medium and ~** يَتَوَفَّرُ في مَقاساتِ صَغيرٍ وَوَسَطٍ وَكَبيرٍ

B (**at large**) *adj phr* **1** (free) ‹*prisoner, killer*› طَليق (طُلَقاءُ), مُطْلَق السَراحِ **2** (in general) ‹*society, population*› كَكُلٍّ, بِشَكْلٍ عامٍّ

(Idiom) **larger than life** ‹*character, personality*› غَيْر عاديٍّ

large intestine *n* مِعًى غَليظ

largely /ˈlɑːdʒli/ *adv* ‹*ignored, unchanged*› إلى حَدٍّ كَبيرٍ, إلى دَرَجةٍ كَبيرةٍ, في الأَغْلَبِ

large-scale /ˈlɑːdʒskeɪl/ *adj* ‹*project, production*› واسِع النِطاقِ

lark /lɑːk/ *n* قُنْبَر (n coll)

larva /ˈlɑːvə/ *n* (*pl* **larvae**) يَرَقة, يَرَقان

laryngitis /ˌlarɪnˈdʒʌɪtɪs/ *n* اِلْتِهاب الحَنْجَرة

larynx /ˈlarɪŋks/ *n* (*pl* **larynxes** or **larynges** /ləˈrɪndʒiːs/) حَنْجَرة (حَناجِرُ)

lasagne, **lasagna** /ləˈzanjə/ *n* لازانْيا (نَوْع من المَعْكَرونة)

laser /ˈleɪzə/ *n* لِيزَر

laser beam *n* شُعاع لِيزَر

laser printer *n* طابِعة لِيزَر

lash /laʃ/ **A** *vt* 1 (to batter) «gale, waves» ضَرَبَ (i; ضَرْب) ‹*the coast, region*›; **gales ~ed the coastal towns** ضَرَبَت العَواصِفُ المُدُنَ الساحِلِيّةَ 2 (to tie up) رَبَطَ (i-u; رَبْط) ‹*the cargo, crates*›; **they ~ed themselves together for safety** رَبَطوا أَنْفُسَهُم مَعاً طَلَباً للأَمانِ 3 (to criticize) هاجَمَ, اِنْتَقَدَ ‹*the manager, coach*› 4 (to whip) ضَرَبَ بالسَوْطِ ‹*a horse, prisoner*›

B *vi* (violently) **the rain ~ed down incessantly** هَطَلَ المَطَرُ بِلا اِنْقِطاعٍ

C *n* 1 (whip) سَوْط (أَسْواط, سِياط) 2 (blow) ضَرْبة, جَلْدة; **he was sentenced to twenty ~es** حُكِمَ عَلَيْهِ بالجَلْد بالسَوْطِ عِشْرينَ جَلْدةً 3 ▸ **eyelash**

Phrasal verb **lash out** 1 (to hit out) «opponent, cats» هَجَمَ (u; هُجوم); **to ~ out at sb** هَجَمَ على شَخْصٍ 2 (verbally) اِنْتَقَدَ, هاجَمَ; **to ~ out at** *or* **against sb** اِنْتَقَدَ \ هاجَمَ شَخْصاً; **the coach ~ed out at his critics** هاجَمَ المُدَرِّبُ مُنْتَقِديه 3 (infml) (to spend freely) أَنْفَقَ بِبَذَخٍ; **to ~ out on a new car** أَنْفَقَ أَمْوالاً طائِلةً لِشِراءِ سَيّارةٍ جَديدةٍ

lass /las/ *n* (BrE liter, dialect) فَتاة (فَتَيات), صَبِيّة (صَبايا), شابّة

lasso /laˈsuː/ *n* (*pl* **lassos** or **lassoes**) وَهْق (حَبْل لِصَيْدِ الحَيَواناتِ)

last /lɑːst/ **A** *adj* 1 (final) ‹*time, hope, novel*› آخِر (dipt); **the ~ time we met, she was not well** لَم تَكُنْ في آخِرِ مَرّةٍ تَقابَلْنا, بِصِحّةٍ جَيِّدةٍ; **in my ~ job** في وَظيفَتي السابِقةِ; **the ~ person to see her alive** آخِر من رَآها وَهِيَ على قَيْدِ الحَياةِ; **what is your ~ name?** ما اسْمُكَ الأَخيرُ؟; **the ~ building but one** المَبْنى قبل الأَخيرِ; **the ~ few children** آخِر مَجْموعةٍ من الأَطْفالِ 2 (describing past time) ماضٍ; **~ week/year** الأُسْبوع \ العام الماضي; **~ Monday** الاثْنَيْن الماضي; **~ night** اللَيْلة الماضِية; **I was in Spain ~ Christmas** كُنْتُ في إِسْبانِيا في عيدِ الميلادِ الماضي; **over the ~ ten years** خلال العَشْرةِ أَعْوامٍ الماضِيةِ; **she has been in Beirut for the ~ eight months** مَكَثَتْ في بَيْروتَ خلال الأَشْهُرِ الثَمانيةِ الماضِيةِ 3 (infml) (least desirable) ‹*place, person, thing*› آخِر; **he's the ~ person I'd ask!** هو آخِرُ مَنْ أَرْغَبُ في سُؤالِهِ!; **the ~ thing we want is publicity!** آخِرُ ما نُريدُ هو الإِشْهارُ!

B *adv* 1 (in final position) **to come in ~** «runner, car, horse» جاءَ في المَرْكَزِ الأَخيرِ; **to leave sth till ~** تَرَكَ شَيْئاً حتّى آخِرَ الوَقْتِ; **~ of all** أَخيراً 2 (most recently) ‹*to visit, hear, see*› آخِرَ مَرّةٍ; **she was ~ in the country in 2005** كانَتْ في البَلَدِ آخِرَ مَرّةٍ عامَ 2005; **when did you ~ see him?** مَتى كانَتْ آخِرَ مَرّةٍ رَأَيْتَهُ فيها؟

C *pron* (final) **the ~** الأَخير; **the ~ but one** قبل الأَخيرِ; **the night before ~** اللَيْلة قبل الماضِيةِ; **the week before ~** الأُسْبوع قبل الماضي; **that was the ~ of the rice** كانَ ذلك آخِرَ ما تَبَقّى من الأَرُزِّ; **the ~ of the guests was just leaving** كانَ آخِرُ الضُيوفِ على وَشْكِ المُغادَرةِ; **this is not the ~ of the matter!** ≈ سَتَدْفَعُ الثَمَنَ!; **I hope we've seen the ~ of him** أَتَمَنّى أَلاّ نَراهُ مَرّةً أُخرى

D *vt* كَفى (i; كِفاية); **a loaf of bread ~s me two days** يَكْفيني رَغيفُ خبزٍ لِيَوْمَيْنِ

E *vi* 1 (to extend in time) «meetings, the ceasefire» اِسْتَمَرَّ, دامَ (u; دَوْم, دَوام); **it won't ~!** لن يَدومَ!; **he won't ~ long in this place** لن يَسْتَمِرَّ طَوِيلاً في هذا المَكانِ; **that delivery didn't ~ long** تِلْكَ الشَحْنةُ لم تَدُمْ طَوِيلاً 2 (to stay in good condition) «shoes, batteries, food» ظَلَّ صالِحاً

F *n* 1 (for shoes) قالَب (قَوالِبُ) 2 (end) **to the ~** حتى النِهايةِ

Phrasal verb **last out** **A** **~ out** 1 (not run out) «money, supplies, batteries» لم يَنْفَدْ 2 (to persist) «competitors, crew» صَمَدَ طوال ‹*a siege*›; **B** **~ out [sth]** صَمَدَ أمام [شَيْءٍ] اسْتَمَرَّ [شَيْءٍ] ‹*the winter, night*›

last-ditch /ˌlɑːstˈdɪtʃ/ *adj* ‹*attempt, appeal*› يائِس

lasting /ˈlɑːstɪŋ/ *adj* ‹*impression, relationship*› دائِم

lastly /ˈlɑːstli/ *adv* أَخيراً, خِتاماً, في النِهايةِ

last-minute /ˌlɑːstˈmɪnɪt/ *adj* ‹*change, shopping*› في اللَحْظةِ الأخيرةِ

last name *n* اسْم العائِلةِ

last rites *n* طُقوس الاحْتِضارِ

latch /latʃ/ *n* [1] (fastening) مِزْلاج (مَزاليجُ) [2] (spring lock) [قُفْل بنابِضٍ]

(Phrasal verb) **latch on** (infml) **A** **~ on to [sb]** تَعَلَّق ب [شَخْصٍ]

B **~ on to [sth]** [1] (to take up) أولِعَ ب [شَيْءٍ] ‹*an idea, a trend*›

[2] (to understand) أدْرَكَ [شَيْئاً]

late /leɪt/ **A** *adj* [1] (after the due time) ‹*arrival, publication, delivery*› مُتَأَخِّر; **to have a ~ lunch** تَناوَلَ الغَداءَ في وَقْتٍ مُتَأَخِّرٍ; **to have a ~ night** سَهِرَ حتى وَقْتٍ مُتَأَخِّرٍ من اللَيْلِ; **sorry I'm ~** آسِفٌ على تَأَخُّري; **to be ~ for work/an appointment** تَأَخَّرَ عن العَمَلِ \ مَوْعِدٍ; **the train/flight was an hour ~** تَأَخَّرَتْ رِحْلةُ القِطارِ \ الطائِرةِ ساعةً; **to be ~ with the rent** تَأَخَّرَ في دَفْعِ الإيجارِ; **if the payment is more than three days ~ ...** إذا تَأَخَّرَ الدَفْعُ لِأَكْثَرَ من ثَلاثةِ أيّامٍ ... [2] (in the day, season, sb's life) ‹*meal, purchase, stage*› مُتَأَخِّر; **to take a ~ holiday** أَخَذَ إجازةً مُتَأَخِّرةً; **in ~r life** في العُمْرِ المُتَقَدِّمِ; **to be in one's ~ fifties** كانَ في أَواخِرِ الخَمْسيناتِ; **at this ~ hour/stage** في هذه الساعةِ \ المَرْحَلةِ المُتَقَدِّمةِ; **in ~ January** في أَواخِرِ يَنايِر; **in the ~ 90s** في أَواخِرِ التِسْعيناتِ; **it was ~ afternoon when I arrived** كانَ الوَقْتُ مُتَأَخِّراً بعد الظُهْرِ عِنْدَما وَصَلْتُ; **the ~st appointment is at 4 pm** آخِرُ مَوْعِدٍ هو 4 مَساءً [3] (in a series) أخير; **in one of her ~r films** في أَحَدِ أَفْلامِها الأَخيرةِ; **his ~st experiments** آخِر تَجارُبِهِ [4] (fml) (deceased) ‹*brother, wife*› راحِل; **my ~ husband** زَوْجي الراحِل; **the ~ President** الرَئيس الراحِل

B *adv* [1] (after expected time) ‹*to leave, start, finish*› مُتَأَخِّراً; **we started three months ~** بَدَأْنا مُتَأَخِّرينَ بِثَلاثةِ شُهورٍ; **the plane landed twenty minutes ~** هَبَطَت الطائِرةُ مُتَأَخِّرةً عِشْرينَ دَقيقةً; **to be running ~** «people, trains» بَدَأَ يَتَأَخَّرُ

[2] (towards the end of a day, season) ‹*to open, get up, end*› في وَقْتٍ مُتَأَخِّرٍ; **he called ~ last night/in the evening** اتَّصَلَ في وَقْتٍ مُتَأَخِّرٍ اللَيْلَةَ الماضِيةَ \ في المَساءِ; **~ last week** في أَواخِرِ الأُسْبوعِ الماضي; **~r on** فيما بَعْدُ; **we must leave no ~r than 6 o'clock** يَجِبُ أنْ نُغادِرَ قبل الساعةِ 6; **they married ~ in life** تَزَوَّجوا في عُمْرٍ مُتَقَدِّمٍ; **he left for Yemen six months ~r** رَحَلَ إلى اليَمَنِ بَعْدَها بِستّةِ أَشْهُرٍ; **see you ~r!** أَراكَ لاحِقاً!; **it's a bit ~ in the day to ask for help** الوَقْتُ مُتَأَخِّرٌ بَعْضَ الشَيْءِ لِطَلَبِ المُساعَدةِ

C (**of late**) *adv phr* (fml) في الآوِنةِ الأَخيرةِ

latecomer /ˈleɪtkʌmə/ *n* مُتَأَخِّر في الوُصولِ

late developer *n* [1] (physically) مُتَأَخِّر النُموِّ

[2] (educationally) [طِفْل مُتَأَخِّر النُموِّ التَحْصيليِّ]

lately /ˈleɪtli/ *adv* حَديثاً, مُؤَخَّراً

late-night /ˈleɪtnʌɪt/ *adj* ‹*show, film*› في وَقْتٍ مُتَأَخِّرٍ من اللَيْلِ

latent /ˈleɪt(ə)nt/ *adj* ‹*infection, racism*› كامِن

later /ˈleɪtə/ **A** *adj* ‹*version, works*› لاحِق; **I caught a ~ train** أَدْرَكْتُ قِطاراً لاحِقاً

B *adv* في وَقْتٍ لاحِقٍ; **please call back ~** اتَّصِلْ في وَقْتٍ لاحِقٍ لو سَمَحْتَ; **~ on** فيما بَعْدُ, لاحِق; بعد حينٍ; **see you ~!** (infml) أَراكَ فيما بَعْدُ!

lateral /ˈlat(ə)r(ə)l/ *adj* ‹*movement, view*› جانِبيّ

latest /ˈleɪtɪst/ **A** *adj* ‹*book, news*› آخِر (dipt), أَحْدَث

B (**at the latest**) *phr* في مَوْعِدٍ أَقْصاهُ

latex /ˈleɪtɛks/ *n* لاتِكْس

lathe /leɪð/ *n* مِخْرَطة (مَخارِطُ)

lather /ˈlɑːðə, ˈlaðə/ **A** *n* رَغْوة (رَغاوٍ)

B *vt* صَبَّنَ ‹*one's hands, body*›

Latin /ˈlatɪn/ **A** *n* (اللُغة) اللاتينيّة

B *adj* ‹*word, grammar*› لاتينيّ; **the ~ temperament** المِزاج اللاتينيّ

Latin America *pr n* أَمْريكا اللاتينيّة

Latin American *n, adj* أَمْريكيّ لاتينيّ

latitude /ˈlatɪtjuːd/ *n* [1] (Geog) خطّ العَرْضِ [2] [u] (freedom) حُرّيّة تَصَرُّفٍ

latter /ˈlatə/ **A** *n* (*pl* latter) **the ~** الثاني, الأخير

B *adj* [1] ‹*part, years*› أخير; **the ~ part of the 20th century** الجُزْء الأَخير من القَرْنِ العِشْرينَ; **in his ~ years** في سَنَواتِهِ الأَخيرةِ [2] ‹*category, option*› ثانٍ

lattice /ˈlatɪs/ *n* شَبَكة (شَبَكات)

Latvia /ˈlatvɪə/ *pr n* لاتْفِيا

Latvian /ˈlatvɪən/ [A] *n* [1] (citizen) لاتْفيّ [2] (language) (اللُغة) اللاتْفيّة

[B] *adj* ‹*ambassador, border, food*› لاتْفيّ

laud /lɔːd/ *vt* (fml) مَدَحَ (a; مَدْح ,مِدْحة), امْتَدَحَ ‹*a production, merits*›

laugh /lɑːf/ [A] *vi* ضَحِكَ (a; ضَحِك ,ضِحْك ,ضَحْك); **to make sb ~** أَضْحَكَ شَخْصاً; **to ~ out loud/quietly** ضَحِكَ بِصَوْتٍ عالٍ \ مُنْخَفِضٍ; **to ~ at sb/sth** ضَحِكَ على شَخْصٍ \ شَيْءٍ; **the children ~ed at the clown** ضَحِكَ الأَطْفالُ على المُهَرِّجِ; **I don't like people ~ing at me** لا أُحِبُّ أَنْ يَسْخَرَ الناسُ مِنّي; **we were ~ing about the things we used to do as kids** كُنّا نَضْحَكُ على الأَشْياءِ الّتي اعْتَدْنا على فِعْلِها وَنَحْنُ صِغارٌ; **I don't know whether to ~ or cry!** لا أَدْري أَأَضْحَكُ أم أَبْكي!

[B] *n* [1] (noise) ضِحْكة; **she gave a loud ~** ضَحِكَتْ ضِحْكةً عالِيَةً; **we like a good ~** نُحِبُّ الفُكاهةَ; **to get** *or* **raise a ~** أَثارَ الضَحِكَ [2] (infml) (source of amusement) مُزاح ,مَرَح; **to do sth for a ~** فَعَلَ شَيْئاً بِقَصْدِ المُزاحِ; **your brother is a real ~** أَخوكَ ظَريفٌ جِدًّا; **let's go to the party, it'll be a ~** دَعْنا نَذْهَبُ إلى الحَفْلِ، سَيَكونُ مَليئاً بالمَرَحِ

(Idioms) **to have the last laugh** كانَتْ لَهُ الضِحْكةُ الأَخيرةُ; **to laugh in sb's face** هَزَأَ بِشَخْصٍ; **to be laughing all the way to the bank** [نالَ ثَرْوةً طائِلةً بِلا عَناءٍ]

(Phrasal verb) **laugh off**: **~ [sth] off, ~ off [sth]** قابَلَ [شَيْئاً] بالسُخْرِيّةِ ‹*a mistake, defeat, a rumour*›; **she ~ed the whole thing off** قابَلَت الأَمْرَ كُلَّهُ بالسُخْرِيّةِ

laughable /ˈlɑːfəb(ə)l/ *adj* ‹*attempt, idea*› مُضْحِك, مُثير لِلضِحْكِ

laughing /ˈlɑːfɪŋ/ *adj* ‹*eyes, face*› ضاحِك; **it's no ~ matter** إنَّهُ أَمْرٌ لا مَجالَ فيهِ للضَحِكِ

laughing stock *n* أُضْحوكة (أَضاحيك)

laughter /ˈlɑːftə/ *n* ضَحِك; **to roar with ~** قَهْقَهَ (i; قَهْقَهة)

launch /lɔːntʃ/ [A] *vt* [1] دَشَّنَ ‹*the lifeboat, a dinghy, ship*› [2] أَطْلَقَ ‹*a rocket, satellite*› [3] (to fire) أَطْلَقَ ‹*a missile, torpedo*› [4] (to start) دَشَّنَ ‹*a campaign, product, magazine*›; فَتَحَ (a; فَتْح) ‹*an investigation*›; شَنَّ هُجوماً; **to ~ an attack on the enemy** شَنَّ هُجوماً على العَدوِّ; **the police have ~ed an investigation into the incident** فَتَحَت الشُرْطةُ تَحْقيقاً في الحادِثِ

[B] *vi* **to ~ into sth** شَرَعَ في شَيْءٍ ‹*a description, speech, song*›

[C] *v refl* **to ~ oneself at sb/sth** أَلْقى بِنَفْسِهِ على شَخْصٍ \ شَيْءٍ

[D] *n* [1] (boat) (also **motor launch**) لَنْش ,زَوْرَق بُخاريّ [2] (of a ship) تَدْشين [3] (of a rocket, missile) إطْلاق (إطْلاقات) [4] (of a publicity campaign, product) إطْلاق ,تَدْشين (إطْلاقات); **the ~ of a new range of models** إطْلاق تَشْكيلةٍ جَديدةٍ من النَماذِجِ; **the ~ of his campaign to win the White House** تَدْشين حَمْلَتِهِ للفَوْزِ بالبَيْتِ الأَبْيَضِ

launch pad, **launching pad** *n* مَنَصّة إطْلاق

launder /ˈlɔːndə/ *vt* [1] (fml) غَسَلَ (i; غَسْل) ‹*clothes*› [2] غَسَلَ (i; غَسْل) ‹*money*›

launderette, **laundrette** /lɔːnˈdret/ *n* (BrE) مَغْسَلة عامّة

laundromat® /ˈlɔːndrəmat/ *n* (AmE) مَغْسَلة عامّة

laundry /ˈlɔːndri/ *n* (*pl* **laundries**) [1] (place for washing in a hotel, house) حُجْرة غَسيل; (commercial place for washing) مَغْسَلة عامّة [2] (clothes) غَسيل

laurel /ˈlɒrəl/ *n* غار (أَغْوار)

lava /ˈlɑːvə/ *n* حُمَم (n coll)

lavatory /ˈlavət(ə)ri/ *n* (*pl* **lavatories**) [1] (in a private house) دَوْرة مِياهٍ [2] (public) دَوْرة مِياهٍ [3] (receptacle) مِرْحاض (مَراحيضُ)

lavender /ˈlav(ə)ndə/ *n* خُزامى (f; n coll; singul n خُزاماة), لاوَنْدة

lavish /ˈlavɪʃ/ [A] *adj* ‹*lifestyle*› مُسْرِف; ‹*party*› فَخْم; ‹*production*› فاخِر

[B] *vt* أَغْدَقَ ,أَسْبَغَ ‹*praise, money*›; **the critics have ~ed praise on her work** أَغْدَقَ النُقّادُ الثَناءَ على عَمَلِها

lavishly /ˈlavɪʃli/ *adv* ‹*illustrated, decorated, to spend*› بِبَذَخٍ

law /lɔː/ *n* [1] [u] (of a nation) قانون; **to study ~** دَرَسَ القانونَ; **to obey/break the ~** أَطاعَ \ خَرَقَ القانونَ; **to be against the ~** كانَ مُخالِفاً للقانونِ; **to be above the ~** كانَ فوق القانونِ; **criminal/employment ~** القانون الجِنائيّ \ قانون العَمَلِ; **under Islamic ~** طِبْقاً للشَريعةِ الإسْلاميّةِ; **by ~ you must report**

a road accident بِموجِبِ القانونِ يَجِبُ الإبْلاغُ عن حادِثِ طَرِيقٍ; **the act becomes ~ in three months** يُصْبِحُ مُقْتَرَحُ القانونِ قانوناً بعد ثَلاثةِ شُهورٍ; **to take the ~ into one's own hands** أَخَذَ حَقَّهُ بِيَدِهِ **2** (rule) قانون (قَوانينُ); **a ~ against gambling** قانون ضدّ القِمارِ; **there's no ~ against prostitution** لَيْسَ هُناكَ قانونٌ ضدّ الدِعارةِ **3** (justice) قانون; **a court of ~** مَحْكَمة قانونيّة; **to go to ~ over sth** لَجَأَ إلى القانونِ بِخُصوصِ شَيْءٍ **4** (principle) قانون (قَوانينُ); **the ~ of diminishing returns** قانون الغَلّة المُتَناقِصة

(Idiom) **to be a law unto oneself** كانَ لَهُ قانونُهُ الخاصّ

law-abiding /ˈlɔːəbʌɪdɪŋ/ ***adj*** ‹*citizen, community*› مُطيع \ مُحْتَرِم مُلْتَزِم بالقانونِ ,للقانونِ

law and order ***n*** القانون والنِظام

law court ***n*** مَحْكَمة (مَحاكِمُ)

lawful /ˈlɔːfʊl/ ***adj*** ‹*activity, conduct*› قانونيّ; ‹*owner, wife*› شَرْعيّ

lawless /ˈlɔːləs/ ***adj*** ‹*area, town*› يَنْعَدِمُ فيهِ القانونُ ,فَوْضَويّ; ‹*gangs, thugs*› خارِج على القانونِ

lawn /lɔːn/ ***n*** مَرْج (مِساحة مَزْروعة بالعُشْبِ الأَخْضرِ في حَديقةٍ)

lawnmower /ˈlɔːnməʊə/ ***n*** جَزّازة عُشْبٍ

lawn tennis ***n*** (fml) تِنِس أَرْضيّ

law school ***n*** كُلّيّة حُقوقٍ

lawsuit /ˈlɔːsuːt/ ***n*** قَضيّة ,دَعْوى قضائيّة (قضايا)

lawyer /ˈlɔːjə/ ***n*** مُحام (مُحامونَ)

lax /laks/ ***adj*** ‹*security, standards*› مُتَراخٍ; ‹*authorities, parents*› مُتَهاوِن ,غَيْر صارِمٍ

laxative /ˈlaksətɪv/ ***n*** مُلَيِّن (مُلَيِّنات)

lay /leɪ/ **A** ***vt*** (*past tense, past participle* **laid**) **1** (to place) وَضَعَ (a; وَضْع) ‹*one's hand, a letter, baby*›; **she laid the baby in the cot** وَضَعَتْ الرَضيعَ في المَهْدِ; **he laid his hand on her shoulder** وَضَعَ يَدَهُ على كَتِفِها; **to ~ the cards face down** وَضَعَ الوَرَقاتِ مَقْلوبةً; **to ~ hands on sb/sth** عَثَرَ على شَخْصٍ \ شَيْءٍ **2** (to spread out) بَسَطَ (u; بَسْط), فَرَشَ (i; فَرْش) ‹*a towel, blanket, newspaper*›; **he laid a blanket over the body** فَرَشَ بَطّانيّةً على الجُثّةِ **3** (for a meal) **to ~ the table** أَعَدَّ المائِدةَ; **to ~ an extra place** أَعَدَّ مَكاناً إضافيًّا **4** (to prepare) أَعَدَّ ‹*a fire*› **5** «hens, fish» وَضَعَ (a; وَضْع) ‹*eggs*› **6** (to put down on surface) رَصَّ (u; رَصّ) ‹*bricks, tiles*›; بَسَطَ (u; بَسْط) ‹*a carpet*›; (to put down underground) دَفَنَ (i; دَفْن) ‹*a cable, sewer*›; **they laid mines along the shore** زَرَعوا أَلْغاماً على طولِ الشاطِئِ **7** (to draw up) وَضَعَ (a; وَضْع) ‹*a plan, foundations*›; نَصَبَ (u; نَصْب) ‹*a trap*›; **the plan aims to ~ the foundations for economic recovery** تَهْدُفُ الخُطّةُ إلى وَضْعِ الأُسُسِ لِتَحْقيقِ الانْتِعاشِ الاقْتِصاديّ **8** (fml) (to bring forward) قَدَّمَ ‹*a charge*›; وَجَّهَ ‹*a complaint*›; **to ~ the blame for a mistake on sb** أَلْقى باللَوْمِ في خَطَإٍ على شَخْصٍ; **to ~ great stress on sth** أَوْلى شَيْئاً اهْتِماماً كَبيراً **9** (to call down) **to ~ a curse/spell on sb** أَصابَ شَخْصاً بِلَعْنةٍ \ بِسِحْرٍ

B ***vi*** (*past tense, past participle* **laid**) «birds» باضَ (i; بَيْض)

C ***past tense*** ▸ **lie** B2

D ***adj*** **1** (unordained) ‹*preacher, member*› غَيْر إكْليريكيّ **2** (non-specialist) ‹*assessor, magistrate*› عاديّ ,غَيْر مُتَخَصِّصٍ; **the ~ reader/person** القارِئ \ الشَخْص العاديّ

(Idiom) **to lay a finger** *or* **hand on sb** مَسَّ شَخْصاً بِأَذًى

(Phrasal verbs) **lay aside**: **~ aside [sth], ~ [sth] aside** **1** (to put to one side) نَحّى [شَيْئاً] جانِباً ‹*a book, toy, one's sewing*› **2** (to give up) نَحّى [شَيْئاً] جانِباً ‹*one's differences, principles, a doubt*› **3** (to save) ادَّخَرَ [شَيْئاً] ‹*food, money*›

• **lay before**: **~ [sth] before sb** طَرَحَ \ عَرَضَ [شَيْئاً] على شَخْصٍ ‹*a case, the facts, evidence*›; **to ~ a bill before parliament/congress** عَرَضَ مُقْتَرَحَ قانونٍ على البَرْلَمان \ الكونْجْرِس

• **lay by**: **~ by [sth], ~ [sth] by** ادَّخَرَ [شَيْئاً] ‹*money, provisions*›

• **lay down**: **~ down [sth], ~ [sth] down** **1** (to put down) وَضَعَ [شَيْئاً] ‹*a baby, the keys, a suitcase*›; **I laid the papers down on his desk** وَضَعْتُ الأَوْراقَ على مَكْتَبِهِ; **to ~ down one's arms** أَلْقى سِلاحَهُ **2** (to stop using) تَرَكَ [شَيْئاً] ‹*spade, book*› **3** (to sacrifice) **to ~ down one's life for sb/sth** ضَحّى بِحَياتِهِ من أَجْلِ شَخْصٍ \ شَيْءٍ **4** (to establish) وَضَعَ [شَيْئاً] ‹*a rule, procedure, condition*›; **it was laid down that ...** تَمَّ النَصُّ على أنّ ...

• **lay in**: ~ **in** [sth] [شَيْئاً] خَزَّنَ ‹*food, drink, firewood*›

• **lay into**: ~ **into** [sb] (to attack physically) [شَخْصاً] هاجَمَ; (verbally) [شَخْصاً] انْتَقَدَ

• **lay off**: **A** ~ **off** [sb], ~ [sb] **off** (to dismiss permanently) سَرَّحَ [شَخْصاً]; (temporarily) أَوْقَفَ [شَخْصاً] عن العَمَلِ **B** ~ **off** [sth] (infml) (to stop using) تَوَقَّفَ عن [شَيْءٍ] ‹*alcohol, fatty foods, criticism*›; **to ~ off drinking/smoking** تَوَقَّفَ عن الشُرْبِ \ التَدْخينِ **C** ~ **off** [sb] (infml) (to leave alone) كَفَّ عن التَعَرُّضِ لِ [شَخْصٍ]

• **lay on**: ~ **on** [sth], ~ [sth] **on** **1** (to provide) وَفَّرَ [شَيْئاً] ‹*transport*›; قَدَّمَ [شَيْئاً] ‹*a meal, entertainment*› **2** (BrE) (to install) وَصَّلَ [شَيْئاً] ‹*gas, electricity*›

• **lay out** **A** ~ [sth] **out**, ~ **out** [sth] **1** (to put on display) عَرَضَ [شَيْئاً] ‹*goods, documents, food*› **2** (to unfold) بَسَطَ \ فَتَحَ [شَيْئاً] ‹*a map*› **3** (to design architecturally) وَضَعَ تَصْميماً مِعْمارِيّاً لِ [شَيْءٍ] ‹*a town, garden*›; (typographically) صَمَّمَ [شَيْئاً] ‹*a magazine, an advertisement, the illustrations*› **4** (to state) عَرَضَ \ ذَكَرَ [شَيْئاً] ‹*one's reasons, demands*› **5** (infml) (to spend) أَنْفَقَ [شَيْئاً] ‹*a fortune, sum of money*› **B** ~ **out** [sb], ~ [sb] **out** **1** (for burial) أَعَدَّ [شَخْصاً] للدَفْنِ ‹*a corpse*› **2** (infml) (in fighting) ضَرَبَ [شَخْصاً] وَأَفْقَدَهُ الوَعْيَ ‹*a boxer, an attacker*›

• **lay up** **A** ~ **up** [sth], ~ [sth] **up** **1** (to store) خَزَّنَ [شَيْئاً] ‹*food, supplies*› **2** (to accumulate) تَرَكَ [شَيْئاً] يَتراكَمُ ‹*trouble, problems*› **B** ~ [sb] **up** جَعَلَ [شَخْصاً] طَريحَ الفِراشِ; **to be laid up with an illness/injury** كانَ طَريحَ الفِراشِ بِسَبَبِ مَرَضٍ \ إصابةٍ

layabout /ˈleɪəbaʊt/ *n* (BrE infml pej) شَخْص مُتَكاسِل

lay-by /ˈleɪbʌɪ/ *n* (BrE) [مَوْقِف مُؤَقَّت للسَيّاراتِ في جانِبِ الطَريقِ]

layer /ˈleɪə/ **A** *n* (of paint, dust, snow, rock) طَبَقة **B** *vt* قَصَّ على شَكْلِ طَبَقاتٍ ‹*hair*›

layman /ˈleɪmən/ *n* (*pl* **-men** /-mən/) **1** (non-specialist) غَيْر مُتَخَصِّصٍ, شَخْص عامّيّ **2** (church member) عَلْمانيّ (شَخْص من غَيْرِ الكَهَنةِ والرُهْبانِ)

lay-off /ˈleɪɒf/ *n* **1** (dismissal) تَسْريح **2** (interruption) فَتْرة انْقِطاعٍ \ تَوَقُّفٍ

layout /ˈleɪaʊt/ *n* **1** (of buildings, towns, gardens) تَخْطيط (تَخْطيطات), تَصْميم (تَصْميمات, تَصاميمُ) **2** (of a page, magazine, newspaper) تَصْميم (تَصْميمات, تَصاميمُ)

layover /ˈleɪəʊvə/ *n* (AmE Transp) تَوَقُّف للاسْتِراحةِ

laze /leɪz/ *vi* (also **laze around**; **laze about** BrE) تَكاسَلَ

lazily /ˈleɪzɪli/ *adv* ‹*to drift, float*› بِبُطْءٍ; ‹*to lie, stretch*› بِتَكاسُلٍ, مُتَكاسِلاً

laziness /ˈleɪzinəs/ *n* كَسَل, خُمول

lazy /ˈleɪzi/ *adj* (**lazier**, **laziest**) **1** ‹*person*› كَسْلان (dipt; كُسالى), كَسول **2** ‹*day, holiday*› باعِث على الكَسَلِ

lazybones /ˈleɪzɪbəʊnz/ *n* (*pl* **lazybones**) (infml) شَخْص كَسول

lb *abbr* = **pound(s)** رَطْل (أَرْطال)

LCD /ɛlsiːˈdiː/ *n* = **liquid crystal display** عَرْض بِلَّوْريّ سائِل

lead¹ /liːd/ **A** *vt* (*past tense, past participle* **led**) **1** (to escort) قادَ (u; قِيادة), أَوْصَلَ ‹*a prisoner, horse*›; **she led the passengers to safety** أَوْصَلَت المُسافِرينَ إلى بَرِّ الأَمانِ; **they led the hostages away** قادوا الرَهائِنَ إلى مَكانِ الأَسْرِ; **he led the conversation to the subject of finance** وَجَّهَ المُحادثَةَ إلى مَوْضوعِ التَمْويلِ **2** (to influence) **to ~ sb to do/think sth** دَفَعَ \ جَعَلَ شَخْصاً يَفْعَلُ \ يَظُنُّ شَيْئاً; **the news led us to expect a disaster/triumph** دَفَعَتْنا الأَخْبارُ إلى تَوَقُّعِ كارِثةٍ \ انْتِصارٍ; **he led them to think it would be very different** جَعَلَهُمْ يَظُنّون أَنَّهُ سَيَكونُ مُخْتَلِفاً جِدّاً **3** «company, animal» قادَ (u; قِيادة) ‹*the team, attack, strike*›; **he led the team to victory** قادَ الفَريقَ إلى الفَوْزِ **4** (to be at the front of) كانَ في الصَدارةِ ‹*the field, race*› **5** (to have) عاشَ (i; عَيْش, عِيشة, مَعاش) ‹*an active life*›; **they ~ a life of luxury/penury** يَعيشونَ حَياةَ التَرَفِ \ في فَقْرٍ مُدْقِعٍ

B *vi* (*past tense, past participle* **led**) **1** **to ~ to** «paths, roads» أَوْصَلَ, أَدّى; **the path ~s to the front door** يُؤَدّي الطَريقُ إلى البابِ الأَماميِّ **2** (to result in) **to ~ to success/ruin** أَدّى إلى النَجاحِ \ الخَرابِ; **his reforms led to recovery/economic ruin** أَدَّتْ إصْلاحاتُهُ إلى الانْتِعاشِ \ الخَرابِ الاقْتِصاديِّ; **one thing ~s to another** شَيْءٌ يَجُرُّ وَراءَهُ شَيْئاً آخَرَ **3** «runner, team» سَبَقَ (i-u; سَبْق), تَقَدَّمَ, تَصَدَّرَ; **to ~ by 15 seconds** تَقَدَّمَ بِفارِقِ 15 ثانِيةً; **Smith is ~ing, Jones**

is second شميث في الصَدارةِ، يَليهِ جونْز **4** (in dancing, gymnastics) قادَ (u; قِيادة); **to lead from the front** قادَ من الأمامِ

C *n* **1** **to be in the ~** كانَ في المُقَدِّمةِ; **to go into the ~** أَصْبَحَ في المُقَدِّمةِ **2** (margin) صَدارة ,سَبْق; **United has a ~ of two goals** يونايْتِد في الصَدارةِ بفارِقِ هَدَفَيْن; **the American yacht had a half-mile ~ over the rest of the field** كانَ اليَخْتُ الأَمْريكيُّ مُتَقدِّماً بِنِصْفِ مِيلٍ على باقي **3** (initiative) **to take the ~** أَخَذَ زِمامَ المُبادَرة; المُتَنافِسينَ; **to follow sb's ~** حَذا حَذْوَ شَخْصٍ **4** (in investigations) خَيْط (خُيوط), دَليل (دَلائِلُ), أَدِلّة, مِفْتاح (مَفاتيحُ); **the police have a number of ~s to follow** لدى الشُرْطةِ عَدَدٌ من الخُيوطِ التّي يَحْتاجونَ تَتَبُّعَها **5** (wire) سِلْك (أَسْلاك) **6** (BrE) (leash) مِقْوَد (مَقاوِدُ); **dogs must be kept on a ~** يَجِبُ أَنْ تَبْقى الكِلابُ في المَقاوِدِ

D *adj* ‹*guitarist, singer*› رَئيسيّ

Idiom **to lead the way** كانَتْ لَهُ الرِيادةُ

Phrasal verbs **lead on: ~ [sb] on** **1** (to give false hope) غَرَّرَ ب [شَخْصٍ] ‹*a buyer*› **2** (sexually) أَغْرى [شَخْصاً]

• **lead up to: ~ up to [sth]** **1** (to precede) سَبَقَ [شَيْئاً]; **the days ~ing up to the wedding** الأَيّامُ السابِقةُ على الزِفافِ **2** (to end in) أَدّى إلى [شَيْءٍ] ‹*an argument, outburst*›; **his comments led up to the argument** أَدَّتْ تَعْليقاتُهُ إلى الجَدَلِ **3** (to introduce) مَهَّدَ إلى [شَيْءٍ] ‹*a topic*›; **I thought you were ~ing up to that** ظَنَنْتُ أَنَّكَ كُنْتَ تُمَهِّدُ لِهَذا

lead² /lɛd/ *n* **1** (metal) رَصاص **2** (in pencils) رَصاص

leaded petrol /ˌlɛdɪd ˈpɛtrəl/ (BrE), **leaded gasoline** (AmE) *n* بَنْزين يَحْتَوي على الرَصاصِ

leader /ˈliːdə/ *n* **1** (of a country, group, gang) رَئيس (رُؤَساءُ), زَعيم (زُعَماءُ), قائِد (قادة ,قوّاد) **2** (in a race, competition, league) مُتَسابِق \ فَريق مُتَقَدِّم

leader board *n* لَوْحة عَرْضِ قائِمةِ الصَدارة

leadership /ˈliːdəʃɪp/ *n* **1** (control of a country, movement) قِيادة, زَعامة, رِئاسة **2** (quality) قِيادة **3** (leaders) قادة ,قِيادة

lead-free /lɛdˈfriː/ *adj* ‹*petrol, paint*› خالٍ من الرَصاصِ

leading /ˈliːdɪŋ/ *adj* **1** (principal, major) ‹*figure*› قِياديّ; ‹*authority, company, brand*› أَساسيّ ,رَئيسيّ; **to play a ~ role in sth** لَعِبَ دَوْراً بارِزاً في شَيْءٍ **2** (Sport) ‹*team, runner, car*› مُتَقَدِّم

leading edge **A** *n* **1** (of a wing, propeller) حافّة أَماميّة **2** (vanguard) رِيادة ,طَليعة ,مُقَدِّمة;

B (**leading-edge**) *adj before n* ‹*technology, design*› مُتَطَوِّر ,رائِد

leading lady *n* بَطَلة (في فيلْم أو مَسْرَحيّةٍ)

leading light *n* رِياديّ ,(روّاد) رائِد

lead poisoning *n* تَسَمُّم بالرَصاص

lead story *n* خَبَر رَئيسيّ

leaf /liːf/ *n* (*pl* **leaves** /liːvz/) **1** (of a plant) وَرَقة (أَوْراق ,وَرَقات) **2** (page, sheet) وَرَقة (أَوْراق ,وَرَقات) **3** (hinged part) دَرْفة جَناح (في الطاوِلةِ); (sliding part) (دَرَفات)

Idioms **to take a leaf out of sb's book** حَذا حَذْوَ شَخْصٍ; **to turn over a new leaf** فَتَحَ صَفْحةً جَديدةً

Phrasal verb **leaf through: ~ through [sth]** تَصَفَّحَ [شَيْئاً] ‹*a book, pages*›

leaflet /ˈliːflɪt/ *n* (informational) نَشْرة (نَشَرات); (political) مَنْشور (مَنْشورات), بَيان (بَيانات)

leafy /ˈliːfi/ *adj* (**leafier, leafiest**) **1** ‹*tree, vegetable*› مورِق **2** ‹*suburb*› مُحاط بالأَشْجارِ

league /liːg/ *n* **1** (alliance) عُصْبة (عُصَب), رابِطة (رَوابِطُ), جامِعة; **to be in ~ with sb** كانَ مُتَواطِئاً مع شَخْصٍ **2** (Sport) دَوْريّ **3** (class, category) طَبَقة ,دَرَجة; **as a director, he's not in the same ~ as Hitchcock** من ناحِيةِ الإِخْراجِ، هو لَيْسَ في طَبَقةِ هيتْشكوك

League of Arab States *n* (also **Arab League**) جامِعة الدُوَلِ العَرَبيّةِ

league table *n* (BrE) جَدْوَل الدَوْريِّ

leak /liːk/ **A** *vt* **1** «engine, tank» سَرَّبَ ‹*oil, effluent*› **2** (to disclose) سَرَّبَ ‹*information, a report*›

B *vi* **1** «container, pipes, boat» رَشَحَ ,سَرَّبَ (a; رَشْح); **the roof ~s** السَقْفُ يَتَسَرَّبُ مِنْهُ الماءُ **2** «oil, water, gas» تَسَرَّبَ; **the acid ~ed into the river/soil** تَسَرَّبَ الحَمْضُ إلى النَهْرِ \ التُرْبةِ

C *n* **1** (in a container, pipe, ship, roof) فُتْحة (فُتَح, فُتْحات), شَقّ (شُقوق); **to spring a ~** بَدَأَ يُسَرِّبُ; **the boat/pipe has sprung a ~** بَدَأَ القارِبُ \ الأُنْبوبُ في التَسْريبِ **2** (of a liquid, gas) تَسَرُّب (تَسَرُّبات); **a gas/radiation ~** تَسَرُّب غازٍ \ إشْعاعٍ **3** (of information) تَسْريب

(Idiom) **to take a leak** (infml) تَبَوَّلَ

(Phrasal verb) **leak out** **1** «water, oil, gas» تَسَرَّبَ **2** «the news, information» تَسَرَّبَ

leakage /ˈliːkɪdʒ/ *n* تَسَرُّب (تَسَرُّبات)

leaky /ˈliːki/ *adj* (**leakier**, **leakiest**) ‹*roof, boat*› بِهِ ثُقوبٌ \ فَتَحاتٌ, يَتَسَرَّبُ مِنْهُ الماءُ

lean /liːn/ **A** *adj* **1** ‹*body, muscle*› نَحيف (نِحاف, نُحَفاءُ), نَحيل (نَحْلى, نُحَل) **2** ‹*meat*› خالٍ من الدُهونِ, بِلا شَحْمٍ \ دُهْنٍ

B *vt* (*past tense, past participle* **leaned** or **leant** BrE) أَسْنَدَ

C *vi* (*past tense, past participle* **leaned** or **leant** BrE) **1** (to bend, incline) «person» اِنْحَنى; «buildings» مالَ (i; مَيْل, مَيَلان); **she ~ed back in her chair** اِنْحَنَتْ في كُرْسِيِّها إلى الوَراءِ; **don't ~ out of the window** لا تُطِلَّ بِجِسْمِكَ من النافِذةِ **2** (for support) اِتَّكَأَ, اِسْتَنَدَ; **to ~ against sth** اِتَّكَأَ على شَيْءٍ; **~ on my arm** اِتَّكِئ على ذِراعي

leant /lɛnt/ *past tense, past participle* ▸ **lean**

leap /liːp/ **A** *vt* (*past tense, past participle* **leapt** or **leaped**) قَفَزَ (i; قَفْز, قَفَزان; فوق), وَثَبَ (i; وَثْب; فوق) ‹*a hedge, stream*›; **he ~t three metres** قَفَزَ ثَلاثةَ أَمْتارٍ

B *vi* (*past tense, past participle* **leapt** or **leaped**) **1** «people, animals» قَفَزَ (i; قَفْز, قَفَزان), وَثَبَ (i; وَثْب); **to ~ out of the bath/to one's feet** قَفَزَ خارِجَ الحَمّامِ \ انْتَفَضَ مُنْتَصِباً على قَدَمَيْهِ; **to ~ over the river/wall** قَفَزَ فوق النَهْرِ \ الجِدارِ; **to ~ out of bed** نَهَضَ من فِراشِهِ مُسْرِعاً; **to ~ to sb's defence** نَهَضَ للدِفاعِ عن شَخْصٍ **2** «one's heart» طارَ (i; طَيَران) **3** (to increase) «prices, profits» قَفَزَ (i; قَفْز, قَفَزان), اِرْتَفَعَ بِشِدّةٍ

C *n* **1** (jump) وَثْبة (وَثَبات), قَفْزة (قَفَزات); **in one ~** في قَفْزةٍ واحِدةٍ **2** (big step) قَفْزة (قَفَزات); **it requires a ~ of the imagination** يَتَطَلَّبُ خَيالاً واسِعاً **3** (in prices, demand) قَفْزة (قَفَزات), اِرْتِفاع كَبير

(Phrasal verbs) **leap around**, **leap about** قَفَزَ (i; قَفْز, قَفَزان), تَنَطَّطَ

• **leap at**: **~ at [sth]** اِقْتَنَصَ [شَيْئاً] ‹*a chance, an offer*›

• **leap in** (with an answer, a remark) قاطَعَ الحَديثَ, أَقْحَمَ نَفْسَهُ في الحَديثِ

• **leap out** **A** (from a hiding place) خَرَجَ فَجْأةً **B ~ out at [sb]** **1** (from a hiding place) باغَتَ [شَخْصاً]; **he hid in the doorway and ~t out at them** اِخْتَبَأَ في المَدْخَلِ وَباغَتَهُمْ **2** (to stand out) لَفَتَ \ خَطَفَ انْتِباهَ [شَخْصٍ]; **the photograph ~t out at me** لَفَتَت الصورةُ انْتِباهي

• **leap up** **1** (to one's feet) نَهَضَ بِسُرْعةٍ; **to ~ up at sb** «dogs» قَفَزَ نحو شَخْصٍ فَجْأةً **2** (to rise) «prices» قَفَزَ (i; قَفْز, قَفَزان), اِرْتَفَعَ

leapfrog /ˈliːpfrɒɡ/ *n* لُعْبة النَطّةِ (لُعْبة يَقْفِزُ فيها بَعْضُ الأَشْخاصِ فوق ظُهورِ بَعْضٍ); **to play ~** لَعِبَ لُعْبةَ النَطّةِ

leapt /lɛpt/ *past tense, past participle* ▸ **leap**

leap year *n* سَنة كَبيسة

learn /lɜːn/ **A** *vt* (*past tense, past participle* **learnt** or **learned**) **1** (through study, practice) تَعَلَّمَ ‹*a language, a skill*›; عَرَفَ (i; مَعْرِفة, عِرْفان), عَلِمَ (a; عِلْم) ‹*the facts*›; **to ~ to solve equations** تَعَلَّمَ حَلَّ المُعادَلاتِ; **to ~ how to swim backstroke** تَعَلَّمَ السِباحةَ على ظَهْرِهِ; **to ~ to live with sth** تَعَلَّمَ كيف يَتَعايَشُ مع شَيْءٍ **2** (to find out) **to ~ that ...** عَلِمَ أنَّ ...

B *vi* (*past tense, past participle* **learnt** or **learned**) **1** (to acquire knowledge) تَعَلَّمَ, عَلِمَ (a; عِلْم); **to ~ about sth** دَرى بِشَيْءٍ; **to ~ from one's mistakes** تَعَلَّمَ من أَخْطائِهِ **2** (to hear information) **to ~ of the accident/sb's death** دَرى \ عَرَفَ بالحادِثِ \ بِمَوْتِ شَخْصٍ

(Idiom) **to live and learn** عاشَ وَتَعَلَّمَ

learned /ˈlɜːnɪd/ *adj* ‹*person*› مُثَقَّف; ‹*society, journal*› عِلْمِيّ

learner /ˈlɜːnə/ *n* (Educ) **1** (student) تِلْميذ (تَلاميذُ, تَلامِذة), طالِب (طُلّاب, طَلَبة), مُتَعَلِّم; **to be a fast/slow ~** كان سَريعَ \ بَطيءَ التَعَلُّمِ **2** (also **learner driver**) سائِق تحت التَدْريبِ

learning /ˈlɜːnɪŋ/ *n* **1** (process) تَعَلُّم, تَحْصيل العِلْمِ **2** (knowledge) عِلْم, مَعْرِفة

learning curve *n* مُنْحَنى التَّعَلُّمِ

learning difficulties (BrE), **learning disabilities** (AmE) *n pl* صُعوبات التَّعَلُّمِ

learnt /lɜːnt/ *past tense, past participle* ▸ **learn**

lease /liːs/ **A** *n* عَقْد إيجارٍ

B *vt* **1** (to grant use of) أَجَّرَ ‹*a property, a vehicle*› **2** (to take under lease) اسْتَأْجَرَ ‹*a property, a vehicle*›

(Idiom) **a new lease of** *or* (AmE) **on life** فُرْصة لِحَياةٍ أَفْضَل

leasehold /ˈliːshəʊld/ **A** *n* **1** [u] (tenure) اسْتِئْجار **2** (property) عَقار مُسْتَأْجَر

B *adj* ‹*property*› مُسْتَأْجَر

leaseholder /ˈliːshəʊldə/ *n* مُسْتَأْجِر

leash /liːʃ/ *n* مِقْوَد (مَقاوِدُ)

leasing /ˈliːsɪŋ/ *n* اسْتِئْجار, إيجار

least /liːst/ **A** *determiner* (*superlative of* ▸ **little**) (**(the) least**) الأَقَلّ; **they have the ~ food** لَدَيْهِمْ أَقَلُّ كَمِّيَّةٍ من الطَعام; **the ~ thing annoys him** أَقَلُّ شَيْءٍ يُضايِقُهُ; **I haven't the ~ idea** لَيْسَ لَدَيَّ أَدْنى فِكْرةٍ; **they haven't the ~ chance of winning** لَيْسَ لَدَيْهِمْ أَدْنى فُرْصة للفَوْزِ; **he wasn't the ~ bit jealous** لم يَشْعُرْ بالغَيْرة على الإطْلاقِ

B *pron* (**(the) least**) الأَقَلّ; **it was the ~ I could do** كانَ هذا أَقَلَّ ما يُمْكِنُ أَنْ أَفْعَلَهُ; **the ~ he could have done was phone the police** أَقَلُّ ما كانَ يُمْكِنُ أَنْ يَفْعَلَهُ هو أَنْ يَتَّصِلَ بالشُرْطةِ; **that's the ~ of our problems!** تِلْكَ أَهْوَنُ مَشاكِلِنا!; **she was surprised, to say the ~ (of it)** أَقَلُّ ما يُقالُ أَنَّها فوجِئَتْ

C *adv* **1** (**(the) least**) (with adj or noun) الأَقَلّ; **the ~ viable solution** أَقَلّ الحُلولِ قابِلِيَّةً للتَطْبيقِ; **the ~ wealthy families** أَقَلّ الأُسَرِ ثَراءً **2** (with verbs) بِأَقَلِّ دَرَجةٍ; **I like that one (the) ~** ذلك أَكْثَرُ شَيْءٍ لا يُعْجِبُني; **just when we ~ expected it** في الوَقْتِ الّذي لم نَكُنْ نَتَوَقَّعُهُ إطْلاقاً; **nobody liked it, John ~ of all, nobody liked it, ~ of all John** لم يُعْجِبْ أَحَداً, وَخُصوصاً جون

D (**at least**) *adv phr* **1** (stating the minimum) على الأَقَلِّ, على أَقَلِّ تَقْديرٍ; **she's at ~ 40** عُمْرُها 40 عاماً على أَقَلِّ تَقْديرٍ; **there were at ~ 50 people in the room** كانَ هُناكَ على الأَقَلِّ 50 شَخْصاً في الغُرْفةِ; **they could at ~ have phoned!** كانَ بِإمْكانِهِمْ على الأَقَلِّ أَنْ يَتَّصِلوا!; **he's at ~ as qualified as she is** هو على أَقَلِّ تَقْديرٍ مُؤَهَّلٌ مِثْلَها تَماماً **2** (qualifying statement) على الأَقَلِّ; **he's gone out—at ~ I think so** لَقَدْ خَرَجَ — على الأَقَلِّ هذا ما أَظُنُّهُ; **he's never been abroad—at ~, that's what he says** لم يُسافِرْ إلى الخارِجِ أَبَداً — على الأَقَلِّ، ذلك ما يَقولُهُ

(Idioms) **in the least** على الإطْلاقِ; **it doesn't matter in the ~** لا يُهِمُّ على الإطْلاقِ; **I'm not worried in the ~, I'm not in the ~ (bit) worried** لَسْتُ قَلِقاً البَتَّةَ; **last but not least** أَخيراً وَلَيْسَ آخِراً

leather /ˈlɛðə/ *n* جِلْد (جُلود)

leave /liːv/ **A** *vt* (*past tense, past participle* **left**) **1** (to depart from) غادَرَ ‹*a house, room, country*›; **he left home early** انْصَرَفَ من البَيْتِ مُبَكِّراً; **to ~ school** تَرَكَ الدِراسةَ; **he left the office for a few minutes** غادَرَ المَكْتَبَ لِبِضْعِ دَقائِقَ; **the plane/train ~s Cairo at 9.00** تُغادِرُ الطائِرةُ \ يُغادِرُ القِطارُ من القاهِرةِ الساعةَ 9.00; **the car left the road** انْحَرَفَت السَيّارةُ عن الطَريقِ; **I left him cleaning his car** تَرَكْتُهُ وَهُوَ يُنَظِّفُ سَيّارَتَهُ **2** (to abandon) تَرَكَ (u; تَرْك), هَجَرَ (u; هَجْر) ‹*a child, one's family*›; **she left her husband** تَرَكَتْ زَوْجَها **3** (to forget) نَسِيَ (a; نَسْي, نِسْيان) ‹*one's glasses, keys*›; **I left my book/gloves on the bus** نَسيتُ كِتابي \ قُفّازاتي في الحافِلةِ **4** (for sb's use) تَرَكَ (u; تَرْك) ‹*money, instructions, a letter*›; **to ~ sb a tip** تَرَكَ بَقْشيشاً لِشَخْصٍ; **to ~ sb/sth in sb's care** تَرَكَ شَخْصاً \ شَيْئاً في عِنايةِ شَخْصٍ **5** (to allow to stay) تَرَكَ (u; تَرْك) ‹*one's food, a gap*›; **to ~ sth tidy/open** تَرَكَ شَيْئاً مُرَتَّباً \ مَفْتوحاً; **to ~ sth lying around** تَرَكَ شَيْئاً مُبَعْثَراً; **we have five minutes left** تَتَبَقّى لَدَيْنا خَمْسُ دَقائِقَ; **it left us short of money** سَبَّبَ لَنا نَقْصاً في المالِ; **the accident left him scarred/an orphan** سَبَّبَ لَهُ الحادِثُ نَدَبةً \ تَرَكَهُ الحادِثُ يَتيماً; **where does that ~ me?** كيف سَيُؤَثِّرُ هذا عَلَيَّ ؟; **you ~ me no choice but to tell your parents** أَنْتَ لا تَدَعُ لي خِياراً سِوى إخْبارِ والِدَيْكَ; **he left us in no doubt as to** *or* **about his feelings** لم يَتْرُكْ لَدَيْنا أَيَّ شَكٍّ في مَشاعِرِهِ **6** (to allow to do sth) **~ it to** *or* **with me** دَعْهُ لي; **to ~ it up to sb to do sth** تَرَكَ لِشَخْصٍ مَسْؤولِيَّةَ فِعْلِ شَيْءٍ; **to ~ the decision to sb**

تَرَكَ القرارَ لِشَخْصٍ; **I'll ~ you to it** سَأَدَعُكَ تُكْمِلُ ذلك; **to ~ sb be** (fml) تَرَكَ شَخْصاً وَشَأْنَهُ **7** (to cause) «the tea, oil» تَرَكَ (u; تَرْك) ‹*a stain, mark*›; **the wheels left marks on the floor** تَرَكَت العَجَلاتُ عَلاماتٍ على الأَرْضيّةِ **8** (to postpone) أَجَّلَ ‹*a task, your homework*›; **don't ~ it till tomorrow/the last day** لا تُؤَجِّلْهُ إلى الغَدِ \ آخِرِ يَوْمٍ **9** (to stop discussing) **let's just ~ it at that** دَعْنا نَتَوَقَّفُ عند هذا الحَدِّ **10** (in inheritance) **to ~ one's money/possessions to sb, to ~ sb one's money/possessions** تَرَكَ مالَهُ \ مُمْتَلَكاتِهِ لِشَخْصٍ

B *vi* (*past tense, past participle* **left**) رَحَلَ, غادَرَ (a; رَحيل); **he left for the airport/for work** ذَهَبَ إلى المَطارِ \ العَمَلِ; **the bus ~s at 10 a.m.** تُغادِرُ الحافلةُ الساعةَ 10 صَباحاً

C *v refl* (*past tense, past participle* **left**) **to ~ oneself time to do sth** تَرَكَ لِنَفْسِهِ وَقْتاً لِفِعْلِ شَيْءٍ; **to ~ oneself short of money** وَضَعَ نَفْسَهُ في ضائِقَةٍ ماليّةٍ

D *n* **1** (from one's job, unit) إجازة; **I took three days' ~** أَخَذْتُ إجازةً ثَلاثةَ أيّامٍ; **to be/go on ~** (from one's job, unit) كانَ في إجازةٍ \ أَخَذَ إجازةً; ▸ **gardening leave**, ▸ **maternity leave**, ▸ **paternity leave**, ▸ **sick leave** **2** (fml) (permission) إِذْن; **to give sb ~ to do sth** أَعْطى شَخْصاً الإِذْنَ بِفِعْلِ شَيْءٍ; **by** *or* **with your ~** بِإِذْنِكَ **3** (fml) (to say goodbye) **to take one's ~ of sb** وَدَّعَ شَخْصاً

Phrasal verbs **leave about** ▸ **leave around**

• **leave around**: **~ [sth] around** تَرَكَ [شَيْئاً] مُتَناثِراً ‹*books, papers*›

• **leave aside**: **~ [sth] aside, ~ aside [sth]** نَحّى [شَيْئاً] جانِباً ‹*a subject, question*›

• **leave behind** **A** **~ [sb/sth] behind** **1** (to go faster than) سَبَقَ [شَخْصاً \ شَيْئاً] ‹*a cyclist, car, runner*›; **our manufacturing industry is in danger of being left behind** يُواجِهُ قِطاعُ التَّصْنيعِ لَدَيْنا خَطَرَ التَّخَلُّفِ عن الرَّكْبِ **2** (to move away from) ابْتَعَدَ عن [شَخْصٍ \ شَيْءٍ] ‹*the coast, port*› **3** (to go without) رَحَلَ دون أنْ يَأْخُذَ [شَخصاً \ شَيْئاً] مَعَهُ ‹*one's keys, phone, a passenger*› **B** **~ [sth] behind** (in its wake) «the earthquake, storm» خَلَّفَ [شَيْئاً] وراءَهُ ‹*damage, flooding*›

• **leave go, leave hold**: (infml) **to ~ go** *or* **hold of sb/sth** أَفْلَتَ شَخْصاً \ شَيْئاً من يَدِهِ

• **leave off** **A** (to stop) «the rain, students» تَوَقَّفَ; **continue where you left off last time** اسْتَمِرَّ من حَيْثُ تَوَقَّفْتَ في المَرّةِ السابِقةِ **B** **~ [sth] off, ~ off [sth]** **1** (to not put on) لم يَرْتَدِ [شَيْئاً] ‹*your coat*›; لم يَضَعْ [شَيْئاً] ‹*the lid, cover*› **2** (without power) تَرَكَ [شَيْئاً] مُغْلَقاً ‹*the light, TV, central heating*› **3** (to omit) أَغْفَلَ [شَيْئاً] ‹*a name, an item*›; **he left my name off the list** لم يُدْرِج اسْمي في القائِمةِ

• **leave on**: **~ [sth] on** **1** (to not remove) ظَلَّ يَرْتَدي [شَيْئاً] ‹*hat, coat*›; تَرَكَ [شَيْئاً] ‹*the lid, cover, bandage*›; **~ the bandage on for three hours** اُتْرُك الضِمادةَ ثَلاثَ ساعاتٍ **2** (activated) تَرَكَ [شَيْئاً] موقَداً ‹*the light, heating, gas*›

• **leave out**: **~ [sb/sth] out, ~ out [sb/sth]** **1** (to omit) أَغْفَلَ [شَخْصاً \ شَيْئاً] ‹*a word, line, name*› **2** (from a group, an activity) اسْتَبْعَدَ [شَخْصاً \ شَيْئاً] ‹*a player, child*›; **he's been left out of the first team** تَمَّ اسْتِبْعادُهُ من الفريقِ الأَوَّلِ; **to feel left out** شَعَرَ بِأَنَّهُ غَيْرُ مَرْغوبٍ فيهِ **3** (outdoors) تَرَكَ [شَخْصاً \ شَيْئاً] خارِجَ البَيْتِ ‹*a bicycle, the washing, milk*›

• **leave over**: **~ [sth] over** (to have unused) **to have some money/cement left over** تَبَقّى لَدَيْهِ بَعْضُ المالِ \ الإسْمَنت; **at the end of the month, there is nothing/some money left over** في نِهايةِ الشَّهْرِ، لم يَتَبَقَّ شَيْءٌ \ تَبَقّى بَعْضُ المالِ

leaven /ˈlev(ə)n/ *vt* **1** أَضافَ خَميرةً إلى, خَمَّرَ ‹*the dough, mixture*› **2** لَطَّفَ ‹*a story, mood*›

leaves /liːvz/ *n pl* ▸ **leaf**

Lebanese /lebəˈniːz/ *n, adj* (*n pl* **Lebanese**) لُبْنانيّ

Lebanon /ˈleb(ə)nən/ *pr n* لُبْنان (dipt f)

lecherous /ˈletʃ(ə)rəs/ *adj* ‹*grin, man*› شَهْوانيّ

lectern /ˈlekt(ə)n/ *n* مِنَصّة القِراءة

lecture /ˈlektʃə/ **A** *n* **1** (talk) مُحاضَرة **2** (reprimand) تَوْبيخ (تَوْبيخات)

B *vt* **1** (Educ) حاضَرَ **2** (to reprimand) وَبَّخَ

C *vi* (Educ) أَلْقى مُحاضَرةً

lecturer /ˈlektʃ(ə)rə/ *n* **1** (speaker) مُتَحَدِّث, مُحاضِر **2** (BrE) (in a university or college) مُحاضِر

lecture theatre (BrE), **lecture theater** (AmE) *n* قاعة مُحاضَراتٍ

led /lɛd/ *past tense, past participle* ▸ **lead¹**

LED /ɛli:'di:/ *n* = **light-emitting diode** صِمام ثُنائيّ باعِث للضَوْء

ledge /lɛdʒ/ *n* 1 (shelf on a building, wall) حافّة بارِزة \ ناتِئة (on a window) (أَعْتاب, عَتَبات) عَتَبة 2 (on a mountain) جُزْء بارِز \ ناتِئ

ledger /'lɛdʒə/ *n* سِجِلّ حِساباتٍ

leech /li:tʃ/ *n* عَلَقة (عَلَقات)

leek /li:k/ *n* كُرّاث

leer /lɪə/ *vi* **to ~ at sb** نَظَرَ إلى شَخْصٍ نَظْرةً خَبيثةً

leeway /'li:weɪ/ *n* حُرّيّة, مُرونة; **they have more ~ in decision-making than I do** لَدَيْهِمْ حُرّيّةٌ أَكْثَرُ مِنّي في اتِّخاذِ القَراراتِ; **the new rules give no ~ for different interpretations** لا تُعْطي القَوانينُ الجَديدةُ مُرونةً في إعْطاءِ تَفْسيراتٍ مُخْتَلِفةٍ

left /lɛft/ **A** *past tense, past participle* ▸ **leave**

B *adj* 1 (as opposed to right) <*hand, shoe*> أَيْسَر (dipt)

2 (remaining) **to be ~** تَبَقّى; **there isn't much time ~** لم يَتَبَقَّ الكَثيرُ من الوَقْتِ

C *adv* <*look, go*> إلى اليَسارِ; **to turn ~** دارَ إلى اليَسارِ

D *n* 1 [u] (side, direction) يَسار; **keep to the ~** ابْقَ على اليَسارِ; **on your ~ is the town hall** تَقَعُ دارُ البَلَدِيّةِ على يَسارِكَ; **he was sitting to the ~ of us** كان جالِساً إلى يَسارِنا 2 (turn) **to take** *or* **make a ~** انْعَطَفَ إلى اليَسارِ 3 (Pol) [u] (**the left, the Left**) اليَسار 4 (in boxing) لَكْمة يَساريّة

Idiom **left, right and centre** في كُلِّ الاتِّجاهاتِ

left-hand /lɛft'hand/ *adj* <*corner, turn*> أَيْسَر (dipt); **on the ~ side** في الجِهةِ اليُسْرى

left-hand drive *adj* <*vehicle*> ذو مِقْوَدٍ على الجانِبِ الأَيْسَرِ

left-handed /lɛft'handɪd/ *adj* 1 <*person*> أَعْسَر (dipt), أَشْوَل (dipt) 2 <*golf club, scissors*> خاصّ للعُسْرِ

leftist /'lɛftɪst/ (Pol) *n, adj* يَساريّ

left luggage *n* (BrE) **left luggage (office)** مَكْتَب حِفْظِ الأَمْتِعةِ

left-of-centre /ˌlɛftəv'sɛntə/ (BrE), **left-of-center** (AmE) *adj* <*politician, party*> يَسار الوَسَطِ

leftover /'lɛftəʊvə/ *adj* <*food, material*> مُتَبَقٍّ, فائِض

leftovers /'lɛftəʊvəz/ *n pl* بَقايا طَعامٍ

left wing *n* 1 (Pol) جَناح يَساريّ 2 (Sport) جَناح أَيْسَر

left-wing /lɛft/ *adj* <*group, views*> يَساريّ, اشْتِراكيّ

left-winger /ˌlɛft'wɪŋə/ *n* (Pol) يَساريّ (شَخْص ذو مُيولٍ يَسارِيّةٍ)

leg /lɛg/ **A** *n* 1 (limb) ساق (f; سيقان), رِجْل (f; أَرْجُل); **to stand on one ~** وَقَفَ على ساقٍ واحِدةٍ 2 (of animal) رِجْل (f; أَرْجُل) 3 (of lamb) رِجْل (f; أَرْجُل) 4 (of chairs, stools) رِجْل (f; أَرْجُل); **a table ~** رِجْل طاوِلةٍ 5 (of trousers, pants) رِجْل (f; أَرْجُل) 6 (of a journey, race) مَرْحَلة (مَراحِلُ) 7 (in a competition) شَوْط (أَشْواط)

B *vt* (**-gg-**) **to ~ it** (infml) (to walk) مَشى (i; مَشْي); (to run) جَرى (i; جَرْي)

C (**-legged**); *in combination* **four-/six-~ged** <*animal, insect*> بِأَرْبَعِ \ بِستِّ أَرْجُلٍ; **long-~ged** <*person*> ذو سيقانٍ طَويلةٍ

Idioms **on one's last legs** «computer, car, person» على مَشارِفِ النِهايةِ; **to give sb a leg up** (infml) (over a wall) رَفَعَ شَخْصاً; (to help) أَعانَ شَخْصاً; **to pull sb's leg** خَدَعَ شَخْصاً بِقَصْدِ المِزاحِ

legacy /'lɛgəsi/ **A** *n* (*pl* **legacies**) 1 (bequest) وَصيّة (وَصايا); **to leave/make a ~ to sb** تَرَكَ وَصيّةً لِشَخْصٍ 2 (from the past) ميراث (مَوارِيث), إِرْث, تَرِكة

B *adj before n* (inherited) <*system, business*> قَديم; **the ~ software needs to be replaced** تَحْتاجُ البَرامِجُ القَديمةُ إلى الاسْتِبْدالِ

legal /'li:g(ə)l/ *adj* 1 (relating to the law) <*system, profession*> قانونيّ; **to take ~ action against sb** اتَّخَذَ اجْراءاتٍ قانونيّةً ضِدَّ شَخْصٍ 2 (lawful) <*right, obligation, owner*> قانونيّ, شَرْعيّ; **what I did was perfectly ~** ما فَعَلْتُهُ كانَ قانونيًّا تَماماً

legal aid *n* مَعونة قانونيّة

legal holiday *n* (AmE) عُطْلة رَسْمِيّة

legality /li:'galəti/ *n* شَرْعيّة, قانونيّة

legalization, **-isation** (BrE) /li:gəlʌɪ'zeɪʃ(ə)n/ *n* إباحة

legalize, **-ise** (BrE) /'li:gəlʌɪz/ *vt* أَضْفى الشَرْعيّةَ على, قَنَّنَ, أَباحَ <*marijuana, abortion*>

legally /ˈliːg(ə)li/ *adv* ‹*binding, responsible*› بِموجِبِ القانونِ، من الناحِيةِ القانونيّةِ، قانوناً

legal tender *n* عُمْلة قانونيّة

legation /lɪˈgeɪʃ(ə)n/ *n* مُفَوَّضيّة

legend /ˈlɛdʒ(ə)nd/ *n* أُسْطورة (أَساطيرُ)

legendary /ˈlɛdʒ(ə)nd(ə)ri/ *adj* ‹*figure, status*› أُسْطوريّ

leggings /ˈlɛgɪŋz/ *n pl* طِماق (كِساء للساقَيْنِ)

legible /ˈlɛdʒɪb(ə)l/ *adj* ‹*handwriting, text*› مَقْروء

legion /ˈliːdʒ(ə)n/ *n* (Mil, Hist) فَيْلَق (فَيالِقُ)

legionnaire /ˌliːdʒəˈnɛː/ *n* (Mil) جُنْديّ في فَيْلَقٍ

legionnaires' disease /ˌlidʒ(ə)nˈɛːz ˌdɪziːs/ *n* داء الفَيالِقِ

legislate /ˈlɛdʒɪsleɪt/ *vi* «parliaments, governments» سَنَّ، شَرَّعَ قَوانينَ; **to ~ against/for sth** سَنَّ قانوناً ضِدّ \ من أَجْلِ شَيْءٍ

legislation /lɛdʒɪsˈleɪʃ(ə)n/ *n* قَوانين، تَشْريعات

legislative /ˈlɛdʒɪslətɪv/ *adj* ‹*process, body*› تَشْريعيّ

legislator /ˈlɛdʒɪsleɪtə/ *n* مُشَرِّع

legislature /ˈlɛdʒɪslətʃə/ *n* (fml) مَجْلِس تَشْريعيّ، هَيْئة تَشْريعيّة

legitimacy /lɪˈdʒɪtɪməsi/ *n* **1** (legality) قانونيّة، شَرْعيّة **2** (justifiability) مَشْروعيّة، صِحّة; **he questioned the ~ of her objections** شَكَّكَ في صِحّةِ اعْتِراضاتِها

legitimate /lɪˈdʒɪtɪmət/ *adj* **1** (justifiable) ‹*concern, interest*› مَنْطِقيّ **2** (lawful) ‹*owner, claim*› قانونيّ، شَرْعيّ **3** (with married parents) ‹*child, son*› شَرْعيّ

legitimize, **-ise** (BrE) /lɪˈdʒɪtɪmʌɪz/ *vt* **1** (to legalize) أَباحَ، قَنَّنَ ‹*a practice*›; أَضْفى الشَرْعيّةَ على ‹*an organization*› **2** (to justify) بَرَّرَ ‹*an action, a policy*›

legroom /ˈlɛgruːm/ *n* [حَيِّز لِمَدِّ الرِجْلَيْنِ أثناء الجُلوسِ]

legume /ˈlɛgjuːm/ *n* بَقْل (n coll; بُقول)

leg warmer *n* [جَوْرَب صوفيّ مَفْتوح]

leisure /ˈlɛʒə/ *n* **1** (free time) وَقْت فَراغ; **take it and read it at your ~** خُذْهُ وَاقْرَأْهُ على مَهْلِكَ **2** (leisure activities) تَرْفيه

leisure centre *n* (BrE) مَرْكَز تَرْفيهيّ

leisurely /ˈlɛʒ(ə)li/ *adj* ‹*stroll, breakfast*› بِدونِ اسْتِعْجالٍ، بِتَمَهُّلٍ; **at a ~ pace** على نَحْوٍ مُتَمَهِّلٍ

leisure time *n* وَقْت فَراغٍ

leisurewear /ˈlɛʒəwɛː/ *n* مَلابِس غَيْر رَسْميّة

lemming /ˈlɛmɪŋ/ *n* لاموس (حَيَوان من القَوارِضِ)

lemon /ˈlɛmən/ *n* **1** (fruit) لَيْمون (n coll) **2** (colour) أَصْفَر لَيْمونيّ، باهِت

lemonade /lɛməˈneɪd/ *n* **1** (still) ليمونادة **2** (BrE) (fizzy) [مَشْروب غازيّ بِطَعْمِ اللَيْمونِ]

lemon curd, **lemon cheese** *n* (BrE) مُهَلَّبيّة اللَيْمونِ

lemon juice *n* عَصير لَيْمونٍ

lemon tea *n* شاي لَيْمونٍ

lemon tree *n* شَجَرة لَيْمونٍ

lend /lɛnd/ *vt* (*past tense, past participle* **lent**) **1** (to loan) أَقْرَضَ ‹*money, a book*›; **I lent him £500** أَقْرَضْتُهُ 500 جُنَيْهٍ **2** (to give) أَضْفى ‹*support, credence*›

lender /ˈlɛndə/ *n* مُقْرِض

lending /ˈlɛndɪŋ/ *n* إِقْراض

length /lɛŋθ/ **A** *n* **1** (longest measurement) طول (أَطْوال); **what is the ~ of the plank?, what ~ is the plank?** ما طولُ اللَوْحِ؟; **to be 15 cm/50 km in ~** كانَ طولُهُ 15 سم \ 50 كم; **it's twice the ~ of the original bridge** طولُهُ ضِعْفُ طولِ الجِسْرِ الأَصْليِّ; **the road runs the ~ of the valley** يَمْتَدُّ الطَريقُ بِطولِ الوادي; **the ~ and breadth of Ireland** في طولِ إِيرْلَنْدا وَعَرْضِها **2** (of a book, movie, list) طول (أَطْوال); **he can't concentrate for any ~ of time** لا يَسْتَطيعُ التَرْكيزَ لأَيِّ فَتْرةٍ من الوَقْتِ; **for a considerable ~ of time** لِفَتْرةٍ طَويلةٍ من الزَمَنِ **3** **notice the ~ of the vowels/notes in …** لاحِظْ طولَ الحُروفِ المُتَحَرِّكةِ \ النَغَماتِ في … **4** (piece of string, cable, wood) قِطْعة (قِطَع); **to cut the cloth into two metre ~s** قَصَّ القُماشَ قِطْعَتَيْنِ طولُ كُلٍّ مِنْهُما مِتْرَيْنِ **5** (in swimming) [طول حَمّامِ السِباحةِ]

B (**lengths**) *n pl* **to go to great ~s to do sth** بَذَلَ قُصارى جُهْدِهِ لِفِعْلِ شَيْءٍ; **the family is willing to go to any ~s to rescue her** الأُسْرةُ مُسْتَعِدّةٌ لِأَنْ تَفْعَلَ أَيَّ شَيْءٍ مُمْكِنٍ لِإِنْقاذِها

C (**at length**) *adv phr* (fml) **1** (for a long time) لِمُدّةٍ طَويلةٍ; **we have examined the issue at ~** دَرَسْنا المَسْأَلةَ بالتَفْصيلِ **2** (at last) أَخيراً

D (**-length**) *in combination*: **shoulder-~ hair** شَعْر طولُهُ للكَتِفِ; **floor-~ curtains** سَتائِر طولُها للأَرْضِيّةِ ▸ **full-length**

lengthen /ˈlɛŋθ(ə)n/ **A** *vt* طَوَّلَ <*a garment*>; أَطالَ <*life, one's stay*>; مَدَّ (u; مَدّ) <*a road*>
B *vi* «shadows» امْتَدَّ; «days» طالَ (u; طول)

lengthwise /ˈlɛŋθwʌɪz/, **lengthways** (BrE) /ˈlɛŋθweɪz/ *adv* <*to cut, fold*> طوليًّا, بالطولِ

lengthy /ˈlɛŋθi/ *adj* (**lengthier**, **lengthiest**) <*process, discussion*> مُطَوَّل, طَويل

lenient /ˈliːnɪənt/ *adj* <*sentence*> مُتَساهِل; <*person*> مُتَسامِح; <*treatment*> رَفيق

lens /lɛnz/ *n* (*pl* **lenses**) **1** (in spectacles) عَدَسة **2** (contact lens) عَدَسة لاصِقة **3** (in a camera) عَدَسة **4** (in optical instruments) عَدَسة

lent /lɛnt/ *past tense, past participle* ▸ **lend**

Lent /lɛnt/ *n* الصَّوْم الكَبير (عند المَسيحيّين)

lentil /ˈlɛnt(ə)l/ *n* عَدَس (n coll)

Leo /ˈliːəʊ/ *n* **1** (sign) بُرْج الأَسَدِ **2** (person) [شَخْص من بُرْج الأَسَدِ]

leopard /ˈlɛpəd/ *n* نَمِر (أَرْقَط); **a ~ cannot change its spots** ≈ الطَبْعُ يَغْلِبُ التَطَبُّعِ

leotard /ˈliːətɑːd/ *n* [ثَوْب ضَيِّق كالّذي تَرْتَديه راقِصةُ الباليه]

leper /ˈlɛpə/ *n* مُصاب بالجُذام, مَجْذوم

leprosy /ˈlɛprəsi/ *n* جُذام

lesbian /ˈlɛzbɪən/ **A** *n* سِحاقيّة, مُساحِقة
B *adj* <*relationship, partner*> سِحاقيّ

lesion /ˈliːʒ(ə)n/ *n* جُرْح (جُروح, جِراح), آفة

Lesotho /ləˈsuːtuː, ləˈsəʊtəʊ/ *pr n* ليسوتو (f)

less /lɛs/ **A** *determiner* (*comparative of* ▸ **little**) أَقَلّ (dipt); **~ beer/information/money** أَقَلّ من البيرةِ \ المَعْلوماتِ \ المالِ; **it took ~ time than we expected** تَطَلَّبَ الأَمْرُ وَقْتاً أَقَلَّ مِمّا تَوَقَّعْنا; **it's of ~ value/importance** هو أَقَلُّ قيمةً \ أَهَمّيّةً
B *pron* أَقَلّ (dipt); **I have ~ than you** عِنْدي أَقَلُّ مِمّا عِنْدَكَ; **in ~ than three hours** في أَقَلَّ من ثَلاثِ ساعاتٍ; **~ than half the class passed** نَجَحَ أَقَلُّ من نِصْفِ الصَفِّ; **no ~ than 30 casualties** لَيْسَ أَقَلَّ من 30 مُصاباً; **we're paid far ~ than they are** نَتَقاضى أَقَلَّ بِكَثيرٍ مِمّا يَتَقاضَوْنَ; **the ~ said about it the better** كُلَّما قَلَّ الكَلامُ عَنْهُ كُلَّما كانَ ذلك أَفْضَلَ; **a sum of not ~ than £1,000** مَبْلَغ لا يَقِلُّ عن 1000 جُنَيْهٍ; **it's nothing ~ than a scandal!** هي فَضيحةٌ بِكُلِّ المَعاييرِ!; **I think no ~ of her for that** لم يَقِلَّ تَقْديري لَها بِسَبَبِ ذلك; **I'll accept £1,000 and not a penny ~!** سَأَقْبَلُ 1000 جُنَيْهٍ وَلَيْسَ أَقَلَّ من ذلك بِفِلْسٍ واحِدٍ!
C *adv* على نَحْوٍ أَقَلَّ, بِدَرَجةٍ أَقَلَّ; **I read ~ these days** أَقْرَأُ أَقَلَّ هذه الأَيّامَ; **they come ~ often now** يَأْتونَ بِدَرَجةٍ أَقَلَّ من المُعْتادِ هذه الأَيّامَ; **I liked it ~ than you did** أَعْجَبَني بِدَرَجةٍ أَقَلَّ مِمّا أَعْجَبَكَ; **that's a ~ serious offence** تِلْكَ جَريمةٌ أَقَلُّ خُطورةً; **she is no ~ qualified than you** لَيْسَتْ أَقَلَّ كَفاءةً مِنْكَ; **the more I have to do with them, the ~ I like them** كُلَّما تَعامَلْتُ مَعَهُمْ أَكْثَرَ كُلَّما قَلَّ حُبّي لَهُمْ; **a ~ well-known director** مُخْرِج أَقَلّ شُهْرةً; **no ~ a person than the president** الرَئيس نَفْسُهُ
D *prep* إلاّ, ناقِصاً مِنْهُ, مَطْروحاً; **it's $750 ~ 15%** هو ب 750 دولار ثُمَّ يُخْصَمُ 15٪; **a salary of £40,000, ~ tax** مُرَتَّب 40,000 جُنَيْهٍ، قبل خَصْمِ الضَريبةِ
E (**less and less**) *adv phr* أَقَلّ وَأَقَلّ; **we see them ~ and ~** تَقِلُّ رُؤْيَتُنا لَهُمْ أَكْثَرَ وَأَكْثَرَ

lessee /lɛˈsiː/ *n* مُسْتَأْجِر

lessen /ˈlɛs(ə)n/ **A** *vt* قَلَّلَ, خَفَّضَ, خَفَّفَ <*a cost, risk*>
B *vi* «interest, feelings» قَلَّ (i; قِلّة), خَفَّ (i; خِفّة), نَقَصَ (u; نُقْصان, نَقْص); «noise» انْخَفَضَ

lesser /ˈlɛsə/ *adj* أَقَلّ (dipt), أَصْغَر (dipt); **to a ~ extent** بِدَرَجةٍ أَقَلَّ

lesson /ˈlɛs(ə)n/ *n* **1** (class) دَرْس (دُروس), حِصّة (حِصَص); **she's having driving ~s** تَأْخُذُ دُروساً في تَعَلُّمِ القِيادةِ **2** (in a textbook) دَرْس (دُروس) **3** (by experience) دَرْس (دُروس); **to learn one's ~** تَعَلَّمَ الدَرْسَ

lessor /lɛˈsɔː/ *n* مُؤَجِّر

lest /lɛst/ *conj* **1** (fml) (in case that) لِكَيْلا, حتّى لا, لِئَلاّ; **~ we forget** حتّى لا نَنْسى **2** (fml) (after expressions of fear) خَشْيةَ, مَخافةَ أَنْ, أَنْ; **she was afraid ~ he might** *or* **should drown** كانَتْ تَخْشى عَلَيْهِ من الغَرَقِ

let¹ /lɛt/ **A** *vt* (*present participle* **-tt-**; *past tense, past participle* **let**)

1 (in suggestions) **~'s go for a swim** لِنَذْهَبْ للسِباحةِ; **~'s give it a try** هَيّا نُجَرِّبُهُ; **ok, ~'s start!** حَسَناً، فَلْنَبْدَأْ!; **~ me see ..., ~'s see ...** دَعْني أرى ...; **~'s pretend that this is the interview** دَعْنا نَتَظاهَرُ أنّ هذه هي المُقابَلةُ; **'~'s dance, Susan' - 'yes, ~'s!'** 'هَيّا نَرْقُصْ، يا سوزان' - 'أَجَلْ، هَيّا!' **2** (in commands, in defiance) **~ there be no doubt about it!** يَجِبُ ألاّ يَكونَ هُناكَ أَيُّ شَكٍّ في هذا!; **~'s not talk about that!** دَعْنا نَتْرُكُ الحَديثَ في هذا الأَمْرِ!; **~ that be a lesson to you!** لِيَكُنْ ذلك دَرْساً لَكَ!; **could you ~ me have that in writing?** هل تَسْمَحُ بِأَنْ تُعْطِيَني ذلك مَكْتوباً؟; **~'s face it; you were wrong** دَعْنا نُواجِهُ الحَقيقةَ؛ لَقَدْ كُنْتَ مُخْطِئاً **3** (to allow) **to ~ sb do sth** سَمَحَ لِشَخْصٍ بِأَنْ يَفْعَلَ شَيْئاً; **they ~ the children feed the animals** يَسْمَحونَ للأَطْفالِ بِإطْعامِ الحَيَواناتِ; **~ me go first** دَعْني أَذْهَبُ أَوَّلاً; **~ me pay for dinner** دَعْني أَدْفَعُ حِسابَ العَشاءِ; **~ me have a look** دَعْني أُلْقي نَظْرةً; **they ~ us in without paying** سَمَحوا لَنا بالدُخولِ دون أنْ نَدْفَعَ; **don't ~ me forget to get the paper** لا تَدَعْني أَنْسى إحْضارَ الجَريدةِ; **don't ~ the milk boil over!** لا تَتْرُكِ الحَليبَ يَفورُ!; **to ~ one's hair grow** أَطالَ شَعْرَهُ; **to ~ one's beard grow** أَطْلَقَ لِحْيَتَهُ **4** (with free movement, passage) **to ~ sb through** أَفْسَحَ الطَريقَ لِشَخْصٍ; **to ~ sb on/off the bus** أَفْسَحَ الطَريقَ لِشَخْصٍ حتّى يَصْعَدَ إلى \ يَنْزِلَ من الحافِلةِ; **can you ~ me off here?** هل يُمْكِنُكَ أنْ تُنْزِلَني هُنا؟; **I let myself in** سَمَحْتُ لِنَفْسي بالدُخولِ; **to ~ air into a room** سَمَحَ للهَواءِ بالدُخولِ إلى الحُجْرةِ; **to ~ the air out of a tyre** أَفْرَغَ إطاراً من الهَواءِ **5** (to insert) **to ~ a door/window into a wall** فَتَحَ باباً \ نافِذةً في حائِطٍ **6** (in propositions) **~ y = 25** افْتَرِضْ أنّ ص = 25

B (**let alone**) *conj phr* فَما بالُكَ ب; **she was too ill to stand ~ alone walk** كانَتْ مَريضةً جِدًّا ولا تَسْتَطيعُ الوُقوفَ فَما بالُكَ بالمَشْيِ

Phrasal verbs **let down A ~ [sb] down** (to disappoint) «organization, person» خَذَلَ [شَخْصاً]; **the satnav has never let me down** لم يَخْذُلْني جِهازُ المِلاحةِ أبداً; **the guide/driver let us down** خَذَلَنا المُرْشِدُ \ السائِقُ; ▸ **side B ~ [sth] down, ~ down [sth] 1** (to lower) أَنْزَلَ [شَيْئاً] *‹a bucket, basket›*; **he ~ down the car window** فَتَحَ نافِذةَ السَيّارةِ **2** (BrE) (to deflate) أَفْرَغَ من الهَواءِ *‹a tyre›* **3** (to lengthen) أَسْبَلَ *‹the hem›*; أَرْخى *‹skirt›*

• **let go A** (to loosen one's grip) خَفَّفَ قَبْضَتَهُ; **don't ~ go!** لا تَدَعْهُ يُفْلِتُ من قَبْضَتِكَ! **B ~ [sb/sth] go, ~ go [sb/sth] 1** (to free) أَطْلَقَ سَراحَ [شَخْصٍ] *‹a hostage, suspect›* **2** (to release) أَفْلَتَ قَبْضَتَهُ عن [شَخْصٍ \ شَيْءٍ] *‹a person, sleeve, arm›*; **~ me go, ~ go of me!** اُتْرُكْني!; **~ go of my arm** اُتْرُكْ ذِراعي **3** (to lay off) فَصَلَ [شَخْصاً] *‹an employee›*; **to be let go** فُصِلَ من عَمَلِهِ **4** **to ~ oneself go** (uninhibitedly) أَطْلَقَ لِنَفْسِهِ العِنانَ **C ~ [sth] go, ~ go [sth]** (to release) أَرْخى قَبْضَتَهُ عن [شَيْءٍ] *‹the rope, bar›*; **she wouldn't ~ go of her bag** لم تُرِدْ أنْ تَتْرُكَ الحَقيبةَ تُفْلِتُ من يَدِها

• **let in A ~ in [sth], ~ [sth] in 1** (to allow to enter) «roof, shoes, window» سَرَّبَ [شَيْئاً] *‹water›* **2** (in scoring) سَمَحَ لِخَصْمِهِ بِتَسْجيلِ [شَيْءٍ] *‹a goal›* **B ~ [sb] in, ~ in [sb] 1** (to admit) سَمَحَ ل [شَخْصٍ] بالدُخولِ *‹a cat, thief›*; **I let the cat in** أَدْخَلْتُ القِطّةَ **2** (to expose oneself to) **to ~ oneself in for trouble/a shock** عَرَّضَ نَفْسَهُ للخَطَرِ \ لِصَدْمةٍ **3** **to ~ sb in on a secret/joke** أَطْلَعَ شَخْصاً على سِرٍّ \ نُكْتةٍ

• **let off A ~ off [sth]** أَطْلَقَ [شَيْئاً] *‹fireworks›*; فَجَّرَ [شَيْئاً] *‹bomb›*; أَطْلَقَ النارَ من [شَيْءٍ] *‹rifle›* ▸ **hook, steam B ~ [sb] off 1** (to leave unpunished) تَرَكَ [شَخْصاً] دون عِقابٍ *‹the culprit›*; **to be ~ off with (just a) fine** لم يَتَلَقَّ أَيَّ عِقابٍ وأُلْزِمَ فَقَطْ بِدَفْعِ غَرامةٍ **2** **to ~ sb off sth** (to excuse) أَعْفى شَخْصاً من شَيْءٍ *‹homework, chores›*

• **let on** (to reveal sth) كَشَفَ (i; كَشْف); **don't ~ on!** لا تُخْبِرْ أَحَداً!; **she knows them better than she ~s on** تَعْرِفُ عَنْهُمْ أَكْثَرَ مِمّا تُخْبِرُ بِهِ

• **let out A ~ out** (AmE) «school» بَدَأَ العُطْلةَ **B ~ out [sth] 1** (to emit) أَطْلَقَ [شَيْئاً] *‹a scream, sigh›*; **to ~ out a scream of terror** أَطْلَقَ صَرْخةَ رُعْبٍ; **he ~ out a sigh of relief** تَنَفَّسَ الصُعَداءَ **2** (BrE) (to reveal) كَشَفَ [شَيْئاً]; **she ~ out that we were leaving** كَشَفَتْ أَنَّنا سَنُغادِرُ **C ~ [sth] out, ~ out [sth] 1** (to release) أَطْلَقَ سَراحَ [شَيْءٍ] *‹an animal›* **2** (to alter)

وَسَّعَ [شَيْئاً] ‹*a skirt, the waist*› **D** ~ **[sb] out** (to release) أَطْلَقَ سَراحَ [شَخْصٍ] ‹*a prisoner*›; سَمَحَ ل [شَخْصٍ] بالخُروجِ ‹*class*›

• **let through**: ~ **[sb] through**, ~ **through [sb]** (in crowds) أَفْسَحَ الطَّريقَ ل [شَخْصٍ]

• **let up** 1 (to ease off) «rain, wind» هَدَأَ (a; هُدوء, هَدْء); **the rain/wind never let up** لم يَهْدَأ المَطَرُ \ تَهْدَأ الريحُ أَبَداً 2 (to slow down) «worker» تَوانى; **he never ~s up** لا يُقَصِّرُ أَبَداً 3 (infml) (to be less severe) **to ~ up on sb** خَفَّفَ الضَغْطَ عن شَخْصٍ

let² /lɛt/ *vt* (*present participle* **-tt-**; *past tense, past participle* **let**) (also **let out** BrE) (to rent out) أَجَّرَ

let-down /ˈlɛtdaʊn/ *n* خَيْبة أَمَل

lethal /ˈliːθ(ə)l/ *adj* 1 (fatal) ‹*injection, weapon*› قاتِل, مُميت, مُهْلِك 2 (dangerous) ‹*cocktail, criticism*› خطير

lethargic /lɪˈθɑːdʒɪk/ *adj* ‹*mood, movement*› خامِل, كَسول

lethargy /ˈlɛθədʒi/ *n* كَسَل, نُعاس, خُمول

let's /lɛts/ *abbr* = **let us**

letter /ˈlɛtə/ **A** *n* 1 (written message) رِسالة (رِسالات, رَسائِلُ), خِطاب (خِطابات, أَخْطِبة); **his ~s to and from his family** رَسائِلُهُ مع أُسْرَتِهِ; **I wrote him a ~ of apology** كَتَبْتُ لَهُ خِطابَ اعْتِذارٍ; **my ~ of resignation** خِطاب اسْتِقالَتي; **~s to the editor** رَسائِل إلى المُحَرِّرِ 2 (of the alphabet) حَرْف (حُروف, أَحْرُف); **to write in capital ~s** كَتَبَ بِحُروفٍ كَبيرةٍ
B (**letters**) *n pl* (fml) (literature) أَدَب (آداب); **a man/woman of ~s** أَديب \ أَديبة

letter bomb *n* رِسالة مُفَخَّخة

letter box *n* 1 (for delivery: in a door) فَتْحة في بابٍ تُسَلَّمُ من خِلالِها الرَسائِلُ 2 (beside an entrance) صُنْدوق رَسائِلَ (بالقُرْبِ من مَسْكَنٍ) 3 (for collection) صُنْدوق بَريدٍ

letterhead /ˈlɛtəhɛd/ *n* رَأْسيّة, تَرْويسة

lettuce /ˈlɛtɪs/ *n* خَسّ

let-up /ˈlɛtʌp/ *n* تَوَقُّف, انْقِطاع

leukaemia (BrE), **leukemia** (AmE) /luːˈkiːmɪə/ *n* لوكيميا, سَرَطان الدَمِ

Levant /lɪˈvant/ *n* (**the Levant**) (old use) بِلاد الشامِ

level /ˈlɛv(ə)l/ **A** *n* 1 (of a building, mine) طابَق (طَوابِقُ), دَوْر (أَدْوار) 2 (of a liquid, the sea) مُسْتَوًى (مُسْتَوَيات); **the ~ of the water at high/low tide** مُسْتَوى الماءِ في المَدِّ العالي \ المُنْخَفِضِ 3 (of difficulty) مُسْتَوًى (مُسْتَوَيات); **to be on the same ~ as sb** كانَ في نَفْسِ مُسْتَوى شَخْصٍ; **at intermediate/advanced ~** في المُسْتَوى المُتَوَسِّطِ \ المُتَقَدِّمِ 4 (equal plane) مُسْتَوًى (مُسْتَوَيات), ارْتِفاع; **to be at** *or* **on the same ~ with sth** كانَ على نَفْسِ مُسْتَوى شَيْءٍ; **the windows are not at** *or* **on the same ~** لَيْسَت النَوافِذُ على نَفْسِ المُسْتَوى; **at street ~** على مُسْتَوى الشارِعِ; **at waist-/knee-~** بارْتِفاعِ الخَصْرِ \ الرُكْبةِ; **on a practical ~** على الصَعيدِ العَمَليِّ 5 (amount of pollution, unemployment, spending) مُسْتَوًى (مُسْتَوَيات); **the ~ of sugar/cholesterol in the blood** مُسْتَوى السُكَّرِ \ الكوليسْتول في الدَمِ 6 (in a hierarchy) مُسْتَوًى (مُسْتَوَيات); **at national/board ~** على المُسْتَوى الوَطَنيِّ \ مُسْتَوى مَجْلِسِ الإدارةِ; **at a higher/lower ~** على مُسْتَوى أَعْلى \ أَدْنى
B *adj* 1 (not sloping) ‹*shelf, surface, floor*› مُسْتَوٍ 2 (not bumpy) ‹*ground, surface, field*› مُسْتَوٍ, مُنْبَسِط 3 ‹*teaspoonful*› مَمْسوح 4 (equally high) **to be ~** «floors, surfaces, windows» كانَ على نَفْسِ المُسْتَوى \ الارْتِفاعِ; **ensure that the door is ~ with the floor** تَأَكَّدْ أنّ البابَ على نَفْسِ مُسْتَوى الأَرْضيّةِ 5 (equal in achievement, rank) **to be ~** «competitors, teams» كانَ مُتَساوياً \ مُتَعادِلاً; **at the half-way stage the teams were ~** كانَت الفِرَقُ مُتَساويةً في المَرْحَلةِ الوُسْطى 6 (stable) **to remain ~** «growth, inflation» ظَلَّ مُسْتَقِرّاً 7 (without emotion) «tone, voice» هادِئ, غَيْر مُنْفَعِلٍ
C *adv* (in competitions) **to draw ~ with sb** أَصْبَحَ مُتَعادِلاً مع شَخْصٍ ‹*a competitor, team, car*›
D *vt* (**-ll-** BrE, **-l-** AmE) 1 سَوّى, مَهَّدَ ‹*the ground, road*›; **the town was ~led by the earthquake** سَوّى الزِلْزالُ المَدينةَ بالأَرْضِ 2 (to aim) صَوَّبَ ‹*a gun, weapon*›; وَجَّهَ ‹*criticism, an accusation*›

Idiom **to be on the level** كانَ فوقَ مُسْتَوى الشُبُهاتِ

Phrasal verb **level off, level out** 1 «prices, rate of growth» اسْتَقَرَّ 2 «planes, pilots» طارَ أُفُقيًّا 3 «paths, roads» اسْتَوى, انْبَسَطَ

level crossing *n* (BrE) مَزْلَقان

level-headed /ˌlev(ə)lˈhedɪd/ *adj* ‹*manner, pragmatist*› مُتَّزِن

lever /ˈliːvə/ **A** *n* **1** (on a machine) ذِراع تَشْغيلٍ **2** (bar) عَتَلَة **B** *vt* رَفَعَ \ حَرَّكَ بِعَتَلَةٍ ‹*a rock, window*›; **to ~ the door open** فَتَحَ البابَ بِعَتَلَةٍ

leverage /ˈliːvərɪdʒ/ *n* **1** (influence) نُفوذ **2** (force of a lever) رَفْع ماليّ **3** (Fin) قوّة رَفْعٍ

levy /ˈlevi/ **A** *vt* (**levies**, **levying**, **levied**) فَرَضَ (i; فَرْض) ‹*a tax, duty*› **B** *n* (*pl* **levies**) **1** (charge) رَسْم (رُسوم) **2** (tax) ضَريبة (ضَرائِبُ)

lewd /ljuːd/ *adj* (**lewder**, **lewdest**) ‹*joke, gesture*› خادِش, خَليع لِلحَياءِ

lexicon /ˈleksɪk(ə)n/ *n* (*pl* **lexicons** or **lexica** /ˈleksɪkə/) **1** (vocabulary) قائِمة كَلِماتٍ, مُعْجَم (مَعاجِمُ) **2** (dictionary) قاموس (قَواميسُ), مُعْجَم (مَعاجِمُ)

LGV /ɛldʒiˈvi/ *n* = **large goods vehicle** سَيّارة نَقْلٍ ثَقيلٍ

liability /lʌɪəˈbɪlɪti/ **A** *n* (*pl* **liabilities**) **1** (responsibility) مَسْؤوليّة; **to deny ~ for sth** نَفى مَسْؤوليَّتَهُ عن شَيْءٍ **2** (drawback) عِبْء (أَعْباء) **B** (**liabilities**) *n pl* خُصوم, دُيون; **assets and liabilities** أُصول وَخُصوم, مَوْجودات وَمَطْلوبات

liable /ˈlʌɪəb(ə)l/ *adj* **1** (likely) مُعَرَّض, عُرْضة; **he is ~ to forget** هو مُعَرَّضٌ لِلنِسْيانِ; **the earlier model was ~ to overheat** كانَ النَموذَجُ السابِقُ عُرْضةً لِارْتِفاعٍ مُفْرِطٍ في دَرَجةِ الحَرارةِ **2** (responsible) مَسْؤول; **to be ~ for the cost of repairs** كانَ مَسْؤولاً عن تَكاليفِ التَصْليحاتِ

liaise /lɪˈeɪz/ *vi* «groups, counterparts» نَسَّقَ; **to ~ with one's counterpart** نَسَّقَ مع نَظيرِهِ

liaison /lɪˈeɪz(ə)n/ *n* **1** [u] (coordination) تَنْسيق **2** (liter) (affair) عَلاقة غَراميّة

liar /ˈlʌɪə/ *n* كاذِب, كَذّاب

libel /ˈlʌɪb(ə)l/ **A** *n* **1** [u] (defamation) سَبّ وقَذْف, تَشْهير **2** (statement) سَبّ (سُباب), تَشْهير, قَذْف **B** *vt* (**-ll-** BrE, **-l-** AmE) قَذَفَ (i; قَذْف), شَهَّرَ (ب) ‹*a politician, witness*›

libellous (BrE), **libelous** (AmE) /ˈlʌɪbələs/ *adj* ‹*allegation, article*› تَشْهيريّ

liberal /ˈlɪb(ə)rəl/ **A** *adj* **1** (tolerant) ‹*ideas, interpretation*› مُتَحَرِّر, تَحَرُّريّ **2** (generous) ‹*amount, supply*› سَخيّ (أَسْخِياءُ), كَريم (كِرام, كُرَماءُ) **3** (**Liberal**) (in politics) لِيبِراليّ **B** *n* **1** (a tolerant person) مُتَحَرِّر, تَحَرُّريّ **2** (**Liberal**) (in politics) لِيبِراليّ

liberal arts *n* فُنون مُتَحَرِّرة \ حُرّة \ لِيبِراليّة

Liberal Democrat *n* (BrE) عُضْو في الحِزْبِ اللِيبِراليّ الديمُقْراطيِّ

liberalism /ˈlɪb(ə)rəlɪz(ə)m/ *n* **1** لِيبِراليّة **2** لِيبِراليّة, الاقْتِصاد الحُرّ

liberalization, **-isation** (BrE) /lɪbrəlʌɪˈzeɪʃ(ə)n/ *n* تَحْرير

liberalize, **-ise** (BrE) /ˈlɪb(ə)rəlʌɪz/ *vt* حَرَّرَ ‹*trade, a market*›

liberally /ˈlɪb(ə)rəli/ *adv* **1** (generously) ‹*to donate*› بِسَخاءٍ, بِكَرَمٍ; ‹*sprinkle*› بِكَثْرةٍ **2** (not literally) ‹*to translate, interpret*› بِشَكْلٍ غَيْرِ حَرْفيٍّ

liberal studies *n* (BrE) دِراسات لِيبِراليّة

liberate /ˈlɪbəreɪt/ *vt* أَعْتَقَ, حَرَّرَ ‹*a prisoner, country*›

liberation /lɪbəˈreɪʃ(ə)n/ *n* تَحْرير

Liberia /lʌɪˈbɪərɪə/ *pr n* لِيبيريا

Liberian /lʌɪˈbɪərɪən/ *n, adj* لِيبيريّ

libertarian /ˌlɪbəˈtɛːrɪən/ *n, adj* تَحَرُّريّ

liberty /ˈlɪbəti/ *n* (*pl* **liberties**) حُرِّيّة; **we are not at ~ to discuss that** لا نَمْلِكُ مُطْلَقَ الحُرِّيّةِ في مُناقَشةِ هذا الأَمْرِ; **may I take the ~ of giving you an invitation?** هل لي أنْ أَسْمَحَ لِنَفْسي بِإِعْطائِكُم دَعْوةً؟

libido /lɪˈbiːdəʊ/ *n* رَغْبة جِنْسيّة, شَبَق, شَهْوة جِنْسيّة

Libra /ˈliːbrə/ *n* **1** (sign) بُرْج الميزانِ **2** (person) شَخْص من بُرْجِ الميزانِ

librarian /lʌɪˈbrɛːrɪən/ *n* أَمين مَكْتَبةٍ

library /ˈlʌɪbrəri/ *n* (*pl* **libraries**) مَكْتَبة (مَكْتَبات); **the public ~** المَكْتَبة العامّة

libretto /lɪˈbretəʊ/ *n* (*pl* **libretti** or **librettos**) نَصّ أوبِرا \ أوبِراليّ

Libya /ˈlɪbɪə/ *pr n* ليبْيا

Libyan /ˈlɪbiən/ *n, adj* ليبيّ

lice /lʌɪs/ *n pl* قَمْل; ▸ **louse**

licence (BrE), **license** (AmE) /ˈlʌɪs(ə)ns/ *n* 1 (a document) رُخْصة (رُخَص); **an import/export ~** رُخْصة اسْتيرادٍ \ تَصْديرٍ; **a television ~** رُخْصة تِلِفِزْيون 2 (fml) (freedom) [u] حُرِّيّة; **artistic/poetic ~** حُرِّيّة فَنِّيّة \ شِعْرِيّة

license /ˈlʌɪs(ə)ns/ A *n* (AmE) ▸ **licence**

B *vt* رَخَّصَ ‹*the software, casino*›; **this certificate ~s him to handle dangerous drugs** تُرَخِّصُ لَهُ هذه الشَهادةُ التَعامُلَ مع العَقاقيرِ الخَطِرةِ

licensed /ˈlʌɪs(ə)nst/ *adj* 1 (permitted under licence) ‹*copy, firearm*› مُرَخَّص 2 (in UK: to sell alcohol) ‹*premises, restaurant*› مُرَخَّص لَهُ بَيْعُ الخُمورِ

licensed practical nurse *n* (AmE) مُمَرِّضة حاصِلة على شَهادةٍ مُعْتَمَدةٍ

licensee /lʌɪs(ə)nˈsiː/ *n* صاحِب رُخْصةٍ

license plate *n* (AmE) لَوْحة أَرْقامِ سَيّارةٍ

licensing laws /ˈlʌɪs(ə)nsɪŋ lɔːz/ *n pl* (BrE) قَوانين تَرْخيصِ بَيْعِ الخُمورِ

licensor /ˈlʌɪs(ə)nsə/ *n* مانِح التَرْخيصِ, مُرَخِّص

licentious /lʌɪˈsɛnʃəs/ *adj* (fml) ‹*behaviour, lifestyle*› مُنْحَلّ, خَليع, ماجِن (مَواجِنُ)

lichen /ˈlʌɪk(ə)n/ *n* أُشْنة (نَبات)

lick /lɪk/ A *vt* 1 لَعِقَ (a; لَعْق), لَحِسَ (a; لَحْس) ‹*a spoon, the ice cream, a stamp*›; **the cat was ~ing its paws** كانَ القِطُّ يَلْعَقُ مَخالِبَهُ; **he ~ed his lips** أَظْهَرَ تَلَهُّفاً 2 (infml) (in games, competitions) سَحَقَ (a; سَحْق) ‹*an opponent, a team*›; **we got ~ed** سُحِقْنا; **we've finally ~ed the problem!** أَخيراً أَنْهَيْنا المُشْكِلةَ

B *n* 1 (with one's tongue) لَعْقة; **to give sth a ~** لَعِقَ شَيْئاً 2 (infml) (of paint) **to give sth a ~ of paint** غَطّى شَيْئاً بِطَبَقةٍ من الطِلاءِ

(Idiom) **to lick sb's boots** (infml) لَعِقَ حِذاءَ شَخْصٍ

licorice (AmE) ▸ **liquorice**

lid /lɪd/ *n* 1 (of a box, jar) غِطاء (أَغْطِية) 2 ▸ **eyelid**

(Idioms) **to blow the lid off sth** (infml) كَشَفَ سِرَّ شَيْءٍ; **to keep the lid on sth** (infml) أَبْقى شَيْئاً سِرّاً

lie /lʌɪ/ A *vt* (*present participle* **lying**; *past tense, past participle* **lied**) **she ~d her way out of trouble** اخْتَلَقَتْ أَكاذيبَ لِلخُروجِ من المُشْكِلةِ

B *vi* 1 (*present participle* **lying**; *past tense, past participle* **lied**) (to tell untruths) كَذَبَ (i; كَذِب, كِذْب); **she ~d to her father about her fiancé** كَذَبَتْ على والِدِها بِخُصوصِ خَطيبِها

2 (*present participle* **lying**; *past tense* **lay**; *past participle* **lain**) (to be horizontal) «people, horses, boats»; **to ~ on one's back/front** رَقَدَ \ اسْتَلْقى على ظَهْرِهِ \ بَطْنِهِ; **to ~ face down** اِسْتَلْقى \ انْبَطَحَ على وَجْهِهِ; **the boat was lying on its side** كانَ القارِبُ مُلْقًى على جانِبِهِ; **don't ~ in the sun too long** لا تَرْقُدْ في الشَمْسِ لِفَتْرةٍ طَويلةٍ; **she lay perfectly still** رَقَدَتْ ساكِنةً تَماماً; **he lay dead** رَقَدَ مَيِّتاً; **here ~s John Brown** هُنا يَرْقُدُ جون بْراوْن 3 (*present participle* **lying**; *past tense* **lay**; *past participle* **lain**) (to be situated) وَقَعَ (a; وُقوع); **the documents lay all over the floor** تَبَعْثَرَت الوَثائِقُ على الأَرْضِيّةِ; **a bright future ~s before you** يَنْتَظِرُكَ مُسْتَقْبَلٌ مُشْرِقٌ; **who knows what ~s ahead for them?** مَنْ يَعْلَمُ ماذا يَنْتَظِرُهُمْ؟; **my horse was lying fifth/in fifth place** كانَ حِصاني في المَرْكَزِ الخامِسِ

4 (*present participle* **lying**; *past tense* **lay**; *past participle* **lain**) (to remain) ظَلَّ (a; ظَلّ, ظُلول; perf ظَلِلْتُ), بَقِيَ (a; بَقاء); **the letter lay on the doormat** بَقِيَ الخِطابُ على مِمْسَحةِ الأَحْذِيةِ; **the factory was lying idle** ظَلَّ المَصْنَعُ مُعَطَّلاً

5 (*present participle* **lying**; *past tense* **lay**; *past participle* **lain**) (fml) (to exist, be found) وَقَعَ (a; وُقوع), كَمَنَ (u; كُمون); **their interests ~ elsewhere** تَكْمُنُ مَصالِحُهُمْ في مَوْضِعٍ آخَرَ; **the fault/secret ~s in the design** يَكْمُنُ الخَطَأُ \ السِرُّ في التَصْميمِ; **the responsibility ~s with the management** تَقَعُ المَسْؤولِيّةُ على عاتِقِ الإِدارةِ; **what lay behind that sudden decision?** ماذا كانَ وراءَ ذلك القَرارِ المُفاجِئِ؟ 6 (*present participle* **lying**; *past tense* **lay**; *past participle* **lain**) «snow» تَراكَمَ; **the snow is/is not lying** يَتَراكَمُ \ لا يَتَراكَمُ الثَلْجُ; **dust lay thick on the furniture** تَرَسَّبَتْ طَبَقةٌ سَميكةٌ من الغُبارِ على الأَثاثِ

[C] *n* كِذْبة, أُكْذوبة (أَكاذيبُ); **to tell a ~** كَذَبَ (i; كِذْب, كَذِب)
▸wait

(Idioms) **to lie low** مَكَثَ بَعيداً عن الأَنْظارِ; **to live a lie** عاشَ كِذْبةً; **to take sth lying down** تَقَبَّلَ شَيْئاً بِاسْتِكانةٍ

(Phrasal verbs) **lie about ▸lie around**

• **lie around** [A] [1] «clothes, papers, toys» تَبَعْثَرَ, تَناثَرَ; **to leave things lying around** تَرَكَ الأَشْياءَ مُبَعْثَرةً [2] «holidaymakers, children, animals» مَكَثَ في, رَقَدَ مُتَكاسِلاً [B] **~ around [sth]** ‹*the house, garden*› [شَيْءٍ] مُتَكاسِلاً

• **lie back** (to recline) أَسْنَدَ ظَهْرَهُ; **she lay back on the pillow** أَسْنَدَتْ ظَهْرَها على الوِسادةِ

• **lie down** (to recover) أَخَذَ قِسْطاً من الراحةِ; (to sleep) نامَ (a; نَوْم, نِيام); **I need to ~ down** أَحْتاجُ إلى الراحةِ

• **lie in** (in bed) بَقِيَ في الفِراشِ

lie detector *n* جِهاز كَشْفِ الكَذِبِ

lie-in /ˈlʌɪɪn/ *n* بَقاء في الفِراشِ; **to have a ~** بَقِيَ في الفِراشِ

lien /ˈliːən/ *n* حَقّ الحَجْزِ

lieu /ljuː/ [A] **(in lieu)** *adv phr* في المُقابِلِ [B] **(in lieu of)** *prep phr* عِوَضاً عن, بَدَلاً من; **they gave him two days off in ~ of payment** أَعْطوهُ يَوْمَيْنِ عُطْلةً بَدَلاً من الدَفْعِ

lieutenant /lɛfˈtɛnənt/ *n* [1] (Mil) (UK army; UK, US navy) مُلازِم أَوَّل; **to promote sb to [the rank of] ~** رَقّى شَخْصاً إلى رُتْبةِ مُلازِمٍ أَوَّلٍ; **a ~ in the army/navy** مُلازِم أَوَّل في الجَيْشِ \ البَحْرِيّةِ [2] (US police) مُلازِم; **a ~ in the police/FBI** مُلازِم في الشُرْطةِ \ مَكْتَبِ التَحْقيقاتِ الفيدراليِّ; **to make sb a ~** رَقّى شَخْصاً إلى رُتْبةِ مُلازِمٍ [3] (assistant) مُساعِد; **Sherlock Holmes' faithful ~, Dr Watson** الدُكْتور واتْسون, المُساعِد الأَمين لِشِرْلوك هولْمِز; **the gang leader entered, flanked by his ~s** دَخَلَ زَعيمُ العِصابةِ مُحاطاً بِرِجالِهِ

lieutenant colonel *n* مُقَدَّم

lieutenant general *n* فَريق

life /lʌɪf/ *n* (*pl* **lives**) [1] (being alive) حَياة (حَيَوات); **it's a matter of ~ and death** هِيَ مَسْأَلةُ حَياةٍ أو مَوْتٍ; **to bring sb back to ~** أَعادَ شَخْصاً إلى الحَياةِ; **to have a love of ~** أَحَبَّ الحَياةَ; **to take one's own ~** اِنْتَحَرَ; **that's ~!** هذه هي الحَياةُ!; **is there ~ on Mars?** هل هُناكَ حَياةٌ على المَرّيخِ؟ [2] (period from birth to death) حَياة (حَيَوات); **throughout his ~** طوالَ حَياتِهِ; **in early/later ~** في أَوائِلِ \ أَواخِرِ العُمْرِ; **the first time in my ~** أَوَّلَ مَرّةٍ في حَياتي; **the ~ and times of Mikhail Gorbachev** حَياة ميخائيل جورْباتْشوف وَعَصْرُهُ [3] (vitality) حَيَوِيّة; **she was full of ~** كانَتْ مَليئةً بالحَيَوِيّةِ; **there's not much ~ in this town** لَيْسَ هُناكَ الكَثيرُ من وَسائِلِ التَرْفيهِ في هذه المَدينةِ; **to come to ~** «characters, parties» دَبَّتْ فيهِ الحَياةُ; **to bring a subject to ~** جَعَلَ مَوْضوعاً مُشَوِّقاً [4] (lifestyle) حَياة (حَيَوات); **my private ~** حَياتي الخاصّة; **his way of ~** أُسْلوب حَياتِهِ; **a ~ of crime** حَياة جَريمةٍ; **to live the good** *or* **high ~** عاشَ حَياةَ التَرَفِ; **it's no ~ for a child** لا تُعْتَبَرُ هذه حَياةً مَقْبولةً بالنِسْبةِ لِطِفْلٍ [5] (living being) روح (mf; أَرْواح); **it sank with the loss of 500 lives** غَرِقَ وَأَدّى إلى وَفاةِ 500 شَخْصٍ; **it crashed without loss of ~** تَحَطَّمَ دون خَسارةٍ في الأَرْواحِ [6] (of machines, vehicles, products) عُمْر (أَعْمار), مُدّة الصَلاحِيّةِ [7] (in sentencing) **to sentence a criminal to ~** حَكَمَ على مُجْرِمٍ بالسَجْنِ المُؤَبَّدِ \ مَدى الحَياةِ; **to serve ~** قَضى عُقوبةَ السَجْنِ المُؤَبَّدِ; **to get ~** (infml) حُكِمَ عَلَيْهِ بالسَجْنِ المُؤَبَّدِ \ مَدى الحَياةِ

(Idioms) **for dear life** (infml) تَشَبُّثاً بالحَياةِ; **get a life!** (infml) [اِشْغَلْ حَياتَكَ بِشَيْءٍ ذي قيمةٍ!]; **this is the life!** [هذه هي الحَياةُ المُمْتِعةُ!]; **to have the time of one's life** عاشَ أَسْعَدَ أَيّامِ حَياتِهِ

lifebelt /ˈlʌɪfbɛlt/ *n* (in rescues) طَوْق نَجاةٍ

lifeboat /ˈlʌɪfbəʊt/ *n* (on the shore) زَوْرَق إنْقاذٍ; (on a ship) قارِب نَجاةٍ

lifebuoy /ˈlʌɪfbɔɪ/ *n* عَوّامة إنْقاذٍ

life cycle *n* دَوْرة حَياةٍ

life drawing *n* [1] [u] (activity) رَسْم الطَبيعةِ [2] (drawing produced) لَوْحة لِمَنْظَرٍ من الطَبيعةِ

life expectancy *n* [1] (of a living thing) مُتَوسِّط العُمْرِ المُتَوَقَّع [2] (of a product) عُمْر افْتِراضيّ

lifeguard /ˈlʌɪfgɑːd/ *n* حارِس إنْقاذٍ; **he is a ~** يَعْمَلُ حارِسَ إنْقاذٍ

life imprisonment *n* سَجْن مَدى الحَياةِ

life insurance, **life assurance** *n* تأمين على الحَياةِ

life jacket *n* (in rescues) سُتْرة نَجاةٍ

lifeless /ˈlʌɪfləs/ *adj* ‹*body, desert*› بِلا حَياةٍ, لا حَياةَ فيهِ

lifelike /ˈlʌɪflʌɪk/ *adj* ‹*portrait, doll*› يُضاهي الحَقيقةَ

lifeline /ˈlʌɪflʌɪn/ *n* (in rescues) حَبْل نَجاةٍ \ إنْقاذٍ; (support) شُرْيان حَياةٍ

lifelong /ˈlʌɪflɒŋ/ *adj* ‹*learning*› مُسْتَمِرّ \ دائِم مَدى الحَياةِ; ‹*friend*› العُمْرِ

life membership *n* عُضْويّة مَدى الحَياةِ

life preserver, **life vest** *n* سُتْرة نَجاةٍ

life raft *n* قارِب نَجاةٍ

lifesaver /ˈlʌɪfseɪvə/ *n* **1** (a lifeguard) حارِس إنْقاذٍ **2** (great help) مُنْقِذ للحَياةِ; **penicillin was literally a ~** كانَ البِنْسِلين سَبَباً في إنْقاذِ الأَرْواحِ بِمَعْنى الكَلِمةِ

life-saving /ˈlʌɪfseɪvɪŋ/ **A** *n* إنْقاذ الغَرْقى **B** *adj* ‹*drugs, treatment*› مُنْقِذ للحَياةِ

life sentence *n* عُقوبة السَجْنِ مَدى الحَياةِ

life-size /ˈlʌɪfsʌɪz/ *adj* ‹*statue, replica*› بالحَجْمِ الطَبيعيِّ

lifespan /ˈlʌɪfspan/ *n* عُمْر (أَعْمار), فَتْرة حَياةٍ \ مُدّة

life story *n* قِصّة حَياةٍ

lifestyle /ˈlʌɪfstʌɪl/ *n* أُسْلوب \ نَمَط حَياةٍ

life-support machine /ˈlʌɪfsəˌpɔːt məʃiːn/ *n* جِهاز تَنَفُّسٍ صِناعيٍّ; **on a ~** على جِهازِ تَنَفُّسٍ صِناعيٍّ

life-threatening /ˈlʌɪfˌθret(ə)nɪŋ/ *adj* ‹*injury, condition*› مُهَدِّد للحَياةِ

lifetime /ˈlʌɪftʌɪm/ *n* عُمْر (أَعْمار); **the chance of a ~** فُرْصة العُمْرِ; **a ~ guarantee** ضَمان مَدى الحَياةِ

lift /lɪft/ **A** *vt* **1** (to pick up) رَفَعَ (a; رَفْع) ‹*a suitcase, box, child*›; **he ~ed the bag onto the table/the child out of the buggy** رَفَعَ الحَقيبةَ على الطاوِلةِ \ أَخْرَجَ الطِفْلَ من العَرَبةِ; **she ~ed the spoon to her lips** رَفَعَت المِلْعَقة إلى فَمِها; **I feel as if a weight has been ~ed from my shoulders** أَشْعُرُ كَما لو أنّ حِمْلاً قد انْزاحَ من على كَتِفَيَّ **2** (to boost) **to ~ sb's spirits** رَفَعَ الروحَ المَعْنَويّةَ لِشَخْصٍ; **the national team's win ~ed the country's spirits** رَفَعَ فَوْزُ الفَريقِ الوَطَنيِّ الروحَ المَعْنَويّةَ للبَلَدِ **3** (infml) (to steal) سَرَقَ (i; سَرِقة) ‹*a file, key, sb's wallet*› **4** (in cosmetic surgery) **to have one's face ~ed** أَجْرى عَمَليّةَ شَدٍّ لِوَجْهِهِ

B *vi* **1** (to improve) «one's mood» حَسَّنَ; «headache» خَفَّفَ **2** (to clear) «the fog, mist» أَزالَ **3** (to rise) «the lid, trapdoor» رَفَعَ (a; رَفْع)

C *n* **1** (BrE) (in a building) مِصْعَد (مَصاعِدُ); **to take the lift to the fifth floor** أَخَذَ المِصْعَدَ إلى الطابَقِ الخامِسِ **2** (in a car) **to give sb a ~ to the station** وَصَّلَ شَخْصاً إلى المَحَطّةِ **3** (infml) (boost) دَفْعة (دَفَعات); **the news gave us all a ~** أَعْطَتْنا الأَخْبارُ دَفْعةً **4** [u] (for flight) قوّة رَفْعٍ

(Phrasal verbs) **lift down**: **~ [sb/sth] down, ~ down [sb/sth]** أَنْزَلَ [شَخْصاً \ شَيْئاً] ‹*a box, jar, child*›

• **lift off** **A** **1** «the top, cover» انْفَكَّ, انْفَصَلَ **2** «rockets» انْطَلَقَ **B** **~ [sth] off, ~ off [sth]** رَفَعَ [شَيْئاً] ‹*a cover, lid*›

• **lift up** **A** (to rise) «curtains, lid» ارْتَفَعَ **B** **~ [sb/sth] up, ~ up [sb/sth]** **1** رَفَعَ [شَخْصاً \ شَيْئاً] ‹*a box, suitcase, child*› **2** رَفَعَ [شَيْئاً] ‹*one's head, gaze*›

lift-off /ˈlɪftɒf/ *n* انْطِلاق (صاروخٍ)

lift-operator /ˈlɪftˌɒpəreɪtə/ *n* (BrE) عامِل مِصْعَدٍ

ligament /ˈlɪgəmənt/ *n* رِباط (أَرْبِطة)

ligature /ˈlɪgətʃə/ *n* **1** (tie) رِباط (أَرْبِطة), ضِمادة **2** (of letters) حَرْف مُزْدَوِج (الرَبْط بين حَرْفَيْنِ في الطِباعةِ)

light /lʌɪt/ **A** *n* **1** (brightness) ضَوْء (أَضْواء), نور (أَنْوار); **by the ~ of the fire/moon** على ضَوْءِ النارِ \ القَمَرِ; **in the ~ of day** في نورِ النَهارِ; **I'd like to get back in the ~** أَوَدُّ أنْ أَعودَ قبلَ حُلولِ الظَلامِ; **to throw** *or* **shed ~ on sth** أَلْقى الضَوْءَ على شَيْءٍ; **to hold sth up to the ~** وَضَعَ شَيْئاً في الضَوْءِ; **with the ~ behind her** والضَوْءُ من وَرائِها **2** (in a building) مِصْباح (مَصابيحُ), لَمْبة; (in the street, on a machine) إشارة; **to put** *or* **switch** *or* **turn a ~ on** أَوْقَدَ النورَ; **to put** *or* **switch** *or* **turn a ~ off** أَطْفَأَ النورَ; **to leave a ~ on** تَرَكَ نوراً موقَداً; **are all the ~s off?** هل أُطْفِئَتْ كُلُّ الأَنْوارِ؟ **3** (on an instrument panel) مِصْباح أَماميّ **4** (Aut) (headlight) نور (أَنْوار), ضَوْء (أَضْواء) (tail light) مِصْباح خَلْفيّ **5** (flame) **have you got a ~?** هل لَدَيْكَ قَدّاحةٌ؟; **to set ~ to sth** أَوْقَدَ شَيْئاً; **to put a ~ to sth**

أَضْرَمَ النارَ في شَيْءٍ **6** (aspect) جانِب (جَوانِبُ), زاوية (زَوايا); **to see sth in a different ~** رَأى شَيْئاً من زاوِيةٍ مُخْتَلِفةٍ; **we reviewed the case in the ~ of new evidence** راجَعْنا القَضيّةَ في ضَوْءِ أَدِلّةٍ جديدةٍ; **to appear in a bad ~** ظَهَرَ في صورةٍ سَيِّئةٍ **7** (public knowledge) **to bring a crime/fact to ~** كَشَفَ النِقابَ عن جَريمةٍ \ حَقيقةٍ; **the details came to ~ a year later** ظَهَرَت التَفاصيلُ بعد عام

B (**lights**) *n pl* **1** (also **traffic lights**) إشارات المُرورِ; **the ~s were red/green** كانَت الإشارةُ حَمْراءَ \ خَضْراءَ; **to jump the ~s** خَرَقَ الإشارةَ **2** (decorative illuminations) ضَوْء زينةٍ

C *vt* (*past tense, past participle* **lit** or (old use) **lighted**) **1** (to set fire to) أَوْقَدَ *‹a candle, cigarette, the oven›*; أَشْعَلَ النارَ في *‹the wood, paper, a firework›*; أَشْعَلَ *‹a match›*; **to ~ a fire** أَوْقَدَ ناراً **2** (to illuminate) أَضاءَ *‹a corridor, room, path›*; **to ~ the way for sb** أَضاءَ الطَريقَ لِشَخْصٍ

D *vi* (*past tense, past participle* **lit** or (old use) **lighted**) «the fire, gas, matches» أوقَدَ

E *adj* **1** (bright) *‹evening, room›* مُضيء, مُنير; **the sky got** *or* **grew ~er** كانَ النورُ يَزْدادُ في السَماءِ; **we will leave as soon as it gets ~** سَنُغادِرُ بِمُجَرَّدِ أنْ يَطْلُعَ الصُبْحُ; **it's still ~** ما زالَ النَهارُ باقِياً **2** (pale) *‹colour, fabric, hair›* فاتِح; **~ blue/grey** أَزْرَق \ رَماديّ فاتِح **3** (not heavy) *‹box, rain›* خَفيف; **she is 8 kg ~er** هي أَخَفُّ ب 8 كجم; **to be a ~ sleeper** كانَ نَوْمُهُ خَفيفاً; **to have a ~ meal** تَناوَلَ وَجْبةً خَفيفةً **4** (not severe) *‹damage, sentence›* بَسيط, خَفيف **5** (delicate) *‹knock, touch›* خَفيف; **to be ~ on one's feet** كانَ خَفيفَ الحَرَكةِ **6** (not tiring) *‹work, exercise›* خَفيف; **to be on ~ duties** كانَتْ عِنْدَهُ واجِباتٌ خَفيفةٌ; **to make ~ work of sth** سَهَّلَ شَيْئاً **7** (not intellectually demanding) *‹music, film›* خَفيف; **a bit of ~ relief** بَعْض من التَرْفيهِ; **some ~ reading on the beach** بَعْض القراءة الخَفيفة على الشاطِئِ **8** (trivial) **it is no ~ matter** لَيْسَ هذا أَمْراً تافِهاً; **to make ~ of a rumour/injury** اسْتَهانَ بإشاعةٍ \ بإصابةٍ **9** (Culin) (low-fat) *‹margarine, cheese, spread›* قَليل الدَسَمِ

Idiom **to see the light** (to understand) اتَّضَحَ لَهُ الأَمْرُ; (to appear) «stories, books, cars» خَرَجَ إلى النورِ

Phrasal verbs **light on**: **~ on [sth]** لَمَحَ (a; لَمْح) *‹a detail, name, key›*

• **light up** (infml) **A** **1** (to light a cigarette) أَشْعَلَ سيجارةً; (to light a pipe) أَشْعَلَ غَلْيوناً **2** «lamps, street lights» اشْتَعَلَ **3** «sb's face, eyes» أَشْرَقَ **B** **~ up [sth]**, **~ [sth] up** **1** أَشْعَلَ [شَيْئاً] *‹a cigarette, pipe›* **2** (to illuminate) أَضاءَ [شَيْئاً] *‹a room, town, the surroundings›*

light bulb *n* مِصْباح كَهْرَبائيّ, لَمْبة

light-emitting diode /ˌlʌɪtəˌmɪtɪŋ ˈdʌɪəʊd/ *n* دايود باعِث للضَوْءِ

lighten /ˈlʌɪt(ə)n/ **A** *vt* **1** أَنارَ, أَضاءَ *‹the sky, room›* **2** خَفَّفَ *‹the load, burden›* **3** خَفَّفَ *‹the mood, atmosphere›*

B *vi* **1** «the sky, room» سَطَعَ (a; سُطوع), تَأَلَّقَ **2** «the workload» تَخَفَّفَ **3** «the atmosphere, her face» انْقَشَعَ, صَفا (u; صَفْو, صَفاء)

Phrasal verb **lighten up**: **~ up** انْشَرَحَ

lighter /ˈlʌɪtə/ *n* قَدّاحة, وَلّاعة

lighter fuel *n* وَقود الوَلّاعاتِ

light-fingered /ˌlʌɪtˈfɪŋɡəd/ *adj* *‹thief, pickpocket›* طَويل اليَدِ

light-hearted /lʌɪtˈhɑːtɪd/ *adj* *‹remark, atmosphere›* خالي البالِ, خالٍ من الهُمومِ

lighthouse /ˈlʌɪthaʊs/ *n* مَنارة (مَناوِرُ), فَنار (فَنارات)

lighting /ˈlʌɪtɪŋ/ *n* (in the streets) إنارة; (in the theatre, etc.) إضاءة

lightly /ˈlʌɪtli/ *adv* **1** (not violently) *‹to touch, knock›* بِرِقّةٍ, بِلُطْفٍ **2** (not copiously) *‹to snow, rain›* قَليلاً **3** *‹to fry, brown›* بِخِفّةٍ, بَعْضَ الشَيْءِ, قَليلاً **4** (lightheartedly) *‹to undertake, dismiss›* بِاسْتِخْفافٍ **5** **to get off/be let off ~** لم يَأْخُذْ ما يَسْتَحِقُّهُ من العِقابِ

lightning /ˈlʌɪtnɪŋ/ **A** *n* بَرْق (بُروق); **a flash of ~** وَميض بَرْقٍ, صاعِقة (صَواعِقُ); **to be struck by ~** صَعَقَهُ البَرْقُ

B *adj before n* *‹visit, raid›* بِسُرْعةِ البَرْقِ; **the calculations were done at ~ speed** تَتِمُّ الحِساباتُ بِسُرْعةِ البَرْقِ

light switch *n* زِرّ الكَهْرَباءِ

lightweight /ˈlʌɪtweɪt/ *adj* **1** *‹jacket, suit›* خَفيف الوَزْنِ **2** *‹champion, crew›* الوَزْنِ الخَفيفِ

light year *n* سَنة ضَوْئيّة

like¹ /laɪk/ **A** *prep* **1** (in the same way as) كَ ,مِثْلَ; **he acted ~ a professional** تَصَرَّفَ كَمُحْتَرِفٍ; **it happened ~ this** حَدَثَ على هذا النَحْوِ; **~ the liar that she is, she ...** وَلِأَنَّ الكَذِبَ طَبْعٌ فيها، فَهِيَ ...; **when I see things ~ that** عِنْدَما أرى أَشْياءَ كَهَذِهِ **2** (similar to) مِثْلَ; **what's she ~?** كَيفَ تَبْدو؟; **what's it ~?** كيف هو؟; **what was the weather ~?** كيف كانَ الطَقْسُ؟; **to be ~ sb/sth** كانَ مِثْلَ شَخْصٍ \ شَيْءٍ; **he's ~ his father** هو مِثْلُ والِدِهِ; **there's nothing ~ a coffee ice cream!** لا شَيْءَ يُضاهي الآيس كْريم بِنَكْهَةِ القَهْوَةِ!; **I've never seen anything ~ it!** لم أَرَ شَيْئاً مِثْلَهُ من قَبْلُ!; **I don't earn anything ~ as much as she does** دَخْلي لا يُضاهي دَخْلَها لا من قَريبٍ وَلا من بَعيدٍ **3** (typical of) **it's just ~ him to forget** من عادَتِهِ أَنْ يَنْسى; **it's not ~ her to be late** لَيْسَ من عادَتِها أَنْ تَتَأَخَّرَ **4** (expressing probability) **it looks ~ rain** يَبْدو أَنَّها سَتُمْطِرُ; **it looks ~ the war will be a long one** يَبْدو أَنَّ الحَرْبَ سَتَكونُ طَويلَةً **5** (close to, akin to) **it cost something ~ $400** كانَ ثَمَنُهُ يُقارِبُ 400 دولار

B *conj* **1** (infml) (as) كَما; **~ I said, I wasn't there** كَما قُلْتُ، لم أَكُنْ هُناكَ; **they don't write songs ~ they used to** لا يَكْتُبونَ الأَغانيَ كَما اعْتادوا أَنْ يَفْعَلوا **2** (infml) (as if) كَما لو; **he acts ~ he owns the place** يَتَصَرَّفُ كَما لو أَنَّهُ يَمْتَلِكُ المَكانَ

C *n* **1** (equivalent) **I've never seen the ~ of it** لم أَرَ مِثْلَهُ من قَبْلُ; **she won't even speak to the ~s of us!** (infml) هي لا تَرْغَبُ حتّى في التَحَدُّثِ مع أَشْخاصٍ مِثْلِنا! **2** (preference) **we were asked to list our ~s and dislikes** طُلِبَ مِنّا أَنْ نَكْتُبَ قائِمَةً بِالأَشْياءِ الّتي نُحِبُّها والأَشْياءِ الّتي لا نُحِبُّها

D *adj* (fml) مُتَشابِه; **to be of ~ mind** كانوا مُتَشابِهينَ في التَفْكيرِ

E (-like); *in combination* **a bird-~ appetite** شَهِيّة ضَعيفة; **a child-~ trust** ثِقة طُفوليّة

F *adv* (nearly) **it's nothing ~ as nice as their previous house** لَيْسَ جَميلاً كَمَنْزِلِهِم السابِقِ على الإِطْلاقِ

like² /laɪk/ *vt* **1** (to get on well with) أَحَبَّ, أُعْجِبَ ب <a person>; **I ~ Paul/Sandra** يُعْجِبُني بول \ تُعْجِبُني ساندرا; **to ~ Arthur best** أَحَبَّ آرْثَر أَكْثَرَ من الجَميعِ; **to ~ Arthur better than Bradley** أَحَبَّ آرْثَر أَكْثَرَ من بْرادْلي; **she's nice, and I ~ her** هي لَطيفَةٌ، وَأَنا مُعْجَبٌ بِها **2** (to find to one's taste) أَحَبَّ, أُعْجِبَ ب <an artist, food, music>; **she ~s Picasso/Woody Allen** تُحِبُّ بيكاسو \ وودي آلان; **how do you ~ your tea?** كيف تُحِبُّ شايَكَ؟; **I ~ my coffee strong** أُحِبُّ قَهْوَتي مُرَكَّزَةً; **we ~ goats' cheese/salsa** نُحِبُّ جُبْنَ الماعِزِ \ الصَلْصَةَ; **to ~ sth better than sth else** أَحَبَّ شَيْئاً أَكْثَرَ من شَيْءٍ آخَرَ; **to ~ sth best** أَحَبَّ شَيْئاً أَكْثَرَ من أَيِّ شَيْءٍ آخَرَ; **what I ~ about him/this car is ...** ما يُعْجِبُني فيهِ \ في هذه السَيّارَةِ هو ...; **we ~ the look of the house** يُعْجِبُنا مَنْظَرُ البَيْتِ; **I don't ~ the look of that man** لا يُعْجِبُني مَنْظَرُ ذلك الرَجُلِ; **I don't ~ the sound of that** لا يُعْجِبُني هذا الكَلامُ; **tomatoes ~ plenty of water** تَحْتاجُ الطَماطِمُ إلى الكَثيرِ من الماءِ **3** (to enjoy) أَحَبَّ <sports, reading, chess>; **how do you ~ your new job?** هل تُحِبُّ وَظيفَتَكَ الجَديدَةَ؟; **how do you ~ living in New York?** هل تُحِبُّ الحَياةَ في نيويورْك؟; **I ~ swimming and tennis** أُحِبُّ السِباحَةَ والتِنِس; **I ~ to play football/bridge** أُحِبُّ أَنْ أَلْعَبَ كُرَةَ القَدَمِ \ البْريدْج **4** (to approve of) أَحَبَّ, أُعْجِبَ ب; (on facebook) أُعْجِبَ ب; **the boss ~s your sales plan** المُديرُ مُعْجَبٌ بِخُطّةِ مَبيعاتِكَ; **I don't ~ your attitude** لا يُعْجِبُني أُسْلوبُكَ في التَعامُلِ; **I ~ to keep fit** أُحِبُّ أَنْ أُحافِظَ على لِياقَتي; **she doesn't ~ to be kept waiting** لا تُحِبُّ الانْتِظارَ; **~ it or not we all pay tax** سَواءٌ أَعْجَبَكَ أم لا كُلُّنا نَدْفَعُ الضَرائِبَ **5** (in requests, wishes) أَحَبَّ, وَدَّ (وِدّ, وَدّ; a); **I would *or* should ~ a ticket to ...** من فَضْلِكَ أُريدُ تَذْكِرَةً إلى ...; **would you ~ to come to dinner?** هل تُحِبُّ أَنْ تَأْتِيَ للعَشاءِ؟; **would you ~ me to come now?** هل تُريدُني أَنْ آتِيَ الآنَ؟; **I would *or* should not ~ to disturb her** لا أُريدُ أَنْ أُزْعِجَها **6** (to want) أَرادَ; **you can do what you ~** يُمْكِنُكَ أَنْ تَفْعَلَ ما تُريدُ; **sit anywhere you ~** اِجْلِسْ أَيْنَما تُريدُ; **say what you ~, I think it's a good idea** قُلْ ما تُريدُ، وَلَكِنّي أَعْتَقِدُ أَنَّها فِكْرَةٌ جَيِّدَةٌ; **where did the money come from, that's what I'd ~ to know** من أَيْنَ أَتى المالُ، ذلك ما أُريدُ أَنْ أَعْرِفَ; **he's a bit of a rebel if you ~** هو مُتَمَرِّدٌ بَعْضَ الشَيْءِ إذا جازَ التَعْبيرُ

likeable, likable /ˈlaɪkəb(ə)l/ *adj* <character, guy> خَفيف الظِلِّ, أَنيس, حُلو المَعْشَر

likelihood /ˈlaɪklihʊd/ *n* أَرْجَحِيّة, اِحْتِمال (اِحْتِمالات) إِمْكانيّة; **in all ~, they will lose the match** على الأَرْجَحِ سَيَخْسَرونَ المُباراةَ; **what is the ~ of a win?** ما هو اِحْتِمالُ الفَوْزِ؟

likely /ˈlaɪkli/ *adj* (**likelier**, **likeliest**) **1** (probable) ‹*explanation, outcome*› مُحْتَمَل, مُرَجَّح; **prices are ~ to rise** من المُرَجَّحِ أنْ تَرْتَفِعَ الأَسْعارُ; **the most ~ explanation is …** التَفْسيرُ الأَكْثَرُ اِحْتِمالاً هو …; **it is/seems ~ that she'll come** من المُرَجَّحِ أنْ تَأْتِيَ **2** (promising) ‹*candidate, target*› مُناسِب

like-minded /laɪkˈmaɪndɪd/ *adj* ‹*people, colleagues*› مُتَشابِه في التَفْكيرِ

liken /ˈlaɪk(ə)n/ *vt* شَبَّهَ ‹*a situation, politician*›; **he ~ed the flood to the tsunami** شَبَّهَ الطوفانَ بالتْسونامي

likeness /ˈlaɪknəs/ *n* **1** (similarity) شَبَه (أَشْباه), تَشابُه; **there is a strong family ~** هُناكَ تَشابُهٌ عائِليٌّ قَوِيٌّ **2** (of a picture) **to be a good ~ of sb** كانَ صورةً شَبيهةً تماماً لِشَخْصٍ

likewise /ˈlaɪkwaɪz/ *adv* ‹*to do, think*› كَذَلِكَ

liking /ˈlaɪkɪŋ/ *n* مَيْل (مُيول), حُبّ; **he took a ~ to her** بَدَأَ يُحِبُّها; **he has a ~ for fast cars** يُحِبُّ السَيّاراتِ السَريعةَ; **is the soup to your ~?** هل الحَساءُ كما تُحِبُّ؟

lilac /ˈlaɪlək/ **A** *n* **1** (the plant) لَيْلَج **2** (the colour) لَيْلَكِيّ (أُرْجُوانيّ فاتِح)

B *adj* ‹*dress, curtain*› لَيْلَكِيّ (أُرْجُوانيّ فاتِح)

lilt /lɪlt/ *n* (of a tune) لَحْن (أَلْحان); (of a voice) لُكْنة; **she spoke with a distinctive Welsh ~** تَكَلَّمَتْ بِلُكْنةٍ ويلزيّةٍ مُمَيَّزةٍ

lilting /ˈlɪltɪŋ/ *adj* ‹*accent, melody*› رَخيم

lily /ˈlɪli/ *n* (*pl* **lilies**) زَنْبَق (n coll; زَنابِق)

lily of the valley *n* زَنْبَق الوادي

limb /lɪm/ *n* **1** (arm, leg) طَرَف الجِسْم **2** (of a tree) غُصْن (غُصون, أَغْصان)

(Idioms) **to be out on a limb** [كانَ لَهُ رَأْيٌ شاذٌّ]; **to go out on a limb** [خاطَرَ بِإِبْداءِ رَأْيٍ مُخْتَلَفٍ عَلَيْهِ]; **to risk life and limb** خاطَرَ بِحَياتِهِ; **to tear sb limb from limb** مَزَّقَ شَخْصاً إِرْباً إِرْباً

limber up /ˈlɪmbə/ *vi* «runners, athletes» أَحْمى العَضَلاتِ

limbo /ˈlɪmbəʊ/ *n* **1** يَمْبوس (مَوْطِن أَرْواحِ الصالِحينَ قبل مَجيءِ المَسيحِ) **2** (uncertainty) عَدَم يَقينٍ; **to be in ~** كانَ في حالةٍ من عَدَمِ اليَقينِ

lime /laɪm/ *n* **1** [u] (calcium) جير جَيّ **2** (citrus) لَيْمون حامِض; **~ juice** عَصير لَيْمونٍ حامِضٍ **3** (also **lime tree**) (linden) زَيْزَفون

lime green **A** *n* [لَوْن أَخْضَر مائِل إلى الصُفْرةِ];

B *adj* ‹*dress, curtain*› [أَخْضَر مائِل إلى الصُفْرةِ]

limelight /ˈlaɪmlaɪt/ *n* **to be in the ~** كانَ مَحَطَّ الأَنْظارِ

limerick /ˈlɪmərɪk/ *n* [قَصيدة هَزْلِيّة من خَمْسةِ أَبْياتٍ]

limestone /ˈlaɪmstəʊn/ *n* حَجَر جير

limit /ˈlɪmɪt/ **A** *n* **1** (boundary) حَدّ (حُدود); **there were no ~s to their hospitality** لم يَكُنْ هُناكَ حَدٌّ لِكَرَمِهِمْ; **within the ~s of what we can do** في حُدودِ ما يُمْكِنُنا فِعْلُهُ; **to push sb to the ~** ضَغَطَ على شَخْصٍ إلى أَقْصى حَدٍّ مُمْكِنٍ **2** **to be off ~s to sb** كانَ خارِجَ النِطاقِ المَسْموحِ بِهِ لِشَخْصٍ **3** (legal restriction) حَدّ (حُدود); **to be over the ~** (of alcohol) كانَتْ نِسْبةُ الكُحولِ لَدَيْهِ فوق الحَدِّ القانونيِّ

B *vt* (to restrict) حَدَّ (u; حَدّ; من), حَصَرَ (i-u; حَصْر), قَيَّدَ ‹*imports, sb's actions, movements*›; **the number of places is ~ed to 60** عَدَدُ الأَماكِنِ مَحْدودٌ ب 60; **to ~ the use of guns** حَدَّ من اسْتِخْدامِ الأَسْلِحةِ

C *v refl* **to ~ oneself to sth** قَصَرَ نَفْسَهُ على شَيْءٍ ‹*an amount, a quantity*›

limitation /lɪmɪˈteɪʃ(ə)n/ *n* **1** (restriction) تَحْديد (تَحْديدات), حَصْر, تَقْييد (تَقْييدات) **2** (shortcoming) عَجْز, قُصور; **to know one's ~s** عَرَفَ مَواطِنَ ضَعْفِهِ

limited /ˈlɪmɪtɪd/ *adj* **1** (restricted) ‹*space, menu, resources*› مَحْدود, مُقَيَّد; **there is a ~ choice of seats** هُناكَ خِيارٌ مَحْدودٌ من المَقاعِدِ **2** (below par) ‹*vocabulary, ambition*› مَحْدود; **a student of ~ ability** طالِب ذو قُدْرةٍ مَحْدودةٍ **3** (in company law) **Nolan Computers Limited** شَرِكة 'نولان للحَواسيبِ' المَحْدودة

limited company *n* (BrE) شَرِكة مَحْدودة

limitless /ˈlɪmɪtləs/ *adj* ‹*possibility, supply*› لا حَدَّ لَهُ, غَيْر مَحْدودٍ

limo /ˈlɪməʊ/ *n* (infml) ليموزين; **a stretch ~** ليموزين طَويل

limousine /ˈlɪməziːn/ *n* ليموزين

limp /lɪmp/ **A** *vi* «patients» عَرَجَ (a-u; عَرَج, عَرَجان)

B *n* عَرَج; **to have a ~** عَرَجَ (a-u; عَرَج, عَرَجان)

C *adj* **1** ‹*body, handshake*› ضَعيف ,لَيِّن ,رَخْو; **her body went ~** ضَعُفَ جَسَدُها **2** ‹*lettuce*› (ذُبُل) ذابِل

limpet /ˈlɪmpɪt/ *n* بِطْلينوس

limpet mine *n* [لَغَم يُلْصَقُ بِسَفينةٍ لِتَفْجيرها في مُدَّةٍ مُحَدَّدَةٍ]

linchpin /ˈlɪntʃpɪn/ *n* (مَحاوِرُ) مِحْوَر

linden, **linden tree** /ˈlɪnd(ə)n/ *n* زَيْزَفون

line /lʌɪn/ **A** *n* **1** (made with a pen, pencil, etc) خَطّ (خُطوط); **a straight/curved ~** خَطّ مُسْتَقيم \ مُنْحَنٍ; **he put a ~ through the word/the calculations** شَطَبَ على الكَلِمةِ \ الحِساباتِ; **the ~ AB** (in geometry) الخَطّ أ ب **2** (of people, cars) صَفّ (صُفوف), (طَوابيرُ) طابور; (of trees) صَفّ (صُفوف); **to sit in straight ~s** جَلَسوا في صُفوفٍ مُسْتَقيمةٍ; **put the desks in ~** ضَع المَكاتِبَ في صَفٍّ **3** (expressing suitability) **to be in ~ for promotion** كانَ عَلَيْهِ الدَوْرُ في التَرْقِيةِ **4** (AmE) (of customers, passengers) صَفّ (صُفوف), (طَوابيرُ) طابور; **to stand** *or* **wait in ~** وَقَفَ أو انْتَظَرَ في الصَفِّ; **to form a ~** شَكَّلَ صَفًّا **5** (on the face) (تَجاعيدُ) تَجْعيد **6** (shape) مُخَطَّط (مُخَطَّطات), (تَصاميمُ ,تَصْميمات) تَصْميم **7** (boundary) حَدّ (حُدود), خَطّ فاصِل; **there's a fine ~ between knowledge and pedantry** هُناكَ خَطٌّ دَقيقٌ يَفْصِلُ بين المَعْرِفةِ والحَذْلَقةِ **8** (rope) (حِبال) حَبْل; (for fishing) (خيطان ,خُيوط) خَيْط; **to put the washing on the ~** وَضَعَ الغَسيلَ على الحَبْلِ **9** (Elec) (cable) (أَسْلاك) سِلْك **10** (Tel) (connection) خَطّ (خُطوط); **it's a very bad ~** هو خَطٌّ سَيِّئٌ جِدًّا; **to be on the ~ to sb** كانَ على الخَطِّ مع شَخْصٍ; **the ~ went dead** تَوَقَّفَ الخَطُّ **11** (route) (خُطوط) خَطّ, (mf; طُرُق) طَريق **12** (track, rails) (خُطوط) خَطّ **13** (in genealogy) (سَلاسِلُ) سِلْسِلة, سُلالة; **the male/female ~** سِلْسِلةُ الذُكورِ \ الإناثِ; **to trace one's ~ back to sb** تَعَقَّبَ نَسْلَهُ حتّى شَخْصٍ; **she is second in ~ to the throne** هي الثانِيةُ في تَرْتيبِ وِلايةِ العَرْشِ **14** (in prose) (of music) (أَسْطُر ,سُطور) سَطْر; (in poetry) (أَبْيات) بَيْت; **a ~ from Shakespeare** بَيْت من شِعْرِ شِكْسْبير; **he has all the best ~s** جَرَتْ على لِسانِهِ أَفْضَلُ العِباراتِ; **to learn one's ~s** (Theat) حَفِظَ دَوْرَهُ **15** (conformity) **to fall into ~ with the rest of the group/the demands of the leadership** كانَ مُتَوافِقاً مع باقي المَجْموعةِ \ مُتَطَلَّباتِ القِيادةِ; **we need to bring our legislation into ~ with the rest of Europe** نَحْنُ بِحاجةٍ لِجَعْلِ تَشْريعِنا مُتَماشِياً مع بَقيّةِ أوروبّا; **to keep sb in ~** أَلْزَمَ شَخْصاً حَدَّهُ **16** (infml) **you're way out of ~!** (infml) تَجاوَزْتَ الحَدَّ! (piece of information) **to have a ~ on sb/sth** كانَ لَدَيْهِ مَعْلومةٌ عن شَخْصٍ \ شَيْءٍ; **don't give me that ~!** لا تَقُصَّ عَلَيَّ هذه الأُكْذوبةَ! **17** (stance) (مَواقِفُ) مَوْقِف; **the official ~** المَوْقِف الرَسْميّ; **to take a firm ~ with sb** اتَّخَذَ مَوْقِفاً حازِماً مع شَخْصٍ; **to be on the right ~s** كانَ على المَسارِ الصَحيحِ **18** (Busn) (type of product) (خُطوط) خَطّ **19** (Mil) **behind enemy ~s** خَلْفَ خُطوطِ العَدوِّ **20** (infml) (of cocaine) خَطّ (خُطوط)

B (**in line with**) *prep phr* بما يَتَناسَبُ مع ‹*a policy, trend, requirement*›; **to increase in ~ with inflation** زادَ بما يَتَناسَبُ مع التَضَخُّمِ

C *vt* **1** (to add a layer to) بَطَّنَ ‹*a dress, box, nest*› **2** (to stand along) اصْطَفَّ على ‹*a route*›

(Idioms) **something along those lines** شَيْء من هذا القَبيلِ; **somewhere along the line** لاحِقاً عند نُقْطةٍ ما; **to be on the line** كانَ مُعَرَّضاً للخَطَرِ; **to put sth on the line** عَرَّضَ شَيْئاً للخَطَرِ; **to sign on the dotted line** وَقَّعَ بالمُوافَقةِ

(Phrasal verb) **line up** **A** **1** (to stand side by side) وَقَفَ جَنْباً إلى جَنْب; (one behind the other) وَقَفَ في طابورٍ **2** (in a competition, dispute) **to ~ up against sb** (Pol) «unions, nations» عارَضَ شَخْصاً; (Sport) «players, teams» لَعِبَ ضدّ شَخْصٍ **B** **~ up [sb]**, **~ [sb] up** (side by side) وَضَعَ [شَخْصاً] في صَفٍّ; (one behind the other) وَضَعَ [شَخْصاً] في طابورٍ **C** **~ [sth] up**, **~ up [sth]** **1** (to align) حاذى [شَيْئاً]; **to ~ sth up with a building/post** وَضَعَ شَيْئاً في مُحاذاةِ مَبْنًى \ عمودٍ **2** (to organize) **to have sb/sth ~d up** ‹*work, an activity, a band*› أَعَدَّ \ رَتَّبَ [شَيْئاً]; **what have you got ~d up for us tonight?** ماذا أَعْدَدْتَ لَنا اللَيْلةَ؟

lineage /ˈlɪnɪɪdʒ/ *n* (أَنْساب) نَسَب, سُلالة

linear /ˈlɪnɪə/ *adj* ‹*progression, narrative*› خَطِّيّ

lined /lʌɪnd/ *adj* **1** ‹*paper, notebook*› مُسَطَّر **2** ‹*face, skin*› مُجَعَّد **3** ‹*jacket, curtains*› مُبَطَّن; **these boots are ~ with fur** هذا الحِذاءُ مُبَطَّنٌ بالفَرْوِ

line judge *n* مُراقِب الخَطِّ

lineman /ˈlʌɪnmən/ *n* (*pl* **-men**) 1 (electrical worker) [ميكانيكيّ الشَّبَكةِ الكَهْرَبائيّةِ] 2 (telephone company worker) [ميكانيكيّ الشَّبَكةِ الهاتِفيّةِ] 3 (AmE) (football player) [لاعِب أماميّ في كُرةِ القَدَمِ الأَمْريكيّةِ]

line manager *n* مُدير خطِّ إنْتاجٍ

linen /ˈlɪnɪn/ *n* 1 (fabric) كَتّان 2 (bedding, etc) بَيّاضات, مُلاءات

linen basket *n* سَلّة غَسيلٍ

linen cupboard (BrE), **linen closet** (AmE) *n* خِزانة بَيّاضاتٍ

liner /ˈlʌɪnə/ *n* 1 (ship) سَفينة رُكّابٍ (تَعْمَلُ على خَطٍّ مِلاحيٍّ مُنْتَظِمٍ) 2 (lining) بِطانة (بِطانات); **a nappy ~** بِطانة حِفاظةٍ; **a (dust) bin ~** كيس قُمامةٍ

linesman /ˈlʌɪnzmən/ *n* (*pl* **-men**) (BrE) مُراقِب, مُساعِد حَكَمِ خُطوطٍ

line-up /ˈlʌɪnʌp/ *n* 1 (of participants) تَشْكيلة, رَتَل (أَرْتال), 2 (of suspects) صَفّ (صُفوف) طابور المُشْتَبَهِ بِهِمْ; **a police ~** طابور المُشْتَبَهِ بِهِمْ

linger /ˈlɪŋgə/ *vi* 1 (to delay) «guests, stragglers» تَلَكَّأَ, تَوانى; **we ~ed over coffee** مَكَثْنا وَقْتاً طَويلاً نَتَناوَلُ القَهْوةَ; **a smile still ~ed on his lips** كانَتْ هُناكَ ابْتِسامةٌ لا تَزالُ باقِيةً على شَفَتَيْهِ 2 (to remain) «memories, smells» بَقِيَ عالِقاً; **I have a ~ing doubt** لَدَيَّ شَكٌّ عالِقٌ في ذِهْني

lingerie /ˈlandʒ(ə)ri/ *n* مَلابِس داخِليّة للنساءِ

linguist /ˈlɪŋgwɪst/ *n* لُغَويّ

linguistic /lɪŋˈgwɪstɪk/ *adj* ‹ability, skill› لُغَويّ

linguistics /lɪŋˈgwɪstɪks/ *n* لِسانيّات, عِلْم اللُغة, لُغَويّات

lining /ˈlʌɪnɪŋ/ *n* بِطانة (بِطانات); **this coat has a fur ~** هذا المِعْطَفُ بِهِ بِطانةٌ من الفِراءِ

link /lɪŋk/ **A** *n* 1 (in a chain) حَلْقة (حَلَقات, حَلَق); **you need to find the weakest ~** يَجِبُ أنْ تَعْثُرَ على الحَلَقةِ الأَضْعَفِ 2 (by rail, road, air) رَبْط 3 (between facts, events) رابِط; **the missing ~** الحَلَقة المَفْقودة 4 (in business, politics) رابِط (رَوابِطُ); **the historical ~s between Qatar and India** الرَوابِط التاريخيّة بين قَطَرَ والهِنْدِ; **to have ~s with** *or* **to extremist groups** كانَ لَهُ صِلاتٌ بِجَماعاتٍ مُتَطَرِّفةٍ 5 (on a web page) رابِط (رَوابِطُ) 6 (in broadcasting) رَبْط

B *vt* 1 (to connect) «roads, tunnels, flights» رَبَطَ (i-u; رَبْط) ‹places, cities, countries›; **the causeway that ~s Bahrain and** *or* **with** *or* **to Saudi Arabia** الجِسْر الّذي يَرْبُطُ بين البَحْرَيْنِ والسَعوديّةِ; **to ~ arms with sb** شَبَّكَ \ وَضَعَ ذِراعَهُ في ذِراعِ شَخْصٍ 2 (to make connections between) **to ~ sth to** *or* **with sth** رَبَطَ \ وَصَّلَ شَيْئاً بِشَيْءٍ; **to ~ high wages with inflation** رَبَطَ ما بين الأُجورِ المُرْتَفِعةِ والتَضَخُّمِ الماليِّ; **their names have been ~ed** تَمَّ الرَبْطُ بين أَسْمائِهِمْ 3 (in broadcasting) رَبَطَ (i-u; رَبْط), أَقامَ خَطَّ اتِّصالٍ بين ‹studios, cities› 4 (in networks) وَصَّلَ ‹terminals, computers›

Phrasal verb **link up** «companies, schools, organizations» أَقامَ رَوابِطَ; **to ~ up with sb/sth** أَقامَ رَوابِطَ مع شَخْصٍ \ شَيْءٍ

linkage /ˈlɪŋkɪdʒ/ *n* صِلة, ارْتِباط (ارْتِباطات)

link road *n* طَريق رابِط (بين مِنْطَقَتَيْنِ أو شارِعَيْنِ)

links /lɪŋks/ *n* + *sing or pl vb* (**links**, *pl*) مَلْعَب غولْف (مُحاذٍ للشاطِئِ)

link-up /ˈlɪŋkʌp/ *n* 1 (on TV, radio) رَبْط 2 (collaboration) ارْتِباط (ارْتِباطات)

linnet /ˈlɪnɪt/ *n* طائِر \ عُصْفور تُفّاحيّ

lino /ˈlʌɪnəʊ/ *n* مُشَمَّع (لِفَرْشِ الأَرْضيّاتِ)

linoleum /lɪˈnəʊlɪəm/ *n* مُشَمَّع (لِفَرْشِ الأَرْضيّاتِ)

linseed /ˈlɪnsiːd/ *n* بَذْرة كَتّانٍ

lint /lɪnt/ *n* 1 (dressing) ضِمادة (ضِمادات) 2 (AmE) (fluff) نُسالة (أَوْبار), وَبَر

lion /ˈlʌɪən/ *n* أَسَد (أُسود), لَيْث (لُيوث)

Idiom **the lion's share** نَصيب \ حِصّة الأَسَدِ

lion cub *n* شِبْل (أَشْبال)

lioness /ˈlʌɪənɛs/ *n* لَبُؤة

lion tamer *n* مُرَوِّض الأُسودِ

lip /lɪp/ *n* 1 (of mouth) شَفة (شِفاه) 2 (of a jug) حافّة

lip gloss *n* مُلَمِّع الشِفاهِ

lipid /ˈlɪpɪd/ *n* دُهْن

liposuction /ˈlɪpəʊsʌkʃ(ə)n/ *n* شَفْط الدُهونِ

lip-read /ˈlɪpriːd/ *vt, vi* (*past tense, past participle* **lip-read** /ˈlɪpred/) قَرَأَ حَرَكاتِ الشِفاهِ

lipsalve /ˈlɪpsalv/ *n* مُرَطِّب \ بَلْسَم \ مَرْهَم الشِفاهِ

lip service *n* **to pay ~ to the rules/feminism** تَشَدَّقَ بالكَلامِ عن القَوانينِ \ الحَرَكةِ النِسْويّةِ

lipstick /ˈlɪpstɪk/ *n* أَحْمَر شِفاهٍ

liquefy /ˈlɪkwɪfʌɪ/ **A** *vt* (**liquefies**, **liquefying**, **liquefied**) أَسالَ, سَيَّلَ ‹*a gas, solid*›

B *vi* «gases, solids» سالَ (i; سَيْل ,سَيَلان), تَحَوَّلَ إلى سائِلٍ

liqueur /lɪˈkjʊə/ *n* ليكور (مَشْروب كُحوليّ مُحَلّى)

liquid /ˈlɪkwɪd/ **A** *n* سائِل (سَوائِل)

B *adj before n* **1** ‹*nitrogen, soap*› سائِل **2** ‹*assets*› سائِل

liquidate /ˈlɪkwɪdeɪt/ *vt* **1** ‹*an asset, a holding*› سَيَّلَ **2** ‹*a partnership, business*› صَفَّى **3** ‹*an opponent, the opposition*› قَضَى, صَفَّى (i; قَضاء على)

liquidation /lɪkwɪˈdeɪʃ(ə)n/ *n* تَصْفِية; **the company has gone into ~** تَمَّ تَصْفِيةُ الشَرِكةِ

liquidator /ˈlɪkwɪdeɪtə/ *n* مَأمور تَصْفِيةٍ, مُصَفٍّ

liquid crystal display *n* عَرْض بِلَّوْرِيّ سائِل

liquidity /lɪˈkwɪdɪti/ *n* سُيولة

liquidize, -ise (BrE) /ˈlɪkwɪdʌɪz/ *vt* (BrE) هَرَسَ (u; هَرْس) ‹*the fruit, vegetables*›

liquidizer, -iser (BrE) /ˈlɪkwɪdʌɪzə/ *n* (BrE) خَلّاط

liquor /ˈlɪkə/ *n* مَشْروب روحيّ \ كُحوليّ

liquorice, licorice (AmE) /ˈlɪkərɪs/ *n* **1** (consumable) عِرْقسوس **2** (plant) عِرْق السوس, عِرْقسوس

liquor store *n* (AmE) مَتْجَر خُمور

Lisbon /ˈlɪzb(ə)n/ *pr n* لِشْبونة

lisp /lɪsp/ *n* لُثْغة; **to speak with a ~** نَطَقَ بِلُثْغةٍ

list /lɪst/ **A** *n* **1** (of names, products, places) قائِمة (قَوائِمُ), كَشْف (كُشوف), قائِمات; **to be at the top of the ~** كانَ في أَعْلى القائِمةِ; **to be high/low on one's ~ of priorities** كانَ في أَعْلى \ أَسْفَلِ قائِمةِ أَوْلَويّاتِه; **to put sb/sth on a ~** وَضَعَ شَخْصاً \ شَيْئاً على قائِمةٍ; ▸**checklist**, ▸**price list**, ▸**waiting list** **2** (of a ship) مَيَلان, مَيْل

B *vt* **1** ‹*names, products, places*› أَضافَ إلى \ وَضَعَ في قائِمةٍ; **it will be ~ed under "Various"** سَتُضافُ تحت فِئة 'مُتَنوِّعاتٍ'; **~ them in alphabetical order/order of size** ضَعْهُمْ في قائِمةٍ مُرَتَّبةٍ تَرْتيباً أَبْجَديًّا \ حَسَبَ الحَجْمِ **2** **to be ~ed on a stock exchange** كانَ مُدْرَجاً \ مُسَجَّلاً في سوقِ الأَوْراقِ الماليّةِ

C *vi* «the ship» مالَ (i; مَيْل, مَيَلان)

D (**listed**) *adj* **1** (Fin) ‹*company*› مُسَجَّل, مُدْرَج **2** (BrE Archit) ‹*building*› مُسَجَّل ضِمْنَ الآثارِ

listen /ˈlɪs(ə)n/ *vi* **1** (to hear) «animals, people» اِسْتَمَعَ, أَنْصَتَ; **to ~ to music/the speech** اِسْتَمَعَ إلى الموسيقى \ الخِطابِ **2** (to take notice) أَصْغى, اِسْتَمَعَ; **to ~ to reason** اِسْتَمَعَ إلى صَوْتِ العَقْلِ

Phrasal verb **listen in** تَصَنَّتَ, تَنَصَّتَ

listener /ˈlɪs(ə)nə/ *n* **1** (to the radio) مُسْتَمِع **2** (in conversation) مُسْتَمِع

listeria /lɪˈstɪərɪə/ *n* لِيسْتيرِيا (بَكْتيريا)

listing /ˈlɪstɪŋ/ **A** *n* (on a stock exchange) تَسْجيل, إِدْراج

B (**listings**) *n pl* جَداوِل البَرامِجِ

listless /ˈlɪstləs/ *adj* ‹*performance*› مُتَراخٍ, فاتِر

list price *n* سِعْر التَجْزِئةِ المُقْتَرَح, سِعْر القائِمةِ

lit /lɪt/ **A** *past tense, past participle* ▸**light**

B *abbr* (infml) = **literature** أَدَب (آداب)

litany /ˈlɪt(ə)ni/ *n* (*pl* **litanies**) **1** (in a religious service) إِفْشين (أَفاشينُ) **2** (of complaints) قائِمة طَويلة

lite /lʌɪt/ *adj* (infml) **1** (low in alcohol) خَفيف ‹*beer*›; (in calories) يَحْتَوي على سُعْراتٍ حَراريّةٍ مُنْخَفِضةٍ ‹*cream, energy drinks*›

2 *after n* (undemanding) مُخَفَّف ‹*jazz, tragedy*›

liter (AmE) *n* ▸**litre**

literacy /ˈlɪt(ə)rəsi/ *n* مَعْرِفة القِراءةِ والكِتابةِ

literal /ˈlɪt(ə)rəl/ *adj* ‹*meaning, translation*› حَرْفيّ

literally /ˈlɪt(ə)rəli/ *adv* ‹*to mean, to translate*› حَرْفيًّا; **to take sth ~** فَهِمَ شَيْئاً فَهْماً حَرْفيًّا

literary /ˈlɪt(ə)rəri/ *adj* ‹*prize, talent*› أَدَبيّ; **his style is very ~** أُسْلوبُهُ أَدَبيٌّ جِدًّا

literary agent *n* وَكيل أَدَبيّ \ نَشْرٍ

literary criticism *n* نَقْد أَدَبِيّ

literate /ˈlɪt(ə)rət/ *adj* ❶ (able to read and write) **to be ~** كانَ يَسْتَطِيعُ القِراءةَ والكِتابةَ ❷ (cultured) ‹*person, readership*› مُثَقَّف

literature /ˈlɪt(ə)rətʃə/ *n* ❶ أَدَب (آداب) ❷ (promotional material) مَنْشورات إعْلانيّة; **read the sales ~** اقْرَأ المَنْشوراتِ الإعْلانيّةَ

lithe /lʌɪð/ *adj* (**lither**, **lithest**) ‹*body*› مَرِن; ‹*dancer*› رَشِيق (رُشَقاءُ)

lithograph /ˈlɪθəgrɑːf/ **A** *n* صورة مَطْبوعة بالطِباعةِ الحَجَرِيّةِ] **B** *vt* طَبَعَ طِباعةً حَجَرِيّةً

Lithuania /ˌlɪθjuːˈeɪnɪə/ *pr n* لِيتُوانِيا

Lithuanian /lɪθjuːˈeɪnɪən/ **A** *adj* ‹*ambassador, border, food*› لِيتُوانِيّ

B *n* ❶ (citizen) لِيتُوانِيّ ❷ (language) (اللُغة) اللِيتُوانيّة

litigant /ˈlɪtɪg(ə)nt/ *n* مُتَقاضٍ

litigation /lɪtɪˈgeɪʃ(ə)n/ *n* تَقاضٍ

litmus /ˈlɪtməs/ *n* صِبْغة عَبّادِ الشَمْسِ

litmus test *n* ❶ (pointer) فاصِل \ اخْتِبار حاسِم ❷ (Chem) [اخْتِبار الحُموضةِ بواسِطةِ وَرَقِ عَبّادِ الشَمْسِ]

litre (BrE), **liter** (AmE) /ˈliːtə/ *n* لِتْر (لِتْرات)

litter /ˈlɪtə/ **A** *n* ❶ (rubbish) نُفايات, قُمامة (قُمامات, قُمام) ❷ (of animals) [مَجْموعة حَيواناتٍ تولَدُ في بَطْنٍ واحِدٍ] ❸ (for pet tray) [مادّة ماصّة يُفْرَشُ بها صُنْدوقُ فَضَلاتٍ]

B *vt* تَناثَرَ, تَبَعْثَرَ (في) ‹*a room, street*›; **the floor was ~ed with books** تَناثَرَت \ تَبَعْثَرت الكُتُبُ على الأَرْضِ

litter bin *n* وِعاء القُمامةِ

litterbug /ˈlɪtəbʌg/, **litter lout** (BrE) *n* (pej) [شَخْص يُلْقي \ يَرْمي القاذوراتِ في الأَماكِنِ العامّةِ]

little /ˈlɪt(ə)l/ **A** *adj* (*comparative* **smaller**, *superlative* **smallest**)

❶ (small) ‹*house, cat, child*› صَغير (صِغار, صُغَراءُ); **they have a ~ cottage by the sea** عِنْدَهُم كوخٌ صَغيرٌ بالقُرْبِ من البَحْرِ

❷ (young) ‹*brother, sister, boy*› صَغير (صِغار, صُغَراءُ); **my ~ brother/sister** أَخي الصَغير \ أُخْتي الصَغيرة; **when I was ~** عِنْدَما كُنْتُ صَغيراً ❸ (pej) (expressing scorn) صَغير (صِغار, صُغَراءُ), تافِه (تَوافِهُ); **what a silly ~ man!** يا لَهُ من رَجُلٍ تافِهٍ سَخيفٍ! ❹ (short) ‹*rest, walk*› قَصير; **we took a ~ break** أَخَذْنا اسْتِراحةً قَصيرةً

B *determiner* (*comparative* **less**, *superlative* **least**) **~ chance** فُرْصة ضَئيلة; **there's so ~ time** الوَقْتُ ضَيِّقٌ جِدًّا; **too ~ money** مال قَليل جِدًّا; **~ or no influence** نُفوذ قَليل أو مَعْدوم; **I have ~ time for reading** لَيْسَ لَدَيَّ وَقْتٌ كَثيرٌ للقِراءةِ

C *pron* **I only ate a ~** لم آكُلْ إلاّ القَليلَ; **I did what ~ I could** فَعَلْتُ القَليلَ الّذي كانَ بوُسْعي عَمَلُهُ; **he remembers very ~** لم يَتَذَكَّرْ إلاّ القَليلَ; **there's ~ I can do** لَيْسَ هُناكَ الكَثيرُ الّذي يُمْكِنُني فِعْلُهُ; **age has ~ to do with it** الأَمْرُ لا يَتَعَلَّقُ بالسِنِّ; **to do as ~ as possible** فَعَلَ أَقَلَّ ما يُمْكِنُ فِعْلُهُ

D *adv* ❶ (not much, rarely) ‹*to say, sleep, eat*› قَليلاً; **I go there very ~** لا أَذْهَبُ هُناكَ إلّا قَليلاً جِدًّا; **the next results were ~ better** كانَت النَتائِجُ التالِيةُ أَحْسَنَ قَليلاً; **~ more than an hour ago** منذ أَكْثَرَ من ساعةٍ بقَليلٍ; **a ~-known novel** رواية غَيْر مَعْروفةٍ \ مَشْهورةٍ ❷ (fml) (not at all) **~ did she realize that the watch was stolen** لم تُلاحِظْ أنّ الساعةَ سُرِقَتْ ❸ (**a little (bit)**) (slightly) قَليلاً; **a ~ less/more** أَقَلّ \ أَكْثَر قَليلاً; **stay a ~ longer** ابْقَ مَعَنا أَكْثَرَ; **she felt a ~ bit anxious** شَعَرَت بقَليلٍ من التَوَتُّرِ

(Idioms) **as little as** ما لا يَزيدُ عن; **for as ~ as $10 a day** مُقابِلَ ما لا يَزيدُ عن $10 في اليَوْمِ; **it can cost as ~ as £60** قد لا يَزيدُ ثَمَنُهُ عن £60; **little by little** شَيْئاً فَشَيْئاً, رُوَيْداً رُوَيْداً; **he's recovering ~ by ~** يَتَعافى تَدْريجيًّا \ شَيْئاً فَشَيْئاً

little finger *n* خِنْصِر (خَناصِرُ)

live¹ /lɪv/ **A** *vt* عاشَ (i; عَيْش, عيشة) ‹*one's life*›; **to ~ a normal/eventful life** عاشَ حَياةً عادِيّةً \ مَليئةً بالأَحْداثِ; **to ~ a life of luxury** عاشَ حَياةً مُتْرَفةً

B *vi* ❶ (to reside) سَكَنَ (u; سَكَن); **they ~ in Tripoli/at number 7** يَسْكُنونَ في طَرابُلُسَ \ المَنْزِلِ رَقْم 7; **to ~ together** عاشا مَعاً (دون زَواج); **have you found somewhere to ~?** هل وَجَدْتَ سَكَناً؟ ❷ (to lead one's life) عاشَ (i; عَيْش, عيشة); **they ~ in poverty** يَعيشونَ في فَقْرٍ; **we ~ in the computer age** نَعيشُ في عَصْرِ الحاسوبِ; **to ~ for one's work/family** عاشَ من أَجْلِ عَمَلِهِ \ أُسْرَتِهِ; **to ~ through a difficult period** مَرَّ بفَتْرةٍ صَعْبةٍ ❸ (to survive) عاشَ (i; عَيْش, عيشة); **to ~ to be eighty** عاشَ لِسِنِّ الثَمانينَ; **his grandfather is still living** ما زالَ جَدُّهُ حَيًّا \ على قَيْدِ الحَياةِ; **I'll never forget you as long**

as I ~ لن أنساكَ طالَما حَييتُ; he will ~ to regret sth سَيَنْدَمُ يَوْماً على شَيْءٍ; long ~ democracy! تَحْيا الديموقراطيّةُ!
4 (to subsist) عاشَ (i; عَيْش, عيشة); to ~ on fruit/a low wage عاشَ على الفاكِهة \ أَجْرٍ مُنْخَفِضٍ; to ~ off the interest/profits عاشَ على الفَوائِدِ \ الأَرْباحِ; to ~ by one's wits عاشَ على الاحْتِيالِ **5** (to put up with) to ~ with an illness/the consequences تَحَمَّلَ مَرَضاً \ التَبِعاتِ; I have to ~ with my failure يَجِبُ أَنْ أَتَعايَشَ مع فَشَلي **6** (to enjoy life) عاشَ حَياتَهُ, تَمَتَّعَ بِحَياتِهِ; you haven't ~d until you've been to Miami لن تَعيشَ حَياتَكَ بِحَقٍّ حتّى تَزورَ مَيامي

(Idioms) live and let live عِشْ ودَعْ غَيْرَكَ يَعيشُ; to live it up (infml) رَفَّهَ عن نَفْسِهِ; to live sth down مَحا ذِكْرى مُحْرِجةً من أَذْهانِ الناسِ

(Phrasal verbs) live in «carer, nannies» [أَقامَ في مَكانِ العَمَلِ]
• live on (to survive) «traditions, sb's reputation» اِسْتَمَرَّ, تَواصَلَ
• live out **A** «carer, maids» [أَقامَ في غَيْرِ مَكانِ العَمَلِ] **B** ~ out [sth] **1** (to spend) to ~ out one's days عاشَ \ قَضى آخِرَ أَيّامِهِ **2** (to enact) عاشَ (i; عَيْش, عيشة) ‹one's fantasies›
• live up to رَقِيَ لِمُسْتَوى ‹one's principles, standards, sb's expectations›

live² /lʌɪv/ **A** adj **1** (alive) ‹animal, snake› حَيّ, (أَحْياء) على قَيْدِ الحَياةِ **2** ‹broadcast, coverage› حَيّ, مُباشِر; coverage will be ~ سَتكونُ التَغْطِيةُ مُباشِرةً \ حَيّةً **3** ‹cable, wire› مُكَهْرَب
B adv ‹to appear, to broadcast› مُباشَرةً, على المُباشِرِ; the ceremony is broadcast ~ تُبَثُّ مَراسِمُ الاحْتِفالِ على المُباشِرِ

live-in /ˈlɪvɪn/ adj ‹maid, gardener› [مُقيم بالمَنْزِلِ الَّذي يَعْمَلُ فيه]; to have a ~ lover أَقامَ مع عَشيقَتِهِ

livelihood /ˈlʌɪvlɪhʊd/ n رِزْق (أَرْزاق), مَعاش (مَعاشات), مَعيشة (مَعايِش)

lively /ˈlʌɪvli/ adj (livelier, liveliest) **1** (active) ‹child, atmosphere› حَيَوِيّ, بالنَشاطِ \ مُفْعَم بالحَيَوِيّةِ **2** (animated) ‹debate, discussion› حَيَوِيّ

(Idiom) look lively! (infml) كُنْ سَريعَ \ خَفيفَ الحَرَكةِ!

liven up /ˈlʌɪv(ə)n/ **A** vi «people, parties» انْتَعَشَ
B vt to ~ sb/sth, to liven sb/sth up نَشَّطَ \ أَنْعَشَ شَخْصاً شَيْئاً ‹a person, evening›; a coat of paint would ~ the office up سَتُضْفي طَبَقةُ طِلاءٍ بَهْجةً \ مَسْحةَ جَمالٍ على المَكْتَبِ

liver /ˈlɪvə/ n كَبِد (f; كُبود, أَكْباد)

livery /ˈlɪv(ə)ri/ n (pl liveries) (uniform) بِزّة

lives /lʌɪvz/ n pl ▸ life

livestock /ˈlʌɪvstɒk/ n ماشِية (مَواشٍ)

live wire n شَخْص مُفْعَم بالحَياةِ \ بالحَيَوِيّةِ

livid /ˈlɪvɪd/ adj **1** (furious) حانِق; I was absolutely ~ كُنْتُ حانِقاً للغايةِ **2** (in colour) ‹face, scar› رَمادِيّ, مُزْرَقّ

living /ˈlɪvɪŋ/ **A** n **1** (income) مَصْدَر عَيْشٍ \ رِزْقٍ; to work for one's ~ عَمِلَ لِكَسْبِ قوتِ اليَوْمِ \ لُقْمةِ العَيْشِ; what do you do for a ~? ما مِهْنَتُكَ؟ **2** (lifestyle) حَياة
B adj ‹organism, person› حَيّ (أَحْياء), على قَيْدِ الحَياةِ

living conditions n ظُروف مَعيشيّة \ الحَياةِ

living expenses n تَكاليف \ نَفَقات المَعيشةِ

living room n غُرْفة جُلوسٍ \ مَعيشةٍ

living standards n مَعايير مَعيشيّة

living will n [وَثيقة يُخْبِرُ فيها الشَخْصُ عن اخْتِياراتِهِ في العلاجِ مُسْتَقْبَلاً]

lizard /ˈlɪzəd/ n سِحْلِيّة (سَحالٍ), عَظاية (عَظايا)

llama /ˈlɑːmə/ n لاما

LLB /ɛlɛlˈbiː/ n = Bachelor of Laws بَكالوريوس في الحُقوقِ (ME), ليسانْس في الحُقوقِ (NA)

load /ləʊd/ **A** n **1** (on trucks, planes) شَحْنة (شِحَن, شِحْنات), (on animals) حِمْل (أَحْمال), حُمولة; a ~ of firewood/scrap metal شَحْنة حَطَبٍ \ خُرْدةٍ مَعْدِنيّةٍ; a plane-load of supplies طائِرة مَليئة بالمُؤَنِ **2** (of clothes) حُمولة **3** (amount of work) عِبْء (أَعْباء), حِمْل (أَحْمال); to lighten/spread the ~ خَفَّفَ \ وَزَّعَ الحِمْلَ; to take a ~ off sb's mind رَفَعَ العِبْءَ عن كاهِلِ شَخْصٍ **4** (maximum weight) وَزْن أَقْصى, حُمولة **5** (infml) (a lot) a ~ or a whole ~ of people عَدَد كَبير من الناسِ; there's a ~ of food on the table هُناكَ الكَثيرُ من الطَعامِ على المائِدةِ
B (loads) n pl (infml) ~s of people/flowers كَثير من الناسِ \ الأَزْهارِ; we've got ~s of time لَدَيْنا الكَثيرُ من الوَقْتِ; there's ~s to eat هُناكَ الكَثيرُ من الطَعامِ

C *vt* **1** حَمَّلَ ‹*a truck, ship, donkey*›; **to ~ the truck with cement** حَمَّلَ الشاحِنةَ بالإسْمَنْت; **to ~ the luggage into the car** حَمَّلَ الأَمْتِعةَ على السَيّارةِ **2** (to prepare) حَشا (u; حَشْو) ‹*a gun*›; مَلأَ, عَبَّأَ (a; مَلْء) ‹*washing machine*› **3** حَمَّلَ ‹*a program, the operating system*›

D *vi* «lorries, ships, planes» حُمِّلَ

(Idiom) **a load of rubbish** *or* **garbage** (infml) كَلام فارِغ

(Phrasal verb) **load down**: **A** ~ **[sb] down** حَمَّلَ [شَخْصاً] بِحِمْلٍ زائِدٍ; **to be ~ed down with luggage/work** كانَ مُثْقَلاً بالأَمْتِعةِ \ بالعَمَلِ **B** ~ **[sth] down** حَمَّلَ [شَيْئاً] بِحِمْلٍ زائِدٍ ‹*a truck, car*›

loaded /ˈləʊdɪd/ *adj* **1** ‹*truck, cart*› مَشْحون, مُحَمَّل **2** ‹*gun*› مَحْشوّ; **make sure the printer is ~ with paper** تأَكَّدْ من تَحْميلِ الوَرَقِ في الطابِعةِ **3** (infml) (rich) مُمْتَلِئ الجُيوبِ, ذو مالٍ وَفيرٍ; **he can afford it, he's ~** في مَقْدورِهِ أنْ يَتَحَمَّلَ النَفَقاتِ، فَلَدَيْهِ مالٌ وَفيرٌ **4** ‹*question*› مَلْغوم

loading /ˈləʊdɪŋ/ *n* **1** (of goods) تَحْميل **2** (Fin) (in insurance) زيادة في قِسْطِ تَأْمينٍ (على إثْرِ تَفاقُمِ الخَطَرِ المُؤَمَّنِ عَلَيْهِ)

loaf /ləʊf/ *n* (*pl* **loaves**) رَغيف (أَرْغِفة); **a ~ of bread** رَغيف خُبْزٍ, خُبْزة

(Phrasal verb) **loaf about**, **loaf around** «students, bystanders» تَسَكَّعَ

loafer /ˈləʊfə/ *n* **1** (shoe) [حِذاء جِلْديّ مُسَطَّح بِدونِ رِباطٍ] **2** (idler) مُتَسَكِّع

loan /ləʊn/ **A** *n* **1** (money) قَرْض (قُروض); **a $40,000 ~/ a ~ of $40,000** قَرْض ب $40000 \ قيمَتُهُ $40000; **a ~ from the IMF** قَرْض من صُنْدوقِ النَقْدِ الدُوَليِّ **2** (temporary use) إعارة; **to be on ~** (books) قَيْدَ الاسْتِعارةِ \ الإعارةِ; (players) كانَ مُعاراً \ انْتَقَلَ على سَبيلِ الإعارة

B *vt* (also **loan out**) سَلَّفَ, أَقْرَضَ ‹*money*›; أَعارَ ‹*equipment*›; **to ~ money to sb** أَقْرَضَ \ أدانَ شَخْصاً مالاً; **to ~ money from the bank** اقْتَرَضَ مالاً \ أَخَذَ قَرْضاً من البَنْكِ

loan shark *n* (infml) مُراب [مُقْرِض بِسِعْرِ فائِدةٍ فاحِشٍ]

loath /ləʊθ/ *adj* (fml) **to be ~ to do sth** مَقَتَ أنْ يَفْعَلَ شَيْئاً

loathe /ləʊð/ *vt* (fml) مَقَتَ (u; مَقْت), تَقَزَّزَ (من), اشْمَأَزَّ (من) ‹*camping, seafood*›; **he ~s the sight of her** تَشْمَئِزُّ \ تَتَقَزَّزُ نَفْسُهُ من رُؤْيَتِها

loathsome /ˈləʊðs(ə)m/ *adj* ‹*sight, food*› بَغيض, كَريه, مُقَزِّز; **James and his ~ fiancée** جيمْس وَخَطيبَتُهُ البَغيضة, مُقْرِف

loaves /ləʊvz/ *n pl* ▸ **loaf**

lob /lɒb/ **A** *vt* **(-bb-)** **1** (to throw) رَمى (i; رَمْي, رِماية), قَذَفَ (i; قَذْف) **2** (in tennis) ضَرَبَ \ قَذَفَ الكُرَةَ على شَكْلِ [قَوْسٍ عالٍ]

B *vi* **(-bb-)** «players» سَدَّدَ كُرةً مُقَوَّسةً

C *n* (in tennis) [ضَرْبة قَوْسيّة \ مُقَوَّسة \ مَرْفوعة]

lobby /ˈlɒbi/ **A** *n* **1** (of a hotel, theatre etc.) رَدْهة (رَدَهات) **2** (pressure group) جَماعة ضَغْطٍ, لوبي

B *vi* (**lobbies**, **lobbying**, **lobbied**) «groups, people» مارَسَ ضَغْطاً (للتَأْثيرِ على قَرارٍ \ لِتَحْقيقِ مَصْلَحةٍ); **to ~ for changes in the law** مارَسَ ضَغْطاً لإِحْداثِ تَغْييراتٍ في القانونِ

lobbying /ˈlɒbiɪŋ/ *n* ضَغْط المَصْلَحة

lobbyist /ˈlɒbiɪst/ *n* [شَخْص ذو نُفوذٍ يُحاوِلُ التَأْثيرَ على السِياسيّينَ لِتَحْقيقِ مَصالِحِهِ \ في سَبيلِ قَضيّةٍ]; **she is a ~ for women's rights** هي مُناضِلةٌ ناشِطةٌ من أَجْلِ حُقوقِ المَرْأةِ

lobe /ləʊb/ *n* **1** (of the ear) شَحْمة **2** (of the brain) فَصّ (فُصوص)

lobster /ˈlɒbstə/ *n* كَرْكَنْد, سَرَطان البَحْرِ

local /ˈləʊk(ə)l/ **A** *adj* ‹*library, park, news*› مَحَلّيّ

B *n* **1** (person) ساكِن مَحَلّيّ; **the ~s** السُكّان المَحَلّيّونَ **2** (pub) حانة مَحَلّيّة

local anaesthetic (BrE), **local anesthetic** (AmE) *n* مُخَدِّر مَوْضِعيّ

local authority *n* (BrE) سُلْطة مَحَلّيّة

local call *n* مُكالَمة هاتِفيّة مَحَلّيّة

locale /ləʊˈkɑːl/ *n* مَكان (أَماكِنُ, أَمْكِنة)

local election *n* انْتِخاب مَحَلّيّ

local government *n* حُكومة \ إدارة \ سُلْطة مَحَلّيّة

locality /ləʊˈkalɪti/ *n* (*pl* **localities**) جِوار, جِهة

localization, **-isation** (BrE) /ləʊkəlʌɪˈzeɪʃ(ə)n/ *n* (Comput) تَوْطين, تَطْويع

localize, **-ise** (BrE) /ˈləʊkəlʌɪz/ *vt* **1** (to pinpoint) حَدَّدَ, عَيَّنَ ‹*the origin, tumour*› **2** (to restrict) حَدَّ (u; حَدّ; من) ‹*the damage, effect*›

localized /ˈləʊkəlʌɪzd/ *adj* 1 ‹*flooding, storms*› مُتَمَرْكِز, مُتَمَوْضِع 2 ‹*tenderness, swelling*› مَوْضِعيّ, مُتَمَوْضِع

locate /ləʊˈkeɪt/ *vt* 1 (find) [حَدَّدَ مَكانَ \ مَوْقِعَ شَيْءٍ] ‹*a file, fault*› 2 (position) وَضَعَ (a; وَضْع) ‹*a site, business*›

location /ləʊˈkeɪʃ(ə)n/ *n* 1 (place) مَوْضِع (مَواقِعُ), مَوْقِع (مَواضِعُ) 2 (Cin) [مَوْقِع تَصْويرٍ خارِجيّ \ خارِجَ الاسْتوديو]; **filmed on ~ in Italy** [صُوِّرَ في مَواقِعَ في إيطاليا]

loch /lɒk, lɒx/ *n* بُحَيْرة (بُحَيْرات)

lock /lɒk/ A *n* 1 (on a door, window) قُفْل (أَقْفال, قُفول); **to put sth under ~ and key** وَضَعَ شَيْئاً في الحِفْظِ والصَوْنِ 2 (of hair) خُصْلة (خُصُلات, خُصَل); **her curly ~s** خُصُلات شَعْرِها المُمَوَّج 3 (in canals, rivers) هَويس (أَهوِسة) 4 (in wrestling) **an arm/a leg ~** حَرَكة قَفْلِ \ تَثْبيتِ الذِراعِ \ الرِجْلِ 5 [u] (of a vehicle) دَرَجة لَفِّ عَجَلةِ القِيادةِ, قُطْر اسْتِدارةٍ; **it has a good ~** دَورانُهُ جَيِّدٌ 6 (on a file) قُفْل, تَأْمين (أَقْفال)

B *vt* 1 (with a key) قَفَلَ (i; قَفْل) ‹*a door, window, box*›; **to ~ sth in a drawer** قَفَلَ على شَيْءٍ في دُرْجٍ 2 وَضَعَ قُفْلاً على ‹*a file*›

C *vi* 1 (securely) «doors, drawers» قُفِلَ 2 (to jam) «wheels, brakes» تَوَقَّفَ عن الحَرَكةِ, عَلَّقَ

(Phrasal verbs) **lock away**: **~ [sth] away, ~ away [sth]** حَفِظَ [شَيْئاً] في مَكانٍ مَأْمونٍ

• **lock in**: **~ [sb] in** (on purpose) حَبَسَ [شَخْصاً]; (by mistake) قَفَلَ على [شَخْصٍ]

• **lock out**: **~ [sb] out** قَفَلَ البابَ مَنْعاً [لِشَخْصٍ] من الدُخولِ; **to be *or* get ~ed out** لم يَقْدِرْ على الدُخولِ بِسَبَبِ غَلْقِ البابِ

• **lock up** A قَفَلَ \ أَغْلَقَ جَميعَ الأَبْوابِ والنَوافِذِ B **~ [sth] up, ~ up [sth]** 1 وَضَعَ [شَيْئاً] في مَكانٍ مَقْفولٍ ‹*documents, jewellery*› 2 أَغْلَقَ بالمِفْتاحِ, قَفَلَ (i; قَفْل) ‹*a house, room*› C **~ [sb] up, ~ up [sb]** 1 (illegally) حَبَسَ [شَخْصاً] ‹*a hostage, captive*› 2 (to imprison) سَجَنَ [شَخْصاً] ‹*a killer, thief*›

locker /ˈlɒkə/ *n* خزانة لِحِفْظِ الأَغْراضِ الشَخْصيّةِ

locker room *n* غُرْفة تَبْديلِ المَلابِسِ (في قاعة رِياضيّةٍ)

locket /ˈlɒkɪt/ *n* دَلاّية (تَحْمِلُ صورةً بِداخِلِها)

lockout /ˈlɒkaʊt/ *n* إغْلاق تَعْجيزيّ

locksmith /ˈlɒksmɪθ/ *n* صانِع أَقْفالٍ, قَفّال

locomotive /ləʊkəˈməʊtɪv/ *n* قاطِرة

locum /ˈləʊkəm/ *n* (BrE) بَديل (بُدَلاءُ), نائِب (نُوّاب)

locus /ˈləʊkəs/ *n* (*pl* **loci**) مَحَلّ, مَوْضِع (مَواضِعُ), مَوْقِع (مَواقِعُ)

locust /ˈləʊkəst/ *n* جَراد (n coll)

lode /ləʊd/ *n* عِرْق مَعْدِنيّ

lodge /lɒdʒ/ A *n* 1 (for porter) [بَيْت صَغير \ غُرْفة (عند مَدْخَلِ مَبْنًى)] 2 (small country house) بَيْت ريفيّ, كوخ (أَكْواخ)

B *vi* 1 «students, tenants» سَكَنَ (u; سَكَن), أَقامَ; **I used to ~ with Mrs Brown** كُنْتُ أَسْكُنُ \ أُقيمُ مع السَيِّدةِ بْراوْن 2 «bullet» وَجَدَ مُسْتَقَرًّا لَهُ, انْغَرَسَ

lodger /ˈlɒdʒə/ *n* مُسْتَأْجِر, نَزيل (نُزَلاءُ)

lodging /ˈlɒdʒɪŋ/ A *n* سَكَن (مُؤَقَّت \ مُسْتَأْجَر); **£50 a week for board and ~** £50 في الأُسْبوعِ مُقابِلَ الطَعامِ والسَكَنِ

B (**lodgings**) *n pl* [غُرْفة \ غُرَف مُسْتَأْجَرة]

loft /lɒft/ *n* 1 (attic) عِلّيّة 2 (apartment) شِقّة (في مَصْنَعٍ \ عَنْبَرٍ سابِقٍ)

loft conversion *n* [عِلّيّة تَمَّ تَحْويلُها إلى غُرْفةٍ إضافيّةٍ]

loftily /ˈlɒftɪli/ *adv* ‹*answer, speak*› بِاسْتِعْلاءٍ, بِغَطْرَسةٍ

lofty /ˈlɒfti/ *adj* (**loftier, loftiest**) 1 ‹*ideals, goals*› سامٍ, نَبيل 2 ‹*manner, tone*› مُتَعالٍ, مُتَغَطْرِس 3 ‹*building, height*› شامِخ (شَوامِخُ, شُمَّخ), شاهِق (شَواهِقُ)

log /lɒg/ A *n* 1 (of wood) جِذْع (أَجْذاع, جُذوع) 2 (of a ship) سِجِلّ (سِجِلاّت)

B *vt* (**-gg-**) 1 (to record) دَوَّنَ ‹*the speed, incident*›; سَجَّلَ ‹*a call*› 2 (also **log up**) (to achieve) حَقَّقَ ‹*miles, average speed*›

(Phrasal verbs) **log on, log in** سَجَّلَ الدُخولَ

• **log off, log out** سَجَّلَ الخُروجَ

loganberry /ˈləʊg(ə)nb(ə)ri/ *n* (*pl* **loganberries**) توت لوغان

logarithm /ˈlɒgərɪð(ə)m/ *n* لوغاريتْم (لوغاريتْمات)

logbook *n* 1 (of a plane, ship) سِجِلّ (سِجِلاّت) 2 (of a car) وَثيقة تَسْجيلٍ \ مِلْكيّةٍ

log cabin *n* تَخْشيبة (تَخْشيبات, تَخاشيبُ)

log fire *n* نار (من) حَطَبٍ

loggerheads /ˈlɒgəhedz/ *n pl* **to be at ~** كانَ على خِلافٍ (حادٍّ)

logging /ˈlɒgɪŋ/ *n* حِطابة, قَطْع الأَشْجارِ

logic /ˈlɒdʒɪk/ *n* مَنْطِق

logical /ˈlɒdʒɪk(ə)l/ *adj* ‹*thought, argument*› مَنْطِقِيّ

logically /ˈlɒdʒɪkli/ *adv* ‹*to act, think*› بِشَكْلٍ مَنْطِقِيٍّ, بِصورةٍ مَنْطِقِيّةٍ

login /ˈlɒgɪn/, **logon** /ˈlɒgɒn/ *n* 1 (act of logging in) تَسْجيل دُخولٍ 2 (code) بَيانات دُخولٍ

logistics /ləˈdʒɪstɪks/ *n* 1 (Mil) لوجِسْتيّة 2 (Busn) الإمْداد والتَّموين

logo /ˈləʊgəʊ/ *n* (*pl* **logos**) شِعار (شِعارات)

logoff /ˈlɒgɒf/ *n* تَسْجيل خُروجٍ

logon /ˈlɒgɒn/ *n* ▸ **login**

loin /lɔɪn/ **A** *n* [قِطْعة لَحْمٍ من الخاصِرةِ]; **~ of beef** [قِطْعة لَحْمٍ من خاصِرةِ البَقَرةِ]

B (**loins**) *n pl* أَصْلاب

loincloth /ˈlɔɪnklɒθ/ *n* وِزْرة (وِزَرات)

loiter /ˈlɔɪtə/ *vi* «youths, gangs» تَسَكَّعَ

loll /lɒl/ *vi* 1 «people» اِسْتَلْقى, اِسْتَرْخى 2 «head, tongue» تَدَلّى

lollipop /ˈlɒlɪpɒp/ *n* مَصّاصة

lolly /ˈlɒli/ *n* (*pl* **lollies**) (BrE) 1 (infml) (money) فُلوس 2 (sweet) مَصّاصة

London /ˈlʌnd(ə)n/ *pr n* لُنْدُن (f)

Londoner /ˈlʌnd(ə)nə/ *n* لُنْدُنيّ

lone /ləʊn/ *adj* ‹*parent*› أَعْزَب (dipt); ‹*woman*› وَحْدانيّ; **a ~ wolf** شَخص مُنْفَرِد بِنَفْسِهِ

loneliness /ˈləʊnlinəs/ *n* (of a person) وَحْدة; (of a place) وَحْشة

lonely /ˈləʊnli/ *adj* (**lonelier**, **loneliest**) 1 (alone) ‹*person*› وَحيد; **a ~ life** حَياة الوَحْدةِ 2 (isolated) ‹*place, cottage*› مُنْعَزِل

lonely hearts' column *n* رُكْن تَعارُفٍ

loner /ˈləʊnə/ *n* وَحْدانيّ

lonesome /ˈləʊns(ə)m/ *adj* (AmE) ‹*person*› وَحيد; ‹*place*› مُنْعَزِل

long /lɒŋ/ **A** *adj* 1 (in distance, extent) ‹*arm, dress, queue*› طَويل (طِوال); **the rug is 1.5 m ~** طولُ السَّجّادةِ 1.5 م; **the grass/your hair is getting ~** أَصْبَحَ العُشْبُ \ شَعْرُكَ طَويلاً; **there is a ~ waiting list** هُناكَ قائِمةُ انْتِظارٍ طَويلةٍ; **to make the sleeves ~er** طَوَّلَ الأَكْمامَ; **to take the ~ way around** أَخَذَ الطَّريقَ الطَّويلَ
2 (lengthy) ‹*process, book, wait*› طَويل; **it's an hour ~** مُدَّتُهُ ساعةٌ; **is an hour ~ enough?** هل تَكْفي ساعةٌ؟; **how ~ is the interval?** كم مُدّةُ الفاصِلِ؟; **the days are getting** *or* **growing ~er** يَزْدادُ النَّهارُ طولاً; **to work ~ hours** عَمِلَ ساعاتٍ طَويلةً
3 ‹*vowel*› طَويل

B *adv* 1 (a long time) طَويلاً; **don't be ~** لا تَغِبْ طَويلاً; **will you be ~?** هل سَتَسْتَغْرِقُ وَقْتاً طَويلاً؟; **how ~ will you be at the market?** كم من الوَقْتِ سَتَقْضي في السوقِ؟; **not very ~** لَيْسَ طَويلاً; **it won't be ~ before he's back** لن يَمُرَّ الكَثيرُ من الوَقْتِ قبل أنْ يَعودَ; **you'll be the manager before ~** سَتُصْبِحُ المُديرَ عن قَريبٍ; **he'll be here before much ~er** سَيَكونُ هُنا بعد فَتْرةٍ وَجيزةٍ; **I can't stand it any ~er** لم أَعُدْ أَتَحَمَّلُهُ; **it's not so ~ since I was a student** لم يَمْضِ وَقْتٌ طَويلٌ منذ كُنْتُ طالِباً; **it wasn't ~ before the money ran out** لم يَمْضِ وَقْتٌ طَويلٌ قبل أنْ يَنْفَدَ المالُ; **I haven't got ~** لَيْسَ لَدَيَّ وَقْتٌ كَثيرٌ; **this won't take ~** لن يَسْتَغْرِقَ هذا وَقْتاً طَويلاً; **how ~ did it take him to find it?** كم اسْتَغْرَقَ من الوَقْتِ لِلعُثورِ عَلَيْهِ؟; **it took me ~er than I thought** اسْتَغْرَقَ مِنّي وَقْتاً أَطْوَلَ مِمّا كُنْتُ أَتَوَقَّعُ; **I can stay for three days at the ~est** يُمْكِنُني البَقاءُ ثَلاثةَ أَيّامٍ على الأَكْثَرِ; **not for ~** لَيْسَ لِفَتْرةٍ طَويلةٍ; **will you be gone for ~?** هل سَتَغيبُ فَتْرةً طَويلةً؟; **~ after the inauguration** بعد الافْتِتاحِ بِفَتْرةٍ طَويلةٍ; **not ~ after my birthday** بعد عيدِ ميلادي بِفَتْرةٍ لَيْسَتْ طَويلةً; **~ ago** منذ زَمَنٍ بَعيدٍ; **he phoned not ~ before lunch** اتَّصَلَ قبل الغَداءِ بِقَليلٍ; **he's no ~er head of the school** لم يَعُدْ مُديرَ المَدْرَسةِ
2 (for a long time) منذ فَتْرةٍ طَويلةٍ; **those days are ~ gone** تِلْكَ الأَيّامُ انْتَهَتْ منذ زَمَنٍ بَعيدٍ; **a ~-forgotten manuscript** مَخْطوطة مَنْسيّة منذ فَتْرةٍ طَويلةٍ 3 (throughout) **all night/day ~** طوال اللَّيْلِ \ النَّهارِ

C (**a long time**) *adv phr* **she's been away a ~ time** غابَتْ لِفَتْرةٍ طَويلةٍ; **they've taken a ~ time to decide** اسْتَغْرَقوا وَقْتاً طَويلاً لِيُقَرِّروا; **the journey takes a ~ time** تَسْتَغْرِقُ الرِّحْلةُ وَقْتاً طَويلاً; **I've been a teacher for a ~ time** أَعْمَلُ مُدَرِّساً منذ زَمَنٍ بَعيدٍ; **a ~ time ago** منذ زَمَنٍ \ عَهْدٍ بَعيدٍ

D (**a long way**) *adv phr* **it's a ~ way to the airport** المَسافةُ

المَسافةُ إلى الأَسْفَلِ إلى المَطارِ طَويلةٌ; **it's a ~ way down** بَعيدةٌ; **January is a ~ way off** يَنايِر ما يَزالُ بَعيداً; **a ~ way down the list** في أَواخِرِ القائِمةِ; **Jack will go a ~ way** سَيُحَقِّقُ جاكْ الكَثيرَ في حَياتِهِ; **we can make the food go a ~ way** يُمْكِنُنا إطْعامُ الكَثيرينَ بِهَذا الطَعامِ; **the donations went a ~ way towards covering the expenses** غَطَّتِ التَبَرُّعاتُ جُزْءاً كَبيراً من المَصاريفِ

[E] (**as long as**) *conj phr* **[1]** (in time) ما دامَ, طالَما; **borrow it for as ~ as you like** اسْتَعِرْهُ للمُدّةِ الّتي تُريدُها; **as ~ as I live** ما دُمْتُ حَيًّا **[2]** (provided that) (also **so long as**) طالَما; **so ~ as you keep me informed** طالَما أَبْقَيْتَني على اطِّلاعٍ

[F] *vi* (liter) (to desire) **to ~ for peace/sb's return** تاقَ إلى السَلام \ اشْتاقَ إلى عَوْدةِ شَخْصٍ; **he ~s for his family** يَشْتاقُ إلى أُسْرَتِهِ; **she ~s to return home** تَشْتاقُ إلى العَوْدةِ للوَطَنِ

(Idiom) **to have a long face** كانَ كالِحَ الوَجْهِ \ مُتَجَهِّماً

long-awaited /lɒŋə'weɪtɪd/ *adj* <*event, arrival*> طالَ انْتِظارُهُ

long-distance /ˌlɒŋ'dɪst(ə)ns/ *adj* <*runner*> المَسافاتِ الطَويلةِ; <*telephone call*> بَعيد المَدى

longevity /lɒn'dʒɛvɪti/ *n* طول العُمْرِ

long-haired /lɒŋ'hɛːd/ *adj* <*teenager, cat*> ذو شَعْرٍ طَويلٍ

longhand /'lɒŋhand/ *n* **in ~** بِخطِّ اليَدِ

long-haul /ˌlɒŋ'hɔːl/ *adj* <*flight, route*> طَويل

longing /'lɒŋɪŋ/ *n* تَوْق, لَهْفة (لَهَفات)

longitude /'lɒŋgɪtjuːd/ *n* خطّ الطولِ

longitudinal /lɒŋgɪ'tjuːdɪn(ə)l/ *adj* <*measurement, axis*> طوليّ

long johns *n* (infml) سِرْوال \ بَنْطَلون داخِليّ طَويل

long jump *n* قَفْز \ وَثْب طَويل

long-life /ˌlɒŋ'lʌɪf/ *adj* <*milk*> ذو فَتْرةِ صَلاحيّةٍ طَويلةٍ; <*battery*> طَويل العُمْرِ

long-lost /ˌlɒŋ'lɒst/ *adj* <*cousin, book*> مَفْقود منذ مُدّةٍ طَويلةٍ

long-playing record /ˌlɒŋˌpleɪɪŋ 'rɛkɔːd/ (BrE), **longplay record** (AmE) *n* أُسْطُوانة ذات 33 دَوْرةً وثُلْثٍ في الدَقيقةِ]

long-range /ˌlɒŋ'reɪndʒ/ *adj* **[1]** (over a long distance) <*missile, shot*> طَويل المَدى **[2]** (over a long time) <*forecast, planning*> طَويل المَدى \ الأَمَدِ

long-running /ˌlɒŋ'rʌnɪŋ/ *adj* <*dispute*> يَطولُ أَمَدُهُ; <*series*> يَسْتَمِرُّ عَرْضُهُ لِفَتْرةٍ طَويلةٍ]

longshoreman /'lɒŋʃɔːmən/ *n* (*pl* **-men**) (AmE) عامِل شَحْنٍ وتَفْريغ بالسُفُنِ]

long-sighted /ˌlɒŋ'sʌɪtɪd/ *adj* <*patient*> طَويل النَظَرِ \ البَصَرِ; **to be ~** كانَ طَويلَ النَظَرِ \ البَصَرِ

long-sleeved /ˌlɒŋ'sliːvd/ *adj* <*shirt, sweater*> طَويل الأَكْمامِ

long-standing /ˌlɒŋ'standɪŋ/ *adj* <*agreement, tradition*> مَوْجود \ مُسْتَمِرّ منذ زَمَنٍ طَويلٍ

long-suffering /ˌlɒŋ'sʌfərɪŋ/ *adj* <*parent, wife*> طالَتْ مُعاناتُهُ

long-term /ˌlɒŋ'təːm/ **[A]** *adj* <*solution, loan*> طَويل الأَجَلِ \ الأَمَدِ **[B]** *adv* <*to plan, think*> على المَدى البَعيد \ الطَويلِ

long-time /'lɒŋtʌɪm/ *adj* <*supporter, friend*> لِفَتْرةٍ طَويلةٍ من الزَمَنِ

long wave *n* المَوْجة الطَويلة

long-winded /ˌlɒŋ'wɪndɪd/ *adj* <*speech, explanation*> مُسْهَب, مُطْنَب

loo /luː/ *n* (BrE infml) **the ~** المِرْحاض

look /lʊk/ **[A]** *vt* **[1]** (to gaze, stare) **to ~ sb in the eye/in the face** نَظَرَ إلى شَخْصٍ في عَيْنَيْ شَخْصٍ; **to ~ sb up and down** نَظَرَ في عَيْنَيْ شَخْصٍ بِنَظْرةٍ فاحِصةٍ; **~ what you've done!** أُنْظُرْ ماذا فَعَلْتَ!; **~ who it is!** أُنْظُرْ مَنْ هذا! **[2]** (to appear to be) **to ~ one's age** كانَ يَبْدو سِنَّهُ; **she's 40 but she doesn't ~ it** عُمْرُها 40 سَنةً ولَكِنَّها تَبْدو أَصْغَرَ; **he ~s about 50** يَبْدو عُمْرُهُ حَوالَيْ 50 سَنةً; **he doesn't ~ himself today** لا يَبْدو على ما يُرامُ اليَوْمَ

[B] *vi* **[1]** نَظَرَ (u; نَظَر); **to ~ away** أَشاحَ بِوَجْهِهِ; **to ~ out of the window** نَظَرَ من النافِذةِ; **to ~ up and down the street** جالَ بِنَظَرِهِ في الشارِعِ; **could you ~ and see who's at the door?** هل يُمْكِنُكَ أنْ تَذْهَبَ لِتَرى مَنْ على البابِ؟ **[2]** (to search) بَحَثَ (a; بَحْث); **we are still ~ing** ما زِلْنا نَبْحَثُ; **I'm just ~ing** أَتَفَرَّجُ فَقَطْ **[3]** (to appear) «person, thing» بَدا (u; بَداء, بُدُوّ); **you ~ hot/cold** تَبْدو كَأَنَّكَ تَشْعُرُ بالحَرِّ \ بالبَرْدِ; **you ~ well/ill** تَبْدو بِصِحّةٍ جَيِّدةٍ \ مَريضاً; **that dress makes you ~ younger** ذلك الفُسْتانُ يَجْعَلُكِ تَبْدينَ أَصْغَرَ سِنًّا; **how do I ~?** كيف أَبْدو؟; **the picture will ~ good in the hall** سَتَبْدو الصورةُ جَيِّدةً في الرَدْهةِ; **it won't ~ good if you refuse** لن تَبْدُوَ جَيِّداً

إذا رَفَضْتَ; **it ~s as if** *or* **as though it is going to snow** يَبْدو أنّ الثّلجَ سَيَتساقَطُ; **it ~s likely/certain that ...** من المُتَوَقَّعِ \ المُؤكَّد أنّ ... **4**▸ **to ~ like sb/sth** أَشْبَهَ شَخْصاً \ شَيْئاً; **that photograph doesn't ~ like you** لا تُشْبِهُكَ تِلْكَ الصورةُ; **it ~s nothing like him** لا تُشْبِهُهُ بَتاتاً!; **what does the house ~ like?** كيف يَبْدو المَنْزِلُ؟; **you ~ like being the only man there** يَبْدو أنَّكَ سَتكونُ الرَجُلَ الوَحيدَ هُناك; **it ~s like being fun/interesting** يَبْدو مُمْتِعاً \ مُثيراً; **it ~s like rain/snow** يَبْدو أنّها سَتُمْطِرُ \ أنّ الثّلجَ سَيَتساقَطُ; **it ~s like a jellyfish to me** يَبْدو لي أنَّهُ قِنْديلُ البَحْرِ **5**▸ (listen) اِسْمَعْ, انْظُرْ; **~, this is ridiculous** اِسْمَعْ, هذا شَيْءٌ سَخيفٌ; **now ~ here!** اسْمَعْني هُنا! **6**▸ (to face) **to ~ north/south** «houses, rooms» واجَهَ الشَمالَ \ الجَنوبَ

C (*in combination* **-looking**) **distinguished-~ing** ذو مَظْهَرٍ مُتَمَيِّزٍ; **a sinister-~ing house** بَيْتٌ ذو مَظْهَرٍ مَشْؤومٍ; **he's not bad-~ing** لَيْسَ قَبيحَ الشَكْلِ

D *n* **1**▸ (glance) نَظْرة (نَظَرات); **one ~ told me that he was ill** عَرَفْتُ من نَظْرةٍ واحِدةٍ أنَّهُ كانَ مَريضاً; **to have** *or* **take a ~ at sb/sth** أَلْقى نَظْرةً على شَخْصٍ \ شَيْءٍ; **let me take a ~ at it for you** دَعْني أُلْقي نَظْرةً عَلَيْهِ; **to have a good ~ at a car/contract** فَحَصَ سَيّارةً \ عَقْداً بِعِنايةٍ; **I didn't get a good ~ at the thief** لم أَرَ اللصَّ بِوُضوحٍ; **to have a ~ inside/behind sth** نَظَرَ داخِلَ \ وراءَ شَيْءٍ; **to have a ~ round the shops/town** تَفَرَّجَ على المَحَلّاتِ \ المَدينةِ **2**▸ (search) **to have a ~ for sth** بَحَثَ عن شَيْءٍ **3**▸ (expression) نَظْرة (نَظَرات); **a ~ of sadness/anger** نَظْرةُ حُزْنٍ \ غَضَبٍ; **from the ~ on his face you knew he was angry** عَرَفْتَ أنَّهُ غاضِبٌ من نَظْرَتِهِ; **to give sb an angry ~** نَظَرَ إلى شَخْصٍ شَزْراً **4**▸ (appearance) مَظْهَر (مَظاهِرُ), شَكْل (أَشْكال); **to have the ~ of a military man** كانَ لَهُ مَظْهَرُ رِجالِ الجَيْشِ; **it has a dated ~** شَكْلُهُ قَديمٌ; **I like the ~ of it** يُعْجِبُني شَكْلُهُ; **I like the ~ of him** أَراهُ مُناسِباً; **I don't like the ~ of him** لَسْتُ مُطْمَئِنّاً لَهُ; **I don't like the ~ of the weather/that rash** لَسْتُ مُطْمَئِنّاً لِحالةِ الطَقْسِ \ لِذَلِكَ الطَفْحِ الجِلْديِّ; **you can't go** *or* **judge by ~s alone** لا يُمْكِنُ الحُكْمُ من المَظاهِرِ فَقَطْ **5**▸ (style) موضة; **this year's ~** موضة هذا العامِ

E (**looks**) *n pl* (outward appearance) مَظْهَر (مَظاهِرُ); **~s aren't everything** لَيْسَت المَظاهِرُ كُلَّ شَيْءٍ; **she's losing her ~s** تَفْقِدُ جَمالَ مَظْهَرِها; **to keep one's ~s** حافَظَ على مَظْهَرِهِ

(Idioms) **look before you leap** انْظُرْ قبل أنْ تَقْفِزَ; **to look right through sb** تَصَرَّفَ كما لو أنَّهُ لم يَرَ شَخْصاً

(Phrasal verbs) **look after** **A** **~ after [sb/sth]** **1**▸ (to care for) اعْتَنى ب [شَخْصٍ \ شَيْءٍ] ‹*a patient, child, animal*›; **she ~ed after me when I came out of hospital** اعْتَنَتْ بي بَعْدَما خَرَجْتُ من المُسْتَشْفى **2**▸ (to be responsible for) رَعى [شَخْصاً \ شَيْئاً] ‹*sb's finances, house, baggage*› **B** **~ after oneself** اعْتَنى بِنَفْسِهِ

• **look around** **A** **1**▸ (to turn around) نَظَرَ حَوْلَهُ **2**▸ (to search) بَحَثَ (a; بَحْث); **to ~ around for sb/sth** بَحَثَ عن شَخْصٍ \ شَيْءٍ **3**▸ (to visit) تَجَوَّلَ **B** **~ around [sth]** **1**▸ (to search) فَتَّشَ [شَيْئاً] ‹*sb's house, office*› **2**▸ (to visit) تَجَوَّلَ في [شَيْءٍ] ‹*the town, church*›

• **look at**: **~ at [sth]** **1**▸ (to focus on) نَظَرَ إلى [شَيْءٍ] ‹*a person, building*›; فَحَصَ [شَيْئاً] ‹*document*›; **what are you ~ing at?** إلى ماذا تَنْظُرُ؟; **he was ~ing at the papers** كانَ يَفْحَصُ الأَوْراقَ **2**▸ (to examine) فَحَصَ [شَيْئاً] ‹*sb's watch, plumbing*›; كَشَفَ على [شَيْءٍ] ‹*wound*› **3**▸ (to consider) فَكَّرَ في [شَيْءٍ] ‹*a problem, the implications, an offer*›; **we ~ed at all the options** دَرَسْنا جَميعَ الخِياراتِ; **try to ~ at it from my point of view** حاوِلْ أنْ تَنْظُرَ إلَيْهِ من وِجْهةِ نَظَري

• **look back** **1**▸ (to glance behind) نَظَرَ إلى الخَلْفِ; **to ~ back at sb/sth** نَظَرَ خَلْفَهُ إلى شَخْصٍ \ شَيْءٍ; **she's never ~ed back** لم تَنْظُرْ إلى الوَراءِ أَبَداً **2**▸ (in time) **to ~ back on an event/experience** تَفَكَّرَ في حَدَثٍ ماضٍ \ تَجْرِبةٍ ماضِيةٍ; **~ing back on it, I think I made the right decision** عِنْدَما أُفَكِّرُ فيه، أَعْتَقِدُ أنّني اتَّخَذْتُ القَرارَ الصائِبَ

• **look down** **A** (focusing downward) نَظَرَ لِأَسْفَلَ **B** **~ down [sth]** (to read) نَظَرَ إلى [شَيْءٍ] ‹*a list, page*› **C** **~ down on [sb/sth]** **1**▸ (to despise) احْتَقَرَ [شَخْصاً \ شَيْئاً] ‹*a neighbour, sb's lifestyle*› **2**▸ (to dominate) «towers, the fortress» أَطَلَّ على [شَيْءٍ] ‹*a town, valley*›

• **look for**: **~ for [sb/sth]** (to search for) بَحَثَ عن [شَخْصٍ \ شَيْءٍ] ‹*a hotel, your keys, a criminal*›

• **look forward**: **~ forward to [sth]** [انْتَظَرَ ,تَطَلَّعَ إلى [شَيْءٍ [شَيْئاً] بِشَوْقٍ ‹*a reunion, an outing, a concert*›; **I'm not ~ing forward to the interview** أَخْشى المُقابَلَةَ; **I ~ forward to hearing from you** أَنْتَظِرُ رَدَّكَ بِشَوْقٍ

• **look in** (to visit) زار (u; زِيارة); **to ~ in on a friend** زارَ صَدِيقاً

• **look into**: **~ into [sth]** حَقَّقَ في [شَيْءٍ] ‹*the problem, sb's accounts, background*›

• **look on** **A** (to watch) «crowd, spectators» تَفَرَّجَ ,شاهَدَ **B** **~ on [sb/sth]** اِعْتَبَرَ [شَخْصاً \ شَيْئاً]; **we ~ on him as a son/a friend** نَعْتَبِرُهُ ابْنَنا \ صَدِيقَنا

• **look onto**: **~ onto [sth]** «houses, rooms» أَطَلَّ على [شَيْءٍ] ‹*the sea, garden*›

• **look out** **A** (to be careful) انْتَبَهَ ,احْتَرَسَ; **~ out!** احْتَرِسْ! **B** **~ out for [sb/sth]** (to be alert for) تَرَقَّبَ [شَخْصاً \ شَيْئاً] ‹*a friend*›; انْتَبَهَ ;‹*bargain*› بَحَثَ عن [شَخْصٍ \ شَيْءٍ] إلى [شَخْصٍ \ شَيْءٍ] ‹*the symptoms*› **C** **~ out over [sth]** «windows, balconies» أَطَلَّ على [شَيْءٍ] ‹*the sea, park*›

• **look over** **A** **~ [sb/sth] over** (to inspect) فَحَصَ [شَخْصاً \ شَيْئاً]; كَشَفَ على [شَخْصٍ \ شَيْءٍ] ‹*a car, the equipment*›; ‹*horse*› **B** **~ over [sth]**, **~ [sth] over** (to read) أَلْقى نَظْرةً على [شَيْءٍ] ‹*a document, contract, the notes*› **C** **~ over [sth]** (to visit) زارَ [شَيْئاً] ‹*a factory, the gardens, house*›

• **look round** ▸ **look around**

• **look through**: **~ through [sth]** **1** (to read) أَلْقى نَظْرةً على [شَيْءٍ] ‹*the file, report, notes*› **2** (to search) بَحَثَ في [شَيْءٍ] ‹*sb's papers, suitcase*›

• **look to** **A** **~ to [sb/sth]** (to turn to) اعْتَمَدَ على [شَخْصٍ \ شَيْءٍ] ‹*a friend, one's family*› **B** **~ to [sth]** (to pay attention to) اهْتَمَّ بِ [شَيْءٍ] ‹*one's interests, problems*› **C** **~ to do sth** (to expect) تَوَقَّعَ أَنْ يَفْعَلَ شَيْئاً; **we're ~ing to break even** نَتَوَقَّعُ أَنْ تَتَساوى الأَرْباحُ والتَكاليفُ

• **look up** **A** **~ up** **1** (to raise one's eyes) رَفَعَ عَيْنَيْهِ; **she ~ed up from her book/at the night sky** رَفَعَتْ عَيْنَيْها عن الكِتابِ \ إلى سَماءِ اللَيْلِ **2** (to improve) «business, the situation, markets» تَحَسَّنَ; **things are ~ing up for us** تَتَحَسَّنُ الأَوْضاعُ بالنِسْبَةِ لَنا **B** **~ [sb/sth] up, ~ up [sb/sth]** **1** (in books, on the Internet) بَحَثَ عن [شَخْصٍ \ شَيْءٍ] ‹*a phone number, price, reference*› **2** (to visit) زارَ [شَخْصاً] ‹*an acquaintance, a friend*› **C** **~ up to [sb]** قَدَّرَ [شَخْصاً] ‹*your father, teacher*›

lookalike /ˈlʊkəlʌɪk/ *n* شَبيه (شِباه)

look-in /ˈlʊkɪn/ *n* (BrE infml) **to get a ~** حَصَلَ على فُرْصةِ المُشارَكَةِ

looking glass /ˈlʊkɪŋ glɑːs/ *n* مِرْآة (مَرايا)

lookout /ˈlʊkaʊt/ *n* **1** **to be on the ~ for a stolen vehicle** بَحَثَ عن سَيّارةٍ مَسْروقةٍ **2** (person) رَقيب (يَرْصُدُ التَحَرُّكاتِ في الخارِجِ لِإبْلاغِ رُفَقائِهِ)

loom /luːm/ **A** *n* مِنْسَج (مَناسِجُ) ,مِنْوال ,نَوْل (أَنْوال)
B *vi* **1** (to appear) (also **loom up**) «cliffs, building» لاحَ (u; لَوْح) **2** (to seem imminent) «wars, deadline» أَوْشَكَ; **decision time ~s** يَلوحُ مَوْعِدُ اتِّخاذِ القَرارِ في الأُفُقِ; **the deadline was ~ing** باتَ المَوْعِدُ الأَخيرُ وَشيكاً

loony /ˈluːni/ (infml) **A** *n* (*pl* **loonies**) مَجْنون (مَجانينُ)
B *adj* (**loonier**, **looniest**) ‹*scheme, idea*› غَريب

loop /luːp/ **A** *n* أُنْشوطة (أَناشيطُ) ,عُقْدة (عُقَد)
B *vt* عَقَدَ (i; عَقْد) ‹*a rope, thread*›
C *vi* «roads, rivers» الْتَفَّ \ الْتَوى في شَكْلِ حَلْقةٍ

(Idiom) **to be in/out of the loop** كانَ على عِلْمٍ \ غَيْرِ عِلْمٍ بِما يَحْصُلُ

loophole /ˈluːphəʊl/ *n* ثُغْرة (ثُغْرات ,ثُغَر)

loose /luːs/ **A** *adj* **1** (not firm or tight) ‹*knot*› غَيْر مُرْتَخٍ; ‹*handle, button*› مَفْكوك ,غَيْر مُحْكَم; ‹*tooth*› مُقَلْقَل, مَشْدودٍ; غَيْر ثابِتٍ; **the handle has come** *or* **worked ~** أَصْبَحَ المِقْبَضُ مَفْكوكاً; **there is a ~ connection** هُناكَ وُصْلةٌ غَيْرُ مُحْكَمَةٍ; **the pages have come ~** أَصْبَحَت الصَفَحاتُ مُفَكَّكَةً **2** (to release) **to let** *or* **set** *or* **turn an animal ~** أَطْلَقَ سَراحَ حَيَوانٍ; **to break ~** «animals» تَحَرَّرَ من أَسْرِهِ **3** (not packaged) ‹*fruit, oatmeal*› [غَيْر مُعَلَّبٍ أو مُكَيَّسٍ]; (individually) ‹*envelopes, cigarettes*› فَرْدي; **~ change** فَكّة **4** (not tight) ‹*jacket, trousers, fit*› واسِع ,غَيْر مَضْغوطٍ; **5** (not compact) ‹*soil*› فَضْفاض; ‹*weave*› فَضْفاض **6** (informal) ‹*alliance, association, structure*› غَيْر فَضْفاض ,هَشّ **7** (inexact) ‹*translation, interpretation*› غَيْر دَقيقٍ ,حَرْفي; ‹*wording*› **8** (old use) (dissolute) ‹*morals, life*› فاسِد ,مُنْحَلّ (فَسْدى)

B *n* **to be on the ~** كانَ طَليقاً; **the killer is still on the ~** ما زالَ القاتِلُ طَليقاً

(Phrasal verb) **loose off**: **~ off [sth]** (to fire) أَطْلَقَ [شَيْئاً] ‹*a shot, round*›

loose-fitting /ˌlu:s'fɪtɪŋ/ *adj* ‹*jacket, trousers*› فَضْفاض

loose-leaf /ˌlu:s'lif/ *adj* ‹*folder, binder*› [ذو أَوْراقٍ مُثَبَّتةٍ بِطَريقةٍ تَسْمَحُ بِسَحْبِها \ إضافةِ أَوْراقٍ أُخْرى]

loosely /'lu:sli/ *adv* **1** (with little pressure) ‹*to hold, wrap*› بِشَكْلٍ رَخْوٍ \ مُرْتَخٍ **2** (vaguely) ‹*connected, organized*› بِشَكْلٍ غَيْرِ دَقيقٍ \ ما **3** (imprecisely) ‹*to translate, describe*› في المُجْمَلِ، ذلك مَضْبوطٍ; **~ speaking, that's correct** صَحيحٌ

loosely knit *adj* ‹*group*› لا تَرْبِطُهُ عَلاقاتٌ وَطيدةٌ; ‹*structure*› غَيْر مُتَماسِكٍ

loosen /'lu:s(ə)n/ *vt* **1** (to make less tight) أَرْخى ‹*a belt, nail*› **2** (to relax) أَرْخى ‹*one's grip*›; خفَّفَ ‹*control*›

(Phrasal verb) **loosen up** **1** (Sport) سَخَّنَ \ أَحْمى العَضَلاتِ **2** (infml) (to relax) اسْتَرْخى

loot /lu:t/ **A** *n* غَنيمة (غَنائِمُ)

B *vt* نَهَبَ (a-u; نَهْب) ‹*a shop, village*›

looter /'lu:tə/ *n* ناهِب

looting /'lu:tɪŋ/ *n* نَهْب (نهاب)

lop /lɒp/ *vt* **(-pp-)** قَلَّمَ (هَذْب ;i) هَذَبَ, شَذَّبَ ‹*a tree, branch*›

(Phrasal verb) **lop off**: **~ [sth] off, ~ off [sth]** قَطَعَ [شَيْئاً] ‹*a branch, sb's head*›

lope /ləʊp/ *vi* «tigers, runners» جَرى (بِخَطَواتٍ كَبيرةٍ واثِبةٍ

lopsided /lɒp'sʌɪdɪd/ *adj* **1** (not symmetrical) ‹*smile, cake*› مائِل **2** (not equal) ‹*contest, score*› غَيْر مُتَكافِئٍ

lord /lɔ:d/ *n* **1** (ruler) سُلْطان (سَلاطينُ) **2** (**Lord**) (peer) لورْد; **the (House of) Lords** مَجْلِس الشُيوخِ **3** (**Lord**) (God) رَبّ (أَرْباب); **may the L~ be with you** كانَ الرَبُّ مَعَكَ **4** (**Lord**) (infml) (in exclamations) **good L~!** يا إِلَهي!

(Idiom) **to lord it over sb** (infml) تَأَمَّرَ \ تَعالى على شَخْصٍ

Lord Mayor *n* [لَقَب لِعُمْدةِ مَدينةٍ مُهِمّةٍ في بَريطانيا]

lordship /'lɔ:dʃɪp/ *n* **your/his ~** جَنابُكَ \ جَنابُهُ

Lord's Prayer *n* (**the Lord's Prayer**) الصَلاة الرَبّانيّة

lore /lɔ:/ *n* مَعارِف تَقْليديّة \ مَوْروثة

lorry /'lɒri/ *n* (*pl* **lorries** BrE) شاحِنة

lorry driver *n* (BrE) سائِق شاحِنةٍ

lose /lu:z/ **A** *vt* (*past tense, past participle* **lost**) **1** (to mislay) فَقَدَ (i; فِقْدان, فَقْد) أَضاعَ ‹*your keys, phone, passport*›; **to ~ one's way** فَقَدَ \ ضَلَّ طَريقَهُ **2** (to not have any longer) فَقَدَ (i; فَقْد, فِقْدان); **to ~ interest in sth** فَقَدَ الاهْتِمامَ بِشَيْءٍ; **I lost the use of my arm** فَقَدْتُ القُدْرةَ على اسْتِخْدامِ ذِراعي; **many lives were lost** فُقِدَت العَديدُ من الأَرْواحِ; **200 jobs will be lost** سَتُفْقَدُ 200 وَظيفةٍ; **she has nothing to ~** لَيْسَ لَدَيْها ما تَخْسَرُهُ; **she has too much to ~** لَدَيْها الكَثيرُ لِتَخْسَرَهُ **3** (to miss, waste) ضَيَّعَ ‹*a chance, time*›; **we're losing valuable time** نُضَيِّعُ وَقْتاً ثَميناً; **there's no time to ~** لَيْسَ هُناكَ وَقْتٌ نُضَيِّعُهُ; **it ~s something in translation** يَفْقِدُ بَعْضَ مَعانيهِ في التَرْجَمةِ; **the significance of the news was not lost on him** لم يَغْفُلْ أَهَمِّيّةَ الخَبَرِ **4** (to be defeated in) خَسِرَ (a; خُسْر) ‹*a war, race, election, an argument*›; **we won the battle but lost the war** كَسَبْنا المَعْرَكةَ وَلَكِنَّنا خَسِرْنا الحَرْبَ **5** (to stop seeing) فَقَدَ (i; فِقْدان, فَقْد) ‹*a fugitive, vehicle*› **6** (to evade) تَمَلَّصَ (من) ‹*a pursuer*›; **you've lost me there!** (infml) لم أَعُدْ أَفْهَمُكَ الآنَ!

7 (to get rid of) فَقَدَ (i; فِقْدان, فَقْد) ‹*weight, your inhibitions, shyness*›; **I've lost two kilos!** فَقَدْتُ كيلوَيْنِ من وَزْني! **8** (in timekeeping) «clocks, watches» أَخَّرَ ‹*minutes, seconds*›; **my watch/clock ~s about a minute a day** ساعَتي تُؤَخِّرُ حوالَيْ دَقيقةً كُلَّ يَوْمٍ **9** (to cost) **to ~ sb sth** تَسَبَّبَ في فِقْدانِ شَخْصٍ لِشَيْءٍ

B *vi* (*past tense, past participle* **lost**) **1** (to be defeated) «competitors, players, teams» خَسِرَ (a; خُسْر); **we lost in the final/to the Qatari team** خَسِرْنا المُباراةَ النِهائيّةَ \ أمام الفَريقِ القَطَرِيِّ **2** (financially) خَسِرَ (a; خُسْر); **overall they have lost on the deal** خَسِروا في الصَفْقةِ بِشَكْلٍ عامٍّ **3** «clocks, watches» تَأَخَّرَ

C *v refl* (*past tense, past participle* **lost**) **to ~ oneself in a book/in contemplation** انْهَمَكَ في قِراءةِ كِتابٍ \ التَفْكيرِ

(Idiom) **to lose it** (infml) فَقَدَ السَيْطَرةَ على نَفْسِهِ

Phrasal verb **lose out** خَسِرَ (a; خُسْر); **to ~ out on a bargain/an offer** خَسِرَ في الصَفْقةِ \ العَرْضِ

loser /ˈluːzə/ *n* 1 (in a contest, battle) خاسِر 2 (infml) (failure) فاشِل

loss /lɒs/ *n* 1 [u] (of an asset, benefit) خَسارة 2 [u] (of blood, hearing) فِقْدان 3 (in business) (خَسائِرُ) خَسارة 4 (of a person) وَفاة 5 (**losses** *n pl*) (casualties) خَسائِر

Idioms **to be at a loss** كانَ في حَيْرةٍ من أَمْرِهِ; **I was at a ~ for words** خانَتْني الكَلِماتُ; **to cut one's losses** حَدَّ من خَسائِرِهِ

loss adjuster *n* خَبير مُعايَنةٍ وتَقْديرِ أَضْرارٍ

loss-leader /ˈlɒsˌliːdə/ *n* [مُنْتَج مُسَعَّر بِسِعْرٍ رَخيصٍ لِجَذْبِ الزَبائِنِ]

lost /lɒst/ A *past tense, past participle* ▸ **lose**

B *adj* 1 ‹*suitcase, child, keys*› (ضِياع ,ضُيَّع) ضائِع ,مَفْقود; **I think we're ~** أَظُنُّ أَنَّنا تُهْنا; **we got ~ in the market** تُهْنا في السوقِ; **get ~!** (infml) أُغْرُبْ عن وَجْهي! 2 (wasted, vanished) ‹*civilisation, city*› مَفْقود 3 (unrecoverable) ‹*opportunity, innocence, youth*› (ضِياع ,ضُيَّع) ضائِع ,مَفْقود; **the novel is about ~ innocence/a ~ youth in another world** الرِوايةُ عن البَراءةِ المَفْقودةِ \ شابٌّ ضائِعٍ في عالَمٍ آخَر 4 (mystified) **to be ~** كانَ تائِهاً \ مُتَحَيِّراً; **I'd be ~ without you/without my calculator** سَأَضيعُ بِدونِكَ \ بِدونِ الآلةِ الحاسِبةِ; **to be ~ for words** لم يَجِدْ ما يَقولُهُ 5 (absorbed) **to be ~ in a book/in thought** كانَ مُنْهَمِكاً في قِراءةِ كِتابٍ \ التَفْكيرِ 6 (hopeless) مَيْؤوس مِنْهُ ,خاسِر; **a ~ cause** قَضيّة خاسِرة; **all is not ~** لم يُفْقَدِ الأَمَلُ تَماماً

lost and found *n* (مَكْتَب) المَفْقودات

lost property *n* (مَكْتَب) المَفْقودات

lot¹ /lɒt/ A *pron* 1 (**a lot**) (great deal) كَثير; **we spent a ~ at the market** أَنْفَقْنا كَثيراً في السوقِ; **to get a ~ out of the visit** اِسْتَفادَ من الزِيارةِ كَثيراً; **he knows a ~ about sport** يَعْرِفُ الكَثيرَ عن الرِياضةِ; **it says a ~ about her** يَكْشِفُ الكَثيرَ عَنْها; **an awful ~** كَثير جِدًّا; **quite a ~** قَدْر \ عَدَد كَبير; **there's a lot to be said for working for yourself** هُناكَ مَزايا كَثيرةٌ للعَمَلِ الحُرِّ; **such a ~** مِثْل هذا القَدْرِ \ العَدَدِ الكَبير; **such a ~ of people can't be wrong** لا يُمْكِنُ أنْ يَكونَ كُلُّ هَؤُلاءِ الناسِ مُخْطِئِينَ 2 (great deal) **a ~ of sth** كَثير من شَيْءٍ; **it took a ~ of money/energy/people** تَطَلَّبَ الكَثيرَ من الأَمْوالِ \ الطاقةِ \ الناسِ; **there were quite a ~ of children/cars/books** كانَ هُناكَ عَدَدٌ كَبيرٌ من الأَطْفالِ \ السَيّاراتِ \ الكُتُبِ; **not a ~ of people know that** لا يَعْرِفُ ذلكَ الكَثيرُ من الناسِ; **I see a ~ of him** أَراهُ كَثيراً; **he spent an awful ~ of time on it** أَمْضى قَدْراً هائِلاً من الوَقْتِ فيهِ; **quite a ~ of our support** قَدْر كَبير من دَعْمِنا; **what a ~ of people!** يا لَلأَعْدادِ الغَفيرةِ! ▸**fat** B3 3 (**lots**) (infml) **~s of people/cars/energy** كَثير من الناسِ \ السَيّارات \ الطاقة; **there are ~s of things to do** هُناكَ الكَثيرُ مِمّا يَنْبَغي عَمَلُهُ; **there were games, competitions and ~s more** كانَ هُناكَ أَلْعابٌ ومُسابَقاتٌ وأَشْياءُ أُخْرى كَثيرةٌ

B *n* 1 (infml) (expressing entirety) **the ~** الجَميع ,الكُلّ; **he paid the ~ in cash** دَفَعَ المَبْلَغَ كُلَّهُ نَقْداً; **the nicest dress of the ~** أَجْمَل فُسْتانٍ فيها جَميعاً; **heartburn, headache, cramps, the ~!** حُرْقة في المِعْدةِ وصُداع وتَقَلُّصات، كُلّ شَيْءٍ! 2 (infml) (group of people) **she's the best of the ~** هي أَحْسَنُهُمْ كُلِّهِمْ; **I don't trust that ~** لا أَثِقُ في أَيٍّ مِنْهُمْ; **they're not a bad ~** لَيْسوا سَيِّئِينَ

C (**lots**) *adv* (infml) **~s better/more interesting** أَفْضَل \ أَكْثَر تَشْويقاً بِكَثيرٍ

D (**a lot**) *adv phr* بِكَثيرٍ ,كَثيراً; **a ~ better/more useful than the other one** أَفْضَل \ أَفْيَد من الآخَرِ بِكَثيرٍ; **I like it a ~** أُحِبُّهُ كَثيراً; **a ~ worse** أَسْوأ بِكَثيرٍ; **an awful ~ cheaper** أَرْخص بِكَثيرٍ جِدًّا; **the situation has improved a ~** تَحَسَّنَ الوَضْعُ كَثيراً; **this happens quite a ~** يَحْدُثُ هذا كَثيراً; **he travels such a ~** يُسافِرُ كَثيراً جِدًّا

lot² /lɒt/ *n* 1 (situation) (أَقْدار) قَدَر ,قِسْمة ,(أَنْصِبة) نَصيب; **to be happy with one's ~** كانَ راضِياً بِنَصيبِهِ; **to throw one's ~ in with sb** رَبَطَ مَصيرَهُ بِشَخْصٍ 2 (AmE) (piece of land) أَرْض فَضاء ,(ساحات) ساحة ,باحة ,قِطْعة أَرْضٍ; **a vacant ~** سوق السَيّاراتِ المُسْتَعْمَلةِ; **the used car ~** 3 (at a studio) [مِنْطَقة مُحيطة باسْتوديو] 4 (at an auction) مَجْموعة; ▸**job lot** 5 (of students, tourists) مَجْموعة

Idiom **to draw lots** سَحَبَ قُرْعةً

loth *adj* ▸ **loath**

lotion /ˈləʊʃ(ə)n/ *n* لوسيون

lottery /ˈlɒt(ə)ri/ *n* (*pl* **lotteries**) يانَصيب

lotus /ˈləʊtəs/ *n* (*pl* **lotuses**) لوتَس

loud /laʊd/ **A** *adj* **1** (noisy) ‹*noise, voice, music, crash*› عالٍ, صاخِب; **he said it in a ~ whisper** قالَهُ بِهَمْسةٍ مَسْموعةٍ **2** (vulgar) ‹*colour*› صارِخ, صاخِب; ‹*pattern*› مُبَهْرَج; ‹*behaviour*› سوقيّ; **the hotel's decor is very ~ and in your face** ديكور الفُنْدُق صارِخٌ ومُبَهْرَجٌ **B** *adv* بِصَوْتٍ مُرْتَفِع \ عالٍ; **they have their radio/TV on very ~** يرفعون صَوْتَ الرادِيو \ التِلِفِزْيون عالِيا جدًّا; **to read out ~** قَرَأَ بِصَوْتٍ مُرْتَفِعٍ; **~ and clear** بِشَكْلٍ واضِحٍ تماما

loudly /ˈlaʊdli/ *adv* ‹*to knock, talk*› بِصَوْتٍ عالٍ

loudmouth /ˈlaʊdmaʊθ/ *n* (infml) ثَرْثار

loudspeaker /laʊdˈspiːkə/ *n* مِجْهار (مَجاهيرُ), مُكَبِّر صَوْتٍ

Louisiana /luːˌiːziˈanə/ *pr n* لُويزِيانا

Louisianan /luːˌiːziˈan(ə)n/, **Louisianian** /luːˌiːziˈanɪən/ *pr n, adj* (شَخْص) من لُويزِيانا

lounge /laʊndʒ/ *n* غُرْفة \ حُجْرة جُلوسٍ

Phrasal verb **lounge about, lounge around** تَكاسَلَ

louse /laʊs/ *n* (*pl* **lice**) (insect) قَمْل (n coll)

Phrasal verb **louse up** (infml): **~ [sth] up, ~ up [sth]** «weather, person» أَفْسَدَ [شَيْئاً] ‹*the plan, attempt*›

lousy /ˈlaʊzi/ *adj* (**lousier, lousiest**) (infml) ‹*weather, job*› سَيِّئ, رَديء (أَرْدِياءُ)

lout /laʊt/ *n* (infml) جِلْف (أَجْلاف), فَظّ (أَفْظاظ), غَليظ (غِلاظ)

loutish /ˈlaʊtɪʃ/ *adj* ‹*youth, behaviour*› غَليظ (غِلاظ), فَظّ (أَفْظاظ), جِلْف (أَجْلاف)

louvre (BrE), **louver** (AmE) /ˈluːvə/ *n* (strip) كوّة

louvred (BrE), **louvered** (AmE) /ˈluːvəd/ *adj* ‹*door, shutter*› مُزَوَّد بِكوّاتٍ

lovable /ˈlʌvəb(ə)l/ *adj* ‹*child, animal*› مَحْبوب

love /lʌv/ **A** *n* **1** (affection) حُبّ, عِشْق, مَحَبّة, غَرام; **his ~ for his children/country** حُبُّهُ لِأَبْنائِهِ \ لِوَطَنِهِ; **to be in ~ with sb** كانَ يَعْشَقُ شَخْصاً; **to fall in ~ with sb** وَقَعَ في حُبِّ شَخْصٍ; **to do sth for the ~ of it** فَعَلَ شَيْئاً حُبًّا فيه; **to make ~ with sb** (to have sex) مارَسَ الجِنْسَ مع شَخْصٍ **2** (in polite formulas) **give my ~ to Jo** أَرْسِلْ سَلامي إلى جو; **Andy sends his ~** يُرْسِلُ آنْدي سَلامَهُ إِلَيْكَ; **~ Bob, with ~ from Bob** (in a letter) مع خالِصِ الحُبِّ من بوب **3** (object of affection) حُبّ; **he/music was my first ~** كانَ هو \ كانَت الموسيقى حُبّي الأَوَّلَ; **she was the ~ of his life** كانَتْ حُبَّ حَياتِهِ **4** (BrE) (infml) (term of address to a child, customer) عَزيزي; (to one's partner, spouse) حَبيبي; **that's 75 pence please, ~** الحسابُ 75 بِنْس من فَضْلِكَ يا عَزيزي **5** (in tennis) صِفْر

B *vt* **1** (to feel affection for) أَحَبَّ, حَبَّ (i; حُبّ) ‹*one's spouse, family, country*›; **to ~ sb very much** أَحَبَّ شَخْصاً جدًّا; **to ~ each other** أَحَبَّ بَعْضُهُمْ بَعْضاً; **she really ~s the children** إِنَّها تُحِبُّ الأَطْفالَ حَقًّا **2** (to enjoy) حَبَّ (i; حُبّ), هَوِيَ (a; هَوًى) ‹*an activity, a place, thing*›; **he ~s tennis/going to the theatre** يَهْوى التِنِس \ الذهابَ إلى المَسْرَحِ; **she ~s Rome** تُحِبُّ روما; **I'd ~ to meet him** أَوَدُّ أَنْ أُقابِلَهُ

Idioms **love at first sight** الحُبُّ من أَوَّلِ نَظْرةٍ; **not for love or for money** مَهْما كانَ الإِغْراءُ; **there's no love lost between them** لا يُكِنّونَ لِبَعْضِهِمْ أَيَّ حُبٍّ

love affair *n* عَلاقة عاطِفيّة \ غَراميّة

loved one /ˈlʌvd wʌn/ *n* شَخص عَزيز, حَبيب (أَحِبّاءُ)

loveless /ˈlʌvləs/ *adj* ‹*marriage, childhood*› خالٍ من الحُبِّ

love life *n* حَياة عاطِفيّة

lovely /ˈlʌvli/ *adj* (**lovelier, loveliest**) **1** (beautiful) ‹*colour, garden*› رائِع; **you look ~** تَبْدينَ رائِعةً **2** (very pleasant) ‹*letter, present, weather*› جَميل جِدًّا; ‹*person*› وَدود; ‹*meal*› شَهيّ; **we had a ~ time** اِسْتَمْتَعْنا بِوَقْتِنا كَثيراً; **that smells ~!** يا لَلْرائِحةِ الشَهيّةِ!

lover /ˈlʌvə/ *n* **1** (in an affair) عَشيق (عُشّاق) **2** (person in love) عاشِق (عُشّاق, عاشِقونَ), مُحِبّ **3** (enthusiast) مُحِبّ; **a jazz ~** مُحِبّ للجاز

love story *n* قِصّة حُبٍّ

loving /ˈlʌvɪŋ/ *adj* ‹*husband*› حَنون, مُحِبّ; ‹*look*› حُبٍّ \ مَحَبّةٍ, حَنانٍ

lovingly /ˈlʌvɪŋli/ *adv* ‹to look, embrace› بِحَنانٍ, بِمَحَبَّةٍ, بِحُبٍّ

low /ləʊ/ **A** *adj* **1** (near the ground) ‹wall, cloud, table› مُنْخَفِض; **the sun is ~ in the sky** الشَّمْسُ مُنْخَفِضةٌ في السَماءِ; **there will be flooding on ~ ground** سَيَحْدُثُ فَيَضانٌ في الأَراضي المُنْخَفِضةِ **2** (nearly depleted) ‹reservoir, level› مُنْخَفِض; **our stocks are ~** مُسْتَوى مَخْزونِنا مُنْخَفِضٌ; **I'm ~ on fuel** وَقودُ سَيّارتي مُنْخَفِضٌ; **the fire was getting ~** كانَت النارُ تَخْبُتُ **3** (minimal) ‹price, output, pressure› مُنْخَفِض; **cook it on a ~ heat** اُطْبُخْهُ على نارٍ هادِئةٍ; **demand is ~ for the time of year** الطَّلَبُ مُنْخَفِضٌ بالنِسْبةِ لِهَذا الوَقْتِ من السَنةِ; **these products are ~ in sugar/fat** هذه المُنْتَجاتُ قَليلةُ السُكَّرِ \ الدَسَمِ; **a number ~er than 50** رَقْم أَقَلّ من 50 **4** (in importance) ‹status, rank, priority› مُنْخَفِض; **a ~er court** مَحْكَمة أَدْنى; **it's very ~ on my list of priorities** هو في ذَيْلِ قائِمةِ أَوْلَوِيّاتي; **to be ~ down in the hierarchy** كانَ في مَرْتَبةٍ مُنْخَفِضةٍ **5** (inferior) ‹mark, score, quality› مُنْخَفِض; **a ~ achiever** [شَخْص إِنْجازُهُ دون المُسْتَوى]; **there is a ~ degree of risk** هُناكَ نِسْبةُ مُخاطَرةٍ مُنْخَفِضةٌ **6** (depressed) مُكْتَئِب; **to feel ~** شَعَرَ باكْتِئابٍ **7** ‹note, tone, voice› مُنْخَفِض; **the radio is too ~** صَوْتُ الراديو مُنْخَفِضٌ جدًّا **8** (base) ‹action, behaviour› غَيْر أَخْلاقيٍّ, وَضيع (وُضَعاءُ), دَنيء (أَدْنِياءُ); **that was a ~ thing to do** كانَ ذلك تَصَرُّفاً دَنيئاً; **~ cunning** خِداع

B *n* **1** (depression) مُنْخَفَض جَوِّيّ **2** (on an index) انْخِفاض (انْخِفاضات); **the price of oil closed at a record ~** سَجَّلَ سِعْرُ النَفْطِ أَدْنى إِغْلاقٍ لَهُ; **turn the oven to ~** اخْفِضْ حَرارةَ الفُرْنِ

C *adv* **1** (not high) ‹to fly, aim, shoot› على مُسْتَوًى مُنْخَفِضٍ; **the plane flew ~ over the desert** طارَت الطائِرةُ على مُسْتَوًى مُنْخَفِضٍ فوق الصَحْراءِ; **I wouldn't sink so ~ as to ask him for money** لن أَتَدَنّى لِمُسْتَوى طَلَبِ المالِ مِنْهُ **2** (near the bottom) **it comes ~ (down) on the list** يَأْتي في ذَيْلِ القائِمةِ; **look ~er down the page** انْظُرْ أَسْفَلَ الصَفْحةِ **3** (at reduced levels) ‹to buy› بِسِعْرٍ مُنْخَفِضٍ; **to turn the heating down ~** خَفَضَ دَرَجةَ التَدْفِئةِ; **stocks are running ~** مُسْتَوى المَخْزونِ آخِذٌ في الانْخِفاضِ; **I rate him pretty ~** رَأْيي فيهِ سَيِّئٌ **4** (of sounds) ‹to sing, play› على دَرَجةٍ مُنْخَفِضةٍ; **the bass part goes very ~** النَغْمةُ العَميقةُ مُنْخَفِضةٌ جِدًّا

D *vi* خارَ (u; خُوار)

Idiom **to be the lowest of the low** كانَ أَسْفَلَ السافِلينَ

low-alcohol /ləʊˈalkəhɒl/ *adj* ‹beer, wine› مُنْخَفِض الكُحولِ

lowbrow /ˈləʊbraʊ/ *adj* ‹comedy, newspaper› مُوَجَّه للعامّةِ (لا يُعَبِّرُ عن مَضْمونٍ فِكْريٍّ \ ثَقافيٍّ)

low-budget /ˌləʊˈbʌdʒət/ *adj* ‹project, film› مُنْخَفِض المِيزانيّةِ

low-calorie /ləʊˈkaləri/ *adj* ‹diet, drink› قَليل السُعُراتِ الحَرارِيّةِ

low-cost /ləʊˈkɒst/ *adj* ‹airline, materials› مُنْخَفِض التَكْلِفةِ

low-cut /ləʊˈkʌt/ *adj* ‹blouse, dress› مَكْشوف الصَدْرِ, مُقَوَّر

low-down /ˈləʊdaʊn/ *adj* (infml) ‹cheat, lie› حَقير (حُقَراءُ), دَنيء (أَدْنِياءُ, أَدْناء)

lower /ˈləʊə/ **A** *adj* (comparative of **low**) ‹jaw, lip› أَسْفَل (dipt; أَسافِلُ); **the ~ back** أَسْفَلُ الظَهْرِ

B *vt* **1** (to bring down) خَفَضَ (i; خَفْض) ‹barrier, a flag, a curtain›; أَنْزَلَ ‹lifeboat›; **as they entered harbour they ~ed the mainsail** خَفَضوا الشِراعَ الرَئيسيَّ عند دُخولِهِم الميناءَ; **to ~ the cargo onto the quay** أَنْزَلَ الحُمولةَ إلى الرَصيفِ; **to ~ one's hand** خَفَضَ يَدَهُ; **she ~ed her eyes** خَفَضَتْ عَيْنَيْها **2** (to reduce) خَفَّضَ ‹the temperature, the price, age limit›; **to ~ one's voice** خَفَضَ صَوْتَهُ **3** (Econ) (to reduce) خَفَّضَ (i; خفض) ‹a trade barrier› **4** (to let down) خفض (i; خفض) ‹one's gun, sword›; **to ~ one's guard** خَفَضَ ذِراعَيْهِ (في المُلاكَمةِ) **5** (in renovations, etc) خفض (i; خَفْض) ‹a ceiling›

C *v refl* **to ~ oneself** **1** (to demean oneself) أَهانَ نَفْسَهُ **2** (in sitting) **to ~ oneself into a chair/the bath** جَلَسَ بِحَذَرٍ على الكُرْسيِّ \ في حَوْضِ الاسْتِحْمامِ

lower case *n* حُروف صَغيرة

lower-case letter *n* حَرْف صَغير

lower class *n* (also **lower classes**) طَبَقة دُنْيا \ سُفْلى

Lower Egypt *n* الوَجْه البَحْريّ, الدِلْتا, مِصْر السُفْلى

lower school *n* مَدْرَسة ابْتِدائيّة

low-fat /ləʊˈfat/ *adj* ‹diet, cheese› قَليل الدُهونِ \ الدَسَمِ

low-flying /ˌləʊˈflʌɪɪŋ/ *adj* ‹aircraft› مُحَلِّق على ارْتِفاعٍ مُنْخَفِضٍ

low-frequency /ləʊˈfriːkwənsi/ *adj* ‹radio wave, signal› ذو تَرَدُّدٍ مُنْخَفِضٍ

low-grade /ˈləʊgreɪd/ *adj* ‹*ore, paper*› مُنْخَفِض الجَوْدة

low-income /ləʊˈɪnkəm/ *adj* ‹*family, taxpayer*› ذو دَخْلٍ مُنْخَفِضٍ \ مَحْدودٍ

low-key /ləʊˈkiː/ *adj* ‹*meeting, celebrations*› مُنْخَفِض المُسْتَوى

lowland /ˈləʊlənd/ *n* (or **lowlands**) أَرْض مُنْخَفِضة \ واطِئة

lowland farming *n* زِراعة في الأراضي المُنْخَفِضة

low-level /ˌləʊˈlev(ə)l/ *adj* **1** (Aviat) ‹*bombing, flight*› على مُسْتَوى مُنْخَفِض **2** (of minor importance) ‹*radiation*› مُنْخَفِض؛ ‹*talks*› مُنْخَفِض المُسْتَوى

lowly /ˈləʊli/ *adj* (**lowlier**, **lowliest**) ‹*occupation, position*› وَضيع (وُضَعاءُ), مُتَواضِع

low-lying /ˌləʊˈlʌɪɪŋ/ *adj* ‹*ground, area*› مُنْخَفِض

low-necked /ˌləʊˈnɛkt/ *adj* ‹*blouse, dress*› مَكْشوف الصَّدْرِ

low-paid /ˌləʊˈpʌɪd/ *adj* ‹*job, worker*› مُنْخَفِض الأَجْر

low-price, **low-priced** /ləʊˈprʌɪs/ *adj* ‹*item, ticket*› مُنْخَفِض السِعْرِ

low profile *adj* ‹*operation, approach*› بعيد عن الأَضْواءِ

low-quality /ləʊˈkwɒləti/ *adj* ‹*goods, cloth*› مُنْخَفِض الجَوْدةِ

low-resolution /ləʊrɛzəˈluːʃ(ə)n/ *adj* ‹*video, screen*› مُنْخَفِض الدِقّةِ

low-rise /ˌləʊˈrʌɪz/ **A** *adj* ‹*building, hotel*› مُنْخَفِض الارْتِفاع **B** *n* مَبْنًى مُنْخَفِض

low-risk /ˌləʊˈrɪsk/ *adj* ‹*investment, operation*› مُنْخَفِض المَخاطِر

low season *n* مَوْسِم مُنْخَفِض

low-tech /ˌləʊˈtɛk/ *adj* ‹*solution, system*› ذو تِقْنِيّة بَسيطة, مُنْخَفِض التِقْنِيّة

low tide, **low water** *n* جَزْر, مَدّ مُنْخَفِض

loyal /ˈlɔɪəl/ *adj* ‹*friend, supporter*› مُخْلِص (أَوْفِياءُ) وَفِيّ

loyalist /ˈlɔɪəlɪst/ **A** *n* مُوالٍ **B** (**Loyalist**) *pr n* [شَخْص يَتَبَنّى فِكْرةَ اسْتِمْرارِ الاتِّحادِ بين بَريطانِيا وَشَمالِ أَيْرِلَنْدا]

loyalty /ˈlɔɪəlti/ *n* (*pl* **loyalties**) وَلاء

loyalty card *n* بِطاقة وَلاءٍ

lozenge /ˈlɒzɪndʒ/ *n* **1** (for coughs) قُرْص لِلمَصِّ **2** (shape) مَعين

LP /ɛlˈpiː/ *n* [أُسْطُوانة ذات 33 دَوْرةً وَثُلْثٍ في الدَقيقةِ]

L-plate /ˈɛlpleɪt/ *n* (BrE) [عَلامة تَدُلُّ على أنّ سائِقَ السَيّارةِ تحت التَعْليمِ]

LSD /ɛlɛsˈdiː/ *n* = **lysergic acid diethylamide** إِلْ إِسْ دي (دَواء لِلهَلْوَسةِ)

Ltd /ˈlɪmɪtɪd/ (BrE) *abbr* = **limited** م (مَحْدودة)

lubricant /ˈluːbrɪk(ə)nt/ *n* مادّة تَشْحيم

lubricate /ˈluːbrɪkeɪt/ *vt* زَيَّتَ, شَحَّمَ ‹*a wheel, machine*›

lucid /ˈluːsɪd/ *adj* **1** (clear) ‹*explanation, style*› واضِح **2** (clear-headed) ‹*moment*› صافٍ؛ ‹*patient*› صافِي الذِهْنِ؛ **to be ~** كانَ صافِيَ الذِهْنِ

luck /lʌk/ *n* **1** (fortune) حَظّ (حُظوظ), بَخْت (بُخوت)؛ **that was good/bad ~** كانَ ذلك حَظًّا سَعيداً \ سَيِّئاً؛ **good ~!** أَتَمَنى لَكَ حَظًّا سَعيداً!؛ **bad or hard ~!** يا لَلْحَظِّ العاثِرِ!؛ **to bring sb good/bad ~** جَلَبَ حَظًّا سَعيداً \ سَيِّئاً لِشَخْصٍ؛ **to try one's ~** جَرَّبَ حَظَّهُ؛ **as ~ would have it ...** وَكانَ من تَصاريفِ القدَرِ أَنّ ...؛ **just my ~!** من سوءِ حَظّي! **2** (good fortune) حَظّ (حُظوظ)؛ **with a bit of ~** مع بَعْضِ الحَظّ \ التَوْفيق؛ **to be in/out of ~** حالَفَهُ \ لم يُحالِفْهُ الحَظُّ؛ **by a stroke of ~** بِضَرْبةِ حَظٍّ؛ **our ~ ran out** خانَنا الحَظُّ؛ **any ~ with the job hunting?** هل وُفِّقْتَ في العُثورِ على عَمَلٍ؟

Idiom **no such luck!** لا لِلأَسَفِ!

Phrasal verb **luck out** (AmE infml) اِبْتَسَمَ لَهُ الحَظُّ

luckily /ˈlʌkɪli/ *adv* لِحُسْنِ الحَظِّ؛ **~ for me, the boss was late too** لِحُسْنِ حَظّي، كانَ رَئيسي مُتَأَخِّراً كَذَلِكَ

lucky /ˈlʌki/ *adj* (**luckier**, **luckiest**) **1** (fortunate) ‹*guy, winner, escape*› مَحْظوظ؛ **they were ~ that the referee did not see the foul** كانوا مَحْظوظينَ لِأَنَّ الحَكَمَ لم يَرَ المُخالَفةَ؛ **you'll be ~ to get a taxi** سَتَكونُ مَحْظوظاً إنْ وَجَدْتَ تاكْسي؛ **it was ~ for me that you came along** كانَ من حُسْنِ حَظّي أَنَّكَ أَتَيْتَ **2** (bringing good luck) ‹*charm, colour, number*› الحَظِّ؛ **it's my ~ day!** هذا يَوْمُ سَعْدي!

Idioms **to strike it lucky** (BrE) (infml) صادَفَهُ الحَظُّ؛ **to thank one's lucky stars** (infml) شَكَرَ حَظَّهُ

lucrative /ˈluːkrətɪv/ *adj* ‹*market, business*› مُرْبِح

ludicrous /ˈluːdɪkrəs/ *adj* ‹*situation, suggestion*› مُضْحِك, سَخيف

lug /lʌg/ **A** *vt* **(-gg-)** (infml) جَرّ (u; جَرّ), سَحَبَ (a; سَحْب) ‹*a suitcase, box*›

B *n* مِقْبَض (مَقابِضُ)

luggage /ˈlʌgɪdʒ/ *n* أَمْتِعة, حَقائِب

luggage handler *n* حَمّال أَمْتِعةٍ

luggage rack *n* رَفّ أَمْتِعةٍ

lugubrious /lʊˈguːbrɪəs/ *adj* ‹*tone, occasion*› حَزين (حُزَناءُ, حَزانى), كَئيب

lukewarm /luːkˈwɔːm/ *adj* **1** (not hot) ‹*coffee, water*› فاتِر

2 (unenthusiastic) ‹*applause, support*› فاتِر

lull /lʌl/ **A** *vt* **1** (to soothe) **to ~ sb to sleep** هَدْهَدَ شَخْصاً لِيَنامَ

2 (to deceive) **to ~ sb into thinking that ...** هَيَّأَ لِشَخْصٍ الاعْتِقادَ بِأَنَّ ... ; **to ~ sb into a false sense of security** جَعَلَ شَخْصاً يَشْعُرُ بِإِحْساسٍ خادِعٍ بالأَمانِ

B *n* هُدوء مُؤَقَّت

lullaby /ˈlʌləbaɪ/ *n* (*pl* **lullabies**) تَهْويدة

lumbago /lʌmˈbeɪgəʊ/ *n* أَلَم أَسْفَلِ الظَّهْرِ

lumbar /ˈlʌmbə/ *adj* ‹*pain, puncture*› في أَسْفَلِ الظَّهْر

lumber /ˈlʌmbə/ **A** *n* (AmE) **1** (wood) خَشَب مَنْشور **2** (junk) أَغْراض مُهْمَلة

B *vt* (BrE) **to get** *or* **be ~ed with sb/sth** كانَ مُثْقَلاً بِعِبْءِ شَخْصٍ \ شَيْءٍ

C *vi* مَشى بِتَثاقُلٍ

lumberjack /ˈlʌmbədʒak/ *n* حَطّاب (حَطّابة), قاطِع الأَخْشابِ

lumberyard /ˈlʌmbəjɑːd/ *n* (AmE) مُسْتَوْدَع أَخْشابٍ

luminous /ˈluːmɪnəs/ *adj* ‹*jacket, glow*› مُضيء

lump /lʌmp/ **A** *n* **1** (of coal, wood, meat) قِطْعة (قِطَع); (of dough, clay) كُتْلة (كُتَل), قالَب (قَوالِبُ) **2** (in cement, a sauce) كُتْلة (كُتَل) **3** (of sugar, butter) قالَب (قَوالِبُ), قِطْعة (قِطَع)

4 (swelling) وَرَم (أَوْرام)

B *vt* (infml) **to ~ different people/items together** جَمَعَ أَشْخاصاً مُخْتَلِفينَ \ أَشْياءَ مُخْتَلِفَةً مَعاً

Idiom **to have a lump in one's throat** شَعَرَ بِغُصَّةٍ في حَلْقِهِ

lump sum *n* مَبْلَغ إِجْماليّ

lumpy /ˈlʌmpi/ *adj* (**lumpier**, **lumpiest**) ‹*sauce, mattress, soil*› مُتَكَتِّل

lunacy /ˈluːnəsi/ *n* (*pl* **lunacies**) جُنون, خَبَل

lunar /ˈluːnə/ *adj* ‹*landscape, eclipse*› قَمَريّ

lunatic /ˈluːnətɪk/ *n* مَخْبول (مَخْبولون, مَخابيلُ), مَجْنون (مَجانينُ), مَعْتوه (مَعاتيهُ)

lunch /lʌntʃ/ *n* غداء (أَغْدِية); **to have ~** تَغَدّى, تَناوَلَ الغداءَ

▸ **packed lunch**

lunch break *n* اسْتِراحة غداءٍ

luncheon /ˈlʌntʃ(ə)n/ *n* (fml) غَداء (أَغْدِية)

lunch hour *n* ساعة غَداءٍ

lunchtime /ˈlʌntʃtaɪm/ *n* وَقْت الغَداءِ

lung /lʌŋ/ *n* رِئة

lung cancer *n* سَرَطان الرِئةِ

lunge /lʌndʒ/ **A** *n* انْدِفاع (انْدِفاعات)

B *vi* «attacker, dog» انْدَفَعَ; **to ~ at sb** انْدَفَعَ نحو شَخْصٍ

lurch /ləːtʃ/ **A** *vi* «vehicle» تَمايَلَ, تَأَرْجَحَ; «person» تَرَنَّحَ

B *n* تَمايُل, تَرَنُّح, تَأَرْجُح

Idiom **to leave sb in the lurch** تَخَلّى عن شَخْصٍ وَقْتَ الشِدّةِ

lure /lʊə/ **A** *vt* أَغْرى ‹*customers, victims*›

B *n* (attraction) إِغْراء (إِغْراءات)

lurid /ˈljʊərɪd/ *adj* **1** ‹*colour*› صارِخ **2** (sensational) ‹*details, tale*› مُثير

lurk /ləːk/ *vi* «killers, animals» تَرَبَّصَ, تَرَصَّدَ; «danger» حَدَّقَ

luscious /ˈlʌʃəs/ *adj* **1** ‹*fruit*› لَذيذ, شَهيّ **2** ‹*woman, lips*› مُثير, مُغْرٍ

lush /lʌʃ/ *adj* ‹*vegetation, forest*› كَثيف, أَغَنّ (dipt), وارِف

lust /lʌst/ **A** *n* **1** (sexual) شَهْوة (شَهَوات) **2** (craving) تَوْق, تَوَقان

B *vi* **1** **to ~ after sb** اشْتَهى شَخْصاً **2** **to ~ after sth** اشْتَهى شَيْئاً

luster (AmE) *n* بَريق, لَمَعان ▸ **lustre**

lustful /ˈlʌstfʊl/ *adj* ‹*thoughts, glance*› شَهْوانيّ

lustre (BrE), **luster** (AmE) /ˈlʌstə/ *n* بَريق, لَمَعان

lusty /ˈlʌsti/ *adj* (**lustier**, **lustiest**) ‹*youth, voice*› مُفْعَم بالحَيَويّة

lute /luːt/ *n* لوت, عود ≈ (عيدان, أعْواد)

luvvy /ˈlʌvi/ *n* (*pl* **luvvies**) (BrE infml) مُمَثِّل مُتَصَنِّع

Luxembourg /ˈlʌksəmbɜːg/ *pr n* لوكْسِمْبورْغ (f)

Luxor /ˈlʌksɔː/ *pr n* الأُقْصُر (f)

luxuriant /lʌgˈʒʊəriənt/ *adj* ‹*vegetation*› أَغَنّ (dipt), وارِف; ‹*hair*› كَثيف (كِثاف)

luxuriate /lʌgˈʒʊərieɪt/ *vi* **to ~ in sth** تَنَعَّمَ بِشَيْءٍ

luxurious /lʌgˈʒʊəriəs/ *adj* ‹*hotel, lifestyle*› مُتْرَف, فَخْم (فِخام)

luxury /ˈlʌkʃ(ə)ri/ **A** *n* (*pl* **luxuries**) **1** [u] (great comfort) تَرَف, رَفاهِية **2** (treat) تَرَف

B *adj* ‹*hotel, goods*› مُتْرَف, فَخْم, فاخِر

lychee /ˈlaɪtʃiː, laɪˈtʃiː/ *n* لِيتْشي (فاكِهة)

lying /ˈlaɪɪŋ/ **A** *present participle* ▸ **lie**

B *adj* كاذِب

lymph /lɪmf/ *n* لِمْف

lymph node *n* عُقْدة لِمْفاويّة

lymphocyte /ˈlɪmfəʊsaɪt/ *n* خَليّة لِمْفاويّة

lynch /lɪntʃ/ *vt* ‹*a rapist, murderer*› [أَعْدَمَ دون مُحاكَمةٍ]

lynch mob *n* [غَوْغاء تُعْدِمُ شَخْصاً دون مُحاكَمةٍ]

lynx /lɪŋks/ *n* (*pl* **lynxes**) وَشَق

lyre /ˈlaɪə/ *n* قيثارة (قَياثيرُ), كَنّارة (كَنّارات, كَنانيرُ)

lyric /ˈlɪrɪk/ **A** *adj* (also **lyrical**) ‹*poet, poetry*› غِنائيّ

B *n* شِعْر غِنائيّ

C (**lyrics**) *n pl* (of song) كَلِمات \ نَصّ أُغْنِية

lyrical /ˈlɪrɪk(ə)l/ *adj* ‹*style, prose*› عاطِفيّ, شاعِريّ

lyricist /ˈlɪrɪsɪst/ *n* مُؤَلِّف أغانٍ \ كاتِب, شاعِر غِنائيّ

lyric writer *n* مُؤَلِّف أغانٍ \ كاتِب, شاعِر غِنائيّ

Mm

M, m /ɛm/ **A** *n* (letter); ميم ≈ (الحَرْف الثالِث عَشَرَ من الأَبْجَدِيّةِ الإنْكليزِيّةِ)

B *abbr* **1** (m) = **metre(s)** (BrE) = **meter(s)** (AmE) م **2** (M) (BrE) = **motorway** [طَرِيق سَرِيع]; **take the M3 as far as ...** خُذْ طَرِيق ال M3 إلى ... **3** (m) = **mile(s)** ميل (أَمْيال) **4** (m) = **million(s)** مِلْيون (مَلايينُ) **5** = **medium** (in clothes sizes) مُتَوسِّط

ma /mɑː/ *n* (infml) ماما

MA **A** *abbr* = **Massachusetts**

B (also **M.A.**) /ɛm'eɪ/ *n* = **Master of Arts** (degree) ماجِسْتير في الآدابِ; **Kate Darby, MA** كَيت دارْبي، ماجِسْتير في الآدابِ

mac /mak/ *n* (infml) [مِعْطَف مَطَرٍ طَويل]

Mac® /mak/ *n* ماكِنْتوش

macabre /mə'kɑːbrə/ *adj* ‹*tale, humour*› مُرِيع ,مُرَوِّع

macaroni /,makə'rəʊni/ *n* مَكْرونة ,مَعْكَرونة

mace /meɪs/ *n* **1** (spice) جَوزة الطِيبِ **2** (staff of office) صَوْلَجان (صَوْلَجانات) **3** (weapon) [قَضيب حَديدِيّ شائِك] **4** (**Mace®**) (chemical) [نَوْع من الغازِ المُسيلِ للدُموعِ (في بَخّاخٍ) لِكَسْرِ الدروعِ]

Macedonia /,masɪ'dəʊnɪə/ *pr n* مَقْدونِيا

machete /mə'ʃɛti/ *n* ساطور ≈ (سِكّين طَويل)

machinations /makɪ'neɪʃ(ə)nz/ *n pl* مُؤامَرات ,مَكائِد ,دَسائِس

machine /mə'ʃiːn/ *n* جِهاز ,آلة (مَكائِنُ ,ماكينات) ماكينة (أَجْهِزة); **the process is carried out by ~** يَتِمُّ تَنْفيذُ العَمَليّةِ بِاسْتِخْدامِ ماكيناتٍ

machine gun *n* مِدْفَع رَشّاش ,بُنْدُقيّة آليّة ,(رَشّاشات) رَشّاش

machine-readable /məʃiːn'riːdəb(ə)l/ *adj* ‹*data, passport*› مَقْروء آليًّا

machinery /mə'ʃiːn(ə)ri/ *n* **1** (machines) ماكينات ,آلات **2** (working parts) أَجْزاء ماكينةٍ

machinist /mə'ʃiːnɪst/ *n* مُشَغِّل ماكيناتٍ

macho /'matʃəʊ/ *adj* ‹*image, culture*› ذُكوريّ

mackerel /'mak(ə)rəl/ *n* (*pl* **mackerel** or **mackerels**) إسْقُمْريّ, ماكْريل

mackintosh, macintosh /'makɪntɒʃ/ *n* [مِعْطَف مَطَرٍ طَويل]

macro /'makrəʊ/ *n* (Comput) ماكْرو

mad /mad/ *adj* (**-dd-**) **1** (insane) ‹*person*› مَجْنون (مَجانينُ), مَعْتوه (مَعاتيهُ); **to go ~** جُنَّ ,أَصْبَحَ مَجْنوناً (a; جُنون ,جَنّ); **to drive sb ~** دَفَعَ شَخْصاً إلى الجُنونِ ,جَنَّنَ شَخْصاً **2** (foolish) ‹*idea, scheme*› مَجْنون (مَجانينُ); **you'd be ~ to turn down the opportunity** سَتكونُ مَجْنوناً إذا أَضَعْتَ هذه الفُرْصةَ **3** (infml) (angry) غاضِب ,مَجْنون (مَجانينُ); **to be ~ at** *or* **with sb** غَضِبَ; **to get ~ at** *or* **with sb** جُنَّ جُنونُهُ على شَخْصٍ; **it makes me ~** يُغْضِبُني من شَخْصٍ **4** (rabid) ‹*dog*› مَسْعور **5** (infml) (enthusiastic) **to be ~ about sth** كانَ مَهْووساً بِشَيْءٍ; **they're ~ about each other** إنَّهُما مَهْووسانِ بِبَعْضِهِما البَعْضِ **6** (frantic) ‹*dash, panic*› مَجْنون (مَجانينُ); **the audience got into a ~ panic** أُصيبَ الجُمْهورُ بِهَلَعٍ كَبيرٍ; **to be in a ~ rush** كانَ في عَجَلةٍ من أَمْرِهِ; **we made a ~ dash for the bus** جَرَيْنا بِسُرْعةٍ جُنونيّةٍ لِلَّحاقِ بالحافِلةِ

Idiom **... like mad** (infml) كالمَجْنونِ ... ; **to work like ~** عَمِلَ كالمَجْنونِ; **to laugh like ~** ضَحِكَ كالمَجْنونِ

Madagascar /,madə'gaskə/ *pr n* مَدَغَشْقَر (f)

madam /'madəm/ *n* سَيِّدة; **Dear M~** (in a letter) سَيِّدَتي العَزيزة

mad cow disease *n* (infml) مَرَض جُنونِ البَقَرِ

madden /'mad(ə)n/ *vt* **1** (to make angry) أَغْضَبَ ,أَحْنَقَ **2** (to drive mad) دَفَعَ \ قادَ إلى الجُنونِ ,جَنَّنَ

maddening /'madnɪŋ/ *adj* ‹*habit, itch*› مُضايِق للغايةِ, مُزْعِج جِدًّا

made /meɪd/ **A** *past tense, past participle* ▸**make**

B *adj* **1** (sure to succeed) **to have it ~** ضَمِنَ تَحْقيقَ النَجاحِ

2 (ideally suited) **to be ~ for each other** خُلِقا لِبَعْضِهِما

Madeira /məˈdɪərə/ *pr n* ماديرا

made to measure /meɪd tə ˈmɛʒə/ *adj* (*before n* **made-to-measure**) ‹*suit, curtains*› مُفَصَّل على المَقاسِ

made-up /meɪdˈʌp/ *adj* **1** (wearing make-up) عَلَيْهِ مَكِياج

2 (invented) مُخْتَلَق

madly /ˈmadli/ *adv* **1** (frantically) ‹*to grin, rush*› كالمَجْنونِ

2 (extremely) بِجُنونٍ; **they fell ~ in love with each other** أَحَبّا بَعْضَهُما بِجُنونٍ

madman /ˈmadmən/ *n* (*pl* **-men**) مَجْنون (مَجانينُ)

madness /ˈmadnəs/ *n* **1** (insanity) جُنون **2** (folly) جُنون, حَماقة

madrasa /məˈdrasə/ *n* مَدْرَسة إِسْلامِيّة

Madrid /məˈdrɪd/ *pr n* مَدْريد (f)

madwoman /ˈmadwʊmən/ *n* (*pl* **-women**) (infml) امْرَأة مَجْنونة \ مَخْبولة

Mafia /ˈmafɪə/ *n* (**the Mafia**) المافِيا; (any organized crime group) عِصابة مُنَظَّمة, مافِيا

magazine /magəˈziːn/ *n* **1** (publication) مَجَلّة **2** (also **magazine programme** or **program** AmE) (on radio, TV) بَرْنامَج مُنَوَّعاتٍ **3** (of a gun) خِزانة (خَزائِنُ, خِزانات), خَزْنة

4 (of a camera) عُلْبة (عُلَب), حُجَيْرة

magenta /məˈdʒɛntə/ *n, adj* أُرْجُوانِيّ

maggot /ˈmagət/ *n* يَرَقانة, يَرَقة

Maghreb /ˈmagrɪb/ *n* (**the Maghreb**) المَغْرِب العَرَبِيّ

magic /ˈmadʒɪk/ **A** *n* سِحْر (أَسْحار); **as if by ~** كَما لو كانَ بِفِعْلِ السِحْرِ

B *adj* **1** ‹*wand, trick*› سِحْرِيّ **2** (wonderful) ساحِر, بَديع

magical /ˈmadʒɪk(ə)l/ *adj* **1** ‹*powers, creature*› سِحْرِيّ

2 (wonderful) ‹*moment, place*› ساحِر, بَديع

magic bullet *n* وَصْفة سِحْرِيّة, حَلّ سِحْرِيّ

magic carpet *n* بِساط سِحْرِيّ, بِساط الريحِ

magician /məˈdʒɪʃ(ə)n/ *n* **1** (conjuror) ساحِر (سَحَرة), حاوٍ (حُواة)

2 (sorcerer) ساحِر (سَحَرة)

magistrate /ˈmadʒɪstreɪt/ *n* قاضٍ (قُضاة)

magistrates' court (BrE) *n* ≈ مَحْكَمة ابْتِدائِيّة

magnanimous /magˈnanɪməs/ *adj* ‹*ruler*› شَهْم (شِهام), نَبيل (نُبَلاءُ); ‹*gesture*› يَنُمُّ عن الشَهامةِ

magnate /ˈmagneɪt/ *n* قُطْب (رَجُل أَعْمالٍ كَبير); **an oil ~** من أَقْطابِ النَفْطِ

magnesium /magˈniːzɪəm/ *n* مَغْنِسيوم

magnet /ˈmagnɪt/ *n* **1** (Phys) مَغْنَطيس **2** (lure) شَخْص \ شَيْء [جَذّاب]; **the city is a ~ for tourists** المَدينةُ مَرْكَزُ جَذْبٍ للسُيّاحِ

magnetic /magˈnɛtɪk/ *adj* **1** ‹*field, strip*› مَغْنَطيسِيّ

2 (alluring) ‹*personality, appeal*› جَذّاب, مَغْنَطيسِيّ

magnetic north *n* الشَمال المَغْنَطيسِيّ

magnetism /ˈmagnɪtɪz(ə)m/ *n* **1** (in physics) مَغْنَطيسِيّة

2 (allure) جاذِبِيّة

magnetize, -ise (BrE) /ˈmagnɪtʌɪz/ *vt* **1** مَغْنَطَ (i; مَغْنَطة) ‹*a needle, an iron bar*› **2** جَذَبَ (i; جَذْب) ‹*an audience, student*›

magnificent /magˈnɪfɪs(ə)nt/ *adj* ‹*view, building*› رائِع, عَظيم (عِظام, عُظَماءُ), فَخْم (فِخام)

magnify /ˈmagnɪfʌɪ/ *vt* (**magnifies, magnifying, magnified**)

1 كَبَّرَ ‹*an image, object*› **2** كَبَّرَ, ضَخَّمَ ‹*an effect, a problem*›

magnifying glass /ˈmagnɪfʌɪɪŋ glɑːs/ *n* عَدَسة مُكَبِّرة

magnitude /ˈmagnɪtjuːd/ *n* **1** (size) حَجْم (أَحْجام), قُوّة (قُوًى)

2 (importance) حَجْم (أَحْجام), ضَخامة

magnolia /magˈnəʊlɪə/ *n* **1** (also **magnolia tree**) مَغْنولِيا, مانولِيا **2** [u] (colour) [لَوْن زَهْرةِ المانولِيا]

magpie /ˈmagpʌɪ/ *n* عَقْعَق (عَقاعِقُ)

Mahdi /ˈmɑːdi/ *n* مَهْدِيّ

mahogany /məˈhɒg(ə)ni/ *n* ماهوجَني

maid /meɪd/ *n* **1** (in a house) خادِمة; (in a hotel) عامِلة **2** (liter) (girl) آنِسة (آنِسات, أَوانِسُ)

maiden /ˈmeɪd(ə)n/ **A** *n* (liter) آنِسة (آنِسات, أَوانِسُ)

B *adj* ‹*voyage, speech*› أَوَّل (dipt; f أولى)

maiden name *n* [لَقَب المَرْأةِ قبل الزَواجِ]

mail /meɪl/ **A** *n* **1** (system) بَريد; **to send sth by ~** أَرْسَلَ شَيْئًا بالبَريدِ; **your cheque is in the ~** أُرْسِلَ شيكُكَ بالبَريدِ;

(to reply) by return ~ رَدَّ) بِرُجوعِ البَريدِ) **2** (letters and parcels) بَريد; **it came in today's ~** جاءَ مع بريدِ اليَوْمِ **3** (armour) تُرْس (تُروس, أَتْراس), دِرْع (دُروع)
B *vt* أَرْسَلَ بالبَريدِ *‹a letter, parcel›*; **to ~ a letter to sb** أَرْسَلَ رِسالةً بالبَريدِ إلى شَخْصٍ

mailbox /ˈmeɪlbɒks/ *n* **1** (AmE) (for in-coming mail) صُنْدوق رَسائِلَ (أمام بَيْتٍ); (for out-going mail) صُنْدوق بَريدٍ **2** (for email) صُنْدوق بَريدٍ إلكْترونيٍّ

mailing /ˈmeɪlɪŋ/ *n* مُراسَلة بالبَريدِ

mailing list *n* قائِمة بَريديّة

mailman /ˈmeɪlmən/ *n* (*pl* **-men**) (AmE) ساعي بَريدٍ

mail order *n* طَلَب بالبريدِ

mail order catalogue (BrE), **mail order catalog** (AmE) *n* [كَتالوج بَضائِعَ يُمْكِنُ طَلَبُها بالبَريدِ]

maim /meɪm/ *vt* سَبَّبَ إعاقةً \ عَجْزاً ل, أَعاق *‹a child, civilian›*

main /meɪn/ **A** *adj ‹reason, objective›* رَئيسيّ; **the ~ thing** الشَيْء المُهِمّ
B *n* **1** (pipe) أُنْبوب \ خطّ رَئيسيّ; **turn the water/gas ~ on** افْتَحْ أُنْبوبَ الماءِ \ الغازِ الرَئيسيِّ **2** (cable) كابِل رَئيسيّ **3** (BrE) (supply) (**the mains**) الخَطّ الرَئيسيّ; **to turn the water/gas off at the ~s** أَغْلَقَ الماءَ \ الغازَ من الخطِّ الرَئيسيِّ
(Idiom) **in the main** بِرُمَّتِهِ

main course *n* طَبَق رَئيسيّ

Maine /meɪn/ *pr n* ماين (f)

Mainer /ˈmeɪnə/ *pr n* [(شَخْص) من ماين]

mainframe /ˈmeɪnfreɪm/ *n* (also **mainframe computer**) كُمْبيوتَر \ حاسوب مَرْكَزيّ

mainland /ˈmeɪnlənd/ *n* (**the mainland**) البَرّ الرَئيسيّ; **~ China** بَرّ الصين الرَئيسيِّ; **~ Europe** أوروبّا القارّيّة

main line *n* خطّ رَئيسيّ

mainly /ˈmeɪnli/ *adv ‹to consist, work›* في الأَساسِ, بِشَكْلٍ رَئيسيٍّ, بِصورةٍ رَئيسيّةٍ

main road *n* طَريق رَئيسيّ

mainstream /ˈmeɪnstriːm/ *adj ‹society, political parties›* تَقْليديّ

main street *n* شارِع رَئيسيّ

maintain /meɪnˈteɪn/ *vt* **1** (to keep up) حافَظَ (على) *‹contact, a relationship, level›* **2** (to look after) أَجْرى صِيانةً على *‹a building, road›* **3** (to support) أَعالَ *‹a family›* **4** (to assert) أَكَّدَ

maintenance /ˈmeɪnt(ə)nəns/ *n* **1** (upkeep) صِيانة **2** (BrE) (alimony) نَفَقة (نَفَقات)

maisonette /ˌmeɪzəˈnɛt/ *n* [شَقّة مُؤَلَّفة من طابِقَيْنِ]

maize /meɪz/ *n* ذُرة

majestic /məˈdʒɛstɪk/ *adj ‹building, animal›* فَخْم (فِخام)

majesty /ˈmadʒɪsti/ *n* (*pl* **majesties**) **1** [u] (grandeur) عَظَمة, فَخامة **2** (as a title) **His/Her Majesty** صاحِب \ صاحِبة الجَلالةِ; **Your Majesty** يا صاحِبَ الجَلالةِ

major /ˈmeɪdʒə/ **A** *adj* **1** (important) *‹change, role, event›* كَبير, رَئيسيّ (كُبَراءُ, كِبار); **it's a ~ undertaking** هي مُهِمّةٌ كَبيرةٌ **2** (main) *‹part, share›* رَئيسيّ **3** (Mus) *‹key, scale›* كَبير
B *n* **1** (Mil) رائِد **2** (subject) مادّة تَخَصُّصٍ
C *vi* (Educ) **to ~ in physics/Russian** دَرَسَ الفيزْياءَ \ الروسيّةَ كَمادّةِ تَخَصُّصٍ

Majorca /məˈjɔːkə/ *pr n* مايورْكا

majority /məˈdʒɒrɪti/ *n* (*pl* **majorities**) **1** (greater number) أَغْلَبيّة, غالِبيّة; **the vast ~** الأَغْلَبيّة الساحِقة, الغالِبيّة العُظْمى; **the ~ is** *or* **are in favour of the proposal** تُؤَيِّدُ الأَغْلَبيّةُ الاقْتِراحَ **2** (Pol) أَغْلَبيّة

majority rule *n* حُكْم الأَغْلَبيّةِ

major league *n* (بيسْبول) دَوْريّ مُمْتاز

major road *n* طَريق رَئيسيّ

make /meɪk/ **A** *vt* (*past tense, past participle* **made**) **1** (to create) صَنَعَ (a; صِناعة) *‹a dress, cake›*; أَخْرَجَ *‹film›*; حَفَرَ (i; حَفْر) *‹hole›*; **they ~ the engines** يَصْنَعونَ المُحَرِّكاتِ; **to ~ sth of/out of sth else** صَنَعَ شَيْئاً من شَيْءٍ آخَرَ; **they make gloves out of leather** يَصْنَعونَ قُفّازاتٍ من الجِلْدِ; **it's made of gold** هو مَصْنوعٌ من الذَهَبِ; **to ~ sth into sth else** حَوَّلَ شَيْئاً إلى شَيْءٍ آخَرَ; **they ~ the raw cotton into cloth** يَصْنَعونَ قُماشاً من القُطْنِ; **to ~ a house into apartments** حَوَّلَ بَيْتاً إلى شِقَقٍ; **to ~ sth for sb, to ~ sb sth** صَنَعَ شَيْئاً لِشَخْصٍ; **it's made a stain on the carpet** لَطَّخَ السَجّادةَ; **they're making a hole in the road** يَحْفِرونَ الطَريقَ; **made in the USA** مَصْنوع في

أَمْريكا; **God made man** خَلَقَ اللهُ الإنْسانَ **2** (to prepare) أَعَدَّ ‹*the coffee, breakfast*›; **to ~ the beds** رَتَّبَ السَرِيرَ **3** (with relationships) صادَقَ ‹*friends*›; عادى ‹*enemies*› **4** (to cause to be) جَعَلَ (a; جَعْل); **to ~ sb happy/jealous** جَعَلَ شَخْصاً سَعيداً \ يَشْعُرُ بالغَيْرةِ; **this work ~s me thirsty** هذا العَمَلُ يَجْعَلُني أَشْعُرُ بالعَطَشِ; **I tried to ~ myself heard/understood** حاوَلْتُ أَنْ أَجْعَلَ نَفْسي مَسْموعاً \ مَفْهوماً; **to ~ the picture bigger/smaller** جَعَلَ الصورةَ أَكْبَرَ \ أَصْغَرَ; **that ~s it possible/ impossible to go** ذلك يَجْعَلُ الذهابَ مُمْكناً \ مُسْتَحيلاً; **it'll ~ your cold better** [سَيَجْعَلُ صِحَّتَكَ تَتَحَسَّنُ] **5** (to cause to do) جَعَلَ (a; جَعْل); **to ~ sb smile/jump** جَعَلَ شَخْصاً يَبْتَسِمُ \ يَقْفِزُ; **it made us laugh** جَعَلَنا نَضْحَكُ; **it ~s me look fat** يَجْعَلُني أَبْدو سَميناً; **I made her listen to me** جَعَلْتُها تُنْصِتُ إِلَيَّ; **he made it start/work** جَعَلَها تَبْدَأُ \ تَعْمَلُ; **it ~s the crops ripen earlier** يَجْعَلُ المَحْصولَ يَنْضَجُ مُبَكِّراً **6** (to compel) **to ~ sb do sth** جَعَلَ شَخْصاً يَفْعَلُ شَيْئاً; **they made me do it** جَعَلوني أَفْعَلُهُ; **I can't ~ them refund the money** لا أَسْتَطيعُ أَنْ أَجْعَلَهُمْ يُعيدونَ إِلَيَّ الأَمْوالَ; **they made us wait an hour** جَعَلونا نَنْتَظِرُ ساعةً **7** **to ~ sb our representative/ leader** (to turn into) جَعَلَ شَخْصاً مُمَثِّلَنا \ قائِدَنا; **we made him club treasurer** جَعَلْناهُ أَمينَ صُنْدوقِ النادي; **she made it her duty to look after them** أَلْزَمَتْ نَفْسَها بِرِعايَتِهِمْ; **she'll ~ a good doctor** سَتَكونُ طَبيبةً جَيِّدةً; **he'll ~ sb a good husband** سَيَكونُ زَوْجاً جَيِّداً لِشَخْصٍ; **to ~ a habit of sth** جَعَلَ من شَيْءٍ عادةً; **she's made a habit of coming in late/ early** جَعَلَتْ من القُدومِ مُتَأَخِّراً \ باكِراً عادةً لَها; **he's made an issue of it** جَعَلَ مِنْهُ مُشْكِلةً **8** (to draw up) كَتَبَ (u; كِتابة) ‹*one's will*› **9** (to add up to) ساوى ‹*a number, total*›; **three and three ~ six** مَجْموعُ ثَلاثةٍ مع ثَلاثةٍ يُساوي سِتّةً; **that ~s ten altogether** ذلك كُلُّهُ يُساوي عَشَرةً **10** (to earn) كَسَبَ (i; كَسْب) ‹*an amount*›; **to ~ $1,500 a week** كَسَبَ $1500 في الأُسْبوعِ; **to ~ a profit/loss** حَقَّقَ رِبْحاً \ خَسارةً; **to ~ a fortune** حَقَّقَ ثَرْوةً; **she makes her living as a designer** تَعيشُ من عَمَلِها كَمُصَمِّمةٍ **11** (to achieve) أَحْرَزَ ‹*first place*›; **to ~ the first team** تَمَكَّنَ من الانْضِمامِ إلى الفَريقِ الأَوَّلِ; **to ~ the front page** تَصَدَّرَ الصَفْحةَ الأولى **12** (to score) سَجَّلَ ‹*runs, home runs*› **13** (to estimate, say) **I ~ it five o'clock** الساعةُ الخامِسةُ الآنَ; **what time do you ~ it?** كم الساعةُ الآنَ؟; **let's ~ it fifty dollars** لِيَكُنِ المَبْلَغُ خَمْسينَ دولاراً; **what do you ~ of it?** ما رَأْيُكَ فيه؟ **14** (to cause success of) جَعَلَ الشَيْءَ جَيِّداً \ حَسَناً ‹*a holiday, day*›; طَيَّبَ ‹*a meal*›; **it made my day** لَقَدْ جَعَلَ يَوْمي سَعيداً; **it really ~s the room** جَعَلَتِ الغُرْفةَ أَجْمَلَ فِعْلاً

B *n* (brand) نَوْع (أَنْواع); **what ~ is your car?** ما هو نَوْعُ سَيّارَتِكَ؟

(Idioms) **to make it** (to be successful) حالَفَهُ النَجاحُ; **he made it/ never made it as an actor** حالَفَهُ \ ما حالَفَهُ النَجاحُ في عَمَلِهِ كَمُمَثِّلٍ; (to get somewhere) [وَصَلَ]; **we made it home before dark** وَصَلْنا إلى البَيْتِ قبل الظَلامِ; **I'm sorry, I can't make it** أَنا آسِفٌ، لن أَسْتَطيعَ الحُضورَ; **to be on the make** (infml) أَعْماهُ الجَشَعُ

(Phrasal verbs) **make after**: **~ after [sb]** لاحَقَ [شَخْصاً] ‹*a vehicle, rioters*›; **the police made after the rioters** لاحَقَت الشُرْطةُ المُشاغبينَ

• **make do**: **~ do** تَدَبَّرَ أَمْرَهُ; **to ~ do with what one has** تَدَبَّرَ أَمْرَهُ بما عِنْدَهُ

• **make for**: **~ for [sth]** **1** (to head for) اتَّجَهَ نحو [شَيْءٍ] ‹*the door, check-out*› **2** (to facilitate) [شَيْئاً] سَهَّلَ ‹*a difficult life, happy marriage*›

• **make good**: **~ good [sth]** **1** (to repair) أَصْلَحَ [شَيْئاً] ‹*the damage*›; [شَيْئاً] عَوَّضَ ‹*losses*› **2** (to keep) حافَظَ على [شَيْءٍ] ‹*one's promise*›

• **make off** (infml) فَرَّ (i; مَفَرّ, فِرار); **to ~ off with the money** فَرَّ بالأَمْوالِ

• **make out** **A** **~ out** **1** (infml) (to manage) تَدَبَّرَ; **how are you making out?** كيف تَتَدَبَّرُ أُمورَكَ؟ **2** (to claim) ادَّعى **3** (AmE) (infml) (sexually) [لامَسَ وَقَبَّلَ] **B** **~ out [sth], ~ [sth] out** **1** (to distinguish) [شَيْئاً] مَيَّزَ ‹*a sign, a signature*› **2** (to understand, work out) [شَيْئاً] فَهِمَ ‹*the meaning*›; **I can't ~ out what he's saying** لا أَسْتَطيعُ أَنْ أَفْهَمَ ما يَقولُ **3** (to write out) [شَيْئاً] كَتَبَ ‹*a cheque*›; [شَيْئاً] حَرَّرَ ‹*a prescription*› **C** **~ sb out to be a sth** ادَّعى أَنَّ شَخْصاً كانَ شَيْئاً

• **make over**: **~ over [sth], ~ [sth] over** 1 (to transform) غَيَّرَ [شَيْئاً] *‹a building, sb's appearance›* 2 (to assign) نَقَلَ مِلْكِيَّة [شَيْءٍ] *‹a property, the assets›*

• **make towards**: **~ towards [sth/sb]** اتَّجَهَ نحو [شَيْءٍ \ شَخْصٍ] *‹the door, check-out›*

• **make up** A **~ up** 1 (after quarrelling) تَصالَحَ 2 (to compensate for) **to ~ up for a loss** عَوَّضَ خَسارةً; **nothing can ~ up for the loss of a parent** لا شَيْءَ يُعَوِّضُ خَسارةَ أَحَدِ الأَبَوَيْنِ B **~ up [sth], ~ [sth] up** 1 (to invent) اخْتَلَقَ [شَيْئاً] *‹an excuse, a story›* 2 (to prepare) أَعَدَّ [شَيْئاً] *‹a parcel, the room›* 3 (to constitute) شَكَّلَ [شَيْئاً] *‹a whole, society›*; **they ~ up the majority of the population** هُمْ يُشَكِّلونَ أَغْلَبِيَّةَ الشَّعْبِ 4 (to compensate for) عَوَّضَ [شَيْئاً] *‹a loss, shortfall›* 5 (to put make-up on) زَيَّنَ [شَيْئاً] *‹a person, one's face›*; **to ~ oneself up** تَزَيَّنَ 6 حَلَّ \ حَسَمَ [شَيْئاً] *‹one's differences›*; **let's ~ it up** هَيّا نَتَصالَحُ

make-believe /ˈmeɪkbɪliːv/ *n* (pretending) ادِّعاء, تَظاهُر (ادِّعاءات); (imagining) تَخَيُّل (تَخَيُّلات) وَهْم (أَوْهام), تَوَهُّم, خِداع النَّفْسِ

makeover /ˈmeɪkəʊvə/ *n* 1 (of a person) تَغْيير شَكْلٍ \ مَظْهَرٍ 2 (of a building) تَجْديد (تَجْديدات)

maker /ˈmeɪkə/ *n* (company that produces) شَرِكة مُصَنِّعة; (person who produces) صانِع (صُنّاع); **one of the world's largest toy ~s** واحِدة من كُبْرى الشَرِكاتِ المُصَنِّعةِ لِلُعَبِ الأَطْفالِ في العالَمِ

makeshift /ˈmeɪkʃɪft/ *adj ‹shelter, bed›* مُؤَقَّت

make-up /ˈmeɪkʌp/ *n* 1 (cosmetics) مَكْياج; **to put one's ~ on** وَضَعَ مَكياجَهُ 2 (composition) تَرْكيبة (تَرْكيبات, تَراكيبُ) 3 (character) تَكْوين

make-up artist *n* فَنّان تَجْميلٍ, ماكْيير

make-up bag *n* حَقيبة ماكياج

make-up remover *n* مُزيل ماكياج

making /ˈmeɪkɪŋ/ *n* (of a product) إِنْتاج, صُنْع; **he died during the ~ of the film** ماتَ خلال إِنْتاجِ الفيلْمِ; **the novel was ten years in the ~** اسْتَغْرَقَتْ كِتابةُ الرِوايةِ عَشْرَ سَنواتٍ

(Idiom) **to have the makings of sth**: **he has the ~s of a world champion** لَدَيْهِ المُقَوِّماتُ لِأَنْ يَصْبَحَ بَطَلاً عالَمِيًّا; **we have the ~s of a great story here** لَدَيْنا هُنا مُكَوِّناتُ قِصّةٍ عَظيمةٍ

maladjusted /ˌmæləˈdʒʌstɪd/ *adj ‹adolescent, child›* غَيْر مُنْسَجِمٍ \ مُتوافِقٍ

maladjustment /mæləˈdʒʌstmənt/ *n* عَدَم, انْعِدام التَكَيُّفِ \ تَوافُقٍ \ انْسِجامٍ

malaria /məˈlɛːrɪə/ *n* مَلاريا

Malawi /məˈlɑːwi/ *pr n* مالاوي (f)

Malawian /məˈlɑːwɪən/ *n, adj* مالاويّ

Malay /məˈleɪ/, **Malayan** /məˈleɪən/ A *n* 1 (inhabitant) ماليزيّ 2 (language) (اللُغة) الماليزيّة \ المَلايُويّة, لُغة المَلايو B *adj ‹peninsula, language, people›* ماليزيّ

Malaysia /məˈleɪzɪə/ *pr n* ماليزِيا

Malaysian /məˈleɪziən/ *n, adj* ماليزيّ

Maldives /ˈmɔːldʌɪvz/ *pr n pl* (**the Maldives** also **the Maldive Islands**) جُزُر المالْديف

male /meɪl/ A *adj* 1 *‹animal›* ذَكَر; **a ~ frog** ضِفْدَع ذَكَر 2 *‹sex, voice, body›* ذَكَر (ذُكور); **a ~ friend** صَديق ذَكَر B *n* 1 (animal) ذَكَر 2 (man, boy) ذَكَر (ذُكور)

malevolent /məˈlɛvələnt/ *adj ‹force, spirit›* خَبيث, (أَشْرار) شِرّير (خُبَثاء, خَبَثة)

malformation /malfɔːˈmeɪʃ(ə)n/ *n* تَشَوُّه (تَشَوُّهات)

malformed /ˌmalˈfɔːmd/ *adj ‹limb, foetus›* مُشَوَّه

malfunction /malˈfʌŋkʃ(ə)n/ A *vi* «machines» حَدَثَ بِهِ خَلَلٌ \ عُطْلٌ; «organs» حَدَثَ بِهِ قُصورٌ B *n* خَلَل (وَظيفيّ), (أَعْطال) عُطْل

Mali /ˈmɑːli/ *pr n* مالي (f)

Malian /ˈmɑːliən/ *n, adj* ماليّ

malice /ˈmalɪs/ *n* شَرّ, غِلّ, (أَحْقاد) حِقْد

malicious /məˈlɪʃəs/ *adj ‹rumour, intent›* خَبيث, (أَشْرار) شِرّير (خَبَثة, خُبَثاء)

malign /məˈlʌɪn/ *vt* انْتَقَدَ بِشِدّةٍ *‹sb's character, work›*

malignant /məˈlɪgnənt/ *adj* 1 *‹tumour, cell›* خَبيث 2 *‹force, spirit›* خَبيث, خُبَثاءُ, خَبَثة, شِرّير (أَشْرار)

Maliki /'malıki/ *adj* مالِكيّ

malinger /mə'lıŋgə/ *vi* (pej) «soldiers, employees» تَمارَضَ

mall /mal, mɔːl/ *n* **1** (also **shopping mall**) (AmE) مَرْكَز تَسَوُّقٍ, مُجَمَّع تِجاريّ **2** (street) مُتَنَزَّه (مُتَنَزَّهات)

mallard /'malɑːd/ *n* (*pl* **mallard, mallards**) بَطّة بَرّيّة

mallet /'malıt/ *n* مِطْرَقة خَشَبيّة

malnutrition /malnjʊ'trıʃ(ə)n/ *n* سوء تَغْذِيةٍ

malpractice /mal'praktıs/ *n* سوء مُمارَسةٍ

malt /mɔːlt/ *n* **1** (grain) شَعير مُخَمَّر, مالْت **2** (whisky) ويسْكي الشَعيرِ

Malta /'mɔːltə/ *pr n* مالْطا

Maltese /mɔːl'tiːz/ **A** *n* (*pl* **Maltese**) **1** (citizen) مالْطيّ **2** (language) (اللُغة) المالْطيّة **B** *adj* <*flag, custom*> مالْطيّ

maltreat /mal'triːt/ *vt* أساءَ المُعامَلةَ <*a prisoner, child*>

mama, mamma /'mamə/ *n* (AmE) ماما

mammal /'mam(ə)l/ *n* ثَدْييّ (ثَدْيِيّات)

mammalian /ma'meılıən/ *adj* <*cell, species*> ثَدْييّ

mammogram /'maməgram/ *n* ماموغْرام, أَشِعّة على الثَدْيِ, تَصوير الثَدْيِ الشُعاعيّ

mammography /ma'mɒgrəfi/ *n* تَصْوير الثَدْيِ بالأَشِعّةِ

mammoth /'maməθ/ **A** *n* ماموث **B** *adj* <*task, organization*> ضَخْم (ضِخام)

man /man/ **A** *n* (*pl* **men** /mɛn/) **1** (adult male) رَجُل (رِجال); **a single/married ~** رَجُل أَعْزَب \ مُتَزَوِّج; **an old ~** شَيْخ (شُيوخ); **a ~ of God** رَجُل دينٍ; **a ~ of the people** رَجُل شَعْبيّ; **~ of the match** رَجُل المُباراةِ; **good ~!** [مُمْتاز!]; **to talk about it ~ to ~** تَحَدَّثَ عَنْهُ بِصَراحةٍ \ رَجُلاً لِرَجُلٍ **2** (husband, partner) رَجُل (رِجال); **he is the right ~ for her** هو الرَجُلُ المُناسِبُ لَها; **to live as ~ and wife** عاشا كَزَوْجٍ وَزَوْجةٍ **3** [u] (person) إنْسان **4** (*also* **Man**) (mankind) إنْسان; **~ is mortal** الإنْسانُ فانٍ **5** (in chess, in draughts) حَجَر (أَحْجار, حِجارة); **to be one ~ up** كانَ مُتَقَدِّماً بِحَجَرةٍ واحِدةٍ **B** (**men**) *n pl* (soldiers, sailors) رِجال; **the colonel addressed the men** خَطَبَ العَقيدُ في رِجالِ الجَيْشِ **C** *vt* (-nn-) (to operate) شَغَّلَ, أَدارَ <*the switchboard, desk, ship*>; **will the switchboard be ~ned?** هل سَيَتِمُّ تَشْغيلُ لَوْحةِ المَفاتيحِ؟; **a ~ned flight/spacecraft** مَرْكَبة فَضائيّة مَأْهولة **D** *excl* **1** (infml) (expressing surprise) يا رَجُل **2** (infml) (addressing somebody) **hey ~!** يا رَجُل!

Idioms **every man for himself** اللّهُمَّ نَفْسي; **to a man** بالإجْماعِ; **to be man enough to do sth** كانَتْ لَدَيْهِ الجُرْأةُ الكافِيةُ لِفِعْلِ شَيْءٍ; **to be one's own man** كانَ يَعْتَمِدُ على نَفْسِهِ; **to sort** *or* **separate the men from the boys** عَرَفَ الغَثَّ من السَمينِ

manage /'manıdʒ/ **A** *vt* **1** (to run) أَدارَ <*a business, company, bank*>; **my sister's company is managing the project** تُديرُ شَرِكةُ أُخْتي المَشْروعَ **2** (to administer) تَصَرَّفَ (في) <*resources, sb's estate, one's time*> **3** (to supervise) تَعامَلَ (مع) <*a patient, an illness*> **4** (to be the manager of) أَدارَ, أَشْرَفَ (على) <*a team, band, player*> **5** (to succeed); **she ~d to finish early** تَمَكَّنَتْ من الانْتِهاءِ باكِراً; **he ~d to offend everybody** اسْتَطاعَ أنْ يُغْضِبَ كُلَّ شَخْصٍ; **she ~d a smile** تَمَكَّنَتْ من رَسْمِ ابْتِسامةٍ على وَجْهِها; **they ~d a draw** تَمَكَّنوا من التَعادُلِ; **I couldn't ~ another thing!** لا أَسْتَطيعُ أنْ أَتَناوَلَ شَيْئاً آخَرَ!; **to ~ to do sth** تَمَكَّنَ من فِعْلِ شَيْءٍ **6** (to negotiate) تَعامَلَ (مع) <*a situation, the controls, group*>; **she ~d the interview very well/badly** كانَ أَداؤُها في المُقابَلةِ جَيِّداً \ سَيِّئاً; **I can't ~ Friday** الجُمْعةُ لَيْسَ يَوْماً مُناسِباً لي **B** *vi* «people, families» تَدَبَّرَ الأَمْرَ; **can you ~?** هل تَسْتَطيعُ أنْ تَتَدَبَّرَ أَمْرَكَ؟; **they have to ~ on £50 a week** عَلَيْهِمْ أنْ يَتَدَبَّروا أُمورَهُمْ بِخَمْسينَ جُنَيْهاً في الأُسْبوعِ

manageable /'manıdʒəb(ə)l/ *adj* <*level, size*> يُمْكِنُ السَيْطَرةُ عَلَيْهِ \ التَحَكُّمُ فيه; <*task*> يُمْكِنُ إدارَتُهُ; <*hair*> سَهْل التَصْفيفِ; <*animal, person*> يُمْكِنُ التَعامُلُ مَعَهُ

management /'manıdʒmənt/ **A** *n* **1** [u] (of a situation) إدارة **2** [u] (of businesses, teams, a shop, project) إدارة; (of resources) تَصَرُّف, إدارة; **'under new ~'** 'تحت إدارةٍ جَديدةٍ' **3** [u] (skill) عِلْم الإدارة **4** [u] (of patients, diseases) تَعامُل (مع) **5** [u] (managers collectively) إدارة; **senior/middle**

~ **and unions** الإدارة والاتِّحادات العُمّاليّة; ~ إدارة عُليا \ وُسْطى

B *modifier* <*company, style, committee*> إداريّ; **the ~ team** الفَريق الإداريّ

management consultant *n* مُسْتَشار إداريّ

management trainee *n* مُتَدَرِّب على الإدارةِ

manager /ˈmanɪdʒə/ *n* **1** (of a company, bank, project) مُدير; **he's the general ~ at Hilton Cairo** هو المُديرُ العامُّ لِفَنادِقِ هيلْتون بالقاهِرةِ **2** (of a performer, boxer, etc) مُدير أَعْمالٍ **3** (of a team) مُدير

manageress /ˌmanɪdʒəˈres/ *n* (BrE) مُديرة

managerial /manəˈdʒiːrɪəl/ *adj* <*position, skills*> إداريّ

managing director /ˌmanədʒɪŋ dɪˈrektə/ *n* مُدير تَنْفيذيّ

Manama /məˈnɑːmə/ *pr n* المَنامة

mandarin, **mandarin orange** /ˈmandərɪn/ *n* مَنْدَرين ,يوسُفيّ

mandate /ˈmandeɪt/ *n* تَفْويض (تَفْويضات)

mandatory /ˈmandət(ə)ri/ *adj* <*sentence, requirement*> إِلْزامي, إجْباريّ; **the sentence for murder is ~** القاضي مُلْزَمٌ بِمُعاقبةِ القاتِلِ

mandolin /mandəˈlɪn/ *n* مَنْدولين

mane /meɪn/ *n* **1** (of a horse, lion) عُرْف (أَعْراف) **2** (person's hair) لُبْدة (لُبَد)

maneuver (AmE) *n, vt, vi* ▸ **manoeuvre**

manganese /ˈmaŋgəniːz/ *n* مَنْجَنيز

mangel /ˈmaŋg(ə)l/, **mangel-wurzel** /ˈmanglwəːz(ə)l/ *n* ▸ **mangold**

manger /ˈmeɪndʒə/ *n* مِعْلَف (مَعالِفُ), مِذْوَد (مَذاوِدُ)

mangetout /mɑːnʒˈtuː/ *n* بازِلاّء خَضْراء عَريضة تُؤْكَل دون [تَقْصيصٍ]

mangle /ˈmaŋg(ə)l/ **A** *n* عَصّارة الثِّيابِ

B *vt* **1** شَوَّهَ <*a body, vehicle*> **2** شَوَّهَ <*a song*>; ارْتَكَبَ أَخْطاءً فادِحةً في <*the grammar*>

mango /ˈmaŋgəʊ/ *n* (*pl* **mangoes** or **mangos**) مانْجو

mangold /ˈmaŋgəʊld/ *n* شَمَنْدَر

mangrove /ˈmaŋgrəʊv/ *n* مانْجْروف ,قُرْم ,أَيكة ساحِلِيّة

mangy /ˈmeɪndʒi/ *adj* (**mangier, mangiest**) <*dog, cat*> أَجْرَب (dipt; جُرْب, جَرْبان)

manhandle /ˈmanhand(ə)l/ *vt* **1** (to treat roughly) عامَلَ بِخُشونةٍ <*protesters, prisoners*> **2** (to move by hand) نَقَلَ \ حَرَّكَ يَدَويًّا <*heavy objects*>

manhole /ˈmanhəʊl/ *n* بالوعة (بالوعات, بَواليعُ)

manhood /ˈmanhʊd/ *n* **1** (adulthood) سِنّ الرُجولةِ **2** (masculinity) رُجولة

man-hour /ˈmanˌaʊə/ *n* ساعة عَمَلٍ

manhunt /ˈmanhʌnt/ *n* مُلاحَقة مُتَّهَمٍ أو هارِبٍ

mania /ˈmeɪnɪə/ *n* **1** (mental illness) هوس **2** (obsession) هَوَس

maniac /ˈmeɪnɪak/ *n* مَهْووس ,مَخبول (مَخْبولون, مَخابيل), مَجْنون (مَجانين)

manic /ˈmanɪk/ *adj* **1** <*episode, symptoms*> هَوَسِيّ **2** <*energy, activity*> مَهْووس

manic depression *n* هَوَس اكْتِئابيّ

manicure /ˈmanɪkjʊə/ **A** *n* مانيكير ,تَجْميل \ تَدْريم أَظافِرِ اليَدِ

B *vt* دَرَّمَ <*sb's nails*>

manicurist /ˈmanɪkjʊərɪst/ *n* خَبير \ عامِل ,مُدَرِّم أَظافِرِ اليَدِ مانيكير

manifest /ˈmanɪfest/ **A** *adj* (fml) <*error, failure*> جَلِيّ ,واضِح

B *vt* (fml) أَبْدى ,أَظْهَرَ <*intention*>; ظَهَرَ عَلَيْهِ <*symptoms*>

C *v refl* (fml) **to ~ itself** «disease, feeling» ظَهَرَ ,تَجَلّى (a; ظُهور)

manifestation /ˌmanɪfeˈsteɪʃ(ə)n/ *n* (fml) مَظْهَر (مَظاهِرُ)

manifesto /manɪˈfestəʊ/ *n* (*pl* **manifestos**) بَيان رَسْميّ

manifold /ˈmanɪfəʊld/ **A** *adj* (fml) <*temptations, benefits*> عَديد, مُتَعَدِّد

B *n* أُنْبوب مُتَفَرِّع \ مُتَشَعِّب

manioc /ˈmanɪɒk/ *n* مَنْهِيوت ,كَسافا

manipulate /məˈnɪpjʊleɪt/ *vt* **1** (unscrupulously) تَلاعَبَ (ب), احْتالَ (على) <*a person, the situation, system*> **2** (to control) تَحَكَّمَ (في) <*the levers, image*> **3** (in computing) عالَجَ <*the data*>

manipulation /məˌnɪpjʊˈleɪʃ(ə)n/ *n* **1** (of figures, facts) تَلاعُب (تَلاعُبات) **2** (of data) مُعالَجة **3** (of bones, limbs) [رَدّ العَظْمِ المَخْلوعِ إلى مَكانِهِ]

manipulative /mə'nɪpjʊlətɪv/ *adj* ‹*parent, tactic*› اسْتِغْلاليّ, مُسَيْطِر (بالدَهاءِ والمَكْرِ)

mankind /man'kʌɪnd/ *n* بَشَريّة, إِنْسانيّة

manly /'manli/ *adj* (**manlier, manliest**) ‹*voice, laugh*› رُجوليّ

man-made /man'meɪd/ *adj* ‹*fibre, fabric*› اصْطِناعيّ, صِناعيّ; ‹*lake, tools*› من صُنْعِ الإِنْسانِ

manna /'manə/ *n* مَنّ

manned /mand/ *adj* ‹*mission, aircraft, crossing*› مَأْهول

manner /'manə/ **A** *n* **1** (way, method) أُسْلوب (أَساليبُ), طَريقة (طَرائِقُ, طُرُق); **in an efficient ~** بِأُسْلوبٍ فَعّالٍ; **in this ~** بِهَذِه الطَريقةِ; **in a ~ of speaking** إذا جازَ التَعْبيرُ **2** (of behaviour) سُلوك; **something in his ~ made her uneasy** شَيْءٌ في سُلوكِهِ جَعَلَها قَلِقةً; **to have a good telephone ~** كانَ لَدَيْهِ أُسْلوبٌ جَيِّدٌ في الحَديثِ على الهاتِفِ **B** (**manners**) *n pl* **1** (social behaviour) أَخْلاق; **good/bad ~s** أَخْلاق جَيِّدة \ سَيِّئة; **he has no ~s** هو غَيْرُ مُؤَدَّبٍ; ▸ **table manners** **2** (fml) (social customs) الأُصول (آداب سُلوكِ فِئةٍ اجْتِماعيّةٍ مُعَيَّنةٍ); **a comedy of ~s** كوميديا الأَخْلاقِ

mannerism /'man(ə)rɪz(ə)m/ *n* (habit) طَريقة (طَرائِقُ, طُرُق), أُسْلوب (أَساليبُ); (quirk) عادة غَريبة

manoeuvre (BrE), **maneuver** (AmE) /mə'nu:və/ **A** *n* **1** مُناوَرة **2** (**manoeuvres** *n pl* (Mil)) مُناوَرات, مُناوَرة **B** *vt* **1** (to move) ناوَرَ (ب) ‹*a vehicle, an object*› **2** (to manipulate) ناوَرَ ‹*an opponent, a candidate*›; أَدارَ ‹*the conversation*› **C** *vi* «lorries, ships» ناوَرَ

manor /'manə/ *n* (also **manor house**) [قَصْر مالِكِ الضَيْعةِ]; **Lord/Lady of the ~** سَيِّد \ سَيِّدة القَصْرِ; **Malsway Manor** قَصْر مالْسْواي

manpower /'manpaʊə/ *n* قُوًى \ أَيْدٍ عامِلة

mansion /'manʃ(ə)n/ *n* قَصْر (قُصور)

manslaughter /'manslɔ:tə/ *n* قَتْل; **to commit ~** ارْتَكَبَ جَريمةَ قَتْلٍ; **to be charged with/found guilty of ~** اُتُّهِمَ \ أُدينَ في جَريمةِ قَتْلٍ

mantelpiece /'mantəlpi:s/ *n* رَفّ مَوْقِدٍ

mantle /'mant(ə)l/ *n* **1** (cloak) عَباءة (أَعْبِئة) **2** (covering) غِطاء (أَغْطِية) **3** (Geol) دِثار (دُثُر)

manual /'manjʊəl/ **A** *adj* ‹*labour, worker, gearbox*› يَدَويّ **B** *n* دَليل (كُتَيِّب)

manually /'manju:əli/ *adv* ‹*to operate, turn*› يَدَوِيًّا

manufacture /manjʊ'faktʃə/ **A** *vt* صَنَعَ (a; صِناعة) ‹*clothes, cars*› **B** *n* (of clothes, cars) صِناعة

manufacturer /ˌmanjʊ'faktʃ(ə)rə/ *n* (person) صانِع (صُنّاع); (enterprise) شَرِكة مُصَنِّعة

manufacturing /manju:'faktʃərɪŋ/ *n* **1** (economic sector) صِناعة **2** (of cars, heavy machinery) تَصْنيع

manufacturing costs *n* تَكاليف تَصْنيعٍ

manufacturing plant *n* مَصْنَع (مَصانِعُ)

manure /mə'njʊə/ *n* رَوْث (أَرْواث), سَماد (أَسْمِدة)

manuscript /'manjʊskrɪpt/ *n* مَخْطوطة (مَخْطوطات)

Manx /maŋks/ **A** *adj* ‹*dances, customs, people*› مانْكْسيّ **B** *n* **1** (Ling) (اللُغة) المانْكْسيّة **2** **the ~** (+ *v pl*) سُكّان جَزيرةِ مان

Manx cat *n* قِطّ مانْكْسيّ

many /'mɛni/ **A** *determiner* ‹*units, things, people*› كَثير, كَثيرونَ, كِثار; **~ people** كَثير من الناسِ; **~ times** أَوْقات كَثيرة; **for ~ years** لِسَنَواتٍ عَديدةٍ; **how ~ people/times?** كم شَخْصاً \ مَرّةً؟; **too ~ visitors** عَدَد زائِد من الزوّارِ; **I have as ~ books as you (do)** لَدَيَّ نَفْسُ عَدَدِ كُتُبِكَ; **so ~ questions** أَسْئِلة كَثيرة جِدًّا; **there are ~ models to choose from** هُناكَ الكَثيرُ من النَماذِجِ للاخْتِيارِ من بَيْنِها; **I don't have very ~ books** لَيْسَ لَدَيَّ الكَثيرُ من الكُتُبِ **B** *pron* (*comparative* **more**; *superlative* **most**) كَثير, كَثيرونَ, كِثار; **not ~** عَدَد قَليل, عَدَد لَيْسَ بِكَثيرٍ; **too ~** كَثير جِدًّا; **how ~?** كَم؟; **as ~ as you like** العَدَدُ الّذي تُريدُهُ; **I didn't know there were so ~** لم أَكُنْ أَعْرِفُ أَنَّهُمْ بِهَذا العَدَدِ الكَبيرِ; **~ of them were genuine/false** الكَثيرُ مِنْها كانَ حَقيقيًّا \ زائِفاً

many-sided *adj* مُتَعَدِّد الجَوانِبِ

Maori /'maʊri/ **A** *n* **1** (person) ماوْريّ **2** (language) (اللُغة) الماوْريّة **B** *adj* ‹*dress, people*› ماوْريّ

map /map/ *n* (of a country, continent) خَريطة (خَرائِطُ); **a street ~** خَريطة شَوارِعَ

Idiom to put sb/sth on the map جَعَلَ شَخْصاً \ شَيْئاً يَتَبَوَّأُ مَكانةً عالِيةً

Phrasal verb **map out**: ~ out [sth], ~ [sth] out «manager» خَطَّطَ [شَيْئاً], حَدَّدَ مَعالِمَ \ مَلامِحَ [شَيْءٍ] ‹a strategy, sb's career›; **the idea of the meeting is to ~ out the sales strategy for the next two years** فِكْرةُ الاجْتِماعِ هي رَسْمُ اسْتراتيجيّةِ المَبيعاتِ للسَّنَتَيْنِ القادِمَتَيْنِ

maple /ˈmeɪp(ə)l/ *n* إسْفِنْدان, قَيْقَب

mar /mɑː/ *vt* (-rr-) أَفْسَدَ ‹career, holiday›

marabou /ˈmarəbuː/ *n* أبو سَعْن الإفْريقيّ

marabout /ˈmarəbuːt/ *n* مُرابِط

marathon /ˈmarəθ(ə)n/ **A** *n* **1** (race) ماراثون; **to run in the New York ~** رَكَضَ في ماراثون نيويورْك **2** (demanding episode) ماراثون; **the interview was a real ~** كانَتْ المُقابَلةُ ماراثوناً حَقيقيّاً

B *adj before n* **1** a ~ runner مُتَسابِق ماراثون **2** (lengthy) ‹session› ماراثونيّ; ‹speech› مُطَوَّل

marauder /məˈrɔːdə/ *n* لِصّ, نَهّاب (لُصوص)

marble /ˈmɑːb(ə)l/ *n* **1** (stone) رُخام; **to be made of ~** كانَ مَصْنوعاً من الرُخامِ **2** (Games) لُعْبة الكُراتِ الزُجاجيّةِ; **to play ~s** لَعِبَ بالكُراتِ الزُجاجيّةِ

Idiom to lose one's marbles (infml) جُنَّ جُنونُه, فَقَدَ عَقْلَهُ

march /mɑːtʃ/ **A** *vt* حَثَّ على السَّيْرِ ‹the prisoners, squad›; **he ~ed the suspect into the police station** اقْتادَ المُتَّهَمَ نحو مَرْكَزِ الشُرْطةِ \ البوليس

B *vi* **1** «soldiers» سارَ (i; مَسير, سَيْر); **forward/quick ~!** إلى الأَمامِ سِرْ! **2** (in protest) «demonstrators, protesters» سارَ (i; مَسير, سَيْر), مَشى (i; مَشْي); **the protesters ~ed through the capital** سارَ \ مَشى المُتَظاهِرونَ عَبْرَ العاصِمةِ **3** (to stride) سارَ (i; مَسير, سَيْر); **she ~ed up to the manager** سارَتْ نحو المُديرِ

C *n* **1** (journey on foot) مارِش عَسْكَريّ, مَسيرة عَسْكَريّة; **a 40 km ~** مَسيرة 40 كلم; **it's a day's ~ from here** إنَّها على مَسيرةِ يَوْمٍ من هُنا; **the ~ of time** مَسيرة الزَمَنِ **2** (demonstration) مُظاهَرة, مَسيرة; **a protest ~** مَسيرة احْتِجاجٍ; **a ~ on the presidential palace** مَسيرة نحو القَصْرِ الرِئاسيِّ **3** (Mus) موسيقى المارِشِ; **a slow/quick ~** مارِش بَطيء \ سَريع

Idioms to give sb their marching orders طَرَدَهُ شَرَّ طَرْدةٍ; **to steal a march on sb** [اسْتَبَقَ شَخْصاً بالحيلةِ والخِداعِ]

March /mɑːtʃ/ *n* مارِس (NA, Gulf), آذار (dipt) (Levant, Iraq); **in ~** في آذارَ \ مارِس; **her birthday is in M~** عيدُ ميلادِها في آذارَ \ مارِس; **our holiday starts on M~ 23rd/23 M~** تَبْدَأُ عُطْلَتُنا 23 آذار \ مارس; **next/last M~** آذارَ \ مارس المُقْبِل \ الماضي; **we visit them every M~** نَزورُهُمْ في شَهْرِ آذارَ \ مارِس من كُلِّ عامٍ; **in mid-M~ /the middle of M~** في مُنْتَصَفِ آذارَ \ مارِس

marcher /ˈmɑːtʃə/ *n* (in demonstration) مُتَظاهِر, مُشارِك في مَسيرةٍ; (in procession) سائِر, مُشارِك في مَوْكِبٍ

march past *n* اسْتِعْراض عَسْكَريّ (مَسيرة الجُنودِ أمامَ قائِدٍ للتَحيّةِ)

mare /mɛː/ *n* (horse) أُنْثى الفَرَسِ, مُهْرة (مُهَر); (donkey) حِمارة, أَتان (أُتُن)

margarine /ˌmɑːdʒəˈriːn/ *n* مَرْغَرين, سَمْن نَباتيّ

margin /ˈmɑːdʒɪn/ *n* (of a page) حاشِية, هامِش (هَوامِش), (حَواشٍ); (edge) حافّة; **by a narrow ~** بِهامِشٍ, بِفارِقٍ بَسيطٍ; **in the ~** في الحاشِيةِ, على الهامِشِ, ضَيِّق

marginal /ˈmɑːdʒɪn(ə)l/ *adj* ‹improvement, change, adjustment› هامِشيّ

marginalize, -ise (BrE) /ˈmɑːdʒɪnəlʌɪz/ *vt* «party, authorities» هَمَّشَ ‹activity, group, issue›

marginally /ˈmɑːdʒɪn(ə)li/ *adv* ‹more successful, kinder, more effective› بِدَرَجةٍ بَسيطةٍ, بِشَكْلٍ طَفيفٍ

marigold /ˈmarɪɡəʊld/ *n* آذَرْيون

marijuana /ˌmarɪˈhwɑːnə/ *n* قِنَّب هِنْديّ, ماريجُوانا; **teenage kids smoking ~** أطْفال مُراهِقونَ يُدَخِّنونَ الماريجُوانا

marinade /ˌmarɪˈneɪd/ *n* [مَحْلول لِتَخْليلِ أو تَتْبيلِ الأَطْعِمةِ]

marine /məˈriːn/ **A** *adj* **1** ‹biology, mammal› بَحْريّ **2** ‹insurance, engineering› بَحْريّ

B *n* جُنْديّ في البَحْريّةِ

marital /ˈmarɪt(ə)l/ *adj* ‹relations, vows› زَوْجيّ

marital status *n* حالة اجْتِماعيّة

maritime /ˈmarɪtʌɪm/ *adj* ‹*museum, law*› بَحْرِيّ

marjoram /ˈmɑːdʒ(ə)rəm/ *n* مَرْدَقوش

mark /mɑːk/ **A** *n* **1** (stain, blemish) بُقْعة (بُقَع ,بِقاع); **to leave one's/its ~ on sth** تَرَكَ بَصْمَتَهُ على شَيْءٍ **2** (distinguishing feature) بُقْعة (بُقَع ,بِقاع), عَلامة (عَلامات ,عَلائِم), سِمة; **it has a distinctive white ~ on its head** عِنْدَها بُقْعةٌ بَيْضاءُ مُمَيَّزَةٌ على رَأْسِها; **to make one's ~** تَرَكَ بَصْمَتَهُ; **it's the ~ of a real professional that ...** إنَّها عَلامةٌ على الاحْتِراف أنْ ... **3** (indicator) مُؤَشِّر (مُؤَشِّرات); **the high-/low-water ~** مُسْتَوى المِياهِ المُرْتَفِع \ المُنْخَفِض; **unemployment has reached the two million ~** لَقَدْ بَلَغَت البِطالةُ مُسْتَوى المَلْيونَيْنِ; **the race is nearing the halfway ~** يَقْتَرِبُ السِباقُ من عَلامةِ المُنْتَصَفِ **4** (symbol) عَلامة (عَلامات ,عَلائِمُ); **as a ~ of respect/appreciation** كَعَلامةِ احْتِرامٍ \ تَقْديرٍ **5** (point) عَلامة (عَلامات); (total) مَجْموع (مَجاميعُ), عَلامة نِهائيّة; **the exam counts towards your final ~** الامْتِحانُ جُزْءٌ من عَلامَتِكَ النِهائيّةِ **6** (in races) نُقْطة انْطِلاقٍ; **on your ~s, get set, go!** خُذْ مَكانَكَ، اسْتَعِدَّ، انْطَلِقْ! **7** (target) هَدَف (أَهْداف), مَرْمًى (مَرامٍ); **to hit/miss its ~** «criticism» أَصابَ \ أخْطأَ هَدَفَهُ; «arrow» أَصابَ \ أخْطأَ مَرْماهُ; **to be wide of the ~** كانَ بَعيداً عن الهَدَفِ المَنْشودِ **8** (also **Marque**) (model) مارْكة; **Jaguar Mark II** جاغْوار مارْك 2 **9** (also **Deutschmark**) (Hist) مارْك (مارْكات)

B *vt* **1** (to stain) لَطَّخ ‹*clothes, paper*›; **to ~ sb for life** أَثَّرَ على حَياةِ شَخْصٍ إلى الأَبَدِ **2** (to indicate) أَشَّرَ ‹*a place, position*›; **the envelope was ~ed 'personal'** وُضِعَت عَلامةُ 'شَخْصِيّ' على الظَرْفِ; **X ~s the spot** حَرْفُ X يَدُلُّ على البُقْعةِ; **fields ~ed with an asterisk are mandatory** يَجِبُ مَلْءُ الحُقولِ الّتي بِجِوارِها نَجْمةٌ **3** (to label) عَلَّمَ (بِعَلامةٍ) ‹*boxes, belongings*› **4** (to represent) كانَ مُؤَشِّراً, رَسَمَ عَلامةً على ‹*the end, a turning point*› **5** (to commemorate) أَحْيا ذِكْرى ‹*an anniversary, occasion*› **6** (to characterize) طَبَعَ (a; طَبْع) ‹*an era*› **7** (to grade) صَحَّحَ, وَضَعَ عَلامةً ‹*an essay, homework*› **8** (to pay attention to) **you'll pay for this, ~ my words** سَتَدْفَعُ ثَمَنَ هذا، تَذَكَّرْ كَلامي **9** (BrE Sport) حاصَرَ ‹*a forward*›

C *vi* (to become stained) «carpet, fabric» تَلَطَّخَ

Idioms **to be fast** *or* **quick/slow off the mark** [تَحَرَّكَ بِسُرْعةٍ \ بِبُطْءٍ]; **to mark time** (in marching) راوَحَ مَكانَهُ, مَشى في المَحَلِّ; (to wait) قَتَلَ الوَقْتَ ▸ **overstep**

Phrasal verbs **mark down A ~ [sth] down, ~ down [sth]** خَفَّضَ [شَيْئاً] ‹*a product, price*› **B ~ [sb] down 1** (to lower the grade of) نَقَّصَ في عَلامةِ [شَخْصٍ] ‹*a student*› **2** (to consider to be) **to ~ sb down as sth** اعْتَبَرَ شَخْصاً شَيْئاً

• **mark out A ~ [sth] out, ~ out [sth]** رَسَمَ حُدودَ [شَيْءٍ] ‹*an area, one's territory*› **B ~ [sb] out, ~ out [sb] 1** (to distinguish) مَيَّزَ [شَخْصاً] ‹*a person*› **2** (to destine) **to ~ sb out for sth** رَشَّحَ [شَخْصاً] لِشَيْءٍ

• **mark up**: **1 ~ [sth] up, ~ up [sth]** رَفَعَ سِعْرَ [شَيْءٍ] ‹*a product, a price*› **2** نَقَّحَ [شَيْئاً] ‹*a text, score*›

marked /mɑːkt/ *adj* ‹*difference, increase*› مَلْحوظ, واضِح, جَلِيّ

markedly /ˈmɑːkɪdli/ *adv* ‹*better, to improve*› بِشَكْلٍ مَلْحوظٍ

marker /ˈmɑːkə/ *n* **1** (also **marker pen**) قَلَم مارْكَر **2** (to indicate position) عَلامة (عَلامات)

market /ˈmɑːkɪt/ **A** *n* **1** (in a town) سوق (mf; أَسْواق) **2** (geographical area) سوق (mf; أَسْواق); **the North American ~** سوق أَمْريكا الشَمالِيّةِ **3** (in a stock, commodity) سوق (mf; أَسْواق); **the property/bond ~** سوق العَقاراتِ \ السَنَداتِ; **to put a house on the ~** عَرَضَ بَيْتاً لِلبَيْعِ; **to corner the ~ in sth** سَيْطَرَ على السوقِ في شَيْءٍ **4** (in stocks and shares) سوق (mf; أَسْواق)

B *vt* سَوَّقَ ‹*a product, drug*›

market analyst *n* مُحَلِّل سوقٍ

market day *n* يَوْم عَمَلٍ لِسوقٍ

market economy *n* اقْتِصاد السوقِ

marketeer /mɑːkɪˈtɪə/ *n* ▸ **black marketeer**

marketer /ˈmɑːkɪtə/ *n* مُسَوِّق

market forces *n* قُوى السوقِ

market gardening *n* [زِراعة فَواكِهَ وَخُضْرَواتٍ بِكَمّيّاتٍ تِجارِيّةٍ]

marketing /ˈmɑːkɪtɪŋ/ *n* تَسْويق

marketing strategy *n* إسْتْراتيجِيّة تَسْويقٍ

market leader *n* قائِد \ رائِد سوقٍ

marketplace /ˈmɑːkɪtpleɪs/ *n* ساحة سوقٍ

market research *n* دِراسة سوقٍ

market researcher *n* باحِث سوقٍ (مُتَخصِّص في بُحوثِ السوقِ)

market share *n* حِصّة في سوقٍ

market town *n* [بَلْدة ريفيّةٍ يُقام فيها سوقٌ]

market trader *n* بائِع في سوقٍ

market value *n* قيمة سوقيّة

marking /ˈmɑːkɪŋ/ *n* **1** (on an animal) عَلامة, (وُسوم) وَسْم (عَلامات); (on an aircraft) (شِعارات) شِعار; **road ~s** عَلامات إرْشادات سَيْرٍ, طَريقٍ **2** (BrE) (of student work) تَصْحيح (تَصْحيحات) **3** (of a player) مُحاصَرة

marksman /ˈmɑːksmən/ *n* (*pl* **-men**) قَنّاص (قَنّاصة)

markup /ˈmɑːkʌp/ *n* هامِش رِبْح; **what is the ~ on goods?** ما هو هامِشُ الرِبْحِ على السِلَعِ؟

marlin /ˈmɑːlɪn/ *n* (سَمَك) مَرْلين

marmalade /ˈmɑːməleɪd/ *n* مُرَبّى البُرْتُقالِ, مَرْمَلاد

Maronite /ˈmarənaɪt/ *n, adj* مارونيّ

maroon /məˈruːn/ **A** *n, adj* كَسْتَنائيّ

B *vt* **to be ~ed on an island** انْقَطَعَتْ بِهِ السُبُلُ في جَزيرةٍ

marquee /mɑːˈkiː/ *n* **1** (BrE) (tent) سُرادِق **2** (AmE) (canopy) (مِظَلّات) مِظَلّة

Marrakech, Marrakesh /ˌmarəˈkɛʃ/ *pr n* مَرّاكُش (dipt f)

marriage /ˈmarɪdʒ/ *n* **1** [u] (state) زَواج **2** (ceremony) زَواج

marriage certificate *n* عَقْد زَواجٍ

marriage vows *n* عُهود الزَواجِ

married /ˈmarɪd/ *adj* ‹*man*› مُتَزَوِّج; ‹*life*› زَوْجيّ; **a young ~ couple** زَوْجانِ شابّانِ

marrow /ˈmarəʊ/ *n* **1** (also **bone marrow**) نُخاع (نُخُع) **2** (BrE) (vegetable) قَرْع, كوسة (نَبات قَرْعيّ)

marry /ˈmari/ **A** *vt* (**marries, marrying, married**) **1** تَزَوَّجَ ‹*one's fiancée, boyfriend*›; **will you ~ me?** هل تَقْبَلُ الزَواجَ مِنّي؟ **2** «priest, registrar» زَوَّجَ ‹*a couple*›

B *vi* تَزَوَّجَ

(Phrasal verb) **marry off**: **~ off [sb]**, **~ [sb] off** زَوَّجَ [شَخْصاً] ‹*a daughter, friend*›

Mars /mɑːz/ *pr n* المِرّيخ

marsh /mɑːʃ/ *n* (also **marshland**) هَوْر (أَهْوار), سَبْخة (سِباخ), مُسْتَنْقَع (مُسْتَنْقَعات)

marshal /ˈmɑːʃ(ə)l/ **A** *n* **1** (at a demonstration, race) مُنَظِّم **2** (AmE) (officer of the law) مارِشال **3** (AmE) (in the fire service) مارِشال **4** (**Marshal**) (Mil) مُشير, مُهيب (Iraq)

B *vt* (**-ll-** BrE, **-l-** AmE) حَشَدَ (i-u; حَشْد) ‹*troops, support*›

marten /ˈmɑːtɪn/ *n* دَلَق

martial /ˈmɑːʃ(ə)l/ *adj* ‹*bravery, exploits*› حَرْبيّ, عَسْكَريّ, قِتاليّ

martial arts *n* فُنون قِتاليّة

martial law *n* أَحْكام عُرْفيّة

martyr /ˈmɑːtə/ **A** *n* شَهيد (شُهَداءُ)

B *vt* قَتَلَ (u; قَتْل), أَعْدَمَ ‹*a saint, bishop*›

martyrdom /ˈmɑːtədəm/ *n* شَهادة

marvel /ˈmɑːv(ə)l/ **A** *vi* (AmE, **-ll-** AmE, **-l-**) **to ~ at sth** تَعَجَّبَ من شَيْءٍ

B *n* مُعْجِزة, أُعْجوبة (أَعاجيبُ)

marvellous (BrE), **marvelous** (AmE) /ˈmɑːvələs/ *adj* ‹*job, sight*› رائِع

Marxism /ˈmɑːksɪz(ə)m/ *n* مارْكْسيّة

Marxist /ˈmɑːksɪst/ *n, adj* مارْكْسيّ

Maryland /ˈmɛːrɪˌland/ *pr n* مارِيلانْد (f)

Marylander /ˈmɛːrɪlandə/ *pr n* [(شَخْص) من مارِيلانْد]

marzipan /ˈmɑːzɪpan, ˌmɑːzɪˈpan/ *n* مَرْزِبان, مَرْصِبان, مَرْزِبانيّة

mascara /maˈskɑːrə/ *n* مَسْكَرة

mascot /ˈmaskət, ˈmaskɒt/ *n* جالِب حَظٍّ, دُمْية حَظٍّ

masculine /ˈmaskjʊlɪn/ *adj* **1** ‹*trait, pride*› ذُكوريّ, رُجوليّ **2** ‹*noun, form*› مُذَكَّر

masculinity /ˌmaskjʊˈlɪnɪti/ *n* ذُكورة, رُجولة

mash /maʃ/ **A** *vt* (also **mash**) هَرَسَ (u; هَرْس) ‹*potatoes, a banana*›

B *n* هَريس, طَعام مَهْروس

mask /mɑːsk/ **A** *n* قِناع (أَقْنِعة)

B *vt* حَجَبَ (u; حَجْب), أَخْفى ‹*one's face, features*›

masking tape /ˈmɑːskɪŋ teɪp/ *n* شَريط لاصِق

masochist /ˈmasəkɪst/ *n* مازوشيّ (شَخص يَتَلَذَّذُ بالتَعْذيبِ الجِنْسيِّ)

masochistic /masəˈkɪstɪk/ *adj* ‹*fantasy, desire*› مازوشيّ (مُتَعَلِّق بالتَلَذُّذِ بالتَعْذيبِ الجِنْسيِّ)

mason /ˈmeɪs(ə)n/ *n* 1 (Constr) بَنّاء 2 (also **Freemason**) ماسونيّ

masonry /ˈmeɪs(ə)nri/ *n* حِجارة (مَبْنِيّة)

Masqat, **Muscat** /ˈmʌskat/ *pr n* مَسْقَط (dipt f)

masquerade /ˌmɑːskəˈreɪd/ **A** *n* 1 (pretence) تَظاهُر, تَصَنُّع 2 (party) حَفْلَة تَنَكُّرِيّة

B *vi* **to ~ as a policeman** تَظاهَرَ بِأَنَّهُ شُرْطِيٌّ

mass /mas/ **A** *n* 1 (body) كُتْلَة (كُتَل); **she had a ~ of black hair** كانَ لَها شَعْرٌ أَسْوَدُ كَثيفٌ 2 (large amount) كَمِّيّة كَبيرة 3 (Rel_Chr) (also **Mass**) قُدّاس (قَداديسُ); **to go to M~** ذَهَبَ إلى القُدّاسِ 4 (Phys) كُتْلَة (كُتَل)

B (**masses**) *n pl* 1 **the ~es** (the people) عامّة الناس, العامّة 2 (BrE infml) (lots) **to have ~es of work/friends** كانَ لَدَيْهِ الكَثيرُ من العَمَلِ \ الأَصْدِقاءِ

C *adj* 1 (large-scale) ‹*protest, destruction*› شامِل; ‹*unemployment*› واسِع, جَماعيّ; **a ~ meeting** لِقاء جَماهيريّ 2 (of or for ordinary people) ‹*communications, culture*› جَماهيريّ; **to have ~ appeal** كانَ لَدَيْهِ قَبولٌ شَعْبيٌّ

D *vi* «troops, clouds» تَجَمَّعَ

Massachusetts /ˌmasəˈtʃuːsɪts/ *pr n* ماساتشوسِتْس (f)

massacre /ˈmasəkə/ **A** *n* مَجْزَرة (مَجازِرُ), مَذْبَحة (مَذابِحُ)

B *vt* ارْتَكَبَ مَجْزَرةً ضِدَّ ‹*the civilians, prisoners*›

massage /ˈmasɑːʒ/ **A** *n* تَمْسيد, مَساج, تَدْليك

B *vt* مَسَّدَ, دَلَّكَ ‹*sb's back, a muscle*›

masseur /maˈsəː/ *n* أَخِصّائيّ \ خَبير مَساج, مُدَلِّك

masseuse /maˈsəːz/ *n* أَخِصّائيّة \ خَبيرة مَساج, مُدَلِّكة

mass grave *n* مَقْبَرة جَماعيّة

massive /ˈmasɪv/ *adj* 1 ‹*wall, factory, earthquake, explosion*› ضَخْم, هائِل 2 ‹*increase, amount*› ضَخْم

massively /ˈmasɪvli/ *adv* ‹*to reduce, increase*› بِشَكْلٍ هائِلٍ; ‹*stretched*› على نِطاقٍ واسِعٍ, على نَحْوٍ هائِلٍ; **to be ~ successful** نَجَحَ نَجاحاً باهِراً; **a ~ complicated system** نِظام مُعَقَّد بِشَكْلٍ كَبيرٍ

mass-marketing /masˈmɑːkɪtɪŋ/ *n* تَسْويق شامِل

mass media *n* (**the mass media**) وَسائِل الإِعْلامِ الجَماهيريّة

mass murderer *n* قَتْل جَماعيّ

mass-produce /masprəˈdjuːs/ *vt* أَنْتَجَ بِكَمِّيّاتٍ ضَخْمةٍ ‹*cars, computers*›

mass production *n* إِنْتاج بِكَمِّيّاتٍ ضَخْمةٍ

mass transit *n* نَقْل جَماعيّ

mast /mɑːst/ *n* 1 (for sails) سارِية (سارِيات), صارٍ (صَوارٍ), 2 (for broadcasting) بُرْج إِرْسالٍ (سَوارٍ) 3 (flagpole) سارِية (سَوارٍ, سارِيات)

mastectomy /maˈstɛktəmi/ *n* اسْتِئْصال الثَدْيِ

master /ˈmɑːstə/ **A** *n* 1 (man in charge) سَيِّد (سادة, أَسْياد); **to be ~ in one's own house** كانَ سَيِّداً في بَيْتِهِ; **to be ~ of the situation** كانَ سَيِّدَ المَوْقِفِ 2 (primary teacher) مُعَلِّم; (secondary teacher) أُسْتاذ (أَساتِذة); **he was the only French/ physics ~ on the staff** كانَ أُسْتاذَ الفِرَنْسيّةِ \ الفيزِياءِ الوَحيدَ ضِمْنَ طاقَمِ المُعَلِّمينَ 3 (painter) **the Dutch/Italian ~s** عَمالِقة الفَنِّ الهولَنْديّونَ \ الإيطاليّونَ; (painting) **an old ~** تُحْفة فَنِّيّة قَديمة 4 (also **master copy**) نُسْخة أَصْلِيّة 5 (**Master's** also **Master's Degree** *n*) ماجِسْتير; **to be working on one's M~'s** كانَ يَدْرُسُ الماجِسْتير 6 (of a ship, boat) رُبّان (رَبابِنةُ, رَبابينُ) 7 (in chess, bridge etc) أُسْتاذ (أَساتِذة); **an international grand ~** أُسْتاذ دُوَليّ كَبير 8 (old use) (title of a young man) سَيِّد (للأَطْفالِ)

B (**Masters**) *n pl + v sg* **the Masters** (in golf, tennis) بُطولة الأَساتِذةِ \ الماسْتِرْز

C *vt* 1 (to learn) «person» بَرَعَ (a-u; بَراعة) (في) ‹*a language, theory, the basics*›; **to ~ the complexities of tax system** بَرَعَ في فَهْمِ تَعْقيداتِ نِظامِ الضَرائِبِ 2 (to control) سَيْطَرَ (i; سَيْطَرة) ‹*the situation, one's feelings*›

master builder *n* كَبير البَنّائينَ

master key *n* مِفْتاح عُموميّ \ رَئيسيّ

masterly /ˈmɑːstəli/ *adj* ‹*display, stroke*› مُتْقَن, بارِع

mastermind /ˈmɑːstəmʌɪnd/ **A** *n* عَقْل مُدَبِّر

B *vt* دَبَّرَ, نَظَّمَ ‹*a robbery, an attack*›

Master of Arts *n* ماجِسْتير في الآدابِ

Master of Business Administration *n* ماجِسْتير في إدارةِ الأَعْمالِ

master of ceremonies *n* رَئيس التَشْريفاتِ

Master of Science *n* ماجِسْتير في العُلومِ

masterpiece /ˈmɑːstəpiːs/ *n* تُحْفة (تُحَف)

master plan *n* خُطّة رَئيسيّة

Master's degree, **master's** *n* ماجِسْتير

master spy *n* جاسوس مُحْتَرِف

mastery /ˈmɑːst(ə)ri/ *n* تَمَكُّن ,مَهارة ,بَراعة

mastitis /maˈstʌɪtɪs/ *n* الْتِهاب الثَدْيِ

masturbate /ˈmastəbeɪt/ *vi* مارَسَ العادةَ السرّيّةَ ,اسْتَمْنى

mat /mat/ *n* **1** (rug) حَصيرة **2** (also **door mat**) مِمْسَحة أَرْجُلٍ **3** (also **place mat**) [مِفْرَش صَغير يوضَعُ تحت الأَواني السَاخِنةِ] **4** ▸ **prayer mat**

match /matʃ/ **A** *n* **1** (for fire-lighting) عود ثِقابٍ; **to put a ~ to the papers** أَشْعَلَ النارَ في الأَوْراقِ بعودِ ثِقابٍ **2** (in sport) مُباراة (مُباريات) ,مُقابَلة; **a boxing ~** مُباراة \ مُقابَلة مُلاكَمةٍ; **a football ~** مُباراة \ مُقابَلة كُرةِ قَدَمٍ **3** (in tennis) مُباراة (مُبارَيات) ,مُقابَلة; **to play a ~ point** لَعِبَ شَوْطاً فاصِلاً **4** (equal) نَظير (نُظَراءُ; f pl نَظائِرُ) ,مَثيل (أَمْثال); **to be a ~ for sb** كانَ مُناسِباً لِشَخْصٍ; **to be no ~ for sb** ما كانَ مُنافِساً من; **to meet one's ~** قابَلَ نِصْفَهُ الآخَرَ; نَفْسِ المُسْتَوى; **to be more than a ~ for sb** كانَ أَقْوى من شَخْصٍ **5** (counterpart) نَظير (نُظَراءُ; f pl نَظائِرُ); **to be a good ~ for sth** تَناسَبَ مع شَيْءٍ; **they're a perfect ~ for each other** يَتَناسَبانِ بَعْضُهُما تَماماً; **no ~ was found for your search terms** لا توجَدُ نَتائِجُ مُطابِقةٌ لِبَحْثِكَ **6** (marriage) زَوج مُناسِب; **to make a good ~** اخْتارَ زَوْجةً مُناسِبةً

B *vt* **1** (to harmonize with) (مع) تَناسَقَ ,(مع) انْسَجَمَ ‹*a colour, an item of clothing*› **2** (in descriptions) (مع) اتَّفَقَ ‹*a description*› **3** (to correspond to) (مع) تَطابَقَ ‹*the specification, sb's requirements*›; **a kitchen that ~es your lifestyle** مَطْبَخ يَتَماشى مع نَمَطِ حَياتِكَ **4** (in science, maths) (مع) تَطابَقَ ‹*sb's blood group, DNA, the data*›; **the DNA sample ~es that of the victim** عَيِّنةُ الحامِضِ النَوَوِيِّ تَتَطابَقُ مع عَيِّنةِ الضَحيّةِ **5** (to equal) وازى ‹*a record, performance*›; **if you find a lower price, we'll ~ it** إذا وَجَدْتَ سِعْراً أَقَلَّ، فَسَنَقومُ بِمُطابَقةِ هذا السِعْرِ \ لا شَيْءَ يَمْنَحُكَ خَصْماً; **nothing can ~ being there yourself** يُماثِلُ أَنْ تَكونَ هُناكَ بِنَفْسِكَ **6** (to place in competition) أَوْقَعَتْهُ القُرْعةُ مع ‹*teams, competitors*› **7** (to find a match for) رَبَطَ (i-u; رَبْط) ‹*words*›; **to ~ potential trainees with companies** لاءَمَ بين مُتَدَرِّبينَ واعِدينَ وَشَرِكاتٍ

C *vi* **1** (to harmonize) «colours, clothes» انْسَجَمَ; **with gloves to ~, with ~ing gloves** مع قُفّازاتٍ مُلائِمةٍ **2** (to correspond) «components, versions» تَطابَقَ

Phrasal verb **match up** **1** «pieces, parts» تَطابَقَ; **to ~ up to sb's expectations** طابَقَ تَوَقُّعاتِ شَخْصٍ **2** **~ up [sth], ~ [sth] up** طابَقَ [شَيْئاً] ‹*words, pieces, candidates*›

matchbox /ˈmatʃbɒks/ *n* عُلْبة كِبْريتٍ \ ثِقابٍ

matchmaker /ˈmatʃmeɪkə/ *n* وَسيط زَواج

match point *n* نُقْطة فَوْزٍ

matchstick /ˈmatʃstɪk/ *n* عود ثِقابٍ

mate /meɪt/ **A** *n* **1** (BrE infml) (friend) زَميل (رِفاق ,رُفَقاءُ) رَفيق **2** (Zool) زَوْج (mf; أَزْواج) **3** (in the navy) وَكيل الرُبّانِ (زُمَلاءُ) **4** (assistant) مُعاوِن ,مُساعِد **5** (in chess) مَوْت الشاه

B *vt* ‹*cattle, birds*› زاوَجَ

C *vi* تَزاوَجَ

material /məˈtɪərɪəl/ **A** *n* **1** [u] (information) مادّة (مَوادُّ); **to collect ~ on a topic** جَمَعَ مادّةَ المَوْضوعِ; **to prepare teaching/publicity ~** جَمَعَ مَوادَّ تَدْريس \ إعْلاناتٍ **2** [u] (substance) مادّة (مَوادُّ); **radioactive ~** مادّة مُشِعّة **3** [u] (fabric) قُماش; **curtain/dress ~** قُماش سِتارةٍ \ فُسْتانٍ; **3 metres of ~** 3 أَمْتارٍ من القُماشِ **4** [u] (potential) واعِد; **he's officer/management ~** هو مَشْروعُ ضابِطٍ \ مُديرٍ واعِدٍ

B (**materials**) *n pl* (basic elements) مَوادّ; **artist's ~s** مَوادّ فَنّانٍ; **building ~s** مَوادّ بِناءٍ; **raw ~s** مَوادّ خام

C *adj* (fml) **1** (real) ‹*assistance, change, effect*› مادّيّ; **the storm caused ~ damage** تَسَبَّبَت العاصِفةُ في خَسائِرَ مادّيّةٍ **2** (important) ‹*evidence, question*› مادّيّ; **she was one of the ~ witnesses in the case** كانَتْ واحِدةً من الشُهودِ المُهِمّينَ

في القَضيَّةِ **3** (concrete) ‹*possessions, comfort*› مادّيّ; **all his ~ needs were catered for** تَمَّ تَلْبِيةُ كُلِّ حاجاتِهِ المادّيّةِ

materialistic /məˌtɪərɪəˈlɪstɪk/ *adj* ‹*society, values*› مادّيّ

materialize, -ise (BrE) /məˈtɪərɪəlʌɪz/ *vi* **1** (to happen) «threats, projects» تَحَقَّقَ **2** (to appear) «people, cars» ظَهَرَ (a; ظُهور); «spirits» تَجَسَّدَ, تَجَسَّمَ

maternal /məˈtəːn(ə)l/ *adj* **1** ‹*concern, love*› أُموميّ **2** ‹*grandmother, DNA*› من جِهةِ الأُمِّ

maternity /məˈtəːnɪti/ *n* أُمومة

maternity leave *n* إجازة أُمومةٍ \ وَضْعٍ

maternity unit *n* قِسْم النِساءِ والتَّوْليدِ

maternity ward *n* عَنْبَر النِساءِ والتَّوْليدِ

math /maθ/ *n* (AmE) ▸ **maths**

mathematical /maθəˈmatɪk(ə)l/ *adj* ‹*formula, precision*› رِياضيّ

mathematician /maθəməˈtɪʃ(ə)n/ *n* عالِم رِياضيّاتٍ

mathematics /maθəˈmatɪks/ *n* رِياضيّات

maths (BrE) /maθs/, **math** (AmE) /maθ/ *n* رِياضيّات

matinee /ˈmatɪneɪ/ *n* عَرْض نَهاريّ

mating season /ˈmeɪtɪŋ ˌsiːz(ə)n/ *n* مَوْسِم تَزاوُجٍ

matriarch /ˈmeɪtrɪɑːk/ *n* أُمّ حاكِمة (رَبّة عائِلةٍ \ قَبيلةٍ)

matrices /ˈmeɪtrɪsiːz/ *n pl* ▸ **matrix**

matriculate /məˈtrɪkjʊleɪt/ *vi* الْتَحَقَ بِجامِعةٍ

matrimony /ˈmatrɪməni/ *n* (fml) زَواج, نِكاح

matrix /ˈmeɪtrɪks/ *n* (*pl* **matrices**) مَصْفوفة

matron /ˈmeɪtrən/ *n* **1** (fml) (married woman) عَقيلة (امْرَأة مُتَزَوِّجة في مُنْتَصَفِ العُمْرِ) **2** (BrE) (in a hospital) رَئيسة مُمَرِّضاتٍ **3** (BrE) (in a school) مَسْؤولة رِعايةٍ **4** (AmE) (in a prison) حارِسة

matt (BrE), **matte** (AmE) /mat/ *adj* ‹*paint, finish*› غَيْر لامِعٍ, مُنْطَفِئ, باهِت

matted /ˈmatɪd/ *adj* ‹*hair, wool*› مُتَعَقِّد, مُتَلَبِّد, مُتَشابِك

matter /ˈmatə/ **A** *n* **1** (subject) مَسْأَلة (مَسائِلُ), قَضيّة (قَضايا); **legal/financial ~s** مَسائِل قانونيّة \ ماليّة; **that's a different ~** تِلْكَ مَسْأَلَةٌ مُخْتَلِفَةٌ; **it is a ~ of concern** إنّها مَسْأَلَةٌ مُثيرةٌ للقَلَقِ; **this is a ~ for the police** هذه مَسْأَلَةٌ تَخُصُّ الشُّرْطَةَ; **the ~ in hand** المَسْأَلة الّتي بين أَيْدينا; **~s arising** (in a meeting) مَسائِل ناشِئة; **this is not the end of the ~** هذه لَيْسَتْ نِهايةَ المَسْأَلةِ; **to let the ~ drop** تَرَكَ المَسْأَلَةَ تَبْرُدُ; **to take the ~ further** [اتَّخَذَ إجْراءاتٍ \ تَدابيرَ]; **the fact** *or* **truth of the ~ is that ...** لُبُّ القَضيّةِ هو ... **2** (**matters** *n pl*) (current situation) وَضْع (أَوْضاع); **to make ~s worse** جَعَلَ الأُمورَ أَسْوَأَ; **you're not helping ~s** أَنْتَ لا تُساعِدُ الوَضْعَ **3** (question) مَسْأَلة (مَسائِلُ); **I refuse to pay as a ~ of principle** أَرْفُضُ أنْ أَدْفَعَ من حَيْثُ المَبْدَأ; **it's only a ~ of time before somebody gets killed** إنّها فَقَطْ مَسْأَلةُ وَقْتٍ قبل أنْ يُقْتَلَ أَحَدٌ; **a ~ of life and death** مَسْأَلة حَياةٍ أو مَوْتٍ **4** (with problems) أَمْر (أُمور); **what's the ~?** ما الأَمْرُ؟; **is anything the ~?** هل هُناكَ مُشْكِلةٌ؟; **there's something the ~ with the engine** هُناكَ مُشْكِلةٌ ما في المُحَرِّكِ; **what's the ~ with Louise?** ما هي المُشْكِلةُ مع لُويز؟ **5** (substance) مادّة (مَوادّ); **the soil is high in organic ~** التُّرْبةُ غَنيّةٌ بالمَوادِّ العُضْويّةِ **6** (printed material) مَطْبوع (مَطْبوعات); **printed ~** مَوادّ مَطْبوعة; **reading ~** مَوادّ للقِراءة **B** (**as a matter of fact**) *adv phr* في حَقيقةِ الأَمْرِ; **as a ~ of fact, it isn't like that at all** في حَقيقةِ الأَمْرِ، هي لَيْسَتْ مِثْلَ ذَلِكَ إطْلاقاً **C** (**for that matter**) *adv phr* على كُلِّ حالٍ **D** (**no matter**) *conj phr* مَهْما, بِغَضِّ النَظَرِ; **no ~ what I do, it's never right** مَهْما فَعَلْتُ، لا يُعْتَبَرُ صَواباً أَبَداً; **no ~ how hard I tried** مَهْما حاوَلْتُ **E** *vi* هَمَّ (u; هَمّ); **it doesn't ~** لا يَهُمُّ; **your opinion ~s to me** يَهُمُّني رَأْيُكَ; **what ~s most is your safety** أَهَمُّ شَيْءٍ هو سَلامَتُكَ

Idioms **as a matter of course** بِطَبيعةِ الحالِ; **no matter!** لا يَهُمُّ!; **to take matters into one's own hands** أَخَذَ حَقَّهُ بِيَدَيْهِ

matter-of-fact /ˌmat(ə)rəvˈfakt/ *adj* ‹*person*› عَمَليّ, واقِعيّ; ‹*tone*› خالٍ من الانْفِعالِ

mattress /ˈmatrɪs/ *n* مَرْتَبة (مَراتِبُ), حَشيّة (حَشيّات, حَشايا)

mature /mə'tʃʊə/ **A** *adj* **1** (fully developed) ‹*tree, animal*› ناضِج ,مُكْتَمِل النموِّ **2** (emotionally) ‹*person, attitude*› ناضِج **3** ‹*cheese, wine*› مُعَتَّق
B *vi* **1** (physically) «trees, animals» بَلَغَ مَرْحَلةَ ,اكْتَمَلَ نُموُّهُ (نَضْج (a; نَضِجَ **2** (emotionally) «teenagers, leaders» نَضِجَ (a; النُضْج) **3** «cheese, wine» عتَّقَ **4** «policies, bonds» اسْتَحَقَّ

mature student *n* [طالِب كَبير في السِنِّ]

maturity /mə'tʃʊərəti/ *n* **1** [u] (in development) نُضْج **2** [u] (emotional) نُضوج ,نُضْج **3** (due date) مَوْعِد الاسْتِحْقاقِ \ الوَفاءِ

maudlin /'mɔːdlɪn/ *adj* ‹*song, drunk*› مُرْهَف الإحْساسِ ,بَكّاء; **to get ~** جاشَتْ عَواطِفُهُ ;جَيّاش العاطِفةِ

maul /mɔːl/ *vt* **1** (to attack) «lions, dogs» هَجَمَ (u; هُجوم ;على) ‹*a child, neighbour*› **2** (to handle roughly) عامَلَ بِخُشونةٍ ‹*a patient, toy*›

Mauritania /ˌmɒrɪ'teɪnɪə/ *pr n* موريتانيا

Mauritanian /mɒrɪ'teɪnɪən/ *n, adj* موريتانيّ

Mauritius /mə'rɪʃəs/ *pr n* موريشيوس (f)

mausoleum /mɔːsə'liːəm/ *n* (*pl* **mausoleums**) ضَريح (أَضْرِحة)

mauve /məʊv/ **A** *adj* ‹*curtains, sunset*› موف ,بَنَفْسَجيّ فاتِح
B *n* لَوْن موف ,لَوْن بَنَفْسَجيّ فاتِح

maverick /'mavərɪk/ *n* مُنْشَقّ ,مُتَمَرِّد

Mawlid /'maʊlɪd/, **Milad** /'miːlɑːd/ *n* مَوْلِد (النَبيِّ)

max /maks/ **A** *n* = **maximum** (infml) حَدّ أَقْصى; **to the ~** إلى الحَدِّ الأَقْصى
B *adv* (infml) على أَقْصى تَقْديرٍ ,بِحَدٍّ أَقْصى

maxim /'maksɪm/ *n* مَقولة ,قَوْل مَأْثور ,حِكْمة (حِكَم)

maximize, **-ise** (BrE) /'maksɪmʌɪz/ *vt* **1** (Fin) كَبَّرَ ,عَظَّمَ (مِن), كَبَّرَ (إلى أَقْصى ‹*profit, sales*› **2** (Comput) حَقَّقَ أَقْصى قَدْرٍ من دَرَجةٍ) ‹*the screen, an application*›

maximum /'maksɪməm/ **A** *n* (*pl* **maximums, maxima**) حَدّ أَقْصى \ أَعْلى; **the ~ of foreign exchange you're allowed is...** الحَدُّ الأَقْصى من النَقْدِ الأَجْنَبيِّ المَسْموحِ لَكَ بِهِ هو ...
B *adj* ‹*speed, amount*› أَقْصى (f قُصْوى); **do not exceed the ~ dosage** لا تَتَجاوَز الجُرْعةَ القُصْوى; **the judge imposed the ~ sentence** فَرَضَ القاضي العُقوبةَ القُصْوى; **at a ~ of 120 km per hour** في سُرْعةٍ أَقْصاها 120 كم في الساعةِ

maximum security prison *n* سِجْن مُشَدَّد الحِراسةِ

may /meɪ/ *modal aux* **1** (expressing possibility) **it ~ rain** قد تُمْطِرُ; **she ~ not have seen him** رُبَّما لم تَرَهُ; **come what ~** مَهْما حَدَثَ **2** (fml) (expressing permission) **you ~ sit down** يُمْكِنُكَ الجُلوسُ; **~ I come in?** هل تَسْمَحُ لي بالدُخولِ؟ **3** (expressing a wish) **~ he rest in peace** تَغَمَّدَهُ اللهُ بِرَحْمَتِهِ, رَحِمَهُ اللهُ ,طَيَّبَ اللهُ ثَراهُ

May /meɪ/ *n* مايو (Mor, Egypt, Gulf), أَيّار (dipt) (Levant, Iraq), ماي (Algeria, Tunisia) ▸ **March**

maybe /'meɪbiː/ *adv* رُبَّما; **~ they'll set out early** رُبَّما يَنْطَلِقونَ في رِحْلَتِهِمْ مُبَكِّراً; **~ he was right** رُبَّما كانَ على حَقٍّ; **~ you could have a look at my computer** رُبَّما يُمْكِنُكَ أنْ تُلْقِيَ نَظْرةً على كُمْبيوتَري; **will you come? — ~ I will, ~ I won't** هل سَتَأْتي؟ — رُبَّما آتي، ورُبَّما لا; **I saw him ~ three weeks ago** رَأَيْتُهُ رُبَّما منذ ثَلاثةِ أَسابيعَ

Mayday /'meɪdeɪ/ *n* إشارة اسْتِغاثةٍ

May Day *n* (spring holiday) أَوَّل مايو (مَهْرَجان الرَبيعِ); (workers' day) عيد العُمّالِ

mayhem /'meɪhɛm/ *n* فَوْضى (f)

mayonnaise /meɪə'neɪz/ *n* مايونيز

mayor /mɛː/ *n* عُمْدة ,رَئيس بَلَديّةٍ (عُمَد)

mayoress /mɛː'rɛs/ *n* **1** (female mayor) رَئيسة بَلَديّةٍ **2** (mayor's wife) زَوْجة رَئيس بَلَديّةٍ

maze /meɪz/ *n* (in a garden) (of streets, corridors) مَتاهة

MB /ɛm'biː/ *n* **1** (BrE) = **Bachelor of Medicine** (degree) بَكالوريوس في الطِبِّ; (person) حاصِل على \ حامِل بَكالوريوس في الطِبِّ; **Jack Smart, ~** جاك سْمارْت، بَكالوريوس في الطِبِّ **2** (also **Mb**) = **megabyte** (unit of information) ميجا بايْت

MBA /ɛmbiː'eɪ/ *n* = **Master of Business Administration** (degree) ماجِسْتير في إدارةِ الأَعْمالِ; (degree holder) حاصِل على \ حامِل ماجِسْتير في إدارةِ الأَعْمالِ

MBO /ɛmbiː'əʊ/ *n* = **management buyout** اسْتِحْواذ إداريّ [شِراء شَرِكةٍ من قِبَلِ الإدارةِ]

MC /ɛm'siː/ *n* = **Master of Ceremonies** 1▸ (at a formal event) رَئيس التَّشريفاتِ 2▸ (rapper) مُغَنّي الراب

MD /ɛm'diː/ **A** *n* 1▸ = **Doctor of Medicine** (degree) دُكْتوراه في الطِبِّ; (degree holder) دُكْتور في الطِبِّ; **Luke Harrison, ~** لوك هاريسون، دُكْتور في الطِبِّ 2▸ = **Managing Director** (position) مُدير تَنْفيذيّ
B *abbr* = **Maryland**

me¹ /miː, mɪ/ *pron* 1▸ (direct object) ـني; **she knows ~** تَعْرِفُني; **he frightens ~** يُخيفُني 2▸ (indirect object) ـي; **he sent ~ a text** أَرْسَلَ لي رِسالةً نَصّيّةً 3▸ (after prepositions) ـي; **is this for ~?** هل هذا لي؟; **she's older than ~** هي أَكْبَرُ مِنّي 4▸ (emphatic) أَنا; **it's ~!** إنَّهُ أَنا!; **'who wants it?' — '~!'** 'مَنْ يُريدُهُ؟' – 'أَنا!'; **Mrs Jones and ~/~ and Mrs Jones** أنا والسَّيِّدة جونز

me² /miː/ *n* (نَغْمة من نَغَماتِ السُّلَّم الموسيقيِّ) مي

ME /ɛm'iː/ **A** *n* 1▸ = **myalgic encephalomyelitis** الْتِهاب الدِماغ والنُخاعِ, مُتَلازِمة التَعَبِ المُزْمِنِ 2▸ (AmE) = **medical examiner ▸ medical examiner**
B *abbr* = **Maine**

meadow /'mɛdəʊ/ *n* مَرْج (مُروج)

meagre (BrE), **meager** (AmE) /'miːɡə/ *adj* ‹portion, meal› ضَئيل

meal /miːl/ *n* 1▸ (intake of food) وَجْبة (وَجَبات) 2▸ (powder) طَحين, دَقيق

mealtime /'miːltaɪm/ *n* وَقْت تَناوُلِ الطَعامِ

mean /miːn/ **A** *vt* (*past tense, past participle* **meant**) 1▸ (to signify) «word, symbol» عَنى (i; عَنْي); **what does 'psychosomatic' ~?** ماذا تَعْني كَلِمةُ 'سيكوسوماتيّ'؟; **the name ~s 'peace' in Arabic** الاسْمُ يَعْني 'السَلام' في العَرَبيّةِ; **the name ~s nothing to me** لا يَعْني الاسْمُ لي شَيْئاً 2▸ (to intend) **to ~ to do sth** قَصَدَ أَنْ يَفْعَلَ شَيْئاً; **I didn't ~ to do it** لم أَقْصِدْ أَنْ أَفْعَلَهُ; **I meant it as a joke** قَصَدْتُ من ورائها المُزاح; **she meant no offence** لم تَقْصِد الإساءةَ; **to ~ well** كانَ حَسَنَ النِيّةِ, قَصَدَ خَيْراً; **to ~ sb to do sth, to ~ for sb to do sth** (AmE) تَوَقَّع من شَخْصٍ أَنْ يَفْعَلَ شَيْئاً; **without ~ing to** دون أَنْ يَقْصِدَهُ 3▸ (to be serious about) قَصَدَ (i; قَصْد); **he ~s what he says** يَقْصِدُ ما يَقولُ 4▸ (to entail) عَنى (i; عَنْي) ‹the end, loss, change›; **the new job ~s having to move house** تَعْني الوَظيفةُ الجَديدةُ أَنْ نَنْتَقِلَ من البَيْتِ 5▸ (to intend to say) قَصَدَ (i; قَصْد); **what do you ~ by that remark?** ماذا تَقْصِدُ بِتِلْكَ المُلاحَظةِ؟; **what do you ~ by opening my letters?** ماذا تَقْصِدُ بِفَتْحِ رَسائِلي؟; **I know what you ~** أَعْرِفُ ما تَقْصِدُ 6▸ (to be of importance) عَنى (i; عَنْي); **his friendship ~s a lot to me** صَداقَتُهُ تَعْني لي الكَثيرَ; **Julie ~t everything to him** عَنَتْ جولي لَهُ كُلَّ شَيْءٍ; **our opinions ~ nothing** لا تَعْني آراؤُنا شَيْئاً 7▸ (supposed to) **to be ~t to do sth** كانَ من المُفْتَرَضِ أَنْ يَفْعَلَ شَيْئاً; **they're meant to be impartial** من المُفْتَرَضِ أَنْ يَكونوا نُزَهاءَ 8▸ (destined) **to be ~t to do sth** كانَ من المَفْروضِ أَنْ يَفْعَلَ شَيْئاً; **it was meant to be** *or* **happen** كانَ من المَفْروضِ أَنْ يَحْدُثَ; **that present was ~t for me** كانَ من المَفْروضِ أَنْ تَكونَ تِلْكَ الهَديّةُ لي; **they were meant for each other** خُلِقا لِيَكونا مَعاً
B *adj* 1▸ (average) ‹age, value› مُتَوَسِّط; **the city has a ~ annual temperature of 25°C** مُتَوَسِّطُ دَرَجةِ الحَرارةِ السَنَويّةِ في المَدينةِ 25 دَرَجةً مِئَويّةً 2▸ (miserly) بَخيل (بُخَلاءُ); **she's ~ with money** هي بَخيلةٌ عِنْدَما يَتَعَلَّقُ الأَمْرُ بالمال 3▸ (unkind, nasty) قاسٍ (قُساة); **to be ~ to sb** كانَ قاسِياً مع شَخْصٍ; **he had a ~ streak** كانَتْ عِنْدَهُ نَزْعةٌ من الحِقْدِ 4▸ (vicious) ‹person, look› شِرّير (أَشْرار) 5▸ (liter) (poor, shabby) ‹hovel, dwelling› رَثّ (رِثاث); **that's no ~ feat!** لَيْسَ ذلكَ بالأَمْرِ الهَيِّنِ! 6▸ (infml) (excellent) ‹cook, guitarist› مُمْتاز
C *n* 1▸ (Math) مُتَوَسِّط; **above/below the ~** فوق \ تحت المُتَوَسِّطِ 2▸ (middle point) وَسَط (أَوْساط)

meander /mɪ'ændə/ *vi* «rivers, roads» تَعَرَّجَ, تَلَوّى

meaning /'miːnɪŋ/ *n* 1▸ (of a word, dream, fable) مَعْنًى (مَعانٍ); **a word with two ~s** كَلِمة ذات مَعْنَيَيْنِ; **what is the ~ of this?** ما مَعْنى هذا؟; **a look/gesture full of ~** نَظْرة \ حَرَكة مَليئة بالمَعْنى 2▸ (purpose) مَعْنًى (مَعانٍ); **what is the ~ of life?** ما مَعْنى الحَياةِ؟

meaningful /'miːnɪŋfʊl/ *adj* 1▸ (having meaning) ‹statistics, word› ذو مَعْنًى 2▸ (significant) ‹relationship, dialogue› جادّ; ‹contribution› ذو مَعْنًى; **the research failed to produce ~ results** فَشِلَ البَحْثُ في العُثورِ على نَتائِجَ ذاتِ مَعْنًى 3▸ (eloquent) ‹look, gesture› ذو مَعْنًى; **she gave me a ~ look** نَظَرَتْ إِلَيَّ نَظْرةً ذاتَ مَعْنًى

meaningless /ˈmiːnɪŋləs/ *adj* **1** (having no meaning) *‹word, phrase›* بلا \ بِدونِ مَعْنًى **2** (without purpose) *‹life, sacrifice›* بلا \ بِدونِ مَعْنًى; **the election was a ~ exercise** كانَت الانْتِخاباتُ مُمارَسةً بِلا مَعْنًى

means /miːnz/ **A** *n pl* (method) وَسيلة (وَسائِلُ); **a ~ of communication/transport** وَسيلة اتِّصالاتٍ \ مُواصَلاتٍ; **by ~ of sth** عن طَريقِ شَيْءٍ; **by peaceful ~** بِوَسائِلَ سِلْميّةٍ; **yes, by all ~** نَعْمْ، بِكُلِّ ما في الكَلِمةِ من مَعْنًى; **a ~ to an end** وَسيلة وَلَيْسَ غايةً في حَدِّ ذاتِهِ

B (resources) دَخْل; **of modest ~** ذو دَخْلٍ مُتَواضِعٍ; **a man of ~** رَجُل صاحِب ثَرْوةٍ; **to live beyond/within one's ~** لم يَعِشْ \ عاشَ على قَدْرِ دَخْلِهِ

means test *n* اسْتِطْلاع المَوارِدِ الماليّةِ

meant /mɛnt/ *past tense, past participle* ▸ **mean**

meantime /ˈmiːntʌɪm/ *adv* (also **in the meantime**) في غُضونِ ذلك; **for the ~** في الوَقْتِ الراهِنِ

meanwhile /ˈmiːnwʌɪl/ *adv* (also **in the meanwhile**) في غُضونِ ذلك

measles /ˈmiːzəlz/ *n sing* حَصْبة

measure /ˈmɛʒə/ **A** *vt* **1** (to take the measurement of) (to determine) قاسَ (i; قِياس, قَيْس) *‹the length, pressure, depth›*; **to ~ sth in centimetres** قاسَ شَيْئاً بالسَّنْتيمِتْراتِ; **to get oneself ~d for a suit** أَخَذَ مَقاساتِهِ لِيُفَصِّلَ بَدْلةً **2** (with units) بَلَغَ قِياسُهُ; **the room ~s only 2.5 metres by 3 metres** تَبْلُغُ قِياساتُ الغُرْفةِ مِتْرَيْنِ وَنِصْفاً على ثَلاثةِ أَمْتارٍ فَقَطْ; **an earth tremor measuring 5.2 on the Richter scale** هَزّة أَرْضيّة بِقوّةِ 5.2 على مِقْياسِ ريخْتِر **3** (to assess) قاسَ (i; قِياس, قَيْس) *‹success, performance›* **4** (to compare) **to ~ sth against sth** قارَنَ شَيْئاً بِشَيْءٍ

B *n* **1** (step) إِجْراء (إِجْراءات); **security/safety ~s** إِجْراءات أَمْنيّة \ سَلامةٍ; **as a precautionary ~** كَإِجْراءٍ وِقائيٍّ; **to take ~s to do sth** أَخَذَ إِجْراءاتٍ لِيَفْعَلَ شَيْئاً **2** (unit) قِياس (أَقْيِسة, قِياسات); **weights and ~s** أَوْزان وَقِياسات **3** [u] (system) نِظام; **a metric/imperial ~** نِظام مِتْريّ \ إِمْبِراطوريّ **4** (fml) (degree) دَرَجة; **we achieved a ~ of success** بَلَغْنا دَرَجةً من النَجاحِ; **this was due in large** *or* **no small ~ to his leadership** يَعودُ هذا بِدَرَجةٍ كَبيرةٍ إلى زَعامَتِهِ \ قِيادَتِهِ **5** (tape measure) شَريط قِياسٍ **6** (yardstick) قِياس (أَقْيِسة, قِياسات); **profit is used as a ~ of performance** يُسْتَعْمَلُ الرِبْحُ لِقِياسِ الأَداءِ; **beyond ~** إلى أَقْصى حَدٍّ; **this is a ~ of how serious the situation is** هذا قِياسٌ دَرَجةٍ لِمَدى جِدّيّةِ الوَضْعيّةِ

(Idioms) **for good measure** زِيادةُ الخَيْرِ بَرَكةٌ; **to get/have the measure of sb** سَبَرَ غَوْرَهُ; **I think I have the ~ of him** أَظُنُّ أنّي قد سَبَرْتُ غَوْرَهُ

(Phrasal verbs) **measure out: ~ out [sth]** كالَ [شَيْئاً] *‹ingredients, flour›*

• **measure up A** بَلَغَ المُسْتَوى; **to ~ up to sb's expectations** بَلَغَ مُسْتَوى تَوَقُّعاتِ شَخْصٍ **B ~ up [sth/sb]** قاسَ [شَيْئاً \ شَخْصاً] *‹a person, room›*

measurement /ˈmɛʒəmənt/ *n* **1** (action of measuring) قِياس **2** (dimension) مِقْياس (مَقاييسُ) (أَقْيِسة, قِياسات)

measuring jug /ˈmɛʒərɪŋ ˌdʒʌg/ *n* إِبْريق قِياسٍ

measuring spoon /ˈmɛʒərɪŋ ˌspuːn/ *n* مِلْعَقة قِياسٍ

measuring tape /ˈmɛʒərɪŋ ˌteɪp/ *n* شَريط قِياسٍ

meat /miːt/ *n* لَحْم (n coll; لُحوم)

meatball /ˈmiːtbɔːl/ *n* **1** (Culin) كُرة لَحْمٍ **2** (AmE infml) (fool) أَبْلَه (dipt) أَحْمَق (dipt; حُمْق, f حَمْقى)

meat-eater /ˈmiːtiːtə/ *n* آكِل لُحومٍ

meat loaf *n* رَغيف لَحْمٍ

meat pie *n* فَطيرة لَحْمٍ

meaty /ˈmiːti/ *adj* (**meatier, meatiest**) **1** *‹flavour, smell›* اللَحْمِ; *‹pie, stew›* كَثير اللَحْمِ **2** *‹article, book›* دَسِم

Mecca /ˈmɛkə/ *pr n* **1** (holy city) مَكّة (المُكَرَّمة); **a pilgrimage to ~** رِحْلة حَجٍّ إلى مَكّةَ المُكَرَّمةِ **2** (popular location) قِبْلة

mechanic /mɪˈkanɪk/ *n* ميكانيكيّ

mechanical /mɪˈkanɪk(ə)l/ *adj ‹instrument, means›* آليّ, ميكانيكيّ

mechanical engineer *n* مُهَنْدِس ميكانيكيّ

mechanical engineering *n* هَنْدَسة ميكانيكيّة

mechanics /mɪˈkanɪks/ **A** *n sing* (field) عِلْم الميكانيكا **B** *n pl* (workings) آليّات

mechanism /ˈmɛk(ə)niz(ə)m/ *n* آليّة

mechanization, -isation (BrE) /mɛk(ə)nʌɪˈzeɪʃ(ə)n/ *n* مَيْكَنة, مَكْنَنة

mechanize, -ise (BrE) /ˈmɛk(ə)nʌɪz/ *vt* مَكْنَنَ (i; مَكْنَنة) ‹*agriculture, production*›

medal /ˈmɛd(ə)l/ *n* ميدالِية, وِسام (أَوْسِمة), نَوْط (أَنْواط)

medallion /mɪˈdaljən/ *n* ميدالِية, وِسام (أَوْسِمة)

medallist (BrE), **medalist** (AmE) /ˈmɛdəlɪst/ *n* \ حامِل وِسامٍ; ميدالِيةٍ; **gold ~** حامِل الميدالِيةِ الذَهَبِيّةِ

meddle /ˈmɛd(ə)l/ *vi* تَطَفَّلَ, تَدَخَّلَ; **to ~ in sb's business/affairs** تَدَخَّلَ في شُؤُونِ شَخْصٍ

media /ˈmiːdɪə/ *n pl* وَسائِل الإعْلام

media coverage *n* تَغْطِية إعْلاميّة

mediaeval /mɛdiˈiːv(ə)l/ *adj* ▸ **medieval**

median /ˈmiːdɪən/ **A** *adj* ‹*price, income*› مُتَوَسِّط

B *n* **1** (Math) مُتَوَسِّط, قيمة مُتَوَسِّطة **2** (AmE Transp) ▸ **median strip**

median strip *n* (AmE) خَطّ الوَسَط (الجَزيرة الوُسْطى للطَريق الفاصِل بين الطُرُق ذاتِ الاتِّجاهَيْنِ)

media reports *n* تَقارير وَسائِلِ الإعْلام

media studies *n* دِراسات وَسائِلِ الإعْلام

mediate /ˈmiːdɪeɪt/ **A** *vt* تَوَسَّطَ في التَوَصُّلِ إلى ‹*a settlement, peace*›

B *vi* تَوَسَّطَ; **to ~ in a dispute/conflict** \ تَوَسَّطَ في خِلافٍ نِزاعٍ; **to ~ between two rivals/nations** \ تَوَسَّطَ بين خَصْمَيْنِ بَلَدَيْنِ

mediation /miːdɪˈeɪʃ(ə)n/ *n* تَوسُّط

mediator /ˈmiːdɪeɪtə/ *n* وَسيط (وُسَطاءُ)

medic /ˈmɛdɪk/ *n* **1** (infml) (doctor) طَبيب (أَطِبّاءُ, أَطِبّة) **2** (infml) (student) طالِب طِبٍّ **3** (AmE) (paramedic) مُسْعِف

Medicaid /ˈmɛdɪkeɪd/ *n* (AmE) ≈ الضَمان الصِحّيّ (بَرْنامَج حُكوميّ للرِعايةِ الصِحّيّةِ للفُقَراء)

medical /ˈmɛdɪk(ə)l/ **A** *adj* ‹*training, staff*› طِبّي

B *n* فَحص طِبّيّ

medical examiner *n* (AmE) طَبيب شَرْعيّ

medical history *n* تاريخ طِبّيّ

medical insurance *n* تَأْمين صِحّيّ

medical practitioner *n* طَبيب (أَطِبّاءُ, أَطِبّة)

medical records *n* سِجِلّات طِبّيّة

medical school *n* كُلّيّة طِبٍّ

medical student *n* طالِب طِبٍّ

Medicare /ˈmɛdɪkɛː/ *n* (AmE) رِعاية صِحّيّة لِكِبارِ السِنِّ في الوِلاياتِ المُتَّحِدةِ

medicated /ˈmɛdɪkeɪtɪd/ *adj* ‹*shampoo, cream*›; مُعالِج, عِلاجيّ, طِبّيّ

medication /mɛdɪˈkeɪʃ(ə)n/ *n* عِلاج, دَواء (أَدْوِية); **to be on ~** كانَ يَتَناوَلُ أَدْوِيةً

medicinal /mɪˈdɪsɪn(ə)l/ *adj* ‹*property, herb*› عِلاجيّ, طِبّيّ

medicine /ˈmɛds(ə)n/ *n* **1** [u] (field) طِبّ **2** (drug, remedy) دَواء (أَدْوِية)

medicine cabinet, medicine cupboard *n* خَزينة دَواءٍ

medicine man *n* طَبيب ساحِر

medieval, mediaeval /mɛdiˈiːv(ə)l/ *adj* ‹*castle, manuscript*› من القُرونِ الوُسْطى; **in ~ times** في العُصورِ الوُسْطى

medievalist /mɛdrˈiːvəlɪst/ *n* مُتَخَصِّص في دِراسةِ العُصورِ الوُسْطى

Medina /mɛˈdiːnə/ *pr n* المَدينة (المُنَوَّرة)

mediocre /ˌmiːdɪˈəʊkə/ *adj* ‹*workmanship, quality*› مُتَواضِع, دون المُتَوَسِّطِ

mediocrity /miːdɪˈɒkrɪti/ *n* تَواضُع, ضَآلة جَوْدةٍ

meditate /ˈmɛdɪteɪt/ *vi* تَأَمَّلَ, تَفَكَّرَ, فَكَّرَ مَليًّا; **to ~ on sth** فَكَّرَ مَليًّا في شَيْءٍ

meditation /mɛdɪˈteɪʃ(ə)n/ *n* تَأَمُّل

Mediterranean /ˌmɛdɪtəˈreɪnɪən/ **A** *pr n* **1** (**the Mediterranean (Sea)**) البَحْر (الأَبْيَض) المُتَوَسِّط **2** (region) (**the Mediterranean**) مِنْطَقة البَحْرِ (الأَبْيَض) المُتَوَسِّطِ

B *adj* ‹*island, vegetation*› مُتَوَسِّطيّ, واقِع بِمِنْطَقةِ البَحْرِ المُتَوَسِّطِ

Mediterranean climate *n* مَناخ البَحْرِ الأَبْيَضِ المُتَوَسِّطِ

Mediterranean diet *n* حِمية البَحْرِ الأَبْيَضِ المُتَوَسِّطِ

medium /ˈmiːdɪəm/ **A** *n* **1** (*pl* **mediums**) (spiritualist) وَسيط روحانيّ **2** (*pl* **media**) (means) وَسيلة (وَسائِلُ)

3 (*pl* **media**) (environment) وَسَط (أَوْساط)

B *adj* ‹*weight, size*› مُتَوَسِّط

(Idiom) **to find** *or* **strike a happy medium** وَجَدَ حَلاً وَسَطاً

medium-dry /miːdɪəmˈdrʌɪ/ *adj* ‹*wine, sherry*› نِصْف جافّ (مَشْروب كُحوليّ لا حُلْو وَلا جافّ)

medium-rare /miːdɪəmˈrɛː/ *adj* ‹*steak, beef*› مُتَوَسِّط النُضْج

medium-sized /ˌmiːdɪəmˈsʌɪzd/ *adj* ‹*business, car*› مُتَوَسِّط الحَجْم

medium-term /miːdɪəmˈtəːm/ **A** *adj* ‹*strategy, plan*› مُتَوَسِّط الأَجَل

B *adv* ‹*to plan, think*› على المَدى المُتَوَسِّط

medley /ˈmɛdli/ *n* **1** (Mus) تَشْكيلة **2** (mixture) مَزيج (مُزُج)، خَليط

meek /miːk/ *adj* ‹*housewife, accountant*› وَديع (وُدَعاءُ); ‹*submission, acceptance*› مُتَواضِع

meet /miːt/ **A** *vt* (*past tense, past participle* **met**) **1** (to encounter by chance) الْتَقى (ب); (by arrangement) قابَلَ; **let's ~ at 10 a.m.** لِنَتَقابَل الساعة العاشِرة صَباحاً; **they met in the street** الْتَقَوْا \ تَقابَلوا صُدْفةً في الشارِع **2** (to get to know) تَعَرَّفَ (على); **Paul, ~ my boss, Janet** بول، أُقَدِّمُ لَكَ رَئيسَتي في العَمَل، جانيت; **pleased to ~ you** تَشَرَّفْتُ بِمَعْرِفَتِكَ; **they met each other in Beirut** تَقابَلا في بَيْروتَ **3** (as opponents) ‹*a team, an opponent*› تَقابَلَ **4** (to wait for) انْتَظَرَ ‹*a train, plane*›; **I'm being met at the airport** سَيَنْتَظِرُني أَحَدٌ في المَطار; **she offered to ~ our plane/flight** عَرَضَتْ عَلَيْنا أَنْ تَنْتَظِرَنا في المَطارِ **5** (to experience) واجَهَ ‹*problems, danger*›; **to ~ one's death** لَقِيَ حَتْفَهُ **6** (in awareness) تَفَطَّنَ (إلى); **his eyes met hers** الْتَقَتْ عَيْناهُ بِعَيْنَيْها; **a wonderful sight met our eyes** قوبِلَتْ عُيونُنا بِمَشْهَدٍ رائِعٍ **7** (to fulfil) حَقَّقَ ‹*a target*›; اسْتَوْفى ‹*standard*›; أَوْفى (ب) ‹*commitment*›; **can they ~ the deadline?** هل يَسْتَطيعونَ أَنْ يوفوا بِالْتِزاماتِهِمْ قبل المَوْعِدِ النِهائيِّ؟; **the product does not ~ safety standards** لا تَتَوَفَّرُ في المُنْتَجِ مَعاييرُ السَلامةِ **8** تَكَفَّلَ (ب) ‹*the cost, expenses*› **9** (to rise to) رَقِيَ إلى المُسْتَوى ‹*a challenge*› **10** (to answer) أَجابَ (عن) ‹*an objection, a criticism*›

B *vi* (*past tense, past participle* **met**) **1** (to come together) «friends, colleagues, committee» الْتَقى; **we met for lunch** الْتَقَيْنا لِنَتَناوَلَ الغَداءَ مَعاً; **till we ~ again!** إلى اللِقاءِ \ حتّى نَلْتَقِيَ مَرّةً أُخْرى! **2** (as opponents) «teams, armies» تَقابَلَ, الْتَقى **3** (for the first time) «people» تَقابَلَ, الْتَقى **4** (to join) «hands, lines» الْتَقى; **their eyes met** الْتَقَتْ عُيونُهُما; **four roads ~ at the central square** تَلْتَقي أَرْبَعةُ طُرُقٍ في الساحةِ المَرْكَزيّةِ

C *n* **1** (Sport) مُسابقات رياضيّة **2** (BrE) (in hunting) اجْتِماع [الصَيّادينَ مَصْحوبينَ بِكِلابِهِمْ قبل الصَيْد]

(Idioms) **there's more to this/him than meets the eye** ما خَفِيَ كانَ أَعْظَمَ; **to make ends meet** عاشَ على الكَفافِ

(Phrasal verbs) **meet up** (infml) «people» الْتَقى, تَقابَلَ; **to ~ up with sb** الْتَقى بِشَخْصٍ

• **meet with: 1** **~ with [sb]** اجْتَمَعَ مع [شَخْصٍ] ‹*leaders, officials*› **2** **~ with [sth]** (to encounter) لاقى [شَيْئاً] ‹*success, resistance*›; **her question met with a stunned silence** قوبِلَ سُؤالُها بِصَمْتٍ مُطْبِقٍ; **he met with an accident** تَعَرَّضَ إلى حادِثٍ

meeting /ˈmiːtɪŋ/ *n* **1** (Busn, Pol) اجْتِماع (اجْتِماعات); **to be in a ~** كانَ في اجْتِماع **2** (BrE Sport) **a race ~** مَهْرَجان سِباقاتِ الخَيْلِ

meeting place *n* مَكان اجْتِماعٍ, مُلْتَقًى (مُلْتَقَيات)

meeting point *n* نُقْطة الْتِقاءٍ

megabyte /ˈmɛgəbʌɪt/ *n* ميجا بايْت

megalomania /ˌmɛgələʊˈmeɪnɪə/ *n* جُنونُ العَظَمةِ

megalomaniac /mɛgələˈmeɪniak/ *n* شَخْص مُصاب بِجُنونِ العَظَمةِ

megaphone /ˈmɛgəfəʊn/ *n* بوق, مُكَبِّر صَوْتٍ (أَبْواق)

megastore /ˈmɛgəstɔː/ *n* مَتْجَر عِمْلاق

melancholy /ˈmɛlənk(ə)li/ **A** *n* حُزْن, كَآبة (أَحْزان)

B *adj* ‹*person, mood*› مُكْتَئِب, كَئيب; ‹*music*› حَزين, يَبْعَثُ على الحُزْنِ

melanoma /ˌmɛləˈnəʊmə/ *n* سَرَطان الخَلايا الصِبْغيّةِ, ميلانوما, وَرَم ميلانينيّ

mellow /ˈmɛləʊ/ **A** *adj* **1** ‹*flavour, wine*› لَذيذ; ‹*sound*› رَخيم, عَذْب; ‹*colour*› ناعِم, رَقيق **2** ‹*person, mood*› رَقيق, هادِئ (رِقاق, أَرِقّاءُ)

B *vt* رَقَّقَ, لَيَّنَ ‹*a person*›

C *vi* **1** «person, attitudes» لانَ (i; لين), لَطُفَ (u; لُطْف, لَطافة); **he has ~ed with age** لانَ طَبْعُهُ مع تَقَدُّمِ العُمْرِ

2 «wine, flavour» نَضِجَ (a; نَضْج)

melodic /mɪˈlɒdɪk/ *adj* **1** ‹*voice, song*› مُطْرِب, رَخيم, شَجِيّ

2 ‹*structure, material*› لَحْنِيّ

melodrama /ˈmɛləʊdrɑːmə/ *n* مَشْجاة, ميلودْراما

melodramatic /mɛlədrəˈmatɪk/ *adj* ‹*story, gesture*› مُثير, ميلودْرامِيّ

melody /ˈmɛlədi/ *n* (*pl* **melodies**) لَحْن (أَلْحان), نَغَم (أَنْغام)

melon /ˈmɛlən/ *n* بِطّيخ (n coll), شَمّام (n coll)

melt /mɛlt/ **A** *vt* **1** ذَوَّبَ, أَذابَ ‹*the butter, snow*›; صَهَرَ (a; صَهْر) ‹*a metal*› **2** (to disarm) رَقَّقَ, أَلانَ; **his smile ~ed my heart** أَلانَت ابْتِسامَتُهُ قَلْبي

B *vi* **1** «snow, wax» ذابَ (u; ذَوَبان); «a metal» انْصَهَرَ

2 (to disappear) **he had ~ed into the crowd** اخْتَفى في الحَشْدِ

Phrasal verbs **melt away** **1** «snow, ice» ذابَ (u; ذَوَبان)

2 (to disappear) «resistance, crowd» تَلاشى

• **melt down**: **~ down [sth], ~ [sth] down** صَهَرَ [شَيْئاً] ‹*the metal, coins*›

meltdown /ˈmɛltdaʊn/ *n* **1** (of a nuclear reactor) انْصِهار (نَوَوِيّ) **2** (collapse) انْهِيار (انْهِيارات)

melting point *n* دَرَجة انْصِهار

member /ˈmɛmbə/ *n* **1** (of a family, club, party, etc) عُضْو (أَعْضاء); **a ~ of staff** أَحَد المُوَظَّفينَ; **we have received complaints from ~s of the public** تَلَقَّيْنا شَكاوى من مُواطِنينَ; **a ~ of the audience** شَخْص من الجُمْهورِ **2** (limb) عُضْو (أَعْضاء)

Member of Congress *n* (AmE) عُضْو في الكونْغِرِس

Member of Parliament *n* (BrE) نائب في البَرْلَمان

membership /ˈmɛmbəʃɪp/ *n* **1** (of an organization, party) عُضْوِيّة; **to apply for ~** تَقَدَّمَ بِطَلَبٍ للعُضْوِيّةِ; **~ is open to all** العُضْوِيّةُ مَفْتوحةٌ للجَميع **2** (members) مَجْموع أَعْضاءٍ

membership card *n* بِطاقة عُضْوِيّةٍ

membership fee *n* رَسْم عُضْوِيّةٍ

member state *n* (also **member country**) دَوْلة عُضْو

membrane /ˈmɛmbreɪn/ *n* غِشاء (أَغْشِية)

memento /mɪˈmɛntəʊ/ *n* (*pl* **mementos** or **mementoes**) تَذْكار (تَذْكارات)

memo /ˈmɛməʊ/ *n* مُذَكِّرة

memoirs /ˈmɛmwɑːz/ *n pl* مُذَكِّرات شَخْصِيّة

memorabilia /ˌmɛm(ə)rəˈbɪlɪə/ *n pl* تَذْكارات, أَشْياء تَذْكارِيّة

memorable /ˈmɛm(ə)rəb(ə)l/ *adj* ‹*moment, experience*› لا يُنْسى

memorandum /mɛməˈrandəm/ *n* (*pl* **memorandums** or **memoranda**) مُذَكِّرة

memorial /mɪˈmɔːrɪəl/ **A** *n* نُصُب تَذْكارِي

B *adj* ‹*service, plaque*› تَذْكارِيّ

Memorial Day *n* (AmE) يَوْم الذِكْرى

memorize, -ise (BrE) /ˈmɛmərʌɪz/ *vt* حَفِظَ (a; حِفْظ), اسْتَظْهَرَ ‹*numbers, words*›

memory /ˈmɛm(ə)ri/ *n* (*pl* **memories**) **1** [u] (faculty) ذاكِرة; **from ~** من الذاكِرةِ **2** [u] (remembrance) ذِكْرى (f); **in ~ of the victims/the disaster** إحْياءً لِذِكْرى الضَحايا \ الكارِثةِ

3 (something remembered) ذِكْرى (f; ذِكْرَيات); **he has no ~ of what happened** لا يَتَذَكَّرُ ما حَدَثَ; **the coldest winter in living ~** أَبْرَد شِتاءٍ في الذاكِرةِ الحَيّةِ **4** (Comput) [u] ذاكِرة

Memory Stick® *n* عصا ذاكِرةٍ

men /mɛn/ *n pl* ▸ **man**

menace /ˈmɛnəs/ **A** *n* **1** (danger) خَطَر (أَخْطار); **that man is a ~ to society** يُشَكِّلُ ذلك الرَجُلُ خَطَراً على المُجْتَمَعِ

2 (threatening quality) تَهْديد (تَهْديدات), وَعيد; **his voice was full of ~** كانَ صَوْتُهُ مَليئاً بالتَهْديدِ

B *vt* تَوَعَّدَ, هَدَّدَ ‹*a neighbourhood, victim*›

menacing /ˈmɛnɪsɪŋ/ *adj* ‹*tone, look*› مُتَوَعِّد, مُهَدِّد, تَهْديدِيّ

menagerie /məˈnadʒ(ə)ri/ *n* مَعْرِض للحَيَوانات البَرِّيّة

mend /mɛnd/ **A** *vt* صَلَّحَ, أَصْلَحَ ‹*clothes, shoes, a roof, road*›

B *vi* «bone, tissue» شُفِيَ

Idiom **to mend one's ways** أَصْلَحَ نَفْسَهُ

menial /ˈmiːnɪəl/ *adj* ‹*job, task*› حَقير, مُتَدَنٍّ, وَضيع

meningitis /ˌmɛnɪnˈdʒʌɪtɪs/ *n* الْتِهاب سِحائيّ \ السَّحايا

menopause /ˈmɛnəpɔːz/ *n* سِنّ ,انْقِطاع الطَمْثِ \ الحَيْضِ اليَأْسِ

men's room *n* (AmE) حَمّام الرِجالِ

menstrual /ˈmɛnstrʊəl/ *adj* <*cycle, blood*> طَمْثٍ ,حَيْضٍ

menstruate /ˈmɛnstrʊeɪt/ *vi* حاض (i; مَحيض ,حَيْض)

menstruation /mɛnstrʊˈeɪʃ(ə)n/ *n* طَمْث ,حَيْض

menswear /ˈmɛnzwɛː/ *n* مَلابِس رِجالٍ

mental /ˈmɛnt(ə)l/ *adj* **1** (of the mind) <*health, illness*> عَقْليّ, ذِهْنيّ **2** (psychiatric) <*hospital*> للأَمْراضِ العَقْليّةِ; <*patient*> يُعاني من مَرَضٍ عَقْليٍّ

mental arithmetic *n* حساب ذِهْنيّ

mental block *n* إغْلاق عَقْليّ (شَلَل مُؤَقَّت بالتَفْكير)

mental breakdown *n* انْهِيار عَصَبيّ

mentality /mɛnˈtalɪti/ *n* (*pl* **mentalities**) عَقْليّة

mentally /ˈmɛnt(ə)li/ *adv* ذِهْنيًّا ,عَقْليًّا; **~ ill** مَريض عَقْليًّا; **to be ~ exhausted** كانَ مُرْهَقاً ذِهْنيًّا

menthol /ˈmɛnθɒl/ *n* مِنْتول (مادّة تُسْتَخْلَصُ من النَعْناعِ)

mentholated /ˈmɛnθəleɪtɪd/ *adj* يَحْتَوي على مِنْتول

mention /ˈmɛnʃ(ə)n/ **A** *vt* **1** (to refer to) ذَكَر (u; ذِكْر) <*a person, name, topic*>; **he didn't ~ money** لم يَذْكُر الأَمْوالَ; **please don't ~ my name** لا تَذْكُر اسْمي من فَضْلِكَ; **she never ~ed her work** لم تَذْكُرْ عَمَلَها أَبداً; **to ~ sb/sth to sb** ذَكَرَ شَخْصاً \ شَيْئاً لِشَخْصٍ; **to ~ that ...** ذَكَرَ أنّ ...; **she ~ed (that) you were coming** ذَكَرَتْ أَنَّكَ كُنْتَ سَتَجيءُ; **not to ~** ناهيكَ عن; **access is difficult, not to ~ finding a parking space** الدُخولُ صَعْبٌ ناهيكَ عن العُثورِ على مَكانٍ لِرَكْنِ سَيّارَتِكَ **2** (to acknowledge) «letter, dispatch, report» نَوَّهَ (ب) <*name*>; اعْتَرَفَ (ب) <*service*>
B *n* **1** (reference) ذِكْر (ذُكور); **there was no ~ of the floods** لم يَكُنْ هُناكَ ذِكْرٌ للفَيْضاناتِ; **at the ~ of his name** عند ذِكْرِ اسْمِهِ **2** (acknowledgement) تَنْويه; **she received a special ~ and a prize of £500** تَلَقَّتْ تَنْويهاً خاصًّا وَجائِزةً قَدْرُها £500

mentor /ˈmɛntɔː/ *n* مُرْشِد ,(نُصَّح ,نُصّاح) ناصِح ,مُعَلِّم

menu /ˈmɛnjuː/ *n* **1** (in a restaurant) قائِمة طَعامٍ **2** (on a computer) قائِمة (قَوائِمُ)

menu bar *n* شَريط قَوائِمَ

meow *n, vi* (AmE) ▸ **miaow**

MEP /ɛmiːˈpiː/ *n* = **Member of the European Parliament** عُضْو في البَرْلَمان الأوروبّيّ

mercenary /ˈməːsɪn(ə)ri/ **A** *adj* <*motive, person*> نَفْعيّ
B *n* (*pl* **mercenaries**) مُرْتَزِق (مُرْتَزِقة)

merchandise /ˈməːtʃ(ə)ndʌɪz/ *n* بِضاعة (بَضائِعُ)

merchandising /ˈməːtʃ(ə)ndʌɪsɪŋ/ *n* (also **merchandizing**) تَسْويق ,تَرْويج

merchant /ˈməːtʃ(ə)nt/ *n* تاجِر (تُجّار); **a wine ~** تاجِر خُمورٍ

merchant bank *n* (BrE) بَنْك اسْتِثْماريّ

merchant navy (BrE), **merchant marine** (AmE) *n* أُسْطول تِجاريّ

merciful /ˈməːsɪfʊl/ *adj* <*god*> رَحيم (رُحَماءُ) ,رَؤوف; <*act*> يَنُمُّ عن الرَحْمةِ

merciless /ˈməːsɪləs/ *adj* <*killer, tyrant*> قاسي ,عَديم الرَحْمةِ ,لا يَرْحَمُ ,القَلْبِ

mercury /ˈməːkjəri/ *n* زِئْبَق

Mercury /ˈməːkjʊri/ *pr n* عُطارِد (dipt)

mercy /ˈməːsi/ *n* (*pl* **mercies**) **1** [u] (clemency) رَأْفة ,رَحْمة; **to have ~ on sb** رَأَفَ بِشَخْصٍ; **farmers are at the ~ of the weather** المُزارِعونَ تحت رَحْمةِ الطَقْسِ **2** (boon) نِعْمة; **it's a ~ that no one was injured** من حُسْنِ الحَظِّ أنّ أَحَداً لم يُصَبْ بِأَذًى

mercy killing *n* قَتْل رَحيم

mere /mɪə/ *adj* (fml) **1** (simple) <*fact, coincidence, formality*> مُجَرَّد, مَحْض; **he's a ~ child** هو مُجَرَّدُ طِفْلٍ; **she gave the ~st hint of a smile** بَدا عَلَيْها أَبْسَطُ مَلامِحِ الابْتِسامِ **2** (very) <*presence, mention*> مُجَرَّد; **he trembles at the ~ mention of her name** يَرْتَعِدُ لِمُجَرَّدِ ذِكْرِ اسْمِها

merely /ˈmɪəli/ *adv* <*to say, ask*> فَحَسْب ,فَقَطْ

merge /məːdʒ/ **A** *vt* **1** دَمَجَ (u; دَمْج) ,أَدْمَجَ <*companies, organizations*>; **to ~ sth with sth** دَمَجَ شَيْئاً بِشَيْءٍ **2** خَلَطَ (i; خَلْط) <*colours, styles*>

B *vi* **1** «companies, organizations» اِنْدَمَجَ **2** «rivers, roads» اِلْتَقى **3** «colours, sounds» اِخْتَلَطَ; **the colours ~ into one another** تَخْتَلِطُ الأَلْوانُ بِبَعْضِها البَعْض

merger /ˈmɜːdʒə/ *n* اِنْدِماج

meringue /məˈraŋ/ *n* ميرانْغ (كَعْكة صَغيرة)

merit /ˈmɛrɪt/ **A** *n* اِسْتِحْقاق, جَدارة; **each case is judged on its own ~s** يُحْكَمُ في كُلِّ قَضيّة وَفْقاً لِحَيْثِيّاتِها

B *vt* اِسْتَحَقَّ, اِسْتأْهَلَ ‹*attention, consideration*›

merlin /ˈmɜːlɪn/ *n* ميرْلين, يُؤْيُؤ (صَقر صَغير)

mermaid /ˈmɜːmeɪd/ *n* عَروس \ حورِيّة بَحْرٍ

merrily /ˈmɛrɪli/ *adv* **1** (happily) بِابْتِهاجٍ, بِمَرَحٍ **2** (unconcernedly) بِلا مُبالاةٍ

merriment /ˈmɛrɪmənt/ *n* **1** (fun) بَهْجة, مَرَح **2** (laughter) ضَحِك

merry /ˈmɛri/ *adj* (**merrier**, **merriest**) **1** (happy) مَرِح (مَرْحى), مُبْتَهِج (سُعَداءُ), سَعيد; **M~ Christmas!** عيد ميلادٍ مَجيد! **2** (infml) (tipsy) ثَمِل

(Idiom) **the more the merrier** [كُلَّما زادَ العَدَدُ كُلَّما زادَ المَرَحُ]

merry-go-round /ˈmɛrɪgəʊraʊnd/ *n* أُرْجوحة, دَوّامة خَيْلٍ دَوّارة

mesh /mɛʃ/ **A** *n* شَبَكة (شِباك, شَبَك)

B *vi* **to ~ with sth** «styles, ideas» تَناغَمَ مع شَيْءٍ

mesmerize, **-ise** (BrE) /ˈmɛzmərʌɪz/ *vt* بَهَرَ (a; بَهْر), سَحَرَ (a; سِحْر), خَلَبَ الأَلْباب ‹*an audience, a crowd*›

Mesopotamia /ˌmɛsəpəˈteɪmɪə/ *pr n* بِلاد ما بين النَّهْرَيْن

mess /mɛs/ *n* **1** (infml) (disorder) فَوْضى (f); **what a ~!** يا لَها من فَوْضى!; **the tenants left the kitchen in a ~** تَرَكَ المُسْتأْجِرون المَطْبَخ في حالةِ فَوْضى; **to make a ~** سَبَّبَ فَوْضى; **my hair is in a ~** شَعْري في حالةٍ مُزْرِيةٍ **2** (infml) (muddle) فَوْضى (f), اِرْتِباك (اِرْتِباكات), كَدَر (أَكْدار); **my life is a ~** حَياتي في حالةٍ من الفَوْضى; **the country/economy is in a ~** البَلَدُ \ الاقْتِصادُ في حالةٍ مُزْرِيةٍ; **to make a ~ of sth** أَفْسَدَ شَيْئاً; **how did you get into this ~?** كيف وَصَلْتَ إلى هذا المَأْزِق؟ **3** (infml) (excrement) بُراز الحَيَوانِ, فَضَلات; **the dog made a ~ on the carpet** تَبَرَّزَ الكَلْبُ على السَّجّادةِ **4** (for recreation) مَطْعَم (مَطاعِمُ); **the officers' ~** مَطْعَم الضُّبّاطِ **5** (AmE infml) (large amount) قَدْر \ عَدَد كَبير; **it's won a whole ~ of awards** حازَ على عَدَدٍ كَبيرٍ من الجَوائِزِ

(Phrasal verbs) **mess around**, **mess about** (BrE infml) **A** **1** (to act the fool) لَعِبَ (a; لِعْب), لَها (u; لَهْو), عَبِثَ (a; عَبَث); **don't ~ around with fireworks** لا تَعْبَثْ بالأَلْعابِ النارِيّةِ **2** (to potter) لَها (u; لَهْو); **he likes ~ing around with cars and motorbikes** يُحِبُّ أنْ يُلْهِي نَفْسَهُ بالسَّيّاراتِ والدَرّاجاتِ النارِيّةِ **3** (sexually) **to ~ around with sb** أَقامَ عَلاقةً غَرامِيّةً مع شَخْصٍ **B** **~ [sb] around** (BrE infml) أَرْبَكَ شَخْصاً

• **mess up** (infml) **A** أَفْسَدَ **B** **~ [sth] up**, **~ up [sth]** **1** (to make untidy) بَعْثَرَ [شَيْئاً] ‹*sb's papers*›; نَكَشَ [شَيْئاً] ‹*sb's hair*› **2** (to dirty) وَسَّخَ [شَيْئاً] ‹*the carpet, one's clothes*› **3** (to spoil) أَفْسَدَ [شَيْئاً] ‹*sb's life, plans, an interview*›

• **mess with** (infml) **A** **~ with [sth]** **1** (to interfere with) عَبِثَ بِ [شَيْءٍ] ‹*a system, settings*› **2** (to get involved with) تَوَرَّطَ في اسْتِعْمالِ [شَيْءٍ] ‹*drugs, explosives*› **B** **~ with [sb]** ضايَقَ [شَخْصاً]

message /ˈmɛsɪdʒ/ *n* **1** (verbal, written) رِسالة (رِسالات, رَسائِلُ); **could you give her a ~?** هل يُمْكِنُكَ أنْ تُبْلِغَها رِسالةً؟ **2** (of a film, speech, etc) رِسالة (رِسالات, رَسائِلُ); **a story with a powerful ~** قِصّة لَها رِسالةٌ قَوِيّةٌ

(Idiom) **to get the message** (infml) فَهِمَ الرِسالةَ

messaging /ˈmɛsɪdʒɪŋ/ *n* إِرْسال رَسائِلَ نَصِّيّةٍ

messenger /ˈmɛsɪndʒə/ *n* رَسول (رُسُل)

messiah /mɪˈsʌɪə/ *n* مَسيح (مَسْحى, مُسَحاءُ); **the Messiah** المَسيح

Messrs /ˈmɛsəz/ *abbr* = **Messieurs** السادة

messy /ˈmɛsi/ *adj* (**messier**, **messiest**) **1** (untidy) ‹*room, house, handwriting*› غَيْر مُرَتَّبٍ \ مُنَظَّمٍ; ‹*hair*› أَشْعَث (dipt), غَيْر مُمَشَّطٍ **2** (involving mess) ‹*job*› غَيْر مُنَظَّمٍ **3** (unpleasantly complicated) ‹*situation, divorce*› فَوْضَوِيّ, مُرْتَبِك, مُعَقَّد

met /mɛt/ *past tense, past participle* ▸ **meet**

metabolic /mɛtəˈbɒlɪk/ *adj* ‹*rate, disorder*› أَيْضِيّ

metabolism /mɪˈtabəlɪz(ə)m/ *n* أَيْض, تَمْثيل غِذائِيّ

metal /ˈmɛt(ə)l/ **A** *n* مَعْدِن (مَعادِنُ)

B *adj before n* ‹*bar, box*› مَعْدِنِيّ

metallic /mɪ'talɪk/ *adj* **1** *<element, object>* مَعْدِنِيّ **2** *<paint, finish>* ميتاليك, لامِع, مَعْدِنِيّ

metallurgist /mə'talədʒɪst/ *n* عالِم بالمَعادِنِ

metalworker /'mɛtlwə:kə/ *n* عامِل مَعادِنَ, حَدّاد, سَمْكَرِيّ

metamorphosis /,mɛtə'mɔ:fəsɪs/ *n* (*pl* **metamorphoses**) تَحَوُّل (تَحَوُّلات)

metaphor /'mɛtəfɔ:/ *n* اسْتِعارة, كِناية, مَجاز

metaphorical /,mɛtə'fɒrɪk(ə)l/ *adj* *<sense, language>* مَجازِيّ

metaphysical /mɛtə'fɪzɪk(ə)l/ *adj* (Philos) *<argument, theory>* ماوَرائِيّ, ميتافيزيقِيّ

meteor /'mi:tɪə/ *n* نَيْزَك (نَيازِك), شِهاب (شُهُب)

meteoric /,mi:tɪ'ɒrɪk/ *adj* **1** (Astron) *<dust, iron>* نَيْزَكِيّ **2** (rapid) *<rise>* صاروخِيّ; *<growth>* سَريع جدًّا

meteorite /'mi:tɪərʌɪt/ *n* حَجَر نَيْزَكِيّ

meteorologist /,mi:tɪə'rɒlədʒɪst/ *n* عالِم, عالِم أَرْصادٍ جَوِّيّةٍ طَقْسٍ

meteorology /,mi:tɪə'rɒlədʒi/ *n* عِلْم الطَقْسِ \ الأَرْصادِ الجَوِّيّةِ

mete out /mi:t/ *vt* **to ~ sth, to mete sth out** فَرَضَ شَيْئًا *<treatment, punishment>*

meter /'mi:tə/ **A** *n* **1** (measuring device) عَدّاد (عَدّادات), مِقْياس (مَقاييسُ), جِهاز قِياس; **a gas/water ~** عَدّاد الغازِ \ الماءِ **2** (also **parking meter**) عَدّاد انْتِظارِ السَيّاراتِ **3** (AmE) ▸ **metre**

B *vt* قاسَ (i; قِياس) *<water, electricity, gas>*

methane /'mi:θeɪn/ *n* ميثان

method /'mɛθəd/ *n* **1** (means) طَريقة (طُرُق), أُسْلوب (أَساليبُ); **a ~ of payment** طَريقة دَفْعٍ **2** [u] (discipline) نِظام (نُظُم), مَنْهَج (مَناهِجُ), (أَنْظِمة; **to lack ~** افْتَقَرَ إِلى النِظامِ; **the scientific ~** المَنْهَج العِلْمِيّ

methodical /mɪ'θɒdɪk(ə)l/ *adj* *<approach, investigation>* مَنْهَجِيّ

Methodism /'mɛθədiz(ə)m/ *n* ميثودِيّة, مَنْهَجِيّة (طائِفة مَسيحِيّة)

Methodist /'mɛθədɪst/ *n, adj* ميثودِيّ (شَخْص) من الكَنيسةِ الميثودِيّةِ)

methodological /mɛθədə'lɒdʒɪk(ə)l/ *adj* *<analysis, problem>* مَنْهَجِيّ

methodology /mɛθə'dɒlədʒi/ *n* (*pl* **methodologies**) (fml) مَنْهَجِيّة

methylated spirit, **methylated spirits** /mɛθəleɪtɪd 'spɪrɪt/ *n* كُحول مُحَوَّل (إيثانول مُعالَج بالميثانول)

meticulous /mɪ'tɪkjʊləs/ *adj* *<planning, research>* دَقيق (دِقاق)

metre (BrE), **meter** (AmE) /'mi:tə/ *n* مِتْر (أَمْتار); **three ~s of cloth** ثَلاثة أَمْتارٍ من القُماشِ; **it's a hundred ~s away** تَبْعُدُ مِئةَ مِتْرٍ; **the 1500 ~s** سِباق 1500 مِتْرٍ

metric /'mɛtrɪk/ *adj* *<system, unit>* مِتْرِيّ

metropolitan /mɛtrə'pɒlɪt(ə)n/ *adj* *<area, city>* حَضَرِيّ, مِتْروبوليتانِيّ (مُتَعَلِّق بِمَدينةٍ عُظْمى)

mettle /'mɛt(ə)l/ *n* هِمّة (هِمَم)

Idiom **to be on one's mettle** شَدَّ الهِمّةَ

mew /mju:/ *vi* «cats» ماءَ (u; مُواء); «seabirds» صاحَ (i; صِيَح, صِياح)

Mexican /'mɛksɪk(ə)n/ *n, adj* مِكْسيكِيّ

Mexico /'mɛksɪkəʊ/ *pr n* المَكْسيك (f)

Mexico City *n* مِكْسيكو سيتي

mezzanine /'mɛtsəni:n/ *n* طابِق مَسْحور, طابِق الشُرْفةِ (Egypt)

mg /ɛm'dʒi:/ *n* = **milligram** مِلّيغرام (مِلّيغرامات)

MI *abbr* = **Michigan**

miaow /mɪ'aʊ/ **A** *n* مُواء (مُواءات)

B *vi* ماءَ (u; مُواء)

mice /mʌɪs/ *n pl* ▸ **mouse**

Michigan /'mɪʃɪg(ə)n/ *pr n* ميشيغان (f)

Michigander /mɪʃɪ'gandə/ *pr n* [(شَخْص) من ميشيغان]

micro /'mʌɪkrəʊ/ **A** *n* (*pl* **micros**) **1** also **~computer** حاسوب دَقيق **2** also **~processor** مُعالِج دَقيق

B (**micro +**); *in combination* دَقيق; **~organisms such as viruses** أَحْياء دَقيقة مِثْل الفيروساتِ

microbe /'mʌɪkrəʊb/ *n* ميكْروب (ميكْروبات), جُرْثوم (جَراثيمُ)

microbiologist /mʌɪkrəʊbʌɪ'ɒlədʒɪst/ *n* أَخِصّائِيّ أَحْياءٍ دَقيقةٍ \ ميكْروبيولوجيا

microbusiness /,mʌɪkrə(ʊ)'bɪznəs/ *n* مَشْروع صَغير

microchip /'mʌɪkrəʊtʃɪp/ *n* رُقاقة مُصَغَّرة

microcomputer /'mʌɪkrəʊkɒm,pju:tə/ *n* حاسوب دَقيق

microcosm /'mʌɪkrəʊkɒzəm/ *n* عالَم مُصَغَّر

microfilm /'mʌɪkrəʊfɪlm/ *n* ميكْروفيلْم

microlight /'mʌɪkrəʊlʌɪt/ *n* طائِرة خَفيفة

microlighting /'mʌɪkrəlʌɪtɪŋ/ *n* قِيادة الطائِراتِ الخَفيفةِ

micromanage /'mʌɪkrəʊmaɛnɪdʒ/ *vt* مارَس الإدارة التَفْصيليّة \ الجُزْئيّة <*a business, subordinate*>

microphone /'mʌɪkrəfəʊn/ *n* ميكْروفون (ميكْروفونات)

microprocessor /mʌɪkrəʊ'prəʊsesə/ *n* مُعالِج دَقيق

microscope /'mʌɪkrəskəʊp/ *n* مِجْهَر (مَجاهيرُ), ميكْروسْكوب (ميكْروسْكوبات)

microscopic /mʌɪkrə'skɒpɪk/ *adj* 1▸ (minute) <*organism, particle*> مِجْهَريّ, ميكْروسْكوبيّ 2▸ (using a microscope) <*examination, analysis*> مِجْهَريّ, ميكْروسْكوبيّ

microscopy /mʌɪ'krɒskəpi/ *n* فَحْص مِجْهَريّ

microwave /'mʌɪkrəʊweɪv/ *n* 1▸ (Phys) مَوْجة دَقيقة, مَوْجة 2▸ (also **microwave oven**) فُرْن ميكْروويف, ميكْرُويّة

micturate /'mɪktjʊreɪt/ *vi* تَبَوَّلَ

mid /mɪd/ *adj* مُنْتَصَف; **in ~ May** في مُنْتَصَفِ مايو; **~ morning** مُنْتَصَف الصَباحِ; **he's in his ~ forties** هو في مُنْتَصَفِ الأَرْبَعيناتِ

mid-air /mɪdɛː/ **A** *n* **in ~** في الجَوِّ **B** *adj* <*collision*> جَوّيّ; <*refuelling*> جَوًّا, في الجَوِّ

midday /mɪd'deɪ/ *n* مُنْتَصَف النَهارِ

middle /'mɪd(ə)l/ **A** *adj* 1▸ <*drawer, house, shelf*> مُتَوَسِّط, أَوْسَط (dipt); **I was the ~ child of five** كُنْتُ الأَوْسَطَ بين خَمْسةِ أَطْفالٍ 2▸ (intermediate) <*height, size*> مُتَوَسِّط; **a man of ~ height** رَجُل مُتَوَسِّط الطولِ

B *n* 1▸ (central point) مُنْتَصَف, وَسْط (أَوْساط); **in the ~ of the room** في وَسْطِ الغُرْفةِ; **to split sth down the ~** قَسَم شَيْئًا نِصْفَيْنِ; **the party is split down the ~ on this issue** انْقَسَم الحِزْبُ إلى فريقَيْنِ بِشَأْنِ هذه المَسْأَلةِ 2▸ (of the day, week, etc) مُنْتَصَف; **in the ~ of the night** في مُنْتَصَفِ اللَيْلِ; **in the ~ of winter** في مُنْتَصَفِ الشتاءِ; **I was in the ~ of cooking dinner** كُنْتُ مُنْهَمِكاً في طَهْيِ العَشاءِ 3▸ (infml) (waist) وَسْط (أَوْساط), بَطْن (بُطون, أَبْطُن)

Idioms **in the middle of nowhere** (infml) في مَكانٍ ناءٍ; **to steer a middle course** تَبَنّى نَهْجاً مُعْتَدِلاً

middle-aged /mɪdəl'eɪdʒd/ *adj* <*man, woman*> في مُنْتَصَفِ العُمْرِ

Middle Ages *n* (**the Middle Ages**) العُصور الوُسْطى

middle class *n* طَبَقة وُسْطى

middle distance **A** *n* مُنْتَصَف المَسافة (في مَشْهَدٍ طَبيعيٍّ أو صورةٍ); **in the ~** في مُنْتَصَفِ المَسافةِ

B (**middle-distance**) *adj* <*runner, race*> مَسافاتٍ مُتَوَسِّطةٍ

middle ear *n* (**the middle ear**) الأُذُن الوُسْطى

Middle East *pr n* (**the Middle East**) الشَرْق الأَوْسَط

Middle Eastern /,mɪdəl 'iːst(ə)n/ *adj* <*country, food*> شرق أَوْسَطي

middle finger *n* وُسْطى

middle ground *n* أَرْضيّة وُسْطى

middleman /'mɪdəlman/ *n* (*pl* **-men**) وَسيط (وُسَطاءُ), سِمْسار (سَماسِرة)

middle management *n* إدارة وُسْطى

middle name *n* اسْم أَوْسَط

middle-of-the-road /,mɪdələvðə'rəʊd/ *adj* 1▸ <*policy, views*> وَسَطيّ 2▸ <*music*> [لَيْسَ فيها مُغامَرةٌ أو تَجْريبٌ]

middle school *n* مَدْرَسة مُتَوَسِّطة, مَدْرَسة إعْداديّة

middle-sized /mɪd(ə)l'sʌɪzd/ *adj* <*company, town*> مُتَوَسِّط الحَجْمِ

middleweight /'mɪdəlweɪt/ *n* وَزْن مُتَوَسِّط

middling /'mɪdəlɪŋ/ *adj* <*quality, success*> مُتَوَسِّط

midfield /mɪd'fiːld/ *n* (in soccer) وَسَط المَيْدانِ

midfielder /'mɪdfiːldə/ *n* لاعِب وَسَطِ المَيْدانِ

midge /mɪdʒ/ *n* بَرْغشة

midget /'mɪdʒɪt/ *n* قَزَم (أَقْزام)

midnight /'mɪdnʌɪt/ *n* مُنْتَصَف اللَيْلِ

midriff /'mɪdrɪf/ *n* بَطْن (بُطون)

midst /mɪdst/ *n* **in the ~ of war/a crisis** في مُنْتَصَفِ الحَرْبِ \ أَزْمةٍ; **in our/their ~** بَيْنَنا \ بَيْنَهُم

midstream /mɪd'striːm/ *phr* (**in midstream**) <*to change, interrupt*> في مُنْتَصَفِ الطَريقِ

midsummer /mɪdˈsʌmə/ *n* مُنْتَصَف الصَيْف

Midsummer Day *n* يَوْم مُنْتَصَفِ الصَيْف

midterm /mɪdˈtɜːm/ **A** *n* (of a government) **in ~** في مُنْتَصَفِ الفَتْرةِ

B *adj before n* ‹*elections*› نِصْفيّ

midterm election *n* انْتِخابات نِصْفيّة

midterm exams *n* امْتِحانات مُنْتَصَفِ الفَصْلِ

midtown /ˈmɪdtaʊn/ *adj before n* (AmE) ‹*office, hotel*› [في وَسَطِ المَدينةِ]

midway /mɪdˈweɪ/ *adv* ‹*to stop, arrive*› في مُنْتَصَفِ الفَتْرةِ; ‹*to lie, be located*› في مُنْتَصَفِ الطَريق; **~ through the film** في مُنْتَصَفِ الفيلْم

midweek /mɪdˈwiːk/ **A** *adj* ‹*game, break*› مُنْتَصَفِ الأُسْبوعِ

B *adv* ‹*to travel, meet*› مُنْتَصَفَ الأُسْبوعِ

Midwest /mɪdˈwest/ *pr n* (**the Midwest**) الغَرْب الأَوْسَط, الوَسَط الغَرْبيّ

midwife /ˈmɪdwʌɪf/ *n* (*pl* **-wives**) قابِلة (قابِلات, قَوابِلُ)

midwinter /mɪdˈwɪntə/ *n* مُنْتَصف الشتاءِ

might¹ /mʌɪt/ *modal aux* (*past tense* **may**; *negative* **might not**, **mightn't**) **1** (indicating possibility) **she ~ be right** قد تَكونُ مُحِقّةً; **the rumour ~ not be true** قد لا تَكونُ الإشاعةُ حَقيقيّةً; **I ~ (well) lose my job** قد أَفْقِدُ وَظيفَتي; **they ~ not go** قد لا يَذْهَبونَ; **'will you go?'—'I ~'** 'هل سَتَذْهَبُ؟' — 'رُبَّما'; **they ~ need to go away** قد يَكونُ عَلَيْهِم الرَحيلُ; **they ~ have got lost** من المُحْتَمَلِ أَنَّهُمْ قد تاهوا; **whatever they ~ think** أَيًّا كانَ ما يُفَكِّرونَ بِهِ; **try as I ~, I couldn't do it** حاوَلْتُ قَدْرَ اسْتِطاعَتي، وَلَكِنّي لم أَسْتَطِعْ أَنْ أَفْعَلَهُ **2** (indicating unrealized possibility) **I ~ have been killed!** كانَ من المُمْكِنِ أَنْ أُقْتَلَ!; **I hate to think what ~ have happened** أَكْرَهُ التَفْكيرَ فيما كانَ من المُمْكِنِ أَنْ يَحْدُثَ; **if I had been there all this ~ not have happened** رُبَّما لو كُنْتُ هُناكَ لَما حَدَثَ كُلُّ هذا **3** (in sequence of tenses, in reported speech) **I thought it ~ rain** ظَنَنْتُ أَنَّها رُبَّما تُمْطِرُ; **they thought she ~ have been his lover** اعْتَقَدوا أَنَّهُ كانَ من المُمْكِنِ أَنْ تَكونَ عَشيقَتَهُ **4** (fml) (when making requests) **~ I make a suggestion?** هل بِإِمْكاني أَنْ أُقَدِّمَ اقْتِراحاً؟; **~ I ask who's calling?** هل يُمْكِنُني أَنْ أَسْأَلَ مَن المُتَّصِلُ؟ **5** (with suggestions) **it ~ be a good idea to phone them** قد تَكونُ مُهاتَفَتُهُمْ فِكْرةً جَيِّدةً; **it ~ be a good idea to leave early** رُبَّما من الأَحْسَنِ المُغادَرةُ مُبَكِّراً **6** (fml) (with statements, arguments) **one ~ argue** *or* **it ~ be argued that . . .** يُمْكِنُ القَوْلُ إنّ; **as you** *or* **one ~ expect** كَما قد تَتَوَقَّعُ \ يَتَوقَّعُ المَرْءُ; **as you ~ imagine, he has conservative tastes** كَما قد تَتَصَوَّرُ، هو صاحِبُ ذَوْقٍ مُحافِظٍ **7** (expressing reproach, irritation) **you ~ try helping!** بِإِمْكانِكَ على الأَقَلِّ أَنْ تُحاوِلَ المُساعَدةَ!; **you ~ have warned me!** كانَ بِإِمْكانِكَ أَنْ تُحَذِّرَني! **8** (in concessions) **they ~ not be fast but they're reliable** قد يَفْتَقِرونَ إلى السُرْعةِ وَلَكِنْ يُمْكِنُ الاعْتِمادُ عَلَيْهِمْ

might² /mʌɪt/ *n* **1** (power) قوّة (قوّات, قُوًى) **2** (physical strength) قوّة (قوّات, قُوًى); **with all his ~** بِكُلِّ ما يَمْلِكُ من قوّةٍ

mightn't /ˈmʌɪt(ə)nt/ *abbr* = **might not** ▸ **might¹**

mighty /ˈmʌɪti/ *adj* (**mightier, mightiest**) **1** (powerful) ‹*army, empire*› قويّ (أَقْوِياءُ), جَبّار (جَبّارون, جَبابِرة); ‹*blow, roar*› قويّ **2** (large, imposing) ‹*river, tree*› عَظيم

migraine /ˈmiːgreɪn/ *n* صُداع نِصْفيّ

migrant /ˈmʌɪgrənt/ **A** *n* **1** (worker) مُهاجِر **2** (bird) طائِر مُهاجِر **3** (animal) حَيَوان مُهاجِر

B *adj* ‹*worker, bird*› مُهاجِر

migrate /mʌɪˈgreɪt/ *vi* **1** «*birds, animals*» هاجَرَ **2** «*workers*» هاجَرَ

migration /mʌɪˈgreɪʃ(ə)n/ *n* **1** (of workers) هِجْرة **2** (Zool) هِجْرة

mihrab /ˈmiːrɑːb/ *n* مِحْراب (مَحاريبُ)

mike /mʌɪk/ *n* (infml) ميكْروفون (ميكْروفونات)

mild /mʌɪld/ *adj* **1** (not serious) ‹*symptoms, illness*› طَفيف, بَسيط **2** (not cold) ‹*climate, winter, weather*› مُعْتَدِل; **it's quite ~ today** الطَقْسُ مُعْتَدِلٌ اليَوْمَ **3** (not harsh) ‹*detergent, sedative*› خَفيف **4** (not intense) ‹*surprise, criticism*› خَفيف, غَيْر حادٍّ **5** (not strong or spicy) ‹*flavour, curry*› غَيْر حارٍّ **6** (gentle) ‹*person, manner*› لَطيف (لِطاف, لُطَفاءُ)

mildew /ˈmɪldjuː/ *n* عَفَن فُطْريّ

mildly /ˈmʌɪldli/ *adv* 1 (slightly) ‹*amusing, annoying*› إلى حَدٍّ ما 2 (gently) ‹*to speak*› بِلُطْفٍ; ‹*to rebuke*› بِرِفْقٍ; **to put it ~** أَقَلُّ ما يُقالُ

mile /mʌɪl/ **A** *n* 1 (Meas) ميل (أَمْيال); **60 ~s per hour** 60 ميلاً في الساعةِ; **a ten-~ journey** رِحْلة مَسافَتُها عَشَرةُ أَمْيالٍ 2 (great distance) **to walk for ~s** مَشى مَسافةً طَويلةً جِدًّا; **it's ~s from anywhere** يَقَعُ على مَسافةٍ بَعيدةٍ من كُلِّ الأَماكِنِ المُجاوِرةِ; **it's not a million ~s from here** هو لا يَبْعُدُ كَثيراً عن هُنا; **to see sth a ~ off** رَأى شَيْئاً بِوُضوحٍ; **to stand** *or* **stick out a ~** ظَهَرَ بِوُضوحٍ; **to be ~s away** كانَ شارِدَ الذِهْنِ 3 (race) **(the mile)** سِباق الميلِ الواحِدِ
B **(miles)** *n pl* (infml) (as intensifier) بِكَثيرٍ جِدًّا; **it's ~s better/bigger** هو أَفْضَلُ \ أَكْبَرُ بِكَثيرٍ جِدًّا; **the calculation is ~s out** الحِسابُ بَعيدٌ كُلَّ البُعْدِ عن الصَواب
(Idiom) **to go the extra mile** بَذَلَ جُهْداً إضافيًّا

mileage /ˈmʌɪlɪdʒ/ *n* 1 (miles covered) المَسافة بالميل 2 (infml) (benefit) فائِدة (فَوائِدُ); **he's getting the maximum political ~ out of the crisis** يُحَقِّقُ أَقْصى فائِدةٍ سِياسيّةٍ من الأَزْمةِ

milestone /ˈmʌɪlstəʊn/ *n* 1 (on a road) عَلامة ميل 2 (significant event) مَعْلَم (مَعالِمُ), عَلامة بارِزة

milieu /ˈmiːljəː/ *n* (*pl* **milieux** or **milieus**) مُحيط (مُحيطات), بيئة

militant /ˈmɪlɪt(ə)nt/ **A** *adj* ‹*group, trade unionist*› مُناضِل
B *n* مُحارِب, مُقاتِل, مُناضِل

militarize, -ise (BrE) /ˈmɪlɪtərʌɪz/ *vt* «government, person» عَسْكَرَ (i; عَسْكَرة) ‹*a zone, society*›

military /ˈmɪlɪt(ə)ri/ **A** *adj* ‹*action, operation*› عَسْكَريّ
B *n* **the ~** الجَيْش, القوّات المُسَلَّحة

military academy *n* (*pl* **military academies**) أَكاديميّة عَسْكَريّة

military police *n* شُرْطة عَسْكَريّة

military service *n* خِدْمة عَسْكَريّة

militia /mɪˈlɪʃə/ *n* ميليشيا

milk /mɪlk/ **A** *n* حَليب (لِبان, أَلْبان) لَبَن; **full-cream** *or* (AmE) **whole ~** لَبَن كامِل الدَسَمِ; **skimmed** *or* (AmE) **skim ~** لَبَن مَنْزوع الدَسَمِ
B *vt* 1 حَلَبَ (i-u; حَلْب) ‹*a cow, goat*› 2 (to exploit) اسْتَنْزَفَ ‹*the banking system*›; اسْتَغَلَّ ‹*a situation*›; **to ~ sb dry** اسْتَنْزَفَ كُلَّ ما لدى شَخْصٍ

milk chocolate *n* شوكولاتة بالحَليبِ

milk fever *n* حُمّى الحَليبِ

milk float *n* سَيّارة الحَليبِ, سَيّارة تَوْزيعِ الحَليبِ

milkman /ˈmɪlkmən/ *n* (*pl* **-men**) بائِع حَليبٍ, مُوَزِّع حَليبٍ

milkshake /ˈmɪlkʃeɪk/ *n* مَخْفوق الحَليبِ, ميلْك شَيْك

milk tooth *n* سِنّ لَبَنيّ, سِنّ الحَليبِ

milky /ˈmɪlki/ *adj* (**milkier**, **milkiest**) 1 ‹*tea, coffee*› [مع الكَثيرِ من الحَليبِ] 2 ‹*skin, liquid*› حَليبيّ

Milky Way *n* **(the Milky Way)** دَرْب التَبّانةِ \ اللَبّانةِ

mill /mɪl/ **A** *n* 1 (factory for grinding grain) طاحونة (طَواحينُ) 2 (factory for steel) مَصْنَع (مَصانِعُ) 3 (device for grinding pepper) مِطْحَنة (مَطاحِنُ)
B *vt* طَحَنَ (a; طَحْن) ‹*grain, pepper*›
(Phrasal verb) **mill around**, **mill about** (BrE) «crowds, guests» تَسَكَّعَ

millennium /mɪˈlɛnɪəm/ *n* (*pl* **millenniums** or **millennia**) أَلْفيّة

miller /ˈmɪlə/ *n* طَحّان

millet /ˈmɪlɪt/ *n* دُخْن

milligram, milligramme /ˈmɪlɪɡram/ *n* مِلّيغرام (مِلّيغرامات)

millilitre (BrE), **milliliter** (AmE) /ˈmɪlɪliːtə/ *n* مِلّيلِتر (مِلّيلِترات)

millimetre (BrE), **millimeter** (AmE) /ˈmɪlɪmiːtə/ *n* مِلّيمِتر (مِلّيمِترات)

milliner /ˈmɪlɪnə/ *n* صانِع \ بائِع قُبَّعاتٍ نِسائيّةٍ

million /ˈmɪljən/ *n, adj* مِلْيون (مَلايينُ)
(Idiom) **to be one in a million** كانَ شَخْصاً لا مَثيلَ لَهُ

millionaire /mɪljəˈnɛː/ *n* مِلْيونير (مِلْيونيرات)

milometer /mʌɪˈlɒmɪtə/ *n* (BrE) عَدّاد السَيّارة

mime /mʌɪm/ **A** *n* 1 [u] (technique) إيماء 2 (performance) مَسْرَحيّة صامِتة, تَمْثيل إيمائيّ 3 (also **mime artist**) مُمَثِّل إيمائيّ
B *vt* مَثَّلَ بِشَكْلٍ صامِتٍ, حاكى ‹*an action, a scene*›
C *vi* «singers» غَنّى بِطَريقةِ البْلاي باك

mimic /ˈmɪmɪk/ *vt* (**-ck-**) قَلَّدَ, حاكى ‹*sb's behaviour, voice*›

min., min /mɪn/ *n* 1 = **minute** دَقيقة (دَقائِقُ) 2 = **minimum** أَدْنى

minaret /ˌmɪnəˈrɛt/ *n* مِئْذَنة (مَآذِنُ)

minbar /ˈmɪnbɑː/ *n* مِنْبَر (مَنابِرُ)

mince /mɪns/ A *vt* فَرَمَ (i; فَرْم) ‹*meat, onions*›

B *n* (BrE) لَحْم مَفْروم

(Idiom) **not to mince one's words** لم يَخفْ في الحَقِّ لَوْمةَ لائِمٍ

mincemeat /ˈmɪnsmiːt/ *n* 1 (without meat) حَشْوة من [الفواكِهِ الجافّة والبَهارات للفطائِر] 2 (BrE) (of meat) لَحْم مَفْروم

mind /mʌɪnd/ A *n* 1 [u] (brain) عَقَل (i; عَقْل), ذِهْن (أَذْهان); **it's all in the ~** كُلُّ هذا في الذِهْنِ فَقَطْ; **what's on your ~?** ماذا يَجولُ في ذِهْنِكَ؟; **that thought was always at the back of my ~** كانَتْ هذه الفِكْرةُ دائِماً تَجولُ في خاطِري; **nothing could be further from my ~** لم يَخْطُرْ لي على بالٍ; **what did you have in ~?** ماذا كُنْتَ تَنْوي؟; **it is designed with children in ~** تَمَّ تَصْميمُهُ مع وَضْعِ الأَطْفال في الاعْتبار; **bear in ~ that ...** ضَعْ في اعْتِبارِكَ أَنَّ ... ; **to set sb's ~ at rest** أَراحَ بالَ شَخْصٍ; **I can't get it out of my ~** لا يُمْكِنُني التَوَقُّفُ عن التَفْكيرِ فيهِ; **my ~'s a blank** عَقْلي مُشَوَّشٌ; **to bring sth to ~** ذَكَّرَ بِشَيْءٍ 2 [u] (intellect) عَقْل, ذَكاء, عَقْلِيّة; **to have a good ~** لَدَيْهِ عَقْلٌ سَليمٌ; **a person with the ~ of a two-year-old** شَخْص بعَقْلِيّةِ طِفْلٍ عُمْرُهُ سَنَتانِ; **it's a case of ~ over matter** هي مَسْأَلةُ سَيْطَرةِ العَقْلِ على المادّةِ 3 (way of thinking) عَقْل (عُقول), عَقْلِيّة; **to have a creative/logical ~** كانَ لَدَيْه عَقْلٌ مُبْدِعٌ \ مَنْطِقيٌّ 4 (opinion) رَأْي (آراء), وِجْهة نَظَرٍ; **to my ~** في رَأْيي; **to make up one's ~ about sth/to do sth** اتَّخَذَ قَراراً بخُصوصِ شَيْءٍ \ فِعْلِ شَيْءٍ; **to change one's ~** غَيَّرَ رَأْيَهُ; **to be of one ~** (fml) كانَ لَهُمْ نَفْسُ الرَأْيِ; **to keep an open ~ about sth** أَبْقى عَقْلَهُ مَفْتوحاً بِخُصوصِ شَيْءٍ; **to know one's own ~** كانَ يَعْرِفُ ما يُريدُ 5 [u] (attention) انْتِباه, تَرْكيز; **to keep one's ~ on sth** رَكَّزَ انْتِباهُهُ على شَيْءٍ; **you can do anything if you put your ~ to it** يُمْكِنُكَ أَنْ تَفْعَلَ أَيَّ شَيْءٍ إذا عَقَدْتَ العَزْمَ عَلَيْهِ; **to take sb's ~ off sth** صَرَفَ ذِهْنَ شَخْصٍ عن شَيْءٍ 6 [u] (infml) (mental faculties) عَقل, تَفْكير, فِكْر; **are you out of your ~?** هل جُنِنْتَ؟; **her ~ is going** صِحَّتُها العَقْلِيّةُ تَتَدَهْوَرُ 7 (intelligent person) شَخْص ذَكِيّ

B *vt* 1 (to pay attention to) انْتَبَهَ (إلى); **~ your head/the step** انْتَبِهْ إلى رَأْسِكَ \ الدَرَجةِ; **~ your manners!** انْتَبِهْ إلى سُلوكِكَ!; **~ your language!** انْتَبِهْ إلى أَلْفاظِكَ!; **~ you don't forget** حاوِلْ أَلاّ تَنْسى; **carry on, don't ~ me** اسْتَمِرَّ، وَلا تَلْتَفِتْ لي 2 (to object to) مانَعَ (في), عارَضَ, اعْتَرَضَ (على); **I don't ~ the cold** لا يُهِمُّني البَرْدُ; **I don't ~ coffee, but I prefer tea** لا أُمانِعُ في القَهْوة، وَلَكِنّي أُفَضِّلُ الشايَ; **would you ~ waiting outside?** هل تُمانِعُ في الانْتِظارِ بالخارِجِ؟; **will they ~ us being late?** هل سَيُمانِعونَ إذا تَأَخَّرْنا؟; **I wouldn't ~ a cup of tea** لا أُمانِعُ في كوبٍ من الشايِ 3 (to concern oneself about) اهْتَمَّ (ب), اعْتَنى (ب); **could you ~ my case?** هل يُمْكِنُكَ أَنْ تَنْتَبِهَ إلى حَقيبَتي؟; **he will ~ the shop, while we're on vacation** سَوْفَ يَعْتَني بالمَتْجَرِ وَنَحْنُ في إجازةٍ; **never ~ that, we have to go now** دَعْكَ من ذلك، عَلَيْنا أَنْ نَذْهَبَ الآنَ; **he can't afford a bike, never ~ a car** لا يَسْتَطيعُ تَوْفيرَ ثَمَنِ دَرّاجةٍ، فَما بالُكَ بِسَيّارةٍ

C *vi* 1 (to object) مانَعَ; **I don't ~ at all** لا أُمانِعُ على الإطْلاقِ 2 (to concern oneself) اهْتَمَّ; **'which one do you want?' — 'I don't ~'** 'أَيُّها تُريدُ؟' — 'لا يُهِمُّ'; **never ~** (don't worry) لا تَقْلَقْ; (it doesn't matter) لا يُهِمُّ; **'how much did it cost?' — 'never you ~!'** 'كَم كانَتْ تَكْلِفَتُها؟' — 'لا تُشْغِلْ بالَكَ!'; **~ you, it won't be easy** هل تَعْرِفُ، هو لن يَكونَ سَهْلاً

(Idioms) **mind your own business!** لا تَتَدَخَّلْ فيما لا يَعْنيكَ!; **to be in** *or* (AmE) **of two minds about sth** كانَ مُتَحَيِّراً بِخُصوصِ شَيْءٍ; **to have a good mind to do sth** كانَ مَيّالاً إلى فِعْلِ شَيْءٍ; **to have a mind of one's own** كانَ لَهُ رَأْيُهُ المُسْتَقِلُّ ▸ **piece**

(Phrasal verb) **mind out** انْتَبَهَ; **~ out!** انْتَبِهْ!; **~ out for the potholes** انْتَبِهْ إلى الحُفَرِ

mind-blowing /ˈmʌɪndbləʊɪŋ/ *adj* (infml) ‹*experience, special effects*› بَديع, مُدْهِش

mind-boggling /ˈmʌɪndbɒglɪŋ/ *adj* (infml) ‹*complexity, stupidity*› مُذْهِل

-minded /ˈmʌɪndɪd/ *adj in combination* **technically~** ذو كَفاءةٍ تِقْنِيّةٍ; **independent~** ذو عَقْلٍ مُسْتَقِلٍّ

mindful /ˈmʌɪndfʊl/ *adj* **to be ~ of one's obligations/promise** كانَ حَريصاً على واجِباتِهِ \ الوَفاءِ بِوَعْدِهِ

mindless /ˈmʌɪndləs/ *adj* 1 ‹*violence, vandalism*› غَيْر طائِش 2 ‹*entertainment*› تافِه 3 ‹*task, repetition*› بَسيط مُبَرَّر

mindset /ˈmʌɪndsɛt/ *n* عَقْلِيّة

mine¹ /mʌɪn/ *pron* **his car is green but ~ is blue** سَيّارَتُهُ خَضْراءُ لَكِنَّ سَيّارَتي زَرْقاءُ; **the green gloves are ~** القُفّازاتُ الخَضْراءُ لي; **she's a friend of ~** هِي واحِدَةٌ من أَصْدِقائي; **it's not ~** لَيْسَ لي; **the furniture is ~ to sell** الأَثاثُ لي وَمِنْ حَقّي أَنْ أَبيعَهُ; **that brother of ~** (infml) أَخي اللَعين ذلك; **~'s a whisky** (infml) أَشْرَبُ ويسْكي; **~ was not an easy task** (fml) مُهِمَّتي لم تَكُنْ مُهِمّةً سَهْلَةً

mine² /mʌɪn/ **A** *n* 1 (for coal, gold, etc) مَنْجَم (مَناجِمُ); **the book was a ~ of information** كانَ الكِتابُ مَنْجَماً من المَعْلوماتِ 2 (bomb) لَغَم (أَلْغام)

B *vt* 1 ‹*coal, gold*› اسْتَخْرَجَ (عن) نَقَّبَ 2 (Mil) ‹*an area*› لَغَّمَ

mine detector *n* كاشِف أَلْغامٍ

minefield /ˈmʌɪnfiːld/ *n* حَقْل أَلْغامٍ

miner /ˈmʌɪnə/ *n* عامِل مَنْجَمٍ

mineral /ˈmɪn(ə)rəl/ **A** *n* مَعْدِن (مَعادِنُ)

B *adj* ‹*resources, content*› مَعْدِنيّ

mineralogist /mɪnəˈralədʒɪst/ *n* عالِم مَعادِنَ

mineral water *n* ماء مَعْدِنيّ

minesweeper /ˈmʌɪnswiːpə/ *n* كاسِحة أَلْغامٍ

mineworker /ˈmʌɪnwəːkə/ *n* عامِل مَنْجَمٍ

mingle /ˈmɪŋg(ə)l/ **A** *vt* مَزَجَ (u; مَزْج)

B *vi* 1 (to associate) خالَطَ اخْتَلَطَ (ب); (at a social function) اخْتَلَطَ 2 «liquids, flavours» اخْتَلَطَ, امْتَزَجَ

mini /ˈmɪni/ **A** *n* also **~skirt** تَنّورة قَصيرة, ميني جيب

B (**mini +**); *in combination* [صَغير]; **we played ~golf** لَعِبْنا ميني غولْف; **we took a ~bus to the airport** أَخَذْنا حافِلَةً صَغيرةً إلى المَطارِ

miniature /ˈmɪnɪtʃə/ **A** *adj* ‹*painting, railway, tree, horse*› صَغير جِدًّا

B *n* نَموذَج مُصَغَّر

minibus /ˈmɪnɪbʌs/ *n* (BrE) حافِلة صَغيرة, ميني باص

minicab /ˈmɪnɪkab/ *n* (BrE) تاكْسي, سَيّارة أُجْرةٍ (يَتِمُّ حَجْزُها مُسَبَّقاً)

minidress /ˈmɪnidrɛs/ *n* فُسْتان قَصير

minim /ˈmɪnɪm/ *n* (BrE) البَيْضاء (نِصْف نَغْمةٍ)

minimal /ˈmɪnɪm(ə)l/ *adj* ‹*amount, impact*› أَقَلّ, أَدْنى (dipt), أَصْغَر (dipt; أَصاغِرُ)

minimalism /ˈmɪnɪməˌlɪz(ə)m/ *n* التَقْليليّة

minimalist /ˈmɪnɪməlɪst/ *n, adj* تَبْسيطيّ, تَقْليليّ, اخْتِزاليّ

minimize, **-ise** (BrE) /ˈmɪnɪmʌɪz/ *vt* 1 (to reduce) خَفَّضَ, قَلَّلَ ‹*a risk, costs*› 2 (in computing) صَغَّرَ (إلى أَدْنى حَدٍّ) ‹*the screen, image*›

minimum /ˈmɪnɪməm/ **A** *n* (*pl* **minima** /-mə/ or **minimums**) الحَدّ الأَدْنى, العَدَد الأَقَلّ; **take the ~ of luggage** خُذْ أَقَلَّ عَدَدٍ من الأَمْتِعةِ; **costs were kept to a ~** أُبْقِيَت المَصاريفُ عند الحَدِّ الأَدْنى

B *adj* ‹*standard, age*› أَقَلّ (dipt), أَدْنى; **the ~ deposit is $1,000** أَقَلُّ وَديعةٍ هي 1000 دولار; **the defence pleaded for the ~ sentence** التَمَسَ الدِفاعُ إِنْزالَ أَدْنى عُقوبةٍ; **the ~ contribution is....** أَقَلُّ مُساهمةٍ هي....

minimum wage *n* حَدّ أَدْنى للأَجْرِ, أَجْر أَدْنى

mining /ˈmʌɪnɪŋ/ **A** *n* تَعْدين

B *adj before n* ‹*company, industry*› مَنْجَميّ; **an Australian ~ town** مَدينة مَنْجَميّة أُسْتُراليّة

miniskirt /ˈmɪnɪskəːt/ *n* تَنّورة قَصيرة, ميني جيب

minister /ˈmɪnɪstə/ **A** *n* 1 (in government) وَزير (وُزَراءُ) 2 (member of the clergy) قِسّيس (قِسّيسون, قَساوِسة)

B *vi* **to ~ to sb** اعْتَنى بِشَخْصٍ

ministerial /mɪnɪˈstɪərɪəl/ *adj* ‹*duties, powers*› وِزاريّ

Minister of State *n* (BrE) وَزير دَوْلةٍ

ministry /ˈmɪnɪstri/ *n* (*pl* **ministries**) 1 (Pol) وِزارة 2 (Rel_Chr) (**the ministry**) الكِهانة

mink /mɪŋk/ *n* (*pl* **minks** or **mink**) مِنْك

Minnesota /ˌmɪnɪˈsəʊtə/ *pr n* مينيسوتا

Minnesotan /ˌmɪnɪˈsəʊt(ə)n/ *pr n, adj* [(شَخْص) من مينيسوتا]

minnow /ˈmɪnəʊ/ *n* مِنْوة (سَمَك)

minor /ˈmaɪnə/ **A** *adj* ‹*injury, problem, change*› صَغير,بَسيط; **that's a ~ detail** ذلك من التَفاصيلِ الهامشيّةِ

B *n* **1** (young person) قاصِر **2** (subject) فَرْعيّ

C *vi* (Educ) **to ~ in chemistry/history** \ تَخَصَّصَ في الكيمياء التاريخ تَخَصُّصاً فَرْعيًا

Minorca /mɪˈnɔːkə/ *pr n* مَنورَقة ,مينورْكا

minority /maɪˈnɒrəti/ *n* (*pl* **minorities**) أَقَلِّيّة; **to be in the ~** كانَ من \ في الأَقَلِّيّةِ

minority government *n* حُكومة أَقَلِّيّة

minority group *n* أَقَلِّيّة

minor league *n* [رابطة لِلاعِبي البيسْبول من الدَرَجة الثانِيةِ

minor offence (BrE), **minor offense** (AmE) *n* (جُنَح) جُنْحة

minor road *n* طَريق فَرْعيّ

minstrel /ˈmɪnstrəl/ *n* (من العُصورِ الوُسْطى) مُغَنٍّ

mint /mɪnt/ **A** *n* **1** (plant) نَعْناع **2** (confectionery) حَلْوى بالنَعْناع **3** (for coins) دار سَكٍّ \ ضَرْبِ نُقودٍ

B *adj* ‹*copy, coin*› جَيِّد, جَديد; **in ~ condition** في حالةٍ جَيِّدةٍ

C *vt* ضَرَبَ (i; ضَرْب), سَكَّ (u; سَكّ) ‹*coins*›

minuet /mɪnjuˈet/ *n* رَقْصة المينْويت

minus /ˈmaɪnəs/ **A** *prep* **1** (Math) إلاّ, ناقِص; **what is 20 ~ 8?** ما هو ناتِجُ 20 ناقِص \ إلاّ 8; **11 degrees ~** 11 دَرَجةً تحت الصِفرِ **2** (infml) (without) بِدونِ ,دون

B *adj* **1** (negative) ‹*number, quantity*› تحت الصِفرِ ,سَلْبيّ **2** (disadvantageous) ‹*point*› سَلْبيّ; **on the ~ side** في الجانِبِ السَلْبيِّ

C *n* (*pl* **minuses**) **1** (also **minus sign**) إلاّ ,ناقِص (NA) **2** (drawback) (عُيوب) عَيْب ,(نَقائِصُ) نَقيصة ,سَلْبيّة

minuscule /ˈmɪnəskjuːl/ *adj* ‹*amount, increase*› صَغير جِدًّا

minute¹ /ˈmɪnɪt/ **A** *n* **1** (sixty seconds) (دَقائِقُ) دَقيقة; **a few ~s earlier/later** قبل \ بعد ذلك بِبِضْعِ دَقائِقَ; **it's five ~s' walk away** هو على مَسافةِ خَمْسِ دَقائِقَ مَشْياً من هُنا **2** (moment) (بُرَه ,بُرْهات) بُرْهة ,(دَقائِقُ) دَقيقة ,(لَحَظات) لَحْظة; **just a ~, please** دَقيقة من فَضْلِكَ; **I'll be ready in a ~** سأكونُ جاهِزاً بعد لَحْظةٍ; **it won't take a ~** لن يَسْتَغْرِقَ أَكْثَر من بُرْهةٍ **3** (exact instant) **I telephoned the ~ I heard the news** اتَّصَلْتُ فَوْرَ سَماعي بالأَخْبارِ; **they're due to arrive any ~ now** سَيَصِلونَ في أيِّ لَحْظةِ الآنَ; **to leave things to the last ~** تَرَكَ الأَشْياءَ لِآخِرِ لَحْظةٍ; **to arrive at the last ~** وَصَلَ في آخِرِ لَحْظةٍ **4** (of an angle) دَقيقة قَوْسيّة

B (**minutes**) *n pl* مَحْضَر اجْتِماعٍ \ جَلْسةٍ; **to take the ~s** كَتَبَ مَحْضَرَ الاجْتِماعِ \ الجَلْسةِ

C *vt* سَجَّلَ في مَحْضَرِ الاجْتِماعِ ‹*a decision, an objection*›; **the chairman directed that the suggestion should be ~d** وَجَّهَ الرَئيسُ بِأَنَّهُ يَنْبَغي كِتابةُ الاقْتِراحِ في مَحْضَرِ الاجْتِماعِ

minute² /maɪˈnjuːt/ *adj* **1** (tiny) ‹*amount, quantity, particle*› دَقيق ,بالِغ الصِغَرِ; **her handwriting is ~** خَطُّها صَغيرٌ جدًّا **2** (meticulous) **in ~ detail** بِأَدَقِّ التَفاصيلِ

minute hand *n* عَقْرَب الدَقائِقِ

miracle /ˈmɪrək(ə)l/ *n* مُعْجِزة; **to work** *or* **perform ~s** صَنَعَ المُعْجِزاتِ

miracle cure *n* دَواء \ عَقار \ عِلاج مُعْجِزة

miraculous /mɪˈrakjʊləs/ *adj* ‹*recovery, powers*› إعْجازيّ ,مُعْجِز

mirage /ˈmɪrɑːʒ, mɪˈrɑːʒ/ *n* سَراب

mirror /ˈmɪrə/ **A** *n* **1** (looking glass) (مَرايا) مِرْآة **2** (for driving) (مَرايا) مِرْآة

B *vt* عَكَسَ (i; عَكْس) ‹*sb's experience, life*›

mirror image *n* صورة مِرْآويّة \ مِرْآتيّة

mirth /mɜːθ/ *n* بَهْجة ,مَرَح

misadventure /mɪsədˈventʃə/ *n* (fml) (مَكْروهات) مَكْروه, (BrE) [u] **death by ~** وَفاة ناتِجة عن حادِثٍ ;حادِث مُؤْسِف

misapprehension /mɪsaprɪˈhenʃ(ə)n/ *n* (fml) فَهْم ,سوء فَهْم; **he's is under the ~ that ...** لَدَيْهِ سوءُ فَهْمٍ مُفادُهُ أن ... ;خاطئ

misappropriate /mɪsəˈprəʊprɪeɪt/ *vt* (fml) اخْتَلَسَ ‹*funds, assets*›

misbehave /mɪsbɪˈheɪv/ *vi* «children, pupils» أساءَ التَصَرُّفَ \ السُلوكَ

miscalculation /ˌmɪskalkjʊˈleɪʃ(ə)n/ *n* خَطأ في التَقْديرِ

miscarriage /ˈmɪskarɪdʒ, mɪsˈkarɪdʒ/ *n* **1** إجْهاض (تِلْقائيّ); **to have a ~** تَعَرَّضَتْ للإجْهاضِ **2** **a ~ of justice** إخْفاق العَدالةِ

miscarry /mɪsˈkari/ *vi* (**miscarries, miscarrying, miscarried**) **1** «woman» تَعَرَّضَتْ للإجْهاضِ **2** (fml) «plan, strategy» أَخْفَقَ

miscellaneous /ˌmɪsəˈleɪnɪəs/ *adj* <*items, assortment*> مُتَنَوِّع; **~ expenses** مَصاريف مُتَنَوِّعة

mischance /mɪsˈtʃɑːns/ *n* (fml) سوء حَظٍّ \ طالِعٍ

mischief /ˈmɪstʃɪf/ *n* 1▸ (naughtiness) شَقاوة; **to get up to ~** قامَ بِأَفْعالٍ شَقِيّةٍ 2▸ (trouble) أَذًى; **to make ~** سَبَّبَ أَذًى

mischievous /ˈmɪstʃɪvəs/ *adj* 1▸ <*child, grin*> شَقِيّ (أَشْقِياءُ) 2▸ <*action, statement*> مُضِرّ, مُؤْذٍ

misconception /mɪskənˈsɛpʃən/ *n* فِكْرة \ اعْتِقاد خاطِئ(ة)

misconduct /mɪsˈkɒndʌkt/ *n* (fml) سوء سُلوكٍ \ تَصَرُّفٍ

misconstrue /mɪskənˈstruː/ *vt* (fml) أَساءَ التَفْسيرَ \ التَأْويلَ <*a remark, criticism*>

misdemeanour (BrE), **misdemeanor** (AmE) /mɪsdɪˈmiːnə/ *n* 1▸ (misdeed) جُنْحة (جُنَح), مُخالَفة 2▸ (AmE) (minor infraction) جُنْحة (جُنَح)

miser /ˈmʌɪzə/ *n* بَخيل (بُخَلاءُ)

miserable /ˈmɪz(ə)rəb(ə)l/ *adj* 1▸ (in low spirits) <*mood, wretch*> تَعيس (تُعَساءُ), مِسْكين (مَساكينُ), بائِس (بُؤَساءُ) 2▸ (depressing) <*weather, prospect*> كَئيب, بائِس 3▸ (wretched, poor) <*existence, dwelling*> شَقِيّ, تَعيس, بائِس 4▸ (inadequate) <*wage, performance*> بائِس

miserably /ˈmɪzrəbli/ *adv* 1▸ (unhappily) <*to sob, stare*> بِشَكْلٍ كَئيبٍ \ بِكَآبةٍ 2▸ (poorly) <*to fail, perform*> بِشَكْلٍ ذَريعٍ \ بائِسٍ

miserly /ˈmʌɪzəli/ *adj* 1▸ (mean) <*character, habit*> شَحيح, بَخيل (بُخَلاءُ), شَحاح (أَشِحّاءُ) 2▸ (meagre) <*amount, allowance*> ضَئيل

misery /ˈmɪz(ə)ri/ *n* (*pl* **miseries**) 1▸ [u] (distress) مُعاناة 2▸ (unhappiness) تَعاسة, شَقاء, بُؤْس; **to make sb's life a ~** جَعَلَ حَياةَ شَخْصٍ شَقاءً 3▸ (infml) (person) تَعِس, بائِس (بُؤَساءُ)

misfire /mɪsˈfʌɪə/ *vi* 1▸ «guns» [أَخْطَأَ في إِطْلاقِ النارِ] 2▸ «engines» [أَخْفَقَ في الاشْتِعالِ] 3▸ «plans, intentions» أَخْفَقَ

misfit /ˈmɪsfɪt/ *n* شاذُّ الطِباعِ, غَريبُ الأَطْوارِ; **he's a social ~** هو غَريبُ الأَطْوارِ اجْتِماعيًّا

misfortune /mɪsˈfɔːtʃuːn/ *n* 1▸ [u] (bad luck) سوء حَظٍّ \ طالِعٍ; **he had the ~ to be orphaned very young** من سوءِ حَظِّهِ أَنَّهُ تَيَتَّمَ عِنْدَما كانَ صَغيراً جِدًّا 2▸ (unfortunate event) شِدّة

misgiving /mɪsˈgɪvɪŋ/ *n* رِيبة (رِيَب), هاجِس (هَواجِسُ); **I felt a sense of ~ at the prospect of retirement** أَحْسَسْتُ بِشَيْءٍ من الريبةِ من فِكْرةِ التَقاعُدِ

misgovern /mɪsˈgʌv(ə)n/ *vt* أَدارَ بِشَكْلٍ سَيِّئٍ, أَساءَ الإِدارةَ <*a country, state*>

misguided /mɪsˈgʌɪdɪd/ *adj* <*strategy, belief*> مُضَلَّل, مَغْلوط

mishandle /mɪsˈhand(ə)l/ *vt* أَساءَ التَعامُلَ مع <*a situation, an operation*>

mishap /ˈmɪshap/ *n* مَكْروه (مَكْروهات); **the journey passed off without ~** مَرَّت الرِحْلةُ دون حُدوثِ أَيِّ مَكْروهٍ

mishear /mɪsˈhɪə/ *vt* (*past tense, past participle* **misheard**) أَساءَ السَمْعَ <*an instruction, a word*>

misinform /mɪsɪnˈfɔːm/ *vt* (fml) ضَلَّلَ <*the public, a reader*>

misinterpret /mɪsɪnˈtəːprɪt/ *vt* أَساءَ التَأْويلَ \ الفَهْمَ <*a statement, the data*>

misinterpretation /mɪsɪntəːprɪˈteɪʃ(ə)n/ *n* سوء تَأْويلٍ, تَأْويل خاطِئ

misjudge /mɪsˈdʒʌdʒ/ *vt* 1▸ (to judge incorrectly) أَخْطَأَ في الحُكْمِ على <*a situation, character*> 2▸ (to miscalculate) أَخْطَأَ في التَقْديرِ <*a speed, distance*>

mislay /mɪsˈleɪ/ *vt* (*past tense, past participle* **mislaid**) فَقَدَ (i; فَقْد, فِقْدان), أَضاعَ <*a document, wallet*>

mislead /mɪsˈliːd/ *vt* (*past tense, past participle* **misled**) <*a court, reader*> ضَلَّلَ, خَدَعَ (a; خَدْع)

misleading /mɪsˈliːdɪŋ/ *adj* <*impression, claim*> مُخادِع, مُضَلِّل

mismanage /mɪsˈmanɪdʒ/ *vt* أَساءَ الإِدارةَ, أَساءَ التَصَرُّفَ في <*a company, one's time*>

mismatch /ˈmɪsmatʃ/ *n* 1▸ (of styles, colours) عَدَم تَوافُقٍ \ انْسِجامٍ 2▸ (of skills) عَدَم نِدِّيّةٍ 3▸ (of personalities) عَدَم تَوافُقٍ \ انْسِجامٍ

misogynist /mɪˈsɒdʒ(ə)nɪst/ *n* كارِه النِساءِ

misplace /mɪsˈpleɪs/ *vt* [فَقَدَ (شَيْئاً) لِأَنَّهُ وَضَعَهُ في غَيْرِ مَوْضِعِهِ] <*the passport, a wallet*>

misprint /ˈmɪsprɪnt/ *n* خَطَأ مَطْبَعِيّ

mispronounce /mɪsprəˈnaʊns/ *vt* أَخْطَأَ النُطْقَ <*a name, word*>

misread /mɪsˈriːd/ *vt* (*past tense, past participle* **misread** /ˌmɪsˈrɛd/) **1** (to read wrongly) ‹*a sentence, map*› أخطأَ القِراءةَ **2** (to misinterpret) ‹*an action, a situation*› أساءَ القِراءةَ

misrepresent /ˌmɪsrɛprɪˈzɛnt/ *vt* أعْطى ,شَوَّهَ ,أساءَ التَمْثيل فِكْرةً خاطِئةً عن ‹*a fact, view*›

misrepresentation /ˌmɪsrɛprɪzɛnˈteɪʃ(ə)n/ *n* ,سوء تَمْثيلٍ إعْطاء فِكْرةٍ خاطِئةٍ ,تَشْويه

miss /mɪs/ **A** *vt* **1** (to fail to hit, reach) لم يُصِبْ ,أخْطأَ ‹*a target*›; **he ~ed the ball** لم يَتَمَكَّنْ من ضَرْبِ الكُرةِ; **he ~ed the other car/a pedestrian by inches** أفْلَتَ من الاصْطِدام بالسَّيّارةِ الأُخْرى \ بأَحَدِ المُشاةِ بِمَسافةٍ ضَئيلةٍ; **the stone just ~ed my head** كادَ الحَجَرُ أنْ يُصيبَ رَأسي **2** (to fail to take) ‹*a bus, train, flight*› أخْفَقَ في اللَّحاقِ ب ,فاتَهُ; **to ~ the post** فاتَهُ مَوْعِدُ تَجْميعِ البَريدِ; **I'm sorry, you just ~ed her** أنا آسِفٌ، لَقَدْ خَرَجَتْ لِتَوِّها أضاعَ **3** (to fail to make use of) ‹*an opportunity, a chance*› فاتَهُ **4** (to fail to be present for) ‹*a game, TV programme*› تَغَيَّبَ عن; **to ~ school** تَغَيَّبَ عن المَدْرَسةِ; **it's wonderful, don't ~ it!** هو رائِعٌ، لا تَدَعْهُ يَفوتُكَ! **5** (to fail to see) ‹*a turning, landmark*› لم يُلاحِظْ; **you can't ~ it** لن تَفوتَكَ **6** (in perception) ‹*a remark, an action*› فاتَهُ مُلاحَظَتُهُ; **she's ~ed the joke!** لم تَفْهم النُّكْتةَ! **7** (to avoid) ‹*the traffic, rush hour*› تَفادى; **she narrowly ~ed being run over** كانَتْ قابَ قَوْسَيْنِ أو أدْنى من أنْ تَصْدِمَها سَيّارةٌ **8** (to omit) ‹*a chapter, line*› غَفَلَ (عن; غُفول ,غَفْلة u;); **he ~ed breakfast today** لم يَتَناوَل الإفْطارَ اليَوْمَ **9** (to notice the absence of) ‹*a possession*› افْتَقَدَ; **when did you first ~ it?** مَتى افْتَقَدْتَهُ أوَّلَ مَرّةٍ؟ **10** (to regret the absence of) ‹*a person, place, an activity*› اشْتاقَ ,افْتَقَدَ (إلى); **I ~ you** أفْتَقِدُكَ; **she doesn't ~ work at all** لا تَشْتاقُ إلى العَمَلِ على الإطْلاقِ; **I ~ having someone to talk to** أفْتَقِدُ وُجودَ شَخْصٍ أتَحَدَّثُ مَعَهُ; **she'll be greatly ~ed** سَوْفَ يَفْتَقِدُها مَنْ حَوْلَها كَثيراً جِدّاً

B *vi* (to fail to hit a target) «marksmen, players» أخْطأَ; **he took a shot at goal, but ~ed** حاوَلَ تَسْديدَ الهَدَفِ، ولَكِنَّهُ أخْطأَ الهَدَفَ

C *n* **1** (failure to hit, reach) خَطأٌ في إصابة ,(إخْفاقات) إخْفاق **2** (BrE) (to decide not to do, have) **to give sth a ~** (infml) ‹*a class, meeting*› لم يَحْضُرْ; ‹*dessert, starter*› تَرَكَ (تَرْك ;u) **3** (**Miss**) (woman's title) آنِسة (آنِسات ,أوانِسُ); (form of address) أُسْتاذة; **M~ Judy Vine** الأُسْتاذة جودي فايْن

Phrasal verb **miss out** **A** (infml) فاتَهُ; **to ~ out on an offer/opportunity** فاتَهُ العَرْضُ \ فاتَتْهُ الفُرْصةُ **B ~ out [sb/sth], ~ [sb/sth] out** (BrE) غَفَلَ عن [شَخْصٍ \ شَيْءٍ] ‹*an important point, a word, step*›

misshapen /mɪsˈʃeɪp(ə)n/ *adj* ‹*limb, object*› مَمْسوخ ,مُشَوَّه

missile /ˈmɪsaɪl/ *n* **1** صاروخ (صَواريخُ) **2** (rock, bottle) قَذيفة (قَذائِفُ)

missing /ˈmɪsɪŋ/ *adj* ‹*piece, component, child*› ضائِع ,مَفْقود; **two pieces are ~** هُناكَ قِطْعَتانِ مَفْقودَتانِ; **fill in the ~ words** أكْتُبِ الكَلِماتِ النَّاقِصةَ; **to go ~** «person» فُقِدَ; «object» ضاعَ (ضَياع ,ضَيْع ;i); **~ in action** فُقِدَ في المَعْرَكةِ

mission /ˈmɪʃ(ə)n/ *n* مَهَمّة (مَهامُّ)

missionary /ˈmɪʃ(ə)n(ə)ri/ *n* مُبَشِّر

Mississippi /ˌmɪsɪˈsɪpi/ *pr n* **1** (**the (river) Mississippi**) (نَهْر) ميسيسيبي **2** (US state) ميسيسيبي (f)

Mississippian /mɪsɪˈsɪpɪən/ *pr n, adj* [(شَخْص) من ميسيسيبي]

Missouri /mɪˈzʊəri/ *pr n* **1** **the (river) ~** (نَهْر) ميسوري **2** (US state) ميسوري (f)

Missourian /mɪˈzʊəriən/ *pr n, adj* [(شَخْص) من ميسوري]

mist /mɪst/ *n* **1** (thin fog) سَديم (سُدُم); **sea ~** سَديم البَحْرِ **2** (spray) رَذاذ

Phrasal verbs **mist over** **1** «fields, landscape» غَطّاهُ السَّديمُ **2** «lenses, mirrors» تَضَبَّبَ ,أصْبَحَ مُغَطّىً بالبُخار • **mist up** «windows, mirrors» تَضَبَّبَ ,أصْبَحَ مُغَطّىً بالبُخار

mistake /mɪˈsteɪk/ **A** *n* **1** (error) خَطأ (أخْطاء) ,غَلْطة (غَلَطات ,أغْلاط); **to make a ~** ارْتَكَبَ خَطأً; **I made the ~ of telling him** أخْطأْتُ عِنْدَما أخْبَرْتُهُ; **to do sth by ~** فَعَلَ شَيْئاً عن طَريقِ الخَطأِ; **sorry, my ~!** آسِفٌ، كانَ هذا خَطَئي!; **make no ~, this is a tough job** (infml) لا يَكُنْ عِنْدَكَ شَكٌّ، هذه وَظيفةٌ قاسِيةٌ **2** (inaccuracy in text, spelling, etc) غَلَط (أغْلاط) ,خَطأ (أخْطاء) ,غَلْطة (أغْلاط ,غَلَطات); **to make a spelling ~** ارْتَكَبَ خَطأً إمْلائيّاً; **the article/assignment is full of ~s** المَقالُ \ الواجِبُ مَليءٌ بالأخْطاءِ; **there must be some ~** لا بُدَّ أنّ هُناكَ خَطأً ما

B *vt* (*past tense* **mistook**; *past participle* **mistaken**) **1** (to confuse) **to ~ sth for sth else** خَلَطَ بين شَيْءٍ وَشَيْءٍ آخَرَ; **to ~ sb for sb else** خَلَطَ بين شَخْصٍ وَشَخْصٍ آخَرَ; **there's no mistaking that voice** لا يُمْكِنُ الخَطَأُ في مَعْرِفَةِ صاحِبِ ذلك الصَّوْتِ **2** (to misinterpret) أَخْطَأَ في الفَهْمِ ‹*sb's meaning, intent*›

mistaken /mɪ'steɪk(ə)n/ *adj* **1** مُخْطِئ; **unless I am (very) much ~** إلاّ إذا كُنْتُ مُخْطِئاً جِدًّا **2** ‹*impression, idea*› خاطِئ

mistakenly /mɪ'steɪk(ə)nli/ *adv* ‹*to think, fear*› بِشَكْلٍ \ على نَحْوٍ خاطِئٍ

mistletoe /'mɪsəltəʊ/ *n* هَدال, دِبْق

mistook /mɪ'stʊk/ *past tense* ▸ **mistake**

mistranslation /mɪstrans'leɪʃ(ə)n/ *n* خَطَأٌ في, إساءة تَرْجَمةٍ التَّرْجَمةِ

mistreat /mɪs'tri:t/ *vt* أَساءَ المُعامَلَةَ ‹*a prisoner, child*›

mistress /'mɪstrɪs/ *n* **1** (woman in charge) مَسْؤولة ,سَيِّدة **2** (lover) خَليلة ,عَشيقة

mistrust /mɪs'trʌst/ **A** *vt* (في) أَساءَ الظَّنَّ ,(في) ارْتابَ ‹*a motive, judgement*›

B *n* ارْتِياب, سوء ظَنٍّ ,عَدَم ثِقةٍ

mistrustful /mɪs'trʌstfʊl/ *adj* سَيِّءُ الظَّنِّ ,مُرْتاب ,عَديم الثِّقةِ

misty /'mɪsti/ *adj* (**mistier, mistiest**) **1** ‹*morning, conditions*› سَديميّ; **it's ~** الجَوُّ سَديميٌّ **2** ‹*window, lens*› مُغَطًّى بالبُخارِ

misunderstand /,mɪsʌndə'stand/ *vt* (*past tense, past participle* **misunderstood**) أَساءَ الفَهْمَ ‹*an intention, instruction*›

misunderstanding /,mɪsʌndə'standɪŋ/ *n*

1 (miscomprehension) سوء فَهْمٍ **2** (slight disagreement) سوء تَفاهُمٍ

misunderstood /mɪsʌndə'stʊd/ *adj* **to feel ~** شَعَرَ أَنَّهُ غَيْرُ مُقَدَّرٍ حَقَّ قَدْرِهِ

misuse **A** /mɪs'ju:z/ *vt* أَساءَ الاسْتِخْدامَ ‹*a word, resources*›

B /mɪs'ju:s/ *n* (of equipment, a word, resources) إساءة اسْتِعْمال سَيِّء ,الاسْتِعْمالِ; (of power, funds) اسْتِغْلال

mite /mʌɪt/ *n* سوس

miter (AmE) *n* ▸ **mitre**

mitigate /'mɪtɪgeɪt/ **A** *vt* خَفَّفَ (من) ‹*an effect, risk*›

B (**mitigating**) *adj* ‹*factor, evidence*› مُخَفِّف; **mitigating circumstances** ظُروف مُخَفِّفة

mitochondrial /mʌɪtəʊ'kɒndriəl/ *adj* ‹*gene, DNA*› المُتَقَدِّراتِ ,الميتوكونْدْرِيا

mitochondrion /,mʌɪtəʊ'kɒndrɪən/ *n* (*pl* **mitochondria**) ميتوكونْدْرِيا ,مُتَقَدِّرة

mitre (BrE), **miter** (AmE) /'mʌɪtə/ *n* تاج الأُسْقُفِ (بَراطِلُ) بُرْطُل

mitt /mɪt/ *n* **1** (mitten) قُفّاز (قُفّازات) **2** (infml) (hand) يَد (f; أَيْدٍ, أَيادٍ) **3** (in baseball) قُفّاز البيسْبول

mitten /'mɪt(ə)n/ *n* قُفّاز (يُغَطّي الإِبْهامَ مُنْفَرِداً والأَصابِعَ الباقِيةَ مَعاً)

mix /mɪks/ **A** *vt* **1** (to combine) خَلَطَ (i; خَلْط), مَزَجَ (u; مَزْج, مِزاج) ‹*colours, ingredients, styles*›; **~ the eggs with** *or* **and the milk** اخْلِط البَيْضَ باللَّبَنِ; **to ~ the eggs into the flour** خَلَطَ البَيْضَ بالدَّقيقِ; **to ~ and match colours/components** مَزَجَ وَوَفَّقَ بين الأَلْوانِ \ المُكَوِّناتِ **2** (to prepare) أَعَدَّ ‹*a drink, cocktail*› **3** (to make) خَلَطَ (i; خَلْط) ‹*cement, concrete*› **4** «producer» دَمَجَ (u; دَمْج) ‹*a track, record*›

B *vi* **1** «substances» (to combine) امْتَزَجَ ,اخْتَلَطَ; **oil and water don't ~** الزَّيْتُ والماءُ لا يَمْتَزِجانِ; **family and business don't ~** الأُسْرةُ والعَمَلُ لا يَتَّفِقانِ **2** (to socialize) اخْتَلَطَ; **to ~ with people** اخْتَلَطَ بالناسِ

C *n* **1** (combination) خَليط ,(مُزُج) مَزيج; **a broad ~ of people/abilities** مَزيج واسِع التَّنَوُّعِ من الناسِ \ القُدُراتِ **2** (for cake, cement) خَلْطة ,خَليط; **add two litres of water to the ~** ضَعْ لِتْرَيْنِ من الماءِ على الخَلْطةِ **3** (Mus) مَزْج ,دَمْج

Phrasal verbs **mix in**: **~ [sth] in, ~ in [sth]** خَلَطَ [شَيْئاً] ‹*an ingredient*›

• **mix up**: **~ [sth/sb] up, ~up [sth/sb]** **1** (to confuse) اخْتَلَطَ عَلَيْهِ [شَيْءٌ \ شَخْصٌ]; **she ~ed up the dates** اخْتَلَطَتْ عَلَيْها التَّواريخُ; **I ~ed you up with your brother** أَخْطَأْتُ بَيْنَكَ وَبَيْنَ أَخيكَ **2** (to put out of order) بَعْثَرَ (i; بَعْثَرة) ‹*papers, clothes*› **3** (to get involved) **to be/get ~ed up in sth** تَوَرَّطَ في شَيْءٍ; **he got ~ed up with the wrong crowd** تَوَرَّطَ مع أُناسٍ سَيِّئينَ

mixed /mɪkst/ *adj* 1 (various) ‹*programme, diet*› مُتَنَوِّع ,مُخْتَلِط 2 (socially, in age) ‹*group, community*› مُتَنَوِّع ,مُخْتَلِط 3 (for both sexes) ‹*bathing, team*› مُخْتَلِط 4 (ambivalent) ‹*reception, emotions*› مُتَبايِن ,مُخْتَلِط; **I have ~ feelings about it** لَدَيَّ مَشاعِرُ مُخْتَلِطةٌ \ مُتَبايِنةٌ حَوْلَها

mixed ability *adj* ‹*class, teaching*› مُتَبايِن القُدُراتِ

mixed farming *n* زِراعة \ فِلاحة مُخْتَلِطة

mixed race /ˌmɪkst'reɪs/ *n* **of ~** من عِرْقٍ مُخْتَلِطٍ

mixed spice *n* تَوابِل \ بَهارات مُخْتَلِطة

mixed up *adj* (*before n* **mixed-up**) ‹*kid, teenager*› مُشَوَّش ,مُضْطَرِب (التَفْكيرِ)

mixer /'mɪksə/ *n* 1 (for food) خَلّاط 2 (drink) [شراب مازج صَوْتٍ] يُضافُ إلى المَشْروباتِ الروحيّةِ 3 (machine) مازج صَوْتٍ 4 (engineer) مُهَنْدس صَوْتٍ 5 (sociable person) اجْتِماعيّ 6 (AmE) (dance) [مُناسَبة اجْتِماعيّة للرَقْصِ للتَعارُفِ]

mixing /'mɪksɪŋ/ *n* (combining) مَزْج ,خَلْط

mixing bowl *n* وِعاء خَلْطٍ

mixture /'mɪkstʃə/ *n* 1 (of ingredients) (مُزُج) مَزيج ,خَليط 2 (of people, styles, etc) (مُزُج) مَزيج ,خَليط; **the city is a ~ of old and new buildings** المَدينةُ خَليطٌ \ مَزيجٌ من البِناياتِ القَديمةِ والجَديدةِ

mix-up /'mɪksʌp/ *n* (infml) (بَلابِلُ) بَلْبَلة

ml *abbr* = **millilitre(s)** (مِلّيلِتْرات) مِلّيلِتْر

mm *abbr* = **millimetre(s)** (مِلّيمِتْرات) مِلّيمِتْر

MN *abbr* = **Minnesota**

MO /ɛm'əʊ/ **A** *n* = **medical officer** مَسْؤول طِبّيّ **B** *abbr* = **Missouri**

moan /məʊn/ **A** *n* 1 (noise) تَأَوُّه ,أَنين 2 (infml) (complaint) (تَذَمُّرات) تَذَمُّر **B** *vi* 1 (to groan) «patients, lovers» أَنَّ (i; أَنين) ,تَأَوَّهَ 2 (infml) (to complain) «workers, students» تَذَمَّرَ; **to ~ (about sth)** تَذَمَّرَ (من شَيْءٍ)

moat /məʊt/ *n* خَنْدَق مَليء بالماءِ

mob /mɒb/ **A** *n* غَوْغاء (dipt f), هَمَج (n coll), (عِصابات) عِصابة **B** *vt* (-bb-) (حول) اِحْتَشَدَ (حول) ,تَجَمْهَرَ ‹*a celebrity, convoy*›

mobile /'məʊbaɪl/ **A** *adj* 1 (moveable) ‹*library, shop*› مُتَنَقِّل, مُتَجَوِّل 2 (able to move) قادِر على الحَرَكةِ; **we try and get the patient ~ as soon as possible** نُحاوِلُ أنْ نُساعِدَ المَريضَ على الحَرَكةِ بِأَسْرَعِ وَقْتٍ مُمْكِنٍ **B** *n* 1 (hanging) [قِطَع مُزَخْرَفة مُتَدَلِّية للزينةِ] 2 (also **mobile phone**) موبايِل ,مَحْمول ,جَوّال

mobile home *n* كَرَفانة ,بَيْت مُتَنَقِّل

mobile phone *n* موبايِل ,هاتِف مَحْمول \ جَوّال

mobility /məʊ'bɪləti/ *n* 1 (ability to move) قابِليّة الحَرَكةِ 2 (in society) **social ~** الحَراك الاجْتِماعيّ

mobilization, -isation (BrE) /məʊbɪlaɪ'zeɪʃ(ə)n/ *n* (of troops) اِسْتِنْفار ,تَعْبِئة; (of resources) تَجْهيز

mobilize, -ise (BrE) /'məʊbɪlaɪz/ *vt* 1 حَشَدَ ,عَبَّأَ (i-u; حَشْد) ‹*troops, an army*› 2 ‹*volunteers, supporters*› دَفَعَ (a; دَفْع) ,شَجَّعَ 3 عَبَّأَ ,حَشَدَ (i-u; حَشْد) ‹*resources, support*›

mob rule *n* [u] قانونُ الغابِ

mocha /'mɒkə/ *n* 1 (coffee) بُنّ يَمَنيّ (نَوْع من أَنْواعِ البُنِّ) 2 (flavour) موكا (ذَوْق الشوكولاتةِ والبُنِّ) المُمْتاز والقَويّ

mock /mɒk/ **A** *vt* 1 (to laugh at) سَخِرَ (a; سُخْريّة) (من) ,هَزَأَ (a; هُزْء ,هَزْء) (من) ‹*an action, effort*› 2 (to ridicule by imitation) قَلَّدَ ‹*a mannerism, defect*› **B** *adj* 1 (not real) ‹*suede, surprise*› كاذِب ,زائِف 2 (practice) ‹*examination, interview*› وَهْميّ ,تَجْريبيّ **C** *n* (BrE) امْتِحان تَجْريبيّ

mockery /'mɒk(ə)ri/ *n* 1 (ridicule) اسْتِهْزاء ,سُخْريّة 2 (travesty) مَهْزَلة (تَقْليل من شَأْنِ شَيْءٍ) (اسْتِهْزاءات); **to make a ~ of sth** [قَلَّلَ من قيمةِ شَيْءٍ]

mocking /'mɒkɪŋ/ **A** *n* تَهَكُّم ,اسْتِهْزاء ,سُخْريّة **B** *adj* ‹*remark, smile*› مُتَهَكِّم ,ساخِر ,اسْتِهْزائيّ

mockingbird /'mɒkɪŋbəːd/ *n* طائِر مُحاكٍ

mod con /mɒd 'kɒn/ *n* = **modern convenience** (BrE infml) [أَداة عَصْريّة مُريحة وَعَمَليّة]

mode /məʊd/ *n* 1 (method) أُسْلوب (طَرائِقُ ,طُرُق) طَريقة (أَساليبُ) 2 (operating method) (أَوْضاع) وَضْع; **I'm in holiday ~** أنا في حالةِ إجازةٍ 3 (style) صيغة

model /ˈmɒd(ə)l/ **A** *n* **1** (scale representation) نموذَج (نَماذِجُ, نموذَجات); **a scale ~ of the new airport** نموذَج مُصَغَّر من المَطارِ الجَديدِ **2** (of a car, plane, ship, etc) نموذَج (نَماذِجُ, نَموذَجات) نَموذَج مُصَغَّر, مُجَسَّم; **a ~ of the Titanic** نَموذَج سَفينةِ تَيْتانيك **3** (of product) موديل (موديلات) تَصْميم (تَصاميمُ, تَصْميمات) طِراز (طُرُز, أَطْرِزة); **the latest ~s are on display** يَتِمُّ عَرْضُ أَحْدَثِ الموديلاتِ **4** (example) نَموذَج (نَماذِجُ, نَموذَجات) مِثال (أَمْثِلة, مُثُل) نَمَط (أَنْماط, نِماط); **a ~ of good practice** نَموذَج يُحْتَذى بِهِ في المُمارَسةِ الجَيِّدةِ; **a legal system based on the American ~** نِظام قانونيّ قائِم على النَمَطِ الأَمْريكيِّ **5** (in the fashion industry) موديل (موديلات) **6** (for an artist) [شَخْص يَقِفُ أمام فَنّانٍ لِيَرسمَ لَهُ صورةً أو يَصْنَعَ لَهُ تِمْثالاً] **7** (simulation) نَموذَج إِلِكْتْرونيّ; **an economic ~** نَموذَج إِلِكْترونيّ للاقْتِصاد

B *adj before n* **1** (scaled down) ‹*railway, soldier*› مُصَغَّر **2** (perfect) ‹*student, spouse*› نَموذَجيّ, مِثاليّ **3** (exemplary) ‹*prison, farm*› نَموذَجيّ, مِثاليّ

C *vt* (**-ll-** BrE, **-l-** AmE) **1** **to ~ sth on sth** صَمَّمَ شَيْئاً على غِرار شَيْءٍ; **our educational system is ~led on the American one** نِظامُنا التَعْليميُّ مُصَمَّمٌ على غِرارِ النِظامِ الأَمْريكيِّ **2** صَمَّمَ ‹*a garment, design*› **3** (to shape) شَكَّلَ ‹*a figure, wax*›; **first he ~led the horse in clay** في البِدايةِ صَنَعَ نَموذَجاً لِلحِصانِ من الصَلْصالِ **4** «researchers» طَوَّرَ نَموذَجاً إِلِكْتْرونيّاً ل ‹*an economy, a process*›

D *vi* (BrE, **-ll-** AmE, **-l-**) **1** «fashion model» عَرَضَ الأَزْياءَ; **she ~s for Europe's top designers** تَعْرِضُ الأَزْياءَ لِأَكْبَرِ المُصَمِّمينَ في أوروبّا **2** «artist's model» [وَقَفَ أمامَ فَنّانٍ لِيَرسمَ لَهُ صورةً أو يَصْنَعَ لَهُ تِمْثالاً] **3** «sculptors» **to ~ in clay/bronze** صَنَعَ تَماثيلَ من الصَلْصالِ \ البْرونْز

E *v refl* **to ~ oneself on sb** اتَّخَذَ من شَخْصٍ قُدْوةً \ مِثالاً لَهُ

modelling (BrE), **modeling** (AmE) /ˈmɒdəlɪŋ/ *n* **1** (in fashion) عَرْض أَزْياءٍ **2** (simulating) نَمْذَجة \ مُحاكاة; **computer ~** نَمْذَجة بالحاسوبِ

modem /ˈməʊdɛm/ *n* مودم

moderate **A** /ˈmɒd(ə)rət/ *adj* **1** (not extreme) ‹*size, success*› مُعْتَدِل, مُتَوسِّط **2** ‹*views, wing*› مُعْتَدِل

B /ˈmɒd(ə)rət/ *n* مُعْتَدِل

C /ˈmɒdəreɪt/ *vt* **1** ‹*a demand, one's language*› لَيَّنَ, خَفَّفَ الحِدّةَ **2** (BrE) ‹*an examination, process*› راجَعَ, عَدَّلَ

D /ˈmɒdəreɪt/ *vi* «winds, weather» هَدَأَ (a; هُدوء, هَدْء)

moderately /ˈmɒd(ə)rətli/ *adv* (averagely) ‹*successful, confident*› نَوْعاً ما, إلى حَدٍّ ما; **this model is quite ~ priced** هذا الطِرازُ سِعْرُهُ مَعْقولٌ

moderation /mɒdəˈreɪʃ(ə)n/ *n* **1** (quality of moderation) اعْتِدال; **drinking in ~** شُرْب الكُحولِ باعْتِدالٍ **2** (action of moderation) تَخْفيف, تَلْيين

moderator /ˈmɒdəreɪtə/ *n* **1** (of a meeting) رَئيس (رُؤَساءُ) **2** (BrE) (of exams) مُشْرِف أَوَّل (على الامْتِحاناتِ) **3** (Rel_Chr) (of a church) [رَئيس مَجالِسِ الكَنائسِ البْروتِسْتانْتيّة]

modern /ˈmɒd(ə)n/ *adj* **1** (contemporary) ‹*society, literature*› حَديث (حِداث, حُدَثاءُ), عَصْريّ **2** (up-to-date) ‹*car, device*› حَديث, عَصْريّ

modern-day /ˌmɒd(ə)nˈdeɪ/ *adj* ‹*entertainment, Romans*› مُعاصِر

modernism /ˈmɒd(ə)nɪz(ə)m/ *n* (also **Modernism**) الحَداثة

modernist /ˈmɒd(ə)nɪst/ *n, adj* (also **Modernist**) مُنْتَمٍ إلى حَرَكةِ الحَداثةِ, حَداثيّ

modernity /məˈdəːnɪti/ *n* عَصْريّة, حَداثة

modernization, **-isation** (BrE) /mɒd(ə)nʌɪˈzeɪʃ(ə)n/ *n* تَحْديث, تَجْديد (تَجْديدات)

modernize, **-ise** (BrE) /ˈmɒd(ə)nʌɪz/ *vt* ‹*a system, factory*› حَدَّثَ, جَدَّدَ

modern languages *n* لُغات مُعاصِرة

Modern Standard Arabic *n* اللُغة العَرَبيّة الفُصْحى الحَديثة

modest /ˈmɒdɪst/ *adj* **1** (not boastful) ‹*remark, character*› مُتَواضِع **2** مُتَوسِّط, مُعْتَدِل, مُتَواضِع **3** (chaste) ‹*woman, clothing*› مُحْتَشِم

modesty /ˈmɒdɪsti/ *n* **1** (in outlook) تَواضُع **2** (restraint) احْتِشام

modicum /ˈmɒdɪkəm/ *n* (fml) قَليل, يَسير; **a ~ of sth** قَليل من شَيْءٍ

modification /ˌmɒdɪfɪˈkeɪʃ(ə)n/ *n* **1** [u] (process of change) تَعْديل **2** (change) تَغْيير (تَغْييرات), تَعْديل (تَعْديلات)

modify /ˈmɒdɪfʌɪ/ *vt* (**modifies, modifying, modified**) عَدَّلَ ‹*a plan, an attitude*›

modular /ˈmɒdjʊlə/ *adj* **1** ‹*design, furniture*› جُزْئِيّ **2** ‹*degree, course*› ذو وَحْداتٍ \ مَوادَّ دِراسِيَّةٍ (مُنْفَصِلةٍ)

modulate /ˈmɒdjʊleɪt/ *vt* **1** عَدَّلَ ‹*a temperature, response*› **2** عَدَّلَ ‹*one's voice, pitch*› **3** غَيَّرَ التَرَدُّدَ, ضَمَّنَ ‹*a wave, signal*›

modulation /mɒdjʊˈleɪʃ(ə)n/ *n* تَعْديل (تَعْديلات), تَغْيير (تَغْييرات)

module /ˈmɒdjuːl/ *n* **1** (unit of study) [مادّة دِراسيّة] **2** (unit) جُزْء (أَجْزاء) **3** (unit of a computer program) وَحْدة

mogul /ˈməʊg(ə)l/ *n* قُطْب (أَقْطاب)

moist /mɔɪst/ *adj* ‹*climate, skin*› رَطْب

moisten /ˈmɔɪs(ə)n/ *vt* رَطَّبَ, بَلَّلَ ‹*a cloth, surface*›

moisture /ˈmɔɪstʃə/ *n* رُطوبة, نَداوة

moisturize, -ise (BrE) /ˈmɔɪstʃərʌɪz/ **A** *vt* رَطَّبَ, لَيَّنَ, لَطَّفَ, طَرّى ‹*one's skin, lips*› **B** (**moisturizing**) *adj* ‹*lotion, product*› مُرَطِّب, مُلَيِّن, مُلَطِّف; **moisturizing cream** كْريم مُرَطِّب

moisturizer, -iser (BrE) /ˈmɔɪstʃərʌɪzə/ *n* مُرَطِّب البَشَرةِ

molar /ˈməʊlə/ *n* ضِرْس (أَضْراس, ضُروس)

molasses /məˈlasɪz/ *n + v sing* دِبْس

mold (AmE) ▸ **mould**

Moldavia /mɒlˈdeɪvɪə/ *pr n* مولْدافِيا

Moldova /mɒlˈdəʊvə/ *pr n* مولْدوفا

moldy (AmE) *adj* ▸ **mouldy**

mole¹ /məʊl/ *n* خُلْد (خُلْدان)

mole² /məʊl/ *n* خال (خيلان), شامة (شامات, شام)

molecular /məˈlɛkjʊlə/ *adj* ‹*biology, weight*› جُزَيْئِيّ

molecule /ˈmɒlɪkjuːl/ *n* جُزَيْء (جُزَيْئات)

molest /məˈlɛst/ *vt* **1** (to harass) ضايَقَ, أَزْعَجَ ‹*a co-worker, celebrity*› **2** (to sexually assault) اعْتَدى (على) ‹*a child, victim*›

mollusc (BrE), **mollusk** (AmE) /ˈmɒləsk/ *n* حَيَوان رِخْوِيّ

mollycoddle /ˈmɒlɪkɒd(ə)l/ *vt* (infml pej) دَلَّلَ, دَلَّعَ ‹*a child, an invalid*›

molt (AmE) *vi* ▸ **moult**

molten /ˈməʊlt(ə)n/ *adj* ‹*steel*› مَصْهور; ‹*lava*› مُنْصَهِر

mom /mɒm/ *n* (AmE infml) ماما

moment /ˈməʊmənt/ *n* **1** (short time) لَحْظة (لَحَظات), بُرْهة (بُرَه, بُراهات); **in a ~** في لَحْظةٍ; **it will only take a ~** لن يَسْتَغْرِق أَكْثَر من لَحْظةٍ; **just a ~** *or* **one ~, please** لَحْظة من فَضْلِك; **I don't believe that for one ~** لا يَنْطَلي ذلك عَلَيَّ وَلَوْ لِوَهْلةٍ **2** (point in time) وَقْت (أَوْقات); **at the ~** في الوَقْتِ الراهِنِ; **at any ~** في أَيِّ لَحْظةٍ; **for the ~** حالِيًّا, في الوَقْتِ الحالِيِّ; **phone me the ~ he arrives** اتَّصِلْ بي فَوْرَ وُصولِهِ; **I've only just this ~ got in** وَصَلْتُ لِتَوِّي **3** [u] (fml) (importance) أَهَمِّيّة

Idiom **to have its/one's moments** كانَتْ لَهُ شُهْرةٌ عَريضةٌ ذاتَ يَوْمٍ

momentarily /ˈməʊmənt(ə)rəli/ *adv* **1** (for an instant) لِلَحْظةٍ ‹*to pause, lapse*› **2** (AmE) (very soon) في لَحْظةٍ ‹*to happen, leave*›

momentary /ˈməʊmənt(ə)ri/ *adj* ‹*lapse, glimpse*› خاطِف

momentous /məʊˈmɛntəs/ *adj* ‹*event*› جَليل; ‹*decision*› حاسِم

momentum /məˈmɛntəm/ *n* (*pl* **momenta** /-tə/ or **momentums**) **1** (in physics) كَمِّيّة التَحَرُّكِ **2** (impetus) زَخْم; **the campaign is gathering ~** تَكْتَسِبُ الحَمْلةُ زَخْماً

mommy /ˈmɒmi/ *n* (*pl* **mommies**) (AmE infml) ماما

Monaco /ˈmɒnəkəʊ/ *pr n* موناكو (f)

monarch /ˈmɒnək/ *n* مَلِك (مُلوك), عاهِل (عَواهِلُ)

monarchist /ˈmɒnəkɪst/ *n, adj* مَلَكِيّ

monarchy /ˈmɒnəki/ *n* مَلَكِيّة

monastery /ˈmɒnəst(ə)ri/ *n* (*pl* **monasteries**) دَيْر (أَدْيِرة)

Monday /ˈmʌndeɪ, ˈmʌndi/ *n* (يَوْم) الاثْنَيْن; ▸ **Wednesday**

monetarism /ˈmʌnɪt(ə)rɪz(ə)m/ *n* نَظَرِيّة نَقْدِيّة \ نُقودِيّة

monetary /ˈmʌnɪt(ə)ri/ *adj* ‹*policy, system*› نَقْدِيّ; **an item of little ~ value** بِضاعة ذات قيمةٍ نَقْدِيّةٍ ضَئيلةٍ

monetary union *n* اتِّحاد نَقْدِيّ

monetize, -ise (BrE) /ˈmʌnɪtʌɪz/ *vt* حَوَّلَ إلى نَقْدٍ \ عُمْلةٍ; **a fully ~d society** مُجْتَمَع تَعْتَمِدُ تِجارَتُهُ كُلِّيًّا على العُمْلةِ

money /ˈmʌni/ **A** *n* **1** [u] (coins, notes) مال (أَمْوال); **to make ~** حَقَّقَ رِبْحاً; **to raise ~** (obtain a loan) اقْتَرَضَ مالاً; (for charity)

جَمَعَ تَبَرُّعاتٍ; **to get one's ~ back** (refund) اِسْتَرَدَّ مالَهُ; (on an investment) عادَ إِلَيْهِ مالُهُ; **to pay good ~ for sth** دَفَعَ مَبْلَغاً كَبِيراً في شَيْءٍ; **there's no ~ in it** لا رِبْحَ فيه **2** [u] (wages) أَجْر (أُجور), مُرَتَّب (مُرَتَّبات); **the ~ was good, but I hated the job** كانَ المُرَتَّبُ جَيِّداً، وَلَكِنّي كَرِهْتُ الوَظيفةَ

B **(monies, moneys)** *n pl* (fml) أَمْوال

(Idioms) **for my money ...** في رَأْيي ...; **to get one's money's worth** وَضَعَ مالَهُ في مَوْضِعِهِ; **to be made of money** (infml) كانَ واسِعَ الثَّراءِ; **money talks** المالُ لَهُ سُلْطانٌ; **it's money well spent** أُنْفِقَ المالُ في مَكانِهِ الصَّحيحِ; **to have money to burn** كانَ لَدَيْهِ فائِضٌ من المالِ; **to put one's money where one's mouth is** (infml) [أَعْطى ما وَعَدَ بِهِ]

money box *n* حَصّالة

money laundering *n* غَسيل \ تَبْييض أَمْوالٍ

moneylender /ˈmʌnɪlendə/ *n* مُرابٍ (مُرابونَ)

moneymaker /ˈmʌnɪmeɪkə/ *n* تِجارة رابحة

moneymaking /ˈmʌnɪˌmeɪkɪŋ/ *adj* ‹*scheme, opportunity*› مُدِرّ للمال

money order *n* حَوالة بَريدِيّة \ ماليّة

money supply *n* مَعْروض نَقْدِيّ

Mongol /ˈmɒŋg(ə)l/ **A** *n* **1** (citizen) مُغوليّ (مُغول) **2** (language) (اللُغة) المُغوليّة

B *adj* ‹*minority, tradition*› مُغوليّ (مُغول)

Mongolia /mɒŋˈgəʊlɪə/ *pr n* مُنْغوليا

Mongolian /mɒŋˈgəʊlɪən/ **A** *n* **1** (citizen) مُغوليّ **2** (language) (اللُغة) المُغوليّة

B *adj* ‹*currency, border*› مُغوليّ

mongoose /ˈmɒŋguːs/ *n* (*pl* **mongooses**) نِمْس (n coll; نُموس)

mongrel /ˈmʌŋgrəl/ *n* كَلْب مُهَجَّن \ هَجين

monitor /ˈmɒnɪtə/ **A** *n* **1** (screen) شاشة; **a computer ~** شاشة كُمْبيوتر **2** (measuring device) جِهاز مُراقَبةٍ; **a heart-rate ~** جِهاز مُراقَبةِ نَبَضاتِ القَلْبِ

B *vt* **1** (to check) تابَعَ, راقَبَ ‹*a situation, patient*› **2** (to listen to) تَنَصَّتَ (على) ‹*communications, a broadcast*›

monitoring /ˈmɒnɪtərɪŋ/ *n* **1** (of patients, employees, trends) مُتابَعة, مُراقَبة **2** (of a broadcast, phone calls) تَنَصُّت, مُراقَبة

monk /mʌŋk/ *n* راهِب (رُهْبان)

monkey /ˈmʌŋki/ *n* قِرْد (قُرود, قِرَدة)

monkey wrench *n* مِفْتاح إِنْجْليزيّ

monkfish /ˈmʌŋkfɪʃ/ *n* (*pl* **monkfish**) سَمَك الراهِبِ

mono /ˈmɒnəʊ/ **A** *adj* ‹*track, sound*› أُحاديّ

B *n* نِظام صَوْتيّ أُحاديّ

monochrome /ˈmɒnəkrəʊm/ *adj* ‹*painting, printer*› أُحاديّ اللَوْنِ

monogamous /məˈnɒgəməs/ *adj* ‹*relationship, species, marriage*› أُحاديّ الزَوْجِ

monogamy /məˈnɒgəmi/ *n* الزَواج الأُحاديّ

monologue (BrE) /ˈmɒnəlɒg/, **monolog** (AmE) /ˈmɒnəlɔːg/ *n* مونولوج

mononucleosis /ˌmɒnəʊnjuːklɪˈəʊsɪs/ *n* كَثْرة الوَحيداتِ العَدْوائيّةِ \ الخَمْجيّةِ

monopolize, -ise (BrE) /məˈnɒpəlʌɪz/ *vt* **1** (trade, etc.) احْتَكَرَ ‹*the market, trade*› **2** (a conversation, etc.) اسْتَحْوَذَ, احْتَكَرَ (على) ‹*a conversation, sb's attention*›

monopoly /məˈnɒp(ə)li/ *n* (*pl* **monopolies**) احْتِكار (احْتِكارات)

monoski /ˈmɒnəʊskiː/ *n* [لَوْح للتَزَلُّجِ يَتِمُّ الوُقوفُ عَلَيْهِ بالقَدَمَيْنِ]

monosyllable /ˈmɒnəʊsɪləb(ə)l/ *n* كَلِمة أُحاديّة المَقْطَعِ

monotone /ˈmɒnətəʊn/ *n* اطِّراد (صَوْت أو نَغَم رَتيب)

monotonous /məˈnɒt(ə)nəs/ *adj* ‹*routine, voice*› رَتيب, مُمِلّ

monotony /məˈnɒt(ə)ni/ *n* رَتابة, مَلَل

monsoon /mɒnˈsuːn/ *n* رِياح مَوْسِمِيّة

monster /ˈmɒnstə/ *n* وَحْش (وُحوش), مَسْخ (مُسوخ)

monstrous /ˈmɒnstrəs/ *adj* **1** (shocking) ‹*injustice, lie*› فَظيع, شَنيع **2** (huge) ‹*building, wave*› رَهيب, هائِل

Montana /mɒnˈtanə/ *pr n* مونْتانا

Montanan /mɒnˈtan(ə)n/ *pr n, adj* [(شَخْص) من مونْتانا]

month /mʌnθ/ *n* شَهْر (أَشْهُر, شُهور); **this ~** هذا الشَهْر; **next/last ~** الشَهْر القادِم \ الماضي; **in the ~ of June** في شَهْرِ حُزَيْرانَ \ يونْيو; **in two ~s' time** بعد شَهْرَيْنِ; **she earns $1500 a ~** تَكْسِبُ 1500 دولار في الشَهْرِ

monthly /ˈmʌnθli/ **A** *adj* **1** (happening once a month) *‹magazine, meeting›* شَهْرِيّ **2** (for one month) *‹payment, salary›* شَهْرِيّ; **it is payable in ~ instalments** يُدْفَعُ بالتَقْسيطِ شَهْرِيًّا; **a ~ season ticket** تَذْكَرة شَهْرِيّة
B *adv ‹to meet, pay›* شَهْرِيًّا
C *n* (*pl* **monthlies**) مَجَلّة شَهْرِيّة; **a literary ~** مَجَلّة أَدَبِيّة شَهْرِيّة

Montreal /ˌmɒntriˈɔːl/ *pr n* مونْتِرْيال (f)

monument /ˈmɒnjʊmənt/ *n* نُصْب \ مَعْلَم تِذْكاريّ

monumental /mɒnjʊˈmɛnt(ə)l/ *adj ‹task, achievement›* جَسيم (جِسام); **a decision of ~ proportions** قَرار ذو أَبْعادٍ خَطيرة

moo /muː/ *vi* (**moos, mooing, mooed**) «cows, calves» خارَ (u; خُوار)

mood /muːd/ *n* **1** (state of mind) مِزاج (أَمْزِجة); **to be in a good/bad ~** كانَ في مِزاجٍ جَيِّدٍ \ سَيِّءٍ; **I'm not in the ~ for dancing** لَيْسَ لي مِزاجٌ للرَقْصِ **2** (of an era) جَوّ (أَجْواء) **3** (in grammar) صيغة (صِيَغ)

mood swing *n* تَقَلُّب المِزاجِ

moody /ˈmuːdi/ *adj* (**moodier, moodiest**) *‹stare, teenager, disposition›* عابِس, نَكَديّ

moon /muːn/ *n* قَمَر (أَقْمار)
(Idioms) **many moons ago** مُنذ زَمَنٍ بَعيدٍ; **once in a blue moon** [نادِراً]

moonbeam /ˈmuːnbiːm/ *n* شُعاع القَمَرِ

moon letter *n* حَرْف قَمَريّ

moonlight /ˈmuːnlʌɪt/ **A** *n* ضَوْء القَمَرِ
B *vi* «illegally, secretly» عَمِلَ عَمَلاً ثانياً (عادةً في الخَفاءِ)

moonlighting /ˈmuːnlʌɪtɪŋ/ *n* القِيام بِعَمَلٍ ثانٍ (عادةً في الخَفاءِ)

moonlit /ˈmuːnlɪt/ *adj ‹night, sky›* مُقْمِر

moor /mɔː/ **A** *n* أَرْض بور
B *vt* أَرْسى *‹a boat, ship›*
C *vi* «boats, ships» رَسا (u; رَسْو)

moorhen /ˈmɔːhɛn/ *n* (BrE) دَجاج ماءٍ, سَحْنون

mooring /ˈmɔːrɪŋ/ *n* **1** مَرْسًى (مَراسٍ) **2** (**moorings** *n pl*) مَراسٍ

moorland /ˈmɔːlənd/ *n* أَرْض بور

moose /muːs/ *n* (*pl* **moose**) إِلْكة (نَوْع من الأَيائِل)

moot /muːt/ **A** *adj before n* قابِل للنِقاشِ *‹point, question›*
B *vt* طَرَحَ (a; طَرْح), عَرَضَ (i; عَرْض) *‹a proposal, an idea›*

mop /mɒp/ **A** *n* (for floors) مِمْسَحة (مَماسِحُ)
B *vt* (**-pp-**) **1** مَسَحَ (a; مَسْح) *‹the floor, kitchen›* **2** **to ~ one's brow** مَسَحَ العَرَقَ عن جَبينِهِ
(Phrasal verb) **mop up A** **~ up [sth], ~ [sth] up** مَسَحَ [شَيْئًا] *‹the mess, spills›* **B** (Mil) «troops» مَشَّطَ **C** **~ up [sth], ~ [sth] up** مَشَّط [شَيْئًا] *‹resistance›*

mope /məʊp/ *vi* اكْتَأَبَ, اغْتَمَّ
(Phrasal verb) **mope about, mope around** هامَ (i; هَيْم, هَيَمان)

moped /ˈməʊpɛd/ *n* دَرّاجة نارِيّة (ذات مُحَرِّكٍ صَغير)

moral /ˈmɒrəl/ **A** *adj ‹dilemma, values›* أَخْلاقِيّ
B *n* مَغْزًى (مَغازٍ)
C (**morals**) *n pl* أَخْلاق

morale /məˈrɑːl/ *n* مَعْنَوِيّات, روح مَعْنَوِيّة

morality /məˈralɪti/ *n* مَبادئ أَخْلاقِيّة

morally /ˈmɒrəli/ *adv ‹wrong, superior›* أَخْلاقِيًّا

moral majority *n* أَغْلَبِيّة أَخْلاقِيّة

moratorium /ˌmɒrəˈtɔːrɪəm/ *n* (*pl* **moratoriums** or **moratoria** /-rɪə/) (تَعْليق العَمَلِ بِشَيْءٍ) وَقْف, موراتورْيوم; **to impose a ~ on arms sales** تَمَّ فَرْضُ وَقْفٍ \ موراتوريوم على بَيْعِ السلاحِ

morbid /ˈmɔːbɪd/ *adj ‹fascination›* مَرَضِيّ; *‹humour›* ≈ كَئيب

morbidity /mɔːˈbɪdəti/ *n* **1** (of outlook) ≈ كَآبة **2** (of an organ, tumour) اعْتِلال

more /mɔː/ **A** *adj ‹people, information›* أَكْثَر (dipt); **I have ~ money than him** لَدَيَّ مالٌ أَكْثَرُ مِنْهُ; **some ~ books** كُتُب أَكْثَر; **there's no ~ bread** لا يوجَدُ المَزيدُ من الخُبْزِ; **have some ~ coffee!** تَفَضَّل المَزيدَ من القَهْوةِ!; **no ~ talking please!** الرَجاءُ التَوَقُّفُ عن الكَلامِ!
B *pron* **1** (a larger amount or number) أَكْثَر (dipt); **it costs ~ to go by bus** الذَهابُ بالحافِلةِ يُكَلِّفُ أَكْثَرَ; **he eats ~ than you** يأْكُلُ أَكْثَرَ مِنْكَ; **there were ~ than 20 people at the workshop** كانَ هُناكَ أَكْثَرُ من 20 شَخْصاً في الوَرْشةِ **2** (an additional amount) المَزيد; **I need ~ of them** أَحْتاجُ

قُلْ لي المَزيدَ **tell me ~**; إلى المَزيدِ مِنْها \ مِنْهُمْ

C *adv* **1** (in comparatives) ‹*expensive, carefully*› أَكْثَر (dipt); **she is ~ intelligent than her sister** هي أَكْثَرُ ذَكاءً من أُخْتِها **2** (to a greater degree) ‹*to know, talk*› أَكْثَر; **you must rest ~** يَجِبُ أنْ تَرْتاحَ أَكْثَر; **she eats ~ than I do** هي تأْكُلُ أَكْثَرَ مِنّي; **I like her ~ than her sister** أُحِبُّها أَكْثَرَ من أُخْتِها **3** (longer) **I don't work there any ~** لم أَعُدْ أَعْمَلُ هُناكَ **4** (again) **once ~** مَرّةً أُخرى

Idioms **and what is/what's more** وَفَوْقَ ذلك; **you're wrong, and what's ~, you know it!** أَنْتَ مُخْطِئٌ، وَفَوْقَ ذلك فَأَنْتَ تَعْرِفُ هذا!; **more or less** (almost) تَقْريباً; **I'm ~ or less ready** أنا تَقْريباً جاهِزٌ; **he earns £200 a day, ~ or less** يَكْسِبُ 200 جُنَيْهٍ اسْتَرْلينيٍّ تَقْريباً في اليَوْمِ; **more and more** أَكْثر فأَكْثر; **~ and ~ work** عَمَل أَكْثر فأَكْثر

moreover /mɔːr'əʊvə/ *adv* (fml) بالإضافة إلى, عِلاوةً على ذلك; **~, no new cases have been reported** عِلاوة على ذلك، لم يَتِمَّ الإبْلاغُ عن أيِّ حالاتٍ جَديدةٍ; **it's expensive, and ~, it's labour-intensive** هو غالٍ، وبالإضافة إلى ذلك، فَهُوَ يَتَطَلَّبُ عِمالةً كَثيفةً

morgue /mɔːg/ *n* مَشْرَحة (مَشارِحُ)

Mormon /'mɔːmən/ *n, adj* مورْمونيّ

morning /'mɔːnɪŋ/ **A** *n* (part of day) صَباح; **every ~** كُلّ صَباحٍ; **early in the ~** في الصَباحِ الباكِرِ; **every Tuesday ~** صَباحَ كُلِّ ثُلاثاءَ; **I'll be in all ~** سَأَبْقى بالمَنْزِلِ طوالَ الصَباحِ; **tomorrow/yesterday ~** غَداً صَباحاً \ صَباحَ أَمْسِ; **at seven o'clock in the ~** في السابِعةِ صَباحاً; **I'll see you tomorrow ~** أَراكَ غَداً صَباحاً; **on Tuesday ~** صَباحَ يَوْمِ الثُلاثاءِ; **on Tuesday ~s** صَباحَ كُلِّ ثُلاثاء; **on the ~ of the 4th May** صَباحَ الرابِعِ من مايو; **to work ~s** كانَ يَعْمَلُ في الفَتْرةِ الصَباحيّةِ

B *excl* (**good morning** also (infml) **morning**) صَباحُ الخَيْرِ; **good ~, madam. Can I help you?** صَباحُ الخَيْرِ يا سَيِّدَتي، هل يُمْكِنُني أنْ أُساعِدَكِ؟; **~, Dave!** صَباحُ الخَيْرِ يا ديف!

morning-after pill /,mɔːnɪŋ'ɑːftə pɪl/ *n* حَبّة الصَباحِ التالي

morning coat *n* مِعْطَف الصَباحِ

morning sickness *n* غَثَيان الصَباحِ

Moroccan /mə'rɒk(ə)n/ *n, adj* مَغْرِبيّ (مَغارِبة)

Morocco /mə'rɒkəʊ/ *pr n* المَغْرِب

moron /'mɔːrɒn/ *n* (infml pej) مُغَفَّل, أَبْلَه (dipt)

morose /mə'rəʊs/ *adj* ‹*mood, silence*› مُتَجَهِّم

morphine /'mɔːfiːn/ *n* مورْفين; **to take ~** تَناوَلَ المورْفين

morph into /mɔːf/ *vt* تَحَوَّلَ إلى ‹*a new shape/personality*›

morphological /mɔːfə'lɒdʒɪk(ə)l/ *adj* **1** (of organism) صَرْفيّ, مورْفولوجيّ **2** (of words) تَشَكُّليّ, مورْفولوجيّ

morphology /mɔː'fɒlədʒi/ *n* **1** (of organism) مورْفولوجيا, عِلْم التَشَكُّلِ **2** (of words) عِلْم الصَرْفِ, مورْفولوجيا

Morse, Morse code /mɔːs/ *n* شَفْرة مورْس

morsel /'mɔːs(ə)l/ *n* لُقْمة (مِقْدار صَغير)

mortal /'mɔːt(ə)l/ **A** *adj* **1** ‹*beings, flesh*› هالِك, فانٍ, هَلْكى (هَوالِكُ) **2** ‹*blow, wound*› قاضٍ, مُهْلِك, مُميت; **she struck the ~ blow** ضَرَبَت الضَرْبةَ القاضِيةَ \ المُميتةَ

B *n* (n coll, no singul n), إنْسان, بَشَر

mortality /mɔː'talɪti/ *n* **1** (state) فَناء, هَلاك **2** (number of deaths) مُعَدَّل الوَفَياتِ; **the infant ~ rate** مُعَدَّل وَفَياتِ الأَطْفالِ الرُضَّعِ

mortar /'mɔːtə/ *n* **1** (for building) مِلاط (مُلُط) **2** (a weapon) مِدْفَع هاوُنٍ; **~ fire/attack** إطْلاق الهاوُنِ \ هُجوم بالهاوُنِ **3** (a bowl) هاوُن (هَوَاوِينُ, أَهْوان), مِهْراس (مَهارِيسُ)

mortgage /'mɔːgɪdʒ/ **A** *n* رَهْن (رُهون, رُهونات); **to take out ~ on a property** أَخَذَ قَرْضاً على عَقارٍ

B *vt* رَهَنَ (a; رَهْن) ‹*your house, land*›

mortgagee /,mɔːgɪ'dʒiː/ *n* دائِن (في عَمَليّةِ الرَهْنِ العَقاريِّ)

mortgage rate *n* نِسْبة التَمْويلِ العَقاريِّ

mortgagor, mortgager /,mɔːgɪ'dʒɔː/ *n* راهِن

mortician /mɔː'tɪʃ(ə)n/ *n* (AmE) مُتَعَهِّد دَفْنٍ, حانوتيّ (حانوتيّة)

mortuary /'mɔːtʃ(ə)ri/ *n* (*pl* **mortuaries**) مَشْرَحة (مَشارِحُ)

mosaic /məʊ'zeɪɪk/ *n* فُسَيْفِساء

Moscow /'mɒskəʊ/ *pr n* موسْكو (f)

Moslem /'mɒzləm/ ▸**Muslim**

mosque /mɒsk/ *n* مَسْجِد (مَساجِدُ), جامِع (جَوامِعُ)

mosquito /mə'skiːtəʊ, mɒ'skiːtəʊ/ *n* (*pl* **mosquitoes**) بَعوض (n coll); **a ~ bite** قَرْصة بَعوضةٍ

mosquito repellent *n* طارِد بَعوضٍ

moss /mɒs/ *n* طُحْلُبُ (طَحالِبُ)

most /məʊst/ **A** *adj* **1** (nearly all) ‹*people, companies*› مُعْظَم; **~ people** مُعْظَم الناسِ \ أَغْلَبِيّة **2** (as superlative) ‹*money, time*› الأَكْثَر, الأَغْلَب; **she got (the) ~ votes** فازَتْ بِأَغْلَبِ الأَصْواتِ

B *pron* **1** (nearly all) أَغْلَب (dipt; غُلْب), مُعْظَم; **~ of the time** مُعْظَم الوَقْتِ; **~ of his friends deserted him** تَرَكَهُ أَغْلَبُ أَصْحابِهِ; **for ~ of the day** خلال مُعْظَم اليَوْم **2** (in superlatives) الأَغْلَب, الأَكْثَر; **John has the ~** جون عِنْدَهُ العَدَدُ الأَكْبَرُ

C *adv* **1** (in superlatives) ‹*beautiful, often*› الأَكْثَر; **the ~ intelligent girl in the class** الفَتاة الأَكْثَر ذَكاءً في الفَصْل **2** (very) ‹*interesting, likely*› للغايةِ, جِدًّا; **~ probably** على الأَرْجَحِ; **a ~ enjoyable evening** أُمْسِيّة مُمْتِعة للغايةِ; **these results are ~ encouraging** هذه النَتائِجُ مُشَجِّعةٌ للغاية **3** (more than the rest) ‹*to talk, enjoy*› الأَكْثَر; **what he liked ~ (of all) was ...** أَكْثَرُ شَيْءٍ أَعْجَبَهُ كانَ ...; **he talked ~** تَكَلَّمَ أَكْثَرَ من غَيْرِهِ

D **(at (the) most)** *phr* على الأَكْثَرِ; **there were 50 people there, at ~** كانَ هُناكَ 50 شَخْصاً على الأَكْثَرِ

E **(for the most part)** *phr* في الأَغْلَبِ; **the waiting staff are, for the ~ part, students** أَغْلَبُ نُدُلِ المَطْعَمِ من الطُلّابِ

(Idiom) **to make the most of sth** اسْتَفادَ من شَيْءٍ إلى أَقْصى حَدٍّ

mostly /ˈməʊstli/ *adv* ‹*to consist of, focus on*› غالِباً, في الأَغْلَبِ; **we rely ~ on advertising for funds** نَعْتَمِدُ في تَمْويلنا غالِباً على الإِعْلاناتِ; **their fans are ~ female** مُعْجَبوهُمْ غالِباً من النِساءِ

Mosul /ˈməʊsʊl/ *pr n* المَوْصِل (f)

MOT /ɛməʊˈtiː/ *n* (also **MOT test**) (BrE) فَحْص دَوْرِيّ للسَيّاراتِ

motel /məʊˈtɛl/ *n* موتيل

moth /mɒθ/ *n* عُثّ (n coll; عُثَث)

mother /ˈmʌðə/ **A** *n* أُمّ (f; أُمَّهات), والدة **B** *vt* ‹*a husband, brother*› دَلَّلَ (مِثْلَ أُمٍّ)

motherboard /ˈmʌðəbɔːd/ *n* لَوْحة أُمّ

motherhood /ˈmʌðəhʊd/ *n* أُمومة

Mothering Sunday /ˈmʌðərɪŋ ˌsʌndeɪ/ *n* (BrE) عيد \ يَوْم الأُمِّ

mother-in-law /ˈmʌðərɪnlɔː/ *n* (*pl* **mothers-in-law**) حَماة (حَمَوات)

motherland /ˈmʌðəland/ *n* وَطَن أُمّ

motherly /ˈmʌðəli/ *adj* ‹*care*› أُمومِيّ; ‹*woman*› عَطوف (عُطُف), حَنون

mother-of-pearl /mʌðərəvˈpəːl/ *n* عِرْق اللُؤْلُؤِ

Mother's Day *n* عيد \ يَوْم الأُمِّ

Mother Superior *n* رَئِيسة الدَيْر

mother-to-be /ˌmʌðətəˈbiː/ *n* (*pl* **mothers-to-be**) امْرَأة حامِل (خاصّةً للمَرّةِ الأولى)

mother tongue *n* لُغة أُمّ

motif /məʊˈtiːf/ *n* موتيف

motion /ˈməʊʃ(ə)n/ **A** *n* **1** [u] (movement) حَرَكة; **to set a plan in ~** وَضَعَ مُخَطَّطاً حَيِّزَ التَنْفيذ **2** (a proposal) اقْتِراح (اقْتِراحات); **to propose a ~** عَرَضَ اقْتِراحاً

B *vi* **I ~ed to him to close the door** أَوْمَأْتُ لَهُ \ أَشَرْتُ لَهُ أَنْ يُغْلِقَ الباب

(Idiom) **to go through the motions (of doing sth)** تَظاهَرَ (بالقِيامِ بِشَيْءٍ)

motionless /ˈməʊʃnləs/ *adj* ‹*to stand, remain*› ساكِن

motion picture *n* فيلْم (أَفْلام)

motivate /ˈməʊtɪveɪt/ *vt* ‹*students, employees*› حَفَّزَ

motivated /ˈməʊtɪveɪtɪd/ *adj* **1** ‹*students, employees*› مُتَحَمِّس **2** **politically/racially ~** بِدَوافِعَ سِياسيّةٍ \ عُنْصُرِيّةٍ; **this was a racially ~ attack** كانَ هُجوماً بِدَوافِعَ عُنْصُرِيّةٍ

motivation /məʊtɪˈveɪʃ(ə)n/ *n* **1** (drive) هِمّة (هِمَم); **to lack ~** افْتَقَرَ إلى الهِمّةِ **2** (reason) دافِع (دَوافِعُ)

motive /ˈməʊtɪv/ *n* دافِع (دَوافِعُ); **the ~ for the crime** الدافِع للجَريمةِ

motley /ˈmɒtli/ *adj* ‹*collection, bunch*› مُتَنافِر

motor /ˈməʊtə/ **A** *n* مُحَرِّك (مُحَرِّكات)

B *adj* **1** ‹*vehicle*› ذو مُحَرِّكٍ; ‹*insurance*› سَيّاراتٍ **2** (of muscles) ‹*nerves, skills*› حَرَكِيّ

motorbike /ˈməʊtəbʌɪk/ *n* دَرّاجة نارِيّة

motor boat *n* (لَنْشات) لَنْش ,قارِب بِمُحَرِّكٍ

motor car *n* (old use) سَيّارة

motorcycle /ˈməʊtəsʌɪk(ə)l/ *n* درّاجة ناريّة

motorcycling /ˈməʊtəsʌɪklɪŋ/ *n* رُكوب الدَرّاجاتِ الناريّةِ

motorcyclist /ˈməʊtəsʌɪklɪst/ *n* سائِق درّاجةٍ ناريّةٍ

motorhome /ˈməʊtəhəʊm/ *n* بَيْت مُتَنَقِّل

motoring /ˈməʊtərɪŋ/ *n* (old use) قِيادة السَيّارةِ

motoring accident *n* حادِث مُرورٍ

motoring magazine *n* مَجَلّة سَيّاراتٍ

motorist /ˈməʊtərɪst/ *n* سائِق سَيّارةٍ

motor racing *n* سِباق سَيّاراتٍ

motorway /ˈməʊtəweɪ/ *n* (BrE) طَريق سَريع

mottled /ˈmɒt(ə)ld/ *adj* ‹*skin, appearance*› مُبَقَّع

motto /ˈmɒtəʊ/ *n* (*pl* **mottoes**) (شِعارات) شِعار

mould (BrE), **mold** (AmE) /məʊld/ [A] *n* [1] (container) قالَب (قَوالِبُ) [2] (fungus) عَفَن (أَعْفان)

[B] *vt* [1] (to shape) قَوْلَبَ (i; قَوْلَبة) ,شَكَّلَ ‹*the plastic, clay*› [2] (to influence) شَكَّلَ ‹*public opinion, sb's personality*›

mouldy (BrE), **moldy** (AmE) /ˈməʊldi/ *adj* (**mouldier, mouldiest**) ‹*smell, cheese*› مُتَعَفِّن; **to become** *or* **go ~** تَعَفَّنَ

moult (BrE), **molt** (AmE) /məʊlt/ *vi* «birds» طَرَحَ \ فَقَدَ ريشَهُ; «cats» طَرَحَ \ فَقَدَ شَعْرَهُ

mound /maʊnd/ *n* [1] (of earth) تَلّ (تِلال) ,رابِية (رَوابٍ) [2] (pile) كَوْم (أَكْوام)

mount /maʊnt/ [A] *vt* [1] (to go up) صَعِدَ (a; صُعود) ‹*the stairs, scaffold*›; **to ~ a horse** اِمْتَطى جَواداً; **the car ~ed the pavement** صَعِدَت السَيّارة على الرَصيفِ [2] (to fix into place) ثَبَّتَ ‹*a jewel, photograph, stamp*› [3] (to set up) أَقامَ ‹*an exhibition*›; أَطْلَقَ ‹*a campaign*›; شَنَّ (u; شَنّ) ‹*an attack*› [4] (in breeding) صَعِدَ على الظَهْرِ ,اِعْتَلى ‹*the mare, female*›

[B] *vi* [1] (to increase) «numbers, concern, temperatures» اِزْدادَ; **the death toll continues to ~** تَسْتَمِرُّ حَصيلةُ الوَفيّاتِ في الاِرْتِفاعِ [2] «climbers» صَعِدَ (a; صُعود)

[C] (**mounting**) *adj* ‹*pressure, problems*› مُتَصاعِد ,مُتَزايِد

[D] *n* [1] (mountain) جَبَل (جِبال ,أَجْبال); **Mount Everest** جَبَل إِفَرِسْت; **the Mount of Olives** جَبَل الزَيْتونِ [2] (horse) مَطِيّة (مَطِيّ ,مَطايا) [3] (support for a jewel) رَكوبة; (for a lens) حامِل (f; حَوامِلُ); **the ~ for the lens is broken** حامِل العَدَساتِ مَكْسورٌ

mountain /ˈmaʊntɪn/ *n* جَبَل (جِبال)

mountain bike *n* درّاجة جَبَليّة \ الجَبَلِ

mountaineer /maʊntɪˈnɪə/ *n* مُتَسَلِّق جِبالٍ

mountaineering /maʊntəˈnɪərɪŋ/ *n* تَسَلُّق الجِبالِ

mountain goat *n* أُرْوِيّة ,ماعِز الجَبَلِ (أَراوِيّ)

mountainous /ˈmaʊntɪnəs/ *adj* [1] (Geog) ‹*terrain, area*› جَبَليّ [2] (huge) ‹*wave, seas*› ضَخْم (ضِخام) ,عِمْلاق (عَمالِقة)

mountaintop /ˈmaʊnt(ə)ntɒp/ *n* قِمّة جَبَلٍ

mourn /mɔːn/ [A] *vt* حَدَّ (i; حِداد) (على) ‹*a friend, sb's death*›

[B] *vi* لَبِسَ الحِدادَ; **to ~ for sb** لَبِسَ الحِدادَ على شَخْصٍ

mourner /ˈmɔːnə/ *n* مُعَزٍّ

mournful /ˈmɔːnfʊl/ *adj* ‹*cry, ballad*› حَزين (حَزانى)

mourning /ˈmɔːnɪŋ/ *n* حِداد; **to be in ~ for sb** كانَ في حِدادٍ على شَخْصٍ

mouse /maʊs/ *n* (*pl* **mice**) [1] (rodent) فَأْر (n coll; فِئْران) [2] (for computer) فَأْرة

mouse mat *n* وِسادة الفَأْرةِ

mouseover /ˈmaʊsəʊvə/ *n* تَمْرير الفَأْرةِ

mousey /ˈmaʊsi/ *adj* ▸ **mousy**

mousse /muːs/ *n* [1] (Culin) موس; **a lemon ~** موس لَيْمونٍ [2] (for hair) موس

moustache, **mustache** (AmE) /məˈstɑːʃ/ *n* شارِب (شَوارِبُ)

mousy, **mousey** /ˈmaʊsi/ *adj* (**mousier, mousiest**) ‹*hair, colour*› بُنّيّ فاتِح

mouth /maʊθ *pl* maʊðz/ [A] *n* [1] (of a human, animal) فَم (أَفْواه); **with his ~ open** (not shut) وَفَمُهُ مَفْتوحٌ; (in surprise, admiration) فاغِراً فاهُ; **you'd better keep your ~ shut about this** (infml) مِن الأَفْضَلِ لَكَ أَنْ تَكْتُمَ ذلك السِرَّ; **now they have another ~ to feed** والآنَ لَدَيْهِم طِفْلٌ جَديدٌ لِيَتَحَمَّلوا أَعْباءَهُ [2] (of a cave, tunnel) مَدْخَل (مَداخِلُ) ,فوّهة [3] (of a river, harbour) مَصَبّ (مَصابُّ ,مَصَبّات) [4] (of a bottle, jar) فُتْحة (فُتَح ,فُتْحات)

B *vt* **1** نَطَقَ (u; نُطْق ,ب) تَفَوَّهَ (ب) ‹*words, obscenities*› **2** تَشَدَّقَ (ب) ‹*platitudes, slogans*›

Idiom **to be all mouth and no trousers** (BrE infml) كانَ كَثيرَ الكَلامِ قَليلَ الفِعْلِ

mouthful /ˈmaʊθfʊl/ *n* **1** (of food) لُقْمة (لُقَم); (of drink) جُرْعة (جُرْعات, جُرَع) **2** (infml) (of abuse) **to give sb a ~** أَوْسَعَ شَخْصاً شَتْماً

mouth organ *n* هارْمونيكا

mouthpiece /ˈmaʊθpiːs/ *n* **1** (of a musical instrument) مَبْسِم, فَم (الآلةِ الموسيقيّةِ); (of a telephone) ميكْروفون (الهاتِفِ) **2** (spokesperson) مُتَحَدِّث ,ناطِق

mouth-to-mouth resuscitation /ˌmaʊθtəˌmaʊθ rɪˌsʌsɪˈteɪʃ(ə)n/ *n* إنْعاش فَماً لِفَمٍ (قُبْلة الحَياةِ)

mouthwash /ˈmaʊθwɒʃ/ *n* غَسول الفَمِ

mouth-watering /ˈmaʊθwɔːtərɪŋ/ *adj* ‹*dish, smell*› مُسيل لِلُعابِ

move /muːv/ **A** *vt* **1** (to a new position) نَقَلَ (u; نَقْل) ‹*the cursor, a car, furniture*›; **to ~ sth further away/closer** نَقَلَ شَيْئًا إلى مَكانٍ أَبْعَدَ \ أَقْرَبَ; **~ your head, I can't see!** أَبْعِدْ رَأْسَكَ، لا يُمْكِنُني أنْ أرى!; **let's ~ the table into the garden** هَيّا نَنْقُل الطاوِلةَ إلى الحَديقةِ; **can you ~ your bike out of the way?** هَل يُمْكِنُكَ أنْ تُبْعِدَ دَرّاجَتَكَ من الطَريقِ؟; **to ~ a patient to a different ward** نَقَلَ مَريضاً إلى عَنْبَرٍ آخَرَ **2** (to a new location) نَقَلَ (u; نَقْل) ‹*one's offices, one's family*›; **to ~ house** غَيَّرَ سَكَنَهُ; **to ~ jobs** غَيَّرَ وَظيفَتَهُ **3** حَرَّكَ ‹*troops, forces*›; **to ~ troops to the front** حَرَّكَ القُوّاتِ إلى المُقَدِّمةِ **4** (emotionally) «story, images» أَثَّرَ, حَرَّكَ المَشاعِرَ; **to be ~d to tears** تَحَرَّكَتْ مَشاعِرُهُ حتّى بَكى **5** (fml) (to motivate) **to ~ sb to do sth** حَمَلَ شَخْصاً على فِعْلِ شَيْءٍ **6** (to propose) اِقْتَرَحَ ‹*an amendment, a resolution*›; **I ~ that the proposal be put to the vote** أَقْتَرِحُ أنْ يُطْرَحَ الاقْتِراحُ للتَصْويتِ

B *vi* **1** (to a position) «person, branch, hand» تَحَرَّكَ; **I ~d a little closer** اِقْتَرَبْتُ قَليلاً; **don't ~!** لا تَتَحَرَّكْ! **2** (to be in motion) «person, vehicle, army» تَحَرَّكَ; **we have to keep moving** عَلَيْنا أنْ نُواصِلَ المُضِيَّ; **the train started moving** بَدَأَ القِطارُ في التَحَرُّكِ; **we're moving in the right direction** نَحْنُ نَتَحَرَّكُ في الاتِّجاهِ الصَحيحِ; **to ~ back/forward** تَراجَعَ للخَلْفِ \ سارَ للأَمامِ **3** (to a new address) «family, firm, employee» اِنْتَقَلَ; **to ~ to the countryside/Dubai** اِنْتَقَلَ إلى الريفِ \ دُبَيٍّ; **I ~d out of my apartment/into a new one** اِنْتَقَلْتُ من شَقَّتي إلى شَقّةٍ أُخْرى; **to ~ to accounts/a different department** اِنْتَقَلَ إلى الحِساباتِ \ إدارةٍ أُخْرى **4** (to act) «government, organization» تَحَرَّكَ; **to ~ to do sth** تَحَرَّكَ لِفِعْلِ شَيْءٍ **5** (in board games) «player» نَقَلَ (u; نَقْل); «piece» اِنْتَقَلَ

C *n* **1** (movement) حَرَكة; **she made a ~ to get up** حاوَلَت النُهوضَ; **he made no ~ to help me** لم يُحَرِّكْ ساكِناً لِمُساعَدَتي **2** (to a new address) اِنْتِقال (اِنْتِقالات), تَغْيير السَكَنِ; **the ~ to the New York went very well** سارَ الانْتِقالُ إلى نْيويورْك على نَحْوٍ طَيِّبٍ جِدًّا **3** (action, step) خَطْوة (خَطَوات); **a good/bad ~** خَطْوة طَيِّبة \ سَيِّئة; **she made the ~ from TV to the stage** اِنْتَقَلَتْ من التِلِفِزْيون إلى المَسْرَحِ; **to make the first ~** أَخَذَ الخَطْوةَ الأولى; **to watch sb's every ~** راقَبَ شَخْصاً في كُلِّ خَطَواتِهِ **4** (in board games) دَوْر (أَدْوار); **it's your ~** هذا دَوْرُكَ **5** (in soccer, hockey) حَرَكة

Idioms **to get a move on** (infml) أَسْرَعَ; **to move with the times** واكَبَ الزَمَنَ; **to make a move on sb** (infml) أَبْدى لِشَخْصٍ رَغْبَتَهُ في الارْتِباطِ بِهِ; **as a businessman he's always on the ~** لِأَنَّهُ رَجُلُ أَعْمالٍ فَهُوَ دائِمُ التَجْوالِ

Phrasal verbs **move along** **1** (to make room) تَقَدَّمَ للأَمامِ **2** (to progress) «story, plot» تَطَوَّرَ; **things are moving along nicely** تَسيرُ الأُمورُ على نَحْوٍ طَيِّبٍ

• **move around, move about** (BrE) **A** **1** (to different positions) (to different positions) «person» تَحَرَّكَ من مَكانٍ لِمَكانٍ **2** (to change residence) «families» تَنَقَّلَ **B** **1** **~ [sth] around** نَقَلَ [شَيْئاً] من مَكانٍ لِمَكانٍ ‹*the furniture, cursor*› **2** **~ [sb] around** نَقَلَ [شَخْصاً] من مَكانٍ لِمَكانٍ ‹*an employee*›; **they ~ him around a lot between branches** يُنَقِّلونَهُ كَثيراً بين الأَفْرُعِ

• **move away** **1** (to move house) تَرَكَ سَكَنَهُ **2** (to one side) نَقَلَ [شَيْئاً] بَعيداً **3** **~ [sth] away, ~ away [sth]** اِبْتَعَدَ ‹*an object, obstacle*›

• **move down** **A** (in ranking) «team, player» نَزَلَ (i; نُزول); **he will benefit from moving down a class** سَيَسْتَفيدُ من النُزولِ إلى صَفٍّ أَدْنى **B** ~ **[sth] down,** ~ **down [sth]** (to a lower shelf, floor, etc) أَنْزَلَ [شَيْئاً] ‹an object›

• **move in** **1** (to a house) اِنْتَقَلَ للسَكَنِ; **to ~ in with a friend/relative** اِنْتَقَلَ للسَكَنِ مع صَديقٍ \ قَريبٍ **2** (for a purpose) «police, state» تَدَخَّلَ; «bulldozers» دَخَلَ (u; دُخول); **police ~d in and evicted the demonstrators** تَدَخَّلَت الشُرْطةُ وَأَجْلَت المُتَظاهِرينَ; **the state ~d in and nationalized the banks** تَدَخَّلَت الدَوْلةُ وَأَمَّمَت البُنوكَ; **the bulldozers have ~d in to clear the site** دَخَلَت الجَرّافاتُ لِإخْلاءِ المِنْطَقةِ

• **move off** «parade, procession, train» بَدأَ في التَحَرُّكِ

• **move on** **1** «travellers, traffic, vehicle» واصَلَ السَيْرَ **2** (to another topic) اِنْتَقَلَ; **to ~ on to the next item on the agenda** اِنْتَقَلَ إلى البَنْدِ التالي في جَدْوَلِ الأَعْمالِ **3** (to progress) تَطَوَّرَ; **time ~s on** يَمْضي الزَمَنُ للأَمامِ; **things have ~d on since then** تَغَيَّرَت الأَوْضاعُ منذ ذلك الوَقْتِ مع الزَمَنِ

• **move out** (of a house) تَرَكَ السَكَنَ

• **move over** (to make room) أَفْسَحَ

• **move up** **A** **1** (to make room) أَفْسَحَ **2** (in ranking) «team, player» اِنْتَقَلَ إلى دَرَجةٍ أَعْلى, تَرَقّى; **she's been ~d up to the top class** نُقِلَتْ إلى الفَصْلِ الأَكْثَرِ تَفَوُّقاً **B** ~ **[sb] up,** ~ **up [sb]** (to promote) رَقّى \ نَقَلَ [شَخْصاً] إلى الدَرَجةِ الأَعْلى ‹a team, pupil, an employee› **C** ~ **[sth] up** (to a higher shelf, floor, etc) نَقَلَ [شَيْئاً] لِأَعْلى

movement /'mu:vmənt/ *n* **1** (act of moving) حَرَكة; **he has restricted ~** حَرَكَتُهُ مَحْدودةٌ **2** (of moving parts) حَرَكة **3** (in prices, situations) حَرَكة; **there was very little ~ on the stock exchange** كانَ هُناكَ حَرَكةٌ بَسيطةٌ جِدًّا في سوقِ الأَوْراقِ المالِيّةِ; **there's a ~ towards deregulation** هُناكَ تَحَرُّكٌ نحو رَفْعِ القُيودِ **4** (ideological) حَرَكة; **a mass ~** حَرَكة شَعْبِيّة; **the women's liberation ~** حَرَكة تَحْريرِ المَرْأةِ **5** (Mus) جُزْء (أَجْزاء); **a symphony in three ~s** سِمْفونِيّة من ثَلاثةِ أَجْزاءٍ **6** (of workers, goods) حَرَكة, تَنَقُّل (تَنَقُّلات); **the free ~ of labour/goods** حُرِّيّة حَرَكةِ العُمّالِ \ البَضائِعِ **7** (fml) (of bowels) تَبَرُّز, تَغَوُّط

mover /'mu:və/ *n* (AmE) حَمّال ≈ (شَخْص يَعْمَلُ لِشَرِكةِ نَقْلِ أَمْتِعةٍ)

movie /'mu:vi/ **A** *n* (film) فيلْم (أَفْلام)

B **(movies)** *n pl* (cinema) **the ~s** السينَما

movie director *n* مُخْرِج سينَمائيّ

movie star *n* نَجْم سينَمائيّ

movie theatre *n* (AmE) سينَما

moving /'mu:vɪŋ/ *adj* **1** (in motion) ‹vehicle, target› مُتَحَرِّك

2 (emotional) ‹scene, speech› مُؤَثِّر

mow /məʊ/ *vt* (*past participle* **mowed** or **mown**) حَصَدَ (i-u; حَصاد) ‹the hay›; قَصَّ \ جَزَّ العُشْبَ ‹lawn›

(Phrasal verb) **mow down ~ down [sb], ~ [sb] down** حَصَدَ روحَ [شَخْصٍ] ‹civilians, a crowd›

mower /'məʊə/ *n* آلة قَصِّ العُشْبِ, جَزّازة

mown /məʊn/ *past participle* ▸ **mow**

Mozambique /,məʊzam'bi:k/ *pr n* موزَمْبيق (f)

MP /ɛm'pi:/ *n* **1** (in UK) = **Member of Parliament** عُضْو في البَرْلَمان **2** = **Military Police** شُرْطة عَسْكَرِيّة

MP3 player /ɛmpi:'θri: ,pleɪə/ *n* مُشَغِّل إم بي ثْري

mph /ɛmpi:'eɪtʃ/ *abbr* = **miles per hour** ميل في الساعة

MPV /ɛmpi:'vi:/ *n* = **multipurpose vehicle** سَيّارة مُتَعَدِّدة الأَغْراضِ \ الاسْتِعْمالات

Mr /'mɪstə/ *abbr* (*pl* **Messrs**) = **Mister** سَيِّد (سادة, أَسْياد)

MRI /ɛma:r'ʌɪ/ *n* **1** = **magnetic resonance imaging** التَصْوير بالرَنينِ المِغْناطيسيِّ **2** (scan) صورة رَنينٍ مِغْناطيسيٍّ

Mrs /'mɪsɪz/ *abbr* سَيِّدة

Ms /mɪz, məz/ *n* [لَقَب احْتِرام للمَرْأةِ العازِبةِ أو المُتَزَوِّجةِ]

MS /ɛm'ɛs/ **A** *n* **1** = **multiple sclerosis** التَصَلُّب المُتَعَدِّد

2 (AmE) (also **M.S.**) = **Master of Science** (degree) ماجِسْتير في العُلومِ; (degree holder) حاصِل على \ حامِل ماجِسْتير في العُلومِ

B *abbr* = **Mississippi**

MSA /ɛmɛs'eɪ/ *n* = **Modern Standard Arabic** اللُغة العَرَبِيّة الفُصْحى الحَديثة

MSc, M.Sc. /ɛmɛs'si:/ *n* = **Master of Science** (degree) ماجِسْتير في العُلومِ; (degree holder) حاصِل على \ حامِل ماجِسْتير في العُلومِ; **Oliver Franklin, MSc** أوليفَر فرَنْكْلين, ماجِسْتير في العُلومِ

MST /ɛmɛs'tiː/ *n* (AmE) = **Mountain Standard Time** التَوْقيت الجَبَليّ

Mt /maʊnt/ *abbr* = **Mount** جَبَل (جِبال)

MT /ɛm'tiː/ *abbr* = **Montana**

much /mʌtʃ/ **A** *determiner* ‹*money, food*› كَثير; **I haven't got ~ time** لَيْسَ لَدَيَّ الكَثيرُ من الوَقْتِ; **you used too ~ flour** اِسْتَعْمَلْتَ الكَثيرَ من الدَقيقِ; **he ate as ~ breakfast as me** أَكَلَ نَفْسَ مِقْدارِ الفُطورِ الّذي أَكَلْتُهُ; **how ~ oil have you got left?** كَم من الزَيْتِ تَبَقّى لَدَيْكَ؟; **don't use so ~ salt** لا تَسْتَخْدِمْ كَثيراً من المِلْحِ

B *pron* كَثير; **we didn't eat ~** لم نَأْكُلْ كَثيراً; **I don't see ~ of them now** لا أَراهُمْ كَثيراً الآنَ; **do as ~ as you can** قُمْ بِقَدْرِ ما تَسْتَطيعُ; **how ~ did you pay?** كَم دَفَعْتَ؟; **it cost too ~** إِنَّهُ يُكَلِّفُ كَثيراً جِدًّا; **is there ~ left?** هل بَقِيَ الكَثيرُ؟

C *adv* كَثيراً, بِكَثيرٍ; **this one is ~ smaller** هذا أَصْغَرُ بِكَثيرٍ; **I like it very ~** أُحِبُّهُ كَثيراً; **she talks too ~** تَتَحَدَّثُ كَثيراً جِدًّا; **does it hurt ~?** هل تَتَأَلَّمُ كَثيراً؟; **they still argue as ~ as ever** ما زالوا يَتَجادَلونَ كَثيراً كَعادَتِهِمْ; **things are ~ the same** لم تَتَغَيَّر الأَشْياءُ كَثيراً

D *combining form* كَثيراً, جِدًّا; **a ~-loved teacher** أُسْتاذ مَحْبوب كَثيراً; **a ~-maligned singer** مُطْرِب مَذْموم جِدًّا; **a ~-needed solution** حَلّ ضَروريّ جِدًّا

muck /mʌk/ *n* **1** (dirt) وَسَخ (أَوْساخ) **2** (excrement) سَماد (حَيَوانيّ)

(Phrasal verbs) **muck about** (infml) **muck around** (infml): **1** **~ about** (to do silly things) عَبَثَ (a; عَبَث) **2** **~ [sb] about** (to waste sb's time) ضَيَّعَ وَقْتَ [شَخْصٍ]

• **muck in** (infml) (to share) تَعاوَنَ

• **muck out**: **~ out [sth]**, **~ [sth] out** نَظَّفَ [شَيْئاً] ‹*a cowshed, stable*›

• **muck up** (infml): **~ up [sth]**, **~ [sth] up** **1** (to spoil) أَفْسَدَ [شَيْئاً] ‹*a plan, holiday*› **2** (to do badly) خَرْبَطَ في [شَيْءٍ] ‹*a job, an exam*›

mucus /'mjuːkəs/ *n* مُخاط (أَمْخِطة)

mud /mʌd/ *n* وَحْل (وُحول, أَوْحال), طين (أَطْيان)

muddle /'mʌd(ə)l/ **A** *n* (infml) **1** [u] (disorder) فَوْضى, اِرْتِباك (f), اِضْطِراب, تَشَوُّش; **to be in a ~** «papers» كانَ في حالةٍ من الفَوْضى; «person» كانَ في حالةٍ من التَشَوُّشِ \ الارْتِباكِ; **to get into a ~** أَصابَهُ ارْتِباكٌ شَديدٌ **2** (mix-up) اِرْتِباك (اِرْتِباكات); **there is a ~ over the booking** هُناكَ ارْتِباكٌ بِخُصوصِ الحَجْزِ, لَخْبَطة

B *vt* ▸ **muddle up**

(Phrasal verbs) **muddle through** سارَ بِتَخَبُّطٍ

• **muddle up**: **1** **~ [sth] up**, **~ up [sth]** (to mix up) بَعْثَرَ [شَيْئاً] ‹*papers, documents*› **2** **~ [sth/sb] up**, **~ up [sth/sb]** (to confuse) اِخْتَلَطَ عَلَيْهِ [شَيْءٌ \ شَخْصٌ]; **to get sth ~d up** اِلْتَبَسَ عَلَيْهِ شَيْءٌ; **I got you ~d up with Martin** أَخْطَأْتُ بَيْنَكَ وَبَيْنَ مارْتِنْ

muddled /'mʌd(ə)ld/ *adj* مُشَوَّش, مُضْطَرِب

muddy /'mʌdi/ *adj* (**muddier**, **muddiest**) ‹*shoes*› مُغَطّى بالطين; ‹*road*› موحِل

(Idiom) **to muddy the waters** عَقَّدَ المَوْقِفَ

mudflap /'mʌdflap/ *n* رَفْرَف (رَفارِفُ)

mudguard /'mʌdgaːd/ *n* واقي العَجَلاتِ (للحِمايةِ من الوَحْلِ والماءِ)

muesli /'mjuːzli/ *n* (BrE) [فُطور يَتَكَوَّنُ من حُبوبٍ وفَواكِهَ جافّةٍ]

muezzin /muː'ɛzɪn/ *n* مُؤَذِّن

muff /mʌf/ **A** *n* [غِطاء أُسْطُوانيّ من الفِراءِ لِتَدْفِئةِ اليَدَيْنِ]

B *vt* (infml) أَخْفَقَ (في) ‹*a shot, catch*›; ضَيَّعَ ‹*a chance, one's lines*›

muffin /'mʌfɪn/ *n* **1** (BrE) (for toasting) [خُبْزة إِسْفَنْجيّة صَغيرة] **2** (AmE) (cake) [كَعْكة إِسْفَنْجيّة صَغيرة]

muffle /'mʌf(ə)l/ *vt* كَتَمَ (u; كَتْم, كِتْمان) ‹*a voice, sound*›

muffler /'mʌflə/, /'mʌflə/ *n* **1** (scarf) وِشاح (أَوْشِحة) **2** (AmE) (on cars) كاتِم الصَوْتِ

mufti /'mʌfti/ *n* **1** (legal expert) مُفْتٍ **2** (infml) لِباس مَدَنيّ; **to wear ~** اِرْتَدى لِباساً مَدَنيًّا

mug /mʌg/ **A** *n* **1** (cup) فِنْجان كَبير **2** (infml) (face) وَجْه (أَوْجُه, وُجوه) **3** (BrE infml) (fool) مُغَفَّل

B *vt* (**-gg-**) سَطا (u; سَطْو) (على) ‹*a pensioner, jogger*›

mugger /'mʌgə/ *n* لِصّ (لُصوص), حَراميّ (حَراميّة)

mugging /'mʌgɪŋ/ *n* سَطْو

muggy /'mʌgi/ *adj* (**muggier**, **muggiest**) (infml) ‹*day, weather*› رَطْب وَحارّ

mugshot /ˈmʌɡʃɒt/ *n* (infml) [صورة المُتَّهَمِ \ المُشْتَبَه فيهِ لدى الشُّرْطةِ]

Muhammad /məˈhamɪd/ *pr n* مُحَمَّد; **~ is the messenger of Allah** مُحَمَّدٌ رَسولُ اللهِ

Muharram /məˈhʌrəm/ *n* مُحَرَّم

mujahideen, **mujahedin** /ˌmʊdʒɑːhɪˈdiːn/ *n pl* مُجاهِدونَ

mujtahid /mʊdʒˈtɑːhɪd/ *n* (*pl* **mujtahids, mujtahidūn**) مُجْتَهِد

mulberry /ˈmʌlb(ə)ri/ *n* (*pl* **mulberries**) توت

mule /mjuːl/ *n* بَغْل (بِغال)

mullah /ˈmʌlə/ *n* مُلاّ

mulled wine /mʌld ˈwʌɪn/ *n* نَبيذ مُتَبَّل (يُقَدَّمُ ساخِناً)

mullet /ˈmʌlɪt/ *n* (*pl* **mullet**) بوريّ

mull over /mʌl/ *vt* **to ~ sth, to mull sth over** فَكَّرَ مَلياً في شَيْءٍ ‹*a question, an issue*›

multicoloured (BrE), **multicolored** (AmE) /ˈmʌltɪkʌləd/ *adj* ‹*umbrella, clothes*› مُتَعَدِّد الأَلْوانِ

multicultural /mʌltɪˈkʌltʃ(ə)rəl/ *adj* ‹*society, school*› مُتَعَدِّد الثَقافاتِ

multidisciplinary /mʌltɪdɪsəˈplɪn(ə)ri/ *adj* ‹*approach, research*› مُتَعَدِّد التَخَصُّصاتِ

multi-ethnic /mʌltɪˈɛθnɪk/ *adj* ‹*society, area*› مُتَعَدِّد العِرْقِيّاتِ

multifunctional /mʌltɪˈfʌŋkʃ(ə)n(ə)l/, **multifunction** /mʌltɪˈfʌŋkʃ(ə)n/ *adj before n* ‹*device, display*› مُتَعَدِّد الوَظائِف

multigym /ˈmʌltɪdʒɪm/ *n* جِهاز رِياضيّ مُتَعَدِّد الاسْتِخْداماتِ

multilateral /mʌltɪˈlat(ə)rəl/ *adj* ‹*agreement, negotiations*› مُتَعَدِّد الأَطْرافِ

multilevel /ˈmʌltɪlɛv(ə)l/ *adj* 1 ‹*building, car park*› مُتَعَدِّد الطَوابِقِ 2 ‹*model, analysis*› مُتَعَدِّد المُسْتَوَياتِ

multimedia /ˈmʌltɪmiːdɪə/ A *adj before n* ‹*resources, course*› ذو وَسائِطَ مُتَعَدِّدةٍ
B *n* وَسائِط الإعْلامِ المُتَعَدِّدة

multinational /mʌltɪˈnaʃ(ə)n(ə)l/ A *adj* ‹*company, force*› مُتَعَدِّد الجِنْسِيّاتِ
B *n* شَرِكة مُتَعَدِّدة الجِنْسِيّاتِ

multiple /ˈmʌltɪp(ə)l/ A *adj* ‹*copies, injuries*› كَثير, مُتَعَدِّد (كِثار, كَثيرونَ)
B *n* مُضاعَف

multiple-choice /mʌltɪp(ə)lˈtʃɔɪs/ *adj* ‹*question, test*› مُتَعَدِّد الاخْتِياراتِ

multiple sclerosis *n* التَصَلُّب المُتَعَدِّد

multiplex /ˈmʌltɪplɛks/ *n* 1 (Cin) مُجَمَّع سينَمائيّ
2 (in telecommunications) قَناة الإرْسالِ المُتَعَدِّد

multiplication /ˌmʌltɪplɪˈkeɪʃ(ə)n/ *n* ضَرْب (في الحِسابِ)

multiply /ˈmʌltɪplʌɪ/ A *vt* (**multiplies, multiplying, multiplied**) ‹*a number*› ضَرَبَ (عَدداً في آخَرَ); **to ~ 5 by 8** ضَرَبَ 5 في 8
B *vi* 1 (in maths) «children, computers» قامَ بِعَمَليّةِ ضَرْبٍ
2 (to increase) «problems, debts» تَضاعَفَ, زادَ (i; زِيادة)

multipurpose /mʌltɪˈpəːpəs/ *adj* ‹*oil, hall*› مُتَعَدِّد الأَغْراضِ \ الاسْتِعْمالاتِ

multipurpose vehicle *n* سَيّارة مُتَعَدِّدة الأَغْراضِ \ الاسْتِعْمالاتِ

multiracial /mʌltɪˈreɪʃ(ə)l/ *adj* ‹*community, society*› مُتَعَدِّد الأَعْراقِ

multistorey /mʌltɪˈstɔːri/ *adj* (BrE) ‹*car park, shopping centre*› مُتَعَدِّد الطَوابِقِ

multitrack /ˈmʌltɪtrak/ *adj* ‹*system, recording*› مُتَعَدِّد المَساراتِ

multitude /ˈmʌltɪtjuːd/ *n* 1 (large number) كَثير, عَديد; **a ~ of reasons/options** عَديد من الأَسْبابِ \ الخِياراتِ 2 (crowd) حَشْد (حُشود)

multivitamin /mʌltiˈvɪtəmɪn/ *n* قُرْص مُتَعَدِّد الفيتاميناتِ

mum, **Mum** /mʌm/ *n* (BrE) ماما

Idiom **to keep mum** (infml) الْتَزَمَ الصَمْتَ

mumble /ˈmʌmb(ə)l/ A *vi* غَمْغَمَ (i; غَمْغَمة), هَمْهَمَ (i; هَمْهَمة)
B *vt* تَمْتَمَ (i; تَمْتَمة ;ب) ‹*a question, reply*›

mumbo jumbo /ˌmʌmbəʊ ˈdʒʌmbəʊ/ *n* (infml) هُراء

mummy /ˈmʌmi/ *n* 1 (infml) (mother) ماما 2 (preserved body) مومِياء (مومِيات)

mumps /mʌmps/ *n sing* نُكاف

munch /mʌntʃ/ *vt* مَضَغَ (a-u; مَضْغ) ‹*popcorn, a sandwich*›

mundane /mʌnˈdeɪn/ *adj* ‹*performance, film*› عاديّ

municipal /mjʊˈnɪsɪp(ə)l/ *adj* ‹*council, offices*› بَلَديّ

municipality /mjʊˌnɪsɪˈpalɪti/ *n* (*pl* **municipalities**)

1 (governing body) بَلَديّة 2 (area) بَلَديّة

munitions /mjuːˈnɪʃ(ə)nz/ *n pl* ذَخيرة (ذَخائِرُ)

munitions factory *n* مَصْنَع ذَخيرةٍ

mural /ˈmjʊ(ə)rəl/ *n* لَوْحة جِدارية

murder /ˈməːdə/ **A** *n* 1 (crime) قَتْل; **to commit ~** ارْتَكَبَ جَريمةَ قَتْلٍ; **attempted ~** مُحاولة قَتْلٍ 2 [u] (infml) (difficult task, experience) شَيْء عَسير; **the traffic/exam was ~** كانَ المُرورُ خانِقاً \ الامْتِحانُ عَسيراً

B *modifier* ‹*case, weapon, victim*› قَتْل

C *vt* 1 (to kill) قَتَلَ (u; قَتْل) ‹*one's wife, civilians, a hostage*›; **the ~ed man/woman** القَتيل \ القَتيلة 2 (infml) (in anger) قَتَلَ (u; قَتْل); **I could ~ that woman!** كُنْتُ على وَشْكِ أنْ أَقْتُلَ تِلْكَ المَرْأةَ! 3 (infml) (to ruin) دَمَّرَ, خَرَّبَ ‹*a piece of music, language*›

(Idiom) **to get away with murder** (infml) فَعَلَ ما بَدا لَهُ

murderer /ˈməːd(ə)rə/ *n* قاتِل (قاتِلونَ, قَتَلة)

murderess /ˈməːdərɛs/ *n* قاتِلة

murder inquiry *n* تَحْقيق في جَريمةِ قَتْلٍ

murderous /ˈməːd(ə)rəs/ *adj* ‹*expression, thoughts*› قاتِل (قَتَلة, قاتِلونَ)

murder scene *n* مَوْقِع جَريمةِ قَتْلٍ

murder victim *n* قَتيل (قَتْلى)

murid /mjʊˈriːd, mʊˈriːd/ *n* مُريد

murky /ˈməːki/ *adj* (**murkier**, **murkiest**) 1 ‹*water*› عَكِر; ‹*darkness*› مُكْفَهِرّ, بَهيم 2 ‹*past*› مُثير للريبةِ; ‹*events*› غامِض

murmur /ˈməːmə/ **A** *n* 1 (in speech) هَمْس (هَمَسات), وَشْوَشة 2 (also **heart murmur**) نَفْخة قَلْبيّة

B *vt* هَمَسَ (i; هَمْس), وَشْوَشَ (i; وَشْوَشة) ‹*words, an apology*›

muscle /ˈmʌs(ə)l/ *n* 1 (Anat) عَضَلة (عَضَلات, عَضَل) 2 (power) عَضَلة (عَضَلات, عَضَل)

(Phrasal verb) **muscle in** (infml): **to ~ in on sb's territory** اقْتَحَمَ مَنْطَقةَ شَخْصٍ; **to ~ in on sb's operation** تَدَخَّلَ في أَعْمالِ شَخْصٍ بالقوّة

Muscovite /ˈmʌskəvʌɪt/ *n, adj* موسْكوفيّ

muscular /ˈmʌskjʊlə/ *adj* 1 ‹*athlete, body*› قَويّ \ مَفْتول 2 ‹*disease, atrophy*› عَضَليّ العَضَلاتِ

muscular dystrophy *n* الضُمور العَضَليّ

muse /mjuːz/ **A** *n* (**Muse**) رَبّة الإلْهامِ

B *vi* تَأَمَّلَ

museum /mjuːˈzɪəm/ *n* مَتْحَف (مَتاحِفُ)

mush /mʌʃ/ *n* عَصيدة (عَصائِدُ)

mushroom /ˈmʌʃrʊm, ˈmʌʃruːm/ **A** *n* فِطْر

B *vi* «towns, companies» انْتَشَرَ كالفِطْرِ

mushy /ˈmʌʃi/ *adj* (**mushier**, **mushiest**) (infml) 1 (soft and wet) ‹*mixture, vegetables*› طَرِيّ, ناعِم 2 (sentimental) ‹*film, story*› عاطِفيّ

music /mjuːzɪk/ *n* موسيقى (f)

(Idioms) **to be music to sb's ears** كانَ لَهُ وَقْعُ الموسيقى على أُذُنِ شَخْصٍ; **to face the music** تَحَمَّلَ عَواقِبَ تَصَرُّفاتِهِ

musical /ˈmjuːzɪk(ə)l/ **A** *adj* 1 (musically gifted) ‹*family*› موسيقيّ; ‹*child*› مولَع بالموسيقى 2 (melodious) ‹*voice, laughter*› موسيقيّ

B *n* (play) مَسْرَحيّة موسيقيّة; (film) فيلْم موسيقيّ

musical box *n* صُنْدوق الموسيقى

musical chairs *n* لُعْبة الكَراسي الموسيقيّةِ

musical instrument *n* آلة موسيقيّة

musically /ˈmjuːzɪkli/ *adv* 1 (regarding music) موسيقيًّا 2 (pleasantly) بنَغْمةٍ موسيقيّةٍ

music box *n* صُنْدوق الموسيقى

music hall *n* (BrE) مَسْرَح غِنائيّ

musician /mjuːˈzɪʃ(ə)n/ *n* موسيقار, موسيقيّ

music video *n* أُغْنِية مُصَوَّرة

musk /mʌsk/ *n* مِسْك

musket /ˈmʌskɪt/ *n* بُنْدُقيّة قَديمة الطِراز, مُسْكيت

Muslim /ˈmʊzlɪm/ **A** *n* مُسْلِم

B *adj* ‹*faith, holiday*› إسْلاميّ

Muslimah /ˈmʌzlɪmə, ˈmʊzlɪmə/ *n* مُسْلِمة

Muslim Brotherhood *n* الإخْوان المُسْلِمونَ

muslin /ˈmʌzlɪn/ *n* موسْلين (نَسيج قُطْنِيّ رَقيق)

muss /mʌs/ (AmE infml) *vt* (also **muss up**) بَعْثَرَ (i; بَعْثَرة)

mussel /ˈmʌs(ə)l/ *n* مَحار ,بَلَح البَحْرِ (n coll)

must /mʌst, məst/ **A** *modal aux* (*negative* **must not, mustn't**) **1** (indicating obligation, prohibition) **all instruments ~ be sterilized** يَجِبُ تَعْقيمُ كُلِّ الأَدَواتِ; **all visitors ~ leave the premises** يَجِبُ على جَميعِ الزوّارِ مُغادَرةُ المَبْنى; **we really ~ get up at 5 a.m.?** هل يَجِبُ عَلَيْنا حَقًّا أنْ نَسْتَيْقِظَ الساعة 5 صَباحاً؟; **you mustn't mention this to anyone** يَجِبُ ألاّ تَذْكُرَ هذا لِأَحَدٍ; **the loan ~ be repaid in one year** يَجِبُ أنْ يُسَدَّدَ القَرْضُ خلال عامٍ واحِدٍ **2** (indicating requirement, condition) **candidates ~ be EU nationals** يَجِبُ أنْ يَكونَ المُرَشَّحونَ من مُواطِني الاتِّحادِ الأوروبِّيِّ; **to qualify you ~ have 40 hours practical experience** لِكَيْ تكونَ مُؤَهَّلاً يَجِبُ أنْ يَكونَ لَدَيْكَ 40 ساعةً من الخِبْرةِ العَمَليّةِ **3** (stressing importance, necessity) **you ~ be patient** يَجِبُ أنْ تَتَحَلّى بالصَبْرِ; **we ~ do more to improve standards** يَجِبُ أنْ نَفْعَلَ المَزيدَ لِتَحْسينِ المَعاييرِ; **tell her she mustn't worry** أَخْبِرْها أنّها لا يَجِبُ أنْ تَقْلَقَ; **we ~ never forget** يَجِبُ ألاّ نَنْسى أبَداً; **I ~ ask you not to smoke** يَجِبُ أنْ أَطْلُبَ مِنْكَ ألاّ تُدَخِّنَ; **it ~ be said that …** … يَجِبُ القَوْلُ إنّ; **I ~ apologize for being late** يَجِبُ أنْ أَعْتَذِرَ عن تَأَخُّري; **I ~ say I was impressed** يَجِبُ أنْ أَقولَ إنّني كُنْتُ مَبْهوراً; **it's very odd I ~ admit** يَجِبُ أنْ أُقِرَّ أنّ هذا غَريبٌ جِدًّا **4** (expressing intention) **we ~ ask them about it** يَجِبُ أنْ نَسْأَلَهُم عَنْهُ; **I really ~ write to her** يَجِبُ عَلَيَّ حَقًّا أنْ أَكْتُبَ لَها **5** (indicating irritation) **well, come in if you ~** حَسَناً، تَعالَ إذا كانَ هذا ضَرورِيًّا; **why ~ she always be so cynical?** لِماذا عَلَيْها أنْ تَكونَ دائِماً شَكّاكةً لِهَذِهِ الدَرَجةِ؟; **he's ill, if you ~ know** هو مَريضٌ، إذا كانَ من الضَروريِّ أنْ تَعْرِفَ **6** (in invitations, suggestions) **you ~ come and visit us!** لا بُدَّ أنْ تَأْتِيَ لِتَزورَنا!; **we really ~ get together soon** يَجِبُ حَقًّا أنْ نَجْتَمِعَ عن قَريبٍ **7** (expressing assumption, probability) **it ~ be difficult living there** لا بُدَّ أنّ الحَياةَ هُناكَ صَعْبةٌ; **it ~ have been very interesting** لا بُدَّ أنّهُ كانَ مُثيراً للاهْتِمامِ جِدًّا; **there ~ be some mistake!** لا بُدَّ أنّ هُناكَ خَطأً ما!; **what ~ people think?** ماذا سَيَظُنُّ الناسُ ؟; **viewers ~ have been surprised** لا بُدَّ أنّ المُشاهِدينَ قد انْدَهَشوا; **you ~ be out of your mind!** لا بُدَّ أنّكَ فَقَدْتَ صَوابَكَ!; **I ~ look ridiculous!** لا بُدَّ أنّني أَبْدو سَخيفاً! **8** (expressing strong interest, desire) **this I ~ see!** لا بُدَّ أنْ أرى هذا حَتْماً!; **we ~ get away from here!** يَجِبُ أنْ نَرْحَلَ من هُنا!

B *n* **to be a ~** كانَ ضَرورِيًّا \ لا بُدَّ مِنْهُ; **a visit to Petra is a ~ for all tourists** زِيارةُ البَتْراءِ هو أَمْرٌ لا بُدَّ مِنْهُ لِكُلِّ السُيّاحِ

mustache /məˈstɑːʃ/ (AmE) ▸ **moustache**

mustard /ˈmʌstəd/ *n* خَرْدَل (n coll)

muster /ˈmʌstə/ *vt* **1** (to bring together) جَنَّدَ ‹*troops, a team*› **2** (also **muster up**) حَشَدَ (i-u; حَشْد) ‹*support, enthusiasm*›

mustn't /ˈmʌs(ə)nt/ *abbr* = **must not** ▸ **must**

musty /ˈmʌsti/ *adj* (**mustier, mustiest**) ‹*smell, basement*› عَفِن

mutant /ˈmjuːt(ə)nt/ *n, adj* مُتَحَوِّر

mutate /mjuːˈteɪt/ *vi* «viruses, genes» تَحَوَّرَ, شَهِدَ طَفْرةً

mutation /mjuːˈteɪʃ(ə)n/ *n* تَحَوُّر, طَفْرة

mute /mjuːt/ **A** *adj* **1** (silent) ‹*spectator, astonishment*› صامِت (صَوامِتُ, صُموت) **2** (old use or offensive) (unable to speak) أَخْرَس (dipt; خُرْس, خُرْسان, f خَرْساءُ), أَبْكَم (dipt; بُكْم, f بَكْماءُ)

B *vt* كَتَمَ (u; كِتْمان, كَتْم), أَسْكَتَ ‹*the sound*›

muted /ˈmjuːtɪd/ *adj* **1** (quiet) ‹*voice, conversation*› خافِت, هادِئ **2** (subdued) ‹*response, celebration*› مُحْتَشِم **3** (Mus) ‹*trumpet*› مَكْتوم الصَوْتِ

mutilate /ˈmjuːtɪleɪt/ *vt* مَثَّلَ (ب), شَوَّهَ ‹*a body, sb's face*›

mutineer /mjuːtɪˈnɪə/ *n* مُتَمَرِّد, عاصٍ (عُصاة)

mutinous /ˈmjuːtɪnəs/ *adj* ‹*soldier, mood*› مُتَمَرِّد, عاصٍ (عُصاة)

mutiny /ˈmjuːtɪni/ **A** *n* (*pl* **mutinies**) تَمَرُّد, عِصْيان

B *vi* (**mutinies, mutinying, mutinied**) تَمَرَّدَ, عَصى (i; عِصْيان)

mutt /mʌt/ *n* (infml) كَلْب مُهَجَّن \ هَجين

mutter /ˈmʌtə/ *vt, vi* غَمْغَمَ (i; غَمْغَمة) ‹*words, a threat*›

mutton /ˈmʌt(ə)n/ *n* لَحْم الضَأْنِ

mutual /ˈmjuːtʃʊəl/ *adj* **1** (reciprocal) ‹*aid, suspicion*› مُتَبادَل **2** (shared) ‹*friend, interests*› مُشْتَرَك

mutual fund *n* صُنْدوق اسْتِثْمارٍ

mutually /ˈmjuːtʃuːəli/ *adv* ‹*convenient*› بِشَكْلٍ مُتَبادَلٍ \ مُشْتَرَكٍ; **the options are ~ exclusive** الخِيارانِ مُتَناقِضانِ

muzzle /ˈmʌz(ə)l/ **A** *n* **1** (snout) خَطْم (خُطوم) **2** (harness) كِمامة (كِمامات ,كَمائِمُ) **3** (of a gun) فوَّهة سِلاحٍ
B *vt* **1** كَمَّمَ ‹*a dog*› **2** كَمَّمَ ‹*the press, a journalist*›

my /mʌɪ/ **A** *determiner* (showing possession) ـي; **I've sold ~ house** بِعْتُ بَيْتي; **I washed ~ feet** غَسَلْتُ رِجْلَيَّ; **this is ~ father** هذا أَبي
B *excl* **~, ~!** يا لَلْعَجَبِ!

myalgic encephalomyelitis /mʌɪˌaldʒɪk ɛnˌsɛfələʊmʌɪəˈlʌɪtɪs/ *n* مُتَلازِمة التَعَبِ المُزْمِنِ

Myanmar /mjanˈmɑː/ *pr n* مِيانْمار (f)

mycosis /mʌɪˈkəʊsɪs/ *n* (*pl* **mycoses**) فُطار

myopic /mʌɪˈɒpɪk/ *adj* **1** (short-sighted) ‹*vision*› حَسير (حَسْرى); ‹*patient*› قصير البَصَرِ **2** (pej) (lacking foresight) ‹*view, policy*› قَصير النَظَرِ

myriad /ˈmɪrɪəd/ **A** *n* عَدَد ضَخْم \ غَفير
B *adj* ‹*problems, opportunities*› لا يُحْصى ,لا حَصْرَ لَهُ

myrrh /məː/ *n* مُرّ (أَمْرار)

myself /mʌɪˈsɛlf, məˈsɛlf/ *pron* **1** (reflexive) نَفْسي; **I cut ~** جَرَحْتُ نَفْسي; **I was talking to ~** كُنْتُ أَتَكَلَّمُ مع نَفْسي **2** (emphatic) بِنَفْسي; **I made it ~** فَعَلْتُهُ بِنَفْسي; **I saw it ~** رَأَيْتُهُ بِنَفْسي **3** (after prepositions) **speaking for ~** هذا رَأْيي الشَخْصيُّ **4** (in expressions) **I'm not ~ today** لَسْتُ على ما يُرامُ اليَوْمَ; **I'm (all) by ~** أنا بِمُفْرَدي

mysterious /mɪˈstɪərɪəs/ *adj* ‹*circumstances, event*› غامِض ,مُلْغَز (غَوامِضُ)

mystery /ˈmɪst(ə)ri/ *n* **1** (puzzle) لُغْز (أَلْغاز) **2** (book, film) قِصّة بوليسيّة

mystical /ˈmɪstɪk(ə)l/ *adj* ‹*experience, rites*› صوفيّ

mystify /ˈmɪstɪfʌɪ/ *vt* (**mystifies, mystifying, mystified**) أَرْبَكَ ,حَيَّرَ ‹*a doctor, the police*›

myth /mɪθ/ *n* أُسْطورة (أَساطيرُ)

mythology /mɪˈθɒlədʒi/ *n* (*pl* **mythologies**) ميثولوجِيا

Nn

N, n /ɛn/ **A** *n* (letter); نون ≈ [الحَرْف الرابِعَ عَشَرَ من الأَبْجَدِيَّة الإنْكليزيَّة]
B *abbr* **1** (**N**) = **North** شَمال **2** (**n**) (Math) [رَقْم مُتَغَيِّر أو غَيْر مُحَدَّدٍ]

NAACP /ɛndʌbəleɪsiːˈpiː/ *n* (AmE) = **National Association for the Advancement of Colored People** الرابِطة الوَطَنِيَّة لِتَقَدُّم المُلَوَّنين

nab /nab/ *vt* **(-bb-)** (infml) **1** (to catch) أَمْسَكَ (ب), قَبَضَ (i; قَبْض على) <*a crook, driver*> **2** (to take, get) أَخَذَ (u; أَخْذ) <*some food, a seat*>

Nablus /ˈnɑːbləs/ *pr n* نابُلُس (f)

nadir /ˈneɪdɪə/ *n* **1** (Astron) نَظير (نُظَراءُ) **2** (low point) حَضيض (حُضُض)

naff /naf/ *adj* (BrE infml) <*clothes, music*> قَبيح, مُزْرٍ

nag /nag/ *vt* **(-gg-)** أَزْعَجَ, ناكَدَ

nagging /ˈnagɪŋ/ *adj* **1** **a ~ wife/husband** زَوْجة مُزْعِجة \ زَوْج مُزْعِج **2** <*pain, doubt*> مُسْتَمِرّ, لا يُقْلِعُ

nail /neɪl/ **A** *n* **1** (of fingers, toes) ظُفْر (أَظْفار, أَظافِرُ); **to bite one's ~s** قَضَمَ أَظافِرَهُ **2** (for wood) مِسْمار (مَساميرُ)
B *vt* **1** (to secure) <*a board, picture*> سَمَّرَ, ثَبَّتَ بِمِسْمارٍ
2 (infml) (to catch) قَبَضَ (i; قَبْض على), ضَبَطَ (i-u; ضَبْط) <*the fraudster, tax evader*> **3** (infml) (to expose) دَحَضَ (a; دَحْض, دُحوض) <*the lie, rumour*>

(Idioms) **to be as tough as nails** كانَ صَلْباً كالصَخْرِ; **to fight tooth and nail** حارَبَ بِكُلِّ طاقَتِهِ \ ما أوتِيَ من قوّةٍ; **to hit the nail on the head** أصابَ كَبِدَ الحَقيقةِ

(Phrasal verbs) **nail down** **A** **~ down [sth], ~ [sth] down** **1** (to secure) ثَبَّتَ [شَيْئاً] بالمَساميرِ <*a floorboard*> **2** (to define) حَدَّدَ مَلامِحَ [شَيْءٍ] <*an agreement, a policy*> **B** **~ [sb] down** (to pressurize) ضَغَطَ على [شَخْصٍ] <*a supplier, contractor*>
• **nail up**: **~ up [sth], ~ [sth] up** **1** (to fix in place) عَلَّقَ [شَيْئاً] بالمَساميرِ <*a sign, picture*> **2** (with boards) سَدَّ [شَيْئاً] <*the window, doors*> **3** (to seal) بَرْشَمَ [شَيْئاً] <*a crate, box*>

nail-biting /ˈneɪlbʌɪtɪŋ/ *adj* <*match, finish*> مُشَوِّق

nail brush *n* فُرْشاة أَظافِرَ

nail clippers *n* مِقَصّ أَظافِرَ

nail file *n* مِبْرَد أَظافِرَ

nail polish, **nail varnish** *n* طِلاء أَظافِرَ

nail polish remover, **nail varnish remover** *n* مُزيل طِلاءِ أَظافِرَ

naive /nʌɪˈiːv/ *adj* <*assumption, fool*> ساذَج (سُذَّج), بَسيط (بُسَطاءُ)

Najaf /ˈnadʒaf/ *n* النَجَف (f)

naked /ˈneɪkɪd/ *adj* <*man, body*> عارٍ (عُراة)

namaz /nəˈmɑːz/ *n* صَلاة (صَلَوات)

name /neɪm/ **A** *n* **1** (title) اسْم (أَسْماء, أَسامٍ); **my ~ is Ibrahim** اسْمي إبْراهيمُ; **he goes by the ~ of Max** هو مَعْروفٌ بِاسْمِ ماكْس; **I only know the company by ~** أَعْرِفُ الشَرِكةَ من اسْمِها فَقَطْ; **he is president in ~ only** هو رَئيسٌ بالاسْمِ فَقَطْ; **she is the manager in all but ~** هي المُديرةُ الفِعْلِيّةُ; **to put one's ~ down for a course/school** سَجَّلَ اسْمَهُ في دَوْرةٍ \ مَدْرَسةٍ **2** (reputation) سُمْعة; **to have a ~ for efficiency/for being strict** كانَ مَعْروفاً بالكَفاءةِ \ بالصَرامةِ; **to give sb a bad ~** أَعْطى شَخْصاً سُمْعةً سَيِّئةً **3** (insult) **to call sb ~s** سَبَّ \ شَتَمَ شَخْصاً
B *vt* **1** (to call) سَمّى <*a baby, city, a boat*>; **they ~d her after** (BrE) *or* **for** (AmE) **her mother** سَمَّياها على اسْمِ أُمِّها; **a boy ~d Joe** وَلَد اسْمُهُ جو; **the product is ~d after** (BrE) *or* **for** (AmE) **its inventor** سُمِّيَ المُنْتَجُ على اسْمِ مُخْتَرِعِهِ **2** (to cite) ذَكَرَ

(u; تَذْكار ,ذِكْر); **~ five European countries with no sea coast** أُذْكُرْ خَمْسَ دُوَلٍ أوروبيّةٍ لا تُطِلُّ على ساحِلٍ **3▸** (to identify) حَدَّدَ الاسْمَ ‹*a suspect, source*›; **to be ~d as a suspect** وَرَدَ اسْمُهُ على أنَّهُ مُتَّهَمٌ; **I'm not going to ~ names** لن أُحَدِّدَ أسْماءً **4▸** (to select) اِخْتارَ ‹*a team*›; **to ~ sb as captain/as your successor** اِخْتارَ شَخْصاً لِيكونَ رَئيسَ الفريق \ خَليفتَكَ **5▸** (to state) حَدَّدَ ‹*a place, time*›; **~ your price** كم تُريدُ؟

(Idiom) **that's the name of the game** (infml) هذا هو صُلْبُ المَوْضوعِ

name-drop /ˈneɪmdrɒp/ *vi* **(-pp-)** [تَباهى بِذِكْرِ أسْماءِ المَشاهيرِ الَّذين يَعْرِفُهُمْ]

nameless /ˈneɪmləs/ *adj* **1▸** (anonymous) ‹*official, grave*› (غَوامِضُ) غامِض ,مُبْهَم **2▸** (indefinable) ‹*fear, dread*› مَجْهول, هُلاميّ

namely /ˈneɪmli/ *adv* (fml) أَلا وَهُوَ ,أَيْ

namesake /ˈneɪmseɪk/ *n* سَمِيّ (شَخْص يَحْمِلُ نَفْسَ الاسْمِ)

Namibia /nəˈmɪbɪə/ *pr n* نامِيبيا

Namibian /nəˈmɪbiən/ *n, adj* ناميبيّ

nanny /ˈnani/ *n* (*pl* **nannies**) **1▸** (employee) مُرَبِّية **2▸** (infml) (grandmother) جَدّة

nanny goat *n* عَنْزة ,مِعْزاة

nanotechnology /ˌnanə(ʊ)tɛkˈnɒlədʒi/ *n* نانوتكنولوجيا

nap /nap/ **A** *vi* **(-pp-)** تَقَيَّلَ ,أَخَذَ قَيْلولةً

B *n* قَيْلولة

(Idiom) **to catch sb napping** فاجَأَ شَخْصاً على حينِ غِرّةٍ

napalm /ˈneɪpɑːm/ *n* نابالْم (مادّة هُلاميّة شَديدة الانْفِجار)

nape /neɪp/ *n* **(nape of the neck)** قَفا العُنُق

napkin /ˈnapkɪn/ *n* فوطة (فُوَط)

nappy /ˈnapi/ *n* (*pl* **nappies**) (BrE) حفاظة

narcotic /nɑːˈkɒtɪk/ *n* **1▸** (illegal drug) مُخَدِّر (مُخَدِّرات) **2▸** (sedative) مُخَدِّر (مُخَدِّرات)

narked /nɑːkt/ *adj* (infml) ‹*expression, tone*› مُنْزَعِج

narrate /nəˈreɪt/ *vt* رَوى (i; رِواية), حَكى (i; حِكاية), سَرَدَ (u; سَرْد) ‹*a story, an adventure*›

narration /nəˈreɪʃ(ə)n/ *n* سَرْد ,حِكاية ,رِواية

narrative /ˈnarətɪv/ **A** *n* سَرْد

B *adj* ‹*prose, poem*› قَصَصيّ ,رِوائيّ

narrator /nəˈreɪtə/ *n* **1▸** (Cin, TV) مُعَلِّق **2▸** (Literat) راوٍ (رُواة)

narrow /ˈnarəʊ/ **A** *adj* **1▸** (in width) ‹*street, gap, bridge*› ضَيِّق; **the road is too ~ for cars to pass** الطَرِيقُ ضَيِّقٌ جِدًّا ولا يَسْمَحُ بِمُرور السَيّاراتِ **2▸** (in degree) ‹*majority, margin*› ضَئيل, بَسيط; **to have a ~ lead** كانَ مُتَقَدِّماً بفارِقٍ ضَئيلٍ; **a ~ victory** فَوْز هَزيل; **we had a ~ escape** نَجَوْنا بأُعْجوبة **3▸** (in scope) ‹*field, range, definition*› مَحْدود ,ضَيِّق

B *vt* **1▸** (to limit) حَدَّ ,ضَيَّقَ (u; حَدّ; من) ‹*sb's choice, range, options*› **2▸** (to reduce) قَلَّلَ ,ضَيَّقَ ‹*a gap, deficit, margin*›; **their lead has been ~ed to five percentage points** تَراجَعَ تَقَدُّمُهُمْ لِيُصْبِحَ خَمْسَ نِقاطٍ مِئَوِيّةٍ **3▸** (with width) ضَيَّقَ ‹*a road, river, sb's arteries*›; **to ~ one's eyes** ضَيَّقَ عَيْنَيْهِ

C *vi* **1▸** «streets, rivers, valleys» (in width) ضاقَ (i; ضِيْق, ضَيْق) **2▸** (to decrease) «gaps, deficits, margins» ضاقَ (i; ضيق, ضَيْق), نَقَصَ (u; نَقْص ,نُقْصان); **the Liberals' lead has ~ed to a single point** تَراجَعَ تَقَدُّمُ الليبراليّينَ لِيُصْبِحَ نُقْطةً واحِدةً

D **(narrows)** *n pl* مَضيق (مَضائِقُ ,مَضايِقُ), بوغاز (بَواغيزُ), مَمَرّ مائيّ

(Idiom) **the straight and narrow** الطَريقُ القَويم

(Phrasal verb) **narrow down: ~ [sth] down, ~ down [sth]** قَلَّلَ [شَيْئاً] ‹*a number, the choices*›; ضَيَّقَ نِطاقَ [شَيْءٍ] ‹*one's research, an investigation*›

narrowly /ˈnarəʊli/ *adv* ‹*to win, miss*› بالكادِ

narrow-minded /narəʊˈmʌɪndɪd/ *adj* ‹*attitude, individual*› مُتَزَمِّت ,ضَيِّقُ الأُفُقِ

NASA /ˈnasə/ *n* = **National Aeronautics and Space Administration** الإدارة الوَطَنيّة للمِلاحةِ الفَضائيّةِ ,ناسا

nasal /ˈneɪz(ə)l/ *adj* **1▸** ‹*passages, congestion*› أَنْفيّ **2▸** (Ling) ‹*vowel, accent*› أَغَنّ (dipt)

nasal spray *n* رَذاذ للأَنْفِ

nasty /ˈnɑːsti/ *adj* **(nastier, nastiest)** **1▸** ‹*surprise, habit*› كَريه ‹*taste*›; مُقْرِف ‹*smell*› **2▸** ‹*man, remark*› قَذِر ,قَبيح

لَئيم (لِئام, لُؤَماءُ), خَبيث (خُبَثاءُ, خَبَثة), مَقيت (مُقْتاءُ) **3** ‹cut, bruise› بَليغ; ‹accident, fall› خَطير

natal /ˈneɪt(ə)l/ *adj* **1** (Astrol) ‹chart, horoscope› [خاصّ بِوَقْتِ الوِلادةِ] **2** (Zool) ‹territory, nest› [خاصّ بِمَكانِ وِلادةِ الحَيَوانِ]

nation /ˈneɪʃ(ə)n/ *n* أُمّة (أُمَم)

national /ˈnaʃ(ə)n(ə)l/ **A** *adj* ‹institution, championship› وَطَنيّ **B** *n* مُواطِن

national anthem *n* نَشيد وَطَنيّ

national curriculum *n* (BrE) نِظام تَعْليمٍ وَطَنيّ, مَنْهَج دِراسيّ وَطَنيّ

national debt *n* دَيْن عامّ

National Health Service *n* (BrE) [نِظام الخَدَماتِ الصِحّيّةِ القَوْميّةِ في بَريطانيا]

National Insurance *n* (in the UK) تَأْمين وَطَنيّ (ضَريبة تُقْتَطَعُ من الراتِبِ تُسْتَخْدَمُ للخَدَماتِ الصِحّيّةِ والمُساعَدةِ الاجْتِماعيّةِ في بَريطانيا)

nationalism /ˈnaʃ(ə)nəlɪz(ə)m/ *n* قَوْميّة

nationalist /ˈnaʃ(ə)nəlɪst/ *n, adj* قَوْميّ, وَطَنيّ

nationality /naʃəˈnalɪti/ *n* (*pl* **nationalities**) جِنْسيّة

nationalize, -ise (BrE) /ˈnaʃ(ə)nəlʌɪz/ *vt* أَمَّمَ ‹an industry, a company›

nationally /ˈnaʃ(ə)n(ə)li/ *adv* ‹to develop, negotiate› على الصَعيدِ الوَطَنيِّ; ‹to broadcast, distribute› في كُلِّ أَنْحاءِ الوَطَنِ

national park *n* مُتَنَزَّه وَطَنيّ, مِنْطَقة مَحْميّة

national security *n* أَمْن قَوْميّ

national service *n* خِدْمة عَسْكَريّة إِلْزاميّة

nation state *n* دَوْلة قَوْميّة

nationwide /neɪʃ(ə)nˈwʌɪd/ **A** *adj* ‹campaign, strike› يَشْمَلُ كُلَّ أَنْحاءِ البَلَدِ **B** *adv* ‹to broadcast, distribute› في كُلِّ أَنْحاءِ البَلَدِ

native /ˈneɪtɪv/ **A** *n* **1** (of a city, country) قاطِن (مِن مَواليد مَدينةٍ أو بَلَدٍ ما) **2** (indigenous person) [واحِد من السُكّانِ الأَصْليّينَ]; (indigenous animal) حَيَوان مَحَلّيّ; (indigenous plant) نَبات مَحَلّيّ **B** *adj* **1** ‹land, language› أَصْليّ; **her ~ Scotland** اسْكُتْلَنْدا مَوْطِنُها الأَصْليّ; **a ~ German speaker** شَخْص لُغَتُهُ الأَصْليّةُ هي الأَلْمانيّةُ **2** ‹flora, fauna› بَلَديّ, مَحَلّيّ

Native American *n* أَمْريكيّ أَصْليّ

nativity /nəˈtɪvɪti/ *n* ميلاد المَسيحِ

NATO /ˈneɪtəʊ/ *n* = **North Atlantic Treaty Organization** مُنَظَّمة حِلْفِ شَمالِ الأَطْلَسيِّ, ناتو

natural /ˈnatʃ(ə)rəl/ **A** *adj* **1** (relating to nature) ‹disaster, phenomenon, process› طَبيعيّ; **the ~ world** عالَم الطَبيعةِ; **the office has no ~ light** لا توجَدُ في المَكْتَبِ إضاءةٌ طَبيعيّةٌ; **to die of ~ causes** ماتَ ميتةً طَبيعيّةً **2** (normal) ‹reaction, consequence› طَبيعيّ, عاديّ; **it's only ~** هذا شَيْءٌ طَبيعيٌّ; **one's ~ reaction is to refuse/complain** رَدُّ الفِعْلِ الطَبيعيّ للمَرْءِ أنْ يَرْفُضَ \ يَشْتَكي **3** (inborn) ‹gift, talent› مَوْهوب, بالفِطْرةِ; **he's a ~ artist/storyteller** هو فَنّانٌ \ قَصّاصٌ بالفِطْرةِ **4** (in manner) ‹person, manner› غَيْر مُتَكَلِّفٍ **5** (Mus) ‹scale, key› [دون رَفْعٍ أو خَفْضٍ] **B** *n* **1** (infml) (skilled person) **to be a ~** امْتَلَكَ مَوْهِبةً طَبيعيّةً **2** (Mus) (sign) عَلامة إِلْغاءٍ \ تَحْويل (عَلامة تُلْغي عَلامةَ الرَفْعِ أو التَخْفيضِ السابِقةَ); (note) [نوتة دون رَفْعٍ أو خَفْضٍ]

natural childbirth *n* وِلادة طَبيعيّة

natural history *n* عِلْم النَباتِ والحَيَوانِ

naturalist /ˈnatʃ(ə)rəlɪst/ *n* مُتَخَصِّص في عِلْم النَباتِ والحَيَوانِ

naturalization, -isation (BrE) /natʃrəlʌɪˈzeɪʃ(ə)n/ *n* **1** (of a person) تَجَنُّس **2** (of a plant, animal) تَأَقْلُم

naturalized /ˈnatʃrəlʌɪzd/ *adj* **1** ‹citizen, immigrant› مُتَجَنِّس **2** ‹species, animal› مُتَأَقْلِم

naturally /ˈnatʃ(ə)rəli/ *adv* **1** (obviously) بالطَبْعِ, طَبْعاً; **~ I stopped to help** طَبْعاً تَوَقَّفْتُ للمُساعَدةِ **2** (by nature) بِحُكْمِ الطَبيعة; **~ occurring radioactivity** نَشاط إشْعاعيّ يَحْدُثُ بِحُكْمِ الطَبيعةِ **3** (in a relaxed fashion) ‹to behave, smile› تِلْقائيًّا

nature /ˈneɪtʃə/ **A** *n* **1** (the natural world) الطَبيعة; **let ~ take its course** دَعِ الطَبيعةَ تَأْخُذُ مَجْراها **2** (character) طَبيعة (طَبائِعُ), طَبْع (طِباع), فِطْرة (فِطَر); **he was a kind man by ~** كانَ رَجُلاً طَيِّباً بِفِطْرَتِهِ; **it's not in her ~ to do that** لَيْسَ من

طَبِيعَتِها أنْ تَفْعَلَ ذلك; **it is in the ~ of things that …** من الطَّبيعيّ أنْ … **3** (fml) (kind, sort) طبيعة (طَبائِع); **matters of a personal/medical ~** مَسائِل ذات طَبِيعةٍ خاصّةٍ \ طِبِّيّة
B **(-natured)**; *in combination* **sweet-/pleasant-~d** لَطيف بِطَبْعِهِ
Idiom **to answer a call of nature** (infml) قَضى حاجَتَهُ

nature conservancy *n* حِفْظ \ حماية الطَّبيعةِ

nature reserve *n* مَحْميّة طَبيعيّة

nature trail *n* مَمَرّ طَبيعيّ

naturist /ˈneɪtʃərɪst/ *n, adj* [مُؤَيِّد مَذْهَبِ العُرْيِ]

naught /nɔːt/ *n* (old use) لا شَيْءَ, عَدَم; **to come to ~** خابَ (i; خَيْبَة), فَشِلَ (a; فَشَل), لم يَأْتِ بِأَيِّ نَتيجةٍ

naughty /ˈnɔːti/ *adj* **(naughtier, naughtiest)** **1** (disobedient) ‹*boy, puppy*› شَقيّ (أَشْقِياءُ), غَيْر مُطيع **2** (rude) ‹*joke, picture*› بَذيء

nausea /ˈnɔːsɪə/ *n* غَثَيان

nauseating /ˈnɔːzieɪtɪŋ/ *adj* ‹*smell, taste*› مُقْرِف, مُقَزِّز

nauseous /ˈnɔːsɪəs/ *adj* ‹*smell, taste*› مُقْرِف, مُقَزِّز; **to feel ~** شَعَرَ بالغَثَيانِ

nautical /ˈnɔːtɪk(ə)l/ *adj* ‹*chart, term*› مِلاحيّ, بَحْرِيّ

nautical mile *n* ميل بَحْرِيّ (حَوالَيْ 1852 مِتْراً)

naval /ˈneɪv(ə)l/ *adj* ‹*battle, officer*› بَحْرِيّ

nave /neɪv/ *n* صَحْن كَنيسةٍ

navel /ˈneɪv(ə)l/ *n* سُرّة (سُرَر)

navel ring *n* خاتَم سُرّةٍ

navigable /ˈnavɪgəb(ə)l/ *adj* ‹*river, waterway*› صالِح لِلمِلاحةِ

navigate /ˈnavɪgeɪt/ **A** *vt* **1** أَبْحَرَ (في) ‹*the oceans, a river*› **2** قادَ (u; قِيادة), وَجَّهَ ‹*a ship*›
B *vi* أَبْحَرَ

navigation /navɪˈgeɪʃ(ə)n/ *n* **1** (on a ship, plane) ملاحة **2** (in a car) ملاحة

navigator /ˈnavɪgeɪtə/ *n* **1** (on a ship, plane) مَلّاح **2** (in a car) مَلّاح

navy /ˈneɪvi/ **A** *n* (*pl* **navies**) **1** (Naut) سِلاح البَحْرِيّةِ **2** (also **navy**) لَوْن كُحْليّ \ أَزْرَق داكِن
B *adj before n* **1** ‹*vessel, diver*› بَحْرِيّ **2** also **~-blue** كُحْليّ, أَزْرَق داكِن ‹*uniform, shirt*›

Nazareth /ˈnazərəθ/ *pr n* النَّاصِرة

Nazi /ˈnɑːtsi/ *n, adj* نازِيّ

NB /ɛnˈbiː/ *abbr* (Latin) = **nota bene: please note** مُلاحَظة, مَلْحوظة

NBC /ɛnbiːˈsiː/ *n* (AmE) = **National Broadcasting Company** شَرِكة إنْ بي سي التِلِفِزْيونيّة

NC *abbr* **1** (Busn) = **no charge** بِدونِ مُقابِلٍ **2** = **North Carolina**

NCO /ɛnsiːˈəʊ/ *n* = **noncommissioned officer** ضابِط صَفٍّ

ND *abbr* = **North Dakota**

NE *abbr* **1** = **northeast** شَمال شَرْقِيّ **2** = **Nebraska**

near /nɪə/ **A** *adv* **1** (in position, time) قَريباً, بالقُرْبِ, على مَقْرُبةٍ; **we live quite ~** نَعيشُ على مَقْرُبةٍ من هُنا; **as the day drew ~er** عِنْدَما اقْتَرَبَ المَوْعِدُ **2** (nearly) تَقْريباً; **a ~ perfect performance** أداء يَقْتَرِبُ من الكَمالِ
B *prep* بالقُرْب من, قَريب من, بِجانِبِ, بِجِوارِ; **~ here** بالقُرْبِ من هُنا; **~ Christmas** قبل عيدِ الميلادِ بِقَليلٍ
C *adj* قَريب, مُجاوِر; **the ~est shops** المَتاجِر الأَقْرَب; **in the ~ future** في المُسْتَقْبَلِ القَريبِ
D *vt* اقْتَرَبَ (من) ‹*a destination, station*›; **to ~ completion** اقْتَرَبَ من الانْتِهاءِ
E **(near to)** *phr* **1** (in position, time) قَريب من; **it's ~ to the school** هو قَريبٌ من المَدْرَسةِ **2** (on the point of) على وَشْكِ; **to be ~ to tears/collapse** كانَ على وَشْكِ البُكاءِ \ الانْهِيارِ

nearby /nɪəˈbʌɪ/ **A** *adj* ‹*town, hospital*› قَريب, مُجاوِر
B *adv* ‹*to live, stand*› على مَقْرَبةٍ

nearly /ˈnɪəli/ *adv* **1** (almost) (almost) تَقْريباً; **have you ~ finished?** هل أَوْشَكْتَ على الانْتِهاءِ؟; **I very ~ gave up a week later** كُنْتُ على وَشْكِ أنْ أَسْتَسْلِمَ بعد ذلك بأُسْبوعٍ تَقْريباً **2** (much less) **not ~** لَيْسَ من قَريبٍ أو بَعيدٍ; **she isn't ~ as talented as you** هي لَيْسَتْ مَوْهوبةً مِثْلَكَ من قريبٍ أو بَعيدٍ

near miss *n* نَجاة بِأُعْجوبةٍ; **to be/have a near miss** نَجا بِأُعْجوبةٍ

nearside /ˈnɪəsʌɪd/ *n* (BrE) [جانِب السَيّارةِ البَعيد عن السائِق]

nearsighted /nɪəˈsʌɪtɪd/ *adj* ‹*patient*› قَصير البَصَرِ \ النَظَرِ; **to be ~** عانى من قِصَرِ النَظَرِ

neat /niːt/ **A** *adj* **1▸** (personally) ‹*hair, appearance*› أنيق **2▸** (tidy) ‹*room, handwriting*› مُنَظَّم, مُرَتَّب; **their house is always very ~ and tidy** بَيْتُهُمْ دائماً مُرَتَّبٌ وَمُنَظَّمٌ **3▸** (elegant) ‹*explanation, solution*› جَيِّد, مُحْكَم, مُتْقَن **4▸** (AmE infml) (good) ‹*movie, time*› جَيِّد **5▸** ‹*whisky, spirits*› نَقِيّ, غَيْر مُخَفَّفٍ \ مَخْلوطٍ

B *adv* **to drink brandy/rum ~** شَرِبَ بْرانْدي \ روم نَقِيًّا

neatly /ˈniːtli/ *adv* **1▸** (tidily) ‹*to dress, fold*› بِعِنايةٍ, بِشَكْلٍ أنيق **2▸** (perfectly) ‹*to illustrate, solve*› تماماً

Nebraska /nɪˈbraskə/ *pr n* نِبْراسْكا

Nebraskan /nɪˈbrask(ə)n/ *pr n, adj* [(شَخص) من نِبْراسْكا]

necessarily /nɛsəˈsɛrəli, ˈnɛsəs(ə)rəli/ *adv* حَتْماً, بالضَرورة

necessary /ˈnɛsəs(ə)ri/ *adj* لازم, ضَروريّ

necessitate /nɪˈsɛsɪteɪt/ *vt* ‹*sb's departure, a change*› اسْتَوْجَبَ, اقْتَضى, تَطَلَّبَ, اسْتَلْزَمَ

necessity /nɪˈsɛsɪti/ *n* (*pl* **necessities**) **1▸** [u] (need) ضَرورة, حاجة; **the ~ for sth** الحاجة إلى شَيْءٍ; **out of ~** بِدافِعِ \ بِحُكْمِ الضَرورةِ **2▸** (essential) شَيْء ضَروريّ \ أساسيّ; **the basic/bare necessities** الضَروريّات الأساسيّة

neck /nɛk/ **A** *n* **1▸** (of people, animals) عُنُق (f; أَعْناق), رَقَبة (رِقاب, رَقَبات); **the back of the ~** مُؤَخِرة العُنُقِ, القَفا **2▸** (of a bottle, flask) عُنُق (f; أَعْناق) **3▸** (of the womb) عُنُق (f; أَعْناق) **4▸** (of pullover, dress, etc) رَقَبة (رِقاب); **a dress with a high/low ~** فُسْتان بِرَقَبةٍ عاليةٍ \ قَصيرةٍ **5▸** (of beef, lamb) رَقَبة (رِقاب), عُنُق (f; أَعْناق)

B *vi* (infml) «pair, couple» [قَبَّلَ]

(Idioms) **to be neck and neck** كانَ رَأْساً لِرَأْسٍ; **to be a pain in the neck** (infml) كانَ شَوْكَةً في الحَلْقِ; **to stick one's neck out** (infml) عَرَّضَ نَفْسَهُ للسُخْرِيّةِ

necklace /ˈnɛklɪs/ *n* عِقْد (عُقود), قِلادة (قَلائِدُ)

neckline /ˈnɛklʌɪn/ *n* خطّ العُنُقِ, تَقْويرة الرَقَبةِ

necktie /ˈnɛktʌɪ/ *n* (AmE) رَبْطة عُنُقٍ

nectar /ˈnɛktə/ *n* رَحيق

nectarine /ˈnɛktərɪn/ *n* نِكْتارين (خَوْخ أَمْلَس القِشْرةِ)

née /neɪ/ *adj* [لَقَب المَرْأةِ قبل الزَواجِ]; **Lisa Smith, ~ Jones** ليزا سْميث, ولَقَبُها قبل الزَواجِ جونز

need /niːd/ **A** *vt* **1▸** (to require) **to ~ sth** احْتاجَ شَيْئاً; **she ~s glasses/a loan** تَحْتاجُ إلى نَظّارةٍ \ قَرْضٍ; **take whatever you ~** خُذْ كُلَّ ما تَحْتاجُ; **you ~ to learn it by heart** عَلَيْكَ أنْ تَحْفَظَهُ عن ظَهْرِ قَلْبٍ; **my shoes ~ to be polished, my shoes ~ polishing** يَحْتاجُ حِذائي إلى تَلْميعٍ; **the figures ~ checking** تَحْتاجُ الأَرْقامُ إلى مُراجَعةٍ; **more money/more time is ~ed** هُناكَ حاجةٌ إلى المَزيد من المالِ \ الوَقْتِ; **it ~s four men to lift it** يَحْتاجُ إلى أَرْبَعة رِجالٍ لِيَرْفَعوهُ; **they ~ to have things explained to them** يَحْتاجونَ إلى مَنْ يَشْرَحُ لَهُم الأَشْياءَ; **everything you ~ to know about computers** كُلّ ما تَحْتاجُ مَعْرِفَتَهُ عن الحَواسيبِ **2▸** (have to) **you'll ~ to work hard** سَيَكونُ عَلَيْكَ العَمَلُ بِجِدٍّ; **something ~s to be done** لا بُدَّ من عَمَلِ شَيْءٍ; **you only ~ to ask** ما عَلَيْكَ إلاّ أنْ تَسْأَلَ; **nobody ~s to know** لا يَجِبُ أنْ يَعْلَمَ أَحَدٌ; **all you ~ to do is complete this form** كُلُّ ما عَلَيْكَ فِعْلُهُ هو أنْ تَمْلأَ هذه الاسْتِمارةَ **3▸** (to want) احْتاجَ; **I ~ a new suit** أَحْتاجُ إلى بَدْلةٍ جَديدةٍ; **we ~ a holiday** نَحْتاجُ إلى إجازةٍ; **she ~s to feel loved** تَحْتاجُ أنْ تَشْعُرَ أنَّها مَحْبوبةٌ

B *modal aux* **1▸** (must, have to) **he didn't ~ to ask permission** لم يَكُنْ بِحاجةٍ إلى طَلَبِ الإذْنِ; **you needn't wait** لَيْسَ عَلَيْكَ الانْتِظارُ; **'I waited for you'—'you needn't have'** 'بَقيتُ في انْتِظارِكَ' — 'لم يَكُنْ هُناكَ داعٍ لِذَلِكَ'; **I needn't have worn a jacket** لم أَكُنْ بِحاجةٍ لِارْتِداءِ سُتْرةٍ; **~ we discuss it now?** هل نَحْنُ بِحاجةٍ إلى مُناقَشَتِهِ الآنَ؟; **~ I say more?** هل أنا بِحاجةٍ لِقَوْلِ المَزيدِ؟; **did you ~ to be so unpleasant to him?** هل كُنْتَ بِحاجةٍ إلى أنْ تَكونَ فَظّاً مَعَهُ بِهذا الشَكْلِ؟; **I ~ hardly remind you that ...** لا أَحْتاجُ إلى تَذْكيرِكَ بِأَنَّ ... **2▸** (be logically inevitable) **it needn't be the case** لَيْسَ بالضَرورةِ أنْ يَكونَ الحالُ هكذا; **it needn't cost a fortune** لَيْسَ بالضَرورةِ أنْ يُكَلِّفَ مَبْلَغاً طائِلاً

C *n* **1▸** (necessity) ضَرورة, حاجة (حاجات); **there is a ~ for it** هُناكَ حاجةٌ لَهُ; **there is no ~ for an inquiry** لَيْسَ هُناكَ حاجةٌ

شَعَرَ بالحاجةِ إلى فِعْلِ شَيْءٍ للتَحْقيقِ; **to feel the ~ to do sth** شَعَرَ بالحاجةِ إلى فِعْلِ شَيْءٍ; **to have no ~ to work** لم يَكُنْ بِحاجةٍ للعَمَلِ; **there's no ~ to wait/hurry** لا حاجةَ للانْتِظارِ \ للعَجَلةِ; **there's no ~ for you to wait** لَسْتَ بِحاجةٍ للانْتِظارِ; **if ~ be, we can go later** إذا دَعَت الحاجةُ; **if the ~ arises** لَزِمَ الأَمْرُ، يُمْكِنُنا أَنْ نَذْهَبَ لاحِقاً **2** (requirement) احْتِياج (احْتِياجات); **the ~s of the children are paramount** احْتِياجاتُ الأَطْفالِ لَها أَهَمِّيّةٌ قُصْوى; **give me a list of your ~s** أَعْطِني قائِمةً باحْتِياجاتِكَ; **to meet the ~s of the elderly** لَبّى احْتِياجاتِ كِبارِ السِنِّ **3** [u] (adversity) **to help sb in times of ~** ساعَدَ شَخْصاً في أَوْقاتِ الضيقِ; **your ~ is greater than mine** أَنْتَ بِحاجةٍ إِلَيْهِ أَكْثَرَ مِني **4** [u] (deprivation) عَوَز, حِرْمان; **to be in ~** كانَ مُحْتاجاً; **children in ~** الأَطْفال المُحْتاجونَ

needle /ˈniːd(ə)l/ **A** *n* **1** (for sewing, knitting) إِبْرة (إِبَر) **2** (for injections) إِبْرة (إِبَر) **3** (on instruments) مُؤَشِّر (مُؤَشِّرات), **4** (on a pine tree) وَرَقة (أَوْراق, وَرَقات) **B** *vt* أَثارَ, أَزْعَجَ, أَغاظَ; **I was ~d by her lack of interest** حفيظَتي عَدَمُ اهْتِمامِها

(Idioms) **a needle in a haystack** إِبْرة في كَوْمةٍ من القَشِّ; **to have pins and needles** شَعَرَ بِوَخْزٍ

needless /ˈniːdləs/ *adj* ‹*suffering, repetition*› غَيْر ضَروريٍّ, غَنِيٌّ عن القَوْلِ; **~ to say, there is no easy solution** لا مُبَرِّرَ لَهُ أَنَّهُ لا يوجَدُ حَلٌّ سَهْلٌ

needlework /ˈniːdlwəːk/ *n* **1** (activity) شُغْل الإِبْرة, تَطْريز **2** (items) أَدَوات التَطْريزِ

needy /ˈniːdi/ *adj* (**needier, neediest**) ‹*child, family*› مُحْتاج, مُعْوِز

negate /nɪˈɡeɪt/ *vt* (fml) أَبْطَلَ, أَلْغى ‹*the effects, need*›

negative /ˈnɛɡətɪv/ **A** *adj* **1** (saying no) ‹*reply, reaction*› سَلْبِيّ **2** (unconstructive) ‹*effect, mood*› سَلْبِيّ **3** (harmful) ‹*effect, publicity*› سَلْبِيّ **4** ‹*number*› سالِب **5** ‹*electrode*› سالِب **6** **to test ~** كانَتْ نَتيجةُ تَحْليلِهِ سَلْبِيّةً **B** *n* **1** (in grammar) نَفْي; **in the ~** بالسَلْبِ **2** (Phot) صورة سالِبة

negatively /ˈnɛɡətɪvli/ *adv* **1** (uncooperatively) ‹*to react, respond*› بِشَكْلٍ سَلْبِيٍّ **2** (harmfully) ‹*to affect, influence*› بِشَكْلٍ سالِبٍ **3** (Phys) ‹*to charge*› بِشَكْلٍ سَلْبِيٍّ

neglect /nɪˈɡlɛkt/ **A** *vt* **1** (to fail to care for) أَهْمَلَ ‹*one's family, house, health*› **2** (not to attend to) تَجاهَلَ ‹*a problem, one's work*› **3** (to fail) **to ~ to do sth** لم يَفْعَلْ شَيْئاً; **she ~ed to mention that she was married** لم تَذْكُرْ أَنَّها مُتَزَوِّجةٌ **B** *v refl* **to ~ oneself** أَهْمَلَ نَفْسَهُ **C** *n* إِهْمال; **to fall into ~** عانى الإِهْمالَ; **~ of duty** تَخَلّي عن الواجِبِ

neglected /nɪˈɡlɛktɪd/ *adj* **1** ‹*building, garden*› مُهْمَل **2** ‹*wife, child*› مُهْمَل; **to feel ~** شَعَرَ بِأَنَّهُ مُهْمَلٌ

neglectful /nɪˈɡlɛktfʊl/ *adj* ‹*parent, parenting*› مُقَصِّر, مُهْمِل

negligee, **négligée** /ˈnɛɡlɪʒeɪ/ *n* مِبْذَل (مَباذِل), قَميص نَوْم

negligence /ˈnɛɡlɪdʒ(ə)ns/ *n* إِهْمال, تَقْصير

negligent /ˈnɛɡlɪdʒ(ə)nt/ *adj* ‹*act, driving*› مُقَصِّر, مُهْمِل

negligible /ˈnɛɡlɪdʒɪb(ə)l/ *adj* ‹*effect, amount*› تافِه, لا يُذْكَرُ

negotiable /nɪˈɡəʊʃɪəb(ə)l/ *adj* **1** (subject to negotiation) ‹*salary, terms*› قابِل للتَفاوُضِ **2** (passable) ‹*road, pass*› يُمْكِنُ اجْتِيازُهُ

negotiate /nɪˈɡəʊʃɪeɪt/ **A** *vt* **1** (to bargain over) تَفاوَضَ (حول) ‹*a contract, treaty*› **2** (fml) (to get past, through) اجْتازَ ‹*a bend, an obstacle*› **B** *vi* «unions, governments» تَفاوَضَ; **to ~ with sb** تَفاوَضَ مع شَخْصٍ; **to ~ for better conditions** تَفاوَضَ من أَجْلِ ظُروفٍ أَفْضَلَ

negotiation /nɪɡəʊʃɪˈeɪʃ(ə)n/ *n* تَفاوُض (تَفاوُضات), مُفاوَضة; **the problem is under ~** المُشْكِلةُ قَيْدُ التَفاوُضِ

negotiator /nɪˈɡəʊʃɪeɪtə/ *n* مُفاوِض

Negro /ˈniːɡrəʊ/ (old use or offensive) **A** *n* (*pl* **Negroes**) زِنْجِيّ (زُنوج, زِنْج), (n coll; زِنْج)

B *adj* ‹*descent, race*› زِنْجِيّ (زِنْج)

neigh /neɪ/ *vi* «horses, mules» صَهَلَ (a-i; صَهيل)

neighbour (BrE), **neighbor** (AmE) /ˈneɪbə/ *n* جار (جيران)

neighbourhood (BrE), **neighborhood** (AmE) /ˈneɪbəhʊd/ *n* **1** (district) حَيّ (أَحْياء), مِنْطَقة (مَناطِقُ); **in the ~ of the village** في جِوارِ القَرْيةِ **2** (people) أَهْل الحَيِّ

neighbouring (BrE), **neighboring** (AmE) /ˈneɪbərɪŋ/ *adj* *‹country, state›* قريب ,مُتاخِم ,مُجاوِر

neither /ˈnaɪðə, ˈniːðə/ **A** *conj* **1** (after negative statements) لا كَذَلِكَ; **she can't read Greek, and ~ can I** هي لا تَسْتَطيعُ قِراءةَ اللُغةِ اليونانيّةِ، ولا أنا كَذَلِكَ; **we don't have broadband, ~ do they** لَيْسَ لَدَيْنا نِطاقٌ عَريضٌ، ولا هُمْ كَذَلِكَ **2** (not either) لا; **~ ... nor ...** لا ... ولا ...; **I have ~ the time nor the money** لَيْسَ لَدَيَّ الوَقْتُ ولا المالُ; **~ he nor his wife were well** لا هو ولا زَوْجَتُهُ كانا على ما يُرامُ

B *determiner* ولا واحِدَ من; **~ book is suitable** ولا واحِدَ من الكتابَيْنِ مُناسِبٌ; **~ answer is correct** ولا إجابةَ من الإجابَتَيْنِ صَحيحةٌ; **~ candidate replied** ولا واحِدَ من المُرَشَّحَيْنِ رَدَّ

C *pron* ولا واحِدَ من; **~ of the two is suitable** ولا واحِدَ مِنْهُما مُناسِبٌ; **~ of the answers is correct** ولا إجابةَ من الإجابَتَيْنِ صَحيحةٌ; **'which one is responsible?'—'~'** 'أيُّهُما المَسْؤولُ؟' — 'لا أَحَدَ مِنْهُما'

neocolonialism /ˌniːəʊkəˈləʊnɪəlɪz(ə)m/ *n* الاسْتِعْمار الجَديد

neoconservative /niːəʊkənˈsɜːvətɪv/ **A** *adj* *‹policy, initiative›* المُحافِظينَ الجُدُدِ

B (Pol) *n* (شَخْص) من المُحافِظينَ الجُدُدِ

neon /ˈniːɒn/ **A** *n* نِيون (عُنْصُر غازيّ)

B *adj before n* *‹lights, sign›* نِيون

neonatal /ˌniːəʊˈneɪt(ə)l/ *adj* *‹unit, mortality›* حَديثي الوِلادةِ

Nepal /nɪˈpɔːl/ *pr n* نيبال (f)

Nepalese /nɛpəˈliːz/, **Nepali** /nɪˈpɔːli/ **A** *n* (*pl* **Nepalese**) **1** (citizen) نيباليّ **2** (language) (اللُغة) النيباليّة

B *adj* *‹custom, river›* نيباليّ

Nepali /nɪˈpɔːli/ **A** *n* **1** (citizen) نيباليّ **2** (language) (اللُغة) النيباليّة

B *adj* *‹custom, food›* نيباليّ

nephew /ˈnɛfjuː, ˈnɛvjuː/ *n* **1** (son of your brother) ابْن أَخٍ; (son of your sister) ابْن أُخْتٍ **2** (son of your brother-in-law) ابْن أخ الزَوجِ \ الزَوْجةِ; (son of your sister-in-law) ابْن أُخْت الزَوجِ \ الزَوْجةِ

nepotism /ˈnɛpətiz(ə)m/ *n* مَحْسوبيّة ,مُحاباة الأَقارِبِ

Neptune /ˈnɛptjuːn/ *pr n* نِبْتون

nerve /nɜːv/ **A** *n* **1** (in the body) عَصَب (أَعْصاب) **2** [u] (infml) (courage) شَجاعة ,جُرْأة ,رَباطة جَأْشٍ; **to lose one's ~** فَقَدَ أَعْصابَهُ **3** [u] (infml) (cheek) جَسارة ,صَفاقة الوَجْهِ ,وَقاحة; **he had the ~ to call me a liar!** تَجَرَّأَ على القَوْلِ بِأَنَّني كَذّابٌ!

B **(nerves)** *n pl* تَوَتُّر ,عَصَبيّة

(Idiom) **to get on sb's nerves** أَثارَ غَضَبَ شَخْصٍ

nerve-racking, **nerve-wracking** /ˈnəvrakɪŋ/ *adj* *‹experience, moment›* مُحَطِّم للأَعْصابِ

nervous /ˈnəːvəs/ *adj* **1** (anxious) *‹laugh, glance›* عَصَبيّ, مُتَوَتِّر; **to feel ~** شَعَرَ بالعَصَبيّةِ; **to be ~ about the interview** شَعَرَ بالعَصَبيّةِ بِخُصوصِ المُقابَلةِ **2** (relating to the nerves) *‹disorder, tissue›* عَصَبيّ

nervous breakdown *n* انْهِيار عَصَبيّ

nervously /ˈnəːvəsli/ *adv* *‹to glance, laugh›* بِعَصَبيّةٍ

nervous system *n* جِهاز عَصَبيّ

nervous wreck *n* (infml) (شَخْص) مُحَطَّم الأَعْصابِ

nest /nɛst/ **A** *n* **1** (of birds) عُشّ (أَعْشاش ,عِشاش) ,وَكْر (أَوْكار) **2** (of ants, wasps) خَلِيّة (خَلايا)

B *vi* «birds, eagles» بَنى عُشًّا ,عَشَّشَ

(Idiom) **to flee/leave the nest** غادَرَ العُشَّ الأُسَريَّ

nest egg *n* (infml) تَحْويشة العُمْرِ (مال مُدَّخَر للحاجة)

nestle /ˈnɛs(ə)l/ *vi* **1** «puppies, children» أوى ,اسْتَكَنَّ (i; أُوِيّ); **the kittens ~d against their mother's body** ارْتَمَت الهُرَيْراتُ على جَسَدِ أُمِّها **2** «villages, houses» وَقَعَ (a; وُقوع); **the village ~s in a secluded valley** تَقَعُ القَرْيةُ في وادٍ مُنْعَزِلٍ

nestling /ˈnɛstlɪŋ/ *n* فَرْخ (فِراخ ,أَفْراخ)

net /nɛt/ **A** *n* **1** (for fish, butterflies) شَبَكة **2** (in sports) شَبَكة; **to come up to the ~** لَعِبَ في ساحةِ الإرْسالِ **3** (trap) فَخّ (فُخوخ ,فِخاخ); **to slip through the ~** قُرْبَ الشَبَكةِ أَفْلَتَ **4** (network) شَبَكة; **neural ~** شَبَكة عَصَبيّة **5** **(the Net)** (the Internet) الإنْتَرْنِت; **to surf the ~** تَصَفَّحَ الإنْتَرْنِت; **look it up on the N~** ابْحَثْ عَنْها على الإنْتَرْنِت **6** [u] (fabric) تُلّ

B *adj* (also **nett**) **1** *‹profit, loss, weight›* صافٍ; **~ of tax** صافي الضَريبةِ; **~ weight: 20 kilos** صافي الوَزْنِ: 20 كيلو

2 ‹*effect, increase, result*› إجْماليّ, نهائيّ

C *vt* (-tt-) **1** اصْطادَ ‹*a fish, butterfly*› **2** حَقَّق ‹*a profit*›

netball /ˈnɛtbɔːl/ *n* [u] كُرة الشَّبَكةِ

net curtain *n* سِتارة شَبَكيّة

Netherlander /ˈnɛðələndə/ *n* (old use) هولَنْديّ

Netherlands /ˈnɛðələndz/ *pr n* (**the Netherlands**) هولَنْدا

netiquette /ˈnɛtɪkɛt/ *n* آداب الإنْتَرْنِت

netspeak /ˈnɛtspiːk/ *n* لُغة الإنْتَرْنِت

nett *adj* (BrE) ▸ **net** B

netting /ˈnɛtɪŋ/ *n* شَبَكة (شِباك, شَبَك)

nettle /ˈnɛt(ə)l/ *n* (also **stinging nettle**) قُرّاص

(Idiom) **to grasp/seize the nettle** أَمْسَكَ بزمامِ الأُمورِ

network /ˈnɛtwəːk/ **A** *n* **1** (system) شَبَكة; **the road/rail ~** شَبَكة الطُرُقِ \ السِكَكِ الحَديديّة **2** (of people) شَبَكة **3** (of computers) شَبَكة **4** (in broadcasting) شَبَكة

B *vt* **1** رَبَطَ (i-u; رَبْط) ‹*the computers, PCs*›; **you can ~ the PCs and share a single Internet connection** يُمْكِنُكَ رَبْطُ أَجْهزة الكومْبيوتر الشَّخْصيّة والاشْتِراكُ في اتّصالٍ واحِدٍ بالإنْتَرْنِت

2 أذاعَ ‹*a TV programme*›

C *vi* **she ~s with buyers throughout Europe** تَتَواصَلُ مع مُشْتَرينَ من جَميعِ أَنْحاءِ أوروبّا

networking /ˈnɛtwəːkɪŋ/ *n* **1** (connecting computers) رَبْط شَبَكيّ; **wireless ~** رَبْط شَبَكيّ لاسِلْكيّ **2** (with contacts) تَواصُل

network television *n* (AmE) شَبَكة تِلِفِزْيون

neural /ˈnjʊ(ə)rəl/ *adj* ‹*functions, networks*› عَصَبيّ

neuralgia /ˌnjʊəˈraldʒə/ *n* أَلَم عَصَبيّ

neurological /njʊərəˈlɒdʒɪk(ə)l/ *adj* ‹*disorder*› عَصَبيّ; ‹*research*› الجِهازِ العَصَبيِّ

neurology /ˌnjʊəˈrɒlədʒi/ *n* طِبّ الجِهازِ العَصَبيِّ

neuron /ˈnjʊərɒn/, **neurone** /ˈnjʊərəʊn/ *n* عَصَبون (عَصابينُ), خَليّة عَصَبيّة

neurosis /ˌnjʊəˈrəʊsɪs/ *n* (*pl* **neuroses**) اضْطِراب عَصَبيّ, عُصاب

neurotic /njʊəˈrɒtɪk/ **A** *adj* ‹*disorder, obsession*› عَصَبيّ, عُصابيّ

B *n* شَخْص يُعاني من اضْطِرابٍ عَصَبيٍّ

neuter /ˈnjuːtə/ **A** *adj* ‹*noun*› مُحايِد (لا جِنْسَ لَهُ)

B *n* اسم مُحايِد (لا جِنْسَ لَهُ)

C *vt* خَصى (i; خِصاء) ‹*a cat, pet*›

neutral /ˈnjuːtrəl/ **A** *adj* **1** ‹*government, observer*› حِياديّ, غَيْر مُتَعادِل **2** ‹*tone, colour*› مُحايِد **3** ‹*wire, connection*› مُحايِد, مُتَعادِل (لا حامِضيّ وَلا قاعِديّ) **4** ‹*substance*› مَشْحونٍ

B *n* وَضْع مُحايِد \ اللاتَعْشيق

neutrality /njuːˈtralɪti/ *n* حِياد

neutralize, **-ise** (BrE) /ˈnjuːtrəlʌɪz/ *vt* أزالَ, أَبْطَلَ, حَيَّدَ ‹*a threat, an advantage*›

neutron /ˈnjuːtrɒn/ *n* نيوتْرون

Nevada /nɪˈvɑːdə/ *pr n* نيفادا

Nevadan /nɪˈvɑːd(ə)n/ *pr n, adj* [(شَخْص) من نيفادا]

never /ˈnɛvə/ *adv* ‹*have, get*› لا ... مُطْلَقاً, لا ... قَطُّ, لا ... أَبداً; **I ~ go to London** لا أَذْهَبُ إلى لُنْدُن أَبَداً; **~ lie to me again!** لا تَكْذِبْ عَلَيَّ مَرّةً أُخْرى أَبَداً!; **I ~ knew that** لَمْ أَعْرِفْ ذَلِكَ مُطْلَقاً

never-ending /nɛvərˈɛndɪŋ/ *adj* ‹*battle, devotion*› لا نِهاية لَهُ, لا يَنْتَهي

nevertheless /nɛvəðəˈlɛs/ *adv* **1** (however) بالرَغْمِ من ذلك, مع ذلك; **he was a just, but ~ powerful ruler** كانَ حاكِماً عادِلاً، وَلَكِنَّهُ مع ذلك كانَ قَويّاً **2** (nonetheless) بالرَغْمِ من ذلك; **~, he remained popular, he remained popular ~** وَبالرَغْمِ من ذلك، ظَلَّ يَتَمَتَّعُ بِشَعْبيّةٍ كَبيرةٍ; **they kept trying ~** وَبالرَغْمِ من ذلك ظَلّوا يُحاوِلونَ

new /njuː/ **A** *n* (**the new** *n pl*) العَصْر الحَديث; **out with the old and in with the ~** مَضى العَهْدُ القَديمُ وَبَدَأَ العَهْدُ الجَديدُ

B *adj* ‹*car, song, joke*› جَديد; **as good as ~** مُسْتَعْمَل كالجَديدِ, شِبْه جَديدٍ; **a ~ product** مُنْتَج جَديد; **I'd like you to meet my ~ friends, the Smiths** أُريدُكَ أَنْ تُقابِلَ أَصْدِقائي الجُدُدَ، عائِلة سْميث; **the ~ town** المَدينة الجَديدة; **to be ~ to a job/town** كانَ حَديثَ عَهْدٍ بِوَظيفةٍ \ بِمَدينةٍ; **the area/subject is ~ to me** المِنْطَقةُ \ المَوْضوعُ جَديدٌ عَلَيَّ; **let's try something ~** هَيّا نُجَرِّبُ شَيْئاً جَديداً

New Age *adj* ‹*music, beliefs*› العَصْر الجَديد

newborn /ˈnju:bɔ:n/ *adj* <*baby, calf*> حَديث الوِلادةِ

new build *n* بِناء جَديد

newcomer /ˈnju:kʌmə/ *n* وافِد \ قادِم جَديد; **he's a ~ to cricket** هو مُبْتَدِئٌ في لُعْبةِ الكْرِيكِت

New Delhi *pr n* نْيودلْهي (f)

newfangled /nju:ˈfaŋgəld/ *adj* (pej) <*invention, notion*> مُسْتَحْدَث, غَيْر مَأْلوفٍ

new-found /ˌnju:ˈfaʊnd/ *adj* <*wealth*> جَديد; <*freedom*> اُكْتُشِفَ \ وُجِدَ حَديثاً

New Guinea *pr n* غينيا الجَديدة

New Hampshire *pr n* نْيو هامْشير (f)

New Jersey *pr n* نْيوجيرْسي (f)

New Jerseyan *pr n, adj* [(شَخْص) من نْيو جيرْسي]

new-look /ˌnju:ˈlʊk/ *adj* <*squad, website*> في مَظْهَرٍ جَديدٍ

newly /ˈnju:li/ *adv* <*formed, elected*> حَديثاً, مُؤَخَّراً; **a ~ released DVD** دي في دي صادِر حَديثاً

newly-weds /ˈnju:liwɛdz/ *n pl* عَروسانِ

New Mexican *pr n, adj* [(شَخْص) من نْيو مِكْسيكو]

New Mexico *pr n* نْيو مِكْسيكو (f)

newness /ˈnju:nəs/ *n* حَداثة

news /nju:z/ *n* **1▸** (in the media) أَنْباء, أَخْبار; **an item** *or* **piece of ~** خَبَر (أَخْبار); **the latest ~ from Damascus** أَحْدَث الأَخْبارِ من دِمَشْق; **~ is just coming in of an explosion** وَرَدَت الأَنْباءُ للتَّوِّ عن وُقوعِ انْفِجارٍ; **today's sports ~** أَخْبار الرِياضةِ اليَوْمَ; **to be in the ~** جاءَ في الأَخْبارِ **2▸** (personal information) أَخْبار; **that's good/bad ~!** ذلك خَبَرٌ طَيِّبٌ \ سَيِّئٌ!; **I have some sad ~** لَدَيَّ بَعْضُ الأَخْبارِ الغَيْرُ سارّةٍ; **a bit of ~ about Uncle Jack** قَليل من الأَخْبارِ عن العَمِّ جاك; **have you heard the ~?** هل سَمِعْتَ الأَخْبارَ؟; **tell me all your ~!** أَخْبِرْني عن كُلِّ أَخْبارِكَ!; **that's ~ to me!** لم أَسْمَعْ ذلك الخَبَرَ من قَبْلُ **3▸** (Radio, TV) (programme) **the ~** نَشْرة الأَخْبارِ; **to see sth/sb on the ~** رَأى شَيْئاً \ شَخْصاً في نَشْرةِ الأَخْبارِ; **to present the national ~** قَدَّمَ نَشْرةَ الأَخْبارِ الوَطَنِيّةِ **4▸** (newspaper section) **financial/home ~** الأَخْبار المالِيّة \ المَحَلِّيّة

news agency *n* وَكالة أَنْباءٍ

newsagent /ˈnju:zeɪdʒ(ə)nt/, **newsagent's** *n* (BrE) بائِع صُحُفٍ

news bulletin *n* (BrE) نَشْرة أَخْبارٍ

newscast /ˈnju:zkɑ:st/ (AmE) *n* نَشْرة أَخْبارٍ

newscaster /ˈnju:zkɑ:stə/ *n* مُذيع \ مُقَدِّم نَشْرةِ أَخْبارٍ

news conference *n* مُؤْتَمَر صُحُفِيّ

newsdealer /ˈnju:zdi:lə/ *n* (AmE) بائِع صُحُفٍ

news editor *n* مُدير أَخْبارٍ \ تَحْريرٍ

newsflash /ˈnju:zflaʃ/ *n* خَبَر عاجِل

newsgroup /ˈnju:zgru:p/ *n* مَجْموعة إِخْبارِيّة

news headlines *n pl* عَناوين الأَخْبارِ

new shekel *n* شيقِل جَديد

news item *n* خَبَر

newsletter /ˈnju:zlɛtə/ *n* رِسالة إِخْبارِيّة

newspaper /ˈnju:zpeɪpə/ *n* جَريدة (جَرائِدُ), صَحيفة (صُحُف)

newsprint /ˈnju:zprɪnt/ *n* وَرَق جَرائِدَ \ صُحُفٍ

newsreader /ˈnju:zri:də/ *n* (BrE) قارِئ أَخْبار

newsreel /ˈnju:zri:l/ *n* [فيلْم إِخْبارِيّ كانَ يُعْرَضُ في دور السينَما]

newsroom /ˈnju:zru:m/ *n* غُرْفة أَخْبارٍ

news stand *n* كُشْك جَرائِدَ

newsvendor /ˈnju:zvɛndə/ *n* صاحِب كُشْك جَرائِدَ

newt /nju:t/ *n* سَمَنْدَل (سَمادِلُ)

New Testament *n* العَهْد الجَديد

new year *n* سَنة جَديدة

New Year's Day (BrE), **New Year's** (AmE) *n* عيد رَأْسِ السَنةِ

New Year's Eve *n* لَيْلة رَأْسِ السَنةِ

New York *n* **1▸** (*also* **New York City**) نيويورْك (f) **2▸** (US state) نيويورْك (f)

New Yorker *n* [(شَخْص) من نيويورْك]

New Zealand *pr n* نيوزيلَنْدا

New Zealander *n* نيوزيلَنْديّ

next /nɛkst/ **A** *pron* تالٍ (تَوالٍ), قادِم, مُقْبِل; **the week after ~** الأُسْبوع بعد القادِمِ; **from one minute to the ~** بين دَقيقةٍ وأُخْرى

B *adj* 1 (in time) ‹*day, train*› تالٍ, قادِم, مُقْبِل; **~ Thursday** الخَميس القادِم; **catch the ~ bus** اسْتَقِلَّ الحافِلَةَ التالِيَةَ; **he got on the ~ train** اسْتَقَلَّ القِطارَ التالِيَ; **you're ~ to speak** أَنْتَ التالي في التَحَدُّثِ 2 (in sequence) ‹*customer, chapter*› تالٍ (تَوالٍ); **take the ~ turning on the right** خُذ المُنْعَطَفَ التالِيَ على اليَمينِ 3 (beside) ‹*room, house*› مُجاوِر; **the ~ house to ours** البَيْتُ المُجاوِر لِبَيْتِنا

C *adv* 1 (in time) ‹*to happen, do*› بعد ذلك; **what happened ~?** ماذا حَدَثَ بعد ذلك؟; **~, we interviewed Mr Jackson** بعد ذلك، أَجْرَيْنا مُقابَلَةً مع السَيِّدِ جاكسون; **~ I'm going to save the files** بعد ذلك سَأُخَزِّنُ المِلَفّاتِ; **what shall we do ~?** ماذا نَفْعَلُ بعد ذلك؟; **when I go there ~** عِنْدما أَذْهَبُ إلى هُناكَ في المَرَّةِ التالِيَةِ 2 (sequentially) ‹*best, most important*› تالٍ (تَوالٍ); **the ~ tallest is Patrick** يَليهِ في الطولِ باتْريك; **which speech comes ~?** ما هو الخِطابُ التالي؟; **it's your turn ~** سَتَكونُ أَنْتَ التالي

D **(next to)** *phr* 1 (beside, close to) بِجانِبِ, إلى جانِبِ, بِجِوارِ; **two seats ~ to each other** مَقْعَدانِ مُتَجاوِرانِ 2 (compared with) مُقارَنَةً ب; **~ to her, the rest of the class seem dull** مُقارَنَةً بها، يَبْدو بَقِيَّةُ الطُلّابِ بَطيئي الفَهْمِ 3 (following) إضافَةً إلى; **~ to riding, I like swimming** أَكْثَرُ ما أُحِبُّ بعد رُكوبِ الخَيْلِ هو السِباحَةُ 4 (almost) **in ~ to no time it was over** انْتَهى ذلك في غَمْضَةِ عَيْنٍ; **to get sth for ~ to nothing** حَصَلَ على شَيْءٍ بِثَمَنٍ بَخْسٍ

next door **A** *adj* (also **next-door**) ‹*flat, house*› مُجاوِر, مُتاخِم; **B** *adv* ‹*to live, move in*› بِجوار; **she lives next door to me** تَسْكُنُ بِجِواري

next-door neighbour (BrE), **next-door neighbor** (AmE) *n* جار مُتاخِم

next of kin *n* أَقْرَب الأَقارِبِ

NGO /ˌendʒiːˈəʊ/ *n* = **Non-Governmental Organization** مُنَظَّمة غَيْر حُكوميَّة

NH *abbr* = **New Hampshire**

NHS /ˌeneɪtʃˈes/ *n* (BrE) = **National Health Service** هَيْئة الخَدَماتِ الصِحّيَّةِ الوَطَنِيَّةِ (في بَريطانيا)

NHS hospital *n* مُسْتَشْفًى تابع لِهَيْئَةِ الخَدَماتِ الصِحّيَّةِ الوَطَنِيَّةِ (في بَريطانيا)

nib /nɪb/ *n* سِنّ قَلَم حِبْر

nibble /ˈnɪb(ə)l/ **A** *vi* «mice, guests» قَضَمَ (a-i; قَضْم), قَرَضَ (i; قَرْض), قَرَمَ (i; قَرْم); **she took a cake from the tray and ~d at it** تَناوَلَتْ حَلْوى من الصينيّةِ وَأَخَذَتْ تَقْضِمُها

B *vt* قَضَمَ (a-i; قَضْم) ‹*a sandwich, sb's ear*›

Nicaragua /ˌnɪkəˈragjʊə/ *pr n* نيكاراغوا

Nicaraguan /nɪkəˈragju:ən/ *n, adj* نيكاراغُويّ

nice /nʌɪs/ *adj* 1 (enjoyable, pleasant) ‹*day, drive, holiday*› لَطيف, مُمْتِع, سارّ; **it will be ~ to see them** سَيَكونُ من اللَطيفِ أنْ نَراهُمْ; **have a ~ day!** أَتَمَنّى لكَ نَهاراً سَعيداً!; **did you have a ~ time?** هل قَضَيْتَ وَقْتاً لَطيفاً؟; **it's ~ and sunny** الجَوُّ لَطيفٌ وَمُشْمِسٌ; **we had a ~ long chat** دارَتْ بَيْنَنا مُحادَثَةٌ طَويلَةٌ لَطيفَةٌ; **~ to have met you** تَشَرَّفْتُ بِمُقابَلَتِكَ 2 (attractive) ‹*house, clothes, painting*› لَطيف, جَميل, جَذّاب; **you look very ~** تَبْدو جَميلاً جِدًّا 3 (tasty) ‹*meal, drink*› لَذيذ; **it tastes ~** طَعْمُهُ لَذيذٌ; **a ~ cool drink** شَراب بارِد لَذيذ 4 (kind) ‹*child, doctor, letter*› لَطيف, رَقيق; **to be ~ to sb** كانَ لَطيفاً مع شَخْصٍ; **he says really ~ things about you** يَقولُ عَنْكَ أَشْياءَ لَطيفَةً حَقًّا 5 (socially acceptable) ‹*neighbourhood, school, behaviour*› لَطيف; **this a ~ suburb to live in** هذه ضاحِيَةٌ لَطيفَةٌ للعَيْشِ فيها 6 (used ironically) **~ friends you've got!** ما أَسْخَفَ أَصْدِقاءَكَ!; **this is a ~ mess you've got us into!** لَقَدْ أَوْقَعْتَنا في هذا المَأْزِقِ السَخيفِ!; **that's a ~ way to talk to your father!** هذا أُسْلوبٌ سَخيفٌ للحَديثِ مع أَبيكَ!

Idiom **nice one!** (infml) (in admiration) أَحْسَنْتَ!

nice-looking /nʌɪsˈlʊkɪŋ/ *adj* ‹*guy, lady*› جَميل المَظْهَرِ, وَسيم (وُسَماءُ, وِسام); **she is nicer-looking than her sister** هي أَجْمَلُ مَظْهَراً من أُخْتِها

nicely /ˈnʌɪsli/ *adv* 1 (attractively) ‹*presented, dressed*› بِشَكْلٍ جَميلٍ 2 (kindly) ‹*to smile, treat*› بِلُطْفٍ 3 (politely) ‹*to behave, ask*› بِأَدَبٍ

niche /nɪtʃ, niːʃ/ *n* كوّة (كُوًى, كوّات)

niche market *n* سوق مُتَخَصِّصة

nick /nɪk/ **A** *n* (حُزوز) حَزّ ,(ثُلَم) ثُلْمة; **there was a small ~ in the edge of the ruler** كانَتْ هُناكَ ثَلْمةٌ في طَرَفِ المِسْطَرةِ

B *vt* **1** (to cut) ثَلَمَ (i; ثَلْم), حَزَّ (u; حَزّ) ‹*yourself, cloth*›; **he ~ed himself shaving** جَرَحَ نَفْسَهُ وَهُوَ يَحْلُقُ ذَقْنَهُ **2** (BrE infml) (to steal) سَرَقَ (i; سَرِقة), اخْتَلَسَ ‹*the food, money*›

(Idiom) **in the nick of time** في آخِرِ لَحْظةٍ

nickel /ˈnɪk(ə)l/ *n* **1** [u] (metal) نَيْكَل **2** (AmE) (coin) (قِطْعة مَعْدِنيّة تُساوي خَمْسة سِنْتاتٍ)

nickname /ˈnɪkneɪm/ **A** *n* لَقَب (أَلْقاب), كُنْية (كُنًى)

B *vt* لَقَّبَ, كَنَّى; **she was ~d 'Bubbles'** كانَتْ تُلَقَّبُ بـ 'بابِلْز'

Nicosia /ˌnɪkəˈsɪə/ *pr n* نيقوسيا

nicotine /ˈnɪkətiːn/ *n* نيكوتين

nicotine patch *n* لَصْقة نيكوتين

niece /niːs/ *n* **1** (daughter of your brother) ابْنة أَخٍ; (daughter of your sister) ابْنة أُخْتٍ **2** (daughter of your brother-in-law) ابْنة أَخِ الزَوْجِ \ الزَوْجةِ; (daughter of your sister-in-law) ابْنة أُخْتِ الزَوْجِ \ الزَوْجةِ

Niger /ˈnʌɪdʒə/ *pr n* النيجِر (f)

Nigeria /nʌɪˈdʒɪərɪə/ *pr n* نَيْجيريا

Nigerian /nʌɪˈdʒɪərɪən/ *n, adj* نَيْجيريّ

niggle /ˈnɪg(ə)l/ **A** *vt* ضايَقَ ‹*the reader, user*›

B *n* اعْتِراض بَسيط

niggling /ˈnɪglɪŋ/ *adj* ‹*doubt, suspicion*› بَسيط (وَمُسْتَمِرّ)

night /nʌɪt/ *n* **1** (part of day) لَيْل (لَيالٍ), لَيْلة (لَيالٍ, لَيْلات), مَساء (أَمْسِيّات, أَمْساء); **every ~** كُلَّ لَيْلةٍ; **every Thursday ~** مَساءَ كُلِّ ثُلاثاءَ; **he was awake all ~** كانَ مُسْتَيْقِظاً طَوالَ اللَيْلِ; **tomorrow ~** غَداً مَساءً; **they arrived in the middle of the ~** وَصَلوا في مُنْتَصَفِ اللَيْلِ; **he left last ~** غادَرَ اللَيْلةَ الماضِيةَ; **the ~ before last** اللَيْلة قَبلَ الماضِيةِ; **on Friday ~** مَساءَ الجُمْعةِ; **on Friday ~s** مَساءَ كُلِّ جُمْعةٍ; **on the ~ of the 9th October** مَساءَ التاسِعِ من أُكْتوبِرَ; **to travel/work at** *or* **by ~** سافَرَ \ عَمِلَ لَيْلاً; **to get an early ~** نامَ مُبَكِّراً; **to see Beirut by ~** رَأى بَيْروتَ لَيْلاً; **to work ~s** عَمِلَ بالفَتْرةِ اللَيْلِيّةِ; **to spend** *or* **stay the ~ in Rome** قَضى اللَيْلةَ في روما; **we stayed for three ~s** مَكَثْنا ثَلاثَ لَيالٍ **2** (evening) مَساء (أَمْسِيّات, أَمْساء), لَيْلة (لَيْلات); **it's his ~ out** هذه هي اللَيْلةُ الّتي يَخْرُجُ فيها; **it's my ~ off** هذه هي اللَيْلةُ الّتي أَسْتَريحُ فيها; **it was a ~ to remember** كانَتْ لَيْلةً لا تُنْسى; **the show will run for three ~s** سَيَسْتَمِرُّ العَرْضُ ثَلاثَ لَيالٍ **3** (darkness) ظَلام; **he left as ~ was falling** غادَرَ عِنْدَما بَدَأَ الظَلامُ يَحُلُّ **4** (in reservations) لَيْلة (لَيْلات, لَيالٍ); **we're booked for three ~s** حَجَزْنا ثَلاثَ لَيالٍ

nightcap /ˈnʌɪtkap/ *n* **1** (for head) طاقيّة نَوْمٍ **2** (drink) [مَشْروب روحيّ يُتَناوَلُ قبل النَوْمِ]; **to have a ~** تَناوَلَ مَشْروباً روحيًّا قبل النَوْمِ

nightclothes /ˈnʌɪtkləʊðz/ *n pl* مَلابِس نَوْمٍ

nightclub /ˈnʌɪtklʌb/ *n* مَلْهًى \ نادٍ لَيْليّ

nightclubbing /ˈnʌɪtklʌbɪŋ/ *n* ارْتِياد النَوادي اللَيْلِيّةِ; **to go ~** ارْتادَ النَوادِيَ اللَيْلِيّةَ

nightdress /ˈnʌɪtdrɛs/ *n* قَميص نَوْمٍ

nightfall /ˈnʌɪtfɔːl/ *n* حُلول اللَيْلِ \ الظَلامِ; **at ~** عند حُلولِ الظَلامِ

nightgown /ˈnʌɪtgaʊn/ *n* قَميص نَوْمٍ

nightie /ˈnʌɪti/ *n* (infml); ▸**nightdress**

nightingale /ˈnʌɪtɪŋˌgeɪl/ *n* عَنْدَليب (عَنادِلُ)

Night Journey *n* إسْراء ومِعْراج

nightlife /ˈnʌɪtlʌɪf/ *n* حَياة لَيْلِيّة

nightly /ˈnʌɪtli/ **A** *adj* ‹*performance, broadcast*› لَيْلي, في كُلِّ لَيْلةٍ

B *adv* ‹*to perform, be broadcast*› لَيْلِيًّا, كُلَّ لَيْلةٍ

nightmare /ˈnʌɪtmɛː/ *n* كابوس (كَوابيسُ)

night school *n* مَدْرَسة \ دُروس مَسائيّة \ لَيْليّة

night shelter *n* [مَأْوًى لَيْليّ للمُشَرَّدين]

night shift *n* **1** (workers) عُمّال النَوْبةِ اللَيْلِيّةِ **2** (period) مُناوَبة \ نَوْبة لَيْليّة

nightshirt /ˈnʌɪtʃəːt/ *n* [قَميص نَوْمٍ للرجالِ]

nightspot /ˈnʌɪtspɒt/ *n* (infml) مَرْقَص \ مَلْهًى \ نادٍ لَيْليّ

nightstick /ˈnʌɪtstɪk/ *n* هِراوة (هَراوى)

night-time /ˈnʌɪttʌɪm/ *n* ساعات \ وَقْت اللَيْلِ

nightwatchman /nʌɪtˈwɒtʃmən/ *n* (*pl* **-men**) حارِس لَيْليّ

nightwear /ˈnʌɪtwɛː/ *n* مَلابِس للنَوْمِ

nikah /nɪˈkɑː/ *n* نِكاح

nil /nɪl/ *n* **1** (nothing) لا شَيْءَ **2** (BrE Sport) صِفْر

Nile /nʌɪl/ *pr n* (**the Nile**) النيل; **the Blue ~** النيل الأَزْرَق **the White ~** النيل الأَبْيَض

nimble /ˈnɪmb(ə)l/ *adj* 1 *<fingers, feet>* خَفيف الحَرَكَةِ, ماهِر; *<person>* حاذِق (حُذّاق) 2 *<mind>* حادّ \ سَريع الذِهْنِ

nine /nʌɪn/ *n, adj* تِسْعة ▸ see also **five**

nineteen /nʌɪnˈtiːn/ *n, adj* تِسْعةَ عَشَرَ

nineteenth /nʌɪnˈtiːnθ/ **A** *n* 1 (in a series) تاسِعَ عَشَرَ 2 (fraction) جُزْء من تِسْعةَ عَشَرَ 3 (**the nineteenth**) (of a month) التاسِعَ عَشَرَ
B *adj <century, day>* تاسِعَ عَشَرَ
C *adv* في المَرْكَزِ التاسِعَ عَشَرَ

nineties /ˈnʌɪntiz/ *n pl* 1 (decade) (**the nineties**) التِسْعينات 2 (age) **to be in one's ~** كانَ في التِسْعينات (من عُمْرِه)

ninetieth /ˈnʌɪntiəθ/ **A** *n* 1 (**the ninetieth**) (in a series) التِسْعونَ 2 (fraction) جُزْء من تِسْعينَ
B *adj <birthday, anniversary>* التِسْعونَ
C *adv* في المَرْكَزِ التِسْعينَ

nine-to-five /nʌɪntəˈfʌɪv/ *adj <job, routine>* من الساعةِ التاسِعةِ إلى الخامِسةِ

ninety /ˈnʌɪnti/ *n* (*pl* **nineties**) (number) تِسْعونَ

ninth /nʌɪnθ/ **A** *n* 1 (in a series) تاسِع 2 (fraction) تُسْع 3 (**the ninth**) (of a month) التاسِع
B *adj <century, day>* تاسِع
C *adv* في المَرْكَزِ التاسِعِ

nip /nɪp/ **A** *vt* (**-pp-**) 1 (to bite) عَضّ (a; عَضّ, عَضيض) *<sb's hand, leg>* 2 (to pinch) قَرَص (u; قَرْص) *<sb's leg, arm>*
B *vi* (**-pp-**) 1 (to bite) «dogs, crabs» عَضّ (a; عَضّ, عَضيض), قَرَص (u; قَرْص) 2 (BrE) (infml) (to go) **to ~ into a shop** خَطَفَ رِجْلَهُ إلى مَتْجَرٍ; **to ~ in front of sb** مَضى مُسْرِعاً أمام شَخْصٍ; **we ~ped over to Aqaba for the weekend** ذَهَبْنا في زِيارةٍ خاطِفةٍ إلى العَقَبةِ في عُطْلةِ نِهاية الأُسْبوعِ
C *n* 1 (bite) عَضّة 2 (pinch) قَرْصة 3 (infml) (chill) **there's a ~ in the air** الجَوُّ فيهِ لَسْعةُ بَرْدٍ
(Idiom) **to be nip and tuck** (infml) (closely contested) كانَت المُنافَسةُ مُحْتَدِمةً; (close to a time limit) كانَ في سِباقٍ مع الزَمَنِ

(Phrasal verbs) **nip along** (to move quickly) أَسْرَعَ في المَسيرِ
• **nip off** 1 (infml) (to go away) ذَهَبَ مُسْرِعاً 2 **~ off [sth]**, **~ [sth] off** (to cut off) قَطَعَ [شَيْئاً] *<a flower, bud>*

nipple /ˈnɪp(ə)l/ *n* 1 (person's) حَلَمة 2 (on a bottle) حَلَمة

nippy /ˈnɪpi/ *adj* (**nippier, nippiest**) (infml) 1 (chilly) بارِد; **it's a bit ~** الجَوُّ بارِدٌ بَعْضَ الشَيْءِ 2 (quick) *<car, forward>* سَريع (سِراع)

niqab /nɪˈkɑːb/ *n* نِقاب (نُقُب, أَنْقِبة)

nit /nɪt/ *n* صُؤاب, بَيْض القَمْل (n coll; صِئْبان, صيبان)

nitpick /ˈnɪtpɪk/ *vi* (infml) [اِهْتَمَّ بالعُيوبِ الصَغيرةِ]

nitpicking /ˈnɪtpɪkɪŋ/ *n* (infml) [الاِهْتِمام بالعُيوبِ الصَغيرةِ \ التَفاصيل]

nitrate /ˈnʌɪtreɪt/ *n* نِتْرات

nitrogen /ˈnʌɪtrədʒ(ə)n/ *n* نِتْروجين

nitty-gritty /nɪtɪˈɡrɪti/ *n* (infml) (**the nitty-gritty**) التَفاصيل الجَوْهَريّة

NJ *abbr* = **New Jersey**

NM *abbr* = **New Mexico**

no /nəʊ/ **A** *determiner* 1 (none, not any) **to have ~ coat/job/money/shoes** لم يكُنْ لَدَيْهِ أيُّ مِعْطَفٍ \ وَظيفةٍ \ مالٍ \ حِذاءٍ; **there's ~ bread left** لم يَتَبَقَّ أَيُّ خُبْزٍ; **~ responsible person would do that** لن يَفْعَلَ ذلك أَيُّ شَخْصٍ مَسْؤولٍ; **~ two dresses are alike** لَيْسَ هُناكَ أَيُّ فُسْتانَيْنِ مُتَشابِهَيْنِ; **it's of ~ interest/importance** لَيس ذا أَهَمِّيةٍ; **with ~ help from anyone** بِدونِ مُساعَدةٍ من أَحَدٍ; **I have ~ wish to go there** لَيْسَتْ لَدَيَّ أَيُّ رَغْبةٍ في الذَهابِ إلى هُناكَ 2 (fml) (with gerunds) **there's ~ knowing what will happen** لَيْسَ من المُمْكِنِ مَعْرِفةُ ما سَيَحْدُثُ; **there's ~ denying that ...** لَيْسَ من المُمْكِنِ إنْكارُ أنّ ... 3 (in prohibitions) **~ smoking** مَمْنوعٌ التَدْخينُ; **~ parking** مَمْنوعٌ رَكْنُ السَيّاراتِ; **~ talking!** مَمْنوعٌ الكَلامُ! 4 (fml) (for emphasis) **she's ~ fool** هي لَيْسَتْ بِحَمْقاءَ; **this is ~ time to complain** لَيْسَ هذا وَقْتَ الشَكْوى; **this is ~ place to stop** لَيْسَ هذا مَكاناً يَصِحُّ التَوَقُّفُ فيه; **it was ~ easy task** لم تَكُنْ بالمُهِمّةِ السَهْلةِ; **at ~ time did I say that** لم أَقُلْ ذلك

أبداً **5** (hardly any) **in ~ time** في لَمحِ البَصَرِ; **it's ~ distance** هي مَسافةٌ لا تُذْكَر

B *excl* لا ,كَلاَّ; **'lend me £10'—'~, I won't'** 'أَقْرِضْني £10' — 'لا, لن أَفْعَلَ'; **~ thank you, ~ thanks** لا شُكْراً; **oh ~! – whatever next?** آه لا! – ماذا بَعْدُ؟; **'Is anything wrong?' - 'No'** 'هل من مُشْكِلةٍ؟' – 'لا'

C *adv* (in negation) **it's ~ further/easier/more interesting than …** لَيْسَ أَبْعَدَ \ أَسْهَلَ \ أَكْثَر إثارةً للاهْتِمامِ من …; **I ~ longer work there** لم أَعُدْ أَعْمَلُ هُناكَ; **~ later than Wednesday** الأَرْبِعاء على أَقْصى تَقْديرٍ; **it's ~ different from driving a car** لا يَخْتَلِفُ أَبداً عن قِيادةِ سَيّارةٍ; **~ fewer than 50 people** ما لا يَقِلُّ عن 50 شَخْصاً

D *n* (*pl* **noes**) (negative response) رَفْض; (negative vote) لا; **can't you give me a straight yes or ~?** أَلا يُمْكِنُكَ أَنْ تُعْطِيَني إجابةً صَريحةً بِنَعَمْ أو لا؟

No., no. *abbr* = **number** رَقْم (أَرْقام)

Nobel Prize /nəʊbɛl ˈprʌɪz/ *n* جائِزة نوبِل

nobility /nəʊˈbɪlɪti/ *n* **1** (of character) شَهامة ,نُبْل **2** (social class) **the ~** النُبَلاء

noble /ˈnəʊb(ə)l/ **A** *adj* ‹*cause, act*› نَبيل (نُبَلاءُ) ,كَريم (كِرام ,كُرَماءُ) ,شَهْم (شِهام)

B *n* نَبيل (نُبَلاءُ) ,شَريف (شُرَفاءُ ,أَشْراف)

nobleman /ˈnəʊb(ə)lmən/ *n* (*pl* **-men**) نَبيل (نُبَلاءُ) ,عَريق النَسَبِ, شَريف (شُرَفاءُ ,أَشْراف)

noblewoman /ˈnəʊb(ə)lwʊmən/ *n* (*pl* **-women**) نَبيلة

nobody /ˈnəʊbədi/ **A** *pron* لا أَحَدَ; **~ saw her** لم يَرَها أَحَدٌ; **~ but me** لا أَحَدَ سِوايَ; **there was ~ at home** لم يَكُنْ هُناكَ أَحَدٌ في المَنْزِلِ; **it's ~'s business but mine** لا شَأْنَ لأَحَدٍ بِهَذا سِوايَ

B *n* (*pl* **nobodies**) (infml) **to be a ~** كانَ شَخْصاً نَكِرةً; **she married a ~** تَزَوَّجَتْ شَخْصاً نَكِرةً; **I knew her when she was a ~** عَرَفْتُها عِنْدَما كانَتْ نَكِرةً

nocturnal /nɒkˈtəːn(ə)l/ *adj* ‹*animal, activity*› لَيْليّ

nod /nɒd/ **A** *vt* (**-dd-**) **to ~ one's head** أَوْمَأَ بِرَأْسِهِ; **he ~ded his approval** أَوْمَأَ بِرَأْسِهِ بالمُوافَقةِ

B *vi* (**-dd-**) **1** أَوْمَأَ بِرَأْسِهِ; **to ~ to sb** أَوْمَأَ بِرَأْسِهِ لِشَخْصٍ **2** (to sway) «flowers, treetops» تَمايَلَ **3** (to fall asleep) أَخَذَتْهُ غَفْوةٌ

C *n* إيماءة; **she gave him a ~** أَوْمَأَتْ لَهُ بِرَأْسِها

Idiom **to get the nod** (BrE) (infml) نالَ المُوافَقةَ

Phrasal verb **nod off** «children, driver» غَفا (u; غُفُو ,غَفْو), نامَ (a; نَوْم ,نِيام)

node /nəʊd/ *n* **1** (for lymph) عُقْدة (عُقَد) **2** (swelling) تَوَرُّم (تَوَرُّمات), وَرَم (أَوْرام) **3** (on plants) عُجْرة (عُجَر) **4** (in networks) عُقْدة (عُقَد)

nodule /ˈnɒdjuːl/ *n* **1** (in the body) وَرَم (أَوْرام) **2** (on roots) [عُقْدة صَغيرة]

no-fly zone /ˌnəʊˈflʌɪ ˌzəʊn/ *n* مِنْطَقة حَظْرِ الطَيَرانِ

no-go area /ˌnəʊˈgəʊ ɛːriə/ *n* مِنْطَقة مَحْظورة \ خَطِرة

no-good /ˌnəʊˈgʊd/ *adj before n* (infml) ‹*husband, sister*› تافِه (تَوافِهُ), عَديم القيمةِ ,خَسيس (أَخِسّاءُ)

no-hoper /nəʊˈhəʊpə/ *n* (infml) [شَخْص لا أَمَلَ فيه]

noise /nɔɪz/ *n* ضَوْضاء ,ضَجيج (f); **to make a ~** (individual sound) أَحْدَثَ صَوْتاً; (din) أَحْدَثَ ضَجّةً

noisily /ˈnɔɪzɪli/ *adv* ‹*to chatter, complain*› بِصَوْتٍ مُرْتَفِعٍ

noisy /ˈnɔɪzi/ *adj* (**noisier, noisiest**) ‹*neighbours, children*› كَثير الضَوْضاءِ \ صاحِب الضَجيجِ ,ضَجوج; **it's very ~ in here** هذا المَكانُ كَثيرُ الضَجّةِ \ ضاجٌّ

nomad /ˈnəʊmad/ *n* بَدَويّ (بَدْو), رَحّال (رُحَّل ,رُحّال)

no man's land /ˈnəʊ manz land/ *n* مِنْطَقة حَرامٍ \ مُتَنازَع عَلَيْها

nominal /ˈnɒmɪn(ə)l/ *adj* **1** (in name only) ‹*leader, government*› اسْميّ **2** (token) ‹*fee, charge*› رَمْزيّ ,ضَئيل (ضِئال ,ضُؤَلاءُ)

nominate /ˈnɒmɪneɪt/ *vt* **1** (to propose) رَشَّحَ ‹*a colleague, film, an actor*›; **to ~ sb for sth** رَشَّحَ شَخْصاً لِشَيْءٍ; **to be ~d for an award** رُشِّحَ لِجائِزةٍ **2** (to choose) اخْتارَ ,سَمّى ‹*a candidate, representative*›

nomination /nɒmɪˈneɪʃ(ə)n/ *n* **1** (proposal) تَرْشيح (تَرْشيحات) **2** (as a candidate) اخْتِيار **3** (appointment) تَعْيين (تَعْيينات)

nominative /ˈnɒmɪnətɪv/ **A** *adj* ‹*case, pronoun*› مَرْفوع

B *n* (**the nominative**) حالة الرَفْعِ

nominee /nɒmɪ'niː/ *n* 1 (person proposed) مُرَشَّح 2 (candidate) شَخْص مُعَيَّن 3 (person appointed) مُرَشَّح

non-addictive /nɒnə'dɪktɪv/ *adj* ‹*drug, substance*› غَيْر مُسَبِّبٍ للإدْمان

non-aggression /nɒnə'greʃ(ə)n/ *n* عَدَم اعْتِداءٍ

non-aggression pact *n* مُعاهَدة عَدَمِ اعْتِداءٍ

non-alcoholic /nɒnalkə'hɒlɪk/ *adj* ‹*drink, beer*› خالٍ من الكُحولِ

non-aligned /nɒnə'lʌɪnd/ *adj* ‹*nation, country*› غَيْر مُنْحازٍ

non-believer /nɒnbɪ'liːvə/ *n* كافِر, غَيْر مُؤْمِنٍ (كَفَرة, كُفّار)

nonchalant /'nɒnʃələnt/ *adj* ‹*attitude, shrug*› غَيْر مُكْتَرِثٍ \ مُبالٍ

non-commissioned officer /ˌnɒnkəˌmɪʃ(ə)nd 'ɒfɪsə/ *n* ضابِط صَفٍّ

non-committal /nɒnkə'mɪt(ə)l/ *adj* ‹*reply, stance*› غَيْر مُلْتَزِمٍ

non-compliance /nɒnkəm'plʌɪəns/ *n* عدم امْتِثالٍ

nonconformist /nɒnkən'fɔːmɪst/ *adj* 1 ‹*minister, church*› غَيْر مُنْشَقّ, [مُنْشَقّ عن الكَنيسة الإنْكليزيّةِ] 2 ‹*attitude, views*› مُلْتَزِمٍ \ مُتَمَسِّكٍ بالتَقاليدِ

non-cooperation /nɒnkəʊɒpə'reɪʃ(ə)n/ *n* عَدَم تعاوُنٍ

non-denominational /nɒndɪnɒmɪ'neɪʃ(ə)n(ə)l/ *adj* ‹*school, church*› غَيْر طائِفِيٍّ

nondescript /'nɒndɪskrɪpt/ *adj* ‹*building*› غَيْر مُمَيِّزٍ; ‹*clothes, person*› غَيْر مُتَمَيِّزٍ, عاديّ

non-disclosure agreement /nɒndɪ'skləʊʒə əˌgriːmənt/ *n* اتِّفاقيّة عَدَمِ الإفْصاح, اتِّفاقيّة المُحافَظة على السرّيّة

none /nʌn/ **A** *pron* 1 (not any, not one) لا شَيْءَ, لا أَحَد; ~ of us/you/them لا أَحَدَ مِنّا \ مِنْكُمْ \ مِنْهُمْ; ~ of the chairs/houses وَلا واحِدَ من الكَراسيّ \ البُيوتِ; 'have you any pens?'—'~ at all' 'هَل لَدَيْكَ أَيُّ أَقْلامٍ؟' — 'لا، البَتَّة'; ~ was more beautiful/interesting than ... لا أَحَدَ \ شَيْءَ كانَ أَجْمَلَ \ أَكْثَر إثارةً للاهْتِمامِ من ...; he saw three dogs, ~ of which was black رَأى ثَلاثةَ كِلابٍ، وَلَمْ يَكُنْ أَيٌّ مِنْهُمْ أَسْوَدَ; he waited for some sign of anger but saw ~ انْتَظَرَ أنْ يَرى عَلامةَ غَضَبٍ وَلَكِنَّهُ لم يَرَ شَيْئاً; her brother has four children, but she has ~ لَدى أخيها أَرْبَعةُ أَطْفالٍ، أَمّا هي فَلَيْسَ لَدَيْها أَطْفالٌ 2 (not any, no part) ~ of the wine/milk ... كُلُّ الخَمْرِ \ الحَليبِ لَيْسَ ... ; ~ of the cheese got eaten لم يُؤْكَل الجُبْنُ إطْلاقاً; 'is there any money left?'—'~ at all' 'هَل تَبَقّى أيُّ مالٍ؟' — 'لا شَيْءَ على الإطْلاقِ'; 'did you have any difficulty?'—'~ whatsoever *or* at all' 'هَل وَجَدْتَ أيَّ صُعوبةٍ؟' — 'لا، مُطْلَقاً'; we have ~ لَيْسَ لَدَيْنا أَيُّ شَيْءٍ; there's ~ left لم يَتَبَقَّ شَيْءٌ; ~ of it was true/of any interest لم يَكُنْ أيٌّ مِنهُ صَحيحاً \ ذا أَهَمِّيّةٍ; he was having ~ of it لم يَحْصُل على أيٍّ مِنْهُ; some money is better than ~ بَعْضُ المالِ أَفْضَلُ من لا شَيْءَ 3 (nobody, not one person) لا أَحَد; ~ can sing so well as her لا أَحَدَ يَسْتَطيعُ أنْ يُغَنّيَ بِمِثْلِ بَراعَتِها; there's ~ so clever/old as Jane لَيسَ هُناكَ أَحَدٌ في مِثْلِ ذَكاءِ \ سِنّ جين; I waited but ~ came انْتَظَرْتُ وَلَكِنْ لم يَأْتِ أَحَدٌ; if you need a lawyer, there's ~ better than George إذا احْتَجْتَ مُحامِياً، فَلَيْسَ هُناكَ أَحَدٌ أَفْضَلُ من جورج; ~ but him/you لا أَحَدَ سِواهُ \ سِواكَ; I told ~ but him/you لم أُخْبِرْ أَحَداً سِواهُ \ سِواكَ; ~ but a fool would do it لا يَفْعَلُ هذا إلا أَحْمَقُ; it was ~ other than Peter/the prime minister كانَ بيتر \ رَئيسَ الوُزَراءِ بِنَفْسِه \ بعَيْنِه; ~ can match (himself) لا يَسْتَطيعُ أَحَدٌ أنْ يُضاهِيَ مَظْهَرَها her looks 4 (on form, questionnaire) لا يوجَدُ; in the box headed 'Dependants' he wrote '~' في مُرَبَّعِ 'المُعالونَ' كَتَبَ 'لا يوجَدُ'; I see you answered '~' to the question on allergies أرى أنَّكَ أَجَبْتَ بـ 'لا يوجَدُ' على السُّؤالِ المُتَعَلِّقِ بالحَسّاسيّةِ

B *adv* (not, not at all) it was ~ too easy/pleasant لم يَكُنْ سَهلاً \ سارًّا على الإطْلاقِ; I was ~ too sure/happy that ... لم أَكُنْ واثِقاً \ سَعيداً جِدًّا أنّ ...; 'I'm here!'—'and ~ too soon!' 'أنا هُنا!' — 'وَفي آخِرِ لَحْظةٍ!'; he was ~ the worse for the experience لم تُقَلِّل الخِبْرةُ من شَأْنِهِ; the play is long, but ~ the worse for that المَسْرَحيّةُ طَويلةٌ، وَلَكِنَّ ذلك لا يُقَلِّلُ من قيمَتِها

nonentity /nɒ'nɛntɪti/ *n* (*pl* **nonentities**) شَخْص عَديم القيمةِ

nonessentials /nɒnɪ'senʃ(ə)lz/ *n pl* أَشْياء غَيْر, كَماليّات ضَروريّةٍ

nonetheless /nʌnðə'lɛs/ *adv* مع ذلك, بالرَغْمِ من ذلك

non-existent /nɒnɪɡ'zɪst(ə)nt/ *adj* ‹*threat, address*› غَيْر مَعْدوم, غَيْر مَوْجودٍ

non-fiction /nɒn'fɪkʃ(ə)n/ *n* نَثْر غَيْر رِوائيٍّ \ قَصَصيٍّ

non-infectious /nɒnɪn'fɛkʃəs/ *adj* ‹*disease, inflammation*› غَيْر مَعْدٍ

non-invasive /nɒnɪn'veɪsɪv/ *adj* (Med) ‹*surgery, method*› غَيْر جِراحيّ

non-iron /nɒn'ʌɪən/ *adj* ‹*shirt, fabric*› [لا يَحْتاجُ للكَيِّ]

no-nonsense /nəʊ'nɒns(ə)ns/ *adj* ‹*approach, coach*› جادّ

nonplussed /nɒn'plʌst/ *adj* ‹*expression, silence*› يَنُمُّ عن الحيرة; ‹*person*› مُتَحَيِّر, مَذْهول, مُرْتَبِك

non-political /nɒnpə'lɪtɪk(ə)l/ *adj* ‹*organisation, appointment*› غَيْر سِياسيٍّ

non-profit /nɒn'prɒfɪt/, **non-profitmaking** /nɒn'prɒfɪtmeɪkɪŋ/ *adj before n* (BrE) ‹*organization*› غَير رِبْحيٍّ \ هادِفٍ للرِبْحِ

non-resident /nɒn'rɛsɪd(ə)nt/ *n* غَيْر مُقيمٍ

nonsense /'nɒns(ə)ns/ *n* **1▸** (rubbish) كَلام فارِغ \ سَخيف, تَفاهة, هُراء; **don't talk ~!** كَفاكَ كَلاماً فارِغاً! **2▸** (foolishness) سُخْف

nonsensical /nɒn'sɛnsɪk(ə)l/ *adj* ‹*idea, argument*› غَيْر مَعْقولٍ, سَخيف

non-smoker /nɒn'sməʊkə/ *n* غَيْر مُدَخِّنٍ

non-smoking /nɒn'sməʊkɪŋ/ *adj* ‹*area, pub*› مَمْنوعٌ التَدْخينُ فيه

non-starter /nɒn'stɑːtə/ *n* (infml) **to be a ~** كانَ مَيْؤوساً من نَجاحِهِ

non-stick /nɒn'stɪk/ *adj* ‹*pan, coating*› غَيْر لاصِقٍ

non-stop /nɒn'stɒp/ **A** *adj* **1▸** (in travel) ‹*flight, train*› مُباشِر, بِدونِ تَوَقُّفٍ **2▸** (continuous) ‹*coverage, music*› مُتَواصِل

B *adv* **1▸** ‹*to work*› (continuously) على نَحْوٍ, بِلا تَوَقُّفٍ, مُتَواصِلٍ **2▸** (in travel) ‹*to fly*› بِلا \ بِدونِ تَوَقُّفٍ

non-taxable /nɒn'taksab(ə)l/ *adj* ‹*income, allowance*› مُعْفًى من, غَيْر خاضِعٍ للضَريبةِ, الضَرائِبِ

noodles /'nuːd(ə)lz/ *n pl* نودِلْز, شَرائِح المَعْكَرونةِ, شَعْرِيّة

nook /nʊk/ *n* مَكان مُنْعَزِل, خَلْوة

Idiom **every nook and cranny** جَميع الأَرْجاءِ

noon /nuːn/ *n* الثانِيَة عَشْرة ظُهْراً, مُنْتَصف النَهارِ, ظَهيرة; **at ~** ظُهْراً, عند الظَهيرةِ; **he works morning, ~ and night** يَعْمَلُ من الصَباحِ حتّى اللَيْلِ

no one, no-one *pron* ▸ **nobody** A

noose /nuːs/ *n* أُحْبولة (أَحابيلُ), أُنْشوطة (أَناشيطُ)

nor /nɔː, nə/ *conj* وَلا; **~ do I** وَلا أنا ▸ see also **neither**

Nordic /'nɔːdɪk/ *adj* [من دُوَلِ شِمالِ أوروبّا]

Nordic skiing *n* التَزَلُّج الشماليّ

norm /nɔːm/ *n* مُعَدَّل عاديّ

normal /'nɔːm(ə)l/ **A** *adj* ‹*life, level, time*› عاديّ, مُعْتاد

B *n* عاديّ, طَبيعيّ; **when things get back to ~** عِنْدَما تَعودُ الأَوْضاعُ إلى حالَتِها الطَبيعيّةِ

normality /nɔː'malɪti/ *n* اعْتِياديّ \ وَضْع طَبيعيّ

normalize, -ise (BrE) /'nɔːməlʌɪz/ **A** *vt* أعادَ إلى, جَعَلَ طَبيعيًّا ‹*a relationship, situation*› الوَضْع الطَبيعيّ

B *vi* «conditions, relations» عادَ إلى طَبيعَتِه

normally /'nɔːm(ə)li/ *adv* ‹*to use, do*› بِشَكْلٍ عاديٍّ, عادةً

normative /'nɔːmətɪv/ *adj* (fml) ‹*data, theory*› مِقْياسيّ, مِعْياريّ

north /nɔːθ/ **A** *n* **1▸** (compass direction) شَمال; **the wind is blowing from the ~** تَهُبُّ الريحُ من الشمالِ; **a village to the ~ of Hebron** قَرْية شَمالَ الخَليلِ **2▸** (**the North**) (part of the world, a country) الشَمال; **in the ~ of Egypt** في شَمالِ مِصْرَ

3▸ (**the North**) (in US history) وِلايات الشَمالِ (في الوِلاياتِ المُتَّحِدةِ إبّانَ الحَرْبِ الأَهْليّةِ)

B *adj* **1▸** ‹*coast, bank, wall*› شَماليّ; **the ~ face of the Eiger** الواجِهة الشَماليّة لِجَبَلِ إيجر **2▸** (from the north) ‹*wind*› شَماليّ

C *adv* **1▸** (to the north) ‹*to go, drive, sail*› في اتِّجاهِ, شَمالاً الشَمالِ; **to travel due ~** سافَرَ بِاتِّجاهِ الشَمالِ **2▸** (on the northern side) ‹*to lie, live*› شَمالاً; **they live ~ of the river** يَعيشونَ شَمالَ النَهْرِ

North Africa *pr n* شَمال إفْريقِيا

North African *n, adj* شَمال إفْريقيّ

North America *pr n* شَمال أَمْريكا

North American *n, adj* شَمال أَمْريكيّ

northbound /ˈnɔːθbaʊnd/ *adj* ‹*lane, train*› مُتَّجِه شَمالاً

North Carolina *pr n* كارولايْنا الشَماليّة

North Carolinian *pr n, adj* [(شَخْص) من كارولايْنا الشَماليَّة]

North Dakota *pr n* داكوتا الشَماليّة

North Dakotan *pr n, adj* [(شَخْص) من داكوتا الشَماليَّة]

north-east /nɔːθˈiːst/ **A** *n* **1** (compass direction) شَمال شَرْقيّ **2** (**the North East**) (of a country) الشَمال الشَرْقيّ

B *adj* ‹*coast, wind*› شَماليّ شَرْقيّ

C *adv* ‹*to face, move*› نحو \ بِاتِّجاهِ الشَمالِ الشَرْقيّ

north-easterly /nɔːθˈiːst(ə)li/ *adj* ‹*direction, wind*› شَماليّ شَرْقيّ

north-eastern /nɔːθˈiːst(ə)n/ *adj* ‹*region, city*› شَماليّ شَرْقيّ

northerly /ˈnɔːðəli/ **A** *adj* ‹*direction, route, wind*› شَماليّ

B *n* (*pl* **northerlies**) رِياح شَماليّة

northern /ˈnɔːð(ə)n/ *adj* ‹*region, accent*› شَماليّ; **~ Europe** شَمال أوروبّا

Northern Ireland *pr n* إيرْلَنْدا الشَماليّة

north-facing /ˈnɔːθfeɪsɪŋ/ *adj* ‹*window, balcony, room*› شَماليّ

North Korea *pr n* كورِيا الشَماليّة

North Korean *n, adj* كوريّ شَماليّ

North Pole *pr n* (**the North Pole**) القُطْب الشَماليّ

North Sea *pr n* (**the North Sea**) بَحْر الشَمال

North Star *n* (**the North Star**) النَجْم القُطْبيّ

northward /ˈnɔːθwəd/ **A** *adj* ‹*migration, journey*› مُتَّجِه شَمالاً

B *adv* (also **northwards** BrE) ‹*to travel, move*› نحو الشَمالِ ,شَمالاً

north-west /nɔːθˈwɛst/ **A** *n* **1** (compass direction) شَمال غَرْبيّ **2** (**the North West**) (of a country) الشَمال الغَرْبيّ

B *adj* ‹*coast, wind*› شَماليّ غَرْبيّ

C *adv* ‹*to face, move*› نحو \ بِاتِّجاهِ الشَمالِ الغَرْبيّ

north-westerly /nɔːθˈwɛst(ə)li/ *adj* ‹*direction, wind*› شَماليّ غَرْبيّ

north-western /nɔːθˈwɛst(ə)n/ *adj* ‹*region, city*› شَماليّ غَرْبيّ

Norway /ˈnɔːweɪ/ *pr n* النُرْويج (f)

Norwegian /nɔːˈwiːdʒ(ə)n/ **A** *adj* ‹*government, food*› نُرْويجيّ

B *n* **1** (citizen) نُرْويجيّ **2** (language) (اللُغة) النُرْويجيّة

nose /nəʊz/ **A** *n* **1** (person's) أَنْف (أُنوف); **to speak through one's ~** تَحَدَّثَ من أَنْفِه **2** (of a plane, boat, car) مُقَدِّمة; **the traffic was ~ to tail** كانَ المُرورُ شَديدَ الزِحامِ **3** (of wine) رائِحة ,شَذاً (رَوائِحُ) **4** (infml) (instinct) **to have a ~ for a good story/bargain** كانَتْ لَدَيْه القُدْرةُ على اكْتِشافِ قِصّةٍ \ صَفْقةٍ جَيِّدةٍ

B *vt* **to ~ one's way forwards** تَحَسَّسَ طَريقَهُ

C *vi* **to ~ into/out of the narrow street** سارَ بِحَذَرٍ وَهُوَ يَدْخُلُ في \ يَخْرُجُ من الشارِعِ الضَيِّقِ; **the boat ~d into/out of the harbour** سارَ القارِبُ بِحَذَرٍ وَهُوَ يَدْخُلُ في \ يَخْرُجُ من المَرْفَأ

Idioms **(right) under sb's nose** (infml) على مَرْأًى وَمَسْمَعٍ من شَخْصٍ; **to get up sb's nose** (infml) عَكَّرَ مِزاجَ شَخْصٍ; **to lead sb by the nose** جَعَلَ شَخْصاً طَوْعَ أَمْرِهِ; **to look down one's nose at sb/sth** نَظَرَ إلى شَخْصٍ \ شَيْءٍ بِازْدِراءٍ; **to pay through the nose for sth** (infml) دَفَعَ ثَمَناً باهِظاً في شَيْءٍ; **to turn one's nose up at sth** (infml) لم يَكْتَرِثْ بِشَيْءٍ

Phrasal verbs **nose about, nose around** «journalists, visitors» تَطَفَّلَ

• **nose out**: **~ out** [**sth**], **~** [**sth**] **out** (to discover) اكْتَشَفَ [شَيْئاً] ‹*the facts, truth, a secret*›; **the investigators ~d out the truth** اكْتَشَفَ المُحَقِّقونَ الحَقيقةَ

nosebleed /ˈnəʊzbliːd/ *n* نَزيف أَنْفيّ \ الأَنْفِ; **to have a ~** عانى من نَزيفٍ بالأَنْفِ

nosedive /ˈnəʊzdaɪv/ **A** *n* **1** (of planes) هُبوط رَأْسيّ \ هُبوط عَموديّ; **to go into a ~** هَبَطَ عَموديًّا **2** (worsening) انْخِفاض مُفاجِئ; **to take a ~** انْخَفَضَ فَجْأةً

B *vi* **1** «aircraft» هَبَطَ عَموديًّا **2** (to worsen) «stock prices, confidence» انْخَفَضَ \ هَبَطَ فَجْأةً

nose ring *n* **1** (for an animal) حَلَقة أَنْفٍ **2** (for a person) حَلَقة \ خاتَم أَنْفٍ

nosey /ˈnəʊzi/ *adj* (infml) ▸ **nosy**

nostalgia /nɒˈstaldʒə/ *n* الحَنين إلى الماضي

nostalgic /nɒˈstaldʒɪk/ *adj* ‹*memory, trip*› مُثير للذِكْرَياتِ; ‹*feeling*› الحَنينِ إلى الماضي

nostril /ˈnɒstrəl/ *n* فَتْحة أَنْفٍ ,(مَناخِرُ) مِنْخَر

nosy /ˈnəʊzi/ *adj* (**nosier**, **nosiest**) (infml) ‹*neighbour, reporter*› مُتَطَفِّل ,فُضوليّ

not /nɒt/ **A** *adv* **1** (negating verb present tense) لا; (past tense) لَمْ; (future tense) لَنْ; **she isn't at home** لَيْسَتْ في البَيْتِ; **they didn't like it** لَمْ يُعْجِبْهُمْ; **we won't need a car** لَنْ نَحْتاجَ إلى سَيّارةٍ; **he's ~ coming** لَنْ يَأْتِيَ **2** (replacing word, clause, sentence etc) **'is he angry?'—'I hope ~'** 'هل هو غاضِبٌ؟' — 'آمُلُ أَلاّ يَكونَ كَذلِكَ'; **'is she married?'—'I think ~'** 'هل هي مُتَزَوِّجةٌ؟' — 'لا أَظُنُّ ذلك'; **'are you coming?' — 'I'm afraid ~'** 'هل أَنْتَ قادِمٌ؟' — 'للأَسَفِ لا'; **'can she come too?' — 'certainly ~!'** 'هل يُمْكِنُها أَنْ تَأْتِيَ هي أَيْضاً؟' — 'بالتَأْكيدِ لا!'; **do you know whether he's coming or ~?** هل تَعْلَمُ ما إذا كانَ سَيأْتي أم لا؟; **whether it rains or ~, I'm going** سَواءٌ أَمْطَرَتْ أم لَمْ تُمْطِرْ، فَأَنا ذاهِبٌ **3** (in contrasts) لَيْسَ (no imperf); **they live in caves, ~ in houses, they live ~ in houses, but in caves** يَعيشونَ في كُهوفٍ، ولَيْسَ في بُيوتٍ; **he's ~ so much aggressive as assertive** هو لَيْسَ عُدْوانِيًّا بِقَدْرِ ما هو حازِمٌ **4** (in suggestions) **hadn't we better pay the bill?** أَلَمْ يَكُنْ من الأَفْضَلِ أَنْ نَدْفَعَ الفاتورةَ؟; **couldn't we tell them later?** أَلَيْسَ بِوُسْعِنا أَنْ نُخْبِرَهُمْ فيما بَعْدُ؟; **why ~ do it now?, why don't we do it now?** لِمَ لا نَفْعَلُهُ الآنَ؟ **5** (fml) (less than) أَقَلّ من; **it's ~ three miles/hours from here** يَقَعُ على بُعْدِ أَقَلَّ من ثَلاثةِ أَمْيالٍ \ ثَلاثِ ساعاتٍ من هُنا **6** (to emphasize opposite) **it's ~ impossible/cheap** لَيْسَ مُسْتَحيلاً \ رَخيصاً; **it's ~ without its problems** هو لَيْسَ بِلا مَشاكِلَ; **you're ~ far wrong** أَنْتَ لَسْتَ بَعيداً عن الصَوابِ **7** (with all, every) **~ all doctors agree, ~ every doctor agrees** لَيْسَ كُلُّ الأَطِبّاءِ مُتَّفِقينَ على ذلك; **~ everyone likes it** لَيْسَ كُلُّ الناسِ يُعْجِبُهُمْ هذا; **it's ~ everyone that can speak several foreign languages** لَيْسَ بِمَقْدورِ كُلِّ واحِدٍ أَنْ يَتَحَدَّثَ عِدّةَ لُغاتٍ أَجْنَبِيّةٍ; **it's ~ every day that ...** لا يَحْدُثُ كُلَّ يَوْمٍ أَنْ ... **8** (with a, one) **~ a** *or* **one** لا أَحَدَ \ شَيْءَ; **~ a sound was heard** لم يُسْمَعْ أَيُّ صَوْتٍ; **~ one** *or* **a single person knew** لم يَعْلَمْ أَحَدٌ; **~ all the poems are serious** لَيْسَتْ كُلُّ القَصائِدِ جادّةً

B (**not at all**) *adv phr* **1** (intensifying negativity) على الإِطْلاقِ; **it's ~ at all certain** لَيْسَ مُؤَكَّداً على الإِطْلاقِ; **it's ~ at all a foregone conclusion** لَيْسَتْ نَتيجةً حَتْمِيّةً على الإِطْلاقِ **2** (fml) (acknowledging thanks) **~ at all!** عَفْواً!, العَفْوَ!; **'thank you very much!' — '~ at all!'** 'أَشْكُرُكَ شُكْراً جَزيلاً!' — 'العَفْوَ!'

C (**not that**) *conj phr* **it's ~ that he hasn't been helpful/friendly** لَيْسَ المَوْضوعُ أَنَّهُ لم يَكُنْ مُفيداً \ وَدوداً; **'was anyone late?' — '~ that I know of'** 'هل تَأَخَّرَ أَحَدٌ؟' — 'لَيْسَ على حَدِّ عِلْمي'

notable /ˈnəʊtəb(ə)l/ *adj* ‹*exception, success*› بارِز ,مَلْحوظ ‹*public figure*› (مَشاهيرُ) مَشْهور ,مَرْموق

notably /ˈnəʊtəbli/ *adv* **1** (markedly) بِصورةٍ مَلْحوظةٍ **2** (in particular) لا سِيَّما ,خاصّةً

notarize, **-ise** (BrE) /ˈnəʊtərʌɪz/ *vt* (على) صَدَّقَ ,وَثَّقَ ‹*a document, copy*›

notary /ˈnəʊt(ə)ri/ *n* (also **notary public**) كاتِب ,مُوَثِّق عُقودٍ مُوَثِّق عامّ ,العَدْل

notation /nəʊˈteɪʃ(ə)n/ *n* تَدْوين

notch /nɒtʃ/ *n* **1** (indentation) (ثُلوم) ثَلْم ,(حُزوز) حَزّ **2** (point, degree) (نِقاط ,نُقَط) نُقْطة ,دَرَجة; **my opinion of her went up a ~** تَحَسَّنَ رَأْيي فيها قَليلاً

Phrasal verb **notch up** (infml): **~ up [sth]** أَحْرَزَ [شَيْئاً] ‹*points, wins*›

note /nəʊt/ **A** *n* **1** (written record) مُلاحَظة مَكْتوبة ,مُذَكِّرة; **to take ~s** دَوَّنَ مُلاحَظاتٍ; **to make a ~ of the date/of sb's address** دَوَّنَ مُلاحَظةً بالتاريخِ \ بِعُنْوانِ شَخْصٍ; **to compare ~s** تَبادَلَ الخِبْراتِ **2** (short letter) رِسالة قَصيرة **3** (annotation) مَلْحوظة; **see ~ below** أُنْظُرِ المَلْحوظةَ أَدْناه; **translator's ~** مَلْحوظة المُتَرْجِمِ **4** (tone) نَبْرة; **to strike the wrong ~** ضَرَبَ على الوَتَرِ الخَطَأِ; **to hit the right ~** ضَرَبَ على الوَتَرِ الصَحيحِ; **on a less serious ~** على صَعيدٍ أَقَلَّ خُطورةٍ **5** (in music) (نَغَمات) نَغْمة ,(نُوَت) نوتة; **a high/low ~** نَغْمة عالِية \ مُنْخَفِضة **6** (banknote) وَرَقة نَقْدِيّة; **a £20 ~** وَرَقة نَقْدِيّة فِئة £20

B (**of note**) *adj phr* ‹*scientist, development, author*› ذو أَهَمِّيّةٍ ,مُهِمّ

C *vt* **1** (to notice) لاحَظَ ‹*a comment, similarity, an increase*›; **it should be ~d that ...** ... تَجدُرُ الإشارةُ إلى أنّ; **I have ~d your remarks** فهِمْتُ مُلاحَظاتِكَ **2** (to write down) دَوَّنَ مُلاحَظةً ب ‹*the date, number, symptoms*›; **~ the date in your diary** دَوِّن التاريخَ في مُفَكِّرَتِكَ

D (**noted**) *adj* ‹*artist, intellectual, criminal*› مَشْهور (مَشاهيرُ); **to be ~d for one's tact/wit** كانَ مَعْروفاً بِلَباقَتِهِ \ بِظُرْفِهِ

(Phrasal verb) **note down**: **~ down [sth], ~ [sth] down** دَوَّنَ [شَيْئاً] ‹*an idea, the details*›

notebook /ˈnəʊtbʊk/ *n* **1** (booklet) دَفْتَر (دَفاتِرُ), مُذَكِّرة **2** (also **notebook computer**) كُمْبيوتر مَحْمول

noted /ˈnəʊtɪd/ *adj* ‹*scholar, author*› مَشْهور (مَشاهيرُ), مَعْروف

notepad /ˈnəʊtpad/ *n* مُفَكِّرة, دَفْتَر مُلاحَظاتٍ

notepaper /ˈnəʊtpeɪpə/ *n* وَرَق رَسائِل

noteworthy /ˈnəʊtwəːði/ *adj* ‹*feature, achievement*› جَدير بالمُلاحَظةِ \ بالانْتِباهِ

nothing /ˈnʌθɪŋ/ **A** *pron* **1** (no item, event, idea) لا شَيْءَ; **she said ~** لم تَقُلْ شَيْئاً; **we've had ~ to eat** لم يَكُنْ لَدَيْنا شَيْءٌ نَأْكُلُهُ; **I know ~ about it** لا أَعْلَمُ شَيْئاً عَنْهُ; **there's ~ in the fridge** لا يوجَدُ شَيْءٌ في الثَلاّجةِ; **there's ~ to drink** لَيْسَ هُناكَ شَيْءٌ يُشْرَبُ; **~ happened** لم يَحْدُثْ شَيْءٌ; **can ~ be done to help?** أَلَيْسَ هُناكَ شَيْءٌ يُمكِنُ فِعْلُهُ للمُساعَدةِ؟; **I have ~ to wear** لَيْسَ لَدَيَّ شَيْءٌ أَرْتَديهِ; **you did ~ at all to stop them** أَنْتَ لم تَفعَلْ شَيْئاً على الإطْلاقِ لإيقافِهِمْ; **she had ~ much to say** لم يَكُنْ لَدَيْها الكَثيرُ لِتَقولَهُ; **we ask for ~ more** لا نَطْلُبُ أَكْثَرَ من ذلك; **is there ~ more you can do?** أَلا يوجَدُ ما يُمْكِنُكَ القِيامُ بِهِ أَكْثَرَ من ذلك؟; **she's just a friend, ~ more** هي مُجَرَّدُ صَديقةٍ، لا أَكْثَرَ; **~ else matters** لا شَيْءَ آخَرَ يُهِمُّ; **to have ~ against sb/sth** لم يَكُنْ لَدَيْهِ أَيُّ شَيْءٍ ضِدّ شَخْصٍ \ شَيْءٍ; **to have ~ to do with sb/sth** لم يَكُنْ لَهُ أَيُّ عَلاقةٍ بِشَخْصٍ \ بِشَيْءٍ; **he had ~ to do with the fraud** لم يَكُنْ لَهُ عَلاقةٌ بِعَمَلِيّةِ الاحْتِيالِ; **that's got ~ to do with it!** لَيْسَ لِذلِكَ عَلاقةٌ بِهِ!; **he wants ~ to do with us** لا يُريدُ أَنْ تَرْبِطَهُ أَيُّ عَلاقةٍ بِنا; **to have ~ on** (no clothes) لم يَكُنْ يَرْتَدي أَيَّ مَلابِسَ; (no commitments) لم يَكُنْ لَدَيْهِ أَيُّ ارْتِباطاتٍ **2** (in significance) لا شَيْءَ, شَيْءٌ لا يُذْكَرُ; **a fuss about ~** ضَجّة حول لا شَيْءَ; **to get upset over ~** انْزَعَجَ بِلا سَبَبٍ; **to count for ~** لم يُعْتَدَّ بِهِ; **our hopes came to ~** خابَتْ آمالُنا; **he means ~ to me** هو لا يَعْني شَيْئاً بالنِسْبةِ لي; **the name meant ~ to him** لم يَعْنِ الاسْمُ شَيْئاً لَهُ; **he thinks ~ of driving there and back in a day** يَظُنُّ أنّ القِيادةَ إلى هُناكَ والعَوْدةَ في نَفْسِ اليَوْمِ أَمْرٌ هَيِّنٌ; **there's ~ to it!** لا صُعوبةَ فيهِ! **3** (very little) لا شَيْءَ يُذْكَرُ; **it cost next to ~** لم يُكَلِّفْ شَيْئاً يُذْكَرُ; **it's money for ~** هو رِبْحٌ سَهْلٌ; **not for ~ is he known as ...** هُناكَ سَبَبٌ وَجيهٌ لِكَوْنِهِ مَعْروفاً بـ ... **4** (indicating absence) **there's ~ new to report** لَيْسَ هُناكَ شَيْءٌ جَديدٌ للإبْلاغِ عَنْهُ; **there's ~ unusual about it** لا يوجَدُ شَيْءٌ غَيْرُ عاديٍّ بِخُصوصِهِ; **I hope it's ~ serious** آمُلُ أَلاّ يَكونَ شَيْئاً خَطيراً **5** (setting up comparisons) **it's ~ like that at all!** هو لا شَيْءَ من هذا القَبيلِ على الإطْلاقِ!; **there's ~ like it!** لَيْسَ لَهُ مَثيلٌ!; **it seems easy/difficult but it's ~ of the kind** يَبْدو سَهْلاً \ صَعْباً وَلَكِنَّهُ لَيْسَ شَيْئاً من هذا القَبيلِ; **there's ~ more ridiculous than that** لَيْسَ هُناكَ أَسْخَفُ من ذلك; **I can think of ~ worse** لا أَسْتَطيعُ أنْ أُفَكِّرَ في شَيْءٍ أَسْوَأَ; **detested by his colleagues to say ~ of the students** مَكْروه من زُمَلائِهِ ناهيكَ عن طُلاّبِهِ **6** (no element, part) **to know ~ of the plan/proposal** لم يَعْرِفْ شَيْئاً عن الخُطّةِ \ الاقْتِراحِ; **he knows ~ of what is involved** لا يَعْرِفُ شَيْئاً عَمّا يَنْطَوي عَلَيْهِ الأَمْرُ; **we heard ~ of what was said** لم نَسْمَعْ شَيْئاً مِمّا قيلَ **7** (no truth, value, use) **there's ~ in it** لَيْسَ لَهُ أَساسٌ من الصِحّةِ; **there's ~ in it for me** لا مَصْلَحةَ لي فيهِ

B *n* عَدَم

C *adv* **1** (in no way) **to be ~ like as important/difficult** لم يَكُنْ على أَيِّ دَرَجةٍ من الأَهَمّيّةِ \ الصُعوبةِ; **it's ~ like enough!** لَيْسَ كافِياً على الإطْلاقِ!; **the portrait looks ~ like him** لا تُشْبِهُهُ الصورةُ لا من قَريبٍ ولا من بَعيدٍ; **the city is ~ like what it was** المَدينةُ لَيْسَتْ كَما كانَتْ على الإطْلاقِ **2** (emphatic: totally, only) **it's ~ short of brilliant/disgraceful** أَقَلُّ ما يُقالُ عَنْهُ أَنَّهُ رائِعٌ \ مُشينٌ; **~ short of a miracle can save them** لن يُنْقِذَهُمْ أَيُّ شَيْءٍ إلاّ مُعْجِزةً **3** (emphatic: decidedly) **she's ~ if not original in her dress** هي لا تَرْتَدي سِوى المَلابِسِ الأَصْليّةِ

D (**nothing but**) *adv phr* **it's caused me ~ but trouble** لم يُسَبِّبْ لي سِوى المَشاكِلِ; **they've done ~ but complain** لم يَفْعَلوا شَيْئاً سِوى التَشَكّي; **she has ~ but praise for them** لا تَتَحَدَّثُ عَنْهُمْ إلاّ بالمَدْحِ

E (**nothing less than**) *adv phr* **it's ~ less than a betrayal** لا يَقِلُّ دَرَجةً عن الخِيانةِ

F (**nothing more than**) *adv phr* **the accusations are ~ more than gossip** لا تَعْدو الاتِّهاماتُ كَوْنَها ثَرْثَرةً; **they'd like ~ more than to get rid of him** لا يَرْغَبونَ في شَيْءٍ أَكْثَرَ من التَخَلُّصِ مِنْهُ

(Idiom) **there's nothing for it** لا حَلَّ لَهُ; **there's ~ for it, but to pay the fine** لا حَلَّ لَهُ، سِوى دَفْعِ الغَرامةِ

notice /ˈnəʊtɪs/ **A** *n* **1▸** (sign) لافِتة (لافِتات, لَوافِتُ) **2▸** (advertisement) إعْلان (إعْلانات) **3▸** [u] (attention) انْتِباه, مُلاحَظة; **to take ~** لاحَظَ; **take no ~, don't take any ~** لا تُعِرْهُ انْتِباهاً **4▸** (**notices** *n pl*) تَعْليقات, نَقْد; (review) **to get good/bad ~s** قوبِلَ باسْتِحْسانٍ \ بِاسْتِهْجانِ النُقّادِ **5▸** [u] (fml) (warning) إخْطار (إخْطارات), إنْذار (إنْذارات), إشْعار (إشْعارات); **we require one month's ~** اشْتَرَطْنا ضَرورةَ الإخْطارِ قَبْلَها بِشَهْرٍ; **to do sth at short ~** فَعَلَ شَيْئاً دون إعْطاءِ مُهْلةٍ كافيةٍ; **to give sb ~ of closure/eviction** أعْطى شَخْصاً إشْعاراً بالإغْلاقِ \ بالإخْلاءِ; **until further ~** حتّى إشْعارٍ آخَرَ **6▸** [u] (of resignation, dismissal) **to hand in one's ~** قَدَّمَ إخْطاراً بِعَزْمِهِ على الاسْتِقالةِ; **we got one month's ~** تَسَلَّمْنا إخْطاراً بإنْهاءِ خِدْمَتِنا بعد شَهْرٍ

B *vt* لاحَظَ, رَأى (a; رَأْي, رُؤْية) ‹*sb's absence, a mark*›; **I ~ that ...** أرى أنّ ...; **to get oneself ~d** حَقَّقَ نَجاحاً مَلْحوظاً

noticeable /ˈnəʊtɪsəb(ə)l/ *adj* **1▸** (easily seen) ‹*flaw, scar*› ظاهِر, واضِح **2▸** (significant) ‹*improvement, deterioration*› مَلْحوظ, جَدير بالمُلاحَظةِ; **a ~ increase/decrease in crime** ارْتِفاع \ انْخِفاض مَلْحوظ في الجَريمةِ

noticeably /ˈnəʊtɪsəbli/ *adv* ‹*to increase, improve*› بِشَكْلٍ مَلْحوظٍ, بِصورةٍ مَلْحوظةٍ; **it has been ~ warmer/colder today** الجَوُّ اليَوْمَ أَدْفَأُ \ أَبْرَدُ بِشَكْلٍ مَلْحوظٍ

noticeboard /ˈnəʊtɪsbɔːd/ *n* (BrE) لَوْحة إعْلاناتٍ

notifiable /ˈnəʊtɪfʌɪəb(ə)l/ *adj* ‹*disease, offence*› يَجِبُ الإبْلاغُ عَنْهُ

notification /ˌnəʊtɪfɪˈkeɪʃ(ə)n/ *n* إعْلام, إبْلاغ (إبْلاغات), إشْعار (إشْعارات)

notify /ˈnəʊtɪfʌɪ/ *vt* (**notifies, notifying, notified**) أَخْطَرَ, أَبْلَغَ, أَعْلَمَ ‹*parents, customers*›; **to ~ sb of sth** أَخْطَرَ شَخْصاً بِشَيْءٍ

notion /ˈnəʊʃ(ə)n/ **A** *n* (concept) مَفْهوم (مَفاهيمُ), فِكْرة (فِكَر); **he has no ~ of time** لَيْسَ لَدَيْهِ تَقْديرٌ لِلوَقْتِ

B (**notions**) *n pl* (AmE) (sewing equipment) لَوازِم الخِياطةِ

notorious /nəʊˈtɔːrɪəs/ *adj* ‹*criminal, case*› رَديء \ سَيِّئ السُمْعةِ

notoriously /nəʊˈtɔːrɪəsli/ *adv* ‹*unreliable, difficult*› على نَحْوٍ مَعْروفٍ \ مَشْهورٍ

notwithstanding /nɒtwɪθˈstandɪŋ/ (fml) **A** *prep* بالرَغْمِ من

B *adv* ‹*to proceed, persevere*› على الرَغْمِ من ذلك

nougat /ˈnuːgɑː, ˈnʌgət/ *n* نوغة (حَلْوى)

nought /nɔːt/ *n* (BrE) صِفْر

noun /naʊn/ *n* اسْم (أَسْماء, أسامٍ)

nourish /ˈnʌrɪʃ/ *vt* غَذّى ‹*the body, one's children*›

nourishing /ˈnʌrɪʃɪŋ/ *adj* ‹*food, meal*› مُغَذٍّ

nourishment /ˈnʌrɪʃmənt/ *n* غِذاء (أَغْذِية), قوت (أَقْوات), طَعام (أَطْعِمة)

novel /ˈnɒv(ə)l/ **A** *n* رِواية, قِصّة طَويلة

B *adj* ‹*idea, approach*› مُبْتَكِر, جَديد (جُدُد), حَديث

novelist /ˈnɒvəlɪst/ *n* رِوائيّ, مُؤَلِّف رِواياتٍ

novelty /ˈnɒvəlti/ *n* (*pl* **novelties**) **1▸** [u] (newness) حَداثة **2▸** (new thing) شَيْء جَديد \ مُسْتَحْدَث

November /nəʊˈvɛmbə/ *n* نوفَمْبر (NA, Gulf), تِشْرين الثاني (Levant, Iraq), نُوَنْبر (Mor) ▸**March**

novice /ˈnɒvɪs/ *n* مُبْتَدِئ

no-vote /ˈnəʊvəʊt/ *n* تَصْويت بِلا

now /naʊ/ **A** *adv* **1▸** (this instant) الآنَ; **you can come in ~** يُمْكِنُكَ الدُخولُ الآنَ; **do it ~** افْعَلْهُ الآنَ; **~ is your opportunity** الآنَ فُرْصَتُكَ; **the flight is expected any time ~** من المُتَوَقَّعِ أنْ تَصِلَ الرِحْلةُ بين لَحْظةٍ وأُخْرى; **(every) ~ and then** *or* **again** بين (كُلِّ) حينٍ وآخَرَ **2▸** (at the present time) الآنَ, في وَقْتِنا \ عَصْرِنا الحاضِرِ; **people expect it ~** يَتَوَقَّعُهُ الناسُ في عَصْرِنا هذا **3▸** (at that time) **it was ~ 4 p.m.**

كانَت الساعةُ في ذلك الوَقْتِ 4 مَساءً; **it was ~ time to say farewell** حانَتْ لَحْظةُ الوَداعِ في ذلك الوَقْتِ; **it was ~ just after 4 o'clock** كانَت الساعةُ في ذلك الوَقْتِ بعد الرابعةِ بِقَليلٍ **4** (with length of time) حتّى الآنَ; **we've lived here ten years ~** عِشْنا هُنا عَشْرَ سَنواتٍ حتّى الآنَ **5** (with a preposition) **you should have phoned him before ~** كانَ يَجِبُ أنْ تَتَّصِلَ بِهِ سَلَفاً; **he should be finished by ~** لا بُدَّ أنَّهُ قد انتهى الآنَ; **by ~ it was too late** كانَ قد فاتَ الأوانُ; **between ~ and next Friday** من الآنَ وَحَتّى الجُمْعةِ المُقْبِلةِ; **between ~ and then** من الآنَ وَحَتّى ذلك الوَقْتِ; **for ~ follow the old procedure** حاليًّا اتَّبِعِ الإجْراءَ القَديمَ; **from ~ on, new rules apply** من الآنَ فصاعِداً، تَنْطَبِقُ قَواعِدُ جَديدةٌ **6** (with commands, warnings) **~, look here!** اسْمَعْني جَيِّداً الآنَ!; **careful ~!** انْتَبِهْ! اِحْتَرِسْ!; **~ then, let's get back to work** والآنَ، فَلْنَعُدْ للعَمَلِ; **~, there's a man I can trust!** حَسَناً، هذا رَجُلٌ أَسْتَطيعُ أنْ أَثِقَ بِهِ!

B *conj* **~ (that)** … الآنَ وَقَدْ …; **~ (that) you're here, we can get set to work** الآنَ وقد وَصَلْتَ، يُمْكِنُنا أنْ نَبْدَأَ العَمَلَ; **~ (that) she's been put in the picture, we can start planning** بما أنَّهُ تَمَّ إعْلامُها الآنَ، يُمْكِنُنا أنْ نَبْدَأَ بالتَخْطيطِ

nowadays /ˈnaʊədeɪz/ *adv* الحاليَّ \ في الوَقْتِ الحاضِرِ, في هذه الأيّامِ

nowhere /ˈnəʊwɛː/ **A** *adv* **1** (with place) لَيْسَ في أيِّ مَكانٍ; **there's ~ to sit down/park** لَيْسَ هُناكَ أيُّ مَكانٍ للجُلوسِ \ لِرَكْنِ السَيّارةِ; **there's ~ better/worse for a holiday** لَيْسَ هُناكَ أيُّ مَكانٍ أفْضَلُ \ أَسْوأُ لِقَضاءِ إجازةٍ; **'where are you going?' —'~ special'** 'إلى أيْنَ أنْتَ ذاهِبٌ؟' — 'لَيْس إلى أيِّ مَكانٍ مُمَيَّزٍ'; **she's ~ to be seen** اخْتَفَتْ; **the key is ~ to be found** لا يُمْكِنُ العُثورُ على المِفتاحِ في أيِّ مَكانٍ; **I have ~ else to go** لَيْس لي مَكانٌ آخَرُ أذْهَبُ إلَيْهِ; **~ but in France, can you find so many cheeses** لا يُمْكِنُكَ أنْ تَجِدَ أَنْواعاً شَتّى من الجُبْنِ في أيِّ مَكانٍ إلاّ فَرَنْسا **2** (with progression) **these negotiations are getting/going ~** لن تُؤَدِّيَ هذه المُفاوَضاتُ إلى أيِّ نَتيجةٍ; **£10 goes ~ these days** لا يُعَدُّ لَها قيمةٌ هذه الأيّامَ £10; **to appear** *or* **come out of ~** ظَهَرَ فَجْأةً; **flattery will get you ~!** لن يوصِلَكَ الإطْراءُ إلى أيِّ شَيْءٍ!

B (nowhere near) *adv phr, prep phr* **it's ~ near sufficient/satisfactory** هو بَعيدٌ كُلَّ البُعْدِ عن كَوْنِهِ كافِياً \ مُرْضِياً; **I'm ~ near finished** أنا بَعيدٌ كُلَّ البُعْدِ عن الانْتِهاءِ; **their office is ~ near the bank** مَكْتَبُهُم بَعيدٌ كُلَّ البُعْدِ عن البَنْكِ; **$50 is ~ near enough** $50 بَعيدةٌ كُلَّ البُعْدِ عن كَوْنِها كافيةً

noxious /ˈnɒkʃəs/ *adj* <*fumes, substance*> (poisonous) ضارٌّ, سامٌّ; (unpleasant) كَريه

nozzle /ˈnɒz(ə)l/ *n* (of a hose, shower) فوَّهة

NSPCC /ɛnespiːsiːˈsiː/ *n* (BrE) = **National Society for the Prevention of Cruelty to Children** [الجَمْعيّة الوَطَنيّة لِمَنْعِ القَسْوةِ ضِدّ الأطْفالِ]

nuance /ˈnjuːɑːns/ *n* فارِق دَقيق

nuclear /ˈnjuːklɪə/ *adj* <*weapons, programme, war*> نَوَويّ

nuclear disarmament *n* نَزْع السِلاحِ النَوَويِّ

nuclear family *n* أُسْرة نَوَويّة \ نَواة

nuclear fission *n* انْشِطار نَوَويّ

nuclear fusion *n* انْدِماج نَوَويّ

nuclear power *n* طاقة نَوَويّة

nuclear-powered /ˌnjuːklɪəˈpaʊəd/ *adj* <*submarine, aircraft carrier*> يَعْمَلُ بالطاقة النَوَويّة

nuclear power station *n* مَحطّة طاقةٍ نَوَويّةٍ

nuclear weapon *n* سِلاح نَوَويّ

nucleus /ˈnjuːklɪəs/ *n* (*pl* **nuclei**) **1** (of an atom) نَواة (نَوَيات), **2** (of group, movement, etc) قَلْب (قُلوب), مَرْكَز (مَراكِزُ) نَوًى

nude /njuːd/ **A** *adj* <*model, bather, statue*> عارٍ (عُراة)

B *n* (Art) [صورة \ تِمْثال لِشَخْصٍ عارٍ]; **to walk around in the ~** تجَوَّلَ عُرْياناً

nudge /nʌdʒ/ *vt* لَكَزَ (u; لَكْز), وَكَزَ (i; وَكْز)

nudist /ˈnjuːdɪst/ *n, adj* عُرْيانيّ (شَخْص يُؤْمِنُ بِفَلْسَفةِ التَعَرّي)

nudity /ˈnjuːdɪti/ *n* عُرْي, تَعَرٍّ

nugget /ˈnʌgɪt/ *n* كُتْلة, شَذْر (من مَعْدِنٍ نَفيسٍ خامٍّ)

nuisance /ˈnjuːs(ə)ns/ *n* مَصْدَر إزْعاجٍ; **to be a ~** كانَ مَصْدَرَ إزْعاجٍ

nuisance call *n* مُعاكَسة تِلِفونيّة

null /nʌl/ *adj* **~ and void** ‹*agreement, contract*› لاغٍ, باطِل

nullify /ˈnʌlɪfʌɪ/ *vt* (**nullifies**, **nullifying**, **nullified**) أَبْطَلَ, أَلْغى ‹*a contract, law*›

numb /nʌm/ **A** *adj* ‹*hand, leg*› مُخَدَّر, فاقِد الحِسِّ \ الإِحْساسِ

B *vt* خَدَّرَ, أَفْقَدَ الحِسَّ \ الإِحْساسَ ‹*one's leg, mouth*›

number /ˈnʌmbə/ **A** *n* **1** (figure) عَدَد (أَعْداد), رَقْم (أَرْقام); **an odd/even ~** رَقْم فَرْدِيّ \ زَوْجِيّ; **a three-figure** *or* **three-digit ~** عَدَد من ثَلاثِة أَرْقام **2** (of a bus, house, page, telephone) رَقْم (أَرْقام); **we live at ~ 18** نَعيشُ في المَنْزِل رَقْم 18; **to get a wrong ~** اتَّصَلَ بالرَقْمِ الخَطَأِ; **to be ~ three on the list** كانَ الثالِثَ في القائِمةِ **3** (amount, quantity) عَدَد (أَعْداد); **for a ~ of reasons** لِعَدَدٍ من الأَسْبابِ; **they were sixteen in ~** كانَ عَدَدُهُمْ سِتَّةَ عَشَرَ; **in equal ~s** بِأَعْدادٍ مُتَساوِيةٍ; **large ~s of people** أَعْداد كَبيرة من الناسِ; **I phoned any ~ of times** اتَّصَلْتُ مَرّاتٍ عَديدةً **4** (group) **one of our ~** أَحَدُنا **5** (of a magazine) عَدَد (أَعْداد) **6** (act) (song) فَقْرة فَنِّيّة **7** (infml) (object of admiration) تُحْفة (تُحَف); **that car is a neat little ~** تِلْكَ السَيّارةُ تُحْفةٌ صَغيرةٌ أَنيقةٌ; **a little black ~** فُسْتان سَهْرةٍ أَسْوَد

B (**numbers**) *n pl* (in a crowd, at a school) أَعْداد; **the ~s are falling/rising** الأَعْداد تَتَناقَصُ \ تَتَزايَدُ; **there is safety in ~s** ≈ الكَثْرةُ تَغْلِبُ الشَجاعةَ; **to win by sheer force** *or* **weight of ~s** انْتَصَرَ بِسَبَبِ الكَثْرةِ العَدَدِيّةِ فَقَطْ

C *vt* **1** (to assign a number to) رَقَّمَ ‹*the copies, sheets, pages*›; **they are ~ed from 1 to 100** هي مُرَقَّمةٌ من 1 إلى 100 **2** (to amount to) بَلَغَ عَدَدُهُ; **the demonstrators ~ed more than 5,000** بَلَغَ عَدَدُ المُتَظاهِرينَ أَكْثَرَ من 5000 مُتَظاهِرٍ **3** (to include) **to ~ sb among one's friends** عَدَّ شَخْصاً من ضِمْنِ أَصْدِقائِهِ **4** (to be limited) **to be ~ed** كانَ مَحْدوداً \ مَعْدوداً; **his options are ~ed** خِياراتُهُ مَحْدودةٌ; **his days are ~ed** أَيّامُهُ مَعْدودةٌ

D *vi* **1** (to comprise) **a crowd ~ing in the thousands** جُمْهور يُقَدَّرُ عَدَدُهُ بالآلافِ **2** (to be included) **to ~ among the great musicians/philosophers** كانَ يُعَدُّ ضِمْنَ الموسيقيِّينَ \ الفَلاسِفةِ العِظامِ

number plate *n* (BrE) لَوْحة رَقْمِ سَيّارةٍ

numeracy /ˈnjuːm(ə)rəsi/ *n* القُدْرة على الحِسابِ

numeral /ˈnjuːm(ə)rəl/ *n* عَدَد (أَعْداد), رَقْم (أَرْقام)

numerical /njuːˈmɛrɪk(ə)l/ *adj* ‹*advantage, order*› رَقْمِيّ, عَدَدِيّ

numerous /ˈnjuːm(ə)rəs/ *adj* ‹*occasions, friends*› كَثير, عَديد

nun /nʌn/ *n* راهِبة

nunation /nuːˈneɪʃ(ə)n/ *n* تَنْوين

nunnery /ˈnʌn(ə)ri/ *n* (*pl* **nunneries**) (old use) دَيْر راهِباتٍ

nurse /nəːs/ **A** *n* **1** (in hospitals) مُمَرِّض **2** ▸ **nursemaid**

B *vt* **1** (to care for) اعْتَنى (ب), رَعى (a; رَعْي, رِعاية), مَرَّضَ ‹*a patient*› **2** (to feed) أَرْضَعَ, رَضَّعَ ‹*a baby*› **3** (to think of) أَضْمَرَ ‹*a grievance*›; كانَ لَدَيْهِ ‹*a hope*›

nursemaid /ˈnəːsmeɪd/ *n* مُرَبِّية أَطْفال

nursery /ˈnəːs(ə)ri/ *n* (*pl* **nurseries**) **1** (Educ) also **day ~** حَضانة **2** (room) غُرْفة أَطْفالٍ **3** (for trees, plants) مَشْتَل (مَشاتِلُ)

nursery rhyme *n* أُغْنِية \ أُنْشودة أَطْفال

nursery school *n* رَوْضة أَطْفالٍ, حَضانة

nursing /ˈnəːsɪŋ/ *n* تَمْريض

nursing home *n* دار رِعايةٍ \ مُسِنّينَ

nurture /ˈnəːtʃə/ *vt* **1** اعْتَنى (ب), رَعى (a; رَعْي, رِعاية), رَبّى ‹*a child, plant*› **2** طَوَّرَ, نَمّى ‹*a talent*›; قَوّى, عَزَّزَ ‹*a hope*›

nut /nʌt/ **A** *n* **1** (kernel) بُنْدُق (n coll), جَوْز (أَجْواز), لَوْز (n coll); **chocolate with ~s in it** شوكولاتة بالمُكَسَّراتِ **2** (for bolt) صامولة (صَواميلُ), صَمولة (صَوامِلُ), حَزْقة; **to tighten/loosen a ~** رَبَطَ \ فَكَّ صامولةً **3** (infml) (mad person) مَجْنون (مَجانينُ) **4** (infml) (enthusiast) شَخْص مُتَحَمِّس **5** (infml) (head) رَأْس (mf; رُؤوس, أَرْؤُس); **use your ~!** اسْتَعْمِلْ عَقْلَكَ!

B (**nuts**) *n pl* (vulg) (testicles) خِصْيَتانِ

C (**nuts**) *adj* **1** (infml) (crazy) مَجْنون (مَجانينُ), أَبْلَه (dipt) **2** (infml) (enthusiastic) **to be ~s about sb** كانَ مولَعاً بِشَخْصٍ; **to be ~s about tennis/acting** كانَ مولَعاً بالتَنس \ بالتَمْثيلِ

Idiom **the nuts and bolts** (infml) النِقاط الأَساسيّة

nut allergy *n* حَسّاسيّة المُكَسَّراتِ

nutcase /ˈnʌtkeɪs/ *n* (infml) مَجْنون (مَجانينُ), أَحْمَق (dipt; حُمْق; f حَمْقى)

nutcracker /ˈnʌtkrakə/, **nutcrackers** /ˈnʌtkrakəz/ *n* كَسّارة بُنْدُقٍ \ جَوْزٍ

nutmeg /ˈnʌtmɛg/ *n* جَوْزة الطيبِ

nutrient /ˈnjuːtrɪənt/ *n* مادّة غِذائيّة

nutrition /njʊˈtrɪʃ(ə)n/ *n* تَغْذِية ,(أَغْذِية) غِذاء

nutritional /njuːˈtrɪʃ(ə)n(ə)l/ *adj* <*value, information*> غِذائيّ

nutritious /njʊˈtrɪʃəs/ *adj* <*meal*> مُغَذٍّ

nutshell /ˈnʌtʃɛl/ *n* قِشْرة جَوْزةٍ

(Idiom) **in a nutshell** بِإيجازٍ ,بِاخْتِصارٍ

nutty /ˈnʌti/ *adj* (**nuttier, nuttiest**) **1** (Culin) <*biscuit*> مَليء بالجَوْزِ; <*flavour*> الجَوْز **2** (infml) (crazy) <*person, plan*> مَجْنون (مَجانينُ)

nuzzle /ˈnʌz(ə)l/ *vt* حَكَّ \ مَسَّ بالأَنْفِ <*sb's neck, hair*>

NV *abbr* = **Nevada**

NVQ /ɛnviːˈkjuː/ *n* = **National Vocational Qualification** التَأْهيل المِهَنيّ الوَطَنيّ (في المَمْلَكةِ المُتَّحِدةِ)

NW *n* = **northwest** شَمال غَرْبيّ

NY *abbr* = **New York**

nylon /ˈnʌɪlɒn/ **A** *n* (fibre) نايْلون
B (**nylons**) *n pl* (stockings, tights) جَوْرَب من النايْلون

nymph /nɪmf/ *n* حورِيّة (حور ,حورِيّات)

Oo

O, o /əʊ/ *n* **1** (letter) [الحَرْف الخامِسَ عَشَرَ من الأَبْجَدِيّة الإنْكليزِيّة] **2** (**O**) (in spoken numbers) صِفْر **3** (**O**) (Med) **blood group O** O فَصيلة الدَمِ

oaf /əʊf/ *n* أَبْلَه (dipt), (أَغْبِياءُ) غَبيّ

oak /əʊk/ **A** *n* بَلّوط (n coll), سِنْدِيان
B *adj* ‹*furniture, beam*› من خَشَبِ البَلّوطِ

OAP /əʊeɪ'piː/ *n* (BrE) = **old age pensioner** [شَخْص كَبير في السِنِّ مُتَقاعِد]

oar /ɔː/ *n* مِجْداف (مَجاديفُ), مِقْذاف (مَقاذيفُ)

oarsman /'ɔːzmən/ *n* (*pl* **-men**) مُجَدِّف

oarswoman /'ɔːzwʊmən/ *n* (*pl* **-women**) مُجَدِّفة

oasis /əʊ'eɪsɪs/ *n* (*pl* **oases**) واحة

oath /əʊθ/ *n* **1** (solemn promise) يَمين (f; أَيْمُن), قَسَم (أَقْسام); **to be under ~** كان تحت القَسَمِ **2** (swear word) تَجْديف, لَعْنة

oatmeal /'əʊtmiːl/ *n* **1** (flour) دَقيق الشوفانِ **2** (AmE) (porridge) عَصيدة الشوفانِ

oats /əʊts/ *n* شوفان

obedience /ə'biːdɪəns/ *n* طاعة, إِذْعان, خُضوع

obedient /ə'biːdɪənt/ *adj* ‹*pupil, dog*› مُطيع, خاضِع (خُضَّع)

obese /əʊ'biːs/ *adj* ‹*patient, child*› بَدين (بُدُن), سَمين (سِمان)

obesity /əʊ'biːsɪti/ *n* بَدانة, سُمْنة مُفْرِطة

obey /əʊ'beɪ/ **A** *vt* أَطاعَ ‹*one's father, teacher*›; انْصاعَ (ل), أَذْعَنَ (ل) ‹*instructions, an order*›
B *vi* [انْصاعَ للأَوامِرِ]

obituary /ə'bɪtʃuːəri/ *n* (*pl* **obituaries**) also **~ notice** نَعْي

object A /'ɒbdʒɪkt/ *n* **1** (item) شَيْء (أَشْياءُ) **2** (goal) هَدَف (أَهْداف), غَرَض (أَغْراض); **with the ~ of doing sth** بِهَدَفِ فِعْلِ شَيْءٍ **3** (focus) **to be the ~ of ridicule/hatred** كانَ مَوْضِعَ السُخْرِيّةِ \ الكَراهِيةِ **4** (in grammar) مَفْعول بِهِ; **the direct/indirect ~** المَفْعول بِهِ المُباشِر \ غَيْر المُباشِرِ
B /əb'dʒɛkt/ *vt* **to ~ that ...** اعْتَرَضَ بِأَنْ ...
C /əb'dʒɛkt/ *vi* اعْتَرَضَ; **'I ~!'** 'أَنا أَعْتَرِضُ!'; **to ~ to a plan/proposal** اعْتَرَضَ على خُطّةٍ \ مُقْتَرَحٍ; **to ~ strongly to sth** اعْتَرَضَ بِشِدّةٍ على شَيْءٍ; **to ~ to sb doing sth** *or* **to sb's doing sth** اعْتَرَضَ على قِيامِ شَخْصٍ بِشَيْءٍ; **I don't ~ to him** *or* **his staying with us** لا أَعْتَرِضُ على بَقائِهِ مَعَنا

objection /əb'dʒɛkʃ(ə)n/ *n* اعْتِراض (اعْتِراضات), مانِع (مَوانِعُ)

objectionable /əb'dʒɛkʃ(ə)nəb(ə)l/ *adj* ‹*remark, behaviour*›; ‹*man, teenager*› بَغيض

objective /əb'dʒɛktɪv/ **A** *adj* ‹*assessment, opinion*› مَوْضوعيّ
B *n* هَدَف (أَهْداف), غاية, غَرَض (أَغْراض)

objectively /əb'dʒɛktɪvli/ *adv* ‹*to view, consider*› بِمَوْضوعيّةٍ

objectivity /ɒbdʒɛk'tɪvəti/ *n* مَوْضوعيّة

obligate /'ɒblɪgeɪt/ *vt* أَلْزَمَ, فَرَضَ (i; فَرْض; على) ‹*a company, an employee*›

obligation /ɒblɪ'geɪʃ(ə)n/ *n* الْتِزام (الْتِزامات), واجِب (واجِبات); **to be under an ~ to do sth** كانَ واجِباً عَلَيْهِ أَنْ يَفْعَلَ شَيْئاً

obligatory /ə'blɪgət(ə)ri/ *adj* ‹*inspection, stop*› إِلْزاميّ, إِجْباريّ

oblige /ə'blʌɪdʒ/ *vt* **1** (to compel) أَلْزَمَ, أَجْبَرَ (على) ‹*a company, tenant*› **2** (fml) (to be helpful to) تَفَضَّلَ (على), أَسْدى مَعْروفاً إلى ‹*a client, neighbour*›; **I'm much ~d to you** أنا مُمْتَنٌّ لَكَ جِدًّا

obliging /ə'blʌɪdʒɪŋ/ *adj* ‹*shop assistant*› خَدوم, مِعْوان (مَعاوينُ), مُساعِد; ‹*manner*› لَطيف

oblique /ə'bliːk/ **A** *adj* **1** (sloping) ‹*line, angle*› مائِل, مُنْحَرِف **2** (indirect) ‹*attack, reference*› غَيْر مُباشِرٍ
B *n* (P&P) خطّ مائِل \ مُنْحَرِف

obliterate /ə'blɪtəreɪt/ *vt* مَحا (u; مَحْو), طَمَسَ (i-u; طَمْس) ‹*an inscription, a memory*›; أَزالَ, مَحَقَ (a; مَحْق) ‹*a city, factory*›

oblivion /əˈblɪvɪən/ *n* نِسْيان

oblivious /əˈblɪvɪəs/ *adj* غافِل (غُفول), ذاهِل, ساهٍ (سُهاة); **to be ~ of** *or* **to sth** كانَ غافِلاً عن شَيْءٍ, كانَ غَيْرَ واعٍ لِشَيْءٍ *‹sb's presence, a danger›*

oblong /ˈɒblɒŋ/ **A** *n* مُسْتَطيل
B *adj ‹shape, table›* مُسْتَطيل

obnoxious /əbˈnɒkʃəs/ *adj ‹behaviour, smell›* بَغيض, كَريه

oboe /ˈəʊbəʊ/ *n* أوبوا

obscene /əbˈsiːn/ *adj ‹publication, picture›* فاحِش, بَذيء

obscenity /əbˈsenɪti/ *n* (*pl* **obscenities**) **1** (rude remark) بَذاءة **2** [u] (offensive nature) فُحْش, بَذاءة

obscure /əbˈskjʊə/ **A** *adj* **1** (difficult to understand) *‹reference, argument›* غامِض, مُبْهَم, عَويص **2** (little known) *‹poet, publication›* مَغْمور, غَيْر مَعْروفٍ
B *vt* **1** *‹a fact, meaning›* أَبْهَمَ **2** حَجَبَ (حَجْب; u), أَخْفى *‹a view, face›*

obscurity /əbˈskjʊərɪti/ *n* (*pl* **obscurities**) **1** (of an argument) غُموض, إبْهام **2** (anonymity) خفاء

obsequious /əbˈsiːkwɪəs/ *adj* (fml) *‹waiter, flattery›* خانِع, مُتَذَلِّل

observant /əbˈzɜːv(ə)nt/ *adj ‹police officer, child›* يَقِظ (أَيْقاظ), مُنْتَبِه, سَريع المُلاحَظةِ

observation /ˌɒbzəˈveɪʃ(ə)n/ *n* **1** (study) مُراقَبة, مُلاحَظة, رَصْد; **to keep a patient under ~** وَضَعَ مَريضاً تحت المُراقَبةِ **2** (remark) مُلاحَظة

observation post *n* مَرْكَز مُراقَبةٍ \ رَصْدٍ

observation satellite *n* [قَمَر صِناعيّ للمُراقَبةِ]

observatory /əbˈzɜːvət(ə)ri/ *n* (*pl* **observatories**) مَرْصَد (مَراصِدُ)

observe /əbˈzɜːv/ *vt* **1** (fml) (to notice) لاحَظَ, رَأى (رُؤْيةٌ; a), *‹a stranger, movement›* **2** (to watch, study) شاهَدَ, راقَبَ, رَصَدَ (رَصْد; u) *‹a patient, suspect›* **3** (to remark) لاحَظَ, ذَكَرَ (ذِكْر; u), عَلَّقَ; **she ~d that I was late** عَلَّقَتْ أَنَّني أَتَيْتُ مُتَأَخِّراً **4** (to adhere to) راعى, امْتَثَلَ *‹a law, custom›*

observer /əbˈzɜːvə/ *n* مُراقِب, مُلاحِظ

obsess /əbˈses/ *vt* اسْتَحْوَذَ (على) *‹a child, parent›*

obsession /əbˈseʃ(ə)n/ *n* هاجِس (هَواجِسُ), اسْتِحْواذ

obsessive /əbˈsesɪv/ *adj ‹thought›* مُلِحّ, مُسْتَحْوِذ; *‹patient›* وَسْواسيّ, مُوَسْوَس, مَهْووس

obsolescence /ˌɒbsəˈles(ə)ns/ *n* تَقادُم

obsolete /ˈɒbsəliːt/ *adj ‹technology›* بالٍ, مِن طِرازٍ قَديمٍ; *‹idea›* مُنْدَثِر, مَهْجور

obstacle /ˈɒbstək(ə)l/ *n* عائِق (عَوائِقُ), عَقَبة (عَقَبات, عِقاب), حائِل (حَوائِلُ)

obstacle course *n* ميدان المَوانِعِ

obstacle race *n* سِباق الحَواجِزِ

obstetric /əbˈstetrɪk/ *adj ‹practice, complications›* تَوْليديّ

obstetrician /ˌɒbstəˈtrɪʃ(ə)n/ *n* طَبيب تَوْليدٍ

obstetrics /əbˈstetrɪks/ *n sing* طِبّ التَّوْليدِ

obstinate /ˈɒbstɪnət/ *adj ‹refusal, child›* عَنيد (عُنُد), صُلْب الرَّأْيِ

obstinately /ˈɒbstənətli/ *adv ‹to refuse, defend›* بِعِنادٍ, بِإصْرارٍ

obstruct /əbˈstrʌkt/ *vt* **1** (to block) عَرْقَلَ (عَرْقَلة; i), سَدَّ (سَدّ; u), أَعاقَ, مَنَعَ (مَنْع; a) *‹the traffic›*; حَجَبَ (حَجْب; u) *‹a view›* **2** (in sports) سَدَّ (سَدّ; u) *‹a player›* **3** أَعاقَ, عَرْقَلَ (عَرْقَلة; i) *‹justice›*

obstruction /əbˈstrʌkʃ(ə)n/ *n* **1** (of traffic, a view) عَقَبة (عَقَبات, عِقاب), عائِق (عَوائِقُ) **2** [u] (of justice) إعاقة, عَرْقَلة **3** [u] (of a player) سَدّ, حَجْز

obtain /əbˈteɪn/ *vt* حَصَلَ (على; حُصول; u), نالَ (نَوْل; u), أَحْرَزَ *‹information, a document›*

obtrusive /əbˈtruːsɪv/ *adj ‹advertising›* [يَظْهَر بِشَكْلٍ مُزْعِجٍ]; *‹building›* ناتِئ

obtuse /əbˈtjuːs/ *adj ‹student, listener›* بَليد, غَبيّ (أَغْبِياءُ); *‹remark, lyrics›* غامِض, مُبْهَم

obvious /ˈɒbvɪəs/ **A** *adj ‹reason, choice›* واضِح, بَيِّن; *‹danger, target›* جَليّ, بارِز
B *n* **to state the ~** ذَكَرَ ما هو مَعْروفٌ

obviously /ˈɒbvɪəsli/ **A** *adv* (clearly) من الواضِحِ \ الجَليِّ, بِشَكْلٍ واضِحٍ, على نَحْوٍ بَيِّنٍ; **she ~ needs help** من الواضِحِ أَنَّها تَحْتاجُ إلى مُساعَدةٍ; **it is ~ wrong** هَذا خَطَأٌ على نَحْوٍ بَيِّنٍ; **~ you have lied to me** من الجَليِّ أَنَّكَ كَذَبْتَ عَلَيَّ
B *excl* (of course) طَبْعاً, بالتَّأْكيدِ; **'did she win?'—'~ not!'** 'هَلْ فازَتْ؟' - 'طَبْعاً لا!'

occasion /əˈkeɪʒ(ə)n/ **A** *n* **1** (particular time) مُناسَبة; **on that ~** في تِلْكَ المُناسَبةِ; **on a previous ~** في مُناسَبةٍ سابِقةٍ; **on one ~** في إحْدى المُناسَباتِ; **on ~** أَحْياناً; **on several ~s** في عِدّةِ مُناسَباتٍ; **on the ~ of his retirement/the opening of the bridge** بِمُناسَبةِ تَقاعُدِهِ \ افْتِتاحِ الجِسْرِ **2** (event, function) مُناسَبة, حَدَث (أَحْداث); **on special ~s** في المُناسَباتِ الخاصّةِ; **the wedding was quite an ~** كانَ العُرْسُ حَدَثاً كَبيراً **3** (opportunity) فُرْصة (فُرَص); **if the ~ arises** إذا سَنَحَت الفُرْصةُ; **to rise to the ~** كانَ على مُسْتوى الحَدَثِ **4** [u] (fml) (reason) سَبَب (أَسْباب), داعٍ (دُعاة, دَواعٍ); **to have ~ to do sth** كانَ لَدَيْهِ سَبَبٌ لِفِعْلِ شَيْءٍ **B** *vt* (fml) <*surprise, a reaction, response*> سَبَّبَ, تَسَبَّبَ (في)

occasional /əˈkeɪʒ(ə)n(ə)l/ *adj* <*visit, storm*> عَرَضيّ, من حينٍ لِآخَرَ

occasionally /əˈkeɪʒ(ə)n(ə)li/ *adv* <*to visit, help*> بين أَحْياناً; **very ~** نادِراً, الفَيْنةِ والفَيْنةِ

occlusion /əˈkluːʒ(ə)n/ *n* انْسِداد, إطْباق

occult /ɒˈkʌlt/ *n* **the ~** عُلوم الغَيْبِ

occupant /ˈɒkjʊp(ə)nt/ *n* **1** (of a house) ساكِن; (of an office) شاغِل **2** (of a vehicle) راكِب (رُكّاب)

occupation /ɒkjʊˈpeɪʃ(ə)n/ *n* **1** (Mil) (of a country, city) احْتِلال **2** (profession) مِهْنة (مِهَن), حِرْفة (حِرَف) **3** (hobby) شُغْل (أَشْغال)

occupational /ɒkjʊˈpeɪʃ(ə)n(ə)l/ *adj* <*pension, safety*> مِهْنيّ

occupational hazard *n* خَطَر مِهْنيّ

occupational therapy *n* العِلاج بالعَمَلِ

occupier /ˈɒkjʊpʌɪə/ *n* ساكِن

occupy /ˈɒkjʊpʌɪ/ *vt* (**occupies, occupying, occupied**) **1** (Mil) <*a country, city*> احْتَلَّ **2** (to live, work in) سَكَنَ (u; سَكَن), أقامَ (في) <*a flat*>; شَغَلَ (a; شُغْل) <*an office*> **3** (to fill) مَلَأَ (a; مَلْء), شَغَلَ (a; شَغْل), قَضى (i; قَضاء) <*an hour, one's time*>; **to keep oneself occupied** شَغَلَ نَفْسَهُ

occur /əˈkəː/ *vi* (**-rr-**) **1** (to happen) وَقَعَ (a; وُقوع) **2** (to be present) وُجِدَ **3** **to ~ to sb** (to come to mind) خطَرَ على بالِ شَخْصٍ

occurrence /əˈkʌrəns/ *n* **1** (event) حادِثة (حَوادِثُ), واقِعة **2** (incidence) وُجود

ocean /ˈəʊʃ(ə)n/ *n* مُحيط (مُحيطات)

ocean-going /ˈəʊʃ(ə)ngəʊɪŋ/ *adj* <*vessel, trawler*> [مُعَدّ \ مُجَهَّز للإبْحارِ في المُحيطِ]; **~ liner** عابِرة مُحيطٍ مُنْتَظِمة

o'clock /əˈklɒk/ *adv* **at one/three ~** في الساعةِ الواحِدةِ \ الثالِثةِ; **it's two/eleven ~** الساعةُ الثانيةُ \ الحادِيةَ عَشْرةَ

octagon /ˈɒktəg(ə)n/ *n* مُثَمَّن

octane /ˈɒkteɪn/ *n* أوكْتان

octave /ˈɒktɪv/ *n* (سِلْسِلة دَرَجاتِ السُّلَّمِ السَّبْعة) أوكْتاف

October /ɒkˈtəʊbə/ *n* أُكْتوبر (NA, Gulf), تِشْرين الأوَّل (Levant, Iraq) ▸**March**

October War *n* ▸**Yom Kippur War**

octopus /ˈɒktəpəs/ *n* أُخْطُبوط

ocular /ˈɒkjʊlə/ *adj* <*hypertension, lens*> عَيْنيّ, بَصَريّ

oculist /ˈɒkjʊlɪst/ *n* (old use) طَبيب عُيونٍ

OD /əʊˈdiː/ *n* (infml) ▸**overdose**

odd /ɒd/ **A** *adj* **1** (strange) <*child, object, occurrence*> غَريب (غُرَباءُ); **that's ~** ذلك غَريبٌ; **there is something ~ about his story/about her** هُناكَ شَيْءٌ غَريبٌ في قِصَّتِهِ \ بِشَأْنِها; **it is ~ how people react** رُدودُ أَفْعالِ الناسِ غَريبةٌ **2** (unmatched) <*sock, glove*> مُخْتَلِف; **he was wearing ~ socks** كانَ يَرْتَدي جَوْرَبَيْنِ مُخْتَلِفَيْنِ **3** (infml) (occasional) <*moment, minute, trip*> غَيْر مُنْتَظِمٍ, عَرَضيّ; **I have the ~ drink** أَشْرَبُ في أَحْيانٍ قَليلةٍ **4** (miscellaneous) <*scrap, piece*> مُتَفَرِّق, مُتَنَوِّع; **a few ~ coins** بِضْع عُمُلاتٍ مُتَنَوِّعةٍ **5** (Math) <*number*> فَرْديّ **6** (different) **to spot the ~ man** *or* **one out** تَعَرَّفَ على الرَّجُلِ \ الواحِدِ الغَريبِ **B** (**-odd**); *in combination* (approximately) **there were sixty-~ people present** كانَ عَدَدُ الحاضِرينَ حَوالَيْ سِتّينَ شَخْصاً; **twenty-~ years later** بعد ذلك بِحَوالَيْ عِشْرينَ سَنةً

oddball /ˈɒdbɔːl/ *n* (infml) غَريب الأَطْوارِ

oddity /ˈɒdɪti/ *n* (*pl* **oddities**) [شَيْء أو حادِث غَريب]

odd job *n* عَمَل (أَعْمال), مَهَمّة (مَهامّ)

odd-job man /ˌɒdˈdʒɒb man/ *n* (*pl* **-men**) [رَجُل كُلِّ المَهَمّاتِ]

oddly /'ɒdli/ *adj* ‹*to behave, dress*› بِشَكْلٍ غَريبٍ \ شاذٍّ

oddment /'ɒdmənt/ *n* (old use) فَضْلَة ,(بَقايا) بَقيّة (فَضَلات)

odds /ɒdz/ *n pl* ⓵ (in betting) اِحْتِمال الفَوْزِ والخَسارةِ, أَرْجَحيّة; **the ~ are 5 to 1 against/on** اِحْتِمالُ الفَوْزِ وَالخَسارةِ 1 إلى 5 بِنِسْبَةِ ضِدَّهُ \ في صالِحِهِ; **to shorten/lengthen the ~ on sth** خَفَّضَ \ زادَ قيمةَ الرِهانِ على شَيْءٍ ⓶ (likelihood) اِحْتِماليّة; **the ~ are against/in favour of sth happening** من المُسْتَبْعَدِ \ المُحْتَمَلِ حُدوثُ شَيْءٍ; **the ~ were against us** كانَتِ الظُروفُ ضِدَّنا; **the ~ are in your favour** الظُروفُ في صالِحِكَ; **to succeed against the ~** تَغَلَّبَ على الظُروفِ

▸ **odds-on**

(Idioms) **to be at odds** كانوا على خِلافٍ; **to pay over the odds for sth** (BrE) دفعَ في شَيْءٍ أَكْثَرَ مِمّا يَنْبَغي

odds and ends *n* (BrE infml) نَثْريّات [أَشْياء صَغيرة مُتَنوِّعة]

odds-on /ɒdz'ɒn/ *adj* ‹*winner*› مُرَجَّح; ‹*favourite*› أَقوى

odious /'əʊdiəs/ *adj* ‹*regime, man*› بَغيض ,كَريه

odometer /əʊ'dɒmɪtə/ *n* (AmE) عَدّاد المَسافاتِ

odontologist /ɒdɒn'tɒlədʒɪst/ *n* أَخِصّائيّ طِبِّ وَجِراحةِ الفَمِ والأَسْنانِ

odour (BrE), **odor** (AmE) /'əʊdə/ *n* رائِحة (رَوائِحُ)

odourless (BrE), **odorless** (AmE) /'əʊdələs/ *adj* ‹*gas, liquid*› لا رائِحةَ لَهُ

oesophagus (BrE), **esophagus** (AmE) /ɪ'sɒfəgəs/ *n* مَرِيء (أَمْرِئة)

oestrogen (BrE), **estrogen** (AmE) /'iːstrədʒ(ə)n/ *n* إِسْتْروجين

of /ɒv, əv/ *prep* ⓵ (expressing part of a whole) مِنْ; **the leg ~ the table** رِجْل الطاوِلةِ; **a member ~ staff** عُضو مِنْ \ في فَريقِ العَمَلِ; **there were six ~ us** كُنّا سِتّةً ⓶ (expressing content, material) مِنْ; **a ring made ~ gold** خاتَم مَصْنوع مِن الذَهَبِ; **a box ~ chocolates** عُلْبة شوكولاتةٍ ⓷ (descriptive use) [أداة إِضافةٍ]; **a friend ~ mine** صَديق لي; **the city ~ Cairo** مَدينة القاهِرةِ

off /ɒf/ **A** *adv* ⓵ (indicating departure) غادَرَ ,مُغادِراً; **to be ~** غادَرَ ~; **well I'd better be ~** عَلَيَّ أَنْ أُغادِرَ ⓶ (indicating removal) [مِنْهُ]; **take the lid ~** اِنْزَع الغِطاءَ; **he broke the tip ~** خَلَعَ ~ الرَأْسَ; **they took 20% ~** خَصَموا ٪20 ⓷ (indicating distance) على مَسافةٍ; **some way ~** في مَكانٍ بَعيدٍ ⓸ (in time) **the conference is still several months ~** لن يَنْعَقِدُ المُؤْتَمَرُ إلاّ بعد شُهورٍ

B *prep* ⓵ (away from) عَنْ; **an island ~ the west coast** جَزيرة على الساحِلِ الغَرْبيِّ; **twenty feet ~ the ground** 20 قَدَماً فوق الأَرْضِ ⓶ (absent from) غائِب عن; **to be ~ work** كانَ غائِباً عن العَمَلِ ⓷ (from) مِنْ ,عَنْ; **to pick sth up ~ the floor/table** اِلْتَقَطَ شَيْئاً عَن الأَرْضِ \ الطاوِلةِ ⓸ (infml) **to be ~ one's food** فَقَدَ شَهيّةَ الأَكْلِ

C *adj* ⓵ (free) **a day ~** يَوْم إِجازةٍ ⓶ (not functioning) **to be ~** «appliances, engine» كانَ غَيْرَ شَغّالٍ; «heating, light» كانَ مُنْطَفِئاً; **the gas/electricity is ~** الغازُ مُنْقَطِعٌ \ الكَهْرَباءُ مُنْقَطِعةٌ ⓷ (cancelled) مُلْغًى; **the match/party is ~** أُلْغِيَت المُباراةُ \ الحَفْلةُ ⓸ (removed) مَكْشوف ,مَنْزوع; **the lid was ~** كانَ الغِطاءُ مَنْزوعاً ⓹ (infml) (of food, drinks) **to be ~** فَسَدَ (i-u; فُسود) ,كانَ رَديئاً \ غَيْرَ طازَجٍ; **the milk was ~** كانَ الحَليبُ فاسِداً; **the cheese/meat is ~** الجُبْنُ \ اللَحْمُ فاسِدٌ

offal /'ɒf(ə)l/ *n* فَضَلات الذَبيحةِ

offbeat /ɒf'biːt/ *adj* ⓵ (unusual) ‹*humour, account*› لافِت للنَظَرِ, غَيْر عاديٍّ ⓶ (Mus) ‹*rhythm*› أَعْرَج (dipt)

off-centre (BrE), **off-center** (AmE) /ɒf'sentə/ *adj, adv* إلى جانِبِ الوَسَطِ

off-chance /'ɒftʃɑːns/ *n* **on the ~ that** على أَمَلِ أَنْ

off colour (BrE), **off color** (AmE) *adj* ⓵ (infml) (unwell) **to be/feel a bit off colour** [لم يَكُنْ بِخَيْرٍ] ⓶ (AmE) (risqué) ‹*joke, story*› غَيْر مُحْتَشِمٍ ,بَذيء

offcut /'ɒfkʌt/ *n* فَضَلات ,بَقايا

offence (BrE), **offense** (AmE) /ə'fens/ *n* ⓵ (crime) مُخالَفة, جُنْحة (جُنَح) ,جَريمة (جَرائِمُ) ⓶ [u] (displeasure) **to cause ~ to sb** أَهانَ شَخْصاً; **to take ~ at sb's words/actions** اِسْتاءَ من كَلِماتِ \ أَفْعالِ شَخْصٍ

offend /ə'fend/ **A** *vt* أَغاظَ ,ضايَقَ ,جَرَحَ المَشاعِرَ ‹*a minority, a friend*›

B *vi* اِرْتَكَبَ جَريمةً

offender /ə'fendə/ *n* مُخالِف للقانونِ ,مُرْتَكِب جَريمةٍ

offense (AmE) *n* ▸**offence**

offensive /ə'fensɪv/ **A** *adj* ‹remark, behaviour› جارِح ,مُؤْذٍ ,مُهين للمَشاعِرِ

B *n* (Mil) مُهاجَمة ,هُجوم

offer /'ɒfə/ **A** *vt* **1** (to proffer) عَرَضَ (i; عَرْض) ‹a drink, advice, help›; **to ~ a drink/help to sb, to ~ sb a drink/help** عَرَضَ شَراباً \ مُساعَدةً على شَخْصٍ; **he ~ed me a cigarette/water** عَرَضَ عَلَيَّ سيجارةً \ ماءً; **he ~ed me an apology/no apology** قَدَّمَ \ لم يُقَدِّمْ لي اعْتِذاراً **2** (in transactions) عَرَضَ (i; عَرْض) ‹money, a job, discount›; **he ~ed me $2,000 for it** عَرَضَ عَلَيَّ 2000 دولار في مُقابِلِهِ; **to ~ sb the position of ...** عَرَضَ على شَخْصٍ مَنْصِبَ ... **3** **to ~ sth for sale** عَرَضَ شَيْئاً لِلبَيْعِ; **laptops are being ~ed at bargain prices** الحاسِباتُ المَحْمولةُ مَعْروضةٌ بِأَسْعارٍ مُخَفَّضةٍ **4** (to volunteer) عَرَضَ (i; عَرْض); **to ~ to do sth** عَرَضَ القِيامَ بِشَيْءٍ **5** (fml) (to provide) قَدَّمَ ‹a service, information, an advantage›; **the service we ~ is second to none** الخِدْمةُ الَّتي نُقَدِّمُها لَيْسَ لَها مَثيلٌ; **it ~s little protection against the rain** لا يَحْمي من المَطَرِ; **the university has a lot to ~** لدى الجامِعةِ الكَثيرُ لِتُقَدِّمَهُ **6** (to possess) امْتَلَكَ ‹specialist knowledge›; أَجادَ ‹a language›

B *vi* (to volunteer) تَطَوَّعَ

C *v refl* (fml) **to ~ oneself** رَشَّحَ نَفْسَهُ; **to ~ oneself for re-election** رَشَّحَ نَفْسَهُ مَرَّةً أُخْرى في الانْتِخاباتِ

D *n* **1** (proposition) عَرْض (عُروض); **a job ~** عَرْض عَمَلٍ; **an ~ of marriage** عَرْض زَواجٍ; **that's my final ~** هَذا هو عَرْضي الأَخير; **to be open to ~s** كانَ مُسْتَعِدًّا لِتَلَقّي العُروضِ; **the house is under ~** هُناكَ عَرْضٌ لِشِراءِ البَيْتِ; **$500 or near ~** 500 دولار أو عَرْض قَريب من هذا السِعْرِ **2** (promotion) عَرْض (عُروض), تَخْفيض (تَخْفيضات); **to be on special ~** كانَ عَلَيْهِ عَرْضٌ خاصٌّ

E (**on offer**) *adj phr* **1** (available) مَعْروض; **they didn't have much on ~** لم يَكُنْ لَدَيْهِم الكَثيرُ من المَعْروضاتِ **2** (at a special price) مُخَفَّض ,عَلَيْهِ عَرْضٌ خاصٌّ; **laptops are on ~ at £349** هُناكَ عَرْضٌ خاصٌّ على الحاسِباتِ المَحْمولةِ بِسِعْرِ 349 جُنَيْهاً

offering /'ɒfərɪŋ/ *n* **1** (Relig, Mythol) تَقْديم قُرْبانٍ \ ذَبيحةٍ **2** (Busn) مَعْروض لِلبَيْعِ

offhand /ɒf'hand/ **A** *adj* ‹remark, manner› فَظّ (أَفْظاظ), خَشِن (خِشان)

B *adv* على البَديهةِ, ارْتِجالاً, من دونِ تَفْكيرٍ; **~, I don't know/I can't say** ارْتِجالاً، لا أَسْتَطيعُ أَنْ أَجْزِمَ

office /'ɒfɪs/ **A** *n* **1** (place of work) مَكْتَب (مَكاتِبُ); **the accounts ~** مَكْتَبُ المُحاسِبينَ; **to go to the ~** ذَهَبَ إلى المَكْتَبِ; **the whole ~ knows** المَكْتَبُ كُلُّهُ يَعْرِفُ **2** (AmE) ▸**dentist's office**, ▸**doctor's office** **3** (position) مَنْصِب (مَناصِبُ), وَظيفة (وَظائِفُ); **to be in ~** «the president» كانَ في السُلْطة «mayor» كانَ في مَنْصِبِهِ; **to take ~** تَوَلّى المَنْصِبَ; **to leave ~** «the president, political parties» تَرَكَ المَنْصِبَ; **to run** *or* **stand** (BrE) **for ~** تَرَشَّحَ لِمَنْصِبٍ

B (**offices**) *n pl* (fml) (services) خِدْمات; **through their good ~s** عن طَريقِ وَساطَتِهِمْ

office block *n* (BrE) عِمارة مَكاتِبَ

office equipment *n* تَجْهيزات مَكْتَبٍ

office party *n* حَفْلة لِلمُوَظَّفينَ في مَكْتَبٍ

officer /'ɒfɪsə/ *n* **1** (in the army, navy) ضابِط (ضُبّاط) **2** (official) مَسْؤول **3** (also **police officer**) شُرْطيّ

office worker *n* مُوَظَّف \ عامِل إداريّ

official /ə'fɪʃ(ə)l/ **A** *adj* ‹sources, inquiry, figures› رَسْميّ

B *n* مُوَظَّف, مَسْؤول

officially /ə'fɪʃ(ə)li/ *adv* ‹to announce, confirm› رَسْميًّا

officiate /ə'fɪʃieɪt/ *vi* (at a ceremony, an event) «priests» أَقامَ القُدّاسَ; «officials, leaders» رَأَسَ (a; رِئاسة); «referee, stewards» تَوَلّى مُهِمّةَ الحَكَمِ

officious /ə'fɪʃəs/ *adj* (pej) ‹customs officer, clerk› مُتَسَلِّط, مُتَأَمِّر

offing /'ɒfɪŋ/ *n* **to be in the ~** على وَشْكِ الحُدوثِ

off key *adj, adv* ناشِز, بِنَشازٍ

off-licence /'ɒflaɪs(ə)ns/ *n* (BrE) مَحَلّ بَيْعِ الخُمورِ

off limits *adj* ‹building, area› مَحْظور \ مَمْنوع الدُخولِ

offline /ɒf'laɪn/ *adj* غَيْر مُتَّصِل (بالإنْتَرْنِت); **to be ~** «users, servers» كانَ غَيْرَ مُتَّصِلٍ (بالإنْتَرْنِت)

offload /ɒf'ləʊd/ *vt* فَرَّغَ ‹goods, a container›

off-message /ɒfˈmɛsɪdʒ/ *adj* (Pol) **to be ~** «opinion, candidates» [خَرَجَ عن الالْتِزامِ الحِزْبِيِّ \ الخِطابِ السِياسيِّ للحِزْبِ]

off-peak /ɒfˈpiːk/ *adj* ‹rate, travel› خارِجَ أَوْقاتِ الذُرْوةِ

off-putting /ɒfˈpʊtɪŋ/ *adj* (BrE) **1** (disconcerting) ‹manner, sensation› مُرْبِك, مُنَفِّر **2** (unpleasant) ‹experience, behaviour› غَيْر مُرِيح, مُضايِق

off-road /ɒfˈrəʊd/ *adj* ‹driving, use› خارِجَ الطريقِ; **an ~ vehicle** سَيّارة دَفْعٍ رُباعيٍّ ≈

off-season /ɒfˈsiːz(ə)n/ *adj* **1** (of holiday time) ‹cruise, holiday› خارِجَ المَوْسِمِ **2** (Sport) ‹signing, training› خارِجَ المَوْسِمِ

offset /ˈɒfsɛt/ *vt* (*present participle* **-tt-**; *past tense, past participle* **offset**) وازَنَ, عَوَّضَ, عادَلَ ‹a cost, loss›

offshoot /ˈɒfʃuːt/ *n* فَرْع (فُروع), شُعْبة (شُعَب)

offshore /ɒfˈʃɔː/ **A** *adj* **1** (in the sea) ‹exploration, island› بَحْرِيّ **2** (towards the open sea) ‹breeze, current› في اتِّجاهِ البَحْرِ **3** (Fin) ‹investments, account› خارِجِيّ, ما وراء البِحارِ, في الخارِجِ

B *adv* **1** (towards the open sea) ‹to blow, drift› في اتِّجاهِ البَحْرِ **2** (Fin) ‹to invest, move› إلى الخارِجِ

offside /ɒfˈsʌɪd/ **A** *adj* ‹player, position, goal› مُتَسَلِّل; **to be ~** كانَ مُتَسَلِّلاً

B *adv* ‹to run, stray› مُتَسَلِّلاً

C *n* (BrE) [جانِب السَيّارةِ القَرِيب من السائِقِ]

offspring /ˈɒfsprɪŋ/ *n* (*pl* **offspring**) (in family) ذُرِّيّة (ذُرِّيّات), نَسْل (أَنْسال), سُلالة; (Zool) صَغير (صِغار)

offstage /ɒfˈsteɪdʒ/ *adj, adv* خارِجَ المَسْرَحِ

off the cuff *adj* (*before n* **off-the-cuff**) ‹remark, speech› ارْتِجاليّ, من دونِ سابِقِ إعْدادٍ \ تَحْضيرٍ

off the peg *adj* (*before n* **off-the-peg**) ‹clothes, suit› جاهِز

off the shelf *adj* (*before n* **off-the-shelf**) ‹goods, software› مُتاح في السوقِ; ‹sale› مُباشِر

off the wall *adj* (*before n* **off-the-wall**) (infml) ‹humour, comedy› غَريب, غَيْر مَأْلوفٍ

off-white /ɒfˈwʌɪt/ *adj* [أَبْيَض مائِل للصُفْرةِ]

often /ˈɒf(ə)n, ˈɒft(ə)n/ *adv* ‹to call, meet› غالِباً, كَثيراً ما, مِراراً; **every so ~** من وَقْتٍ لآخَرَ, بين الفَيْنةِ والأُخْرى; **once too ~** مِراراً وتَكْراراً; **how ~ do you meet?** كم مَرّةً تَلْتَقونَ؟

ogle /ˈəʊg(ə)l/ *vt* بَصْبَصَ (i; بَصْبَصة ل) ‹a woman, girl›

ogre /ˈəʊgə/ *n* **1** (giant) غول (أَغْوال) **2** (cruel person) [شَخْص وَحْشيّ \ فَظّ جِدًّا]

oh /əʊ/ *excl* آخ, أوف, أوه, يا; **~ dear!** يا إلَهي!

OH *abbr* = **Ohio**

Ohio /əʊˈhʌɪəʊ/ *pr n* أوهايو (f)

Ohioan /əʊˈhʌɪəʊən/ *pr n, adj* [(شَخْص) من أوهايو]

oil /ɔɪl/ **A** *n* **1** (for fuel) نَفْط; (for lubrication) زَيْت (زُيوت); **heating ~** زَيْت تَدْفِئة; **to check the ~** فَحَصَ الزَيْتَ; **to change the ~** غَيَّرَ الزَيْتَ; **to strike ~** عَثَرَ على النَفْطِ **2** (for cooking) زَيْت (زُيوت); **olive/sunflower ~** زَيْت الزَيْتونِ \ عَبّادِ الشَمْسِ; **to cook with ~** طَبَخَ بالزَيْتِ **3** (oil paint) **to work in ~s** رَسَمَ بالأَلْوانِ الزَيْتيّة **4** (in cosmetics) زَيْت (زُيوت); **essential ~s** الزُيوت الأساسيّة **5** (AmE infml) (flattery) إطْراء

B *vt* زَيَّتَ ‹a mechanism, the moving parts›

oilcan /ˈɔɪlkan/ *n* مِزْيَتة

oil change *n* تَغْيير زَيْتِ السَيّارةِ

oilcloth /ˈɔɪlklɒθ/ *n* مُشَمَّع

oil derrick *n* ▸ **derrick 2**

oil exploration *n* تَنْقيب عن النَفْطِ

oilfield /ˈɔɪlfiːld/ *n* حَقْل نَفْطٍ

oil industry *n* صِناعة النَفْطِ, صِناعات بِتْروليّة

oil paint *n* أَلْوان زَيْتيّة

oil painting *n* **1** (painting) لَوْحة \ صورة زَيْتيّة **2** [u] (activity) التَصْوير \ الرَسْم بالزَيْتِ

oil refinery *n* مِصْفاة نَفْطٍ

oil rig *n* مَنَصّة للتَنْقيب عن النَفْطِ

oilseed rape /ˌɔɪlsiːd ˈreɪp/ *n* لِفْت زَيْتيّ, سَلْجَم

oilskins /ˈɔɪlskɪnz/ *n pl* (BrE) بِزّة واقِية من المَطَرِ

oil slick *n* بُقْعة زَيْتٍ \ نَفْطٍ

oil tanker *n* ناقِلة نَفْطٍ \ زَيْتٍ

oil terminal *n* ميناء بِتْروليّ

oil well *n* بِئْر زَيْتٍ \ نَفْطٍ

oily /ˈɔɪli/ *adj* (**oilier**, **oiliest**) 1 ‹*liquid, pool*› مُزَيَّت ,زَيْتيّ 2 ‹*hair, skin*› دُهْنيّ 3 ‹*clothes, rag*› مُلَطَّخ بالزَيْتِ 4 ‹*food, chips*› مُشَبَّع بالزَيْتِ

oily fish *n* سَمَك زَيْتيّ \ دُهْنيّ \ غَنيّ بالزُيوتِ

ointment /ˈɔɪntmənt/ *n* مَرْهَم (مَراهِمُ)

OK¹ /əʊˈkeɪ/ (infml) **A** *adj* **are you ~?** هل أَنْت بخَيْرٍ؟ ;**is it ~ to use this?** هل من المُمْكِنِ اسْتِعْمالُ هذا؟ ;**'how was the concert?'—'~'** 'كيف كانَت الحَفْلةُ الموسيقيّةُ؟' -'لا بَأْسَ' **B** *adv* ‹*to play, work out*› بِشَكْلٍ مَقْبولٍ ,بِطَريقةٍ لا بَأْسَ بِها ;**it went ~** جَرى بِطَريقةٍ جَيِّدةٍ **C** *n* **to give sb the ~** أَعْطى شَخْصاً المُوافَقةَ \ الضَوْءَ الأَخْضَرَ **D** *excl* حَسَناً; **'can I borrow your car?'—'~'** 'هل يُمْكِنُني اسْتِعارةُ سَيّارَتِكَ؟' -'حَسَناً'

OK² *abbr* = **Oklahoma**

okay /əʊˈkeɪ/ *adj, adv, n, excl* ▸**OK¹**

Oklahoma /ˌəʊkləˈhəʊmə/ *pr n* أوكْلاهوما

Oklahoman /ˌəʊkləˈhəʊm(ə)n/ *pr n, adj* [(شَخْص) من أوكْلاهوما]

okra /ˈəʊkrə/ *n* بامِية

old /əʊld/ **A** *n* 1 (**the old** *n pl*) (old people) كِبار السِنِّ 2 (earlier era) **in days of ~** في قَديمِ الزَمانِ; **I know him of ~** أَعْرِفُهُ منذ زَمَنٍ بَعيدٍ **B** *adj* 1 (elderly, not young) ‹*person, horse, tiger*› عَجوز (mf; عَجائِزُ), مُسِنّ; **an ~ man/woman** رَجُل \ امْرَأة عَجوز; **~ people** المُسِنّونَ ,الكِبار; **to get** *or* **grow ~** كَبِرَ (a; كِبَر), تَقَدَّمَ في السِنِّ; **~ before one's time** عَجوز قبل أَوانِهِ 2 (fml) (of a particular age) **how ~ are you?** كم عُمْرُكَ؟; **a six-year-~ boy** هذا صَبيّ عُمْرُهُ سِتُّ سَنَواتٍ; **this bread is a week ~** الخُبْزُ عُمْرُهُ أُسْبوعٌ; **to be as ~ as sb else** كانَ في نَفْسِ عُمْرِ شَخْصٍ آخَرَ; **we don't know how ~ it is** لا نَعْرِفُ عُمْرَهُ; **my ~er brother** أَخي الأَكْبَر; **she is 10 years ~er than him** هي أَكْبَرُ مِنْهُ بِعَشْرِ سَنَواتٍ; **the ~er children play here** الأَطْفالُ الأَكْبَرُ سِنّاً يَلْعَبونَ هُنا; **I'm the ~est in my class** أنا الأَكْبَرُ في فَصْلي; **to be ~ enough to do sth** كانَ كَبيراً بما فيه الكِفايةُ لِيَفْعَلَ شَيْئاً; **you're ~ enough to know better** أَنْتَ كَبيرٌ بما يَكْفي لِئَلاّ تَفْعَلَ هَذا الخَطأَ 3 (not new) ‹*clothes, song, joke*› قَديم (قُدامى ,قُدَماءُ); **we're ~ friends** نَحْنُ أَصْدِقاءُ قُدامى; **a famous ~ company** شَرِكة قَديمة مَشْهورة; **the ~ town** البَلْدة القَديمة 4 (former, previous) ‹*address, job, system*› قَديم; **in the ~ days** في الأَيّامِ الخَوالي; **just like ~ times** كَما كانَ في الماضي; **this is the ~ road to London** هذا هو الطَريقُ القَديمُ إلى لَنْدَن 5 (infml) (expressing affection) ‹*car, cat*› قَديم (قُدامى ,قُدَماءُ); **poor ~ George died at 62** ماتَ صَديقُنا المِسْكينُ جورْج عن عُمْرِ 62 عاماً 6 (infml) (as an intensifier) **a right ~ mess** فَوْضى تامّة; **just put them down any ~ how/where** ضَعْها كَيْفَما \ حَيْثُما شِئْتَ

old age *n* شَيْخوخة

old-age pensioner /ˌəʊldeɪdʒ ˈpenʃ(ə)nə/ *n* (BrE) مُتَقاعِد (مُحال على مَعاشِ الشَيْخوخةِ)

old boy *n* 1 (ex-pupil) تِلْميذ سابِق 2 (infml) (old man) مُسِنّ, عَجوز (mf; عَجائِزُ)

olden /ˈəʊld(ə)n/ *adj* **in ~ times, in the ~ days** في أَيّامَ زَمانٍ الماضي

old-fashioned /əʊldˈfaʃ(ə)nd/ *adj* ‹*detective, method*› على الطِرازِ القَديمِ; ‹*idea, attitude*› مُحافِظ ,قَديم; ‹*suitcase, typewriter*› عَتيق, من طِرازٍ قَديمٍ

old girl *n* 1 (ex-pupil) تِلْميذة سابِقة 2 (infml) (old lady) امْرَأة عَجوز ,مُسِنّة (mf; عَجائِزُ)

old people's home *n* بَيْت العَجَزةِ \ المُسِنّينَ

Old Testament *n* (**the Old Testament**) العَهْد القَديم

old wives' tale *n* خُرافة

oligarchy /ˈɒlɪgɑːki/ *n* (*pl* **oligarchies**) 1 [u] (rule) أوليغارْشيّة, حُكْم القِلّةِ 2 (state) دَوْلة أوليغارْشيّة

olive /ˈɒlɪv/ **A** *n* 1 (fruit) زَيْتون (n coll) 2 (also **olive tree**) شَجَرة زَيْتونٍ **B** *adj* (also **olive green**) ‹*eyes, dress*› زَيْتيّ ,زَيْتونيّ

olive oil *n* زَيْت زَيْتونٍ

Olympic /əˈlɪmpɪk/ **A** *adj* ‹*medal, torch*› أولِمْبيّ **B** *n pl* **the ~s** الأَلْعاب الأولِمْبيّة

Olympic Games *n* (**the Olympic Games**) الأَلْعاب الأولِمْبيّة

Olympics *n pl* ▸ **Olympic Games**

Oman /əʊˈmɑːn/ *pr n* عُمان (dipt f)

Omani /əʊˈmɑːni/ *n, adj* عُمانيّ

ombudsman /ˈɒmbʊdzmən/ *n* (*pl* **ombudsmen** /ˈɒmbʊdzmɛn/) [وسيط قانونيّ]

omelette, **omelet** /ˈɒmlɪt/ *n* أومْليت, عُجّة بَيْضٍ; **a plain/cheese ~** أومْليت سادة \ بالجُبْنِ

omen /ˈəʊmən/ *n* (good) (فُؤول) فَأْل; (bad) (نُذُر) نَذير, طيرة

ominous /ˈɒmɪnəs/ *adj* <*sign, cloud*> مُنْذِر بِسوءٍ, مَشْؤوم

omission /əʊˈmɪʃ(ə)n/ *n* إهْمال, حَذْف, (إغْفالات) إغْفال; **it was an ~ on our part** كانَ ذلكَ سَهْواً من جانِبِنا

omit /əʊˈmɪt/ *vt* (**-tt-**) 1 حَذَفَ (i; حَذْف) <*words, details*>; **the composer's name was ~ted from the programme** حُذِفَ اسْمُ المُؤَلِّفِ من البَرْنامَجِ 2 **to ~ to do sth** أَهْمَلَ فِعْلَ شَيْءٍ

omnibus /ˈɒmnɪbəs/ *n* (*pl* **omnibuses**) 1 (also **omnibus edition** BrE) (of a TV or radio programme) [سِلْسِلة حَلَقاتٍ] 2 (also **omnibus volume**) (a book) [مَجْموعة كُتُبٍ \ مَجلّاتٍ في غِلافٍ واحِدٍ]

omnipotent /ɒmˈnɪpət(ə)nt/ *adj* <*God, tyrant*> مُطْلَق السُلْطةِ, قَهّار, جَبّار

omnipresent /ɒmnɪˈprɛz(ə)nt/ *adj* <*threat, surveillance*> كُلّيّ مَوْجود في كُلِّ مَكانٍ, الوجودِ

omnivorous /ɒmˈnɪv(ə)rəs/ *adj* <*diet, mammal*> قارِت

on /ɒn/ **A** *prep* 1 (showing position) عَلى; **~ the floor/table** عَلى الأَرْضِ \ المائِدةِ; **~ top of the cupboard** عَلى \ فوق الخِزانةِ; **there's a stain ~ it** يوجَدُ عَلَيْهِ بُقْعةٌ; **to live ~ Park Avenue** سَكَنَ في (شارع) بارْك آفِنْيو; **to live ~ the coast** سَكَنَ على الساحِلِ; **the paintings ~ the wall** اللَوْحات على الحائِطِ 2 (indicating attachment, contact) **to hang sth ~ a nail** عَلَّقَ شَيْئاً على مِسْمارٍ; **to punch sb ~ the nose/on the chin** ضَرَبَ شَخْصاً على أَنْفِه \ ذَقْنِهِ 3 (about one's person) **to have a ring ~ one's finger** لَبِسَ خاتَماً في إصْبَعِهِ; **to have a smile ~ one's face** ارْتَسَمَت ابْتِسامةٌ على وَجْهِهِ; **I have $50 ~ me** في حَوْزَتي 50 دولار 4 (about) عَنْ; **a programme ~ Africa** بَرْنامَج عَنْ إفريقيا; **we're ~ fractions in maths** وَصَلْنا إلى دَرْسِ الكُسورِ في الرِياضيّاتِ 5 (employed, active) **to be ~ sth** كانَ ضِمْنَ شَيْءٍ; كانَ عُضْواً في شَيْءٍ <*a team*> <*a board, committee, council*>; **to be ~ the Gazette** عَمِلَ في (جَريدةِ) الجازيت; **a job ~ the railways** وَظيفة في السِكَكِ الحَديديّةِ; **there's a guard ~ the door** هُناكَ حارِسٌ على البابِ 6 (in time expressions) **~ 22 February, ~ February 22** في 22 فِبْرايِر; **~ Saturdays** كُلَّ يَوْمِ سَبْتٍ; **~ sunny days** في الأَيّامِ المُشْمِسةِ; **~ Independence Day** في عيدِ الاسْتِقْلالِ 7 (immediately) **~ his arrival** فَوْرَ وُصولِهِ; **~ hearing the truth she ...** فَوْرَ سَماعِها الحَقيقةَ ... 8 (taking) **to be ~ antibiotics/morphine** كانَ يَتَناوَلُ مُضادّاتٍ حَيَويّةً \ المورْفين; **to be ~ drugs** تَعاطى المُخَدِّراتِ; **to be ~ 40 cigarettes a day** دَخَّنَ 40 سيجارةً في اليَوْمِ 9 (powered by) **to run ~ electricity** عَمِلَ بالكَهْرَباءِ 10 (indicating support) عَلى; **to stand ~ one leg** وَقَفَ على رِجْلٍ واحِدةٍ 11 (indicating a medium) **to be ~ TV/the radio** ظَهَرَ على التِلِفِزْيون \ تَحَدَّثَ على الراديو; **to store data ~ disk** حَفِظَ مَعْلوماتٍ على قُرْصٍ; **I heard it ~ the news** سَمِعْتُ هذا في (نَشْرةِ) الأَخْبارِ 12 (with earnings) **to be ~ a high/low salary** كانَ دَخْلُهُ مُرْتَفِعاً \ مُنْخَفِضاً; **to be ~ an income of $35,000 per year** كانَ دَخْلُهُ 35000 دولار في السَنةِ 13 (infml) (paid for by) **this meal is ~ me** هذه الوَجْبةُ على حِسابي; **have a beer ~ me** تَناوَلْ بيرةً على حِسابي 14 (Transp) **to be ~ the plane** كانَ على مَتْنِ الطائِرةِ; **to be ~ one's bike** كانَ على مَتْنِ دَرّاجَتِهِ; **to leave ~ the first train/flight** رَحَلَ على مَتْنِ أَوَّلِ قِطارٍ \ طائِرةٍ

B *adj* 1 (taking place) **is the match still ~?** هل ما تَزالُ المُباراةُ مُسْتَمِرّةً؟; **while the meeting is ~** أثناء انْعِقادِ الاجْتِماعِ; **there's a war ~** هُناكَ حَرْبٌ دائِرةٌ; **I have nothing ~ this weekend** لَيْسَ لَدَيَّ أَيُّ ارْتِباطاتٍ في عُطْلَةِ نِهايةِ هذا الأُسْبوعِ; **we have got a lot ~** لَدَيْنا الكَثيرُ من المَشاغِلِ \ الارْتِباطاتِ 2 (being broadcast, performed, displayed) **the news is ~ in 10 minutes** سَتَبْدَأُ نَشْرةُ الأَخْبارِ بعد 10 دَقائِقَ; **what's ~?** ما الّذي يُعْرَضُ الآنَ؟; **there's nothing ~** لَيْسَ هُناكَ شَيْءٌ جَيِّدٌ (يُعْرَضُ على التِلِفِزيون مَثَلاً) 3 (functioning) **to be ~** كانَ في وَضْعِ التَشْغيلِ; كانَ دائِراً «engine»; «iron»; كانَ مَفْتوحاً «tap, gas, radio»; كانَ مَضْغوطاً «brakes»; **the gas/electricity is ~** الغازُ مَفْتوحٌ \ الكَهْرَباءُ في وَضْعِ التَشْغيلِ;

the lights are ~ الأنوارُ مُضاءةٌ; **the power is back ~** عادَ التَيّارُ الكَهْرَبائيُّ; **the brakes are ~** دَوّاسةُ الفَرامِلِ مَضْغوطةٌ ④ (in place) **to be ~** ‹*lid, top*› كانَ في مَكانِهِ; **the cap isn't properly ~** الغِطاءُ لَيْسَ في مَكانِهِ \ وَضْعِهِ الصَحيح; **once the roof is ~** عند بِناءِ السَقْفِ ⑤ (BrE) (permissible) **it's just** *or* **simply not ~** هذا غَيْرُ مَقْبولٍ إطْلاقاً

C *adv* ① (on or about one's person) **to have a hat ~** ارْتَدى قُبَّعةً; **to have one's glasses ~** ارْتَدى نَظّارَتَهُ; **to have make-up ~** وَضَعَ ماكياج; **with his slippers ~** مُرْتَدِياً خُفَّهُ

② (ahead in time) **20 years ~ he was still the same** بعد 20 عاماً ظَلَّ على ما هو عَلَيْهِ; **a few years ~ from now** بعد بِضْعِ سَنَواتٍ من الآنَ; **to be well ~ in years** كانَ مُتَقَدِّماً في السِنِّ

③ (further) **to walk ~** تابَعَ السَيْرَ; **it's a little further ~** هو إلى الأَمامِ قَليلاً ④ (on stage) **I'm ~ after the juggler** سَأُقَدِّمُ عَرْضي بعد البَهْلَوانِ; **to come ~** ظَهَرَ على المَسْرَحِ

D **(on and off)** *adv phr* (also **off and on**) **to see sb ~ and off** رَأى شَخْصاً من حينٍ إلى آخَرَ

E **(on and on)** *adv phr* **to go ~ and ~** «speaker» تَحَدَّثَ بِاسْتِمْرارٍ \ دون تَوَقُّفٍ; «speech» اسْتَمَرَّ \ تواصَلَ دون تَوَقُّفٍ; **the list goes ~ and ~** القائِمةُ لا تَنْتَهي

on-board /ˈɒnbɔːd/ *adj* ‹*navigation, catering*› على مَتْنِ السَيّارةِ \ السَفينةِ \ الطائِرةِ

once /wʌns/ **A** *n* (infml) (single occasion) **I've only been there the ~** لم أَذْهَبْ إلى هُناكَ غَيْرَ مَرّةٍ واحِدةٍ; **I'll do it just this ~** سَأَقومُ بِذلِكَ هذه المَرّةَ فَقَطْ; **for ~** لِمَرّةٍ واحِدةٍ

B *adv* ① (on a single occasion) ‹*to say sth, do sth, happen*› مَرّةً واحِدةً; **~ a day/year** مَرّةً في اليَوْمِ \ السَنةِ; **~ before** مَرّةً قبل ذلك; **~ every six months** مَرّةً كُلَّ سِتّةِ أَشْهُرٍ; **I've seen him ~ or twice** رَأَيْتُهُ مَرّةً أو مَرَّتَيْنِ; **I will say this ~ only** سَأَقولُها لِلمَرّةِ الأولى والأَخيرةِ; **(for) ~ and for all** مَرّةً واحِدةً فَقَطْ; **not ~ did he offer to help** لم يَعْرِضِ المُساعَدةَ وَلا حتّى مَرّةً واحِدةً; **you've done that ~ too often** إيّاكَ وَفِعْلُ ذلك مَرّةً أُخْرى; **a ~-in-a-lifetime experience** تَجْرُبة لم وَلَنْ تَتَكَرَّرَ

② (formerly) يَوْماً ما; **she was ~ very famous** كانَتْ يَوْماً ما مَشْهورةً جِدًّا; **~ upon a time ...** كانَ يا ما كانَ ... ; **I'm not as young as I ~ was** لم أَعُدْ شابًّا كَما كُنْتُ

C **(at once)** *adv phr* ① (immediately) ‹*to leave, start*› حالاً, على الفَوْرِ; **come here at ~!** تَعالَ هُنا حالاً!; **all at ~ the door flew open** فَجْأةً انْفَتَحَ البابُ ② (simultaneously) في آنٍ واحِدٍ; **don't all talk at ~!** لا تَتَكَلَّموا في آنٍ واحِدٍ!

D *conj* حالَما, بِمُجَرَّدِ أنْ; **~ he had eaten, he felt better** بِمُجَرَّد أنْ أَكَلَ، شَعَرَ بِتَحَسُّنٍ

once-over /ˈwʌnsəʊvə/ *n* (infml) نَظْرة سَريعة; **to give the house the/a ~** أَخَذَ نَظْرةً سَريعةً على البَيْتِ

oncologist /ɒŋˈkɒlədʒɪst/ *n* أَخِصّائيّ أَوْرامٍ

oncology /ɒŋˈkɒlədʒi/ *n* عِلْمُ الأَوْرامِ

oncoming /ˈɒnkʌmɪŋ/ *adj* ‹*car, traffic*› قادِمٌ

one /wʌn/ **A** *determiner* ① (single) واحِد; **~ car/hat** سَيّارة \ قُبَّعة واحِدة; **chapter ~** الفَصْلُ الأَوَّل; **two offers in ~ day** عَرْضانِ في يَوْمٍ واحِدٍ ② (unique, sole) وَحيد; **her ~ pleasure** مُتْعَتُها الوَحيدة; **my ~ and only wish** أُمْنِيَتي الأولى والأَخيرة; **the ~ and only Kylie Minogue** الفَنّانة الّتي لَيْسَ لَها مَثيلٌ: كايْلي مينوغ ③ (in expressions of time) **at ~ (o'clock)** في (الساعةِ) الواحِدةِ; **~ day in summer, ~ summer's day** في أَحَدِ أَيّامِ الصَيْفِ; **~ of these days** في يَوْمٍ من الأَيّامِ ④ (fml) (same) **to be of ~ mind** كانوا مُتَّفِقينَ

B *pron* ① (thing or person) أَحَد, واحِد; **can you lend me ~?** هل بِإمْكانِكَ أنْ تُعيرَني واحِداً؟; **~ of them must know** لا بُدَّ أنّ أَحَدَهُمْ يَعْرِفُ; **she's ~ of our best customers** هي إحْدى أَفْضَلِ زَبائِنِنا; **she's ~ of us** هي واحِدةٌ مِنّا; **~ after another** واحِد بعد الآخَرِ; **I can't tell ~ from the other** لا أَسْتَطيعُ أنْ أُفَرِّقَ بَيْنَهُما; **~'s grey and the other's black** أَحَدُهُما رَماديٌّ والآخَرُ أَسْوَدُ; ▸ **any** ② (impersonal) المَرْء; **~ would like to think that they are honest** يَوَدُّ المَرْءُ أنْ يَعْتَقِدَ أَنَّهُمْ شُرَفاءُ; **it's enough to make ~ give up** يَكْفي لِجَعْلِ المَرْءِ يَسْتَسْلِمُ

③ (someone: specified) **he's the ~ when it comes to football** هو الشَخْصُ الّذي يَعْرِفُ الكَثيرَ عن كُرةِ القَدَمِ; **I'm not ~ for literature** لَسْتُ بالشَخْصِ الخَبيرِ بالأَدَبِ; (: unspecified) **for ~ who claims to be an expert** لِمَنْ يَدَّعي أَنَّهُ خَبيرٌ

④ (demonstrative) **this ~** هذا الواحِد; **that ~** ذلك الواحِد; **the grey ~** الواحِد الرَماديّ; **the black ~s** السَوْداء; **which ~?** أَيّ واحِدٍ؟; **that's the ~** ذلك هو; **the new model is more** economical than the old ~ النوعُ الجَديدُ اقْتِصاديٌّ أَكْثَرُ من القَديمِ

C *n* واحِد; ~, two, three, go! واحِد، اثْنان، ثَلاثة، انْطَلِقْ! it cost ~ seventy-five ثَمَنُهُ واحِدٌ وَخَمْسَةٌ وَسَبْعونَ

D (as one) *adv phr* ‹to reply, shout› كَرَجُلٍ واحِدٍ

E (in one) *adv phr* you've got it in ~ أَصَبْتَ عَيْنَ الحَقيقَةِ

F (one by one) *adv phr* واحِداً بعد \ تِلْوَ الآخَرِ; they left ~ by ~ غادَروا واحِداً تِلْوَ الآخَرِ; he picked them up ~ by ~ الْتَقَطَهُمْ واحِداً واحِداً

(Idioms) to be at one with sb كانَ مُتَّفِقاً مع شَخْصٍ; to be one up on sb تَقَدَّمَ على شَخْصٍ; to go one better than sb تَفَوَّقَ على شَخْصٍ

one another *pron* (also **each other**) بَعْضُهُمْ بَعْضاً; they love one another يُحِبّونَ بَعْضُهُم البَعْض

one-armed /ˌwʌnˈɑːmd/ *adj* ‹hug, veteran› بِذِراعٍ واحِدَةٍ

one-day /ˈwʌndeɪ/ *adj before n* ‹conference, match› لِيَوْمٍ واحِدٍ

one-man /ˈwʌnman/ *adj* ‹show, crusade› فَرْدِيّ

one-off /wʌnˈɒf/ **A** *adj* ‹payment, incident› فريد من نَوْعِهِ, لِمَرَّةٍ واحِدَةٍ

B *n* [حادِث فَريد من نَوْعِهِ]

one-on-one *adj* ▸ **one-to-one**

one-parent family /wʌnˌpɛːrənt ˈfamli/ *n* [أُسْرة ذات والِدٍ واحِدٍ]

one-piece /ˈwʌnpiːs/ *adj* ‹swimsuit, jumpsuit› ذو قِطْعَةٍ واحِدَةٍ

onerous /ˈəʊn(ə)rəs/ *adj* (fml) ‹task, duty› شاقّ, مُرْهِق

one's /wʌnz/ **A** = **one is**, = **one has**

B *determiner* ـُهُ; ~ books/friends كُتُبُهُ \ أَصْدِقاؤُهُ; a house of ~ own بَيْتُهُ الخاصُّ; one tries to do ~ best يُحاوِلُ الواحِدُ أَنْ يَفْعَلَ أَحْسَنَ ما لَدَيْهِ

oneself /wʌnˈsɛlf/ *pron* **1** (reflexive) نَفْسَهُ; to wash/cut ~ غَسَلَ \ جَرَحَ نَفْسَهُ **2** (emphatic) بِنَفْسِهِ; it's important to read it ~ من المُهِمِّ أَنْ تَقْرَأَهُ بِنَفْسِكَ **3** (after prepositions) to be sure of ~ كانَ مُتَأَكِّداً من نَفْسِهِ; to talk to ~ تَكَلَّمَ مع نَفْسِهِ **4** (in expressions) to live (all) by ~ عاشَ وَحيداً; to do sth (all) by ~ فَعَلَ شَيْئاً بِنَفْسِهِ; to have the house all to ~ كانَ البَيْتُ لَهُ بِمُفْرَدِهِ

one-sided /wʌnˈsʌɪdɪd/ *adj* ‹account, reporting› من طَرَفٍ \ جانِبٍ واحِدٍ, مُتَحَيِّز; ‹contest, encounter› غَيْر مُتَكافِئٍ

one-stop shopping /ˌwʌnstɒp ˈʃɒpɪŋ/ *n* التَسَوُّق من مَكانٍ واحِدٍ

one-time /ˈwʌntʌɪm/ *adj* ‹ally, stronghold› سابِق, في ما مَضى \ من زَمانٍ

one-to-one /wʌntəˈwʌn/ *adj* ‹tuition, basis› فَرْدِيّ, واحِد لِواحِدٍ

one-upmanship /wʌnˈʌpmənʃɪp/ *n* مُزايَدة

one-way /wʌnˈweɪ/ *adj* **1** ‹traffic, street› ب \ ذو اتِّجاهٍ واحِدٍ; Privet Street is ~/a ~ street شارِعُ بْريفِت هو شارِعٌ ذو اتِّجاهٍ واحِدٍ **2** ‹ticket, trip› ذَهاب

one-woman /ˈwʌnˌwʊmən/ *adj* (for one person) ‹job› [لامْرَأَةٍ واحِدَةٍ]; a ~ show [عَرْض فَنِّيّ تُقَدِّمُهُ امْرَأَةٌ واحِدَةٌ]

ongoing /ˈɒŋgəʊɪŋ/ *adj* ‹investigation, debate› جارٍ, مُسْتَمِرّ

onion /ˈʌnjən/ *n* بَصَل (n coll)

online, on-line /ɒnˈlʌɪn/ **A** *adj* ‹shopping, service› على الشَبَكَةِ \ الخَطّ, من خِلالِ \ بِواسِطَةِ \ عَبْرَ الإنْتَرْنِت; are you ~ at the moment? هل أَنْتَ على الخطِّ الآنَ؟

B *adv* ‹to go, search› على الإِنْتَرْنِت, من خِلالِ \ بِواسِطَةِ \ عَبْرَ الإِنْتَرْنِت; the majority of businesses do their banking ~ تُجْري غالِبِيَّةُ الشَرِكاتِ مُعامَلاتِها المَصْرِفيَّةَ على الإِنْتَرْنِت; I do most of my shopping ~ أَشْتَري مُعْظَمَ أَشْيائي من الإِنْتَرْنِت

online dating *n* التَعارُف عن طَريقِ الإِنْتَرْنِت

onlooker /ˈɒnlʊkə/ *n* مُتَفَرِّج, مُشاهِد; curious ~s مُتَفَرِّجونَ فُضوليّونَ

only /ˈəʊnli/ **A** *adv* **1** (exclusively) ‹to apply, exist› فَقَطْ, فَحَسْبُ; it applies ~ to pensioners هذا يَنْطَبِقُ على المُتَقاعِدينَ فَقَطْ; I'm ~ interested in flowers أَنا مُهْتَمٌّ بالوُرودِ فَقَطْ; 'members ~' 'للأَعْضاءِ فَقَطْ' **2** (nothing more than) ‹natural, fair› مُجَرَّد, لَيْسَ إِلّا من بابِ; it's ~ polite to ask permission لا ... إِلّا الأَدَبِ طَلَبُ الإِذْنِ **3** (in expressions of time) ‹yesterday, then› فَقَطْ, لا ... إِلّا, مُنْذُ ... فَقَط; ~ last week, she said she would do it مُنْذُ أُسْبوعٍ فَقَطْ قالَتْ إِنَّها سَتَقومُ بِهِ **4** (merely) فَقَطْ, مُجَرَّد; he's ~ a baby هو مُجَرَّدُ طِفْلٍ; Mark is ~ sixteen عُمْرُ مارْك

16 عاماً فَقَطْ; **I ~ earn £7 an hour** أَكْسَبُ 7 جُنَيْهاتٍ فَقَطْ في الساعةِ; **you'll ~ make him angry** سَتُغْضِبُهُ فَقَطْ

B (**only just**) *adv phr* **1** (very recently) لِتَوِّهِ, تَوًّا, لا ... إلّا; **I've ~ just arrived** لم أَصِلْ إلّا هذه اللَحْظَةَ **2** (barely) بالكاد; **the amount is ~ just enough** المَبْلَغُ بالكادِ يَكْفي

C *adj* (sole) ‹*way, time*› وَحيد; **it's the ~ one left** هو الوَحيدُ المُتَبَقّي; **he's an ~ child** هو طِفْلٌ وَحيدٌ; **she's the ~ one for me** هي الوَحيدةُ بالنِسْبةِ لي; **the ~ place to find it, is ...** المَكانُ الوَحيدُ الّذي يُمْكِنُكَ أنْ تَجِدَهُ فيهِ هو ...

D *conj* (infml) لَكِنْ, غَيْرَ أَنَّ, إلّا أَنَّ; **you can hold the baby, ~ don't drop him** يُمْكِنُكَ حَمْلُ الطِفْلِ لَكِنْ لا تُسْقِطْهُ; **it's like hang-gliding ~ safer** هو مِثْلَ الطَيَرانِ الشِراعيِّ المُعَلَّقِ إلّا أَنَّهُ أَكْثَرُ أَماناً; **I'd come ~ I'm working tonight** أَوَدُّ الحُضورَ إلا أَنّني أَعْمَلُ اللَيْلَةَ

(Idioms) **goodness/God/Heaven only knows!** (infml) اللّهُ أَعْلَمُ!; **not only ... but (also) ...** لا ... فَقَطْ ... بَلْ (أَيْضاً); **she's not ~ charming but also intelligent** لَيْسَتْ فاتِنةً فَقَطْ بَلْ هي ذَكيّةٌ أَيْضاً; **only too** جِدًّا; **I remember it ~ too well** أَتَذَكَّرُهُ جَيِّداً جِدًّا; **they were ~ too pleased to help** كانَ يَسُرُّهُمْ كُلَّ السُرورِ أنْ يُساعِدوا

on-message /ɒn'mesɪdʒ/ *adj* ‹*soundbite, politician*› [على مَسارِ \ نَهْجِ الحِزْبِ]

o.n.o. /əʊen'əʊ/ *abbr* (BrE) = **or near(est) offer**; **guitar £200 ~** قيثار ب 200 جُنَيْهٍ أو أَقْرَبِ سِعْرٍ

on-screen /ɒn'skri:n/ *adj* ‹*romance, character*› على الشاشةِ

onset /'ɒnset/ *n* (of symptoms, a disease) بَدْء; (of winter) مَطْلَع, أَوَّل; (of war) بِداية, مُسْتَهَلّ

onshore /'ɒnʃɔ:/ **A** *adj* **1** (on land) ‹*pipeline, terminal*› في البَرِّ, بَرِّيّ **2** (towards land) ‹*wind, current*› آتٍ من البَحْرِ

B *adv* (towards land) ‹*to blow, drift*› باتِّجاهِ البَرِّ

onside /ɒn'saɪd/ **A** *adj* ‹*player*› خارِجَ مَنْطِقةِ التَسَلُّلِ

B *adv* ‹*to get*› خارِجاً عن مَنْطِقةِ التَسَلُّلِ

on-site /ɒn'saɪt/ *adj* ‹*visit, service*› في المَوْقِعِ

onslaught /'ɒnslɔ:t/ *n* انْقِضاض, سَطْو, هُجوم ضارٍ

onstage /ɒn'steɪdʒ/ *adv* على المَسْرَحِ; **to go/come ~** بَرَزَ \ ظَهَرَ على المَسْرَحِ

on-target earnings /ɒntɑ:gɪt 'ɜ:nɪŋz/ *n pl* [راتِب على أَساسِ نِسْبةِ المَبيعاتِ المُسْتَهْدَفةِ]

on the spot **A** *adj before n* ‹*repairs, decision*› مُباشِر

B *adv* **1** (immediately) ‹*to decide, be killed*› على الفَوْرِ, حالاً, مُباشَرةً **2** (at the scene) في المَكانِ نَفْسِهِ, في عَيْنِ المَكانِ

on to, onto /'ɒntu:/ *prep* **1** (on) فَوْقَ, عَلى; **he climbed up ~ the roof** صَعَدَ فَوْقَ السَقْفِ; **I fell ~ the bed** وَقَعْتُ عَلى السَريرِ **2** (on the trail of) على وَشْكِ الاكْتِشافِ; **we knew we were ~ something big** عَرَفْنا أَنّنا كُنّا على وَشْكِ أنْ نَكْتَشِفَ شَيْئاً كَبيراً; **the police are ~ him** الشُرْطةُ على وَشْكِ اكْتِشافِ أَفْعالِهِ

onus /'əʊnəs/ *n* عِبْء (أَعْباء), مَسْؤوليّة, واجِب (واجِبات); **the ~ is on employers to protect their workers** يَحْمِلُ أَرْبابُ العَمَلِ مَسْؤوليّةَ حِمايةِ عُمّالِهِمْ

onward /'ɒnwəd/ **A** *adv* (BrE also **onwards**) ‹*to move, continue*› إلى الأَمامِ, قُدُماً, فَصاعِداً; **from now ~** من الآنَ فَصاعِداً

B *adj* ‹*journey, flight*› تَكْميليّ

ooh /u:/ *excl* آه, ياي; **~, that is wonderful!** ~, ياي، هذا جَميلٌ!; **~, my feet are killing me!** آه، قَدَمايَ تُؤْلِمانِي!

oops /u:ps, ʊps/ *excl* (infml) يا ساتِرُ

ooze /u:z/ **A** *vt* **1** (to discharge) أَفْرَزَ, نَزَّ (i; نَزّ); **the sore was oozing pus** نَزَّ الدُمَّلُ قَيْحاً **2** (to exude) شَعَّ, تَدَفَّقَ; **to ~ confidence/charm** شَعَّ ثِقةً بالنَفْسِ \ جاذِبيّةً

B *vi* **tortillas oozing with melted cheese** التورْتيلا الّذي يَتَصَبَّبُ الجُبْنُ المُذابُ مِنْهُ; **his voice ~d with sarcasm** [كانَ التَهَكُّمُ في صَوْتِهِ واضِحاً]

op /ɒp/ = **operation** *n* (infml) **1** (medical) عَمَليّة (جِراحيّة) **2** (on computers) عَمَليّة

opal /'əʊp(ə)l/ *n* أوبال

opaque /əʊ'peɪk/ *adj* ‹*glass, tights*› غَيْرُ شَفّافٍ, مُعْتِم

OPEC /'əʊpek/ *n* = **Organization of Petroleum Exporting Countries** مُنَظَّمةُ الدُوَلِ المُصَدِّرةِ لِلبِتْرولِ (f), أوبِك

open /'əʊp(ə)n/ **A** *adj* **1** (not closed) ‹*door, curtains, letter, eyes*› مَفْتوح; **the window was half ~** كانَ الشُبّاكُ نِصْفَ مَفْتوحٍ; **to get the door/safe ~** فَتَحَ البابَ \ الخِزانةَ; **the door burst ~** انْفَتَحَ البابُ فَجْأةً; **the book lay ~ at page 21** كانَ الكِتابُ

21 مَفْتوحاً على صَفْحَةِ; **he welcomed me with ~ arms** اِسْتَقْبَلَني بِذِراعَيْنِ مَفْتوحَيْنِ; **in ~ court** في مُحاكَمةٍ عَلَنِيّةٍ **2** (for business) ‹*bank, shop, bar*› مَفْتوح; **to be ~ for business/to the public** كانَ مَفْتوحاً للعَمَلِ \ للجُمْهورِ; **~ 24/7** مَفْتوح 24 ساعةً في اليَوْم 7 أيّامٍ في الأُسْبوعِ **3** (not obstructed) مَفْتوح; **the road/line is ~ again** الطَريقُ \ الخطُّ مَفْتوحٌ مَرّةً أُخرى; **in the ~ air** في الهَواءِ الطَلْقِ; **the ~ sea** أَعالي البِحارِ; **the wide ~ spaces** المَساحات المَفْتوحة الواسِعة; **an ~ view** مَنْظَر مَفْتوح **4** (not covered) ‹*car, carriage*› مَكْشوف; ‹*mine, sewer*› خارِجيّ; **an ~ fire** نار مَكْشوفة **5** (susceptible) **~ to the air/the elements** مُعَرَّض للهَواءِ \ للعَوامِلِ الجَوِّيّةِ; **~ to attack** مُعَرَّض للهُجومِ; **to leave oneself ~ to criticism** تَرَكَ نَفْسَهُ عُرْضةً للانْتِقادِ; **to be ~ to offers/suggestions** كانَ مُسْتَعِدًّا لِتَلَقّي العُروضِ \ للمُقْتَرَحاتِ; **that's ~ to question** ذلك مَوْضِعٌ للتَسائُلِ **6** (unrestricted) ‹*competition, meeting*› مَفْتوح; **the position is still ~** لا يَزالُ المَنْصِبُ شاغِراً; **there are several courses of action ~ to us** هُناكَ عِدّةُ مَساراتٍ مَفْتوحةٌ لَنا **7** (honest) ‹*person, discussion, statement*› صَريح (صُرَحاءُ); **to be ~ with sb about sth** كانَ صَريحاً مع شَخْصٍ حول شَيْءٍ **8** (undisguised) ‹*hostility, rivalry, disagreement*› عَلَنيّ **9** (undecided) ‹*question, date*› مَفْتوح; **we left the date ~** تَرَكْنا التاريخَ مَفْتوحاً; **the election is wide ~** لا يُمْكِنُ التَنَبُّؤُ بِنَتائِجِ الانْتِخاباتِ; **to keep an ~ mind about sth** تَقَبَّلَ جَميعَ الأَفْكارِ بِشَأْنِ شَيْءٍ بِعَقْلٍ مَفْتوحٍ; **~ ticket** تَذْكِرة مَفْتوحة **10** (with spaces) **~ weave** نَسيج بِفَتْحاتٍ واسِعةٍ **11** (Sport) ‹*tournament*› مَفْتوح **12** ‹*vowel*› مَفْتوح

B *vt* **1** (to cause to be not shut) فَتَحَ (a; فَتْح) ‹*a door, letter, shop*›; **could you ~ the window?** هلّا فَتَحْتَ الشُبّاكَ؟ **2** (to inaugurate) دَشَّنَ, افْتَتَحَ ‹*a bridge, an exhibition, a museum*› **3** (to set up) فَتَحَ (a; فَتْح), أَنْشَأَ ‹*a store, branch, business*› **4** فَتَحَ (a; فَتْح) ‹*an account*› **5** (to begin) بَدَأَ (a; بَدْء), دَشَّنَ ‹*negotiations, a meeting, debate*›

C *vi* **1** (to stop being shut) «doors, flowers, curtains» انْفَتَحَ; **his eyes ~ed** انْفَتَحَتْ عَيْناه; **~ wide!** افْتَحْ على الآخِرِ; **to ~ into** *or* **onto the courtyard** «rooms, windows» انْفَتَحَ على الفِناءِ **2** (to become wider) «gaps, cracks» اتَّسَعَ **3** (for trading) «shops, banks» فَتَحَ (a; فَتْح); **the power station ~ed in 2009** اُفْتُتِحَتْ مَحطّةُ تَوْليدِ الطاقةِ الكَهْرَبائيّةِ في 2009 **4** (to begin) «the meeting, conference» اُفْتُتِحَ; **the session/conference ~ed with a short presentation by the president** اُفْتُتِحَت الجَلْسةُ \ اُفْتُتِحَ المُؤْتَمَرُ بِعَرْضٍ قَصيرٍ من الرَئيسِ **5** «the movie, exhibition» اُفْتُتِحَ; **the play ~s on the 25th** سَتُفْتَتَحُ المَسْرَحيّةُ في الخامِسِ والعِشْرينَ **6** (in court proceedings, debates) اُفْتُتِحَ; **to ~ for the defence/the prosecution** اُفْتُتِحَ للدِفاعِ \ للنِيابةِ **7** «shares, trading» فُتِحَ

D *n* **1** (outside) **in the ~** في الهَواءِ الطَلْقِ, في العَراءِ \ الخَلاءِ **2** (exposed area) مِنْطَقة مَكْشوفة; **to be out in the ~** كانَ مَكْشوفاً; **don't move out into the ~** لا تَذْهَبْ إلى المَكانِ المَكْشوفِ; **to bring sth out into the ~** أَخْرَجَ شَيْئاً إلى العَلَنِ **3** (also **Open**) (Sport) بُطولة مَفْتوحة

(Phrasal verbs) **open out A** (to become broader) «paths, rivers» اِتَّسَعَ; **the tunnel ~s out into a cave** يُؤدّي النَفَقُ إلى كَهْفٍ **B ~ [sth] out, ~ out [sth]** (to unfold) فَتَحَ \ فَرَدَ [شَيْئاً] ‹*a map, newspaper*›

• **open up A ~ up 1** (to unlock a building) فَتَحَ (a; فَتْح); **I'll ~ up for you** سَأَفْتَحُ لَكَ **2** (to enlarge) «gaps, cracks» اِتَّسَعَ; **his wound ~ed up overnight** اتَّسَعَ جُرْحُهُ خلال ساعاتِ اللَيْلِ **3** (to start up) «businesses, branches» اُفْتُتِحَ **4** (economically) «markets, possibilities, opportunities» فُتِحَ **5** (to speak freely) صارَحَ; **to ~ up to sb about sth** صارَحَ شَخْصاً بِشَيْءٍ **B ~ [sth] up, ~ up [sth] 1** (for access) فَتَحَ [شَيْئاً] ‹*a parcel, suitcase*› **2** (to enlarge) وَسَّعَ [شَيْئاً] ‹*a gap, crack*›; **he ~ed up a three-metre lead over the other runners** وَسَّعَ المَسافةَ بَيْنَهُ وَبَيْنَ المُتَسابِقينَ الآخَرينَ بِثَلاثةِ أَمْتارٍ **3** (to unlock) فَتَحَ [شَيْئاً] ‹*a shop, building*› **4** (to start up) أَقامَ \ افْتَتَحَ [شَيْئاً] ‹*a shop, business, factory*› **5** (economically) فَتَحَ [شَيْئاً] ‹*an area, a country, desert*›; **the agreement ~ed up new trading opportunities** فَتَحَت الاتِّفاقيّةُ فُرَصاً تِجاريّةً جَديدةً

open-air /əʊp(ə)nˈɛː/ *adj* ‹*market, swimming pool*› مَكْشوف, في الهَواءِ الطَلْقِ, مَفْتوح

open-and-shut /ˌəʊp(ə)nənˈʃʌt/ *adj*; **an ~ case** أَمْر مَفْروغ مِنْهُ

open day *n* يَوْم مَفْتوح

open-ended /əʊp(ə)nˈɛndɪd/ *adj* **1** ‹*question*› مَفْتوح **2** ‹*contract*› مَفْتوح, غَير مَحْدودٍ; ‹*discussion*› مَفْتوح

opener /ˈəʊp(ə)nə/ *n* (for bottles and cans) فَتّاحة

open-heart surgery /ˌəʊp(ə)nˌhɑːt ˈsəːdʒ(ə)ri/ *n* جِراحة قَلْبٍ مَفْتوحٍ

open house *n* **1** (for entertaining) **to have an open house** وَجَّهَ دَعْوةً مَفْتوحةً **2** (AmE) (for the public) يَوْم \ بَيْت مَفْتوح

opening /ˈəʊp(ə)nɪŋ/ **A** *n* **1** (gap) فَتْحة **2** (of an exhibition, building) افْتِتاح **3** (of a film, play) افْتِتاحيّة **4** (start) بِداية **5** (opportunity) فُرْصة (فُرَص)

B *adj* ‹*ceremony, scene, speech*› افْتِتاحي

opening hours *n* ساعات العَمَلِ, مَواعيد \ أَوْقات الدَوامِ

opening night *n* لَيْلة افْتِتاحيّة

open learning *n* تَعْليم مَفْتوح

openly /ˈəʊp(ə)nli/ *adv* ‹*to admit, discuss*› بِصَراحةٍ, عَلَنيًّا, مُجاهَرةً

open market *n* سوق مَفْتوحة

open-minded /əʊp(ə)nˈmʌɪndɪd/ *adj* ‹*person*› مُنْفَتِح الفِكْرِ \ مُتَحَرِّر, مُتَفَتِّح; ‹*approach, attitude*› واسِع الأُفُقِ, الذِهْنِ

open-mouthed /əʊp(ə)nˈmaʊðd/ *adj* ‹*of a person*› فاغِر الفَمِ, مَشْدوه; ‹*astonishment, horror*› شَديد, بالِغ

open-necked /əʊp(ə)nˈnɛkt/ *adj* ‹*shirt*› مَفْتوح الياقةِ

openness /əʊp(ə)nnəs/ *n* **1** (frankness) عَلانيّة, صَراحة **2** (to ideas, innovation) انْفِتاح **3** (of the landscape) [المِساحة الواسِعة]

open-plan /əʊp(ə)nˈplan/ *adj* ‹*office, living area*› ذو مُخَطَّطٍ مَفْتوحٍ

open-source /əʊp(ə)nˈsɔːs/ *adj* (Comput) مَفْتوح المَصْدَرِ; **~ software** بَرْمَجيّات مَفْتوحة المَصْدَرِ

open ticket *n* تَذْكِرة مَفْتوحة

Open University *n* (BrE) الجامِعة المَفْتوحة

opera /ˈɒp(ə)rə/ *n* (*pl* **operas**) أوبرا

opera house *n* دار أوبرا

operate /ˈɒpəreɪt/ **A** *vt* **1** ‹*a machine, vehicle*› أَدارَ, شَغَّلَ **2** (to manage) ‹*a business, franchise*› سَيَّرَ, أَدارَ **3** (to run) ‹*a system, a service*› أَدارَ

B *vi* **1** (to function) «machinery, mechanism» عَمِلَ (a; عَمَل) **2** (to do business) «companies, organizations» عَمِلَ (a; عَمَل), كانَ ناشِطاً **3** (to run) «systems, service» عَمِلَ (a; عَمَل), اشْتَغَلَ **4** (Med) أَجْرى عَمَليّةً جِراحيّةً; **the doctors decided to ~** قَرَّرَ الأَطِبّاءُ إِجْراءَ عَمَليّةٍ; **they ~ on her knee** يُجْرونَ عَمَليّةً لَها في رُكْبَتِها; **she was ~d on for a tumour** أُجْرِيَتْ لَها عَمَليّةٌ جِراحيّةٌ لاسْتِئْصالِ وَرَمٍ

operatic /ɒpəˈratɪk/ *adj* ‹*voice, role*› [مُتَعَلِّق بالأوبرا]

operating /ˈɒpəreɪtɪŋ/ *adj* ‹*costs*› تَشْغيليّ

operating system *n* نِظام تَشْغيلٍ

operating theatre (BrE), **operating room** (AmE) *n* غُرْفة العَمَليّاتِ الجِراحيّةِ

operation /ɒpəˈreɪʃ(ə)n/ *n* **1** (functioning) تَشْغيل; **to be in ~** «machines» كانَ شَغّالاً \ في وَضْعِ تَشْغيلٍ; «systems» كانَ مَعْمولاً بِهِ **2** (of equipment) عَمَل, اسْتِعْمال, تَشْغيل **3** (activity) عَمَليّة **4** (Med) عَمَليّة جِراحيّة; **a heart ~** عَمَليّة جِراحيّة للقَلْبِ; **an ~ to remove a tumour** عَمَليّة لإِزالة وَرَمٍ; **to perform major/minor ~** أَجْرى عَمَليّةً كُبْرى / صُغْرى

operational /ɒpəˈreɪʃ(ə)n(ə)l/ *adj* **1** (functional) ‹*system, unit*› جاهِز للاسْتِعْمالِ **2** ‹*costs, capability*› عَمَليّاتيّ, تَشْغيليّ

operative /ˈɒp(ə)rətɪv/ **A** *adj* فَعّال, ساري المَفْعولِ; **the ban/decree remains ~** يَبْقى الحَظْرُ \ الحُكْمُ سارِيَ المَفْعولِ; **the ~ word** الكَلِمة الأَساسيّة \ الرَئيسيّة

B *n* **1** (worker) عامِل **2** (secret agent) عَميل سِرّيّ

operator /ˈɒpəreɪtə/ *n* **1** (in telephone exchange) مَأمور بَدّالةٍ **2** (of equipment) عامِل (عُمّال), مُشَغِّل **3** (company) مُؤَسَّسة, شَرِكة

operetta /ɒpəˈrɛtə/ *n* أوبريت

ophthalmic optician /ɒfˌθalmɪk ɒpˈtɪʃ(ə)n/ *n* إِخْصائيّ بَصَريّاتٍ

ophthalmologist /ɒfθalˈmɒlədʒɪst/ *n* أَخِصّائيّ عُيونٍ

ophthalmology /ˌɒfθalˈmɒlədʒi/ *n* طِبّ العُيونِ

ophthalmoscope /ɒfˈθalməskəʊp/ *n* مِنْظار العَيْنِ

opinion /əˈpɪnjən/ *n* **1** (view) رَأْي (آراء); **in my ~** في رَأْيي; **what is your ~ of his new show?** ما رَأْيُكَ في عَرْضِهِ الجَديدِ؟; **that's a matter of ~** تِلْكَ مَسْأَلةُ رَأْيٍ; **to have a**

high/low ~ of sb أَكَنَّ \ لم يَكُنَّ تَقْديراً لِشَخْصٍ; we hold conflicting ~s on this issue آراؤُنا مُتَعارِضةٌ في هذا الشَأْنِ; to be of the ~ that ... رَأى أنّ ... ; we had a difference of ~ اخْتَلَفْنا في الرَأْيِ **2** (evaluation) اسْتِشارة; to get a second ~ حَصَلَ على اسْتِشارةٍ من طَرَفٍ ثانٍ; in my professional ~ بِرَأْيي المِهَنيِّ **3** [u] (general assessment) رَأْي (آراء); ~ is divided الآراءُ مُنْقَسِمةٌ

opinionated /əˈpɪnjəneɪtɪd/ *adj* ‹*journalist*› مُتَشَبِّثٌ بِرَأْيِه; ‹*commentary*› مُنْحاز; his ideas are sound but he's so ~! أَفْكارُهُ سَليمةٌ لَكِنَّهُ مُفْرِطٌ في الاعْتِدادِ بِرَأْيِه!

opinion poll *n* اسْتِطْلاع لِلرَأْيِ

opium /ˈəʊpɪəm/ *n* أَفْيون

opponent /əˈpəʊnənt/ *n* **1** (of a regime, policy) مُعارِض, مُناوِئ; ~s of abortion مُعارِضونَ لِلإجْهاضِ **2** (in sport, in a debate or contest) خَصْم (خُصوم)

opportune /ˈɒpətjuːn/ *adj* ‹*time, encounter*› مُواتٍ, مُناسِب

opportunist /ɒpəˈtjuːnɪst/ **A** *n* نَفْعيّ, انْتِهازيّ
B *adj* (*also* **opportunistic**) ‹*thief, goal*› نَفْعيّ, انْتِهازيّ

opportunity /ɒpəˈtjuːnɪti/ *n* (*pl* **opportunities**) فُرْصة (فُرَص), مُناسَبة; a missed ~ فُرْصة ضائِعة; I had the ~ of studying in the States سَنَحَتْ لي الفُرْصةُ أنْ أَدْرُسَ في الوِلاياتِ المُتَّحِدةِ; to take the ~ of thanking all the contributors انْتَهَزَ الفُرْصةَ لِيَشْكُرَ جَميعَ المُساهِمين

oppose /əˈpəʊz/ **A** *vt* كان (على), اعْتَرَضَ, ناهَضَ, ناوَأَ, عارَضَ ضِدّ ‹*a bill, the war*›; they are strongly ~d to identity cards يُعارِضونَ بِقوّةٍ إدْخالَ بِطاقاتِ الهُوِيّةِ
B (**as opposed to**) *phr* خِلافاً عن, مُقابِلَ; 200 attended, as ~d to 300 last year حَضَرَ 200 شَخْصٍ مُقابِلَ 300 شَخْصٍ في السَنةِ الماضِيةِ

opposing /əˈpəʊzɪŋ/ *adj* **1** (against each other) ‹*team, faction*› مُقابِل; the ~ side الفَريق المُقابِل **2** (very different) ‹*view, ideologies*› مُتَعارِض

opposite /ˈɒpəzɪt/ **A** *adj* **1** (facing) ‹*direction, side*› مُعاكِس, مُقابِل; at ~ ends of the table/street في جِهَتَيْنِ مُتَقابِلَتَيْنِ من الطاوِلةِ \ الشارِعِ; to live at ~ ends of the town عاشا في طَرَفَيْنِ مُتَباعِدَيْنِ من المَدينةِ; we live on the ~ side of the road to each other نَعيشُ في جِهَتَيْنِ مُتَقابِلَتَيْنِ من الطَريقِ **2** (different) ‹*attitude, viewpoint*› مُضادّ; her appeals had the ~ effect to what she intended كانَ لِمُناشَداتِها تَأْثيرٌ مُضادٌّ لِما أَرادَتْ; a word that is ~ in meaning (to another) كَلِمة مُضادّة في المَعْنى (لِكَلِمةٍ أُخْرى)
B *n* نَقيض, (أَضْداد) ضِدّ, عَكْس; fat is the ~ of thin كَلِمة سَمين هي نَقيضُ كَلِمةِ نَحيف; it's the ~ to what you would expect هو عَكْسُ ما يَتَوَقَّعُهُ المَرْءُ; she's the ~ of me هي عَكْسي
C *adv* ‹*to live, stand*› في الجِهةِ المُقابِلةِ; he was standing directly ~ كانَ يَقِفُ في الجِهةِ المُقابِلةِ مُباشَرةً; immediately/nearly/almost ~ في الجِهةِ المُقابِلةِ تَماماً \ تَقْريباً \ غالِباً; we live directly ~ نَحْنُ نَعيشُ مُقابِلَ بَعْضِنا البَعْضَ مُباشَرةً
D *prep* **1** (facing) أَمامَ, في المُقابِل; to live/sit ~ sb/sth عاشَ \ جَلَسَ في مُقابِلِ شَخْصٍ \ شَيْءٍ; we live ~ the park نَعيشُ أمامَ الحَديقةِ العامّةِ **2** (acting) to play ~ an actor مَثَّلَ أمامَ مُمَثِّلٍ

opposite number *n* نَظير (نُظَراءُ), نِدّ (أَنْداد)

opposition /ɒpəˈzɪʃ(ə)n/ *n* **1** (resistance) [u] مُعارَضة, مُقاوَمة; there was considerable ~ to the proposal قوبِلَ الاقْتِراحُ بِمُعارَضةٍ كَبيرةٍ **2** (**the opposition**) (in politics) المُعارَضة; (in business) المُنافِس, المُنافَسة; (in a competition) الخَصْم; the leader of the O~ زَعيم المُعارَضةِ; O~ MPs/parties أَعْضاء البَرْلَمان \ أَحْزاب من المُعارَضةِ

oppress /əˈprɛs/ *vt* ‹*women, the masses*› قَمَعَ (a; قَمْع), اضْطَهَدَ

oppression /əˈprɛʃ(ə)n/ *n* **1** (tyranny) قَمْع, اضْطِهاد **2** (mental suffering) ضَغْط نَفْسيّ

oppressive /əˈprɛsɪv/ *adj* **1** ‹*regime, conduct*› مُسْتَبِدّ, جائِر **2** ‹*heat, atmosphere*› خانِق

oppressor /əˈprɛsə/ *n* ظالِم, طاغِية, مُضْطَهِد (ظَلَمة)

opt /ɒpt/ *vi* «customers, voters» آثَرَ, فَضَّلَ, اخْتارَ (imperf يُؤْثِرُ); after graduating, she ~ed for a career in music بعد التَخَرُّجِ اخْتارَتْ مِهْنةً موسيقيّةً; customers can ~ to buy either model يُمْكِنُ لِلزَبائِنِ أنْ يَخْتاروا شِراءَ أَيٍّ من الموديلَيْنِ
Phrasal verb **opt out** «workers, countries» انْسَحَبَ; employees may ~ out of the company's pension plan يُمْكِنُ لِلمُوَظَّفينَ أنْ يَنْسَحِبوا من خُطّةِ المَعاشِ التَقاعُديِّ لِلشَرِكةِ

optic /ˈɒptɪk/ **A** *adj* ‹*nerve, disc*› بَصَرِيّ

B *n* (BrE) (in a bar) [مِكْيال للمَشْروباتِ الكُحوليّةِ (يُثَبَّتُ في عُنُقِ زُجاجةٍ مَقْلوبةٍ)]

optical /ˈɒptɪk(ə)l/ *adj* ‹*sensor, lens*› بَصَرِيّ

optical illusion *n* خِداع بَصَرِيّ

optician /ɒpˈtɪʃ(ə)n/ *n* **1** (eye specialist) فَنِّيّ بَصَرِيّاتٍ, نَظّاراتِيّ **2** (seller of glasses) نَظّاراتِيّ

optics /ˈɒptɪks/ *n sing* عِلْم البَصَرِيّاتِ

optimal /ˈɒptɪm(ə)l/ *adj* (fml) ‹*temperature, conditions*› أَمْثَل (dipt; f مُثْلى; f pl مُثْلَيات; أَماثِل); **the ~ temperature in the lab is 22º Celsius** دَرَجةُ الحَرارةِ المُثْلى في المُخْتَبَرِ هي 22 دَرَجةً مِئَوِيّةً

optimism /ˈɒptɪmɪz(ə)m/ *n* تَفاؤُل

optimist /ˈɒptɪmɪst/ *n* مُتَفائِل

optimistic /ɒptɪˈmɪstɪk/ *adj* ‹*outlook, estimate*› مُتَفائِل; **I am not ~ about my chances of success** لَسْتُ مُتَفائِلاً بالنِّسْبةِ لِفُرَصِ نَجاحي

optimization, -isation (BrE) /ɒptɪmʌɪˈzeɪʃ(ə)n/ *n* (fml) تَحْقيق الاسْتِخْدامِ الأَمْثَلِ, تَحْسين (تَحْسينات)

optimize, -ise (BrE) /ˈɒptɪmʌɪz/ *vt* ‹*performance, benefits*› حَسَّنَ

optimum /ˈɒptɪməm/ **A** *adj* ‹*conditions, performance*› أَمْثَل (dipt; f مُثْلى; f pl مُثْلَيات; أَماثِل)

B *n* (*pl* **optima**) ذُرْوة, أَوْج (ذُرًى); **at 35 his mathematical creativity was at its ~** في سِنِّ الخامسةِ والثَّلاثينَ بَلَغَ إِبْداعُهُ في الرِّياضِيّاتِ ذُرْوَتَهُ

option /ˈɒpʃ(ə)n/ *n* [u] (freedom to choose) حَقّ \ حُرِّيّة الاخْتِيارِ; (choice) خِيار; **do I really have the ~ to refuse?** هل لَدَيَّ فِعْلاً حُرِّيّةُ الرَّفْضِ؟

optional /ˈɒpʃ(ə)n(ə)l/ *adj* ‹*extra, accessory*› اخْتِيارِيّ, خِيارِيّ

optometry /ɒpˈtɒmɪtri/ *n* قِياس مَدى البَصَرِ

opulence /ˈɒpjʊləns/ *n* (fml) بَذَخ, تَرَف

opulent /ˈɒpjʊlənt/ *adj* (fml) ‹*lifestyle*› باذِخ, مُتْرَف; ‹*palace*› فَخْم, فاخِر

opus /ˈəʊpəs/ *n* (*pl* **opuses** or **opera**) (fml) عَمَل فَنِّيّ \ موسيقِيّ

or /ɔː/ *conj* **1** (offering an alternative) أَمْ, أَوْ; **black ~ white?** أَسْوَد أَمْ أَبْيَض؟; **either here ~ at Dave's** إِمّا هُنا أَوْ عند ديف; **in a week ~ so** في أُسْبوعٍ أَوْ نحو ذلك **2** (linking alternatives in the negative) وَلا; **I can't come today ~ tomorrow** لا أَسْتَطيعُ المَجيءَ اليَوْمَ وَلا غَداً; **without food ~ lodgings** دون طَعامٍ وَلا سَكَنٍ **3** (otherwise) وَإِلاّ; **hurry up, ~ you'll miss it all** أَسْرِعْ، وَإِلاّ سَيفوتُكَ الأَمْرُ كُلُّهُ

OR *abbr* = **Oregon**

oracle /ˈɒrək(ə)l/ *n* وَسيط الوَحْي

oral /ˈɔːrəl/ **A** *adj* **1** ‹*history, exam, evidence*› شَفَوِيّ, شَفَهِيّ **2** ‹*contraceptive, hygiene*› فَمَوِيّ

B *n* امْتِحان شَفَوِيّ \ شَفَهِيّ

Oran /ɔːˈrɑːn/ *pr n* وَهْران (dipt f)

orange /ˈɒrɪndʒ/ **A** *n* **1** (fruit) بُرْتُقال (n coll; بُرْتُقالات) **2** (colour) لَوْن بُرْتُقالِيّ

B *adj* ‹*glow, flame*› بُرْتُقالِيّ; **to paint the cupboard ~** دَهَنَ الخِزانةَ باللَّوْنِ البُرْتُقالِيِّ

orangeade /ɒrɪndʒˈeɪd/ *n* [عَصير بُرْتُقالٍ مُحَلًّى]

orange juice *n* عَصير بُرْتُقالٍ

orator /ˈɒrətə/ *n* (fml) خَطيب (خُطَباءُ)

orbit /ˈɔːbɪt/ **A** *n* مَدار (مَدارات)

B *vt* ‹*the earth, planets*› دارَ (u; دَوَران) حول

C *vi* «planets, spacecraft» دارَ في فَلَكٍ

orchard /ˈɔːtʃəd/ *n* بُسْتان فَواكِهَ

orchestra /ˈɔːkɪstrə/ *n* أورْكِسْترا

orchestral /ɔːˈkɛstrəl/ *adj* **1** ‹*concert, instrument*› أورْكِسْترالِيّ **2** ‹*work, music*› أورْكِسْترالِيّ

orchestrate /ˈɔːkɪstreɪt/ *vt* **1** ‹*a piece of music*› وَزَّعَ **2** ‹*a campaign, an attack*› خَطَّطَ (ل)

orchid /ˈɔːkɪd/ *n* أورْكيد

ordain /ɔːˈdeɪn/ *vt* **1** ‹*a priest*› رَسَمَ (u; رَسْم), سامَ (u; سِيامة); **she was ~ed as a deacon** عُيِّنَتْ شَمّاسةً **2** (to decree) «rulers» أَصْدَرَ أَمْراً; **it was ~ed that the square should be renamed ....** صَدَرَ أَمْرٌ بِإِعادةِ تَسْمِيةِ المَيْدانِ ....

ordeal /ɔːˈdiːəl/ *n* مِحْنة (مِحَن)

order /ˈɔːdə/ **A** *n* **1** (logical arrangement) نِظام; **to set** *or* **put one's life in ~** نَظَّمَ حَياتَهُ **2** (sequence) تَرْتيب (تَرْتيبات);

in the right/wrong ~ بالتَرْتيبِ الصَحيح \ الخَطأ; to do things in ~ فَعَلَ الأَشْياءَ بالتَرْتيبِ; the files are out of ~ المِلَفّاتُ غَيْرُ مُرَتَّبةٍ; in ascending/descending ~ بِتَرْتيبٍ تَصاعُديٍّ \ تَنازُليٍّ; to be in alphabetical ~ كانَ مُرَتَّباً تَرْتيباً هِجائيًّا **3** (discipline, control) انْضِباط ,نِظام; to restore ~ «teachers, the police» اسْتَعادَ النِظامَ **4** (command) أَمْر (أَوامِرُ); to give *or* issue an ~ أَعْطى \ أَصْدَرَ أَمْراً; to carry out an ~ نَفَّذَ أَمْراً; to have ~s to do sth كانَتْ لَدَيْهِ أَوامِرُ بِفِعْلِ شَيْءٍ **5** (in business) طَلَبِيّة; made to ~ مَصْنوع حَسَبَ الطَلَبِ; the spares are on ~ طَلَبِيّة مُسْتَعْجَلة \ a rush/repeat ~ تَمَّ طَلَبُ قِطَعِ الغِيارِ; to place an ~ for a new car مُكَرَّرة وَضَعَ طَلَبِيَّةً لِشِراءِ سَيّارةٍ جَديدةٍ **6** (operational state) to be in working *or* running ~ كانَ يَعْمَلُ بِشَكْلٍ جَيِّدٍ; to be out of ~ كانَ مُتَعَطِّلاً \ لا يَعْمَلُ **7** (established state) نِظام (أَنْظِمة ,نُظُم); the existing ~ النِظام الحاليّ **8** (to be correct) to be in ~ «documents, accounts» كانَ سَليماً; are her documents in ~? هل وَثائِقُها سَليمةٌ؟; would it be out of ~ for me to phone her at home? هل سَيكونُ خَطأً مِني إنْ اتَّصَلْتُ بِها في البَيْتِ؟; I hear that congratulations are in ~ سَمِعْتُ أنَّهُ من الواجِبِ تَقْديمُ التَهاني; austerity is the ~ of the day التَقَشُّفُ من مُتَطَلَّباتِ الوَقْتِ **9** (of monks, nuns) رَهْبَنة **10** (rank, scale) دَرَجة, مَرْتَبة (مَراتِبُ); craftsmen of the highest ~ حِرَفِيّونَ من الدَرَجةِ الأولى **11** (Fin) (on cheques, draft) pay to the ~ of T. Williams ادْفَعوا لِأَمْرِ ت. ويليامْز; ▸ money order, ▸ postal order, ▸ standing order

B (orders) *n pl* سِيامة ,رِسامة; to take holy ~s رُسِمَ كاهِناً

C (in order that) *conj phr* مِن أَجْلِ أنْ ,لِكَيْ; he brought the proofs in ~ that I might check them جاءَ بالأدِلّةِ لِكَيْ أَفْحَصَها

D (in order to) *prep phr* لِ ,لِكَيْ; he telephoned in ~ to talk to me اتَّصَلَ لِيَتَحَدَّثَ مَعي

E *vt* **1** (to command) أَمَرَ (u; أَمْر) ‹*a retrial, an inquiry, investigation*›; to ~ sb to do sth أَمَرَ شَخْصاً بِفِعْلِ شَيْءٍ; the inspectors ~ed them to demolish the building أَمَرَهُم المُفَتِّشونَ بِهَدْمِ المَنْزِلِ **2** (to obtain) طَلَبَ (u; طَلَب) ‹*goods, a meal*›; I ~ed an omelette/a cream tea طَلَبْتُ عُجّةَ بَيْضٍ \ شاياً بالحَليبِ; please ~ me a taxi لَوْ سَمَحْتَ، اُطْلُبْ لي تاكْسي **3** (to arrange) رَتَّبَ ,نَظَّمَ ‹*the files, names*›; I ~ed them by surname followed by first name قُمْتُ بِتَرْتيبِهِمْ حَسَبَ اللَقَبِ ثُمَّ الاسْمِ الأَوَّلِ

F *vi* «diners, customers» طَلَبَ (u; طَلَب); are you ready to ~? هل أَنْتَ جاهِزٌ لِتَطْلُبَ؟

(Idiom) in short order فَوْراً ,بِسُرْعةٍ

(Phrasal verbs) order about, order around: ~ [sb] about (infml) أَمْلى أَوامِرَهُ على [شَخْصٍ] ‹*a colleague, an employee*›

• order off: ~ [sb] off (from one's land, a bus) طَرَدَ [شَخْصاً]

order book *n* دَفْتَر \ سِجِلّ طَلَبِيّاتٍ

ordered /ˈɔːdəd/ *adj* ‹*structure, list*› مُنَظَّم ,مُنْتَظِم

order form *n* اسْتِمارة طَلَبٍ

orderly /ˈɔːd(ə)li/ **A** *adj* **1** (neat) ‹*rows, arrangement*› مُنَظَّم, مُرَتَّب **2** (disciplined) ‹*queue*› مُنَظَّم; ‹*process*› مَنْهَجيّ; in an ~ fashion بِطَريقةٍ مُنَظَّمةٍ

B *n* (*pl* **orderlies**) **1** (in a hospital) عامِل نَظافةٍ في المُسْتَشْفى [عُمّال] **2** (soldier) جُنْديّ (جُنود)

ordinance /ˈɔːdɪnəns/ *n* قرار رَسْميّ ,مَرْسوم

ordinarily /ˈɔːd(ə)nrəli/ *adv* في العادةِ ,عادةً

ordinary /ˈɔːd(ə)nri/ **A** *adj* **1** (normal, average) ‹*people, life*› عاديّ **2** (commonplace) عاديّ

B *n* اعْتِياديّ ,عاديّ; out of the ~ خارِج عن العادةِ \ المَأْلوفِ

ore /ɔː/ *n* خام (مَعْدِن)

oregano /ˌɒrɪˈgɑːnəʊ/ *n* أوريجانو

Oregon /ˈɒrɪg(ə)n/ *pr n* أوريغون (f)

organ /ˈɔːg(ə)n/ *n* **1** (Anat) عُضْو (أَعْضاء) **2** (Mus) أُرْغُن (أَراغِنُ)

organ donor *n* مُتَبَرِّع بالأَعْضاءِ

organic /ɔːˈganɪk/ *adj* **1** ‹*matter, compound*› عُضْويّ **2** ‹*farming, produce*› عُضْويّ

organism /ˈɔːg(ə)nɪz(ə)m/ *n* كائِن حَيّ

organist /ˈɔːg(ə)nɪst/ *n* عازِف أُرْغُن

organization, **-isation** (BrE) /ɔːg(ə)nʌɪˈzeɪʃ(ə)n/ *n* **1** (group) مُنَظَّمة **2** [u] (organizing) تَنْظيم

organizational /ɔːg(ə)nʌɪˈzeɪʃ(ə)n(ə)l/ *adj* **1** ‹*skill, problem*› تَنْظيميّ **2** ‹*structure, chart*› تَنْظيميّ

Organization of American States *n* مُنَظَّمة الدُوَلِ الأَمْريكيّةِ

Organization of Arab Petroleum Exporting Countries *n* مُنَظَّمة الدُوَلِ العَرَبيّةِ المُصَدِّرةِ للنَفْطِ

organize, -ise (BrE) /ˈɔːg(ə)nʌɪz/ *vt* [1] (to arrange) نَظَّمَ ‹*an event, a protest*›; **I'll ~ the drinks** سَأَهْتَمُّ بالمَشْروباتِ [2] (to put in order) رَتَّبَ ‹*books, papers*›; نَظَّمَ ‹*one's life*›; **to ~ oneself** نَظَّمَ نَفْسَهُ

organized /ˈɔːg(ə)nʌɪzd/ *adj* [1] (arranged) ‹*group, tour*› مُنَظَّم [2] (methodical, efficient) ‹*person*› مُنَظَّم; **to get ~** نَظَّمَ نَفْسَهُ [3] ‹*labour, workers*› نِقابيّ

organized crime *n* جَريمة مُنَظَّمة

organizer, -iser (BrE) /ˈɔːg(ə)nʌɪzə/ *n* مُنَظِّم

organ transplant *n* زَرْع \ زراعة أَعْضاءٍ

orgasm /ˈɔːgazəm/ *n* هَزّة الجِماع; **to reach/achieve ~** وَصَلَ إلى هَزّةِ الجِماعِ

orgy /ˈɔːdʒi/ *n* (*pl* **orgies**) حَفْلة ماجنة

orient /ˈɔːrɪənt/ [A] *n* **(the Orient)** الشَرْق

[B] *vt* [1] (to align) وَجَّهَ ‹*a building, an object*› [2] (to aim, intend) وَجَّهَ ‹*a product, course*›; **to be ~ed towards sth** كانَ مُوَجَّهاً نحو شَيْءٍ

[C] *v refl* (AmE) ▸**orientate**

oriental /ɔːriˈɛnt(ə)l/ *adj* ‹*language, medicine*› شَرْقيّ

orientate /ˈɔːrɪənteɪt/ [A] *vt* (**orientates, orientating, orientated**) (BrE) ▸**orient**

[B] *v refl* **to ~** *or* (AmE) **orient oneself** حَدَّدَ مَوْقِعَهُ

orientation /ɔːriənˈteɪʃ(ə)n/ *n* [1] (guidance) إِرْشاد, تَوجيه [2] (inclination) مَيْل (مُيول)

orienteering /ɔːriənˈtɪərɪŋ/ *n* سِباق تَوجيهٍ (باسْتِخدامِ الخَرائِطِ والبوصَلةِ)

orifice /ˈɒrɪfɪs/ *n* فُوْهة, فُتْحة (فُتَح, فُتْحات)

origin /ˈɒrɪdʒɪn/ *n* [1] (source) مَنْشَأ (مَناشِئُ), مَصْدَر (مَصادِرُ) [2] (ancestry) أَصْل (أُصول)

original /əˈrɪdʒ(ə)n(ə)l/ [A] *adj* [1] (first) أَصْليّ; **the ~ owners/inhabitants** المالِكونَ \ السُكّان الأَصْليّونَ [2] (not copied) أَصْليّ [3] (inventive) مُبْتَكَر, أَصيل (أُصَلاءُ)

[B] *n* (artwork, document) نُسْخة أَصْليّة

originality /ərɪdʒɪˈnalɪti/ *n* أَصالة, ابْتِكار

originally /əˈrɪdʒɪn(ə)li/ *adv* [1] (initially) أَصْلاً, في الأَصْلِ [2] (inventively) على نَحْوٍ أَصيلٍ \ مُبْتَكَرٍ

originate /əˈrɪdʒɪneɪt/ *vi* «custom, idea» نَبَعَ (a-i-u; نَبْع, نُبوع), نَشَأَ «fire, epidemic» بَدَأَ (a; بَدْء); «name, term» انْبَعَثَ; «family, ancestors» انْحَدَرَ (a; نَشْأة, نُشوء, نَشْء)

originator /əˈrɪdʒɪneɪtə/ *n* مُبْتَكِر

Orkney /ˈɔːkni/ *pr n* (**the Orkney Islands** or **the Orkneys**) جُزُر أوركْني

ornament /ˈɔːnəmənt/ *n* حِلْية (حِلًى, حُلًى), زينة, زُخْرُف (زَخارِفُ)

ornamental /ɔːnəˈment(ə)l/ *adj* ‹*plant, lake*› زُخْرُفيّ

ornate /ɔːˈneɪt/ *adj* ‹*building, ceiling*› مُنَمَّق, مُزَخْرَف

ornithologist /ɔːnɪˈθɒlədʒɪst/ *n* عالِم الطُيور

ornithology /ˌɔːnɪˈθɒlədʒi/ *n* عِلْم الطُيورِ

orphan /ˈɔːf(ə)n/ [A] *n* يَتيم (أَيْتام, يَتامى)

[B] *vt* يَتَّمَ; **to be ~ed** يَتُمَ (a-i-u; يُتْم), صارَ يَتيماً

orphanage /ˈɔːf(ə)nɪdʒ/ *n* دار أَيْتامٍ

orthodontics /ˌɔːθəˈdɒntɪks/ *n sing* تَقْويم الأَسْنانِ

orthodontist /ɔːθəˈdɒntɪst/ *n* أخصّائيّ تَقْويمِ الأَسْنانِ

orthodox /ˈɔːθədɒks/ *adj* ‹*view, medicine*› تَقْليديّ; ‹*Jew, Christianity*› أُرْثوذُكْسيّ

orthodoxy /ˈɔːθədɒksi/ *n* (*pl* **orthodoxies**) [1] (of belief, doctrine) أُرْثوذُكْسيّة [2] (conventionality) اصْطِلاح, عُرْف

orthopaedic (BrE), **orthopedic** (AmE) /ɔːθəˈpiːdɪk/ *adj* ‹*surgeon*› جِراحة العِظامِ; ‹*ward*› العِظامِ

orthopaedics (BrE), **orthopedics** (AmE) /ɔːθəˈpiːdɪks/ *n sing* جِراحة العِظامِ

oryx /ˈɒrɪks/ *n* (*pl* **oryx**) مَهاة (مَهاً, مَهَوات)

Oscar® /ˈɒskə/ *n* (جائِزة) أوسْكار; **to be nominated for/awarded an ~** رُشِّحَ لِجائِزةِ \ فازَ بِجائِزةِ أوسْكار

oscillate /ˈɒsɪleɪt/ *vi* «needles, current» تَذَبْذَبَ, تَأَرْجَحَ

Oslo /ˈɒzləʊ/ *pr n* أوسْلو (f)

ostensible /ɒˈstɛnsɪb(ə)l/ *adj* (fml) ‹*reason, purpose*› ظاهِر, ظاهِريّ, مَزْعوم

ostensibly /ɒˈstɛnsɪbli/ *adv* (fml) ‹*intended, designed*› على ما \ ظاهِريًّا, فيما يَبْدو

ostentatious /ˌɒstɛnˈteɪʃəs/ *adj* ‹*display*› مُبَهْرَج; ‹*wealth*› فاحِش

osteopath /ˈɒstiəpaθ/ *n* أَخِصّائيّ تَقْويم العِظام

osteopathy /ˌɒstiˈɒpəθi/ *n* تَقْويم العِظام

osteoporosis /ˌɒstiəʊpəˈrəʊsɪs/ *n* هشاشة العِظام

ostracize, -ise (BrE) /ˈɒstrəsʌɪz/ *vt* (fml) نَبَذَ (i; نَبْذ) ‹*a colleague, minority group*›

ostrich /ˈɒstrɪtʃ/ *n* نَعام (n coll; نَعائِمُ)

other /ˈʌðə/ **A** *adj* ‹*people, way*› آخر (f pl أُخْرَيات); **are there any ~ questions?** هل هُناكَ أَيَّةُ أَسْئِلَةٍ أُخْرى؟; **he went the ~ way** ذَهَبَ في الاتِّجاهِ الآخَرِ

B *pron* (*pl* **others**) آخر (f pl أُخْرَيات); **these coats are red, but the ~s are blue** هذه المَعاطِفُ حَمْراءُ، أَمّا الأُخْرى فَهِيَ زَرْقاءُ; **answer the first three questions and one ~** أَجِبْ على الأَسْئِلَةِ الثَّلاثَةِ الأولى إضافةً إلى سُؤالٍ آخَرَ; **I went swimming while the ~s played tennis** ذَهَبْتُ للسِباحةِ بَيْنَما لَعِبَ الآخَرونَ التِنِس

C (**other than**) *phr* (apart from) ما عَدا; (different from) غَيْر; **nobody knows ~ than you** لا أَحَدَ غَيْرُكَ يَعْرِفُ; **I have never known him to behave ~ than selfishly** لم أَشْهَدْهُ يَتَصَرَّفُ إلاّ بِأَنانِيَّةٍ

(Idioms) **my other half** نِصْفي الثاني \ الآخَر; **the other day/week** منذ بِضْعةِ أَيّامٍ \ أَسابيعَ

otherwise /ˈʌðəwʌɪz/ (fml) **A** *adv* **1** (differently) **I have no reason to think ~** لَيْس لَدَيَّ أَيُّ سَبَبٍ للتَفْكيرِ بِشَكْلٍ مُخْتَلِفٍ; **unless we are told ~, we will continue the work** ما لم يُطْلَبْ مِنّا خِلافُ ذلك، سَنَسْتَمِرُّ في العَمَلِ; **he says he's 29, but I know ~** يَقولُ إنّ عُمْرَهُ 29 سَنةً، وَلَكِنّي أَعْلَمُ خِلافَ ذلك

2 (in other respects) فيما عَدا هذا; **there was less damage than might ~ have been the case** وَقَعَ ضَرَرٌ أَقَلُّ مِمّا كانَ يُمْكِنُ أَنْ يَكونَ عَلَيْهِ الوَضْعُ

B *conj* (or else) وَإلاّ; **it's quite safe, ~ I wouldn't do it** هو آمِنٌ تَماماً، وَإلاّ لَما فَعَلْتُهُ

OTT *abbr* (infml) = **over the top** ▸**top**

Ottawa /ˈɒtəwə/ *pr n* أوتاوا

otter /ˈɒtə/ *n* كَلْب \ ثَعْلَب ماءٍ, قُضاعة

Ottoman /ˈɒtəmən/ *n, adj* (*pl* **Ottomans**) عُثْمانيّ

ouch /aʊtʃ/ *excl* آيْ; **~! that hurt (me)!** آيْ! أَوْجَعَني هذا!

oud /uːd/ *n* عود (أَعْواد)

ought /ɔːt/ *modal aux* **1** (expressing probability, expectation) **that ~ to fix it** مِن المُفْتَرَضِ أَنّ هذا سَيُصْلِحُهُ; **he ~ to be back by now** مِن المُفْتَرَضِ أَنْ يَكونَ قد عادَ الآنَ; **it ~ not to give a negative reading** لَيْسَ من المُفْتَرَضِ أَنْ يُعْطِيَ قِراءةً سَلْبيّةً **2** (with polite suggestions) **you ~ to be in bed** يَنْبَغي أَنْ تَكونَ في السَريرِ; **she ~ to see a doctor** يَنْبَغي عَلَيْها أَنْ تَرى طَبيباً; **you ~n't to be here** لا يَنْبَغي أَنْ تكونَ هُنا; **~n't we to consult them first?** أَلا يَنْبَغي أَنْ نَسْتَشيرَهُم أَوَّلاً؟

3 (indicating moral obligation) **we ~ to help** يَجِبُ عَلَيْنا تَقْديمُ المُساعَدةِ; **you ~ not to say such things** لا يَجِبُ أَنْ تَقولَ مِثْلَ هذه الأَشْياءِ **4** (when prefacing an important point) **I ~ to say that ...** يَتَعَيَّنُ عَلَيَّ أَنْ أَقولَ إنّ ...; **I think you ~ to know that ...** أَعْتَقِدُ أَنَّهُ يَنْبَغي عَلَيْكَ أَنْ تَعْرِفَ أَنّ ...

ounce /aʊns/ *n* أَوْنْصة, آوْنْس; **he hasn't got an ~ of common sense** لَيْسَ لَدَيْهِ ذَرّةٌ من الحِسِّ السَليمِ

our /aʊə, ɑː/ *determiner* ـنا; **~ children are grown up** أَطْفالُنا كِبارٌ; **we've sold ~ car** بِعْنا سَيّارَتَنا; **this is ~ son, Bradley** هذا ابْنُنا بْرادْلي

ours /aʊəz/ *pron* **their car is red but ~ is blue** سَيّارَتُهُمْ حَمْراءُ لَكِنَّ سَيّارَتَنا زَرْقاءُ; **those tickets are ~** هذه التَذاكِرُ لَنا; **she's a friend of ~** هِيَ واحِدةٌ من أَصْدِقائِنا; **it's not ~** لَيْسَ لَنا; **the money was not ~ to spend** الأَمْوالُ لم تَكُنْ لَنا حتّى نُنْفِقَها; **that dog of ~** (infml) كَلْبُنا اللَعين ذلك; **~ is not an easy task** (fml) مُهِمَّتُنا لَيْسَتْ مُهِمّةً سَهْلةً

ourselves /aʊəˈsɛlvz, ɑːˈsɛlvz/ *pron* **1** (reflexive) أَنْفُسَنا; **we've exhausted ~** أَنْهَكْنا أَنْفُسَنا **2** (emphatic) (we ourselves) نَحْنُ أَنْفُسُنا; (by ourselves) بِأَنْفُسِنا; **we ~ realized that ...** أَنْفُسُنا أَدْرَكْنا أَنّ ...; **we painted it ~** دَهَنّاهُ بِأَنْفُسِنا **3** (after prepositions) **we can look after ~** نَسْتَطيعُ أَنْ نَعْتَنِيَ بِأَنْفُسِنا **4** (in expressions) **we're (all) by ~** نَحْنُ بِمُفْرَدِنا; **we had the beach all to ~** كانَ الشاطِئُ كُلُّهُ لَنا

oust /aʊst/ *vt* طَرَدَ (u; طَرْد), خَلَعَ (a; خَلْع) <*a leader, regime, chairman*>

out /aʊt/ **A** *adv* **1** (outside) في الخارِجِ; **to be ~ in the garden** كانَ في الحَديقةِ; **to leave sth ~ in the rain** تَرَكَ شَيْئاً في الخارِجِ تحت المَطَرِ; **it's cold/hot ~ there** الطَّقْسُ بارِدٌ \ حارٌّ; **we're better off ~ here** نَحْنُ بِحالٍ أَفْضَلَ هُنا (في الخارِجِ); **he called while you were ~** اتَّصَلَ عِنْدَما كُنْتَ في الخارِجِ; **2** (from within) **to go** *or* **walk ~** خَرَجَ (u; خُروج); **to pull/take a splinter ~** أَخْرَجَ شَظِيَّةً; **to tear a page ~** اقْتَلَعَ صَفْحةً; **3** (away base) **two days ~ from port** يَوْمانِ بَعيداً عَن \ خارِجَ الميناءِ; **the fishing boats are ~ at sea** خَرَجَتْ مَراكِبُ الصَّيْدِ إلى البَحْرِ; **when the tide is ~** في حالةِ الجَزْرِ; **4** (in the world at large) **there are a lot of people ~ there looking for work** هُناكَ الكَثيرُ من الناسِ في كُلِّ مَكانٍ يَبْحَثونَ عن العَمَلِ; (infml) **he's the kindest/stupidest person ~ there** هو أَطْيَبُ \ أَغْبى شَخْصٍ على الإطْلاقِ; **5** (socially) **to invite sb ~ to dinner** دَعا شَخْصاً على العَشاءِ; **a day ~ at the seaside** يَوْم على شاطِئِ البَحْرِ; **6** (published, now public) **to be ~** «book» نُشِرَ; «exam results» أُعْلِنَ; **my secret is ~** اُفْتُضِحَ سِرّي; **7** (in bloom) **to be ~** «blossom, flowers» أَزْهَرَ, تَفَتَّحَ; **8** (extinguished) **to be ~** «fire, light» اِنْطَفَأَ; **lights ~ at 10.30 pm** إطْفاء الأَنْوارِ الساعةَ 10.30 مَساءً (اسْتِعْداداً للنَوْمِ); **9** (in view) **to be ~** «sun, moon, stars» ظَهَرَ (a; ظُهور), طَلَعَ (u; طُلوع, مَطْلَع); **10** (dismissed) **to be ~** «player» أُخْرِجَ; **the ball/shot was ~** وَقَعَت الكُرةُ \ الضَرْبةُ خارِجَ المَلْعَبِ; **11** (not at work) **to be ~** «strikers» كانَ مُضْرِباً عن العَمَلِ; **12** (infml) (unconscious) **to be ~ (cold)** كانَ فاقِدَ الوَعْيِ; **13** (over, finished) **before the week/year is ~** قبل نِهايةِ الأُسْبوعِ \ السَنةِ; **14** (BrE) (incorrect) **to be ~ in one's calculations** أَخْطَأَ في حِساباتِهِ; **my watch is two minutes ~** (slow) ساعَتي مُتَأَخِّرةٌ بدَقيقَتَيْنِ; (fast) ساعَتي مُتَقَدِّمةٌ بدَقيقَتَيْنِ; **15** (infml) (not possible) **no, that option is ~** لا، هذا الخِيارُ غَيْرُ وارِدٍ; **16** (infml) (in search of) **to be ~ to do sth** سَعى لِفِعْلِ شَيْءٍ; **he's just ~ for what he can get** يَبْحَثُ عن مَصْلَحَتِهِ فَقَطْ; **he's ~ to get me** يُريدُ النَيْلَ مِنّي \ إيذائي; **17** (infml) (not in fashion) **to be ~** «style, colour» لم يَعُدْ على الموضةِ, أَصْبَحَ موضةً قَديمةً; **18** (Law) **to be ~** «jury» تَداوَلَ الحُكْمَ \ في القَضِيّةِ

B (**out of**) *prep phr* **1** (from) **to go** *or* **walk** *or* **come ~ of the house** خَرَجَ من البَيْتِ; **get ~ of here!** اُخْرُجْ من هُنا!; **to jump ~ of bed/of the window** قَفَزَ من السَريرِ \ النافِذةِ; **to take sth ~ of a box/of a drawer** أَخْرَجَ شَيْئاً من صُنْدوقٍ \ دُرْجٍ; **2** (in ratios) مِنْ; **two ~ of every three people** اثْنانِ من كُلِّ ثَلاثةِ أَشْخاصٍ; **3** (of whole) **a paragraph ~ of a book** فَقْرة من كِتابٍ; **4** (beyond) **to be ~ of reach/sight** كانَ بَعيدَ المَنالِ \ بَعيداً عن الأَنْظارِ; **5** (away from) **to be ~ of hospital/of prison** خَرَجَ من المُسْتَشْفى \ السِجْنِ; **to be ~ of the water/city** كانَ خارِجَ الماءِ \ المَدينةِ; **6** (not exposed to) **to be ~ of the sun/the rain** لم يَكُنْ مُعَرَّضاً للشَمْسِ \ للمَطَرِ; **7** (lacking) **to be (right) ~ of coffee/batteries** نَفِدَتْ القَهْوةُ \ البَطّاريّاتُ (تَماماً); **8** (made from) **to be made ~ of wood/metal** كانَ مَصْنوعاً من الخَشَبِ \ المَعْدِنِ; **9** (from) **they did it ~ of malice/respect** فَعَلوهُ من بابِ الحِقْدِ \ الاحْتِرامِ

C *vt* [كَشَفَ أَنَّ شَخْصاً مِثْليٌّ] <*a politician, celebrity*>

Idioms **to want out** (infml) أَرادَ أَنْ يَخْرُجَ \ يَتَحَرَّرَ من وَضْعٍ; **I want ~!** أُريدُ أَنْ أَخْرُجَ \ أَتَحَرَّرَ من هذا الوَضْعِ!; **the cat wants ~** يُريدُ القِطُّ الخُروجَ; **to be out and about** كانَ نَشيطاً \ كَثيرَ الحَرَكةِ; **to be out of it** شَعَرَ بارْتِباكٍ \ باضْطِرابٍ; **after the long flight we felt a bit ~ of it** بعد الرِحْلةِ الجَوِّيّةِ الطَويلةِ شَعَرْنا بِبَعْضِ الارْتِباكِ

outage /ˈaʊtɪdʒ/ *n* انْقِطاع

out-and-out /aʊt(ə)nˈaʊt/ *adj attrib* <*liar, feminist*> بِكُلِّ مَعْنى الكَلِمةِ; <*defeat, disgrace*> تامّ, مُطْلَق

outback /ˈaʊtbak/ *n* (**the outback**) [مَناطِق ريفيّة نائِية في أُسْتُرالِيا]

outbid /aʊtˈbɪd/ *vt* (*present participle* **-dd-**; *past tense, past participle* **outbid**) زايَدَ (قَدَّمَ عَرْضَ سِعْرٍ أَعْلى) <*a rival, developer*>

outboard motor /ˌaʊtbɔːd ˈməʊtə/ *n* مُحَرِّك زَوْرَقٍ خارِجيّ

outbreak /ˈaʊtbreɪk/ *n* **1** (of war) نُشوب, انْدِلاع; **at the ~ of the war** عند نُشوبِ الحَرْبِ; **2** (of disease) تَفَشٍّ; **3** (of rain) هُطول, سُقوط

outbuilding /ˈaʊtbɪldɪŋ/ *n* مَبْنًى إضافيّ \ مُلْحَق

outburst /'aʊtbə:st/ *n* جَيَشان, فَوْرة ,سَوْرة; **an angry/emotional ~** سَوْرة غَضَبٍ \ جَيَشان عاطِفيّ

outcast /'aʊtkɑ:st/ *n* مَنْبوذ

outcome /'aʊtkʌm/ *n* (حَصائِلُ) حَصيلة ,(نَتائِجُ) نَتيجة; **what was the ~ of the talks?** ماذا كانَتْ نَتيجةُ المُحادَثاتِ؟

outcrop /'aʊtkrɒp/ *n* نُتوء \ بُروز صَخْري

outcry /'aʊtkraɪ/ *n* (*pl* **outcries**) عاصِفة ,(احْتِجاجات) احْتِجاج مِن الغَضَبِ; **there was an ~ about/against the new car park** كانَ هُناكَ احْتِجاجٌ حول \ ضِدّ مَوْقِفِ السَيّاراتِ الجَديدِ

outdated /aʊt'deɪtɪd/ *adj* ‹*concept, attitude*› بالٍ; ‹*clothing, equipment*› قَديم الطِرازِ

outdistance /aʊt'dɪst(ə)ns/ *vt* سَبَقَ (i-u; سَبْق) ‹*a rival, runner*›

outdo /aʊt'du:/ *vt* (*3rd person present sing* **outdoes**, *past tense* **outdid**, *past participle* **outdone**) (على) امْتازَ ,(على) تَفَوَّقَ ‹*a rival, competitor*›; (فَواق) فاقَ ‹*a result, achievement*›

outdoor /'aʊtdɔ:/ *adj attrib* ‹*activity, concert*› في الهَواءِ الطَلْقِ; **he really thrives on the ~ life** [تَجْعَلُهُ حَياةُ الهَواءِ الطَلْقِ يَشْعُرُ بانْتِعاشٍ وَسَعادةٍ كَبيرةٍ]

outdoors /aʊt'dɔ:z/ *adv* ‹*to work, play*› في ,في الهَواءِ الطَلْقِ العَراءِ

outer /'aʊtə/ *adj* 1 (outside) ‹*layer, wall*› بَرّانيّ ,خارِجيّ 2 (more remote) ‹*limits, regions*› الأَبْعَد

outer space *n* فَضاء خارِجيّ

outfit /'aʊtfɪt/ *n* 1 (set of clothes) (طُقوم) طَقْم ,(بَدْلات) بَدْلة 2 (infml) (company) شَرِكة

outfitter /'aʊtfɪtə/ *n* 1 (BrE fml) (for clothes) مَحَلّ مَلابِسَ 2 (AmE) (for equipment) [مَحَلّ لَوازِمِ الأَنْشِطةِ الرِجاليّةِ الخارِجيّةِ]

outflank /aʊt'flaŋk/ *vt* طَوَّقَ (على سَبيلِ المُناوَرةِ) ‹*the enemy*›

outflow /'aʊtfləʊ/ *n* 1 (of funds) (تَدَفُّقات) تَدَفُّق 2 (of water) (تَدَفُّقات) تَدَفُّق

outgoing /'aʊtgəʊɪŋ/ *adj* 1 (sociable) ‹*personality, type*› مُنْفَتِح, اجْتِماعيّ 2 ‹*president, government*› مُنْصَرِف ,مُغادِر 3 ‹*calls*› مُغادِر; ‹*flights*› صادِر

outgoings /'aʊtgəʊɪŋz/ *n pl* (BrE) مَصْروفات نَثْريّة ,نَثْريّات

outgrow /aʊt'grəʊ/ *vt* (*past tense* **outgrew**; *past participle* **outgrown**) 1 (grow too big for) كَبُرَ (a; كِبَر) (على) ‹*clothes, premises*›; **he's ~n his new shoes already** ضاقَ عَلَيْهِ الحِذاءُ الجَديدُ 2 (to grow too old for) تَجاوَزَ ,تَخَطّى; **I thought she'd ~n that stage** ظَنَنْتُ أَنَّها تَخَطَّتْ تِلْكَ المَرْحَلةَ

outhouse /'aʊthaʊs/ *n* مَبْنًى إضافيّ \ مُلْحَق

outing /'aʊtɪŋ/ *n* (نُزْهات ,نُزَه) نُزْهة

outlandish /aʊt'landɪʃ/ *adj* ‹*clothes, ideas*› غَريب

outlast /aʊt'lɑ:st/ *vt* 1 (to last longer than) دامَ لِفَتْرةٍ أَطْوَلَ 2 (to live longer than) عاشَ لِفَتْرةٍ أَطْوَلَ

outlaw /'aʊtlɔ:/ **A** *n* خارِج عن القانونِ **B** *vt* حَظَرَ (u; حَظْر) ‹*a practice, an organization*›

outlay /'aʊtleɪ/ *n* نَفَقة ,(نَفَقات) مَصْروف ,(مَصْروفات ,مَصاريفُ)

outlet /'aʊtlɛt/ *n* 1 (in retail trade) (مَتاجِرُ) مَتْجَر; **a retail ~** مَحَلّ للبَيْعِ بالتَجْزِئةِ \ بالمُفَرَّقِ 2 (for emotions, talent) مُتَنَفَّس 3 (for water, gas) (مَنافِذُ) مَنْفَذ 4 (AmE) (for plug) مِقْبَس

outline /'aʊtlʌɪn/ **A** *n* 1 (shape) (مَعالِمُ) مَعْلَم; (drawing) خَطّ 2 (of a plan, policy) مَعالِم; (of a book, story) خُطوط عَريضة ,كِفافيّ **B** *vt* 1 (to summarize) لَخَّصَ ,أَوْجَزَ 2 (to silhouette) حَدَّدَ المَعالِمَ; (to draw round) رَسَمَ المَعالِمَ

outlive /aʊt'lɪv/ *vt* عَمَّرَ أَكْثَرَ من ‹*one's husband, children*›

outlook /'aʊtlʊk/ *n* 1 (attitude) (نَظَرات) نَظْرة ,وُجْهة نَظَرٍ, 2 (prospects) (مَواقِفُ) مَوْقِف ,تَوَقُّعات

outlying /'aʊtlʌɪɪŋ/ *adj* 1 (remote) ‹*areas, islands*› ناءٍ 2 (away from city centre) ‹*suburbs, neighbourhoods*› بَعيد عن وَسَطِ المَدينةِ

outnumber /aʊt'nʌmbə/ *vt* فاقَ عَدَداً ‹*the enemy, protesters*›

out-of-body experience /ˌaʊtəvˌbɒdi ɪk'spɪəriəns/ *n* تَجْرِبة الخُروجِ من الجَسَدِ

out of date *adj* (*before n* **out-of-date**) 1 (not valid) ‹*passport, information*› مُنْتَهي الصَلاحيّةِ 2 (old-fashioned) ‹*clothes*› قَديم الطِرازِ; ‹*concept, technology*› بالٍ

out of the way *adj* (*before n* **out-of-the-way**) ‹*place*› ناءٍ; ‹*hotel*› مَعْزول

outpatient /'aʊtpeɪʃ(ə)nt/ *n* مَريض عِيادةٍ خارِجيّةٍ (يَخْرُجُ من المُسْتَشْفى في نَفْسِ اليَوْمِ)

outpost /'aʊtpəʊst/ *n* **1** (Mil) [نُقْطة أَمْنيّة حُدوديّة \ في مِنْطَقةٍ مَعْزولةٍ] **2** (settlement) مُسْتَوْطَنة نائِية

output /'aʊtpʊt/ *n* **1** (production of a factory) إِنْتاج; (of a machine) قُدْرة; (of a writer) نِتاج; **manufacturing ~ is up/down** الإِنْتاجُ الصِناعيُّ عالٍ \ مُنْخَفِضٌ **2** (of an engine, a power plant) قُدْرة فِعْليّة

outrage /'aʊtreɪdʒ/ **A** *n* **1** (indignation) غَضَب شَديد; **many expressed their ~ at the decision** عَبَّرَ الكَثيرُ من الناسِ عن غَضَبِهم الشَديدِ إِزاءَ القَرارِ **2** (atrocity) عَمَل وَحْشيّ **3** (scandal) فَضيحة (فَضائِحُ)

B *vt* أَثارَ غَضَباً شَديداً لدى ‹the public›

outrageous /aʊt'reɪdʒəs/ *adj* **1** ‹claim, behaviour› شَنيع (شَنائِعُ), شائِن; ‹price› باهِظ, فاحِش **2** ‹clothing, hairstyle› غَيْر مَأْلوفٍ, غَريب

outreach /'aʊtriːtʃ/ *n* امْتِداد (امْتِدادات), تَواصُل, تَوْعِية

outreach worker *n* [عامل في مَجالِ التَّوْعِيةِ والتَّواصُلِ]

outright /'aʊtrʌɪt/ **A** *adv* **1** (completely) ‹to own, ban› كُلِّيّةً, على نَحْوٍ مُطْلَقٍ **2** (directly) ‹to reject, deny› بِشَكْلٍ مُباشِرٍ \ صَريح; ‹to lie› على نَحْوٍ سافِرٍ **3** (instantly) ‹to be killed› على الفَوْرِ

B *adj* **1** ‹ban, control› كُلّيّ, تامّ **2** ‹hostility, denial› صَريح; ‹lie› سافِر **3** ‹winner› دون مُنازِعٍ; ‹victory› مُطْلَق

outrun /aʊt'rʌn/ *vt* (*present participle* **outrunning**; *past tense* **outran**; *past participle* **outrun**) سَبَقَ (i-u; سَبْق), تَجاوَزَ ‹a pursuer, an opponent›

outset /'aʊtset/ *n* بَدْء, بِداية, مُسْتَهَلّ; **at/from the ~** في \ منذ البِدايةِ

outshine /aʊt'ʃʌɪn/ *vt* (*past tense, past participle* **outshone**) تَفَوَّقَ (على), تَمَيَّزَ (على) ‹one's competitors, colleagues›

outside /aʊt'sʌɪd, 'aʊtsʌɪd/ **A** *n* **1** (of a building, fruit) خارِج; **the ~ of the building is in disrepair** المَبْنى في حالةٍ سَيِّئةٍ من الخارِجِ; **it's hard on the ~** هو صُلْبٌ من الخارِجِ; **you can only open the door from the ~** يُمْكِنُكَ أَنْ تَفْتَحَ البابَ من الخارِجِ فَقَطْ **2** (maximum) **at the ~** على أَكْثَرِ تَقْديرٍ

B *adj before n* **1** (outdoor) ‹temperature, broadcast› خارِجيّ **2** (outer) ‹measurement, edge, wall› خارِجيّ **3** (Tel) ‹line› خارِجيّ **4** (beyond usual environment) خارِجيّ; **he has no ~ interests** (business) لَيْسَ لَهُ مَصالِحُ خارِجيّةٌ; (hobbies) لَيْسَ لَهُ اهْتِماماتٌ خارِجيّةٌ; **the ~ world doesn't care** العالَمُ الخارِجيُّ لا يَهْتَمُّ **5** (from elsewhere) ‹help, opinion› خارِجيّ **6** **to be in the ~ lane** كانَ في الحارةِ الخارِجيّةِ **7** (faint) **an ~ chance** فُرْصة صَغيرة

C *prep* (also **outside of**) **1** (not within) خارِجَ ‹a city, harbour, prison›; **it's just ~ Richmond** إِنَّهُ خارِجَ ريتْشْموند تَحْديداً; **he's not allowed ~ the prison boundary** لا يُسْمَحُ لَهُ بالخُروجِ عن حُدودِ السِجْنِ **2** (in front of) أَمامَ ‹a house, shop›; **I'll meet you ~ the café** سَأُقابِلُكَ أَمامَ المَقْهى **3** (over) **to wear a shirt ~ one's trousers** لَبِسَ قَميصاً يَتَدَلّى خارِجَ سِرْوالِهِ **4** (not within) **~ office hours** خارِجَ مَواعيدِ المَكْتَبِ \ العَمَلِ; **her life ~ the family circle** حَياتُها خارِجَ نِطاقِ الأُسْرةِ

D *adv* ‹to wait, play› خارِجاً; **wait for me ~** انْتَظِرْني خارِجاً; **to go** *or* **come ~** خَرَجَ (u; خُروج); **to take the chairs/washing ~** أَخْرَجَ الكَراسيَّ \ الغَسيلَ

outsider /aʊt'sʌɪdə/ *n* **1** (person not belonging) أَجْنَبيّ (أَجْنَبيّونَ, أَجانِبُ), دَخيل (دُخَلاءُ), غَريب (غُرَباءُ) **2** (in a competition) [مُنافِس ذو حُظوظٍ ضَئيلةٍ في الفَوْزِ]

outsize /'aʊtsʌɪz/, **outsized** /'aʊtsʌɪzd/ *adj* ‹clothes› واسِع \ عِمْلاق; ‹screen› عَريض جِدًّا

outskirts /'aʊtskəːts/ *n pl* أَطْراف, ضَواحٍ

outsmart /aʊt'smɑːt/ *vt* [غَلَبَ بالحيلةِ \ بالدَهاءِ] ‹one's opponent, enemy›

outsource /aʊt'sɔːs/ *vt* أَسْنَدَ إلى مَصادِرَ خارِجيّةٍ ‹work, services›

outsourcing /'aʊtsɔːsɪŋ/ *n* اسْتِعانة بِمَصادِرَ خارِجيّةٍ; تَعاقُد من الباطِنِ

outspoken /aʊt'spəʊk(ə)n/ *adj* ‹critic, opponent› صَريح (صُرَحاءُ)

outspread /aʊt'spred/ *adj* ‹wings, arms› مَمْدود, مَبْسوط

outstanding /aʊt'standɪŋ/ *adj* **1** (praiseworthy) ‹achievement, player› مُمْتاز; (striking) ‹contribution, beauty› باهِر **2** (prominent) ‹features, display› بارِز, مَرْموق **3** (not yet dealt with/carried out) ‹debt, loan› مُسْتَحَقّ; ‹work, jobs›

<*issue, problem*> عالِق, مُعَلَّق; **a good deal of work is still ~** ما زالَ قَدْرٌ كَبيرٌ من العَمَلِ مُعَلَّقاً

outstay /aʊt'steɪ/ *vt* <*one's time, guest*> مَكَثَ \ بَقِيَ مُدَّةً أَطْوَلَ من

(Idiom) **to outstay one's welcome** أطالَ المُقامَ (عند مُضيفِهِ)

outstretched /aʊt'stretʃt/ *adj* <*hands, wings*> مَمْدود, مَبْسوط

outstrip /aʊt'strɪp/ *vt* **(-pp-)** **1** (to run faster than) سَبَقَ (i-u; سَبْق) <*a runner, competitor*> **2** (to surpass) فاقَ (u; فَوْق, فَواق), <*a rival, counterpart*> **3** (to become larger than) تَفَوَّقَ (على) <*supply, demand*> تَجاوَزَ

outvote /aʊt'vəʊt/ *vt* فازَ بِأَغْلَبِيَّةِ الأَصْواتِ على <*a politician, proposal*>

outward /'aʊtwəd/ **A** *adj* **1** (outside) <*appearance, calm*> خارِجيّ, ظاهِريّ **2** (travelling away) <*journey, voyage*> ذَهابِ; **the ~ journey takes longer than the return** تَسْتَغْرِقُ رِحْلَةُ الذَهابِ وَقْتاً أَطْوَلَ من رِحْلَةِ العَوْدةِ

B *adv* (BrE also **outwards**) <*to radiate, spread*> نحو الخارِجِ

outwardly /'aʊtwədli/ *adv* <*to appear, express*> ظاهِرِيًّا

outwards /'aʊtwədz/ (BrE) ▸**outward** B

outweigh /aʊt'weɪ/ *vt* فاقَ (u; فَوْق, فَواق) <*the benefit, risk*>

outwit /aʊt'wɪt/ *vt* **(-tt-)** غَلَبَ بالحيلةِ والدَهاءِ <*an opponent, enemy*>

outworker /'aʊtwɜːkə/ *n* [شَخْص يَعْمَلُ عن بُعْدٍ \ من البَيْتِ]

oval /'əʊv(ə)l/ **A** *adj* <*shape, mirror*> بَيْضَوِيّ, بَيْضاوِيّ

B *n* شَكْل بَيْضَوِيّ

ovarian /əʊ'veːrɪən/ *adj* <*cancer, cyst*> المَبيضِ

ovary /'əʊv(ə)ri/ *n* (*pl* **ovaries**) مَبيض (مَبايِضُ)

ovation /əʊ'veɪʃ(ə)n/ *n* تَصْفيق حارّ; **the audience gave him a standing ~** وَقَفَ الجُمْهورُ وَصَفَّقَ لَهُ بِحَرارةٍ; **to give sb an ~** صَفَّقَ لِشَخْصٍ تَصْفيقاً حارًّا

oven /'ʌv(ə)n/ *n* فُرْن (أَفْران); **a gas/an electric ~** فُرْن غازٍ \ كَهْرَبائيّ

oven glove *n* قُفّاز فُرْنٍ

ovenproof /'ʌv(ə)npruːf/ *adj* <*dish, casserole*> مُقاوِم لِحَرارةِ الفُرْنِ

oven-ready /ˌʌv(ə)n'redi/ *adj* <*meal, pizza*> جاهِز للطَبْخِ

over¹ /'əʊvə/ **A** *prep* **1** (across the top of) فَوْقَ; **he jumped ~ the fence** قَفَزَ فَوْقَ السِياجِ; **a bridge ~ the river** جِسْر فَوْقَ النَهْرِ **2** (from or on the other side of) **the house ~ the road** البَيْت في الجِهةِ المُقابِلةِ من الشارِعِ; **it's ~ here/there** إنَّهُ هُنا \ هُناكَ; **come ~ here!** تَعالَ هُنا! **3** (on top of) فَوْقَ; **they live ~ the shop** يَسْكُنونَ فَوْقَ المَحَلِّ; **to wear a sweater ~ one's shirt** لَبِسَ سُتْرةً فَوْقَ قَميصِهِ; **shutters ~ the windows** مَصاريع على النَوافِذِ **4** (above) **the water came ~ my ankles** وَصَلَ مُسْتَوى المِياهِ إلى ما فوق كَواحِلي **5** (more than) فَوْقَ; **children (of) ~ six** الأَطْفال فَوْقَ سِنِّ السادِسةِ; **temperatures ~ 40°** دَرَجات الحَرارةِ فَوْقَ 40° **6** (in the course of) **~ the weekend/the summer** <*event, period of time*> خِلالَ عُطْلةِ نِهايةِ الأُسْبوعِ \ الصَيْفِ; **~ a period of ... ~** خِلالَ فَتْرةِ ...; **~ the last few days** خِلالَ الأَيّامِ القَليلةِ الماضِيةِ; **he has changed ~ the years** تَغَيَّرَ بِمُرورِ السِنينِ; **to do sth ~ the weekend** فَعَلَ شَيْئاً خِلالَ عُطْلةِ نِهايةِ الأُسْبوعِ **7** (in recovery from) **to be ~ an illness/operation/a loss** تَعافى من مَرَضٍ \ عَمَلِيّةٍ جِراحِيّةٍ \ خسارةٍ; **to be ~ the worst** تَخَطّى الأَسْوَأَ **8** (by means of) **~ the phone** على الهاتِفِ; **~ the radio** على الراديو **9** (everywhere in) **to travel all ~ the world/Africa** سافَرَ في جَميعِ أَنْحاءِ العالَمِ \ إفْريقيا; **to search all ~ the house** بَحَثَ في البَيْتِ كُلِّهِ **10** (Math) (in divisions) **12 ~ 3 is 4** 12 على 3 يُساوي 4

B (**over and above**) *prep phr* (fml) **~ and above that** فوق كُلِّ ذلك; **it goes ~ and above the minimum requirement** يَفوقُ الحَدَّ الأَدْنى من المُتَطَلَّباتِ

C *adj, adv* **1** (finished) **to be ~** «meeting, event» انْتَهى; **to get sth ~ with** انْتَهى من شَيْءٍ **2** (more) **children of six and ~** الأَطْفال من سِنِّ السادِسةِ فَأَكْثَرَ **3** (infml) (remaining) **to be ~** تَبَقّى; كانَ زائِداً عن اللُزومِ \ الحاجةِ; **we're one ~** لَدَيْنا واحِدٌ زائِدٌ **4** (to one's house) **to invite or ask sb ~** دَعا شَخْصاً لِبَيْتِه; **we had them ~ on Sunday** اسْتَقْبَلْناهُمْ في بَيْتِنا يَوْمَ الأَحَدِ **5** (in broadcasting) **~ to you** إلَيْكَ الخَطُّ **6** (showing repetition) **to start all ~ again** بَدَأَ من جَديدٍ; **I've told you ~ and ~ (again) ...** قُلْتُ لَكَ مِراراً وَتِكْراراً ...; **I had to do it ~** اضْطَرَرْتُ لِإعادةِ فِعْلِهِ من جَديدٍ

over² /ˈəʊvə/ *n* [رَمْي سِتّةِ كُراتٍ مُتَتالِيةٍ في لُعْبةِ الكْرِيكِت]

overact /əʊvərˈakt/ *vi* «actors, performers» بالَغَ في تَمْثِيلِ دَوْرٍ

overall /ˈəʊvərɔːl/ **A** /əʊvərˈɔːl/ *adj* ‹winner› نِهائيّ; ‹effect› كُلّيّ, شامِل; **an ~ increase in poverty** زِيادة عامّة \ إجْماليّة في حالاتِ الفَقْرِ

B *adv* ‹to win, increase› عُموماً; **~, prices are still rising** عُموماً، ما زالَت الأَسْعارُ في ارْتِفاعٍ

C *n* (BrE) مِئْزَر (مَآزِرُ)

D (**overalls**) *n pl* (a boiler suit) (BrE) أَفَرول, بَدْلة وَرْشةٍ; (AmE) ▸**dungarees**

overarm /ˈəʊvərɑːm/ **A** *adj* ‹stroke, bowling› [يُؤَدّى بِأَرْجَحةِ الذِراعِ فوق الكَتِفِ]

B *adv* ‹to throw, bowl› [بِأَرْجَحةِ الذِراعِ فوق الكَتِفِ]

overate /əʊvərˈet/ *past tense* ▸**overeat**

overawe /əʊvərˈɔː/ *vt* ‹a child› أَدْهَش; **the child was ~d by the occasion** انْدَهَشَ الطِفْلُ بالاحْتِفالِ

overbalance /əʊvəˈbaləns/ *vi* «skaters, piles of objects» فَقَد التَوازُنَ

overboard /ˈəʊvəbɔːd/ *adv* ‹to throw sth, fall› في الماءِ (من على مَتْنِ سَفِينةٍ); **man ~!** [سَقَطَ رَجُلٌ من السَفِينةِ!]

Idiom **to go overboard about sth** كانَ مُتَحمِّساً جِدًّا لِشَيْءٍ

overbook /əʊvəˈbʊk/ *vt* ‹a hotel, flight› [حَجَزَ فوق الطاقةِ الاسْتِيعابيّةِ]; **the hotel was ~ed** كانَ الفُنْدُقُ مَحْجوزاً فوق طاقَتِه الاسْتِيعابيّةِ

overcast /əʊvəˈkɑːst/ *adj* ‹sky, day› غائِم, مُلَبَّد بالغُيومِ

overcharge /əʊvəˈtʃɑːdʒ/ **A** *vt* ‹a customer, company› غالى في السِعْرِ على, طَلَبَ سِعْراً باهِظاً من; **to ~ a customer for sth** غالى على الزَبونِ في سِعْرِ شَيْءٍ

B *vi* «assistants, shops» غالى في السِعْرِ, طَلَبَ سِعْراً باهِظاً; **they often ~ for materials** غالِباً ما يُغالونَ في أَسْعارِ المَوادِّ

overcoat /ˈəʊvəkəʊt/ *n* مِعْطَف (مَعاطِفُ)

overcome /əʊvəˈkʌm/ **A** *vt* (*past tense* **overcame**; *past participle* **overcome**) **1** (to defeat) انْتَصَرَ (على), تَغَلَّبَ (على), هَزَمَ (هَزْم; i) ‹an opponent, enemy›; تَخَطّى ‹an obstacle, a fear› **2** (to overwhelm) أَنْهَكَ ‹an occupant, a passenger›; غَمَرَ (غَمْر; u), قَهَرَ (قَهْر; a) ‹a mourner, criminal›; **he was ~ by/with jealousy** اسْتَحْوَذَتْ عَلَيْه الغَيْرةُ

B *vi* (*past tense* **overcame**; *past participle* **overcome**) «teams, sides» انْتَصَرَ

overcook /əʊvəˈkʊk/ *vt* ‹pasta, vegetables› طَهى أَكْثَرَ من اللازِمِ

overcrowded /əʊvəˈkraʊdɪd/ *adj* ‹train, prison, city› مُكْتَظّ

overcrowding /əʊvəˈkraʊdɪŋ/ *n* اكْتِظاظ; **~ in classrooms** الاكْتِظاظ في قاعاتِ الدِراسةِ

overdo /əʊvəˈduː/ *vt* (*3rd person present sing* **overdoes**; *past tense* **overdid**; *past participle* **overdone**) **1** (to exaggerate) بالَغَ (في), أَفْرَطَ (في) ‹praise, an accent›; **it's good to exercise, but don't ~ it** من الجَيِّدِ أنْ تَقومَ بِتَمارِينَ رِياضيّةٍ، وَلَكِنْ لا تُفْرِطْ في ذلك **2** (to overcook) طَهى أَكْثَرَ من اللازِمِ ‹vegetables, steak›; **this fish is ~ne** هذا السَمَكُ مَطْهوٌّ أَكْثَرَ من اللازِمِ

overdose /ˈəʊvədəʊs/ **A** *n* جُرْعة زائِدة; **to take an ~** أَخَذَ جُرْعةً زائِدةً

B *vi* «addicts, suicides» أَخَذَ جُرْعةً زائِدةً; **to ~ on cocaine** تَناوَلَ جُرْعةً زائِدةً من الكوكايين

overdraft /ˈəʊvədrɑːft/ *n* سَحْب على المَكْشوفِ

overdraw /əʊvəˈdrɔː/ *vt* (*past tense* **overdrew**; *past participle* **overdrawn**) سَحَبَ على المَكْشوفِ من ‹one's bank account›; **to ~ one's account** سَحَبَ على المَكْشوفِ من رَصِيدِهِ

overdrawn /əʊvəˈdrɔːn/ *adj* ‹account, customer› ذو حِساب مَكْشوفٍ; **to be ~ by $1000** كانَ حِسابُهُ مَكْشوفاً ب $1000

overdressed /əʊvəˈdrest/ *adj* [مُتَأنِّق في مَلْبَسِهِ بِشَكْلٍ مُبالَغٍ فيه]

overdrive /ˈəʊvədraɪv/ *n* تُرْس زِيادةِ السُرْعةِ

Idiom **to go into overdrive** [أَصْبَحَ نَشِطاً \ نَشِطَ إلى أَقْصى الحُدودِ]

overdue /əʊvəˈdjuː/ *adj* ‹bill, payment› لم يُسَدَّدْ في تاريخِ الاسْتِحْقاقِ; **this measure is long ~** كانَتْ هُناكَ حاجةٌ لاتِّخاذِ هذا الإجْراءِ منذ مُدّةٍ طَوِيلةٍ

overeat /əʊvərˈiːt/ *vi* (*past tense* **overate**; *past participle* **overeaten**) أَكَلَ كَثيراً, أَفْرَطَ في الأَكْلِ

overestimate /əʊvərˈestɪmeɪt/ *vt* بالَغَ في التَقْديرِ ‹the number, importance›

overexcited /əʊvərɪk'sʌɪtɪd/ *adj* ‹*puppy, child*› شَديد التَهَيُّج

overfeed /əʊvə'fiːd/ *vt* (*past tense, past participle* **overfed**) أَطْعَمَ, أَفْرَطَ في الإِطْعامِ, أَكْثَرَ من اللازِمِ ‹*a child, pet*›

overfish /əʊvə'fɪʃ/ *vt* اسْتَنْزَفَ بالصَيْدِ الجائِرِ ‹*a species, cod*›

overflow **A** /əʊvə'fləʊ/ *vt* فاضَ (i; فَيَضان, فَيْض); **the river ~ed its banks** فاضَ \ طَفَحَ النَهْرُ من جَوانِبِهِ
B /əʊvə'fləʊ/ *vi* **1** «river, water» فاضَ (i; فَيَضان, فَيْض), طَفَحَ (a; طَفْح) **2** «bath, rubbish bin» فاضَ (i; فَيَضان, فَيْض); **hospitals were ~ing with the injured** كانَت المُسْتَشْفَياتُ تَعُجُّ بالجَرْحى
C /'əʊvəfləʊ/ *n* **1** (flowing over) فَيَضان **2** (excess) فائِض **3** (outlet) (also **overflow pipe**) ماسورة \ أُنْبوب الفائِضِ

overgrown /əʊvə'grəʊn/ *adj* **1** ‹*garden*› مُغَطًّى بالنَباتاتِ البَرِّيَّةِ **2** ‹*kid*› مُفْرِط في النُموِّ

overhand /'əʊvəhand/ *adj, adv* (AmE) ▸**overarm**

overhang **A** /əʊvə'haŋ/ *vt* (*past tense, past participle* **overhung**) أَطَلَّ (على) ‹*a street, river*›
B /əʊvə'haŋ/ *vi* «branches» تَدَلّى; «roofs» بَرَزَ (u; بُروز)
C /'əʊvəhaŋ/ *n* (of a cliff) بُروز, نُتوء; (of a roof) إِفْريز (أَفاريزُ), طَنْف (طُنوف, أَطْناف)

overhaul **A** /əʊvə'hɔːl/ *vt* **1** [فَحَصَ وَأَصْلَحَ] ‹*an engine, a machine*› **2** [فَحَصَ وَعَدَّلَ] ‹*a system, procedures*›
B /'əʊvəhɔːl/ *n* **1** (technical) [فَحْص وَإِصْلاح]; **an engine ~** عَمْرة المُحَرِّكِ **2** (organizational) [فَحْص وَتَعْديل]

overhead **A** /əʊvə'hɛd/ *adv* ‹*to fly, pass*› فوق الرُؤوسِ, في السَماءِ; **bats flew ~** طارَت الخَفافيشُ فوق الرُؤوسِ
B *adj* /'əʊvəhɛd/ ‹*cable*› هَوائيّ; ‹*light*› عُلْويّ; ‹*railway*› مُرْتَفِع
C /'əʊvəhɛd/ *n* (AmE) ▸**overheads**

overheads /'əʊvəhɛdz/ (BrE), **overhead** (AmE) /'əʊvəhɛd/ *n pl* نَفَقات عامّة

overhear /əʊvə'hɪə/ *vt* (*past tense, past participle* **overheard**) سَمِعَ بالصُدْفةِ \ دون قَصْدٍ ‹*a conversation, person*›

overheat /əʊvə'hiːt/ *vi* «cars, engines» حَمِيَ (a; حَمْيَة), سَخُنَ بِشِدّةٍ

overindulge /əʊvərɪn'dʌldʒ/ *vi* أَسْرَفَ في المَلَذّاتِ

overjoyed /əʊvə'dʒɔɪd/ *adj* مُبْتَهِج \ مُغْتَبِط للغايةِ

overkill /'əʊvəkɪl/ *n* مُبالَغة, إِفْراط

overland **A** *adj before n* /'əʊvəland/ ‹*route, journey*› بَرِّيّ
B *adv* /ˌəʊvə'land/ ‹*to travel*› بَرًّا

overlap **A** /əʊvə'lap/ *vi* **(-pp-)** **1** «edges, tiles» تَداخَلَ **2** «responsibilities, categories» تَطابَقَ
B /'əʊvəlap/ *n* **1** (of edges, tiles) تَطابُق (تَطابُقات) **2** (common area) شَيْء مُشْتَرَك

overleaf /əʊvə'liːf/ *adv* على ظَهْرِ الصَفْحةِ

overload **A** /əʊvə'ləʊd/ *vt* أَثْقَلَ (على), حَمَّلَ فوق طاقَتِهِ ‹*a system, vehicle*›
B /'əʊvələʊd/ *n* حِمْل زائِد

overlook /əʊvə'lʊk/ *vt* **1** (to have a view over) أَطَلَّ (على), أَشْرَفَ (على); **a large window ~ing the garden** نافِذة كَبيرة تُطِلُّ على الحَديقةِ **2** (to fail to notice) أَغْفَلَ **3** (to disregard) تَغاضى (عن)

overly /'əʊvəli/ *adv* ‹*optimistic, aggressive*› بِشَكْلٍ مُفْرِطٍ, أَكْثَرَ من اللازِمِ

overnight /'əʊvənʌɪt/ **A** /əʊvə'nʌɪt/ *adv* **1** (through the night) ‹*to work, detain*› خلال \ أثناء اللَيْلِ; **to stay ~** باتَ لَيْلَةً; **I left the washing to dry ~** تَرَكْتُ الغَسيلَ لِيَجِفَّ أثناء اللَيْلِ **2** (suddenly) ‹*to happen, change*› فَجْأةً, بين عَشِيّةٍ وَضُحاها
B *adj* **1** ‹*stay, journey, train*› لَيْليّ **2** ‹*success*› فَوْريّ, سَريع

overnight bag *n* حَقيبة مَبيتٍ (للرَحَلاتِ القَصيرةِ)

overpaid /əʊvə'peɪd/ *adj* ‹*executives, consultants*› [يَتَقاضى أَجْراً \ راتِباً مُبالَغٌ فيهِ]; **they're ~** رَواتِبُهُمْ مُبالَغٌ فيها

overpass /'əʊvəpɑːs/ *n* جِسْر عُلْويّ

overpopulated /əʊvə'pɒpjuːleɪtɪd/ *adj* ‹*country, planet*› مُكْتَظّ بالسُكّانِ

overpopulation /əʊvəpɒpjuː'leɪʃ(ə)n/ *n* انْفِجار \ اكْتِظاظ سُكّانيّ, زِيادة سُكّانِيّة

overpower /əʊvə'paʊə/ *vt* **1** (to render helpless) تَغَلَّبَ (على) ‹*an opponent, a guard*› **2** (to overwhelm) «smell, heat» تَغَلَّبَ (على)

overpowering /ˌəʊvə'paʊərɪŋ/ *adj* ‹*smell*› نَفّاذ; ‹*desire*› غامِر, قَوِيّ; ‹*heat, smoke*› خانِق

overprescribe /əʊvəprɪˈskrʌɪb/ *vt* (من [وَصَفَ كَمّيّاتٍ الأَدْوِيةِ) أَكْثَرَ من اللازِمِ] ‹*antibiotics, medication*›

overpriced /əʊvəˈprʌɪst/ *adj* ‹*drinks, products*› مُبالَغ في سِعْرِهِ, فاحِش الثَّمَنِ

overqualified /əʊvəˈkwɒlɪfʌɪd/ *adj* ‹*applicant, graduate*› مُؤَهِّلاتُهُ أَعْلى من المَطْلوبِ

overrated /əʊvəˈreɪtɪd/ *adj* ‹*player, film*› مُبالَغ في تَقْديرِهِ

overreach /əʊvəˈriːtʃ/ *v refl* **to ~ oneself** حَمَّلَ نَفْسَهُ ما لا يُطيقُ

overreact /əʊvərɪˈakt/ *vi* «governments, the media» بالَغَ في رَدِّ الفِعْلِ

override /əʊvəˈrʌɪd/ *vt* (*past tense* **overrode**; *past participle* **overridden**) **1** (to overturn) أَبْطَلَ, أَلْغى ‹*a decision, an objection*› **2** (to be more important than) هَيْمَنَ, تَجاوَزَ (i; هَيْمَنَة ;على), طَغى (a; طُغْيان ;على); **this consideration ~s all others** يَطْغى هذا الاعْتِبارُ على كُلِّ الاعْتِباراتِ الأُخْرى

overriding /əʊvəˈrʌɪdɪŋ/ *adj* ‹*concern, objective*› رَئيسيّ, أَساسيّ, جَوْهَريّ

overripe /əʊvəˈrʌɪp/ *adj* ‹*fruit*› زائِد, ناضِج أَكْثَرَ مِمّا يَنْبَغي النُّضجِ

overrule /əʊvəˈruːl/ *vt* نَقَضَ (u; نَقْض), أَبْطَلَ ‹*a decision, an objection*›

overrun /əʊvəˈrʌn/ **A** *vt* (*present participle* **-nn-**, *past tense* **-ran**, *past participle* **-run**) **1** (to invade) اكْتَسَحَ, اجْتاحَ ‹*a country, town*›; **the town was ~ by tourists/rebels** انْتَشَرَ السُّيّاحُ \ المُتَمَرِّدونَ في البَلْدَةِ **2** (to exceed) تَجاوَزَ ‹*a budget, allotted time*›
B *vi* (*present participle* **-nn-**, *past tense* **-ran**, *past participle* **-run**) «meeting, performer» [اسْتَمَرَّ بعد انْتِهاءِ الوَقْتِ المُحَدَّدِ]

overseas /əʊvəˈsiːz/ **A** *adv* ‹*to go, live*› في الخارِجِ, وراء البِحارِ
B *adj* **1** (from abroad) ‹*visitors, students*› من (أَجانِبُ) أَجْنَبيّ **2** (in or to other countries) ‹*trade, travel*› خارِجيّ, الخارِجِ عَبْرَ البِحارِ, في الخارِجِ

oversee /əʊvəˈsiː/ *vt* (*past tense* **oversaw**; *past participle* **overseen**) أَشْرَفَ (على), راقَبَ ‹*a project, process*›

overseer /ˈəʊvəsɪə/ *n* رَئيس عُمّالٍ, مُراقِب, مُشْرِف

overshadow /əʊvəˈʃadəʊ/ *vt* طَغى (a; طُغْيان ;على) ‹*sb's work, achievements*›

overshoot /əʊvəˈʃuːt/ *vt* (*past tense, past participle* **overshot**); **to ~ the runway** «planes» تَخَطّى \ تَجاوَزَ المَدْرَجَ

oversight /ˈəʊvəsʌɪt/ *n* **1** (omission) سَهْو **2** (supervision) مُراقَبة, إِشْراف

oversimplify /əʊvəˈsɪmplɪfʌɪ/ *vt* (**oversimplifies, oversimplifying, oversimplified**) بالَغَ في التَّبْسيطِ ‹*an issue, a situation*›

oversleep /əʊvəˈsliːp/ *vi* (*past tense, past participle* **overslept**) أَفْرَطَ في النَّوْمِ

overspend /əʊvəˈspend/ **A** *vt* (*past tense, past participle* **overspent**) أَسْرَفَ في الإِنْفاقِ, بَذَّرَ ‹*one's budget*›
B *vi* (*past tense, past participle* **overspent**) أَسْرَفَ, بَذَّرَ

overspill /ˈəʊvəspɪl/ *n* (BrE) فائِض السُّكّانِ (سُكّان يُضْطَرّونَ للانْتِقالِ من مَدينةٍ مُزْدَحِمةٍ إلى مَناطِقَ مُجاوِرةٍ)

overstaffed /əʊvəˈstɑːft/ *adj* ‹*company, department*› بِهِ عِمالةٌ زائِدةٌ

overstate /əʊvəˈsteɪt/ *vt* بالَغَ (في), غالى (في) ‹*the importance, problem*›

overstay /əʊvəˈsteɪ/ *vt* تَجاوَزَ مُدّةَ الإِقامةِ ‹*one's visa*›

overstep /əʊvəˈstep/ *vt* (**-pp-**) تَخَطّى, تَجاوَزَ ‹*the bounds, limits*›
(Idiom) **to overstep the mark** تَجاوَزَ حُدودَهُ

overt /ˈəʊvəːt/ *adj* ‹*racism, hostility*› صَريح, عَلَنيّ, (صُرَحاءُ) غَيْر مُسْتَتِرٍ

overtake /əʊvəˈteɪk/ **A** *vt* (*past tense* **overtook**, *past participle* **overtaken**) **1** (to go past) تَخَطّى, تَجاوَزَ **2** (to surpass) تَفَوَّقَ (على)
B *vi* (*past tense* **overtook**, *past participle* **overtaken**) تَخطّى السَّيّارةَ الّتي أَمامَهُ

overtax /əʊvəˈtaks/ *vt* **1** (to strain) أَنْهَكَ, أَجْهَدَ, أَرْهَقَ ‹*a system, resources*› **2** (to tax excessively) أَرْهَقَ بالضَرائِبِ ‹*a product, the citizens*›

over-the-counter /ˌəʊvəðəˈkaʊntə/ **A** *adj* ‹*medicines*› مُتاح دون وَصْفةٍ طِبّيّةٍ
B *adv* (**over the counter**) ‹*to buy, sell*› دون وَصْفةٍ طِبّيّةٍ

over the top *adj* (*before n* **over-the-top**) (infml) ‹*performance, reaction*› مُبالَغ فيهِ

overthrow **A** /əʊvə'θrəʊ/ *vt* (*past tense* **overthrew**; *past participle* **overthrown**) أَسْقَطَ ,(ب) أَطاحَ ‹*a government, ruler*›
B /'əʊvəθrəʊ/ *n* إسْقاط, إطاحة

overtime /'əʊvətʌɪm/ **A** *n* وَقت إضافيّ
B *adv* **to work ~** عَمِلَ وَقْتاً إضافيّاً

overtly /'əʊvə:tli/ *adv* ‹*to threaten, comment*› جَهْراً ,عَلانيَّةً

overtone /'əʊvətəʊn/ *n* لَمْحة (لَمَحات), إيحاء, نَبْرة

overture /'əʊvətjʊə/ *n* **1** (Mus) افْتِتاحيّة \ مُقَدِّمة موسيقيّة, تَمْهيد موسيقيّ **2** (approach, proposal); **to make ~s to sb** (for negotiation) قَدَّمَ مُبادَراتٍ لِشَخْصٍ; (sexually) فاتَحَ شَخْصاً في رَغْبَتِهِ في الارْتِباطِ

overturn /əʊvə'tɜ:n/ **A** *vt* **1** (to tip over) قَلَبَ (قَلْب ;i) ‹*a car, table*› **2** (to reverse) أَبْطَلَ, أَلْغى ‹*a decision, verdict*›
B *vi* «car, boat» انْقَلَبَ رَأْساً على عَقِبٍ

overview /'əʊvəvju:/ *n* اسْتِعْراض ,نَظْرة \ لَمْحة عامّة (اسْتِعْراضات)

overweight /əʊvə'weɪt/ *adj* ‹*person*› سَمين ,(بُدْن ,بُدُن) بَدين (سِمان), زائِد الوَزْنِ; **he's ~** يُعاني من زِيادةِ الوَزْنِ; **my case is 5 kilos ~** حَقيبَتي زائِدةٌ عن الوَزْنِ المَسْموحِ بِخَمْسةِ كيلوغراماتٍ

overwhelm /əʊvə'wɛlm/ *vt* **1** (to stretch) غَمَرَ (غَمْر ;u) ‹*a system, call centre*›; اجْتاحَ ,اكْتَسَحَ ‹*a city*›; **we have been ~ed by the number of applications/the response** غَمَرَتْنا الطَّلَباتُ \ الرُدودُ **2** (emotionally) اسْتَحْوَذَ (على); **to be ~ed by** *or* **with joy** غَمَرَتْهُ النَّشْوةُ; **to be ~ed by** *or* **with grief** قَهَرَهُ الحُزْنُ **3** (in battle, sport) قَهَرَ (قَهْر ;a), هَزَمَ (هَزْم ;i) تَغَلَّبَ (على)

overwhelming /əʊvə'wɛlmɪŋ/ *adj* ‹*response, majority, victory*› ساحِق

overwhelmingly /əʊvə'wɛlmɪŋli/ *adv* ‹*to vote, win*› بِشَكْلٍ ساحِقٍ

overwork /əʊvə'wɜ:k/ **A** *vi* أَجْهَدَ نَفْسَهُ في العَمَلِ
B *n* عَمَل زائِد, إفْراط في العَمَلِ

overworked /əʊvə'wɜ:kt/ *adj* ‹*staff, parents*› مُرْهَق ,مُنْهَك

ovulate /'ɒvjʊleɪt/ *vi* «females» حَدَثَ لَها تَبْويضٌ \ أَباضَ, إباضةٌ

ovulation /ɒvju:'leɪʃ(ə)n/ *n* تَبْويض, إباضة

owe /əʊ/ *vt* **1** (to be in debt to) دانَ (دَيْن ;i) (ب) ‹*money*›; **how much do I ~ you?** بِكَمْ أنا مَدينٌ لَكَ؟ **2** (to feel obliged for) دانَ (دَيْن ;i) (ب) ‹*one's life, success*›; **to ~ one's life to sb** دانَ بِحَياتِهِ لِشَخْصٍ; **to ~ sb one's happiness** دانَ لِشَخْصٍ بِسَعادَتِهِ **3** (to be under obligation to) دانَ (دَيْن ;i) (ب) ‹*an apology, a favour*›

owing /'əʊɪŋ/ **A** *adj* مُسْتَحَقّ; **to be ~ to sb** كانَ مُسْتَحَقّاً لِشَخْصٍ
B (**owing to**) *prep* نَظَراً ل, بِسَبَبِ; **~ to circumstances outside our control...** نَظَراً لِظُروفٍ خارِجةٍ عن سَيْطَرَتِنا ...

owl /aʊl/ *n* بومة

own /əʊn/ **A** *adj* (belonging to particular person, group etc) خاصّ; **his ~ car/house** سَيّارَتُهُ الخاصّة \ بَيْتُهُ الخاصّ; **my ~ sister/son** أُخْتي \ ابْني من لَحْمي وَدَمي; **his ~ children** أَبْناؤُهُ من صُلْبِهِ; **to start one's ~ business** بَدَأَ عَمَلَهُ الخاصَّ; **for your ~ safety use ...** لِسَلامَتِكُم الشَخْصيّةِ اسْتَخْدِموا ...; **the house has its ~ garage/garden** البَيْتُ لَهُ حَديقةٌ خاصّةٌ \ جَراجٌ خاصٌّ; **he has his ~ ideas about that** لَدَيْهِ أَفْكارُهُ الخاصّةُ بِخُصوصِ ذلك; **he's very nice in his ~ way** هو لَطيفٌ جِدًّا بِطَريقَتِهِ الخاصّةِ; **I saw it with my ~ eyes** رَأَيْتُهُ بِأُمِّ عَيْنَيَّ; **she does her ~ cooking/washing** تَقومُ بالطَهْيِ \ بِغَسيلِ المَلابِسِ بِنَفْسِها; **my ~ view is that ...** وِجْهةُ نَظَري الخاصّةُ هي أنّ ...
B *pron* **it's not a company laptop; I use my ~** هذا الكُمْبْيوتَر المَحْمولُ لَيْسَ مِلْكاً للشَرِكةِ؛ فَأَنا أَسْتَخْدِمُ جِهازي الخاصَّ; **she borrowed my book, because she'd lost her ~** اسْتَعارَتْ كِتابي، لِأَنَّها فَقَدَتْ كِتابَها; **they have problems of their ~** لَدَيْهِمْ مَشاكِلُهُم الخاصّةُ; **when you have children of your ~** عِنْدَما تُنْجِبُ أَطْفالاً; **a house/a garden of our (very) ~** بَيْت خاصّ \ حَديقة خاصّة بِنا وَحْدَنا
C *vt* **1** (to possess) «institution, organization, person» امْتَلَكَ ‹*a car, house, dog*›; **she ~s three shops and a café** تَمْتَلِكُ ثَلاثةَ مَتاجِرٍ وَمَقْهًى; **who ~s this house/car?** مَنْ صاحِبُ هذا

المَنْزِلِ \ هذه السَّيّارةِ؟ **2** (fml) (to admit) اِعْتَرَفَ, أَقَرَّ; **he ~ed that it was his mistake** أَقَرَّ أَنَّهُ كانَ خَطَأَهُ

D *vi* (fml) **to ~ to a mistake** أَقَرَّ بِخَطَأٍ

(Idioms) **on one's own** وَحْدَهُ, بِمُفْرَدِهِ; **she's on her ~** تَعيشُ وَحْدَها; **I did it on my ~** فَعَلْتُهُ بِمُفْرَدي; **you're on your ~ now** الأَمْرُ على عاتِقِكَ الآنَ; **to come into one's own** أَظْهَرَ قُدُراتِهِ; **to do one's own thing** (infml) فَعَلَ الشَّيْءَ الّذي يَهْواهُ; الخاصّةَ; **to get one's own back** انْتَقَمَ لِنَفْسِهِ ▸ **hold**

(Phrasal verb) **own up to sth** أَقَرَّ بِشَيْءٍ صَراحةً; **to ~ up to having done sth** أَقَرَّ صَراحةً أَنَّهُ فَعَلَ شَيْئاً

own brand *n* (BrE) عَلامة تِجاريّة خاصّة

owner /ˈəʊnə/ *n* مالِك (مُلاّك), صاحِب (أَصْحاب)

ownership /ˈəʊnəʃɪp/ *n* مِلْكيّة; **to be in private/public ~** كانَ في مِلْكيّةٍ خاصّةٍ \ عامّةٍ

ox /ɒks/ *n* (*pl* **oxen**) ثَوْر (ثيران)

oxen /ˈɒks(ə)n/ *n pl* ▸ **ox**

oxide /ˈɒksʌɪd/ *n* أوكْسيد (أَكاسيدُ)

oxygen /ˈɒksɪdʒ(ə)n/ *n* أُكْسجين

oyster /ˈɔɪstə/ *n* مَحار (n coll)

(Idiom) **the world is my/your oyster** العالَمُ طَوْعَ أَمْري \ أَمْرِكَ

oystercatcher /ˈɔɪstəkatʃə/ *n* صائِد المَحارِ (طائِر بَحْرِيّ)

oz *abbr* = **ounce(s)** أونْصة, أوقيّة

ozone /ˈəʊzəʊn/ *n* أوزون

ozone layer *n* (**the ozone layer**) طَبَقة الأوزون

Pp

P, p /piː/ **A** *n* (letter) [الحَرْف السادِسَ عَشَرَ من الأَبْجَدِيَّةِ الإِنْكليزِيَّةِ]

B *abbr* **1** (BrE) (**p**) = **penny** بِنْس (بِنْسات) = **pence** بِنسات

2 (**p.**; *pl* **pp.**) = **page(s)** صَفْحة

(Idiom) **to mind one's p's and q's** وَزَنَ \ راعى كَلامَهُ

pa /pɑː/ *n* (infml) بابا ,أب ,والِد

PA /piːˈeɪ/ **A** *n* **1** ~ **system** = **public address system** نِظام الإِذاعةِ الداخِلِيَّةِ \ النِداءِ العامِّ **2** (BrE) = **personal assistant** مُساعِد شَخْصِيّ \ خاصّ

B *abbr* = **Pennsylvania**

pace /peɪs/ **A** *n* **1** (step) خَطْوة (خَطَوات) **2** (rate of walking) سُرْعة; (of change, life) وَتيرة (وَتائِر) ,مُعَدَّل (مُعَدَّلات); **at a fast/slow** ~ بِوَتيرةٍ سَريعة \ بَطيئةٍ; **to quicken/slow one's** ~ أَسْرَعَ \ أَبْطَأَ خُطاهُ; **to gather** ~ «trend, process» تَسارَعَ خُطاهُ; **the company can't keep** ~ **with demand** لا تَسْتَطيعُ الشَرِكةُ أَنْ تُواكِبَ الطَلَبَ; **to set the** ~ (in a race) سَبَقَ (i-u; سَبْق), تَقَدَّمَ; (to establish a standard) أَرْسى مِعْياراً; **I can't stand the** ~ لا يُمْكِنُني أَنْ أُواكِبَ مَنْ حَوْلي

B *vt* [سارَ بِخُطواتٍ وَئيدةٍ في] ‹the room, floor›

C *vi* مَشى ,تَجَوَّلَ (i; مَشْي); **to** ~ **back and forth/up and down** ذَرَعَ المَكانَ جيئةً وَذَهاباً

D *v refl* **to** ~ **oneself** سارَ بِوَتيرةٍ ثابِتةٍ

(Idiom) **to put sb through their paces** اخْتَبَرَ قُدُراتِ شَخْصٍ

pacemaker /ˈpeɪsmeɪkə/ *n* **1** (for the heart) جِهاز تَنْظيم ضَرَباتِ القَلْبِ **2** (in races) [شَخْص \ حَيَوان يَفْرِضُ وَتيرةً مُعَيَّنةً في بِدايةِ السِباقِ]

pacesetter /ˈpeɪssetə/ *n* **1** (in a race) [شَخْص \ حَيَوان يَفْرِضُ وَتيرةً مُعَيَّنةً في بِدايةِ السِباقِ] **2** (in a field, an industry) رائِد (رَوّاد), قُدْوة ,شَخْص يُرْسي مِعْياراً

Pacific /pəˈsɪfɪk/ **A** *pr n* (**the Pacific**) المُحيط الهادِئ

B *adj* ‹coast› على المُحيطِ الهادِئِ; ‹island› في المُحيطِ الهادِئِ

Pacific Ocean *pr n* (**the Pacific Ocean**) المُحيط الهادِئ

pacifier /ˈpasɪfʌɪə/ *n* (AmE) مُسْكِتة ,سَكّاتة ,لَهّاية ,مَصّاصة

pacifism /ˈpasɪfɪz(ə)m/ *n* سِلْمِيّة ,مُسالَمة

pacifist /ˈpasɪfɪst/ *n* [شَخْص مُسالِم \ سِلْمِيّ]

pacify /ˈpasɪfʌɪ/ *vt* (**pacifies, pacifying, pacified**) **1** هَدَّأَ الرَوْعَ ‹a person, crowd› **2** أَحَلَّ السَلامَ في ‹a country, region›

pack /pak/ **A** *n* **1** (container) عُلْبة (عِلاب ,عُلَب); **a** ~ **of lies** مَجْموعة من الأَكاذيبِ **2** (rucksack) حَقيبة ظَهْر **3** (of wolves, hounds) قَطيع (قُطْعان) **4** (of undesirables) زُمْرة (زُمَر), طُغْمة, مَجْموعة (مَجاميعُ ,مَجْموعات); **he left, pursued by a** ~ **of journalists** غادَرَ وَتَعَقَّبَهُ زُمْرةٌ من الصُحُفِيِّينَ **5** (in a race) زُمْرة المُتَسابِقينَ \ المُتَنافِسينَ **6** (in rugby) لاعِبو الهُجومِ **7** (BrE) (of cards) رِزْمة (رِزَم), مَجْموعة كامِلة

B *vt* **1** (for a journey) حَزَمَ (i; حَزْم) ‹one's clothes›; (for storage) عَبَّأَ ‹the books, ornaments›; **to** ~ **one's case/suitcase** حَزَمَ حَقيبَتَهُ; **to** ~ **one's bags** عَبَّأَ حَقائِبَهُ **2** (commercially) عَبَّأَ, غَلَّفَ ‹food, perishables, software› **3** (to crowd into) كَدَّسَ ‹a room, stadium›; **the book is** ~**ed with information** الكِتابُ زاخِرٌ بالمَعْلوماتِ **4** (to compact) ضَغَطَ (a; ضَغْط), كَبَسَ (i; كَبْس) ‹snow, earth›

C *vi* **1** (for a journey) حَزَمَ حَقائِبَهُ **2** (into a space) **to** ~ **into a room/car** تَكَدَّسَ \ احْتَشَدَ في غُرْفةٍ \ سَيّارةٍ

(Idiom) **to send sb packing** (infml) طَرَدَ شَخْصاً من العَمَلِ

(Phrasal verbs) **pack in:** ~ **[sth] in,** ~ **in [sth]** **1** (to cram in) حَشَرَ [شَيْئاً] ‹people, objects› **2** (infml) (to give up) تَرَكَ [شَيْئاً] ‹a job, one's boyfriend›; ~ **it in!** كُفَّ عن هذا!

• **pack off**: ~ [**sb**] **off**, ~ **off** [**sb**] (infml) أَرْسَلَ [شَخْصاً] على عَجَلٍ؛ **to ~ sb off to school/bed** أَرْسَلَ شَخْصاً على عَجَلٍ إلى المَدْرَسةِ \ الفِراشِ

• **pack up** **A** **1** (to prepare to move house) حَزَمَ أَمْتِعَتَهُ **2** (infml) (to finish work) أَنْهى عَمَلَهُ **3** (infml) (to stop working) «radio, computer» تَعَطَّلَ؛ «heart» تَوَقَّفَ **B** ~ [**sth**] **up**, ~ **up** [**sth**] **1** (for a journey) حَزَمَ [شَيْئاً] ‹*the equipment, tent*› **2** (for storage) عَبَّأَ [شَيْئاً] ‹*belongings, possessions*›

package /ˈpakɪdʒ/ **A** *n* **1** (parcel) طَرْد (طُرود)، رِزْمة (رِزَم) **2** (of measures, aid) حُزْمة (حُزَم) **3** (Comput) حُزْمة (حُزَم) **B** *vt* رَزَمَ (a-i-u; رَزْم)، عَبَّأَ ‹*products, goods*›

package holiday, **package tour** *n* رِحْلة مُنَظَّمة (من قِبَلِ وَكالةٍ سِياحيّةٍ)

packaging /ˈpakɪdʒɪŋ/ *n* **1** (materials) غِلاف (أَغْلِفة) **2** (packing process) تَغْليف

packed /p[a]kt/ *adj* ‹*hall, train*› مُكْتَظّ؛ **the streets were ~ with people** كانَت الشَوارِعُ مُكْتَظّةً بالناس

packed lunch *n* وَجْبة غَداءٍ مُغَلَّفة

packet /ˈpakɪt/ *n* **1** (BrE) (of cigarettes, biscuits) عُلْبة (عُلَب)؛ (of crisps) كيس (أَكْياس) **2** (of seeds) ظَرْف (ظُروف)

packing /ˈpakɪŋ/ *n* **1** (of a suitcase) حَزْم، رَزْم؛ **to do one's ~** حَزَمَ أَمْتِعَتَهُ **2** (in a factory) تَعْبِئة، تَعْليب

packing case *n* صُنْدوق تَعْبِئةٍ

pact /pakt/ *n* اتِّفاقيّة، حِلْف، ميثاق (مَواثيقُ)

pad /pad/ **A** *n* **1** (of paper) مُفَكِّرة، كُرّاسة (كُرّاسات)، كَراريسُ) **2** (of gauze, cloth) إضْمامة، حَشْوة، لِفافة (لِفافات، لَفائِفُ) **3** (as cushion) وِسادة (وِسادات، وَسائِدُ) **4** (in jacket, etc) بِطانة (بِطانات، بَطائِنُ) **5** (Sport) (for protection) واقٍ (أَوْقِية)؛ **to wear ~s** ارْتَدى أَوْقِيةً **6** (on paw) طَرَف الإصْبَعِ؛ (on finger) أُنْمُلة (أَنامِلُ) **7** (for helicopters) مَهْبِط (مَهابِطُ)؛ (for rockets) قاعِدة (قَواعِدُ)، مِنَصّة (مِنَصّات، مَناصُّ)
B *vt* (-dd-) **1** (to put padding in) بَطَّنَ، حَشا (u; حَشْو) ‹*a seat, the shoulders*› **2** (to make longer) ▸ **pad out**
C *vi* (-dd-) مَشى بِهُدوءٍ؛ **to ~ downstairs** نَزَلَ الدَرَجَ بِهُدوءٍ
D (**padded**) *adj* ‹*bra, jacket*› مُبَطَّن

(Phrasal verb) **pad out**: ~ **out** [**sth**], ~ [**sth**] **out** أَطالَ في \ أَسْهَبَ [شَيْءٍ] ‹*a speech, an essay*›

padded cell *n* غُرْفة مُبَطَّنة (لِحِمايةِ مَرْضى الأَمْراضِ العَقْلِيّةِ من إيذاءِ أَنْفُسِهِمْ)

padded envelope /ˌpadɪd ˈɛnvələʊp/ *n* ظَرْف مُبَطَّن

padding /ˈpadɪŋ/ *n* **1** (material) بِطانة (بِطانات) **2** (in an essay, a speech) حَشْو

paddle /ˈpad(ə)l/ **A** *n* **1** (oar) مِجْداف (مَجاديفُ) **2** [u] (walk in the water) [مَشْي بدونِ حِذاءٍ في المِياهِ الضَحْلةِ]؛ **to go for a ~** [مَشى حافِياً في المِياهِ الضَحْلةِ]
B *vt* جَدَّفَ ‹*a canoe, boat*›
C *vi* **1** (in canoes) جَدَّفَ **2** (in the water) [مَشى حافِياً في المِياهِ الضَحْلةِ] **3** «ducks, dogs» [سَبَحَ بِضَرَباتٍ سَريعةٍ في الماءِ]

paddling pool *n* حَوْض سِباحةٍ للأَطْفالِ

paddock /ˈpadək/ *n* [حَقْل صَغير لِتَرْويضِ الخُيولِ]

paddy /ˈpadi/, **paddy field** /ˈpadi fiːld/ *n* (*pl* **paddies**) حَقْل أَرُزٍّ

padlock /ˈpadlɒk/ **A** *n* قُفْل (أَقْفال، قُفول)
B *vt* قَفَلَ (i; قَفْل)، أَغْلَقَ بِقُفْلٍ ‹*a gate*›؛ وَضَعَ قُفْلاً على ‹*a bicycle*›

padre /ˈpɑːdreɪ/ *n* **1** (civilian) قِسّيس (قِسّيسونَ، قَساوِسة) **2** (military) [قِسّيس مُلْحَق بالجَيْشِ]

paediatric (BrE), **pediatric** (AmE) /piːdɪˈatrɪk/ *adj* ‹*nurse, ward*› طِبِّ الأَطْفالِ

paediatrician (BrE), **pediatrician** (AmE) /ˌpiːdɪəˈtrɪʃ(ə)n/ *n* طَبيب أَطْفال

paediatrics (BrE), **pediatrics** (AmE) /ˌpiːdɪˈatrɪks/ *n sing* طِبّ الأَطْفالِ

paedophile (BrE), **pedophile** (AmE) /ˈpiːdəʊfʌɪl/ *n* [شَخْص يَسْتَغِلُّ الأَطْفالَ جِنْسيّاً]

pagan /ˈpeɪg(ə)n/ *n*, *adj* وَثَنِيّ

page /peɪdʒ/ **A** *n* **1** (of a book, newspaper) صَفْحة (صَفَحات)؛ **on ~ two** في الصَفْحةِ الثانيةِ **2** (attendant at a wedding) [طِفْل يُرافِقُ العَروسَ في الزِفافِ]؛ (in a hotel) [خادِم يَرْتَدي بِزّةً رَسْمِيّةً]

B *vt* (over a loudspeaker) اِسْتَدْعى \ نادى عَبْرَ مُكَبِّرِ صَوْتٍ; (on a pager) اِتَّصَلَ على البَيْجَر

pageant /ˈpadʒ(ə)nt/ *n* **1** (show, parade) مَوْكِب (مَواكِبُ) **2** (historical tableau) عَرْض (عُروض) عَرْض خارِجِيّ \ في عَرَبةٍ مُتَحَرِّكةٍ لِمَشْهَدٍ تاريخيٍّ]

pageboy /ˈpeɪdʒbɔɪ/ *n* (at a wedding) طِفْل يُرافِقُ العَروسَ في الزِفافِ]

pager /ˈpeɪdʒə/ *n* بَيْجَر (جِهاز النِداءِ الآلِيِّ)

page view *n* (Comput) مُشاهَدة صَفْحةٍ; **the site gets 10,000 page views per day** 10000 يَحْصُلُ المَوْقِعُ على مُشاهَدةٍ في اليَوْمِ

paid /peɪd/ **A** *past tense, past participle* ▸ **pay**

B *adj* **1** ‹work› بِأَجْرٍ; ‹leave› مَدْفوعُ الأَجْرِ **2** ‹worker› بِراتِبٍ

Idiom **to put paid to sth** (BrE infml) قَضى على شَيْءٍ

pail /peɪl/ *n* سَطْل (سُطول, أَسْطال), دَلْو (mf; دِلاء)

pain /peɪn/ **A** *n* **1** (physical) أَلَم (آلام), وَجَع (وِجاع, أَوْجاع); **to be in ~** كانَ يَتَأَلَّمُ; **to suffer from back/chest ~** عانى من أَلَمٍ في الظَهْرِ \ الصَدْرِ; **where is the ~?** أَيْنَ الأَلَمُ؟ **2** [u] (mental) مُعاناة, أَلَم; **he caused me a lot of ~** سَبَّبَ لي أَلَماً كَبيراً **3** (infml) (annoying person, thing) شَخْص مُزْعِج; **she is a real ~** هي حَقّاً إِنْسانةٌ مُزْعِجةٌ; **it's a ~ having to read the whole thing** من المُزْعِجِ أَنْ تُضْطَرَّ إلى قِراءةِ هذا الشَيْءِ كُلِّهِ **4** (fml) **on ~ of death/expulsion** وَإلاّ تَعَرَّضَ للقَتْلِ \ للطَرْدِ

B (pains) *n pl*; **to be at ~s to do sth** بَذَلَ قُصارى جُهْدِهِ لِفِعْلِ; **to take great ~s over** *or* **with sth** تَوَخّى الحِرْصَ مع شَيْءٍ

C *vt* (fml) (to grieve) آلَمَ, أَحْزَنَ (Form IV; imperf يُؤْلِمُ); **it ~s me to say this, but ...** يُؤْلِمُني أَنْ أَقولَ هذا, وَلٰكِنْ . . .

D (pained) *adj* ‹expression, sigh› يَنُمُّ عن الأَلَمِ; **to be a pain in the neck** كانَ شَوْكةً في الحَلْقِ; **your friend Betty's becoming a real pain in the ~** بَدَأَتْ صَديقَتُكَ بيتي تُصْبِحُ مَصْدَراً حَقيقيًّا للإزْعاجِ

painful /ˈpeɪnfʊl/ *adj* **1** (physically) ‹illness, part of the body› موجِع, مُؤْلِم; **her shoulder is still ~** ما زالَتْ كَتِفُها تُؤْلِمُها **2** (mentally) ‹experience, memory› مُؤْلِم, أَليم

painfully /ˈpeɪnf(ə)li/ *adv* **1** (excruciatingly) على نَحْوٍ مُؤْلِم \ موجِع; **her head throbbed ~** أُصيبَتْ بِصُداعٍ مُؤْلِمٍ **2** (exceedingly) ‹obvious› لِلغايةِ; ‹slow› بِصورةٍ مُزْعِجةٍ; **he was ~ shy** كانَ خَجولاً للغايةِ

painkiller /ˈpeɪnkɪlə/ *n* مُسَكِّن (مُسَكِّنات)

painless /ˈpeɪnləs/ *adj* **1** (pain-free) غَيْر مُؤْلِم **2** (trouble-free) خالٍ من المَتاعِبِ

painstaking /ˈpeɪnzteɪkɪŋ/ *adj* ‹work, research› دَقيق; ‹process› مُضْنٍ

paint /peɪnt/ **A** *n* دِهان, طِلاء (أَدْهِنة, دِهانات); **a fresh coat of ~** طَبَقة طِلاءٍ جَديدة

B (paints) *n pl* أَصْباغ, أَلْوان

C *vt* **1** «painter» دَهَنَ (u; دَهْن), طَلى (i; طَلْي) ‹a wall, house›; «artist» رَسَمَ (u; رَسْم) ‹a picture›; رَسَمَ صورةً ل ‹a person›; **to ~ sth blue/green** طَلى شَيْئاً باللَوْنِ الأَزْرَقِ \ الأَخْضَرِ; **to ~ sb's portrait** رَسَمَ لَوْحةً لِشَخْصٍ; **to ~ one's face/nails** وَضَعَ ماكياج على وَجْهِهِ \ طَلى أَظافِرَهُ **2** (to describe) رَسَمَ (u; رَسْم); **she ~ed a gloomy/positive picture of the future** رَسَمَتْ صورةً كَئيبةً \ إيجابيّةً للمُسْتَقْبَلِ

D *vi* رَسَمَ (u; رَسْم); **to ~ in oils/watercolours** رَسَمَ بالزَيْتِ \ بالأَلْوانِ المائيّةِ

paintbox /ˈpeɪntbɒks/ *n* عُلْبة أَلْوانٍ للرَسْمِ

paintbrush /ˈpeɪntbrʌʃ/ *n* (artist's) فُرْشاة رَسْمٍ; (decorator's) فُرْشاة دِهانٍ

painter /ˈpeɪntə/ *n* **1** (artist) رَسّام **2** (decorator) دَهّان

painting /ˈpeɪntɪŋ/ *n* **1** (picture) لَوْحة (أَلْواح, لَوْحات) **2** (activity) دَهْن

paint stripper *n* مُزيل دِهانٍ

paintwork /ˈpeɪntwəːk/ *n* دِهان (أَدْهِنة, دِهانات)

pair /peː/ **A** *n* **1** (of shoes, socks, gloves) زَوْج (mf; أَزْواج); **to be one of a ~** كانَ واحِداً من اثْنَيْنِ **2** (item of two parts) **a ~ of scissors** مِقَصّ (مَقاصُّ); **a ~ of jeans** بَنْطَلون جينز **3** (two people) زَوْجانِ; (two animals) زَوْج (mf; أَزْواج); **to work in ~s** عَمِلَ في أَزْواجٍ \ مَجْموعاتٍ ثُنائيّةٍ; **get out, the ~ of you!** أُخْرُجا, كِلاكُما!; **a breeding ~** زَوْج تَرْبِيةٍ

B *vt* قَرَنَ (i; قَرْن), قَسَّمَ إلى أَزْواجٍ (ب) ‹students, garments›; **we were ~ed to play together** وُضِعْنا مَعاً كَثُنائيٍّ في اللَعِبِ; **a leather jacket ~ed with jeans** سُتْرة جِلْديّة مع بَنْطَلون جينز;

tips on how to ~ wine with food نَصائِح حول كَيْفِيّةِ إقْرانِ الخَمْرِ مع الطَعامِ

(Phrasal verbs) **pair off** **A** «couples» بَدَأَ عَلاقةً عاطِفيّةً; «dancers» اقْتَرَنَ ب \ تَزامَلَ مع شَخْصٍ **B** **~ [sb] off, ~ off [sb]** (for a relationship) وَفَّق بين [شَخْصَيْنِ] في عَلاقةٍ عاطِفيّةٍ; (for an activity) قَسَّمَ [أَشْخاصاً] إلى مَجْموعاتٍ ثُنائيّةٍ

• **pair up** **A** «dancers, students» تَزامَلَ **B** **~ [sb] up, ~ up [sb]** ‹*students, participants*› وَضَعَ [أَشْخاصاً] في مَجْموعاتٍ ثُنائيّةٍ

paisley /ˈpeɪzli/ *n* تَصْميم هِنْديّ

pajamas (AmE) *n pl* ▸ **pyjamas**

Pakistan /pɑːkɪˈstɑːn/ *pr n* باكِسْتان (f)

Pakistani /pakɪˈstɑːni/ *n, adj* باكِسْتانيّ

pal /pal/ *n* (infml) رَفيق (رُفَقاءُ, رِفاق), صَديق (أَصْدِقاءُ)

palace /ˈpalɪs/ *n* قَصْر (قُصور)

palatable /ˈpalətəb(ə)l/ *adj* ‹*food, wine*› سائِغ

palate /ˈpalət/ *n* **1▸** (roof of the mouth) حَنَك (أَحْناك), سَقْف الفَم **2▸** (sense of taste) حاسّة الذَوْق \ التَذَوُّق

pale /peɪl/ **A** *adj* **1▸** (light) ‹*colour*› باهِت; ‹*skin, complexion*› شاحِب; **~ blue/green** أَزْرَق \ أَخْضَر باهت **2▸** (pallid) شاحِب, مُمْتَقِع; **to turn** *or* **go ~** شَحَبَ (a-u; شُحوبة, شُحوب), اِمْتَقَعَ **3▸** (not bright) ‹*light, dawn*› خافِت

B *vi* **1▸** «person, face» شَحَبَ (a-u; شُحوب, شُحوبة), اِمْتَقَعَ, اِصْفَرَّ **2▸** (to seem minor) بَدا أَقَلَّ أَهَمّيّةً; **to ~ in comparison to** *or* **with sth** بَدا أَقَلَّ أَهَمّيّةً مُقارَنةً بِشَيْءٍ

(Idiom) **to be beyond the pale** كانَ خارِجَ نِطاقِ المَقْبولِ

Palestine /ˈpalɪstʌɪn/ *pr n* فِلَسْطين (dipt f)

Palestine Liberation Organization *n* مُنَظَّمة التَحْرير الفِلَسْطينيّة

Palestinian /ˌpaləˈstɪnɪən/ *n, adj* فِلَسْطينيّ

Palestinian National Authority *n* السُلْطة الوَطَنيّة الفِلَسْطينيّة

palette /ˈpalɪt/ *n* **1▸** (for mixing paint) لَوْح أَلْوانٍ **2▸** (colours) مَجْموعة أَلْوانٍ

pall /pɔːl/ **A** *n* **1▸** (over a coffin) غِطاء نَعْشٍ **2▸** (of smoke, dust) سَحابة

B *vi* أَصْبَحَ مُمِلاً

pallet /ˈpalɪt/ *n* (for loading) [مِنَصّة لِتَحْميلِ البَضائِعِ]

pallid /ˈpalɪd/ *adj* ‹*face, skin*› شاحِب, مُمْتَقِع

palm /pɑːm/ *n* **1▸** (of the hand) راحة (راحات), كَفّ (mf; أَكُفّ, كُفوف) **2▸** (also **palm tree**) نَخْل (n coll; نَخيل) **3▸** (also **palm leaf**) سَعَف (سَعَفات)

(Phrasal verb) **palm off** (infml): **to ~ sth off on sb** باعَ شَخْصاً شَيْئاً بالغِشّ; **he tried to ~ me off with a copy** حاوَلَ أنْ يُسَلِّمَني نُسْخةً مُزَيَّفةً

palmistry /ˈpɑːmɪstri/ *n* قِراءة الكَفّ

Palm Sunday *n* شَعانين

palmtop /ˈpɑːmtɒp/ *n* (also **palmtop computer**) حاسوب كَفّيّ

Palmyra /palˈmʌɪrə/ *pr n* تَدْمُر (f)

palpable /ˈpalpəb(ə)l/ *adj* ‹*tension, fear*› مَلْموس

palpate /palˈpeɪt/ *vt* جَسَّ (u; جَسّ)

palpitate /ˈpalpɪteɪt/ *vi* «heart» خَفَقَ بِسُرْعةٍ

palpitation /palpɪˈteɪʃ(ə)n/ *n* خَفَقان

palsy /ˈpɔːlzi/ *n* (old use) شَلَل

paltry /ˈpɔːltri/ *adj* (**paltrier, paltriest**) ‹*sum, amount*› زَهيد

pamper /ˈpampə/ *vt* ‹*a guest, pet*› دَلَّلَ, دَلَّعَ

pamphlet /ˈpamflɪt/ *n* (informative) كُرّاسة (كُرّاسات, كَراريسُ), كُتَيِّب (كُتَيِّبات); (political) مَنْشور (مَنْشورات, مَناشيرُ)

pan¹ /pan/ *n* **1▸** (saucepan) مِقْلاة (مَقال); (for baking) قِدْر (قُدور), طَنْجَرة (طَناجِرُ) **2▸** (BrE) (toilet bowl) حَوْض مِرْحاضٍ

pan² /pan/ **A** *vt* (**-nn-**) (infml) ‹*a show, play*› اِنْتَقَدَ بِشِدّةٍ

B *vi* **1▸** (Cin) «cameras» دارَ أُفُقيًّا \ عَموديًّا **2▸** (to prospect) **to ~ for gold** [غَسَلَ الحَصى لِفَصْلِ ذَرّاتِ الذَهَبِ]

panacea /ˌpanəˈsiːə/ *n* (fml) عِلاج ناجِع, دَواء لِكُلِّ داءٍ

panache /pəˈnaʃ/ *n* [أُسْلوب مُمَيَّز جِدًّا]

Panama /ˈpanəmɑː/ *pr n* بَنَما

Panama Canal *pr n* (**the Panama Canal**) قَناة بَنَما

Panamanian /panəˈmeɪnɪən/ *n, adj* بَنَميّ

pancake /ˈpankeɪk/ *n* فَطيرة (مُسَطَّحة ومَقْليّة في مِقْلاةٍ)

pancreas /ˈpaŋkrɪəs/ *n* بَنْكِرِياس

panda /ˈpandə/ *n* بَنْدا

pandemic /pan'dɛmɪk/ *n* وَباء (أَوْبِئة)

pandemonium /ˌpandɪ'məʊnɪəm/ *n* صَخَب ,جَلَبة ,ضَجّة

pander /'pandə/ *vi* **to ~ to sb's tastes/prejudices** رَضَخَ لِذَوْق \ لِأَفْكارِ شَخْصٍ

pane /peɪn/ *n* لَوْح زُجاجيّ (في نافِذةٍ \ بابٍ)

panel /'pan(ə)l/ *n* **1** (of judges) لَجْنة (لِجان ,لَجْنات) ,هَيْئة **2** (in a door) لَوْح (أَلْواح) **3** (of a car body) لَوْح (أَلْواح) **4** (of a garment) كُلْفة (من نَسيجٍ) **5** (of instruments) لَوْحة (أَلْواح ,لَوْحات); **an instrument/control ~** لَوْحةُ العَدّاداتِ \ التحَكُّمِ

panel beater *n* حَدّاد \ سَمْكَريّ سَيّاراتٍ

panel truck *n* (AmE) [شاحِنة تَوْصيلٍ صَغيرة دون نَوافِذَ خَلْفيّةٍ]

pang /paŋ/ *n* **1** (emotional) غُصّة (غُصَص ,غُصّات); **a ~ of conscience** وَخْزة ضَميرٍ; **a ~ of jealousy** [شُعور بالغَيْرةِ] **2** (physical) أَلَم مُفاجِئ; **hunger ~s** قَرَصات الجوعِ

panhandler /'panhandlə/ *n* (AmE infml) شَحّاذ ,مُتَسَوِّل

panic /'panɪk/ **A** *n* ذُعْر ,هَلَع; **to be in a ~** كانَ في حالةِ ذُعْرٍ; **there was ~ in the stadium** كانَتْ هُناكَ حالةُ هَلَعٍ \ ذُعْرٍ في المَلْعَبِ

B *adj before n* [ناتِج عن حالةِ هَلَعٍ \ ذُعْرٍ] ‹*buying, reaction*›

C *vt* (**-ck-**) ‹*a crowd, an audience*› أَصابَ بالهَلَعِ \ بالذُعْرِ

D *vi* (**-ck-**) «crowd, herd» هَلِعَ (هَلَع ;a) ذُعِرَ; **don't ~!** لا تَهْلَعْ!

panic buying *n* حُمّى الشِراءِ \ التَسَوُّقِ (خَوْفاً من حُدوثِ نَقْصٍ في السِلَعِ)

panicky /'panɪki/ *adj* ‹*feeling*› مُرْعِب; ‹*reaction*› مُتَّسِم بالذُعْرِ \ مَذْعور ,بالهَلَعِ

panic-stricken /'panɪkstrɪk(ə)n/ *adj* ‹*crowd, victim, children*› مَذْعور

pannier /'panɪə/ *n* **1** (on a bike) سَلّة دَرّاجةٍ **2** (on a mule) خُرْج (خِرَجة)

panorama /ˌpanə'rɑːmə/ *n* نَظْرة شامِلة ,مَنْظَر عامّ ,بانوراما

panoramic /ˌpanə'ramɪk/ *adj* ‹*view, shot*› شامِل ,بانوراميّ

pansy /'panzi/ *n* (*pl* **pansies**) زَهْرة الثالوثِ

pant /pant/ *vi* «runners, dogs» لَهِثَ (a; لُهاث ,لَهْث)

pantechnicon /pan'tɛknɪk(ə)n/ *n* (BrE) [شاحِنة كَبيرة مُغْلَقة لِنَقْلِ الأَثاثِ]

pantheon /'panθɪən/ *n* بانْثِيون

panther /'panθə/ *n* **1** (leopard) نَمِر (نُمور) **2** (AmE) (puma) أَسَد الجِبالِ; (jaguar) نَمِر أَمْريكيّ

panties /'pantɪz/ *n pl* سِرْوال داخِليّ (للنِساءِ)

pantomime /'pantəmʌɪm/ *n* (BrE) [مَسْرَحيّة غِنائيّة خَفيفة للأَطْفالِ]

pantry /'pantri/ *n* (*pl* **pantries**) غُرْفة \ خِزانة المُؤونة

pants /pants/ *n pl* **1** (AmE) (trousers) بَنْطَلون (بَنْطَلونات), سِرْوال داخِليّ **2** (BrE) (underwear) سِرْوال (سَراويلُ)

Idiom **to wear the pants** [تَوَلّى زِمامَ الأُمورِ في المَنْزِلِ]

pantsuit /'pantsuːt/ *n* (AmE) بَدْلة نِسائيّة (بِسِرْوالٍ)

pantyhose /'pantɪhəʊz/ *n* (AmE) جَوْرَب نِسائيّ

panty-liner /'pantilʌɪnə/ *n* [فوطة صِحّيّة صَغيرة للاسْتِعْمالِ اليَوْميِّ]

papa /pə'pɑː/ *n* (AmE) *or* (fml) بابا

paparazzi /papə'ratsi/ *n pl* باباراتْزي (مُصَوِّرونَ يُطارِدونَ المَشاهيرَ)

papaw (AmE) *n* ▸ **pawpaw**

papaya /pə'pʌɪə/ *n* **1** (fruit) بابايا **2** (tree) شَجَرة بابايا

paper /'peɪpə/ **A** *n* **1** [u] (material) وَرَق (أَوْراق); **a piece/sheet of ~** قِطْعة \ فَرْخ وَرَقٍ; **to get** *or* **put sth down on ~** كَتَبَ شَيْئاً على قِطْعةِ وَرَقٍ; **it's a good idea on ~** هي فِكْرةٌ جَيِّدةٌ على الوَرَقِ; **the agreement isn't worth the ~ it's written on** الاتِّفاقُ لا يُساوي الوَرَقَ الّذي كُتِبَ عَلَيْهِ

2 (also **wallpaper**) وَرَق حائِطٍ \ جُدْرانٍ **3** (newspaper) جَريدة (جَرائِدُ); **to take the local ~** تابَعَ الجَريدةَ المَحَلّيّةَ

4 (published) بَحْث (عِلْميّ) ,وَرَقة بَحْثيّة \ عِلْميّة; (presented orally) مُحاضَرة; **to present a ~** عَرَضَ وَرَقةً بَحْثيّةً **5** (BrE) (examination) وَرَقة امْتِحانٍ **6** (blueprint) تَقْرير (تَقاريرُ), وَثيقة (وَثائِقُ)

B (**papers**) *n pl* (documents) وَثائِق (for identification) أَوْراق ثُبوتيّة

C *modifier* ‹*cup, handkerchief*› وَرَقيّ; ‹*industry*› الوَرَقِ

D *vt* (also **wallpaper**) ‹*a wall, room*› رَكَّبَ وَرَقَ حائِطٍ \ جُدْرانٍ في

(Phrasal verb) **paper over**: **~ over [sth], ~ [sth] over** تَكَتَّمَ على [شَيْءٍ] ‹*the differences, a difficult situation*›; **to ~ over the cracks** دارى على المَشاكِلِ

paperback /ˈpeɪpəbak/ *n* كتاب بِغِلافٍ وَرَقِيٍّ

paper bag *n* كيس وَرَقِيّ

paper clip *n* مِشْبَك وَرَقٍ

paperknife /ˈpeɪpənʌɪf/ *n* مِقْطَع الوَرَق

paper round *n* [تَوْصيل الجَرائِد لِلبُيوتِ عن طَريقِ الأَطْفال]

paper shop *n* مَحَلّ بَيْعِ الصُحُف

paper towel *n* مِنْشَفة وَرَقِيّة

paperweight /ˈpeɪpəweɪt/ *n* ثَقّالة أَوْراقٍ

paperwork /ˈpeɪpəwəːk/ *n* (form-filling) عَمَل إداريّ; (documentation) تَوْثيق

paprika /ˈpaprɪkə/ *n* بابْريكا

Pap smear /ˈpap smɪə/, **Pap test** *n* (AmE) مَسْحة عُنُقِ الرَحِمِ

Papuan /ˈpapʊən/ **A** *n* (person) [شَخْص من بابُوا غينِيا الجَديدةِ] **B** *adj* ‹*culture, language*› بابُوا غينِيا الجَديدةِ

Papua New Guinea /papjuːə njuː ˈgɪniː/ *pr n* بابُوا غينِيا الجَديدة

papyrus /pəˈpʌɪrəs/ *n* (*pl* **papyruses** or **papyri**) وَرَق البَرْديّ

par /pɑː/ *n* **1** **to be on a ~ with sb/sth** كانَ على قَدَمِ المُساواةِ مع شَخْصٍ \ شَيْءٍ; **the service is on a ~ with that of the best hotels** الخِدْمةُ على نَفْسِ مُسْتَوى الخَدَماتِ المُتاحةِ في أَفْضَلِ الفَنادِقِ; **to be up to/below ~** كانَ على \ دونَ المُسْتَوى المَطْلوبِ; **the team's performance was not up to ~** لم يَكُنْ أداءُ الفَريقِ على المُسْتَوى المَطْلوبِ; **her singing was definitely below ~** كانَ غِناؤُها بِلا رَيْبٍ دونَ المُسْتَوى المَطْلوبِ **2** (in golf) [عَدَد الضَرَباتِ المُتَوَقَّعةِ لِمَسارٍ مُعَيَّنٍ]

(Idiom) **to be par for the course** [كانَ أَمْراً مُتَوَقَّعاً مِنْهُ]

para /ˈparə/ *n* **1** = **paragraph** فِقْرة **2** (infml) = **paratrooper** جُنْديّ مِظَلّاتٍ

parable /ˈparəb(ə)l/ *n* مَثَل (أَمْثال)

parachute /ˈparəʃuːt/ **A** *n* مِظَلّة **B** *vi* «troops, soldiers» هَبَطَ بالمِظَلّةِ

parachute drop *n* إِنْزال مِظَلّيّ, إِبْرار جَوّيّ

parachute jump *n* هُبوط \ قَفْز بالمِظَلّةِ

parachuting /ˈparəʃuːtɪŋ/ *n* قَفْز بالمِظَلّةِ

parachutist /ˈparəʃuːtɪst/ *n* مِظَلّيّ

parade /pəˈreɪd/ **A** *n* **1** (procession) مَوْكِب (مَواكِبُ), اِسْتِعْراض (اِسْتِعْراضات) **2** (Mil) (soldiers') اِسْتِعْراض; **to be on ~** عَسْكَرِيٌّ اِشْتَرَكَ في اِسْتِعْراضٍ عَسْكَرِيّ **B** *vt* **1** (to march) [سارَ في صَفٍّ] ‹*the troops, prisoners*› **2** (to display) اِسْتَعْرَضَ ‹*a trophy, banner*› **C** *vi* «soldiers, demonstrators» سارَ في مَوْكِبٍ

parade ground *n* مَيْدان الاسْتِعْراضاتِ العَسْكَرِيّة

paradigm /ˈparədʌɪm/ *n* نَموذَج (نَماذِجُ), مِثال (أَمْثِلة)

paradise /ˈparədʌɪs/ *n* جَنّة (جِنّات, جَنّات), فِرْدَوْس (فَراديسُ)

paradox /ˈparədɒks/ *n* تَناقُض ظاهِرِيّ, مُفارَقة

paradoxical /ˌparəˈdɒksɪk(ə)l/ *adj* ‹*statement, nature*› مُتَناقِض, تَناقُضيّ

paradoxically /parəˈdɒksɪkli/ *adv* (fml) من المُفارَقاتِ; **~, the more he worked, the less tired he felt** إِنَّها لَمُفارَقةٌ أَنَّهُ كُلَّما عَمِلَ أَكْثَرَ كُلَّما قَلَّ شُعورُهُ بالتَعَبِ

paraffin /ˈparəfɪn/ *n* **1** (BrE) (for heating and light) كيروسين **2** (also **paraffin wax**) بَرافين

paragliding /ˈparəglʌɪdɪŋ/ *n* طَيَران شِراعيّ

paragon /ˈparəg(ə)n/ *n* قُدْوة, أُسْوة, نَموذَج (نَماذِجُ); **she's a ~ of virtue** هي مِثالٌ يُقْتَدى بِهِ في الفَضيلة

paragraph /ˈparəgrɑːf/ *n* فِقْرة

Paraguay /ˈparəgwʌɪ/ *pr n* باراغْواي (f)

Paraguayan /parəˈgwʌɪən/ *n, adj* باراغْويّ

parakeet /ˈparəkiːt/ *n* بَبَّغاء الدُرّة

parallel /ˈparəlɛl/ **A** *adj* **1** (Math) ‹*lines, planes*› مُتَوازٍ, مُوازٍ **2** (similar) ‹*situation, case*› مُشابِه, مُماثِل **B** *adv* **to run ~ with sth** «lines, runners» رَكَضَ بِشَكْلٍ مُتَوازٍ مع شَيْءٍ **C** *n* **1** (similarity) تَوازٍ, مُوازاة, تَشابُه; **they were developed in ~** تَمَّ تَطْويرُها في وَقْتٍ واحِدٍ **2** (Maths) خَطّ مُوازٍ \ مُتَوازٍ **3** (Geog) خَطّ العَرْضِ

parallel bars *n* مُتَوازِيانِ (في الجُمْبازِ)

Paralympic Games, **Paralympics** /parəˌlɪmpɪk ˈgeɪmz/ *n pl* أَلْعاب أولِمْبِيّة لِلمُعاقينَ

paralyse (BrE), **paralyze** (AmE) /ˈparəlʌɪz/ *vt* **1** شَلَّ (شَلَل)، أَشَلَّ ‹*a leg, limb*› **2** أصابَ بالشَلَلِ ‹*a city, government*›

paralysis /pəˈralɪsɪs/ *n* (*pl* **paralyses** /-siːz/) شَلَل

paralyze (AmE) *vt* ▸ **paralyse**

paramedic /ˌparəˈmɛdɪk/ *n* مُسْعِف

parameter /pəˈramɪtə/ *n* مَعْلَمة، وَسيط (وُسَطاءُ)، مُتَغَيِّر

paramilitary /ˌparəˈmɪlɪt(ə)ri/ **A** *adj* ‹*force, group*› [شِبْه عَسْكَرِيٍّ]
B *n* [عُضْو في مُنَظَّمةٍ شِبْهِ عَسْكَرِيّةٍ]

paramount /ˈparəmaʊnt/ *adj* **to be ~**, **to be of ~ importance** كانَ ذا أَهَمِّيّةٍ قُصوى

paranoia /ˌparəˈnɔɪə/ *n* **1** (mental illness) جُنون بارانويا **2** (obsession) (هَواجِسُ) هاجِس، الاضْطِهادِ

paranoic, **paranoiac** /parəˈnɔɪɪk/ *n, adj* ▸ **paranoid**

paranoid /ˈparənɔɪd/ *adj* **1** ‹*schizophrenia*› البارانويا؛ ‹*schizophrenic*› مُصاب بالبارانويا **2** (obsessed) مَهْووس، مُوَسْوَس

parapet /ˈparəpɪt/ *n* (of roof) سور (أَسْوار)؛ (of bridge) حاجِز (حَواجِزُ)

paraphernalia /ˌparəfəˈneɪlɪə/ *n* مُعَدّات

paraphrase /ˈparəfreɪz/ *vt* أَعادَ الصِياغةَ ‹*a text, sb's words*›

paraplegia /ˌparəˈpliːdʒə/ *n* شَلَل سُفْلِيّ

paraplegic /parəˈpliːdʒɪk/ **A** *n* مَشْلول من الجُزْءِ السُفْلِيِّ
B *adj* ‹*patient, athlete*› مُصاب بِشَلَلٍ سُفْلِيٍّ

parascending /ˈparəsɛndɪŋ/ *n* طَيَران شِراعِيّ

parasite /ˈparəsʌɪt/ *n* طُفَيْلِيّ (طُفَيْلِيّات)

parasitic /parəˈsɪtɪk/, **parasitical** /parəˈsɪtɪk(ə)l/ *adj* **1** ‹*insect, animal, plant*› طُفَيْلِيّ **2** ‹*disease, infection*› طُفَيْلِيّ

parasiticide /ˌparəˈsɪtɪsʌɪd/ *n* مُبيد طُفَيْلِيّاتٍ

parasol /ˈparəsɒl/ *n* **1** (portable) شَمْسِيّة **2** (for a table) مِظَلّة، شَمْسِيّة (مَظالُّ، مِظَلّات)

paratrooper /ˈparətruːpə/ *n* جُنْدِيّ مِظَلّاتٍ

paratyphoid /parəˈtʌɪfɔɪd/ *n* (also **paratyphoid fever**) حُمّى الباراتيفوئيد

parcel /ˈpɑːs(ə)l/ *n* **1** (package) طَرْد (طُرود) **2** (of land) قِطْعة أَرْضٍ

(Phrasal verbs) **parcel out**: **~ out [sth]**, **~ [sth] out** قَسَّم [شَيْئًا] ‹*work, supplies*›
• **parcel up**: **~ up [sth]**, **~ [sth] up** غَلَّفَ \ لَفَّ [شَيْئًا] ‹*goods, food*›

parcel bomb *n* طَرْد مَلْغوم

parched /pɑːtʃt/ *adj* **1** (dry) ‹*landscape, terrain*› قاحِل، جافّ **2** (thirsty) **to be ~** كانَ ظَمْآنًا

parchment /ˈpɑːtʃmənt/ *n* **1** [u] (material) رَقّ **2** [u] (paper) وَرَق البَرْشُمانِ **3** (document) [مَخْطوطة مَكْتوبة على (جِلْدِ) الرَقِّ]

pardon /ˈpɑːd(ə)n/ **A** *n* **1** [u] (forgiveness) صَفْح، عَفْو، مُسامَحة؛ **I beg your ~?** أَسْتَميحُكَ عُذْرًا؟، عَفْوًا؟، إعْذِرْني؟ **2** (Law) عَفْو؛ **to grant a general ~** منح عَفْوًا عامًّا
B *vt* عَفا (u؛ عَفْو؛ عن) ‹*a criminal*›
C *excl* (also **pardon me**) **1** (what?) عَفْوًا **2** (sorry!) آسِف، مُتَأَسِّف

pare /pɛː/ *vt* **1** (to peel) قَشَرَ (i-u؛ قَشْر)، قَشَّرَ ‹*an apple*› **2** (to trim) قَلَّمَ ‹*nails*› **3** (to reduce) ▸ **pare down**

(Phrasal verbs) **pare down**: **~ [sth] down**, **~ down [sth]** خَفَّضَ [شَيْئًا] بالتَدْريج ‹*the budget, spending*›
• **pare off**: **~ [sth] off**, **~ off [sth]** قَشَرَ \ قَشَّرَ [شَيْئًا] ‹*the rind, peel*›

parent /ˈpɛːrənt/ *n* والِد

parental /pəˈrɛnt(ə)l/ *adj* ‹*responsibility, care*› أَبَوِيّ

parent company *n* شَرِكة أُمّ

parenthesis /pəˈrɛnθɪsɪs/ *n* (*pl* **parentheses**) قَوْس (أَقْواس)

parenthood /ˈpɛːrənthʊd/ *n* (fatherhood) أُبُوّة؛ (motherhood) أُمومة

parenting /ˈpɛːrəntɪŋ/ *n* تَرْبِية الأَوْلادِ

parents' evening *n* [اجْتِماع لِأَوْلياءِ الأُمورِ والأَساتِذةِ]

parent–teacher association /ˌpɛːrəntˈtiːtʃə əsəʊsɪˌeɪʃ(ə)n/ *n* جَمْعِيّة الآباءِ والمُعَلِّمينَ

Paris /ˈparɪs/ *pr n* باريس (f)

parish /ˈparɪʃ/ *n* **1** (Rel_Chr) أَبْرَشِيّة **2** (BrE) (administrative) أَبْرَشِيّة (أَصْغَرُ وَحْدةٍ إدارِيّةٍ في المَناطِقِ الريفِيّةِ)

parishioner /pəˈrɪʃ(ə)nə/ *n* (Rel_Chr) [أَحَد رَعايا أَبْرَشِيّةٍ]

Parisian /pəˈrɪzɪən/ *n, adj* باريسيّ

parity /ˈparɪti/ *n* (equality) تَساوٍ, تَكافُؤ

park /pɑːk/ **A** *n* **1** (public garden) مُتَنَزَّه (مُتَنَزَّهات), مُنْتَزَه (مُتَنَزَّهات), حَديقة عامّة **2** (estate) عِزْبة (عِزَب)

B *vt* رَكَنَ (u; رُكون), صَفَّ (u; صَفّ) ‹*a car, caravan*›

C *vi* «drivers» رَكَنَ \ صَفَّ سَيّارةً

park-and-ride /ˌpɑːk(ə)ndˈrʌɪd/ *n* (BrE) [مَوْقِف سَيّاراتٍ يَتَضَمَّنُ شَبَكةَ نَقْلٍ بالحافِلاتِ إلى وَسَطِ المَدينةِ (لِتَخْفيفِ الازْدِحامِ المُروريِّ)]

parking /ˈpɑːkɪŋ/ *n* رَكْن \ صَفّ سَيّارةٍ; **'No ~'** 'مَمْنوعٌ رَكْنُ السَّيّاراتِ'

parking attendant *n* [عامِل \ حارِس في مَوْقِف سَيّاراتٍ]

parking garage *n* (AmE) **1** (multi-storey) مَوْقِف سَيّاراتٍ مُتَعَدِّد الطَوابِقِ **2** (underground) مَوْقِف سَيّاراتٍ تحت الأَرْضِ

parking light *n* [ضَوْء جانِبيّ صَغير يُسْتَعْمَلُ لِرَكْنِ السَّيّارةِ في اللَّيْلِ]

parking lot *n* (AmE) مَوْقِف سَيّاراتٍ

parking meter *n* عَدّاد مَواقِفِ السَّيّاراتِ

parking space, **parking place** *n* [مَكان لِرَكْنِ سَيّارةٍ]

parking ticket *n* **1** (for parking) تَذْكِرة مَوْقِفِ سَيّاراتٍ **2** (for offenders) [مُخالَفة صَفِّ السَّيّارةِ بِشَكْلٍ غَيْرِ قانونيٍّ]

Parkinson's disease /ˈpɑːkɪns(ə)nz dɪˌziːz/ *n* مَرَض شَلَل رُعاشيّ, بارْكِنْسون

park keeper *n* حارِس حَديقةٍ عامّةٍ

park ranger, **park warden** *n* حارِس الغاباتِ \ المُتَنَزَّهاتِ

parkway /ˈpɑːkweɪ/ *n* **1** (AmE) (avenue) [طَريق واسِع مُشَجَّر] **2** (BrE) (for cars) مَوْقِف مَحَطّةِ سِكّةٍ حَديديّةٍ

parliament /ˈpɑːləmənt/ *n* بَرْلَمان; **a hung ~** بَرْلَمان مُعَلَّق

parliamentary /ˌpɑːləˈmɛnt(ə)ri/ *adj* ‹*election, democracy*› نِيابيّ, بَرْلَمانيّ

parliamentary privilege *n* حَصانة بَرْلَمانيّة \ نِيابيّة

parlour (BrE), **parlor** (AmE) /ˈpɑːlə/ *n* **1** (sitting room) قاعة اسْتِقْبالٍ \ جُلوسٍ **2** (shop) مَحَلّ

parochial /pəˈrəʊkɪəl/ *adj* **1** (pej) (narrow-minded) ‹*outlook, interest*› ضَيِّق الأُفُقِ **2** (of a parish) ‹*council, business*› الأَبْرَشيّةِ

parody /ˈparədi/ **A** *n* (*pl* **parodies**) مُحاكاة تَهَكُّميّة

B *vt* (**parodies**, **parodying**, **parodied**) قَلَّدَ بِطَريقةٍ تَهَكُّميّةٍ ‹*a person, style*›

parole /pəˈrəʊl/ *n* إخْلاء سَبيلٍ مَشْروط; **to release a prisoner on ~** مَنَحَ السَّجينَ إخْلاءَ سَبيلٍ مَشْروطٍ

paroxysm /ˈparəksɪz(ə)m/ *n* نَوْبة (نَوْبات)

parquet /ˈpɑːkeɪ/ **A** *n* **1** (flooring) أَرْضيّة خَشَبيّة, بارْكيه **2** (AmE) (seating) مَقاعِد أَماميّة (قُرْبَ مِنَصّة مَسْرَح); **two seats in the ~** [مَقْعَدانِ أَماميّانِ قُرْبَ المِنَصّة]

B *vt* فَرَشَ بالبارْكيه ‹*a hall, floor*›

parrot /ˈparət/ *n* بَبَّغاء (dipt; بَبَّغاوات)

parry /ˈpari/ *vt* (**parries**, **parrying**, **parried**) **1** تَجَنَّبَ, تَفادى ‹*a thrust, blow*› **2** تَجَنَّبَ, تَفادى ‹*a question, an attack*›

parsley /ˈpɑːsli/ *n* بَقْدونس

parsnip /ˈpɑːsnɪp/ *n* جَزَر أَبْيَض

parson /ˈpɑːs(ə)n/ *n* راعي أَبْرَشيّةٍ

part /pɑːt/ **A** *n* **1** (of a whole) جُزْء (أَجْزاء), قِسْم (أَقْسام); **that's the best/hardest ~** ذلك هو أَفْضَلُ \ أَصْعَبُ جُزْءٍ; **in the early ~ of the century** في بِداياتِ القَرْنِ; **~ of the reason is ...** أَحَدُ الأَسْبابِ هو ...; **in ~** إلى حَدٍّ ما, جُزْئيًّا; **he's become ~ of the family** أَصْبَحَ جُزْءاً من العائِلةِ; **to be/feel ~ of sth** كانَ جُزْءاً \ شَعَرَ أَنَّهُ جُزْءٌ من شَيْءٍ; **in** *or* **around these ~s** في هذه المِنْطَقةِ; **it took the best ~ of an hour** اسْتَغْرَقَ ما يَقْرُبُ من ساعةٍ **2** (component) قِطْعة (قِطَع); **spare ~s** قِطَع غِيارٍ **3** (of a serial, programme) جُزْء (أَجْزاء); **a six-~ series** مُسَلْسَل من سِتّةِ أَجْزاءٍ **4** (role, share) دَوْر (أَدْوار); **technology plays a major ~ in our lives** تَلْعَبُ التِكنولوجيا دَوْراً أَساسيًّا في حَياتِنا; **to take ~ in sth** شارَكَ في شَيْءٍ; **to do one's ~** أَدّى دَوْرَهُ, فَعَلَ ما عَلَيْهِ; **I want no ~ in it, I don't want any ~ of it** لا أُريدُ أَنْ يَكونَ لي أَيُّ عَلاقةٍ بِهِ **5** (in acting) دَوْر (أَدْوار) **6** (for voice, instrument) دَوْر (أَدْوار) **7** (equal measure) مِقْدار (مَقاديرُ); **a mixture of one part cement to four ~s sand** خَليط مُكَوَّن من مِقْدارِ إِسْمَنْت مع أَرْبَعةِ مَقاديرِ رَمْلٍ **8** (fml) (side) **to take sb's ~** تَحَيَّزَ \ انْحازَ إلى شَخْصٍ; **for my/his ~** من جانِبي \ جانِبِهِ; **it was an error on my ~** كانَ خَطَأً من جِهَتي **9** (AmE) (in one's hair) فَرْق (فُروق)

B *vt* **1** (to separate) فَصَلَ (i; فَصْل) ‹*the boxers, a couple*›; **to ~ one's lips** فَتَحَ شَفَتَيْهِ; **to ~ company** افْتَرَقَ; **to be ~ed from sb** افْتَرَقَ عن شَخْصٍ **2** (in hairdressing) **to ~ one's hair** فَرَقَ شَعْرَهُ

C *vi* **1** (to separate) «partners, couples» انْفَصَلَ; **we ~ed amicably/on bad terms** انْفَصَلْنا بِشَكْلٍ وُدّيٍّ \ على عَلاقةٍ سَيِّئةٍ **2** (to divide) «lips, curtains» انْفَتَحَ; «clouds, crowds» تَفَرَّقَ

D *adv* (partly) جُزْئِيًّا; **it was ~ fear, ~ greed** كانَ جُزْئِيًّا بدافِعِ الخَوْفِ، وَجُزْئِيًّا بِدافِعِ الطَمَعِ; **the project is ~ funded by an NGO** المَشْروعُ مُمَوَّلٌ جُزْئِيًّا من قِبَلِ مُنَظَّمةٍ غَيْرِ حُكوميّةٍ

(Idioms) **to look the part** ظَهَرَ بالمَظْهَرِ المُلائِم; **to be part and parcel of sth** كانَ جُزْءاً لا يَتَجَزَّأُ من شَيْءٍ

(Phrasal verb) **part with: ~ with [sth]** تَخلّى عن [شَيْءٍ] ‹*one's money, a possession*›

part exchange *n* (BrE) [نِظام يَحْتَسِبُ قيمةَ المُنْتَجِ المُسْتَبْدَلِ كَجُزْءٍ من قيمةِ المُنْتَجِ الجَديدِ]; **to take the old car in part exchange for the new one** [احْتَسَبَ قيمةَ السَيّارة المُسْتَبْدَلَةِ كَجُزْءٍ من قيمةِ السَيّارة الجَديدةِ]

partial /ˈpɑːʃ(ə)l/ *adj* **1** (not complete) ‹*recovery, victory*› جُزْئِيّ **2** (biased) ‹*advice, judge*› مُنْحاز, مُتَحَيِّز **3** (fond) **to be ~ to caviar** كانَ مولَعاً بالكافيار

partially /ˈpɑːʃ(ə)li/ *adv* ‹*funded*› جُزْئِيًّا; ‹*obscured*› إلى حَدٍّ ما

partially sighted *n* **the ~** ضِعاف البَصَرِ

participant /pɑːˈtɪsɪp(ə)nt/ *n* مُشارِك, مُشْتَرِك

participate /pɑːˈtɪsɪpeɪt/ *vi* «organizations, groups» شارَكَ, اشْتَرَكَ; **to ~ in the discussions** شارَكَ في النِقاشاتِ

participation /pɑːˌtɪsɪˈpeɪʃ(ə)n/ *n* اشْتِراك, مُشارَكة

participle /ˈpɑːtɪsɪp(ə)l/ *n* **the present/past ~** اسْم الفاعِلِ \ المَفْعولِ

particle /ˈpɑːtɪk(ə)l/ *n* **1** (small piece) جُزَيْء (جُزَيْئات) **2** (Phys) جُزَيْء (جُزَيْئات), جُسَيْم (جُسَيْمات)

particular /pəˈtɪkjʊlə/ **A** *adj* **1** (specific) ‹*case, type*› مُعَيَّن, مُحَدَّد; **for no ~ reason** بِدونِ سَبَبٍ مُحَدَّدٍ; **do you have anywhere ~ in mind?** هل تُفَكِّرُ في مَكانٍ مُعَيَّنٍ؟; **no ~ time was mentioned** لم يُذْكَرْ أيَّ وَقْتٍ مُحَدَّدٍ **2** (exceptional) ‹*interest, attention*› اسْتِثْنائِيّ, خاصّ; **to take ~ care over sth** اهْتَمَّ بِشَيْءٍ اهْتِماماً خاصًّا; **he is a ~ friend of mine** هو صَديقٌ خاصٌّ لي **3** (fml) (fussy) صَعْب الإرْضاءِ; **to be ~ about cleanliness/punctuality** كانَ شَديدَ الحِرْصِ على النَظافةِ \ الالْتِزام بالمَواعيدِ; **'any special time?' — 'no, I'm not ~'** 'أيَّ وَقْتٍ مُعَيَّنٍ؟' — 'لا، هذا لا يَعْنيني كَثيراً'

B *n* **1** (fml) (detail) تَفْصيل (تَفْصيلات) تَفاصيلُ; **in every ~** من كافّةِ الجَوانِبِ; **to go into ~s** دَخَلَ في التَفاصيلِ **2** (**in particular**) على وَجْهِ الخُصوصِ; **are you looking for anything in ~?** هل تَبْحَثُ عن أيِّ شَيْءٍ مُعَيَّنٍ؟; **nothing in ~** لا شَيْءَ على وَجْهِ الخُصوصِ

C (**particulars**) *n pl* (information) تَفاصيل; **for further ~s please contact ...** لِمَزيدٍ من التَفاصيلِ اتَّصِلْ ب ...; **the policeman took down his ~s** دَوَّنَ الشُرْطيُّ بَياناتِهِ

particularly /pəˈtɪkjʊləli/ *adv* **1** (specifically) ‹*to remember, like*› تَحْديداً, على وَجْهِ التَحْديد **2** (especially) ‹*important, useful*› على وَجْهِ الخُصوصِ

particulars /pəˈtɪkjʊləz/ *n pl* (fml) بَيانات

parting /ˈpɑːtɪŋ/ *n* **1** (separation) فِراق **2** (BrE) (in hair) مَفْرِق الشَعْرِ

partisan /ˈpɑːtɪzan, ˌpɑːtɪˈzan/ *n* **1** (supporter) نَصير (نُصَراءُ) **2** (Mil) مُوالٍ, [عُضوفي القوّاتِ المُقاوِمةِ للاحْتِلالِ] (أَنْصار)

partition /pɑːˈtɪʃ(ə)n/ **A** *n* **1** (in a room, house) فاصِل **2** (of a country) تَقْسيم (تَقْسيمات)

B *vt* **1** (Constr) فَصَلَ بِحاجِزٍ ‹*an area, a room*› **2** (Pol) قَسَّمَ ‹*a country, territory*›

partly /ˈpɑːtli/ *adv* ‹*open, true*› جُزْئِيًّا; **I'm ~ to blame for the delay** يَقَعُ اللَوْمُ على التَأْخيرِ جُزْئِيًّا على عاتِقي

partner /ˈpɑːtnə/ **A** *n* **1** (Busn) شَريك (شُرَكاءُ) **2** (Sport) شَريك (شُرَكاءُ); (for a dance) مُراقِص **3** (in a relationship) شَريك حَياةٍ

B *vt* (Sport) شارَكَ; (for a dance) راقَصَ

C *vi* (Busn) **to ~ with sb** تَشارَكَ مع شَخْصٍ

partnership /ˈpɑːtnəʃɪp/ *n* (Busn) (relationship) شَراكة; (firm) شَرِكة تَضامُنيّة

part of speech *n* قِسْم من أقْسامِ الكَلامِ

partridge /ˈpɑːtrɪdʒ/ *n* (*pl* **partridges** or **partridge**) حَجَل (n coll; حِجْلى ,حِجْلان)

part-time /pɑːtˈtaɪm/ **A** *adj* ‹*job, employment*› جُزْئيّ **B** *adv* ‹*to work, study*› بِدَوامٍ جُزْئيٍّ

party /ˈpɑːti/ **A** *n* 1 (social event) حَفْل; **to have** *or* **throw a ~** أَقامَ حَفْلاً; **a birthday/leaving ~** حَفْل عيد ميلادٍ \ وَداعٍ 2 (Pol) حِزْب (أَحْزاب) 3 (group) مَجْموعة ,فَريق مَجْموعات); **an advance/a rescue ~** فَريق اسْتِطلاعٍ \ انْقاذٍ (مَجاميعُ 4 (in a dispute, etc) طَرَف (أَطْراف); **to be ~ to a contract/an agreement** كانَ طَرَفاً في عَقْدٍ \ اتِّفاقٍ; **I won't be ~ to any violence** لن أُشارِكَ في أَيِّ عُنْفٍ
B *modifier* ‹*leader, member, conference*› الحِزْبِ
C *vi* (**parties, partying, partied**) (infml) شارَكَ في حَفْلٍ ,احْتَفَلَ

party dress *n* ثَوْب حَفَلاتٍ للأَطْفالِ

party game *n* [لُعْبة لِتَسْلِيةِ الضُيوفِ في حَفْلةٍ]

party line *n* سِياسة \ اتِّجاه حِزْبٍ; **to follow the party** سارَ على نَهْجِ الحِزْبِ

party political broadcast *n* [بَرْنامَج تِلِفِزْيونيّ \ إذاعيّ يَسْتَضيفُ مُمَثِّل حِزْبٍ سِياسيٍّ]

Pashto /ˈpʌʃtəʊ/ *n* (لُغة) البَشْتو

pass /pɑːs/ **A** *vt* 1 (to go in front of) مَرَّ ,تَجاوَزَ ,تَخَطّى (u; مُرور; ب) ‹*a building, place*›; **~ the post office and continue ...** تَخَطّى مَكْتَبَ البَريدِ ثُمَّ اسْتَمِرَّ ....; **the convoy ~ed the refugees coming in the opposite direction** مَرَّت القافِلةُ باللاجِئينَ القادِمينَ في الاتِّجاهِ المُعاكِسِ 2 (to overtake) تَجاوَزَ ,تَخَطّى ‹*a vehicle, runner*›; **to ~ sb in the street** مَرَّ بِشَخْصٍ في الطَريقِ 3 (to exceed) تَجاوَزَ, تَخَطّى ‹*a level, limit*›; **the milk has ~ed its sell-by date** تَجاوَزَ اللَبَنُ تاريخَ عَرْضِ المُنْتَجِ للبَيْعِ 4 (to hand over) نَقَلَ (u; نَقْل) ناوَلَ شَخْصاً ‹*an object, information*›; **to ~ sth to sb, to ~ sb sth** شَيْئاً; **~ me your plate** ناوِلْني طَبَقَكَ; **I ~ed the letter to Jane** أَعْطَيْتُ الخِطابَ لِجين 5 (to move) مَرَّرَ ‹*a rope, thread*›; **she ~ed a hand over her eyes** وَضَعَتْ يَدَها أمامَ عَيْنَيْها 6 مَرَّرَ ‹*the ball*›; **to ~ the ball backwards/forwards** مَرَّرَ الكُرةَ للأَمامِ \ للخَلْفِ 7 (to succeed in) نَجَحَ (a; نَجاح; في) ,اجْتازَ ‹*an exam, a test*› 8 (to spend) قَضى ,أَمْضى (i; قَضاء) ‹*the time*›; **how do you ~ your time?** كيف تُمْضي وَقْتَكَ؟; **it ~es the time** يُساعِدُ في تَمْضِيةِ الوَقْتِ 9 (to declare satisfactory) أَعْطى إجازةً ل ,أَجازَ ‹*a patient, candidate, drug*›; **he has been ~ed fit to play** صُرِّحَ أَنَّهُ لائِقٌ طِبِّيّاً للَّعِبِ 10 (to approve) وافَقَ (على) ‹*a law, resolution*›; **the amendment was ~ed by 51 votes to 17** تَمَّت المُوافَقةُ على التَعْديلِ ب 51 صَوْتاً في مُقابِلِ 17 صَوْتاً للرَفْضِ 11 (to deliver) أَصْدَرَ ‹*a verdict, sentence*›; **he ~ed no comment** لم يُصْدِرْ أَيَّ تَعْليقٍ 12 (to discharge) **to ~ water** تَبَوَّلَ
B *vi* 1 (to go by) «people, vehicles» مَرَّ (u; مُرور) 2 (to overtake) «cars, drivers» تَخَطّى 3 (to move) «people, storms» مَرَّ (u; مُرور); **~ down the bus please** من فَضْلِكَ تَحَرَّكْ إلى داخِلِ الحافِلةِ; **the helicopter ~ed overhead** حَلَّقَت المَرْوَحِيّةُ فوق الرُؤوسِ 4 (to elapse) «time, years» مَرَّ (u; مُرور); **how time ~es!** ما أَسْرَعَ مُرورَ الزَمَنِ! 5 (to disappear) «feeling, pain» زالَ ,انْتَهى (a; زَوال) 6 (to change hands) «ownership, control» انْتَقَلَ; **ownership of the house ~ed to his widow** انْتَقَلَتْ مِلْكيّةُ البَيْتِ إلى أَرْمَلَتِهِ 7 (Sport) مَرَّرَ; **to ~ to sb** مَرَّرَ الكُرةَ إلى شَخْصٍ 8 (in exams) «candidates, students» نَجَحَ (a; نَجاح) 9 (to accept) **to let sth ~** غَضَّ الطَرَفَ عن شَيْءٍ; **to ~ unnoticed** مَرَّ دون أنْ يُلاحِظَهُ أَحَدٌ 10 (not take one's turn) تَخَلّى عن دَوْرِهِ; **I think I'll ~ on that** أَعْتَقِدُ أَنَّني لن أُشارِكَ في ذلك 11 (to happen) حَدَثَ (u; حُدوث); **to come to ~** حَدَثَ (u; حُدوث)
C *n* 1 (permit) تَصْريح (تَصْريحات), بِطاقة مُرورٍ; **please have your boarding ~es ready** الرَجاءُ إظْهارُ بِطاقةِ الصُعودِ إلى الطائِرةِ 2 (for travel) تَذْكِرة (تَذاكِرُ), بِطاقة (بِطاقات) 3 (in exams) نَجاح (نَجاحات); **to get a ~** نَجَحَ (a; نَجاح) 4 (in ball games) تَمْريرة; **to make a ~** قامَ بِتَمْريرةٍ 5 (in mountains) شِعْب (شِعاب), مَمَرّ (مَمَرّات) 6 (by aircraft) تَحْليق; **the helicopter made a low ~ over the town** حَلَّقَت المَرْوَحِيّةُ على ارْتِفاعٍ مُنْخَفِضٍ فوق المَدينةِ 7 (infml) (sexual advance) مُغازَلة; **to make a ~ at sb** غازَلَ شَخْصاً
D (**in passing**) *adv phr* بِشَكْلٍ عابِرٍ; **her achievement was only mentioned in ~ing** لم يُذْكَرْ إنْجازُها إلّا بِشَكْلٍ عابِرٍ

(Phrasal verbs) **pass around**, **pass round** (BrE): **~ [sth] around**, **~ around [sth]** مَرَّرَ [شَيْئاً] (على الحاضِرينَ) ‹*photos, plates*›

• **pass away** (euph) ماتَ (u; مَوْت), فارَقَ الحَياةَ, لَقِيَ حَتْفَهُ

• **pass by** «people, processions, hours» مَرَّ (u; مُرور)

• **pass down**: **~ [sth] down**, **~ down [sth]** نَقَلَ [شَيْئاً] إلى الأَجْيالِ اللاحِقة ‹*a tradition, knowledge*›

• **pass for**: **~ for [sb/sth]** حَسِبَ \ تَخَيَّلَ الناسُ أَنَّهُ [شَخْصٌ \ شَيْءٌ]; **she could ~ for a thirty-year old** قد يَحْسِبُ الناسُ أَنَّ عُمْرَها ثَلاثون عاماً

• **pass off** A (BrE) «events, demonstrations» انْقَضَى, انْفَضَّ
B **~ [sb/sth] off as sth**, **~ off [sb/sth] as sth** قَدَّمَ [شَخْصاً \ شَيْئاً] على أَنَّهُ شَيْءٌ

• **pass on**: A **to ~ on to sth** انْتَقَلَ إلى شَيْءٍ B **~ [sth] on**, **~ on [sth]** 1 بَلَّغَ [شَيْئاً] ‹*information, a message*› 2 نَقَلَ [شَيْئاً] ‹*genes, a disease*› 3 تَرَكَ عِبْءَ [شَيْءٍ] إلى غَيْرِه ‹*costs*›

• **pass out** A **~ [sth] out**, **~ out [sth]** وَزَّعَ [شَيْئاً] ‹*leaflets*›
B 1 (to faint) فَقَدَ وَعْيَهُ 2 (BrE Mil) (to graduate) تَخَرَّجَ

• **pass over**: 1 **~ [sb] over** تَخَطَّى [شَخْصاً] (في التَرْقِية) ‹*an employee, a candidate*›; **she was ~ed over for promotion** تَمَّ تَخَطّيها في التَرْقِية 2 **~ over [sth]** أَغْفَلَ [شَيْئاً] ‹*a subject, fact*›

• **pass through** A «travellers» مَرَّ (u; مُرور); **I'm just ~ing through** أنا فَقَطْ أَمُرُّ من هُنا B **~ through [sth]** مَرَّ من خلالِ [شَيْءٍ] ‹*an area, a door, town*›

• **pass up** (infml): **~ up [sth]** ضَيَّعَ [شَيْئاً] ‹*an opportunity, offer*›

passable /ˈpɑːsəb(ə)l/ *adj* 1 (acceptable) ‹*standard, performance*› لا بَأْسَ بِه, مَقْبول 2 ‹*river, road*› سالِك

passage /ˈpasɪdʒ/ *n* 1 (also **passageway**) (corridor) مَمَرّ (مَمَرّات) 2 **the ~ of time** مُرور الزَمَنِ 3 (journey) رِحْلة 4 (Anat) مَسْلَك (مَسالِكُ)

passenger /ˈpasɪndʒə/ *n* راكِب (رُكّاب)

passer-by /pɑːsəˈbʌɪ/ *n* (*pl* **passers-by**) مارّ (مارّة, مارّونَ)

passing /ˈpɑːsɪŋ/ *adj before n* 1 ‹*motorist, policeman*› عابِر 2 (brief) ‹*fad, whim, look*› عابِر 3 (casual) ‹*reference, comment*› عابِر

passing grade *n* تَقْدير مَقْبول

passion /ˈpaʃ(ə)n/ *n* شَغَف, وَلَع

passionate /ˈpaʃ(ə)nət/ *adj* 1 ‹*affair*› عاطِفِيّ; ‹*love*› جامِح, جارِف 2 ‹*supporter, plea*› حَماسِيّ; ‹*hatred, opposition*› شَديد, حادّ

passionately /ˈpaʃ(ə)nətli/ *adv* 1 ‹*to love, kiss*› بِشَغَفٍ 2 ‹*to write, defend*› بِحَماسٍ; ‹*to hate, oppose*› بِشِدّةٍ

passion fruit *n* ماراجويا, ثَمْرة زَهْرة الآلام

passive /ˈpasɪv/ A *adj* ‹*response, spectator*› سَلْبِيّ
B *n* **the ~** المَبْني لِلمَجْهول

passive smoking *n* تَدْخين سَلْبِيّ \ قَسْرِيّ

pass key *n* مِفْتاح دُخولٍ

pass lane, **passing lane** *n* (AmE) حارة التَخَطّي

pass mark *n* تَقْدير مَقْبول

Passover /ˈpɑːsəʊvə/ *n* عيد الفِصْحِ (عند اليَهودِ)

passport /ˈpɑːspɔːt/ *n* جَواز سَفَرٍ

password /ˈpɑːswəːd/ *n* كَلِمة سِرٍّ

past /pɑːst/ A *adj* 1 (most recent) ‹*weeks, months*› ماضٍ; **in the ~ two years** في العامَيْنِ الماضِيَيْنِ 2 (former) ‹*experience, times*› ماضٍ; **in ~ times** في الأَزْمِنةِ السالِفةِ 3 (finished) **summer is ~** وَلّى الصَيْفُ
B *n* 1 (former times) ماضٍ (مَواضٍ); **in the ~** في الماضي; **that's a thing of the ~** ذلك شَيْءٌ من الماضي; **in the recent ~** في الماضي القَريبِ 2 (of a person, city, country) ماضٍ (مَواضٍ), تاريخ; **to have a shady ~** كانَ لَهُ ماضٍ \ تاريخٌ مَشْبوهٌ 3 (also **past tense**) صيغة الماضي; **put the verb in the ~** *or* **into the ~ tense** ضَعِ الفِعْلَ في صيغةِ الماضي
C *prep* 1 (indicating movement) **to walk ~ sb/sth** مَرَّ بِمُحاذاةِ شَخْصٍ \ شَيْءٍ; **to drive ~ sb/sth** مَرَّ أَمامَ شَخْصٍ \ شَيْءٍ بالسَيّارةِ 2 (beyond) وَراءَ, بَعْدَ; **it is just ~ the school** يَقَعُ بَعْدَ المَدْرَسةِ تَماماً; **I'm ~ caring** لم يَعُدْ يُهِمُّني شَيْءٌ; **this cheese is ~ its best** لم يَعُدْ هذا الجُبْنُ في أَحْسَنِ حالاتِهِ 3 (in time expressions) **at twenty ~ five** في الخامِسةِ والثُلْثِ; **it's half/a quarter ~ seven** إنَّها السابِعةُ والنِصْفُ \ والرُبْعُ; **it's ~ my bedtime** مَرَّ مَوْعِدُ نَوْمي
D *adv* **to go ~** مَرَّ (u; مُرور); **to drive ~** مَرَّ بالسَيّارةِ; **he hurried ~** مَرَّ مُسْرِعاً

pasta /ˈpastə/ *n* مَكَرونة, مَعْكَرونة, باسْتا

paste /peɪst/ **A** *n* **1** (mixture) مَعْجون (مَعاجينُ), عَجينة (عَجائِنُ) **2** (glue) مادّة لاصِقة, مَعْجون لاصِق **3** (Culin) صَلْصة
B *vt* **1** (to glue) أَلْصَقَ ‹*a label, wallpaper*› **2** أَلْصَقَ ‹*text, an image*›

pastel /ˈpast(ə)l/ **A** *n* ≈ قَلَم باسْتيل, لَوْن شَمْع
B *adj* ‹*colour, pink*› فاتِح

pasteurize, -ise (BrE) /ˈpɑːstʃərʌɪz/ *vt* بَسْتَرَ (i; بَسْتَرة) ‹*milk, beer*›

pastille /ˈpast(ə)l/ *n* قُرْص للمَصِّ

pastime /ˈpɑːstʌɪm/ *n* هِواية, تَسْلِية (تَسْليات, تَسالٍ)

pastor /ˈpɑːstə/ *n* قَسّ (قُسوس, قُسُس), قِسّيس (قِسّيسونَ, قَساوِسة), راعي كَنيسةٍ

pastoral /ˈpɑːst(ə)rəl/ *n* **1** (Art) ‹*scene, painting*› ريفيّ
2 (Rel_Chr) ‹*role, work*› رَعَويّ

pastrami /paˈstrɑːmi/ *n* بَسْطُرْمة

pastry /ˈpeɪstri/ *n* (*pl* **pastries**) **1** (mixture) عجينة فطائر
2 (cake) فَطيرة (فَطائِرُ), كَعْكة (كَعْك)

pasture /ˈpɑːstʃə/ *n* مَرْعًى (مَراعٍ), مَرْج (مُروج)
Idiom **to put sb out to pasture** أَرْغَمَ شخْصاً على التَقاعُدِ

pasty¹ /ˈpasti/ *n* (*pl* **pasties**) (BrE Culin) فَطيرة لَحْم مَفْروم [وخُضَر]

pasty² /ˈpeɪsti/ *adj* (**pastier, pastiest**) ‹*face, skin*› شاحِب (شَواحِبُ)

pat /pat/ **A** *vt* (**-tt-**) رَبَّتَ (على), طَبْطَبَ (i; طَبْطَبة; على) ‹*a dog, horse*›; **to ~ sb on the back/head** رَبَّتَ على ظَهْرِ \ رَأْسِ شَخْصٍ
B *n* **1** (touch) تَرْبيتة **2** (of butter) قالَب (قَوالِبُ)
Idiom **to have sth off** (BrE) *or* **down** (AmE) **pat** أَتْقَنَ شَيْئاً على أَكْمَلِ وَجْهٍ

patch /patʃ/ **A** *n* **1** (material for repair on clothing, a tyre) رُقْعة (رُقَع, رِقاع) **2** (badge) شارة **3** (for eyes) عِصابة (عَصائِبُ, عِصابات), ضِمادة (ضِمادات, ضَمائِدُ), رِباط (رُبُط, أَرْبِطة) **4** (small area) رُقْعة (رُقَع, رِقاع), بُقْعة (بُقَع, بِقاع); **a damp ~ on the ceiling** بُقْعة رَطِبة في السَقْفِ **5** (area of ground) رُقْعة (رُقَع, رِقاع), بُقْعة (بُقَع, بِقاع); **a ~ of land** قِطْعة أَرْضٍ; **a vegetable ~** قِطْعة أَرْضٍ مَزْروعة بالخُضْرَواتِ; من الأَرْضِ **6** (BrE infml) (own territory) مِنْطَقة (مَناطِقُ), ناحِية (نَواحٍ) **7** (infml) (period) فَتْرة (فَتَرات); **to go through a bad ~** مَرَّ بِفَتْرةٍ عَصيبةٍ **8** (in computing) مِلَفّ تَصْليحٍ
B *vt* (to repair) رَقَّعَ, رَتَقَ (i-u; رَتْق) ‹*a garment*›; رَدَمَ (i-u; رَدْم), أَصْلَحَ ‹*hole*›
Idiom **not to be a patch on sth** (BrE infml) كانَ لا يَرْقى إلى شَيْءٍ
Phrasal verbs **patch together**: **~ [sth] together, ~ together [sth]** (infml) أَعَدَّ [شَيْئاً] على عَجَلٍ ‹*an agreement, alliance*›
• **patch up**: **1** **~ up [sth]** سَوّى [شَيْئاً] ‹*one's differences, a quarrel*›; **we've ~ed things up** سَوَّينا خِلافاتِنا **2** **~ [sth] up, ~ up [sth]** أَصْلَحَ \ رَمَّمَ [شَيْئاً] بِشَكْلٍ مُؤَقَّتٍ ‹*a hole*› **3** **~ [sth/sb] up** عالَجَ [شَيْئاً \ شَخْصاً] ‹*an injury, a wound*›

patchwork /ˈpatʃwəːk/ *n* تَرْقيع [فَنّ خِياطة قِطَعٍ مُخْتَلِفةِ الأَلْوانِ والأَحْجامِ]

patchwork quilt *n* لِحاف مُرَقَّع

patchy /ˈpatʃi/ *adj* (**patchier, patchiest**) **1** (uneven) ‹*cloud, fog*› مُتَناثِر; ‹*paint, colour*› مُرَقَّع **2** (inconsistent) ‹*knowledge, performance*› غَيْر تامٍّ \ مُكْتَمِلٍ

pâté, paté /ˈpateɪ/ *n* (عجين لَحْمٍ أو سَمَكٍ مَفْروم)

patent /ˈpat(ə)nt, ˈpeɪt(ə)nt/ **A** *n* براءة اخْتِراعٍ; **to hold the ~ on a process** امْتَلَكَ براءة اخْتِراعٍ لِعَمَليّةٍ
B *adj* (obvious) ‹*impossibility, defect*› واضِح, ظاهِر
C *vt* سَجَّلَ بَراءةَ اخْتِراعٍ ل ‹*a process, an invention*›

patent leather *n* جِلْد لامِع

patently /ˈpeɪt(ə)ntli/ *adv* ‹*false, obvious*› بِشَكْلٍ واضِحٍ \ جَليٍّ

paternal /pəˈtəːn(ə)l/ *adj* **1** ‹*concern, pride*› أَبَويّ
2 ‹*grandfather, DNA*› من جِهة الأَبِ

paternity /pəˈtəːnɪti/ *n* أُبوّة

paternity leave *n* إجازة أُبوّةٍ

path /pɑːθ/ *n* **1** (also **pathway**) (track) مَمَرّ (مَمَرّات), دَرْب (دُروب), طَريق (mf; طُرُق, طُرُقات) **2** (course of a projectile, river, hurricane) مَسار (مَسارات)

pathetic /pəˈθɛtɪk/ *adj* **1** (infml) (terrible) ‹*performance, attempt*› رَديء, يُرْثى لَهُ **2** (moving) مُثير للشَفَقةِ ‹*sight, cry*›

pathological /paθəˈlɒdʒɪk(ə)l/ *adj* ‹*fear, hatred*› باثولوجيّ, مَرَضيّ

pathologist /pəˈθɒlədʒɪst/ *n* (clinical) أَخِصّائيّ في عِلْمِ الأَمْراضِ; (forensic) طَبيب شَرْعيّ

pathology /pəˈθɒlədʒi/ *n* باثولوجيا, عِلْم الأَمْراضِ

pathos /ˈpeɪθɒs/ *n* [بَواعِث الرِّثاءِ \ الشَّفَقة]

patience /ˈpeɪʃ(ə)ns/ *n* 1▸ (of a person) حِلْم, أَناة, صَبْر; **to lose ~ with sb/sth** نَفِدَ صَبْرُهُ على شَخْصٍ \ شَيْءٍ 2▸ (BrE) (card game) سوليتير (لُعْبة وَرَق)

patient /ˈpeɪʃ(ə)nt/ **A** *adj* طَويل البالِ, صابِر, صَبور ‹*teacher, assistant*›

B *n* مَريض (مَرْضى)

patiently /ˈpeɪʃ(ə)ntli/ *adv* ‹*to wait, watch*› بِأَناةٍ, بِصَبْرٍ

patio /ˈpatɪəʊ/ *n* صَحْن دارٍ, باحة, فِناء (أَفْنِية)

patio doors *n* باب فِناءٍ

patriarch /ˈpeɪtrɪɑːk/ *n* 1▸ (of a family) شَيْخ قبيلةٍ \ رَبّ عائلةٍ 2▸ (Rel_Chr) (**Patriarch**) بَطْرِيَرك, بَطْرَك (بَطارِكة) عَشيرةٍ

patriarchal /peɪtrɪˈɑːk(ə)l/ *adj* 1▸ ‹*society, system*› ذُكوريّ

2▸ ‹*figure, beard*› بَطْرِيَركيّ

patriot /ˈpatrɪət, ˈpeɪtrɪət/ *n* شَخْص وَطَنيّ \ مُحِبّ لِوَطَنِهِ

patriotic /patrɪˈɒtɪk, peɪtrɪˈɒtɪk/ *adj* ‹*duty, song*› وَطَنيّ; ‹*soldier, citizen*› مُحِبّ لِوَطَنِهِ

patriotism /ˈpatrɪətɪz(ə)m, ˈpeɪtrɪətɪz(ə)m/ *n* وَطَنيّة, حُبّ الوَطَنِ

patrol /pəˈtrəʊl/ **A** *n* دَوْريّة أَمْنيّة \ حِراسة; **to be on ~** كانَ في دَوْريّةٍ أَمْنيّةٍ

B *vt* (**-ll-**) «soldiers, police» حَرَسَ, قامَ بِدَوْريّةٍ في (u; حِراسة) ‹*an area, the border*›

patrol boat *n* زَوْرَق خَفَرِ السَّواحِلِ

patrol car *n* سَيّارة دَوْريّةِ الشُّرْطةِ

patrolman /pəˈtrəʊlmən/ *n* (*pl* **-men**) 1▸ (AmE) (policeman) شُرْطيّ دَوْريّة, حارِس (حُرّاس), خَفير (خُفَراءُ) 2▸ (BrE Aut) [شَخْص يَعْمَلُ في شَرِكةٍ لِمُساعَدةِ السَّيّاراتِ على الطَّريقِ]

patrol plane *n* طائِرة دَوْريّة

patron /ˈpeɪtrən/ *n* 1▸ (of an artist, a charity) داعِم, راعٍ (رُعاة) 2▸ (fml) (client) زَبون (زَبائِنُ), عَميل (عُمَلاءُ)

patronage /ˈpatrənɪdʒ/ *n* (of an artist, charity) دَعْم, رِعاية

patronize, -ise (BrE) /ˈpatrənʌɪz/ *vt* 1▸ (to condescend to) عامَلَ بِاسْتِعْلاءٍ ‹*an employee, a friend*› 2▸ (fml) (to be a client of) تَرَدَّدَ (على), تَعَجْرَفَ (على) ‹*a restaurant, shop*›

patronizing, -ising (BrE) /ˈpatrənʌɪzɪŋ/ *adj* ‹*remark, behaviour*› مُتَعالٍ

patron saint *n* قِدّيس حامٍ \ راعٍ

patter /ˈpatə/ **A** *vi* «rain, drops» طَقْطَقَ (i; طَقْطَقة), نَقَرَ (u; نَقْر); «children, mice» [أَصْدَرَ صَوْتَ وَقْعِ أَقْدامٍ خَفيفٍ]

B *n* 1▸ (of rain) طَقْطَقة, صَوْت نَقْرٍ; (of footsteps) وَقْع

2▸ (speech) كَلام دِعايةٍ \ تَسْويقٍ

pattern /ˈpat(ə)n/ *n* 1▸ (design) شَكْل (أَشْكال, شُكول), نَقْش (نُقوش), رَسْم (رُسوم, رُسومات), تَصْميم (تَصْميمات, تَصاميمُ); **a striped/floral ~** شَكْل مُخَطَّط \ زَخْرَفة نَباتيّة; **a geometrical ~** نَمَط هَنْدَسيّ 2▸ (of events, behaviour) نَمَط (أَنْماط, نِماط), وَتيرة (وَتائِرُ), تَتَبُّع; **the protests/performances follow a set ~** الاحْتِجاجاتُ \ العُروضُ الفَنّيّةُ نَمَطاً ثابِتاً; **weather ~s are constantly evolving** تَتَغَيَّرُ أَنْماطُ الطَقْسِ بِشَكْلٍ دائِمٍ 3▸ (in dressmaking, knitting) نَموذَج (نَماذِجُ, نَموذَجات)

patterned /ˈpat(ə)nd/ *adj* ‹*fabric, wallpaper*› مَنْقوش, مُزَخْرَف

paunch /pɔːntʃ/ *n* كِرْش (كُروش), بَطْن كَبير

pauper /ˈpɔːpə/ *n* فَقير مُعْدِم

pause /pɔːz/ **A** *vi* 1▸ (to stop) تَوَقَّفَ (بِشَكْلٍ مُؤَقَّتٍ) 2▸ (to stop speaking) صَمَتَ (بِشَكْلٍ مُؤَقَّتٍ)

B *vt* (to stop) أَوْقَفَ (مُؤَقَّتاً) ‹*a recording, video*›

C *n* 1▸ (stop) تَوَقُّف قَصير \ مُؤَقَّت 2▸ (silence) صَمْت مُؤَقَّت

pave /peɪv/ *vt* رَصَفَ (u; رَصْف) ‹*a road, square*›

Idiom **to pave the way for sb/sth** مَهَّدَ الطَريقَ لِشَخْصٍ \ لِشَيْءٍ

pavement /ˈpeɪvmənt/ *n* 1▸ (BrE) (footpath) رَصيف (أَرْصِفة) 2▸ (AmE) (of roads) أَرْضيّة مَرْصوفة

pavement cafe *n* (BrE) مَقْهًى على رَصيفٍ

pavilion /pəˈvɪljən/ *n* [جَناح خاصّ في مَلْعَبٍ رِياضيٍّ لِتَبْديلِ المَلابِسِ والاسْتِراحةِ]

paving /ˈpeɪvɪŋ/ *n* أَرْضيّة مَرْصوفة \ مُبَلَّطة

paving stone, paving slab (BrE) *n* حَجَر الرَصْفِ \ التَبْليطِ

paw /pɔː/ **A** *n* قَدَم (f; أَقْدام)

B *vt* [ضَرَبَ \ حَكَّ بِقَدَمِهِ] ‹*a mouse, bone*›; **to ~ the ground** ضَرَبَ الأَرْضَ بِقَدَمِهِ

pawn /pɔːn/ **A** *n* (بَيادِق) بَيْدَق

B *vt* رَهَنَ (a; رَهْن) ‹*jewellery, a watch*›

pawnbroker /ˈpɔːnbrəʊkə/ *n* مُرْتَهِن

pawnshop /ˈpɔːnʃɒp/ *n* مَحَلّ رُهوناتٍ

pawpaw (BrE), **papaw** (AmE) /ˈpɔːpɔː/ *n* بابايا

pay /peɪ/ **A** *vt* (*past tense, past participle* **paid**) **1** دَفَعَ (a; دَفْع) ‹*tax, a bill, a fine*›; **to ~ cash** دَفَعَ نَقْداً; **to ~ cash/a cheque into an account** أَوْدَعَ نَقْداً \ شيكاً في حِسابٍ; **to ~ one's way** «person» تَكَفَّلَ بِنَفْسِه; **to ~ high/low wages** دَفَعَ أُجوراً مُرْتَفِعةً \ مُنْخَفِضةً **2** دَفَعَ (a; دَفْع) ‹*a worker, tradesman, creditor*›; **to ~ sb for sth** دَفَعَ لِشَخْصٍ ثَمَنَ شَيْءٍ; **she paid him £300 to repair the roof** دَفَعَتْ لَهُ £300 لِإِصْلاحِ السَقْفِ; **I'm paid weekly/monthly** أَحْصُلُ على أَجْرٍ أُسْبوعيٍّ \ شَهْريٍّ; **she is well paid** تَحْصُلُ على أَجْرٍ مُجْزٍ **3** «investments» أَعْطى ‹*interest*› **4** (to give) **to ~ attention to sth/sb** أَوْلى اهْتِماماً بِشَيْءٍ \ بِشَخْصٍ; **to ~ tribute to sth/sb** أَشادَ بِشَيْءٍ \ بِشَخْصٍ; **to ~ sb a compliment** جامَلَ شَخْصاً; **to ~ sb a visit** زارَ شَخْصاً **5** (to benefit) **it ~s to do sth** من المُفيدِ فِعْلُ شَيْءٍ; **it ~s to keep up to date** من المُفيدِ الاطِّلاعُ على أَحْدَثِ التَطَوُّراتِ

B *vi* (*past tense, past participle* **paid**) **1** (to give money) «companies, customers» دَفَعَ (a; دَفْع); **to ~ for sth** دَفَعَ مُقابِلَ شَيْءٍ; **to ~ in cash/by cheque** دَفَعَ نَقْداً \ بِشيكٍ; **they're paying for him to go to college** يَدْفعون لَهُ مَصاريفَ الكُلِّيَةِ; **the work doesn't ~ very well** العَمَلُ لا يُعْطي أَجْراً مُجْزياً جِدّاً; **the new system will ~ for itself within four years** سَيُغَطّي النِظامُ الجَديدُ تَكْلِفَتَهُ خلال أَرْبَعِ سِنينَ **2** (to deliver profits) «business, activity» أَفادَ; **it ~s to be honest** من المُفيدِ التَعامُلُ بِأَمانةٍ **3** (for errors, crimes) دَفَعَ الثَمَنَ; **he paid dearly for his mistake** دَفَعَ ثَمَناً فادِحاً لِخَطَئِهِ

C *n* (رَواتِبُ) راتِب ,(أُجور) أَجْر; **the ~ is good/bad** الأَجْرُ جَيِّدٌ \ قَليلٌ; **basic/take-home ~** مُرَتَّب أَساسيّ \ صافٍ; **to lose a day's ~** خُصِمَ مِنْهُ أَجْرُ يَوْمٍ; **to be in the ~ of sb** كانَ يَعْمَلُ لدى شَخْصٍ

D *modifier* ‹*increase, deal, scale*› الأَجْرِ

(Idioms) **to pay the price/penalty for sth** دَفَعَ ثَمَنَ شَيْءٍ; **to pay through the nose** (infml) دَفَعَ ثَمَناً باهِظاً

(Phrasal verbs) **pay back** **A** **~ [sb] back** **1** (to reimburse) سَدَّدَ [لِشَخْصٍ] **2** (for a misdeed) انْتَقَمَ من [شَخْصٍ] ما عَلَيْهِ **B** **~ [sth] back, ~ back [sth]** سَدَّدَ [شَيْئاً] ‹*the money, loan*›

• **pay in ~ [sth] in, ~ in [sth]** أَوْدَعَ [شَيْئاً] ‹*the money, cheque*›

• **pay off** **A** «work, gamble» عادَ بالنَفْعِ ,آتى ثِمارَهُ **B** **~ off [sth], ~ [sth] off** سَدَّدَ [شَيْئاً] بِكامِلِه ‹*a debt, mortgage*› **C** **~ [sb] off, ~ off [sb]** **1** (in dismissals) فَصَلَ [شَخْصاً] ‹*a worker*› **2** (infml) (to bribe) اشْتَرى سُكوتَ [شَخْصٍ]

• **pay out**: **1** **~ out [sth]** (to deliver money to) أَنْفَقَ [شَيْئاً] ‹*money, a sum*› **2** **~ [sth] out, ~ out [sth]** (to let out) (بِبَذَخٍ) أَرْخى [شَيْئاً] ‹*a rope*›

• **pay up** (infml) سَدَّ دَيْناً بِكامِلِه

payable /ˈpeɪəb(ə)l/ *adj* ‹*invoice, cheque*› مُسْتَحِقّ (الدَفْعِ)

pay and display *adj* **pay and display car park** [مَوْقِف سَيّاراتٍ خاصّ يَتِمُّ فيه شِراءُ بِطاقةٍ للوُقوفِ]

pay cheque (BrE), **pay check** (AmE) *n* شيك \ صَكّ راتِبٍ

pay cut *n* تَخْفيض \ اقْتِطاع أُجورٍ

payday /ˈpeɪdeɪ/ *n* يَوْم الدَفْعِ

payee /peɪˈiː/ *n* مُسْتَفيد ,شَخْص مَدْفوع لَهُ

payload /ˈpeɪləʊd/ *n* **1** (of aircraft, spaceships) حُمولة صافِية \ نافِعة **2** (of bombs, missiles) شِحْنة مُتَفَجِّرة **3** (of a virus) حُمولة فيروس

paymaster /ˈpeɪmɑːstə/ *n* **1** (payer of military) صَرّاف رَواتِبَ (للعَسْكَرِيّين) **2** (provider of funds) مُمَوِّل

payment /ˈpeɪmənt/ *n* دَفْع (دُفوع) ,تَسْديد

pay-off /ˈpeɪɒf/ *n* مَكْسَب (مَكاسِبُ)

pay packet *n* (envelope) [ظَرْف يَحْتَوي على راتِبٍ]; (wages) راتِب (رَواتِبُ)

payphone /ˈpeɪfəʊn/ *n* هاتِف عُموميّ (يَعْمَلُ بالعُمْلةِ أو بالبِطاقةِ)

pay rise (BrE), **pay raise** (AmE) *n* زِيادة في الأَجْرِ \ الراتِبِ

payroll /ˈpeɪrəʊl/ *n* كَشْف مُرَتَّباتٍ ,جَدْوَل رَواتِبَ

payslip /ˈpeɪslɪp/ *n* قَسيمة راتِبٍ

pay TV, pay television *n* [قَنَوات تِلِفِزْيونِيّة مَدْفوعة \ بِاشْتِراكٍ]

PC, pc /piːˈsiː/ **A** *n* **1** = **personal computer** حاسوب شَخْصيّ **2** (BrE) = **police constable** شُرْطيّ

B *abbr* = **politically correct** لائِق سِياسيًّا

PDF /piːdiːˈɛf/ *n* = **Portable Document Format** بي دي أف [نَسَق المُسْتَنَدات المَنْقولة]

PDT /piːdiːˈtiː/ *abbr* (AmE) = **Pacific Daylight Time** التَوْقيت الصَيْفيّ الباسِفيكيّ

PE /piːˈiː/ *n* = **physical education** تَرْبِية رِياضيّة

pea /piː/ *n* بازِلاّء, بِسِلّة

peace /piːs/ **A** *n* **1** (between nations, communities) سَلام; **at ~** في سَلامٍ; **to sue for ~** (fml) بَحَثَ عن السَلامِ **2** (absence of civil disorder) **to keep/disturb the ~** «police, citizens» حافَظَ على السَلامِ \ زَعْزَعَ السَلامَ **3** (tranquillity) اطْمِئْنان, أمان, طُمَأْنينة; **I felt at ~** شَعَرْتُ بالأَمانِ; **I need a bit of ~ and quiet** أنا في حاجةٍ إلى القَليلِ من الهُدوءِ والسَكينةِ; **~ of mind** راحة البالِ

B *adj before n* ‹movement, plan, conference› السَلام

Idioms **to hold one's peace** الْتَزَمَ الصَمْتَ; **to make peace with sb** تَصالَحَ مع شَخْصٍ

peace agreement *n* اتِّفاق سَلام

peaceful /ˈpiːsfʊl/ *adj* **1** (tranquil) ‹place, atmosphere› هادِئ **2** (non-violent) ‹demonstration, solution› سِلْميّ

peacefully /ˈpiːsfʊli/ *adv* **1** (tranquilly) ‹to sleep, live› بِهُدوءٍ **2** (without violence) ‹to protest, demonstrate› دون عُنْفٍ, بِشَكْلٍ سِلْميٍّ

peacekeeping /ˈpiːskiːpɪŋ/ *n* حِفْظ سَلامٍ

peacekeeping force *n* قوّة حِفْظِ سَلامٍ

peacemaker /ˈpiːsmeɪkə/ *n* صانِع سَلامٍ

peace process *n* عَمَليّة سَلامٍ

peace talks *n* مُحادَثات سَلامٍ

peacetime /ˈpiːstʌɪm/ *n* زَمَن \ وَقْت سِلْمٍ

peace treaty *n* مُعاهَدة صُلْحٍ \ سَلامٍ

peach /piːtʃ/ *n* **1** (fruit) خَوْخ (n coll), دُرّاق (Levant) **2** also **~ tree** شَجَرة الدُرّاقِ \ الخَوْخِ

peacock /ˈpiːkɒk/ *n* طاووس (طَواويسُ)

peahen /ˈpiːhɛn/ *n* طاووسة, أُنْثى الطاووسِ

peak /piːk/ **A** *n* **1** (mountain) جَبَل (جِبال); (of a mountain) قِمّة (قِمَم), ذُرْوة (ذُرًى) **2** (point) قِمّة (قِمَم) **3** (high point in one's power, popularity) قِمّة, أَوْج, ذُرْوة (ذُرًى); (in unemployment, inflation) ذُرْوة (ذُرًى); **her fame was at its ~** كانَتْ في أَوْجِ شُهْرَتِها; **he's past his ~** وَلّى زَمَنُ مَجْدِهِ **4** (on graphs) ذُرْوة (ذُرًى) **5** (BrE) (on caps) مِنْقار (مَناقيرُ), رَفْراف (حَوافٍ, حافات) حافة

B *vi* «production, population, popularity» وَصَلَ إلى الذُرْوة; **interest rates ~ed at 7.75%** بَلَغَتْ أَسْعارُ الفائدةِ ذُرْوَتَها عند ٪7.75; **sales have ~ed** وَصَلَتْ المَبيعاتُ إلى ذُرْوَتِها; **his popularity ~ed after the election** بَلَغَتْ شَعْبيّتُهُ أَوْجَها بعد الانْتِخاباتِ

C *adj before n* **1** (optimum) ‹performance› الأَمْثَل, الأَفْضَل **2** (most intense) ‹period› الذُرْوة; **a programme shown at ~ time** بَرْنامَج يُعْرَضُ في وَقْتِ الذُرْوةِ; **the ~ season is July and August** مَوْسِم الذُرْوةِ هو شَهْرَيْ يولْيو وَأَغُسْطُس

peak condition *n* أَعْلى مُسْتَوًى من اللِياقةِ; **to be in peak condition** كانَ في أَعْلى مُسْتَوًى من اللِياقةِ

peaked /piːkt/ *adj* ‹cap, hat› [لَهُ حافّةٌ أَماميّةٌ]

peak performance *n* ذُرْوة الأَداءِ

peak period, **peak hours** *n* فَتْرة ذُرْوةٍ

peak rate *n* سِعْر وَقْتِ الذُرْوةِ

peak season *n* مَوْسِم ذُرْوةٍ

peak time *n* وَقْت ذُرْوةٍ

peaky /ˈpiːki/ *adj* (**peakier**, **peakiest**) (infml) **to look ~** بَدا شاحِباً

peal /piːl/ *n* **1** (of bells) رَنين, جَلْجَلة **2** (of laughter) جَلْجَلة

peanut /ˈpiːnʌt/ **A** *n* **1** (plant) فول سودانيّ **2** (seed) فول سودانيّ, فُسْتُق عَبيد

B (**peanuts**) *n pl* (infml) مَبْلَغ تافِه \ زَهيد; **to pay sb ~s** دَفَعَ لِشَخْصٍ مَبْلَغاً ضَئيلاً \ زَهيداً

peanut butter *n* زُبْدة فولٍ سودانيٍّ

pear /pɛː/ *n* **1** (fruit) كُمَّثْرى (f), إجّاص **2** (also **pear tree**) شَجَرة كُمَّثْرى \ إجّاصٍ

Idiom **to go pear-shaped** (infml) أَخْفَقَ

pearl /pəːl/ *n* لُؤْلُؤ (n coll; لَآلِئُ)

peasant /ˈpɛz(ə)nt/ *n* فَلّاح

peat /piːt/ *n* خُثّ

pebble /ˈpɛb(ə)l/ *n* حَصاة (حَصَيات)

pecan /ˈpiːk(ə)n, prˈkan/ *n* جَوْز البَقّان

peck /pɛk/ **A** *vt* «birds» نَقَرَ (u; نَقْر) ‹*a nut*›
B *vi* **1** «birds» نَقَرَ (u; نَقْر); **to ~ at sth** نَقَرَ شَيْئاً **2** (infml) **to ~ at one's food** «children, patients» أَكَلَ قَدْراً قليلاً من طَعامِهِ
C *n* **1** (from a bird) نُقْرة (نُقَر) **2** (infml) (kiss) **to give sb a ~ on the cheek** طَبَعَ على خَدِّ شَخْصٍ قُبْلةً سريعةً

pecking order /ˈpɛkɪŋ ɔːdə/ *n* هَرَم السُلْطةِ

peckish /ˈpɛkɪʃ/ *adj* (infml) **to be ~** شَعَرَ ببَعْضِ الجوعِ

pecs /pɛks/ *n pl* (infml) ▸**pectorals**

pectorals /ˈpɛkt(ə)rəlz/ *n pl* عَضَلات الصَدْرِ

peculiar /prˈkjuːlɪə/ *adj* **1** (odd) ‹*noise, smell*› غَريب (غُرَباءُ), غَيْر مَأْلوفٍ **2** (unique) **to be ~ to sb/sth** كانَ خاصًّا بِشَخْصٍ \ بِشَيْءٍ

peculiarity /pɪˌkjuːlɪˈarɪti/ *n* (*pl* **peculiarities**)
1 (characteristic) خُصوصيّة, خاصّيّة (خاصّيّات), خَصائِص
2 (strangeness) غَرابة

pedagogy /ˈpɛdəgɒdʒi/ *n* (fml) عِلْم أُصول التَدْريس, عِلْم التَرْبِيةِ

pedal /ˈpɛd(ə)l/ **A** *n* دَوّاسة
B *vi* (**-ll-** BrE, **-l-** AmE) «cyclists» حَرَّكَ عَجَلةَ الدَرّاجةِ [بِقَدَمَيْهِ]

pedal bin *n* (BrE) صُنْدوق قُمامةٍ بِدَوّاسةٍ

pedal boat *n* قارِب بِدَوّاساتٍ

pedantic /prˈdantɪk/ *adj* ‹*interpretation, teacher*› مُتَحَذْلِق

peddle /ˈpɛd(ə)l/ *vt* ‹*wares, brushes*› باعَ مُتَجَوِّلاً; **to ~ drugs** تاجَرَ في المُخَدِّراتِ

pedestal /ˈpɛdɪst(ə)l/ *n* قاعِدة (قَواعِدُ)

(Idiom) **to put sb on a pedestal** رَفَعَ من قَدْرِ شَخْصٍ

pedestrian /prˈdɛstrɪən/ **A** *n* ماشٍ (مُشاة)
B *adj* **1** ‹*street, area*› خاصّ لِعُبور المُشاةِ **2** (uninteresting) ‹*article, account*› مُبْتَذَل, رَديء

pedestrian crossing *n* مَعْبَر مُشاةٍ

pedestrian precinct *n* (BrE) مِنْطَقة مُشاةٍ

pediatric (AmE) *adj* ▸**paediatric**

pediatrician (AmE) *n* ▸**paediatrician**

pediatrics (AmE) ▸**paediatrics**

pedicure /ˈpɛdɪkjʊə/ *n* باديكير (العِناية بالأَقْدام)

pedigree /ˈpɛdɪgriː/ **A** *n* (of a dog, person) سُلالة, أَصْل (أُصول)
B *adj* ‹*dog, cattle*› أَصيل (أُصَلاءُ)

pedlar /ˈpɛdlə/ *n* (of brushes, household goods) بائِع مُتَجَوِّل; **a drug ~** بائِع مُخَدِّراتٍ

pedophile (AmE) *n* ▸**paedophile**

pee /piː/ **A** *vi* (*past tense, past participle* **peed**) (infml) تَبَوَّلَ
B *n* (infml) بَوْل (أَبْوال); **to have a ~** تَبَوَّلَ

peek /piːk/ *n* **to have** *or* **take a ~ at sth** اخْتَلَسَ النَظَرَ على شَيْءٍ

peel /piːl/ **A** *vt* قَشَّرَ ‹*an orange, a potato*›
B *vi* «paint, varnish» تَقَشَّرَ, انْقَشَرَ; «skin» انْسَلَخَ
C *n* (of an orange, a potato) قِشْر (قُشور)

(Phrasal verbs) **peel away** ▸**peel off**

• **peel back** ▸**peel off**

• **peel off** **A** «labels, paint» سَقَطَ (u; سُقوط), تَساقَطَ; «skin» انْسَلَخَ **B** **~ off [sth], ~ [sth] off** نَزَعَ [شَيْئاً] ‹*a label, paint*›

peeler /ˈpiːlə/ *n* مِقْشَرة (مَقاشِرُ), قَشّارة

peelings /ˈpiːlɪŋz/ *n pl* قُشارة, قِشْر (قُشور)

peep /piːp/ **A** *vi* (to look) اخْتَلَس النَظَرَ \ أَلْقى نَظْرةً سريعةً; **to ~ at sth/sb** أَلْقى نَظْرةً خاطِفةً على شَيْءٍ \ شَخْصٍ خاطِفةً; **the sun ~ed through the clouds** تَسَلَّلَتْ أَشِعّةُ الشَمْسِ من خِلالِ السُحُبِ
B *n* **1** (quick look) نَظْرة سَريعة \ خاطِفة; **to have/take a ~ at sth** أَلْقى نَظْرةً سَريعةً على شَيْءٍ **2** (sound) صَوْت خافِت \ ضَعيف; (of a chick) زَقْزَقة, سَقْسَقة; **I don't want to hear another ~ out of you!** لا أُريدُ أنْ أَسْمَعَ هَمْسةً أُخْرى مِنْكَ!

(Phrasal verb) **peep out** **1** (be visible) «toes, head» بَرَزَ (u; بُروز) **2** (to appear) «sun, person» ظَهَرَ (a; ظُهور)

peephole /ˈpiːphəʊl/ *n* ثُقْب (للتَلَصُّصِ)

peer /pɪə/ **A** *vi* **to ~ at sb/sth** نَظَرَ مَلِيًّا إلى شَخْصٍ \ شَيْءٍ
B *n* **1** (in status) نَظير (نُظَراءُ) **2** (in age) قَرين (قُرَناءُ), زَميل (زُمَلاءُ) **3** (BrE) (noble) نَبيل (نُبَلاءُ)

peerage /ˈpɪərɪdʒ/ *n* (BrE) **1** (title) رُتْبة النَبالةِ **2** (group) طائِفة النُبَلاءِ

peer group *n* مَجْموعة الأَقْرانِ

peer group pressure *n* ضَغْط الأَقْرانِ

peer review *n* مُراجَعة الأَقْرانِ

peeved /piːvd/ *adj* (infml) <customer> مُتَكَدِّر, مُنْزَعِج; <expression> يُعَبِّرُ عن الإنْزِعاجِ

peevish /ˈpiːvɪʃ/ *adj* <child> مُتَبَرِّم (شُكْس), شَكِس (أَنْكاد) نَكِد; <tone> مُتَّسِم بالشَكاسَةِ \ بِضيقِ الخُلْقِ

peg /pɛg/ **A** *n* **1** (for clothes, hats, etc) شَمّاعة; **he buys his suits off the ~** يَشْتَري بَدَلاتِهِ جاهِزةً **2** (also **clothes peg**) (BrE) مِشْبَك (مَشابِكُ), مِلْقَط (مَلاقِطُ) **3** (also **tent peg**) وَتَد (أَوْتاد), إسْفين (أَسافينُ) **4** (in the ground) عَلامة (عَلامات, عَلائِمُ) **5** (in construction, carpentry) كُلاّب (كَلاليبُ) **6** (on violins, guitars, etc) مِفْتاح (مَفاتيحُ)

B *vt* (-gg-) **1** (to secure) ثَبَّتَ بِوَتَدٍ <a tent, tarpaulin>; **to ~ sth down** *or* **in place** ثَبَّتَ شَيْئاً بِوَتَدٍ **2** (to hang) **to ~ the washing on the line** عَلَّقَ الغَسيلَ على الحَبْلِ **3** (to fix) ثَبَّتَ <a currency, rate>; **its currency is ~ged to the dollar** عُمْلَتُهُ مَرْبوطةٌ بالدولار

Idiom **to take** *or* **bring sb down a peg or two** عَرَّفَ شَخْصاً حَجْمَهُ الحَقيقيَّ

Phrasal verb **peg out** **A** (BrE infml) (to die) فارَقَ الحَياةَ, تُوُفِّيَ **B** **~ [sth] out, ~ out [sth]** **1** (to mark) عَلَّمَ [شَيْئاً] <a plot, boundary> **2** (to hang) عَلَّقَ [شَيْئاً] <washing>

pejorative /pɪˈdʒɒrətɪv/ *adj* <word, expression> تَحْقيريّ, ازْدرائيّ

pelican /ˈpɛlɪk(ə)n/ *n* بَجَع (n coll)

pelican crossing *n* (BrE) [مَعْبَر مُشاة فيه زِرٌّ لِتَشْغيل إشارةِ العُبورِ]

pellagra /pəˈlagrə/ *n* بِلاّغرا, حُصاف

pellet /ˈpɛlɪt/ *n* **1** (shot) خُرْدُق (خَرادِقُ) **2** (of paper, wax) كُرَيّة

pelmet /ˈpɛlmɪt/ *n* بُرْقُع سِتارةٍ (إفْريز يُغَطّي أَعْلى السِتارةِ)

pelt /pɛlt/ **A** *vt* **to ~ sb with tomatoes/cushions** قَذَفَ شَخْصاً بالطَماطِمِ \ بالوَسائِدِ

B *vi* **1** (to rain) also **~ down** انْهَمَرَ المَطَرُ **2** (to move quickly) **to ~ along the road/down the hill** رَكَضَ مُسْرِعاً على طولِ الطَريقِ \ إلى أَسْفَلِ التَلِّ

C *n* (fur) إهاب (أُهُب), جِلْد حَيَوانٍ

Idiom **at full pelt** بِأَقْصى سُرْعةٍ

pelvic /ˈpɛlvɪk/ *adj* <injury, fracture> حَوْضيّ (خاصّ بالحَوْضِ)

pelvis /ˈpɛlvɪs/ *n* (*pl* **pelvises**) حَوْض (أَحْواض)

pen /pɛn/ *n* **1** (for writing) قَلَم (أَقْلام) **2** (for animals) حَظيرة (حَظائِرُ), زَريبة (زَرائِبُ)

penal /ˈpiːn(ə)l/ *adj* <system, law> جَزائيّ; <colony> [مُخَصَّص لِحَبْسِ المُجْرِمينَ]

penalize, -ise (BrE) /ˈpiːnəlʌɪz/ *vt* **1** (Law) عاقَبَ <a lawbreaker, an offence> **2** (Sport) احْتَسَبَ مُخالَفةً على <a player>

penalty /ˈpɛnəlti/ *n* (*pl* **penalties**) **1** (Law) (for an offence) عُقوبة, عِقاب, جَزاء (جَزاءات) **2** (Sport) ضَرْبة جَزاءٍ

penalty area *n* مِنْطَقة الجَزاء

penalty kick *n* رَكْلة جَزاءٍ

penalty shoot-out *n* رَكَلات تَرْجيحٍ

penalty spot *n* نُقْطة ضَرْبةِ الجَزاءِ

penance /ˈpɛnəns/ *n* كَفّارة

pence /pɛns/ (BrE) *n pl* ▸ **penny**

penchant /ˈpɒ̃ʃɒ̃/ *n* مَيْل شَديد, وَلَع; **to have a ~ for sth** كانَ مولَعاً بِشَيْءٍ

pencil /ˈpɛns(ə)l/ *n* قلم رَصاصٍ; **written in ~** مَكْتوب بِقَلَمِ رَصاصٍ

Phrasal verb **pencil in: ~ [sth] in, ~ in [sth]** **1** (to write) كَتَبَ [شَيْئاً] بِقَلَمِ رَصاصٍ <a word, name> **2** (to arrange) رَتَّبَ <a date, an appointment>

pencil case *n* مِقْلَمة

pencil sharpener *n* مِبْراة (مَبارٍ), بَرّاية

pendant /ˈpɛnd(ə)nt/ *n* دَلاّية (حِلْية مُتَدَلِّية)

pending /ˈpɛndɪŋ/ **A** *adj* **1** (incomplete) <matter, case> مُعَلَّق, قَيْدَ النَظَرِ **2** (imminent) <dismissal, result> وَشيك

B *prep* <a decision, trial> في انْتِظارِ, إلى حينِ

pen drive *n* قَلَم ذاكِرةٍ \ عَصا

pendulum /ˈpɛndjʊləm/ *n* (*pl* **pendulums**) بَنْدول, رَقّاص (رَقّاصات)

penetrate /ˈpɛnɪtreɪt/ **A** *vt* **1** اخْتَرَقَ <the skin, a wall, the defences> **2** (to infiltrate) اخْتَرَقَ <an organization, a system> **3** (to begin to sell in) غَزا (u; غَزْو) <a market>

B *vi* **1** نَفَذَ (u; نُفوذ, نَفاذ), تَغَلْغَلَ, تَسَرَّبَ; **to ~ into sth** نَفَذَ

لم يَنْفُذْ أَيُّ ضَوْءٍ إلى شَيْءٍ; **no light ~d into the room** تَتَسَرَّبُ الغُرْفَةِ; **the damp is penetrating through the walls** الرُطوبةُ من خِلالِ الجُدْرانِ; **the troops ~d far behind enemy lines** تَوَغَّلَت القوّاتُ إلى ما وَراءِ خُطوطِ العَدوِّ بِمَسافةٍ كَبيرةٍ

2 (to be understood) «words, meaning» تَمَّ اسْتيعابُهُ \ فَهْمُهُ; **what she said hadn't ~d** لم يُفْهَمْ ما قالَتْ

penetrating /'pɛnɪtreɪtɪŋ/ *adj* **1** ‹*eyes, gaze, voice*› حادّ **2** ‹*insight, question*› ثاقِب

penetration /pɛnɪ'treɪʃ(ə)n/ *n* اخْتِراق (اخْتِراقات), نَفاذ, تَسَلُّل

penfriend /'pɛnfrɛnd/ *n* صَديق بالمُراسَلةِ

penguin /'pɛŋgwɪn/ *n* بِطْريق (بَطارِقة, بَطاريقُ)

penicillin /pɛnɪ'sɪlɪn/ *n* بِنْسِلين

peninsula /pɪ'nɪnsjʊlə/ *n* شِبْه جَزيرةٍ

penis /'piːnɪs/ *n* قَضيب (قُضْبان), عُضْو ذَكَريّ

penitent /'pɛnɪt(ə)nt/ *adj* ‹*sinner, expression*› تائِب, نادِم (نُدّام)

penitentiary /,pɛnɪ'tɛnʃ(ə)ri/ *n* (*pl* **penitentiaries**) (AmE) سِجْن (سُجون)

penknife /'pɛnnʌɪf/ *n* (*pl* **penknives**) سِكّين جَيْبٍ, مِطْواة (مَطاوٍ)

pen name *n* اسْم مُسْتَعار

pennant /'pɛnənt/ *n* **1** (flag) [راية تَرْفَعُها السَفينةُ لإعْطاءِ إشارةٍ] **2** (of teams) [عَلَم مُثَلَّث الشَكْلِ يَحْمِلُ شِعارَ فَريقٍ] **3** (AmE) (championship) بُطولة

penniless /'pɛnɪləs/ *adj* ‹*writer, orphan*› مُفْلِس (مَفاليسُ), مُعْدِم, مُعْوِز

Pennsylvania /,pɛnsɪl'veɪnɪə/ *pr n* بِنْسِلْفانيا

Pennsylvanian /,pɛnsɪl'veɪnɪən/ *pr n, adj* بِنْسِلْفانيّ

penny /'pɛni/ *n* **1** (*pl* **pennies, pence**) (in UK:100th of pound) بِنْس; (in US: 100th of dollar) سِنْت **2** (*pl* **pennies**) (small amount) مَبْلَغ ضَئيل, مِلّيم (مِلّيمات, مَلاليمُ); **it will only cost you a ~ or two** لن يُكَلِّفَكَ إلا مَبْلَغاً ضَئيلاً; **when he died she didn't get a ~** عِنْدَما ماتَ لم تَحْصُلْ على مِلّيمٍ واحِدٍ; **it was worth every ~** كانَ يَسْتَحِقُّ كُلَّ قِرْشٍ دُفِعَ فيهِ

(Idioms) **not to have a penny to one's name** كانَ فَقيراً مُعْدِماً; **he hasn't a ~ to his name** هو فَقيرٌ مُعْدِمٌ; **in for a penny, in for a pound** إذا بَدَأْتَ فَأَكْمِلْ; **the penny dropped** (BrE infml) أخيراً فَهِمَ; **to spend a penny** (BrE infml euph) تَبَوَّلَ, قَضى حاجَتَهُ

penny-pinching /'pɛnɪpɪntʃɪŋ/ *adj* ‹*person*› شَحيح (أَشِحّاءُ), بَخيل (بُخَلاءُ); ‹*approach, government*› مُتَقَشِّف

pen pal *n* صَديق بالمُراسَلةِ

pension /'pɛnʃ(ə)n/ *n* مَعاش (مَعاشات)

pensioner /'pɛnʃ(ə)nə/ *n* مُتَقاعِد, شَخْص على المَعاشِ

pension plan, pension scheme *n* خُطّة مَعاشٍ \ تَقاعُدٍ

pensive /'pɛnsɪv/ *adj* ‹*mood, expression*› تَأَمُّليّ

pentagon /'pɛntəg(ə)n/ *n* **1** (shape) مُخَمَّس (مُخَمَّسات), شَكْل خُماسيّ **2** (in the US) (**the Pentagon**) البِنْتاغون (وِزارة الدِفاعِ الأمْريكيّة)

pentathlon /pɛn'taθlən, pɛn'taθlɒn/ *n* مُباراة خُماسيّة (تَتألّفُ من خَمْسةِ سِباقاتٍ مُخْتَلِفةٍ)

Pentecost /'pɛntɪkɒst/ *n* **1** (in Judaism) عيد الخَمْسين \ **2** (in Christianity) عيد الخَمْسينَ العَنْصَرة

penthouse /'pɛnthaʊs/ *n* [شِقّة فَخْمة في الطابَقِ الأعلى]

pent-up /pɛnt'ʌp/ *adj* ‹*frustration, anger*› مَكْظوم; ‹*energy*› مَكْبوت

penultimate /pɪ'nʌltɪmət/ *adj* ‹*chapter, day*› قبل الأخيرِ

people /'piːp(ə)l/ **A** *n* (nation) شَعْب (n coll, no sing n; شُعوب); **an ancient ~** شَعْب قَديم; **the Arabic-speaking ~s** الشُعوب الناطِقة بالعَرَبيّةِ

B *n pl* **1** (men and women) ناس, أشْخاص; **young/old ~** الشَباب \ كِبار السِنِّ; **~ say that he is dead** يَقولُ الناسُ إنَّهُ مَيِّتٌ; **what will ~ say?** ماذا سَيَقولُ الناسُ ؟; **you of all ~ should know that ...** أَنْتَ على وَجْهِ الخُصوصِ يَنْبَغي أَنْ تَعْلَمَ أَنَّ ... **2** (inhabitants of a town) سُكّان, أَهْل; (of a country) شَعْب (n coll, no singul n; شُعوب), سُكّان; **the ~ of Amman** أهل عَمّانَ; **the Egyptian/Russian ~** الشَعْب المِصْريّ \ الروسيّ **3** (citizens, subjects) (**the people**) الشَعْب, المُواطِنونَ; **a man of the ~** رَجُل من الشَعْبِ **4** (infml) (family) أَهْل (n coll, no singul n; أهالٍ, أَهْلون) **5** (Relig) **P~ of the Book** أَهْل الكِتابِ; **the Chosen P~** الشَعْب المُخْتار

C *vt* (to populate) سَكَنَ (u; سَكَن, في), قَطَنَ (u; قُطون, في, ب) ‹*the planet, country*›

people carrier *n* سْتيشَن \ سَيّارة عائِلية, ميني فان

people's democracy *n* ديمُقراطيّة الشَعْب

People's Republic of China *pr n* (**the People's Republic of China**) جُمْهوريّة الصين الشَعْبيّة

people trafficker *n* مُتاجِر بالبَشَر, مُهَرِّب بَشَر

pepper /ˈpɛpə/ **A** *n* **1** (spice) فُلْفُل (فَلافِل); **black/white ~** فُلْفُل أَسْوَد \ أَبْيَض **2** (vegetable) فُلْفُل (فَلافِل)

B *vt* (to sprinkle) رَشَّ (u; رَشّ); **to be ~ed with sth** أُمْطِرَ بوابِل من شَيْء

peppercorn /ˈpɛpəkɔːn/ *n* حَبّة فُلْفُل

pepper mill *n* مِطْحَنة فُلْفُل

peppermint /ˈpɛpəmɪnt/ **A** *n* **1** (plant) نَعْناع **2** (flavour) نَكْهة نَعْناع **3** (sweet) حَلْوى النَعْناع

B *adj before n* ‹*tea, flavour*› النَعْناع

pepper pot (BrE), **pepper shaker** (AmE) *n* مَبْهَرة \ رَشّاشة فُلْفُل

pep talk *n* خِطاب حَماسيّ \ تَشْجيعيّ

pep up /pɛp/ *vt* (infml) **to ~ sb/sth, to pep sb/sth up** أَنْعَش ‹*a person, an event*›; أَضْفى مَذاقاً طَيِّباً على شَيْء ‹*a meal*› شَخْصاً \ شَيْئاً

per /pɜː/ *prep* لِكُلّ, في; **80 km ~ hour** 80 كلم في الساعة; **rooms are £50 ~ person ~ night** الغُرَف ب 50 جُنَيْهاً للشَخْص في اللَيْلة

per annum /pər ˈanəm/ *adv* سَنَويًّا, كُلّ سَنة \ عام

per capita *adj, adv* للفَرْد, لِكُلّ فَرْد

perceive /pəˈsiːv/ *vt* **1** (with the senses) أَحَسَّ (ب), شَعَرَ (u; شُعور ب) ‹*an object*›; رَأى (a; رُؤْيَة, رَأْي) ‹*a colour*›; سَمِعَ (a; سَمْع) ‹*a sound*› **2** (to realize) أَدْرَكَ **3** (to interpret, view) رَأى (a; رُؤْيَة, رَأْي)

per cent **A** *n* بالمِائة, في المِائة; **half of one per cent** نِصْف في المِائة;

B *adj* بالمِائة, في المِائة; **a five per cent price increase** زِيادة في السِعْر بِمِقْدار خَمْسة في المِائة;

C *adv* بالمِائة, في المِائة; **to increase/decrease 20 per cent** زادَ \ نَقَص بِنِسْبة 20 بالمِائة

percentage /pəˈsɛntɪdʒ/ *n* نِسْبة مِئَويّة; **to express a figure as a ~** عَبَّرَ عن رَقْم كَنِسْبة مِئَويّة; **a high/low ~ of the population** نِسْبة مِئَويّة عالِية \ مُنْخَفِضة من السُكّان

perceptible /pəˈsɛptɪb(ə)l/ *adj* ‹*change, difference*› مَلْحوظ, مَرْئيّ, ظاهِر

perception /pəˈsɛpʃ(ə)n/ *n* **1** (with the senses) إِدْراك **2** (view) بَصيرة (بَصائِر), إِدْراك, فَهْم (أَفْهام) **3** (insight) فَهْم (أَفْهام)

perceptive /pəˈsɛptɪv/ *adj* ‹*comment, observer*› فَطِن, مُتَبَصِّر

perch /pəːtʃ/ **A** *n* **1** (for a bird) مَجْثَم (مَجاثِم) **2** (*pl* **perch** or **perches**) (fish) سَمَك \ فَرْخ نَهْريّ

B *vt* **to be ~ed on a stool/on top of a wall** كانَ جالِساً على مَقْعَد مُرْتَفِع \ حافّة جِدار

C *vi* «bird» حَطَّ (u; حَطّ)

percolate /ˈpəːkəleɪt/ *vi* **1** «water, gas» تَرَشَّحَ, انْسابَ; «information, rumours» تَسَرَّبَ **2** «coffee» أُعِدَّ في إِبْريق [في داخِلِه مِصْفاةٌ]

percolator /ˈpəːkəleɪtə/ *n* إِبْريق قَهْوة بِداخِلِه مِصْفاةٌ]

percussion /pəˈkʌʃ(ə)n/ *n* آلة إِيقاعيّة

peregrine falcon /pɛrɪgrɪn ˈfɔːlk(ə)n/ *n* شاهين (شَواهين), صَقْر جَوّال

perennial /pəˈrɛnɪəl/ **A** *adj* **1** ‹*flower, grass*› مُعَمِّر **2** (enduring) ‹*problem, favourite*› دائِم, مُتَكَرِّر

B *n* نَبات مُعَمِّر

perfect /ˈpəːfɪkt/ **A** *adj* **1** (flawless) ‹*condition, fit*› مُمْتاز **2** (ideal) ‹*example, opportunity*› مِثاليّ **3** (complete) تامّ, يَبْدو الأَمْرُ مَنْطِقيًّا بِمَعْنى الكَلِمة; **it makes ~ sense to me** جِدًّا بالنِسْبة لي

B /pəˈfɛkt/ *vt* أَحْكَمَ, أَتْقَنَ ‹*a technique, skill*›

C *n* **the ~** الزَمَن التامّ

perfection /pəˈfɛkʃ(ə)n/ *n* **1** (state, quality) كَمال **2** (refinement) إِحْكام, إِتْقان

perfectionist /pəˈfɛkʃ(ə)nɪst/ *n* شَخْص يَنْشُدُ الكَمالَ

perfectly /ˈpəːfɪktli/ *adv* **1** (faultlessly) بِإِتْقان **2** (exactly) بالضَبْط, على نَحْوٍ تامّ, تَماماً; **the ring fitted ~** كانَ الخاتَمُ على المَقاسِ تَماماً **3** (completely) تَماماً; **there's a ~ good reason for it** هُناكَ سَبَبٌ وَجيهٌ جِدًّا لِذَلِك

perfect pitch /ˌpəːfɪkt ˈpɪtʃ/ *n* القُدْرة على التَعَرُّف على \ ضَبْط النَغَمات]

perforate /ˈpɜːfəreɪt/ *vt* ثَقَبَ (u; ثَقْب) ‹*an eardrum, paper*›

perforation /ˌpɜːfəˈreɪʃ(ə)n/ *n* 1 (hole) ثُقْب (أَثْقاب, ثُقوب) 2 (to aid tearing) خَطّ مُثَقَّب في وَرَقةٍ لِتَسْهيلِ القَطْعِ

perform /pəˈfɔːm/ **A** *vt* 1 (to carry out) نَفَّذَ ‹*a task*›; أَنْجَزَ ‹*a function, role*›; أَدّى ‹*duties*›; أَجْرى ‹*an experiment, operation*›; أَقامَ ‹*a ceremony*› 2 (to present) قَدَّمَ ‹*a play*›; أَدّى ‹*a part, dance*›; عَزَفَ (i; عَزْف) ‹*a piece of music*›

B *vi* 1 «actors» أَدّى دَوْراً; «musicians» أَحْيا حَفْلاً; «dancer» قَدَّمَ عَرْضاً 2 «team, machine, economy» أَدّى وَظيفةً

performance /pəˈfɔːməns/ *n* 1 (rendition) أَداء (أَداءات); **it was a good ~ of the symphony** كانَ أَداءً جَيِّداً لِلسِمْفونِيّةِ 2 (concert, play, show) عَرْض (عُروض) 3 [u] (of a vehicle, team, company) أَداء (أَداءات) 4 [u] (of duties, a task) أَداء, تَأْدِية (أَداءات)

performer /pəˈfɔːmə/ *n* مُؤَدٍّ, فَنّان

performing /pəˈfɔːmɪŋ/ *adj* ‹*seal, elephant*› مُدَرَّب (على تَقْديمِ عَرْضٍ أمامَ جُمْهورٍ)

performing arts *n* فُنون تَعْبيريّة \ أَدائيّة

perfume /ˈpɜːfjuːm/ **A** *n* عِطْر (عُطور)

B *vt* عَطَّرَ ‹*the air, a room*›

perfunctory /pəˈfʌŋkt(ə)ri/ *adj* ‹*greeting, nod*› غَيْر مُكْتَرِثٍ \ مُبالٍ; ‹*inspection*› شَكْليّ, روتينيّ

perhaps /pəˈhaps/ *adv* لَعَلَّ, رُبَّما; **~ she's forgotten the appointment** لَعَلَّها نَسِيَت المَوْعِدَ

peril /ˈpɛrəl/ *n* خَطَر (أَخْطار); **ignore this advice at your ~** تَجاهَلْ هذه النَصيحةَ على مَسْؤوليَّتِكَ

perilous /ˈpɛrɪləs/ *adj* (fml) ‹*journey, situation*› مَحْفوف بالمَخاطِرِ, خَطير

perimeter /pəˈrɪmɪtə/ *n* مُحيط (خَطّ)

period /ˈpɪərɪəd/ **A** *n* 1 (length of time) فَتْرة (فَتَرات), مُدّة (مُدَد); **for a short/long ~ of time** لِفَتْرةٍ زَمَنيّةٍ قَصيرةٍ \ طَويلةٍ; **a three-year/three-week ~** مُدّة ثَلاثةِ أَعْوامٍ \ أَسابيعَ 2 (in history) عَصْر (عُصور) 3 (menstruation) دَوْرة طَمْثٍ; **to have one's ~** جاءَتْها الدَوْرةُ الشَهْريّةُ; عادة \ دَوْرة شَهْريّة 4 (lesson) حِصّة (حِصَص) 5 (AmE) (point) نُقْطة (نِقاط, نُقَط); **she's wrong, ~!** هي مُخْطِئةٌ, نُقْطة على السَطْرِ!

B *adj before n* (of a certain era) ‹*costume, furniture*› تاريخيّ

periodic /ˌpɪərɪˈɒdɪk/ *adj* ‹*reports, inspections*› دَوْريّ

periodical /pɪərɪˈɒdɪk(ə)l/ **A** *n* دَوْريّة (مَجَلّة)

B *adj* ‹*payment, inspection, publication*› دَوْريّ

periodically /pɪərɪˈɒdɪkli/ *adv* ‹*to happen, appear*› بِشَكْلٍ دَوْريٍّ, دَوْريّاً

periodic table *n* الجَدْوَل الدَوْريّ للعَناصِرِ

peripheral /pəˈrɪf(ə)rəl/ *adj* 1 ‹*area*› طَرَفيّ, هامِشيّ; ‹*vision*› مُحيطيّ 2 (minor) ‹*issue, role*› هامِشيّ 3 (Comput) ‹*device*› طَرَفيّ, مُلْحَق

periphery /pəˈrɪf(ə)ri/ *n* (*pl* **peripheries**) (of a city) طَرَف (أَطْراف); (of society) هامِش (هَوامِش)

periscope /ˈpɛrɪskəʊp/ *n* مِنْظار أُفُق, بَريسْكوب

perish /ˈpɛrɪʃ/ *vi* 1 (liter) (to die) «civilians, crew» هَلَكَ (i; هَلاك), ماتَ (u; مَوْت) 2 (to decay) «rubber, food» تَلِفَ (a; تَلَف)

perishable /ˈpɛrɪʃəb(ə)l/ **A** *adj* ‹*food, goods*› قابِل, سَريع التَلَفِ للتَلَفِ

B (**perishables**) *n pl* أَطْعِمة سَريعة التَلَفِ

peritonitis /ˌpɛrɪtəˈnʌɪtɪs/ *n* اِلْتِهاب الصِفاقِ

perjure /ˈpɜːdʒə/ *v refl* **to ~ oneself** حَلَفَ يَميناً, حَنَثَ بِقَسَمِهِ كاذِبةً

perjury /ˈpɜːdʒ(ə)ri/ *n* يَمين كاذِبة, شَهادة زورٍ, حِنْث بالقَسَمِ

perk /pɜːk/ *n* (infml) (in a job) حافِز إِضافيّ, عِلاوة إِضافيّة

Phrasal verb **perk up** (infml) 1 «person» اِبْتَهَجَ 2 «business, weather» تَحَسَّنَ

perky /ˈpɜːki/ *adj* (**perkier, perkiest**) ‹*voice, mood*› مَرِح, مُبْتَهِج, مُفْعَم بالنَشاطِ (مَرْحى)

perm /pɜːm/ **A** *n* تَمْويج \ تَجْعيد شَعْرٍ

B *vt* مَوَّجَ, جَعَّدَ; **I had my hair ~ed** مَوَّجْتُ شَعْري

permalink /ˈpɜːməlɪŋk/ *n* (Comput) رابِط ثابِت

permanent /ˈpɜːmənənt/ **A** *adj* ‹*job, resident*› دائِم; ‹*dye, ink*› ثابِت (ثُبوت)

B *n* (AmE) ▸ **perm** A

permanently /ˈpɜːmənəntli/ *adv* <*to live, settle*> بِشَكْلٍ دائِمٍ; <*damaged, disabled*> بِشَكْلٍ دائِمٍ; **her sight was ~ damaged** أُصيبَتْ بِقُصورٍ دائِمٍ في نَظَرِها

permeate /ˈpɜːmɪeɪt/ *vt* **1** تَخَلَّلَ, نَفَذَ من خِلالِ, اخْتَرَقَ <*the membrane*> **2** (في) انْتَشَرَ, (في) تَغَلْغَلَ <*the house, room*> **3** «ideas» (في) انْتَشَرَ <*society*>

permissible /pəˈmɪsɪb(ə)l/ *adj* **1** (allowed) <*limit, level*> مَسْموح **2** (acceptable) <*error, conduct*> مَقْبول

permission /pəˈmɪʃ(ə)n/ *n* تَصْريحات) تَصْريح, إجازة, إِذْن (تَصاريح); **to give** *or* **grant sb ~ to do sth** أَعطى \ مَنَحَ شَخصاً الإِذْنَ بِفِعْلِ شَيْءٍ; **to do sth without ~** فَعَلَ شَيْئاً بِدونِ إِذْنٍ; **to get ~ to do sth** حَصَلَ على تَصْريحٍ بِفِعْلِ شَيْءٍ

permissive /pəˈmɪsɪv/ *adj* <*society, attitude*> مُتَسامِح, مُتَساهِل

permit **A** /pəˈmɪt/ *vt* (-tt-) سَمَحَ (a; سَماح ب) <*the use of sth, access*>; **smoking/photography is not ~ted** التَدْخينُ \ التَصويرُ الفوتوغرافيُّ غَيْرُ مَسْموحٍ بِهِ; **to ~ sb to do sth** سَمَحَ لِشَخصٍ أَنْ يَفْعَلَ شَيْئاً

B /pəˈmɪt/ *vi* (-tt-) سَمَحَ (a; سَماح); **weather ~ting, we'll go to the final** إذا سَمَحَتْ ظُروفُ الطَقْسِ، سَنَذْهَبُ إلى المُباراةِ النِهائيَّةِ

C /ˈpɜːmɪt/ *n* تَصْريحات, تَصاريح), رُخْصة (رُخَص) تَصْريح; **to apply for a ~** قَدَّمَ طَلَباً لِلحُصولِ على تَصْريحٍ

permutation /pɜːmjʊˈteɪʃ(ə)n/ *n* تَبْديل

pernickety (BrE) /pəˈnɪkɪti/, **persnickety** (AmE) /pəˈsnɪkɪti/ *adj* (infml) صَعْبُ الإِرْضاءِ, نَزِق

peroxide /pəˈrɒksʌɪd/ *n* بيروكْسيد

perpendicular /ˌpɜːp(ə)nˈdɪkjʊlə/ *adj* **1** <*line, axis*> عَموديّ, مُتَعامِد; **~ to sth** مُتَعامِد مع شَيْءٍ **2** <*cliff, rock face*> شِبْه عَموديّ, شَديد الانْحِدارِ

perpetrate /ˈpɜːpɪtreɪt/ *vt* ارْتَكَبَ <*a crime, fraud*>

perpetrator /ˈpɜːpətreɪtə/ *n* جُناة) جانٍ, مُرْتَكِب جَريمةٍ)

perpetual /pəˈpɛtʃʊəl/ *adj* <*war, struggle*> دائِم, مُسْتَمِرّ

perpetuate /pəˈpɛtʃʊeɪt/ *vt* خَلَّدَ, أَدامَ <*a myth, stereotype*>

perplex /pəˈplɛks/ *vt* أَرْبَكَ, حَيَّرَ <*scientists, mankind*>

perplexed /pəˈplɛkst/ *adj* <*look, reaction*> مُرْتَبِك, حائِر

per se /pɜː ˈseɪ/ *adv* في حَدِّ ذاتِهِ

persecute /ˈpɜːsɪkjuːt/ *vt* اضْطَهَدَ <*minorities, opponents*>

persecution /pɜːsɪˈkjuːʃ(ə)n/ *n* اضْطِهاد (اضْطِهادات)

perseverance /pɜːsɪˈvɪərəns/ *n* مُواظَبَة, مُثابَرة

persevere /pɜːsɪˈvɪə/ *vi* واظَبَ, ثابَرَ

Persia /ˈpɜːʃə/ *pr n* (Hist) فارِس (dipt), بِلاد الفُرْسِ

Persian /ˈpɜːʃ(ə)n/ **A** *n* **1** (Hist) (inhabitant) فارِسيّ (فُرْس) **2** (language) (اللُغة) الفارِسيّة

B *adj* <*carpet, cat*>; فارِسيّ (فُرْس), إيرانيّ

Persian Gulf *pr n* (**the Persian Gulf**) الخَليج الفارِسيّ

persist /pəˈsɪst/ *vi* **1** «person» أَصَرَّ, ثابَرَ; **to ~ in doing sth** ثابَرَ, أَصَرَّ على فِعْلِ شَيْءٍ; **he ~ed in his efforts to free them** اسْتَمَرَّ في جُهودِهِ لِإِطْلاقِ سَراحِهِمْ **2** «problem, symptoms» اسْتَمَرَّ

persistence /pəˈsɪst(ə)ns/ *n* مُواظَبَة, إِصْرار, مُثابَرة

persistent /pəˈsɪst(ə)nt/ *adj* **1** (continual) <*pain, cough, rain*> مُسْتَمِرّ, مُتَواصِل; <*problem, questions*> مُلِحّ **2** (persevering) دَؤوب, مُواظِب, مُثابِر

persnickety /pəˈsnɪkəti/ *adj* (AmE infml) ▸ **pernickety**

person /ˈpɜːs(ə)n/ *n* **1** (*pl* **people, persons**) (human being) شَخْص (mf; أَشْخاص, شُخوص), إِنْسان, امْرُؤ; **a young ~** شابّ (شَباب); **a single ~** شَخْص أَعْزَب; **in ~** شَخْصيًّا; **he's the only ~ who could have done it** هو الشَخْصُ الوَحيدُ الّذي كانَ بِإِمْكانِهِ أَنْ يَفْعَلَهُ; **what kind of ~ would do a thing like that?** أَيُّ بَشَرٍ هذا الّذي يَفْعَلُ شَيْئاً كَهذا؟; **there's no such ~** لا يوجَدُ مِثْلُ هذا الشَخْصِ; **what's she like as a ~?** كيف هي كَإِنْسانةٍ؟; **the very ~ I was looking for!** الشَخْص الّذي كُنْتُ أَبْحَثُ عَنْهُ بِالضَبْطِ!; **the ~ concerned** الشَخْص المَعْنيّ **2** (fml) (individual) شَخْص (mf; أَشْخاص, شُخوص); **to have sth on** *or* **about one's ~** كانَ يَحْمِلُ مَعَهُ شَيْئاً; **with drugs concealed about his ~** مع مُخَدِّراتٍ يَخْبَّئُها مَعَهُ; **a ~ or ~s unknown** شَخْص غَيْر مَعْلومِ الهُوِيّة **3** (in grammar) ضَمير (ضَمائِرُ); **the first ~ singular** ضَمير المُتَكَلِّمِ المُفْرَدِ

persona /pəˈsəʊnə/ *n* (*pl* **personae** or **personas**) شَخْصيّة

personable /ˈpɜːs(ə)nəb(ə)l/ *adj* <*young man, manner*> جَذّاب

personal /ˈpɜːs(ə)n(ə)l/ **A** *adj* **1** (of a person) <*belongings, effects*> شَخْصيّ; **my ~ best is 3 hours** أَفْضَلُ رَقَمٍ حَقَّقْتُهُ شَخْصيًّا هو 3 ساعاتٍ **2** (private) <*opinion, problem, information*> شَخْصيّ,

خاصّ; **for ~ reasons** لِأَسْبابٍ شَخْصِيّةٍ; **on** *or* **at a ~ level** على المُسْتَوى الشَخْصيّ; **to make a ~ call** أَجْرى مُكالَمةً خاصّةً; **as a ~ favour to you** كَمُجامَلةٍ شَخْصِيّةٍ لَكَ **3** (in person) ‹*appearance, visit*› بِنَفْسِه ,بِشَخْصِه
B *n* (AmE) إعْلان تَعارُفٍ

personal ad *n* (infml) إعْلان تَعارُفٍ

personal assistant *n* **1** (secretary) سِكْرتير **2** (assistant) مُساعِد شَخْصيّ

personal best *n* رَقْم قِياسيّ شَخْصيّ

personal column *n* [قِسْم في جَريدةٍ لِإعْلاناتِ التَعارُف]

personal computer *n* حاسوب \ كُمْبيوتَر شَخْصيّ

personality /pəːsə'nalɪti/ *n* (*pl* **personalities**) شَخْصيّة

personalize, -ise (BrE) /'pəːs(ə)nəlʌɪz/ *vt* **1** (according to requirement) [جَعَلَ يَتَناسَبُ مع مُتَطَلَّباتٍ فَرْدِيّةٍ] ‹*stationery, clothing*›; **a ~d number plate** [لَوْحة تَرْقيمٍ تَحْمِلُ عَلاماتٍ اخْتارَها صاحِبُ السَيّارةِ] **2** (in disputes, arguments) جَعَلَ شَخْصَنَ ,مَسْأَلةً شَخْصيّةً ‹*an issue, a discussion*›

personal loan *n* قَرْض شَخْصيّ

personally /'pəːs(ə)n(ə)li/ *adv* **1** (in person) ‹*to meet, apologize*› شَخْصِيًّا **2** (as an individual) ‹*to speak, experience*› شَخْصِيًّا, بِصورةٍ شَخْصيّةٍ; **I don't know her ~** لا أَعْرِفُها شَخْصِيًّا

personal organizer *n* مُفَكِّرة ,مُنَظِّم شَخْصيّ

personal property *n* مُمْتَلَكات مَنْقولة

personal stereo *n* سْتيريو صَغير \ مَحْمول

personification /pəˌsɒnɪfɪ'keɪʃ(ə)n/ *n* تَشْخيص ,تَجْسيد

personify /pə'sɒnɪfʌɪ/ *vt* (**personifies, personifying, personified**) جَسَّدَ ,شَخَّصَ ‹*an ideal, evil*›

personnel /pəːsə'nɛl/ *n* **1** + *pl v* (staff) طاقِم مُوَظَّفينَ \ عُمّالٍ **2** + *sing v* (also **Personnel**) (department) قِسْم \ دائِرة شُؤونِ المُوَظَّفينَ

personnel manager *n* مُدير شُؤونِ المُوَظَّفينَ

personnel officer *n* مَسْؤول عن شُؤونِ المُوَظَّفينَ

perspective /pə'spɛktɪv/ *n* **1** (in art) مَنْظور **2** (attitude) وُجْهة نَظَرٍ ,مَنْظور; **to put things into ~** وَضَعَ الأُمورَ في نِصابِها \ مَنْظورِها الصَحيحِ

Perspex® /'pəːspɛks/ *n* بِرْسْبيكْس (بْلاسْتيك شَفّاف)

perspiration /pəːspɪ'reɪʃ(ə)n/ *n* عَرَق

perspire /pə'spʌɪə/ *vi* عَرِقَ (a; عَرَق)

persuade /pə'sweɪd/ *vt* **1** (to induce) حَثَّ (u; حَثّ); **to ~ sb to do sth** حَثَّ شَخْصاً على فِعْلِ شَيْءٍ **2** (to convince) أَقْنَعَ (ب)

persuasion /pə'sweɪʒ(ə)n/ *n* **1** (persuading, persuasiveness) إقْناع **2** (beliefs) قناعات

persuasive /pə'sweɪsɪv/ *adj* ‹*person, manner, argument*› مُقْنِع

pert /pəːt/ *adj* **1** ‹*young woman*› [مُفْعَم بالحَيَويّةِ \ بالنَشاطِ] **2** ‹*nose, breasts*› [صَغير وَذو شَكْلٍ جَميلٍ \ جَذّابٍ]

pertain /pə'teɪn/ *vi* (fml) **to ~ to a case/subject** «evidence, documents» خَصَّ قَضيّةً \ مَوْضوعاً

pertinent /'pəːtɪnənt/ *adj* ‹*question, information*› [ذو صِلةٍ وَثيقةٍ بِمَوْضوعٍ]; **to be ~ to sth** كانَ وَثيقَ الصلةِ بِشَيْءٍ

perturb /pə'təːb/ *vt* شَوَّشَ الفِكْرَ ,أَقْلَقَ

perturbing /pə'təːbɪŋ/ *adj* ‹*news, reports*› مُشَوِّش ,مُقْلِق

pertussis /pə'tʌsɪs/ *n* سُعال ديكيّ

Peru /pə'ruː/ *pr n* بيرو (f)

peruse /pə'ruːz/ *vt* (fml) تَمَعَّنَ (في) ‹*a menu, document*›

Peruvian /pə'ruːviən/ *n, adj* بيروفيّ

pervade /pə'veɪd/ *vt* **1** «smell» فاحَ (u; فَوْح ,فَوَحان) **2** «attitudes, themes» سادَ (u; سِيادة) ,عَمَّ (u; عُموم)

pervasive /pə'veɪsɪv/ *adj* **1** ‹*smell*› مُخْتَرِق ,مُنْتَشِر **2** ‹*influence, problem*› واسِع الانْتِشارِ ,مُتَغَلْغِل

perverse /pə'vəːs/ *adj* **1** (unreasonable) ‹*pleasure, desire*› غَيْر عَقْلانيٍّ ,جامِح **2** (contradictory) ‹*effect, logic*› مُعاكِس, مُناقِض

perversion /pə'vəːʃ(ə)n/ *n* **1** (distortion of justice) تَشْويه (تَشْويهات); (of the truth) تَحْريف (تَحْريفات) **2** (deviation) شُذوذ ,(انْحِرافات) انْحِراف

pervert **A** *vt* /pə'vəːt/ **1** (to corrupt) ضَلَّلَ ,أَفْسَدَ **2** (to distort) حَرَّفَ ,شَوَّهَ ‹*the truth, the meaning of sth*›
B *n* /'pəːvəːt/ شاذّ (جِنْسيًّا)

perverted /pə'vəːtɪd/ *adj* ‹*mind, pleasure*› يَتَّسِم بِشُذوذٍ جِنْسيٍّ

peseta /pə'seɪtə/ *n* بيزيتا

pesky /'pɛski/ *adj* (**peskier**, **peskiest**) (AmE infml) ‹*kid, questions*› مُزْعِج

peso /'peɪsəʊ/ *n* (*pl* **pesos**) بيزو

pessary /'pɛs(ə)ri/ *n* (*pl* **pessaries**) لَبوس مَهْبَليّ

pessimism /'pɛsɪmɪz(ə)m/ *n* تَشاؤُم

pessimist /'pɛsɪmɪst/ *n* مُتَشائِم

pessimistic /ˌpɛsɪ'mɪstɪk/ *adj* ‹*view, forecast*› مُتَشائِم, تَشاؤُميّ

pest /pɛst/ *n* 1 (animal) حَيَوان ضارّ; (insect) حَشَرة ضارّة 2 (infml) (annoying person) [شَخْص مُزْعِج \ بَغيض]

pester /'pɛstə/ *vt* أَضْجَر, ضايَق, أَزْعَج ‹*parents, tourists*›

pesticide /'pɛstɪsʌɪd/ *n* مُبيد حَشَراتٍ

pestle /'pɛs(ə)l/ *n* يَد الهاوُنِ, مِدَقّة

pet /pɛt/ **A** *n* 1 (animal) حَيَوان أَليف 2 (favourite) [شَخْص يَحْظى بِمُعامَلةٍ خاصّةٍ]; **she's teacher's ~** [هي تَحْظى بِمُعامَلةٍ خاصّةٍ من المُدَرِّس]

B *adj before n* 1 (favourite) ‹*theory, project*› مُفَضَّل 2 أَليف; **~ dog** كَلْب أَليف (أُلَفاءُ)

C *vt* (**-tt-**) رَبَّتَ ‹*an animal*›

D *vi* (**-tt-**) «teenagers, lovers» [تَلامَسَ بِطَريقةٍ حَميمةٍ]

petal /'pɛt(ə)l/ *n* تُوَيْجيّة, بَتَلة (وَرَقة من تاجِ الزَهْرةِ)

peter out /'piːtə/ *vt* «conversation» نَفِدَ تَدْريجيًّا; «road» تَضاءَلَ; «supplies» اخْتَفى تَدْريجيًّا

pet food *n* طَعام الحَيَواناتِ الأَليفةِ

pet hate *n* [شَخْص \ شَيْء مَبْغوض]

petition /pɪ'tɪʃ(ə)n/ **A** *n* 1 (with signatures) عَريضة (عَرائِضُ) 2 (to a court of law) الْتِماس (الْتِماسات), طَلَب لِلمَحْكَمةِ

B *vt* رَفَعَ عَريضةً إلى ‹*a government, court*›

petrified /'pɛtrɪfʌɪd/ *adj* 1 (terrified) ‹*person, silence*› مُرْتَعِب, مُرْعَب, مَشْلول من الخَوْفِ 2 (Geol) ‹*wood, remains*› مُتَحَجِّر

petrochemical /pɛtrəʊ'kɛmɪk(ə)l/ **A** *adj before n* ‹*industry, plant*› بِتْروكيماويّ

B *n* مادّة بِتْروكيماويّة

petrol /'pɛtrəl/ *n* (BrE) بَنْزين

petroleum /pɪ'trəʊlɪəm/ *n* نَفْط, بِتْرول

petrol pump *n* (BrE) مِضَخّة وَقودٍ \ بَنْزينٍ

petrol station *n* (BrE) مَحَطّة وَقودٍ \ بَنْزينٍ

pet shop *n* مَحَلّ بَيْعِ الحَيَواناتِ الأَليفةِ

petticoat /'pɛtɪkəʊt/ *n* (waist slip) تَنّورة داخِليّة \ تَحْتيّة; (BrE) (full-length) [لِباس داخِليّ نِسائيّ]

petty /'pɛti/ *adj* (**pettier**, **pettiest**) 1 (small-minded) ضَيِّق الأُفُقِ \ التَفْكير 2 (unimportant) غَيْر مُهِمٍّ

petty cash *n* صُنْدوق النَثْرِيّاتِ

petty crime *n* جُنْحة صَغيرة

petulant /'pɛtjʊlənt/ *adj* ‹*child, behaviour*› شَكِس

pew /pjuː/ *n* [مَقْعَد خَشَبيّ طَويل في كَنيسةٍ]

pewter /'pjuːtə/ *n* بيوتَر (أُشابة من القَصْديرِ والرَصاصِ والإثْمِدِ)

PG /piː'dʒiː/ *n* = **Parental Guidance** [تَصْنيف أَفْلامٍ يَنْصَحُ بِرَقابةٍ أَبَويّةٍ (لاحْتِواءِ الفيلْمِ على مَشاهِدَ قد لا تُناسِبُ الأَطْفالَ)]

PGCE /piːdʒiːsiː'iː/ *n* (BrE) = **Postgraduate Certificate of Education** شَهادة الدِراساتِ العُلْيا في التَعْليمِ

phantom /'fantəm/ **A** *n* (ghost) شَبَح (أَشْباح), طَيْف (أَطْياف, طُيوف)

B *adj before n* 1 (ghostly) ‹*ship, army*› شَبَحيّ 2 (imaginary) ‹*pain, pregnancy*› خَياليّ, وَهْميّ

pharaoh /'fɛːrəʊ/ *n* (also **the Pharaoh**) فِرْعَوْن (فَراعِنة)

pharmaceutical /fɑːmə'suːtɪk(ə)l/ *adj* ‹*company, industry, product*› صَيْدَلانيّ, دَوائيّ

pharmaceuticals /fɑːmə'suːtɪk(ə)lz/ *n pl* مُسْتَحْضَرات صَيْدَلانيّة \ دَوائيّة; **the ~ industry** صِناعة المُسْتَحْضَراتِ الصَيْدَلانيّة

pharmacist /'fɑːməsɪst/ *n* صَيْدَليّ (صَيادِلة)

pharmacy /'fɑːməsi/ *n* (*pl* **pharmacies**) 1 (shop) صَيْدَليّة; (dispensary) صَيْدَليّة مُسْتَشْفًى 2 [u] (discipline) صَيْدَلة

pharyngitis /ˌfarɪn'dʒʌɪtɪs/ *n* الْتِهاب البُلْعومِ

pharynx /'farɪŋks/ *n* بُلْعوم (بَلاعيمُ)

phase /feɪz/ **A** *n* مَرْحَلة (مَراحِلُ), طَوْر (أَطْوار)

B *vt* نَفَّذَ على مَراحِلَ ‹*a process, plan*›

(Phrasal verbs) **phase in**: **~ in [sth]**, **~ [sth] in** أَدْخَلَ [شَيْئًا] تَدْريجيًّا ‹*changes, measures*›

• **phase out**: ~ **out** [**sth**], ~ [**sth**] **out** سَحَبَ [شَيْئاً] تَدْريجيًّا ‹*subsidies, old products*›

PhD /piːeɪtʃˈdiː/ *n* = **Doctor of Philosophy** (award) دُكْتوراه; **she is doing/has a ~ in Engineering** تُحَضِّرُ رِسالةَ دُكْتوراه \ تَحْمِلُ شهادةَ دُكْتوراه في الهَنْدَسةِ; (degree holder) دُكْتور

pheasant /ˈfɛz(ə)nt/ *n* (*pl* **pheasants** or **pheasant**) تُدْرُج (تَدارِجُ)

phenomena /fəˈnɒmɪnə/ *n pl* ▸ **phenomenon**

phenomenal /fɪˈnɒmɪn(ə)l/ *adj* ‹*success, increase*› هائِل, ضَخْم

phenomenon /fɪˈnɒmɪnən/ *n* (*pl* **phenomena**) ظاهِرة (ظَواهِرُ)

phew /fjuː/ *excl* أُفّ; **~, I'm glad that's over** أُفّ، أنا سَعيدٌ أنّ ذلك انْتَهى; **~, it's hot today!** أُفّ، الجَوُّ حارٌّ اليَوْمَ!

phial /ˈfʌɪəl/ *n* قِنّينة (قَنانٍ), قارورة (قَواريرُ)

philanderer /fɪˈland(ə)rə/ *n* (fml) زير نِساءٍ

philanthropic /ˌfɪlənˈθrɒpɪk/ *adj* ‹*organization, activities*› خَيْرِيّ

philanthropist /fɪˈlanθrəpɪst/ *n* مُحِبّ الخَيْر, مُحْسِن, فاعِل خَيْرٍ

philately /fɪˈlat(ə)li/ *n* [دِراسة وَجَمْع طَوابِع البَريدِ]

Philippine /ˈfɪlɪpiːn/ *adj* ‹*islands, military*› فِلِبّينيّ

Philippines /ˈfɪlɪpiːnz/ *pr n* (**the Philippines**) الفِلِبّين (f)

philistine /ˈfɪlɪstʌɪn/ *n* [شَخْص لا يُحِبُّ الثَّقافةَ والفُنونَ]

Phillips screw® *n* بُرْغيّ فيليبْس

Phillips screwdriver® *n* مِفَكّ فيليبْس

philosopher /fɪˈlɒsəfə/ *n* فَيْلَسوف (فَلاسِفة)

philosophic /fɪləˈsɒfɪk/ *adj* ‹*question, argument*› فَلْسَفيّ

philosophical /fɪləˈsɒfɪk(ə)l/ *adj* ‹*outlook, attitude*› رَصين (رِصان); **she was quite ~ about the robbery** كانَتْ رَدّةُ فِعْلِها على السَرِقةِ رَصينةً

philosophy /fɪˈlɒsəfi/ *n* فَلْسَفة

phishing /ˈfɪʃɪŋ/ *n* تَصَيُّد (أَحَد أَشْكالِ الاحْتِيالِ الإلكْترونيِّ)

phlebitis /flɪˈbʌɪtɪs/ *n* اِلْتِهاب الأَوْرِدةِ

phlegm /flɛm/ *n* بَلْغَم (بَلاغِمُ)

phobia /ˈfəʊbɪə/ *n* رُهاب, فوبْيا; **to have a ~ about spiders** كانَ لَدَيْه فوبْيا العَناكِبِ

phoenix /ˈfiːnɪks/ *n* عَنْقاء (dipt f)

phone /fəʊn/ **A** *n* هاتِف (هَواتِفُ), تِلِفون (تِلِفونات); **to be on the ~** كانَ على الهاتِفِ; **he put the ~ down on me** أَغْلَقَ الخَطَّ في وَجْهي

B *vt* (also **phone up**) تَلْفَنَ (i; تَلْفَنة; ل), اِتَّصَلَ هاتِفيًّا ب ‹*the police, a helpline*›

C *vi* (also **phone up**) «callers, friends» اِتَّصَلَ هاتِفيًّا; **to ~ for a taxi** اِتَّصَلَ هاتِفيًّا لِطَلَبِ سَيّارةِ أُجْرةٍ; **why didn't you ~?** لِماذا لم تَتَّصِلْ؟

Phrasal verbs **phone in** **1** «employees, listeners» أَجْرى مُداخَلةً هاتِفيّةً; **she ~d in sick** اِتَّصَلَتْ هاتِفيًّا بِمَكانِ عَمَلِها [لِتُبْلِغَ بِأَنَّها مَريضةٌ] **2** ~ **in** [**sth**], ~ [**sth**] **in** أَبْلَغَ [شَيْئاً] عَبْرَ الهاتِفِ ‹*a comment, the answer*›

• **phone up** **1** «callers, listeners» اِتَّصَلَ هاتِفيًّا **2** ~ **up** [**sb/sth**], ~ [**sb/sth**] **up** اِتَّصَلَ هاتِفيًّا ب [شَخْصٍ \ شَيْءٍ] ‹*the bank, help line*›

phone book *n* دَليل هاتِفٍ

phone booth *n* كُشْك هاتِفٍ

phone box *n* كُشْك هاتِفٍ

phone call *n* اِتِّصال هاتِفيّ, مُكالَمة هاتِفيّة

phonecard /ˈfəʊnkɑːd/ *n* (BrE) بِطاقة هاتِفٍ; **a £5 ~** بِطاقة هاتِفٍ بِقيمةِ £5

phone-in /ˈfəʊnɪn/ *n* مُداخَلة هاتِفيّة

phone link *n* رابِط هاتِفيّ

phone number *n* رَقْم هاتِفٍ

phonetic /fəˈnɛtɪk/ *adj* صَوْتيّ; **a ~ alphabet** أَلِفْبائيّة صَوْتيّة

phonetics /fəˈnɛtɪks/ *n sing* عِلْم الصَوْتيّاتِ

phoney /ˈfəʊni/ (infml) **A** *adj* (**phonier**, **phoniest**) (not genuine) ‹*passport*› مُزَيَّف; ‹*accent*› مُصْطَنَع

B *n* (*pl* **phoneys** or **phonies**) **1** (insincere person) مُنافِق **2** (impostor) دَجّال, مُحْتال **3** (forgery) تَزْييف, تَزْوير

phosphate /ˈfɒsfeɪt/ **A** *n* فوسْفات

B (**phosphates**) *n pl* سَماد فوسْفاتيّ

phosphorus /ˈfɒsf(ə)rəs/ *n* فُسْفور

photo /ˈfəʊtəʊ/ *n* صورة (صُوَر)

photo album *n* أَلْبوم صُوَرٍ

photo booth *n* كُشْك تَصْويرٍ

photocall /ˈfəʊtəʊkɔːl/ *n* جَلْسة تَصْوِيرٍ

photocopier /ˈfəʊtəʊkɒpiə/ *n* آلة نَسْخٍ

photocopy /ˈfəʊtəʊkɒpi/ **A** *n* (*pl* **photocopies**) نُسْخة مُصَوَّرة \ ضَوْئيّة

B *vt* (**photocopies**, **photocopying**, **photocopied**) اسْتَخْرَجَ نُسْخةً مُصَوَّرةً من ‹*a document, page*›

photo finish *n* سَبْق ضَوْئيّ

photofit® /ˈfəʊtəʊfɪt/ *n* (BrE) صورة مُرَكَّبة (لِمُشْتَبَهٍ بِهِ)

photogenic /ˌfəʊtəʊˈdʒenɪk/ *adj* ‹*looks, model*› [يَبْدو جَذّاباً في الصُّوَرِ]

photograph /ˈfəʊtəɡrɑːf/ **A** *n* (also **photo**) صورة (فوتوغرافيّة); **take a ~ of me/the procession** اِلْتَقِطْ صورةً لي \ للمَوْكِبِ; **a colour/black and white ~** صورة مُلَوَّنة \ بالأَبْيَضِ والأَسْوَدِ

B *vt* الْتَقَطَ صورةً ل, صَوَّرَ ‹*a wedding, bird*›

photographer /fəˈtɒɡrəfə/ *n* مُصَوِّرٌ

photographic /ˌfəʊtəˈɡrafɪk/ *adj* ‹*equipment, evidence*› فوتوغرافيّ; **she has a ~ memory** لَدَيْها ذاكِرةٌ فوتوغْرافيّةٌ

photography /fəˈtɒɡrəfi/ *n* تَصْوير فوتوغْرافيّ

photon /ˈfəʊtɒn/ *n* فوتون

photo opportunity *n* مُناسَبة للتَصْويرِ \ لالْتِقاطِ الصُّوَرِ

photo session *n* جَلْسة اِلْتِقاطِ صُوَرٍ

photosynthesis /ˌfəʊtəʊˈsɪnθɪsɪs/ *n* تَمْثيل \ تَخْليق \ تَرْكيب ضَوْئيّ

photovoltaic /ˌfəʊtəʊvɒlˈteɪɪk/ *adj* ‹*cell, panel*› كَهْروضَوْئيّ

phrasal verb /ˌfreɪzəl ˈvəːb/ *n* فِعْل مُرَكَّب

phrase /freɪz/ **A** *n* شِبْه جُمْلةٍ, تَعْبير, عِبارة

B *vt* صاغَ (u; صِياغة, صَوْغ) ‹*a question, statement*›

phrase book *n* كِتاب عِباراتٍ

physical /ˈfɪzɪk(ə)l/ **A** *adj* 1 (of the body) ‹*strength, disability, violence*› جُسْمانيّ, جَسَديّ 2 (material) ‹*world*› مادّيّ, مَلْموس; ‹*condition*› فِعْليّ

B *n* فَحْص طِبّيّ

physical fitness *n* لِياقة بَدَنيّة

physically /ˈfɪzɪkli/ *adv* ‹*active, demanding*› بَدَنيًّا, جَسَديًّا; **to be ~ exhausted** كانَ مُرْهَقاً \ مُنْهَكاً جَسَديًّا; **their son is ~ handicapped** ابْنُهُمْ مُعاقٌ جَسَديًّا

physical therapist *n* (AmE) أَخِصّائيّ العِلاجِ الطَبيعيِّ

physical therapy *n* (AmE) عِلاج طَبيعيّ

physical training *n* تَدْريب بَدَنيّ, تَرْبية بَدَنيّة

physician /fɪˈzɪʃ(ə)n/ *n* طَبيب (أَطِبّة, أَطِبّاءُ)

physicist /ˈfɪzɪsɪst/ *n* فيزيائيّ

physics /ˈfɪzɪks/ *n sing* فيزياء

physio /ˈfɪzɪəʊ/ *n* (BrE infml) 1 ▸ **physiotherapist** أَخِصّائيّ عِلاجٍ طَبيعيٍّ 2 ▸ **physiotherapy**

physiological /fɪzɪəˈlɒdʒɪk(ə)l/ *adj* ‹*functions, condition*› فيزيولوجيّ

physiology /ˌfɪzɪˈɒlədʒi/ *n* عِلْم وَظائِفِ الأَعْضاءِ, فِسيولوجيا

physiotherapist /fɪzɪəʊˈθerəpɪst/ *n* أَخِصّائيّ عِلاجٍ طَبيعيٍّ

physiotherapy /ˌfɪzɪəʊˈθerəpi/ *n* (discipline) عِلاج طَبيعيّ

physique /fɪˈziːk/ *n* بِنْية جَسَديّة \ جُسْمانيّة

pianist /ˈpɪənɪst/ *n* عازِف بيانو

piano /pɪˈanəʊ/ *n* (*pl* **pianos**) بيانو (بيانوهات)

pic /pɪk/ *n* (infml) 1 (movie) فيلم سينمائيّ 2 (photo) صورة (صُوَر)

piccolo /ˈpɪkələʊ/ *n* بيكُلو (فْلوت من الحَجْمِ الصَغيرِ)

pick /pɪk/ **A** *vt* 1 (to select) انْتَقى, اخْتارَ ‹*a player, card, winner*›; **~ any card from the pack** اِخْتَرْ أَيَّ بِطاقةٍ من الحُزْمةِ; **to be ~ed to play for the first team** أُخْتيرَ للَّعِبِ في الفريقِ الأَوَّلِ; **you ~ed the right candidate** اخْتَرْتَ المُرَشَّحَ الصَحيحَ 2 (to go carefully) **to ~ one's way through the rubble/mines** تَلَمَّسَ طَريقَهُ بين الأَنْقاضِ \ الأَلْغامِ 3 (to gather) قَطَفَ (i; قَطْف, قُطوف) ‹*fruit, flowers*›; **it's time to ~ the strawberries** حانَ وَقْتُ قَطْفِ الفَراوْلةِ 4 **to ~ a fight/quarrel with sb** افْتَعَلَ شِجاراً مع شَخْصٍ 5 (to scratch) حَكَّ (u; حَكّ), نَكَشَ \ نَبَشَ (u; هَرْش) هَرَشَ ‹*a spot, scab*›; **to ~ one's nose** أَنْفَهُ; **to ~ one's teeth** خَلَّلَ أَسْنانَهُ 6 «thief» سَرَقَ (i; سَرِقة) ‹*a lock, safe*›; **to ~ sb's pocket** سَرَقَ \ نَشَلَ جَيْبَ شَخْصٍ

B *vi* (to select) انْتَقى, اخْتارَ; **you can't afford to ~ and choose** لَيْسَ بِمَقْدورِكَ أَنْ تَنْتَقِيَ ما يَروقُ لَكَ

C *n* 1 (for digging) مِعْوَل (مَعاوِلُ) 2 (choice) اخْتِيار; **take your ~** اخْتَرْ واحِداً 3 (best) أَفْضَل; **the ~ of the crop** أَفْضَل المَحْصولِ; **the ~ of the week's programmes** أَفْضَل بَرامِجِ الأُسْبوعِ

Idiom **to pick up the bill** دَفَعَ الفاتورةَ

Phrasal verbs **pick at** **A** **~ at** [**sth**] 1 أَكَلَ قليلاً من [شَيْءٍ] *‹the grain, crumbs›* 2 أَكَلَ من [شَيْءٍ] بِدونِ شَهِيَّةٍ *‹one's food›* 3 حَكَّ [شَيْئاً] *‹a spot, scab›* **B** **~ at** [**sb**] (AmE) ▸**pick on**

• **pick off**: 1 **~** [**sth**] **off sth** قَطَفَ [شَيْئاً] من شَيْءٍ *‹an apple, the dates›* 2 **~** [**sb**] **off**, **~ off** [**sb**] (to kill) «snipers, gunmen» قَتَلَ [شَخْصاً] *‹an enemy›*

• **pick on**: **~ on** [**sb**] (to victimize) ضايَقَ [شَخْصاً] *‹a younger brother›*

• **pick out**: **~** [**sb/sth**] **out**, **~ out** [**sb/sth**] 1 (to select) انْتَقى [شَخْصاً \ شَيْئاً] *‹the best, a winner, an article›*; **to be ~ed out in red/bold** أُبْرِزَ \ مُيِّزَ باللَوْنِ الأَحْمَرِ \ بالخطِّ السَميكِ 2 (to identify) *‹a suspect, landmark, person in crowd›*; تَعَرَّفَ على [شَخْصٍ \ شَيْءٍ]

• **pick over**: **~** [**sth**] **over**, **~ over** [**sth**] (to examine) تَفَحَّصَ [شَيْئاً] *‹the clothes, items on display›*

• **pick up** **A** **~ up** 1 (to improve) «business, weather, health» تَحَسَّنَ 2 (to resume) اسْتَأْنَفَ; **to pick up (from) where one left off** اسْتَأْنَفَ من حَيْثُ تَوَقَّفَ **B** **~** [**sb/sth**] **up**, **~ up** [**sb/sth**] 1 (to lift) الْتَقَطَ \ حمَلَ [شَخْصاً \ شَيْئاً] *‹one's clothes, a child, letter›*; **to ~ up the receiver** التَقطَ \ رَفَعَ سَمّاعةَ الهاتِفِ 2 (to collect) الْتَقطَ \ أَخذَ [شَخْصاً \ شَيْئاً] *‹a passenger, cargo, the tickets›*; **could you ~ me up from the station?** هل يُمْكِنُكَ أنْ تُقِلَّني بِسَيّارَتِكَ من المَحطّةِ؟ **C** **~** [**sth**] **up**, **~ up** [**sth**] 1 (to learn) «person» اكْتَسَبَ \ تَعَلَّمَ [شَيْئاً] *‹a language, an accent, a habit›*; **I'm hoping to ~ up some tips** آمُلُ أنْ أَتَعَلَّمَ بَعْضَ الإرْشاداتِ; **it's not difficult, you'll soon ~ it up** هو لَيْسَ صَعْباً، سَتَتَعَلَّمُهُ بِسُرْعةٍ 2 (to catch) «animal, person» أُصيبَ ب [شَيْءٍ] *‹a cold, bug›* 3 (to detect) الْتَقطَ \ اسْتَقْبَلَ [شَيْئاً] *‹a signal, an aircraft›* 4 (to gain) «participant» حَصَلَ على [شَيْءٍ] *‹a point, qualifications›* **D** **~** [**sb**] **up**, **~ up** [**sb**] 1 (to arrest) أَلْقى القَبْضَ على [شَخْصٍ] *‹a suspect, spy›* 2 (infml) (to meet) أَقامَ عَلاقةً مع [شَخْصٍ] *‹a girl, boy›* **E** **~ oneself up** (to recover) «company, patient» تَعافى، اسْتَعادَ عافِيَتَهُ

pickaxe (BrE), **pickax** (AmE) /ˈpɪkaks/ *n* مِعْوَل (مَعاوِلُ)

picket /ˈpɪkɪt/ **A** *n* اعْتِصام (اعْتِصامات) **B** *vt* اعْتَصَمَ أمامَ *‹an office, factory›*

pickings /ˈpɪkɪŋz/ *n pl* أَرْباح

pickle /ˈpɪk(ə)l/ **A** *n* 1 [u] (sauce) مُخَلَّل; **cheese and ~** جُبْن ومُخَلَّل 2 (AmE) (gherkin) خِيار مُخَلَّل **B** *vt* خَلَّلَ *‹cabbage, beetroot›*

pick-me-up /ˈpɪkmiʌp/ *n* (infml) [شَيْء مُنْعِش \ مُنَشِّط]

pickpocket /ˈpɪkpɒkɪt/ *n* نَشّال; **beware of ~s** احْتَرِسْ من النَشّالينَ

pickup /ˈpɪkʌp/ *n* 1 (vehicle) ▸**pickup truck** 2 (stop) مَحَطّة 3 (increase) انْتِعاش (انْتِعاشات); **a ~ in the housing market** انْتِعاش في سوقِ العَقارِ 4 (infml) (partner) [شَخْص يَتِمُّ التَعَرُّفُ عَلَيْهِ لِإقامةِ عَلاقةٍ عابرةٍ]

pickup truck *n* [شاحِنة صَغيرة مَفْتوحة من الخَلْفِ]

picky /ˈpɪki/ *adj* (**pickier**, **pickiest**) (infml) *‹eater, shopper›* نَيِّق، صَعْبُ الإرْضاءِ

picnic /ˈpɪknɪk/ **A** *n* (meal) [وَجْبة في الهَواءِ الطَلْقِ]; **to go for/on a ~** [خَرَجَ لِتَناوُلِ الطَعامِ في الهَواءِ الطَلْقِ]; **a ~ lunch** غَداء في الهَواءِ الطَلْقِ **B** *vi* [تَناوَلَ وَجْبَتَهُ في الهَواءِ الطَلْقِ]

Idiom **it's no picnic!** هو لَيْسَ بالأَمْرِ الهَيِّنِ!

pictorial /pɪkˈtɔːrɪəl/ *adj* (in pictures) *‹representation, history›* تَصْويريّ

picture /ˈpɪktʃə/ **A** *n* 1 صورة (صُوَر); **to draw/paint a ~ of sb/sth** رَسَمَ صورةً لِشَخْصٍ \ لِشَيْءٍ; **to paint sb's ~** رَسَمَ لَوْحةً لِشَخْصٍ 2 (photograph) صورة (فوتوغْرافيّة); **to take a ~ of sb/sth** الْتَقَطَ صورةً لِشَخْصٍ \ شَيْءٍ 3 (in the mind) صورة (صُوَر) 4 (impression) صورة (صُوَر); **he paints a gloomy ~ of the future** يَرْسُمُ صورةً كَئيبةً للمُسْتَقْبَلِ; **to give a clear ~ of sth** أَعْطى صورةً واضِحةً عن شَيْءٍ 5 (situation) صورة (صُوَر)، وَضْع (أَوْضاع); **the ~ is very different in the UK** الصورةُ مُخْتَلِفةٌ جِدًّا في المَمْلَكةِ المُتَّحِدةِ 6 (movie) فيلْم (أَفْلام) 7 (TV image) صورة (صُوَر) **B** (**pictures**) *n pl* (BrE) (infml) **to go to the ~s** ذَهَبَ إلى السينَما **C** *vt* 1 (to represent) صَوَّرَ *‹a person, place›*; **the winners (~d above) each receive £5,000** اسْتَلَمَ كُلُّ واحِدٍ من المُتَسابِقينَ

في الصورة أعلاهُ) 5000 جُنَيْهٍ); **rich men were often ~d as fat** تَصَوَّرَ كانَ يَتِمُّ تَصْويرُ الأثْرِياء على أنَّهُمْ بُدَناءُ **2** (to imagine) *<the scene, sb's face>*

(Idioms) **to be/look the picture of health** كانَ في كامِلِ الصِحّةِ والعافِيةِ; **to get the picture** (infml) فَهِمَ الصورةَ; **to put sb in the picture** وَضَعَ شَخْصاً في الصورة

picture frame *n* إطار صورةٍ \ لَوْحةٍ

picture framer *n* [صانِعُ بَراويزَ \ إطاراتِ صُوَرٍ]

picture hook *n* عَلّاقة \ مِعْلاق صُوَرٍ

picture postcard *n* بِطاقة بَريديّة مُصَوَّرة

picturesque /ˌpɪktʃəˈrɛsk/ *adj* *<village, setting>* خَلّاب, بَديع

pie /pʌɪ/ *n* فَطيرة (فَطائِرُ); **a meat ~** فَطيرة لَحْمٍ

piece /piːs/ **A** *n* **1** (portion of paper, rope, bread) قِطْعة (قِطَع); **the vase lay in ~s** تَناثَرَت المِزْهَريّةُ قِطَعاً على الأَرْضِ; **to fall to ~s** «building» تَداعى; «furniture» اهْتَرَأَ; «argument, marriage» انْهارَ **2** (unit) **a ~ of furniture** قِطْعة أثاثٍ; **a ~ of advice** نَصيحة (نَصائِحُ); **a ~ of information** مَعْلومة; **a ~ of legislation** تَشْريع (تَشْريعات); **a compass is an essential ~ of equipment** البَوْصَلةُ قِطْعةٌ أساسيّةٌ من العُدّةِ; **a ~ of land** قِطْعة أَرْضٍ; **his latest film is a fine ~ of work** فيلْمُهُ الأخيرُ تُحْفةٌ فَنّيّةٌ رائِعةٌ **3** (of a jigsaw, machine, model) قِطْعة (قِطَع); **~ by ~** قِطْعةً قِطْعةً; **to take sth to ~s** فَكَّكَ شَيْئاً **4** (instance) **a superb ~ of acting** لَقْطة تَمْثيلٍ رائِعة; **a superb ~ of engineering** قِطْعة هَنْدَسيّة رائِعة; **a ~ of luck** ضَرْبة حَظٍّ; **the script is a brilliant ~ of writing** السيناريو قِطْعةٌ أدَبيّةٌ بَديعةٌ **5** (of music) قِطْعة (قِطَع); (article) مَقالة **6** (coin) قِطْعة; **a 50c ~** قِطْعة فِئة 50 سِنْتاً **7** (in chess, draughts) قِطْعة (قِطَع), حَجَر (أَحْجار), حِجارة **8** (AmE) (infml) (gun) مُسَدَّس (مُسَدَّسات)

B (**-piece**) *in combination* **a 60-~ cutlery set** طاقِم أدَواتِ مائِدةٍ من 60 قِطْعةً; **a 5-~ band** فِرْقة موسيقيّة من خَمْسةِ عازِفينَ

(Idioms) **to give sb a piece of one's mind** لَقَّنَ شَخْصاً دَرْساً لن يَنْساهُ; **to go to pieces** خارَتْ قُواهُ; **in one piece** *<person, object>* سالِم; **to pick up the pieces** اِسْتَجْمَعَ قُواهُ; **to say one's piece** أدْلى بِدَلْوِهِ ▸ **action, cake**

(Phrasal verb) **piece together**: **~ [sth] together, ~ together [sth]** **1** رَبَطَ [شَيْئاً] مَعاً *<fragments>* **2** جَمَعَ [شَيْئاً] *<the evidence, events>*

piecemeal /ˈpiːsmiːl/ **A** *adj* *<approach, development>* [تَدْريجيّ وغَيْر مُنْتَظِمٍ] **B** *adv* *<to evolve, plan>* على مَراحِلَ غَيْرِ مُنْتَظِمةٍ

piecework /ˈpiːswəːk/ *n* عَقْد مُقاوَلةٍ; **to be on ~** [حَصَلَ على أَجْرٍ مُقابِلَ العَمَلِ المُنْجَزِ]

pie chart *n* رَسْم بَيانيّ دائِريّ

pier /pɪə/ *n* **1** (for ships) رَصيف (أَرْصِفة) **2** (support) دِعامة (دَعائِمُ, دِعامات)

pierce /pɪəs/ *vt* (to make a hole in) ثَقَبَ (u; ثَقْب), اخْتَرَقَ *<the armour, walls>*; **the shells can ~ the armour of any tank** يُمْكِنُ للقَذائِفِ أنْ تَخْتَرِقَ أيَّ مُدَرَّعةٍ; **she's had her ears ~d** ثَقَبَتْ أُذُنَيْها

piercing /ˈpɪəsɪŋ/ *adj* (penetrating) *<look>* نافِذ, ثاقِب; *<scream>* حادّ; *<wind>* صَرْصَر, عاتٍ

piety /ˈpʌɪəti/ *n* تَقْوى (f), وَرَع

pig /pɪg/ **A** *n* **1** (animal) خِنْزير (خَنازيرُ); **to keep ~s** رَبّى الخَنازيرَ **2** (infml) (glutton) خِنْزير (خَنازيرُ); **to eat like a ~** أَكَلَ بِشَراهةٍ; **to make a ~ of oneself** أكَلَ حتّى التُخْمةِ; **you ~!** أنْتَ خِنْزيرٌ! **3** (Tech) خِنْزيرة أنابيبَ **4** (BrE infml) (task) **this is a real ~ to do!** [هذه مُهِمّةٌ يَصْعُبُ إنْجازُها]

B *v refl* **to ~ oneself** (infml) أَتْخَمَ نَفْسَهُ

(Phrasal verb) **pig out** (infml) أَكَلَ حتّى التُخْمةِ

pigeon /ˈpɪdʒɪn/ *n* حَمام (n coll; حَمائِمُ, حَمامات)

pigeonhole /ˈpɪdʒɪnhəʊl/ **A** *n* [صُنْدوق بَريدٍ مَفْتوح (داخِلَ مَقَرِّ العَمَلِ)]

B *vt* صَنَّفَ *<a character, style>*; **I mistakenly ~d him as a troublemaker** صَنَّفْتُهُ بالخَطَأِ بِأنَّهُ مُشاغِبٌ

pigeon-toed /ˈpɪdʒ(ə)ntəʊd/ *adj* *<child, walk>* [بِقَدَمَيْنِ مُلْتَوِيَتَيْنِ \ حَنْفاوَيْنِ]

piggy /ˈpɪgi/ **A** *n* (*pl* **piggies**) خِنْزير (خَنازيرُ)

B *adj* (infml) *before n* *<eyes, face>* يُشْبِهُ الخِنْزيرَ

piggyback /ˈpɪgɪbak/ *n* (infml) حَمْل على الظَهْرِ والكَتِفَيْنِ; **to give sb a ~** حَمَلَ شَخْصاً على الظَهْرِ والكَتِفَيْنِ

piggy bank *n* حَصّالة

pig-headed /pɪg'hedɪd/ *adj* ‹*stubbornness*› أَحْمَق (f حَمْقى); ‹*fool*› عَنيد جِدًّا

piglet /'pɪglət/ *n* خِنَّوص (خَنانيص)، خِنْزير صَغير

pigment /'pɪgmənt/ *n* خِضاب، صِبْغ (أَصْباغ)

pigmentation /pɪgmən'teɪʃ(ə)n/ *n* اصْطِباغ، تَخَضُّب

pigmy ▸ **pygmy**

pigpen /'pɪgpen/ *n* (AmE) ▸ **pigsty**

pigskin /'pɪgskɪn/ *n* جِلْد خِنْزيرٍ مَدْبوغ

pigsty /'pɪgstʌɪ/ *n* (*pl* **pigsties**) **1** (for pigs) حَظيرة \ زَريبة خنازير **2** (infml) (untidy place) [مَكان قَذِر \ غَيْر مُرَتَّب]

pigtail /'pɪgteɪl/ *n* (plaits) ضَفيرة (في مُؤَخَّرة الرَّأْسِ); (bunches) [ضَفيرة على جانِبِ الرَّأْسِ]

pike /pʌɪk/ *n* (*pl* **pike**) سَمَك الكَراكيّ

Pilates /pɪ'lɑːtiːz/ *n* بيلاتس (نظام تَمارينِ اللِياقة البَدَنِيّة)

pilchard /'pɪltʃəd/ *n* سَرْدين

pile /pʌɪl/ **A** *n* **1** (heap) كُوْم (أَكْوام)، كُدْس (أَكْداس); **in a ~** مُكَوَّماً \ مُكَدَّساً **2** (infml) (large amount) كَثير; **I have ~s or a ~ of work to do** عِنْدي عَمَلٌ كَثيرٌ لأَفْعَلَهُ \ لأُنْجِزَهُ; **to have ~s of money** كانَ عِنْدَهُ أَكْوامٌ من المال **3** (of carpets, velvet) زِئْبَر، وَبَر (أَوْبار) **4** (post, pillar) عَمود (أَعْمِدة) **5** (infml) (building) مَجْموعة بِناياتٍ ضَخْمةٍ **6** (Elec) بَطّارِيّة

B (**piles**) *n pl* (Med) بَواسير

C *vt* كَدَّسَ، كَوَّمَ ‹*the books, bodies*›; **a plate ~d high with cakes** طَبَق بِهِ كَوْمةٌ كَبيرةٌ من الكَعْكِ

D *vi* (infml) **1** (to get in) **to ~ into a car/bus** تَكَدَّسَ داخِلَ سَيّارةٍ \ حافِلةٍ **2** (to crash) **to ~ into sth** اصْطَدَمَ بِشَيْءٍ

Phrasal verbs **pile in** (infml) تَكَدَّسَ (في)

• **pile on**: **~ [sth] on, ~ on [sth]** (infml) كَثَّفَ [شَيْئاً]; **to ~ on the pressure** كَثَّفَ الضَغْطَ

• **pile up** **A** **1** «snow, rubbish» تَكَدَّسَ، تَكَوَّمَ **2** «bills, evidence, work» تَكَدَّسَ، تَكَوَّمَ **B** **~ [sth] up, ~ up [sth]** كَوَّمَ \ كَدَّسَ [شَيْئاً] ‹*snow, dishes*›

pile-up /'pʌɪlʌp/ *n* [تَصادُم عِدّةِ مَرْكَباتٍ]

pilfer /'pɪlfə/ **A** *vt* سَرَقَ (i; سَرِقة) ‹*stationery, parts*›

B *vi* «employees, shoppers» سَرَقَ (i; سَرِقة)، اخْتَلَسَ

pilfering /'pɪlfərɪŋ/ *n* سَرِقة، اخْتِلاس (اخْتِلاسات)

pilgrim /'pɪlgrɪm/ *n* حاجّ (حُجّاج، حَجيج); **a ~ to Mecca** حاجّ إلى مَكّةَ

pilgrimage /'pɪlgrɪmɪdʒ/ *n* حَجّ (حَجّات، حِجَج); **to perform the ~ to Mecca** حَجَّ إلى مَكّةَ

pill /pɪl/ *n* **1** (tablet) حَبّة (حُبوب) **2** ((contraceptive) **the pill**) حَبّة مَنْعِ الحَمْلِ; **to be on the ~** تناوَلَ حُبوبَ مَنْعِ الحَمْلِ

pillage /'pɪlɪdʒ/ **A** *vt* سَلَبَ (u; سَلْب)، نَهَبَ (a-u; نَهْب) ‹*the countryside, village*›

B *vi* «looters» سَلَبَ (u; سَلْب)، غَنِمَ (a; غُنْم، غَنيمة)

pillar /'pɪlə/ *n* **1** (of a building) عَمود (أَعْمِدة)، دِعامة (دِعامات) **2** (رَكيزة (رَكائِزُ)، دَعائِمُ); **the Five P~s of Islam** أَرْكان الإِسْلامِ الخَمْسة

pillar box *n* (BrE) صُنْدوق بَريدٍ عُموميّ

pillion /'pɪljən/ **A** *n* (also **pillion seat**) [مَقْعَد خَلْفيّ لِدَرّاجةٍ نارِيّةٍ]

B *adv* **to ride ~** [رَكِبَ في المَقْعَدِ الخَلْفيّ لِدَرّاجةٍ نارِيّةٍ]

pillory /'pɪləri/ **A** *n* (*pl* **pillories**) [أَداة تَعْذيبٍ خَشَبيّة لِتَكْبيلِ الرَّأْسِ واليَدَيْنِ (في وَضْعِيّةِ الوُقوفِ)]

B *vt* (**pillories, pillorying, pilloried**) اسْتَهْزَأَ عَلَناً ب ‹*sb's methods, views*›

pillow /'pɪləʊ/ *n* وِسادة (وِسادات، وَسائِدُ)، مِخَدّة

pillowcase /'pɪləʊkeɪs/ *n* غِطاء \ كيس وِسادةٍ

pilot /'pʌɪlət/ **A** *n* **1** (of aircraft) طَيّار; **an airline ~** طَيّار خَطٍّ جَوّيٍّ; **a fighter ~** طَيّار مُقاتِل **2** (of ships) مَلاّح بَحْريّ **3** (radio/TV programme) بَرْنامَج تَجْريبيّ

B *adj before n* ‹*project, study*› تَجْريبيّ

C *vt* **1** (to fly) قادَ (u; قِيادة) ‹*a plane, ship*› **2** (to test) [جَرَّبَ بِشَكْلٍ مَحْدودٍ (قبل تَعْميمِه)] ‹*a scheme, project*›

pilot light *n* **1** (with gas) شُعْلة غازٍ دائمة **2** (with electricity) [ضَوْء يُشيرُ إلى أنّ الجِهازَ في وَضْعِ التَشْغيلِ]

pilot scheme *n* مَشْروع تَجْريبيّ

pimiento /pɪmɪ'entəʊ/, **pimento** /pɪ'mentəʊ/ *n* (vegetable) فُلْفُل أَحْمَر صَغير; [u] (spice) [بَهار \ تابِل من الفُلْفُلِ الأَحْمَرِ]

pimp /pɪmp/ *n* قَوّاد

pimple /'pɪmp(ə)l/ *n* بَثْر (n coll; بُثور)

pimply /ˈpɪmpli/ *adj* (**pimplier**, **pimpliest**) ‹*skin, teenager*› مَليء بالبُثورِ

pin /pɪn/ **A** *n* **1** (for cloth, paper) دَبّوس (دَبابيسُ) **2** (AmE) (brooch, badge) بْروش **3** (in surgery) مِسْمار (مَساميرُ) **4** (of a plug) قابِس (أَقْباس); **a three-~ plug** قابِس ثُلاثيّ **5** (of a grenade) دَبّوس (دَبابيسُ) **6** (in bowling) قارورة ,(قَنانٍ) قِنّينة (قَواريرُ) **7** (in golf) عَلَم (أَعْلام) **8** (for attaching wood, metal) مِسْمار (مَساميرُ)

B (**pins**) *n pl* (infml) (legs) ساقانِ

C *vt* (**-nn-**) **1** (to secure with pins) شَدَّ بِدَبّوسٍ ‹*a hem*›; **there was a note ~ned to the door** كانَ هُناكَ رِسالةٌ على البابِ **2** (to immobilize) شَلَّ الحَرَكةَ ‹*sb's arms, an opponent*›; **to ~ sb against the wall/to the ground** شَلَّ حَرَكةَ شَخْصٍ وَثَبَّتَهُ على الحائِطِ \ الأَرْضِ **3** (to attribute) **to ~ the blame on sb** أَلْقى اللَّوْمَ على شَخْصٍ; **to ~ the crime on sb** أَلْصَقَ الجَريمةَ بِشَخْصٍ ▸ **hope** A1

(Phrasal verbs) **pin down** **A** **~ down [sb], ~ [sb] down** **1** (physically) ثَبَّتَ [شَخْصاً] أَرْضاً **2** (to force to commit) أَلْزَمَ [شَخْصاً]; **to ~ sb down to a date** أَلْزَمَ شَخْصاً بِمَوْعِدٍ **B** **~ down [sth], ~ [sth] down** حَدَّدَ [شَيْئاً] ‹*the cause, meaning*›

• **pin up**: **~ up [sth], ~ [sth] up** **1** شَدَّ [شَيْئاً] بِدَبّوسٍ ‹*a notice, one's hair*›

PIN /pɪn/ *n* (also **PIN number**) = **personal identification number** رَقْم سِرّيّ

pinafore /ˈpɪnəfɔː/ *n* (BrE) **1** (a dress) مَرْيول **2** (an apron) ميدَعة (مَوادِعُ)

pinball /ˈpɪnbɔːl/ *n* [u] لُعْبة الكُرةِ والدَّبابيسِ

pincer /ˈpɪnsə/ **A** *n* مِخْلَب السَّرَطانِ الأَماميّ

B (**pincers**) *n pl* كُلّاب (كَلاليبُ), كَمّاشة

pinch /pɪntʃ/ **A** *vt* **1** (to squeeze) قَرَصَ (u; قَرْص) ‹*sb's arm, bottom*› **2** (infml) (to steal) نَشَلَ (u; نَشْل), سَرَقَ (i; سَرِقة) ‹*a wallet, food*›

B *vi* «shoes, sandals» آلَمَ القَدَمَ (لِأَنَّهُ ضَيِّق)

C *n* **1** (with fingers) قَرْصة; **to give sb a ~** قَرَصَ شَخْصاً **2** (of salt, spice) قَبْصة; **add a ~ of salt** أَضِفْ رَشّةَ مِلْحٍ

(Idioms) **at a pinch** إذا اقْتَضَت الحاجةُ \ الضَرورةُ القُصْوى; **to feel the pinch** مَرَّ بِضائِقةٍ ماليّةٍ

pinched /pɪntʃt/ *adj* ‹*expression, face*› شاحِب

pincushion /ˈpɪnkʊʃ(ə)n/ *n* وِسادة دَبابيسَ, مِدْبَسة

pine /pʌɪn/ **A** *n* (the tree) شَجَرة الصَّنَوْبَرِ; (the wood) [u] خَشَب الصَّنَوْبَرِ

B *adj* ‹*furniture, table*› صَنَوْبَريّ

C *vi* «lovers, exiles» حَنَّ (i; حَنين ,(إلى)), اشْتاقَ (إلى), تاقَ (u; تَوْق ,تَوَقان (إلى)); **the lovers ~d for each other while they were apart** اشْتاقَ العَشيقانِ لِبَعْضِهِما البَعْضَ عِنْدَما كانا مُفْتَرِقَيْنِ

(Phrasal verb) **pine away** «lovers, mourners» الْتاعَ قَلْبُهُ

pineapple /ˈpʌɪnap(ə)l/ *n* أَناناس

pine cone *n* كوز \ حَبّة صَنَوْبَرٍ

ping-pong® /ˈpɪŋpɒŋ/ *n* كُرة \ تِنِس الطاوِلةِ; **to play ~** لَعِبَ كُرةَ الطاوِلةِ

pinion /ˈpɪnjən/ *vt* قَيَّدَ, أَوْثَقَ, كَبَّلَ ‹*sb's arms, body*›

pink /pɪŋk/ **A** *adj* (**pinker**, **pinkest**) ‹*dress, flower*› زَهْريّ, وَرْديّ; **to turn ~ with embarrassment** احْمَرَّ وَجْهُهُ من الإحْراجِ

B *n* **1** (colour) لَوْن وَرْديّ \ زَهْريّ **2** (flower) قَرَنْفُل

pinking shears /ˈpɪŋkɪŋ ʃɪəz/, **pinking scissors** *n pl* مِقَصّ مُشَرْشَر

pin money *n* مَصْروف جَيْبٍ

pinnacle /ˈpɪnək(ə)l/ *n* **1** (on a building) قِمّة مُسْتَدِقّة (بُرْج صَغير مُزَخْرَف) **2** (of a rock) قِمّة (قِمَم), قُنّة (قُنَن, قِنان) **3** (climax) ذُرْوة (ذُرًى), أَوْج

pinpoint /ˈpɪnpɔɪnt/ *vt* **1** (to find) وَجَدَ \ عَيَّنَ بِدِقّةٍ ‹*a location, target*› **2** (to identify) حَدَّدَ بِدِقّةٍ ‹*the cause of sth, a problem*›

pinprick /ˈpɪnprɪk/ *n* وَخْزة دَبّوسٍ

pinstripe /ˈpɪnstrʌɪp/, **pinstriped** /ˈpɪnstrʌɪpt/ *adj* ‹*suit, shirt*› مُقَلَّم, مُخَطَّط

pint /pʌɪnt/ *n* بايْنت (نِصْف لِتْرٍ)

pin-up /ˈpɪnʌp/ *n* **1** (poster) مُلْصَق (لِشَخْصٍ مَشْهورٍ) **2** (person) [شَخْص يَظْهَرُ في مُلْصَقٍ]

pioneer /pʌɪəˈnɪə/ **A** *n* رائِد (رُوّاد)

B *vt* ابْتَكَرَ ‹*a technique, concept*›

pioneering /pʌɪəˈnɪərɪŋ/ *adj* <*work, study*> رياديّ

pious /ˈpʌɪəs/ *adj* **1** (devout) <*person, prayer*> تقيّ (أَتْقِياءُ)، وَرِع (أَوْراع) **2** (sanctimonious) <*platitudes*> مُتَظاهِر بالتَّقْوى

pip /pɪp/ *n* **1** (seed) بَذْرة (بَذْرات) **2** (BrE) **the ~s** (in time signals) [إشارة صَوْتيّة في الراديو تُشيرُ إلى الساعةِ]

pipe /pʌɪp/ **A** *n* **1** (for water, gas) أُنْبوب (أَنابيبُ)، ماسورة (مَواسيرُ) **2** (for smokers) غَلْيون (غَلايينُ)؛ **to smoke a ~** دَخَّنَ الغَلْيونَ **3** (flute) ناي (نايات) **4** (on an organ) أُنْبوب (أَنابيبُ) **B** (**pipes**) *n pl* (bagpipes) مِزْمار القِرْبة، مِزْوَد (مَزاوِدُ) (Tunisia) **C** *vt* **1** (to supply) نَقَلَ بالأنابيبِ <*water, gas, oil*>; **the village now has ~d water** في القَرْيةِ الآنَ ماءٌ جارٍ في الأنابيبِ **2** (to transmit) بَثَّ (i-u; بَثّ) <*music*> **3** (in sewing) [زَيَّنَ الحَواشيَ بالخُيوطِ] <*a cushion, garment*> **4** (in greeting) **to ~ sb aboard** [عَزَفَ على النايِ أو المِزْمارِ عند اسْتِقْبالِ شَخْصٍ]

Phrasal verbs **pipe down** (infml) صَمَتَ (u; صَمْت، صُموت)، هَدَأَ (a; هُدوء)

• **pipe up** صَرَخَ (u; صُراخ)؛ **'I know the answer!' Jake ~d up** أَعرِفُ الجوابَ! صَرَخَ جايك

pipe bomb *n* قُنْبُلة أُنْبوبيّة

piped music /ˌpʌɪpt ˈmjuːzɪk/ *n* [موسيقى خَلْفيّة مُسَجَّلة]

pipe dream *n* أَمَل صَعْب المَنالِ

pipeline /ˈpʌɪplʌɪn/ *n* خَطّ أَنابيبَ

Idiom **to be in the pipeline** كانَ في طَوْرِ التَّخْطيطِ

piper /ˈpʌɪpə/ *n* عازِف مِزْمارِ القِرْبةِ

piping /ˈpʌɪpɪŋ/ *n* **1** (pipes) أَنابيبُ، مَواسيرُ **2** (on clothing, cushions) حَبْل رَقيق مَلْفوف بالنَّسيجِ (لِتَزْيينِ المَلابِسِ \ الوِساداتِ)]

piping hot *adj* <*tea, soup*> حارّ \ ساخِن جِدًّا

pique /piːk/ **A** *n* اسْتِياء (لِسَبَبٍ يَمُسُّ الكِبْرياءَ) **B** *vt* أَثارَ <*sb's interest, curiosity*>

pir /pɪə/ *n* [رَجُل مُسْلِم من الأَوْلِياءِ]

piracy /ˈpʌɪrəsi/ *n* **1** (at sea) قَرْصَنة **2** (of software, music) قَرْصَنة

pirate /ˈpʌɪrət/ **A** *n* **1** (at sea) قُرْصان (قَراصِنة) **2** (of software, music) قُرْصان (قَراصِنة) **B** *vt* [نَسَخَ بِطَريقةٍ غَيْرِ قانونيّةٍ] <*a DVD, software*>

pirated /ˈpʌɪrətɪd/ *adj* <*software, music*> مُقَرْصَن (مَنْسوخ بِطَريقةٍ غَيْرِ مَشْروعةٍ)

pirouette /ˌpɪruˈɛt/ **A** *n* [دَوَران على قَدَمٍ واحِدةٍ] **B** *vi* [دارَ على قَدَمٍ واحِدةٍ]

Pisa /ˈpiːzə/ *pr n* بيزا

Pisces /ˈpʌɪsiːz/ *n* **1** (sign) بُرْج الحوتِ **2** (person) [من مَواليدِ بُرْجِ الحوتِ]

piss /pɪs/ (infml) **A** *n* **1** [u] (urine) بَوْل (أَبْوال) **2** (urination) تَبَوُّل؛ **to have** *or* (AmE) **take a ~** بالَ (u; بَوْل)، تَبَوَّلَ (أَبْوال) بَوْل **B** *vt* تَبَوَّلَ \ بالَ في <*one's pants, the bed*> **C** *vi* «person, animal» بالَ (u; بَوْل) **D** *v refl* **to ~ oneself** بالَ على نَفْسِه

Idiom **to take the piss out of sb/sth** (BrE) سَخِرَ من شَخْصٍ \ شَيْءٍ

Phrasal verb **piss off A** انْصَرَفَ **B ~ [sb] off, ~ off [sb]** أَزْعَجَ [شَخْصاً]

pissed /pɪst/ *adj* (vulg) **1** (BrE) (drunk) سَكْران (dipt; سُكارى، سَكارى) **2** (AmE) (annoyed) مُنْزَعِج، مُتَضايِق

pistachio /pɪˈstaʃiəʊ/ *n* (also **pistachio nut**) فُسْتُق

pistol /ˈpɪst(ə)l/ *n* مُسَدَّس (مُسَدَّسات)

piston /ˈpɪst(ə)n/ *n* مِكْبَس (مَكابِسُ)

pit /pɪt/ **A** *n* **1** (hole) حُفْرة (حُفَر)، بُؤْرة (بُؤَر)؛ (as a grave) قَبْر (قُبور) **2** (mine) مَنْجَم (مَناجِمُ)؛ **to work down the ~** عَمِلَ في المَنْجَمِ **3** (for gravel) مَحْجَر (مَحاجِرُ)، مَقْلَع (مَقالِعُ)؛ **a gravel ~** مَحْجَر \ مَقْلَع حَصى **4** (hollow) تَجْويف (تَجاويفُ)؛ **the ~ of one's stomach** التَّجْويف في مَعِدَتِه **5** (in theatres) مَوْضَع الأوركِسْترا؛ **the orchestra ~** مَوْضَع الأوركِسْترا **6** (in motor racing) **the ~s** حَلْبة الصِيانةِ **7** (for car servicing) حُفْرة الصِيانةِ **8** (AmE) (in fruit) نَواة (نَوًى) **B** *vt* (**-tt-**) **1** (in competition) **to ~ sb against sb/sth** حَرَّضَ \ أَلَّبَ شَخْصاً على شَخْصٍ \ شَيْءٍ؛ **to ~ oneself against sb/sth** تَشَجَّعَ على مُنافَسةِ شَخْصٍ \ شَيْءٍ؛ **to ~ one's wits against sb** نافَسَ شَخْصاً بالحيلةِ والدَهاءِ **2** (to mark) حَفَرَ (i; حَفْر) <*a road, skin*> **3** (AmE) (to remove the stone from) اسْتَخْرَجَ النَواةَ من <*a peach, an olive*>

Idiom **to be the pits** (infml) كانَ أَسْوَأَ مِمّا تَتَصَوَّرُ

pit bull *n* كَلْب بيتْبول

pitch /pɪtʃ/ **A** *n* **1** (BrE) (playing field) مَلْعَب مُعَشَّب; **a football/cricket ~** مَلْعَب كُرةِ قَدَمٍ \ كْرِيكِت **2** (of a note, sb's voice) نَبْرة, نَغْمة (نَغَمات) **3** (degree) دَرَجة; **excitement was at fever ~** كانَتْ الإثارةُ في ذَرْوَتِها **4** (sales talk) دِعاية تَرْويجيّة; **his sales ~ was very convincing** كانَتْ دِعايَتُهُ التَرْويجيّةُ مُقْنِعةً جِدًّا **5** (tar) قُطْران, قار, زِفْت **6** (BrE) (in street trading) مَكان في الشارِعِ يَعْرِضُ فيهِ بائِعٌ مُتَجَوِّلٌ [بِضاعَتَهُ] **7** (in baseball) رَمْيَة **8** [u] (of a roof) انْحِدار (انْحِدارات)

B *vt* **1** (to throw) رَمى (i; رِماية, رَمْي), قَذَفَ (i; قَذْف) ‹*a stone, bag*› **2** (in baseball) رَمى (i; رِماية, رَمْي) ‹*the ball*› **3** (to aim) اسْتَهْدَفَ ‹*a speech, campaign, the publicity*›; **the programme is ~ed at young people** اسْتَهْدَفَ البَرْنامَجُ الشَبابَ; **the exam was ~ed at a high level** وُضِعَ الامْتِحانُ لِيَسْتَهْدِفَ ذَوي المُسْتَوياتِ العالِيَةِ **4** «singers, musicians» ضَبَطَ (i-u; ضَبْط) ‹*a note*›; **to ~ one's voice higher/lower** ضَبَطَ صَوْتَهُ على نَبْرةٍ عالِيةٍ \ مُنْخَفِضةٍ **5** (to set up) **to ~ the tent** نَصَبَ الخَيْمَةَ; **to ~ camp** أَقامَ مُخَيَّماً

C *vi* **1** «riders, passengers» (to be thrown) انْقَذَفَ; **the cyclist ~ed over the handlebars/into the water** انْقَذَفَ راكِبُ الدَرّاجةِ فوق مِقْوَدِ الدَرّاجةِ \ في الماءِ **2** «the boat, ship» تَأَرْجَحَ; **to ~ and roll** تَأَرْجَحَ وتَمايَلَ **3** (in baseball) رَمى (i; رِماية, رَمْي), قَذَفَ (i; قَذْف)

Phrasal verbs **pitch in** (infml) (to join in) «volunteers, the group» مَدَّ يَدَ المُساعَدةِ; **we all ~ed in together** مَدَدْنا كُلُّنا يَدَ المُساعَدةِ

• **pitch into A ~ into [sb/sth] 1** (to attack) اعْتَدى على [شَخْصٍ \ شَيْءٍ] ‹*an opponent, your victim*› **2** (to launch into) بَدَأَ [شَيْئاً] بِنَشاطٍ ‹*the work, a job*› **B ~ [sb] into sth** زَجَّ ب [شَخْصٍ] في شَيْءٍ ‹*a situation, dispute*›

• **pitch out** (infml): **~ out [sb/sth], ~ [sb/sth] out 1** رَمى \ أَلْقى ب [شَخْصٍ \ شَيْءٍ] خارِجاً ‹*a troublemaker, drunk*› **2** تَخَلَّصَ من [شَيْءٍ] ‹*one's belongings, luggage*›

pitch-black /pɪtʃˈblak/, **pitch-dark** /pɪtʃˈdɑːk/ *adj* ‹*night, room*› حالِك (حَوالِكُ)

pitched battle /pɪtʃd ˈbat(ə)l/ *n* مَعْرَكة ضارِية

pitcher /ˈpɪtʃə/ *n* **1** (jug) إِبْريق (أَباريقُ); (BrE) (large clay jug) جَرّة كَبيرة من الطينِ **2** (AmE) (in baseball) رامٍ (رُماة)

pitchfork /ˈpɪtʃfɔːk/ *n* مِذْراة (مَذارٍ)

pitfall /ˈpɪtfɔːl/ *n* خَطَر كامِن \ غَيْر مُتَوَقَّع

pith /pɪθ/ *n* لُبّ (لُبوب)

pithy /ˈpɪθi/ *adj* (**pithier, pithiest**) ‹*comment, style*› موجَز ومُعَبِّر جِدًّا

pitiful /ˈpɪtɪfʊl/ *adj* **1** (arousing pity) ‹*sight, cry*› مُثير للشَفَقةِ **2** (wretched, inadequate) ‹*state, attempt*› مُؤْسِف, يُرْثى لَهُ

pitiless /ˈpɪtɪləs/ *adj* ‹*gaze*› قاسٍ; ‹*tyrant*› عَديم الرَحْمةِ \ الشَفَقةِ

pit stop *n* نُقْطة تَوَقُّفٍ في حَلْبةِ سِباقٍ (لِتَزْويدِ السَيّاراتِ بالوَقودِ)

pitta bread, pitta /ˈpɪtə brɛd/ *n* خُبْز بيتا

pittance /ˈpɪt(ə)ns/ *n* مَبْلَغ زَهيد

pity /ˈpɪti/ **A** *n* **1** (compassion) شَفَقة, إِشْفاق; **to take ~ on sb** أَشْفَقَ على شَخْصٍ **2** (cause for regret) أَسَف; **what a ~!** يا لَلأَسَف!; **it's a ~ that you have to leave** من المُؤْسِفِ أَنَّهُ عَلَيْكَ أَنْ تُغادِرَ

B *vt* (**pities, pitying, pitied**) شَفِقَ (a; شَفَق, على), أَشْفَقَ (على) ‹*a person, an animal*›

pivot /ˈpɪvət/ **A** *n* مِحْوَر (مَحاوِرُ)

B *vi* «door, device» لَفَّ \ دارَ على مِحْوَرٍ; **he ~ed on his heel** الْتَفَّ على كَعْبِهِ

pivotal /ˈpɪvət(ə)l/ *adj* ‹*role, decision*› مِحْوَريّ, بالِغ الأَهَمِّيّةِ

pixel /ˈpɪks(ə)l/ *n* بِكْسِل

pixie /ˈpɪksi/ *n* شَخْصيّة خُرافيّة

pizza /ˈpiːtsə/ *n* بيتْزا

pizzeria /ˌpiːtsəˈriːə/ *n* مَحَلّ \ مَطْعَم بيتْزا

placard /ˈplakɑːd/ *n* (at a demonstration) يافِطة, لافِتة, مَنْشور (مَنْشورات); (on a wall) مُلْصَق (مُلْصَقات), إِعْلان (إِعْلانات)

placate /pləˈkeɪt/ *vt* هَدَّأَ, اسْتَرْضى ‹*one's critics, the public*›

place /pleɪs/ **A** *n* **1** (location, position) مَكان (أَمْكِنة, أَماكِنُ); **your ~ of birth/work** مَكان وِلادَتِكَ \ عَمَلِكَ; **her leg was broken in several ~s** كانَت ساقُها مَكْسورةً في أَماكِنَ عَديدةٍ;

to move from ~ to ~ انْتَقَلَ من مَكانٍ إلى مَكانٍ; **is this the right ~?** هل هذا هو المَكانُ الصَحيحُ؟; **to be in the right ~ at the right time** كانَ في المَكانِ المُناسِبِ في الوَقْتِ المُناسِبِ; **to lose/find one's ~** فَقَدَ \ وَجَدَ مَكانَهُ **2** (infml) (town, hotel, etc) مَكان (أَماكِنُ, أَمْكِنة); **a good ~ to eat** مَكان جَيِّد للأَكْلِ; **there isn't much to do in this ~** لَيْسَ هُناكَ الكَثيرُ لِنَفْعَلَهُ في هذا المَكانِ; **a little ~ called Kingsthorpe** مَكان صَغير يُدْعى كينْغسْثورْب; **to be seen in all the right ~s** تَواجَدَ دائماً في المَكانِ المُناسِبِ; **new houses are going up all over the ~** هُناكَ بُيوتٌ جَديدةٌ في كُلِّ مَكانٍ; **your hair is all over the ~!** شَعْرُكَ مُبَعْثَرٌ! **3** (home) بَيْت (بُيوت); **David's ~** بَيْت دايْفِد; **a ~ by the sea** بَيْت على البَحْرِ; **I want a ~ of my own** أُريدُ بَيْتاً خاصًّا بي **4** (on a bus, at a table, in a queue) مَكان (أَماكِنُ, أَمْكِنة); **to keep a ~ for sb** حَجَزَ مَكاناً لِشَخْصٍ; **I couldn't find a ~ to park** لم أَسْتَطِعْ أَنْ أَجِدَ مَكاناً في المُنْتَزَهِ; **please take your ~s** خُذوا أَماكِنَكُمْ من فَضْلِكُمْ; **to change ~s with sb** تَبادَلَ مَكانَهُ مع شَخْصٍ; **to lay *or* set a ~ for sb** تَرَكَ مَكاناً لِشَخْصٍ **5** (in a team) مَوْقِع (مَواقِعُ); (on a committee) وَظيفة (وَظائِفُ) **6** (on a course) مَكان (أَماكِنُ, أَمْكِنة); **to get a ~ at Cambridge** قُبِلَ في كَمْبْريدج **7** (in competitions, races) مَرْتَبة (مَراتِبُ); **to finish in first/third ~** انْتَهى في المَرْتَبةِ الأولى \ الثالِثةِ; **to take second ~ to sth** جاءَ في المَرْتَبةِ الثانِيةِ بعد شَخْصٍ **8** **in the first ~** في المَرْتَبةِ الأولى **9** (in the correct position) **everything is in its ~** كُلُّ شَيْءٍ في مَكانِهِ; **to hold sth in ~** حافَظَ على شَيْءٍ في مَكانِهِ; **to put a system/procedure in ~** وَضَعَ نِظاماً \ إجْراءً; **to put sb in their ~** عَرَّفَ شَخْصاً قَدْرَهُ **10** (role) مَكان (أَماكِنُ, أَمْكِنة); **to take sb's ~** أَخَذَ مَكانَ شَخْصٍ; **it's not my ~ to tell her** لَيْسَتْ مُهِمَّتي أَنْ أُخْبِرَها; **people like that have no ~ in this organization** ناسٌ كَأولَئِكَ لَيْسَ لَهُمْ مَكانٌ في هذه المُنَظَّمةِ **11** (situation) **in my/his ~** في مَكاني \ مَكانِهِ **12** (AmE) (infml) (unspecified location) **some ~** مَكان ما; **it'll turn up some ~** سَيَظْهَرُ في مَكانٍ ما

B (**out of place**) *adj phr* ‹*remark, behaviour, language*› لَيْسَ في مَحَلِّهِ \ مَكانِهِ; **to look out of ~** «building, person» بَدا خارِجَ المَكانِ, بَدا مُتَناقِضاً; **to feel out of ~** شَعَرَ أَنَّهُ لَيْسَ في مَكانِهِ

C (**in place of**) *prep phr* عِوَضاً عن ‹*a player, material, an object*›; **he spoke in my ~** تَكَلَّمَ بَدَلاً مِنّي

D *vt* **1** (to put carefully) وَضَعَ (a; وَضْع) ‹*a book, glass, one's hand*›; **I ~d the clock/glass on the shelf** وَضَعْتُ الساعةَ \ الكَأْسَ على الرَفِّ **2** (to arrange) وَضَعَ (a; وَضْع) ‹*the cards, chairs, slices*›; **to ~ the cards face down on the table** وَضَعَ الأَوْراقَ مَقْلوبةً على الطاوِلةِ; **to ~ the chairs in a ring** وَضَعَ الكَراسِيَ في شَكْلِ دائِرةٍ **3** (to locate) حَدَّدَ; **to ~ sb in charge of a project** أَوْلى شَخْصاً المَسْؤوليّةَ عن مَشْروعٍ; **to be strategically/awkwardly ~d** وُضِعَ بِشَكْلٍ اسْتراتيجيٍّ \ غَريبٍ; **to ~ sb at risk** وَضَعَ حَياةَ شَخْصٍ في خَطَرٍ; **he is not well ~d to judge** لَيْسَ في إمْكانِهِ أَنْ يَحْكُمَ **4** (to make arrangements for) **to ~ an advertisement in the paper** وَضَعَ إعْلاناً في الجَريدةِ; **to ~ an order for sth** طَلَبَ شَيْئاً; **to ~ a bet on a horse** راهَنَ على حِصانٍ **5** (to attach) وَضَعَ (a; وَضْع) ‹*confidence, reliance, emphasis*›; **I ~d my trust in him** وَضَعْتُ ثِقَتي فيه; **we ~ great emphasis on technical skills** نُؤَكِّدُ كَثيراً على المَهاراتِ التَقْنِيّةِ **6** (to rank) صَنَّفَ, رَتَّبَ ‹*competitor, a company, product*›; **the Kenyan runner was ~d third** احْتَلَّ مَرْتَبةً; صُنِّفَ العَدّاءُ الكينيُّ ثالِثاً; **the merger ~s the company in the top 10** جَعَلَ الانْدِماجُ الشَرِكةَ تَحْتَلُّ مَرْتَبةً في قائِمةِ أَفْضَلِ 10 شَرِكاتٍ **7** (to identify) تَعَرَّفَ (على) ‹*a person, an accent*›; **I can't ~ him/his face** لا أَسْتَطيعُ أَنْ أَتَعَرَّفَ عَلَيْهِ \ على مَلامِحِ وَجْهِهِ **8** (to find a good spot for) وَضَعَ (a; وَضْع) ‹*a child, trainee*›

(Idioms) **to fall *or* fit into place** [أَصْبَحَ واضِحاً]; **to have friends in high places** كانَ عِنْدَهُ مَعارِفُ في مَراكِزَ مُهِمّةٍ; **to take place** [حَدَثَ]

placebo /plə'si:bəʊ/ *n* (*pl* **placebos**) بْلاسيبو, دَواء وَهْمِيّ

place mat *n* مَفْرَش أَطْباقٍ

placement /'pleɪsmənt/ *n* **1** (positioning) وَضْع **2** (also **work placement**) (BrE) تَدْريب عَمَليّ

place name *n* اسْم مَكانٍ

placenta /plə'sɛntə/ *n* (*pl* **placentas** or **placentae** /-ti:/) مَشيمة, خَلاص

placid /'plasɪd/ *adj* ‹*lake, nature*› هادِئ

plagiarism /ˈpleɪdʒ(ə)riz(ə)m/ *n* انْتِحال, سَرِقة أَدَبيّة

plagiarize, -ise (BrE) /ˈpleɪdʒəraɪz/ *vt* انْتَحَلَ ‹*sb's work, an essay*›

plague /pleɪɡ/ **A** *n* **1** (disease) طاعون (طَواعينُ); **one of the ~s which devastated Europe** واحِد من الطَواعينِ الّتي عَصِفَتْ بِأوروبّا **2** (of ants, vermin, etc) جَيْش (جُيوش); **a ~ of locusts/wasps** جَيْش جَرادٍ \ دَبابيرَ **3** (nuisance) إزْعاج; **these tourists are such a ~!** هَؤُلاءُ السُيّاحُ مُزْعِجونَ!; **what a ~ that boy is!** يا لَهُ من مُصيبةٍ ذلك الطِفْلُ!

B *vt* **to be ~d by doubt/pain** بُلِيَ بالشَكِّ \ الألَمِ; **the team was ~d by injury** بُلِيَ الفَريقُ بالإصاباتِ; **the press ~d her with impertinent questions** أَحْرَجَها الصِحافيّونَ بِأَسْئِلةٍ وَقِحةٍ

Idiom **to avoid sb/sth like the plague** تَجَنَّبَ شَخْصاً \ شَيْئاً كَأَنَّهُ مَوْبوءٌ

plaice /pleɪs/ *n* (*pl* **plaice**) سَمَك بْلايس

plaid /plad/ **A** *n* قُماش من الصوفِ مَنْقوش بِمُرَبَّعاتٍ

B *adj before n* ‹*shirt, skirt*› مَنْقوش بِمُرَبَّعاتٍ

plain /pleɪn/ **A** *adj* **1** (simple) ‹*decor, food, living*› بَسيط (بُسَطاءُ); **the decor is ~ and functional** الديكورُ بَسيطٌ ولَكِنَّهُ عَمَليٌّ; **~ cooking** طَبْخ بَسيط; **the food in the hotel is plentiful but ~** الطَعامُ في الفُنْدُقِ كَثيرٌ ولَكِنَّهُ بَسيطٌ; **give me a ~ envelope** أَعْطِني ظَرْفاً عاديًّا; **she wore a ~ blue dress** ارْتَدَتْ فُسْتاناً أَزْرَقَ بَسيطاً **2** (obvious) واضِح; **it's the ~ truth** إنَّها الحَقيقةُ الواضِحةُ; **it's a ~ fact that ...** إنَّها حَقيقةٌ واضِحةٌ أنّ ...; **it was ~ to everyone that he was lying** كانَ واضِحاً للجَميعِ أنَّهُ كانَ يَكْذِبُ **3** (in looks) ‹*woman*› عاديّ; **she's rather ~, but very bright** هي امْرَأةٌ عاديّةٌ نَوْعاً ما ولَكِنَّها ذَكيّةٌ **4** (direct) ‹*language, answer*› واضِح, بَسيط; **in ~ English, this means it's over** هذا يَعْني، بِبَساطةٍ، أنّ كُلَّ شَيْءٍ قد انْتَهى; **at least we got a ~ answer** حَصَلْنا على جَوابٍ واضِحٍ على الأَقَلِّ **5** *before n* (downright) ‹*common sense, laziness, ignorance*› مُجَرَّد, مَحْض; **all you need is ~ common sense** التَفْكيرُ السَليمُ فَقَطْ هو كُلُّ ما تَحْتاجُ إلَيْهِ **6** *before n* (ordinary) **I'm not Dr, I'm ~ Mr Williams** لَسْتُ الدُكْتورَ وِلْيامز، اسْمي بِبَساطةٍ هو السَيِّدُ وِلْيامز **7** *before n* (unflavoured) ‹*rice, yoghurt*› بِدونِ نَكْهاتٍ مُضافةٍ

B *adv* **1** (infml) (completely) ‹*stupid, wrong*› تَماماً; **he's not ill, he's just ~ lazy!** هو لَيْسَ مَريضاً، هو فَقَطْ كَسولٌ تَماماً **2** (directly) **I can't put it any ~er than that** لا أَسْتَطيعُ أنْ أَقولَهُ بِشَكْلٍ أَوْضَحَ من ذلك

C *n* سَهْل (سُهولة, سُهول); **on the ~** في السَهْلِ; **the Great Plains** السُهول الكُبْرى

Idiom **to be plain sailing** كانَتِ الريحُ مُؤاتِيةً

plain chocolate *n* شوكولاتة خالِصة

plain clothes *n pl* مَلابِس مَدَنيّة; **in ~** في مَلابِسَ مَدَنيّةٍ

plainly /ˈpleɪnli/ *adv* **1** (obviously) ‹*wrong, right*› بِوُضوحٍ, بِجَلاءٍ **2** (distinctly) ‹*to see, remember*› بِوُضوحٍ **3** (frankly) ‹*to speak*› بِصَراحةٍ **4** (simply) ‹*to dress, eat*› بِبَساطةٍ

plaintiff /ˈpleɪntɪf/ *n* مُدَّعٍ

plaintive /ˈpleɪntɪv/ *adj* ‹*cry, melody*› نائِح, حَزين

plait /plat/ **A** *n* (BrE) ضَفيرة (ضَفائِرُ), جَديلة (جَدائِلُ)

B *vt* ‹*sb's hair, a mane*› ضَفَّرَ, جَدَّلَ

plan /plan/ **A** *n* **1** (scheme, course of action) خُطّة (خُطَط, خِطَط), بَرْنامَج (بَرامِجُ); **the ~ is to leave at six in the morning** الخُطّةُ هي أنْ نُغادِرَ على الساعةِ السادِسةِ صَباحاً; **everything went according to ~** سارَ كُلُّ شَيْءٍ وِفْقاً للخُطّةِ; **we have a ~ to deal with this problem** لَدَيْنا خُطّةٌ للتَعامُلِ مع هذه المُشْكِلةِ **2** (intention) خُطّة (خُطَط, خِطَط); **my ~ is to visit Europe next year** خُطّتي أنْ أَزورَ أوروبّا السنةَ القادِمةَ **3** (for essays, a books) خُطّة (خُطَط, خِطَط), مُخَطَّط (مُخَطَّطات) **4** (map) خَريطة (خَرائِطُ)

B (**plans**) *n pl* **1** (arrangements) مُخَطَّط (مُخَطَّطات), بَرْنامَج (بَرامِجُ), مَشْروع (مَشْروعات, مَشاريعُ); **what are your ~s for the future?** ما هي مَشاريعُكَ للمُسْتَقْبَلِ؟; **I have no ~s for tonight** لَيْسَ لَدَيَّ ارْتِباطاتٌ اللَيْلةَ; **to make ~s for the wedding/holiday** خَطَّطَ للزَواجِ \ للعُطْلةِ; **... but Paul had other ~s** ... لَكِنَّ بول كانَ عِنْدَهُ خُطَطٌ أُخْرى **2** (Archit) **the ~s** التَصاميم

C *vt* (**-nn-**) **1** (to prepare, organize) ‹*an operation, holiday, one's day*› خَطَّطَ, نَظَّمَ (ل); **he ~ned it so he could leave early** خَطَّطَ لِيُغادِرَ باكِراً; **we ~ned the event down to the last detail** خَطَّطْنا للحَدَثِ حتّى أَدَقِّ التَفاصيلِ; **I rarely ~ my working day in advance** نادِراً ما أُخَطِّطُ مُقَدَّماً لِيَوْمِ عَمَلي

when do you ~ to retire? مَتى تُخَطِّطُ للتَقاعُدِ؟ **2** (to design) صَمَّمَ *‹a kitchen, garden›* **3** (to structure) خَطَّطَ *‹an essay, a book›*

D *vi* (-nn-) «government, organization, management» خَطَّطَ; **to ~ for changes/for an increase** خَطَّطَ لِتَغْييراتٍ \ لِزِيادةٍ; **to ~ on going away** خَطَّطَ للمُغادَرةِ

plane /pleɪn/ **A** *n* **1** (aircraft) طائِرة **2** (tool) فَأْرة, مِسْحاج (مَساحيجُ) **3** (in geometry) سَطْح مُسْتوٍ **4** (also **plane tree**) دُلْب

B *vt* سَحَجَ (a; سَحْج), قَشَطَ (i; قَشْط) *‹wood, edges›*

planet /ˈplanɪt/ *n* كَوْكَب (كَواكِبُ), كَوْكَب سَيّار

planetarium /ˌplanɪˈtɛːrɪəm/ *n* (*pl* **planetariums** or **planetaria**) بْلانِتاريوم (نَموذَج النِظامِ الشَمْسيِّ)

planetary /ˈplanɪt(ə)ri/ *adj* *‹science, exploration›* كَوْكَبيّ

plank /plaŋk/ *n* **1** (of wood) لَوْح (خَشَبٍ) **2** (of a policy, campaign) نُقْطة أَساسيّة

plankton /ˈplaŋkt(ə)n/ *n* عَوالِق

planned /pland/ *adj* **1** *‹attack, change›* مُخَطَّط; *‹visit, meeting›* مُرْتَقَب **2** *‹economy›* مُخَطَّط

planner /ˈplanə/ *n* **1** (of projects) مُنَظِّم, مُخَطِّط **2** (town planner) اخْتِصاصيّ في التَخْطيطِ

planning /ˈplanɪŋ/ *n* **1** (of a project, an event) تَدْبير, تَنْظيم, تَخْطيط **2** (town planning) تَخْطيط

planning permission *n* رُخْصة \ تَصْريح بِناءٍ

plant /plɑːnt/ **A** *n* **1** (Bot) نَبات (n coll), نَبْتة (نَبَتات); **to water the ~s** سَقى النَباتاتِ **2** (factory) مَصْنَع (مَصانِعُ); (power station) مَحَطّة تَوْليدٍ كَهْرَبائيٍّ; **a steel/car ~** مَصْنَع صُلْبٍ \ سَيّاراتٍ; **the car ~ will begin production in …** سَيَبْدَأُ مَصْنَعُ السَيّاراتِ الإنْتاجَ في … **3** [u] (buildings and fixtures) مُنْشَأة صِناعيّة **4** [u] (industrial machinery) آلة صِناعيّة **5** (informer) عَميل (عُمَلاءُ), مُخْبِر

B *vt* **1** «gardener» زَرَعَ (a; زَرْع) *‹a tree, potato, seed›*; **to ~ a field with carrots/wheat** زَرَعَ حَقْلاً بالجَزَرِ \ بالحُبوبِ **2** (to sow) **to ~ doubt/an idea in sb's mind** زَرَعَ الشَكَّ \ فِكْرةً في رَأْسِ شَخْصٍ **3** (to position) زَرَعَ (a; زَرْع) *‹a bomb, explosives›*; **to ~ drugs/a weapon on sb** خَبَأَ مُخَدِّراتٍ \ سِلاحاً في حِيازةِ شَخْصٍ **4** (to place) **to ~ a kiss/kick on sth** قَبَّلَ \ رَكَلَ شَخْصاً

C *v refl* **to ~ oneself between/in front of sth** تَمَرْكَزَ بين \ أمام شَيْءٍ

(Phrasal verb) **plant out**: **~ [sth] out, ~ out [sth]** زَرَعَ [شَيْئاً] *‹seedlings, lettuces›*

plantain /ˈplantɪn/ *n* **1** (fruit) مَوْز الجَنّةِ **2** (plant) نَبات مَوْزِ الجَنّةِ

plantation /plɑːnˈteɪʃ(ə)n/ *n* مَزْرَعة (مَزارِعُ), مَغْرِس (مَغارِسُ)

planter /ˈplɑːntə/ *n* **1** (for plants) أَصيص (أُصُص), حَوْض زُهورٍ **2** (plantation owner) صاحِب مَزْرَعةٍ

plant life *n* عالَم النَباتاتِ

plant pot *n* أَصيص (أُصُص)

plaque /plɑːk/ *n* **1** (on a wall, monument) لافِتة (لَوافِتُ), لَوْحة (أَلْواح) **2** [u] (on teeth) بْلاك (الأَسْنانِ), لُوَيْحة سِنِّيّة

plasma /ˈplazmə/ *n* بِلازْما

plasma screen *n* شاشة بِلازْما

plasma TV *n* تِلِفِزْيون بلازْما

plaster /ˈplɑːstə/ **A** *n* **1** (for walls, ceilings) جِبْس (أَجْباس), جِصّ **2** (also **plaster of Paris**) (for broken bones) جِبْس (أَجْباس); **his leg is in ~** رِجْلُهُ في الجِبْسِ **3** (also **sticking plaster**) (BrE) (for cuts) لَزْقة (لَزَقات)

B *vt* **1** جَبَّسَ, جَصَّصَ, كَلَّسَ *‹a wall, ceiling›* **2** (to cover with) لَطَّخَ *‹one's face, hair›* **3** (to display) أَلْصَقَ *‹a poster, photo›*; **the walls are ~ed with election posters** الحيطانُ مُغَطّاةٌ بِمُلْصَقاتِ الانْتِخاباتِ

plaster cast *n* **1** (for a bone) جِبْس (أَجْباس) **2** (for a sculpture) قالِب من الجِبْسِ

plasterer /ˈplɑːst(ə)rə/ *n* جَصّاص, جَبّاس, مُبَيِّض

plastic /ˈplastɪk/ **A** *n* بْلاسْتيك

B *adj* **1** (made of plastic) *‹bag, bottle›* بْلاسْتيكيّ, من البْلاسْتيكِ **2** (malleable) *‹substance, material›* لَيِّن

plastic bullet *n* رَصاص مَطّاطيّ

plastic explosive *n* مُتَفَجِّر بلاسْتيكيّ

plasticine® /ˈplastɪsiːn/ *n* بْلاسْتيسين (طين لَدائِنيّ)

plastic surgeon *n* جَرّاح تَجْميليّ \ تَقْويميّ

plastic surgery *n* جِراحة تَجْميل

plate /pleɪt/ **A** **1** (dish) صَحْن (صُحون) أوانٍ **2** [u] (dishes) أوانٍ **3** (sheet of metal) صَفيحة (مَعْدِنيّة) مَعْدِنيّة **4** (plaque) لَوْحة رَقْمٍ **5** (number plate) لَوْحة (أَلْواح ,لَوْحات) لَوْحة سَيّارةٍ **6** (illustration) صورة (صُوَر) رَسْم (رُسوم) **7** (in photography) لَوْح (أَلْواح) **8** (in the earth's crust) صَفيحة (أَرْضيّة)

B *vt* طَلى (i; طَلْي)

plateau /ˈplatəʊ/ *n* (*pl* **plateaus** or **plateaux**) هَضْبة (هِضاب)

plate glass *n* زُجاج مُسَطَّح

platelet /ˈpleɪtlɪt/ *n* صُفَيْحة \ لُوَيْحة دَمٍ

platform /ˈplatfɔːm/ *n* **1** (raised level surface) مِنَصّة (مِنَصّات, مَناصُّ) **2** (stage) مِنْبَر (مَنابِرُ) مِنَصّة (مِنَصّات, مَناصُّ) **3** (in rail stations) رَصيف المَحَطّة \ القِطار **4** (for gas, oil) مِنَصّة (مِنَصّات, مَناصُّ) **5** (to express views) مِنَصّة (مِنَصّات, مَناصُّ) مِنْبَر (مَنابِرُ) **6** (manifesto) بَرْنامَج (بَرامِجُ) **7** (for programs) نِظام \ مِنَصّة تَشْغيلٍ

platform shoes *n* أَحْذِية ذات نَعْلٍ سَميكٍ

platinum /ˈplatɪnəm/ *n* بلاتين

platitude /ˈplatɪtjuːd/ *n* كَلام مُبْتَذَل \ تافِه

platonic /pləˈtɒnɪk/ *adj* ‹*relationship, friend*› عُذْريّ, أَفْلاطونيّ

platoon /pləˈtuːn/ *n* فَصيلة (فَصائِلُ)

platter /ˈplatə/ *n* صينيّة (صَوانيّ)

platypus /ˈplatɪpəs/ *n* مِنْقار البَطِّ, خُلْد الماءِ

plausible /ˈplɔːzɪb(ə)l/ *adj* **1** ‹*explanation, argument*› مَقْبول, قابِل للتَّصْديق **2** ‹*liar*› مَنْطِقيّ, مَعْقول

play /pleɪ/ **A** *vt* **1** (for amusement) لَعِبَ (a; لَعِب, لِعْب) ‹*a game*›; **to ~ hide-and-seek** لَعِبَ الغُمَّيْضةَ; **to ~ cards/a computer game** لَعِبَ الوَرَقَ \ على الكُمْبيوتر; **to ~ a joke on sb** مازَحَ \ عابَثَ شَخْصاً **2** (Sport) لَعِبَ (a; لَعِب, لِعْب) ‹*tennis, football, basketball*› **3** (to compete against) لَعِبَ ضِدّ ‹*a friend, rival, team*›; **to ~ chess/tennis with sb, to ~ sb at chess/at tennis** لَعِبَ الشِّطْرَنْجَ \ التِنِس ضِدّ شَخْصٍ; **Manchester United ~ Liverpool tomorrow** سَيَلْعَبُ فَريقُ مانْشَسْتَر يونايْتِد ضِدّ فَريقِ ليفَرْبول غَداً **4** «the selectors» أَشْرَكَ ‹*a player*› **5** (to hit, kick) ضَرَبَ (i; ضَرْب), قَذَفَ (i; قَذْف), رَمى (i; رَمْي), مَرَّرَ الكُرةَ إلى شَخْصٍ ‹*the ball*›; **to ~ the ball to sb** رِماية **6** «musicians» عَزَفَ (i; عَزْف) ‹*a symphony, chord, song*›; **to ~ the guitar/the piano** عَزَفَ على الجيتار \ البيانو; **she ~ed a tune on the clarinet** عَزَفَتْ مَقْطوعةً على الكلارينيت **7** شَغَّلَ ‹*a DVD, CD*›; **we ~ed their latest album** اسْتَمَعْنا إلى أَلْبومِهِم الأَخيرِ; **let me ~ the DVD for you** دَعْني أُشَغِّلُ لَكَ الفيلْمَ **8** «actor» لَعِبَ (a; لَعِب, لِعْب), قامَ (u; قِيام) بـ ‹*a role, part*›; **he ~s a young naval officer** يَقومُ بِدَوْرِ ضابِطِ بَحْريّةٍ شابٍّ **9** (in cards) لَعِبَ (a; لَعِب, لِعْب) ‹*an ace, a king, five*› **10** (Fin) **to ~ the stock market** ضارَبَ في البورْصة

B *vi* **1** (for entertainment) «children» لَعِبَ (a; لَعِب, لِعْب); **to ~ at doctors and nurses** لَعِبَ لُعْبةَ الطَبيبِ والمَريضِ **2** (in amateur way) **to ~ at being a manager/an artist** تَقَمَّصَ صِفةَ مُديرٍ \ فَنّانٍ بِغَرَضِ المِزاحِ **3** (Sport) (to take part) لَعِبَ (a; لَعِب, لِعْب); **have you ~ed yet?** هل لَعِبْتَ؟; **to ~ fair** لَعِبَ بِشَكْلٍ عادِلٍ; **to ~ for one's country** مَثَّلَ بِلادَهُ; **to ~ in goal/on the wing** لَعِبَ كَحارِسِ المَرْمى \ في الجَناحِ; **Egypt ~ against Tunisia tomorrow** سَتَلْعَبُ مِصْرُ ضِدّ تونسَ غَداً **4** (to hit the ball) **to ~ into the net** سَدَّدَ \ قَدَّمَ الكُرةَ نحو المَرْمى **5** «musicians, band, orchestra» عَزَفَ **6** «actors» قامَ بِدَوْرٍ, مَثَّلَ; **she ~s opposite him in 'The Cherry Orchard'** تُشارِكُهُ البُطولةَ في 'بُسْتانِ الكَرَزِ' **7** «music» عُزِفَ; «CDs» انْبَعَثَ الموسيقى

C *n* **1** (drama) مَسْرَحيّة; **a ~ in three acts** مَسْرَحيّة من ثَلاثةِ فُصولٍ; **a radio ~** مَسْرَحيّة إذاعيّة **2** [u] (recreation) **the sound of children at ~** صَوْتُ الأَطْفالِ عند اللَعِبِ; **to learn through ~** تَعَلَّمَ من خِلالِ اللَعِبِ **3** (Sport) [u] **~ starts at 3.15** تَبْدَأُ المُباراةُ الساعةَ 3:15; **the ball is out of/in ~** الكُرةُ خارِجَ \ داخِلَ المَيْدانِ **4** [u] (movement, interaction) **to come into ~** بَدَأَ يَلْعَبُ دَوْراً; **it has brought new factors into ~** جاءَ بِعَوامِلَ جَديدةٍ إلى الساحةِ **5** (move) [سِلْسِلة من الحَرَكاتِ والمُناوَراتِ في لُعْبةٍ] **6** (Ling) **a ~ on words** لَعِب بالكَلِماتِ **7** [u] (movement) خَلْخَلة; **there is too much ~ in the steering** هُناكَ الكَثيرُ من الخَلْخَلةِ في المِقْوَدِ

(Idioms) **all work and no play (makes Jack a dull boy)** رَوِّحْ عن نَفْسِكَ; **to make a play for sb** (infml) [غازَلَ شَخْصاً];

to play for time حاوَلَ أنْ يَكْسِبَ الوَقْتَ; **to play into sb's hands** [تَصَرَّفَ بِشَكْلٍ يَخْدِمُ مَصالِحَ شَخْصٍ]; **to play it cool** (infml) [تَصَرَّفَ بِهُدوءٍ]

(Phrasal verbs) **play along A** (on the piano, guitar, etc) رافَقَ في العَزْفِ **B to ~ along with sb** (to cooperate) نَزَلَ عند إرادةِ شَخْصٍ

• **play around** (infml) ① (to act the fool) عَبِثَ (a; عَبَث) ② (experimentally) **let's ~ around with the dates** [لِنُحاوِلْ أنْ نُعَدِّلَ في جَدْوَلِ المَواعيدِ]; **how much money do we have to ~ around with?** [كم من المالِ عِنْدَنا نَسْتَطيعُ أنْ نَتَصَرَّفَ فيهِ؟] ③ (to fiddle with) لَعِبَ (a; لُعْب, لِعْب), عَبِثَ (a; عَبَث) ‹a paperclip, knife›; **he spent the day ~ around with his computer** قَضى اليَوْمَ كُلَّهُ يَلْعَبُ على الحاسوبِ

• **play back**: **~ [sth] back, ~ back [sth]** أعادَ تَشْغيلَ [شَيْءٍ] ‹a song, tape, video›

• **play down**: **~ down [sth], ~ [sth] down** قَلَّلَ من أَهَمِّيَّةِ [شَيْءٍ] ‹a defeat, disaster, the effects›

• **play off**: **to ~ sb off against sb** وَضَعَ شَخْصاً في مُواجَهةِ شَخْصٍ

• **play on A** «musicians» واصَلَ العَزْفَ; «players» واصَلَ اللَعِبَ **B ~ on [sth]** لَعِبَ على وَتَرِ [شَيْءٍ] ‹sb's fears, prejudices›

• **play out**: **~ out [sth]** مَثَّلَ [شَيْئاً] ‹drama›; عاشَ [شَيْئاً] ‹a fantasy›

• **play up** (infml) **A** (to cause problems) «computers, children, sb's back» [سَبَّبَ مَشاكِلَ] **B ~ up [sth]** بالَغَ في [شَيْءٍ] ‹the dangers, advantages›

• **play upon** ▸**play on** B

play-acting /ˈpleɪaktɪŋ/ *n* مُراءاة

playback /ˈpleɪbak/ *n* تَشْغيل الصَوتِ أو الفيديو

playboy /ˈpleɪbɔɪ/ *n* زير نِساءٍ

play-by-play /ˌpleɪbʌɪˈpleɪ/ *n* (AmE Sport) تَعْليق مُباشِر

player /ˈpleɪə/ *n* ① (in sport, games) لاعِب; **she's a good tennis/chess ~** هي لاعِبةُ تِنِس \ شَطْرَنْجٍ جَيِّدةٌ ② (in music) عازِف

playful /ˈpleɪfʊl/ *adj* ① (boisterous) ‹child, puppy› لَعوب (لَعائِبُ) ② (not serious) ‹remark, punch› هازِل, مازِح

playfully /ˈpleɪf(ə)li/ *adv* ① (boisterously) ‹to dance, chase› على سَبيلِ اللَعْبِ ② (humorously) ‹to wink, punch› على سَبيلِ المُزاحِ

playground /ˈpleɪgraʊnd/ *n* ساحة اللَعِبِ, حَديقة أَطْفالٍ

playgroup /ˈpleɪgruːp/ *n* مَجْموعة اللَعْبِ (ما قبل المَدْرَسةِ)

playhouse /ˈpleɪhaʊs/ *n* ① (theatre) مَسْرَح (مَسارِحُ) ② (toy house) بَيْت دُمًى

playing card /ˈpleɪɪŋ kɑːd/ *n* وَرَقة لَعِبٍ

playing field /ˈpleɪɪŋ fiːld/ *n* مَلْعَب (مَلاعِبُ)

playlist /ˈpleɪlɪst/ *n* قائِمة تَشْغيلٍ

playmate /ˈpleɪmeɪt/ *n* صَديق (أَصْدِقاءُ)

play-off /ˈpleɪɒf/ *n* مُباراة فاصِلة \ حاسِمة

playpen /ˈpleɪpɛn/ *n* قَفَص لَعِبٍ (للأَطْفالِ)

playroom /ˈpleɪruːm/ *n* غُرْفة لَعِبٍ (للأَطْفالِ)

playschool /ˈpleɪskuːl/ *n* (BrE) حَضانة \ رَوْضة للأَطْفالِ

plaything /ˈpleɪθɪŋ/ *n* ① (toy) لُعْبة (لُعَب) ② (person) أُلْعوبة (أَلاعيبُ)

playtime /ˈpleɪtʌɪm/ *n* اسْتِراحة

playwright /ˈpleɪrʌɪt/ *n* كاتِب مَسْرَحِيّ

plaza /ˈplɑːzə/ *n* ① (square) ساحة (ساحات, ساح) ② (AmE) (shopping centre) مُجَمَّع تِجاريّ

plc, **PLC** /piːɛlˈsiː/ *abbr* (BrE) = **public limited company** شَرِكة عُموميّة مَحْدودة (شَرِكة مُساهَمةٍ تُباعُ أَسْهُمُها بالمَزادِ العَلَنيِّ للادِّخارِ)

plea /pliː/ *n* ① (appeal) دَعْوة, الْتِماس (الْتِماسات); **he made a ~ for tolerance and understanding** وَجَّهَ دَعْوةً للتَسامُحِ والتَفَهُّمِ ② (Law) دَفْع; **to enter a ~ of guilty/not guilty** أَقَرَّ بالذَنْبِ \ دَفَعَ بالبَراءةِ

plea bargaining *n* مُساوَمة قَضائيّة

plead /pliːd/ **A** *vt* (*past tense, past participle* **pleaded** or **pled** AmE) ① (to beg, implore) تَوَسَّلَ, تَرَجّى (إلى); **'don't go,' he ~ed** قال مُتَوَسِّلاً: 'لا تَذْهَبْ' ② (to give as an excuse) تَذَرَّعَ, تَعَلَّلَ; **you cannot ~ ignorance as an excuse** لا يُمْكِنُكَ أنْ تَتَذَرَّعَ بالجَهْلِ

B *vi* (*past tense, past participle* **pleaded** or **pled** AmE) ① (to beg, implore) «victims, children» تَرَجّى, الْتَمَسَ; **she ~ed with**

me to buy it for her تَرَجَّتْني أَنْ أَشْتَرِيَهُ لَها; **an injured man ~ing for help** رَجُل جَريح يَلْتَمِسُ المُساعَدةَ ② (Law) **to ~ guilty/not guilty** «defendants, the accused» أَقَرَّ بالذَنْبِ \ دَفَعَ بالبَراءةِ

pleasant /ˈplɛz(ə)nt/ *adj* ① (enjoyable) ‹*surprise*› سارّ; ‹*experience, evening*› مُسَلٍّ, مُمْتِع; ‹*climate*› لَطيف ② (likeable) ‹*person*› لَطيف (لُطَفاءُ, لِطاف), دَمِث (دِماث)

pleasantly /ˈplɛz(ə)ntli/ *adv* ① (enjoyably) ‹*situated, decorated*› بِسُرورٍ, بِشَكْلٍ مُمْتِعٍ, بِشَكْلٍ جَميلٍ; **I was ~ surprised by what I found** كانَ ما وَجَدْتُ مُفاجَأةً سارّةً لي ② (in a friendly way) ‹*to smile, to say, reply*› بِلُطْفٍ

pleasantry /ˈplɛz(ə)ntri/ *n* (*pl* **pleasantries**) مُجامَلة

please /pliːz/ **A** *vt* (to make happy) سَرَّ, أَسْعَدَ (u; سُرور, مَسَرّة); **she is easy/hard to ~** من السَهْلِ \ من الصَعْبِ إسْعادُها; **the results ~d us all** أَسْعَدَتْنا النَتائِجُ جَميعاً
B *vi* ① (to make sb happy) أَسْعَدَ, أَرْضى; **we aim to ~** نَسْعى إلى إرْضائِكَ ② (to like, choose) **do as you ~** افْعَلْ ما تَشاءُ
C *v refl* **to ~ oneself** فَعَلَ ما يَحْلو لَهُ
D *adv* مِن فَضْلِكَ, لو سَمَحْتَ, أَرْجوكَ; **two coffees, ~** كوبانِ من القَهْوةِ من فَضْلِكَ; **tell me if you need anything ~** أَخْبِرْني من فَضْلِكَ إنْ احْتَجْتَ إلى أيِّ شَيْءٍ; **may I borrow the car, ~?, ~, may I borrow the car?** هل يُمْكِنُني أنْ أَسْتَعيرَ السَيّارةَ, من فَضْلِكَ؟; **~ be seated** (fml) تَفَضَّلْ بالجُلوسِ; **~, come in** تَفَضَّلْ بالدُخولِ; **'may I come in?'—'~ do'** (fml) هل أَسْتَطيعُ الدُخولَ؟ 'تَفَضَّلْ'
E (**if you please**) *adv phr* (fml) (in indignation) **he came to the wedding, if you ~!** جاءَ إلى حَفْلِ الزِفافِ, للأَسَفِ!

pleased /pliːzd/ *adj* ① (happy) سَعيد, مَسْرور (سُعَداءُ); **he seemed ~ to see me** بَدا مَسْروراً لِرُؤْيَتي; **I'm so ~ for you!** أنا سَعيدٌ جِدًّا لَكَ!; **~ to meet you** تَشَرَّفْتُ بِمَعْرِفَتِكَ ② (satisfied) راضٍ (رُضاة); **we're ~ with the results** تُرْضينا النَتائِجُ; **she looked very ~ with herself** بَدَتْ وَكَأَنَّها مُعْجَبةٌ بِنَفْسِها

pleasing /ˈpliːzɪŋ/ *adj* ‹*manner*› سارّ, مُريح; ‹*colour, appearance*› مُرْضٍ; ‹*result*› مُحَبَّب للنَفْسِ

pleasurable /ˈplɛʒ(ə)rəb(ə)l/ *adj* ‹*experience, sensation*› سارّ, مُسَلٍّ, مُمْتِع

pleasure /ˈplɛʒə/ *n* ① [u] (enjoyment) مُتْعة, سُرور; **to take ~ in sth** تَمَتَّعَ بِشَيْءٍ; **it gives me great ~ to announce the winner** يَسُرُّني جِدًّا أنْ أُعْلِنَ لَكُمْ عن اسْمِ الفائِزِ; **'thank you!' — 'my ~'** 'شُكْراً!' - 'بِكُلِّ سُرورٍ' ② (source of pleasure) مُتْعة (مُتَع); **it's always a ~ to see her** يُسْعِدُني دائِماً أنْ أَراها ③ [u] (recreation) مُتْعة (مُتَع); **I only read for ~** أَقْرأُ للمُتْعةِ فَقَطْ

pleasure boat *n* قارِب تَنَزُّه

pleat /pliːt/ *n* طَيّة, ثَنْية (ثَنَيات)

pleated /ˈpliːtɪd/ *adj* ‹*skirt, fabric*› مَطْويّ, مَثْنيّ

plebiscite /ˈplɛbɪsɪt/ *n* اسْتِفْتاء (اسْتِفْتاءات)

plectrum /ˈplɛktrəm/ *n* (*pl* **plectrums** or **plectra**) ريشة

pled /plɛd/ (AmE) *past tense, past participle* ▸ **plead**

pledge /plɛdʒ/ **A** *n* ① (promise) تَعَهُّد (تَعَهُّدات); **to give** *or* **make a ~ to do sth** أَعْطى \ قَدَّمَ تَعَهُّداً بِأَنْ يَفْعَلَ شَيْئاً ② (guarantee) رَهْن (رُهون, رُهونات), ضَمان ③ (of one's love, friendship) عُرْبون (عَرابينُ) ④ (donation) تَبَرُّع (تَبَرُّعات) ⑤ (AmE) (in fraternities, sororities) طالِب مُرَشَّح للانْضِمامِ [إلى أَخَويّةٍ]
B *vt* ① (to promise) ‹*allegiance, aid, support*› تَعَهَّدَ; **to ~ to do sth, to ~ oneself to do sth** تَعَهَّدَ بِأَنْ يَفْعَلَ شَيْئاً; **the family has ~d $10,000 to the research fund** تَعَهَّدَت العائِلةُ بِأَنْ تَتَبَرَّعَ بـ $10000 للبَحْثِ ② (to oblige) أَلْزَمَ; **to be ~d to secrecy** أُخِذَ مِنْهُ تَعَهُّدٌ بالسِرّيّةِ ③ (to deposit) ‹*jewellery, valuables, a ring*› رَهَنَ (a; رَهْن) ④ (AmE) (in fraternities, sororities) **to ~ a fraternity/sorority** انْضَمَّ إلى أَخَويّةٍ \ نادي طالِباتٍ

plentiful /ˈplɛntɪfʊl/ *adj* ‹*supply, food*› وافِر, غَزير (غِزار)

plenty /ˈplɛnti/ **A** *pron* ① (more than enough) كَثْرة, وَفْرة; **we have ~ of time/food** لَدَيْنا مُتَّسَعٌ من الوَقْتِ \ وَفْرةٌ من الطَعامِ; **there's ~ to do** هُناكَ الكَثيرُ لِنَفْعَلَهُ ② (sufficient) كِفاية; **that's ~, thank you** هذا كِفايةٌ, شُكْراً
B *adv* بِغَزارةٍ; **there'll be ~ more opportunities** سَيَكونُ هُناكَ المَزيدُ من الفُرَصِ الجَديدةِ

plethora /ˈplɛθ(ə)rə/ *n* وَفْرة, مَزيد; **a ~ of information/choices** قَدْر هائِل من المَعْلوماتِ \ الخِياراتِ

pleurisy /ˈplʊərɪsi/ *n* ذات الجَنْبِ

pliable /ˈplʌɪəb(ə)l/ *adj* **1** ‹*plastic, dough*› طَيِّع ,لَيِّن **2** ‹*person, mind*› (خُضُع) خَضوع ,مَرِن

pliers /ˈplʌɪəz/ *n pl* كَمّاشة

plight /plʌɪt/ *n* مَوْقِف حَرِج ,(مَآزِق) مَأْزِق ,(وِراط) وَرْطة

plimsoll /ˈplɪms(ə)l/ *n* (BrE) حِذاء رِياضةٍ

plinth /plɪnθ/ *n* **1** (of a statue) (قَواعِدُ) قاعِدة **2** (of a column) (قَواعِدُ) قاعِدة

plod /plɒd/ *vi* (**-dd-**) **1** (to walk heavily) «person, animal» مَشى بِخَطَواتٍ مُتَثاقِلةٍ **2** (to work slowly) «student, worker» سارَ بِبُطْءٍ

plodder /ˈplɒdə/ *n* (infml) ≈ كادِح

plonk /plɒŋk/ **A** *vt* (also **plonk down**) طَرَحَ (a; طَرْح), رَمى (i; رَمْي) ‹*a plate, books*›

B *n* (infml) [خَمْر رَخيص وَرَديء]

plot /plɒt/ **A** *n* **1** (conspiracy) (خِطَط ,خُطَط) خُطّة ,مُؤامَرة **2** (of movies, novels, plays) (عُقَد) عُقْدة ,حَبْكة **3** (piece of land) قِطْعة أَرْضٍ

B *vt* (**-tt-**) **1** (to plan) دَبَّرَ ,خَطَّطَ ‹*an attack, a coup*› **2** (on graphs) رَسَمَ (u; رَسْم) ‹*a curve*›

C *vi* (**-tt-**) «terrorists, groups» تَآمَرَ (على); **to ~ against sb** تَآمَرَ على شَخْصٍ

plotter /ˈplɒtə/ *n* **1** (conspirator) مُدَبِّر ,مُخَطِّط ,مُتآمِر **2** (device) راسِمة

plough (BrE), **plow** (AmE) /plaʊ/ **A** *n* (مَحاريثُ) مِحْراث

B (**the Plough**) *pr n* الدُبّ الأَكْبَر

C *vt* **1** (Agric) حَرَثَ (i-u; حَرْث) ‹*the land, a field*›; شَقَّ في ‹*a furrow*› الأَرْضِ بالمِحْراثِ **2** (to invest) **to ~ money into a project/company** اسْتَثْمَرَ أَمْوالاً في مَشْروعٍ \ شَرِكةٍ

D *vi* حَرَثَ (i-u; حَرْث)

(Phrasal verbs) **plough back**: **~ [sth] back, ~ back [sth]** أَعادَ اسْتِثْمار [شَيْءٍ] ‹*the profits, money*›

• **plough into**: **~ into [sth]** **1** (to crash into) اصْطَدَمَ بـ [شَيْءٍ] ‹*a tree, wall, crowd*› **2** (AmE) (with enthusiasm) أَقْبَلَ على [شَيْءٍ] ‹*one's work, a job*›

• **plough through**: **~ through sth** **1** تَقَدَّمَ بِصُعوبةٍ خلال شَيْءٍ ‹*mud, snow*› **2** قَرَأَ شَيْئاً بِصُعوبةٍ ‹*a book*›; قامَ بِشَيْءٍ بِصُعوبةٍ ‹*a task*›

• **plough up**: **~ [sth] up, ~ up [sth]** **1** (to turn over) «farmer» قَلَبَ [شَيْئاً] ‹*a field, the land*› **2** (to make muddy) «vehicles» جَعَلَ [شَيْئاً] موحِلاً ‹*the ground, entrance*›

ploughman (BrE), **plowman** (AmE) /ˈplaʊmən/ *n* (*pl* **-men**) فَلّاح ,(حُرّاث) حارِث

plover /ˈplʌvə/ *n* (*pl* **plovers** or **plover**) قَطْقاط ,زَقْزاق

ploy /plɔɪ/ *n* (حِيَل) حيلة ,(خُدَع) خُدْعة

pluck /plʌk/ **A** *vt* **1** اقْتَطَفَ ‹*a fruit, flower*› **2** نَتَفَ (i; نَتْف) ‹*a chicken*›; **to ~ one's eyebrows** نَتَفَ الحَواجِبَ **3** نَقَرَ (u; نَقْر) ‹*an instrument, strings*›

B *n* إقْدام ,شَجاعة ,جُرْأة

plucky /ˈplʌki/ *adj* (**pluckier**, **pluckiest**) ‹*youngster, performance*› (أَجْرِياءُ) جَريء ,(مَقاديمُ) مِقْدام ,(بُسَلاءُ) باسِل ,(شَجَعة) شُجاع

plug /plʌɡ/ **A** *n* **1** (on appliances) (قَوابِسُ) قابِس; **an electric ~** قابِس كَهْرَبائيّ; **to change a ~** غَيَّرَ قابِساً **2** (socket) مِقْبَس; **a mains ~** مِقْبَس; **he ran the machine off a mains ~** شَغَّلَ الماكينةَ من المِقْبَسِ; **use the ~ in the corridor** اسْتَخْدِمْ المِقْبَسَ المَوْجودَ في الرِواقِ **3** (connecting device) قابِس **4** (in sinks, baths) سِدادة; **to pull out the ~** نَزَعَ وَصْلٍ **5** (for screws) (خَوابيرُ) خابور **6** (stopper) سِدادة; **he removed the ~ from the empty barrel** نَزَعَ السِدادةَ عن البِرْميلِ الفارِغِ **7** (in engines) ▸ **spark plug** **8** (mention) دِعاية; **to give a product a ~ on the early morning show** قَدَّمَ دِعايةً لِمُنْتَجٍ في البَرْنامَجِ الّذي يُبَثُّ في الصَباحِ الباكِرِ **9** (Geol) (also **volcanic plug**) نَصْلة \ سِدادة بُرْكانيّة

B *vt* (**-gg-**) **1** (to block) سَدَّ (u; سَدّ) ‹*a leak, hole*›; **that ~s the gap very well** ذلك يَسُدُّ الفَجْوةَ بِشَكْلٍ جَيِّدٍ **2** (to promote) رَوَّجَ ‹*the show, product*›; **to ~ a record on a programme** رَوَّجَ لِأَلْبوم في \ على بَرْنامَجٍ **3** (to insert) **to ~ an appliance into another one** وَصَلَ \ رَبَطَ جِهازاً بِجِهازٍ آخَرَ; **to ~ the keyboard into the computer** وَصَلَ \ رَبَطَ لَوْحةَ المَفاتيحِ بالحاسوبِ

C *vi* (**-gg-**) **to ~ into a TV/computer** «cable, appliance» أَمْكَنَ تَوْصيلُهُ بالتِلِفِزْيون \ بالحاسوبِ

plug and play *n* التَوْصيل والتَشْغيل

plughole /ˈplʌɡhəʊl/ *n* (BrE) فَتْحة تَصْريفِ المِياهِ

plug-in /ˈplʌɡɪn/ **A** *adj* **1** ‹*appliance*› بِقابِسٍ **2** ‹*software, application*› تَكْميليّ ,مُساعِد ,إضافيّ

B *n* مُلْحَق (مَلاحِقُ)

plum /plʌm/ *n* **1** (fruit) بَرْقوق (n coll), خَوْخ (n coll) (Syria) **2** (also **plum tree**) شَجَرة البَرْقوقِ

plumage /ˈpluːmɪdʒ/ *n* ريش (رياش)

plumb /plʌm/ *vt* **1** (measure) قاسَ (i; قَيْس) ‹*depth*›; سَبَرَ (i-u; سَبْر) ‹*water*› **2** (liter) (explore fully) أَدْرَكَ عُمْقَهُ ‹*soul, mystery*›; **to ~ the depths of despair/bad taste** غارَ في عُمْقِ الأَسى \ جَرَّبَ قِمّةَ الذَوْقِ السَيِّئِ

plumber /ˈplʌmə/ *n* سَمْكَريّ ,سَبّاك

plumbing /ˈplʌmɪŋ/ *n* **1** (system of pipes) سِباكة **2** (installation work) سِباكة

plume /pluːm/ *n* **1** (feather) ريش (n coll; أَرْياش) **2** (cluster of feathers) خُصْلة من الريشِ **3** (of smoke, steam etc.) عَمود (أَعْمِدة)

plummet /ˈplʌmɪt/ *vi* **1** (through the air) «aircraft, bird» هَوى (i; هُوِيّ) **2** (in value, amount) «prices, temperatures» هَبَطَ بِشِدّةٍ

plump /plʌmp/ *adj* ‹*person, tomato, chicken*› بَدين ,مُمْتَلِئ (بُدْن ,بُدُن)

Phrasal verbs **plump for**: **~ for [sth]** (infml) (to choose) اخْتارَ [شَيْئاً] ‹*an option*›

• **plump up**: **~ up [sth]** نَفَضَ [شَيْئاً] ‹*a pillow, cushion*›

plunder /ˈplʌndə/ **A** *vt* **1** (to steal) نَهَبَ (a-u; نَهْب), سَلَبَ (u; سَلْب) ‹*resources, wealth*› **2** (to steal from) سَلَبَ (u; سَلْب), نَهَبَ (a-u; نَهْب) ‹*a country, town*›

B *n* **1** (act of stealing) نَهْب (نهاب), سَلْب **2** (booty) غَنيمة (غَنائِمُ)

plunge /plʌndʒ/ **A** *vt* (to thrust) **to ~ sth into sth** غَرَزَ شَيْئاً في شَيْءٍ; **to be ~d into debt/crisis** كانَ غارِقاً في الدُيونِ \ أَزْمةٍ; **the city was ~d into darkness** كانَت المَدينةُ غارِقةً في الظَلامِ

B *vi* **1** (to fall) «river, roads» انْهارَ; **the plane ~d to the ground** سَقَطَت الطائِرةُ على الأَرْضِ **2** (to dive) «birds» انْقَضَّ; «divers» غاصَ (u; غَوْص), غَطَسَ (i; غَطْس); **the country has ~d into crisis** غَرِقَت البِلادُ في أَزْمةٍ **3** (to fall) «rates, shares, prices» انْهارَ **4** (to embark on) **to ~ into a new venture/job** انْغَمَسَ في مُغامَرةٍ \ وَظيفةٍ جَديدةٍ

C *n* **1** (dive) غَوْص ,غَطْس **2** (fall) سُقوط **3** (in prices, values) انْهِيار (انْهِيارات)

Idiom **to take the plunge** اتَّخَذَ خُطْوةً جَريئةً

Phrasal verb **plunge in** **1** (into water) غَطَسَ (i; غَطْس), غاصَ (u; غَوْص) **2** (into an activity) انْغَمَسَ

plunger /ˈplʌndʒə/ *n* **1** (of syringes, coffee makers, etc) مِكْبَس (مَكابِسُ) **2** (for unblocking pipes) سَلاّكة حَوْضٍ

plunk /plʌŋk/ *vt* (AmE infml) ▸ **plonk**

pluperfect /pluːˈpɜːfɪkt/ *n* صيغة الماضي التامّ

plural /ˈplʊ(ə)rəl/ **A** *adj* ‹*form, noun*› في (صيغةِ) الجَمْعِ; ‹*ending*› الجَمْعِ

B *n* جَمْع (جُموع); **in the ~** في صيغةِ الجَمْعِ; **the noun has a broken ~** للاسْمِ جَمْعُ تَكْسيرٍ

pluralism /ˈplʊ(ə)rəliz(ə)m/ *n* تَعَدُّديّة

plus /plʌs/ **A** *prep* زائِدَ; **6 ~ 7 equals 13** 6 زائِدَ 7 يُساوي 13; **four bedrooms ~ a study** أَرْبَع غُرَفِ نَوْمٍ زائِدَ غُرْفةِ دِراسةٍ

B *adj* **1** (and more) أَكْثَر من; **he is 50 ~** عُمْرُهُ أَكْثَرُ من 50 سَنةً; **it will cost $10,000 ~** سَيُكَلِّفُ أَكْثَرَ من 10000 دولار **2** (infml) (advantageous) ‹*point, factor*› حَسَن ,إيجابيّ; **on the ~ side** من ناحيةٍ إيجابيةٍ

C *n* (*pl* **pluses**) **1** (sign) (also **plus sign**) علامة زائِدٍ **2** (advantage) ميزة; **consider the ~es and minuses of the proposal** خُذْ بِعَيْنِ الاعْتِبارِ إيجابيّاتِ وَسَلْبيّاتِ العَرْضِ

plush /plʌʃ/ *adj* (infml) ‹*hotel, office*› فَخْم ,مُتْرَف

plus-size /ˈplʌssʌɪz/ *adj* ‹*swimwear, clothing*› ذو مَقاساتٍ كَبيرةٍ

Pluto /ˈpluːtəʊ/ *pr n* بْلوتو

plutonium /pluːˈtəʊnɪəm/ *n* بْلوتونيوم

ply /plʌɪ/ *vt* (**plies, plying, plied**) **1** (fml) (to carry on) **to ~ one's trade** مارَسَ مِهْنَتَهُ **2** (to offer) **to ~ sb with drink** زَوَّدَ شَخْصاً بالمَشْروبِ **3** (to work) «boat, bus» سارَ بِانْتِظام ‹*a route*›

plywood /ˈplʌɪwʊd/ *n* أَبْلَكاج ,خَشَب رَقائِقيّ

p.m. /piː'em/ *adv* = **post meridiem**; **at two pm** في الثانِية بعد الظُهرِ; **nine pm** التاسِعة مَساءً

PMS /piːem'es:/ *n* = **premenstrual syndrome** أعْراض ما قبل الحَيْضِ

PMT /piːem'tiː/ *n* = **premenstrual tension** أعْراض ما قبل الحَيْضِ

pneumatic drill /njuː,matɪk 'drɪl/ *n* مِثْقاب هوائيّ

pneumonia /njuː'məʊnɪə/ *n* اِلتِهاب رِئَويّ

poach /pəʊtʃ/ **A** *vt* **1** اصْطادَ بِدونِ تَرْخيصٍ ‹salmon, big game› **2** سَلَقَ (u; سَلْق) ‹an egg›

B *vi* «hunters» اصطادَ بِدونِ تَرْخيصٍ

poacher /'pəʊtʃə/ *n* صَيّاد بدونِ رُخْصةٍ

PO box /pi,əʊ 'bɒks/, **post office box** *n* صُنْدوق بَريدٍ

pocket /'pɒkɪt/ **A** *n* **1** (in garments) جَيْب (جُيوب); **to go through sb's ~s** فَتَّشَ جُيوبَ شَخْصٍ; **he paid for it out of his own ~** دَفَعَ ثَمَنَها من جَيْبِهِ الخاصّ; **prices to suit every ~** أسْعار تُلائِمُ كُلَّ جَيْبٍ **2** (small area) **~s of resistance/ unemployment** جُيوب مُقاوَمةٍ \ أماكِن بِطالةٍ **3** (in snooker, pool) جَيْب (جُيوب)

B *vt* (to keep) وَضَعَ في جَيْبِهِ ‹the money, profits›

Idioms **to be in sb's pocket** يُسَيْطِرُ عَلَيْهِ شَخْصٌ; **to be out of pocket** أصْبَحَتْ جُيوبُهُ خاوِيةً; **to line one's pockets** انْتَفَخَتْ جُيوبُهُ

pocketbook /'pɒkɪtbʊk/ *n* **1** (BrE) (notebook) دَفْتَر جَيْبٍ **2** (AmE) (wallet) مَحْفَظة (مَحافِظُ); (handbag) شَنْطة \ حَقيبة يَدٍ **3** (AmE) (spending money) دَخْل **4** (AmE) (paperback) كِتاب جَيْبٍ

pocket dictionary *n* قاموس جَيْبٍ

pocketknife /'pɒkɪtnaɪf/ *n* (*pl* **pocketknives**) سِكّين جَيْبٍ, مِطْواة (مَطاوٍ)

pocket money *n* مَصْروف جَيْبٍ

pockmark /'pɒkmaːk/ *n* [أثَر البَثَراتِ أو الجُدَريّ]

pod /pɒd/ *n* **1** (of peas, beans) قَرْن (قُرون) **2** (for an engine, fuel) حُجَيْرة (وَقودٍ \ مُحَرِّكٍ)

POD *n* ▸ **print-on-demand**

podcast /'pɒdkaːst/ **A** *n* بودْكاسْت

B *vt* نَشَرَ بِتَقْنِيّةِ البودْكاسْت ‹a show, an interview›

podgy /'pɒdʒi/ *adj* (**podgier, podgiest**) (infml) ‹arms, child› [سَمين وَقَصير]

podiatrist /pə'dʌɪətrɪst/ *n* مُعالِج أقْدامٍ

podiatry /pəʊ'dʌɪətri/ *n* عِلاج الأقْدامِ

podium /'pəʊdɪəm/ *n* (*pl* **podiums, podia**) مِنَصّة (مَناصّ, مِنَصّات)

poem /'pəʊɪm/ *n* قَصيدة (قَصائِدُ), شِعْر (أشْعار); **to write/recite a ~** كَتَبَ \ ألْقى قَصيدةً

poet /'pəʊɪt/ *n* شاعِر (شُعَراءُ)

poetic /pəʊ'etɪk/ *adj* ‹language, imagination› شِعْريّ

Poet Laureate *n* شاعِر البَلاطِ, الشاعِر الأوَّل

poetry /'pəʊɪtri/ *n* شِعْر (أشْعار)

poignant /'pɔɪnjənt/ *adj* (fml) ‹reminder, moment› مُثير, مُؤَثِّر للعاطِفةِ

point /pɔɪnt/ **A** *n* **1** (of a knife, needle, pencil) ذُؤابة (ذَوائِبُ) **2** (place) نُقْطة (نِقاط, نُقَط); **~ of entry** (into a country, building) مَكان دُخولٍ; نُقْطة دُخولٍ \ عُبورٍ; (in a wound) **the ~ of no return** نُقْطة اللاعَوْدةِ \ اللارَجْعةِ **3** (extent, degree) نُقْطة (نِقاط, نُقَط); **I've reached the ~ where I can't take any more** وَصَلْتُ إلى النُقْطةِ الّتي لا أسْتَطيعُ أنْ أتَحَمَّلَ فيها أكْثَرَ; **up to a ~** إلى دَرَجةٍ ما **4** (in time) **to be on the ~ of doing sth** كادَ أنْ يَفْعَلَ شَيْئاً; **at this ~ I gave up** عند هذه النُقْطةِ \ في هذه اللَحْظةِ اسْتَسْلَمْتُ; **at some ~ in the future** في وَقْتٍ ما في المُسْتَقْبَلِ; **at one ~** في لَحْظةٍ ما; **when it came to the ~ of deciding** عِنْدَما جاءَتْ لَحْظةُ اتِّخاذِ القَرارِ; **at this ~ in time** في هذه اللَحْظةِ **5** (in discussions, debates) نُقْطة (نِقاط, نُقَط); **to raise a ~ about sth** أثارَ نُقْطةً تَتَعَلَّقُ بِشَيْءٍ; **he made a valid ~** قال كَلاماً وَجيهاً; **to make a ~ of doing sth** حَرِصَ على فِعْلِ شَيْءٍ; **you have a ~ there** مَعَكَ حَقٌّ في ذلك; **I take your ~, but ...** أفْهَمُ ما تَقولُ, لَكِنْ .... **6** (pivotal issue) لُبّ المَسْألةِ; **that's the whole ~** ذلك هو لُبُّ المَسْألةِ; **that's not the ~** لَيْسَ ذلك بَيْتَ القَصيدِ; **to come straight to the ~** عَبَّرَ بِشَكْلٍ مُباشِرٍ عن جَوْهَرِ المَوْضوعِ; **to keep to**

or **stick to the ~** اِلْتَزَمَ بِصُلْبِ المَوْضوعِ; **to get the ~** فَهِمَ المَوْضوعَ; **to miss the ~** أَساءَ فَهْمَ المَوْضوعِ; **what she said was to the ~** ما قالَتْهُ كانَ وَثيقَ الصِلةِ بالمَوْضوعِ; **that's beside the ~** لَيْسَ لِذَلِكَ عَلاقةٌ بالمَوْضوعِ **7** (purpose) غاية; **what's the ~ of doing that?** ما الغايةُ من فِعْلِ ذلك؟; **there's no ~ in phoning her** لَيْسَ هُناكَ مَعْنًى للاتِّصالِ بها; **I don't see the ~ of repeating the experiment** لا أرى غايةً من إعادةِ التَجْرِبةِ **8** (characteristic) ميزة; **punctuality is not her strong ~** الدِقّةُ في المَواعيدِ لَيْسَتْ ميزَتَها القَوِيّةَ **9** (in scoring) نُقْطة (نُقَط, نِقاط); **to win by 10 ~s** اِنْتَصَرَ بِعَشْرِ نِقاطٍ; **to win on ~s** (in boxing) اِنْتَصَرَ بالنِقاطِ **10** (headland) رَأْس, لِسان بَحْرِيّ (mf; رُؤوس) **11** (in text, figures) نُقْطة (نُقَط, نِقاط) **12** (Fin) (on index) نُقْطة (نُقَط, نِقاط) **13** ((in typography) also **point size**) حَجْمُ النُقْطةِ

B (**points**) *n pl* **1** (BrE) (on a railway tracks) تَحْويلة (تَحاويلُ) **2** (Aut) مَقابِس

C *vt* **1** (to aim, direct) **to ~ a camera/gun at sb** صَوَّبَ; **to ~ one's finger at sb** وَجَّهَ إِصْبَعَهُ إلى شَخْصٍ; **to ~ the finger at sb** (to accuse) وَجَّهَ أَصابِعَ الاتِّهامِ إلى شَخْصٍ **2** (to show) «signposts, arrows» أَشارَ (إلى); **the report ~s the way to a fairer system** يُشيرُ التَقْريرُ إلى الطَريقِ نحو نِظامٍ أَكْثَرَ عَدالةً **3** (Constr) [مَلأَ الشُقوقَ بالاسْمَنْتِ] ‹a wall, house›

D *vi* **1** (with one's finger) أَشارَ; **to ~ at sb/sth** أَشارَ إلى شَخْصٍ \ شَيْءٍ **2** (to be directed) «signposts, arrows» صُوِّبَ; **the camera was ~ing in my direction** كانت الكاميرا مُوَجَّهةً نَحْوي; **the arrows ~ to the exit** تُشيرُ الأَسْهُمُ إلى المَخْرَجِ **3** (to suggest) **to ~ to a conclusion/result** أَشارَ إلى اسْتِنْتاجٍ \ نَتيجةٍ; **everything ~s in that direction** كُلُّ شَيْءٍ يُشيرُ إلى ذلك الاتِّجاهِ; **to ~ to sth as evidence of success** أَشارَ إلى شَيْءٍ كَبُرْهانٍ على النَجاحِ

(Idioms) **not to put too fine a point on it** بِكُلِّ صَراحةٍ وَبِدونِ مُوارَبةٍ; **to be a sore point** كانَتْ نُقْطةً حَسّاسةً

(Phrasal verbs) **point out**: **A** **~ out [sth/sb]**, **~ [sth/sb] out** (to indicate) أَشارَ إلى [شَيْءٍ \ شَخْصٍ] ‹an object, animal, a person› **B** **~ out [sth]** (to remark on) أَشارَ إلى [شَيْءٍ] ‹a fact, discrepancy›

• **point up**: **~ up [sth]** أَكَّدَ على أَهَمِّيّةِ [شَيْءٍ] ‹a contrast, similarity, need›

point-blank /pɔɪnt'blaŋk/ **A** *adj* **1** **at ~ range** عن كَثَبٍ **2** ‹refusal, question› مُباشِر

B *adv* **1** ‹to shoot› من مَسافةٍ قَريبةٍ **2** ‹to refuse, to deny› بِطَريقةٍ مُباشِرةٍ

pointed /'pɔɪntɪd/ *adj* **1** ‹hat, stick› حادّ, مُدَبَّب, مُسَنَّن **2** ‹remark› حادّ, لاذِع, ثاقِب

pointer /'pɔɪntə/ *n* **1** (piece of information) إشارة, تَلْميح (تَلْميحات), نَصيحة (نَصائِحُ) **2** (on dial) مُؤَشِّر (مُؤَشِّرات); (on clock) عَقْرَب (mf; عَقارِبُ) **3** (on projector screen) عَصاً (f; عِصِيّ) **4** (cursor) مُؤَشِّر (مُؤَشِّرات) **5** (dog) بوينْتِر

pointless /'pɔɪntləs/ *adj* ‹request, activity› غير مُجْدٍ, لا فائِدةَ مِنْهُ; **it's ~ to go** من العَبَثِ الذَهابُ

point of view *n* وِجْهة نَظَرٍ, مَوْقِف (مَواقِفُ)

poise /pɔɪz/ *n* **1** (composure) رَزانة, وَقار **2** (in movement) تَوازُن

poised /pɔɪzd/ *adj* **1** (ready) مُسْتَعِدّ, مُتَأَهِّب; **to be ~ to do sth** كانَ مُسْتَعِدًّا للقِيامِ بِشَيْءٍ **2** (self-assured) ‹performance› مُتَّزِن **3** (in movement) ‹dancer, gymnast› مُتَوازِن

poison /'pɔɪz(ə)n/ **A** *n* سَمّ (سُموم, سِمام)

B *vt* **1** (to kill) سَمَّ (u; سَمّ), سَمَّمَ ‹an enemy, a rat› **2** (to contaminate) لَوَّثَ ‹a river, soil›

poisoning /'pɔɪz(ə)nɪŋ/ *n* تَسَمُّم

poisonous /'pɔɪz(ə)nəs/ *adj* **1** ‹chemical, snake› سامّ (سَوامُّ) **2** ‹rumour› مُغْرِض; ‹atmosphere› مُلَوَّث; **these allegations are absolutely ~** هذه ادِّعاءاتٌ هَدّامةٌ تَماماً

poison pen letter *n* رِسالة قَذْفٍ وسَبٍّ

poke /pəʊk/ **A** *vt* **1** (to jab) هَمَزَ (i-u; هَمْز), وَخَزَ (i; وَخْز) ‹a friend, colleague›; **he ~d his food with his fork** غَرَسَ شَوْكَتَهُ في طَعامِهِ; **to ~ sb in the ribs** نَكَزَ شَخْصاً في جَنْبِهِ; **to ~ the fire** حَرَّكَ النارَ **2** (to push, put) **to ~ sth into a hole/pot** دَفَعَ شَيْئاً داخِلَ حُفْرةٍ \ قِدْرٍ; **to ~ one's head round the door** أَخْرَجَ رَأْسَهُ من وَراءِ البابِ **3** (to pierce) **to ~ a hole in a bag/the cloth** أَحْدَثَ ثُقْباً في حَقيبةٍ \ القُماشِ

B *vi* ▸**poke out**

C *n* (prod) وَخز ,هَمْز (n coll)

(Idiom) **better than a poke in the eye with a sharp stick** (infml) أَحْسَن من لا شَيْءَ

(Phrasal verbs) **poke around, poke about** (BrE) فَتَّش

• **poke at**: ~ **at [sb/sth]** نَقَرَ \ لَكَزَ [شَخْصاً \ شَيْئاً] ‹*your food, a snake*›

• **poke out** **A** «flowers, one's toe» بَرَزَ (u; بُروز) **B** **to ~ [sth] out** **1** أَخْرَجَ [شَيْئاً] ‹*one's head, nose*› **2** **to ~ sb's eye out** فَقَأَ عَيْنَ شَخْصٍ

poker /ˈpəʊkə/ *n* **1** (for fire) مِحَسّ (قَضيب حَديديّ لِتَحْريكِ الفَحْمِ \ الخَشَبِ في النارِ) **2** (card game) بوكَر

poker-faced /ˈpəʊkəfeɪst/ *adj* ‹*gambler, negotiator*› بِوَجْهِ البوكَر (بِوَجْهٍ خالٍ من التَعابيرِ)

poky /ˈpəʊki/ *adj* (**pokier, pokiest**) (infml) ‹*room, apartment*› ضَيِّق; **we lived in a ~ little house** سَكَنّا في بَيْتٍ ضَيِّقٍ

Poland /ˈpəʊlənd/ *pr n* بولَنْدا

polar /ˈpəʊlə/ *adj* **1** ‹*region, orbit*› قُطْبيّ **2** ‹*opposites*› مُتَناقِض, مُتَضادّ

polar bear *n* دُبّ قُطْبيّ

polarity /pəʊˈlarɪti/ *n* (*pl* **polarities**) قُطْبيّة

polarize, -ise (BrE) /ˈpəʊlərʌɪz/ *vt* **1** (to divide) قَسَّمَ ,فَرَّقَ ‹*opinions, a society*› **2** (Phys) اسْتَقْطَبَ ‹*light*›

pole /pəʊl/ *n* **1** (support for plants, a tent) عَمود (أَعْمِدة); (for a flag) سارية (سَوارٍ, ساريات) **2** (for a boat) سارية (ساريات, سَوارٍ) **3** ▸**ski pole** **4** (in navigation) قُطْب (أَقْطاب); **magnetic North P~** القُطْبُ الشَماليّ المِغْناطيسيّ; **the negative/positive ~s** الأَقْطاب الإيجابيّة \ السَلْبيّة

(Idiom) **to be poles apart** كانَ يَقِفُ على طَرَفَيْ نَقيضٍ; **the two sides are ~s apart** الجانِبانِ يَقِفانِ على طَرَفَيْ نَقيضٍ

Pole /pəʊl/ *n* بولَنْديّ

polecat /ˈpəʊlkat/ *n* **1** (weasel-like) فَأر الخَيْل **2** (AmE) (skunk) ظَرِبان أَمْريكيّ

pole dancing *n* الرَقْص على العَمودِ (بِغَرَضِ الإثارةِ الجِنْسيّةِ)

polemical /pəˈlɛmɪk(ə)l/ *adj* ‹*writing, style*› جَدَليّ

pole position *n* [مَوْقِع في المُقَدِّمةِ \ الصَدارةِ]

Pole Star *n* (**the Pole Star**) النَجْم القُطْبيّ

pole vault *n* القَفْز بالزانة

police /pəˈliːs/ **A** *n* شُرْطة

B *vt* **1** ضَبَطَ ,راقَبَ ‹*a town, the streets*›; حَفِظَ النِظامَ في (i-u; ضَبْط) ‹*a demonstration, an event*› **2** أَشْرَفَ ‹*an industry, a system*›

police car *n* سَيّارة شُرْطةٍ

police chief *n* ▸**chief of police**

police constable *n* (BrE) شُرْطيّ

police court (AmE) *n* مَحْكَمة الشُرْطةِ \ الجُنَحِ

Police Department *n* (AmE) شُرْطة

police dog *n* كَلْب بوليسيّ

police force *n* قوّات الشُرْطةِ

policeman /pəˈliːsmən/ *n* (*pl* **-men**) شُرْطيّ

police officer *n* ضابِط شُرْطةٍ

police record *n* صَحيفة سَوابق

police state *n* (pej) دَوْلة بوليسيّة

police station *n* مَرْكَز شُرْطةٍ

policewoman /pəˈliːswʊmən/ *n* (*pl* **-women**) شُرْطيّة

policing /pəˈliːsɪŋ/ *n* **1** (by the police) حِفظ النِظام **2** (supervision) إشْراف

policy /ˈpɒlɪsi/ *n* (*pl* **policies**) **1** (plan, rule) سِياسة; **foreign/economic ~** السِياسة الخارجيّة \ الاقْتِصاديّة **2** (insurance document) بوليصة

policyholder /ˈpɒlɪsɪˌhəʊldə/ *n* حامِل سَنَدِ, شَخْص مُؤَمَّن عَلَيْهِ تأْمينٍ

polio /ˈpəʊlɪəʊ/ *n* شَلَل الأَطْفالِ

poliomyelitis /pəʊliəʊmʌɪəˈlʌɪtɪs/ *n* شَلَل الأَطْفالِ

polish /ˈpɒlɪʃ/ **A** *vt* **1** لَمَّعَ ‹*the furniture, one's shoes, the a car*› **2** (to refine) حَسَّنَ ‹*one's performance, style, image*›

B *vi* لَمَّعَ

C *n* **1** (for furniture, shoes, cars) وَرْنيش **2** (application) **to give the furniture/one's shoes a ~** لَمَّعَ الأَثاثَ \ حِذاءَهُ **3** (shiny surface) بَريق ,لَمَعان **4** (sophistication) أَناقة

(Phrasal verbs) **polish off**: ~ **off [sth]**, ~ **[sth] off** (infml) **1** (to eat) أَنْهى [شَيْئاً] أَتى على [شَيْءٍ] *<the food, a meal>* **2** (to finish) *<a job, task>*

• **polish up**: ~ **up [sth]**, ~ **[sth] up** **1** (to make shiny) لَمَّعَ [شَيْئاً] *<the furniture, one's glasses, the car>* **2** (infml) (to perfect) صَقَلَ [شَيْئاً] *<one's Arabic, one's serve>*

Polish /ˈpəʊlɪʃ/ **A** *adj <government, army, embassy>* بولَنْديّ **B** *n* (language) (اللُغة) البولَنْديّة

polished /ˈpɒlɪʃt/ *adj* **1** (shiny) *<floor, stone>* مَصْقول **2** (accomplished) *<performance, production>* مُتْقَن **3** (refined) *<style, person>* مُهَذَّب

polite /pəˈlʌɪt/ *adj <receptionist, pupil>* مُؤَدَّب, مُهَذَّب; **to be ~ to sb/about sth** كانَ مُهَذَّباً مع شَخْصٍ \ في شَيْءٍ; **to make ~ conversation** أَجْرى مُحادَثةً وِدّيّةً; **in ~ company** في صُحْبَةِ أُناسٍ مُحْتَرَمينَ; (Ling) **to use the ~ form** اسْتَعْمَلَ صيغةَ الاحْتِرامِ

politely /pəˈlʌɪtli/ *adv <to ask, say>* بِشَكْلٍ مُهَذَّبٍ, بِأَدَبٍ

politeness /pəˈlʌɪtnəs/ *n* كِياسة, أَدَب

political /pəˈlɪtɪk(ə)l/ *adj <party, system, prisoner>* سِياسيّ

political correctness *n* الصَواب السِياسيّ

politically /pəˈlɪtɪkli/ *adv <motivated, biased>* سِياسيًّا

politician /pɒlɪˈtɪʃ(ə)n/ *n* سِياسيّ

politicize, **-ise** (BrE) /pəˈlɪtɪsʌɪz/ *vt* سَيَّسَ *<education, an issue>*

politics /ˈpɒlɪtɪks/ *n* **1** + *v sing* (activity, science) سِياسة; **to enter ~** أَصْبَحَ سِياسيًّا **2** + *v pl* (views) مُعْتَقَدات سِياسيّة

polka /ˈpɒlkə/ *n* بولْكا (رَقْصة)

polka dot *n* نُقْطة (نقاط ,نُقَط)

poll /pəʊl/ **A** *n* **1** [u] (process of voting) اقْتِراع (اقْتِراعات); **the result of the ~** نَتائِج الاقْتِراعِ **2** (number of votes cast) تَصْويت; **to go to the ~s** ذَهَبَ إلى صَناديقِ الاقْتِراعِ **3** (survey) اسْتِطْلاع (اسْتِطْلاعات); **to conduct** *or* **take a ~ of teachers' views** قامَ بِاسْتِطْلاعِ آراءِ الأَساتِذةِ

B *vt* **1** (in an election) تَحَصَّلَ (على) *<votes>* **2** (to canvass) اسْتَطْلَعَ آراءَ *<viewers, readers>*

C *vi* (to obtain votes) **to ~ badly/well** حَقَّقَ نَتائِجَ سَيِّئةً \ جَيِّدةً

pollack, **pollock** /ˈpɒlək/ *n* (*pl* **pollack** or **pollacks**) بُلوق (سَمَك)

pollen /ˈpɒlən/ *n* لَقاح

pollen count *n* مُعَدَّل اللَقاحِ

pollinate /ˈpɒlɪneɪt/ *vt* لَقَّحَ *<a flower, crop>*

pollination /pɒləˈneɪʃ(ə)n/ *n* تَلْقيح

polling /ˈpəʊlɪŋ/ *n* (voting) اقْتِراع (اقْتِراعات), تَصْويت

polling booth *n* غُرْفة اقْتِراعٍ

polling day *n* يَوْم الاقْتِراعِ \ التَصْويتِ

polling station (BrE), **polling place** (AmE) *n* مَكْتَب \ مَرْكَز اقْتِراعٍ

poll tax *n* (BrE) ضَريبة الرُؤوسِ

pollutant /pəˈljuːt(ə)nt/ *n* مادّة مُلَوِّثة

pollute /pəˈluːt/ *vt* لَوَّثَ *<water, the air>*

polluter /pəˈluːtə/ *n* مُلَوِّث

pollution /pəˈluːʃ(ə)n/ *n* تَلَوُّث

polo /ˈpəʊləʊ/ *n* بولو (لُعْبة رِياضيّة)

polo neck *n* (BrE) ياقة عالِية

poltergeist /ˈpɒltəgʌɪst/ *n* شَبَح (أَشْباح, شُبوح)

poly /ˈpɒli/ *n* (BrE infml) ▸ **polytechnic**

polyester /ˌpɒliˈɛstə/ *n* بوليسْتَر

polyethylene /ˌpɒliˈɛθɪliːn/ *n* ▸ **polythene**

polygamy /pəˈlɪgəmi/ *n* تَعَدُّد الزَوْجاتِ

polymer /ˈpɒlɪmə/ *n* بوليمَر, مُكَوْثَر

polymorphism /ˌpɒlɪˈmɔːfɪz(ə)m/ *n* تَعَدُّد أَشْكالٍ

Polynesia /ˌpɒlɪˈniːʒə/ *pr n* بولينيزيا

Polynesian /pɒlɪˈniːʒ(ə)n/ **A** *adj <island, culture>* بولينيزيّ **B** *n* **1** (inhabitant) بولينيزيّ **2** (language) (اللُغة) البولينيزيّة

polyp /ˈpɒlɪp/ *n* سَليلة (سَلائِل)

polystyrene /ˌpɒlɪˈstʌɪriːn/ *n* بوليسْتَيْرين

polytechnic /ˌpɒlɪˈtɛknɪk/ *n* (BrE) مَعْهَد العُلوم التَطْبيقيّة

polytheism /ˈpɒliˌθiːɪz(ə)m/ *n* الاعْتِقاد بِتَعَدُّدِ الآلِهةِ

polythene /ˈpɒlɪθiːn/ *n* (BrE) بوليثين, بولي إثيلين, مُتَعَدِّد \ عَديد الإثيلين

polyunsaturated /ˌpɒlɪʌnˈsatʃərеɪtɪd/ *adj <fat, oil>* عَديد اللاتَشَبُّعِ

pomegranate /ˈpɒmɪgranɪt/ *n* رُمّان (n coll)

pomp /pɒmp/ *n* أُبَّهة

pom-pom /ˈpɒmpɒm/, **pompon** /ˈpɒmpɒn/ *n* [كُرة مَنْفوشة من الخُيوطِ للزينةِ]

pompous /ˈpɒmpəs/ *adj* ‹*fool*› مُتَغَطْرِس, مَغْرور; ‹*speech*› طَنّان, رَنّان

pond /pɒnd/ *n* بِرْكة (بِرَك)

ponder /ˈpɒndə/ *vi* أَمْعَنَ التَفْكير, فَكَّر; **to ~ on** *or* **over sth** أَمْعَنَ التَفْكيرَ في شَيْءٍ

ponderous /ˈpɒnd(ə)rəs/ *adj* ‹*movement, pace*› بَطيء, مُتَثاقِل (بَطيئونَ, بِطاء)

pong /pɒŋ/ (BrE infml) **A** *n* رائِحة كَريهة **B** *vi* «factories, feet» بَعَثَ رائِحةً كَريهةً

pontiff /ˈpɒntɪf/ *n* (**the (supreme) pontiff**) البابا

pontoon /pɒnˈtuːn/ *n* (jetty) جِسْر عائِم

pony /ˈpəʊni/ *n* (*pl* **ponies**) حُصان قَزَم, سيسي (Egypt, ME), (Jordan, Leb)

ponytail /ˈpəʊnɪteɪl/ *n* تَسْريحة ذَيْلِ الحُصانِ

poodle /ˈpuːd(ə)l/ *n* بودْل (نَوْع من الكِلابِ)

pooh-pooh /puːˈpuː/ *vt* (infml) اِسْتَخَفَّ (ب), اِزْدَرى ‹*an idea, a suggestion*›

pool /puːl/ **A** *n* [1] (of water, blood) بِرْكة (بِرَك) [2] (also **swimming pool**) حَمّام سِباحةٍ [3] (of money, resources) صُنْدوق (ماليّ) مُشْتَرَك [4] (game) بِلْيارْدو
B (**the pools**) *n pl* (BrE) (also **the football pool**) المُراهَنات
C *vt* أَسْهَمَ (في صُنْدوقٍ مُشْتَرَكٍ) ‹*the money, resources*›

pool attendant *n* مُنْقِذ

pool cue *n* عَصا البِلْيارْدو

poolroom /ˈpuːlruːm/ *n* صالة \ قاعة بِلْيارْدو

pool table *n* طاوِلة بِلْيارْدو

poor /pɔː/ **A** *n* **the ~** + *v pl* الفُقَراء, المساكين
B *adj* [1] ‹*country, family*› فَقير (فُقَراءُ); **to become** *or* **grow ~** أَصْبَحَ فَقيراً; **the country's ~est communities** المُجْتَمَعات الأَكْثَر فَقْراً في البَلَدِ [2] (inferior) ‹*performance, weather, communications*› رَديء (أَرْدِياءُ); ‹*soldier, manager*› سَيِّء, عَديم الكَفاءةِ; ‹*health, appetite, chances*› ضَعيف; **~ housing conditions** ظُروف سَكَنيَّة سَيِّئة; **to be ~ at physics** كانَ ضَعيفاً في الفيزْياءِ [3] (deserving pity) مِسْكين (مَساكينُ, مِسْكينونَ), مُثير للشَفَقةِ; **~ thing!** يا لَهُ من مِسْكينٍ!; **~ Hassan!** مِسْكين حَسَن! [4] ‹*soil, diet*› فَقير; **a soil ~ in nitrogen** تُرْبة فَقيرة النِتْروجين

poorly /ˈpɔːli/ **A** *adv* (badly) ‹*written, paid*› على نَحْوٍ سَيِّءٍ \ رَديءٍ
B *adj* (infml) (ill) **to be/feel ~** شَعَرَ بِتَوَعُّكٍ

pop /pɒp/ **A** *vt* (**-pp-**) [1] (infml) (to burst) فَرْقَعَ (i; فَرْقَعة) ‹*a balloon, bubble*› [2] (to remove) أَزالَ (مُحْدِثاً فَرْقَعةً) ‹*a cork*› [3] (infml) (to put) **to ~ sth in the oven/in one's mouth** أَلْقى شَيْئاً في الفُرْنِ \ في فَمِهِ; **to ~ one's head through the window/round the door** أَطَلَّ بِرَأْسِهِ من خِلالِ النافِذةِ \ من وَراءِ البابِ [4] (infml) (to take) ‹*a pill, painkiller*› تَناوَلَ
B *vi* (**-pp-**) [1] (to go bang) «balloons, corks» فَرْقَعَ (i; فَرْقَعة); **her eyes were ~ping out of her head** كادَتْ عَيْناها تَقْفِزانِ من مُقْلَتَيْهِما; **one of her buttons ~ped open** سَقَطَ أَحَدُ أَزْرارِ ثَوْبِها فَجْأةً [2] «ears» طَقْطَقَ (i; طَقْطَقة) [3] (infml) (to go) **to ~ next door** [قامَ بِزيارةٍ خاطِفةٍ إلى الجيرانِ]; **I'll ~ back later** سَأَعودُ عَمّا قَليلٍ; **she ~ped out for some bread** ذَهَبَتْ لِشِراءِ بَعْضِ الخُبْزِ
C *n* [1] (sound) فَرْقَعة (فَرْقَعات, فَراقِعُ), طَقْطَقة; **to go ~** «balloons» فَرْقَعَ (i; فَرْقَعة), اِنْفَجَرَ; «corks» فَرْقَعَ (i; فَرْقَعة) [2] (infml) (drink) مَشْروب غازيّ [3] (popular music) موسيقى البوب [4] (infml) (dad) أَب (آباء)

Idiom **to pop the question** طَلَبَ يَدَ شَخْصٍ للزَواجِ

Phrasal verbs **pop in A** (infml) (to visit) مَرَّ (u; مُرور; ب); **I'll ~ in later** سَأَقومُ بِزيارةٍ خاطِفةٍ لاحِقاً **B pop [sth] in** (infml) (to put in) «وَضَعَ [شَيْئاً] في شَيْءٍ» ‹*a coin, chicken*›
• **pop off** (infml) [1] (to die) ماتَ (u; مَوْت); **she ~ped off on her eightieth birthday** ماتَتْ في عيدِ ميلادِها الثَمانينَ [2] (BrE) (to leave) غادَرَ; **they have ~ped off to my aunt's for a day or two** ذَهَبوا إلى عَمَّتي في زِيارةٍ خاطِفةٍ تَسْتَغْرِقُ يَوْماً أَو يَوْمَيْنِ
• **pop up** (infml) «problems, a long-lost cousin» ظَهَرَ (فَجْأةً);

pop concert *n* حَفْل موسيقى البوب

popcorn /ˈpɒpkɔːn/ *n* فُشار

pope, Pope /pəʊp/ *n* بابا (بابَوات); **P~ Benedict** البابا بِنِديكْت

pop group *n* فِرْقة البوب

poplar /ˈpɒplə/ *n* حَوْر

pop music *n* موسيقى البوب

poppy /ˈpɒpi/ *n* (*pl* **poppies**) خَشْخاش (خَشاخيش)

Popsicle® /ˈpɒpsɪk(ə)l/ *n* (AmE) أَيس كْريم

popsock /ˈpɒpsɒk/ *n* [جَوْرَب نَيْلون للرُّكْبَةِ]

pop star *n* نَجْم البوب

populace /ˈpɒpjʊləs/ *n* عامّة (عَوامُّ), جَماهير

popular /ˈpɒpjʊlə/ *adj* ① (generally liked) ‹*actor, drink, design, politician*› شَعْبيّ; **he was a ~ choice as chairman** كانَ يُمَثِّلُ خِياراً شَعْبيًّا كَرَئيسٍ; **she's ~ with the public** لَها شَعْبيّةٌ عند الجَماهير ② (of or for the people) ‹*music, science, movement, support*› شَعْبيّ; **contrary to ~ belief** على عَكْسِ المُعْتَقَدِ الشَّعْبيّ; **the ~ view** *or* **perception of sth** الرَّأْيُ الشَّعْبيّ في شَيْءٍ; **by ~ demand** *or* **request** بِطَلَبٍ شَعْبيٍّ; **the ~ press** الصَحافة الشَعْبيّة

popularity /pɒpjʊˈlarəti/ *n* شَعْبيّة

popularize, -ise (BrE) /ˈpɒpjʊlərʌɪz/ *vt* نَشَرَ (u; نَشْر), رَوَّجَ, جَعَلَ شَعْبيًّا ‹*a fashion, sport*›

populate /ˈpɒpjʊleɪt/ *vt* سَكَنَ (u; سَكَن), قَطَنَ (u; قُطون; في, ب) ‹*a city, an area*›

population /pɒpjʊˈleɪʃ(ə)n/ *n* سُكّان

populist /ˈpɒpjʊlɪst/ *n, adj* شَعْبيّ, جَماهيريّ

pop-up /ˈpɒpʌp/ *n* نافِذة مُنْبَثِقة

pop-up blocker *n* مانِع النَوافِذ المُنْبَثِقة

pop-up menu *n* قائِمة مُنْبَثِقة

pop-up window *n* إطار مُنْبَثِق, نافِذة مُنْبَثِقة

porcelain /ˈpɔːsəlɪn/ *n* بورْسلين (خَزَف صينيّ)

porch /pɔːtʃ/ *n* ① (of a house, church) مَدْخَل (مَسْقوف) ② (AmE) (veranda) فَرانْدة

porcupine /ˈpɔːkjʊpʌɪn/ *n* شَيْهَم, نَيْص

pore /pɔː/ *n* مَسَمّ (مَسامُّ)

(Phrasal verb) **pore over**: **~ over [sth]** طالَعَ [شَيْئاً] ‹*a book, map*›

pork /pɔːk/ *n* لَحْم خِنْزير

porn /pɔːn/ *n* (infml) = **pornography** مَوادّ إباحيّة

pornographic /ˌpɔːnəˈgrafɪk/ *adj* ‹*material, film*› إباحيّ

pornography /pɔːˈnɒgrəfi/ *n* مَوادّ إباحيّة

porous /ˈpɔːrəs/ *adj* ‹*material, rock*› مَساميّ

porpoise /ˈpɔːpəs/ *n* خِنْزير البَحْرِ

porridge /ˈpɒrɪdʒ/ *n* عَصيدة

port /pɔːt/ **A** *n* ① (harbour, town) ميناء (f; مَوانٍ, مَوانِئُ), مَرْفَأ (مَرافِئُ); **~ of call** ميناء تَوَقُّفٍ ② (on computers) مَنْفَذ (مَنافِذُ); **a USB/parallel ~** مَنْفَذ يو إس بي \ مُتَوازٍ ③ (left side) المَيْسَرة ④ (drink) بورْت (نَبيذ بُرْتُغاليّ)

B *adj before n* ‹*engine, side*› أَيْسَر (dipt; يُسْر)

portable /ˈpɔːtəb(ə)l/ *adj* ‹*CD player, TV*› مَحْمول, نَقّال

portable media player *n* مُشَغِّل وَسائِطَ مَحْمول

portal /ˈpɔːt(ə)l/ *n* مَدْخَل (مَداخِلُ), بَوّابة

port authority *n* هَيْئة ميناءٍ

portcullis /pɔːtˈkʌlɪs/ *n* شَعْريّة تَحْصينٍ (نَوْع من بَوّاباتِ القِلاعِ)

portend /pɔːˈtɛnd/ *vt* (liter) أَنْبَأَ (ب) ‹*change, disaster*›

portent /ˈpɔːtɛnt/ *n* (liter) (of good) فَأْل (فُؤول, أَفْؤُل); (of bad) نَذير (نُذُر)

porter /ˈpɔːtə/ *n* ① (in a station, airport, hotel) شَيّال, حَمّال ② (in hospitals) عَتّال [عامِل يَنْقُلُ المُعَدّاتِ والمَرْضى] ③ (in apartment block) بَوّاب; (in hotel or college) حارِس (حُرّاس, حَرَس) ④ (on an expedition) شَيّال, حَمّال, عَتّال

portfolio /pɔːtˈfəʊlɪəʊ/ *n* ① (case) حافِظة (حَوافِظُ), مِحْفَظة (مَحافِظُ), حَقيبة (حَقائِبُ) ② (samples of work) [مَجْموعة أَعْمالٍ فَنّيّةٍ \ رُسوماتٍ \ مُصَوَّراتٍ] ③ (Pol) حَقيبة (وِزاريّة)

porthole /ˈpɔːthəʊl/ *n* كَوّة

portion /ˈpɔːʃ(ə)n/ *n* ① (part) جُزْء (أَجْزاء), قِسْم (أَقْسام) ② (share) حِصّة (حِصَص), نَصيب (أَنْصِبة, نُصُب), نِسْبة (نِسَب) ③ (at a meal) حِصّة (حِصَص), كَمّيّة

portrait /ˈpɔːtreɪt, ˈpɔːtrət/ *n* ① (picture) صورة, لَوْحة (لِشَخْصٍ) ② (impression) وَصْف (أَوْصاف), تَصْوير (تَصاويرُ)

portrait painter *n* رَسّام لَوْحاتٍ (أَشْخاصٍ)

portray /pɔːˈtreɪ/ *vt* ① (to depict) «picture, artist» صَوَّرَ ‹*a scene, person*› ② (to play the part of) «actor» صَوَّرَ, مَثَّلَ ‹*a character*› ③ (to describe) «films, authors» صَوَّرَ, وَصَفَ (i; وَصْف) ‹*people, events*›

portrayal /pɔ:'treɪəl/ *n* 1 (by an artist) تَصْوير (تَصاويرُ) 2 (by an actor) تَمْثيل, (تَصاويرُ) تَصْوير 3 (by an author, filmmaker) وَصْف (أَوْصاف), (تَصاويرُ) تَصْوير

Portugal /'pɔ:tʃʊg(ə)l/ *pr n* البُرْتُغال (f)

Portuguese /pɔ:tʃʊ'gi:z/ **A** *adj* ‹*ambassador, food, lesson*› بُرْتُغاليّ

B *n* (*pl* **Portuguese**) 1 (citizen) بُرْتُغاليّ 2 (language) (اللُغة) البُرْتُغاليّة

pose /pəʊz/ **A** *vt* 1 شَكَّلَ ‹*a threat, risk*›; مَثَّلَ ‹*a problem, challenge*› 2 طَرَحَ (a; طَرْح) ‹*a question*›

B *vi* 1 (for a painting, photograph) اتَّخَذَ وَضْعاً مُعَيَّناً [للتَصْويرِ أو الرَسْمِ] 2 (to behave affectedly) تَصَنَّعَ 3 (to pretend to be) تَظاهَرَ, انْتَحَلَ الشَخْصيّةَ; **to ~ as sb/sth** تَظاهَرَ بِأَنَّهُ شَخْصٌ \ شَيْءٌ ما

poser¹ /'pəʊzə/ *n* مُتَصَنِّع, مُتَكَلِّف

poser² /'pəʊzə/ *n* (difficult question) سُؤال صَعْب \ مُحَيِّر; (problem) مُشْكِلة عَويصة \ مُحَيِّرة

poseur /pəʊ'zə:/ *n* ▸ **poser¹**

posh /pɒʃ/ *adj* (infml) فاخِر, راقٍ

posit /'pɒzɪt/ *vt* (fml) افْتَرَضَ ‹*a theory, the existence of sth*›

position /pə'zɪʃ(ə)n/ **A** *n* 1 (situation) مَوْقِف (مَواقِفُ), وَضْعيّة; **if I were in your ~, I would ...** لَوْ كُنْتُ مَكانَكَ لَ ...; **to be in a strong/weak ~** كانَ في مَوْقِفٍ قَويٍّ \ ضَعيفٍ; **to be in a good ~ to do sth** كانَ في مَوْقِفٍ جَيِّدٍ لِيَفْعَلَ شَيْئاً; **to be in no ~ to do sth** كانَ في وَضْعيّةٍ لا تَسْمَحُ لَهُ بِأَنْ يَفْعَلَ شَيْئاً; **the ~ is changing hour by hour** الوَضْعُ يَتَغَيَّرُ ساعةً بعد ساعةٍ 2 (attitude, stance) مَوْقِف (مَواقِفُ); **the official ~ on the matter** المَوْقِف الرَسْميّ حول المَسْأَلةِ; **to make one's ~ very clear** جَعَلَ مَوْقِفَهُ واضِحاً جدًّا 3 (location) مَكان (أَماكِنُ, أَمْكِنة), مَوْضِع (مَواضِعُ); **the house is in a good ~** البَيْتُ في مَكانٍ جَيِّدٍ; **to be in ~** كانَ جاهِزاً في مَكانِ العَمَليّةِ; **to get into ~** وَصَلَ إلى مَكانِ العَمَليّةِ 4 (posture) وَضْعيّة, وَضْع (أَوْضاع); **to be in a sitting/kneeling ~** كانَ في وَضْعيّةِ جُلوسٍ \ رُكوعٍ 5 (of a lever, switch) وَضْع (أَوْضاع) 6 (in a ranking) مَرْتَبة (مَراتِبُ); **to be in third ~** كانَ في المَرْتَبةِ الثالِثةِ 7 (job) وَظيفة (وَظائِفُ), مَنْصِب (مَناصِبُ); **to hold** *or* **occupy a senior ~** شَغَلَ مَنْصِباً عالِياً; **the ~ of chief accountant** مَنْصِب رَئيسِ المُحاسِبينَ 8 (in a team) مَرْكَز (مَراكِزُ), خُطّة (خُطَط) (Tunisia); **what ~ does he play?** في أَيِّ مَرْكَزٍ يَلْعَبُ؟ 9 (Mil) مَوْقِع (مَواقِعُ) 10 (counter) شُبّاك (شَبابيكُ); **'~ closed'** الشُبّاكُ مُغْلَقٌ

B *vt* 1 (to station) نَشَرَ (u; نَشْر) ‹*troops, artillery, a lookout*› 2 (to situate) وَضَعَ (a; وَضْع) ‹*a camera, the cursor*›; بَنى (في) مِنْطَقةٍ ‹*building*›

C *v refl* **to ~ oneself** تَمَوْضَعَ في مَكانٍ

positive /'pɒzɪtɪv/ *adj* 1 (affirmative) ‹*reply, reaction*› إيجابيّ 2 (constructive) ‹*effect, attitude*› إيجابيّ 3 (definite) ‹*evidence, identification*› مُتَيَقِّن, مُتَأَكِّد 4 (certain) أَكيد, حاسِم, قاطِع, واثِق; **'are you sure?' — '~'** 'هل أَنْتَ واثِقٌ؟'—'بكُلِّ تَأْكيد'; كانَتْ **to test ~** 5 ‹*number*› موجَب 6 ‹*electrode*› موجَب 7 نَتيجةُ اخْتِبارِهِ إيجابيّةً 8 (infml) (absolute) ‹*disgrace, genius*› بِلا شَكٍّ, بالتَأْكيدِ, تَماماً

positive discrimination *n* تَمْييز إيجابيّ

positively /'pɒzətɪvli/ *adv* 1 (constructively) ‹*to react, think*› بِصورةٍ إيجابيّةٍ; **they responded ~ to the suggestion** اسْتَجابوا للاقْتِراحِ بِصورةٍ 2 (definitely) ‹*to identify, prove*› قاطِعةٍ \ حاسِمةٍ 3 (absolutely) ‹*dangerous, misleading*› تَماماً, إلى أَبْعَدِ حَدٍّ, بالتَأْكيدِ

posse /'pɒsi/ *n* 1 (AmE) (sheriff's) جَماعة تُعاوِنُ الشُرْطةَ عند [الطَوارِئِ] 2 (group) زُمْرة (زُمَر), حَشْد (حُشود), جَماعة

possess /pə'zes/ *vt* 1 (to own) امْتَلَكَ ‹*property, a weapon*› 2 (to take control of) «anger, fury» تَمَلَّكَ, سَيْطَرَ (i; سَيْطَرة); «demons» مَسَّ (u; مَسّ), تَلَبَّسَ (ب) ‹*a person*›; **what ~ed you to do that?** ماذا دَهاكَ لِتَفْعَلَ ذلكَ؟; **to be ~ed by demons/the devil** مَسَّتْهُ الشَياطينُ \ مَسَّهُ الشَيْطانُ

possession /pə'zeʃ(ə)n/ *n* 1 (something owned) مِلْك (أَمْلاك), مُمْتَلَك (مُمْتَلَكات) 2 (ownership) امْتِلاك (امْتِلاكات), تَمَلُّك, حِيازة; **to be in the ~ of sb, to be in sb's ~** كانَ في حَوْزةِ شَخْصٍ; **to take ~ of sth** وَضَعَ يَدَهُ على شَيْءٍ ‹*land, property*› 3 (of arms, drugs etc.) حِيازة

possessive /pə'zesɪv/ *adj* ‹*lover, attitude*› مُحِبّ التَمَلُّكِ

possessor /pə'zesə/ *n* مالِك (مُلّاك), صاحِب (أَصْحاب), حائِز

possibility /ˌpɒsɪˈbɪlɪti/ **A** *n* (احْتِمالات) احْتِمال **B** (**possibilities** *n pl*) (potential) إمْكانات

possible /ˈpɒsɪb(ə)l/ **A** *adj* **1** (potential) ‹*consequence, candidate, explanation*› مُحْتَمَل; **it's quite ~** هو مُمْكِنٌ جِدًّا **2** (achievable) مُمْكِن; **he did as much as ~** فَعَلَ كُلَّ ما في وِسْعِهِ; **as far as ~** إلى أقْصى حَدٍّ مُمْكِن; **I'll do it as soon as ~** سَأَفْعَلُهُ في أَسْرَعِ وَقْتٍ مُمْكِنٍ; **as quickly as ~** بِأَسْرَعِ ما يُمْكِنُ; **the experiment is technically ~** التَّجْرِبَةُ مُمْكِنَةٌ فَنِّيًّا **3** (for emphasis) **what ~ good is it to you?** ما الّذي سَتَجْنيهِ مِنْهُ؟ **4** (when conjecturing); **it is ~ that he took it** من المُمْكِنِ أنْ يَكونَ قَدْ أَخَذَها **B** *n* (candidate) مُرَشَّح

possibly /ˈpɒsɪbli/ *adv* **1** (perhaps) رُبَّما **2** (conceivably) من المُمْكِن \ المُحْتَمَل; **we can't ~ afford it** لا يُمْكِنُنا بِأَيّة حال تَحَمُّلُ ذلك ماليًّا; **could you ~ help me with this?** هل يُمْكِنُكَ مُساعَدَتي في ذلك إذا أَمْكَنَ؟

post /pəʊst/ **A** *n* **1** (for fences, street lamps, etc) (أعْمِدة) عَمود; **the starting/finishing ~** نُقْطة البِدايةِ \ النِّهايةِ; **to be beaten at the ~** خَسِرَ في اللَّحْظةِ الأَخيرةِ; **to be (the) first past the ~** كانَ أوَّلَ الفائِزينَ **2** (job) (وَظائِفُ) وَظيفة, (مَناصِبُ) مَنْصِب; **an academic/administrative ~** وَظيفة أكاديميّة \ إداريّة; **to hold the ~ of chief accountant** تَوَلّى وَظيفةَ رَئيس المُحاسِبينَ **3** (BrE) (delivery system) بَريد; **to send sth by ~** أَرْسَلَ شَيْئاً بالبَريدِ; **to catch/miss the ~** لَحِقَ مَوْعِدَ \ تَأَخَّرَ على مَوْعِدِ جَمْعِ البَريد; **your cheque is in the ~** صَكُّكَ في طَريقِهِ إلَيْكَ بالبَريدِ; **(to reply) by return of ~** أَرْسَلَ الرَّدَّ في أَقْرَبِ وَقْتٍ **4** (letters and parcels) بريد; **it came in today's ~** وَصَلَ في بَريدِ اليَوْمِ; **to deal with the ~** تَصَرَّفَ مع البَريدِ **5** (duty station) (مَواقِعُ) مَوْقِع, مَكان الخِدْمةِ; **to remain at/desert one's ~** بَقِيَ في \ هَجَرَ مَوْقِعه **6** (on a blog, social network) رِسالة, مُشارَكة

B (**post-**) *in combination* بَعْدَ; **~-9/11, everything changed** بَعْدَ 11 سِبْتَمْبِر، تَغَيَّرَ كُلُّ شَيْءٍ

C *vt* **1** (BrE) (to send by post) أَرْسَلَ بالبَريد ‹*a parcel, letter*› **2** (on wall, notice board) وَضَعَ (a; وَضْع), أَلْصَقَ ‹*a notice, advertisement*›; **~ no bills** مَمْنوعٌ وَضْعُ المُلْصَقاتِ **3** (on a blog, social network) وَضَعَ (a; وَضْع) ‹*a comment, photo*› **4** (to send) بَعَثَ, أَرْسَلَ (a; بَعْث); **to be ~ed to Amman** أُرْسِلَ إلى عَمّانَ **5** (to station) وَضَعَ (a; وَضْع) ‹*a sentry, guard*›; **sentries were ~ed at all the gates** وُضِعَ الحُرّاسُ على كُلِّ البَوّاباتِ **6** أَدْخَلَ ‹*an entry*›

Idiom **to keep sb posted (about sth)** أَبْقى شَخْصاً على دِرايةٍ (بِشَيْءٍ)

postage /ˈpəʊstɪdʒ/ *n* رُسوم \ أُجْرة بَريدٍ; **~ and packing** *or* (AmE) **handling** رُسوم الشَّحْنِ

postage paid *adj, adv* خالِص أُجْرةِ البَريدِ

postage stamp *n* طابِع بَريديّ

postal /ˈpəʊst(ə)l/ *adj* ‹*worker, service*› بَريديّ; ‹*vote, survey*› بالبَريدِ

postal order *n* (BrE) حَوالة بَريديّة

postbox /ˈpəʊstbɒks/ *n* (BrE) صُنْدوق بَريدٍ

postcard /ˈpəʊstkɑːd/ *n* بطاقة بَريديّة

postcode /ˈpəʊstkəʊd/ *n* (BrE) رَمْز بَريديّ

post-date /pəʊstˈdeɪt/ *vt* أَرَّخَ بتاريخٍ لاحِقٍ ‹*a cheque, document*›

poster /ˈpəʊstə/ *n* (مُلْصَقات) مُلْصَق

posterior /pɒˈstɪərɪə/ **A** *adj* ‹*auricle, artery*› خَلْفيّ **B** *n* (hum) مَقْعَدة, (أكْفال) كَفَل, مُؤَخَّرة

posterity /pɒˈsterɪti/ *n* الأَجْيال القادِمة

poster paint *n* لَوْن جُواش

postgraduate /pəʊstˈgradjʊət/ **A** *adj* ‹*student, course*› دِراساتٍ عُلْيا; f (عُلْيا) ‹*studies*› أَعْلى, (عُلًى) أَعالٍ, عُلْيا **B** *n* طالِب دِراساتٍ عُلْيا

posthumous /ˈpɒstjʊməs/ *adj* ‹*publication, award*› بعد الوَفاةِ \ المَوْتِ

posting /ˈpəʊstɪŋ/ *n* **1** (تَعْيينات) تَعْيين **2** (on a blog) رِسالة

postman /ˈpəʊstmən/ *n* (*pl* **-men**) ساعي بَريدٍ

postmark /ˈpəʊstmɑːk/ **A** *n* خَتْم بَريدٍ **B** *vt* خَتَمَ بِخَتْمِ بَريد

postmaster /ˈpəʊstmɑːstə/ *n* مُدير مَكْتَبِ بَريدٍ

postmistress /ˈpəʊstmɪstrɪs/ *n* مُديرة مَكْتَبِ بَريدٍ

postmodern /pəʊstˈmɒd(ə)n/ *adj* ‹*approach, design*› ما بعد الحَداثةِ

post-mortem /pəʊstˈmɔːtəm/ *n* تَشْريح جُثّةٍ

postnatal /pəʊstˈneɪt(ə)l/ *adj* ‹*depression, care*› ما بعد الوِلادةِ

post office *n* مَكْتَب بَريدٍ

post-operative /pəʊstˈɒp(ə)rətɪv/ *adj* ‹*complications, care*› ما بعد الجِراحةِ

postpone /pəˈspəʊn/ *vt* أَرْجَأ ,أَجَّل ‹*a decision, trip*›

postponement /pəʊstˈpəʊnmənt/ *n* إرْجاء ,تَأْجيل

postscript /ˈpəʊstskrɪpt/ *n* (to a letter) حاشية (حَواشٍ), (to a book) مَلْحوظة ;مُلْحَق (مَلاحِقُ) ,ذَيْل (أَذْيال ,ذُيول) ,تَذْيِيل (مُلْحَقات)

postulate **A** /ˈpɒstjʊleɪt/ *vt* سَلَّمَ (جَدَلاً) (ب) ‹*an idea, the need*› **B** /ˈpɒstjʊlət/ *n* بَديهيّة ,مُسَلَّمة

posture /ˈpɒstʃə/ *n* **1** (position) وَضْعيّة ,(أَوْضاع) وَضْع **2** (bearing) وَضْعيّة

post-viral fatigue syndrome /ˌpəʊstˌvʌɪrəl fəˈtiːg ˌsɪndrəʊm/, **post-viral syndrome** *n* مُتلازِمة التعَبِ بعد العَدْوى الفَيْروسيّةِ

post-war /pəʊstˈwɔː/ *adj* ‹*period, reconstruction*› بعد الحَرْبِ

postwoman /ˈpəʊstwʊmən/ *n* (*pl* **-women**) ساعِية بَريدٍ

posy /ˈpəʊzi/ *n* (*pl* **posies**) باقة

pot /pɒt/ **A** *n* **1** (saucepan) إناء (آنِية ,أَوانٍ) ,وِعاء (أَوْعِية ,أَواعٍ); **the ~s and pans** أَواني الطَبْخِ **2** (also **tea pot**) إبْريق شايٍ (also **coffee pot**) إبْريق \ رَكْوة قَهْوةٍ; **to make a ~ of tea/ coffee** حَضَّرَ إبْريقاً من الشايِ \ القَهْوةِ **3** (piece of pottery) إناء فَخّاريّ **4** (for paint, glue) وِعاء (أَوْعِية ,أَواعٍ) **5** (also **plant pot**) أُصيص (أُصُص) **6** [u] (infml) (cannabis) قِنَّب ,حَشيش; **to smoke ~** دَخَّنَ الحَشيشَ **7** (funds) وِعاء (أَوْعِية); **there is $300 in the ~** هُناكَ 300 دولار في الوِعاءِ
B *vt* (**-tt-**) also **~ up** وَضَعَ في أُصيصٍ ‹*a plant*›
C (**potted**) *adj* **1** (condensed) ‹*biography, history*› مُخْتَصَر **2** (BrE Culin) **~ted meat** لَحْم مُعَلَّب; **~ted shrimps** جَمْبَريّ مُعَلَّب

Idioms **to go to pot** (infml) أَصابَهُ الخَرابُ; **to have pots of sth** (infml) لَدَيْهِ الكَثيرِ والكَثيرِ من شَيْءٍ

potash /ˈpɒtaʃ/ *n* بوتاس

potassium /pəˈtasɪəm/ *n* بوتاسِيوم

potato /pəˈteɪtəʊ/ *n* (*pl* **potatoes**) بَطاطِس (dipt) (Egypt, Gulf), بَطاطا (Levant)

potato chip *n* (wafer) رُقاقة بَطاطِسَ مَقْليّةٍ

potato crisp (BrE), **potato chip** (AmE) *n* رُقاقة بَطاطِسَ مَقْليّةٍ

potato peeler *n* مِقْشَرة بَطاطِسَ

pot belly *n* كِرْش (كُروش ,أَكْراش)

potency /ˈpəʊt(ə)nsi/ *n* **1** (strength) قوّة ,(قُدُرات) قُدْرة ,فَعّاليّة **2** (sexual ability) قُدْرة ,فُحولة (جِنْسيّة) (قُوًى ,قوّات)

potent /ˈpəʊt(ə)nt/ *adj* **1** ‹*drug, drink*› (أَقْوِياءُ) قَويّ ,فَعّال **2** (sexually) قَويّ جِنْسيًّا

potential /pəʊˈtɛnʃ(ə)l/ **A** *adj* ‹*problem, champion*› مُحْتَمَل **B** *n* قُدُرات ,إمْكانيّات

potentially /pəˈtɛnʃ(ə)li/ *adv* ‹*dangerous, fatal*› على نَحْوٍ مُحْتَمَلٍ

pothole /ˈpɒthəʊl/ *n* **1** (cave) [كَهْف عَموديّ] **2** (in a road) حُفْرة وِعائيّة ,(نُقَر) نُقْرة ,(حُفَر) حُفْرة (SA)

potholing /ˈpɒthəʊlɪŋ/ *n* (BrE) رِياضة اسْتِكْشافِ الكُهوفِ

potion /ˈpəʊʃ(ə)n/ *n* شَراب سِحْريّ

pot plant *n* نَبات مَنْزِليّ

potshot /ˈpɒtʃɒt/ *n* [طَلْقة من مَسافةٍ قَريبةٍ]

potter /ˈpɒtə/ *n* فاخوريّ ,فَخّاريّ ,خَزّاف

Phrasal verb **potter about, potter around** (BrE) «gardeners, people» عَبِثَ (a; عَبَث)

pottery /ˈpɒt(ə)ri/ *n* (*pl* **potteries**) **1** [u] (vessels) فَخّاريّات, صِناعة الفَخّارِ ,فِخارة **2** [u] (craft) أَوانٍ فَخّاريّة ,فَخّار **3** (workshop, factory) مَصْنَع \ وَرْشة فَخّارٍ

potting compost /ˈpɒtɪŋ ˌkɒmpɒst/ *n* تُرْبة أَصيصٍ

potty /ˈpɒti/ **A** *n* (*pl* **potties**) (قَصارٍ) قَصْريّة ,نونيّة (Egypt) **B** *adj* (**pottier, pottiest**) (BrE infml) ‹*person, idea*› مَجْنون (مَجانينُ) ,مَخْبول (مَخابيلُ ,مَخْبولونَ)

pouch /paʊtʃ/ *n* **1** (small bag) كيس ,(جُرُب ,أَجْرِبة) جِراب (أَكْياس) **2** (for mail) حَقيبة (حَقائِبُ) ,شَنْطة (شُنَط) **3** (of a marsupial) جِراب (جُرُب ,أَجْرِبة)

poultice /ˈpəʊltɪs/ *n* لَبْخة

poultry /ˈpəʊltri/ *n* 1 (birds) طُيور داجِنة ,دَواجِن 2 (meat) لَحْم دَواجِن

pounce /paʊns/ *vi* انْقَضَّ; **to ~ on sb/sth** انْقَضَّ على شَخْصٍ \ شَيْءٍ

pound /paʊnd/ **A** *n* 1 (unit of weight) رَطْل (أَرْطال); **pears are £1.50 a** *or* **per ~** الكُمَّثْرى بـ 1.50 جُنَيْهٍ للرَطْلِ; **he weighs 210 ~s** وَزْنُهُ 210 أَرْطالٍ 2 (unit of currency) جُنَيْه (جُنَيْهات); **the Egyptian/Turkish ~** الجُنَيْه المِصْريّ \ التُرْكيّ; **a twenty-~ note** وَرَقة نَقْديّة من فِئةِ عِشْرينَ جُنَيْهاً 3 (for cars) مُسْتَوْدَع (مُسْتَوْدَعات), مَخْزَن (مَخازِنُ); (for dogs) مَلْجَأ (مَلاجِئُ)

B *vt* 1 (to crush) طَحَنَ (a; طَحْن), سَحَقَ (a; سَحْق) ‹*spices*›; **to ~ sth into a powder** طَحَنَ شَيْئاً حتّى صارَ مَسْحوقاً 2 (to beat) «waves» ضَرَبَ (i; ضَرْب) ‹*the rocks, wreck*›; **to ~ the door** طَرَقَ على البابِ بِشِدّةٍ 3 (to bombard) قَصَفَ (i; قَصْف) ‹*a city, port*›

C *vi* 1 (to knock loudly) **to ~ on the door** ضَرَبَ على البابِ بقوّةٍ 2 (to run noisily) **to ~ up/down the stairs** صَعَدَ \ نَزَلَ الدَرَجَ مُحْدِثاً جَلَبةً 3 (to throb) «heart, head» خفَقَ بِشِدّةٍ 4 (to crash) **to ~ on the beach/rocks** تَحَطَّمَ على الشاطِئِ \ الصُخورِ

(Phrasal verbs) **pound away** (on a piano, keyboard) «keyboarder, pianist» انْهَمكَ في العَزْفِ

• **pound out A ~ out** «music» كانَ صَوْتُهُ صاخِباً **B ~ sth out, ~ out sth** 1 (to play) عَزَفَ شَيْئاً بِصَوْتٍ عالٍ ‹*the tune, song*› 2 (infml) (to produce) كَتَبَ (u; كِتابة) ‹*a script, novel*›

pound sign *n* 1 (BrE) (for currency: the sign £) عَلامة جُنَيْه 2 (AmE) (the sign #) عَلامة شُبّاكٍ \ مُرَبَّع

pound sterling *n* جُنَيْه إِسْتِرْلينيّ

pour /pɔː/ **A** *vt* 1 (to make flow) سَكَبَ (u; سَكْب), صَبَّ (u; صَبّ) ‹*water, cement, molten iron*› 2 (to serve) صَبَّ (u; صَبّ) ‹*tea, water*›; **can I ~ you some more coffee?** هل أَصُبُّ لَكَ المَزيدَ من القَهْوةِ؟; **to ~ oneself a drink** صَبَّ لِنَفْسِهِ شَراباً 3 (to supply freely) **to ~ money/resources into a project** ضَخَّ مالاً \ سَخَّرَ مَوارِدَ في مَشْروعٍ

B *vi* 1 (to flow) تَدَفَّقَ; **water ~ed into the house** تَدَفَّقَ الماءُ إلى البَيْتِ; **smoke was ~ing out of the building** تَصاعَدَ الدُخانُ من المَبْنى; **water ~ed over the dam** تَدَفَّقَ الماءُ فوق السَدِّ; **light ~ed through the window** تَدَفَّقَ الضَوْءُ من خِلالِ النافِذةِ; **tears ~ed down her face** انْهالَت الدُموعُ على وَجْهِها 2 «people, cars, supplies» تَدَفَّقَ; **refugees ~ed across the border/bridge** تَدَفَّقَ اللاجِئونَ عَبْرَ الحُدودِ \ الجِسْرِ; **money/supplies ~ed into the country** تَدَفَّقَ المالُ \ تَدَفَّقَت الإِمْداداتُ إلى البَلَدِ 3 (to serve tea, coffee) صَبَّ (u; صَبّ)

C (**pouring**) *adj* **in the ~ing rain** تحت المَطَرِ المُنْهَمِرِ

D *v impers* (Meteorol) **it's ~ing, it's ~ing with rain** المَطَرُ يَنْهَمِرُ

(Idiom) **to pour cold water on sth** ثَبَّطَ الهِمَمَ بِخُصوصِ شَيْءٍ

(Phrasal verbs) **pour away**: **~ away [sth], ~ [sth] away** سَكَبَ [شَيْئاً] ‹*milk, oil*›

• **pour down** «the rain» انْهَمَرَ; **the rain was** *or* **it was ~ing down** كانَ المَطَرُ يَنْهَمِرُ

• **pour in A** 1 (to flow in) «water» تَدَفَّقَ إلى الداخِلِ 2 «letters, requests, supplies» انْهالَ **B ~ in [sth], ~ [sth] in** سَكَبَ [شَيْئاً] ‹*water, cream*›

• **pour off**: **~ off [sth], ~ [sth] off** تَخَلَّصَ من [شَيْءٍ] ‹*the water, fat*›

• **pour out A ~ out** ▸**pour** A1, ▸**pour** A2 **B ~ out [sth], ~ [sth] out** 1 (to serve) صَبَّ [شَيْئاً] ‹*coffee, wine*› 2 (to get rid of) تَخَلَّصَ من [شَيْءٍ] ‹*fumes, sewage*› 3 أَطْلَقَ العِنانَ لـ [شَيْءٍ] ‹*one's feelings, anger*›; **to ~ out one's troubles/heart to sb** فَتَحَ قَلْبَهُ لِشَخْصٍ

pout /paʊt/ *vi* (in annoyance) «child» بَرْطَمَ (i; بَرْطَمة), بَوَّزَ; (seductively) «woman» أَبْرَزَتْ شَفَتَيْها

poverty /ˈpɒvəti/ *n* فَقْر, فاقة, إِمْلاق

poverty line *n* خَطّ الفَقْرِ

poverty-stricken /ˈpɒvətiˌstrɪk(ə)n/ *adj* ‹*family, village*› مُعْدِم, شَديد الفَقْرِ

POW /piːəʊˈdʌbljuː/ *n* = **prisoner of war** أَسير حَرْبٍ

powder /ˈpaʊdə/ **A** *n* مَسْحوق (مَساحيقُ)

B *vt* وَضَعَ \ رَشَّ بودْرةً على ‹*your face, body*›

(Idiom) **to powder your nose** [ذَهَبَ إلى الحَمّامِ]

powdered /ˈpaʊdəd/ *adj* ‹*egg, milk*› مُجَفَّف, بودْرة

powdery /ˈpaʊd(ə)riː/ *adj* ‹*substance*› مَسْحوق; ‹*snow, chalk*› شَبيه بالمَسْحوقِ

power /ˈpaʊə/ **A** *n* **1** [u] (political control) سُلْطة (سُلْطات, سُلُطات); **to be in/come to ~** كانَ في \ جاءَ إلى السُلْطةِ; **to seize ~** اسْتَوْلى على السُلْطةِ; **to be returned/swept to ~** أُعيدَ \ وَصَلَ إلى السُلْطةِ; **~ to the people!** السُلْطةُ للشَعْبِ! **2** (influence) نُفوذ, تَأْثير; **to do everything in one's ~ to change the plan** قامَ بِكُلِّ ما في وُسْعِهِ لِتَغْيِيرِ الخُطّةِ; **to have ~ over the committee/over how the money is spent** كانَ لَهُ تَأْثيرٌ على اللَجْنةِ \ كَيْفيّةِ صَرْفِ المالِ **3** (authority) سُلْطة (سُلْطات, سُلُطات), صَلاحيّة; **the act gives new ~s to the tax authorities** يُعْطي القانونُ صَلاحيّاتٍ جَديدةً لِسُلُطاتِ الضَرائِبِ; **the police have the ~ to arrest anyone on suspicion** لدى الشُرْطةِ سُلْطةُ اعْتِقالِ أيِّ شَخْصٍ بِناءً على الاشْتِباهِ **4** (conviction) تَأْثير; **a poem/speech of great ~** قَصيدة \ خُطْبة ذات تَأْثيرٍ عَظيمٍ **5** (capability) قُدْرة (قُدُرات); **to lose the ~ of speech** فَقَدَ القُدْرة على النُطْقِ; **~ of concentration/persuasion** القُدْرة على التَرْكيزِ \ الإقْناعِ; **to be at the height of one's ~s** كانَ في قِمّةِ \ أَوْجِ قوّتِهِ **6** (nation) قوّة (قُوًى); **the great/emergent ~s** القُوى العُظْمى \ الناشِئة; **Turkey was a great sea ~** كانَتْ تُرْكيا قوّةً بَحْريّةً عَظيمةً **7** (physical force) قوّة (قُوًى); **the ~ of the storm/waves** قوّة العاصِفةِ \ الأَمْواجِ **8** (electrical) كَهْرَباء (f); **switch on/off the ~ now** أَطْفِئ \ شَغِّل الكَهْرَباءَ الآنَ **9** (of engines, planes) قوّة (قُوًى); **to be running at full/half ~** سارَ بكامِلِ \ بِنِصْفِ قوّتِهِ **10** (in maths) قوّة, أُسّ (قُوًى); **8 to the ~ of 3** 8 أُسّ 3

B *vt* شَغَّلَ ‹*a reactor, ship*›; **the smelter is ~ed by coal** يَعْمَلُ المَصْهَرُ بالفَحْمِ

Idiom **the powers that be** الإدارة, المَسْؤولونَ

power base *n* مَصْدَر \ مَرْكَز دَعْمٍ

powerboat /ˈpaʊəbəʊt/ *n* لانْش (زَوْرَق بِمُحَرِّكٍ قَويٍّ)

power cut *n* انْقِطاع كَهْرَباءٍ

power drill *n* مِثْقاب كَهْرَبائيّ

powerful /ˈpaʊəfʊl/ *adj* **1** (influential) ‹*nation, ally*› ذو تَأْثيرٍ \ نُفوذٍ **2** (with great force) ‹*engine, weapon*› قَويّ (أَقْوِياءُ) **3** (effective) ‹*drug*› فَعّال; ‹*argument*› قَويّ, دامِغ **4** (strong) ‹*body, athlete*› قَويّ (أَقْوِياءُ)

powerfully /ˈpaʊəf(ə)li/ *adv* **1** (strongly) ‹*to attack*› بِقوّةٍ; **to be ~ built** كانَ ذا بُنْيانٍ قَويٍّ; **he struck the ball ~** ضَرَبَ الكُرةَ بقوّةٍ **2** (convincingly) ‹*to argue, portray*› بِصورةٍ مُؤَثِّرةٍ \ مُقْنِعةٍ, بقوّةٍ

powerless /ˈpaʊələs/ *adj* ‹*victim, position*› عاجِز (عَجَزة), عَديم الحيلةِ; **we were ~ to prevent the accident** كُنّا عاجِزينَ عن مَنْعِ الحادِثِ

power line *n* خَطّ كَهْرَباءٍ

power of attorney *n* **1** (authority) وَكالة **2** (written authorization) تَوْكيل (رَسْميّ)

power-sharing /ˈpaʊəʃɛːrɪŋ/ *n* تَقاسُم السُلْطةِ

power station, power plant *n* مَحطّة طاقةٍ \ كَهْرَباءٍ \ قُدْرةٍ

power steering *n* نِظام قِيادةٍ كَهْرَبائيّ \ مُعَزَّز (آليًّا)

power supply *n* (*pl* **supplies**) **1** [u] (electricity) كَهْرَباء (f) **2** (of a computer) مُزَوِّد \ مَصْدَر طاقةٍ

power user *n* مُسْتَخْدِم مُتَقَدِّم \ مُتَمَرِّس \ مُتَمَيِّز

pp /piːˈpiː/ *abbr* **1** (on a document) = **per procurationem** بالنِيابةِ عن **2** (in a book) = **pages** ص; **see ~ 12-15** أُنْظُر ص 12–15

PR /piːˈɑː/ *n* **1** = **public relations** عَلاقات عامّة **2** = **proportional representation** تَمْثيل نِسْبيّ

practicable /ˈpraktɪkəb(ə)l/ *adj* ‹*option, measure*› مُمْكِن

practical /ˈpraktɪk(ə)l/ **A** *adj* **1** (not theoretical) ‹*advice, purpose*› عَمَليّ; **what ~ skills do you have?** ما المَهاراتُ العَمَليّةُ الّتي تَمْتَلِكُها؟ **2** (feasible) ‹*plan, solution*› عَمَليّ

B *n* (exam) امْتِحان عَمَليّ; (lesson) دَرْس عَمَليّ

practicality /ˌpraktɪˈkalɪti/ *n* **1** [u] (of a person) قُدْرة عَمَليّة; (of an idea, project) تَطْبيق عَمَليّ **2** (**practicalities** *n pl*) (real facts) جَوانِب عَمَليّة

practical joke *n* مَزْحة عَمَليّة, مَقْلَب (مَقالِبُ)

practically /ˈpraktɪk(ə)li/ *adv* **1** (almost) ‹*dead, empty*› تَقْريباً; **he comes ~ everyday** يَأْتي كُلَّ يَوْمٍ تَقْريباً **2** (in a practical way) ‹*to think, mean*› عَمَليًّا, بِطَريقةٍ عَمَليّةٍ, مِن الناحِيةِ العَمَليّةِ;

what can we do to help ~? ما الّذي يُمْكِنُنا القِيامُ بِهِ لِتَقْدِيمِ المُساعَدةِ بِطَرِيقةٍ عَمَلِيّةٍ؟

practice /'praktɪs/ **A** *n* **1** [u] (exercises) تَدْرِيب, تَمْرِين; **to do one's piano ~** تَمَرَّنَ على البِيانو; **to be in ~/out of ~** كانَ مُحافِظاً على \ مُتَوَقِّفاً عن التَدْرِيبِ; **to have had a lot of ~ in sth** اكْتَسَبَ خِبْرةً في شَيْءٍ **2** (training session) حِصّة (تَدْرِيبِيّة) **3** [u] (procedure) مُمارَسة, إجْراء; **it's standard ~ to make a report** الإجْراءُ المُتَّبَعُ هو كِتابةُ تَقْرِيرٍ; **that's good business ~** تِلْكَ مُمارَسةٌ تِجارِيّةٌ جَيِّدةٌ **4** [u] (habit, custom) عادة; **as is my usual ~** كَما هي عادَتي **5** (business of a doctor) عِيادة; (of a lawyer) مَكْتَب (مَكاتِبُ); **to set up a legal/medical ~** فَتَحَ مَكْتَبَ مُحاماةٍ \ عِيادةً **6** [u] (work of a doctor, lawyer) مُمارَسة; **to be in private ~** امْتَلَكَ مَكْتَباً خاصّاً \ عِيادةً خاصّةً **7** [u] (not theory) تَطْبِيق; **in ~, it doesn't work** عَمَلِيّاً, لا جَدْوى مِنْهُ

B *vt, vi* (AmE) ▸ **practise**

(Idiom) **practice makes perfect** المُمارَسةُ تُؤَدِّي إلى الإتْقانِ

practice match *n* مُباراة تَدْرِيبِيّة

practicing (AmE) *adj* ▸ **practising**

practise (BrE), **practice** (AmE) /'praktɪs/ **A** *vt* **1** (to improve) تَمَرَّنَ (على) *‹a skill, speech›*; **I'm practising my speech/serve** أتَمَرَّنُ على الكَلِمةِ \ ضَرَباتِ الإرْسالِ **2** (with professions) مارَسَ *‹medicine, law›* **3** (to observe) اتَّبَعَ *‹a religion›*; مارَسَ *‹ritual›*

B *vi* **1** (to rehearse) «performers, sportspeople» تَدَرَّبَ, تَمَرَّنَ; **how often do you ~?** كَمْ مَرّةً تَتَمَرَّنُ؟ **2** (to work) «lawyers, doctors» عَمِلَ (a; عَمَل); **to ~ as an architect/lawyer** عَمِلَ كَمُهَنْدِسٍ مِعْمارِيٍّ \ مُحامٍ

practising (BrE), **practicing** (AmE) /'praktɪsɪŋ/ *adj* **1** *‹Christian, Muslim›* مُلْتَزِم **2** *‹doctor, lawyer›* مُمارِس

practitioner /prak'tɪʃ(ə)nə/ *n* **1** (in law, medicine) مُمارِس (مِهْنةٍ); **a dental ~** طَبِيبُ أسْنانٍ مُمارِس **2** (any professional) مُمارِس (مِهْنةٍ)

pragmatic /prag'matɪk/ *adj ‹approach, solution›* عَمَلِيّ, بْراغْماتِيّ

pragmatism /'pragmətɪz(ə)m/ *n* تَفْكِير عَمَلِيّ, بْراغْماتِيّ

pragmatist /'pragmətɪst/ *n* بْراغْماتِيّ

Prague /prɑːg/ *pr n* بْراغ (f)

prairie /'prɛːri/ *n* مَرْج بَرارِيّ (مُرُوج)

prairie dog *n* كَلْب البَرارِيّ \ المُرُوجِ

praise /preɪz/ **A** *vt* **1** (to compliment) مَدَحَ (a; مَدْح), أثْنى (على), أطْرى *‹sb's work, courage›* **2** (to worship) حَمِدَ (a; حَمْد), سَبَّحَ *‹God, Allah›*

B *n* **1** (approval) مَدْح, إطْراء, ثَناء **2** (in worship) تَسْبِيح (تَسابِيحُ)

praiseworthy /'preɪzwəːði/ *adj ‹attempt, achievement›* جَدِير بالثَناءِ \ بالإطْراءِ \ بالمَدِيح

pram /pram/ *n* (BrE) عَرَبة طِفْلٍ

prance /prɑːns/ *vi* **1** «horses, ponies» وَثَبَ (i; وَثْب), قَفَزَ (i; قَفْز) **2** «performers» تَبَخْتَرَ, اخْتالَ في مِشْيَتِهِ

prank /praŋk/ *n* (infml) مَقْلَب (مَقالِبُ), مَزْحة ثَقِيلة

prat /prat/ *n* (BrE infml) غَبِيّ (أغْبِياءُ), أحْمَق (dipt; حُمْق; f حَمْقى), مُغَفَّل

prattle /'prat(ə)l/ *vi* «children» ثَرْثَرَ (i; ثَرْثَرة), هَذَرَ (i-u; هَذْر)

prawn /prɔːn/ *n* جَمْبَرِيّ, قُرَيْدِس

prawn cocktail *n* كوكْتيل جَمْبَرِيّ

pray /preɪ/ *vi* «worshippers, congregation» دَعا (u; دُعاء), صَلّى, تَضَرَّعَ; **to ~ to God** دَعا اللّهَ; **let us ~ for the sick/peace** لِنُصَلِّ من أجْلِ المَرْضى \ السَلام

prayer /prɛː/ *n* **1** دُعاء, ابْتِهال (ابْتِهالات), صَلاة (صَلَوات); **to say a ~ for peace** دَعا من أجْلِ السَلامِ **2** (**prayers** *n pl*) صَلاة (صَلَوات); **to go to morning/evening ~s** ذَهَبَ لأداءِ صَلاةِ الصَباحِ \ المَساءِ

prayer mat, prayer rug *n* سَجّادة صَلاةٍ

preach /priːtʃ/ **A** *vt* **1** *‹a sermon›* ألْقى **2** (to advocate) دَعا (u; دُعاء) (إلى) *‹tolerance›*; حَرَّضَ (على) *‹hatred›*

B *vi* «priests, preachers» وَعَظَ (i; وَعْظ, عِظة), ألْقى عِظةً \ خُطْبةً دِينِيّةً; **she ~ed about sin** ألْقَتْ عِظةً حول الخَطِيئةِ

(Idiom) **to preach to the converted** حاوَلَ إقْناعَ المُقْتَنِعِينَ

preacher /'priːtʃə/ *n* **1** (of a sermon) واعِظ (وُعّاظ), خَطِيب (دِينِيّ) **2** (AmE) (minister of religion) قَسّ (قُسُوس, قُسُس)

prearranged /priːə'reɪndʒd/ *adj ‹time, signal›* مُتَّفَق عَلَيْهِ

precarious /prɪˈkɛːrɪəs/ *adj* ‹*existence, position*› مَحْفوف بالمَخاطِرِ, خَطير; ‹*balance*› مُتَزَعْزِع, مُتَقَلْقِل, غَيْر ثابِتٍ \ مُسْتَقِرٍّ

precaution /prɪˈkɔːʃ(ə)n/ *n* اِحْتِياط, تَدْبير \ إِجْراء اِحْتِياطيّ \ وِقائيّ; **take the tablets as a ~** تناوَل الأَقْراصَ على سَبيلِ الوِقايةِ

precautionary /prɪˈkɔːʃ(ə)n(ə)ri/ *adj* ‹*measure, approach*› وِقائيّ, اِحْتِرازيّ, اِحْتِياطيّ

precede /prɪˈsiːd/ *vt* سَبَقَ (i-u; سَبْق) ‹*the onset, arrival*›

precedence /ˈprɛsɪd(ə)ns/ *n* أَوْلَويّة, أَسْبَقيّة; **their needs take ~ over everything else** حاجاتُهُمْ لَها الأَوْلَويّةُ على أَيِّ شَيْءٍ آخَرَ

precedent /ˈprɛsɪd(ə)nt/ *n* سابِقة (سَوابِقُ, سابِقات); **the ruling sets a ~ for similar cases** يُشَكِّلُ الحُكْمُ سابِقةً لِلقَضايا المُماثِلةِ

preceding /prɪˈsiːdɪŋ/ *adj* ‹*year, paragraph*› سابِق

precept /ˈpriːsɛpt/ *n* (fml) مَبْدَأ (مَبادِئُ)

precinct /ˈpriːsɪŋkt/ *n* 1 (also **shopping precinct, pedestrian precinct**) (BrE) (area) مِنْطَقة تِجاريّة \ تَسَوُّقٍ (لِلمُشاةِ فَقَطْ) 2 (AmE) (for elections) دائِرة اِنْتِخابيّة 3 (AmE) (police district) دائِرة شُرْطةٍ 4 (**precincts**); *pl* (surroundings of city, castle etc.) مُحيط; (of holy buildings, university) حَرَم (أَحْرام)

precious /ˈprɛʃəs/ **A** *adj* 1 (valuable) ‹*commodity, resources*› ثَمين, نَفيس (نِفاس), قَيِّم; **~ metals have been traded here since ...** ... يَتاجِرُ النّاسُ في المَعادِنِ الثَّمينةِ هُنا مُنذ 2 (held dear) ‹*moment, memory*› عَزيز (أَعِزّاءُ, أَعِزّة), غالٍ 3 (affected) ‹*style, mannerism*› مُتَكَلِّف, مُتَصَنِّع

B *adv* (for emphasis) جِدًّا, إِلى حَدٍّ بَعيدٍ; **we've had ~ few inquiries** تَلَقَّيْنا عَدَداً قَليلاً جِدًّا من الاِسْتِفْساراتِ; **we got ~ little work done** لَم نُنْجِزْ من العَمَلِ إِلاّ أَقَلَّ القَليلِ

precipice /ˈprɛsɪpɪs/ *n* (fml) حافّة جُرُفٍ

precipitate /prɪˈsɪpɪteɪt/ *vt* (fml) عَجَّلَ (ب) ‹*a crisis, sb's resignation*›

precipitation /prɪˌsɪpɪˈteɪʃ(ə)n/ *n* 1 (rain, snow, etc) هُطول \ سُقوط الأَمْطارِ 2 (chemical) تَرْسيب

precis /ˈpreɪsi/ *n* مُلَخَّص (مُلَخَّصات), تَلْخيص (تَلْخيصات)

precise /prɪˈsʌɪs/ *adj* ‹*measurement, worker*› دَقيق

precisely /prɪˈsʌɪsli/ *adv* 1 (exactly) ‹*to know, mean*› بِدِقّةٍ, بالضَّبْطِ, تَماماً; **at ten o'clock ~** في تَمامِ (الساعة) العاشِرةِ 2 (accurately) ‹*to define, measure*› بِدِقّةٍ, بالضَّبْطِ

precision /prɪˈsɪʒ(ə)n/ **A** *n* دِقّة

B *adj before n* بالِغ الدِقّةِ ‹*tools, instruments*›

preclude /prɪˈkluːd/ *vt* (fml) مَنَعَ (a; مَنْع), حالَ (u; حَيْلولة; دون) ‹*a possibility, use*›

precocious /prɪˈkəʊʃəs/ *adj* ‹*child, talent*› مُبَكِّر النُّضْجِ

preconceived /priːkənˈsiːvd/ *adj* ‹*idea, opinion*› مُسْبَق, مُكَوَّن سَلَفاً

preconception /priːkənˈsɛpʃən/ *n* (Philos) تَصَوُّر مُسْبَق

precondition /priːkənˈdɪʃən/ *n* شَرْط مُسْبَق

precursor /prɪˈkəːsə/ *n* (person) بَشير (بُشَراءُ), نَذير (نُذُر); (thing or event) مُقَدِّمة

predate /priːˈdeɪt/ *vt* 1 (to precede) سَبَقَ (i-u; سَبْق) ‹*an arrival, invention*› 2 (to give an earlier date) أَرَّخَ بِتاريخٍ سابِقٍ ‹*a cheque, document*›

predator /ˈprɛdətə/ *n* (animal) مُفْتَرِس (حَيَوان), ضارٍ (حَيَوان); (bird) جارِح (طائِر), كاسِر (طائِر)

predatory /ˈprɛdət(ə)ri/ *adj* 1 ‹*fish, insect*› مُفْتَرِس, ضارٍ; ‹*bird*› جارِح, كاسِر 2 (of people) ‹*lender, paedophile*› اِسْتِغْلاليّ

predecessor /ˈpriːdɪsɛsə/ *n* سَلَف (أَسْلاف)

predestine /priːˈdɛstɪn/ *vt* قَدَّرَ, كَتَبَ (u; كِتابة) ‹*salvation, failure*›

predetermine /priːdɪˈtəːmɪn/ *vt* حَدَّدَ (سَلَفاً) ‹*an outcome, fate*›

predicament /prɪˈdɪkəmənt/ *n* مَأْزِق (مَآزِقُ), وَرْطة (وَرَطات)

predicate **A** /ˈprɛdɪkət/ *n* مُسْنَد (مَسانِدُ), خَبَر (أَخْبار)

B /ˈprɛdɪkeɪt/ *vt* (to base) بَنى (i; بِناء) ‹*a theory, project*›

predicative /prɪˈdɪkətɪv/ *adj* ‹*adjective, noun*› خَبَريّ

predict /prɪˈdɪkt/ *vt* تَنَبَّأَ (ب) ‹*an outcome, the future*›

predictable /prɪˈdɪktəb(ə)l/ *adj* ‹*outcome, result*› مُتَوَقَّع, يُمْكِنُ التَنَبُّؤُ بِهِ

predictably /prɪˈdɪktəbli/ *adv* ‹*to behave, react*› على نَحْوٍ مُتَوَقَّعٍ, كَما هو مُتَوَقَّعٌ

prediction /prɪˈdɪkʃ(ə)n/ *n* نُبوءة, تَنَبُّؤ (تَنَبُّؤات)

predictive /prɪˈdɪktɪv/ *adj* ‹*ability, model*› تَنَبُّؤِيّ

predictive text *n* نَصّ تَنَبُّؤِيّ

predispose /ˌpriːdɪˈspəʊz/ *vt* هَيَّأَ, أَهَّبَ, عَرَّضَ ‹*a patient, individuals*›; **to be ~d to an illness** كانَ عُرْضةً للإصابةِ بِمَرَضٍ

predominance /prɪˈdɒmɪnəns/ *n* غَلَبة, هَيْمَنة, سَيْطَرة

predominant /prɪˈdɒmɪnənt/ *adj* ‹*symptom, colour*› مُسَيْطِر, سائِد, غالِب

predominantly /prɪˈdɒmɪnəntli/ *adv* ‹*rural, middle-class*› في الغالِبِ, على الأَغْلَبِ

predominate /prɪˈdɒmɪneɪt/ *vi* «the elderly, males» غَلَبَ (i; غَلَبة), سادَ (u; سِيادة), هَيْمَنَ (i; هَيْمَنة)

pre-eclampsia /priːɪˈklampsɪə/ *n* تَسَمُّم الحَمْل

pre-eminent /priːˈɛmɪnənt/ *adj* ‹*scholar, historian*› مُتَفَوِّق, بارِز

pre-empt /priˈɛmpt/ *vt* تَجَنَّبَ, تفادى (بِاتِّخاذِ إِجْراءٍ اسْتِباقِيٍّ) ‹*an attack, decision*›

pre-emptive /priˈɛmptɪv/ *adj* ‹*attack, action*› اسْتِباقِيّ, وِقائِيّ

preen /priːn/ **A** *vt* [سَوّى بِمِنْقارِهِ] ‹*feathers*› **B** *v refl* **to ~ oneself** «narcissists» تَأَنَّقَ, تَهَنْدَمَ, هَنْدَمَ نَفْسَهُ; «birds» [سَوّى ريشَهُ بِمِنْقارِهِ]

pre-existing /priːɪɡˈzɪstɪŋ/ *adj before n* ‹*condition, illness*› مَوْجود مُسْبَقاً

prefabricated /priːˈfabrɪkeɪtɪd/ *adj* ‹*section, bridge*› سابِق التَجْهيز

preface /ˈprɛfəs/ *n* مُقَدِّمة, تَمْهيد (تَمْهيدات), تَوْطِئة

prefect /ˈpriːfɛkt/ *n* **1** (a senior pupil) (BrE) رائِد (فَصْلٍ) **2** (an official) حاكِم (إِقْليمٍ أو مُقاطَعةٍ)

prefer /prɪˈfəː/ *vt* (**-rr-**) فَضَّلَ, آثَرَ (imperf يُؤْثِرُ) ‹*an approach, version*›; **I ~ the red one to the black one** أُفَضِّلُ الأَحْمَرَ على الأَسْوَدِ; **the donor ~s to remain anonymous** يُفَضِّلُ المانِحُ عَدَمَ الكَشْفِ عن هُوِيَّتِهِ

preferable /ˈprɛf(ə)rəb(ə)l/ *adj* ‹*option, approach*› أَفْضَل (dipt; أَفاضِلُ; f فُضْلى; f pl فُضْلَيات); **for him classical music is ~ to rock** يُفَضِّلُ الموسيقى الكْلاسيكيّةَ على الروك

preferably /ˈprɛfrəbli/ *adv* وَيُفَضَّلُ, مِن المُفَضَّلِ; **I need it quickly, ~ today** أَحْتاجُهُ بِسُرْعةٍ وَيُفَضَّلُ اليَوْمَ

preference /ˈprɛf(ə)rəns/ *n* أَفْضَلِيّة; **his ~ is for bright colours** يُفَضِّلُ الأَلْوانَ الفاقِعةَ; **list them in order of ~** رَتِّبْها حَسَبَ الأَفْضَلِيّةِ

preferential /ˌprɛfəˈrɛnʃ(ə)l/ *adj before n* ‹*treatment, rate*› تَفْضيلِيّ

prefigure /priːˈfɪɡə/ *vt* أَنْذَرَ (ب) ‹*the fate, defeat*›

prefix /ˈpriːfɪks/ *n* (*pl* **prefixes**) بادِئة

pregnancy /ˈprɛɡnənsi/ *n* (*pl* **pregnancies**) حَمْل

pregnant /ˈprɛɡnənt/ *adj* **1** ‹*woman, mare*› حامِل (f; حَوامِلُ), حُبْلى (f; حَبالى); **she's six months' ~** هي حامِلٌ \ حُبْلى في شَهْرِها السادِسِ **2** ‹*silence, pause*› ثَقيل

preheat /priːˈhiːt/ *vt* سَخَّنَ (مُسْبَقاً) ‹*an oven, grill*›; **~ the oven to 400°** سَخِّنِ الفُرْنَ مُسْبَقاً حتّى 400 دَرَجةً

prehistoric /priːhɪˈstɒrɪk/ *adj* ‹*creature, cave*› مِن حِقْبةِ ما قبل التاريخ

prejudge /priːˈdʒʌdʒ/ *vt* حَكَمَ مُسْبَقاً على ‹*an outcome, a defendant*›

prejudice /ˈprɛdʒʊdɪs/ **A** *n* تَحامُل; **victims of racial/political ~** ضَحايا التَعَصُّبِ العِرْقِيِّ \ السِياسِيِّ; **there was a lot of ~ against women in the army** كانَ هُناكَ الكَثيرُ من التَعَصُّبِ ضِدّ المَرْأةِ في الجَيْشِ **B** *vt* **1** (to influence) أَثَّرَ (على) ‹*a jury, the public*› **2** (to harm) أَضَرَّ (ب), آذى (Form IV; imperf يُؤْذي) ‹*a trial, claim*›

prejudiced /ˈprɛdʒədɪst/ *adj* ‹*view, society*› مُتَحَيِّز; **they are ~ against foreigners** هُمْ مُتَحامِلونَ على الأَجانِبِ

preliminary /prɪˈlɪmɪn(ə)ri/ **A** *adj* ‹*result, hearing*› تَمْهيدِيّ **B** *n* (*pl* **preliminaries**) مُقَدِّمة, تَمْهيد (تَمْهيدات) **C** (**preliminaries**) *n pl* (in a competition) أَدْوار تَمْهيدِيّة

prelude /ˈprɛljuːd/ *n* **1** (an introduction) مُقَدِّمة, فاتِحة (فَواتِحُ) **2** (in music) مَطْلَع موسيقِيّ, فاتِحة موسيقِيّة

premarital /priːˈmarɪt(ə)l/ *adj before n* ‹*sex, agreement*› ما قبل الزَواج

premature /ˈprɛmətjʊə/ *adj* **1** ‹*death, report*› مُبَكِّر **2** ‹*baby*› مَوْلود قبل أَوانِهِ, خَديج (خُدُج); ‹*birth*› مُبَكِّر; **the baby was six weeks ~** وُلِدَ الطِفْلُ قبل مَوْعِدِهِ بِسِتّةِ أَسابيعَ

prematurely /ˈprɛmətʃ(ə)li/ *adv* ‹*to die, end*› قبل أَوانِهِ

pre-med /priːˈmɛd/ **A** *n* **1** (BrE) (premedication) تَمْهيد التَخْدير **2** (AmE) (premedical studies) [دِراسات تَحْضيريّة في الطِبِّ] **B** *adj* (AmE) ‹*student, course*› [دِراساتٍ تَحْضيريّةٍ في الطِبِّ]

premedication /ˌpriːmɛdɪˈkeɪʃ(ə)n/ *n* تَمْهيد التَخْدير

premeditated /priːˈmɛdɪteɪtɪd/ *adj* ‹*murder, act*› مُتَعَمَّد, مع سَبْق الإصْرارِ والتَرَصُّدِ

premenstrual /priːˈmɛnstrʊəl/ *adj* ‹*symptom, disorder*› ما قبل الحَيْض

premier /ˈprɛmɪə/ **A** *adj* ‹*league, destination*› أَوَّل (dipt; أَوائِلُ; f أُولى; f pl أُولَيات), أَهَمّ **B** *n* وَزير أَوَّل, رَئيس وُزَراءَ

premiere /ˈprɛmɪɛː/ **A** *n* عَرْض أَوَّل; **the world/British ~** العَرْض الأَوَّل في بَريطانيا \ العالَمِ **B** *vt* عَرَض لأَوَّلِ مَرّةٍ ‹*a film, work*› **C** *vi* «shows, plays» عُرِضَ لِأَوَّلِ مَرّةٍ

premiership /ˈprɛmɪəʃɪp/ *n* **1** (of a prime minister) فَتْرة رِئاسة وُزَراءَ **2** (BrE) (in football, rugby) also (**the Premiership**) الدَوْريّ المُمْتاز

premise /ˈprɛmɪs/ *n* (also **premiss**) افْتِراض, فَرْضيّة (افْتِراضات), مُقَدِّمة مَنْطِقيّة

premises /ˈprɛmɪsɪz/ *n pl* مَبْنًى (وَما حَوْلَهُ); **on the ~** في المَبْنى; **off the ~** خارِجَ المَبْنى; **private ~** مَبْنًى خاصّ; **they've moved the business to new ~** نَقَلوا الشَرِكةَ إلى مَقَرٍّ جَديدٍ

premium /ˈpriːmɪəm/ *n* **1** (bonus) مُكافَأة, عِلاوة; (surcharge) رَسْم إضافيّ **2** (in insurance) قِسْط (أَقْساط) **at a premium** (in short supply) [غَيْر مُتَوَفِّرٍ بِشَكْلٍ كافٍ]; (at a high price) بِسِعْرٍ غالٍ

Idiom **to put/set a (high) premium on sb/sth** أَعْلى من شَأْنِ شَخْصٍ \ قيمةِ شَيْءٍ

Premium Bond *n* (BrE) [سَنَد حُكوميّ بَريطانيّ بِدونِ فائِدةٍ يُخَوِّلُ لِحامِلِهِ دُخولَ سَحْبٍ على جَوائِزَ نَقْديّةٍ]

premonition /priːməˈnɪʃ(ə)n, prɛməˈnɪʃ(ə)n/ *n* هاجِس (هَواجِسُ)

prenatal /priːˈneɪt(ə)l/ *adj* ‹*care, testing*› ما قبل الوِلادةِ

prenatal class *n* دُروس ما قبل الوِلادةِ

prenup /ˈpriːnʌp/ *n* ▸ **prenuptial agreement**

prenuptial /priːˈnʌpʃ(ə)l/ *adj* ‹*nerves, contract*› قبل الزَواجِ

prenuptial agreement *n* [اتِّفاق قبل الزَواجِ على المَسائِلِ الماليّةِ]

preoccupation /prɪˌɒkjʊˈpeɪʃ(ə)n/ *n* **1** (obsession) انْهِماك **2** (concern) شُغْل شاغِل (انْهِماكات)

preoccupied /prɪˈɒkjuːpʌɪd/ *adj* ‹*look, frown*› مَشْغول البالِ, مُنْغَمِس

preoccupy /priːˈɒkjʊpʌɪ/ *vt* (**preoccupies, preoccupying, preoccupied**) شَغَلَ البالَ ‹*a politician, journalist*›

prep /prɛp/ *n* (BrE infml) (homework) واجِبات

prepaid /priːˈpeɪd/ *adj* ‹*phone card, envelope*› مَدْفوع, مُسْبَق الدَفْعِ مُسَبَّقاً

prepaid credit card *n* بِطاقة ائْتِمانٍ مُسْبَقة الدَفْعِ

preparation /ˌprɛpəˈreɪʃ(ə)n/ *n* **1** [U] (of food, of a venue) تَحْضير, إعْداد; (for an event, a trip) اسْتِعْداد; **in ~ for the journey/visit** اسْتِعْداداً للرِحْلةِ \ للزِيارةِ **2** (**preparations** *n pl*) (arrangements) اسْتِعْدادات

preparatory /prɪˈparət(ə)ri/ *adj* ‹*meeting, work*› تَمْهيديّ, تَحْضيريّ

preparatory school *n* **1** (BrE) (for pupils aged seven to thirteen) مَدْرَسة إعْداديّة **2** (AmE) (preparing students for university) [مَدْرَسة تَحْضيريّة خاصّة قبل الجامِعةِ]

prepare /prɪˈpɛː/ **A** *vt* **1** حَضَّر, أَعَدَّ ‹*a speech, plan*›; **to ~ sb for a shock/some bad news** هَيَّأَ شَخْصاً لِسَماعِ خَبَرٍ صادِمٍ \ بَعْضِ الأَخْبارِ السَيِّئةِ; **~ the ground before sowing the seeds** أَعَدَّ الأَرْض قبل زِراعةِ البُذورِ **2** حَضَّر, أَعَدَّ ‹*food, a meal*›; **to ~ a dinner for fifteen people** حَضَّرَ عَشاءً لِخَمْسةَ عَشَرَ شَخْصاً **B** *vi* اسْتَعَدَّ; **to ~ to leave** اسْتَعَدَّ لِيُغادِرَ \ للمُغادَرةِ; **to ~ for a trip/an exam** اسْتَعَدَّ لِرِحْلةٍ \ لِامْتِحانٍ

prepared /prɪˈpɛːd/ *adj* **1** (ready) **to be ~ for emergencies/a surprise** كانَ مُسْتَعِدًّا للطَوارِئِ \ لِمُفاجَأةٍ **2** (willing) **to be ~ to do sth** كانَ مُسْتَعِدًّا لِيَفْعَلَ شَيْئاً

preposition /ˌprɛpəˈzɪʃ(ə)n/ *n* حَرْف جَرٍّ

prepossessing /priːpəˈzɛsɪŋ/ *adj* ‹*appearance, manner*› فاتِن

preposterous /prɪˈpɒst(ə)rəs/ *adj* ‹*claim, idea*› مُنافٍ للعَقْلِ

prep school *n* ▸ **preparatory school**

prerequisite /priːˈrɛkwɪzɪt/ *n* شَرْط أَساسيّ \ مُسَبَّق

prerogative /prɪˈrɒɡətɪv/ *n* صَلاحيّة, امْتِياز (امْتِيازات); **that's your ~** ذلك حَقُّكَ

Presbyterian /ˌprɛzbɪˈtɪərɪən/ *n, adj* مَشْيَخيّ

preschool /priːskuːl/ **A** *adj* ‹children, education› ما قبل المَدْرَسةِ **B** *n* (AmE) رَوْضة أَطْفالٍ

prescribe /prɪˈskrʌɪb/ *vt* وَصَفَ (i; وَصْف) ‹a drug, medication›

prescription /prɪˈskrɪpʃ(ə)n/ *n* روشتّة, وَصْفة طِبّيّة

prescriptive /prɪˈskrɪptɪv/ *adj* ‹grammar, dictionary› مِعْياريّ, تَوْجيهيّ

presence /ˈprɛz(ə)ns/ *n* حُضور

Idiom **to make one's presence felt** جَعَلَ حُضورَهُ مَحْسوساً

presence of mind *n* حُضور الذِهْنِ

present¹ /ˈprɛz(ə)nt/ *adj* **1** (in a specified place) حاضِر, مَوْجود; **to be ~ at a meeting/funeral** كانَ حاضِراً في اجْتِماعٍ \ جَنازةٍ; **all ~ and correct!** حاضِر ومُسْتَعِدّ! **2** (current) ‹address, leadership, situation› حالِيّ, حاضِر; **up to the ~ day** إلى يَوْمِنا هذا; **at the ~ time** *or* **moment** في الوَقْتِ الراهِنِ; **the ~ owner of the house** صاحِب البَيْتِ الحاليّ **3** (Ling) ‹tense, participle› مُضارِع

present² /prɪˈzɛnt/ **A** *vt* **1** (to raise) طَرَحَ (a; طَرْح) ‹a problem, challenge, an obstacle›; **their offer ~s us with some interesting options** يَطْرَحُ عَرْضُهُمْ أَمامَنا خَياراتٍ مُثيرة للاهْتِمامِ **2** (to show) أَظْهَرَ ‹a ticket, passport› **3** (to submit for consideration) قَدَّمَ, عَرَضَ (i; عَرْض), طَرَحَ (a; طَرْح) ‹a plan, report, figures›; **the plan will be ~ed to the board** سَتُعْرَضُ الخُطّةُ على مَجْلِسِ الإدارةِ **4** قَدَّمَ ‹a programme, show› **5** (to give) قَدَّمَ, أَعْطى ‹a prize, medal, cheque›; **I was ~ed with a huge bill** قُدِّمَتْ لي فاتورةٌ ضَخْمةٌ; **to ~ sb with a choice** أَعْطى شَخْصاً خِياراً **6** (to portray) قَدَّمَ, صَوَّرَ, عَرَضَ (i; عَرْض) ‹a person, situation›; **to ~ sb/sth in a different light** قَدَّمَ شَخْصاً \ شَيْئاً بِشَكْلٍ مُغايِرٍ **7** (to put on, produce) قَدَّمَ ‹a production, play› **8** (fml) (to introduce) قَدَّمَ ‹a friend, one's spouse, daughter›; **may I ~ my son Piers?** هَلاّ سَمَحْتَ لي بِتَقْديمِ ابْني بيرْس ؟

9 (Mil) **to ~ arms** أَشْهَرَ \ رَفَعَ سِلاحَهُ (في اسْتِعْراضٍ عَسْكَريٍّ) **B** *vi* (Med) «patients» عانى; «symptoms» ظَهَرَ (a; ظُهور) **C** *v refl* **1** **to ~ oneself** قَدَّمَ نَفْسَهُ; **to learn how to ~ oneself** تَعَلَّمَ كيف يُقَدِّمُ نَفْسَهُ; **to ~ oneself as sth** قَدَّمَ نَفْسَهُ كَشَيْءٍ **2** (to arise) **when the opportunity ~ed itself** عِنْدَما سَنَحَت الفُرْصةُ

present³ /ˈprɛz(ə)nt/ **A** *n* **1** (gift) هَدِيّة (هَدايا); **to give sb sth as a ~** أَعْطى شَخْصاً شَيْئاً كَهَدِيّةٍ; **a Christmas/birthday ~** هَدِيّة أَعْيادِ الميلادِ \ عيد ميلادٍ **2** (current time) **the ~** الوَقْت الحاضِر; **for the ~** في الوَقْتِ الحاليِّ **3** (also **present tense**) زَمَن المُضارِعِ; **put the verb in the ~** *or* **into the ~ tense** ضَعِ الفِعْلَ في زَمَنِ المُضارِعِ **B** (**at present**) *adv phr* (at this moment) في الوَقْتِ الحاليِّ

presentable /prɪˈzɛntəb(ə)l/ *adj* ‹clothes, young man› لائِق

presentation /prɛz(ə)nˈteɪʃ(ə)n/ *n* **1** (of a gift, prize) تَقْديم (تَقْديمات), تَسْليم; (of a letter, petition) تَقْديم (تَقْديمات), تَسْليم **2** (talk) تَقْديم (تَقْديمات), عَرْض (عُروض); **to give a ~ on the new methodology** قَدَّمَ عَرْضاً عن المَنْهَجيّةِ الجَديدةِ

present-day /ˌprɛz(ə)ntˈdeɪ/ *adj* ‹conditions, attitudes› الوَقْتِ الحاضِرِ \ الراهِنِ

presenter /prɪˈzɛntə/ *n* مُقَدِّم (بَرامِجَ)

presently /ˈprɛz(ə)ntli/ *adv* **1** (currently) ‹to exist, work› الآنَ, حاليًّا, في الوَقْتِ الراهِنِ **2** (soon) ‹to arrive, buy› عاجِلاً, قَريباً, بعد قَليلٍ

preservation /prɛzəˈveɪʃ(ə)n/ *n* حِماية, مُحافَظة

preservative /prɪˈzəːvətɪv/ *n* مادّة حافِظة

preserve /prɪˈzəːv/ **A** *vt* **1** (to save) حَفِظَ (a; حِفْظ), حافَظَ (على), حَمى (i; حِماية) ‹a building, species› **2** (to maintain) حافَظَ (على) ‹the peace, a right› **3** حَفِظَ (a; حِفْظ), صَبَّرَ ‹meat, fruit›; حَفِظَ (a; حِفْظ) ‹wood, a painting, an organ› **B** *n* **1** (jam) مُرَبّى (مُرَبّيات), مَعْجون (مَعاجينُ) **2** (area of activity) نَشاط (أَنْشِطة); **it's the ~ of the rich/middle classes** إنَّها لُعْبةُ الأَغْنِياءِ \ الطَبَقةِ الوُسْطى

preset /priːˈset/ **A** *vt* (present participle **-tt-**, past tense, past participle **preset**) ضَبَطَ مُسْبَقاً ‹a timer, thermostat› **B** *n* إعْداد مُسْبَق

preside /prɪˈzʌɪd/ *vi* **to ~ over a ceremony/meeting** تَرَأَّسَ حَفْلاً \ اجْتِماعاً

presidency /ˈprɛzɪd(ə)nsi/ *n* (*pl* **presidencies**) رِئاسة; **Greece takes over the ~ of the EU** تَتَوَلَّى اليونان رِئاسةَ الاتِّحادِ الأوروبِّيِّ

president /ˈprɛzɪd(ə)nt/ *n* 1 (of a nation) رَئيس (رُؤَساءُ); **to run for ~** تَرَشَّحَ لِلرِئاسةِ 2 (AmE) (of a corporation) رَئيس (رُؤَساءُ)

president-elect /ˌprɛzəd(ə)ntɪˈlɛkt/ *n* الرَئيس المُنْتَخَب

presidential /prɛzɪˈdɛnʃ(ə)l/ *adj* ‹*campaign, palace*› رِئاسيّ

press /prɛs/ **A** *vt* 1 (to push) ضَغَط (a; ضَغْط; على) ‹*a button, switch*› داسَ (u; دَوْس; على) ‹*pedal*›; **~ the pedal down** داسَ على الدَوّاسةِ; **to ~ a wound** ضَغَطَ على جُرْحٍ 2 (to squeeze) ضَغَطَ (a; ضَغْط; على) ‹*sb's arm, hand*›; **she ~ed the baby to her breast** ضَمَّت الطِفْلَ إلى صَدْرِها; **he ~ed his knees/lips together** ضَمَّ رُكْبَتَيْهِ \ شَفَتَيْهِ 3 (to iron) كَوى (i; كَيّ) ‹*a suit, shirt*› 4 (to urge) ضَغَطَ (a; ضَغْط; على) ‹*an employee, a witness*›; **to ~ sb to do sth** ضَغَطَ على شَخْصٍ لِفِعْلِ شَيْءٍ; **to ~ sb into doing sth** ضَغَطَ على شَخْصٍ لِكَيْ يَفْعَلَ شَيْئاً; **I must ~ you for an answer** أنا مُضْطَرٌّ لِأَنْ أُلِحَّ عَلَيْكَ للحُصولِ على جَوابٍ; **when ~ed, he admitted that ...** عِنْدَما ضُغِطَ عَلَيْهِ، أَقَرَّ أنَّ ...; **to ~ one's point/case** أَكَّدَ على وُجْهةِ نَظَرِهِ \ قَضيَّتِهِ 5 (Tech) كَبَسَ (i; كَبْس) ‹*a panel, a CD, shape*›; **all the doors/panels are ~ed at the Milton plant** صُنِعَتْ كُلُّ الأَبْوابِ \ الأَلْواحِ في مَصْنَعِ ميلْتون

B *vi* 1 (with one's hand, foot, etc) **to ~ down** ضَغَطَ لِأَسْفَلَ 2 (to crowd) تَدافَعَ; **the crowd was ~ing against the barrier** كانَ الحَشْدُ يَتَدافَعُ على الحاجِزِ; **they all tried to ~ through the entrance** حاوَلوا كُلُّهُمْ التَدافُعَ من خِلالِ البَوّابةِ

C *v refl* **to ~ oneself against sb/sth** ضَغَطَ بِجِسْمِهِ على شَخْصٍ \ شَيْءٍ

D *n* 1 (P&P) (**the press, the Press**) (journalists) الصِحافيّونَ; (publications) الصِحافة; **the story appeared in the ~** ظَهَرَت القِصّةُ في الصِحافةِ; **to get a good/bad ~** حَصَلَ على تَغْطِيةٍ جَيِّدةٍ \ سَيِّئةٍ من الصِحافةِ 2 (also **printing press**) مِطْبَعة (مَطابِعُ); **to go to ~** ذَهَبَ \ أُرْسِلَ إلى المِطْبَعةِ 3 (publishing house) دار نَشْرٍ; **published by Yale University Press** نَشَرَتْهُ دارُ نَشْرِ جامِعةِ ييل 4 (printing works) مَطْبَعة (مَطابِعُ); **printed at the Eastern Star Printing Press** طَبَعَتْهُ مُؤَسَّسةُ إيسْتيرْن سْتار للطِباعةِ 5 (act of pushing) ضَغْط (ضُغوط); **at the ~ of a button** بِضَغْطةِ زِرٍّ; **to give the doorbell/accelerator a ~** ضَغَطَ على جَرَسِ البابِ \ زِرِّ المِصْعَدِ 6 (crowd) زِحام 7 (with an iron) كَيّ 8 (for panels, plates) آلة كَبْسٍ

(Phrasal verbs) **press ahead** مَضى قُدُماً; **to ~ ahead with the reform/plan** مَضى قُدُماً في الإِصْلاحِ \ الخُطّةِ

• **press for**: 1 **~ for [sth]** ضَغَطَ من أَجْلِ [شَيْءٍ] ‹*a change, sb's release*› 2 (to be short of) **to be ~ed for time/money** نَقَصَهُ الوَقْتُ \ المالُ

• **press on** **A** 1 (on a journey) واصَلَ, تابَعَ 2 (with a task) تابَعَ; **let's ~ on to the next item** دَعْنا نَنْتَقِلُ إلى الفَقْرةِ التاليةِ; **to ~ on regardless** تابَعَ بِغَضِّ النَظَرِ عن أيِّ شَيْءٍ **B** **~ [sth] on sb** فَرَضَ [شَيْئاً] على شَخْصٍ ‹*gifts, food, money*›

press agency *n* وَكالةُ أَنْباءٍ

press conference *n* نَدْوة صَحَفيّة

pressing /ˈprɛsɪŋ/ *adj* ‹*need, problem*› مُلِحّ, مُسْتَعْجَل

press officer *n* (BrE) مُلْحَق صَحَفِيّ

press release *n* بَيان صَحَفيّ

press stud *n* (BrE) زِرّ مَعْدِنيّ (يَتَكَوَّنُ من قِطْعَتَيْنِ)

press-up /ˈprɛsʌp/ *n* تَمْرين الضَغْطِ

pressure /ˈprɛʃə/ **A** *n* 1 (force) ضَغْط (ضُغوط); **a ~ of 1 kg per cm2** ضَغْط بِقوّةِ 1 كغ لِكُلِّ سم مُرَبَّعٍ; **~ is high/low over the eastern Mediterranean** الضَغْطُ عالٍ \ مُنْخَفِضٌ على شَرْقِ المُتَوَسِّطِ; **to store sth under ~** خَزَنَ شَيْئاً في صورةٍ مَضْغوطةٍ 2 (on a person) ضَغْط (ضُغوط); **the ~s of modern life** ضُغوط الحَياةِ المُعاصِرةِ; **to work well/badly under ~** عَمِلَ بِشَكْلٍ جَيِّدٍ \ سَيِّئٍ تحت الضَغْطِ; **to put ~ on sb to agree** ضَغَطَ على شَخْصٍ لِكَيْ يُوافِقَ 3 (of traffic, tourists, visitors) ضَغْط (ضُغوط)

B *vt* ▸ **pressurize**

pressure cooker *n* قِدْر \ طَنْجَرة الضَغْطِ

pressure group *n* جَماعة ضَغْطٍ

pressure point *n* نُقْطة ضَغْطٍ

pressurize, -ise (BrE) /ˈprɛʃərʌɪz/ *vt* **1** كَيَّفَ الضَغْط ‹*a cabin, gas*› **2** (to coerce) ضَغَطَ (a; ضَغْط; على), أَرْغَمَ (على) ‹*an employee, a friend*›

prestige /prɛˈstiːdʒ/ *n* وَجاهة, هَيْبة, مَكانة مَرْموقة; **to have great ~** كانَ لَهُ هَيْبةٌ عَظيمةٌ

prestigious /prɛˈstɪdʒəs/ *adj* ‹*university, prize*› مَرْموق

presumably /prɪˈzjuːməbli/ *adv* مِن المُفْتَرَضِ, يُفْتَرَضُ; **~ you still have the receipt** مِن المُفْتَرَضِ أنّ الإيصالَ ما زالَ مَعَكَ

presume /prɪˈzjuːm/ *vt* **1** (to assume) اِفْتَرَضَ; **I ~ that she'll accept** أَفْتَرِضُ أنَّها سَتُوافِقُ; **I ~ that this is your house** أَفْتَرِضُ أنّ هذا هو بَيْتُكَ **2** (to dare) **to ~ to do sth** تَجَرَّأَ على فِعْلِ شَيْءٍ

presumption /prɪˈzʌmpʃ(ə)n/ *n* **1** (supposition) اِفْتِراض (اِفْتِراضات) **2** (impudence) وَقاحة

presumptuous /prɪˈzʌmptʃʊəs/ *adj* ‹*letter, behaviour*› وَقِح (وُقُح)

presuppose /priːsəˈpəʊz/ *vt* اِفْتَرَضَ سَلَفاً \ مُسَبَّقاً ‹*knowledge, existence*›

pre-tax /priːˈtaks/ *adj* ‹*profit, income*› قبل الضَريبةِ

pretence (BrE), **pretense** (AmE) /prɪˈtɛns/ *n* اِدِّعاء (اِدِّعاءات), تَظاهُر; **let's drop the ~** لِنَتَوَقَّفْ عن الادِّعاءِ; **under false ~s** تحت ادِّعاءٍ زائِفٍ

pretend /prɪˈtɛnd/ **A** *vt* تَظاهَرَ, اِدَّعى (ب) ‹*innocence, ignorance*›; **he was ~ing to be ill** كانَ يَتَظاهَرُ بالمَرَضِ; **we ~ed that we had never met her** تَظاهَرْنا بِأنَّنا لم نَلْتَقِ بها أبَداً

B *vi* تَظاهَرَ

C *adj* (infml) ‹*gun, money*› غَيْر حَقيقيٍّ

pretender /prɪˈtɛndə/ *n* مُدَّعٍ

pretense (AmE) *n* ▸ **pretence**

pretension /prɪˈtɛnʃ(ə)n/ *n* اِدِّعاء (اِدِّعاءات)

pretentious /prɪˈtɛnʃəs/ *adj* ‹*artist, rubbish*› مُدَّعٍ

preterite /ˈprɛtərɪt/ *n* ماضٍ (الزَمَن الماضي)

pretext /ˈpriːtɛkst/ *n* ذَريعة (ذَرائِعُ)

pretty /ˈprɪti/ **A** *adj* (**prettier, prettiest**) **1** (in looks) ‹*face, woman, child*› جَميل **2** (attractive) ‹*dress, village, view*› جَميل; **it was not a ~ sight** لم يَكُنْ مَنْظَراً جَميلاً

B *adv* (infml) (very) جِدًّا; (fairly) إلى حَدٍّ ما; **that's ~ good!** ذلك جَيِّدٌ جِدًّا!; **he's ~ good but not as good as me** هو ماهِرٌ إلى حَدٍّ ما ولَكِنْ لَيْسَ في مِثْلِ مَهارَتي; **~ well everyone knows** الكُلُّ تَقْريباً يَعْرِفُ

Idiom **to be sitting pretty** كانَ في وَضْعٍ جَيِّدٍ

Phrasal verb **pretty up**: **~ [sth] up, ~ up [sth]** جَمَّلَ \ زَيَّنَ [شَيْئاً] ‹*a village, room*›

prevail /prɪˈveɪl/ *vi* **1** (to triumph) «justice, common sense» اِنْتَصَرَ, (غَلَبة; i) غَلَبَ; «troops, allies» سادَ (u; سِيادة) **2** (to exist) طَغى (a; طُغْيان)

Phrasal verb **prevail upon**: **~ upon [sb]** أَقْنَعَ [شَخْصاً]

prevailing /prɪˈveɪlɪŋ/ *adj* (current) ‹*attitude, conditions*› سائِد, مُهَيْمِن

prevalence /ˈprɛvələns/ *n* (rate) اِنْتِشار

prevalent /ˈprɛvələnt/ *adj* (common) ‹*disease, belief*› سائِد

prevaricate /prɪˈvarɪkeɪt/ *vi* «politicians, employees» راوَغَ, لَفَّ وَدارَ (حول المَوْضوع)

prevent /prɪˈvɛnt/ *vt* مَنَعَ (a; مَنْع) ‹*a fire, an illness*›; **to ~ sb/sth from doing sth** مَنَعَ شَخْصاً \ شَيْئاً من فِعْلِ شَيْءٍ

preventable /prɪˈvɛntəb(ə)l/ *adj* ‹*accident*› مِن المُمْكِنِ تَفاديه; ‹*disease*› مِن المُمْكِنِ الوِقايةُ مِنْهُ

preventative /prɪˈvɛntətɪv/ *adj* ▸ **preventive**

prevention /prɪˈvɛnʃ(ə)n/ *n* وِقاية, مَنْع

preventive /prɪˈvɛntɪv/ *adj* ‹*measure, medicine*› وِقائيّ

preview /ˈpriːvjuː/ *n* **1** (advance showing) عَرْض مُسَبَّق **2** (trailer) عَرْض \ شَريط دِعائيّ

previous /ˈpriːvɪəs/ *adj* ‹*day, owner, experience*› سابِق; **we met the ~ day/evening** اِلْتَقَيْنا في اليَوْمِ \ المَساءِ السابِقِ; **he had no ~ experience of book-keeping** لم تَكُنْ لَدَيْهِ خِبْرةٌ سابِقةٌ في تَسْجيلِ الحِسابات

previously /ˈpriːvɪəsli/ *adv* ‹*to mention, work*› سابِقاً

pre-war /priːˈwɔː/ *adj* ‹*vehicles, plumbing*› ما قبل الحَرْبِ

prey /preɪ/ *n* فَريسة (فَرائِسُ)

(Phrasal verb) **prey on A ~ on [sth] 1** (to hunt) افْتَرَس [شَيْئاً] <*rodents, birds*> **2** (to exploit) اسْتَغَلَّ [شَيْئاً] <*sb's fear, worries*> **3** (to worry) **to ~ on sb's mind** نَهَش عَقْلَ شَخْصٍ **B ~ on [sb]** اعْتَدى على [شَخْصٍ] <*children*>; اسْتَغَلَّ [شَخْصاً] <*the elderly*>

price /praɪs/ **A** *n* **1** (cost) سِعْر (أَسْعار), ثَمَن (أَثْمان); **the ~ per kilo** سِعْر الكيلو الواحِدِ; **'we pay top ~s for gold'** 'نَشْتَري الذَهَبَ بِأَفْضَلِ الأَسْعارِ'; **cars have gone up in/fallen in ~** ارْتَفَعَتْ \ انْخَفَضَتْ أَسْعارُ السَيّاراتِ; **to pay half/full ~ for sth** اشْتَرى شَيْئاً بِنِصْفِ \ بِكامِلِ الثَمَنِ; **what sort of ~ did you have to pay?** كم دَفَعْتَ فيه؟; **to pay a high ~ for sth** دَفَعَ ثَمَناً غالِياً في شَيْءٍ; **that was a small ~ to pay for peace of mind** كانَ ذلك ثَمَناً رَخيصاً لِراحةِ البالِ **2** (value) سِعْر (أَسْعار), قِيَم (أَثْمان) ثَمَن; **to put a ~ on an antique/a car** قَيَّمَ سِعْرَ تُحْفَةٍ \ سَيّارةٍ; **to put** *or* **set a high ~ on loyalty/hard work** قَدَّرَ قيمة الوَلاءِ \ المُثابَرةِ في العَمَلِ **3** (in betting) احْتِمالات الفَوْزِ; **the starting ~** الاحْتِمال المَبْدَئيّ
B *vt* **1** (to value) سَعَّرَ <*a car, house, computer*>; **a dress ~d at $400** فُسْتان مُسَعَّر ب 400 دولار **2** (with a label) وَضَعَ تَسْعيرةً على <*a product*> **3** (in estimates) «tradesmen, valuers» قَدَّرَ السِعْرَ <*an object, a job*>

(Phrasal verb) **price out: to ~ oneself** *or* **one's goods out of the market** عَرَضَ بَضائِعَهُ بِأَسْعارٍ تَفوقُ أَسْعارَ السوقِ

price cut *n* تَخْفيض السِعْرِ

price-fixing /ˈpraɪsfɪksɪŋ/ *n* اتِّفاق تَحْديد السِعْرِ

price freeze *n* تَثْبيت \ تَجْميد الأَسْعارِ

priceless /ˈpraɪsləs/ *adj* **1** (valuable) <*treasure, painting*> نَفيس, لا يُقَدَّرُ بِثَمَنٍ **2** (infml) (amusing) <*remark, scene*> ظَريف (ظُرَفاءُ)

price list *n* **1** (in a shop, catalogue) قائِمة الأَسْعارِ **2** (in a bar, restaurant) قائِمة الطَعامِ

price rise *n* ارْتِفاع الأَسْعارِ

price tag *n* (label) بِطاقة سِعْرٍ

price war *n* حَرْب أَسْعارٍ

pricey /ˈpraɪsi/ *adj* (**pricier, priciest**) (infml) <*tickets, restaurant*> غالٍ, باهِظ الثَمَنِ

prick /prɪk/ **A** *vt* وَخَزَ (وَخْز; i) <*plastic film, sb's hand*>; **I ~ed my finger** وَخَزْتُ إِصْبَعي; **her conscience ~ed her** وَخَزَها ضَميرُها; **to ~ a hole in sth** ثَقَبَ شَيْئاً
B *vi* شاكَ (شَوْك; u)
C *n* **1** (with a needle, etc) وَخْز **2** (penis) قَضيب الرَجُلِ

(Phrasal verbs) **prick out: ~ out [sth], ~ [sth] out** (Agric) نَقَلَ [شَيْئاً] <*seedlings*>
• **prick up: A ~ up** «ears» انْتَصَبَ **B ~ [sth] up, ~ up [sth]: to ~ up one's ears** نَصَبَ أُذُنَيْهِ

prickle /ˈprɪk(ə)l/ **A** *n* **1** (thorn) شَوْكة, شَوْك (أَشْواك) **2** (of a hedgehog) شَوْكة, شَوْك (أَشْواك)
B *vi* «wool, beard» وَخَزَ (وَخْز; i)

prickly /ˈprɪkli/ *adj* (**pricklier, prickliest**) **1** <*hedge, leaf*> شَوْكيّ **2** <*hedgehog, spines*> شَوْكيّ **3** (itchy) <*wool, beard*> واخِز, مُثير للحَكّةِ **4** (infml) (touchy) <*relationship, mood*> نَزِق (نَزَق, نُزوق; a-i)

pride /praɪd/ **A** *n* **1** (in one's work, home, etc) افْتِخار, اعْتِزاز; **to take ~ in one's achievements/appearance** افْتَخَرَ بِانْجازاتِهِ \ بِمَظْهَرِهِ; **to be sb's ~ and joy** كانَ مَصْدَرَ فَخْرٍ وَسَعادةٍ لِشَخْصٍ **2** (self-respect) كَرامة, كِبْرِياء (dipt); **national ~** كَرامة وَطَنيّة; **to hurt sb's ~** جَرَحَ كَرامةَ شَخْصٍ **3** (arrogance) اسْتِكْبار, غَطْرَسة, تَكَبُّر **4** (group of lions) قَطيع (من الأُسودِ)
B *v refl* **to ~ oneself on sth/on doing sth** تَفاخَرَ بِشَيْءٍ \ بِفِعْلِ شَيْءٍ

(Idioms) **pride comes before a fall** [التَكَبُّرُ عاقِبَتُهُ وَخيمةٌ]; **pride of place** مَكان الشَرَفِ

priest /priːst/ *n* قِسّيس (قِسّيسونَ, قَساوِسة), كاهِن (كُهّان, كَهَنة), خوريّ (خَوارِنة)

priestess /ˈpriːstɪs/ *n* قِسّيسة, كاهِنة

priesthood /ˈpriːsthʊd/ *n* **1** (position) قُسوسة, كِهانة **2** (clergy) قَساوِسة, كَهَنة

prig /prɪɡ/ *n* مَزْهوّ بِنَفْسِهِ

prim /prɪm/ *adj* (**-mm-**) <*clothing, school teacher*> مُتَزَمِّت

prima ballerina /ˌpriːmə baləˈriːnə/ *n* راقِصة, الباليرينا الأولى, الباليه الأولى

primaeval *adj* (BrE) ▸ **primeval**

primarily /ˈprʌɪm(ə)rəli/ *adv* (chiefly) ‹*to consist, focus*› أَوَّلاً, بِشَكْلٍ أَساسِيٍّ

primary /ˈprʌɪm(ə)ri/ **A** *adj* **1** (most important) ‹*source, concern*› أَساسِيّ, رَئِيسِيّ **2** (Educ) ‹*education, teacher*› اِبْتِدائِيّ
B *n* (*pl* **primaries**) (AmE Pol) اِنْتِخابات تَمْهِيدِيَّة

primary colour (BrE), **primary color** (AmE) *n* لَوْن أَوَّلِيّ

primary school *n* (BrE) مَدْرَسة اِبْتِدائِيَّة

primate /ˈprʌɪmeɪt/ *n* **1** (mammal) حَيَوان رَئِيسِيّ **2** (archbishop) رَئِيس \ كَبِير أَساقِفةٍ

prime /prʌɪm/ **A** *adj before n* **1** (chief) ‹*aim, suspect, concern*› رَئِيسِيّ; **to be of ~ importance** كانَ ذا أَهَمِّيَّةٍ بالِغةٍ; **it's a ~ example of what not to do!** هو مِثالٌ ساطِعٌ لِما يَجِبُ الاِمْتِناعُ عن فِعْلِهِ! **2** (of top quality) ‹*beef, investment*› مُمْتاز; **the shop occupies a ~ position** يَحْتَلُّ المَتْجَرُ مَوْقِعاً مُمْتازاً; **bonds of ~ quality** سَنَدات من أَفْضَلِ الأَنْواعِ; **~ cuts of meat** أَفْضَلُ قِطَعِ اللَحْمِ
B *n* **1** (at one's best) **to be in one's ~** كانَ في أَفْضَلِ حالاتِهِ; **to be past one's ~** وَلَّتْ فَتْرةُ تَأَلُّقِهِ; **this cheese is past its ~** لم يَعُدْ هذا الجُبْنُ في أَفْضَلِ حالاتِهِ **2** ▸ **prime number**
C *vt* **1** (to brief) «advisers» أَحاطَ عِلْماً, أَطْلَعَ ‹*a witness, an interviewee*›; **to ~ sb about possible problems** حَذَّرَ شَخْصاً من مَشاكِلَ مُحْتَمَلةٍ **2** (with paint) طَلَى طِلاءً أَوَّلِيًّا, وَضَعَ بِطانةَ طِلاءٍ ‹*the wood, metal*› **3** جَهَّزَ \ حَضَّرَ للعَمَلِ ‹*the pump*› **4** جَهَّزَ للتَشْغيلِ ‹*device*›; أَعَدَّ للتَفْجيرِ ‹*a bomb*›; **the bomb was ~d, ready to explode** تَمَّ تَجْهيزُ القُنْبُلةِ للاِنْفِجارِ

prime minister *n* رَئِيس وُزَراءَ, وَزِير أَوَّل

prime mover *n* مُحَرِّك رَئِيسِيّ

prime number *n* عَدَد أَوَّلِيّ

primer /ˈprʌɪmə/ *n* **1** (paint) طِلاء أَوَّلِيّ **2** (old use) (book) تَمْهِيدِيّ

prime time *n* وَقْت الذُرْوةِ

primeval, **primaeval** /prʌɪˈmiːv(ə)l/ *adj* ‹*rocks, forest*› بُدائِيّ

primitive /ˈprɪmɪtɪv/ *adj* ‹*people, tribe, organism*› بُدائِيّ

primitive man /ˌprɪmətɪv ˈman/ *n* [u] إِنْسان بُدائِيّ

primrose /ˈprɪmrəʊz/ *n* كَعْب الثَلْج, زَهْرة الرَبيع

Primus® /ˈprʌɪməs/, **~ stove** *n* مَوْقِد كيروسين

prince /prɪns/ *n* أَمِير (أُمَراءُ)

princess /prɪnˈsɛs/ *n* أَمِيرة

principal /ˈprɪnsɪp(ə)l/ **A** *adj* ‹*component, reason*› رَئِيسِيّ
B *n* (of a school) مُدِير; (of a university, college) رَئِيس (رُؤَساءُ)

principality /ˌprɪnsɪˈpalɪti/ *n* (*pl* **principalities**) إِمارة

principally /ˈprɪnsɪp(ə)li/ *adv* ‹*to consist, focus*› أَساساً

principle /ˈprɪnsɪp(ə)l/ *n* **1** (basic rule) مَبْدَأ (مَبادِئُ); **in ~ it will work** سَيَعْمَلُ من حَيْثُ المَبْدَأِ **2** (belief) مَبْدَأ (مَبادِئُ); **to do sth on ~** فَعَلَ شَيْئاً يَتَماشَى مع مَبادِئِهِ; **it is against my ~s** يَتَنافَى ومَبادِئي

print /prɪnt/ **A** *vt* **1** طَبَعَ (a; طَبْع) ‹*a poster, book, banknote*›; **to ~ sth in italics** طَبَعَ شَيْئاً بِحُروفٍ مائِلةٍ; **'~ed in Hong Kong'** 'طُبِعَ في هونْغ كونْغ' **2** (to write) كَتَبَ (u; كِتابة) ‹*letters*›; **'~ your name in block capitals'** 'أُكْتُبْ اسْمَكَ بِحُروفٍ كَبيرةٍ' **3** (to make public) نَشَرَ (u; نَشْر) ‹*a report, story*›; **the article was ~ed in the local press** نُشِرَت المَقالةُ في الصحافة المَحَلِّيَّةِ **4** (from negatives) طَبَعَ (a; طَبْع) ‹*the photos, a copy*›
B *vi* **1** (P&P) «printer, printing machines» طَبَعَ (a; طَبْع) **2** (to write) «child» كَتَبَ (u; كِتابة)
C (printed) *adj* ‹*fabric, design*› مَطْبوع; **'~ed matter'** 'مَطْبوعات'
D *n* **1** [u] (typeface) خَطّ (خُطوط); **the ~ is very small/large** الخَطُّ صَغيرٌ \ كَبيرٌ جِدًّا; **make sure you read the small *or* fine ~** احْرِصْ على أَنْ تَقْرَأَ الشُروطَ والأَحْكامَ **2** (published form) **to be in/out of ~** كانَ \ لم يَكُنْ مُتَوَفِّرًا في الأَسْواقِ; **to go into ~** نُشِرَ **3** (picture) صورة (صُوَر) **4** (photograph) صورة (صُوَر) **5** (cloth) قُماش مُلَوَّن; **light summer ~s** قُماش صَيْفيّ خَفيف ومُلَوَّن

Phrasal verbs **print off: ~ off [sth], ~ [sth] off** طَبَعَ [شَيْئاً] ‹*the copies*›
• **print out: ~ out [sth], ~ [sth] out** طَبَعَ [شَيْئاً] ‹*the data, copy*›

print dress *n* فُسْتان مُزَرْكَش

printer /ˈprɪntə/ *n* **1** (machine) طابِعة **2** (operator) طَبّاع, عامِل طِباعةٍ **3** (company) مَطْبَعة (مَطابِعُ); **it's at the ~'s** الكِتابُ تحت الطَبْعِ

printing /ˈprɪntɪŋ/ *n* طِباعة

printing press *n* مِطْبَعة (مَطابِعُ)

print-on-demand /ˌprɪntɒndɪˈmɑːnd/ *n* الطِباعة عند الطَلَبِ

printout /ˈprɪntaʊt/ *n* نُسْخة مَطْبوعة

print preview *n* مُعايَنة الطِباعةِ

print run *n* طَبْعة (عَدَد النُسَخِ المَطْبوعةِ في كُلِّ طَبْعةٍ)

prior¹ /ˈprʌɪə/ *adj* **1** (previous) ‹*arrangements, experience*› سابِق **2** **prior to sth** قبل شَيْءٍ

prior² /ˈprʌɪə/ *n* (Rel_Chr) رَئيس دَيْرٍ

priority /prʌɪˈɒrɪti/ *n* (*pl* **priorities**) أَوْلَوِيّة

priory /ˈprʌɪəri/ *n* (*pl* **priories**) دَيْر (صَغير)

prise off /prʌɪz/ *vt* **to ~ sth, to prise sth off** فَتَحَ شَيْئاً (بِصُعوبةٍ أو بِاسْتِعْمالِ أَداةٍ) ‹*a lid, cover*›

prise open *vt* **to ~ sth, to prise sth open** فَتَحَ شَيْئاً (بِصُعوبةٍ أو بِاسْتِعْمالِ أَداةٍ) ‹*a container, door*›

prism /ˈprɪz(ə)m/ *n* مَنْشور (مَناشيرُ)، مَوْشور (مَواشيرُ)

prison /ˈprɪz(ə)n/ *n* سِجْن (سُجون)؛ **to put sb in ~** وَضَعَ شَخْصاً في سِجْنٍ، سَجَنَ شَخْصاً

prison camp *n* مُعَسْكَر سُجَناء \ اعْتِقالٍ

prisoner /ˈprɪz(ə)nə/ *n* (sentenced) سَجين (سُجَناءُ)؛ (captured) أسير (أَسْرى)؛ **to take sb ~** أَسَرَ شَخْصاً

prisoner of war *n* أسير \ سَجين حَرْبٍ

prisoner of war camp *n* مُعَسْكَر أَسْرى حَرْبٍ

prison guard *n* (AmE) سَجّان، حارِسُ سِجْنٍ

prison officer *n* (BrE) ضابِط سِجْنٍ

prison sentence *n* حُكْم بالسِجْنِ

prissy /ˈprɪsi/ *adj* (**prissier**, **prissiest**) ‹*girl, teacher*› نَيِّق (مُفْرِط في التَأَنُّقِ واللِياقةِ)

pristine /ˈprɪstiːn/ *adj* ‹*condition*› مِثاليّ؛ ‹*car*› في حالةٍ مُمْتازةٍ

privacy /ˈprɪvəsi, ˈprʌɪvəsi/ *n* خُصوصيّة

private /ˈprʌɪvət/ **A** *adj* **1** (not for the general public) ‹*property, land, jet*› خاصّ؛ **a room with a ~ bathroom** غُرْفة مع حَمّام خاصٍّ؛ **the funeral will be ~** سَتكونُ الجَنازةُ للأَهْلِ فَقَطْ **2** (personal) ‹*letter, phone call, investment*› خاصّ، شَخْصيّ؛ **~ citizens** المُواطِنونَ العاديّونَ؛ **as a public figure, she doesn't have much ~ life** كَشَخْصيّةٍ عامّةٍ، لَيْسَتْ لَدَيْها حَياةٌ خاصّةٌ **3** (not public, not state-run) ‹*education, school, hospital*› خاصّ؛ **the ~ sector** القِطاع الخاصّ؛ **~ lessons** دُروس خاصّة \ خُصوصيّة **4** (quiet, free from intrusion) ‹*place, room*› خاصّ **5** (confidential) ‹*conversation, meeting, matter*› خاصّ، سِرّيّ؛ **a ~ joke** [نُكْتة يَفْهَمُها المُطَّلِعونَ فَقَطْ]؛ **to keep a matter ~** حافَظَ على خُصوصيّةِ شَيْءٍ؛ **to come to a ~ understanding** وَصَلوا إلى تَفاهُمٍ خاصٍّ **6** (secretive) ‹*person*› كَتوم (كُتُم)

B *n* (Mil) جُنْديّ (جُنود)، عَسْكَريّ (عَساكِرُ)

C (**in private**) *adv phr* على انْفِرادٍ

private company *n* شَرِكة خاصّة

private detective *n* مُحَقِّق \ مُخْبِر خاصّ

private enterprise *n* مُؤَسَّسة خاصّة

private equity firm *n* شَرِكة اسْتِثْمارٍ خاصٍّ

private eye, private investigator *n* مُحَقِّق \ مُخْبِر خاصّ

privately /ˈprʌɪvɪtli/ *adv* **1** (not publicly) ‹*to talk, admit, question*› سِرًّا، في السِرِّ **2** (inwardly) ‹*to feel, believe, doubt*› في السِرِّ **3** (not publicly funded) ‹*to be educated, be treated*› بِشَكْلٍ خاصٍّ؛ **the project was ~ funded** *or* **financed** المَشْروعُ مُمَوَّلٌ من (قِبَلِ) القِطاعِ الخاصِّ؛ **she's being treated ~** تَدْفَعُ مَصاريفَ عِلاجِها على نَفَقَتِها الخاصّةِ **4** (without agents) ‹*to sell, rent*› بِنَفْسِهِ

private parts *n* (euph) أَعْضاء تَناسُليّة

private practice *n* (BrE) عَمَل حُرّ \ خاصّ

privation /prʌɪˈveɪʃ(ə)n/ *n* (fml) حِرْمان، عَوَز

privatization, -isation (BrE) /ˌprʌɪvətʌɪˈzeɪʃ(ə)n/ *n* خَصْخَصة، خَوْصَصة

privatize, -ise (BrE) /ˈprʌɪvətʌɪz/ *vt* خَصْخَصَ (i; خَصْخَصة)، (Mor) خَوْصَصَ (i; خَوْصَصة) ‹*the railways, a utility*›

privilege /ˈprɪvɪlɪdʒ/ *n* **1** (special right) امْتِياز (امْتِيازات) **2** (honour) شَرَف

privileged /ˈprɪvəlɪdʒd/ *adj* **1** (having special rights) ‹*background, elite*› ذو امْتِيازٍ **2** (honoured) لَهُ الشَرَفُ؛ **to be ~ to do sth** كانَ لَهُ الشَرَفُ أَنْ يَفْعَلَ شَيْئاً

privy /ˈprɪvi/ **A** *adj* **to be ~ to sth** كانَ مُطَّلِعاً على شَيْءٍ

B *n* (*pl* **privies**) (old use) مِرْحاض (مَراحيضُ)

prize /prʌɪz/ **A** *n* **1** (in a competition) جائِزة (جَوائِزُ) **2** (in a lottery) جائِزة (جَوائِزُ)

B *adj* **1** (award-winning) ‹*vegetable, bull*› حائِز على جائِزةٍ

2 (treasured) ‹*possession*› عَزيز (أَعِزّة ,أَعِزّاءُ) **3** (complete) **a ~ idiot** غَبيّ بِشَكْلٍ مُطْلَقٍ

prize draw *n* سَحْب اليانَصيب

prize-giving /ˈprʌɪzgɪvɪŋ/ *n* حَفْل تَوْزيع جَوائِز

prize money *n* جائِزة ماليّة

prizewinner /ˈprʌɪzwɪnə/ *n* فائِز بِجائِزةٍ

pro /prəʊ/ **A** *n* **1** (infml) (professional) مُحْتَرِف **2** (advantage) **to weigh up the ~s and cons** وَزَنَ الإيجابيّاتِ والسَلْبيّاتِ

B *prep* (in favour of) مُؤَيِّد

pro- /prəʊ/ *prefix* مُنْحاز

proactive /prəʊˈaktɪv/ *adj* ‹*approach*› اسْتِباقيّ; ‹*management*› مُبادِر

probability /prɒbəˈbɪlɪti/ *n* (*pl* **probabilities**) احْتِمال (احْتِمالات), إمْكانيّة (إمْكانيّات, إمْكانات)

probable /ˈprɒbəb(ə)l/ *adj* ‹*cause, outcome*› مُحْتَمَل

probably /ˈprɒbəbli/ *adv* رُبَّما ,من المُحْتَمَلِ ,على الأَرْجَحِ

probate /ˈprəʊbeɪt/ **A** *n* إثْبات صِحّةِ وَصيّةٍ; **to grant ~** أَكَّدَ على صِحّةِ الوَصيّةِ وَأَثْبَتَها

B *vt* (AmE) أَثْبَتَ الصِحّةَ ‹*a will*›; **if you don't ~ her will, you won't have access to the money** إذا لم تُثْبِتْ صِحّةَ وَصيّتِها، فَلَنْ تَحْصُلَ على الأَمْوالِ

probation /prəˈbeɪʃ(ə)n/ *n* **1** (Law) إخْلاء السَبيلِ المَشْروط بِحُسْنِ السُلوكِ **2** (trial period) فَتْرة اخْتِبارٍ

probationary /prəˈbeɪʃ(ə)nri/ *adj* ‹*period*› اخْتِبارٍ; ‹*teacher*› في فَتْرةِ اخْتِبارٍ

probation officer *n* مُراقِب سُلوكٍ

probe /prəʊb/ **A** *n* **1** (investigation) تَحْقيق (تَحْقيقات)

2 (instrument) مِسْبار (مَسابيرُ)

B *vt* **1** (to investigate) «journalists» أَجْرى تَحْقيقاً \ اسْتِطْلاعاً في ‹*scandal*›; «police» حَقَّقَ (في) ‹*a mystery*›

2 فَحَصَ (بِمِسْبارٍ) ‹*a wound*›

probing /ˈprəʊbɪŋ/ *adj* ‹*question, look*› فاحِص

problem /ˈprɒbləm/ *n* **1** (difficulty) مُشْكِلة (مُشْكِلات, مَشاكِلُ); **to have ~s with sb/sth** كانَتْ لَدَيْهِ مَشاكِلُ مع شَخْصٍ \ شَيْءٍ; **his family have had real ~s with him** كانَتْ لدى عائِلَتِه مَشاكِلُ حَقيقيّةٌ مَعَهُ; **I have a ~ with the car/ mixer** هُناكَ مُشْكِلةٌ في السَيّارة \ الخَلاّطِ; **to have a drink ~** كانَتْ لَدَيْهِ مُشْكِلةٌ مع الشُرْبِ; **that's not my ~!** تِلْكَ لَيْسَتْ مُشْكِلَتي! **2** (mathematical task) مَسْأَلة (مَسائِلُ); **to solve a ~** حَلَّ مَسْأَلةً

problematic /prɒbləˈmatɪk/, **problematical** /prɒbləˈmatɪk(ə)l/ *adj* ‹*behaviour, situation*› إشْكاليّ

problem child *n* طِفْل مُثير للمَشاكِلِ

problem page *n* صَفْحة مَشاكِلَ خاصّة

procedural /prəˈsiːdʒ(ə)rəl/ *adj* ‹*detail, dispute*› إجْرائيّ

procedure /prəˈsiːdʒə/ *n* مَنْهَج (مَناهِجُ), إجْراء (إجْراءات)

proceed /prəˈsiːd, prəʊˈsiːd/ (fml) **A** *vt* **to ~ to do sth** شَرَعَ في فِعْلِ شَيْءٍ

B *vi* **1** (to continue) تابَعَ; **to ~ with the sale/plan** قامَ بِعَمَليّةِ البَيْعِ \ بِتَنْفيذِ الخُطّةِ; **let's ~ to the third item/problem** دَعْنا نَنْتَقِلُ إلى الفَقَرةِ \ المَسْأَلةِ الثالِثةِ; **you may ~** تَسْتَطيعُ المُتابَعةَ

2 (to move forward) «drivers, vehicles» تَقَدَّمَ إلى الأَمامِ

3 (to develop) «work, projects, talks» مَضى ,مَضى قُدُماً (يَمْضي ;i, مُضيّ) ,تَقَدَّمَ; **everything is ~ing according to plan** كُلُّ شَيْءٍ قُدُماً حَسَبَ الخُطّةِ **4** (to act) أَقْدَمَ على \ قامَ ب **5** (Law) **to ~ against sb** «prosecution» رَفَعَ \ أَقامَ دَعْوى على شَخْصٍ

proceedings /prəˈsiːdɪŋz/ *n pl* **1** (events) إجْراءات ,وَقائِع

2 (Law) ادِّعاء (ادِّعاءات) ,مُقاضاة; **to take** *or* **bring ~ against sb** قاضى أو ادَّعى على شَخْصٍ

proceeds /ˈprəʊsiːdz/ *n pl* مَداخيل ,عائِدات

process¹ /ˈprəʊses/ *n* **1** (procedure) عَمَليّة ,إجْراء (إجْراءات); **to begin the ~ of re-evaluation** قامَ بِإجْراءاتِ إعادةِ التَقْييمِ; **to be in the ~ of restructuring the business** كانَ يَقومُ بِعَمَليّةِ إعادةِ هَيْكَلةِ المَشْروعِ التِجاريِّ; **recovery is a long ~** التَعافي عَمَليّةٌ طَويلةٌ **2** (method) أُسْلوب (طُرُق) ,طَريقة (أَساليبُ); **the Bessemer ~ of steel production** طَريقة بيسيمَر لِصِناعةِ الفولاذِ **3** (summons) اسْتِدْعاء (اسْتِدْعاءات) **4** (legal procedure) إجْراء قانونيّ]; **to observe due ~** اتَّبَعَ الإجْراءاتِ القانونيّةَ السَليمةَ

process² /ˈprəʊses/ **A** *vt* **1** (to resolve) تَعامَلَ (مع) ‹*an order, application*› **2** (by program) عالَجَ ‹*the data*› **3** (industrially) «factory» عالَجَ ‹*raw materials, waste*› **4** (in food preparation) جَهَّزَ, حَضَّرَ ‹*food, cheese*› **5** (to develop) حَمَّضَ ‹*a film*›
B /prəˈses/ *vi* (fml) (to move) **to ~ from one place to another** سارَ من مَكانٍ لِآخَرَ

processing /ˈprəʊsesɪŋ/ *n* مُعالَجة

procession /prəˈseʃ(ə)n/ *n* مَوْكِب (مَواكِبُ); **a funeral ~** مَوْكِب جَنازةٍ

processor /ˈprəʊsesə/ *n* **1** (Comput) مُعالِج **2** (machine) ماكينة مُعالَجةٍ **3** (person) [عامِل في صِناعاتٍ تَحْويليّةٍ]; (company) شَرِكة صِناعاتٍ تَحْويليّةٍ

pro-choice /prəʊˈtʃɔɪs/ *adj* مُؤَيِّد الاخْتِيارِ (يُؤَيِّدُ إباحةَ الإجْهاضِ)

proclaim /prəˈkleɪm/ *vt* أَعْلَنَ ‹*independence, a state of emergency*›

proclamation /prɒkləˈmeɪʃ(ə)n/ *n* إعْلان (إعْلانات)

procrastinate /prəʊˈkrastɪneɪt/ *vi* سَوَّفَ, ماطَلَ

procreation /prəʊkriˈeɪʃ(ə)n/ *n* إنْجاب

procure /prəˈkjʊə/ *vt* تَحَصَّلَ (على) ‹*alcohol, equipment*›

procurement /prəˈkjʊəmənt/ *n* [u] حُصول

prod /prɒd/ **A** *vt* (-dd-) **1** (with one's foot) رَكَلَ (u; رَكْل) ‹*a package, snake, body*›; (with a stick) نَخَسَ (a-u; نَخْس); (with one's finger, elbow) نَكَزَ (u; نَكْز) ‹*a friend, the driver*›; **stop ~ding me!** تَوَقَّفْ عن نَكْزي! **2** (infml) (to remind, encourage) ذَكَّرَ; **to ~ sb into doing sth** ذَكَّرَ شَخْصاً بِأَنْ يَفْعَلَ شَيْئاً
B *n* **1** (poke) نَكْزة; **to give sb/sth a ~** نَكَزَ شَخْصاً \ شَيْئاً
2 **to give sb a ~** (infml) ذَكَّرَ شَخْصاً

prodigal /ˈprɒdɪɡ(ə)l/ *adj* (liter) ‹*expenditure, brother*› مُبَذِّر; **the ~ son** الابْن الضالّ

prodigious /prəˈdɪdʒəs/ *adj* ‹*talent, amount*› هائِل

prodigy /ˈprɒdɪdʒi/ *n* (*pl* **prodigies**) عَبْقَريّ (عَباقِرة), أُعْجوبة (أَعاجيبُ)

produce **A** /prəˈdjuːs/ *vt* **1** (to cause) أَحْدَثَ, أَدّى (إلى), أَسْفَرَ (عن) ‹*an effect, agreement, a result*› **2** (to manufacture) صَنَعَ (a; صِناعة) ‹*components, cars, computers*› **3** (to write, create) كَتَبَ (u; كِتابة) ‹*a timetable, report*› **4** «farmers» أَنْتَجَ ‹*corn, honey, meat*›; **each cow ~s six gallons of milk per day** تُنْتِجُ كُلُّ بَقَرةٍ سِتّةَ غالوناتٍ من الحَليبِ يَوْميًّا; **she ~d four kittens** وَلَدَتْ أَرْبَعَ هِرّاتٍ **5** (to generate) وَلَّدَ ‹*heat, electricity*›; أَحْدَثَ ‹*sound*› **6** (to present, show) قَدَّمَ ‹*evidence, a passport*›; عَرَضَ (i; عَرْض) ‹*a gun*›; **no evidence was ~d** لم يُقَدَّمْ أَيُّ دَليلٍ **7** «backers» أَنْتَجَ ‹*a movie, series*› **8** أَنْتَجَ ‹*a play*›
B /ˈprɒdjuːs/ *n* مُنْتَج (مُنْتَجات)

producer /prəˈdjuːsə/ *n* **1** (of fruit, oil) مُنْتِج; (of furniture, cars) مُصَنِّع **2** (of movies, programmes, CDs) مُنْتِج

product /ˈprɒdʌkt/ *n* مُنْتَج (مُنْتَجات), مَنْتوج (مَنْتوجات)

product designer *n* مُصَمِّم مُنْتَجاتٍ

production /prəˈdʌkʃ(ə)n/ *n* **1** (of fruit, meat) إنْتاج; (of furniture, cars) صِناعة (صِناعات); (of oil, coal) إنْتاج **2** (of movies, programmes, operas) إنْتاج; **to see the new ~ of Hamlet** شاهَدَ مَسْرَحيّةَ هامْلِت الجَديدةَ; **to go into record ~** اتَّجَهَ للعَمَلِ في الإنْتاجِ الموسيقيِّ

production line *n* خطّ إنْتاجٍ

production manager *n* **1** (in a factory) مُدير إنْتاجٍ **2** (for movies, plays, etc.) مُدير إنْتاجٍ

productive /prəˈdʌktɪv/ *adj* **1** ‹*factory, land*› غَزير \ كَثير الإنْتاجِ **2** ‹*meeting, day*› مُثْمِر

productively /prəˈdʌktɪvli/ *adv* ‹*to work, farm*› بِشَكْلٍ فَعّالٍ; **to spend one's time ~** قَضى وَقْتَهُ بِشَكْلٍ مُثْمِرٍ

productivity /prɒdʌkˈtɪvɪti/ *n* إنْتاجيّة

product manager *n* مُدير مُنْتَجٍ

profane /prəˈfeɪn/ **A** *adj* **1** (blasphemous) ‹*language, act*› مُدَنَّس **2** (secular) ‹*music, literature*› دُنْيَويّ
B *vt* (to desecrate) ‹*a church, tomb*› دَنَّسَ

profanity /prəˈfanɪti/ *n* (*pl* **profanities**) **1** (oath) شَتيمة (شَتائِمُ) **2** [u] (blasphemous language) تَجْديف, أَلْفاظ كُفْريّة

profess /prəˈfɛs/ *vt* (fml) **1** (to claim) ادَّعى ‹*understanding, knowledge*› **2** (to declare) أَعْلَنَ ‹*one's faith, love*›

profession /prəˈfɛʃ(ə)n/ *n* **1** (job) مِهْنة (مِهَن), حِرْفة (حِرَف); **by ~** من حَيْثُ المِهْنةِ **2** (group) أَهْل المِهْنةِ; **the medical/**

teaching ~ التَدْرِيسِ \ العامِلونَ في الطِبِّ **3** (declaration) اعْتِراف

professional /prəˈfɛʃ(ə)n(ə)l/ **A** *adj* ‹*association, qualification*› مُحْتَرِف ,مِهْنيّ; ‹*golfer, footballer*› مُحْتَرِف
B *n* مُحْتَرِف

professionalism /prəˈfɛʃ(ə)nəlɪz(ə)m/ *n* مِهْنيّة ,حِرَفيّة ,احْتِرافيّة

professionally /prəˈfɛʃ(ə)n(ə)li/ *adv* **1** (by a professional) ‹*designed, installed*› بِشَكْلٍ مُحْتَرِفٍ **2** (as a profession) ‹*to play, sing*› بِشَكْلٍ مُحْتَرِفٍ **3** (to a high standard) ‹*to behave, work*› بِشَكْلٍ مُحْتَرِفٍ

professor /prəˈfɛsə/ *n* **1** (head of department) رَئيس ,أُسْتاذ (قِسْمٍ (في الجامِعةِ **2** (AmE) (teacher) أُسْتاذ جامِعيّ

proffer /ˈprɒfə/ *vt* (fml) قَدَّمَ ‹*one's hand, a pen*›

proficiency /prəˈfɪʃ(ə)nsi/ *n* مَهارة ,كَفاءة

proficient /prəˈfɪʃ(ə)nt/ *adj* ‹*musician, negotiator*› بارِع ,(مَهَرة) ماهِر

profile /ˈprəʊfʌɪl/ *n* **1** (side view) بُروفيل (صورة جانِبيّة للوَجْه)**;** **in ~** جانِبيّةً \ من الجانِبِ **2** (in perceptions) بُروفيل ,شُهْرة; **to keep a high ~** حافَظَ على مَكانةٍ عالِيةٍ; **to keep a low ~** تَجَنَّبَ لَفْتَ الانْتِباهِ إلَيْهِ **3** (personal details) بَيانات شَخْصيّة **4** (of a suspect) بُروفيل ,مِبْيان نَفْسيّ

profiling /ˈprəʊfʌɪlɪŋ/ *n* [رَسْم وَتَحْليل مَلامِح شَخْصيّةٍ]

profit /ˈprɒfɪt/ **A** *n* رِبْح (أَرْباح); **they made a ~ of £3 million** حَقَّقوا رِبْحًا بِقيمةِ 3 مَلايينَ جُنَيْهٍ
B *vi* **to ~ from sth** (financially) اسْتَفادَ مادِّيًا من شَيْءٍ; (to derive benefit) اسْتَفادَ من شَيْءٍ

profitability /prɒfɪtəˈbɪləti/ *n* رِبْحيّة ,رِبْح (أَرْباح)

profitable /ˈprɒfɪtəb(ə)l/ *adj* **1** ‹*company, investment*› مُرْبِح **2** (beneficial) ‹*use, day*› مُفيد

profitably /ˈprɒfɪtəbli/ *adv* **1** ‹*to operate, trade*› بِشَكْلٍ \ على نَحْوٍ مُرْبِحٍ; ‹*to sell*› بِشَكْلٍ \ على نَحْوٍ مُرْبِحٍ **2** (beneficially) ‹*to use, spend one's time*› بِشَكْلٍ \ على نَحْوٍ مُثْمِرٍ

profit and loss account *n* حساب أَرْباحٍ وَخَسائِرَ

profiteer /prɒfɪˈtɪə/ *n* (pej) انْتِهازيّ

profiteering /prɒfɪˈtɪərɪŋ/ *n* (pej) إثْراء غَيْر مَشْروعٍ

profit margin *n* هامِش رِبْحٍ

profit-sharing /ˈprɒfɪtʃɛːrɪŋ/ *n* اقْتِسام أَرْباحٍ

profound /prəˈfaʊnd/ *adj* ‹*effect, change*› عَميق

profoundly /prəˈfaʊndli/ *adv* ‹*different, important*› بِشَكْلٍ عَميقٍ

profuse /prəˈfjuːs/ *adj* ‹*apologies*› عَميق; ‹*thanks*› جَزيل; ‹*sweating, bleeding*› غَزير

profusely /prəˈfjuːsli/ *adv* ‹*to apologize*› بِشِدّةٍ; ‹*to thank*› شُكْرًا جَزيلاً; ‹*to sweat, bleed*› بِغَزارةٍ \ بِشَكْلٍ غَزيرٍ

profusion /prəˈfjuːʒ(ə)n/ *n* وَفْرة

progeny /ˈprɒdʒ(ə)ni/ *n sing* (fml) (human) ذُرّيّة (ذُرّيّات ,ذَراريّ); (animal) سُلالة (أَنْسال), نَسْل

prognosis /prɒgˈnəʊsɪs/ *n* (*pl* **prognoses** /-siːz/) تَخْمين مَسارِ مَرَضٍ

prognostic /prɒgˈnɒstɪk/ *adj* ‹*factor, significance*› مُنْبِئ بِمَسارِ مَرَضٍ

program /ˈprəʊgram/ **A** *n* **1** (in computing) بَرْنامَج (بَرامِجُ); **to install/uninstall a ~** تَثْبيت \ إزالة بَرْنامَجٍ **2** (AmE) ▸ **programme** A
B *vt* (-mm- or -m-) **1** بَرْمَجَ (i; بَرْمَجة) ‹*a computer*› **2** (AmE) ▸ **programme** B

programme (BrE), **program** (AmE) /ˈprəʊgram/ **A** *n* **1** (on TV, radio) بَرْنامَج (بَرامِجُ) **2** (schedule) بَرْنامَج (بَرامِجُ) **3** (for plays, concerts) بَرْنامَج (بَرامِجُ)
B *vt* **1** بَرْمَجَ (i; بَرْمَجة) ‹*a computer, robot*› **2** بَرْمَجَ (i; بَرْمَجة) ‹*a video recorder, device*› **3** (to schedule) بَرْمَجَ (i; بَرْمَجة), نَظَّمَ ‹*an event, activities*›

programmer /ˈprəʊgramə/ *n* مُبَرْمِج

programming (BrE), **programing** (AmE) /ˈprəʊgramɪŋ/ *n* **1** (for computers) بَرْمَجة **2** (for radio, TV, etc) بَرْمَجة

progress **A** /ˈprəʊgrɛs/ *n* **1** (forward movement) تَقَدُّم; **we made slow/steady ~ across the desert** تَقَدَّمْنا بِشَكْلٍ بَطيءٍ \ ثابِتٍ عَبْرَ الصَحْراءِ **2** (improvement) تَحَسُّن; **the patient is making ~** المَريض في تَحَسُّنٍ; **he has made steady ~ in all subjects** حَقَّقَ تَحَسُّنًا مُسْتَمِرًّا في جَميعِ المَوادِّ **3** (development, evolution) تَطَوُّر (تَطَوُّرات); **to monitor the ~ of the disease/crisis** راقَبَ تَطَوُّرَ المَرَضِ \ الأَزْمةِ

4 (**in progress**) مُسْتَمِرّ; **the meeting is still in ~** لا يَزالُ الاجْتِماعُ مُنْعَقِداً

B /prəˈgrɛs/ *vi* **1** (to move forward) «vehicles, boats» تَقَدَّمَ; **we ~ed slowly up the river** تَقَدَّمْنا بِبُطْءٍ في النَهْرِ **2** (to advance) «project, students, society» تَقَدَّمَ; **our research is ~ing** بَحْثُنا يُحْرِزُ تَقَدُّماً **3** (to evolve) «pregnancy, disputes» تَطَوَّرَ; **as the day/meeting ~ed** مع تَقَدُّمِ النَهارِ \ الاجْتِماعِ

C /prəˈgrɛs/ *vt* (to bring forward) أَحْرَزَ تَقَدُّماً في ‹*a matter, report, an investigation*›

progression /prəˈgrɛʃ(ə)n/ *n* **1** (advance) تَقَدُّم **2** (series) سِلْسِلة (سَلاسِلُ) **3** (in music) تَتابُع

progressive /prəˈgrɛsɪv/ *adj* **1** (forward-looking) ‹*policy, ideas*› تَقَدُّمِيّ **2** (gradual) ‹*change, loss*› مُتَدَرِّج **3** (in severity) ‹*disease, loss*› مُسْتَفْحِل, يَتَطَوَّرُ بِشَكْلٍ تَدْرِيجِيٍّ

progressively /prəˈgrɛsɪvli/ *adv* ‹*more difficult, worse*› تَدْرِيجيًّا \ بِشَكْلٍ تَدْرِيجِيٍّ

progress report *n* تَقْرِير عن التَطَوُّرِ

prohibit /prəʊˈhɪbɪt/ *vt* **1** (to forbid) حَظَرَ (u; حَظْر), مَنَعَ (a; مَنْع) ‹*the use of sth, an activity*› **2** (to prevent) مَنَعَ (a; مَنْع), حالَ دون

prohibition /prəʊɪˈbɪʃ(ə)n/ *n* **1** مَنْع, حَظْر **2** (**Prohibition**) (AmE Hist) مَنْع الكُحُولِ (في الوِلاياتِ المُتَّحِدةِ)

prohibitive /prəʊˈhɪbɪtɪv/ *adj* ‹*cost, price*› باهِظ

project **A** /ˈprɒdʒɛkt/ *n* **1** (scheme) مَشْروع (مَشْروعات, مَشاريعُ) **2** (at school, university) مَشْروع (مَشْروعات, مَشاريعُ) **3** (AmE) (state housing) سَكَن مَدْعوم حُكومِيًّا (في الوِلاياتِ المُتَّحِدةِ)

B /prəˈdʒɛkt/ *vt* **1** عَرَضَ (i; عَرْض) ‹*an image, a film*› **2** (to propel) قَذَفَ (i; قَذْف), أَطْلَقَ ‹*the debris, ash*› **3** رَفَعَ (a; رَفْع) ‹*one's voice*› **4** (to present) عَرَضَ (i; عَرْض) ‹*an image, idea*› **5** (to forecast) تَوَقَّعَ ‹*growth, a deficit*›; **the ~ed cost of the project** التَكالِيف المُتَوَقَّعة لِلمَشْروع

C *vi* «shelves, balcony» امْتَدَّ

projecting /prəˈdʒɛktɪŋ/ *adj* ‹*roof, eaves*› بارِز, ناتِئ

projection /prəˈdʒɛkʃ(ə)n/ *n* **1** (forecast) تَوَقُّع **2** (of images, movies) عَرْض (عُروض) **3** (in map-making) إِسْقاط

projector /prəˈdʒɛktə/ *n* مِسْلاط, عارِض ضَوْئِيّ

proletarian /ˌprəʊlɪˈtɛːrɪən/ *adj* ‹*revolution, dictatorship*› بْروليتارِيّ

pro-life /prəʊˈlʌɪf/ *adj* مُؤَيِّد الحَياةِ (يُعارِضُ الإِجْهاضَ)

proliferate /prəˈlɪfəreɪt/ *vi* «cells, nuclear weapons» انْتَشَرَ, تَكاثَرَ

proliferation /prəlɪfəˈreɪʃ(ə)n/ *n* (fml) انْتِشار, تَكاثُر

prolific /prəˈlɪfɪk/ *adj* ‹*writer, composer*› غَزِير الإِنْتاجِ

prologue /ˈprəʊlɒg/ *n* مُقَدِّمة, تَمْهِيد

prolong /prəˈlɒŋ/ *vt* أَطالَ, مَدَّدَ ‹*life, a war*›

prom /prɒm/ *n* (infml) **1** (AmE) (school dance) حَفْلة راقِصة (في نِهايةِ العامِ الدِراسِيِّ) **2** (BrE) (at the seaside) كورْنِيش

promenade /ˌprɒməˈnɑːd/ *n* (at the seaside) كورْنِيش

prominence /ˈprɒmɪnəns/ *n* **1** (importance) أَهَمِّيّة **2** (conspicuousness) بُروز

prominent /ˈprɒmɪnənt/ *adj* **1** (important) ‹*figure, politician, role, part*› بارِز, مُهِمّ **2** (conspicuous) ‹*position, feature*› بارِز **3** (projecting) ‹*nose, cheekbones*› بارِز, ناتِئ

prominently /ˈprɒmɪnəntli/ *adv* **1** (importantly) بِشَكْلٍ \ على نَحْوٍ مُهِمٍّ; **to figure ~ in sth** لَعِبَ دَوْراً مُهِمًّا في شَيْءٍ **2** (conspicuously) ‹*displayed, placed*› بِشَكْلٍ بارِزٍ

promiscuity /prɒmɪˈskjuːɪti/ *n* [تَعَدُّد العَلاقاتِ الجِنْسِيّةِ]

promiscuous /prəˈmɪskjʊəs/ *adj* ‹*behaviour*› داعِر, مُنْحَل; ‹*sex*› غَيْر شَرْعِيٍّ

promise /ˈprɒmɪs/ **A** *n* **1** (undertaking) وَعْد (وُعود); **to break one's ~** أَخْلَفَ وَعْدَهُ; **they held him to his ~** أَلْزَموهُ بِوَعْدِهِ **2** [u] (for the future) دَلِيل (دَلائِلُ), مُؤَشِّر (مُؤَشِّرات); **he shows great ~** تَظْهَرُ عَلَيْه مُؤَشِّراتُ النَجاحِ بِدَرَجةٍ كَبِيرةٍ; **there seems little ~ of an improvement** لا يَبْدو أَنَّ هُناكَ أَمَلٌ كَبِيرٌ في التَحَسُّنِ; **a team which is full of ~** فَرِيق مَلِيء بِالمَواهِبِ

B *vt* **1** (to pledge) **to ~ sb sth** وَعَدَ شَخْصاً بِشَيْءٍ; **she ~d to help/write** وَعَدَتْ أَنْ تُساعِدَ \ تُراسِلَ; **as ~d** كَما وُعِدَ **2** (to offer the prospect of) **it ~s to be a fine day** يَبْدو أَنَّ اليَوْمَ سَيَكونُ جَمِيلاً **3** (to assure) أَكَّدَ; **it won't be easy, I ~ you** لن يَكونَ الأَمْرُ سَهْلاً, أُؤَكِّدُ لَكَ

C *vi* **1** (to give a pledge) وَعَدَ (i; وَعْد), تَعَهَّدَ; **do you ~?** هل تَعِدُ بِهَذا؟ **2** (for the future) **to ~ well/badly** «candidate, results» بَشَّرَ بِخَيْرٍ \ بِشَرٍّ; **this doesn't ~ well for the future** لا يُبَشِّرُ هذا بِخَيْرٍ لِلمُسْتَقْبَلِ

promising /ˈprɒmɪsɪŋ/ *adj* ‹*career, player, future*› واعِد

promote /prəˈməʊt/ *vt* **1** (in rank) رَقَّى ‹*an officer, employee*› **2** (to publicize) رَوَّجَ ‹*a product, book*› **3** (to encourage) عَزَّزَ, شَجَّعَ ‹*growth, awareness*› **4** (BrE) (in football) **to be ~d** صَعِدَ (a; صُعود); **Wigan were ~d to the first division** صَعِدَ نادي ويغان إلى الدَوْرِ الأَوَّلِ المُمْتازِ

promoter /prəˈməʊtə/ *n* مُنَظِّم, مُتَعَهِّد

promotion /prəˈməʊʃ(ə)n/ *n* **1** (of an employee, a team) تَرْقِية **2** [u] (encouragement) تَشْجيع (تَشْجيعات), تَعْزيز (تَعْزيزات) **3** [u] (publicizing) تَرْويج **4** (publicity campaign) حَمْلة دِعائيّة

promotional /prəˈməʊʃ(ə)n(ə)l/ *adj* ‹*campaign, video*› تَرْويجيّ, دِعائيّ

prompt /prɒmpt/ **A** *vt* **1** أَثارَ ‹*a question, response*›; **to ~ sb to do sth** حَثَّ شَخْصاً على فِعْلِ شَيْءٍ **2** لَقَّنَ ‹*an actor, student*› **B** *n* **1** (hint) تَلْميح (تَلْميحات, تَلاميحُ), إشارة **2** (for actors) تَلْقين **C** *adj* ‹*action, reply*› عاجِل, فَوْريّ **D** *adv* (BrE); **at ten o'clock ~** في الساعةِ العاشِرةِ تَماماً

prompter /ˈprɒmptə/ *n* مُلَقِّن

promptly /ˈprɒmptli/ *adv* **1** (punctually) ‹*to start, leave*› دون تَأْخيرٍ **2** (speedily) ‹*to act, reply*› بِسُرْعةٍ **3** (immediately) ‹*to fall asleep, forget*› فَوْراً, على الفَوْرِ

prone /prəʊn/ *adj* **1** (liable) **to be ~ to sth** كانَ عُرْضةً لِشَيْءٍ **2** (face down) ‹*position, body*› مُنْبَطِح

prong /prɒŋ/ *n* سِنّ (mf; أَسْنان), إِبْرة (إِبَر, إِبْرات), فَرْع (فُروع, أَفْرُع), شُعْبة (شُعَب)

pronoun /ˈprəʊnaʊn/ *n* ضَمير (ضَمائِرُ)

pronounce /prəˈnaʊns/ *vt* **1** نَطَقَ (u; نُطْق), تَلَفَّظَ (ب) ‹*a word, name*› **2** (to declare) أَعْلَنَ (بِشَكْلٍ رَسْميٍّ); **to ~ sentence/judgement** أَصْدَرَ عُقوبةً \ حُكْماً; **the doctor ~d him dead** أَعْلَنَ الطَبيبُ أَنَّهُ قد ماتَ

pronounced /prəˈnaʊnst/ *adj* ‹*accent, limp*› واضِح, مَلْحوظ

pronouncement /prəˈnaʊnsmənt/ *n* تَصْريح (تَصْريحات), بَيان (بَيانات)

pronunciation /prəˌnʌnsiˈeɪʃ(ə)n/ *n* نُطْق, تَلَفُّظ

proof /pruːf/ **A** *n* **1** [u] (evidence) دَليل (أَدِلّة, دَلائِلُ), إِثْبات (إِثْباتات); **we have ~ that he is alive** لَدَيْنا دَليلٌ بِأَنَّهُ حَيٌّ; **there is no ~ that he did it** لَيْسَ هُناكَ دَليلٌ على أَنَّهُ فَعَلَها; **to produce sth as ~** قَدَّمَ شَيْئاً كَدَليلٍ; **bring your passport as ~ of identity** اصْطَحِبْ مَعَكَ جَوازَ سَفَرِكَ كَإِثْباتِ شَخْصيّةٍ **2** (in printing) مُسَوَّدة طَبْع, بُروفة; **to check/correct the ~s** راجَعَ \ صَحَّحَ مُسَوَّدةَ الطَبْعِ **3** (of a photo) نُسْخة تَجْريبيّة **4** (of alcohol) نِسْبة الكُحولِ; **to be 70°** *or* **70 ~** كانَتْ نِسْبةُ الكُحولِ فيهِ 35 بالمِائةِ **B** *adj* **to be ~ against the cold/rain** كانَ مُقاوِماً لِلبَرْدِ \ لِلمَطَرِ **C** **(-proof)** *in combination* (resistant to) **rust-~** مُقاوِم لِلصَدَأِ; **moth-~** مُقاوِم لِلعُثِّ **D** *vt* **1** (to make waterproof) جَعَلَ مُقاوِماً لِلماءِ ‹*a coat, fabric*› **2** (to correct) صَحَّحَ طَبْعةً تَجْريبيّةً \ مُسَوَّدةً ‹*a book, text*›

proof of purchase *n* إِثْبات شِراءٍ

proofread /ˈpruːfriːd/ **A** *vt* (*past tense, past participle* **proofread** /ˈpruːfrɛd/) راجَعَ, صَحَّحَ, دَقَّقَ **B** *vi* [قامَ بِالمُراجَعةِ اللُغَويّةِ]

proofreader /ˈpruːfriːdə/ *n* مُصَحِّح / مُدَقِّق لُغَويّ

prop /prɒp/ **A** *n* **1** (support) دِعامة (دِعامات, دَعائِمُ) **2** (in theatre, film) مُلْحَق إِكْسِسْوار (في المَسْرَحِ والسينَما) **B** *vt* **(-pp-)** (also **prop up**) **to ~ sth against sth** أَسْنَدَ شَيْئاً على شَيْءٍ

Phrasal verb **prop up**: **~ [sth] up, ~ up [sth]** **1** (to hold up) دَعَمَ [شَيْئاً] ‹*a wall, roof*› **2** (to give support to) دَعَمَ (a; دَعْم), سانَدَ ‹*a regime, an economy*›

propaganda /prɒpəˈgandə/ *n* دِعاية, بْروباغَنْدا

propagandist /prɒpəˈgandɪst/ *n* بوق دِعايةٍ

propagate /ˈprɒpəgeɪt/ **A** *vt* **1** كَثَّرَ ‹*plants, species*› **2** رَوَّجَ ‹*an idea, a myth*› **B** *vi* «plants» تَكاثَرَ

propel /prəˈpɛl/ *vt* **(-ll-)** دَفَعَ (a; دَفْع) ‹*a boat, vehicle*›

propeller /prəˈpɛlə/ *n* مِرْوَحة (مَراوِحُ)

propensity /prəˈpɛnsɪti/ *n* (*pl* **propensities**) (fml) مَيْل (مُيول), نَزْعة (نَزَعات)

proper /ˈprɒpə/ *adj* 1 (correct, right) ‹*response, clothing, tool*› صَحيح (صِحاح), سَليم, مُناسِب; **the ~ response would have been ...** كانَ الرَدُّ المُناسِبُ هو ...; **that's not its ~ place** لَيْسَ ذلك مَكانَهُ الصَحيحَ; **to go through the ~ channels** مَرَّ عَبْرَ القَنواتِ الصَحيحةِ; **it's only ~ for her to keep the money** من الصَحيح أنْ تَحْتَفِظَ بالمالِ 2 (fml) (fitting) مُلائِم, مُناسِب, لائِق ‹*respect, courtesy*›; **to show ~ respect for tradition/for the dead** أَظْهَرَ الاحْتِرامَ الواجِبَ للتَقاليدِ \ للأَمْواتِ; **I did as I thought ~** فَعَلْتُ ما ظَنَنْتُ أَنَّهُ مُناسِبٌ 3 (adequate) ‹*recognition, funding*› مُناسِب; **she never had a ~ education** لم تَتَلَقَّ أَبَداً تَعْليماً مُناسِباً 4 (socially correct) ‹*person, behaviour*› مُهَذَّب, مُؤَدَّب; **he's very ~** هو مُهَذَّبٌ جِدًّا 5 (real) ‹*doctor, job, holiday*› حَقيقيّ; **the competition ~** المُسابَقة الحَقيقيّة 6 (infml) (complete) ‹*mess, disaster*› حَقيقيّ; **I felt a ~ idiot!** شَعَرْتُ بِأَنّي أَبْلَهٌ تَماماً!

properly /ˈprɒp(ə)li/ *adv* 1 (correctly) ‹*to work, do*› كَما يَنْبَغي, بِشَكْلٍ صَحيحٍ 2 (appropriately) ‹*to behave, treat*› بِشَكْلٍ لائِقٍ 3 (adequately) ‹*to sleep, eat*› بِشَكْلٍ مُناسِبٍ

proper name, **proper noun** *n* اسْم عَلَمٍ

property /ˈprɒpəti/ *n* 1 (possessions) مِلْكيّة, مُمْتَلَكات 2 [U] (buildings, land) عَقار (عَقارات) 3 (building) مَبْنًى (مَبانٍ), بِناية 4 (piece of land) قِطْعة أَرْضٍ; **this land is private ~** هذه الأَرْضُ مِلْكٌ خاصٌّ 5 (quality) خاصّيّة (خاصّيّات, خَصائِصُ)

property developer *n* مُطَوِّر عَقاراتٍ

property owner *n* مالِك عَقارٍ, صاحِب أَمْلاكٍ

prophecy /ˈprɒfɪsi/ *n* (*pl* **prophecies**) نُبوءة

prophesy /ˈprɒfɪsʌɪ/ *vt* (**prophesies, sying, prophesied**) ‹*the future, an event*› تَنَبَّأَ (ب)

prophet /ˈprɒfɪt/ *n* نَبيّ (أَنْبِياءُ, نَبِيّونَ); **the P~ Muhammad** النَبيّ مُحَمَّد

prophetic /prəˈfɛtɪk/ *adj* ‹*words, vision*› نَبَويّ

prophylactic /ˌprɒfɪˈlaktɪk/ A *adj* ‹*treatment, medication*› وِقائيّ B *n* 1 (medicine) دَواء وِقائيّ 2 (AmE) (condom) واقٍ ذَكَريّ

prophylaxis /ˌprɒfɪˈlaksɪs/ *n* وِقاية

proponent /prəˈpəʊnənt/ *n* (fml) مُؤَيِّد, مُناصِر

proportion /prəˈpɔːʃ(ə)n/ A *n* 1 (of a group, population) نِسْبة (نِسَب); **a large/small ~ of the students** نِسْبة كَبيرة \ صَغيرة من الطُلّابِ; **the vast ~ of work/profits is ...** النِسْبةُ العُظْمى من العَمَلِ \ الأَرْباحِ هي ... 2 (ratio) نِسْبة (نِسَب); **the ~ of pupils to teachers is 25:1** نِسْبةُ الطُلّابِ إلى المُدَرِّسينَ هي 25:1; **tax is levied in ~ to income** يَتِمُّ فَرْضُ الضَريبةِ بِما يَتَناسَبُ مع الدَخْلِ 3 (harmony, symmetry) **to be out of/in ~ with sth** لم يَتَناسَبْ \ تَناسَبَ مع شَيْءٍ 4 (perspective) قَدْر (أَقْدار), حَجْم (أَحْجام); **to get sth out of ~** أَعْطى شَيْئاً أَهَمِّيّةً لا يَسْتَحِقُّها; **you've got to have a sense of ~** يَجِبُ أنْ تَكونَ لَدَيْكَ القُدْرةُ على تَقْديرِ الأَهَمِّيّةِ النِسْبيّةِ للأَشْياءِ B (**proportions**) *n pl* (of a building, ship, machine) أَبْعاد; (of a problem, project) حَجْم; **the problem has reached alarming ~s** وَصَلَت المُشْكِلةُ إلى دَرَجةٍ مُقْلِقةٍ C (**proportioned**); *in combination* **well-/badly-~ed** مُتَناسِق \ غَيْر مُتَناسِقٍ

proportional /prəˈpɔːʃ(ə)n(ə)l/ *adj* ‹*increase, reduction*› مُتَناسِب

proportional representation *n* تَمْثيل نِسْبيّ

proportionate /prəˈpɔːʃ(ə)nət/ *adj* ‹*response, share*› مُتَناسِب

proposal /prəˈpəʊz(ə)l/ *n* 1 (suggestion) اقْتِراح (اقْتِراحات), مَشْروع (مَشْروعات, مَشاريعُ) 2 (also **proposal of marriage**) عَرْض \ طَلَب زَواجٍ

propose /prəˈpəʊz/ A *vt* 1 (to suggest) ‹*a solution, plan*› اقْتَرَحَ; **he ~d extending the house** اقْتَرَحَ تَوْسيعَ البَيْتِ 2 (to present) ‹*a motion, an amendment*› اقْتَرَحَ, تَقَدَّمَ (ب) 3 (to intend) **to ~ to do sth** نَوى فِعْلَ شَيْءٍ B *vi* «suitor, man» عَرَضَ الزَواجَ, طَلَبَ الزَواجَ; **to ~ to sb** عَرَضَ على شَخْصٍ الزَواجَ C (**proposed**) *adj* ‹*change, legislation*› مُقْتَرَح; **the ~d changes** التَغْييرات المُقْتَرَحة

proposition /prɒpəˈzɪʃ(ə)n/ A *n* 1 (assertion) ادِّعاء (ادِّعاءات), افْتِراض (افْتِراضات) 2 (suggestion) اقْتِراح (اقْتِراحات) 3 (enterprise) مَشْروع (مَشْروعات, مَشاريعُ); **the site is an attractive ~ for developers** يُعْتَبَرُ المَوْقِعُ مَشْروعاً جَذّاباً

للمُطوِّرين العقاريّين

B *vt* راوَدَ ‹*a woman, man*›

proprietary /prəˈprʌɪət(ə)ri/ *adj* **1**▸ ‹*interest, rights*› مِلْكِيّ

2▸ ‹*software, system*› احْتِكاريّ

proprietor /prəˈprʌɪətə/ *n* مالِك (مُلاّك)

propriety /prəˈprʌɪəti/ *n* (fml) احْتِشام ,لِياقة

propulsion /prəˈpʌlʃ(ə)n/ *n* دَفْع

pro rata *adj, adv* بالتَناسُبِ

prosaic /prəʊˈzeɪɪk/ *adj* ‹*reality, explanation*› مُبْتَذَل

proscribe /prəʊˈskrʌɪb/ *vt* حَظَرَ (u; حَظْر) ,مَنَعَ (a; مَنْع) ‹*an organization, activity*›

prose /prəʊz/ *n* نَثْر

prosecute /ˈprɒsɪkjuːt/ **A** *vt* أقامَ \ رَفَعَ دَعْوى على ,قاضى ‹*a criminal, company*›; **to ~ sb for sth** قاضى شَخْصاً على شَيْءٍ

B *vi* «police, authorities» أقامَ \ رَفَعَ دَعْوى

prosecution /prɒsɪˈkjuːʃ(ə)n/ *n* **1**▸ (bringing to trial) مُقاضاة

2▸ (prosecuting side) **the ~** النِيابة

prosecutor /ˈprɒsɪkjuːtə/ *n* **1**▸ (instituting prosecution) مُدَّعٍ عامّ ,نائِب عامّ (Egypt), وَكيل المَلِكِ \ النِيابةِ العامّةِ (Mor), الجُمْهوريّةِ (Tunisia, Algeria) **2**▸ (in court) مُدَّعٍ

prospect **A** /ˈprɒspɛkt/ *n* (fml) **1**▸ (expectation) إمْكانيّة, احْتِماليّة ,فُرْصة (فُرَص); **what are the ~s of success/failure?** ما هي فُرَصُ النَجاحِ \ الفَشَلِ؟; **there is some/little ~ of improvement** هُناكَ بَعْضُ الأمَلِ \ أمَلٌ ضَعيفٌ في حُدوثِ تَحَسُّنٍ **2**▸ (outlook) تَوَقُّعات; **a bleak/gloomy ~** تَوَقُّعات لا تُبَشِّرُ بِخَيْرٍ; **various changes are in ~** من المُرْتَقَبِ حُدوثُ تَغَيُّراتٍ مُخْتَلِفةٍ **3**▸ (candidate) مُرَشَّح **4**▸ (likely client) زَبون مُحْتَمَل **5**▸ (view) مَنْظَر (مَناظِرُ), مَشْهَد

B (**prospects**) *n pl* /ˈprɒspɛkts/ فُرَص نَجاح; **she has good career ~s** مُسْتَقْبَلُها المِهَنيُّ يُبَشِّرُ بالخَيْرِ; **to have no ~s** «employees» لم تَكُنْ لَدَيْهِ فُرَصٌ للنَجاحِ

C /prəˈspɛkt/ *vt* نَقَّبَ (في) ‹*the land, a region*›

D /prəˈspɛkt/ *vi* «mining companies, oil companies, miners» نَقَّبَ; **to ~ for oil/diamonds** نَقَّبَ عن النَفْطِ \ الماسِ

prospective /prəˈspɛktɪv/ *adj* ‹*buyer, student*› مُتَوَقَّع; ‹*bride, husband*› مُنْتَظَر

prospector /prəˈspɛktə/ *n* مُنَقِّب

prospectus /prəˈspɛktəs/ *n* **1**▸ نَشْرة إصْدارٍ **2**▸ دَليل جامِعيّ

prosper /ˈprɒspə/ *vi* «businesses, economies» ازْدَهَرَ

prosperity /prɒˈspɛrɪti/ *n* ازْدِهار (ازْدِهارات)

prosperous /ˈprɒsp(ə)rəs/ *adj* ‹*country, future*› مُزْدَهِر

prostate /ˈprɒsteɪt/ *n* (also **prostate gland**) بُروسْتاتا, موثة

prostitute /ˈprɒstɪtjuːt/ **A** *n* مومِس (مومِسات), بائِعة هَوى

B *vt* (**prostitutes, prostituting, prostituted**) امْتَهَنَ ‹*one's talents*›

C *v refl* **to ~ oneself** امْتَهَنَ نَفْسَهُ

prostitution /ˌprɒstɪˈtjuːʃ(ə)n/ *n* بِغاء

prostrate /ˈprɒstreɪt/ *adj* ‹*form, body*› (stretched out) مُنْبَطِح; (kneeling and bending in reverence) ساجِد (سُجَّد, سُجود)

protagonist /prəˈtag(ə)nɪst/ *n* بَطَل (أبْطال), شَخْصيّة رَئيسيّة

protect /prəˈtɛkt/ **A** *vt* حَمى (i; حِماية) ‹*rights, children*›; **to ~ sb/sth from sth** حَمى شَخْصاً \ شَيْئاً من شَيْءٍ; **he was too weak to ~ himself** كانَ أضْعَفَ من أنْ يَحْمِيَ نَفْسَهُ

B *vi* **to ~ against disease/attack** وَقى من المَرَضِ \ الهُجومِ

protection /prəˈtɛkʃ(ə)n/ *n* حِماية

protectionism /prəˈtɛkʃ(ə)niz(ə)m/ *n* حِمائيّة

protection racket *n* إتاوة (تُدْفَعُ للعِصاباتِ تَجَنُّباً لأذاها)

protective /prəˈtɛktɪv/ *adj* **1**▸ ‹*clothing, coating*› واقٍ **2**▸ ‹*feelings, parents*› غَيور (غُيُر)

protector /prəˈtɛktə/ *n* حامٍ (حُماة), واقٍ

protein /ˈprəʊtiːn/ *n* بْروتين (بْروتينات); **a diet that is high/low in ~** حِمْية تَعْتَمِدُ على الكَثيرِ \ القَليلِ من البْروتين

protest **A** /ˈprəʊtɛst/ *n* **1**▸ [u] (disagreement) احْتِجاج (احْتِجاجات), اعْتِراض (اعْتِراضات); **to resign in ~ against the policy** اسْتَقالَ احْتِجاجاً على السِياسةِ المُتَّبَعةِ; **to do sth without ~** فَعَلَ شَيْئاً دون اعْتِراضٍ; **I stayed under ~** بَقَيْتُ مُعْتَرِضاً **2**▸ (complaint) احْتِجاج (احْتِجاجات), اعْتِراض شَكْوى (f; شَكاوى), (اعْتِراضات); **as a ~ against *or* about sth** إعْراباً عن الاحْتِجاجِ على شَيْءٍ; **to lodge a ~** قَدَّمَ احْتِجاجاً **3**▸ (demonstration) مُظاهَرة; **the ~ will take place at …** سَتَكونُ المُظاهَرةُ في …; **to mount *or* stage a ~ against the reforms** نَظَّمَ مُظاهَرةً ضدّ الإصْلاحاتِ

B /prəˈtɛst/ *vt* 1 (to declare) **to ~ one's innocence** أَعْلَنَ أَنَّهُ بَرِيءٌ 2 (to complain) **'that's unfair!' they ~ed** احْتَجّوا قائِلِينَ 'لَيْسَ ذلك عَدْلاً!'; **to ~ that …** اعْتَرَضَ على أنّ … 3 (AmE) (to complain about) احْتَجَّ (على), اعْتَرَضَ (على) ‹*an injustice, a decision*›

C /prəˈtɛst/ *vi* 1 (to complain) اعْتَرَضَ, شَكا (u; شَكْوى); **he ~ed at being selected** اعْتَرَضَ على اخْتِيارِه; **we ~ed about** *or* **over the noise** شَكَوْنا من الضَوْضاء 2 (to demonstrate) «demonstrators, strikers» تَظاهَرَ, خَرَجَ في مُظاهَرةٍ; **to ~ against a war/the regime** تَظاهَرَ ضدّ حَرْبٍ \ النِظامِ

Protestant /ˈprɒtɪst(ə)nt/ *n, adj* بْروتِسْتانْتِيّ

Protestantism /ˈprɒtɪst(ə)ntɪz(ə)m/ *n* بْروتِسْتانْتِيّة

protester /prəˈtɛstə/ *n* مُتَظاهِر, مُحْتَجّ

protocol /ˈprəʊtəkɒl/ *n* 1 (Pol, Admin) بُروتوكول, مَراسِم 2 (Comput) بُروتوكول

proton /ˈprəʊtɒn/ *n* بْروتون (بْروتونات)

prototype /ˈprəʊtətʌɪp/ *n* نَموذَج أَوَّلِيّ

protract /prəˈtrakt/ *vt* (fml) أَطالَ ‹*a discussion, the negotiation*›

protracted /prəˈtraktɪd/ *adj* ‹*war, negotiations*› طَويل

protrude /prəˈtruːd/ *vi* «head, tongue» بَرَزَ (u; بُروز)

protruding /prəˈtruːdɪŋ/ *adj* ‹*eyes*› جاحِظ (جُحَظ); ‹*teeth, belly, rock, nail*› بارِز

proud /praʊd/ *adj* 1 (feeling pride) ‹*owner, parent*› فَخور; **to be ~ of sth/sb** كانَ فَخوراً بِشَيْءٍ \ بِشَخْصٍ 2 (causing pride) ‹*moment, tradition*› باعِث على الفَخْرِ 3 (pej) (arrogant) ‹*person*› مُتَكَبِّر

proudly /ˈpraʊdli/ *adv* 1 (with satisfaction) ‹*to display, announce*› بِفَخْرٍ 2 (arrogantly) ‹*to boast*› بِتَكَبُّرٍ, بِغَطْرَسةٍ

prove /pruːv/ A *vt* (*past tense* **proved**, *past participle* **proved** or **proven**) بَرْهَنَ (i; بَرْهَنة; على), أَثْبَتَ ‹*a theory, sb's innocence*›; **to ~ his point he gave an example** أَعْطى مِثالاً لِيُثْبِتَ وِجْهةَ نَظَرِهِ

B *vi* «product, event» تَبَيَّنَ, اِتَّضَحَ; **the show ~d very popular with audiences** تَبَيَّنَ أنّ العَرْضَ مَحْبوبٌ لدى الجَماهير

C *v refl* **to ~ oneself** أَثْبَتَ نَفْسَهُ; **she ~d herself worthy of our trust** أَثْبَتَتْ أنّها جَديرةٌ بِثِقَتِنا

proven /ˈpruːv(ə)n/ *adj* ‹*track record*› حافِل; ‹*reliability*› مُؤَكَّد

proverb /ˈprɒvəːb/ *n* مَثَل (أَمْثال), قَوْل مَأْثور

proverbial /prəˈvəːbɪəl/ *adj* ‹*saying, wisdom*› مَأْثور

provide /prəˈvʌɪd/ A *vt* 1 (to supply) قَدَّمَ, وَفَّرَ ‹*services, food, an opportunity*›; **a meal is ~d on the flight** تُقَدَّمُ وَجْبةٌ أثناء الرِحْلةِ; **to ~ sb with sth, to ~ sth for sb** وَفَّرَ شَيْئاً لِشَخْصٍ; **the state ~s the citizens with education and medical services, the state ~s education and medical services for the citizens** تُوَفِّرُ الدَوْلةُ التَعْليمَ والخَدَماتِ الطِبِّيّةَ للمُواطِنينَ; **they were ~d with everything they needed** تَمَّ تَزْويدُهُمْ بِكُلِّ ما يَحْتاجونَهُ; **it ~d the perfect excuse to …** وَفَّرَ الحُجّةَ المُناسِبةَ ل … 2 (to stipulate) «law, agreement» نَصَّ (u; نَصّ); **the contract ~s that the rent is paid in advance** يَنُصُّ العَقْدُ على دَفْعِ الإيجارِ مُقَدَّماً

B *vi* «the state» وَفَّرَ سُبُلَ العَيْشِ; «God» رَزَقَ (u; رِزْق)

(Phrasal verbs) **provide against**: **~ against [sth]** اتَّخَذَ التَدابيرَ اللازِمةَ ل [شَيْءٍ] ‹*hardship, a disaster*›

• **provide for** A **~ for [sth]** 1 (to make arrangements for) تَحَسَّبَ \ احْتاطَ ل [شَيْءٍ] ‹*a contingency, expenses, an eventuality*› 2 (to foresee) «insurance policies, laws, agreements» نَصَّ (u; نَصّ; على), اشْتَرَطَ ‹*action, help*› B **~ for [sb]** أَعالَ [شَخْصاً] ‹*one's family, a child*›; **to be well ~d for** اُعْتُنِيَ به بِشَكْلٍ جَيِّدٍ

provided /prəˈvʌɪdɪd/, **providing** /prəˈvʌɪdɪŋ/ *conj* (also **provided that**) ما دامَ, طالَما

providence /ˈprɒvɪd(ə)ns/ *n* (fate) قَدَر (أَقْدار), عِناية إِلَهِيّة

provider /prəˈvʌɪdə/ *n* 1 (of products, services) مُزَوِّد 2 (in families) مُعيل, عائِل

province /ˈprɒvɪns/ *n* 1 (administrative unit) إِقْليم (أَقاليمُ), مُقاطَعة 2 (area of responsibility) دائِرة اخْتِصاصٍ; (area of interest) دائِرة اهْتِمامٍ

provincial /prəˈvɪnʃ(ə)l/ *adj* 1 ‹*government, election*› إِقْليمِيّ 2 (outside the capital) ‹*town, newspaper*› إِقْليمِيّ 3 (pej) (parochial) ‹*attitude, life*› ضَيِّق الأُفُق

provision /prəˈvɪʒ(ə)n/ A *n* 1 (of housing, meals, training) تَوْفير; **to be responsible for the ~ of transport** كانَ مَسْؤولاً

عن تَوْفيرِ خِدمةِ النَقْلِ; **health care ~** تَوْفير الرِعايةِ الصِحّيّةِ **2** (for the future) تَدابير **3** (stipulation) نَصّ (نُصوص), شَرْط (شُروط); **under the ~s of the will** طِبْقاً لِنُصوصِ الوَصيّةِ

B (**provisions**) *n pl* (food and drink) مُؤَن

provisional /prəˈvɪʒ(ə)n(ə)l/ *adj* ‹*measures, government*› مُؤَقَّت

proviso /prəˈvʌɪzəʊ/ *n* (*pl* **provisos**) شَرْط (شُروط)

provocation /ˌprɒvəˈkeɪʃ(ə)n/ *n* اسْتِفْزاز (اسْتِفْزازات)

provocative /prəˈvɒkətɪv/ *adj* **1** (causing trouble, controversy) ‹*question, action*› اسْتِفْزازيّ **2** (suggestive) ‹*dress, smile*› مُثير

provoke /prəˈvəʊk/ *vt* **1** (to annoy) اسْتَفَزَّ ‹*a victim, crowd*›; **he was ~d into a fight** جُرَّ إلى مَعْرَكةٍ **2** (to cause) تَسَبَّبَ (في) ‹*a reaction, criticism*›; أثارَ ‹*outrage, anger*›; أدّى (إلى) ‹*a debate, discussion*›

prow /praʊ/ *n* جُؤْجُؤ (جَآجِئ), مُقَدَّمة سَفينةٍ

prowess /ˈpraʊɪs/ *n* مَهارة, بَراعة

prowl /praʊl/ **A** *vt* جاسَ (u; جَوْس, جَوَسان), تَجَوَّلَ خُفْيةً في ‹*the streets, a neighbourhood*›

B *vi* «wild animals, burglars» طافَ (بَحْثاً عن فَريسةٍ)

proximity /prɒkˈsɪmɪti/ *n* قُرْب

proxy /ˈprɒksi/ *n* (*pl* **proxies**) **1** (person) وَكيل (وُكَلاءُ) **2** (authorization) تَوْكيل (تَوْكيلات), تَفْويض (تَفْويضات); **by ~** بالوَكالةِ \ بالنِيابةِ

prude /pruːd/ *n* [شَخْص شَديد الاحْتِشام]

prudence /ˈpruːd(ə)ns/ *n* حِكْمة, حَصافة

prudent /ˈpruːd(ə)nt/ *adj* ‹*management, decision*› حَكيم (حُكَماءُ), رَشيد (رُشَداءُ)

prudish /ˈpruːdɪʃ/ *adj* ‹*attitude, person*› شَديد الاحْتِشامِ

prune /pruːn/ **A** *n* بَرْقوق مُجَفَّف

B *vt* **1** قَلَّمَ, شَذَّبَ ‹*a tree, plant*› **2** اخْتَزَلَ ‹*a text*›; قَلَّصَ (في) ‹*budget*›

pry /prʌɪ/ **A** *vi* (**pries**, **prying**, **pried**) «journalists, nosey people» تَطَفَّلَ; **to ~ into sb's life/affairs** تَطَفَّلَ على حَياةِ \ شُؤونِ شَخْصٍ

B *vt* (**pries**, **prying**, **pried**) (AmE) ▸ **prise off**

PS /piːˈes/ *n* = **postscript** مُلاحَظة (في آخِرِ الرِسالةِ)

psalm /sɑːm/ *n* مَزْمور (مَزامير)

pseudonym /ˈsjuːd(ə)nɪm/ *n* اسْم مُسْتَعار

psittacosis /ˌsɪtəˈkəʊsɪs/ *n* بَبَّغائيّة (مَرَض مُعْدٍ)

psoriasis /sɒˈrʌɪəsɪs/ *n* صَدَفيّة

PST /piːesˈtiː/ *abbr* (AmE) = **Pacific Standard Time** تَوْقيت المُحيطِ الهادِئِ, التَوْقيت الباسيفيكيّ

psyche /ˈsʌɪki/ *n* نَفْس (f; أَنْفُس, نُفوس)

psychiatric /ˌsʌɪkiˈatrɪk/ *adj* ‹*disorder, hospital*› نَفْسيّ

psychiatrist /sʌɪˈkʌɪətrɪst/ *n* طَبيب نَفْسيّ

psychiatry /sʌɪˈkʌɪətri/ *n* طِبّ نَفْسيّ

psychic /ˈsʌɪkɪk/ **A** *adj* **1** (paranormal) ‹*powers, phenomena*› روحانيّ **2** (telepathic) ‹*person*› روحانيّ

B *n* وَسيط روحانيّ

psychoanalysis /ˌsʌɪkəʊəˈnalɪsɪs/ *n* تَحْليل نَفْسيّ

psychoanalyst /sʌɪkəʊˈanəlɪst/ *n* مُحَلِّل نَفْسيّ

psychological /sʌɪkəˈlɒdʒɪk(ə)l/ *adj* ‹*problem, effect*› نَفْسيّ, سيكولوجيّ

psychologically /sʌɪkəˈlɒdʒɪkli/ *adv* ‹*to suffer, affect*› نَفْسيًّا, سيكولوجيًّا; **~, it was a clever move** كانَتْ خُطوةً ذَكيّةً من الناحِيةِ النَفْسيّةِ

psychologist /sʌɪˈkɒlədʒɪst/ *n* طَبيب, أَخِصّائيّ \ عالِم نَفْسيّ نَفْسانيّ

psychology /sʌɪˈkɒlədʒi/ *n* (*pl* **psychologies**) عِلْم النَفْسِ

psychopath /ˈsʌɪkəpaθ/ *n* سيكوباتيّ (شَخْص مُضْطَرِب عَقْليًّا)

psychosis /sʌɪˈkəʊsɪs/ *n* (*pl* **psychoses** /-siːz/) ذُهان (اضْطِراب عَقْليّ)

psychosomatic /ˌsʌɪkəʊsəˈmatɪk/ *adj* ‹*illness, symptoms*› نَفْسيّ جَسَديّ, سيكوسوماتيّ

psychotherapist /sʌɪkəʊˈθɛrəpɪst/ *n* مُعالِج نَفْسيّ

psychotherapy /sʌɪkəʊˈθɛrəpi/ *n* (*pl* **psychotherapies**) عِلاج نَفْسيّ

psychotic /sʌɪˈkɒtɪk/ *adj* ‹*symptoms, disorder*› ذُهانيّ

psych out /sʌɪk/ *vt* (infml) **to ~ sb, to psych sb out** أَثَّرَ على شَخْصٍ نَفْسيًّا ‹*an opponent, person*›

psych up *vt* (infml) **to psych oneself up** أَعَدَّ نَفْسَهُ مَعْنَويًّا \ هَيَّأَ

PTA /piːtiː'eɪ/ *n* = **Parent-Teacher Association** رابِطة الآباءِ والمُعَلِّمين

PTO /piːtiː'əʊ/ *abbr* = **please turn over** من فَضْلِكَ اقْلِب الصَفْحة

pub /pʌb/ *n* (BrE) حانة, بار (بارات)

puberty /'pjuːbəti/ *n* بُلوغ

pubic /'pjuːbɪk/ *adj* ‹*hair, bone, area*› العانةِ

pubis /'pjuːbɪs/ *n* عَظْم العانةِ

public /'pʌblɪk/ **A** *adj* **1** (open to all) ‹*park, library, footpath*› عامّ; **to make one's views ~** صَرَّحَ بِآرائِهِ في العَلَنِ; **to live in the ~ eye** عاشَ تحت الأَضْواءِ; **it is ~ knowledge that** القاصي والداني يَعْرِفُ أنّ ... ; **let's go somewhere less ~** هَيّا نَذْهَبُ إلى مَكانٍ بَعيدٍ عن الأَنْظارِ **2** (of collective responsibility) ‹*health, expenditure*› عامّ; **to be in the ~ interest** كانَ في المَصْلَحةِ العامّةِ; **the ports are in ~ ownership** المَوانِئُ مَمْلوكةٌ للدَوْلةِ; **at ~ expense** على حِساب الدَوْلةِ; **the ~ sector** القِطاع العامّ **3** (open) ‹*announcement, inquiry, execution*› عَلَنيّ; **the decree was made ~ yesterday** أُعْلِنَ عن المَرْسوم البارِحة; **a ~ enquiry is needed to establish the facts** هُناكَ حاجةٌ إلى إجْراءِ تَحْقيقٍ عَلَنيٍّ للوُقوفِ على الحَقائِقِ; **she has decided to go ~ with her story** قَرَّرَتْ أنْ تَرْوي قِصَّتَها على المَلأِ

B *n* **the ~** الجُمْهور; **open to the ~** مَفْتوح للجُمْهورِ

C (**in public**) *adv phr* في العَلَنِ; **her first appearance in ~** أوّل ظُهورٍ عَلَنيٍّ لَها

public address system *n* نِظام مُكَبِّراتِ الصَوْتِ

publican /'pʌblɪk(ə)n/ *n* (BrE) صاحِب حانةٍ \ بارٍ

public assistance *n* (AmE) إعانات \ مُساعَدات حُكوميّة (للمُحْتاجينَ)

publication /ˌpʌblɪ'keɪʃ(ə)n/ *n* **1** [u] (publishing) نَشْر **2** (book, journal etc.) مَطْبوعة

public company *n* شَرِكة مُساهَمةٍ عامّة

public convenience *n* (BrE) مِرْحاض عامّ

public holiday *n* (BrE) عُطْلة عامّة

public house *n* (BrE) حانة, بار (بارات)

publicity /pʌb'lɪsɪti/ *n* دِعاية

publicity campaign *n* حَمْلة إعْلانيّة \ دِعائيّة

publicity stunt *n* حيلة دِعائيّة

publicize, -ise (BrE) /'pʌblɪsaɪz/ *vt* **1** (to make public) أَعْلَنَ, نَشَرَ (u; نَشْر) ‹*information*›; عَرَّفَ (ب) ‹*a problem*› **2** (to advertise) رَوَّجَ (ل) ‹*an event, a book*›

publicly /'pʌblɪkli/ *adv* **1** (in public) ‹*to speak, apologize*› عَلَناً, عَلانيّةً; **the information is ~ available** المَعْلوماتُ مُتاحةٌ عَلَناً للجُمْهورِ **2** (by the state) ‹*funded, owned*› حُكوميًّا; **the project is ~ funded** المَشْروعُ مُمَوَّلٌ حُكوميًّا

public office *n* وَظيفة عامّة

public opinion *n* رَأْي عامّ

public prosecutor *n* نائِب عامّ, مُدَّعٍ عامّ (Egypt), وَكيل الجُمْهوريّةِ (Tunisia, Algeria), المَلِكِ \ النِيابةِ (Mor)

public relations *n* عَلاقات عامّة

public school *n* **1** (in UK, fee-paying) مَدْرَسة ثانَويّة خاصّة (في بَريطانيا) **2** (state-funded) مَدْرَسة عامّة \ حُكوميّة

public sector *n* قِطاع عامّ

public spending *n* الإنْفاق العامّ

public-spirited /ˌpʌblɪk'spɪrɪtɪd/ *adj* ‹*citizen, gesture*› حَريص على المَصْلَحةِ العامّةِ

public transport *n* مُواصَلات عامّة \ عُموميّة

publish /'pʌblɪʃ/ *vt* **1** نَشَرَ (u; نَشْر) ‹*a book, an article*› **2** (to make known) أَعْلَنَ ‹*results, findings*›

publisher /'pʌblɪʃə/ *n* **1** (company) دار نَشْرٍ **2** (person) ناشِر

publishing /'pʌblɪʃɪŋ/ *n* نَشْر

publishing house *n* دار نَشْرٍ

pucker /'pʌkə/ *vt* زَمَّ (u; زَمّ) ‹*one's lips*›; قَطَّبَ ‹*brow*›

pudding /'pʊdɪŋ/ *n* **1** (sweet cooked dish) بودِنْج (طَبَق حَلْوى مَطْهيّة) **2** (BrE) (hot savoury dish) بودِنْج (أُكْلة من الدَقيقِ واللَحْمِ أو الخَضْراوات) **3** [u] (BrE) (dessert course) طَبَق حَلْوى (يُخْتَتَمُ بِهِ الطَعامُ)

puddle /'pʌd(ə)l/ *n* بِرْكة (بِرَك)

Puerto Rican /ˌpwɛːtə 'riːk(ə)n/ *n, adj* بورْتوريكيّ

Puerto Rico /ˌpwɛːtə 'riːkəʊ/ *pr n* بورْتوريكو (f)

puff /pʌf/ **A** *n* **1** (of air) نَفْحة (نَفَحات); (of smoke, steam) نَفْثة (نَفَثات), نَفْخة; **there wasn't the slightest ~ of wind** لم تَكُنْ

هُناكَ وَلا نَفْحةٌ من الهَواءِ في الجَوّ; **to disappear in a ~ of smoke** اختَفى في سَحابةٍ من الدُخانِ **2** (BrE) [u] (infml) (breath) نَفَس (أَنْفاس); **I'm out of ~** أَشْعُرُ بِضيقٍ في النَفَسِ **3** (Culin) [فَطيرة مُنْتَفِخة] **4** (infml) (favourable review) مَديح, إطْراء (مَدائِحُ)

B *vt* نَفَثَ الدُخانَ ‹*a pipe, cigarette*›; **to ~ smoke into sb's face** نَفَثَ الدُخانَ في وَجْهِ شَخْصٍ

C *vi* **1** (to blow) هَبَّ (u; هَبّ, هُبوب); **smoke ~ed from the chimney** تَصاعَدَ الدُخانُ من المَدْخَنةِ **2** (on a cigarette, pipe) أَخَذَ \ سَحَبَ نَفَساً; **he ~ed at *or* on his pipe/cigarette** أَخَذَ نَفَساً من غَلْيونِهِ \ سيجارَتِهِ **3** (to pant) «runners, workers» لَهَثَ (a; لَهْث, لُهاثة); **to ~ and pant *or* blow** لَهَثَ بِشِدّةٍ

(Phrasal verbs) **puff out A** «sails, sleeves» انْتَفَخَ, امْتَلأَ بالهَواءِ **B ~ out [sth], ~ [sth] out 1** (to swell) نَفَخَ [شَيْئاً], مَلأَ [شَيْئاً] بالهَواءِ ‹*the sails*›; **to ~ out one's cheeks** نَفَخَ وَجْنَتَيْهِ; **to ~ out one's chest** نَفَخَ صَدْرَهُ; **the bird ~ed out its feathers** نَفَشَ الطائِرُ ريشَهُ **2** (to belch out) **to ~ out smoke** نَفَثَ الدُخانَ **C ~ [sb] out** (infml) (to exhaust) أَنْهَكَ \ أَرْهَقَ [شَخْصاً]

• **puff up A** «feathers» انْتَفَشَ, انْتَفَخَ **B ~ up [sth], ~ [sth] up** نَفَشَ \ نَفَخَ [شَيْئاً] ‹*feathers, fur*›; **to be ~ed up with pride** كانَ مَليئاً بالفَخْرِ

puffed /pʌfd/ *adj* ‹*sleeve*› مُنْتَفِخ

puffin /ˈpʌfɪn/ *n* طائِر البَفَن

puff pastry *n* فَطائِر هِشّة

puffy /ˈpʌfi/ *adj* (**puffier**, **puffiest**) ‹*eyes, face*› مُنْتَفِخ, مُتَوَرِّم

puke /pjuːk/ *vi* (infml) تَقَيَّأَ

pull /pʊl/ **A** *vt* **1** (to tug) جَرَّ (u; جَرّ), شَدَّ (i-u; شَدّ) ‹*a rope, sb's hair, a chain*›; **don't ~ the cat's tail** لا تَشُدَّ ذَيْلَ القِطِّ; **to ~ the sheets over one's head** غَطّى رَأْسَهُ بالشَراشِفِ; **to ~ a sweater over one's head** (to put it on) لَبِسَ سُتْرةً; (to take it off) نَزَعَ سُتْرةً **2** (to move, drag) جَرَّ (u; جَرّ) ‹*a sack, body, chair*›; **he ~ed me to the window** جَرَّني إلى الشُبّاكِ; **to ~ sth out of one's pocket/a drawer** أَخْرَجَ شَيْئاً من جَيْبِهِ \ دُرْجٍ; **to ~ sb out of the rubble** أَخْرَجَ شَخْصاً من بَيْنِ الأَنْقاضِ; **he ~ed the dog off her** شَدَّ الكَلْبَ بَعيداً عَنْها **3** (to draw) جَرَّ (u; جَرّ) ‹*a caravan, cart, sled*› **4** (to operate) جَذَبَ (i; جَذْب) ‹*a lever, switch*›; ضَغَطَ (a; ضَغْط) على ‹*the trigger*› **5** (to strain) مَزَّقَ ‹*a muscle, ligament*› **6** (to harvest) حَصَدَ (i-u; حَصاد) ‹*beans, potatoes*› **7** (infml) (to produce) أَخْرَجَ ‹*a gun, knife*›; **to ~ a gun on sb** رَفَعَ بُنْدُقِيّةً على شَخْصٍ **8** (to steer, guide) قادَ (u; قِيادة) ‹*the car, bicycle*›; **he ~ed the car to the side of the road** قادَ السَيّارةَ إلى جانِبِ الطَريقِ **9** (BrE) (infml) (to serve) صَبَّ (u; صَبّ) ‹*a pint*› **10** (to attract) جَذَبَ (i; جَذْب) ‹*an audience, voters*› **11** (infml) (to pick up) كَسَبَ الوِدَّ, أَوْقَعَ في حِبالِهِ ‹*a woman, man*› **12** (to make) **to ~ a face** [رَسَمَ تَعْبيراً على وَجْهِهِ]

B *vi* **1** (to tug) جَرَّ (u; جَرّ), شَدَّ (i-u; شَدّ); **she ~ed at my sleeve** شَدَّتْني من كُمّي; **stop ~ing on the rope** تَوَقَّفْ عن شَدِّ الحَبْلِ **2** (to struggle) «dogs, horses» شَدَّ (i-u; شَدّ) **3** (to move) تَحَرَّكَ; **to ~ ahead of sb** «athletes, drivers» سَبَقَ شَخْصاً **4** (to smoke) **to ~ at *or* on a pipe/cigarette** دَخَّنَ غَلْيوناً \ سيجارةً **5** (to drink) **to ~ at a bottle** شَرِبَ من زُجاجةٍ **6** (in rowing) شَدَّ بِقوّةٍ

C *n* **1** (tug) شَدّ, جَرّ, سَحْب; **to give a rope a ~** شَدَّ حَبْلاً **2** (attraction) جَذْب **3** (infml) (influence) تَأْثير, نُفوذ; **he has a lot of ~ in the party** لَدَيْهِ نُفوذٌ كَبيرٌ في الحِزْبِ **4** (infml) (swig) جُرْعة كَبيرة **5** (infml) (on a cigarette, pipe) نَفَس (أَنْفاس) **6** (prolonged effort) **to be a long/hard ~** كانَتْ مُهِمّةً شاقّةً

(Phrasal verbs) **pull along**: **~ [sth] along, ~ along [sth]** جَرَّ [شَيْئاً] ‹*a sled, cart*›

• **pull apart A** «components, furniture» فَكَّكَ **B ~ [sb/sth] apart 1** (to separate fighters) فَضَّ الاشْتِباكَ بين [أَشْخاصٍ \ أَشْياءَ] ‹*the boxers, dogs*›; (to separate objects) فَصَلَ بين [أَشْياءَ] ‹*the pages, layers, wires*› **2** (to destroy) «children, vandals» حَطَّمَ [شَيْئاً] ‹*the furniture, a toy*› **3** (critically) هاجَمَ [شَخْصاً \ شَيْئاً] ‹*an idea, a person, proposal*›

• **pull away A 1** (to move off) «cars, trains» انْطَلَقَ **2** (to move away) «person» ابْتَعَدَ **3** (from rivals) «leader, runners, cars» أَحْرَزَ تَقَدُّماً **B ~ [sb/sth] away** أَبْعَدَ [شَخْصاً \ شَيْئاً] ‹*a person, one's hand*›; **to ~ sb/sth away from the window** جَذَبَ شَخْصاً \ شَيْئاً بَعيداً عن الشُبّاكِ **C ~ away from [sb/sth] 1** «drivers, vehicles» تَحَرَّكَ بَعيداً عن [شَخْصٍ \ شَيْءٍ] ‹*the lights, the kerb*›

2 (to move away from) ابْتَعَدَ عن [شَخْصٍ \ شَيْءٍ] ‹a person› 3 (to take a lead over) «leader, runners, driver» أَحْرَزَ تَقَدُّماً على [شَخْصٍ \ شَيْءٍ] ‹the competition, rest›

• **pull back** A 1 (to withdraw) «troops» انْسَحَبَ 2 (from fear, surprise) «children, spectators» تَراجَعَ للخَلْفِ B ~ **[sb/sth] back, ~ back [sb/sth]** 1 (to move back) جَذَبَ [شَخْصاً \ شَيْئاً] إلى الخَلْفِ ‹a curtain, chair› 2 (to restrain) جَذَبَ [شخصاً \ شَيْئاً] إلى الوَراءِ ‹a child, dog› 3 (to withdraw) سَحَبَ [شَخْصاً \ شَيْئاً] ‹troops, artillery›

• **pull down**: ~ **[sth] down, ~ down [sth]** 1 (to demolish) هَدَمَ [شَيْئاً] ‹a building› 2 (to lower) أَنْزَلَ [شَيْئاً] ‹a blind, flag›; **to ~ down one's trousers** نَزَعَ سِرْوالَهُ 3 (to reduce) «mistakes» أَنْقَصَ [شَيْئاً] ‹grades, results› 4 (to weaken) «illnesses» أَضْعَفَ [شَخْصاً] ‹a person› 5 (to damage) «losses, errors» أَضَرَّ ب [شَخْصٍ \ شَيْءٍ] ‹a person, one's reputation, the organization›

• **pull in** A 1 (to park) «cars, drivers» تَوَقَّفَ; **~ in just here** تَوَقَّفْ هُنا 2 (to arrive) «buses, trains» وَصَلَ (i; وُصول) B **~ [sb] in, ~ in [sb]** 1 (to detain) احْتَجَزَ [شَخْصاً] ‹a suspect› 2 (to attract) شَدَّ انْتِباهَ [شَخْصٍ] ‹an audience, a crowd, tourists› C **~ [sth] in, ~ in [sth]** 1 (to retract) سَحَبَ [شَيْئاً] إلى الداخِلِ ‹claws, tentacles› 2 (infml) (to earn) سَحَبَ [شَيْئاً] ‹a sum, salary›

• **pull off** A «handles, tops» أَمْكَنَ نَزْعُهُ B **~ off [sth]** (to leave) خَرَجَ من [شَيْءٍ] ‹a motorway, road› C **~ off [sth], ~ [sth] off** 1 (to remove clothes) نَزَعَ \ خَلَعَ [شَيْئاً] ‹one's coat, shoes› 2 (infml) (to carry out) أَبْرَمَ [شَيْئاً] ‹a deal›; شَنَّ [شَيْئاً] ‹a raid›; قامَ ب [شَيْءٍ] ‹a robbery›

• **pull out** A 1 (into the road) «cars, drivers» تَخَطَّى; (from a station) «buses, trains» انْطَلَقَ, بَدَأَ في التَحَرُّكِ 2 (to start off) «trains, buses» غادَرَ 3 (from a competition, race) «competitors, negotiators, candidates» انْسَحَبَ 4 (to withdraw) «troops, the army» انْسَحَبَ 5 (to come out) «drawers» خَرَجَ (u; خُروج) B **~ [sth] out, ~ out [sth]** 1 (to extract) خَلَعَ [شَيْئاً] ‹a tooth›; أَخْرَجَ [شَيْئاً] ‹a splinter›; نَزَعَ [شَيْئاً] ‹a plug› 2 (from a pocket, bag) أَخْرَجَ [شَيْئاً] ‹one's wallet, mobile, a gun› 3 (to withdraw) سَحَبَ [شَيْئاً] ‹the troops, a team›

• **pull over** A «drivers, vehicles» تَوَقَّفَ على جانِبِ الطَريقِ B **~ [sb/sth] over** 1 (to stop) «police officers» أَوْقَفَ [شَخْصاً \ شَيْئاً] ‹a driver, vehicle› 2 (to knock over) أَسْقَطَ [شَخْصاً \ شَيْئاً] على الأَرْضِ ‹a statue, person›

• **pull through** «victims» اجْتازَ الصِعابَ; «patients» تَغَلَّبَ على المَرَضِ

• **pull together** A (to cooperate) تَكاتَفَ B **~ [sth] together** 1 جَمَعَ [شَيْئاً] مَعاً ‹the chairs, ends, the parts› 2 **~ oneself together** تَمالَكَ نَفْسَهُ

• **pull up** A (to stop) «drivers, vehicles» تَوَقَّفَ B **~ up [sth], ~ [sth] up** 1 (to uproot) اقْتَلَعَ [شَيْئاً] ‹weeds, a crop› 2 (to draw up) رَفَعَ [شَيْئاً] ‹an anchor, a drawbridge› 3 (to bring closer) قَرَّبَ [شَيْئاً] ‹a chair, stool› C **~ [sb] up** 1 (to raise) رَفَعَ [شَخْصاً]; **we ~ed him up out of the water** انْتَشَلْناهُ من الماءِ 2 (to reprimand) وَبَّخَ [شَخْصاً] 3 (to stop) أَوْقَفَ [شَخْصاً] ‹a driver, vehicle›

pull-down menu /ˌpʊlˌdaʊn ˈmɛnjuː/ *n* (Comput) قائمة مُنْسَدِلة

pulley /ˈpʊli/ *n* بَكَرة (بَكَرات, بَكَر)

pull-out /ˈpʊlaʊt/ A *adj* ‹section, supplement› مُلْحَق B *n* انْسِحاب (انْسِحابات)

pullover /ˈpʊləʊvə/ *n* بُلوفَر

pull-up /ˈpʊlʌp/ *n* [تَمارين رَفْعِ الجِسْمِ بِإمْساكِ قَضيبٍ مُعَلَّقٍ]

pulmonary /ˈpʌlmən(ə)ri/ *adj* ‹artery, disease› رِئَوِيّ

pulp /pʌlp/ *n* 1 (of fruit) لُبّ 2 (for paper) لُبّ (الخَشَبِ \ الوَرَقِ) 3 (crushed mass) عَجينة (عَجائِنُ)

pulp fiction *n* [أَدَب مُبْتَذَل]

pulpit /ˈpʊlpɪt/ *n* مِنْبَر (مَنابِرُ)

pulsate /pʌlˈseɪt/ *vi* «veins, heart» نَبَضَ (i; نَبْض, نَبَضان); «music, room» اهْتَزَّ

pulse /pʌls/ *n* 1 (of the blood) نَبْض (أَنْباض); **to take sb's ~** قاسَ نَبْضَ شَخْصٍ; **the patient had no ~** لم يَكُنْ للمَريضِ نَبْضٌ 2 (rhythm) إيقاع (إيقاعات) 3 (of sound, light, electricity) مَوْجة نابِضة 4 (food) (**pulses** *n pl*) حُبوب البُقولِ

pulse rate *n* مُعَدَّل النَبْضِ

pulverize, **-ise** (BrE) /'pʌlvərʌɪz/ *vt* سَحَقَ (a; سَحْق) ‹*rock, a city*›

puma /'pju:mə/ *n* أَسَد الجِبالِ

pummel /'pʌm(ə)l/ *vt* (**-ll-** AmE, **-l-**) لَكَمَ (مِراراً) ‹*an opponent, a surface*›

pump /pʌmp/ **A** *n* 1 (for water, air) مِضَخّة; **a bicycle ~** مِنْفاخ عَجَلةِ دَرّاجةٍ 2 (also **gas pump** AmE, **petrol pump** BrE) مِضَخّة 3 (BrE) (woman's flat shoe) [حِذاء نِسائيّ ذو كَعْبٍ مُنْخَفِضٍ] 4 (AmE) (plain shoe) [حِذاء ذو كَعْبٍ مُنْخَفِضٍ] **B** *vt* 1 ضَخَّ (u; ضَخّ) ‹*air, gas, water*›; **to ~ air into a tyre** ضَخَّ الهَواءَ في إطارٍ; **to ~ the cellar dry** نَزَحَ الماءَ من القَبْوِ بِمِضَخّةٍ 2 (to move) حَرَّكَ لِأَعْلى وَلِأَسْفَلَ ‹*a handle, lever*›; **he ~ed my hand in congratulation** صافَحَني بِحَرارةٍ مُهَنِّئاً لي 3 (infml) (to question) اِسْتَجْوَبَ, أَمْطَرَ بالأَسْئِلةِ ‹*a person*›; **to ~ sb for information/news** اِسْتَجْوَبَ شَخْصاً للحُصولِ على مَعْلوماتٍ \ أَخْبارٍ 4 **to ~ sb's stomach out** غَسَلَ مَعِدةَ شَخْصٍ

C *vi* 1 (to work hard) «pistons» تَحَرَّكَ لِأَعْلى وَلِأَسْفَلَ «heart» نَبَضَ (i; نَبْض, نَبَضان) بِشَكْلٍ دَوْرِيٍّ 2 (to flow) «blood» تَدَفَّقَ

Phrasal verbs **pump out**: **~ out [sth], ~ [sth] out** 1 (to empty) أَفْرَغَ [شَيْئاً] بالضخ ‹*a pool, boat*› 2 (to emit) نَفَثَ [شَيْئاً] ‹*smoke*›; أَصْدَرَ الكَثيرَ من [شَيْءٍ] ‹*legislation*›

• **pump up**: **~ up [sth], ~ [sth] up** 1 (to inflate) نَفَخَ [شَيْئاً] ‹*a tyre, air bed*› 2 (infml) (to exaggerate) ضَخَّمَ [شَيْئاً], بالَغَ في [شَيْءٍ] ‹*the figures, volume*›

pumpkin /'pʌmpkɪn/ *n* قَرْع, يَقْطين (n coll)

pun /pʌn/ *n* تَوْرِية

punch /pʌntʃ/ **A** *vt* 1 (to hit) **to ~ sb in the face/on the jaw** لَكَمَ شَخْصاً في وَجْهِهِ \ فَكِّهِ 2 ضَغَطَ (a; ضَغْط) (على) ‹*the keys*› 3 خَرَمَ (i; خَرْم), ثَقَبَ (u; ثَقْب) ‹*the cards, tickets*›; **to ~ a ticket** ثَقَبَ تَذْكِرةً

B *vi* «boxer, person» لَكَمَ (u; لَكْم), سَدَّدَ لَكْمةً

C *n* 1 (blow) لَكْمة (لَكَمات); **to give sb a ~ on the jaw/in the ribs** لَكَمَ شَخْصاً على فَكِّهِ \ في الأَضْلاعِ; **to throw a ~ at sb** وَجَّهَ \ سَدَّدَ لَكْمةً لِشَخْصٍ 2 (effectiveness) حَيَوِيّة; **it lacks ~** تَنْقُصُهُ الحَيَوِيّةُ; **it has plenty of ~** هو مَليءٌ بالحَيَوِيّةِ 3 (drink) [شَراب كُحوليّ] 4 (tool for leather, metal) خَرّامة, آلة تَثْقيبٍ

Idioms **to pack a punch** (infml) سَدَّدَ ضَرْبةً موجِعةً; **to pull no punches** تَحَدَّثَ دون تَحَفُّظٍ

Phrasal verb **punch in**: **~ in [sth], ~ [sth] in** «keyboarder» أَدْخَلَ [شَيْئاً] في الحاسوبِ ‹*the data, code*›

Punch-and-Judy show *n* عَرْض بَنْش وَجودي (مَسْرَح عَرائِس)

punchbag (BrE) /'pʌntʃbag/, **punching bag** (AmE) /'pʌntʃɪŋ bag/ *n* كيس مُلاكَمةٍ

punchball /'pʌntʃbɔ:l/ *n* 1 (BrE) (equipment) كُرة مُلاكَمةٍ 2 [u] (AmE) (game) كُرة المُلاكَمةِ (لُعْبة)

punch-drunk /'pʌntʃdrʌnk/ *adj* (in boxing) ‹*opponent*› مُتَرَنِّح

punchline /'pʌntʃlʌɪn/ *n* ذُرْوة النُكْتةِ

punch-up /'pʌntʃʌp/ *n* (BrE infml) تَلاكُم, عِراك بالأَيْدي

punctual /'pʌŋktʃʊəl/ *adj* ‹*payment, train*› في الوَقْتِ المُحَدَّدِ

punctuality /pʌŋktʃu:'aləti/ *n* دِقّة المَواعيدِ

punctually /'pʌŋktʃʊəli/ *adv* ‹*to arrive, leave*› في الوَقْتِ المُحَدَّدِ, في حينِهِ

punctuate /'pʌŋktʃʊeɪt/ **A** *vt* 1 (to insert punctuation) رَقَّمَ ‹*a sentence, text*› 2 (to interrupt) قاطَعَ ‹*a conversation, speech*› **B** *vi* «students, children» رَقَّمَ

punctuation /pʌŋktʃu:'eɪʃ(ə)n/ *n* تَرْقيم

punctuation mark *n* عَلامة تَرْقيمٍ

puncture /'pʌŋktʃə/ **A** *n* ثُقْب (ثُقوب); **we had a ~ on the way** ثُقِبَ الإطارُ في الطَريقِ **B** *vt* ثَقَبَ (u; ثَقْب) ‹*a tyre, lung*›

puncture repair kit *n* عُدّة إِصْلاحِ الثُقوبِ (للدَرّاجةِ)

pundit /'pʌndɪt/ *n* خَبير (خُبَراءُ)

pungent /'pʌndʒ(ə)nt/ *adj* ‹*smell*› لاذِع, حادّ; ‹*cheese*› حادّ \ لاذِع النَكْهةِ

punish /'pʌnɪʃ/ *vt* عاقَبَ ‹*a criminal, child*›

punishable /'pʌnɪʃəb(ə)l/ *adj* ‹*crime, act*› يُعاقِبُ عَلَيْهِ القانونُ; **shop lifting is ~ by a fine or imprisonment** سَرِقةُ المَتاجِرِ جَريمةٌ يُعاقِبُ عَلَيْها القانونُ بالغَرامةِ أو الحَبْسِ

punishing /ˈpʌnɪʃɪŋ/ *adj* ‹*schedule, pace*› قاسٍ; **they suffered a ~ defeat** عانوا من هَزيمةٍ قاسِيةٍ

punishment /ˈpʌnɪʃmənt/ *n* عُقوبة, عِقاب

punitive /ˈpjuːnɪtɪv/ *adj* ‹*measure, action*› عِقابيّ, تَأْديبيّ

punk /pʌŋk/ *n* **1** (music) موسيقى البانْك **2** (punk rocker) [شابّ من شَبابِ البانْك] **3** (AmE infml) (lout) أَوْغاد) وَغْد)

punnet /ˈpʌnɪt/ *n* (BrE) سَلّة (صَغيرة); **a ~ of strawberries** سَلّة صَغيرة من الفَراوْلةِ

punt /pʌnt/ **A** *n* **1** (boat) قارِب البَنْط **2** (BrE infml) (bet) رِهان **B** *vi* «punters, holidaymakers» [رَكِبَ قارِبَ البَنْط]

punter /ˈpʌntə/ *n* (BrE infml) **1** (gambler) مُقامِر **2** (average client) زَبون (عاديّ)

puny /ˈpjuːni/ *adj* (**punier**, **puniest**) **1** ‹*weakling, baby*› هَزيل **2** ‹*salary, effort*› زَهيد, ضَئيل (وُهاة) واهٍ, (هَزْلى)

pup /pʌp/ *n* **1** (also **puppy**) (dog) جَرْو (جِراء) **2** (seal, otter) جَرْو (جِراء)

pupil /ˈpjuːpɪl/ *n* **1** (at school) تِلْميذ (تَلاميذُ, تَلامِذة) **2** (student) تِلْميذ (تَلاميذُ, تَلامِذة) **3** (in the eye) بُؤْبُؤ, إنسان العَيْنِ

puppet /ˈpʌpɪt/ *n* **1** (toy) دُمْية (دُمًى), عَروسة (عَرائِسُ) **2** (stooge) دُمْية (شَخْص أو شَيْء واقِع تحت سَيْطرةٍ خارجيّةٍ)

puppeteer /ˌpʌpɪˈtɪə/ *n* مُحَرِّك الدُمى

puppy /ˈpʌpi/ *n* (*pl* **puppies**) جَرْو (جِراء)

purchase /ˈpəːtʃɪs/ **A** *vt* اشْتَرى ‹*a product, property*› **B** *n* (fml) شِراء

purchaser /ˈpəːtʃɪsə/ *n* (fml) مُشْترٍ (مُشْتَرون)

purchasing power /ˈpəːtʃəsɪŋ ˌpaʊə/ *n* قُوّة شِرائيّة

purdah /ˈpəːdə/ *n*; **to go into ~** اتَّخَذَ حِجاباً

pure /pjʊə/ *adj* ‹*gold, form*› نَقيّ, خالِص; **the ~ water from the spring** الماء النَقيّ من النَبْع; **it's guaranteed to be ~ wool** مَضْمونٌ أَنّهُ صوفٌ خالِصٌ

puree /ˈpjʊəreɪ/ *n* بوريه (هَريسة الفَواكِهِ أو الخُضَر)

purely /ˈpjʊəli/ *adv* ‹*decorative, coincidental*› كُلّيًا, تماماً; **we met ~ by chance** تقابَلْنا بِمَحْضِ الصُدْفةِ

purgatory /ˈpəːgət(ə)ri/ *n* **1** (for souls of the dead) مَطْهَر (في الكَنيسةِ الكاثوليكيّة) **2** (unpleasant experience) مُعاناة

purge /pəːdʒ/ *vt* طَهَّرَ ‹*a party, government*›; **he ~d the party of extremists** طَهَّرَ الحِزْبَ من المُتَطَرِّفينَ

purify /ˈpjʊərɪfʌɪ/ *vt* (**purifies**, **purifying**, **purified**) نَقّى ‹*water, chemicals*›

purist /ˈpjʊərɪst/ *n* ذو نَزْعةٍ صَفائيّةٍ

puritan /ˈpjʊərɪt(ə)n/ *n* بيوريتاني

puritanical /pjʊərɪˈtanɪk(ə)l/ *adj* ‹*attitude, sect*› مُتَشَدِّد, مُتَزمِّت

purity /ˈpjʊərɪti/ *n* صَفاء, نَقاء

purl /pəːl/ *n* تَطْريز عَكْسيّ

purple /ˈpəːp(ə)l/ **A** *n* اللَوْن الأَرْجُوانيّ; **to wear ~** ارْتَدى مَلابِسَ أُرْجُوانيّةً **B** *adj* ‹*flower, velvet*› أُرْجُوانيّ; **he went ~ with rage** احْمَرَّ وَجْهُهُ من شِدّةِ الغَضَبِ

purport /pəˈpɔːt/ *vt* (fml) **to ~ to be sth** «claimants» زَعَمَ \ ادَّعى أنَّهُ شَيْءٌ

purpose /ˈpəːpəs/ **A** *n* **1** (fml) (objective) غَرَض (أَغْراض), غاية, هَدَف (أَهْداف); **what is the ~ of your trip?** ما الغَرَضُ \ الهَدَفُ من رِحْلَتِكَ لِهَذِهِ؟; **for our ~s, we can assume that ...** الأَهْداف \ الدَوافِع، بِإمْكانِنا أنْ نَفْتَرِضَ أنّ ...; **it must serve some ~** لا بُدَّ أنّ لَهُ وَظيفةً; **put it in the bin provided for the ~** ضَعْهُ في سَلّةِ المُهْمَلاتِ المُخَصَّصةِ لِذلِكَ الغَرَضِ; **it was all to no ~** ذَهَبَ عَناؤُنا هَباءً **2** [u] (determination) عَزْم, تَصْميم; **to have a sense of ~** كانَ لَدَيْهِ شُعورٌ بالهَدَفِ **B** (**on purpose**) *adv phr* (deliberately) عَمْداً, عن قَصْدٍ; **I didn't do it on ~** لم أَفْعَلْ ذلك عن قَصْدٍ

purpose-built /ˌpəːpəsˈbɪlt/ *adj* ‹*module, product*› مَبْنيّ لِغَرَضٍ مُعَيَّنٍ

purposeful /ˈpəːpəsfʊl/ *adj* ‹*manner, expression*› يَنُمُّ عن الإصْرارِ

purposely /ˈpəːpəsli/ *adv* ‹*to avoid, mislead*› عَمْداً, عن قَصْدٍ

purr /pəː/ **A** *vi* **1** «cats» خَرْخَرَ (خَرْخَرة; i) **2** «engines» قَرْقَرَ (قَرْقَرة; i), خَرْخَرَ (خَرْخَرة; i) **B** *n* **1** (of cats) خَرْخَرة **2** (of engines) [صَوْت اهْتِزازٍ خافِتٍ]

purse /pəːs/ *n* 1 (for money) كيس نُقودٍ ,(جِزْدانات) جِزْدان 2 (AmE) (handbag) حَقيبة يَدٍ

Idiom **to purse one's lips** مَطَّ شَفَتَيْهِ

purser /ˈpəːsə/ *n* 1 (on ship) ضابِط المُحاسَبةِ 2 (on aircraft) ضابِط المُحاسَبةِ

pursuant /pəˈsjuːənt/ *adj* (fml) **~ to a law/regulation** وَفْقاً لِقانونٍ \ للائِحةِ

pursue /pəˈsjuː/ *vt* 1 (to chase) لاحَقَ, طارَدَ ‹*a thief, fox*› 2 (to seek) سَعى (a; سَعْي; وراء) ‹*happiness, a goal*› 3 (to further) عَزَّزَ, طَوَّرَ ‹*a career, policy*›

pursuer /pəˈsjuːə/ *n* مُلاحِق, مُطارِد

pursuit /pəˈsjuːt/ *n* 1 مُطارَدة, مُلاحَقة; **they set off in ~ of the mugger** انطَلَقوا يُلاحِقون قاطِعَ الطَريقِ; **the ~ of happiness/knowledge** السَعْي وراء السَعادةِ \ المَعْرِفةِ 2 (hobby) هِواية

pus /pʌs/ *n* قَيْح, صَديد (قُيوح)

push /pʊʃ/ A *vt* 1 (vigorously) دَفَعَ (a; دَفْع) ‹*a person, a thing*›; **to ~ sb/sth away** دَفَعَ شَخْصاً \ شَيْئاً بَعيداً; **she ~ed him down the stairs** دَفَعَتْهُ من على الدَرَجِ; **to ~ sb/sth out of the way** أَزاحَ شَخْصاً \ شَيْئاً من الطَريقِ; **to ~ one's way through the crowd** شَقَّ طَريقَهُ في الزِحامِ 2 (to insert) أَدْخَلَ ‹*a stick, one's finger*›; **to ~ the stick into the ground** غَرَسَ العَصا في الأَرْضِ; **to ~ one's finger into sth** أَدْخَلَ إِصْبَعَهُ في شَيْءٍ 3 (to impel) دَفَعَ (a; دَفْع) ‹*a car, pram, door*›; **we had to ~ the car to get it started** اُضْطُرِرْنا إلى دَفْعِ السَيّارةِ لِكَيْ تَعْمَلَ; **to ~ the window open/shut** فَتَحَ \ أَغْلَقَ الشُبّاكَ 4 (to activate) ضَغَطَ (a; ضَغْط) على ‹*a button, switch*›; **to ~ the button** ضَغَطَ الزِرَّ 5 (to drive) دَفَعَ (a; دَفْع) ‹*a pupil, an employee, the troops*›; **to ~ sb into doing sth** دَفَعَ شَخْصاً لِلقِيامِ بِشَيْءٍ; **to ~ sb too far** ضَغَطَ على شَخْصٍ أَكْثَرَ من اللازِمِ 6 (infml) (to promote) رَوَّجَ (ل) ‹*a product, theory*› 7 (infml) (to sell) تاجَرَ (في) ‹*drugs, cocaine*›

B *vi* دَفَعَ (a; دَفْع); **to ~ against the door/fence** دَفَعَ البابَ \ السِياجَ; **to ~ past sb** دَفَعَ شَخْصاً أثناء مُرورِهِ; **to ~ through a crowd** شَقَّ طَريقَهُ في الزِحامِ

C *v refl* 1 (physically) دَفَعَ (a; دَفْع); **to ~ oneself out of the water** دَفَعَ نَفْسَهُ خارِجَ الماءِ 2 (mentally) **to ~ oneself to do sth** ضَغَطَ على نَفْسِهِ لِفِعْلِ شَيْءٍ; **they really ~ed themselves to finish on time** في الحَقيقةِ ضَغَطوا على أَنْفُسِهِمْ لِكَيْ يُنْهوا في الوَقْتِ المُحَدَّدِ

D *adj* (infml) (short, lacking) **I'm a bit ~ed today** أنا مَشْغولٌ اليَوْمَ; **to be ~ed for money/time/space** عانى من ضيقٍ في المالِ \ الوَقْتِ \ المَكانِ

E *n* 1 (shove) دَفْعة (دَفَعات); **to give sb/sth a ~** دَفَعَ شَخْصاً \ شَيْئاً; **at the ~ of a button** بِضَغْطةِ زِرٍّ 2 (stimulus) دَفْعة (دَفَعات); **to give sth a ~ in the right direction** أَعْطى شَيْئاً دَفْعةً في الاتِّجاهِ الصَحيحِ 3 (offensive) هَجْمة (هَجَمات); **the big ~** الهُجوم الكَبير 4 (campaign) حَمْلة (حَمَلات); **a ~ to recruit more teachers** حَمْلة لِتَعْيينِ المَزيدِ من المُدَرِّسينَ

Idioms **to push one's luck** (infml) اِعْتَمَدَ على الحَظِّ; **to give sb the push** (BrE) (infml) فَصَلَ شَخْصاً ‹*an employee*›; أَخْرَجَ شَخْصاً من حَياتِهِ ‹*one's boyfriend, girlfriend*›; **when push comes to shove** عِنْدَما تَحينُ ساعةُ الحَسْمِ

Phrasal verbs **push about** (infml) ▸**push around**

• **push ahead** (with a project) مَضى قُدُماً

• **push around** (infml): **~ [sb] around** 1 (physically) تَعامَلَ مع [شَخْصٍ] بِعُنْفٍ ‹*a boy, passer-by*› 2 (to give orders to) فَرَضَ أَوامِرَهُ على [شَخْصٍ] ‹*a colleague, one's brother*›

• **push back**: **~ [sb/sth] back, ~ back [sb/sth]** 1 (to move) دَفَعَ [شَخْصاً \ شَيْئاً] بَعيداً ‹*the furniture, a box, a car*› 2 (to repel) أَجْبَرَ [شَخْصاً \ شَيْئاً] على التَراجُعِ ‹*an army, the enemy, the front line*›

• **push down**: **~ [sb/sth] down, ~ down [sb/sth]** 1 (to reduce) خَفَّضَ [شَيْئاً] ‹*a price, rate, temperature*› 2 (to cause to fall) أَوْقَعَ [شَخْصاً \ شَيْئاً] ‹*a person*›; (to cause to sit) أَجْلَسَ [شَخْصاً] ‹*a person*›

• **push for ~ for [sth]** ضَغَطَ من أَجْلِ [شَيْءٍ] ‹*an improvement, changes*›

• **push forward** A 1 (with a project) مَضى قُدُماً 2 (on a journey) واصَلَ B **~ [sb/sth] forward** 1 صَمَّمَ على [شَيْءٍ] ‹*an idea, a plan*› 2 **to ~ oneself forward as sth** طَرَحَ نَفْسَهُ كَشَيْءٍ

• **push in** A (to jump the queue) تَجاوَزَ طابوراً B **~ [sth] in,**

~ in [sth] **1** (to press in) ضَغَطَ على [شَيْءٍ] ‹*a button, bell*› **2** (to break down) كَسَرَ [شَيْئاً] ‹*a door, window*›

• **push off** **1** (in a boat) جَدَّفَ مُبْتَعِداً **2** (BrE) (infml) (to go away) رَحَلَ, غادَرَ (a; رَحيل)

• **push on** **1** (on a journey) واصَلَ **2** (with a project) مَضى قُدُماً

• **push over** **A** (infml) (to move over) أَفْسَحَ **B** **~ over [sth/sb], ~ [sth/sb] over** أَوْقَعَ [شَخْصاً \ شَيْئاً] ‹*a person, table, car*›

• **push through**: **~ [sth] through, ~ through [sth]** مَرَّرَ [شَيْئاً] ‹*legislation*›; أَتَمَّ \ أَنْجَزَ [شَيْئاً] ‹*an application*›; مَلأَ [شَيْئاً] ‹*a sale*›

• **push up**: **~ up [sth], ~ [sth] up** رَفَعَ [شَيْئاً] ‹*prices, unemployment*›

pushbike /ˈpʊʃbʌɪk/ *n* (BrE infml) دَرّاجة (هَوائيّة)

push-button /ˈpʊʃbʌt(ə)n/ *adj before n* ‹*switch, telephone*› يَعْمَلُ بالضَغْطِ على الأَزْرارِ

pushchair /ˈpʊʃtʃɛː/ *n* (BrE) عَرَبة الطِفْلِ

pusher /ˈpʊʃə/ *n* (infml) (also **drug pusher**) بائِع مُخَدِّراتٍ

pushover /ˈpʊʃəʊvə/ *n* (infml) **1** (game, task) شَيْء سَهْل; **the game will be a ~** سَوْفَ تَكونُ اللُعْبةُ سَهْلةً **2** (client, opponent) شَخْص سَهْل المِراسِ

push-start /pʊʃˈstɑːt/ *vt* شَغَّلَ بالدَفع اليَدَويِّ ‹*a car*›

push-up /ˈpʊʃʌp/ *n* تَمْرين الضَغْطِ

pushy /ˈpʊʃi/ *adj* (**pushier**, **pushiest**) (infml) ‹*parent, salesman*› فارِض نَفْسَهُ \ رَأْيَهُ

pussy /ˈpʊsi/ *n* (*pl* **pussies**) **1** (also **pussycat**) قِطّة (قِطَط), هِرّة (هِرَر) **2** (vulg) (coward) شَخْص جَبان **3** (vulg) (vagina) فَرْج [المَرْأَةِ]

put /pʊt/ **A** *vt* (*present participle* **-tt-**; *past tense, past participle* **put**) **1** (to place) وَضَعَ (a; وَضْع) ‹*the shopping, letters, one's hand*›; **I ~ sugar in his tea by mistake** وَضَعْتُ سُكَّراً في كوبِ الشايِ الخاصِّ بِهِ بِالخَطَأِ; **~ the boxes on the shelf, please** ضَع الصَناديقَ على الرَفِّ من فَضْلِكَ; **I ~ my hand in my pocket** وَضَعْتُ يَدي في جَيْبي; **to ~ a satellite into space** وَضَعَ قَمَراً صِناعيًّا في الفَضاءِ **2** (to push) **to ~ sth through the window/letterbox** أَدْخَلَ شَيْئاً من النافِذةِ \ صُنْدوقِ الرَسائِلِ; **to ~ one's head through the window** أَخْرَجَ رَأْسَهُ من النافِذةِ **3** (in procedures) **to ~ the car/camera through some tests** أَجْرى بَعْضَ الاخْتِباراتِ على السَيّارةِ \ الكاميرا; **to ~ sb through college/university** دَفَعَ مَصاريفَ كُلّيّةٍ \ جامعةٍ لِشَخْصٍ; **after all you've ~ me through** بعد كُلِّ ما عانَيْتُ مِنْهُ بِسَبَبِكَ; **to ~ sb in a difficult position** وَضَعَ شَخْصاً في مَوْقِفٍ صَعْبٍ; **to ~ sb to work** جَعَلَ شَخْصاً يَعْمَلُ; **to ~ sb to death** أَعْدَمَ شَخْصاً; **to ~ sb's life at risk** عَرَّضَ حَياةَ شَخْصٍ للخَطَرِ **4** (to devote, invest) **to ~ money/energy into sth** بَذَلَ مالاً \ جُهْداً في شَيْءٍ; **we all ~ a lot into the project** بَذَلْنا جَميعاً الكَثيرَ في المَشْروعِ **5** (to add) **~ this money towards some new clothes** ادَّخِرْ هذا المالَ من أَجْلِ شِراءِ مَلابِسَ جَديدةٍ; **to ~ tax/duty on sth** فَرَضَ ضَريبةً \ رَسْماً على شَيْءٍ **6** (to express) **he ~ it very well/badly** عَبَّرَ عَنْهُ بِشَكْلٍ جَيِّدٍ \ سَيِّءٍ; **let me ~ it another way** دَعْني أَشْرَحُهُ بِطَريقةٍ أُخرى; **to ~ it bluntly** بِصَراحةٍ, بدونِ مُجامَلةٍ; **that was very well ~** أَحْسَنْتَ القَوْلَ; **it is difficult to ~ that in Arabic** يَصْعُبُ قَوْلُ ذلك باللُغةِ العَرَبيةِ; **to ~ sth in writing** كَتَبَ شَيْئاً; **to ~ one's feelings into words** عَبَّرَ عن مَشاعِرِه كِتابةً **7** (to offer for consideration) طَرَحَ (a; طَرْح) ‹*an argument, a point of view, proposal*›; **to ~ sth to the committee** طَرَحَ شَيْئاً على اللَجْنةِ; **to ~ the proposal to the vote** طَرَحَ الاقْتِراحَ للتَصْويتِ **8** (to rank) **to ~ an artist/a player at the top of the rankings** صَنَّفَ فَنّاناً \ لاعِباً في أَعْلى مَرْتَبةٍ; **to ~ safety first** وَضعَ السَلامةَ أَوَّلاً **9** (to ascribe, estimate) **to ~ the value at £500** قَدَّرَ الثَمَنَ بِـ£500; **I ~ his age at about 40** أَظُنُّ أنّ عُمْرَهُ 40 عاماً تَقْريباً **10** (Sport) **to ~ the shot** رَمى الجُلّةَ

B *v refl* (*present participle* **-tt-**; *past tense, past participle* **put**) **to ~ oneself in a strong/difficult position** وَضَعَ نَفْسَهُ في وَضْعٍ قَويٍّ \ صَعْبٍ; **to ~ oneself in sb's place** *or* **position** وَضَعَ نَفْسَهُ في مَكانِ شَخْصٍ

Idioms **I wouldn't put it past him/you!** (infml) لا أَسْتَبْعِدُ ذلك عَنْهُ \ عَنْكَ!; **to put one over** *or* **across on sb** (infml) خَدَعَ شَخْصاً

(Phrasal verbs) **put about**: **~ [sth] about, ~ about [sth]** (to spread) [شَيْئاً] نَشَرَ ‹gossip, a rumour, story›; **they ~ it about that he was dead** رَوَّجوا شائِعةً بِأَنَّهُ تُوُفِّيَ

• **put across**: **~ across [sth], ~ [sth] across** عَبَّرَ عن [شَيْءٍ] ‹an idea, a message, concept›

• **put aside**: **~ aside [sth], ~ [sth] aside** 1 (to place on one side) وَضَعَ [شَيْئاً] جانِباً ‹a book, gun› 2 (to set aside) نَحّى [شَيْئاً] جانِباً ‹one's differences, mistrust› 3 (to save) ادَّخَرَ [شَيْئاً] ‹money, food›

• **put away** **A** **~ away [sth], ~ [sth] away** 1 (to tidy away) أعادَ [شَيْئاً] إلى مَكانِهِ ‹toys, the dishes› 2 (to save) ادَّخَرَ [شَيْئاً] ‹money, supplies› 3 (infml) (to consume) اسْتَهْلَكَ [شَيْئاً] ‹food, drink› **B** **~ [sb] away, ~ away [sb]** (infml) 1 (in a psychiatric hospital) أَوْدَعَ \ حَجَزَ [شَخْصاً] ‹a patient› 2 (in prison) سَجَنَ \ حَبَسَ [شَخْصاً] ‹a murderer, burglar›

• **put back**: **~ back [sth], ~ [sth] back** 1 (to return, restore) أعادَ [شَيْئاً] ‹an ornament, a painting, necklace›; **to ~ sth back where it belongs** أعادَ شَيْئاً لِمَكانِهِ 2 (to postpone) أَخَّرَ \ أَجَّلَ [شَيْئاً] ‹a meeting, one's departure›; **we ~ back the date of the launch** أَجَّلْنا مَوْعِدَ الإطْلاقِ 3 أَخَّرَ [شَيْئاً] ‹a clock, watch› 4 (to delay) أَخَّرَ [شَيْئاً] ‹a project, delivery› 5 (infml) (to knock back) احْتَسى [شَيْئاً] ‹one's drink, a bottle›

• **put by**: **~ [sth] by, ~ by [sth]** (BrE) ادَّخَرَ [شَيْئاً] ‹money, food›

• **put down** **A** (to land) «pilots, aircraft» هَبَطَ (i-u; هُبوط) **B** **~ [sth] down, ~ down [sth]** 1 (to deposit) وَضَعَ [شَيْئاً] (على الأَرْضِ) ‹a bag, the shopping› 2 (as bait) وَضَعَ [شَيْئاً] ‹rat poison› 3 (to suppress) قَمَعَ [شَيْئاً] ‹dissent, an uprising› 4 (to write down) دَوَّنَ \ كَتَبَ [شَيْئاً] ‹a date, detail, name› 5 (to attribute) **to ~ sth down to incompetence/human error** اعْتَبَرَ أنّ شَيْئاً نَتيجةُ عَدَمِ الكَفاءةِ \ خَطَأٍ بَشَريٍّ; **I ~ her success down to the fact that she works hard** أَعْتَبِرُ أنّ نَجاحَها نَتيجةٌ لِجُهْدِها في العَمَلِ 6 (to kill) أَجْهَزَ على [شَيْءٍ] ‹a horse, cat› 7 (as surety) دَفَعَ [شَيْئاً] ‹a deposit›; **I ~ £50 down on the bike** دَفَعْتُ £50 عُرْبوناً على الدَّرّاجةِ 8 (to mature) خَزَّنَ [شَيْئاً] لِيَنْضَجَ ‹wine, cheese› 9 (for debate) طَرَحَ [شَيْئاً] ‹a motion› **C** **~ [sb] down, ~ down [sb]** 1 (infml) (to humiliate) أهانَ [شَخْصاً] ‹a rival, classmate, co-worker› 2 (into a lower class) نَزَّلَ [شَخْصاً] دَرَجةً ‹a pupil› 3 (into a lower league) نَزَّلَ [شَخْصاً] إلى مَرْتَبةٍ أَقَلّ ‹a team› 4 (to classify, take into account) **to ~ sb down as sth** اعْتَبَرَ شَخْصاً شَيْئاً ‹a possibility, candidate, fool›; **to ~ sb down for a school/club** وَضَعَ شَخْصاً على قائِمةِ انْتِظارِ مَدْرَسةٍ \ نادٍ; **to ~ sb down for three tickets** عَمِلَ حِسابَ ثَلاثِ تَذاكِرَ لِشَخْصٍ 5 (to drop off) أَنْزَلَ [شَخْصاً] ‹a passenger›

• **put forward** **A** **~ forward [sth], ~ [sth] forward** 1 (to propose) قَدَّمَ \ طَرَحَ [شَيْئاً] ‹an idea, a plan, suggestion› 2 (to hold earlier) قَدَّمَ ميعادَ [شَيْءٍ] ‹a meeting› 3 قَدَّمَ [شَيْئاً] ‹a watch, clock› **B** **~ [sb] forward, ~ forward [sb]** رَشَّحَ [شَخْصاً]; **to ~ oneself forward as a candidate** قَدَّمَ نَفْسَهُ كَمُرَشَّحٍ

• **put in** **A** 1 «ships» رَسا (u; رَسْو) 2 (to apply) **to ~ in for sth** قَدَّمَ طَلَباً لِلحُصولِ على شَيْءٍ ‹a job, promotion, subsidy› **B** **~ in [sth], ~ [sth] in** 1 (to fit, install) رَكَّبَ [شَيْئاً] ‹a shower, kitchen›; **I forgot to ~ my contact lenses in** نَسيتُ أن أَضَعَ عَدَساتي اللاصِقةَ 2 (to submit) قَدَّمَ [شَيْئاً] ‹a request, claim, an offer›; **to ~ in an application for a visa/job** قَدَّمَ طَلَباً لِلحُصولِ على تَأْشيرةٍ \ وَظيفةٍ 3 (to dedicate) خَصَّصَ \ كَرَّسَ [شَيْئاً] ‹time, hours, work›; **to ~ in a lot of time doing sth** قَضى وَقْتاً كَبيراً في عَمَلِ شَيْءٍ; **to ~ in a good day's work** قَضى يَوْماً طَويلاً في العَمَلِ; **to ~ in $500** ساهَمَ \ تَبَرَّعَ بـ $500 4 (to interject) أَضافَ [شَيْئاً] **C** **~ [sb] in for sth** سَجَّلَ اسْمَ [شَخْصٍ] في شَيْءٍ ‹a competition, an exam›; رَشَّحَ [شَخْصاً] لِشَيْءٍ ‹an award›

• **put off** **A** **~ off [sth], ~ [sth] off** (to delay) أَجَّلَ [شَيْئاً] ‹a wedding, meeting› **B** **~ off [sb], ~ [sb] off** 1 (to delay a meeting with) أَجَّلَ \ أَلْغى مَوْعِداً مع [شَخْصٍ] ‹a friend, visitor, colleague› 2 (to repel) «appearance, smell, manner» أَثارَ اشْمِئْزازَ [شَخْصٍ] 3 (to distract) شَتَّتَ انْتِباهَ [شَخْصٍ] ‹a player, student› 4 (to drop off) أَنْزَلَ [شَخْصاً] ‹a passenger›

• **put on** **A** **~ on [sth], ~ [sth] on** 1 لَبِسَ \ ارْتَدى [شَيْئاً] ‹one's shirt, shoes, hat›; وَضَعَ [شَيْئاً] ‹cream, lipstick› 2 (to switch on, operate) فَتَحَ [شَيْئاً] ‹the light›; شَغَّلَ [شَيْئاً] ‹washing machine, music›; **to ~ the kettle on** شَغَّلَ الغَلّايةَ 3 (to gain) زادَ [شَيْئاً]

‹weight, a kilo› **4** (to add) فَرَضَ [شَيْئاً] ‹extra duty, tax› **5** (to produce) قَدَّمَ [شَيْئاً] ‹a play, an exhibition› **6** (to assume, adopt) تَظاهَرَ [بِشَيْءٍ], اِصْطَنَعَ [شَيْئاً] ‹an air, accent, expression›; **he's ~ting it on** هو يَتَظاهَرُ **7** (to lay on, offer) وَفَّرَ [شَيْئاً] ‹an extra train, a bus service›; قَدَّمَ [شَيْئاً] ‹a meal, dish› **8** (to put forward) قَدَّمَ [شَيْئاً] ‹a clock, watch› **9** (to bet) راهَنَ على [شَيْءٍ] ‹a bet, an amount› **B** ~ **[sb] on** **1** (Tel) أَعْطى سَمّاعَةَ الهاتِفِ [لِشَخْصٍ]; **I'll ~ him on** سَأُعْطي لَهُ السَمّاعَةَ **2** (to recommend) **to ~ sb on to a supplier/a good offer** دَلَّ شَخْصاً على مُوَرِّدٍ \ عَرْضٍ جَيِّدٍ **3** (to put on the trail of) **to ~ sb on to the thief/killer** بَلَّغَ شَخْصاً بِمَكانِ اللِصِّ \ القاتِلِ

• **put out** **A** (Naut) **to ~ out to sea/from port** أَبْحَرَ في البَحْرِ \ من الميناءِ **B** ~ **out [sth]**, ~ **[sth] out** **1** (to extend) مَدَّ [شَيْئاً] ‹one's hand, arm, leg› **2** (to extinguish) أَطْفَأَ [شَيْئاً] ‹a fire, cigarette, the light› **3** (to take outside) أَخْرَجَ [شَيْئاً] ‹garbage, the cat› **4** (to issue) أَصْدَرَ [شَيْئاً] ‹a description, warning, communiqué› **5** (to put on display) وَضَعَ [شَيْئاً] ‹food, bottles of water, towels› **6** (to sprout) نَبَتَ مِنْهُ [شَيْءٌ] ‹a shoot, buds, roots› **7** (to cause to be wrong) أَدّى إلى الخَطَإِ [في شَيْءٍ] ‹a figure, an estimate› **8** (to dislocate) خَلَعَ [شَيْئاً] ‹one's shoulder, ankle, hip› **9** (to subcontract) تَعاقَدَ على [شَيْءٍ] من الباطِنِ ‹work›; **to ~ work out to subcontractors** أَعْطى عَمَلاً لِمُقاوِلينَ من الباطِنِ; **to ~ a project out to tender** طَرَحَ مُناقَصةً لِمَشروعٍ **C** ~ **[sb] out** **1** (to inconvenience) أَزْعَجَ [شَخْصاً]; **to ~ oneself out for sb** جاءَ على نَفْسِهِ من أَجْلِ شَخْصٍ **2** **to be ~ out** (to be upset) تَضايَقَ, اِنْزَعَجَ **3** (to evict) طَرَدَ [شَخْصاً] ‹a tenant, squatter›

• **put over**: ~ **over [sth]**, ~ **[sth] over** عَبَّرَ عن [شَيْءٍ] ‹an idea, a message, point of view›

• **put through** **A** ~ **[sth] through**, ~ **through [sth]** **1** (to implement) نَفَّذَ [شَيْئاً] ‹an amendment, a reform, change› **2** (to transfer) حَوَّلَ [شَيْئاً] ‹a call› **B** ~ **[sb] through** (on the phone) وَصَّلَ [شَخْصاً] ‹a caller›

• **put together**: ~ **[sb/sth] together**, ~ **together [sb/sth]** **1** (to assemble) جَمَّعَ [شَيْئاً] ‹parts, components›; رَكَّبَ [شَيْئاً] ‹furniture, a desk, machine›; **to ~ sth together again, to ~ sth back together** أَعادَ تَجْميعَ شَيْءٍ **2** (to place together) جَمَّعَ [شَيْئاً] ‹animals, objects, people›; **to be better/smarter than all the rest ~ together** كانَ أَفْضَلَ \ أَذْكى من الجَميعِ مُجْتَمِعينَ **3** (to form) شَكَّلَ [شَيْئاً] ‹a coalition, team, an orchestra› **4** (to edit, make) عَمِلَ [شَيْئاً] ‹a file, list, film›; جَمَعَ [شَيْئاً] ‹an anthology› **5** (to concoct) أَعَدَّ [شَيْئاً] ‹a meal› **6** (to present) قَدَّمَ [شَيْئاً] ‹a case, an argument› **7** **to ~ one's hands together for sb** (to applaud) صَفَّقَ لِشَخْصٍ

• **put up** **A** (to stay) **to ~ up in a hotel/at sb's house** أَقامَ في فُنْدُقٍ \ مَنْزِلِ شَخْصٍ **B** ~ **[sth] up**, ~ **up [sth]** **1** (to raise) رَفَعَ [شَيْئاً] ‹a flag, sail›; **~ your hands up!** ارْفَعْ يَدَيْكَ! **2** (to display) عَلَّقَ [شَيْئاً] ‹a sign, list, decorations› **3** (to build, erect) نَصَبَ [شَيْئاً] ‹a fence, barrier, tent›; أَنْشَأَ \ بَنى [شَيْئاً] ‹a building, memorial› **4** (to increase, raise) رَفَعَ [شَيْئاً] ‹the rent, price, tax› **5** (to provide) أَقْرَضَ [شَيْئاً] ‹the money, an amount› **6** (to offer) أَبْدى [شَيْئاً] ‹resistance›; شَنَّ [شَيْئاً] ‹a fight›; **to ~ up a struggle** كافَحَ; **the team ~ up a good performance** أَدّى الفَريقُ أَداءً جَيِّداً **7** (to put in orbit) وَضَعَ [شَيْئاً] (في مَدارٍ) ‹a satellite› **C** ~ **[sb] up**, ~ **up [sb]** **1** (to lodge) اِسْتَضافَ [شَخْصاً] ‹a visitor, guest› **2** (as a candidate) رَشَّحَ [شَخْصاً] ‹a candidate›; **to ~ sb up for sth** رَشَّحَ شَخْصاً لِشَيْءٍ ‹chairman, promotion› **3** (to a higher class) صَعَّدَ [شَخْصاً] ‹a pupil› **4** (to a higher league) صَعَّدَ [شَخْصاً] ‹a team› **5** (to incite) **to ~ sb up to sth/to doing sth** حَرَّضَ شَخْصاً على شَيْءٍ \ فِعْلِ شَيْءٍ

• **put up with**: ~ **up with [sb/sth]** (to tolerate) تَحَمَّلَ [شَخْصاً \ شَيْئاً]

• **put upon**: ~ **upon [sb]** اِسْتَغَلَّ [شَخْصاً] ‹a relative, colleague›

putative /ˈpjuːtətɪv/ *adj* (fml) ‹author, origin› مُفْتَرَض

put-down /ˈpʊtdaʊn/ *n* (infml) تَجْريح, اِسْتِخْفاف, اِزْدِراء

put out *adj after n* (infml) **to be ~** مُسْتاء, مُنْزَعِج

putrid /ˈpjuːtrɪd/ *adj* ‹smell, flesh› مُتَعَفِّن, مُنْتِن

putt /pʌt/ **A** *vi* «players» ضَرَبَ الكُرة بِرِفْقٍ
B *vt* ضَرَبَ بِرِفْقٍ ‹the ball›
C *n* [في الجولْفِ: ضَرْبة خفيفة عِنْدَما تكونُ الكُرةُ قَريبةً من الحُفْرةِ]

putter /ˈpʌtə/ **A** *n* [مِضْرَب جولْف يُسْتَعْمَلُ للضَرَباتِ الخَفيفةِ]

B *vi* (AmE) ▸ **potter about**

putting green /ˈpʌtɪŋ griːn/ *n* المِنْطَقة الخَضْراء (في الجولْف)

putty /ˈpʌti/ *n* مَعْجون تَثْبيتِ زُجاجِ النَوافِذِ

puzzle /ˈpʌz(ə)l/ **A** *vt* ‹*a commentator, reader*› أَرْبَكَ, حَيَّرَ

B *n* **1** (mystery) لُغْز (أَلْغاز) **2** (game) أُحْجِيّة (أَحاجٍ, أَحاجيّ)

puzzle book *n* كِتاب أَلْغازٍ

puzzled /ˈpʌz(ə)ld/ *adj* ‹*look, reader*› مُرْتَبِك, مُتَحَيِّر

puzzling /ˈpʌzlɪŋ/ *adj* ‹*aspect, behaviour*› غامِض, مُحَيِّر

PVC /piːviːˈsiː/ *n* = **polyvinyl chloride** بولي فينيل كْلوريد

pygmy /ˈpɪgmi/ **A** *n* (*pl* **pygmies**) بيغْمي (أَحَد الزُنوجِ الأَقْزامِ في إفْريقيا الاسْتِوائيّةِ)

B *adj* ‹*chimpanzee, hippo*› قَزَم (أَقْزام)

pyjamas (BrE), **pajamas** (AmE) /pəˈdʒɑːməz/ *n pl* بيجاما; **a pair of ~** طَقْم بيجاما

pylon /ˈpʌɪlən, ˈpʌɪlɑːn/ *n* **1** (for cables) بُرْج أَسْلاكٍ **2** (AmE) (traffic cone) مَخْروط المُرورِ

pyramid /ˈpɪrəmɪd/ *n* هَرَم (أَهْرام, أَهْرامات)

pyre /pʌɪə/ *n* [كَوْم حَطَبٍ مُعَدّ لِإِحْراقِ جُثَثِ المَوْتى في جَنازةٍ]

Pyrenees /ˌpɪrəˈniːz/ *pr n pl* (**the Pyrenees**) جِبال البَرانِسِ

Pyrex® /ˈpʌɪrɛks/ *n* بايْرِكْس (زُجاج مُضادّ للحَرارة)

python /ˈpʌɪθ(ə)n/ *n* أَصَلة (ثُعْبان)

Qq

Q, **q** /kjuː/ *n* [الحَرْف السابِعَ عَشَرَ من الأَبْجَدِيّةِ الإِنْكْليزِيّة]

Qatar /ka'tɑː/ *pr n* قَطَر (dipt f)

Qatari /ka'tɑːri/ *n*, *adj* قَطَرِيّ

qawwali /ka'wɑːli/ *n* قَوّالِيّ (نَوْع من الموسيقى الصوفيّة)

QE *n* (Fin) (**quantitative easing**) التَيْسير الكَمّيّ

QED /kjuːiː'diː/ *abbr* = **quod erat demonstrandum** وَهُوَ المَطْلوبُ إِثْباتُهُ

qiblah, **kiblah** /'kɪblə/ *n* قِبْلة

Qom /kʊm/ *pr n* قُمّ (f)

quack /kwak/ **A** *n* **1** (of a duck) بَطْبَطة (صَوْت البَطّ) **2** (BrE) (infml) (fake doctor) مُدّعي الطِبّ

B *vi* «ducks, drakes» بَطْبَطَ, أَصْدَرَ صَوْتَ البَطّ (i; بَطْبَطة)

quad /kwɒd/ *n* (infml) **1** = **quadrangle** [ساحة مُرَبَّعة تُحيطُ بِها المَباني] **2** = **quadruplet** [أَحَد أَرْبَعة تَوائِم]

quad bike *n* دَرّاجة رُباعيّة

quadrangle /'kwɒdraŋg(ə)l/ *n* [ساحة مُرَبَّعة تُحيطُ بِها المَباني]

quadrant /'kwɒdrənt/ *n* رُبْع دائِرةٍ

quadrilateral /ˌkwɒdrɪ'lat(ə)rəl/ **A** *n* مُضَلَّع رُباعيّ

B *adj* ‹*shape, figure*› رُباعيّ الأَضْلاع

quadriplegia /ˌkwɒdrɪ'pliːdʒə/ *n* شَلَل رُباعيّ

quadruped /'kwɒdrʊpɛd/ *n* (fml) حَيَوان من ذَواتِ الأَرْبَع

quadruple **A** /'kwɒdrʊp(ə)l/ *adj* ‹*bypass, homicide*› رُباعيّ

B /kwɒ'druːp(ə)l/ *vt* ضاعَفَ أَرْبَعَ مَرّاتٍ ‹*the number, price*›

C /kwɒ'druːp(ə)l/ *vi* «populations, sales» تَضاعَفَ أَرْبَعَ مَرّاتٍ

D /'kwɒdrʊp(ə)l/ *n* أَرْبَعة أَضْعافٍ; **the number 16 is a ~ of 4** العَدَدُ 16 هو أَرْبَعةُ أَضْعافِ العَدَدِ 4

quadruplet /'kwɒdrʊplət/ *n* [أَحَد أَرْبَعةِ تَوائِمَ]

quaff /kwɒf/ *vt* عَبَّ (أَفْرَطَ في الشُرْبِ) ‹*beer, champagne*›

quagmire /'kwɒgmʌɪə, 'kwagmʌɪə/ *n* **1** (bog) مُسْتَنْقَع **2** (difficult situation) مُسْتَنْقَع (مُسْتَنْقَعات), وَرْطة (وَرَطات), مَأْزِق (مَآزِق)

quail /kweɪl/ **A** *n* (*pl* **quails** or *collective n* **quail**) سُماني (f; سُمانَيات), سَلْوى (n coll; sing n سَلْواة; سَلاوى)

B *vi* «spirits, children» فَزِعَ (a; فَزَع), ارْتَعَدَ

quaint /kweɪnt/ *adj* (**quainter**, **quaintest**) ‹*village, customs*› غَيْر مَأْلوفٍ, طَريف, غَريب

quake /kweɪk/ *vi* «voices» اهْتَزَّ, ارْتَجَفَ, ارْتَعَشَ; «the earth» اهْتَزَّ, تَزَلْزَلَ

Quaker /'kweɪkə/ *n* [عُضْو في جَمْعيّةِ الأَصْدِقاءِ الدينيّةِ]

qualification /ˌkwɒlɪfɪ'keɪʃ(ə)n/ *n* **1** (diploma, degree) مُؤَهِّل, دَرَجة عِلْميّة; **do you have a ~ in teaching?** هل لَدَيْكَ مُؤَهِّلٌ في التَدْريسِ؟ **2** (experience, skill) مُؤَهِّل, مَهارة **3** (modification) تَعْديل (تَعْديلات); **the report was accepted with/without ~** قُبِلَ التَقْريرُ ب \ بِدونِ تَعْديلاتٍ **4** [u] (eligibility) تَأَهُّل

qualified /'kwɒlɪfʌɪd/ *adj* **1** (having a diploma) ‹*teacher, candidate*› مُؤَهَّل; **she's a ~ teacher/doctor** هي مُدَرِّسةٌ \ طَبيبةٌ مُؤَهَّلةٌ; **to be ~ to do sth** كانَ مُؤَهَّلاً لِأَنْ يَفْعَلَ شَيْئاً; **I am not ~ to comment on this** لَسْتُ مُؤَهَّلاً لِأَنْ أُعَلِّقَ على هذا **2** (partly endorsed) ‹*success, praise*› مُقَيَّد, مَشْروط

qualifier /'kwɒlɪfʌɪə/ *n* **1** (game) مُباراة تَأْهيليّة **2** (player) [لاعِب تَأَهَّلَ لِلَّعِبِ في مُباراةٍ] **3** (in language) قَيْد (قُيود), مُعَدِّل

qualify /'kwɒlɪfʌɪ/ **A** *vt* (**qualifies**, **qualifying**, **qualified**) **1** (to entitle) أَهَّلَ, أَعْطى الحَقَّ; **to ~ sb to receive a subsidy/to reside in the country** أَهَّلَ شَخْصاً للحُصولِ على دَعْمٍ \ للإقامةِ في الدَوْلةِ **2** (to equip) **to ~ sb for a role/job**

«experience, skills» أَهَّلَ شَخْصاً لِدَوْرٍ \ لِوَظيفةٍ; **20 years' experience qualifies him to lead the mission** تُؤَهِّلُهُ خِبْرةُ 20 عاماً لِقيادةِ البَعْثةِ **3** (fml) (to modify) وَضَّحَ, حَدَّدَ ‹remark, a statement›; قَيَّدَ ‹one's approval› **4** (Ling) وَصَفَ (i; وَصْف), ‹a verb, noun› نَعَتَ (a; نَعْت) **5** «auditor» شَكَّكَ (في) ‹the accounts›

B vi (**qualifies**, **qualifying**, **qualified**) **1** (to obtain a diploma, degree etc) حَصَلَ على مُؤَهِّلٍ; **to ~ as an engineer/a doctor** حَصَلَ على مُؤَهِّلٍ في الهَنْدَسةِ \ الطِبِّ; **to ~ to teach/practise law** حَصَلَ على مُؤَهِّلٍ لِتَدْريسِ \ لِمُمارَسةِ القانونِ **2** (to meet the requirements for) انطَبَقَتْ عَلَيْهِ الشُروطُ; **to ~ for aid/ membership** انطَبَقَتْ عَلَيْهِ شُروطُ المَعونةِ \ العُضْويّةِ **3** (in competitions) تَأَهَّلَ; **to ~ for the championship/the next round** تَأَهَّلَ للبُطولةِ \ للدَوْرِ التالي

qualitative /ˈkwɒlɪtətɪv/ *adj* ‹research, difference› كَيْفيّ, نَوْعيّ

quality /ˈkwɒlɪti/ *n* (*pl* **qualities**) **1** [u] (worth) جَوْدة; **goods of high/low ~** بَضائع ذات جَوْدةٍ عاليةٍ \ مُنْخَفِضةٍ; **an improvement/decline in water ~** تَحَسُّن \ تَراجُع في جَوْدة المِياهِ **2** (characteristic) خاصِّيّة, صِفة (خَصائِصُ); **he has the qualities needed for the job** لَدَيْهِ الصِفاتُ الّتي تَتَطَلَّبُها للوَظيفةِ

quality assurance *n* ضَمان الجَوْدةِ

quality control *n* مُراقَبة الجَوْدةِ

quality controller *n* مُراقِب الجَوْدةِ

qualm /kwɑːm/ *n* هاجِس (هَواجِسُ), ريبة (رِيَب), شَكّ (شُكوك); **to have no ~s about sth** لَيْسَ لَدَيْهِ أَيُّ شَكٍّ حول شَيْءٍ

quandary /ˈkwɒnd(ə)ri/ *n usu sing* (*pl* **quandaries**) حَيْرة, تَرَدُّد, ارْتِباك (ارْتِباكات); **to be in a ~ about sth** كانَ في حَيْرةٍ من أَمْرِهِ بِخُصوصِ شَيْءٍ; **I'm in a ~ about whether to take the job** أنا في حَيْرةٍ من أَمْري بِخُصوصِ قُبولِ الوَظيفةِ

quango /ˈkwaŋgəʊ/ *n* (*pl* **quangos** BrE) [مُنَظَّمة غَيْر حُكوميّةٍ شِبْه مُسْتَقِلّةٍ]

quantifiable /kwɒntɪˈfʌɪəb(ə)l/ *adj* ‹data, results› قابِل للقِياسِ, يُمْكِنُ قِياسُهُ

quantify /ˈkwɒntɪfʌɪ/ *vt* (**quantifies**, **quantifying**, **quantified**) ‹the effect, damage› قاسَ \ حَدَّدَ كَمّيّةً

quantitative /ˈkwɒntɪtətɪv/ *adj* ‹analysis, methods› كَمّيّ, مُتَعَلِّق بالكَمّيّةِ

quantity /ˈkwɒntɪti/ *n* (*pl* **quantities**) كَمّيّة, مِقْدار (مَقاديرُ); **the emphasis is on quality rather than ~ of the products** يَتِمُّ التَرْكيزُ في المُنْتَجاتِ على الكَيْفِ وَلَيْسَ الكَمِّ; **to buy goods in ~** اشْتَرى السِلَعَ بِكَمّيّاتٍ كَبيرةٍ; **large quantities of food were wasted** أُهْدِرَتْ كَمّيّاتٌ كَبيرةٌ من الطَعامِ

quantity surveyor *n* مَسّاح كَمّيّاتٍ (شَخْص مُخْتَصّ بِتَقْديرِ تَكاليفِ البِناءِ)

quantum /ˈkwɒntəm/ *n* (*pl* **quanta**) كَمّ (أَصْغَر جُزْءٍ يُمْكِنُ تَقْسيمُ الأَشْياءِ إِلَيْهِ)

quantum leap, **quantum jump** *n* طَفْرة هائِلة, قَفْزة نَوْعيّة

quantum mechanics *n* ميكانيكا الكَمِّ

quantum theory *n* نَظَرِيّة الكَمِّ

quarantine /ˈkwɒrəntiːn/ **A** *n* حَجْر صِحّيّ; **she was put in ~ for a month** وُضِعَتْ في الحَجْرِ الصِحّيِّ لِمُدّةِ شَهْرٍ

B *vt* ‹a patient, an animal› وَضَعَ في الحَجْرِ الصِحّيِّ

quarrel /ˈkwɒrəl/ **A** *n* **1** (argument) شِجار, نِزاع (نِزاعات); **to have a ~ about/over money** تَشاجَرَ حول المالِ; **a ~ between neighbours** شِجار بين الجيرانِ; **I've had a ~ with my boyfriend** تَشاجَرْتُ مع صَديقي **2** [u] (fml) (disagreement) اعْتِراض; **to have no ~ with sth/sb** لَيْسَ لَدَيْهِ اعْتِراضٌ على شَيْءٍ \ شَخْصٍ

B *vi* (**-ll-** BrE, **-l-** AmE) تَشاجَرَ, تَنازَعَ; **to ~ over sth** تَشاجَرَ حول شَيْءٍ; **they ~led over their father's will** تَشاجَروا حول وَصيّةِ أَبيهِمْ

quarrelling (BrE), **quarreling** (AmE) /ˈkwɒrəlɪŋ/ *n* تَشاجُر, تَنازُع (تَنازُعات)

quarrelsome /ˈkwɒrəls(ə)m/ *adj* ‹temperament, individual› مُحِبّ للشِجارِ, مُشاكِس

quarry /ˈkwɒri/ **A** *n* (*pl* **quarries**) **1** (for stone) مَحْجَر (مَحاجِرُ), مَقْلَع أَحْجارٍ **2** (prey) فَريسة (فَرائِسُ), طَريدة (طَرائِدُ)

B *vt* (**quarries**, **quarrying**, **quarried**) ‹stone, limestone› اسْتَخْرَجَ; **the area is quarried for slate** يُسْتَخْرَجُ الأَرْدُوازُ من المِنْطَقةِ

quarry tile *n* بَلاطة مَحاجِرَ (بَلاطة أَرْضيّةٍ غَيْر مَصْقولةٍ)

quart /kwɔːt/ *n* (BrE = 1.13 l) (AmE = 0.94 l) كوارْت (رُبْع غالون)

quarter /ˈkwɔːtə/ **A** *n* **1** (fourth part) رُبْع (أَرْباع); **a ~ of the population** رُبْع السُكّانِ; **in a ~ of an hour** خلال رُبْعِ ساعةٍ **2** (Fin) (three months) فَصْل (فُصول), رُبْع سَنةٍ **3** (area) حَيّ (أَحْياء), مِنْطَقة (مَناطِق); **a rich/poor residential ~** حَيّ سَكَنيّ غَنيّ \ فَقير; **the Empty Q~** الرُبْع الخالي **4** (in basketball, American football) رُبْع (أَرْباع), شَوْط (أَشْواط) **5** (fml) (source of help, information) جِهة (شَخْص أو مَجموعة); **don't expect any help from that ~** لا تَتَوَقَّعْ أَيَّ مُساعَدةٍ من تِلْكَ الجِهةِ **6** [u] (fml) (mercy) **to give/receive no ~** لم يُظْهِرْ \ يَتلَقَّ أَيَّ تَعاطُفٍ **7** (of a dollar) رُبْع دولار

B (**quarters**) *n pl* (accommodation) سَكَن, مَساكِن; **the officers' ~s** مَساكِن الضُبّاطِ; **the living ~s** أَماكِن المَعيشةِ

C *pron* **1** (one fourth) رُبْع (أَرْباع); **only a ~ passed** لم يَنْجَحْ سِوى الرُبْعِ **2** (in time phrases) **an hour and a ~** ساعة وَرُبْع; **at a ~ to 11** (BrE), **at a ~ of 11** (AmE) الحادِيةَ عَشَرةَ إلاّ الرُبْعَ; **at a ~ past 2** (BrE), **at a ~ after 2** (AmE) الثانِيةَ والرُبْعَ; **she's ten and a ~** عُمْرُها عَشْرُ سَنواتٍ وَثَلاثةُ شُهورٍ

D *adj before n* ‹*pound, mile, inch*› رُبْع; **a ~ share in the company** رُبْع أَسْهُمِ الشَرِكةِ; **a ~ century** رُبْع قَرْنٍ

E *adv* **a ~ full** مَليء إلى رُبْعِه; **a ~ as big** أَكْبَر بِمِقْدار الرُبْعِ; **it isn't worth ~ the price** لا يَسْتَحِقُّ رُبْعَ الثَمَنِ

F (**at close quarters**) *adv phr* من مَسافةٍ قَريبةٍ, عن قُرْبٍ; **to fight at close ~s** قاتَلَ من مَسافةٍ قَريبةٍ

G *vt* **1** (to divide into four) قَسَّمَ إلى أَرْبَعةِ أَرْباعٍ ‹*a cake, an apple*›; **to be hung, drawn and ~ed** [قُتِل وَمُثِّل بِجُثَّتِه] **2** (fml) (to accommodate) وَفَّرَ سَكَناً لـ, أَسْكَنَ ‹*troops, a refugee*›

quarterback /ˈkwɔːtəbak/ *n* (AmE) ظَهير رُبْعيّ (في كُرةِ القَدَمِ الأَمْريكيّةِ)

quarter-final /kwɔːtəˈfʌɪn(ə)l/ *n* دَوْر رُبْع نِهائيّ

quarterly /ˈkwɔːt(ə)li/ **A** *adj* ‹*newsletter, earnings*› رُبْع سَنَويّ, فَصْليّ

B *adv* ‹*to publish, meet*› بِشَكْلٍ فَصْليٍّ, بِشَكْلٍ رُبْع سَنَويٍّ

quartermaster /ˈkwɔːtəmɑːstə/ *n* **1** (in the army) ضابِط عُهْدةٍ **2** (in the navy) رَئيس بَحَريّ

quarter note *n* (AmE) نَغْمة رُبْعيّة

quartet /kwɔːˈtɛt/ *n* موسيقى رُباعيّة (موسيقى يَعْزِفُها أَرْبَعةُ عازِفينَ); **a jazz/string ~** موسيقى رُباعيّة للجازِ \ للآلاتِ الوَتَريّة

quartz /kwɔːts/ *n* مَرْو, كَوارْتْز

quash /kwɒʃ/ *vt* **1** أَلْغى (a; فَسْخ), فَسَخَ (a; فَسْخ) ‹*a conviction, sentence*› **2** سَحَقَ (a; سَحْق), قَمَعَ (a; قَمْع) ‹*a protest, rebellion*›

quasi- /ˈkweɪzʌɪ/ *prefix* شِبْه; **a ~scientific explanation** تَفْسير شِبْه عِلْميٍّ

quaver /ˈkweɪvə/ **A** *vi* «voices» اِرْتَعَدَ, تَهَدَّجَ, اِرْتَعَشَ; **his voice ~ed with emotion** تَهَدَّجَ صَوْتُهُ بِسَبَبِ غَلَبةِ العاطِفةِ

B *n* **1** (BrE) (musical note) ذات السِنِّ (نوتة موسيقيّة خاصّة) **2** (trembling) اِرْتِعاش, تَهَدُّج

quay /kiː/ *n* رَصيف مَرْفَأٍ

quayside /ˈkiːsʌɪd/ *n* [المِنْطَقة المُحيطة بِرَصيفِ المَرْفَأِ]

queasiness /ˈkwiːzinəs/ *n* غَثَيان

queasy /ˈkwiːzi/ *adj* (**queasier, queasiest**) ‹*feeling, stomach*› مُصاب بالغَثَيانِ; **to feel ~** شَعَرَ بالغَثَيانِ

Quebec /kwɪˈbɛk/ *pr n* (province) كيبِك (f); (city) كيبِك (f)

queen /kwiːn/ *n* **1** (ruler) مَلِكة **2** (in cards) بِنْت (f; بَنات)

queen bee *n* مَلِكة النَحْلِ

queen mother *n* المَلِكة الأُمّ

Queen's Counsel *n* (BrE) مُسْتَشار المَلِكةِ

queer /kwɪə/ **A** *adj* **1** (often offensive) (homosexual) يَدُلُّ على الشُذوذِ الجِنْسيِّ **2** (gay) ‹*studies, activism*› مِثْليّ **3** (old use) (strange) ‹*feeling, event*› عَجيب, غَريب

B *n* (offensive) (homosexual) لوطيّ, شاذّ جِنْسيًّا

quell /kwɛl/ *vt* أَخْمَدَ, كَبَحَ (a; كَبْح) ‹*a rebellion, anxieties*›

quench /kwɛntʃ/ *vt* **1** رَوى (i; رَيّ, رِيّ) ‹*sb's thirst*› **2** أَطْفَأَ, أَخْمَدَ ‹*flames, a fire*›

querulous /ˈkwɛrʊləs/ *adj* ‹*character, remark*› كَثير التَشَكّي, كَثير التَذَمُّرِ

query /ˈkwɪəri/ **A** *n* (*pl* **queries**) **1** (fml) (question) سُؤال (أَسْئِلة), اِسْتِعْلام (اِسْتِعْلامات), اِسْتِفْسار (اِسْتِفْسارات); **to answer queries from customers/parents** أَجابَ على اِسْتِفْساراتِ

العُمَلاءِ \ الآباءِ; **a ~ about sb's expenses** اسْتِفْسار عن نَفَقاتِ شَخْصٍ **2** (Comput) اسْتِعْلام (اسْتِعْلامات)

B *vt* (**queries**, **querying**, **queried**) (fml) تَشَكَّكَ (في) ‹*a bill, sb's judgement, a decision*›; **to ~ whether ...** تَشَكَّكَ فيما إذا ... ; **to ~ sb's ability** تَشَكَّكَ في مَقْدِرةِ شَخْصٍ

quest /kwɛst/ *n* سَعْي ,بَحْث; **the ~ for happiness/knowledge** البَحْث عن السَعادةِ \ المَعْرِفةِ

question /ˈkwɛstʃ(ə)n/ **A** *n* **1** (requiring an answer) سُؤال (أَسْئِلة); **to ask sb a ~** سَأَلَ شَخْصاً سُؤالاً; **to do sth without ~** فَعَلَ شَيْئاً دون تَرَدُّدٍ; **what a ~!** يا لَهُ من سُؤالٍ! **2** (problem) مَسْأَلة (مَسائِل), قَضية (قَضايا); **it's a ~ of saving money** هي مَسْأَلةُ تَوْفيرِ المالِ; **the Palestinian ~** القَضيّة الفِلَسْطينيّة; **the ~ of the environment** مَسْأَلة البيئةِ; **the person in ~** الشخص المَعْنيّ; **that's another ~** تِلْكَ مَسْأَلةٌ أُخرى; **that's out of the ~** ذلك غَيْرُ وارِدٍ **3** [u] (fml) (uncertainty) شَكّ (شُكوك), ريبة (رِيَب); **to call sth into ~** شَكَّكَ في شَيْءٍ; **to prove beyond ~ that ...** أَثْبَتَ بِما لا يَدَعُ مَجالاً للشَكِّ أنّ ... ; **it's open to ~** هو مَشْكوكٌ فيهِ; **his integrity was never in ~** لم تَكُنْ نَزاهَتُهُ أَبَداً مَوْضِعَ شَكٍّ

B *vt* **1** (to interrogate) اسْتَجْوَبَ ‹*a suspect, driver, politician*› **2** (to doubt) شَكَّكَ (في) ‹*tactics, a method, figures*›; **no one is ~ing your judgement** لا يُشكُّ أَحَدٌ في قُدْرَتِكَ على الحُكْمِ على الأَشْياءِ

questionable /ˈkwɛstʃ(ə)nəb(ə)l/ *adj* **1** (debatable) ‹*decision, assumption*› قابِل للنِقاشِ, فيهِ نَظَرٌ **2** (dubious) ‹*practices, motive*› مَشْكوك فيهِ, مُريب

questioner /ˈkwɛstʃ(ə)nə/ *n* مُحقِّق, مُسْتَجْوِب, سائِل

questioning /ˈkwɛstʃ(ə)nɪŋ/ **A** *n* اسْتِجْواب (اسْتِجْوابات), تَحْقيق (تَحْقيقات)

B *adj* ‹*look, tone*› تَساؤُليّ, اسْتِفْهاميّ

question mark *n* علامة اسْتِفْهامٍ

questionnaire /kwɛstʃəˈnɛː/ *n* اسْتِبْيان, نَموذَج اسْتِطْلاعٍ; **to fill in/answer the ~** مَلأَ الاسْتِبْيانَ \ أَجابَ على أَسْئِلة الاسْتِبْيانِ

queue /kjuː/ (BrE) **A** *n* (of customers) (vehicles) طابور (طَوابيرُ), صَفّ (صُفوف); **to stand/wait in a ~** وَقَفَ \ انْتَظَرَ في طابورٍ; **to jump the ~** تَجاوَزَ الطابورَ; **there was a long ~ at the check-out** كانَ هُناكَ طابورٌ طَويلٌ عند مَكانِ تَسْجيلِ الخُروجِ

B *vi* (also **queue up**) «fans, traffic» اصْطَفَّ في طابورٍ

queue-jump /ˈkjuːdʒʌmp/ *vi* «customers, vehicles» تَجاوَزَ الطابورَ

quibble /ˈkwɪb(ə)l/ **A** *n* جِدال (في أُمورٍ تافِهةٍ)

B *vi* «customers, sellers» جادَلَ (في أُمورٍ تافِهةٍ); **he's quibbling about/over tiny details** يُجادِلُ حول تَفاصيلَ ضَئيلةٍ

quick /kwɪk/ **A** *adj* **1** (speedy) ‹*turnaround, profit*› سَريع; ‹*break*› قَصير; **to make a ~ phone call** أَجْرى مُكالَمةً تِلِفونيّةً قَصيرةً \ سَريعةً; **they had three children in ~ succession** أَنْجَبوا ثَلاثةَ أَطْفالٍ في تَتابُعٍ سَريعٍ; **we need to make a ~ decision** نَحْنُ في حاجةٍ إلى اتِّخاذِ قَرارٍ سَريعٍ; **she's a ~ worker** تَعْمَلُ بِسُرْعةٍ; **the ~est way to get there is ...** أَسْرَعُ طَريقةٍ للوُصولِ إلى هُناكَ هي ... ; **it's ~er by train** هو أَسْرَعُ بالقِطارِ; **to make a ~ recovery** تَعافى بِسُرْعةٍ **2** (clever) ‹*student, learner*› سَريع الفَهْم, ذَكيّ (أَذْكِياءُ); **she's very ~ on the uptake** هي سَريعةُ الاسْتيعابِ جِدًّا **3** (prompt) **to be ~ to anger/take offence** كانَ سَريعَ الغَضَبِ \ الشُعورِ بالإهانةِ; **to have a ~ wit** كانَ سَريعَ البَديهةِ

B *adv* (come) **~!** تَعالَ بِسُرْعةٍ! احْضَرْ!; **come as ~ as you can!** في أَقْرَبِ وَقْتٍ مُمْكِنٍ!; **(as) ~ as a flash** بِسُرْعةِ البَرْقِ

C *n* [اللَحْم تحت الظُفْرِ]

(Idioms) **to be quick off the mark** كانَ سَبّاقاً; **to make a quick buck** حَقَّقَ رِبْحاً سَريعاً; **their sole aim is to make a ~ buck** هَدَفُهُم الوَحيدُ هو تَحْقيقُ الرِبْحِ السَريعِ

quicken /ˈkwɪk(ə)n/ **A** *vt* عَجَّلَ, سَرَّعَ ‹*one's pace, a process*›

B *vi* «the pace, rhythm» تَسارَعَ, أَسْرَعَ

quick-fire /ˌkwɪkˈfʌɪə/ *adj before n* ‹*dialogue, assault*› (quick) سَريع, فَوْريّ; (in rapid succession) مُتَوالٍ, مُتَتابِع

quicklime /ˈkwɪklʌɪm/ *n* جير حَيّ, أوكْسيد الكالْسِيوم

quickly /ˈkwɪkli/ *adv* ‹*to talk, to realize*› بِسُرْعةٍ; **children grow up so ~** يَنْمو الأَطْفالُ بِسُرْعةٍ كَبيرةٍ; **come ~!** تَعالَ بِسُرْعةٍ!

quick march *n* خَطْوة سَريعة

quickness /ˈkwɪknəs/ *n* **1** (in thought, speech) سُرْعة **2** (nimbleness) سُرْعة

quicksand /ˈkwɪksand/ *n* رِمال مُتَحَرِّكة

quicksilver /ˈkwɪksɪlvə/ *n* زِئْبَق

quick-tempered /ˌkwɪkˈtɛmpəd/ *adj* ‹*person*› سَرِيع الغَضَب, حادّ الطَبْع; **to be very ~** كانَ سَرِيعَ الغَضَبِ جِدًّا

quick time *n* (AmE) خُطًى مُتسارِعة (سَيْر المُجَنَّدِ بِسُرْعةِ 120 خَطْوةً في الدَقيقةِ)

quick-witted /kwɪkˈwɪtɪd/ *adj* ‹*comedian, retort*› سَرِيع البَدِيهةِ, حادّ الذِهْنِ; **to be very ~** كانَ سَرِيعَ البَدِيهةِ جِدًّا

quid /kwɪd/ *n* (*pl* **quid**) (BrE) (infml) جُنَيْه إسْتِرْلِينيّ

quiet /ˈkwʌɪət/ **A** *adj* **1** (not noisy) ‹*office, area*› هادِئ; **they live in a ~ suburban road** يَعِيشُونَ في شارِعٍ جانِبِيٍّ هادِئٍ; **be ~!** اُصْمُتْ!; **to keep ~** اِلْتَزَمَ الصَمْتَ **2** (reserved) ‹*pupil, neighbours*› هادِئ **3** (not loud) ‹*voice, laugh, engine*› هادِئ; **he spoke in a ~ voice** تَحَدَّثَ بِصَوْتٍ هادِئٍ **4** (low-key) ‹*weekend, life, wedding*› هادِئ; **business is ~** التِجارةُ هادِئةٌ **5** (discreet) ‹*diplomacy, chat, confidence*› هادِئ; **to have a ~ word with sb** عاتَبَ شَخْصاً على انْفِرادٍ **6** (secret) **to keep one's plan ~** احْتَفَظَ بِخُطَّتِهِ سِرًّا

B *n* **1** (silence) صَمْت, هُدوء; **~ please!** رَجاءً الهُدوء! **2** (lack of activity) هُدوء; **we need some peace and ~** نَحْنُ في حاجةٍ إلى بَعْضِ الهُدوءِ والسَكِينةِ **3** (infml) (secret) **to do sth on the ~** فَعَلَ شَيْئاً في الخَفاءِ

C *vt* (AmE) ▸ **quieten**

quieten /ˈkwʌɪət(ə)n/ *vt* **1** (to silence) هَدَّأَ ‹*a class, crowd*› **2** (to calm) هَدَّأَ, طَمْأَنَ (i; طَمْأَنة) ‹*a patient, an animal*›; **I need something to ~ my nerves** أَحْتاجُ لِشَيْءٍ يُهَدِّئُ أَعْصابي

Phrasal verb **quieten down** **A** **~ down** **1** (to become calm) «queue, situation» هَدَأَ (a; هُدوء) **2** (to fall silent) «crowd, class» صَمَتَ (u; صَمْت) **B** **~ down [sb/sth], ~ [sb/sth] down** (to calm) هَدَّأَ [شَخْصاً \ شَيْئاً] ‹*a baby, crowd*›

quietly /ˈkwʌɪətli/ *adv* **1** (not noisily) ‹*to move, speak*› بِهُدوءٍ **2** (silently) ‹*to play, read*› في صَمْتٍ, بِهُدوءٍ **3** (unobtrusively) ‹*to go, mention*› بِطَمَأْنينةٍ, بِهُدوءٍ

quietness /ˈkwʌɪətnəs/ *n* **1** (of a place) هُدوء **2** (of a voice) خُفوت, هُدوء

quiff /kwɪf/ *n* (BrE) [تَسْرِيحة شَعْرٍ لِلرِجالِ يُرْفَعُ فِيها الشَعْرُ عند مُقَدِّمةِ الرَأْسِ]

quill /kwɪl/ *n* **1** (feather) رِيشة **2** (porcupine's) شَوْكة (أَشْواك) **3** (also **quill pen**) رِيشةِ (قَلَم)

quilt /kwɪlt/ *n* **1** (BrE) ▸ **duvet** **2** (bed cover) لِحاف (لُحُف, أَلْحِفة)

quin /kwɪn/ *n* (BrE infml) ▸ **quintuplet**

quince /kwɪns/ *n* **1** (fruit) سَفَرْجَل (n coll; سَفارِجُ) **2** (tree) سَفَرْجَل (n coll; سَفارِجُ)

quinine /kwɪˈniːn/ *n* كِينِين

quint /kwɪnt/ *n* (AmE infml) ▸ **quintuplet**

quintessential /ˌkwɪntɪˈsɛnʃ(ə)l/ *adj* (fml) ‹*gentleman, example*› نَمُوذَجِيّ

quintet /kwɪnˈtɛt/ *n* **1** (of players) خُماسيّ [فِرْقة مُكَوَّنة من خَمْسةِ مُطْرِبِينَ أو عازِفِينَ] **2** (unit of five) خُماسيّ [مَجْموعة من خَمْسةِ أَشْخاصٍ أو أَشْياءَ]

quintuplet /kwɪnˈtjuːplət/ *n* [أَحَد خَمْسة تَوائِمَ]

quip /kwɪp/ **A** *n* تَعْلِيق طَرِيف \ ساخِر **B** *vi* (**-pp-**) «comedians, writers» [أَطْلَقَ تَعْلِيقاً طَرِيفاً \ ساخِراً]

quirk /kwəːk/ *n* **1** (of person) عادة غَرِيبة, هَوَس **2** (circumstance) مُصادَفة غَرِيبة; **it was a ~ of fate that they met** كانَ من مُصادَفاتِ القَدَرِ الغَرِيبةِ أَنَّهُمْ تَقابَلوا

quirky /ˈkwəːki/ *adj* (**quirkier**, **quirkiest**) ‹*humour, character*› غَيْر مُعْتادٍ, غَرِيب

quit /kwɪt/ **A** *vt* (*present participle* **-tt-**, *past tense, past participle* **quit** or **quitted**) **1** تَوَقَّفَ (عن), تَرَكَ (u; تَرْك) ‹*drinking, smoking*› **2** تَرَكَ (u; تَرْك) ‹*a job, school*›

B *vi* **1** (to give up) «drinker, smoker» تَوَقَّفَ **2** (to resign) «worker» اسْتَقالَ; «politician» اعْتَزَلَ; «student» تَرَكَ الدِراسة

quite /kwʌɪt/ *adv* **1** (completely) ‹*new, ready, differently*› تَماماً, كُلِّيّةً; **I ~ agree** أنا مُوافِقٌ تَماماً; **I ~ understand** أَفْهَمُ تَماماً; **you're ~ right** أَنْتَ مُحِقٌّ تَماماً; **it's ~ out of the question** هو غَيْرُ وارِدٍ مُطْلَقاً; **are you ~ sure?** هل أَنْتَ واثِقٌ تَماماً؟; (replying to apology) **it's ~ all right** لا عَلَيْكَ **2** (exactly) **not ~** لَيْسَ بالضَبْطِ; **nobody knows ~ what he means** لا أَحَدَ يَعْلَمُ ماذا يَقْصِدُ بالضَبْطِ; **I don't ~ know** لا أَعْلَمُ بالضَبْطِ;

not ~ so much لَيْسَ تَماماً; **that's not ~ all** لَيْسَ ذلك كُلَّ شَيْءٍ بالضَبْطِ **3** (fml) (definitely) **it was ~ the best answer** كانَتْ بالتَأْكيدِ أَفْضَلَ إجابةٍ; **our whisky is ~ simply the best!** الويسكي عِنْدَنا هو بِصَراحةٍ الأَفْضَلُ على الإِطْلاقِ! **4** (rather) ‹*big, easily, often*› نَوْعاً ما, إلى حَدٍّ ما; **it's ~ small** (a bit small) هو صَغيرٌ بَعْضَ الشَيْءِ; (very small) هو صَغيرٌ جِدًّا; **it's ~ warm today** (very hot) الجَوُّ اليَوْمَ حارٌّ جِدًّا; (comparatively hot) الجَوُّ اليَوْمَ دافِئٌ نَوْعاً ما; **it's ~ likely that ...** من المُحْتَمَلِ جِدًّا أنْ ...; **I ~ like Chinese food** أُحِبُّ الطَعامَ الصِينيَّ; **a few ~** عَدَد لا بَأْسَ بِهِ; **there is ~ a lot of opposition** هُناكَ الكَثيرُ من المُعارَضةِ **5** (infml) (giving emphasis) **that's ~ a difference** هذا اخْتِلافٌ كَبيرٌ; **that will be ~ a change for you** سَوْفَ يَكونُ ذلك تَغْييراً كَبيراً بالنِسْبةِ لَكَ; **their house is ~ something** بَيْتُهُمْ مُبْهِرٌ جِدًّا **6** (BrE) (expressing agreement) تَماماً; **'he could have told us'—'~ (so)'** 'كانَ بِوِسْعِهِ أنْ يُخْبِرَنا' — 'تَماماً'

quits /kwɪts/ *adj* (infml) **1** **to be ~** (to be even) كانا مُتَخالِصَيْنِ \ مُتَعادِلَيْنِ **2** **to call it ~** (in conclusion) اتَّفَقا على أَنَّهُما مُتَخالِصانِ; (in disagreement) اتَّفَقا على فَضِّ المَوْضوعِ

quitter /ˈkwɪtə/ *n* (infml) سَريع الاسْتِسْلامِ

quiver /ˈkwɪvə/ **A** *vi* «voice, lips» ارْتَعَشَ, اهْتَزَّ

B *n* **1** (for arrows) كِنانة \ جَعْبة سِهامٍ **2** (in sb's voice) تَهَدُّج, (ارْتِعاشات) ارْتِعاش, ارْتِجاف

quiz /kwɪz/ **A** *n* (*pl* **-zes**) **1** (competition) مُسابَقة (في المَعْلوماتِ) **2** (AmE Educ) (test) اخْتِبار قَصير

B *vt* (**-zz-**) ‹*a suspect*› اسْتَجْوَبَ; ‹*candidate*› حاوَرَ

quiz show, **quiz game** *n* مُسابَقة (في المَعْلوماتِ)

quizzical /ˈkwɪzɪk(ə)l/ *adj* (fml) ‹*look, expression*› فُضوليّ, حائر

quorum /ˈkwɔːrəm/ *n* نِصاب قانونيّ

quota /ˈkwəʊtə/ *n* (*pl* **quotas**) **1** (limited amount) حِصّة (حِصَص), كوتة **2** (target) قَدْر مُسْتَهْدَف

quotation /kwəʊˈteɪʃ(ə)n/ *n* **1** (citation) اقْتِباس (اقْتِباسات), اسْتِشْهاد (اسْتِشْهادات) **2** (of costs) عَرْض أَسْعارٍ

quotation marks /kwəʊˈteɪʃ(ə)n mɑːks/ *n pl* (also **quotes**) عَلامات الاقْتِباسِ \ التَنْصيصِ

quote /kwəʊt/ **A** *vt* **1** (to repeat) اسْتَشْهَدَ, اقْتَبَسَ (ب) ‹*a person, author*›; ذَكَرَ (u; ذِكْر, تَذْكار) ‹*a reference number*›; **to ~ Shakespeare** اقْتَبَسَ كَلامَ شِكْسْبير; **don't ~ me on this, but ...** لا تَسْتَشْهِدْ بِكَلامي في هذا الأَمْرِ, ولَكِنْ ...; **she was ~d as saying they were an item** نُقِلَ عَنْها قَوْلُها إِنَّهُما كانا على عَلاقةٍ عاطِفيّةٍ **2** (for a job, service, product) قَدَّمَ عَرْضاً ب ‹*a price, figure*›; **they ~d us £400 to repair the car** قَدَّموا لَنا عَرْضاً بِإِصْلاحِ السَيّارة مُقابِلَ £400 **3** (on the stock exchange) عَرَضَ سِعْراً ل ‹*a share, stock*›; **to be ~d on the Stock Exchange** «companies» عُرِضَتْ أَسْهُمُهُ للتَداوُلِ في سوقِ الأَوْراقِ الماليّةِ; **the shares are being ~d at €12.6** تُعْرَضُ الأَسْهُمُ بِسِعْرِ €12.6

B *vi* **1** (from a text, speech) اسْتَشْهَدَ, اقْتَبَسَ; **to ~ from Keats** اقْتَبَسَ من كيتْس; **he's in Beirut on ~ 'business' unquote** هو في بَيْروتَ في, بين قَوْسَيْنِ, 'مُهِمّةِ عَمَلٍ' **2** (for a job, service, product) عَرَضَ سِعْراً; **to ~ for a job** عَرَضَ سِعْراً للقِيامِ بِعَمَلٍ

C *n* **1** (from a text, speech) اسْتِشْهاد, (اقْتِباسات) اقْتِباس (اسْتِشْهادات) **2** (for a job, service, product) عَرْض سِعْرٍ **3** (for stocks and shares) عَرْض سِعْرٍ

D (**quotes**) *n pl* ▸ **quotation marks**

quotient /ˈkwəʊʃ(ə)nt/ *n* حاصِل \ خارِج \ ناتِج القِسْمةِ

Qur'an, **Quran** /kəˈrɑːn/ *n* (**the Qur'an**) القُرْآن

Rr

R, **r** /ɑː/ *n* (letter) راء = (الحَرْف الثامِن عَشَر من الأَبْجَديّة الإنْكْليزيّة)

Rabat /rə'bat/ *pr n* الرِباط (f)

rabbi /'rabʌɪ/ *n* (*pl* **rabbis**) حَبْر ,حاخام (عند اليَهود)

rabbit /'rabɪt/ *n* 1 (animal) أَرْنَب (أَرانِبُ) 2 [u] (meat) لَحْم أَرانِبَ

rabble /'rab(ə)l/ *n* 1 (mob) حَشْد من الغَوْغاءِ 2 (pej) (common people) **the ~** الدَهْماء ,عامّة الناسِ

Rabi al-Awwal /rabiː alə'wal/ *n* رَبيع الأَوَّل

Rabi al-Thani /rabiː al'θɑːni/ *n* رَبيع الثاني

rabid /'rabɪd/ *adj* 1 (with rabies) ‹*dog, animal*› مَسْعور 2 (fanatical) مُصاب بداءِ الكَلْبِ ,مَسْعور (مَساعيرُ ,مَسْعورونَ) ‹*fan, supporter*› مُتَعَصِّب

rabies /'reɪbiːz/ *n* سُعار ,داء الكَلْبِ

RAC /ɑːreɪ'siː/ *n* (BrE) = **Royal Automobile Club** [شَرِكة بَريطانيّة تُوَفِّرُ خَدَماتٍ لِقائِدي السَيّاراتِ]

raccoon /rə'kuːn/ *n* (*pl* **raccoons** or **raccoon**) راكون

race /reɪs/ **A** *n* 1 (in sport) سِباق (سِباقات); **to run a ~** اِشْتَرَكَ في سِباقٍ; **let's have a ~!** هَيّا نَتَسابَقُ! 2 (contest) سِباق (سِباقات); **a ~ against time** سِباق مع الزَمَنِ; **the ~ for the presidency** سِباق الرِئاسةِ 3 (for horses, dogs) **the ~s** [سِباق الخَيْلِ أو الكِلابِ] 4 (human group) جِنْس (أَجْناس), عِرْق (أَعْراق); **the human ~** الجِنْس البَشَريّ

B *vt* 1 (to compete with) ‹*a person, car*› سابَقَ ,تَسابَقَ (مع) 2 (to enter in races) ‹*a horse, car, boat*› أَدْخَلَ في سِباقٍ; **he ~s his horses internationally** اِشْتَرَكَ بِخَيْلِهِ في سِباقاتٍ عالَميّةٍ 3 (to rev) ‹*an engine*› سَرَّعَ الدَوَرانَ ,زادَ السُرْعةَ

C *vi* 1 (to compete) «cars, athletes» تَسابَقَ 2 (to rush) هَرْوَلَ (i; هَرْوَلة), أَسْرَعَ ,اِنْطَلَقَ بِسُرْعةٍ; **to ~ down/up the stairs** نَزَلَ \ صَعَدَ الدَرَجَ مُهَرْوِلاً; **to ~ in/out of the house** دَخَلَ المَنْزِلَ \ خَرَجَ من المَنْزِلِ مُهَرْوِلاً; **he ~d through his homework** عَمِلَ واجِباتِهِ المَنْزِليّةَ على عَجَلٍ; **my mind was racing** كُنْتُ مُسْتَغْرِقاً في التَفْكيرِ 3 «heart, pulse» تَسارَعَ 4 «engine» أَسْرَعَ

(Phrasal verb) **race by** «time, vehicles» مَرَّ بِسُرْعةٍ

race car *n* (AmE) سَيّارة سِباقٍ

racecourse /'reɪskɔːs/ *n* 1 (BrE) (for horses, dogs) حَلَبة \ مِضْمار \ مَيْدان سِباقٍ 2 (AmE) (for cars) حَلَبة \ مِضْمار \ مَيْدان سِباقٍ

racehorse /'reɪshɔːs/ *n* حِصان سِباقٍ

race meeting *n* (BrE) مَجْموعة سِباقاتٍ

racer /'reɪsə/ *n* 1 (bike) دَرّاجة سِباقٍ; (motorbike) دَرّاجة سِباقٍ نارِيّة 2 (driver, cyclist) مُتَسابِق

race relations *n* عَلاقات بين الأَعْراقِ ,عَلاقات عِرْقِيّة

racetrack /'reɪstrak/ *n* (for cars) (for horses) (for runners, dogs) حَلَبة \ مِضْمار سِباقٍ

racial /'reɪʃ(ə)l/ *adj* ‹*discrimination, group*› عُنْصُريّ ,عِرْقيّ

racially /'reɪʃ(ə)li/ *adv* ‹*diverse, motivated*› عِرْقِيّاً

racial profiling *n* تَنْميط عُنْصُريّ

racing /'reɪsɪŋ/ *n* 1 (with horses) سِباق (سِباقات) 2 (with cars, yachts etc.) سِباق (سِباقات)

racing car *n* سَيّارة سِباقٍ

racing driver *n* سائِق سَيّارة سِباقٍ ,مُتَسابِق

racism /'reɪsɪz(ə)m/ *n* تَمْييز عُنْصُريّ ,عُنْصُريّة

racist /'reɪsɪst/ **A** *n* عُنْصُريّ

B *adj* ‹*attack, views*› عُنْصُريّ

rack /rak/ **A** *n* 1 (for bottles, plates, luggage) رَفّ (رُفوف); (for clothes) حامِل (حَمَلة) 2 (for torture) (**the Rack**) المِخْلَعة

(آلة تَعْذيبِ تُسْتَعْمَلُ لِشَدِّ الجِسْمِ والأَطْرافِ)

B *vt* «sobs, pain» عَذَّبَ ,يُؤْلِمُ (Form IV; imperf أَلَمَ ,أَوْجَعَ) *<sb's body>*; **she was ~ed with guilt** عَذَّبَها النَدَمُ

(Idiom) **to rack one's brains** كَدَّ ذِهْنَهُ

racket /'rakɪt/ *n* **1** (also **racquet**) (for tennis, squash etc.) مِضْرَب (مَضارِبُ) **2** (infml) (noise) جَلَبَة (جَلَب), صَخَب **3** (infml) (scam) احْتِيال (احْتِيالات), نَصْب; **a protection ~** إتاوة (أَتاوى)

racketeer /rakɪ'tɪə/ *n* مُحْتال, نَصّاب

racketeering /rakə'tɪərɪŋ/ *n* احْتِيال (احْتِيالات), نَصْب

rackets /'rakɪts/ *n* + *v sing* لُعْبة الراحِ \ الراكيت (لُعْبة تُشْبِهُ الإسْكْواش)

racquet /'rakɪt/ *n* ▸ **racket** 1

racquetball /'rakɪtbɔːl/ *n* [u] لُعْبة الراحِ \ الراكيت

racy /'reɪsi/ *adj* (**racier**, **raciest**) **1** (lively) *<style, thriller>* مُفْعَم بالحَيَوِيّة **2** (risqué) *<images, novel>* مُثير جِنْسيًّا

radar /'reɪdɑː/ *n* رادار (رادارات)

radial /'reɪdɪəl/ *adj* *<pattern, lines>* شُعاعيّ, نِصْف قُطْريّ

radial tyre (BrE), **radial tire** (AmE) *n* إطار شُعاعيّ \ قُطْريّ \ نِصْف قُطْريّ

radiant /'reɪdɪənt/ *adj* **1** *<light, sun>* مُضيء ,(سَواطِعُ) ساطِع **2** *<smile, beauty>* مُشْرِق, مُتَأَلِّق

radiate /'reɪdɪeɪt/ *vt* **1** أَشَعَّ *<energy, happiness>* **2** أَشَعَّ *<heat, light>*

radiation /reɪdɪ'eɪʃ(ə)n/ *n* إشْعاع (إشْعاعات)

radiation sickness *n* داء الإشْعاعِ ,تَسَمُّم إشْعاعيّ

radiator /'reɪdɪeɪtə/ *n* مِشْعاع (جِهاز تَدْفِئةٍ)

radical /'radɪk(ə)l/ **A** *adj* **1** (far-reaching) *<change, reform>* جِذْريّ **2** (in politics) *<group, ideas>* مُتَطَرِّف ,راديكاليّ; **his ideas were too ~ for his colleagues** كانَتْ أَفْكارُهُ مُتَطَرِّفةً جِدًّا من وُجْهة نَظَرِ زُمَلائِهِ

B *n* **1** (in politics) راديكاليّ **2** (in Semitic languages) حَرْف أَصْليّ (أَحَد حُروفِ جِذْرِ الكَلِمةِ)

radicalization, **-isation** (BrE) /,radɪkəlʌɪ'zeɪʃ(ə)n/ *n* دَفْع نحو التَطَرُّفِ

radically /'radɪkli/ *adv* *<different, opposed>* بِصورةٍ جِذْرِيّةٍ; *<to change, improve>* جَوْهَريًّا ,جِذْريًّا

radii /'reɪdɪʌɪ/ *n pl* ▸ **radius**

radio /'reɪdɪəʊ/ **A** *n* (*pl* **radios**) **1** [u] (medium) رادِيو; **to contact sb by ~** اتَّصَلَ بِشَخْصٍ عَبْرَ جِهازِ اللاسِلْكيِّ **2** (receiver) رادِيو ,مِذْياع (مَذاييعُ); (transmitter) رادِيو ,جِهاز اتِّصالٍ لاسِلْكيٍّ; **to hear sth on the ~** سَمِعَ شَيْئاً في الراديو; **to listen to the ~** اسْتَمَعَ إلى الراديو; **a two-way ~** جِهاز إرْسالٍ وَاسْتِقْبالٍ

B *vt* (*3rd person present sing* **radios**; *past tense, past participle* **radioed**) أَبْرَق \ أَرْسَلَ لاسِلْكيًّا *<a control tower, colleague>*

C *vi* **to ~ for help** «pilots, crew» أَرْسَلَ رِسالةَ اسْتِنْجادٍ باللاسِلْكيِّ

radioactive /,reɪdɪəʊ'aktɪv/ *adj* *<material, waste>* مُشِعّ

radioactivity /,reɪdɪəʊak'tɪvɪti/ *n* نَشاط إشْعاعيّ

radiochemistry /,reɪdɪəʊ'kɛmɪstri/ *n* كيمْياء إشْعاعيّة

radio-controlled /,reɪdɪəʊkən'trəʊld/ *adj* *<car, toy>* مُوَجَّه عن بُعْدٍ

radiogram /'reɪdɪəʊgram/ *n* (BrE) [جِهاز يَحْتَوي على راديو وَجْرامافون]

radiograph /'reɪdɪəʊgrɑːf/ *n* صورة بالأَشِعّةِ

radiographer /reɪdi'ɒgrəfə/ *n* فَنّيّ تَصْوير بالأَشِعّةِ

radiography /,reɪdɪ'ɒgrəfi/ *n* تَصْوير شُعاعيّ \ بالأَشِعّةِ

radiologist /reɪdi'ɒlədʒɪst/ *n* أَخِصّائيّ أَشِعّةٍ

radiology /reɪdɪ'ɒlədʒi/ *n* عِلْم الأَشِعّةِ

radio station *n* مَحَطّة إذاعيّة

radiotherapy /,reɪdɪəʊ'θɛrəpi/ *n* عِلاج إشْعاعيّ \ بالأَشِعّة

radish /'radɪʃ/ *n* فُجْل (فُجول)

radius /'reɪdɪəs/ *n* (*pl* **radii** or **radiuses**) شُعاع ,نِصف قُطْرٍ (n coll; أَشِعّة)

radon /'reɪdɒn/ *n* رادون (غاز مُشِعّ)

RAF /raf/ *n* (BrE) = **Royal Air Force** سِلاح الجَوِّ المَلَكيّ البَريطانيّ

raffle /'raf(ə)l/ **A** *n* قُرْعة ,يانَصيب (قُرَع)

B *vt* [عَرَضَ شَيْئاً كَجائزةٍ لليانَصيبِ]

raft /rɑːft/ *n* طَوْف (أَطْواف)

rafter /ˈrɑːftə/ *n* رافِدة (دِعامة خَشَبيّة لِسَقْفٍ)

rag /raɡ/ *n* 1 (piece of cloth) خِرْقة (خِرَق) 2 **rags** *n pl* (clothes) ثِياب بالِية 3 (pej) (newspaper) جَريدة مُبْتَذَلة

Idiom **to go from rags to riches** انْتَقَلَ من الفَقْرِ المُدْقِعِ إلى الثَراءِ الفاحِشِ

ragamuffin /ˈraɡəmʌfɪn/ *n* طِفْل شَوارِعَ

rag doll *n* دُمْية من القُماشِ

rage /reɪdʒ/ **A** *n* 1 [u] (violent anger) حَنَق, غَيْظ, غَضَب شَديد 2 (fit of fury) فَوْرة \ نَوْبة غَضَبٍ; **to fly into a ~** اسْتَشاطَ غَضَباً 3 [u] (infml) (fashion) **to be all the ~** لَقِيَ رَواجاً كَبيراً

B *vi* 1 «storm» هاجَ, اشْتَدَّ (i; هَيَجان); «battle» اسْتَعَرَ, اشْتَدَّ, «debate» احْتَدَمَ; «fire» انْدَلَعَ; «epidemic» حَمِيَ وَطيسُهُ, تَفَشّى 2 «person» اسْتَشاطَ \ اشْتاطَ غَضَباً

ragged /ˈraɡɪd/ *adj* 1 ‹person› رَثّ المَظْهَرِ; ‹appearance, clothes› رَثّ (رِثاث) 2 ‹edge, outline› خَشِن (خِشان)

raging /ˈreɪdʒɪŋ/ *adj* 1 ‹headache› حادّ; ‹thirst› شَديد; ‹argument, debate› مُحْتَدِم 2 ‹storm› أَهْوَج; ‹sea› هائِج; ‹fire› مُلْتَهِب

rag trade *n* (infml) صِناعة المَلابِسِ

raid /reɪd/ **A** *n* 1 (military) غارة, هُجوم 2 (by thieves) هُجوم, مُداهَمة 3 (by police, customs) حَمْلة (حَمَلات), اقْتِحام, مُداهَمة

B *vt* 1 (to attack) اقْتَحَمَ, هاجَمَ ‹a village, a bank, house› 2 (to attack) «troops» شَنَّ غارةً على ‹enemy positions, camp› 3 (to rob) «robbers» سَطا (u; سَطْو; على), اقْتَحَمَ ‹a bank, shop› 4 (in security operations) «police» اقْتَحَمَ, داهَمَ, قامَ بِحَمْلةٍ على ‹a house, premises› 5 (infml) لَجَأَ (a; لَجْء, لُجوء) إلى ‹one's savings› 6 (hum) أَغارَ (على) ‹the fridge, larder›

raider /ˈreɪdə/ *n* 1 (marauder) مُغير, مُهاجِم 2 (robber) مُداهِم, لِصّ مُسَلَّح

rail /reɪl/ *n* 1 (for support) دَرابَزين 2 (for safety) حاجِز (حَواجِز), سِياج (سِياجات) 3 (for clothes) حامِل (حَمَلة); (for curtains) قَضيب سِتارةٍ 4 (for trains) قَضيب سِكّةِ حَديدٍ 5 [u] (railway system) السِكّة الحَديديّة; **to send sth by ~** أَرْسَلَ شَيْئاً بالقِطارِ

railing /ˈreɪlɪŋ/ *n* (also **railings**) دَرابَزين, سور, سِياج (مَعْدِنيّ أو حَديديّ)

railroad /ˈreɪlrəʊd/ **A** *n* (AmE) ▸ **railway**

B *vt* (to compel) فَرَضَ (i; فَرْض) ‹the legislation›; أَجْبَرَ ‹a witness›; **to ~ sb into agreeing to sth** أَجْبَرَ شَخْصاً على المُوافَقةِ على شَيْءٍ

railroad man *n* (*pl* **-men**) (AmE) عامِل \ مُوَظَّف بالسِكَكِ الحَديديّة

railroad station *n* (AmE) مَحَطّة قِطارٍ \ سِكَكٍ حَديديّة

railway /ˈreɪlweɪ/ *n* (BrE) 1 (network) سِكّة حَديديّة 2 (track) خطّ سِكّةٍ حَديديّةٍ

railway line *n* (BrE) 1 (track) خطّ سِكّةٍ حَديديّةٍ 2 (route) مَسار سِكّةٍ حَديديّةٍ

railwayman /ˈreɪlweɪmən/ *n* (*pl* **-men**) (BrE) عامِل \ مُوَظَّف سِكَكٍ حَديديّة

railway station *n* (BrE) مَحَطّة قِطارٍ \ سِكَكٍ حَديديّة

rain /reɪn/ **A** *n* مَطَر (أَمْطار); **in the ~** في المَطَرِ; **it looks like ~** يَبْدو أَنَّها سَتُمْطِرُ; **the ~ started/stopped** بَدَأَ \ تَوَقَّفَ المَطَرُ; **the ~s** (season) مَوْسِم الأَمْطارِ

B *vt* **to ~ blows/bombs on sb** أَمْطَرَ شَخْصاً بوابِلٍ من الضَرَباتِ \ القَنابِلِ

C *v impers* أَمْطَرَ; **it's ~ing** السَماءُ تُمْطِرُ

Idiom **come rain or shine** مَهْما تَكُن الظُروفُ

Phrasal verbs **rain down** «bombs, debris» انْهالَ \ تَساقَطَ بِغَزارةٍ

• **rain off** (AmE) • **rain out** **the game/event was ~ed off** (cancelled) أُلْغِيَت المُباراةُ \ الحَفْلةُ بِسَبَبِ المَطَرِ; (stopped) أوقِفَت المُباراةُ \ الحَفْلةُ بِسَبَبِ المَطَرِ

rainbow /ˈreɪnbəʊ/ *n* قَوْس قُزَح

rainbow trout *n* تَراوْت قَوْس قُزَح (سَمَك)

rain cloud *n* غَيْمة مَطَرٍ, سَحابة مُمْطِرة

raincoat /ˈreɪnkəʊt/ *n* مِعْطَف مَطَرٍ

raindrop /ˈreɪndrɒp/ *n* قَطْرة مَطَرٍ

rainfall /ˈreɪnfɔːl/ *n* 1 (in statistics) كَمّيّة, مُعَدَّل سُقوطِ الأَمْطارِ 2 (rain) سُقوط \ هُطول المَطَرِ

rainforest /ˈreɪnfɒrɪst/ *n* غابة اسْتِوائيّة

rainwater /ˈreɪnwɔːtə/ *n* مِياه المَطَرِ

rainy /ˈreɪni/ *adj* (**rainier**, **rainiest**) ‹*day, weather*› ماطِر ,مُمْطِر, مَطير

rainy season *n* مَوْسِم مَطير \ مُمْطِر

raise /reɪz/ **A** *vt* **1** (to lift) رَفَعَ (a; رَفْع) ‹*a barrier, flag, the blinds*›; **to ~ one's hand/head** رَفَعَ يَدَهُ \ رَأْسَهُ; **he ~d his glass to his lips** رَفَعَ كوبَهُ إلى شَفَتَيْهِ; **the guard ~d the barrier to let the cars through** رَفَعَ الحارِسُ الحاجِزَ للسَماحِ لِلسَيّاراتِ بالمُرورِ; **he ~d his eyes** رَفَعَ عَيْنَيْهِ; **as they left harbour they ~d the mainsail** بِمُجَرَّدِ أنْ غادَروا الميناءَ رَفَعوا الشِراعَ الرَئيسيَّ **2** (to increase) رَفَعَ (a; رَفْع), زادَ (i; زِيادة) ‹*interest rates, prices, the age limit*›; **to ~ one's voice** رَفَعَ صَوْتَهُ; **to raise awareness of sth** زادَ الوَعْيَ بِشَيْءٍ; **to raise educational standards** رَفَعَ مُسْتَوَياتِ التَعْليمِ; **we need to ~ the profile of the company** نَحْنُ في حاجةٍ إلى رَفْعِ سُمْعةِ الشَرِكةِ **3** رَفَعَ ,اِنْتَشَلَ (a; رَفْع), سَحَبَ (a; سَحْب) ‹*a sunken ship*› **4** (to broach) طَرَحَ (a; طَرْح) ‹*an issue, the question*›; أَبْدى ‹*an objection*›; **the incident ~s questions about airport safety** يَطْرَحُ الحادِثُ التَساؤُلاتِ حول مُسْتَوى السَلامةِ في المَطارِ **5** (to bring about) أَثارَ ‹*doubts, fears*›; **to ~ a smile** جَعَلَ الحاضِرينَ يَبْتَسِمونَ; **to ~ the alarm** دَقَّ جَرَسَ الإنْذارِ **6** (to collect) جَمَعَ (a; جَمْع) ‹*money, funds*›; **the money ~d from the concert** المال الّذي جُمِعَ من الحَفْلِ الغِنائيِّ **7** (fml) (to collect) حَصَّلَ (u; حُصول على) ‹*a loan, capital*› **8** (to form) شَكَّلَ ,كَوَّنَ ‹*a team*› **9** (to bring up) نَشَّأَ ,رَبّى ‹*a child, family*›; **I was ~d a Muslim/Catholic** نَشَأْتُ كَمُسْلِمٍ \ كَكاثوليكيٍّ **10** (to breed) رَبّى ‹*livestock*› **11** (to erect) بَنى (i; بُنْيان ,بِناء) ‹*a monument, statue*›; **to ~ a ceiling** علّى سَقْفاً **12** (to resurrect) **to ~ sb from the dead** بَعَثَ شَخْصاً بعد مَوْتِهِ **13** (to end) رَفَعَ (a; رَفْع), أَنْهى ‹*an embargo, a siege*› **14** (Math) **to ~ a number to the power of three/four** رَفَعَ رَقْماً إلى أُسِّ ثَلاثةٍ \ أَرْبَعةٍ

B *n* (AmE) (pay increase) زِيادة (في المُرَتَّبِ)

raised /reɪzd/ *adj* **1** ‹*platform, area*› مُرْتَفِع **2** ‹*voice, pressure*› مُرْتَفِع ,عالٍ

raisin /ˈreɪz(ə)n/ *n* زَبيب (n coll)

Rajab /ˈradʒab/ *n* رَجَب

rake /reɪk/ **A** *n* شَوْكة حَديقةٍ ,مِدَمّة **B** *vt* جَمَعَ ,كَنَسَ (بالمِدَمّةِ) ‹*the hay, leaves*›

(Phrasal verbs) **rake in** (infml): **~ in [sth]** جَنى قَدْراً كَبيراً من [شَيْءٍ] ‹*the money, profits*›; **he's raking it in!** يَجْني أَمْوالاً طائِلةً!

• **rake up**: **~ up [sth]**, **~ [sth] up** جَمَعَ [شَيْئاً] بالمِدَمّةِ ‹*the leaves, grass cuttings*›

rakish /ˈreɪkɪʃ/ *adj* (jaunty) ‹*charm, air*› مُثير

rally /ˈrali/ **A** *vt* (**rallies**, **rallying**, **rallied**) **1** حَشَدَ (i-u; حَشْد) ‹*support, his supporters*› **2** أَعادَ الحَشْدَ ‹*the troops, forces*›

B *vi* **1** (to assemble) «workers, protesters» اِحْتَشَدَ ,تَجَمَّعَ **2** (to unite) «friends, supporters» اِتَّحَدَ **3** (to improve) «patients» تَعافى **4** (to recover) «currencies, markets» اِنْتَعَشَ

C *n* (*pl* **rallies**) **1** (of supporters) اِجْتِماع حاشِد ,تَجَمُّع; (of protesters) مُظاهَرة **2** (race) رالي ,سِباق سَيّاراتٍ **3** (in racket sports) [تَبادُل ضَرْبِ الكُرةِ بالمِضْرَبِ لِفَتْرةٍ طَويلةٍ] **4** (recovery) اِنْتِعاش (اِنْتِعاشات)

(Phrasal verb) **rally round**, **rally around** «friends, neighbours» تَكاتَفَ; **everyone rallied round to help** تَكاتَفَ الجَميعُ لِتَقْديمِ يَدِ العَوْنِ

rallying cry /ˈraliɪŋ ˌkrʌɪ/ *n* صَيْحة اسْتِنْفارٍ ,(صَرْخة) نِداء

ram /ram/ **A** *n* **1** (male sheep) خَروف (أَكْباش ,كِباش) ,كَبْش **2** (implement) مِدَكّ (مِدَكّات) ,(خِرْفان ,خِراف)

B *vt* (**-mm-**) **1** (to crash into) صَدَمَ (بِقوّةٍ) ‹*a car, boat*› **2** (to thrust) حَشَرَ ,دَفَعَ (بِقوّةٍ) ‹*one's fist, clothes*›; **he ~med his fist through the door** دَحَمَ قَبْضَتَهُ عَبْرَ البابِ; **she ~med some clothes into a case** حَشَرَتْ بَعْضَ الثِيابِ في حَقيبةٍ; **to ~ home the point/message** أَكَّدَ وُجْهةَ النَظَرِ \ الرِسالةَ

C *vi* **to ~ into sth** اِصْطَدَمَ بِشَيْءٍ بِقوّةٍ

RAM /ram/ *n* (Comput) = **random access memory** ذاكِرة رام ,الوُصولِ العَشْوائيِّ

Ramadan /ˈramədan, ˌraməˈdan, raməˈdɑːn/ *n* رَمَضان (dipt)

Ramallah /rəˈmalə/ *pr n* رام الله (f)

ramble /ˈramb(ə)l/ **A** *vi* **1** (to walk) «ramblers, holidaymakers» تَجَوَّلَ ,تَنَزَّهَ **2** (in speech, writing) «speakers, writers» تَحَدَّثَ بِدونِ تَفْكيرٍ \ تَرْكيزٍ

B *n* نُزْهة ريفيّة

(Phrasal verb) **ramble on** «speakers, writers» اسْتَرْسَلَ أَكْثَر من اللازِم

rambler /ˈramblə/ *n* [هاوي التَنَزُّهِ في الريفِ]

rambling /ˈramblɪŋ/ *adj* **1** ‹*house, building*› [ذو غُرَفٍ وَدَهاليزَ مُتَفَرِّقةٍ] **2** ‹*speech, story*› [مُسْتَرْسِل [يَتَّسِم بالإطالةِ والإعادةِ

ramification /ˌramɪfɪˈkeɪʃ(ə)n/ *n* عاقِبة (عَواقِبُ), تَداعٍ (تَداعِيات)

ramp /ramp/ *n* **1** (slope) مُنْحَدَر (مُنْحَدَرات); **the hall has a ~ for wheelchair access** يوجَدُ أمامَ القاعةِ رَصيفٌ مُنْحَدِرٌ يُسَهِّلُ دُخولَ الكَراسي المُتَحَرِّكةِ **2** (to a plane) سُلَّم نَقّال **3** (BrE) (in a road) مَطَبّ (صِناعِيّ) **4** (AmE) (access or exit road) مَمَرّ \ رَصيف مُنْحَدِر; **an entrance/exit ~** مُنْحَدَر الدُخول \ الخُروج

rampage /ˈrampeɪdʒ/ *n*; **to be/go on the ~** كانَ في حالةٍ \ انْتابَتْهُ حالةٌ من الهَياجِ

rampant /ˈramp(ə)nt/ *adj* ‹*corruption, disease*› مُتَفَشٍّ, مُسْتَشْرٍ, مُنْتَشِر

rampart /ˈrampɑːt/ *n* (wall) سور (أَسْوار); (bank) مِتْراس (مَتاريسُ)

ram raid *n* (BrE) [السَطْو على مَحَلٍّ تِجاريٍّ عن طَريقِ تَحْطيمِ واجِهَتِهِ الزُجاجِيّةِ]

ramshackle /ˈramʃak(ə)l/ *adj* ‹*house, hut*› آيِل للسُقوطِ

ran /ran/ *past tense* ▸ **run**

ranch /rɑːntʃ/ *n* مَزْرَعة (مَزارِعُ)

rancher /ˈrɑːntʃə/ *n* صاحِب مَزْرَعةٍ

rancid /ˈransɪd/ *adj* ‹*butter, smell*› زَنِخ, عَفِن, مُنْتِن

rancour (BrE), **rancor** (AmE) /ˈraŋkə/ *n* حِقْد (أَحْقاد, حُقود), ضَغينة (ضَغائِنُ), غِلّ

rand /rand/ *n* (*pl* **rand**) راند (عُمْلة جُمْهورِيّة جَنوبِ إفْريقِيا)

random /ˈrandəm/ *adj* **1** ‹*sample, number*› عَشْوائِيّ **2** **at ~** (as adv) عَشْوائِيًّا, جُزافاً

randomize, -ise (BrE) /ˈrandəmʌɪz/ *vt* ‹*trials, patients*› رَتَّبَ \ اخْتارَ عَشْوائِيًّا

randomly /ˈrandəmli/ *adv* ‹*to select*› عَشْوائِيًّا, جُزافاً

rang /raŋ/ *past tense* ▸ **ring**

range /reɪndʒ/ **A** *n* **1** (of options, activities, colours, etc) نِطاق (نُطُق); **a wide age ~** شَريحة عُمْرِيّة واسِعة; **there is a wide ~ of options/prices** هُناكَ مَجْموعةٌ مُتَنَوِّعةٌ من الخِياراتِ \ الأَسْعارِ; **they come in a wide ~ of colours** هِيَ مُتاحةٌ في تَشْكيلةٍ كَبيرةٍ من الأَلْوانِ; **what is your price ~?** ما حُدودُ سِعْرِكَ؟ **2** (of prices, products) مَجْموعة (مَجاميعُ, مَجْموعات); **the latest model in the ~** أَحْدَث طِرازٍ في المَجْموعةِ **3** (of vision, hearing) نِطاق (نُطُق), مَجال (مَجالات), مَدًى; **to be within hearing ~** كانَ داخِلَ نِطاقِ السَمْعِ **4** (of a gun, radar) مَدًى, مَسافة; **to be in/out of ~** كانَ داخِلَ \ خارِجَ المَدى; **to shoot sb at close ~** أَطْلَقَ النارَ على شَخْصٍ من مَسافةٍ قَريبةٍ **5** (of operation) مَدًى, مَسافة; **the aircraft has a ~ of 4,000 miles** يَصِلُ مَدى الطائِرةِ إلى 4000 ميلاً **6** (AmE) (prairie) مَرْعًى (مَراعٍ), مَرْج (مُروج) **7** (of mountains) سِلْسِلة جِبالٍ; **the Atlas R~** سِلْسِلة جِبالِ الأَطْلَسِ **8** (firing area) مَيْدان الرَمْيِ \ الرِمايةِ **9** (of voice) طَبَقات; (of instrument) مَجال صَوْتِيّ

B *vt* (to draw up) صَفَّ (u; صَفّ) ‹*the forces, troops*›; **riot police were ~d in front of the parliament building** اصْطَفَّتْ شُرْطةُ مُكافَحةِ الشَغَبِ أمامَ مَبْنى البَرْلَمان

C *vi* **1** (to vary) «increases, ages, price» تَراوَحَ; **the students' ages ~ between 16 and 30** تَتَراوَحُ أَعْمارُ الطُلّابِ بين 16 و 30 عاماً **2** (to cover) **to ~ over sth** «topics, issues, problems» تَناوَلَ \ غَطّى شَيْئاً; **his speech ~d over a variety of issues** تَناوَلَ حَديثُهُ مَجْموعةً مُتَنَوِّعةً من القَضايا **3** (to roam) «travellers, animals» تَجَوَّلَ

ranger /ˈreɪndʒə/ *n* حارِس (في حَديقةٍ أو غابةٍ)

rank /raŋk/ **A** *n* **1** (status in the military, police) رُتْبة (رُتَب); (in an organization) مَنْصِب (مَناصِبُ); (in society) طَبَقة, دَرَجة, مَنْزِلة (مَنازِلُ), مَرْكَز (مَراكِزُ); **to pull ~** اسْتَغَلَّ عِلاقاتِهِ **2** (row of soldiers, objects) صَفّ (صُفوف); **to break ~s** «soldiers» خَرَجَ من الصَفِّ; «politicians» خَرَجَ عن الخَطِّ \ الالْتِزام; **to close ~s** «soldiers» وَقَفَ في صَفٍّ مُتَلاصِقٍ; «politicians» اتَّحَدَ **3** (for taxis) مَوْقِف (مَواقِفُ)

B (**ranks**) *n pl* **1** (members) صُفوف **2** (soldiers) جُنود, أَفْراد; **to rise through the ~s** تَرَقّى في الرُتَبِ

C *adj* **1** (absolute) ‹*outsider, amateur*› تَماماً; ‹*hypocrisy, stupidity*› تامّ **2** (foul) ‹*odour*› كَريه الرائِحةِ ,مُنْتِن **3** (profuse) ‹*grass, weeds*› كَثيف

D *vt* **1** (to classify) صَنَّفَ ‹*a player, country*› **2** (AmE) (to outrank) تفوَّقَ \ تقدَّمَ في المَرْتَبةِ على ‹*a colleague*›

E *vi* «players, countries» جاءَ في المَرْتَبةِ; **they ~ed 23rd out of 142 countries** جاؤوا في المَرْتَبةِ الثالِثةِ والعِشْرينَ من بَيْنِ 142 دَوْلةً; **a general ~s above a colonel** رُتْبةُ الجِنرال أَعْلى من العَقيدِ; **this has to ~ as one of the worst films I've ever seen** هذا يُعَدُّ من أَسْوَأ الأَفْلامِ الّتي رَأَيْتُها في حَياتي

rank and file *n* (**the rank and file**) المُوَظَّفونَ العاديّونَ

ranking /ˈraŋkɪŋ/ *n* مَرْتَبة ,تَصْنيف ,تَرْتيب (مَراتِبُ)

rankle /ˈraŋk(ə)l/ *vi* «defeat, comment» تَرَكَ ,حَزَّ في النَّفْسِ شُعوراً بالمَرارةِ

ransack /ˈransak/ *vt* **1** (to plunder) نَهَبَ (a-u; نَهْب) ‹*a house, building*› **2** (to search) فَتَّشَ (وَبَعْثَرَ المُحْتَوياتِ) ‹*drawers, cupboards*›

ransom /ˈransəm/ *n* فِدْية (فِدْيات)

(Idiom) **to hold sb to ransom** (BrE) ابْتَزَّ شَخْصاً

rant /rant/ *vi* «politicians, preachers» جَعْجَعَ (i; جَعْجَعة), تَحَدَّثَ بِعُنْفٍ

rap /rap/ **A** *vt* (**-pp-**) طَرَقَ (u; طَرْق) ,قَرَعَ (a; قَرْع) ,نَقَرَ (u; نَقْر) ‹*a table, door*›

B *vi* طَرَقَ (u; طَرْق) ,ضَرَبَ (i; ضَرْب)

C *n* **1** (tap) دَقّة ,خَبْطة ,طَرْقة (طَرَقات) **2** [u] (also **rap music**) موسيقى الراب **3** (AmE infml) (treatment) **to get a bad/bum ~** انْتُقِدَ بِقَسْوةٍ

(Idiom) **to take the rap for sth** (infml) تَحَمَّلَ خَطأً لم يَرْتَكِبْهُ

rape /reɪp/ **A** *n* **1** (crime) اغْتِصاب (اغْتِصابات) **2** [u] (plant) سَلْجَم

B *vt* اغْتَصَبَ ‹*a woman, man*›

rapid /ˈrapɪd/ *adj* ‹*growth, change*› سَريع (سِراع)

rapidly /ˈrapɪdli/ *adv* ‹*to grow, change*› بِسُرْعةٍ

rapids /ˈrapɪdz/ *n pl* مُنْحَدَر (في نَهْرٍ)

rapist /ˈreɪpɪst/ *n* مُغْتَصِب

rapper /ˈrapə/ *n* فَنّان الراب

rapport /raˈpɔː/ *n* اتِّصال وَثيق ,أُلْفة ,وِئام

rapprochement /raˈprɒʃmɒ̃, raˈprəʊʃmɒ̃/ *n* تَقارُب (تَقارُبات), إقامة عَلاقاتٍ وِدّيّةٍ

rapt /rapt/ *adj* ‹*audience*› مُنْهمِك ,مَشْدود الانْتِباهِ ,مُسْتَغْرِق; ‹*attention*› مَشْدود

rapture /ˈraptʃə/ *n* طَرَب ,نَشْوة (أَطْراب); **to go into ~s over sth** كادَ يَطيرُ فَرَحاً بِشَيْءٍ

rapturous /ˈraptʃ(ə)rəs/ *adj* ‹*applause*› مُتَحَمِّس ,حَماسيّ; ‹*reception*› حافِل

rare /rɛː/ *adj* (**rarer, rarest**) **1** (uncommon) ‹*species, book, occasion, opportunity*› نادِر **2** ‹*steak*› غَيْر ناضِجٍ

rarely /ˈrɛːli/ *adv* ‹*to see, have*› نادِراً

raring /ˈrɛːrɪŋ/ *adj* **to be ~ to go** كانَ مُتَشَوِّقاً \ تَوّاقاً للذَهابِ

rarity /ˈrɛːrɪti/ *n* (*pl* **rarities**) **1** (rare thing, occurrence) شَيْء نادِر; **to be a ~** كانَ شَيْئاً نادِراً **2** [u] (rareness) قِلّة ,نُدْرة

rascal /ˈrɑːsk(ə)l/ *n* شَخْص مُشاغِب

rash /raʃ/ **A** *n* طَفْح جِلْديّ

B *adj* ‹*decision, behaviour*› مُتَهَوِّر ,طائِش ,مُتَسَرِّع

rasher /ˈraʃə/ *n* شَريحة (من لَحْمِ الخِنْزيرِ)

rashly /ˈraʃli/ *adv* ‹*to promise, assume*› بدونِ تَرَوٍّ ,بِتَسَرُّعٍ

rasp /rɑːsp/ **A** *n* **1** (sound) صَوْت خَشِن \ أَجَشّ **2** (for wood, metal) مِبْرَد (مَبارِدُ) ,مِقْشَط (مَقاشِطُ)

B *vt* (to say hoarsely) قالَ بِصَوْتٍ خَشِنٍ

raspberry /ˈrɑːzb(ə)ri/ *n* (*pl* **raspberries**) توت العُلَّيْق

rasping /ˈrɑːspɪŋ/ *adj* ‹*voice, sound*› خَشِن (خِشان) ,غَليظ (غِلاظ)

Rastafarian /rastəˈfɛːriən/ *n, adj* راسْتافاريّ

rat /rat/ *n* **1** (animal) جُرَذ (جِرْذان ,جُرْذان) ,فَأْر (n coll; فِئْران) **2** (infml) (despicable person) خائِن (خَوَنة)

rate /reɪt/ **A** *n* **1** (speed) مُعَدَّل (مُعَدَّلات); **his ~ of improvement has increased/decreased** ارْتَفَعَ \ انْخَفَضَ مُعَدَّلُ تَحَسُّنِهِ; **they are being produced at a ~ of 5 a month** يَتِمُّ انْتاجُها بِمُعَدَّلِ 5 قِطَعٍ في الشَهْرِ; **the ~ at which children learn** المُعَدَّل الّذي يَتَعَلَّمُ بِهِ الأَطْفالُ **2** (ratio) مُعَدَّل (مُعَدَّلات) ,نِسْبة (نِسَب); **the ~ of growth/inflation has fallen/risen** ارْتَفَعَ \ انْخَفَضَ

(كُلَف؛ كُلْفة ,(أَسْعار) سِعْر (charge) **3** مُعَدَّلُ النموِّ \ التضخُّمِ **advertising ~s** أَسْعار الإعْلاناتِ؛ **his hourly ~ is £30** أَجْرُهُ في الساعةِ 30 جُنَيْهاً **4** (in foreign exchange) سِعْرُ الصَّرْفِ

B (**rates**) *n pl* (BrE) **1** (also **business rates**) (local tax) ضَريبة مَحَلّيّة **2** (**the rates**) (local personal tax) الضَريبة العَقاريّة

C *vt* **1** (to classify) صَنَّفَ ,قَيَّمَ؛ **I ~ his work very highly** أُثَمِّنُ عَمَلَهُ بِدَرَجةٍ كَبيرةٍ؛ **~ its quality on a scale of 1 to 10** قَيِّمْ جَوْدَتَهُ على مِقْياسٍ من 1 إلى 10؛ **he is ~d number two in the world** هو مُصَنَّفٌ في المَرْتَبةِ الثانيةِ عالَمِيًّا **2** (to qualify for) **this hotel ~s three stars** هذا الفُنْدُقُ يَسْتَحِقُّ ثَلاثةَ نُجومٍ

D *vi* (to rank) وَقَعَ في مَرْتَبةٍ؛ **that doesn't ~ high on my priority list** لا يَحْتَلُّ ذلك أَهَمِّيّةً كَبيرةً في قائِمةِ أَوْلَويّاتي؛ **she ~s among the top ten tennis players** تُعَدُّ من ضِمْنِ أَفْضَلِ عَشَرِ لاعِباتِ تِنِس

Idiom **at any rate** مَهْما حَدَثَ

ratepayer /'reɪtpeɪə/ *n* (BrE) دافِعُ ضَرائِبَ

rather /'rɑːðə/ *adv* **1** (preferably) مُفَضَّلاً؛ **which would you ~ have?** ماذا تُفَضِّلُ ؟؛ **I'd ~ not go** أُفَضِّلُ عَدَمَ الذَهابِ؛ **~ you than me!** [من حُسْنِ حَظّي أنّي لَسْتُ مُضْطَرًّا للقِيامِ بِعَمَلِكَ] **2** (somewhat) نَوْعاً ما ,إلى حَدٍّ ما ,بَعْضَ الشَيْءِ؛ **it's ~ like an apple** إنَّهُ يُشْبِهُ تُفّاحةً إلى حَدٍّ ما **3** (quite) إلى حَدٍّ كَبيرٍ؛ **I ~ like him** يُعْجِبُني إلى حَدٍّ كَبيرٍ؛ **it's ~ a long way** المَسافةُ بَعيدةٌ جِدًّا **4** (more exactly) على الأَصَحِّ ,بالأَحْرى؛ **or ~** وَبالأَحْرى؛ **let's have actions ~ than words** عَلَيْنا بالأَفْعالِ بَدَلاً من الأَقْوالِ

ratification /ratɪfɪ'keɪʃ(ə)n/ *n* تَصْديق ,إقْرار ,إبْرام

ratify /'ratɪfʌɪ/ *vt* (**ratifies, ratifying, ratified**) صَدَّقَ (على), صادَقَ (على) ‹a treaty, an agreement›

rating /'reɪtɪŋ/ *n* **1** (of quality, performance) تَصْنيف ,دَرَجة؛ **an A ~ for energy efficiency** دَرَجة 'أ' لِمُسْتَوى كَفاءةِ الطاقةِ **2** (**ratings** *n pl*) (of programmes) نِسْبةُ المُشاهَدةِ؛ **the show's ~ fell/rose** هَبَطَتْ \ ارْتَفَعَتْ نِسْبةُ مُشاهَدةِ البَرْنامَجِ

ratio /'reɪʃɪəʊ/ *n* (*pl* **ratios**) نِسْبة (نِسَب)؛ **in a ~ of two to one** بِنِسْبةِ اثْنَيْنِ إلى واحِدٍ؛ **the pupil-teacher ~** نِسْبةُ التَلاميذِ إلى الأَساتِذةِ

ration /'raʃ(ə)n/ **A** *n* **1** (allowance) حِصّة (حِصَص) ,جِراية **2** (**rations** *n pl*) جِرايات ,مُؤَن

B *vt* وَزَّعَ بِكَمِّيّاتٍ مُحَدَّدةٍ ‹food, water›

rational /'raʃ(ə)n(ə)l/ *adj* **1** (sensible, logical) ‹thought, decision› مَنْطِقيّ **2** (sane) ‹person› مَنْطِقيّ ,عَقْلانيّ **3** (able to reason) ‹being› عاقِل (عُقَلاءُ ,عاقِلونَ)

rationale /ˌraʃə'nɑːl/ *n* أَسْباب جَوْهَريّة ,أَساس مَنْطِقيّ

rationality /raʃə'nalətɪ/ *n* تَفْكير مَنْطِقيّ ,عَقْلانيّة

rationalize, -ise (BrE) /'raʃ(ə)nəlʌɪz/ *vt* **1** (to justify) بَرَّرَ, سَوَّغَ ,عَلَّلَ ‹actions, decisions› **2** (to streamline) رَشَّدَ ,نَظَّمَ ‹production, an industry›

rationally /'raʃ(ə)n(ə)lɪ/ *adv* ‹to think, act› بِشَكْلٍ ,بِعَقْلانيّةٍ مَنْطِقيٍّ

rationing /'raʃnɪŋ/ *n* تَوْزيع بالحِصّةِ ,تَقْنين

rat poison *n* سَمّ فِئْرانٍ

rat race *n* (**the rat race**) سِباق الفِئْرانِ (التَنافُس من أَجْلِ التَرَقّي الاجْتِماعيِّ)

rat run *n* طَريق جانِبيّ (يُسْتَخْدَمُ للهُروبِ من الزِحامِ)

rattle /'rat(ə)l/ **A** *vt* **1** (to shake) خَشْخَشَ (خَشْخَشة ;i), جَلْجَلَ (جَلْجَلة ;i) ‹chains, crockery›؛ صَرَّ (صَرير ,صَرّ ;i), هَزَّ (هَزّ ;u) ‹a window, door› **2** (infml) (to disconcert) ضايَقَ ,أَزْعَجَ ‹a person›

B *vi* «chains, crockery» خَشْخَشَ (خَشْخَشة ;i), جَلْجَلَ (جَلْجَلة ;i)؛ «windows, doors» صَرَّ (صَرير ,صَرّ ;i), اهْتَزَّ؛ **a train ~d past** مَرَّ القِطارُ بِسُرْعةٍ فائِقةٍ

C *n* **1** (noise of chains, crockery) جَلْجَلة ,خَشْخَشة؛ (of wheels, a train) احْتِكاك (احْتِكاكات) ,صَرير؛ (of a window, door) اهْتِزاز (اهْتِزازات)؛ (of gunfire) قَعْقَعة (قَراقِعُ ,قَرْقَعات) ,قَرْقَعة ,دَويّ **2** (baby's toy) شُخْشيخة (شَخاشِخُ) **3** (BrE) (of a sports fan) شُخْشيخة (شَخاشِخُ) **4** (rattlesnake's tail) جَرَس جُلْجُل (أَجْراس)

Phrasal verb **rattle off**: **~ [sth] off, ~ off [sth]** سَرَدَ \ تَلا [شَيْئاً] بِسُرْعةٍ ‹a list, names›

rattlesnake /'ratəlsneɪk/ *n* أَفْعى جَرَسيّة ,أَفْعى الجَلْجَلةِ

raucous /'rɔːkəs/ *adj* **1** (strident) ‹laughter, cheers› صاخِب **2** (loud and boisterous) ‹crowd, behaviour› صاخِب

raunchy /ˈrɔːntʃi/ *adj* (**raunchier, raunchiest**) (infml) ‹*scene, humour*› يَتَضَمَّنُ تَلْميحاتٍ جِنسيّةً

ravage /ˈravɪdʒ/ *vt* دَمَّرَ, خَرَّبَ ‹*a country, an area*›

ravages /ˈravɪdʒɪz/ *n pl* خراب (أَخْرِبة)

rave /reɪv/ **A** *vi* **1** (incoherently) «drunkards, mad people» هَذى (i; هَذيان, هَذْي) **2** (angrily) «protesters, speakers» تَحَدَّثَ بغَضَبٍ **3** (enthusiastically) «critics, fans» أَفْرَطَ في المَديح

B *adj* (full of praise) شَديد الإِطْراء \ الثناء; **~ reviews** إطراء النُّقّادِ

C *n* (infml) حَفْلة صاخِبة

raven /ˈreɪv(ə)n/ *n* غُراب أَسْوَد, غُداف (غِدْفان)

ravenous /ˈrav(ə)nəs/ *adj* ‹*appetite, wolf*› شَديد الجوع; **to be ~** كانَ جائعاً جِدًّا

ravine /rəˈviːn/ *n* [وادٍ ضَيِّق عَميق]

raving /ˈreɪvɪŋ/ **A** *n* هَذَيان

B *adj* (infml) (as intensifier) **1** يَهْذي; **a ~ lunatic** مَجْنون يَهْذي **2** *as adv* **he's stark ~ mad** هو مَجْنونٌ تَماماً

ravioli /ˌravɪˈəʊli/ *n* رافيولي (فَطيرة مَحْشوّة)

ravish /ˈravɪʃ/ *vt* (old use) (to rape) اغْتَصَبَ ‹*a woman, girl*›

ravishing /ˈravɪʃɪŋ/ *adj* ‹*beauty, melody*› فاتِن (فَواتِنُ), أَخّاذ, ساحِر

raw /rɔː/ *adj* **1** (uncooked) ‹*meat*› نيء; ‹*vegetables*› غَيْر مَطْبوخٍ **2** (unrefined) ‹*sugar, cotton*› خام (mf) **3** (unstructured) ‹*data*› خام, أَوَّليّ (mf) **4** (unpurified) ‹*sewage*› خام (mf), غَيْر مُعالَج **5** (strong) ‹*emotion, energy*› شَديد **6** (sore) ‹*skin, patch*› مُلْتَهِب **7** (inexperienced) ‹*recruit, reporter*› عَديم الخِبْرة

raw material *n* مادّة خام \ أَوَّلِيّة

ray /reɪ/ *n* **1** (beam) شُعاع (n coll; أَشِعّة); **a ~ of hope** بَصيص من الأَمَل **2** (fish) (سَمَك) شِفْنين, راي

rayon /ˈreɪɒn/ *n* حَرير صِناعيّ, رايون

raze /reɪz/ *vt* **to ~ a building/village to the ground** سَوّى مَبْنًى \ قَرْيةً بالأَرْض

razor /ˈreɪzə/ *n* موسى (الحِلاقةِ)

razor blade *n* شَفْرة موسى (الحِلاقة)

razzmatazz /razməˈtaz/ *n* (infml) صَخَب

Rd *abbr* = **road** شارِع (شَوارِعُ)

re¹ /reɪ/ *n* ري (النوتة الثانِية في السُّلَّمِ الموسيقيِّ)

re² /riː, reɪ/ *prep* = **with reference to** بِشَأْنِ, بِخُصوصِ, بالنِسْبةِ \ بالإشارة إلى

RE /ɑːrˈiː/ *n* = **Religious Education** التَعْليم الدينيّ

reach /riːtʃ/ **A** *vt* **1** (with hands) وَصَلَ (i; وُصول; إلى) ‹*a shelf, switch*› **2** (to arrive at) وَصَلَ (i; وُصول; إلى) ‹*a place, one's destination*›; **the letter never ~ed her** لم يَصِلْ إلَيْها الخِطابُ أَبداً; **it's easily ~ed by bus** يُمْكِنُ الوُصولُ إلَيْهِ بِسُهولةٍ بالحافِلةِ **3** (to attain) وَصَلَ (i; وُصول; إلى), بَلَغَ (u; بُلوغ) ‹*a level, goal, an age*›; **to ~ retirement age/the age of 40** وَصَلَ إلى سِنِّ التَقاعُدِ \ ال 40; **to ~ the finals** وَصَلَ إلى النِهائيّاتِ; **we want to ~ a wider audience** نُريدُ الوُصولَ إلى جُمْهورٍ أَوْسَعَ **4** (to come to) تَوَصَّلَ (إلى) ‹*an agreement, a conclusion*› **5** (to extend to) وَصَلَ (i; وُصول; إلى) ‹*the floor, ceiling*› **6** (to contact) اتَّصَلَ (ب) ‹*a person*›

B *vi* **1** (to stretch far enough) وَصَلَ (i; وُصول) **2** (with one's arm) **to ~ up/down** مَدَّ يَدَهُ لِأَعْلى \ لِأَسْفَلَ; **she ~ed over and turned it off** مَدَّتْ ذِراعَها نَحْوَهُ وَأَغْلَقَتْهُ; **he ~ed for her hand** مَدَّ يَدَهُ لِيُمْسِكَ يَدَها **3** (to extend to) وَصَلَ (i; وُصول), امْتَدَّ; **the water ~ed up to our knees** وَصَلَ الماءُ إلى رُكَبِنا

C *n* **1** (of one's arm) مُتَناوَل; **within arm's ~** في مُتَناوَلِ اليَدِ; **it's within easy ~ of the town centre** هو على مَقْرُبةٍ من وَسَطِ المَدينةِ; **out of ~** بَعيد, لا يُمْكِنُ الوُصولُ إلَيْهِ; **a house like that is out of our ~** بَيْتٌ كَهذا بَعيدُ المَنالِ عَلَيْنا; **beyond the ~ of ...** بَعيد عن مُتَناوَلِ ... **2** (influence) امْتِداد (امْتِدادات), انْتِشار

D (**reaches**) *n pl* (of a river) امْتِداد, لِسان (أَلْسِنة, أَلْسُن); **the upper/lower ~es of the river** امْتِداد النَهْرِ عند المَنْبَعِ \ المَصَبِّ

(Phrasal verb) **reach out** **A** **1** (to extend one's arm) مَدَّ ذِراعَهُ **2** (to seek) **to ~ out for help** طَلَبَ العَوْنَ \ المُساعَدةَ **3** **to ~ out to sb** (to help) مَدَّ يَدَ العَوْنِ لِشَخْصٍ; (to make contact) تَواصَلَ مع شَخْصٍ **B** **~ [sth] out, ~ out [sth]** مَدَّ \ بَسَطَ [شَيْئاً] ‹*one's hand, arm*›

react /rɪ'akt/ *vi* 1 (to respond) رَدَّ, اسْتَجابَ, أَبْدى رَدَّ فِعْلٍ (u; رَدّ) 2 (chemically) تَفاعَلَ

reaction /rɪ'akʃ(ə)n/ *n* 1 (response) رَدّ فِعْلٍ 2 (in chemistry) تَفاعُل (تَفاعُلات); **to suffer an adverse ~ to the drug** عانى من تَأْثِيرٍ سَلْبِيٍّ لِلدَواءِ

reactionary /rɪ'akʃ(ə)n(ə)ri/ **A** *adj* ‹party, views› رَجْعِيّ **B** *n* (*pl* **reactionaries**) رَجْعِيّ

reactive /rɪ'aktɪv/ *adj* ‹substance, metal› مُتَفاعِل, تَفاعُلِيّ

reactor /rɪ'aktə/ *n* also **nuclear ~** مُفاعِل (مُفاعِلات)

read **A** /riːd/ *vt* (*past tense, past participle* **read** /rɛd/) 1 قَرَأَ (a; قِراءة) ‹a book, an article, music›; **I can ~ Russian** أَسْتَطِيعُ أَنْ أَقْرَأَ الروسيّةَ; **can you ~ his writing?** هل يُمْكِنُكَ أَنْ تَقْرَأَ خَطَّهُ؟ 2 (aloud) قَرَأَ (a; قِراءة), تَلا (u; تِلاوة) ‹a poem, statement›; **to ~ sb sth, to ~ sth to sb** قَرَأَ شَيْئاً لِشَخْصٍ 3 (to say) «headline, sign» قالَ (u; قَوْل); **the card ~s 'Happy Birthday'** تَقولُ البِطاقةُ 'عيد ميلادٍ سَعيد' 4 (to interpret) قَرَأَ (a; قِراءة), فَهِمَ (a; فَهْم), فَسَّرَ ‹the signs, situation›; **to ~ sb's thoughts** *or* **mind** قَرَأَ أَفْكارَ شَخْصٍ; **his restraint was ~ as a sign of weakness** فُسِّرَ ضَبْطُهُ لِنَفْسِهِ على أَنَّهُ ضَعْفٌ; **don't ~ too much into these results** لا تُحَمِّلِ النَتائِجَ من المَعاني أَكْثَرَ مِمّا تَحْتَمِلُ 5 (BrE) (to study) دَرَسَ (u; دَرْس) ‹law, classics› 6 (to inspect) قَرَأَ (a; قِراءة) ‹a meter› 7 (in computing) قَرَأَ (a; قِراءة) ‹data, a disk› 8 (in radio) سَمِعَ (وَفَهِمَ) ‹a person›; **I ~ you loud and clear** أَسْمَعُكَ بِكُلِّ وُضوحٍ

B /riːd/ *vi* (*past tense, past participle* **read** /rɛd/) 1 «person» قَرَأَ (a; قِراءة); **to ~ about sth** قَرَأَ عن شَيْءٍ; **she ~ to him from the Bible** قَرَأَتْ لَهُ من الكِتابِ المُقَدَّسِ; **to ~ aloud** قَرَأَ بِصَوْتٍ عالٍ 2 (to say) **the sentence should ~ as follows** من المُفْتَرَضِ أَنْ تَقولَ الجُمْلةُ ما يَلي 3 (to convey an impression) **the document ~s well/awkwardly** تُعْطي الوَثيقةُ انْطِباعاً جَيِّداً \ سَيِّئاً

C /riːd/ *n* قِراءة, مُطالَعة; **the book is a good/an interesting ~** قِراءةُ الكِتابِ مُمْتِعةٌ \ مُشَوِّقةٌ; **I had a quick ~ of it** قَرَأْتُهُ قِراءةً سَريعةً

(Idioms) **to read between the lines** قَرَأَ بين السُطورِ; **to take sth as read** اعْتَبَرَ شَيْئاً أَمْراً مُسَلَّماً بِهِ

(Phrasal verbs) **read back**: **~ [sth] back, ~ back [sth]** راجَعَ [شَيْئاً] ‹a sentence, message›

• **read on** واصَلَ القِراءةَ

• **read out**: **~ [sth] out, ~ out [sth]** قَرَأَ [شَيْئاً] بِصَوْتٍ مُرْتَفِعٍ ‹a statement, names›

• **read over**: **~ over [sth], ~ [sth] over** 1 (to reread) راجَعَ [شَيْئاً] ‹one's notes, a speech› 2 (for the first time) قَرَأَ [شَيْئاً] كُلَّهُ ‹a book, letter›

• **read through**: **~ through [sth], ~ [sth] through** قَرَأَ [شَيْئاً] كُلَّهُ ‹a book, list›

• **read up**: **to ~ up on sth/sb** قَرَأَ عن شَيْءٍ \ شَخْصٍ

readable /'riːdəb(ə)l/ *adj* 1 (legible) ‹text, handwriting› مَقْروء, واضِح 2 (enjoyable) ‹article, essay› مُمْتِع, سَهْل القِراءةِ

reader /'riːdə/ *n* 1 (person who reads) قارِئ (قُرّاء, قارِئونَ) 2 (book) [كِتاب لِتَعْليمِ القِراءةِ]

readership /'riːdəʃɪp/ *n* جُمْهور القُرّاءِ

readily /'rɛdɪli/ *adv* 1 (willingly) ‹to respond, accept› عن طيبِ خاطِرٍ \ نَفْسٍ, بدونِ تَرَدُّدٍ 2 (easily) ‹accessible, available› بِسُهولةٍ

readiness /'rɛdinəs/ *n* 1 (preparedness) اسْتِعْداد (اسْتِعْدادات), تَأَهُّب; **to be in a state of ~** كانَ في حالةِ تَأَهُّبٍ 2 (willingness) رَغْبة (رَغَبات)

reading /'riːdɪŋ/ *n* 1 (ability) القِراءة; **~ and writing** القِراءة والكِتابة 2 (books) قِراءة; **these books are required ~ for the course** قِراءةُ هذه الكُتُبِ من مُتَطَلَّباتِ الدَوْرةِ; **her novels make light/heavy ~** رِواياتُها خَفيفةٌ \ ثَقيلةٌ في القِراءةِ; **a woman of wide ~** امْرَأة واسِعة الاطِّلاعِ 3 (on instruments) قِراءة; **to take a ~** أَخَذَ القِراءةَ; **the gas ~** قِراءة الغازِ 4 (interpretation) قِراءة, فَهْم (أَفْهام), تَفْسير (تَفاسيرُ); **a literal ~ of the text** قِراءة حَرْفيّة لِلنَصِّ; **my ~ of the situation is that...** قِراءَتي لِلوَضْعِ هي أَنّ ... 5 (extract) نَصّ (نُصوص); **the first ~ is taken from ...** النَصُّ الأَوَّلُ مَأْخوذٌ من ... 6 (of wills, banns) قِراءة; **the ~ of the banns** قِراءة إِعْلانِ الزَواجِ; **the family had gathered for the ~ of the will** اجْتَمَعَت الأُسْرةُ لِقِراءةِ الوَصيّةِ 7 (BrE) (of a bill) مُناقَشة; **the first ~ of the Finance Bill** أَوَّل مُناقَشةٍ لِمَشْروعِ قانونِ الماليّةِ

reading glasses *n* نَظّارة قِراءةٍ

reading group *n* [مَجموعة تَجْتَمِعُ لمُناقَشةِ كِتابٍ ما]

reading list *n* قائِمة للقِراءةِ

readjust /riːəˈdʒʌst/ **A** *vt* **1** أعادَ الضَبْطَ \ التَعْديلَ ‹*an instrument, the gauge*› **2** ضَبَطَ, عَدَّلَ (i-u; ضَبْط) ‹*one's hat, belt*›
B *vi* تَكَيَّفَ, تَأَقْلَمَ

re-advertise /riːˈadvətʌɪz/ *vt* أعادَ الإعْلانَ عن ‹*a post, car*›

ready /ˈrɛdi/ **A** *adj* (**readier**, **readiest**) **1** (prepared) مُسْتَعِدّ, مُتَأَهِّب, جاهِز; **to get ~** تَأَهَّبَ, اسْتَعَدَّ; **to get sth/sb ~** جَهَّزَ شَيْئاً \ شَخْصاً; **to be ~ to go/come** كانَ جاهِزاً للذَهابِ \ للحُضورِ; **the vehicles are kept ~ for use** يَتِمُّ الاحْتِفاظُ بالمَرْكَباتِ جاهِزةً للاسْتِخدامِ; **~, steady, go!** (خُذْ) مَكانَكَ, اسْتَعِدَّ, انْطَلِقْ! **2** (willing) (رَغْبة) راغِب, مُسْتَعِدّ; **to be ~ to help** كانَ مُسْتَعِدًّا للمُساعَدةِ; **she's ~ to admit when she's wrong** هي مُسْتَعِدّةٌ للاعْتِرافِ عِنْدَما تُخْطِئُ **3** (quick) ‹*answer, smile*› حاضِر; **he has a ~ wit** هو حاضِرُ البَديهةِ **4** (available, easy) ‹*supply, market*› مُتاح, جاهِز; **~ cash, ~ money** نُقود جاهِزة
B *n* **to be at the ~** كانَ على أُهْبةِ الاسْتِعْدادِ
C *vt* (*3rd person present sing* **readies**, *present participle* **readying**, *past tense, past participle* **readied**) هَيَّأَ, أَعَدَّ, جَهَّزَ ‹*one's weapons, troops*›
D *v refl* (*3rd person present sing* **readies**, *present participle* **readying**, *past tense, past participle* **readied**) **to ~ oneself for sth/to do sth** جَهَّزَ نَفْسَهُ لشَيْءٍ \ لِفِعْلِ شَيْءٍ

ready-made /rɛdɪˈmeɪd/ *adj* جاهِز

ready meal *n* وَجْبة جاهِزة

ready-to-wear /ˌrɛditəˈwɛː/ *adj* ‹*clothes, suit*› جاهِز للارْتِداءِ

reaffirm /riːəˈfəːm/ *vt* أَكَّدَ ثانيةً \ من جَديدٍ, أعادَ التَأكيدَ ‹*one's intention, determination*›

real /rɪəl/ **A** *n* واقِع
B *adj* **1** (not imaginary) ‹*person, threat*› حَقيقيّ; **the ~ world** العالَم الحَقيقيّ; **in ~ life** في الحَياةِ الحَقيقيّةِ; **in ~ terms, nothing has changed** في الواقِعِ، لم يَتَغَيَّرْ شَيْءٌ; **in ~ terms, inflation has increased by...** من حَيْثُ القيمةِ الحَقيقيّةِ، زادَ التَضَخُّمُ بِنِسْبةِ ... **2** (not artificial) ‹*diamond*› أَصْليّ, حَقيقيّ; ‹*leather*› طَبيعيّ; **the gloves are made of ~ leather** القُفّازاتُ مَصْنوعةٌ من الجِلْدِ الطَبيعيِّ; **the ~ thing, the ~ McCoy** (infml) الشَيْءُ الأَصْليّ \ الحَقيقيّ **3** (true, proper) ‹*reason, friend, name*› حَقيقيّ; **the ~ Africa** إفْريقيا الحَقيقيّة; **it's ages since I had a ~ holiday** لم أَحْصُلْ على إجازةٍ حَقيقيّةٍ منذ أَمَدٍ بَعيدٍ; **Johnson isn't his ~ surname** جونسون لَيْسَ هو اسْمَ عائِلَتِهِ **4** (infml) (for emphasis) ‹*pleasure, surprise*› حَقيقيّ; **it's a ~ shame** هو عارٌ بِحَقٍّ
C *adv* (AmE) (infml) (very) ‹*quick, bad*› فِعْلاً, حَقًّا; **that coffee smells ~ good** رائِحةُ هذه القَهْوةِ طَيِّبةٌ حَقًّا
Idiom **for real** (infml) حَقيقيّ

real estate *n* عَقارات

real estate agent *n* (AmE) سِمْسار عَقاراتٍ, وَكيل عَقاريّ

real-estate broker /ˈrɪələsteɪt ˌbrəʊkə/ *n* (AmE) سِمْسار عَقاراتٍ

realism /ˈrɪəliz(ə)m/ *n* واقِعيّة

realist /ˈriːəlɪst/ *n* شَخْص واقِعيّ

realistic /rɪəˈlɪstɪk/ *adj* ‹*person, attitude, goal*› واقِعيّ

realistically /rɪəˈlɪstɪkli/ *adv* **1** (reasonably) ‹*to expect, afford*› بِشَكْلٍ \ على نَحْوٍ واقِعيٍّ **2** (factually) ‹*to portray, describe*› طِبْقاً للواقِعِ

reality /rɪˈalɪti/ *n* (*pl* **realities**) حَقيقة (حَقائِقُ), واقِع; **in ~** في الواقِعِ

reality TV *n* تِلِفِزْيون الواقِعِ

realization, -isation (BrE) /riːəlʌɪˈzeɪʃ(ə)n/ *n* **1** (of a fact, the truth) إدْراك **2** (of a plan, dream) تَحْقيق

realize, -ise (BrE) /ˈrɪəlʌɪz/ *vt* **1** أَدْرَكَ ‹*a fact, the truth*› **2** حَقَّقَ ‹*an idea, a dream*›; **to ~ one's potential** حَقَّقَ إمْكاناتِهِ

reallocate /riːˈaləkeɪt/ *vt* أعادَ التَخْصيصَ ‹*space, funds*›

really /ˈrɪəli/ **A** *adv* **1** (in actual fact) في الحَقيقةِ, في الواقِعِ, حَقًّا, بالفِعْلِ; **I'll tell you what ~ happened** سَأُخْبِرُكَ بِما حَدَثَ بالفِعْلِ; **he's a good teacher ~** هو مُدَرِّسٌ جَيِّدٌ بالفِعْلِ; **'do you want to go?' — 'not ~'** 'هل تُريدُ الذَهابَ؟' — 'في الحَقيقةِ لا'; **I don't ~ know him that well** في الواقِعِ لا أَعْرِفُهُ بِشَكْلٍ جَيِّدٍ **2** (for emphasis) حَقًّا, فِعْلاً; **they ~ enjoyed the**

film لَقَد اسْتَمْتَعوا حَقًّا بالفيلم; I ~ must be going حَقًّا يَجِبُ عَلَيْكَ حَقًّا أنْ; you ~ ought to see a doctor عَلَيَّ أنْ أذْهَبَ تَرى طَبيباً **3** (infml) (very) ‹*good, important, interesting*› جِدًّا; **the food/weather was ~ good** كانَ الطَعامُ \ الطَقسُ جَيِّدٌ جِدًّا; **the service is ~ bad** الخِدْمةُ سَيِّئةٌ جِدًّا **4** (seriously) حَقًّا, جِدّيًّا; **are you sure you ~ want to do this?** هل أنْتَ مُتَأَكِّدٌ أَنَّكَ تُريدُ جِدّيًّا أنْ تَفْعَلَ هذا؟; **does she ~?** هل هي حَقًّا تَفْعَلُ ذلك؟

B *excl* **1** **~?** (expressing surprise, interest) حَقًّا \ صَحيح \ مَعْقول؟ **2** (also **well really**) (expressing annoyance) حَقًّا; **~! you could have told me!** حَقًّا! كانَ بِوسْعِكَ أنْ تُخْبِرَني !

realm /rɛlm/ *n* **1** (liter) (kingdom) مَمْلَكة (مَمالِكُ) **2** (sphere) **in the ~ of fantasy/speculation** في عالَمِ الخَيال \ التَأَمُّلِ

real time *n* وَقْت حَقيقيّ

realtor® /ˈrɪəltə/, /ˈriːəltə/ *n* (AmE) وَكيل عَقاريّ, سِمْسار عَقاراتٍ

ream /riːm/ *n* (of paper) ماعون (رزمة وَرَق تَتَألَّفُ من 500 وَرَقةٍ)

reamer /ˈriːmə/ *n* **1** (tool) مُوَسِّع ثُقوبٍ **2** (AmE) (for fruit) عَصّارة (فَواكِهَ)

reap /riːp/ *vt* **1** حَصَدَ (i-u; حَصْد, حَصاد), جَنى (i; جَنْي) ‹*corn, a crop*› **2** حَصَدَ (i-u; حَصْد, حَصاد), جَنى (i; جَنْي) ‹*a reward, benefit*›

reappear /riːəˈpɪə/ *vi* عادَ إلى الظُهورِ, ظَهَرَ ثانيةً \ من جَديدٍ

reappearance /riːəˈpɪərəns/ *n* عَوْدة ظُهورٍ, ظُهور مَرّة أُخرى

reapply /riːəˈplʌɪ/ **A** *vi* (**reapplies, reapplying, reapplied**) (for a job, visa) أعادَ تَقْديمَ طَلَبٍ

B *vt* (**reapplies, reapplying, reapplied**) أعادَ الوَضْعَ ‹*a weedkiller, paint*›

reappraise /riːəˈpreɪz/ *vt* أعادَ التَقْييمَ ‹*a decision, rule*›

rear /rɪə/ **A** *n* **1** (of a building, car, room) مُؤَخَّرة **2** (infml) (buttocks) مُؤَخَّرة, عَجُز (أَعْجاز), دُبُر (أَدْبار)

B *adj* ‹*door, wheel, garden*› خَلْفيّ

C *vt* ‹*poultry, a family*› رَبّى

D *vi* also **~ up** «horses» شَبَّ (شِباب, شَبيب)

rearguard /ˈrɪəgɑːd/ *n* مُؤَخَّرة الجَيْشِ, حَرَس المُؤَخَّرةِ, ساقة

rearm /riːˈɑːm/ **A** *vt* أعادَ التَسْليحَ ‹*forces, troops*›

B *vi* «country, guerrillas» أعاد التَسَلُّحَ

rearmament /riˈɑːməmənt/ *n* إعادة التَسْليحِ \ التَسَلُّحِ

rearrange /riːəˈreɪndʒ/ *vt* **1** أعادَ التَنْظيمَ ‹*furniture, a room*›; أعادَ التَرْتيبَ ‹*clothes*›; أعادَ التَصْفيفَ ‹*one's hair*› **2** غَيَّرَ الوَقْتَ \ المَوْعِدَ ‹*a meeting, game, an appointment*›

rear-view mirror /ˌrɪəvjuː ˈmɪrə/ *n* مِرْآة الرُؤْيةِ الخَلْفيّةِ, مِرْآة داخِليّة

reason /ˈriːz(ə)n/ **A** *n* **1** (cause) سَبَب (أَسْباب), داعٍ (دَواعٍ), دافِع (دَوافِعُ); **the ~ is that ...** السَبَبُ هو أنّ ...; **what was his ~ for resigning?** ما السَبَبُ الّذي دَفَعَهُ للاسْتِقالةِ؟; **for no good ~, without good ~** بِدونِ \ بلا سَبَبٍ وَجيهٍ; **if, for any ~, you can't come** إذا لم تَسْتَطِعِ الحُضورَ لأيِّ سَبَبٍ من الأَسْبابِ; **if he doesn't do it, I shall want to know the ~ why** إذا لم يَفْعَلْهُ، سَأَحْتاجُ إلى مَعْرِفةِ السَبَبِ; **by ~ of** (fml) بِسَبَبِ **2** [u] (grounds) سَبَب (أَسْباب), مُبَرِّر (مُبَرِّرات), دافِع (دَوافِعُ); **they had good** *or* **every ~ to be worried** لَدَيْهِمْ كُلُّ الحَقِّ في القَلَقِ; **I have ~ to believe that ...** لَدَيَّ أَسْبابي في الاعْتِقادِ بِأنَّ ...; **I had no ~ to doubt him** لم يَكُنْ لَدَيَّ سَبَبٌ للشَكِّ فيهِ; **all the more ~ to insist on it** مِمّا يَزيدُ من أَسْبابِ الإصْرارِ عَلَيْهِ **3** [u] (fml) (common sense) المَنْطِقيّ, المَعْقول; **to listen to** *or* **see ~** اسْتَمَعَ لِصَوْتِ العَقْلِ; **it stands to ~** هو أمْرٌ مَعْقولٌ \ مَنْطِقيٌّ; **within ~** في حُدودِ المَعْقولِ **4** [u] (fml) (faculty) عَقْل (عُقول); **to lose one's ~** فَقَدَ صَوابَهُ

B *vt* (fml) اسْتَنْتَجَ, فَكَّرَ

C *vi* (fml) فَكَّرَ (بِشَكْلٍ مَنْطِقيٍّ); **to ~ with sb** ناقَشَ شَخْصاً

D (**reasoned**) *adj* (fml) ‹*argument, decision*› مَنْطِقيّ

reasonable /ˈriːz(ə)nəb(ə)l/ *adj* **1** (sensible) ‹*person*› عاقِل (عُقَلاءُ, عاقِلونَ), رَشيد (رُشَداءُ); ‹*request*› مَعْقول, مَنْطِقيّ **2** (moderately good) ‹*food, weather*› مَقْبول

reasonably /ˈriːznəbli/ *adv* **1** (sensibly) ‹*to talk, act*› بِعَقْلانيّةٍ, بِشَكْلٍ عَقْلانيٍّ **2** (moderately) ‹*safe, accurate*› على نَحْوٍ مَقْبولٍ, بِدَرَجةٍ مَعْقولةٍ; **it went ~ well** سارَ بِشَكْلٍ مَعْقولٍ

reasoning /ˈriːz(ə)nɪŋ/ *n* تَفْكير (مَنْطِقيّ)

reassemble /riːəˈsɛmb(ə)l/ **A** *vt* **1** (to put together again) أعادَ التَرْكيبَ \ التَجْميعَ ‹*a machine, an engine*› **2** (to bring together again) أعادَ جَمْعَ ‹*pupils*›; أعادَ الانْعِقادَ ‹*the committee*›

B *vi* «team members, troops» اجْتَمَعَ من جَديدٍ

reassert /riːəˈsɜːt/ *vt* أعادَ التَّأْكيد, أَكَّدَ مُجَدَّداً *‹one's authority, a claim›*

reassess /riːəˈses/ *vt* أَعادَ التَّقْييمَ *‹a result, probability›*

reassurance /riːəˈʃʊərəns/ *n* [1] (guarantee) تطْمين ,طَمْأَنة (تَطْمينات) [2] [u] (comfort) اطْمِئْنان ,طُمَأْنينة

reassure /riːəˈʃʊə/ *vt* طَمْأَنَ (i; طَمْأَنة) *‹a victim, an employee›*

reassuring /riːəˈʃɔːrɪŋ/ *adj ‹smile, words›* مُطَمْئِن

rebate /ˈriːbeɪt/ *n* مُسْتَرَدّات (جُزْء مُسْتَرَدّ من مَبْلَغٍ تَمَّ دَفْعُهُ كَضَريبةٍ أو إيجارٍ إلَخ)

rebel [A] /ˈreb(ə)l/ *n* (ثُوّار) ثائِر ,مُتَمَرِّد

[B] /rɪˈbel/ *vi* (**-ll-**) «armed forces, children» تَمَرَّدَ

rebellion /rɪˈbeljən/ *n* تَمَرُّد

rebellious /rɪˈbeljəs/ *adj ‹child, tribe›* مُتَمَرِّد

rebirth /riːˈbɜːθ/ *n* [1] (of nationalism, confidence) تَجَدُّد ,بَعْث, تَناسُخ [2] (after death) ميلاد جَديد

reboot /riːˈbuːt/ *vt* أَعادَ التَّشْغيلَ *‹a computer, system›*

rebound [A] /rɪˈbaʊnd/ *vi* [1] (to bounce) «shots, balls» ارْتَدَّ [2] (to affect adversely) **to ~ on sb** ارْتَدَّ عكسياً على شَخْصٍ [3] (to recover) «prices, currencies» انْتَعَشَ

[B] /ˈriːbaʊnd/ *n* (of a ball) (ارْتِدادات) ارْتِداد

Idiom **to be on the rebound** «prices, figures» انْتَعَشَ; «men, women» كانَ مُضْطَرِباً (بعد انْهيارِ عَلاقةٍ زَوْجيّةٍ أو عاطِفيّةٍ)

rebuff /rɪˈbʌf/ [A] *vt* رَفَضَ (i-u; رَفْض) ,صَدَّ (u; صَدّ) *‹a suitor, an offer›*

[B] *n* رَفْض ,صَدّ

rebuild /riːˈbɪld/ *vt* (*past tense, past participle* **rebuilt** /riːˈbɪlt/) أَعادَ البِناءَ *‹a town, house›*

rebuke /rɪˈbjuːk/ [A] *vt* أَنَّبَ ,وَبَّخَ *‹a pupil, member of staff›*

[B] *n* تَأْنيب ,(تَوْبيخات) تَوْبيخ

rebut /rɪˈbʌt/ *vt* (**-tt-**) دَحَضَ (a; دَحْض) ,فَنَّدَ *‹a criticism, an accusation›*

recall [A] /rɪˈkɔːl/ *vt* [1] (fml) (to remember) تَذَكَّرَ *‹an occasion, incident›* [2] (to summon) سَحَبَ (a; سَحْب) *‹troops, an ambassador›* [3] سَحَبَ من السوق ,اسْتَرْجَعَ *‹cars, toys›*

[B] /ˈriːkɔːl/ *n* [1] (memory) تَذَكُّر [2] (of troops, an ambassador) سَحْب [3] (of cars, toys) (اسْتِرْجاعات) اسْتِرْجاع ,سَحْب من السوقِ

recant /rɪˈkant/ [A] *vt* (عن) تَراجَعَ ,(من) تَنَصَّلَ *‹a heresy, statement›*

[B] *vi* تَراجَعَ

recap [A] /riːˈkap, ˈriːkap/ *vt* (**-pp-**) (infml) لَخَّصَ *‹a situation, story›*

[B] /ˈriːkap/ *n* (infml) (مُلَخَّصات) مُلَخَّص

recapitulate /ˌriːkəˈpɪtjʊleɪt/ *vt* لَخَّصَ *‹points, a situation›*

recapitulation /ˌriːkəpɪtjʊˈleɪʃ(ə)n/ *n* (تَلْخيصات) تَلْخيص

recapture /riːˈkaptʃə/ *vt* [1] (to return to captivity) أَعادَ القَبْضَ على *‹a prisoner›*; اسْتَعادَ السَيْطَرةَ على *‹town›* [2] (to recover) اسْتَعادَ *‹one's youth, an atmosphere›*

recede /rɪˈsiːd/ *vi* [1] (to retreat) تَراجَعَ; **the lights/cliffs ~d into the distance** تَراجَعَت الأَضْواءُ \ الأَجْرافُ في الأُفُقِ البَعيد [2] (gradually to diminish) «hope» تَبَدَّدَ ,انْحَسَرَ [3] (of hair) تَراجَعَ; **a receding hairline** خطّ شَعْرٍ مُتَراجِع

receding /rɪˈsiːdɪŋ/ *adj ‹chin, hairline›* مُنْحَسِر

receipt /rɪˈsiːt/ [A] *n* [1] (for purchases) وَصْل ,(إيصالات) إيصال [2] (of letters, packages) اسْتِلام (وُصولات)

[B] (**receipts**) *n pl* (income) إيرادات; **net/gross ~s** صافي \ إجْماليّ الإيراداتِ

receive /rɪˈsiːv/ [A] *vt* [1] (to get) تَلَقّى ,اسْتَقْبَلَ *‹a letter, telephone call, funds›*; اسْتَلَمَ *‹payment›*; **he ~d a 30-year sentence** حُكِمَ عَلَيْهِ بالسَجْنِ 30 عاما; **payment has not yet been ~d** لم يَتِمّ اسْتِلامُ المَبْلَغِ بَعْدُ [2] (to be given) تَلَقّى *‹medical treatment›*; **he ~d no treatment for three hours** لم يَتَلَقَّ أيّ عِلاجٍ لِثَلاثِ ساعاتٍ [3] (for resale) اشْتَرى *‹stolen goods›* [4] (to welcome) اسْتَقْبَلَ *‹a visitor, delegation›*; **to be ~d into the Church** قُبِلَ عُضْواً بالكَنيسةِ [5] (in broadcasting) اسْتَقْبَلَ *‹a channel, signal›*

[B] (**received**) *adj ‹opinions, ideas›* (سَوائِدُ) سائِد; **~d wisdom** حِكْمة سائِدة

Idiom **to be on the receiving end of sth** (infml) كانَ في الطَرَفِ المُتَلَقّي لِشَيْءٍ

receiver /rɪˈsiːvə/ *n* [1] (of a telephone) سَمّاعة; **to pick up/put down the ~** رَفَعَ \ أَغْلَقَ سَمّاعةَ التِلِفون [2] (in radio, TV) جِهاز اسْتِقْبالٍ [3] (in insolvency) حارِس قَضائيّ [4] (of stolen goods) [شَخْص يَسْتَلِمُ السِلَعَ المَسْروقةَ لِإعادةِ بَيْعِها]

receivership /rɪ'siːvəʃɪp/ *n* **to go into ~** خَضَعَ للحِراسةِ القَضائيّةِ

recent /'riːs(ə)nt/ *adj* <*event, arrival*> حَديث; **in ~ years** في السَنَواتِ الأخيرةِ; **the ~ past** في الماضي القَريبِ

recently /'riːs(ə)ntli/ *adv* <*discovered, bereaved*> حَديثاً, مُؤَخَّراً; **until ~** حتّى وَقْتٍ قَريبٍ

receptacle /rɪ'sɛptək(ə)l/ *n* (fml) وِعاء (أَوْعِية), إناء (آنِية, أَوانٍ)

reception /rɪ'sɛpʃ(ə)n/ *n* 1 also **~ desk** مَكْتَب اسْتِقْبالٍ 2 (gathering) حَفْل اسْتِقْبالٍ 3 (welcome) اسْتِقْبال (اسْتِقْبالات); **to receive a friendly/cool ~** لَقِيَ اسْتِقْبالاً وِدِّيًا \ فاتِراً 4 (signal) اسْتِقْبال

receptionist /rɪ'sɛpʃ(ə)nɪst/ *n* مُوَظَّف اسْتِقْبالٍ

receptive /rɪ'sɛptɪv/ *adj* <*attitude, mind*> مُتَقَبِّل, مُتَفَتِّح

receptor /rɪ'sɛptə/ *n* مُسْتَقْبِل

recess /rɪ'sɛs, 'riːsɛs/ *n* 1 (in parliament) عُطْلة (عُطُلات) 2 (AmE) (in school) اسْتِراحة 3 (alcove) تَجْويف (تَجاويفُ)

recession /rɪ'sɛʃ(ə)n/ *n* رُكود

recharge /riː'tʃɑːdʒ/ *vt* أَعادَ الشَحْنَ <*a battery, phone*>

rechargeable /riː'tʃɑːdʒəb(ə)l/ *adj* <*battery, device*> قابِل لِإعادةِ الشَحْنِ

recipe /'rɛsɪpi/ *n* وَصْفة (وَصَفات)

recipient /rɪ'sɪpɪənt/ *n* (of a letter, package) مُسْتَلِم, مُتَلَقٍّ; (of a prize) فائِز

reciprocal /rɪ'sɪprək(ə)l/ *adj* <*trade, help*> تَبادُليّ, مُتَبادَل, ثُنائيّ

reciprocate /rɪ'sɪprəkeɪt/ **A** *vt* بادَلَ <*love, a compliment*> **B** *vi* رَدَّ (u; رَدّ)

recital /rɪ'sʌɪt(ə)l/ *n* حَفْلة فَنِّيّة

recitation /ˌrɛsɪ'teɪʃ(ə)n/ *n* قِراءة, تَرْتيل, تَجْويد

recite /rɪ'sʌɪt/ *vt* 1 (to declaim) أَلْقى <*poem*>; قَرَأَ (a; قِراءة) <*a passage*>; تَلا (u; تِلاوة) <*the Koran*> 2 (to list) سَرَدَ (u; سَرْد), تَلا (u; تِلاوة) <*names, facts*>

reckless /'rɛkləs/ *adj* <*driving, gamble*> مُتَهَوِّر, طائِش, مُسْتَهْتِر

recklessly /'rɛklɪsli/ *adv* <*to drive, gamble*> بِتَهَوُّرٍ, باسْتِهْتارٍ

reckon /'rɛk(ə)n/ *vt* 1 (infml) (to think) **to ~ (that)** اِعْتَقَدَ (أَنَّ); **what do you ~?** ما رَأْيُكَ ؟ 2 (to judge) اِعْتَبَرَ, ظَنَّ (u; ظَنّ), حَسِبَ (a-i; حِسْبان); **it's ~ed to be the best in the country** يُعْتَبَرُ الأَفْضَلَ في البَلَدِ; **I ~ he's about 50** أَظُنُّ أنّ عُمْرَهُ حَوالَيْ 50 عاماً 3 (to calculate) حَسَبَ (u; حِساب) <*the cost, number*>; **~ your answer to two places of decimals** احْسِبْ إجابَتَكَ إلى أَقْرَبِ رَقْمَيْنِ عَشْرِيَّيْنِ 4 (to expect) **to ~ to do sth** تَوَقَّعَ أنْ يَفْعَلَ شَيْئاً

Phrasal verbs **reckon on** (infml): **~ on [sth]** 1 (to count on) اِعْتَمَدَ \ عَوَّلَ على [شَيْءٍ] 2 (to expect) تَوَقَّعَ [شَيْئاً]; **I hadn't ~ed on having to pay** لم أَتَوَقَّعْ أنْ أُضْطَرَّ للدَفْعِ

• **reckon up**: **~ [sth] up, ~ up [sth]** حَسَبَ [شَيْئاً] <*the cost, takings*>

• **reckon with**: **~ with [sb/sth]** أَخَذَ [شَخْصاً \ شَيْئاً] في الحُسْبانِ <*a problem, an opponent*>

• **reckon without**: **~ without [sb/sth]** لم يَضَعْ [شَخْصاً \ شَيْئاً] في اعْتِبارِهِ; **I thought we'd won, but I ~ed without her stubbornness** كُنْتُ أَعْتَقِدُ أَنَّنا انْتَصَرْنا وَلَكِنَّني لم أَضَعْ عِنادَها في اعْتِباري

reckoning /'rɛk(ə)nɪŋ/ *n* تَقْدير (تَقْديرات), حِساب (حِسابات)

Idiom **the day of reckoning** يَوْم الحِسابِ

reclaim /rɪ'kleɪm/ *vt* 1 اسْتَصْلَحَ <*land, marshland*> 2 أَعادَ الاسْتِعْمالَ <*glass, bricks*> 3 اسْتَرَدَّ <*a deposit, tax*> 4 اسْتَلَمَ <*a suitcase, baggage*>

reclaimable /rɪ'kleɪməb(ə)l/ *adj* 1 <*glass, metal*> قابِل لِإعادةِ الاسْتِعْمالِ 2 <*land*> قابِل للاسْتِصْلاحِ

recline /rɪ'klʌɪn/ *vi* 1 (to lie back) اسْتَرْخى, اضْطَجَعَ 2 (to tilt back) «seats» أَمْكَنَ دَفْعُهُ إلى الخَلْفِ

reclining /rɪ'klʌɪnɪŋ/ *adj* 1 <*figure, nude*> مُسْتَرْخٍ, مُضْطَجِع 2 <*seat, chair*> يُمْكِنُ دَفْعُهُ إلى الخَلْفِ

recluse /rɪ'kluːs/ *n* (شَخْص) مُنْعَزِل عن العالَمِ

reclusive /rɪ'kluːsɪv/ *adj* <*millionaire, lifestyle*> مُنْعَزِل, يُفَضِّلُ الوَحْدةَ

recognition /rɛkəg'nɪʃ(ə)n/ *n* (identification) تَعَرُّف; (acceptance) اعْتِراف

recognizable /rɛkəg'nʌɪzəb(ə)l, 'rɛkəgnʌɪzəb(ə)l/ *adj* <*face, landmark*> يُمْكِنُ التَعَرُّفُ عَلَيْهِ

recognize, **-ise** (BrE) /ˈrɛkəgnʌɪz/ **A** *vt* **1** (to identify) تَعَرَّفَ (على) ‹*a person, sign*›; **to ~ the symptoms of malaria** تَعَرَّفَ على أَعْراضِ المَلارِيا **2** (to acknowledge) أَقَرَّ, اعْتَرَفَ (ب) ‹*a problem, contribution*›; **his discovery was ~d for what it was** تَمَّ تَقْديرُ اكْتِشافِهِ لِأَهَمِّيَّتِهِ **3** (in diplomacy) اعْتَرَفَ (ب) ‹*a country, government*› **4** (AmE) (in a debate) أَعْطى فُرْصةً للتَحَدُّثِ ‹*a speaker, representative*›
B (**recognized**) *adj* **1** (acknowledged) ‹*expert, charity*› مُعْتَرَف بِهِ **2** (with accreditation) ‹*firm, agent*› مُعْتَرَف بِهِ

recoil /rɪˈkɔɪl/ *vi* **1** (to move away) تَراجَعَ للوَراءِ **2** (when firing) «guns, cannon» ارْتَدَّ للخَلْفِ

recollect /ˌrɛkəˈlɛkt/ **A** *vt* تَذَكَّرَ ‹*a date, name*›
B *vi* تَذَكَّرَ

recollection /ˌrɛkəˈlɛkʃ(ə)n/ *n* تَذَكُّر (تَذَكُّرات), ذِكْرى (f; ذِكْرَيات)

recommend /rɛkəˈmɛnd/ *vt* **1** (to praise) زَكّى, رَشَّحَ ‹*a book, restaurant*› **2** (to advise, suggest) أَوْصى (ب), نَصَحَ (a; نُصْح, نَصيحة; ب) ‹*a change, closure*›; **to ~ sth/doing sth** أَوْصى بِشَيْءٍ \ بِفِعْلِ شَيْءٍ

recommendation /ˌrɛkəmɛnˈdeɪʃ(ə)n/ *n* **1** (approval) تَوْصِية, تَزْكِية **2** (suggestion) اقْتِراح (اقْتِراحات), تَوْصِية

recommended reading /rɛkəˌmɛndɪd ˈriːdɪŋ/ *n* قِراءات مُقْتَرحة

recommended retail price /rɛkəˌmɛndɪd ˈriːteɪl ˌprʌɪs/ *n* سِعْر التَجْزِئة المُقْتَرح

recompense /ˈrɛkəmpɛns/ *n* (fml) تَعْويض (تَعْويضات)

reconcile /ˈrɛk(ə)nsʌɪl/ *vt* **1** أَصْلَحَ (بين) ‹*brothers, enemies*› **2** وَفَّقَ (بين) ‹*attitudes, theories*› **3** **to become ~d to sth** رَضِيَ بِشَيْءٍ

reconciliation /ˌrɛk(ə)nsɪliˈeɪʃ(ə)n/ *n* **1** (between enemies, brothers) مُصالَحة **2** (of ideas) تَوْفيق

recondition /riːkənˈdɪʃ(ə)n/ *vt* أَصْلَحَ, جَدَّدَ, ضَبَطَ أو اسْتَبْدَلَ الأَجْزاءَ التالِفةَ في آلةٍ ‹*an engine, a part*›

reconnaissance /rɪˈkɒnɪs(ə)ns/ *n* اسْتِطْلاع (اسْتِطْلاعات)

reconnoitre (BrE), **reconnoiter** (AmE) /ˌrɛkəˈnɔɪtə/ *vt* اسْتَطْلَعَ, اسْتَكْشَفَ ‹*terrain, an area*›

reconsider /riːk(ə)nˈsɪdə/ *vt* أَعادَ النَظَرَ في ‹*a decision, position*›

reconstruct /riːk(ə)nˈstrʌkt/ *vt* **1** (to rebuild) أَعادَ البِناءَ ‹*a building, city*› **2** (to recreate) أَعادَ التَمْثيلَ ‹*a crime, an accident*›

reconstruction /riːk(ə)nˈstrʌkʃ(ə)n/ *n* **1** (of a building, city) إعادة البِناءِ **2** (of a crime, an accident) إعادة التَمْثيلِ

record **A** /ˈrɛkɔːd/ *n* **1** (account of events, life) سِجِلّ (سِجِلّات); (of meetings, proceedings) مَحْضَر (مَحاضِرُ); **to keep a ~ of expenditure** احْتَفَظَ بِسِجِلٍّ للمَصْروفاتِ; **we have no ~ of your application** طَلَبُكَ لَيْسَ في سِجِلّاتِنا; **the hottest summer on ~** أَحَرُّ صَيْفٍ على الإطْلاقِ; **he is on ~ as saying that ...** صَرَّحَ رَسْميًّا أَنَّ ... ; **this is strictly off the ~** هذا لَيْسَ للنَشْرِ قَطْعيًّا; **I'd like to set the ~ straight** أَوَدُّ أَنْ أَضَعَ الأُمورَ في نِصابِها (الصَحيحِ) **2** (also **records**) (data in archives) سِجِلّ (سِجِلّات), وَثيقة (وَثائِقُ) **3** (history of an individual, organization) سِجِلّ (سِجِلّات), تاريخ (تَواريخُ); **to have a good ~ on safety/human rights** كانَ لَهُ سِجِلٌّ طَيِّبٌ فيما يَتَعَلَّقُ بالأَمانِ \ بِحُقوقِ الإنْسانِ **4** (also **criminal record**) سِجِلّ جِنائيّ **5** (best performance) رَقْم قِياسيّ; **to set/break a ~** حَقَّقَ \ حَطَّمَ رَقْماً قِياسيًّا; **to hold the ~ for the marathon** كانَ صاحِبَ الرَقْمِ القِياسيِّ في الماراثون **6** (disc) أُسْطُوانة; **to play a ~** شَغَّلَ أُسْطُوانةً **7** (unit of data) سِجِلّ (سِجِلّات)
B /ˈrɛkɔːd/ *adj* ‹*number, level, time*› قِياسيّ; **to be at a ~ high/low** كانَ في أَعْلى \ أَدْنى مُسْتَوًى قِياسيٍّ لَهُ
C /rɪˈkɔːd/ *vt* **1** (to note) سَجَّلَ, دَوَّنَ ‹*the details, time, a transaction*›; **the data is ~ed electronically** يَتِمُّ تَسْجيلُ البَياناتِ إلِكْترونيًّا; **the highest/lowest temperature ~ed was...** أَعْلى \ أَدْنى دَرَجةِ حَرارةٍ تَمَّ تَسْجيلُها كانَتْ ... **2** (officially) سَجَّلَ ‹*a verdict, death*› **3** (to be a record of) سَجَّلَ, وَثَّقَ ‹*events, conditions*› **4** (on CD, DVD, etc) سَجَّلَ ‹*an album, interview*›
D *vi* «bands, recording equipment» سَجَّلَ

record book *n* سِجِلّ الأَرْقامِ القِياسيّةِ

record card *n* بِطاقة بَياناتٍ

record company *n* شَرِكة إنْتاجٍ موسيقيٍّ

recorded /rɪˈkɔːdɪd/ *adj* **1** (preserved on tape, disk, etc.) ‹*music, interview*› مُسَجَّل **2** (documented) ‹*case, sighting*› مُوَثَّق

recorded delivery *n* (BrE) بَريد مُسَجَّل

recorder /rɪ'kɔːdə/ *n* (Mus) ريكورْد

record holder *n* صاحِب رَقْمٍ قِياسيٍّ

recording /rɪ'kɔːdɪŋ/ *n* تَسْجيل (تَسْجيلات)

record label *n* شَرِكة تَسْجيلاتٍ موسيقيّةٍ \ إِنْتاج موسيقيٍّ

record player *n* فونوغْراف (فونوغْرافات)

recount¹ /rɪ'kaʊnt/ *vt* (fml) حَكى (i; حِكاية)، رَوى (i; رِواية)، سَرَد (u; سَرْد) <*the story*>

recount² **A** /riː'kaʊnt/ *vt* أَعادَ العَدَّ <*passengers, votes*> **B** /'riːkaʊnt/ *n* إعادة العَدِّ

recoup /rɪ'kuːp/ *vt* اسْتَرَدَّ، عَوَّض <*losses, costs*>

recourse /rɪ'kɔːs/ *n* اِسْتِعانة، لُجوء; **without ~ to sth** دون اللُّجوءِ إلى شَيْءٍ

recover /rɪ'kʌvə/ **A** *vt* **1** (to get back) اسْتَرَدَّ، اسْتَعادَ <*a vehicle, the money*> **2** (to find) انْتَشَلَ <*a body*>; اسْتَعادَ، اسْتَرَدَّ <*a weapon*> **3** (to recoup) اسْتَرَدَّ، عَوَّض <*losses, costs*> **4** (to regain) اسْتَعادَ <*consciousness, one's mobility*>; **she ~ed the use of her arm** اِسْتَعادَتِ القُدْرةَ على تَحْريكِ ذِراعِها; **to ~ consciousness** اسْتَعادَ وَعْيَهُ
B *vi* **1** (from illness, injury) «patients, athletes» شُفِيَ، تَعافى **2** «demand, economy, country» انْتَعَش، تَعافى

recovery /rɪ'kʌv(ə)ri/ *n* **1** (from illness, injury) تَعافٍ، شِفاء **2** (of money, stolen goods) اسْتِعادة، اسْتِرْداد **3** (of a body) اِنْتِشال; (of a weapon) اسْتِعادة، اسْتِرْداد **4** (of losses) تَعْويض **5** (economic) تَعافٍ، انْتِعاش

recovery vehicle *n* وِنْش إِنْقاذِ السَّيّاراتِ

recreate /riːkri'eɪt/ *vt* أَعادَ التَّجْسيدَ <*an atmosphere, a battle*>

recreation /rɛkri'eɪʃ(ə)n/ *n* تَسْلية، تَرْفيه

recreational /rɛkri'eɪʃ(ə)n(ə)l/ *adj* <*facilities, amenities*> تَرْفيهيّ

recreational drug *n* مُخَدِّر تَرْفيهيّ

recrimination /rɪˌkrɪmɪ'neɪʃ(ə)n/ *n* اتِّهام مُضادّ

recruit /rɪ'kruːt/ **A** *vt* جَنَّدَ <*a soldier*>; وَظَّفَ، عَيَّنَ <*new member*> **B** *n* **1** (new soldier, policeman) مُجَنَّد **2** (new employee) مُوَظَّف جديد

recruiting officer /rɪ'kruːtɪŋ ˌɒfɪsə/ *n* مَسْؤول التَّجْنيدِ

recruitment /rɪ'kruːtmənt/ *n* **1** (into the army, navy) تَجْنيد **2** (into a firm) تَوْظيف

rectal /'rɛkt(ə)l/ *adj* <*examination, cancer*> شَرَجيّ

rectangle /'rɛktaŋg(ə)l/ *n* مُسْتَطيل

rectangular /rɛk'taŋgjʊlə/ *adj* <*shape, frame*> مُسْتَطيل

rectify /'rɛktɪfʌɪ/ *vt* (**rectifies, rectifying, rectified**) صَحَّحَ، صَوَّبَ <*an error, a record*>

rector /'rɛktə/ *n* راعي أَبْرَشيّةٍ

rectum /'rɛktəm/ *n* (*pl* **rectums** or **recta**) مُسْتَقيم (مُسْتَقيمات)

recuperate /rɪ'kuːpəreɪt/ *vi* تَماثَلَ لِلشِفاءِ، تَعافى

recuperation /rɪkuːpə'reɪʃ(ə)n/ *n* شِفاء، تَعافٍ

recur /rɪ'kəː/ *vi* (**-rr-**) «infection, errors, events» تَكَرَّرَ

recurrence /rɪ'kʌrəns/ *n* (fml) مُعاوَدة، تَكْرار

recurrent /rɪ'kʌrənt/ *adj* <*theme, problem, infection*> مُعاوِد، مُتَكَرِّر

recyclable /riː'sʌɪkləb(ə)l/ *adj* <*product, plastic*> قابِل لِإعادة التَّدْويرِ

recycle /riː'sʌɪk(ə)l/ *vt* أَعادَ التَّدْويرَ <*paper, waste*>

recycling /riː'sʌɪklɪŋ/ *n* إعادة التَّدْويرِ

red /rɛd/ **A** *adj* (**-dd-**) **1** (primary colour) <*flag, rose, car*> أَحْمَر (dipt); **to paint the doors ~** طَلى الأَبْوابَ باللَّوْنِ الأَحْمَرِ; **the lights went ~** تَحَوَّلَتْ إشارةُ المُرورِ إلى الضَوْءِ الأَحْمَرِ; **~ blood cells** خَلايا الدَمِ الحَمْراء **2** (in the face) <*face, cheeks*> أَحْمَر (dipt); **he went ~ when I asked him** احْمَرَّ وَجْهُهُ عِنْدَما سَأَلْتُهُ; **to be ~ in the face** كانَ وَجْهُهُ مُحْمَرًّا; **her eyes were ~ from crying** كانَتْ عَيْناها مُحْمَرَّتَيْنِ من البُكاءِ **3** (of hair) أَحْمَر (dipt); **to have ~ hair** كانَ شَعْرُهُ أَحْمَرَ **4** <*wine*> أَحْمَر (dipt)
B *n* **1** (primary colour) اللَّوْن الأَحْمَر; **do you have this in ~?** هل يَتَوَفَّرُ هذا لَدَيْكَ باللَّوْنِ الأَحْمَرِ؟; **to be dressed in ~** كانَ يَرْتَدي مَلابِسَ حَمْراءَ **2** (also **Red**) (pej) (communist) شَخْص شُيوعيّ **3** (in deficit) **to be in the ~** «account, company» كانَ رَصيدُهُ مَديناً **4** (wine) خَمْر \ نَبيذ أَحْمر

Idioms **to be caught red-handed** ضُبِطَ مُتَلَبِّساً; **to see red** (infml) اشْتاطَ غَضَباً

red admiral *n* فَراشة الأَميرالِ الحَمْراءِ

red alert *n* حالة الاسْتِعْدادِ القُصْوى

red card *n* بِطاقة حَمْراء; **to show a player the red card** أعْطى لاعِباً بِطاقة حَمْراءَ

red carpet *n* بِساط أَحْمَر; **to roll out the red carpet for sb** اسْتَقْبَلَ شَخْصاً اسْتِقْبالاً حافِلاً

Red Crescent *n* (**the Red Crescent**) الهِلال الأَحْمَر

Red Cross *n* (**the Red Cross**) الصَّليب الأَحْمَر

redcurrant /rɛd'kʌrənt/ *n* كِشْمِش أَحْمَر

redden /'rɛd(ə)n/ **A** *vi* «water, sky» احْمَرَّ **B** *vt* حَمَّرَ ‹*waters, a river*›

reddish /'rɛdɪʃ/ *adj* ‹*glow, light*› ضارِب إلى الحُمْرة ,مُحْمَرّ

redecorate /riː'dɛkəreɪt/ *vt* أعادَ الطِلاء ‹*a room, shop*›

redeem /rɪ'diːm/ *vt* **1** (to save) خَلَّصَ ‹*a sinner*› **2** (to pay off) سَدَّدَ ‹*a mortgage, a bond*› **3** (to convert into) اسْتَبْدَل ‹*one's points, a voucher*› **4** (from a pawnshop) فَكَّ الرَّهْنَ عن ‹*a watch, ring*›

redefine /riːdɪ'fʌɪn/ *vt* أعادَ التَعْريف ‹*a concept, problem*›

redemption /rɪ'dɛmpʃ(ə)n/ *n* **1** (Relig) خَلاص; **to be beyond ~** كانَ غَيْرَ قابِلٍ لِلإصْلاحِ **2** (of a mortgage, loan) سَداد **3** (in a pawnshop) فَكّ

redeploy /riːdɪ'plɔɪ/ *vt* أعادَ النَشْرَ ‹*troops*›; أعادَ التَوْزيعَ ‹*resources*›

redesign /riːdɪ'zʌɪn/ *vt* أعادَ التَصْميمَ ‹*a building, website*›

redevelop /riːdɪ'vɛləp/ *vt* «builders, council» أعادَ التَطْويرَ ‹*a site, the docks*›

redevelopment /riːdɪ'vɛləpmənt/ *n* إعادة التَطْوير

red-faced /rɛd'feɪst/ *adj* **to be ~** احْمَرَّ وَجْهُهُ (خَجَلاً)

red-haired /'rɛdhɛːd/ *adj* ‹*girl, boy*› أَحْمَر الشَعْر

red-handed *adj* **to be caught ~** قُبِضَ عَلَيْهِ مُتَلَبِّساً

redhead /'rɛdhɛd/ *n* شَخْص أَحْمَر الشَعْرِ

red herring *n* ذَرّ الرَمادِ في العُيونِ ,إشارة مُضَلِّلة

red-hot /rɛd'hɒt/ *adj* **1** ‹*metal, coal*› مُتَوَهِّج ,مُلْتَهِب **2** ‹*favourite*› ذائِع الصيتِ ,شَهير

redial **A** *vt* /riː'dʌɪl/ أعادَ الاتِّصالَ ب ‹*a number*› **B** *vi* /riː'dʌɪl/ «callers, operators» أعادَ الاتِّصالَ **C** *n* /'riːˌdʌɪl/ إعادة الاتِّصالِ

redial button *n* زِرّ إعادةِ الاتِّصالِ

redirect /riːdɪ'rɛkt/ *vt* **1** (with mail) أعادَ التَوْجيهَ ‹*the mail, letters*› **2** «police» حَوَّلَ ‹*the traffic*› **3** (on Internet) «websites» حَوَّلَ ‹*a visitor*› **4** «government, company, country» حَوَّلَ ‹*one's energy, resources*›

rediscover /riːdɪ'skʌvə/ *vt* أعادَ الاكْتِشافَ ‹*the manuscript, oneself*›

redistribute /ˌriːdɪ'strɪbjuːt/ *vt* أعادَ التَوْزيعَ ‹*wealth, land, resources*›

red light *n* ضَوْء أَحْمَر; **to go through a red light** كَسَرَ الإشارةَ الحَمْراءَ

red-light district *n* حَيّ أَحْمَر (مِنْطَقة تَنْتَشِرُ فيها بُيوتُ الدِعارة والأَنْشِطةُ الإباحيّةُ)

red meat *n* لَحْم أَحْمَر

red mullet *n* (*pl* **red mullet**) سُلْطان إبْراهيم ,بَرْبوني ,بَرْبون

redneck /'rɛdnɛk/ *n* (infml) [شَخْص أَبْيَض من الريفِ في جَنوبِ الوِلاياتِ المُتَّحِدةِ غَيْر مُتَعَلِّمٍ وَلَهُ أَفْكارٌ رَجْعيّةٌ]

redo /riː'duː/ *vt* (*3rd person present sing* **redoes**; *past tense* **redid**; *past participle* **redone**) أعادَ ‹*the calculation, job*›

redouble /riː'dʌb(ə)l/ *vt* ضاعَفَ ‹*efforts*›; **to ~ one's efforts** ضاعَفَ جُهودَهُ

red pepper *n* فِلْفِل أَحْمَر

redraft /riː'drɑːft/ *vt* أعادَ الصِياغةَ ‹*a contract, legislation*›

redress /rɪ'drɛs/ **A** *vt* صَحَّحَ ,عَوَّضَ ,أَصْلَحَ ‹*an injustice, grievances*›; **to ~ the balance** عالَجَ الخَلَلَ في التَوازُنِ **B** *n* (of a wrong) إصْلاح (إصْلاحات) ,تَعْويض (تَعويضات)

Red Sea *pr n* (**the Red Sea**) البَحْر الأَحْمَر

red squirrel *n* سِنْجاب أَحْمَر

red tape *n* الروتين الإداريّ

reduce /rɪ'djuːs/ **A** *vt* **1** (in size) صَغَّرَ ‹*the dimensions, the image*›; خَفَّضَ ,قَلَّلَ ‹*the number/amount, costs*›; **~ the number of words to 500** قَلَّلَ عَدَدَ الكَلِماتِ إلى 500 **2** (in scope) قَلَّلَ ,خَفَّفَ ‹*the impact, the pressure*›; خَفَّضَ ‹*a number*›; **all prices have been ~d by 30%** خُفِّضَتْ كُلُّ الأَسْعارِ بِنِسْبة 30٪; **'~ speed now'** 'خَفِّض السُرْعةَ الآنَ' **3** (to shorten) قَصَّرَ ‹*a sentence*› **4** (in intensity) خَفَّفَ ‹*the discomfort, swelling*› **5** (in rank) **to be ~d to the ranks** جُرِّدَ من رُتْبَتِهِ **6** (to alter the state of) **to ~ sb to tears/silence** دَفَعَ شَخْصاً إلى البُكاءِ \ اِلْتِزامِ الصَّمْتِ; **to ~ the village to ashes** حَوَّلَ المَدينةَ إلى رَمادٍ; **to be ~d to begging/stealing** آلَ بِهِ الحالُ إلى التَسَوُّلِ \ السَرِقةِ **7** (to simplify) اِخْتَصَرَ ,لَخَّصَ ‹an argument, a policy› **8** غَلى (حتّى يُقَلِّلَ الحَجْمَ) ‹a sauce, stock›

B *vi* **1** (AmE) (to lose weight) أَنْقَصَ وَزْنَهُ; **she's reducing again** تُنْقِصُ وَزْنَها مَرّةً أُخرى **2** «sauces, stock» غَلى (حتّى قَلَّ حَجْمُهُ)

C **(reduced)** *adj* **1** (in price) مُخَفَّض; **all prices ~d** كُلُّ الأَسْعارِ مُخَفَّضةٌ **2** ‹scale, rate› مُنْخَفِض **3** (fml) (straitened) **to live in ~d circumstances** عانى من ضيقِ العَيْشِ

reduction /rɪ'dʌkʃ(ə)n/ *n* **1** (in number, quantity) اِنْخِفاض (اِنْخِفاضات), تَخْفيض, إِنْقاص, تَقْليل, خَفْض **2** (discount) تَخْفيض (تَخْفيضات), تَنْزيل (تَنْزيلات)

redundancy /rɪ'dʌnd(ə)nsi/ **A** *n* (*pl* **redundancies**) **1** [u] (superfluousness) زِيادة عن الحاجةِ **2** (BrE) [u] (in employment) تَسْريح ,فَصْل من العَمَلِ; **to be given compulsory ~** تَعَرَّضَ لِتَسْريحٍ إجْباريٍّ; **to take voluntary ~** تَقَدَّمَ بِطَلَبِ تَسْريحٍ طَوْعيٍّ **3** (dismissal) تَسْريح ,فَصْل

B *adj before n* (in dismissals) التَّسْريحِ, الإقالةِ ‹payment, package›

redundant /rɪ'dʌnd(ə)nt/ *adj* **1** (superfluous) ‹skills, words› غَيْر ضَروريٍّ ,زائِد عن الحاجةِ **2** (BrE) (in the workplace) ‹staff, worker› مَفْصول; **to make workers ~** فَصَلَ العُمّالَ من عَمَلِهِمْ

reed /ri:d/ *n* (plant) قَصَب (n coll), بوص (n coll)

re-educate /ri:'edʒʊkeɪt/ *vt* أَعادَ التَعْليمَ ‹the public›; أَعادَ التَرْبِيةَ ‹an offender›

reef /ri:f/ *n* شِعْب (شِعاب)

reek /ri:k/ *vi* **1** (to stink) **to ~ of tobacco smoke/drink** فاحَتْ مِنْهُ رائِحةُ دُخانِ التَبْغِ \ الشَرابِ **2** (to have the air of) **to ~ of corruption/nepotism** فاحَتْ مِنْهُ رائِحةُ الفَسادِ \ المَحْسوبِيّةِ

reel /ri:l/ **A** *n* **1** (for cable, cotton, film, tape) بَكَرة (بَكَرات), بَكَر **2** (also **fishing reel**) بَكَرة (بَكَر ,بَكَرات) **3** (dance) ريل (رَقْصة إسْكُتْلَنْدِيّة)

B *vi* تَرَنَّحَ; **the blow sent him ~ing** جَعَلَتْهُ الضَرْبةُ يَتَرَنَّحُ; **I am still ~ing from the shock** ما أَزالُ أُعاني من آثارِ الصَدْمةِ

Phrasal verbs **reel in**: ~ in [sth], ~ [sth] in جَرَّ \ سَحَبَ [شَيْئاً] ‹a fish›

• **reel off**: ~ off [sth] سَرَدَ \ تَلا [شَيْئاً] ‹a list, names›

re-elect /ri:ɪ'lɛkt/ *vt* اِنْتَخَبَ مَرّةً ثانِيةً ,أَعادَ الانْتِخابَ ‹the mayor, politician›

re-emerge /ri:ɪ'mə:dʒ/ *vi* **1** (to reappear) «sun, divers» عاوَدَ ظَهَرَ مَرّةً أُخرى ,الظُهورَ **2** (to reoccur) «problems, diseases» ظَهَرَ مَرّةً أُخرى ,عاوَدَ الظُهورَ

re-enact /ri:ɪ'nakt/ *vt* **1** أَعادَ التَمْثيلَ ‹a battle, crime› **2** أَعادَ السَنَّ \ التَشْريعَ ‹a law, statute›

re-enter /ri:'ɛntə/ **A** *vt* دَخَلَ مَرّةً أُخْرى ‹a country, the atmosphere›

B *vi* (to come back in) «people, vehicles» عادَ (u; عَوْدة)

re-examine /ri:ɪg'zamɪn/ *vt* **1** فَحَصَ ثانِيةً ,أَعادَ الفَحْصَ ‹the evidence, problem› **2** أَعادَ الاسْتِجْوابَ ‹a witness›

ref /rɛf/ **A** *n* (infml) = **referee** حَكَم (حُكّام)

B *abbr* = **reference** رَقْم مَرْجِعيّ

C *vt* (infml) حَكَّمَ ‹a contest, match›

D *vi* (infml) حَكَّمَ

refectory /rɪ'fɛkt(ə)ri/ *n* (*pl* **refectories**) قاعة طَعامٍ

refer /rɪ'fə:/ *vt* **(-rr-)** **1** (to pass on) أَحالَ ‹a matter, case› **2** (to direct) وَجَّهَ ,أَحالَ ‹a reader›; **the reader is ~red to chapter 13** يُوَجَّهُ القارِئُ إلى الفَصْلِ 13 **3** (to send to) أَرْسَلَ ‹friend›; حَوَّلَ ,أَحالَ ‹a patient›; **to ~ a patient to a specialist** حَوَّلَ مَريضاً إلى أَخِصّائيٍّ

Phrasal verb **refer to** **A** ~ **to** [sth/sb] (to allude to) أَشارَ إلى [شَيْءٍ] ‹a person, fact›; **she ~s to him as Bob** أَشارَتْ إِلَيْهِ بِاسْمِ بوب **B** ~ **to** [sth] **1** (to consult) رَجَعَ إلى [شَيْءٍ] ‹one's notes, a dictionary› **2** (to signify) «term, number» أَشارَ إلى [شَيْءٍ]

referee /rɛfə'ri:/ **A** *n* **1** (umpire) حَكَم (حُكّام) **2** (BrE) (in job applications) مَرْجِع (شَخْص يُمْكِنُ الرُجوعُ إِلَيْهِ لِلاسْتِفْسارِ عن مُقَدِّمِ الطَلَبِ)

B *vt* حَكَّمَ ‹a game, fight›

C *vi* «person» حَكَّمَ

reference /'rɛf(ə)rəns/ **A** *n* **1** (allusion) إِشارة; **to make ~ to sth** أَشارَ إلى شَيْءٍ; **there are three ~s to him in the book** أُشيرَ إِلَيْهِ ثَلاثَ مَرّاتٍ في الكِتابِ **2** [u] (consultation)

رُجوع ,اسْتِشارة; **to do sth without ~ to sb/sth** فَعَلَ شَيْئاً دون الرُجوعِ إلى شَخْصٍ \ شَيْءٍ; **'for ~ only'** (on a library book) 'للاطِّلاعِ فَقَطْ'; **for future ~** للرُجوعِ إِلَيْهِ مُسْتَقْبَلاً

3 (information source) مَرْجِع (مَراجِعُ) 4 (citation) اسْتِشْهاد (اسْتِشْهادات) 5 (for identification) رَقْم مَرْجِعيّ \ اسْتِدْلاليّ; **please quote this ~** رَجاءً اُذْكُرْ هذا الرَقْمَ المَرْجِعيَّ 6 (for a job candidate) خِطاب تَوْصِيةٍ; **a map ~** دَليل \ مِفْتاح خَريطةٍ; **to give sb a ~** أَعْطى شَخْصاً خِطابَ تَوْصِيةٍ; **to take up ~s** تَحَقَّق من المَراجِعِ

B (**with reference to**) *prep phr* (fml) بالإشارةِ إلى; **with ~ to your letter/request** بالإشارةِ إلى خِطابِكَ \ طَلَبِكَ

C *vt* 1 (fml) (to mention) أَشارَ (إلى) *<a subject, writer>* 2 (to provide with citations) ذَكَرَ كَمَرْجِعٍ *<a book>*

reference book *n* كِتاب مَرْجِعيّ

reference number *n* رَقْم مَرْجِعيّ

reference point, point of reference *n* نُقْطة مَرْجِعيّة

referendum /ˌrɛfəˈrɛndəm/ *n* (*pl* **referenda**) اسْتِفْتاء (اسْتِفْتاءات); **to hold a ~** أَجْرى اسْتِفْتاءً

referral /rɪˈfəːrəl/ *n* إحالة

refill **A** /riːˈfɪl/ *vt* أَعادَ التَعْبِئةَ ,أَعادَ المَلْءَ *<a glass, lighter>*

B /ˈriːfɪl/ *n* 1 (for a pen, lighter) إعادة تَعْبِئةٍ ,إعادة مَلْءٍ 2 (drink) إعادة مَلْءٍ; **would you like a ~?** هل تَرْغَبُ في إعادةِ مَلْءِ الكوبِ؟

refine /rɪˈfʌɪn/ *vt* 1 (to purify) كَرَّرَ *<oil, sugar>* 2 (to improve) جَوَّدَ ,حَسَّنَ *<a technique, formula>*

refined /rɪˈfʌɪnd/ *adj* 1 *<manners, taste>* رَقيق ,رَفيع 2 *<oil, sugar>* مُكَرَّر

refinement /rɪˈfʌɪnmənt/ *n* 1 (of a formula, design) تَحْسين (تَحْسينات) ,تَجْويد 2 [u] (in manners, taste) دَماثة ,رِقّة ,رِفْعة 3 [u] (of sugar, oil) تَكْرير

refinery /rɪˈfʌɪn(ə)ri/ *n* (*pl* **refineries**) مِصْفاة (مَصافٍ) ,مَعْمَل تَكْرير; **he works at a sugar/an oil ~** يَعْمَلُ في مِصْفاةٍ للسُكَّرِ \ للبِتْرول

reflect /rɪˈflɛkt/ **A** *vt* 1 (with images) عَكَسَ (عَكْس; i) *<an image, a face>*; **the trees were ~ed in the water** انْعَكَسَتْ صورةُ الأَشْجارِ في الماءِ 2 (with heat, light) عَكَسَ (عَكْس; i) *<the light, heat>* 3 (to be a sign of) عَكَسَ (عَكْس; i) *<a fact, view>*

B *vi* 1 (to think) «characters, narrators» تَأَمَّلَ ,تَفَكَّرَ ,فَكَّرَ; **she went off by herself to ~ on the situation** غادَرَتْ بِمُفْرَدِها لِتَتَفَكَّرَ في الوَضْعِ 2 (to beam back) «light, heat» انْعَكَسَ

(Idiom) **to reflect well/badly on sb/sth** انْعَكَسَ بِشَكْلٍ جَيِّدٍ \ سَيِّئٍ على شَخْصٍ \ شَيْءٍ

reflection /rɪˈflɛkʃ(ə)n/ *n* 1 [u] (of images) صورة مُنْعَكِسة; **the ~ of the trees in the water** صورة الأَشْجارِ المُنْعَكِسة على الماءِ 2 [u] (of light, heat) انْعِكاس 3 [u] (contemplation) تَأَمُّل ,تَفْكير ,تَفَكُّر; **on ~, I have decided to forgive him** بعد تَفْكيرٍ، قَرَّرْتُ أَنْ أُسامِحَهُ 4 (sign) عَلامة (عَلامات), انْعِكاس (انْعِكاسات) 5 (comment) تَعْليق ,(آراء) رَأْي (تَعْليقات)

reflective /rɪˈflɛktɪv/ *adj* 1 (thoughtful) *<mood, style>* تَأَمُّليّ

2 (with light, heat) *<surface, clothing>* عاكِس

reflector /rɪˈflɛktə/ *n* 1 (on a vehicle) عاكِس (عَواكِسُ)

2 (of light, heat) عاكِس (عَواكِسُ)

reflex /ˈriːflɛks/ **A** *n* رَدّ فِعْلٍ مُنْعَكِس

B *adj* *<action, response>* مُنْعَكِس

reflexive /rɪˈflɛksɪv/ **A** *adj* *<construction, pronoun>* انْعِكاسيّ

B *n* 1 (also **reflexive verb**) ≈ فِعْل انْعِكاسيّ ,فِعْل مُطاوَعةٍ [فِعْل يَكونُ مَفْعولُهُ ضَميراً يَعودُ على الفاعِلِ]; **'to wash oneself' is a ~** 'to wash oneself' هو فِعْلٌ انْعِكاسيٌّ 2 (also **reflexive form**) صيغة انْعِكاسيّة; **the verb 'wash' can be used transitively or in the ~** يُمْكِنُ اسْتِخْدامُ الفِعْلِ 'wash' كَفِعْلٍ مُتَعَدٍّ أو في الصيغةِ الانْعِكاسيّةِ

reflexologist /riːflɛkˈsɒlədʒɪst/ *n* أَخِصّائيّ الطِبِّ الانْعِكاسيِّ, أَخِصّائيّ طِبِّ المُنْعَكَساتِ

reflux /ˈriːflʌks/ *n* ارْتِجاع

reform /rɪˈfɔːm/ **A** *vt* أَصْلَحَ *<the law, a system>*

B *n* إصْلاح (إصْلاحات)

reformation /rɛfəˈmeɪʃ(ə)n/ *n* 1 (act of reforming) إصْلاح

2 (**the Reformation**) (16th century movement) حَرَكة الإصْلاحِ الدينيِّ

reformatory /rɪˈfɔːmət(ə)ri/ *n* (*pl* **reformatories**) إصْلاحيّة, دارُ الأحْداثِ

reformer /rɪˈfɔːmə/ *n* مُصْلِح

reformist /rɪˈfɔːmɪst/ **A** *adj* ‹*zeal, government*› إصْلاحيّ **B** *n* شَخْص إصْلاحيّ

refrain /rɪˈfreɪn/ **A** *n* **B** *vi* (fml) «politicians, committees» أَحْجَمَ, امْتَنَعَ; **he ~ed from comment** امْتَنَعَ عن التَعْليق; **she was going to object, but ~ed** كانَتْ سَتَعْتَرِضُ، وَلَكِنَّها أَحْجَمَتْ عن ذلك

refresh /rɪˈfreʃ/ *vt* **1** نَشَّطَ, أَنْعَشَ ‹*oneself, one's mind*› **2** حَدَّثَ ‹*the data*›

refresher course /rɪˈfreʃə ˌkɔːs/ *n* دَوْرة تَنْشيطيّة

refreshing /rɪˈfreʃɪŋ/ *adj* **1** (restorative) ‹*drink, shower*› مُنْعِش, مُنَشِّط **2** (welcome) ‹*change, honesty*› لَطيف, مُريح

refreshment /rɪˈfreʃmənt/ **A** *n* (restoration) إنْعاش, انْتِعاش **B** (**refreshments**) *n pl* (drinks) مُرَطِّبات; **light ~s will be served** سَوْفَ يَتِمُّ تَقْديمُ مُرَطِّباتٍ خَفيفةٍ

refrigerate /rɪˈfrɪdʒəreɪt/ *vt* ثَلَّجَ, بَرَّدَ ‹*food, meat*›

refrigerator /rɪˈfrɪdʒəreɪtə/ *n* بَرّاد, ثَلّاجة

refuel /riːˈfjʊəl/ **A** *vt* (**-ll-** BrE, **-l-** AmE) زَوَّدَ بالوَقودِ ‹*an aircraft, ship*› **B** *vi* «aircraft, tankers» تَزَوَّدَ بالوَقودِ

refuge /ˈrefjuːdʒ/ *n* **1** [u] (protection) مَلاذ, حِماية, احْتِماء; **they took ~ from the storm in the barn** لَجَأوا إلى الحَظيرةِ احْتِماءً من العاصِفةِ **2** (hostel) مَلْجَأ (مَلاجِئُ); **a women's ~** مَلْجَأ للنِساءِ

refugee /refjʊˈdʒiː/ *n* لاجِئ

refugee camp *n* مُخَيَّم للاجِئينَ

refugee status *n* وَضْع لاجِئٍ

refund **A** /rɪˈfʌnd/ *vt* رَدَّ (u; رَدّ), أعادَ ‹*the money, fee*›; **your expenses will be ~ed** سَوْفَ يَتِمُّ رَدُّ النَفَقاتِ إلَيْكَ **B** /ˈriːfʌnd/ *n* مَبْلَغ مُسْتَرَدّ; **to be entitled to a ~** كانَ يَحِقُّ لَهُ اسْتِرْدادُ مَبْلَغٍ

refurbish /riːˈfəːbɪʃ/ *vt* رَمَّمَ, جَدَّدَ ‹*a building, property*›

refurbishment /riːˈfəːbɪʃmənt/ *n* تَرْميم (تَرْميمات), تَجْديد (تَجْديدات)

refusal /rɪˈfjuːz(ə)l/ *n* **1** (of a request) رَفْض **2** (of an offer) رَفْض; **her ~ of his offer of help** رَفْضُها عَرْضَهُ للمُساعَدةِ **3** (of permission) رَفْض; **the ~ of permission for development** رَفْض السَماحِ بالبِناءِ

refuse¹ /rɪˈfjuːz/ **A** *vt* **1** (to choose not to) رَفَضَ (i-u; رَفْض); **they ~d to leave** رَفَضوا الانْصِرافَ **2** (to turn down) رَفَضَ (i-u; رَفْض) ‹*an offer, treatment*›; **the job offer was too good to ~** كانَ عَرْضُ العَمَلِ جَيِّداً جِدًّا وَلا يُمْكِنُ رَفْضُهُ **3** (to deny) رَفَضَ (i-u; رَفْض) ‹*permission, a request*›; **the authorities ~d him a visa** رَفَضَت السُلُطاتِ إعْطاءَهُ تَأْشيرةً **B** *vi* «employers, governments» رَفَضَ (i-u; رَفْض)

refuse² /ˈrefjuːs/ *n* مُخَلَّفات, نُفايات; **household/garden ~** مُخَلَّفات المَنازِلِ \ الحَدائِقِ

refuse collector *n* جامِعُ نُفاياتٍ, عامِل قُمامةٍ

refute /rɪˈfjuːt/ *vt* دَحَضَ (a; دَحْض), فَنَّدَ ‹*a claim, an argument*›

regain /rɪˈɡeɪn/ *vt* **1** (to get back use of) اسْتَرَدَّ, اسْتَعادَ, اسْتَرْجَعَ ‹*one's strength, composure*›; **to ~ consciousness** اسْتَعادَ وَعْيَهُ **2** (to get back) اسْتَعادَ ‹*control, a lead*›

regal /ˈriːɡ(ə)l/ *adj* ‹*bearing, splendour*› فَخْم, مَلَكيّ

regale /rɪˈɡeɪl/ *vt* أَبْهَجَ, مَتَّعَ ‹*an audience, guests*›; **he ~d his guests with hilarious stories** أَبْهَجَ ضُيوفَهُ بِقَصَصٍ مَرِحةٍ

regalia /rɪˈɡeɪlɪə/ *n pl* [الشِعارات والرُموز الدالّة على مَنْصِبٍ]

regard /rɪˈɡɑːd/ **A** *vt* **1** (to consider) اعْتَبَرَ ‹*an issue, sb's behaviour*›; **capital punishment was ~ed as normal** كانَتْ عُقوبةُ الإعْدامِ تُعْتَبَرُ عُقوبةً عاديّةً; **her work is very highly ~ed** يُنْظَرُ إلى عَمَلِها باحْتِرامٍ كَبيرٍ **2** (to look at) نَظَرَ (u; نَظَر إلى) ‹*a friend, colleague*›

B *n* **1** (consideration) اهْتِمام, اعْتِبار; **the rescuers worked without ~ for their safety** عَمِلَ عُمّالُ الإنْقاذِ دون مُراعاةٍ لِسَلامَتِهِمْ **2** (esteem) احْتِرام, تَقْدير; **I have a high ~ for him** أُكِنُّ لَهُ تَقْديراً كَبيراً **3** (**regards**, *pl*) (greeting) تَحيّات

(Idioms) **in/with regard to sb/sth** فيما يَتَعَلَّقُ بِشَخْصٍ \ بِشَيْءٍ; **as regards sb/sth** (fml) بِخُصوصِ شَخْصٍ \ شَيْءٍ

regarding /rɪˈɡɑːdɪŋ/ *prep* فيما يَتَعَلَّقُ ب, بِخُصوصِ; **did she say anything ~ our comments?** هل قالَتْ أَيَّ شَيْءٍ بِخُصوصِ تَعْليقاتِنا؟

regardless /rɪˈɡɑːdləs/ **A** *prep* (**regardless of sb/sth**) بِغَضِّ النَظَرِ عن ,دون الالْتِفاتِ إلى; **all candidates are treated the same, ~ of age, sex or origin** يَتِمُّ مُعامَلَةُ كُلِّ المُرَشَّحينَ بالمِثْلِ, بِغَضِّ النَظَرِ عن السِنِّ أو الجِنْسِ أو الأَصْلِ **B** *adv* ‹to carry on, continue› دون الالْتِفاتِ إلى ذلك; **he protested, but they carried on ~** احْتَجَّ، ولَكِنَّهُمْ استَمَرّوا دون الالْتِفاتِ إلى ذلك

regatta /rɪˈɡatə/ *n* سِباقات الزَوارِق

regenerate /rɪˈdʒɛnəreɪt/ **A** *vt* **1** (to revive) أَنْعَشَ ,أَحْيا ‹a city, industry› **2** (to grow) جَدَّدَ ‹tissue, an organ› **B** *vi* «cells, forests» تَجَدَّدَ

regeneration /rɪdʒɛnəˈreɪʃ(ə)n/ *n* **1** (economic, political) تَحْديث ,إِنْعاش ,إحْياء; **urban ~** تَحْديث المَناطِق الحَضَرِيّة **2** (biological) تَجَدُّد

regent /ˈriːdʒ(ə)nt/ *n* وَصِيّ على العَرْشِ

reggae /ˈrɛɡeɪ/ *n* (موسيقى) ريغي

regime /reɪˈʒiːm/ *n* **1** (government) نِظام حُكْمٍ **2** (system) نِظام (أَنْظِمة)

regiment /ˈrɛdʒɪmənt/ *n* فَوْج عَسْكَرِيّ, كَتيبة (كَتائِبُ)

regimental /rɛdʒɪˈmɛnt(ə)l/ *adj* ‹commander, band› فَوْجِ, كَتيبةِ

region /ˈriːdʒ(ə)n/ *n* مِنْطَقة (مَناطِقُ), إقْليم (أَقاليمُ) (Idiom) **in the region of** في حُدودِ, قُرابةَ

regional /ˈriːdʒ(ə)n(ə)l/ *adj* ‹development, director› إقْليمي

regionalism /ˈriːdʒ(ə)nəliz(ə)m/ *n* نَزْعة إقْليميّة

register /ˈrɛdʒɪstə/ **A** *n* **1** (list) سِجِلّ (سِجِلّات), قائِمة (قَوائِمُ); **to make an entry in a ~** أَضاف خانة في سِجِلّ; **~ of births, marriages and deaths** سِجِلّ المَواليدِ والزَواجِ والوَفَيّاتِ **2** **to call/take the ~** نادى كَشْفَ الحُضورِ **3** (of sound) قُدْرة صَوْتِيّة **B** *vt* **1** (to record) سَجَّلَ, دَوَّنَ في سِجِلٍّ ‹a birth, death›; **to ~ the marriage** سَجَّلَ الزَواجَ; **everybody must be ~ed before they can vote** يَجِبُ على الجَميعِ أنْ يُسَجِّلوا أَنْفُسَهُمْ قبل أنْ يَتَمَكَّنوا من التَصْويتِ; **to ~ a protest** قَدَّمَ احْتِجاجاً **2** (for licensing) سَجَّلَ ‹a trademark, patent, vehicle› **3** (with instruments) سَجَّلَ ‹the speed, temperature›; **the earthquake ~ed six on the Richter scale** سَجَّلَ الزِلْزالُ سِتَّ دَرَجاتٍ على مِقْياسِ ريخْتر **4** (to show) عَبَّرَ (عن), نَمَّ (عن) (i-u; نَمّ) ‹anger, surprise, relief›; **his face ~ed no emotion** لم يُعَبِّرْ وَجْهُهُ عن أَيِّ مَشاعِرَ **5** (to achieve, record) حَقَّقَ ‹victory›; مُنِيَ ب ‹a loss›; **the party has ~ed a significant success** حَقَّقَ \ سَجَّلَ الحِزْبُ نَجاحاً كَبيراً **6** (in postage) أَرْسَلَ بالبَريدِ المُسَجَّلِ ‹a letter, parcel› **C** *vi* **1** (put name on a register) سَجَّلَ نَفْسَهُ \ اسْمَهُ; **to ~ as a voter** سَجَّلَ نَفْسَهُ كَناخِبٍ; **to ~ with social security** سَجَّلَ نَفْسَهُ في الضَمانِ الاجْتِماعيِّ; **to ~ with a doctor/dentist** سَجَّلَ نَفْسَهُ مع طَبيبٍ \ طَبيبِ أَسْنانٍ **2** (to show) «temperatures, earthquakes» ظَهَرَ أَثَرُهُ **3** (mentally) **the importance of the news did not ~** لم يَتِمَّ اسْتيعابُ \ إدْراكُ أَهَمِّيّةِ الأَخْبارِ

registered /ˈrɛdʒɪstəd/ *adj* **1** ‹voter, trademark› مُسَجَّل; **to be ~ as disabled/blind** كانَ مُسَجَّلاً كَمُعاقٍ \ كَأَعْمى **2** ‹letter› مُسَجَّل

registered nurse *n* (AmE) مُمَرِّض مُسَجَّل

registered trademark *n* عَلامة تِجارِيّة مُسَجَّلة

register office *n* (BrE) مَكْتَب سِجِلٍّ مَدَنِيٍّ

registrar /rɛdʒɪˈstrɑː, ˈrɛdʒɪstrɑː/ *n* **1** (record keeper) أمين السِجِلِّ **2** (academic) مُسَجِّل الجامِعةِ **3** (in UK: doctor) نائِب الأَخِصّائيِّ

registration /rɛdʒɪˈstreɪʃ(ə)n/ *n* **1** (of births, voters, vehicles) تَسْجيل (تَسْجيلات) **2** (of trademarks, patents, companies) تَسْجيل (تَسْجيلات) **3** [u] (for participants) تَسْجيل

registration number *n* رَقْم تَسْجيلٍ (في المَرْكَباتِ)

registration plate *n* لَوْحة تَسْجيلٍ (في المَرْكَباتِ)

registry /ˈrɛdʒɪstri/ *n* (*pl* **registries**) **1** (for records) مَكْتَب التَسْجيلِ **2** (AmE) (list) سِجِلّ (سِجِلّات) **3** (in a church) مَكْتَب السِجِلّاتِ

registry office *n* (BrE) ▸ **register office**

regress /ˈriːɡrɛs/ *vi* «patients, old people» تَراجَعَ, انْتَكَسَ, تَدَهْوَرَ

regression /rɪˈɡrɛʃ(ə)n/ *n* تَدَهْوُر, انْتِكاسة

regret /rɪˈgrɛt/ **A** *vt* (**-tt-**) **1** (to feel remorse over) نَدِمَ (a; نَدَم, نَدامة ;على) ‹*a decision, fact*›; **this could be a decision that you live to ~** قد يَكونُ هذا قراراً تَنْدَمُ عَلَيْهِ فيما بَعْدُ **2** (fml) (to be sorry about) أَسِفَ (a; أَسَف ;على) ‹*an inconvenience, error*›; **I ~ that I am unable to attend** أنا آسِفٌ أَنَّني لا أَسْتَطيعُ الحُضورَ

B *n* **1** (sadness) أَسَف, حُزْن (أَحْزان) **2** (remorse) نَدَم; **what is your greatest ~?** ما هي أَكْثَرُ الأَشْياءِ الّتي نَدِمْتَ عَلَيْها؟

regretful /rɪˈgrɛtfʊl/ *adj* ‹*tone, sigh*› آسِف, نادِم

regretfully /rɪˈgrɛtf(ə)li/ *adv* ‹*to announce, decline*› مع الأَسَفِ, للأَسَفِ; **~, I have to tell you that this is my last visit** مع الأَسَفِ، أنا مُضْطَرٌّ لأَنْ أُخْبِرَكَ بِأَنَّ هذه سَتَكونُ آخِرَ زِيارةٍ لي

regrettable /rɪˈgrɛtəb(ə)l/ *adj* ‹*mistake, necessity*› مُؤْسِف, يُؤْسَفُ لَهُ

regrettably /rɪˈgrɛtəbli/ *adv* (sadly) بِشَكْلٍ يَدْعو للأَسَفِ, للأَسَفِ; **~, I will not be available to meet them** للأَسَفِ، لن أَكونَ مُتاحاً لِمُقابَلَتِهِمْ

regroup /riːˈgruːp/ **A** *vt* أَعادَ التَجْميعَ \ التَوْزيعَ \ التَنْظيمَ ‹*the forces, soldiers*›

B *vi* «fighters, soldiers» أَعادَ ,انْتَظَمَ في مَجْموعةٍ من جَديدٍ تَنْظيمَ صُفوفِهِ

regular /ˈrɛgjʊlə/ **A** *adj* **1** (periodic) ‹*meetings, exercise*› دَوْرِيّ; **at ~ intervals** (in time) على فَتَراتٍ مُنْتَظِمةٍ; (in space) على فَواصِلَ \ مَسافاتٍ مُتَساوِيةٍ \ مُنْتَظِمةٍ; **to take ~ exercise** مارَسَ التَمارينَ الرياضيّةَ بِانْتِظام **2** (frequent) ‹*visitor, customer, contact*› مُنْتَظِم; **they are in ~ contact with each other** يَتَّصِلُ بَعْضُهُمْ بِبَعْضٍ بِشَكْلٍ مُنْتَظِمٍ **3** (constant) ‹*job, income*› دائِم, ثابِت **4** (uninterrupted) ‹*breathing, pulse*› مُنْتَظِم **5** (usual) ‹*supplier, teacher*› أَساسِيّ **6** (medium-sized) ‹*portion*› مُتَوَسِّط الحَجْمِ; **a burger with ~ fries** بيرْجِر مع بَطاطِس مَقْلِيّةٍ مُتَوَسِّطةِ الحَجْمِ **7** ‹*army, soldier*› نِظامِيّ **8** ‹*verb, conjugation*› قِياسِيّ **9** (AmE) (infml) (unpretentious) غَيْر مُتَكَلِّفٍ; **he's a ~ guy** هو شَخْصٌ غَيْرُ مُتَكَلِّفٍ

B *n* **1** (customer) زَبون \ عُضْو دائِم **2** (soldier) جُنْديّ نِظامِيّ **3** (AmE) (gasoline) بَنْزين عادِيّ

regularity /rɛgjʊˈlarəti/ *n* اطِّراد, انْتِظام

regularly /ˈrɛgjələli/ *adv* ‹*to meet, exercise*› بِاطِّرادٍ, بِانْتِظامٍ

regulate /ˈrɛgjʊleɪt/ *vt* **1** (with rules) نَظَّمَ ‹*an industry, activities*› **2** (to adjust) ضَبَطَ (i-u; ضَبْط) ‹*temperature, flow*›

regulation /rɛgjʊˈleɪʃ(ə)n/ **A** *n* **1** (rule) قاعِدة (قَواعِدُ), قانون (قَوانينُ), لائِحة (لَوائِحُ ,لائِحات), إِرْشاد; **safety/building ~s** إِرْشادات الحِمايةِ من الحَريقِ \ لَوائِح \ قَوانين السلامةِ \ البِناءِ; **fire ~s** لَوائِح الاتِّحادِ الأوروبِّيِّ; **EU ~s** لَوائِح; **it's against the ~s** هو مُخالِفٌ للقَواعِدِ **2** [u] (control) ضَبْط, تَنْظيم

B *adj before n* ‹*size, width*› مُطابِق للقَواعِدِ

regulation haircut *n* حِلاقة عَسْكَرِيّة (حِلاقة شَعْرٍ قَصيرة)

regulation uniform *n* زِيّ عَسْكَرِيّ \ نِظامِيّ

regulator /ˈrɛgjʊleɪtə/ *n* **1** (device) مُنَظِّم **2** (of an industry) (a person) ضابِط, مُنَظِّم (ضُبّاط); (a body) هَيْئة تَنْظيمِيّة

regulatory /ˈrɛgjələt(ə)ri/ *adj* ‹*body, approval*› تَنْظيمِيّ

regurgitate /rɪˈgəːdʒɪteɪt/ *vt* **1** (to vomit) تَقَيَّأَ ‹*food, bones*› **2** (to repeat) رَدَّدَ (دون تَحْليلٍ \ فَهْمٍ) ‹*propaganda, clichés*›

rehab /ˈriːhab/ *n* = **rehabilitation** إِعادة تَأْهيلِ المُدْمِنينَ; **to go into ~** دَخَلَ مَرْكَزَ إِعادةِ تَأْهيلِ المُدْمِنينَ

rehabilitate /riːhəˈbɪlɪteɪt/ *vt* أَعادَ التَأْهيلَ ‹*an offender, a victim*›

rehabilitation /riːəbɪlɪˈteɪʃ(ə)n/ *n* إِعادة تَأْهيلٍ

rehabilitation centre (BrE), **rehabilitation center** (AmE) *n* مَرْكَز إِعادةِ تَأْهيلٍ

rehearsal /rɪˈhəːs(ə)l/ *n* بُروفة; **they're having the dress ~ for the show on Saturday afternoon** عِنْدَهُمْ بُروفةُ مَلابِسَ لِعَرْضِ يَوْمِ السَبْتِ مَساءً

rehearse /rɪˈhəːs/ **A** *vt* تَدَرَّبَ (على), تَمَرَّنَ (على) ‹*a play, scene*›; **to ~ a routine for the show** تَدَرَّبَ على مَقْطَعٍ من العَرْضِ

B *vi* «bands, actors» تَمَرَّنَ, قامَ بِبُروفةٍ; **the choir is rehearsing for the concert** تَقومُ الجَوْقةُ بِبُروفةٍ للحَفْلةِ

reheat /riːˈhiːt/ *vt* أَعادَ التَسْخينَ ‹*leftovers, a sauce*›

rehouse /riːˈhaʊz/ *vt* أَعادَ التَسْكينَ ‹*a victim, tenant*›

reign /reɪn/ **A** *vi* «queens, kings» تَوَلّى الحُكْمَ; **Herod ~ed over Palestine** حَكَمَ هيرود فِلَسْطين

B *n* عَهْد (عُهود), فَتْرة حُكْمٍ

reigning /ˈreɪnɪŋ/ *adj* **1** (in power) ‹*monarch, king*› على سُدّةِ الحُكْمِ **2** (holding a title) ‹*champion, medallist*› حامِل لَقَبٍ

reimburse /ˌriːɪmˈbɜːs/ *vt* عَوَّض ‹*an expense, cost*›; رَدَّ, أعادَ (u; رَدّ) ‹*an employee, a customer*›

rein /reɪn/ *n* عِنان (أَعِنَّة)

(Idiom) **to give sb free rein** أَطْلَقَ العِنانَ لِشَخْصٍ

reincarnation /ˌriːɪnkɑːˈneɪʃ(ə)n/ *n* **1** [u] (after death) تَناسُخ \ تَقَمُّص الأَرْواحِ **2** (person, animal) [روح تَتَقَمَّصُ جَسَداً آخَرَ]

reindeer /ˈreɪndɪə/ *n* (*pl* **reindeer**) حَيَوان الرَّنَّة

reinforce /riːɪnˈfɔːs/ *vt* **1** (to stress) رَسَّخ ‹*a message, stereotype*› **2** (militarily) دَعَّم ‹*troops, a garrison*› **3** (to make stronger) عَزَّزَ, قَوّى ‹*the foundations, plastic*›

reinforced concrete /ˌriɪnfɔːst ˈkɒŋkriːt/ *n* إسْمَنْت مُسَلَّح, خَرَسانة مُسَلَّحة

reinforcement /riːɪnˈfɔːsmənt/ *n* **1** (of a structure) تَرْسيخ, تَدْعيم **2** (of ideas, impressions) تَعْزيز, تَقْوية **3** (**reinforcements** *n pl*) (forces) تَعْزيزات \ إمْدادات عَسْكَرِيّة

reinstate /riːɪnˈsteɪt/ *vt* **1** (in the workplace) أعادَ إلى مَنْصِبِهِ السابِقِ ‹*an employee, official*› **2** (to reactivate) أعادَ (بعد أنْ كانَ مُعَلَّقاً) ‹*ban, licence*›

reintegrate /riːˈɪntɪɡreɪt/ *vt* أعاد الدَمْج \ الإدْماجَ ‹*offenders, former soldiers*›; **the scheme helps ~ former prisoners into society** يُساعِدُ المُخَطَّطُ في إعادةِ دَمْجِ السُجَناءِ السابِقينَ في المُجْتَمَعِ

reintegration /riːɪntɪˈɡreɪʃ(ə)n/ *n* إعادة إدْماج

reissue /riːˈɪʃuː/ **A** *vt* أعادَ الإصْدارَ \ التَوْزيعَ ‹*an album, book, ticket*›; **to ~ the tickets to the passengers** أعادَ إصْدارَ البِطاقاتِ للمُسافِرينَ

B *n* **1** (republication) إعادة إصْدارٍ \ طَبْعٍ **2** (new version) طَبْعة جَديدة

reiterate /riːˈɪtəreɪt/ *vt* (fml) أَكَّدَ ‹*a commitment*›; كَرَّر ‹*demand*›

reject **A** /rɪˈdʒɛkt/ *vt* رَفَضَ (i-u; رَفْض) ‹*an offer, claim*›

B /ˈriːdʒɛkt/ *n* [سِلْعة مَعيبة تُباعُ بِثَمَنٍ رَخيصٍ]

rejection /rɪˈdʒɛkʃ(ə)n/ *n* **1** (of proposals, offers) رَفْض **2** (of a candidate) رَفْض

rejection letter *n* رِسالة رَفْضٍ

reject shop *n* [مَحَلّ لِبَيْعِ السِلَعِ المَعيبةِ بِثَمَنٍ رَخيصٍ]

rejoice /rɪˈdʒɔɪs/ *vi* «fans, families» فَرِحَ, اِبْتَهَجَ (a; فَرْح)

rejuvenate /rɪˈdʒuːv(ə)neɪt/ *vt* أَنْعَشَ ‹*one's spirits, one's skin*›

rekindle /riːˈkɪnd(ə)l/ *vt* (to revive) أَحْيا من جَديدٍ ‹*a dispute, an interest*›

relapse **A** /rɪˈlaps/ *vi* «patients, invalids» اِنْتَكَسَ; **to ~ into a coma** دَخَلَ في غَيْبوبةٍ إثْرَ انْتِكاسةٍ

B /ˈriːlaps/ *n* انْتِكاس

relate /rɪˈleɪt/ **A** *vt* **1** (to connect) رَبَطَ (i-u; رَبْط; بين) ‹*incidents, ideas*›; **to ~ sth to sth** رَبَطَ بين شَيْءٍ وَشَيْءٍ **2** (to recount) حَكى (i; حِكاية), قَصَّ (u; قَصَص) ‹*a story, an experience*›; **to ~ how ...** حَكى كيف

B *vi* **1** (to be concerned with) **to ~ to sth/sb** تَعَلَّقَ بِشَيْءٍ \ بِشَخْصٍ; **matters relating to health** الأُمور المُتَعَلِّقة بالصِحّةِ **2** (to communicate) **she has problems relating to other people** لَدَيْها مُشاكِلُ في التَواصُلِ مع الآخَرينَ **3** (to identify with) **to ~ to sth/sb** تَعاطَفَ مع شَيْءٍ \ شَخْصٍ; **I can't ~ to the character** لا أَسْتَطيعُ أنْ أَتَعاطَفَ مع الشَخْصيّةِ; **I can ~ to that!** ذلك يَنْطَبِقُ عَلَيَّ أنا أَيْضاً!

related /rɪˈleɪtɪd/ *adj* **1** (by blood) قَريب (أَقْرِباءُ, أَقارِبُ); **are you ~ to Mary?** هل لَكَ صِلةُ قَرابةٍ بماري؟ **2** (connected) مُرْتَبِط, مُتَّصِل ‹*problem, incident*›; **a drug-~ crime** جَريمة مُرْتَبِطة بالمُخَدِّراتِ

relation /rɪˈleɪʃ(ə)n/ **A** *n* **1** (relative) قَريب (أَقْرِباءُ, أَقارِبُ), نَسيب (أَنْسِباءُ) **2** (connection) عَلاقة, صِلة (عَلاقات); **the sentence bore no ~ to the crime** كانَت العُقوبةُ لا تَمُتُّ للجَريمةِ بِأَيّةِ صِلةٍ

B (**relations**) *n pl* عَلاقات; **to break off/establish commercial/diplomatic ~s** قَطَعَ \ أَسَّسَ عَلاقاتٍ تِجاريّةً \ دِبْلوماسيّةً

(Idiom) **in relation to sb/sth** بالنِسْبةِ لِشَخْصٍ \ لِشَيْءٍ

relationship /rɪˈleɪʃ(ə)nʃɪp/ *n* **1** (between people) عَلاقة (عَلاقات); **she has a very close ~ with her sister** لَدَيْها عَلاقةٌ وَثيقةٌ جِدًّا مع أُخْتِها; **~s between the two communities have improved** تَحَسَّنَت العَلاقاتُ بين الجَماعَتَيْنِ **2** (connection) عَلاقة (عَلاقات), صِلة; **the ~ between mental and physical illness** العَلاقة بين المَرَضِ العَقْليِّ والجَسَديِّ **3** (involvement) عَلاقة (عاطِفيّة); **are you in a ~?** هل أَنْتَ مُرْتَبِطٌ؟ **4** (in a family) صِلة قَرابةٍ

relative /ˈrɛlətɪv/ **A** *adj* 1 (respective) ‹*merits, ability*› خاصّ 2 (comparative) ‹*poverty, ease*› نِسْبِيّ **B** *n* (by blood) قَرِيب (أَقارِبُ, أَقْرِباءُ); **she's a distant/close ~** تَرْبِطُني بِها صِلةُ قَرابةٍ بَعِيدةٌ \ مُباشِرةٌ Idiom **relative to sth** بالنِسْبةِ إلى شَيْءٍ

relatively /ˈrɛlətɪvli/ *adv* ‹*small, safe*› نِسْبِيًّا

relax /rɪˈlaks/ **A** *vt* 1 (to loosen) ‹*a muscle, your grip*› أَرْخى 2 (to make less strict) ‹*the rules, a ban*› خَفَّفَ **B** *vi* 1 (to rest) «visitors, passengers» اِسْتَراحَ 2 (to loosen) «muscles, bodies» اِسْتَرْخى

relaxation /riːlakˈseɪʃ(ə)n/ *n* 1 (for rest) اِسْتِرْخاء 2 (of restrictions, discipline) تَخْفِيف

relaxed /rɪˈlakst/ *adj* ‹*atmosphere, attitude*› هادِئ

relaxing /rɪˈlaksɪŋ/ *adj* ‹*atmosphere, activity*› مُرِيح

relay /ˈriːleɪ/ **A** *n* 1 (of workers) عُمّال مُناوِبة; **to work in ~s** عَمِلَ بالتَناوُبِ 2 (also **relay race**) سِباق تَتابُعٍ **B** *vt* 1 نَقَلَ (u; نَقْل) ‹*a signal, images*› 2 بَعَثَ (a; بَعْث), أَرْسَلَ ‹*a message*›

release /rɪˈliːs/ **A** *vt* 1 (to set free) أَفْرَجَ (عن), أَطْلَقَ السَراحَ ‹*a prisoner, hostage*›; أَطْلَقَ ‹*an animal*›; **she was ~d from hospital today** سُمِحَ لَها بالخُروجِ من المُسْتَشْفى اليَوْمَ 2 (from contracts) أَعْفى ‹*a player, an employee*›; **to ~ sb from a contract/an obligation** أَعْفى شَخْصاً من عَقْدٍ \ اِلْتِزامٍ 3 (to emit) أَطْلَقَ, اِنْبَعَثَ مِنْهُ ‹*energy, gases*› 4 (to disengage) حَرَّرَ, أَطْلَقَ ‹*a catch, the clutch, handbrake*› 5 (to launch) أَطْلَقَ ‹*a bomb, missile*› 6 (to let go of) تَرَكَ (u; تَرْك), أَرْخى قَبْضَتَهُ عن ‹*sb's hand, arm*› 7 (to make public) أَعْلَنَ, أَصْدَرَ ‹*a statement, information*› 8 (to put on sale) أَصْدَرَ ‹*an album, a film*› **B** *n* 1 [u] (of a prisoner, hostage) إِطْلاق السَراحِ, تَحْرِير, إِفْراج (عن); **on his ~ from prison** بعد إِطْلاقِ سَراحِهِ من السِجْنِ 2 [u] (relief) شُعور بالارْتِياحِ; **death came as a merciful ~** جاءَ المَوْتُ كَنِهايةٍ رَحِيمةٍ لَهُ 3 [u] (of energy, gas) إِطْلاق, اِنْبِعاث 4 [u] (of information) نَشْر, إِفْراج (عن) 5 (announcement) بَيان (بَيانات); **a news ~** بَيان صَحَفِيّ 6 [u] (of an album, a film) إِصْدار; **the film is now on general ~** الفِيلْم الآنَ مُتاحٌ للجُمْهورِ 7 (album, film) إِصْدار (إِصْدارات); **new film/DVD ~s** إِصْدارات جَدِيدة للفِيلْمِ \ للدِي في دي

release mechanism *n* آلِيّة إِعْتاقٍ

relegate /ˈrɛlɪɡeɪt/ *vt* 1 (to give a lower rank to) [مَنَحَ مَرْتَبةً أَدْنى] ‹*a topic, women*› 2 (BrE) (in sport) [أَنْزَلَ إلى قِسْمٍ أَدْنى] ‹*a team, club*›; **to be ~d from the second to the third division** أُنْزِلَ من القِسْمِ الثاني إلى الثالِثِ

relegation /rɛlɪˈɡeɪʃ(ə)n/ *n* 1 (to a lower rank) تَخْفِيض المَنْزِلةِ 2 (in sport) [إِنْزال إلى قِسْمٍ أَدْنى]; **the team's ~ to the second division** إِنْزال الفَرِيقِ إلى القِسْمِ الثاني

relent /rɪˈlɛnt/ *vi* (fml) «authorities, parents» رَضَخَ (a-i; رُضوخ)

relentless /rɪˈlɛntləs/ *adj* 1 (never ending) ‹*policy, pressure*› لا يَعْرِفُ الهَوادةَ 2 (implacable) ‹*pursuer, enemy*› دَؤوب

relentlessly /rɪˈlɛntlɪsli/ *adv* ‹*to campaign, attack*› بِلا هَوادةٍ

relevance /ˈrɛləv(ə)ns/ *n* صِلة; **what is the ~ of his comments?** ما عَلاقةُ تَعْلِيقاتِهِ بالمَوْضوعِ؟

relevant /ˈrɛlɪv(ə)nt/ *adj* ‹*information, document*› مُتَعَلِّق, مُرْتَبِط, ذو صِلةٍ; **the data are not ~ to the issue** لَيْسَ للمَعْلوماتِ صِلةٌ بالمَسْأَلةِ

reliability /rɪlʌɪəˈbɪlɪti/ *n* 1 (of a witness, data) اِعْتِمادِيّة 2 (of employees) مَوْثوقِيّة 3 (of cars, machines) اِعْتِمادِيّة

reliable /rɪˈlʌɪəb(ə)l/ *adj* 1 (accurate) ‹*information, witness*› دَقِيق 2 (trustworthy) ‹*employee, firm*› مَوْثوق بِهِ 3 (in performance) ‹*car, service*› يُعْتَمَدُ عَلَيْهِ

reliably /rɪˈlʌɪəbli/ *adv* ‹*to inform*› من مَصْدَرٍ مَوْثوقٍ بِهِ \ مُطَّلِعٍ; **I am ~ informed that the airport will be open** لَدَيَّ مَعْلوماتٌ من مَصْدَرٍ مَوْثوقٍ بِهِ أنّ المَطارَ سَيَكونُ مَفْتوحاً

reliance /rɪˈlʌɪəns/ *n* اِعْتِماد, اِتِّكال; **to put one's ~ on sth** وَضَعَ ثِقَتَهُ في شَيْءٍ

reliant /rɪˈlʌɪənt/ *adj* مُعْتَمِد (على), مُتَّكِل (على); **to be ~ on sb/sth** كانَ مُعْتَمِداً على شَخْصٍ \ شَيْءٍ

relic /ˈrɛlɪk/ *n* 1 (object) أَثَر (آثار) 2 (of holy person) رُفات

relief /rɪˈliːf/ *n* 1 (from tension) اِرْتِياح 2 (from pain) تَخْفِيف 3 (aid) إِعانة, مَعونة, غَوْث

relief agency *n* وَكالة غَوْثٍ

relief fund *n* صُنْدوق إِغاثةٍ \ مَعونةٍ

relief road *n* طَريق جانبيّ لا يَختَرِقُ قَلْبَ المَدينةِ (لِتجَنُّبِ الزِحامِ)

relief supplies *n* مَوادّ \ إمْدادات إغاثةٍ

relief work *n* أَعْمال إغاثةٍ

relief worker *n* عامِل إغاثةٍ

relieve /rɪˈliːv/ *vt* 1 (to alleviate) خَفَّفَ ‹pain, suffering› 2 (fml) **to ~ sb of sth** أَراحَ شَخْصاً من شَيْءٍ 3 (in duties) سَرَّحَ ‹a worker, sentry› 4 (fml) **to ~ oneself** قَضى حاجَتَهُ

religion /rɪˈlɪdʒ(ə)n/ *n* دين (أَدْيان)

religious /rɪˈlɪdʒəs/ *adj* ‹belief, leader› دينيّ; **~ observance is increasing/decreasing** الالْتِزامُ الدينيُّ في ازْدِيادٍ \ نُقْصانٍ

religiously /rɪˈlɪdʒəsli/ *adv* 1 (connected with religion) ‹diverse, motivated› دينيًّا 2 (conscientiously) ‹to follow instructions, exercise› بِانْتِظامٍ, بِالْتِزامٍ

relinquish /rɪˈlɪŋkwɪʃ/ *vt* تَخَلّى (عن), تَنازَلَ (عن) ‹a right, responsibility›; **to ~ control of sth** تَخَلّى عن زِمامِ التَحَكُّمِ في شَيْءٍ

relish /ˈrelɪʃ/ A *n* 1 **with ~** ‹to eat, devour› بِلَذَّةٍ, بِتَلَذُّذٍ; ‹to say, perform› بِاسْتِمْتاعٍ 2 (Culin) (piquant sauce) صَلْصة قَوِيّةُ النَكْهةِ; (pickle) مُخَلَّل

B *vt* 1 (to enjoy) اسْتَمْتَعَ (بِ), تَلَذَّذَ (بِ) ‹one's food, freedom› 2 (to look forward to) تَطَلَّعَ (إلى) ‹the prospect, thought›; **she is ~ing the prospect of retirement** تَتَطَلَّعُ إلى احْتِمالِ التَقاعُدِ

relive /riːˈlɪv/ *vt* «person» اسْتَذْكَرَ (في ذِهْنِهِ) ‹an experience, the past›

relocate /riːləʊˈkeɪt/ A *vt* نَقَلَ (إلى مَكانٍ جَديدٍ) ‹an office, a family›

B *vi* «companies, employees» انْتَقَلَ (إلى مَكانٍ جَديدٍ)

relocation /riːləʊˈkeɪʃ(ə)n/ *n* انْتِقال, نَقْل (إلى مَكانٍ جَديدٍ)

reluctance /rɪˈlʌkt(ə)ns/ *n* تَرَدُّد, إحْجام, عَدَم حَماسٍ

reluctant /rɪˈlʌkt(ə)nt/ *adj* ‹hero, participant› مُتَرَدِّد, غَيْر مُتَحَمِّسٍ; **to be ~ to do sth** كانَ مُتَرَدِّداً في فِعْلِ شَيْءٍ

reluctantly /rɪˈlʌkt(ə)ntli/ *adv* ‹to agree, admit› على مَضَضٍ

rely /rɪˈlaɪ/ *vi* (**relies**, **relying**, **relied**) 1 (to be dependent on) اعْتَمَدَ (على), اتَّكَلَ; **to ~ on or upon sb/sth** اعْتَمَدَ على شَخْصٍ \ شَيْءٍ; **she relies on her children for transport** تَعْتَمِدُ على أَوْلادِها في المُواصَلاتِ 2 (to count on) عَوَّلَ, اتَّكَلَ (على), اعْتَمَدَ; **to ~ on or upon sb/sth** عَوَّلَ \ اتَّكَلَ على شَخْصٍ \ شَيْءٍ; **you can ~ on me** يُمْكِنُكَ الاتِّكالُ عَلَيَّ; **buses can't be relied upon to arrive on time** لا يُمْكِنُ الاعْتِمادُ على الحافِلاتِ للوُصولِ في المَوْعِدِ

remain /rɪˈmeɪn/ *vi* 1 (to continue to be) «person, situation» ظَلَّ (a; ظُلول; perf ظَلِلْتُ), بَقِيَ (a; بَقاء); **she ~ed silent** ظَلَّتْ صامِتةً; **the question ~s: is it worth it?** وَيَبْقى السُؤالُ: هل يَسْتَحِقُّ الأَمْرُ ذلك؟; **his identity ~s a mystery** تَبْقى هُوِيَّتُهُ لُغْزاً 2 (to stay) «person» مَكَثَ (u; مُكوث); **to ~ behind** مَكَثَ في الخَلْفِ 3 (to be left) «tasks, ruins» بَقِيَ (a; بَقاء); **the fact ~s that he lied to me** الحَقيقةُ هي أَنَّهُ كَذَبَ عَلَيَّ; **that ~s to be seen** إنّ غَداً لِناظِرِهِ قَريبٌ

remainder /rɪˈmeɪndə/ *n* **the ~** البَقِيّةُ

remains /rɪˈmeɪnz/ *n pl* 1 (of a building) مُخَلَّفات; (of a meal) بَقايا 2 (of a corpse) رُفات

remake A /riːˈmeɪk/ *vt* (*past tense, past participle* **remade**) «person» أَعادَ الإنْتاجَ ‹a film›; أَعادَ التَرْتيبَ ‹a bed›

B /ˈriːmeɪk/ *n* طَبْعة جَديدة

remand /rɪˈmɑːnd/ A *vt* **to be ~ed in custody** وُضِعَ رَهْنَ الحَبْسِ الاحْتِياطيِّ; **to be ~ed on bail** أُفْرِجَ عَنْهُ بِكَفالةٍ ماليّةٍ

B *n* **to be on ~** كانَ في الحَبْسِ الاحْتِياطيِّ

remand centre *n* (BrE) مَرْكَز حَبْسٍ احْتِياطيٍّ

remark /rɪˈmɑːk/ A *vt* لاحَظَ, عَلَّقَ

B *vi* **to ~ on or upon sth** «observers, speakers» أَبْدى مُلاحَظةً على شَيْءٍ

C *n* مُلاحَظة, تَعْليق

remarkable /rɪˈmɑːkəb(ə)l/ *adj* ‹achievement, success› مَلْحوظ; ‹story, ability› مُلْفِت; ‹man, woman› رائِع

remarkably /rɪˈmɑːkəbli/ *adv* ‹similar, good› بِشَكْلٍ مَلْحوظٍ \ مُلْفِتٍ

remarry /riːˈmari/ *vi* (**remarries**, **remarrying**, **remarried**) «widower, widow» تَزَوَّجَ مَرّةً أُخْرى

remedial /rɪˈmiːdɪəl/ *adj* 1 ‹work, action› إصْلاحيّ 2 ‹treatment› عِلاجيّ 3 ‹class, course› تَعْويضيّ

remedy /ˈremɪdi/ A *n* (*pl* **remedies**) عِلاج

B *vt* (**remedies, remedying, remedied**) صَحَّحَ ‹*a situation, problem*›

remember /rɪˈmɛmbə/ **A** *vt* **1** (to recall) تَذَكَّرَ ‹*a fact, place, name*›; **to ~ doing sth** تَذَكَّرَ أَنَّهُ فَعَلَ شَيْئاً; **I ~ meeting him last year** أَتَذَكَّرُ أَنَّني قابَلْتُهُ العامَ الماضِيَ; **I don't ~ anything about it** لا أَتَذَكَّرُ أَيَّ شَيْءٍ عَنْهُ; **~ that he was only 20 at the time** ضَعْ في اعْتِبارِكَ أَنّ عُمْرَهُ وَقْتَها كانَ 20 عاماً فَقَطْ **2** (not to forget) تَذَكَّرَ ‹*an anniversary, a birthday*›; **to ~ to do sth** تَذَكَّرَ أَنْ يَفْعَلَ شَيْئاً; **~ to bring the keys** تَذَكَّرْ أَنْ تُحْضِرَ المَفاتيحَ; **~ that it's fragile** تَذَكَّرْ أَنَّهُ قابِلٌ للكَسْرِ; **~ where you are!** احْتَرِمِ المَكانَ الّذي أَنْتَ فيهِ! **3** (to commemorate) حَيّا الذِكْرى ‹*a battle, the dead*› **4** (fml) (to leave money to) أَوْصى (بِنَصيبٍ) لِ; **to ~ sb in one's will** جَعَلَ لِشَخْصٍ نَصيباً في وَصيَّتِهِ **5** (fml) (to convey greetings from) **to ~ sb to sb** حَمَلَ تَحيّاتِ شَخْصٍ إلى شَخْصٍ; **~ me to your parents** بَلِّغْ تَحيّاتي لِوالِدَيْكَ

B *vi* تَذَكَّرَ; **they all claimed they could not ~** كُلُّهُمْ زَعَموا أَنَّهُمْ لم يَسْتَطيعوا التَذَكُّرَ; **if I ~ correctly** إذا لم تَخُنّي الذاكِرةُ; **as far as I can ~** على ما أَتَذَكَّرُ; **not as far as I ~** لَيْسَ على حَدِّ ما أَتَذَكَّرُ

remembrance /rɪˈmɛmbrəns/ *n* (fml) إحْياء \ تَخْليد ذِكْرى; **in ~ of sb/sth** إحْياءً لِذِكْرى شَخْصٍ \ شَيْءٍ

Remembrance Day *n* **Remembrance Sunday** (BrE) [ذِكْرى شُهَداءِ الحَرْبَيْنِ العالَمِيَّتَيْنِ في بَريطانيا]

remind /rɪˈmaɪnd/ *vt* **1** (to cause to remember) ذَكَّرَ; **to ~ sb to do sth** ذَكَّرَ شَخْصاً بِفِعْلِ شَيْءٍ; **oh! that ~s me** آه! هذا يُذَكِّرُني **2** (to bring to mind) **to ~ sb of sth/sb** «person, voice» ذَكَّرَ شَخْصاً بِشَيْءٍ \ بِشَخْصٍ; **he ~s me of my father** يُذَكِّرُني بِوالِدي

reminder /rɪˈmaɪndə/ *n* **1** (memory jerker) تَذْكير; **to serve as a ~ of sth** كانَ بِمَثابَةِ تَذْكيرٍ بِشَيْءٍ **2** (for payment) رِسالة تَذْكيرٍ

reminisce /ˌrɛmɪˈnɪs/ *vi* اسْتَعادَ الذِكْرَياتِ; **to ~ about sth** اسْتَعادَ ذِكْرَياتِ شَيْءٍ

reminiscence /rɛmɪˈnɪs(ə)ns/ *n* [ذِكْرى \ قِصّة من الماضي]

reminiscent /rɛmɪˈnɪs(ə)nt/ *adj* **to be ~ of sb/sth** ذَكَّرَ بِشَخْصٍ \ بِشَيْءٍ

remiss /rɪˈmɪs/ *adj* مُقَصِّر, مُهْمِل

remission /rɪˈmɪʃ(ə)n/ *n* **1** (reduction of a sentence) تَخْفيف; (of a debt) إعْفاء **2** (from disease) اسْتِقْرار, خُمود; **to be in ~ from cancer** كانَ لَدَيْهِ سَرَطانٌ في حالةِ خُمودٍ

remit **A** /rɪˈmɪt/ *vt* (**-tt-**) **1** أَلْغى ‹*a sentence, debt*› **2** حَوَّلَ ‹*money, funds*›

B /ˈriːmɪt/ *n* صَلاحيّة

remittance /rɪˈmɪt(ə)ns/ *n* تَحْويل ماليّ, حَوالة ماليّة

remix /riːˈmɪks/ **A** *vt* [أَعادَ صِياغةَ نُسْخةٍ موسيقيّةٍ] ‹*a track, song*›

B *n* ريمِكْس (صيغة مُخْتَلِفة لِنُسْخةٍ موسيقيّةٍ)

remnant /rɛmnənt/ *n* **1** (leftover) بَقيّة (بَقايا); **a ~ of the past** أَثَر من الماضي; **the ~s of his army** فُلول جَيْشِهِ **2** (of fabric) [قِطْعة مُتَبَقِّية من قُماشٍ]

remodel /riːˈmɒd(ə)l/ *vt* (**-ll-** BrE, **-l-** AmE) أَعادَ التَصْميمَ ‹*a house, kitchen*›

remold (AmE) *n*, *vt* ▸ **remould**

remonstrate /ˈrɛmənstreɪt/ *vi* (fml) احْتَجَّ (على); **to ~ with sb** عَنَّفَ \ وَبَّخَ شَخْصاً

remorse /rɪˈmɔːs/ *n* نَدامة, نَدَم

remorseful /rɪˈmɔːsfʊl/ *adj* نادِم, مُتَّسِم بالنَدَمِ (نُدّام); **to be ~** كانَ مُتَّسِماً بالنَدَمِ

remorseless /rɪˈmɔːsləs/ *adj* **1** (unrepentant) ‹*killer, enemy*› لا يَعْرِفُ النَدَمَ **2** (relentless) ‹*progress, determination*› لا يَعْرِفُ الهَوادةَ

remote /rɪˈməʊt/ *adj* **1** (isolated) ‹*area, village*› ناءٍ, بَعيد **2** (aloof) ‹*person*› غَيْر وَدودٍ **3** (slight) ‹*chance, possibility*› ضَئيل

remote control *n* **1** [u] (system) تَحَكُّم عن بُعْدٍ **2** (device) جِهاز ريموت كُنْتْرول, جِهاز تَحَكُّمٍ عن بُعْدٍ

remote-controlled /rɪˌməʊtk(ə)nˈtrəʊld/ *adj* ‹*bomb, car*› يَتِمُّ التَحَكُّمُ فيهِ عن بُعْدٍ

remotely /rɪˈməʊtli/ *adv* **1** (in the least) ‹*interested, resembling*› لا من قَريبٍ وَلا من بَعيدٍ **2** (from a distance) ‹*to control, operate*› عن بُعْدٍ

remould (BrE), **remold** (AmE) **A** /riːˈməʊld/ *vt* **1** (BrE) [وَضَعَ طَبَقةً جَديدةً من المَطّاطِ على] ‹*a tyre*› **2** (to transform) أَعادَ الصِياغةَ ‹*a society, attitudes*›

B /ˈriːməʊld/ *n* (BrE) إطار مُجَدَّد

removable /rɪˈmuːvəb(ə)l/ *adj* ‹*media, battery*› قابِل للإزالةِ

removal /rɪˈmuːv(ə)l/ *n* **1** (taking away of refuse, graffiti) إزاحة; (of stains, unwanted hair) إزالة; (of a tumour, an organ) اسْتِئْصال **2** (abolishing of barriers, restrictions) إزالة **3** (BrE) (change of home) نَقْل (نُقَل), نُقْلة

remove /rɪˈmuːv/ **A** *vt* **1** (to take off) خَلَعَ (a; خَلْع), نَزَعَ (i; نَزْع) ‹*sb's clothes, shoes, a bandage*›; **I ~d my jacket** خَلَعْتُ سُتْرَتي; **the nurses ~d his shirt** خَلَعَت المُمَرِّضاتُ قَميصَهُ; **to ~ one's make-up** أزالَ مَكياجَهُ **2** (in operations) اسْتَأْصَلَ, أزالَ ‹*a tumour, an organ*› **3** (to take away) أزالَ ‹*a stain, an obstacle*›; حَذَفَ (i; حَذْف) ‹*a word*›; **to ~ sb's name from a list** حَذَفَ اسْمَ شَخْصٍ من قائِمةٍ; **to ~ a product from the market** سَحَبَ مُنْتَجاً من السوقِ **4** (to dispel) أزالَ ‹*a suspicion, doubt*› **5** (to oust) عَزَلَ (i; عَزْل), فَصَلَ (i; فَصْل), أقالَ ‹*a director, politician, an employee*›; **to ~ a minister from office** عَزَلَ وَزيراً من مَنْصِبِهِ **B** (**removed**) *adj* **1** **to be far ~d from reality/the truth** كانَ بَعيداً كُلَّ البُعْدِ عن الواقِعِ \ الحَقيقةِ **2** (in kinship) **my cousin once/twice ~d** ابْن \ حَفيد ابْنِ عَمّي **C** *n* (fml) **to be at one ~ from sth** فَصَلَتْ بَيْنَهُ وَبَيْنَ شَيْءٍ خَطْوةٌ \ شَعْرةٌ واحِدةٌ

remover /rɪˈmuːvə/ *n* مُزيل

remuneration /rɪˌmjuːnəˈreɪʃ(ə)n/ *n* (fml) أَجْر, أَتْعاب

Renaissance /rɪˈneɪs(ə)ns/ *n* **1** (movement) **the R~** عَصْر النَّهْضةِ (الأوروبّيّةِ) **2** (revival) **a r~** نَهْضة

renal /ˈriːn(ə)l/ *adj* ‹*failure, function*› كُلَوِيّ

rename /riːˈneɪm/ *vt* أعادَ التَّسْمِيةَ ‹*a street, computer file*›

render /ˈrɛndə/ *vt* (fml) **1** (to cause to become) **to ~ sth impossible/harmless** جَعَلَ شَيْئاً مُسْتَحيلاً \ عَديمَ الضَرَرِ; **to ~ sb unconscious/speechless** أفْقَدَ شَخْصاً الوَعْيَ \ النُطْقَ **2** (to provide) قَدَّمَ ‹*assistance, a service*›; **for services ~ed** عن الخَدَماتِ المُقَدَّمةِ **3** (to depict) صَوَّرَ ‹*sb's hands*›; وَصَفَ (i; وَصْف) ‹*mood*› **4** (to translate) تَرْجَمَ (i; تَرْجَمة) ‹*a text, phrase*› **5** (Constr) غَطّى \ طَلى بِطَبَقةٍ من المَعْجونِ ‹*a wall*›

rendering /ˈrɛndərɪŋ/ *n* **1** (performance) أداء (فَنّيّ) **2** (translation) تَرْجَمة (تَراجِمُ) **3** (on exterior wall) طِلاء [خارِجيّ من الجِبْسِ]

rendezvous /ˈrɒndɪvuː/ *n* (*pl* **rendezvous**) **1** (meeting) مَوْعِد (مَواعِدُ), لِقاء (لِقاءات) **2** (place) مُلْتَقًى (مُلْتَقَيات)

rendition /rɛnˈdɪʃ(ə)n/ *n* أداء (فَنّيّ), تَقْديم

renegade /ˈrɛnɪɡeɪd/ *n* مُرْتَدّ, مُنْشَقّ

renew /rɪˈnjuː/ *vt* **1** جَدَّدَ ‹*a contract, licence*›; جَدَّدَ الإعارةَ ‹*a library book*› **2** اسْتَأْنَفَ ‹*one's efforts, an attack*› **3** جَدَّدَ ‹*an acquaintance, a friendship*›

renewable /rɪˈnjuːəb(ə)l/ *adj* ‹*energy, contract*› قابِل للتَجْديدِ

renewal /rɪˈnjuːəl/ *n* **1** (of a licence, contract, passport) تَجْديد **2** (of interest) تَجْديد; (of talks, negotiations) اسْتِئْناف; (of hostilities) تَجَدُّد

renewed /rɪˈnjuːd/ *adj* ‹*interest, vigour*› مُتَجَدِّد

renminbi /ˈrɛnmɪnbi/ *n* (*pl* **renminbi**) رِنْمينْبي (العُمْلة الصينيّة)

renounce /rɪˈnaʊns/ *vt* **1** (to abandon) تَخَلّى (عن), تنازَلَ (عن) ‹*a claim, one's citizenship*› **2** (to abjure) نَبَذَ (i; نَبْذ) ‹*violence*›; ارْتَدّ (عن) ‹*one's faith*›

renovate /ˈrɛnəveɪt/ *vt* رَمَّمَ ‹*a building, house*›

renovation /ˌrɛnəˈveɪʃ(ə)n/ *n* تَرْميم (تَرْميمات)

renown /rɪˈnaʊn/ *n* صيت, شُهْرة

renowned /rɪˈnaʊnd/ *adj* ‹*artist, expert*› ذائِع الصيتِ

rent /rɛnt/ **A** *n* إيجار; **for ~** للإيجارِ; **~s have risen/fallen** ارْتَفَعَتْ \ انْخَفَضَتْ الإيجاراتُ **B** *vt* **1** (taking) اسْتَأْجَرَ ‹*a house, car, DVD*› **2** (providing) أَجَّرَ ‹*a house, car*› **3** ▸ **rent out**

Phrasal verb **rent out**: **~ [sth] out, ~ out [sth]** أَجَّرَ [شَيْئاً] ‹*a room, boat*›

rental /ˈrɛnt(ə)l/ *n* **1** (act of renting) تَأْجير **2** (payment) إيجار

renunciation /rɪnʌnsɪˈeɪʃ(ə)n/ *n* (rejection of claims, citizenship) تَخَلٍّ; (of violence) نَبْذ; (of one's faith) ارْتِداد

reoffend /riːəˈfɛnd/ *vi* «offenders, inmates» ارْتَكَبَ جَريمةً أُخْرى

reopen /riːˈəʊp(ə)n/ **A** *vt* **1** أعادَ الفَتْحَ ‹*a case, road*› **2** اسْتَأْنَفَ, عاوَدَ ‹*negotiations, talks*› **B** *vi* «building, border» أُعيدَ فَتْحُهُ

reorganization, **-isation** (BrE) /riɔːɡ(ə)nʌɪˈzeɪʃ(ə)n/ *n* إعادة تَنْظيمٍ

reorganize, -ise (BrE) /riː'ɔːg(ə)nʌɪz/ *vt* أَعادَ التَّنْظِيمَ ‹*a system, company*›

rep /rɛp/ *n* (infml) مُمَثِّل (يَنوبُ عن مَجْموعةٍ)؛ **a union ~** مُمَثِّل نَقابةٍ

repair /rɪ'pɛː/ **A** *vt* **1** أَصْلَحَ ‹*a clock, road, clothes*› **2** أَصْلَحَ ‹*relations, the damage*›

B *n* **1** [u] (restoration) صِيانة, إِصْلاح؛ **the boat/AC system is under ~** القاربُ \ جهازُ التَّكْييفِ قَيْدُ الإصْلاحِ؛ **it was damaged beyond ~** تَعَرَّضَ للتَّلَفِ بِدَرَجةٍ يَتَعَذَّرُ مَعَها إِصْلاحُهُ **2** (measure) إِصْلاح (إِصْلاحات)؛ **the cost of ~s amounted to ...** بَلَغَتْ تَكْلِفَةُ الإِصْلاحاتِ ...؛ **to carry out the ~s to sth** أَجْرى إِصْلاحاتٍ على شَيْءٍ **3** [u] (condition) **to be in good/bad ~** كانَ في حالةٍ جَيِّدةٍ \ سَيِّئةٍ؛ **to keep sth in good/bad ~** احْتَفَظَ بِشَيْءٍ في حالةٍ جَيِّدةٍ \ سَيِّئةٍ

repairer /rɪ'pɛːrə/ *n* مُصَلِّح؛ **a shoe/watch ~** مُصَلِّح أَحْذِيةٍ \ ساعاتٍ

repairman /rɪ'pɛːmən/ *n* (*pl* **-men**) مُصَلِّح

repatriate /riː'patrɪeɪt/ *vt* رَحَّلَ, أَعادَ إلى وَطَنِهِ ‹*a refugee, an immigrant*›

repatriation /riːpatrɪ'eɪʃ(ə)n/ *n* تَرْحيل (تَراحيلُ), إِعادة إلى الوَطَنِ

repay /rɪ'peɪ/ *vt* (*past tense, past participle* **repaid**) **1** سَدَّدَ ‹*the loan, money*› **2** سَدَّدَ الدَّيْنَ ل ‹*a person, creditor*› **3** رَدَّ (u; رَدّ) ‹*a favour*›؛ جازى (على), كافَأَ (على) ‹*kindness*›

repayment /rɪ'peɪmənt/ *n* **1** [u] (of a loan, debt) تَسْديد **2** (amount) قِسْط (أَقْساط), دُفْعة (دُفُعات)

repeal /rɪ'piːl/ **A** *vt* أَلْغى, أَبْطَلَ ‹*a law, legislation*›

B *n* إِلْغاء, إِبْطال (قانونٍ)

repeat /rɪ'piːt/ **A** *vt* **1** «speaker» كَرَّرَ, أَعادَ, رَدَّدَ ‹*a word, sentence*›؛ **~ the words after me** رَدِّدِ الكَلِماتِ وَرائي؛ **this programme will be ~ed on Friday** سَيُعادُ هذا البَرْنامَجُ يَوْمَ الجُمْعةِ **2** كَرَّرَ ‹*a test, one's success*›؛ **they were unable to ~ the experiment** لم يَسْتَطيعوا أَنْ يُكَرِّروا التَّجْرِبةَ **3** «student» أَعادَ ‹*a year, course*›

B *vi* **1** (to do sth again) كَرَّرَ **2** (infml) (to cause indigestion) **to ~ on sb** سَبَّبَ عُسْرَ هَضْمٍ لِشَخْصٍ

C *v refl* **to ~ oneself** «speaker, old people» كَرَّرَ \ أَعادَ ما قالَهُ؛ **history is ~ing itself** التاريخُ يُعيدُ نَفْسَهُ

D *n* (of an event, act, broadcast) إِعادة, تَكْرار؛ **the final is a ~ of last year's game** المُباراةُ النِهائيَّةُ هي تَكْرارٌ لِمُباراةِ العامِ السابِقِ؛ **there are too many ~s on TV** هُناكَ الكَثيرُ جِدًّا من البَرامِجِ المُعادةِ في التِلِفِزْيون

repeated /rɪ'piːtɪd/ *adj* ‹*attempts, requests, phone calls*› مُتَكَرِّر

repeatedly /rɪ'piːtɪdli/ *adv* ‹*to say, ask*› تَكْراراً, مِراراً وَتَكْراراً

repel /rɪ'pɛl/ *vt* (**-ll-**) **1** صَدَّ (u; صَدّ, صُدود) ‹*an attack, invasion*› **2** أَبْعَدَ ‹*insects, pests*› **3** (to disgust) «sight, idea» نَفَّرَ, أَثارَ الاشْمِئْزازَ ‹*a person*›

repellent /rɪ'pɛlənt/ **A** *adj* **1** (able to repel) ‹*spray, finish*› طارِد, صادّ **2** (disgusting) ‹*smell, person*› كَريه, بَغيض, مُثير للاشْمِئْزازِ

B *n* **1** (repelling substance) طارِد حَشَراتٍ **2** (waterproofing substance) مادّة مُقاوِمة \ مُضادّة للماءِ

repent /rɪ'pɛnt/ *vi* «people, sinners» تابَ (u; تَوْب), نَدِمَ (a; نَدَم؛ على)

repentance /rɪ'pɛnt(ə)ns/ *n* تَوْبة, نَدَم

repentant /rɪ'pɛnt(ə)nt/ *adj* ‹*sinner, criminal*› تائِب, نادِم (نُدّام)

repercussion /riːpə'kʌʃ(ə)n/ *n* عاقِبة (عَواقِبُ), تَبِعة

repertoire /'rɛpətwɑː/ *n* [مَجْموعة عُروضٍ فَنِّيَّةٍ تَدَرَّبَ عَلَيْها فَنّانٌ]

repertory /'rɛpət(ə)ri/ *n* **1** [تَقْديم عُروضٍ فَنِّيَّةٍ مُخْتَلِفةٍ من طَرَفِ شَرِكةٍ]؛ **to be/work in ~** [كانَ \ عَمِلَ في فِرْقةٍ مَسْرَحِيَّةٍ تُقَدِّمُ عُروضاً مُخْتَلِفةً] **2** ▸ **repertoire**

repetition /rɛpɪ'tɪʃ(ə)n/ *n* تَكْرار

repetitious /rɛpɪ'tɪʃəs/ *adj* ‹*work, style*› حافِل بالتَكْرارِ, تَكْراريّ

repetitive /rɪ'pɛtɪtɪv/ *adj* ‹*work, movement*› حافِل بالتَكْرارِ, تَكْراريّ

repetitive strain injury *n* إِصابة الإِجْهادِ المُتَكَرِّرِ

rephrase /riː'freɪz/ *vt* أَعادَ الصِياغةَ ‹*a question, sentence*›

replace /rɪ'pleɪs/ *vt* **1** (to substitute for) أَبْدَلَ ‹*a part, broken window*›؛ اسْتَبْدَلَ ‹*a lost item*›؛ حَلَّ المَحَلَّ ‹*an employee, official*› **2** (to put back) وَضَعَ ثانِيةً ‹*a lid, cork*›؛ أَعادَ إلى مَكانِهِ, رَجَّعَ ‹*a book, an ornament*›؛ وَضَعَ (a; وَضْع) ‹*the receiver*›

replacement /rɪ'pleɪsmənt/ *n* 1 [u] (act) اسْتِبْدال 2 (person) (بُدَلاءُ) بَديل 3 (object) (بَدائِلُ) بَديل

replay A /riː'pleɪ/ *vt* 1 لَعِبَ من جَديدٍ ‹a match, game› 2 ‹a tape› اسْتَمَعَ مَرَّةً أُخرى إلى; ‹a scene› شاهَدَ مَرَّةً أُخرى
B /'riːpleɪ/ *n* 1 (of an incident, event) إعادة; **action** *or* (AmE) **instant ~** [إعادة بَثٍّ لِقَطْعةٍ من حَدَثٍ رِياضيٍّ] 2 (match, game) مُباراة مُعادة \ إعادةٍ

replenish /rɪ'plenɪʃ/ *vt* مَلأَ ثانِيةً ‹supplies, stocks›

replete /rɪ'pliːt/ *adj* **~ with sth** مَليء بِشَيْءٍ

replica /'replɪkə/ *n* نُسْخة طِبْقَ الأَصْلِ

replicate /'replɪkeɪt/ *vt* 1 (to copy) نَسَخَ (a; نَسْخ) ‹the data, original› 2 (to repeat) كَرَّرَ ‹an experiment, the findings›

replication /replɪ'keɪʃ(ə)n/ *n* 1 (copy) نَسْخ 2 (reproduction) إعادة, تَكْرار

reply /rɪ'plʌɪ/ A *vt* (**replies**, **replying**, **replied**) رَدَّ, أَجابَ (u; رَدّ)
B *vi* «person» رَدَّ, أَجابَ (u; رَدّ); **she didn't ~ to my question/letter** لم تُجِبْ على سُؤالي \ رِسالَتي
C *n* (*pl* **replies**) جَواب (أَجْوِبة), إجابة, رَدّ (رُدود); **in ~ to a question/your letter** رَدًّا على سُؤالٍ \ رِسالَتِكُمْ

report /rɪ'pɔːt/ A *vt* 1 (to give news of) أَعْلَنَ (عن), أَبْلَغَ (عن) ‹an increase, a result, sb's success›; **all departments ~ed a decline in sales** أَبْلَغَتْ جَميعُ الإداراتِ عن انْخِفاضٍ في المَبيعاتِ; **he ~s that my parents are well** يَقولُ إنَّ والِدَيَّ بِخَيْرٍ 2 (to give an account of) قَدَّمَ تَقْريراً عن ‹a debate, sb's death, an incident›; **local TV is ~ing that the town has been captured** يُفيدُ التِلِفِزيون المَحَلِّيُّ أنَّ المَدينة تَمَّ الاسْتيلاءُ عَلَيْها; **five people are ~ed to be dead** تُفيدُ التَقاريرُ أنَّ خَمْسةَ أَشْخاصٍ قد لَقوا مَصْرَعَهُمْ 3 (to notify) أَبْلَغَ (عن) ‹a theft, death, an accident›; **15 new cases of cholera have been ~ed** تَمَّ الإبْلاغُ عن 15 حالةً جَديدةً للإصابةِ بالكوليرا 4 (to allege) يُقالُ (u; قَوْل), زَعَمَ (u; زَعْم); **she is ~ed to have resigned** قالَ إنَّها اسْتَقالَتْ 5 (to inform about) أَبْلَغَ (عن) ‹a company, thief, vandal›
B *vi* 1 (to give an account) نَقَلَ \ غَطّى الأَخْبارَ; **to ~ on the talks/battle** نَقَلَ أَخْبارَ المُحادَثاتِ \ المَعْرَكةِ 2 (to present findings) «committee, inquiry» قَدَّمَ تَقْريراً 3 (to present oneself) قَدَّمَ \ سَجَّلَ نَفْسَهُ; **please ~ to reception** يُرْجى إعْلامُ مَكْتَبِ الاسْتِقْبالِ بِحُضورِكَ; **to ~ for duty** حَضَرَ \ قَدَّمَ نَفْسَهُ للخِدْمةِ; **to ~ sick** أَبْلَغَ جِهةَ العَمَلِ أَنَّهُ مَريضٌ 4 (in hierarchies) **to ~ to the finance director/area manager** كانَ تحت رئاسةِ المُديرِ الماليِّ \ مُديرِ المِنْطَقةِ
C *n* 1 (on an event, situation) تَقْرير (تَقاريرُ); **the monthly sales ~** تَقْرير المَبيعاتِ الشَهْرِيّة 2 (of an incident, accident) مَحْضَر (مَحاضِرُ), تَقْرير (تَقاريرُ); **both drivers need to sign the accident ~** يَجِبُ على كِلا السائِقَيْنِ التَوْقيعُ على مَحْضَرِ الحادِثِ 3 (in newspapers) تَحْقيق صُحُفِيّ; (on broadcast news) تَقْرير إخْبارِيّ 4 (BrE) (from school) تَقْرير دِراسِيّ, شَهادة مَدْرَسِيّة 5 (AmE) (review) تَقْرير (تَقاريرُ) 6 (of a shot, an explosion) دَوِيّ
D (**reports**) *n pl* (unconfirmed information) تَقارير, أَنْباء; **~s are coming in of an explosion in Main Street** تَرِدُ التَقاريرُ عن وُقوعِ انْفِجارٍ في شارِعِ 'مين'

Phrasal verb **report back** 1 (after an absence) «employees» عادَ إلى عَمَلِهِ; «soldiers» عادَ إلى ثَكَناتِهِ 2 (with findings) قَدَّمَ تَقْريراً

report card *n* (AmE) بِطاقة تَقْييم تِلْميذٍ

reportedly /rɪ'pɔːtɪdli/ *adv* حَسْبَما يُقالُ, طِبْقاً لِما يُقالُ

reported speech /rɪ,pɔːtɪd 'spiːtʃ/ *n* خِطاب مَنْقول \ غَيْر مُباشِرٍ

reporter /rɪ'pɔːtə/ *n* مُراسِل صُحُفِيّ

reporting /rɪ'pɔːtɪŋ/ *n* تَغْطِية (إعْلامِيّة)

repose /rɪ'pəʊz/ *n* (liter) هُدوء, سُكون, اسْتِراحة; **in ~** في حالةِ سُكونٍ

repository /rɪ'pɒzɪt(ə)ri/ *n* (*pl* **repositories**) (fml) 1 (for information, books, waste) مَخْزَن (مَخازِنُ) 2 (of knowledge, power) مُسْتَوْدَع (مُسْتَوْدَعات)

repossess /,riːpə'zes/ *vt* اسْتَعادَ المِلْكِيّةَ, اسْتَرَدَّ, اسْتَرْجَعَ ‹a house, car›

repossession /riːpə'zeʃ(ə)n/ *n* اسْتِرْجاع (اسْتِرْجاعات), اسْتِعادة مِلْكِيّةٍ, اسْتِرْداد

reprehensible /,reprɪ'hensɪb(ə)l/ *adj* ‹act, conduct› مُسْتَهْجَن, مَعيب, ذَميم

represent /rɛprɪˈzɛnt/ *vt* [1] (to act for) مَثَّلَ ‹*a country, client*› [2] (to stand for) رَمَزَ (i-u; رَمْز) (إلى [3] (to constitute) مَثَّلَ, شَكَّلَ ‹*a threat, an opportunity*› [4] (to describe) وَصَفَ (i; وَصْف), صَوَّرَ ‹*a person, situation*›

representation /ˌrɛprɪzɛnˈteɪʃ(ə)n/ *n* [1] تَمْثيل [2] (**representations** *n pl*) شَكاوى رَسْميّة; **to make ~s to sb** تَقَدَّمَ بِشَكاوى رَسْميّة لدى شَخْصٍ

representative /rɛprɪˈzɛntətɪv/ **A** *adj* ‹*sample, example*› نموذَجيّ, تَمْثيليّ; **to be ~ of a group** مَثَّلَ مَجْموعةً **B** *n* [1] (of a person, group) مَنْدوب, مُمَثِّل [2] (of a company) وَكيل (وُكَلاءُ) [3] (in US government) نائِب (نوّاب)

repress /rɪˈprɛs/ *vt* [1] قَمَعَ (a; قَمْع) ‹*dissent, opposition*›; **all dissent was brutally ~ed** قُمِعَ كُلّ المُعارِضينَ بِوَحْشيّةٍ [2] كَبَتَ (i; كَبْت), كَبَحَ (a; كَبْح) ‹*a memory, desire*›

repression /rɪˈprɛʃ(ə)n/ *n* [1] (of a people, movement) قَمْع [2] (of feelings) كَبْت

repressive /rɪˈprɛsɪv/ *adj* ‹*regime, measures*› تَعَسُّفيّ, قَمْعيّ

reprieve /rɪˈpriːv/ **A** *vt* أَوْقَفَ تَنْفيذَ العُقوبةِ على ‹*a prisoner, criminal*› **B** *n* [1] (of a prisoner) إيقاف تَنْفيذ (عُقوبةٍ); **to grant/receive a ~** مَنَحَ \ أُعْطِيَ وَقْفاً للعُقوبةِ [2] (respite) مُهْلة (مُهَل)

reprimand /ˈrɛprɪmɑːnd/ **A** *n* تَوْبيخ (تَوْبيخات), تأْنيب **B** *vt* أَنَّبَ, وَبَّخَ ‹*an employee, a child*›

reprint **A** /riːˈprɪnt/ *vt* أَعادَ الطَبْعَ ‹*an article, a book*› **B** /ˈriːprɪnt/ *n* (book) (photograph) إعادة الطَبْع

reprisal /rɪˈprʌɪz(ə)l/ *n* ثَأْر (ثَأْرات), انْتِقام, إجْراء انْتِقاميّ

reproach /rɪˈprəʊtʃ/ **A** *vt* لامَ (u; لَوْم), وَبَّخَ, عاتَبَ ‹*a child, wrongdoer*›; **she ~ed me for not telling her sooner** لامَتْني لِأَنّني لم أُخْبِرْها قبل ذلك **B** *n* تَوْبيخ (تَوْبيخات), لَوْم, عِتاب; **to be above** *or* **beyond ~** كانَ فوق مُسْتَوى الشُبُهاتِ

reproachful /rɪˈprəʊtʃfʊl/ *adj* ‹*look, tone*› تأْنيبيّ, مُعاتِب, تَوْبيخيّ

reprocessing plant /riˈprəʊsɛsɪŋ ˌplɑːnt/ *n* مَحَطّة إعادةِ مُعالَجةِ الوَقود النَوَويّ

reproduce /riːprəˈdjuːs/ **A** *vt* نَسَخَ (a; نَسْخ) ‹*an image*›; أَعادَ الإنْتاجَ ‹*a sound*›; أَعادَ الإحْداثَ ‹*an effect*› **B** *vi* «species, cells» تَوالَدَ, تَكاثَرَ, تَناسَلَ

reproduction /riːprəˈdʌkʃ(ə)n/ *n* [1] (of paintings, photos, documents) نُسْخة (نُسَخ), صورة (صُوَر) [2] [u] (of humans, animals, plants) تَكاثُر, تَناسُل, تَوالُد

reproductive /ˌriːprəˈdʌktɪv/ *adj* ‹*organs, system*› تَناسُليّ

reproof /rɪˈpruːf/ *n* لَوْم, تَوْبيخ (تَوْبيخات), تأْنيب

reprove /rɪˈpruːv/ *vt* وَبَّخَ, أَنَّبَ

reptile /ˈrɛptʌɪl/ *n* زاحِف (زَواحِفُ)

republic /rɪˈpʌblɪk/ *n* جُمْهوريّة

republican /rɪˈpʌblɪk(ə)n/ **A** *adj* [1] (of a republic) ‹*government, principles*› جُمْهوريّ [2] (**Republican**) (in US politics) ‹*candidate, senator*› من الحِزْبِ الجُمْهوريِّ **B** *n* [1] (supporter of a republic) مُؤَيِّد للنِظام الجُمْهوريِّ [2] (**Republican**) (in US politics) مُؤَيِّد للحِزْبِ الجُمْهوريِّ

Republican Party *n* (in US politics) الحِزْب الجُمْهوريّ

repudiate /rɪˈpjuːdɪeɪt/ *vt* [1] (to deny) أَنْكَرَ ‹*a claim, an accusation*› [2] (to reject) رَفَضَ (i-u; رَفْض), أَنْكَرَ ‹*beliefs, values*›

repugnance /rɪˈpʌgnəns/ *n* اشْمِئْزاز, نُفور, امْتِعاض (امْتِعاضات)

repugnant /rɪˈpʌgnənt/ *adj* ‹*appearance, views*› كَريه, بَغيض, مُثير للاشْمِئْزازِ

repulse /rɪˈpʌls/ *vt* صَدَّ (u; صَدّ), رَدَّ (u; رَدّ) ‹*an attack, the enemy*›

repulsion /rɪˈpʌlʃ(ə)n/ *n* نُفور, اشْمِئْزاز

repulsive /rɪˈpʌlsɪv/ *adj* ‹*behaviour, sight*› مُثير للاشْمِئْزازِ, كَريه, بَغيض

reputable /ˈrɛpjʊtəb(ə)l/ *adj* ‹*company, publication*› حَسَن \ طَيِّب السُمْعة

reputation /rɛpjʊˈteɪʃ(ə)n/ *n* صيت, سُمْعة, شُهْرة; **to have a good/bad ~** كانَتْ لَهُ سُمْعةٌ طَيِّبةٌ \ سَيِّئةٌ; **a ~ for quality/violence** بالجَوْدة \ بالعُنْف

repute /rɪˈpjuːt/ *n* صيت, سُمْعة; **an author of ~** كاتِبٌ ذو سُمْعةٍ مُحْتَرَمةٍ

reputed /rɪˈpjuːtɪd/ *adj* ‹*leader, father*› مَعْروف, شَهير; **he is ~ to be very rich** مَشْهورٌ عَنْهُ أَنَّهُ غَنيٌّ جِدًّا

reputedly /rɪ'pjuːtɪdli/ *adv* حَسْبَما يُقالُ ,كَما هو مَعْروفٌ

request /rɪ'kwɛst/ **A** *n* **1** (polite demand) طَلَب (طَلَبات), الْتِماس (الْتِماسات), مَطْلَب (مَطالِبُ); **to make a ~ for sth** طَلَبَ شَيْئاً; **further information is available on ~** المَزيدُ من المَعْلوماتِ مُتاحٌ عند الطَلَبِ **2** (on radio) طَلَب (طَلَبات) **B** *vt* طَلَبَ (u; طَلَب, مَطْلَب) ‹*information, permission*›; **to ~ sb to do sth** طَلَبَ من شَخْصٍ القِيامَ بِشَيْءٍ

requiem /'rɛkwiəm/ *n* قُدّاس المَوْتى

require /rɪ'kwʌɪə/ *vt* **1** (to need) احْتاجَ ‹*treatment, information*› **2** (to call for) تَطَلَّبَ ‹*effort, skill*› **3** (to demand) طَلَبَ (u; طَلَب, مَطْلَب) ‹*payment, qualifications*›; **parents are ~d by law to send their children to school** الآباءُ مُطالَبونَ قانونيًا بِإِرْسالِ أَبْنائِهِمْ إلى المَدْرَسةِ; **they did not understand what was ~d of them** لم يَفْهَموا المَطْلوبَ مِنْهُمْ

required /rɪ'kwʌɪəd/ *adj* **1** (stipulated) ‹*standard, number*› مَطْلوب **2** (compulsory) ‹*reading, course*› لازِم ,إِجْبارِيّ

requirement /rɪ'kwʌɪəmənt/ *n* **1** (need) حاجة (حاجات) **2** (condition) شَرْط (شُروط), مَطْلَب (مَطالِبُ); **to meet** *or* **satisfy the ~s** اسْتَوفى المُتَطَلَّباتِ

requisite /'rɛkwɪzɪt/ *adj* ‹*number, skills*› لازِم ,ضَروريّ

requisition /ˌrɛkwɪ'zɪʃ(ə)n/ *vt* صادَرَ (بِغَرَضِ الاسْتِخْدام الحَرْبِيِّ) ‹*a vehicle, supplies*›

reroute /riː'ruːt/ *vt* **1** حَوَّلَ المَسارَ ‹*a flight, the traffic*› **2** أَعادَ التَوْجيه ‹*a telephone call*›

reschedule /riː'ʃɛdjuːl/ *vt* حَدَّدَ وَقْتاً ,غَيَّرَ الوَقْتَ \ التاريخَ جَديداً ل ‹*a meeting, flight*›

rescind /rɪ'sɪnd/ *vt* فَسَخَ (a; فَسْخ), أَلْغى ‹*a decision, a contract, an order*›

rescue /'rɛskjuː/ **A** *vt* أَنْقَذَ ‹*survivors, victims*› **B** *n* نَجْدة ,إِنْقاذ; **to come/go to sb's ~** أَتى \ ذَهَبَ لِنَجْدةِ شَخْصٍ

rescuer /'rɛskjuːə/ *n* مُنْجِد ,مُسْعِف ,مُنْقِذ

rescue worker *n* رَجُل \ عامِل إِنْقاذٍ

research /rɪ'səːtʃ, 'riːsəːtʃ/ **A** *n* بَحْث (أَبْحاث ,بُحوث); **~ into the effects of the drug** البَحْثُ في آثارِ العَقّارِ; **very little ~ has been done on this subject** أُجْرِيَ القَليلُ من البَحْثِ في هذا المَوْضوعِ **B** *vt* **1** (to gather data on) بَحَثَ (a; بَحْث), أَجْرى بَحْثاً عن ‹*a subject, an issue*›; **she ~ed the family's history** بَحَثَتْ في تاريخِ العائِلةِ **2** (to gather data for) جَمَعَ ,أَجْرى بَحْثاً (عن) مَعْلوماتٍ (عن) ‹*a book, an article*›; **the book is well ~ed** أُجْرِيَ على الكِتابِ الكَثيرُ من الأَبْحاثِ **C** *vi* بَحَثَ (a; بَحْث), أَجْرى بَحْثاً; **to ~ into possible cures for the disease** أَجْرى بَحْثاً عن أَساليبَ العِلاجِ المُمْكِنةِ للمَرَضِ

researcher /rɪ'səːtʃə, 'riːsəːtʃə/ *n* باحِث

resemblance /rɪ'zɛmbləns/ *n* شَبَه ,تَشابُه (أَشْباه); **he bears a strong ~ to his father** يُشْبِهُ والِدَهُ كَثيراً

resemble /rɪ'zɛmb(ə)l/ *vt* ماثَلَ ,أَشْبَهَ ,شابَهَ ‹*a person, an object*›

resend /riː'sɛnd/ *vt* أَعادَ الإِرْسالَ

resent /rɪ'zɛnt/ *vt* اسْتاءَ (من), امْتَعَضَ (من), كَرِهَ (a; كُرْه ,كَراهِية) ‹*a person, sb's presence, success*›; **she ~ed my success** اسْتاءَتْ من نَجاحي; **I ~ having to pay for it** أَكْرَهُ أَنْ أُضْطَرَّ إلى دَفْعِ ثَمَنِهِ

resentful /rɪ'zɛntfʊl/ *adj* ‹*person*› ساخِط ,مُسْتاء ,مُمْتَعِض; ‹*silence, tone*› يَنُمُّ عن السُخْطِ \ الاسْتِياءِ

resentment /rɪ'zɛntmənt/ *n* امْتِعاض ,(اسْتِياءات) اسْتِياء ,(امْتِعاضات) سُخْط

reservation /ˌrɛzə'veɪʃ(ə)n/ *n* **1** (booking) حَجْز; **to make a ~ for a double room/a table for four** حَجَزَ غُرْفةَ نَوْمٍ مُزْدَوِجةً \ مائِدةً لِأَرْبَعةِ أَشْخاصٍ **2** (doubt) تَحَفُّظ (تَحَفُّظات); **without ~** دون تَحَفُّظٍ **3** (land set aside) مَحْمِيّة

reserve /rɪ'zəːv/ **A** *vt* **1** (to keep back) احْتَفَظَ (ب), ادَّخَرَ ‹*praise, blame*›; **she ~s her fiercest criticism for her ex-husband** تَخُصُّ زَوْجَها السابِقَ بِأَعْنَفِ انْتِقاداتِها; **to ~ one's strength** ادَّخَرَ قوّتَهُ; **to ~ the right to do sth** احْتَفَظَ بالحَقِّ في فِعْلِ شَيْءٍ **2** (to book) حَجَزَ (i-u; حَجْز) ‹*a room, seat, table*› **B** *n* **1** (of a commodity) احْتِياطِيّ; (of food, water, ammunition) مَخْزون (مَخْزونات); (of patience) قَدْر كَبير; **oil ~s are high/low** احْتِياطِيّاتُ النَفْطِ مُرْتَفِعةٌ \ مُنْخَفِضةٌ; **to keep sth in ~** احْتَفَظَ بِشَيْءٍ كَاحْتِياطِيٍّ **2** [u] (shyness) تَحَفُّظ; **to lose one's ~** تَخَلّى عن تَحَفُّظِهِ; **to break through sb's ~** جَعَلَ شَخْصاً يَتَخَلّى عن تَحَفُّظِهِ **3** (fml) (doubt, qualification)

قَبِلَ ~ to accept an explanation without ;(تَحَفُّظات) تَحَفُّظ **4** (additional forces) the ~, the ~s قوّات تَوْضيحاً دون تَحَفُّظٍ **5** (additional player) لاعِب احْتِياطٍ **6** (for wild life, etc) الاحْتِياطِ مَحْمِيّة

reserved /rɪ'zɜ:vd/ *adj* ‹*disposition, manner*› مُتَحَفِّظ

reserve player *n* لاعِب احْتِياطيّ

reserve price *n* سِعْر تَحَفُّظيّ \ احْتِياطيّ (سِعْر يَشْتَرِطُهُ البائِعُ كَحَدٍّ أَدْنى للبَيْع); **to put a reserve on sth** وَضَعَ سِعْراً تَحَفُّظيًّا على شَيْءٍ; **the painting has a reserve price of £5,000** هُناكَ سِعْرٌ تَحَفُّظيٌّ على اللَوْحَةِ بِمِقْدارِ £5000

reserve supplies *n* إمْدادات احْتِياطيّة

reservist /rɪ'zɜ:vɪst/ *n* جُنْديّ احْتِياطٍ

reservoir /'rɛzəvwɑ:/ *n* خَزّان (خَزّانات), مُسْتَوْدَع (مُسْتَوْدَعات)

reset /ri:'sɛt/ *vt* (*present participle* **-tt-**; *past tense, past participle* **reset**) **1** (to adjust) أعادَ الضَبْطَ \ الإعْدادَ ‹*the alarm, a counter, watch*› **2** (to realign) عَدَّلَ ‹*a bone*›

reshuffle /ri:'ʃʌf(ə)l/ *n* **1** (in cards) إعادة خَلْطِ أَوْراقِ اللَعِبِ **2** (of posts) تَعْديل (تَعْديلات); **cabinet ~** (BrE) تَعْديل وِزاريّ

reside /rɪ'zʌɪd/ *vi* **1** (to live) «family, citizen» سَكَنَ, أقامَ (u; سُكْنى, سَكَن) **2** (to be present in) «power, value» كَمَنَ (u; كُمون)

residence /'rɛzɪd(ə)ns/ *n* **1** (fml) (a home) مَسْكَن (مَساكِنُ), بَيْت (بُيوت) **2** (in a country) إقامة

residence permit *n* تَصْريح إقامةٍ

residency /'rɛzɪd(ə)nsi/ *n* **1** (fml) (residence) إقامة **2** (for artists, orchestra) [مَنْصِب لِفَنّانٍ في الجامِعةِ للتَدْريسِ] **3** (in US: for doctors) فَتْرة نِيابةٍ

resident /'rɛzɪd(ə)nt/ **A** *n* **1** (of a neighbourhood) مُقيم **2** (of country) مُقيم **3** (of a hotel, etc) نَزيل (نُزَلاءُ) **4** (in US: doctor) طَبيب مُقيم

B *adj* **1** ‹*population, species*› مُسْتَوْطِن, مُقيم; **are you ~ or non-resident for tax purposes** هل أَنْتَ مُقيمٌ أو غَيْرُ مُقيمٍ لِأَسْبابٍ تَتَعَلَّقُ بالضَرائِبِ **2** ‹*doctor, tutor*› مُقيم

residential /rɛzɪ'dɛnʃ(ə)l/ *adj* **1** (suburban) ‹*area, development*› سَكَنيّ **2** (with accommodation) ‹*course, treatment*› داخِليّ; **to be in ~ care** كانَ في دارِ رِعايةٍ

residual /rɪ'zɪdjʊəl/ *adj* ‹*income, fear*› مُتَبَقٍّ

residue /'rɛzɪdju:/ *n* **1** (remainder) بَقيّة (بَقايا) **2** (substance) راسِب (رَواسِبُ)

resign /rɪ'zʌɪn/ **A** *vt* اسْتَقالَ (من) ‹*a position, one's membership*›

B *vi* «employee, leader» اسْتَقالَ

C *v refl* **to ~ oneself to sth** كَيَّفَ \ أَقْلَمَ نَفْسَهُ على شَيْءٍ

resignation /rɛzɪg'neɪʃ(ə)n/ *n* **1** (from post) اسْتِقالة **2** (acceptance) تَأَقْلُم, تَكَيُّف, تَقَبُّل

resigned /rɪ'zʌɪnd/ *adj* ‹*acceptance, expression*› مُذْعِن, خاضِع

resilience /rɪ'zɪlɪəns/ *n* **1** (of person) قُدْرة على, مُرونة **2** (of substance, material) قُدْرة على, لُيونة التَحَمُّلِ \ الصُمودِ التَحَمُّلِ

resilient /rɪ'zɪlɪənt/ *adj* **1** ‹*nature, character*› قادِر على, مَرِن التَحَمُّلِ **2** ‹*material, fabric*› قادِر على التَحَمُّلِ, لَيِّن

resin /'rɛzɪn/ *n* **1** (from tree) راتينَج (مادّة صَمْغيّة) **2** (synthetic) راتينَج (مادّة صَمْغيّة)

resist /rɪ'zɪst/ **A** *vt* **1** (to fight against) قاوَمَ ‹*an attacker, the enemy*› **2** (to oppose) عارَضَ ‹*change, a plan*› **3** (to refrain from) قاوَمَ ‹*an urge, a temptation*›; **I couldn't ~ taking a look** لم أَسْتَطِعْ أنْ أُقاوِمَ الرَغْبةَ في إلْقاءِ نَظْرةٍ

B *vi* «defenders, rebels» صَمَدَ, قاوَمَ (u; صُمود)

resistance /rɪ'zɪst(ə)ns/ *n* **1** (to drugs, diseases) مُقاوَمة **2** (to change, new ideas) مُعارَضة **3** (armed opposition) مُقاوَمة **4** (**the Resistance**) (in France) المُقاوَمة الفَرَنْسيّة

resistance fighter *n* مُقاتِل في المُقاوَمةِ

resistant /rɪ'zɪst(ə)nt/ *adj* **1** **to be ~ to change** كانَ مُقاوِماً \ مُناهِضاً للتَغْييرِ **2** (to drugs, diseases) ‹*strain, organism*› مُقاوِم

resit **A** /ri:'sɪt/ *vt* (*past tense, past participle* **resat**) أَعادَ ‹*an exam*›

B /'ri:sɪt/ *n* (BrE) امْتِحان إعادةٍ \ مُلْحَقٍ

reskill /ri:'skɪl/ *vt* أَعادَ التَأْهيلَ, دَرَّبَ (على مَهاراتٍ جَديدةٍ) ‹*a workforce, the unemployed*›

resolute /'rɛzəlu:t/ *adj* ‹*action*› حاسِم, حازِم; ‹*opponent*› عَنيد (عُنُد)

resolution /rɛzə'lu:ʃ(ə)n/ *n* **1** (pledge) عَهْد (عُهود), وَعْد (وُعود); **a new year's ~** عَهْد العامِ الجَديدِ; **to make a ~ to lose weight** اتَّخَذَ قَراراً بِتَخْسيسِ الوَزْنِ **2** [u] (determination)

دَرَجة النَّقاءِ ,دِقّة (of monitors, screens) **3** عَزْم ,تَصْميم

4 (passed by legislature) (قرارات) قَرار

resolve /rɪˈzɒlv/ **A** *vt* (fml) **1** (to solve) (حُلول ,حَلّ (i-u; حَلَّ سَوّى *‹a problem›*; (على) تَغَلَّبَ ,ذَلَّلَ *‹a difficulty›* **2** (to decide) **to ~ to do sth** قَرَّرَ فعل شَيْءٍ

B *n* (fml) **1** (determination) تَصْميم ,عَزيمة **2** (pledge) وَعْد (وُعود) ,عَهْد (عُهود)

resonance /ˈrɛz(ə)nəns/ *n* (fml) **1** (of voices, sounds) رَنين **2** (power to evoke) صَدًى

resonant /ˈrɛz(ə)nənt/ *adj ‹voice, sound›* مُدَوٍّ ,طَنّان ,رَنّان

resonate /ˈrɛz(ə)neɪt/ *vi* (fml) «voice, footsteps» تَرَدَّدَ صَداهُ; **the slogan ~d with the voters** لاقى الشِعارُ قُبولاً بين الناخِبينَ

resort /rɪˈzɔːt/ **A** *n* **1** (holiday town) مُنْتَجَع (مُنْتَجَعات) **2** (fml) (recourse) مَسار (مَسارات) ,إجْراء (إجْراءات); **as a last ~** كَمَلْجَإٍ أخيرٍ

B *vi* (fml) **to ~ to** لَجَأَ (a; لُجوء) (إلى) *‹force, violence›*

resound /rɪˈzaʊnd/ *vi* «voice, laughter» دَوّى ,جَلْجَلَ (i; جَلْجَلة)

resounding /rɪˈzaʊndɪŋ/ *adj before n* **1** *‹applause, explosion›* مُدَوٍّ **2** *‹success, failure›* مُدَوٍّ

resource /rɪˈsɔːs/ *n* (also **resources**) مَوْرِد (مَوارِدُ) ,مَصْدَر (مَصادِرُ)

resource centre (BrE), **resource center** (AmE) *n* مَرْكَز المَوارِدِ

resourceful /rɪˈsɔːsfʊl/ *adj ‹manager, housewife›* واسِع الحيلة, ذَكيّ (أذْكِياءُ)

respect /rɪˈspɛkt/ **A** *n* **1** (appreciation) احْتِرام (احْتِرامات), تَقْدير (تَقْديرات) ,(تَقاديرُ); **to win sb's ~** نالَ احْتِرام شَخْصٍ; **to command ~** حَظِيَ بالاحْتِرام **2** (consideration) احْتِرام (احْتِرامات); **out of ~ for the victims** مِن مُنْطَلَقِ الاحْتِرام للضَحايا; **they have no ~ for their elders** لا يَحْتَرِمون كِبارَ السِنِّ بَيْنَهُم; **with all due ~** مع كامِلِ ,مع كُلِّ الاحْتِرام الواجِبِ الاحْتِرامِ **3** (for human rights, the law) احْتِرام (احْتِرامات)

4 (aspect, detail) **in this ~** في هذا الصَدَدِ \ الخُصوصِ; **in ~ of sth** فيما يَتَعَلَّقُ بِشَيْءٍ; **in what ~?** من أيِّ ناحِيةٍ؟; **in many/several ~s** من نَواحٍ عَديدةٍ; **with ~ to sth** بِخُصوصِ شَيْءٍ

B (**respects**) *n pl* تَحِيّات; **to pay one's ~s to sb** قَدَّمَ تَحِيّاتِهِ لِشَخْصٍ; **to pay one's last ~s to sb** وَدَّعَ شَخْصاً الوَداعَ الأخيرَ

C *vt* **1** (to appreciate) احْتَرَمَ *‹a colleague, one's elders, an organization›* **2** (to abide by) احْتَرَمَ *‹sb's wishes, feelings, rights›*; **to ~ the law** احْتَرَمَ القانونَ; **we must ~ the patient's wishes** يَجِبُ عَلَيْنا أنْ نَحْتَرِمَ رَغَباتِ المَريضِ

respectable /rɪˈspɛktəb(ə)l/ *adj* **1** (socially acceptable) *‹family, career›* مُحْتَرَم **2** (fairly good) *‹amount›* كَبير; *‹score›* جَيِّد

respectful /rɪˈspɛktfʊl/ *adj ‹manner›* يَتَّسِمُ بالاحْتِرام; *‹voice›* يَدُلُّ على الاحْتِرام

respecting /rɪˈspɛktɪŋ/ *prep* (fml) بِخُصوص ,بِصَدَدِ ,بِشَأْنِ; **the rules ~ personal imports are very complex** القَواعِدُ المُتَعَلِّقةُ بالوارداتِ الشَخْصيّةِ مُعَقَّدةٌ جِدًّا

respective /rɪˈspɛktɪv/ *adj before n* خاصّ ,خُصوصيّ

respectively /rɪˈspɛktɪvli/ *adv* على التَوالي ,على التَعاقُبِ; **the price of flour and oil has risen by 5 and 7 per cent ~** زادَ سِعْرُ الدَقيقِ والزَيْتِ بنِسْبة 5 و 7 بالمائة على التَوالي

respiration /rɛspɪˈreɪʃ(ə)n/ *n* **1** (patient's) تَنَفُّس **2** (of plants) تَنَفُّس

respirator /ˈrɛspɪreɪtə/ *n* **1** (Med) جِهاز تَنَفُّسٍ صِناعيٍّ **2** (mask) كِمامة (كِمامات ,كَمائِمُ)

respiratory /rəˈspɪrətri/ *adj ‹organ, infection›* تَنَفُّسيّ

respite /ˈrɛspʌɪt/ *n sing* فَتْرة راحةٍ; **without ~** دون تَوَقُّفٍ

respite care *n* رِعاية مُؤَقَّتة

resplendent /rɪˈsplɛnd(ə)nt/ *adj* (fml) *‹gown, decorations›* مُتَأَلِّق ,زاهٍ

respond /rɪˈspɒnd/ *vi* (fml) **1** (to answer) «government, organisation» رَدَّ (u; رَدّ) ,أجابَ; **to ~ to sth** رَدَّ على شَيْءٍ **2** (to react) «patient, audience» اسْتَجابَ ,تَجاوَبَ; **the patient is ~ing well/badly to treatment** يَسْتَجيبُ \ لا يَسْتَجيبُ المَريضُ للعِلاج بِشَكْلٍ جَيِّدٍ

respondent /rɪˈspɒnd(ə)nt/ *n* **1** (to questionnaires, advertisements) مُجيب **2** (in a legal case) مُدَّعًى عَلَيْهِ

response /rɪˈspɒns/ *n* **1** (answer) رَدّ (رُدود) ,جَواب (أجْوِبة); **in ~ to your letter** رَدًّا على رِسالَتِكَ **2** (reaction) اسْتِجابة, رَدّ فِعْلٍ

responsibility /rɪˌspɒnsɪˈbɪlɪti/ *n* (*pl* **responsibilities**)
1 [u] (accountability) مَسْؤوليّة; **to take ~ for sth** تَحمَّلَ مَسْؤوليّةَ شَيْءٍ **2** (task, duty) مَسْؤوليّة, واجِب (واجِبات) **3** [u] (liability, blame) مَسْؤوليّة; **to accept ~ for an accident** أَقَرَّ بِمَسْؤوليَّتِه عن حادِثٍ

responsible /rɪˈspɒnsɪb(ə)l/ *adj* **1** (accountable) ‹*police, parents*› مَسْؤول; **to be ~ for sb/sth** كانَ مَسْؤولاً عن شَخْصٍ \ شَيْءٍ **2** (in management) **to be ~ for a building/ cleanliness** كانَ مَسْؤولاً عن مَبْنًى \ التَنْظيفِ; **to be ~ to sb** كانَ مَسْؤولاً أمام شَخْصٍ **3** (trustworthy) ‹*citizen, attitude*› مَسْؤول, جَدير بالثِقةِ **4** *before n* ‹*job, position*› ذو مَسْؤوليّةٍ كَبيرةٍ

responsibly /rɪˈspɒnsəbli/ *adv* ‹*behave, to work*› بِمَسْؤوليّةٍ, بِشَكْلٍ مَسْؤولٍ

responsive /rɪˈspɒnsɪv/ *adj* **1** (receptive) ‹*patient, audience*› مُتَجاوِب **2** (quick to react) ‹*brakes, engine*› سَريع الاسْتِجابة

rest /rest/ **A** *vt* **1** (to allow to relax) أَراحَ ‹*one's legs, feet, a player*›; **Sharp will be ~ed for this game** سَيَسْتَريحُ \ سَيُرْتاحُ شارْب في هذه المُباراةِ **2** (Agric) أَراحَ (تَرَكَ أَرْضاً بِلا زِراعةٍ لِتَرْتاحَ) ‹*land, fields*›
B *vi* **1** (to relax) اسْتَراحَ, أَخَذَ قِسْطاً من الراحةِ; **we ~ed once on the way to the top** تَوَقَّفْنا للاسْتِراحةِ مَرّةً في طَريقِنا إلى القِمّةِ; **I won't ~ until I know the truth** لن أَسْتَريحَ حتّى أَعْلَمَ الحَقيقةَ **2** (to be supported) **to ~ on sth** «one's hands, the weight, shelves» اسْتَنَدَ على شَيْءٍ **3** (of the dead) **to ~ in peace** رَقَدَ بِسَلامٍ; **may his soul ~ in peace** رَحِمَهُ اللهُ **4** **to let the matter** *or* **things ~** تَرَكَ الأُمورَ تَهْدَأُ
C *n* **1** [u] (remainder) **the ~** البَقيّة, الباقي; **for the ~ of my life** حتّى آخِرِ عُمْري \ حَياتي; **you can keep the ~** يُمْكِنُكَ أَنْ تَحْتَفِظَ بالباقي; **you know the ~** أَنْتَ تَعْلَمُ الباقي **2** [u] (other people) **the ~** الباقونَ; **he is no different from the ~** هو لا يَخْتَلِفُ عن الباقينَ; **the ~ passed** نَجَحَ الباقونَ **3** [u] (relaxation, inactivity) راحة, اسْتِراحة; **after a few hours' ~** بعد اسْتِراحةٍ لِبِضْعِ ساعاتٍ; **to put sb's mind at ~** طَمْأَنَ شَخْصاً **4** (break) اسْتِراحة; **we stopped for a ~** تَوَقَّفْنا للاسْتِراحةِ; **to have an afternoon ~** أَخَذَ قَيْلولةً بعد الظُهْرِ **5** (support) مِسْنَد (مَسانِدُ) **6** [u] (immobility) **to come to ~** تَوَقَّفَ عن الحَرَكةِ

(Idiom) **give it a rest!** (BrE) (infml) كَفاكَ حَديثاً عن هذا الأَمْرِ!

(Phrasal verbs) **rest on**: **~ on [sb/sth]** **1** «sb's eyes, gaze» اسْتَقَرَّ على [شَخْصٍ \ شَيْءٍ] **2** (fml) (to depend on) «decisions, actions» تَوَقَّفَ \ اعْتَمَدَ على [شَخْصٍ \ شَيْءٍ]
• **rest up** اسْتَراحَ, اسْتَجَمَّ
• **rest with**: **~ with [sb]** (fml) كانَ من شأنِ \ رَجَعَ إلى [شَخْصٍ] اخْتِصاصِ [شَخْصٍ]

rest area *n* اسْتِراحة

restart /riːˈstɑːt/ *vt* **1** (to set going) أَعادَ التَشْغيلَ ‹*the engine, computer*› **2** (to resume) اسْتَأْنَفَ ‹*talks, a race*›

restaurant /ˈrɛstrɒnt/ *n* مَطْعَم (مَطاعِمُ)

restaurant car *n* (BrE) عَرَبة طَعامٍ (في قِطارٍ)

restaurateur /ˌrɛst(ə)rəˈtəː/ *n* صاحِب مَطْعَمٍ

restful /ˈrɛstfʊl/ *adj* ‹*holiday, sleep*› هادِئ, مُريح

rest home *n* دار للمُسِنّينَ

restless /ˈrɛstləs/ *adj* **1** (fidgety) ‹*audience, child*› ضَجِر, مُتَمَلْمِل **2** (unable to settle) ‹*patient, mind*› قَلِق, مُتَوَتِّر; ‹*night, sleep*› مُضْطَرِب

restock /riːˈstɒk/ *vt* **1** (with goods) أَعادَ التَخْزينَ ‹*a shop*›; أَعادَ المَلْءَ ‹*a shelf*› **2** (with fish) أَعادَ المَلْءَ ‹*a river, pond*› **3** (with groceries) أَعادَ التَعْبِئةَ \ المَلْءَ ‹*the freezer, larder*›

restoration /rɛstəˈreɪʃ(ə)n/ *n* **1** (of democracy, order, etc) اسْتِعادة, إرْجاع **2** (of buildings, paintings) تَرْميم (تَرْميمات), تَجْديد (تَجْديدات)

restorative /rɪˈstɒrətɪv/ **A** *adj* ‹*effect, power*› مُجَدِّد للنَشاطِ, مُنَشِّط
B *n* (fml) شَيْء مُجَدِّد للنَشاطِ

restore /rɪˈstɔː/ *vt* **1** (to resupply) أَعادَ, اسْتَعادَ ‹*the supply, power*› **2** (to reinstate) أَعادَ, اسْتَعادَ ‹*order, peace, democracy*›; **the president was ~d to power** أُعيدَ الرَئيسُ إلى الحُكْمِ **3** (to give back) اسْتَعادَ, اسْتَرَدَّ ‹*one's confidence, sight*› **4** (to recover) اسْتَرَدَّ ‹*a file, data*› **5** (to repair) رَمَّمَ, جَدَّدَ ‹*a building, painting*›

restrain /rɪˈstreɪn/ **A** ***vt*** **1** (to hold back) كَبَحَ (a; كَبْح) ‹*an urge, impulse*› **2** (to control) كَبَحَ (a; كَبْح), سَيْطَرَ (i; سَيْطَرة; على) ‹*a prisoner, crowd*›
B ***v refl*** **to ~ oneself** كَبَحَ جِماحَ نَفْسِهِ

restrained /rɪˈstreɪnd/ ***adj*** **1** (self-controlled) ‹*behaviour, language*› يَتَّسِمُ بِضَبْطِ النَفْسِ **2** (understated) ‹*style, elegance*› مُتَحَفِّظ

restraint /rɪˈstreɪnt/ ***n*** **1** [u] (self-control) ضَبْط النَفْس; **to exercise ~ in sth** تَحَلّى بِضَبْطِ النَفْسِ في شَيْءٍ
2 (restriction) تَقْييد (تَقْييدات), سَيْطَرة

restrict /rɪˈstrɪkt/ ***vt*** حَدَّ (u; حَدّ; من), قَيَّدَ ‹*an activity, a freedom, movement*›; **to be ~ed to sth** اقْتَصَرَ على شَيْءٍ

restricted /rɪˈstrɪktɪd/ ***adj*** **1** (limited) ‹*space, number, movement*› مَحْدود **2** (confidential) ‹*document, data*› سِرّيّ, مَحْظور
3 (confidential) ‹*area, zone*› مَحْظور

restriction /rɪˈstrɪkʃ(ə)n/ ***n*** تَقْييد (تَقْييدات)

restrictive /rɪˈstrɪktɪv/ ***adj*** ‹*law, measure, practice*› تَقْييديّ, مُقَيِّد

restring /riːˈstrɪŋ/ ***vt*** (*past tense, past participle* **restrung**)
1 ‹*a guitar, violin*› جَدَّدَ الأَوْتارَ **2** ‹*a necklace, pearls*› جَدَّدَ الخَيْطَ

restroom /ˈrɛstruːm/ ***n*** (AmE) مِرْحاض (مَراحيض), حَمّام (حَمّامات), دَوْرة مِياهٍ

result /rɪˈzʌlt/ **A** ***n*** **1** (effect) نَتيجة (نَتائِجُ); **she lost her leg as a ~ of the accident** فَقَدَتْ ساقَها إِثْرَ الحادِثِ; **what was the ~ of the game?** ماذا كانَتْ نَتيجةُ المُباراةِ؟; **as a ~, we did not meet** نَتيجةً لِذَلِكَ، لم نَلْتَقِ **2** (of calculations, tests) نَتيجة (نَتائِجُ) **3** (of exams) نَتيجة (نَتائِجُ)
B ***vi*** «damage, problem» نَتَجَ (i; نِتاج); **to ~ in success/failure** أَدّى إلى النَجاحِ \ الفَشَلِ

resultant /rɪˈzʌlt(ə)nt/ ***adj before n*** ‹*change, effect*› ناتِج, ناجِم

resume /rɪˈzjuːm/ **A** ***vt*** (fml) **1** (to begin again) اسْتَأْنَفَ ‹*work, the journey*› **2** (to occupy again) عادَ (u; عَوْدة; إلى), رَجَعَ (i; رُجوع; إلى) ‹*a seat, position*›
B ***vi*** «service, talks» اُسْتُؤْنِفَ

résumé /ˈrɛzjʊmeɪ/ ***n*** **1** (summary) مُلَخَّص (مُلَخَّصات), نُبْذة (نُبَذ) **2** (AmE) (for job applications) سيرة ذاتيّة

resumption /rɪˈzʌmpʃ(ə)n/ ***n*** اسْتِئْناف (اسْتِئْنافات); **the ~ of the negotiations** اسْتِئْناف المُفاوَضاتِ

resurface /riːˈsəːfɪs/ **A** ***vt*** أَعادَ الرَصْفَ ‹*a road, runway*›; غَيَّرَ الأَرْضيّةَ ‹*a track*›
B ***vi*** **1** (from the water) «submarine, divers» ظَهَرَ \ طَفى على السَطْحِ **2** (to recur) «rumour, doubt» ظَهَرَ من جَديدٍ, عادَ مُجَدَّداً

resurgence /rɪˈsəːdʒ(ə)ns/ ***n*** انْبِعاث (انْبِعاثات), عَوْدة

resurrect /rɛzəˈrɛkt/ ***vt*** **1** (to revive) أَحْيا ‹*a tradition, career*›
2 (to restore to life) بَعَثَ (a; بَعْث), أَحْيا ‹*a dead person*›

resurrection /rɛzəˈrɛkʃ(ə)n/ ***n*** **1** (of a body, spirit) بَعْث; **the Resurrection** قِيامة يَسوعَ **2** (of a tradition, career) إِحْياء

resuscitate /rɪˈsʌsɪteɪt/ ***vt*** **1** (to bring round) أَفاقَ, أَنْعَشَ ‹*a patient, victim*› **2** (to revive) أَحْيا, أَنْعَشَ ‹*the economy, a career*›

resuscitation /rɪˌsʌsɪˈteɪʃ(ə)n/ ***n*** إِفاقة, إِنْعاش

retail /ˈriːteɪl/ **A** ***n*** ▸ **retail trade**
B ***adj*** ‹*price, trade*› التَجْزِئةِ
C ***adv*** ‹*to sell, buy*› بالتَجْزِئةِ
D ***vi*** **to ~ at** *or* **for £25** كانَ سِعْرُ تَجزِئتِهِ £25

retailer /ˈriːteɪlə/ ***n*** تاجِر تَجْزِئةٍ

retail price ***n*** سِعْر تَجْزِئةٍ

retail price index ***n*** (also **RPI**) مُؤَشِّر سِعْرِ التَجْزِئةِ

retain /rɪˈteɪn/ ***vt*** **1** (to keep) احْتَفَظَ (ب) ‹*control, a position*›
2 (to remember) تَذَكَّرَ ‹*information, a fact*›

retake **A** /riːˈteɪk/ ***vt*** (*past tense* **retook**; *past participle* **retaken**)
1 (Mil) اسْتَعادَ, اسْتَرَدَّ ‹*a town, an island*› **2** (Educ) أَعادَ ‹*an exam, a test*›
B /ˈriːteɪk/ ***n*** إِعادة امْتِحانٍ

retaliate /rɪˈtalɪeɪt/ ***vi*** انْتَقَمَ, ثَأَرَ (a; ثَأْر)

retaliation /rɪˌtalɪˈeɪʃ(ə)n/ ***n*** انْتِقام, ثَأْر

retarded /rɪˈtɑːdɪd/ ***adj*** (old use or offensive) ‹*child*› مُتَخَلِّف; ‹*development*› مُتَأَخِّر

retch /rɛtʃ/ ***vi*** حاوَلَ التَقَيُّؤَ

retention /rɪˈtɛnʃ(ə)n/ ***n*** (fml) **1** (of employees, etc) احْتِفاظ, اسْتِبْقاء **2** (of fluids) احْتِباس **3** (of information, facts) ذاكِرة, قُدْرة على التَذَكُّرِ

retentive /rɪ'tentɪv/ *adj* ‹memory› قَوِيّ الذاكِرة, قادِر على التَذَكُّرِ

rethink /ri:θɪŋk/ *n* **to have a ~** أعادَ التَفْكيرَ \ النَظَرَ

reticence /'rɛtɪs(ə)ns/ *n* تَحَفُّظ, تَكَتُّم

reticent /'rɛtɪs(ə)nt/ *adj* مُتَحَفِّظ, (كُتُم) كَتوم

retina /'rɛtɪnə/ *n* (*pl* **retinas** or **retinae**) شَبَكِيّة

retinue /'rɛtɪnju:/ *n* حاشِية (حَواشٍ), بِطانة (بِطانات)

retire /rɪ'tʌɪə/ *vi* 1 (from work) تَقاعَدَ 2 (from a competition) انْسَحَبَ

retired /rɪ'tʌɪəd/ *adj* ‹teacher, civil servant› مُتَقاعِد

retiree /rɪtʌɪə'ri:/ *n* مُحال على المَعاشِ, مُتَقاعِد

retirement /rɪ'tʌɪəmənt/ *n* تَقاعُد, خُروج على المَعاشِ

retirement age *n* سِنّ التَقاعُدِ

retirement home *n* دار مُسِنّينَ

retiring /rɪ'tʌɪərɪŋ/ *adj* ‹nature, child› خَجول, مُنْطَوٍ على نَفْسِهِ

retort /rɪ'tɔ:t/ A *vt* رَدَّ بِسُرْعةٍ

B *n* رَدّ \ جَواب سَريع

retrace /rɪ'treɪs/ *vt* تَتَبَّعَ ‹a path, route›; **to ~ one's steps** تَتَبَّعَ خَطَواتِهِ

retract /rɪ'trakt/ *vt* 1 تَراجَعَ (عن), سَحَبَ (a; سَحْب) ‹an allegation, a statement› 2 «pilots» أعادَ إلى مَكانِهِ ‹the landing gear› 3 «cats» ضَمَّ (u; ضَمّ) ‹its claws›

retrain /ri:'treɪn/ A *vt* أعادَ التَدْريبَ ‹staff, workers›

B *vi* تَدَرَّبَ مُجَدَّداً

retraining /ri:'treɪnɪŋ/ *n* إعادة تَدْريبٍ

retread A /ri:'trɛd/ *vt* (*past tense, past participle* **retreaded**) [جَدَّدَ سَطْحَ إطارٍ بِوَضْعِ طَبَقةٍ جَديدةٍ من المَطّاطِ عَلَيْهِ] ‹a tyre›

B /'ri:trɛd/ *n* إطار مُجَدَّد (أُلْصِقَتْ بِسَطْحِهِ طَبَقةٌ جَديدةٌ من المَطّاطِ)

retreat /rɪ'tri:t/ A *vi* «troops, army» انْسَحَبَ, تَقَهْقَرَ, تَراجَعَ; «flood waters, ice» انْحَسَرَ

B *n* انْسِحاب (انْسِحابات), تَراجُع (تَراجُعات), تَقَهْقُر

retrench /rɪ'trentʃ/ *vi* (fml) اقْتَصَدَ, خَفَّضَ النَفَقاتِ

retrial /ri:'trʌɪəl/ *n* إعادة مُحاكَمةٍ

retribution /rɛtrɪ'bju:ʃ(ə)n/ *n* (fml) انْتِقام

retrieval /rɪ'tri:v(ə)l/ *n* 1 (of property, money) اسْتِعادة, اسْتِرْداد 2 (of data) اسْتِرْجاع, اسْتِرْداد

retrieve /rɪ'tri:v/ *vt* 1 (fml) اسْتَرَدَّ, اسْتَعادَ, اسْتَرْجَعَ ‹money, a bag› 2 أنْقَذَ ‹a body› 3 اسْتَرْجَعَ ‹the data, information›

retriever /rɪ'tri:və/ *n* كَلْب اسْتِرْدادٍ (كَلْب صَيْدٍ يُعيدُ الطَريدةَ إلى الصَيّادِ)

retro /'rɛtrəʊ/ A *adj* ‹clothes, music› [مُقَلِّد لِشَيْءٍ من الماضي]

B *n* [تَقْليد لِشَيْءٍ من الماضي]

retroactive /rɛtrəʊ'aktɪv/ *adj* ‹agreement, legislation› ذو أثَرٍ رَجْعِيٍّ

retrograde /'rɛtrəgreɪd/ *adj* 1 عَكْسِيّ ‹orbit, motion› 2 رَجْعِيّ, انْتِكاسِيّ ‹step, act›

retrospect /'rɛtrəspɛkt/ *n* **in ~** [عند التَدَبُّرِ في الأحْداثِ الماضِيةِ]

retrospective /rɛtrəʊ'spɛktɪv/ A *adj* 1 اسْتِعادِيّ ‹study, review› 2 ذو أثَرٍ رَجْعِيٍّ ‹law, permission›

B *n* also **~ exhibition** مَعْرِض اسْتِعادِيّ

return /rɪ'tə:n/ A *vt* 1 (to give back) أرْجَعَ, رَدَّ (u; رَدّ), أعادَ, رَجَّعَ ‹a book, the money, DVD›; **the car was ~ed with a full tank** أُعيدَت السَيّارةُ وَخَزّانُ وَقودِها مُمْتَلِئٌ 2 (referring to unwanted, defective goods) أعادَ, رَدَّ (u; رَدّ), أرْجَعَ, رَجَّعَ ‹a purchase, garment, an item›; **if it doesn't work, you can ~ it** إذا لم يَعْمَلْ، يُمْكِنُكَ أنْ تَرُدَّهُ 3 (to put back) أعادَ ‹a file, book› 4 (to send back) أعادَ ‹a parcel, sample›; **'~ to sender'** 'يُعادُ إلى المُرْسِلِ' 5 (to reciprocate) رَدَّ (u; رَدّ) ‹a greeting, an invitation›; بادَلَ ‹sb's love, feelings, affection›; **to ~ the favour** رَدَّ الجَميلَ 6 (Mil) **to ~ fire** رَدَّ على مَصْدَرِ إطْلاقِ النارِ 7 «player» أرْجَعَ, رَجَّعَ ‹the ball, a shot, serve› 8 «the jury» أصْدَرَ ‹a verdict› 9 (to yield) «stocks, investments» حَقَّقَ ‹a profit, loss›; **the company has ~ed a profit/loss** حَقَّقَت الشَرِكةُ رِبْحاً \ خَسارةً 10 (to elect) انْتَخَبَ ‹a candidate› 11 (Tel) **to ~ sb's call** اتَّصَلَ بِشَخْصٍ رَدًّا على مُكالَمَتِهِ

B *vi* 1 (to go back, come back) «vehicles, animals, people» عادَ (u; عَوْد, عَوْدة), رَجَعَ (i; رُجوع); **to ~ to/from a place** عادَ إلى \ من مَكانٍ; **what time do you plan to ~?** ما الوَقْتُ الذي تُخَطِّطُ للعَوْدةِ فيه؟ 2 (to resume) **to ~ to teaching/to power**

عادَ إلى التَّدْريسِ \ السُّلْطةِ **3** (to recur) «symptoms, feeling, doubt» عادَ من جَديدٍ

C *n* **1** (to a place) عَوْدة, رُجوع; **on my ~ to work/from Syria** عند عَوْدَتي إلى العَمَلِ \ من سوريا **2** (recurrence) عَوْدة **3** (of belongings) رَدّ, إعادة, إرْجاع **4** (reinstatement) عَوْدة, إعادة التَّطْبيقِ **5** (on an investment) عائِد (عَوائِدُ, عائِدات); **the law of diminishing ~s** قانون تَناقُصِ الغَلّةِ **6** (BrE) (ticket) (تَذْكِرة) ذَهابٍ وَعَوْدةٍ; **two ~s to Glasgow** تَذْكِرَتا ذَهابٍ وَعَوْدةٍ إلى جْلاسْجو **7** (unwanted ticket, product) مُرْتَجَع **8** (in tennis, badminton) ضَرْبة إرْجاع

D (**in return**) *adv phr* في المُقابِل

Idiom **many happy returns!** (fml) كُلّ عامٍ وَأَنْتَ بِخَيْر!

returnable /rɪˈtəːnəb(ə)l/ *adj* **1** ‹*bottle, goods*› قابِل للإعادةِ \ الإرْجاعِ **2** ‹*deposit, money*› واجِب الرَّدِّ

return fare *n* سِعْر تَذْكِرة ذَهابٍ وَإيابٍ

return flight *n* رِحْلة ذَهابٍ وَإيابٍ (بالطائِرة)

return ticket *n* تَذْكِرة ذَهابٍ وَإيابٍ

return trip *n* رِحْلة عَوْدةٍ

reunification /riːjuːnɪfɪˈkeɪʃ(ə)n/ *n* إعادة تَوْحيدٍ

reunify /riːˈjuːnɪfʌɪ/ *vt* (**reunifies, reunifying, reunified**) ‹*a country, party*› أَعادَ التَّوْحيدَ, وَحَّدَ ثانِيةً

reunion /riːˈjuːniən/ *n* اجْتِماع لَمِّ شَمْلٍ

reunite /riːjʊˈnʌɪt/ *vt* ‹*a family, group*› لَمَّ الشَّمْلَ, جَمَّعَ

reusable /riːˈjuːzəb(ə)l/ *adj* ‹*bag, nappy*› قابِل لِإعادةِ الاسْتِخْدامِ, يُمْكِنُ إعادةُ اسْتِعْمالِهِ

reuse /riːˈjuːz/ *vt* ‹*a bag, the wood*› أَعادَ الاسْتِخْدامَ

rev /rɛv/ *vt* (**-vv-**) (infml) ‹*an engine, a motorbike*› زادَ السُّرْعةَ, سَرَّعَ الدَّوَرانَ

revaluation /riːvaljuːˈeɪʃ(ə)n/ *n* **1** (of a currency) إعادة تَقْييمٍ **2** (of an asset) إعادة تَقْديرٍ

revalue /riːˈvaljuː/ *vt* **1** ‹*a currency*› أَعادَ التَّقْييمَ **2** ‹*an asset*› أَعادَ التَّقْديرَ

revamp /riːˈvamp/ *vt* ‹*a website, system*› جَدَّدَ, حَدَّثَ

reveal /rɪˈviːl/ *vt* **1** (to disclose) كَشَفَ (i; كَشْف) ‹*information, a secret*› **2** (to make visible) أَظْهَرَ, كَشَفَ (i; كَشْف) ‹*a mosaic, message*›

revealing /rɪˈviːlɪŋ/ *adj* ‹*remark, report*› كاشِف, مُوَضِّح

reveille /rɪˈvali/ *n* صَفير الاسْتيقاظِ (صَوْت لِإيقاظِ الجُنودِ)

revel /ˈrɛv(ə)l/ *vi* (**-ll-** BrE, **-l-** AmE) **1** (to have fun) مَرِحَ (بِشَكْلٍ صاخِبٍ) **2** (to take pleasure) **to ~ in sth** وَجَدَ مُتْعةً بالِغةً في شَيْءٍ

revelation /rɛvəˈleɪʃ(ə)n/ *n* كَشْف, إظْهار, إفْشاء

reveller (BrE), **reveler** (AmE) /ˈrɛv(ə)lə/ *n* شَخْص مُحِبّ للمَرَحِ [والصَخَبِ]

revelry /ˈrɛv(ə)lri/ *n* (*pl* **revelries**) احْتِفال صاخِب

revenge /rɪˈvɛndʒ/ **A** *n* ثَأْر (ثَأْرات), انْتِقام; **to get one's ~ on sb for sth** أَخَذَ بِثَأْرِه من شَخْصٍ بِسَبَبِ شَيْءٍ

B *v refl* (**revenges, revenging, revenged**) ثَأَرَ (a; ثَأْر) (ل) ‹*sb's death, a defeat*›

revenue /ˈrɛv(ə)njuː/ *n* (income) دَخْل, إيراد (إيرادات)

reverberate /rɪˈvəːbəreɪt/ *vi* دَوّى, تَرَدَّدَ صَداهُ

revere /rɪˈvɪə/ *vt* (fml) بَجَّلَ, وَقَّرَ ‹*sb's teachings, a cleric*›

reverence /ˈrɛv(ə)rəns/ *n* تَوْقير, تَبْجيل

reverend /ˈrɛv(ə)rənd/ *n* كاهن, قِسّيس (قِسّيسونَ, قَساوِسة)

reverent /ˈrɛv(ə)rənt/ *adj* ‹*silence, tone*› يَنُمُّ عن التَّوْقيرِ \ التَّبْجيلِ

reverie /ˈrɛv(ə)ri/ *n* حُلْم يَقَظةٍ

reversal /rɪˈvəːs(ə)l/ *n* (of policy, a trend) تَحَوُّل عَكْسِيّ; (of roles) عَكْس; (of fortune) انْقِلاب (انْقِلابات), انْعِكاس (انْعِكاسات)

reverse /rɪˈvəːs/ **A** *vt* **1** أَرْجَعَ للوَراءِ ‹*a car, truck*›; **to ~ the car out of the garage** رَجَعَ بالسَّيّارةِ للخَلْفِ إلى خارجِ الجَراجِ **2** (to invert) عَكَسَ (i; عَكْس) ‹*the order, polarity, a process*› **3** (to exchange, switch) تَبادَلَ, عَكَسَ (i; عَكْس) ‹*roles*› **4** نَقَضَ (u; نَقْض) ‹*a decision, verdict*› **5** (BrE) عَكَسَ (i; عَكْس) ‹*a defeat, result*› **6** (Tel) **to ~ the charges** أَجْرى مُكالَمةً على حِسابِ المُسْتَقْبِلِ

B *vi* «drivers, vehicles» رَجَعَ للخَلْفِ; **to ~ down the lane/into a parking space** رَجَعَ بالسَّيّارةِ للخَلْفِ في المَمَرِّ \ إلى مَكانٍ لِوُقوفِ السَيّاراتِ

C *adj* **1** (opposite) ‹*argument*› نَقيض; ‹*direction, effect, trend*› عَكْس **2** (of a coin, fabric) **the ~ side** الظَّهْر **3** (backwards) ‹*somersault*› مَعْكوس, عَكْسِيّ; **in ~ order** في تَرْتيبٍ عَكْسِيٍّ

D *n* 1 (opposite) **the ~** العَكْس 2 (back) **the ~** الظَهْر 3 (fml) (setback) انْتِكاسة 4 (also **reverse gear**) تُرْس الرُجوعِ للخَلْفِ; **to put the car in ~** نَقَلَ السُرْعَةَ إلى تُرْسِ \ غِيارِ الرُجوعِ للخَلْفِ

E (**in reverse**) *adv phr* 1 ‹*to drive, enter*› إلى الوَراءِ \ الخَلْفِ 2 ‹*to work, happen*› بِشَكْلٍ عَكْسيٍّ

reverse charge call *n* (BrE) مُكالَمة على حِسابِ المُتَلَقّي

reversible /rɪˈvəːsɪb(ə)l/ *adj* ‹*process*› يُمْكِنُ عَكْسُهُ; ‹*coat*› ذو وَجْهَيْنِ (يُلْبَسُ على أيٍّ من وَجْهَيْهِ)

reversion /rɪˈvəːʃ(ə)n/ *n* عَوْدة, رُجوع

revert /rɪˈvəːt/ *vi* **to ~ to sth** عادَ \ رَجِعَ إلى شَيْءٍ

review /rɪˈvjuː/ **A** *n* 1 (reconsideration) فَحْص, مُراجَعة (فُحوص); **the policy is under ~** السِياسةُ قَيْدُ المُراجَعةِ; **to be subject to ~** خَضَعَ للمُراجَعةِ 2 (report) تَقْرير (تَقارير) 3 (assessment) اسْتِعْراض (اسْتِعْراضات); **to get good/bad ~s** لاقى اسْتِحْساناً \ اسْتِهْجاناً من النُقّادِ; **to get rave ~s** نالَ اسْتِحْساناً واسِعاً من قِبَلِ النُقّادِ 4 (magazine) مَجَلّة 5 (of soldiers, etc) اسْتِعْراض (اسْتِعْراضات) 6 (AmE) (of a lesson) مُراجَعة

B *vt* 1 (to evaluate) فَحَصَ, راجَعَ (a; فَحْص) ‹*the facts, a case, sb's salary, progress*› 2 (to critique) كَتَبَ اسْتِعْراضاً لِ ‹*a book, film, play*› 3 (to inspect) اسْتَعْرَضَ ‹*the troops, guard*› 4 (AmE) (to revise) راجَعَ ‹*a subject, lesson*›

reviewer /rɪˈvjuːə/ *n* ناقِد (نُقّاد, ناقِدونَ)

revise /rɪˈvʌɪz/ **A** *vt* 1 (to reconsider) أعادَ النَظَرَ في, راجَعَ ‹*an estimate, opinion*›; **to ~ one's opinion of sb/sth** راجَعَ رَأْيَهُ في شَخْصٍ \ شَيْءٍ 2 (to correct) صَحَّحَ, نَقَّحَ, راجَعَ ‹*a text*›

B *vi* (BrE) (for exams) «students, pupils» راجَعَ

revision /rɪˈvɪʒ(ə)n/ *n* 1 (of estimates, texts) مُراجَعة 2 (to a text) تَصْحيح (تَصْحيحات), تَنْقيح (تَنْقيحات), مُراجَعة 3 (BrE) (for exams) مُراجَعة

revisit /riːˈvɪzɪt/ *vt* 1 زارَ مَرّةً ثانيةً, أعادَ الزِيارةَ ‹*a place, museum*› 2 ‹*a subject*› أعادَ النَظَرَ في; ‹*a memory*› اسْتَدْعى

revitalize, -ise (BrE) /riːˈvʌɪtəlʌɪz/ *vt* نَشَّطَ, بَعَثَ الحَياةَ في ‹*a party, an economy*›

revival /rɪˈvʌɪv(ə)l/ *n* 1 (of interest, enthusiasm) تَجْديد (تَجْديدات); (of a custom, language) إحْياء; **the economic ~** الانْتِعاش الاقْتِصاديّ 2 (from unconsciousness) اسْتِعادة الوَعْي

revive /rɪˈvʌɪv/ **A** *vt* 1 (to reestablish) جَدَّدَ ‹*sb's interest, enthusiasm*›; أحْيا ‹*a custom, a language*› 2 (from unconsciousness) أفاقَ, أنْعَشَ ‹*a patient, victim*›

B *vi* 1 «one's interest, enthusiasm» تَجَدَّدَ; «the economy, language» انْتَعَشَ 2 (from unconsciousness) «patient» اسْتَعادَ الوَعْيَ

revoke /rɪˈvəʊk/ *vt* سَحَبَ (a; سَحْب), ألْغى ‹*a licence, decision*›

revolt /rɪˈvəʊlt/ **A** *vt* (to disgust) أثارَ الاشْمِئْزازَ

B *vi* (to rebel) ثارَ (u; ثَوْرة, ثَوَران), تَمَرَّدَ

C *n* ثَوْرة, تَمَرُّد

revolting /rɪˈvəʊltɪŋ/ *adj* ‹*food, sight, man, habit*› مُثير, مُقَزِّز للاشْمِئْزازِ

revolution /rɛvəˈluːʃ(ə)n/ *n* 1 (against a government) ثَوْرة; **the 1917 Russian R~** الثَوْرة الروسيّة في عامِ 1917 2 (dramatic change) ثَوْرة 3 (movement of planets, engine parts) دَوَران

revolutionary /rɛvəˈluːʃ(ə)n(ə)ri/ **A** *adj* 1 ‹*movement, troops*› ثَوْريّ 2 ‹*design, approach*› مُبْتَكَر, ثَوْريّ

B *n* (*pl* **revolutionaries**) ثائِر (ثائِرونَ, ثُوّار)

revolutionize, -ise (BrE) /rɛvəˈluːʃ(ə)nʌɪz/ *vt* أحْدَثَ ثَوْرةً في, طَوَّرَ تَطْويراً جَذْريًّا ‹*an industry, a process*›

revolve /rɪˈvɒlv/ *vi* دارَ (u; دَوْر, دَوَران), لَفَّ (u; لَفّ)

revolver /rɪˈvɒlvə/ *n* مُسَدَّس (مُسَدَّسات)

revolving /rɪˈvɒlvɪŋ/ *adj* ‹*chair, door*› دَوّار

revue /rɪˈvjuː/ *n* [عَمَل مَسْرَحيّ ساخِر]

revulsion /rɪˈvʌlʃ(ə)n/ *n* نُفور, اشْمِئْزاز

reward /rɪˈwɔːd/ **A** *n* مُكافَأة; **a ~ for information/one's contribution** مُكافَأة للمَعْلوماتِ \ لِمُساهَمَتِهِ

B *vt* كافَأَ ‹*an employee, sb's loyalty, sb's efforts*›

rewarding /rɪˈwɔːdɪŋ/ *adj* ‹*experience, job*› مُجْزٍ, مُمْتِع, مُرْضٍ

rewind /riːˈwʌɪnd/ *vt* (*past tense, past participle* **rewound**) رَجَّعَ, أعادَ \ أرْجَعَ إلى الوَراءِ ‹*a tape, film*›

rewind button *n* زِرّ التَرْجيعِ \ الإرْجاعِ

rewire /riːˈwʌɪə/ *vt* [جَهَّزَ بِأَسْلاكٍ جَديدةٍ] ‹*a house, building*›

reword /riːˈwəːd/ *vt* صاغَ بِعِبارةٍ أُخْرى ,أَعادَ الصِياغة ‹*a speech, sentence*›

rework /riːˈwəːk/ *vt* صاغَ بِشَكْلٍ مُخْتَلِفٍ ,عَدَّلَ ‹*a theme, song*›

rewound /riːˈwaʊnd/ *past tense, past participle* ▸ **rewind**

rewrite /riːˈrʌɪt/ *vt* (*past tense* **rewrote**; *past participle* **rewritten**) أَعادَ الكِتابة \ الصِياغة ‹*a story, contract*›

Reykjavik /ˈreɪkjəvɪk/ *pr n* ريكْيافيك (f)

Rh *abbr* = **rhesus** عامِل ريسوس; ▸ **rhesus factor**, **rhesus negative**, **rhesus positive**

rhapsody /ˈrapsədi/ *n* (*pl* **rhapsodies**) [لَحْن موسيقيّ مُرْتَجَل وَغَيْر تَقْليديّ]

rhesus baby *n* طِفْل ريسوس

rhesus factor *n* عامِل ريسوس

rhesus negative *adj* ‹*blood, mother*› عامِل ريسوس سَلْبيّ

rhesus positive *adj* ‹*blood, mother*› عامل ريسوس إيجابيّ

rhetoric /ˈretərɪk/ *n* عِلم البَلاغةِ \ البَيانِ

rhetorical /rɪˈtɒrɪk(ə)l/ *adj* ‹*device, eloquence*› بَيانيّ ,بَلاغيّ

rheumatic /rʊˈmatɪk/ *adj* ‹*condition, pain*› روماتِزميّ

rheumatic fever *n* حُمّى روماتِزْميّة

rheumatism /ˈruːmətiz(ə)m/ *n* روماتِزْم

rheumatoid arthritis /ruːmətɔɪd ɑːˈθrʌɪtɪs/ *n* اِلْتِهاب المَفاصِل الروماتويْديّ

rheumatologist /ruːməˈtɒlədʒɪst/ *n* أَخِصائيّ روماتِزْم

rheumatology /ˌruːməˈtɒlədʒi/ *n* طِبّ الروماتِزْم

Rhine /rʌɪn/ *pr n* (**the Rhine**) نَهْر الرايْن

rhino /ˈrʌɪnəʊ/ *n* (*pl* **rhinos** or **rhino**) كَرْكَدَنّ ,وَحيد القَرْنِ

rhinoceros /rʌɪˈnɒs(ə)rəs/ *n* (*pl* **rhinoceroses** or **rhinoceros**) كَرْكَدَنّ ,وَحيد القَرْنِ

Rhode Island /ˈrəʊd ʌɪlənd/ *pr n* رود آيْلانْد (f)

Rhode Islander /ˈrəʊd ˌʌɪləndə/ *pr n* [مُواطِن من رود آيْلانْد]

rhubarb /ˈruːbɑːb/ *n* راوَنْد

rhyme /rʌɪm/ **A** *n* **1** (in poetry) قافِية (قَوافٍ) **2** (poem) قَصيدة مُقَفّاة

B *vi* «words, lines» كانَ على نَفْسِ القافِيةِ

rhythm /ˈrɪð(ə)m/ *n* إيقاع (إيقاعات), نَغَم (أَنْغام)

rhythmic /ˈrɪðmɪk/, **rhythmical** /ˈrɪðmɪk(ə)l/ *adj* ‹*movement, beat*› مُتَناغِم إيقاعيّ

RI *abbr* = **Rhode Island**

rial /ˈriːɑːl/ *n* ريال

rib /rɪb/ *n* ضِلْع (ضُلوع, أَضْلاع, أَضْلُع)

ribald /ˈrɪb(ə)ld/ *adj* ‹*laughter, comment*› فاحِش ,بَذيء

ribbed /rɪbd/ *adj* **1** ‹*jumper, neck*› مُضَلَّع **2** ‹*ceiling, vault*› مُضَلَّع

ribbon /ˈrɪb(ə)n/ *n* شَريط (شَرائِط, أَشْرِطة)

ribcage /ˈrɪbkeɪdʒ/ *n* قَفَص صَدْريّ

rice /rʌɪs/ *n* أُرْز

rice field *n* حَقْل أُرْزٍ

rice paddy *n* [حَقْل مَغْمور بالماءِ لِزراعةِ الأَرُز]

rice paper *n* وَرَق أُرْزٍ

rich /rɪtʃ/ **A** *n* **1** (**the rich** *n pl*) الأَغْنِياء **2** (**the riches** *n pl*) ثَروات

B *adj* **1** ‹*country, family*› غَنيّ (أَغْنِياءُ); **to grow/become ~** أَثْرى ,(ثَراء ;a) ثَرِيَ ,أَصْبَحَ غَنيًّا; **to make sb ~** أَثْرى شَخْصاً **2** ‹*heritage, vocabulary*› غَنيّ **3** ‹*soil*› خِصْب; ‹*food*› مُغَذٍّ; **lemons are ~ in vitamin C** اللَيْمونُ غَنيٌّ بِفيتامين ج **4** ‹*sauce, milk*› دَسِم; **the chocolate mousse was delicious but very ~** كانَ موس الشوكولاتةِ لَذيذاً وَلَكِنَّهُ كانَ كَثيرَ الدَسَم **5** ‹*colour*› غَنيّ ,بَهيّ; ‹*texture*› غَنيّ بالأَلْوانِ; **the ~ colours of the New England fall** الأَلْوان البَهيّة للخريفِ في نيو إِنْجْلانْد

Idioms **that's a bit rich!** ذَلِكَ يَتَجاوَزُ حُدودَ اللِياقةِ!; **to strike it rich** ظَفَرَ بِثَرْوةٍ هائلةٍ

riches /ˈrɪtʃɪz/ *n pl* ثَرَوات

richly /ˈrɪtʃli/ *adv* **1** ‹*dressed, furnished*› بِشَكْلٍ فَخْم ,بِتَرَف; ‹*ornamented*› بِسَخاءٍ ,بِوَفْرةٍ **2** ‹*to deserve*› عن جَدارةٍ; ‹*to reward*› بِسَخاءٍ; **he ~ deserved his fate/the award** هو يَسْتَحِقُّ مَصيرَهُ \ المُكافَأةَ بِجَدارةٍ

richness /ˈrɪtʃnəs/ *n* **1** (wealth) ثَراء ,غِنًى **2** (of prose, style) غِنًى ,ثَراء

rickets /ˈrɪkɪts/ *n sing* كُساح الأَطْفالِ

rickety /ˈrɪkɪti/ *adj* ‹*bed, stairs*› مُتَهالِك, مُتَداعٍ

rickshaw /ˈrɪkʃɔː/ *n* [عَرَبة هِنْدِيّة ذات عَجَلَتَيْن]

ricochet /ˈrɪkəʃeɪ/ *vi* (*past tense, past participle* **ricocheted** BrE, **ricochetted** AmE) نَبا (u; نَبْو ,نُبُوّ), اِرْتَدَّ; **to ~ off sth** اِرْتَدَّ بعد اِرْتِطامِهِ بِشَيْءٍ

rid /rɪd/ *vt* (*present participle* **-dd-**; *past tense, past participle* **rid**)
1 **to ~ a town/the world of sth** خَلَّصَ البَلْدةَ \ العالَمَ من شَيْءٍ **2** **to get ~ of an old car/some rubbish** تَخَلَّصَ من سَيّارةٍ قَديمةٍ \ بَعْضِ النِفاياتِ; **to get ~ of a dictator/salesman** تَخَلَّصَ من دِيكْتاتور \ بائِعٍ

riddance /ˈrɪd(ə)ns/ *n*
Idiom **good riddance (to bad rubbish)!** راحَ إلى بِئْسِ المَصير!, وَأَراحَ! في داهِيةٍ!

ridden /ˈrɪd(ə)n/ *past participle* ▸ **ride**

riddle /ˈrɪd(ə)l/ **A** *n* **1** (question, puzzle) لُغْز (أَلْغاز), أُحْجِيّة (أَحاج, أَحاجِيّ) **2** (mystery) لُغْز (أَلْغاز), مُعْضِلة (مُعْضِلات) مَعاضِلُ)
B *vt* **to be ~d with bullets** أُمْطِرَ جَسَدُهُ بوابِلٍ من الرَصاص

ride /raɪd/ **A** *vt* (*past tense* **rode**; *past participle* **ridden**) **1** رَكِبَ (a; رُكوب) ‹*a horse, a bike, motorbike*›; **he ~s his bike to school** يَرْكَبُ دَرّاجَتَهُ الهَوائِيّةَ إلى المَدْرَسةِ; **to ~ one's bike up/down the road** قادَ دَرّاجَتَهُ على طولِ الطَريقِ; **do you want to ~ my horse?** هل تُريدُ أنْ تَمْتَطِيَ حِصاني؟; **he rode a good race** أَبْلى بَلاءً حَسَناً في سِباقِ الخَيْلِ **2** (AmE) (to travel on) رَكِبَ (a; رُكوب) ‹*the subway, bus*› **3** «surfer» تَزَلَّجَ (على) رَكِبَ (a; رُكوب) ‹*a wave*› **4** (AmE) (infml) (to criticize) **to ~ sb** سَخِرَ من شَخْصٍ
B *vi* (*past tense* **rode**; *past participle* **ridden**) **1** (on a horse, bike, motorbike) رَكِبَ (a; رُكوب); **she was riding on a camel/his shoulders** كانَتْ تَرْكَبُ على جَمَلٍ \ كَتِفَيْهِ; **she rode to London on her bike** ذَهَبَتْ إلى لَنْدَن على دَرّاجَتِها; **to ~ across the desert/country** عَبَرَ البَلَدَ \ الصَحْراءَ راكِباً; **to ~ along the road/cycle path** رَكِبَ الدَرّاجةَ على طولِ الطَريقِ \ مَسارِ الدَرّاجاتِ **2** (in horse and cycle races) اِشْتَرَكَ; **he rode in last year's Dubai World Cup** اِشْتَرَكَ في سِباقِ كَأْسِ دُبَيِّ العالَمِيِّ **3** (Transp) (to travel) **to ~ on a bus/in a taxi** اِسْتَقَلَّ حافِلةً \ تاكسي **4** (to be carried) **to ~ on a wave** «surfers» تَزَلَّجَ \ رَكِبَ على مَوْجةٍ; **he is riding on a wave of popularity** يَشْعُرُ بالنَشْوةِ بِسَبَبِ شَعْبِيَّتِهِ **5** (to be at stake) **to ~ on sth** «money, sb's future» تَوَقَّفَ على شَيْءٍ; **a lot of money is riding on this project** يَتَوَقَّفُ الكَثيرُ من المالِ على هذا المَشْروعِ
C *n* **1** (journey) رِحْلة (رِحَل, رِحْلات); **it's a twenty-minute ~ by taxi** تَسْتَغْرِقُ الرِحْلةُ عِشْرينَ دَقيقةً بالتاكسي; **we went for a ~ along the coast** ذَهَبْنا في جَوْلةٍ بالسَيّارةِ على طولِ الساحِلِ; **to give sb a ~** (AmE) وَصَّلَ شَخْصاً بالسَيّارة **2** (on a horse, bicycle) رُكوب **3** [u] (of a car) رُكوب
Idioms **to be riding high** (to be successful) كانَ نَجْمُهُ في صُعودٍ; **to be/go along for the ride** (infml) رافَقَ شَخْصاً في رِحْلةٍ بالسَيّارة; **to give sb an easy/rough ride** عامَلَ شَخْصاً بِرِفْقٍ \ بِخُشونةٍ; **to take sb for a ride** (infml) (to trick sb) اِحْتالَ على شَخْصٍ
Phrasal verbs **ride about, ride around** «horseriders, cyclists, motorcyclists» تَجَوَّلَ راكِباً (حِصاناً أو دَرّاجةً)
• **ride off** «horseriders, bikers» غادَرَ راكِباً (حِصاناً أو دَرّاجةً); **to ~ off to the next village** غادَرَ إلى القَرْيةِ التالِيةِ
• **ride out**: **~ [sth] out, ~ out [sth]** اِجْتازَ [شَيْئاً] ‹*a crisis, recession*›; **to ~ out the storm** اِجْتازَ الأَزْمةَ
• **ride up** **1** (to approach) «horseriders, cyclists, motorcyclists» اِقْتَرَبَ راكِباً (حِصاناً أو دَرّاجةً) **2** «skirts, sweaters» (to rise) اِرْتَفَعَ لِأَعْلى

rider /ˈraɪdə/ *n* **1** (on a horse, bicycle, motorbike) راكِب (رُكّاب) **2** (condition) فِقْرة إضافِيّة

ridge /rɪdʒ/ *n* **1** (on a hill, mountain) حافّة (حافات, حَوافٍ), **2** (on a bone, stone) نُتوء **3** (on a roof) [الحافّة العُلْوِيّة للسَطْحِ المُنْحَدِرِ]

ridicule /ˈrɪdɪkjuːl/ **A** *n* اِسْتِهْزاء, سُخْرِيّة (اِسْتِهْزاءات)
B *vt* سَخِرَ (a; سُخْرِيّة; من), اِسْتَهْزَأَ (ب) ‹*an idea, a proposal*›

ridiculous /rɪˈdɪkjʊləs/ *adj* ‹*idea*› سَخيف (سِخاف), مُثير لِلسُخْرِيّةِ; ‹*amount*› تافِه

riding /ˈraɪdɪŋ/ *n* رُكوب الخَيْلِ; **to go ~** ذَهَبَ لِرُكوبِ الخَيْلِ

riding lesson *n* دَرْس في رُكوبِ الخَيْلِ

riding school *n* مَدْرَسة لِتَعْليمِ رُكوبِ الخَيْلِ

rife /rʌɪf/ *adj* **to be ~** «speculation, corruption» كانَ شائِعاً \ مُنْتَشِراً \ مُتَفَشِّياً

riff /rɪf/ *n* [نَغْمة مُتَكَرِّرة في موسيقى]

riff-raff /ˈrɪfraf/ *n* هَمَج (n coll), أَوْباش

rifle /ˈrʌɪf(ə)l/ *n* بُنْدُقيّة (بَنادِق)

(Phrasal verb) **rifle through**: **~ through [sth]** فَتَّش في [شَيْءٍ] ‹a bag, drawer›

rift /rɪft/ *n* **1** (disagreement) خِلاف (خِلافات) **2** (in rock) شَقّ (شُقوق), صَدْع (صُدوع)

rig /rɪɡ/ **A** *vt* **(-gg-)** **1** ‹an election, a result› (في) تَلاعَبَ, زَوَّرَ **2** ‹a ship, boat› أَعَدَّ (من حَيْثُ شَكْلِ الأَشْرِعة والصَواري) **B** *n* **1** (for oil, gas) بَرِّيمة, مَنَصّة (لِلحَفْرِ) **2** (of a boat) [شَكْل السَفينةِ من حَيْثُ الأَشْرِعةِ والصَواري]

(Phrasal verbs) **rig out**: **~ [sb/sth] out, ~ out [sb/sth]** (to equip) ‹a soldier, house› جَهَّزَ [شَخْصاً \ شَيْئاً]

• **rig up**: **~ [sth] up, ~ up [sth]** ‹the antenna› ثَبَّتَ [شَيْئاً]; أَنْشَأَ [شَيْئاً] ‹a system›

rigger /ˈrɪɡə/ *n* **1** (on oil rigs) عامِل بِمَنَصّة \ بِبَرِّيمةِ حَفْرٍ **2** (AmE) (industrial mover) [شَرِكة نَقْلِ مُعَدّاتٍ ثَقيلةٍ]

rigging /ˈrɪɡɪŋ/ *n* **1** (on a ship, yacht) تَجْهيزات (من أَشْرِعةٍ وَحِبالٍ إلخ) **2** [u] (of an election, a result) تَلاعُب (تَلاعُبات), تَزْوير

right /rʌɪt/ **A** *adj* **1** (as opposed to left) ‹eye, shoe› أَيْمَن (dipt) **2** (morally correct, fair) صَواب; **it's never ~ to steal** السَرِقةُ لَيْسَتْ صَواباً أَبَداً; **it's only ~ that they should know first** عَيْنُ الصَوابِ أَنْ يَتِمَّ إِخْبارُهُمْ أَوَّلاً; **I thought it ~ to tell him** اِعْتَقَدْتُ أَنَّهُ من الصَوابِ إِخْبارُهُ; **to do the ~ thing** فَعَلَ الصَوابَ **3** (correct, true) ‹answer, direction, choice› صَحيح; **you are ~** أَنْتَ مُحِقٌّ; **that's ~** ذلك صَحيحٌ; **that can't be ~** لا يُمْكِنُ أَنْ يَكونَ ذلك صَحيحاً; **so you're a student, is that ~?** إِذَنْ أَنْتَ طالِبٌ، هل هذا صَحيحٌ؟; **what's the ~ time?** ما الوَقْتُ المُناسِبُ \ الصَحيحُ؟; **is this the ~ train for Latakia?** هل هذا هو القِطارُ الصَحيحُ إلى لاذِقِيا؟; **is this the ~ way to the market?** هل هذا هو الطَريقُ الصَحيحُ إلى السوقِ؟; **to get one's facts ~** تَحَقَّقَ من مَعْلوماتِهِ; **you've got the spelling ~** كَتَبْتَ \ قُلْتَ الهِجاءَ الصَحيحَ; **it wouldn't look ~ if we didn't attend** لن يَبْدو ذلك لائِقاً إذا لم نَحْضُرْ **4** (most suitable) أَمْثَل, مُناسِب (dipt; f مُثْلى; pl أَماثِلُ; f pl مُثْلَيات); **the ~ person for the job** الشَخْصُ الأَمْثَلُ لِلوَظيفةِ; **you need to have the ~ equipment** تَحْتاجُ أَنْ تَكونَ مَعَكَ المُعَدّاتُ المُناسِبةُ; **when the time is ~** عِنْدَما يَكونُ الوَقْتُ مُناسِباً; **to be in the ~ place at the ~ time** كانَ في المَكانِ المُناسِبِ في الوَقْتِ المُناسِبِ; **to know the ~ people** كانَتْ لَهُ عَلاقاتٍ جَيِّدةٍ **5** (as it should be) ‹machine, situation› على ما يُرامُ, كَما يَنْبَغي أَنْ يَكونَ; **things are not quite ~** لَيْسَت الأُمورُ على ما يُرامُ; **the engine isn't quite ~** لا يَعْمَلُ المُحَرِّكُ كَما يَنْبَغي **6** (in order) **to put** *or* **set sth ~** وَضَعَ شَيْئاً في نِصابِهِ الصَحيحِ ‹the situation›; صَحَّحَ \ رَفَعَ \ أَزالَ شَيْئاً ‹a mistake›; صَوَّبَ شَيْئاً ‹an injustice›; **to put one's watch ~** ضَبَطَ ساعَتَهُ; **they gave him a month to put things ~** أَمْهَلوهُ شَهْراً لِوَضْعِ الأُمورِ في نِصابِها الصَحيحِ **7** (BrE) (infml) (complete) كامِل, تامّ; **he's a ~ idiot!** هو أَحْمَقُ تَماماً

B *adv* **1** ‹to look, go› يَميناً; **to turn ~** انْعَطَفَ \ اسْتَدارَ يَميناً **2** (directly) مُباشَرةً; **it's ~ in front of you** هو أَمامَكَ مُباشَرةً; **the path goes ~ down to the river** يُؤَدّي المَمَرُّ مُباشَرةً إلى النَهْرِ; **I'll be ~ back** سَأَعودُ على الفَوْرِ; **~ after dinner/Christmas** بعد الغَداءِ \ عيدِ الميلادِ مُباشَرةً; **he walked ~ up to her and said hello** مَشى نَحْوَها مُباشَرةً وَقالَ أَهْلاً **3** (exactly) بِالضَبْطِ, تَماماً; **~ in the middle of the room** في مُنْتَصَفِ الغُرْفةِ تَماماً; **I'm staying ~ here** لن أُبارِحَ هذا المَكانَ; **your book's ~ there on the desk** كِتابُكَ مَوْجودٌ هُناكَ على المَكْتَبِ; **come back, ~ now!** عُدْ حالاً \ فَوْراً!; **~ now, we have no funds** في الوَقْتِ الحالِيِّ، لَيْسَ لَدَيْنا أَيُّ أَمْوالٍ **4** (correctly) بِشَكْلٍ صَحيحٍ; **I guessed ~** أَصَبْتُ في تَخْميني; **if I remember ~** لو لم تَخُنّي ذاكِرَتي; **you're not doing it ~** أَنْتَ لا تَفْعَلُهُ بالطَريقةِ الصَحيحةِ **5** (completely) تَماماً; **~ at the bottom** في القاعِ تَماماً; **the wall goes ~ around the park** يُحيطُ السورُ بالحَديقةِ كُلِّها; **~ up until the 1950s** وُصولاً حَتّى الخَمْسيناتِ; **we're ~ behind you!** نَحْنُ نَدْعَمُكَ بِشَكْلٍ كامِلٍ! **6** (BrE) (in Parliament) **the Right Honourable Gentleman/**

Lady مَعالي الوَزير \ الوَزيرة **7** (infml) (OK) حَسَناً; **~, let's go!** حَسَناً، هَيّا نَذْهَبُ!

C *n* **1** [u] (side, direction) يَمين (f); **keep to the ~** ابْقَ على اليَمينِ; **on your ~ is the presidential palace** على يَمِينِكَ يوجَدُ القَصْرُ الرِئاسيُّ; **I was standing to the ~ of the door** كُنْتُ واقِفاً على يَمينِ الباب **2** (turn) انْعِطاف \ اسْتِدارة; **to take** *or* **make a ~** انْعَطَفَ \ اسْتَدارَ يَميناً للْيَمينِ **3** [u] (**the right**, **the Right**) اليَمين (السِياسيّ) **4** [u] (what is good or correct) صَواب, حَقّ; **to be in the ~** كانَ على حَقٍّ \ صَوابٍ **5** (entitlement) حَقّ (حُقوق); **to have the ~ to free speech** كانَ لَهُ الحَقُّ في حُرِّيّةِ التَعْبيرِ; **to be within one's ~s** كانَ من حَقِّهِ; **she has no ~ to treat you like that** لا يَحِقُّ لَها أنْ تُعامِلَكَ بِهَذا الشَكْلِ; **what ~ have you to criticize me?** بِأيِّ حَقٍّ تَنْتَقِدُني؟; **her husband is famous in his own ~** زَوْجُها مَشْهورٌ بِذاتِهِ **6** (in boxing) لَكْمة باليَدِ اليُمْنى

D (**rights**) *n pl* **1** (to exploit sth) حُقوق; **exploration ~s** حُقوق التَنْقيبِ; **the film ~s of a book** حُقوق تَحْويلِ الكِتابِ إلى فيلْم **2** (moral) **the ~s and wrongs of the matter** جَوانِب الصَواب والخَطأ في المَسْألَةِ

E *vt* **1** عَدَلَ (i; عَدْل) ‹*a vehicle, yacht*› **2** (fml) (to correct) رَفَعَ (a; رَفْع), أزالَ ‹*an injustice*›; **to ~ a wrong** أصْلَحَ خَطأً

F *v refl* **1** (Naut) **the boat ~ed itself** عادَ القارِبُ إلى وَضْعِهِ الصَحيح **2** (to correct itself) **the situation/problem will ~ itself** سَيُصَحِّحُ الوَضْعُ نَفْسَهُ بِنَفْسِهِ \ سَتَحِلُّ المُشْكِلةُ نَفْسَها بِنَفْسِها

(Idioms) **right enough** (infml) بالتَأْكيدِ; **by rights** إذا أرَدْنا الحَقَّ

right angle *n* زاوِية قائِمة

right away *adv* ‹*to leave, reply*› في الحالِ, فَوْراً, تَوّاً

righteous /ˈrʌɪtʃəs/ *adj* **1** ‹*indignation, anger*› لَهُ ما يُبَرِّرُهُ **2** ‹*man, king*› صالِح (صَوالِحُ)

righteousness /ˈrʌɪtʃəsnəs/ *n* اسْتِقامة, صَلاح

rightful /ˈrʌɪtfʊl/ *adj* ‹*claim, owner*› قانونيّ, شَرْعيّ

right hand *n* مُساعِد مُقَرَّب, ذِراع أيْمَن, يَد يُمْنى

right-hand /ˈrʌɪthand/ *adj before n* ‹*corner, door*› أيْمَن (dipt); **on the ~ side** على الجانِبِ الأيْمَنِ, على الجِهةِ اليُمْنى

right-hand drive *adj* ‹*vehicle*› [مُزَوَّد بِعَجَلةِ القِيادةِ على اليَمينِ]

right-handed /rʌɪtˈhandɪd/ *adj* **1** ‹*child, batsman*› أيْمَن (dipt; f يُمْنى), [مُعَدّ للاسْتِخْدامِ باليَدِ اليُمْنى] **2** ‹*golf club, scissors*› يَمينيّ

right-hand man *n* مُساعِد مُقَرَّب, ذِراع أيْمَن, يَد يُمْنى

right-hand woman *n* مُساعِدة مُقَرَّبة, ذِراع أيْمَن, يَد يُمْنى

rightly /ˈrʌɪtli/ *adv* **1** (accurately) ‹*to describe, point out*› بِحَقٍّ **2** (justifiably) ‹*upset, indignant, furious*› عن حَقٍّ; **and quite ~** وَلَهُ كُلُّ الحَقِّ \ العُذْرِ; **~ or wrongly** عن حَقٍّ أو عن باطِلٍ **3** (for sure) عن يَقينٍ, يَقيناً; **I don't ~ know** لا أعْلَمُ يَقيناً; **I can't ~ say** لا أسْتَطيعُ أنْ أجْزِمَ

right-of-centre /ˌrʌɪtəvˈsɛntə/ (BrE), **right-of-center** (AmE) *adj* ‹*politician, party*› يَمين الوَسَط

right of way *n* **1** [u] (in driving) أوْلَويّة المُرورِ **2** (over land) [حَقّ المُرورِ عَبْرَ مُمْتَلَكاتِ الآخَرينَ]

right-on /rʌɪtˈɒn/ **A** *adj* (infml) ‹*views, parents*› مُتَماشٍ \ مُتَوافِق مع روحِ العَصْرِ

B (**right on**) *excl* (AmE infml) أنْتَ على حَقٍّ, تَماماً

right-thinking /ˈrʌɪtˌθɪŋkɪŋ/ *adj* ‹*people, investor*› سَليم التَفْكير, مُتَعَقِّل, سَديد الرَأْيِ

right-to-life /ˌrʌɪttəˈlʌɪf/ *adj* ‹*movement, protester*› مُعارِض للإجْهاضِ, مُؤَيِّد للحَقِّ في الحَياةِ

right wing **A** *n* **1** (Pol) جَناح يَمينيّ **2** (Sport) جَناح أيْمَن;

B (**right-wing**) *adj* (Pol) ‹*policies, politician*› يَمينيّ

right-winger /ˌrʌɪtˈwɪŋə/ *n* **1** (Pol) شَخْص يَمينيّ **2** (Sport) لاعِب في الجَناحِ الأيْمَنِ

rigid /ˈrɪdʒɪd/ *adj* **1** (stiff) ‹*material, structure*› صُلْب (أصْلاب), جامِد (جَوامِدُ); **she was ~ with fear** تَجَمَّدَتْ مَكانَها من الخَوْفِ **2** (inflexible) ‹*discipline, adherence*› صارِم (صَوارِمُ)

rigidly /ˈrɪdʒɪdli/ *adv* ‹*to enforce, stick to*› بِصَلابةٍ, بِصَرامةٍ

rigmarole /ˈrɪgm(ə)rəʊl/ *n* (infml) إجْراء مُعَقَّد

rigor (AmE) *n* ▸ **rigour**

rigor mortis *n* تَيَبُّس المَيِّتِ

rigorous /ˈrɪg(ə)rəs/ *adj* ‹*standards, training*› شَديد, قاسٍ, صارِم

rigour (BrE), **rigor** (AmE) /ˈrɪgə/ *n* **1** (strictness) شِدّة, صَرامة, قَسْوة **2** (thoroughness) دِقّة

rile /rʌɪl/ *vt* (infml) أزْعَجَ, أثارَ, أغْضَبَ ‹*a neighbour, colleague*›

rim /rɪm/ *n* 1 (of cups, bowls) حافة (حافات, حَوافٍ) 2 (on a wheel) (of a car) جُنْط (جُنوط)؛ (of a bicycle) طَوْق (أَطْواق)

rind /raɪnd/ *n* 1 (on cheese) قِشْرة (قِشْر) 2 (on fruit) قِشْرة (قِشْر) 3 (on bacon) [طَبَقة خارِجيّة]

ring /rɪŋ/ A *n* 1 (for one's finger) خاتَم (خَواتِمُ)، دُبْلة; **a wedding ~** خاتَم الزَواجِ \ دُبْلة; **a diamond ~** خاتَم ماسٍ 2 (of a doorbell) دَقّة; (of a phone) رَنّة 3 (BrE) (phone call) اِتِّصال (اِتِّصالات)، مُهاتَفة; **to give sb a ~** هاتَفَ \ اِتَّصَلَ بِشَخْصٍ 4 [u] (resonance) نَبْرة; **that story has a familiar ~ to it** تِلْكَ القِصّةُ لَها نَبْرةٌ مَأْلوفةٌ; **the name has a nice ~ to it** الاسْمُ لَهُ رَنّةٌ لَطيفةٌ 5 (circle) دائِرة (دَوائِرُ); **to draw a ~ around an advertisement** وَضَعَ دائِرةً حول إعْلانٍ; **to have ~s under one's eyes** كانَتْ لَدَيْهِ تَجاعيدُ تحت عَيْنَيْهِ 6 (for boxing, wrestling) حَلْبة (حَلَبات) 7 (of drug dealers, pornographers) عِصابة (عِصابات, عَصائِبُ) 8 (for identification) طَوْق (أَطْواق)، حَلْقة (حَلَقات, حَلَق) 9 (around a planet) حَلْقة (حَلَق, حَلَقات) 10 (on a cooker) رَأْس الموقِد

B *vt* 1 (*past tense* **rang**; *past participle* **rung**) (to cause to sound) دَقَّ (u; دَقّ) ‹*a bell*›; **to ~ the doorbell** دَقَّ جَرَسَ البابِ 2 (BrE Tel) (*past tense* **rang**; *past participle* **rung**) اِتَّصَلَ (ب)، هاتَفَ ‹*a friend, number, the station*› 3 (to encircle) (*past tense, past participle* **ringed**) طَوَّقَ، أَحاطَ (ب) ‹*a building, park, vehicle*› 4 (Zool) (*past tense, past participle* **ringed**) عَلَّمَ بِحَلَقةٍ مَعْدِنيّةٍ ‹*a bird*›

C *vi* (*past tense* **rang**; *past participle* **rung**) 1 (to sound) «doorbells, telephones» دَقَّ (u; دَقّ) 2 (to sound a bell) دَقَّ (u; دَقّ); **to ~ at the door** دَقَّ جَرَسَ البابِ; **'please ~ for service'** 'يُرْجى دَقُّ الجَرَسِ لِطَلَبِ الخِدْمةِ' 3 (BrE Tel) (to telephone) اِتَّصَلَ، أَجْرى مُكالَمةً هاتِفيّةً; **to ~ for a taxi/an ambulance** اِتَّصَلَ لِطَلَبِ تاكسي \ سَيّارة إسْعافٍ 4 (to resonate) «laughter, words» رَنَّ (i; رَنين)، تَرَدَّدَ صَداهُ; **her laughter rang in my ears** رَنَّتْ ضِحْكَتُها في أُذُني; **his explanation ~s true/false** يَبْدو تَبْريرُهُ مُقْنِعاً \ غَيْرَ مُقْنِعٍ

Phrasal verbs **ring back** (BrE) 1 (to phone again) عاوَدَ الاتِّصالَ 2 **~ [sb] back** (to phone again) عاوَدَ الاتِّصالَ [بِشَخْصٍ]; (to return a call) رَدَّ المُكالَمةَ ل [شَخْصٍ]

• **ring in** (BrE) 1 (to a phone-in show) اِتَّصَلَ، هاتَفَ 2 (to one's place of work) اِتَّصَلَ، هاتَفَ; **I had to ~ in sick** اُضْطُرِرْتُ للاتِّصالِ للإبْلاغِ بِأَنّي مَريضٌ

• **ring off** (BrE) أَنْهى مُكالَمةً

• **ring out** 1 «voice, shots» دَوّى 2 «bells» دَقَّ عالِياً

• **ring up** (BrE) A (to telephone) اِتَّصَلَ، هاتَفَ B **~ up [sb/sth]**, **~ [sb/sth] up** 1 (on the phone) اِتَّصَلَ ب [شَخْصٍ \ شَيْءٍ] ‹*a friend, the station*› 2 (on the cash register) سَجَّلَ [شَيْئاً] ‹*a figure, total*›

ring binder *n* مِلَفٌ بِهِ حَلَقاتٌ مَعْدِنيّةٌ لِتَثْبيتِ الوَرَقِ

ringing /ˈrɪŋɪŋ/ *n* 1 (of a bell, an alarm) رَنين 2 (in the ears) طَنين، رَنين

ringleader /ˈrɪŋliːdə/ *n* زَعيم عِصابةٍ

ringlet /ˈrɪŋlɪt/ *n* عِقْصة شَعْرٍ \ جَعْدة

ring road *n* (BrE) طَريق دائِريّ

ringtone /ˈrɪŋtəʊn/ *n* رَنّة هاتِفٍ \ نَغْمة

ringworm /ˈrɪŋwɜːm/ *n* قوباء حَلَقيّة

rink /rɪŋk/ *n* 1 (for ice skating) حَلَبة التَزَلُّج 2 (for roller skating) حَلَبة التَزَلُّج

rinse /rɪns/ A *vt* 1 (with water) شَطَفَ (u; شَطْف) ‹*rice, a jar*› 2 (to remove soap) شَطَفَ (u; شَطْف) ‹*clothes, the dishes*› 3 (to wash out) شَطَفَ (u; شَطْف) ‹*dishes*›; **to ~ out one's mouth** تَمَضْمَضَ

B *n* 1 (wash) شَطْف 2 (removal of soap) شَطْف 3 (solution for hair) غَسول

riot /ˈraɪət/ A *n* شَغَب، أَعْمال شَغَبٍ \ أَحْداث; **a food ~** أَعْمال شَغَبٍ بِسَبَبِ ارْتِفاعِ أَسْعارِ الغِذاءِ

B *vi* «prisoners, fans» قامَ بِأَعْمالِ شَغَبٍ

Idioms **a riot of colour** مَجْموعة من الأَلْوانِ المُتَنَوِّعةِ; **to run riot** خَرَجَ عن السَيْطَرةِ

rioter /ˈraɪətə/ *n* مُشاغِب، مُثير شَغَبٍ

riot gear *n* زيّ مُكافَحةِ الشَغَبِ

rioting /ˈraɪətɪŋ/ *n* أَعْمال شَغَبٍ

riotous /ˈraɪətəs/ *adj* 1 ‹*laughter, lunch*› (boisterous) صاخِب 2 (noisy and violent) ‹*behaviour, crowd*› غَوْغائيّ، مُشاغِب

riot police *n* قوّات مُكافَحةِ الشَغَبِ

rip /rɪp/ **A** *vt* **(-pp-)** **1** (to tear) شَقَّ (u; شَقّ), مَزَّق *<one's skirt, trousers, clothing>*; **to ~ a hole in sth** شَقَّ فَتْحةً في شَيْءٍ; **to ~ sth/sb to pieces** *or* **shreds** مَزَّق شَيْئاً \ شَخْصاً إرباً **2** (to snatch away) خَطَفَ (i; خَطْف); **to ~ away the wrapping/tape** مَزَّق الغِلافَ \ الشَريطَ بِسُرْعةٍ; **to ~ the flag/ fence down** أَسْقطَ العَلَمَ \ الجِدارَ

B *vi* **(-pp-)** «fabric, dress, shirt» انْشَقَّ, تَمَزَّقَ

C *n* شَقّ, مَزْق (شُقوق)

(Idiom) **to let rip** (infml) (to not restrain oneself) أَطْلَقَ لِنَفْسِهِ العَنانَ; (to go fast) انْطَلَقَ بِأَقْصى سُرْعةٍ; **to let ~ at sb** كالَ الانْتِقاداتِ لِشَخْصٍ

(Phrasal verbs) **rip apart**: **~ [sb/sth] apart** **1** دَمَّرَ [شَيْئاً] تَماماً *<a car, building>* **2** قَطَّعَ [شَخْصاً \ شَيْئاً] إرباً *<one's prey, a person, garment>* **3** (infml) (to defeat) هَزَمَ [شَخْصاً \ شَيْئاً] هَزيمةً مُنْكَرةً *<a team, sb's defence>*

• **rip off** **A** **~ off [sth]**, **~ [sth] off** **1** (to detach) أَزالَ [شَيْئاً] بِعُنْفٍ *<a wrapping>*; أَسْقطَ [شَيْئاً] *<a door handle, the roof>* **2** (infml) (to steal) سَرَقَ [شَيْئاً] *<a computer, clothes, design>* **B** **~ off [sb]**, **~ [sb] off** (infml) (to cheat) غَشَّ, تَقاضى من [شَخْصاً] [شَخْصٍ] ثَمَناً فاحِشاً

• **rip open**: **~ open [sth]**, **~ [sth] open** فَتَحَ [شَيْئاً] بِعُنْفٍ *<an envelope, a bag>*

• **rip through**: **~ through [sth]** «the fire, explosion» اخْتَرَقَ [شَيْئاً] *<a building>*

• **rip up**: **~ up [sth]**, **~ [sth] up** **1** (into pieces) مَزَّقَ [شَيْئاً] إرباً *<a letter, contract>* **2** (to remove) أَزالَ [شَيْئاً] بِعُنْفٍ *<the floorboards, carpet>*

RIP /ɑːrʌɪ'piː/ *abbr* (Latin) = **requiescat in pace** رَحْمةُ اللهِ عَلَيْهِ, طَيَّبَ اللهُ ثَراهُ

ripcord /'rɪpkɔːd/ *n* حَبْل إطْلاقِ المَظَلّةِ \ الباراشوت

ripe /rʌɪp/ *adj* **1** (of fruit) *<pear, tomato>* ناضِج; **to harvest the ~ crop** حَصَدَ المَحْصولَ الناضِجَ **2** (of cheese) *<cheese, brie>* مُعَتَّق, قَديم

ripen /'rʌɪp(ə)n/ **A** *vt* أَنْضَجَ *<fruit, crops>*; **sun-~ed tomatoes** طَماطِم أَنْضَجَتْها الشَمْسُ

B *vi* «fruit, crops» نَضِجَ (a; نُضْج)

rip-off /'rɪpɒf/ *n* (infml) **1** (swindle) نَصْب, احْتِيال (احْتِيالات) **2** (copy) نُسْخة مُقَلَّدة

ripple /'rɪp(ə)l/ **A** *n* **1** (on water) تَمَوُّج **2** (of applause, fear) مَوْجة; **a ~ of laughter/applause** مَوْجة ضِحْكٍ \ تَصْفيقٍ

B *vi* **1** «waves, water» تَمَوَّجَ **2** «muscles, corn» تَمَوَّجَ

rise /rʌɪz/ **A** *vi* (*past tense* **rose**; *past participle* **risen**) **1** (to become higher) «prices, temperatures, waters» زادَ, ارْتَفَعَ (i; زِيادة), ازْدادَ, صَعِدَ (a; صُعود); **his voice rose in anger** ارْتَفَعَ صَوْتُهُ غَضَباً; **the temperature rose above 48°** ارْتَفَعَتْ دَرَجةُ الحَرارة فوق 48 دَرَجةً **2** (to intensify) «tension, frustration, anger» اشْتَدَّ, تَزايَدَ, ازْدادَ; **hopes of a solution are rising** تَتَزايَدُ الآمالُ في الوُصولِ إلى حَلٍّ **3** (to get up) اسْتَيْقَظَ; (from seat) نَهَضَ (a; نُهوض, نَهْض), وَقَفَ (i; وُقوف, وَقْف) **4** (to be successful) **to ~ to the occasion/challenge** ارْتَفَعَ إلى مُسْتَوى الحَدَثِ \ التَحَدّي **5** (to progress) **to ~ to fame/ power** صَعِدَ إلى الشُهْرةِ \ السُلْطةِ; **he rose from office boy to general manager** تَحَوَّلَ من ساعٍ إلى مُديرٍ عامٍّ **6** (to slope upwards) «the ground, road» ارْتَفَعَ **7** (to appear) «the sun, moon» طَلَعَ (u; طُلوع, مَطْلَع) **8** «rivers» نَبَعَ (a-i-u; نَبْع, نُبوع, نَبَعان); **the Euphrates ~s in Turkey** يَنْبُعُ نَهْرُ الفُراتِ من تُرْكيا **9** (Culin) «dough, cakes» اخْتَمَرَ, انْتَفَخَ, ارْتَفَعَ **10** «court» رُفِعَ; «committee» أَنْهى أَعْمالَهُ

B *n* **1** (in an amount, a number, rate) زِيادة; (in prices, pressure, temperature) ارْتِفاع **2** (BrE) (also **pay rise**) زِيادة (في الراتِبِ) **3** (of empires, companies, ideologies) صُعود, ازْدِهار (ازْدِهارات); **her ~ to fame/power** صُعودُها إلى الشُهْرةِ \ السُلْطةِ **4** (hill) تَلّ صَغير **5** (to be the origin of) **to give ~ to speculation/a rumour** أَثارَ التَكَهُّناتِ \ شائِعةً

(Phrasal verbs) **rise above**: **~ above [sth]** (to overcome) تَغَلَّبَ على [شَيْءٍ] *<a problem, disability>*

• **rise up** **1** (to ascend) «aircraft, birds, smoke» عَلا, ارْتَفَعَ (u; عُلُوّ) **2** (to tower up) «mountains, buildings» عَلا, ارْتَفَعَ (u; عُلُوّ) **3** (to rebel) «tribes, cities» ثارَ, تَمَرَّدَ (u; ثَوْرة, ثَوَران)

rising /'rʌɪzɪŋ/ **A** *n* انْتِفاضة, ثَوْرة

B *adj* **1** (getting higher) *<sun, tide>* آخِذ في الارْتِفاعِ **2** (increasing) *<prices, interest rates>* مُتَصاعِد, آخِذ في الارْتِفاعِ

3 (intensifying) ‹*temperature, tensions*› مُتَزايِد **4** (sloping upwards) ‹*slope, path*› صاعِد لِأَعْلى

rising damp *n* اِنْتِقال الرُّطوبةِ من الأَرْضِ إلى الجُدْرانِ

risk /rɪsk/ **A** *n* **1** (potential for negative result) مُخاطَرة; **the ~ is minimal/very high** المُخاطَرةُ مُتَدَنِّيةٌ \ عاليةٌ جِدًّا; **to run the ~ of failure** عَرَّض نَفْسَهُ للفَشَلِ; **to take ~s** جازَفَ; **it's worth/not worth the ~** يَسْتَحِقُّ \ لا يَسْتَحِقُّ المُخاطَرة; **their jobs are at ~** وَظائِفُهُمْ في خَطَرٍ; **to put sb's health at ~** عَرَّض صِحّةَ شَخْصٍ للخَطَرِ **2** (in banking, insurance) مُخاطَرة; **to be a good/bad ~** كانَ مُخاطَرةً مَقْبولةً \ غَيْرَ مَقْبولةٍ; **an all-~s policy** بوليصة \ وَثيقة تَأْمينٍ ضِدَّ جَميعِ المَخاطِرِ

B *vt* **1** (to endanger) عَرَّضَ للخَطَرِ; **to ~ one's life/one's health** عَرَّضَ حَياتَهُ \ صِحَّتَهُ للخَطَرِ **2** (to take a chance with) خاطَرَ (ب); **to ~ missing the train** خاطَرَ بِأَنْ يَفوتَهُ القِطارُ; **we decided to ~ it** قَرَّرْنا أَنْ نَخوضَ المُخاطَرة

risk assessment *n* تَقْييم مَخاطِرَ

risk manager *n* مُدير مَخاطِرَ

risky /ˈrɪski/ *adj* (**riskier**, **riskiest**) ‹*business, investment*› مَحْفوف بالمَخاطِرِ

risqué /ˈriːskeɪ/ *adj* ‹*joke, photo*› مُبْتَذَل ,غَيْر مُحْتَشِمٍ \ لائِق

rite /rʌɪt/ *n* طَقْس (طُقوس) ,شَعيرة (شَعائِرُ)

ritual /ˈrɪtʃʊəl/ **A** *n* طَقْس (طُقوس) ,شَعيرة (شَعائِرُ)

B *adj* ‹*sacrifice, dance*› شَعائِريّ

rival /ˈrʌɪv(ə)l/ **A** *n* خَصْم (خُصوم ,أَخْصام) ,مُنافِس

B *adj before n* ‹*gang, firm*› مُنافِس

C *vt* (**-ll-** BrE, **-l-** AmE) ضاهى ,نافَسَ ‹*the best*›

rivalry /ˈrʌɪvəlri/ *n* (*pl* **rivalries**) مُنافَسة; **a bitter ~ between the two clubs/companies** مُنافَسة مُحْتَدِمة بين النادِيَيْنِ \ الشَرِكَتَيْنِ

river /ˈrɪvə/ *n* نَهْر (أَنْهُر ,أَنْهار); **the R~ Jordan, the Jordan R~** نَهْر الأُرْدُنِ

(Idiom) **to sell sb down the river** غَدَرَ بِشَخْصٍ

riverbank /ˈrɪvəbaŋk/ *n* ضِفّة نَهْرٍ

riverbed /ˈrɪvəbɛd/ *n* قاع نَهْرٍ

riverside /ˈrɪvəsʌɪd/ **A** *n* ضِفّة نَهْرٍ

B *adj before n* ‹*walk, path*› على ضِفّةِ النَهْرِ

rivet /ˈrɪvɪt/ **A** *n* مِسْمار بِرْشامٍ

B *vt* (to attach) بَرْشَمَ ,ثَبَّتَ (بِمِسْمارِ بِرْشامٍ) ‹*a plate, girder*›; **my attention was ~ed by her story** شَدَّت انْتِباهي بِقِصَّتِها

(Idiom) **to be riveted to the spot/ground** تَسَمَّرَ مَكانَهُ

riveting /ˈrɪvɪtɪŋ/ *adj* ‹*story, performance*› يَشُدُّ \ يَجْذِبُ الانْتِباه

riviera /ˌrɪvɪˈɛːrə/ *n* (**the Riviera**) الريفْييرا; **the French R~** الريفْييرا الفَرَنْسيّة

Riyadh /riːˈɑːd/ *pr n* الرياض (f)

riyal /ˈriːɑːl/ *n* رِيال

RN /ɑːrˈɛn/ *n* **1** (in US) = **registered nurse** مُمَرِّض مُسَجَّل \ مُعْتَمَد **2** (in UK) = **Royal Navy** البَحْرِيّة المَلَكيّة البَريطانيّة

RNA /ɑːrɛnˈeɪ/ *n* = **ribonucleic acid** الحَمْض النَوَويّ الريبيّ

roach /rəʊtʃ/ *n* **1** (*pl* **roach**) (fish) روش (سَمَك نَهْريّ) **2** (AmE) (infml) (insect) صُرْصور (صَراصيرُ)

road /rəʊd/ *n* **1** (between towns, places) طَريق (mf; طُرُق); **the ~ to/from Birmingham** الطَريق إلى \ من بِرْمِنْجْهام; **the ~ north** الطَريق المُتَّجِه شَمالاً; **the ~ home** الطَريق إلى البَيْتِ; **the ~ back to Beirut** طَريق العَوْدةِ إلى بَيْروت; **are we on the right ~ for Springfield?** هل نَحْنُ على الطَريقِ الصَحيحِ إلى سْبرينْجْفيلْد؟; **after a week on the ~** بعد أُسْبوعٍ من السَفَرِ; **goods transported by ~** بَضائِع مَنْقولة بَرًّا \ على الطَريقِ; **to be off the ~** «vehicles» كانَ مَرْفوعاً \ مُتَوَقِّفاً \ لا يُسْتَخْدَمُ **2** (in a built-up area) طَريق (mf; طُرُق) ,شارِع (شَوارِعُ); **it's across the ~** هو على الجانِبِ الآخَرِ من الطَريقِ; **go to the end of this ~** اذْهَبْ إلى آخِرِ هذا الطَريقِ; **cross the ~ at the pedestrian crossing** اُعْبُر الطَريقَ من مَمَرِّ المُشاةِ; **he lives just along** *or* **down the ~** يَعيشُ في الجِوارِ **3** (way) طَريق (mf; طُرُق); **to be on the ~ to disaster/victory** كانَ في طَريقِهِ إلى كارِثةٍ \ نَصْرٍ; **we think we're on the right ~** نَظُنُّ أَنَّنا على المَسارِ الصَحيحِ; **we don't want to go down that ~** لا نُريدُ أَنْ نَسيرَ في هذا المَسارِ; **to reach the end of the ~** وَصَلَ إلى نِهايةِ المَطافِ

roadblock /ˈrəʊdblɒk/ *n* مِتْراس ,حاجِز طَريقٍ (مَتاريسُ); **a police ~** حاجِز طَريقٍ تابِع للشُرْطةِ

road haulier *n* (BrE) **1** (person) سائِق شاحِنةِ نَقْلٍ بَرّيٍّ **2** (company) شَرِكة نَقْلٍ بَرّيٍّ

road hog *n* سائِق مُسْتَهْتِر

road hump *n* مَطَبّات صِناعيّة

road map *n* 1 (to find your way) خَريطة طُرُق 2 (plan) خارِطة طَريقٍ

road rage *n* الغَضَب ,الغَضَب أثناء القِيادة ,غَضَب الطَريق على الطَريقِ

roadshow /ˈrəʊdʃəʊ/ *n* 1 (show, programme) [بَرنامَج تِلِفِزْيونيّ 2 (publicity tour) جَوْلة تَرْويجيّة \ دِعائيّة] أو إذاعيّ مُتَجَوِّل

roadside /ˈrəʊdsʌɪd/ A *n* جانِب الطَريق

B *adj* ‹stall, verge› (واقِع) على جانِب الطَريق

road sign *n* عَلامة طَريقٍ ,إشارة مُرور

roadster /ˈrəʊdstə/ *n* رودْسْتَر (سَيّارة صَغيرة مَكْشوفة تَتَّسِع لِراكِبَيْن فَقَط)

road sweeper *n* 1 (person) كَنّاس \ مُنَظِّف شَوارِعَ

2 (machine) سَيّارة كَنْس شَوارِعَ

road tax *n* (BrE) ضَريبة طَريقٍ

road tax disc *n* (BrE) [وَثيقة إثْباتِ دَفْعِ ضَريبةِ الطَريق]

roadworks (BrE), **roadwork** (AmE) /ˈrəʊdwəːk(s)/ *n pl* أَعْمال طُرُقٍ

roadworthy /ˈrəʊdwəːði/ *adj* ‹car, vehicle› صالِح لِلسَيْر

roam /rəʊm/ A *vt* تَجَوَّلَ (في) ,طافَ (u; طَواف ;في) ‹the streets, countryside›

B *vi* «deer, tigers» حامَ (u; حَوْم ,حَوَمان) ,هامَ (i; هَيْم)

(Phrasal verb) **roam around** «animals» حامَ ,جالَ (u; جَوْل ,حول)

roaming /ˈrəʊmɪŋ/ *n* 1 (for phoning) خِدْمة التَجْوالِ

2 (wandering) تَجْوال ,تَنَقُّل ,تَرْحال

roar /rɔː/ A *n* (of lions) زَئير ;(of bears) زَمْجَرة ,قَهْقاع ;(of a person, crowd) صِياح ;(of engines, traffic) ضَجيج ;(of the sea) هَدير ;(of wind) صَفير

B *vi* 1 «lions» زَأَرَ (a-i; زَئير ,زَأْر) ;«bears» زَمْجَرَ (i; زَمْجَرة)

2 (to cry out) **to ~ with anger/pain** صَرَخَ غاضِباً \ مِن شِدّة الأَلَمِ ;**we all ~ed with laughter** انْفَجَرْنا كُلّنا في الضَحِكِ

3 (to make a loud noise) «the sea, wind, traffic» أَصْدَرَ ضَجيجاً عالِياً ;**the convoy ~ed past** مَرَّ المَوْكِبُ مُسْرِعاً وَهُوَ يُصْدِرُ ضَجّةً عالِيةً

roaring /ˈrɔːrɪŋ/ *adj before n* 1 (noisy) ‹engine, waterfall› صاخِب 2 (burning) ‹fire, flames› مُلْتَهِب 3 (infml) (successful) ‹success› باهِر ,مُدَوٍّ ‹trade› مُزْدَهِر ;**supermarkets are doing a ~ trade in snacks** الأَطْعِمةُ الخَفيفةُ هي تِجارةٌ مُزْدَهِرةٌ في مَحَلّاتِ السوبَر مارْكيت

roast /rəʊst/ A *vt* شَوى (i; شَيّ) ‹meat, potatoes›; حَمَّصَ ‹coffee beans›

B *vi* «meat» انْشَوى ;«chestnuts» تَحَمَّصَ

C *adj* ‹meat, potatoes› مَشْوِيّ

D *n* لَحْم شِواءٍ

roasting /ˈrəʊstɪŋ/ A *n* (infml) انْتِقاد لاذِع ,تَوْبيخ شَديد ;**to give sb a ~** وَبَّخَ شَخْصاً بِشِدّةٍ

B *adj* 1 ‹tin, pan› لِلشَيِّ 2 (infml) ‹day, weather› حارّ جِدّاً ;**I must take off my coat - I'm ~!** لا بُدَّ أَنْ أَنْزِعَ مِعْطَفي – أَكادُ أَغْلي من شِدّةِ الحَرِّ!

rob /rɒb/ *vt* (-bb-) 1 (to take valuables from a person) سَرَقَ (i; سَرِقة) ‹the tourist, passers-by›; (a bank, safe, etc) سَطا (u; سَطْو; سَرِقَ (على) ‹a bank, grave, safe›; **she was ~bed of her phone** تَعَرَّضَ مِنْها هاتِفُها ;**the bank was ~bed by masked men** البَنْكُ لِلسَرِقة من قِبَلِ رِجالٍ مُقَنَّعين ;**the tomb was ~bed centuries ago** نُهِبَت المَقْبَرةُ مُنذ قُرونٍ 2 (to deprive) **to ~ sb/sth of sth** حَرَمَ شَخْصاً \ شَيْئاً ,سَلَبَ شَيْئاً من شَخْصٍ \ شَيْءٍ مِن شَيْءٍ

robber /ˈrɒbə/ *n* سارِق (لُصوص) ,لِصّ

robbery /ˈrɒb(ə)ri/ *n* (*pl* **robberies**) سَطْو ,سَرِقة

robe /rəʊb/, /rəʊb/ *n* 1 (ceremonial garment) ثَوْب (ثِياب) , رِداء (أَرْدِية) 2 (AmE) (bathrobe) ثَوْب \ روب حَمّام (أَثْواب)

robin /ˈrɒbɪn/ *n* 1 (also **robin redbreast**) (European) أَبو الحِنّاء

2 (North American) أَبو الحِنّاء (الأَمْريكيّ الشَماليّ)

robot /ˈrəʊbɒt/ *n* روبوت ,إِنْسان آلِيّ

robust /rəʊˈbʌst/ *adj* ‹child, health› قَوِيّ (أَقْوِياءُ) ,مَتين (مِتان)

rock /rɒk/ A *n* 1 [u] (substance) صَخْر (n coll); **a layer of ~** طَبَقة من الصَخْرِ ;**molten ~** صَخْر مُنْصَهِر 2 (stone) صَخْر (n coll; صُخور) ;**~s blocked the road** سَدَّت الصُخورُ الطَريقَ ;**to throw ~s at sb** أَلْقى صُخوراً على شَخْصٍ 3 (piece of stone) صَخْر (n coll; صُخور) ;**the ship went on the ~s** اصْطَدَمَت السَفينةُ بالصُخورِ ;**the marriage is on the ~s** الزَواجُ مُتَعَثِّرٌ \ غَيْرُ مُسْتَقِرٍّ ;**the castle is built on a ~** القَلْعةُ

مَبْنِيَّةٌ على صَخْرةٍ 4 (also **rock music**) الروك (موسيقى)
5 (infml) (jewel) *usu pl* حَجَر ماس

B *vt* 1 (to move gently) «waves, wind, person» هَزَّ (u; هَزّ) ‹*a cradle, baby*›; **the boat was gently ~ed by the waves** هَزَّت الأَمْواجُ القارِبَ بِرِفقٍ 2 (to shake) هَزَّ (u; هَزّ), رَجَّ (u; رَجّ) ‹*a city, building*› 3 (to weaken) «scandal» هَزَّ (u; هَزّ) ‹*the government, party*›; **the country was ~ed by a series of political scandals** هَزَّت البِلادَ سِلْسِلةٌ من الفَضائِحِ السِياسيَّةِ

C *vi* 1 (to sway) «cradle, person» اِهْتَزَّ, تَأَرْجَحَ; **to ~ to and fro** تَأَرْجَحَ للأَمامِ والخَلْفِ; **the hammock ~ed gently in the breeze** تَأَرْجَحَت الأُرجوحةُ الشَّبَكيَّةُ بِرِفقٍ في النَسيمِ 2 (to shake) «buildings, ground» اِهْتَزَّ, اِرْتَجَّ 3 (infml) (to dance) **to ~ (away)** [رَقَصَ على موسيقى الروك]; **the place was ~ing** [كانَ الناسُ في المَكانِ يَرْقُصونَ على أَنْغامِ موسيقى الروك]

Idioms **between a rock and a hard place** بين المِطْرَقةِ والسِنْدانِ; **on the rocks** مع مُكَعَّباتِ الثَلْجِ

rock and roll, **rock 'n' roll** *n* روك أَنْد رول

rock band *n* فِرْقة روك

rock-bottom /rɒkˈbɒtəm/ **A** *adj before n* ‹*price*› مُتَدَنٍّ جِدًّا, بَخْس; **to sell at ~ prices** باعَ بِأَدْنى الأَسْعارِ

B *n* قاع (قيعان); **to reach ~** وَصَلَ إلى أَدْنى مُسْتَوًى

rock climber *n* مُتَسَلِّق صُخورٍ

rock climbing *n* تَسَلُّق صُخورٍ

rock concert *n* حَفْلة روك

rocker /ˈrɒkə/ *n* 1 (on a cradle, chair) [إِحْدى قاعِدَتَيِ الكُرْسيِّ الهَزّازِ] 2 (AmE) (chair) كُرْسيّ هَزّاز 3 (infml) (performer) مُغَنّي روك; (fan) مُحِبّ لِموسيقى الروك

Idiom **to be off one's rocker** (infml) كانَ فاقِداً لِصَوابِهِ

rockery /ˈrɒk(ə)ri/ *n* (*pl* **rockeries**) (BrE) [جُزْء من حَديقةٍ بِهِ صُخورٌ وَنَباتاتٌ صَخْرِيَّةٌ]

rocket /ˈrɒkɪt/ **A** *n* 1 (spacecraft) صاروخ (صَواريخُ) 2 (weapon) صاروخ (صَواريخُ); **a ~ attack** هُجوم بالصَواريخِ; **an anti-tank ~** صاروخ مُضادّ للدَبّاباتِ 3 (firework) صاروخ أَلْعابٍ نارِيَّةٍ 4 (salad) جِرْجير

B *vi* «prices, unemployment» قَفَزَ (i; قَفْز), اِرْتَفَعَ بِشَكْلٍ حادٍّ

rocket launcher *n* قاذِفة \ راجِمة صَواريخَ

rocket science *n* عِلْم الصَواريخ; (hum) **that's hardly rocket science!** لَيْسَ ذلك مُعَقَّداً كَما تَتَخَيَّلُ!

rock face *n* واجِهة صَخْرِيّة

rockfall /ˈrɒkfɔːl/ *n* اِنْهِيار صَخْريّ

rock-hard /rɒkˈhɑːd/ *adj* ‹*ground, biscuit*› شَديد الصَلابةِ

rocking chair /ˈrɒkɪŋ tʃɛː/ *n* كُرْسيّ هَزّاز

rocking horse /ˈrɒkɪŋ hɔːs/ *n* حِصان هَزّاز

rock music *n* موسيقى الروك

rock salmon *n* (BrE) نَهّاش أَحْمَر (سَلْمون)

rock star *n* نَجْم موسيقى الروك

rocky /ˈrɒki/ *adj* (**rockier**, **rockiest**) 1 (full of rocks) ‹*shore, terrain*› صَخْريّ, كَثير الصُخورِ 2 (unsteady) ‹*base*› مُتَزَعْزِع, غَيْر ثابِتٍ; ‹*toddler*› مُتَرَنِّح في مِشْيَتِهِ 3 (full of problems) ‹*relationship, period*› مُتَقَلْقِل, غَيْر مُسْتَقِرٍّ

Rocky Mountains *pr n* (**the Rocky Mountains**) جِبال روكي

rod /rɒd/ *n* 1 (bar) قَضيب (قُضْبان); **a curtain ~** قَضيب سِتارةٍ 2 (for fishing) قَصَبة, صِنّارة (صَنانيرُ)

rode /rəʊd/ *past tense* ▸ **ride**

rodent /ˈrəʊd(ə)nt/ *n* قارِض (قَوارِضُ)

rodeo /ˈrəʊdɪəʊ/ *n* (*pl* **rodeos**) [مُسابَقات رُعاةِ البَقَرِ]

roe /rəʊ/ *n* بَطْرَخ (بَطارِخُ)

roe deer *n* يَحْمور

rogue /rəʊg/ *n* (liter) وَغْد (أَوْغاد), شَقيّ (أَشْقِياءُ)

roguish /ˈrəʊgɪʃ/ *adj* (liter) ‹*smile, charm*› خَبيث (خُبَثاءُ, خُبَثة), لَئيم (لُؤَماءُ, لِئام)

role /rəʊl/ *n* 1 (in a film, play) دَوْر (أَدْوار); **Sir Laurence Olivier played the ~ of Hamlet** لَعِبَ السَيِّدُ لورَنْس أوليفْيير دَوْرَ هامْلِت 2 (function) دَوْر (أَدْوار), وَظيفة (وَظائِفُ)

role model *n* قُدْوة, نَموذَج يُحْتَذى بِهِ

role-play /ˈrəʊlpleɪ/ *n* لَعِب \ تَمْثيل أَدْوارٍ

roll /rəʊl/ **A** *vt* 1 (to push) دَحْرَجَ (i; دَحْرَجة) ‹*a ball, barrel, log*›; **to ~ sth away** دَحْرَجَ شَيْئاً بَعيداً; **to ~ sth downhill** دَحْرَجَ شَيْئاً إلى أَسْفَلَ 2 (to make) لَفَّ (u; لَفّ) ‹*a cigarette*›; **to ~ string/clay into a ball** لَفَّ الخَيْطَ \ شَكَّلَ الصَلْصالَ إلى كُرةٍ 3 (in foundries) دَرْفَلَ (i; دَرْفَلة) ‹*steel, metal, pipes*›

4 (in breadmaking) فَرَدَ (u; فَرْد) ‹dough› **5** (to turn) **to ~ one's eyes** دارَتْ عَيْناهُ **6** (in games) رَمى (i; رَمْي, رِماية), أَلْقى ‹the dice› **7** (in pronunciation) **to ~ one's ‘r’s** [نَطَقَ حَرْفَ الراءِ بِجَعْلِ طَرَفِ اللِسانِ يَصِلُ إلى سَقْفِ الحَلْقِ]

B *vi* **1** (to move) «balls, coins, rocks» تَدَحْرَجَ; **the car ~ed down the hill** تَدَحْرَجَت السَيّارةُ إلى أَسْفَلِ التَلِّ; **the ball ~ed over the line** تَدَحْرَجَت الكُرةُ فوق الخَطِّ; **the tanks ~ed into the square** دَخَلَت الدَبّاباتُ إلى المَيْدانِ; **I ~ed off the couch/out of bed** نَهَضْتُ من على الأَريكةِ \ السَريرِ **2** (to sway) «ships, trains» تَمايَلَ **3** (to turn over) «planes» انْعَطَفَ, **4** (thunder, drums) دَوّى **5** (to operate) «cameras» دارَ (u; دَوَران, دَوْر), اشْتَغَلَ

C (**rolling**) *adj* **1** ‹countryside, hills› مُتَعَرِّج **2** ‹programme, reform, news service› مُتَواصِل

D *n* **1** (of paper, cloth, banknotes) لَفّة, لِفافة (لِفافات, لَفائِفُ) **2** (of fat) كُتْلة (كُتَل) **3** (bread) خُبْزة; **cheese ~** خُبْزة بالجُبْنِ **4** (register) سِجِلّ (سِجِلاّت), كَشْف (كُشوف); **to be on the electoral ~** كانَ اسْمُهُ في سِجِلِّ \ كُشوفِ النَّاخِبينَ; **to call the ~** نادى كَشْفَ الحُضورِ **5** [u] (of a ship, train) تَمايُل, تَأَرْجُح **6** (by a plane) عُطوف, انْعِطاف (انْعِطافات) **7** (in gymnastics) دَوَران, تَدَحْرُج; **forward/backward ~** تَدَحْرُج للأَمامِ \ للخَلْفِ **8** (of dice) لَفّة **9** (of drums, thunder) دَوِيّ

Idioms **to be on a roll** (infml) حالَفَهُ التَوْفيقُ; **to be rolling in it** (infml) كانَ واسِعَ الثَراءِ; **rolled into one** مَجْموعة \ مَجْموعونَ في واحِدٍ

Phrasal verbs **roll about** (BrE), **roll around** **1** (while playing, in pain) تَمَرَّغَ على الأَرْضِ **2** «marbles, cans, balls» تَدَحْرَجَ

• **roll back**: **~ [sth] back, ~ back [sth]** **1** (to push back) طَوى (i; طَيّ) ‹the carpet›; شَمَّرَ ‹one's sleeve› **2** (to reverse) أَلْغى, أَبْطَلَ ‹a reform, the improvements›; **to ~ back the years** *or* **the clock** أَعادَ الزَمَنَ إلى الوَراءِ

• **roll down**: **~ [sth] down, ~ down [sth]** فَرَدَ [شَيْئاً] ‹one's sleeves›; **to ~ down the window** أَنْزَلَ زُجاجَ النافِذةِ

• **roll in** **1** (to arrive in great numbers) «tourists» تَدَفَّقَ, تَوافَدَ; «orders, money» انْهالَ **2** (infml) (to turn up) جاءَ (i; مَجيء), حَضَرَ (u; حُضور); **she ~ed in 20 minutes late** جاءَتْ مُتَأَخِّرةً 20 دَقيقةً

• **roll off**: **~ off [sth]**: **the cars/computers ~ed off the production line** دَخَلَت السَيّاراتُ \ أَجْهِزةُ الحاسوبِ في خَطِّ الإِنْتاجِ

• **roll out**: **~ [sth] out, ~ out [sth]** **1** (to flatten) فَرَدَ \ رَقَّقَ [شَيْئاً] ‹the pastry, the lumps› **2** (to unroll) فَرَدَ \ بَسَطَ [شَيْئاً] ‹a carpet, the cloth› **3** (to introduce) طَرَحَ \ دَشَّنَ [شَيْئاً] ‹a new model, prototype›

• **roll over** **A** (to turn over) «cars, boats» انْقَلَبَ; **to ~ over on one's back/stomach** اسْتَلْقى على ظَهْرِهِ \ بَطْنِهِ **B** **~ [sb] over** قَلَبَ [شَخْصاً] (في فِراشِهِ) ‹a patient, an invalid›

• **roll up** **A** (infml) (to arrive) «guests, visitors» حَضَرَ (u; حُضور); **~ up!** (for a show, spectacle) هَلُمَّ احْضَروا! **B** **~ up [sth], ~ [sth] up** طَوى \ لَفَّ [شَيْئاً] ‹a rug, poster›; **to ~ up one's sleeves** شَمَّرَ أَكْمامَهُ

roll bar *n* [قَضيب حَديديّ يُرَكَّبُ خلف السَيّاراتِ المَكْشوفةِ لِحِمايةِ الرُكّابِ]

roll call *n* مُناداة على الحُضورِ

rolled gold /ˌrəʊld ˈɡəʊld/ *n* [مَعْدِن مُغَطًّى بِطَبَقةٍ من الذَهَبِ]

roller /ˈrəʊlə/ *n* **1** (in a machine) أُسْطُوانة, بَكَرة (بَكَرات, بَكَر) **2** (for painting) رولّة (فُرْشاة أُسْطُوانيّة); **a paint ~** رولّة **3** (for a lawn) مِدْحَلة (آلة أُسْطُوانيّة لِتَسْوِيةِ الأَرْضِ) **4** (curler) بَكَرة (بَكَرات, بَكَر) **5** (infml) (wave) مَوْجة كَبيرة

Rollerblade® /ˈrəʊlbleɪd/ **A** *n* حِذاء بِعَجَلاتٍ **B** *vi* تَزَحْلَقَ على حِذاءٍ بِعَجَلاتٍ

roller blind *n* سِتارة لَفّافة

roller coaster *n* قِطار المَلاهي, أُفْعُوانيّة

roller-skate /ˈrəʊləskeɪt/ **A** *n* حِذاء تَزَلُّجٍ, مِزْلَجة **B** *vi* تَزَحْلَقَ على المِزْلَجةِ

roller skating *n* تَزَلُّج بالعَجَلاتِ

rolling pin /ˈrəʊlɪŋ ˌpɪn/ *n* شَوْبَك (شَوابِكُ), مِرْقاق (مَراقيقُ), نَشّابة

roll-neck /ˈrəʊlnɛk/ *n* **1** (collar) رَقَبة عالِية **2** (garment) كَنْزة ذات رَقَبةٍ عالِيةٍ

roll-on /ˈrəʊlɒn/ *adj before n* بِلْيةٍ دَوّارة; **a ~ deodorant** مُزيل عَرَقٍ بِبِلْيةٍ دَوّارةٍ

ROM /rɒm/ *n* = **read-only memory** ذاكِرة القِراءةِ فَقَطْ (ذاكِرة داخِليّة في الحاسوبِ)

Roman /ˈrəʊmən/ *n, adj* رومانيّ (رومان)

Roman Catholic *n, adj* كاثوليكيّ رومانيّ

romance /rəʊˈmans/ *n* 1 [u] (liter) (emotion) شاعِرِيّة ,رومانْسيّة 2 [u] (love) غرام ,حُبّ 3 (love affair) عَلاقة عاطِفيّة 4 (novel) (film) قِصّة غراميّة \ عاطِفيّة

Romance /rəʊˈmans/ *adj before n ‹language, literature›* رومانْسيّ

Romania /rəʊˈmeɪnɪə/ *pr n* رومانيا

Romanian /rəʊˈmeɪnɪən/ A *adj ‹ambassador, food›* رومانيّ (رومان)

B *n* 1 (citizen) رومانيّ (رومان) 2 (language) (اللُغة) الرومانيّة

romantic /rəʊˈmantɪk/ A *adj* 1 (showing love) *‹husband, wife›* رومانْسيّ 2 (connected with love) *‹love, relationship›* عاطِفيّ 3 **R~** من الفَتْرةِ الرومانْسيّةِ *‹poet›*; رومانْسيّ *‹movement, era›*

B *n* 1 (person) شَخص رومانْسيّ 2 (writer, artist, etc) [أديب \ فَنّان من الفَتْرةِ الرومانْسيّةِ]

romantic fiction *n* القِصص الرومانْسيّة \ العاطِفيّة

romanticize, -ise (BrE) /rəʊˈmantɪsʌɪz/ *vt* صَوَّرَ بِطَريقةٍ رومانْسيّةٍ *‹the past, facts›*

Romany /ˈrɒməni/ A *n* (*pl* **Romanies**) 1 (person) غَجَريّ (غَجَر) 2 (language) (اللُغة) الغَجَريّة

B *adj ‹culture, custom›* غَجَريّ (غَجَر)

Rome /rəʊm/ *pr n* روما

romp /rɒmp/ (infml) A *vi* «children, animals» لَها (u; لَهْو)

B **~ through [sth]** اجْتازَ [شَيْئاً] بِسُهولةٍ *‹an exam, qualifying round›*

C *n* 1 (play) نَزْوة (جِنْسيّة) 2 (sexual) (أَلْعاب) لَعِب ,لَهْو

rompers /ˈrɒmpəz/ *n pl* سالوبيت ≈ (ثَوْب فَضْفاض للأَطْفال)

roof /ruːf/ *n* (*pl* **roofs** /ruːfs, ruːvz/) 1 (on a building) سَقْف (أَسْقُف ,سُقوف); **a flat/sloping ~** سَقْف مُسْتَوٍ \ مائِل 2 (on a car) سَقف (أَسْقُف ,سُقوف) 3 **the ~ of the mouth** سَقْف الحَلْقِ

Idioms **to go through** *or* **hit the roof** اِشْتاطَ غَضَباً; **to raise the roof** أَحْدَثَ ضَجّةً صاخِبةً

roofer /ˈruːfə/ *n* سَقّاف (شَخْص مِهْنَتُهُ بِناءُ الأَسْقُفِ)

roofing /ˈruːfɪŋ/ *n* 1 (material) مَوادّ التَسْقيفِ 2 (process) تَسْقيف

roof rack *n* رَفّ سَقْفِ سَيّارةٍ

rooftop /ˈruːftɒp/ *n* سَطْح (أَسْطُح ,سُطوح)

Idiom **to shout sth from the rooftops** أَذاعَ شَيْئاً على المَلأ

rook /rʊk/ *n* 1 (bird) غُداف شائِع ,غُراب القَيْظِ 2 (in chess) طابِية ,(رِخاخ) رُخّ (Egypt)

rookie /ˈrʊki/ (AmE) *n* (infml) (in the army or police) مُجَنَّد جَديد; (in sports) لاعِب مُبْتَدِئ

room /ruːm, rʊm/ A *n* 1 (part of a house, building) غُرْفة (غُرُفات ,غُرَف), حُجْرة (حُجَر ,حُجَرات); **she's waiting in the next ~** هي مُنْتَظِرةٌ في الغُرْفةِ المُجاورة; **I'm in ~ 159** أنا في الغُرْفةِ 159; **can I use this ~ for a training session?** هل يُمْكِنُني أنْ أَسْتَخْدِمَ هذه الحُجْرة لِجَلْسةٍ تَدْريبيّةٍ؟; **~ and board** المَبيت والطَعام; **'~s to let'** 'غُرَف للإيجار' 2 [u] (space) مَكان ,مِساحة; **this table takes up too much ~** هذه الطاوِلةُ تَحْتَلّ مِساحةً كَبيرةً; **to make ~ for sth** أَفْسَحَ مَكاناً لِشَيْءٍ; **to be short of ~** لا يوجَدُ لَدَيْهِ مَكانٌ 3 [u] (opportunity) **there is ~ for improvement** هُناكَ مَجالٌ للتَحْسينِ; **we have no ~ for manoeuvre** لَيْسَ لَدَيْنا مِساحةٌ للحَرَكةِ

B *vi* (AmE) (to lodge) أَقامَ; **to ~ with sb** أَقامَ مع شَخْصٍ

C **(-roomed)** *in combination* **four-~ed apartment** شَقّة من أَرْبَعِ غُرَفٍ

room clerk *n* (AmE) مَسْؤول حَجْزِ الغُرَفِ (في فُنْدُقٍ)

room-mate /ˈruːmmeɪt/ *n* 1 (sharing a room) رَفيق حُجْرةٍ, 2 (AmE) (sharing an apartment) رَفيق مَنْزِلٍ \ شَقّةٍ شَريك غُرْفةٍ

room service *n* خِدْمة غُرَفٍ

room temperature *n* دَرَجة حَرارةِ الغُرْفةِ

roomy /ˈruːmi/ *adj* (**roomier, roomiest**) *‹car, accommodation›* رَحْب ,مُتَّسِع ,فَسيح

roost /ruːst/ A *n* مَحَطّ (مَحاطّ), مَأْوًى (مَآوٍ)

B *vi* «birds, bats» جَثَمَ (i-u; جُثوم ,جَثْم), حَطَّ (u; حَطّ), أَوى (i; أُوِيّ)

Idiom **to rule the roost** أَمْسَكَ بِزِمامِ الأُمورِ

rooster /ˈruːstə/ *n* ديك (دُيوك ,دِيَكة)

root /ruːt/ **A** *n* **1** (of a plant) جِذْر (جُذور) **2** (of a word) جِذْر (جُذور) **3** (of a tooth) جِذْر (جُذور) **4** (of a hair) جِذْر (جُذور) **5** (of a problem) جِذْر (جُذور), مَصْدَر (مَصادِرُ), أَصْل (أُصول) **6** (**roots** *n pl*) (origin) جُذور, أُصول; **their family ~s are in Italy** جُذورُ عائِلَتِهِمْ من إيطاليا
B *vt* غَرَسَ (i; غِراسة, غَرْس) ‹*a plant, cutting*›
C *vi* (to grow roots) «plants, trees» كَوَّنَ جِذْراً
Idiom **to take root** (of plants) مَدَّ جُذورَهُ; (of ideas) تَرَسَّخَ
Phrasal verbs **root around for**: **~ around for [sb/sth]** (infml) فَتَّشَ عن [شَخْصٍ \ شَيْءٍ] ‹*one's glasses, food*›
• **root for**: **~ for [sb/sth]** (infml) شَجَّعَ [شَخْصاً \ شَيْئاً] ‹*a team, contestant*›
• **root out**: **~ out [sth]**, **~ [sth] out** اقْتَلَعَ جُذورَ, اسْتَأْصَلَ [شَيْئاً \ شَيْءٍ] ‹*corruption, terrorists*›

root beer *n* (AmE) جِعة الجُذورِ

root crop *n* مَحْصول جَذْرِيّ

rootless /ˈruːtləs/ *adj* ‹*family, young people*› بِلا جُذور

rope /rəʊp/ **A** *n* حَبْل (حِبال); **a 20-metre ~, a 20-metre length of ~** حَبْل طولُهُ 20 مِتْراً
B *vt* **1** (to tie) **to ~ a prisoner/donkey to sb/sth** رَبَطَ سَجيناً \ حِماراً بِحَبْلٍ مع شَخْصٍ \ في شَيْءٍ; **to ~ a trunk/ladder to sth** رَبَطَ صُنْدوقاً \ سُلَّماً بِحَبْلٍ في شَيْءٍ; **to be ~d together** رُبِطوا مَعاً بِحَبْلٍ **2** (AmE) (to lasso) رَبَطَ بِحَبْلٍ حول العُنُقِ ‹*cattle, a steer*›
Idioms **to be on the ropes** (boxers) كانَ مُحاصَراً في جانِبِ الحَلَبةِ; (ministers, governments) كانَ في أَزْمةٍ صَعْبةٍ \ وَضْعٍ لا يُحْسَدُ عَلَيْهِ; **to show sb the ropes** بَيَّنَ لِشَخْصٍ الأُمورَ الهامَّةِ
Phrasal verbs **rope in**: **~ [sb] in, ~ in [sb]** (infml) (for a task) دَفَعَ [شَخْصاً] إلى المُشارَكةِ
• **rope off**: **~ off [sth]**, **~ [sth] off** وَضَعَ شَريطاً أَمْنِيًّا, طَوَّقَ [شَيْئاً] حول [شَيْءٍ] ‹*a street, an area*›

rope ladder *n* سُلَّم حَبْلٍ

ropy, ropey /ˈrəʊpi/ *adj* (**ropier, ropiest**) (BrE infml) ‹*performance, health*› هَزيل (هَزْلى), ضَعيف (ضُعَفاءُ, ضِعاف); **to feel a bit ~** شَعَرَ بِشَيْءٍ من الوَهَنِ

rosary /ˈrəʊz(ə)ri/ *n* (*pl* **rosaries**) (prayer) تَسْبيح (تَسابيحُ); (beads) مِسْبَحة (مَسابِحُ); **to say the ~** قالَ التَسابيحَ

rose /rəʊz/ **A** *past tense* ▸**rise**
B *n* **1** (plant) (flower) وَرْد (n coll; وُرود) **2** (colour) (اللَوْن) الوَرْدِيّ

rosé /ˈrəʊzeɪ/ *n* نَبيذ وَرْدِيّ

rosebud /ˈrəʊzbʌd/ *n* بُرْعُم وَرْدةٍ

rose hip *n* ثَمَر وَرْدٍ بَرِّيٍّ

rosemary /ˈrəʊzm(ə)ri/ *n* روزماري, إكْليل الجَبَلِ

rose-tinted /ˈrəʊztɪntɪd/ *adj* ‹*clouds, glow*› وَرْدِيّ
Idiom **to see things through rose-tinted glasses** *or* **spectacles** نَظَرَ إلى الأُمورِ بِنَظْرةٍ وَرْدِيّةٍ

rosette /rəʊˈzet/ *n* [شِعار على شَكْلِ وَرْدةٍ \ شارة]

roster /ˈrɒstə/ *n* جَدْوَل خِدْمةٍ

rostrum /ˈrɒstrəm/ *n* (*pl* **rostrums** or **rostra**) مِنَصّة, مِنْبَر (مَنابِرُ)

rosy /ˈrəʊzi/ *adj* (**rosier, rosiest**) **1** ‹*cheeks, light*› وَرْدِيّ, مُتَوَرِّد **2** ‹*picture, future*› مُشْرِق

rot /rɒt/ **A** (-tt-) *vt* نَخَرَ (i-u; نَخْر, نَخير), سَبَّبَ التَسَوُّسَ ‹*teeth*›; أَفْسَدَ, عَفَّنَ ‹*wood*›
B *vi* (also **rot away**) «teeth» تَسَوَّسَ; «wood» تَعَفَّنَ
C *n* عَفَن, تَعَفُّن
Idiom **to stop the rot** حَدَّ من تَدَهْوُرِ \ تَفاقُمِ الوَضْعِ

rota /ˈrəʊtə/ *n* (BrE) جَدْوَل \ لائِحة مُناوَبةٍ

rotary /ˈrəʊt(ə)ri/ **A** *adj* ‹*engine, motion*› دَوَرانِيّ, دَوّار
B *n* (AmE) مَمَرّ دائِرِيّ, دَوَران, دَوّار (دَوّارات) (Gulf), صينِيّة (صَوانِيّ) (Egypt)

rotate /rəʊˈteɪt/ **A** *vt* **1** (to turn) لَفَّ (u; لَفّ), أَدارَ ‹*one's body, an image*› **2** (to alternate) تَناوَبَ \ تَعاقَبَ في الزَرْعِ ‹*crops*›
B *vi* **1** «the Earth, blades» دارَ (u; دَوْر, دَوَران), لَفَّ (u; لَفّ) **2** «presidency, job» سارَ بِنِظامِ التَناوُبِ

rotation /rəʊˈteɪʃ(ə)n/ *n* دَوَران

rote /rəʊt/ *n* **by ~** (التَعَلُّم أو الحِفْظ) عن ظَهْرِ قَلْبٍ

rotten /ˈrɒt(ə)n/ *adj* **1** ‹*egg, apple*› نَتِن, فاسِد, مُتَعَفِّن; ‹*teeth*› مُسَوَّس, مَنْخور **2** (infml) (very bad) ‹*weather, luck, job*› سَيِّئ جِدًّا

rotund /rəʊˈtʌnd/ *adj* ‹*person, stomach*› مُمْتَلِئ

rouble (BrE), **ruble** (AmE) /ˈruːb(ə)l/ *n* روبِل (العُمْلة الروسيّة)

rouge /ruːʒ/ *n* أَحْمَر خُدودٍ \ شِفاهٍ

rough /rʌf/ **A** *adj* 1 (not smooth) ‹*hands, fabric, surface*› خَشِن; ‹*terrain, landscape*› وَعْر; **to smooth off the ~ edges** نَعَّمَ \ صَقَلَ الحَوافَّ الخَشِنة; **the terrain is very ~** التَضاريسُ وَعْرةٌ جِدًّا 2 (uncivilized, violent) ‹*man, treatment, sport*› خَشِن, عَنيف; **he got ~ with me** تَعامَلَ مَعي بِخُشونةٍ 3 (stormy) ‹*sea, crossing*› هائِج, عاصِف; ‹*weather*› سَيِّء, مُضْطَرِب 4 (not law-abiding) ‹*area, district*› تَكْثُرُ فيه الجَريمةُ 5 (approximate) ‹*description, translation, calculation*› تَقْريبيّ; **give me a ~ idea of the cost** أَعْطِني فِكْرةً تَقْريبيّةً عن التَكْلِفةِ 6 (difficult) ‹*life, period*› عَصيب, صَعْب; **we're having a ~ time** نَمُرُّ بوَقْتٍ عَصيبٍ; **it's ~ on the children** هو صَعْبٌ على الأَطْفالِ; **to give sb a ~ ride** سَبَّبَ لِشَخْصٍ قَدْراً كَبيراً من المُعاناةِ 7 (unrefined) ‹*hut, table*› بُدائيّ, بَسيط 8 **he told us to leave in a ~ voice** خاطَبَنا بِصَوْتٍ خَشِنٍ وَطَلَبَ مِنّا أَنْ نَرْحَلَ 9 (unfair) ‹*deal, treatment*› غَيْر عادِلٍ; **~ justice** إِفْراط \ مُبالَغة في العِقابِ

B *adv* (in the open) ‹*to sleep, live*› في العَراءِ

C *n* 1 (of drawings, designs) رَسْم \ تَصْميم أَوَّليّ; **to write out the report in ~** كَتَبَ مُسَوَّدةً للتَقْريرِ 2 (in golf) **the ~** مِنْطَقة العُشْبِ الطَويلِ

(Idioms) **to rough it** عاشَ حَياةً خَشِنةً; **to take the rough with the smooth** تَقَبَّلَ الأَشْياءَ حُلْوَها ومُرَّها, قَبِلَ الأَشْياءَ على عِلّاتِها

(Phrasal verbs) **rough out**: **~ out [sth]** 1 (to sketch) وَضَعَ الخُطوطَ العَريضةَ ل [شَيْءٍ] ‹*a plan, drawing*› 2 (to jot down) كَتَبَ مُسَوَّدةً أَوَّليّةً ل [شَيْءٍ] ‹*an idea, a proposal*›

• **rough up**: **~ [sb] up, ~ up [sb]** (infml) (to beat up) ضَرَبَ [شَخْصاً]

roughage /ˈrʌfɪdʒ/ *n* أَلْياف غِذائيّة, أَطْعِمة خَشِنة

rough and ready *adj* (before *n* **rough-and-ready**) 1 ‹*method, system*› بَسيط, غَيْر مُتَطَوِّرٍ 2 ‹*person, conditions*› خَشِن

roughen /ˈrʌf(ə)n/ *vt* خَشَّنَ ‹*a surface, hands*›

roughly /ˈrʌfli/ *adv* 1 (approximately) ‹*equal, comparable*› تَقْريباً 2 (not gently) ‹*to handle, push*› بِفَظاظةٍ, بِخُشونةٍ, بِقَسْوةٍ 3 (crudely) ‹*made, hewn*› بِدونِ دِقّةٍ \ إِتْقانٍ

roughness /ˈrʌfnəs/ *n* 1 (of skin, fabrics, surface) خُشونة; (of the terrain) وُعورة 2 (of sb's manners) خُشونة, غِلْظة, فَظاظة, قَسْوة 3 (violence) عُنْف, خُشونة 4 (of the furnishings, finish) بَساطة, بُدائيّة 5 (of the sea, wind) هَيَجان; **the ~ of the weather forced them to turn back** اضْطَرَّهُمْ سوءُ الأَحْوالِ الجَوّيّةِ إلى العَوْدةِ

rough paper *n* مُسَوَّدة, وَرَقة تَحْضيريّة

roughshod /ˈrʌfʃɒd/ *adv*

(Idiom) **to ride roughshod over sth/sb** مَضى قُدُماً غَيْر عابِئٍ بِشَيْءٍ \ بِشَخْصٍ

roulette /ruˈlɛt/ *n* روليت (لُعْبة قِمارٍ)

round /raʊnd/ **A** *adj* 1 (circular) ‹*building, glasses, face*› مُسْتَدير 2 (curved) ‹*arch, handwriting*› مُنْحَنٍ, مُقَوَّس; **to have ~ shoulders** كانَ مُقَوَّسَ الكَتِفَيْنِ 3 (complete) ‹*figure*› صَحيح; **in ~ figures, that's £300** النَتيجةُ £300 بالتَقْريبِ

B *n* 1 (of activities) سِلْسِلة أَحْداثٍ \ أَعْمالٍ روتينيّةٍ; **the daily ~ of events** الأَحْداث اليَوْميّة المُعْتادة \ الروتينيّة 2 (of a tournament) جَوْلة; **the qualifying ~s** جَوْلات التَصْفِية, التَصْفِيات 3 (in golf) مُباراة (مُبارَيات); (in cards) لُعْبة (لُعَب) 4 (in boxing, wrestling) جَوْلة 5 (in elections) جَوْلة 6 (of drinks) [مَجْموعة مَشْروباتٍ كُحوليّةٍ يَشْتَريها شَخْصٌ لِجَماعةٍ في الحانةِ] 7 (of ammunition) طَلْقة (طَلَقات) 8 (of clapping) تَصْفيق; **the dancers got a great ~ of applause** نالَ الراقِصونَ تَصْفيقاً حارًّا 9 (of bread) شَريحة (شَرائِحُ), قِطْعة (قِطَع); **a ~ of toast** شَريحة خُبْزٍ مُحَمَّصٍ 10 (route) جَوْلة; **Dr Findlay is out on his ~s** [يَقومُ د. فينْدْلي بِزياراتٍ للمَرْضى في بُيوتِهِم]

C *adv* 1 (BrE) (on all sides) **all ~** من كُلِّ ناحيةٍ \ النَواحي; **whisky all ~!** ويِسْكي للجَميعِ!; **to go all the way ~** «fence, moat, wall» امْتَدَّ من كُلِّ ناحيةٍ 2 (BrE) (circular movement) **to go ~ and ~** «wheels, carousel» دارَ (u; دَوْر, دَوَران) 3 (BrE) (to specific place, home) **to go ~ to sb's house/office/school** ذَهَبَ إلى بَيْتِ \ مَكْتَبِ \ مَدْرَسةِ شَخْصٍ; **to ask sb (to come) ~** دَعا شَخْصاً (للمَجيءِ) إلى بَيْتِه; **to invite sb ~ for lunch** دَعا شَخْصاً على الغَداءِ; **I'll be ~ in a minute** سَآتي بعد قَليلٍ 4 (BrE) (in circumference) **three metres ~** مُحيطُهُ ثَلاثة أَمْتارٍ

5 (BrE) (part of a cycle) **all year ~** على مَدارِ العامِ; **this time** ~ هذه المَرّةَ

D (**round about**) *adv phr* 1 (approximately) «number, time» تَقْريباً; «place» حَوالَيْ; **it happened ~ about here** حَدَثَ هُنا تَقْريباً 2 (in the vicinity) **the people ~ about** الناس في هذه النَواحي \ الضَواحي

E *prep* (BrE) 1 (expressing location) حَوْلَ; **let's sit ~ the table** لِنَجْلِسْ حول المائِدةِ; **they sat ~ the fire** جَلَسوا حول النارِ; **the wall goes right ~ the house** يَمْتَدُّ السورُ حول كامِلِ المَنْزِلِ 2 (expressing direction) **to go ~ the corner** انْعَطَفَ عند الناصِيةِ; **to go ~ a bend** انْعَطَفَ مع الطَريقِ; **to go ~ an obstacle** تَفادى حاجِزاً 3 (on tour, visit) **her sister took us ~ York** أَخَذَتْنا أُخْتُها في جَوْلةٍ حول (مَدينةِ) يورْكَ; **to go ~ the shops** تَسَوَّقَ في المَحَلاّتِ

F *vt* (to leave behind) «ship» انْعَطَفَ (عند) ‹a point, headland›; **to ~ the corner** انْعَطَفَ عند الناصِيةِ; **to ~ a bend** انْعَطَفَ مع الطَريقِ

(Phrasal verbs) **round down**: **~ [sth] down, ~ down [sth]** قَرَّبَ [شَيْئاً] إلى أَقَلِّ عَدَدٍ صَحيحٍ ‹a figure›

• **round off**: **~ off [sth], ~ [sth] off** 1 (to finish off) خَتَمَ [شَيْئاً] ‹the meal, evening, season› مِسْكَ خِتامٍ 2 (to make smooth) صَنْفَرَ \ نَعَّمَ [شَيْئاً] ‹a corner, an edge›; اسْتَخْدَمَ وَرَقَ الصَنْفَرةِ لِتَنْعيمِ الحافّاتِ الحادّةِ 3 (to change) قَرَّبَ [شَيْئاً] إلى أَقْرَبِ عَدَدٍ صَحيحٍ ‹a figure, number›

• **round on** (BrE): **~ on [sb]** هاجَمَ [شَخْصاً] ‹a critic, an opponent›; **suddenly she ~ed on me** هاجَمَتْني فَجْأةً

• **round up** A **~ up [sb], ~ [sb] up** (to detain) «police, soldiers» اعْتَقَلَ [شَخْصاً] ‹protesters, inhabitants, suspects›; **to be ~ed up** اعْتُقِلَ B **~ up [sth], ~ [sth] up** 1 (in farming) جَمَعَ [شَيْئاً] ‹the cattle, sheep› 2 قَرَّبَ [شَيْئاً] إلى أَكْبَرِ عَدَدٍ صَحيحٍ ‹a figure›

roundabout /ˈraʊndəbaʊt/ A *n* 1 (BrE) (for traffic) مَمَرّ دائِريّ, دَوَران, دَوّار (دَوّارات) (Gulf), صِينيّة (Egypt) صَوانيّ 2 (at fairgrounds) دَوّامة خَيْلٍ, أُرْجوحة دَوّارة 3 (in a playground) لُعْبة على شَكْلِ مُسَطَّحٍ دائِريٍّ

B *adj* ‹route› غَيْر مُباشِرٍ, مُلْتَوٍ; **he explained it in a ~ way** شَرَحَهُ بِطَريقةٍ غَيْرِ مُباشِرةٍ

rounded /ˈraʊndɪd/ *adj* ‹corner, shape› مُدَوَّر, مُسْتَدير

rounders /ˈraʊndəz/ *n* (BrE) لُعْبة إنْجْليزيّة تُشْبِهُ البيسْبول

round-necked sweater /ˌraʊndnɛkt ˈswɛtə/, **round-neck sweater** /ˌraʊndnɛk ˈswɛtə/ *n* كَنْزة بِرَقَبةٍ دائِريّةٍ

round table, **round-table discussion** *n* مُناقَشة حول مائِدةٍ مُسْتَديرةٍ

round-the-clock /ˌraʊndðəˈklɒk/ A *adj* (BrE) ‹care, coverage› مُتَواصِل, على مَدارِ الأَرْبَعِ والعِشْرينَ ساعةً, على مَدارِ الساعةِ

B (**round the clock**) *adv phr* ‹to work, operate› على مَدارِ الساعةِ, على مَدارِ الأَرْبَعِ والعِشْرينَ ساعةً, بِشَكْلٍ مُتَواصِلٍ

round-the-world /ˌraʊndðəˈwəːld/ *adj before n* ‹trip, race› حول العالَمِ

round trip *n* رِحْلة ذَهابٍ وَإيابٍ \ وَعَوْدةٍ

round-up /ˈraʊndʌp/ *n* 1 (detention of criminals, dissidents) اعْتِقال (اعْتِقالات); (of cattle, horses) حَشْد, تَجْميع (حُشود) 2 (of the news, events) مُلَخَّص, موجَز

rouse /raʊz/ *vt* 1 أَيْقَظَ ‹a sleeper, household› 2 حَرَّكَ, أَثارَ ‹interest, anger›

rousing /ˈraʊzɪŋ/ *adj* ‹speech, chorus› مُحَرِّك للمَشاعِرِ, مُثير, حافِل ‹reception, send-off› حَماسيّ

rout /raʊt/ A *n* انْدِحار, هَزيمة مُنْكَرة (انْدِحارات)

B *vt* 1 (to defeat) هَزَمَ هَزيمةً مُنْكَرةً ‹the enemy, opponents› 2 (to put to flight) دَحَرَ (a; دَحْر, دُحور) ‹the enemy, an army›

route /ruːt/ A *n* 1 (to/from a place) طَريق (mf; طُرُق, طُرُقات), مَسار (مَسارات); **the fastest/shortest ~ to Riyadh** أَسْرَع \ أَقْصَر طَريقٍ إلى الرِياضِ; **to plan a ~** خَطَّطَ مَسارَ رِحْلةٍ; **it's not on my ~** هو لَيْسَ في مَسارِ رِحْلَتي 2 (line, service) خَطّ (خُطوط), طَريق (mf; طُرُق, طُرُقات); **a little-used bus/rail ~** خَطّ حافِلاتٍ \ قِطاراتٍ لا يُسْتَخْدَمُ إلاّ قَليلاً; **a shipping ~** طَريق شَحْنٍ; **domestic ~s** خُطوط مَحَلّيّة 3 (US road) طَريق (mf; طُرُق, طُرُقات); **R~ 86** الطَريق 86 4 (to power, success, fame) طَريق (mf; طُرُق, طُرُقات)

B *vt* أَرْسَلَ ‹the goods, supplies, a flight›; **the flight was ~d to Beirut via Rome** كانَ مَسارُ الرِحْلةِ إلى بَيْروتَ عن طَريقِ روما

router¹ /ˈruːtə/ *n* (tool) مِسْحاج تَخْديدٍ (آلة حَفْرٍ على الخَشَبِ)

router² /ˈruːtə/ *n* (Comput) راوْتَر, جِهاز تَوْجيهٍ, مُوَجِّه

routine /ru:ˈti:n/ **A** *n* **1** (regular pattern) روتين (أَعْمال مُعْتادة) **2** (of a performer, comedian) نَمَط فَنِّيّ

B *adj* **1** (regular, usual) ‹*maintenance, test*› اعْتِيادِيّ, روتينِيّ

2 (dull) ‹*life, task*› رَتيب, مُمِلّ

routinely /ru:ˈti:nli/ *adv* ‹*to use, carry out*› بِشَكْلٍ بِانْتِظامٍ دَوْرِيٍّ \ روتينِيٍّ

routing number /ˈru:tɪŋ ˌnʌmbə/ *n* (AmE) رَقْم, رَقْم \ رَمْز البَنْك التَّوْجيه المَصْرِفِيّ (رَقْم للتَعْريف بِأَفْرُع البُنوكِ)

roving /ˈrəʊvɪŋ/ *adj* ‹*reporter*› مُتَجَوِّل; ‹*ambassador*› مُتَنَقِّل

row¹ /rəʊ/ **A** *n* **1** (of houses, trees, seats) (of people) صَفّ (صُفوف); **in a ~/in ~s** في صَفٍّ \ في صُفوفٍ **2** (in knitting) خَطّ (خُطوط) **3** (succession) **four times in a ~** أَرْبَعَ مَرّاتٍ على التَوالي

B *vt* **1** ‹*a boat*› جَدَّفَ **2** ‹*a passenger*› نَقَلَ (في قارِبٍ)

C *vi* جَدَّفَ; **to go ~ing** رَكِبَ قارِبَ تَجْديفٍ

row² /raʊ/ **A** *n* **1** (quarrel) تَشاجُر, شِجار; **to have a ~ with sb** تَشاجَرَ مع شَخْصٍ **2** (public dispute) نِزاع (نِزاعات) **3** (noise) ضَجّة, جَلَبة (جَلَب)

B *vi* تَشاجَرَ

rowboat /ˈrəʊbəʊt/ *n* (AmE) زَوْرَق \ قارِب تَجْديفٍ

rowdy /ˈraʊdi/ *adj* (**rowdier, rowdiest**) ‹*behaviour, crowd*› صاخِب; ‹*teenagers, children*› مُشاكِس, مُشاغِب

rower /ˈrəʊə/ *n* مُجَدِّف

row house (AmE) *n* [بَيْت في صَفٍّ من البُيوتِ المُتَلاصِقةِ]

rowing /ˈrəʊɪŋ/ *n* تَجْديف

rowing boat (BrE) *n* زَوْرَق \ قارِب تَجْديفٍ

rowing machine *n* جِهاز تَجْديفٍ

royal /ˈrɔɪəl/ *adj* **1** ‹*family, palace*› مَلَكِيّ **2** (splendid) ‹*welcome*› فَخْم (فِخام)

royal blue **A** *n* لَوْن أَزْرَق غامِق;

B *adj* أَزْرَق غامِق

Royal Highness *n* **His/Her Royal Highness** صاحِب \ صاحِبة السُمُوِّ المَلَكِيِّ

royalist /ˈrɔɪəlɪst/ *n, adj* مُؤَيِّد للنِظامِ المَلَكِيِّ

royalty /ˈrɔɪəlti/ *n* (*pl* **royalties**) **1** (payment) رَسْم امْتِيازٍ **2** [u] (persons) أَفْراد العائِلةِ المالِكةِ

rpm /ɑ:pi:ˈɛm/ *abbr* = **revolutions per minute** لَفّة \ دَوْرة في الدَقيقةِ (مُعَدَّل سُرْعةِ المُحَرِّكِ)

RSPCA /ɑ:rɛspi:si:ˈeɪ/ *n* (in the UK) = **Royal Society for the Prevention of Cruelty to Animals** الجَمْعِيّة المَلَكِيّة لِمَنْعِ القَسْوةِ على الحَيَوانِ

RSVP /ɑ:rɛsvi:ˈpi:/ *abbr* = **répondez s'il vous plaît** يُرْجى الرَدُّ

rub /rʌb/ **A** *vt* (**-bb-**) **1** (with fingers, hands) حَكَّ (u; حَكّ) ‹*one's arm, eyes, head*›; **to ~ sb's back/shoulders** دَلَّكَ ظَهْرَ \ كَتِفَيْ شَخْصٍ; **to ~ one's hands with glee** فَرَكَ يَدَيْهِ فَرَحاً **2** (to polish) حَكَّ (u; حَكّ) ‹*a stain, surface, knife*›; **to ~ a stain away** أَزالَ بُقْعةً **3** (to apply) **to ~ a cream/lotion on** *or* **into one's skin** دَهَنَ جِسْمَهُ بِكْريم \ بِلوسْيون; **can you ~ some lotion on my back?** هل يُمْكِنُكَ أَنْ تَدْهَنَ ظَهْري بِبَعْضِ اللوسْيون؟ **4** (to chafe) «shoes» احْتَكَّ (ب) ‹*one's heel, ankle*›

B *vi* (**-bb-**) **1** (to scrub) حَكَّ (u; حَكّ) **2** (to chafe) احْتَكَّ; **these shoes ~** هذا الحِذاءُ يَحْتَكُّ بالقَدَمِ; **to ~ against sth** احْتَكَّ بِشَيْءٍ

C *n* **1** (massage) تَدْليك; **to give sb's back a ~** دَلَّكَ ظَهْرَ شَخْصٍ **2** (while cleaning) دَعْك; **to give the knife/tabletop a ~** لَمَّعَ السِكّينَ \ سَطْحَ الطاوِلةِ

(Idioms) **to rub sb's nose in it** (infml) عَيَّرَ شَخْصاً; **to rub sb up the wrong way** (infml) اسْتَفَزَّ شَخْصاً

(Phrasal verbs) **rub along** **1** (infml) (to manage, get by) تَدَبَّرَ أُمورَهُ **2** (to get along) تَكَيَّفَ, تعايَشَ; **to ~ along with one's flatmates/co-workers** كَيَّفَ نَفْسَهُ على الحَياةِ مع زُمَلائِهِ في السَكَنِ \ العَمَلِ

• **rub down**: **~ [sb/sth] down, ~ down [sb/sth]** **1** (after exercise) ‹*an athlete*› جَفَّفَ \ نَشَّفَ [شَخْصاً \ شَيْئاً] **2** (to smooth) ‹*a wall, the plaster, wood*› صَقَلَ [شَيْئاً]

• **rub in**: **~ [sth] in, ~ in [sth]** **1** ‹*lotion, cream*› دَلَّكَ [شَيْئاً] **2** (infml) (to remind) **to ~ it in** [ذَكَّرَ بِشَيْءٍ غَيْرِ مُسْتَحَبٍّ] **there's no need to ~ it in!** لا داعِيَ للمُعايَرةِ!

• **rub off** **A** (to come off) «dye, ink» زالَ (a; زَوال); **this chalk ~s off easily** يُمْكِنُ مَسْحُ هذا الطَباشيرِ بِسُهولةٍ **B** **~ [sth] off, ~ off [sth]** ‹*a stain, pattern*› أَزالَ [شَيْئاً]

• **rub out** **A** «chalk, pencil» يُمْكِنُ مَسْحُهُ **B** **~ [sth] out, ~ out [sth]** ‹*a word, drawing*› مَسَحَ \ مَحى [شَيْئاً]

rubber /ˈrʌbə/ *n* **1** (substance) مَطّاط **2** (BrE) (eraser) مِمْحاة (مَماحٍ)

rubber band *n* رِباط \ شَريط مَطّاطيّ

rubber bullet *n* رَصاصة مَطّاطيّة

rubber gloves *n* قُفّاز مَطّاطيّ

rubber plant *n* تين المَطّاط

rubber stamp *n* خَتْم مَطّاطيّ

rubber tree *n* شَجَرة مَطّاط

rubbery /ˈrʌb(ə)ri/ *adj* ‹*material, texture*› شَبيه بالمَطّاطِ

rubbish /ˈrʌbɪʃ/ *n* **1** (refuse) قُمامة (قُمامات)، نُفاية، زُبالة **2** (junk) سَقَط المَتاعِ، خُرْدة (خُرْدَوات)، مُهْمَلات **3** (infml) (nonsense) هُراء، كَلام فارِغ; **how can you believe such ~?** كيف تُصَدِّقُ مِثْلَ هذا الكَلامِ الفارِغِ؟

rubbish bag *n* (BrE) كيس قُمامةٍ

rubbish bin *n* (BrE) صُنْدوق قُمامةٍ

rubbish dump *n* (BrE) مَكَبّ \ مَقْلَب نُفاياتٍ

rubble /ˈrʌb(ə)l/ *n* أَنْقاض; **to pull a victim from the ~** سَحَبَ ضَحيّةً من تَحْتِ الأَنْقاضِ

rubella /ruˈbɛlə/ *n* الحَصْبة الأَلْمانيّة

ruble (AmE) *n* ▸ **rouble**

ruby /ˈruːbi/ *n* (*pl* **rubies**) ياقوت (يَواقيتُ)

rucksack /ˈrʌksak/ *n* حَقيبة ظَهْرٍ

ructions /ˈrʌkʃ(ə)nz/ *n pl* (BrE infml) هِياج، اضْطِراب (اضْطِرابات)

rudder /ˈrʌdə/ *n* **1** (on ships, boats) دَفّة **2** (on a plane) دَفّة

ruddy /ˈrʌdi/ *adj* (**ruddier, ruddiest**) ‹*complexion, cheeks*› مُتَوَرِّد، ضارِب للحُمْرة

rude /ruːd/ *adj* **1** (impolite) ‹*person, comment, behaviour*› وَقِح (وُقُح)، غَيْر مُهَذَّبٍ; **to be ~ to sb** كانَ وَقِحاً مع شَخْصٍ **2** (BrE) (indecent) ‹*word, gesture*› بَذيء **3** (abrupt) **a ~ awakening** صَدْمة عَنيفة، مُفاجَأة مُذْهِلة

rudely /ˈruːdli/ *adv* **1** (impolitely) ‹*to behave, reply*› بِوَقاحةٍ، على نَحْوٍ فَجٍّ **2** (abruptly) ‹*awakened, shattered*› بِأُسْلوبٍ مُفاجِئٍ

rudeness /ˈruːdnəs/ *n* وَقاحة، فَظاظة

rudimentary /ˌruːdɪˈmɛnt(ə)ri/ *adj* ‹*form, knowledge*› بُدائيّ، أَوَّليّ

rudiments /ˈruːdɪmənts/ *n pl* أَوَّليّة، مَبادِئ، بُدائيّات، أَساسيّات

rue /ruː/ *vt* ‹*a missed opportunity*› تَحَسَّرَ (على)، تَنَدَّمَ; تَأَسَّفَ (على) ‹*a decision*›

rueful /ˈruːfʊl/ *adj* ‹*smile, look*› مُتَحَسِّر، نادِم (نُدّام)، مُتَأَسِّف

ruff /rʌf/ *n* **1** (frill) [ياقة مُكَشْكَشة كانَتْ تُلْبَسُ حول العُنُقِ قَديماً] **2** (on a bird) [طَوْق من الريشِ حول عُنُقِ الطائِرِ]; (on an animal) [طَوْق من الشَعْرِ حول عُنُقِ الحَيَوانِ]

ruffian /ˈrʌfɪən/ *n* شَخْص هَمَجيّ

ruffle /ˈrʌf(ə)l/ **A** *vt* **1** نَكَشَ (u; نَكْش) ‹*hair, fur*›; أَحْدَثَ اضْطِراباً في ‹*the surface, water*› **2** (to disconcert) أَرْبَكَ، شَوَّشَ (على) ‹*an opponent, interviewee*›

B *n* كَشْكَشة

rug /rʌg/ *n* **1** (small carpet) سَجّادة (سَجّادات، سَجاجيدُ)، بِساط (بُسُط، بِساطات) **2** (BrE) (blanket) بَطّانيّة (بَطّانيّات)، غِطاء (أَغْطِية)

rugby /ˈrʌgbi/ *n* رُغْبي

rugby league *n* دَوْريّ الرُغْبي

rugby union *n* اتِّحاد الرُغْبي

rugged /ˈrʌgɪd/ *adj* **1** ‹*terrain, landscape, mountains*› وَعْر، غَيْر مُسْتَوٍ **2** ‹*features, looks*› صارِم (صَوارِمُ)، حادّ

ruin /ˈruːɪn/ **A** *n* **1** [u] (destruction) خَراب (أَخْرِبة)، دَمار، انْهِيار (انْهِيارات); **to face financial ~** واجَهَ انْهِياراً مالِيّاً **2** (of a building) أَنْقاض، أَطْلال; **to be in ~s** «city» كانَ في دَمارٍ; «career» تَدَمَّرَ، تَحَطَّمَ

B *vt* **1** (to destroy) دَمَّرَ، خَرَّبَ ‹*sb's life, career*› **2** (to spoil) أَفْسَدَ، أَتْلَفَ ‹*a dress, an event, the food*› **3** (financially) أَفْقَرَ، تَسَبَّبَ في إِفْقارٍ ‹*a person, company*›

ruined /ˈruːɪnd/ *adj* **1** ‹*city, building*› مُهَدَّم **2** ‹*life, career*› مُحَطَّم

rule /ruːl/ **A** *n* **1** (of grammar) قاعِدة (قَواعِدُ); (of games, schools, institutions) قاعِدة (قَواعِدُ)، قانون (قَوانينُ); **the ~s of the game** قَوانين \ قَواعِد اللُعْبة; **to obey/break the ~s** الْتَزَمَ ب \ خالَفَ القَواعِدَ; **it's against the ~s** هو مُخالِفٌ للقَواعِدِ; **to bend the ~s** تَساهَلَ في تَطْبيقِ القَوانينِ **2** (normal practice) قاعِدة (قَواعِدُ)، كَقاعِدةٍ عامّةٍ; **as a ~ we work a 37-hour week** نَحْنُ نَعْمَلُ 37 ساعة في الأُسْبوعِ; **I make it a ~ to always**

check the pressure أُواظِبُ دائماً على الكَشْفِ على الضَغْطِ
3 [u] (control, authority) سِيادة ,حُكْم; **the ~ of law** سِيادة القانونِ **4** (for measuring) مِسْطَرة (مَساطِرُ)
B *vt* **1** (to govern) «the president, king, army» حَكَمَ (u; حُكْم) ‹*the country, people*› **2** (to control) «feelings, money» تَحَكَّمَ (في) ,سَيْطَرَ (على ;سَيْطَرة (i; ‹*sb's behaviour, life*›; **to let one's heart ~ one's head** تَرَكَ قَلْبَهُ يُسَيْطِرُ على عَقْلِهِ
3 (to decide) **to ~ that ...** «judge» حَكَمَ بِأَنْ ... ;«referee» قَرَّرَ أَنّ ...
C *vi* **1** (to govern) «the president, king» حَكَمَ (u; حُكْم); **anarchy/chaos ~s outside the capital** تَسودُ الفَوْضى خارِجَ العاصِمةِ **2** **to ~ in favour of/against sb** «judges, referees» حَكَمَ في صالِحِ \ ضدّ شَخْصٍ
(Phrasal verb) **rule out**: **~ out [sth], ~ [sth] out** **1** (to exclude) اسْتَبْعَدَ ‹*a possibility, an option*›; **to ~ out doing sth** اسْتَبْعَدَ [شَيْئاً] **2** (to prevent) مَنَعَ [شَيْئاً] ‹*an activity*› فِعْلَ شَيْءٍ

rule of law *n* سِيادة القانونِ

ruler /ˈruːlə/ *n* **1** (leader) حاكِم (حاكِمونَ ,حُكّام) **2** (for measuring) مِسْطَرة (مَساطِرُ)

ruling /ˈruːlɪŋ/ **A** *n* حُكْم (أَحْكام) ,قرار (قَرارات)
B *adj* **1** (in power) ‹*party, class*› حاكِم **2** (dominant) ‹*principle*› مُسَيْطِر ,غالِب ,حاكِم ;‹*passion*› غالِب

rum /rʌm/ *n* روم (شَراب كُحوليّ)

Rumania *pr n* ▸ **Romania**

rumble /ˈrʌmb(ə)l/ **A** *vi* «thunder» دَوّى ;«trains, trucks» هَدَرَ (i; هَدير ,هَدْر); «stomach» قَرْقَرَ (i; قَرْقَرة)
B *n* (of thunder, gunfire) دَوِيّ; (of trains, trucks) هَدير; (of sb's stomach) قَرْقَرة (قَراقِرُ)

rumble strip *n* [شَرائِط مُروريّة لِتَهْدِئةِ السُرْعةِ]

ruminate /ˈruːmɪneɪt/ *vi* **1** (fml) (to ponder) **to ~ on** *or* **about sth** «person» فَكَّرَ مَلِيًّا في شَيْءٍ **2** «cows, sheep» اجْتَرَّ

rummage /ˈrʌmɪdʒ/ *vi* **to ~ through/in sth** فَتَّشَ في شَيْءٍ

rummy /ˈrʌmi/ *n* رومي (لُعْبة وَرَق)

rumour (BrE), **rumor** (AmE) /ˈruːmə/ **A** *n* شائِعة (شائِعات), إِشاعة
B *vt* **it is ~ed that...** يُشاعُ أَنّ ...

rumoured (BrE), **rumored** (AmE) /ˈruːməd/ *adj* ‹*deal, affair*› الّذي يُشاعُ عَنْهُ

rump /rʌmp/ *n* **1** (hind part) كَفَل (أَكْفال), رِدْف (أَرْداف), **2** (meat) [قِطْعة لَحْم من فَخْذِ البَقَرِ] **3** (infml hum) (buttocks) مُؤَخَّرة, رِدْف (أَرْداف)

rumple /ˈrʌmp(ə)l/ *vt* جَعَّدَ ‹*clothes, sheets*›

rump steak *n* [شَريحة لَحْمٍ من فَخْذِ البَقَرِ]

rumpus /ˈrʌmpəs/ *n* (infml) جَلَبة ,ضَجّة

run /rʌn/ **A** *vt* (*present participle* **-nn-**; *past tense* **ran**; *past participle* **run**) **1** (to cover on foot) جرى (i; جَرْي), رَكَض (u; رَكْض) ‹*a race, distance, marathon*›; **she ran two miles to get help** جَرَتْ مِيلَيْنِ للحُصولِ على المُساعَدةِ; **he ran the fastest time** قَطَعَ سِباقَ العَدْوِ في أَسْرَعِ وَقْتٍ **2** (to drive) أَوْصَلَ, أَوْصَلَ ,وَصَّلَ ‹*a person, package, vehicle*›; **to ~ sb to the station** وَصَّلَ شَخْصاً إلى المَحطّةِ; **I have to ~ these boxes over to the warehouse** عَلَيَّ أن أُوَصِّلَ هذه الصَناديقَ إلى المُسْتَوْدَعِ **3** (to pass, move) **to ~ one's hand over sth** مَرَّرَ يَدَهُ فوق شَيْءٍ; **to ~ one's eye over sth** جالَ بِنَظَرِهِ في شَيْءٍ; **to ~ a duster over sth** نَفَّضَ شَيْئاً بالمِنْفَضةِ; **to ~ one's pen through sth** شَطَبَ شَيْئاً بِقَلَمِهِ **4** (to manage) أَدارَ ‹*a business, hotel, service*›; **stop trying to ~ my life!** كَفاكَ تَدَخُّلاً في شُؤوني!; **the company ~s management courses** تُقَدِّمُ الشَرِكةُ دَوْراتٍ في الإدارةِ; **a well-~/badly ~ organization** مُنَظَّمة تُدارُ بِشَكْلٍ جَيِّدٍ \ سَيِّءٍ **5** (to operate) أَدارَ ,شَغَّلَ ‹*a machine, an engine*› **6** (to execute) شَغَّلَ ‹*a program*› **7** (to carry out) أَجْرى ‹*a test, check*› **8** (to install) مَدَّ (u; مَدّ) ‹*a cable, pipe, rope*› **9** (to cause to flow) فَتَحَ ‹*water, tap*›; مَلَأَ (a; مَلْء) ‹*a bath*› **10** «newspapers, editors» نَشَرَ (u; نَشْر) ‹*a story, an article*› **11** (to smuggle) هَرَّبَ ‹*guns, drugs*›
B *vi* (*present participle* **-nn-**; *past tense* **ran**; *past participle* **run**) **1** (to move quickly) «children, joggers, camels» جَرى (i; جَرْي); **to ~ across the field/along the beach** جَرى عَبْرَ الحَقْلِ \ على طولِ الشاطِئِ; **to ~ around the house/garden** جَرى حول البَيْتِ \ الحَديقةِ; **to ~ for the bus** جَرى للِّحاقِ بالحافِلةِ; **to ~ for the exit** جَرى نحو مَكانِ الخُروجِ; **she came ~ning towards me** جاءَتْ نَحْوي وَهِيَ تَجْري

2 (to compete) **to ~ in a race** «athletes, horses» اشْتَرَكَ في سِباقٍ للعَدْوِ **3** (to flee) هَرَبَ (u; هُروب), فَرَّ (i; فَرّ, فِرار, مَفَرّ); **to ~ for one's life** هَرَبَ لِيَنْجُوَ بِحَياتِهِ; **~ for it!** (infml) أُهْرُبْ وانْجُ بِحَياتِكَ!; **she went ~ning to her parents** فَرَّتْ إلى أَبَوَيْها **4** (to function) «machines, generators, engines» دارَ (u; دَوْر, دَوَران), اشْتَغَلَ; **to leave the engine ~ning** تَرَكَ المُحَرِّكَ دائِراً; **to ~ off the mains/off batteries** كانَ يَعْمَلُ بالكَهْرَباءِ \ بالبَطّاريّاتِ; **it ~s on diesel** هو يَعْمَلُ بالديزل; **this clock is ~ning fast/slow** هذه الساعةُ مُتَقَدِّمةٌ \ مُتَأَخِّرةٌ; **the organization ~s very smoothly** تَعْمَلُ المُنَظَّمةُ بِسَلاسةٍ كَبيرةٍ **5** (to continue, last) «contracts, leases» اِسْتَمَرَّ; **the season ~s from September to May** يَسْتَمِرُّ المَوْسِمُ من سِبْتَمْبِر حتّى مايو **6** (to be performed) «plays, musicals, movies» عُرِضَ; **this show will ~ and ~!** هذا العَرْضُ سَيَسْتَمِرُّ وَيَسْتَمِرُّ! **7** (to go, pass) **to ~ past/through sth** «the frontier, paths, lines» اِمْتَدَّ; مَرَّ ب \ من خِلالِ شَيْءٍ; **to ~ from east to west** من الشَرْقِ إلى الغَرْبِ; **to ~ parallel to sth** سارَ في خَطٍّ مُتَوازٍ مع شَيْءٍ **8** (to move) «sledges, vehicles» انْزَلَقَ; **the rope ran through my hands** تَفَلَّتَ الحَبْلُ من يَدي; **a pain ran up my leg** سَرى أَلَمٌ في رِجْلي; **a wave of excitement ran through the crowd** انْتابَت الحَشْدُ مَوْجةٌ من الإثارة **9** (to operate) «buses, trains» سارَ (i; سَيْر, مَسير); **a ferry service ~s between Nuweiba and Aqaba** هُناكَ خَطُّ عَبّاراتٍ يَسيرُ بين نُوَيبِع والعَقَبة; **the train is ~ning late** يَبْدَأُ القِطارُ في التَأَخُّرِ **10** (to flow) «water, streams» تَدَفَّقَ; «tap» سالَ الماءُ \ تَدَفَّقَ من; **my nose is ~ning** أَنْفي يَسيلُ \ يَرْشَحُ; **tears ran down his cheeks** سالَت الدُموعُ على خَدَّيْهِ **11** (to spread) «colours, dyes, garments» ساحَ (i; سِياحة), سالَ (i; سَيْل, سَيَلان) **12** (as a candidate) رَشَّحَ نَفْسَهُ; **to ~ for mayor/president** رَشَّحَ نَفْسَهُ لِرِئاسةِ البَلَدِيّةِ \ للرِئاسةِ **13** (to be worded) «message» قالَ (u; قَوْل); **the argument ~s as follows ...** نَصُّ الحُجّةِ كَما يَلي ... **14** (to snag) «tights, stockings» نَسَلَ (u; نَسْل, نُسول)

C *n* **1** (act of running) جَرْي, عَدْو, رَكْض; **a two-mile ~** جَرْي لِمَسافةِ ميلَيْن; **to go for a ~** مارَسَ الرَكْضَ **2** **to be on the ~** كانَ هارِباً; **to be on the ~ from jail/the police** كانَ هارِباً من السِجْنِ \ الشُرْطةِ; **to have the enemy/one's opponent on the ~** حَقَّقَ انْتِصاراتٍ ضِدّ العَدُوِّ \ خَصْمِهِ; **to make a ~ for it** حاوَلَ الفِرارَ جَرْياً على الأَقْدامِ **3** (sequence) سِلْسِلة مُتَعاقِبة; **to have a ~ of luck/of bad luck** لازَمَهُ الحَظُّ الطَيِّبُ \ العاثِرُ لِفَتْرةٍ **4** (of performances) عَرْض (عُروض); **to have a six-month ~** اسْتَمَرَّ لِمُدّةِ سِتّةِ أَشْهُرٍ **5** (trend) مَجْرًى (مَجْرَيات), اتّجاه (اتّجاهات), مَسار (مَسارات); **in the normal ~ of events** في الظُروفِ الطَبيعيّةِ; **the ~ of the dice was against me** كانَ الحَظُّ ضِدّي **6** (in printing) [عَدَد النُسَخ في الطَبْعةِ \ الإصْدارِ الواحِدِ]; (in manufacturing) [عَدَد القِطَع في الدُفْعةِ الواحِدةِ] **7** (on banks, stock exchanges) **there was a ~ on the banks** كانَ هُناكَ إقْبالٌ كَبيرٌ على السَحْبِ في البُنوكِ **8** (trip) رِحْلة (رِحَل, رِحْلات), جَوْلة; **to do the school ~** أَوْصَلَ الأَوْلادَ إلى \ من المَدْرَسةِ **9** (in cricket, baseball) نُقْطة (نُقَط, نِقاط) **10** (for chickens, rabbits etc) حَظيرة (حَظائِرُ) **11** (in tights, stockings) نَسْل, تَنْسيل **12** (for skiing, etc) مَسار (مَسارات) **13** (attempt, chance) مُحاوَلة; **to give sb a clear ~ at sth** مَنَحَ شَخْصاً فُرْصةً ذَهَبيّةً للفَوْزِ بِشَيْءٍ

D **(runs)** *n pl* (infml) (diarrhoea) **the ~s** الإسْهال

Idioms **in the long run** على المَدى البَعيدِ; **in the short run** على المَدى القَصيرِ; **to have the run of the house/garden** كانَ لَهُ حُرِّيّةُ التَصَرُّفِ في البَيْتِ \ الحَديقةِ

Phrasal verbs **run about, run around** **1** (to rush) جَرى هُنا وَهُناكَ **2** (to keep company) **to ~ about** *or* **around with sb** صاحَبَ شَخْصاً

• **run across**: **~ across [sth/sb]** (infml) **1** قابَلَ [شَيْئاً \ شَخْصاً] بالصُدْفةِ ‹*an acquaintance, sb's brother*› **2** عَثَرَ على [شَيْءٍ] بالصُدْفةِ ‹*a document, reference*›

• **run along** (infml) (to go away) انْصَرَفَ, رَحَلَ (a; رَحيل)

• **run at**: **~ at [sb/sth]** **1** (to charge towards) هَجَمَ على [شَخْصٍ \ شَيْءٍ] ‹*a door, person*› **2** (to be at) بَلَغَ [شَيْئاً] ‹*a percentage, figure*›

• **run away** **A** **1** (to flee) «robbers, vandals» فَرَّ (i; فِرار, فَرّ, مَفَرّ), هَرَبَ (u; هُروب); **the would-be thieves ran away** فَرَّ الَّذينَ كانوا يُحاوِلونَ السَرِقةَ **2** (from problems) «children, animals» هَرَبَ (u; هُروب); **to ~ away from home** هَرَبَ

③ «water, liquids» انْصَرَفَ من البَيْتِ **B** ~ **away with [sb]** (to flee with) هَرَبَ مع [شَخْصٍ] ‹sb's daughter› **C** ~ **away with [sth]** ① (to steal) سَرَقَ [شَيْئاً] ‹the money, jewellery› ② (to get carried away) **to ~ away with the idea that ...** انْساقَ وراء فِكْرَةِ أنّ ...; **she let her emotions ~ away with her** انْساقَتْ وراء عواطِفِها

• **run down** **A** «batteries» فَرَغَ شَحْنُهُ **B** ~ **down [sth/sb]**, ~ **[sth/sb] down** ① (in a vehicle) صَدَمَ [شَيْئاً \ شَخْصاً] ② (to reduce) خَفَّضَ \ قَلَّلَ [شَيْئاً] ‹production, an industry, one's defences› ③ (to disparage) حَطَّ من شَأْنِ \ قَدْرِ [شَخْصٍ] ‹a person›; حَطَّ من قيمةِ [شَيْءٍ] ‹sb's work› ④ (to find) عَثَرَ على [شَيْءٍ] ‹a component, painting›

• **run in**: ~ **in [sth]**, ~ **[sth] in** لَيَّنَ \ مَرَّنَ [شَيْئاً] ‹a car, engine›

• **run into**: ~ **into [sth/sb]** ① (to collide with) اصْطَدَمَ ب [شَيْءٍ \ شَخْصٍ] ‹a car, wall, person›; **we ran into the car in front** اصْطَدَمْنا بالسَيّارةِ الّتي أمامَنا ② (to meet) قابَلَ [شَخْصاً] ‹a person› ③ (to encounter) تَعَرَّضَ ل [شَيْءٍ] مُصادَفةً ‹opposition, bad weather, a difficulty›; **to ~ into debt** أُثْقِلَ بالدُيونِ ④ (to amount to) «sales» بَلَغَ [شَيْئاً] ‹hundreds of dollars, millions of pounds›

• **run off** **A** ① (to make off) «robbers, vandals» فَرَّ هارِباً ② «water, liquids» انْصَرَفَ **B** ~ **off with [sth]** (to steal) سَرَقَ [شَيْئاً] ‹the money, jewellery› **C** ~ **off with [sb]** (to flee with) هَرَبَ مع [شَخْصٍ] ‹sb's daughter›

• **run on** (to last too long) تَواصَلَ, امْتَدَّ

• **run out** **A** ① (to become exhausted) «supplies, resources» نَفِدَ (a; نَفْد, نَفاد); **time is ~ning out** بَدَأَ الوَقْتُ يَنْفَدُ ② (to have no more) نَفِدَ ما عِنْدَهُ; **sorry, we've ~ out** آسِفٌ، فَقَدْ نَفِدَ ما عِنْدَنا ③ (to expire) «passports, licences» انْتَهَتْ صَلاحِيَّتُهُ; «leases» انْتَهى أَجَلُهُ **B** ~ **out of [sth]** لم يَعُدْ لَدَيْهِ [شَيْءٌ] ‹ideas, time›; **we've ~ out of fuel/money** نَفَدَ ما لَدَيْنا من وَقودٍ \ مالٍ

• **run out on**: ~ **out on [sb]** (infml) هَجَرَ [شَخْصاً] ‹one's family, wife›

• **run over** **A** ① (to last too long) «meetings, events» تَواصَلَ, امْتَدَّ; **to ~ over by an hour** امْتَدَّ ساعةً بعد مَوْعِدِهِ ② (to overflow) «the sink, bath, cups» طَفَحَ (a; طَفْح), فاضَ (i; فَيْض, فَيَضان) **B** ~ **over [sth]** ① ▸**run through** 1 ② ▸**run through** 2 **C** ~ **over [sth/sb]**, ~ **[sth/sb] over** (drive over a person, animal) دَهَسَ [شَيْئاً \ شَخْصاً] ‹a child, cat›; (travel over a thing) سارَ فوق [شَيْءٍ] ‹a bump, stone›

• **run through**: ~ **through [sth]** ① (to look through) تَصَفَّحَ [شَيْئاً] ‹an agenda, the details, figures› ② (to discuss briefly) راجَعَ \ اسْتَعْرَضَ [شَيْئاً] ‹the main points, schedule, list› ③ (to be present in) سَرى \ شاعَ في [شَيْءٍ] ‹a society, sb's work› ④ (to use up) اسْتَهْلَكَ \ اسْتَنْفَدَ [شَيْئاً] ‹one's savings, the supplies›

• **run to**: ~ **to [sth]** ① (to extend as far as) بَلَغَ [شَيْئاً] ‹a number of pages, words› ② (to provide money for) كَفى لِشِراءِ [شَيْءٍ] ‹a new car, gift›

• **run up**: ~ **up [sth]**, ~ **[sth] up** ① (to accumulate) تَرَكَ [شَيْئاً] يَتَراكَمُ ‹a bill, debt› ② (to make) خاطَ \ حاكَ [شَيْئاً] بِسُرْعةٍ ‹a dress, pair of curtains› ③ (to raise) رَفَعَ [شَيْئاً] ‹a flag, sail›

• **run up against**: ~ **up against [sth]** لَقِيَ \ واجَهَ [شَيْئاً] ‹opposition, a difficulty, a problem›

runabout /ˈrʌnəbaʊt/ *n* (infml) سَيّارة صَغيرة (للرَحَلاتِ القَصيرةِ)

runaway /ˈrʌnəweɪ/ **A** *n* شَخْص هارِب

B *adj before n* ① ‹spouse, slave› هارِب ② ‹train, truck› جامِح, خارِج عن السَيْطَرةِ ③ ‹success› كاسِح; ‹winner› مُكْتَسِح

rundown /ˈrʌndaʊn/ **A** *n* تَقْرير موجَز

B (**run-down**) /rʌnˈdaʊn/ *adj* ① (tired and unwell) مُرْهَق, مُجْهَد, مُنْهَك ② (shabby) ‹area, neighbourhood› مُتَرَدٍّ; ‹building, house› مُتَهالِك

rung /rʌŋ/ **A** *past participle* ▸**ring**

B *n* ① (of a ladder) دَرَجة ② (in hierarchies) مَرْتَبة (مَراتِبُ), دَرَجة

run-in /ˈrʌnɪn/ *n* (infml) خِلاف (خِلافات), صِدام

runner /ˈrʌnə/ *n* ① (athlete) عَدّاء ② (messenger) ساعٍ (سُعاة, ساعونَ), ③ (for a drawer) مَجْرًى (مَجارٍ); (on a sledge) أَحَد المِزْلاقَيْنِ في أَسْفَلِ الزَحّافةِ

runner bean *n* (BrE) فاصولْيا إِسْبانيّة

runner-up /rʌnərˈʌp/ *n* (*pl* **runners-up**) فائِز بالمَرْكَزِ الثاني

running /ˈrʌnɪŋ/ **A** *n* ① (sport, exercise) رَكْض, عَدْو, جَرْي ② (of a company, project) إدارة

B *adj* **1** (flowing) ‹water› جارٍ; **~ sore** جُرْح لا يَنْدَمِلُ **2** (consecutive) **for five days ~** لِخَمْسَةِ أَيّامٍ مُتَوالِيَةٍ

Idioms **to be in the running** كانَ لَدَيْهِ فُرْصَةٌ في الفَوْزِ; **to be out of the running** لم يَكُنْ لَدَيْهِ فُرْصَةٌ في الفَوْزِ; **to make the running** (BrE) (in a race) سَبَقَ مَنْ مَعَهُ; (in an activity) أَرْسى مِعْياراً

running battle *n* **1** (Mil) (military) مَعْرَكة مُتَنَقِّلة **2** (Pol) (confrontation) مُواجَهة طَويلة الأَمَدِ

running commentary *n* تَعْليق مُباشِر

running costs *n* **1** (of organizations) تكاليف جارِية **2** (of machines, vehicles) تكاليف تَشْغيلٍ

running shoes *n* أَحْذِية الرَّكْضِ

running total *n* إجْماليّ مُتَحَرِّك

runny /ˈrʌni/ *adj* (**runnier, runniest**) **1** ‹sauce, honey› مائِع **2** ‹nose› سَيّال; **he's got a ~ nose** يُعاني من سَيَلانِ الأَنْفِ

run-off /ˈrʌnɒf/ *n* **1** (in an election) جَوْلة إعادةٍ \ نهائيّة, مَرْحَلة حاسِمة **2** (water, liquid) الماء \ السائِل المُتَدَفِّق

run-of-the-mill /ˌrʌnəvðəˈmɪl/ *adj* ‹film, thriller› عاديّ, غَيْر مُتَمَيِّزٍ

runt /rʌnt/ *n* [أَصْغَر حَيَوانٍ بين أَقْرانِهِ]

run-up /ˈrʌnʌp/ *n* (preceding period) فَتْرة اسْتِعْدادٍ; **in the ~ to the elections** في الفَتْرةِ الّتي تَسْبِقُ الانْتِخاباتِ

runway /ˈrʌnweɪ/ *n* مَدْرَج (مَدارِجُ), مَمَرّ الإقْلاعِ والهُبوطِ

rupee /ruːˈpiː/ *n* روبِيّة

rupture /ˈrʌptʃə/ **A** *vt* فَتَقَ (u; فَتْق), مَزَّقَ ‹a ligament›; شَقَّ (u; شَقّ) ‹fuel tank›

B *n* **1** (of an organ, blood vessel) فَتْق (فُتوق), تَمَزُّق **2** (in relationships) قَطْع

rural /ˈrʊ(ə)rəl/ *adj* ‹area, community› قَرَويّ, ريفيّ

ruse /ruːz/ *n* خُدْعة (خُدَع, خُدْعات), حيلة (حِيَل)

rush /rʌʃ/ **A** *vt* **1** (to transport urgently) أَرْسَلَ \ نَقَلَ على عَجَلٍ ‹supplies, equipment, troops›; **to ~ aid workers/supplies to the area** نَقَلَ مُوَظَّفي الإغاثةِ \ المُؤَنَ على عَجَلٍ إلى المِنْطَقةِ; **the patient was ~ed to hospital** نُقِلَ المَريضُ بِسُرْعةٍ إلى المُسْتَشْفى; **I'll ~ the documents to you** سَأُرْسِلُ الوَثائِقَ لَكَ بِسُرْعةٍ **2** (to do hastily) فَعَلَ على عَجَلٍ \ بِاسْتِعْجالٍ ‹a repair, an essay›; **don't try to ~ things** لا تَتَعَجَّلْ في عَمَلِكَ **3** (to pressurize) تَعَجَّلَ, اسْتَعْجَلَ ‹a colleague, worker, client› **4** (to charge at) انْقَضَّ (على), باغَتَ, هاجَمَ بَغْتةً ‹a guard, kidnapper, the checkpoint› **5** (AmE) «student» حاوَلَ الالْتِحاقَ بـ ‹a sorority, fraternity›

B *vi* **1** (to make haste) تَعَجَّلَ, اسْتَعْجَلَ; **there is no need to ~** لا داعِيَ للعَجَلةِ **2** (to move hastily) انْدَفَعَ; **to ~ for the exits** انْدَفَعَ نحو أماكِنِ الخُروجِ; **to ~ down the stairs/out of the room** نَزَلَ الدَرَجَ \ خَرَجَ من الغُرْفةِ على عَجَلٍ; **he ~ed past** مَرَّ على عَجَلٍ; **to ~ off** رَحَلَ \ غادَرَ على عَجَلٍ; **to ~ up to sb/sth** هَرَعَ \ أَسْرَعَ إلى شَخْصٍ \ شَيْءٍ; **water ~ed in through the door** انْدَفَعَ الماءُ إلى الداخِلِ من خِلالِ البابِ

C *n* **1** [u] (haste, hurry) عَجَلة, تَسَرُّع; **there's no ~** لا داعِيَ للعَجَلةِ; **to be in a ~** كانَ على عَجَلةٍ من أَمْرِهِ; **to do sth in a ~** فَعَلَ شَيْئاً على عَجَلٍ **2** (by a crowd) انْدِفاع (انْدِفاعات), تَزاحُم; (of air, water) تَدَفُّق (تَدَفُّقات); (of complaints, e-mails, adrenaline) زِيادة; (of anger) اشْتِداد; **everybody made a ~ for the exit** انْدَفَعَ الجَميعُ نحو مَكانِ الخُروجِ; **she was hurt in the ~** جُرِحَتْ أثناء انْدِفاعِ الجَماهيرِ \ الزَبائِنِ **3** (of activity, traffic) ساعة ذُرْوةٍ; (in trading) فَتْرة زِحامٍ; **the morning/evening ~** ساعة الذُرْوةِ الصَباحيّة \ المَسائيّة; **the summer/Christmas ~** زِحام الصَيْفِ \ عيدِ الميلادِ; **order now and beat the ~!** اُطْلُب الآنَ وتَفادَ الزِحامَ! **4** (Bot) أَسَل, سَمار

D (**rushes**) *n pl* النُسْخة المُتَعَجِّلة

Phrasal verbs **rush into**: **A ~ into [sth]** تَعَجَّلَ في [شَيْءٍ] ‹an agreement, a purchase, sale›; **to ~ into marriage** تَعَجَّلَ في الزَواجِ **B ~ [sb] into sth** تَعَجَّلَ \ اسْتَعْجَلَ [شَخْصاً] في شَيْءٍ; **don't be ~ed into signing anything** لا تَدَعْ أَحَداً يَتَعَجَّلُكَ في التَوْقيعِ على أَيِّ شَيْءٍ

• **rush out**: **~ out [sth], ~ [sth] out** **1** أَصْدَرَ [شَيْئاً] على عَجَلٍ ‹a pamphlet›; صَمَّمَ [شَيْئاً] على عَجَلٍ ‹new model› **2** أَصْدَرَ [شَيْئاً] على عَجَلٍ ‹a version, fix›

• **rush through**: **A ~ through [sth]** (to read, finish quickly) تَناوَلَ [شَيْئاً] بِاسْتِعْجالٍ ‹a task, an article, the agenda› **B ~ [sth] through, ~ through [sth]** **1** (to approve quickly) مَرَّرَ [شَيْئاً]

على عَجَلٍ ‹the legislation, a bill, an amendment› **2** (to process quickly) نَظَرَ في [شَيْءٍ] على عَجَلٍ ‹an order, application›

rushed /rʌʃt/ *adj* ‹decision› مُتَعَجِّل, مُتَسَرِّع; ‹job› مُسْتَعْجَل

rush hour *n* ساعة الازْدِحامِ \ الذُرْوة

rush job, **rushed job** *n* عَمَل مُسْتَعْجَل

rusk /rʌsk/ *n* (dry biscuit) بُقْسُماط (كَعْك مُجَفَّف); (baby biscuit) [بَسْكَويت أَطْفالٍ]

russet /ˈrʌsɪt/ *adj* ‹hair, leaves› خَمْرِيّ اللَوْنِ

Russia /ˈrʌʃə/ *pr n* روسِيا

Russian /ˈrʌʃ(ə)n/ **A** *adj* ‹class, culture, embassy› روسيّ (روس)
B *n* **1** (citizen) روسيّ (روس) **2** (language) (اللُغة) الروسيّة

Russian roulette *n* روليت روسيّ

rust /rʌst/ **A** *n* صَدَأ
B *vt* أَصابَ بالصَدَأِ, أَصْدَأَ ‹the metalwork, machinery›
C *vi* «metal, machinery» صَدِئَ (a; صَداءة), أُصيبَ بالصَدَأِ

rustic /ˈrʌstɪk/ *adj* ‹charm, style› ريفيّ, قَرَوِيّ, بَسيط (بُسَطاءُ)

rustle /ˈrʌs(ə)l/ **A** *vt* **1** «wind» خَشْخَشَ (i; خَشْخَشة) ‹leaves, papers› **2** (to steal) سَرَقَ (i; سَرِقة) ‹cattle, horses›
B *vi* «leaves, papers» خَشْخَشَ (i; خَشْخَشة), حَفَّ (i; حَفيف)
C *n* (sound of paper, leaves) خَشْخَشة; (of skirts, silk) حَفيف

rustler /ˈrʌslə/ *n* لِصّ \ سارِق مَواشٍ

rustproof /ˈrʌstpruːf/ **A** *adj* ‹steel, screw› غَيْر قابِلٍ للصَدَأِ; ‹coating, paint› مُقاوِم للصَدَأِ
B *vt* [عالَجَ ضدّ الصَدَأِ] ‹vehicle, bodywork›

rusty /ˈrʌsti/ *adj* (**rustier**, **rustiest**) **1** ‹nail, gate› صَدِئ
2 ‹French, skills› صَدِئ, يَنْقُصُهُ التَمْرينُ; **I'm a bit ~** أنا مُتَوَقِّفٌ عن التَدْريب بَعْضَ الشَيْءِ

rut /rʌt/ *n* **1** (in the ground) أُخْدود (أَخاديدُ; dipt) ثَلْم (ثُلوم)
2 (of deer, bears) وِداق, مَوْسِم التَزاوُج

Idiom **to be (stuck) in a rut** وَقَعَ في دائِرةِ الرَتابةِ

rutabaga /ˌruːtəˈbeɪɡə/ *n* (AmE) لِفْت سُويديّ

ruthless /ˈruːθləs/ *adj* ‹killer› قاسي القَلْبِ, عَديم الرَحْمةِ; ‹repression› وَحْشيّ; ‹ambition› جامِح

RV /ɑːˈviː/ *n* (AmE) = **recreational vehicle** سَيّارة تَرْفيهيّة

Rwanda /ruːˈandə/ *pr n* رُوانْدا

Rwandan /ruːˈand(ə)n/ *n, adj* رُوانْديّ

rye /raɪ/ *n* سُلْت, جاوْدار, شَيْلَم

rye bread *n* خُبْز الجاوْدار

rye whiskey *n* ويسْكي الجاوْدار

Ss

S, **s** /es/ **A** *n* (letter) سين ≈ (الحَرْف التاسِعَ عَشَرَ من الأَبْجَدِيَّةِ الإِنْكليزِيَّةِ)
B *abbr* (**S**) **1** = **South** جَنوب **2** = **small** حَجْم صَغير

sabbath /ˈsabəθ/ *n* (Jewish) سَبْت (يَوْم السَبْتِ); (Christian) (يَوْم الأَحَدِ); **to observe/to break the ~** حَفِظَ \ لم يَحْفَظ السَبْتَ

sabbatical /səˈbatɪk(ə)l/ *n* إجازة تفَرُّغ عِلْمِيّ; **to be/go on ~** كانَ \ ذَهَب في إجازةِ تَفَرُّغٍ عِلْميٍّ

Sabian /ˈseɪbɪən/ *n* صابِئ

sabotage /ˈsabətɑːʒ/ **A** *vt* خَرَّبَ ‹*the equipment, factory*›
B *n* تَخْريب

saboteur /ˌsabəˈtəː/ *n* مُخَرِّب

sabre, **saber** (AmE) /ˈseɪbə/ *n* سَيْف مُنْحَنٍ

sac /sak/ *n* كيس (أَكْياس)

saccharin /ˈsakərɪn/ *n* سُكَّرين

saccharine /ˈsak(ə)riːn/ *adj* (pej) ‹*sweetness*› زائِد; ‹*smile*› ≈ مُداهِن, زائِف ≈

sachet /ˈsaʃeɪ/ *n* [كيس صَغير]; **a ~ of shampoo/sugar** [كيس صَغير من الشامْبو \ السُكَّرِ]

sack /sak/ **A** *n* **1** (of flour, potatoes, coal) كيس (أَكْياس)
2 (AmE) (paper bag) كيس وَرَقيّ **3** (infml) **to hit the ~** ارْتَمى في السَريرِ **4** (BrE) (infml) (dismissal) فَصْل; **to get the ~** فُصِلَ من عَمَلِهِ; **to give sb the ~** فَصَلَ شَخْصاً من عَمَلِهِ
B *vt* **1** (BrE) (infml) (to dismiss) فَصَلَ (i; فَصْل) ‹*an employee, the workforce*› **2** (to destroy) دَمَّرَ ‹*a town, city*›

sacrament /ˈsakrəmənt/ *n* سِرّ مُقَدَّس

sacred /ˈseɪkrɪd/ *adj* ‹*text, rite*› مُقَدَّس; **the site at Eleusis is ~ to Demeter** المَوْقِعُ في إلِفْسينا مَوْقِعٌ مُقَدَّسٌ للإلاهةِ ديميتير

sacrifice /ˈsakrɪfʌɪs/ **A** *n* **1** (offering) قُرْبان (قَرابينُ); **a ~ to the gods** قُرْبان للآلِهةِ **2** (of important things) تَضْحِية; **to make ~s** قَدَّمَ تَضْحِياتٍ
B *vt* **1** (to the gods) ضَحّى (ب) ‹*an animal*› قَدَّمَ قُرْباناً ‹*a virgin*› **2** (to give up) ضَحّى (ب) ‹*your liberty, happiness*›; **to ~ one's career for one's family** ضَحّى بِمُسْتَقْبَلِهِ المِهَنيّ من أَجْلِ عائِلَتِهِ

sacrilege /ˈsakrɪlɪdʒ/ *n* تَدْنيس حُرْمةٍ

sacrilegious /ˌsakrɪˈlɪdʒəs/ *adj* ‹*act, imagery*› مُسيء (لِشَيْءٍ مُقَدَّسٍ)

sacrosanct /ˈsakrəʊsaŋkt/ *adj* ‹*principle, idea*› مُقَدَّس

sad /sad/ *adj* (**-dd-**) **1** (unhappy) ‹*person, story, face*› حَزين (حَزانى); **I'll be very ~ to see her go** سَأكونُ حَزيناً جِدًّا لِرُؤْيَتِها تُغادِرُ; **to feel ~** شَعَرَ بالحُزْنِ; **it makes me ~** يَجْعَلُني حَزيناً; **it's so ~ that he died young** إِنَّهُ لَأَمْرٌ مُحْزِنٌ \ مُؤْسِفٌ أَنَّهُ ماتَ شابًّا **2** (unfortunate) ‹*fact, truth*› مُؤْسِف; **~ to say, she never lived to see it** من المُؤْسِفِ أَنَّها لم تَعِشْ لِتَراهُ
3 (deplorable) ‹*situation*› مُحْزِن; **it's a ~ state of affairs when honesty counts for so little** إِنَّهُ أَمْرٌ مُحْزِنٌ أن تَكونَ النَزاهةُ قَليلةَ الأَهَمِّيَّةِ **4** (infml) (pathetic) مُحْزِن, مِسْكين (مِسْكينونَ, مَساكينُ), بائِس (بُؤَساءُ); **he's a ~ little man** هو رَجُلٌ بائِسٌ

sadden /ˈsad(ə)n/ *vt* أَحْزَنَ ‹*a community, friend*›; **I was ~ed by her uncaring attitude** أَحْزَنَني مَوْقِفُها اللامُبالي

saddle /ˈsad(ə)l/ **A** *n* **1** (for horses) سَرْج (أَسْرِجة, سُروج)
2 (for bicycles) سَرْج (أَسْرِجة, سُروج), مَقْعَد (مَقاعِدُ)
B *vt* **1** (to put a saddle on) سَرَّجَ ‹*a horse, donkey*› **2** (to burden) حَمَّلَ أَعْباءً, أَثْقَلَ الكاهِلَ ‹*a taxpayer, generation*›; **to ~ sb with a responsibility** حَمَّلَ شَخْصاً أَعْباءَ مَسْؤوليّةٍ;

the company is ~d with huge debts الشَرِكةُ مُثْقَلةٌ بِدُيونٍ ضَخْمةٍ

saddlebag /ˈsadəlbag/ *n* **1** (for horses) (عُدول, أَعْدال) عِدْل, **2** (for bicycles) (حَقائِبُ) حَقيبة (جِعاب) جَعْبة

sadism /ˈseɪdɪz(ə)m/ *n* سادِيّة

sadist /ˈseɪdɪst/ *n* ساديّ

sadistic /səˈdɪstɪk/ *adj* ‹*pleasure, killer*› ساديّ

sadly /ˈsadli/ *adv* **1** (with sadness) ‹*to say, smile*› بِحُزْنٍ **2** (unfortunately) لِلأَسَفِ; **~, it was not to be** لِلأَسَفِ, لم يُقَدَّرْ لَهُ أَنْ يَكونَ; **you are ~ mistaken** أَنْتَ مُخْطِئٌ لِلأَسَفِ الشَديدِ

sadness /ˈsadnəs/ *n* (أَحْزان) حُزْن

sae /ɛseɪˈiː/ *n* (BrE) = **stamped addressed envelope, self-addressed envelope** [ظَرْف مُعَنْوَن وَمُزَوَّد بِطابِعٍ]

Safar /ˈsafɑː/ *n* صَفَر

safari /səˈfɑːri/ *n* رِحْلة سَفاري; **to go/be on ~** ذَهَبَ \ كانَ في رِحْلةِ سَفاري

safari park *n* حديقة سَفاري

Safavid /ˈsafəvɪd/ *n, adj* صَفَويّ

safe /seɪf/ **A** *adj* **1** (not in danger) آمِن; **to feel ~** شَعَرَ بالأَمْنِ; **is the bike ~ here?** هل الدَرّاجةُ آمِنةٌ هُنا؟; **keep this key/money ~** ضَعْ هذا المِفْتاحَ \ هذه الأَمْوالَ في مَكانٍ آمِنٍ; **to keep one's children ~ from harm** حافَظَ على أَطْفالِهِ آمِنين من الأَذى; **no city was ~ from attack** لم تَكُنْ أَيُّ مَدينةٍ آمِنةً من الهُجومِ; **your secret is ~ with me** سِرُّكَ آمِنٌ مَعي **2** (secure) ‹*place, environment*› آمِن; **~ passage** مَمَرٌّ آمِن **3** (not dangerous) ‹*product, drug, building*› آمِن; **is the water ~ to drink?** هل الماءُ صالِحٌ للشُرْبِ؟; **the beach is ~ for children** الشاطِئُ آمِنٌ للأَطْفالِ; **it's not ~ to go out at night** الخُروجُ في اللَيْلِ لَيْسَ آمِناً; **the bomb was made ~** تَمَّ تَعْطيلُ القُنْبُلةِ; **that car is not ~ to drive** تِلْكَ السَيّارةُ لَيْسَتْ آمِنةً لِلقِيادةِ; **(have a) ~ journey!** أَتَمَنّى لَكَ رِحْلةً آمِنةً! **4** (unharmed) (سُلَماءُ) سَليم ,سالِم; **~ and sound** سَليم وَمُعافًى; **we are praying for her ~ return** نُصَلّي من أَجْلِ عَوْدَتِها سالِمةً **5** (not risky) ‹*investment, option*› آمِن; **it is ~ to say/assume that ...** بِوُسْعِنا أن نَقولَ \ نَفْتَرِضَ أَنّ ...; **we kept to ~ subjects** تَكَلَّمْنا في مَواضيعَ غَيْرِ خِلافيّةٍ **6** (prudent) ‹*driver*› حَذِر; **to be in ~ hands** كانَ في أَيْدٍ أَمينةٍ **B** *n* صُنْدوق وَدائِعَ

(Idioms) **better safe than sorry!** السَلامةُ غَنيمةٌ; **to be on the safe side** من بابِ الحيطةِ والحَذَرِ; **to play safe** تَصَرَّفَ بِحَذَرٍ

safe conduct *n* ضَمان مُرورٍ آمِنٍ

safe-deposit box /ˌseɪfdɪˈpɒsɪt ˌbɒks/ *n* صُنْدوق الأَماناتِ

safeguard /ˈseɪfgɑːd/ **A** *n* ضَمان; **a legal/constitutional ~** ضَمان قانونيّ \ دُسْتوريّ **B** *vt* (على) حافَظَ ‹*rights, the constitution*›

safe haven *n* (مَلاجِئُ) مَلْجأ

safe house *n* بَيْت سِرّيّ, مَلْجأ سِرّيّ

safekeeping /ˌseɪfˈkiːpɪŋ/ *n* عُهْدة

safely /ˈseɪfli/ *adv* **1** (without danger) ‹*to use, dispose of*› بِشَكْلٍ آمِنٍ; **an area where children can play ~** مِنْطَقة يَسْتَطيعُ الأَطْفالُ أن يَلْعَبوا فيها بِشَكْلٍ آمِنٍ **2** (unharmed) ‹*to return, to land*› سالِماً; **to arrive ~** «person, cheque» وَصَلَ سالِماً **3** (securely) ‹*stored, hidden*› بِشَكْلٍ آمِنٍ; **to be ~ tucked up in bed** وُضِعَ في السَريرِ بِشَكْلٍ آمِنٍ; **you can ~ leave your car in the street** تَسْتَطيعُ أن تَتْرُكَ سَيّارَتَكَ في الطَريقِ بِأَمانٍ **4** (without risk) ‹*to say, assume*› بِثِقةٍ **5** (prudently) ‹*to drive*› بِحَذَرٍ

safe sex *n* الجِنْس الآمِن

safety /ˈseɪfti/ *n* (*pl* **safeties**) أَمان ,سَلامة

(Idiom) **there's safety in numbers** ≈ في الاتِّحادِ قوّةٌ

safety belt *n* حِزام أَمانٍ \ سَلامةٍ

safety catch *n* عَتَلة الأَمانِ

safety net *n* **1** (for acrobats) شَبَكة أَمانٍ **2** (safeguard) شَبَكة أَمانٍ

safety pin *n* دَبّوس أَمانٍ

saffron /ˈsafrən/ **A** *n* **1** (flower) زَعْفَران **2** (spice) زَعْفَران **3** (colour) لَوْن الزَعْفَرانِ **B** *adj* ‹*robes, cloth*› زَعْفَرانيّ اللَوْنِ

sag /sag/ *vi* **(-gg-)** **1** (to sink) «beams» انْثَنى; «mattresses» تَقَعَّرَ **2** (to drop) «demand, support» (قِلّة) قَلَّ, تَناقَصَ, **3** (to droop) «breasts, face» تَدَلّى تَلاشى

saga /ˈsɑːɡə/ *n* **1** (heroic tale) قِصّة مَلْحَمِيّة ,مَلْحَمة **2** (infml) (long story) قِصّة طَويلة

sage /seɪdʒ/ *n* **1** [u] (herb) مَرْيَمِيّة ,(نَواعِمُ) ناعِمة ,قُوَيْسة **2** (fml) (wise person) (حُكَماءُ) حَكيم

Sagittarius /ˌsadʒɪˈtɛːrɪəs/ *n* **1** (sign) بُرْج القَوْسِ **2** (person) [مِن مَواليد بُرْجِ القَوْسِ]

Sahara /səˈhɑːrə/ *pr n* (**the Sahara (Desert)**) الصَّحْراء الكُبْرى

said /sɛd/ *past tense, past participle* ▸ **say**

sail /seɪl/ **A** *n* **1** (on boats, ships) قِلْع ,(أَشْرِعة ,شُرُع) شِراع (قِلاع ,قُلوع); **to set ~** «ship» أَبْحَرَ ,أَقْلَعَ ,أَبْحَرَ «person» أَبْحَرَ; **under ~** أَبْحَرَ ,جاهِزة للإِبْحارِ **2** (journey) **to go for a ~** ذَهَبَ في رِحْلةٍ بَحْرِيّةٍ **3** (on a windmill) ريشة طاحونةٍ هوائيّةٍ

B *vt* **1** قادَ (u; قِيادة) ,أَبْحَرَ (ب) ‹*a boat, ship*›; **we ~ed the boat up-river** أَبْحَرْنا بالمَرْكَبِ باتِّجاهِ مَنْبَعِ النَّهرِ **2** (to travel across) أَبْحَرَ (في) ‹*the seas, ocean*›

C *vi* **1** (to travel) «ship, boat» أَبْحَرَ; **she is ~ing around the world** تُبْحِرُ حول العالَمِ **2** (to leave port) «ship» أَبْحَرَ ,أَقْلَعَ; «person» أَبْحَرَ; **the boat ~s at 10 a.m.** تُقْلِعُ \ تُبْحِرُ السَفينةُ الساعةَ العاشِرةَ صَباحاً; **he ~ed for America** أَبْحَرَ إلى أَمْريكا **3** (as a hobby) **to go ~ing** أَبْحَرَ على مَرْكَبٍ شِراعيٍّ **4** (to move past, go by) **a bus ~ed past me** مَرَّتْ حافِلةٌ بِجانِبي; **the ball ~ed over the crossbar** مَرَّت الكُرةُ فوق العارِضةِ الأُفُقيّةِ

(Phrasal verb) **sail through**: **~ through [sth]** (infml) نَجَحَ بِسُهولةٍ في [شَيْءٍ] ‹*an exam, interview*›

sailboard /ˈseɪlbɔːd/ *n* لَوْح شِراعيّ

sailboarder /ˈseɪlbɔːdə/ *n* راكِب أَمْواجٍ (باسْتِخْدام شِراعٍ)

sailing /ˈseɪlɪŋ/ *n* إِبْحار

sailing boat (BrE), **sailboat** (AmE) *n* قارِب شِراعيّ

sailing ship *n* سَفينة شِراعيّة

sailor /ˈseɪlə/ *n* مَلّاح ,(بَحّارة) بَحّار

saint /seɪnt, s(ə)nt/ *n* قِدّيس; **Saint Mark** القِدّيس مُرْقُس; **Saint Anne** القِدّيسة حَنّة

sake /seɪk/ *n* **for the ~ of sth** (on account of) في ,لِأَجْلِ شَيْءٍ سَبيلِ شَيْءٍ; **she carried on working for the ~ of the children** اِسْتَمَرَّتْ تَعْمَلُ لِأَجْلِ الأَطْفالِ; **I believe in education for its own ~** أُؤْمِنُ بالتَّعْليمِ لِذاتِهِ

salad /ˈsaləd/ *n* سَلَطة; **egg ~** سَلَطة البَيْضِ

salad bar *n* طاوِلة السَلَطاتِ

salad bowl *n* سُلْطانيّة السَلَطةِ

salad cream *n* (BrE) [صَلْصة سَلَطةٍ قِشْديّة]

salad dressing *n* صَلْصة سَلَطةٍ

Salafi /səˈlɑːfi/ *n* (*pl* **Salafis**) سَلَفيّ

salamander /ˈsaləˌmandə/ *n* سَمَنْدَر ,(سَمادِلُ) سَمَنْدَل

salami /səˈlɑːmi/ *n* (*pl* **salamis**) سَلامي (سُجُقّ بالثَّوْمِ)

salaried /ˈsalərɪːd/ *adj* ‹*staff, post*› بِراتِبٍ

salary /ˈsaləri/ **A** *n* (*pl* **salaries**) (رَواتِبُ) راتِب ,(مُرَتَّبات) مُرَتَّب; **to be on a high/low ~** كانَ مُرَتَّبُهُ عالياً \ مُنْخَفِضاً

B *modifier* ‹*increase, freeze*› الراتِبِ

salat /səˈlɑːt/ *n* (صَلَوات) صَلاة

sale /seɪl/ **A** *n* **1** (act of selling) (بُيوعات ,بُيوع) بَيْع; **regulations governing the ~ of drugs** اللَوائِح الّتي تَحْكُمُ بَيْعَ العَقاقيرِ **2** (occasion of selling) (بُيوعات ,بُيوع) بَيْع **3** (auction) مَزاد **4** (with bargains) تَنْزيلات عَلَنيّ

B (**sales**) *n pl* **1** (number sold) مَبيعات; **~s fell/rose by 5% in November** انْخَفَضَتْ \ ارْتَفَعَتْ المَبيعاتُ ب 5٪ في نوفَمْبر **2** (department) قِسْم المَبيعاتِ

(Idiom) **for sale** للبَيْعِ

(Idiom) **to be on sale** (available to buy) كانَ للبَيْعِ; (AmE) (at a reduced price) كانَ مُخَفَّضَ السِعْرِ

sale price *n* سِعْر بعد التَخْفيضِ ,سِعْر مُخَفَّض

saleroom /ˈseɪlruːm/, **salesroom** /ˈseɪlzruːm/ *n* صالة \ قاعة مَزادٍ

sales assistant (BrE), **sales clerk** (AmE) *n* مُساعِد مَبيعاتٍ

sales director *n* مُدير مَبيعاتٍ

sales executive *n* (باعة ,بائِعونَ) بائِع

sales force *n* فَريق مَبيعاتٍ

salesman /ˈseɪlzmən/ *n* (*pl* **-men**) (باعة ,بائِعونَ) بائِع; **a travelling ~** بائِع مُتَجَوِّل

salesperson /ˈseɪlzpəːs(ə)n/ *n* (*pl* **salespersons** or **-people**) (باعة ,بائِعونَ) بائِع

sales pitch *n* [كَلام البائِع لِإقْناع الزَبونِ]

sales representative *n* مَنْدوب مَبيعاتٍ

sales tax *n* (AmE) ضَريبة المَبيعاتِ

saleswoman /ˈseɪlzwʊmən/ *n* (*pl* **-women**) بائِعة

saline /ˈseɪlʌɪn/ **A** *adj* ‹*drip, solution*› مِلْحيّ

B *n* (also **saline solution**) مَحْلول مِلْحيّ

saliva /səˈlʌɪvə/ *n* لُعاب

salivate /ˈsalɪveɪt/ *vi* «dogs, hungry people» سالَ لُعابُهُ

sallow /ˈsaləʊ/ *adj* (**sallower**, **sallowest**) ‹*complexion, skin*› (شَواحِبُ) شاحِب

salmon /ˈsamən/ *n* (*pl* **salmon**) سَلْمون

salmonella /ˌsalməˈnɛlə/ *n* (*pl* **salmonellae**) **1** (bacterium) بَكْتيرِيا السالْمونيلا **2** (disease) مَرَض السالْمونيلا

salmonella poisoning *n* تَسَمُّم السالْمونيلا

salon /ˈsalɒn/ *n* صالون (صالونات); **a hairdressing/beauty ~** صالون حِلاقةٍ \ تَجْميلٍ

saloon /səˈluːn/ *n* **1** (also **saloon car**) (BrE) (car) سَيّارة صالون **2** (on a ship) صالون (صالونات) **3** (AmE) (bar) بار (بارات), خَمّارة, حانة

salsify /ˈsalsɪfi/ *n* (plant) سَلْسَفى

salt /sɔːlt/ **A** *n* مِلْح (أَمْلاح); **a kilo of common ~** كيلو من المِلْحِ العادِيِّ

B *vt* **1** (for flavour) أَضافَ المِلْحَ إلى ‹*the vegetables, soup*› **2** (to prevent freezing) رَشّ بالمِلْحِ ‹*a road, path*› **3** (with foods) مَلَّحَ ‹*meat, fish*›

salt cellar *n* مِمْلَحة (مَمالِحُ)

saltwater /ˈsɔːltwɔːtə/ *adj before n* **1** (of salt water) ‹*lake, marsh*› مالِح **2** (in habitat) ‹*fish, plant*› المِياهِ المالِحة

salty /ˈsɔːlti/ *adj* (**saltier**, **saltiest**) ‹*taste, food*› مالِح

salubrious /səˈluːbrɪəs/ *adj* (fml) **1** (healthy) ‹*climate, weather*› صِحّيّ **2** (wholesome) ‹*surroundings, establishment*› راقٍ

salutary /ˈsaljʊt(ə)ri/ *adj* (fml) ‹*experience, reminder*› مُفيد

salute /səˈljuːt/ **A** *n* **1** (greeting) تَحيّة عَسْكَريّة **2** (with guns) طَلْقة تَرْحيبيّة

B *vt* **1** (to greet) قَدَّمَ التَحيّةَ ل ‹*an officer*›; حَيّا ‹*visitor*› **2** (to pay tribute to) أَشادَ (ب) ‹*an achievement*›; حَيّا ‹*hero*›

C *vi* «soldiers» أَدّى التَحيّةَ

Salvadorean /ˌsalvəˈdɔːrɪən/, **Salvadoran** /salvəˈdɔːrən/ *n*, *adj* سَلْفادوريّ

salvage /ˈsalvɪdʒ/ **A** *vt* **1** (to rescue) اِنْتَشَلَ ‹*a wreck, belongings*› **2** (to regain) «teams» اِسْتَرَدَّ, أَنْقَذَ ‹*one's pride, a game*› **3** (for recycling) حافَظَ على (لِإعادةِ اسْتِعْمالِهِ \ تَدْويرِهِ) ‹*metal, paper*›

B *n* **1** (rescue) اِنْتِشال **2** (goods rescued) بَضائِع مُنْتَشَلة

salvation /salˈveɪʃ(ə)n/ *n* **1** (from evil) خَلاص **2** (from harm) إنْقاذ

Salvation Army *n* جَيْش الخَلاصِ

salve /salv/ **A** *n* مَرْهَم (مَراهِمُ)

B *vt* أَراحَ ‹*your conscience*›; داوى ‹*injured pride*›

Samaritan /səˈmarɪt(ə)n/ *n* سامِريّ

(Idiom) **a good Samaritan** شَخْص خَيِّر

same /seɪm/ **A** *adj* **1** (identical) نَفْس (f; أَنْفُس); **they look the ~** يَتَشابَهوا; **to be the ~ as sth** طابَقَ شَيْئاً; **people are the ~ everywhere** الناسُ مُتَشابِهونَ في كُلِّ مَكانٍ; **it's the ~ with the latest model** نَفْس الشَيْءِ مع آخِرِ نَموذَجٍ; **at the ~ time last week/year** في نَفْسِ الوَقْتِ من الأُسْبوعِ \ العامِ الماضي; **it amounts** *or* **comes to the ~ thing** [سَيُؤَدّي كِلاهُما إلى نَفْسِ النَتيجةِ]; **it's all the ~ to me** لَيْسَ هُناكَ فَرْقٌ عِنْدي; **if it's all the ~ to you** إنْ لم يَكُنْ عِنْدَكَ أَيُّ مانِعٍ **2** (emphatic) ذات (f) نَفْس; **~ day delivery guaranteed** نَضْمَنُ التَسْليمَ في نَفْسِ اليَوْمِ; **he's the very ~ one, who ...** هو نَفْسُهُ الّذي; **they are one and the ~ (person)** هُما شَخْصٌ واحِدٌ **3** (unchanged) كَما هو; **to be still the ~** ما زالَ كَما هو; **things are just the ~ as before** الأَشْياءُ كَما هي لم تَعُدْ; **she's not the ~ woman** لم تَعُدْ نَفْسَ المَرْأةِ; **things were never the ~ again** لم تَعُدِ الأَشْياءُ إلى حالِها أَبَداً; **it's/he's the ~ as ever** هو كَما هو دائِماً

B **(the same)** *adv phr* ‹*to act, speak, dress*› بِنَفْسِ الطَريقةِ; **they're pronounced the ~** لَهُما نَفْسُ اللَفْظِ; **to feel the ~ about sb/sth** فَكَّرَ في شَخْصٍ \ شَيْءٍ بِنَفْسِ الطَريقةِ

C **(the same)** *pron* **1** (the identical thing) ذات, نَفْس الشَيْءِ; **I'll have the ~** أُريدُ نَفْسَ الشَيْءِ; **the ~ goes for you** الشَيْءُ ذاتُهُ يَنْطَبِقُ عَلَيْكَ أَنْتَ; **you would do the ~ for me**

كُنْتَ سَتَفْعَلُ نَفْسَ الشَيْءِ لي; **the ~ to you!** (of insult) أَنْتَ مَنْ يَسْتَحِقُّ ذلك!; (to well-wisher) وَأَنْتَ كَذَلِكَ! ② (Busn) المَذْكور (سابِقاً)

(Idiom) **all the same, …** … بالرَغْمِ من ذلك،

same-day /ˈseɪmdeɪ/ *adj before n* ‹*delivery, service*› في نَفْسِ اليَوْمِ

same-sex /ˈseɪmseks/ *adj* ‹*couple, marriage*› مِثْلِيّ

Samoa /səˈməʊə/ *pr n* ساموا

sample /ˈsɑːmp(ə)l/ **A** *n* ① (of DNA, tissue, soil) عَيِّنَة; **to take a blood ~** أَخَذَ عَيِّنَةً من دَمٍ ② (of work, fabric) عَيِّنَة, نموذَج (نَماذِجُ) ③ (of a product) عَيِّنَة, نموذَج (نَماذِجُ) ④ (in research) عَيِّنَة; **a representative ~ of the population** عَيِّنَة مُمَثِّلة للسُّكّانِ

B *vt* ① (to try out) أَخَذَ عَيِّنَةً \ نموذَجاً من ‹*food, wine*› ② (in research) أَخَذَ عَيِّنَةً من ‹*public opinion, the population*› ③ أَخَذَ عَيِّنَةً من ‹*genes, species*›

sample pack *n* عَيِّنَة

sampling /ˈsɑːmplɪŋ/ *n* عَيِّنَة

Sana'a /saˈnɑː/ *pr n* صَنْعاء (dipt f)

sanatorium (BrE), **sanitarium** (AmE) /ˌsanəˈtɔːrɪəm/ *n* (*pl* **sanatoriums** or **sanatoria**) مَصَحّة

sanctify /ˈsaŋktɪfʌɪ/ *vt* (**sanctifies**, **sanctifying**, **sanctified**) بارَكَ ‹*an occasion, marriage*›

sanctimonious /ˌsaŋktɪˈməʊnɪəs/ *adj* (pej) ‹*condemnation, hypocrite*› مُنافِق, مُراءٍ (مُراؤونَ)

sanction /ˈsaŋkʃ(ə)n/ **A** *n* ① (permission) مُوافَقة ② (penalty) عُقوبة; **to impose ~s on a country** فَرَضَ عُقوباتٍ على بَلَدٍ; **to lift ~s on a country** رَفَعَ العُقوباتِ عن بَلَدٍ

B *vt* وافَقَ (على) ‹*a loan, an agreement*›

sanctity /ˈsaŋktɪti/ *n* ① (holiness) حُرْمة, قَداسة, قُدْسيّة ② (inviolability) حُرْمة, قُدْسيّة; **the ~ of marriage** حُرْمة \ قُدْسيّة الزَواجِ

sanctuary /ˈsaŋktjʊəri/ *n* (*pl* **sanctuaries**) ① [u] (safety) مَلاذ آمِن ② (safe place) مَلاذ آمِن ③ (for wildlife) مَحْمِيّة

sand /sand/ **A** *n* رَمْل (رِمال)

B *vt* (also **sand down**) كَشَطَ (i; كَشْط) ‹*the floor, surface*›

(Idiom) **to bury your head in the sand** دَفَنَ رَأْسَهُ في الرَمْلِ

sandal /ˈsand(ə)l/ *n* صَنْدَل (صَنادِلُ)

sandbag /ˈsandbag/ *n* كيس من الرَمْلِ

sandbank /ˈsandbaŋk/ *n* [رُكام رَمْلٍ في البَحْرِ]

sandcastle /ˈsandkɑːs(ə)l/ *n* قَلْعة رَمْليّة

sand dune *n* تَلّ رَمْليّ

sandfly /ˈsandflʌɪ/ *n* ذُباب الرَمْلِ, فاصِدة (فَواصِدُ)

sandlot /ˈsandlɒt/ (AmE) *n* [أَرْض مَتْروكة يَلْعَبُ فيها الأَطْفالُ]

sandpaper /ˈsandpeɪpə/ **A** *n* وَرَق الصَنْفَرةِ

B *vt* كَشَطَ (i; كَشْط) ‹*the wood, surface*›

sandpit /ˈsandpɪt/ *n* [مُرَبَّع الرَمْلِ (يَلْعَبُ فيهِ الأَطْفالُ)]

sandstone /ˈsandstəʊn/ *n* حَجَر \ صَخْر رَمْليّ

sandstorm /ˈsandstɔːm/ *n* عاصِفة رَمْليّة

sandwich /ˈsanwɪdʒ/ **A** *n* (*pl* **sandwiches**) شَطيرة (شَطائِرُ), سَنْدويتْش (سَنْدويتْشات)

B *vt* **to be ~ed between two people/things** [وَقَعَ \ كانَ بين شَخْصَيْنِ \ شَيْئَيْنِ]

sandwich bar *n* مَحَلّ سانْدويتْشاتٍ

sandwich course *n* (BrE) [دِراسة نَظَريّة يَتَخَلَّلُها تَطْبيقٌ عَمَليٌّ]

sandy /ˈsandi/ *adj* (**sandier**, **sandiest**) ① (of sand) ‹*beach, soil*› رَمْليّ ② (in colour) ‹*hair, colour*› أَصْهَب (dipt; صُهْب)

sane /seɪn/ *adj* (**saner**, **sanest**) ① (not mad) ‹*person*› عاقِل (عُقَلاءُ), بِكامِلِ قُواهِ العَقْليّةِ; ‹*mind*› سَليم ② (sensible) ‹*response, advice*› حَكيم, عَقْلانيّ, حَصيف

San Francisco /ˌsan franˈsɪskəʊ/ *pr n* سان فْرانْسيسْكو (f)

sang /saŋ/ *past tense* ▸ **sing**

sanitarium (AmE) *n* ▸ **sanatorium**

sanitary /ˈsanɪt(ə)ri/ *adj* ① *before n* (concerning health) ‹*conditions, facility*› صِحّيّ ② (hygienic) ‹*ward, house*› صِحّيّ

sanitary engineer *n* مُهَنْدِس صِحّيّ

sanitary napkin *n* (AmE) فوطة صِحّيّة

sanitary towel *n* فوطة صِحّيّة

sanitation /sanɪˈteɪʃ(ə)n/ *n* المَرافِق الصِحّيّة

sanitize, -ise (BrE) /ˈsanɪtʌɪz/ *vt* ① (pej) (to make inoffensive) نَقَّحَ (a; نَقْح) ‹*a proposal, report*› ② (to disinfect) طَهَّرَ, عَقَّمَ ‹*a toilet, container*›

sanity /'sanɪti/ *n* 1 (mental health) سَلامة العَقْلِ 2 (good sense) التَفْكير السَليم

sank /saŋk/ *past tense* ▸ **sink**

Santa Claus /'santə klɔːz/, **Santa** *pr n* بابا نُويل

sap /sap/ A *n* نُسْغ
B *vt* (-pp-) اسْتَنْفَد ‹sb's energy, strength›

sapling /'saplɪŋ/ *n* شَتْلة (شُتول, شَتائِل)

sapper /'sapə/ *n* (BrE) مُهَنْدِس عَسْكَرِيّ

sapphire /'safʌɪə/ A *n* 1 (stone) ياقوت أَزْرَق, صَفِير 2 (colour) أَزْرَق ياقوتِيّ
B *adj* ‹eyes, dress› أَزْرَق ياقوتِيّ

sarcasm /'sɑːkazəm/ *n* سُخْرِيّة, تَهَكُّم (تَهَكُّمات)

sarcastic /sɑː'kastɪk/ *adj* ‹comment, smile› ساخِر, تَهَكُّمِيّ

sarcoma /sɑː'kəʊmə/ *n* سَرْكوما

sarcomatosis /sɑː,kəʊmə'təʊsɪs/ *n* [مَرَض السَرْقوم]

sardine /sɑː'diːn/ *n* سَرْدين

Sardinia /sɑː'dɪnɪə/ *pr n* سَرْدينيا

sardonic /sɑː'dɒnɪk/ *adj* ‹wit, smile› ساخِر, تَهَكُّمِيّ

sari /'sɑːri/ *n* (*pl* **saris**) ساري

SARS /sɑːz/ *n* سارْس (مَرَض)

SAS /ɛseɪ'ɛs/ *n* (BrE) = **Special Air Service** القوّات الجَوّيّة الخاصّة

sash /saʃ/ *n* (round waist) [قِطْعة قُماشٍ طَويلة تُلَفُّ حول الخَصْرِ]; (over shoulder) وِشاح (أَوْشِحة)

sash window *n* نافذة مُنْزَلِقة

sassy /'sasi/ *adj* (**sassier, sassiest**) (infml) 1 (stylish) ‹woman, outfit› على الموضةِ 2 (AmE) (cheeky) ‹girl, attitude› وَقِح (وُقُح)

sat /sat/ *past tense, past participle* ▸ **sit**

SAT *n* 1 /sat/ (in UK) = **Standard Assessment Task** [اخْتِبار قِياسيّ لِطُلّابِ المَدارِسِ] 2 (**SAT®**) /ɛseɪ'tiː/ (in US) = **Scholastic Aptitude Test** [اخْتِبار القَبولِ في كُلِّيّةٍ]

Satan /'seɪt(ə)n/ *pr n* شَيْطان (شَياطينُ), إِبْليس (أَبالِسة)

satanic /sə'tanɪk/ *adj* ‹cult, ritual› شَيْطانيّ

satchel /'satʃ(ə)l/ *n* حَقيبة كُتُبٍ (تُعَلَّقُ بالكَتِفِ)

sate /seɪt/ *vt* (fml) سَكَّنَ ‹one's appetite, hunger›

satellite /'satəlʌɪt/ *n* 1 (man-made) قَمَر صِناعيّ 2 (natural) قَمَر (أَقْمار)

satellite dish *n* صَحْن لاقِط, طَبَق قَمَرٍ صِناعيٍّ

satellite town *n* مَدينة تابِعة

satellite TV *n* تِلِفِزْيون فَضائيّ

satin /'satɪn/ *n* ساتان

satire /'satʌɪə/ *n* هِجاء, تَهَكُّم

satiric /sə'tɪrɪk/, **satirical** /sə'tɪrɪk(ə)l/ *adj* ‹novel, comedy› هِجائيّ, تَهَكُّميّ

satirize, -ise (BrE) /'satɪrʌɪz/ *vt* هَجا (u; هِجاء), تَهَكَّمَ (على) ‹society, leader›

satisfaction /satɪs'fakʃ(ə)n/ *n* 1 (pleasure) رِضًى, رِضاء; **to express ~ with sth** عَبَّرَ عن رِضاهُ عن شَيْءٍ; **to get ~ from sth** شَعَرَ بالرِضا بِفَضْلِ شَيْءٍ; **the matter has been resolved to the ~ of all concerned** لَقَدْ حُلَّتْ المَسْأَلةُ بِرِضا جَميعِ الأَطْرافِ المَعْنيّةِ; **he had the ~ of knowing that he had succeeded** شَعَرَ بالرِضا لِمَعْرِفةِ أَنَّهُ قد نَجَحَ 2 (fml) (fulfilment of a need, desire) رِضًى, رِضاء 3 (fml) (redress) تَعْويض (تَعْويضات)

satisfactory /satɪs'fakt(ə)ri/ *adj* ‹outcome, answer› مُرْضٍ

satisfied /'satɪsfʌɪd/ *adj* 1 (pleased) ‹customer, audience› راضٍ, قانِع 2 (convinced) ‹judge, authorities› مُقْتَنِع

satisfy /'satɪsfʌɪ/ *vt* (**satisfies, satisfying, satisfied**) 1 (to gratify) أَرْضى, أَشْبَعَ ‹a need, one's appetite› 2 (to meet) اسْتَجابَ (ل) ‹a demand, the requirements› 3 (to convince) أَقْنَعَ ‹public opinion, a judge›

satisfying /'satɪsfʌɪɪŋ/ *adj* 1 (filling) ‹meal› مُشْبِع 2 (rewarding) ‹job, experience› باعِث على الرِضا \ السَعادة

satnav /'satnav/ *n* ساتْناف (مِلاحة بِواسِطةِ الأَقْمارِ الاصْطِناعيّةِ)

satphone /'satfəʊn/ *n* هاتِف فَضائيّ

satsuma /sat'suːmə/ *n* بُرْتُقال ساتْسوما

saturate /'satʃəreɪt/ *vt* 1 (to soak) رَوى (i; رَيّ, رِيّ) ‹soil›; غَمَرَ (u; غَمْر), نَقَعَ (a; نَقْع) ‹clothes› 2 (to overload) أَغْرَقَ ‹the market›

saturated /ˈsatʃəreɪtɪd/ *adj* **1** (soaked) ‹*soil*› (بالماءِ) مُشْبَع; ‹*clothes*› مَنْقوع **2** ‹*fat, oil*› مُشْبَع, مُشَبَّع

saturation /satʃəˈreɪʃ(ə)n/ *n* تَشَبُّع

saturation coverage *n* تَغْطِية إعلاميّة مُكَثَّفة

saturation point *n* نُقْطة التَشَبُّع

Saturday /ˈsatədeɪ, ˈsatədi/ *n* (يَوْم) السَبْتِ; ▸**Wednesday**

Saturn /ˈsat(ə)n/ *pr n* زُحَل (dipt)

sauce /sɔːs/ *n* صَلْصة

saucepan /ˈsɔːsp(ə)n/ *n* قِدْر (قُدور), طَنْجَرة (طَناجِرُ)

saucer /ˈsɔːsə/ *n* صَحْن فِنْجانٍ

saucy /ˈsɔːsi/ *adj* (**saucier**, **sauciest**) ‹*postcard, underwear*› [ذو إيحاءٍ جِنْسيٍّ]

Saudi /ˈsaʊdi/ *n, adj* سَعوديّ

Saudi Arabia *pr n* (المَمْلَكة العَرَبيّة) السَعوديّة

Saudi Arabian *n, adj* ▸**Saudi**

sauna /ˈsɔːnə, ˈsaʊnə/ *n* ساوْنا

saunter /ˈsɔːntə/ *vi* «pedestrians» تَمَشّى

sausage /ˈsɒsɪdʒ/ *n* سُجُقّ

sausage dog *n* (infml) ▸**dachshund**

sausage roll *n* لَفّة سُجُقّ

sauté /ˈsəʊteɪ/ **A** *adj* (also **sautéd** or **sautéed**) مَقْليّ (قَلْياً خفيفاً) **B** *vt* (*present participle* **sautéing**; *past tense, past participle* **sautéd** or **sautéed**) ‹*mushrooms, onions*› قَلى (قَلْياً خفيفاً)

savage /ˈsavɪdʒ/ **A** *adj* **1** (vicious) ‹*attack, criticism*› وَحْشيّ, شَرِس **2** (old use) (uncivilized) ‹*tribe, race*› مُتَوَحِّش

B *n* مُتَوَحِّش

C *vt* **1** ‹*the sheep, child*› هاجَمَ بِوَحْشيّةٍ \ بِشَراسةٍ **2** (verbally) ‹*a show, an opponent*› انْتَقَدَ بِشَراسةٍ

savagely /ˈsavɪdʒli/ *adv* ‹*to beat, attack*› بِشَكْلٍ وَحْشيٍّ

savagery /ˈsavɪdʒ(ə)ri/ *n* (fml) هَمَجيّة, وَحْشيّة

save /seɪv/ **A** *vt* **1** (to rescue) ‹*people, jobs*› أَنْقَذَ; **to ~ sb's life** أَنْقَذَ حَياةَ شَخْصٍ; **she ~d him from drowning** أَنْقَذَتْهُ من الغَرَقِ; **she is the one person who can ~ him from himself** هي الشَخْصُ الّذي يَسْتَطيعُ أنْ يَحْمِيَهُ من نَفْسِهِ; **to ~ the day** *or* **the situation** أَنْقَذَ المَوْقِف **2** (for future use) ‹*money, food*› ادَّخَرَ; **to ~ money for one's retirement** ادَّخَرَ الأَمْوالَ لِتَقاعُدِهِ; **will you ~ a place for me?** هل سَتَحْجِزُ لي مَكاناً؟ **3** (to be economical with) ‹*time, money, energy*› وَفَّرَ; **to ~ time by booking on line** وَفَّرَ الوَقْتَ من خِلالِ الحَجْزِ عَبْرَ الإِنْتَرْنَت; **I ~d myself $40** وَفَّرْتُ على نَفْسي $40; **to ~ one's energy/ voice** =preserve it by not using it حافَظَ على طاقَتِهِ \ صَوْتِهِ

4 (to avoid) ‹*trouble, expense*› تَجَنَّبَ; **I could have ~ myself the trouble** كُنْتُ أَسْتَطيعُ أنْ أَتَجَنَّبَ المَشاكِلَ; **if I get it, you can ~ the bus fare** إذا تَحَصَّلْتُ عَلَيْهِ فَسَيَكونُ بِإِمْكانِكَ أنْ تُوَفِّرَ ثَمَنَ تَذْكِرةِ الحافِلةِ **5** (in sport) تَصَدّى (ل) ‹*a penalty, shot*› **6** (in computing) حَفِظَ (a; حِفْظ) ‹*a file, one's work*› **7** خَلَّصَ ‹*a sinner, soul*›

B *vi* **1** (to put money aside) ادَّخَرَ; **to save to buy a house** ادَّخَرَ لِشراءِ بَيْتٍ; **to save for one's retirement** ادَّخَرَ لِتَقاعُدِهِ **2** (to avoid expense) اقْتَصَدَ, وَفَّرَ; **to ~ on transport costs/ fuel bills** اقْتَصَدَ في تَكاليفِ التَنَقُّلِ \ فَواتيرِ الوَقودِ

C *n* (in sport) [إنْقاذ المَرْمى]

Phrasal verb **save up** **A** ادَّخَرَ; **to ~ up for sth/to do sth** ادَّخَرَ لِشَيْءٍ \ لِفِعْلِ شَيْءٍ **B** **~ up** [sth], **~** [sth] **up** ادَّخَرَ [شَيْئاً] ‹*money, tokens*›

saver /ˈseɪvə/ *n* مُدَّخِر

saving /ˈseɪvɪŋ/ **A** *n* **1** (in time) تَوْفير; (expenses) اقْتِصاد; **to make ~s on expenditure** اقْتَصَدَ في الإِنْفاقِ **2** [u] (of money) ادِّخار

B (**savings**) *n pl* مُدَّخَرات

saving grace *n* فَضيلة وَحيدة; **his humour is his saving grace** روحُ الفُكاهةِ لَدَيْهِ هي فَضيلَتُهُ الوَحيدةُ

savings account *n* حِساب ادِّخارٍ

savings and loan, **savings and loan association** *n* (AmE) جَمْعيّة بِناءٍ (تَقومُ بِتَقْديمِ فَوائِدَ على المُدَّخَراتِ وقُروضٍ)

savings bank *n* بَنْك ادِّخارٍ

saviour (BrE), **savior** (AmE) /ˈseɪvjə/ *n* **1** (rescuer) مُنْقِذ, المُخَلِّص \ مُخَلِّصنا **2** (in Christianity) **the/our S~** مُخَلِّص

savour (BrE), **savor** (AmE) /ˈseɪvə/ **A** *vt* **1** (to relish) تَلَذَّذَ (ب) ‹*food, drink*› **2** (to enjoy) اسْتَمْتَعَ (ب) ‹*a moment, victory*›

B *n* نَكْهة; **to lose its ~** فَقَدَ نَكْهَتَهُ

savoury (BrE), **savory** (AmE) /ˈseɪv(ə)ri/ *adj* **1** (not sweet) ‹*dish, snack*› مُتَبَّل **2** (appetizing) ‹*smell, taste*› شَهِيّ **3** (of character) ‹*character, aspect*› [مَقْبول أَخْلاقيًّا]; **he's not a very ~ character** هو شَخْصِيَّةٌ لَيْسَتْ مَقْبولةً جِدًّا أَخْلاقيًّا

savvy /ˈsavi/ (infml) *adj* (**savvier, savviest**) ‹*investor, consumer*› حاذِق, عارِف (حُذّاق)

saw /sɔː/ **A** *past tense* ▸ **see**

B *n* مِنْشار (مَناشيرُ)

C *vt* (*past tense* **sawed**; *past participle* **sawn** and **sawed** AmE) ‹*a plank, logs*› قَصَّ بالمِنْشارِ, نَشَرَ (u; نَشْر); **to ~ through a plank/cable** قَصَّ لَوْحاً خَشَبيًّا \ سِلْكاً بالمِنْشارِ

sawdust /ˈsɔːdʌst/ *n* نُشارة

sawed-off /sɔːdˈɒf/ *adj* (AmE) ▸ **sawn-off**

sawm /saʊm/ *n* صَوْم

sawn /sɔːn/ *past participle* ▸ **saw**

sawn-off /sɔːnˈɒf/ *adj* (BrE) ‹*gun, shotgun*› ذو فوَّهةٍ مَقْصوصةٍ

sawn-off shotgun (BrE), **sawed-off shotgun** (AmE) *n* [بُنْدُقيّة ذات فوَّهةٍ مَقْصوصةٍ]

saxophone /ˈsaksəfəʊn/ *n* ساكْسوفون, ساكْس

saxophonist /sakˈsɒf(ə)nɪst/ *n* عازِف ساكْسوفون \ ساكْس

say /seɪ/ **A** *vt* (*past tense, past participle* **said**) **1** «person» قالَ (u; قَوْل) ‹*the words, a prayer*›; **what did he ~ to you?** ماذا قالَ لَكَ؟; **to ~ hello/goodbye to sb** قالَ مَرْحَباً \ مع السَلامة لِشَخْصٍ; **I'm sure she'll ~ yes/no** أنا مُتَأَكِّدٌ أنّها سَتَقولُ نَعَمْ \ لا; **she didn't ~ a word** لَمْ تَقُلْ كَلِمةً; **that's a stupid thing to ~** مِن الغَباءِ قَوْلُ ذلك; **she ~s he's ill** تَقولُ إنَّهُ مَريضٌ; **I don't care what anyone ~s** لا أَهْتَمُّ بِما يَقولُ أَيُّ شَخْصٍ; **if you ~ so** إذا أَرَدْتَ; **it looks pretty good, if** *or* **though I do ~ so myself!** يَبْدو رائعاً إذا جازَ لي القَوْلُ; **I wouldn't ~ no to an ice cream** (infml) لا أَسْتَطيعُ أَنْ أَقولَ لا لِشَيْءٍ من البوظةِ; **you said it!** (infml) أُوافِقُكَ القَوْلَ \ الرَأْيَ; **you can ~ that again!** (infml) أَتَّفِقُ مَعَكَ تَماماً!; **~ no more** (infml) لا حاجةَ لِقَوْلِ المَزيدِ; **I'm disappointed, I must ~, I must ~, I'm disappointed** لا أَسْتَطيعُ أن أَقولَ إلاّ أنّي أَشْعُرُ بِخَيْبةِ أَمَلٍ; **what have you got to ~ for yourself?** ماذا سَتَقولُ لِنَفْسِكَ؟ **2** «report, sign» قالَ (u; قَوْل); **it ~s in the paper/on the label that ...** تَقولُ الجَريدةُ \ العَلامةُ إنّ ... **3** «clock, dial» أَشارَ (إلى); **my watch ~s two o'clock** تُشيرُ ساعَتي إلى الثانِيةِ **4** (to be significant to) «music, art» عَنى (i; عَنْي); **this music ~s nothing to me** لا تَعْني لي الموسيقى شَيْئاً **5** (to assert, allege) زَعَمَ (u; زَعْم); **they ~ he's quite poor** يَزْعَمونَ أَنَّهُ فِعْلاً فَقيرٌ; **she is said to be very rich** يُقالُ إنَّها غَنيَّةٌ جِدًّا; **the story is true, or so they ~** القِصّةُ حَقيقيَّةٌ، أو هذا ما يَزْعَمونَ **6** (to decide) قَرَّرَ; **that's for the committee to ~** ذلك القَرارُ يَعودُ لِلَّجْنةِ; **it's not for me to ~** لَيْسَ من شَأْني أنْ أُقَرِّرَ **7** (to estimate) خَمَّنَ; **how high would you ~ it is?** ما ارْتِفاعُهُ في رَأْيِك؟; **I'd ~ she's about twenty-five** أُخَمِّنُ أنَّها تَبْلُغُ خَمْساً وَعِشْرينَ سَنةً **8** (to assume) **let's ~ that we win ...** لِنَقُلْ إنَّنا انْتَصَرْنا ...; **~ you have an accident** افْتَرِضْ أنَّكَ تَعَرَّضْتَ لِحادِثٍ; **you'll need, ~, £50 for petrol** سَتَحْتاجُ، رُبَّما، إلى £50 لِلبِنْزينِ

B *vi* (*past tense, past participle* **said**) قالَ (u; قَوْل); **stop when I ~** قِفْ عِنْدَما أَطْلُبُ مِنْكَ ذلك; **I'd rather not ~** من الأَحْرى ألّا أَقولَ; **as you ~, we have to be realistic** كَما تَقولُ، يَجِبُ أن نَكونَ واقِعيّينَ; **you don't ~!** (infml) حَقًّا!; **~s who?, who ~s?** (infml) مَنْ قالَ؟

C *excl* (AmE) [تُقالُ للتَعَجُّبِ وَلَفْتِ الانْتِباهِ]; **~, don't I know you?** أَظُنُّ أَنّي أَعْرِفُكَ، أَلَيْسَ كَذلِكَ؟

D *n* **to have one's ~** قالَ كَلِمَتَهُ, أَعْطى رَأْيَهُ; **he has the final ~ on it** لَهُ الكَلِمةُ الأَخيرةُ فيهِ

Idioms **it/that goes without saying** غَنِيٌّ عن القَوْلِ; **that says it all** ذلك يُلَخِّصُ كُلَّ شَيْءٍ; **when all is said and done** إذا ما أَخَذْنا كُلَّ شَيْءٍ بِعَيْنِ الاعْتِبارِ

saying /ˈseɪɪŋ/ *n* قَوْل (أَقْوال)

sayyid, sayid /ˈseɪjɪd, ˈsʌɪɪd/ *n* سَيِّد (سادة)

SC *abbr* = **South Carolina**

scab /skab/ *n* **1** (over wound) قِشْرة (قِشَر) **2** (pej) (strike-breaker) [مَنْ يُواصِلُ العَمَلَ أثناءَ إضْرابٍ]

scabies /ˈskeɪbiːz/ *n* جَرَب

scaffold /ˈskafəʊld/ *n* ① (for building) سِقالة (سَقائِلُ) ② (for execution) مِنَصّة إعْدامٍ

scaffolder /ˈskafəʊldə/ *n* عامِل سِقالاتٍ

scaffolding /ˈskafəldɪŋ/ *n* سِقالة (سَقائِلُ)

scald /skɔːld/ *vt* أَحْرَقَ ‹*one's skin, tongue*›

scalding /ˈskɔːldɪŋ/ *adj* ‹*water, coffee*› ساخِن \ حارّ جِدًّا

scale /skeɪl/ **A** *n* ① [u] (of a problem, disaster, challenge, change, task) حَجْم ,مَدًى (أَحْجام); **on a large/small ~** على نِطاقٍ واسِعٍ \ ضَيِّقٍ; **we have never had unemployment on this ~** لم تَكُنْ عِنْدَنا بِطالةٌ بِهَذا الحَجْمِ أَبَداً; **the company is expanding its ~ of operations** تَقومُ الشَرِكةُ بِتَوْسيعِ نِطاقِ عَمَليّاتِها ② (grading system) مِقْياس (مَقاييسُ); **a pay/salary ~** سُلَّم أُجورٍ \ رَواتِبَ; **on a ~ of 1 to 10** على مِقْياسٍ يَتَراوَحُ من 1 إلى 10 ③ (for maps, models) مِقْياس (مَقاييسُ), سُلَّم (سَلالِمُ); **on a ~ of 2 km to 1 cm** على مِقْياسِ 2 كم لِكُلِّ 1 سم; **the plan is not to ~** التَخْطيطُ لَيْسَ دَقيقاً ④ (on gauges) مِقْياس \ سُلَّم (سَلالِمُ), مِقْياس (مَقاييسُ); **the Richter ~** سُلَّم ريخْتِر ⑤ (for weighing) ▸B ⑥ (in music) سُلَّم موسيقيّ ⑦ (on fish, insects) قِشْرة (قُشور), قِشْرة (قِشْر) ⑧ [u] (in pipes) قِشْرة ⑨ [u] (on teeth) كِلْس

B (**scales**) *n pl* ميزان (مَوازينُ); **bathroom/kitchen ~s** ميزان حَمّام \ مَطْبَخ

C *vt* ① (to climb) تَسَلَّقَ ‹*a wall, peak*› ② (in food preparation) قَشَّرَ ‹*a fish*›

(Phrasal verbs) **scale back, scale down**: **~ [sth] down, ~ down [sth]** قَلَّصَ \ خَفَّضَ [شَيْئاً] ‹*plans, operations*›

• **scale up**: **~ [sth] up, ~ up [sth]** وَسَّعَ [شَيْئاً] ‹*production, operations*›

scale drawing *n* مِقْياس رَسْم

scale model *n* نموذَج مُصَغَّر

scallion /ˈskalɪən/ *n* (AmE) بَصَل أَخْضَر \ رَبيعي

scallop, scollop /ˈskɒləp/ *n* مَحار مِرْوَحيّ, إِسْقَلوب

scalp /skalp/ **A** *n* ① (on top of head) جِلْد \ فَرْوة الرَأْسِ ② (as a trophy) [جُزْء من فَرْوةِ رَأْسِ العَدوِّ يَنْتَزِعُهُ الهُنودُ الحُمْرُ كَعَلامةٍ على النَصْرِ]

B *vt* [سَلَخَ فَرْوةَ الرَأْسِ] ‹*an enemy*›

scalpel /ˈskalp(ə)l/ *n* مِشْرَط (مَشارِطُ), مِبْضَع (مَباضِعُ)

scaly /ˈskeɪli/ *adj* (**scalier, scaliest**) ① (covered in scales) ‹*fish, lizard*› حَرْشَفيّ ② (flaking) ‹*skin, rash*› قِشْريّ

scam /skam/ *n* (infml) احْتِيال (احْتِيالات), نَصْب

scamper /ˈskampə/ *vi* «children, puppy» نَطَّ (u; نَطّ), وَثَبَ (i; وَثْب)

scampi /ˈskampi/ *n pl* [أُكْلة جَرادِ البَحْرِ]

scan /skan/ **A** *vt* (**-nn-**) ① (to read quickly) أَلْقَى نَظْرةً سَريعةً (على) ‹*a page, newspaper*› ② (to scrutinize) تَفَحَّصَ ‹*the horizon, faces*› ③ (electronically) مَسَحَ (a; مَسْح) ‹*space, the airwaves*›; **to ~ a barcode** مَسَحَ \ قَرَأَ بارْكود ④ (Med) قامَ بِمَسْحٍ ضَوْئيٍّ ل ‹*an organ, a patient*› ⑤ (Comput) قامَ بِمَسْحٍ ضَوْئيٍّ ل ‹*a document, an image*›

B *n* ① (examination) مَسْح ضَوْئيّ; **to have a brain ~** أُجْرِيَ لَهُ مَسْحٌ ضَوْئيٌّ على المُخِّ ② (image) صورة بالأَشِعّةِ

scandal /ˈskand(ə)l/ *n* ① (in public life) فَضيحة (فَضائِحُ); **the ~ over award of contracts** فَضيحة على خَلْفيّةِ مَنْحِ عُقودٍ; **the amount of compensation is a ~** مَبْلَغُ التَعْويضِ فَضيحةٌ ② [u] (gossip) فَضيحة (فَضائِحُ)

scandalize, -ise (BrE) /ˈskandəlaɪz/ *vt* صَدَمَ (بِعَمَلٍ غَيْرِ أَخْلاقيٍّ) ‹*the nation, the neighbours*›

scandalous /ˈskandələs/ *adj* ① (disgraceful) ‹*waste, failure*› فاضِح ,مَعيب ② (immoral) ‹*behaviour, affair*› مُخْزٍ, شائِن

Scandinavia /ˌskandɪˈneɪvɪə/ *pr n* اسْكَنْدينافيا

Scandinavian /skandɪˈneɪvɪən/ *n, adj* اسْكَنْدينافيّ

scanner /ˈskanə/ *n* ① (for diagnoses) مِفْراس, ماسِح ضَوْئيّ (Iraq) ② (for security) ماسِح ضَوْئيّ ③ (for barcodes) قارِئ ماسِح ضَوْئيّ البارْكود ④ (for documents) ماسِح ضَوْئيّ

scanning /ˈskanɪŋ/ *n* مَسْح ضَوْئيّ

scant /skant/ *adj before n* ‹*attention, supply*› ضَئيل (ضِئال)

scanty /ˈskanti/ *adj* (**scantier, scantiest**) ① ‹*evidence, supply*› ضَعيف (ضُعَفاءُ) ② (skimpy) ‹*swimsuit, costume*› كاشِف (كَشَفة), فاضِح

scapegoat /ˈskeɪpgəʊt/ *n* كَبْش فِداءٍ

scar /skɑː/ **A** *n* **1** (on the skin) نَدْبة (نُدوب) **2** (emotional) نَدْبة (نُدوب)

B *vt* (-rr-) **1** (to mark) تَرَكَ نُدوباً على *<one's face, skin>*
2 (to traumatize) تَرَكَ نُدوباً على *<one's mind, childhood>*

scarab /'skarəb/ *n* **1** (also **scarab beetle**) جُعَل (جِعْلان), جُعْران **2** (amulet) تميمة (في شَكْلِ جُعَلٍ)

scarce /skɛːs/ *adj* *<resource, book>* نادِر; **I made myself ~** اخْتَفَيْتُ عن الأَنْظارِ

scarcely /'skɛːsli/ *adv* *<remember, believe>* بالكادِ, نادِراً; **~ anybody will believe you** بالكادِ سَتَجِدُ مَنْ يُصَدِّقُكَ

scarcity /'skɛːsɪti/ *n* (*pl* **scarcities**) نُدْرة

scare /skɛː/ **A** *vt* أَخافَ, أَفْزَعَ *<a child, horse>*

B *n* **1** (fright) رُعْب, فَزَع **2** (alert) ذُعْر; **there was a bomb ~ at the bus station** كانَ هُناكَ ذُعْرٌ من وُجودِ قُنْبُلةٍ في مَحَطّةِ الحافِلاتِ

Phrasal verb **scare away, scare off**: **~ away [sth/sb], ~ [sth/sb] away** أَخافَ [شَيْئاً \ شَخْصاً] *<investors, an animal>*

scarecrow /'skɛːkrəʊ/ *n* فَزّاعة (فَزازيعُ)

scared /skɛːd/ *adj* *<child, animal>* خائِف; **to be ~ of sb/snakes** كانَ خائِفاً من شَخْصٍ \ الثَعابينِ

scaremongering /'skɛːmʌŋgərɪŋ/ *n* إثارة الذُعْرِ

scarf /skɑːf/ *n* (*pl* **scarves**) وِشاح (أَوْشِحة, وَشائِحُ)

scarlet /'skɑːlɪt/ *adj, n* قِرْمِزيّ

scarlet fever *n* حُمّى قِرْمِزيّة

scarlet woman *n* داعِرة

scarves /skɑːvz/ *n pl* ▸ **scarf**

scary /'skɛːri/ *adj* (**scarier, scariest**) (infml) *<story, thought>* مُخيف

scathing /'skeɪðɪŋ/ *adj* *<attack, look>* لاذِع (لَوَاذِعُ)

scatter /'skatə/ **A** *vt* **1** (also **scatter around**) (to strew) بَعْثَرَ (i; بَعْثَرة) *<books, clothes>* **2** (to throw) بَذَرَ (u; بَذْر) *<seeds>*; نَثَرَ (i-u; نَثْر, نِثار) *<salt>* **3** (to disperse) فَرَّقَ *<a crowd, herd>*

B *vi* «the crowd, birds» تَفَرَّقَ

scatterbrained /'skatəbreɪnd/ *adj* (infml) *<assistant>* مُشَتَّت الذِهْنِ; (infml) *<idea>* مُشَوَّش

scattered /'skatəd/ *adj before n* *<population, trees>* مُتَفَرِّق, مُتَناثِر; **~ showers** أَمْطار مُتَفَرِّقة

scatty /'skati/ *adj* (**scattier, scattiest**) (BrE) (infml) *<behaviour>* طائِش; *<woman>* شارِد الذِهْنِ

scavenge /'skavɪndʒ/ *vi* «birds, animals» نَبَشَ النُفاياتِ; **to ~ for food/scrap metal** نَبَشَ النُفاياتِ بَحْثاً عن الطَعامِ \ خُرْدةِ المَعادِنِ

scavenger /'skavɪndʒə/ *n* **1** (bird, animal) آكِل الجيفة **2** (person) نابِش النُفاياتِ

scenario /sɪ'nɑːrɪəʊ/ *n* (*pl* **scenarios**) **1** (situation) سيناريو (سيناريُوات); **in the best-case/worst-case ~** في أَفْضَلِ \ أَسْوَأِ الأَحْوالِ **2** (of films, plays) سيناريو (سيناريُوات)

scene /siːn/ *n* **1** (location) مَكان (أَماكِنُ, أَمْكِنة); **the ~ of the crime/accident** مَكان الجَريمةِ \ الحادِثِ; **the opening paragraph sets the ~** تُهَيِّئُ الفَقْرةُ الافْتِتاحيّةُ المَشْهَدَ; **the ~ was set for a major confrontation** تَمَّتْ تَهْيِئةُ الجَوِّ لِمُواجَهةٍ كَبيرةٍ; **to arrive** *or* **come on the ~** وَصَلَ إلى مَسْرَحِ العَمَليّةِ; **you need a change of ~** تَحْتاجُ إلى تَغْييرِ الجَوِّ **2** (in plays films, etc) مَشْهَد (مَشاهِدُ), مَنْظَر (مَناظِرُ) **3** (stage scenery) كَواليس; **behind the ~s** وراء الكَواليسِ **4** (image, sight) مَشْهَد (مَشاهِدُ), مَنْظَر (مَناظِرُ); **the film contains ~s of violence** يَحْتَوي الفيلْمُ على مَشاهِدَ عُنْفٍ **5** (emotional incident) ضَجّة; **to make a ~** أَحْدَثَ ضَجّةً على المَلأِ **6** (sphere, field) مَشْهَد (مَشاهِدُ); **the music/political ~** المَشْهَد الموسيقيّ \ السِياسيّ; **it's not my ~** (infml) لَيْسَ من هِواياتي **7** (landscape) مَشْهَد (مَشاهِدُ), مَنْظَر (مَناظِرُ)

scenery /'siːn(ə)ri/ *n* **1** (landscape) مَناظِر طَبيعيّة **2** (on a set) خَلْفيّة

scenic /'siːnɪk/ *adj* *<route, location>* ذو مَناظِرَ طَبيعيّةٍ خَلّابةٍ

scent /sent/ **A** *n* **1** (smell) رائِحة (رَوائِحُ) **2** (perfume) عِطْر (عُطور, عُطورات) **3** (trail) أَثَر (آثار); **to throw sb off the ~** ضَلَّلَ \ خَدَعَ شَخْصاً

B *vt* **1** (to smell) شَمَّ (a-u; شَمّ; perf شَمِمْتُ, شَمَمْتُ), اشْتَمَّ *<blood, a prey>* **2** (to perfume) عَطَّرَ *<the air, a room>* **3** (to sense) اسْتَشْعَرَ *<danger, victory>*

scepter (AmE) *n* ▸ **sceptre**

sceptic (BrE), **skeptic** (AmE) /ˈskɛptɪk/ *n* شُكوكيّ

sceptical (BrE), **skeptical** (AmE) /ˈskɛptɪk(ə)l/ *adj* ‹*remark, look*› مُرْتاب

scepticism (BrE), **skepticism** (AmE) /ˈskɛptɪsɪz(ə)m/ *n* (شُكوك) شَكّ ,ارْتِياب

sceptre (BrE), **scepter** (AmE) /ˈsɛptə/ *n* (صَوْلَجانات) صَوْلَجان

schedule /ˈʃɛdjuːl/ **A** *n* **1** (programme, plan) (جَداوِلُ) جَدْوَل; **a ~ of events** جَدْوَل أَحْداثٍ; **we're running behind ~** نُحْنُ مُتَخَلِّفونَ عن الجَدْوَلِ الزَمَنيِّ; **to work to a tight ~** عَمِلَ تحت الضَغْطِ; **the flight departed on/behind ~** انْطَلَقَت الرِحْلةُ في مَوْعِدِها \ مُتَأَخِّرةً عن مَوْعِدِها; **work was completed on ~/two months ahead of ~** انْتَهى العَمَلُ في مَوْعِدِهِ \ قبل مَوْعِدِهِ بِشَهْرَيْنِ; **according to ~** وِفْقاً للجَدْوَلِ **2** (of appointments) (جَداوِلُ) جَدْوَل, (بَرامِجُ) بَرْنامَج; **he has a busy ~** عِنْدَهُ جَدْوَلٌ مُزْدَحِمٌ **3** (of TV, radio programmes) (بَرامِجُ) بَرْنامَج **4** (AmE) (of services) (جَداوِلُ) جَدْوَل, (بَرامِجُ) بَرْنامَج **5** (list of charges) (لَوائِحُ, لائِحات) لائِحة, (قَوائِمُ) قائِمة; (of payments, costs) (جَداوِلُ) جَدْوَل **6** (to a contract, will) (مُلْحَقات, مَلاحِقُ) مُلْحَق

B *vt* حَدَّدَ المَوْعِدَ ‹*a meeting, an election*›; **the plane is ~d to arrive at 2.00 p.m.** من المُقَرَّرِ أن تَصِلَ الطائِرةُ الساعةَ الثانِيةَ بعد الظُهْرِ; **the next Games are ~d for 2016** من المُقَرَّرِ أنْ تَكونَ الدَوْرةُ القادِمةُ للأَلْعابِ في سَنةِ 2016; **the station is ~d for completion in 2013** من المُقَرَّرِ أنْ تَنْتَهِيَ الأَشْغالُ في المَحَطّةِ سَنةَ 2013

scheduled flight *n* رِحْلة مُبَرْمَجة \ مُقَرَّرة

scheduling /ˈʃɛdjuːlɪŋ/ *n* **1** (of a project, work) جَدْوَلة **2** (for radio, TV) بَرْمَجة

scheme /skiːm/ **A** *n* **1** (plan) (خِطَط, خُطَط) خُطّة **2** (plot) مُؤامَرة

B *vi* «plotters, criminals» تآمَرَ

(Idiom) **in the scheme of things** إذا أَخَذْنا كُلَّ شَيْءٍ بِعَيْنِ الاعْتِبارِ

scheming /ˈskiːmɪŋ/ **A** *adj before n* ‹*liar, vixen*› ماكِر, مُخادِع (مَكَرة)

B *n* مَكْر, خِداع, تَآمُر

schism /ˈsɪz(ə)m/ *n* (صُدوع) صَدْع, (انْقِسامات) انْقِسام

schistosomiasis /ˌʃɪstəʊsəˈmʌɪəsɪs/ *n* داء المُنْشَقّاتِ, بِلْهارْسِيا

schizophrenia /ˌskɪtsəʊˈfriːnɪə/ *n* فُصام, انْفِصام الشَخْصيّةِ

schizophrenic /skɪtsəˈfrɛnɪk/ *n, adj* فُصاميّ

schmaltz, **schmalz** /ʃmɔːlts/ *n* (infml) [عاطِفيّة مُبالَغ فيها]

schmaltzy, **schmalzy** /ˈʃmɔːltsi/ *adj* (infml) ‹*lovesong, ending*› [عاطِفيّ جِدًّا]

scholar /ˈskɒlə/ *n* **1** (learned person) (عُلَماءُ) عالِم **2** (scholarship holder) [طالِب حائِز على مِنْحةٍ دِراسيّةٍ]

scholarly /ˈskɒləli/ *adj* **1** ‹*work, journal*› عِلْميّ **2** (erudite) ‹*community, writer*› واسِع المَعْرِفةِ

scholarship /ˈskɒləʃɪp/ *n* **1** (grant) مِنْحة دِراسيّة **2** [u] (learning) تَحْصيل عِلْميّ

school /skuːl/ **A** *n* **1** (for primary and secondary education) (مَدارِسُ) مَدْرَسة; **to go to ~** ذَهَبَ إلى المَدْرَسةِ; **Jack is still at ~** ما زالَ جاك في المَدْرَسةِ; **he left ~ at 16** غادَرَ المَدْرَسةَ الثانَويّةَ في سِنِّ السادِسةِ عَشْرةَ; **there's no ~ today** المَدْرَسةُ مُغْلَقةٌ اليَوْمَ **2** (of music, art, etc) مَدْرَسة (مَدارِسُ), كُلّيّة **3** (university department) (مَدارِسُ) مَدْرَسة, (أَقْسام) قِسْم; **she is applying to law/medical ~** قَدَّمَتْ طَلَباً للالْتِحاقِ بِكُلّيّةِ الحُقوقِ \ الطِبِّ **4** (AmE) (university, college) جامِعة **5** (of painting, literature, thought) (مَدارِسُ) مَدْرَسة; **there are two ~s of thought on this** هُناكَ مَدْرَسَتانِ فِكْريَّتانِ في هذا المَوْضوعِ **6** (of fish, whales, etc) (أَسْراب) سِرْب, (قُطْعان) قَطيع

B *vt* (fml) (to train) **to ~ sb in sth** دَرَّبَ شَخْصاً على شَيْءٍ

school age *n* سِنّ الدِراسةِ

schoolbag /ˈskuːlbag/ *n* (مَحافِظُ, مَحْفَظات) مَحْفَظة, حَقيبة مَدْرَسيّة

school board *n* (AmE) مَجْلِس الآباءِ والمُعَلِّمينَ

schoolboy /ˈskuːlbɔɪ/ *n* (تَلامِذة, تَلاميذُ) تِلْميذ

schoolchild /ˈskuːltʃʌɪld/ *n* (*pl* **-children** /-ˈtʃɪldrən/) تِلْميذ (تَلامِذة, تَلاميذُ)

school friend *n* صَديق مَدْرَسةٍ

schoolgirl /ˈskuːlɡəːl/ *n* تِلْميذة

school holidays *n* عُطْلة مَدْرَسيّة

schooling /ˈskuːlɪŋ/ *n* تَعْليم

school-leaver /ˈskuːlliːvə/ *n* (BrE) [مَنْ أَنْهى الدِراسةَ الثانويّةَ حَديثاً]

school-leaving age /ˌskuːlˈliːvɪŋ ˌeɪdʒ/ *n* سِنّ تَرْكِ المَدْرَسةِ

schoolmaster /ˈskuːlmɑːstə/ *n* (primary) مُعَلِّم; (secondary) أُسْتاذ (أَساتِذة)

schoolmate /ˈskuːlmeɪt/ *n* زَميل مَدْرَسةٍ

school meal *n* وَجْبة مَدْرَسيّة

schoolmistress /ˈskuːlmɪstrɪs/ *n* (primary) مُعَلِّمة; (secondary) أُسْتاذة

schoolroom /ˈskuːlruːm/ *n* صَفّ, قاعة دَرْس, قِسْم (أَقْسام) (NA)

schoolteacher /ˈskuːltiːtʃə/ *n* (primary) مُعَلِّم; (secondary) أُسْتاذ (أَساتِذة)

school uniform *n* لِباس \ زيّ مَدْرَسيّ

schoolwork /ˈskuːlwəːk/ *n* واجِبات مَدْرَسيّة

school year *n* سَنة دِراسيّة

sciatic /sʌɪˈatɪk/ *adj* ‹*nerve, pain*› وِرْكيّ

sciatica /sʌɪˈatɪkə/ *n* أَلَم عِرْقِ النَسا, أَلَم العَصَبِ الوِرْكيّ

science /ˈsʌɪəns/ *n* عِلْم (عُلوم); **to teach/study ~** دَرَّسَ \ دَرَسَ العُلومَ; **he studies earth ~s** يَدْرُسُ عُلومَ الأَرْضِ

science fiction *n* الخَيال العِلْميّ

scientific /sʌɪənˈtɪfɪk/ *adj* ‹*research, community*› عِلْميّ

scientifically /sʌɪənˈtɪfɪkli/ *adv* ‹*proven, trained*› عِلْميًّا

scientist /ˈsʌɪəntɪst/ *n* عالِم (عُلَماءُ)

sci-fi /ˈsʌɪfʌɪ/ *n* (infml) الخَيال العِلْميّ

sci-fi film, sci-fi movie *n* فيلْم خَيالٍ عِلْميٍّ

Scilly Isles /ˈsɪli ʌɪlz/, **Scillies** /ˈsɪliz/ *pr n* (**the Scilly Isles**) جُزُر سيلي

scintillating /ˈsɪntɪleɪtɪŋ/ *adj* ‹*performance, conversation*› مُتَأَلِّق

scissors /ˈsɪzəz/ *n pl* مِقَصّ (مَقاصُّ); **a pair of ~** مِقَصّ (مَقاصُّ)

sclerosis /sklɪəˈrəʊsɪs/ *n* (*pl* **scleroses** /-siːz/) تَصَلُّب

sclerotic /sklɪəˈrɒtɪk/ *adj* ‹*lesion, tissue*› مُتَصَلِّب

scoff /skɒf/ **A** *vt* (BrE infml) اِلْتَهَمَ ‹*food*›

B *vi* «critics, skeptics» سَخِرَ, اِسْتَهْزَأَ (a; سُخْرِيّة); **she ~ed at the idea** اِسْتَهْزَأَتْ بالفِكْرةِ

scold /skəʊld/ *vt* عَنَّفَ, وَبَّخَ ‹*a child, servant*›

scone /skɒn, skəʊn/ *n* (BrE) [كَعْكة صَغيرة]

scoop /skuːp/ *n* **1** (utensil) مِغْرَفة (مَغارِفُ) **2** (portion of ice cream, mashed potato) مِغْرَفة (مَغارِفُ) **3** (in journalism) سَبْق صُحُفيّ

(Phrasal verbs) **scoop out**: **~ out [sth], ~ [sth] out** **1** غَرَفَ [شَيْئاً] ‹*the seeds, pulp*› **2** حَفَرَ [شَيْئاً] ‹*a hole, hollow*›

• **scoop up**: **~ [sth] up, ~ up [sth]** اِلْتَقَطَ [شَيْئاً] ‹*the earth*›; غَرَفَ [شَيْئاً] ‹*water*›

scooter /ˈskuːtə/ *n* سْكوتِر

scope /skəʊp/ *n* **1** (extent) مَجال (مَجالات) **2** (opportunity) مَجال (مَجالات)

scorch /skɔːtʃ/ *vt* **1** أَحْرَقَ (حَرْقاً سَطْحيًّا) ‹*fabric, skin*› **2** جَفَّفَ ‹*grass, the landscape*›

scorching /ˈskɔːtʃɪŋ/ *adj* ‹*sun, heat*› حارِق, لافِح; **it was a ~ hot day** كانَ يَوْماً شَديدَ الحَرِّ

score /skɔː/ **A** *n* **1** (in sports, games) نَتيجة (نَتائِجُ); **there is still no ~** ما زالَت النَتيجةُ سَلْبيّةً; **the final ~ was 3–1** كانَت النَتيجةُ النِهائيّةُ 3–1; **what's the ~?** كم \ ما هي النَتيجةُ؟ **2** (in exams, tests, quizzes) عَلامة (عَلامات) **3** (written music) قِطْعة موسيقيّة **4** (for films) موسيقى تَصْويريّة **5** (twenty) **a ~** عِشْرونَ; **~s of people/complaints** عَشَرات الأَشْخاصِ \ الشَكاوى **6** (reason) سَبَب (أَسْباب); **on this/that ~** بِناءً على هذا \ ذلك الأَساسِ

B *vt* **1** (to register) سَجَّلَ ‹*a goal, point*›; **who ~d the first goal?** مَنْ سَجَّلَ الهَدَفَ الأَوَّلَ؟; **you ~d 9 out of 10** سَجَّلْتَ 9 من 10; **each correct answer ~s five points** يَتَحَصَّلُ كُلُّ جوابٍ صَحيحٍ على خَمْسِ نِقاطٍ; **to ~ a hit** «missile, marksman» أَصابَ المَرْمى; «singer, film» حَقَّقَ \ أَحْرَزَ نَجاحاً **2** (infml) أَحْرَزَ ‹*a victory, success*› **3** (to orchestrate) أَلَّفَ ‹*a piece of music*› **4** (to compose music for) وَضَعَ \ أَلَّفَ موسيقى ‹*a film*› **5** خَدَشَ (خَدْش i;) ‹*the surface*›; (to cut into) قَطَعَ (قَطْع a;) ‹*wood*› **6** (infml) اِقْتَنى (بِشَكْلٍ غَيْرِ قانونيٍّ) ‹*heroin, crack*›

C *vi* **1** (to gain a point) «teams, players» سَجَّلَ; **she ~d well in the IQ test** تَحَصَّلَتْ على مَجْموعٍ عالٍ في اخْتِبارِ الذَكاءِ **2** (to keep a tally) سَجَّلَ النِقاطَ المُحْرَزة **3** (infml) (to be successful) «companies, products» لاقى نَجاحاً; **the movie ~d with the critics** لاقى الفيلْمُ نَجاحاً بين النُقّادِ; **this is where they ~ over all their rivals** هذا هو المَجالُ الّذي تَغَلَّبوا فيه على كُلِّ مُنافِسيهِمْ **4** (infml) (sexually) [مارَسَ الجِنْسَ بِشَكْلٍ عابِرٍ]

(Idioms) **to know the score** (infml) أَدْرَكَ حَقيقةَ المَوْقِفِ; **to settle a score** صَفّى حِساباتٍ

scoreboard /ˈskɔːbɔːd/ *n* لَوْحة نَتائِجَ

scorer /ˈskɔːrə/ *n* **1** (of goals, points) هَدّاف **2** (recorder) مُسَجِّل الإصاباتِ

scoring /ˈskɔːrɪŋ/ *n* **1** (of goals, points) تَهْديف, تَسْجيل; **to open the ~** أَحْرَزَ الهَدَفَ الأَوَّلَ **2** (of music) تَدْوين (موسيقيّ)

scorn /skɔːn/ **A** *n* احْتِقار, ازْدِراء; **to pour ~ on sth** ازْدَرى شَخْصاً

B *vt* احْتَقَرَ, ازْدَرى ‹*an idea, offer*›

scornful /ˈskɔːnfʊl/ *adj* ‹*tone, look*› مُحْتَقِر, مُزْدَرٍ; **to be ~ of sth/sb** احْتَقَرَ شَيْئاً \ شَخْصاً

Scorpio /ˈskɔːpɪəʊ/ *n* (*pl* **Scorpios**) **1** (sign) بُرْج العَقْرَبِ **2** (person) [من مَواليدِ بُرْجِ العَقْرَبِ]

scorpion /ˈskɔːpɪən/ *n* عَقْرَب (mf; عَقارِبُ)

Scot /skɒt/ *n* اسْكُتْلَنْديّ

scotch /skɒtʃ/ *vt* دَحَضَ (a; دَحْض, دُحوض), فَنَّدَ ‹*rumours, suggestions*›; أَحْبَطَ ‹*plans*›

Scotch /skɒtʃ/ *n* (also **scotch**) ويسْكي اسْكُتْلَنْديّ

Scotch egg *n* (BrE) بَيْض اسْكُتْلَنْديّ (طَبَق من البَيْضِ المَسْلوقِ المُغَطّى بِلَحْمِ السُجُقِّ وَفُتاتِ الخُبْزِ)

Scotch tape® *n* (AmE) شَريط لاصِق شَفّاف

Scotch whisky *n* (*pl* **Scotch whiskies**) ويسْكي اسْكُتْلَنْديّ

scot-free /skɒtˈfriː/ *adj* (infml) **to get off ~** نَجا من العِقابِ

Scotland /ˈskɒtlənd/ *pr n* اسْكُتْلَنْدا

Scots /skɒts/ *adj* ‹*law, parliament*› اسْكُتْلَنْديّ

Scotsman /ˈskɒtsmən/ *n* (*pl* **-men**) اسْكُتْلَنْديّ

Scotswoman /ˈskɒtswʊmən/ *n* (*pl* **-women** /-wɪmɪn/) اسْكُتْلَنْديّة

Scottish /ˈskɒtɪʃ/ *adj* ‹*city*› اسْكُتْلَنْديّ

scoundrel /ˈskaʊndrəl/ *n* وَغْد (أَوْغاد), نَذْل (أَنْذال)

scour /ˈskaʊə/ *vt* **1** (to scrub) حَكَّ (u; حَكّ), فَرَكَ (u; فَرْك) ‹*a sink, pan*› **2** (to search) مَشَّطَ ‹*an area*›; فَتَّشَ ‹*shops, the Internet*›

scourer /ˈskaʊərə/ *n* ليفة

scourge /skɜːdʒ/ *n* كارِثة (كَوارِثُ), بَلِيّة (بَلايا)

scouring powder /ˈskaʊərɪŋ ˌpaʊdə/ *n* مَسْحوق تَنْظيفٍ

scout /skaʊt/ *n* **1** (Mil) (person) كَشّاف (كَشّافة), وَحَداتٍ عُضْو الاسْتِطْلاعِ **2** (also **Scout**) (boy scout) كَشّاف (كَشّافة) **3** (AmE) (for sports players) كَشّاف مَواهِبَ

(Phrasal verb) **scout around**: **to ~ around for sth** بَحَثَ عن شَيْءٍ في كُلِّ مَكانٍ

scowl /skaʊl/ **A** *n* تَجَهُّم, عُبوس

B *vi* «person» تَجَهَّمَ, عَبَسَ (i; عُبوس); **to ~ at sb** عَبَسَ في وَجْهِ شَخْصٍ

scrabble /ˈskrab(ə)l/ *vi* «dogs, chickens» نَبَشَ (u; نَبْش); **she was scrabbling around for her keys** كانَتْ تُفَتِّشُ بِأَصابِعِها عن مَفاتيحِها

scraggy /ˈskragi/ *adj* (**scraggier, scraggiest**) **1** (scrawny) ‹*neck*› نَحيف (نُحَفاءُ, نِحاف), نَحيل (نُحَّل); ‹*bird, animal*› هَزيل (هَزْلى) **2** (ragged) ‹*beard, hair*› أَشْعَثُ (dipt; شُعْث)

scram /skram/ *vi* (infml) (**-mm-**) «animals, people» انْصَرَفَ مُسْرِعاً; **~!** انْصَرِفْ حالاً!

scramble /ˈskramb(ə)l/ **A** *vt* **1** **to ~ eggs** خَفَقَ (i-u; خَفْق, خفقان) **2** [أَعطى الأوامِرَ بالإقْلاعِ الفَوْريِّ] ‹*a squadron, helicopter*› **3** (in broadcasting) شَفَّرَ ‹*a signal, message*›

B *vi* **1** (to clamber) تَسَلَّقَ; **we ~d up the hillside** تَسلَّقنا مُنْحَدَرَ التَلِّ; **to ~ to one's feet** انْدَفَعَ مَذْعوراً واقِفاً على رِجْلَيْهِ **2** (to struggle, compete) تَدافَعَ; **to ~ for a seat** تَدافَعَ لِأَجْلِ الحُصولِ على كُرْسيٍّ **3** (to rush) انْدَفَعَ; **everyone ~d out of**

the way تَدافَعوا مُفْسِحينَ الطَريقَ

C *n* **1** (rush) تَدافُع; **there was a mad ~ to get on board** كانَ هُناكَ تَدافُعٌ مَسْعورٌ للصُعودِ إلى الطائِرةِ **2** (climb) تَسَلُّق

scrambled egg /ˌskrambəld ˈɛg/ *n* (also **scrambled eggs**) بَيْض مَخْفوق مَقْليّ

scrambling /ˈskramblɪŋ/ *n* **1** (motor racing) [سِباق دَرّاجاتٍ ناريّةٍ في طَريقٍ وَعْرٍ] **2** (rock climbing) [تَسَلُّق الصُخورِ]

scrap /skrap/ **A** *n* **1** (of cloth) قِطْعة (قِطَع); (of paper) قُصاصة; (of news) نُبْذة (نُبَذ); **they ate every ~ of food** أَكَلوا كُلَّ الطَعام; **there isn't a ~ of evidence** لَيْسَ هُناكَ أَيُّ دَليلٍ **2** (infml) (fight) مُشاجَرة; **he got into a ~ in the playground** تَوَرَّطَ في مُشاجَرةٍ في ساحةِ اللَعِبِ **3** (waste metal) خُرْدة (خُرْدَوات); **to sell sth for ~** باعَ شَيْئاً للخُرْدةِ

B (**scraps**) *n pl* فَضَلات

C *vt* (**-pp-**) **1** (infml) (to abandon) تَخَلَّصَ (مِن) ‹*an agreement, a system, tax*›; **let's ~ the whole idea** دَعْنا نَتَخَلّى عن الفِكْرةِ كُلِّها **2** (to take out of service) تَخَلَّصَ (مِن) ‹*a ship, the equipment*›

D *vi* (**-pp-**) (infml) (to fight) «children, dogs» (infml) تَعارَكَ

scrapbook /ˈskrapbʊk/ *n* سِجِلّ قُصاصاتٍ

scrap dealer, **scrap merchant** *n* تاجِر خُرْدةٍ

scrape /skreɪp/ **A** *vt* **1** (to clean) كَشَطَ (i; كَشْط) ‹*the ice, paint*›; نَظَّفَ ‹*one's shoes*› **2** (to damage) خَدَشَ (i; خَدْش) ‹*a car, the paintwork*› **3** (to graze) خَدَشَ (i; خَدْش), جَرَحَ (a; جَرْح) ‹*one's knees, knuckles*›

B *vi* **to ~ against sth** (damaging) خَدَشَ شَيْئاً; (making noise) [احْتَكَّ بِشَيْءٍ مُحْدِثاً صَوْتاً مُزْعِجاً]

C *n* **1** (graze) خَدْش (خُدوش) **2** (infml) (predicament) وَرْطة (وَرَطات), مَأْزِق (مَآزِق); **to get into a ~** وَقَعَ في وَرْطةٍ

(Phrasal verbs) **scrape by** (financially) عاشَ على الكَفافِ

• **scrape off**: **~ off [sth]**, **~ [sth] off** كَشَطَ [شَيْئاً] ‹*the paint, mud*›

• **scrape through**: **1** **~ through** نَجَحَ بِشَقِّ الأَنْفُسِ **2** **~ through [sth]** نَجَحَ بِشَقِّ الأَنْفُسِ في [شَيْءٍ] ‹*an exam*›

• **scrape together**: **~ [sth] together**, **~ together [sth]** حَصَّلَ [شَيْئاً] بِصُعوبةٍ ‹*money*›

scraper /ˈskreɪpə/ *n* مِقْشَط (مَقاشِطُ), مِكْشَط (مَكاشِطُ)

scrapheap /ˈskraphi:p/ *n* كَوْمة خُرْدةٍ

(Idiom) **to be thrown on the scrapheap** (infml) كانَ غَيْرَ مَرْغوبٍ فيهِ

scrap iron *n* خُرْدة الحَديدِ

scrap metal *n* نُفايات مَعادِنَ

scrap paper *n* وَرَق مُسَوَّدةٍ

scrap value *n* قيمة الخُرْدةِ

scrapyard /ˈskrapjɑ:d/ *n* مُسْتَوْدَع خُرْدةٍ

scratch /skratʃ/ **A** *vt* **1** (to damage) خَدَشَ (i; خَدْش), خَرْبَشَ (خَرْبَشة ;i) ‹*the furniture, a car*› **2** (to wound) خَدَشَ (i; خَدْش), خَمَشَ (i-u; خَمْش) ‹*sb's face, skin*›; **I ~ed my arm on the thorns** خَدَشَت الأَشْواكُ ذِراعي **3** (to rub) حَكَّ (u; حَكّ) ‹*a spot, an itch*›; **to ~ one's head** حَكَّ رَأْسَهُ **4** (to trace) **to ~ one's initials on sth** حَفَرَ حُروفَ اسْمِهِ على شَيْءٍ **5** (to withdraw) انْسَحَبَ ‹*a horse, competitor*›

B *vi* **1** (to make wounds) «cats, animal» خَدَشَ (i; خَدْش), خَمَشَ (i-u; خَمْش) **2** (to relieve an itch) حَكَّ (u; حَكّ) **3** (to make a noise) «dog, cat» أَحْدَثَ صَريراً **4** (to claw the ground) «hens» نَقَرَ (u; نَقْر)

C *v refl* **to ~ oneself** (to rub) حَكَّ نَفْسَهُ; (to injure) خَدَشَ نَفْسَهُ

D *n* **1** (on metal, furniture, glass, lens) خَدْش (خُدوش) **2** (wound) خَدْش (خُدوش); **he just had a few ~es and bruises** أُصيبَ بِخُدوشٍ قَليلةٍ وَكَدَماتٍ فَقَطْ **3** (to relieve an itch) حِكّة **4** (sound) صَرير

E *adj before n* ‹*team, crew*› مُلَفَّق

(Idioms) **to be up to scratch** كانَ في المُسْتَوى; **from scratch** مِن الصِفْرِ; **to scratch the surface** عالَجَ المَوْضوعَ بِشَكْلٍ سَطْحيٍّ; **the report barely ~es the surface of the problem** عالَجَ التَقْريرُ المُشْكِلةَ بِشَكْلٍ سَطْحيٍّ; **you scratch my back (and I'll scratch yours)** حُكَّ لي ظَهْري أَحُكُّ لَكَ ظَهْرَكَ

scratch card *n* بِطاقة يانَصيبٍ فَوْريٍّ

scratch pad *n* دَفْتَر مُلاحَظاتٍ

scrawl /skrɔ:l/ **A** *vt* خَرْبَشَ (i; خَرْبَشة) ‹*graffiti, a note*›

B *vi* «writers, children» خَرْبَشَ (i; خَرْبَشة)

C *n* خَرْبَشة

scrawny /ˈskrɔːni/ *adj* (**scrawnier, scrawniest**) ‹*person*› هَزيل (هَزْلى); ‹*animal*› أَعْجَف (dipt)

scream /skriːm/ **A** *vt* صاحَ (i; صِياح ,صَيْح) ‹*sb's name, abuse*› **B** *vi* **1** «person, animal, bird» صَرَخَ (u; صَريخ ,صُراخ); **to ~ at sb** صَرَخَ على شَخْصٍ; **to ~ with pain** صَرَخَ مُتَأَلِّماً; **I ~ed for help** صَرَخْتُ طَلَباً للنَجْدةِ **2** «tyres» أَطْلَقَ صَريراً; «sirens, engines» أَطْلَقَ صَفّارةَ الإِنْذارِ **C** *n* **1** (person's) صُراخ; (animal's, bird's) صِياح; **~s of laughter** ضَحَكات صارِخة **2** (of tyres) صَرير; (of engines, sirens) صَفّارة **3** (infml) (funny person or thing) **he/it was a ~** [كانَ مُضْحِكاً بِشَكْلٍ لا يوصَفُ]

screech /skriːtʃ/ **A** *vi* **1** «person, animal, bird» صاحَ (i; صِياح ,صَيْح) **2** «tyres, brakes» أَطْلَقَ صَريراً **B** *n* **1** (of a person, animal, bird) صَيْحة **2** (of tyres, brakes) صَرير

screen /skriːn/ **A** *n* **1** (for televisions, computers) شاشة; **on ~** على الشاشةِ **2** (for films) شاشة (كَبيرة); **adapted for the ~** أُعِدَّ للسينَما **3** (as divider, for privacy) سِتار (سُتُر); **a bullet-proof ~** سِتار واقٍ من الرَصاصِ **4** (for doors, windows) شَبَك **5** (for concealment) سِياج (سِياجات); **a ~ of trees** سِياج من الأَشْجارِ **6** (for disease) كَشْف (كُشوف), فَحْص (فُحوص) **B** *vt* **1** (to show) عَرَضَ (i; عَرْض) ‹*a movie*› **2** (to broadcast) بَثَّ (i-u; بَثّ) ‹*a programme, documentary*› **3** (to conceal) حَجَبَ (u; حَجْب) ‹*a house, palace*› **4** (from the sun) حَمى (i; حِماية) ‹*one's face, eyes*› **5** (in selection procedures) فَحَصَ (a; فَحْص) ‹*an applicant, a candidate*› **6** (electronically) فَحَصَ (a; فَحْص) ‹*a passenger, baggage*› **7** (for disease) فَحَصَ (a; فَحْص) ‹*a patient*›; **to ~ sb for cancer** أَجْرى فَحْصَ السَرَطانِ على شَخْصٍ

(Phrasal verb) **screen off**: **~ off [sth], ~ [sth] off** فَصَلَ [شَيْئاً] عن ‹*part of a room, garden*›

screen debut *n* [أَوَّل ظُهورٍ في السينَما]

screen door *n* باب مُشَبَّك

screening /ˈskriːnɪŋ/ *n* **1** (showing in a cinema) عَرْض سينَمائيّ; (on TV) عَرْض تِلِفِزْيونيّ **2** [u] (of candidates) فَحْص **3** (of patients) فَحْص (فُحوص)

screenplay /ˈskriːnpleɪ/ *n* سيناريو (سينارِيُوات)

screen saver *n* شاشة تَوَقُّفٍ

screen test *n* [اخْتِبار صَلاحيّةِ مُمَثِّلٍ على الشاشةِ]

screenwash /ˈskriːnwɒʃ/ *n* [سائِل مَسّاحاتِ زُجاجِ السَيّاراتِ]

screenwriter /ˈskriːnraɪtə/ *n* كاتِب سيناريو

screw /skruː/ **A** *n* **1** (fastener) بُرْغيّ **2** (propellor) مِرْوَحة (مَراوِحُ) **3** (infml) (prison guard) سَجّان **4** (vulg) (sex) **to have a ~** مارَسَ الجِنْسَ **B** *vt* **1** (with a screwdriver) **to ~ a picture onto a wall** عَلَّقَ صورةً على الجِدارِ **2** **to ~ a lid onto a jar** أَغْلَقَ جَرّةً **3** (infml) (to extort) **to ~ sth out of sb** انْتَزَعَ شَيْئاً من شَخْصٍ; **I had to ~ the money out of him, he's so tight-fisted** كانَ عَلَيَّ أن أَنْتَزِعَ الأَمْوالَ مِنْهُ، إنَّهُ بَخيلٌ جِدًّا; **she ~ed that promise out of him by threatening to show the letters to his wife** انْتَزَعَتْ ذلك الوَعْدَ مِنْهُ عن طَريقِ تَهْديدِهِ بِعَرْضِ الرسائِلِ على زَوْجَتِهِ **4** (infml) (to swindle) احْتالَ (على), خَدَعَ (a; خَدْع, خَديعة, خُدْعة) ‹*a tourist, an investor*›; **the gullible investors were ~ed** خُدِعَ المُسْتَثْمِرونَ السُذَّجُ **5** (vulg) (to have sex with) ناكَ (i; نيك) ‹*her, him*› **C** *vi* **1** (Tech) **to ~ onto/into sth** «parts, fitments» الْتَصَقَ بِشَيْءٍ; **this piece ~s into/onto that piece** هذه القِطْعةُ تَلْتَصِقُ بِتِلْكَ القِطْعةِ **2** (vulg) (to have sex) مارَسَ الجِنْسَ

(Phrasal verbs) **screw around**: **~ around** **1** (infml) (to sleep around) [كانَ لَهُ عَلاقاتٌ جِنْسيّةٌ عابِرةٌ] **2** (AmE) (infml) (to be idle) تَسَكَّعَ

• **screw down**: **~ [sth] down, ~ down [sth]** أَغْلَقَ [شَيْئاً] بِإِحْكامٍ ‹*a lid, hatch*›

• **screw in**: **~ [sth] in, ~ in [sth]** ثَبَّتَ [شَيْئاً] ‹*a bolt, screw*›

• **screw on**: **~ [sth] on, ~ on [sth]** **1** أَغْلَقَ [شَيْئاً] ‹*a lid, cap*› **2** سَمَّرَ [شَيْئاً] ‹*the handle, guard*›

• **screw together**: **1** **~ together** «parts» شَدَّ مَعاً **2** **~ [sth] together, ~ together [sth]** جَمَّعَ [شَيْئاً] بالبَراغي ‹*a table, the parts*›

• **screw up** **A** **~ up** (infml) (to mess up) «person, company» لَخْبَطَ (i; لَخْبَطة) **B** **~ [sth] up, ~ up [sth]** **1** (to crumple) ضَغَطَ [شَيْئاً] ‹*a paper, material*›; **to ~ up one's eyes** أَغْمَضَ

عَيْنَيْهِ 2 (infml) (to make a mess of) [شَيْئاً] خَرْبَطَ ‹*the plan, sb's preparations*› 3 (to summon) **to ~ up one's courage to do sth** اِسْتَجْمَعَ شَجاعَتَهُ لِيَفْعَلَ شَيْئاً

screwball /ˈskruːbɔːl/ *n* (infml) أَحْمَق (dipt; حُمْق; f حَمْقى)

screwdriver /ˈskruːdrʌɪvə/ *n* مِفَكّ بَراغٍ; **a Phillips ~** مِفَكّ فيليبس

scribble /ˈskrɪb(ə)l/ A *vt* خَرْبَش (i; خَرْبَشة), كَتَبَ \ دَوَّنَ على عَجَلٍ ‹*a note, message*›; **I ~d down a few notes** دَوَّنْتُ على عَجَلٍ بَعْضَ المُلاحَظاتِ
B *vi* «writers, children» خَرْبَش (i; خَرْبَشة)
C *n* خَرْبَشة

scrimp /skrɪmp/ *vi* «families, companies» اِقْتَصَدَ; **to ~ on sth** اِقْتَصَدَ في شَيْءٍ; **to ~ and save** اِقْتَصَدَ وادَّخَرَ

script /skrɪpt/ *n* 1 (for a film, play) سيناريو (سيناريُوات) 2 [u] (handwriting) خَطّ يَدَويّ 3 (typeface) خَطّ (خُطوط) 4 (alphabet) كِتابة, خَطّ (خُطوط)

scripture /ˈskrɪptʃə/ *n* (also **Scripture**, **the Scriptures**) كِتاب مُقَدَّس

scriptwriter /ˈskrɪptrʌɪtə/ *n* كاتِب سيناريو \ حِوارٍ

scroll /skrəʊl/ *n* 1 (of paper, parchment) لِفافة (لِفافات, لَفائِفُ), طامور (طَواميرُ) 2 (ancient document) لِفافة (لِفافات, لَفائِفُ), لَوْح (أَلْواح), مَخْطوط (مَخْطوطات); **the Dead Sea ~s** مَخْطوطات \ لَفائِف البَحْرِ المَيِّتِ

Phrasal verbs **scroll down** «computer user» اِنْتَقَلَ إلى الأَسْفَلِ
• **scroll up** «computer user» اِنْتَقَلَ إلى الأَعْلى

scroll bar *n* شَريط تَمْريرٍ

scrounge /skraʊndʒ/ (infml pej) A *vt* **to ~ sth off sb** اِسْتَجْدى شَيْئاً من شَخْصٍ ‹*a cigarette, drink*›
B *vi* «poor people, students» تَطَفَّلَ; **to ~ off sb** تَطَفَّلَ على شَخْصٍ

scrounger /ˈskraʊndʒə/ *n* (infml pej) طُفَيْليّ

scrub /skrʌb/ A *vt* (-bb-) 1 (to clean) غَسَلَ (i; غَسْل) ‹*the floor, potatoes, one's hands*›; **to ~ the floor/shirt clean** غَسَلَ الأَرْضِيّةَ \ القَميصَ 2 (infml) (to cancel) أَلْغى ‹*the meeting, idea*›
B *vi* (-bb-) فَرَكَ (u; فَرْك)
C *n* 1 (clean) **to give sth a (good) ~** نَظَّفَ شَيْئاً (تَنْظيفاً جَيِّداً)
2 [u] (undergrowth) أَجَم (n coll)

Phrasal verbs **scrub down**: **~ down [sth/sb]**, **~ [sth/sb] down** نَظَّفَ [شَيْئاً] ‹*a table, wall, surface*›
• **scrub off**: **~ off [sth]**, **~ [sth] off** مَحا [شَيْئاً] ‹*a stain, the graffiti*›
• **scrub out**: **~ out [sth]**, **~ [sth] out** 1 (to clean) نَظَّفَ [شَيْئاً] ‹*a pan, sink*› 2 (to rub out) مَحا [شَيْئاً] ‹*a mark, word*›
• **scrub up** «surgeons» غَسَلَ يَدَهُ قبل الجِراحة

scrubbing brush /ˈskrʌbɪŋ ˌbrʌʃ/ (BrE), **scrub brush** (AmE) *n* فُرْشاة تَنْظيفٍ

scruff /skrʌf/ *n*; **by the ~ of the neck** من مُؤَخَّرةِ العُنُقِ

scruffy /ˈskrʌfi/ *adj* (**scruffier**, **scruffiest**) ‹*person*› رَثّ الهَيْئةِ \ الثِيابِ; ‹*clothes, appearance*› رَثّ

scrum /skrʌm/, **scrummage** /ˈskrʌmɪdʒ/ *n* (in rugby) [تَشابُك اللاعِبينَ بالأَكْتافِ في لُعْبةِ الرُّجْبي]

scrumptious /ˈskrʌmpʃəs/ *adj* (infml) ‹*meal, cake*› شَهِيّ \ لَذيذ جِدّاً

scrunchy /ˈskrʌntʃi/, **scrunchie** *n* رَبْطة شَعْرٍ

scruple /ˈskruːp(ə)l/ *n* تَرَدُّد, تَحَرُّج

scrupulous /ˈskruːpjʊləs/ *adj* ‹*care, fairness*› دَقيق

scrupulously /ˈskruːpjʊləsli/ *adv* ‹*to avoid, maintain*› على نَحْوٍ دَقيقٍ, بِدِقّةٍ; **~ clean** نَظيف إلى أَقْصى حَدٍّ

scrutinize, **-ise** (BrE) /ˈskruːtɪnʌɪz/ *vt* فَحَصَ (a; فَحْص) ‹*documents, evidence*›; تَأَمَّلَ, تَمَعَّنَ (في) ‹*sb's face*›

scrutiny /ˈskruːtɪni/ *n* (*pl* **scrutinies**) فَحْص (فُحوص), مُعايَنة

scuba diving /ˈskuːbə dʌɪvɪŋ/ *n* غَوْص (بِجِهازِ تَنَفُّسٍ)

scuff /skʌf/ *vt* حَكَّ (u; حَكّ) ‹*one's shoes*›; [تَرَكَ أَثَراً من جَرّاءِ الحَكِّ على] ‹*the floor, furniture*›

scuffle /ˈskʌf(ə)l/ *n* اِشْتِباك (اِشْتِباكات), شِجار

scullery /ˈskʌləri/ *n* (*pl* **sculleries**) [مَطْبَخ صَغير أو حُجْرة خَلْفيّة لِغَسْلِ الأَواني]

sculpt /skʌlpt/ A *vt* نَحَتَ (i-u; نَحْت) ‹*a figure, statue*›
B *vi* «sculptors, artists» نَحَتَ (i-u; نَحْت)

sculptor /ˈskʌlptə/ *n* نَحّات

sculptress /ˈskʌlptrəs/ *n* نَحّاتة

sculpture /ˈskʌlptʃə/ *n* **1** [u] (art) نَحْت **2** (object) مَنْحوتة

scum /skʌm/ *n* **1** (on liquid) غُثاء ,رَغاوٍ) رَغْوة (n coll; أَغْثاء) **2** (infml pej) (people) حُثالة; **the ~ of the earth** حُثالة المُجْتَمَع

scupper /ˈskʌpə/ *vt* (BrE) **1** (infml) (to ruin) أَفْسَدَ ‹*sb's plans, a deal*› **2** أَغْرَقَ ‹*a ship, boat*›

scurf /skəːf/ *n* قِشْرة الجِلْد

scurry /ˈskʌri/ *vi* (*past tense, past participle* **scurried**) «rats» جرى (i; جَرْي); «waiters» هَرْوَلَ (i; هَرْوَلة); **he scurried back to the kitchen** هَرْوَلَ عائداً إلى المَطْبَخ; **I saw rats ~ing around** رَأَيْتُ الجُرْذانَ تَجْري في كُلِّ اتِّجاهٍ

scuttle /ˈskʌt(ə)l/ **A** *n* (also **coal scuttle**) سَطْل لِجَمْعِ الفَحْمِ وَحِفْظِه
B *vt* **1** أَغْرَقَ ‹*a ship, boat*› **2** أَفْشَلَ ‹*sb's plans, a deal*›
C *vi* «servant» هَرْوَلَ (i; هَرْوَلة); «rat, insect» جَرى (i; جَرْي); **she bowed and ~d away/off** انْحَنَتْ وَهَرْوَلَتْ مُبْتَعِدةً

scythe /sʌɪð/ *n* مِنْجَل (مَناجِلُ)

SD *abbr* = **South Dakota**

SE *abbr* = **south-east** الجَنوب الشَرْقيّ; **~ Asia** جَنوب شَرْق آسيا

sea /siː/ **A** *n* **1** (as opposed to land) بَحْر (بِحار ,بُحور ,أَبْحُر); **the open ~** عَرْض البَحْرِ; **they live by the ~** يَسْكُنونَ على البَحْرِ; **to put to ~** أَبْحَرَ; **to be at ~** سافَرَ بَحْراً; **to travel by ~** سافَرَ بَحْراً; **a long way out to ~** بَعيداً في عَرْضِ البَحْرِ; **the ~ is calm/rough** البَحْرُ هادِئٌ \ هائِجٌ **2** (also **Sea**) **the Mediterranean S~** البَحْر الأَبْيَض المُتَوَسِّط; **the ~ of Galilee** بَحْر الجَليل ,بُحَيْرة طَبَرِيّا \ طَبَرِيّة **3** (as a career) **to go to ~** عَمِلَ في البَحْرِ; **after three months at ~** (as a passenger) بعد ثَلاثَةِ أَشْهُرٍ قَضّاها مُسافِراً في البَحْرِ; (as a seaman) بعد ثَلاثَةِ أَشْهُرٍ من الإِبْحارِ **4** (large quantity) **a ~ of faces/banners** عَدَد هائِل من الوُجوهِ \ الأَعْلامِ
B (**seas**) *n pl* **the high ~s** مِياه دَوْلِيّة ,أَعالي البِحارِ; **to sink in heavy ~s** غَرِقَ في المِياهِ الهائِجَةِ; **to sail the seven ~s** أَبْحَرَ في البُحورِ السَبْعَةِ

(Idiom) **to be all at sea** [كانَ مُرْتَبِكاً]

sea anemone *n* شَقيق \ شَقائِق البَحْرِ

sea bass *n* قاروس (n coll)

seabed /ˈsiːbɛd/ *n* قاع \ قَعْر بَحْرٍ

seafood /ˈsiːfuːd/ *n* غِلال البَحْرِ ,مَأْكولات بَحْرِيّة (NA)

seafront /ˈsiːfrʌnt/ *n* واجِهة البَحْرِ

seagull /ˈsiːgʌl/ *n* نَوْرَس (نَوارِسُ)

seahorse /ˈsiːhɔːs/ *n* فَرَس البَحْرِ

seal /siːl/ **A** *n* **1** (animal) فُقْمة (فُقَم) **2** (stamp) خَتْم (أَخْتام, خُتوم); **to set the ~ on a friendship/victory** وَقَّعَ على مُعاهَدةِ صَداقةٍ \ انْتِصارٍ; **to give sth one's ~ of approval** وَضَعَ خَتْمَ المُوافَقَةِ على شَيْءٍ **3** (on letters, packaging) خَتْم (أَخْتام, خُتوم) **4** (on pipes, joints, a door) مانِع تَسَرُّبٍ
B *vt* **1** (to close) خَتَمَ (i; خَتْم) ‹*an envelope, a package*› **2** أَغْلَقَ ‹*a border*› **3** (to make airtight, watertight) أَغْلَقَ بِإِحْكامٍ ‹*a jar, container*› **4** (to coat) غَطّى \ طَلى بِطَبَقةٍ عازِلةٍ ‹*a surface, wood*› **5** (to authenticate) خَتَمَ (i; خَتْم) (على) ‹*a document*› **6** (to settle) «negotiators» عَقَدَ (i; عَقْد) ‹*a deal*›; «players» حَقَّقَ ‹*a victory*›; «governments» عَقَدَ (i; عَقْد) ‹*an alliance, a friendship*›; **to ~ sb's fate** حَسَمَ مَصيرَ \ نِهايةَ شَخْصٍ

(Phrasal verbs) **seal off**: **~ [sth] off, ~ off [sth]** أَغْلَقَ [شَيْئاً] ‹*an area, a road*›
• **seal up**: **~ [sth] up, ~ up [sth]** سَدَّ \ أَغْلَقَ [شَيْئاً] ‹*an entrance, a house, a door*›

sealant /ˈsiːlənt/ *n* مادّة سادّة

sea level *n* مُسْتَوى سَطْحِ البَحْرِ

sealing wax /ˈsiːlɪŋ waks/ *n* شَمْع الخَتْمِ ,الشَمْع الأَحْمَر

sea lion *n* أَسَد البَحْرِ

seam /siːm/ *n* **1** (of garments) دَرْز (دُروز) **2** (of coal, gold) طَبَقة أَرْضِيّة

seaman /ˈsiːmən/ *n* (*pl* **-men**) **1** (professional) بَحّار (رُتْبة في البَحْرِيّة) **2** (amateur) بَحّار (بَحّارة)

seamless /ˈsiːmləs/ *adj* **1** ‹*stockings, fabric*› بدونِ ,بِلا دَرْزٍ **2** ‹*transition, integration*› سَلِس

seamstress /ˈsiːmstrɪs/ *n* خَيّاطة

seamy /ˈsiːmi/ *adj* (**seamier**, **seamiest**) ‹*area, motel*› وَضيع (وُضَعاءُ), حَقير (حُقَراءُ)

seance /ˈseɪɒ̃s/ *n* جَلْسة اسْتِحْضارِ أَرْواحٍ

seaplane /ˈsiːpleɪn/ *n* طائِرة بَحْرِيّة \ مائيّة

sear /sɪə/ *vt* 1 (to seal) قَلى (بِسُرْعةٍ) ‹*the meat*› 2 (to scorch) لَفَحَ (a; لَفْح, لَفَحان) ‹*the paintwork, flesh*›

search /sɜːtʃ/ **A** *vt* 1 (to hunt through) فَتَّشَ ‹*an area, a room, the woods*›; **~ me!** (infml) اللهُ أَعْلَمُ! 2 (looking for sth) فَتَّشَ ‹*a house, car*› 3 بَحَثَ (a; بَحْث; في) ‹*the records, archives*› 4 بَحَثَ (a; بَحْث; في) ‹*a database, the Internet*›

B *vi* **to ~ for one's glasses/a needle** بَحَثَ عن نَظّارَتِهِ \ إِبْرةٍ; **we ~ed through the rubble/our records** بَحَثْنا في الأَنْقاضِ \ سِجِلاّتِنا; **I started ~ing around on the Internet** بَدَأْتُ أَبْحَثُ في الإِنْتِرْنِت

C *n* 1 (hunt) بَحْث (بُحوث, أَبْحاث); **the ~ for survivors continues** يَتَواصَلُ البَحْثُ عن ناجينَ; **to go in ~ of sb/sth** ذَهَبَ للبَحْثِ عن شَخْصٍ \ شَيْءٍ; **he went off in ~ of adventure/his son** ذَهَبَ باحِثاً \ للبَحْثِ عن مُغامَرةٍ \ ابْنِهِ 2 (of a building, person) تَفْتيش (تَفْتيشات); **to carry out a ~ of sth** قامَ بِتَفْتيشِ شَيْءٍ 3 (of records) بَحْث (بُحوث, أَبْحاث) 4 (by computer) بَحْث (بُحوث, أَبْحاث); **I did a ~ on** *or* **for 'cheap flights'** قُمْتُ بِبَحْثٍ عن 'رِحْلات رَخيصة'

(Phrasal verb) **search out**: **~ [sb/sth] out, ~ out [sb/sth]**

1 (to look for) تَقَصّى [شَخْصاً \ شَيْئاً] ‹*new methods, the truth*›

2 (to find) اكْتَشَفَ [شَخْصاً \ شَيْئاً] ‹*an article, a garment*›

search engine *n* مُحَرِّك بَحْثٍ

searching /ˈsɜːtʃɪŋ/ *adj* ‹*question, inquiry*› فاحِص; ‹*look*› ثاقِب

searchlight /ˈsɜːtʃlʌɪt/ *n* نور كَشّاف

search party *n* فَريق بَحْثٍ وَإِنْقاذٍ

search warrant *n* مُذَكِّرة تَفْتيشٍ

sea salt *n* مِلْح بَحْرِيّ

seascape /ˈsiːskeɪp/ *n* مَنْظَر بَحْرِيّ

seashell /ˈsiːʃel/ *n* صَدَف (n coll; أَصْداف)

seashore /ˈsiːʃɔː/ *n* شاطِئ (شَواطِئُ, شُطْآن)

seasick /ˈsiːsɪk/ *adj* مُصاب بِدُوارِ البَحْرِ; **to feel ~** شَعَرَ بِدُوارِ البَحْرِ

seasickness /ˈsiːsɪknəs/ *n* دُوار البَحْرِ

seaside /ˈsiːsʌɪd/ *n* شاطِئ البَحْرِ; **a day at the ~** يَوْم على شاطِئِ البَحْرِ

seaside resort *n* مُنْتَجَع بَحْرِيّ

season /ˈsiːz(ə)n/ **A** *n* 1 (time of year) فَصْل (فُصول); **the four ~s** الفُصول الأَرْبَعة; **in the dry/rainy ~** في الفَصْلِ الجافّ \ المُمْطِرِ; **the growing/planting ~** فَصْل النُموّ \ الزِراعةِ; **strawberries are in/out of ~** هذا هو مَوْسِمُ \ لَيْسَ مَوْسِمَ الفَراوْلةِ; **it's the tulip ~** إِنَّهُ مَوْسِمُ التوليب 2 (specific period) مَوْسِم (مَواسِمُ); **early/late in the tourist ~** باكِراً \ مُتَأَخِّراً في المَوْسِمِ السِياحيِّ; **the football ~** المَوْسِم الكُرَوِيّ; **hotels are full during the ~** تَكونُ الفَنادِقُ مُمْتَلِئةً في المَوْسِمِ السِياحيِّ; **the town is quiet out of ~** المَدينةُ فارِغةٌ في غَيْرِ المَوْسِمِ السِياحيِّ 3 (festive period) **the ~ of Lent** مَوْسِم الصَوْمِ الكَبيرِ; **Season's greetings!** (on Christmas cards) أَجْمَل التَحيّاتِ بِمُناسَبةِ مَواسِمِ الأَعْيادِ 4 (in entertainment) مَوْسِم (مَواسِمُ); **a ~ of French films** مَوْسِم الأَفْلامِ الفِرَنْسِيّةِ 5 (of female animals) مَوْسِم التَزاوُجِ

B *vt* 1 (with spices) تَبَّلَ ‹*a dish, food*›; **~ with salt and pepper** تَبَّلَ بالمِلْحِ والفُلْفُلِ 2 (to mature) جَفَّفَ ‹*timber*›

seasonal /ˈsiːz(ə)n(ə)l/ *adj* ‹*fruit, pattern, work*› مَوْسِمِيّ

seasoned /ˈsiːz(ə)nd/ *adj* 1 (experienced) ‹*professional, traveller*› مُحَنَّك, ذو خِبْرةٍ طَويلةٍ 2 ‹*food, flour*› مُتَبَّل, مُبَهَّر 3 ‹*wood*› خَشَب مُجَفَّف

seasoning /ˈsiːz(ə)nɪŋ/ *n* تَوابِل

season ticket *n* 1 (for travel) تَذْكِرة مَوْسِمِيّة (للسَفَرِ) 2 (for football clubs, etc) تَذْكِرة مَوْسِمِيّة (لِدُخولِ المَلاعِبِ)

seat /siːt/ **A** *n* 1 (place to sit) كُرْسِيّ (كَراسِيّ, كَراسٍ), مَقْعَد (مَقاعِدُ); **let's find a ~** لِنَبْحَثْ عن مَقْعَدٍ; **to book** *or* **reserve a ~** حَجَزَ مَكاناً; **there are no ~s left** لَيْسَ هُناكَ أَماكِنُ; **could you keep me a ~?** هل تَسْتَطيعُ أن تَحْجِزَ لي مَكاناً؟ 2 (place to sit) مَقْعَد (مَقاعِدُ); **the front/back ~** المَقْعَد الأَماميّ \ الخَلْفِيّ 3 (in a parliament) مَقْعَد (مَقاعِدُ); **a safe/marginal ~** مَقْعَد بالبَرْلَمان يُمْكِنُ \ يَصْعُبُ الحِفاظُ عَلَيْهِ; **to win/hold/lose a ~** رَبِحَ \ حافَظَ على \ خَسِرَ مَقْعَداً; **a ~ on the New**

York Stock Exchange عُضْويّة \ مَقْعَد في بورْصةِ نِيويورْك

4 (part of a chair) (مَقاعِدُ) مَقْعَد **5** (of trousers) مُؤَخَّرة; **you've got a hole in the ~ of your jeans** هُناكَ ثُقْبٌ في مُؤَخَّرةِ سِرْوالِكَ **6** (centre) (مَراكِزُ) مَرْكَز; **Washington DC is the ~ of government** واشِنْطُن العاصِمةُ هي مَرْكَزُ الحُكومةِ **7** (residence) (مَقارُّ) مَقَرّ

B (**-seat**) *in combination* **a 150-~ plane/cinema** طائِرة \ قاعة سِينَما ذات 150 مَقْعَداً

C *vt* **1** (to place) أَجْلَسَ ‹*a guest*›; **I'll ~ you next to Mrs Henwood** سَأُجْلِسُكَ بِجوارِ السَيِّدةِ هِينْوود **2** (to have places for) اتَّسَعَ (ل) ‹*people*›; **the room ~s thirty (people)** الغُرْفةُ تَتَّسِعُ لِثَلاثِينَ شَخْصاً

D (**seated**) *adj* (fml) (جُلوس) جالِس; **to be ~ed at the high table** أُجْلِسَ إلى الطاوِلةِ العالِيةِ; **please remain ~ed** أَرْجوكَ ابْقَ جالِساً

(Idioms) **to be in the hot seat** كانَ في مَوْقِفٍ لا يُحْسَدُ عَلَيْهِ; **to take a back seat** قامَ بِدَوْرٍ ثانَوِيٍّ

seat belt *n* حِزام الأَمانِ

-seater /'si:tə/ *combining form* ذو ... مَقاعِدَ; **a two~ plane/sports car** طائِرة \ سَيّارة رِياضيّة ذات مَقْعَدَيْنِ

seating /'si:tɪŋ/ *n* **1** (seats) مَقاعِد; **the restaurant has ~ for 80 people** في المَطْعَمِ مَقاعِدُ لِثَمانِينَ شَخْصاً **2** (seating arrangements) تَرْتيب نِظامِ الجُلوسِ

sea urchin *n* قُنْفُذ البَحْرِ

sea view *n* مَنْظَر البَحْرِ

seawater *n* مِياه البَحْرِ

seaway /'si:weɪ/ *n* طَريق بَحْرِيّ

seaweed /'si:wi:d/ *n* عُشْب \ طُحْلُب بَحْرِيّ

seaworthy /'si:wə:ði/ *adj* ‹*boat*› صالِح لِلإِبْحارِ

sec /sɛk/ **A** *abbr* = **second(s)** (ثَوانٍ) ثانِية

B *n* (infml) (moment) (لَحَظات) لَحْظة

secateurs /ˌsɛkə'tə:z, 'sɛkətə:z/ *n pl* (BrE) مِقَصّ تَقْليم

secede /sɪ'si:d/ *vi* «states, provinces» انْفَصَلَ (عن)

secession /sɪ'sɛʃ(ə)n/ *n* (انْفِصالات) انْفِصال

secluded /sɪ'klu:dɪd/ *adj* ‹*beach, life*› مَعْزول, مُنْعَزِل

seclusion /sɪ'klu:ʒ(ə)n/ *n* انْعِزال, عُزْلة

second[1] /'sɛk(ə)nd/ **A** *n* **1** (ordinal number) ثانٍ; **she came ~** حَلَّتْ \ جاءَتْ في المَرْتَبةِ الثانِيةِ; **crime is seen as ~ only in importance to unemployment** تَأْتي الجَريمةُ في المَرْتَبةِ الثانِيةِ فَقَطْ بعد البِطالةِ من حَيْثُ الأَهَمّيّةِ **2** (**the second**) (of a month) **the ~ of May, May the ~** الثاني من مايو **3** (BrE) (in degree classification) **upper/lower ~** تَقْييم جَيِّد جِدًّا \ جَيِّد (دَرَجة جامِعيّة); **a ~ in chemistry** جَيِّد جِدًّا في الكيمِياء **4** (also **second gear**) (Aut) التِرْس \ الغِيار الثاني **5** (item for sale) بِضاعة من الدَرَجةِ الثانِيةِ **6** (in boxing) مُعاوِن, مُساعِد

B (**seconds**) *n pl* (infml) (at meals) مُؤَن إضافِيّة

C *adj* ثانٍ; **for the ~ time** لِلمَرّةِ الثانِيةِ; **every ~ day/Monday** كُلَّ يَوْمٍ وَيَوْم \ ثاني اثْنَيْنِ; **to have a ~ chance to do sth** كانَ عِنْدَهُ فُرْصةٌ ثانِيةٌ لِفِعْلِ شَيْءٍ; **he was the ~ child in a family of six** كانَ الطِفْلَ الثانِيَ في عائِلةٍ تَتَكَوَّنُ من سِتّةِ أَطْفالٍ

D *adv* **1** (in second place) ثانِياً; **to come** *or* **finish ~** حَلَّ \ جاءَ ثانِياً; **I spoke ~** تَكَلَّمْتُ ثانِياً; **to travel ~** سافَرَ على الدَرَجةِ الثانِيةِ; **the ~ tallest building in the world** ثاني أَعْلى بِنايةٍ في العالَمِ **2** (also **secondly**) ثانِياً; **~, I have to say ...** ثانِياً, يَجِبُ أَنْ أَقولَ ...

E *vt* **1** (in debates, etc) سانَدَ, أَيَّدَ ‹*the motion, speaker*›; **the motion was ~ed by Mr Glover** أَيَّدَ السَيِّدُ غْلوفَر المُذَكِّرةَ **2** (in boxing) سانَدَ ‹*a boxer, duellist*›

(Idioms) **to be second nature** كانَ شَيْئاً طَبيعيًّا; **in two weeks, this will be ~ nature to you** سَيَكونُ هذا شَيْئاً طَبيعيًّا لَكَ خِلالَ أُسْبوعَيْنِ; **to be second to none** كانَ لا يُضاهى; **to have second thoughts** ساوَرَتْهُ الشُكوكُ; **on second thoughts** بعد إعادةِ التَفْكيرِ في الأَمْرِ

second[2] /'sɛk(ə)nd/ *n* **1** (sixtieth of a minute) (ثَوانٍ) ثانِية **2** (infml) (an instant) (لَحَظات) لَحْظة; **just a ~!** لَحْظةٌ فَقَطْ!; **this won't take a ~** الأَمْرُ لن يَسْتَغْرِقَ أَكْثَرَ من لَحْظةٍ; **they'll arrive any ~ now** قد يَأْتونَ في أَيِّ لَحْظةٍ الآنَ

second[3] /sɪ'kɒnd/ *vt* (in work) أَعارَ ‹*a manager, an employee*›

secondary /'sɛk(ə)nd(ə)ri/ *adj* **1** (subordinate) ‹*role, importance*› ثانَوِيّ **2** (not primary or original) ‹*source*› ثانَوِيّ; ‹*effect*› جانِبِيّ **3** ‹*education, student*› ثانَوِيّ

secondary school *n* مَعْهَد ثانَويّ ,مَدْرَسة ثانَويّة

second best **A** *n* الخَيار الثاني; **she refuses to settle for second best** تَرْفُض أنْ تَقْبَلَ بالخَيارِ الثاني;

B *adj* (*before n* **second-best**) ثاني أَحْسَن;

C *adv* **to come off second best** خَسِرَ المُباراةَ

second class **A** *n* 1 (on a train, ship) دَرَجة ثانِية

2 (for mail) (BrE) بَريد الدَرَجةِ الثانِيةِ; (AmE) [بَريد خاصّ بِتَوْزيعِ الجَرائِدِ والمَجَلّاتِ];

B (**second-class**) *adj* 1 ‹*passenger, ticket*› الدَرَجةِ الثانِيةِ

2 (BrE) ‹*stamp, letter*› الدَرَجةِ الثانِيةِ 3 (inferior) ‹*citizen, status*› من الدَرَجةِ الثانِيةِ;

C *adv* 1 ‹*to travel, go*› في الدَرَجةِ الثانِيةِ 2 ‹*to send*› بِبَريدِ الدَرَجةِ الثانِيةِ

second-class mail, **second-class post** (BrE) *n* بَريد الدَرَجةِ الثانِيةِ

second-degree /ˌsɛk(ə)nddɪˈgriː/ *adj* 1 ‹*burn*› من الدَرَجةِ الثانِيةِ 2 (AmE) ‹*murder, manslaughter*› من الدَرَجةِ الثانِيةِ

second hand /ˈsɛk(ə)nd hand/ **A** *n* عَقْرَب \ مُؤَشِّر ثَوانٍ

B (**second-hand**) *adj* 1 (not new) ‹*clothes, car*› مُسْتَعْمَل

2 *before n* (selling used goods) ‹*shop, bookstore*› لِبَيْعِ البَضائِعِ المُسْتَعْمَلةِ

C *adv* (not new) ‹*to buy, get*› [من مَصْدَرٍ يَبيعُ بَضائِعَ مُسْتَعْمَلةً]

second in command *n* الرَجُل الثاني في قِيادة عَسْكَرِيّة

secondly /ˈsɛk(ə)ndli/ *adv* ثانِياً; **firstly, the engine is too small and ~, the bodywork is rusty** أَوَّلاً، المُحَرِّكُ صَغيرٌ جِدًّا وَثانِياً، الهَيْكَلُ صَدِئٌ

second name *n* 1 (surname) اسْم العائِلةِ 2 (second forename) اسْم الأَبِ

second-rate /ˌsɛk(ə)ndˈreɪt/ *adj* (pej) ‹*service, version*› من الدَرَجةِ الثانِيةِ

secrecy /ˈsiːkrɪsi/ *n* تَكَتُّم ,سِرِّيّة

secret /ˈsiːkrɪt/ **A** *adj* 1 (not known by many) ‹*meeting, location*› سِرِّيّ 2 (anonymous) ‹*ballot*› سِرِّيّ 3 (hidden) ‹*door*› مَخْفِيّ ,سِرِّيّ

B *n* سِرّ (أَسْرار); **to tell sb a ~** أَخْبَرَ شَخْصاً سِرًّا; **to keep a ~** كَتَمَ سِرًّا

C (**in secret**) *phr* بِشَكْلٍ سِرِّيٍّ ,سِرًّا

secretarial /sɛkrəˈtɛːriəl/ *adj* ‹*work, course, staff*› سِكْرِتيرِيّ

secretariat /ˌsɛkrɪˈtɛːrɪət/ *n* أَمانة سِكْرِتارِية

secretary /ˈsɛkrɪt(ə)ri/ *n* (*pl* **secretaries**) 1 (in an office) سِكْرِتير 2 (of a club) أَمين سِكْرِتير (أُمَناءُ) 3 (also **Secretary**) (in government) وَزير (وُزَراءُ); **the S~ of State** (in USA) وَزير الخارِجِيّةِ; **the Foreign S~** (in UK) وَزير الخارِجِيّةِ

secretary general *n* (*pl* **secretaries general**) أَمين عامّ

secrete /sɪˈkriːt/ *vt* 1 (to produce) أَفْرَزَ ‹*fluid, a hormone*›

2 (to hide) خَبَّأَ ,أَخْفى ‹*the valuables, money*›

secretion /sɪˈkriːʃ(ə)n/ *n* 1 [u] (process) إِفْراز 2 (substance) إِفْراز (إِفْرازات); **bodily ~s** إِفْرازات الجِسْمِ

secretive /ˈsiːkrɪtɪv/ *adj* ‹*organization, nature*› كَتوم; **to be ~ about one's work** أَحاطَ عَمَلَهُ بالسِرِّيّةِ

secretly /ˈsiːkrɪtli/ *adv* ‹*to film, plot*› خُفْيةً ,بِشَكْلٍ سِرِّيٍّ ,سِرًّا

secret police *n* شُرْطة سِرِّيّة

secret service *n* 1 (dealing with espionage) جِهاز إِدارة اسْتِخْباراتٍ ,مُخابَراتٍ 2 (**the Secret Service**) (US office dealing with presidential security) جِهاز الخِدْمةِ السِرِّيّةِ (مُكَلَّف بِحِمايةِ الرَئيسِ)

secret weapon *n* سِلاح سِرِّيّ

sect /sɛkt/ *n* طائِفة (طَوائِفُ) ,شيعة (شِيَع)

sectarian /sɛkˈtɛːrɪən/ *adj* (pej) ‹*violence, division*› طائِفِيّ

section /ˈsɛkʃ(ə)n/ **A** *n* 1 (part, unit) جُزْء (أَجْزاء) ,قِسْم (أَقْسام); **this ~ of the plane is reserved** هذا الجُزْءُ من الطائِرةِ مَحْجوزٌ 2 (of a road, river, pipe) جُزْء (أَجْزاء) ,قِسْم (أَقْسام) 3 (of an orange, grapefruit) فَصّ (فُصوص) 4 (of society, the population) شَريحة (شَرائِحُ) 5 (of an organization) قِسْم (أَقْسام); (of a store, library) قِسْم (أَقْسام) ,جُزْء (أَجْزاء) 6 (of a book) قِسْم (أَقْسام) ,جُزْء (أَجْزاء) 7 (of a newspaper) قِسْم (أَقْسام) 8 (of an act, a bill, report) بَنْد (بُنود); **it is an offence under ~ 24 of the Act** هو جَريمةٌ تحت البَنْدِ 24 من القانونِ 9 (of an orchestra) مَجْموعة (مَجْموعات) 10 (in geometry, drawing) مَقْطَع (مَقاطِعُ) 11 (in surgery) عَمَلِيّة 12 (Mil) حَظيرة (وِحْدة عَسْكَرِيّة)

B *vt* **1** (to cut) قَطَّعَ ‹*a specimen, tissue*› **2** (BrE) (to commit to a psychiatric hospital) [أَوْدَعَ في مُسْتَشْفى الأَمْراضِ العَقْلِيّةِ] ‹*a patient*›

Phrasal verb **section off**: **~ off [sth], ~ [sth] off** اقْتَطَعَ [شَيْئاً] (من) ‹*a part, an area*›

sector /ˈsɛktə/ *n* قِطاع (قِطاعات); **the public/private ~** القِطاع العامّ \ الخاصّ; **the manufacturing/banking ~** قِطاع الصناعة \ البُنوك

secular /ˈsɛkjʊlə/ *adj* ‹*society, education*› عَلْمانيّ

secularism /ˈsɛkjələriz(ə)m/ *n* عَلْمانيّة

secularization, **-isation** (BrE) /sɛkjələrʌɪˈzeɪʃ(ə)n/ *n* عَلْمَنة

secure /sɪˈkjʊə/ **A** *adj* **1** (not threatened) ‹*job, marriage, income*› مُسْتَقِرّ, آمِن; **a ~ old age** أَمان ماليّ في سِنِّ الشَّيْخوخةِ; **I'm looking for a ~ investment** أَبْحَثُ عن اسْتِثمارٍ آمِنٍ **2** (safe) ‹*building, route*› مَأْمون, مُؤَمَّن, آمِن; **to make the airport ~ against attack** أَمَّنَ المَطارَ ضِدَّ الهُجوم **3** (strong, robust) ‹*lock, doors*› مُحْكَم, مَتين, مُثَبَّت; **make sure the tent is ~** تَأَكَّدْ من أَنّ الخَيْمة مُثَبّتةٌ بِإحْكام **4** (emotionally) ‹*family, background, future*› آمِن; **to feel ~** شَعَرَ بالأَمانِ **5** (from hackers) ‹*web page, transaction*› آمِن

B *vt* **1** (to obtain) تَوَصَّلَ (إلى) ‹*an agreement*›; ضَمِنَ (a; ضَمان) ‹*sb's release*›; حَصَلَ (u; حُصول; على) ‹*a majority, money*› **2** (to make firm) ثَبَّتَ ‹*a ladder*›; أَحْكَمَ الإغْلاق \ القُفْلَ ‹*a door, window*› **3** (to make safe) أَمَّنَ ‹*a house, one's position*› **4** «borrower» أَعْطى ضَماناً لِ ‹*a loan, debt*›; **the loan is ~d on** *or* **against the value of the house** القَرْضُ مَضْمونٌ بِقيمةِ البَيْتِ **5** أَمَّنَ ‹*a bridge, an exit*›; **once the bridge had been ~d, reinforcements and supplies were sent in** بِمُجَرَّدِ تَأْمينِ الجِسْرِ, تَمَّ إرْسالُ التَعْزيزاتِ والإمْداداتِ

secure unit *n* سِجْن الأَحْداثِ

securities /sɪˈkjʊərətiz/ *n pl* سَنَدات ضَمانٍ, أَوْراق ماليّة

security /sɪˈkjʊərəti/ **A** *n* **1** [u] (protection) أَمْن; **national ~ is at risk** الأَمْنُ القَوْميُّ في خَطَرٍ; **to go through ~** مَرَّ بِأَمْنِ المَطارِ **2** (future stability) أَمان; **job ~ is a myth** الأَمْنُ الوَظيفيُّ وَهْمٌ **3** (emotional) اطْمِئْنان, أَمان; **the ~ of a happy home** أَمان البَيْتِ السَعيدِ **4** (guarantee) ضَمانة, ضَمان **5** (bond) سَنَد (سَنَدات)

B *adj before n* ‹*measures, staff*› أَمْنيّ

security camera *n* كاميرا مُراقَبةٍ أَمْنيّةٍ

security check *n* تَحَرِّيات أَمْنِيّة (عن شَخْصٍ)

security clearance *n* تَصْريح أَمْنيّ

security code *n* رَقْم سِرّيّ

Security Council *n* مَجْلِس الأَمْنِ

security forces *n* قوّات أَمْنيّة

security guard *n* حارِس (حَرَس, حُرّاس)

security leak *n* تَسْريب وَثائِقَ أَمْنِيةٍ

security officer *n* ضابِط أَمْنٍ

security risk *n* خَطَر أَمْنيّ \ على الأَمْنِ

sedan /sɪˈdan/ *n* (AmE) (car) سَيّارة من طِرازِ سيدان

sedate /sɪˈdeɪt/ **A** *adj* ‹*pace, surroundings*› هادِئ

B *vt* أَعْطى مُسَكِّناً ‹*a patient*›

sedation /sɪˈdeɪʃ(ə)n/ *n* اسْتِخْدام مُسَكِّناتٍ

sedative /ˈsɛdətɪv/ *n* مُسَكِّن (مُسَكِّنات), مُهَدِّئ (مُهَدِّئات)

sediment /ˈsɛdɪmənt/ *n* **1** (deposit) ثُفْل (أَثْفال) **2** (geological) راسِب (رَواسِبُ)

seduce /sɪˈdjuːs/ *vt* **1** (sexually) أَغْوى ‹*a woman, minor*› **2** (to tempt) أَغْرى ‹*an electorate, applicant*›; **the applicants were ~d by the prospect of easy money** أَغْرَتْ إمْكانيّةُ الحُصولِ على المالِ بِطَريقةٍ سَهْلةٍ المُتَقَدِّمينَ بالطَلَباتِ

seduction /sɪˈdʌkʃ(ə)n/ *n* **1** (of a woman) إغْواء **2** (temptation) إغْراء (إغْراءات); **the ~s of city life** إغْراءات حَياةِ المَدينةِ

seductive /sɪˈdʌktɪv/ *adj* **1** (tempting) ‹*idea, power*› مُغْرٍ; **the American Dream has an enormously ~ power for the oppressed worldwide** يَتَمَتَّعُ الحُلْمُ الأَمْريكيُّ بِقوّةِ إغْراءٍ هائِلةٍ لِكُلِّ المُضْطَهَدينَ في أَنْحاءِ العالَمِ **2** (sexually attractive) ‹*charm, woman*› مُغْوٍ

see /siː/ **A** *vt* (*past tense* **saw**; *past participle* **seen**) **1** (to perceive) رَأى (a; رَأْي, رُؤْية); **I didn't ~ the bike** لم أَرَ الدَرّاجةَ; **can you ~ the hotel?** هل تَسْتَطيعُ أَنْ تَرى الفُنْدُقَ؟; **we saw him steal** *or* **stealing a car** رَأَيْناهُ يَسْرِقُ سَيّارةً; **there was nobody to be seen** لم يَكُنْ هُناكَ أَحَدٌ; **you should have ~n**

that coming كانَ يَنْبَغي أنْ تَتَوَقَّعَ هذا; **2** (to witness) شاهَدَ, رَأى (a; رَأْي, رُؤْية) ‹*a movie, programme*›; **~ page 156** أُنْظُر الصَفْحةَ رَقْمَ 156; **the official asked to ~ his passport** طَلَبَ المُوَظَّفُ أنْ يَرى جَوازَ سَفَرِهِ; **ask to ~ his work before you make an order** أُطْلُبْ أنْ تَرى عَمَلَهُ قبل أنْ تُقَدِّمَ طَلَبيّةً **3** (to visit) زارَ (u; زِيارة) ‹*an exhibition, a country, the palace*›; **to ~ the sights** زارَ المَعالِمَ السِياحيّةَ **4** (to meet) قابَلَ ‹*one's parents, a friend*›; (to consult) اسْتَشارَ ‹*a lawyer, doctor*›; **we used to ~ a lot of them** كُنّا نُقابِلُهُمْ كَثيراً; **I saw Pete and his family last week** قابَلْتُ بيت وَأُسْرَتَهُ الأُسْبوعَ الماضيَ; **they ~ each other all the time now** يَتَواعَدونَ باسْتِمْرار هذه الأيّام; **I'm ~ing a psychiatrist** أَسْتَشيرُ طَبيباً نَفْسيًّا; **~ you!** (infml) أراكَ!, إلى اللِقاءِ; **~ you next week!** (infml) على خَيْرٍ!, إلى اللِقاءِ في الأُسْبوعِ القادِمِ! **5** (to receive) قابَلَ, اسْتَقْبَلَ ‹*a patient, a client, student*› **6** (to accompany) **to ~ sb to the station** وَصَّلَ شَخْصاً إلى المَحَطّة; **to ~ sb home** وَصَّلَ شَخْصاً إلى بَيْتِهِ **7** (to understand) رَأى (a; رَأْي, رُؤْية), أَدْرَكَ, فَهِمَ (a; فَهْم) ‹*the relevance, advantage, problem*›; **do you ~ what I mean?** هل تَفْهَمُ ما أَعْنيهِ؟; **she didn't ~ the joke** لم تَفْهَم النُكْتةَ; **you can ~ from this example that …** تَسْتَطيعُ أنْ تَرى من هذا المِثالِ أنّ … **8** (to consider) **to ~ sb as a leader/hero** نَظَرَ إلى شَخْصٍ كَقائِدٍ \ كَبَطَل; **I ~ this as an opportunity** أَعْتَبِرُ أنّ هذه فُرْصةٌ **9** (to envisage) تَصَوَّرَ, تَخَيَّلَ ‹*a scenario, situation*›; **I can't ~ him winning the race/marrying her** لا أَسْتَطيعُ أنْ أَتَصَوَّرَ أنْ يَفوزَ في السِباقِ \ يَتَزَوَّجَها **10** (to make sure) **to ~ that sth is done** تَأَكَّدَ أنّ شَيْئاً قد فُعِلَ **11** (to find out) **~ what they want** أُنْظُرْ ماذا يُريدونَ; **I'll ~ if I they can deliver it** سَأرى ما إذا كانَ بِإمْكانِهِمْ أنْ يُرْسِلوهُ **12** (to witness) شَهِدَ (a; شُهود), رَأى (a; رَأْي, رُؤْية), لاقى ‹*change, progress*›; ‹*hardship*›; **next year will ~ the completion of the road** سَوْفَ يَشْهَدُ العامُ القادِمُ إتْمامَ الطَريقِ

B *vi* (*past tense* **saw**; *past participle* **seen**) **1** (with your eyes) رَأى (a; رَأْي, رُؤْية); **I can't ~** لا يُمْكِنُني أنْ أَرى; **you can ~ for miles** يُمْكِنُكَ أنْ تَرى لِمَسافةِ عِدّةِ أَمْيالٍ **2** (to understand) فَهِمَ (a; فَهْم); **I ~** مَفْهوم; **as far as I can ~ …** حَسْبَما أَرى … **3** (to check, find out) **I'll go and ~** سَأَذْهَبُ وَأَرى; **we'll just have to wait and ~** ما عَلَيْنا سِوى أنْ نَنْتَظِرَ وَنَرى **4** (to think, consider) **I'll have to ~** سَأَنْظُرُ في الأَمْرِ; **let's ~, let me ~** دَعْني أُفَكِّرُ

C *v refl* (*past tense* **saw**; *past participle* **seen**) **to ~ oneself** تَخَيَّلَ \ تَصَوَّرَ نَفْسَهُ; **I can't ~ myself being chosen/as a famous ballerina** لا أَتَصَوَّرُ أنْ يَقَعَ الاخْتِيارُ عَلَيَّ \ أنْ أُصْبِحَ راقِصةَ باليه مَشْهورةً

D *n* أُسْقُفيّة, أَبْرَشيّة; **the Holy S~** الكُرْسيّ الرَسوليّ \ البابَويّ

(Idiom) **seeing is believing** المُشاهَدةُ خَيْرُ بُرْهانٍ

(Phrasal verbs) **see about**: **~ about [sth]** تَدَبَّرَ أَمْرَ [شَيْءٍ]; **to ~ about a loan/getting a job** تَدَبَّرَ أَمْرَ الحُصولِ على قَرْضٍ \ وَظيفةٍ

• **see off**: **~ [sb] off, ~ [off] sb** **1** (to say goodbye to) وَدَّعَ **2** (to defeat) هَزَمَ [شَخْصاً] **3** (to get rid of) طَرَدَ [شَخْصاً]

• **see out** **A** **~ [sth] out, ~ out [sth]** اسْتَمَرَّ طوال [شَيْءٍ] ‹*the winter*›; أَكْمَلَ [شَيْئاً] ‹*a campaign*› **B** **~ [sb] out** صَحِبَ \ وَصَّلَ [شَخْصاً] إلى الباب; **I'll ~ myself out** سَأُغادِرُ بِنَفْسي

• **see through**: **A** **~ [sth] through, ~ through [sth]** (to finish) أَكْمَلَ [شَيْئاً] حتى النِهايةِ ‹*a project, task*› **B** **~ through [sth/sb]** فَطِنَ إلى حَقيقةِ [شَيْءٍ \ شَخْصٍ] ‹*an excuse, a lie*›; **I saw through him immediately** فَطِنْتُ إلى حَقيقَتِهِ على الفَوْرِ **C** **~ [sb] through** ساعَدَ [شَخْصاً] على الاسْتِمْرارِ; **this money will ~ you through** سَيَسُدُّ هذا المالُ احْتياجاتِكَ; **there's enough food to ~ us through the week** لَدَيْنا من الطَعامِ ما يَكْفينا طوال الأُسْبوعِ

• **see to**: **~ to [sth]** **1** (to deal with) تَوَلّى أَمْرَ [شَيْءٍ] ‹*the horses, baby, the washing*› **2** (to fix) أَصْلَحَ [شَيْئاً] ‹*the washers, a broken window*›

seed /siːd/ **A** *n* **1** (of plants) بَذْرة (بَذَرات); **to sow ~s** زَرَعَ \ بَذَرَ \ غَرَسَ بَذْرةً **2** [u] (for sowing) بُذور; **to buy ~ in bulk** اشْتَرى بُذوراً بِكَمّيّاتٍ كَبيرةٍ; **to go to ~** بَدَأَ في تَكْوينِ البُذورِ **3** (AmE) (of fruit) بَذْرة (بَذَرات) **4** (of doubt, discontent) بَذْرة (بَذَرات), أَصْل (أُصول), مَنْشَأ (مَناشِئُ); **to sow the ~s of discontent/hope in sb's mind** زَرَعَ بُذورَ السُخْطِ \ الأَمَلِ في عَقْلِ شَخْصٍ **5** (in tennis) لاعِب مُصَنَّف; **the top ~** اللاعِب

اللاعِب المُصَنَّف ~ **the fifth** *or* **number five** ;المُصَنَّف الأَوَّل الخامِس

B *vt* **1** (to sow with) زَرَعَ (a; زَرْع) ‹*a field, lawn*›; **to ~ a field with wheat** زَرَعَ حَقْلاً بالقَمْح **2** (in tennis) صَنَّفَ ‹*a player*›; **to be ~ed sixth** *or* **number six** كانَ مُصَنَّفاً سادِساً **3** «planes» لَقَّحَ ‹*the clouds*›; **planes ~ed the clouds in an attempt to bring rain to the area** لَقَّحَت الطائِراتُ السَحابَ في مُحاوَلةٍ لِإنْزالِ المَطَرِ على المِنْطَقةِ

C *vi* «plants» بَدَأَ في تَكْوينِ البُذورِ; **allow one healthy plant to ~** اُتْرُكْ نَباتاً صَحيحاً يُكَوِّنُ البُذورَ

seedless /ˈsiːdləs/ *adj* ‹*grape, variety*› بِدونِ بُذورٍ

seedling /ˈsiːdlɪŋ/ *n* شَتْلة (شَتائِلُ, شُتول)

seedy /ˈsiːdi/ *adj* (**seedier**, **seediest**) ‹*area, bar*› مَشْبوه ,قَذِر

seeing /ˈsiːɪŋ/ *conj* **~ that, ~ as** نَظَراً ل ,بِما أنّ; **~ that/as they can't swim, a boat trip is not a good idea** بِما أنَّهُم لا يَعْرِفونَ السِباحة، فَإنَّ رِحْلةً بالقارِبِ لَيْسَتْ فِكْرةً جَيِّدةً

Idiom **seeing is believing** المُعايَنةُ خَيْرُ بُرْهانٍ

seek /siːk/ *vt* (*past tense, past participle* **sought**) **1** (fml) (to look for) بَحَثَ (a; بَحْث; عن) ‹*shelter, a criminal*› **2** (to try to obtain) نَشَدَ (u; نَشْد ,نَشْدة ,نِشْدان), سَعَى (a; سَعْي; إلى) ‹*agreement, employment*› **3** (to request) طَلَبَ ,اِلْتَمَسَ (u; طَلَب ,مَطْلَب) ‹*advice, help*›

Phrasal verb **seek out**: **~ out [sth/sb], ~ [sth/sb] out** سَعى لِلبَحْثِ عن [شَيْءٍ \ شَخْصٍ] ‹*information, a customer*›

seeker /ˈsiːkə/ *n* باحِث (باحِثونَ); **a ~ after** *or* **for truth/happiness** باحِث عن الحَقيقةِ \ السَعادةِ

seem /siːm/ *vi* **1** (to appear, give an impression) ظَهَرَ (a; ظُهور), بَدا (u; بُدُوّ ,بَداء); **he ~ed angry, he ~ed to be angry** بَدا غاضِباً; **things are not always what they ~** لَيْسَت الأَشْياءُ دائِماً كَما تَبْدو; **how does she ~ today?** كيف تَبْدو اليَوْمَ؟; **I ~ to have offended him/to have forgotten my wallet** يَبْدو أَنَّني أَغْضَبْتُهُ \ نَسيتُ مَحْفَظَتي; **there ~s to be a mistake** يَبْدو أنّ هُناكَ خَطَأً; **what ~s to be the problem?** ما هي المُشْكِلةُ في ظَنِّكَ؟; **it ~s to me that we are lost** يَبْدو لي أَنَّنا تُهْنا; **it ~s as if** *or* **as though nothing can be done about it** يَبْدو كَما لو أنَّهُ لا يُمْكِنُ فِعْلُ شَيْءٍ حِيالَ ذلك; **it ~s years since we last saw you** يَبْدو كَما لو أَنَّنا لم نَرَكَ منذ سَنَواتٍ; **it ~ed like a good idea at the time** تَراءى لَنا وَقْتَها أَنَّها فِكْرةٌ جَيِّدةٌ **2** (despite trying) **we ~ unable to find the right person** يَبْدو أَنَّنا غَيْرُ قادِرينَ على العُثورِ على الشَخْصِ المُناسِبِ; **I just can't ~ to communicate with them** يَبْدو أَنَّني فَقَطْ لا أَسْتَطيعُ التَواصُلَ مَعَهُمْ

seemingly /ˈsiːmɪŋli/ *adv* ‹*endless, random*› على ما يَبْدو

seen /siːn/ *past participle* ▸ **see**

seep /siːp/ *vi* «water, blood» نَزَّ (i; نَزّ ,نَزيز), تَسَرَّبَ

see-saw /ˈsiːsɔː/ *n* أُرْجوحة (أَراجيحُ)

seethe /siːð/ *vi* **1** (to be angry) «parents, victims» اِسْتَشاطَ غَضَباً; **she walked out, seething with rage** خَرَجَتْ تَسْتَشيطُ غَضَباً **2** (of a place) غَصَّ (a; غَصّ ,غُصّة), عَجَّ (i; عَجيج); (of a crowd of people) [سارَ بِسُرْعةٍ وِبِشَكْلٍ غَيْرِ مُنَظَّمٍ]ب; **the streets were seething with tourists** كانَت الشَوارِعُ تَغُصُّ بالسائِحينَ

see-through /ˈsiːθruː/ *adj* ‹*dress, plastic*› شَفّاف

segment /ˈsɛgmənt/ *n* **1** (section) جُزْء (أَجْزاء); **a ~ of a circle** جُزْء من دائِرةٍ **2** (of citrus fruit) فَصّ (فُصوص)

segregate /ˈsɛgrɪgeɪt/ *vt* **1** (by race, sex) فَرَّقَ (بين), مَيَّزَ (بين) ‹*the sexes, races*› **2** (into different groups) عَزَلَ (i; عَزْل) ‹*an area, group*›

segregated /ˈsɛgrɪgeɪtɪd/ *adj* ‹*education, society*› يَفْصِلُ \ يُمَيِّزُ بين الأَعْراقِ

segregation /ˌsɛgrɪˈgeɪʃ(ə)n/ *n* تَفْرِقة عُنْصُرِيّة

seismic /ˈsʌɪzmɪk/ *adj* ‹*tremor, activity*› زِلْزالِيّ; **there has been a ~ shift in attitude** كانَ هُناكَ تَحَوُّلٌ جِذْرِيٌّ في المَوْقِفِ

seize /siːz/ *vt* **1** (to grab) اِنْتَزَعَ ‹*the gun*›; أَمْسَكَ ‹*sb's arm*› **2** (to take advantage of) اِنْتَهَزَ ,اِغْتَنَمَ ‹*an opportunity*›; اِسْتَغَلَّ ‹*the initiative*› **3** (to confiscate) صادَرَ ‹*the assets, drugs*› **4** (to capture) اِسْتَوْلى (على) ‹*land, power*›

Phrasal verbs **seize on, seize upon**: **~ on [sth]** اِسْتَغَلَّ [شَيْئاً] ‹*an idea, opportunity*›

• **seize up** «engines» تَوَقَّفَ عن العَمَلِ; «muscles» تَجَمَّدَ

seizure /ˈsiːʒə/ *n* 1 (of territory, power) اسْتيلاء 2 (of arms, property) حَجْز, مُصادَرة 3 (fit) نَوْبة (نَوْبات)

seldom /ˈsɛldəm/ *adv* <*to see, mention*> قَلَّما, قَليلاً ما, نادِراً

select /sɪˈlɛkt/ A *vt* (to choose) انْتَقى, اخْتارَ <*a gift, the best*>; **the ~ed works of ...** الأَعْمال المُخْتارة ل ...

B *adj* 1 (carefully chosen) <*group, wine*> مُنْتَقًى 2 (exclusive) <*area, hotel*> مَقْصور على الأَغْنِياءِ \ النُخْبةِ

selection /sɪˈlɛkʃ(ə)n/ *n* 1 (of a team, short list) انْتِقاء, اخْتِيار 2 (thing chosen) اخْتِيار; **a wide/poor ~ of goods** تَشْكيلة واسِعة \ سَيِّئة من السِلَع

selective /sɪˈlɛktɪv/ *adj* 1 (restrictive) <*education, breeding*> انْتِقائيّ 2 (partial) <*memory, account*> انْتِقائيّ

selectively /sɪˈlɛktɪvli/ *adv* 1 <*to target*> بِصورةٍ انْتِقائيَّةٍ 2 <*to quote*> بانْحِيازٍ

selector /sɪˈlɛktə/ *n* 1 (BrE) (of a team) [شَخْص مُهِمَّتُهُ اخْتِيارُ اللاعِبينَ لِمُنْتَخَبٍ] 2 (device) جِهاز انْتِقاءٍ

self /sɛlf/ *n* (*pl* **selves**) طَبيعة (طَبائِعُ); **you'll soon be feeling your old ~ again** سَتَعودُ عَمّا قَريبٍ كَما كُنْتَ من قَبْلُ

self-addressed envelope /ˌsɛlfəˌdrɛst ˈɛnvələʊp/ *n* [ظَرْف عَلَيْهِ عُنْوانُ المُرْسِلِ]

self-adhesive /ˌsɛlfədˈhiːsɪv/ *adj* <*label, tile*> ذاتيّ الالْتِصاقِ

self-assembly /ˌsɛlfəˈsɛmbli/ *adj before n* <*kit, furniture*> ذاتيّ التَرْكيبِ

self-assured /ˌsɛlfəˈʃɔːd/ *adj* <*performer, smile*> واثِق بِنَفْسِهِ \ بِقُدُراتِهِ

self-catering /ˌsɛlfˈkeɪtərɪŋ/ *adj before n* <*accommodation, holiday*> يُوَفِّرُ خِدْمةً ذاتيَّةً

self-centred (BrE), **self-centered** (AmE) /ˌsɛlfˈsɛntəd/ *adj* <*attitude, lifestyle*> أَنانيّ

self-confessed /ˌsɛlfkənˈfɛst/ *adj before n* <*liar, addict*> مُقِرّ بِذَنْبِهِ

self-confidence /ˌsɛlfˈkɒnfɪd(ə)ns/ *n* ثِقة بالنَفْسِ

self-confident /ˌsɛlfˈkɒnfɪd(ə)nt/ *adj* <*child*> واثِق بِنَفْسِهِ; <*attitude*> يُظْهِرُ ثِقةً بالنَفْسِ

self-conscious /ˌsɛlfˈkɒnʃəs/ *adj* 1 (shy) <*adolescent, smile*> خَجول 2 (unnatural) <*style, artifice*> مُتَكَلَّف

self-contained /ˌsɛlfkənˈteɪnd/ *adj* 1 (complete) <*resort, unit*> مُكْتَفٍ ذاتيًّا 2 (with own kitchen, bathroom) <*apartment, accommodation*> [ذو مَطْبَخٍ وَحَمّامٍ مُسْتَقِلٍّ] 3 (independent) <*child, man*> مُسْتَقِلّ

self-control /ˌsɛlfkənˈtrəʊl/ *n* ضَبْط النَفْسِ; **to lose/regain one's ~** فَقَدَ \ اسْتَعادَ رَباطةَ جَأْشِهِ

self-defence (BrE), **self-defense** (AmE) /sɛlfdɪˈfɛns/ *n* 1 (lawful force) دِفاع عن النَفْسِ; **to act in ~** تَصَرَّفَ بِداعي الدِفاعِ عن النَفْسِ 2 (self-protection) دِفاع عن النَفْسِ

self-destruct /ˌsɛlfdɪˈstrʌkt/ A *vi* «storage device, mines» دَمَّرَ ذاتَهُ بِذاتِهِ, تَدَمَّرَ ذاتيًّا

B *adj* <*button, program*> التَدْميرِ الذاتيِّ

self-destructive /ˌsɛlfdɪˈstrʌktɪv/ *adj* <*urge, behaviour*> مُدَمِّر لِلذاتِ

self-determination /ˌsɛlfdɪtəːmɪˈneɪʃ(ə)n/ *n* تَقْرير المَصير

self-discipline /ˌsɛlfˈdɪsəplɪn/ *n* انْضِباط النَفْسِ

self-disciplined /ˌsɛlfˈdɪsəplɪnd/ *adj* <*attitude, learner*> مُنْضَبِط

self-drive /ˌsɛlfˈdrʌɪv/ *adj before n* (BrE) 1 (in rentals) <*car, van*> بِدونِ سائِقٍ (يَقودُهُ المُسْتَأْجِرُ نَفْسُهُ) 2 (using your own car) <*holiday, tour*> [بِسَيّارةٍ شَخْصيّةٍ]

self-effacing /ˌsɛlfɪˈfeɪsɪŋ/ *adj* <*hero*> مُتَواضِع; <*humour*> [يَعْتَمِدُ على السُخْرِيّةِ من النَفْسِ]

self-employed /ˌsɛlfɪmˈplɔɪd/ *adj* <*worker*> صاحِب مِهْنةٍ حُرّةٍ, يَعْمَلُ لِحِسابِهِ الخاصّ

self-esteem /ˌsɛlfɛˈstiːm/ *n* اعْتِداد بالنَفْسِ

self-evident /ˌsɛlfˈɛvɪd(ə)nt/ *adj* <*truth, fact*> بَديهيّ, لا يَحْتاجُ إلى بُرْهانٍ

self-examination /ˌsɛlfɪgzamɪˈneɪʃ(ə)n/ *n* 1 (of your behaviour, motives) مُحاسَبة النَفْسِ 2 (of your body) فَحْص ذاتيّ

self-explanatory /ˌsɛlfɪkˈsplanətri/ *adj* <*title, instructions*> واضِح, لا يَحْتاجُ إلى شَرْحٍ

self-expression /ˌsɛlfɪkˈsprɛʃ(ə)n/ *n* تَعْبير عن الذاتِ \ النَفْسِ

self-governing /ˌsɛlfˈɡʌv(ə)nɪŋ/ *adj* ‹*institution, colony*› ذو حُكْمٍ ذاتيٍّ

self-government /ˌsɛlfˈɡʌv(ə)nmənt/ *n* حُكْم ذاتيّ

self-harm /ˌsɛlfˈhɑːm/ *n* إيذاء الذاتِ

self-help /ˌsɛlfˈhɛlp/ *n* اعْتِماد على النَفْسِ

self-help book *n* كِتاب المُساعَدةِ الذاتيّةِ

self-help group *n* جَماعة المُساعَدةِ الذاتيّةِ

selfie /ˈsɛlfi/ *n* (infml) صورة ذاتيّة

self-image /ˌsɛlfˈɪmɪdʒ/ *n* صورة ذاتية

self-important /ˌsɛlfɪmˈpɔːt(ə)nt/ *adj* (pej) ‹*manner*› مَغْرور; ‹*official*› مَزْهوّ بِنَفْسِهِ

self-imposed /ˌsɛlfɪmˈpəʊzd/ *adj* ‹*exile, silence*› مَفْروض ذاتيًا

self-induced /ˌsɛlfɪnˈdjuːst/ *adj* ‹*vomiting, trance*› [يُحْدِثُهُ الشَخْصُ بِنَفْسِهِ]

self-indulgent /ˌsɛlfɪnˈdʌldʒ(ə)nt/ *adj* (pej) ‹*behaviour*› [يَتَّسِمُ بالانْغِماسِ في المَلَذّاتِ]; ‹*excuse*› [ذو دَوافِعَ أنانيّةٍ]

self-interest /ˌsɛlfˈɪntrɛst/ *n* مَصْلَحة ذاتيّة \ شَخْصيّة

self-interested /ˌsɛlfˈɪntrɛstɪd/ *adj* (pej) ‹*politician, behaviour*› نَفْعيّ (تَدْفَعُهُ المَصْلَحةُ الشَخْصيّةُ)

selfish /ˈsɛlfɪʃ/ *adj* (pej) ‹*motive, behaviour*› أنانيّ

selfishly /ˈsɛlfɪʃli/ *adv* ‹*to act, pursue*› بِأنانيّةٍ

selfishness /ˈsɛlfɪʃnəs/ *n* أنانيّة

selfless /ˈsɛlfləs/ *adj* ‹*act, devotion*› غَيْر أنانيّ, يَتَّسِمُ بالإيثارِ

self-made /ˌsɛlfˈmeɪd/ *adj* ‹*man, millionaire*› عِصاميّ

self-pity /ˌsɛlfˈpɪti/ *n* إشْفاق على الذاتِ \ النَفْسِ

self-portrait /ˌsɛlfˈpɔːtreɪt/ *n* صورة ذاتيّة

self-preservation /ˌsɛlfprɛzəˈveɪʃ(ə)n/ *n* حِفْظ الذاتِ

self-raising flour /ˌsɛlfˈreɪzɪŋ ˌflaʊə/ (BrE), **self-rising flour** (AmE) *n* دَقيق ذاتيّ الاخْتِمارِ

self-reliant /ˌsɛlfrɪˈlʌɪənt/ *adj* ‹*lifestyle*› يَتَّسِمُ بالاعْتِمادِ على الذاتِ; ‹*individual*› مُعْتَمِد على نَفْسِهِ

self-respect /ˌsɛlfrɪˈspɛkt/ *n* احْتِرام الذاتِ \ النَفْسِ

self-respecting /ˌsɛlfrɪˈspɛktɪŋ/ *adj before n* ‹*teacher, journalist*› يَحْتَرِمُ نَفْسَهُ

self-righteous /ˌsɛlfˈrʌɪtʃəs/ *adj* (pej) ‹*indignation, hypocrite*› مُتَعالٍ

self-rule /ˌsɛlfˈruːl/ *n* حُكْم ذاتيّ

self-sacrifice /ˌsɛlfˈsakrɪfʌɪs/ *n* تَضْحِية بالنَفْسِ

selfsame /ˈsɛlfseɪm/ *adj before n* ‹*day, place*› بِعَيْنِهِ, نَفْسُهُ

self-satisfied /ˌsɛlfˈsatɪsfʌɪd/ *adj* (pej) ‹*smile, smugness*› إعْجابٍ بالنَفْسِ

self-service /ˌsɛlfˈsəːvɪs/ **A** *adj before n* ‹*restaurant, machine*› ذو خِدْمةٍ ذاتيّةٍ
B *n* خِدْمة ذاتيّة

self-sufficiency /ˌsɛlfsəˈfɪʃ(ə)nsi/ *n* **1** (in resources) اكْتِفاء ذاتيّ; **to achieve ~ in fuel** حَقَّقَ اكْتِفاءً ذاتيًّا في الوَقودِ **2** (emotional, intellectual) اسْتِقْلاليّة

self-sufficient /ˌsɛlfsəˈfɪʃ(ə)nt/ *adj* **1** (in resources) مُكْتَفٍ ذاتيًّا; **to be ~ in minerals/oil** كانَ مُكْتَفِياً ذاتيًّا في المَعادِنِ \ النَفْطِ **2** (emotionally) مُسْتَقِلّ

self-taught /ˌsɛlfˈtɔːt/ *adj* ‹*artist, musician*› عِصاميّ

sell /sɛl/ **A** *vt* (*past tense, past participle* **sold**) **1** باعَ (i; مَبيع, بَيْع) ‹*insurance, a house, washing machine*›; **to ~ sth at** *or* **for $25** باعَ شَيْئاً ب \ مُقابِلَ 25 دولار; **to ~ sth at a loss** باعَ شَيْئًا بِخَسارةٍ; **to ~ sth to sb, to ~ sb sth** باعَ شَيْئاً لِشَخْصٍ; **his latest novel has sold a million copies** باعَتْ رِوايَتُهُ الأخيرةُ مِلْيون نُسْخةٍ
2 (to promote) (ل) رَوَّجَ, سَوَّقَ ‹*a product, book, newspaper*›; **her name will help to ~ the film** سَيُساعِدُ اسْمُها في تَسْويقِ الفيلْمِ; **the party failed to ~ its policies to the electorate** فَشِلَ الحِزْبُ في تَسْويقِ سِياساتِهِ للناخِبينَ **3** (to surrender) باعَ (i; مَبيع, بَيْع) ‹*one's integrity, reputation, country*›
B *vi* (*past tense, past participle* **sold**) **1** «traders, staff» باعَ (i; مَبيع, بَيْع); **we have to ~ to survive** عَلَيْنا أنْ نَبيعَ من أجْلِ الاسْتِمْرارِ; **'~ by June 27th'** 'صالِح للبَيْعِ حتّى 27 يونْيو'
2 «goods, houses, books» وَجَدَ إقْبالاً; **the new model isn't ~ing well** النَموذَجُ الجَديدُ لا يَجِدُ إقْبالاً كَبيراً; **they are ~ing at a loss/a profit** تُباعُ بِخَسارةٍ \ بِرِبْحٍ
C *v refl* (*past tense, past participle* **sold**) **1** (to prostitute oneself) **to ~ oneself** باعَ جَسَدَهُ **2** (infml) (in interviews) **to ~ oneself** سَوَّقَ نَفْسَهُ

(Idiom) **to be sold on an idea/plan** (infml) اسْتَهْوَتْهُ فِكْرَةٌ \ خُطَّةٌ

(Phrasal verbs) **sell off**: **~ [sth] off, ~ off [sth]** باعَ [شَيْئاً] بِثَمَنٍ بَخْسٍ \ زَهيدٍ ‹goods, land, furniture›

• **sell out** **A** **1** «tickets, newspapers» بيعَ كُلُّهُ \ عن آخِرِه; **the small bottles have sold out** بيعَتْ كُلّ الزُّجاجاتِ الصَّغيرةِ; **sorry, we've sold out** آسِفٌ، لَقَدْ نَفِدَتْ كُلُّ الكَمِّيَّةِ **2** (to liquidate stocks) باعَ حِصَّتَهُ **3** (infml) (to betray one's principles) خانَ مَبادِئَهُ **B** **~ [sth] out, ~ out [sth]** باعَ كُلَّ [شَيْءٍ]; **the concert is sold out** بيعَتْ كُلُّ تَذاكِرِ الحَفْلِ

• **sell up** **A** صَفّى \ باعَ كُلَّ مُمْتَلَكاتِهِ **B** **~ up [sth]** باعَ [شَيْئاً]

sell-by date /ˈselbaɪ deɪt/ *n* (BrE) تاريخ انْتِهاءِ الصَّلاحيَّةِ

seller /ˈselə/ *n* **1** (vendor) بائِع (باعة, بائِعونَ) **2** (item for sale) بِضاعة (بَضائِعُ); **it's a good/poor ~** بِضاعة جَيِّدة \ سَيِّئة

seller's market *n* سوق البائِعين (يكون فيها الطَّلَبُ أَكْبَرَ من العَرْضِ مِمّا يَسْمَحُ للباعةِ بالتَحَكُّمِ في الأَسْعارِ)

selling /ˈselɪŋ/ *n* بَيْع

selling point *n* [ميزة تَجْذِبُ الزَّبائِنَ لِمُنْتَجٍ]

selling price *n* سِعْر بَيْعٍ

Sellotape® /ˈseləʊteɪp/ (BrE) **A** *n* شَريط لاصِق شَفّاف **B** (**sellotape**) *vt* [أَلْصَقَ بِشَريطٍ لاصِقٍ شَفّافٍ] ‹a notice, page›

sell-out /ˈselaʊt/ *n* **1** (performance) عَرْض نَفِدَتْ \ بيعَتْ كُلُّ [تَذاكِرِه] **2** (infml) (betrayal) خِيانة (المَبادِئِ \ القِيَمِ)

sell-out performance *n* [عَرْض نفِدتْ \ بيعَتْ كُلُّ تَذاكِرِه]

selves /selvz/ *n pl* ▸ **self**

semantic /sɪˈmæntɪk/ *adj* ‹analysis, change› دَلالِيّ

semantics /sɪˈmæntɪks/ *n pl* **1** (branch of linguistics) عِلْم الدَّلالَةِ **2** (meaning) مَعْنًى (مَعانٍ)

semaphore /ˈseməfɔː/ *n* سيمافور (نِظام إشاراتٍ بالأَعْلام \ بالذِراعَيْنِ)

semblance /ˈsembləns/ *n* مَظْهَر \ شَكْل خارِجيّ; **to maintain some ~ of order/normality** حافَظَ على مَظْهَرٍ من مَظاهِرِ النِّظامِ \ السُلوكِ السَوِيِّ

semen /ˈsiːmən/ *n* سائِل مَنَوِيّ, مَنِيّ (مُنْي)

semester /sɪˈmestə/ *n* (AmE) فَصْل دِراسِيّ

semi /ˈsemi/ **A** *n* **1** (BrE) (house) بَيْت مُلاصِق لِبَيْتٍ آخَرَ من جِهةٍ واحِدةٍ **2** (AmE) (truck) مَقْطورة **3** (infml) (semi-final) مُباراة نِصْفِ النِهائيِّ

B (**semi-**); *pref* **1** (partly) شِبْه; **in the ~-darkness** في عَتَمةٍ نِصْفِ كُلِّيَّةٍ **2** (half) نِصْف شِبْه كُلِّيَّةٍ

semi-automatic /ˌsemiɔːtəˈmætɪk/ **A** *adj* **1** ‹pistol, weapon› نِصْف أوتوماتيكيّ **2** ‹gearbox› نِصْف أوتوماتيكيّ **B** *n* سِلاح نِصْف أوتوماتيكيّ

semibreve /ˈsemɪbriːv/ *n* (BrE) مُسْتَديرة

semicircle /ˈsemɪsɜːk(ə)l/ *n* نِصْف دائِرةٍ

semicolon /ˌsemɪˈkəʊlən/ *n* فاصِلة مَنْقوطة

semiconductor /ˌsemɪkənˈdʌktə/ *n* شِبْه مُوَصِّل

semi-conscious /semɪˈkɒnʃəs/ *adj* ‹state› شِبْه وَعْيٍ; ‹person› شِبْه واعٍ

semi-darkness /semɪˈdɑːknəs/ *n* شِبْه ظُلْمةٍ

semi-detached /semidɪˈtætʃt/ *adj* (BrE Archit) شِبْه مُسْتَقِلٍّ; **a ~ house** بَيْت شِبْه مُسْتَقِلٍّ

semi-final /semiˈfaɪn(ə)l/ *n* نِصْف نِهائيٍّ

semi-finalist /semiˈfaɪnəlɪst/ *n* [لاعِب \ فريق يَلْعَبُ في نِصفِ نِهائيٍّ]

seminal /ˈsemɪn(ə)l/ *adj* **1** (very influential) ‹work, research› ذو تَأْثيرٍ عَميقٍ **2** ‹fluid, vesicle› مَنَوِيّ

seminar /ˈsemɪnɑː/ *n* مُؤْتَمَر (مُؤْتَمَرات)

seminary /ˈsemɪn(ə)ri/ *n* (*pl* **seminaries**) كُلِّيّة لاهوتِيّة / إكْليريكيّة

semiquaver /ˈsemɪˌkweɪvə/ *n* (BrE) ذات السِّنَّيْنِ (نوتة موسيقيّة)

semi-skilled /semɪˈskɪld/ *adj* ‹worker, labour› شِبْه ماهِرٍ

semi-skimmed /semɪˈskɪmd/ *adj* (BrE) ‹milk› نِصْف دَسَمٍ

Semitic /sɪˈmɪtɪk/ *adj* ‹languages› سامِيّ

semitone /ˈsemɪtəʊn/ *n* (BrE) نِصْف نَغْمةٍ

semi-trailer /ˈsemʌɪtreɪlə/ *n* (AmE) مَقْطورة

semolina /seməˈliːnə/ *n* سَميد

senate, Senate /ˈsenɪt/ *n* **1** (in government) مَجْلِس الشُيوخِ **2** (of a university) المَجْلِس الأَعْلى

senator /ˈsenətə/ *n* عُضْو في مَجْلِسِ الشُيوخِ, سيناتور

send /sɛnd/ *vt* (*past tense, past participle* **sent**) 1 (to dispatch) أَرْسَلَ, بَعَثَ (a; بَعْث) *<a parcel, message, person>*; **to ~ sth to sb, to ~ sb sth** أَرْسَلَ شَيْئاً إلى شَخْصٍ; **they'll ~ a car for you** سَيُرْسِلونَ لَكَ سَيّارة; **to ~ sb home** أَعادَ شَخْصاً إلى بَيْتِه; **to ~ sb to prison** سَجَنَ شَخْصاً; **she sent him to buy some bread** أَرْسَلَتْهُ لِشِراءِ بَعْضِ الخُبْز; **~ her my love!** بَلِّغْها حُبّي!; **~ them my regards** بَلِّغْهُمْ تَحِيّاتي 2 (to be the cause of) أَدّى (إلى), سَبَّبَ; **the news sent share prices soaring/plummeting** أَدَّت الأَخْبارُ إلى ارْتِفاعِ \ انْخِفاضِ أَسْعارِ الأَسْهُمِ بِشَكْلٍ حادٍّ; **the explosion sent debris in all directions** أَدّى الانْفِجارُ إلى تَناثُرِ الحُطامِ في كُلِّ الاتِّجاهاتِ 3 (in changes of state) جَعَلَ (a; جَعْل); **to ~ sb mad** أَدّى \ دَفَعَ بِشَخْصٍ إلى الجُنونِ; **to ~ sb into a rage** جَعَلَ شَخْصاً يَشْتاطُ غَضَباً; **to ~ sb to sleep** جَعَلَ شَخْصاً يَنامُ

Phrasal verbs **send around** A **~ [sth] around, ~ around [sth]** (to circulate) نَشَرَ \ وَزَّعَ [شَيْئاً] *<a letter, message, an e-mail>* B **~ [sb/sth] around** (to cause to go) أَرْسَلَ [شَخْصاً \ شَيْئاً] *<a person, envelope, package>*

• **send away**: A **~ [sb/sth] away** طَلَبَ من [شَخْصٍ] المُغادَرةَ, أَرْسَلَ [شَيْئاً]; **to ~ a salesman away** طَلَبَ من مَنْدوبِ مَبيعاتٍ أَنْ يَرْحَلَ B **~ away for [sth]** طَلَبَ [شَيْئاً] بالبَريدِ *<a book, product>*

• **send down**: **~ [sb] down** 1 (BrE) (infml) (to imprison) سَجَنَ 2 (BrE) (to expel) طَرَدَ [شَخْصاً] (من الجامِعةِ) [شَخْصاً]

• **send for**: **~ for [sb/sth]** أَرْسَلَ في طَلَبِ [شَخْصٍ \ شَيْءٍ] *<a doctor, taxi>*

• **send in**: **~ [sb/sth] in, ~ in [sb/sth]** 1 أَرْسَلَ [شَخْصاً \ شَيْئاً] *<a letter, entry>* 2 أَرْسَلَ [شَخْصاً \ شَيْئاً] *<the police, troops>*

• **send off** A **~ [sth/sb] off, ~ off [sth/sb]** 1 (to a place) أَرْسَلَ [شَيْئاً \ شَخْصاً] *<a child, an employee>*; **I sent them off to school/to his office** أَرْسَلْتُهُمْ إلى المَدْرَسةِ \ مَكْتَبِهِ 2 (to post) أَرْسَلَ [شَيْئاً] بالبَريدِ *<a letter, an application>* B **~ off for [sth]** (to order) طَلَبَ [شَيْئاً] بالبَريدِ *<a DVD, catalogue>* C **~ [sb] off, ~ off [sb]** طَرَدَ [شَخْصاً] *<a player>*

• **send out** A **~ [sth] out, ~ out [sth]** 1 (to post) وَزَّعَ [شَيْئاً] بالبَريدِ *<the invitations, leaflets>* 2 (to emit) أَصْدَرَ [شَيْئاً] *<a signal, light>* B **~ [sb] out** طَلَبَ من [شَخْصٍ] أَنْ يُغادِرَ *<a pupil, messenger>* C **~ out for [sth]** أَرْسَلَ في طَلَبِ [شَيْءٍ] *<a sandwich, pizza>*

• **send round** (BrE) ▸ **send around**

• **send up**: **~ [sb/sth] up, ~ up [sb/sth]** 1 (into the sky, into space) أَطْلَقَ [شَخْصاً \ شَيْئاً] *<an astronaut, a rocket>* 2 (BrE) (infml) (to parody) قَلَّدَ [شَخْصاً] *<a person>* 3 (AmE) (infml) (to put in prison) سَجَنَ [شَخْصاً]

sender /ˈsɛndə/ *n* مُرْسِل

send-off /ˈsɛndɒf/ *n* (infml) حَفْلة تَوْديع \ وَداع

send-up /ˈsɛndʌp/ *n* (BrE infml) مُحاكاة تَهَكُّمِيّة

Senegal /ˌsɛnɪˈgɔːl/ *pr n* السِنِغال (f)

Senegalese /sɛnɪgəˈliz/ *n, adj* (*n pl* **Senegalese**) سِنِغاليّ

senile /ˈsiːnʌɪl/ *adj* *<person>* خَرِف; *<decay>* شَيْخوخيّ

senile dementia *n* خَرَف الشَّيْخوخةِ

senior /ˈsiːnɪə/ A *adj* 1 (older) أَكْبَر سِنّاً; **he's two years ~ to Mark** هو يَكْبُرُ مارْك بِسَنَتَيْنِ; **Robert King, S~** روبِرْت كينغ، الأَب 2 (in rank) *<officer, manager>* ذو رُتْبةٍ عالية; **a ~ government official** مَسْؤول حُكوميّ رَفيع المُسْتَوى B *n* 1 (older person) شَخْص أَكْبَر سِنّاً 2 (person of higher rank) شَخْص أَعْلى مَرْتَبةً 3 (AmE) مُسِنّ (مُسِنّونَ); ▸ **senior citizen** 4 (student) طالِب في آخِرِ سَنةٍ

senior citizen *n* مُسِنّ (مُسِنّونَ)

senior high school *n* (AmE) [مَدْرَسة ثانَوِيّة تَضُمُّ الصُفوفَ الثَلاثةَ العُلْيا (بين 16–19)]

seniority /siːnɪˈɒrɪti/ *n* 1 (in rank) أَسْبَقِيّة 2 (in years of service) أَقْدَمِيّة

senior school *n* (BrE) مَدْرَسة ثانَوِيّة

sensation /sɛnˈseɪʃ(ə)n/ *n* 1 (feeling, impression) شُعور, إِحْساس (إِحْساسات, أَحاسِيسُ) 2 (furore) ضَجّة, اهْتِمام كَبير 3 (great success) [شَخْص \ حَدَث يُثيرُ ضَجّةً كَبيرةً]; **the book became an overnight ~** أَصْبَحَ الكِتابُ حَدَثاً مُثيراً بين عَشِيّةٍ وَضُحاها

sensational /sɛnˈseɪʃ(ə)n(ə)l/ *adj* 1 (causing furore) *<case, trial>* مُثير للضَجّةِ 2 (sensationalist) *<headline, story>* مُثير للأَحاسيسِ 3 (infml) (very good) *<performance, film>* رائِع, مُمْتاز

sensationalist /sɛn'seɪʃ(ə)nəlɪst/ *adj* ‹*headline, story*› مُثير للأَحاسيسِ

sensationalize, **-ise** (BrE) /sɛn'seɪʃ(ə)nəlʌɪz/ *vt* هَوَّلَ ‹*a story, an incident*›

sense /sens/ **A** *n* **1** (faculty) حاسّة (حَواسُّ); **~ of hearing/taste** حاسّة السَمْعِ \ التَذَوُّقِ; **to lose one's ~ of smell** فَقَدَ حاسّةَ الشَمِّ; **to dull/sharpen the ~s** أَضْعَفَ \ شَحَذَ الحَواسَّ **2** (mental aptitude for) إحْساس (إحْساسات), إدْراك, وَعْي, شُعور (أَحاسيسُ); **a ~ of direction/of rhythm** إحْساس بالاتِّجاهِ \ بالنَغْمةِ; **to lose all ~ of time** فَقَدَ الإحْساسَ بالوَقْتِ **3** (feeling) إحْساس (إحْساسات), شُعور (أَحاسيسُ), إدْراك; **a ~ of security/identity** شُعور بالأَمْنِ \ بالهُوِيّةِ; **a ~ of purpose** إحْساس بالهَدَفِ; **the town has a great ~ of community** المَدينةُ لَدَيْها إحْساسٌ عَظيمٌ بالانْتِماءِ للمُجْتَمَعِ **4** (wisdom) حِكْمة, عَقْل, تَمْييز, تَقْدير, حِسّ; **to have the good ~ to do sth** كانَ لَدَيْهِ من حُسْنِ التَقْديرِ ما يَجْعَلُهُ يَفْعَلُ شَيْئاً; **he had more ~ than to buy it** كانَ لَدَيْهِ من الحِكْمةِ ما يَمْنَعُهُ من شِرائِهِ; **he has more more money than ~** لَدَيْهِ من المالِ أَكْثَرُ مِمّا لَدَيْهِ من العَقْلِ **5** (purpose) هَدَف (أَهْداف), مَغْزًى (مَغازٍ); **there's no ~ in getting angry** لَيْسَ هُناكَ سَبَبٌ لِأَنْ تَغْضَبَ; **what's the ~ in leaving now?** ما المَغْزى من الرَحيلِ الآنَ؟ **6** (meaning) مَعْنًى (مَعانٍ); **in the literal/figurative ~ of the word** بالمَعْنى الحَرْفيِّ \ المَجازيِّ للكَلِمةِ; **to make ~** كانَ مَنْطِقيًّا; **what he said didn't make much ~ to me** ما قالَهُ لم يَكُنْ مَنْطِقيًّا بالنِسْبةِ لي; **it makes ~ to work together** من المَنْطِقيِّ أنْ نَعْمَلَ مَعاً; **to make ~ of sth** فَهِمَ مَغْزى شَيْءٍ; **I can't make ~ of this article** لا أَسْتَطيعُ أنْ أَفْهَمَ مَغْزى هذه المَقالةِ

B (**senses**); *npl* (sanity) عَقْل (عُقول), اتِّزان; **to come to one's ~s** ثابَ إلى رُشْدِهِ; **to take leave of one's ~s** فَقَدَ صَوابَهُ; **the news brought him to his ~s** أَعادَتْهُ الأَخْبارُ إلى صَوابِهِ \ رُشْدِهِ

C *vt* **1** (to be aware of) شَعَرَ (u; شُعور), أَحَسَّ (ب); **to ~ danger** شَعَرَ \ أَحَسَّ بالخَطَرِ; **he ~d that she was worried** شَعَرَ أَنّها كانَتْ قَلِقةً **2** (to detect) اسْتَشْعَرَ ‹*movement, heat, light*›

(Idioms) **to see sense** أَدْرَكَ خَطَأَهُ; **to talk sense** تَحَدَّثَ بِكَلامٍ مَنْطِقيٍّ \ مَعْقولٍ

senseless /'sɛnsləs/ *adj* **1** (pointless) ‹*violence, waste*› لا مَعْنًى لَهُ **2** (unconscious) فاقِد الوَعْيِ

sensibility /ˌsɛnsɪ'bɪlɪti/ **A** *n* شُعور مُرْهَف **B** (**sensibilities**) *n pl* حَسّاسيّات

sensible /'sɛnsɪb(ə)l/ *adj* **1** ‹*decision, approach*› رَشيد; **she's a very ~ person** هي إنْسانةٌ عاقِلةٌ جِدًّا **2** ‹*clothes, shoes*› [بَسيط وعَمَليّ]

sensitive /'sɛnsɪtɪv/ *adj* **1** (physically) ‹*skin, instrument*› حَسّاس; **it's ~ to light** هو حَسّاسٌ للضَوْءِ **2** (perceptive, discerning) ‹*person*› بَصير (بُصَراءُ) **3** (touchy) ‹*person, personality*› حَسّاس **4** (requiring tact) ‹*issue, subject*› حَسّاس **5** (confidential) ‹*information, documents*› حَسّاس

sensitivity /sɛnsɪ'tɪvɪti/ *n* **1** (physical) حَسّاسيّة **2** (perceptiveness, discernment) حَسّاسيّة **3** (touchiness) الإفْراط في الحَسّاسيّةِ, سُرْعة تَأَثُّرٍ

sensor /'sɛnsə/ *n* جِهاز اسْتِشْعارٍ \ تَحَسُّسٍ

sensory /'sɛns(ə)ri/ *adj* ‹*experience, deprivation*› حِسّيّ

sensual /'sɛnʃuːəl/ *adj* ‹*pleasure, desire*› شَهْوانيّ

sensuous /'sɛnʃʊəs/ *adj* ‹*texture, sound*› حِسّيّ

sent /sɛnt/ *past tense, past participle* ▸ **send**

sentence /'sɛnt(ə)ns/ **A** *n* **1** (in grammar) جُمْلة (جُمَل) **2** (punishment) عُقوبة, حُكْم (أَحْكام); **to pass ~ on sb** أَصْدَرَ حُكْماً على شَخْصٍ; **to serve a life ~** قَضى حُكْماً بالسِجْنِ مَدى الحَياةِ

B *vt* ‹*an offender, a defendant*› أَصْدَرَ حُكْماً على; **he was ~d to two years hard labour** حُكِمَ عَلَيْهِ بالأَشْغالِ الشاقّةِ لِمُدّةِ عامَيْنِ

sentiment /'sɛntɪmənt/ *n* **1** (opinion) رَأْي (آراء), مَوْقِف (مَواقِفُ) **2** (feeling) شُعور

sentimental /sɛntɪ'mɛnt(ə)l/ *adj* **1** ‹*value, reasons*› عاطِفيّ **2** (overemotional) ‹*song, plot*› عاطِفيّ جِدًّا

sentry /'sɛntri/ *n* (*pl* **sentries**) [جُنْديّ مُكَلَّف بالحِراسةِ]

Seoul /səʊl/ *pr n* سيئول (f), سْيول (f)

separate **A** /ˈsɛp(ə)rət/ *adj* **1** (individual) ‹*lives, bank accounts, holidays*› مُنْفَصِل; **they asked for ~ bills** طَلَبوا فَواتيرَ مُنْفَصِلةً; **they have ~ rooms** لَدَيْهِمْ غُرَفٌ مُسْتَقِلّةٌ; **a ~ appointment for each child** مَوْعِد مُنْفَصِل لِكُلِّ طِفْلٍ **2** (distinct) ‹*issue, occasion, organization*› مُنْفَصِل ,مُسْتَقِلّ ,مُخْتَلِف; **the money he owes is a ~ issue** المالُ الّذي اقْتَرَضَهُ هو أَمْرٌ مُخْتَلِفٌ; **he visited the property on three ~ occasions** زارَ العَقارَ في ثَلاثِ مُناسَباتٍ مُتَفَرِّقةٍ; **to send sth under ~ cover** أَرْسَلَ شَيْئاً بِشَكْلٍ مُنْفَصِلٍ ,مُسْتَقِلّ **3** (apart) ‹*piece, section, building*› مُنْفَصِل; **the department is housed in three ~ buildings** توجَدُ مَقَرّاتُ الإدارةِ في ثَلاثةِ مَبانٍ مُنْفَصِلةٍ

B /ˈsɛp(ə)rət/ *adv* مُنْفَصِل; **keep the knives ~** أَبْقِ السَكاكينَ مُنْفَصِلةً

C /ˈsɛpəreɪt/ *vt* **1** (to set apart) فَصَلَ (i; فَصْل) (بين) ‹*people*›; **the referee had to ~ them** اُضْطُرَّ الحَكَمُ إلى الفَصْلِ بَيْنَهُمْ; **the child became ~d from his mother** انْفَصَلَ الطِفْلُ عن أُمِّهِ; **~ the cream from the milk** افْصِلِ الزُبْدةَ عن اللَبَنِ; **we cannot ~ the issue of pay from that of working hours** لا يُمْكِنُ أَنْ نَفْصِلَ بين مَسْأَلَتَي الأَجْرِ وَساعاتِ العَمَلِ **2** (to keep apart) فَصَلَ (i; فَصْل) ‹*a country, city, building*›; **the river ~s the old city from the new** يَفْصِلُ النَهْرُ المَدينةَ القَديمةَ عن المَدينةِ الجَديدةِ; **the issue of a wealth tax ~s the two parties** تَفْصِلُ مَسْأَلةُ ضَريبةِ الثَروةِ بين الحِزْبَيْنِ **3** (also **separate out**) (to sort) فَرَزَ (i; فَرْز) ‹*fruit, seeds, components*›

D /ˈsɛpəreɪt/ *vi* (to end a relationship) «couple» انْفَصَلَ; **we have ~d** انْفَصَلْنا; **he has ~d from his wife** انْفَصَلَ عن زَوْجَتِهِ; **to be ~d** «man» كانَ مُنْفَصِلاً عن زَوْجَتِهِ; «couple» كانا مُنْفَصِلَيْنِ

separately /ˈsɛp(ə)rətli/ *adv* **1** (apart) ‹*to live, work*› بِشَكْلٍ مُنْفَصِلٍ **2** (individually) ‹*to analyze, purchase*› على حِدةٍ

separates /ˈsɛprəts/ *n pl* [قِطَع مَلابِسَ يُمْكِنُ تَنْسيقُها بِطُرُقٍ مُخْتَلِفةٍ]

separation /sɛpəˈreɪʃ(ə)n/ *n* **1** (division) فَصْل **2** (of a couple) انْفِصال

separatism /ˈsɛp(ə)rətiz(ə)m/ *n* انْفِصاليّة

separatist /ˈsɛp(ə)rətɪst/ *n, adj* انْفِصاليّ

sepsis /ˈsɛpsɪs/ *n* إنْتان ,تَقَيُّح ,تَلَوُّث الدَمِ

September /sɛpˈtɛmbə/ *n* سِبْتَمْبِر (NA, Gulf), أَيْلول (dipt) (Levant, Iraq), شُتَمْبِر (Mor) ▸**March**

septic /ˈsɛptɪk/ *adj* ‹*wound, infection*› مُتَقَيِّح; **to go ~** تَعَفَّنَ

septicaemia (BrE), **septicemia** (AmE) /ˌsɛptɪˈsiːmɪə/ *n* تَسَمُّم الدَمِ

septic tank *n* خَزّان صَرْفٍ صِحّيٍّ

sequel /ˈsiːkwəl/ *n* **1** (film, book) تَكْمِلة ,تَتِمّة **2** (later event) (نَتائِجُ) نَتيجة ,(عَواقِبُ) عاقِبة

sequence /ˈsiːkwəns/ *n* **1** (series) (سَلاسِلُ) سِلْسِلة; **the ~ of events which led to his death** سِلْسِلةُ الأَحْداثِ الّتي أَدَّتْ إلى مَوْتِهِ **2** (order) تَعاقُب ,تَتابُع ,تَسَلْسُل; **the images were shown in ~** عُرِضَتْ الصُوَرُ بالتَسَلْسُلِ **3** (in a film) مَشْهَد (مَشاهِدُ)

sequential /sɪˈkwɛnʃ(ə)l/ *adj* ‹*order, numbers*› مُتَسَلْسِل ,مُتَتابِع ,تَتابُعِيّ

sequestration /ˌsiːkwəˈstreɪʃ(ə)n/ *n* حَجْز ,مُصادَرة ,نَزْع المِلْكيّةِ

sequin /ˈsiːkwɪn/ *n* تِرْتِر

seraglio /sɛˈrɑːlɪəʊ/ *n* (*pl* **seraglios**) [الحَريم في سَراي السُلْطانِ]

Serb /səːb/ *n, adj* صِرْبِيّ (صِرْبِيّونَ)

Serbia /ˈsəːbɪə/ *pr n* الصِرْب ,صِرْبِيا

Serbian /ˈsəːbɪən/ **A** *n* **1** ▸**Serb** **2** (Ling) (اللُغة) الصِرْبِيّة

B *adj* ▸**Serb**

Serbo-Croat /ˌsəːbəʊˈkrəʊat/, **Serbo-Croatian** /səːbəʊkrəʊˈeɪʃ(ə)n/ *n* (Ling) اللُغة الصِرْبِيّة الكُرْواتيّة

serenade /sɛrəˈneɪd/ **A** *n* سِرِناد (قِطْعة موسيقيّة هادِئة تُعْزَفُ مَساءً على شَرَفِ شَخْصٍ)

B *vt* ‹*a girl, guests*› [عَزَفَ سِرِناد ل]

serene /sɪˈriːn/ *adj* ‹*beauty*› رائِق; ‹*smile*› هادِئ

sergeant /ˈsɑːdʒ(ə)nt/ *n* **1** (in the army, air force) رَقيب (رُقَباءُ) **2** (in the police) ضابِط شُرْطةٍ

sergeant major *n* **1** (in the British army) ضابِط صَفٍّ بِرُتْبةٍ رَقيب أَوَّل **2** (in the US army) مُساعِدٍ أَوَّلِ

serial /ˈsɪərɪəl/ **A** *adj* **1** *<publication>* مُتَسَلْسِل **2** *<killer, offender>* مُتَعَدِّد الجَرائِم **3** *<port, interface>* تَسَلْسُليّ
B *n* (story delivered on TV, radio) مُسَلْسَل (مُسَلْسَلات); (in magazines) رِواية \ قِصّة مُسَلْسَلة

serialize, -ise (BrE) /ˈsɪərɪəlaɪz/ *vt* نَشَرَ بِشَكْلٍ مُتَسَلْسِلٍ *<a book, story>*

serial killer *n* سَفّاح ,قاتِل مُتَسَلْسِل

serial number *n* رَقْم تَسَلْسُليّ

series /ˈsɪəriːz/ *n* (*pl* **series**) **1** (succession) سِلْسِلة (سَلاسِلُ) **2** (on TV, radio) مُسَلْسَل (مُسَلْسَلات)

serious /ˈsɪərɪəs/ *adj* **1** (not frivolous) *<discussion, issue, offer>* جادّ; **being a parent is ~ business** كَوْنُكَ والِداً لَيس بالأَمْرِ الهَيِّنِ; **it's a ~ attempt to reach a compromise** هي مُحاوَلةٌ جادّةٌ للوُصولِ إلى حَلٍّ وَسَطٍ; **there is a ~ message behind the comedy** هُناكَ رِسالةٌ جادّةٌ وراء الكوميدْيا; **he wore a ~ expression** كانَتْ تَعْبيراتُ وَجْهِهِ جادّةٌ **2** (committed) **to be ~ about sth** كانَ جادًّا بِخُصوصِ شَيْءٍ; **is he ~ about going to America?** هَل هو جادٌّ بِخُصوصِ الذَهابِ إلى أَمْريكا؟; **this is a ~ offer** هذا عَرْضٌ جادٌّ; **to be ~ about sb** كانَ جادًّا في مَشاعِرِهِ تُجاهَ شَخْصٍ **3** (important) *<accident, condition, crime>* خَطير; **his condition is ~** حالَتُهُ خَطيرةٌ; **this is a very ~ error** هذا خَطأٌ خَطيرٌ جِدًّا **4** (infml) (plenty) *<money>* كَثير ,وَفير; **to make ~ money** رَبِحَ مالاً كَثيراً

seriously /ˈsɪərɪəsli/ *adv* **1** (not frivolously) *<to think, consider>* بِجِدّيّة ,جِدّيًّا; **to take sth/sb ~** أَخَذَ شَيْئاً \ شَخْصاً على مَحْمَلِ الجِدِّ **2** (genuinely, sincerely) *<to believe, suggest>* على نَحْوٍ جادٍّ; **you can't ~ believe that** لا يُمْكِنُكَ أَنْ تُصَدِّقَ ذلك فِعْلاً **3** (gravely) *<injured, ill>* على نَحْوٍ خَطيرٍ ,بِشَكْلٍ خَطِرٍ; *<to affect, undermine>* بِصورةٍ بالِغةٍ

seriousness /ˈsɪərɪəsnəs/ *n* **1** (of intentions, tone, manner) جِدّيّة; **in all ~** بِكُلِّ جِدّيّةٍ **2** (of an injury, illness) خُطورة

sermon /ˈsɜːmən/ *n* خُطْبة ,عِظة (خُطَب)

seropositive /ˌsɪərəʊˈpɒzɪtɪv/ *adj* *<patient, status>* إيجابيّ المَصْلِ

serpent /ˈsɜːp(ə)nt/ *n* (liter) ثُعْبان (ثَعابينُ)

serrated /səˈreɪtɪd/ *adj* *<edge, knife>* مُسَنَّن

serum /ˈsɪərəm/ *n* (*pl* **serums** or **sera**) مَصْل (مُصول)

servant /ˈsɜːv(ə)nt/ *n* خادِم (m; خُدّام)

serve /sɜːv/ **A** *vt* **1** (to work for) خَدَمَ (i-u; خِدْمة) *<one's country, the community, company>*; **to ~ the corporation faithfully for forty years** خَدَمَ الشَرِكةَ بِإِخْلاصٍ لِمُدّةِ أَرْبَعينَ عاماً **2** (to attend to) خَدَمَ (i-u; خِدْمة) *<a customer>*; **are you being ~d?** هل هُناكَ مَنْ يَقومُ على خِدْمَتِكَ؟ **3** (at table) قَدَّمَ الطَعامَ لِ *<a guest>*; قَدَّمَ *<meal, dish>*; **let me ~ you some beef** دَعْني أُقَدِّمُ لَكَ بَعْضَ لَحْمِ البَقَرِ; **lunch is ~d** يَتِمُّ تَقْديمُ الغَداءِ; **~ it hot or cold** يُقَدَّمُ ساخِناً أو بارِداً **4** (to supply) خَدَمَ (i-u; خِدْمة) *<an area, a county, community>*; **the reservoir ~s the south-eastern area** يَخْدِمُ الخَزّانُ المِنْطَقةَ الشَماليّةَ الشَرْقيّةَ; **the area is well/poorly ~d with transport** المِنْطَقةُ بِها خِدْمةُ مُواصَلاتٍ جَيِّدةٌ \ سَيِّئةٌ **5** (to assist) خَدَمَ (i-u; خِدْمة), ساعَدَ; **he was badly ~d by his advisers** لم يُحْسِنْ مُسْتَشاريهِ في تَقْديمِ النُصْحِ لَهُ; **if my memory ~s me well** إذا أَسْعَفَتْني الذاكِرةُ; **the Volvo has ~d me well** خَدَمَتْني السَيّارةُ الفولْفو بِشَكْلٍ طَيِّبٍ; **to ~ a useful purpose/no useful purpose** يَخْدِمُ غَرَضاً مُفيداً \ لا يَخْدِمُ أَيَّ غَرَضٍ مُفيدٍ; **this map will ~ my purpose** سَتَفي هذه الخَريطةُ بِغَرَضي **6** (to work out) أَتَمَّ, قَضى (i; قَضاء) *<one's sentence, term of office>*; **he ~d his sentence in a high security jail** قَضى فَتْرةَ عُقوبَتِهِ في سِجْنٍ بِهِ حِراسةٌ مُشَدَّدةٌ; **Clinton ~d two terms as President** خَدَمَ كْلينْتون فَتْرَتَيْنِ رِئاسيَّتَيْنِ **7** **to ~ a summons on sb, to ~ sb with a summons** أَرْسَلَ اسْتِدْعاءً لِشَخْصٍ; **the landlord ~d them with notice to quit** أَرْسَلَ صاحِبُ العَقارِ لَهُمْ إِنْذاراً بالإخْلاءِ **8** (in tennis, squash) ضَرَبَ ضَرْبةَ الإِرْسالِ *<the ball, an ace>* **9** (fml) (to mate with) «bull, stallion» نَزا (u; نَزْو, نُزوّ, نَزَوان), جامَعَ (على) *<a cow, mare>*
B *vi* **1** (in retail) خَدَمَ الزَبائِنَ; **is anyone serving?** هل هُناكَ مَنْ يَقومُ على خِدْمةِ الزَبائِنِ؟ **2** (at table) قَدَّمَ الطَعامَ; **would you like to ~?** هل تُحِبُّ أَنْ تُقَدِّمَ الطَعامَ؟ **3** (to fulfil a role) شَغَلَ وَظيفةً; **he's serving as general secretary** يَشْغَلُ وَظيفةَ الأَمينِ العامِّ; **to ~ in the army/navy** خَدَمَ في الجَيْشِ \ البَحْريّةِ; **she ~d two years on the finance committee** عَمِلَتْ سَنَتَيْنِ في اللَجْنةِ الماليّةِ **4** (to meet a need) أَدّى وَظيفةً;

this room ~s as an extra office تُسْتَغَلُّ هذه الغُرْفَةُ كَمَكْتَبٍ إضافيٍّ; **it will ~ as a warning** سَيَكونُ بِمَثابَةِ تَحْذيرٍ **5** (in tennis, squash) سَدَّدَ ضَرْبَةَ الإِرْسالِ; **Evans to ~** سَيَضْرِبُ إيفانْز ضَرْبَةَ الإِرْسالِ

C *n* (in tennis, squash, etc) ضَرْبَة إِرْسالٍ; **it's your ~** هذا دَوْرُكَ في تَسْديدِ ضَرْبَةِ الإِرْسالِ

Phrasal verbs **serve out**: **~ out [sth], ~ [sth] out** **1** قَدَّمَ [شَيْئاً] ‹the meal, food› **2** (to finish) أَنْهى \ أَتَمَّ [شَيْئاً] ‹one's tour of duty, a prison sentence›

• **serve up** **A** (infml) قَدَّمَ الطَّعامَ **B** **~ up [sth], ~ [sth] up** (infml) قَدَّمَ [شَيْئاً]

server /ˈsəːvə/ *n* **1** (computer) خادوم ,مُلَقِّم ,سيرْفِر **2** (in tennis) [المُبْتَدِئ في ضَرْبِ كُرةِ التِنِس]

service /ˈsəːvɪs/ **A** *n* **1** (department) إدارة ,(أَجْهِزة) جِهاز; **the diplomatic ~** السِلْك الدِبْلوماسيّ; **the intelligence ~** جِهاز المُخابَراتِ; **the emergency ~s** أَجْهِزة \ خَدَمات الطَوارِئِ **2** (facility offered, work done) خِدْمة (خِدْمات); **we run an advisory/a public ~** نُقَدِّمُ خِدْمَةً اسْتِشارِيّةً \ عامّةً; **it's all part of the ~** كُلُّ هذا جُزْءٌ من الخِدْمَةِ; **'normal ~ will be resumed as soon as possible'** 'سَيَتِمُّ اسْتِئْنافُ الخِدْمَةِ بِشَكْلٍ طَبيعيٍّ في أَقْرَبِ وَقْتٍ مُمْكِنٍ'; **I'm at your ~** أَنا في خِدْمَتِكَ; **to put** *or* **place sth at sb's ~** وَضَعَ شَيْئاً في خِدْمة شَخْصٍ; **he gave his life in the ~ of his country** ضَحّى بِحَياتِهِ في سَبيلِ وَطَنِهِ; **to be in ~** كانَ في الخِدْمَةِ **3** [u] (customer care) خِدْمة; **the ~ was atrocious/excellent** كانَت الخِدْمَةُ فَظيعةً \ رائِعةً **4** [u] (on a bill) خِدْمة; **~ included/not included** شامِلٍ \ غَيْر شامِلِ الخِدْمَةِ; **they add on 12.5% for ~** يُضيفونَ ٪12.5 للخِدْمَةِ **5** [u] (from machines, vehicles, products) خِدْمة; **it went out of ~ years ago** خَرَجَ من الخِدْمَةِ منذ عِدّةِ سَنَواتٍ **6** (transport facility) خِدْمة نَقْلٍ \ مُواصَلاتٍ; **to run a regular ~** وَفَّرَ خِدْمَةَ نَقْلٍ مُنْتَظِمةً (رِحْلة); **an hourly bus/train ~** حافِلةٍ \ قِطارٍ كُلَّ ساعةٍ تَمُرُّ; **this ~ runs via Birmingham** هذه الرِحْلةُ عَبْرَ بِرْمِنْجْهام **7** (overhaul) صِيانة **8** (in church) قُدّاس (قَداديسُ ,قُدّاسات); **to go to morning/Sunday ~** ذَهَبَ إلى قُدّاسِ الصَباحِ \ الأَحَدِ; **the marriage ~** قُدّاس الزَواجِ **9** (of crockery) طَقْم المائِدةِ **10** (in tennis) ضَرْبة إِرْسالٍ

B (**services**) *n pl* **1** (Mil) **the ~s** القُوّات المُسَلَّحة **2** (on a motorway) مَحَطّة خِدْمةِ السَيّاراتِ

C *vt* **1** (to maintain, overhaul) أَجْرى صِيانةً على \ ل ‹a vehicle, machine›; **to have one's car ~d** أَجْرى صِيانةً على سَيّارَتِهِ **2** دَفَعَ \ سَدَّدَ الخِدْمةَ ‹a debt, loan›

service centre (BrE), **service center** (AmE) *n* مَرْكَز خِدْماتٍ

service charge *n* **1** (in restaurants) رَسْم الخِدْمةِ; **service charge included/not included** شامِل \ غَيْر شامِلٍ رَسْمَ الخِدْمةِ **2** (for common benefits) رَسْم صِيانةٍ **3** (in banking) رَسْم خِدْماتٍ مَصْرِفيّةٍ

service engineer *n* مُهَنْدِس صِيانةٍ

service industry *n* قِطاع الخِدْماتِ

serviceman /ˈsəːvɪsmən/ *n* (*pl* **-men**) جُنْديّ (جُنود)

service provider *n* مُزَوِّد خِدْمةِ الإِنْتَرْنِت

service station *n* مَحَطّة وَقودٍ

servicewoman /ˈsəːrvɪswʊmən/ *n* (*pl* **-women** /-wɪmɪn/) جُنْديّة

serviette /ˌsəːvɪˈɛt/ *n* (BrE) فوطة مائِدةٍ

servile /ˈsəːvʌɪl/ *adj* ذَليل ,خَنوع ,خانِع (أَذِلّة ,أَذِلّاءُ)

serving /ˈsəːvɪŋ/ *n* [حِصّة من طَعامٍ]

serving dish *n* طَبَق لِتَقْديمِ الطَعامِ

serving spoon *n* مِغْرَفة (مَغارِفُ)

session /ˈsɛʃ(ə)n/ *n* **1** (activity time) حِصّة (حِصَص); **a training ~** حِصّة تَدْريبٍ; **the morning/afternoon ~** حِصّة الصَباحِ \ بعد الظُهْرِ **2** (sitting) جَلْسة; **to be in ~** كانَ في جَلْسةٍ «parliament, court» **3** (AmE) (of academic year) فَصْل دِراسيّ

set /sɛt/ **A** *n* **1** (of keys, stamps, data) مَجْموعة (مَجْموعات, مَجاميعُ); (of cutlery, crockery) طَقْم (طُقوم); **a clean ~ of clothes** مَجْموعة نَظيفة من المَلابِسِ; **they're sold in ~s of 10** تُباعُ في مَجْموعاتٍ من 10 قِطَعٍ; **a ~ of fingerprints** بَصَمات أَصابِعِ اليَدَيْنِ; **a ~ of traffic lights** إشارة مُرورٍ **2** (kit, game) مَجْموعة (مَجاميعُ ,مَجْموعات); **a chess ~** مَجْموعة الشَطْرَنْج (قِطَع وَلَوْحة الشَطْرَنْج) **3** (pair) **a ~ of sheets** صَفْحَتانِ مُتَجاوِرَتانِ; **a ~ of false teeth** طَقَم أَسْنانٍ صِناعيّةٍ; **both ~s**

of parents agreed with us اتَّفَقَ كُلٌّ من والِدَي الزَوْجِ ووالِدَي الزَوْجةِ مَعَنا **4** (in tennis) مَجْموعة (مَجْموعات، مَجاميعُ) **5** (group) مَجْموعة (مَجْموعات، مَجاميعُ)، جَماعة; **a member of the racing/yachting ~** عُضْو في مَجْموعةِ السِباقِ \ الإِبْحارِ باليُخوتِ **6** (stage decoration) مَناظِر **7** (receiver) جِهاز اسْتِقْبالٍ **8** (Math) مَجْموعة (مَجْموعات، مَجاميعُ) **9** (BrE) (ability group) [مَجْموعة مُتَجانِسة القُدُراتِ] **10** (in hairdressing) تَصْفيف; **to have a shampoo and ~** غَسَلَ وَصَفَّفَ شَعْرَهُ

B *adj* **1** (fixed) ‹*procedure, time, formula*› مُحَدَّد; **to be ~ in one's ways** كانَ مُتَشَبِّثًا بِرَأْيِهِ; **~ phrase, ~ expression** تَعْبير اصْطِلاحيّ \ ثابِت; **we meet at a ~ time each week** نَتَقابَلُ في وَقْتٍ مُحَدَّدٍ كُلَّ أُسْبوعٍ **2** (prescribed) ‹*book, text*› مُقَرَّر **3** (ready) مُسْتَعِدّ، جاهِز; **to be ~ to leave** كانَ مُسْتَعِدًّا للمُغادَرةِ; **ready, get ~, go!** قِفْ، اسْتَعِدَّ، انْطَلِقْ! **4** (determined) **to be ~ on/against sth** كانَ مُصِرًّا على شَيْءٍ \ مُتَصَلِّبًا في مَوْقِفِهِ ضدّ شَيْءٍ; **he is ~ against closing the office/against the reform** هو مُتَصَلِّبٌ في مَوْقِفِهِ ضدّ إِغْلاقِ المَكْتَبِ \ الإِصْلاحِ; **they are ~ on changing the system/on military intervention** هُمْ مُصِرّونَ على تَغْييرِ النِظامِ \ التَدَخُّلِ العَسْكَريِّ

C *vt* (*present participle* **-tt-**; *past tense, past participle* **set**) **1** (to place, position) وَضَعَ (وَضْع ;a) ‹*a chair, an ornament, a computer*›; **he ~ the chairs in a circle** وَضَعَ الكَراسيَّ في حَلَقةٍ; **to ~ sth upright** وَضَعَ شَيْئاً في وَضْعٍ مُنْتَصِبٍ; **to ~ a post in the ground** نَصَبَ عَموداً في الأَرْضِ; **to ~ the tray in front of sb** وَضَعَ الصينيّةَ أمامَ شَخْصٍ; **a house ~ among the trees/back from the road** بَيْت مَبْنيّ بين الأَشْجارِ \ بَعيداً عن الطَريقِ **2** (to prepare) نَصَبَ (نَصْب ;u)، أَعَدَّ ‹*a trap, an ambush*›; **he ~ a trap for the minister** نَصَبَ فَخًّا للوَزيرِ; **to ~ the table for dinner** أَعَدَّ المائِدةَ للغَداءِ **3** (to establish) حَدَّدَ ‹*a date, price, fashion*›; **to ~ a good/bad example to sb** كانَ قُدْوةً حَسَنةً \ سَيِّئةً لِشَخْصٍ; **to ~ a new Olympic record** حَقَّقَ رَقْماً قِياسيًّا جَديداً في الأولِمْبِياد **4** (in specified operations) ضَبَطَ (ضَبْط ;i-u) ‹*a clock, the alarm, DVR*›; **to ~ the oven to 180°** ضَبَطَ الفُرْنَ على 180 دَرَجةً; **to ~ the alarm for 4 a.m.** ضَبَطَ المُنَبِّهَ على 4 صَباحاً **5** (to cause to start) شَغَّلَ الجِهازَ \ جَعَلَ يَبْدَأُ; **to ~ the machine/engine going** شَغَّلَ المُحَرِّكَ; **he ~ me to work cleaning floors** جَعَلَني أَشْرَعُ في تَنْظيفِ الأَرْضيّاتِ **6** (to prescribe) وَضَعَ (وَضْع ;a) ‹*exam*›; طَلَبَ (طَلَب، مَطْلَب ;u) ‹*an essay*›; أَعْطى ‹*the homework*›; **to ~ sb a task** أَعْطى شَخْصاً مُهِمّةً; **a ~ book** كِتاب مُقَرَّر **7** (to place) وَضَعَ (وَضْع ;a); **the film is ~ in Istanbul** مَشاهِدُ الفيلْمِ مُصَوَّرةٌ في إِسْتَنْبول; **he ~ the book in the sixties** وَضَعَ أَحْداثَ الرِوايةِ في السِتّيناتِ **8** ثَبَّتَ، رَكَّبَ ‹*a ruby, diamond*› **9** **to ~ sth to music** لَحَّنَ شَيْئاً ‹*a libretto, poem, the lyrics*› **10** «compositor» نَضَّدَ، جَهَّزَ للطِباعةِ ‹*type*› **11** «surgeon» جَبَرَ (جَبْر ;u) ‹*a bone, broken leg*› **12** (to style) **to ~ sb's hair** صَفَّفَ شَعْرَ شَخْصٍ

D *vi* (*present participle* **-tt-**; *past tense, past participle* **set**) **1** «the sun» غَرَبَ (غُروب ;u) **2** (to harden) «jam, concrete, glue» تَماسَكَ

(Phrasal verbs) **set about**: **~ about [sth]** شَرَعَ \ بَدَأَ في [شَيْءٍ] ‹*the work, one's duties*›; **to ~ about painting the bedroom/cleaning up** بَدَأَ في طِلاءِ غُرْفةِ النَوْمِ \ التَنْظيفِ; **they ~ about the job** *or* **task of rebuilding the city** شَرَعوا في مُهِمّةِ إِعادةِ بِناءِ المَدينةِ

• **set against**: **A** **~ [sb] against sb** أَثارَ [شَخْصاً] ضدّ شَخْصٍ **B** **~ [sth] against sth** (to balance) وازَنَ \ عادَلَ [شَيْئاً] بِشَيْءٍ ‹*an advantage, the profits*›; **the advantages seem small when ~ against the risks** تَبْدو المَزايا صَغيرةً عِنْدَما تُقارَنُ بالمَخاطِرِ

• **set apart**: **~ [sb/sth] apart** أَفْرَدَ \ مَيَّزَ [شَخْصاً \ شَيْئاً] ‹*a player, book, hotel*›

• **set aside**: **~ [sth] aside, ~ aside [sth]** **1** (to put down) نَحّى \ حَجَزَ [شَيْئاً] جانِباً ‹*a book, one's knitting*› **2** (to reserve) وَفَّرَ \ ادَّخَرَ [شَيْئاً] خَصَّصَ [شَيْئاً] ‹*an area, a room, time*›; ‹*money, supplies*› **3** (to disregard) نَحّى [شَيْئاً] جانِباً ‹*one's differences, prejudices*› **4** (Law) أَلْغى \ أَبْطَلَ [شَيْئاً] ‹*a decision, verdict*›

• **set back** **A** **~ [sth] back** (to position towards the rear) حَرَّكَ [شَيْئاً] للخَلْفِ ‹*a chair, table*›; **the house is set back from the road** البَيْتُ في مَكانٍ بَعيدٍ عن الطَريقِ **B** **~ back [sth], ~ [sth]**

back (to delay) أَخَّرَ [شَيْئاً] *‹production, sb's recovery, work›* **C ~ [sb] back** (infml) (to cost) كَلَّفَ [شَخْصاً]

• **set by**: **~ [sth] by, ~ by [sth]** *‹money, supplies›* ادَّخَرَ [شَيْئاً]

• **set down A ~ [sb] down** أَنْزَلَ [شَخْصاً] *‹a passenger›* **B ~ down [sth], ~ [sth] down 1▸** (to put on the floor, on a table, etc) وَضَعَ [شَيْئاً] *‹a suitcase, vase›* **2▸** (to establish) حَدَّدَ \ قَرَّرَ \ وَضَعَ [شَيْئاً] *‹the conditions, criteria, rules›* **3▸** (to record) دَوَّنَ \ سَجَّلَ [شَيْئاً] *‹an event, fact›*; **to ~ down one's thoughts** دَوَّنَ أَفْكارَهُ

• **set in 1▸** (to take hold) «gangrene» اِنْتَشَرَ; «complications» كَثُرَ (u; كَثْرة), تَزايَدَ **2▸** (to begin) «winter, bad weather» حَلَّ (i-u; حَلّ, حُلول)

• **set off A** اِنْطَلَقَ, رَحَلَ (a; رَحيل); **to ~ off on a journey/an expedition** اِنْطَلَقَ في رِحْلةٍ \ بَعْثةٍ; **she ~ off for the market/station** غادَرَتْ إلى السوقِ \ المَحَطّةِ **B ~ [off] sth, ~ [sth] off 1▸** (to trigger) أَطْلَقَ \ قَرَعَ [شَيْئاً] *‹an alarm›*; فَجَّرَ [شَيْئاً] *‹a bomb›*; أَشْعَلَ فَتيلَ \ نيرانَ [شَيْءٍ] *‹riot›* **2▸** (to enhance) أَبْرَزَ \ أَظْهَرَ حُسْنَ [شَيْءٍ] *‹a design, colour›* **3▸** (Fin) **to ~ one's losses/costs off against profits** أَسْقَطَ خَسائِرَهُ \ تَكاليفَهُ من الأَرْباحِ **C ~ [sb] off** (infml) (to cause to laugh) جَعَلَ [شَخْصاً] يَنْفَجِرُ في الضَحِكِ; (to cry) جَعَلَ [شَخْصاً] يَنْفَجِرُ في البُكاءِ; **be quiet or you'll ~ the baby off** اِلْتَزِم الهُدوءَ وإلاّ بَدَأَ الطِفْلُ في البُكاءِ

• **set on**: **A ~ [sb/sth] on sb** أَطْلَقَ [شَخْصاً \ شَيْئاً] على شَخْصٍ *‹a dog, the riot police›* **B ~ [sb] onto sb/sth** أَرْشَدَ [شَخْصاً] عن شَخْصٍ \ شَيْءٍ *‹a detective, the police›*; **a tip ~ the police onto them/onto their trail** مَعْلومة أَرْشَدَت الشُرْطةَ عَنْهُمْ \ عن طَريقةِ الوُصولِ إلَيْهِمْ

• **set out A 1▸** (to leave) اِنْطَلَقَ; **to ~ out on a journey** اِنْطَلَقَ في رِحْلةٍ **2▸** (to have as one's intention) **to ~ out to do sth** عَزَمَ على أنْ يَفْعَلَ شَيْئاً **B ~ [sth] out, ~ out [sth] 1▸** (to display) عَرَضَ [شَيْئاً] *‹chairs, items for sale, food›*; **the information is clearly ~ out** عُرِضَت المَعْلوماتُ بِشَكْلٍ واضِحٍ **2▸** (to present) شَرَحَ \ عَرَضَ \ قَدَّمَ [شَيْئاً] *‹one's conclusions, objections, ideas›*

• **set up A** (to establish oneself) «trader, entrepreneur» بَدَأَ عَمَلاً خاصًّا; **to ~ up in business** بَدَأَ عَمَلاً خاصًّا \ حُرًّا; **to ~ up on one's own** بَدَأَ عَمَلاً خاصًّا بِمُفْرَدِهِ في التِجارةِ; **to ~ up as a decorator** بَدَأَ عَمَلاً خاصًّا كَنَقّاشٍ **B ~ [sth] up, ~ up [sth] 1▸** (to erect) نَصَبَ [شَيْئاً] *‹a stand›*; أَعَدَّ [شَيْئاً] *‹one's equipment›*; أَنْشَأَ \ أَقامَ [شَيْئاً] *‹a roadblock›*; **to ~ up camp/a tent** نَصَبَ خَيْمةً; **to ~ up house** أَسَّسَ بَيْتاً **2▸** (to organize) أَعَدَّ [شَيْئاً] *‹a meeting, an experiment›* **3▸** (to found, establish) أَنْشَأَ [شَيْئاً] *‹a business, charity, commission›* **4▸** (to configure) نَصَّبَ \ أَعَدَّ [شَيْئاً] *‹a printer, modem, laptop›* **5▸** (to start) تَسَبَّبَ في [شَيْءٍ], أَدّى إلى [شَيْءٍ] *‹a reaction, vibrations›* **C ~ [sb] up 1▸** (in business) **to ~ sb up in business as a plumber** أَعانَ شَخْصاً على إقامةِ عَمَلٍ خاصٍّ كَسَبّاكٍ **2▸** (to improve materially) **that deal ~ her up for life** وَفَّرَتْ لَها تِلْكَ الصَفْقةُ مَعيشةً كَريمةً لِبَقِيّةِ عُمْرِها **D ~ [oneself] up 1▸ to ~ oneself up in business** أَنْشَأَ لِنَفْسِهِ عَمَلاً تِجارِيًّا خاصًّا; **she ~ herself up as a financial adviser** بَدَأَتْ عَمَلاً خاصًّا بِها كَمُسْتَشارٍ ماليٍّ **2▸** (to claim to be) **I don't ~ myself up as an expert** لا أَدَّعي أَنَّني خَبيرٌ

• **set upon**: **~ upon [sb]** هَجَمَ \ اِنْقَضَّ على [شَخْصٍ]

setback /ˈsɛtbak/ *n* نَكْسة (نَكَسات)

set menu *n* قائِمة طَعامٍ مُحَدَّدة (بِأَسْعارٍ ثابِتةٍ)

set square *n* كوس (كوسات)

settee /sɛˈtiː/ *n* كَنَبة

setting /ˈsɛtɪŋ/ *n* **1▸** (location) مَوْقِع (مَواقِعُ), مَكان (أَماكِنُ, أَمْكِنة); **a house in an urban/rural ~** بَيْت في مَوْقِعٍ حَضَريٍّ \ ريفيٍّ; **Dublin is the ~ for the novel** دَبْلِن هي المَدينةُ الّتي تَجْري فيها أَحْداثُ الرِوايةِ **2▸** (of a mechanism) وَضْع (أَوْضاع); **to adjust the ~s** ضَبَطَ الإعْداداتِ **3▸** (of a jewel) إطار (إطارات, أُطُر), **4▸** (of cement, glue, jam) تَماسُك **5▸** (of a piece of music) لَحْن (أَلْحان) حَمَلة) حامِل) **6▸** (Meteorol) **the ~ of the sun** غُروب الشَمْسِ

setting-up /sɛtɪŋˈʌp/ *n* إنْشاء, تَأْسيس

settle /ˈsɛt(ə)l/ **A** *vt* (**settles, settling, settled**) **1▸** (to accommodate) [وَضَعَ في مَكانٍ مُريحٍ] *‹a child, laptop›*; **to ~ the children for the night** جَهَّزَ الأَطْفالَ للنَوْمِ; **to get one's guests ~d** أَجْلَسَ الضُيوفَ في أَماكِنِهِمْ **2▸** (to calm) هَدَّأَ *‹your nerves, stomach›* **3▸** (to resolve) حَلَّ (u; حَلّ), سَوّى, حَسَمَ

(i; حَسْم) ‹*the problem, disagreement, dispute*›; **well, that's ~d** حَسَناً، لَقَدْ تَمَّ تَسْوِيةُ ذلك; **we've ~d the terms of the loan** وَصَلْنا إلى اتِّفاقٍ حول شُروطِ القَرْضِ; **we should try to ~ the case out of court** يَنْبَغي أنْ نُحاوِلَ تَسْوِيةَ القَضيّةِ خارج المَحْكَمةِ **4** (to pay) دَفَعَ ,سَدَّدَ (a; دَفْع) ‹*a bill, debt, claims*› **5** (to put in order) **to ~ one's affairs** رَتَّبَ \ نَظَّمَ شُؤونَهُ **6** (to colonize) اسْتَوْطَنَ ‹*a territory, an island*› **7** (to leave to) **to ~ money on sb** وَهَبَ مالاً لِشَخْصٍ

B *vi* (**settles, settling, settled**) **1** (to come to rest) «dust, dregs, sediment» اسْتَقَرَّ; **let the dregs ~** أُتْرُك الرَواسِبَ حتّى تَسْتَقِرّ; **the boat ~d on the bottom** اسْتَقَرَّ القارِبُ في القاعِ **2** (to alight) «birds, insects» حَطَّ (u; حَطّ) ,هَبَطَ (i-u; هُبوط) **3** (of snow) تَراكَمَ **4** (to become resident) اسْتَقَرَّ **5** (to become firm) «foundations, ground» اسْتَقَرَّ ,ثَبَتَ (u; ثَبات) ,رَسَخَ (u; رُسوخ ,ثُبوت) **6** «child, baby» (to calm down) هَدَأَ (a; هُدوء ,هَدْء) **7** (to become stable) «weather» اسْتَقَرَّ **8** (to agree) تَوَصَّلَ إلى تَسْوِيةٍ; **to ~ out of court** تَوَصَّلَ إلى تَسْوِيةٍ خارج المَحْكَمةِ

C *v refl* (**settles, settling, settled**) **to ~ oneself in a chair/bed** اسْتَلْقى \ اسْتَرْخى على الكُرْسيِّ \ السَريرِ

D *n* مَقْعد خَشَبيّ لَهُ ظَهْرٌ عالٍ

Phrasal verbs **settle back**: **~ back** أَسْنَدَ ظَهْرَهُ; **to ~ back in a chair** أَسْنَدَ ظَهْرَهُ على الكُرْسيِّ

• **settle down**: **~ down** **1** (to calm down) «country, situation, person» هَدَأَ (a; هُدوء ,هَدْء); **the country is settling down after the disturbances** تَهْدَأُ الأَوْضاعُ في البِلادِ بعد الاضْطِراباتِ; **to ~ down to work** فَرَّغَ \ هَيَّأَ نَفْسَهُ للعَمَلِ **2** (to marry) «person» تَزَوَّجَ

• **settle for**: **~ for [sth]** رَضِيَ ب [شَيْءٍ] ‹*an alternative, the poorer option*›; **why ~ for less?** لِماذا تَرْضى بالقَليلِ ؟

• **settle in** **1** (in the home) اسْتَقَرَّ ,تَكَيَّفَ **2** (at work) اسْتَقَرَّ, تَكَيَّفَ

• **settle on**: **~ on [sth]** اسْتَقَرَّ اخْتِيارُهُ على [شَيْءٍ] ‹*a name, colour*›

• **settle up**: **~ up** **1** (to pay) سَدَّدَ \ دَفَعَ الحِسابَ; **to ~ up with the waiter/the hotel** سَدَّدَ الحِسابَ إلى النادِلِ \ الفُنْدُقِ **2** (between several people) سَوّى الحِسابَ ,تَحاسَبَ; **let's ~ up later** لِنَتَحاسَبَ فيما بَعْدُ

settled /ˈset(ə)ld/ *adj pred* **1** ‹*life, relationship*› مُسْتَقِرّ; **I feel ~ here** أَشْعُرُ بالاسْتِقْرارِ هُنا **2** ‹*problem, issue*› مَبْتوت فيهِ **3** ‹*weather*› مُسْتَقِرّ

settlement /ˈsetəlmənt/ *n* **1** (agreement) اتِّفاق (اتِّفاقات), تَسْوِية; **a pay/wage ~** تَسْوِية راتِبٍ **2** [u] (of a dispute) تَسْوِية, اتِّفاق صُلْحٍ **3** [u] (of invoices, a bills) سَداد; **~ is due within 30 days** السَدادُ واجِبٌ خلال 30 يَوْماً **4** (village) مُسْتَوْطَنة

settler /ˈsetlə/ *n* مُسْتَوْطِن

set-top box /ˌsettɒp ˈbɒks/ *n* جِهاز اسْتِقْبالٍ

set-up /ˈsetʌp/ *n* (infml) **1** (system, arrangement) نِظام (نِظامات, أَنْظِمة ,نُظُم) **2** (trick, trap) خُدْعة (خُدَع ,خُدْعات), فَخّ (فِخاخ)

seven /ˈsev(ə)n/ *n, adj* سَبْعة ▸ see also **five**

seventeen /sev(ə)nˈtiːn/ *n, adj* سَبْعة عَشَرَ

seventeenth /sev(ə)nˈtiːnθ/ **A** *n* **1** (in a series) سابِع عَشَرَ **2** (fraction) جُزْء من سَبْعةَ عَشَرَ **3** (**the seventeenth**) (of a month) السابِع عَشَرَ

B *adj* سابِعَ عَشَرَ

C *adv* في المَرْكَزِ السابِعَ عَشَرَ

seventh /ˈsev(ə)nθ/ **A** *n* **1** (in a series) سابِع **2** (fraction) سُبْع **3** (**the seventh**) (of a month) السابِع

B *adj* ‹*century, day*› سابِع

C *adv* في المَرْكَزِ السابِعِ

seventies /ˈsev(ə)ntɪz/ *n pl* **1** (decade) (**the seventies**) السَبْعينات **2** (age) **to be in one's ~** كانَ في السَبْعيناتِ (من عُمْرِه)

seventieth /ˈsev(ə)ntiəθ/ **A** *n* **1** (**the seventieth**) (in a series) السَبْعونَ **2** (fraction) جُزْء من سَبْعينَ

B *adj* ‹*birthday, anniversary*› السَبْعونَ

C *adv* في المَرْكَزِ السَبْعينَ

seventy /ˈsev(ə)nti/ *n, adj* سَبْعونَ

sever /ˈsevə/ *vt* **1** بَتَرَ (u; بَتْر) ‹*sb's head, an artery*›; قَطَعَ (a; قَطْع) ‹*a rope, branch*›; **her head was ~ed from her body** فُصِلَ رَأْسُها عن جَسَدِها **2** قَطَعَ (a; قَطْع) ,أَنْهى ‹*ties, relations*›

several /ˈsɛv(ə)rəl/ **A** *determiner* عِدّة

B *pron* بِضع

severance /ˈsɛv(ə)rəns/ *n* **1** (of relations, ties) إنْهاء ,قَطْع

2 (also **severance pay**) تَعْويض إنْهاءِ الخِدْمةِ

severe /sɪˈvɪə/ *adj* **1** (serious) <*injury, problem*> خَطير; <*pain, headache*> شَديد ,حادّ **2** (bad, extreme) <*weather*> عاصِف; <*winter*> قارِس; <*weather conditions*> سَيِّئ جِدًّا ,قاسٍ **3** (harsh) <*punishment, person*> صارِم ,(قُساة) قاسٍ **4** (austere) <*style, clothes*> بَسيط جِدًّا

severely /sɪˈvɪəli/ *adv* **1** (seriously) <*injured, ill*> على نَحْوٍ خَطيرٍ; **her son is ~ disabled** اِبْنُها مُصابٌ بِإعاقةٍ خَطيرةٍ; **they were ~ affected by the measures** تَأَثَّروا تَأَثُّراً شَديداً بالإجْراءاتِ **2** (harshly) <*to punish, criticize*> بِشِدّةٍ ,بِقَسْوةٍ

severity /sɪˈvɛrɪti/ *n* **1** (seriousness of an injury, illness) حِدّة; (of a problem, damage) خُطورة **2** (harshness) شِدّة ,قَسْوة

sew /səʊ/ **A** *vt* (*past tense* **sewed**, *past participle* **sewn** or **sewed**) <*a seam, hem*> دَرَزَ (u; دَرْز); <*clothes, a dress*> خاطَ (i; خَيْط), خَيَّطَ

B *vi* «seamstress, machine» خاطَ (i; خَيْط)

(Phrasal verb) **sew up**: **~ [sth] up, ~ up [sth]** <*a hole, tear*> رَتَقَ [شَيْئاً]; <*a wound*> خاطَ [شَيْئاً]

sewage /ˈsuːɪdʒ/ *n* مِياه المَجاري

sewer /ˈsuːə/ *n* مَصْرِف (مَصارِفُ), مَجْرى تَصْريفٍ

sewing /ˈsəʊɪŋ/ *n* **1** (activity) خِياطة **2** (piece of work) [قِطْعة قُماشٍ \ نَسيج للخِياطةِ]

sewing machine *n* آلة \ ماكينة خِياطةٍ

sewn /səʊn/ *past participle* ▸ **sew**

sex /sɛks/ **A** *n* **1** [u] (sexual matters) الجِنْس **2** [u] (intercourse) جِماع ,جِنْس; **to have ~** مارَسَ الجِنْسَ **3** (gender) جِنْس (أَجْناس); **the opposite ~** الجِنْس الآخَر; **the battle between the ~es** المَعْرَكة بين الأَجْناسِ

B *adj before n* <*organ*> جِنْسيّ; <*industry*> الجِنْسِ

sex appeal *n* جاذِبيّة جِنْسيّة

sex discrimination *n* تَمْييز جِنْسيّ

sex education *n* تَرْبِية جِنْسيّة

sexism /ˈsɛksɪz(ə)m/ *n* تَفْرِقة جِنْسيّة

sexist /ˈsɛksɪst/ **A** *n* شَخْص مُتَحَيِّز جِنْسيًّا, شَخْص مُتَحَيِّز ضدّ المَرْأة

B *adj* <*comment, attitude*> مُتَحَيِّز جِنْسيًّا, مُتَحَيِّز ضدّ المَرْأةِ

sex life *n* حَياة جِنْسيّة

sex offender *n* مُرْتَكِب جَريمةٍ جِنْسيّةٍ

sextet /sɛksˈtɛt/ *n* فِرْقة موسيقيّة سُداسيّة

sexual /ˈsɛkʃʊəl/ *adj* **1** <*reproduction*> جِنْسيّ **2** <*relationship, orientation*> جِنْسيّ

sexual abuse *n* اِعْتِداء جِنْسيّ, إساءة جِنْسيّة

sexual equality *n* مُساواة جِنْسيّة

sexual harassment *n* تَحَرُّش جِنْسيّ

sexual intercourse *n* (fml) اِتِّصال جِنْسيّ, جِماع, عَمَليّة جِنْسيّة

sexuality /sɛkʃuːˈaləti/ *n* نَشاط جِنْسيّ, جِنْسانيّة

sexually /ˈsɛkʃuːəli/ *adv* <*to abuse, assault*> جِنْسيًّا

sexually transmitted disease *n* مَرَض مَنْقول جِنْسيًّا

sexy /ˈsɛksi/ *adj* (**sexier**, **sexiest**) (infml) **1** (sexually attractive) <*woman, voice*> مُثير جِنْسيًّا, مُغْرٍ **2** (erotic) <*DVD, underwear*> مُثير جِنْسيًّا, مُثير للشَّهْوةِ

Seychelles /seɪˈʃɛlz/ *pr n* (**the Seychelles**) سيشيل (f)

Shaaban /ʃaːˈban/ *n* شَعْبان (dipt)

shabby /ˈʃabi/ *adj* (**shabbier**, **shabbiest**) **1** <*clothes*> رَثّ, بالٍ; <*person*> رَثّ المَلْبَسِ; <*room, building*> مُتَهالِك, مُهْتَرِئ **2** <*treatment, manner*> سَيِّئ, رَديء

shack /ʃak/ *n* كوخ (أَكْواخ), كُشْك (أَكْشاك)

shackle /ˈʃak(ə)l/ **A** (**shackles**) *n pl* غُلّ (أَغْلال), غُلول, قَيْد (قُيود), صَفَد (أَصْفاد)

B *vt* <*a prisoner, an animal*> قَيَّدَ, كَبَّلَ بالسَلاسِلِ

shade /ʃeɪd/ **A** *n* **1** [u] (out of sunlight) ظِلّ (ظِلال); **to sit in the ~** جَلَسَ في الظِلِّ **2** (of colour) دَرَجة; **an attractive ~ of blue** دَرَجة جَذّابة من دَرَجاتِ اللَوْنِ الأَزْرَق; **all ~s of political opinion** كُلّ أَطْيافِ الآراءِ السِياسيّةِ **3** [u] (small amount, degree) **a ~ too loud** أَعْلى من اللازِمِ بِدَرَجةٍ بَسيطةٍ; **a ~ of resentment** لَمْحة اسْتِياءٍ

B (**shades**) *n pl* **1** (infml) (sunglasses) نَظارة شَمْسيّة

2 (undertones) **with ~s of Mozart/of the sixties** بِلَوْنِ موزارْت \ السِّتّيناتِ

C *vt* **1** (to screen) ظَلَّلَ, حَجَبَ *<a place, one's eyes>*; **the hat ~d her face** سَتَرَت القُبَّعةُ وَجْهَها عن الشَّمْسِ; **to ~ one's eyes with one's hand** ظَلَّلَ عَيْنَيْهِ بِيَدِهِ **2** ▸ **shade in**

D *vi* (to blend) **to ~ into sth** «colours, tones» تَحَوَّلَ تَدْريجيًّا إلى شَيْءٍ

E **(shaded)** *adj* **1** (shady) *<place, garden>* مُظَلَّل **2** (Art) *<area, background>* مُظَلَّل

(Idiom) **to put sb/sth in the shade** نَحّى شَخْصاً \ شَيْئاً جانِباً

(Phrasal verb) **shade in**: **~ in [sth], ~ [sth] in** ظَلَّلَ [شَيْئاً] *<a drawing, the background>*

shadow /ˈʃadəʊ/ **A** *n* **1** (area of shade) ظِلّ (ظِلال); **to live in the ~ of the power station/factory** عاش قَريباً من مَحَطّةِ الكَهْرَباءِ \ المَصْنَعِ; **to cast a ~ over the event** ألْقى بِظِلالِهِ على الحَدَثِ; **she's a ~ of her former self** لم يَبْقَ مِنْها سِوى ظِلٍّ باهِتٍ; **they live in the ~ of war/famine** يَعيشونَ في ظِلِّ الحَرْبِ \ المَجاعةِ **2** (person who follows sb) شَخْص يُراقِبُ شَخْصاً آخَرَ في كُلِّ تَحَرُّكاتِهِ **3** (trace, hint) أَثَر (آثار), لَمْحة (لَمَحات); **there is not a ~ of suspicion** لَيْسَ هُناكَ ذَرّةُ شَكٍّ; **without a ~ of a doubt** دون أدْنى شَكٍّ

B **(shadows)** *n pl* (liter) (darkness) ظَلام

C *vt* **1** (to darken) ظَلَّلَ *<a garden, square>* **2** (to follow) تَتَبَّعَ, راقَبَ *<a person>*

shadow cabinet *n* حُكومة ظِلٍّ

shadowy /ˈʃadəʊi/ *adj* **1** (full of shadows) *<corner, corridor>* مُظَلَّل, مُعْتِم **2** (indistinct) *<figure, form>* مُبْهَم, غامِض, غَيْر واضِحِ المَعالِمِ

shady /ˈʃeɪdi/ *adj* **(shadier, shadiest)** **1** (giving shade) *<spot, garden, tree>* ظَليل **2** (infml) (disreputable) *<deal, business>* مَشْبوه; *<character>* مُريب, مَشْكوك فيه

Shafi'i /ˈʃafiʔiː/ *adj* شافِعِيّ

shaft /ʃɑːft/ *n* **1** (of axes) عَمود (أعْمِدة); (of a spear) قَصَبة; (of an arrow) عود (أعْواد, عيدان); (of a golf club) عَصاً (f; عِصِيّ) **2** (of light) شُعاع (n coll; أشِعّة) **3** (in mines) مَدْخَل (مَداخِلُ), بِئْر المِصْعَدِ **4** (in buildings) نَفَق الدُخولِ **5** (in an engine, machine) عَمود الدَوَرانِ

shaggy /ˈʃagi/ *adj* **(shaggier, shaggiest)** **1** *<hair, beard>* أَشْعَث (dipt; شُعْث), غَيْر مُهَنْدَمٍ **2** *<dog, pony, sheep>* أَشْعَث (dipt)

shaggy dog story *n* [قِصّة طَويلة وَمُمِلّة]

shahada, shahadah /ʃəˈhɑːda/ *n* شَهادة

shahid, shaheed /ʃəˈhiːd/ *n* شَهيد (شُهَداءُ)

Shaitan /ʃeɪˈtɑːn/ *n* شَيْطان (شَياطينُ)

shake /ʃeɪk/ **A** *vt* (*past tense* **shook**; *past participle* **shaken**) **1** هَزَّ (u; هَزّ) *<a duster, branch>*; رَجَّ (u; رَجّ) *<a bottle>*; **~ the pepper over the food** هُزَّ الفُلْفُلَ فوق الطعامِ; **'~ before use'** 'يُرَجُّ قبل الاسْتِخْدامِ' **2** (with people) هَزَّ (u; هَزّ) *<a person>*; **I shook him to wake him up** هَزَزْتُهُ لأوقظَهُ; **to ~ hands with sb, to ~ sb's hand** صافَحَ شَخْصاً; **to ~ hands on the deal** أعْطى مُوافَقَتَهُ على الاتِّفاقِ; **to ~ one's fist** رفَعَ قَبْضَتَهُ في تَحَدٍّ; **to ~ one's head** هَزَّ رَأْسَهُ بالرَفْضِ **3** «earthquakes, explosions» هَزَّ (u; هَزّ) *<a building, town>* **4** (to shock) صَدَمَ (i; صَدْم), هَزَّ (u; هَزّ) *<the nation, a person>*; **the earthquake shook my faith** هَزَّ الزِلْزالُ إيماني **5** (AmE) (to get rid of) ▸ **shake off**

B *vi* (*past tense* **shook**; *past participle* **shaken**) **1** (to tremble) «a person, sb's hand» ارْتَعَشَ, ارْتَجَفَ; «a building» اهْتَزَّ; **she was shaking with fear/cold** كانَتْ تَرْتَجِفُ من الخَوْفِ \ البَرْدِ; **the ground shook violently** كانَت الأرْضُ تَهْتَزُّ بِعُنْفٍ **2** (to shake hands) تَصافَحَ; **they shook on it** أعْطوا مُوافَقَتَهُمْ عَلَيْهِ

C *v refl* (*past tense* **shook**; *past participle* **shaken**) **to ~ oneself** هَزَّ نَفْسَهُ

D *n* **1** **to give sth a ~** نَفَّضَ شَيْئاً *<cloth, duster>*; رَجَّ شَيْئاً *<a bottle, medicine>*; **with a ~ of one's head** وَهُوَ يَهُزُّ رَأْسَهُ بالنَفْيِ **2** (also **milkshake**) حَليب مَخْفوق

(Idiom) **to be no great shakes** (infml) كانَ مُتَواضِعَ المُسْتَوى

(Phrasal verbs) **shake about** = **shake around**

• **shake around** **A** «planes, cars» اهْتَزَّ **B** **~ [sb/sth] around** هَزَّ [شَخْصاً \ شَيْئاً] بِعُنْفٍ *<a passenger, package, laptop>*

• **shake off**: **~ [sb/sth] off, ~ off [sb/sth]** **1** نَفَّضَ [شَيْئاً] *<dust,*

dirt> **2** (to get rid of) شُفِيَ \ تَعافى من [شَيْءٍ] *<a cough,*
cold> **3** (infml) (to escape from) هَرَبَ من [شَخْصٍ \ شَيْءٍ]
<a pursuer>

• **shake out**: **A** ~ **[sth] out**, ~ **out [sth]** **1** نَفَضَ [شَيْئاً]
<the tablecloth, rug> **2** رَشَّ [شَيْئاً] *<some flour, the seeds>* **B** ~
[sb] out of sth *<a depressive>* ساعَدَ [شَخْصاً] على التَخلُّصِ
من شَيْءٍ

• **shake up** **A** ~ **up [sth]**, ~ **[sth] up** رَجَّ [شَيْئاً] *<a bottle, mixture>*
B ~ **[sb/sth] up**, ~ **up [sb/sth]** **1** (to jolt) هَزَّ [شَخْصاً \ شَيْئاً]
<a passenger, package> **2** (to reorganize) أَعادَ تَنْظيمَ [شَيْءٍ] بقوّةٍ
<a company, department>

shaken /ˈʃeɪk(ə)n/ **A** *past participle* ▸ **shake**
B *adj* (disconcerted, upset) مَهْزوز ,مُرْتَبِك ,مُضْطَرِب

shaker /ˈʃeɪkə/ *n* **1** (for cocktails) [وِعاء لِمَزْجِ السَوائِلِ]
2 (for salt) مَمْلَحة (مَمالِحُ); (for pepper) رَشّاشة الفُلْفُلِ;
(for sugar) سُكَّريّة **3** (for dice) عُلْبة لِهَزِّ النَرْدِ

shake-up /ˈʃeɪkʌp/ *n* إعادة تَنْظيمٍ شامِلة ,تَغْيير جِذْريّ

shaky /ˈʃeɪki/ *adj* (**shakier, shakiest**) **1** (trembling)
<hands, voice> مُرْتَعِش **2** (unsteady) *<table, chair>* مُتَزَعْزِع,
غَيْر ثابِتٍ ,مُهْتَزّ ,مُتَخَلْخِل; **I feel a bit ~** أَشْعُرُ بِبَعْضِ التَوَتُّرِ
3 (unreliable, faltering) *<start>* مُتَزَعْزِع ,مَهْزوز; *<economy,*
government> غَيْر مُسْتَقِرّ ,هَشّ; *<evidence, argument>* ضَعيف

shale /ʃeɪl/ *n* طَفْل صَفْحيّ ,صَخْر طينيّ

shall /ʃal, ʃ(ə)l/ *modal aux* (*also* **'ll**; *negative* **shan't, shall not**)
1 (for the future tense) **I ~** *or* **I'll see you tomorrow**
سَأُقابِلُكَ \ سَوْفَ أُقابِلُكَ غَداً; **we ~ not** *or* **shan't have a reply**
before Friday لن يَصِلَنا رَدٌّ قبل يَوْمِ الجُمُعةِ **2** (in suggestions)
~ I set the table? هل أُعِدُّ المائدةَ؟; **~ we go to the cinema**
tonight? هل نَذْهَبُ إلى السينَما اللَيْلةَ؟ **3** (fml) (in commands,
contracts etc) **you ~ do as I say** يَجِبُ أَنْ تَفْعَلَ كَما أقولُ لَكَ;
the balance ~ be paid on delivery of the goods يَجِبُ دَفْعُ
المَبْلَغِ المُتَبَقّي عند اسْتِلامِ البَضائِعِ

shallot /ʃəˈlɒt/ *n* قُفْلوط ,كُرّاث أَنْدَلُسيّ

shallow /ˈʃaləʊ/ *adj* **1** *<water>* ضَحْل; *<dish>* مُسَطَّح
2 *<breathing>* ضَحْل ,سَطْحيّ **3** *<person, relationship>* سَطْحيّ

shallows /ˈʃaləʊz/ *n pl* مِياه ضَحْلة

sham /ʃam/ **A** *n* خُدْعة (خُدْعات ,خُدَع)
B *adj* *<marriage, trial>* زائِف ,صوريّ
C *vt* (**-mm-**) ادَّعى (ب) ,تَظاهَرَ *<indifference, interest>*
D *vi* ادَّعى ,تَظاهَرَ «person»

shambles /ˈʃambəlz/ *n* (infml) فَوْضى (f)

shame /ʃeɪm/ **A** *n* **1** [u] (guilt) شُعور بالذَنْبِ ,خَجَل; **he has**
no ~ لَيْسَ لَدَيْهِ حَياءٌ; **to feel ~ at sth** شَعَرَ بالخَجَلِ من شَيْءٍ
2 (fml) (disgrace) عار ,خِزْي (أَعْيار); **to my eternal ~** مِمّا
يُؤْسِفُني دائِماً; **to bring ~ on oneself/one's family** جَلَبَ
العارَ على نَفْسِه \ عائِلَتِهِ; **the ~ of it!** يا لَلْعارِ! **3** (pity) أَسَف,
أَسًى; **what a ~!** يا لَلأَسَفِ!; **it's a ~ that we can't be at the**
wedding من المُؤْسِفِ أَنّنا لا نَسْتَطيعُ حُضورَ الزِفافِ; **it was**
such a ~ that she lost كانَ من المُؤْسِفِ جِدّاً أَنّها خَسِرَتْ;
it's a ~ about Dave's father من دَواعي الأَسى ما حَدَثَ
لِوالِدِ ديف

B *vt* **1** (to embarrass) أَخْجَلَ ,أَحْرَجَ *<a person>*; **I was ~d by**
her words أَحْرَجَتْني كَلِماتُها; **to ~ sb into doing sth** حَمَلَ
شخصاً على فِعْلِ شَيْءٍ بِدافِعِ الإحْراجِ **2** (to disgrace) جَلَبَ
العارَ لِ *<one's family, country>*; **they ~d the nation** جَلَبوا العارَ
لِلبِلادِ

Idiom **to put sb to shame** أَظْهَرَ تَفَوُّقاً كَبيراً على شَخْصٍ

shamefaced /ʃeɪmˈfeɪst/ *adj* *<grin, confession>* يَعْتَريهِ الخَجَلُ

shameful /ˈʃeɪmfʊl/ *adj* *<secret, behaviour>* مُخْزٍ ,مُخْجِل

shameless /ˈʃeɪmləs/ *adj* *<behaviour, exploitation>* مُخْزٍ ,وَقِح;
<liar, cheat> قَليل الحَياءِ ,صَفيق الوَجْهِ

shampoo /ʃamˈpuː/ **A** *n* (*pl* **shampoos**) شامْبو (شامْبُوات)
B *vt* (*present tense* **shampoos**; *past tense, past participle*
shampooed) غَسَلَ بالشامْبو *<one's hair>*; نَظَّفَ بالشامْبو
<carpets, upholstery>

shamrock /ˈʃamrɒk/ *n* نَفَل (نَبات يُشْبِهُ البِرْسيمَ)

shandy (BrE) /ˈʃandi/, **shandygaff** (AmE) /ˈʃandigaf/ *n*
(*pl* **shandies**) [جِعة مَمْزوجة بالليمونادة]

shan't /ʃɑːnt/ *abbr* = **shall not** ▸ **shall**

shanty /ˈʃanti/ *n* (*pl* **shanties**) **1** (hut) كوخ (أَكْواخ) **2** (also
sea shanty) (song) أُنْشودة البَحّارة

shanty town *n* مِنْطَقة عَشْوائيّة ,مَدينة أَكْواخٍ \ صَفيحٍ

shape /ʃeɪp/ **A** *n* **1** (of an object, a building, etc) شَكْل (شُكول ,أَشْكال); **a square/triangular ~** شَكْل مُرَبَّع \ مُثَلَّث; **what ~ is it?** ما شَكْلُهُ؟; **it was an odd ~** كانَ شَكْلاً غَريباً; **they are the right/wrong ~** هي على الشَكْلِ الصَحيحِ \ الخَطَإ; **to be round/square in ~** كانَ شَكْلُهُ دائِريًّا \ مُرَبَّعاً; **it's in the ~ of a star** هو على شَكْلِ نَجْمةٍ; **to lose its ~** «sweater, sock» فَقَدَ شَكْلَهُ; **in all ~s and sizes** بكُلِّ الأَشْكالِ والأَحْجامِ **2** (form) شَكْل (شُكول ,أَشْكال) **3** (infml) (optimum condition) شَكْل أَمْثَل; **to be out of ~** كانَ فاقِداً لِلِّياقةِ البَدَنيّةِ; **to get/keep in ~** اسْتَعادَ لياقَتَهُ \ احْتَفَظَ بِلِياقَتِهِ; **to knock the report/team into ~** حَسَّنَ شَكْلَ التَقْرير \ لِياقةَ الفَريقِ **4** (character, structure) هَيْئة (شُكول ,أَشْكال); **the ~ of things to come** تَطَوُّرات الأَحْداثِ القادِمةِ; **to take ~** «plan, ideas» بَدَأَتْ تَتَّضِحُ مَعالِمُهُ; **I condemn violence in any ~ or form** أُدينُ العُنْفَ بِكُلِّ أَشْكالِهِ وَصُوَرِهِ **5** (guise) **in the ~ of sth** على هَيْئةِ شَيْءٍ; **help arrived in the ~ of a policeman/a large sum of money** وَصَلَت المُساعَدةُ في شَكْلِ شُرْطيٍّ \ كَمّيّةٍ كَبيرةٍ من المالِ **6** (mould) قالِب (قَوالِبُ)
B *vt* **1** (to fashion, mould) شَكَّلَ ‹*the clay, stone, wood*›; **~ the clay/dough into a ball** شَكِّل الصَلْصالَ \ العَجينة في شَكْلِ كُرةٍ; **to ~ the stone into a triangle** شَكَّلَ الحَجَرَ في شَكْلِ مُثَلَّثٍ **2** (to influence) «leader, events» شَكَّلَ ‹*a policy, an organization, sb's future*›; **he played a part in shaping the country's future** لَعِبَ دَوْراً في تَشْكيلِ مُسْتَقْبَلِ البَلَدِ **3** (to fit closely) فَصَّلَ على المَقاسِ ‹*a garment*›

(Phrasal verb) **shape up** (infml) **1** (to develop) «employees, recruits» تَحَسَّنَ; **how are things shaping up at head office?** كيف تَتَطَوَّرُ الأُمورُ في المَكْتَبِ الرَئيسيِّ؟ **2** (to meet expectations) لَبّى التَوَقُّعاتِ

shaped /ʃeɪpt/ *adj* **to be ~ like a vase/pipe** كانَ على شَكْلِ مِزْهَريّةٍ \ ماسورةٍ

-shaped /-ʃeɪpt/ *suffix* على شَكْلِ \ هَيْئةِ ...; **star-/V~** على شَكْلِ نَجْمةٍ \ حَرْفِ V

shapeless /ˈʃeɪpləs/ *adj* ‹*mass, dress*› عَديم الشَكْلِ, غَيْر واضِحِ المَعالِمِ

shapely /ˈʃeɪpli/ *adj* (**shapelier, shapeliest**) ‹*legs, figure*› مَمْشوق ,رَشيق

share /ʃɛː/ **A** *n* **1** [u] (of money, food, blame) نَصيب (نُصُب, أَنْصِبة); **her ~ of the inheritance was too big** نَصيبُها من الميراثِ كانَ كَبيراً جِدًّا; **he did his ~ of the work** أَدّى ما عَلَيْهِ من العَمَلِ; **to pay one's fair ~** دَفَعَ حِصَّتَهُ العادِلةَ; **to have a ~ in sb's success/in a result** كانَ لَهُ إِسْهامٌ في نَجاحِ شَخْصٍ \ في الوُصولِ إلى نَتيجةٍ **2** (in a company) سَهْم (أَسْهُم); **to own ~s in a company** امْتَلَكَ أَسْهُماً في شَرِكةٍ; **~s closed higher/lower** أَغْلَقَت الأَسْهُمُ على ارْتِفاعٍ \ انْخِفاضٍ
B *vt* اشْتَرَكَ (في) ‹*money, a prize, room, taxi*›; **to ~ the food/taxi** اشْتَرَكَ في الطَعامِ \ سَيّارةِ الأُجْرةِ; **the prize was ~d between the two students** تَقاسَمَ الطالِبانِ الجائِزةَ; **we ~ the responsibility for her care** نَتَقاسَمُ مَسْؤوليّةَ رِعايَتِها; **we ~ a birthday** عيدُ ميلادِنا في نَفْسِ اليَوْمِ; **we ~ many interests** نَشْتَرِكُ في العَديدِ من الاهْتِماماتِ
C *vi* **to ~ in sth** اشْتَرَكَ في شَيْءٍ ‹*the success, sb's happiness, the benefits*›

(Phrasal verb) **share out**: **~ [sth] out, ~ out [sth]** (to apportion) وَزَّعَ \ قَسَّمَ [شَيْئاً] ‹*food, profits, supplies*›

shared /ʃɛːd/ *adj* **1** ‹*house, entrance*› مُشْتَرَك **2** ‹*experience, values*› مُشْتَرَك

shareholder /ˈʃɛːhəʊldə/ *n* حامِل أَسْهُمٍ ,مُساهِم

share option plan, share option scheme *n* نِظام خِيارِ شِراءِ الأَسْهُمِ

shareware /ˈʃɛːwɛː/ *n* بَرامِج تَجْريبيّة

sharia /ʃəˈriːə/ *n* (also **sharia law**) الشَريعة الإِسْلاميّة

sharif /ʃəˈriːf/ *n* شَريف (أَشْراف)

shark /ʃɑːk/ *n* قِرْش (سَمَك)

sharp /ʃɑːp/ **A** *adj* **1** (good for cutting) ‹*knife, razor, scissors*› حادّ; **you need a ~ blade** تَحْتاجُ إلى شَفْرةٍ حادّةٍ **2** (pointed) ‹*needle, pencil*› حادّ; ‹*nose*› مُدَبَّب **3** (abrupt) ‹*bend, turning, angle*› حادّ ,شَديد الانْحِناء; **there were ~ falls/rises on the stock markets** كانَ هُناكَ انْخِفاضاتٌ \ ارْتِفاعاتٌ حادّةٌ في سوقِ الأَوْراقِ الماليّةِ **4** (acidic) ‹*taste, fruit*› حامِض ,لاذِع

5 (severe) <*frost, cold, wind*> قارِس 6 (intense) <*pain, blow*> شَديد ,حادّ 7 (alert) <*person*> مُتَّقِد الذِهْنِ ,(أَذْكِياءُ) ذَكِيّ, حادّ الذَكاءِ; <*mind*> ثاقِب ,مُتَّقِد; **he is known for his ~ wit** مَعْروفٌ عَنْهُ سُرْعةُ بَديهَتِهِ 8 (of senses) <*eyesight, hearing*> حادّ; **to have a ~ eye for sth** كانَ لَدَيْهِ قُدْرةٌ كَبيرةٌ على اكْتِشافِ شَيْءٍ; **he has a ~ eye for mistakes/bargains** لَدَيْهِ قُدْرةٌ كَبيرةٌ على اكْتِشافِ الأَخْطاءِ \ الصَفَقاتِ 9 (astute) <*businessman, dealer*> بارِع ,ماهِر (مَهَرة); **she is extremely ~** هي بارِعةٌ للغايةِ 10 (clearly defined) <*image, outline*> شَديد الوُضوحِ; **to be in ~ contrast with sth** كانَ في تَناقُضٍ حادٍّ مع شَيْءٍ 11 (aggressive) <*rebuke, words*> حادّ ,لاذِع 12 (infml) (stylish) <*dresser, style, suit*> أَنيق

B *adv* 1 (abruptly) <*to stop, pull up*> فَجْأةً ,بِشَكْلٍ مُفاجِئٍ; **to turn ~ left/right** انْعَطَفَ شِمالاً \ يَميناً بِشَكْلٍ حادٍّ 2 (promptly) تَماماً ,بالضَبْطِ; **be there at 9 a.m. ~** كُنْ هُناكَ الساعةَ 9 صَباحاً بالضَبْطِ

C *n* عَلامة الرَفْعِ (في التَدْوينِ الموسيقيِّ)

Idioms **to be at the sharp end** كانَ في اللَحَظاتِ الحاسِمةِ; **to look sharp** أَسْرَعَ

sharpen /ˈʃɑːp(ə)n/ *vt* شَحَذَ (a; شَحْذ), سَنَّ (u; سَنّ) <*a knife, pair of scissors*>; بَرى (i; بَري) <*a pencil*>

sharpener /ˈʃɑːpnə/ *n* (for knives) مِسَنّ ,(مَشاحِذُ) مِشْحَذ (مِسَنّات); (for pencils) بَرّاية ,(مَبارٍ) مِبْراة

sharply /ˈʃɑːpli/ *adv* 1 <*to rise, to fall*> بِشَكْلٍ حادٍّ ,بِحِدّةٍ <*to bend, to turn*> بِسُرْعةٍ ,فَجْأةً 2 <*to speak, to criticize*> بِصَرامةٍ, بِخُشونةٍ ,بِفَظاظةٍ 3 <*outlined, defined*> بِوُضوحٍ

shat /ʃat/ *past tense, past participle* ▸ **shit**

shatter /ˈʃatə/ **A** *vt* 1 حَطَّمَ ,هَشَّمَ ,كَسَّرَ <*a window, glass*> 2 <*hope, confidence*>; قَضى (i; قَضاء) (على) <*peace*>; كَسَرَ (i; كَسْر) <*silence*>; أَتْلَفَ <*nerves, health*>

B *vi* «windows, glass» تَهَشَّمَ ,تَكَسَّرَ

shattered /ˈʃatəd/ *adj* 1 <*confidence, dream*> مُحَطَّم; <*plate, window*> مُكَسَّر ,مُهَشَّم 2 (devastated) مُنْزَعِج ,مُتَضايِق; (infml) (tired) مُرْهَق ,مُنْهَك ,مُتْعَب

shave /ʃeɪv/ **A** *vt* (*past participle* **shaved** or **shaven**) حَلَقَ (i; حَلْق) <*one's face, legs*>

B *vi* (*past participle* **shaved** or **shaven**) «men» حَلَقَ ذَقْنَهُ

C *n* حِلاقة الذَقْنِ; **to have a ~** حَلَقَ ذَقْنَهُ

shaver /ˈʃeɪvə/ *n* (also **electric shaver**) ماكينة حِلاقةٍ كَهْرَبائيّة

shaving /ˈʃeɪvɪŋ/ *n* 1 [u] (action) حِلاقة 2 **~s** (of wood) نُجارة; (of metal) قُصاصات

shaving brush *n* فُرْشاة حِلاقةٍ

shaving cream *n* كْريم \ مَعْجون حِلاقةٍ

shaving foam *n* رَغْوة حِلاقةٍ

shaving mirror *n* مِرْآة حِلاقةٍ

shawl /ʃɔːl/ *n* شال (شالات)

Shawwal /ʃaˈwal/ *n* شوّال

she /ʃiː, ʃi/ *pron* هِيَ; **here ~ is** ها هِيَ ذي; **~'s a judge** هِيَ قاضِيةٌ; **~ didn't say that, I did** هِيَ لم تَقُلْ ذلك، أنا مَنْ قالَهُ; **her brother's poor, but ~'s rich** أَخوها فَقيرٌ، لَكِنَّها غَنيّةٌ; **~ and I eat there often** أنا وَهِيَ نَأْكُلُ هُناكَ غالِباً

sheaf /ʃiːf/ *n* (*pl* **sheaves**) (of corn, flowers) حُزْمة (حُزَم); (of papers) رِزْمة (رِزَم)

shear /ʃɪə/ *vt* (*past tense* **sheared**; *past participle* **shorn** or **sheared**) جَزَّ الصوفَ <*sheep*>

shears /ʃɪəz/ *n pl* 1 (for gardening) مِقَصّ تَشْذيبٍ 2 (for sheep) مِجَزّ

sheath /ʃiːθ/ *n* (*pl* **sheaths** /ʃiːðz/) 1 (Bot, Zool) غِمْد (غُمود), جِراب ,(أَغْماد ,غُمود) 2 (case of a sword, knife) غِمْد (أَغْماد), (أَجْرِبة); (of a cable) غِلاف (أَغْلِفة) 3 (condom) واقٍ \ عازِل ذَكَريّ

sheaves /ʃiːvz/ *n pl* ▸ **sheaf**

shed /ʃɛd/ **A** *n* 1 (in a garden) سَقيفة ,(سَقائِفُ) عَريش (عُرُش) 2 (at a factory, port) مُسْتَوْدَع (مُسْتَوْدَعات)

B *vt* (*past tense, past participle* **shed**) 1 (to make flow) ذَرَفَ (i; ذَرْف ,ذَرَفان), سَكَبَ (u; سَكْب) <*tears*>; سَفَكَ (i-u; سَفْك), أَراقَ <*blood*> 2 (to lose) أَسْقَطَ <*leaves*>; انْسَلَخَ (من) <*skin*>; فَقَدَ (i; فَقْد ,فِقْدان) <*jobs, weight*> 3 (to emit) بَثَّ (i-u; بَثّ), أَشَعَّ ,بَعَثَ (a; بَعْث) <*light, happiness*>

she'd /ʃiːd, ʃɪd/ *abbr* = **she had**, = **she would**

sheen /ʃiːn/ *n* بَريق ,لَمَعان

sheep /ʃiːp/ *n* (*pl* **sheep**) خَروف (خِرْفان ,خِراف)

sheepdog /ˈʃiːpdɒɡ/ *n* كَلْب الراعي

sheepish /ˈʃiːpɪʃ/ *adj* <*grin, look*> يَنُمُّ عن الخَجَلِ; <*person*> خَجول

sheepskin /ˈʃiːpskɪn/ *n* فَرْوة خَروفٍ

sheer /ʃɪə/ *adj* (**sheerer, sheerest**) 1 <*size, madness*> مُجَرَّد, مَحْض; **the ~ size of the task overwhelmed them** أَثْقَلَت المُشْكِلةُ بِحَجْمِها الهائِلِ كاهِلَهُمْ 2 <*cliff, drop*> عَموديّ, شَديد الانْحِدارِ 3 <*fabric, stockings*> رَقيق

sheet /ʃiːt/ *n* 1 (for a bed) مُلاءة, شَرْشَف (شَراشِفُ); **a single/double ~** مُلاءة لِسَريرٍ فَرْديٍّ \ مُزْدَوَجٍ; **he was as white as a ~** كانَ لَوْنُهُ أَصْفَرَ مِثْلَ الكُرْكُمِ 2 (of paper) صَفْحة (صَفَحات), صَحيفة (صَحائِفُ ,صُحُف), فَرْخ (فُروخ ,أَفْراخ); **a blank/loose ~** صَفْحة فارِغة \ مُنْفَصِلة; **a ~ of stamps** صَفْحة طَوابِعَ بَريديّةٍ 3 (piece of plastic) وَرَقة (أَوْراق ,وَرَقات); (of metal) صَفيحة (صَفائِحُ); (of glass) لَوْح (أَلْواح ,أَلاويحُ); **wrap it in a plastic ~ to keep it dry** غَلِّفْهُ في وَرَقةٍ من البْلاسْتيك لِيَظَلَّ جافًّا 4 (of snow, ice, water, etc) صَفْحة (صَفَحات); **a ~ of ice covered the road** غَطَّتْ صَفْحةٌ من الجَليدِ الطَريقَ; **~s of flame came from the roof** خَرَجَتْ أَلْسِنةُ اللَهَبِ من السَطْحِ; **the rain was coming down in ~s** كانَ المَطَرُ يَنْهَمِرُ بِشِدّةٍ 5 (printed paper) صَفْحة (صَفَحات)

(Idiom) **to have a clean sheet** كانَ سِجِلُّهُ نَظيفًا

sheet lightning *n* بَرْق صَفْحيّ

sheet metal *n* صَفيحة مَعْدِنيّة

sheet music *n* موسيقى مَكْتوبة

sheikh /ʃeɪk/ *n* 1 (ruler) شَيْخ (شُيوخ), رَئيس \ زَعيم قَبيلةٍ 2 (scholar) شَيْخ (شُيوخ)

shekel /ˈʃek(ə)l/ *n* شيقِل

shelf /ʃelf/ *n* (*pl* **shelves**) 1 (for books, etc) رَفّ (رُفوف ,أَرْفُف) 2 (in rock, ice) حافة (حافات ,حَوافٍ)

shelf life *n* 1 (of foods, medicine, etc) فَتْرة صَلاحيّةٍ 2 (of technology, pop music, etc) [فَتْرة رَواجِ سِلْعةٍ]

shell /ʃel/ A *n* 1 (of an egg, a nut, shrimp) قِشْرة (قِشْر); (of a snail) صَدَف (n coll; أَصْداف), قَوْقَعة (قَواقِعُ); (of a tortoise) تُرْس (تُروس ,أَتْراس), دَرَقة; **sea ~s** أَصْداف \ قَواقِع بَحْريّة 2 (bomb) قُنْبُلة (قَنابِلُ), قَذيفة (قَذائِفُ) 3 (of a building) هَيْكَل (هَياكِلُ)

B *vt* 1 (Mil) قَصَفَ (i; قَصْف), ضَرَبَ بالمَدافِعِ <*a town, an installation*> 2 (Culin) قَشَّرَ <*peas, a prawn*>

(Idiom) **to come out of/go back into one's shell** خَرَجَ من \ عادَ إلى قَوْقَعَتِهِ

(Phrasal verb) **shell out** (infml): 1 **~ out** أَنْفَقَ 2 **~ out [sth]** دَفَعَ [شَيْئًا] <*a sum*>

she'll /ʃiːl/ *abbr* = **she will**

shellfish /ˈʃelfɪʃ/ *n pl* 1 (Zool) مَحاريّات 2 (Culin) مَحاريّات

shell shock *n* صَدْمة القَصْفِ \ القَنابِلِ (اضْطِراب عَصَبيّ نَتيجةَ التَعَرُّضِ للقَصْفِ)

shell suit *n* بَدْلة رِياضيّة

shelter /ˈʃeltə/ A *n* 1 [u] (protection) مَلْجَأ, مَلاذ (مَآوٍ), مَأْوًى (مَلاجِئُ), مَخْبَأ (مَخابِئُ) 2 (a building) مَلْجَأ (مَلاجِئُ)

B *vt* 1 (against the weather) حَمى (i; حِماية), سَتَرَ (i-u; سَتْر) <*a garden, person*> 2 (from sth difficult) حَمى (i; حِماية ,حَمْي), وَقى (i; وِقاية ,وَقْي) <*a criminal, child*>

C *vi* «animals, people» احْتَمى (ب), اتَّخَذَ ساتِرًا

sheltered /ˈʃeltəd/ *adj* 1 (of a place) <*valley, spot*> مَسْتور, مَحْميّ 2 (of circumstances) <*life, childhood*> مَحْميّ; **to lead a ~ life** عاشَ حَياةً مَعْزولةً 3 (for the disabled) <*workshop, work*> للمُعاقينَ

sheltered housing, **sheltered accommodation** *n* دار إيواءٍ

shelve /ʃelv/ A *vt* 1 (to postpone) عَلَّقَ, أَرْجَأَ, أَجَّلَ <*a plan, project*> 2 (to store on a shelf) وَضَعَ على الرَفِّ <*books, products*> 3 (to provide with shelves) زَوَّدَ بِرُفوفٍ <*a wall, room*>

B *vi* «beach, ground» انْحَدَرَ

shelves /ʃelvz/ *n pl* ▸ **shelf**

shelving /ˈʃelvɪŋ/ *n* رُفوف, أَرْفُف

shepherd /ˈʃepəd/ *n* راعي غَنَمٍ

shepherdess /ʃepəˈdes/ *n* راعِية غَنَمٍ

shepherd's pie *n* فَطيرة الراعي

sherbet /ˈʃɜ:bət/ *n* 1 (BrE) (powder) [مَسْحوق حُلْو فَوّار] 2 (AmE) (sorbet) [عَصير فاكِهةٍ مُثَلَّج]

sheriff /ˈʃerɪf/ *n* 1 (BrE) عُمْدة (عُمَد) 2 (AmE) ≈ مَأمور

sherry /ˈʃeri/ *n* (*pl* **sherries**) [خَمْر \ نَبيذ إسْبانيّ]

she's /ʃi:z/ *abbr* = **she is**, = **she has**

shh /ʃ/ *excl* (تَعْبير لِطَلَبِ الهُدوءِ) هُدوءاً ,هُسّ

Shia, **Shiah** /ˈʃɪə/ A *n* 1 [u] (religion) المَذْهَب الشيعيّ 2 (*pl* **Shia**, **Shias**) (adherent) شيعيّ (شيعة)

B *adj* ‹*cleric, Muslim*› شيعيّ (شيعة)

shield /ʃi:ld/ A *n* 1 (Hist, Mil) دِرْع (دُروع, أدْرُع) 2 (on a machine) غِطاء واقٍ ,(أحْجِبة ,حُجُب) حِجاب 3 (AmE) (police officer's badge) شارة الشُرْطةِ

B *vt* حَمى (i; حِماية) ,وَقى (i; وِقاية ,وَقْي) ‹*eyes, a child*›

shift /ʃɪft/ A *vt* 1 (to move) نَقَل ,حَرَّكَ (u; نَقْل) ‹*furniture*›; غَيَّر ‹*scenery*›; **I can't ~ this lid** لا أسْتَطيعُ أنْ أُحَرِّكَ هذا الغِطاءَ; **they are ~ing production to Asia** يَنْقُلونَ الإنْتاجَ إلى آسيا; **to ~ one's ground** *or* **position** غَيَّر \ حَوَّلَ مَوْقِفَهُ 2 (infml) (to get rid of) تَخَلَّصَ (مِن) ‹*a stain, cold*› 3 (to refocus) ألْقى ‹*the blame, responsibility*›; **he's trying to ~ the blame onto us** يُحاوِلُ أنْ يُلْقِيَ اللَوْمَ عَلَيْنا 4 (AmE Aut) **to ~ gear** نَقَل الغِيارَ 5 (BrE) (infml) (to sell) باعَ (i; بَيْع ,مَبيع) ‹*the stock, goods*›

B *vi* 1 (to move) «cargo, contents» انْتَقَل; **the cargo had ~ed in the storm** تَحَرَّكَت الحُمولةُ بِسَبَبِ العاصِفةِ; **to ~ uneasily in one's chair** تَمَلْمَلَ في كُرْسيِّهِ 2 (to change) «public opinion, winds» تَحَوَّلَ ,تَغَيَّرَ 3 «wall, foundations» تَزَحْزَحَ, ارْتَحَلَ; **the foundations had ~ed over the years** تَزَحْزَحَت الأساساتُ مع مُرورِ السِنينَ 4 «keyboarder» [ضَغَطَ على زِرِّ 'العالي'] 5 (in location) «scene» تَغَيَّرَ 6 (AmE Auto) **to ~ from first into second** نَقَل الغِيارَ من الأوَّلِ إلى الثاني

C *n* 1 (change) تَغَيُّر (تَغَيُّرات) ,تَحَوُّل (تَحَوُّلات); **a ~ in public opinion/policy** تَحَوُّل في الرَأْيِ العامِّ \ السِياسةِ; **the ~ from agriculture to industry** التَحَوُّل من الزِراعةِ إلى الصِناعةِ; **a ~ to the left/right** تَحَوُّل إلى اليَسارِ \ اليَمينِ 2 (time) مُناوَبة, وَرْديّة ,نَوْبة (نَوْبات); (workers) فَريق مُناوَبةٍ; **to be on the day/night ~** كانَ في مُناوَبةٍ نَهاريّةٍ \ لَيْليّةٍ; **to work an eight-hour ~** عَمِلَ في وَرْديّةٍ من ثَماني ساعاتٍ 3 (woman's dress) قَميص داخِليّ 4 (Comput) ▸ **shift key** 5 (AmE Aut) ▸ **gear lever**

shift key *n* مِفْتاح الإزاحةِ (مِفْتاح الحُروفِ العالِيةِ)

shiftless /ˈʃɪftləs/ *adj* ‹*layabout, gambler*› مُتَراخٍ ,كَسول

shift work *n* عَمَل مُتَناوِب \ بالوَرْديّةِ

shifty /ˈʃɪfti/ *adj* (**shiftier**, **shiftiest**) (infml) ‹*manner, expression*› مُخادِع ,(مَكَرة) ماكِر ,مُراوِغ

Shiism /ˈʃi:ɪz(ə)m/ *n* المَذْهَب الشيعيّ

Shiite /ˈʃi:ʌɪt/ A *n* شيعيّ (شيعة)

B *adj* ‹*cleric, Muslim*› شيعيّ (شيعة)

shilling /ˈʃɪlɪŋ/ *n* شِلِن (1/20 من الجُنَيْهِ الاسْتِرْلينيِّ)

shimmer /ˈʃɪmə/ *vi* «jewels, water» وَمَضَ (i; وَمْض) ,تَلأْلأَ ,بَرَق (u; بَرْق); «silk» لَمَعَ (a; لَمْع ,لَمَعان)

shin /ʃɪn/, **shinbone** /ˈʃɪnbəʊn/ *n* 1 (person's) عَظْم الساقِ \ القَصَبة 2 (of beef) لَحْم الساقِ

shine /ʃʌɪn/ A *vt* (*past tense, past participle* **shone** or **shined**) 1 (to direct a light) صَوَّبَ ,وَجَّهَ ,سَلَّطَ ‹*a light, torch*› 2 (to polish) صَقَلَ (u; صَقْل ,صِقال) ,جَلا (i; جِلاء) ,لَمَّعَ ‹*shoes*›; ‹*silver*›

B *vi* (*past tense, past participle* **shone**) 1 (with light) «sun» أشْرَقَ; «light» سَطَعَ (a; سُطوع); «hair» لَمَعَ (a; لَمْع ,لَمَعان); «brass, floor» تَألَّقَ ,أضاءَ 2 (with emotion) «eyes» تَألَّقَ 3 (to excel) «employees, students» نَبَغَ ,تَفَوَّقَ ,تَألَّقَ (a-i-u; نُبوغ)

C *n* 1 (brightness) بَريق ,لَمَعان (بَرائِقُ) 2 (act) تَلْميع (تَلْميعات)

Idiom **to take a shine to sb** (infml) أُعْجِبَ بِشَخْصٍ

Phrasal verbs **shine in** «light, sun» أضاءَ

• **shine through** «talent, beauty» ظَهَرَ بِوُضوحٍ

shingle /ˈʃɪŋg(ə)l/ A *n* 1 (on a beach) حَصًى (n coll) 2 (on a roof) لَوْح خَشَبيّ

B *n pl* قوباء مِنْطَقيّة (مَرَض جِلْديّ)

shining /ˈʃʌɪnɪŋ/ *adj* 1 (shiny) ‹*hair, metal*› بَرّاق ,لامِع (لَوامِعُ) 2 (happy) ‹*face, eyes*› بَرّاق ,مُشْرِق 3 (excellent) ‹*talent*› ساطِع (سَواطِعُ) ,مُتَألِّق; ‹*example*›

shiny /ˈʃaɪni/ *adj* (**shinier**, **shiniest**) ‹*hair, surface, shoes*› لامِع, بَرّاق

ship /ʃɪp/ **A** *n* سَفينة (سُفُن, سَفائِنُ); **a passenger ~** سَفينة رُكّابٍ; **a container ~** سَفينة حاوِياتٍ

B *vt* **(-pp-)** **1** (to send by sea) «exporters» شَحَنَ بَحْراً ‹*goods, a consignment*›; (to transport) **to ~ the goods from the warehouse** شَحَنَ البَضائِعَ مِن المَخْزَنِ **2** (to take on board) **to ~ water** [امْتَلأَ بالماءَ من الداخِلِ (بِفِعْلِ الأَمْواجِ)]

Phrasal verb **ship off**: **~ [sth/sb] off**, **~ off [sth/sb]** (infml) (to send away) تَخَلَّصَ من [شَيْءٍ \ شَخْصٍ] بِإِرْسالِهِ بَعيداً ‹*a child*›

shipbroker /ˈʃɪpbrəʊkə/ *n* سِمْسار \ وسيط بَحْري

shipbuilder /ˈʃɪpbɪldə/ *n* صانِع سُفُنٍ

shipbuilding /ˈʃɪpbɪldɪŋ/ *n* بِناء سُفُنٍ

shipload /ˈʃɪpləʊd/ *n* حُمولة سَفينةٍ

shipment /ˈʃɪpmənt/ *n* **1** (goods) شُحْنة (شُحْنات, شِحَن), حُمولة **2** [u] (action) شَحْن

shipowner /ˈʃɪpəʊnə/ *n* صاحِب \ مالِك سَفينةٍ

shipper /ˈʃɪpə/ *n* **1** (person) شاحِن بَضائِعَ **2** (company) شَرِكة شَحْنِ بَضائِعَ

shipping /ˈʃɪpɪŋ/ *n* **1** (ships) سُفُن **2** (transport) شَحْن

shipping company *n* شَرِكة شَحْنٍ

shipshape /ˈʃɪpʃeɪp/ *adj* (BrE) ‹*house, room*› مُنَظَّم, مُرَتَّب

shipwreck /ˈʃɪprɛk/ **A** *n* **1** (event) غَرَق \ تَحَطُّم سَفينة **2** (ship) حُطام سَفينةٍ

B *vt* **to be ~ed** «ships, sailors» غَرِق, تَحَطَّمَ (غَرَق; a)

shipyard /ˈʃɪpjɑːd/ *n* حَوْض بِناءِ سُفُنٍ

shirk /ʃɜːk/ *vt* تَهَرَّبَ (مِن), تَنَصَّلَ (مِن), تَمَلَّصَ (مِن) ‹*a task, responsibility*›

shirt /ʃɜːt/ *n* (for a man) قَميص (قُمْصان, أَقْمِصة); (for a woman) بْلوزة; (for sport) قَميص رِياضيّ

Idiom **to lose one's shirt** خَسِرَ كُلَّ ما يَمْلِكُ

shirtsleeve /ˈʃɜːtsliːv/ *n* كُمّ قَميصٍ; **he was in his ~s in the kitchen** كانَ في المَطْبَخِ مُرْتَدياً قَميصَهُ (دون سُتْرةٍ)

shirty /ˈʃɜːti/ *adj* (**shirtier**, **shirtiest**) (BrE) (infml) سَريع الغَضَبِ, عَصَبيّ المِزاجِ

shit /ʃɪt/ (vulg) **A** *n* **1** [u] (excrement) بِراز; **there's a lot of dog ~ in the park** هُناكَ الكَثيرُ من بِرازِ الكِلابِ في الحَديقةِ **2** (also **bullshit**) كَلام فارِغ, هُراء; **to talk bull~** قالَ كَلاماً فارِغاً; **he's full of ~** هو مَليءٌ بالعُيوبِ **3** (nasty person) شَخْص حَقير; **he's a real ~** هو شَخْصٌ حَقيرٌ جِدًّا

B *vi* (*present participle* **-tt-**; *past tense, past participle* **shitted** or **shit** or **shat**) تَغَوَّطَ

C *v refl* (*present participle* **-tt-**; *past tense, past participle* **shitted** or **shit** or **shat**) **to ~ oneself** نَجَّسَ نَفْسَهُ بالغائِطِ

D *excl* تَبًّا, اللَّعْنة

Idioms **I don't give a shit about sb/sth** لا أُعيرُ شَخْصاً \ شَيْئاً أَيَّ اهْتِمامٍ; **to be in the shit** كانَ في وَرْطةٍ; **to beat the shit out of sb** ضَرَبَ شَخْصاً بِشِدّةٍ

shiver /ˈʃɪvə/ **A** *vi* «people, animals» (with cold) ارْتَعَشَ, ارْتَعَدَ, ارْتَجَفَ; (with fear) اقْشَعَرَّ

B *n* رَجْفة (رَجَفات), رَعْشة (رَعَشات); **to give sb the ~s** جَعَلَ شَخْصاً يَرْتَعِدُ خَوْفاً

shivery /ˈʃɪv(ə)ri/ *adj* ‹*animal*› مُرْتَجِف, مُرْتَعِش

shoal /ʃəʊl/ *n* سِرْب (مِن السَّمَكِ)

shock /ʃɒk/ **A** *n* **1** (unpleasant surprise) صَدْمة (صَدَمات); **to give sb a ~** أَصابَ شَخْصاً بِصَدْمةٍ; **her death was a tremendous ~ to the family** كانَتْ وَفاتُها صَدْمةً هائِلةً لِعائِلَتِها; **to recover from** *or* **get over the ~** تَغَلَّبَ على الصَّدْمةِ

2 [u] (Med) صَدْمة; **to be in (a state of) ~** كانَ في حالةِ صَدْمةٍ; **to treat sb for ~** عالَجَ شَخْصاً من صَدْمةٍ **3** ▸ **electric shock** **4** (impact) صَدْمة, رَجّة, هَزّة (صَدَمات) **5** (of hair) خُصْلة (خُصَل, خُصْلات) **6** (Aut infml) ▸ **shock absorber**

B *vt* (to surprise) صَدَمَ (صَدْم, i; ل), سَبَّبَ صَدْمةً ل; **we were ~ed by the news** صَدَمَتْنا الأَخْبارُ; **she's not easily ~ed** هي لا تُصْدَمُ بِسُهولةٍ

shock absorber *n* مُمْتَصّ الصَّدَماتِ

shocking /ˈʃɒkɪŋ/ *adj* **1** (surprising) ‹*sight, news*› مُريع, مُرَوِّع, مُثير للاشْمِئْزازِ **2** (disgusting) ‹*behaviour, film*› مَشين, صادِم **3** (BrE) (infml) (very bad) ‹*weather, match*› رَديء, فَظيع (فُظَعاءُ), سَيِّئ

shock result *n* نَتيجة صادِمة

shock wave *n* 1 (from explosions) مَوْجة صَدْمةٍ \ صَدْميّة 2 (effect) مَوْجة \ آثار صَدْمةٍ

shod /ʃɒd/ **A** *past tense, past participle* ▸ **shoe** B

B *adj* مُرْتَدي حِذاء, مُنْتَعِل

shoddy /ˈʃɒdi/ *adj* (**shoddier, shoddiest**) (infml) ‹*product, goods, work*› رَديء

shoe /ʃu:/ **A** *n* 1 (footwear) حِذاء (أَحْذِية), نَعْل (mf; نِعال, أَنْعُل); **a pair of ~s** حِذاء; **to take off/put on one's ~s** خَلَعَ \ ارْتَدى حِذاءَهُ 2 (horse's) حُذْوة 3 (Aut) (also **brake shoe**) حِذاء الفَرامِلِ \ المِكْبَح

B *vt* (*present participle* **shoeing**; *past tense, past participle* **shod**) رَكَّبَ حُذْوةً ل ‹*a horse*›; **take the horse to the blacksmith to be shod** خُذ الحِصانَ إلى الحَدّادِ لِيُرَكِّبَ لَهُ حُذْوةً

(Idioms) **to be in sb's shoes** كانَ في مَكانِ شَخْصٍ; **to fill sb's shoes** حَلَّ مَحَلَّ شَخصٍ

shoehorn /ˈʃu:hɔ:n/ *n* لَبِّيسة أَحْذِيةٍ

shoelace /ˈʃu:leɪs/ *n* رِباط حِذاءٍ

shoe polish *n* وَرْنيش أَحْذِية

shoe repairer *n* عامِل تَصْليح أَحْذِيةٍ, إسْكافيّ

shoe shop *n* مَتْجَر \ دُكّان أَحْذِيةٍ

shoe size *n* مَقاس حِذاءٍ

shoestring /ˈʃu:strɪŋ/ *n* (AmE) رِباط حِذاءٍ

(Idiom) **on a shoestring** بِميزانيّةٍ ضَئيلةٍ; **the film was made on a ~** أُنْتِجَ الفيلْمُ بِميزانيّةٍ ضَئيلةٍ

shone /ʃɒn/ *past tense, past participle* ▸ **shine**

shoo /ʃu:/ *vt* (also **shoo away**) أَبْعَدَ ‹*a child, an animal*›

shook /ʃʊk/ *past tense* ▸ **shake**

shoot /ʃu:t/ **A** *vt* (*past tense, past participle* **shot**) 1 (to wound) أَصابَ بالرَصاصِ ‹*a person, an animal*›; (to kill) قَتَلَ بالرَصاصِ ‹*a person, an animal*›; **she shot him in the foot** أَصابَتْهُ في قَدَمِهِ بالرَصاصِ; **he was shot in the back** أُصيبَ في ظَهْرِهِ بالرَصاصِ; **to ~ sb dead** قَتَلَ شَخْصاً بالرَصاصِ; **to ~ a soldier for desertion** أَعْدَمَ جُنْديًّا رَمْياً بالرَصاصِ لِهُروبِهِ من الخِدْمةِ 2 (to fire) أَطْلَقَ ‹*a bullet, arrow, missile*›; أَطْلَقَ النارَ من ‹*a gun*› 3 (to hunt) اصْطادَ ‹*game, rabbits*› 4 (to direct) وَجَّهَ ‹*a glance, smile*›; **to ~ questions at sb** أَمْطَرَ شَخْصاً بِوابِلٍ من الأَسْئِلةِ 5 (to film) صَوَّرَ ‹*a movie, scene*› 6 (with doors, shutters) جَرَّ (u; جَرّ) ‹*a bolt*› 7 (in canoeing) **to ~ the rapids** أَبْحَرَ في المِياهِ المُنْحَدِرةِ 8 (infml) (to pass when red) **to ~ the lights** تَجاوَزَ إشارةَ المُرورِ الحَمْراءَ 9 (in golf) **to ~ 75** حَقَّقَ \ سَجَّلَ 75 ضَرْبةً 10 (AmE) (infml) (to play) **to ~ pool/dice** لَعِبَ البِلْيارْدو \ النَرْدَ 11 (infml) (to inject) حَقَنَ (i-u; حَقْن) ‹*drugs, heroin*›

B *vi* (*past tense, past participle* **shot**) 1 (with weapons) «marksman, soldier, police» أَطْلَقَ النارَ; **to ~ at sb/sth** أَطْلَقَ النارَ على شَخْصٍ \ شَيْءٍ; **the soldiers were ordered to ~ to kill** أُعْطِيَ الجُنودُ أوامِرَ بِإطْلاقِ النارِ في أماكِنَ قاتِلةٍ 2 (to hunt) اصْطادَ 3 (to move suddenly) انْدَفَعَ; **he shot forward in his seat** انْدَفَعَ للأَمامِ في مَقْعَدِهِ; **flames shot into the air** تَطايَرَتْ أَلْسِنةُ اللَهَبِ في الهَواءِ; **a car shot past** مَرَّتْ سَيّارةٌ مُسْرِعةً 4 (to film) «directors, film companies» صَوَّرَ 5 (in football, hockey, etc) «player» سَدَّدَ

C *v refl* (*past tense, past participle* **shot**) **to ~ oneself** أَطْلَقَ النارَ على نَفْسِهِ

D *n* 1 (young growth) غُصْن جَديد 2 (in photography) تَصْوير (تَصاويرُ) 3 (in movies) تَصْوير (تَصاويرُ) 4 (hunters' outing) رِحْلة صَيْدٍ

(Phrasal verbs) **shoot down: ~ down [sth], ~ [sth] down** 1 أَسْقَطَ [شَيْئاً] ‹*a plane, missile*› 2 نَسَفَ [شَيْئاً] ‹*an idea, a proposal*›

• **shoot out A** «car, cyclist» خَرَجَ مُنْدَفِعاً **B ~ out [sth], ~ [sth] out** 1 مَدَّ [شَيْئاً] بِسُرْعةٍ ‹*one's hand, arm*› 2 أَطْفَأَ [شَيْئاً] بِإطْلاقِ النارِ عَلَيْهِ ‹*the light*›

• **shoot up** 1 (to increase rapidly) «prices, rates» ارْتَفَعَ بِسُرْعةٍ 2 (to grow rapidly) «children, plants» نَما بِسُرْعةٍ 3 (infml) (to inject oneself with drugs) حَقَنَ نَفْسَهُ بِمُخَدِّرٍ

shooter /ˈʃu:tə/ *n* (infml) 1 (pistol) مُسَدَّس (مُسَدَّسات) 2 (gunman) مُطْلِق النارِ

shooting /ˈʃu:tɪŋ/ **A** *n* 1 (of a person) إصابة \ قَتْل بالرَصاصِ 2 [u] (of shots) إطْلاق النارِ \ الرَصاصِ, رِماية

3 [u] (as a sport, pastime) صَيْد ,رماية

B *adj* ‹*pain*› حادّ

shooting range *n* **1** (area) مَيْدان رِمايةٍ **2** (of a gun) مَدى إطْلاقٍ \ تَصْويبٍ

shooting star *n* شِهاب (شُهُب), شُهْبان

shoot-out /ˈʃuːtaʊt/ *n* تَبادُل إطْلاقِ النارِ

shop /ʃɒp/ **A** *n* **1** (retail outlet) مَتْجَر (مَتاجِرُ), مَحَلّ (مَحَلّات), دُكّان (mf; دَكاكينُ); **to go to the ~s** ذَهَبَ للتَسَوُّقِ; **to set up ~** فَتَحَ مَحَلاً; **to shut up ~** تَوَقَّفَ عن العَمَلِ **2** (BrE) (infml) (shopping) تَسَوُّق; **to do the weekly ~** قامَ بالتَسَوُّقِ الأُسْبوعيِّ **3** (workshop) وَرْشة (وَرْشات, وِرَش) **4** (AmE) [u] (technical training) تَدْريب فَنّيّ

B *vt* (-pp-) (BrE) (infml) (to inform on) بَلَّغَ (عن) ‹*a criminal, wrongdoer*›

C *vi* (-pp-) «person» تَسَوَّقَ; **to go ~ping** ذَهَبَ للتَسَوُّقِ; **where do you ~ for clothes?** من أَيْنَ تَشْتَري مَلابِسَكَ؟

(Idioms) **all over the shop** (infml) (everywhere) مُبَعْثَر; (in disarray) في حالةٍ من الفَوْضى; **to talk shop** تَحَدَّثَ عن العَمَلِ (في غَيْرِ مَوْضِعِهِ)

(Phrasal verb) **shop around** بَحَثَ عن أَفْضَلِ العُروضِ \ الأَسْعارِ

shopaholic /ʃɒpəˈhɒlɪk/ *n* (infml) مُحِبّ \ مُدْمِن التَسَوُّقِ

shop assistant *n* (BrE) عامِل \ بائِع في مَتْجَرٍ

shop floor *n* وَرْشة (وَرْشات, وِرَش), مَشْغَل (مَشاغِلُ)

shopkeeper /ˈʃɒpkiːpə/ *n* صاحِب مَتْجَرٍ

shoplifter /ˈʃɒplɪftə/ *n* سارِق مَعْروضاتٍ (من المَتاجِرِ)

shoplifting /ˈʃɒplɪftɪŋ/ *n* سَرِقة مَعْروضاتٍ (من المَتاجِرِ)

shopper /ˈʃɒpə/ *n* مُتَسَوِّق, مُتَبَضِّع

shopping /ˈʃɒpɪŋ/ *n* **1** (activity) تَسَوُّق, تَبَضُّع; **to do the ~** تَسَوَّقَ, تَبَضَّعَ **2** (purchases) مُشْتَرَيات

shopping bag *n* حَقيبة \ كيس تَسَوُّقٍ

shopping cart *n* عَرَبة تَسَوُّقٍ

shopping centre (BrE), **shopping center** (AmE) *n* مَرْكَز تَسَوُّقٍ \ تِجاريّ

shopping list *n* قائِمة تَسَوُّقٍ

shopping mall *n* مَجْمَع تِجاريّ, مول (مولات)

shopping trolley *n* عَرَبة تَسَوُّقٍ

shop-soiled /ˈʃɒpsɔɪld/ *adj* (BrE) ‹*goods, towels*› بالٍ \ مُتَّسِخ بِسَبَبِ بَقائِهِ في المَتْجَرِ

shop steward *n* مُمَثِّل نِقابةِ العُمّالِ

shop window *n* نافِذة \ واجِهة عَرْضٍ (في مَتْجَرٍ)

shopworn /ˈʃɒpwɔːn/ *adj* (AmE) ▸ **shop-soiled**

shore /ʃɔː/ *n* **1** (of a sea, lake) ساحِل (سَواحِلُ), شاطِئ (شَواطِئُ) **2** (land) بَرّ, يابِسة; **on ~** على اليابِسةِ

(Phrasal verb) **shore up**: **1** **~ up [sth], ~ [sth] up** رَكَّبَ دِعاماتٍ ل [شَيْءٍ] ‹*a building, wall*› **2** عَزَّزَ \ دَعَمَ [شَيْئاً] ‹*economy, confidence*›

shorn /ʃɔːn/ *past participle* ▸ **shear**

short /ʃɔːt/ **A** *adj* **1** (not long-lasting) ‹*time, stay, course, conversation*› قَصير; **a ~ time** *or* **while ago** منذ وَقْتٍ قَصيرٍ; **you have a ~ memory** ذاكِرَتُكَ ضَعيفةٌ; **the days are getting ~er** يَزْدادُ النَهارُ قِصَراً; **to work ~er hours** عَمِلَ ساعاتٍ أَقَلَّ **2** (in length) ‹*distance, hair, list*› قَصير; **a ~ distance away** على بُعْدِ مَسافةٍ قَصيرةٍ; **the house is a ~ walk from the beach** يَقَعُ المَنْزِلُ على بُعْدِ مَسافةٍ قَصيرةٍ من الشاطِئِ سَيْراً على الأَقْدامِ; **to have one's hair cut ~** قَصَّ شَعْرَهُ قَصيراً **3** (in height) ‹*man, woman*› قَصير (قِصار), قَصير القامةِ **4** (scarce, deficient) لَيْسَ لَدَيَّ مالٌ \ وَقْتٌ; **I'm a bit ~ of money/time** لَدَيْهِ نَقْصٌ; **to be in ~ supply** كانَ غَيْرَ كافٍ; **my wages are £30 ~** أَجْري ناقِصٌ 30 جُنَيْهاً; **he gave me ~ measure** (in a shop) لم يُعْطِني حَقّي في الميزانِ **5** (in abbreviations) **Tom is ~ for Thomas** توم هو اخْتِصارُ توماس; **this is Nicholas, Nick for ~!** هذا نيكولاس، أو نيك اخْتِصاراً! **6** (abrupt) فَظّ (أَفْظاظ), جافّ; **to be ~ with sb** كانَ فَظّاً مع شَخْصٍ **7** ‹*pastry*› هَشّ **8** ‹*vowel*› قَصير

B *adv* **1** (abruptly) فَجْأةً, بِشَكْلٍ فُجائيٍّ; **to stop ~** تَوَقَّفَ فَجْأةً **2** (indicating insufficiency) **to go ~ of money/food** عانى من نَقْصٍ في المالِ \ الطَعامِ; **time is running ~** الوَقْتُ يَنْفَدُ; **to fall ~ of expectations/the required standard** جاءَ أَدْنى من التَوَقُّعاتِ \ المُسْتَوى المَطْلوبِ **3** (in distance, duration) **the ball landed just ~ of the green** لم تَصِلِ الكُرةُ إلى المِنْطَقةِ الخَضْراءِ; **we had to cut our holiday ~** اُضْطُرِرْنا

لم يَصِلْ إلى حَدِّ فِعْلِ; **to stop ~ of doing sth** إلى قَطْعِ إجازَتِنا شَيْءٍ

C (**in short**) *adv phr* بِإيجازٍ, بِاخْتِصارٍ

D (**short of**) *prep phr* **1** (less than) أَقَلّ من; **that's nothing ~ of blackmail!** لَيْسَ ذلك إلاّ ابْتِزازاً! **2** (except) إلاّ; **~ of locking him in, I can't stop him leaving** بِاسْتِثْناءِ إغْلاقِ البابِ عَلَيْهِ، فَلا يَسَعُني أنْ أَمْنَعَهُ من المُغادَرةِ

E *n* **1** (drink) [مَشْروب كُحوليّ مُرَكَّز] **2** (movie) فيلْم قَصير **3** (Elec) ▸ **short circuit**

F (**shorts**) *n pl* **1** (short trousers) شورْت, سِرْوال قَصير; **a pair of cycling ~s** شورْت رُكوبِ الدَرّاجاتِ **2** (AmE) (men's underwear) سِرْوال داخِليّ

G *vt* ▸ **short circuit**

(Idioms) **to be caught short** فوجِئ (وَهُوَ غَيْرُ مُسْتَعِدٍّ); **to make short work of sth** قَضى على شَيْءٍ; **short and sweet** قَصير وحُلْو

shortage /'ʃɔːtɪdʒ/ *n* عَجْز, نَقْص

shortbread /'ʃɔːtbred/, **shortcake** /'ʃɔːtkeɪk/ *n* شورْت كيك (بَسْكويت \ كَعْك بِسَمْنٍ وسُكَّرٍ)

short-change /ʃɔːt'tʃeɪndʒ/ *vt* [أعْطى باقِياً أَقَلّ من المُسْتَحَقّ] ‹*a customer*›; عامَلَ بِشَكْلٍ غَيْرِ مُنْصِفٍ ‹*a fan*›

short circuit **A** *n* ماسّ كَهْرَبائيّ;

B (**short-circuit**) *vt* **1** (Elec) سَبَّبَ ماسًّا كَهْرَبائيًّا في ‹*a motor, circuit board*› **2** (to shorten) قَصَّرَ, اخْتَصَرَ ‹*a process, system*›;

C (**short-circuit**) *vi* «lights, batteries» أُصيبَ بِعُطْلٍ \ بِماسٍّ كَهْرَبائيٍّ

shortcoming /'ʃɔːtkʌmɪŋ/ *n* عَيْب (عُيوب), نَقيصة (نَقائِص)

shortcomings /'ʃɔːtkʌmɪŋz/ *n pl* عُيوب, نَقائِص, مَواطِن ضَعْفٍ

shortcrust pastry /ʃɔːtkrʌst 'peɪstri/ *n* عَجينة المِلْفيه \ الشورْت كَرْسْت

shortcut /'ʃɔːtkʌt/ *n* **1** (shorter route) طَريق مُخْتَصَر; **to take a ~** أَخَذَ طَريقاً مُخْتَصَراً **2** (quicker method) طَريقة سَريعة, طَريق مُخْتَصَر **3** (to folders) أيْقونة اخْتِصارٍ, اخْتِصار; **a keyboard ~** اخْتِصار من لَوْحةِ المَفاتيحِ

shorten /'ʃɔːt(ə)n/ **A** *vt* قَصَّرَ; قَلَّلَ, اخْتَصَرَ ‹*length, distance*› ‹*a skirt, talk*›

B *vi* «days» قَصُرَ (u; قِصَر); «odds» قَلَّ (i; قِلّة)

shortfall /'ʃɔːtfɔːl/ *n* عَجْز, نَقْص; **a ~ in arts funding** عَجْز في تَمْويلِ الفُنونِ

short-haired /ʃɔːt'hɛːd/ *adj* ‹*boy, terrier*› قَصير الشَعْرِ

shorthand /'ʃɔːthand/ *n* كِتابة مُخْتَزَلة, (اخْتِزالات) اخْتِزال

shorthand typist *n* [شَخْص مُؤَهَّل في الكِتابةِ المُخْتَزَلةِ]

short-haul /'ʃɔːthɔːl/ *adj pred* ‹*flight, route*› قَصير المَدى

shortlist /'ʃɔːtlɪst/ **A** *n* قائِمة مُخْتَصَرة (بِأَفْضَلِ المُرَشَّحينَ); **a ~ of applicants for the job** قائِمة مُخْتَصَرة بِأَفْضَلِ المُتَقَدِّمين للوَظيفةِ

B *vt* وَضَعَ في قائِمةٍ مُخْتَصَرةٍ (بِأَفْضَلِ المُرَشَّحينَ) ‹*a candidate, novel*›

short-lived /ʃɔːt'lɪvd/ *adj* ‹*success, recovery*› قَصير الأَجَلِ, لم يَدُمْ طَويلاً

shortly /'ʃɔːtli/ *adv* **1** (soon) ‹*to follow, arrive*› قَريباً, بعد قَليلٍ **2** **~ after/before** بعد \ قبل ذلك بِقَليلٍ, عن قَريبٍ **3** (abruptly) بِاقْتِضابٍ

short-sighted /ʃɔːt'sʌɪtɪd/ *adj* **1** ‹*patient*› قَصير البَصَرِ \ النَظَرِ; **to be ~** عانى من قِصَرِ البَصَرِ **2** (lacking foresight) ‹*policy, politician*› قَصير النَظَرِ

short-sleeved /ʃɔːt'sliːvd/ *adj* ‹*shirt, dress*› قَصير الأَكْمامِ

short-staffed /ʃɔːt'stɑːft/ *adj* **to be ~** عانى من نَقْصٍ المُوَظَّفينَ

short story *n* قِصّة قَصيرة

short-tempered /ʃɔːt'tɛmpəd/ *adj* ‹*man, animal*› سَريع الغَضَبِ

short-term /ʃɔːt'təːm/ **A** *adj* ‹*solution, loan*› قَصير الأَجَلِ \ الأَمَدِ

B *adv* ‹*to plan, think*› على المَدى القَصيرِ, مُؤَقَّتاً

short wave *n* مَوْجة قَصيرة

shot /ʃɒt/ **A** *past tense, past participle* ▸ **shoot**

B *n* **1** (from guns) طَلْقة (طَلَقات); **~s were heard in the street** سُمِعَ صَوْتُ طَلَقاتٍ في الشارِعِ; **to take a ~ at sb/sth**

أَطْلَقَ النارَ على شَخْصٍ \ شَيْءٍ **2▸** (infml) (attempt) **to have a ~ at doing sth** قامَ بِمُحاوَلةٍ لِفِعْلِ شَيْءٍ; **would you like to have a ~ at it?** هل تُحِبُّ أنْ تُجَرِّبَهُ؟; **I'll give it my best ~** سَأَبْذُلُ قُصارى جُهْدي مَعَهُ **3▸** (in sports) تَسْديدة; **to take a ~ at goal** صَوَّبَ تَسْديدةً نحو الهَدَفِ; **'good ~!'** 'تَسْديدة جَيِّدة!' **4▸** (track event) **the shot** الجُلّة; **to put the ~** رَمى الجُلّةَ **5▸** (photograph) لَقْطة (لَقَطات), صورة (صُوَر); **a ~ of the palace** صورة للقَصْرِ **6▸** (injection) حُقْنة (حُقَن) **7▸** [u] (pellets) خُرْدُق **8▸** (person who shoots) **to be a good/poor ~** كانَ رامِياً ماهِراً \ ضَعيفَ المُسْتَوى **9▸** (infml) (of liquor) جُرْعة (جُرَع, جُرْعات)

C *adj* (also **shot through**) (streaked) ‹*cloth, silk*› مُمَوَّه, مُتَمَوِّج الأَلْوانِ; **~ (through) with gold** بِهِ خُيوطٌ ذَهَبِيّةٌ

Idioms **a shot in the dark** تَخْمين بِدونِ دَليل; **to be shot of sb/sth** (infml) تَخَلَّصَ من شَخْصٍ \ شَيْءٍ; **to call the shots** تَوَلّى الزِمامَ

shotgun /ˈʃɒtgʌn/ *n* بُنْدُقيّة رَشّ, شوزَن; **a sawn-off ~** بُنْدُقيّة رَشّ ذات ماسورةٍ قَصيرةٍ

shot-put /ˈʃɒtˌpʊt/ *n* رَمْي \ دَفْع الجُلّةِ

should /ʃʊd, ʃəd/ *modal aux* (*conditional* **shall**) **1▸** (expressing probability, expectation) **that ~ fix it** من المُفْتَرِضِ أنّ ذلك سَيُصْلِحُهُ; **it ~n't be difficult to convince them** من المُفْتَرِضِ أنّهُ لن يَكونَ من الصَعْبِ إقْناعُهُم; **how ~ I know?** كيف لي أنْ أعْرِفَ؟; **his hearing is not as good as it ~ be** حاسّةُ السَمْعِ لَدَيْهِ لَيْسَتْ جَيِّدةً كما يَنْبَغي أنْ تَكونَ **2▸** (indicating moral obligation) **we ~ help them** عَلَيْنا أنْ نُساعِدَهُمْ; **you ~ have told me before** كانَ يَنْبَغي أنْ تُخْبِرَني من قَبْلُ; **you ~ not say things like that** لا يَنْبَغي أنْ تَقولَ أشْياءَ مِثْلَ هذه; **someone ~ have accompanied her** كانَ يَنْبَغي أنْ يُرافِقَها أَحَدٌ ما **3▸** (in polite suggestions) **she ~ see a doctor** يَنْبَغي أنْ تَرى طَبيباً; **~ I put this in the safe?** هل أَضَعُ هذا في الخَزْنةِ؟ **4▸** (in conditional sentences) **if he had asked me, I ~ have accepted** لو أنّهُ سَأَلَني, لَكُنْتُ قد قَبِلْتُ; **~ anybody phone, tell them I'm out** إذا اتَّصَلَ أَحَدٌ, أَخْبِرْهُ أنّي قد خَرَجْتُ; **~ the opportunity arise** إذا سَنَحَت الفُرْصةُ **5▸** (expressing purpose) **we are anxious that he ~ succeed** نَحْنُ مُتَلَهِّفونَ على نَجاحِهِ **6▸** (in polite requests) **I ~ like a mint tea** أُريدُ كوباً من الشايِ بالنَعْناعِ من فَضْلِكَ; **I ~ like to visit the town** أَوَدُّ أنْ أَزورَ المَدينةَ **7▸** (expressing opinion) **I ~ think so!** أنا مُوافِقٌ على ذلك تَماماً!; **I ~ think not!** لا أَظُنُّ ذلك على الإطْلاقِ!; **'how long will it take?'—'an hour, I ~ think'** 'كم سَيَسْتَغْرِقُ هذا؟' — 'ساعة, على ما أَظُنُّ'; **I ~n't worry about it if I were you** لو كُنْتُ مَكانَكَ لَما قَلِقْتُ بِخُصوصِ هذا **8▸** (when prefacing an important point) **I ~ say that ...** يَجِبُ أنْ أقولَ إنّ ...; **I think you ~ know that ...** أَعْتَقِدُ أنّهُ يَجِبُ أنْ تَعْلَمَ أنّ ...

shoulder /ˈʃəʊldə/ **A** *n* **1▸** (person's) كَتِف (mf; أَكْتاف, كِتَفة), مَنْكِب (مَناكِبُ); **this jacket is too tight across the ~s** هذه السُتْرةُ ضَيِّقةٌ جِدًّا عند الكَتِفَيْنِ; **to straighten one's ~s** فَرَدَ \ صَلَبَ ظَهْرَهُ; **to look over sb's ~** نَظَرَ من خَلْفِ \ وَراءِ شَخْصٍ **2▸** (of a jacket) كَتِف (mf; أَكْتاف) **3▸** (AmE) (of a road) حافّة **4▸** (Culin) كَتِف (mf; أَكْتاف)

B *vt* **1▸** حَمَلَ على كَتِفِهِ ‹*a bag, an implement*›; **to ~ one's rifle** حَمَلَ بُنْدُقيّتَهُ على كَتِفِهِ; **squad, ~ arms!** فِرْقة, كَتِفاً سِلاح! **2▸** تَحَمَّلَ ‹*the burden, expense, responsibility*› **3▸** (to push) **to ~ one's way through/past** شَقَّ طَريقَهُ بِكَتِفَيْهِ عَبْرَ الزِحامِ; **she ~ed her way to the front of the queue** دَفَعَت الناسَ بِكَتِفِها حتّى وَصَلَتْ إلى مُقَدِّمةِ الطابورِ

Idioms **to be head and shoulders above sb/sth** كانَ أَفْضَلَ بِمَراحِلَ من شَخْصٍ \ شَيْءٍ; **a shoulder to cry on** صَدْر حَنون; **I'm always there if you need a ~ to cry on** سَأَكونُ دائِماً إلى جِوارِكَ إذا احْتَجْتَ إلى صَدْرٍ حَنونٍ; **to rub shoulders with sb** اخْتَلَطَ بِشَخْصٍ; **to stand shoulder to shoulder with sb** وَقَفَ جَنْباً إلى جَنْبٍ مع شَخْصٍ ▸ **cold**

shoulder bag *n* حَقيبة كَتِفٍ

shoulder blade *n* عَظْم \ لَوْح الكَتِفِ

shoulder-length /ˈʃəʊldəlɛŋθ/ *adj* ‹*hair*› طولُهُ للكَتِفِ

shoulder pad *n* كَتّافة, بِطانة كَتِفٍ

shoulder strap *n* **1▸** (on a garment) حَمّالة كَتِفٍ **2▸** (on a bag) حِزام كَتِفٍ

shouldn't /ˈʃʊd(ə)nt/ *abbr* = **should not** ▸ **should**

shout /ʃaʊt/ **A** *vt* رَدَّدَ, هَتَفَ (i; هُتاف, ب) رَفَعَ (a; رَفْع) ‹*slogans*›; نادى ‹*sb's name*›; صاحَ (i; صِياح, صَيْح, ب) ‹*abuse*›

B *vi* صَرَخ (u; صُراخ), صاحَ (i; صِياح, صَيْح); **to ~ at sb** صاحَ \ صَرَخ في وَجْهِ شَخْصٍ; **he ~ed at us to go away** صاحَ في وَجْهِنا وَطَلَبَ مِنّا الرَحيلَ; **to ~ for help** صَرَخَ طَلَباً لِلمُساعَدةِ

C *n* (cry) صَرْخة (صَرَخات); **give me a ~ if you need any help** نادِ عَلَيَّ إذا احْتَجْتَ إلى مُساعَدةٍ (infml)

Phrasal verbs **shout down**: **~ down [sb], ~ [sb] down** «crowd, audience» صاحَ لِيُغَطِّيَ على صَوْتِ [شَخْصٍ] ‹a speaker›

• **shout out** **A** «person, voice» صاحَ (i; صِياح, صَيْح) **B** **~ out [sth], ~ [sth] out** قالَ [شَيْئاً] بِصَوْتٍ عالٍ ‹sb's name, the answer›

shouting /ˈʃaʊtɪŋ/ *n* صُراخ, صِياح; **there was a lot of yelling and ~** كانَ هُناكَ الكَثيرُ من الصِياحِ والصُراخِ

shove /ʃʌv/ **A** *vt* **1** (infml) (to put) دَسَّ, وَضَعَ (بِغَلاظةٍ) ‹a bag, notebook› **2** (to push) دَفَعَ (بِشِدّةٍ) ‹a person, door›

B *vi* «fans, supporters» تَزاحَمَ, تَدافَعَ

C *n* (infml) دَفْعة قَوِيّة

Phrasal verbs **shove off** (BrE) **1** (infml) (leave) انْصَرَفَ **2** (in a boat) انْطَلَقَ \ انْدَفَعَ إلى الماءِ

• **shove over** (infml): **1** **~ over** «people, children» أَفْسَحَ المَكانَ **2** **~ [sth] over, ~ over [sth]** دَفَعَ [شَيْئاً] ‹a book, plate›

• **shove up** (infml) «people, children» تَزَحْزَحَ

shovel /ˈʃʌv(ə)l/ **A** *n* مِجْرَفة (مَجارِفُ), جاروف (جَواريفُ)

B *vt* (**-ll** BrE, **-l-** AmE) جَرَفَ (u; جَرْف), نَقَلَ بالجاروفِ ‹snow, earth›

show /ʃəʊ/ **A** *vt* (*past tense* **showed**; *past participle* **shown** or **showed**) **1** (to offer for inspection) أَظْهَرَ ‹a ticket, photo›; **to ~ sb sth, to ~ sth to sb** أَطْلَعَ شَخْصاً على شَيْءٍ **2** (to screen) عَرَضَ (i; عَرْض) ‹a movie, programme› **3** (to exhibit) عَرَضَ (i; عَرْض) ‹a painting, sb's work› **4** (to reveal) كشفَ (i; كَشْف), أَظْهَرَ ‹the dirt, one's underclothes›; **to ~ one's age** كشفَ سِنَّهُ **5** (to demonstrate) أَظْهَرَ, بَيَّنَ; **studies ~ that ...** تُبَيِّنُ الدِراساتُ أنّ ...; **she has ~n herself very capable** أَظْهَرَتْ أنّها قادِرةٌ جِدّاً; **it just goes to ~ that you can't trust anyone** هذا يُثْبِتُ أنّهُ لا يُمْكِنُكَ أنْ تَثِقَ بِأَيِّ شَخْصٍ **6** (to record) أَظْهَرَ ‹the time, a reading›; **the lights are ~ing red** الإشارةُ حَمْراءُ **7** (to report) أَظْهَرَ ‹an increase, a profit› **8** (to depict) بَيَّنَ «pictures, maps»; **as shown in figure 1** كَما هو مُبَيَّنٌ في الشَكْلِ 1 **9** (to express) أَبْدى, أَظْهَرَ ‹interest, emotion›; **she ~ed interest in the proposal** أَبْدَت اهْتِماماً بالمُقْتَرَحِ; **he ~ed no emotion as he was sentenced** لم يُظْهِرْ أَيَّ انْفِعالٍ بَيْنَما كانَ الحَكْمُ يَصْدُرُ عَلَيْهِ **10** (to explain) **to ~ sb how to do sth** بَيَّنَ لِشَخْصٍ كيف يَفْعَلُ شَيْئاً **11** (to conduct) **to ~ sb to their seat** أَرْشَدَ شَخْصاً إلى مَقْعَدِهِ; **he ~ed us to our room** صَحِبَنا إلى غُرْفَتِنا; **to ~ sb to the door** وَصَّلَ شَخْصاً إلى البابِ

B *vi* (*past tense* **showed**; *past participle* **shown** or **showed**) **1** «label, stain» ظَهَرَ (a; ظُهور) **2** «disappointment, anger» ظَهَرَ (a; ظُهور); **her nervousness ~ed on her face** ظَهَرَ تَوَتُّرُها على وَجْهِها **3** «movie» عُرِضَ; **what's ~ing at the local cinema?** ما الفيلْمُ الّذي يَتِمُّ عَرْضُهُ في السينَما المَحَلِّيّةِ؟

C *n* **1** (stage production) عَرْض (عُروض); **the ~ must go on** يَجِبُ أنْ تَسْتَمِرَّ الحَياةُ; **to put up a good ~** قَدَّمَ عَرْضاً جَيِّداً **2** (on television, radio) بَرْنامَج (بَرامِجُ); **he's been invited to be a guest in a TV/radio ~** دُعِيَ كَضَيْفٍ في بَرْنامَجٍ تلِفِزْيونيٍّ \ إذاعيٍّ **3** (trade event) مَعْرِض (مَعارِضُ) **4** (exhibition) مَعْرِض (مَعارِضُ); **to be on ~** كانَ مَعْروضاً **5** (display) عَرْض (عُروض), اسْتِعْراض (اسْتِعْراضات), إظْهار; **a ~ of force/affection** اسْتِعْراض للقوّةِ \ إظْهار للمَحَبّةِ **6** (of concern, impatience) إظْهار, إبْداء; **he made a ~ of concern** أَبْدى قَلَقَهُ; **it's just for ~** هو للزينة فقطْ **7** (infml) (business, undertaking) عَمَل (أَعْمال); **it's clear who's running the ~** من الواضِحِ مَن الّذي يُديرُ العَمَلَ

Idioms **to show one's face** ظَهَرَ على المَلَأِ; **to show one's hand** كَشَفَ أَوْراقَهُ; **to show the way** بَيَّنَ الطَريقَ; **to have nothing to show for sth** لم يَكُنْ لَدَيْهِ ما يَعْرِضُهُ بِخُصوصِ شَيْءٍ; **to steal the show** خَطَفَ الانْتِباهَ

Phrasal verbs **show around** (AmE) ▸ **show round**

• **show in**: **~ [sb] in** أَدْخَلَ [شَخْصاً]

• **show off** **A** (infml) تَفاخَرَ \ تَباهى بِنَفْسِهِ **B** **1** **~ [sb/sth] off, ~ off [sb/sth]** (to display) تَباهى بـ [شَخْصٍ \ شَيْءٍ] ‹one's skills, talents› **2** **~ [sth] off, ~ off [sth]** (to advantage) «a style» أَبْرَزَ [شَيْئاً] ‹one's figure›

• **show out**: **~ [sb] out** صَحِبَ [شَخْصاً] إلى البابِ

• **show round**: **~ [sb] round** صَحِبَ [شَخْصاً] في جَوْلةٍ

• **show up** **A** **1** (to stand out) «marks, patterns» ظَهَرَ (a; ظُهور), بَرَزَ (u; بُروز) **2** (infml) (to arrive) حَضَرَ (u; حُضور)
B **~ up [sth/sb], ~ [sth/sb] up** (to expose) كَشَفَ [شَيْئاً \ شَخْصاً] ‹*a weakness, flaw*›; **to ~ sb up for what they are** كَشَفَ حَقيقةَ شَخْصٍ

show business *n* عالَم العُروضِ الفَنِّيّةِ

showcase /ˈʃəʊkeɪs/ *n* **1** (for objects) واجِهة عَرْضٍ **2** (for artists or ideas) مَعْرِض (مَعارِضُ)

showdown /ˈʃəʊdaʊn/ *n* مُواجَهة حاسِمة

shower /ˈʃaʊə/ **A** *n* **1** (for washing) دُشّ (أَدْشاش); **he's in the ~** هو تحت الدُشِّ; **to have** *or* **take a ~** أَخَذَ دُشًّا, اِسْتَحَمَّ **2** (of rain) مَطْرة, هَمْرة (هَمَرات), زَخّة; **there will be heavy/scattered ~s** سَتكونُ هُناكَ أَمْطارٌ غَزيرةٌ \ مُتَقَطِّعةٌ **3** (of stones, sparks) وابِل **4** (AmE) (for a bride/mother to be) حَفْل [لِتَقْديمِ الهَدايا]
B *vt* **1** (to spray) **to ~ confetti on** *or* **over sb/sth, to ~ sb/sth with confetti** نَثَرَ قُصاصاتِ الوَرَقِ المُلَوَّنِ على شَخْصٍ \ شَيْءٍ; **the volcano ~ed dust over the surrounding area** أَمْطَرَ البُرْكانُ المِنْطَقَةَ المُحيطةَ بالغُبارِ **2** (to bestow lavishly) **to ~ sb with gifts/praise, to ~ gifts/praise on sb** أَغْدَقَ على شَخْصٍ بالهَدايا \ بالمَديحِ
C *vi* **1** (to wash) «person» أَخَذَ دُشًّا **2** (to pour) «ash, petals, sparks» اِنْهَمَرَ, نَزَلَ كالمَطَرِ \ اِنْهالَ; **ash ~ed down** تَساقَطَ الرَمادُ كالمَطَرِ

shower curtain *n* سِتارة حَمّام

showground /ˈʃəʊɡraʊnd/ *n* (for displays) ساحة \ أَرْض مَعارِضَ; (for competitions) ساحة مُسابَقاتٍ

show house *n* مَنْزِل للعَرْضِ

showing /ˈʃəʊɪŋ/ *n* **1** (individual screening) عَرْض (عُروض) **2** (performance) أَداء (أَداءات)

showjumping /ˈʃəʊdʒʌmpɪŋ/ *n* قَفْز الحَواجِزِ

shown /ʃəʊn/ *past participle* ▸ **show**

show-off /ˈʃəʊɒf/ *n* (infml) شَخْص يُحِبُّ التَفاخُرَ \ التَباهِيَ

show of hands *n* تَصْويت بِرَفْعِ الأَيْدي

showroom /ˈʃəʊruːm, ˈʃəʊrʊm/ *n* مَعْرِض, صالة عَرْضٍ (مَعارِضُ)

show trial *n* مُحاكَمة شَكْلِيّة \ صورِيّة \ اسْتِعْراضِيّة

showy /ˈʃəʊi/ *adj* (**showier, showiest**) **1** (infml) (ostentatious) ‹*clothing, design*› مُبَهْرَج **2** (colourful) ‹*flower, foliage*› زاهي اللَوْنِ

shrank /ʃræŋk/ *past tense* ▸ **shrink**

shrapnel /ˈʃræpn(ə)l/ *n* شَظِيّة (شَظايا)

shred /ʃred/ **A** *n* **1** (of paper, fabric) قُصاصة, مِزْقة (مِزَق); **to tear the cloth to ~s** مَزَّقَ القُماشَ إِرْباً إِرْباً; **to be in ~s** كانَ مُمَزَّقاً **2** (of evidence, truth) ذَرّة; **there is not a ~ of truth in the accusation** لَيْسَ هُناكَ ذَرّةٌ من الحَقيقةِ في الاتِّهامِ
B *vt* (**-dd-**) مَزَّقَ ‹*a document*›; فَرَمَ (i; فَرْم) ‹*branches*›

shredder /ˈʃredə/ *n* (for paper) ماكينة تَمْزيقٍ \ فَرْمِ الوَرَقِ; (for garden waste) ماكينة فَرْمِ المُخَلَّفاتِ الزِراعِيّةِ

shrew /ʃruː/ *n* زَباب (حَيَوان يُشْبِهُ الفَأْرَ) (n coll)

shrewd /ʃruːd/ *adj* (**shrewder, shrewdest**) ‹*move, businessman*› داهِية (mf), حاذِق (حُذّاق), حَصيف (حُصَفاءُ)

shriek /ʃriːk/ **A** *vi* «children, birds» زَعَقَ (a; زَعْق), صَرَخَ (u; صُراخ, صَريخ), صاحَ (i; صَيْح, صِياح)
B *n* **1** (of pain, fear) صَرْخة (صَرَخات), زَعْقة (زَعَقات), صُراخ **2** (of delight) صَيْحة

shrift /ʃrɪft/ *n* **to give sb/sth short ~** لم يُعِرْ شَخْصاً \ شَيْئاً أَيَّ اِهْتِمامٍ; **he gave me/my proposal short ~** لم يُعِرْني \ يُعِرِ اقْتِراحي أَيَّ اهْتِمامٍ

shrill /ʃrɪl/ *adj* (**shriller, shrillest**) ‹*voice, whistle*› حادّ, عالٍ, صاخِب

shrimp /ʃrɪmp/ *n* (*pl* **shrimp** or **shrimps** BrE) **1** (in UK: small shellfish) رُوبيان, جَمْبَرِيّ صَغير **2** (in US: larger shellfish) جَمْبَرِيّ

shrine /ʃraɪn/ *n* **1** (holy place) ضَريح (أَضْرِحة), مَزار (مَزارات), مَقام (مَقامات); **a ~ of St Thomas** ضَريحُ القِدّيسِ توماس **2** (memorial) ضَريح (أَضْرِحة); **little ~s by the side of the road** أَضْرِحة صَغيرة على جانِبِ الطَريقِ

shrink /ʃrɪŋk/ **A** *vt* (*past tense* **shrank** or **shrunk**; *past participle* **shrunk** or **shrunken**) ‹*a garment, fabric*› جَعَلَ يَنْكَمِشُ, تَسَبَّبَ في الانْكِماشِ

B *vi* (*past tense* **shrank** or **shrunk**; *past participle* **shrunk** or **shrunken**) **1** «fabric, garment, wool» انْكَمَش; **my sweater shrank in the wash** انْكَمَشَتْ كَنْزَتي في الغَسيلِ **2** «economy, demand, profits» تَقَلَّص ,انْكَمَش; **our profits have shrunk by 45%** انْكَمَشَتْ أَرْباحُنا بِنِسْبةِ 45٪ **3** «population, budget» انْخَفَض ,انْكَمَش; **the workforce has shrunk from 200 to 50** انْكَمَشَت القوَّةُ العامِلةُ من 200 إلى 50 مُوَظَّفاً **4** «tumour, person» قَلَّ حَجْمُهُ **5** (to move back) **to ~ back** *or* **away from sth/sb** تراجَعَ مُبْتَعِداً عن شَيْءٍ \ شَخْصٍ **6** (to shy away) **to ~ from doing sth** تَمَلَّصَ من فِعْل شَيْءٍ; **she is not one to ~ from a challenge** لَيْسَت الشَخْصَ الّذي يَتَهَرَّبُ من التَحَدّي

C *n* (infml) طَبيب نَفْسانِيّ

shrinkage /ʃrɪŋkɪdʒ/ *n* **1** (of clothes, fabric) انْكِماش **2** (of profits, output) هُبوط (تَراجُعات) ,تَراجُع (تَقَلُّصات) ,تَقَلُّص

shrink-wrap /ˈʃrɪŋkrap/ *vt* (-pp-) لَفَّ بِغُلافٍ بْلاسْتيكِيٍّ شَفّافٍ ‹CDs, food›

shrivel /ˈʃrɪv(ə)l/ **A** *vt* (-ll- BrE, -l- AmE) جَفَّفَ \ سَبَّبَ الجَفافَ الذُبولَ ‹a plant, leaf›

B *vi* (also **shrivel up**) «skin, plants» جَفَّ (i; جَفاف) ,ذَبَلَ (u; ذُبول)

shroud /ʃraʊd/ **A** *n* كَفَن (أَكْفان)

B *vt* **1** (to envelop) لَفَّ (u; لَفّ) ,أَحاطَ (ب) ,اكْتَنَفَ ,غَطّى ‹mountains, landscape› **2** (to obscure) سَتَرَ (i-u; سَتْر) ,أَخْفى ,اكْتَنَفَ ‹origin, identity›

Shrove Tuesday /ʃrəʊv ˈtjuːsdeɪ/ *n* ثُلاثاء المَرافِع

shrub /ʃrʌb/ *n* شُجَيْرة

shrubbery /ˈʃrʌb(ə)ri/ *n* (*pl* **shrubberies**) [أَرْض تَكْسوها الشُجَيْراتُ]

shrug /ʃrʌg/ **A** *vt* (-gg-) **to ~ one's shoulders** هَزَّ كَتِفَيْهِ

B *vi* (-gg-) هَزَّ كَتِفَيْهِ

C *n* (showing indifference) هَزّ الكَتِفَيْن

(Phrasal verb) **shrug off: ~ off [sth], ~ [sth] off** قَلَّلَ من أَهَمِّيّةِ [شَيْءٍ] ‹criticism, disappointment›

shrunk /ʃrʌŋk/ *past participle* ▸ **shrink**

shrunken /ˈʃrʌŋk(ə)n/ *past participle* ▸ **shrink**

shudder /ˈʃʌdə/ **A** *vi* **1** «person» ارْتَجَفَ ,ارْتَعَشَ ,ارْتَعَدَ; **to ~ with fear/cold** ارْتَعَشَ من الخَوْفِ \ البَرْدِ; **I ~ to think!** يَقْشَعِرُّ بَدَني عِنْدَما أُفَكِّرُ في ذلك! **2** (to shake) «vehicle, engine» ارْتَجَّ ,اهْتَزَّ; **to ~ to a halt** ارْتَجَّ ثُمَّ تَوَقَّفَ

B *n* **1** (of a person) ارْتِعاش ,(ارْتِعاشات) ,رَعْشة (رَعَشات) ,رَجْفة (رَجَفات); **with a ~** مُرْتَعِشاً ,مُرْتَجِفاً **2** (of a vehicle, an engine) هَزّة ,رَجّة; **to give a ~** ارْتَجَّ

shuffle /ˈʃʌf(ə)l/ **A** *vt* **1** (to mix up) خَلَطَ (i; خَلْط) ‹the pack, deck, cards› **2** (to move around) أَعادَ التَرْتيبَ ‹papers› **3** (with feet) **to ~ one's feet** جَرَّ \ جَرْجَرَ قَدَمَيْهِ **4** (in politics) عَدَّلَ, أَجْرى تَعْديلاً في ‹ministers, cabinet›; **the prime minister has ~d his cabinet** أَجْرى رَئيسُ الوُزَراءِ تَعْديلاً وِزاريًّا

B *vi* (to walk) «old woman, patient» مَشى بِخُطًى مُتَثاقِلة

shun /ʃʌn/ *vt* (-nn-) تَهَرَّبَ (من) ,تَحاشى ,تَجَنَّبَ ‹publicity, responsibility›

shunt /ʃʌnt/ *vt* حَوَّلَ ‹a wagon, coach›

shura /ˈʃʊərə/ *n* **1** [u] (consultation) شورى (f) **2** (assembly) مَجْلِس الشورى

shush /ʃʊʃ/ (infml) **A** *excl* اُسْكُتْ! ,صَهْ!

B *vt* أَسْكَتَ ‹a baby, classroom›

shut /ʃʌt/ **A** *adj* «eyes, door, shop» موصَد ,مُغْلَق; **the doors are ~ but not locked** الأَبوابُ مُغْلَقةٌ وَلَكِنَّها غَيْرُ مُقْفَلةٍ; **to slam** *or* **bang ~** انْغَلَقَ بِقوّةٍ بالمَزاليجِ

B *vt* (*present participle* **-tt-**; *past tense, past participle* **shut**) **1** أَغْلَقَ ‹a door, one's mouth, eyes›; **~ your mouth!** (infml) أَغْلِقْ فَمَكَ! **2** أَغْلَقَ ‹a school, factory, shop› **3** (to trap) أَغْلَقَ (على) ‹my finger›

C *vi* (*present participle* **-tt-**; *past tense, past participle* **shut**) **1** «door, eyes, mouth» انْغَلَقَ **2** «factory, shop» أَغْلَقَ أَبْوابَهُ

(Phrasal verbs) **shut away: ~ [sb/sth] away, ~ away [sb/sth]** **1** (for safety) حَفِظَ [شَيْئاً] في مَكانٍ مُغْلَقٍ ‹valuables› **2** (in isolation) حَجَزَ \ حَبَسَ [شَخْصاً] ‹a person›

• **shut down** **A** **1** «factory, plant» أَغْلَقَ أَبْوابَهُ **2** «computer, machinery» تَوَقَّفَ **B** **~ [sth] down, ~ down [sth]** **1** أَغْلَقَ

[شَيْئاً] ‹a factory, website› **2** أَوْقَفَ تَشْغيلَ [شَيْءٍ] ‹machinery, a reactor›

• **shut in**: **~ [sb/sth] in** أَغْلَقَ البابَ على [شَخْصٍ \ شَيْءٍ], حَبَسَ [شَخْصاً \ شَيْئاً] ‹a person, an animal›

• **shut off**: **~ [sth] off, ~ off [sth]** **1** قَطَعَ [شَيْئاً] ‹the water, supply› **2** أَوْقَفَ تَشْغيلَ [شَيْءٍ] ‹the engine, a machine›

• **shut out**: **~ out [sth/sb], ~ [sth/sb] out** **1** (to keep out) أَغْلَقَ البابَ في وَجْهِ [شَيْءٍ \ شَخْصٍ] ‹a person, an animal›; **I've ~ myself out** أَغْلَقْتُ البابَ وَنَسيتُ المَفاتيحَ بالداخِلِ **2** (to screen) حَجَبَ [شَيْئاً \ شَخْصاً] ‹the light, noise› **3** (to exclude) أَخْرَجَ [شَيْئاً \ شَخْصاً] من رَأْسِهِ ‹a thought, memory›; **to ~ out the world** عَزَلَ نَفْسَهُ عن العالَمِ **4** (to cut out) اسْتَبْعَدَ [شَيْئاً \ شَخْصاً] ‹a person, spouse›; **to feel ~ out** شَعَرَ بِأَنَّهُ مُسْتَبْعَدٌ \ مَعْزولٌ

• **shut up** **A** (infml) اخْرَسْ! **~ up!** ;تَوَقَّفَ عن الكَلامِ **B** **~ [sth] up, ~ up [sth]** أَغْلَقَ [شَيْئاً] ‹a house, business› **C** **~ [sb] up, ~ up [sb]** **1** (to confine) حَبَسَ [شَخْصاً] ‹an animal› **2** (infml) (to silence) أَخْرَسَ [شَخْصاً] ‹one's critics, a child›

shutdown /ˈʃʌtdaʊn/ *n* إيقافُ العَمَلِ \ التَّشْغيلِ, إغْلاقٌ

shutter /ˈʃʌtə/ *n* **1** (for windows, shop fronts) مِصْراعٌ (مَصاريعُ) **2** (on a camera) غالِقٌ

shuttle /ˈʃʌt(ə)l/ **A** *n* **1** (bus, train) حافِلَةٌ مَكّوكيّةٌ **2** (also **shuttlecock**) كُرةُ الريشةِ

B *vt* نَقَلَ في رِحْلَةٍ مَكّوكيّةٍ ‹the commuters, passengers›

shuttlecock /ˈʃʌtəlkɒk/ *n* كُرةُ الريشةِ

shuttle service *n* خِدْمةُ نَقْلٍ مَكّوكيّةٌ

shy /ʃʌɪ/ **A** *adj* (**shyer, shyest**) ‹child, smile› خَجولٌ, مُسْتَحٍ

B *vi* (**shies, shying, shied**) «horses» جَفَلَ (i-u; جُفولٌ, جَفْلٌ), نَفَرَ (i-u; نَفْرٌ)

(Phrasal verb) **shy away**: **~ away from sth** «backers, consumers» أَحْجَمَ عن شَيْءٍ

shyly /ˈʃʌɪli/ *adv* ‹to smile, say› على اسْتِحْياءٍ, بِحَياءٍ, بِخَجَلٍ

shyness /ˈʃʌɪnəs/ *n* خَجَلٌ, حَياءٌ

Siamese /ˌsʌɪəˈmiːz/ *n* (*pl* **Siamese**) (also **Siamese cat**) قِطٌّ سِياميٌّ

Siamese twins *n* تَوْأَمانِ سِياميّانِ \ مُلْتَصِقانِ

Siberia /sʌɪˈbɪərɪə/ *pr n* سيبيريا

sibling /ˈsɪblɪŋ/ *n* [شَقيقٌ]; **~ rivalry/affection** مُنافَسةٌ \ مَوَدّةٌ بين الإخْوةِ

sic /sɪk/ *adv* كَذا, هكَذا (تَعْبيرٌ يُشيرُ إلى أنّ الجُمْلَةَ نُقِلَتْ بِأَخْطائِها دونَ تَعْديلٍ)

Sicily /ˈsɪsɪli/ *pr n* صِقِلّيّةُ

sick /sɪk/ **A** *adj* **1** (ill) ‹worker, patient› مَريضٌ (مَرْضى); **to feel too ~ to work** شَعَرَ أَنّهُ مَريضٌ جِدًّا وَلا يَسْتَطيعُ العَمَلَ; **to be off ~** (BrE) كانَ في إجازةٍ مَرَضيّةٍ **2** (nauseous) **to feel ~** شَعَرَ بالغَثَيانِ; **she was ~ on the bus** تَقَيّأَتْ في الحافِلَةِ **3** (disgusted) مُتَقَزِّزٌ, شاعِرٌ بالاشْمِئْزازِ; **it's enough to make you ~!** يَكْفي لِجَعْلِ المَرْءِ يَشْعُرُ بالاشْمِئْزازِ!; **you make me ~!** أَشْعُرُ!أَنْتَ تُثيرُ اشْمِئْزازي; **I'm ~ and tired of all this gossip!** بالسَّأَمِ والمَلَلِ من كُلِّ هذه النَّميمةِ!; **we're ~ to death of her excuses** نَشْعُرُ بالسَّأَمِ الشَّديدِ من أَعْذارِها **4** (tasteless) ‹joke, story› سَخيفٌ; **his ~ jokes fell completely flat** نِكاتُهُ السَّخيفةُ لم تُعْجِبْ أَحَداً **5** (perverted) ‹mind, society› مُنْحَرِفٌ; **many people just regarded him as ~** اعْتَبَرَهُ الكَثيرُ من الناسِ مُنْحَرِفاً; **our society has become very ~** أَصْبَحَ مُجْتَمَعُنا مُنْحَرِفاً جِدًّا

B *n* **1** (**the sick** *n pl*) المَرْضى **2** (BrE) (infml) (vomit) قَيْءٌ

sickbay /ˈsɪkbeɪ/ *n* مَصَحّةٌ, جَناحُ المَرْضى, عِيادةٌ

sickbed /ˈsɪkbɛd/ *n* (liter) فِراشُ المَرَضِ

sick building syndrome *n* مُتَلازِمةُ مَرَضِ المَباني

sicken /ˈsɪk(ə)n/ **A** *vt* أَصابَ بالسَّأَمِ, أَثارَ الاشْمِئْزازَ ‹the viewers, reader›

B *vi* «patient, child» سَقِمَ (a; سَقَمٌ), مَرِضَ (a; مَرَضٌ)

sickening /ˈsɪk(ə)nɪŋ/ *adj* ‹sight, sound› مُقَزِّزٌ, مُثيرٌ للاشْمِئْزازِ

sickie /ˈsɪki/ *n* **1** (infml) (time off work) إجازةٌ مَرَضيّةٌ **2** (AmE infml) (psychotic) مَخْبولٌ, مَخْبولونَ, مَخابيلُ, مَعْتوهٌ (مَعاتيهُ)

sickle /ˈsɪk(ə)l/ *n* مِنْجَلٌ (مَناجِلُ)

sick leave *n* إجازةٌ مَرَضيّةٌ

sickle-cell anaemia /ˌsɪkəlsel əˈniːmiə/ (BrE), **sickle-cell anemia** (AmE) *n* فَقْرُ الدَمِ المِنْجَليّ

sickly /ˈsɪkli/ *adj* (**sicklier, sickliest**) 1 (unhealthy) واهِن, ضَعيف ‹*plant*›; (سُقُم, أَعِلاّءُ) سَقيم, عَليل ‹*child*› 2 (unpleasant) ‹*smell, taste*› مُثير للغَثَيان, كَريه

sickness /ˈsɪknəs/ *n* 1 (illness) مَرَض (أَمْراض) 2 (nausea) غَثَيان

sickness benefit *n* (in UK) مُساعَدة حُكوميّة للمَرْضى

sick note *n* شَهادة مَرَضيّة

sick pay *n* تَعْويض الأَجْرِ خلال فَتْرة المَرَض

sickroom /ˈsɪkruːm/ *n* غُرْفة المَرْضى

side /sʌɪd/ A *n* 1 (of a road) جانِب (جَوانِبُ); (of a river, lake) ضِفّة (ضِفاف); **at the ~ of the road** على جانِبِ الطَّريق 2 (adjacent area) جانِب (جَوانِبُ); **the gate at the ~ of the house** البَوّابة إلى جانِبِ البَيْت; **she tilted her head to one ~** أَمالَتْ رَأْسَها جانِباً; **the north/south ~ of town** الجانِب الشَّماليّ \ الجَنوبيّ من المَدينة; **from ~ to ~** من جانِبٍ إلى آخَر; **on/from all ~s** على \ من كُلِّ الجَوانِب 3 (surface of a box, building, hill) جانِب (جَوانِبُ); **'this ~ up'** (on a package) 'هذا الجانِبُ لأَعْلى' 4 (of a person, animal) جانِب (جَوانِبُ), جَنْب (أَجْناب, جُنوب); **he was lying on his ~** كانَ مُسْتَلْقِياً على جَنْبِه; **she never left my ~** لم تَتْرُكْني وَحْدي أَبَداً; **he was always at the president's ~** كانَ دائِماً إلى جانِبِ الرَّئيس; **~ by ~** جَنْباً إلى جَنْبٍ 5 (of a paper, coin) وَجْه (وُجوه, أَوْجُه); **write on both ~s of the paper** أُكْتُبْ على وَجْهَي الوَرَقة 6 (aspect) جانِب (جَوانِبُ); **let him tell his ~ of the story** دَعْهُ يَرْوي القِصّةَ من وُجْهةِ نَظَرِهِ هو; **she runs the business ~ of things** تَتَوَلّى الشُّؤونَ الإداريّة; **on the positive ~** من الناحِيةِ الإيجابيّة 7 (of sb's character) جانِب (جَوانِبُ) 8 (in disputes) جانِب (جَوانِبُ); **whose ~ are you on?** مع أَيِّ جانِبٍ تَقِفُ؟; **to take ~s** انْحازَ إلى أَحَدِ الأَطْرافِ 9 (BrE) (team) فَريق 10 (page) صَفْحة (صَفَحات) 11 (in descent) ناحِية (نَواحٍ), جِهة; **on/from his mother's ~** من جِهةِ أُمِّه

B (**sided**) *in combination* **a six-~d figure** شَكْل سُداسيّ; **double-~d adhesive tape** شَريط لاصِق من الوَجْهَيْن

C (**on the side**) *adv phr* 1 (in addition) **she does a bit of translation on the ~** تَقومُ بِبَعْضِ أَعْمالِ التَّرْجَمةِ كَعَمَلٍ إضافيّ 2 (AmE) (with servings) **a steak with salad on the ~** بِفْتيك مع سَلَطةٍ كَطَبَقٍ إضافيّ

(Idioms) **to be a bit on the big/small side** كانَ كَبيراً \ صَغيراً بَعْضَ الشَّيْءِ; **to let the side down** (BrE) لم يَكُنْ في مُسْتَوى التَّوَقُّعاتِ, خَيَّبَ الآمالَ; **to put sth to one side** (to place) وَضَعَ شَيْئاً جانِباً; (to postpone) نَحّى شَيْئاً جانِباً

(Phrasal verb) **side with: side with [sb/sth]** انْحازَ إلى [شَخْصٍ \ شَيْءٍ] ‹*the government, opposition*›

sideboard /ˈsʌɪdbɔːd/ *n* نَضَد المائِدةِ, صِوان السُّفْرة

sideburns /ˈsʌɪdbəːnz/ *n pl* سالِفان, عِذاران (الشَّعْرُ الّذي يُحاذي الأُذُنَ)

sidecar /ˈsʌɪdkɑː/ *n* عَرَبة جانِبيّة لِدَرّاجةٍ ناريّةٍ (تَتَّسِعُ لِراكِبٍ واحِدٍ)

side dish *n* طَبَق جانِبيّ (يُقَدَّمُ مع الطَّبَقِ الرَّئيسيّ)

side effect *n* عَرَض جانِبيّ

side entrance *n* مَدْخَل جانِبيّ

sidekick /ˈsʌɪdkɪk/ *n* (infml) مُساعِد شَخْصيّ

sidelight /ˈsʌɪdlʌɪt/ *n* 1 (BrE) (on cars) ضَوْء \ مِصْباح جانِبيّ 2 (aspect) مَعْلومة تَوْضيحيّة

sideline /ˈsʌɪdlʌɪn/ *n* 1 (secondary activity) عَمَل إضافيّ 2 (on courts, pitches) خَطّ التَّماسّ; **to be on the ~s** وَقَفَ على الهامِشِ \ مُتَفَرِّجاً

sidelong /ˈsʌɪdlɒŋ/ *adj before n* ‹*glance, look*› جانِبيّ

side plate *n* صَحْن جانِبيّ صَغير (يَحْتَوي على خُبْزٍ ومَأْكولاتٍ مُصاحِبةٍ للطَّبَقِ الرَّئيسيّ)

side-saddle /ˈsʌɪdsadl/ *adv* ‹*to ride*› واضِعاً كِلْتا رِجْلَيْهِ على جانِبٍ واحِدٍ من الحِصانِ

sideshow /ˈsʌɪdʃəʊ/ *n* 1 (at a fair) عَرْض صَغير مُنْفَصِل (في سِرْكٍ \ مَهْرَجانٍ تَرْفيهيٍّ) 2 حَدَث ثانَويّ

sidestep /ˈsʌɪdstɛp/ *vt* (**-pp-**) 1 (to avoid) تَفادى, تَجَنَّبَ ‹*a blow, an obstruction*› 2 (to evade) تَهَرَّبَ (من) ‹*a question, an issue*›

side street *n* شارِع جانِبيّ

sidestroke /ˈsʌɪdstrəʊk/ *n* سِباحة على الجانِبِ

sidetrack /ˈsʌɪdtrak/ *vt* صَرَفَ عن المَوْضوعِ ‹*a meeting, the chairman*›

sidewalk /ˈsʌɪdwɔːk/ *n* (AmE) رَصيف (أَرْصِفة)

sidewalk cafe *n* (AmE) مَقْهًى على رَصيفٍ

sideways /ˈsʌɪdweɪz/ **A** *adv* **1** (to or from the side) ‹*to move, look*› باتِّجاهِ أَحَدِ الجَوانِبِ **2** (with side part forward) ‹*to stand, turn*› جانِبيًّا

B *adj* ‹*glance, movement*› جانِبيّ

siding /ˈsʌɪdɪŋ/ *n* خَطّ تَخْزينٍ جانِبِيّ

sidle /ˈsʌɪd(ə)l/ *vi* «animal, person» مَشى جانِبياً; **to ~ up to sb** [اقْتَرَبَ بِهُدوءٍ \ بِحَياءٍ مِن شَخْصٍ]

SIDS /ɛsʌɪdiːˈɛs/ *n* = **sudden infant death syndrome** مَوْت الوَليدِ المُفاجِئ

siege /siːdʒ/ *n* حِصار (حُصُر); **to be under ~** كانَ تحت الحِصارِ

Sierra Leone /si,ɛrə lɪˈəʊn/ *pr n* سيراليون (f)

siesta /sɪˈɛstə/ *n* قَيْلولة

sieve /sɪv/ **A** *n* مُنْخَل (مَناخِل), غِرْبال (غَرابيل)

B *vt* نَخَلَ (نَخْل; u), غَرْبَلَ (غَرْبَلة; i) ‹*the flour, soil*›

sift /sɪft/ *vt* **1** (to sieve) نَخَلَ (نَخْل; u), غَرْبَلَ (غَرْبَلة; i) ‹*flour, soil*›

2 (to examine) مَحَّصَ (في), دَقَّقَ ‹*the evidence, information*›

(Phrasal verbs) **sift out**: **1** **~ [sb] out, ~ out [sb]** (to eliminate) اسْتَبْعَدَ [شَخْصاً] ‹*troublemakers, candidates*› **2** **~ [sth] out, ~ out [sth]** (to filter out) غَرْبَلَ [شَيْئاً] ‹*gold, wheat*›

• **sift through**: **~ through [sth]** دَقَّقَ في [شَيْءٍ] ‹*applications, rubble*›

sigh /sʌɪ/ **A** *vi* «speaker» تَنَهَّدَ; «the wind» زَفْزَفَ; **to ~ with relief/regret** تَنَهَّدَ تَنْهيدة ارْتِياحٍ \ حَسْرة

B *n* تَنْهيدة, زَفْرة; **a ~ of relief/despair** تَنْهيدة ارْتِياحٍ \ حَسْرةٍ; **to breathe a ~ of relief** تَنَفَّسَ الصُّعَداءَ

sight /sʌɪt/ **A** *n* **1** [u] (faculty) بَصَر (أَبْصار); **his ~ is good/poor** بَصَرُهُ جَيِّدٌ \ ضَعيفٌ **2** [u] (act of seeing) رُؤْية (رُؤًى); **it was my first ~ of the city** كانَت المَرّةَ الأولى الّتي أرى فيها المَدينةَ; **at first ~** مِن النَّظْرةِ الأولى; **he faints at the ~ of blood** يَفْقِدُ وَعْيَهُ عند رُؤْيةِ الدَمِ; **to catch ~ of sb/sth** لَمَحَ شَخْصاً \ شَيْئاً; **to know sb by ~** عَرَفَ شَخْصاً بالشَكْلِ; **I can't stand the ~ of him!** لا أُطيقُ رُؤْيَتَهُ! **3** [u] (range of vision) مَدى الرُؤْيةِ; **land/victory was in ~** كانَ الشَطُّ \ النَصْرُ يَلوحُ في الأُفُقِ; **the end is in ~!** النِهايةُ تَلوحُ في الأُفُقِ!; **there wasn't a soul in ~** لم يَكُنْ هُناكَ من مَخْلوقٍ; **to come into ~** ظَهَرَ للعَيانِ; **to keep** *or* **stay out of ~** بَقِيَ بَعيداً عن الأَنْظارِ; **to keep sth/sb out of ~** أَبْقى شَيْئاً \ شَخْصاً بَعيداً عن الأَنْظارِ; **I watched the car disappear out of ~** راقَبْتُ السَيّارةَ وَهِيَ تَخْتَفي عن الأَنْظارِ; **don't let her out of your ~!** لا تَدَعْها تَغيبُ عن نَظَرِكَ! **4** (thing seen) مَنْظَر (مَناظِرُ), مَشْهَد (مَشاهِدُ); **to be a common/familiar ~** كانَ مَنْظَراً شائِعاً \ مَأْلوفاً **5** (infml) (a shock to see) مَنْظَر فَظيع; **I look a ~!** مَنْظَري فَظيعٌ!; **your bedroom is a ~!** غُرْفةُ نَوْمِكَ مَنْظَرُها فَظيعٌ!

B **(sights)** *n pl* **1** (places of interest) مَعالِم (سِياحيّة); **to see the ~s** رَأى المَعالِمَ السِياحيّةَ; **to show sb the ~s** أرى شَخْصاً المَعالِمَ السِياحيّةَ **2** (on a rifle, telescope) مِهْداف

C *vt* رَأى, أَبْصَرَ (رُؤْية, رَأْي; a), لَمَحَ (لَمْح; a) ‹*a whale, land*›

(Idioms) **to have sth in one's sights** وَضَعَ عَيْنَهُ على شَيْءٍ; **to lose sight of the fact that ...** أَغْفَلَ حَقيقةَ أنّ ...; **out of sight, out of mind** البُعْدُ, البَعيدُ عن العَيْنِ بَعيدٌ عن القَلْبِ; **to raise/lower one's sights** رَفَعَ \ خَفَضَ سَقْفَ طُموحاتِهِ; **to set one's sights on sth/doing sth** وَضَعَ شَيْئاً \ فِعْلَ شَيْءٍ نُصْبَ عَيْنَيْهِ

sighted /ˈsʌɪtɪd/ *adj* ‹*person, guide*› مُبْصِر; ▸ **far-sighted**, ▸ **nearsighted**, ▸ **partially sighted**

sighting /ˈsʌɪtɪŋ/ *n* رُؤْية (رُؤًى), مُشاهَدة

sight-read /ˈsʌɪtriːd/ **A** *vt* (*past tense, past participle* **-read** /ˈsʌɪtrɛd/) [عَزَفَ بِمُجَرَّدِ النَظَرِ إلى وَرَقةِ الموسيقى (دون تَحْضير)] ‹*music*›

B *vi* «musician, singer» [عَزَفَ بِمُجَرَّدِ النَظَرِ إلى وَرَقةِ الموسيقى (دون تَحْضير)]

sightseeing /ˈsʌɪtsiːɪŋ/ *n* زِيارة المَعالِمِ السِياحيّةِ

sightseer /ˈsʌɪt,siːə/ *n* سائِح (سائِحونَ, سُيّاح, سُوّاح)

sign /sʌɪn/ **A** *n* **1** (indication) عَلامة, إشارة, دَلالة; **that's a good ~** تِلْكَ عَلامةٌ جَيِّدةٌ; **there is no ~ of any improvement** لَيْسَ هُناكَ مُؤَشِّرٌ على أَيِّ تَحَسُّنٍ; **there is no ~ of life** لَيْسَتْ هُناكَ عَلامةٌ على الحَياةِ; **the storm showed no ~s of abating** لم تَكُنْ هُناكَ أَيّةُ مُؤَشِّراتٍ على تراجُعِ العاصِفةِ; **the ~s are that ...** تُشيرُ الدَلائِلُ إلى أنّ ... **2** (gesture) إشارة, إيماءة;

to make the ~ of the cross رَسَمَ عَلامةَ الصَليب **3** (notice) إشارة ,عَلامة **4** (symbol) عَلامة, رَمْز (رُموز); **the dollar ~** عَلامة الدولار **5** (of the zodiac) بُرْج (بُروج ,أبراج); **what ~ are you?** من أيّ بُرْجٍ أنْتَ؟

B *vt* **1** (with a signature) وَقَّعَ (على) ‹*a letter, treaty, petition*›; **to ~ one's name** وَقَّعَ بِاسْمِهِ; **the letter was ~ed by the manager** كانَت الرِسالةُ مُوَقَّعةً من قِبَلِ المُديرِ **2** (to engage) تعاقَدَ (مع) ‹*a player, musician*›

C *vi* **1** (with one's signature) وَقَّعَ **2** (to agree a contract) «player, musician» تعاقَدَ **3** (to signal) **to ~ to sb to do sth** أشارَ إلى شَخْصٍ أنْ يَفْعَلَ شَيْئاً **4** (using sign language) تَحَدَّثَ بِلُغةِ الإشارةِ

(Phrasal verbs) **sign away**: **~ away [sth], ~ [sth] away** وَقَّعَ على تَنازُلٍ عن [شَيْءٍ] ‹*one's rights, an inheritance*›

• **sign for**: **~ for [sth]** وَقَّعَ على اسْتِلامِ [شَيْءٍ] ‹*a package, equipment*›

• **sign in** **1** وَقَّعَ عند الحُضور **2** **~ in [sb], ~ [sb] in** سَجَّلَ حُضور [شَخْصٍ] ‹*a guest, visitor*›

• **sign off** **A** **1** (from a radio or TV show) أَنْهى **2** (to end a letter) خَتَمَ (i; خَتْم) **B** **~ off [sth], ~ [sth] off** صَدَّقَ على [شَيْءٍ] ‹*accounts, expenses*›

• **sign off on**: **~ off on [sth]** ▸ **sign off**

• **sign on** **A** **1** (in commitments) وَقَّعَ عَقْداً **2** (for courses) قَيَّدَ اسْمَهُ **3** (BrE) (for benefit) سَجَّلَ اسْمَهُ في سِجِلِّ العاطِلينَ **B** **~ on [sb], ~ [sb] on** تَعاقَدَ مع [شَخْصٍ] ‹*an employee, a player*›

• **sign out** **A** «guests, visitors» سَجَّلَ اسْمَهُ عند المُغادَرة **B** **~ [sth] out, ~ out [sth]** وَقَّعَ عند اسْتِعارة [شَيْءٍ] ‹*a book, equipment*›

• **sign up** **A** **1** (for a service, an activity) تَعاقَدَ **2** (for a course) اشْتَرَكَ **3** (with club, teams) تَعاقَدَ **4** (in the armed forces) تَطَوَّعَ **B** **~ up [sb], ~ [sb] up** **1** سَجَّلَ [شَخْصاً] ‹*a customer, member*› **2** تَعاقَدَ مع [شَخْصٍ] ‹*a player, band, worker*›

signal /ˈsɪɡn(ə)l/ **A** *n* **1** (gesture) إشارة; **to give the ~ to start** أعْطى إشارةَ البَدْءِ **2** (cue) إشارة; **this was my ~ to leave** كانَتْ هذه إشارَتي للمُغادَرة **3** (indication) إشارة; **he gave a ~ that all is not well** أعْطى إشارةً بِأَنَّ كُلَّ شَيْءٍ لَيْسَ على ما يُرامُ; **to send the wrong ~s** أَرْسَلَ إشاراتٍ خاطِئةً **4** (for trains) إشارة **5** (in broadcasting, telephony) إشارة; **a weak/strong ~** إشارة قَوِيّة \ ضَعيفة; **to send/receive ~s** أَرْسَلَ \ اسْتَقْبَلَ إشاراتٍ

B *vt* (**-ll-** BrE, **-l-** AmE) **1** (to gesture to) **to ~ sb to do sth** أَوْمَأَ إلى شَخْصٍ بِفعْلِ شَيْءٍ; **she ~led that she was ready to leave** أشارَتْ إلى أنَّها كانَتْ جاهِزةً للمُغادَرة **2** (to indicate) أشارَ (إلى) ‹*a change, the start*›; **this ~led the end of an era** كانَ ذلك إشارةً بانْتِهاءِ عَهْدٍ; **to ~ one's intention to do sth** أشارَ إلى اعْتِزامِهِ فِعْلَ شَيْءٍ

C *vi* (**-ll-** BrE, **-l-** AmE) **1** (to gesture) أَوْمَأَ ,أشارَ; **he ~led to me to stop** أشارَ لي بالتَوَقُّفِ **2** (to indicate) «drivers, cyclists» أعْطى إشارةً

signalman /ˈsɪɡnəlmən/ *n* (*pl* **-men**) **1** (on railways) عامِل [مَسْؤول عن الإشاراتِ والتَحْويلاتِ] **2** (in the army, navy) [شخص يُرسِلُ وَيَسْتَقْبِلُ الإشاراتِ العَسْكَرِيّةِ]

signatory /ˈsɪɡnət(ə)ri/ *n* (*pl* **signatories**) مُوَقِّع

signature /ˈsɪɡnətʃə/ *n* تَوْقيع (تَوْقيعات), إمْضاء

signature tune *n* [لَحْن يَرْتَبِطُ ذِكْرُهُ باسْمِ فَنّانٍ \ بَرْنامَجٍ]

signboard /ˈsʌɪnbɔːd/ *n* لافِتة (مَحَلٍّ تِجارِيٍّ \ مُنْتَجٍ)

significance /sɪɡˈnɪfɪk(ə)ns/ *n* **1** (importance) أَهَمِّيّة; **to be of ~** كانَ كَبيرَ الأَهَمِّيّةِ **2** (meaning) مَعْنًى, مَغْزًى, فَحْوى (f)

significant /sɪɡˈnɪfɪk(ə)nt/ *adj* **1** (noticeable) ‹*impact, amount*› مَلْحوظ **2** (notable) ‹*musician, figure*› مُهِمّ; **does she have a ~ other?** هل هُناكَ شَخْصٌ في حَياتِها؟

significantly /sɪɡˈnɪfɪk(ə)ntli/ *adv* **1** (considerably) ‹*to differ, increase*› بِشَكْلٍ مَلْحوظٍ **2** (meaningfully) ‹*to smile, look*› بِطَريقةٍ ذاتِ مَعْنًى \ دَلالةٍ; **~, he arrived late** وَصَلَ مُتَأَخِّراً لِسَبَبٍ مُهِمٍّ

signify /ˈsɪɡnɪfʌɪ/ *vt* (**signifies, signifying, signified**) دَلَّ (على; دَلالة; u), أشارَ (إلى) ‹*the end, a victory*›

signing /ˈsʌɪnɪŋ/ *n* **1** [u] (of treaties, agreements) تَوْقيع **2** (of footballers, musicians) تَعاقُد

sign language *n* لُغة الإشارة

signpost /ˈsaɪnpəʊst/ **A** *n* لافِتة مُروريّة

B *vt* زَوَّدَ بِلافِتاتٍ مُروريّةٍ ‹*a road, route*›; **the route was well ~ed** [كانَ الطَريقُ مُزَوَّداً بِلافِتاتٍ مُروريّةٍ بِشَكْلٍ جَيِّدٍ]

Sikh /siːk/ **A** *n* سيخيّ (من أَتْباعِ السيخيّة)

B *adj* ‹*temple, faith*› سيخيّ

silage /ˈsaɪlɪdʒ/ *n* سيلاج (عَلَف أَخْضَر مَحْفوظ)

silence /ˈsaɪləns/ **A** *n* سُكوت ,صَمْت; **in ~** بِصَمْتٍ

B *vt* **1** (to quieten) أَسْكَتَ ‹*an audience, crowd*› **2** (to stop) أَسْكَتَ ‹*critics, opposition*›

silencer /ˈsaɪlənsə/ *n* **1** (BrE) (on cars) كاتِم صَوْتٍ **2** (on guns) كاتِم صَوْتٍ

silent /ˈsaɪlənt/ *adj* **1** (noiseless) ‹*night, crowd*› هادِئ ,ساكِن **2** (not speaking) ‹*prayer, protest*› صامت **3** (of films) ‹*film, screen*› صامت

silently /ˈsaɪləntli/ *adv* **1** ‹*to appear, creep*› دون إحْداثِ ,بِهُدوءٍ ضَجّةٍ **2** ‹*to pray, thank*› بِصَمْتٍ

silent partner *n* (AmE) شَريك موصٍ

silhouette /ˌsɪluˈet/ *n* صورة ظِلّيّة

silicon /ˈsɪlɪk(ə)n/ *n* سيليكون

silicon chip *n* رُقاقة \ شَريحة سيليكون

silicosis /ˌsɪlɪˈkəʊsɪs/ *n* سُحار رَمْليّ

silk /sɪlk/ *n* (حَرائِرُ) حَرير

silkworm /ˈsɪlkwɜːm/ *n* دودة حَرير \ قَزٌّ

silky /ˈsɪlki/ *adj* (**silkier, silkiest**) ‹*fabric, skin*› حَريريّ

sill /sɪl/ *n* عَتَبة \ سناد نافذة

silly /ˈsɪli/ *adj* (**sillier, silliest**) **1** (foolish) ‹*mistake, question*› أَحْمَق (dipt; حُمْق; f حَمْقى) **2** (infantile) ‹*clothes, behaviour*› سَخيف

silo /ˈsaɪləʊ/ *n* (*pl* **silos**) **1** (for grain) (صَوامِعُ) صَوْمَعة **2** (for missiles) مَخْزَن صَواريخ نَوَويّةٍ

silt /sɪlt/ *n* طَمْي ,غَرين

silver /ˈsɪlvə/ **A** *n* **1** (metal) فِضّة; (colour) لَوْن فِضّيّ; **a ring made of ~** خاتَم مَصْنوع من فِضّةٍ **2** (silverware) فِضّيّات; **to clean the ~** غَسَلَ الفِضّيّاتِ **3** (also **silver medal**) ميدالية فِضّيّة; **to win** *or* **take ~** *or* **a ~ medal** فازَ بِميداليةٍ فِضّيّةٍ

B *adj* **1** (made of silver) ‹*ring, coin*› فِضّيّ; **a ~ spoon** مِلْعَقة فِضّية **2** (in colour) ‹*hair, paint*› فِضّيّ

silver birch *n* بَتولا فِضّيّة

silverfish /ˈsɪlvəfɪʃ/ *n* (*pl* **silverfish**) سَمَك فِضّيّ ,لاحِسة السُكَّرِ

silver foil *n* (BrE) وَرَق أَلومِنيوم

silver jubilee *n* يوبيل فِضّيّ

silver plate *n* أَوانٍ فِضّيّة

silversmith /ˈsɪlvəsmɪθ/ *n* صائِغ فِضّة

silverware /ˈsɪlvəweː/ *n* **1** (tableware) أَدَوات مائِدةٍ **2** (AmE) (cutlery) فِضّيّات

silver wedding *n* العيد الخامِسُ والعِشْرونَ لِزَواجٍ

SIM /sɪm/ *n* (also **SIM card**) بِطاقة وَحْدةِ تَعْريفِ ,بِطاقة سيم مُشْتَرِكٍ

similar /ˈsɪmɪlə/ *adj* ‹*result, price*› مُماثِل ,مُتَشابِه ,مُشابِه; **to be ~ to sth** كانَ مُشابِهاً لِشَيْءٍ

similarity /sɪməˈlarəti/ *n* (*pl* **similarities**) تَشابُه ,(أَشْباه) شَبَه, (تَماثُلات) تَماثُل; **there is a marked ~ between the brothers** هُناكَ شَبَهٌ واضِحٌ بين الاخْوة

similarly /ˈsɪmələli/ *adv* **1** (in a similar way) ‹*to dress, react*› كَذَلِكَ ,على نَحْوٍ مُماثِلٍ ,بِشَكْلٍ مُتَشابِهٍ **2** (likewise) كَذَلِكَ

simile /ˈsɪmɪli/ *n* (تَشْبيهات) تَشْبيه

simmer /ˈsɪmə/ *vi* **1** (of liquids) «water, soup» غَلى على نارٍ هادِئةٍ **2** (of emotions) «resentment, anger» جاشَ (i; جَيَشان)

simple /ˈsɪmp(ə)l/ *adj* (**simpler, simplest**) **1** (uncomplicated) ‹*fact, question*› بَسيط; **keep it ~** لا تُعَقِّد الأُمورَ **2** (plain) ‹*dress, food*› بَسيط **3** (old use or offensive) (very unintelligent) ذو ذَكاءٍ مَحْدودٍ; **he's a bit ~** هو ذو ذَكاءٍ مَحْدودٍ بَعْضَ الشَيْءِ

simplicity /sɪmˈplɪsɪti/ *n* **1** (easiness) سُهولة **2** (of design, structure) بَساطة

simplify /ˈsɪmplɪfaɪ/ *vt* (**simplifies, simplifying, simplified**) بَسَّطَ ‹*a process, task*›

simplistic /sɪmˈplɪstɪk/ *adj* ‹*view, explanation*› ساذَج

simply /ˈsɪmpli/ *adv* **1** (in an easy way) ‹*to explain, express oneself*› بِشَكْلٍ بَسيطٍ; **to put it ~ …** المَسْأَلةُ بِبَساطةٍ هي … **2** (plainly) ‹*to dress, live*› بِبَساطةٍ **3** (just) فَقَطْ; **~ complete the application form** امْلأ الاسْتِمارةَ فَقَطْ

simulate /ˈsɪmjʊleɪt/ *vt* **1** (to feign) تَظاهَرَ (بِ) <*interest, illness*> **2** (to replicate) حاكى <*a scenario, the conditions*>

simulation /sɪmjuːˈleɪʃ(ə)n/ *n* مُحاكاة

simulator /ˈsɪmjʊleɪtə/ *n* جِهاز مُحاكاةٍ

simultaneous /ˌsɪməlˈteɪnɪəs/ *adj* <*attack*> مُتَزامِن; <*translation*> فَوْريّ

simultaneously /ˌsɪm(ə)lˈteɪnɪəsli/ *adv* <*to take place, broadcast*> في آنٍ واحِدٍ, في نَفْسِ الوَقْتِ

sin /sɪn/ **A** *n* إثْم (آثام), خَطيئة (خَطايا), مَعْصِية (مَعاصٍ) **B** *vi* (**-nn-**) «faithful, mortals» أَثِمَ (a; إثْم), أَذْنَبَ, ارْتَكَبَ مَعْصِيةً

Sinai /ˈsʌɪnʌɪ/ *pr n* (also **the Sinai Peninsula**) سيناء (dipt f); **Mount ~** طور سيناءَ

sin bin *n* (infml) [مَقْعَد يُرْسَلُ إلَيْهِ لاعِبٌ ارْتَكَبَ مُخالَفةً]

since /sɪns/ **A** *prep* مُنْذُ; **she's been waiting ~ 10 a.m.** تَنْتَظِرُ مُنْذُ العاشِرةِ صَباحاً; **she'd been a teacher ~ 1995; I haven't seen him ~ then** لم أَرَهُ منذ ذلك الحينِ; **~ arriving** *or* **~ his arrival he …** منذ وُصولِهِ وَهُوَ … **B** *conj* **1** (from the time when) مُنْذُ, منذ أنْ; **~ he's been away** غابَ; **ever ~ I married him** منذ أنْ تَزَوَّجْتُهُ; **it's 10 years ~ we last met** مَرَّتْ 10 سَنَواتٍ منذ أنْ الْتَقَيْنا آخِرَ مَرَّةٍ **2** (because) لِأَنَّ, بِما أنّ **C** *adv* (subsequently) بَعْدَئِذٍ, منذ ذلك الوَقْتِ \ الحينِ; **she has ~ qualified** تَأَهَّلَتْ بَعْدَئِذٍ; **we've kept in touch ever ~** بَقينا على اتِّصالٍ منذ ذلك الوَقْتِ

sincere /sɪnˈsɪə/ *adj* (**sincerer, sincerest**) <*thanks, apology*> صادِق, مُخْلِص; **please accept our ~st apologies/ condolences** تَقَبَّلْ من فَضْلِكَ خالِصَ اعْتِذاراتِنا \ تَعازينا

sincerely /sɪnˈsɪəli/ *adv* **1** (truly, honestly) <*to apologize, hope*> بِصِدْقٍ, بِإخْلاصٍ **2** (in letter endings) **Yours ~, Jean Gonzalez** (BrE), **S~ yours, Jean Gonzalez, S~, Jean Gonzalez** (AmE) المُخْلِص، جين غونْزاليز

sincerity /sɪnˈserəti/ *n* صِدْق, إخْلاص

sinew /ˈsɪnjuː/ *n* وَتَر (أَوْتار)

sinful /ˈsɪnfʊl/ *adj* <*thoughts, nature*> آثِم, أثيم

sing /sɪŋ/ **A** *vt* (*past tense* **sang**; *past participle* **sung**) «singers» غَنّى <*a song, hymn*> غَنّى, أنْشَدَ; **to ~ the national anthem** غَنّى النَشيدَ الوَطَنيَّ; **why don't you ~ something for us?** لِماذا لا تُغَنّي لَنا شَيْئاً؟ **B** *vi* (*past tense* **sang**; *past participle* **sung**) **1** «singer» غَنّى; **to ~ in/out of tune** غَنّى بِشَكْلٍ مُتَوافِقٍ \ غَيْرِ مُتَوافِقٍ مع اللَحْنِ **2** «birds» زَقْزَقَ (i; زَقْزَقة), غَرَّدَ; «crickets» صَرَّ (i; صَرير) **3** «kettles» صَفَرَ; **to make sb's ears ~** جَعَلَ أُذُنَيْ شَخْصٍ تَطِنّانِ

(Idiom) **to sing sb's/sth's praises** كالَ المَديحَ لِشَخْصٍ \ لِشَيْءٍ

(Phrasal verb) **sing along** شارَكَ في الغِناءِ; **to ~ along to sth/with sb** غَنّى مع شَيْءٍ \ شَخْصٍ

Singapore /ˌsɪŋəˈpɔː/ *pr n* سِنْغافورة

singe /sɪndʒ/ *vt* (*present participle* **singeing**) شَيَّطَ, أَحْرَقَ قَليلاً <*one's hair, clothes*>

singer /ˈsɪŋə/ *n* مُغَنٍّ, مُطْرِب

singing /ˈsɪŋɪŋ/ *n* غِناء

single /ˈsɪŋg(ə)l/ **A** *adj* **1** (sole) وَحيد, واحِد; **a ~ rose** وَرْدة واحِدة **2** (not double) <*sheet, sink, unit*> فَرْديّ **3** (for one) <*bed*> فَرْديّ; <*portion*> لِشَخْصٍ واحِدٍ; **the hotel only has two ~ rooms left** لم يَبْقَ إلاّ غُرْفتانِ فَرْديَّتانِ في الفُنْدُقِ **4** (unmarried) <*man, woman, person*> أَعْزَب (dipt), عازِب (عُزّاب); **are you married or ~?** هل أنْتَ مُتَزَوِّجٌ أم أعْزَبُ؟ **5** (with numbers) **inflation is in ~ figures** نِسْبةُ التَضَخُّمِ في أَرْقامٍ أُحاديّةٍ **6** (for emphasis) **the ~ most important factor is …** العامِلُ الوَحيدُ الأكْثَرُ أَهَمّيّةً هو …; **she earns more in a ~ day than I do in a week** تَكْسِبُ في اليَوْمِ الواحِدِ أَكْثَرَ مِمّا أَكْسِبُهُ أنا في أُسْبوعٍ **B** *n* **1** (record) أُسْطوانة فَرْديّة **2** (also **single room**) غُرْفة فَرْديّة **3** (also **single ticket**) تَذْكِرة ذَهابٍ **4** (AmE) (dollar) دولار واحِد **5** (in baseball) [ضَرْبة تَسْمَحُ لِلضارِبِ بالرَكْضِ إلى أَوَّلِ قاعِدةٍ]; (in cricket) [ضَرْبة تُحَقِّقُ نُقْطةً واحِدةً لِحامِلِ المِضْرَبِ] **6** (seat) تَذْكِرة لِكُرْسيٍّ مُنْفَرِدٍ **C** (**singles**) *n pl* **1** (in tennis) فَرْديّ; **the men's/ladies' ~s** فَرْديّ الرِجالِ \ السَيِّداتِ **2** (the unattached) عُزّاب

(Phrasal verb) **single out**: ~ [sb/sth] out, ~ out [sb/sth] اخْتارَ \ انْتقى [شَخْصاً \ شَيْئاً] *<a competitor, candidate, novel>*; **to ~ sb out for punishment** اخْتَصَّ شَخْصاً بالعُقوبةِ; **to be ~d out for blame** أُلْقِيَ عَلَيْهِ اللَوْمُ وَحْدَهُ

single-breasted /ˌsɪŋɡəlˈbrɛstɪd/ *adj* *<suit, jacket>* [ذو صَفٍّ واحِدٍ من الأَزْرارِ]

single cream *n* كْريم مُنْخَفِض الدُهونِ

single currency *n* (**the Single currency**) العُمْلة المُوَحَّدة

single file *adv* *<to proceed, walk>* الواحد تِلْوَ الآخَر

single-handed /ˌsɪŋɡ(ə)lˈhandɪd/, **single-handedly** /ˌsɪŋɡ(ə)lˈhandɪdli/ *adv* *<to manage, rescue>* دون مُساعَدةٍ من أَحَدٍ, بِمُفْرَدِهِ

single market *n* (**the Single market**) السوق المُوَحَّدة

single-minded /ˌsɪŋɡ(ə)lˈmʌɪndɪd/ *adj* *<determination>* يُرَكِّزُ على هَدَفٍ واحِدٍ; *<attitude>* أُحاديّ النَهْجِ

single mother *n* أُمّ عازِبة

single parent *n* والِد أَعْزَب (يُرَبّي أَطْفالَهُ بِمُفْرَدِهِ)

single-parent family *n* [أُسْرة تَضُمُّ أَحَدَ الوالِدَيْنِ فَقَطْ]

singles /ˈsɪŋɡ(ə)lz/ *n pl* فَرْديّ; **the women's/men's ~** فَرْديّ السَيِّداتِ \ الرِجالِ

singles bar *n* [بار للعُزّابِ]

singles charts *n* [لائِحة أُسْبوعيّة لِأَغاني البوب الأَكْثَر مَبيعاً]

single-sex /ˌsɪŋɡ(ə)lˈsɛks/ *adj* *<school, accommodation>* غَيْر مُخْتَلِطٍ (للإناثِ أو الذُكورِ)

singlet /ˈsɪŋɡlɪt/ *n* (BrE) 1 (vest) [قَميص داخِليّ دون أَكْمامٍ] 2 (for runners) [قَميص رِياضيّ دون أَكْمامٍ]

sing-song /ˈsɪŋsɒŋ/ (BrE) **A** *adj* *<voice, accent>* رَتيب **B** *n* [غِناء جَماعيّ تَرْفيهيّ]

singular /ˈsɪŋɡjʊlə/ **A** *adj* 1 (in language) *<noun, verb>* مُفْرَد 2 (fml) (outstanding) *<achievement, beauty>* باهِر, بارِز **B** *n* صيغة المُفْرَدِ

sinister /ˈsɪnɪstə/ *adj* *<character, motive, plot>* خَبيث, شِرّير

sink /sɪŋk/ **A** *n* 1 (in kitchens) مَجْلًى (مَجالٍ), حَوْض (أَحْواض); **a double ~** حَوْض مُزْدَوَج 2 (in bathrooms) مِغْسَلة (مَغاسِلُ), حَوْض (أَحْواض) **B** *vt* (*past tense* **sank**; *past participle* **sunk**) 1 (in war) أَغْرَقَ *<a ship>* 2 (in mining, exploration) حَفَرَ (حَفْر; i) *<a well, shaft>* 3 (to embed) نَصَبَ (نَصْب; u), غَرَسَ (غَرْس, غِراسة; i) *<a post, pillar>*; **the dog sank its teeth into my arm** غَرَسَ الكَلْبُ أَسْنانَهُ في ذِراعي 4 (to cause to fail) قَضى (قَضاء; i) (على), أَغْرَقَ *<a government, company>*; **the cancellation could ~ the company** الإلْغاءُ قد يَقْضي على الشَرِكةِ 5 (to invest) **to ~ money into a project/company** ضَخَّ مالاً في مَشْروعٍ \ شَرِكةٍ **C** *vi* (*past tense* **sank**; *past participle* **sunk**) 1 (in water, mud) غَرِقَ (غَرَق; a), غاصَ (غَوْص; u); **the car sank into the mud** غاصَت السَيّارةُ في الوَحْلِ 2 (to drop) «water level» انْخَفَضَ, هَبَطَ (هُبوط; i-u); **to ~ into a chair** غاصَ في كُرْسيٍّ; **to ~ to one's knees** رَكَعَ (رُكوع; a), جَثا على رُكْبَتَيْهِ 3 «sun» غابَ (غِياب, غَيْبة; i), اخْتَفى 4 (to relapse) **to ~ into a deep sleep** اسْتَغْرَقَ في نَوْمٍ عَميقٍ; **to ~ into despair** مَلَأَهُ اليَأْسُ; **to ~ into oblivion** طَواهُ النِسْيانُ 5 (in value) «shares, profits» هَبَطَ (هُبوط; i-u), انْخَفَضَ; **he has sunk in my estimation** سَقَطَ من نَظَري

(Idioms) **to sink or swim** [تَحَتَّمَ عَلَيْهِ أَنْ يُدَبِّرَ أَمْرَهُ بِنَفْسِهِ]; **that sinking feeling** (infml) [الشُعور بالقَلَقِ]; **to sink without trace** اخْتَفى بِلا أَثَرٍ

(Phrasal verb) **sink in** 1 «water, lotion» تَمَّ امْتِصاصُهُ 2 «words, news» اسْتُوعِبَ

sinner /ˈsɪnə/ *n* آثِم (أَثَمة), أَثيم (أُثَماءُ)

sinus /ˈsʌɪnəs/ *n* (*pl* **sinuses**) جَيْب (جُيوب), تَجْويف (تَجاويفُ)

sinusitis /ˌsʌɪnəˈsʌɪtɪs/ *n* الْتِهاب الجُيوبِ الأَنْفيّةِ

sip /sɪp/ **A** *vt* (**-pp-**) احْتَسى, ارْتَشَفَ *<one's tea, medicine>* **B** *n* رَشْفة, حُسْوة (حُسُوات, أَحْسِية)

siphon, **syphon** /ˈsʌɪf(ə)n/ **A** *n* مِمَصّ (مِمَصّات) **B** *vt* (also **siphon off**) 1 (to draw out) سَحَبَ بِمِمَصٍّ *<the fuel, beer>* 2 (to divert) سَحَبَ \ حَوَّلَ بِشَكْلٍ غَيْر قانونيٍّ *<money, resources>*

sir /səː/ *n* 1 (fml) (address to a male customer) سَيِّدي; (to a male teacher) أُسْتاذ 2 (in a letter) سَيِّدي; **Dear Sir, ...** سَيِّدي العَزيز، ... 3 (**Sir** BrE (title of a knight)) **S~ Elton John** سير إلْتون جون

sire /sʌɪə/ **A** *n* (fml) فَحْل (الوالِد الذكَرِ لِحَيَوانٍ)
B *vt* (fml) أَنْجَبَ ‹*a foal, offspring*›

siren /ˈsʌɪrən/ *n* صَفّارة إِنْذارٍ

sirloin /ˈsəːlɔɪn/ *n* لَحْم خاصِرة البَقَرِ

sister /ˈsɪstə/ **A** *n* **1** (female sibling) أُخْت (f; أَخَوات), شَقيقة (شَقيقات); **my eldest/youngest ~** شَقيقَتي الكُبْرى \ الصُغْرى; **my elder ~** شَقيقَتي الأَكْبَرُ مِنّي **2** (also **Sister**) (BrE) (nurse) رَئيسة هَيْئَةِ تَمْريضٍ **3** (also **Sister**) (nun) راهِبة
B *adj before n* ‹*company, ship*› شَقيق

sister city *n* (AmE) مَدينة شَقيقة \ تَوْأَم

sisterhood /ˈsɪstəhʊd/ *n* **1** [u] (bond) عَلاقة أُخُوّةٍ (بين النِساءِ) **2** (of nuns) جَماعة راهِباتٍ **3** (women's association) جَمْعيّة نِسائيّة

sister-in-law /ˈsɪstərɪnlɔː/ *n* (*pl* **sisters-in-law**) **1** (on wife's side) أُخْت الزَوْجِ; (on husband's side) أُخْت الزَوْجةِ **2** (your brother's wife) زَوْجة أَخٍ

sisterly /ˈsɪst(ə)li/ *adj* ‹*love, kiss*› أَخَويّ

sit /sɪt/ **A** *vi* (*present participle* **-tt-**, *past tense, past participle* **sat**)
1 (on chairs, seats, etc) جَلَسَ (i; جُلوس); **come and ~ next to me** تَعالَ واجْلِسْ بِجانِبي; **to ~ on the floor** جَلَسَ على الأَرْضِ **2** (to be seated) جَلَسَ (i; جُلوس); **to be ~ting reading** كانَ جالِساً يَقْرَأُ; **she was ~ting at her desk** كانَتْ جالِسةً في مَكْتَبِها; **~ still!** اِجْلِسْ ساكِناً!; **to ~ at home** جَلَسَ في البَيْتِ **3** (to be located) وَقَعَ (a; وُقوع); **the house ~s at the top the hill** يَقَعُ البَيْتُ على قِمّةِ التَلِّ; **the keys are ~ting where you left them** توجَدُ المَفاتيحُ حَيْثُ تَرَكْتَها **4** (to meet) «court, parliament» عَقَدَ جَلْساتِهِ, اِنْعَقَدَ; **the court ~s twice a month** تَنْعَقِدُ المَحْكَمةُ مَرَّتَيْنِ في الشَهْرِ **5** (to hold office) شَغَلَ مَنْصِباً; **to ~ as a judge** شَغَلَ مَنْصِبَ القاضي; **to ~ on a committee/jury** كانَ عُضْواً في لَجْنةٍ \ هَيْئةِ مُحَلَّفينَ **6** (to be an MP) **to ~ for a constituency** كانَ نائِباً عن دائِرةٍ اِنْتِخابيّةٍ **7** (as an artist's model) [جَلَسَ \ وَقَفَ أَمامَ رَسّامٍ \ مُصَوِّرٍ] **8** (to fit) **the jacket ~s well across the shoulders** مَقاسُ هذه السُتْرةِ مُناسِبٌ على الكَتِفَيْنِ; **his statements don't ~ well with his lifestyle** أَقْوالُهُ لا تَتَناسَبُ مع أُسْلوبِ حَياتِهِ **9** (on eggs) رَقَدَ (u; رُقود)
B *vt* (*present participle* **-tt-**, *past tense, past participle* **sat**) **1** (to cause to be seated) أَجْلَسَ; **to ~ sb in/on a chair** أَجْلَسَ شَخْصاً على كُرْسيٍّ **2** (to put) وَضَعَ (a; وَضْع); **~ the dish in a pan of water** ضَعِ الطَبَقَ في قِدْرٍ من الماءِ **3** (BrE) «candidates» أَدّى ‹*an exam*›

Phrasal verbs **sit around** تَكاسَلَ, أَمْضى وَقْتَهُ بِلا فائِدةٍ
• **sit back** **1** (to relax) اِسْتَرْخى **2** (to take no action) جَلَسَ مُتَفَرِّجاً
• **sit down** جَلَسَ (i; جُلوس); **to ~ down to dinner** جَلَسَ لِيَتَعَشّى; **do ~ down!** تَفَضَّلْ بالجُلوسِ
• **sit in**: **to ~ in on a meeting/discussion** حَضَرَ اجْتِماعاً \ نِقاشاً
• **sit in for**: **~ in for [sb]** نابَ عن [شَخْصٍ]
• **sit on** (infml): **~ on [sth]** (not to deal with) تَباطَأَ في التَعامُلِ مع [شَيْءٍ] ‹*an application*›; تَكَتَّمَ على [شَيْءٍ] ‹*information*›
• **sit out**: **~ [sth] out** **1** (not to take part in) لم يُشارِكْ في [شَيْءٍ] ‹*a game, dance*› **2** (until the end of) اِنْتَظَرَ إلى نِهايةِ [شَيْءٍ] ‹*the recession, storm*›; **to ~ it out** اِنْتَظَرَ إلى نِهايَتِهِ
• **sit through**: **~ through [sth]** بَقِيَ جالِساً إلى نِهايةِ [شَيْءٍ] ‹*a lecture, movie*›
• **sit up** **1** (vertically) اِعْتَدَلَ في جِلْسَتِهِ, جَلَسَ مُسْتَقيمَ الظَهْرِ; **she was ~ting up in bed reading** كانَتْ جالِسةً على السَريرِ تَقْرَأُ; **~ up straight!** اِعْتَدِلْ في جِلْسَتِكَ!; **to make sb ~ up and take notice** (infml) لَفَتَ انْتِباهَ شَخْصٍ **2** (not to go to bed) سَهِرَ (a; سَهَر); **we sat up late, watching a film** سَهِرْنا إلى وَقْتٍ مُتَأَخِّرٍ, نُشاهِدُ فيلْماً

sitar /ˈsɪtɑː, sɪˈtɑː/ *n* سيتار

sitcom /ˈsɪtkɒm/ *n* (infml) سيتْكوم (مُسَلْسَل يَعْتَمِدُ على كوميديا المَوْقِفِ)

site /sʌɪt/ *n* **1** (location) مَوْقِع (مَواقِعُ); **the ~ of the castle** مَوْقِع القَصْرِ; **the ~ for the new school** مَوْقِع للمَدْرَسةِ الجَديدةِ **2** (also **building site**) (for building work) مَوْقِع بِناءٍ **3** (for a dig) مَوْقِع حَفْرٍ **4** (also **website**) (on the Internet) مَوْقِع (إلِكْترونيّ)

sit-in /ˈsɪtɪn/ *n* اِعْتِصام (اِعْتِصامات)

sitting /ˈsɪtɪŋ/ **A** *n* **1** (in a restaurant) مَوْعِد خِدْمةِ الطَعامِ **2** (of a court, parliament) جَلْسة **3** (for a portrait) [الجُلوس

[في وَضْعٍ مُعَيَّنٍ أمامَ رَسّامٍ

B *adj before n* **1** (seated) *‹position, area›* جُلوسٍ **2** (present) *‹member, president›* حاليّ

sitting duck *n* (infml) هَدَف سَهْل

sitting room *n* غُرْفة جُلوسٍ

sitting target *n* هَدَف سَهْل

situate /ˈsɪtʃʊeɪt/ *vt* وَضَعَ (وَضْع ;a) *‹a hotel, development›*; **to be ~d** كانَ يَقَعُ; **the hotel is ~d on the banks of the river** يَقَعُ الفُنْدُقُ على ضِفّةِ النَهْرِ

situation /sɪtjʊˈeɪʃ(ə)n/ *n* **1** (circumstances) حالة, ظُروف **2** (location) مَوْقِع (مَواقِع) **3** (job section) **~s vacant** قِسْم الوَظائِفِ الشاغِرة (في جَريدةٍ)

situation comedy *n* كوميديا المَوْقِف

sit-ups /ˈsɪtʌps/ *n pl* [تَمارين لِتَقْوِيةِ عَضَلاتِ البَطْنِ]

six /sɪks/ *n, adj* سِتّة ▸ see also **five**

Idioms **to hit/knock sb for six** صَدَمَ \ فاجَأَ شَخْصاً; **to be at sixes and sevens** كانَ في حالةِ ارْتِباكٍ شَديدٍ

Six Day War, June War *n* النَكْسة, 1967 حَرْب

sixteen /sɪksˈtiːn/ *n, adj* سِتّةَ عَشَرَ

sixteenth /sɪksˈtiːnθ/ **A** *n* **1** (in a series) سادِسَ عَشَرَ **2** (fraction) جُزْء من سِتّةَ عَشَرَ **3** (**the sixteenth**) (of a month) السادِسَ عَشَرَ

B *adj ‹century, day›* سادِسَ عَشَرَ

C *adv ‹to come, finish›* في المَرْكَزِ السادِسَ عَشَرَ

sixth /sɪksθ/ **A** *n* **1** (in a series) سادِس **2** (fraction) سُدْس **3** (**the sixth**) (of a month) السادِس **4** (BrE) ▸ **sixth form**

B *adj ‹century, day›* سادِس

C *adv ‹to come, finish›* في المَرْكَزِ السادِسِ

sixth form (BrE) *n* [صَفّ تَحْضيريّ للشَهادةِ الثانَويّةِ]

sixth-form college *n* (BrE) [مَدْرَسة تَحْضيريّة لامْتِحانِ الشَهادةِ الثانَويّةِ]

sixth sense *n* حاسّة سادِسة

sixties /ˈsɪkstiz/ *n pl* **1** (decade) (**the sixties**) السِتّينات **2** (age) **to be in one's ~** كانَ في السِتّيناتِ (من عُمْرِهِ)

sixtieth /ˈsɪkstiəθ/ **A** *n* **1** (**the sixtieth**) (in a series) السِتّونَ **2** (fraction) جُزْء من سِتّينَ

B *adj* السِتّونَ

C *adv* في المَرْكَزِ السِتّينَ

sixty /ˈsɪksti/ *n, adj* سِتّونَ

size /saɪz/ **A** *n* **1** (dimensions) حَجْم (حُجوم, أَحْجام); **it's the ~ of an egg/of this room** هو بِحَجْمِ بَيْضةٍ \ هذه الغُرْفةِ; **he's about your ~** هو بِحَجْمِكَ تَقْريباً; **the files vary in ~** تَخْتَلِفُ المَلَفّاتُ من حَيْثُ الحَجْمِ; **they're the same ~** هُمْ في نَفْسِ الحَجْمِ **2** (of the population, a group, family) حَجْم (حُجوم, أَحْجام) عَدَد (أَعْداد) **3** (of a problem) حَجْم (حُجوم, أَحْجام) **4** (of clothes, shoes) مَقاس (مَقاسات); **what ~ do you take?, what ~ are you?** ما مَقاسُكَ؟; **I'm a ~ 12** مَقاسي 12; **I take ~ 6/39 in shoes** مَقاسي في الأَحْذِيةِ هو 6/39; **try this for ~** جَرِّبْ هذا المَقاسَ

B *vt* **1** حَدَّدَ الحَجْمَ *‹an image, a window›* **2** فَرَزَ حَسَبَ الحَجْمِ *‹eggs, fruit›*

Idiom **to cut sb down to size** وَضَعَ شَخْصاً في حَجْمِه الحَقيقيِّ

Phrasal verb **size up** (infml): **1** **~ up [sth], ~ [sth] up** قَدَّرَ حَجْمَ [شَيْءٍ] *‹a situation, the competition›* **2** **~ up [sb], ~ [sb] up** قَدَّرَ حَجْمَ [شَخْصٍ] *‹an opponent, enemy›*

sizeable /ˈsaɪzəb(ə)l/ *adj ‹amount, house›* ضَخْم

sizzle /ˈsɪz(ə)l/ *vi* «sausages, eggs» نَشَّ (نَشّ, نَشيش ;i), أَزَّ (i-u; أَزيز)

skate /skeɪt/ **A** *n* **1** (also **ice skate**) (for ice skating) مِزْلَجة (also **roller skate**) (for roller skating) حِذاء تَزَلُّجٍ; **a pair of ~s** جِذاء تَزَلُّجٍ **2** (fish) وَرْنَك **3** (food) وَرْنَك

B *vi* «skaters, children» تَزَلَّجَ, تَزَحْلَقَ

skateboard /ˈskeɪtbɔːd/ *n* لَوح تَزَحْلُقٍ \ تَزَلُّجٍ

skateboarder /ˈskeɪtbɔːdə/ *n* مُتَزَلِّج, مُتَزَحْلِق

skateboarding /ˈskeɪtbɔːdɪŋ/ *n* تَزَحْلُق \ تَزَلُّج على اللَوْحِ

skater /ˈskeɪtə/ *n* مُتَزَلِّج

skating /ˈskeɪtɪŋ/ *n* تَزَلُّج

skating rink *n* **1** (of ice) حَلْبة تَزَلُّجٍ **2** (for roller skating) أَرْضيّة تَزَلُّجٍ

skeletal /ˈskɛlət(ə)l/ *adj ‹muscle, remains›* هَيْكَليّ

skeleton /ˈskɛlɪt(ə)n/ *n* 1 (of a body) هَيْكَل عَظْميّ 2 (of buildings, vehicles) هَيْكَل (هَياكِل)

Idiom **the skeleton in the cupboard** (BrE) **closet** (AmE) [سِرّ مُخْزٍ \ مُحْرِج]

skeleton key *n* [مِفْتاح يَفْتَح سِلْسِلَةً مُخْتَلِفَةً من الأَقْفال]

skeptic (AmE) *n* ▸**sceptic**

skeptical (AmE) *adj* ▸**sceptical**

skepticism (AmE) *n* ▸**scepticism**

sketch /skɛtʃ/ A *n* 1 (drawing) رَسْم ,مُخَطَّط ,سْكيتْش; **a rough ~** رَسْم \ مُخَطَّط تَقْريبيّ ;تَخْطيطيّ \ أَوَّليّ 2 (comic depiction) (مَشْهَد مَسْرَحيّ هَزْليّ) سْكيتْش مَسْرَحيّ 3 (brief account) وَصْف مُخْتَصِر \ موجَز

B *vt* 1 (to draw) رَسَمَ (u; رَسْم) ‹*a person, scene*› 2 (also **sketch out**) (to describe) وَصَفَ (i; وَصْف) ‹*a plan, the outlines*›

C *vi* (in pencil, ink) «artists, cartoonists» رَسَمَ مُخَطَّطاً

Phrasal verb **sketch in**: **~ in [sth], ~ [sth] in** 1 (to draw) رَسَمَ (u; رَسْم) ‹*the outlines, trees*› 2 (to describe) وَصَفَ (i; وَصْف) ‹*the detail, background*›

sketchbook /ˈskɛtʃbʊk/ *n* كُرّاسة رُسومٍ تَخْطيطيّةٍ

sketchpad /ˈskɛtʃpad/ *n* ▸**sketchbook**

sketchy /ˈskɛtʃi/ *adj* (**sketchier**, **sketchiest**) ‹*information, knowledge*› غَيْر كافٍ ,ناقِص

skew /skjuː/ *vt* حَرَّفَ ‹*a result, statistics*›

skewer /ˈskjuːə/ *n* (أَسْياخ) سيخ

ski /skiː/ A *n* زَلّاجة

B *vi* (*3rd person present sing* **skis**, *past tense* **skied**, *past participle* **skiing**) «skiers, holidaymakers» تَزَلَّجَ; **to go ~ing** ذَهَبَ للتزلُّجِ

ski boot *n* حِذاء تَزَلُّجٍ

skid /skɪd/ A *vi* (**-dd-**) «cars, feet» انْزَلَقَ

B *n* انْزِلاق

Idiom **to be on the skids** (BrE) **to hit the skids** (AmE infml) كانَ في حالةٍ حَرِجةٍ

skier /ˈskiːə/ *n* مُتَزَلِّج

skiing /ˈskiːɪŋ/ *n* تَزَلُّج

skiing holiday *n* عُطْلة تَزَلُّجٍ

ski instructor *n* مُدَرِّب التَزَلُّجِ

ski jump *n* [مَسار مُنْحَدِر لِمُمارَسةِ القَفْزِ التَزَلُّجيّ]

skilful (BrE), **skillful** (AmE) /ˈskɪlfʊl/ *adj* 1 (having skill) ‹*craftsman, negotiator*› بارِع ,(مَهَرة) ماهِر; **she is very ~ at needlework** هي ماهِرةٌ جِدًّا في التَطْريز 2 (accomplished) ‹*diplomacy*› بارِع; ‹*handling*› مُتْقَن

ski lift *n* مِصْعَد تَزَلُّجٍ

skill /skɪl/ *n* 1 [u] (ability) بَراعة ,مَهارة 2 (technique) مَهارة; **to learn new ~s** تَعَلَّمَ مَهاراتٍ جَديدةً

skilled /skɪld/ *adj* 1 (trained) ‹*worker, labour*› (مَهَرة) ماهِر مُدَرَّب 2 (talented) ‹*craftsman, negotiator*› بارِع; **he is ~ in the arts of diplomacy** هو بارِعٌ في فُنونِ الدِبْلوماسيّةِ

skillet /ˈskɪlɪt/ *n* (AmE) (مَقالٍ) مِقْلاة

skillful (AmE) *adj* ▸**skilful**

skim /skɪm/ A *vt* (**-mm-**) 1 فَصَلَ القِشْدة عن ,نَزَعَ الدَسَمَ من ‹*milk*› 2 قَشَطَ الرَغْوةَ من ‹*stock, soup*› 3 (to remove) **to ~ the fat/oil off sth** قَشَطَ الدُهْنَ \ الزَيْتَ من شَيْءٍ 4 (to touch lightly) لامَسَ ‹*the surface, treetops*› 5 (to read quickly) تَصَفَّحَ ‹*the pages, a book*›

B *vi* (**-mm-**) 1 **to ~ over** *or* **across sth** «planes, birds» حَلَّقَ فوق شَيْءٍ; **the report ~s over the issue** يَتناوَلُ التَقْريرُ القَضيّةَ بِشَكْلٍ سَطْحيٍّ 2 **to ~ through sth** (to read quickly) تَصَفَّحَ شَيْئاً بِسُرْعةٍ

Idiom **to skim the surface of sth** تناوَلَ شَيْئاً بشَكْلٍ سَطْحيٍّ

skimmed milk, **skim milk** *n* حَليب مَقْشود

skimp /skɪmp/ *vi* «cooks, companies» تَبَخَّلَ ,اقْتَصَدَ ,قَتَّرَ; **to ~ on quality/investment** تَبَخَّلَ في النَوْعيّة \ الاسْتِثْمارِ

skimpy /ˈskɪmpi/ *adj* (**skimpier**, **skimpiest**) 1 (brief) ‹*outfit, bikini*› [ضَيِّق وَفاضِح] 2 (mean) ‹*allowance, portion*› هَزيل, ضَئيل

skin /skɪn/ A *n* 1 (of a person) (جُلود) جِلْد; **she has fair ~** لَدَيْها بَشَرةٌ فاتِحةٌ 2 (of an animal, fish) (جُلود) جِلْد 3 (of fruit, vegetables) (قُشور) قِشْر 4 (of sausages) (قِشْر) قِشْرة 5 (on liquids) [طَبَقة رَقيقة تَتَشَكَّلُ على سَطْحِ سائِلٍ بارِدٍ]

B *vt* (**-nn-**) **1** (in meat preparation) سَلَخَ (a-u; سَلْخ) ‹*a rabbit, cow*› **2** (to peel) قَشَّرَ ‹*a tomato, an onion*› **3** (to graze) ‹*one's knuckles, knee*› خَدَشَ (i; خَدْش)

Idioms **by the skin of your teeth** (infml) بالكادِ; **to get under sb's skin** (infml) أَثارَ أَعْصابَ شَخْصٍ; **to have a thick/thin skin** كانَ عَديمَ \ مُرْهَفَ الحِسِّ; **to save one's (own) skin** نَجا بِجِلْدِهِ

skin cancer *n* سَرَطان الجِلْد

skin-deep /skɪnˈdiːp/ *adj* ‹*emotion, quality*› سَطْحيّ; **his political commitment is only ~** اِلْتِزامُهُ السِياسيُّ لَيْسَ إلاّ شَيْئاً سَطْحيًّا

skin-diver *n* [غَطّاس مُزَوَّد بجهاز \ بقَصَبةِ تَنَفُّسٍ]

skin-diving *n* غَطْس بجهازٍ \ بِقَصَبةِ تَنَفُّسٍ

skinhead /ˈskɪnhɛd/ *n* (BrE) [شَخْص من جَماعة حَليقي الرُؤوس]

skinny /ˈskɪni/ *adj* (**skinnier, skinniest**) (infml) ‹*legs, child*› نَحيل (نَحْلى, نُحَّل), هَزيل (هَزْلى), نَحيف (نحاف, نُحَفاءُ)

skint /skɪnt/ *adj* (BrE) (infml) **to be ~** كانَ مُفْلِساً

skintight /skɪnˈtʌɪt/ *adj* ‹*jeans, dress*› ضَيِّق جدًّا

skip /skɪp/ **A** *vt* (**-pp-**) **1** (not to attend) فَوَّتَ, تَخَطّى ‹*a meal*›; تَغَيَّبَ (عن) ‹*a meeting*›; **to ~ school/class** تَغَيَّبَ عن المَدْرَسة \ الصَفِّ **2** (to leave out) تَرَكَ (u; تَرْك), تَخَطّى ‹*a step, chapter*›; **let's ~ the formalities** دَعْنا نَتَخَطّى الرَسْميّاتِ; **~ it!** (infml) دَعْكَ من هذا! **3** (infml) (to leave) **to ~ town/the country** غادَرَ مَدينةً \ البَلَدَ خُلْسةً

B *vi* (**-pp-**) **1** (to jump) وَثَبَ (i; وُثوب, وَثَبان), قفز (i; قفز) **2** (BrE) (with a rope) قَفَزَ على الحَبْل, نَطَّ الحَبْلَ **3** (to move) قَفَزَ (i; قَفْز, قَفَزان), اِنْتَقَلَ; **to ~ from one subject to another** قَفَزَ من مَوْضوع إلى آخَرَ

C *n* **1** (jump) قَفْزة (قَفَزات) **2** (BrE) (container) حاوِية

ski pants *n* سِرْوال تَزَلُّجٍ

ski pass *n* [بِطاقة دُخولٍ لِمَحَطّةِ تَزَلُّجٍ]

ski pole *n* عَصا تَزَلُّجٍ

skipper /ˈskɪpə/ **A** *n* (infml) **1** (of a boat) رُبّان (رَبابين, رَبابِنة) **2** (of a team) قائِد فَريق

B *vt* قادَ (u; قِيادة) ‹*the team, boat*›; **he ~ed the first team for five seasons** قادَ الفَريقَ الأَوَّلَ لِخَمْسةِ مَواسِمَ

skipping rope /ˈskɪpɪŋ ˌrəʊp/ *n* (BrE) حَبْل قَفْزٍ

ski resort *n* مُنْتَجع تَزَلُّجٍ

skirmish /ˈskəːmɪʃ/ *n* (fight) اشْتِباك (مُسَلَّح)

skirt /skəːt/ **A** *n* تَنّورة (تَنانيرُ)

B *vt* (also **skirt around, skirt round** BrE) **1** (to go around) سارَ مُحاذِياً ل ‹*a wood, village*› **2** (to ignore) تَمَلَّصَ (من), تَجاهَلَ ‹*a problem, an issue*›

skirting /ˈskəːtɪŋ/, **skirting board** *n* (BrE) [لَوْحة خَشَبيّة تُثَبَّتُ على طولِ الجُزْءِ السُفْليِّ لِجِدارٍ]

ski slope *n* مُنْحَدَر للتَزَلُّجِ

ski suit *n* بَدْلة تَزَلُّجٍ

skittle /ˈskɪt(ə)l/ **A** *n* [قِنّينة خَشَبيّة تُسْتَعْمَلُ في لُعْبةِ القَناني]

B (**skittles**) *n pl* [لُعْبة القَناني الخَشَبيّة]

skive /skʌɪv/ *vi* (also **skive off**) (BrE infml) **1** (from school) «students, pupils» تَهَرَّبَ من المَدْرَسة **2** (from work) «workers, employees» تَهَرَّبَ من العَمَلِ

skulk /skʌlk/ *vi* «pickpockets, youths» تَوارى

skull /skʌl/ *n* جُمْجُمة (جَماجِمُ)

skullcap /ˈskʌlkap/ *n* (Catholic) قَلَنْسُوة (قَلانِسُ, قَلانيس); (Jewish) طاقيّة

skunk /skʌŋk/ *n* ظَرِبان أَمْريكيّ

sky /skʌɪ/ **A** *n* (*pl* **skies**) (above the earth) سَماء (f; سَماوات); **a clear/cloudy ~** سَماء صافية \ غائمة; **a patch of blue ~** رُقْعة من سَماءٍ زَرْقاءَ; **the night ~** سَماء اللَيْلِ; **the plane rose high into the ~** اِرْتَفَعَت الطائِرةُ عالِياً في السَماءِ

B (**skies**) *n pl* (in forecasts) سَماء (f; سَماوات); **a day of rain and cloudy skies** يَوْم مُمْطِر وَسَماء غائِمة; **clear skies spreading from the west after early rain** سَماء صافية تَنْتَشِرُ من ناحِيةِ الغَرْبِ بعد أَمْطارٍ مُبَكِّرةٍ

C *vt* (*3rd person present sing* **skies**, *present participle* **skying**, *past tense, past participle* **skied**) (Sport) **to ~ a ball/shot** «golfers, batters» ضَرَبَ كُرةً \ طَلْقةً في السَماءِ

Idiom **the sky's the limit** لَيْسَ هُناكَ حُدودٌ

skydiving /ˈskʌɪdʌɪvɪŋ/ *n* قَفْز بالمِظَلّاتِ

sky-high /skʌɪˈhʌɪ/ *adj* ‹*prices, rates*› مُرْتَفِع جدًّا

skyjack /ˈskʌɪdʒak/ *vt* اخْتَطَفَ *‹airliner, an aeroplane›*

skyjacker /ˈskʌɪdʒakə/ *n* مُخْتَطِف طائِرةٍ

skyjacking /ˈskʌɪdʒakɪŋ/ *n* اخْتِطاف (اخْتِطافات)

skylark /ˈskʌɪlɑːk/ *n* قُنْبَر (n coll)

skylight /ˈskʌɪlʌɪt/ *n* مَنْوَر

skyline /ˈskʌɪlʌɪn/ *n* أُفُق (آفاق); **the Manhattan ~** أُفُق مَدينةِ مانْهاتَن

sky marshal *n* [رَجُل أَمْنٍ مُتَخَفٍّ على مَتْنِ بَعْضِ الرِحْلاتِ الدَوْلِيّةِ (لِمُكافَحةِ اخْتِطافِ الطائِراتِ)]

Skype® /skʌɪp/ **A** *n* سْكايْب

B *vt* تَحَدَّثَ عَبْرَ سْكايْب مع

skyscraper /ˈskʌɪskreɪpə/ *n* ناطِحة سَحابٍ

slab /slab/ *n* **1** (of stone) لَوْح سَميك; (of marble) بَلاطة (أَبْلِطة, بَلاطات) **2** (of cheese, cake) شَريحة سَميكة

slack /slak/ **A** *adj* **1** (loose, limp) *‹rope, fishing line›* رَخْو; **to go ~** «rope, fishing line» ارْتَخى **2** (careless) *‹attitude, work›* غَيْر مُبالٍ, مُهْمِل; **to be ~ about doing sth** أَهْمَلَ في فِعْلِ شَيْءٍ **3** (not busy) *‹period, season, demand›* ضَعيف; **business is ~** حَرَكةُ التِجارة ضَعيفةٌ

B *n* (in ropes, cables) [الجُزْء غَيْر المَشْدودِ \ الرَخْو]; **to take up the ~** سَدَّ الفَجْوةَ \ الخَلَلَ

C (**slacks**) *n pl* سِرْوال (سَراويلُ); **a pair of ~s** سِرْوال (سَراويلُ)

D *vi* «workers» تَكاسَلَ

(Idiom) **to cut sb some slack** (infml) تَساهَلَ \ تَسامَحَ مع شَخْصٍ

(Phrasal verb) **slack off** **1** «business, trade» تَباطَأَ **2** «rain» خَفَّ (i; خَفّ)

slacken /ˈslak(ə)n/ **A** *vt* **1** (to loosen) *‹a rope, one's grip›* أَرْخى **2** (to free) *‹a nut, bolt›* فَكَّ (u; فَكّ), حَلَّ (u; حَلّ) **3** (to reduce) *‹the pace, speed›* خَفَّفَ

B *vi* **1** (to loosen) «ropes, sb's grip» تَراخى **2** (to slow down) «sb's pace, speed» تَباطَأَ **3** (to diminish) «demand, business» تَباطَأَ

(Phrasal verb) **slacken off**: **1** **~ off** (to lessen) «demand, business» تَباطَأَ **2** (to die down) «gales, rain» هَدَأَ (a; هَدْء, هُدوء)

slag /slag/ *n* **1** خَبَث (أَخْباث) **2** (BrE pej) (slut) فاجِرة (فَواجِرُ)

(Phrasal verb) **slag off** (infml): **~ off [sb/sth], ~ [sb/sth] off** (BrE) ذَمَّ [شَخْصاً \ شَيْئاً] *‹the government, performance›*

slag heap *n* كَوْمة نُفاياتٍ مَعْدِنيّةٍ

slain /sleɪn/ *past participle* ▸ **slay**

slake /sleɪk/ *vt* **to ~ one's thirst** أَرْوى ظَمَأَهُ

slalom /ˈslɑːləm/ *n* (on snow) سِباق التَزَلُّجِ المُتَعَرِّجِ

slam /slam/ **A** *vt* (**-mm-**) **1** (to shut) «person» أَغْلَقَ بِقوّةٍ *‹a door›*; **don't ~ the door!** لا تُغْلِقِ البابَ بِقوّةٍ!; **to ~ the door in sb's face** أَغْلَقَ البابَ في وَجْهِ شَخْصٍ **2** (with violence) ضَرَبَ بِقوّةٍ; **I ~med the phone down** أَغْلَقْتُ سَمّاعةَ الهاتِفِ بِقوّةٍ; **to ~ one's fist on the table** ضَرَبَ الطاوِلةَ بِقَبْضَتِهِ بِقوّةٍ; **to ~ on the brakes** (infml) داسَ على الفَرامِلِ بِقوّةٍ **3** (infml) (to criticize) انْتَقَدَ بِشِدّةٍ *‹the plan, a decision›*

B *vi* (**-mm-**) **1** «door, window» انْغَلَقَ بِقوّةٍ; **to ~ shut** انْغَلَقَ بِقوّةٍ **2** **to ~ into sth** «vehicle, missile» اصْطَدَمَ \ ارْتَطَمَ بِقوّةٍ بِشَيْءٍ

C *n* **1** (of a door) دَوِيّ **2** (in bridge) [طَريقة لِلفَوْزِ في لُعْبةِ البْريدْج]

slander /ˈslɑːndə/ **A** *n* قَذْف, تَشْهير

B *vt* شَهَّرَ (ب) *‹sb's name, reputation›*

slang /slaŋ/ *n* لُغة دارِجة \ عامّيّة

slangy /ˈslaŋi/ *adj* (**slangier, slangiest**) *‹expression, style›* عامّيّ

slant /slɑːnt/ **A** *vt* **1** (to bias) *‹the facts, story›* حَرَّفَ **2** (to orientate) *‹a picture, rail›* أَمالَ

B *vi* «floor, ground, handwriting» مالَ (i; مَيْل, مَيَلان)

C *n* **1** (perspective) وُجْهة نَظَرٍ, مَنْظور, تَوَجُّه; **a European ~ on the crisis** وُجْهة نَظَرٍ أوروبّيّة بِشَأْنِ الأَزْمةِ; **his writing betrays a right-wing ~** ما كَتَبَهُ يَكْشِفُ \ يُفْشي عن تَوَجُّهٍ يَمينيٍّ **2** (angle) مائِل; **the floor has a ~** الأَرْضيّةُ مائِلةٌ; **the curtain is at a ~** السِتارُ مائِلٌ \ مُنْحَرِفٌ

slanting /ˈslɑːntɪŋ/ *adj* *‹eyes, roof, rays›* مائِل

slap /slap/ **A** *vt* (**-pp-**) **1** (to hit) صَفَعَ (a; صَفْع), لَطَمَ (i; لَطْم) *‹a child, sb's face›*; **to ~ sb for sth/for doing sth** صَفَعَ شَخْصاً لِشَيْءٍ \ لِفِعْلِهِ شَيْئاً; **to ~ sb on the leg, to ~ sb's leg** ضَرَبَ

رَبَّتَ على ظَهْرِ شَخْصاً على رِجْلِه; **to ~ sb on the back** شَخْصٍ; **to ~ sb in the face** صَفَعَ شَخْصاً على وَجْهِهِ ❷ (to put) رَمى (i; رَمْي), أَلْقى; **he ~ped the money on the table** أَلْقى بالمالِ على الطاولةِ; **she ~ped some make-up on her face** وَضَعَتْ بَعْضَ المَكِياجِ على وَجْهِها على عَجَلٍ; **they have ~ped a tax on it** لَقَدْ فَرَضوا ضَريبةً عَلَيْهِ

B *n* (blow) صَفْعة, لَطْمة (لَطَمات); **a ~ in the face** لَطْمة على الوَجْهِ; **it was a real ~ in the face for the government** كانَتْ صَفْعةً حَقيقيّةً في وَجْهِ الحُكومةِ; **to give sb a ~ on the back** رَبَّتَ على كَتْفِ شَخْصٍ; **a ~ on the wrist** تَوْبيخ

C *adv* (forcefully) **to walk/drive ~ into sb/sth** سارَ \ قادَ السَّيّارة حتّى اصْطَدَمَ بِشَخْصٍ \ بِشَيْءٍ; **I ran ~ bang into my old headmaster** [تَقابَلْتُ مع مُدير مَدْرَستي السابِقِ بالصُدْفةِ]

(Phrasal verb) **slap down**: **~ [sb] down** عَرَّفَ [شَخْصاً] حَجْمَهُ الحَقيقيَّ

slap bang *adv* (infml) ❶ (with force) [بَغْتة وَمُباشرةً] ❷ (exactly) تَماماً بالضَبْطِ

slapdash /ˈslapdaʃ/ *adj* (infml) ‹*approach, work*› أَهْوَج (dipt), مُتَسَرِّع

slapstick /ˈslapstɪk/ *n* (also **slapstick comedy**) كوميديا تَهْريجيّة

slash /slaʃ/ **A** *vt* ❶ (to wound) جَرَحَ (a; جَرْح), قَطَعَ (a; قَطْع) ‹*sb's face, throat*›; **she had ~ed her wrists** كانَتْ قد قَطَعَتْ شَرايينَ يَدَيْها ❷ (to cut) قَطَعَ (a; قَطْع), شَقَّ (u; شَقّ) ‹*fabric, tyres*›; **to ~ one's way through the undergrowth** شَقَّ طَريقَهُ في الأَحْراشِ ❸ (to reduce) خَفَّضَ ‹*the price, budget*›; **falling demand has caused the company to ~ output** الانْخِفاضُ في الطَلَبِ جَعَلَ الشَرِكةَ تُخَفِّضُ الإنْتاجَ

B *n* ❶ (in fabric, seat, tyre) شَقّ, قَطْع; **a ~ in the canvas** شَقّ في اللَوْحةِ ❷ (diagonal stroke) شَرْطة مائلة للأمامِ ❸ (cutting movement) ضَرْبة (ضَرَبات)

slat /slat/ *n* (of a blind, shutter, bench) قِدّة (قِدَد)

slate /sleɪt/ **A** *n* ❶ [u] (stone) أَرْدُواز ❷ (tile) قِرْميد (قَراميدُ)

B *vt* ❶ غَطّى بالقِرْميد ‹*a roof*› ❷ (BrE infml) (to criticize) انْتَقَدَ (بِشِدّةٍ) ‹*a film, show*› ❸ (AmE) (to schedule) حَدَّدَ المَوْعِدَ; **the election is ~d for June** حُدِّدَ شَهْرُ يونيو مَوْعِداً للانْتِخابِ

slater /ˈsleɪtə/ *n* (roofer) [شَخْص مِهْنَتُهُ بِناءُ الأَسْقُفِ]

slaughter /ˈslɔːtə/ **A** *vt* ❶ ذَبَحَ (a; ذَبْح) ‹*animals*› ❷ قَتَلَ بِوَحْشيّةٍ ‹*people*›

B *n* ❶ (in butchery) ذَبْح ❷ (massacre) مَجْزَرة (مَجازِرُ)

slaughterhouse /ˈslɔːtəhaʊs/ *n* مَسْلَخ (مَسالِخُ)

Slav /slɑːv/ *n, adj* صَقْلَب (صَقالِبة)

slave /sleɪv/ **A** *n* عَبْد (عَبيد); **to be a ~ to fashion** كانَ عَبْداً للموضة

B *vi* (also **slave away**) «workers, housewives» كَدَّ (u; كَدّ), عَمِلَ بِجُهْدٍ كَبيرٍ; **I've been slaving away all day in the kitchen** عَمِلْتُ بِجُهْدٍ كَبيرٍ في المَطْبَخِ طوالَ اليومِ

slave driver *n* ❶ (infml) (taskmaster) [شَخْص مُتَسَلِّط على الآخرينَ في العَمَلِ] ❷ (slaver) نَخّاس

slave labour, **slave labor** (AmE) *n* (work) سُخْرة

slaver¹ /ˈsleɪvə/ *n* ❶ (trader) نَخّاس, تاجِر رَقيقٍ ❷ (ship) سَفينة نَقْلِ العَبيدِ

slaver² /ˈsleɪvə/ *vi* «dog» سالَ لُعابُهُ, رالَ (i; رَيْل); **to ~ over sth** سالَ لُعابُهُ أمامَ شَيْءٍ; **he was ~ing over the prospect of winning the government contract** سالَ لُعابُهُ أمامَ إمْكانيّةِ الفَوْزِ بالعَقْدِ الحُكوميِّ

slavery /ˈsleɪv(ə)ri/ *n* رِقّ (رُقوق)

slaw /slɔː/ *n* (AmE) ▸ **coleslaw**

slay /sleɪ/ *vt* (*past tense* **slew** or **slayed**; *past participle* **slain**) (liter) قَتَلَ (u; قَتْل) ‹*a dragon, the enemy*›

sleaze /sliːz/ *n* (infml) فَساد (أَخْلاقيّ)

sleazy /ˈsliːzi/ *adj* (**sleazier**, **sleaziest**) (infml) ❶ ‹*character*› مَشْبوه, قَذِر ❷ ‹*bar, area*› فاسِد

sledge (BrE) /slɛdʒ/, **sled** (AmE) /slɛd/ **A** *n* مِزْلَجة

B *vi* رَكِبَ مِزْلَجةً

sledgehammer /ˈslɛdʒhamə/ *n* مِرْزَبّة (مَرازِبُ)

(Idiom) **like taking a sledgehammer to crack a nut** مِثْل سِتّ وَجارِيَتَيْنِ على قَلْي بَيْضَتَيْنِ (colloq Egypt)

sleek /sliːk/ *adj* ❶ (glossy) ‹*hair, fur*› أَمْلَس (dipt; مُلْس), ناعِم (نَواعِمُ), حَريريّ ❷ (streamlined) ‹*design, lines*› انْسِيابيّ ❸ (well-groomed) ‹*person*› أَنيق

sleep /sli:p/ **A** *n* **1** نَوْم; **to go to ~** ذَهَبَ إلى النَوْمِ; **to go back to ~** رَجَعَ إلى النَوْمِ; **I couldn't get to ~** لم أَسْتَطِع النَوْمَ; **my leg has gone to ~** خَدِرَتْ رِجْلي; **the film sent** *or* **put me to ~** جَعَلَني الفيلْم أَشْعُرُ بالنُعاسِ; **to have a ~** حَصَلَ على قِسْطٍ من النَوْمِ; **to have a good night's ~** نامَ لَيْلَةً هادِئةً; **to get some ~** أَخَذَ قِسْطاً من النَوْمِ **2** (infml) (to kill) **to put an animal to ~** قَتَلَ حَيَواناً

B *vt* (*past tense, past participle* **slept**) **the house ~s six people** يَسَعُ البَيْتُ لَمَبيت سِتّةِ أَفْرادٍ

C *vi* (*past tense, past participle* **slept**) **1** نامَ (a; نَوْم ,نِيام); **how did you ~?** كيف كانَ نَوْمُكَ؟; **to ~ soundly** نامَ نَوْماً عَميقاً **2** (to stay the night) باتَ (i; مَبيت); **to ~ at a friend's house** باتَ في مَنْزِلِ صَديقٍ; **to ~ with sb** ضاجَعَ شَخْصاً

(Idiom) **to cry oneself to sleep** بَكى إلى أنْ نامَ

(Phrasal verbs) **sleep around** (infml) مارَسَ الجِنْسَ مع أَشْخاصٍ كَثيرينَ

• **sleep in** (to stay in bed late) أَطالَ النَوْمَ

• **sleep on** **A** (to stay in bed late) أَطالَ النَوْمَ **B** **~ on a problem/decison** (to take time over) أَخَذَ وَقْتاً للتَفْكير في مُشْكِلةٍ \ قَرارٍ; **I'd like to ~ on it/on my decision** أَوَدُّ أنْ آخُذَ بَعْضَ الوَقْتِ للتَفْكير في الأَمْرِ \ قراري

• **sleep out** (in the open) باتَ في العَراءِ

• **sleep over** نامَ خارِجَ البَيْتِ; **to ~ over at sb's house** نامَ في بَيْتِ شَخْصٍ

sleeper /'sli:pə/ *n* **1** (person) نائِم (نِيام); **to be a heavy/light ~** كانَ ثَقيل \ خَفيفَ النَوْمِ **2** (train) قِطار نَوْم **3** (sleeping car) عَرَبة نَوْمٍ (بالقِطار) **4** (sleeping space) سَرير نَوْمٍ (بِقِطارٍ أو سَفينةٍ) **5** (on a rail track) عارضة (عَوارِضُ), راقِدة

sleeping bag *n* كيس \ حَقيبة نَوْمٍ

sleeping car *n* عَرَبة نَوْمٍ

sleeping partner *n* (BrE) شَريك بالمالِ, شَريك موصٍ

sleeping pill, sleeping tablet (BrE) *n* حَبّة, قُرْص مُنَوِّم مُنَوِّمة

sleeping sickness *n* مَرَض النَوْمِ

sleepless /'sli:pləs/ *adj* ‹*night*› مُؤَرَّق; **to have a ~ night** قَضى لَيْلةً مُؤَرَّقةً

sleepover /'sli:pəʊvə/ *n* [قَضاء لَيْلَةٍ في بَيْتِ صَديقٍ]

sleepwalk /'sli:pwɔ:k/ *vi* «sleeper» سارَ أَثْناء نَوْمِهِ

sleepy /'sli:pi/ *adj* (**sleepier, sleepiest**) **1** ‹*person*› نَعْسان (dipt; نَعْسى f), وَسْنان, شَعَرَ بالنُعاسِ; **to feel/be ~** شَعَرَ بالنُعاسِ, نِعاس **2** ‹*eyes, voice*› ناعِس (نُعْس) (a-u; نَعْس) نَعَسَ **3** ‹*town, village*› ساكِن, هادِئ, ناعِس

sleet /sli:t/ *n* (مَطَر فيه بَرَدٌ) قِطْقِط

sleeve /sli:v/ **A** *n* **1** (of garments) كُمّ (أَكْمام), رُدْن (أَرْدان); **to pull at sb's ~** شَدَّ شَخْصاً من كُمِّهِ; **to roll up one's ~s** شَمَّرَ أَكْمامَهُ **2** (for a CD, record) غِلاف (أَغْلِفة); (for documents) ظَرْف **3** (for cables, wires) غِلاف (أَغْلِفة), غِطاء (أَغْطِية)

B (**sleeved**) *in combination* **long-/short-~d** طَويل \ قَصير الأَكْمامِ

(Idioms) **to have sth up one's sleeve** احْتَفَظَ بِشَيْءٍ في جَعْبَتِهِ; **to wear one's heart on one's sleeve** كانَ ما في قَلْبِهِ على لِسانِهِ

sleeveless /'sli:vləs/ *adj* ‹*top, dress*› بلا أَكْمامٍ

sleigh /sleɪ/ *n* مِزْلَقة (مَزالِقُ)

sleight of hand /slʌɪt əv 'hand/ *n* خِفّة يَدٍ

slender /'slɛndə/ *adj* (**slenderer, slenderest**) **1** ‹*figure, neck*› مَمْشوق, أَهْيَف (dipt); ‹*fingers*› رَفيع, نَحيف **2** ‹*lead, majority*› ضَئيل, بَسيط (بُسَطاءُ); ‹*hope, chance*› ضَعيف

slept /slept/ *past tense, past participle* ▸ **sleep**

sleuth /slu:θ/ *n* (infml) مُخْبِر

slew /slu:/ *past tense* ▸ **slay**

slice /slʌɪs/ **A** *n* **1** (of bread, meat, cake, lemon) شَريحة (شَرائِحُ), قِطْعة (قِطَع); **to cut a loaf into ~s** قَطَّعَ رَغيفاً إلى شَرائِحَ **2** (part) حِصّة (حِصَص), شَريحة (شَرائِحُ); **they wanted a ~ of the Asian market** أَرادوا حِصّةً من السوقِ الأَسْيَويّةِ; ▸ **action 3** (for cake) مِلْوَق (مَلاوِقُ); (in frying) ▸ **fish slice**

B *vt* **1** (to cut into pieces) قَطَّعَ إلى شَرائِحَ ‹*a loaf, roast, cucumber*›; **could you ~ the bread/beef?** هَلاّ قَطَّعْتَ الخُبْزَ \ لَحْمَ البَقَرِ إلى شَرائِحَ؟ **2** (to cut through) «knives, blades» ‹*sb's skin, cheek*› قَطَعَ (a; قَطْع), جَرَحَ (a; جَرْح)

C *vi* **1** (to be cut) «meat, cake, bread» قُطِّعَ إلى شَرائِحَ **2** (to cut) **to ~ through sth** «axes, blades» قَطَّعَ شَيْئاً إلى شَرائِحَ ‹*the meat*›; قَطَّعَ شَيْئاً إلى قِطَعٍ ‹*rope, timber*›

sliced bread /ˌslʌɪst ˈbrɛd/ *n* خُبْزٌ شَرائِحَ
Idiom **the best thing since sliced bread** (infml) [ابْتِكار مُمْتاز]

slice of life *n* شريحة من الحَياةِ

slick /slɪk/ **A** *adj* **1** (shiny) ‹*hair*› أَمْلَس (dipt; مُلْس) **2** (infml) (stylish) ‹*movement, operation*› (مَهَرة) ماهِر, بارِع **3** (pej) (deceptive) ‹*marketing, salesman*› (مَكَرة) ماكِر, مُراوِغ **4** (slippery) ‹*surface, road*› زَلِق
B *n* (also **oil slick**) بُقْعة (نَفْطيّة)

slide /slʌɪd/ **A** *vt* (*past tense, past participle* **slid**) (to propel) دَفَعَ (a; دَفْع) ‹*a book, chair, glass*›; **to ~ a letter under the door** دَفَعَ رِسالةً من تَحْتِ البابِ; **he slid the bolt across/back** أَغْلَقَ \ فَتَحَ المِزْلاجَ; **~ the seat back** اسْحَب الكُرْسيَّ إلى الخَلْفِ; **they slid the boat into the water** دَفَعوا القارِبَ إلى الماءِ
B *vi* (*past tense, past participle* **slid**) **1** (to move smoothly) **to ~ in and out** «drawers, trays, covers» انْزَلَقَ إلى الداخِلِ والخارِجِ; **to ~ up and down** «windows, blinds» انْزَلَقَ إلى أَعْلى وَأَسْفَلَ; **to ~ down a rope** انْزَلَقَ نازِلاً على حَبْلٍ; **to ~ out of/into one's seat** نَهَضَ من \ جَلَسَ في كُرْسيِّهِ **2** (to slip) «cars, pedestrians» انْزَلَقَ; **the car slid off the road** انْزَلَقَت السَيّارةُ وَخَرَجَتْ عن الطَريقِ; **the boxes slid around in the back** انْزَلَقَت الصَناديقُ في الخَلْفِ **3** (to decline) «prices, shares» انْخَفَضَ, تَراجَعَ; **the economy is sliding into recession** يَنْحَدِرُ الاقْتِصادُ إلى الكَسادِ; **you mustn't let things ~** لا تَدَعِ الأَشياءَ تُفْلِتُ من بَيْنِ يَدَيْكَ
C *n* **1** (in value, popularity) انْخِفاض (انْخِفاضات), تَراجُع (تَراجُعات); **a ~ in demand/stock prices** انْخِفاض في الطَلَبِ \ أَسْعارِ الأَسْهُمِ; **the ~ into civil war** الانْزِلاق إلى الحَرْبِ الأَهْليّةِ; **the ~ in the president's approval ratings** الانْخِفاض في شَعْبيّةِ الرَئيسِ **2** (in playgrounds) مَزْلَقة (مَزالِقُ), زَلّاقة **3** (skid) انْزِلاق **4** (transparency) شَريحة (شَرائِحُ) **5** (microscope plate) شَريحة, رَقيقة (زُجاجيّة) شَفّافة **6** (BrE) (for one's hair) مِشْبَك \ توكة شَعْرٍ; ►**hairslide** **7** (of trombones) [الجُزْء المُنْزَلِق في الترومْبون]

slide projector *n* جهاز عَرْضِ شَرائِحَ

slide rule (BrE), **slide ruler** (AmE) *n* مِسْطَرة حاسِبة

slide show *n* عَرْض شَرائِحَ

sliding /ˈslʌɪdɪŋ/ *adj* انْزِلاقيّ, مُنْزَلِق

sliding scale *n* مِقْياس مُتَحَرِّك

slight /slʌɪt/ **A** *adj* **1** ‹*increase, change*› طَفيف, لا يُذْكَرُ; **he has a ~ stutter** يُعاني من تَلَعْثُمٍ بَسيطٍ \ خَفيفٍ; **I haven't the ~est idea** لَيْسَ لَدَيَّ أَدْنى فِكْرةٍ **2** (in build) نَحيف
B *vt* (ب) اسْتَخَفَّ, تَجاهَلَ ‹*a country, suitor*›
C *n* إساءة, إهانة

slightly /ˈslʌɪtli/ *adv* ‹*different, disappointed*› بَعْضَ الشَيْءِ, قَليلاً

slim /slɪm/ **A** *adj* (**-mm-**) **1** ‹*build, waist*› أَهْيَف, مَمْشوق (dipt) **2** ‹*volume, case*› رَقيق, نَحيف, رَفيع **3** ‹*chance, hope*› ضَعيف; ‹*majority, margin*› ضَئيل, بَسيط
B *vi* (**-mm-** BrE) «overweight people, slimmers» نَحُفَ (u; نَحافة)

slime /slʌɪm/ *n* **1** (viscous substance) [مادّة لَزِجة (كالوَحْلِ)] **2** (of a slug, snail) [مادّة لَزِجة (يُفْرِزُها الحَلَزونُ)]

slimmer /ˈslɪmə/ *n* (BrE) [راغِب في النَحافةِ]

slimy /ˈslʌɪmi/ *adj* (**slimier, slimiest**) **1** ‹*substance*› لَزِج; ‹*rock*› زَلِق **2** (pej) (obsequious) ‹*politician, lawyer*› مُتَزَلِّف, مُتَمَلِّق, مُداهِن

sling /slɪŋ/ **A** *n* **1** (weapon) (مَقاليعُ) مِقْلاع **2** (for a broken arm) حَمّالة ذِراعٍ **3** (for a baby) حَمّالة طِفْلٍ **4** (for lifting) (رَوافِعُ) رافِعة
B *vt* (*past tense, past participle* **slung**) **1** (to hang) عَلَّقَ ‹*a hammock, rope*›; **to ~ a hammock from the beams** عَلَّقَ أُرْجوحةً على العَوارِضِ; **to be slung over/across sth** كانَ مُعَلَّقاً على \ فوق شَيْءٍ; **to ~ a rifle over one's shoulder** عَلَّقَ بُنْدُقيّةً على كَتِفِهِ **2** (infml) (to throw) رَمى (i; رَمْي), أَلْقى ‹*a ball, stone*›; **he slung a brick through the window** رَمى قالِبَ طوبٍ من خِلالِ النافِذةِ; **he slung the cases into the car** أَلْقى الحَقائِبَ في السَيّارةِ
Phrasal verb **sling out**: **A** ~ [**sth**] **out**, ~ **out** [**sth**] (infml) (to throw away) تَخَلَّصَ من [شَيْءٍ] **B** ~ [**sb**] **out** (infml) (to eject) طَرَدَ [شَخْصاً]

slink /slɪŋk/ *vi* (*past tense, past participle* **slunk**) **to ~ off** *or* **away** «person, dog» انْسَلَّ

slip /slɪp/ A *vt* (**-pp-**) 1 (to slide) **to ~ an envelope/document into/under sth** دَفَعَ ظَرْفاً \ وَثيقةً في \ تحت شَيْءٍ; **he ~ped a present into her case** دَسَّ هَدِيَّةً في حَقيبَتِها; **she ~ped her feet into her shoes** ارْتَدَتْ حِذاءَها بِسُرْعةٍ; **she ~ped the shirt over her head** (putting on) لَبِسَت القَميصَ بِسُرْعةٍ; (taking off) نَزَعَت القَميصَ بِسُرْعةٍ 2 (infml) (to pass surreptitiously) **to ~ sb sth, to ~ sth to sb** مَرَّرَ شَيْئاً إلى شَخْصٍ سِرًّا ‹money, a note› 3 (to escape) **to ~ sb's notice** *or* **attention** غَفَلَ عَنْهُ شَخْصٌ; **to ~ sb's mind** نَسِيَهُ شَخْصٌ; **the dog ~ped its lead** أَفْلَتَ الكَلْبُ من الحَبْلِ 4 (Med) **to ~ a disc** أُصيبَ بِانْزِلاقٍ في الفِقْراتِ

B *vi* (**-pp-**) 1 (to lose footing) «walkers, cyclists» انْزَلَقَ 2 (to slide accidentally) «the load, cargo» انْفَلَتَ, انْزَلَقَ; **the case ~ped off the rack and fell to the floor** انْزَلَقَت الحَقيبةُ من الرَفِّ وَوَقَعَتْ على الأَرْضِ 3 (to escape) **to ~ through sb's fingers** «victory, opportunity» فَلَتَ \ أَفْلَتَ من يَدَيْ شَخْصٍ; **the glass ~ped out of his hand** أَفْلَتَ الكَأْسُ من يَدِهِ; **to let ~ a chance** ضَيَّعَ فُرْصةً; **to let ~ a remark** أَفْلَتَ مِنْهُ تَعْليقٌ 4 (to dress quickly) **to ~ into a costume** لَبِسَ ثَوْباً بِسُرْعةٍ; **to ~ out of one's dress** خَلَعَتْ فُسْتانَها بِسُرْعةٍ 5 (to move quietly) **to ~ into/out of a building** تَسَلَّلَ إلى داخِلِ \ خارِجِ مَبْنًى; **we ~ped across/over the border** تَسَلَّلْنا عَبْرَ الحُدودِ; **I just ~ped back to warn you** رَجَعْتُ للتوِّ مُتَسَلِّلاً لِكَيْ أُحَذِّرَكَ 6 (to descend) انْزَلَقَ; **to ~ into chaos** انْزَلَقَ \ انْحَدَرَ إلى الفَوْضى; **to ~ into a coma** دَخَلَ في غَيْبوبةٍ 7 (infml) (to be losing one's skills) **to be ~ping** فَقَدَ مَهاراتِه

C *n* 1 (error) خَطَأ, زَلّة (أَخْطاء); **to make a ~** وَقَعَ في زَلّةٍ, ارْتَكَبَ خَطَأً; **a ~ of the tongue** زَلّة لِسانٍ 2 (of paper) قِطْعة وَرَقٍ, قُصاصة; **a voting ~** بطاقة تَصْويتٍ \ انْتِخابٍ; **my wage ~** كَشْف راتِبي 3 (fall) انْزِلاق 4 (petticoat) تَنّورة داخِلِيّة 5 (infml) (slender person) **a ~ of a child** طِفْل نَحيف \ نَحيل

Idiom **to give sb the slip** (infml) هَرَبَ من شَخْصٍ

Phrasal verbs **slip away** 1 (to leave unnoticed) «guests, children, boats» تَسَلَّلَ مُغادِراً 2 (to leave gradually) «sb's life, strength» تَلاشى

- **slip by** «months, time, life» انْقَضى
- **slip in** A (to enter unnoticed) «children, mistakes» تَسَلَّلَ B ~ [sth] in, ~ in [sth] ذَكَرَ [شَيْئاً] بِشَكْلٍ عارِضٍ ‹a remark, joke›
- **slip off** A ▸ **slip away** B ~ [sth] off, ~ off [sth] نَزَعَ [شَيْئاً] بِسُرْعةٍ ‹one's coat, dress, ring›
- **slip on**: ~ [sth] on, ~ on [sth] لَبِسَ [شَيْئاً] بِسُرْعةٍ ‹one's coat, ring›
- **slip out** 1 (to leave quietly) «person» انْسَلَّ, خَرَجَ بِهُدوءٍ 2 (to come out accidentally) «words, statement» فَلَتَ, أَفْلَتَ (i; فَلْت); **it just ~ped out!** أَفْلَتَتْ مِنّي دون قَصْدٍ!
- **slip up** (infml) وَقَعَ في زَلّةٍ

slip knot عُقْدة مُنْزَلِقة

slipped disc /slɪpt 'dɪsk/ *n* قُرْص مُنْزَلِق, انْزِلاق غُضْروفيّ

slipper /'slɪpə/ *n* 1 (indoor shoe) خُفّ (أَخْفاف), شِبْشِب (شَباشِبُ) 2 (dancing shoe) حِذاء باليه

slippery /'slɪp(ə)ri/ *adj* 1 ‹surface, road› زَلِق 2 (untrustworthy) ‹person› مُراوِغ 3 (unclear) ‹concept, term› مُلْتَبِس

slip road *n* (BrE) طَريق فَرْعيّ \ جانِبيّ

slipshod /'slɪpʃɒd/ *adj* ‹work, presentation› غَيْر مُتْقَنٍ

slip-up *n* (infml) هَفْوة, زَلّة (هَفَوات)

slit /slɪt/ A *n* 1 (opening) شَقّ (شُقوق) 2 (cut) شَقّ (شُقوق)

B *vt* (*past tense, past participle* **slit**) شَقَّ (u; شَقّ), قَطَعَ (a; قَطْع) ‹skin, fabric›; **to ~ sb's throat** ذَبَحَ شَخْصاً

slither /'slɪðə/ *vi* «snake» انْزَلَقَ, زَحَفَ (مُتَلَوِّياً)

sliver /'slɪvə/ *n* (of glass, bone) كِسْرة (كِسْرات, كِسَر), شَظِيّة (شَظايا); (of meat, cake) شَريحة (شَرائِحُ), شُطْفة

slob /slɒb/ *n* (infml) شَخْص قَذِر

slobber /'slɒbə/ *vi* «dog, baby» رَيَّلَ, سالَ لُعابُهُ

slog /slɒg/ A *vt* (**-gg-**) 1 (to progress with difficulty) **to ~ one's way up the hill/over the dune** شَقَّ طَريقَهُ بِصُعوبةٍ وَهُوَ يَصْعَدُ على التَلِّ \ يَعْبُرُ الكَثيبَ 2 (infml) (to hit hard) ضَرَبَ بِشِدّةٍ ‹the ball›; **to ~ it out** قاتَلَ حتّى النِهايةِ

B *vi* (**-gg-**) 1 (to progress with difficulty) **to ~ up a hill/dune** صَعَدَ تَلاً \ كَثيباً بِمَشَقّةٍ 2 (infml) (to work hard) عَمِلَ بِجِدٍّ

C *n* **1** (hard work) كَدّ, كَدْح; **this week has been a hard ~** بَذَلْنا جُهْداً مُضْنِياً هذا الأُسْبوعَ; **the long ~ up the last hill** الجُهْد الطَّوِيل عند صُعودِ آخِرِ تَلٍّ **2** (infml) (hard shot) ضَرْبة شَديدة

(Phrasal verb) **slog away** اِجْتَهَدَ, بَذَلَ جُهْداً كَبيراً

slogan /ˈsləʊg(ə)n/ *n* شِعار (شِعارات)

slop /slɒp/ **A** *vt* (-pp-) سَكَبَ (u; سَكْب), دَلَقَ (u; دَلْق) ‹*a drink, paint*›

B *vi* (-pp-) «drinks, water» اِنْسَكَبَ, اِنْدَلَقَ

slope /sləʊp/ **A** *n* **1** (sloping surface) مُنْحَدَر (مُنْحَدَرات), اِنْحِدار (اِنْحِدارات) **2** (mountainside) مُنْحَدَر (مُنْحَدَرات), اِنْحِدار (اِنْحِدارات) **3** (also **ski slope**) مُنْحَدَر تَزَلُّج; **to spend the day on the ~s** قَضى اليَوْمَ في التَزَلُّجِ على المُنْحَدَراتِ

B *vi* **1** «ground, roof» اِنْحَدَرَ, مالَ (i; مَيْل, مَيَلان); **the path ~s upwards/downwards** يَنْحَدِرُ المَسارُ لأَعْلى \ لأَسْفَلَ **2** «writing» مالَ (i; مَيْل, مَيَلان); **his handwriting ~s backwards/forwards** كِتابَتُهُ مائِلةٌ للخَلْفِ \ للأَمامِ

sloping /ˈsləʊpɪŋ/ *adj* ‹*roof, writing*› مائِل; ‹*floor, ground*› مُنْحَدِر

sloppy /ˈslɒpi/ *adj* (**sloppier**, **sloppiest**) **1** (careless) ‹*work*› غَيْر مُتْقَن \ دَقيق; ‹*thinking*› غَيْر سَليم \ مُنَظَّم **2** (loose-fitting) ‹*sweater*› فَضْفاض **3** ‹*kiss*› رَطْب, مُبَلَّل

slosh /slɒʃ/ **A** *vt* دَلَقَ (u; دَلْق), سَكَبَ (u; سَكْب) ‹*beer*›; طَرْطَشَ (طَرْطَشة), لَطَّخَ (i; ‹*paint*›

B *vi* **to ~ around** *or* **about** «water, drink» اِنْسَكَبَ, اِنْدَلَقَ; «person» خاضَ (في الماءِ)

slot /slɒt/ **A** *n* **1** (for a coin, ticket) فَتْحة **2** (groove) فَتْحة **3** (in a schedule, timetable) مَكان مُخَصَّص, وَقْت مُخَصَّص; **a prime-time ~** فَتْرة في ساعاتِ الذُرْوةِ **4** (position, job) وَظيفة (وَظائِفُ)

B *vt* (-tt-) **to ~ a battery/card into sth** وَضَعَ البَطّارِيّةَ \ البِطاقةَ في مَكانِها في شَيْءٍ; **to ~ a appointment into a schedule/timetable** أَدْرَجَ مَوْعِداً في جَدْوَلِ مَواعيدَ

C *vi* (-tt-) **to ~ into a groove/machine** «cards, components» ثَبَّتَ في فَتْحةٍ مُخَصَّصةٍ \ آلةٍ; **to ~ into place** *or* **position** ناسَبَ مَكاناً; **to ~ into a role/an organization** «employees» اِنْسَجَمَ مع وَظيفةٍ \ مُؤَسَّسةٍ

(Phrasal verbs) **slot in A** «cards, batteries, components» ناسَبَ

B ~ [sth] in, **~ in [sth] 1** وَضَعَ [شَيْئاً] في مَكانِهِ المَكانَ **2** خَصَّصَ وَقْتاً ل [شَيْءٍ] ‹*a coin, battery, component*› المُخَصَّصِ ‹*a film, programme*› **C ~ [sb] in** خَصَّصَ مَوْعِداً ل [شَخْصٍ] ‹*a patient, client*›

• **slot together 1** تَلاحَمَ مَعاً **2 ~ [sth] together** رَكَّبَ [شَيْئاً] ‹*parts, a box, bookcase*›

sloth /sləʊθ/ *n* كَسْلان (حَيْوان ثَدْيِيّ يَعيشُ على الأَشْجارِ)

slot machine *n* **1** (for gambling) ماكينة قِمارٍ **2** (vending machine) ماكينة بَيْعٍ آلِيٍّ (تَعْمَلُ بالنُقودِ المَعْدِنِيّةِ)

slouch /slaʊtʃ/ *vi* «person» (when sitting) جَلَسَ مُتَثاقِلاً; (when standing) وَقَفَ مُتَثاقِلاً; (when walking) مَشى بِخُطًى مُتَثاقِلةٍ; **he ~ed in his chair** جَلَسَ مُتَثاقِلاً على كُرْسِيِّهِ

Slovak /ˈsləʊvak/ **A** *n* **1** (also **Slovakian** /sləˈvakɪən/) (citizen) سْلوفاكِيّ **2** (language) (اللُغة) السْلوفاكِيّة

B *adj* (also **Slovakian**) ‹*capital, people*› سْلوفاكِيّ

Slovakia /sləˈvakɪə/ *pr n* سْلوفاكِيا

Slovene /ˈsləʊviːn/, **Slovenian** /sləˈviːniən/ **A** *n* **1** (citizen) سْلوفينِيّ **2** (language) (اللُغة) السْلوفينِيّة

B *adj* ‹*capital, minority*› سْلوفينِيّ

Slovenia /sləˈviːnɪə/ *pr n* سْلوفينِيا

slovenly /ˈslʌv(ə)nli/ *adj* **1** (untidy and dirty) ‹*person*› رَثّ الهَيْئةِ, غَيْر مُهَنْدَمٍ; ‹*habits*› قَذِر **2** (careless) ‹*work*› غَيْر مُتْقَنٍ; ‹*worker*› مُهْمِل

slow /sləʊ/ **A** *adj* **1** (not quick) ‹*reader, train, speed*› بَطيء; **a ~ time** وَقْت بَطيء; **to take the ~ train** أَخَذَ القِطارَ البَطيءَ; **to make ~ progress** حَقَّقَ تَقَدُّماً بَطيئاً; **to be ~ to react/develop** كانَ بَطيئاً في الرَدِّ \ التَطَوُّرِ; **change was ~ in coming** التَغْييرُ يَأْتي بِبُطْءٍ **2** (not quick to learn) ‹*learner, pupil*› بَطيء الفَهْمِ **3** (behind correct time) **to be ~** «clocks, watches» كانَ مُتَأَخِّراً; **to be 10 minutes ~** كانَ مُتَأَخِّراً ب 10 دَقائِقَ **4** (lacking activity) ‹*business, trade, the market*› بَطيء **5** (not too hot) ‹*oven*› مُنْخَفِض الحَرارةِ **6** (for ease of play) ‹*court, pitch*› [مُبْطِئ لِحَرَكةِ الكُرةِ]

B *adv* ‹*to drive, travel*› بِبُطْءٍ; **to work ~** عَمِلَ بِبُطْءٍ

C *vt, vi* ▸ **slow down**

(Phrasal verbs) **slow down** A 1 «trains, runners» أَبْطَأَ; **traffic ~ed down to a crawl** تَباطَأَتْ حَرَكةُ المُرورِ حتّى صارَتْ كالزَحْفِ 2 «growth, output, the economy» تَباطَأَ; **the economy is ~ing down** يَتَباطَأُ الاقْتِصادُ B **~ down [sth/sb], ~ [sth/sb] down** (to reduce the speed of) أَبْطَأَ من سُرْعَةِ [شَيْءٍ \ شَخْصٍ] ‹a car, runner, production›

• **slow up** ▸ **slow down**

slowdown /ˈsləʊdaʊn/ *n* بُطْء, تَباطُؤ

slowly /ˈsləʊli/ *adv* ‹to walk, speak› بِبُطْءٍ; **~ but surely** بِبُطْءٍ وَلَكِنْ بِثَباتٍ

slow motion *n* حَرَكة بَطيئة, تَصْوير بَطيء

slow-moving /ˌsləʊˈmuːvɪŋ/ *adj* ‹vehicle, traffic› بَطيء الحَرَكةِ

slowness /ˈsləʊnəs/ *n* 1 (of movement, a vehicle, reaction) بُطْء 2 (of the market, economy) بُطْء, تَباطُؤ 3 (of a child, pupil) بُطْء الفَهْمِ 4 (of a plot, the action) بُطْء الوَتيرة 5 (of courts, surfaces) بُطْء (إبْطاء لِحَرَكةِ الكُرة)

slow-worm /ˈsləʊwɜːm/ *n* دودة بَطيئة, عَظاية عَمْياء

sludge /slʌdʒ/ *n* راسِب طينيّ (من مُخَلَّفاتِ المَصانِعِ)

slug /slʌg/ *n* بَزّاقة (كائِن رَخويّ عَديم القَوْقَعةِ)

sluggish /ˈslʌgɪʃ/ *adj* 1 ‹person› خامِل, بَليد, كَسول 2 ‹river, pace› بَطيء الحَرَكةِ 3 ‹economy› راكِد (رَواكِدُ); ‹growth› بَطيء, مُتَباطِئ

sluice /sluːs/ *n* (also **sluice gate**) بَوّابة هَويسٍ

slum /slʌm/ *n* 1 (area) مِنْطَقة عَشْوائيّة, حَيّ شَعْبيّ \ فَقير 2 (dwelling) مَسْكَن وَضيع \ غَيْر آدَميٍّ

slumber /ˈslʌmbə/ (liter) A *vi* «person» نامَ (a; نَوْم, نِيام) B *n* نَوْم, سُبات, هُجوع

slump /slʌmp/ A *vi* 1 «sales, demand» هَبَطَ (i-u; هُبوط), انْخَفَضَ, تَراجَعَ 2 «person, body» سَقَطَ, تَهاوى (u; سُقوط); **he was found ~ed at his desk** عُثِرَ عَلَيْه مُنْكَفِئاً على مَكْتَبِه B *n* 1 (economic depression) تَدَهْوُر, هُبوط, رُكود 2 (steep decline in sales, demand) انْخِفاض (انْخِفاضات); (in support, popularity) تَراجُع (تَراجُعات)

slung /slʌŋ/ *past tense, past participle* ▸ **sling**

slunk /slʌŋk/ *past tense, past participle* ▸ **slink**

slur /slɜː/ A *vt* (**-rr-**) 1 **to ~ one's words** تَمْتَمَ \ غَمْغَمَ بِكَلامٍ غَيْرِ مَفْهومٍ 2 (Mus) ‹notes, chords› عَزَفَ عَزْفاً مُتَّصِلاً B (**slurred**) *adj* ‹speech, voice› مُبْهَم C *n* 1 (insult) سَبّ, قَدْح (سُباب), افْتِراء (افْتِراءات); **to cast a ~ on sth/sb** قَدَحَ في شَيْءٍ \ شَخْصٍ 2 (Mus) عَلامة رَبْطٍ

slurp /slɜːp/ *vt* ‹one's soup, drink› [أَكَلَ أو شَرِبَ مُحْدِثاً صَوْتاً]

slush /slʌʃ/ *n* 1 (melting snow) وَحْل جَليديّ (ثَلْج نِصْف ذائِبٍ) 2 (infml) [u] (sentimentality) عَواطِف مُبْتَذَلة

slush fund *n* مال رَشْوةٍ

slut /slʌt/ *n* (pej) عاهِرة (عاهِرات, عَواهِرُ), فاجِرة (فَواجِرُ)

sly /slaɪ/ *adj* (**slier**, **sliest**) 1 (cunning) ‹person› ماكِرَ, مُخادِع 2 (knowing) ‹smile, look› خَبيث (خُبَثاءُ, خُبَثة)

(Idiom) **on the sly** في الخَفاءِ

smack /smak/ A *n* ضَرْبة (ضَرَبات), لَطْمة (لَطَمات) B *vt* 1 ‹a child› ضَرَبَ (i; ضَرْب), لَطَمَ (i; لَطْم) 2 **to ~ one's lips** تَلَمَّظَ, تَمَطَّقَ C *vi* **to ~ of sth** فاحَتْ مِنْهُ رائِحةُ شَيْءٍ, نَمَّ عن شَيْءٍ

small /smɔːl/ A *adj* (**smaller**, **smallest**) 1 (not big) ‹car, ears, apartment› صَغير; **the portions are very ~** القِطَعُ صَغيرةٌ جِدًّا; **the dress is too ~ for her** الفُسْتانُ صَغيرٌ جِدًّا عَلَيْها; **sizes come in ~, medium and large** يَأْتي في مَقاساتٍ صَغيرٍ وَمُتَوَسِّطٍ وَكَبيرٍ; **it's a ~ world!** يا لَهُ من عالَمٍ صَغيرٍ!; **he's ~ for his age** هو قَصيرٌ بالنِسْبةِ لِسِنِّهِ 2 (insubstantial) ‹appetite› ضَعيف; ‹crowd, fortune› قَليل; **only a ~ proportion of them smoke** نِسْبةٌ قَليلةٌ مِنْهُمْ فَقَطْ هي الّتي تُدَخِّنُ; **they won by a ~ majority** فازوا بِأَغْلَبيّةٍ قَليلةٍ; **add a ~ amount of pepper** أَضِفْ قَليلاً من الفُلْفُلِ; **it would cost a ~ fortune** سَيَتَكَلَّفُ مالاً كَثيراً; **he belongs to a ~ family** يَنْتَمي إلى أُسْرةٍ صَغيرةٍ 3 (not much) ‹chance, consolation, cause› بَسيط; **it is ~ comfort to know that** لا عَزاءَ في مَعْرِفةِ أنَّ; **they have a ~ chance of winning** لَدَيْهِمْ فُرْصةٌ بَسيطةٌ في الفَوْزِ; **~ wonder he left!** لا غَرْوَ أَنَّهُ رَحَلَ! 4 (quiet) ‹voice, noise› هادِئ 5 (humiliated) **to make sb look ~** جَعَلَ شَخْصاً يَشْعُرُ بالمَهانةِ; **by losing so badly we were made to look very ~** بعد أن خَسِرْنا هذه الخَسارةَ الكَبيرةَ شَعَرْنا بِكَثيرٍ من المَهانةِ B *n* **the ~ of the back** أَسْفَل الظَهْرِ

C *adv* ‹*to write*› بِخَطٍّ صَغِيرٍ; **cut them up ~** قَطِّعْها إلى قِطَعٍ صَغِيرةٍ

small ad *n* إعْلان مُبَوَّب

small businessman *n* رَجُل أَعْمالٍ صَغِير

small change *n* فَكّة

smallholder /'smɔːlhəʊldə/ *n* (BrE) صاحِب مَزْرَعةٍ صَغِيرةٍ, مُزارِع صَغِير

smallholding /'smɔːlhəʊldɪŋ/ *n* (BrE) أَرْض ,حِيازة صَغِيرة زراعيّة صَغِيرة

small hours *n pl* [الساعات الأولى بعد مُنْتَصَفِ اللَّيْلِ]

small intestine *n* مِعًى دَقِيق ,أَمْعاء دَقِيقة

small-minded /smɔː'lmaɪndɪd/ *adj* ‹*person, attitude*› ضَيِّق الأُفُق \ التَّفْكِير

smallpox /'smɔːlpɒks/ *n* جُدَرِيّ

small print *n* (**the small print**) الشُّروط والأَحْكام (المَطْبوعة بِحُروفٍ صَغِيرةٍ)

small-scale /smɔː'lskeɪl/ *adj* ‹*project, business*› صَغِير الحَجْم \ النِطاقِ

small talk *n* دَرْدَشة ,مُحادَثة خَفِيفة; **to make small talk** دَرْدَشَ (i; دَرْدَشة)

small-time /'smɔːltaɪm/ *adj* (infml) ‹*businessman, crook*› تافِه (تَوافِهُ)

small-town /'smɔːltaʊn/ *adj* (pej) ‹*life, mentality*› قَرَوِيّ ,رِيفِيّ [مُتَعَلِّق بِبَلْدةٍ صَغِيرةٍ]

smart /smɑːt/ **A** *adj* **1** (elegant) ‹*suit, businessman, appearance*› أَنِيق **2** (infml) (clever) ‹*kid, journalist, decision*› ذَكِيّ; **that was a ~ choice/move** كانَ ذلك اخْتِياراً \ تَحَرُّكاً ذَكِيّاً **3** (upmarket) ‹*restaurant, hotel, street*› مُتْرَف ,راقٍ; **the ~ set** أَصْحاب الأَناقةِ **4** (stinging) ‹*slap*› قَوِيّ; ‹*rebuke, retort*› لاذِع **5** (brisk) **to walk** *or* **go at a ~ pace** مَشَى \ مَضَى بِخُطُواتٍ سَرِيعةٍ; **that was ~ work!** لَقَدْ أَنْجَزْتَ العَمَلَ بِسُرْعةٍ! **6** ‹*technology, system, meter*› ذَكِيّ

B *vi* **1** (to sting) «eyes, cuts» آلَمَ (Form IV; imperf يُؤْلِمُ), أَوْجَعَ **2** (from an insult, defeat) شَعَرَ بالمَرارة; **they are still ~ing over their defeat** ما زالوا يَشْعُرونَ بِمَرارةِ هَزِيمَتِهِمْ

smart bomb *n* قُنْبُلة ذَكِيّة

smart card *n* بِطاقة ذَكِيّة

smarten up /'smɑːt(ə)n/ **A** *vt* **to ~ sth, to smarten sth up** حَسَّنَ صورة / مَنْظَرَ شَيْءٍ ,جَمَّلَ شَيْئاً ‹*a property, town*›

B *vi* **1** (in appearance) «person» تَهَنْدَمَ ,تَزَيَّنَ ,تَأَنَّقَ **2** (to behave more wisely) «person, company» تَصَرَّفَ بِحِكْمةٍ

smartly /'smɑːtli/ *adv* **1** (elegantly) ‹*to dress, decorate*› بِأَناقةٍ **2** (infml) (cleverly) ‹*to choose, buy, decide*› بِذَكاءٍ **3** (quickly) ‹*to move, walk, finish*› بِسُرْعةٍ

smartphone /'smɑːtfəʊn/ *n* هاتِف ذَكِيّ

smash /smaʃ/ **A** *vt* **1** (to break) هَشَّمَ ,حَطَّمَ ‹*a glass, window*›; **the thieves ~ed their way into the shop** حَطَّمَ اللُّصوصُ مَدْخَلَ المَتْجَرِ وَاقْتَحَموهُ; **she ~ed the vase as she pushed by** حطَّمت المَزْهَرِيّةَ بَيْنَما كانَتْ تَمُرُّ بِجِوارِها **2** (to hit hard) **to ~ the ball** ضَرَبَ الكُرةَ بِقُوّةٍ **3** (to break up) فَضَّ (u; فَضّ) ‹*a demonstration, protest*›; قَضَى (i; قَضاء; على) ‹*gang*› **4** (to break) حَطَّمَ ‹*a record, time*›

B *vi* **1** (to disintegrate) «glasses, windows» تَحَطَّمَ ,تَهَشَّمَ **2** (to crash) **to ~ into a wall/truck** اصْطَدَمَ بِحائِطٍ \ بِشاحِنةٍ **3** (using violence) **to ~ through a wall/door** اخْتَرَقَ حائِطاً \ باباً

C *n* **1** (sound of breaking glass, china) [صَوْت تَحَطُّم] **2** (also **smash-up**) (infml) (accident) حادِث تَصادُم **3** (in tennis, badminton, etc) ضَرْبة ساحِقة **4** (infml) (also **smash hit**) (record, film) [شَيْء حَقَّقَ نَجاحاً ساحِقاً]

(Phrasal verbs) **smash down**: **~ [sth] down, ~ down [sth]** حَطَّمَ [شَيْئاً] ‹*a door, fence, wall*›

• **smash in**: **~ [sth] in, ~ in [sth]** هَشَّمَ [شَيْئاً] ‹*a door, window*›

• **smash open**: **~ [sth] open, ~ open [sth]** حَطَّمَ [شَيْئاً] ‹*a door, box*›

• **smash up**: **~ [sth] up, ~ up [sth]** **1** (deliberately) حَطَّمَ \ كَسَّرَ [شَيْئاً] ‹*a bar, shop, the furniture*› **2** (in accidents) حَطَّمَ [شَيْئاً] ‹*a vehicle*›

smashing /'smaʃɪŋ/ *adj* (BrE infml) ‹*present, person*› هائِل ,رائِع ,مُبْهِر

smattering /'smatərɪŋ/ *n* مَعْرِفة سَطْحِيّة \ بَسِيطة

smear /smɪə/ **A** *vt* **1** (to dirty) وَسَّخَ ,لَطَّخَ ‹*one's face, a wall*›; **her face was ~ed with jam** كانَ وَجْهُها مُلَطَّخاً بالمُرَبّى

2 (to spread) **to ~ sth on/over sth** فَرَشَ \ فَرَدَ \ وَضَعَ شَيْئاً على شَيْءٍ ‹*paint*›; لَطَّخَ شَيْئاً بِشَيْءٍ ‹*blood*›; **she ~ed the lotion onto her back** وَضَعَت الغَسولَ على ظَهْرِها 3 (to slander) شَوَّهَ السُمْعَة ‹*an opponent, sb's reputation*›

B *vi* «make-up, ink» سالَ (i; سَيْل ,سَيَلان)

C *n* 1 (of grease, paint) لَطْخة (لَطَخات) ,بُقْعة (بُقَع) 2 (slander) تَشْويه سُمْعةٍ ,تَشْهير 3 (also **smear test**) اخْتِبار مَسْحةِ عُنُقِ الرَحِم

smell /smɛl/ **A** *n* 1 (odour) رائِحة (رَوائِحُ); **the ~ of roasted coffee** رائِحة البُنِّ المُحَمَّصِ; **what a horrible ~!** يا لَلْرائِحة البَشِعةِ! 2 (sense) **to have a good sense of ~** كانَ لَدَيْهِ حاسّةُ شَمٍّ جَيِّدةٍ

B *vt* (*past tense, past participle* **smelled** or **smelt** BrE) 1 (to notice) شَمَّ (a-u; شَمّ ,شَميم; perf شَمَمْتُ ,شَمِمْتُ) ‹*alcohol, onions*›; **I can ~ burning** أَشُمُّ رائِحةَ حَريقٍ 2 (to sniff at) شَمَّ (a-u; شَمّ ,شَميم; perf شَمَمْتُ ,شَمِمْتُ) ,اشْتَمَّ ‹*a flower, perfume*› 3 (to detect) أَحَسَّ (ب) ,اشْتَمَّ \ شَمَّ الرائِحةَ ‹*danger, success, a problem*›

C *vi* (*past tense, past participle* **smelled** or **smelt** BrE) 1 (to have an odour) «liquid, gases» فاحَتْ \ انْبَعَثَتْ مِنْهُ رائِحةٌ; **this gas doesn't ~** هذا الغازُ عَديمُ الرائِحة; **to ~ of roses** فاحَتْ مِنْهُ رائِحةُ الوُرود; **that ~s like curry** رائِحَتُهُ مِثْلُ رائِحةِ الكاري 2 (to have a sense of smell) شَمَّ (a-u; شَمّ ,شَميم; perf شَمَمْتُ ,شَمِمْتُ)

(Phrasal verb) **smell out**: **~ [sth] out, ~ out [sth]** 1 (to discover) «dogs» اكْتَشَفَ [شَيْئاً] عن طَريقِ الشَمِّ ‹*drugs, explosives*› 2 (infml) (to cause to stink) نَشَرَ رائِحةً كَريهةً في [شَيْءٍ] ‹*a room, house*›

smelling salts /ˈsmɛlɪŋ sɔːlts/ *n pl* نُشادِر

smelly /ˈsmɛli/ *adj* (**smellier, smelliest**) ‹*feet, cheese*› كَريه الرائِحةِ

smelt /smɛlt/ **A** *past tense, past participle* ▸ **smell**

B *vt* صَهَرَ (a; صَهْر) ,اسْتَخْرَجَ بالصَهْرِ ‹*ore, iron*›

smile /smʌɪl/ **A** *vt* ‹*one's thanks, approval*› عَبَّرَ بِابْتِسامةٍ; **to ~ one's thanks** عَبَّرَ عن شُكْرِهِ بِابْتِسامةٍ

B *vi* ابْتَسَمَ; **they ~d at each other** ابْتَسَموا لِبَعْضِهِم البَعْض; **I ~d at the idea** ابْتَسَمْتُ عند سَماعي للفِكْرةِ; **to ~ with satisfaction** ابْتَسَمَ تَعْبيراً عن الرِضا; **to ~ to oneself** ابْتَسَمَ بَيْنَهُ وبَيْنَ نَفْسِهِ

C *n* ابْتِسام (ابْتِسامات) ,ابْتِسامة ,بَسْمة (بَسَمات); **to give sb a ~** ابْتَسَمَ في وَجْهِ شَخْصٍ; **he said it with a ~** قالَ ذلك مُبْتَسِماً

(Phrasal verb) **smile on**: **~ on [sb/sth]** «fortune, the weather» ابْتَسَم ل [شَخْصٍ \ شَيْءٍ] ‹*a person, team, project*›

smiley /ˈsmʌɪli/ *n* (infml) وَجه مُبْتَسِم (تَعْليق رَمْزِيّ)

smirk /smɜːk/ **A** *vi* «person» ابْتَسَم ابْتِسامةً مُصْطَنَعةً

B *n* ابْتِسامة مُتَكَلِّفة \ صَفْراء

smith /smɪθ/ *n* حَدّاد

smithereens /ˌsmɪðəˈriːnz/ *n pl* قِطَع صَغيرة; **to blow/smash sth to ~** فَجَّرَ \ حَطَّمَ شَيْئاً إلى فُتاتٍ

smock /smɒk/ *n* 1 (woman's garment) [ثَوْب نِسائيّ فَضْفاض] 2 (of a farmer, an artist) [ثَوْب عَمَلٍ فَضْفاض]

smog /smɒg/ *n* ضَبْخان ,ضَباب دُخانيّ

smoke /sməʊk/ **A** *n* 1 [u] (from a fire, chimney) دُخان; **all our hopes went up in ~** تَبَخَّرَتْ كُلُّ آمالُنا 2 (infml) (cigarette) سيجارة (سَجايِرُ); **to have a ~** دَخَّنَ سيجارةً

B *vt* 1 (to consume) دَخَّنَ ‹*tobacco, marijuana, a cigarette*›; **he ~s a hookah** يَشْرَبُ \ يُدَخِّنُ شيشةً 2 (to preserve) دَخَّنَ ‹*fish, meat*›

C *vi* 1 «smokers, patients» دَخَّنَ; **do you ~?** هل تُدَخِّنُ؟ 2 (to emit fumes) «fires, wood» انْبَعَثَ \ صَدَرَ مِنْهُ دُخانٌ

(Phrasal verb) **smoke out** **A** **~ [sb/sth] out, ~ out [sb/sth]** 1 (to remove) أَجْبَرَ [شَخْصاً \ شَيْئاً] على الخُروجِ بِاسْتِخْدام الدُخانِ ‹*a nest, bees, a fugitive*› 2 (to find) عَثَرَ على [شَخْصٍ \ شَيْءٍ] ‹*a traitor, culprit, sniper*› **B** **~ [sth] out** (to fill with smoke) مَلأَ [شَيْئاً] بالدُخان ‹*a room, house*›

smoke alarm *n* جِهاز إِنْذار الدُخانِ

smoke bomb *n* قُنْبُلة دُخانيّة \ دُخانٍ

smoked /sməʊkt/ *adj* 1 ‹*fish, meat*› مُدَخَّن 2 ‹*glass*› مُدَخَّن, فيميه

smokeless /ˈsməʊkləs/ *adj* ‹*fuel*› عَديم الدُخان ,بِلا دُخان

smoker /ˈsməʊkə/ *n* مُدَخِّن; **he's a heavy ~** هو مُدَخِّنٌ شَرِهٌ

smokescreen /ˈsməʊkskriːn/ *n* سِتار من الدُخان (للمُداراةِ على شَيْءٍ)

smoke signal *n* (a column of smoke) إشارة دُخانٍ; (an indication) دَليل (أَدِلّة ,دَلائِلُ) ,مُؤَشِّر (مُؤَشِّرات)

smoking /ˈsməʊkɪŋ/ *n* تَدْخين; **'no ~'** 'مَمْنوعٌ التَدْخينُ'; **to give up ~** أَقْلَع عن التَدْخينِ

smoking car *n* (AmE) عَرَبة تَدْخينٍ (بالقِطارِ)

smoking compartment *n* (BrE) مَقْصورة تَدْخينٍ (بالقِطارِ)

smoking-related /ˈsməʊkɪŋrɪˌleɪtɪd/ *adj* ‹*disease, death*› مُرْتَبِط ب \ ناجِم عن التَدْخينِ

smoky /ˈsməʊki/ *adj* (**smokier, smokiest**) **1** ‹*bar, room*› مُعَبَّأ \ مُمْتَلِئ بالدُخانِ; ‹*atmosphere, environment*› كَثير الدُخانِ **2** ‹*fire, chimney*› مُدَخِّن [مُتَصاعِد مِنْهُ دُخانٌ كَثيفٌ] **3** ‹*flavour, taste*› تَفوحُ \ تَنْبَعِثُ مِنْهُ رائِحةُ الدُخانِ

smolder /ˈsməʊldə/ (AmE) *vi* ▸ **smoulder**

smooth /smuːð/ **A** *adj* **1** (even) ‹*surface*› مُسْتَوٍ; ‹*sea*› هادِئ; ‹*skin, fabric*› أَمْلَس (dipt), ناعِم; ‹*crossing, road*› سَلِس الحَرَكةِ; **the tyres were worn ~** بَلِيَت الإطاراتُ وأَصْبَحَتْ ناعِمةً; **the car has very ~ acceleration** تَسارُعُ السَيّارةِ سَلِسٌ جِداً; **beat the mixture until it's ~** اضْرِب الخَليطَ حتّى يُصْبِحَ ناعِماً **2** (problem-free) ‹*transition, journey*› سَلِس; **the bill had a ~ passage through Parliament** تَمَّ تَمْريرُ مَشْروعِ القانونِ بِسَلاسةٍ في البَرْلَمان **3** (pleasant) ‹*taste, wine, whisky*› مُسْتَساغ **4** (suave) ‹*politician, salesman*› مُداهِن ,مُمالِق ,مُتَمَلِّق; سائِغ; **to be a ~ talker** كانَ مُحَدِّثاً مُتَمَلِّقاً; **a ~ operator** شَخْص شَديد الدَهاءِ

B *vt* **1** (to flatten out) ‹*one's hair*› نَعَّمَ; ‹*a road*› مَهَّدَ; ‹*a surface*› صَقَلَ (u; صِقال ,صَقْل); **~ the cream into your skin** اُدْهُن الكَريم في بَشْرَتِك **2** (to make easier) ‹*a process, transition, path*› سَهَّلَ

Phrasal verbs **smooth away**: **~ away [sth], ~ [sth] away** ‹*wrinkles, a crease*› فَرَدَ [شَيْئاً]; ‹*a problem*› أزالَ [شَيْئاً]

• **smooth down**: **~ [sth] down, ~ down [sth]** ‹*wood, a surface*› سَوّى [شَيْئاً]; ‹*one's hair, skirt*› فَرَدَ [شَيْئاً]

• **smooth out**: **~ [sth] out, ~ out [sth]** (to remove the creases from) ‹*a map, sheet, one's skirt*› فَرَدَ [شَيْئاً]

• **smooth over**: **~ [sth] over, ~ over [sth]** ‹*differences, problems*› خَفَّفَ من حِدّةِ [شَيْءٍ]; **to ~ things over** لَطَّفَ الأَجْواءَ

smoothly /ˈsmuːðli/ *adv* **1** (without jerks, steadily) ‹*to operate, move*› بانْسِيابِيّةٍ ,بِسُهولةٍ ,بِسَلاسةٍ **2** (without problems) ‹*to go, run*› بِسُهولةٍ ,بِسَلاسةٍ **3** (suavely) ‹*to say, reply*› بِدَهاءٍ ,بِلَباقةٍ

smooth-running /ˌsmuːðˈrʌnɪŋ/ *adj* ‹*system, engine*› سَلِس العَمَلِ; **this car has an exceptionally ~ engine** هذه السَيّارةُ لَدَيْها مُحَرِّكٌ سَلِسُ الأَداءِ للغاية

smother /ˈsmʌðə/ *vt* **1** (to kill) خَنَقَ (u; خَنْق) ,كَتَمَ الأَنْفاسَ ‹*a baby, patient*› **2** (to extinguish) أَخْمَدَ ‹*the flames, a fire*› **3** (to suppress) كَتَمَ (u; كِتْمان) ,كَبَتَ (i; كَبْت) ‹*a laugh, yawn*› **4** (to cover) غَطّى ‹*a surface, food*›

smoulder (BrE), **smolder** (AmE) /ˈsməʊldə/ *vi* **1** «embers, cigarette» احْتَرَقَ (بِبُطْءٍ دون لَهَبٍ) **2** «eyes» جاشَ (i; جَيْشان)

SMS /ɛsɛmˈɛs/ *n* **1** = **Short Message Service** خِدْمة الرَسائِل القَصيرة **2** (message) رِسالة قَصيرة

smudge /smʌdʒ/ **A** *vt* ‹*one's face, make-up, ink*› لَطَّخَ

B *vi* «lipstick, ink» تَلَطَّخَ

C *n* بُقْعة (بُقَع) ,لَطْخة (لَطَخات)

smug /smʌg/ *adj* (**-gg-**) ‹*smile, look, person*› مُتَعَجْرِف

smuggle /ˈsmʌg(ə)l/ *vt* ‹*drugs, arms*› هَرَّبَ; **to ~ sb into/out of the country** هَرَّبَ شَخْصاً إلى \ خارِجَ البِلادِ

smuggler /ˈsmʌglə/ *n* مُهَرِّب

smuggling /ˈsmʌglɪŋ/ *n* تَهْريب (تَهْريبات)

smut /smʌt/ *n* **1** (vulgarity) بَذاءات **2** (dirt) سُخام

smutty /ˈsmʌti/ *adj* (**smuttier, smuttiest**) (crude) ‹*joke, humour*› بَذيء

snack /snak/ *n* **1** (light meal) وَجْبة خَفيفة; **to have a ~** تَناوَلَ وَجْبةً خَفيفةً **2** (crisps, peanuts etc) مُقَرْمِشات ,تَسالٍ

snack bar *n* مَطْعَم وَجَباتٍ خَفيفةٍ

snag /snag/ **A** *n* **1** (problem) عَقَبة (عَقَبات) ,عائِق (عَوائِقُ) **2** (tear) اهْتِراء ,تَنَسُّل ,تَمَزُّق

B *vt* (**-gg-**) ‹*a garment, fishing net*› جَعَلَهُ يَعْلَقُ

snail /sneɪl/ *n* حَلَزون (حَلَزونات) ,قَوْقَع (n coll)

snail mail *n* (infml) بَريد عاديّ \ وَرَقيّ

snake /sneɪk/ *n* حَيّة ,(أَفاعٍ ;f) أَفعى ,(ثَعابينُ) ثُعْبان

snakebite /ˈsneɪkbʌɪt/ *n* عَضّة ثُعْبانٍ ,لَدْغة أَفْعى

snake charmer *n* ساحِر الأَفاعي (شَخْص يَجْعَلُ الأَفْعى تَرْقُصُ على عَزْفِهِ)

snap /snap/ **A** *vt* **(-pp-)** **1** (to click) طَقَّ (طَقّ ;u), طَقْطَقَ (i; طَقْطَقة), فَرْقَعَ (i; فَرْقَعة) ‹*one's fingers, jaws*›; **to ~ the lid shut** كَبَسَ الغِطاءَ لِإِغْلاقِهِ **2** (to break) كَسَرَ (i; كَسْر) ‹*a stick, branch*› **3** (to say angrily) قالَ مُحْتَدًّا **4** (infml) الْتَقَطَ صورةً سَريعةً ل ‹*a baby, building*›

B *vi* **(-pp-)** **1** (to break) «branches, bones» انْكَسَرَ **2** (to click) **to ~ open/shut** «handbag, lid» انْفَتَحَ \ انْغَلَقَ **3** (infml) (to lose control) «person» فَقَدَ أَعْصابَهُ; **my patience finally ~ped** أَخيراً نَفِدَ صَبْري **4** (to speak angrily) تَحَدَّثَ بِحِدّةٍ

C *n* **1** (of a branch, one's fingers, elastic) فَرْقَعة (فَرْقَعات), طَقْطَقة (فَراقِعُ) **2** (bite) قَضْم **3** (BrE) (infml); ▸**snapshot** **4** [u] (card game) سْناب (لُعْبة وَرَق)

D *adj before n* (quick) ‹*decision, judgement, vote*› عاجِل; **to call a ~ election** دَعا إلى انتِخاباتٍ عاجِلةٍ

(Idiom) **snap out of it!** (infml) أَخْرِجْ نَفْسَكَ من هذه الحالةِ النَفْسيّة!

(Phrasal verbs) **snap at**: **~ at [sb/sth]** **1** (to speak sharply to) احْتَدَّ على [شَخْصٍ \ شَيْءٍ] **2** (to bite) حاوَلَ عَضَّ [شَخْصٍ \ شَيْءٍ] ‹*sb's ankles, a fly*›

• **snap off** **A** (to break) «branches, handles» كَسَرَ (i; كَسْر) **B** ~ **off [sth]**, **~ [sth] off** كَسَرَ [شَيْئاً] ‹*a branch, handle*›

• **snap out**: **~ [sth] out**, **~ out [sth]** قالَ [شَيْئاً] بِحِدّةٍ ‹*an order, a reply*›

• **snap up**: **~ up [sth]**, **~ [sth] up** تَلَقَّفَ [شَيْئاً] ‹*a bargain*›

snappy /ˈsnapi/ *adj* **(snappier, snappiest)** **1** ‹*person*› سَريع الانْفِعالِ \ الغَضَبِ **2** ‹*dialogue, title*› جَذّاب ,أَنيق ,لَبِق

snapshot /ˈsnapʃɒt/ *n* لَقْطة (فوتوغْرافيّة)

snare /snɛː/ **A** *n* شَرَك (شِراك), فَخّ (فِخاخ), مِصْيَدة (مَصايِدُ)

B *vt* صادَ (بِشَرَكٍ) ‹*an animal, a bird*›

snarl /snɑːl/ **A** *vt* قالَ بِصَوْتٍ غَليظٍ ‹*an order, a threat*›; **'forget it' he ~ed** قالَ بِصَوْتٍ غَليظٍ 'انْسَ هذا الأَمْرَ'

B *vi* «dog, person» زَمْجَرَ (i; زَمْجَرة); **the dog ~ed at me** زَمْجَرَ الكَلْبُ في وَجْهي

C *n* زَمْجَرة

(Phrasal verb) **snarl up** **A** «ropes, wool» تَعَقَّدَ, تَشابَكَ **B** ~ **up [sth]** «accident» عَرْقَلَ حَرَكَةَ [شَيْءٍ] ‹*the traffic, a road*›; **the roads were/the traffic was ~ed up for hours** تَعَرْقَلَتْ حَرَكةُ الطُرُقِ \ المُرورِ لِعدّةِ ساعاتٍ; **I got ~ed up in the traffic** تَعَطَّلْتُ في المُرورِ

snarl-up /ˈsnɑːlʌp/ *n* (BrE infml) اخْتِناق مُروريّ

snatch /snatʃ/ **A** *vt* **1** (to grab) انْتَزَعَ, اخْتَطَفَ ‹*a book, key*›; **to ~ a coin from sb** خَطَفَ قِطْعةَ نُقودٍ من شَخْصٍ **2** (to take) خَطَفَ (i; خَطْف) ‹*a victory, the lead*›; **to ~ a kiss** خَطَفَ قُبْلةً **3** (infml) (to steal) سَرَقَ (i; سَرِقة), خَطَفَ (i; خَطْف) ‹*the handbag, jewels*› **4** (infml) (to kidnap) خَطَفَ (i; خَطْف) ‹*a baby, heiress*› **5** (to take hurriedly) **to ~ some sleep** اخْتَلَسَ بَعْضَ الوَقْتِ للنَوْمِ; **have we got time to ~ a meal?** هل لَدَيْنا وَقْتٌ لِنَتَناوَلَ وَجْبةً سَريعةً؟

B *vi* **to ~ at a rope/letter** أَمْسَكَ بالحَبْلِ \ بالخِطابِ

C *n* **1** (of a conversation, song) جُزْء \ مَقْطَع صَغير **2** (infml) (grab) **to make a ~ at sth** حاوَلَ انْتِزاعَ \ خَطْفَ شَيْءٍ **3** (infml) (kidnapping) خَطْف, اخْتِطاف (اخْتِطافات) **4** (in weightlifting) خَطْف

(Phrasal verbs) **snatch away**: **~ [sth] away** خَطَفَ [شَيْئاً] ‹*a letter, one's hand, the phone*›

• **snatch up**: **~ up [sth]** جَمَعَ [شَيْئاً] على عَجَلٍ ‹*one's clothes, papers*›; **to ~ up a bargain** اقْتَنَصَ صَفْقةً

sneak /sniːk/ **A** *vt* (*past tense, past participle* **sneaked, snuck**) **1** (infml) (to have secretly) اخْتَلَسَ, أَخَذَ خِلْسةً ‹*a cigarette, sweet, drink*›; **to ~ a look at sth** اخْتَلَسَ نَظْرةً على شَيْءٍ **2** (to steal) سَرَقَ (i; سَرِقة), نَشَلَ (u; نَشْل) ‹*food, fruit, money*›; **to ~ sth out of/into a place** أَخَذَ شَيْئاً من \ أَدْخَلَ شَيْئاً إلى مَكانٍ خِلْسةً

B *vi* (*past tense, past participle* **sneaked, snuck**) **1** (to move furtively) **to ~ in/out of sb's room** تَسَلَّلَ إلى \ من غُرْفةِ شَخْصٍ; **he ~ed up behind me** جاءَ من وَرائي خِلْسةً; **he ~ed in through the back door** تَسَلَّلَ من البابِ الخَلْفيِّ; **to ~ away**

تَسَلَّلَ بَعيداً **2** (BrE) (infml) (to tell tales) وَشى (i; وَشْي, وِشاية); **to ~ on sb** وَشى بِشَخْصٍ

C *n* (BrE) (infml) (betrayer) شَخْص نَمّام \ واشٍ

sneaker /ˈsniːkə/ *n* (AmE) [حِذاء رِياضيّ خَفيف]

sneaking /ˈsniːkɪŋ/ *adj* ‹*suspicion, feeling*› كامِن, خَفيّ

sneak preview *n* عَرْض مُسْبَق

sneak thief *n* [لِصّ يَتَسَلَّلُ عَبْرَ مَنافِذَ مَفْتوحة]

sneaky /ˈsniːki/ *adj* (**sneakier**, **sneakiest**) (infml) ‹*trick, person*› ماكِر; ‹*peek*› مُخْتَلَس

sneer /snɪə/ **A** *n* اِسْتِهْزاء, اِزْدِراء, سُخْرِيّة (اِسْتِهْزاءات)

B *vt* قالَ ساخِراً

C *vi* «critics, cynics» سَخِرَ (a; سُخْرِيّة), تَهَكَّمَ, اِسْتَهْزَأَ

sneeze /sniːz/ **A** *vi* «person, cat» عَطَسَ (i-u; عَطْس, عُطاس)

B *n* عَطْسة

snide /snaɪd/ *adj* ‹*remark, tone*› ساخِر, مُتَهَكِّم, مُسْتَهْزِئ

sniff /snɪf/ **A** *vt* **1** (using sense of smell) شَمَّ (a-u; شَمّ, شَميم; perf شَمَمْتُ, شَمِمْتُ), اِشْتَمَّ ‹*the air, perfume, a flower*›; **the police dogs ~ed the luggage** شَمَّت الكِلابُ البوليسيّةُ الحَقائِبَ **2** (to inhale) اِسْتَنْشَقَ ‹*glue, cocaine*›

B *vi* شَهَقَ من أَنْفِهِ; **he was ~ing all day at the office** كانَ يَشْهَقُ من أَنْفِهِ طوال النَهارِ في المَكْتَبِ

C *n* **1** (when crying) تَهَنُّف, إِجْهاش; (when clearing one's nose) شَهيق من الأَنْفِ **2** (of a smell) شَمّة; **take a good ~ of this cheese!** شُمَّ هذا الجُبْنَ جَيِّداً! **3** (infml) (trace, hint) رائحة (رَوائِحُ), دَليل (دَلائِلُ, أَدِلّة), أَثَر (آثار), إِشارة, مُؤَشِّر (مُؤَشِّرات); **there has never been a ~ of scandal** لم يَكُنْ هُناكَ أَبَداً أَيُّ مُؤَشِّرٍ على فَضيحةٍ

Phrasal verbs **sniff at**: **~ at [sth]** **1** شَمَّ [شَيْئاً] ‹*the air, food, a flower*›; **I couldn't resist the temptation to ~ at the roses as we went in** لم أَسْتَطِعْ أَنْ أُقاوِمَ الرَغْبةَ في شَمِّ الوُرودِ عِنْدَما دَخَلْنا **2** قابَلَ [شَيْئاً] بِازْدِراءٍ ‹*a suggestion, an idea*›; **the prize is not to be ~ed at** الجائِزةُ لا يُسْتَهانُ بِها

• **sniff out**: **~ out [sth]** **1** «dog» اِكْتَشَفَ [شَيْئاً] عن طَريقِ الشَمِّ ‹*explosives, drugs*› **2** (to detect) اِكْتَشَفَ [شَيْئاً] ‹*a scandal, bargain*›

sniffer dog /ˈsnɪfə dɒɡ/ *n* كَلْب بوليسيّ

sniffle /ˈsnɪf(ə)l/ **A** *vi* (when crying) شَهَقَ (a; شَهيق); (with a cold) تَنَشَّقَ

B *n* (infml) (cold) زُكام, بَرْد

snigger /ˈsnɪɡə/ **A** *vi* «children, colleagues» ضَحِكَ ضِحْكةً مَكْتومةً

B *n* ضِحْكة مَكْتومة

snip /snɪp/ **A** *vt* (**-pp-**) قَصَّ (بِضَرْبةِ مِقَصٍّ سَريعةٍ) ‹*thread, wire*›

B *n* **1** (action) ضَرْبة مِقَصٍّ **2** (sound) [صَوْت مِقَصٍّ]

snipe /snʌɪp/ **A** *n* (*pl* **snipes** or **snipe**) جُهْلول, شُنْقُب (طائِر)

B *vi* **to ~ at sb** **1** (to shoot) «marksmen, soldiers» قَنَصَ شَخْصاً **2** (to criticize) «critics, opponents» اِنْتَقَدَ \ هاجَمَ شَخْصاً

sniper /ˈsnʌɪpə/ *n* قَنّاص (قَنّاصة)

snippet /ˈsnɪpɪt/ *n* مُقْتَطَف (مُقْتَطَفات), مَقْطَع (مَقاطِعُ); **~s of information/conversation** مُقْتَطَفات من المَعْلوماتِ \ المُحادَثة

snitch /snɪtʃ/ **A** *vt* (to steal) اِخْتَلَسَ ‹*food, candy, money*›

B *vi* **to ~ on sb** وَشى بِشَخْصٍ

C *n* (infml) (betrayer) واشٍ (وُشاة, واشونَ), خائِن (خَوَنة)

snivel /ˈsnɪv(ə)l/ *vi* (**-ll-** BrE, **-l-** AmE) «child, coward» تَباكى

snob /snɒb/ *n* شَخْص مُتَكَبِّر \ مُتَغَطْرِس

snobbery /ˈsnɒb(ə)ri/ *n* تَكَبُّر, اِسْتِعْلاء, غَطْرَسة

snobbish /ˈsnɒbɪʃ/ *adj* ‹*attitude, accent*› مُتَكَبِّر, مُتَغَطْرِس, مُتَعَجْرِف

snog /snɒɡ/ **A** *vt* (**-gg-**) (infml) قَبَّلَ (بِحَرارةٍ) ‹*one's girlfriend, boyfriend*›

B *vi* (**-gg-**) (infml) «lovers» تَبادَلَ القُبُلاتِ (بِحَرارةٍ)

C *n* (infml) تَقْبيل بِحَرارة

snooker /ˈsnuːkə/ *n* سْنوكَر (لُعْبة شَبيهة بالبِلْيارْدو)

snoop /snuːp/ (infml) **A** *vi* «police, journalists» تَجَسَّسَ, تَلَصَّصَ; **to ~ on sb** تَجَسَّسَ \ تَلَصَّصَ على شَخْصٍ

B *n* نَظْرة فُضوليّة \ مُخْتَلَسة

snooper /ˈsnuːpə/ *n* (infml) شَخْص مُتَلَصِّص \ فُضوليّ

snooze /snuːz/ **A** *n* غَفْوة, قَيْلولة

B *vi* «person, animal» غَفا (u; غَفْو, غُفُوّ), أَخَذَ قَيْلولةً

snooze button *n* زِرّ الانْتِظارِ \ الغَفْوةِ

snore /snɔː/ **A** *n* غَطيط ,شَخير

B *vi* غَطَّ ,شَخَّرَ (أثناء النَوْم)

snoring /ˈsnɔːrɪŋ/ *n* غَطيط ,شَخير

snorkel /ˈsnɔːk(ə)l/ *n* قَصَبة تَنَفُّسٍ (تُسْتَخْدَمُ في الغَوْصِ)

snorkelling (BrE), **snorkeling** (AmE) /ˈsnɔːklɪŋ/ *n* غَوْص [بِاسْتِخْدامِ قَصَبةِ التَنَفُّسِ]; **to go ~** [ذَهَب للغَوْصِ بِاسْتِخْدامِ قَصَبةِ التَنَفُّسِ]

snort /snɔːt/ **A** *n* شَخير ,نَخير

B *vt* **1** (to utter) [قالَ هازِئاً] ‹*a reply, remark*› **2** (to inhale) شَمَّ (a-u; شَمّ), اسْتَنْشَقَ ‹*cocaine, heroin*›

C *vi* «horse, bull» [زَفَرَ بِمِنْخارِه]; **to ~ with laughter** [ضَحِكَ بِشَكْلٍ غَيْرِ مُهَذَّبٍ]

snout /snaʊt/ *n* خَطْم (خُطوم)

snow /snəʊ/ **A** *n* ثَلْج (ثُلوج)

B *v impers* أَثْلَجَ ,أَمْطَرَ ثَلْجاً; **it's ~ing** تَتَساقَطُ الثُلوجُ

Phrasal verbs **snow in**: **to be ~ed in** «houses, family» حوصِرَ بالثُلوجِ

• **snow under**: **to be ~ed under** **1** (with snow) «cars, garden» غَطَّتْهُ الثُلوجُ **2** (with work) كانَ مُثْقَلاً بالعَمَلِ

snowball /ˈsnəʊbɔːl/ **A** *n* كُرة ثَلْج

B *vi* «debts, demand» تَفاقَمَ ,تَضَخَّمَ

snowboard /ˈsnəʊbɔːd/ **A** *n* لَوْح تَزَلُّجٍ على الجَليد

B *vi* «snowboarders» تَزَلَّجَ على الجَليدِ; **do you ~?** هل تُمارِسُ التَزَلُّجَ على الجَليدِ؟

snowboarding /ˈsnəʊbɔːdɪŋ/ *n* تَزَلُّج على الجَليد

snowbound /ˈsnəʊbaʊnd/ *adj* ‹*airport, village*› مُحاصَر بالثُلوج

snow chains *n* سَلاسِل إطاراتٍ ,سَلاسِل ثَلْجٍ

snowdrift /ˈsnəʊdrɪft/ *n* كَوْمة جَليدٍ ,رُكام ثَلْجيّ

snowdrop /ˈsnəʊdrɒp/ *n* زَهْرة اللَبَنِ الثَلْجيّة

snowfall /ˈsnəʊfɔːl/ *n* تَساقُط ثُلوجٍ

snowflake /ˈsnəʊfleɪk/ *n* نُدْفة \ رُقاقة ثَلْجٍ

snowman /ˈsnəʊman/ *n* (*pl* **-men**) رَجُل ثَلْجٍ

snowmobile /ˈsnəʊməbiːl/ *n* زَلاّقة جَليدٍ آليّة ,مَرْكَبة جَليدٍ

snowplough (BrE), **snowplow** (AmE) /ˈsnəʊplaʊ/ *n* كاسِحة \ جَرّافة ثُلوجٍ

snowshoe /ˈsnəʊʃuː/ *n* [حِذاء للسَيْرِ على الثُلوجِ]

snowstorm /ˈsnəʊstɔːm/ *n* عاصِفة ثَلْجيّة

snowsuit /ˈsnəʊsuːt/ *n* بَدْلة ثَلْجٍ

snowy /ˈsnəʊi/ *adj* (**snowier**, **snowiest**) ‹*landscape, mountain*› مُغَطًّى بالثُلوجِ \ مَكْسوّ; ‹*day*› ثَلْجيّ ,كَثير الثُلوجِ

snub /snʌb/ **A** *vt* (**-bb-**) صَدَّ (u; صَدّ ,صُدود), تَجاهَلَ ‹*an offer, invitation*›

B *n* صَدّ ,تَجاهُل

snub-nosed /ˌsnʌbˈnəʊzd/ *adj* ‹*girl, child*› أَفْطَس الأَنْفِ

snuck /snʌk/ (infml) *past tense, past participle* ▸ **sneak**

snuff /snʌf/ *n* سَعوط ,نَشوق

Phrasal verb **snuff out**: **~ [sth] out, ~ out [sth]** **1** (to extinguish) أَطْفَأَ [شَيْئاً] ‹*a candle, flame*› **2** (to suppress) قَضى على [شَيْءٍ] ‹*hope, opposition*›

snuffbox /ˈsnʌfbɒks/ *n* عُلْبة نَشوقٍ \ سَعوطٍ

snug /snʌg/ *adj* **1** ‹*room, bed*› [دافِئ وَمُريح] **2** ‹*jeans, T-shirt*› ضَيِّق ,مُحْكَم

snuggle /ˈsnʌg(ə)l/ *vi* **to ~ up to sb** «animals» اقْتَرَبَ من / رَكَنَ إلى شَخْصٍ

so /səʊ/ **A** *adv* **1** (for emphasis) جِدًّا; **she is ~ happy/sad** هي سَعيدةٌ \ حَزينةٌ جِدًّا; **he does worry ~** هو بالفِعْلِ يَقْلَقُ كَثيراً; **he treated us ~ well/badly** عامَلَنا مُعامَلةً حَسَنةً \ سَيِّئةً جِدًّا; **it happened ~ quickly/slowly** حَدَثَ بِسُرْعةٍ كَبيرةٍ \ بِبُطْءٍ شَديدٍ; **they are ~ looking forward to meeting you** يَتَطَلَّعونَ بِشِدّةٍ لِلِقائِكَ; **I'm not feeling ~ good** لا أَشْعُرُ أَنّني على ما يُرامُ **2** (infml) (in comparisons) بِنَفْسِ الدَرَجةِ / القَدْرِ; **he's not ~ good as you think** لَيْسَ طَيِّباً بِقَدْرِ ما تَظُنُّ; **they escaped, but the rest were not ~ lucky** هَرَبوا، لَكِنَّ الباقينَ لم يكونوا مَحْظوظينَ بِنَفْسِ الدَرَجةِ **3** (for that reason) لِذَلِكَ ,لِذا ,لِهَذا; **~ it was that ...** وَهَكَذا ...; **she was young and ~ lacked experience** كانَتْ صَغيرةً وَلِذَلِكَ فَهِيَ كانَتْ تَفْتَقِرُ إلى الخِبْرةِ **4** (true) **is that ~?** هل ذلك صَحيحٌ ؟; **if (that's) ~, then ...** إذا كانَ الأَمْرُ كَذَلِكَ، إذَنْ ...; **I'm afraid ~** للأَسَفِ هذا

صَحيحٌ; **I believe ~** أَعْتَقِدُ ذلك; **who says ~?** مَنْ قالَ ذلك؟; **perhaps ~** رُبَّما يَكونُ كَذَلِكَ **5▸** (as well) أَيْضاً, كَذَلِكَ; **~ is she** وَكَذَلِكَ هي; **he's Iraqi, and ~ is she** هو عِراقِيٌّ، وَكَذَلِكَ هي; **if they agree to pay, ~ do I** إذا وافَقوا على الدَفْعِ، كَذَلِكَ سَأَفْعَلُ أنا **6▸** (**or so**) (infml) (thereabouts) أو ما يُقارِبُ ذلك; **20 or ~** 20 أو ما يُقارِبُ ذلك; **a year or ~ ago** قبل عامٍ أو ما يُقارِبُ ذلك **7▸** (with limitation) **we can only work ~ fast and no faster** لا يُمْكِنُنا أنْ نَعْمَلَ بِسُرْعةٍ أَكْبَرَ من ذلك; **you can only do ~ much (and no more)** لا يُمْكِنُكَ أنْ تَفْعَلَ أَكْثَرَ من هذا **8▸** (as introductory remark) **~ there you are** حَسَناً **9▸** إذَنْ ذلك هو السَبَبُ; **~ that's the reason** هذا هو الحالُ (in such a way) **hold it ~** أُمْسُكْهُ هكذا; **she likes everything to be just ~** تُحِبُّ أنْ يَكونَ كُلُّ شَيْءٍ مُرَتَّباً وَمُنَظَّماً; **just as in the 20th century, ~ today** تَماماً كَما كانَ في القَرْنِ العِشْرينَ، كَذَلِكَ اليَوْمَ; **~ be it!** فَلْيَكُنْ ما يَكونُ!; **and ~ on and ~ forth** هَكَذا وَهَلُمَّ جَرًّا, وَهَكَذا دَوالَيْكَ **10▸** (to avoid repetition) هَكَذا; **I told you ~** لَقَدْ حَذَّرْتُكَ من قَبْلُ; **~ it appears** هذا ما يَبْدو; **he's the owner or ~ he claims** هو المالِكُ أو هكذا يَدَّعي; **~ to speak** إذا جازَ التَعْبيرُ **11▸** (infml) (refuting a statement) **'he didn't hit you'—'he did ~!'** 'لم يَضْرِبْكَ' — 'بَلْ فَعَلَ!' **12▸** (infml) (as casual response) إذَنْ; **'I'm leaving'—'~?'** 'سَأُغادِرُ' — 'وَماذا إذَنْ؟'; **~ why worry!** إذَنْ لِمَ القَلَقُ! **13▸** (reinforcing a statement) **'I'm sorry'—'~ you should be'** 'أنا آسِفٌ' — 'هذا هو المَفْروضُ'; **'it's broken'—'~ it is'** 'مَكْسورٌ' — 'إنَّهُ حَقًّا كَذَلِكَ'

B (**so (that)**) *conj phr* من أَجْلِ أنْ, حتّى; **she wrote out the instructions ~ that she had a copy** كَتَبَت التَعْليماتِ حتى تَحْتَفِظَ بِنُسْخةٍ

C (**so as**) *conj phr* لِكَيْ, حَتّى; **he got up early ~ as not to miss them** اسْتَيْقَظَ مُبَكِّراً حتّى لا يَفوتَهُ لِقاؤُهُمْ

D (**so much**) *adv phr, pronoun phr* **1▸** (also **so many**) (such large quantity) الكَثير; **~ much of her life** فَتْرةٌ طَويلة من حَياتِها; **~ many of her friends** الكَثير من أَصْدِقائِها **2▸** (to such an extent) جِدًّا; **~ much worse/better** أَسْوأ\ أَفْضَل بِكَثيرٍ جِدًّا; **~ much ~ that ...** جِدًّا لِدَرَجةِ أنّ... **3▸** (in contrasts) **not ~ much X as Y** لَيْسَ كَذا بَلْ بالأَحْرى كَذا

E (**so much for**) *prep phr* **1▸** (with finality) **~ much for the accounts, now for ...** كَفانا حَديثاً عن الحِساباتِ، والآنَ بالنِسْبةِ ل... **2▸** (disparagingly) **~ much for equality** لم يَتِمَّ مُراعاةُ المُساواةِ; **~ much for saying you'd help** لم تُساعِدْني كَما قُلْتَ

(Idioms) **so long as** (infml) ▸ **long** E; **so much as** (even) حَتّى; **he never ~ much as apologized** هو حتّى لم يَعْتَذِرْ أَبَداً; **so so** لا بَأْسَ بِهِ; **so there!** (infml) هذا نِهائيٌّ!

soak /səʊk/ **A** *vt* **1▸** (to wet) بَلَّلَ <*a person, sb's clothes*>; **to get ~ed** ابْتَلَّ **2▸** (to immerse) نَقَعَ (a; نَقْع) <*clothes, lentils*>

B *vi* **1▸** (to be immersed) «clothes, lentils» انْتَقَعَ; **to leave the lentils/washing to ~** نَقَعَ العَدَسَ \ الغَسيلَ **2▸** **to ~ into the paper/fabric** «water, blood» تَشَرَّبَهُ الوَرَقُ \ القُماشُ; **the blood ~ed through the bandage** تَشَرَّبَت الضِمادةُ الدَمَ

C (**soaked**) *in combination* **blood-~ed** <*bandages*> مُضَمَّخ بالدَمِ; **sweat-~ed** <*shirt*> مُشَبَّع بالعَرَقِ; **rain-~ed** <*ground, track*> غارِق في ماءِ المَطَرِ

D *n* **to have a ~** (infml) اغْتَسَلَ في حَوْضِ الاسْتِحْمامِ; **to give sth a ~** (BrE) نَقَعَ شَيْئاً

(Phrasal verbs) **soak away** «water» جَفَّ (i; جَفاف, جُفوف)

• **soak in** «ink, water, blood» جَفَّ (i; جَفاف, جُفوف)

• **soak up**: **A** **~ [sth] up, ~ up [sth]** (to absorb) امْتَصَّ \ تَشَرَّبَ [شَيْئاً] <*water, blood*> **B** **~ up [sth]** (to enjoy) **to ~ up the sun/atmosphere** «visitors, tourists» تَمَتَّعَ بالشَمْسِ \ بالجَوِّ

soaked /səʊkt/ *adj* <*garment, hair*> مُبْتَلّ \ شَديد البَلَلِ, مَنْقوع; **to be ~ through** *or* **~ to the skin** كانَ مُبْتَلاً تَماماً مَبْلول جِدًّا

soaking /ˈsəʊkɪŋ/ *adj* <*garment, hair*> مُبْتَلّ \ شَديد البَلَلِ, مَبْلول جِدًّا

so-and-so /ˈsəʊ(ə)nsəʊ/ *n* **1▸** (unknown person) فُلان **2▸** (disliked person) نَذْل (أَنْذال)

soap /səʊp/ *n* صابون

soap flakes *n* رَقائِق صابون, صابون مَبْشور

soap opera *n* أوبِرا الصابون (مُسَلْسَل اجْتِماعيّ طَويل)

soap powder *n* مَسْحوق غَسيل

soapsuds /ˈsəʊpsʌdz/ *n pl* رَغْوة صابون

soapy /ˈsəʊpi/ *adj* (**soapier**, **soapiest**) ‹*water, hands*› بِهِ صابون

soar /sɔː/ *vi* 1 (to glide) «birds, planes» حَلَّقَ, حامَ (u; حَوْم, حَوَمان) 2 (to increase) «costs, temperatures» اِرْتَفَعَ بِشِدَّةٍ, قَفَزَ (i; قَفْز) 3 (to tower) «skyscrapers, mountains» شَمَخَ (a; شُموخ), سَمَقَ (u; سُموق), اِرْتَفَعَ

soaring /ˈsɔːrɪŋ/ *adj* ‹*prices, temperatures*› مُرْتَفِع بِشَكْلٍ حادٍّ

sob /sɒb/ **A** *vi* (**-bb-**) اِنْتَحَبَ, نَشَجَ (i; نَشيج), تَنَهَّدَ (تَنَهُّد) **B** *n* نَحيب, نَشيج (نُشُج), تَنَهُّد (تَنَهُّدات)

sober /ˈsəʊbə/ *adj* 1 (Law) (not drunk) «man, driver» واعٍ, غَيْر ثَمِلٍ 2 (serious) ‹*expression, occasion*› جادّ 3 (subdued) ‹*suit, colours*› غَيْر زاهٍ

Phrasal verb **sober up**: 1 **~ up** أفاقَ (مِن سُكْرِهِ) 2 **~ [sb] up** ‹*a drunk*› جَعَلَ [شَخْصاً] يُفيقُ مِن سُكْرِهِ

sobriety /səˈbraɪəti/ *n* 1 (soberness) اِعْتِدال (في الشرابِ) 2 (seriousness) رَزانة, وَقار 3 (simplicity of dress, decor) بَساطة

sobriety test *n* اِخْتِبار ثَمالةٍ (اِخْتِبارَ يَكْشِفُ عن تَعاطي الكُحولِ والمُخَدِّراتِ)

sob story *n* (infml) قِصّة مُثيرة لِلشَفَقةِ

so-called *adj* 1 (commonly designated) مَدْعوّ, مُسَمًّى 2 (inappropriately named) مَزْعوم

soccer /ˈsɒkə/ *n* كُرة القَدَمِ

sociable /ˈsəʊʃəb(ə)l/ *adj* ‹*person, evening*› اِجْتِماعيّ

social /ˈsəʊʃ(ə)l/ *adj* 1 (recreational) ‹*event, visit*› اِجْتِماعيّ 2 (relating to society) ‹*issue, change*› اِجْتِماعيّ

social climber *n* شَخْص وُصوليّ \ اِنْتِهازيّ

social club *n* نادٍ اِجْتِماعيّ

social democracy *n* ديموقْراطيّة اشْتِراكيّة

social democrat *n* [شَخْص يَتَبَنّى فِكْرةَ الديموقْراطيّةِ الاشْتِراكيّةِ]

social entrepreneur *n* رائِد أَعْمالٍ اِجْتِماعيّ

social gathering *n* لِقاء \ تَجَمُّع اِجْتِماعيّ

socialism /ˈsəʊʃəliz(ə)m/ *n* اشْتِراكيّة

socialist /ˈsəʊʃəlɪst/ *n, adj* اشْتِراكيّ

socialite /ˈsəʊʃəlaɪt/ *n* شَخْصيّة اِجْتِماعيّة

socialize, **-ise** (BrE) /ˈsəʊʃəlaɪz/ *vi* عاشَرَ, اِخْتَلَطَ, كَوَّنَ صَداقةً; **to ~ with sb** عاشَرَ شَخْصاً

social life *n* حَياة اِجْتِماعيّة

socially /ˈsəʊʃ(ə)li/ *adv* ‹*to meet, mix*› في إطارٍ اِجْتِماعيٍّ; **I know him ~** أَعْرِفُهُ من الناحِيةِ الاجْتِماعيّةِ

social media *n* إعْلام اِجْتِماعيّ

social mobility *n* حَراك اِجْتِماعيّ

social network, **social networking site** *n* مَوْقِع تَواصُلٍ اِجْتِماعيٍّ

social science *n* عِلْم اِجْتِماعيّ

social security *n* 1 (in the UK) ضَمان اِجْتِماعيّ 2 (in the US) تَأْمين اِجْتِماعيّ

social service *n* خِدْمة مُجْتَمَعيّة \ اِجْتِماعيّة

social services *n pl* خِدْمات اِجْتِماعيّة

social status *n* مَكانة اِجْتِماعيّة

social work *n* خِدْمة اِجْتِماعيّة, عَمَل اِجْتِماعيّ

social worker *n* أَخِصّائيّ اِجْتِماعيّ, عامِل اِجْتِماعيّ

societal /səˈsaɪət(ə)l/ *adj* ‹*change, norm*› مُجْتَمَعيّ, اِجْتِماعيّ

society /səˈsaɪəti/ *n* (*pl* **societies**) 1 (community) مُجْتَمَع 2 (organization) جَمْعيّة 3 [u] (also **high society**) الطَبَقة الراقِية

socio-economic /ˌsəʊsiəʊˌiːkəˈnɒmɪk/ *adj* ‹*factor, group*› اقْتِصاديّ اِجْتِماعيّ

sociological /ˌsəʊsiəˈlɒdʒɪk(ə)l/ *adj* ‹*study, issue*› سوسيولوجيّ, اِجْتِماعيّ

sociologist /ˌsəʊsiˈɒlədʒɪst/ *n* عالِم اِجْتِماعٍ, مُتَخَصِّص في عِلْمِ الاجْتِماعِ

sociology /ˌsəʊsɪˈɒlədʒi/ *n* عِلْم الاجْتِماعِ, سوسيولوجيا

sociopath /ˈsəʊsiəʊpæθ/ *n* شَخْص مَريض \ مُعْتَلّ اِجْتِماعيًّا

sock /sɒk/ *n* جَوْرَب (جَوارِبُ)

socket /ˈsɒkɪt/ *n* 1 (for plugs) مِقْبَس, مَأْخَذ تَوْصيلٍ 2 (for bulbs) مَقْبِس (مَصْباحٍ) 3 (of tooth, eye) تَجْويف (تَجاويفُ)

Socotra /səˈkəʊtrə/ *pr n* سُقُطْرى (f)

sod /sɒd/ *n* 1 (turf) طَبَقة من العُشْبِ 2 (BrE vulg) (unpleasant person) رَجُل بَغيض

Phrasal verb **sod off**: (BrE vulg) **~ off!** أُغْرُب عن وَجْهي!

soda /ˈsəʊdə/ *n* **1** (chemical) كَرْبونات الصوديوم, صودا **2** (also **soda water**) مِياه غازيّة; **a whisky and ~** ويسكي وَمِياه غازيّة **3** (also **soda pop**) (AmE) مَشْروب غازيّ **4** (also **ice-cream soda**) (AmE) [أَيْس كْريم في مَشْروبٍ غازيٍّ]

sodden /ˈsɒd(ə)n/ *adj* ‹*ground, clothes*› مَغْمور \ مُشَبَّع بالماءِ

sodium /ˈsəʊdiəm/ *n* صوديوم

sodium bicarbonate *n* بيكَرْبونات الصوديوم

sodium chloride *n* كْلوريد الصوديوم

sofa /ˈsəʊfə/ *n* أَريكة (أَرائِك), كَنَبة

sofa bed *n* كَنَبة سَرير (أَريكة تَتَحَوَّلُ إِلى سَرير)

Sofia /ˈsəʊfiə/ *pr n* صوفيا

soft /sɒft/ *adj* (**softer, softest**) **1** (yielding, not firm) ‹*mattress*› لَيِّن; ‹*ground*› رَخْو; ‹*butter*› طَرِيّ; ‹*hair*› ناعِم; ‹*snow*› هَشّ; **the leather is ~ to the touch** الجِلْدُ ناعِمُ المَلْمَس; **the ground is getting ~** بَدَأَت الأَرْضُ تَلين; **~ ice cream** أَيس كْريم لَيِّن; **the ground is too ~ for the wheels to grip** الأَرْضُ لَيِّنةٌ جِدًّا بِحَيْثُ لا تَثْبُتُ عَلَيْها العَجَلاتُ **2** (smooth) ‹*skin, hands*› ناعِم **3** (in lighting, colour) ‹*colour, light*› هادِئ **4** (in sounds) ‹*note, laugh*› هادِئ; **~ music is played to callers** يَتِمُّ تَشْغيلُ موسيقى هادِئةٍ لِلمُتَّصِلينَ **5** (gentle) ‹*climate*› مُعْتَدِل; ‹*breeze, rain*› خَفيف; **a ~ sea breeze** نَسيم بَحْرٍ خَفيف **6** (not sharp) ‹*outline, profile*› باهِت **7** (easy) ‹*subject, question*› سَهْل; **there are no ~ options** لا توجَدُ خِياراتٌ سَهْلَةٌ **8** (weak in price) ‹*prices, market*› ضَعيف **9** (undemanding) ‹*loan*› مُيَسَّر **10** (infml) (lenient) ‹*parent, teacher*› لَيِّن, مُتَساهِل; **to take a ~ line with sb** تَبَنّى مَوْقِفاً مُتَسامِحاً مع شَخْصٍ **11** (infml) (stupid) **to be ~ in the head** كانَ ضَعيفَ العَقْلِ **12** (infml) (agreeable) ‹*life, job*› سَهْل **13** (not most harmful) ‹*drug, porn*› خَفيف **14** ‹*water*› يَسِر **15** ‹*consonant*› خَفيف

softa /ˈsɒftə/ *n* [طالِب عُلومٍ دينيّةٍ]

softball /ˈsɒftbɔːl/ *n* **1** [u] (game) كُرة لَيِّنة **2** (ball) كُرة لَيِّنة

soft cheese *n* جُبْن طَرِيّ

soft copy *n* نُسْخة إِلِكْتْرونيّة

soft drink *n* مَشْروب غَيْر كُحوليٍّ

soften /ˈsɒf(ə)n/ **A** *vt* **1** (to make soft) ‹*skin*› نَعَّمَ, لَيَّنَ; [جَعَلَ لَيِّنَ القَوامِ] ‹*butter*› **2** (to alleviate) خَفَّفَ ‹*an impact, a shock*›; **to ~ the blow** خَفَّفَ الضَّرْبَةَ **3** (of water quality) أَزالَ العُسْرَ \ الصَّلابةَ ‹*the water*›

B *vi* **1** «light» خَفَتَ (u; خُفوت); «outline» بَهِتَ (a; بَهْت) **2** (to mellow) «attitudes, one's manner» لانَ (i; لين, لِيان), أَصْبَحَ أَكْثَرَ لُطْفاً

Phrasal verb **soften up**: **1** **~ up** «butter, leather» لانَ (i; لين, لِيان), طَرِيَ (a; طَراوة, طَرِيَ), أَصْبَحَ أَكْثَرَ لُيونةً **2** **~ up [sb], ~ [sb] up** أَضْعَفَ [شَخْصاً] ‹*the opposition, electorate*›

softener /ˈsɒfnə/ *n* **1** (also **fabric softener**) مُنَعِّم أَقْمِشةٍ **2** (also **water softener**) جِهاز إِزالةِ عُسْرِ الماءِ

softly /ˈsɒftli/ *adv* ‹*to speak, touch*› بِلُطْفٍ, بِرِفْقٍ

soft option *n* **to take the soft option** أَخَذَ الخِيارَ الأَسْهَل

soft skills *n* مَهارات ناعِمة

soft-spoken /sɒftˈspəʊk(ə)n/ *adj* مَعْسول اللِسانِ; **to be ~** كانَ مَعْسولَ اللِسانِ

soft spot *n* (infml) **to have a soft spot for sb** كانَ لَدَيْهِ نُقْطةُ ضَعْفٍ تُجاهَ شَخْصٍ

soft-top *n* **1** (car) سَيّارة بِسَقْفٍ قابِلٍ للطَيِّ **2** (roof) سَقْف قابِل للطَيِّ

soft touch *n* (infml) شَخْص لَيِّن الجانِبِ \ سَهْل المِراسِ; **to be a soft touch** كانَ لَيِّناً

soft toy *n* دُمْية لَيِّنة \ طَرِيّة

software /ˈsɒftwɛː/ *n* بَرْمَجيّات, بَرامِج (كُمْبيوتَر)

software house *n* شِرِكة بَرامِج كُمْبيوتَر \ بَرْمَجيّاتٍ

software package *n* حُزْمة بَرامِجَ

software piracy *n* قَرْصَنة البَرْمَجيّاتِ \ بَرامِجِ الكُمْبيوتَر

soggy /ˈsɒgi/ *adj* (**soggier, soggiest**) ‹*ground*› شَديد البَلَلِ; ‹*bread*› رَطْب

soh /səʊ/ *n* صول (النَغْمة الموسيقيّة الخامِسة من السُلَّمِ الموسيقيِّ)

soil /sɔɪl/ **A** *n* **1** (earth) تُرْبة (تُرَب), أَرْض (f; أَراضٍ) **2** (AmE) (filth) وَسَخ (أَوْساخ)

B *vt* **1** (with dirt) وَسَّخَ, لَطَّخَ ‹*one's clothes, the laundry*› **2** (with faeces) نَجَّسَ ‹*one's underwear, bed*›

soiled /sɔɪld/ *adj* 1 (dirty) ‹*clothes, nappy*› مُلَطَّخ ,مُتَّسِخ 2 (also **shop-soiled**) (BrE) [مُتَّسِخ \ بالٍ بِسَبَبِ بَقائِهِ في المَتْجَرِ]

solace /'sɒləs/ *n* (fml) عَزاء ,سُلْوان

solar /'səʊlə/ *adj* ‹*radiation, cycle*› شَمْسيّ

solar eclipse *n* كُسوف شَمْسيّ

solar energy, **solar power** *n* طاقة شَمْسيّة

solar plexus *n* ضَفيرة شَمْسيّة

solar system *n* نِظام شَمْسيّ ,مَجْموعة شَمْسيّة

sold /səʊld/ *past tense, past participle* ▸ **sell**

solder /'səʊldə, 'sɒldə/ A *vt* لَحَمَ (u; لَحْم) ‹*a wire, connection*› B *vi* «electrician» لَحَمَ (u; لَحْم)

soldier /'səʊldʒə/ *n* جُنْديّ (جُنود)

Phrasal verb **soldier on** «workers, volunteers» صَمَدَ (u; صُمود) واصَلَ ,ثابَرَ

sole /səʊl/ A *n* 1 (*pl* **sole** or **soles**) (fish) سَمَك موسى 2 (of foot) باطِن القَدَم 3 (of shoe, sock) نَعْل (mf; نِعال ,أَنْعُل) B *adj before n* 1 (only) ‹*purpose, wish*› مُفْرَد ,واحِد ,وَحيد 2 (exclusive) ‹*agent, right*› مُنْفَرِد ,حَصْريّ ,وَحيد

solely /'səʊlli/ *adv* ‹*to use, base*› حَصْريًّا ,كُلّيّةً ,بِشَكْلٍ مُنْفَرِدٍ; **I'm ~ responsible** أنا وَحْدي المَسْؤولُ

solemn /'sɒləm/ *adj* 1 (sincere) ‹*promise, duty*› رَسْمي 2 (serious) ‹*occasion, expression*› جِدّيّ ,جادّ

sole trader *n* تاجِر مُنْفَرِد ,مُنْشَأة فَرْديّة

sol-fa /'sɒlfɑː/ *n* الصولفيج (قِراءة المَقاطِع الغِنائيّة حَسَبَ النوتاتِ الموسيقيّة)

solicit /sə'lɪsɪt/ A *vt* (fml) طَلَبَ ,الْتَمَسَ (u; طَلَب ,مَطْلَب) ‹*information, help*› B *vi* «prostitutes» [عَرَضَتْ نَفْسَها على شَخْصٍ مُقابِلَ المالِ]

soliciting /sə'lɪsɪtɪŋ/ *n* [عَرْض الجِنْسِ على شَخْصٍ مُقابِلَ المالِ]

solicitor /sə'lɪsɪtə/ *n* 1 (in UK: lawyer) مُحامٍ (مُحامونَ) 2 (in US: law officer) مُحامٍ عامّ

solid /'sɒlɪd/ A *adj* 1 (not liquid or gaseous) ‹*metal, lava*› صُلْب; **to become ~** تَصَلَّبَ 2 (of materials) ‹*granite, teak*› مُصْمَت; ‹*gold*› خالِص; **a ~ gold ring** خاتَم من الذَهَبِ الخالِصِ; **a tunnel cut through ~ rock** نَفَق تَمَّ شَقُّهُ في الصَخْرِ المُصْمَتِ 3 (strong) ‹*foundations, relationship, argument*› قَويّ, مَتين; **doctors need a ~ foundation in chemistry** يَحْتاجُ الأَطِبّاءُ إلى أَساسٍ قَويٍّ في الكيمْياءِ; **despite the problems, their marriage remained ~** بالرَغْمِ من المَشاكِلِ, بَقِيَ زَواجُهُما قَوِيًّا 4 (reliable) ‹*evidence, information*› مُوَثَّق ,ثابِت; **no ~ evidence was produced** لَم يُقَدَّمْ دَليلٌ ثابِتٌ; **a ~ piece of work** عَمَل مُوَثَّق; **the team gave another ~ performance** قَدَّمَ الفَريقُ أَداءً قَوِيًّا آخَرَ; **Elsie has turned in a ~ term's work** سَلَّمَتْ إِلْسي عَمَلاً قَوِيًّا للفَصْلِ الدِراسيِّ لَدَيْهِمْ 5 (in appearance) ‹*person*› قَويّ (البِنْيَة); **they have some ~ defenders** بَعْضُ المُدافِعينَ الأَقْوِياءِ 6 (dense) ‹*traffic, crowd, expanse*› كَثيف; **the traffic is ~ as far as the lights** المُرورُ مُزْدَحِمٌ حتّى إِشارةَ المُرورِ; **the streets were ~ with people** كانَتْ الشَوارِعُ مُزْدَحِمةً بالسُكّانِ; **a ~ area of red** مِنْطَقة يُغَطّيها اللَوْنُ الأَحْمَرُ بِكَثافةٍ 7 (uninterrupted) **five ~ days, five days** خَمْسة أَيّامٍ مُتَواصِلة ~ 8 (loyal) ‹*support, supporter*› قَويّ; **to have the ~ support of the party** سانَدَهُ الحِزْبُ بِقوّةٍ; **the strike has remained ~** ظَلَّ الإِضْرابُ قَوِيًّا 9 (respectable) ‹*citizen*› شَريف (أَشْراف ,شُرَفاءُ); **despite his childhood of crime, he became a ~ citizen** بالرَغْمِ من انْخِراطِهِ في حَياةِ الجَريمةِ في طُفولَتِهِ, فَقَدْ أَصْبَحَ مُواطِناً شَريفاً B *adv* ‹*to freeze*› كُلّيّةً ,تَماماً ,عن آخِرِهِ; **the play is booked ~** المَسْرحيّةُ مَحْجوزةٌ عن آخِرِها C *n* 1 (figure) مُجَسَّم (جِسْم); **a tetrahedron is a four-sided ~ with triangular faces** رُباعي الأَسْطُحِ هو مُجَسَّمٌ مُؤَلَّفٌ من أَرْبَعةِ أَوْجُهٍ مُثَلَّثةٍ 2 (substance) مادّة صُلْبة D (**solids**) *n pl* (food) أَطْعِمة صُلْبة; **to be on ~s** تَغَذّى بالأَطْعِمةِ الصُلْبةِ; **to take ~s** تَناوَلَ الأَطْعِمةَ الصُلْبةَ

solidarity /ˌsɒlɪ'dærɪtɪ/ *n* تَضامُن; **to express one's ~ for sb** أَعْرَبَ عن تَضامُنِهِ مع شَخْصٍ

solidify /sə'lɪdɪfaɪ/ A *vi* «liquid, wax» تَصَلَّبَ ,تَجَمَّدَ B *vt* (**solidifies**, **solidifying**, **solidified**) قَوّى ,مَتَّنَ ,رَسَّخَ ,وَطَّدَ ‹*a position, one's identity*›

solidly /'sɒlɪdli/ *adv* 1 (strongly) ‹*built, made*› بِمَتانةٍ ,بِصَلابةٍ 2 (continuously) ‹*to work, rain*› بِدونِ تَوَقُّفٍ ,باسْتِمْرارٍ

3 (staunchly) <conservative, socialist> بِثَباتٍ ,بِقوّةٍ; **Milton voted ~ for the Radicals** صَوَّتَ ناخِبو ميلتون بالإجْماعِ لِصالِحِ الراديكاليّينَ

solitaire /sɒlɪˈtɛː/ *n* 1 (gemstone) خاتَم حَجَر كَريم; (ring) سوليتير\ بِهِ حَجَرٌ كَريمٌ 2 (AmE) (with cards) سوليتير (لُعْبة) لُعْبة من ألْعابِ الطاوِلةِ) 3 (board game) وَرَق)

solitary /ˈsɒlɪt(ə)ri/ *adj* 1 (unaccompanied) <walk, pastime> (مُنْزَوونَ) مُنْزَوٍ 2 (lonely) <person, animal> وَحيد ,مُنْفَرِد 3 (isolated) <farm, house> مُنْعَزِل 4 (infml) (single) <reason, question> وَحيد ,مُنْطَوٍ أَوْحَد ,وَحيد (dipt)

solitary confinement *n* حَبْس انْفِراديّ

solitude /ˈsɒlɪtjuːd/ *n* عُزْلة ,وَحْدة

solo /ˈsəʊləʊ/ A *n* (*pl* **solos**) سولو (لَحْن يُؤَدّيه فَنّانٌ مُنْفَرِدٌ)

B *adj* 1 (unaccompanied) <piece, section> مُنْفَرِد 2 (single-handed) <flight, album> مُنْفَرِد ,مُسْتَقِلّ

C *adv* <to fly, sail> وَحيداً ,مُنْفَرِداً

soloist /ˈsəʊləʊɪst/ *n* مُغَنٍّ\ عازِف مُنْفَرِد

solstice /ˈsɒlstɪs/ *n* انْقِلاب الشَّمْسِ; **the summer/winter ~** انْقِلاب الشَّمْسِ الصَّيْفيّ\ الشَّتْويّ

soluble /ˈsɒljʊb(ə)l/ *adj* <compound, vitamin> قابِل لِلذَّوَبانِ

solution /səˈluːʃ(ə)n/ *n* 1 (to a problem) حَلّ (حُلول), إجابة 2 (liquid) مَحْلول (مَحاليلُ)

solve /sɒlv/ *vt* 1 (to work out) حَلَّ (u; حَلّ) <an equation, a crossword>; **money alone will not ~ social ills** المالُ وَحْدَهُ لن يُعالِجَ الأمْراضَ الاجْتِماعيّةَ 2 (to explain) حَلَّ ,فَكَّ اللُّغْزَ (u; حَلّ) <a crime, mystery>

solvent /ˈsɒlv(ə)nt/ A *adj* <company, bank> قادِر على سَدادِ دُيونِهِ

B *n* مادّة مُذيبة ,مُذيب

Somali /səˈmɑːli/ A *n* 1 (*pl* **Somali** or **Somalis**) (citizen) صوماليّ 2 (language) (اللُّغة) الصوماليّة

B *adj* <currency, custom> صوماليّ

Somalia /səˈmɑːlɪə/ *pr n* الصومال (f)

sombre (BrE), **somber** (AmE) /ˈsɒmbə/ *adj* 1 (dark) <colours, clothes> قاتِم ,داكِن 2 (solemn) <mood, ceremony> كَئيب

some /sʌm/ A *determiner* 1 (an unspecified amount or number) بَعْض; **I bought ~ cheese** اشْتَرَيْتُ بَعْضَ الجُبْنِ; **I brought ~ money** أَحْضَرْتُ بَعْضَ المالِ; **she gave her ~ apples** أَعْطَتْها بَعْضَ التُّفّاحِ 2 (certain) بَعْض; **~ children like it** بَعْضُ الأطْفالِ يُحِبّونَهُ; **~ shops won't stock this product** بَعْضُ المَحَلاّتِ تَرْفُضُ تخْزينَ هذا المُنْتَجِ; **in ~ parts of Europe** في بَعْضِ الأجْزاءِ من أوروبّا; **in ~ cases, people have had to wait years for compensation/a work permit** في بَعْضِ الحالاتِ، اضْطُرَّ الناسُ للانْتِظارِ لِسَنواتٍ للحُصولِ على تَعْويضٍ\ تَصْريحِ عَمَلٍ 3 (a considerable amount or number) قَدْر كَبير من; **we stayed there for ~ time** مَكَثْنا هُناكَ لِوَقْتٍ طَويلٍ; **she managed it with ~ ease/difficulty** اسْتَطاعَتْ فِعْلَهُ بِسُهولةٍ\ بِصُعوبةٍ شَديدةٍ; **it will take ~ doing** سَيَكونُ من الصَّعْبِ فِعْلُهُ; **we waited for ~ hours/days** انْتَظَرْنا لِساعاتٍ\ أيّامٍ طَويلةٍ; **candidates need to have ~ knowledge of computers** يَجِبُ أنْ يَكونَ المُتَقَدِّمونَ على قَدْرٍ من المَعْرِفةِ بالحَواسيبِ; **the award will go ~ way towards compensating her for her injuries** سَوْفَ تُساهِمُ الجائِزةُ إلى حَدٍّ ما في تَعْويضِها عن إصاباتِها 4 (a little, a slight) **the meeting did have ~ value** كانَ للاجْتِماعِ بَعْضُ القيمةِ فِعْلاً; **you must have ~ idea where the house is** لا بُدَّ أنّ لَدَيْكَ فِكْرةٌ ما عن مَكانِ البَيْتِ; **well that's ~ consolation anyway!** حَسَناً، في ذلكَ بَعْضُ العَزاءِ على أيِّ حالٍ!; **to ~ extent he's right** إلى حَدٍّ ما هو مُحِقٌّ 5 (pej) (an unspecified, unknown) شَيْء\ شَخْص ما; **she married ~ poet** تَزَوَّجَتْ شاعِراً ما; **he's doing ~ course** يَأْخُذُ دَوْرةً ما; **~ man came to the house** جاءَ رَجُلٌ ما إلى البَيْتِ 6 (infml) (a remarkable) **that was ~ car!** كانَتْ تِلْكَ سَيّارةً رائِعةً!; **that's ~ woman/man!** ذلكَ امْرَأةٌ رائِعةٌ\ رَجُلٌ رائِعٌ! 7 (infml) (not much) **~ help you are!** أَتُسَمّي هذه مُساعَدةً!; **'I'd like the work to be finished by Monday'—'~ hope!'** 'أُريدُ أنْ يَنْتَهِيَ العَمَلُ بِحُلولِ يَوْمِ الاثْنَيْنِ' — 'يَبْقى بَصيصٌ من الأمَلِ!'

B *pron* 1 (an unspecified amount or number) **I'd like ~ of those** أُريدُ بَعْضاً من تِلْكَ; **would you like ~?** هل تُريدُ بَعْضاً؟; **(do) have ~ more!** تَفَضَّل المَزيدَ!; من هذا؟ 2 (certain ones: in contrast to others) **~ (of them) are blue** بَعْضُهُمْ أزْرَقُ;

~ (of them) arrived early وَصَلَ بَعْضُهُمْ مُبَكِّراً; ~ say that ... يَقولُ البَعْضُ إنّ ...; I agree with ~ of what you say أتَّفِقُ مع بَعْضِ ما قُلْتَ

C *adv* **1** (approximately) حَوالَيْ, تَقْريباً; ~ 20 people/buses حَوالَيْ 20 شَخْصاً \ حافِلةً; that was ~ 20 years ago كانَ ذلك منذ ما يَقْرُبُ من 20 عاماً; ~ 70% of the population voted صَوَّتَ 70٪ من السُكّانِ تَقْريباً **2** (AmE) (infml) (a lot) كَثير; from here to Washington Street in 5 minutes; that's going ~ من هُنا إلى شارِعِ واشِنْطون في 5 دَقائِقَ؛ هذا إنْجازٌ كَبيرٌ

Idiom and then some! (infml) وَأكْثَر من ذلك بِكَثيرٍ!

somebody /ˈsʌmbədi/ *pron* **1** (unspecified person) شَخْص ما, أحَد; ~ came to see me جاءَ شَخْصٌ ما لِرُؤْيَتي; there's ~ at the door هُناكَ شَخْصٌ ما على البابِ; we need ~ who speaks Japanese نَحْتاجُ شَخْصاً يَتَكَلَّمُ اليابانيّةَ; ask John or Henry or ~ اِسْألْ جون أو هِنْري أو أيَّ شَخْصٍ; it's always ~ else's fault يَقَعُ اللَوْمُ دَوْماً على شَخْصٍ آخَرَ **2** (infml) (important person) he (really) thinks he's ~ يَظُنُّ نَفْسَهُ (حَقًّا) شَخْصاً مُهِمًّا; now she's a manager, she really is a ~ in the film industry هي الآنَ مُديرةٌ, وَهِيَ حَقًّا شَخْصيّةٌ مُهِمّةٌ في صِناعةِ الأفْلامِ

somehow /ˈsʌmhaʊ/, **someway** (AmE) /ˈsʌmweɪ/ *adv* **1** (also somehow or other) (by some means) بِطَريقةٍ أو بِأُخْرى, بِطَريقةٍ ما; we'll get there ~ سَنَصِلُ هُناكَ بِطَريقةٍ ما **2** (for some reason) لِسَبَبٍ ما; ~ it doesn't seem necessary لا يَبْدو هذا ضَروريًّا لِسَبَبٍ ما

someone /ˈsʌmwʌn/ *pron* ▸ **somebody**

someplace /ˈsʌmpleɪs/ *adv* (AmE) ▸ **somewhere**

somersault /ˈsʌməsɒlt/ **A** *n* شَقْلَبة; to do/turn a ~ تَشَقْلَبَ

B *vi* «gymnasts, vehicles» تَشَقْلَبَ

something /ˈsʌmθɪŋ/ **A** *pron* **1** (unspecified thing) شَيْء ما; ~ new/interesting شَيْءٌ جَديد \ مُثير للاهْتِمامِ; they need ~ to do/eat يَحْتاجونَ إلى شَيْءٍ يَفْعَلونَهُ \ يَأْكُلونَهُ; to say ~ قالَ شَيْئاً; ~ made him laugh شَيْءٌ ما جَعَلَهُ يَضْحَكُ; there's ~ wrong هُناكَ شَيْءٌ خَطَأٌ; there's ~ odd about her هُناكَ شَيْءٌ غَريبٌ فيها; there's ~ funny going on هُناكَ شَيْءٌ مُضْحِكٌ يَحْدُثُ; he said ~ or other before leaving قالَ شَيْئاً ما قبل أنْ يَرْحَلَ **2** (thing of importance, value etc) it proves ~ يُثْبِتُ شَيْئاً هامًّا; to make ~ of oneself *or* one's life حَقَّقَ \ أثْبَتَ ذاتَهُ; he got ~ out of it اِسْتَفادَ مِنْهُ; he is quite *or* really ~! هو حَقًّا شَخْصٌ مُثيرٌ للإعْجابِ!; their house/car is really ~! بَيْتُهُمْ مُبْهِرٌ \ سَيّارَتُهُمْ مُبْهِرةٌ حَقًّا!; there's ~ in what he says هُناكَ بَعْضُ الصِدْقِ فيما يَقولُ; you have ~ there! ما قُلْتَهُ جَديرٌ بالاهْتِمامِ!; she has a certain ~ لَدَيْها ميزةٌ ما; 'I've found the key'—'well that's ~' 'لَقَدْ وَجَدْتُ المِفْتاحَ' — 'حَسَناً, هذا شَيْءٌ جَيِّدٌ' **3** (forgotten, unknown name, amount etc) his name's Andy ~ اِسْمُهُ آنْدي شَيْءٍ ما; in twenty-~ عامَ ألْفَيْن وَشَيْءٍ ما; he's six foot ~ طولُهُ سِتّةُ أقْدامٍ وَكُسورٌ; she's gone shopping or ~ خَرَجَتْ للتَسَوُّقِ أو لِغَرَضٍ ما

B *adv* **1** (a bit) بِقَليلٍ, قَليلاً; ~ over/under $400 أكْثَر \ أقَلّ من 400 دولارٍ بِقَليلٍ **2** (infml) (a lot) it was blowing ~ awful *or* terrible كانَ يَهُبُّ بِشَكْلٍ فَظيعٍ

C (something of) *adv phr* (rather, quite) he is ~ of an actor/expert هو مُمَثِّلٌ مَوْهوبٌ \ خَبيرٌ نَوْعاً ما; she is ~ of an expert on ... هي خَبيرةٌ بَعْضَ الشَيْءِ في ...; it was ~ of a surprise/mystery كانَ أمْراً مُفاجِئاً \ غامِضاً بِدَرَجةٍ كَبيرةٍ

sometime /ˈsʌmtaɪm/ *adv* في وَقْتٍ \ يَوْم ما; I'll tell you about it ~, ~ I'll tell you about it سَأُحَدِّثُكَ عَنْهُ يَوْماً ما

sometimes /ˈsʌmtaɪmz/ *adv* في بَعْضِ الأحْيانِ, أحْياناً

someway /ˈsʌmweɪ/ *adv* ▸ **somehow**

somewhat /ˈsʌmwɒt/ *adv* <surprised, annoyed> بَعْضَ, إلى حَدٍّ ما, نَوْعاً ما, الشَيْءِ

somewhere /ˈsʌmweə/ *adv* **1** (some place) مَكان ما; I read ~ that ... قَرَأْتُ في مَكانٍ ما أنّ ...; he needs ~ to live in Cairo يَحْتاجُ إلى مَكانٍ ما لِيَعيشَ فيهِ في القاهِرةِ; it's ~ downstairs/in the office هو في مَكانٍ ما في الطابَقِ السُفْليِّ \ المَكْتَبِ; she's ~ about *or* around هي في مَكانٍ ما قَريبٍ من هُنا; let's go ~ else دَعْنا نَذْهَبُ إلى مَكانٍ آخَرَ; it's ~ or other in the garage هو في مَكانٍ ما في الجَراجِ; they live in Manchester or ~ يَعيشونَ في مانْشِسْتَر أو في مَكانٍ ما **2** (in approximations) ~ between 50 and 100 people يَتَراوَحُ بين 50 وَ100 شَخْصٍ; ~ around 10 a.m./$500 حَوالَيْ 10 صَباحاً \ 500 دولارٍ; he's ~ in his sixties هو في السِتّيناتِ من عُمْرِهِ

son /sʌn/ *n* ابْن (أَبْناء ,بَنون)

sonata /səˈnɑːtə/ *n* (*pl* **sonatas**) سوناتا (قِطْعة موسيقيّة مَكْتوبة لِآلَةٍ أو آلَتَيْنِ)

song /sɒŋ/ *n* 1 (singer's) أُغْنِيّة (أَغانيٌّ); **to sing a ~** غَنّى أُغْنِيّةً; **to burst into ~** بَدَأَ بالغِناءِ 2 (bird's) تَغْريد ,شَدْو

(Idiom) **for a song** (infml) بِسِعْرٍ زَهيدٍ ,بِسِعْرِ التُرابِ

songbird /ˈsɒŋbɜːd/ *n* طائِر مُغَرِّد \ صَدّاح

songwriter /ˈsɒŋraɪtə/ *n* شاعِر غِنائيّ ,مُؤَلِّف أَغانٍ

sonic /ˈsɒnɪk/ *adj* ‹*vibration, measurement*› صَوْتيّ

sonic boom *n* دَويّ اخْتِراقِ حاجِزِ الصَوْتِ

son-in-law /ˈsʌnɪnlɔː/ *n* (*pl* **sons-in-law**) صِهْر ,زَوْج الابْنةِ (أَصْهار)

sonnet /ˈsɒnɪt/ *n* سونيتّة (قَصيدة من أَرْبَعة عَشَرَ بَيْتاً)

son of a bitch A *n* 1 (pej) ابْن العاهِرةِ \ الساقِطةِ 2 (jocular) وَغْد 3 (difficult task) عَمَل صَعْب \ شاقّ; B *excl* يا لَلْعَجَبِ!

soon /suːn/ *adv* 1 (shortly) سَريعاً ,عاجِلاً ,حالاً ,قَريباً; **he left ~ afterwards** غادَرَ بعد ذلك بِقَليل; **~ after midday** بعد مُنْتَصَفِ النَهارِ بِفَتْرةٍ وَجيزةٍ; **it ~ became clear that she wasn't coming back** سُرْعان ما اتَّضَحَ أنّها لن تَعودَ; **it will ~ be five years since he died** عَمّا قَريبٍ سَيَكونُ قد مَرَّ على وَفاتِهِ خَمْسُ سِنينَ; **see you ~!** أَراكَ عَمّا قَريبٍ!; **no ~er had I hung the washing out than it started raining** لم أَكَدْ أَنْشُرُ الغَسيلَ حتّى بَدأَت تُمْطِرُ 2 (quickly) قَريباً ,بِسُرْعةٍ; **you'll find out ~ enough** سَتَكْتَشِفُ عَمّا قَريبٍ; **as ~ as possible** بِأَسْرَعِ ما يُمْكِنُ; **~er or later** عاجِلاً أم آجِلاً; **the ~er the better** خَيْرُ البِرِّ عاجِلُهُ; **the ~er we leave, the ~er we'll get there** كُلَّما أَسْرَعْنا في الرَحيلِ، كُلّما وَصَلْنا باكِراً إلى هُناك; **it's not going to happen anytime ~** لَن يَحْدُثَ هذا في أَيِّ وَقْتٍ قَريبٍ; **as ~ as he arrives** بِمُجَرَّدِ أَنْ يَصِلَ; **I spoke too ~!** كُنْتُ مُخْطِئاً!; **Friday at the ~est** الجُمْعة على أَقْرَبِ تَقْديرٍ; **and not a moment too ~!** في آخِرِ لَحْظةٍ! 3 (indicating preference) **I would just as ~ eat now as later** سِيّانِ عِنْدي أَنْ آكُلَ الآنَ أَم لاحِقاً; **he would ~er die than ask for help** يُفَضِّلُ المَوْتَ على طَلَبِ المُساعَدةِ; **~er him than me!** [أُفَضِّلُ أَنْ يُصيبَهُ الحَظُّ العاثِرُ قبل أَنْ يُصيبَني!]

(Idiom) **no sooner said than done** تَمَّ التَنْفيذُ على الفَوْرِ

soot /sʊt/ *n* سُخام ,سِناج (أَسْنِجة ,سُنُج)

soothe /suːð/ *vt* 1 (to calm) هَدَّأَ ‹*nerves, a baby*› 2 (to ease) لَطَّفَ ,خَفَّفَ ,سَكَّنَ ‹*pain, sunburn, a cough*›

soothing /ˈsuːðɪŋ/ *adj* 1 (reassuring) ‹*music, voice*› مُهَدِّئ, مُسَكِّن ‹*words*› مُطَمْئِن 2 (easing) ‹*cream, syrup*› مُريح, مُخَفِّف للأَلَمِ ,مُلَطِّف

sophisticated /səˈfɪstɪkeɪtɪd/ *adj* 1 (elegant) ‹*tastes, restaurant*› أَنيق ,راقٍ 2 (complex) ‹*technology, argument*› مُتَقَدِّم ,مُتَطَوِّر

sophistication /səˌfɪstɪˈkeɪʃ(ə)n/ *n* 1 (complexity) تَقَدُّم ,تَطَوُّر 2 (understanding) (تَطَوُّرات) تَمَرُّس ,حُنْكة 3 (worldliness) رُقيّ

sophomore /ˈsɒfəmɔː/ *n* (AmE) [طالِب كُلّيّةٍ بالسَنةِ الثانيةِ]

soporific /ˌsɒpəˈrɪfɪk/ *adj* ‹*drug, play*› يَبْعَثُ على النُعاسِ ,مُنَوِّم

sopping /ˈsɒpɪŋ/ *adj* (also **sopping wet**) ‹*clothes, hair*› مَنْقوع \ شَديد البَلَل ,مُشَبَّع بالماءِ

soprano /səˈprɑːnəʊ/ *n* (*pl* **sopranos**) (voice, instrument) سوبرانو (طَبَقة صَوْتيّة مُرْتَفِعة); (person) مُغَنّي سوبرانو

sorbet /ˈsɔːbeɪ/ *n* [عَصير فاكِهةٍ مُثَلَّج]

sorcerer /ˈsɔːs(ə)rə/ *n* ساحِر (سَحَرة)

sordid /ˈsɔːdɪd/ *adj* 1 (ignoble) ‹*story, affair*› خَسيس ,حَقير, مُثير للاشْمِئْزاز ,دَنيء 2 (squalid) ‹*conditions, hovel*› مُزْرٍ ,قَذِر

sore /sɔː/ A *adj* (**sorer**, **sorest**) 1 (painful) ‹*eyes, gums*› مُلْتَهِب, مُؤْلِم; **I have a ~ throat** أُعاني من احْتِقانٍ بالحَلْقِ 2 (AmE) (infml) (angry) غاضِب ,مُغْتاظ B *n* قَرْحة (قُرَح) ,الْتِهاب (الْتِهابات)

sorghum /ˈsɔːgəm/ *n* سورْغَم (نَبات يُشْبِهُ الذُرةَ)

sorority /səˈrɒrɪti/ *n* (*pl* **sororities**) 1 (AmE) (in colleges) رابِطة جَمْعيّة \ رابِطة نِسائيّة 2 (sisterhood) اتِّحاد للطالِباتِ ,للفَتَياتِ

sorrow /ˈsɒrəʊ/ *n* حُزْن (أَحْزان) ,أَسًى

sorrowful /ˈsɒrəʊfʊl/ *adj* ‹*expression, glance, voice*› حَزين (حَزانى), مَهْموم

sorry /ˈsɒri/ A *adj* (**sorrier**, **sorriest**) 1 (in apologies) آسِف, مُتَأَسِّف; **I'm very/terribly ~** أَنا آسِفٌ جِدًّا; **I'm ~ I'm late**

نَأْسَفُ على التَّأْخيرِ ;we are ~ for the delay آسِفٌ أنّي تَأَخَّرْتُ; I'm ~ to bother you but ... آسِف على الإزْعاجِ وَلَكِنْ ... ; ~ about that! عَفْواً على ذلك! ; to say ~ اعْتَذَرَ **2** (expressing regret) (حَزانى) حَزين ,شاعِر بالأَسى \ بالأَسَفِ; I was ~ to hear that you've been ill تَأَسَّفْتُ لِسَماعِ أَنَّكَ كُنْتَ مَريضاً; I'm so ~ about your father أَشْعُرُ بالأَسى لِما حَدَثَ لأَبيكَ; I felt ~ about it afterwards نَدِمْتُ على ذلك فيما بَعْدُ; will you be ~ to leave? هل سَتَحْزَنُ عِنْدَما تَرْحَلُ؟; no one will be ~ to see him go! لن يَأْسَفَ أَحَدٌ عَلَيْهِ عِنْدَما يَرْحَلُ! **3** (expressing pity) to be/feel ~ for sb شَعَرَ بالأَسى على شَخْصٍ; to feel ~ for oneself حَزِنَ على نَفْسِه **4** (pathetic, deplorable) ‹*state, sight, business*› بائِس ,مُحْزِن ,مُؤْسِف; this is a ~ state of affairs! هذه هي حالةٌ مُؤْسِفةٌ!

B *excl* **1** (in apologies) عُذْراً ,عَفْواً ,آسِف **2** (asking for a repeat) ~? عَفْواً؟ **3** (correcting oneself) so we have two, ~, three options وَهَكَذا لَدَيْنا خِياران، عَفْواً، ثَلاثةُ خِياراتٍ **4** (excusing oneself) ~, could I get past? عَفْواً، هل يُمْكِنُني أنْ أَمُرَّ؟

sort /sɔːt/ **A** *n* **1** (kind) (أَنْواع) نَوْع ,(أَصْناف) صِنْف ,(صُنوف); all ~s of people/reasons كُلّ أَنْواعِ البَشَرِ \ الأَسْبابِ; books, records — that ~ of thing كُتُب وَأُسْطُوانات — وَمِثْل هذه الأَشْياءِ; you know the ~ of thing I mean أَنْتَ تَعْلَمُ ما الّذي أَقْصِدُهُ; what ~ of person would do such a thing? أَيّ صِنْفٍ من النّاسِ يَفْعَلُ مِثْلَ هذا الشَّيْءِ؟; any ~ of knife will do أَيُّ سِكّينٍ سَيَفي بالغَرَضِ; it's a strange ~ of honeymoon هذا شَهْرُ عَسَلٍ من نَوْعٍ غَريبٍ; that's the ~ of food I like ذلك هو نَوْعُ الطَّعامِ الّذي أُحِبُّهُ; this must be some ~ of joke لا بُدَّ أَنّ هذه مِزْحةٌ من نَوْعٍ ما; the same ~ of thing نَفْس الشَّيْءِ; something of that *or* the ~ شَيْء من هذا القَبيلِ; I didn't say anything of the ~! لم أَقُلْ أَيَّ شَيْءٍ من هذا القَبيلِ!; 'I'll pay' — 'you'll do nothing of the ~!' 'سَأَدْفَعُ' — 'لن تَفْعَلَ شَيْئاً كَهَذا!' **2** (infml) (type of person) (صُنوف ,أَصْناف) صِنْف; I know his ~ أَعْرِفُ هذا الصِّنْفَ من البَشَرِ; he's a good ~ هو شَخْصٌ طَيِّبٌ; we see all ~s here نَرى كُلّ أَصْنافِ البَشَرِ هُنا

B (of sorts, of a sort) *adv phr* at least I have a bed of ~s *or* of a ~ على الأَقَلِّ لَدَيَّ سَريرٌ من نَوْعٍ ما; a compromise of ~s was reached تَمَّ التَوَصُّلُ إلى اتِّفاقٍ من نَوْعٍ ما

C (sort of) *adv phr* (infml) **1** (a bit) إلى حَدٍّ ما ,نَوْعاً ما; 'were you disappointed?' — '~ of' 'هل كُنْتَ مُحْبَطاً؟' — 'نَوْعاً ما' **2** (in a way) it's ~ of bluey green لَوْنُهُ يُشْبِهُ الأَخْضَرَ المائِلَ إلى الزُّرْقةِ; it just ~ of happened حَدَثَ ذلك فَجْأةً نَوْعاً ما; it's ~ of a secret هو سِرٌّ إلى حَدٍّ ما

D *vt* **1** (to classify) (فَرْز ;i) فَرَزَ ,صَنَّفَ ‹*mail, waste*›; I ~ed the books into piles قَسَّمْتُ الكُتُبَ في أَكْوامٍ; to ~ the good fruit from the bad فَصَلَ الفاكِهةَ الجَيِّدةَ عن الرَديئةِ **2** (to order) رَتَّبَ ‹*data, a list*› **3** (BrE) (infml) (to resolve) (حَلّ ;u) حَلَّ ,سَوّى; that's ~ed تَمَّ التَعامُلُ مع ذلك الأَمْرِ

(Idiom) to be/feel out of sorts (unwell) كانَ مُتَوَعِّكاً \ شَعَرَ بِوَعْكةٍ; (upset) كانَ مُتَعَكِّرَ المِزاجِ \ شَعَرَ بِتَعَكُّرِ المِزاجِ

(Phrasal verbs) **sort out** **A** ~ [sth] out, ~ out [sth] **1** (to resolve) سَوّى [شَيْئاً] ‹*a problem, an issue*›; it's their responsibility to ~ the problem out إنّها مَسْؤوليّتُهُمْ أنْ يَحُلّوا المُشْكِلةَ **2** (to put in order) رَتَّبَ [شَيْئاً] ‹*a cupboard, one's desk, affairs*›; you need to ~ out your priorities تَحْتاجُ إلى أنْ تُرَتِّبَ أَوْلَوِيّاتِكَ **3** (to arrange, organize) رَتَّبَ [شَيْئاً] ‹*the details, accommodation*›; have you ~ed out who's coming to pick me up? هل رَتَّبْتَ مَنْ سَيُقِلُّني؟ **B** ~ out [sth] **1** (to separate out) فَرَزَ [شَيْئاً] ‹*clothes, photos*›; to ~ out the truth from the lies مَيَّزَ بين الحَقيقةِ والأَكاذيبِ **2** (to establish) تَحَقَّقَ من [شَيْءٍ]; we're still trying to ~ out what happened ما زِلْنا نُحاوِلُ التَحَقُّقَ مِمّا حَدَثَ **C** ~ [sb] out (infml) **1** (to help) «receptionist» ساعَدَ [شَخْصاً]; the doctor will soon ~ you out سَيَحُلُّ الطَبيبُ مُشْكِلَتَكَ حالاً **2** (to punish) عاقَبَ [شَخْصاً]

• **sort through**: ~ through [sth] تَفَحَّصَ [شَيْئاً] ‹*a pile, papers*›

sort code, sorting code *n* رَقْم \ رَمْز البَنْك (رَقْم للتَعْريفِ بِأَفْرُعِ البُنوكِ)

sortie /'sɔːtiː/ *n* **1** (Mil) هُجوم خاطِف \ مُباغِت (لِفَكِّ الحِصارِ) **2** (hum) رِحْلة قَصيرة

SOS /ɛsəʊ'ɛs/ *n* [إشارة اسْتِغاثةٍ]

so-so /səʊ'səʊ/ (infml) **A** *adj* مَقْبول ,لَيْسَ جَيِّداً أو سَيِّئاً ,بَيْنَ بَيْنَ **B** *adv* بِشَكْلٍ مَقْبولٍ

soufflé /'suːfleɪ/ *n* سوفْليه (كَعْكة خَفيفة)

sought /sɔːt/ *past tense, past participle* ▸ **seek**

sought after *adj* ‹brand, area› مَرْغوب, مَطْلوب

soul /səʊl/ *n* ① (of a person) روح (mf; أَرْواح), نَفْس (f; نُفوس, أَنْفُس) ② (also **soul music**) [u] موسيقى السول

(Idiom) **it's good for the soul** هو بَلْسَمٌ للروح

soul-destroying /ˈsəʊldɪˌstrɔɪɪŋ/ *adj* ‹work, job› روتينيّ قاتِل

soulful /ˈsəʊlfʊl/ *adj* ‹eyes, expression› مُفْعَم بالعاطِفةِ, جيّاش العاطِفةِ

soulmate /ˈsəʊlmeɪt/ *n* تَوْأم الروح

soul-searching /ˈsəʊlsɜːtʃɪŋ/ *n* بَحْث عن الذاتِ, مُراجعة النَّفْسِ

sound /saʊnd/ **A** *n* ① [u] (Phys) صَوْت; **to fly at the speed of sound** طارَ بِسُرْعةِ الصَوْتِ ② (of voices, footsteps, gunfire) صوت (أَصْوات); **the engine is making a grating ~** يُصْدِرُ المُحَرِّكُ صَوْتاً خَشِناً; **without a ~** بِدونِ صَوْتٍ; **there was not a ~ to be heard** لم يَكُنْ هُناكَ صَوْتٌ يُسْمَعُ ③ [u] (in broadcasting, movies) صَوْت ④ (impression conveyed) مَغْزًى (مَغازٍ), مَضْمون (مَضامينُ); **I don't like the ~ of that!** ذلك أَمْرٌ غَيْرُ مُطَمْئِنٍ!; **you've got enough problems, by the ~ of it** على ما يَبْدو لديكَ ما يَكْفيكَ من المَشاكِلِ ⑤ (distinctive style) أُسْلوب (أَساليبُ); **the Motown ~** أُسْلوب موتاوْن ⑥ (stretch of water) مَضيق

B *adj* ① (healthy) ‹heart› سَليم, في صِحةٍ جَيِّدةٍ; **to be of ~ mind** كانَ سَليمَ العَقْلِ ② (structurally) ‹building, structure› في حالةٍ جَيِّدةٍ ③ (well-founded) ‹argument, reasons› سَليم ④ (reliable, competent) ‹policy, judgement› سَليم; **he gave me very ~ advice** أَعْطاني نَصيحةً سَديدةً جِدًّا; **you can trust him, he's very ~** يُمْكِنُكَ أنْ تَثِقَ بِهِ، فَهُوَ كُفْءٌ جِدًّا; **all our products are environmentally ~** كُلُّ مُنْتَجاتُنا سَليمةٌ بيئيًّا ⑤ (financially secure) ‹investment, economy› سَليم; **she got the business on a ~ footing** وَضَعَتِ الشَرِكةَ على مَسارٍ سَليمٍ ⑥ (deep) ‹sleep› عَميق; **to be a ~ sleeper** كانَ يَنامُ بِعُمْقٍ ⑦ (thorough) ‹beating, thrashing› شَديد

C *adv* **to be ~ asleep** كانَ مُسْتَغْرِقاً في نَوْمِهِ

D *vt* ① ‹a siren, foghorn› اسْتَخْدَمَ, اسْتَعْمَلَ; **to ~ one's horn** اسْتَعْمَلَ بوق سَيّارَتِهِ; **to ~ the alarm** شَغَّلَ جَرَسَ الإنْذارِ ② ‹a trumpet› نَفَخَ (a; نَفْخ في); عَزَفَ (i; عَزْف) ‹the retreat› ③ (to express) أَطْلَقَ, وَجَّهَ ‹a warning›; **to ~ a note of caution** أَطْلَقَ تَحْذيراً ④ (to pronounce) نَطَقَ (u; نُطْق) ‹a letter›

E *vi* ① (of things heard) «voice, music» بَدا (u; بُدوّ, بَداء); **your voice ~s like your mother's** صَوْتُكَ يُشْبِهُ صَوْتَ أُمِّكَ; **that tune ~s familiar** تَبْدو تِلْكَ النَغَمةُ مَأْلوفةً ② (to seem) «idea, person» بَدا (u; بُدوّ, بَداء); **it ~s like fun!** يَبْدو هذا مُمْتِعاً!; **she ~s like a nice person** يَبْدو أنَّها إنسانةٌ لَطيفةٌ; **it ~s as though he needs help** يَبْدو الأَمْرُ كَما لو أَنَّهُ يَحْتاجُ إلى مُساعَدةٍ; **it doesn't ~ to me as if she's interested** لا يَبْدو لي أَنَّها مُهْتَمّةٌ; **you make it ~ interesting** تَجْعَلُهُ يَبْدو مُشَوِّقاً; **'how about eating out?' — '~s good to me'** 'ما رَأْيُكَ في تَناوُلِ الطَعامِ خارِجَ البَيْتِ؟' — 'هذه فِكْرةٌ جَيِّدةٌ بالنِسْبةِ لي' ③ (to make a noise) «alarm, trumpet» انْطَلَقَ

(Phrasal verbs) **sound off** (infml) جَهَرَ بِرَأْيِهِ

• **sound out**: ~ out [sb], ~ [sb] out اسْتَطْلَعَ رَأْيَ [شَخْص] ‹a colleague, potential investor›

sound barrier *n* حاجِز \ جِدار الصَوْتِ; **to break the sound barrier** اخْتَرَقَ حاجِزَ الصَوْتِ

sound bite *n* مُقْتَطَف صَوْتيّ

sound card *n* بِطاقة صَوْتٍ

sound effects *n pl* مُؤَثِّرات صَوْتيّة

sound engineer *n* مُهَنْدِس صَوْتٍ

sounding /ˈsaʊndɪŋ/ **A** *n* ① (of depth) سَبْرُ الأَغْوار (قِياس الأَعْماقِ بِواسِطةِ الصَدى) ② [u] (of trumpets, etc) صَوْت (من آلةٍ موسيقيّةٍ)

B (**soundings**) *n pl* (of opinions) اسْتِطْلاعات لِلرَأْيِ; **he took ~s about the possibility of raising the tax** أَجْرى اسْتِطْلاعاتٍ لِلرَأْيِ حول إمْكانيّةِ زِيادةِ الضَرائِبِ

C (**sounding**) *in combination* **an English-~ name** اسْم يَبْدو إنْجليزيًّا

soundly /ˈsaʊndli/ *adv* ① ‹to sleep› بِعُمْقٍ ② ‹to defeat, beat› بِشَكْلٍ ساحِقٍ, تَماماً

sound plural *n* جَمْع سالِم

soundproof /ˈsaʊndpruːf/ **A** *adj* ‹room, walls› عازِل لِلصَوْتِ

B *vt* (use) ‹a room, studio› عَزَلَ الصَوْتَ في

sound system *n* نِظام صَوْتيّ

soundtrack /ˈsaʊndtrak/ *n* موسيقى فيلْم

soup /suːp/ *n* مَرَق (شُرَب) شُرْبة (أَحْسِية) حَساء

soup kitchen *n* تَكِيّة (مَكان لِإطْعام الفُقَراءِ بالمَجّانِ)

soup plate *n* طَبَق حَساءٍ \ شُرْبة

soup spoon *n* مِلْعَقة حَساءٍ \ شُرْبة

sour /saʊə/ **A** *adj* (**sourer**, **sourest**) **1** (acidic) <*cherry, taste*> حامِض **2** (bad) <*milk, cream*> فاسِد **3** (bad-tempered) <*expression, note*> فَجّ (فِجاج) فَظّ (أَفْظاظ)

B *vt* **1** حَمَّض <*cream, a drink*> **2** عَكَّر <*an atmosphere, a mood*>

source /sɔːs/ *n* **1** (origin, cause) مَصْدَر (مَصادِرُ) مَنْبَع (مَنابِعُ) سَبَب (أَسْباب); **you must declare all ~s of income** يَجِبُ أَنْ تُعْلِنَ عن كُلِّ مَصادِرِ دَخْلِكَ **2** (of information) مَصْدَر (مَصادِرُ)

sourdough /ˈsaʊədəʊ/ *n* عَجينة مُتَخَمِّرة

south /saʊθ/ **A** *n* **1** (compass direction) جَنوب **2** (**the South**) (part of the world, a country) الجَنوب **3** (in US history) (**the South**) جَنوب الوِلاياتِ المُتَّحِدةِ الأَمْريكيّة (أثناء الحَرْبِ الأَهْلِيّة)

B *adj* <*coast, wind*> جَنوبيّ

C *adv* (to the south) <*to face, move*> نحو \ بِاتِّجاهِ الجَنوبِ (on the southern side) <*to lie, live*> في النّاحِيةِ الجَنوبيّةِ; **they live ~ of the river** يَسْكُنونَ في النّاحِيةِ الجَنوبيّةِ من النَّهْرِ

South Africa *pr n* جَنوب إفْريقِيا

South African *n, adj* جَنوب إفْريقيّ

South America *pr n* أَمْريكا الجَنوبيّة

South American *n, adj* أَمْريكيّ جَنوبيّ

southbound /ˈsaʊθbaʊnd/ *adj* <*lane, train*> مُتَّجِه جَنوباً

South Carolina *pr n* كارولايْنا الجَنوبيّة

South Carolinian *pr n, adj* [(شَخْص) من كارولايْنا الجَنوبيّةِ]

South Dakota *pr n* داكوتا الجَنوبيّة

South Dakotan *pr n, adj* [(شَخْص) من داكوتا الجَنوبيّةِ]

south-east /saʊθˈiːst/ **A** *n* **1** (compass direction) جَنوب شَرْقيّ **2** (also **the South East**) (of a country) الجَنوب الشَّرْقيّ

B *adj* <*coast, wind*> جَنوبيّ شَرْقيّ

C *adv* <*to move, travel*> نحو \ بِاتِّجاهِ الجَنوبِ الشَّرْقيِّ

south-easterly /saʊθˈiːst(ə)li/ **A** *adj* <*direction, wind*> جَنوبيّ شَرْقيّ

B *n* (*pl* **south-easterlies**) رِياح جَنوبيّة شَرْقيّة

south-eastern /saʊθˈiːst(ə)n/ *adj* <*accent, town*> جَنوبيّ شَرْقيّ

southerly /ˈsʌðəli/ **A** *adj* <*coast, wind*> جَنوبيّ

B *n* (*pl* **southerlies**) رِياح جَنوبيّة

southern /ˈsʌð(ə)n/ *adj* <*coast, accent*> جَنوبيّ

south-facing /ˈsaʊθfeɪsɪŋ/ *adj* <*window, balcony, room*> بِاتِّجاهِ الجَنوبِ

South Korea *pr n* كوريا الجَنوبيّة

South Korean *n, adj* كوريّ جَنوبيّ

South Pole *pr n* (**the South Pole**) القُطْب الجَنوبيّ

South Sudan *pr n* جَنوب السودانِ

South Sudanese *n, adj* سودانيّ جَنوبيّ

southward /ˈsaʊθwəd/ **A** *adj* <*expansion, journey*> نحو \ بِاتِّجاهِ الجَنوبِ

B *adv* (also **southwards**) <*to travel, move*> نحو \ بِاتِّجاهِ الجَنوبِ, جَنوباً

south-west /saʊθˈwɛst/ **A** *n* **1** (compass direction) جَنوب غَرْبيّ **2** (also **the South West**) (of a country) الجَنوب الغَرْبيّ

B *adj* <*coast, wind*> جَنوبيّ غَرْبيّ

C *adv* <*to face, move*> نحو \ بِاتِّجاهِ الجَنوبِ الغَرْبيِّ

south-westerly /ˌsaʊθˈwɛst(ə)li/ **A** *adj* <*city, wind*> جَنوبيّ غَرْبيّ

B *n* (*pl* **south-westerlies**) رِياح جَنوبيّة غَرْبيّة

south-western /ˌsaʊθˈwɛst(ə)n/ *adj* <*accent, town*> جَنوبيّ غَرْبيّ

souvenir /ˌsuːvəˈnɪə/ *n* تَذْكار (تَذْكارات)

sovereign /ˈsɒvrɪn/ **A** *n* **1** (monarch) عاهِل (مُلوك) مَلِك, (عَواهِلُ) **2** (coin) سُفْرِن (جُنَيْه إنْجْليزيّ ذَهَبيّ قَديم)

B *adj* <*state*> ذو سِيادةٍ; <*rights*> سِياديّ

sovereign debt **A** *n* دَيْن سِياديّ;

B *adj before n* <*crisis, rating*> الدُّيونِ السِّياديّةِ

sovereignty /ˈsɒvrɪnti/ *n* سِيادة

sovereign wealth fund *n* صُنْدوق ثَرْوةٍ سِياديّةٍ

Soviet /ˈsəʊviət, ˈsɒviət/ (Hist) **A** *adj* ‹*Russia, bloc*› سوفْياتيّ (سوفْيات)

B *n* (**the Soviets** *n pl*) السوفْيات

Soviet Union *pr n* (**the Soviet Union**) الاتّحاد السوفْياتيّ

sow¹ /saʊ/ *n* أُنْثى الخِنْزير

sow² /səʊ/ *vt* (*past tense* **sowed**; *past participle* **sowed** or **sown**)

1 بَذَرَ (u; بَذْر) ‹*seeds, corn*›; **to ~ the seeds in the ground** بَذَرَ الحُبوبَ في الأَرْضِ **2** زَرَعَ (a; زَرْع) ‹*a field, flowerbed*›; **to ~ a field with wheat** زَرَعَ حَقْلاً قَمْحاً **3** (to cause) أَثار ‹*doubt, discontent*›

sown /səʊn/ *past participle* ▸ **sow²**

soya /ˈsɔɪə/ *n* صويا

soya milk *n* حليب الصويا

soya sauce, **soy sauce** *n* صَلْصة الصويا

soybean, **soya bean** *n* فول الصويا

spa /spɑː/ *n* **1** (town) مُنْتَجَع للمِياهِ المَعْدِنِيَّة **2** (health club) مُنْتَجَع صِحّيّ

space /speɪs/ **A** *n* **1** [u] (room) مَكان ,حَيِّز ,مساحة; **to take up little/a lot of ~** شَغَل حَيِّزاً صَغيراً \ كَبيراً; **the flat has plenty of storage ~** الشَقّةُ بِها مِساحةٌ كَبيرةٌ للتَخْزين; **500 square metres of office ~** 500 مِتْرٍ مُرَبَّعٍ مَكاتِب في مِساحةِ; **I need my ~** أُريدُ بَعْضَ الخُصوصيّةِ; **to invade sb's personal ~** اعْتَدى على خُصوصيّةِ شَخْصٍ **2** (gap) مِساحة; **sign in the ~ provided** وَقِّعْ في المساحةِ المُخَصَّصةِ **3** (area of land) مِساحات مَفْتوحة \ عامّة; **open/public ~s** مِساحات **4** (interval of time) فَتْرة (فَتَرات); **in the ~ of five minutes** في فَتْرةِ خَمْسِ دَقائِقَ; **in a short ~ of time** في فَتْرةٍ زَمَنيّةٍ قَصيرةٍ **5** (in text) مَسافة **6** [u] (outer space) فَضاء

B *vt* باعَدَ (بين) ‹*plants, holes*›; **the posts were ~d 10 metres apart** تُرِكَتْ مَسافةُ 10 أَمْتارٍ بين الأَعْمِدةِ

Phrasal verb **space out**: **~ out [sth], ~ [sth] out** باعَدَ بين [شَيْءٍ] ‹*plants, events*›

space age *n* عَصْر الفَضاءِ

space bar *n* مِفْتاح المَسافةِ (على لَوْحةِ المَفاتيح)

spacecraft /ˈspeɪskrɑːft/ *n* (*pl* **spacecraft**) مَرْكَبة فَضائيّة

spaced out /speɪst ˈaʊt/ *adj* (infml) ‹*teenagers, junkies*› غَيْر واعٍ, فاقِد للتَرْكيز

space exploration *n* اسْتِكْشاف الفَضاءِ

spaceman /ˈspeɪsman/ *n* (*pl* **-men**) رائِد \ رَجُل الفَضاءِ

spaceship /ˈspeɪsʃɪp/ *n* سَفينة فَضائيّة

space shuttle *n* مَكوك فَضائيّ

space station *n* مَحَطّة فَضائيّة

spacesuit /ˈspeɪssuːt/ *n* بَدْلة فَضاءٍ

spacing /ˈspeɪsɪŋ/ *n* تَباعُد الكَلِماتِ \ الأَسْطُرِ

spacious /ˈspeɪʃəs/ *adj* ‹*house, room*› رَحْب ,واسِع ,فسيح

spade /speɪd/ *n* **1** (implement) مِسْحاة ,(مَجارِفُ) مِجْرَفة (مَساحٍ), جاروف (جَواريفُ) **2** (**spades** *n pl*) (in cards) بَسْتونيّ

Idioms **to call a spade a spade** سَمّى الأَشْياءَ بِمُسَمَّياتِها \ بِأَسْمائِها; **in spades** بِوَفْرةٍ ,بِغَزارةٍ; **he has charm in ~s, but little integrity** لَدَيْهِ جاذِبيّةٌ فائِقةٌ، ولَكِنْ تَنْقُصُهُ النَزاهةُ

spaghetti /spəˈɡɛti/ *n* مَعْكَرونة أَعْوادٍ ,سْباغيتي

Spain /speɪn/ *pr n* إِسْبانيا

spam /spam/ **A** *n* **1** (in emails) بَريد مُزْعِج \ غَيْر مَرْغوبٍ فيه, **2** ®(food) سْبام [لَحْم خِنْزيرٍ مَحْفوظ]

B *vt* (**-mm-**) أَرْسَلَ سْبام \ بَريداً مُزْعِجاً إلى ‹*an organization, a newsgroup, person*›

spammer /ˈspamə/ *n* مُرْسِل السْبام \ الرَسائِلِ المُزْعِجة

spamming /ˈspamɪŋ/ *n* إِرْسال السْبام \ الرَسائِلِ المُزْعِجةِ

span /span/ **A** *n* **1** (of time) فَتْرة (فَتَرات), مُدّة (مُدَد) **2** (length) اتِّساع (اتِّساعات) ,امْتِداد (امْتِدادات)

B *vt* (*present participle* **-nn-**) **1** (physically) قَطَعَ ,(عَبْرَ) امْتَدَّ (a; قَطْع) ‹*a valley, river*› **2** (fig) غَطّى ,(عَبْرَ) امْتَدَّ ‹*a range, the world*›

Spaniard /ˈspanjəd/ *n* إِسْبانيّ (إسْبان)

spaniel /ˈspanjəl/ *n* سْبانيل (نَوْع من الكِلابِ)

Spanish /ˈspanɪʃ/ **A** *adj* ‹*ambassador, food, lesson*› إِسْبانيّ (إسْبان); **he is ~** هو إِسْبانيٌّ

B *n* **1** (citizens) **the ~** الإِسْبان ,الإِسْبانيّونَ **2** (language) (اللُغة) الإِسْبانيّة

Spanish omelette *n* أومْليت إسْبانيّ

spank /spaŋk/ *vt* ضَرَبَ (شَخْصاً على مُؤَخَّرَتِهِ للتَّأْديبِ) <*a bottom, child*>

spanner /ˈspanə/ *n* (BrE) مِفْتاح رَبْطٍ; **an adjustable ~** مِفْتاح إنْجليزيّ

spar /spɑː/ *vi* (**-rr-**) 1 (to fight) «boxers» تَناوَشَ 2 (to argue) «politicians» تَجادَلَ

spare /spɛː/ **A** *adj* 1 (surplus) <*cash, capacity, copy*> احْتِياطيّ, فائِض, زائِد, إضافيّ; **I have a ~ ticket** لَدَيَّ تَذْكِرةٌ إضافيّةٌ; **how much ~ cash do you have?** كم لَدَيْكَ من المالِ الفائِضِ عن حاجَتِكَ؟ 2 (in reserve) <*bulb, fuse, wheel*> احْتِياطيّ 3 (not in use) <*land, chair*> فارِغ; **there's a ~ seat next to me** هُناكَ كُرْسِيٌّ فارِغٌ بِجواري 4 (in physique) <*build*> نَحيف (نِحاف, نُحَفاءُ); **a tall, ~ man** رَجُل طَويل نَحيف 5 (BrE) (infml) (wild) غاضِب; **to go ~** جُنَّ جُنونُهُ

B *n* (part) قِطْعة غِيارٍ; **the equipment comes with a complete set of ~s** يَأْتي الجِهازُ مع مَجْموعةٍ كامِلةٍ من قِطَعِ الغِيارِ; **use my pen, I've got a ~** اسْتَخْدِمْ قَلَمي، فَلَدَيَّ واحِدٌ آخَرُ

C *vt* (**spares**, **sparing**, **spared**) 1 (with surpluses) **to have milk/a ticket to ~** كانَ لَدَيْهِ فائِضٌ من اللَّبَنِ \ تَذْكِرةٌ إضافيّةٌ; **have this one, I've got one to ~** خُذْ هذا، فَلَدَيَّ واحِدٌ آخَرُ; **to check in with five minutes to ~** سَجَّلَ الدُخولَ قبل المَوْعِدِ بخَمْسِ دَقائِقَ; **to have time to ~ at the airport** كانَ لَدَيْهِ وَقْتٌ إضافيٌّ في المَطارِ 2 (to have mercy on) رَأَفَ (a-u; رَأْفة, رَآفة) (ب), أَبْقى (على) <*an enemy, animal*>; **to ~ sb's life** أَبْقى على حَياةِ شَخْصٍ; **to ~ sb sth** وَفَّرَ على شَخْصٍ عَناءَ شَيْءٍ; **I will ~ you the details** سَأُوَفِّرُ عَلَيْكَ عَناءَ الدُخولِ في التَفاصيلِ 3 (to afford) دَبَّرَ <*the money, time*>; **I can't ~ the cash** لا أَسْتَطيعُ أنْ أُدَبِّرَ المالَ; **can you ~ a couple of minutes?** هل يُمْكِنُكَ أنْ تُعْطِيَني دَقيقَتَيْنِ من وَقْتِكَ؟; **could you ~ us one of your staff for a day?** هل يُمْكِنُكَ أنْ تُعيرَنا أَحَدَ مُوَظَّفيكَ لِيَوْمٍ واحِدٍ؟

D *v refl* (**spares, sparing, spared**) **to ~ oneself sth** وَفَّرَ على نَفْسِهِ شَيْئاً; **I ~d myself the trouble of going there** وَفَّرْتُ على نَفْسي عَناءَ الذَهابِ إلى هُناكَ

Idiom **to spare no effort** لم يَدَّخِرْ جُهْداً

spare part *n* قِطْعة غِيارٍ

spare room *n* غُرْفة نَوْم إضافيّة

spare time *n* وَقْت فَراغٍ

spare tyre (BrE), **spare tire** (AmE) *n* 1 (Aut) عَجَلة احْتِياطيّة 2 (hum) (roll of fat) دُهون حول الخَصْرِ

sparingly /ˈspɛːrɪŋli/ *adv* <*to use, add*> بِكَمّيّاتٍ قَليلةٍ, باقْتِصادٍ

spark /spɑːk/ **A** *n* شَرار (n coll)

B *vt* (BrE also **spark off**) 1 أَشْعَلَ <*a fire*> 2 أَثارَ <*a reaction, riot, debate*>

sparkle /ˈspɑːk(ə)l/ **A** *vi* 1 «flames, lights» اتَّقَدَ; «jewels, water, eyes» تَلَأْلَأَ, بَرَقَ (u; بَرْق) 2 «a script, performance» فاضَ بالحَيَويّةِ, تَأَلَّقَ

B *n* 1 (of light) (in eye) تَلَأْلُؤ (تَلَأْلُؤات), تَأَلُّق 2 (animation) حَيَويّة

sparkler /ˈspɑːklə/ *n* [نَوْع من الألْعابِ النارِيّةِ يُطْلِقُ شَراراتٍ لامِعةً]

sparkling /ˈspɑːklɪŋ/ *adj* 1 <*jewels, eyes*> مُتَلَأْلِئ, بَرّاق 2 <*wit, conversation*> مُفْعَم بالحَيَويّةِ 3 <*wine, water*> فَوّار

spark plug *n* شَمْعة الإشْعالِ

sparrow /ˈsparəʊ/ *n* عُصْفور دوريّ

sparse /spɑːs/ *adj* <*population*> ضَئيل, قَليل; <*vegetation*> مُتَناثِر, مُتَفَرِّق

sparsely /ˈspɑːsli/ *adv* <*furnished*> بِشَكْلٍ خَفيفٍ; <*populated*> بِكَثافةٍ قَليلةٍ

spasm /ˈspazəm/ *n* تَشَنُّج (تَشَنُّجات)

spasmodic /spazˈmɒdɪk/ *adj* 1 (intermittent) <*activity, fighting*> مُتَقَطِّع 2 <*coughing, cramp*> تَشَنُّجيّ

spat /spat/ **A** *past participle, past tense* ▸ **spit**

B *n* 1 (infml) (quarrel) مُشاحَنة, مُشاجَرة صَغيرة 2 (on a shoe) [غِطاء واقٍ لِمُشْطِ القَدَمِ والكاحِلِ]

spate /speɪt/ *n* 1 **in full ~** (BrE) في أَوْجِ عُنْفُوانِهِ 2 **a ~ of attacks/incidents** سِلْسِلة \ مَوْجة من الهَجَماتِ \ الأَحْداثِ

spatial /ˈspeɪʃ(ə)l/ *adj* <*awareness, distribution*> حَيِّزيّ, مَكانيّ

spatter /ˈspatə/ **A** *vt* **to ~ sb/sth with sth, to ~ sth over sb/sth** طَرْطَشَ \ رَشَّ شَيْئاً على شَخْصٍ \ شَيْءٍ

B *vi* «bullets, rain» تَساقَطَ

C (**spattered**) *adj* مُلَطَّخ; **blood-/paint-~ed overalls** سُتْرة مُلَطَّخة بالدِماءِ \ بالدِهانِ

D *n* **1** (of liquid) رَشّة ,طَرْطَشة **2** (sound) صَوْت الطَرْطَشةِ **3** (small amount) كَمّيّة قَليلة

spatula /ˈspatjʊlə/ *n* **1** (in cooking) سْباتْيولا ,مَلاوِق) مِلْوَق) **2** (for tongue) خافِض اللِسانِ

spawn /spɔːn/ **A** *vt* **1** (pej) أَدّى إلى الظُهور ,أَنْتَجَ ‹*a craze, an imitation*› **2** وَضَعَ (a; وَضْع) ‹*eggs, young*›

B *vi* «frogs, salmon» باضَ (i; بَيْض)

C *n* **1** (of fish, frogs) بَيْض (n coll; بُيوض) **2** (of fungi) غَزْل فِطْرِيّ ,مَشيجة فِطْرِيّة

spay /speɪ/ *vt* عَقَّمَ ‹*a cat, pet*›

SPCA /ɛspiːsiːˈeɪ/ *n* (AmE) = **Society for the Prevention of Cruelty to Animals** جَمْعِيّة مَنْع القَسْوةِ على الحَيَواناتِ

SPCC /ɛspiːsiːˈsiː/ *n* (AmE) = **Society for the Prevention of Cruelty to Children** جَمْعِيّة مَنْع القَسْوةِ على الأَطْفالِ

speak /spiːk/ **A** (**-speak**) *in combination* لُغة (اصْطِلاحيّة); **computer-/management-~** لُغة الحاسوب \ الإدارة

B *vt* (*past tense* **spoke**; *past participle* **spoken**) **1** تَحَدَّثَ ,تَكَلَّمَ ‹*a language*›; **do you ~ English?** هَل تَتَحَدَّثُ الإِنْجِليزِيّةَ؟; **'Arabic spoken'** 'ناطِق بالعَرَبِيّةِ'; **she ~s four languages fluently** تَتَحَدَّثُ أَرْبَعَ لُغاتٍ بِطَلاقةٍ **2** (to express) قالَ (u; قَوْل) ‹*the truth, a word, one's name*›; **he's ~ing the truth** يَقولُ الحَقيقةَ; **she never spoke a word** لَم تَنْبِس بِبِنْتِ شَفةٍ; **to ~ one's mind** أَفْصَحَ عن رَأْيِهِ

C *vi* (*past tense* **spoke**; *past participle* **spoken**) **1** (to talk) تَحَدَّثَ ,تَكَلَّمَ; **she spoke to him about it** تَحَدَّثَتْ مَعَهُ عَنْهُ; **they didn't ~ about it** لَم يَتَحَدَّثوا عَنْهُ; **to ~ in a whisper** تَحَدَّثَ هَمْساً; **please ~ more slowly/loudly** من فَضْلِكَ تَحَدَّثْ بِبُطْءٍ أَكْثَرَ \ بِصَوْتٍ أَعْلى; **to ~ in Farsi/Russian** تَحَدَّثَ بالفارِسيّةِ \ بالروسيّةِ; **they're not ~ing to each other** لا يَتَحَدَّثونَ إلى بَعْضِهِم البَعْضُ; **he spoke very highly of her/ her achievements** أَشادَ بِها \ بِإنْجازاتِها كَثيراً; **generally ~ing** بِشَكْلٍ عامٍّ; **we've had no trouble to ~ of** لم يَكُنْ لَدَيْنا أَيُّ مَشاكِلَ تُذْكَرُ; **~ing as a layman …** بِصِفَتي شَخْصاً عادِيًّا … **this is your captain ~ing** أنا كابْتِن الطائِرةِ أَتَحَدَّثُ إِلَيْكُمْ **2** (on the phone) تَحَدَّثَ; **who's ~ing please?** من فَضْلِكَ مَن المُتَحَدِّثُ؟; **(this is) Jamilla ~ing** أنا جَميلةُ مَعَكَ على الهاتِفِ; **'is that Mr Reed?'—'~ing!'** 'هل هذا هو السَيِّدُ ريد؟' — 'أَجَلْ!' **3** (to make a speech) أَلْقى كَلِمةً; **to ~ for/ in support of the motion** أَلْقى كَلِمةً دَعْماً لِمَشْروعِ القَرارِ; **I've been asked to ~ at the meeting/in the debate** طُلِبَ مِنّي أنْ أُلْقِيَ كَلِمةً في الاجْتِماعِ \ في المُناقَشةِ; **the president spoke against the proposal** عارَضَ الرَئيسُ المُقْتَرَحَ في كَلِمَتِهِ

Phrasal verbs **speak for**: **~ for [sth/sb]** **1** (on behalf of) تَحَدَّثَ \ دافَعَ بالنِيابةِ عن [شَيْءٍ \ شَخْصٍ] ‹*a person*›; **to ~ for oneself** تَحَدَّثَ عن نَفْسِهِ; **the facts ~ for themselves** الحَقائِقُ تَتَحَدَّثُ عن نَفْسِها **2** (to reserve) **to be spoken for** «exhibits» كانَ مَحْجوزاً

• **speak out** «activists, representatives» عَبَّرَ عن رَأْيِهِ; **she spoke out against the changes** أَعْلَنَتْ مُعارَضَتَها للتَغْييراتِ

• **speak up** **1** (louder) تَحَدَّثَ بِصَوْتٍ مُرْتَفِعٍ; **please ~ up!** من فَضْلِكَ ارْفَعْ صَوْتَكَ! **2** (to support) **to ~ up for sb/sth** أَيَّدَ في حَديثِهِ شَخْصاً \ شَيْئاً

speaker /ˈspiːkə/ *n* **1** (person talking) مُتَحَدِّث ,مُتَكَلِّم; (public speaker) خَطيب (خُطَباءُ) **2** (of a language) مُتَحَدِّث ,مُتَكَلِّم **3** (on a sound system) مُكَبِّر الصَوْتِ **4** (**Speaker**) (in parliament) رَئيس مَجْلِسٍ نِيابيٍّ

-speaking /-ˈspiːkɪŋ/ *combining form* **English-/French-~** ناطِق باللُغةِ الإنْجليزيّةِ \ الفَرَنْسيّةِ

spear /spɪə/ *n* رُمْح (أَرْماح ,رِماح)

spearhead /ˈspɪəhɛd/ *vt* كانَ رَأْسَ الحَرْبةِ ل ,قادَ (u; قِيادة) ‹*a campaign, revolt*›

spearmint /ˈspɪəmɪnt/ *n* نَعْناع مُدَبَّب \ سُنْبُلِيّ \ بَلَدِيّ

spec /spɛk/ (infml) **A** *n* **1** = **specification** مُواصَفة **2** = **speculation**; **on ~** بِدافِعِ الأَمَلِ; **we called in on ~** ذَهَبْنا إِلَيْهِمْ على أَمَلِ أنْ نَجِدَهُمْ

B (**specs**) *n pl* (infml) = **spectacles** نَظّارة

special /ˈspɛʃ(ə)l/ **A** *adj* **1** (exceptional) ‹*guest, feature, case, edition*› خاصّ; **to pay ~ attention to sth** أَوْلى اهْتِماماً خاصًّا

لا نَسْتَخْدِمُها إلاّ لِشَيْءٍ; **we only use them for ~ occasions** في المُناسَباتِ الخاصّةِ; **what's so ~ about it?** ما الشَّيْءُ المُمَيَّزُ فيهِ؟; **'what are you doing this weekend?' — 'nothing ~'** 'ماذا سَتَفْعَلُ في عُطْلَةِ نِهايةِ الأُسْبوعِ القادِمةِ؟' 'لا شَيْءَ على وَجْهِ الخُصوصِ' **2** (for a purpose) ‹*arrangements, equipment*› خاصّ; **the police have been given ~ powers to control the situation** مُنِحَت الشُّرْطةُ صَلاحيّاتٍ خاصّةً للسَيْطَرةِ على المَوْقِفِ **3** (overriding) ‹*interest, reason*› خاصّ **4** (valued) ‹*friend*› عَزيز (أَعِزّة ,أَعِزّاءُ), حَميم (أَحِمّاءُ); **my aunt was very ~ to me** كانَتْ لِعَمَّتي مَعَزّةٌ خاصّةٌ عِنْدي **5** (individual) ‹*qualities, methods*› خاصّ

B *n* **1** (in a restaurant) طَبَق خاصّ; **the chef's ~** طَبَق خاصّ من الشيف **2** (programme) بَرْنامَج خاصّ, حَلَقة خاصّة **3** (infml) (discounted offer); ▸**special offer** **4** (bus) حافِلة خاصّة; (train) قِطار خاصّ

special delivery *n* **1** (in UK: guaranteed delivery) تَسْليم خاصّ \ بالبَريدِ السَريعِ **2** (in US: distance delivery) بَريد مُسْتَعْجَل, خِدْمة بَريديّة خاصّة

special effects *n* مُؤَثِّرات خاصّة

special interest group *n* مَجْموعة ذات مَصالِحَ خاصّة

specialist /'spɛʃəlɪst/ *n* أَخِصّائيّ

speciality /ˌspɛʃɪ'alɪti/ (BrE) *n* (*pl* **specialities**) **1** (in cooking) خاصّيّة (خاصّيّات, خَصائِصُ) **2** (in studies, skill) اخْتِصاص (اخْتِصاصات), تَخَصُّص

specialization, -isation (BrE) /spɛʃəlʌɪ'zeɪʃ(ə)n/ *n* **1** [u] (in education, research) تَخَصُّص **2** (area, field) تَخَصُّص (تَخَصُّصات), اخْتِصاص (اخْتِصاصات)

specialize, -ise (BrE) /'spɛʃəlʌɪz/ *vi* «consultants, firms» تَخَصَّصَ; **a financial consultant specializing in risk management** مُسْتَشار ماليّ مُتَخَصِّص في إدارة المَخاطِرِ

specially /'spɛʃ(ə)li/ *adv* **1** (specifically) ‹*altered, designed, made*› خاصّةً, خِصّيصاً **2** (particularly) ‹*good, difficult, to like*› بِشَكْلٍ خاصٍّ

special needs *n* احْتِياجات خاصّة

special offer *n* عَرْض خاصّ; **to be on special offer** كانَ عَلَيْهِ عَرْضٌ خاصٌّ

special school *n* مَدْرَسة لِذَوي الاحْتِياجاتِ الخاصّةِ, مَدْرَسة للتَرْبِيةِ الخاصّةِ

specialty /'spɛʃəlti/ *n* (*pl* **specialties**) **1** (in cooking) خاصّيّة (خاصّيّات, خَصائِصُ) **2** (in studies, skill) اخْتِصاص (اخْتِصاصات), تَخَصُّص

species /'spiːʃiːz/ *n* (*pl* **species**) نَوْع (أَنْواع), صِنْف (أَصْناف, صُنوف)

specific /spə'sɪfɪk/ *adj* ‹*requirements, area, details*› مُحَدَّد, مُعَيَّن

specifically /spə'sɪfɪkli/ *adv* **1** (specially) ‹*to plan, design*› خُصوصاً, خِصّيصاً **2** (explicitly) ‹*to state, warn*› على وَجْهِ خُصوصاً **3** (in particular) تَحْديداً, التَحْديدِ, على وَجْهِ الخُصوصِ

specification /ˌspɛsɪfɪ'keɪʃ(ə)n/ *n* (also **specifications**) (of a design, building) مُواصَفات

specify /'spɛsɪfʌɪ/ *vt* (**specifies, specifying, specified**) ‹*a date, conditions*› حَدَّدَ

specimen /'spɛsɪmɪn/ *n* **1** (sample) عَيِّنة **2** (example) عَيِّنة

speck /spɛk/ *n* **1** (particle) (of dust, dirt) ذَرّة, مِقْدار ضَئيل **2** (stain) (of blood, mud, paint) لَطْخة (لَطَخات), بُقْعة (بُقَع) **3** (in the distance) نُقْطة (نُقَط, نِقاط)

speckle /'spɛk(ə)l/ **A** *vt* ‹*a surface, skin*› نَقَّطَ, بَقَّعَ

B (**speckled**) *adj* ‹*egg, hen*› مُنَقَّط, أَرْقَط, مُبَرْقَش

spectacle /'spɛktək(ə)l/ **A** *n* مَشْهَد (مَشاهِدُ)

B (**spectacles**) *n pl* نَظّارة

spectacular /spɛk'takjʊlə/ *adj* ‹*view, display*› مُذْهِل, مُدْهِش, باهِر

spectator /spɛk'teɪtə/ *n* مُشاهِد, مُتَفَرِّج

specter (AmE) *n* ▸**spectre**

spectra /'spɛktrə/ *n pl* ▸**spectrum**

spectral /'spɛktrəl/ *adj* **1** (ghostlike) ‹*figure, voice*› طَيْفيّ, شَبَحيّ **2** ‹*analysis, change*› طَيْفيّ

spectre (BrE), **specter** (AmE) /'spɛktə/ *n* **1** (ghost) شَبَح (أَشْباح, شُبوح), طَيْف (أَطْياف, طُيوف) **2** (prospect) شَبَح (أَشْباح, شُبوح); **the ~ of war/famine** شَبَح الحَرْبِ \ المَجاعةِ

spectrum /ˈspɛktrəm/ *n* (*pl* **spectra**) 1 (of colours) طَيْف (طُيوف ,أَطْياف) 2 (range) طَيْف ,(طُيوف ,أَطْياف) نِطاق ,نُطُق; **the political ~** الأَطْياف السِياسيّة ,أَلْوان الطَيْف السِياسيّ

speculate /ˈspɛkjʊleɪt/ *vi* 1 (to conjecture) «people, the media» تَكَهَّنَ ,خَمَّنَ ,تَوَقَّعَ; **to ~ on/about sth** تَكَهَّنَ حول شَيْءٍ 2 (pej) (in commodities, futures) ضارَبَ

speculation /ˌspɛkjʊˈleɪʃ(ə)n/ *n* 1 (conjecture) تَكَهُّن (تَكَهُّنات) ,تَوَقُّع ,تَخْمين (تَخْمينات) 2 [u] (pej) (in commodities, futures) مُضارَبة

speculative /ˈspɛkjʊlətɪv/ *adj* 1 ‹*statement, theory*› تَخْمينيّ, نَظَريّ 2 ‹*investment, finance*› مُضارَبيّ

speculator /ˈspɛkjuːleɪtə/ *n* (pej) مُضارِب

speculum /ˈspɛkjʊləm/ *n* (*pl* **specula**) مِنْظار طِبِّيّ

sped /spɛd/ *past tense, past participle* ▸ **speed** B, C

speech /spiːtʃ/ *n* 1 (to an audience) خُطْبة ,خِطاب (خِطابات) ,(خُطَب) كَلِمة; **to give** *or* **make a ~** أَلْقى خِطاباً 2 [u] (faculty) قُدْرة على الكَلام ,كَلام ,نُطْق 3 (language) كَلام (n coll, no singul n); **colloquial ~** اللُغة العامِّيّة 4 (manner of speaking) أُسْلوب كَلامٍ 5 (in plays) مونولوج

speech impediment *n* إعاقة النُطْقِ

speechless /ˈspiːtʃləs/ *adj* عاجِز عن الكَلامِ ,مَشْدوه ,واجِم ,مَعْقود اللِسانِ; **she was ~ with surprise** أَخْرَسَتْها المُفاجَأةُ; **I'm ~!** أنا عاجِزٌ عن الكَلامِ!

speech recognition *n* التَعَرُّف على الكَلامِ

speech therapy *n* (*pl* **speech therapies**) تَقْويم النُطْقِ

speech-writer /ˈspiːtʃrʌɪtə/ *n* كاتِب خِطاباتٍ

speed /spiːd/ **A** *n* 1 (of vehicles, responses, the wind) سُرْعة; **to gain/lose ~** زادَتْ \ انْخَفَضَتْ سُرْعَتُهُ; **winds reaching ~s of ... ...** رِياح تَصِلُ سُرْعَتُها إلى; **to go faster than the ~ of sound** سارَ بِسُرْعةٍ أَسْرَعَ من سُرْعةِ الصَوْتِ 2 (gear) سُرْعة; **a five-~ bicycle** دَرّاجة بِخَمْسِ سُرْعاتٍ 3 (of the film, shutter) سُرْعة 4 (infml) (amphetamine) أَمْفيتامين

B *vt* (*past tense, past participle* **sped** or **speeded**) سَرَّعَ ‹*the recovery, process*›; **take this, it'll ~ your recovery** خُذْ هذا، فَسَيُساعِدُكَ على التَعافي بِسُرْعةٍ; **to ~ sb on their way** تَمَنّى لِشَخْصٍ رِحْلةً سَعيدةً

C *vi* 1 (*past tense, past participle* **sped**) (infml) (to move fast) **to ~ along** أَسْرَعَ; **to ~ away/off** أَسْرَعَ مُبْتَعِداً; **the train sped past/by** مَرَّ القِطارُ مُسْرِعاً 2 (*past tense, past participle* **speeded**) (to drive too fast) «drivers, vehicles» تَجاوَزَ السُرْعةَ المُحَدَّدةَ; **he was ~ing in a restricted area** تَجاوَزَ السُرْعةَ في مِنْطَقةٍ مَحْظورةٍ

Idiom **to be up to speed** (infml) كانَ على اطِّلاعٍ بِكافّةِ المُسْتَجَدّاتِ

Phrasal verb **speed up**: 1 **~ up** «runners, cars» أَسْرَعَ 2 **~ up [sth], ~ [sth] up** سَرَّعَ [شَيْئاً] ‹*the process, output*›

speedboat /ˈspiːdbəʊt/ *n* زَوْرَق سَريع

speed bump, **speed hump** *n* مَطَبّ

speed camera *n* كاميرا مُراقَبةِ السُرْعةِ (مُثَبَّتة على جانِبِ الطَريق)

speed dating *n* تَواعُد سَريع (سِلْسِلة من المُحادَثاتِ القَصيرةِ لِتَحْديدِ إمْكانيّةِ إقامةِ علاقةٍ عاطِفيّةٍ)

speed dial *n* الاتِّصال السَريع

speeding /ˈspiːdɪŋ/ *n* تَجاوُز السُرْعةِ المُحَدَّدةِ

speed limit *n* الحَدّ الأَقْصى للسُرْعةِ

speedometer /spiːˈdɒmɪtə/ *n* عَدّاد السُرْعةِ

speed skating *n* التَزَلُّج السَريع

speedway /ˈspiːdweɪ/ *n* (Sport) 1 [u] (BrE) (sport) سْبيدْواي [سِباق دَرّاجاتٍ نارِيّةٍ] 2 (AmE) (track) حَلْبة سِباقٍ

speedy /ˈspiːdi/ *adj* (**speedier**, **speediest**) ‹*recovery, resolution, response*› سَريع ,عاجِل

spell /spɛl/ **A** *n* 1 (period) فَتْرة (فَتَرات) ,مُدّة (مُدَد); **a ~ in prison/hospital** فَتْرة في السِجْنِ \ المُسْتَشْفى; **a cold/dry ~** فَتْرة من الطَقْسِ البارِدِ \ الجافّ; **she has dizzy ~s** تَنابُها نَوْباتٌ من الدُوارِ 2 (witch's) تَعْويذة (تَعاويذ); **a magic ~** تَعْويذة سِحْرِيّة; **to cast** *or* **put a ~ on sb** سَحَرَ شَخْصاً; **to be under a ~** كانَ واقِعاً تحت تَأْثيرِ السِحْرِ; **to be/fall under sb's ~** كانَ \ وَقَعَ تحت تَأْثيرِ شَخْصٍ; **to break the ~** أَنْهى تَأْثيرَ السِحْرِ

B *vt* (*past tense, past participle* **spelled** or **spelt** BrE) 1 (in letters) «pupil» هَجّى ,تَهَجّى ‹*a word*›; **how do you ~ Madagascar?** كيف تَتَهَجّى كَلِمةَ مَدَغَشْقَر؟ 2 (to mean)

عَنَى (i; عَنْي) ‹*the end, disaster*›

C *vi* (*past tense, past participle* **spelled** or **spelt** BrE) تَهَجَّى, هَجَّى; **he can't ~ very well** لا يَسْتَطِيعُ التَهَجِّي جَيِّداً

(Phrasal verb) **spell out**: **~ out [sth], ~ [sth] out** **1** تَهَجَّى [شَيْئاً] ‹*a word, name*› **2** شَرَحَ [شَيْئاً] ‹*one's plans, the details, implications*›; **the president ~ed out the recovery plan** شَرَحَ الرَئِيسُ خُطَّةَ الإِنْعاشِ

spellbinding /'spɛlbʌɪndɪŋ/ *adj* ‹*performance, story*› أَخّاذ, خَلّاب

spellbound /'spɛlbaʊnd/ *adj* ‹*audience, fascination*› مَسْحور, مَأْخوذ, مَفْتون

spellcheck /'spɛltʃɛk/ *vt* دَقَّقَ إِمْلائيًّا (بِواسِطَةِ مُدَقِّقٍ إِمْلائِيٍّ) ‹*a document, text*›

spellchecker /'spɛltʃɛkə/ *n* مُدَقِّق إِمْلائيّ

spelling /'spɛlɪŋ/ *n* **1** (ability) هِجاء, تَهْجِئة; **to be good/bad at ~** أَجادَ \ لم يُجِدْ التَهْجِئةَ **2** (of a word) تَهْجِئة, هِجاء

spelling mistake *n* خَطَأ إِمْلائيّ

spelt /spɛlt/ (BrE) *past tense, past participle* ▸ **spell** B, C

spelunking /spɪ'lʌŋkɪŋ/ *n* (AmE) اسْتِكْشاف الكُهوف

spend /spɛnd/ **A** *vt* (*past tense, past participle* **spent**) **1** أَنْفَقَ, صَرَفَ (i; صَرْف) ‹*money, fifty pounds*›; **to ~ money on clothes/food** أَنْفَقَ مالاً على المَلابِسِ \ الطَعامِ; **I spent $2,000 on the house repairs** أَنْفَقْتُ 2000 دولار على إِصْلاحاتِ المَنْزِل **2** قَضى (i; قَضاء), أَمْضى ‹*time, two years*›; **don't ~ too long on the report** لا تَسْتَغْرِقْ وَقْتاً طَويلاً في التَقْريرِ; **he spent ten years in prison/at IBM** قَضى عَشْرَ سِنينَ في السِجْنِ \ شَرِكةِ آي بي إم

B *vi* (*past tense, past participle* **spent**) أَنْفَقَ

C *n* مَصْروف (مَصاريفُ, مَصْروفات)

spending /'spɛndɪŋ/ *n* إِنْفاق; **~ on education/defence** الإِنْفاق على التَعْليمِ \ الدِفاعِ

spending cut *n* خَفض الإِنْفاقِ

spending money *n* مَصْروف الجَيْبِ

spending power *n* القُدْرة الشِرائيّة \ الصَرْفيّة \ على الإِنْفاقِ

spendthrift /'spɛndθrɪft/ *n* (pej) مُبَذِّر

spent /spɛnt/ **A** *past tense, past participle* ▸ **spend**

B *adj* ‹*fuel, bullet*› مُسْتَهْلَك

sperm /spɜːm/ *n* (*pl* **sperm** or **sperms**) **1** [u] (semen) سائِل مَنَويّ **2** (spermatozoon) حَيَوان مَنَويّ

spew /spjuː/ **A** *vt* (also **spew out**) نَفَثَ (i-u; نَفْث) ‹*smoke, lava*›

B *vi* **1** «lava, oil» تَدَفَّقَ; «smoke» انْبَعَثَ **2** (also **spew up**) (infml) (to vomit) تَقَيَّأَ

sphere /sfɪə/ *n* **1** (shape) كُرة (كُرات), جِسْم كُرَويّ **2** (of activity, interest) مَجال (مَجالات), نِطاق (نُطُق); **Brazil's growing ~ of influence** تَزايُد نِطاقِ نُفوذِ البَرازيلِ

spherical /'sfɛrɪk(ə)l/ *adj* ‹*shape, object*› كُرَويّ

sphinx /sfɪŋks/ *n* [تِمْثال أَبي الهَوْلِ]; **the S~** أَبو الهَوْل

spice /spʌɪs/ **A** *n* **1** (seasoning) بَهار (بَهارات), تابِل (تَوابِلُ) **2** (excitement, interest) حَيَويّة, إِثارة, عُنْصُر

B *vt* **1** (to season) تَبَّلَ **2** (also **spice up**) (to add interest to) أَنْعَشَ

spick and span /spɪk ən 'span/ *adj* ‹*house, room*› في غايةِ التَرْتيبِ والنَظافةِ

spicy /'spʌɪsi/ *adj* (**spicier**, **spiciest**) **1** ‹*food, sauce*› (with spices) مُتَبَّل, كَثير البَهاراتِ; (hot) حِرّيف, حارّ, مُفَلْفَل **2** (racy) ‹*details, story*› مُثير, لاذِع

spider /'spʌɪdə/ *n* عَنْكَبوت (mf; عَناكِبُ)

spider's web (BrE), **spiderweb** (AmE) *n* نَسيج \ بَيْت عَنْكَبوتٍ

spike /spʌɪk/ **A** *n* **1** (pointed object) مِسْماريّ \ نُتوء مَعْدِنيّ **2** (on track shoes) مِسْمار (في النَعْلِ لِمَنْعِ الانْزِلاقِ) **3** (in prices, costs) ارْتِفاع مُفاجِئ **4** (**spikes** *n pl*) حِذاء أَلْعابِ القُوى (ذو رُؤوسٍ مَعْدِنيّةٍ في أَسْفَلِها)

B *vt* **1** (to pierce) ثَقَبَ (u; ثَقْب) ‹*the meat, one's hand*› **2** (infml) (to add alcohol, drugs to) خَلَطَ بالكُحولِ \ بالمُخَدِّراتِ ‹*a drink*›; **her drink had been ~d with drugs** كانَ مَشْروبُها مَخْلوطاً بالمُخَدِّراتِ

spiky /'spʌɪki/ *adj* (**spikier**, **spikiest**) **1** (with spikes) ‹*plant, leaf*› شائِك **2** (pointed) ‹*tail, high heels*› مُدَبَّب, حادّ **3** ‹*hair*› شائِك

spill /spɪl/ **A** *vt* (*past tense, past participle* **spilled**, **spilt**) **1** (with liquids) سَكَبَ (u; سَكْب), أَراقَ ‹*coffee, the contents, one's drink*›; **she spilt coffee on** *or* **over the keyboard** سَكَبَت القَهْوة على لَوْحِةِ المَفاتيحِ; **too much blood has been spilled** \ سُفِكَتْ دِماءٌ كَثيرةٌ أُريقَتْ **2** (to disgorge) أَنْزَلَ, فَرَّغَ ‹*passengers*›; ‹*a load*›

B *vi* **1** (*past tense, past participle* **spilled**, **spilt**) «water, oil, contents» طَفَحَ (a; طَفْح), اِنْسَكَبَ; **thousands of tons of crude oil ~ed into the sea** اِنْسَكَبَتْ آلافُ الأَطْنانِ من النَفْطِ الخامِ في البَحْرِ **2** ▸ **spill out**

C *n* **1** (of oil, milk, etc) تَسَرُّب (تَسَرُّبات) **2** (infml) (from a horse, bike) وُقوع, سُقوط

(Idiom) **to spill the beans** (infml) أَفْشى السِرَّ

(Phrasal verbs) **spill out** «crowds, passengers» خَرَجَ مُنْدَفِعاً; **the audience ~ed out into** *or* **onto the street** خَرَجَ الجُمْهورُ مُنْدَفِعاً إلى الشارِعِ

• **spill over** «violence, conflict» اِنْتَشَرَ, تَفَشّى

spillage /ˈspɪlɪdʒ/ *n* تَسَرُّب (تَسَرُّبات)

spilt /spɪlt/ *past tense, past participle* ▸ **spill** A, B

spin /spɪn/ **A** *vt* (*present participle* **-nn-**; *past tense, past participle* **spun**) **1** (to rotate) لَفَّ (u; لَفّ), دَوَّرَ ‹*a wheel, top*› **2** (in ball games) لَفَّ (u; لَفّ), دَوَّرَ ‹*the ball*› **3** (to toss) **to ~ a coin** قَذَفَ قِطْعَةَ نُقودٍ **4** غَزَلَ (i; غَزْل) ‹*wool, thread*›; **to ~ cotton into thread** غَزَلَ القُطْنَ إلى خَيْطٍ **5** غَزَلَ (i; غَزْل) ‹*a web, cocoon*› **6** (to tell) قَصَّ (u; قَصَص), حَكى (i; حِكاية) ‹*a tale, story*›; **to ~ a yarn** نَسَجَ قِصَّةً **7** ▸ **spin-dry**

B *vi* (*present participle* **-nn-**; *past tense, past participle* **spun**) **1** (to go round) «wheels, discs, dancers» لَفَّ (u; لَفّ), دارَ (u; دَوْر, دَوَران) **2** (with dizziness) لَفَّ (u; لَفّ), دارَ (u; دَوْر, دَوَران); **my head is ~ning** رَأْسي يَدورُ; **the room was ~ning** كانَت الغُرْفةُ تَدورُ **3** (to move quickly) «car» لَفَّ (u; لَفّ), دارَ (u; دَوْر, دَوَران); **the car spun out of control** لَفَّت السَيّارةُ وَخَرَجَتْ عن السَيْطَرةِ; **the stone went ~ning through the air** أَخَذَ الحَجَرُ يَدورُ في الهَواءِ **4** (to make yarn) غَزَلَ (i; غَزْل)

C *n* **1** (turn) لَفّ \ دَوَّرَ; **to give sth a ~** لَفَّ \ دَوَّرَ شَيْئاً بِسُرْعةٍ **2** [u] (on a ball) لَفّ, دَوَران; **to put ~ on a ball** جَعَلَ كُرةً تَلُفُّ \ تَدورُ **3** (of an aircraft) لَفّ, دَوَران; **to go into a ~** أَخَذَ في الدَوَرانِ حول نَفْسِهِ **4** (drive, ride, etc) جَوْلة, رِحْلة (رِحْلات, رِحَل); **to go for** *or* **take a ~** ذَهَبَ في جَوْلةٍ **5** (interpretation) **to put a positive/new ~ on sth** وَضَعَ تَحْليلاً إيجابيّاً \ جَديداً لِشَيْءٍ

(Idiom) **to be in a spin** (infml) كانَ في حالةٍ من الذُهولِ

(Phrasal verbs) **spin around**, **spin round A 1** (to turn around) اِسْتَدارَ للخَلْفِ; **she spun round to face him** اِسْتَدارَتْ للخَلْفِ لِتَكونَ في مُواجَهَتِهِ **2** (in dancing) لَفَّ \ دارَ حول نَفْسِهِ **B 1** ~ [sth] around لَفَّ \ أَدارَ [شَيْئاً] ‹*a wheel*› **2** ~ [sb] round (to turn around) أَدارَ [شَخْصاً]; (in dancing) جَعَلَ [شَخْصاً] يَلُفُّ \ يَدورُ

• **spin out**: ~ [sth] out, ~ out [sth] أَطالَ أَمَدَ [شَيْءٍ] ‹*the negotiations, debate, the suspense*›

spina bifida /ˌspʌɪnə ˈbɪfɪdə/ *n* الصُلب الأَشْرَم

spinach /ˈspɪnɪdʒ/ *n* سَبانِخ

spinal /ˈspʌɪn(ə)l/ *adj* ‹*injury, surgery*› شَوْكيّ, فِقْريّ

spinal column *n* عمود فِقْريّ \ شَوْكيّ

spinal cord *n* نُخاع شَوْكيّ

spindle /ˈspɪnd(ə)l/ *n* **1** (for spinning) مِغْزَل (مَغازِلُ) **2** (machine part) عَمود الإدارةِ

spindly /ˈspɪndli/ *adj* (**spindlier**, **spindliest**) ‹*arms, tree*› [طَويل وَنَحيل]

spin doctor *n* خَبير دِعائيّ

spin-dry /ˌspɪnˈdrʌɪ/ *vt* (**-dries**, **-drying**, **-dried**) جَفَّفَ بِآلةِ تَجْفيفٍ

spin dryer, **spin drier** *n* آلة تَجْفيفٍ

spine /spʌɪn/ *n* **1** (backbone) عَمود فَقْريّ **2** (of a book) كَعْب (كِتابٍ) **3** (on an animal, fish) حَسَك (n coll); (on a cactus) شَوْك (أَشْواك)

spine-chilling /ˈspʌɪnˌtʃɪlɪŋ/ *adj* ‹*tale, scream*› تَقْشَعِرُّ لَهُ الأَبْدانُ

spineless /ˈspʌɪnləs/ *adj* **1** (weak) ‹*politician, coward*› ضَعيف (ضُعَفاءُ) **2** (Zool) ‹*creature, worm*› لا فَقاريّ

spinner /ˈspɪnə/ *n* **1** (of thread) غَزّال **2** (fishing lure) طُعْم صِناعيّ (لِصَيْدِ السَمَكِ)

spinning /ˈspɪnɪŋ/ *n* 1 (Clothing) غَزْل (غُزول) 2 ®(Sport) سْبينينغ (الرِياضة على دَرّاجةٍ مَنْزِليّةٍ)

spinning wheel *n* دولاب غَزْلٍ

spin-off /ˈspɪnɒf/ *n* 1 (incidental benefit) فائِدة جانِبيّة 2 (from a TV programme, film) [كِتاب أو مُسَلْسَل مُنْبَثِق من كِتابٍ أو مُسَلْسَلٍ آخَرَ] 3 (company) شَرِكة مُنْبَثِقة

spinster /ˈspɪnstə/ *n* 1 (pej) عانِس (f; عَوانِسُ) 2 (old use) امْرَأة غَيْر مُتَزَوِّجةٍ \ عَزْباءَ

spiral /ˈspʌɪrəl/ **A** *adj* ‹*pattern, shape*› حَلَزونيّ ,لَوْلَبيّ

B *n* 1 (shape, pattern) لَوْلَب (لَوالِبُ) ,حَلَزون (حَلَزونات)

2 (of violence, depression) دَوّامة

C *vi* (**-ll-** BrE, **-l-** AmE) 1 «smoke, leaves» اتَّخَذَ مَساراً لَوْلَبيًّا

2 «costs, prices» تَصاعَدَ

spiral staircase *n* سُلَّم حَلَزونيّ \ لَوْلَبيّ

spire /spʌɪə/ *n* قِمّة (قِمَم)

spirit /ˈspɪrɪt/ **A** *n* 1 (mood, attitude) روح (mf; أَرْواح), مِزاج (أَمْزِجة), جَوّ (أَجْواء, جِواء); **in a ~ of cooperation** بِروح من التَعاوُنِ; **he took my criticism in the right/wrong ~** اسْتَقْبَلَ نَقْدي بِشَكْلٍ إيجابيٍّ \ سَلْبيٍّ; **to enter into the ~ of sth** دَخَلَ في جَوِّ شَيْءٍ 2 [u] (courage, determination) حَماسة ,عَزيمة; **to have/show great ~** كانَتْ لَدَيْهِ عَزيمةٌ كَبيرةٌ \ أَظْهَرَ عَزيمةً كَبيرةً; **to break sb's ~** كَسَرَ روحَ شَخْصٍ 3 (essence) روح (mf; أَرْواح); **we abide by the ~ as well as the letter of the law** نَلْتَزِمُ بِروحِ القانونِ كَما نَلْتَزِمُ بِنَصِّهِ 4 (soul) روح (mf; أَرْواح) 5 (ghost) شَبَح (أَشْباح ,شُبوح); **the Holy S~** الروح القُدُس

B (**spirits**) *n pl* 1 (emotional state) روح \ حالة مَعْنَويّة; **to be in good/low ~s** كانَ في حالةٍ مَعْنَويّةٍ جَيِّدةٍ \ سَيِّئةٍ; **to be in high ~s** كانَ في روحٍ مَعْنَويّةٍ عاليةٍ; **to keep one's ~s up** احْتَفَظَ بِروحٍ مَعْنَويّةٍ مُرْتَفِعةٍ; **to raise sb's ~s** رَفَعَ روحَ شَخْصٍ المَعْنَويّةَ 2 (alcoholic drink) مَشْروبات كُحوليّة \ روحيّة

C *vt* **to ~ sb/sth away** هَرَّبَ شَخْصاً \ شَيْئاً

spirited /ˈspɪrɪtɪd/ *adj* ‹*horse*› نَشيط (نِشاط); ‹*performance, defence*› مُتَحَمِّس; ‹*debate*› مُفْعَم بالحَيَويّةِ

spirit level *n* ميزان تَسْوِيةٍ \ ماءٍ

spiritual /ˈspɪrɪtʃʊəl/ **A** *adj* ‹*life, leader*› روحيّ ,روحانيّ

B *n* (also **Negro spiritual**) [أُغْنِية ذات طابعٍ دينيٍّ عند زُنوجِ أَمْريكا]

spiritualism /ˈspɪrɪtʃʊəliz(ə)m/ *n* 1 (occult) تَحْضير الأَرْواحِ 2 (philosophy) روحانيّة

spirituality /spɪrɪtʃuːˈaləti/ *n* روحانيّة ,قِيَم روحيّة

spiritually /ˈspɪrɪtʃuːəli/ *adv* ‹*uplifting, impoverished*› روحانيًّا

spit /spɪt/ **A** *vt* (*present participle* **-tt-**; *past tense, past participle* **spat**) 1 ‹*blood, food, venom*› بَصَقَ (u; بَصْق) 2 (to utter) تَفَوَّهَ (ب), تَلَفَّظَ (ب) ‹*insults, a curse*›

B *vi* (*present participle* **-tt-**; *past tense, past participle* **spat**) 1 «person» بَصَقَ (u; بَصْق), تَفَلَ (i-u; تَفْل); **he spat on the floor** بَصَقَ على الأَرْضيّةِ; **to ~ in sb's face** بَصَقَ على وَجْهِ شَخْصٍ 2 «cat» هَرَّ (i; هَرير), هَسْهَسَ (هَسْهَسة) 3 «hot fat, sausages» طَشْطَشَ (i; طَشْطَشة) 4 «fire, logs» فَرْقَعَ (i; فَرْقَعة)

C *v impers* **it's ~ting with rain** تُمْطِرُ رَذاذاً

D *n* 1 (infml) (saliva) بُصاق ,بَصْقة 2 (for roasting) سيخ (أَسْياخ) ,سَفّود (سَفافيدُ) 3 (of land) لِسان (أَلْسِنة ,أَلْسُن)

(Idioms) **to be the spitting image of sb** (infml) كانَ صورةً طِبْقَ الأَصْلِ من شَخْصٍ; **to be within spitting distance** (infml) كانَ على مَسافةٍ قَريبةٍ جِدًّا

(Phrasal verb) **spit out**: **~ [sth] out, ~ out [sth]** 1 ‹*water, food*› بَصَقَ [شَيْئاً] 2 ‹*an insult, a curse*› تَفَوَّهَ \ تَلَفَّظَ ب [شَيْءٍ]; **~ it out!** (infml) هات \ قُلْ ما عِنْدَكَ!

spite /spʌɪt/ **A** *n* حِقْد (أَحْقاد), ضَغينة (ضَغائِنُ), سوء نيّةٍ

B *vt* آذى (Form IV; imperf يُؤْذي), ضايَقَ ‹*a person*›

C (**in spite of**) *phr* رَغْمَ, على الرَغْمِ من

spiteful /ˈspʌɪtfʊl/ *adj* ‹*person*› حَقود (حُقُد), خَبيث (خُبُث); ‹*remark*› جارِح

spittle /ˈspɪt(ə)l/ *n* بُصاق ,لُعاب

splash /splaʃ/ **A** *vt* 1 (to spatter, spray) رَشَّ (u; رَشّ) ‹*a person, surface*›; **to ~ water on one's face, to ~ one's face with water** رَشَّ الماءَ على وَجْهِهِ 2 (to print) طَبَعَ (a; طَبْع) ‹*a story, picture*›; **the news was ~ed across the front page** كانَت الأَخْبارُ مَطْبوعةً على كامِلِ الصَفْحةِ الأولى

B *vi* 1 «water, blood» تَدَفَّقَ ,تَناثَرَ; **water was ~ing from a**

fountain كانَ الماءُ يَتَناثَرُ من نافورةٍ; **2** «person» خَبَطَ الماءَ; **to ~ through the puddles** خَبَطَ ماءَ البِرَكِ

C *n* **1** (sound) صَوْتُ الارْتِطامِ بالماءِ; **I heard a ~** سَمِعْتُ صَوْتَ ارْتِطامٍ بالماءِ **2** (of blood, paint, etc) بُقْعة (بُقَع ,بِقاع) **3** (small amount) مِقْدار قَليل; **a ~ of soda/milk** مِقْدار قَليل من المِياهِ الغازيّةِ \ الحَليبِ **4** (of colour) بُقْعة (بُقَع ,بِقاع)

Idiom **to make a splash** (infml) أَثارَ الانْتِباهَ

Phrasal verbs **splash around, splash about** (BrE) **A** خَبَطَ الماءَ **B ~ [sth] around** (infml) نَثَرَ [شَيْئاً] ‹money›

• **splash down** «spacecraft» حَطَّ على الماءِ

• **splash out** (infml) أَنْفَقَ (بِسَخاءٍ); **to ~ out on a new outfit** أَنْفَقَ بِسَخاءٍ على شِراءِ بَدْلَةٍ جديدةٍ

splatter /ˈsplatə/ **A** *vt* طَرْطَشَ (i; طَرْطَشَة), رَشَّ (u; رَشّ) ‹blood, paint›

B *vi* «blood, rain» تَناثَرَ, تَرَشْرَشَ, تَرَشَّشَ

splay /spleɪ/ *vt* مَدَّ (u; مَدّ), بَسَطَ (u; بَسْط), فَلْطَحَ (i; فَلْطَحة) ‹one's fingers, feet›; **he sat with his legs ~ed out** جَلَسَ مُمَدِّداً ساقَيْهِ

spleen /spliːn/ *n* طِحال (طِحالات, طُحُل)

splendid /ˈsplɛndɪd/ *adj* **1** (excellent) ‹performance, idea› مُمْتاز, رائع **2** (imposing) ‹building, display› باهِر

splendour (BrE), **splendor** (AmE) /ˈsplɛndə/ *n* بَهاء, رَوْعة

splice /splʌɪs/ *vt* **1** وَصَلَ (بالجِدْلِ) ‹a rope› **2** وَصَلَ (i; وَصْل) ‹a tape, film›

splint /splɪnt/ *n* جَبيرة (جَبائِرُ)

splinter /ˈsplɪntə/ **A** *n* (of wood, bone) فَسْخة; (of glass, metal) شَظيّة (شَظايا), فُتات (mf; فَتائِتُ)

B *vi* **1** «wood, bone» تَشَظَّى; «glass, metal» تَشَتَّتَ **2** «parties, organizations» تَفَكَّكَ

splinter group *n* جَماعة مُنْشَقّة

split /splɪt/ **A** *vt* (*present participle* **-tt-**; *past tense, past participle* **split**) **1** (to break) شَقَّ (u; شَقّ) ‹the wood, stone›; **to ~ the atom** شَطَرَ الذَرّةَ **2** (to tear) مَزَّقَ ‹one's trousers, a seam› **3** (to divide) قَسَّمَ ‹a group, the participants›; **we were ~ into two teams** قُسِّمْنا إلى فَريقَيْنِ **4** (to cause dissent in) قَسَّمَ ‹a party, family›; **the new candidate ~ the vote** قَسَّمَ المُرَشَّحُ الجَديدُ الأَصْواتَ **5** (to divide) تَقاسَمَ ‹the cost, money›; **they ~ the profits equally** تَقاسَموا الأَرْباحَ بالتَساوي

B *adj* **1** (divided) مُنْقَسِم ‹vote, decision›; **opinion is ~ over this issue** الآراءُ مُنْقَسِمةٌ حول هذه القَضيّةِ **2** (cut) شَقّ ‹lip›

C *vi* (*present participle* **-tt-**; *past tense, past participle* **split**) **1** «wood» انْشَطَرَ, انْقَسَمَ, انْشَقَّ **2** «garment, seam» تَمَزَّقَ; **the box ~ open when he dropped it** انْفَتَحَ الصُنْدوقُ عِنْدَما أَسْقَطَهُ **3** «road, river» تَفَرَّعَ **4** «party, coalition» انْشَقَّ; **the voters ~ along ethnic lines** انْقَسَمَ الناخِبونَ على أُسُسٍ عِرْقيّةٍ **5** (infml) (in relationships) «couple, band» انْفَصَلَ **6** (BrE) (infml) (to inform) **to ~ on sb** أَخْبَرَ عن شَخْصٍ

D *n* **1** (division) قِسْمة; **they agreed on a 50-50 ~ of the profits** اِتَّفَقوا على اقْتِسامِ الأَرْباحِ مُناصَفةً; **there was a three-way ~ in the vote** تَوَزَّعَت الأَصْواتُ على ثَلاثةِ أَقْسامٍ **2** (in parties, movements) انْقِسام (انْقِسامات); **the issue caused a major ~ in the coalition** تَسَبَّبَت القَضيّةُ في انْقِسامٍ حادٍّ في التَحالُفِ **3** (infml) (break-up) انْفِصال (انْفِصالات) **4** (opening) شَقّ (شُقوق) **5** (in wood) شَقّ (شُقوق)

E (**splits**) *n pl* **to do the ~s** قامَ بِتَمارينِ فَتْحِ الحَوْضِ

Idiom **to split the difference** تَقاسَمَ الباقي

Phrasal verb **split up A 1** «couple, band» انْفَصَلَ; **she's ~ up with her boyfriend** انْفَصَلَتْ عن صَديقِها **2** «group, crowd» انْقَسَمَ, تَفَرَّقَ; **to ~ up into five groups** انْقَسَموا إلى خَمْسِ فِرَقٍ **B ~ [sb] up: to ~ the group/a family up** قَسَّمَ الفَريقَ \ عائِلةً إلى قِسْمَيْنِ \ أَقْسامٍ **C ~ [sth] up, ~ up [sth]** اقْتَسَمَ \ تَقاسَمَ [شَيْئاً] ‹the profits, work›

split ends *n* أَطْراف شَعْرٍ مُتَقَصِّفة

split-level /splɪtˈlɛv(ə)l/ *adj* ‹house, apartment› بِمُسْتَوَيَيْنِ

split peas *n* بِسِلّة مُجَفَّفة

split second *n* جُزْء من الثانية

splitting /ˈsplɪtɪŋ/ *adj* (infml) **I've got a ~ headache** أُعاني من صُداعٍ فَظيعٍ

splutter /ˈsplʌtə/ *vi* **1** «person» غَمْغَمَ (i; غَمْغَمة), دَمْدَمَ (i; دَمْدَمة) **2** «engine» [أَحْدَثَ صَوْتاً مُفَرْقِعاً]; «candle, flames» زَفَرَ (i; زَفير)

spoil /spɔɪl/ **A** *vt* (*past tense, past participle* **spoiled** or **spoilt** BrE) **1** (to mar) أَفْسَدَ ‹*sb's enjoyment, a surprise, the view*›; **to ~ sb's fun** أَفْسَدَ فَرْحَةَ شَخْصٍ; **he's ~ing the trip for everybody else** يُفْسِدُ الرِحْلَةَ على الجَميعِ; **it will ~ your appetite** سَتُفْسِدُ شَهِيَّتَكَ; **injury ~ed his chances of winning the championship** أَفْسَدَتْ إصابَتُهُ حُظوظَهُ في الحُصولِ على البُطولةِ **2** (to indulge) دَلَّلَ ‹*a child*›; **he was the ~ed child of aging parents** كانَ طِفلاً مُدَلَّلاً لِأَبَوَيْنِ كَبيرَيْنِ; **to ~ sb rotten** (infml) دَلَّلَ شَخْصاً تَدْليلاً كَثيراً **3** (in voting) أَبْطَلَ ‹*a ballot paper*›

B *vi* (*past tense, past participle* **spoiled** or **spoilt** BrE) «food, meat» فَسَدَ (i-u; فَساد); **your dinner will ~!** سَيَفْسُدُ عَشاؤُكَ!

C (**spoils**) *n pl* غَنيمة (غَنائِمُ)

(Idioms) **to be spoiling for a fight** سَعى جاهداً إلى القِتالِ; **to be spoilt for choice** (BrE) احْتارَ من كَثْرةِ الاخْتياراتِ

spoiled /spɔɪld/, **spoilt** /spɔɪlt/ (BrE) *adj* ‹*child, dog*› مُدَلَّل; **a ~ rich kid** طِفْل غَنِيّ مُدَلَّل

spoiler /ˈspɔɪlə/ *n* **1** (on cars, planes) سْبويْلَر **2** (in elections) [مُرَشَّح يَهْدُفُ إلى تَشْتيتِ الأَصْواتِ] **3** (plot details) تَسْريب [يُفْسِدُ الاسْتِمْتاعَ بِأَحْداثِ القِصّةِ]

spoils /spɔɪlz/ *n pl* (of war, crime) سَلَب (أَسْلاب), غَنيمة (غَنائِمُ)

spoilsport /ˈspɔɪlspɔːt/ *n* (infml) [شَخْص يُعَكِّرُ أَفْراحَ الآخَرينَ]

spoilt /spɔɪlt/ (BrE) **A** *past tense, past participle* ▸**spoil**

B ▸**spoiled**

spoke /spəʊk/ **A** *past tense* ▸**speak**

B *n* بَرْمَق, شُعاع عَجَلةٍ

(Idiom) **to put a spoke in sb's wheel** عَرْقَلَ \ أَحْبَطَ خُطّةَ شَخْصٍ

spoken /ˈspəʊk(ə)n/ **A** *past participle* ▸**speak**

B *adj* ‹*word, language*› مَنْطوق

spokesman /ˈspəʊksmən/ *n* (*pl* **-men**) مُتَحَدِّث (بالاسْمِ), ناطِق (باللِسانِ)

spokesperson /ˈspəʊkspɜːs(ə)n/ *n* مُتَحَدِّث (بالاسْمِ), ناطِق (باللِسانِ)

sponge /spʌndʒ/ **A** *n* **1** (for washing, cleaning) إسْفَنْج **2** (Zool) إسْفَنْج **3** (also **sponge cake**) (BrE) كَعْكة إسْفَنْجيّة

B *vt* **1** (to clean) نَظَّفَ (بِإسْفَنْجةٍ) ‹*a surface, stain*› **2** (infml) (to scrounge) **to ~ sth off** *or* **from sb** تَسَوَّلَ شَيْئاً من شَخْصٍ

C *vi* (infml) **to ~ off** *or* **on sb** عاشَ عالةً على شَخْصٍ

(Phrasal verb) **sponge down: ~ [sth] down, ~ down [sth]** نَظَّفَ [شَيْئاً] بِإسْفَنْجةٍ ‹*a surface, an animal*›

sponge bag *n* حَقيبة حَمّامٍ

sponsor /ˈspɒnsə/ **A** *n* **1** (of a sporting event, show) راعٍ (رُعاة), مُمَوِّل **2** (for charity) راعٍ (رُعاة), مُتَبَرِّع **3** (guarantor) كَفيل (كُفَلاءُ) **4** (of a bill, legislation) مُؤَيِّد (لِقَرارٍ أو قانونٍ)

B *vt* **1** رَعى (a; رِعاية) ‹*an event, a team*› **2** رَعى (a; رِعاية), مَوَّلَ ‹*a project, research*› **3** (for charity) رَعى (بِتَقْديمِ الدَعْمِ المالِيِّ) ‹*a participant, walker*› **4** قَدَّمَ, اقْتَرَحَ ‹*a bill, legislation*›

sponsorship /ˈspɒnsəʃɪp/ *n* (of an event, a team, a project, the arts) رِعاية, تَمْويل

spontaneous /spɒnˈteɪnɪəs/ *adj* ‹*applause, reaction*› عَفْوِيّ, تِلْقائِيّ

spontaneously /spɒnˈteɪnɪəsli/ *adv* ‹*to occur, respond*› تِلْقائِيًّا

spoof /spuːf/ *n* (infml) مُحاكاة تَهَكُّمِيّة, تَقْليد ساخِر

spooky /ˈspuːki/ *adj* (**spookier, spookiest**) (infml) ‹*story, music*› مُرْعِب, مُخيف

spool /spuːl/ *n* بَكَرة

spoon /spuːn/ *n* مِلْعَقة (مَلاعِقُ)

spoon-feed /ˈspuːnfiːd/ *vt* (*past tense, past participle* **-fed** /-fɛd/) **1** لَقَّمَ بِمِلْعَقةٍ ‹*a baby, an invalid*› **2** (pej) (to help too much) لَقَّمَ, لَقَّنَ ‹*students, audiences*›

spoonful /ˈspuːnfʊl/ *n* (*pl* **spoonfuls**) مِلْءُ مِلْعَقةٍ

sporadic /spəˈradɪk/ *adj* ‹*violence, outbreaks*› مُتَقَطِّع, مُتَفَرِّق

spore /spɔː/ *n* بَوْغ (أَبْواغ)

sport /spɔːt/ *n* **1** [u] (BrE) (**sports** *n pl* AmE) (sporting activities) رِياضة **2** (individual sport) رِياضة **3** (understanding person) **he's a good ~** [هو رَجُل طَيِّب]

sporting /ˈspɔːtɪŋ/ *adj* **1** (relating to sport) ‹*event, achievement*› رِياضيّ **2** (fair) ‹*person, spirit*› ذو روحٍ رِياضيّةٍ

sports car *n* سَيّارة رِياضيّة

sports centre (BrE), **sports center** (AmE) *n* مَرْكَز رِياضيّ

sports club *n* نادٍ رِياضيّ

sports ground *n* مَلْعَب (مَلاعِبُ)

sports jacket *n* سُتْرة (سُتَر)

sportsman /ˈspɔːtsmən/ *n* (*pl* **-men**) رِياضيّ

sportsmanship /ˈspɔːtsmənʃɪp/ *n* روح رِياضيّة

sportswear /ˈspɔːtsweː/ *n* مَلابِس رِياضيّة

sportswoman /ˈspɔːtswʊmən/ *n* (*pl* **-women**) (لاعِبة) رِياضيّة

sporty /ˈspɔːti/ *adj* (**sportier**, **sportiest**) (infml) **1** ‹*person*› رِياضيّ **2** ‹*car*› رِياضيّ

spot /spɒt/ **A** *n* **1** (on animals) بُقْعة (بِقاع ,بُقَع); (on fabric) بُقْعة (بِقاع ,بُقَع); **to see ~s before one's eyes** رَأى بُقَعاً أمام عَيْنَيْه **2** (stain) بُقْعة (بِقاع ,بُقَع) **3** (pimple) بَثْر (n coll; بُثُور); **to come out in ~s** أُصيبَ بِحَبِّ الشَّبابِ **4** (place) بُقْعة (بُقَع, بِقاع); **to look for a shady/sunny ~** بَحَثَ عن بُقْعةٍ ظَليلةٍ \ مُشْمِسةٍ; **the ambulance was on the ~ in no time** كانَتْ سَيّارةُ الإسْعافِ في المَكانِ في لَمْحِ البَصَرِ; **he was sacked on the ~** أُقيلَ من مَنْصِبِه فَوْراً; **the album held the top ~ for ten weeks** حافَظَ الألْبوم على المَرْتَبةِ الأولى لِعَشَرةِ أسابيعَ **5** (infml) (small amount) مِقْدار قَليل; **I did a ~ of shopping/gardening** اشْتَرَيْتُ أشْياءَ قَليلةً \ عَمِلْتُ قَليلاً في الحَديقةِ; **he got into a ~ of bother with the police** دَخَلَ في مُناوَشةٍ صَغيرةٍ مع الشُّرْطةِ **6** (TV appearance) فَقْرة تِلِفِزْيونيّة **7** (in advertising) فاصِل إعْلانيّ **8** (for penalty kicks) نُقْطة ضَرْبةِ الجَزاءِ
B *vt* (**-tt**) **1** (to see) لَمَحَ (a; لَمْح) ‹*a person, road sign*›; **to ~ sb doing sth** لَمَحَ شَخْصاً يَفْعَلُ شَيْئاً; **well ~ted!** قُوّة مُلاحَظةٍ مُمْتازة! **2** (to recognize) لاحَظَ ‹*a problem, bargain, the signs*›; رَصَدَ (u; رَصْد) ‹*an opportunity, a bargain*›; **can you ~ the difference between the photos?** هل تَسْتَطيعُ أن تُلاحِظَ الاخْتِلافَ بين الصورَتَيْنِ؟; **he was ~ted as he tried to board a plane** رُصِدَ عِنْدَما كانَ يُحاوِلُ الصُعودَ إلى طائِرةٍ **3** (to mark) بَقَّعَ ‹*a shirt, carpet*›

Idioms **to be in a tight spot** (infml) كانَ في وَرْطةٍ \ مَأْزِقٍ; **to have a soft spot for sb** كانَ مُغْرَماً \ مولَعاً بِشَخْصٍ; **to put sb on the spot** وَضَعَ شَخْصاً في الزاوِيةِ

spot check *n* عَيِّنة عَشْوائيّة

spotless /ˈspɒtləs/ *adj* **1** ‹*kitchen, floor*› في غايةِ النَظافةِ; ‹*suit, uniform*› في غايةِ النَصاعةِ **2** ‹*record, reputation*› لا عَيْبَ فيهِ, نَقيّ لا غُبارَ عَلَيْه

spotlight /ˈspɒtlaɪt/ *n* (in a theatre) ضَوْء مَسْرَحٍ; (on a building, vehicle) ضَوْء كَشّاف; (in the home) مِصْباح مَوْضِعيّ; **she is once again in the media ~** أصْبَحَتْ مَرّةً أُخْرى مَحَطَّ اهْتِمامِ وَسائِلِ الإعْلامِ

spot price *n* السِعْرُ الفَوْريّ \ الآنيّ

spotted /ˈspɒtɪd/ *adj* **1** ‹*fur, dog*› أَرْقَط (dipt), مُنَقَّط **2** ‹*tie, dress*› مُنَقَّط

spotter plane /ˈspɒtə pleɪn/ *n* طائِرة اسْتِطْلاعٍ

spotty /ˈspɒti/ *adj* (**spottier**, **spottiest**) **1** ‹*dog, pattern*› مُرَقَّط **2** (BrE) (pimply) ‹*skin, complexion*› مَليء بالبُثورِ, نَمِش; ‹*teenager, youth*› أَنْمَش (dipt; نُمْش)

spouse /spaʊz/ *n* زَوْج (mf; أزْواج), قَرين (قُرَناءُ)

spout /spaʊt/ **A** *n* **1** (of a teapot, kettle) فُوَهة, بُزْبوز (بَزابيزُ) **2** (pipe on a gutter, fountain) ماسورة (مَواسيرُ) **3** (jet) دَفْق
B *vt* **1** (to spurt) دَفَقَ (i-u; دُفوق) ‹*water, blood*› **2** (to recite) تَفَوَّهَ (ب) ‹*nonsense, platitudes*›
C *vi* «water, blood» تَدَفَّقَ, انْبَجَسَ

sprain /spreɪn/ **A** *vt* لَوى (i; لَيّ), وَثَأَ (a; وَثْء) ‹*your ankle, a joint*›
B *n* الْتِواء (الْتِواءات), وَثْء

sprang /spraŋ/ *past tense* ▸ **spring**

sprawl /sprɔːl/ **A** *vi* «passengers, children» اسْتَلْقى (باسِطاً ذِراعَيْه وساقَيْه)
B *n* انْتِشار بِدونِ تَنْظيمٍ

spray /spreɪ/ **A** *n* **1** [u] (from the sea) رَذاذ البَحْرِ **2** [u] (of water, perfume) رَذاذ **3** (aerosol) بَخّاخ; **a nasal ~** بَخّاخ أنْفٍ **4** (for perfume) رَشّاشة عِطْرٍ **5** (posy) باقة أزْهارٍ
B *vt* رَشّ (u; رَشّ), بَخَّ (u; بَخّ) ‹*water, paint*›; **they ~ed the fields with insecticide** رَشّوا الحُقولَ بِمُبيدِ الحَشَراتِ; **to ~ insecticide onto/over the plants** رَشَّ مُبيدَ الحَشَراتِ على النَباتاتِ; **to ~ sb/sth with bullets** رَشَّ شَخْصاً بالرَصاصِ
C *vi* «blood, water» تَدَفَّقَ; **water ~ed from the hydrant** تَدَفَّقَ الماءُ من خُرْطومِ المَطافِئِ

spray can *n* مِرَشّة, بَخّاخ (مَراشّ)

spray paint *n* دِهان \ طَلاء رَشّ

spread /sprɛd/ **A** *vt* (*past tense, past participle* **spread**) **1** (to open out) فَتَحَ (a; فَتْح) ‹*a cloth, map*›; **to ~ a cloth on the table** بَسَطَ سِماطاً على الطاوِلةِ **2** (to stretch out) «bird» مَدَّ (u; مَدّ) ‹*its wings*›; **to ~ one's arms/legs** مَدَّ ذِراعَيْهِ \ ساقَيْهِ **3** (to propagate) نَشَرَ (u; نَشْر) ‹*disease, infection*›; **a strong wind ~ the blaze** نَشَرَتْ ريحٌ قَوِيّةٌ الحَريقَ **4** (in layers) دَهَنَ (u; دَهْن) ‹*butter, jam*›; **to ~ the cake with cream** دَهَنَ الكَعْكَ بالقِشْدةِ **5** (to distribute) وَزَّعَ ‹*manure, sand*› **6** (to disseminate) نَشَرَ (u; نَشْر) ‹*a rumour, the news*›; **to ~ the word about sth** نَشَرَ خَبَراً حول شَيْءٍ **7** (to stagger) وَزَّعَ ‹*the cost, payments*› **8** (to share out) تَقاسَمَ ‹*the workload, wealth*›; **we have to ~ our resources very thinly** يَجِبُ أن نوَزِّعَ المَوارِدَ بَيْننا بِشَكْلٍ مُتَحَفِّظٍ

B *vi* (*past tense, past participle* **spread**) **1** (to proliferate) «disease, infection» اِنْتَشَرَ, تَفَشّى; **fires ~ quickly in the dry conditions** تَنْتَشِرُ النيرانُ بِسُرْعةٍ في الظُروفِ الجافّةِ **2** (to extend) «fame, species, forest» اِنْتَشَرَ, اِمْتَدَّ; **the cancer has ~ to her liver** اِنْتَشَرَ السَرَطانُ إلى كَبِدِها; **rain will ~ to most areas during the night** سَتَمْتَدُّ الأَمْطارُ إلى مُعْظَمِ المَناطِقِ أثناء اللَيْلِ **3** (to be disseminated) «rumours, news» اِنْتَشَرَ; «panic, fear» تَفَشّى; **rumours ~ that the prisoners were going to be freed** اِنْتَشَرَت الإشاعاتُ بِأَنَّ الأَسْرى سَيُحَرَّرونَ **4** «butter, jam» دُهِنَ

C *n* **1** (of diseases) تَفَشٍّ **2** (of fashions, nuclear weapons, etc) اِنْتِشار; **the ~ of mobile phone use** اِنْتِشار اسْتِخْدام الهاتِفِ المَحْمولِ; **the ~ of secularism in Europe** اِنْتِشار العَلْمانيّةِ في أوروبّا **3** (of ideas) اِنْتِشار **4** (of wings, branches) اِمْتِداد (اِمْتِدادات) **5** (range) مَجال (مَجالات); **to have a wide/narrow ~ of interests** كانَ عِنْدَهُ مَجالُ اِهْتِماماتٍ واسِعٌ \ ضَيِّقٌ **6** (in a newspaper) **a double-page ~** مَنْشور على صَفْحَتَيْنِ **7** (for bread) [مَعْجون للدَهْن] **8** (infml) (large meal) مَأْدُبة (مَآدِبُ) **9** (AmE) (ranch) مَزْرَعة (مَزارِعُ)

(Idiom) **to spread one's wings** وَسَّعَ آفاقَهُ \ دائِرةَ اِهْتِماماتِهِ

(Phrasal verb) **spread out** **A** **1** (to move apart) «troops, search party» اِنْتَشَرَ, تَوَزَّعَ **2** (to extend) «city, fields» اِمْتَدَّ **B** ~ [sth] out, ~ out [sth] **1** (to open out) فَتَحَ \ بَسَطَ [شَيْئاً] ‹*a cloth, map*› **2** (to stretch out) مَدَّ [شَيْئاً] ‹*one's arms, hands*› **3** (over an area) نَشَرَ [شَيْئاً] ‹*cards, papers*›

spreadeagled /sprɛdˈiːg(ə)ld/ *adj* ‹*arms, legs*› مُنْفَرِجِ الذِراعَيْنِ والساقَيْنِ

spreadsheet /ˈsprɛdʃiːt/ *n* جَدْوَل حِسابِيّ

spree /spriː/ *n* [اِنْغِماس في نَشاطٍ ما]; **to go on a shopping ~** خَرَجَ في جَوْلةِ شِراءٍ في المَتاجِرِ

sprig /sprɪg/ *n* عُسْلوج (عَسالِجُ)

sprightly /ˈsprʌɪtli/ *adj* (**sprightlier**, **sprightliest**) **1** (of people) ‹*pensioner, old lady*› مُفْعَم بالحَيَويّةِ, نَشيط **2** (of movements) ‹*walk, dance*› خَفيفُ الحَرَكةِ, نَشيط

spring /sprɪŋ/ **A** *vt* (*past tense* **sprang** or **sprung**; *past participle* **sprung**) **1** (to produce unexpectedly) فاجَأَ (ب); **I'm sorry to ~ the news on you like this** أَعْتَذِرُ أنّي فاجَأْتُكَ بالأَخْبارِ على هذا النَحْوِ; **to ~ a surprise on sb** فاجَأَ شَخْصاً **2** (to set off) ‹*a trap*›; **to ~ a trap on sb** أَوْقَعَ شَخْصاً في الفَخِّ **3** (to develop) **to ~ a leak** أَغْلَقَ اِنْثَقَبَ

B *vi* (*past tense* **sprang** or **sprung**; *past participle* **sprung**) **1** (to jump) قَفَزَ (i; قَفْز, قَفَزان); **I sprang out of bed** قَفَزْتُ من السَريرِ; **he sprang to his feet** قَفَزَ واقِفاً على رِجْلَيْهِ; **to ~ at sb** اِرْتَمى على شَخْصٍ **2** (to activate) **the door/suitcase sprang open** اِنْفَتَحَ البابُ \ اِنْفَتَحَت الحَقيبةُ فَجْأةً; **to ~ into action** هَبَّ إلى العَمَلِ; **the engine sprang to life** اِنْطَلَقَ المُحَرِّكُ بِقوّةٍ **3** (to originate) **to ~ from sth** «idea, problem» اِنْبَثَقَ من شَيْءٍ **4** (to appear) ظَهَرَ (a; ظُهور); **where did you ~ from?** مِن أَيْنَ خَرَجْتَ؟; **one example that ~s to mind is Japan** أَحَدُ الأَمْثِلةِ الّتي تَخْطُرُ على البالِ هو اليابان

C *n* **1** (season) رَبيع (أَرْبِعة); ▸ **summer** **2** (metal coil) زُنْبُرُك (زَنابِكُ), لَوْلَب (لَوالِبُ) **3** (jump) قَفْزة (قَفَزات) **4** (water source) عَيْن (f; عُيون, أَعْيُن), نَبْع (نُبوع) **5** [u] (elasticity) مُرونة; **to have a ~ in one's step** [اِمْتَلَأَ طاقةً وَحَيَويّةً]

(Phrasal verb) **spring up** **1** (to jump to one's feet) قَفَزَ واقِفاً **2** (to appear) «buildings, groups, weeds» بَرَزَ (u; بُروز); **a cold wind had sprung up** هَبَّتْ ريحٌ بارِدةٌ

springboard /'sprɪŋbɔːd/ *n* (in gymnastics) مَنَصّة وَثْبٍ; (for diving) لَوْح غَطْسٍ

spring-clean /ˌsprɪŋ'kliːn/ *vt* نَظَّفَ تَنْظيفاً تامّاً ‹a house, room›

spring-cleaning /sprɪŋ'kliːnɪŋ/ *n* تَنْظيف تامّ

spring flower *n* زَهْرة الرَبيع

spring onion *n* (BrE) بَصَل أَخْضر

springtime /'sprɪŋtʌɪm/ *n* فَصْل \ مَوْسِم الرَبيع

springy /'sprɪŋi/ *adj* (**springier, springiest**) ‹mattress, floor› مَرِن

sprinkle /'sprɪŋk(ə)l/ *vt* ذَرَّ (u; ذَرّ), رَشَّ (u; رَشّ) ‹salt, water›; **to ~ salt on/over her food** ذَرَّ المِلْحَ على طَعامِها

sprinkler /'sprɪŋklə/ *n* 1 (in gardens) رَشّاشة \ مِرَشّة زِراعيّة 2 (in buildings) رَشّاش حَريقٍ \ مِياهٍ إِرْوائيّة

sprint /sprɪnt/ A *vi* 1 (in athletics) «runners, athletes» عَدا (مَسافةً قَصيرةً بِأَقْصى السُرْعةِ) 2 (to run fast) «children, men» رَكَضَ (u; رَكْض)
B *n* 1 (short race) عَدْو 2 (fast run) جَرْي سَريع

sprout /spraʊt/ A *vt* 1 ‹leaves, shoots› بَرْعَمَ (i; بَرْعمة) 2 ‹a beard› رَبّى; ‹wings, horns› نَما لَهُ
B *vi* 1 (to grow) «leaves, weeds, hair» نَما (u; نُمُوّ) 2 (to germinate) «seeds» نَبَتَ (u; نَبْت) 3 (to appear) ▸ **sprout up**
C *n* 1 (on a plant) بُرْعُم (بَراعِمُ) 2 (also **Brussels sprout**) كُرُنْب بْروكْسَل
Phrasal verb **sprout up** «buildings, companies» بَرَزَ فَجْأةً

spruce /spruːs/ A *n* (also **spruce tree**) تَنّوب, شوح
B *adj* (**-cer, -cest**) «clothes, house» مُهَنْدَم
Phrasal verb **spruce up**: ~ **up** [**sth/sb**], ~ [**sth/sb**] **up** هَنْدَمَ [شَيْئاً \ شَخْصاً] ‹a house, oneself›

sprung /sprʌŋ/ *past participle* ▸ **spring**

spry /sprʌɪ/ *adj* (**-er, -est**) ‹grandmother, old man› نَشيط (نِشاط), مُفْعَم بالحَيَويّةِ

spud /spʌd/ *n* (infml) بَطاطا (dipt), بَطاطِس

spun /spʌn/ *past tense, past participle* ▸ **spin**

spur /spɜː/ A *n* 1 (stimulus) حافِز (حَوافِزُ); **competition acts as a ~ for** *or* **to innovation** تَعْمَلُ المُنافَسةُ كَحافِزٍ للابْتِكارِ 2 (in horse riding) مِهْماز (مَهاميزُ) 3 (of mountain) نُتوء جَبَليّ 4 (branch line) فَرْع سِكَكٍ حَديديّةٍ قَصير 5 (cockerel's) مِهْماز (مَهاميزُ)
B *vt* (**-rr-**) 1 (to encourage) حَفَّزَ; **to ~ sb to do sth** حَفَّزَ شَخْصاً على فِعْلِ شَيْءٍ; **fear ~red me into action** دَفَعَني الخَوْفُ إلى العَمَلِ; **~red on by his success, he is writing more songs** يَكْتُبُ أُغْنياتٍ أَكْثَرَ مَدْفوعاً بِنَجاحِهِ 2 (to promote) ‹growth, development› شَجَّعَ 3 (to urge forward) ‹a horse› حَثَّ (u; حَثّ) (على)
Idiom **on the spur of the moment** دون سابق تَخْطيطٍ

spurious /'spjʊərɪəs/ (pej) *adj* (unconvincing) ‹excuse, evidence› غَيْر مُقْنِعٍ

spurn /spɜːn/ *vt* ‹an offer, an opportunity› رَفَضَ (i-u; رَفْض), أَبى (a; إباء, إباءة)

spurt /spɜːt/ A *vi* (also **spurt out**) «water, blood» تَدَفَّقَ, انْبَجَس
B *n* 1 (of water, blood) تَدَفُّق (تَدَفُّقات), دُفْقة (دُفُقات, دُفْقات) 2 (of activity, energy) طَفْرة (نَشاطٍ)

sputum /'spjuːtəm/ *n* بَلْغَم (بَلاغِمُ)

spy /spʌɪ/ A *n* (*pl* **spies**) جاسوس (جَواسيسُ)
B *vt* (**spies, spying, spied**) (fml) لَمَحَ (a; لَمْح), رَأى (a; رُؤْية), لاحَظَ ‹a figure, an object›
C *vi* **to ~ on sb/sth** «informers, neighbours» تَجَسَّسَ على شَخْصٍ \ شَيْءٍ; **to ~ for a foreign power** تَجَسَّسَ لِصالِحِ قوّةٍ خارِجيّةٍ

spying /'spʌɪɪŋ/ *n* تَجَسُّس

sq. *abbr* = **square** مَيْدان (مَيادينُ)

squabble /'skwɒb(ə)l/ *vi* (infml) «children, families» تَنازَعَ, ناقَرَ, تَشاجَرَ; **he's squabbling with his sister again** ها هو يَتَشاجَرُ مع أُخْتِهِ ثانِيةً

squad /skwɒd/ *n* 1 (of soldiers) فِرْقة (فِرَق), فَصيلة (فَصائِلُ) 2 (of players) فَريق 3 (of the police) فَريق, فِرْقة (فِرَق); **the fraud ~** فَريق مُكافَحةِ جَرائِمِ الاحْتِيالِ

squad car *n* سَيّارة دَوْريّةٍ

squadron /'skwɒdrən/ *n* 1 (of planes) سِرْب (أَسْراب); **a fighter/bomber ~** سِرْب طائِراتٍ حَرْبيّةٍ \ قاذِفاتِ قَنابِلَ 2 (division of a regiment) سَرِيّة (سَرايا) 3 (of ships) أُسْطول (أَساطيلُ)

squadron leader *n* (BrE) رائِد (روّاد)

squalid /ˈskwɒlɪd/ *adj* **1** (dirty) ‹*apartment, condition*› وَسِخ, قَذِر **2** (sordid) ‹*story, affair*› دَنيء

squall /skwɔːl/ *n* (أَنْواء) نَوْء ,عَصْفة

squalor /ˈskwɒlə/ *n* دَناءة ,وَساخة, قَذارة

squander /ˈskwɒndə/ *vt* **1** (to waste) بَدَّد, بَذَّر ‹*a fortune, resources*› **2** (to misuse) ضَيَّعَ ‹*an opportunity*›

square /skwɛː/ **A** *n* **1** (in a town) ساحة (ساح, ساحات) مَيْدان (مَيادينُ); **the main ~** الساحة الرَّئيسيّة **2** (in maths) مُرَبَّع (مُرَبَّعات); (in board games, crosswords) خانة ,(مُرَبَّعات) مُرَبَّع; (of cloth, wood) قِطْعة مُرَبَّعة; **to divide a page up into ~s** قَسَّمَ صَفْحةً إلى مُرَبَّعاتٍ **3** (number) مُرَبَّع; **9 is the ~ of 3** 9 هو مُرَبَّعُ العَدَدِ 3 **4** (instrument) كوس (كوسات) **5** (old use infml) (old-fashioned person) [شَخْص تَقْليديّ]

B *adj* **1** (in shape) ‹*hole, box*› مُرَبَّع **2** (right-angled) ‹*corner, frame*› زاوِية قائِمة; **to be ~ with the wall/edge** كَوَّنَ زاوِيةً قائِمةً مع الجِدارِ \ الحافةِ **3** (in area measurement) ‹*metre, kilometre, inch*› مُرَبَّع; **the lake covers four ~ kilometres** تُغَطّي البُحَيْرةُ مِساحةَ أَرْبَعةِ كيلومِتْراتٍ مُرَبَّعةٍ; **an area four metres ~** مِساحة أَرْبَعة أَمْتارٍ مُرَبَّعةٍ **4** (on equal terms) **to be all ~** «clients, friends» كانوا مُتَخالِصين; **after 45 minutes they were all ~ at two-two** «teams» بعد 45 دَقيقةً كانوا مُتَعادِلينَ **5** (honest) **to give sb/to get a ~ deal** أَعْطى شَخْصاً سِعْراً مَعْقولاً \ حَصَلَ على سِعْرٍ مَعْقولٍ

C *adv* (directly) ‹*to fall, hit*› مُباشَرةً; **she looked him ~ in the eye** نَظَرَتْ إلَيْهِ مُباشَرةً في العَيْنَيْنِ; **he hit me ~ on the jaw** ضَرَبَني مُباشَرةً على الفَكِّ

D *vt* **1** (to make right-angled) رَبَّعَ ‹*timber, a block*› **2** (to settle) سَدَّدَ ‹*an account, a debt*›; **to ~ one's account with sb** صَفّى حِسابَهُ مع شَخْصٍ **3** (to make equal) عَدَّلَ ‹*a game, score, series*›

E (**squared**) *adj* **1** ‹*paper*› مُرَبَّع **2** (Math) ‹*number*› مُرَبَّع; **6 ~d is 36** 36 هو العَدَدُ 6 مُرَبَّعُ العَدَدِ

(Phrasal verbs) **square up** **1** (to prepare to fight) واجَهَ **2** (to settle up) صَفّى حِساباً; **to ~ up with sb** صَفّى حِساباً مع شَخْصٍ

• **square with**: **A ~ with sth** (to be consistent with) اتَّفَقَ مع شَيْءٍ ‹*the facts, a statement*› **B ~ sth with sb** (to obtain permission for) اسْتَأْذَنَ من شَخْصٍ ‹*the idea, plan*›; **I'll ~ it with the manager** سَأَسْتَأْذِنُ من المُديرِ

square brackets *n* قَوْسانِ مُرَبَّعانِ

squarely /ˈskwɛːli/ *adv* ‹*to stand, land*› بِشَكْلٍ مُسْتَقيم; **she looked him ~ in the eye** نَظَرَتْ إلَيْهِ وَجْهاً لِوَجْهٍ

square root *n* جَذْر تَرْبيعيّ

squash /skwɒʃ/ **A** *vt* **1** (to crush) سَحَقَ (a; سَحْق), هَرَسَ (u; هَرْس) ‹*an insect, fruit*› **2** (to press) كَبَسَ (i; كَبْس), حَشَرَ (i-u; حَشْر) ‹*clothes, passengers*›

B *vi* «passengers, children» انْحَشَرَ

C *n* **1** [u] (game) لُعْبة الإسْكُواش **2** (BrE) (drink) عَصير فاكِهةٍ **3** (vegetable) يَقْطين, قَرْع (n coll)

squashy /ˈskwɒʃi/ *adj* (**-shier**, **-shiest**) (infml) ‹*sofa, fruit*› ناعِم, لَيِّن

squat /skwɒt/ **A** *vi* (**-tt-**) **1** (to crouch) «children, animals» جَلَسَ القُرْفُصاءَ, قَرْفَصَ (i; قَرْفَصة) **2** (in a building, on land) «homeless, travellers» [أَقامَ في مَكانٍ بِدونِ إِذْنٍ]

B *adj* (**-tt-**) ‹*man, tower*› بُحْتُر, قَصير وَعَريض

squatter /ˈskwɒtə/ *n* [مُحْتَلّ عِقارٍ بالاغْتِصابِ]

squawk /skwɔːk/ **A** *vi* «parrots, birds» صَرَخَ (u; صُراخ)

B *n* صُراخ

squeak /skwiːk/ **A** *n* **1** (of a child) صُراخ; (of a mouse) صَرير **2** (of a hinge, chalk) صَرير **3** (of shoes, floorboards) صَرير

B *vi* **1** «doors, hinges» صَرَّ (i; صَرير, صَرّ) **2** «children» صَرَخَ (u; صُراخ); «mice» صَرَّ (i; صَرير) **3** «floorboards, shoes» صَرَّ (i; صَرير)

squeaky /ˈskwiːki/ *adj* (**squeakier**, **squeakiest**) ‹*voice*› ذو صَوْتٍ حادٍّ; ‹*gate*› ذو صَريرٍ

squeal /skwiːl/ **A** *n* **1** (of children, pigs) زَعْق, صِياح **2** (of brakes, tyres) صَفير, أَزيز, صَرير

B *vi* **1** «children, pigs» صاحَ (i; صِياح), زَعَقَ (a; زَعْق) **2** «brakes, cars» صَرَّ (i; صَرير), أَزَّ (i-u; أَزيز), صَفَرَ **3** (infml) (to inform) «suspects, members» وَشى (i; وَشْي), أَدْلى بِمَعْلوماتٍ

squeamish /ˈskwiːmɪʃ/ *adj* ‹*disposition, viewer*› سَريع الغَثَيانِ

squeeze /skwi:z/ **A** *vt* **1** (to press) ضَغَطَ (a; ضَغْط (على) ‹*a lemon, tube, sb's hand*›; **to ~ some glue onto sth** ضَغَطَ بَعْضَ الغِراءِ على شَيْءٍ; **she ~d my hand** ضَغَطَتْ على يَدي **2** (to press) ضَغَطَ (a; ضَغْط (على) ‹*the trigger*› **3** (to make fit) **to ~ sth into sth** زَجَّ بِشَيْءٍ في شَيْءٍ; **to ~ the clothes into the case/drawer** ضَغَطَ المَلابِسَ في الحقيبةِ \ الدُرْجِ **4** (infml) (to extract) انْتَزَعَ; **I ~d a loan out of my dad** انْتَزَعْتُ قَرْضاً من أَبي; **to ~ the truth/a confession out of sb** انْتَزَعَ الحَقيقةَ \ اعْتِرافاً من شَخْصٍ **5** (to reduce) قَلَّلَ ‹*profits, margins*›
B *vi* (into a space, room) دَخَلَ بِصُعوبةٍ; **to ~ into a dress** لَبِسَتْ فُسْتاناً بِصُعوبةٍ; **to manage to ~ through the gap** تَمَكَّنَ من العُبورِ من خِلالِ الفَجْوةِ بِصُعوبةٍ
C *n* **1** (pressing) ضَغْط (ضُغوط); **to give the tube/sb's hand a ~** ضَغَطَ على الأُنْبوبِ \ يَدِ شَخْصٍ; **to give sb a ~** عانَقَ شَخْصاً **2** (small amount) **a ~ of lemon** قَليل من اللَيْمونِ **3** (on spending, salaries) قَيْد (قُيود); **to impose a ~ on lending** فَرَضَ قُيوداً على الإِقْراضِ **4** (infml) (crush) **to be a tight ~** كانَ مُكْتَظّاً

Phrasal verbs **squeeze in**: **~ [sb] in** حَشَرَ [شَخْصاً] في الجَدْوَلِ ‹*a patient, client*›
• **squeeze out** **A** **~ [sth] out, ~ out [sth]** عَصَرَ [شَيْئاً] ‹*a cloth, mop*› **B** **~ [sb] out, ~ out [sb]** ضَيَّقَ على [شَخْصٍ] ‹*a competitor, company*›
• **squeeze past**: **~ past [sth/sb]** مَرَّ بِصُعوبةٍ قَريباً من [شَيْءٍ \ شَخْصٍ] ‹*an obstacle, a person*›

squelch /skweltʃ/ **A** *vt* (infml) ‹*the opposition, protest*› سَحَقَ (a; سَحْق)
B *vi* «mud, boots» بَقْبَقَ (i; بَقْبَقة)

squid /skwɪd/ *n* (*pl* **squid**) (creature) حَبّار

squiggle /ˈskwɪg(ə)l/ *n* خَرْبَشة

squint /skwɪnt/ **A** *vi* **1** (to blink) «old people, eyes» ضَيَّقَ عَيْنَيْهِ (عند النَظَرِ) **2** (to be cross-eyed) «patients» حَوِلَ (a; حَوَل), كانَ أَحْوَلَ
B *n* حَوَل

squire /skwʌɪə/ *n* (BrE) **1** (landowner) مالِك ضَيْعةٍ **2** (infml) (as form of address) أَخي

squirm /skwəːm/ *vi* «worms, children» تَلَوّى

squirrel /ˈskwɪrəl/ *n* سِنْجاب (سَناجيبُ)

squirt /skwəːt/ **A** *vt* رَشَّ (u; رَشّ), بَخَّ (u; بَخّ), ثَجَّ (u; ثَجّ) ‹*ink, water*›
B *vi* «oil, juice» سالَ (i; سَيْل, سَيَلان), انْصَبَّ, تَدَفَّقَ, انْبَجَسَ

Sr /ˈsiːnjə/ *abbr* = **senior** (in a family) الأَب; **Harry Fenton, S~** هاري فينْتون الأَب

Sri Lanka /sri ˈlaŋkə/ *pr n* سِريلانْكا

Sri Lankan /sri ˈlaŋk(ə)n/ *n, adj* سِريلانْكيّ

St /seɪnt/ *abbr* **1** = **Saint** القِدّيس **2** = **Street** شارِع

stab /stab/ **A** *vt* (**-bb-**) طَعَنَ (a-u; طَعْن) ‹*a teenager, policeman*›
B *n* **1** (with a knife) طَعْنة **2** (of pain) وَخْز **3** (infml) (attempt) مُحاوَلة; **to have a ~ at sth/doing sth** حاوَلَ شَيْئاً

stabbing /ˈstabɪŋ/ **A** *n* مُشاجَرة بالسَكاكين
B *adj* ‹*pain, sensation*› واخِز

stability /stəˈbɪlɪti/ *n* اسْتِقْرار

stabilization, -isation (BrE) /steɪbəlʌɪˈzeɪʃ(ə)n/ *n* **1** (Fin) تَثْبيت **2** (Med) العَمَل على اسْتِقْرارِ (المَريضِ)

stabilize, -ise (BrE) /ˈsteɪbɪlʌɪz/ **A** *vt* **1** ثَبَّتَ, جَعَلَ مُسْتَقِرًّا ‹*an economy, prices*› **2** جَعَلَ الحالةَ مُسْتَقِرّةً ‹*the patient*›
B *vi* **1** «demand, prices» اسْتَقَرَّ, أَصْبَحَ مُسْتَقِرًّا **2** «patient, condition» اسْتَقَرَّ

stable /ˈsteɪb(ə)l/ **A** *n* إِصْطَبْل
B *adj* (**stabler, stablest**) **1** (steady) ‹*environment, relationship*› مُسْتَقِرّ; **the political situation is now ~** الوَضْعُ السِياسيُّ مُسْتَقِرٌّ الآنَ **2** (in illness) ‹*condition*› مُسْتَقِرّ **3** (well-balanced) ‹*temperament, character*› مُتَّزِن

staccato /stəˈkɑːtəʊ/ **A** *adv* ‹*to play, sing*› على نَحْوٍ مُتَقَطِّعٍ
B *adj* ‹*note, rhythm*› مُتَقَطِّع

stack /stak/ **A** *n* **1** (of hay, straw) كَوْم (أَكْوام); (of books, chairs, plates) كَوْم (أَكْوام), كُدْس (أَكْداس) **2** (in a library) صَفّ خَزائِنَ الكُتُبِ في مَكْتَبةٍ **3** (infml) (lots of) **~s of sth, a ~ of sth** كُدْس من شَيْءٍ; **there was a ~ of letters to be read** كانَ هُناكَ كَوْمةٌ من الرَسائِلِ للقِراءةِ; **we've got ~s of time** عِنْدَنا الكَثيرُ من الوَقْتِ

B *vt* **1** (to pile) كَوَّمَ ,كَدَّسَ ‹*boxes, books, plates*› **2** (to fill) مَلَأَ (a; مَلْء) ‹*shelves*› **3** نَظَّمَ \ عَلَّقَ على ارْتِفاعٍ مُعَيَّنٍ ‹*planes*›

Phrasal verb **stack up A** (to make sense) عَنَى (i; عَنْي) ‹*facts, figures*› **B ~ up** [sth], **~** [sth] **up** كَدَّسَ \ كَوَّمَ [شَيْئاً] ‹*boxes, books, plates*›

stadium /ˈsteɪdɪəm/ *n* (*pl* **stadiums** or **stadia**) إسْتاد (إسْتادات), مَلْعَب (مَلاعِبُ); **the Olympic ~** المَلْعَب الأولِمْبيّ

staff /stɑːf/ **A** *n* **1** (employees) فَريق العَمَلِ ,(طَواقِمُ) طاقِم مُوَظَّفونَ; **a member of ~** أَحَد أَفْراد طاقِمٍ; **a small business with a ~ of ten** شَرِكة صَغيرة ذات طاقِمٍ من عَشَرة أَفْرادٍ **2** (*pl* **staffs**; also **teaching staff**) هَيْئة تَدْريسٍ **3** (Mil) هَيْئة الأَرْكانِ **4** (*pl* **staves**) (for walking) عَصاً (f; عِصِيّ), عُكّاز (عَكاكيزُ) **5** (*pl* **staves**) (Mus) سُطور موسيقيّة

B *vt* وَفَّرَ عامِلينَ ل ‹*a business, school, restaurant*›; **the restaurant is entirely ~ed by students** كُلُّ الَّذينَ يَعْمَلونَ في المَطْعَمِ طُلّابٌ

staff college *n* كُلِّيّة أَرْكانِ الحَرْبِ

staff meeting *n* اجْتِماع مُوَظَّفينَ

staff nurse *n* مُمَرِّض مُؤَهَّل

staffroom /ˈstɑːfruːm/ *n* (BrE) غُرْفة الأَساتِذةِ

stag /stag/ *n* أَيِّل (أَيائِلُ)

stage /steɪdʒ/ **A** *n* **1** (of an illness, sb's career) مَرْحَلة (مَراحِلُ), طور (أَطْوار); (of a match) شَوْط (أَشْواط); **at this ~ in the process** في هذه المَرْحَلةِ من العَمَليّةِ; **at every ~ of the journey** في كُلِّ طَوْرٍ من الرِحْلةِ; **the project is in the design ~** المَشْروعُ في طَوْرِ التَصْميمِ; **we built the theatre in ~s** بَنَيْنا المَسْرَحَ على مَراحِلَ **2** (in a theatre) مِنَصّة (مِنَصّات), رُكْح (أَرْكاح); **to go** *or* **appear on ~** صَعِدَ على الرُكْحِ \ المِنَصّةِ; **to set the ~ for sth** هَيَّأَ الجَوَّ لِشَيْءٍ **3** (activity) **the Stage** المَسْرَح; **to go on the ~** بَدَأَ يَعْمَلُ في المَسْرَحِ **4** (for an event, conference) مَسْرَح (مَسارِحُ)

B *vt* **1** (Theat) قَدَّمَ على المَسْرَحِ ‹*a play, performance*› **2** (to organize) نَظَّمَ ‹*a competition, a strike*›; قامَ (u; قِيام ;ب) ‹*a coup, rebellion*› **3** (to fake) تَظاهَرَ (ب) ‹*a quarrel, fight*›; **the whole thing was ~d** كانَ كُلُّ شَيْءٍ تَمْثيليّةً

stagecoach /ˈsteɪdʒkəʊtʃ/ *n* عَرَبة خُيولٍ

stage fright *n* رَهْبة المَسْرَحِ

stagehand /ˈsteɪdʒhand/ *n* عامِل مَسْرَحٍ

stage-manage /ˈsteɪdʒˌmanɪdʒ/ *vt* دَبَّرَ ,أَدارَ ‹*a campaign, an event*›

stage manager *n* مُدير مَسْرَحٍ

stagger /ˈstagə/ **A** *vt* **1** (to astonish) فاجَأَ ‹*those present, the viewers*› **2** (to spread out) وَزَّعَ ‹*the repayments, holidays*›

B *vi* (to move unsteadily) تَرَنَّحَ; **to ~ to the door/car** مَشى مُتَرَنِّحاً إلى البابِ \ السَيّارةِ; **to ~ to one's feet** تَرَنَّحَ واقِفاً على رِجْلَيْهِ

C (**staggered**) *past participle, adj* **1** (astonished) **to be ~ed by the news** فوجِئَ بالأَخْبارِ **2** (carefully timed) **~ed departures/arrivals** مَواقيت الانْطِلاقِ \ الوُصولِ مُعَدّة بِعِنايةٍ

D *n* (movement) **to walk with a ~** مَشى مُتَرَنِّحاً

staggering /ˈstagərɪŋ/ *adj* ‹*amount, achievement*› مُذْهِل

stagnant /ˈstagnənt/ *adj* ‹*water, pool*› آسِن ,راكِد

stagnate /stagˈneɪt/ *vi* **1** (to become stagnant) «water, pools» أَسِنَ (a; أَسَن), رَكَدَ (u; رُكود) **2** (to become inactive) «economies, growth» كَسَدَ ,تَراخى (u; كَساد), رَكَدَ (u; رُكود)

stag night, **stag party** *n* حَفْلة للعَريسِ في اللَيْلةِ قبل الزَواجِ

staid /steɪd/ *adj* (**staider**, **staidest**) ‹*image, atmosphere*› رَزين, باهِت ,رَصين

stain /steɪn/ **A** *vt* **1** (to mark) لَطَّخَ ,بَقَّعَ ‹*clothes, a carpet*› **2** (to dye) صَبَغَ (a-i-u; صَبْغ) ‹*wood, fabric*›

B *vi* «ink, wine» سَبَّبَ بُقْعةً \ بُقَعاً

C *n* **1** (mark) لَطْخة (لَطَخات), بُقْعة (بُقَع) **2** (dye) صِبْغ (أَصْباغ) **3** (on sb's character) شائِبة ,وَصْمة (عار); **to leave a ~ on sb's reputation** تَرَكَ وَصْمةَ عارٍ على سُمْعةِ شَخْصٍ

stained glass /ˌsteɪnd ˈglɑːs/ *n* [u] زُجاج مُلَوَّن

stained glass window *n* نافِذة بِزُجاجٍ مُلَوَّنٍ

stainless steel /steɪnləs ˈstiːl/ *n* [u] فولاذ مُقاوِم \ غَيْر قابِلٍ للصَدَأ

stain remover *n* مُزيل البُقَعِ

stair /stɛː/ **A** *n* دَرَجة

B (**stairs**) *n pl* دَرَج (أَدْراج), سُلَّم (سَلالِمُ); **to fall down the ~s** سَقَطَ من الدَرَجِ

staircase /ˈsteːkeɪs/, **stairway** /ˈsteːweɪ/ *n* سُلَّم ,(أَدْراج) دَرَج (سَلالِمُ)

stairwell /ˈsteːwel/ *n* بِئْر السُلَّمِ ,بَيْت الدَرَجِ

stake /steɪk/ **A** *n* **1** (in gambling) مَبْلَغ الرِهانِ **2** (interest) (حِصَص) حِصّة; **to have a large/small ~ in a business** كانَ لَدَيْه حِصّةٌ كَبيرةٌ \ صَغيرةٌ في مَشْروعٍ تِجاريٍّ **3** (post) وَتَد ,خازوق (مُدَبَّب الرَأْسِ)

B *vt* **1** (to risk) قامَرَ ,جازَفَ (ب) خاطَرَ ,راهَنَ ‹*money, your reputation*› **2** (to support) دَعَّمَ ,سَنَّدَ ‹*a tree, plant*›

(Idioms) **to be at stake** كانَ في خَطَرٍ; **to stake your claim to sth** طالَبَ بِحَقِّهِ في شَيْءٍ

(Phrasal verb) **stake out**: **~ out [sth]**, **~ [sth] out** حَدَّدَ [شَيْئاً] (بالأَوْتادِ) ‹*a plot, an area*›

stakeholder /ˈsteɪkhəʊldə/ *n* **1** (interested party) طَرَف صاحِب مَصْلَحةٍ ,جِهة مَعْنيّة ,مَعْني **2** (in projects, businesses) مُساهِم ,حامِل أَسْهُمٍ **3** (in betting) أَمين \ مُتَسَلِّم رِهانٍ

stalactite /ˈstaləktʌɪt/ *n* نازِلة (نَوازِلُ) ,هابِطة (هَوابِط) ,حُلَيْمات عُلْيا

stalagmite /ˈstaləgmʌɪt/ *n* صاعِدة (صَواعِد) ,حُلَيْمات سُفْلى

stale /steɪl/ *adj* (**staler**, **stalest**) **1** (not fresh) ‹*bread, beer*› غَيْر طازَجٍ **2** (unpleasant) ‹*smell*› كَريه; ‹*smoke*› كَريه الرائحةِ **3** (overused) ‹*joke, idea*› مُبْتَذَل ,قَديم

stalemate /ˈsteɪlmeɪt/ *n* **1** (in chess) إِحْراج الشاهِ **2** (deadlock) طَريق مَسْدود; **to reach a ~ in the negotiations** وَصَلَ إلى طَريقٍ مَسْدودٍ في المُفاوَضاتِ

stalk /stɔːk/ **A** *n* (of grass, plants) ساق (f; سيقان); (of leaves, apples) عُنُق (f; أَعْناق); (of mushrooms) ساق (f; سيقان)

B *vt* **1** (in hunting) «animals, hunters» تَرَبَّصَ (ب) ‹*a prey, an animal*› **2** (fml) (to threaten) «danger, fear, killer» هَدَّدَ ‹*the streets, the neighbourhood*› **3** (to harass) تَحَرَّشَ (ب) ‹*a woman, celebrity*›

C *vi* (to walk) **to ~ in/out** دَخَلَ \ خَرَجَ يَمْشي مُخْتالاً; **to ~ out of the room** خَرَجَ من الغُرْفةِ يَمْشي مُخْتالاً

stalker /ˈstɔːkə/ *n* مُعاكِس

stall /stɔːl/ **A** *n* **1** (in markets) كُشْك (أَكْشاك) \ طاوِلة بَيْعٍ **2** (for horses) مَرْبَط (مَرابِطُ); (for pigs) حَظيرة (حَظائِرُ) مَبيعاتٍ

B (**stalls**) *n pl* (BrE) صَفّ أَماميّ (في صالةِ المَسْرَحِ); **two seats in the ~s** مَقْعَدانِ في الصَفِّ الأَماميِّ

C *vt* أَوْقَفَ فَجْأَةً ‹*the engine, car*›

D *vi* «cars, aircraft» تَوَقَّفَ \ تَعَطَّلَ فَجْأَةً

stallholder /ˈstɔːlhəʊldə/ *n* صاحِب كُشْكٍ \ طاوِلةِ بَيْعٍ

stallion /ˈstaljən/ *n* فَحْل خَيْلٍ

stalwart /ˈstɔːlwət/ **A** *adj* ‹*supporter, defender*› شَديد ,مُتَحَمِّس (شداد ,أَشِدّاءُ)

B *n* نَصير (أَنْصار)

stamina /ˈstamɪnə/ *n* قوّة ,قُدْرة على الاحْتِمالِ ,جَلَد

stammer /ˈstamə/ **A** *vi* «speakers» تَلَجْلَجَ ,(تَأْتَأَة ;i) تَأْتَأَ ,تَلَعْثَمَ

B *n* لَجْلَجة ,تَأْتَأة ,تَلَعْثُم; **to have a ~** عانى من اللَعْثَمةِ

stamp /stamp/ **A** *vt* **1** (to mark) طَبَعَ (a; طَبْع) ‹*the date, a number*›; خَتَمَ (i; خَتْم) ‹*a passport*›; **to ~ the date/time on sth, to ~ sth with the date/time** طَبَعَ التاريخَ \ الوَقْتَ على شَيْءٍ; **to ~ one's authority on a project/competition** تَرَكَ بَصْمَتَهُ على مَشْروعٍ \ مُنافَسةٍ **2** (in anger, to keep warm) **to ~ one's foot** ضَرَبَ الأَرْضَ بِرِجْلِهِ **3** وَضَعَ طابِعاً بَريديًّا على ‹*an envelope, a letter*›

B *vi* **1** (with one's feet) «children, protesters» ضَرَبَ الأَرْضَ بِرِجْلَيْهِ **2** (to walk heavily) **to ~ out of the room** خَرَجَ من الغُرْفةِ قارِعاً الأَرْضيّةَ بِقَدَمَيْهِ **3** (to crush) **to ~ on a toy/sb's foot** داسَ على لُعْبةٍ \ قَدَمِ شَخْصٍ

C *n* **1** (for letters) طابِع بَريديّ; **a 60p ~** طابِع بَريديّ من فِئةِ 60 بِنْساً; **'no ~ needed'** 'مَدْفوع الرُسومِ البَريديّةِ' **2** (for marking letters, bills, passports) خَتْم (خُتوم ,أَخْتام); **a date ~** خَتْم تاريخٍ **3** (characteristic mark) **to set one's ~ on a film/company** وَضَعَ بَصْمَتَهُ على فيلْمٍ \ شَرِكةٍ **4** (for gold, silver) خَتْم ,دَمْغة (أَخْتام); **without a ~ it's difficult to know the quality of the silver/gold** تَصْعُبُ مَعْرِفةُ جَوْدةِ الفِضّةِ \ الذَهَبِ دون خَتْمٍ **5** (of one's foot) وَقْع أَقْدامٍ; **with a ~ of her foot** بِوَقْعِ قَدَمِها

(Phrasal verb) **stamp out**: **~ out [sth]**, **~ [sth] out** **1** (to put out) أَطْفَأَ [شَيْئاً] ‹*a fire, the flames*› **2** (to crush) قَضى على [شَيْءٍ] ‹*the opposition, crime, a revolt*›

stamp album *n* أَلْبوم طَوابِعَ

stamp collection *n* مَجْموعة طَوابِعَ

stamp duty *n* (in UK) رَسْم دَمْغةٍ \ طابَعٍ

stamped addressed envelope /ˌstampt əˌdrɛst ˈɛnvələʊp/ *n* (BrE) ▸ **sae**

stampede /stamˈpiːd/ **A** *n* تَزاحُم ,تَدافُع **B** *vi* «horses, crowds» تَزاحَمَ ,تَدافَعَ

stance /stɑːns/ *n* **1** (posture) وَضْعيّة ,(أَوْضاع) وَضْع ,وَقْفة **2** (attitude) (مَواقِفُ) مَوْقِف

stand /stand/ **A** *vt* (*past tense, past participle* **stood**) **1** (to place) أَوْقَفَ ‹*a child*›; وَضَعَ (بِشَكْلٍ عَموديٍّ) ‹*ladder, bottle*›; **~ the lamp on that table** ضِعِ المِصْباحَ على تِلْكَ الطاوِلةِ; **he stood the ladder against the wall** أَسْنَدَ السُلَّمَ على الحائِطِ **2** (to tolerate) تَحَمَّلَ ‹*the pain, noise, a person*›; **I can't ~ the sight of him** لا أَسْتَطيعُ أَنْ أَتَحَمَّلَ رُؤْيَتَهُ; **he can't ~ losing** *or* **to lose** لا يَتَحَمَّلُ الخسارةَ; **she won't ~ any nonsense** لن تَتَحَمَّلَ أَيَّ هُراءٍ **3** (to pay for) **to ~ sb a drink/meal** تَكَفَّلَ بِمَشْروبٍ \ وَجْبةٍ لِشَخْصٍ **4** (to be liable) **to ~ to lose/gain sth** تَحَمَّلَ مَسْؤوليّةَ خسارةٍ \ رِبْحِ شَيْءٍ

B *vi* (*past tense, past participle* **stood**) **1** (also **stand up**) (to rise) وَقَفَ (i; وُقوف ,وَقْف) **2** (to be upright) «people» وَقَفَ (i; وُقوف ,وَقْف); **to remain ~ing** ظَلَّ واقِفاً; **she's too weak to ~** هي ضَعيفةٌ جِدًّا على الوُقوفِ **3** (to be positioned) «buildings, villages» وَقَعَ (a; وُقوع); **the train ~ing at platform 4, will leave in …** القِطارُ الواقِفُ على الرَصيفِ 4، سَيُغادِرُ في … **4** (to step) **to ~ on sb's foot/on a piece of glass** داسَ على قَدَمِ شَخْصٍ \ قِطْعةٍ من الزُجاجِ **5** (to be) كانَ (u; كَيْنونة ,كَوْن); **the house stood empty for years** كانَ البَيْتُ فارِغاً لِسَنَواتٍ; **as things ~, we have no other options** يَبْدو أَنَّهُ لَيْسَتْ عِنْدَنا اخْتِياراتٌ أُخْرى; **to ~ in sb's way** وَقَفَ في طَريقِ شَخْصٍ; **I want to know where I ~** أُريدُ أَنْ أَعرِفَ أَيْنَ أَقِفُ; **the score ~s at 3-0** النَتيجةُ 3−0; **where do you ~ on educational reform?** ما رَأْيُكَ في إصْلاحِ التَعْليمِ؟ **6** (to remain valid) «offers, agreements, records» ما زالَ صالِحاً **7** (to be a candidate) تَرَشَّحَ; **to ~ as a candidate/for mayor** تَرَشَّحَ \ تَرَشَّحَ لِرئاسةِ البَلَديّةِ; **to ~ for parliament** تَرَشَّحَ للبَرْلَمان **8** (to stay still) «water» رَكَدَ (u; رُكود); «mixture» ارْتاحَ

C *n* **1** (attitude) (مَواقِفُ) مَوْقِف; **to take a ~ on an issue** أَخَذَ مَوْقِفاً من قَضيّةٍ **2** (against attack) مُقاوَمة; **to make one's last ~** خاضَ مَعْرَكَتَهُ الأخيرةَ **3** (at a market) مِنَصّة ,طاوِلة; (in a trade fair) جَناح (أَجْنِحة) **4** (in stadiums) مَدْرَج (مَدارِجُ) **5** (in a court) مِنَصّة; **to take the ~** وَقَفَ \ مَثُلَ أمام المِنَصّةِ **6** (for coats, hats) مِشْجَب ,شَمّاعة (مَشاجِبُ); (for music, plants) طاوِلة

Idiom **to leave sb standing** تَرَكَ شَخْصاً وَراءَهُ

Phrasal verbs **stand about**, **stand around** انْتَظَرَ

- **stand aside** **1** (to move to one side) وَقَفَ جانِباً **2** (to do nothing) وَقَفَ مُتَفَرِّجاً
- **stand back** **1** (to move back) «person, crowd» تَراجَعَ **2** (to be situated) «houses» وَقَعَ (a; وُقوع)
- **stand by** **A** **1** (to be prepared) «doctors, soldiers» تَأَهَّبَ, اسْتَعَدَّ; **the army is ~ing by to evacuate people** الجَيْشُ مُتَأَهِّبٌ لِإجْلاءِ الناسِ **2** (to do nothing) وَقَفَ مُتَفَرِّجاً; **we cannot ~ by and allow this to happen** لا نَسْتَطيعُ أَنْ نَقِفَ مُتَفَرِّجينَ وَنَسْمَحَ بِحُدوثِ هذا **B** **~ by** [sb/sth] (to be loyal to) ناصَرَ [شَخْصاً \ شَيْئاً] ‹*an ally, a friend, one's decision*›
- **stand down** (to resign) «the president, candidate» اسْتَقالَ, تَنازَلَ ,انْسَحَبَ
- **stand for**: **~ for** [sth] **1** (to denote) رَمَزَ لِ [شَيْءٍ] ‹*a name, word, term*›; **VIP ~s for Very Important Person** 'في آي بي' تَرْمُزُ إلى شَخْصٍ مُهِمٍّ جِدًّا **2** (to uphold) أَيَّدَ [شَيْئاً] ‹*justice, equality, an ideal*› **3** (to tolerate) تَسامَحَ مع [شَيْءٍ] ‹*sb's rudeness, an insult*›; **I will not ~ for that!** لن أَتَسامَحَ مع ذلك!
- **stand in** عَوَّضَ; **to ~ in for sb** حَلَّ مَحَلَّ شَخْصٍ
- **stand off** (to keep away) ظَلَّ بَعيداً
- **stand out** **1** (to be noticeable) «musicians, designs, achievements» بَرَزَ (u; بُروز); **he ~s out from the group** يَبْرُزُ من بَيْنِ الفَريقِ **2** (to protrude) «veins, shapes, structures» بَرَزَ (u; بُروز)
- **stand up** **A** **1** (to get up) وَقَفَ (i; وُقوف ,وَقْف) **2** (to stay upright) «lamps, ladders» بَقِيَ قائِماً **3** (to be convincing) «arguments, theories» كانَ مُقْنِعاً; **to ~ up to scrutiny/**

investigation صَمَدَ أمام الفَحْصِ \ التَّحْقِيق **4** (to resist) **to ~ up to sb** واجَهَ شَخْصاً **5** (to defend) **to ~ up for sb/one's rights** دافَعَ عن شَخْصٍ \ حُقُوقِهِ ;**to ~ up for oneself** دافَعَ عن نَفْسِهِ **B** ~ **[sb/sth] up** **1** (to place upright) أَوْقَفَ [شَخْصاً \ شَيْئاً] <a child>; وَضَعَ [شَخْصاً \ شَيْئاً] بِشَكْلٍ عَموديّ <ladder, bottle>; **to ~ sth up against/on sth** أَسْنَدَ شَيْئاً على شَيْءٍ **2** (infml) (to fail to meet) خَلَفَ المَوْعِد مع [شَخْصٍ \ شَيْءٍ] <a girlfriend, boyfriend>

stand-alone /'standələʊn/ *adj before n* <PC, application> مُسْتَقِلّ قائِم بِذاتِهِ ,مُنْفَصِل

standard /'standəd/ **A** *n* **1** (of candidates, products) مِعْيار مَعايِيرُ ;**~s of service have improved/declined** الجَوْدَةِ ;جَوْدَةِ الخَدَماتِ قد تَحَسَّنَتْ \ تَراجَعَتْ ;**the candidates are of a high/low ~** المَرَشَّحونَ يَنْتَمونَ إلى فِئَةٍ عالِيَةٍ \ قَليلَةِ الجَوْدَةِ ;**this is excellent/unacceptable by any ~s** هذا مُمْتازٌ \ غَيْرُ مَقْبولٍ بِكُلِّ المَعايِيرِ ;**by today's ~s** بِمَعايِيرِ اليَوْمِ ;**to set high/low ~s for others to follow** وَضَعَ مَعايِيرَ عالِيَةً \ مُنْخَفِضةً للآخَرينَ لِيَتْبَعوها ;**to have double ~s** كالَ بِمِكْيالَيْن **2** (specification) مِعْيار (مَعايِيرُ) ;**to comply with the EU ~ of safety** اسْتَجابَ لِمَعايِيرِ السَّلامَةِ الأوروبِّيَّةِ **3** (banner) عَلَم (أَعْلام) ,راية **4** (Mus) [أَعْمال موسيقيّة رائِدة]

B *adj* **1** (normal) <size, equipment, rate> مُتَعارَف عَلَيْهِ ;**this model includes satnav as ~** هذا الطِرازُ يَحْتَوي على نِظام المِلاحة بالأَقْمار الصِناعيّة ;**broadcasters must be fluent in ~ English** يَجِبُ أنْ يَكونَ المُذيعونَ فَصيحينَ في اللُغةِ الإنْجليزِيّةِ الرَسْميّةِ وِفْقاً للمَعايِيرِ **2** (authoritative) <work, manual> مَرْجِعيّ ,رَسْميّ **3** (BrE) (also **standard class**) <ticket, return> دَرَجة عاديّة

standard assessment task *n* (BrE) [اخْتِبار قِياسيّ لِتَقْييمِ مُسْتَوى الطالِبِ]

standardization, **-isation** (BrE) /standədʌɪ'zeɪʃ(ə)n/ *n* تَوْحيد تَقْييس ,تَوْحيد قِياسيّ ,مَعايِير / مُواصَفاتٍ

standardize, **-ise** (BrE) /'standədʌɪz/ *vt* وَحَّدَ المَعايِيرَ / المُواصَفاتِ <a procedure, system>

standard lamp *n* (BrE) مِصْباح أَرْضيّ (مَحْمول على عَمودٍ)

standard of living *n* مُسْتَوى مَعيشةٍ

standby /'standbʌɪ/ **A** *n* (*pl* **standbys**) بَديل ,احْتِياطيّ (بُدَلاءُ)

B *adj before n* <ticket> احْتِياطيّ

C *adj before n* **1** (unreserved) <ticket, seat> احْتِياطيّ **2** (for emergencies) <generator, childminder> احْتِياطيّ

Idiom **on standby** (ready to be used) في حالةِ تَأَهُّبٍ ;(for a journey, performance) على قائِمةِ الانْتِظارِ

stand-in /'standɪn/ *n* بَديل ,دوبْلير (بُدَلاءُ)

standing /'standɪŋ/ **A** *n* **1** (reputation) مَنْزِلة ,مَكانة (مَنازِلُ) **2** (position) وَضع (أَوْضاع) **3** (length of time) أَمَد (آماد) ,فَتْرة (فَتَرات) ;**a friendship of long ~** صَداقة طَوِيلة الأَمَدِ

B *adj* **1** (permanent) <committee> دائِم ;<invitation> مَفْتوح **2** (not seated) <passenger, jump> واقِف (وُقوف ,واقِفونَ)

standing charge *n* رَسْم ثابت

standing joke *n* مَحَلّ تَنَدُّرٍ

standing order *n* **1** (general ordinance) تَعْليمات دائِمة **2** (with suppliers) طَلَب شِراءٍ دائِم **3** (BrE) (with banks) طَلَب اسْتِقْطاع دائِم ,أَمْر (دَفْع) مُسْتَديم

standing ovation *n* [الوُقوف والتَّصْفيق لِشَخْصٍ حَفاوةً بِهِ]

stand-off /'standɒf/ *n* نُقْطة جُمودٍ ,طَريق مَسْدود

standpoint /'standpɔɪnt/ *n* وُجْهة نَظَر ;**try to see it from my ~** حاوِلْ أنْ تَراهُ من وُجْهة نَظَري

standstill /'standstɪl/ *n* [u] **1** (inactivity) رُكود ,تَوَقُّف تامّ **2** (of vehicles) تَوَقُّف تامّ ;**the car came to a ~** تَوَقَّفَت السَيّارةُ تَماماً

stand-up /'standʌp/ **A** *adj* <comedian, routine> على ,مَسْرَحيّ المَسْرَحِ

B *n* [u] (also **stand-up comedy**) كوميدْيا الوُقوف (عَرْض لِفَنّانٍ يُلْقي نُكَتاً على المَسْرَحِ)

stank /staŋk/ *past tense* ▸ **stink**

Stanley knife® /'stanli nʌɪf/ *n* سِكّين قَطْعٍ

staple /'steɪp(ə)l/ **A** *n* **1** (for papers) دَبّوس (دَبابيسُ) **2** (for wood) مِسْمار مُزْدَوِج السِنِّ **3** (basic food) غِذاء رَئيسيّ

B *adj* <crop, food> أَساسيّ ,رَئيسيّ

C *vt* <paper> دَبَّسَ ;<wire> ثَبَّتَ

stapler /'steɪplə/ *n* دَبّاسة

star /stɑː/ **A** *n* **1** (in the sky) نَجْم (n coll; أَنْجُم ,نُجوم); **the ~s are out** ظَهَرَت النُجومُ **2** (actor, player, etc) نَجْم (n coll; نُجوم); **a movie/rock ~** نَجْم فيلْمٍ \ موسيقى الروك **3** (asterisk) نَجْمة (نَجْمات) **4** (award) نَجْمة (نُجوم); **this hotel has three ~s** هذا الفُنْدُقُ من فئة ثَلاثِ نُجومٍ **5** (in generals' ranking) نَجْمة (نُجوم); **a four-~ general** عَقيد بِأَرْبَعِ نُجومٍ

B (**stars**) *n pl* نُجوم; **what do my ~s say?** ماذا تَقولُ النُجومُ لي؟

C (**-star**) *in combination* (in grading) **a three-/four-~ hotel/restaurant** فُنْدُق \ مَطْعَم ثَلاثِ \ أَرْبَعِ نُجومٍ

D *vt* (**-rr-**) **1** «films, plays» مَثَّل دَوْرَ البُطولةِ فيهِ ‹an actor, actress›; **a movie ~ring Tom Cruise and Demi Moore** فيلْم مَثَّل دَوْرَ البُطولةِ فيه توم كْروز وديمي مور **2** *usu passive* (to mark with a star) وَضَعَ عَلَيْهِ نَجْمةً; **the ~red items/dishes are ...** العَناصِرُ \ الصُحونُ الّتي عَلَيْها نَجْمةٌ...

E *vi* (**-rr-**) «actors» قامَ بِدورٍ رَئيسيٍّ; **Hal Henderson ~s as Dracula** قامَ هال هِنْدِرسون بِدورِ دْراكولا

Idioms **to reach for the stars** أَرادَ أَنْ يَلْمَسَ النُجومَ بِيَدَيْهِ; **to have stars in one's eyes** [كانَ يَحْدوهُ أَمَلٌ كَبيرٌ]

starboard /ˈstɑːbəd/ **A** *n* الجانِب الأَيْمَن ,المَيْمَنة

B *adj before n* ‹side, engine› أَيْمَن (dipt)

starch /stɑːtʃ/ *n* **1** (carbohydrate) نَشاء ,نَشاً **2** (for clothes) نَشاً

starchy /ˈstɑːtʃi/ *adj* (**starchier, starchiest**) ‹food, diet› نَشَويّ

stardom /ˈstɑːdəm/ *n* نُجوميّة

stare /steː/ **A** *vi* حَدَّقَ (في) ,تَفَرَّسَ (إلى ,في); **it's rude to ~** مِن العَيْبِ أَنْ تُحَدِّقَ; **to ~ at sb/sth** حَدَّقَ في شَخْصٍ \ شَيْءٍ; **we all ~d at her in disbelief** حَدَّقْنا كُلُّنا بِأَعْيُنِنا فيها غَيْرَ مُصَدِّقينَ; **to ~ into space** حَدَّقَ في الفَضاءِ

B *n* تَحْديق

Idiom **to be staring sb in the face** (to be obvious) «the solution» كانَ واضِحاً وُضوحَ الشَمْسِ; (to be imminent) «disaster» كانَ لا مَهْرَبَ مِنْهُ

Phrasal verbs **stare down**: **~ [sb] down** تَحَدّى شَخْصاً بالنَظَرِ [في عَيْنَيْهِ لِمُدّةٍ طَويلةٍ]

• **stare out** ▸ **stare down**

starfish /ˈstɑːfɪʃ/ *n* (*pl* **starfish**) نَجْم البَحْرِ

stark /stɑːk/ *adj* (**starker, starkest**) **1** (severe) ‹landscape› مُقْفِر; ‹room› كَئيب **2** (extreme) ‹contrast, difference› صارِخ **3** (unpleasantly clear) ‹warning, reality› صارِخ ,واضِح

Idiom **stark naked** عارٍ تَماماً

starlet /ˈstɑːlɪt/ *n* مُمَثِّلة ناشِئة

starling /ˈstɑːlɪŋ/ *n* زُرْزور (زَرازيرُ)

star quality *n* صِفات النُجوميّةِ

starry /ˈstɑːri/ *adj* (**starrier, starriest**) ‹night, sky› مُرَصَّع \ مُضيء بالنُجومِ

starry-eyed /ˌstɑːriˈʌɪd/ *adj* ‹idealist, optimism› حالِم

Stars and Stripes *pr n* (**the Stars and Stripes**) عَلَم النُجومِ والخُطوطِ (عَلَم الوِلاياتِ المُتَّحِدةِ)

star sign *n* بُرْج فَلَكِيّ

Star-spangled Banner /stɑːspaŋɡəld ˈbanə/ *n* الراية المُوَشَّحة بالنُجومِ (النَشيد الوَطَنيّ للوِلاياتِ المُتَّحِدةِ)

star-studded /ˈstɑːˌstʌdɪd/ *adj* ‹event, cast› مَليء بالنُجومِ

start /stɑːt/ **A** *vt* **1** (to begin) بَدَأَ (a; بَدْء) ‹an exercise, activity›; **to ~ to do sth, to ~ doing sth** بَدَأَ فِعْلَ شَيْءٍ; **he's just ~ed a new job** بَدَأَ للتَوِّ عَمَلاً جَديداً; **she ~ed her working life as a clerk** بَدَأَتْ حَياتَها العَمَليّةَ كَمُوَظَّفةٍ عاديّةٍ; **to ~ a family** بَدَأَ في تَكْوينِ أُسْرةٍ; **don't ~ that again!** لا تَفْتَحْ ذلكَ المَوْضوعَ مَرّةً أُخْرى! **2** (to begin to use) بَدَأَ في الاسْتِعْمالِ ‹a bottle, packet, notebook› **3** (to cause, initiate) بَدَأَ (a; بَدْء) ‹a quarrel, rumour, war, fire›; **who ~ed it?** مَن بَدَأَهُ؟ **4** (to activate) شَغَّل ‹a car, machine, engine›

B (**to start with**) *adv phr* **1** (at first) أَوَّلاً; **I didn't understand to ~ with** أَوَّلاً أنا لم أَفْهَمْ; **she wasn't keen on the idea to ~ with** أَوَّلاً هي لم تَكُنْ مُتَحَمِّسةً لِلفِكْرةِ **2** (giving reasons) **to ~ with, it's more expensive** أَوَّلاً، هو أَغْلى

C *vi* **1** (to begin) «journeys, stories, work» بَدَأَ (a; بَدْء); **to ~ by doing sth** بَدَأَ بِفِعْلِ شَيْءٍ; **to ~ again** بَدَأَ من جَديدٍ; **she ~ed as a secretary** بَدَأَتْ كَسِكْرِتيرةٍ; **I'll ~ with the salmon** سَأَبْدَأُ بالسَلْمونِ; **when can you ~?** متى تَسْتَطيعُ أَنْ تَبْدَأَ؟; **let's ~ at the beginning** لِنَبْدَأْ من البِدايةِ **2** «cars, machines» (to become operational) عَمِلَ ,اشْتَغَلَ (a; عَمَل)

3 (to jump) (قَفْزٌ ,قَفَزان ;i) قَفَزَ

D *n* **1** (beginning) بداية; **right from the ~** منذ البِدايةِ; **at the ~ of the project** في بِدايةِ المَشْروعِ; **to make a ~ on the task** انْطَلَقَ في العَمَلِ على المُهِمّةِ; **to make an early ~** بَدَأَ مُبَكِّراً; **for a ~** أَوَّلاً **2** (advantage) أَسْبَقِيّة **3** (departure point) نُقْطة انْطِلاقٍ **4** (out of surprise, fear) **to wake with a ~** صَحا \ اسْتَيْقَظَ بِسَبَبِ رَعْشةٍ مُفاجِئةٍ; **you gave me a ~!** أَخَفْتَني!

(Phrasal verbs) **start back** **1** (to begin one's return) بَدَأَ يَعودُ **2** (to jump back) قَفَزَ إلى الوَراءِ

• **start off** **A** **1** (to begin) «speakers» (بَدْء ;a) بَدَأَ; **he ~ed off by saying how much he admired her work** بَدَأَ بالتَعْبيرِ عن مَدى إعْجابِهِ بِعَمَلِها **2** (to get going) «trains, runners» انْطَلَقَ

B ~ [sb/sth] **off**, ~ **off** [sb/sth] **1** (to begin) بَدَأَ [شَيْئاً] ‹*a visit, talk*› **2** (BrE infml) (with laughter) أَضْحَكَ [شَخْصاً]; (with tears) أَبْكى [شَخْصاً]; **she giggled and that ~ed me off** قَهْقَهَتْ وذلك ما جَعَلَني أَضْحَكُ **3** (to set to work on) أَعْطى [شَخْصاً] عَمَلاً ‹*an employee, student*›

• **start on**: ~ **on** [sth] (to begin) بَدَأَ ب [شَيْءٍ] ‹*the laundry, a book, journey*›

• **start out** **1** (on journeys) انْطَلَقَ **2** (in life, work) بَدَأَ مِشْوارَهُ **3** (to begin) **to ~ out as sth** «occasions, employees, discussions» بَدَأَ كَشَيْءٍ

• **start over** (infml) (to begin again) بَدَأَ من جَديدٍ

• **start up** **A** **1** «engines, machines» اشْتَغَلَ **2** «the music, shouting» انْطَلَقَ **3** «companies, entrepreneurs» (بَدْء ;a) بَدَأَ

B ~ [sth] **up**, ~ **up** [sth] **1** شَغَّلَ [شَيْئاً] ‹*a car, machine*› **2** بَدَأَ [شَيْئاً] ‹*a business, shop*›

starter /ˈstɑːtə/ *n* **1** (in races) مُتَسابِق (مُشارِك من بِداية السِباقِ) **2** (dish) طَبَق أَوَّل **3** (also **starter motor**) بادِئ تَشْغيلٍ \ مُشَغِّل حَرَكةٍ

(Idiom) **for starters** (infml) بادِئ ذي بَدْءٍ, أَوَّلاً

starting line /ˈstɑːtɪŋ ˌlaɪn/ *n* (Sport) خطّ بِدايةٍ \ انْطِلاقٍ

starting point /ˈstɑːtɪŋ ˌpɔɪnt/ *n* نُقْطة انْطِلاقٍ \ بِدايةٍ

startle /ˈstɑːt(ə)l/ *vt* رَوَّعَ, أَفْزَعَ, أَجْفَلَ ‹*a person, an animal*›

startling /ˈstɑːtlɪŋ/ *adj* ‹*news, likeness*› مُذْهِل

start-up /ˈstɑːtʌp/ *n* **1** (process) بَدْء, إنْشاء (عَمَلٍ تِجاريٍّ) **2** (business) شَرِكة ناشِئة \ مُبْتَدِئة

starvation /stɑːˈveɪʃ(ə)n/ *n* مَجاعة; **to die of** *or* **from ~** ماتَ من الجوعِ

starve /stɑːv/ **A** *vt* **1** (to deny food to) جَوَّعَ ‹*a child, a prisoner*› **2** (to deprive of) **to ~ sb of funds/information** حَرَمَ شَخْصاً من التَمْويلِ \ المَعْلوماتِ

B *vi* «prisoners, animals» جاعَ (u; جَوْع), عانى من الجوعِ; **I'm starving!** أَكادُ أَموتُ من الجوعِ!

starving /ˈstɑːvɪŋ/ *adj* ‹*child, animal*› جائِع جِدًّا, مُتَضَوِّر جوعاً

stash /stæʃ/ (infml) **A** *vt* (infml) خَبَّأَ, أَخْفى ‹*money, drugs*›; **to ~ sth in/under sth** خَبَّأَ شَيْئاً في \ تحت شَيْءٍ

B *n* مخزون (سِرّيّ)

(Phrasal verb) **stash away** (infml): ~ [sth] **away**, ~ **away** [sth] (infml) خَبَّأَ [شَيْئاً] ‹*money, drugs*›

state /steɪt/ **A** *n* **1** (condition) حال (mf; أَحْوال), حالة; **to be in a good/bad ~** كانَ في حالٍ جَيِّدٍ \ سَيِّئٍ; **what ~ is the car in?** ما هي الحالةُ الّتي عَلَيْها السَيّارةُ؟; **the present ~ of affairs** الوَضْع الراهِن للأَشْياءِ; **in my present ~ of mind** في حالَتي الراهِنةِ; **he's not in a fit ~ to drive** هو لَيس في حالةٍ تَسْمَحُ لَهُ بِقِيادةِ السَيّارة; **in a liquid/solid ~** في حالةٍ سائلةٍ \ صَلْبةٍ **2** (of a country) وِلاية; **the ~ of Kansas** وِلاية كانْساس **3** (nation) دَوْلة (دُوَل); **the Baltic States** دُوَل البَلْطيق **4** [u] (political entity) **the State** الدَوْلة; **the railways are owned by the S~** تَمْلِكُ الدَوْلةُ سِكَكَ الحَديدِ **5** [u] (in ceremonial) **to lie in ~** سُجِّيَ لإلْقاءِ النَظْرةِ الأَخيرةِ عَلَيْهِ

B (**the States**) *n pl* الوِلايات المُتَّحِدة الأَمْريكيّة

C *vt* (to say) صَرَّحَ, أَعْلَنَ ‹*one's age, income, opinion*›; **you must ~ all your sources of income** يَجِبُ أنْ تُعْلِنَ عن كُلِّ مَصادِرِ دَخْلِكَ; **to ~ one's case** عَرَضَ قَضيَّتَهُ; **as ~d above/below** كما هو مُوَضَّحٌ أَعْلاهُ \ أَسْفَلَهُ

state capitalism *n* رَأْسْماليّة الدَوْلةِ

State Department *n* (**the State Department**) وِزارة الخارِجيّة (الأَمْريكيّة)

state education *n* تَعْليم حُكوميّ

state-funded /ˈsteɪtfʌndɪd/ *adj* ‹*education, pension*› مُمَوَّل من الحُكومةِ \ الدَّولةِ

stateless /ˈsteɪtləs/ *adj* ‹*refugee, person*› عَديم الجِنْسيّةِ

stately /ˈsteɪtli/ *adj* (**statelier, stateliest**) 1 (dignified) ‹*pace, procession*› مَهيب ,جَليل 2 (impressive) ‹*mansion, building*› عَظيم ,فَخْم

stately home *n* قَصْر (قُصور)

statement /ˈsteɪtmənt/ *n* 1 (of facts, opinions) بَيان (بَيانات), تَصْريح (تَصْريحات) 2 (also **bank statement**) كَشْف حِسابٍ بَنْكيّ

state of emergency *n* حالة طَوارِئ; **to declare a state of emergency** أَعْلَنَ حالةَ الطَوارِئ

state-of-the-art /ˌsteɪtəvðiˈɑːt/ *adj* ‹*equipment, technology*› مُتَقَدِّم ,حَديث

state-owned /ˈsteɪtəʊnd/ *adj* ‹*company, bank*› مَمْلوك للدَّوْلة

state school *n* مَدْرَسة حُكوميّة

stateside /ˈsteɪtsʌɪd/ **A** *adj* (AmE) ‹*debut, posting*› في الولاياتِ المُتَّحدة
B *adv* ‹*to return, head*› إلى الولاياتِ المُتَّحدة

statesman /ˈsteɪtsmən/ *n* (*pl* **-men**) رَجُل دَوْلةٍ

stateswoman /ˈsteɪtswʊmən/ *n* (*pl* **-women**) امْرَأة دَوْلةٍ

statewide /ˈsteɪtwʌɪd/ (AmE) **A** *adj* ‹*ban, referendum*› على مُسْتَوى \ نِطاقِ الوِلايةِ
B *adv* ‹*to distribute, implement*› في ,على مُسْتَوى \ نِطاقِ الوِلايةِ كُلِّ أَنْحاءِ الوِلايةِ

static /ˈstatɪk/ **A** *adj* 1 (stationary) ‹*image, traffic*› غَيْر ,ثابِت مُتَحَرِّكٍ 2 (stable) ‹*population, prices*› مُسْتَقِرّ
B *n* 1 ~ **electricity** كَهْرَباء ساكِنة \ اسْتاتيكيّة 2 (interference) تَشْويش

station /ˈsteɪʃ(ə)n/ **A** *n* 1 (for trains, buses, etc) مَحَطّة 2 (in broadcasting) مَحَطّة; **a local/national radio ~** مَحَطّة إذاعيّة مَحَلّيّة \ وَطَنيّة 3 (also **police station**) مَرْكَز شُرْطةٍ 4 (Mil) (base) قاعِدة (قَواعِدُ) 5 (Mil) (post) مَرْكَز (مَراكِزُ) 6 (Australian ranch) مَزْرَعة أُسْتُراليّة
B *vt* 1 (to post to) أَرْسَلَ ‹*an officer, a guard, troops*›; **to be ~ed in the south/on the coast** تَمَرْكَزَ في الجَنوبِ \ الساحِلِ 2 (with a task) أَرْسَلَ في مُهِمّةٍ ‹*a guard, tank, sentry*›; **to ~ a guard at the crossroads** أَرْسَلَ عَوْنَ حَرَسٍ إلى مُفْتَرَقِ الطُرُقِ
C *v refl* **to ~ oneself** تَمَرْكَزَ

stationary /ˈsteɪʃ(ə)n(ə)ri/ *adj* ‹*target, traffic*› ثابِت (ثَوابِتُ), ساكِن, غَيْر مُتَحَرِّكٍ

stationer /ˈsteɪʃ(ə)nə/, **stationer's** /ˈsteɪʃ(ə)nɛrz/ *n* بائِع أَدَواتٍ قِرْطاسيّ ,مَكْتَبيّةٍ

stationery /ˈsteɪʃ(ə)n(ə)ri/ *n* 1 (writing paper) وَرَق كِتابةٍ 2 (office materials) قِرْطاسيّة ,أَدَوات مَكْتَبيّة

stationery shop (BrE), **stationery store** (AmE) *n* مَحَلّ مَحَلّ قِرْطاسيّةٍ ,أَدَواتٍ مَكْتَبيّةٍ

stationmaster /ˈsteɪʃ(ə)nmɑːstə/ *n* ناظِر \ مُدير مَحَطّةِ قِطارٍ

station wagon *n* (AmE) سَيّارة صالون عائِليّة ,سَيّارة سْتيشَن واجَن

statistic /stəˈtɪstɪk/ *n* إحْصائيّة

statistical /stəˈtɪstɪk(ə)l/ *adj* ‹*analysis, evidence*› إحْصائيّ

statistically /stəˈtɪstɪkli/ *adv* ‹*reliable, representative*› إحْصائيًّا; **~, the risk is very low** إحْصائيًّا، نِسْبةُ المُخاطَرة قَليلةٌ جِدًّا

statistician /statɪˈstɪʃ(ə)n/ *n* خَبير إحْصاءٍ ,إحْصائيّ

statistics /stəˈtɪstɪks/ **A** *n sing* (subject) عِلْم الإحْصاءِ
B *n pl* (data) إحْصائيّات

stats /stats/ *n pl* (infml) = **statistics** (data) إحْصائيّات

statue /ˈstatʃuː/ *n* تِمْثال (تَماثيلُ)

stature /ˈstatʃə/ *n* 1 (height) قامة 2 (status) مَكانة ,مَنْزِلة (مَنازِلُ), مَقام (مَقامات)

status /ˈsteɪtəs/ *n* 1 (for legal, tax purposes) وَضْع (أَوْضاع); **what is his tax/legal ~?** ما وَضْعُهُ القانونيُّ \ الضريبيُّ ؟ 2 (in a community) مَنْزِلة (مَنازِلُ), مَكانة 3 (prestige) مَكانة, مَرْكَز (مَراكِزُ)

status symbol *n* رَمْز الوَجاهةِ

statute /ˈstatʃuːt/ *n* قانون (قَوانينُ), تَشْريع (تَشْريعات), مَرْسوم (مَراسيمُ)

statutory /ˈstatʃətri/ *adj* ‹*duty, right*› قانونيّ

staunch /stɔːntʃ/ *adj* ‹*supporter, Catholic*› مُخْلِص ,وَفيّ (أَوْفِياءُ)

stave /steɪv/ *n* 1 (stick, club) هِراوة (هَراوى), عَصاً (f; عِصيّ) 2 (of a barrel) لَوْح (أَلْواح) 3 (Mus) مُدَرَّج موسيقيّ

(Phrasal verbs) **stave in**: **~ in [sth], ~ [sth] in** حَطَّم [شَيْئاً] *<a door, hull>*

• **stave off** (*past tense, past participle* **staved**): **~ [sth] off, ~ off [sth]** تَجَنَّبَ \ تَفادى [شَيْئاً] *<hunger, defeat>*; دَرَأَ [شَيْئاً] *<an attack, a threat>*

staves /steɪvz/ *n pl* ▸ **staff** A4, A5, **stave**

stay /steɪ/ **A** *vi* 1 (to remain) بَقِيَ (a; بَقاء); **please ~ for lunch** اِبْقَ من فَضْلِكَ للغَداءِ; **to ~ in bed/at home** بَقِيَ في الفِراشِ \ في البَيْتِ; **please ~ calm** اِبْقَ هادِئاً من فَضْلِكَ; **to ~ put** بَقِيَ في مَكانِهِ; **digital technology is here to ~** التِكْنولوجيا الرَقْمِيَّةُ وُجِدَتْ لِتَبْقى 2 (to have accommodation) أَقامَ; **to ~ in a hotel/at a friend's house** أَقامَ في فُنْدُقٍ \ في بَيْتِ صَديقٍ 3 (to visit) **to come to ~** جاءَ للزِيارةِ

B *n* 1 (period of visit) إقامة; **enjoy your ~!** اِسْتَمْتِعْ بِإقامَتِكَ!; **a short ~ in hospital** إقامة قَصيرة في المُسْتَشْفى 2 (Law) (also **stay of execution**) وَقْفُ التَنْفيذِ; **a ~ of execution in the extradition proceedings** وَقْفُ التَنْفيذِ في إجْراءاتِ التَسْليمِ

(Phrasal verbs) **stay away** 1 (to remain distant) بَقِيَ بَعيداً; **to ~ away from the water's edge** بَقِيَ بَعيداً عن حافَّةِ الماءِ 2 (not to attend) تَغَيَّبَ (عن); **to ~ away from classes/work** تَغَيَّبَ عن الدِراسةِ \ العَمَلِ

• **stay behind** «students, workers» تَخَلَّفَ

• **stay in** (not to go out) «children, family» بَقِيَ في البَيْتِ

• **stay out**: 1 (to remain away) **to ~ out late/all night** بَقِيَ خارِجاً لِساعةٍ مُتَأَخِّرةٍ \ طوال اللَيْلِ; **to ~ out of sight** بَقِيَ بَعيداً عن الأَنْظارِ; **~ out of his way** اِبْقَ بَعيداً عن طَريقِهِ 2 (to continue on strike) «workers» واصَلَ الإضْرابَ

• **stay up** 1 (not go to bed) سَهِرَ (a; سَهَر); **we ~ed up all night** سَهِرْنا طوال اللَيْلِ 2 (not to fall down) «buildings» بَقِيَ قائِماً

staying power /ˈsteɪɪŋ ˌpaʊə/ *n* قُدْرة على الاحْتِمالِ

STD /ˌɛstiːˈdiː/ *n* = **sexually transmitted disease** مَرَض مَنْقول جِنْسِيّاً

stead /stɛd/ *n* (fml) **to do sth/go somewhere in sb's ~** فَعَلَ شَيْئاً \ ذَهَبَ إلى مَكانٍ بَدَلاً من شَخْصٍ

(Idiom) **to stand sb in good stead** كانَ مُفيداً لِشَخْصٍ

steadfast /ˈstɛdfɑːst/ *adj* *<determination>* راسِخ, ثابِت; *<supporter>* مُخْلِص, وَفيّ (أَوْفِياءُ)

steadily /ˈstɛdɪli/ *adv* 1 (gradually) *<to fall, increase>* بِشَكْلٍ ثابِتٍ \ مُطَّرِدٍ 2 (without stopping) *<to work, rain>* دون تَوَقُّفٍ

steady /ˈstɛdi/ **A** *adj* (**steadier, steadiest**) 1 (constant) *<speed, improvement, breathing>* مُسْتَقِرّ, مُنْتَظِم; **a ~ stream of cars** مَوْكِب مُنْتَظِم من السَيّاراتِ; **to drive at a ~ 110 kmh** قادَ سَيّارةً بِسُرْعةٍ ثابِتةٍ عند 110 كلم في الساعةِ; **a ~ increase/decline in numbers** زِيادة ثابِتة \ تَراجُع ثابِت في الأَرْقامِ 2 (firm, unwavering) *<handwriting>* ثابِت (ثَوابِتُ); **hold the camera ~** اِمْسِكْ الكاميرا بِإحْكامٍ; **he isn't very ~ on his feet** لا يَسْتَطيعُ الوُقوفَ بِشَكْلٍ ثابِتٍ 3 (calm) *<voice, nerves, gaze>* هادِئ 4 (with continuity) *<job, income, employment>* ثابِت (ثَوابِتُ); **does she have a ~ boyfriend?** هل لَها صَديقٌ دائِمٌ؟

B *vt* (**steadies, steadying, steadied**) 1 (to keep firm) ثَبَّتَ *<a camera, ladder>* 2 (to control) **to ~ one's nerves** سَيْطَرَ على أَعْصابِهِ

C *vi* (**steadies, steadying, steadied**) 1 «hands, voice» هَدَأَ (a; هُدوء) 2 «prices, interest rates, inflation» اِسْتَقَرَّ

D *v refl* **to ~ oneself** تَماسَكَ, ثَبَّتَ نَفْسَهُ

E *excl* (BrE) (infml) **~!** كُنْ حَذِراً!; **~ on!** (in reproach) رُوَيْدَكَ!

(Idiom) **to go steady with sb** كانَ في عَلاقةٍ عاطِفِيّةٍ مُسْتَقِرّةٍ

steak /steɪk/ *n* (of beef) شَريحة لَحْمٍ بَقَريٍّ; (of fish) شَريحة سَمَكٍ

steal /stiːl/ **A** *vt* (*past tense* **stole**, *past participle* **stolen**) سَرَقَ (i; سَرِقة) *<jewellery, money>*; **to ~ sth from sb** سَرَقَ شَيْئاً من شَخْصٍ; **stolen property** مَسْروقات, مُمْتَلَكات مَسْروقة

B *vi* 1 (committing theft) سَرَقَ (i; سَرِقة); **to ~ from sb** سَرَقَ من شَخْصٍ 2 (to move stealthily) **to ~ out of a room** اِنْسَلَّ من غُرْفةٍ; **to ~ into a room** تَسَلَّلَ إلى غُرْفةٍ

stealth /stɛlθ/ *n* (of a cat, burglar) تَسَلُّل, اِنْسِلال, تَخَفٍّ

stealth bomber *n* قاذِفة القَنابِلِ الشَبَح

stealthy /'stɛlθi/ *adj* (**stealthier, stealthiest**) ‹*approach*› سِرّيّ; ‹*killer*› خَفيّ

steam /sti:m/ **A** *n* **1** (vapour) (أَبْخِرة) بُخار; **a ~-powered machine** آلة تَعْمَلُ بالبُخارِ **2** (in a room, on a window) بُخار (أَبْخِرة)

B *vt* طَها \ طَبَخ على البُخارِ ‹*the vegetables, a pudding*›

C *vi* **1** (to give off vapour) «water, pan, soup» خَرَجَ \ تصاعَدَ **2** (Transp) «ships, trains» سارَ (i; سَيْر, مَسير, مَسيرة) مِنْهُ البُخارُ

Idioms **to get up** *or* **pick up steam** اكْتَسَبَ زَخماً; **to let off steam** نَفَّسَ عن نَفْسِهِ; **to run out of steam** نَفَذَتْ طاقَتُهُ; **the economy is running out of ~** يَبْدَأُ الاقْتِصادُ في التَباطُؤِ

Phrasal verbs **steam open**: **~ [sth] open, ~ open [sth]** فَتَحَ شَيْئاً بالبُخارِ ‹*an envelope, a letter*›

• **steam up** «windows, glasses» غَطّاهُ البُخارُ

steamboat /'sti:mbəʊt/ *n* باخِرة, قارِب \ مَرْكَب بُخاريّ (بَواخِرُ)

steam engine *n* مُحَرِّك بُخاريّ

steamer /'sti:mə/ *n* **1** (Culin) حَلّة بُخارٍ **2** (Naut) سَفينة بُخاريّة, باخِرة (بَواخِرُ)

steamroller /'sti:mrəʊlə/ *n* مِحْدَلة \ مِدْحَلة بُخاريّة

steamship /'sti:mʃɪp/ *n* سَفينة بُخاريّة, باخِرة (بَواخِرُ)

steamy /'sti:mi/ *adj* (**steamier, steamiest**) **1** ‹*bathroom, jungle*› مُشَبَّع بالبُخارِ **2** (passionate) ‹*scene, affair*› مُثير جِنْسيًّا

steel /sti:l/ **A** *n* فولاذ, صُلْب

B *v refl* **to ~ oneself** أَعَدَّ \ جَهَّزَ نَفْسَهُ

steel wool *n* سِلْك غَسيلِ الأَواني

steelworker /'sti:lwə:kə/ *n* عامِل بِمَصْنَعِ صُلْبٍ

steelworks /'sti:lwə:ks/ *n* (*pl* **steelworks**) مَصْنَع صُلْبٍ

steely /'sti:li/ *adj* (**steelier, steeliest**) **1** ‹*determination, resolve*› لا يَلينُ, صُلْب, فولاذيّ; ‹*gaze, stare*› صارِم, حادّ **2** ‹*sky, clouds*› رَماديّ

steep /sti:p/ **A** *adj* **1** ‹*stairs, hill*› شَديد الانْحِدارِ **2** ‹*rise, fall*› حادّ **3** (infml) (expensive) ‹*price, charge*› باهِظ

B *vt* (to soak) **to ~ sth in sth** نَقَعَ \ غَمَسَ شَيْئاً في شَيْءٍ ‹*fruit, tea*›

steeple /'sti:p(ə)l/ *n* قِمّة بُرْجٍ (لِكَنيسةٍ)

steeplechase /'sti:pəltʃeɪs/ *n* سِباق حَواجِزَ

steeplejack /'sti:pəldʒak/ *n* [عامِل تَرْميمِ الأَبْراجِ والمُنْشَآتِ المُرْتَفِعةِ]

steeply /'sti:pli/ *adv* ‹*to rise, fall*› بِحِدّةٍ

steer /stɪə/ **A** *vt* **1** (in navigation) قادَ (u; قِيادة) ‹*a car, bicycle, boat*› **2** (to guide) وَجَّهَ ‹*a person*›; **to ~ a course through the problem** تَبَنّى مَساراً للتَعامُلِ مع المُشْكِلةِ; **to ~ a bill through parliament** أَشْرَفَ على تَمْريرِ مَشْروعِ قانونٍ في البَرْلَمان; **to ~ a conversation onto a different subject** حَوَّلَ المُحادَثةَ إلى مَوْضوعٍ مُخْتَلِفٍ

B *vi* **to ~ towards** *or* **for sth** سارَ بِاتِّجاهِ شَيْءٍ

C *n* **1** (bullock) عِجْل مَخْصيّ **2** (infml) (tip) نَصيحة (نَصائِحُ)

Idiom **to steer clear of sth/sb** ابْتَعَدَ عن شَيْءٍ \ شَخْصٍ

steering /'stɪərɪŋ/ *n* تَوْجيه

steering column *n* عَمود التَوْجيهِ \ عَجَلةِ القِيادةِ

steering lock *n* قُفْل المِقْوَدِ \ عَجَلةِ القِيادةِ

steering wheel *n* عَجَلة قِيادةٍ, مِقْوَد (مَقاوِدُ)

stellar /'stɛlə/ *adj* **1** ‹*astronomy, explosion*› نَجْميّ **2** (in show business) ‹*performance, cast*› مِن الطِرازِ الأَوَّلِ, رائِع, مُمْتاز

stem /stɛm/ **A** *n* **1** (of a flower, leaf) ساق (f; سيقان) **2** (of a glass) ساق (f; سيقان), عُنُق (f; أَعْناق)

B *vt* (**-mm-**) حَجَّمَ, أَوْقَفَ ‹*a flow, an advance*›

C *vi* (**-mm-**) **to ~ from sth** نَشَأَ \ تَوَلَّدَ عن شَيْءٍ

stem cell *n* خَليّة جِذْعيّة

stem ginger *n* [زَنْجَبيل حُلْو مَحْفوظ]

stench /stɛntʃ/ *n* رائِحة كَريهة \ مُنْتِنة

stencil /'stɛnsɪl/ **A** *n* اسْتِنْسِل, مِرْسام (مَراسيمُ)

B *vt* (**-ll-** BrE, **-l-** AmE) طَبَعَ بِمِرْسامٍ \ باسْتِنْسِل ‹*a number, picture*›

stenographer /stə'nɒgrəfə/ *n* (AmE) كاتِب اخْتِزالٍ, مُخْتَزِل

stenography /stɪ'nɒgrəfi/ *n* (AmE) اخْتِزال (اخْتِزالات)

step /stɛp/ **A** *n* **1** (pace) خَطْوة (خَطَوات); **to take a ~** خطا \ اتَّخَذَ خَطْوةً; **I was a few ~s behind her** كُنْتُ خَلْفَها بِخَطَواتٍ قَليلةٍ; **to watch one's ~** (when walking) مَشى بِحِرْصٍ; (to be careful) تَوَخّى الحَذَرَ **2** (in marching, walking) **to walk** *or*

keep in ~ سارَ في خَطواتٍ مُنْتَظِمةٍ; **to be out of ~ with the times** لم يَتماشَ مع الزَمَنِ **3** (sound) وَقْع خَطَواتٍ **4** (move, stage) خَطْوة (خَطَوات); **the first ~ is to make a plan** أَوَّلُ خَطْوةٍ هي وَضْعُ خُطَّةٍ; **it's a ~ in the right direction** هي خَطْوةٌ في الاتِّجاهِ الصَحيحِ; **to be one ~ closer to winning** اِقْتَرَبَ خَطْوةً أُخْرى من الفَوْزِ; **to be one ~ ahead of the competition** اِحْتَلَّ الصَدارةَ في المُسابَقةِ; **it is a ~ forward/backward** هي خَطْوةٌ للأَمام \ للخَلْفِ; **to take ~s to do sth** اتَّخَذَ عِدّةَ خَطَواتٍ لِفِعْلِ شَيْءٍ **5** (way of walking) خَطْوة (خَطَوات), مِشْية **6** (of a dance) خَطْوة (خَطَوات) **7** (on a staircase) دَرَجة; **a flight of ~s** دَرَج (أَدْراج, دِراج)

B (**steps**) *n pl* **1** (stairs) دَرَج (أَدْراج, دِراج) **2** (ladder) سُلَّم (سَلالِمُ)

C *vi* (**-pp-**) خَطا (u; خَطْو); **to ~ into the lift/doorway** دَخَلَ إلى المِصْعَدِ \ المَدْخَلِ; **to ~ onto the scales/bus** صَعَدَ على الميزانِ \ إلى الحافِلةِ; **would you ~ this way?** تَفَضَّلْ من هذا الطَريقِ; **to ~ off the plane/pavement** نَزَلَ من على الطائِرةِ \ الرَصيفِ; **to ~ on sb's foot** داسَ \ وطِئَ على قَدَمِ شَخْصٍ; **to ~ over a fence/stream** تَخَطَّى سِياجاً \ مَجْرًى; **to ~ up to the microphone** تَقَدَّمَ إلى الميكْروفون

Idioms **one step at a time** خَطْوةً خَطْوةً; **to step on it** (infml) أَسْرَعَ

Phrasal verbs **step aside** (to move to one side) تَنَحَّى جانِباً

- **step back** **1** (to move back) رجعَ \ تراجَعَ للخَلْفِ **2** (from a situation) اِبْتَعَدَ; **to ~ back from the brink** تجنب السُقوط في الهاوِيةِ
- **step down** (to resign) «executive, minister» اِسْتَقالَ
- **step in** (to take action) تَدَخَّلَ
- **step up**: **~ up** [**sth**] (to increase) زادَ [شَيْئاً] ‹*production, one's efforts*›

step aerobics *n* [تَمارين الأَيروبيكْس بِاسْتِخْدام منَصّةٍ صَغيرةٍ]

stepbrother /ˈstɛpbrʌðə/ *n* أَخ غَيْر شَقيقٍ

step-by-step /ˌstɛpbʌɪˈstɛp/ **A** *adj* ‹*instructions, programme*› خَطْوة بِخَطْوةٍ; ‹*reduction*› تَدْريجيّ

B (**step by step**) *adv* ‹*to transform, explain*› خَطْوةً خَطْوةً, تَدْريجيًّا; **to take things step by step** تَعامَلَ مع الأُمورِ تَدْريجيًّا

stepchild /ˈstɛptʃʌɪld/ *n* (*pl* **-children**) رَبيب (طِفْل الزَوْجِ أو الزَوْجةِ)

stepdaughter /ˈstɛpdɔːtə/ *n* رَبيبة (بِنْت الزَوْجِ \ الزَوْجةِ)

stepfather /ˈstɛpfɑːðə/ *n* زَوْجُ الأُمِّ

stepladder /ˈstɛpladə/ *n* سُلَّم نَقّال

stepmother /ˈstɛpmʌðə/ *n* زَوْجة الأَبِ

step-parent /ˈstɛpˌpɛːrənt/ *n* (mother) زَوْجة الأَبِ; (father) زَوْج الأُمِّ

stepping stone /ˈstɛpɪŋ stəʊn/ *n* (stone) [حَجَر يوضَعُ في مَخاضةٍ للعُبورِ عَلَيْهِ]; (starting point) نُقْطة انْطِلاقٍ

stepsister /ˈstɛpsɪstə/ *n* أُخْت غَيْر شَقيقةٍ

stepson /ˈstɛpsʌn/ *n* رَبيب (اِبْن الزَوْجِ \ الزَوْجةِ)

stereo /ˈstɛrɪəʊ/ *n* **1** (sound) سْتيريو, صَوْت مُجَسَّم; **in ~** بِصَوْتٍ مُجَسَّمٍ **2** (device) **~ system** نِظام سْتيريو \ صَوْتيّ مُجَسَّم

stereotype /ˈstɛriətʌɪp/ *n* قالَب نَمَطيّ, صورة نَمَطيّة

sterile /ˈstɛrʌɪl/ *adj* **1** ‹*male*› عَقيم (عِقام); ‹*female*› عاقِر (mf; f pl عَواقِرُ) **2** ‹*dressing, instruments*› مُعَقَّم **3** ‹*discussion, argument*› عَقيم, غَيْر مُثْمِرٍ

sterility /stəˈrɪlɪti/ *n* **1** (germ-free state) تَعْقيم, خُلوّ من الجَراثيم **2** (infertility) عُقْم **3** (of ideas, debate) عُقْم

sterilize, -ise (BrE) /ˈstɛrɪlʌɪz/ *vt* **1** ‹*a needle, wound*› عَقَّمَ, طَهَّرَ **2** ‹*a patient, cat*› عَقَّمَ, جَعَلَ عَقيماً

sterling /ˈstəːlɪŋ/ *n* جُنَيْه اسْتِرْلينيّ

stern /stəːn/ **A** *n* (Naut) مُؤَخَّرة (سَفينة)

B *adj* ‹*teacher, father*› صارِم (صَوارِمُ), جادّ

sternum /ˈstəːnəm/ *n* (*pl* **sternums** or **sterna**) عَظْمة القَصِّ

steroid /ˈstɛrɔɪd/ *n* سْتيرويْد (سْتيرويْدات)

stethoscope /ˈstɛθəskəʊp/ *n* سَمّاعة طِبِّيّة \ طَبيبٍ, مِسْماع

stevedore /ˈstiːvədɔː/ *n* عامِل شَحْنٍ وَتَفْريغٍ

stew /stjuː/ **A** *n* يَخْنة

B *vt* ‹*beef, apples*› [طَهى في مَرَقٍ على نارٍ هادِئةٍ]

steward /ˈstjuːəd/ *n* **1** (on a ship, train) مُضيف **2** (at a demonstration, sporting event) مُنَظِّم, مُشْرِف, مُنَسِّق

stewardess /stjuːəˈdɛs/ *n* (on a ship, plane) مُضيفة

stg *abbr* = **sterling** جُنَيْه اسْتِرْلينيّ

stick /stɪk/ **A** *n* 1 (piece of wood) عَصاً (f; عِصِيّ) 2 (also **walking stick**) عَصاً (f; عِصِيّ), عُكّاز (عَكاكيز) 3 (piece) **a ~ of chalk/dynamite** إصْبَع طَباشيرٍ \ ديناميت; **a ~ of celery/rhubarb** عود كَرَفْسٍ \ راوَنْدٍ 4 (in hockey) عَصاً (f; عِصِيّ) 5 (infml) (piece of furniture) **a few ~s of furniture** بَعْض قِطَع الأَثاثِ البالي 6 (BrE) [u] (infml) (criticism) انْتِقاد, نَقْد; **to get** *or* **take some ~** نالَهُ بَعْضُ النَّقْدِ; **to give sb some ~** وَجَّهَ إلى شَخْصٍ بَعْضَ النَّقْدِ

B (**sticks**) *n pl* (infml) (rural area) **in the ~s** في الأَرْياف

C *vt* (*past tense, past participle* **stuck**) 1 (to push) **to ~ a pin/knife into sth** غَرَزَ دَبّوساً \ سِكّيناً في شَيْءٍ; **she stuck her fork into the meat** غَرَزَتْ شَوْكَتَها في اللَحْمِ 2 (infml) (to put) وَضَعَ (a; وَضْع); **~ the shopping on the table** ضَع المُشْتَرَياتِ على الطاوِلَةِ; **she stuck her hands in her pockets** وَضَعَتْ يَدَيْها في جُيوبِها; **to ~ an advert in the paper** وَضَعَ إعْلاناً في الجَريدةِ; **to ~ sb in a home** وَضَعَ شَخْصاً في دارِ رِعايةٍ 3 (to fix in place) لَصِقَ (a; لَصْق, لُصوق) ‹*the wood, poster, stamp*›; **will this glue ~ plastic?** هل يَعْمَلُ هذا اللَصْقُ مع البَلاسْتيك؟; **I stuck the two ends together** لَصَقْتُ الطَرَفَيْنِ مَعاً 4 (infml) (to impose) **to ~ an extra £10 on the price** أضاف 10 جُنَيْهاتٍ على السِعْرِ; **I was stuck with Frank** اضْطُرِرْتُ إلى البَقاءِ مع فِرانك 5 (BrE) (infml) (to bear) تَحَمَّلَ ‹*a person, situation*›; **I couldn't ~ the noise any longer** لم أعُدْ أُطيقُ الضَوْضاءَ

D *vi* (*past tense, past participle* **stuck**) 1 (to adhere) «stamps, glue» الْتَصَقَ; **the sauce/rice had stuck to the pan** الْتَصَقَتِ الصَلْصةُ \ الْتَصَقَ الأُرْزُ بالمَقْلاةِ 2 (to jam) «drawers, doors» تَوَقَّفَ عن الحَرَكةِ 3 (to remain) الْتَصَقَ, بَقِيَ (a; بَقاء), ثَبَتَ (u; ثُبوت, ثَبات); **the name stuck** الْتَصَقَ بِهِ الاسْمُ; **to ~ in sb's memory** *or* **mind** رَسَخَ في ذاكِرةِ شَخْصٍ; **the police couldn't make the charges ~** لم تَسْتَطِعِ الشُرْطةُ أنْ تُثْبِتَ التُهَمَ; **to ~ close to sb** بَقِيَ قَريباً من شَخْصٍ

Phrasal verbs **stick around** (infml) (to stay) مَكَثَ (u; مُكْث, مُكوث), بَقِيَ (a; بَقاء)

• **stick at**: **~ at [sth]** عَكَفَ على [شَيْءٍ] ‹*a task*›

• **stick by**: **~ by [sb]** وَقَفَ بِجِوارِ [شَخْصٍ] ‹*one's spouse, a friend*›

• **stick out A** (to protrude) «nails, rocks, sb's hair» بَرَزَ للخارِجِ; **his ears ~ out** تَبْرُزُ أُذُنَيْهِ للخارِجِ **B ~ [sth] out, ~ out [sth]** 1 (to push outwards) **to ~ out one's hand/foot** مَدَّ يَدَهُ \ قَدَمَهُ; **to ~ one's tongue out** أَخْرَجَ لِسانَهُ 2 (infml) (to endure) تَحَمَّلَ [شَيْئاً] ‹*tough times, a job*›; **we decided to ~ it out/~ things out** قَرَّرْنا أنْ نَسْتَمِرَّ في المُحاوَلةِ

• **stick to**: **~ to [sth/sb]** 1 (to keep to) تَمَسَّكَ ب [شَيْءٍ \ شَخْصٍ] ‹*the facts, point, a plan*›; **I stuck to my diet** الْتَزَمْتُ بِحِمْيَتي الغِذائيّةِ 2 (to stay close to) لازَمَ [شَيْئاً \ شَخْصاً] ‹*a person, path, river*› 3 (to stay faithful to) بَقِيَ على وَلائِهِ ل [شَيْءٍ \ شَخْصٍ] ‹*a brand, shop, one's principles*›

• **stick together A** 1 (to adhere) «pages, tablets» الْتَصَقَ 2 (infml) (to stay loyal) تَكاتَفَ, تَعاضَدَ مَعاً 3 (infml) (not to separate) بَقِيَ مَعاً **B ~ [sth] together, ~ together [sth]** لَصَّقَ [شَيْئاً] ‹*a toy, plate, the pieces*›; **to ~ sth back together, to ~ sth together again** لَصَّقَ شَيْئاً مَرَّةً أُخرى

• **stick up A** 1 (to protrude) «posts, rocks, sb's hair» بَرَزَ للخارِجِ 2 (to defend) **to ~ up for sb** دافَعَ عن شَخْصٍ; **you have to ~ up for yourself** لا بُدَّ أنْ تُدافِعَ عن نَفْسِكَ **B ~ [sth] up, ~ up [sth]** 1 (to fix) عَلَّقَ [شَيْئاً] ‹*a poster, notice*› 2 (to raise) رَفَعَ [شَيْئاً] ‹*one's hand, head*›; **~ 'em up!** (infml) ارْفَعْ يَدَيْكَ!

sticker /ˈstɪkə/ *n* مُلْصَق (مُلْصَقات), لاصِقة

sticking plaster /ˈstɪkɪŋ ˌplɑːstə/ *n* لَزْقة (جُروحٍ), لَصْقة

stick insect *n* حَشَرة عَصَوِيّة, حَشَرة العَصا \ العيدانِ

stick-in-the-mud /ˈstɪkɪnðəˌmʌd/ *n* (infml) شَخْص رَجْعِيّ

stickler /ˈstɪklə/ *n* **to be a ~ for discipline/detail** كانَ شَديدَ التَمَسُّكِ بالنِظامِ \ بالتَفاصيلِ

stick-on /ˈstɪkɒn/ *adj* ‹*label, tattoo*› لاصِق

stick shift *n* (AmE) ناقِل حَرَكةٍ \ سُرْعةٍ يَدَوِيّ

stick-up /ˈstɪkʌp/ *n* (infml) سَطْو مُسَلَّح, سَرِقة مُسَلَّحة

sticky /ˈstɪki/ *adj* (**stickier, stickiest**) 1 ‹*label*› لاصِق; ‹*sweet*› لَزِج 2 (difficult) ‹*situation, problem*› شائِك, صَعْب (صِعاب)

sticky tape *n* (infml) شَريط لاصِق

stiff /stɪf/ **A** *adj* 1 (from age, illness, exercise) مُتَصَلِّب; **to have a ~ neck** كانَ لَدَيْهِ تَصَلُّبٌ في الرَقَبةِ; **my legs are ~**

لَدَيَّ تَصَلُّبٌ في الساقَيْنِ **2** (hard to move) ‹*drawer, door, lever*› خَشِن, صَعْب الحَرَكةِ **3** (rigid) ‹*cardboard, fabric, collar*› مُتَيَبِّس, مُتَخَشِّب **4** (Culin) ‹*mixture*› مُتَماسِك; **beat the egg whites until ~** أُخْفُقْ بَياضَ البَيْضِ حتّى يَتَماسَكَ **5** (not relaxed) ‹*manner, atmosphere*› صارِم, حادّ, جافّ; **it was a ~ and formal occasion** كانَتْ مُناسَبةً رَسْميّةً جافّةً **6** (harsh) ‹*letter*› شَديد اللَهْجةِ; ‹*fine, sentence*› مُشَدَّد **7** (difficult) ‹*exam, challenge, climb*› صَعْب; **they put up ~ opposition** قاوَموا مُقاوَمةً شَديدةً **8** (strong) ‹*breeze*› قَويّ, شَديد; **I need a ~ drink** أَحْتاجُ إلى مَشْروبٍ قَويٍّ

B *adv* (infml) **to be bored ~** شَعَرَ بِمَلَلٍ شَديدٍ; **to be frozen ~** شَعَرَ بِبَرْدٍ شَديدٍ; **he scared us ~** أَفْزَعَنا بِشِدّةٍ

C *n* **1** (infml) (corpse) جُثّة (جُثَث, أَجْثاث) **2** (AmE) (infml) (boring person) [شَخْص مُمِلّ] **3** (AmE) (infml) (guy) شَخْص (شُخوص, أَشْخاص; mf)

stiffen /ˈstɪf(ə)n/ **A** *vt* **1** (to make rigid) صَلَّبَ ‹*fabric, a frame*› **2** (to make more severe) غَلَّظَ ‹*a penalty, punishment*› **3** (to make stronger) قَوّى ‹*sb's resolve, resistance*›

B *vi* **1** «muscles, joints» تَصَلَّبَ **2** «sb's resolve, resistance» اِشْتَدَّ, قَوِيَ (a; قوّة)

stiffly /ˈstɪfli/ *adv* **1** (in a rigid way) ‹*to walk, move*› بِصُعوبةٍ **2** (formally) ‹*to say, bow*› بِتَصَنُّعٍ, بِجَفاءٍ

stifle /ˈstaɪf(ə)l/ *vt* **1** خَنَقَ (u; خَنْق), كَبَتَ (i; كَبْت), قَيَّدَ ‹*innovation, creativity*›; **to ~ dissent** قَمَعَ المُعارَضةَ; **to ~ debate** أَفْسَدَ النِقاشَ **2** كَتَمَ (u; كَتْم, كِتْمان) ‹*a yawn, laugh*›

stifling /ˈstaɪflɪŋ/ *adj* ‹*heat, climate*› خانِق

stigma /ˈstɪɡmə/ *n* (*pl* **stigmas** or **stigmata**) وَصْمة عارٍ

stigmatize, -ise (BrE) /ˈstɪɡmətaɪz/ *vt* وَصَمَ (i; وَصْم) ‹*a minority, person*›

stile /staɪl/ *n* مَرْقًى, دَرَج (مُخَصَّص لِعُبورِ سِياجٍ)

stiletto /stɪˈletəʊ/ *n* (*pl* **stilettos**) حِذاء سْتيليتو (حِذاء بِكَعْبٍ عالٍ); **~ heel** كَعْب عالٍ

still /stɪl/ **A** *adj* **1** (motionless) ‹*air*› ساكِن; ‹*water*› راكِد (رَواكِد); **to stand/sit ~** وَقَفَ \ جَلَسَ بِلا حَراكٍ; **keep ~!** لا تَتَحَرَّكْ! **2** (not fizzy) ‹*water, orange drink*› غَيْر غازيٍّ

B *n* **1** (for making alcohol) جِهاز تَقْطيرٍ, إنْبيق **2** (photograph) صورة (صُوَر), لَقْطة (لَقَطات)

C *adv* **1** (even now, even then) ‹*to work, think*› ما زالَ; **he's ~ as crazy as ever!** ما زالَ مَجْنوناً كَما كانَ!; **I ~ have four miles to go** ما زالَ أَمامي أَرْبَعةُ أَمْيالٍ; **do you ~ live at the same address?** أَما زِلْتَ تَعيشُ في نَفْسِ العُنْوانِ؟; **we ~ don't know what happened** ما زِلْنا لا نَعْرِفُ ما حَدَثَ; **they ~ haven't replied** لم يَرُدّوا بَعْدُ **2** (used for emphasis) أَكْثَر; **that's better/worse ~!** ذلك أَفْضَلُ \ أَسْوَأُ بِكَثيرٍ! **3** (nevertheless) لَكِنَّ, وَمَعَ ذلك; **~, you can't blame him for being angry** وَمَعَ ذلك، لا يُمْكِنُكَ أَنْ تَلومَهُ على غَضَبِهِ; **it ~ doesn't explain why he never returned** لَكِنَّ هذا لا يُفَسِّرُ لِماذا لم يَعُدْ مُطْلَقاً

stillbirth /ˈstɪlbɜːθ/ *n* وِلادة جَنينٍ مَيِّتٍ

stillborn /ˈstɪlbɔːn/ *adj* ‹*child, baby*› مَوْلود مَيِّتاً

still life *n* (*pl* **still-lifes**) صورة لِلطَبيعةِ الصامِتةِ \ لِلحَياةِ الساكِنةِ

stilt /stɪlt/ *n* **1** (pole) طَوّالة (إحْدى ساقَيْنِ خَشَبِيَّتَيْنِ يُمْشى عَلَيْهِما) **2** (Constr) رَكيزة (رَكائِزُ), دِعامة (دَعائِمُ, دِعامات)

stilted /ˈstɪltɪd/ *adj* ‹*conversation, English*› مُتَكَلَّف, مُصْطَنَع

stimulant /ˈstɪmjʊlənt/ *n* مُنَبِّه (مُنَبِّهات), مُنَشِّط (مُنَشِّطات)

stimulate /ˈstɪmjʊleɪt/ *vt* **1** أَثارَ ‹*the imagination, discussion*›; حَفَّزَ, شَجَّعَ ‹*students, children*› **2** نَشَّطَ, حَفَّزَ ‹*the economy, demand*›

stimulating /ˈstɪmjʊleɪtɪŋ/ *adj* ‹*discussion*› مُثير; ‹*environment*› مُحَفِّز, مُشَجِّع

stimulation /stɪmjuːˈleɪʃ(ə)n/ *n* **1** (of the mind) تَنْشيط, إثارة **2** (of the economy) تَنْشيط, تَحْفيز

stimulus /ˈstɪmjʊləs/ *n* (*pl* **stimuli**) **1** (physical) مُنَبِّه (مُنَبِّهات), مُثير, مُحَفِّز **2** (incentive) حافِز (حَوافِزُ)

sting /stɪŋ/ **A** *n* **1** (of bees, wasps) إبْرة (إبَر), شَوْكة (شَوْكات, شُوَك) **2** (wound) لَسْعة, لَدْغة (لَدَغات)

B *vt* (*past tense, past participle* **stung**) **1** (to wound) «bees» لَسَعَ (a; لَسْع); «nettles» وَخَزَ (i; وَخْز), شَوَّكَ ‹*a person, sb's hand*› **2** (to irritate) آلَمَ (Form IV; imperf يُؤْلِمُ) ‹*your eyes, skin*›

C *vi* (*past tense, past participle* **stung**) **1** (to wound) «wasps» لَسَعَ (a; لَسْع); «nettles» وَخَزَ (i; وَخْز), شَوَّكَ **2** (to hurt) «cuts, eyes» آلَمَ (Form IV; imperf يُؤْلِمُ)

Idiom **to have a sting in the tail** كانَ لَهُ جانِبٌ سَلْبيٌّ

stinging nettle /ˈstɪŋɪŋ ˌnɛt(ə)l/ *n* (نَبات) قُرّاص

stingy /ˈstɪndʒi/ *adj* (**stingier**, **stingiest**) (infml) 1 (mean) ‹*employer, parent*› بَخيل (بُخَلاءُ)، شَحيح (أَشِحّاءُ، أَشِحّة) 2 (scant) ‹*portion, tip*› ضَئيل، هَزيل

stink /stɪŋk/ A *vi* (*past tense* **stank** or **stunk**; *past participle* **stunk**) «drains, rubbish» نَتَنَ (a-i-u; نَتْن، نَتانة)، فاحَتْ مِنْهُ رائِحةٌ كَريهةٌ \ نَتِنةٌ

B *n* 1 (foul smell) رائِحة كَريهة \ نَتِنة \ خبيثة، نَتْن، نَتانة 2 (infml) (fuss) جَلَب، جَلَبة، اهْتِياج (اهْتِجاجات) احْتِجاج; **to make/kick up a ~** مَلأَ الدُّنْيا ضَجيجاً

stink bomb *n* قُنْبُلة رائِحةٍ كَريهةٍ

stinking /ˈstɪŋkɪŋ/ *adj before n* 1 (foul-smelling) ‹*sewage, clothes*› كَريه الرائِحةِ، نَتِن 2 (infml) (horrible) ‹*cold*› شَديد; ‹*place*› كَريه، بَغيض

stint /stɪnt/ A *vi* «organizations, chefs» بَخِلَ (a; بُخْل); **they didn't ~ over the wedding arrangements** لم يَبْخَلوا في تَرْتيباتِ حَفْلِ الزِفافِ

B *n* فَتْرة عَمَلٍ (مُحَدَّدةٍ)

stipulate /ˈstɪpjʊleɪt/ *vt* اشْتَرَطَ، نَصَّ (u; نَصّ) على ‹*a condition, penalty*›

stipulation /ˌstɪpjʊˈleɪʃ(ə)n/ *n* شَرْط (شُروط)

stir /stəː/ A *vt* (**-rr-**) 1 (to mix) حَرَّكَ، قَلَّبَ ‹*a mixture, sauce, paint*›; **to ~ sth into the mixture/sauce** قَلَّبَ شَيْئاً مع الخَليطِ \ حَرَّكَ الصَّلْصةِ 2 (to move slightly) «breeze» هَزَّ (u; هَزّ) ‹*the leaves, papers*› 3 (to arouse) أَثارَ، هَيَّجَ المَشاعِرَ ‹*a person*›; **to ~ sb to pity/into action** أَثارَ شَفَقةَ شَخْصٍ \ دَفَعَ شَخْصاً إلى القِيامِ بِفِعْلٍ; **what she said ~red my curiosity** ما قالَتْهُ أَثارَ فُضولي

B *vi* (**-rr-**) 1 (to move gently) «leaves, papers» تَحَرَّكَ، اهْتَزَّ; **nothing ~red in the house** لم تَكُنْ هُناكَ أَيُّ حَرَكةٍ في البَيْتِ 2 (in one's sleep) تَحَرَّكَ; **the patient ~red at 5.30 a.m.** تَحَرَّكَ المَريضُ الساعةَ 5.30 صَباحاً

C *v refl* (**-rr-**) **to ~ oneself** حَرَّكَ نَفْسَهُ

D *n* 1 (in mixing) **to give the sauce/mixture a ~** حَرَّكَ الصَّلْصةَ \ الخَليطَ 2 (commotion) اضْطِراب (اضْطِرابات)، هِياج; **to cause a ~** أَحْدَثَ اضْطِراباً

(Phrasal verb) **stir up** A **~ [sth] up, ~ up [sth]** 1 (to whip up) أَثارَ [شَيْئاً] ‹*the dust, leaves*› 2 (to arouse) أَثارَ [شَيْئاً] ‹*trouble, hatred, memories*› B **~ [sb] up, ~ up [sb]** هَيَّجَ \ أَثارَ [شَخْصاً] ‹*the crowd, residents, workers*›

stir-fry /ˈstəːfrʌɪ/ A *vt* (*past tense, past participle* **-fried**) قَلى سَريعاً ‹*vegetables, noodles*›

B *n* وَجْبة قَلْيٍ سَريعٍ

stirring /ˈstəːrɪŋ/ *adj* ‹*speech, rendition*› مُؤَثِّر

stirrup /ˈstɪrəp/ *n* رِكاب (حَلْقة في سَرْجٍ)

stitch /stɪtʃ/ A *n* 1 (in sewing) غُرْزة (غُرَز)، دَرْزة 2 (in a wound) غُرْزة (غُرَز) 3 [u] (pain) أَلَم، وَخْز (بالجَنْبِ أو الصَدْرِ)

B *vt* 1 (to sew) دَرَزَ (u; دَرْز)، خاطَ (i; خَيْط) ‹*clothes, a seam*› 2 خاطَ (i; خَيْط) ‹*a wound, patient*›

(Idioms) **to be in stitches** ضَحِكَ بِشَكْلٍ هيسْتيريٍّ; **a stitch in time (saves nine)** الوِقايةُ خَيْرٌ من العِلاجِ، دِرْهَمُ وِقايةٍ خَيْرٌ من قِنْطارِ عِلاجٍ

STM /ɛstiˈɛm/ *n* = **scanning tunnelling microscope** مِجْهَر مَسْحٍ نَفَقيّ

stoat /stəʊt/ *n* قاقُم (حَيَوان من جِنْسِ ابْنِ عِرْسٍ)

stock /stɒk/ A *n* 1 [u] (in shops, warehouses) مَخْزون; **to have sth in ~** كانَ لَدَيْهِ شَيْءٌ مُتاحٌ لِلبَيْعِ; **to be out of ~** نَفِدَ (a; نَفْد، نَفاد) 2 (supply, store) مَخْزون (مَخْزونات); **~s are running low** بَدَأَ المَخْزونُ يَنْقُصُ; **to get in a ~ of food** جَمَعَ مَخْزوناً من الطَعامِ; **while ~s last** حتّى نَفادِ الكَمّيّةِ 3 (in a company) سَهْم (أَسْهُم); **he owns 10% of the corporation's ~** يَمْتَلِكُ 10٪ من أَسْهُمِ الشَرِكةِ; **~s closed higher/lower** أَغْلَقَت الأَسْهُمُ على ارْتِفاعٍ \ انْخِفاضٍ 4 [u] (descent) أَصْل; **to be of peasant ~** كانَ من أَصْلٍ ريفيٍّ 5 [u] (livestock) ماشِية 6 [u] (standing) مَكانة; **his ~ has risen/fallen** ارْتَفَعَتْ \ انْخَفَضَتْ مَكانَتُهُ 7 [u] (Culin) مَرَق; **beef ~** مَرَق لَحْمِ بَقَرٍ 8 (in grafting) [ساق النَّبْتةِ الَّذي يوضَعُ فيهِ الطُّعْمُ]

B (**stocks**) *n pl* **the ~s** [أَداة تَعْذيبٍ خَشَبيّة تُعَلَّقُ فيها الأَقْدامُ]

C *adj before n* 1 ‹*answer, excuse*› شائِع، مُعْتاد 2 ‹*size, colour*› أَساسيّ، قِياسيّ

D *vt* 1 (to have available) تَوَفَّرَ لَدَيْهِ ‹*a make, model, size*›;

I'm sorry, we don't ~ that model آسِف، لا يَتوَفَّر لَدَيْنا هذا النَموذَجُ **2** (to replenish with supplies) مَلأَ (a; مَلْء) ‹*the larder, fridge*›; (with sale items) عَبَّأَ زَوَّدَ بالبِضاعةِ ‹*a shop*›; ‹*the shelves*›; **a well-~ed garden/library** حَديقة \ مَكْتَبة مُجَهَّزة بِشَكْلٍ جَيِّدٍ **3** (to put fish into) زَوَّدَ ‹*a lake, river*›

(Idiom) **to take stock** (to check inventories) جَرَدَ المَخْزون; (of a situation) قَيَّمَ المَوْقِف

(Phrasal verb) **stock up** خَزَّنَ; **to ~ up on/with food** خَزَّنَ طعاما

stockbreeder /ˈstɒkbriːdə/ *n* مُرَبّي ماشِيةٍ

stockbroker /ˈstɒkbrəʊkə/ *n* سِمْسار بورْصةٍ \ أَوْراقٍ مالِيّةٍ

stock car *n* **1** (in motor racing) سَيّارة سِباق **2** (AmE) (waggon) عَرَبة نَقْل ماشِيةٍ

stock company *n* شَرِكة مُساهِمة

stock control *n* مُراقَبة مَخْزوناتٍ

stock cube *n* مُكَعَّب مَرَقةٍ \ حَساءٍ

stock exchange *n* (**the stock exchange**) سوق ,بورْصة أَوْراقٍ مالِيّةٍ

stockholder /ˈstɒkhəʊldə/ *n* حامِل أَسْهُمٍ ,مُساهِم

Stockholm /ˈstɒkhəʊm/ *pr n* سْتوكْهولْم (f)

stocking /ˈstɒkɪŋ/ *n* (woman's garment) جَوْرَب طَويل

stock-in-trade /ˌstɒkɪnˈtreɪd/ *n* سِلْعة \ مادّة رائِجة

stockist /ˈstɒkɪst/ *n* (BrE) تاجِر جُمْلةٍ

stock market *n* سوق أَوْراقٍ مالِيّةٍ ,بورْصة

stock option plan *n* نِظام خِيارِ شِراءِ الأَسْهُمِ

stockpile /ˈstɒkpaɪl/ **A** *n* مَخْزون (مَخْزونات)

B *vt* خَزَّنَ ‹*weapons, food*›

stockroom /ˈstɒkruːm/ *n* مَخْزَن (مَخازِن)

stock-still /stɒkˈstɪl/ *adv* ‹*to stand, remain*› بِلا حَراكٍ; **we stood ~ as the dog ran towards us** وَقَفْنا بِلا حَراكٍ عِنْدَما جَرى الكَلْبُ نَحْوَنا

stocktaking /ˈstɒkteɪkɪŋ/ *n* جَرْد (جُرود), حَصْر المَخْزونِ

stocky /ˈstɒki/ *adj* (**stockier**, **stockiest**) ‹*build, man*› مُكْتَنِز ,مُمْتَلِئ (وَقَوِيّ البِنْيةِ)

stockyard /ˈstɒkjɑːd/ *n* (AmE) حَظيرة (حَظائِرُ), زَريبة (زَرائِبُ)

stodgy /ˈstɒdʒi/ *adj* (**stodgier**, **stodgiest**) (infml) ‹*food, pudding*› ثَقيل ,صَعْب الهَضْمِ

stoical /ˈstəʊɪk(ə)l/ *adj* ‹*attitude, acceptance*› صَبور (صُبُر), حَمول

stoke /stəʊk/ *vt* (also **stoke up**) زَوَّدَ بالوَقودِ ‹*a furnace*›; أَذْكى, أَجَّجَ ‹*the fire*›

stole /stəʊl/ **A** *past tense* ▸ **steal**

B *n* شال (شالات)

stolen /ˈstəʊlən/ *past participle* ▸ **steal**

stolid /ˈstɒlɪd/ *adj* ‹*character, policeman*› بارِد ,مُتَبَلِّد الحِسِّ (الطَبْعِ)

stomach /ˈstʌmək/ **A** *n* **1** (digestive organ) مَعِدة (مِعَد); **to have a pain in one's ~** كانَ لَدَيْهِ أَلَمٌ في مَعِدَتِهِ; **to do sth on a full/an empty ~** فَعَلَ شَيْئاً على مَعِدةٍ مُمْتَلِئةٍ \ خاوِيةٍ; **to have a strong ~** (infml) [كانَ لَدَيْهِ القُدْرةُ على تَحَمُّلِ الأَشْياءِ المُقَزِّزة] **2** (belly) بَطْن (أَبْطُن ,بُطون); **to lie on one's ~** رَقَدَ على بَطْنِهِ

B *vt* **1** (infml) (to eat) أَطاقَ \ تَحَمَّلَ الأَكْلَ ‹*fatty food, raw fish*› **2** (to endure) تَحَمَّلَ ,أَطاقَ ‹*a person, sb's attitude, violence*›; **I can't ~ that guy!** لا أُطيقُ هذا الشَخْصَ!

stomach ache *n* أَلَم في المَعِدةِ ,مَغَص (أَمْغاص); **I've got a stomach ache!** أُعاني من أَلَمٍ في المَعِدةِ!

stomach pump *n* جِهاز غَسيلِ المَعِدةِ

stomach ulcer *n* قُرْحة المَعِدةِ

stomp /stɒmp/ *vi* (infml) «angry people, feet» ضَرَبَ الأَرْضَ; **to ~ in/out of the room** دَخَلَ إلى \ خَرَجَ من الغُرْفةِ بِقَدَمَيْهِ ضارِباً الأَرْضَ بِقَدَمَيْهِ

stone /stəʊn/ **A** *n* **1** [u] (material) صَخْر ,حَجَر (n coll); **made of ~** مَصْنوع من الحَجَرِ; **to have a heart of ~** كانَ قَلْبُهُ من حَجَرٍ **2** (piece of rock) حَجَر (حِجارة ,أَحْجار); **to throw a ~** أَلْقى حَجَراً **3** (in building) حَجَر (حِجارة ,أَحْجار); **to lay the first ~** وَضَعَ حَجَرَ الأَساسِ **4** (also **precious stone**) جَوْهَر (جَواهِرُ) ,حَجَر كَريم **5** (in fruit) نَواة (نَوَيات ,نَوًى), بَذْرة (بَذَرات) **6** (in the kidney, gall bladder) حَصْوة **7** (BrE) (*pl* **stone** or **stones**) (6.35 كج) حَجَر; **he weighs 12 stone 3 pounds** يَزِنُ 12 حَجَراً و 3 أَرْطالٍ

B *vt* **1** (to throw stones at) أَلْقى حِجارةً على ‹*a person, bus, car*›; **to ~ sb to death** رَجَمَ شَخْصاً حتّى المَوْتِ

[2] (to remove stones from) نَزَعَ النَواةَ من ‹a peach, an olive, cherry›

(Idioms) **to be set in (tablets of) stone** كانَ مَنْحوتاً في الصَخْرِ; **to cast the first stone** أَلْقى الحَجَرَ الأَوَّلَ; **to leave no stone unturned** بَذَلَ قُصارى جُهْدِهِ

Stone Age *n* العَصْر الحَجَرِيّ

stone circle *n* دائِرة الحِجارةِ (أَثَر على شَكْلِ دائِرةٍ مُتَراصّةٍ من الحِجارةِ)

stone cold *adj* بارِد جِدًّا

stoned /stəʊnd/ *adj* [1] (infml) ‹teenager, hippie› مُغَيَّب, مَسْطول العَقْلِ; **to get ~** تَغَيَّبَ عَقْلُهُ, انْسَطَلَ [2] ‹olive, date› مَنْزوع النَوى

stone deaf *adj* أَصَمّ تَماماً

stonemason /ˈstəʊnmeɪs(ə)n/ *n* بَنّاء بالحِجارةِ

stonewall /stəʊnˈwɔːl/ *vi* «governments, committees» راوَغَ

stonewashed /ˈstəʊnwɒʃd/ *adj* ‹jeans, denim› [مَغْسول بِمادّةٍ كاشِطةٍ لِيَبْدُوَ باهِتاً وبالِياً]

stony /ˈstəʊni/ *adj* (**stonier, stoniest**) [1] (rocky) ‹ground, path› كَثير الحِجارة [2] (unfriendly) ‹look, silence› بارِد

stood /stʊd/ *past tense, past participle* ▸ **stand** A, B

stool /stuːl/ *n* [1] (seat) كُرْسِيّ (بِلا ظَهْرٍ أو ذِراعَيْنِ) [2] (faecal) غائِط, بِراز

stoop /stuːp/ [A] *vi* [1] (to have a stoop) «old people» كانَ مُنْحَنِيَ الظَهْرِ [2] (to bend down) «tall people» انْحَنى [3] (to demean oneself) **to ~ to do sth** انْحَدَرَ \ انْحَطَّ لِدَرَجةِ أَنْ يَفْعَلَ شَيْئاً

[B] *n* انْحِناء الظَهْرِ; **to have a ~** كانَ لَدَيْهِ انْحِناءٌ بالظَهْرِ

stop /stɒp/ [A] *vt* (**-pp-**) [1] (to cease) أَوْقَفَ, تَوَقَّفَ (عن) ‹one's work, an activity›; **they ~ped the game/debate** أَوْقَفوا اللُعْبةَ \ المُناظَرةَ; **to ~ talking/digging** تَوَقَّفَ عن الكَلامِ \ الحَفْرِ; **I have to ~ smoking** عَلَيَّ أَنْ أَتَوَقَّفَ عن التَدْخينِ; **~ that noise!** أَوْقِفْ ذلك الضَجيجَ! [2] (to bring to a halt) أَوْقَفَ ‹a person, vehicle, trial›; **they ~ped me at the gate** اسْتَوْقَفوني عند البَوّابة; **rain ~ped play** أَوْقَفَ المَطَرُ اللَعِبَ [3] (to prevent) مَنَعَ, أَوْقَفَ (a; مَنْع) ‹publication, an event, attack›; **the protests ~ped the ceremony** أَوْقَفَت الاحْتِجاجاتُ الاحْتِفالَ; **to ~ sb doing sth, to ~ sb from doing sth** مَنَعَ شَخْصاً من فِعْلِ شَيْءٍ; **there's nothing to ~ you calling him** لَيْسَ هُناكَ ما يَمْنَعُكَ من الاتِّصالِ بِهِ; **what's ~ping you from leaving?** ما الّذي يَمْنَعُكَ من المُغادَرةِ؟ [4] (to cancel) أَلْغى, أَوْقَفَ ‹payments, deliveries, a service›; **to ~ a cheque/subscription** أَمَرَ بِعَدَمِ صَرْفِ شيك \ أَلْغى اشْتِراكاً; **they ~ped free travel for pensioners** أَلْغَوْا السَفَرَ المَجّانِيَّ لِأَصْحابِ المَعاشاتِ [5] (to plug) سَدَّ (u; سَدّ) ‹a gap, hole›; **to ~ a leak** سَدَّ تَسَرُّباً; **to ~ one's ears** سَدَّ أُذُنَيْهِ

[B] *vi* (**-pp-**) [1] (to cease moving) «vehicles, trains» تَوَقَّفَ; (functioning) «engines, workers, clocks» تَوَقَّفَ عن العَمَلِ; **the train ~ped outside the station** تَوَقَّفَ القِطارُ خارِجَ المَحَطّةِ; **my watch has ~ped** تَوَقَّفَتْ ساعَتي; **his heart ~ped** تَوَقَّفَ قَلْبُهُ; **we ~ped for a chat/for lunch** تَوَقَّفْنا لِتَبادُلِ الحَديثِ \ لِتَناوُلِ الغَداءِ [2] (to cease happening) «pain, negotiations, music» انْتَهى, تَوَقَّفَ; **the rain/wind finally ~ped** أَخيراً تَوَقَّفَ المَطَرُ \ الريحُ [3] (to take a break) «workers, walkers» تَوَقَّفَ; **I can't ~ now** لا يُمْكِنُني أَنْ أَتَوَقَّفَ الآنَ; **to ~ for a break/meal** تَوَقَّفَ للراحةِ \ لِتَناوُلِ وَجْبةٍ

[C] *v refl* (**-pp-**) مَنَعَ نَفْسَهُ, امْتَنَعَ; **I can't ~ myself** لا يُمْكِنُني أَنْ أَمْنَعَ نَفْسي

[D] *n* [1] (halt) تَوَقُّف; **to bring activities to a ~** أَوْقَفَ الأَنْشِطةَ; **to come to a ~** تَوَقَّفَ; **to put a ~ to sth** وَضَعَ حَدًّا لِلشَيْءِ [2] (in itineraries) وُقوف; **the train makes three ~s** يَقِفُ القِطارُ ثَلاثَ مَرّاتٍ [3] (for a buses, trains) مَحَطّة [4] (on a drawer, door) حاجِز (حَواجِزُ), صَدّادة

(Idiom) **to pull out all the stops** (infml) لم يَدَّخِرْ وُسْعاً

(Phrasal verbs) **stop by** [A] (infml) (to call in) زارَ (u; زِيارة, زَوْر)

[B] **~ by [sth]** (infml) زارَ [شَيْئاً] ‹the office, café, sb's house›

• **stop off** (to interrupt a journey) تَوَقَّفَ; **to ~ off in Bristol/at Paul's house** تَوَقَّفَ لِزِيارةِ بريسْتول \ مَنْزِلِ بول

• **stop over** (to break a journey) تَوَقَّفَ

• **stop up**: **~ [sth] up, ~ up [sth]** سَدَّ [شَيْئاً] ‹a hole, gap›

stop button *n* زِرّ إِيقافٍ

stopcock /ˈstɒpkɒk/ *n* مَحْبِس (مَحابِسُ)

stopgap /ˈstɒpgap/ *n* بَديل مُؤَقَّت

stop light *n* **1** (on a car) ضَوْء فَرامِلَ \ مَكابِحَ **2** (on a traffic light) إشارة حَمْراء

stop-off /ˈstɒpɒf/ *n* تَوَقُّف للاسْتِراحةِ (أثناء السَفَرِ)

stopover /ˈstɒpəʊvə/ *n* اسْتِراحة ,تَوَقُّف (أثناء السَفَرِ)

stoppage /ˈstɒpɪdʒ/ *n* **1** (in games) تَوَقُّف **2** (interruption) إضْراب (عن العَمَلِ) **3** (strike) تَعَطُّل ,تَوَقُّف

stoppage time *n* وَقْت بَدَلِ الضائِعِ

stopper /ˈstɒpə/ *n* سِدادة

stopping train /ˈstɒpɪŋ ˌtreɪn/ *n* قِطار بَطيء (قِطار يَتَوَقَّفُ في مُعْظَمِ المَحَطّاتِ)

stop press *n* آخِر خَبَرٍ

stop sign *n* عَلامة \ لافِتة تَوَقُّفٍ

stopwatch /ˈstɒpwɒtʃ/ *n* ساعة تَوْقيتٍ \ إيقافٍ \ تَوقيفٍ

storage /ˈstɔːrɪdʒ/ *n* **1** (of goods) تَخْزين (تَخْزينات); **our furniture is in ~** أثاثُنا مُخَزَّنٌ **2** (also **storage space**) (space for storing) مِساحة للتَخْزينِ **3** (on a computer) تَخْزين (تَخْزينات)

storage heater *n* مِدْفَأة كَهْربائيّة تُخَزِّنُ الحَرارةَ

store /stɔː/ **A** *n* **1** (large retail outlet) مَتْجَر (مَتاجِرُ), مَحَلّ; (smaller retail outlet) دُكّان (mf; دَكاكينُ); **an electrical ~** مَتْجَر للأَدَواتِ الكَهْرَبائيّة **2** (of food, fuel, information) مَخْزون (مَخْزونات) **3** (for food, fuel) مَخْزَن (مَخازِنُ), مُسْتَوْدَع (مُسْتَوْدَعات) **4** [u] (storage) **to put sth into ~** خَزَّنَ شَيْئاً <*furniture, food, goods*>; **our furniture is in ~** أثاثُنا مُخَزَّنٌ; **what does the future have in ~ for us?** ماذا يُخَبِّئُ المُسْتَقْبَلُ لَنا؟

B (**stores**) *n pl* (supply centre) المُؤَن والإمْدادات

C *vt* **1** (to put away) خَزَّنَ <*food, furniture, chemicals*>; **what temperature should the meat be ~d at?** ما دَرَجةُ الحَرارةِ التّي يَنْبَغي حِفظُ اللُحومِ عِنْدَها؟ **2** حَفِظَ (a; حِفْظ), خَزَّنَ <*data, a record*>

(Phrasal verb) **store up**: **~ up [sth]** خَزَّنَ [شَيْئاً] <*food, water, supplies*>; **you're storing up problems for yourself** أنْتَ تَجْعَلُ المَشاكِلَ تَتَراكَمُ عَلَيْكَ

store brand *n* (AmE) عَلامة تِجاريّة خاصّة

store detective *n* حارِس مَتْجَرٍ

storehouse /ˈstɔːhaʊs/ *n* **1** (warehouse) مَخْزَن (مَخازِنُ), مُسْتَوْدَع (مُسْتَوْدَعات) **2** (source) مَصْدَر (مَصادِرُ)

storekeeper /ˈstɔːkiːpə/ *n* (AmE) صاحِب مَتْجَرٍ

store manager *n* مُدير مَتْجَرٍ

storeroom /ˈstɔːruːm/ *n* (in a house, factory) مَخْزَن (مَخازِنُ)

storey (BrE), **story** (AmE) /ˈstɔːri/ *n* (*pl* **storeys** BrE, **stories** AmE) طابَق (طَوابِقُ), دَوْر (أدْوار)

stork /stɔːk/ *n* لَقْلَق (لَقالِقُ)

storm /stɔːm/ **A** *n* **1** عاصِفة (عَواصِفُ); **the ~ broke** هَبَّتْ العاصِفةُ; **to weather the ~** تَجاوَزَ الظَرْفَ العَصيبَ **2** (violent assault) **to take a town by ~** شَنَّ هُجوماً كاسِحاً على مَدينةٍ; **she took Broadway by ~** اجْتاحَتْ شُهْرَتُها بْرودْواي **3** (outburst) مَوْجة, عاصِفة (عَواصِفُ); **a ~ of criticism/protest** عاصِفة من النَقْدِ \ الاحْتِجاجِ

B *vt* (to attack) اجْتاحَ <*a town, prison*>

C *vi* (to move angrily) **to ~ in/out** دَخَلَ \ خَرَجَ غاضِباً

stormy /ˈstɔːmi/ *adj* (**stormier**, **stormiest**) **1** (with strong winds, rain) <*weather, sea*> عاصِف **2** (emotional) <*relationship, encounter*> عاصِف, مُضْطَرِب

story /ˈstɔːri/ *n* **1** قِصّة (قِصَص); **a true ~** قِصّة حَقيقيّة; **to stick to/change one's ~** تَمَسَّكَ بِروايَتِهِ \ غَيَّرَ روايَتَهُ; **to tell a ghost ~** حَكى حِكاية عن الأشْباحِ; **to read a detective ~** قَرَأَ رِوايةً بوليسيّةً **2** (in journalism) قِصّة (قِصَص); **an exclusive ~** قِصّة حَصْريّة **3** (untruthful) قِصّة (قِصَص); **to make up a ~** اخْتَلَقَ قِصّةً **4** (rumour) إشاعة **5** (also **story line**) (of a novel, play) حَبْكة; (of a film) سيناريو (سيناريُوات) **6** (AmE) (floor) ▸ **storey**

(Idioms) **to be a different** *or* **another story** كانَ قِصّةً أُخرى; **... and I met her sister, but that's another ~!** (avoiding detail) ... وَقابَلْتُ أُخْتَها، وَلَكِنَّ تِلْكَ قِصّةٌ أُخْرى!; **at £500 each, that's another ~** (expressing reluctance, rejection) بِسِعْرِ 500 جُنَيْهٍ هذا أمْرٌ مُسْتَبْعَدٌ; **the story goes that/has it that ...** تَقولُ القِصّةُ إنّ ...

storybook /ˈstɔːribʊk/ *n* كِتاب قَصَصيّ (للأَطْفالِ)

storyteller /ˈstɔːrɪtelə/ *n* قاصّ (قُصّاص), قَصّاص (قُصّاص), راوي قَصَصٍ

stout /staʊt/ *adj* (**stouter**, **stoutest**) 1 (fat) ‹*gentleman, build*› بدين ,مُمْتَلِئ (بُدَناءُ) 2 (strong) ‹*footwear, material*› مَتين (مِتان), قَويّ (أَقْوِياءُ)

stove /stəʊv/ *n* 1 (cooker) مَوْقِد (مَواقِدُ), بوتاجاز (بوتاجازات) (Egypt) 2 (heater) مِدْفَأة (مَدافِئُ)

stovetop /ˈstəʊvtɒp/ *n* سَطْح المَوْقِد

stow /stəʊ/ *vt* خَزَّنَ ‹*one's gear, bags*›

Phrasal verb **stow away**: 1 **~ away** «refugees, escapees» سافَرَ مُتَخَفِياً 2 **~** [**sth**] **away**, **~ away** [**sth**] خَزَّنَ [شَيْئاً] ‹*provisions, baggage*›

stowaway /ˈstəʊəweɪ/ *n* مُسافِر مُتَخَفٍّ

straddle /ˈstrad(ə)l/ *vt* 1 رَكِبَ (مُباعِداً ما بين رِجْلَيْهِ) ‹*a horse, bike*› 2 (to cover) غَطّى \ تَناوَلَ جانِبَيْنِ من ‹*a subject*›

strafe /strɑːf, streɪf/ *vt* قَصَفَ جَوّاً ‹*a column, the troops*›

straggle /ˈstrag(ə)l/ *vi* 1 (to dawdle) «hikers, children, cattle» تَخَلَّفَ ,تَلَكَّأَ 2 (to spread) «houses, plants» [انْتَشَرَ بِشَكْلٍ عَشْوائيٍّ]

straggler /ˈstraglə/ *n* مُتَأَخِّر ,مُتَلَكِّئ

straggly /ˈstragli/ *adj* (**stragglier**, **straggliest**) ‹*hair*› أَشْعَث (dipt; شُعْث) ‹*bush*› غَيْر مُنْتَظِم الشَّكْلِ

straight /streɪt/ **A** *adj* 1 (not bent) ‹*line, road, hair*› مُسْتَقيم; **in a ~ line** في خطٍّ مُسْتَقيم; **the road was dead ~** كانَ الطَريقُ مُسْتَقيماً تَماماً 2 (in alignment) ‹*post, shelf, wall*› مُسْتَوٍ ,مُسْتَقيم; **the picture/your tie isn't ~** الصورة \ رابطةُ عُنُقِك غَيْرُ مَضْبوطةٍ 3 (in order) ‹*room, one's affairs, accounts*› مُنَظَّم ,مُرَتَّب; **to put the house ~** رَتَّبَ المَنْزِلَ; **I must get my accounts ~ before I leave** يَجِبُ أَنْ أُنَظِّمَ حِساباتي قبل أَنْ أُغادِرَ 4 (clear) **to get the facts/figures ~** تَأَكَّدَ من الحَقائِقِ \ الأَرْقام; **now let's get one thing ~** والآنَ دَعْني أُوَضِّحُ شَيْئاً واحِداً; **to put** *or* **set sb ~ about sth** بَيَّنَ \ أَوْضَحَ لِشَخْصٍ حَقيقةَ شَيْءٍ; **to put** *or* **set the record ~** وَضَعَ الأُمورَ في نِصابِها الصَحيح 5 (honest) ‹*person*› صادِق, أَمين (أُمَناءُ); **to be ~ with sb** كانَ أَميناً مع شَخْصٍ 6 (direct) ‹*question, talking, rejection*› صَريح (صُرَحاءُ ,صَرائِحُ), مُباشِر; **to give sb a ~ answer** أَعْطى شَخْصاً إجابةً مُباشِرةً; **the time has come for some ~ talking** آنَ الأَوانُ للحَديثِ بِصَراحةٍ 7 (unconditional) ‹*choice*› بين شَخْصَيْنِ \ شَيْئَيْنِ; ‹*majority*› مُطْلَق; **to do a ~ swap** بَدَّلَ بين شَخْصَيْنِ \ شَيْئَيْنِ; **it was a ~ choice between the two options** كانَ الاخْتِيارُ مُحَدَّداً بين خِيارَيْنِ 8 (undiluted) ‹*gin, brandy*› خالِص ,صِرْف (غَيْر مُخَفَّفٍ أو مَمْزوجٍ) 9 (consecutive) ‹*win, defeat, profit*› مُتَتالٍ, مُتَتابِع; **she got ~ 'A's** حَصَلَتْ على تَقْديرِ مُمْتازٍ في كُلِّ المَوادِّ; **to win in ~ sets** فازَ بِمَجْموعاتٍ مُتَتالِيةٍ 10 (Theat) ‹*actor, role*› جادّ 11 (infml) (heterosexual) ‹*man, relationship*› غَيْرِيّ

B *adv* 1 (in a direct line) ‹*to walk, steer, fly*› في خطٍّ مُسْتَقيم; (in an upright position) ‹*to stand up, sit up*› مُنْتَصِبَ الظَهْرِ, مُسْتَقيماً; **to go ~ ahead** ذَهَبَ للأَمامِ مُباشَرةً; **sit up ~!** اجْلِسْ مُسْتَقيماً!; **she was looking ~ at me** كانَتْ تَنْظُرُ إِلَيَّ مُباشَرةً; **they drove ~ past me** ساروا بالسَيّارة أَمامي مُباشَرةً; **the bullet went ~ through him** اخْتَرَقَت الرَصاصةُ جَسَدَهُ مُباشَرةً; **she drove ~ into a tree** قادَت السَيّارةَ مُباشَرةً نحو شَجَرةٍ 2 (accurately) ‹*to shoot, throw, cut*› بِدقّةٍ; **cut the cloth ~** قُصَّ القُماشَ بدقّةٍ 3 (without delay) مُباشَرةً, دون تَوانٍ ,على الفَوْرِ; **to go ~ home** ذَهَبَ إلى البَيْتِ مُباشَرةً; **to go ~ to bed** ذَهَبَ إلى الفِراشِ على الفَوْرِ; **to come ~ to the point** دَخَلَ في صَميمِ المَوضوعِ مُباشَرةً; **~ away, ~ off** حالاً, للتَوِّ ,على الفَوْرِ; **she told him ~ out that she was leaving** أَخْبَرَتْهُ على الفَوْرِ أَنَّها راحِلةٌ 4 (infml) (frankly) بِصَراحةٍ, دون تَكَلُّفٍ; **I'll tell you ~** سَأُخْبِرُكَ بِصَراحةٍ 5 ‹*to act*› بِشَكْلٍ مُباشِرٍ 6 (neat) **to drink one's whisky/gin ~** تَناوَلَ شَرابَهُ من الويسْكي \ النَبيذِ خالِصاً

C *n* (in races) [مِنْطَقة مُسْتَقيمة]; **the back ~** المِنْطَقة المُسْتَقيمة في الخَلْفِ; **the home ~** المَرْحَلة الأَخيرة; **to be on the home ~** كانَ في المَرْحَلةِ الأَخيرةِ

Idiom **to keep a straight face** أَحْجَمَ عن الابْتِسامِ

straightaway /ˌstreɪtəˈweɪ/ *adv* (also **straight away**) ‹*to do sth, realise*› فَوْراً ,في الحالِ ,حالاً

straighten /ˈstreɪt(ə)n/ *vt* 1 (to make straight) سَوّى ‹*a road, wire, nail*›; (to extend) مَدَّ (u; مَدّ) ‹*one's arm, leg*›; **to ~ one's back** قَوَّمَ ,نَصَبَ ظَهْرَهُ; **to have one's nose/teeth ~ed** قَوَّمَ أَنْفَهُ \ أَسْنانَهُ; **to ~ one's hair** فَرَدَ شَعْرَهُ 2 (to put upright, level) وَضَعَ في شَكْلٍ مُسْتَقيمٍ ‹*a post, shelf, a picture*›; ضَبَطَ (i-u; ضَبْط) ‹*one's tie, hat*› **3** (to tidy) رَتَّبَ ‹*a room, one's desk, the bedclothes*›

Phrasal verbs **straighten out** **A** «roads, rivers» سارَ ,اسْتَقامَ بِشَكْلٍ مُسْتَقيمٍ **B** **~ out** [**sth**], **~** [**sth**] **out** **1** (to make straight) سَوّى [شَيْئاً] ‹*a bend, wire, nail*› **2** (to clear up) سَوّى [شَيْئاً] ‹*a misunderstanding, problem*›; **to ~ out a misunderstanding** أَزالَ سوءَ تَفاهُمٍ **C** **~ out** [**sb**], **~** [**sb**] **out** (to help over a problem) أَصْلَحَ شَأْنَ [شَخْصٍ]

• **straighten up** **A** **1** (to stand up straight) وَقَفَ مُنْتَصِباً **2** (to tidy up) رَتَّبَ [شَيْئاً] **B** **~ up** [**sth**], **~** [**sth**] **up** (to tidy) رَتَّبَ ‹*a room, toys, papers*›

straight-faced /ˌstreɪtˈfeɪst/ *adj* ‹*expression*› جادّ

straightforward /streɪtˈfɔːwəd/ *adj* **1** (honest) ‹*man*› أَمين (أُمَناءُ); ‹*answer*› مُباشِر, صَريح (صَرائِحُ ,صُرَحاءُ) **2** (uncomplicated) ‹*account, task*› سَهْل ,بَسيط (بُسَطاءُ)

strain /streɪn/ **A** *vt* **1** (to stretch) شَدَّ \ جَذَبَ بِقوّةٍ ‹*a rope, cable*› **2** ضَغَطَ (a; ضَغْط ;على) ‹*sb's resources, a relationship, an alliance*›; **their debt ~ed the marriage to breaking point** ضَغَطَتْ دُيونُهُما على حَياتِهِما الزَوْجِيّةِ وَدَفَعَتْ بِها إلى حافّةِ الهاوِيةِ; **she ~ed her ears to hear them** أَرْخَتْ أُذُنَيْها لِتَسْمَعَهُمْ **3** (to overwork) أَجْهَدَ ‹*one's heart*› **4** (to injure) ‹*a ligament, muscle*› أَصابَ بِشَدٍّ \ تَمَزُّقٍ في العَضَلاتِ; **to ~ one's back** أُصيبَ بِشَدٍّ في عَضَلاتِ الظَهْرِ **5** (to filter) صَفّى ‹*the tea, stock, rice*›

B *vi* **to ~ at the leash/rope** جَذَبَ المِقْوَدَ \ الحَبْلَ بِقوّةٍ; **to ~ to see/hear** حاوَلَ جاهِداً أنْ يَرى \ يَسْمَعَ

C *n* **1** [u] (force) ضَغْط; **to put a ~ on sth** سَبَّبَ ضَغْطاً على شَيْءٍ ‹*a beam, bridge*›; أَجْهَدَ شَيْئاً ‹*sb's heart, lungs*›; **to take the ~** «beams, ropes» تَحَمَّلَ الضَغْطَ **2** [u] (demands) ضَغْط; **he can/can't take the ~** يَسْتَطيعُ \ لا يَسْتَطيعُ تَحَمُّلَ الضَغْطِ; **the relationship is under great ~** العَلاقةُ تحت ضَغْطٍ شَديدٍ; **it has put a great ~ on our resources** سَبَّبَتْ ضَغْطاً كَبيراً على مَوارِدِنا **3** (injury) شَدّ \ تَمَزُّق عَضَلِيّ; **a groin/back ~** شَدّ عَضَلِيّ في الفَخْذِ \ الظَهْرِ **4** (of plant, virus) سُلالة **D** (**strains**) *n pl* أَلْحان ,أَنْغام; **to the ~s of ...** على أَنْغامِ ...

Phrasal verb **strain off**: **~** [**sth**] **off**, **~ off** [**sth**] صَفّى [شَيْئاً] ‹*the water, liquid, fat*›

strained /streɪnd/ *adj* **1** (tense) ‹*relations, atmosphere*› مُتَوَتِّر **2** (injured) ‹*muscle, hamstring*› مُمَزَّق ,مَشْدود

strainer /ˈstreɪnə/ *n* مِصْفاة (مَصافٍ)

strait /streɪt/ *n* **1** (in the sea) بوغاز (بَواغيزُ), مَضيق (مَضايِقُ ,مَضائِقُ) **2** (**straits** *n pl*) (difficult situation) ضائِقة (ضَوائِقُ); **to be in dire ~s** كانَ في ضائِقةٍ شَديدةٍ

straitjacket /ˈstreɪtdʒakɪt/ *n* قَميص المَجانينِ (سُتْرة بِأَكْمامٍ طَويلةٍ لِتَقْييدِ الحَرَكةِ)

strait-laced /streɪtˈleɪst/ *adj* ‹*attitude, businessman*› مُتَزَمِّت

strand /strand/ **A** *vt* **1** (to be driven aground) **to be ~ed at the airport/beside the road** «passenger» عَلِقَ في المَطارِ \ جانِبِ الطَريقِ **2** (to be driven aground) **to be ~ed on the shore** «whale» عَلِقَ على رِمالِ الشاطِئِ; «ship» جَنَحَ إلى الشاطِئِ

B *n* **1** (of thread, wire) شَعْرة; (hair) خُصْلة (خُصَل ,خُصْلات) **2** (of a story, problem) جانِب (جَوانِبُ)

strange /streɪndʒ/ *adj* **1** (unfamiliar) ‹*situation, face*› غَريب (غُرَباءُ) **2** (odd) ‹*behaviour, clothes*› غَيْر مَأْلوفٍ ,غَريب (غُرَباءُ), عَجيب; **it is ~ that we've never met her parents** من الغَريبِ أَنّنا لم نَلْتَقِ والِدَيْها قَطُّ

strangely /ˈstreɪndʒli/ *adv* ‹*to act, dress*› بِشَكْلٍ غَريبٍ; **~ enough, I feel confident** خِلافاً للعادةِ والغَريبُ أَنّني أَشْعُرُ بالثِقةِ

stranger /ˈstreɪndʒə/ *n* **1** (unknown person) غَريب (غُرَباءُ) **2** (outsider) غَريب (غُرَباءُ), أَجْنَبِيّ (أَجانِبُ)

strangle /ˈstraŋɡ(ə)l/ *vt* خَنَقَ (u; خَنْق) ‹*a victim*›

stranglehold /ˈstraŋɡəlhəʊld/ *n* **1** (grip) قَبْضة خانِقة **2** (control) سَيْطَرة كامِلة

strangulated /ˈstraŋɡjuːleɪtɪd/ *adj* ‹*hernia, bowel*› مُخْتَنِق

strangulation /straŋɡjʊˈleɪʃ(ə)n/ *n* **1** (of a victim) خَنْق **2** (Anat) (of a hernia) اخْتِناق (اخْتِناقات); **the ~ of a vein/hernia** اخْتِناق الوَريدِ \ الفَتْقِ

strap /strap/ **A** *n* **1** (on shoes, sandals) سَيْر (سُيور); (on a case, helmet) حِزام (أَحْزِمة); (on a watch) سِوار (أَساوِرُ ,أَسْوِرة)

2 (on a handbag) حِزام (أَحْزِمة); (on a dress, bra) حَمّالة
3 (for passengers) [شَريط يَتَدَلّى من سَقْفِ مَرْكَبةٍ يَتَشَبَّثُ بِهِ الراكِبُ لِحِفْظِ تَوازُنِهِ] 4 (**the Strap**) (as punishment) الجَلْد

B *vt* (**-pp-**) 1 (to secure) ثَبَّتَ بِشَريطٍ \ بِحِزامٍ; **to ~ the cases/furniture to the roof of the car** رَبَطَ الحَقائِبَ \ الأَثاثَ على سَقْفِ السَيّارةِ; **to ~ sb into a seat** قَيَّدَ شَخْصاً في مَقْعَدٍ 2 (to bandage) رَبَطَ بِعِصابةٍ, ضَمَّدَ <*sb's ankle, thigh*>

strapless /'straplas/ *adj* <*dress, bra*> بدونِ حَمّالاتٍ

strapped /strapt/ *adj* (infml) <*borrower, homeowner*> يُعاني من ضائِقةٍ ماليّةٍ; **to be ~ for cash** عانى من نَقْصٍ في السُيولةِ الماليّةِ

strapping /'strapɪŋ/ *adj* <*lad, youngster*> ضَخْم (ضِخام)

strata /'strɑːtə/ *n pl* ▸ **stratum**

stratagem /'stratədʒəm/ *n* خُدْعة (خُدَع), حيلة (حِيَل), مَكيدة (مَكايِدُ)

strategic /strə'tiːdʒɪk/ *adj* 1 (in planning) <*plan, decision*> إِسْتْراتيجيّ 2 (important) <*location, point*> إِسْتْراتيجيّ; **the ~ bombing of the enemy's communications centres** القَصْفُ الإِسْتْراتيجيّ لِمَراكِزِ الاتِّصالاتِ التابعةِ للعَدوِّ

strategically /strə'tiːdʒɪkli/ *adv* <*to deploy, to place*> إِسْتْراتيجيًّا; **to vote ~** صَوَّتَ تَصْويتاً إِسْتْراتيجيًّا

strategist /'stratədʒɪst/ *n* خَبير إِسْتْراتيجيّ

strategy /'stratɪdʒi/ *n* (*pl* **strategies**) خُطّة إِسْتْراتيجيّة; **a ~ to deal with the financial crisis** خُطّة إِسْتْراتيجيّة للتَعامُلِ مع الأَزْمةِ الماليّةِ

stratify /'stratɪfʌɪ/ *vt* (**stratifies, stratifying, stratified**) قَسَّمَ إلى طَبَقاتٍ <*data, a society*>

stratum /'strɑːtəm/ *n* (*pl* **strata**) 1 (of rock) طَبَقة 2 (social) طَبَقة, شَريحة (شَرائِحُ), فِئة

straw /strɔː/ *n* 1 (stalks) قَشّ (قُشوش); (single stalk) قَشّة 2 (for drinking) شَفّاطة, قَصَبة شُرْبٍ \ مَصّاصة

(Idioms) **the last straw** القَشّة الأَخيرة; **to clutch at straws** تَعَلَّقَ بِقَشّةٍ

strawberry /'strɔːb(ə)ri/ **A** *n* (*pl* **strawberries**) 1 (plant) فَراوْلة 2 (fruit) فَراوْلة
B *adj* <*jam, ice cream*> الفَراوْلةِ

straw poll *n* اسْتِطْلاع رَأْيٍ أَوَّليّ \ غَيْر رَسْميٍّ

stray /streɪ/ **A** *vi* 1 (to wander) «sheep, tourists» تاهَ (i; تَيْه, تَيَهان, تيه), شَرَدَ (u; شُرود, شِراد); **to ~ from the house** تاهَ عن البَيْتِ; **to ~ onto the road** سارَ في الطَريقِ تائِهاً; **to ~ from the path** انْحَرَفَ عن المَسارِ 2 «thoughts, eyes, mind» شَرَدَ (u; شُرود, شِراد); **to ~ from the point** ابْتَعَدَ عن المَوْضوعِ
B *adj* 1 (lost) <*dog, cat, sheep*> ضالّ, شارِد 2 (isolated) <*bullet*> طائِش; <*tourist*> تائِه; **he was hit by a ~ bullet** أُصيبَ بِرَصاصةٍ طائِشةٍ
C *n* (animal) حَيَوان ضالّ

streak /striːk/ **A** *n* 1 (in sb's character) نَزْعة (نَزَعات), مَسْحة (مَسَحات) 2 (of luck) فَتْرة مُتَواصِلة; **to be on a winning ~** حالَفَهُ الفَوْزُ لِفَتْرةٍ; **a ~ of good luck** مُحالَفة الحَظِّ 3 (mark) خَطّ (خُطوط) 4 (in hair) خَطّ (خُطوط)
B *vt* رَسَمَ خُطوطاً على <*sb's face, hair*>
C *vi* انْدَفَعَ \ انْطَلَقَ بِسُرْعةٍ; **to ~ past** مَرَقَ بِسُرْعةٍ فائِقةٍ; **to ~ across sth** اخْتَرَقَ شَيْئاً بِسُرْعةٍ فائِقةٍ

streaky /'striːki/ *adj* (**streakier, streakiest**) <*paint, mirror*> عَلَيْهِ خُطوطٌ

streaky bacon *n* (BrE) [شَريحة من لَحْمِ الخِنْزيرِ بها طَبَقاتٌ من اللَحْمِ والشَحْمِ]

stream /striːm/ **A** *n* 1 (small river) غَدير (غُدْران, غُدُر), نُهَيْر (نُهَيْرات), جَدْوَل (جَداوِلُ), مَجْرًى (مَجارٍ, مَجْرَيات) 2 (flow of traffic, questions) تَدَفُّق (تَدَفُّقات); (of water, lava) سَيْل (سُيول); **a ~ of abuse** إساءات مُسْتَمِرّة 3 (Comput) دَفْق, تَدَفُّق (تَدَفُّقات), بَثّ 4 (BrE) (ability group) [مَجْموعة مُتَجانِسة القُدُراتِ]; **the top/bottom ~** المَجْموعة ذات المُسْتَوى الأَعْلى \ الأَدْنى
B *vt* 1 (to send) بَثَّ (i-u; بَثّ), أَرْسَلَ <*music, a movie*>; (to receive) اسْتَقْبَلَ البَثَّ <*music, a movie*> 2 (BrE) (according to ability) [قَسَّمَ إلى مَجْموعاتٍ حَسَبَ القُدْرةِ] <*a class, pupils*>
C *vi* 1 (to flow) «tears, blood, water» سالَ (i; سَيْل, سَيَلان); **tears were ~ing down his face** كانَتْ الدُموعُ تَسيلُ على وَجْهِهِ; **sunlight ~ed into the room** تَسَلَّلَتْ أَشِعّةُ الشَمْسِ إلى الحُجْرةِ 2 (to move) «cars, people» تَدَفَّقَ; **the fans ~ed through the gates** تَدَفَّقَ المُشَجِّعونَ من البَوّاباتِ 3 (in the

wind) «banners, hair» رَفْرَف (i; رَفْرَفة) 4 «eyes, nose» سالَ (i; سَيَلان, سَيْل); **my eyes were ~ing** سالَتْ عَيْنايَ بالدُموعِ; **his face was ~ing with blood** كانَ الدَمُ يَسيلُ من وَجْهِهِ

Idiom **to come on stream** دَخَلَ في مَرْحَلةِ التَشْغيلِ

streamer /ˈstriːmə/ *n* شَريط (للتَزْيين)

streamline /ˈstriːmlʌɪn/ *vt* 1 (in design) جَعَلَ انْسيابِيًّا ‹*a car, design*› 2 (in efficiency) بَسَّطَ, جَعَلَ أَكْثَرَ فاعِلِيَّةً ‹*a process, production*›

streamlined /ˈstriːmlʌɪnd/ *adj* 1 (causing minimal resistance) ‹*design, hull*› مُبَسَّط, انْسِيابِيّ 2 (efficient) ‹*process, structure*› مُبَسَّط, أَكْثَر فاعِلِيَّةً

street /striːt/ *n* شارِع (شَوارِعُ); **to play in/on the ~** لَعِبَ في الشارِعِ; **to take to the ~s** خَرَجوا إلى الشوارِعِ مُحْتَجّينَ

streetcar /ˈstriːtkɑː/ *n* (AmE) تْرام (تْرامات)

street cleaner, **street sweeper** *n* 1 (person) مُنَظِّف \ كَنّاس شَوارِعَ 2 (machine) شاحِنة \ ماكينة كَنْس الشَوارِعِ

street corner *n* ناصِية \ زاوِية شارِعٍ

street cred, **street credibility** *n* مِصْداقِيّة في الشارِعِ; **to have street cred** كانَتْ لَهُ مِصْداقِيّةٌ (خاصّةً لدى الشَباب) في الشارِعِ

streetlamp /ˈstriːtlamp/ *n* مِصْباح شارِعٍ

street level *n* مُسْتَوى الشارِعِ; **my office is at street level** مَكْتَبي في الطابَقِ الأَرْضيِّ

street light *n* ضَوْء شارِعٍ

street lighting *n* إنارة الشَوارِعِ

street map, **street plan** *n* خَريطة شَوارِعَ

street market *n* سوق مَفْتوح, سوق في الهَواءِ الطَلْقِ

street theatre *n* مَسْرَح الهَواءِ الطَلْقِ

street value *n* سِعْر الشارِعِ (للسِلَعِ غَيْرِ المَشْروعة)

streetwise /ˈstriːtwʌɪz/ *adj* (infml) ‹*kid, teenager*› مُواكِب للحَياةِ [في الشارِعِ]

strength /strɛŋθ/ *n* 1 [u] (of a person, of sb's arms, etc) قُوّة; (of the wind, a current) شِدّة; **to build up one's ~** عَزَّزَ قُوَّتَهُ; **to save one's ~** ادَّخَرَ قُوَّتَهُ 2 [u] (of the government, army) قُوّة; **to gain/lose ~** اكْتَسَبَ قوّةً \ فَقَدَ قوَّتَهُ 3 [u] (of a bridge, girder) قُدْرة على التَحَمُّلِ, قُوّة, طاقة 4 (of a solution) تَرْكيز; (of a dose) قوّة 5 [u] (of a bond, relationship) مَتانة; (of feelings, reactions) شِدّة, قوّة 6 [u] (of currencies, economies) قوّة 7 [u] (resolution) قوّة; **~ of character** قوّة الشَخْصيّةِ; **~ of purpose** إصْرار, قوّة العَزيمةِ 8 [u] (of an argument, case) قوّة; **he was convicted on the ~ of the evidence** أُدينَ بِناءً على الدَليلِ 9 [u] (total size) **the workforce is at full ~** القُوى العامِلة بِكامِلِ قِوامِها; **the team is below ~** الفَريقُ لَيْسَ بِكامِلِ قوّتِه

Idiom **to go from strength to strength** انْتَقَلَ من نَجاحٍ إلى نَجاحٍ

strengthen /ˈstrɛŋθ(ə)n/ *vt* 1 (to make stronger) قَوّى ‹*a muscle*›; دَعَّمَ ‹*a building*› 2 (to reinforce) دَعَّمَ, عَزَّزَ ‹*a position, an economy*›

strenuous /ˈstrɛnjʊəs/ *adj* 1 (arduous) ‹*exercise, activity*› مُضْنٍ, شاقّ, مُجْهِد 2 (determined) ‹*objection*› قَوِيّ (أَقْوِياءُ); ‹*efforts*› حَثيث

stress /strɛs/ **A** *n* 1 (mental strain) ضَغْط عَصَبيّ \ نَفْسيّ; **to be under ~** كانَ تحت ضَغْطٍ عَصَبيٍّ; **to suffer from ~** عانى من ضَغْطٍ نَفْسيٍّ 2 (physical strain) إجْهاد 3 (emphasis) تَرْكيز, تَأْكيد (تَأْكيدات); **to lay ~ on a feature/proposal** رَكَّزَ على خاصّيّةٍ \ مُقْتَرَحٍ 4 (on a syllable) نَبْرة, نَبْر

B *vt* 1 (to emphasize) أَكَّدَ (على) ‹*a difficulty*›; **to ~ the importance of sth** أَكَّدَ \ شَدَّدَ على أَهَمّيّةِ شَيْءٍ 2 (Ling) «speaker» ‹*a word, syllable*› نَطَقَ بِنَبْرةٍ

Phrasal verb **stress out** **A** (infml) (to become anxious) قَلِقَ, تَوَتَّرَ (a; قَلَق) **B** **~ [sb] out** (infml) (to make anxious) «lifestyle, work» جَعَلَ [شَخْصاً] يَتَوَتَّرُ

stressed /strɛst/ *adj* 1 (also **stressed out**) (infml) (anxious) ‹*mother, worker*› مُنْهَك, مُرْهَق, مُجْهَد 2 (emphasized) ‹*syllable, vowel*› مُشَدَّد

stress fracture *n* كَسْر إجْهادٍ (كَسْر يَحْدُثُ بِسَبَبِ الإجْهادِ المُتَكَرِّرِ)

stressful /ˈstrɛsfʊl/ *adj* ‹*job*› مُرْهِق, مُجْهِد; ‹*life*› مَليء بالضُغوطِ; ‹*situation*› عَصيب

stretch /strɛtʃ/ **A** *vt* **1** (to extend) مَدَّ (u; مَدّ) ,بَسَطَ (u; بَسْط) ‹*a rope, net*›; **to ~ one's arms** مَدَّ ذِراعَيْهِ; **to ~ one's legs** تَمَشّى; **to ~ one's wings** فَرَدَ \ بَسَطَ جَناحَيْهِ **2** (in elasticity) شَدَّ (i-u; شَدّ) ‹*a spring, fabric*›; مَطَّ (u; مَطّ) ‹*a pullover, sock*›; **they ~ed their lead to 5-2** زادوا فارِق تَقَدُّمِهِمْ إلى 5–2 **3** (to extend) اِلْتَفَّ (حول) ‹*the truth, rules*›; **to ~ a point** بالَغَ في التَقْديرِ **4** (to challenge) دَفَعَ إلى بَذْلِ جُهْدٍ كَبيرٍ ‹*a pupil, an employee*›; **she isn't ~ed at school** لَيْسَ في المَدْرَسةِ ما يَدْفَعُها إلى بَذْلِ جُهْدٍ كَبيرٍ **5** (to test) أَنْفَدَ ‹*sb's patience, tolerance*›; **your stubbornness is ~ing her patience** عِنادُكَ يُنْفِدُ صَبْرَها **6** (to make demands on) ضَغَطَ (a; ضَغْط; على) ‹*the budget, resources*›; **the system is ~ed to the limit** يَتِمُّ الضَغْطُ على النِظامِ إلى أَقْصى حَدٍّ **7** (to eke out) اِقْتَصَدَ في الاسْتِخْدامِ ‹*supplies, food*›

B *vi* **1** (to extend one's limbs) مَطَّ \ مَدَّ \ مَدَّدَ جِسْمَهُ **2** (to extend) «road, track, forest» اِمْتَدَّ; **the plain/desert ~es for miles** يَمْتَدُّ السَهْلُ \ تَمْتَدُّ الصَحْراءُ لِعِدّةِ أَمْيالٍ; **the queue ~ed around the corner** اِمْتَدَّ الطابورُ حول الرُكْنِ; **the course ~es over three years** تَسْتَغْرِقُ الدَورةُ ثَلاثَ سَنَواتٍ **3** (to become larger) «elastic, shoes, sweater» تَمَطَّطَ **4** (infml) (to afford) **to ~ to an expense** وَفَّرَ \ دَبَّرَ تَكاليفاً; **the budget won't ~ to a new computer** لن تَتَحَمَّلَ الميزانيّةُ حاسوباً جَديداً

C *n* **1** (of one's leg, body, etc) تَمْديد ,مَطّ ,مَدّ; **to have a ~** تَمَطَّعَ ,تَمَطَّطَ ,تَمَطّى ,تَمَدَّدَ **2** [u] (elasticity) مُرونة; **at a ~** مع بَلَغَ أَقْصى; بَذْلِ كُلِّ ما في الوُسْعِ; **to be at full ~** «factories» بَذَلَ أَقْصى جُهْدَهُ «workers»; طاقَتِهِ **3** (of road, coastline) مِساحة ,(رِقاع ,رُقَع) رُقْعة **4** (expanse) (اِمْتِدادات) اِمْتِداد **5** (period) فَتْرة مُتَواصِلة; **to work for 12 hours at a ~** عَمِلَ لِمُدّةِ 12 ساعةً مُتَواصِلةً

D *adj before n* ‹*cover, fabric*› قابِل للمَطِّ

(Phrasal verb) **stretch out** **A** **1** (to lie down) اِسْتَرْخى ,تَمَدَّدَ **2** (to extend) «plains, road» اِمْتَدَّ **B** **~ out [sth]**, **~ [sth] out** **1** (to extend) مَدَّ [شَيْئاً] ‹*one's hand, arm*› **2** (to lay out) فَرَدَ \ بَسَطَ [شَيْئاً] ‹*the nets, sheets*›

stretcher /ˈstrɛtʃə/ *n* نَقّالة (إسْعافٍ)

stretch limo, **stretch limousine** *n* سَيّارة ليموزين طَويلة

stretch mark *n* تَشَقُّق جِلْديّ ,خَطّ تَثَلُّمٍ \ أَثْلامٍ ,عَلامة تَمَدُّدٍ

stretchy /ˈstrɛtʃi/ *adj* (**stretchier**, **stretchiest**) ‹*fabric, dough*› مَرِن ,قابِل للمَطِّ

strew /struː/ *vt* (*past tense* **strewed**; *past participle* **strewed** or **strewn**) بَعْثَرَ (i; بَعْثَرة) ,نَثَرَ (i-u; نَثْر) ‹*rubbish, petals*›

stricken /ˈstrɪk(ə)n/ *adj* **1** (afflicted) مُصاب; **her father was ~ with cancer** كانَ والِدُها مُصاباً بالسَرَطانِ; **I was suddenly ~ by conscience** أُصِبْتُ فَجْأةً بِوَخْزِ الضَميرِ **2** (incapacitated) ‹*vessel, plane*› مُتَضَرِّر ,مُصاب ,مَنْكوب

strict /strɪkt/ *adj* **1** (severe) ‹*person, rule*› صارِم (صَوارِمُ), مُتَشَدِّد **2** (rigorous) ‹*vegetarian, Catholic*› حازِم (حَزَمة) ,مُتَشَدِّد **3** (precise) ‹*sense, meaning*› دَقيق (دِقاق); **in the ~ sense of the word** بالمَعْنى الدَقيقِ للكَلِمةِ **4** (absolute) ‹*secrecy, silence*› تامّ; **in the ~est confidence** بِسِرّيّةٍ تامّةٍ

strictly /ˈstrɪktli/ *adv* **1** (severely) ‹*to treat, educate*› بِصَرامةٍ, بِشَكْلٍ صارِمٍ **2** (rigorously) ‹*enforced, controlled*› بِشِدّةٍ; **~ speaking…** على وَجْهِ الدِقّةِ …; **eating meat was ~ forbidden** كانَ أَكْلُ اللَحْمِ مَمْنوعاً مَنْعاً باتّاً **3** (absolutely) ‹*necessary, true*› للغايةِ ,تَماماً; **that is not ~ true** ذلك غَيْرُ صَحيحٍ تَماماً

stride /strʌɪd/ **A** *vi* (*past tense* **strode**; *past participle* **stridden**) «walkers, hikers»; **he strode across the room** عَبَرَ الغُرْفةَ بِخُطًى واسِعةٍ; **she turned on her heels and strode out** اِسْتَدارَتْ للخَلْفِ وخَرَجَتْ بِخُطًى سَريعةٍ

B *n* خُطْوة واسِعة

(Idioms) **to make great strides** قَطَعَ أَشْواطاً كَبيرةً; **to take sth in one's stride** *or* (AmE) **in stride** واجَهَ شَيْئاً بِثِقةٍ وَثَباتٍ

strident /ˈstrʌɪd(ə)nt/ *adj* ‹*voice, tone*› حادّ

strife /strʌɪf/ *n* نِزاع (نِزاعات) ,صِراع (صِراعات)

strike /strʌɪk/ **A** *vt* (*past tense, past participle* **struck**) **1** (to hit) ضَرَبَ (i; ضَرْب) ‹*the ball, a person*›; «torpedo, missiles» ضَرَبَ ‹*the ship, target*› أَصابَ; **to ~ sth with a stick/hammer** ضَرَبَ شَيْئاً بِعَصاً \ بِمِطْرَقةٍ; **to ~ a blow for sth** اِتَّخَذَ مَوْقِفاً داعِماً لِشَيْءٍ; **to ~ sb dead** ضَرَبَ شَخْصاً ضَرْبةً أَوْدَتْ بِحَياتِهِ; **to be struck by lightning** أُصيبَ بِصاعِقةٍ; **to be struck dumb with amazement** أَخْرَسَتْهُ الدَهْشةُ **2** (to crash into) اِرْتَطَمَ (ب)

‹a rock, tree, pedestrian›; **he struck his head on the beam** اصْطَدَمَ رَأْسُهُ بالعارِضةِ الخَشَبيّةِ **3** (to afflict) ضَرَبَ (i; ضَرْب), أَصابَ ‹an area, a family, community›; **disaster struck the town** أُصيبَت المَدينةُ بكارِثةٍ; **the decree struck terror into the inhabitants** أَصابَ القَرارُ السُكّانَ بالفَزَعِ **4** (to impress) «ideas, thoughts, resemblance» تَراءى (ل); **it ~s me that it's very important** أَظُنُّ أنَّهُ مُهِمٌّ جِدًّا; **how does the idea ~ you?** كيف تَبْدو لَكَ الفِكْرةُ؟; **how did he ~ you?** ما رَأْيُكَ فيهِ؟; **I was struck with him** تَرَكَ لَدَيَّ انْطِباعاً حَسَناً **5** (to discover) اكْتَشَفَ ‹oil, gold, rock› **6** (to conclude) عَقَدَ (i; عَقْد), أَبْرَمَ ‹a bargain, deal›; **to ~ a balance** حَقَّقَ تَوازُناً **7** (to ignite) أَشْعَلَ ‹a match› **8** «clocks» دَقَّ (u; دَقّ) ‹the hour, six›; **it had just struck two** دَقَّت الساعةُ الثانيةُ للتَوِّ **9** **to ~ a name/item from a list** حَذَفَ اسْماً \ بَنْداً من قائِمةٍ **10** (to take down) فَكَّ (u; فَكّ) ‹a tent, scaffolding›; **to ~ camp** فَكَّ الخَيْمةَ **11** (to mint) سَكَّ (u; سَكّ), ضَرَبَ (i; ضَرْب) ‹a coin›

B *vi* (*past tense, past participle* **struck**) **1** (to hit) «bombs» أُطْلِقَ; **my head struck against the beam** اصْطَدَمَ رَأْسي بالعارِضةِ **2** (to attack) «killers, robbers» هَجَمَ, هاجَمَ (u; هُجوم); «storms» هَبَّ (u; هَبّ, هُبوب); **the terrorists have struck again** قامَ الإرْهابيّونَ بِهُجومٍ آخَرَ; **disaster struck** وَقَعَتْ كارِثةٌ; **to ~ at a target/an enemy** هاجَمَ هَدَفاً \ عَدوًّا **3** (in labour disputes) «workers» أَضْرَبَ; **to ~ for better wages/against the cuts** أَضْرَبَ (عن العَمَلِ) للمُطالَبةِ بِتَحْسينِ الأُجورِ \ اعْتِراضاً على تَخْفيضِ الأُجورِ **4** «clock» دَقَّ (u; دَقّ); **six o'clock struck** دَقَّت الساعةُ السادِسةُ **5** (to go somewhere) **to ~ north** مَضى نحو الشَمالِ; **to ~ out across the desert** مَضى عَبْرَ الصَحْراءِ

C *n* **1** (by workers) إضْراب (إضْرابات); **to be on/come out on ~** كانَ مُضْرِباً \ قامَ بإضْرابٍ (عن العَمَلِ) **2** (attack) غارة, هُجوم; **the air force launched a ~ against the port** شَنَّت القوّاتُ الجَوّيّةُ هُجوماً على الميناءِ **3** (in mining, drilling) اكْتِشاف مُفاجِئ; **it was a lucky ~** كانَ ضَرْبةَ حَظٍّ **4** (in baseball) ضَرْبة فاشِلة

Phrasal verbs **strike back** (to retaliate) «defence force» انْتَقَمَ, رَدَّ (u; رَدّ)

• **strike down**: **~ [sb] down, ~ down [sb]** **1** (to kill) «cancer, bullets» قَتَلَ [شَخْصاً] **2** (to incapacitate) «malaria» أَقْعَدَ [شَخْصاً]

• **strike off** **A** (to go off) انْطَلَقَ **B** **~ [sth] off, ~ off [sth]** (to delete) حَذَفَ [شَيْئاً] ‹an item, a name› **C** **~ [sb] off** شَطَبَ اسْمَ [شَخْصٍ] ‹a doctor›

• **strike out** **A** **1** (to hit out) هاجَمَ; **to ~ out at one's critics** هاجَمَ مُنْتَقِديهِ **2** (to head for) **to ~ out towards sth** اتَّجَهَ نحو شَيْءٍ; **to ~ out on one's own** بَدَأَ مَشْروعاً مُسْتَقِلاًّ **B** **~ [sth] out, ~ out [sth]** (to delete) حَذَفَ \ شَطَبَ [شَيْئاً] ‹a name, an item›

• **strike up** **A** «band, musician» بَدَأَ في العَزْفِ **B** **~ up [sth]** «band, musicians» عَزَفَ [شَيْئاً] ‹a tune, waltz›; **to ~ up a conversation with sb** اسْتَهَلَّ \ بَدَأَ مُحادَثةً مع شَخْصٍ

strike action *n* إضْراب (إضْرابات)

strike-breaker /ˈstrʌɪkbreɪkə/ *n* مُفْسِد إضْرابٍ (عامِل مُسْتَأْجَر لِيَحِلَّ مَحَلَّ العامِلِ المُضْرِبِ)

strike-breaking /ˈstrʌɪkbreɪkɪŋ/ *n* كَسْر \ خَرْق \ إفْساد إضْرابٍ

strike force *n* قُوّة ضارِبة

striker /ˈstrʌɪkə/ *n* **1** (person on strike) مُضْرِب **2** (in soccer) مُهاجِم, لاعِب هُجوم

striking /ˈstrʌɪkɪŋ/ *adj* **1** (noticeable) ‹similarity, colour, contrast› لافِت للنَظَرِ, مُدْهِش **2** (good-looking) ‹person› رائِع, مُبْهِر **3** (on strike) ‹worker› مُضْرِب

strikingly /ˈstrʌɪkɪŋli/ *adv* ‹similar, beautiful› على نَحْوٍ لافِتٍ للنَظَرِ, بِشَكْلٍ مُبْهِرٍ

string /strɪŋ/ **A** *n* **1** [u] (twine) خَيْط (خُيوط), دوبارة (دوبار), حَبْل (حِبال), رِباط (رُبُط, أَرْبِطة); **a piece of ~** قِطْعة خَيْطٍ; **tied up with ~** مُقَيَّد بِرِباطٍ **2** (on hoods, etc) رِباط (رُبُط, أَرْبِطة) **3** (on bows, rackets) وَتَر (أَوْتار); **to pull the ~s** كانَ العَقْلَ المُدَبِّرَ **4** (Mus) (on instruments) وَتَر (أَوْتار) **5** (series) **a ~ of visitors/victories** أَفْواج من الزوّارِ \ سِلْسِلة من الانْتِصاراتِ; **he's had a ~ of convictions** أُدينَ في عَدَدٍ من التُهَمِ **6** (set, group) **a ~ of onions** حُزْمة بَصَلٍ; **a ~ of pearls** لُؤْلُؤ مَنْظوم في خَيْطٍ; **a ~ of islands** سِلْسِلة من الجُزُرِ **7** (of characters)

سِلْسِلة أَحْرُفٍ; **a searchable ~** سِلْسِلة أَحْرُفٍ قابِلة للبَحْث

B (**strings**) *n pl* **1** (Mus) **the ~s** عازِفو الآلاتِ الوَتَرِيّة **2** (infml) (conditions) قُيود, شُروط

C *vt* (*past tense, past participle* **strung**) **1** (to fit string to) شَدَّ الأَوْتارَ ‹*a racket, guitar*› **2** (to thread) نَظَمَ في خَيْطٍ ‹*beads, pearls*› **3** (to hang) **to ~ sth across the street** عَلَّقَ شَيْئاً عَبْرَ الشارِعِ; **to ~ a hammock between two trees** عَلَّقَ أُرْجوحةً شَبَكِيّةً بين شَجَرَتَيْن

Idioms **to pull strings** (infml) اِسْتَغَلَّ نُفوذَهُ; **with no strings attached** دون قَيْدٍ أو شَرْطٍ

Phrasal verbs **string along** **A** (infml) (to accompany) صَحِبَ (صُحْبة, صَحابة; a), رافَقَ; **to ~ along with sb** رافَقَ شَخْصاً **B ~ [sb] along** (infml) خَدَعَ [شَخْصاً]

• **string out**: **~ [sth] out, ~ out [sth]** **1** (infml) أَطالَ \ مَطَّ [شَيْئاً] ‹*a story, series*› **2** وَضَعَ [شَيْئاً] في صَفٍّ ‹*guards*›; **the tents were strung out along the river** وُضِعَت الخِيامُ في صَفٍّ مُوازٍ للنَهْرِ

• **string together**: **~ [sth] together, ~ together [sth]** (infml) رَبَطَ [شَيْئاً] ‹*sentences, words*›

• **string up**: **~ [sb] up** (infml) شَنَقَ [شَخْصاً]

string bean *n* فاصولِية

stringed instrument /ˌstrɪŋd ˈɪnstrəmənt/ *n* آلة وَتَرِيّة

stringent /ˈstrɪndʒ(ə)nt/ *adj* ‹*requirements, rules*› صارِم (صَوارِمُ), مُشَدَّد

strip /strɪp/ **A** *vt* (**-pp-**) **1** (to remove) نَزَعَ (نَزْع; i), أَزالَ ‹*the paint, a layer*›; **to ~ the paint off the door** أَزالَ الطِلاءَ من على البابِ; **to ~ a bed** نَزَعَ فَرْشَ سَريرٍ **2** (with clothing) عَرّى, جَرَّدَ من مَلابِسِهِ ‹*a prisoner, patient*›; **to ~ the suspect naked** جَرَّدَ المُتَّهَمَ من مَلابِسِهِ **3** (to plunder) «thieves, looters» جَرَّدَ من مُحْتَوَياتِهِ ‹*a house, store*›; **the looters ~ped the store bare** جَرَّدَ اللُصوصُ المَتْجَرَ من كُلِّ مُحْتَوَياتِهِ **4** «painter» أَزالَ الطِلاءَ عن ‹*a door, table, the iron-work*› **5** (to deprive of) **to ~ sb of a title/an award** جَرَّدَ شَخْصاً من لَقَبٍ \ اسْتَرَدَّ جائِزةً من شَخْصٍ; **he was ~ped of his title** جُرِّدَ من لَقَبِهِ

B *vi* (**-pp-**) **1** (to undress) تَعَرّى; **to ~ to the waist** تَعَرّى إلى وَسَطِهِ; **to ~ naked** تَعَرّى, تَجَرَّدَ من ثِيابِهِ **2** (in striptease) «stripper» رَقَصَ مُتَعَرِّياً

C *n* **1** (of fabric, paper, carpet) شَريط (أَشْرِطة, شَرائِطُ); **a ~ of land/beach** شَريط من الأَرْضِ \ ساحِلِيّ; **cut the meat into thin ~s** قَطِّع اللَحْمَ إلى شَرائِحَ رَقيقةٍ **2** (AmE) (street) شارِع (شَوارِعُ) **3** (BrE) (club colours) زِيّ (أَزْياء)

Phrasal verbs **strip down** **A** (to undress) خَلَعَ مَلابِسَهُ **B ~ [sth] down, ~ down [sth]** **1** (to dismantle) فَكَّكَ [شَيْئاً] ‹*an engine*› **2** «painter» أَزالَ الطِلاءَ من [شَيْءٍ] ‹*a door, table, the iron-work*›

• **strip off** **A** (to remove clothing) تَخَفَّفَ من مَلابِسِهِ **B ~ [sth] off, ~ off [sth]** **1** أَزالَ [شَيْئاً] ‹*paint, wallpaper*› **2** خَلَعَ [شَيْئاً] ‹*one's clothes*›

strip cartoon *n* قِصّة كَرْتونِيّة, رُسوم هَزْلِيّة مُسَلْسَلة

stripe /straɪp/ *n* خَطّ (خُطوط)

striped /straɪpt/ *adj* ‹*shirt, suit*› مُخَطَّط, مُقَلَّم

strip lighting *n* [الإنارة بِمَصابيح الفْلورسَنْت \ النيون]

stripper /ˈstrɪpə/ *n* راقِصة مُتَعَرِّية (في مَلْهًى لَيْلِيّ)

strip-search /ˈstrɪpsəːtʃ/ *vt* [التَجْريد من المَلابِس للتَفْتيش]

striptease /ˈstrɪptiːz/ *n* رَقْص مُتَعَرٍّ

striptease artist *n* راقِصة مُتَعَرِّية (في مَلْهًى لَيْلِيّ)

strive /straɪv/ *vi* (*past tense* **strove**; *past participle* **striven**) «companies, individuals» سَعى (جاهداً); **to ~ to do sth** سَعى جاهداً لِفِعْلِ شَيْءٍ; **we ~ for excellence in everything we do** نَسْعى من أَجْلِ التَفَوُّقِ في كُلِّ شَيْءٍ نَفْعَلُهُ

strode /strəʊd/ *past tense* ▸**stride**

stroke /strəʊk/ **A** *n* **1** (with a racket, bat) ضَرْبة (ضَرَبات); **to practise one's ~s** تَمَرَّنَ على تَسْديدِ الضَرَباتِ **2** (of a cane) ضَرْبة (ضَرَبات) **3** (touch, piece) لَمْسة; **at a ~** على الفَوْرِ; **it was a ~ of luck** كانَ ضَرْبةَ حَظٍّ; **a ~ of genius** لَمْسة \ نَفْحة من العَبْقَرِيّة; **he didn't do a ~ of work** لم يُؤَدِّ أَيَّ عَمَلٍ على الإطْلاقِ **4** (in swimming) ضَرْبة (ضَرَبات) **5** (of a clock) دَقّة; **at the ~ of midnight** عند دَقّاتِ مُنْتَصَفِ اللَيْلِ; **to begin/end on the ~ of four** بَدَأَ \ انْتَهى عند دَقّاتِ الساعةِ الرابِعةِ **6** (brain damage) سَكْتة دِماغِيّة **7** (of a pen) جَرّة (جَرّات); (of a brush) ضَرْبة (ضَرَبات) **8** (in alternatives) شَرْطة **9** (of pistons) شَوْط (أَشْواط); **a two-~ engine** مُحَرِّك

ثُنائيّ الأَشْواطِ **10** (caress) تَرْبيت; **to give sb/sth a ~** رَبَّتَ على شَخْصٍ \ شَيْءٍ

B *vt* (to caress) رَبَّتَ (على) ‹*an animal, sb's hair, cheek*›

stroll /strəʊl/ **A** *vi* «tourists, couples» تَنَزَّه, تَمَشّى, تَجَوَّلَ

B *n* تَنَزُّه (تَنَزُّهات), تَمَشٍّ; **to go for** *or* **take a ~** تَمَشّى

stroller /ˈstrəʊlə/ *n* **1** (walker) مُتَنَزِّه, مُتَجَوِّل **2** (AmE) (for child) عَرَبة أَطْفالٍ

strong /strɒŋ/ *adj* **1** (in body) ‹*arm, muscle, runner*› قَويّ; **she's a very ~ swimmer** هي سَبّاحةٌ قَويّةٌ **2** (with force) ‹*wind, current*› قَويّ, شَديد; **~ winds are expected** من المُتَوَقَّع هُبوبُ رياحٍ شَديدةٍ **3** (in health) ‹*eyesight, nerves*› قَويّ; ‹*health*› جَيِّد; **to become/grow ~er** أَصْبَحَ أَقْوى **4** (convincing) ‹*plot, candidate, evidence*› قَويّ **5** (in leadership) ‹*management, leader*› قَويّ **6** (exercising power) ‹*army, government, magnet*› قَويّ; **the unions have always been ~ in this industry** كانَت النِقاباتُ دائِماً قَويّةً في هذه الصِناعةِ **7** ‹*foundations, bridge, girder*› قَويّ, مَتين **8** (durable) ‹*rope, relationship, fabric*› قَويّ, مَتين **9** (buoyant) ‹*currency, economy, demand*› قَويّ **10** (concentrated) ‹*acid, pain-killer, solution*› قَويّ; **at midday the sun's rays are at their ~est** في مُنْتَصَفِ النهارِ تكونُ أَشِعّةُ الشَمْسِ في أَقْوى حالاتِها; **to like ~ tea/coffee** أَحَبَّ الشايَ القَويَّ \ القَهْوةَ القَويّةَ; **a ~ solution of sulphuric acid** مَحْلول مُرَكَّز من حَمْضِ الكِبْريتيك **11** (alcoholic) ‹*drink*› كُحوليّ **12** (noticeable) ‹*smell*› نَفّاذ; ‹*taste*› قَويّ; ‹*colour*› صارِخ **13** (heartfelt) ‹*reaction, support, conviction*› قَويّ; **the news aroused ~ feelings** أَثارَت الأَخْبارُ مَشاعِرَ قَويّةً; **the report caused a ~ reaction** سَبَّبَ التَقْريرُ رَدَّ فِعْلٍ قَويّاً **14** (pronounced) ‹*accent, resemblance*› قَويّ; **she has a ~ resemblance to her father** فيها شَبَهٌ قَويٌّ من أَبيها **15** (resolute) ‹*person, parent*› قَويّ; **try to be ~** حاوِلْ أَنْ تكونَ قَويّاً **16** (very likely) ‹*chance, probability*› كَبير; **there's a ~ possibility that it's true** هُناكَ احْتِمالٌ كَبيرٌ أَنْ يَكونَ صَحيحاً **17** (having ability) قَويّ; **he's ~ in chemistry** هو قَويٌّ في الكيمْياءِ; **what are his ~ points?** ما نِقاطُ قُوَّتِه؟ **18** (immoderate) **~ language** لُغة عَنيفة **19** ‹*verb*› (in English: irregular) شاذّ; (in Arabic: with no weak radicals) صَحيح **20** (in number) **there was a ~ police presence at the demonstration** كانَ هُناكَ تَواجُدٌ كَثيفٌ للشُرْطةِ في المُظاهَرةِ; **the workforce is 500 ~** الأَيْدي العامِلةُ قِوامُها 500 شَخْصٍ

(Idiom) **to be still going strong** ما زالَ في حالةٍ جَيِّدةٍ

strongbox /ˈstrɒŋbɒks/ *n* خِزانة حَديديّة

stronghold /ˈstrɒŋhəʊld/ *n* **1** (fortress) حِصْن (حُصون), قَلْعة (قِلاع) **2** (centre of support) مَعْقِل (مَعاقِلُ)

strongly /ˈstrɒŋli/ *adv* **1** (powerfully) ‹*to beat, blow*› بِشِدّةٍ, بقوّةٍ **2** (solidly) ‹*built, reinforced*› بِشَكْلٍ مَتينٍ **3** (deeply) ‹*to feel, believe*› بِشِدّةٍ, بقوّةٍ **4** (forcefully) ‹*to suggest, oppose*› بِقوّةٍ, بِشِدّةٍ; **I ~ recommend this book** أَنْصَحُ بِشِدّةٍ بِقراءةِ هذا الكِتابِ

strongroom /ˈstrɒŋruːm/ *n* غُرْفة مُحَصَّنة

strong-willed /ˌstrɒŋˈwɪld/ *adj* ‹*woman, individual*› قَويّ الإرادةِ

strove /strəʊv/ *past tense* ▸ **strive**

struck /strʌk/ *past tense, past participle* ▸ **strike**

structural /ˈstrʌktʃ(ə)rəl/ *adj* **1** (organizational) ‹*change, problem*› هَيْكَليّ, بِنْيَويّ **2** (in construction) ‹*damage, defect*› هَيْكَليّ, إنْشائيّ

structure /ˈstrʌktʃə/ **A** *n* **1** (organization) هَيْكَل (هَياكِلُ), بِنْية (بِنًى, بُنًى) **2** (building) بُنْيان, بِناء (أَبْنِية), مَبْنًى (مَبانٍ)

B *vt* ‹*a novel, society*› نَظَّمَ

structured /ˈstrʌktʃəd/ *adj* ‹*interview, course*› مُنَظَّم

struggle /ˈstrʌɡ(ə)l/ **A** *vi* **1** (physically) تَصارَعَ; **he ~d with his attackers** تَصارَعَ مع مُهاجِميهِ; **to ~ free** قاوَمَ حتّى حَرَّرَ نَفْسَهُ **2** (mentally) عانى; **to ~ with a problem/one's conscience** عانى من مُشْكِلةٍ \ تَأْنيبِ الضَميرِ **3** (to have difficulties) «family, company» وَجَدَ صُعوبةً; **to ~ financially** عانى من صُعوباتٍ ماليّةٍ; **to ~ to keep up** وَجَدَ صُعوبةً في الاسْتِمْرارِ **4** (to move with difficulty) **he ~d into his trousers** ارْتَدى سِرْوالَهُ بِصُعوبةٍ; **to ~ to one's feet** وَقَفَ على قَدَمَيْه بِمَشَقّةٍ; **to ~ back to the house** عادَ إلى المَنْزِلِ بِصُعوبةٍ

B *n* **1** (scuffle) صِراع (صِراعات), نِزاع (نِزاعات); **to put up a ~** قاوَمَ بِشِدّةٍ **2** (for freedom, etc) كِفاح (كِفاحات), نِضال (نِضالات); **our ~ for democracy/survival** كِفاحُنا من أَجْلِ الديمُقْراطيّةِ \ البَقاءِ; **to join/give up the ~** انْضَمَّ إلى \ تَوَقَّفَ

عن النِضالِ **3** (difficult task) مَهَمّة شاقّة; **they had a ~ moving it** *or* **to move it** وَجَدوا صُعوبةً في تَحْريكِهِ; **it was a ~ but it was worth it** كانَ أَمْراً شاقًّا وَلَكِنَّهُ كانَ يَسْتَحِقُّ العَناءَ

(Phrasal verbs) **struggle along**, **struggle on** **1** (on a journey) تَقَدَّمَ بِصُعوبةٍ, ثابَرَ **2** (with life, a task) دَبَّرَ أُمورَهُ بِصُعوبةٍ

• **struggle through**: **~ through [sth]** **1** تَقَدَّمَ بِصُعوبةٍ وَسْطَ [شَيْءٍ] *<the snow, jungle, crowd>* **2** انْتَهى من [شَيْءٍ] بِصُعوبةٍ *<a book, an exam>*

struggling /ˈstrʌglɪŋ/ *adj* *<economy, artist>* يُعاني من صُعوباتٍ

strum /strʌm/ *vt* (**-mm-**) عَزَفَ (i; عَزْف) (على) *<a guitar>*; عَزَفَ (i; عَزْف) *<a tune>*

strung /strʌŋ/ *past tense, past participle* ▸ **string**

strung out *adj* (infml) **1** (stressed) *<person>* مُتَوَتِّر **2** (under the influence) *<alcoholic>* سَكْران, ثَمِل (dipt; سَكارى); *<addict>* مُغَيَّب العَقْلِ, مَسْطول; **to be strung out on drugs** كانَ تحت تَأْثيرِ المُخَدِّراتِ

strut /strʌt/ **A** *n* دِعامة (دِعامات, دَعائِمُ), عَمود داعِم, قائِم انْضِغاطٍ

B *vi* (**-tt-**) «models, peacocks» تَبَخْتَرَ, اخْتالَ (في مَشْيِهِ); **to ~ around** *or* **about** مَشى مُتَبَخْتِراً

stub /stʌb/ **A** *n* **1** (of a pencil, candle, cigarette) عُقْب (أَعْقاب) **2** (of a cheque) أَرومة; (of a ticket) كَعْب (كِعاب, كُعوب)

B *vt* (**-bb-**) **to ~ one's toe** اصْطَدَمَ إِصْبَعُ قَدَمِهِ

(Phrasal verb) **stub out**: **~ [sth] out**, **~ out [sth]** أَطْفَأَ [شَيْئاً] *<a cigarette>*

stubble /ˈstʌb(ə)l/ *n* **1** (in a field) جُذامة (عيدان الزَرْعِ المُتَبَقّية في الأَرْضِ بعد الحَصادِ) **2** (of a beard) شَعْر الذَقْنِ (قبل حَلْقِهِ); **he had three days' ~ on his face** لم يَحْلِقْ ذَقْنَهُ لِثَلاثةِ أَيّامٍ

stubborn /ˈstʌb(ə)n/ *adj* **1** *<person, animal>* عَنيد (عُنُد); *<resistance>* شَديد; *<refusal>* مُتَعَنِّت **2** *<stain, problem>* مُسْتَعْصٍ

stuck /stʌk/ **A** *past tense, past participle* ▸ **stick**

B *adj* **1** (unable to move) عالِق, مَحْصور; **this drawer is ~** هَذا الدُرْجُ عالِقٌ; **we were ~ in traffic** كُنّا مَحْصورينَ في زِحامِ المُرورِ; **I'm ~ at home with the baby** أَنا حَبيسٌ في المَنْزِلِ مع الرَضيعِ **2** (at a loss) **I was ~ for words** عَجَزْتُ عن إيجادِ الكَلِماتِ; **she's never ~ for an answer** لا تَعْجَزُ أَبَداً عن الرَدِّ

3 (infml) (lumbered) **to be ~ with sth/sb** لم يَسْتَطِع التَخَلُّصَ من شَخْصٍ \ شَيْءٍ

(Idiom) **to get stuck into sth** (BrE infml) انْهَمَكَ \ اسْتَغْرَقَ في شَيْءٍ

stuck-up /stʌkˈʌp/ *adj* (infml) *<person>* مُتَعَجْرِف, مَغْرور, مُتَكَبِّر

stud /stʌd/ **A** *n* **1** (for decoration) مِسْمار زينةٍ; (for a collar, shirt) زِرّ زينةٍ; (BrE) (on a sports boot) مِسْمار أَحْذيةٍ **2** (piece of jewellery) قُرْط (أَقْراط, قِراط) **3** (stallion) فَحْل خَيْلٍ; (horse farm) مَزْرَعة لِتَرْبِيةِ الخُيولِ

B *vt* رَصَّعَ; **the sky was ~ded with stars** كانَتْ السَماءُ مُرَصَّعةً بالنُجومِ

student /ˈstju:d(ə)nt/ *n* (at university) طالِب (طُلّاب, طَلَبة); (at school) تِلْميذ (تَلاميذُ, تَلامِذة)

student loan *n* قَرْض طُلّابيّ

student nurse *n* طالِب تَمْريضٍ

student teacher *n* مُدَرِّس تحت التَدْريبِ

student union, **students' union** *n* (BrE) **1** (building) مَبْنى اتِّحادِ طُلّابٍ **2** (BrE) (association) اتِّحاد طُلّابٍ

studio /ˈstju:dɪəʊ/ *n* **1** (of an artist, photographer) اسْتوديو (اسْتوديوهات) **2** (for recording) اسْتودِيو (اسْتوديوهات) **3** (also **studio flat** BrE, **studio apartment** AmE) شَقّة اسْتودِيو \ بغُرْفةٍ واحِدةٍ

studious /ˈstju:dɪəs/ *adj* *<pupil, classmate>* مُجْتَهِد

study /ˈstʌdi/ **A** *n* (*pl* **studies**) **1** [u] (academic work) دِراسة **2** (piece of research) بَحْث (بُحوث, أَبْحاث) **3** (room) غُرْفة مَكْتَبٍ (في مَنْزِلٍ) **4** (a musical composition) قِطْعة موسيقيّة تَجْريبيّة; (a drawing) رَسْم تَجْريبيّ

B (**studies**) *n pl* **1** (student's work) دِراسة **2** (academic subject) **social studies** الدِراسات الاجْتِماعيّة; **business studies** الدِراسات التِجاريّة

C *vt* (**studies**, **studying**, **studied**) **1** (at school, university) دَرَسَ (u; دَرْس) *<history, law>* **2** (to investigate, research into) بَحَثَ (a; بَحْث), فَحَصَ (a; فَحْص) *<effects, processes>* **3** (to scrutinize) تَفَحَّصَ *<an object, sb's face>*

D *vi* «students, pupils» دَرَسَ (u; دَرْس)

study aid *n* وَسيلة تَعْليميّة

stuff /stʌf/ **A** *n* (infml) **1** (unnamed substance) شَيْء (أَشْياءُ); **we sell lots of the ~** نَبيعُ الكَثيرَ من هذا الشَيْءِ; **what's that ~ in the bottle?** ما ذلك الشَيْءُ في الزُجاجةِ; **caviar is expensive ~** الكافِيار غالي الثَمَنِ; **this detergent/marijuana is strong ~** هذه المادّةُ المُنَظِّفةُ \ الماريجُوانا قَوِيّةُ المَفْعولِ **2** (unnamed objects) أَشْياءُ; **sort out all the ~ in the garage** رَتِّبْ كُلَّ الأَشْياءِ في الكَراج; **leave your ~ in the hall** اُتْرُكْ أَغْراضَكَ في القاعةِ **3** (content of a speech, book, etc) شَيْء (أَشْياءُ); **have you read much of her ~?** هل قَرَأْتَ الكَثيرَ من أَعْمالِها؟; **who wrote this ~?** مَنْ كَتَبَ هذا الشَيْءَ؟; **do you believe all that ~ about his private life?** هل تُصَدِّقُ كُلَّ تلكَ الأَشْياءِ عن حَياتِهِ الشَخْصِيّةِ؟ **4** (material) مادّةٌ (مَوادُّ); **to be made of (much) sterner ~** كانَتْ شَخصِيَّتُهُ أَقْوى (بِكَثِير)
B *vt* **1** (to fill) سَدَّ (u; سَدّ) ‹*a hole, crack*›; **to ~ a cushion with wool** حَشا \ بَطَّنَ وِسادةً بالصوفِ; **she ~ed his pockets with change** عَبَّأَتْ جُيوبَهُ بِقِطَعٍ نَقْدِيّةٍ صَغيرةٍ; **a book ~ed with useful information** كِتاب مَليء بِمَعْلوماتٍ مُفيدةٍ **2** (infml) (to wedge in) دَسَّ (u; دَسّ), حَشَرَ (i-u; حَشْر) ‹*clothes, paper*›; **to ~ the boxes under the bed** حَشَرَ الصَناديقَ تحت السَريرِ; **he managed to ~ it all into the suitcase** اِسْتَطاعَ أَنْ يَدُسَّهُ كُلَّهُ في الحَقيبةِ; **I ~ed the letters into my pocket** حَشَرْتُ الخِطاباتِ في جَيْبي **3** «cook» حَشا (u; حَشْو) ‹*a turkey, pepper*› **4** «taxidermist» حَنَّطَ ‹*an animal, a bird*›
Idioms **to do one's stuff** (infml) قامَ بِعَمَلِهِ; **to know one's stuff** (infml) كانَ خَبيراً بِعَمَلِهِ

stuffed /stʌft/ *adj* **1** ‹*peppers, olives*› مَحْشوّ **2** ‹*animal, bird*› مُحَنَّط; ‹*toy*› مَحْشوّ

stuffing /ˈstʌfɪŋ/ *n* **1** (for turkey, chicken etc.) حَشْو **2** (of furniture, pillow etc.) حَشْوة, بِطانة (بَطائِنُ, بِطانات)

stuffy /ˈstʌfi/ *adj* (**stuffier, stuffiest**) **1** (airless) ‹*room, office*› خانِق, سَيِّءُ التَهْوِيةِ; **it's very ~ in here** الجَوُّ خانِقٌ جِدًّا هُنا **2** (infml) (blocked) ‹*nose*› مَسْدود **3** (staid) ‹*person, institution*› مُنْغَلِق

stumble /ˈstʌmb(ə)l/ *vi* **1** (to trip) «injured person, animal» تَعَثَّرَ **2** (in speech) «speaker» تَلَعْثَمَ; **to ~ over one's words** تَلَعْثَمَ في كَلامِهِ
Phrasal verbs **stumble across ▸ stumble on**
• **stumble on, stumble upon: ~ on** *or* **upon [sth]** عَثَرَ على [شَيْءٍ] صُدْفةً ‹*an article*›; خَطَرَ على بالِهِ [شَيْءٌ] ‹*an idea*›; اِكْتَشَفَ [شَيْئاً] بالصُدْفةِ ‹*the truth*›

stumbling block /ˈstʌmblɪŋ blɒk/ *n* عَقَبة, حَجَر عَثْرةٍ (عَقَبات)

stump /stʌmp/ **A** *n* **1** (of a tree) جِذْل (أَجْذال, جُذول), جِذْع (جُذوع, أَجْذاع) **2** (of a candle, pencil) الجُزْء المُتَبَقّي من [الشَيْءِ بعد اسْتِخْدامِهِ] **3** (of a limb) بَقِيّةُ الطَرَفِ المَبْتورِ
B *vt* **1** (infml) (to perplex) أَرْبَكَ ‹*a person, an expert*›; **to be ~ed by the question** أَرْبَكَهُ السُؤالُ **2** (AmE) «candidate» قامَ بِجَوْلةٍ انْتِخابيّةٍ في ‹*a state, region*›
C *vi* (AmE) «candidate» قامَ بِجَوْلةٍ انْتِخابيّةٍ
Phrasal verb **stump up A** (BrE infml) (for a present, event) دَفَعَ (a; دَفْع) **B ~ up [sth], ~ [sth] up** (BrE) (infml) دَفَعَ [شَيْئاً] ‹*the money, an amount*›

stun /stʌn/ *vt* (**-nn-**) **1** (to make unconscious) أَفْقَدَ الوَعْيَ ‹*an animal, opponent*› **2** (to amaze) أَذْهَلَ, أَدْهَشَ ‹*an audience, a community*›

stung /stʌŋ/ *past tense, past participle* ▸ **sting** B, C

stunk /stʌŋk/ *past participle* ▸ **stink** A

stunned /stʌnd/ *adj* **1** (dazed) ‹*victim, survivor*› دائِخ, فاقِد الوَعْيِ **2** (amazed) ‹*audience, crowd*› مَشْدوه, مَذْهول; ‹*silence, disbelief*› يَنُمّ عن الذُهولِ

stunning /ˈstʌnɪŋ/ *adj* ‹*view*› خَلّاب, فاتِن; ‹*performance*› مُذْهِل, مُدْهِش; ‹*woman, man*› شَديد الجاذِبِيّةِ

stunt /stʌnt/ **A** *n* **1** (also **publicity stunt**) حيلة دِعائيّة **2** (feat of daring) حَرَكة بَهْلَوانيّة, مُغامَرة جَريئة **3** (in films) مَشْهَد خَطير; **he did his own ~s** أَدّى المَشاهِدَ الخَطيرةَ بِنَفْسِهِ
B *vt* أَعاقَ ‹*growth, development*›

stunted /ˈstʌntɪd/ *adj* ‹*plant, child*› غَيْر مُكْتَمِلِ النُموِّ; ‹*growth*› مُتَوَقِّف, غَيْر مُكْتَمِلٍ

stuntman /ˈstʌntman/ *n* (*pl* **-men**) مُمَثِّل بَديل, دوبْلير

stupefy /ˈstjuːpɪfʌɪ/ *vt* (**stupefies, stupefying, stupefied**) أَذْهَلَ, أَبْهَرَ ‹*an audience, the nation*›

stupefying /ˈstjuːpɪfʌɪɪŋ/ *adj* ‹*banality, boredom*› مُضْجِر

stupendous /stjuːˈpɛndəs/ *adj* ‹success, view› هائِل (هَوائِلُ), مُبْهِر

stupid /ˈstjuːpɪd/ *adj* **1** (foolish) ‹idea, question› غَبيّ, أَحْمَق (حُمْق; f حَمْقى; dipt) **2** (unintelligent) ‹person› غَبيّ (أَغْبياءُ), أَبْلَه (dipt)

stupidity /stjuːˈpɪdəti/ *n* غَباء, حَماقة, بَلاهة

stupor /ˈstjuːpə/ *n* غَيْبوبة, غِياب العَقْلِ; **in a drunken ~** في حالةِ سُكْرٍ

sturdy /ˈstəːdi/ *adj* (**sturdier, sturdiest**) **1** ‹shoes, table› مَتين, قَوِيّ **2** ‹legs, build› قَوِيّ; ‹person, animal› قَوِيّ البِنْيةِ

sturgeon /ˈstəːdʒ(ə)n/ *n* (*pl* **sturgeon**) حَفْش (سَمَك)

stutter /ˈstʌtə/ **A** *vt* تَلَعْثَمَ (في) ‹a reply, an apology›
B *vi* «person» تَلَعْثَمَ, تَأْتَأَ (i; تَأْتَأة, تَأْتاء), تَعْتَعَ (i; تَعْتَعة)
C *n* تَلَعْثُم, تَأْتَأة, تَعْتَعة

St Valentine's Day /seɪnt ˈvaləntʌɪnz deɪ/ *n* عيد الحُبّ, يَوْم القِدّيس فالِنْتَيْن

sty /stʌɪ/ *n* **1** (for pigs) زَريبة (زَرائِبُ), حَظيرة (حَظائِرُ) **2** (also **stye**) شَحّاذ العَيْنِ (دُمَّل بِجَفْنِ العَيْنِ)

style /stʌɪl/ **A** *n* **1** (manner) أُسْلوب (أَساليبُ), طَريقة (طُرُق, طَرائِقُ); **that's not my ~** لَيْسَ ذلك أُسْلوبي **2** (in art, music etc) طِراز (طُرُز, أَطْرِزة), نَمَط (أَنْماط, نِماط), أُسْلوب (أَساليبُ) **3** (elegance) أَناقة, ذَوْق رَفيع, فَخامة, أُبَّهة; **to live/travel in ~** عاشَ \ سافَرَ في أُبَّهةٍ **4** (type, design) تَصْميم (تَصْميمات, تَصاميمُ), شَكْل (أَشْكال) **5** (fashion) موضة; **to come into ~** أَصْبَحَ موضةً; **to go out of ~** مَضى وَقْتُهُ **6** (hairstyle) تَصْفيفة, تَسْريحة
B (**-style**) *suffix* على الطِرازِ \ النَمَطِ; **Chinese-/Italian-~** على الطِرازِ الصينيِّ \ الإيطاليِّ
C *vt* صَفَّفَ ‹hair›

styling /ˈstʌɪlɪŋ/ *n* تَصْميم (تَصْميمات, تَصاميمُ)

stylish /ˈstʌɪlɪʃ/ *adj* ‹clothes, person, restaurant› أَنيق

stylist /ˈstʌɪlɪst/ *n* مُصَفِّف شَعْرٍ

stylistic /stʌɪˈlɪstɪk/ *adj* ‹choice, difference› من حَيْثُ الأُسْلوبِ

stylized /ˈstʌɪlʌɪzd/ *adj* ‹form› مُصْطَنَع; ‹representation› مُتَكَلَّف

stylus /ˈstʌɪləs/ *n* (*pl* **styli** or **styluses**) **1** (on a record player) إِبْرة الفونوغْراف **2** (input device) قَلَم سْتايْلُس \ إِلِكْترونيّ

styrofoam® /ˈstʌɪrəfəʊm/ *n* (AmE) السْتيروفوم (مادّة عازِلة)

suave /swɑːv/ *adj* ‹man, manner› رَقيق (أَرِقّاءُ, رِقاق), لَطيف (لِطاف, لُطَفاءُ)

sub /sʌb/ *n* **1** (submarine) غَوّاصة **2** (infml) (substitute) بَديل (بُدَلاءُ) **3** (infml) (subscription) اشْتِراك (اشْتِراكات)

subcommittee /ˈsʌbkəmɪti/ *n* لَجْنة فَرْعيّة

subconscious /sʌbˈkɒnʃəs/ **A** *adj* ‹mind, desire› لا شُعوريّ [خاصّ بالعَقْلِ الباطِنِ]
B *n* (**the Subconscious**) اللاوَعْي, العَقْل الباطِن

subcontinent /sʌbˈkɒntɪnənt/ *n* شِبْه قارّةٍ

subcontract /sʌbkənˈtrakt/ *vt* تَعاقَدَ من الباطِنِ على ‹the work, maintenance›

subcontracting /sʌbkənˈtraktɪŋ/ *n* تَعاقُد من الباطِنِ, مُقاوَلة فَرْعيّة

subcontractor /sʌbkənˈtraktə/ *n* مُقاوِل من الباطِنِ \ فَرْعيّ, مُتَعَهِّد فَرْعيّ

subcutaneous /sʌbkjuːˈteɪnɪəs/ *adj* ‹tissue, injection› تحت الجِلْدِ

subdivide /sʌbdɪˈvʌɪd/ *vt* قَسَّمَ إلى أَجْزاءٍ أَصْغَرَ, جَزَّأَ ‹land, property, a building›

subdivision /sʌbdɪˈvɪʒ(ə)n/ *n* تَقْسيم إلى أَجْزاءٍ أَصْغَرَ, تَقْسيم فَرْعيّ

subdue /səbˈdjuː/ *vt* **1** كَبَتَ (i; كَبْت) ‹one's passion, excitement› **2** قَهَرَ (a; قَهْر), أَخْضَعَ ‹an enemy, opponent›; قَمَعَ (a; قَمْع) ‹a rebellion, resistance›

subdued /səbˈdjuːd/ *adj* **1** ‹person› مُسْتَكين, حَزين (حُزَناءُ, حَزانى); ‹atmosphere› هادِئ **2** ‹lighting› خافِت; ‹colour› باهِت

subgroup /ˈsʌbɡruːp/ *n* مَجْموعة فَرْعيّة

subheading /ˈsʌbhɛdɪŋ/ *n* عُنْوان فَرْعيّ

subject **A** /ˈsʌbdʒɪkt/ *n* **1** (topic) مَوْضوع (مَوْضوعات, مَواضيعُ); **to change the ~** غَيَّرَ المَوْضوعَ; **to raise a ~** أَثارَ مَوْضوعاً; **can we drop the ~?** هل يُمْكِنُنا أَنْ نَتْرُكَ هذا المَوْضوعَ؟; **while we're on the ~ …** في مَعْرِضِ حَديثِنا عن

… المَوْضوعِ **2** (of study) مَوادُّ مادّة **3** (of a picture, photo) شَخْص] (in an experiment) **4** (مَواضِيعُ ,مَوْضوعات) مَوْضوع مَوْضوعات) مَوْضوع (focus) **5** أو شَيْء يَخْضَعُ للتَجْرِبةِ] (مَواضيعُ); **to be the ~ of an inquiry** كانَ تحت التَحْقيقِ **6** (in grammar) فاعِل **7** (citizen) مُواطِن; **Saudi ~s** مُواطِنونَ سَعوديّونَ

B /'sʌbdʒɪkt/ *adj* **1** (obliged to obey) **to be ~ to a law/rule** «group» كانَ خاضِعاً لِقانونٍ \ لِقاعِدةٍ **2** (liable) **to be ~ to flooding/tax** كانَ عُرْضةً للفَيَضانِ \ لِدَفْعِ ضَريبةٍ; **prices are ~ to increases** الأَسْعارُ مُعَرَّضةٌ للزِيادةِ; **flights are ~ to delay** الرِحْلاتُ عُرْضةٌ للتَأْخيرِ **3** (dependent on) **to be ~ to approval/contract** «decisions, plans» كانَ مُتَوَقِّفاً على المُوافَقةِ \ التَعاقُدِ; '~ **to availability**' رَهْن التَوافُرِ'; **the offer is ~ to availability** العَرْضُ رَهْنُ التَوافُرِ **4** (politically) ‹*people, race*› مُسْتَعْمَر; **they were the first ~ people to break free from their rulers** كانوا أَوَّلَ شَعْبٍ مُسْتَعْمَرٍ يَنْفَصِلُ عن حُكّامِهِ

C /səb'dʒɛkt/ *vt* (to inflict on) **to ~ sb to abuse/insults** عَرَّضَ شَخْصاً لِسوءِ المُعامَلةِ \ للإهانةِ; **to be ~ed to torture** تَعَرَّضَ للتَعْذيبِ

subject heading *n* عُنْوان المَوْضوعِ

subject index *n* (in a book, library) فِهْرِس مَوْضوعاتٍ

subjective /səb'dʒɛktɪv/ *adj* ‹*assessment, opinion*› ذاتيّ, شَخْصيّ

subjectivity /sʌbdʒɛk'tɪvəti/ *n* عَدَم مَوْضوعيّةٍ \ ,تَحَيُّز شَخْصيّ تَجَرُّدٍ

subject matter *n* مَوْضوع البَحْثِ \ الدِراسةِ

subjugate /'sʌbdʒʊgeɪt/ *vt* اسْتَعْبَدَ, قَهَرَ (a; قَهْر), أَخْضَعَ ‹*women, a nation*›

subjunctive /səb'dʒʌŋktɪv/ **A** *adj* ‹*mood, clause*› (in European grammar) احْتِماليّ; (in Arabic grammar) مَنْصوب

B *n* (in European grammar) صيغة الاحْتِمال; (in Arabic grammar) المُضارِع المَنْصوب

sublet /sʌb'lɛt/ *vt* (*present participle* **-tt-**, *past tense, past participle* **sublet**) أَجَّرَ من الباطِنِ ‹*a flat, house*›

sublime /sə'blʌɪm/ *adj* ‹*beauty, music*› سامٍ (سُماة), رائِع, راقٍ

subliminal /sə'blɪmɪn(ə)l/ *adj* ‹*message, level*› لا شُعوريّ, خارِجَ حَيِّزِ الإِدْراكِ

sub-machine gun /sʌbmə'ʃiːn gʌn/ *n* مُسَدَّس رَشّاش

submarine /sʌbmə'riːn/ *n* غَوّاصة

submerge /səb'məːdʒ/ **A** *vt* **1** (to flood) غَمَرَ (u; غَمْر) **2** (to plunge); **to ~ sth in sth** غَطَّسَ شَيْئاً في شَيْءٍ

B *vi* «submarine» غاصَ (u; غَوْص)

submission /səb'mɪʃ(ə)n/ *n* **1** [u] (surrender) خُضوع, إِذْعان, اسْتِسْلام **2** (proposal) عَرْض (عُروض); (application) طَلَب (طَلَبات); (report) تَقْرير (تَقارير)

submissive /səb'mɪsɪv/ *adj* ‹*person, behaviour*› خاضِع (خُضَّع), خانِع, مُذْعِن (خُضْعان)

submit /səb'mɪt/ **A** *vt* (**-tt-**) **1** قَدَّمَ ‹*an application, a report, claim*› **2** (fml) (to suggest) **to ~ that…** … اقْتَرَحَ أَنْ

B *vi* (**-tt-**) (fml) «army, opponent» خَضَعَ (a; خُضوع), اسْتَسْلَمَ; **to ~ to sb/sth** خَضَعَ لِشَخْصٍ \ لِشَيْءٍ

subnormal /sʌb'nɔːm(ə)l/ *adj* **1** ‹*temperatures, reading*› دون المُسْتَوى العاديّ, أَقَلّ تحت المُعَدَّلِ الطَبيعيِّ **2** ‹*intelligence*› من المُعَدَّلِ الطَبيعيِّ; ‹*person*› يُعاني من الضَعْفِ العَقْليِّ

subordinate /sə'bɔːdɪnət/ **A** *adj* ‹*position, officer*› صَغير (صُغَراءُ ,صِغار)

B *n* تابِع, مَرْؤوس (تَبَعة)

subpoena /sə'piːnə/ **A** *n* مُذَكِّرة إِحْضارٍ, أَمْر اسْتِدْعاءٍ (للمَحْكَمةِ)

B *vt* اسْتُدْعِيَ للمَحْكَمةِ ‹*a witness, an official*›

sub-prime /'sʌbprʌɪm/ *adj* ‹*mortgage, loan*› [مُتَعَلِّق بِشَخْصٍ لَهُ تاريخ ائْتِمانيٌّ سَيِّئٌ]

subscribe /səb'skrʌɪb/ *vi* **1** **to ~ to a service/publication** اشْتَرَكَ في خِدْمةٍ \ دَوْريّةٍ; **to ~ to a magazine** اشْتَرَكَ في مَجَلّةٍ; **to ~ to a podcast/email alert** \ اشْتَرَكَ في بودكاسْت نظامِ تَنْبيهٍ بالبَريدِ الإِلكْترونيِّ **2** **to ~ to a theory/view** أَيَّدَ نَظَريّةً \ وُجْهةَ نَظَرٍ

subscriber /səb'skrʌɪbə/ *n* مُشْتَرِك

subscription /səb'skrɪpʃ(ə)n/ *n* اشْتِراك (اشْتِراكات)

subsection /'sʌbsɛkʃ(ə)n/ *n* فِقْرة فَرْعيّة, بَنْد فَرْعيّ

subsequent /ˈsʌbsɪkwənt/ *adj* ‹*years, analysis*› لاحِق ,(تَوالٍ) تالٍ

subsequently /ˈsʌbsɪkwəntli/ *adv* ‹*to become, find*› فيما بَعْدُ, لاحِقاً ,بعد ذلك

subservient /səbˈsəːvɪənt/ *adj* ‹*behaviour, relationship*› خُضوعٍ, خانِع ,(خُضْعان ,خُضَّع) خاضِع ‹*person*›; إذْعانٍ

subset /ˈsʌbsɛt/ *n* مَجْموعة فَرْعيّة \ جُزْئيّة

subside /səbˈsʌɪd/ *vi* 1 «laughter, noise» سَكَنَ (u; سُكون), هَدَأَ (a; هُدوء); **she felt her anger ~** شَعَرَتْ بِغَضَبِها يَهْدَأُ 2 «storm, wind» سَكَنَ (u; سُكون), هَدَأَ (a; هُدوء) 3 «building, land» هَبَطَ (i-u; هُبوط) 4 «floods, water» انْحَسَرَ 5 «swelling, fever, pain» خَفَّ (i; خَفّ), هَدَأَ (a; هَدْء, هُدوء)

subsidence /səbˈsʌɪd(ə)ns, ˈsʌbsɪd(ə)ns/ *n* هُبوط

subsidiary /səbˈsɪdɪəri/ **A** *adj* ‹*role, issue*› فَرْعيّ ,ثانَويّ **B** *n* (also **subsidiary company**) شَرِكة فَرْعيّة

subsidize, -ise (BrE) /ˈsʌbsɪdʌɪz/ *vt* دَعَّمَ ,مَوَّلَ ‹*a service, an industry*›

subsidy /ˈsʌbsɪdi/ *n* (*pl* **subsidies**) دَعْم ماليّ ,إعانة ماليّة

subsist /səbˈsɪst/ *vi* «family, animal» تَقَوَّتَ ,اقْتاتَ ,أعالَ نَفْسَهُ

subsistence /səbˈsɪst(ə)ns/ *n* إعالة \ إعاشة النَفْسِ

subsistence farming *n* زِراعة كَفافٍ \ مَعاشيّة

subsistence level *n* حَدّ \ مُسْتوى الكَفافِ

subsistence wage *n* أجْر كَفافٍ

subsoil /ˈsʌbsɔɪl/ *n* تُرْبة تَحتيّة \ سُفْليّة

substance /ˈsʌbst(ə)ns/ *n* 1 (matter) مادّة (مَوادُّ) 2 (essence) لُبّ (لُبوب) ,جَوْهَر (جَواهِرُ) ,صَميم 3 (weight, validity) ثِقْل (أثْقال) ,وَزْن (أوْزان)

substance abuse *n* إساءة اسْتِخْدامِ ,تَعاطي المُخَدِّراتِ المَوادِّ المُخَدِّرةِ

substandard /sʌbˈstandəd/ *adj* ‹*housing, performance*› دونَ المُسْتوى المَطْلوبِ ,ذو مُسْتَوًى مُتَدَنٍّ

substantial /səbˈstanʃ(ə)l/ *adj* 1 (large) ‹*amount, number*› كَبير, ضَخْم; **two million dollars is a ~ sum** مِلْيونا دولار هو مَبْلَغٌ ضَخْمٌ 2 (significant) ‹*change, difference*› جَوْهَريّ ,أساسيّ; **he made a ~ contribution to our knowledge in this field** أَسْهَمَ إسْهاماً جَوْهَريًّا في زِيادةِ مَعْرِفَتِنا في هذا المَجالِ 3 (solid) ‹*building, furniture*› مَتين 4 (filling) ‹*meal*› ضَخْم ,كَبير

substantially /səbˈstanʃ(ə)li/ *adv* 1 (considerably) ‹*higher, better*› بِدَرَجةٍ كَبيرةٍ ,بِشَكْلٍ هائِلٍ 2 (for the most part) ‹*similar, complete*› إلى حَدٍّ بَعيدٍ ,بِشَكْلٍ جَوْهَريٍّ

substantiate /səbˈstanʃɪeɪt/ *vt* أكَّدَ الصِحّةَ ,أثْبَتَ ‹*a claim, an allegation*›

substantive /ˈsʌbstəntɪv/ *adj* (fml) ‹*issue, evidence*› جَوْهَريّ, أساسيّ

substation /ˈsʌbsteɪʃ(ə)n/ *n* مَحَطّة فَرْعيّة; **a public inquiry will consider the siting of the ~** سَيَكونُ هُناكَ تَحْقيقٌ عامٌّ للنَظَرِ في تَحْديدِ مَوْقِعِ المَحَطّةِ الفَرْعيّةِ

substitute /ˈsʌbstɪtjuːt/ **A** *n* 1 (person) بَديل (بُدَلاءُ) 2 (product, substance) بَديل (بَدائِلُ); **a sugar ~** بَديل للسُكَّرِ; **there is no ~ for a good education** لا بَديلَ عن تَعْليمٍ جَيِّدٍ **B** *vt* 1 (to use instead of) اسْتَبْدَلَ ‹*a component, an ingredient*›; **you can ~ sugar for honey in this recipe** يُمْكِنُكَ أنْ تَسْتَخْدِمَ السُكَّرَ بَدَلاً من العَسَلِ في هذه الوَصْفةِ 2 (to replace with) اسْتَبْدَلَ (ب) ‹*a word, player, a material*›; **to ~ a player** اسْتَبْدَلَ لاعِباً **C** *vi* 1 **to ~ for sth** «ingredients, materials» أغْنى عن شَيْءٍ 2 **to ~ for sb** «players, colleagues» حَلَّ مَحَلَّ شَخْصٍ

substitute family *n* أُسْرة بَديلة

substitute player *n* لاعِب بَديل

substitute teacher *n* مُدَرِّس بَديل

substitution /sʌbstɪˈtjuːʃ(ə)n/ *n* اسْتِبْدال (اسْتِبْدالات), اسْتِعاضة

subterfuge /ˈsʌbtəfjuːdʒ/ *n* 1 [u] (trickery) خِداع ,تَحايُل 2 (trick) حيلة (حِيَل) ,خُدْعة (خُدَع ,خُدُعات)

subterranean /ˌsʌbtəˈreɪnɪən/ *adj* ‹*passage, chamber*› تحت الأرْضِ; ‹*water*› جَوْفيّ

subtitle /ˈsʌbtʌɪt(ə)l/ **A** *n* 1 (subordinate title) عُنْوان فَرْعيّ 2 (**subtitles** *n pl*) (captions) تَرْجمة (تُعْرَضُ على الشاشة) **B** *vt* 1 تَرْجَمَ (للعَرْضِ على الشاشة) ‹*a film, DVD*› 2 وَضَعَ عُنْواناً فَرْعيًّا ل ‹*a book*›

subtitled /ˈsʌbtʌɪt(ə)ld/ *adj* مُتَرْجَم ‹*movie*›

subtle /'sʌt(ə)l/ *adj* (**subtler**, **subtlest**) **1** (not obvious) <*change, difference*> طَفِيف ,دَقِيق; **his humour is very ~** روحُ الدُعابةِ عِنْدَهُ خَفيفةٌ جِدًّا **2** (delicate) <*flavour, effect*> خَفِيف (خِفاف), **3** (indirect) <*approach*> غَيْر مُباشِرٍ; <*hint*> رَقِيق (رِقاق ,أَرِقّاءُ) خَفيّ

subtlety /'sʌtəlti/ *n* (*pl* **subtleties**) **1** [u] (delicacy) رِقّة ,خِفّة **2** [u] (tact) كِياسة ,بَراعة ,حِذْق **3** (distinction, nuance) خَفيّة (خَفايا) ,بُعْد خَفيّ ,أَمْر دَقِيق

subtly /'sʌtli/ *adv* **1** (not obviously) <*to change, shift*> على نَحْوٍ غَيْر مَلْحوظٍ **2** (delicately) <*coloured, flavoured*> بِشَكْلٍ طَفيفٍ, بِدَرجةٍ خَفيفةٍ **3** (indirectly, tactfully) <*to suggest, influence*> بِشَكْلٍ غَيْر مُباشِرٍ

subtotal /'sʌbtəʊt(ə)l/ *n* مَجْموع جُزْئيّ ,إجْماليّ فَرْعيّ

subtract /səb'trakt/ *vt* طَرَحَ (في الحِسابِ) <*a number, an amount*>; **~ nine from thirty** اطْرَحْ تِسْعةً من ثَلاثينَ

subtraction /səb'trakʃ(ə)n/ *n* طَرْح (في الحِسابِ)

suburb /'sʌbəːb/ *n* ضاحِية (ضَواحٍ); **the ~s** الضَواحي

suburban /sə'bəːb(ə)n/ *adj* <*area, home, street*> في ضاحِيةٍ

suburbia /sə'bəːbɪə/ *n* (suburbs) الضَواحي; (inhabitants) سُكّان \ أَهْل الضَواحي

subversive /səb'vəːsɪv/ *adj* <*activity, organization*> هَدّام ,تَخْريبيّ

subvert /səb'vəːt/ *vt* قَوَّضَ ,أَفْسَدَ ,خَرَّبَ <*a policy, system*>

subway /'sʌbweɪ/ *n* **1** (AmE) (underground railway) مِترو \ قِطار أَنْفاقٍ; **the New York S~** قِطار أَنْفاقِ نيويورْك **2** (BrE) (for pedestrians) نَفَق مُشاةٍ

sub-zero /sʌb'zɪərəʊ/ *adj* <*temperatures, conditions*> تحت الصِفْرِ, دون دَرَجة التَجَمُّدِ

succeed /sək'siːd/ **A** *vt* خَلَفَ (u; خَلَف) <*a president, monarch*>; **he ~ed his father as king** خَلَفَ والِدَهُ على العَرْشِ

B *vi* **1** «person, government, plan, efforts» نَجَحَ (a; نَجاح), أَفْلَحَ; **he only ~ed in making things worse** لم يَنْجَحْ إلاّ في جَعْلِ الأُمورِ أَكْثَرَ سوءاً; **they tried to get in, but didn't ~** حاوَلوا الدُخولَ، وَلَكِنَّهُمْ لم يَنْجَحوا; **I knew the plan would never ~** كُنْتُ أَعْلَمُ أنّ المَشْروعَ لن يَنْجَحَ أَبَداً; **to ~ in life** نَجَحَ في حَياتِهِ **2** **to ~ to the throne** وَرِثَ العَرْشَ; **to ~ to a title** وَرِثَ لَقَباً

succeeding /sək'siːdɪŋ/ *adj* <*generations, years*> لاحِق ,تالٍ (تَوالٍ)

success /sək'ses/ *n* **1** [u] (achievement, prosperity) نَجاح (نَجاحات) ,تَوْفيق; **we have had some ~ with this treatment** حَقَّقْنا بَعْضَ النَجاحِ مع هذا العِلاجِ; **I tried to convince her, without much ~** حاوَلْتُ إقْناعَها دون نَجاحٍ يُذْكَرُ **2** (successful thing) شَيْء ناجِح; (successful person) شَخْص ناجِح; **to be a ~** كانَ ناجِحاً

successful /sək'sɛsfʊl/ *adj* **1** <*operation, campaign*> ناجِح, مُوَفَّق; **how to be ~ in business** كيف تَكونُ ناجِحاً في التِجارةِ; **~ candidates/applicants** المُرَشَّحونَ \ المُتَقَدِّمونَ الناجِحونَ **2** <*career, writer, film*> ناجِح

successfully /sək'sɛsf(ə)li/ *adv* <*to complete, use*> بِنَجاحٍ

succession /sək'sɛʃ(ə)n/ *n* **1** (act of following) تَوالٍ, تَتابُع (تَعاقُبات) تَعاقُب; **he won for the third year in ~** فازَ للعامِ الثالِثِ على التَوالي; **in quick *or* rapid ~** في تَتابُعٍ سَريعٍ **2** (series) سِلْسِلة (سَلاسِلُ) **3** (to the throne, title, presidency) خِلافة

successive /sək'sesɪv/ *adj* <*victory, year*> مُتَتابِع ,مُتَعاقِب ,مُتَتالٍ

successor /sək'sesə/ *n* خَليفة (خُلَفاءُ) ,خَلَف (أَخْلاف); **the ~ to the throne/position** خَليفة للعَرْشِ \ للمَنْصِبِ

success rate *n* مُعَدَّل \ نِسْبة نَجاحٍ

success story *n* قِصّة نَجاحٍ

succinct /sək'sɪŋkt/ *adj* (fml) <*answer, description*> موجَز ,مُقْتَضَب

succulent /'sʌkjʊlənt/ *adj* **1** (of food) <*fruit, meat*> غَضّ **2** (of plants) <*leaf, stem*> كَثير العُصارة ,عُصاريّ

succumb /sə'kʌm/ *vi* (fml) (to fail to resist) **to ~ to temptation/pressure** اسْتَسْلَمَ للإغْراءِ \ للضُغوطِ

such /sʌtʃ/ **A** *determiner* **1** (as previously indicated) مِثْل هذا, كَهَذا; **there has never been ~ a situation** لم يَحْدُثْ مِثْلُ هذا المَوْقِفِ أَبَداً; **we have to work together at ~ a time** عَلَيْنا أنْ نَعْمَلَ مَعاً في مِثْلِ هذا الوَقْتِ; **food, clothing and ~ basic necessities are in short supply** هُناكَ نَقْصٌ في الطَعامِ والمَلْبَسِ وَمِثْلِ هذه الاحْتياجاتِ الأَساسيّةِ; **a clerk or some ~ functionary** كاتِب أو مُوَظَّف في مِثْلِ هذا المَنْصِبِ; **there's no ~ person** لا يوجَدُ شَخْصٌ بِهَذا الوَصْفِ; **there was ~ a post I believe** أَعْتَقِدُ أَنَّهُ كانَ هُناكَ وَظيفةٌ كَهَذِهِ; **there's no ~ thing**

لم أَسْمَعْ بِمِثْلِ هذا الشَّيْءِ أَبَداً; لا يوجَدُ شَيْءٌ كَهَذا; **I've never heard of ~ a thing** لم أَقُلْ شَيْئاً من هذا القَبيلِ; **I didn't say any ~ thing** لن تَفْعَلَ شَيْئاً كَهَذا! **you'll do no ~ thing!** ② (fml) (of specific kind) **to be ~ that ...** كانَ كَبيراً \ كَثيراً لِدَرَجةِ أَنّ ...; **the pain was ~ that drugs were prescribed** كانَ الأَلَمُ شَديداً لِدَرَجةِ أَنَّهُ تَمَّ وَصْفُ أَدْوِيةٍ; **he asked in ~ a way that it was very difficult to say no** سَأَلَ بطَريقةٍ جَعَلَتْ من الصَّعْبِ جِدًّا الإجابة بِلا ③ (any possible) **~ money as I have** كُلّ ما لَدَيَّ من المالِ; **until ~ time as ...** حتّى يَأْتِيَ الوَقْتُ الّذي ... ④ (so great) شَديد, هائِل, عَظيم; **I had ~ a headache!** كانَ لَدَيَّ صُداعٌ شَديدٌ!; **there was ~ chaos!** كانَتْ هُناكَ فَوْضى عارِمةٌ!; **we had ~ fun** اسْتَمْتَعْنا كَثيراً; **to be in ~ despair/in ~ a rage** كانَ في حالةِ يَأْسٍ \ غَضَبٍ شَديدٍ; **we are having ~ problems** لَدَيْنا مَشاكِلُ كَبيرةٌ; **she's ~ a nice girl** هي فَتاةٌ لَطيفةٌ جِدًّا ⑤ (infml) (of such small worth, quantity) **you can borrow my boots ~ as they are** يُمْكِنُكَ أَنْ تَسْتَعيرَ حِذائي على عِلاّتِهِ; **we picked the apples ~ as there were** قَطَفْنا التُفّاحَ مع رَداءَتِهِ

B *adv* (to a great degree) بِدَرَجةٍ كَبيرةٍ, إلى حَدٍّ كَبيرٍ; **~ excellent meals** وَجَبات مُمْتازة جِدًّا; **~ good quality as this** بِمِثْلِ هذه الدَرَجةِ من الجَوْدةِ العالِيةِ; **it was ~ a lot of fun** كانَ مُمْتِعاً جِدًّا

C *pron* ① (to be indicated) هَكَذا; **she's talented and recognized as ~** هي مَوْهوبةٌ وَيُعْتَرَفُ لَها بِذلِكَ; **the damage was ~ that it cost $5,000 to repair** كانَ الضَرَرُ بالِغاً لِدَرَجةِ أَنّ إصْلاحَهُ تَكَلَّفَ 5,000 دولارٍ; **~ is life** هَكَذا هي الحَياةُ ② ▸ **suchlike** A

D (**such as**) *determiner phr, conj phr* مِثْل; **a house ~ as this one, ~ a house as this one** بَيْت مِثْل هذا; **we need a person ~ as her** نَحْتاجُ إلى شَخْصٍ مِثْلِها; **it was on ~ a night as this that ...** كانَ ذلك في لَيْلةٍ كَهَذِهِ عِنْدَما ...; **there is no ~ thing as a free lunch** لا يوجَدُ شَيْءٌ بِلا مُقابِلٍ; **'some of his songs are very poor' — '~ as?'** 'بَعْضُ أَغانيهِ رَديئةٌ' — 'مِثْلُ ماذا؟'; **have you ~ a thing as a screwdriver?** هل أَجِدُ لَدَيْكَ مِفَكًّا؟

such-and-such /'sʌtʃ(ə)n,sʌtʃ/ *adj* كَذا وَكَذا, كَيْتَ وَكَيْتَ

suchlike /'sʌtʃlʌɪk/ (infml) **A** *pron* وَما إلى ذلك, ما شابَهَ ذلك; **lions, tigers, and ~** أُسود وَنُمور، وَما شابَهَ ذلك

B *adj* مُشابِه; **caviar, salmon, and ~ delicacies** كافِيار وَسَلْمون، وَما شابَهَ ذلك من الأَطْعِمةِ الشَهيّةِ

suck /sʌk/ **A** *vt* ① (to draw in) شَفَطَ (i; شَفْط), امْتَصَّ ‹*liquid, air*›; **to ~ milk through a straw** شَرِبَ اللَبَنَ بِمَصّاصةٍ \ بِشَفّاطةٍ ② (to extract) شَفَطَ (i; شَفْط), امْتَصَّ; **to ~ poison from a wound** شَفَطَ السُمَّ من الجُرْحِ ③ «baby» مَصَّ (a-u; مَصّ), رَضَعَ (a-i; رَضْع, رَضاع, رَضاعة; من) ‹*the breast*› ④ (in one's mouth) مَصَّ (a-u; مَصّ) ‹*an orange, a sweet*›; **he still ~s his thumb** ما زالَ يَمُصُّ إبْهامَهُ ⑤ (to pull) «currents, quicksand, mud» شَدَّ (i-u; شَدّ), جَذَبَ (i; جَذْب) ‹*a person*›; **to be ~ed under the water** انْجَرَفَ تحت الماءِ; **to get ~ed into the argument** انْجَرَفَ إلى الجَدَلِ

B *vi* ① (with the mouth) مَصَّ (a-u; مَصّ); **to ~ on a pipe/sweet** دَخَّنَ غَلْيوناً \ مَصَّ حَلْوى; **to ~ at the bottle/breast** رَضَعَ من الزُجاجةِ \ الثَدْيِ ② (infml) (to be terrible) **that ~s!** ذلك فَظيعٌ!; **the new goal keeper ~s** حارِسُ المَرْمى الجَديدُ فَظيعٌ

C *n* مَصّ

(Idioms) **to suck it up** (AmE) (infml) لَمْلَمَ جُرْحَهُ; **to suck sb dry** (infml) سَحَبَ \ اسْتَنْزَفَ من شَخْصٍ كُلَّ أَمْوالِهِ

(Phrasal verbs) **suck in** **A** **~ in [sth], ~ [sth] in** (to draw in) شَفَطَ [شَيْئاً] ‹*air, dirt, liquid*›; **to ~ in one's cheeks** شَفَطَ خَدَّيْهِ **B** **~ in [sb], ~ [sb] in** (to involve) وَرَّطَ [شَخْصاً] ‹*a person*›

• **suck up** **A** (infml) (to be obsequious) تَمَلَّقَ, داهَنَ, تَزَلَّفَ (إلى); **to ~ up to sb** تَمَلَّقَ \ داهَنَ شَخْصاً **B** **~ [sth] up, ~ up [sth]** امْتَصَّ \ شَفَطَ [شَيْئاً] ‹*dirt, liquid*›

sucker /'sʌkə/ *n* ① (on plants) فَرْع (مُنْبَثِق من الجِذْرِ) ② (infml) (fool) شَخْص أَبْلَه \ مُغَفَّل

(Idiom) **to be a sucker for punishment** كانَ يُحِبُّ الإتْقانَ

suckle /'sʌk(ə)l/ **A** *vt* أَرْضَعَ ‹*a baby, calf*›

B *vi* «babies, calves» رَضَعَ (a-i; رَضْع, رَضاع, رَضاعة)

sucrose /'su:krəʊz, 'su:krəʊs/ *n* سَكَروز

suction /'sʌkʃ(ə)n/ *n* شَفْط, سَحْب, مَصّ, امْتِصاص (امْتِصاصات)

suction pad *n* قاعِدة شَفْطٍ

Sudan /suːˈdɑːn/ *pr n* (also **the Sudan**) السودان (f); **the Republic of ~** جُمْهوريّة السودان

Sudanese /suːdəˈniːz/ *n, adj* (*n pl* **Sudanese**) سودانيّ

sudden /ˈsʌd(ə)n/ *adj* ‹*movement, increase*› مُفاجِئ, مُباغِت; **all of a ~** فَجْأةً

sudden death *n* شَوْط كَسْرِ التَعادُلِ

suddenly /ˈsʌd(ə)nli/ *adv* ‹*to die, realize*› فَجْأةً, على نَحْوٍ مُفاجِئٍ, بَغْتَةً

sudoku /suːˈdəʊkuː/ *n* سودوكو (لُعْبة)

suds /sʌdz/ *n pl* (also **soapsuds**) رَغْوة الصابون

sue /sjuː/ **A** *vt* أقامَ دَعْوى على, قاضى ‹*an employer, a newspaper*›; **to ~ sb for divorce/damages** رَفَعَ دَعْوى طَلاقٍ \ تَعْويضاتٍ على شَخْصٍ **B** *vi* «victims, plaintiffs» رَفَعَ دَعْوى قَضائيّةً

suede /sweɪd/ *n* جِلْد سُويديّ

suet /ˈsuːɪt, ˈsjuːɪt/ *n* كُظْر (شَحْم كُلْيَتَيِ الخَروفِ أو البَقَرِ)

suffer /ˈsʌfə/ **A** *vt* (to experience) عانى (من) ‹*pain, loss, a defeat*›; **to ~ a heart attack** أُصيبَ بِنَوْبةٍ قَلْبيّةٍ; **she ~ed a great deal of pain** عانَتْ من قَدْرٍ كَبيرٍ من الألَمِ; **our forces have ~ed heavy losses** تَكَبَّدَتْ قوّاتُنا خَسائِرَ ثَقيلةً; **to ~ the consequences** عانى من العَواقِبِ

B *vi* **1** (with illnesses) **to ~ from an illness/condition** عانى من مَرَضٍ \ حالةٍ; **she ~s from depression** تُعاني من الاكْتِئابِ; **do you ~ from high blood pressure?** هل تُعاني من ارْتِفاعِ ضَغْطِ الدَمِ؟ **2** (to have negative experiences) عانى, قاسى; **the civilian population ~ed most** كانَ السُكّانُ المَدَنيّونَ الأكْثَرَ مُعاناةً **3** (to do badly) «companies, profits, sb's popularity» تَدَهْوَرَ; **her health is beginning to ~** تَبْدَأُ صِحَّتُها في التَدَهْوُرِ; **the minister's popularity ~ed** تَراجَعَتْ شَعْبيّةُ الوَزيرِ

sufferer /ˈsʌf(ə)rə/ *n* مُعانٍ; **arthritis ~s, ~s of arthritis** مُعانونَ من الْتِهابِ المَفاصِلِ

suffering /ˈsʌfərɪŋ/ *n* مُعاناة

suffice /səˈfaɪs/ *vi* (fml) «sum, warning» كَفى (i; كِفاية), وَفى بالغَرَضِ; **~ to say, that ...** يَكْفي القَوْلُ إنّ ...

sufficient /səˈfɪʃ(ə)nt/ *adj* ‹*resources, time*› كافٍ (كُفاة); **to be ~ for our needs** كانَ كافِياً لِاحْتِياجاتِنا

sufficiently /səˈfɪʃ(ə)ntli/ *adv* ‹*to develop, recover*› على نَحْوٍ \ بِشَكْلٍ كافٍ

suffix /ˈsʌfɪks/ *n* لاحِقة (لَواحِقُ)

suffocate /ˈsʌfəkeɪt/ **A** *vt* **1** (to smother) خَنَقَ (u; خَنْق) ‹*a victim, baby*› **2** (emotionally) خَنَقَ (u; خَنْق) ‹*a loved one*› **B** *vi* **1** (from lack of oxygen) «people» اخْتَنَقَ **2** (mentally) «young people» شَعَرَ بالاخْتِناقِ

suffocating /ˈsʌfəkeɪtɪŋ/ *adj* **1** (stifling) ‹*smoke, heat*› خانِق **2** (emotionally) ‹*marriage, conventions*› خانِق

suffocation /sʌfəˈkeɪʃ(ə)n/ *n* اخْتِناق (اخْتِناقات)

suffrage /ˈsʌfrɪdʒ/ *n* حَقّ الانْتِخابِ \ التَصْويتِ \ الاقْتِراعِ; **to fight for universal ~** كافَحَ من أجْلِ حَقِّ التَصْويتِ العامِّ

Sufi /ˈsuːfi/ (*pl* **Sufi, Sufis**) *n* صوفيّ

Sufism /ˈsuːfɪz(ə)m/ *n* صوفيّة

sugar /ˈʃʊgə/ *n* سُكَّر; **granulated ~** سُكَّر مُحَبَّب

sugar beet *n* شَمَنْدَر السُكَّرِ \ بَنْجَر, لِفْت سُكَّريّ (Tunisia)

sugar cane *n* قَصَب السُكَّرِ

sugar-free /ʃʊgəˈfriː/ *adj* ‹*drink, diet*› خالٍ من السُكَّرِ

sugar lump *n* قِطْعة سُكَّرٍ

sugar refinery *n* مَعْمَل \ مَصْنَع تَكْرير السُكَّرِ

sugary /ˈʃʊg(ə)ri/ *adj* **1** (sweet) ‹*snack, cereal*› حُلْو (مُحَلّى بالسُكَّرِ أكْثَرَ من اللازِمِ) **2** (sentimental) ‹*smile, words*› مَعْسول

suggest /səˈdʒest/ *vt* **1** (to put forward) اقْتَرَحَ ‹*a solution, possibility, an idea*›; **what are you ~ing?** ماذا تَقْتَرِحُ؟; **I ~ that we get rid of it** أَقْتَرِحُ أنْ نَتَخَلَّصَ مِنْهُ; **she ~ed a fifteen-minute break** اقْتَرَحَتْ راحة لِمُدّةِ خَمْسَ عشرة دَقيقة; **can you ~ how it happened?** هل يُمْكِنُكَ أنْ تُفَسِّرَ كيف حدث ذلك؟ **2** (to recommend) رَشَّحَ, اقْتَرَحَ ‹*a place, candidate*›; **can you ~ a place to meet?** هل يُمْكِنُكَ أنْ تُرَشِّحَ مَكاناً للمُقابَلةِ؟; **I ~ed him for the job** رَشَّحْتُهُ للوَظيفةِ; **I ~ that you leave at once** أَقْتَرِحُ أنْ تَرْحَلَ على الفَوْرِ **3** (fml) (to indicate) «the evidence, tests, results» أشارَ; **the evidence ~s that ...** يُشيرُ الدَليلُ إلى أنّ ...; **an idea ~ed itself to me** تَراءَتْ لي فِكْرةٌ **4** (to evoke) «style, images» نَمَّ (i-u; نَمّ) (عن) ‹*an influence, origin*›

suggestion /sə'dʒestʃ(ə)n/ *n* 1 (proposal) اقْتِراح (اقْتِراحات); **to make a ~** تَقَدَّمَ بِاقْتِراحٍ; **to be open to ~s** كانَ مُنْفَتِحاً على كُلِّ الاقْتِراحاتِ 2 (trace) أَثَر (آثار) 3 (insinuation) إشارة

suggestive /sə'dʒestɪv/ *adj* 1 (evocative) ‹*style, writing*› موحٍ; **to be ~ of sth** كانَ موحِياً بِشَيْءٍ 2 (indecent) ‹*outfit*› مُثير; ‹*remark*› ذو إيحاءاتٍ جِنْسيّةٍ

suicidal /suːɪ'sʌɪd(ə)l/ *adj* ‹*tendency, thoughts*› انْتِحاريّ

suicide /'suːɪsʌɪd/ *n* انْتِحار (انْتِحارات); **to commit ~** انْتَحَرَ

suicide attack *n* هُجوم انْتِحاريّ

suicide bomb *n* تَفْجير انْتِحاريّ

suicide bomber *n* انْتِحاريّ

suit /suːt/ A *n* 1 بَدْلة (بَدَلات)، بِذْلة (بِذَل)، بِزّة; **to wear a ~ and tie** ارْتَدى بَدْلةً وَرَبْطةَ عُنُقٍ; **two-/three-piece ~** بَدْلة من قِطْعَتَيْنِ \ ثَلاثِ قِطَعٍ; **a ~ of armour** دِرْع (دُروع، أَدْرُع) 2 (legal action) ▸ **lawsuit** 3 (in cards) أَوْراق اللَّعِبِ ذات النَّقْشِ الواحِدِ[

B *vt* 1 (to flatter) «colours, outfits» ناسَبَ ‹*a person*›; **red doesn't ~ you** الأَحْمَرُ لا يُناسِبُكَ 2 (to be convenient) «dates, arrangements» ناسَبَ، لاءَمَ ‹*a person*›; **does Sunday ~ you?** هل يُناسِبُكَ الأَحَدُ؟; **it's an arrangement that ~s my needs** هذا تَرْتيبٌ يُناسِبُ احْتِياجاتي 3 (to be beneficial) «sea air, the change» لاءَمَ ‹*a person*›; **this climate doesn't ~ me** هذا المَناخُ لا يُلائِمُني

C *vi* «time, date, day» كانَ مُناسِباً; **does 9.30 ~?** هل 9.30 مُناسِبٌ؟

D *v refl* **to ~ oneself** فَعَلَ ما رَآهُ مُناسِباً; **~ yourself!** افْعَلْ ما تَراهُ مُناسِباً!

(Idioms) **to be sb's strong suit** كانَ نُقْطةَ القُوّةِ لدى شَخْصٍ; **to suit sb down to the ground** لاءَمَ شَخْصاً إلى أَبْعَدِ حَدٍّ

suitable /'suːtəb(ə)l/ *adj* ‹*accommodation, candidate, clothing*› مُناسِب، مُلائِم

suitably /'suːtəbli/ *adv* ‹*qualified, equipped*› بِشَكْلٍ مُناسِبٍ \ مُلائِمٍ

suitcase /'suːtkeɪs/ *n* حَقيبة (لِلسَّفَرِ)

suite /swiːt/ *n* 1 (of rooms) جَناح (أَجْنِحة) 2 (of furniture) طَقْم مَفْروشاتٍ

suited /'suːtɪd/ *adj* **to be ~ to a job** كانَ مُناسِباً لِعَمَلٍ; **they are very well ~** هُما مُتَناسِبانِ جِدًّا

suitor /'suːtə/ *n* مُتَقَدِّم للزَواجِ (خُطّاب)، خاطِب

sulk /sʌlk/ *vi* «children, adolescents» عَبَسَ (i; عُبوس، عَبْس)، تَجَهَّمَ

sulky /'sʌlki/ *adj* (**sulkier**, **sulkiest**) ‹*mood, teenager*› عابِس

sullen /'sʌlən/ *adj* ‹*mood, silence*› مُتَجَهِّم

sulphur (BrE), **sulfur** (AmE) /'sʌlfə/ *n* كِبْريت

sulphuric acid (BrE), **sulfuric acid** (AmE) /sʌlfjʊərɪk 'asɪd/ *n* زَيْت الزاجِ، حَمْض الكِبْريتيك \ الكِبْريتِ

sultan /'sʌlt(ə)n/ *n* سُلْطان (سَلاطينُ)

sultana /sʌl'tɑːnə/ *n* 1 (fruit) كِشْمِش (زَبيب خالٍ من البُذورِ) 2 (sultan's wife) زَوْجة السُلْطانِ، سُلْطانة; (sultan's sister) أُخْت السُلْطانِ; (sultan's daughter) بِنْت السُلْطانِ

sultry /'sʌltri/ *adj* (**sultrier**, **sultriest**) 1 (humid) ‹*weather, night*› شَديد الحَرارةِ والرُطوبةِ 2 (sensual) ‹*voice, look*› مُثير (جِنْسيًّا)

sum /sʌm/ *n* 1 (of money) مَبْلَغ (مَبالِغُ); **a large/small ~ of money** مَبْلَغ كَبير \ صَغير من المالِ 2 (calculation) حِساب (حِسابات); **to be good at ~s** كانَ جَيِّداً في الحِسابِ; **to do one's ~s** حَسَبَ حِساباتِهِ 3 ▸ **sum total**

(Phrasal verb) **sum up** A (in a speech) «speaker» لَخَّصَ; **to ~ up, I'd like to say ...** لِتَلْخيصِ ما سَبَقَ، أُحِبُّ أَنْ أَقولَ ... B **~ up [sth]** 1 (to summarize) لَخَّصَ [شَيْئاً] ‹*an argument, the pros and cons*› 2 (to assess) قَيَّمَ [شَيْئاً] ‹*a situation, person*›

Sumatra /sʊ'mɑːtrə/ *pr n* سومَطْرة

summarize, -ise (BrE) /'sʌmərʌɪz/ *vt* لَخَّصَ ‹*an article, the evidence*›

summary /'sʌm(ə)ri/ *n* (*pl* **summaries**) مُلَخَّص (مُلَخَّصات)

summer /'sʌmə/ A *n* صَيْف (أَصْياف); **last/next ~** الصَيْف الأَخير \ القادِم; **in the ~ of 2010** في صَيْفِ 2010; **in ~ we use less electricity** نَسْتَخْدِمُ كَمّيّةً أَقَلَّ من الكَهْرَباءِ في الصَيْفِ; **to spend the ~ on the French Riviera** قَضى الصَيْفَ في الريفييرا الفَرَنْسيّةِ

B *adj before n* ‹*evening, clothes*› صَيْفيّ; **where are you going to buy your ~ clothes?** من أَيْنَ سَتَشْتَري ثِيابَكَ الصَيْفيّةَ؟

summer camp *n* (AmE) مُخَيَّم صَيْفِيّ

summer holiday (BrE), **summer vacation** (AmE) *n* عُطْلة صَيْفِيّة; **where are you spending your summer holiday** (BrE)/**vacation** (AmE)? أَيْنَ سَتَقْضي عُطْلَتَكَ الصَيْفِيّةَ؟

summer house *n* [كوخ في الحَديقة أو المُنْتَزَه لِاتِّقاءِ حَرارة الشَمْسِ صَيفاً]

summer school *n* مَدْرَسة صَيْفِيّة

summertime /'sʌmətʌɪm/ *n* صَيْف (أَصْياف)

summery /'sʌm(ə)ri/ *adj* ‹*dress, weather*› صَيْفِيّ

summing-up /sʌmɪŋ'ʌp/ *n* (*pl* **summings-up**) اِسْتِعْراض شامِل (يُقَدِّمُ فيه القاضي الأَدِلّةَ والبَراهينَ)

summit /'sʌmɪt/ *n* **1** (of mountain) قِمّة (قِمَم) **2** (meeting) قِمّة (قِمَم)

summon /'sʌmən/ *vt* **1** (fml) (to send for) اِسْتَدْعى ‹*a doctor, servant*› **2** (to serve with a summons) اِسْتَدْعى ‹*a witness, defendant*›

(Phrasal verb) **summon up**: ~ **up [sth] 1** (to gather) اِسْتَجْمَعَ [شَيْئاً] ‹*one's enthusiasm, energy*› **2** (to evoke) اِسْتَحْضَرَ [شَيْئاً] ‹*a memory, an image*›

summons /'sʌmənz/ **A** *n* (*pl* **summonses**) اِسْتِدْعاء (مِن المَحْكَمة)

B *vt* اِسْتَدْعى ‹*a witness, defendant*›

sumo /'su:məʊ/ *n* (also **sumo wrestling**) سومو (مُصارَعة يابانِيّة)

sumptuous /'sʌmptjʊəs/ *adj* ‹*feast, surroundings*› باذِخ, فاخِر

sum total *n* **1** (of money) مَبْلَغ إجْمالِيّ **2** (of achievements) مَجْموع; **the sum total of his achievements** مَجْموع إنْجازاتِهِ

sun /sʌn/ **A** *n* شَمْس (f; شُموس); **to sit in the ~** جَلَسَ في الشَمْسِ; **come in out of the ~** اُدْخُل بَعيدا عن الشَمْسِ; **the ~ has come out/gone in** ظَهَرت \ تَوارت الشَمْسُ; **they sell everything under the ~** يَبيعونَ كُلَّ ما يَخْطُرُ على البالِ

B *v refl* **(-nn-) to ~ oneself** «people, animals» تَشَمَّسَ

sunbathe /'sʌnbeɪð/ *vi* «holidaymakers, lizards» تَشَمَّسَ

sunbeam /'sʌnbi:m/ *n* شُعاع شَمْسٍ

sunbed /'sʌnbɛd/ *n* (BrE) **1** (lounger) كُرْسِيّ تَشَمُّسٍ **2** (with sunlamp) سَرير تَسْمير البَشَرة

sunblock /'sʌnblɒk/ *n* واقٍ شَمْسِيّ

sunburn /'sʌnbə:n/ *n* حُروق الشَمْسِ

sunburned, **sunburnt** /'sʌnbə:nd/ *adj* ‹*one's back, face*› مُصاب بِحُروقِ الشَمْسِ

sundae /'sʌndeɪ/ *n* [بوظة بالفَواكِهِ والمُكَسَّراتِ]

Sunday /'sʌndeɪ, 'sʌndi/ *n* (يَوْم) الأَحَد; **to go to church on ~s** ذَهَبَ إلى الكَنيسةِ أَيّامَ الأَحَدِ; ▸ **Wednesday**

Sunday best *n* [أَفْضَل المَلابِسِ للصَلاة في الكَنيسة]

sundial /'sʌndʌɪəl/ *n* مِزْوَلة (ساعة شَمْسِيّة)

sundown /'sʌndaʊn/ *n* مَغيب, غُروب

sundress /'sʌndrɛs/ *n* [فُسْتان عاري الظَهْرِ والذِراعَيْنِ]

sundries /'sʌndriz/ *n pl* **1** (expenses) مَصاريف نَثْرِيّة **2** (fml) (goods) مَوادّ مُتَنَوِّعة

sundry /'sʌndri/ *adj* ‹*items, expenses*› مُتَنَوِّع; **all and ~** الجَميع دون اسْتِثْناءٍ

sunflower /'sʌnflaʊə/ *n* عَبّاد \ دَوّار الشَمْس

sung /sʌŋ/ *past participle* ▸ **sing**

sunglasses /'sʌnglɑ:sɪz/ *n pl* نَظّارات شَمْسِيّة

sun hat *n* قُبَّعة شَمْسِيّة

sunk /sʌŋk/ *past participle* ▸ **sink**

sunken /'sʌŋk(ə)n/ *adj* **1** (in the sea) ‹*treasure, wreck*› غارِق, مَغْمور **2** (hollow) ‹*eyes, cheeks*› غائِر **3** (low-level) ‹*bath, garden*› مُنْخَفِض

sunlamp /'sʌnlamp/ *n* مِصْباح شَمْسِيّ

sun letter *n* حَرْف شَمْسِيّ

sunlight /'sʌnlʌɪt/ *n* ضَوْء \ نور الشَمْسِ

sunlit /'sʌnlɪt/ *adj* ‹*room, garden*› مُشْمِس, مُنار بِضَوْءِ الشَمْسِ

Sunna /'sʊnə, 'sʌnə/ *n* سُنّة

Sunni /'sʌni/ **A** *n* **1** [u] (religion) المَذْهَب السُنّيّ **2** (*pl* **Sunni**, **Sunnis**) (adherent) سُنّيّ

B *adj* ‹*cleric, Muslim*› سُنّيّ

sunny /'sʌni/ *adj* (**sunnier, sunniest**) **1** (bright) ‹*day, room*› مُشْمِس **2** (cheerful) ‹*disposition, smile*› مَرِح, مُشْرِق; **to look on the ~ side** نَظَرَ إلى الجانِبِ المُشْرِقِ

sunrise /'sʌnrʌɪz/ *n* الشُروق, وَقْت شُروقِ الشَمْسِ; **at/before ~** عند \ قبل الشُروقِ

sunroof /ˈsʌnruːf/ *n* نافِذة السَّقْفِ (في السَّيّارةِ)

sunscreen /ˈsʌnskriːn/ *n* واقٍ شَمْسيّ

sunset /ˈsʌnset/ *n* مَغيب ,غُروب ,وَقْت غُروبِ الشَّمْسِ; **at/before ~** عند \ قبل الغُروبِ

sunshade /ˈsʌnʃeɪd/ *n* 1 شَمْسيّة ,(مِظَلّات) مِظَلّة 2 (**sunshades** *n pl*) نَظّارات شَمْسيّة

sunshine /ˈsʌnʃʌɪn/ *n* ضوء \ أَشِعّة الشَّمْسِ

sunspot /ˈsʌnspɒt/ *n* كَلْفة \ بُقْعة شَمْسيّة

sunstroke /ˈsʌnstrəʊk/ *n* ضَرْبة شَمْسٍ

suntan /ˈsʌntan/ *n* اسْمِرار (بِسَبَبِ التَعَرُّضِ لِأَشِعّةِ الشَّمْسِ); **to get a ~** اسْمَرّ

suntan lotion *n* كَريم الحِمايةِ من الشَّمْسِ

suntanned /ˈsʌntand/ *adj* ‹*face, body*› أَسْمَر (بِسَبَبِ التَعَرُّضِ لِأَشِعّةِ الشَّمْسِ)

suntan oil *n* زَيْت الحِمايةِ من الشَّمْسِ

suntrap /ˈsʌntrap/ *n* بُقْعة مُشْمِسة

super /ˈsuːpə/ (infml) **A** *adj* ‹*time, person*› رائِع **B** *excl* مُمْتاز

superb /suːˈpəːb/ *adj* ‹*performance, quality*› رائِع ,مُمْتاز

superbly /suːˈpəːbli/ *adv* ‹*to perform, recover*› بِشَكْلٍ رائِعٍ \ مُمْتازٍ

superbug /ˈsuːpəbʌg/ *n* بَكْتيريا مُقاوِمة للمُضادّاتِ الحَيَويّةِ

supercilious /suːpəˈsɪlɪəs/ *adj* (fml) ‹*manner, smile*› مُتَكَبِّر, مُتَعَجْرِف

supercomputer /ˈsuːpəkəmpjuːtə/ *n* كُمْبيوتَر \ حاسوب عِمْلاق

superficial /suːpəˈfɪʃ(ə)l/ *adj* 1 (not serious) ‹*wound, damage*› سَطْحيّ 2 (apparent) ‹*resemblance, impression*› ظاهِريّ 3 (shallow) ‹*character, friendship*› سَطْحيّ

superfluous /suːˈpəːflʊəs/ *adj* ‹*detail, remark*› زائِد (عن الحاجةِ)

superglue /ˈsuːpəgluː/ *n* غِراء ,صَمْغ (سَريع المَفْعولِ)

superhighway /ˈsuːpəhʌɪweɪ/ *n* (AmE) طَريق سَريع \ سَيّار

superhuman /ˌsuːpəˈhjuːmən/ *adj* ‹*effort, strength*› فوق طاقةِ البَشَرِ \ مُسْتَوى ,جَبّار (جَبّارونَ ,جَبابِرة)

superimpose /ˌsuːpərɪmˈpəʊz/ *vt* رَكَّبَ (شَيْئاً على شَيْءٍ آخَرَ) ‹*an image, a soundtrack*›

superintend /suːpərɪnˈtɛnd/ *vt* (fml) أَشْرَفَ (على) ‹*a department, a process*›

superintendent /suːpərɪnˈtɛnd(ə)nt/ *n* 1 (fml) (supervisor) مُشْرِف 2 (also **police superintendent**) (in UK) مُدير شُرْطةٍ; (in US) مُفَوَّض شُرْطةٍ 3 (AmE) (caretaker) مُشْرِف على عِمارةٍ 4 (also **school superintendent**) (AmE) مَنْدوب جِهَويّ للتَعْليمِ (Tunisia), مُدير إدارةٍ تَعْليميّةٍ (Egypt)

superior /suːˈpɪərɪə/ **A** *adj* 1 (better) ‹*quality, product*› مُتَفَوِّق; **to be ~ to sth/sb** كانَ مُتَفَوِّقاً على شَيْءٍ \ شَخْصٍ 2 (arrogant) ‹*attitude, smile*› مُتَكَبِّر 3 (in rank) ‹*officer, official*› أَرْفَع \ أَعْلى مَرْتَبةً **B** *n* رَئيس (رُؤَساءُ)

superiority /suːpɪəriˈɒrəti/ *n* 1 (in quality, power) تَفَوُّق 2 (towards others) تَفَوُّق

superlative /suːˈpəːlətɪv/ **A** *adj* 1 (excellent) ‹*performance, service*› رائِع ,مُمْتاز 2 (in grammar) ‹*adjective, adverb*› أَفْعَل التَفْضيلِ **B** *n* صيغة \ اسْم التَفْضيلِ; **'best' is the ~ of 'good'** 'أَحْسَن' اسْمُ تَفْضيلٍ لِكَلِمةِ 'جَيِّد'

superman /ˈsuːpəman/ *n* (*pl* **-men**) سوبِرْمان ,إِنْسان خارِق

supermarket /ˈsuːpəmɑːkɪt/ *n* سوبِرْمارْكِت

supermodel /ˈsuːpəmɒd(ə)l/ *n* عارِضة أَزْياءٍ مَشْهورة

supernatural /suːpəˈnatʃrəl/ **A** *adj* ‹*phenomenon, powers*› خارِق (خَوارِقُ) **B** *n* (**the Supernatural**) الغَيْبيّات

superpower /ˈsuːpəpaʊə/ *n* قوّة عُظْمى

supersede /ˌsuːpəˈsiːd/ *vt* ‹*a model, law*› اسْتَبْدَلَ

supersonic /suːpəˈsɒnɪk/ *adj* ‹*jet, speed*› أَسْرَع من الصَوْتِ, خارِق للصَوْتِ

superstar /ˈsuːpəstɑː/ *n* نَجْم (نُجوم)

superstition /suːpəˈstɪʃ(ə)n/ *n* خُرافة

superstitious /suːpəˈstɪʃəs/ *adj* ‹*belief, nonsense*› خُرافيّ

superstore /ˈsuːpəstɔː/ *n* سوبِرْمارْكِت كَبير

supertanker /ˈsuːpətæŋkə/ *n* ناقِلة نَفْطٍ ضَخْمة

supervise /ˈsuːpəvʌɪz/ *vt* **1** (to check work) (to oversee) راقَبَ, أَشْرَفَ (على) ‹*the construction, staff*› **2** (to keep safe) اعْتَنى (ب) ‹*a child, patient*›

supervision /ˌsuːpəˈvɪʒ(ə)n/ *n* **1** (of staff, work) إِشْراف, **2** (of a child, patient) عِناية, مُراقَبة; **under medical ~** تحت العِناية الطِبِّيّة

supervisor /ˈsuːpəvʌɪzə/ *n* **1** (for staff) مُشْرِف, مُراقِب **2** (of a post-grad student) مُشْرِف (على رِسالةٍ جامِعيّة)

superwoman /ˈsuːpəwʊmən/ *n* (*pl* **-women**) امْرأة خارِقة

supper /ˈsʌpə/ *n* عَشاء (أَعْشِية); **the Last Supper** العَشاء الأَخير \ السِرّيّ \ الرَبّانيّ

supplant /səˈplɑːnt/ *vt* اسْتَأْصَلَ (لِيَحِلَّ مَحَلَّهُ), حَلَّ المَحَلَّ ‹*a rival, theory*›

supple /ˈsʌp(ə)l/ *adj* (**suppler, supplest**) **1** (flexible) ‹*limbs, gymnast*› مَرِن **2** (not hard) ‹*skin, leather*› لَيِّن

supplement **A** /ˈsʌplɪmənt/ *n* **1** (fee) رُسوم إِضافيّة \ تَكْميليّة **2** (dietary) مُكَمِّل **3** (to one's income) مَبْلَغ إِضافيّ \ تَكْميليّ **4** (of newspapers, magazines) مُلْحَق (جَريدةٍ أو مَجَلّةٍ)

B *vt* أَضافَ, أَكْمَلَ ‹*your diet, income*›

supplementary /ˌsʌplɪˈmɛnt(ə)ri/ *adj* ‹*question, material*› تَكْميليّ, إِضافيّ, مُلْحَق

supplementation /sʌplɪmɛnˈteɪʃ(ə)n/ *n* إِضافة, تَكْميل (تَكْميلات)

supplication /ˌsʌplɪˈkeɪʃ(ə)n/ *n* دَعْوة, تَضَرُّع (تَضَرُّعات), ابْتِهال (ابْتِهالات)

supplier /səˈplʌɪə/ *n* مُوَرِّد, مُزَوِّد

supply /səˈplʌɪ/ **A** *vt* (*3rd person present sing* **supplies**, *present participle* **supplying**, *past tense, past participle* **supplied**) **1** (to provide) وَفَّرَ, وَصَّلَ, أَمَدَّ (ب) ‹*food, water, goods*›; قَدَّمَ ‹*services*›; **to ~ arms to sb, to ~ sb with arms** أَمَدَّ شَخْصاً بالأَسْلِحةِ; **the farm supplies meat to local restaurants** تُوَفِّرُ المَزْرَعةُ اللُحومَ للمَطاعِمِ المَحَلِّيّةِ; **we kept them supplied with drinks** اسْتَمْرَرْنا في تَقْديمِ المَشْروباتِ لَهُمْ **2** (to satisfy) لَبّى ‹*sb's needs, requirements*›

B *n* (*pl* **supplies**) **1** (stock) مَخْزون (مَخْزونات); **a year's/month's ~ of sth** مَخْزون من شَيْءٍ يَكْفي لِعام \ لِشَهْرٍ; **nurses/books are in short ~** هُناكَ نَقْصٌ في المُمَرِّضاتِ \ الكُتُبِ; **their food ~ was running out** كانَ مَخْزونُهُمْ من الطَعامِ يَأْخُذُ في النَفادِ **2** [u] (provision) إِمْداد; **the blood ~ to the heart** إِمْداد الدَمِ إلى القَلْبِ; **a contract for the ~ of water to the town** عَقْد لِتَوْصيلِ المِياهِ إلى المَدينةِ **3** [u] (in economics) عَرْض; **the laws of ~ and demand** قَوانين العَرْضِ والطَلَبِ

C (**supplies**) *n pl* مُؤَن; **office/art supplies** لَوازِم مَكْتَبيّة \ فَنّيّة; **to deliver supplies to the disaster area** وَصَّلَ الإِمْداداتِ إلى المَناطِقِ المَنْكوبة

supply ship *n* سَفينة إِمْدادٍ

supply teacher *n* (BrE) مُدَرِّس \ أُسْتاذ بَديل

support /səˈpɔːt/ **A** *vt* **1** (to back) دَعَمَ (a; دَعْم), أَيَّدَ, سانَدَ ‹*a cause, person, bill*› **2** (financially) دَعَمَ (a; دَعْم) ‹*a project, sb's work*› **3** (to provide for) أَنْفَقَ (على), أَعالَ ‹*a family, child*›; **he has a wife and children to ~** يُعيلُ زَوْجةً وأَطْفالاً **4** (in sport) شَجَّعَ ‹*a team*›; **who do you ~?** مَنْ تُشَجِّعُ؟ **5** (to hold up) حَمَلَ (i; حَمْل), سَنَدَ (u; سُنود) ‹*a weight*›; **they ~ed him up the steps** سانَدوهُ في صُعودِ الدَرَجاتِ **6** (to confirm) أَيَّدَ, أَكَّدَ ‹*an argument, a claim*›; **all the evidence ~s this conclusion** تُؤَكِّدُ كُلُّ الأَدِلّةِ هذه النَتيجةَ **7** (to sustain) ساعَدَ (على) ‹*life*› **8** (to work with) اعْتَمَدَ, دَعَمَ (a; دَعْم), عَمِلَ (a; عَمَل) (مع) ‹*a program, format*›

B *v refl* **to ~ oneself** أَعالَ نَفْسَهُ

C *n* **1** [u] (moral, political) دَعْم, مُسانَدة, مُؤازَرة; **there is little public ~ for this policy** هُناكَ دَعْمٌ شَعْبيٌّ ضَئيلٌ لِهَذِهِ السِياسةِ; **he has the full ~ of the board** لَدَيْهِ الدَعْمُ الكامِلُ من مَجْلِسِ الإِدارةِ; **to give one's ~ to sth/sb** أَعْطى دَعْمَهُ لِشَيْءٍ \ لِشَخْصٍ; **to speak in ~ of sb/sth** أَلْقى كَلِمةً دَعْماً لِشَخْصٍ \ لِشَيْءٍ **2** [u] (financial, material) دَعْم; **online technical ~** الدَعْم الفَنّيّ على الإِنْتَرْنت; **the government gives financial ~ to farmers** تُقَدِّمُ الحُكومةُ دَعْماً ماليًّا للمُزارِعينَ; **a collection in ~ of the disaster victims** جَمْع تَبَرُّعاتٍ لِصالِحِ ضَحايا الكارِثةِ; **she has no means of ~** لَيْسَ لَها مَصْدَرُ دَخْلٍ **3** (prop) دِعامة (دِعامات, دَعائِم); **use a stick**

as a ~ مُساندة (u) (ability to hold up) **4▸** اسْتَخْدِمْ عَصاً كَدِعامةٍ **5▸** (u) (corroboration) تَأْييد ,دَعْم; **these figures lend ~ to his argument** تُؤَيِّدُ هذه الأَرْقامُ حُجَّتَهُ **6▸** (person) [شَخْص داعِم]; **to be a ~ to sb** كانَ داعِماً لِشَخْصٍ

support band *n* بَرْنامَج تَمْهيديّ

supporter /sə'pɔːtə/ *n* **1▸** (political) مُؤَيِّد **2▸** (in sports) مُشَجِّع

support group *n* مَجْموعة داعِمة

supporting /sə'pɔːtɪŋ/ *adj before n* ‹*role, cast*› ثانويّ

supportive /sə'pɔːtɪv/ *adj* ‹*environment, wife*› مُسانِد

suppose /sə'pəʊz/ *vt* **1▸** (to assume) اِفْتَرَضَ; **let us ~ that …** لِنَفْتَرِضْ أنّ … ; **I ~ so** أَظُنُّ ذلك; **I ~ not** لا أَظُنُّ ذلك; **I don't ~ you know where he is?** ظَنَّ **2▸** (to think) هل تَعْلَمُ مَكانَهُ؟ (u; ظَنّ), تَصَوَّرَ; **what do you ~ will happen?** ماذا سَيَحْدُثُ في ظَنِّكَ؟ **3▸** (to imagine) اِفْتَرَضَ ,تَخَيَّلَ ,تَصَوَّرَ; **~ he doesn't come?** ماذا إذا لم يَأْتِ؟ **4▸** (indicating obligation) **to be ~d to do sth** كانَ من المُفْتَرَضِ أنْ يَفْعَلَ شَيْئاً; **you are ~d to be at work** من المُفْتَرَضِ أنْ تَكونَ في العَمَلِ; **you're ~d to buy a ticket before you get on the train** من المُفْتَرَضِ أنْ تَشْتَرِيَ تَذْكِرةً قبل رُكوبِ القِطارِ; **I don't know what I'm ~d to be doing** لا أَدْري ماذا عَلَيَّ أنْ أَفْعَلَ **5▸** (indicating intention) قَصَدَ (i; قَصْد); **what's that ~d to mean?** ما المَقْصودُ بِهذا؟ **6▸** (indicating general opinion) **to be ~d to be sth** كانَ من المُفْتَرَضِ أنْ يَكونَ شَيْئاً; **it's ~d to be a good hotel** من المُفْتَرَضِ أنَّهُ فُنْدُقٌ جَيِّدٌ **7▸** (to require) «theory» اِفْتَرَضَ ‹*the existence, possibility*›

supposed /sə'pəʊzd/ *adj* ‹*father, owner*› مَزْعوم; ‹*threat, benefit*› مُفْتَرَض

supposedly /sə'pəʊzɪdli/ *adv* ‹*to represent, belong*› على ما يُظَنُّ \ يُعْتَقَدُ \ يُقالُ

supposing /sə'pəʊzɪŋ/ *conj* هَبْ ,لِنَفْرِضْ; **~ (that) he says no?** لِنَفْرِضْ أَنَّهُ يَقولُ لا؟

supposition /ˌsʌpə'zɪʃ(ə)n/ *n* افْتِراض (افْتِراضات)

suppository /sə'pɒzɪt(ə)ri/ *n* (*pl* **suppositories**) تَحْميلة (تَحاميلُ)

suppress /sə'prɛs/ *vt* **1▸** (not to express) كَبَتَ (i; كَبْت), كَبَحَ (a; كَبْح) ‹*laughter, anger*› **2▸** (to quash) قَمَعَ (a; قَمْع) ‹*a rebellion, opposition*› **3▸** (to keep secret) كَتَمَ (u; كِتْمان ,كَتْم), أَخْفى ‹*evidence, report*› **4▸** (to restrain) أَوْقَفَ ,أَخْمَدَ ‹*the appetite, inflammation, weeds*›

suppression /sə'prɛʃ(ə)n/ *n* **1▸** (of information) إخْفاء ,كِتْمان **2▸** (of emotions) كَبْت **3▸** (of a rebellion) قَمْع **4▸** (of growth, development) إيقاف ,إخْماد

suppurate /'sʌpjʊreɪt/ *vi* «sores, wounds» أَفْرَزَ قَيْحاً ,تَقَيَّحَ

supranational /suːprə'naʃn(ə)l/ *adj* (fml) ‹*organization, institution*› مُتَجاوِز \ مُتَخَطٍّ لِلحُدودِ القَوْمِيّةِ ,دُوَليّ

supremacy /suː'prɛməsi/ *n* هَيْمَنة ,سِيادة ,سَيْطَرة

supreme /suː'priːm/ *adj* **1▸** (in rank) ‹*leader, ruling*› أَعْلى (عُلى) **2▸** (very great) ‹*confidence, sacrifice*› بالِغ ,فائِق

supreme court *n* المَحْكَمة العُلْيا

sura /'sʊərə/ *n* سورة (سُوَر)

surcharge /'səːtʃɑːdʒ/ *n* رُسوم إضافيّة

sure /ʃɔː/ **A** *adj* **1▸** (convinced) مُتَيَقِّن ,واثِق ,مُتَأَكِّد; **to be ~ about sth** أنا واثِقٌ من كانَ مُتَأَكِّداً من شَيْءٍ; **I'm ~ of my facts** مَعْلوماتي; **I feel ~ I've made the right choice** أَشْعُرُ بالثِقةِ أَنّي اتَّخَذْتُ الخِيارَ الصَحيحَ; **I'm not ~ if** *or* **whether it was him** لَسْتُ مُتَيَقِّناً ما إذا كانَ هو; **the one thing you can be ~ of is …** الشَيْءُ الوَحيدُ الّذي يُمْكِنُكَ الوُثوقُ بِهِ هو … **2▸** (certain) مُؤَكَّد ,أَكيد; **nobody knows for ~** لا أَحَدَ يَعْلَمُ على وَجْهِ اليَقينِ; **to make ~ that …** تَأَكَّدَ من أنّ … ; **I won't invite them again, that's for ~!** (infml) لن أَدْعُوَهُمْ مَرّةً أُخرى، بِكُلِّ تَأْكيدٍ!; **he is, to be ~, a very charming man** (fml) هو بالتَأْكيدِ رَجُلٌ جَذّابٌ جِدّاً **3▸** (without doubt) مَحْتوم ,مُحَقَّق ,مُؤَكَّد; **he's ~ to fail/win** من المُؤَكَّدِ أَنَّهُ سَيَفْشَلُ \ سَيَفوزُ; **they're ~ of a place in the final** ضَمِنوا مَكاناً في الدَوْرِ النِهائيِّ; **~ thing!** (infml) بالتَأْكيدِ!; **to be a ~ thing** كانَ أَمْراً مُحَقَّقاً **4▸** (confident) واثِق; **to be ~ of oneself** كانَ واثِقاً من نَفْسِهِ **5▸** (reliable) ‹*sign, method*› مَضْمون ,مَوْثوق; **the ~st way to succeed** أَضْمَنُ طَريقةٍ للنَجاحِ **6▸** (steady) ‹*hand, footing*› ثابِت; **now the business is on a ~r footing** تَقِفُ التِجارةُ الآنَ على أَرْضٍ أَكْثَرَ ثَباتاً

B *adv* **1▸** (infml) (of course) بالطَبْعِ ,بالتَأْكيدِ; **'are you coming?' — '~'** 'هل سَتَأْتي؟' — 'بالتَأْكيدِ!' **2▸** (infml) (for emphasis) بالتَأْكيدِ;

I ~ hope so أَتَمَنَّى ذلك بالتَّأْكيدِ; **it ~ is cold** الجَوُّ بارِدٌ بالتَّأْكيدِ **3** ~ **enough** كَما هو مُتَوَقَّعٌ

sure-fire /ˈsɔːfʌɪə/ *adj* ‹*way, winner*› مَضْمون النَتيجةِ

sure-footed /ˌsɔːˈfʊtɪd/ *adj* ‹*goat, cat*› ثابِت القَدَمِ

surely /ˈʃɔːli/ *adv* **1** (expressing certainty) بالطَبْعِ, بالتَّأْكيدِ, قَطْعاً; **she must ~ have known, ~ she must have known** لا بُدَّ أنَّها كانَتْ تَعْلَمُ بالتَّأْكيدِ; **~ you can understand that?** يُمْكِنُكَ أنْ تَفْهَمَ ذلك، أَلَيْسَ كَذلِكَ؟ **2** (expressing surprise, disbelief) بالتَّأْكيدِ; **~ you don't mean that!** لا أنْتَ بالتَّأْكيدِ لا! تَعْني ذلك! **~ not!** بالتَّأْكيد لا!; **'it happened in 2010' — '~ 2011'** 'حَدَثَ ذلك في 2010' — 'بَلْ بالتَّأْكيدِ في 2011' **3** (without doubt) قَطْعيًّا, بِلا شَكٍّ **4** (AmE) (infml) (of course) بالطَبْعِ, طَبْعاً

surety /ˈʃɔːrəti/ *n* (*pl* **sureties**) **1** (money) كَفالة, ضَمان **2** (person) كَفيل ضامِن

surf /səːf/ **A** *n* أَمْواج مُتَكَسِّرة **B** *vt* (مَواقِعَ الإنْتَرْنِت) اسْتَعْرَضَ, تَصَفَّحَ ‹*the Internet, Web*›; **he spent his evenings ~ing the Internet** قَضى أُمْسِياتِهِ في تَصَفُّحِ الإنْتَرْنِت **C** *vi* «surfers» مارَسَ رِياضةَ رُكوبِ الأَمْواجِ \ الرَكْمَجةِ

surface /ˈsəːfɪs/ **A** *n* **1** (upper layer) وَجْه, (أَسْطُح) سَطْح (وُجوه, أَوْجُه); **the road ~** سَطْح الطَريقِ; **500m below the earth's ~** 500 م تحت سَطْحِ الأَرْضِ **2** (of a lake, the sea) (أَسْطُح) سَطْح **3** (outer appearance) (مَظاهِرُ) مَظْهَر; **on the ~** في الظاهِرِ, ظاهِريًّا; **all his resentment came to the ~** طَفَتْ كُلُّ كَراهِيَتِهِ على السَطْحِ **4** (also **surface area**) مِساحة **5** (of a solid, cube) سَطْح (أَسْطُح), وَجْه (وُجوه, أَوْجُه) **6** (worktop) سَطْح عَمَلٍ **B** *vt* ‹*a road, an area*› غَطّى; **to ~ a path with concrete** غَطّى مَمَرًّا بالخَرَسانةِ **C** *vi* **1** (to emerge) «diver, submarine, whale» صَعَدَ إلى السَطْحِ **2** (to appear) «problem, report, tension» ظَهَرَ (ظُهور; a) **3** (to reappear) «people» عاوَدَ الظُهورَ **4** (infml) (to get up) اسْتَيْقَظَ

surface area *n* مَساحة سَطْحِيّة

surface-to-air *adj before n* ‹*missile*› أَرْض–جَوّ

surface-to-surface *adj before n* ‹*missile*› أَرْض–أَرْض, سَطْح–سَطْح

surface vessel *n* سَفينة سَطْحٍ

surface wound *n* جُرْح سَطْحيّ

surfboard /ˈsəːfbɔːd/ *n* لَوْح رُكوبِ الأَمْواجِ

surfeit /ˈsəːfɪt/ *n* كَمِّيّة هائِلة \ مُفْرِطة

surfer /ˈsəːfə/ *n* **1** (on sea) راكِب أَمْواجٍ **2** (on the Internet) مُسْتَعْرِض (لِمَواقِعِ إنْتَرْنِت)

surfing /ˈsəːfɪŋ/ *n* رِياضة رُكوبِ الأَمْواجِ

surge /səːdʒ/ **A** *n* **1** (of water, people) انْدِفاع (انْدِفاعات); **there was a ~ towards the exit** كانَ هُناكَ انْدِفاعٌ نحو المَخْرَجِ **2** (of interest, support, anger) مَوْجة; **she felt a ~ of anger/remorse** شَعَرَتْ بِحالةٍ شَديدةٍ من الغَضَبِ \ النَدَمِ **3** (in prices, demand, sales) ارْتِفاع حادّ **4** (also **power surge**) (in electricity) ارْتِفاع مُفاجِئ للتَيّارِ الكَهْرَبائيِّ **B** *vi* **1** (to move powerfully) «crowds, water» انْدَفَعَ; **the crowd ~d forward** انْدَفَعَ الحَشْدُ إلى الأَمامِ; **panic ~d up inside her** دَبَّ الذُعْرُ في قَلْبِها; **he was surging ahead in the polls** كانَ يَتَقَدَّمُ بِقوّةٍ في اسْتِطْلاعاتِ الرَأْيِ **2** (to increase) «prices, sales, share prices» ارْتَفَعَ بِشَكْلٍ حادّ **C** (**surging**) *adj* ‹*prices, demand*› مُتَصاعِد

surgeon /ˈsəːdʒ(ə)n/ *n* جَرّاح

surgeon general *n* (AmE) لِواء جَرّاح

surgery /ˈsəːdʒ(ə)ri/ *n* (*pl* **surgeries**) **1** [u] (procedures) جِراحة; **to have/undergo ~** خَضَعَ لِعَمَليّةٍ جِراحيّةٍ **2** (BrE) (premises) عِيادة (غُرْفة الاسْتِشارة الطِبّيّة) **3** (BrE) (consulting time) عِيادة, مَواعيد الزِيارة; **the morning/afternoon ~** العِيادة الصَباحيّة \ المَسائيّة

surgical /ˈsəːdʒɪk(ə)l/ *adj* **1** (relating to surgery) ‹*procedure, instrument*› جِراحيّ **2** (worn after surgery) ‹*stocking, appliance*› طِبّيّ

surgical spirit *n* (BrE) كُحول جِراحيّ \ طِبّيّ

Suriname /ˌsʊərɪˈnam/ *pr n* السورينام (f)

surly /ˈsəːli/ *adj* (**surlier, surliest**) ‹*mood, teenager*› فَظّ (أَفْظاظ), شَكِس (شُكْس), مُتَذَمِّر

surmise /sə'mʌɪz/ (fml) **A** *vt* حَزَرَ ,خَمَّنَ ,قَدَّرَ (i-u; حَزْر); **to ~ that ...** ظَنَّ أَنَّ ... ; **police ~d that he had died of a drug overdose** افْتَرَضَت الشُّرْطَةُ أَنَّهُ ماتَ نَتيجةَ جُرْعةٍ زائِدةٍ من المُخَدِّراتِ

B *n* تَقْدير (تَقْديرات) ,تَخْمين (تَخْمينات)

surmount /sə'maʊnt/ *vt* (fml) **1** (to overcome) تَغَلَّبَ (على), قَهَرَ (a; قَهْر) ‹*an obstacle, a challenge*› **2** **to be ~ed by sth** كانَ يَعْلوهُ شَيْءٌ

surname /'sə:neɪm/ *n* اسْم العائِلةِ; **what's your ~?** ما اسْمُ عائِلَتِكَ؟

surpass /sə'pɑ:s/ **A** *vt* فاقَ (u; فَوْق ,فَواق), جاوَزَ ,تَجاوَزَ, تَخَطّى ‹*expectations, a record*›

B *v refl* **to ~ yourself** تَجاوَزَ نَفْسَهُ

surplus /'sə:pləs/ **A** *n* (*pl* **surpluses**) (excess of material) (of funds) (of produce) فائِض (فَوائِض) ,زِيادة

B *adj* ‹*funds, stock*› زائِد ,فائِض; **it's ~ to our requirements** هو فائِضٌ عن احْتِياجاتِنا

surprise /sə'prʌɪz/ **A** *n* **1** (unexpected event) مُفاجَأة; **to give sb a ~** فاجَأَ شَخْصاً; **to have a big ~** حَدَثَتْ لَهُ مُفاجَأةٌ كَبِيرةٌ; **what a nice/unpleasant ~!** يا لَها من مُفاجَأةٍ لَطِيفةٍ \ غَيْرِ سارَّةٍ!; **it was** *or* **came as no ~ to anyone to hear that ...** لم يُفاجَأْ أَحَدٌ لِسَماعِ أَنَّ ... ; **there were no ~s in the 1,500 metres** لم تَكُنْ هُناكَ أَيُّ مُفاجَآتٍ في سِباقِ ال 1500 مِتْرٍ **2** [u] (astonishment) دَهْشة; **much to my ~** مِمّا أَثارَ دَهْشَتي; **to express ~ at sth** عَبَّرَ عن دَهْشَتِهِ من شَيْءٍ; **to take sb by ~** (unawares) فاجَأَ شَخْصاً; (in war) باغَتَ شَخْصاً

B *vt* **1** (to astonish) «results, decision» أَدْهَشَ; **it wouldn't ~ me if she won** لن أَنْدَهِشَ إذا فازَتْ; **nothing ~s me any more!** لم يَعُدْ هُناكَ ما يُدْهِشُني!; **they were ~d to hear/see that ...** انْدَهشوا عِنْدَما سَمِعوا \ رَأَوْا أَنَّ ... **2** (to come upon) فاجَأَ ,باغَتَ ‹*an intruder, a burglar*›

surprise announcement *n* إعْلان مُفاجِئ

surprise attack *n* هُجوم مُباغِت \ مُفاجِئ

surprised /sə'prʌɪzd/ *adj* ‹*look, observer*› مُتَفاجِئ ,مُنْدَهِش; **to be ~ at/about sth** كانَ مُنْدَهِشاً من شَيْءٍ; **I'm not ~** لَسْتُ مُنْدَهِشاً

surprise visit *n* زِيارة مُفاجِئة

surprising /sə'prʌɪzɪŋ/ *adj* ‹*result, number*› مُدْهِش ,مُفاجِئ, مُذْهِل

surprisingly /sə'prʌɪzɪŋli/ *adv* ‹*easy, effective*› بِصورةٍ تُثيرُ الدَهْشَةَ

surreal /sə'rɪəl/ *adj* ‹*moment, experience*› سُرْيالِيّ

surrealism /sə'rɪəliz(ə)m/ *n* سُرْيالِيّة

surrealist /sə'rɪəlɪst/ *n, adj* سُرْيالِيّ

surrender /sə'rɛndə/ **A** *vt* **1** سَلَّمَ ‹*a town, garrison*› **2** (to give up) تَنازَلَ (عن) ‹*one's rights, power, sovereignty*› **3** (to hand over) سَلَّمَ ,تَنازَلَ (عن) ‹*one's weapons, passport*› **4** (to discontinue) أَلْغى ‹*a lease*› **5** ‹*a life insurance policy*›

B *vi* (to stop resisting) «army, country, soldiers» اسْتَسْلَمَ; **to ~ to the enemy/police** اسْتَسْلَمَ للعَدُوِّ \ للشُّرْطَةِ

C *v refl* **to ~ oneself to sth** سَلَّمَ \ تَرَكَ نَفْسَهُ لِشَيْءٍ

D *n* **1** (to an opponent) اسْتِسْلام; **to negotiate a ~** تَفاوَضَ على الاسْتِسْلام; **to demand unconditional ~** طَلَبَ اسْتِسْلاماً غَيْرَ مَشْروطٍ **2** (of weapons, documents) تَسْليم **3** (of sovereignty, rights) تَنازُل (تَنازُلات) **4** (of a lease) تَنازُل (تَنازُلات)

surreptitious /ˌsʌrəp'tɪʃəs/ *adj* ‹*glance, recording*› خَفِيّ ,مُخْتَلِس

surrogate /'sʌrəgət/ *n* بَديل (بُدَلاءُ)

surrogate mother *n* **1** (bearer of a child) أُمّ ,رَحْم ظِئْر **2** (child carer) وَكيل رِعايةٍ بَديلة

surround /sə'raʊnd/ *vt* **1** (to encircle) أَحاطَ ‹*a house, lake*› **2** (with troops, police) طَوَّقَ ,حاصَرَ ‹*a building, suspect*›

surrounding /sə'raʊndɪŋ/ *adj* ‹*area, countryside*› مُجاوِر ,مُحيط

surroundings /sə'raʊndɪŋz/ *n pl* بيئة ,مُحيط ,ضاحِية (ضَواحٍ)

surveillance /sə:'veɪləns/ *n* مُراقَبة

survey **A** /sə'veɪ/ *vt* **1** (to poll) اسْتَطْلَعَ الرَأْيَ ‹*people, informants*›; **95 per cent of respondents ~ed were satisfied with the service** 95 في المِائةِ من المُشارِكينَ في اسْتِطْلاعِ الرَأْيِ كانوا راضِينَ عن الخِدْمةِ **2** (to look at) فَحَصَ (a; فَحْص) ,تَفَحَّصَ ‹*a room, the landscape*› **3** (to give an overview of) اسْتَعْرَضَ ‹*sb's work, the literature*› **4** (to inspect) مَسَحَ (a; مَسْح) ‹*a site,* *the land›* **5** (BrE) (in house buying) عايَنَ (a; فَحْص)، فَحَصَ *‹a property, building›*

B /ˈsəːveɪ/ *n* **1** (of opinion) اسْتِطْلاع (اسْتِطْلاعات) **2** (overview) اسْتِعْراض (اسْتِعراضات) **3** (of land, terrain) مَسْح **4** (BrE) (inspection) فَحْص (فُحوص)، مُعايَنة; (report) تَقْرير (تَقارير)

surveyor /səˈveɪə/ *n* **1** (of land) مَسّاح **2** (BrE) (of buildings) مُراقِب

survival /səˈvʌɪv(ə)l/ *n* البَقاء على قَيْدِ الحَياةِ

survive /səˈvʌɪv/ **A** *vt* **1** (to live after) نَجا (u; نَجاة؛ من) *‹a disaster, an attack›* **2** (to outlive) بَقِيَ \ عاش أطْوَلَ من *‹a child, husband›*; **he is ~d by his wife and children** تَرَكَ وَراءَهُ زَوْجَتَهُ وَأَوْلادَهُ

B *vi* «plants, human beings» عاشَ (i; عَيْش، مَعيشة؛ على)، بَقِيَ على قَيْدِ الحَياةِ; **to ~ on $100 a week** عاشَ على 100 دولار في الأسْبوع

surviving /səˈvʌɪvɪŋ/ *adj before n ‹relative, children›* باقٍ (على قَيْدِ الحَياةِ)

survivor /səˈvʌɪvə/ *n* ناجٍ (ناجونَ)

susceptibility /səˌsɛptɪˈbɪlɪti/ *n* **1** (to disease) قابِليّة **2** (to flattery, corruption) حَسّاسيّة

susceptible /səˈsɛptɪb(ə)l/ *adj* **1** (likely to be affected) *‹patient, animal›* قابِل، سَريع التَعَرُّضِ; **to be ~ to infection** كانَ عُرْضةً \ سَريع التَعَرُّضِ للعَدْوى **2** (easily swayed) *‹person›* سَريع \ سَهْل التَأثُّرِ; **to be ~ to flattery/corruption** كانَ ضَعيفاً أمام الإطْراءِ \ الرَشْوةِ

suspect A /səˈspɛkt/ *vt* **1** (to believe likely) اشْتَبَهَ (بِ)، ظَنَّ (u; ظَنّ)، اعْتَقَدَ *‹murder, a plot›*; **I ~ (that) he doesn't want to pay for it** أعْتَقِدُ أنَّهُ لا يُريدُ أنْ يَدْفَعَ ثَمَنَهُ; **to ~ sb of theft/treason** اشْتَبَهَ شَخْصاً بالسَرِقةِ \ الخيانةِ **2** (to question) شَكَّ (u; شَكّ؛ في)، ارْتابَ *‹sb's motives, sincerity›*

B (**suspected**) /səˈspɛkt/ *adj ‹criminal, fracture›* مُحْتَمَل

C /ˈsʌspɛkt/ *n* مُشْتَبَه فيهِ، مُتَّهَم

D /ˈsʌspɛkt/ *adj* (suspicious) *‹package, behaviour, story›* مَشْبوه، مَوْضِع رَيْبةٍ \ شُبْهةٍ، مُثير للرَيْبةِ، مُشْتَبَه فيهِ

suspend /səˈspɛnd/ *vt* **1** (to hang) عَلَّقَ *‹a rope, lamp›* **2** **to be ~ed in sth** «particles» كانَ عالِقاً في شَيْءٍ **3** (to discontinue) أوْقَفَ، عَلَّقَ *‹operations, services›*; **the company has ~ed operations because of the weather** عَلَّقَت الشَرِكةُ عَمَليّاتِها بِسَبَبِ الطَقْسِ **4** (to ban) أوْقَفَ *‹an employee, player, student›*; **to be ~ed from duty** أوقِفَ عن العَمَلِ **5** (not to enforce) أوْقَفَ التَنْفيذَ *‹a sentence›*; **her sentence was ~ed** أوقِفَ تَنْفيذُ الحُكْمِ ضِدَّها **6** (to defer) **to ~ disbelief** عَلَّقَ الشَكَّ \ نَزْعةَ عَدَمِ التَصْديقِ; **to ~ judgement** أَجَّلَ الحُكْمَ

suspended sentence /səˌspɛndɪd ˈsɛnt(ə)ns/ *n* حُكْم قَضائيّ مع وَقْفِ التَنْفيذِ; **to be given a ~** تَمَّ إصْدارُ حُكْمٍ بِحَقِّهِ مع وَقْفِ التَنْفيذِ

suspender belt /səˈspɛndə bɛlt/ *n* (BrE) حَمّالة جَوارِبَ

suspenders /səˈspɛndəz/ *n pl* **1** (BrE) (for stockings) حَمّالة جَوارِبَ **2** (AmE) (for trousers) حَمّالة بَنْطَلون

suspense /səˈspɛns/ *n* تَشْويق، تَرَقُّب، حَيْرة، قَلَق; **to leave/keep sb in ~** تَرَكَ \ أبْقى شَخْصاً في حَيْرةٍ

suspension /səˈspɛnʃ(ə)n/ *n* **1** (of a vehicle) ماصّ صَدَماتٍ، نِظام تَعْليقٍ **2** (of a student, team member) حِرْمان مُؤَقَّت، إيقاف **3** [u] (delay) تَعْليق

suspension bridge *n* جِسْر مُعَلَّق

suspension points *n* ثَلاث نُقَطٍ مُتَتالية

suspicion /səˈspɪʃ(ə)n/ *n* **1** (mistrust) اشْتِباه (اشْتِباهات)، شُبْهة (شُبُهات)، تُهْمة; **to be under ~ of treason** كانَ مُتَّهَماً بالخِيانةِ **2** (doubt) ارْتِياب، ريبة، شَكّ

suspicious /səˈspɪʃəs/ *adj* **1** (mistrustful) *‹mind, glance›* مُسيء للظَنِّ **2** (causing suspicion) *‹activity, package›* مُريب، مُرْتاب، مُثير للشَكِّ

suspiciously /səˈspɪʃəsli/ *adv* **1** (mistrustfully) *‹to ask, stare›* بِشَكْلٍ مُرْتابٍ **2** (causing suspicion) *‹to act, behave›* على نَحْوٍ مُريبٍ \ مُثيرٍ للشَكِّ

sustain /səˈsteɪn/ (fml) *vt* **1** (to maintain) حافَظَ (على) *‹life, interest›* **2** (to suffer) تَحَمَّلَ، تَكَبَّدَ، تَلَقّى *‹an injury, a loss›*

sustainable /səˈsteɪnəb(ə)l/ *adj* **1** (in conservation) *‹development, agriculture›* مُسْتَدام **2** (able to be maintained) *‹growth, level›* مُسْتَدام

sustenance /ˈsʌst(ə)nəns/ *n* (fml) غِذاء (أغْذِية)، تَغْذِية

SUV /ɛsjuːˈviː/ *n* = **Sports Utility Vehicle** سَيّارة دَفْعٍ رُباعيٍّ

SW *n* **1** = **south-west** جَنوب غَرْبِيّ **2** = **short wave** مَوْجة قَصيرة

swab /swɒb/ **A** *n* **1** (of cotton, gauze) قِطْعة من القُطْنِ الطِبِّيِّ **2** (specimen) عَيِّنة

B *vt* **1** مَسَحَ (a; مَسْح) ‹*the floor, deck*› **2** مَسَحَ (a; مَسْح), نَظَّفَ ‹*a cut, wound*›

swagger /ˈswagə/ *vi* رَفَلَ (u; رَفْل), تَخَطَّرَ

Swahili /swəˈhiːli/ *n* **1** (language) (اللُغة) السَواحيليّة **2** (person) سَواحيليّ

swallow /ˈswɒləʊ/ **A** *vt* **1** (in eating) بَلَعَ (a; بَلْع), اِبْتَلَعَ, اِزْدَرَدَ ‹*food, a drink*› **2** (to repress) تَنازَلَ (عن) ‹*one's pride*›; تَغَلَّبَ (على) ‹*one's disappointment*› **3** (infml) (to believe) صَدَّقَ ‹*sb's story, explanation*› **4** (infml) (to bear) تَحَمَّلَ ‹*an insult, bad treatment*›

B *vi* **1** «patients, animals» بَلَعَ (a; بَلْع) **2** (nervously) «speaker» بَلَعَ \ اِبْتَلَعَ ريقَهُ

C *n* **1** (bird) سُنونو **2** (in eating, drinking) بَلْعة

(Phrasal verb) **swallow up**: **~ up [sth]**, **~ [sth] up** «countries, organizations, companies» اِسْتَوْلى على [شَيْءٍ] ‹*a country, an organization, a company*›; **I wanted the ground to ~ me up** تَمَنَّيْتُ أنْ تَبْتَلِعَني الأَرْضُ

swam /swam/ *past tense* ▸ **swim**

swamp /swɒmp/ **A** *n* مُسْتَنْقَع (مُسْتَنْقَعات)

B *vt* **1** (to flood) غَمَرَ (u; غَمْر), أَغْرَقَ ‹*an area, a boat*› **2** (to overwhelm) غَمَرَ (u; غَمْر), أَغْرَقَ ‹*a market, village*›; **I'm completely ~ed with work at the moment** أنا غارِقٌ في العَمَلِ في هذه اللَحْظةِ; **to ~ a market with imports** أَغْرَقَ سوقاً بالسِلَعِ المُسْتَوْرَدةِ

swan /swɒn/ *n* تَمّ, إِوَز عِراقيّ

swanky /ˈswaŋki/ *adj* (**swankier**, **swankiest**) (infml) ‹*hotel, resort*› فاخِر, راقٍ

swap, **swop** /swɒp/ **A** *vt* (**-pp-**) قايَضَ, بادَلَ, تَبادَلَ ‹*a shirt, story*›; **to ~ sth for sth else** اِسْتَبْدَلَ شَيْئاً بِشَيْءٍ آخَرَ; **would you mind ~ping places with me?** هل تُمانِعُ في تَبادُلِ مَكانِكَ مَعي؟

B *n* مُقايَضة, مُبادَلة

swarm /swɔːm/ **A** *n* سِرْب (أَسْراب), جَماعة ‹*of birds, flies*›; رِجْل (أَرْجال) ‹*of locusts*›; ثَوْل (أَثْوال), خَشْرَم (خَشارِمُ) ‹*of bees*›

B *vi* «bees» تَجَمَّعَ; «tourists» تَزاحَمَ; **the market was ~ing with people** اِكْتَظَّتِ السوقُ بالناسِ

swarthy /ˈswɔːði/ *adj* (**swarthier**, **swarthiest**) ‹*complexion, man*› داكِن البَشَرة, أَسْمَر اللَوْنِ

swastika /ˈswɒstɪkə/ *n* صَليب مَعْقوف

swat /swɒt/ *vt* (**-tt-**) ضَرَبَ (الذُباب بِمِنَشّةٍ إلخ) ‹*a fly, mosquito*›

sway /sweɪ/ **A** *vt* (to influence) أَثَّرَ (على), اِسْتَمالَ ‹*public opinion, voters*›; **the voters were not ~ed by her policies** لم يَقْتَنِعِ الناخِبون بِسِياساتِها; **that ~ed the decision in our favour** حَوَّلَ ذلك القَرارَ إلى صالِحِنا

B *vi* «trees, branches, buildings» تَمايَلَ; **he ~ed as he walked down the path** تَرَنَّحَ وَهُوَ يَمْشي في المَمَرِّ; **the dancers ~ed to the music** تَمايَلَ الراقِصونَ مع الموسيقى

C *n* **to hold ~** «ideas, values» سَيْطَرَ (i; سَيْطَرة), هَيْمَنَ (i; هَيْمَنة); **to hold ~ over sb/sth** «rulers» سَيْطَرَ على شَخْصٍ \ شَيْءٍ

Swaziland /ˈswɑːzɪland/ *pr n* سْوازيلانْد (f)

swear /swɛː/ **A** *vt* (*past tense* **swore**, *past participle* **sworn**)

1 (to promise) حَلَفَ (i; حِلْف, حَلْف), أَقْسَمَ ‹*an oath, allegiance*›; **the president ~s to uphold the constitution** يُقْسِمُ الرَئيسُ على المُحافَظةِ على الدُسْتورِ; **to ~ allegiance to the flag** حَلَفَ يَمينَ الوَلاءِ لِلعَلَمِ; **he swore revenge on his father's killer** أَقْسَمَ على الانْتِقامِ من قاتِلِ والِدِهِ; **I could have sworn it was there** كِدْتُ أَجْزِمُ أَنَّهُ كانَ هُناكَ **2** (to make sb promise) **to ~ sb to secrecy** اِسْتَحْلَفَ شَخْصاً أَنْ يُحافِظَ على السِرِّيّة

B *vi* (*past tense* **swore**, *past participle* **sworn**) **1** (to curse) سَبَّ (u; سَبّ), شَتَمَ (i-u; شَتْم); **to ~ at sb** سَبَّ \ شَتَمَ شَخْصاً; **he never ~s** لا يَشْتُمُ أَبَداً **2** (to vow) «witness» حَلَفَ, أَقْسَمَ اليَمينَ; **I couldn't ~ to it** لم أَسْتَطِعْ أَنْ أَجْزِمَ بِهِ

(Phrasal verbs) **swear by**: **~ by [sth]** (infml) وَثِقَ ب [شَيْءٍ] ثِقةً تامّةً ‹*a remedy*›

• **swear in**: **~ in [sb]**, **~ [sb] in** جَعَلَ [شَخْصاً] يُؤَدّي اليَمينَ ‹*a president, witness*›; **to be sworn in** أَدّى اليَمينَ

swearing /'swɛːrɪŋ/ *n* شَتْم ,(سُباب) سَبّ

swear word *n* كَلِمة بَذيئة

sweat /swɛt/ **A** *n* **1** (perspiration) عَرَق; **he woke in a ~** اسْتَيْقَظَ وَهُوَ غارِقٌ في عَرَقِهِ; **to break into a ~** بَدَأَ يَعْرَق; **to break out in a cold ~** تَصَبَّبَ مِنْهُ العَرَقُ البارِدُ **2** (infml) (in anxiety) **to be in/get into a ~ about sth** شَعَرَ بالتَوَتُّرِ بِخُصوصِ شَيْءٍ

B (**sweats**) *n pl* (AmE) **1** (sweatsuit) بَدْلة رِياضيّة **2** (sweatpants) سِرْوال رِياضيّ

C *vt* (*past tense, past participle* **sweated** or **sweat** AmE) «cook» [طَهى طَهْياً بَطيئاً] ‹*vegetables*›

D *vi* (*past tense, past participle* **sweated** or **sweat** AmE) **1** (to perspire) «people, animals» عَرِقَ (a; عَرَق) **2** (infml) (to wait anxiously) انْتَظَرَ بِحَرارةٍ; **to make sb ~** تَرَكَ شَخْصاً يَنْتَظِرُ على أَحَرَّ من الجَمْرِ

Idioms **no sweat!** (infml) شَيْء بَسيط!; **to sweat blood over sth** (infml) بَذَلَ جُهْداً مُضْنِياً في شَيْءٍ

Phrasal verb **sweat out**: **~ [sth] out, ~ out [sth]** **1** تَخَلَّصَ من [شَيْءٍ] مع العَرَق ‹*toxins, a fever*› **2** **to ~ it out** (infml) تَعِبَتْ أَعْصابُهُ من الانْتِظار

sweatband /'swɛtband/ *n* عُصابة الرَأْسِ

sweater /'swɛtə/ *n* كَنْزة

sweat gland *n* غُدّة عَرَقيّة

sweatpants /'swɛtpants/ *n pl* سِرْوال \ بَنْطَلون رِياضيّ

sweatshirt /'swɛtʃəːt/ *n* سْويت شيرْت (كَنْزة قُطْنيّة سَميكة)

sweatshop /'swɛtʃɒp/ *n* (pej) مَعْمَل اسْتِغْلاليّ (يُسَخِّرُ فيه العُمّالُ بِأَجْرٍ زَهيدٍ)

sweatsuit /'swɛtsuːt/ *n* بَدْلة رِياضيّة

sweaty /'swɛti/ *adj* (**sweatier, sweatiest**) ‹*palm, player*› مُبْتَلّ بالعَرَق, عَرْقان (dipt)

swede /swiːd/ *n* (BrE) كُرُنْب لِفْتيّ

Swede /swiːd/ *n* سُويديّ

Sweden /'swiːd(ə)n/ *pr n* السُويد (f)

Swedish /'swiːdɪʃ/ **A** *adj* ‹*ambassador, food*› سُويديّ

B *n* **1** (language) السُويديّة (اللُغة) **2** (**the Swedish**) (people) السُويديّونَ

sweep /swiːp/ **A** *vt* (*past tense, past participle* **swept**) **1** (to clean) كَنَسَ (u; كَنْس) ‹*a floor, the streets*›; نَظَّفَ ‹*a chimney*› **2** (to move with a broom) كَنَسَ (u; كَنْس) ‹*dust, snow*›; (with the hand) أَزاحَ; **she swept the hair from her face** رَفَعَتْ شَعْرَها عن وَجْهِها **3** (to move with force) جَرَفَ ,(دَفْع ;a) دَفَعَ ,اجْتاحَ (u; جَرْف) ‹*a person, an object*›; **he swept the pieces off the board** أَزاحَ القِطَعَ من على الطاوِلةِ; **I swept him into my arms** ضَمَمْتُهُ بين ذِراعَيَّ; **to ~ sb overboard** جَرَفَ شَخْصاً إلى الماءِ **4** (to spread through) «storms, epidemics, rumours» اجْتاحَ ,(في) انْتَشَرَ; **the new craze that swept the nation** مَوْجة الهَوَسِ الجَديدة الّتي اجْتاحَت \ اكْتَسَحَت البِلادَ **5** (to search, survey) «police, guards» مَشَّطَ; «searchlights, beams» سَطَعَ (a; سُطوع) (في); **her eyes swept the room** جالَتْ عَيْناها في الغُرْفةِ

B *vi* (*past tense, past participle* **swept**) **1** (to clean) كَنَسَ (u; كَنْس) **2** (to move swiftly) هَبَّ (u; هُبوب ,هَبّ); **the wind swept in from the east** هَبَّت الرِياحُ من الشَرْقِ; **a wave of fear/pain swept over him** اجْتاحَتْهُ نَوْبةٌ من الخَوْفِ \ الأَلَمِ; **to ~ to power** وَصَلَ إلى السُلْطةِ; **to ~ to victory** حَقَّقَ نَصْراً كاسِحاً **3** (to move confidently, majestically) **to ~ in/out** دَخَلَ \ خَرَجَ بِخَطَواتٍ واثِقةٍ **4** (to affect) **bushfires/a storm swept through the area** اجْتاحَتْ حَرائِقُ \ عاصِفةٌ المِنْطَقةَ; **the virus swept through the population** تَفَشّى الفَيْروس بين السُكّانِ **5** (to extend) **the road ~s north** يَمْتَدُّ الطَريقُ شَمالاً; **the mountains ~ down to the sea** تَمْتَدُّ الجِبالُ حتّى البَحْرِ

C *n* **1** (action) كَنْس; **to give the floor a ~** كَنَسَ الأَرْضيّةَ **2** (curving movement) تَلْويح; **with a ~ of his arm** مُلَوِّحاً بِذِراعِهِ **3** (search) تَمْشيط; **to make a ~ of the area** مَشَّطَ المِنْطَقةَ **4** (of a bay, river, the landscape) امْتِداد (امْتِدادات); (of lawn, gravel) مِساحة **5** (scope, range of history, events, opinion) نِطاق (نُطُق) **6** (also **chimney sweep**) مُنَظِّف مَداخِنَ

Idioms **to sweep sb off their feet** خَطَفَ قَلْبَ شَخْصٍ; **to sweep sth under the carpet** *or* (AmE) **rug** دارى على شَيْءٍ; **to sweep the board** اكْتَسَحَ الجَوائِزَ

Phrasal verbs **sweep aside**: **~ [sb/sth] aside, ~ aside [sb/sth]** نَحّى [شَخْصاً \ شَيْئاً] جانِباً ‹*opposition, a suggestion*›

• **sweep away**: ~ **[sb/sth] away**, ~ **away [sb/sth]** 1 (to carry away) [شَخصاً \ شَيْئاً] اجْتاحَ *‹a person, bridge›*; **he was swept away by the music/her enthusiasm** بَهَرَتْهُ الموسيقى \ حَماسَتُها 2 (to get rid of) [شَخصٍ \ شَيْءٍ] تَخَلَّصَ من *‹barriers, obstacles›*

• **sweep up** **A** كَنَسَ (u; كَنْس) **B** ~ **up [sth]**, ~ **[sth] up** 1 (with a broom) [شَيْئاً] كَنَسَ *‹broken glass, leaves›* 2 (with one's arms) [شَيْئاً] حَمَلَ *‹a child, pile of clothes›* 3 (to involve) **to get swept up in a story/the drama of the moment** سَيْطَرَتْ قِصَّةٌ \ لَحْظَةُ الإثارةِ على تَفْكيرِهِ

sweeper /ˈswiːpə/ *n* 1 (road-cleaning person) مُنَظِّف \ كَنّاس شَوارِعَ; (road-cleaning machine) شاحِنة تَنْظيفٍ, مِكْنَسة شَوارِعَ 2 (in soccer) مُدافِع حُرّ

sweeping /ˈswiːpɪŋ/ *adj* 1 (far-reaching) *‹change, powers›* واسِع النِطاقِ, جَسيم 2 (emphatic) *‹victory›* كاسِح; **they won a ~ victory at the polls** فازوا فَوْزاً كاسِحاً في الانْتِخاباتِ 3 (imprecise) *‹statement, generalization›* غَيْر دَقيقٍ, جُزاف 4 (curved) *‹gesture›* مُنْحَنٍ

sweet /swiːt/ **A** *adj* 1 *‹taste, drink, melon›* حُلْو; **a cup of hot, ~ tea** كوب من الشايِ الساخِنِ الحُلْوِ 2 *‹wine, cider›* حُلْو 3 *‹smile›* جَذّاب, جَميل; **the baby has a ~ smile** الرَضيعُ لَهُ اِبْتِسامةٌ جَذّابةٌ 4 *‹note, voice›* عَذْب, جَميل 5 (infml) (for emphasis) **do it in your own ~ time!** افْعَلْهُ في الوَقْتِ الّذي يُلائِمُكَ!

B *adv* **to taste ~** كانَ طَعْمُهُ حُلْواً

C *n* (BrE) 1 (eatable) حَلْوى (f; حَلاوى) 2 (dessert) حُلْو, طَبَق حَلْوى

Idioms **to have a sweet tooth** كانَ مولَعاً بالأَطْعِمةِ الحُلْوةِ; **to keep sb sweet** تَوَدَّدَ إلى شَخْصٍ

sweet-and-sour /ˌswiːt(ə)nˈsaʊə/ *adj before n ‹sauce, pork›* حُلْو وحامِض

sweetbread /ˈswiːtbrɛd/ *n* بَنْكِرِياس العِجْلِ \ الحَمَلِ

sweetcorn /ˈswiːtkɔːn/ *n* 1 (plant) ذُرة سُكَّرِيّة 2 (BrE) (as food) ذُرة حُلْوة

sweeten /ˈswiːt(ə)n/ *vt* 1 حَلّى *‹tea, coffee›* 2 (infml) (to improve) جَعَلَ أَكْثَرَ قُبولاً *‹an offer, the conditions›*; **if we ~ our offer, they are sure to agree** إذا جَعَلْنا عَرْضَنا أَكْثَرَ قُبولاً فَلا بُدَّ أنْ يُوافِقوا

sweetener /ˈswiːt(ə)nə/ *n* 1 (additive) بَديل السُكَّرِ 2 (infml) (bribe) رَشْوة (رُشًى)

sweetheart /ˈswiːthɑːt/ *n* 1 (boyfriend) حَبيب (أَحِبّاءُ); (girlfriend) حَبيبة 2 (dear, darling) حَبيبي, حَبيبَتي

sweetly /ˈswiːtli/ *adv ‹to smile, ask›* بِلُطْفٍ, بِعُذوبةٍ

sweet pepper *n* فِلْفِل حُلْو

sweet potato *n* بَطاطا حُلْوة

sweet shop *n* (BrE) دُكّان حَلْوَياتٍ

sweet-talk *vt* (infml) داهَنَ

swell /swɛl/ **A** *n* 1 (of the sea) عُباب, مَوْج (n coll; أَمْواج); **a heavy ~** أَمْواج مُرْتَفِعة, عُباب جارِف 2 (upsurge) اِزْدِياد (اِزْدِيادات), اِرْتِفاع 3 (rounded shape) اِنْتِفاخ (اِنْتِفاخات) 4 (in sound) اِرْتِفاع تَدْريجيّ

B *adj* (AmE infml old use) *‹guy, party, idea›* رائِع, مُمْتاز

C *vt* (*past tense* **swelled**, *past participle* **swollen** or **swelled**)
1 (to increase) ضَخَّمَ, زادَ (i; زِيادة) *‹the numbers, population›*
2 (to make larger) نَفَخَ (a; نَفْخ), زادَ الحَجْمَ *‹the wood, grain›*
3 (to cause to rise) «rain» زادَ المَنْسوبَ \ المُسْتَوى *‹a river›*

D *vi* (*past tense* **swelled**, *past participle* **swollen** or **swelled**)
1 (to expand) «wood, door, buds» اِنْتَفَخَ; **her heart ~ed with pride** اِمْتَلأَتْ بالفَخْرِ 2 «feet, glands» تَوَرَّمَ 3 (to increase) «numbers, population» اِزْدادَ (اِزْدِياد), زادَ (i; زِيادة), تَضَخَّمَ; **the crowd ~ed to over 3,000** اِزْدادَ الحَشْدُ إلى أَكْثَرَ من 3000 شَخْصٍ 4 «rivers» اِرْتَفَعَ مَنْسوبُ الماءِ بِهِ 5 «sails» اِنْتَفَخَ, اِرْتَفَعَ 6 (to grow louder) «music, singing» اِمْتَلأَ بالهَواءِ

Phrasal verb **swell up** «face, ankles» تَوَرَّمَ

swelling /ˈswɛlɪŋ/ *n* تَوَرُّم (تَوَرُّمات)

sweltering /ˈswɛltərɪŋ/ *adj ‹heat, day›* قائِظ, حارّ جِدّاً

swept /swɛpt/ *past tense, past participle* ▸ **sweep**

swerve /swəːv/ *vi* «cars, driver» اِنْحَرَفَ, حادَ (على نَحْوٍ مُفاجِئٍ)

swift /swɪft/ **A** *adj* 1 *‹action, response›* عاجِل, سَريع, خاطِف 2 *‹movement, animal›* سَريع (سِراع)

B *n* سَمامة

swiftly /ˈswɪftli/ *adv* 1 (rapidly) ‹*to move, run*› بِسُرْعةٍ 2 (promptly) ‹*to act, respond*› بِدونِ تَأْخيرٍ

swig /swɪɡ/ (infml) **A** *vt* (-gg-) تَجَرَّعَ ‹*beer, wine*› **B** *n* جُرْعة (جُرَع)

swill /swɪl/ (infml) **A** *vt* 1 (to drink) عَبَّ (u; عَبّ), شَرِبَ بِنَهَمٍ ‹*beer, tea, wine*› 2 (to rinse) غَسَلَ (i; غَسْل), شَطَفَ (u; شَطْف) ‹*glass, cup*›

B *n* 1 (also **pig swill**) طَعام خَنازيرَ 2 (food) طَعام رَديء; (drink) شَراب رَديء

(Phrasal verbs) **swill around, swill about** (BrE) «liquids» تَقَلَّبَ

• **swill down**: **~ [sth] down, ~ down [sth]** (infml) (to accompany) تَناوَلَ شَراباً مع [شَيْءٍ] ‹*food, a meal*›

swim /swɪm/ **A** *vt* (*present participle* **-mm-**; *past tense* **swam**; *past participle* **swum**) 1 سَبَحَ (a; سِباحة), عامَ (u; عَوْم) ‹*a mile, length*›; **to ~ breaststroke/backstroke** سَبَحَ على صَدْرِهِ \ ظَهْرِهِ 2 عَبَرَ سِباحةً ‹*the Channel, a river*› 3 سَبَحَ (a; سِباحة) في ‹*a race*›

B *vi* (*present participle* **-mm-**; *past tense* **swam**; *past participle* **swum**) 1 «people, fish, animals» سَبَحَ (a; سِباحة), عامَ (u; عَوْم); **to go ~ming** ذَهَبَ للسباحة; **we swam across the river and back** سَبَحْنا إلى الضفَةِ الأُخرى من النَهْرِ ثُمَّ عُدْنا; **to ~ out to sea** سَبَحَ في البَحْرِ بَعيداً عن الشاطِئِ 2 (to be immersed) **the salad was ~ming in olive oil** كانَتْ السَلَطةُ تَعومُ في زَيْتِ الزَيْتونِ; **her eyes were ~ming with tears** كانَتْ عَيْناها غارِقَتَيْنِ في الدُموعِ 3 (to reel, whirl) «one's head, the room» دارَ (u; دَوْر, دَوَران)

C *n* عَوْم, سِباحة; **to go for a ~** ذَهَبَ للسِباحةِ

(Idiom) **to swim against/with the tide** سَبَحَ مع \ ضِدّ التَيّارِ

swimmer /ˈswɪmə/ *n* سَبّاح

swimming /ˈswɪmɪŋ/ *n* سِباحة

swimming costume *n* (BrE) مايوه, زِيّ \ ثَوْب سِباحةٍ (مايوهات)

swimming pool *n* حَوْض سِباحةٍ

swimming trunks *n* سِرْوال سِباحةٍ

swimsuit /ˈswɪmsuːt/ *n* مايوه, زِيّ \ ثَوْب سِباحةٍ (مايوهات)

swindle /ˈswɪnd(ə)l/ **A** *vt* نَصَبَ (u; نَصْب), احْتالَ (على), غَشَّ (u; غِشّ), اخْتَلَسَ ‹*investors, clients*› **B** *n* نَصْب (أَنْصاب), احْتِيال (احْتِيالات), غِشّ, اخْتِلاس (اخْتِلاسات)

swindler /ˈswɪndlə/ *n* مُحْتال, نَصّاب

swine /swʌɪn/ *n* 1 (*pl* **swine**) (pig) خِنْزير (خَنازيرُ) 2 (*pl* **swine** or **swines**) (infml pej) (contemptible person) خِنْزير (خَنازيرُ), وَغْد (أَوْغاد)

swine flu *n* انْفْلُوَنْزا الخَنازيرِ

swing /swɪŋ/ **A** *vt* (*past tense, past participle* **swung**) 1 (to and fro) أَرْجَحَ ‹*a bucket, lantern*›; **to ~ one's legs** أَرْجَحَ رِجْلَيْهِ; **the soldiers swung their arms as they marched** أَرْجَحَ الجُنودُ أَيْديَهُمْ وَهُمْ يَسيرونَ في المارْشِ العَسْكَريِّ 2 (in a curve) لَفَّ (u; لَفّ), أَدارَ, أَرْجَحَ (dipt) ‹*a golf club, bat*›; **she swung the bag over her shoulder** عَلَّقَت الحَقيبةَ على كَتِفِها 3 (to influence) غَيَّرَ, حَوَّلَ ‹*an election, the vote*› 4 (infml) (to bring off) ظَفِرَ (a; ظَفَر) (ب), أَنْجَزَ ‹*a deal*›; **I think we can ~ it** أَعْتَقِدُ أَنَّنا نَسْتَطيعُ أَنْ نَظْفَرَ بِهِ

B *vi* (*past tense, past participle* **swung**) 1 (to and fro) «pendulum, legs» تَأَرْجَحَ; **the door swung open/shut** تَأَرْجَحَ البابُ وَانْفَتَحَ \ وَانْغَلَقَ 2 (in a curve) انْعَطَفَ; **the car swung into the drive** انْعَطَفَت السَيّارةُ إلى المَمَرِّ; **she swung around to face me** اسْتَدارَتْ نَحْوي; **to ~ into action** بَدَأَ في العَمَلِ بِهِمّةٍ 3 (infml) (to attempt to hit) **to ~ at sb** وَجَّهَ لَكْمةً لِشَخْصٍ; **he swung at the ball and missed** حاوَلَ أَنْ يَضْرِبَ الكُرةَ وَلَكِنَّهُ أَخْطَأَ 4 (to shift) «moods, opinions» تَغَيَّرَ, تَحَوَّلَ; **the party has swung to the left/right** تَحَوَّلَ الحِزْبُ إلى اليَسارِ \ اليَمينِ; **the game could ~ either way** قد تَتَحَوَّلُ المُباراةُ لِصالِحِ أَيٍّ من الفَريقَيْنِ 5 (infml) (to be lively) **a club which really ~s** نادٍ يَتَأَلَّقُ حَقّاً

C *n* 1 (of a pendulum) تَأَرْجُح; (of the hips) تَمايُل 2 (infml) (punch) ضَرْبة (ضَرَبات); **he took a ~ at me** وَجَّهَ لَكْمةً لي 3 (in voting, public opinion) تَغَيُّر (تَغَيُّرات), تَحَوُّل (تَحَوُّلات); **a 10% ~ to the Liberals/against the government** تَغَيُّر بِنِسْبةِ 10٪ لِصالِحِ الليبراليّينَ \ ضِدّ الحُكومةِ 4 (in prices, demand) تَذَبْذُب, تَقَلُّب (تَقَلُّبات) 5 (in playgrounds) أُرْجوحة (أَراجيحُ) 6 [u] (in golf) تَأَرْجُح 7 (rhythm) إيقاع (إيقاعات)

8 [u] (style of jazz) موسيقى السْوينْغ; **the era of ~** عَصْر موسيقى السْوينْغ 9 (tour) جَوْلة; **a ~ through the southern states** جَوْلة في الوِلاياتِ الجَنوبيّةِ

(Idioms) **to be in full swing** كانَ في أَوْجِهِ; **to get into the swing of things** (infml) بَدَأَ يَتَأَقْلَمُ

swingbin /ˈswɪŋbɪn/ *n* صُنْدوق قُمامةٍ

swing bridge *n* جِسْر دوّار \ مُتَحرِّك

swing door (BrE), **swinging door** (AmE) *n* باب مِرْوَحة

swipe /swʌɪp/ **A** *vt* 1 (to hit) صَفَعَ (a; صَفْع) ‹*sb's face, hand*› 2 (for validation) أَدْخَل, مَرَّر (بِطاقةً مَغْنَطيسيّةً في قارِئةِ بِطاقاتٍ) ‹*a credit card*› 3 (infml) (to steal) سَرَقَ (i; سَرِقة) ‹*the bag, cash*›

B *n* صَفْعة; **to take a ~ at sth/sb** صَفَعَ شَيْئاً \ شخصاً

swipe card *n* بِطاقة مَغْنَطيسيّة

swirl /swɜːl/ **A** *vi* «dust, leaves, water» اِلْتَفَّ في دَوّامةٍ; «skirts, dancers» دارَ, اِلْتَفَّ (u; دَوَران)

B *n* (of cream, smoke) دَوّامة

swish /swɪʃ/ **A** *vi* «skirt, tail, cane» [أَحْدَثَ صَوْتاً كالصَفيرِ أو الحَفيفِ]

B *n* صَفير, حَفيف

Swiss /swɪs/ *n, adj* (*n pl* **Swiss**) سُويسْريّ

switch /swɪtʃ/ **A** *n* 1 (change) تَغْيير, (تَحَوُّلات) تَحَوُّل (اِنْتِقالات) اِنْتِقال, (تَغْييرات); **the ~ from analogue to digital TV** الاِنْتِقال من التِلِفِزْيون التَماثُليِّ إلى التِلِفِزْيون الرَقْميِّ; **a ~ in tactics** تَغْيير في السِياساتِ 2 (electrical) مِفْتاح (مَفاتيحُ); **the on-off ~** مِفْتاح التَشْغيلِ والغَلْقِ

B *vt* 1 (to change) غَيَّرَ ‹*one's allegiance, attention, jobs*›; **to ~ sides/brands** تَحَوَّلَ من جانِبٍ إلى آخَرَ \ سِلْعةٍ إلى أُخْرى; **it's easy to ~ your account from one bank to another** من السَهْلِ أَنْ تُحَوِّلَ حِسابَكَ من بَنْكٍ إلى آخَرَ 2 (to exchange) بَدَّلَ, غَيَّرَ ‹*places, objects*›; **I've ~ed the furniture round** غَيَّرْتُ تَرْتيبَ الأَثاثِ

C *vi* 1 (to change) «voters, consumers» تَحَوَّلَ; **she ~ed from the violin to the viola** تَحَوَّلَتْ من الكَمانِ إلى الكَمانِ المُتَوَسِّطِ; **this button lets you ~ between applications** هذا الزِرُّ يَجْعَلُكَ تُحَوِّلُ بين التَطْبيقاتِ 2 (to change roles) **to ~ with sb** بَدَّلَ مع شَخْصٍ

(Phrasal verbs) **switch off** **A** 1 (to turn off) «lights, heating» أَطْفَأَ, أَغْلَقَ 2 (infml) (to stop listening, viewing) تَوَقَّفَ عن المُتابَعةِ; **when he talks about the old days, I just ~ off** عِنْدَما يَتَحَدَّثُ عن الأَيّامِ الخَوالي، أَتَوَقَّفُ عن الإِصْغاءِ إِلَيْهِ **B ~ off** [sth], **~** [sth] **off** 1 أَطْفَأَ \ أَغْلَقَ [شَيْئاً] ‹*a light, an appliance, engine*›; **please ~ off your phones** يُرْجى إِغْلاقُ الهَواتِفِ 2 أَغْلَقَ [شَيْئاً] ‹*the water, electricity*›

• **switch on** **A** «lights» أَضاءَ; «heating» اِشْتَغَلَ **B ~ on** [sth], **~** [sth] **on** أَضاءَ [شَيْئاً] ‹*a light*›; شَغَّلَ [شَيْئاً] ‹*an appliance, engine*›

• **switch over** 1 (to change channels) حَوَّلَ 2 (to change) حَوَّلَ; **we have ~ed over from oil to gas** حَوَّلْنا من النَفْطِ إلى الغازِ

switchblade /ˈswɪtʃbleɪd/ *n* (AmE) مِطْواة (مَطاوٍ)

switchboard /ˈswɪtʃbɔːd/ *n* بَدّالة الهاتِفِ

switchboard operator *n* مُشَغِّل بَدّالةِ, عامِل الهاتِفِ الهاتِفِ

switchover /ˈswɪtʃˌəʊvə/ *n* تَحَوُّل (تَحَوُّلات), اِنْتِقال (اِنْتِقالات)

Switzerland /ˈswɪtsələnd/ *pr n* سُويسْرا

swivel /ˈswɪv(ə)l/ **A** *vt* (**-ll-** BrE, **-l-** AmE) أَدارَ ‹*one's head, chair*›

B *vi* (**-ll-** BrE, **-l-** AmE) «head, camera» دارَ (u; دَوَران)

swivel chair *n* كُرْسيّ دَوّار

swollen /ˈswəʊlən/ **A** *past participle* ▸ **swell**

B *adj* ‹*glands*› مُتَوَرِّم; ‹*eyes, ankle*› مَنْفوخ, مُنْتَفِخ; ‹*river*› مُتَدَفِّق

swoon /swuːn/ *vi* (liter) «girl, woman» اِنْتَشى, أُغْمِيَ عَلَيْهِ (لِشِدّةِ إِعْجابِهِ); **to ~ over sb** اِنْتَشى لِمَرْأى شَخْصٍ

swoop /swuːp/ **A** *vi* 1 «bird, plane» اِنْقَضَّ 2 «police, detectives» داهَمَ

B *n* 1 (of a bird, plane) اِنْقِضاض (اِنْقِضاضات) 2 (raid) مُداهَمة, اِنْقِضاض (اِنْقِضاضات)

(Idiom) **in one fell swoop** في ضَرْبةٍ واحِدةٍ, مَرّةً واحِدةً

swop /swɒp/ *n, vt* ▸ **swap**

sword /sɔːd/ *n* سَيْف (أَسْيَاف ,سُيُوف)

Idioms **to be a double-edged sword** كانَ سَيْفاً ذا حَدَّيْنِ; **to cross swords with sb** تَجادَلَ \ تَخاصَمَ مع شَخْصٍ

swordfish /ˈsɔːdfɪʃ/ *n* (*pl* **swordfish**) سَمَك \ أَبو سَيْفٍ

swordsman /ˈsɔːdzmən/ *n* (*pl* **-men**) سَيّاف (سَيّافة)

swore /swɔː/ *past tense* ▸ **swear**

sworn /swɔːn/ **A** *past participle* ▸ **swear**

B *adj* **1** ‹*statement, testimony*› بعد اليَمين ,تحت القَسَم **2** ‹*enemy, brother*› لدود (أَلِدّاءُ)

swot /swɒt/ (BrE infml) **A** *vi* (**-tt-**) «student, child» جَدَّ (i; جَدّ) **B** *n* (pej) [شَخْص مُجْتَهِد في الدِراسةِ]

swum /swʌm/ *past participle* ▸ **swim**

swung /swʌŋ/ *past tense, past participle* ▸ **swing** A, B

sycamore /ˈsɪkəmɔː/ *n* (also **sycamore tree**) **1** (BrE) (maple) دُلْب ,جُمَّيْز **2** (AmE) (plane tree) قَيْقَب ,إِسْفِنْدان

sycophantic /ˌsɪkəˈfantɪk/ *adj* ‹*interview, praise*› مُتَزَلِّف ,مُداهِن

Sydney /ˈsɪdni/ *pr n* سيدْني (f)

syllable /ˈsɪləb(ə)l/ *n* مَقْطَع (الكَلِمة)

syllabus /ˈsɪləbəs/ *n* (*pl* **syllabuses** or **syllabi**) مِنْهاج دِراسيّ

symbiosis /sɪmbʌɪˈəʊsɪs/ *n* (*pl* **symbioses** /-ˈəʊsiːz/) تَكافُل, تَعايُش

symbiotic /sɪmbʌɪˈɒtɪk/ *adj* ‹*relationship, association*› تَكافُليّ

symbol /ˈsɪmb(ə)l/ *n* رَمْز (رُموز)

symbolic /sɪmˈbɒlɪk/ *adj* ‹*gesture, meaning*› رَمْزِيّ; **to be ~ of sth** كانَ رَمْزاً لِشَيْءٍ

symbolism /ˈsɪmbəliz(ə)m/ *n* رَمْزِيّة

symbolize, -ise (BrE) /ˈsɪmbəlʌɪz/ *vt* رَمَزَ (i-u; رَمْز ;إِلى) ‹*power, peace*›

symmetrical /sɪˈmɛtrɪk(ə)l/, **symmetric** /sɪˈmɛtrɪk/ *adj* ‹*pattern, structure*› مُتَناسِق ,مُتَناسِب ,مُتَماثِل

symmetry /ˈsɪmɪtri/ *n* تَناسُق ,تَناسُب ,تَماثُل

sympathetic /sɪmpəˈθɛtɪk/ *adj* **1** (caring) ‹*response, look*› حَنون ,مُتَعاطِف; **she was very ~ when I explained the problem** كانَتْ مُتَعاطِفةً جِدًّا عِنْدَما شَرَحْتُ لَها المُشْكِلةَ **2** (favourably inclined) ‹*audience, crowd*› مُؤَيِّد ,(رُضاة) راضٍ; **I am ~ to or towards their aims** أَدْعَمُ أَهْدافَهُمْ

sympathetically /sɪmpəˈθɛtɪkli/ *adv* **1** (with compassion) بِتَفَهُّمٍ; (with understanding) ‹*to nod, listen*› بِتَعاطُفٍ **2** (favourably) ‹*to treat, respond*› بِصورةٍ إيجابيّةٍ

sympathize, -ise (BrE) /ˈsɪmpəθʌɪz/ *vi* **1** «person» (to show compassion) تَعاطَفَ (مع); (to understand) تَفَهَّمَ; **I do ~ with you** إِنّي أُشارِكُكَ شُعورَكَ **2** (to support) **to ~ with sth/sb** «person, organization» أَيَّدَ شَيْئاً \ شَخْصاً

sympathizer, -iser (BrE) /ˈsɪmpəθʌɪzə/ *n* مُؤَيِّد

sympathy /ˈsɪmpəθi/ *n* **1** (compassion) عَطْف ,تَعاطُف; **I have no ~ for him** لا أَتَعاطَفُ مَعَهُ **2** (condolence) مُواساة ,عَزاء; **we extend our deepest ~ to your family** نُقَدِّمُ أَحَرَّ التَعازي والمُواساةِ لِعائِلَتِكُمْ **3** (support) تَأْييد (تَأْييدات); **I have some ~ for or with that viewpoint** أُؤَيِّدُ وُجْهةَ النَظَرِتِلْكَ بَعْضَ الشَيْءِ **4** (affinity) تَفَهُّم **5** (**sympathies** *n pl*) (loyalty, leanings) وَلاء

symphony /ˈsɪmf(ə)ni/ *n* (*pl* **symphonies**) سِمْفونيّة

symphony orchestra *n* أورْكِسْترا \ فِرْقة سِمْفونيّة

symposium /sɪmˈpəʊzɪəm/ *n* (*pl* **symposiums** or **symposia** /-zɪə/) نَدْوة (نَدَوات)

symptom /ˈsɪmptəm/ *n* عَرَض (أَعْراض)

symptomatic /sɪmptəˈmatɪk/ *adj* عَرَضِيّ; **to be ~ of sth** كانَ دالًّا على شَيْءٍ

synagogue /ˈsɪnəgɒg/ *n* كَنيس \ مَعْبَد يَهوديّ

synchronize, -ise (BrE) /ˈsɪŋkrənʌɪz/ *vt* جَعَلَ مُتَزامِناً ,زامَنَ ‹*clocks, movements*›

synchronized swimming /ˌsɪŋkrənʌɪzd ˈswɪmɪŋ/ *n* سِباحة مُتَزامِنة

syncope /ˈsɪŋkəpi/ *n* غَشْي ,(إِغْماءات) إِغْماء

syndicate **A** /ˈsɪndɪkət/ *n* **1** (interest group) مَجْموعة \ اتِّحاد شَرِكاتٍ; **a crime ~** مَجْموعة إِجْراميّة **2** (news agency) وِكالة أَنْباءٍ

B *vt* (in journalism) [نَشَرَ في وَسائِلِ إِعْلامٍ مُتَعَدِّدةٍ] ‹*a column, the photographs*›

syndrome /ˈsɪndrəʊm/ *n* مُتَلازِمة

synonymous /sɪˈnɒnɪməs/ *adj* ‹*word, term*› مُتَرادِف, مُرادِف; **to be ~ with sth** كانَ مُرادِفاً لِشَيْءٍ

synopsis /sɪˈnɒpsɪs/ *n* (*pl* **synopses**) مُلَخَّص (مُلَخَّصات), مُخْتَصَر (مُخْتَصَرات), موجَز (مَواجِزُ)

syntax /ˈsɪntaks/ *n* نَحْو

synthesis /ˈsɪnθɪsɪs/ *n* (*pl* **syntheses**) 1 (of elements) تَخْليق, تَرْكيب 2 (of ideas) مَزْج, جَمْع, تَوْليف

synthesize, **-ise** (BrE), **-ise** (BrE) /ˈsɪnθɪsʌɪz/ *vt* رَكَّبَ, أَنْتَجَ ‹*proteins, elements*›

synthesizer, **-iser** (BrE) /ˈsɪnθɪsʌɪzə/ *n* سِنْثْسَيْزِر (آلة موسيقيّة إلِكْترونيّة)

synthetic /sɪnˈθetɪk/ A *adj* ‹*material, fibre*› اصْطِناعيّ
B (**synthetics**) *n pl* مَوادّ اصْطِناعيّة

syphilis /ˈsɪfɪlɪs/ *n* سِفْلِس, زُهْرِيّ

syphon *n, vt* ▸ **siphon**

Syria /ˈsɪrɪə/ *pr n* سوريا

Syrian /ˈsɪrɪən/ *n, adj* سوريّ

syringe /sɪˈrɪndʒ/ A *n* مِحْقَنة (مَحاقِنُ)
B *vt* [شَطَفَ \ غَسَلَ بِإبْرة طِبِّيّة] ‹*ears, a wound*›

syrup /ˈsɪrəp/ *n* 1 (sweet liquid) قَطْر (قِطار), شَراب (أَشْرِبة) 2 (medicinal) شَراب (أَشْرِبة)

system /ˈsɪstəm/ *n* 1 (structure) نِظام (نُظُم, أَنْظِمة); **the banking/justice ~** النِظام المَصْرَفيّ \ القَضائيّ; **to reform the tax ~** أَصْلَحَ النِظامَ الضَريبيّ; **a ~ for organizing my accounts** نِظام لِتَنْظيم حِساباتي 2 (technical, mechanical) نِظام (نُظُم), جِهاز (أَجْهِزة, أَنْظِمة); **a stereo ~** جِهاز سْتيريو (أَجْهِزة); **the brake ~** نِظام الفَرامِل \ المَكابِح 3 (of humans, animals) جِهاز (أَجْهِزة); **the reproductive/respiratory ~** الجِهاز التَناسُليّ \ التَنَفُّسيّ; **to get sth out of one's ~** (infml) نَفَّسَ عن شَيْءٍ يُضايِقُهُ 4 (in computing) جِهاز (أَجْهِزة) 5 (**the System**) (establishment) النِظام; **to beat the ~** تَغَلَّبَ على النِظام 6 (for classification) نِظام (نُظُم, أَنْظِمة); **the metric ~** النِظام المِتْريّ

systematic /sɪstəˈmatɪk/ *adj* ‹*approach, person*› نِظاميّ, مَنْهَجيّ

systematically /sɪstəˈmatɪkli/ *adv* ‹*to examine, work*› بِصورةٍ مَنْهَجيّة

systemic /sɪˈstemɪk/ *adj* 1 ‹*insecticide, fungicide*› جِهازيّ 2 ‹*disease, symptom*› جِهازيّ, مَجْموعيّ 3 ‹*failure, change*› عامّ, شامِل

systems analyst *n* مُحَلِّل أَنْظِمةٍ

systems engineer *n* مُهَنْدِس نُظُمٍ

systems programmer (BrE), **systems programer** (AmE) *n* مُبَرمِج نُظُمِ مَعْلوماتٍ

Tt

T, t /tiː/ *n* تاء ≈ (الحَرْف العِشرونَ من الأَبْجَدِيّة الإنْكْليزيّة)

Idiom **to a T** (infml) تماماً

tab /tab/ *n* 1 (on files) عَلامة تَبْويبٍ 2 (on gloves, rucksack) مِقْبَض (مَقابِضُ) 3 (for securing) مِشْبَك (للشَدِّ) 4 (on drinks can, bag) [عُرْوة صَغيرة على غِطاءِ العُلْبةِ تُرْفَعُ لِفَتْحِها] 5 (infml) (bill) فاتورة (فَواتيرُ); **to pick up the ~ for the drinks** دَفَعَ فاتورةَ المَشْروباتِ 6 (in typing) عَلامة تَبْويبٍ \ جَدْوَلة (على لَوْحةِ المَفاتيحِ) 7 (in web browsers, spreadsheets) [صَفْحة على شاشةِ الحاسوبِ]

Idiom **to keep tabs on sth/sb** راقَبَ شَيْئاً \ شَخْصاً

tabbouleh /təˈbuːleɪ, ˈtabuːleɪ/ *n* تَبّولة

tabby /ˈtabi/ *n* (also **tabby cat**) قِطّ (أَرْقَط)

table /ˈteɪb(ə)l/ **A** *n* 1 (piece of furniture) طاولة, مائدة, مَنْضَدة (مَناضِدُ ,مَنْضَدات); **a kitchen/dining-room ~** مائِدة \ طاوِلة; **at ~** على المائدة \ الطاوِلةِ; **to lay/set the ~** أَعَدَّ المائِدة \ طاوِلةَ الطَعامِ; **to clear the ~** نَظَّفَ المائِدة \ طاوِلةَ الطَعامِ; **to put an offer on the ~** وَضَعَ عَرْضاً على الطاوِلةِ; **the plan is to get the parties round the ~** الخُطّةُ هي أنْ نَجْمَعَ كُلَّ الأَطْرافِ حول الطاوِلةِ 2 (list) جَدْوَل (جَداوِلُ); **to present the information in a ~** قَدَّمَ المَعْلوماتِ في جَدْوَلٍ; **a conversion ~** جَدْول تَحْويلٍ; **~ of contents** جَدْوَل مُحْتَوَياتٍ 3 (also **multiplication tables**) جَدْوَل الضَرْبِ; **the six-times ~** جَدْوَل ضَرْبِ العَدَدِ 6 4 (also **league table**) [لائِحة أَنْدِيةٍ رِياضِيّةٍ مَدْرَسِيّةٍ في المَمْلَكةِ المُتَّحِدةِ]; **to be at the top/bottom of the ~** كانَ في أَعْلى \ أَسْفَلِ التَرْتيبِ

B *vt* 1 (BrE) (to present) قَدَّمَ ‹*a proposal, an amendment*›; **to ~ an amendment to the bill** قَدَّمَ تَعْديلاً على مَشْروعِ قانونٍ 2 (AmE) (to postpone) أَجَّلَ ‹*the issue, plan*›

Idiom **to turn the tables on sb** قَلَبَ الطاوِلةَ على شَخْصٍ

tablecloth /ˈteɪbəlklɒθ/ *n* غِطاء المائِدةِ

table linen *n* مِفْرَش مائِدةٍ

table manners *n pl* آداب المائِدةِ

table mat *n* [حَصيرة صَغيرة توضَعُ تحت الصَحْنِ]

tablespoon /ˈteɪbəlspuːn/ *n* 1 (utensil) مِلْعَقة (مَلاعِقُ) 2 (also **tablespoonful**) مِلْعَقة كَبيرة

tablet /ˈtablɪt/ *n* 1 (pill) حَبّة \ قُرْص دَواءٍ 2 ® (computer) كُمْبيوتر لَوْحِيّ 3 (with inscription) لَوْح (أَلْواح)

table tennis *n* تِنِس الطاوِلةِ

tableware /ˈteɪbəlwɛː/ *n* أَدَوات مائِدةٍ

tabloid /ˈtablɔɪd/ **A** *n* صَحيفة تابْلويْد

B *adj before n* ‹*press, journalism*› تابْلويْد ,مُبْتَذَل

taboo /təˈbuː/ **A** *n, adj*

B *n* تابو (تابوهات)

C *adj* ‹*subject, word*› من المُحَرَّماتِ

tabulate /ˈtabjʊleɪt/ *vt* وَضَعَ في جَداوِلَ ,بَوَّبَ ‹*results, data*›

tachograph /ˈtakəgrɑːf/ *n* تاكوغْراف (عَدّاد لِقِياسِ سُرْعةِ السَيّارةِ لِفَتْرةٍ مُعَيَّنةٍ)

tachometer /taˈkɒmɪtə/ *n* عَدّاد الدَوَرانِ

tacit /ˈtasɪt/ *adj* ‹*support, agreement*› ضِمْنِيّ

taciturn /ˈtasɪtəːn/ *adj* ‹*disposition, person*› قَليل الكَلامِ ,مُتَحَفِّظ

tack /tak/ **A** *n* 1 (small nail) مِسْمار تَنْجيدٍ 2 (AmE) (drawing pin) دَبّوس (دَبابيسُ) 3 (approach) مُقارَبة; **to take** *or* **try a different ~** جَرَّبَ مُقارَبةً مُخْتَلِفةً; **to change ~** غَيَّرَ المُقارَبةَ 4 (in sailing) [إبْحار بِطَريقةٍ مُتَعَرِّجةٍ] 5 (stitch) رَتَق; **to put a ~ into the hem** رَتَقَ قَطْعَتَي القُماشِ 6 [u] (for horses) [عُدّة الحِصانِ من سَرْجٍ وَرِكابٍ وَلِجامٍ]

B *vt* 1 (to attach) **to ~ sth to the wall** ثَبَّتَ شَيْئاً على الجِدارِ

ثَبَّتَ سَجّاداً بِمَسامِيرَ تَنْجيدٍ; بِدَبّوسٍ **to ~ a carpet down**

2 رَتَقَ (i-u; رَتْق) ‹*a hem, sheet*›

C *vi* «yacht, sailor» أَبْحَرَ بِشَكْلٍ مُتَعَرِّجٍ; **to ~ to port/starboard** اتَّخَذَ مَساراً مُتَعَرِّجاً نحو اليَسارِ \ اليَمين

(Phrasal verb) **tack on**: **~ [sth] on, ~ on [sth]** (infml) أَلْحَقَ [شَيْئاً] ‹*a clause, building*›

tackle /'tak(ə)l/ **A** *n* **1** (on an opponent) تَصَدٍّ (تَصَدِّيات), **2** (also **fishing tackle**) أَدَوات \ عُدَّة صَيْدِ السَمَكِ **2** مُواجَهة **3** (for lifting) بَكَرة (بَكَرات, بَكَر)

B *vt* **1** (to face up to) عالَجَ ‹*a problem, task*›; **firefighters ~d the blaze** واجَهَ رِجالُ الإِطْفاءِ الحَريقَ; **to ~ sb about sth** واجَهَ شَخْصاً بِشَيْءٍ **2** (to confront) تَصَدّى, واجَهَ ‹*an intruder*› **3** (in football, hockey, etc) ‹*a forward, player*› [حاوَلَ افْتِكاكَ الكُرةِ]

tacky /'taki/ *adj* (**tackier**, **tackiest**) **1** (infml) (cheap and tasteless) ‹*souvenir, clothes*› مُبْتَذَل, رَديء **2** (sticky) ‹*surface, paint*› دَبِق

tact /takt/ *n* بَراعة, لَباقة

tactful /'taktfʊl/ *adj* ‹*manner, person, reply*› لَبِق

tactfully /'taktf(ə)li/ *adv* ‹*to suggest, decline*› بِلَباقةٍ

tactic /'taktɪk/ *n* تَكْتيك; (**tactics** *n pl*) (Mil) تَكْتيكات

tactical /'taktɪk(ə)l/ *adj* ‹*advantage, error*› تَكْتيكيّ

tactically /'taktɪkli/ *adv* ‹*to plan*› بِطَريقةٍ تَكْتيكيّةٍ; **to vote ~** صَوَّتَ تَكْتيكيًّا \ إِسْتْراتيجيًّا

tactical voting *n* تَصْويت تَكْتيكيّ

tactician /tak'tɪʃ(ə)n/ *n* مُناوِر ماهِر, خَبير في التَكْتيك

tactless /'taktləs/ *adj* ‹*remark, person*› أَخْرَق (dipt; خُرْق)

tad /tad/ *n* (infml) **a ~ risky/embarrassing** خَطِر \ مُحْرِج بَعْضَ الشَيْءِ

tadpole /'tadpəʊl/ *n* شُرْغوف (شَراغيفُ)

Tadzhikistan, **Tajikistan** /tɑːdʒɪkɪ'stɑːn/ *pr n* طاجيكِسْتان (f)

tae kwon do /ˌtʌɪ kwɒn 'dəʊ/ *n* تكْوانْدو

taffeta /'tafɪtə/ *n* تَفْتة (نَسيج حَريريّ صَقيل)

taffy /'tafi/ *n* (AmE) تافي (حَلْوى لَيِّنة)

tag /tag/ **A** *n* **1** (on products, luggage) بِطاقة (بِطاقات, بَطائِقُ); (for pets) [صَفيحة فيها مَعْلوماتٌ عن حَيَوانٍ مَنْزِليٍّ] **2** (phrase) عِبارة **3** (for criminals) حَلْقة إِلِكْتْرونيّة **4** (form of words) سُؤال ذَيْليّ; **a ~ question** [كَلِمة أو جُمْلة تُسْتَعْمَلُ كَأَداةِ تَأْكيدٍ] **5** [u] (children's game) [لُعْبة يُطارِدُ فيها الأَطْفالُ بَعْضَهُمْ بَعْضاً]; **to play ~** [لَعِبَ لُعْبةَ المُطارَدةِ] **6** (name) كُنْية (كُنًى) **7** (Comput) عَلامة (عَلامات, عَلائِمُ) **8** (piece of graffiti) تَوْقيع **9** (AmE) (infml) (for cars) عَلامة تَسْجيلِ السَيّارةِ جُرافيتي

B *vt* (**-gg-**) **1** (to label) وَضَعَ عَلامةً على ‹*goods, clothing*›

2 (to describe) وَسَمَ (i; وَسْم, سِمة) ‹*a colleague, celebrity*›

3 «police» وَضَعَ حَلْقةً إِلِكْتْرونيّةً ‹*a criminal*› **4** (in mark-up) وَضَعَ عَلامةً على ‹*a paragraph, an image*› **5** (in graffiti) وَقَّعَ اسْمَهُ على ‹*a wall, bus*›

(Phrasal verbs) **tag along** (infml) رافَقَ; **to ~ along with sb** رافَقَ شَخْصاً

• **tag on**: **~ [sth] on** أَضافَ [شَيْئاً] ‹*a question, phrase*›; **I ~ged an extra day onto my holiday** أَضَفْتُ يَوْماً آخَرَ إِلى عُطْلَتي

tagine /tə'ʒiːn, tə'dʒiːn/ *n* **1** (stew) طاجِن (طَواجِنُ) **2** (utensil) طاجِن (طَواجِنُ)

tahini /tɑː'hiːni/, **tahina** /tɑː'hiːnə/ *n* طَحينة

Tahiti /tə'hiːti/ *pr n* تاهيتي (f)

tail /teɪl/ **A** *n* **1** (of mammals, birds, fish) ذَيْل (ذُيول, أَذْيال) **2** (of an aircraft) ذَيْل (ذُيول, أَذْيال); **only the ~ remained** بَقِيَ الذَيْلُ فَقَطْ **3** (infml) (police observer) رَقيب (رُقَباءُ); **to put a ~ on sb** وَضَعَ رَقيباً على شَخْصٍ

B (**tails**) *n pl* **1** (formal wear) مِعْطَف ذو ذَيْلٍ مَشْقوقٍ; **to wear ~s** لَبِسَ مِعْطَفاً ذا ذَيْلٍ مَشْقوقٍ **2** (with coins) قَفا العُمْلةِ المَعْدِنيّةِ; **heads or ~s?** الوَجْهُ أَم القَفا؟

C *vt* «detective, policeman» تَعَقَّبَ ‹*a suspect, car*›

(Idioms) **to be on sb's tail** لازَمَ شَخْصاً كَخَيالِهِ; **the tail is wagging the dog** الذَيْلُ الّذي يَهُزُّ الكَلْبَ; **to turn tail** أَطْلَقَ ساقَيْهِ للريحِ; **as soon as they saw the police they turned ~** ما إِنْ رَأَوْا الشُرْطةَ حتّى أَطْلَقوا سيقانَهُمْ للريحِ

(Phrasal verb) **tail off** **1** (to reduce) «output, demand» تَضاءَلَ, تَراجَعَ **2** (to fade) «voices, conversation» تَلاشى

tailback /ˈteɪlbak/ *n* (BrE) ازْدِحام مُروريّ

tail end *n* (of a season, film) نِهاية; (of a procession, queue) مُؤَخَّرة

tail fin *n* 1 (of a fish) زَعْنِفة الذَيْل 2 (on aircraft) زَعْنِفة خَلْفيّة 3 (on cars) زَعْنِفة خَلْفيّة (كانَتْ شائِعةً في السَيّاراتِ القَديمةِ)

tailgate /ˈteɪlgeɪt/ *n* باب خَلْفيّ

tail light *n* ضَوْء خَلْفيّ

tail-off /ˈteɪlɒf/ *n* تضاؤُل

tailor /ˈteɪlə/ A *n* خيّاط, تَرْزيّ
B *vt* 1 (to make) فصَّل ‹*a suit, clothing*› 2 (to adapt) كَيَّفَ ‹*a service, course*›
C (**tailored**) *adj* ‹*suit, jacket*› مُفَصَّل

tailor-made /teɪləˈmeɪd/ *adj* 1 ‹*suit, shirt*› مُفَصَّل 2 ‹*solution, holiday*› مُصَمَّم (خِصّيصاً)

tailpipe /ˈteɪlpʌɪp/ *n* (AmE) أُنْبوب العادِمِ

taint /teɪnt/ *vt* 1 ‹*sb's image, reputation*› لَطَّخَ 2 ‹*the food, water*› لَوَّثَ

tainted /ˈteɪntɪd/ *adj* 1 ‹*food, water*› مُلَوَّث 2 ‹*image, reputation*› مُلَطَّخ

Taiwan /tʌɪˈwɑːn/ *pr n* تايْوان (f)

Taiwanese /tʌɪwəˈniːz/ *n, adj* (*n pl* **Taiwanese**) تايْوانيّ

Tajikistan /tadʒiːkɪˈstɑːn/ *pr n* ▸ **Tadzhikistan**

takaful /ˈtɑːkəfuːl/ *n* تكافُل

take /teɪk/ A *vt* (*past tense* **took**; *past participle* **taken**) 1 (to pick up) أَخَذَ (u; أَخْذ) ‹*an object, money*›; **he took the book off the shelf** أَخَذَ الكِتابَ من الرَفِّ; **she took a chocolate from the box** أَخَذَتْ قِطْعَةَ شوكولاتةٍ من الصُنْدوقِ; **he took his glasses out of his pocket** أَخْرَجَ نَظّارَتِهِ من جَيْبِهِ 2 (to carry with one) أَخَذَ (u; أَخْذ) ‹*an object*›; **to ~ sb a present, to ~ a present to sb** أَخَذَ هَدِيّةً إلى شَخْصٍ; **he took his umbrella with him** أَخَذَ مَطَرِيَّتَهُ مَعَهُ; **to ~ sth upstairs/downstairs** أَخَذَ شَيْئاً إلى الطابِقِ العُلْويِّ \ السُفْليِّ; **she forgot to ~ her passport** نَسِيَتْ أَنْ تَأْخُذَ جَوازَ سَفَرِها; **to ~ the letter to the post office** أَخَذَ الرِسالةَ إلى مَرْكَزِ البَريدِ; **to ~ the car to the garage** أَخَذَ السَيّارةَ إلى الكَراجِ 3 (accompanying) أَخَذَ (u; أَخْذ) ‹*one's son, a visitor*›; **I'll ~ you to your room** سَآخُذُكَ إلى غُرْفَتِكَ; **to ~ sb to the station** أَخَذَ شَخْصاً إلى المَحَطّةِ; **this road ~s you straight to the stadium** هذا الطَريقُ يَأْخُذُكَ مُباشَرةً إلى المَلْعَبِ; **to ~ the dog for a walk** أَخَذَ الكَلْبَ في نُزْهةٍ; **I'll ~ you through the procedure** سَأُريكَ كيف تَقومُ بالإجْراءِ; **his work ~s him to many different countries** يَجْعَلُهُ عَمَلُهُ يُسافِرُ إلى دُوَلٍ مُخْتَلِفةٍ كَثيرةٍ 4 (to go by) أَخَذَ (u; أَخْذ) ‹*a bus, taxi, road*› 5 (to negotiate) «drivers, cars» عَبَرَ (u; عَبْر, عُبور) ‹*a corner, bend*› 6 (to capture, win) اسْتَوْلى (على) ‹*a town, chess piece*›; **he took my queen in three moves** اسْتَوْلى على مَلِكَتي في ثَلاثِ نَقْلاتٍ 7 (to have) أَخَذَ (u; أَخْذ) ‹*a bath, shower, holiday*›; **to ~ a photo** أَخَذَ صورةً 8 **do you ~ milk and sugar in your coffee?** هل تَتَناوَلُ \ تَشْرَبُ قَهْوَتَكَ بالحَليبِ والسُكَّرِ؟ 9 تَناوَلَ ‹*aspirin, amphetamine*›; **he ~s daily medication for hay fever** يَأْخُذُ يَوْميًّا الدَواءَ لِحُمّى القَشِّ 10 (to accept) أَخَذَ (u; أَخْذ) ‹*a bribe, phone call*›; «machine» قَبِلَ (a; قَبول, قُبول) ‹*a credit card, coins*›; **do you ~ credit cards?** هل تَقْبَلُ بِطاقاتِ الائْتِمانِ؟; **they are taking fifty more pupils at the school next year** سَيَأْخُذونَ خَمْسينَ تِلْميذاً إضافيًّا في المَدْرَسةِ السَنةَ القادِمةَ; **will you ~ $100 for this watch?** هل تَأْخُذُ 100$ مُقابِلَ هذه الساعةِ؟ 11 (to endure) تَحَمَّلَ ‹*pain, criticism*›; **she can't ~ a joke** لا تَسْتَطيعُ أَنْ تَتَحَمَّلَ المُزاحَ; **I can't ~ any more!** لا أَسْتَطيعُ أَنْ أَتَحَمَّلَ أَكْثَرَ! 12 (to require) «activity, course of action» تَطَلَّبَ ‹*time, courage, skill*›; **learning a new language ~s time and patience** يَتَطَلَّبُ تَعَلُّمُ لُغةٍ جَديدةٍ وَقْتاً وَصَبْراً; **it ~s three hours to get there** يَسْتَغْرِقُ الوُصولُ إلى هُناكَ ثَلاثَ ساعاتٍ; **it ~s a lot of skill to do that** يَتَطَلَّبُ إنْجازُ ذلك الكَثيرَ من المَوْهِبةِ 13 (to govern) تَعَدّى (إلى) ‹*a preposition, an object*›; أَخَذَ (u; أَخْذ) ‹*a case*›; **the preposition ~s the genitive** حَرْفُ الجَرِّ يَجُرُّ ما يَأْتي بَعْدَهُ 14 (to deal with) تَعامَلَ ‹*a matter, the news, comments*›; **to ~ things one step at a time** تَعامَلَ مع الأَشْياءِ على مَهْلٍ 15 (to adopt) **to ~ the view** *or* **attitude that ...** تَبَنّى الرَأْيَ القائِلَ إنّ ... 16 (to assume)

I ~ it that ... أَفْتَرِضُ أنّ ... ; **to ~ sb for *or* to be sth** ظَنَّ أنّ شَخْصاً كانَ شَيْئاً; **what do you ~ me for?** ماذا تَحْسَبُني؟; **what do you ~ this poem to mean?** ماذا تَظُنُّ أنّ هذه القَصيدةَ تَعْني؟ **17** (to consider) أَخَذَ (u; أَخْذ) ‹*a person, an example, a case*›; **~ John, for instance** خُذْ جون، مَثَلاً **18** أَخَذَ (u; أَخْذ) ‹*the form, shape*›; **our next class will ~ the form of a debate** سَيَأْخُذُ صَفُّنا القادِمُ شَكْلَ مُناظَرةٍ **19** (to record) أَخَذَ (u; أَخْذ) ‹*notes, a statement*›; **to have one's blood pressure taken** أُخِذَ ضَغْطُ دَمِهِ **20** (to have room for) «hall, bus» اِتَّسَعَ (ل) ‹*50 people*›; **the tank ~s 500 litres** يَتَّسِعُ الخَزّانُ لـ500 لِتْرٍ; **the suitcase won't ~ any more clothes** لن تَتَّسِعَ الحَقيبةُ لِمَلابِسَ أَكْثَرَ **21** (to study) أَخَذَ (u; أَخْذ) ‹*a subject, course, lessons*›; **she ~s music lessons weekly** تَأْخُذُ دُروساً في الموسيقى أُسْبوعيًّا **22** «student» أَخَذَ (u; أَخْذ) ‹*an exam, a test*› **23** (to suit) ناسَبَ ‹*a size 10*›; **what size do you ~?** (in clothes, shoes) أَيُّ مَقاسٍ يُناسِبُكَ؟ **24** (to subtract) طَرَحَ (a; طَرْح) ‹*a number, quantity*›; **to ~ five away from 32** طَرَحَ خَمْسةً من 32; **~ twenty from the total and add six** اطْرَحْ عِشْرينَ من المَجْموعِ وَأَضِفْ سِتّةً **25** (to officiate at) رَأَسَ (a; رِئاسة) ‹*a service, mass*›

B *vi* (*past tense* **took**; *past participle* **taken**) «plant, dye» نَجَحَ (a; نَجاح); **have the cuttings ~n?** هل نَجَحَ التَعْقيلُ؟

C *n* (in film-making) لَقْطة (لَقَطات)

Phrasal verbs **take aback**: **~ [sb] aback** صَدَمَ \ فاجَأَ [شَخْصاً]

• **take after**: **~ after [sb]** اِقْتَدى بـ[شَخْصٍ] ‹*one's parent*›

• **take against**: **~ against [sb]** عادى [شَخْصاً]

• **take along**: **~ [sb/sth] along, ~ along [sb/sth]** أَخَذَ [شَخْصاً \ شَيْئاً] مَعَهُ ‹*a friend, sample*›

• **take apart** **A** **~ apart** فُكِّكَ إلى أَجْزاءٍ **B** **~ [sb/sth] apart** **1** (to dismantle) فَكَّكَ [شَيْئاً] إلى أَجْزاءٍ ‹*an engine, clock*› **2** (infml) (critically) اِنْتَقَدَ [شَخْصاً \ شَيْئاً] بِشِدّةٍ ‹*an essay, movie, book*› **3** (to defeat) (infml) هَزَمَ [شَخْصاً \ شَيْئاً] ‹*a team, an opponent*›

• **take aside**: **~ [sb] aside** أَخَذَ [شَخْصاً] جانِباً

• **take away**: **~ [sb/sth] away, ~ away [sb/sth]** **1** (to remove) أَخَذَ [شَخْصاً \ شَيْئاً] ‹*a suspect, the food, pain*›; **to ~ away sb's appetite** أَفْقَدَ شَخْصاً شَهيَّتَهُ; **this medicine will ~ away the pain** سَيَقْضي هذا الدَواءُ على الأَلَمِ **2** (to subtract) طَرَحَ [شَيْئاً] ‹*a number*›; **ten ~ away seven is three** إذا طَرَحْتَ سَبْعةً من عَشَرةٍ تَحْصُلُ على ثَلاثةٍ; **we don't ~ anything away from his achievement** لا نُنْقِصُ من إنْجازاتِهِ

• **take back** **A** **~ [sth] back, ~ back [sth]** **1** (to return) «customer» أَعادَ [شَيْئاً] ‹*faulty goods*› **2** (to retract) تَراجَعَ عن [شَيْءٍ] ‹*a statement, one's words*› **B** **~ [sb] back** (to provoke memories) «sight, smell, song» ذَكَّرَ [شَخْصاً] **C** **~ [sb/sth] back, ~ back [sb/sth]** (to accept again) اسْتَعادَ [شَخْصاً \ شَيْئاً] ‹*an employee, a spouse*›

• **take down**: **~ [sth] down, ~ down [sth]** **1** (to remove) أَزالَ [شَيْئاً] ‹*a picture, poster*› **2** (to dismantle) فَكَّكَ [شَيْئاً] ‹*a tent, the scaffolding*› **3** (to write down) «reporters» دَوَّنَ [شَيْئاً] ‹*sb's name, a statement, the details*›

• **take hold**: **~ hold** «disease» اِسْتَحْكَمَ; «ideas» تَرَسَّخَ; «flames» سَيْطَرَ (i; سَيْطَرة); **to ~ hold of sb's hands/an axe** أَمْسَكَ بِيَدَيْ شَخْصٍ \ بِفَأْسٍ

• **take in** **A** **~ [sb] in, ~ in [sb]** **1** (to deceive) خَدَعَ [شَخْصاً]; **we were completely taken in!** لَقَدْ خُدِعْنا! **2** (to allow to stay) أَسْكَنَ [شَخْصاً] في بَيْتِهِ ‹*a relative, lodger, refugee*› **B** **~ [sth] in, ~ in [sth]** **1** (to understand) اسْتَوْعَبَ [شَيْئاً] ‹*a situation*› **2** (to observe) لاحَظَ [شَيْئاً] ‹*the details, scene*› **3** (to cover, include) غَطّى [شَيْئاً] ‹*a place, the latest developments*›; **we'll ~ in a show when we're in New York** سَنُشاهِدُ عَرْضاً عِنْدَما نَكونُ في نِيويورْك **4** (to absorb) «roots» امْتَصَّ [شَيْئاً] ‹*nutrients, oxygen*› **5** «boat, ship» تَسَرَّبَ [شَيْءٌ] إلَيْهِ ‹*water*› **6** «dressmaker» ضَيَّقَ في [شَيْءٍ] ‹*a skirt, the waist*› **7** (for payment) [قَبِلَ أنْ يَعْمَلَ [شَيْئاً] في بَيْتِ شَخْصٍ] ‹*washing, mending*›

• **take off** **A** **~ off** **1** (to leave the ground) «aircraft» أَقْلَعَ **2** (to succeed) «ideas» نَجَحَ (a; نَجاح); «sales» ارْتَفَعَ **3** (infml) (to leave) انْصَرَفَ **B** **~ [sth] off** **1** (to deduct) **to ~ 15% off the price** خَصَمَ 15٪ من السِعْرِ **2** (to have as holiday) **to ~ a week off** أَخَذَ عُطْلةً لِأُسْبوعٍ **C** **~ [sth] off, ~ off [sth]** **1** (to remove) نَزَعَ [شَيْئاً] ‹*a hat, coat, one's shoes*›

2 (to withdraw) [شَيْئاً] سَحَبَ ‹*a show, play*› **D** **~ [sb] off, ~ off [sb]** (BrE) (infml) (to imitate) «comedian» [شَخْصاً] قَلَّدَ **E** **~ [sb] off sth** (to stop) «doctor» أَوْقَفَ [شَخْصاً] عن شَيْءٍ ‹*a patient*›; **he was taken off the treatment/medication** تَوَقَّفَ عن تَناوُلِ العِلاجِ \ الدَواءِ

• **take on**: **~ [sb/sth] on, ~ on [sb/sth]** **1** (to employ) «company, employer» وَظَّفَ [شَخْصاً \ شَيْئاً] ‹*staff, a worker*› **2** (to accept) قَبِلَ [شَخْصاً \ شَيْئاً] ‹*work, a task, responsibilities*› **3** (in competitions) نافَسَ [شَخْصاً \ شَيْئاً] ‹*a team, an opponent*›; **they took on Arsenal in the cup** نافَسوا أَرْسِنال في الكَأْسِ **4** (to assume) أَخَذَ [شَيْئاً] ‹*meaning, a colour, look*›

• **take out**: **~ [sb/sth] out, ~ out [sb/sth]** **1** اِقْتَلَعَ \ نَزَعَ [شَخْصاً \ شَيْئاً] (to remove) ‹*a thorn, splinter, a tooth*›; **I had to have a tooth/my appendix ~n out** كانَ من اللازم أن أَقْتَلِعَ سِنّي \ أَسْتَأْصِلَ الزائدة الدوديّةَ; **I want to ~ out $400** أُريدُ أَنْ أَسْحَبَ $400 **2** (socially) دَعا [شَخْصاً] للتَسْلِية أو العَشاءِ خارِجَ البَيْتِ ‹*a visitor, girlfriend, one's wife*›; **to ~ sb out to dinner** دَعا شَخصا للعَشاءِ خارِجَ البَيْتِ **3** (to go out with) خَرَجَ مع [شَخْصٍ \ شَيْءٍ] ‹*the children, dog*› **4** (to destroy) دَمَّرَ [شَخْصاً \ شَيْئاً] ‹*the tank, fighter, bunker*› **5** **to ~ it out on sb** صَبَّ جامَ غَضَبِهِ على شَخْصٍ ‹*anger, frustration*›; **she took it out on her family** صَبَّتْ جامَ غَضَبِها على عائِلَتِها

• **take over** **A** **~ over** (to take control) «army, faction» تَوَلّى **B** **~ over [sth]** (to take control of) سَيْطَرَ على [شَيْءٍ] مَسْؤوليّةً \ سُلْطةً ‹*a town, country, a business*›; **shall I ~ over the driving for a while?** هل عَلَيَّ أَنْ أَتَوَلّى القِيادة لِبَعْضِ الوَقْتِ؟

• **take to**: **~ to [sb/sth]** **1** (infml) (to develop liking for) **he has ~n to her** بَدَأَ يَتَعَلَّقُ بها **2** (to begin) **to ~ to drink** بَدَأَ يَشْرَبُ; **he's ~n to smoking** بَدَأَ التَدْخينَ **3** (to go to) ذَهَبَ إلى [شَيْءٍ] ‹*the forest, hills*›; **to ~ to one's bed** أَوى إلى فِراشِهِ; ▸ **street**

• **take up** **A** **~ up** (to continue) تَوَلّى; **to ~ up where someone else left off** تَوَلّى المَسْؤوليّة من حَيْثُ انْتَهى شَخْصٌ آخَرُ **B** **~ up [sth]** **1** (to pull up) انْتَزَعَ [شَيْئاً] ‹*a carpet*›; أَزالَ [شَيْئاً] ‹*track, pathway*› **2** (to start) بَدَأَ [شَيْئاً] ‹*golf, the guitar*›; **to ~ up one's duties** بَدَأَ في القِيامِ بِمَسْؤوليّاتِهِ **3** (to continue) واصَلَ [شَيْئاً] ‹*a story, discussion*› **4** (to accept) قَبِلَ [شَيْئاً] ‹*a challenge, an offer, invitation*›; **to ~ up sb's case** تَبَنّى قَضيّةَ شَخصٍ **5** (to raise) **to ~ sth up with sb** لَفَتَ انْتِباهَ شَخْصٍ إلى شَيْءٍ **6** (to fill) اسْتَحْوَذَ على [شَيْءٍ] ‹*sb's time, space, energy*› **7** (to adopt) تَبَنّى [شَيْئاً] ‹*a position, stance*› **8** (to shorten) ثَنى [شَيْئاً] ‹*a skirt, hem, the curtains*› **C** **~ [sb] up** **1** (to adopt) تَبَنّى [شَخْصاً]; **she was taken up by the surrealists** تَبَنّاها السِرْياليّونَ **2** (to accept) **to ~ sb up on an invitation** قَبِلَ دَعْوة [شَخْصٍ]

takeaway /ˈteɪkəweɪ/ (BrE) **A** *n* **1** (meal) وَجْبة جاهِزة **2** (restaurant) مَطْعَم الوَجَباتِ الجاهِزةِ **B** *adj* ‹*food, pizza*› جاهِز; ‹*restaurant*› وَجَباتٍ جاهِزةٍ

take-home pay /ˈteɪkhəʊm peɪ/ *n* صافي المُرَتَّب

taken /ˈteɪk(ə)n/ **A** *past participle* ▸ **take**
B *adj* **1** (occupied) مَحْجوز; **is this seat ~?** هل هذا الكُرْسيُّ مَحْجوزٌ؟ **2** (impressed) **to be ~ with sth/sb** كانَ مَأْخوذاً بِشَيْءٍ \ بِشَخْصٍ; **they seem very ~ with you** يَبْدو أَنَّهُمْ مَأْخوذونَ بِكَ; **I was so ~ with it that I bought it** كُنْتُ مَأْخوذاً جِدًّا بِهِ فَاشْتَرَيْتُهُ

take-off /ˈteɪkɒf/ *n* **1** (of aircraft) إِقْلاع **2** (infml) (imitation) تَقْليد ساخِر

takeout /ˈteɪkaʊt/ (AmE) **A** *n* وَجْبة جاهِزة
B *adj* ‹*food, pizza*› جاهِز; ‹*restaurant*› وَجَباتٍ جاهِزةٍ

takeover /ˈteɪkəʊvə/ *n* **1** (of a company) اسْتِحْواذ **2** (of power) اسْتيلاء

takeover bid *n* عَرْض اسْتِحْواذٍ

taker /ˈteɪkə/ *n* [مَنْ يَقْبَلُ عَرْضاً أو رِهاناً]; **any ~s?** هل من أَحَدٍ يَقْبَلُ العَرْضَ؟

takings /ˈteɪkɪŋz/ *n pl* إيرادات

talaq /taˈlɑːk/ *n* طَلاق

talc /talk/, **talcum powder** /ˈtalkəm paʊdə/ *n* مَسْحوق الطَلْقِ

tale /teɪl/ *n* حِكاية
(Idiom) **to tell tales** نَشَرَ الإشاعاتِ

talent /ˈtalənt/ *n* **1** (aptitude, skill) مَوْهِبة (مَواهِبُ)
2 [u] (talented people) مَواهِب

talent contest *n* مُسابَقة مَواهِبَ

talented /ˈtaləntɪd/ *adj* ‹player, musician› مَوْهوب

Taliban /ˈtalɪban/ *n* **(the Taliban)** طالِبان

talisman /ˈtalɪzmən/ *n* (*pl* **talismans**) طِلَسْم (طَلاسِمُ)

talk /tɔːk/ **A** *vt* **1** (to discuss) تَحَدَّثَ (في); **to ~ business/sport** تَحَدَّثَ في التِجارة \ الرِياضةِ **2** (to speak) تَحَدَّثَ ‹Arabic, French›; **to ~ sense/nonsense** قالَ كَلاماً ذا مَعْنًى \ بِلا مَعْنى
3 (infml) (to envisage) تَصَوَّرَ ‹an amount, a period of time, disaster›; **we're ~ing three years/a million pounds to finish the project** نَتَصَوَّرُ أَنَّنا سَنَنْتَهي من المَشْروعِ خلال ثَلاثِ سَنواتٍ \ بعد إِنْفاقِ مَلْيونِ جُنَيْهٍ **4** (to persuade) **to ~ sb into/out of doing sth** أَقْنَعَ شَخْصاً بِفِعْلِ شَيْءٍ \ بِعَدَمِ فِعْلِ شَيْءٍ; **he ~ed his way out of it** [اِسْتَطاعَ بِلَباقَتِهِ أَنْ يَتَخَلَّصَ من المُشْكِلةِ]
B *vi* (to converse) تَحَدَّثَ; **to ~ to** *or* **with sb** تَحَدَّثَ مع شَخْصٍ; **to ~ to oneself** تَحَدَّثَ مع نَفْسِهِ; **to ~ about sth/ about doing sth** تَكَلَّمَ عن شَيْءٍ \ عن فِعْلِ شَيْءٍ; **to ~ at sb** تَكَلَّمَ إلى شَخْصٍ; **now you're ~ing!** (infml) الآنَ تَتَكَلَّمُ كَلاماً صَواباً
C *n* **1** [u] (reports, gossip) كَلام ,حَديث (n coll, no singul n); **there is ~ of a petrol shortage** هُناكَ حَديثٌ عن نَقْصٍ في البِتْرول; **he's all ~ and no action** يَتَكَلَّمُ كَثيراً وَيَفْعَلُ قَليلاً; **to be the ~ of the town** كانَ حَديثَ المَدينةِ **2** (conversation) مُحادَثة ,حَديث; **to have a ~ with sb** كانَ لَهُ حَديثٌ مع شَخْصٍ; **to have a ~ about sth/sb** كانَ لَهُ حَديثٌ عن شَيْءٍ \ شَخْصٍ; **to make small ~** [تَحَدَّثَ عن أُمورٍ تافِهةٍ] **3** (lecture) مُحاضَرة ,مُحادَثة ,حَديث; **to give a ~ about local history** أَلْقى مُحاضَرةً عن التاريخِ المَحَلّيِّ
D **(talks)** *n pl* (discussions) مُحادَثات; **the peace ~s broke down** تَوَقَّفَتْ مُحادَثاتُ السَلامِ; **to hold ~s with sb** أَجْرى مُحادَثاتٍ مع شَخْصٍ

(Phrasal verbs) **talk back** رَدَّ بِوَقاحةٍ

• **talk down**: **~ down to sb** تَكَلَّمَ مع شَخْصٍ بِتَعالٍ

• **talk over**: **~ [sth] over** (to discuss) ناقَشَ [شَيْئاً] ‹a matter, problem›

• **talk round**: **A ~ [sb] round** (to persuade) أَقْنَعَ [شَخْصاً]
B ~ round [sth] (to avoid) تَجَنَّبَ الخَوْضَ في [شَيْءٍ] ‹a subject, problem›

• **talk through**: **~ [sth] through** (to discuss) ناقَشَ [شَيْئاً] ‹a problem, situation›

talkative /ˈtɔːkətɪv/ *adj* ‹person, mood› ≈ كَثير الكَلامِ

talker /ˈtɔːkə/ *n* مُتَكَلِّم ,مُتَحَدِّث

talking /ˈtɔːkɪŋ/ *n*; **I'll do the ~** سَأَقومُ بِالحَديثِ

talking point *n* مَوْضوع حَديثٍ

talking-to /ˈtɔːkɪŋtuː/ *n* (*pl* **talking-tos**) (infml) تَوْبيخ (تَوْبيخات), تَعْنيف; **I gave him a good ~** وَبَّخْتُهُ أَشَدَّ التَوْبيخِ

talk show *n* بَرْنامَج حِواريّ

tall /tɔːl/ *adj* ‹person› طَويل (طِوال); ‹building, tree› عالٍ; **how ~ are you?** كَم طولُكَ؟; **he's six feet/one metre ninety-five** يَبْلُغُ طولُهُ سِتّةَ أَقْدامٍ \ مِتْراً و95 سم; **he's ~er than you** هو أَطْوَلُ مِنْكَ; **she's ~ for her age** هي طَويلةٌ مُقارَنةً بِعُمْرِها

(Idioms) **that's a tall order** (infml) ذلك طَلَبٌ صَعْبُ التَحْقيقِ; **to walk tall** (infml) كانَ فَخوراً

tall story, **tall tale** *n* حِكاية يَصْعُبُ تَصْديقُها

tally /ˈtali/ **A** *n* (*pl* **tallies**) سِجِلّ (سِجِلّات)
B *vi* (**tallies, tallying, tallied**) «figures, stories» تَطابَقَ

Talmud /ˈtalmʊd/ *pr n* **(the Talmud)** التَلْمود

talon /ˈtalən/ *n* مِخْلَب (مَخالِبُ)

tambourine /ˌtambəˈriːn/ *n* دَفّ (دُفوف), رِقّ (رُقوق)

tame /teɪm/ **A** *adj* **1** ‹lion, monkey› أَليف; ‹bird, squirrel› داجِن
2 (unadventurous) ‹film, experience› عاديّ
B *vt* دَجَّنَ ‹a wild animal›

Tamil /ˈtamɪl/ **A** *n* **1** (person) تاميليّ **2** (language) (اللُغة) التاميليّة
B *adj* ‹people, language› تاميليّ

tamper with /ˈtampə/ *vt* **1** عَبِثَ (a; عَبَث ب) ‹a lock, machinery› **2** تَلاعَبَ (ب) ‹evidence›

tampon /ˈtampɒn/ *n* سَدّادة قُطْنيّة (تُسْتَعْمَلُ أثناء العادةِ الشَهْريّةِ)

tan /tan/ **A** *n* (also **suntan**) سُمْرة (بِسَبَبِ التَعَرُّضِ لِأَشِعّةِ الشَمْسِ); **to get a ~** اِسْمَرَّ

B *vt* (**-nn-**) **1** سَمَّرَ ‹*sb's skin, face*› **2** دَبَغَ (a-i-u; دَبْغ) ‹*hide, leather*›

C *vi* (**-nn-**) «person, skin» اسْمَرَّ

D *adj* ‹*shoes, trousers*› بُنِّيّ فاتِح

tandem /ˈtandəm/ *n* دَرّاجة ذات مَقْعَدَيْن

(Idiom) **to work/run in tandem** عَمِلا \ رَكَضا مَعاً

tang /taŋ/ *n* **1** (strong taste) طَعْم قَوِيّ; (acid taste) طَعْم حامِض **2** (smell) رائِحة قَوِيّة

tangent /ˈtandʒ(ə)nt/ *n* مُماسّ

(Idiom) **to go off at** *or* (AmE) **on a tangent** خَرَجَ عن المَوْضوع

tangerine /tandʒəˈriːn/ *n* مَنْدَرين, يوسُفِيّ

tangible /ˈtandʒɪb(ə)l/ *adj* **1** (real) ‹*assets*› مادِّيّ **2** (real) ‹*results, progress*› مَحْسوس, مَلْموس

Tangier /tanˈdʒɪə/ *pr n* طَنْجة (dipt)

tangle /ˈtaŋg(ə)l/ **A** *vi* «hair, string» تَشابَكَ

B *n* كُتْلة مُتَشابِكة

(Phrasal verbs) **tangle up**: **1** ~ **up** تَشابَكَ; **to get ~d up** «hair, string» تَشابَكَ **2** ~ **up** [**sth**], ~ [**sth**] **up** شَبَّكَ [شَيْئاً] ‹*the wires, string*›; **to get ~d up in somebody's problem** تَوَرَّطَ في مُشْكِلةِ شَخْصٍ

• **tangle with**: ~ **with** [**sb**] تَشابَكَ \ اشْتَبَكَ مع [شَخْصٍ]

tangled /ˈtaŋg(ə)ld/ *adj* ‹*hair, wool*› مُتَشابِك

tango /ˈtaŋgəʊ/ **A** *n* (*pl* **tangos**) تانْغو (رَقْصة من أمْريكا اللاتينِيّة)

B *vi* (**tangoes, tangoing, tangoed**) «dancers» رَقَصَ التانْغو

(Idiom) **it takes two to tango** [لا يَجِبُ إلْقاءُ اللَوْمِ على طَرَفٍ واحِدٍ]; **in all cases of corruption, it takes two to ~** [في كُلِّ حالاتِ الفَسادِ, لا يَجِبُ إلْقاءُ اللَوْمِ على طَرَفٍ واحِدٍ]

tangy /ˈtaŋi/ *adj* (**tangier, tangiest**) ‹*flavour, smell*› لاذِع

tank /taŋk/ *n* **1** (container for water, fuel) خَزّان (خَزّانات), صِهْريج (صَهاريجُ); **an oil storage ~** خَزّان النَفْطِ **2** (in vehicles) خَزّان (خَزّانات) **3** (military) مُدَرَّعة, دَبّابة

tankard /ˈtaŋkəd/ *n* كوز (أكْواز)

tanker /ˈtaŋkə/ *n* **1** (ship) ناقِلة نَفْطٍ **2** (vehicle) صِهْريج (صَهاريجُ) **3** (aircraft) طائِرة التَزْويدِ بالوَقودِ

tanned /tand/ *adj* (also **suntanned**) ‹*back, legs*› مُسْمَرّ (بالتَعَرُّضِ لأشِعّةِ الشَمْسِ)

tanning bed /ˈtanɪŋ bɛd/ *n* (AmE) سَرير التَسْميرِ

tannoy® /ˈtanɔɪ/ *n* (BrE) مُكَبِّر الصَوْتِ; **over the ~** عَبْرَ مُكَبِّرِ الصَوْتِ

tantalizing, -ising (BrE) /ˈtantəlʌɪzɪŋ/ *adj* ‹*glimpse, possibility*› مُحَيِّر

tantamount /ˈtantəmaʊnt/ *adj* **to be ~ to fraud/treason** كانَ بِمَثابةِ احْتِيالٍ \ خِيانةٍ

tantrum /ˈtantrəm/ *n* سَوْرة \ نَوْبة غَضَبٍ; **to have a ~** أُصيبَ بِنَوْبةِ غَضَبٍ

Tanzania /ˌtanzəˈnɪə/ *pr n* تَنْزانِيا

Tanzanian /tanzəˈniːən/ *n, adj* تَنْزانِيّ

Taoism /ˈtaʊiz(ə)m, ˈdaʊiz(ə)m/ *n* طاوِيّة (عَقيدة صينِيّة)

Taoist /ˈtaʊɪst/ *n, adj* طاوِيّ

tap /tap/ **A** *n* **1** (for water, gas) حَنَفِيّة, صُنْبور (صَنابيرُ); **the cold/hot ~** صُنْبور الماءِ البارِدِ \ الساخِنِ; **to turn the ~ on/off** فَتَحَ \ أَغْلَقَ الصُنْبورَ; **to wash one's hands under the ~** غَسَلَ يَدَيْهِ بِماءِ الصُنْبورِ; **beer on ~** بيرة من البِرْميلِ **2** (blow) طَرْق خَفيف; **there was a ~ at the door** كانَ هُناكَ طَرْقٌ خَفيفٌ على البابِ; **he felt a ~ on his shoulder** شَعَرَ بِلَمْسةٍ على كَتِفِه

3 (also **telephone tap**) جِهاز تَنَصُّتٍ

B *vt* (**-pp-**) **1** (to hit) نَقَرَ (u; نَقْر) ‹*the window, radio*›; **to ~ sb on the shoulder** لَمَسَ كَتِفَ شَخْصٍ; **to ~ one's fingers on the table** نَقَرَ بِأَصابِعِهِ على الطاوِلةِ; **to ~ one's feet to the music** نَقَرَ بِرِجْلَيْهِ على نَغَماتِ الموسيقى **2** (to extract) اسْتَغَلَّ ‹*the resources, market, talent*›; **to ~ the country's natural resources** اسْتَغَلَّ الثَرَواتِ الطَبيعيّةَ لِلبِلادِ **3** (in keyboarding) نَقَرَ (u; نَقْر; على) ‹*any key, the space bar*› **4** (in spying) تَنَصَّتَ (على) ‹*sb's telephone, an embassy*› **5** (for sap) اسْتَخْلَصَ النُسْغَ ‹*a tree*›

C *vi* (**- pp-**) «person, fingers, foot» نَقَرَ (u; نَقْر); **to ~ on the window/door** نَقَرَ على النافِذةِ \ البابِ

(Phrasal verbs) **tap in**: ~ [**sth**] **in**, ~ **in** [**sth**] **1** ضَرَبَ [شَيْئاً] بِرِفْقٍ ‹*a nail, tack*› **2** أَدْخَلَ [شَيْئاً] ‹*the number, PIN*›

• **tap out**: ~ [sth] out, ~ out [sth] 1 [شَيْئاً] كَتَبَ ‹*an email, password*› 2 [شَيْئاً] عَزَفَ ‹*a tune, song*›

tapas /'tapas/ *n pl* (طَبَق) مَزّة (وَجْبة صَغيرة خَفيفة)

tap dance *n* 1 (single dance) رَقْصة نَقْريّة 2 [u] (type of dancing) رَقْص نَقْريّ

tap-dancing *n* رَقْص نَقْريّ

tape /teɪp/ A *n* 1 [u] (also **adhesive tape**) شَريط لاصِق 2 (for measuring) شَريط قِياس 3 (for securing, fastening) شَريط (أَشْرِطة, شَرائِطُ); (for labelling) مُلْصَق تِجاريّ 4 (at start, finish lines) شَريط خَطِّ النِهايةِ; (in inaugurations) شَريط تَدْشينٍ; (to prevent access) شريط حِماية مَكانِ الجَريمةِ 5 [u] (for recording) شَريط (أَشْرِطة, شَرائِطُ); **to get sth on** ~ سَجَّلَ شَيْئاً على شَريطٍ 6 (for data) شَريط (أَشْرِطة, شَرائِطُ)

B *vt* 1 (to stick) رَبَطَ بِاسْتِعْمالِ شَريطٍ لاصِقٍ ‹*a parcel*›; **to ~ a sb's hands together** رَبَطَ يَدَيْ شَخْصٍ بِشَريطٍ لاصِقٍ; **to ~ a notice to the door** أَلْصَقَ وَرَقةَ مُلاحَظاتٍ بِشَريطٍ لاصِقٍ على البابِ 2 (a programme) سَجَّلَ; **to ~ sth from the radio/TV** سَجَّلَ شَيْئاً من الراديو \ التَلْفَزة

(Phrasal verb) **tape off**: ~ [sth] off, ~ off [sth] وَضَعَ شَريطَ حِمايةٍ حول [شَيْءٍ] ‹*a building, an entrance*›

(Phrasal verb) **tape up**: ~ [sth] up, ~ up [sth] [شَيْئاً] رَبَطَ \ أَغْلَقَ بِشَريطٍ لاصِقٍ ‹*a parcel, box*›

tape deck *n* جِهاز تَسْجيلٍ

tape measure *n* شَريط قِياسٍ

taper /'teɪpə/ A *vt* أَنْقَصَ تَدْريجيًّا ‹*the medication, dose*›

B *vi* «sleeves, trouser legs» ضاقَ تَدْريجيًّا

(Phrasal verb) **taper off**: ~ off «sales, enthusiasm» تَراجَعَ

tape-record /'teɪprɪˌkɔːd/ *vt* سَجَّلَ (على شَريطٍ) ‹*an interview, a conversation*›

tape recorder *n* مُسَجِّلة, آلة \ جِهاز تَسْجيلٍ

tapestry /'tapɪstri/ *n* (*pl* **tapestries**) 1 (wall hanging) نَجْد (نَسيج مُطَرَّز بالرُسومِ) 2 [u] (art form) فَنّ النُجودِ \ تَطْريزِ النَسيجِ

tapeworm /'teɪpwəːm/ *n* دودة شَريطيّة

tap water *n* ماء الحَنَفيّةِ \ الصُنْبورِ

tar /tɑː/ *n* قار, قَطْران

tarboosh, **tarbush** /tɑː'buːʃ/ *n* طَرْبوش (طَرابيشُ)

target /'tɑːɡɪt/ A *n* 1 (in shooting) هَدَف (أَهْداف) مَرْمًى (مَرام) 2 (for bombs, missiles, attacks) هَدَف (أَهْداف); **to be on ~** كانَ مُوَجَّهاً نحو الهَدَفِ 3 (of criticism, insults) عُرْضة; **to be the ~ of abuse/ridicule** كانَ عُرْضةً للاعْتِداءِ \ الاسْتِهْزاءِ 4 (goal, objective) هَدَف (أَهْداف); **to meet/miss one's ~s** حَقَّقَ \ لم يُحَقِّقْ أَهْدافَهُ; **the figures are above/below ~** الأَرْقامُ فوق \ دون الهَدَفِ المَنْشودِ

B *vt* 1 (Mil) (to aim) **to ~ a missile at sth** وَجَّهَ صاروخاً إلى شَيْءٍ; **to ~ a city/factory** اسْتَهْدَفَ مَدينةً \ مَصْنَعاً 2 (to select) اسْتَهْدَفَ ‹*a group, sector*›; **the magazine ~s affluent young people** تَسْتَهْدِفُ المَجَلّةُ الشبابَ الأَغْنِياءَ

target audience *n* جُمْهور مُسْتَهْدَف

target language *n* لُغة مُسْتَهْدَفة (الّتي يُتَرْجَمُ إلَيْها من لُغةٍ أُخْرى)

target practice *n* تَدْريب على الرِمايةِ

tariff /'tarɪf/ *n* 1 (price list) قائِمة الأَسْعارِ, تَعْريفة, تَعْرِفة 2 (customs duty) تَعْرِفة \ تَعْريفة جُمْرُكيّة

tariqa /ta'riːkə/ *n* طَريقة (طُرُق)

tarmac /'tɑːmak/ A ®*n* 1 (also **Tarmac**) (tar mixture) [خَليط من الزِفْتِ والحِجارةِ لِتَعْبيدِ الطُرُقاتِ] 2 (at airports) مَدْرَج (مَدارِجُ)

B *vt* (-ck-) عَبَّدَ, زَفَّتَ ‹*a road, footpath*›

tarmac road *n* طَريق مُزَفَّتة

tarmac surface *n* سَطْح مُزَفَّت

tarnish /'tɑːnɪʃ/ A *vt* 1 (to discolour) جَعَلَ باهِتاً ‹*the metal, cutlery*› 2 (to sully) شَوَّهَ, لَوَّثَ ‹*sb's reputation, image*›

B *vi* «metal, brass» أَصْبَحَ باهِتاً, بَهِتَ (a; بَهْت)

taro /'tɑːrəʊ/ *n* قُلْقاس

tarpaulin /tɑː'pɔːlɪn/ *n* قُماش مُشَمَّع

tarragon /'tarəɡ(ə)n/ *n* طَرْخون

tarry /'tari/ *vi* مَهَلَ, مادَّ, تَباطَأَ (a; مَهْل)

tart /tɑːt/ A *n* 1 (pastry) فَطيرة فاكِهةٍ 2 (infml) (provocative woman) قَحْبة (قِحاب) 3 (infml) (prostitute) مومِس (مومِسات), بائِعة هَوًى

B *adj* ‹*flavour, fruit*› لاذِع (لَواذِعُ), قارِص

(Phrasal verb) **tart up** (infml): **1** **~ oneself up** تَزَيَّنَ **2** **~ [sth] up, ~ up [sth]** زَيَّنَ [شيئاً] *‹a house, garden›*

tartan /ˈtɑːt(ə)n/ *n* **1** [u] (cloth) قُماش الطَّرْطان (قُماش [تَصْميم ذو مُرَبَّعاتٍ وَخُطوطٍ (pattern) **2** اسْكُتْلَنْديّ مُتَقاطِعةٍ]

tartar /ˈtɑːtə/ *n* **1** (on teeth) جير الأَسْنانِ **2** (taskmaster) مُتَغَطْرِس

task /tɑːsk/ *n* مُهِمّة; **a hard/easy ~** مُهِمّة شاقّة \ سَهْلة

(Idiom) **to take sb to task** وَبَّخَ شَخْصاً بِشِدّةٍ

taskbar *n* شَريط المَهامِّ (في الحاسوبِ)

task force *n* فِرْقة عَمَلٍ

taskmaster /ˈtɑːskmɑːstə/ *n* مُشْرِف مُتَشَدِّد

Tasmania /tazˈmeɪnɪə/ *pr n* تَسْمانيا

tassel /ˈtas(ə)l/ *n* شَرّابة (شَراريبُ)

taste /teɪst/ **A** *n* **1** (flavour) طَعْم (طُعوم), مَذاق, نَكْهة; **to leave a bad *or* nasty ~ in the mouth** تَرَكَ طَعْماً سَيِّئاً في الفَمِ **2** [u] (sense) ذَوْق; **to be bitter/sweet to the ~** كانَ مُرَّ \ حُلْوَ المَذاقِ **3** (small quantity) [مِقْدار قَليل للتَذَوُّقِ]; **have a ~ of this** خُذْ قَليلاً من هذا **4** (experience) تَجْرِبة (تَجارِبُ); **a ~ of life in a big city** فِكْرة عن تَجْرِبةِ الحَياةِ في مَدينةٍ كَبيرةٍ **5** (liking, preference) ذائِقة; **to acquire *or* develop a ~ for sth** طَوَّرَ ذائِقةً لِشَيْءٍ; **to add salt/sugar to ~** أَضافَ مِلْحاً \ سُكَّراً بما يُناسِبُ ذائِقَتَهُ; **is it to your ~?** هَل هو مُناسِبٌ لِذائِقَتِكَ؟; **there's no accounting for ~** للناسِ فيما يَعْشَقونَ مَذاهِبُ **6** [u] (appropriateness) ذَوْق; **she has exquisite ~ in clothes** عِنْدَها ذَوْقٌ رَفيعٌ في المَلابِسِ; **it's a matter of ~** إِنَّها مَسْأَلةُ ذَوْقٍ; **it would be in bad *or* poor ~ to refuse** سَيَكونُ من قِلّةِ الذَوْقِ أَنْ نَرْفُضَ

B *vt* **1** (in detecting) تَطَعَّمَ *‹garlic, pepper›* **2** (in testing) تَذَوَّقَ *‹the soup, sauce›* **3** (to experience) ذاقَ الطَعْمَ *‹freedom, failure, power›*

C *vi* (to have a flavour) كانَ مَذاقُهُ; **to ~ sweet/sour** كانَ مَذاقُهُ حُلْوَ \ حامِضَ المَذاقِ; **to ~ like bananas/chicken** كانَ مَذاقُهُ كالمَوْزِ \ كالدَجاجِ; **it ~s of pineapple/honey** كانَ مَذاقُهُ كالأَناناسِ \ كالعَسَلِ

taste bud *n* بُرْعُم ذَوْقيّ

tasteful /ˈteɪstfʊl/ *adj ‹colour scheme, design›* [يَدُلُّ على حُسْنِ الذَوْقِ]

tastefully /ˈteɪstf(ə)li/ *adv ‹to furnish, dress›* [بِشَكْلٍ يَدُلُّ على حُسْنِ الذَوْقِ]

tasteless /ˈteɪstləs/ *adj* **1** (crude) *‹remark, joke›* عَديم الذَوْق **2** (flavourless) *‹food, liquid›* لا مَذاقَ لَهُ, عَديم الطَعْم

tasty /ˈteɪsti/ *adj* (**tastier**, **tastiest**) *‹snack, recipe›* لَذيذ

tattered /ˈtatəd/ *adj* **1** (worn) *‹clothes, flag›* مُهْتَرِئ, بالٍ **2** (in ruins) *‹reputation, image›* مُحَطَّم

tatters /ˈtatəz/ *n pl* (in ruins) **to be in ~** «reputation, career» كانَ مُحَطَّماً; **his jacket was in ~** كانَتْ سُتْرَتُهُ بالِيةً

tattoo /təˈtuː/ **A** *n* (*pl* **tattoos**) **1** (on arms, chest, etc) وَشْم (وُشوم) **2** (display) اسْتِعْراض عَسْكَريّ

B *vt* (**tattoos**, **tattooing**, **tattooed**) وَشَّمَ *‹sb's arm, chest›*

tattooist /təˈtuːɪst/ *n* رَسّام وَشْمٍ

tatty /ˈtati/ *adj* (**tattier**, **tattiest**) (infml) *‹carpet, clothes›* مُهْتَرِئ, رَثّ, بالٍ

taught /tɔːt/ *past tense, past participle* ▸**teach**

taunt /tɔːnt/ *vt* تَهَكَّمَ (على), اسْتَهْزَأَ (ب) *‹an opponent, a crowd›*

Taurus /ˈtɔːrəs/ *n* **1** (sign) بُرْج الثَوْر **2** (person) [من مَواليد بُرْجِ الثَوْرِ]

taut /tɔːt/ *adj* **1** (tight) *‹rope, muscles, wire›* مَشْدود **2** (tense) *‹thriller, plot›* مُثير

tauten /ˈtɔːt(ə)n/ **A** *vt* شَدَّ (i-u; شَدّ) *‹a cable, rope›*

B *vi* «rope, muscles» انْشَدَّ

tavern /ˈtav(ə)n/ *n* (fml) حانة

tawdry /ˈtɔːdri/ *adj* (**tawdrier**, **tawdriest**) **1** (showy) *‹jewellery, furnishings›* مُبَهْرَج **2** (sordid) *‹tale, affair›* بَغيض

tawny /ˈtɔːni/ *adj* (**tawnier**, **tawniest**) *‹coat, fur›* أَصْفَر بُنّيّ

tax /taks/ **A** *n* (state revenue) ضَريبة (ضَرائِبُ); **a ~ on luxury goods** ضَريبة على السِلَعِ الكَماليّةِ; **to increase/raise ~es** زادَ في الضَرائِبِ; **to cut ~es** خَفَّضَ في الضَرائِبِ; **to levy a ~ on imports** فَرَضَ ضَريبةً على الوارِداتِ; **income before ~**

صافي الرِبْح بعد ~ **profits after** ;صافي الدَخْلِ قبل الضَرائِبِ الضَرائِبِ; **to be liable for ~** كانَ مُطالَباً بِدَفْعِ الضَرائِبِ; **to pay $1,000 per year in ~** دَفَعَ 1000$ في السَنةِ ضَريبةً

B *vt* **1** فَرَضَ ضَريبةً على ‹*one's earnings, profits*›; **profits are ~ed at (a rate of) 28%** تُفْرَضُ ضَريبةُ 28٪ على الأَرْباحِ; **luxury cars are ~ed heavily** تُفْرَضُ ضَرائِبُ عالِيةٌ على السَيّاراتِ الفاخِرةِ **2** **to ~ a vehicle** دَفَعَ الضَريبةَ على سَيّارةٍ **3** (to test) «crisis» اخْتَبَرَ ‹*one's patience, goodwill*›; **his delays ~ed our patience** اخْتَبَرَتْ تأخيراتُهُ صَبْرَنا

taxable /ˈtaksəb(ə)l/ *adj* ‹*income, profit*› خاضِع للضَريبةِ

taxation /takˈseɪʃ(ə)n/ *n* **1** (imposition of taxes) ضَريبة (ضَرائِبُ), جِباية **2** (government revenue) مَداخيل ضَريبيّة

tax avoidance *n* تَهَرُّب \ تَجَنُّب ضَريبيّ

tax bracket *n* شريحة ضَريبيّة

tax collector *n* جابي الضَرائِبِ

tax disc *n* (BrE) مُلْصَق ضَريبيّ (على السَيّارة)

tax dodger *n* (infml) مُتَهَرِّب من الضَرائِبِ

tax evasion *n* تَهَرُّب \ تَجَنُّب ضَريبيّ

tax exile *n* مَنْفيّ ضَريبيّ

tax-free /ˌtaksˈfriː/ *adj* ‹*sum, allowance*› مُعْفًى من الضَريبةِ

tax haven *n* مَلاذ ضَريبيّ

taxi /ˈtaksi/ **A** *n* (*pl* **taxis**) سَيّارة أُجْرةٍ, تاكْسي (تاكْسيات); **to go by ~** ذَهَبَ بالتاكْسي

B *vi* (**taxis**, **taxiing**, **taxied**) «aircraft, pilots» سارَ على مَدْرَجِ المَطارِ (قبل الإقْلاعِ أو بعد الهُبوطِ)

taxicab /ˈtaksɪkab/ *n* ▸ **taxi**

taxidermy /ˈtaksɪˌdəːmi/ *n* تَحْنيط (الحَيْوانِ)

taxi driver *n* سائِق سَيّارةِ أُجْرةٍ \ تاكْسي

taxing /ˈtaksɪŋ/ *adj* ‹*role, job*› مُجْهِد

tax inspector *n* مُفَتِّش الضَرائِبِ

taxi rank (BrE), **taxi stand** (AmE) *n* مَوْقِف سَيّاراتِ الأُجْرةِ \ التاكْسي

taxman /ˈtaksman/ *n* (BrE) (**the Taxman**) (infml) دائِرة \ مَصْلَحة الضَرائِبِ

tax office *n* مَكْتَب الضَرائِبِ

taxpayer /ˈtakspeɪə/ *n* دافِع الضَرائِبِ

tax return *n* إقْرار \ كَشْف ضَريبيّ

TB /tiːˈbiː/ *n* = **tuberculosis** مَرَض السُلِّ

tbsp *abbr* = **tablespoon(s)ful** مِلْعَقة كَبيرة

te /tiː/ *n* (also **ti**) تي (النوتة السابِعة في السُلَّمِ الموسيقيِّ الكَبيرِ)

tea /tiː/ *n* **1** (drink) شاي **2** (BrE) (afternoon meal) شاي ما بعد الظَهيرةِ **3** (BrE) (evening meal) عَشاء

Idioms **he/it's not my cup of tea** (infml) لا يَروقُ لي, لا أَسْتَسيغُهُ

teabag *n* كيس شايٍ

tea break *n* (BrE) اسْتِراحة شايٍ

teach /tiːtʃ/ **A** *vt* (*past tense, past participle* **taught**) **1** (to instruct) عَلَّمَ, دَرَّسَ ‹*children, students, adults*›; **to ~ sb about sth** دَرَّسَ شَخْصاً شَيْئاً; **he taught me to drive/how to operate the machine** عَلَّمَني كيف أَقودُ \ أُشَغِّلُ الماكينة **2** (to give lessons in) عَلَّمَ, دَرَّسَ ‹*a subject, skill*›; **to ~ Russian/woodwork** عَلَّمَ الروسيّةَ \ أَشْغالَ الخَشَبِ; **to ~ school** (AmE) عَمِلَ مُدَرِّساً **3** (infml) (as correction) **to ~ sb a lesson** «friends, parents» لَقَّنَ شَخْصاً دَرْساً; **it taught me a lesson I'll never forget** لَقَّنَني دَرْساً لن أَنْساهُ **4** (to advocate) عَلَّمَ ‹*a doctrine, the virtues of*›

B *vi* (*past tense, past participle* **taught**) (to work as a teacher) دَرَّسَ

C *v refl* (*past tense, past participle* **taught**) **to ~ oneself sth/to do sth** عَلَّمَ نَفْسَهُ شَيْئاً \ أَنْ يَفْعَلَ شَيْئاً; **to ~ oneself Spanish/to type** عَلَّمَ نَفْسَهُ الإسْبانيّةَ \ الكِتابةَ على الآلةِ الطابِعةِ \ الكُمْبيوتَر

teacher /ˈtiːtʃə/ *n* مُدَرِّس, مُعَلِّم, أُسْتاذ (أَساتِذة)

teacher training *n* إعْداد المُعَلِّمينَ

tea chest *n* صُنْدوق الشايِ

teaching /ˈtiːtʃɪŋ/ *n* **1** (profession) تَدْريس, تَعْليم **2** (doctrine) تَعْليم (تَعاليمُ)

teaching assistant *n* **1** (in GB: in a school) مُساعِد مُدَرِّسٍ **2** (in US: at college, university) مُعيد

teaching hospital *n* مُسْتَشْفًى تَعْليميّ

teaching practice *n* (BrE) تَدْريب على التَدْريسِ

tea cloth *n* (BrE) فوطة المَطْبَخ

tea cosy (BrE), **tea cozy** (AmE) *n* غَطاء إبْريقِ الشاي

teacup /ˈtiːkʌp/ *n* فِنْجان شايٍ

(Idiom) **a storm** *or* (AmE) **tempest in a teacup** زَوْبعة في فِنْجانٍ

teak /tiːk/ *n* ساج (سيجان)

tea lady *n* (BrE) امْرَأة مَسْؤولة عن إعْدادِ الشاي وَتَقْديمِهِ [للمُوظَّفين]

tea leaf *n* ثُفْل الشاي

team /tiːm/ *n* 1 (in sports) فريق (فِرَق) 2 (in business) فريق عَمَلٍ

(Phrasal verbs) **team up** تَعاوَنَ

• **team up with** تَعاوَنَ (مع)

teammate /ˈtiːmmeɪt/ *n* زَميل (في نَفْسِ الفَريق)

team member *n* عُضْو فريق

team spirit *n* روح الفَريقِ

teamster /ˈtiːmstə/ *n* (AmE) سائِق شاحِنَةٍ

teamwork /ˈtiːmwəːk/ *n* عَمَل جَماعيّ

tea party *n* حَفْلة شايٍ

teapot /ˈtiːpɒt/ *n* إبْريق الشاي

(Idiom) **a storm** *or* (AmE) **tempest in a teapot** زَوْبَعة في فِنْجانٍ

tear[1] /tɛː/ **A** *vt* (*past tense* **tore**; *past participle* **torn**) 1 (to rip) مَزَّقَ ‹*a cloth, letter*›; **to ~ a page out of a book** مَزَّقَ صَفْحةً من كِتابٍ 2 (to rupture) مَزَّقَ ‹*a ligament, muscle*›

B *vi* (*past tense* **tore**; *past participle* **torn**) 1 (to rip) «cloth, paper» تَمَزَّقَ 2 (infml) (to rush) **to ~ out/off** «vehicle, person» انْدَفَعَ, أَسْرَعَ; **we were ~ing along at eighty miles an hour** كُنّا مُنْدَفِعين بِسُرْعةِ ثَمانينَ ميلاً في الساعةِ

C *n* تَمَزُّق

(Phrasal verbs) **tear apart A ~ [sth] apart, ~ apart [sth]** (in pieces) مَزَّقَ [شَيْئاً] ‹*a building, country, the prey*› **B ~ [sb] apart** 1 (to separate) فَرَّقَ [شَخْصاً] ‹*a family, lovers*› 2 (infml) (to upset) أَحْزَنَ [شَخْصاً]

• **tear away A ~ away [sth], ~ [sth] away** مَزَّقَ [شَيْئاً] ‹*a wrapper, bandage*› **B ~ [sb] away** أَبْعَدَ [شَخْصاً] ‹*a child*›; **to ~ oneself away from sth** أَجْبَرَ نَفْسَهُ على تَرْكِ شَيْءٍ

• **tear down: ~ [sth] down, ~ down [sth]** هَدَمَ [شَيْئاً] ‹*a building, statue*›

• **tear off: ~ [sth] off, ~ off [sth]** انْتَزَعَ [شَيْئاً] ‹*a label, the wrapping paper*›

• **tear open: ~ [sth] open, ~ open [sth]** مَزَّقَ [شَيْئاً] ‹*an envelope, a packet*›

• **tear out: ~ [sth] out, ~ out [sth]** مَزَّقَ [شَيْئاً] ‹*a page, picture*›

• **tear up: ~ [sth] up, ~ up [sth]** 1 (to destroy) مَزَّقَ [شَيْئاً] تَمْزيقاً ‹*the document, letter*› 2 (to reject) أَنْهى [شَيْئاً] ‹*a contract, treaty*›

tear[2] /tɪə/ *n* دَمْع (n coll; دُموع); **to burst into ~s** أَجْهَشَ \ انْفَجَرَ بالبُكاءِ

(Idiom) **to end in tears** انْتَهى بالدُموعِ

teardrop /ˈtɪədrɒp/ *n* دَمْعة

tear duct *n* قَناة دَمْعيّة

tearful /ˈtɪəfʊl/ *adj* ‹*farewell, voice*› دامِع

tear gas *n* غاز مُسَيِّل للدُموعِ

tea room, **tea shop** *n* صالون شايٍ

tease /tiːz/ *vt* عاكَسَ ‹*one's brother, classmate*›

tea service, **tea set** *n* طَقْم الشاي

teasing /ˈtiːzɪŋ/ *n* مُعاكَسة

teaspoon /ˈtiːspuːn/ *n* 1 (utensil) مِلْعَقة شايٍ 2 (also **teaspoonful**) مِلْعَقة صَغيرة

teaspoonful /ˈtiːspuːnfʊl/ *n* مِلْعَقة صَغيرة

tea strainer *n* مِصْفاة شايٍ

teat /tiːt/ *n* 1 (cow's, goat's, etc) حَلَم (n coll), طُبْي (أَطْباء) 2 (BrE) (on baby's bottle) حَلَم (n coll)

teatime /ˈtiːtʌɪm/ *n* شاي ما بعد الظَهيرةِ (وَجْبة خَفيفة)

tea towel *n* مَنْشَفة المَطْبَخ

tech /tɛk/ *n* 1 (BrE infml) 2 ▸**technical college**

technical /ˈtɛknɪk(ə)l/ *adj* ‹*knowledge, issue*› تِقْنيّ, فَنّيّ

technical college *n* كُلّيّة تِقْنيّة \ مِهَنيّة

technical drawing *n* (technique) رَسْم تِقْنيّ \ صِناعيّ

technical hitch *n* (infml) خَلَل فَنّيّ

technicality /ˌtɛknɪˈkalɪti/ *n* (*pl* **technicalities**) ناحِية فَنّيّة

technically /ˈtɛknɪkli/ *adv* 1 (strictly speaking) بالمَعْنى الدَقيقِ للكَلِمةِ طِبْقاً; **~ you have committed an offence** طِبْقاً لِنَصِّ القانونِ فَقَدْ ارْتَكَبْتَ جُرْماً 2 (technologically) ‹*feasible, advanced*› من الناحيةِ الفَنّيّةِ

technician /tɛkˈnɪʃ(ə)n/ *n* تِقْنيّ

technique /tɛkˈniːk/ *n* أُسْلوب ,تِقْنيّة (أَساليبُ)

techno /ˈtɛknəʊ/ *n* موسيقى التِكْنو (موسيقى إلِكْترونيّة راقِصة)

technocrat /ˈtɛknəkrat/ *n* تِكْنوقْراط

technological /tɛknəˈlɒdʒɪk(ə)l/ *adj* ‹*advance, innovation*› تِقْنيّ, تِكْنولوجيّ

technology /tɛkˈnɒlədʒi/ *n* (*pl* **technologies**) تِقْنيّة ,تِكْنولوجِيا

teddy /ˈtɛdi/ *n* (also **teddy bear**) دَبْدوب

tedious /ˈtiːdɪəs/ *adj* ‹*task, process*› مُضْجِر ,مُمِلّ

tedium /ˈtiːdɪəm/ *n* ضَجَر ,مَلَل

tee /tiː/ *n* 1 (for the ball) [حامِل توضَعُ عَلَيْهِ كُرةُ الغولْف] 2 (on golf course) [مِنْطَقة الانْطِلاقِ في مَلْعَبِ الغولْف قبل ضَرْبِها]

Phrasal verb **tee off**: 1 **~ off** [اِسْتَهَلَّ جَوْلةً في لُعْبةِ الغولْف] 2 **~ [sb] off** (AmE) (infml) أَغاظَ [بِدَفْعِ الكُرةِ من فَوْقِ حامِلِها] [شَخْصاً]

teem /tiːm/ *vi* 1 **to ~ with fish/tourists** عَجَّ بالسَمَكِ \ السُيّاحِ; **the mall was ~ing with people** كانَ مَرْكَزُ التَسَوُّقِ يَعُجُّ بالناسِ 2 (to pour) «rain» هَطَلَ (i; هَطْل) ,انْهَمَرَ

teen /tiːn/ *adj* (infml) ‹*fashion, magazine*› المُراهِقينَ

teenage /ˈtiːneɪdʒ/ *adj* 1 (adolescent) ‹*son, daughter*› مُراهِق 2 (for teenagers) ‹*fashion, magazine*› المُراهِقينَ

teenager /ˈtiːneɪdʒə/ *n* مُراهِق

teens /tiːnz/ *n pl* **to be in one's ~** كانَ في سِنِّ المُراهَقةِ

teeter /ˈtiːtə/ *vi* «pile» تَمايَلَ; «economy» تَرَنَّحَ; **to ~ on the brink of failure/bankruptcy** كانَ على حافّةِ الفَشَلِ \ الإفْلاسِ

teeth /tiːθ/ *n pl* ▸ **tooth**

teethe /tiːð/ *vi* «babies, toddlers» نَبَتَت أَسْنانُهُ ,أَثْغَرَ; **teething problems** صُعوبات البِداية

teetotal /tiːˈtəʊt(ə)l/ *adj* ‹*lifestyle, group*› [مُمْتَنِع عن شُرْبِ الكُحولِ]

teetotaller (BrE), **teetotaler** (AmE) /tiːˈtəʊt(ə)lə/ *n* [مُمْتَنِع عن شُرْبِ الكُحولِ]

TEFL /ˈtɛf(ə)l/ *n* = **Teaching of English as a Foreign Language** تَعْليم اللُغةِ الإنْجْليزيّةِ كَلُغةٍ أَجْنَبيّةٍ

Tehran /tɛːˈrɑːn/ *pr n* طَهْران (f)

tekke /ˈtɛkeɪ/ *n* تَكيّة (تَكايا)

tel *abbr* = **telephone** هاتِف (هَواتِفُ), تِلِفون (تِليفونات)

Tel Aviv /ˌtɛl əˈviːv/ *pr n* تَلّ أَبيب (f)

telebanking /ˈtɛlɪbaŋkɪŋ/ *n* صَيْرَفة إلِكْترونيّة

telecommunications /tɛlɪkəmjuːnɪˈkeɪʃ(ə)nz/ *n pl* اتِّصالات

telecommuting /tɛlɪkəˈmjuːtɪŋ/ *n* عَمَل عن بُعْدٍ

teleconference /ˈtɛlɪkɒnf(ə)rəns/ *n* اجْتِماع عن بُعْدٍ

telegram /ˈtɛlɪgram/ *n* بَرْقيّة

telegraph /ˈtɛlɪgrɑːf/ *n* تِلِغْراف (تِلِغْرافات)

telegraph pole *n* عَمود تِلِغْراف

telemarketer /ˈtɛlimɑːkɪtə/ *n* مُسَوِّق عَبْرَ الهاتِفِ

telemarketing /ˈtɛlimɑːkɪtɪŋ/ *n* تَسْويق عَبْرَ الهاتِفِ

telepathic /tɛlɪˈpaθɪk/ *adj* 1 (having capability) ‹*person*› [قادِر على التَخاطُرِ] 2 (describing means) ‹*powers, communication*› تَخاطُريّ

telepathy /tɪˈlɛpəθi/ *n* تَوارُد الخَواطِرِ

telephone /ˈtɛlɪfəʊn/ **A** *n* هاتِف (هَواتِفُ), تِلِفون (تِليفونات); **to be on the ~** (talking) كانَ على الهاتِفِ \ التِلِفون; (connected) كانَ عِنْدَهُ خَطٌّ تِلِفونيٌّ **B** *vt* اتَّصَلَ هاتِفيًّا ,تَلْفَنَ (i; تَلْفَنة), هاتَفَ ‹*a friend, the police*› **C** *vi* «caller» تَلْفَنَ (i; تَلْفَنة); **to ~d for help/a taxi** تَلْفَنَ طالِباً المُساعَدةَ \ تاكْسي

telephone booth *n* هاتِف عُموميّ

telephone box *n* (BrE) هاتِف عُموميّ

telephone call *n* اتِّصال هاتِفيّ ,مُكالَمة هاتِفيّة

telephone directory *n* دَليل الهاتِفِ

telephone exchange *n* سِنْتْرال ,بَدّالة الهاتِفِ

telephone number *n* رَقْم هاتِفٍ \ تِلِفون

telephone operator *n* عامِل التِلِفون

telephonist /tɪˈlɛf(ə)nɪst/ *n* (BrE) عامِل التِلِفون

telephoto /ˈtelɪfəʊtəʊ/, **telephoto lens** *n* عَدَسة تَصْوير مُقَرِّبة

telesales /ˈtelɪseɪlz/ *n pl* مَبيعات عَبْرَ الهاتِفِ

telescope /ˈtelɪskəʊp/ *n* تِلِسْكوب

telescopic /telɪˈskɒpɪk/ *adj* **1** ‹*sight, lens*› تِلِسكوبيّ **2** ‹*aerial, umbrella*› مُتَداخِل

teleshopping /ˈtelɪʃɒpɪŋ/ *n* (selling through television) تَسَوُّق عَبْرَ التِلِفِزْيون; (by phone) تَسَوُّق عَبْرَ الهاتِفِ

teletext /ˈtelɪtekst/ *n* تيليتِكْسْت (نظام المَعْلومات المَرْئيّة على التِلِفِزْيون)

televise /ˈtelɪvaɪz/ *vt* تَلْفَزَ (i; تَلْفَزة) ‹*a game, an event*›

television /ˈtelɪvɪʒ(ə)n/ *n* **1** [u] (medium, industry) تلفِزْيون (تِلِفِزْيونات)، تِلْفاز (تِلْفازات)، تَلْفَزة; **to watch ~** شاهَدَ التِلِفِزْيون; **to see sth on ~** شاهَدَ شَيْئاً في \ على التِلِفِزْيون; **the Olympic games are on ~** يَجْري بَثُّ الألعاب الأولَمْبيّة على التِلِفِزْيون; **to work in ~** عَمِلَ في التِلِفِزْيون **2** (set) تِلِفِزْيون (تِلِفِزْيونات)، تِلْفاز (تِلْفازات)، تَلْفَزة

television licence *n* (BrE) رُخصة تِلِفِزْيون

television set *n* جِهاز تِلِفِزْيون

teleworking /ˈtelɪwɜːkɪŋ/ *n* عَمَل عن بُعْدٍ

telex /ˈteleks/ *n* تِلِكْس

tell /tel/ **A** *vt* (*past tense, past participle* **told**) **1** (to communicate) قالَ (u; قَوْل) ‹*a lie, the truth*›; (to communicate to) قالَ (u; قَوْل) ل ‹*a person*›; **he's ~ing the truth** يَقولُ الحَقيقةَ; **can you ~ me the time, please?** هل يُمْكِنُكَ أن تقولَ لي كم الوَقْتُ، من فَضْلِكَ؟; **I told him the way to the station** قُلْتُ لَهُ كيفَ يَصِلُ إلى المَحطّةِ; **I was told that you are looking for work** قيلَ لي إنّكَ تَبْحثُ عن عَمَلٍ; **to ~ sb how to do sth** قالَ لِشَخْصٍ كيفَ يَفْعَلُ شَيْئاً; **I told you so!** أَلَمْ أَقُلْ لَكَ؟ **2** (to narrate, recount) «narrators, comedians» حَكى (i; حِكاية) ‹*a joke, story*›; **the book ~s the story of two brothers** يَحْكي الكِتابُ قِصّةَ أخَوَيْنِ; **to ~ sb about sth** حَكى لِشَخْصٍ عن شَيْءٍ; **I could ~ you a thing or two about her!** أَسْتَطيعُ أن أقولَ لَكَ شَيْئاً أو شَيْئَيْنِ عَنْها! **3** (to order) **to ~ sb to do sth/not to do sth** أَمَرَ شَخْصاً أنْ يَفْعَلَ شَيْئاً \ أنْ لا يَفْعَلَ شَيْئاً; **she told them not to go** قالَتْ لَهُمْ لا تَذْهَبوا; **do as you are told!** افْعَلْ كما قيلَ لَكَ! **4** (to indicate to) «manual, map, gauges» أَعْلَمَ; **the user guide ~s you what to do** يُقَدِّمُ دَليلُ المُسْتَخْدِمِ مَعْلوماتٍ عَمّا يَجِبُ فِعْلُهُ; **his behaviour ~s us a lot about his character** يَقولُ سُلوكُهُ لَنا الكَثيرَ عن شَخْصيّتِهِ; **the old clock still ~s the right time** ما زالَت الساعةُ القَديمةُ تُشيرُ إلى الوَقْتِ الصَحيح **5** (to deduce) **you can ~ he's lying** تَسْتَطيعُ القَوْلَ إنّهُ يَكْذِبُ; **I could ~ that he was disappointed** أَسْتَطيعُ أنْ أقولَ إنّهُ يَشْعُرُ بِخَيْبةِ أَمَلٍ **6** (to distinguish) **to ~ sth from sth else** مَيَّزَ شَيْئاً من شَيْءٍ آخَرَ; **he can't ~ right from wrong** لا يَسْتَطيعُ أنْ يُمَيِّزَ الصَوابَ من الخَطَأِ; **can you ~ the difference between them?** هل تَسْتَطيعُ أنْ تُمَيِّزَ الفَرْقَ بَيْنَهُما؟; **how can you ~ them apart?** كيفَ تَسْتَطيعُ أنْ تُمَيِّزَ بَيْنَهُما؟

B *vi* (*past tense, past participle* **told**) **1** (to reveal a secret) **promise me you won't ~!** عِدْني أنّكَ لن تقولَ! **2** (to ascertain, know for certain) تَأَكَّدَ; **how can you ~?** كيفَ تَسْتَطيعُ أنْ تَتأَكَّدَ؟; **you never can ~** لَيْسَ بِاسْتِطاعَتِكَ أنْ تَتأَكَّدَ; **as far as I can ~** على حَدِّ عِلْمي **3** (liter) (to be evidence of) **to ~ of happiness/hardship** «sb's expression, face, the ruins» دَلَّ على السَعادةِ \ الشَقاءِ **4** (to count) **his tiredness was beginning to ~** كانَ تَعَبُهُ قد بَدَأَ يَظْهَرُ; **her lack of experience told against her** وَقَفَ افْتِقارُها لِلخِبْرةِ حَجَرَ عَثْرةٍ في طَريقِها

C *v refl* (*past tense, past participle* **told**) **to ~ oneself that ...** قالَ لِنَفْسِهِ إنّ ...

(Idioms) **time will tell** الوَقْتُ وَحْدَهُ كَفيلٌ بِذَلِكَ; **to tell it like it is** (infml) قالَ الحَقيقةَ كما هي; **to tell the whole world about sth** قالَ شَيْئاً لِكُلِّ العالَمِ

(Phrasal verbs) **tell off: ~ [sb] off** (to rebuke) وَبَّخَ [شَخْصاً] ‹*a pupil, child, an employee*›; **she got told off for being late** وُبِّخَتْ لِتَأَخُّرِها

• **tell on: ~ on [sb]** **1** (to betray) أَخْبَرَ عن [شَخْصٍ] **2** (to have an effect on) أَثَّرَ على [شَخْصٍ]; **the strain is beginning to ~ on him** بَدَأَ الإرْهاقُ يُؤَثِّرُ عَلَيْهِ

teller /ˈtelə/ *n* **1** (in banking) أمين صُنْدوقٍ **2** (in elections) مُحْصي أَصْواتِ المُقْتَرِعينَ

telling /ˈtelɪŋ/ *adj* ‹*example, comment*› مُعَبِّر

telltale /ˈtelteɪl/ **A** *adj* ‹*sign, sound*› مُخْبِر, كاشِف (كَشَفة), موحٍ
B *n* (BrE) واشٍ (وُشاة, واشونَ)

telly /ˈteli/ *n* (*pl* **tellies**) (BrE infml) تِلِفِزْيون (تِلِفِزْيونات), تِلْفاز (تِلْفازات)

temp /temp/ **A** *n* عامِل \ مُوَظَّف مُؤَقَّت
B *vi* (infml) عَمِلَ بِشَكْلٍ مُؤَقَّتٍ

temper /ˈtempə/ **A** *n* **1** (mood) مِزاج (أَمْزِجة); **to be in a bad/good ~** كانَ في مِزاجٍ سَيِّءٍ \ حَسَنٍ **2** (nature) طَبْع (طِباع); **to have a short/quick ~** كانَ حادَّ الطَبْعِ **3** (rage) غَيْظ, جَيَشان; **to be in/fly into a ~** اغْتاظَ **4** (good humour) **to lose/keep one's ~** فَقَدَ \ تَمالَكَ أَعْصابَهُ
B *vt* **1** (to moderate) خَفَّفَ ‹*one's enthusiasm, criticism*›
2 قَسّى ‹*steel*›

temperament /ˈtemp(ə)rəmənt/ *n* مِزاج (أَمْزِجة), طَبْع (طِباع)

temperamental /ˌtemp(ə)rəˈment(ə)l/ *adj* ‹*star, actor*› مِزاجِيّ, مُتَقَلِّب

temperance /ˈtemp(ə)rəns/ *n* **1** (moderation) اعْتِدال
2 (abstinence from alcohol) الامْتِناع عن الخَمْرِ

temperate /ˈtemp(ə)rət/ *adj* ‹*climate, zone*› مُعْتَدِل

temperature /ˈtemp(ə)rətʃə/ *n* **1** (degree of heat or cold) دَرَجة الحَرارة; **what's the ~ inside/outside?** ما هِيَ دَرَجةُ الحَرارةِ في الداخِلِ \ الخارِجِ؟ **2** (of the body) دَرَجة الحَرارة; **to take sb's ~** أَخَذَ دَرَجةَ حَرارةِ شَخْصٍ; **to have a ~** كانَ لَدَيْهِ دَرَجةُ حَرارةٍ مُرْتَفِعةٌ

temper tantrum *n* نَوْبة غَضَبٍ

tempest /ˈtempɪst/ *n* (liter) عاصِفة (عَواصِفُ), زَوْبَعة (زَوابِعُ)

tempestuous /temˈpestjʊəs/ *adj* **1** ‹*relationship, affair*› عاصِف **2** (liter) ‹*sea, weather*› عاصِف, هائِج

template /ˈtempleɪt/ *n* **1** (pattern) قالَب (قَوالِبُ)
2 (document format) قالَب (قَوالِبُ)

temple /ˈtemp(ə)l/ *n* **1** (building) مَعْبَد (مَعابِدُ), هَيْكَل (هَياكِلُ)
2 (on the head) صُدْغ (أَصْداغ)

tempo /ˈtempəʊ/ *n* (*pl* **tempos** or **tempi**) **1** (speed) سُرْعة
2 (in music) سُرْعة الإيقاعِ \ العَزْفِ

temporal[1] /ˈtemp(ə)rəl/ *adj* (fml) ‹*pattern, dimension*› زَمَنِيّ

temporal[2] /ˈtemp(ə)rəl/ *adj* ‹*lobe, bone*› صُدْغِيّ

temporarily /ˈtempr(ə)rəli/ *adv* ‹*to suspend, close*› مُؤَقَّتاً

temporary /ˈtemp(ə)rəri/ *adj* ‹*worker, accommodation*› مُؤَقَّت

tempt /tempt/ *vt* أَغْرى, أَغْوى ‹*customers, investors*›; **to be ~ed to do sth** أُغْرِيَ بالقِيامِ بِشَيْءٍ

temptation /tempˈteɪʃ(ə)n/ *n* إغْراء (إغْراءات), إغْواء (إغْواءات)

tempting /ˈtemptɪŋ/ *adj* ‹*offer, prospect*› مُغْرٍ, فاتِن (فَواتِنُ)

ten /ten/ *n, adj* عَشَرة ▸ see also **five**

tenable /ˈtenəb(ə)l/ *adj* ‹*theory, argument*› مُمْكِن الدِفاعُ عَنْهُ

tenacious /tɪˈneɪʃəs/ *adj* ‹*opponent, resistance*› مُصِرّ, مُتَمَسِّك, مُتَشَبِّث

tenacity /tɪˈnasɪti/ *n* إصْرار, عِناد, تَماسُك, تَشَبُّث

tenancy /ˈtenənsi/ *n* (*pl* **tenancies**) **1** (use) اسْتِئْجار, إيجار **2** (period) مُدّة الاسْتِئْجارِ (إيجارات)

tenant /ˈtenənt/ *n* مُسْتَأْجِر

tench /tentʃ/ *n* (*pl* **tench**) [سَمَك نَهْرِيّ]

tend /tend/ **A** *vt* اهْتَمَّ (ب) ‹*a garden, fields*›; رَعى (a; رَعْي, رِعاية) ‹*sheep, flocks*›; اعْتَنى (ب) ‹*a patient, the wounded*›
B *vi* **1** (to be inclined) **to ~ to do sth** مالَ إلى فِعْلِ شَيْءٍ
2 (to attend) **to ~ to sth/sb** «nurses, gardeners» اعْتَنى \ اهْتَمَّ بِشَيْءٍ \ بِشَخْصٍ

tendency /ˈtend(ə)nsi/ *n* (*pl* **tendencies**) مَيْل (مُيول), نَزْعة (نَزَعات)

tender /ˈtendə/ **A** *n* (bid) عَرْض (عُروض), عَطاء
B *adj* **1** (soft) ‹*meat, vegetables*› طَرِيّ, غَضّ **2** (fond) ‹*look, feelings*› لَطيف (لُطَفاءُ), حَنون, رَقيق (أَرِقّاءُ) **3** (sensitive) ‹*swelling, wound*› حَسّاس **4** (young) **at the ~ age of three** في سِنٍّ مُبَكِّرةٍ في الثالِثةِ من العُمْرِ; **he spoke with a wisdom far beyond his ~ years** تَكَلَّمَ بِحِكْمةٍ غَيْرِ مُتَوَقَّعةٍ من شَخْصٍ [في سِنٍّ مُبَكِّرةٍ]
C *vt* (fml) قَدَّمَ ‹*one's resignation*›

tenderize, -ise (BrE) /ˈtendərʌɪz/ *vt* طَرّى, لَيَّنَ ‹*meat, steak*›

tenderly /ˈtend(ə)li/ *adv* ‹*to kiss, smile*› بِرِقّةٍ, بِحَنانٍ, بِعَطْفٍ

tendon /ˈtend(ə)n/ *n* وَتَر (أَوْتار)

tendril /ˈtendrɪl/ *n* مِحْلاق (عُضْو نَباتِيّ ذو شَكْلٍ لَوْلَبِيٍّ تَتَعَلَّقُ بِهِ النَبْتةُ المُعَرِّشةُ)

tenement /ˈtɛnəmənt/ *n* عِمارة (عِمارات)

tenet /ˈtɛnɪt/ *n* مَبْدَأ (مَبادِئ)

tenfold /ˈtɛnfəʊld/ **A** *adj* ‹*increase, growth*› عَشْرة أَضْعافٍ

B *adv* ‹*to increase, multiply*› بِعَشْرة أَضْعافٍ

tenner /ˈtɛnə/ *n* (infml) **1** (BrE) وَرَقة عَشْرةِ جُنَيْهاتٍ **2** (AmE) وَرَقة عَشْرة دولاراتٍ

Tennessean, **Tennesseean** /tɛnəˈsiːən/ *pr n, adj* [(شخص) من تينيسي]

Tennessee /ˌtɛnəˈsiː/ *pr n* تينيسي (f)

tennis /ˈtɛnɪs/ *n* كُرة المِضْرَب, تِنِس

tennis court *n* مَلْعَب تِنِس

tennis player *n* لاعِب كُرة المِضْرَب \ تِنِس

tenor /ˈtɛnə/ **A** *n* **1** (singer) تينور **2** (sense, content) فَحْوى (f; فَحاوٍ), مَضْمون

B *adj* **1** ‹*voice, aria*› تينور **2** ‹*saxophone, horn*› تينور

tenpin bowling /ˌtɛnpɪn ˈbəʊlɪŋ/ (BrE), **tenpins** (AmE) /ˈtɛnpɪnz/ *n* لُعْبة البولِنغ العَشْريّة (تُسْتَخْدَمُ فيها عَشْرُ قَوارير)

tense /tɛns/ **A** *n* صيغة الفِعْل (زَمَن الفِعْل); **the present/past ~** صيغة المُضارِع \ الماضي

B *adj* **1** ‹*person*› مُتَوَتِّر **2** ‹*situation, moment*› مُتَوَتِّر **3** ‹*finish, game*› مُثير **4** ‹*muscles, shoulders*› مَشْدود

C *vt* شَدَّ (i-u; شَدّ) ‹*one's muscles*›

(Phrasal verb) **tense up** «candidates» تَوَتَّرَ

tension /ˈtɛnʃ(ə)n/ *n* **1** (between communities) تَوَتُّر (تَوَتُّرات) **2** (between people) تَوَتُّر (تَوَتُّرات); **nervous ~ leads to stress** يُؤَدّي التَوَتُّرُ العَصَبيُّ إلى الإرْهاقِ **3** (excitement) إثارة; **the ~ was almost too much** كانَت الإثارةُ تَقْريباً أَكْثَر مِمّا يَنْبَغي **4** (of a rope, wire, etc) شَدّ

tent /tɛnt/ *n* خَيْمة (خِيَم, خِيام)

tentacle /ˈtɛntək(ə)l/ *n* مِجَسّ (مِجَسّات, مَجاسّ)

tentative /ˈtɛntətɪv/ *adj* **1** (provisional) ‹*agreement, plan*› مُؤَقَّت, مَبْدَئي **2** (hesitant) ‹*person, steps*› مُتَرَدِّد

tenterhooks /ˈtɛntəhʊks/ *n pl* **to be on ~** انْتَظَرَ بِفارِغِ الصَبْرِ

tenth /tɛnθ/ **A** *n* **1** (in a series) عاشِر **2** (fraction) عُشْر (أَعْشار) **3** (**the tenth**) (of a month) العاشِر

B *adj* ‹*day, place*› عاشِر

C *adv* في المَرْكَزِ العاشِرِ

tenuous /ˈtɛnjʊəs/ *adj* ‹*link, connection*› ضَعيف; ‹*hold, grip*› خَفيف

tenure /ˈtɛnjə/ *n* **1** (fml) (period in office) فَتْرة \ مُدّة تَوَلّي مَنْصِب **2** [u] (job security) تَثْبيت وَظيفيّ **3** [u] (of property, land) حِيازة, مِلْكيّة

tepid /ˈtɛpɪd/ *adj* ‹*water, bath*› فاتِر

term /təːm/ **A** *n* **1** (in office) وِلاية; (in academic year) فَصْل دِراسيّ; **his first ~ of office** وِلايَتُهُ الأولى; **a ~ of imprisonment** فَتْرة قَضاءِ عُقوبةٍ في السِجْنِ; **the spring/summer ~** الفَصْل الدِراسيّ الرَبيعيّ \ الصَيْفيّ; **in the long/short ~** في المَدى البَعيدِ \ القَريبِ **2** (word, phrase) مُصْطَلَح (مُصْطَلَحات); **~ of abuse** مُصْطَلَحُ تَحْقيرٍ; **we discussed it in general ~s** ناقَشْناهُ بِشَكْلٍ عامٍّ; **she condemned their action in the strongest possible ~s** أَدانَتْ عَمَلَهُمْ بِأَشَدِّ العِباراتِ المُمْكِنةِ **3** (of a contract, lease) بَنْد (بُنود) **4** (Math) حَدّ (حُدود)

B (**terms**) *n pl* **1** (conditions) شُروط; **to get a loan on favourable ~s** حَصَلَ على قَرْضٍ بِشُروطٍ مُناسِبةٍ; **~s of reference** صَلاحيّات **2** (to accept) **to come to ~s with defeat/the past** تَصالَحَ مع الهَزيمةِ \ الماضي; **to come to ~s with the idea that ...** قَبِلَ فِكْرةَ ... **3** (in relationships) عَلاقة (عَلاقات); **they are on first-name ~s** تَرْبِطُهُمْ عَلاقةُ صَداقةٍ; **to be on good/bad ~s with sb** كانَ على عَلاقةٍ جَيِّدةٍ \ سَيِّئةٍ مع شَخْصٍ

C (**in terms of**) *prep phr* (from the point of view of) مِن حَيْثُ; **it is difficult to justify in ~s of cost** مِن الصَعْبِ التَبْريرُ مِن حَيْثُ التَكْلِفةِ

D *vt* (fml) سَمّى ‹*an action, a decision*›; **the offer was ~ed derisory** اُعْتُبِرَ العَرْضُ باعِثاً على السُخْريّةِ

terminal /ˈtəːmɪn(ə)l/ **A** *adj* ‹*illness*› قاتِل, مُميت; ‹*patient*› [لا أَمَلَ في شِفائِه]; **he has ~ cancer** هو مُصابٌ بِسَرَطانٍ قاتِلٍ \ مُميتٍ

B *n* 1 (for buses, ships, aircraft) مَحَطّة (أَخيرة) 2 (computer) وِحْدة طَرَفيّة (في شَبَكةِ كُمْبيوتَراتٍ) 3 (for electricity) [أَحَد طَرَفي الدائِرةِ الكَهْرَبائيّة]

terminally /ˈtɜːmɪn(ə)li/ *adv* **to be ~ ill with cancer** كانَ شِفاؤُهُ من السَرَطانِ مَيْؤوساً مِنْهُ

terminate /ˈtɜːmɪneɪt/ **A** *vt* 1 ‹*a contract, a lease*› أَنْهى 2 ‹*a pregnancy*› أَنْهى 3 (AmE) ‹*an employee*› فَصَلَ (i; فَصْل)
B *vi* 1 «lease, employment» انْتَهى 2 «train, service» تَوَقَّفَ (في المَحَطّةِ الأَخيرةِ)

termination /tɜːmɪˈneɪʃ(ə)n/ *n* 1 (ending of a contract, employment) إنْهاء 2 (of a pregnancy) إجْهاض, (إجْهاضات)

terminology /ˌtɜːmɪˈnɒlədʒi/ *n* (*pl* **terminologies**) مُصْطَلَح (مُصْطَلَحات)

terminus /ˈtɜːmɪnəs/ *n* (*pl* **terminuses** or **termini**) (BrE fml) مَحَطّة

termite /ˈtɜːmʌɪt/ *n* نَمْل أَبْيَض, أَرَضة

terrace /ˈtɛrəs/ **A** *n* 1 (patio) باحة, فناء (أَفْنِية) 2 (BrE) (row of houses) صَفّ من البُيوتِ \ المَنازِلِ المُتَلاصِقةِ
B (**terraces**) *n pl* (BrE) (in a stadium) مُدَرَّج (مُدَرَّجات)

terraced house /ˌtɛrɪst ˈhaʊs/, **terrace house** *n* (BrE) [بَيْت في صَفٍّ من البُيوتِ المُتَلاصِقةِ]

terracotta /ˌtɛrəˈkɒtə/ *n* طين نَضيج, تيراكوتا

terrain /tɛˈreɪn/ *n* تَضاريس

terrapin /ˈtɛrəpɪn/ *n* سُلَحْفاة (المِياهِ العَذْبة)

terrestrial /təˈrɛstrɪəl/ *adj* 1 ‹*species, ecosystem*› بَرّيّ, أَرْضيّ 2 ‹*television, channel*› أَرْضيّ

terrible /ˈtɛrɪb(ə)l/ *adj* 1 (serious, severe) ‹*crime, accident, mistake, pain*› فَظيع, رَهيب 2 (infml) (very bad) ‹*food, weather*› فَظيع (فُظَعاءُ)

terribly /ˈtɛrɪbli/ *adv* 1 (very) ‹*important, sorry*› جِدًّا, للغاية 2 (badly) ‹*to treat, behave*› بِشَكْلٍ فَظيعٍ \ رَهيبٍ 3 (very much) ‹*to suffer, hurt*› كَثيراً جِدًّا

terrier /ˈtɛrɪə/ *n* [كَلْب صَغير من كِلابِ الصَيْدِ]

terrific /təˈrɪfɪk/ *adj* 1 (infml) (very good) ‹*performance, idea*› رائِع, بَديع 2 (very great) ‹*amount*› ضَخْم; ‹*noise*› شَديد, حادّ; ‹*force, impact*› عَظيم, هائِل

terrifically /təˈrɪfɪkli/ *adv* (infml) ‹*well, talented*› بِشَكْلٍ رائِعٍ \ بَديع; **we get on ~ well** نَنْسَجِمُ بِشَكْلٍ رائِع

terrified /ˈtɛrɪfʌɪd/ *adj* ‹*child, animal*› مَذْعور, مَرْعوب; **he's ~ of heights/dogs** تُرْعِبُهُ المُرْتَفَعاتُ \ الكِلابُ

terrify /ˈtɛrɪfʌɪ/ *vt* (**terrifies, terrifying, terrified**) ‹*a child, an animal*› أَرْعَبَ, أَفْزَعَ, رَوَّعَ

terrifying /ˈtɛrɪfʌɪɪŋ/ *adj* ‹*ordeal, experience*› مُرْعِب, مُرَوِّع, مُفْزِع

territorial /ˌtɛrɪˈtɔːrɪəl/ *adj* ‹*dispute, claim*› إقْليميّ

territorial waters *n* مِياه إقْليميّة

territory /ˈtɛrɪt(ə)ri/ *n* (*pl* **territories**) أَرْض (f; أَراضٍ), إقْليم

terror /ˈtɛrə/ *n* رُعْب, هَوْل (أَهْوال), ذُعْر; **to flee in ~** فَرَّ مَرْعوباً

terrorism /ˈtɛrərɪz(ə)m/ *n* إرْهاب; **the threat posed by international ~** التَهْديد الّذي يُشَكِّلُهُ الإرْهابُ الدُوَليُّ

terrorist /ˈtɛrərɪst/ *n* إرْهابيّ

terrorize, -ise (BrE) /ˈtɛrərʌɪz/ *vt* ‹*the population, community*› أَرْهَبَ, أَرْعَبَ, رَوَّعَ

terry /ˈtɛri/ *n* (also **terry towelling** BrE; **terry cloth** AmE) قُماش المَناشِفِ

terse /tɜːs/ *adj* ‹*statement, reply*› مُقْتَضَب, موجَز, وَجيز

tertiary /ˈtɜːʃ(ə)ri/ *adj* 1 ‹*education*› عالٍ 2 (Econ) ‹*sector*› الخَدَماتِ

TESL /ˈtɛs(ə)l/ *n* = **Teaching of English as a Second Language**

TESOL /ˈtɛsɒl/ *n* = **teaching of English to speakers of other languages** تَعْليم اللُغةِ الإنْجليزيّةِ لِغَيْرِ الناطِقينَ بها

test /tɛst/ **A** *n* 1 (trial) اخْتِبار (اخْتِبارات); **it was a good ~ of his determination** كانَ اخْتِباراً جَيِّداً لِعَزيمَتِهِ; **to put the safety procedures to the ~** اخْتَبَرَ إجْراءاتِ السَلامةِ; **to stand the ~ of time** صَمَدَ أمامَ عَوامِلِ \ اخْتِبارِ الزَمَنِ; **the poll should be a good ~ of popular opinion** يَجِبُ أنْ يَكونَ اسْتِطْلاعُ الرَأْيِ اخْتِباراً جَيِّداً للرَأْيِ العامِّ 2 (examination) اخْتِبار (اخْتِبارات);

to pass/fail the ~ نَجَحَ \ فَشِلَ في الاخْتِبارِ; **an intelligence/ personality ~** اخْتِبار ذَكاءٍ \ شَخْصِيَّةٍ **3** (of equipment, machines, etc) اخْتِبار (اخْتِبارات), فَحْص (فُحوص) **4** (of blood, urine) اخْتِبار (اخْتِبارات), فَحْص (فُحوص); **to have an eye/hearing ~** كان عِنْدَهُ اخْتِبارُ عُيونٍ \ سَمْعٍ **5** (also **driving test**) امْتِحان \ اخْتِبار القِيادةِ **6** ▸ **Test match**

B *vt* **1** (educationally) امْتَحَنَ, اخْتَبَرَ ‹*a student, class*› **2** (to assess) فَحَصَ (a; فَحْص), اخْتَبَرَ ‹*the engine, equipment, efficiency*›; **the equipment has been ~ed for faults** تَمَّ اخْتِبارُ المُعِدّاتِ للكَشْفِ عن أيِّ خَلَلٍ **3** فَحَصَ (a; فَحْص), اخْتَبَرَ ‹*the sample, blood, drug*›; **he was ~ed for leukaemia** أُجْرِيَ لَهُ فَحْصُ لوكيميا; **to have one's eyes ~ed** كانَ عِنْدَهُ اخْتِبارُ عُيونٍ; **to ~ new drugs on volunteers** اخْتَبَرَ دَواءً جَديداً على مُتَطَوِّعينَ **4** (for weaknesses) اخْتَبَرَ ‹*one's endurance, courage, strength*›; **the conditions ~ed our confidence and endurance** اخْتَبَرت الظُروفُ ثِقَتنا بِأَنْفُسِنا وَطاقة تَحَمُّلِنا; **he set out to ~ the system's effectiveness** عَقَدَ العَزْمَ على اخْتِبارِ فاعِلِيَّةِ النِظامِ

C *vi* **1** (in laboratories) **to ~ for alcohol/pollution** قامَ بِاخْتِبارٍ; **to ~ positive/negative** كانَتْ نَتيجةُ اخْتِبارِهِ الكُحولِ \ التَلَوُّثِ إيجابِيَّةً \ سَلْبِيَّةً **2** «operators, engineers» جَرَّبَ

testament /ˈtɛstəmənt/ *n* **1** (proof) دَليل (بَراهين) بُرْهان (أدِلَّة); **to be a ~ to sth** كانَ دَليلاً على شَيْءٍ **2** (of the Bible) عَهْد (عُهود); ▸ **New Testament**, ▸ **Old Testament** **3** (fml) (will) وَصِيَّة (وَصايا); **his last will and ~** وَصِيَّتُهُ الأخيرة

testator /tɛˈsteɪtə/ *n* مُوَرِّث, تارك الوَصِيّة, موصٍ

test ban *n* (اتِّفاقيّة) حَظْر التَجارِبِ النَوَوِيّة

test case *n* قَضِيّة اخْتِبارِيّة (قَضِيّة قد تُصْبِحُ سابِقَةً قانونِيّةً)

test drive **A** *n* قِيادة تَجْرِيبِيّة;

B *vt* (**test-drive**) جَرَّبَ ‹*a car*›

testicle /ˈtɛstɪk(ə)l/ *n* خُصْيَة (خُصًى); **the ~s** الخُصْيَتانِ

testify /ˈtɛstɪfʌɪ/ **A** *vt* (**testifies, testifying, testified**) **to ~ that ...** شَهِدَ أنَّ . . .

B *vi* (**testifies, testifying, testified**) «witness, defendant» شَهِدَ (a; شَهادة), أَدْلى بِشَهادةٍ; **to ~ for/against sb** شَهِدَ لِصالِحِ \ ضِدَّ شَخْصٍ

testimonial /ˌtɛstɪˈməʊnɪəl/ *n* شَهادة (تَقْديراً أو اعْتِرافاً بالجَميلِ)

testimony /ˈtɛstɪməni/ *n* (*pl* **testimonies**) شَهادة

testing /ˈtɛstɪŋ/ **A** *n* اخْتِبار (اخْتِبارات), فَحْص (فُحوص)

B *adj* (challenging) ‹*conditions, experience*› ≈ صَعْب (صِعاب); **it's been a ~ time for us** كانَتْ فَتْرةً صَعْبَةً لَنا

Test match *n* (in cricket, rugby) مُباراة تَصْفِياتٍ

testosterone /tɛˈstɒstərəʊn/ *n* تَسْتوسْتيرون

test paper *n* **1** (examination) وَرَقة امْتِحانٍ **2** (Chem) وَرَقة اخْتِبارٍ

test pilot *n* طَيّار اخْتِبارٍ

test tube *n* أُنْبوب اخْتِبارٍ

test-tube baby /ˌtɛstjuːb ˈbeɪbi/ *n* طِفْل الأَنابيب

tetanus /ˈtɛt(ə)nəs/ *n* التيتانوس, كُزاز

tether /ˈtɛðə/ **A** *vt* رَبَطَ (i-u; رَبْط), عَقَلَ (i; عَقْل), قَيَّدَ ‹*a horse*›; رَبَطَ (i-u; رَبْط) ‹*balloon*›

B *n* قَيْد (قُيود), رِباط (أَرْبِطة)

(Idiom) **to be at the end of your tether** (BrE) **to be at the end of your rope** (AmE) بَلَغَ السَيْلُ الزُبى, طَفَحَ الكَيْلُ

Texan /ˈtɛks(ə)n/ *pr n, adj* تِكْساسِيّ (شَخْص من تِكْساس)

Texas /ˈtɛksəs/ *pr n* تِكْساس (f)

text /tɛkst/ **A** *n* **1** (of a speech, letter) نَصّ (نُصوص) **2** (also **set text**) (for exam) نَصّ أَدَبِيّ مُقَرَّر في الامْتِحاناتِ **3** (also **text message**) رِسالة نَصِّيّة

B *vt* أَرْسَلَ رِسالةً نَصِّيّةً إلى ‹*a friend*›

textbook /ˈtɛkstbʊk/ **A** *n* كِتاب مَدْرَسِيّ

B *adj before n* ‹*case*› نَموذَجِيّ

textile /ˈtɛkstʌɪl/ *n* نَسيج (أَنْسِجة)

text message *n* رِسالة نَصِّيّة

textphone /ˈtɛkstfəʊn/ *n* هاتف نَصِّيّ (هاتف مُطَوَّر لِمُتَطَلَّباتِ الصُمِّ والبُكْمِ)

textual /ˈtɛkstjʊəl/ *adj* ‹*analysis, evidence*› نَصِّيّ

texture /ˈtɛkstʃə/ *n* مَلْمَس (مَلامِسُ)

Thai /tʌɪ/ **A** *adj* ‹*government, restaurant*› تايْلَنْدِيّ

B *n* **1** (citizen) تايْلَنْدِيّ **2** (language) (اللُغة) التايْلَنْدِيّة

Thailand /ˈtʌɪland/ *pr n* تايْلانْدا

thalassaemia (BrE), **thalassemia** (AmE) /ˌθaləˈsiːmɪə/ *n* الثَلاسيمْيا

thalidomide /θəˈlɪdəmʌɪd/ *n* ثاليدوميد

Thames /tɛmz/ *pr n* (**the Thames**) (نَهر) التايْمز

than /ðan, ðən/ **A** *conj* **1▸** (in comparisons) مِمّا, مِنْ; **he's older ~ I am** هو أكْبَرُ منّي; **it took us longer ~ we thought it would** أَخَذَ مِنّا وَقْتاً أَطْوَلَ مِمّا كُنّا نَظُنُّ; **it was further away ~ I remembered** كانَ أَبْعَدَ مِمّا كُنْتُ أَتَذَكَّرُ **2▸** (expressing preferences) **I would rather do this ~ (do) that** أُفَضِّلُ أنْ أَفْعَلَ هذا على أنْ أَفْعَلَ ذلك **3▸** (when) **hardly** *or* **no sooner had he left ~ the phone rang** بِمُجَرَّدِ أنْ غادَرَ رَنَّ جَرَسُ الهاتِفِ

B *prep* **1▸** (in comparisons) مِنْ; **thinner ~ him** أَنْحَف مِنْهُ; **he has more ~ me** عِنْدَهُ \ لَدَيْهِ أَكْثَرُ مِنّي; **I was more surprised ~ annoyed** كُنْتُ مُنْدهِشاً أَكْثَر مِمّا كُنْتُ مُتَضايِقاً **2▸** (expressing quantity, degree, value) مِنْ; **more/less ~ half** أَكْثَر \ أَقَلّ من النصْف; **more/less ~ 100** أَكْثَر \ أَقَلّ من 100; **more/less ~ $1,000** أَكْثَر \ أَقَلّ من $1000

thank /θaŋk/ *vt* شَكَرَ (u; شُكْر) ‹*the staff, hosts*›; **~ you so much** شُكْراً جَزيلاً; **to ~ sb for sth** شَكَرَ شَخْصاً على شَيْءٍ; **~ God!, ~ goodness!** الحَمْدُ لله!

thankful /ˈθaŋkfʊl/ *adj* ‹*smile, prayer*› مَمْنون, شاكِر

thankfully /ˈθaŋkf(ə)li/ *adv* **1▸** (luckily) لِحُسْنِ الحَظِّ **2▸** (with gratitude) ‹*to smile, accept*› بِكُلِّ امْتِنانٍ

thankless /ˈθaŋkləs/ *adj* ‹*task, job*› صَعْب ≈ (لا يُتَوَقَّعُ من جَرّائِهِ الشُكْرُ)

thanks /θaŋks/ **A** *n pl* شُكْر

B *excl* **~!** شُكْراً!; **~ very much, ~ a lot** شُكْراً جزيلاً; **many ~** شُكْراً جزيلاً

C (**thanks to**) *phr* بِفَضْلِ

Thanksgiving, **Thanksgiving Day** /θaŋksˈɡɪvɪŋ/ *n* (in the US) عيد الشُكْرِ (عيد وَطَنِيّ في أَمْريكا)

thank you *excl* شُكْراً; **thank you very much** شُكْراً جَزيلاً; **to say thank you** قالَ شُكْراً; **thank you for coming/for the flowers** شُكْراً على الحُضور \ الزُهورِ

that /ðat/ **A** *demonstrative pronoun* (*pl* **those**) **1▸** (that one) ذَلِكَ (f تِلْكَ; أولَئِكَ); **what's ~?** ما ذَلِكَ؟; **we prefer this to ~** نُفَضِّلُ هذا على ذَلِكَ; **who's ~ speaking?** مَنْ المُتَحَدِّثُ؟; **who was ~?** (on telephone) مَنْ كانَ ذَلِكَ؟; **~'s my Uncle Hassan** ذَلِكَ عَمّي حَسَنٌ; **'which boys?' — 'those over there'** 'أَيُّ أَوْلادٍ؟' — 'أولَئِكَ الَّذين هُناكَ'; **those are the less popular models** تِلْكَ هي الموديلاتُ الأَقَلُّ شَعْبيَّةً **2▸** (sth observed or mentioned) ذَلِكَ; **~'s wonderful/dreadful!** ذَلِكَ رائِعٌ \ مُخيفٌ!; **~'s where I live** ذَلِكَ هو المَكانُ الَّذي أَعيشُ فيهِ; **who told you ~?** مَنْ قالَ لَكَ ذَلِكَ؟; **~'s not true/fair** ذَلِكَ غَيْرُ صَحيحٍ \ عادِلٍ; **~'s what he said** ذَلِكَ هو ما قالَهُ; **~'s how he did it** تِلْكَ هي الطَريقةُ الَّتي فَعَلَهُ بها; **what did he mean by ~?** ماذا كانَ يَقْصِدُ بِذَلِكَ؟; **before ~, we lived in Beirut** قبل ذَلِكَ، عِشْنا في بَيْروتَ; **he never went there again after ~** لم يَذْهَبْ هُناكَ مَرّةً أُخْرى أَبَداً بعد ذَلِكَ; **he's not as greedy as (all) ~!** هو لَيْسَ طَمّاعاً لِكُلِّ هذه الدَرَجةِ! **3▸** (before relative pronoun) **those who** أولَئِكَ الَّذينَ

B also ðat/ *relative pronoun* الَّذي (f الَّتي; f pl اللاّتي, اللَّواتي; m du اللَّذانِ; f du اللَّتانِ); **the man ~ lost** الرَّجُل الَّذي خَسِرَ; **the men ~ emigrated** الرجال الَّذينَ هاجَروا; **the woman ~ won** المَرْأة الَّتي فازَتْ; **the women ~ stayed behind** النساء اللاّتي بَقينَ في الخَلْف; **the house ~ they live in** البَيْتُ الَّذي يَعيشونَ فيهِ; **the reason ~ I phoned** السَبَبُ الَّذي اتَّصَلْتُ من أَجْلِهِ

C *determiner* (*pl* **those**) ذَلِكَ (f تِلْكَ; أولَئِكَ); **~ chair/those chairs** ذَلِكَ الكُرسيّ \ تِلْكَ الكَراسيّ; **~ horse/those horses** ذَلِكَ الحِصان \ تِلْكَ الأَحْصِنة; **~ woman/those women** تِلْكَ المَرْأة \ أولَئِكَ النِساء; **~ man/those men** ذَلِكَ الرَجُل \ أولَئِكَ الرِجال; **do it this way, not ~ way** افْعَلْهُ بِهَذِهِ الطَريقة، وَلَيْسَ بِتِلْكَ; **I said ~ dress!** قُلْتُ ذَلِكَ الفُسْتانَ!; **I prefer ~ colour to this one** أُفَضِّلُ ذَلِكَ اللَوْنَ على هذا; **he left ~ same day** غادَرَ في نَفْسِ ذَلِكَ اليَوْمِ; **he went ~ way** ذَهَبَ من ذَلِكَ الطَريقِ; **at ~ moment** في تِلْكَ اللَحْظةِ

D *adv* (to the extent shown) **it's about ~ thick** هو بِهَذا السُمْكِ تَقْريباً; **he's ~ tall** هو بِهَذا الطولِ; **she's not ~ clever**

هي لَيْسَتْ بِهذا الذَكاءِ; **she's ~ much smaller than me** هي أَصْغَرُ مِني بِهَذا القَدْرِ; **I can't do ~ much work in one day** لا يُمْكِنُني أَنْ أَقومَ بِكُلِّ هذا القَدْرِ من العَمَلِ في يَوْمٍ واحِدٍ; **he can't swim ~ far** لا يَسْتَطيعُ أَنْ يَسْبَحَ كُلَّ تِلْكَ المَسافَةِ
E also ðət/ *conj* **1** (between clauses) أَنْ, إنَّ, أَنَّ; **he said ~ he had finished** قالَ إنَّهُ قد انْتَهى من عَمَلِهِ; **it's likely ~ they are out** من المُحْتَمَلِ أَنَّهُمْ بالخارِجِ; **we realize ~ it's difficult** نُدْرِكُ أَنَّهُ صَعْبٌ **2** (fml) (expressing wish) **oh ~ he would come!** آهِ لو يَأْتي!; (expressing surprise) **~ it should come to this!** عَجَباً أَنَّهُ آلَ لِهَذا!

(Idiom) **... and all that** (infml) ... وَكُلّ تِلْكَ الأَشْياءِ

thatch /θatʃ/ *n* سَقْف من القَشِّ

thatched /θatʃt/ *adj* ‹*roof*› مَسْقوف بالقَشِّ; ‹*cottage*› مَصْنوع من القَشِّ

thaw /θɔː/ **A** *vt* **1** أَذابَ ‹*the ice, snow*› **2** أَذابَ ‹*frozen food*›
B *vi* **1** «ice, snow» ذابَ (u; ذَوَبان) **2** «frozen food» ذابَ **3** «relations» اسْتَعادَ الدِفْءَ
C *n* **1** (warmer weather) ذَوَبان الثَلْجِ **2** (in relations) عَوْدة الدِفْءِ

the /ðiː, ðə/ *determiner* **1** (specifying, identifying etc) الْ (أَداة التَعْريفِ); **two chapters of ~ book** فَصْلانِ من الكِتابِ; **I met them at ~ supermarket** قابَلْتُهُمْ في المَرْكَزِ التِجاريِّ; **~ wounded** الجَرْحى; **~ Smiths are coming to tea** سَتَأْتي عائِلَةُ سْميث لِتَناوُلِ الشاي مَعَنا **2** (for emphasis) **it's ~ place to buy shoes/vegetables** هو أَفْضَلُ مَكانٍ لِشِراءِ الأَحْذِيَة \ الخُضْرَواتِ; **it's ~ Chinese restaurant** هو أَفْضَلُ مَطْعَمٍ صينيٍّ **3** (enough) **he hadn't ~ courage to refuse** لم تَكُنْ لَدَيْهِ الشَجاعةُ الكافِيةُ لِيَرْفُضَ; **we don't have ~ money for the repairs** لَيْس لَدَيْنا المالُ الكافي للإِصْلاحاتِ **4** (with eras) **~ fifties** الخَمْسينِيّات; **~ nineteenth and twentieth centuries** القَرْنانِ التاسِعَ عَشَرَ والعِشْرونَ **5** (with comparatives) **the news made her all ~ sadder** زادَتْها الأَخْبارُ حُزْناً; **~ more I learn ~ less I understand** كُلَّما ازْدَدْتُ عِلْماً ازْدَدْتُ جَهْلاً; **~ sooner ~ better** كُلَّما كانَ أَبْكَرَ كُلَّما كانَ أَفْضَلَ **6** (with superlatives) **~ fastest train** أَسْرَع قِطارٍ; **she buys only ~ best** هي لا تَشْتَري سِوى الأَفْضَلِ

theatre (BrE), **theater** (AmE) /ˈθɪətə/ *n* **1** (building) مَسْرَح (مَسارِحُ); **to go to the ~** ذَهَبَ إلى المَسْرَحِ **2** [u] (activity, profession) مَسْرَح; **she loves the ~** تُحِبُّ المَسْرَحَ **3** (BrE) (also **operating theatre**) غُرْفة العَمَلِيّاتِ **4** (AmE) (also **movie theater**) سينَما (قاعة)

theatregoer (BrE), **theatergoer** (AmE) /ˈθɪətəgəʊə/ *n* مُرْتاد المَسْرَحِ

theatrical /θɪˈatrɪk(ə)l/ *adj* ‹*performance, production*› مَسْرَحيّ

Thebes /θiːbz/ *pr n* طيبة (الاسْم القَديم لِمَدينةِ الأُقْصُرِ)

thee /ðiː/ *pron* (old use) ▸ **you** 1

theft /θɛft/ *n* سَرِقة, اخْتِلاس (اخْتِلاسات)

their /ðɛː/ *determiner* (masculine or mixed) ـهُمْ; (feminine) ـهُنَّ; (dual) ـهُما; (non-human) ـها; **they came in ~ cars** جاؤوا في سَيّاراتِهِمْ; **everyone should bring ~ own food** يَجِبُ على كُلِّ واحِدٍ أَنْ يُحْضِرَ مَعَهُ أَكْلَهُ

theirs /ðɛːz/ *pron* **my car is red but ~ is blue** سَيّارَتي حَمْراءُ لَكِنَّ سَيّارَتَهُمْ زَرْقاءُ; **which house is ~?** أَيُّ بَيْتٍ بَيْتُهُمْ؟; **I'm a friend of ~** أَنا أَحَدُ أَصْدِقائِهِمْ; **the money wasn't ~ to give away** الأَمْوالُ لم تَكُنْ لَهُمْ حتّى يُفَرِّطوا فيها

them /ðɛm, ðəm/ *pron* **1** (as direct object) (masculine or mixed) ـهُمْ; (feminine) ـهُنَّ; (dual) ـهُما; (non-human) ـها; **he bought ~** اشْتَراها; **she invited ~** اسْتَدْعَتْهُمْ **2** (as indirect object) (masculine or mixed) ـهُمْ; (feminine) ـهُنَّ; (dual) ـهُما; (non-human) ـها; **he bought ~ some presents** اشْتَرى لَهُم بَعْضَ الهَدايا; **give ~ the forms** أَعْطِهِم الاسْتِماراتِ; **he bought it for ~** اشْتَراها لَهُمْ **3** (with prep) (masculine or mixed) ـهُمْ; (feminine) ـهُنَّ; (dual) ـهُما; (non-human) ـها; **it's for ~** إنَّهُ لَهُمْ; **both of ~ came** جاءَ كِلاهُما; **buy both of ~** اشْتَرِ كِلَيْهِما; **there were four of ~** كانَ هُناكَ أَرْبَعةٌ مِنْهُمْ **4** (for emphasis) (masculine or mixed) هُمْ; (feminine) هُنَّ; (dual) هُما; (non-human) هِيَ; **it's ~** إنَّهُمْ هُمْ; **that will be ~** أولَئِكَ سَيَكونونَ هُمْ **5** (indefinite person) هُوَ; **there's someone at the door. — shall I let ~ in?** هُناكَ شَخْصٌ على البابِ. - هل أُدْخِلُهُ؟; **if anyone calls, what should I tell ~?** إذا اتَّصَلَ أَيُّ شَخْصٍ, ماذا أَقولُ لَهُ؟

thematic /θɪ'matɪk/ *adj* <*material, content*> مواضيعيّ

theme /θiːm/ *n* ثيمة ,مَوْضوع

theme park *n* مَدينة تَرْفيهيّة \ مَلاهٍ (ذات مَوْضوع مُحَدَّدٍ)

theme song *n* أُغْنِية البِدايةِ والنِهايةِ (في فيلْمٍ أو مُسَلْسَلٍ)

theme tune *n* موسيقى البِدايةِ والنِهايةِ (في فيلْمٍ أو مُسَلْسَلٍ)

themselves /ðəm'selvz/ *pron* **1** (reflexive) أَنْفُسَهُمْ; **they washed ~** غَسَلوا أَنْفُسَهُمْ **2** (emphatic) (they themselves) هُمْ أَنْفُسُهُمْ; (by themselves) بِأَنْفُسِهِمْ; **they ~ said so** أَنْفُسُهُمْ قالوا ذلك; **they did it ~** فَعَلوها بِأَنْفُسِهِمْ **3** (after prepositions) أَنْفُسِهِمْ; **they kept the money for ~** احْتَفَظوا بالأَمْوالِ لأَنْفُسِهِمْ; **they did it (all) by ~** فَعَلوهُ بِأَنفُسِهِمْ **4** (in expressions) **they're not ~ today** لَيْسوا على ما يُرامُ اليَوْمَ

then /ðɛn/ **A** *adv* **1** (at that time) في ذلك الوَقْتِ; (in those days) في تِلْكَ الأَيّامِ ,وَقْتَئِذٍ; **since ~** مُنْذُ ذلك الوَقْتِ \ الحينِ; **by ~** عِنْدَئِذٍ; **from ~ on** مُنْذُئِذٍ ,مُنْذُ تلك اللحْظةِ; **till** *or* **until ~** حتى ذلك الوَقْتِ \ الحينِ ▸ see also **there** C **2** (next, afterwards) بعد ذلك ,ثُمَّ **3** (in that case, therefore) في ,إذَنْ تِلْكَ الحالةِ; **that's OK ~** حَسَناً إذَنْ **4** (in addition, besides) بالإضافةِ إلى ذلك ,وَفَوْقَ ذلك; **and ~ there's the fare to consider** وَفَوْقَ ذلك \ بالإضافةِ إلى ذلك لا بُدَّ من أَخْذِ الأُجْرةِ بِعَيْنِ الاعْتِبارِ; **~ again** عَلاوةً على ذلك **B** *adj* آنَذاكَ; **the ~ prime minister** رَئيس الوُزَراءِ آنَذاكَ

thence /ðɛns/ *adv* (fml) <*to depart, proceed*> من هُناكَ \ ثُمَّ

theologian /θiːə'ləʊdʒ(ə)n/ *n* عالِم لاهوتٍ ,لاهوتيّ

theological /θɪə'lɒdʒɪk(ə)l/ *adj* <*issue, study*> لاهوتيّ

theology /θiː'ɒlədʒi/ *n* (*pl* **theologies**) عِلْم اللاهوتِ

theorem /'θɪərəm/ *n* مُبَرْهَنة ,نَظَرِيّة

theoretical /θɪə'rɛtɪk(ə)l/ *adj* <*approach, study*> نَظَرِيّ

theoretically /θɪə'rɛtɪkli/ *adv* <*possible, correct*> نَظَرِيًّا

theorize, -ise (BrE) /'θɪərʌɪz/ **A** *vt* نَظَّرَ **B** *vi* نَظَّرَ

theory /'θɪəri/ *n* (*pl* **theories**) نَظَرِيّة; **the ~ of evolution** نَظَرِيّة التَطَوُّرِ; **in ~ everyone will benefit** نَظَرِيًّا سَيَسْتَفيدُ الجَميعُ

therapeutic /ˌθɛrə'pjuːtɪk/ *adj* <*effect, drug*> عِلاجيّ

therapist /'θɛrəpɪst/ *n* اخْتِصاصيّ عِلاجٍ \ مُعالَجةٍ ,مُعالِج

therapy /'θɛrəpi/ *n* (*pl* **therapies**) عِلاج

there /ðɛː/ **A** *pron* (as impersonal subject) هُناكَ ,ثَمّةَ; **~ is a horse in the field** ثَمّةَ حِصانٌ في الحَقْلِ; **~ is some left** هُناكَ بَعْضٌ مِنْهُ تَبَقّى; **~ are horses in the field** هُناكَ خُيولٌ في الحَقْلِ; **~ are many reasons** ثَمّةَ عِدّةُ أَسْبابٍ; **~ seems** *or* **appears to be a mistake** يَبْدو أنّ هُناكَ خَطأً; **~ was a house here once** كانَ يوجَدُ بَيْتٌ هُنا فيما مَضى; **~'ll be dancing later** سَيَكونُ هُناكَ رَقْصٌ فيما بَعْدُ; **~'s no denying that ...** لا يُمْكِنُ أنْ نُنْكِرَ أنّ ...
B *adv* **1** (that place or point) هُناكَ; **put it ~** ضَعْهُ هُناكَ; **put it over ~** ضَعْهُ هُنالِكَ; **stand ~** قِفْ هُناكَ; **go over ~** اذْهَبْ إلى هُنالِكَ; **up to ~** إلى هذا الحَدِّ; **take the offer while it's ~** اقْبَلِ العَرْضَ طالَما لا يَزالُ قائِماً **2** (at or to that place) هُناكَ; **since we were last ~** مُذْ كُنّا هُناكَ آخِرَ مَرّةٍ; **to go ~ and back in an hour** ذَهَبَ هُناكَ وَعادَ في غُضونِ ساعةٍ **3** (drawing attention to sth) ها; **~'s a taxi coming** ها هي سَيّارةُ أُجْرةٍ آتِيةٌ; **~ goes the bus** ها هي الحافِلةُ تُغادِرُ; **~ you go again** [ها أَنْتَ تَتَصَرَّفُ بِنَفْسِ الطَريقةِ مَرّةً أُخْرى]; **ah, ~ you are!** آه، ها قد وَصَلْتَ!; **~ you are!** تَفَضَّلْ!; **what have you got ~?** ما هذا؟; **which one? this one or that one ~?** أَيّ الّذي تَحْمِلُهُ مَعَكَ؟ واحِدٍ؟ هذا أم ذاكَ الّذي هُناكَ؟ **4** (indicating presence) هُناكَ; **they will all be ~** سَوْفَ يَكونُ الجَميعُ هُناكَ; **is she ~ yet?** أَلَمْ تَصِلْ بَعْدُ؟; **we are always ~ if you need us** نَحْنُ دائِماً هُنا إنْ احْتَجْتَنا **5** (indicating juncture) هُنا; **we must stop ~** يَجِبُ أنْ نَتَوَقَّفَ هُنا; **I think you're wrong ~** أَعْتَقِدُ أَنَّكَ مُخْطِئٌ في هذه النُقْطةِ **6** (infml) (emphatic) **hello ~!** أَهْلاً! (نداء من بَعيدٍ)
C (**there and then**) *adv phr* في التَوِّ واللَحْظةِ; **she fired him ~ and then** طَرَدَتْهُ في التَوِّ واللَحْظةِ
D (**there again**) *adv phr* من جِهةٍ أُخْرى; **~ again, our team was better prepared** من جِهةٍ أُخْرى، كانَ فَريقُنا أَفْضَلَ اسْتِعْداداً
E *excl* **~, ~!** لا عَلَيْكَ!; **~! you see, I'm right!** أَرَأَيْتَ؟ الحَقُّ مَعي!; **~, you've broken it!** ها قد كَسَرْتَهُ!

thereabouts /ðɛːrə'baʊts/, **thereabout** (AmE) /ðɛːrə'baʊt/ *adv* **1** (near that figure, time) حَوالَيْ \ نَحْوَ ذلك ,تَقْريباً;

it costs $500 or ~ يُكَلِّفُ 500 دولار أو ما يُقارِبُ ذلك **2** (near that place) قَريباً من ذلك ,بالجِوارِ ,على مَقْرُبةٍ المَكانِ; **they own some land ~** يَمْلِكونَ بَعْضَ الأَراضي بالجِوارِ

thereafter /ðɛːr'ɑːftə/ *adv* (fml) بعد ذلك ,بَعْدَئِذٍ

thereby /ðɛː'bʌɪ/ *adv* (fml) بِذَلِكَ

therefore /'ðɛːfɔː/ *adv* بِناءً على ذلك ,وبالتالي ,لِذَلِكَ; **he had lived there and ~ knew what to expect** كانَ قد عاشَ هُناكَ وبالتالي كانَ يَعْرِفُ ما يُمْكِنُ تَوَقُّعُهُ

therein /ðɛːr'ɪn/ *adv* (fml) **1** (in that respect) في تِلْكَ (المَسْأَلةِ); **~ lies the problem** هُنا تَكْمُنُ المُشْكِلةُ **2** (in that document) في تِلْكَ الوَثيقةِ

thereof /ðɛːr'ɒv/ *adv* (fml) من ذلك ,مُتَعَلِّق بِهِ

there's /ðɛːz/ *abbr* = **there is**, = **there has**

thermal /'θəːm(ə)l/ *adj* **1** ‹*energy, reactor*› حَراريّ **2** ‹*underwear*› [طَويل]; ‹*gloves*› عازِل (عَوازِل)

thermal imaging *n* تَصْوير حَراريّ

thermometer /θə'mɒmɪtə/ *n* مِحْرار ,ميزان \ مِقْياس الحَرارةِ

thermos® /'θəːmɒs/ *n* (also **thermos flask**) تُرْمُس (تَرامِس)

thermostat /'θəːməstat/ *n* تِرْموسْتات ,مُنَظِّم الحَرارة

thesaurus /θɪ'sɔːrəs/ *n* (*pl* **thesauruses** or **thesauri**) مَكْنَز (مَكانِز)

these /ðiːz/ *pl* ▸**this**

thesis /'θiːsɪs/ *n* (*pl* **theses**) **1** (for a university degree) رِسالة جامعيّة ,أُطْروحة **2** (theory) نَظَرِيّة ,فَرْضِيّة

they /ðeɪ/ *pron* **1** (masculine or mixed) هُمْ; (feminine) هُنَّ; (dual) هُما; (non-human) هِيَ; **~ have gone** لَقَدْ ذَهَبوا; **where are ~?** أَيْنَ هُمْ؟ **2** (unspecified person, people) هُوَ; **someone called, but ~ didn't give their name** أَحَدُهُم اتَّصَلَ, لَكِنَّهُ لم يَذْكُر اسْمَهُ; **~'ve started the road repairs** لَقَدْ بَدَؤوا في تَصْليح الطَريقِ; **~ say she's an actress** يُقالُ إنَّها مُمَثِّلةٌ

they'd /ðeɪd/ *abbr* = **they had**, = **they would**

they'll /ðeɪl/ *abbr* = **they will**

they're /ðɛː/ *abbr* = **they are**

they've /ðeɪv/ *abbr* = **they have**

thick /θɪk/ **A** *adj* **1** (in width, depth) ‹*layer, snow, line, cable*› سَميك ,(غِلاظ) غَليظ; **use a ~er paper/sandpaper** اسْتَعْمِلْ وَرَقةً \ وَرَقةَ صَنْفَرةٍ أَغْلَظ; **the glass is 6 mm ~** سُمْكُ البِلَّوْر 6 ملم; **how ~ is the wall?** كم يَبْلُغُ سُمْكُ الجِدارِ؟ **2** (in consistency, density) ‹*sauce, paste, mud*› خاثِر; **to make the soup/sauce ~er** جَعَلَ الحَساءَ \ المَرَقَ أَخْثَرَ; **~ mud made progress slow** جَعَلَ الطينُ السَميكُ التَقَدُّمَ بَطيئاً; **to be ~ with mud/smoke** كانَ غارِقاً في الوَحَلِ \ مَليئاً بالدُخانِ **3** (for warmth) ‹*blanket, overcoat, jumper*› سَميك **4** (impenetrable) ‹*forest, fog, vegetation*› كَثيف; **it's an area of ~ forest** هي مِنْطَقةٌ ذاتُ غاباتٍ كَثيفةٍ; **his ~ beard made him easy to recognize** جَعَلَتْ لِحْيَتُهُ الكَثيفةُ التعَرُّفَ عَلَيْهِ سَهْلاً; **the city was ~ with police** كانَتْ المَدينةُ تَعُجُّ بالبوليس **5** (strong) ‹*accent*› قَوِيّ **6** (infml) (stupid) ‹*person*› بَليد; **I can't get it into his ~ head** لا أَسْتَطيعُ أنْ أوصِلَها إلى رَأْسِهِ البَليدِ **7** (infml) (close) قَريب; **he's very ~ with the boss** هو قَريبٌ جِدًّا من رَئيسِهِ في العَمَلِ

B *adv* ‹*to slice, lie, spread*› بِشَكْلٍ سَميكٍ; **don't spread the butter on too ~** لا تَدْهُنِ الكَثيرَ من الزُبْدةِ على الخُبْزِ; **the snow lies ~ on the ground** هُناكَ طَبَقةٌ سَميكةٌ من الثَلْجِ على الأَرْضِ

Idioms **through thick and thin** في السَرّاءِ والضَرّاءِ; **to be in the thick of sth** كانَ في خِضَمِّ شَيْءٍ ▸**blood**, ▸**brick**, ▸**plank**, ▸**thief**

thicken /'θɪk(ə)n/ **A** *vt* ثَخَّنَ ,كَثَّفَ ‹*a sauce, the air*› **B** *vi* «sauce, mixture» ثَخُنَ (u; ثُخونة); «cloud, fog» تَكَثَّفَ

thicket /'θɪkɪt/ *n* دَغَل (أَدْغال), أَجَم (n coll)

thickly /'θɪkli/ *adv* **1** (in a thick layer) ‹*to spread*› بِكَثافةٍ; ‹*slice*› قِطَعاً \ شَرائِحَ سَميكةً **2** (densely) ‹*populated, forested*› بِكَثافةٍ

thickness /'θɪknəs/ *n* (of a wall, layer, paper, fabric) سُمْك

thickset /θɪk'sɛt/ *adj* ‹*person, animal*› ضَخْم الجُثّةِ ,مُمْتَلِئ الجِسْم

thick-skinned /ˌθɪk'skɪnd/ *adj* ‹*person*› صَفيق ,قَليل الإِحْساسِ الوَجْهِ

thief /θiːf/ *n* (*pl* **thieves**) سارِق ,(لُصوص) لِصّ

Idiom **to be as thick as thieves** [جَمَعَتْ بَيْنَهُما عَلاقةٌ قَوِيّةٌ] ▸**blood**, ▸**brick**, ▸**plank**

thieve /θiːv/ *vi* سَرَقَ (i; سَرِقة)

thigh /θaɪ/ *n* فَخِذ (f; أَفْخاذ)

thimble /ˈθɪmb(ə)l/ *n* كُشْتُبان (كَشاتِبينُ), قِمْع الخِياطةِ

thin /θɪn/ **A** *adj* **(-nn-)** **1** (in width, depth) ‹*layer, wire, wall*› رَقيق; **a ~ film of oil** غِشاء رَقيق من الزَيْتِ; **the roof is very ~** السَقْفُ رَقيقٌ جدًّا **2** (for comfort) ‹*dress, blanket, cardigan*› خفيف **3** (sparse) ‹*hair, beard*› خَفيف; **his hair was going ~** أَصْبَحَ شَعْرُهُ خفيفاً; **a ~ crowd** جُمْهور قليل **4** (in consistency) ‹*sauce, paste, mixture*› خَفيف; **to make the soup/mixture ~ner** جَعَلَ الحَساءَ \ الخَليطَ أَخَفَّ **5** ‹*air*› قَليل الأُكْسيجين **6** (lean, not fat) ‹*face, arm, leg*› نَحيف; **she has very ~ wrists** لَها مِعْصَمانِ رَفيعانِ **7** (unconvincing) ‹*excuse, evidence, plot*› ضَعيف; **his jokes/excuses are wearing ~** أَصْبَحَتْ نِكاتُهُ \ أَعْذارُهُ قديمةً; **my patience is wearing ~** صَبْري يَنْفَدُ **8** (weak) ‹*voice, tone*› ضَعيف

B *adv* (infml) ‹*to slice, spread, lie*› بِشَكْلٍ خَفيفٍ; **I spread the butter very ~** أَدْهُنُ الزُبْدةَ على الخُبْزِ بِشَكْلٍ خَفيفٍ

C *vt* **(-nn-)** **1** (to dilute) خَفَّفَ ‹*paint, sauce*› **2** ▸**thin out**

D *vi* **(-nn-)** «fog, crowds» تَلاشى; «hair» خَفَّ (i; خَفّ)

(Idiom) **to be thin on the ground** كانَ نادِرَ الوُجودِ

(Phrasal verbs) **thin down A** (AmE) (to lose weight) خفَّضَ الوَزْنَ

B ~ [sth] down, ~ down [sth] (to dilute) خَفَّفَ [شَيْئاً] ‹*paint, soup*›

• **thin out A** «fog, crowds» تَلاشى; «hair» خَفَّ (i; خَفّ) **B ~ [sth] out, ~ out [sth]** **1** خَفَّفَ [شَيْئاً] ‹*a hedge, traffic*› **2** قَلَّلَ في [شَيْءٍ] ‹*the population, candidates*›

thing /θɪŋ/ **A** *n* **1** (object) شَيْء (أَشْياءُ); **what's this ~ for?** ماذا سَتَفْعَلُ بِهذا الشَيْءِ؟; **there isn't a ~ to eat in the house!** لا يوجَدُ شَيْءٌ في البَيْتِ لِأَكْلِهِ!; **the one ~ he wants is a bike** الشَيْءُ الوَحيدُ الّذي يُريدُ الحُصولَ عَلَيْهِ هو دَرّاجةٌ **2** (action, task, event) شَيْء (أَشْياءُ); **I've got ~s to do** عِنْدي أَشْياءُ لا بُدَّ من قَضائِها; **there wasn't a ~ I could do** لم يَكُنْ هُناكَ شَيْءٌ أَسْتَطيعُ فِعْلَهُ; **she went on to great ~s in life** أَصْبَحَتْ شَخْصيّةً مُهِمّةً; **it's a good ~ you came** إنَّهُ لَشَيْءٌ جَميلٌ أَنَّكَ أَتَيْتَ; **the ~ to do is to listen carefully** الشَيْءُ الّذي يَجِبُ فِعْلُهُ هو الإنْصاتُ بانْتِباهٍ; **the best ~ to do would be to explain what happened** أَفْضَلُ شَيْءٍ يَجِبُ فِعْلُهُ هو أنْ نُفَسِّرَ ما حَدَثَ; **that's the worst ~ you could have said** ذلك هو أَسْوَأُ شَيْءٍ كانَ بِإمْكانِكَ قَوْلُهُ **3** (matter, fact) شَيْء (أَشْياءُ); **the ~ to remember is ...** الشَيْءُ الّذي يَجِبُ تَذَكُّرُهُ هو ...; **I couldn't hear a ~ he said** لم أَسْتَطِعْ أنْ أَسْمَعَ أَيَّ شَيْءٍ مِمّا قالَ; **I said/did no such ~!** لم أَقُلْ \ أَفْعَلْ شَيْئاً مِثْلَ ذلك!; **the ~ is, ...** كُلّ ما في الأَمْرِ هو أَنّ ...; **the good ~ is that ...** الشَيْءُ الجَيِّدُ هو أَنّ ... **4** (infml) (person) شَخْص (mf; أَشْخاص); **she's a pretty little ~** يا لَها من امْرَأةٍ جَميلةٍ; **you lucky ~!** يا لَكَ من شَخْصٍ مَحْظوظٍ!

B **(things)** *n pl* **1** (personal belongings) أَشْياء; **I've come to collect my ~s** جِئْتُ لِأَجْمَعَ أَشْيائي; **to wash up the breakfast ~s** غَسَلَ أَوانِيَ الفُطورِ **2** (matters) أُمور ,أَشْياء, أَحول; **~s are getting better/worse** تَتَحَسَّنُ \ تَسوءُ الأَشْياءُ; **how are ~s with you?, how are ~s going?** كَيفَ الأَحْوالُ؟; **as ~s are** *or* **stand** كَما تَبْدو الأَشْياءُ; **all ~s considered** كُلّ الأَشْياءِ مَأْخوذة بِعَيْنِ الاعْتِبارِ

(Idioms) **first things first** الأَهَمّ ثُمَّ المُهِمّ; **it was just one of those things** كانَ مُجَرَّدَ حادِثٍ; **it's a girl/guy thing** (infml) إنَّهُ شَأْنٌ نِسائيٌّ \ رِجاليٌّ; **that's just the thing!** ذلك هو الشَيْءُ المَطْلوبُ!; **to have a thing about sth** (infml) (to be obsessive about) كانَ مَهْووساً بِشَيْءٍ; **he has a ~ about roses** هو مَهْووسٌ بالوُرودِ; **to know a thing or two about sth** (infml) كانَ لَهُ عِلْمٌ بِشَيْءٍ

thingamajig /ˈθɪŋəmədʒɪɡ/, **thingamabob** /ˈθɪŋəməbɒb/ *n* (infml) شَيْء مَجْهول الاسْمِ

think /θɪŋk/ **A** *vt* (*past tense, past participle* **thought**) **1** (to believe) اعْتَقَدَ; **I ~ it's going to rain** أَعْتَقِدُ أَنّها سَتُمْطِرُ; **how much do you ~ it will cost?** كم تَظُنُّ أَنّها سَتُكَلِّفُ؟; **I ~ so** أَعْتَقِدُ ذلك; **I don't ~ so, I ~ not** لا أَعْتَقِدُ ذلك; **we thought it best to tell her** اعْتَقَدْنا أَنَّهُ من الأَفْضَلِ أنْ نَقولَهُ لَها **2** (to imagine) تَخَيَّلَ; **who would have thought it!** مَنْ كانَ يَتَخَيَّلُ ذلك!; **I didn't ~ you meant that!** لم أَكُنْ أَعْتَقِدُ أَنَّكَ قَصَدْتَ ذلك; **I can't ~ how he did it** لا أَسْتَطيعُ أنْ أَتَخَيَّلَ كيف فَعَلَهُ; **who do you ~ you are?** مَنْ تَظُنُّ نَفْسَكَ؟; **what on earth do**

you ~ you're doing? ماذا تظُنُّ أنّكَ فاعِلٌ؟ **3** (to have an idea) فَكَّرَ; **I ~ I'll take the car/go for a swim** أُفَكِّرُ أنّي سآخُذُ السَّيّارة \ سأذهَبُ للسِباحةِ; **I didn't ~ to check** لم أُفَكِّرْ في التأكُّدِ **4** (in assessments) **to ~ a lot of a person/of sb's work** قَدَّرَ شخصاً \ عَمَلَ شخصٍ تقديراً كبيراً; **I don't think much of the food** لا أظُنُّ أنّ الطَعامَ جيِّدٌ; **I don't think much of her boyfriend** لا أُقَدِّرُ صاحِبَها; ▸**world** **5** (to remember) افْتكَرَ, تَذَكَّرَ; **I can't ~ where I've put my keys** لا أتذكَّرُ أينَ وضعْتُ مفاتيحي; **try to ~ what he was wearing** حاوِلْ أنْ تتذكَّرَ ما كانَ يَلْبَسُ

B *vi* (*past tense, past participle* **thought**) **1** (to engage in thought) فَكَّرَ; **I'll have to ~ about it** يَجِبُ أنْ أُفكِّرَ فيهِ; **she couldn't ~ clearly** لم تستطِعْ أنْ تُفكِّرَ بِشَكْلٍ واضِحٍ; **to ~ hard** فكَّرَ مليًّا; **to ~ for oneself** فكَّرَ بِشكلٍ مُستقِلٍّ **2** (to take into account) **to ~ about** *or* **of sb/sth** فكَّرَ في شخصٍ \ شيْءٍ; **~ of your family/about the future** فكِّرْ في عائِلَتِكَ \ في مُستقبَلِكَ; **I can't ~ of everything!** لا أستطيعُ أنْ أُفكِّرَ في كُلِّ شيْءٍ! **3** (to regard) **to ~ of sb/sth as sth** اعْتَبَرَ شخصاً \ شيْئاً شيْئاً; **he ~s of himself as an expert** يَعْتبِرُ نفسَهُ خبيراً; **I always thought of it as a challenge** لَطالما اعتَبَرْتُهُ تحدِّياً **4** (to consider) **to ~ of** *or* **about sth** فكَّرَ في شيْءٍ; **he's ~ing of resigning** يُفكِّرُ في الاسْتِقالةِ; **I was ~ing about a trip to Egypt** كُنْتُ أُفكِّرُ في رِحْلةٍ إلى مِصْرَ; **what were you ~ing of?** فيمَ كُنتَ تُفكِّرُ؟; **I wouldn't ~ of going there** لا يُمْكِنُني التفْكيرُ في الذهابِ هُناكَ **5** (to imagine) **to ~ of sth** تخيَّلَ \ تصَوَّرَ شيْئاً; **a million pounds, ~ of that!** مليون جُنَيْهٍ، تخيَّلْ ذلكَ! **6** (to remember) **to ~ of sth** تذكَّرَ شيْئاً; **I can't ~ of his name** لا أستطيعُ أنْ أتذكَّرَ اسْمَهُ; **if you ~ of anything else** إذا تذكَّرْتَ أيَّ شيْءٍ آخَرَ

C *n* (BrE) **to have a ~ about sth** كانَ لدَيْهِ تفكيرٌ في شيْءٍ

Idioms **to think better of sth** أعادَ النظَرَ في شيْءٍ; **to think on one's feet** كانَ سريعَ البديهةِ; **to think well** *or* **highly of sb** قدَّرَ شخصاً تقديراً كبيراً

Phrasal verbs **think again** (to reconsider) أعادَ التفْكيرَ

• **think ahead** (in planning) فكَّرَ في المُستقبَلِ

• **think back** حاوَلَ أنْ يتذكَّرَ

• **think out**: **~ out [sth], ~ [sth] out** درَسَ \ مَحَّصَ [شيْئاً] ‹*a plan, design, the implications*›; **to be well/badly thought out** كانَ مَدْروساً بِشكْلٍ جيِّدٍ \ سيِّئٍ

• **think over**: **~ over [sth], ~ [sth] over** درَسَ [شيْئاً] بِرَوِيَّةٍ ‹*a proposal, conversation, situation*›

• **think through**: **~ through [sth], ~ [sth] through** درَسَ \ مَحَّصَ [شيْئاً] ‹*a proposal, plan, the consequences*›; **to be well/badly thought through** كانَ مَدْروساً بِشكْلٍ جيِّدٍ \ سيِّئٍ

• **think up**: **~ up [sth]** اخْترَعَ \ ابْتكَرَ [شيْئاً] ‹*a plan, an idea, a name*›; **he thought up a way of making it work** ابْتكَرَ طريقةً لِجَعْلِهِ يَعْمَلُ

thinker /ˈθɪŋkə/ *n* مُفكِّرٌ

thinking /ˈθɪŋkɪŋ/ *n* **1** (reflection) تفْكيرٌ; **to do some ~ about sth** قامَ بالتفْكيرِ في شيْءٍ; **quick ~** سُرْعةُ البديهةِ **2** (ideas, opinions) رأيٌ (آراء); **to my way of ~** في رأيي \ اعْتِقادي

think tank *n* مُؤسَّسةٌ فِكْرِيَّةٌ

thinly /ˈθɪnli/ *adv* **1** (in a thin layer) ‹*to spread, slice*› بِشكْلٍ رقيقٍ \ خفيفٍ **2** (not densely) ‹*populated*› بِشكْلٍ قليلٍ \ خفيفٍ

thinner /ˈθɪnə/ *n* **1** (also **paint thinner**) مُرقِّقٌ \ مُخفِّفٌ للدِهانِ **2** (also **blood thinner**) عقاقيرُ منْعِ تجلُّطِ الدمِ

third /θɜːd/ **A** *n* **1** (in a series) ثالثٌ **2** (fraction) ثُلْثٌ (أثْلاث) **3** (**the third**) (of a month) الثالِثُ **4** (Aut) (also **third gear**) التُرْسُ الثالثُ

B *adj* ‹*day, time*› ثالثٌ

C *adv* **1** (in position, time, order) ‹*to come, finish*› في المركَزِ الثالثِ **2** (thirdly) ثالِثاً

third-class /θɜːdˈklɑːs/ *adj* **1** (inferior) ‹*citizen*› من الدرَجةِ الثالثةِ; **they were treated like ~ citizens** كانوا يُعامَلونَ كمُواطِنينَ من الدرَجةِ الثالثةِ **2** (BrE) ‹*degree*› مقبولٌ

third-degree /θɜːdəˈgriː/ *adj* ‹*burn*› من الدرَجةِ الثالثةِ

thirdly /ˈθɜːdli/ *adv* ثالثاً

third party **A** *n* طرَفٌ ثالثٌ;

B (**third-party**) *adj before n* ‹*insurance*› الطرَفِ الثالثِ

Third World *pr n* (**the Third World**) العالَم الثالِث

thirst /θɜːst/ *n* ظَمَأ, عَطَش; **his ~ for knowledge/revenge** تَعَطُّشُهُ للمَعْرِفةِ \ للثأْرِ

thirsty /ˈθɜːsti/ *adj* (**thirstier, thirstiest**) ‹*traveller, animal*› ظَمْآن (dipt), عَطْشان (dipt; عِطاش, f عَطْشى); **to be ~** كانَ عَطْشانَ \ ظَمْآنَ

thirteen /θɜːˈtiːn/ *n, adj* ثَلاثةَ عَشَر

thirteenth /θɜːˈtiːnθ/ **A** *n* **1** (in a series) ثالِثَ عَشَرَ **2** (fraction) جُزْء من ثَلاثةَ عَشَر **3** (**the thirteenth**) (of a month) ثالِثَ عَشَرَ

B *adj* ‹*century, day*› ثالِثَ عَشَرَ

C *adv* في المَرْكَزِ الثالِثَ عَشَرَ

thirties /ˈθɜːtiz/ *n pl* **1** (decade) (**the thirties**) الثَلاثينات

2 (age) **to be in one's ~** كانَ في الثَلاثيناتِ (من عُمْرِه)

3 (in amounts) **temperatures were in the ~** كانَتْ دَرَجةُ الحَرارةِ في الثَلاثيناتِ

thirtieth /ˈθɜːtiəθ/ **A** *n* **1** (**the thirtieth**) (in a series) الثَلاثونَ

2 (fraction) جُزْء من ثَلاثينَ **3** (**the thirtieth**) (of a month) الثَلاثونَ

B *adj* ‹*birthday, anniversary*› الثَلاثونَ

C *adv* في المَرْكَزِ الثَلاثينَ

thirty /ˈθɜːti/ *n, adj* ثَلاثونَ

this /ðɪs/ **A** *demonstrative pronoun* (*pl* **these**) هَذا (هَؤُلاءِ; f هَذِهِ; m du هَذانِ; f du هاتانِ); **what's ~?** ما هذا؟; **~ is the book I was talking about** هذا هو الكِتابُ الّذي كُنْتُ أَتَكَلَّمُ عَنْهُ; **~ is Jack Farrier** مَعَكَ جاك فارْيير; **~ is Janet Ridley** مَعَكِ جانيت ريدْلي; **whose is ~?** لِمَنْ هذا؟; **~ is the dining room** هذه (هي) غُرْفةُ الطَعامِ; **~ is my sister, Pauline** هذه (هي) أُخْتي، بولين; **where's ~?** (on photo) أَيْنَ كانَ هذا؟; **after ~ we'll have lunch** وَبَعْدَ هذا سَنَتَناوَلُ الغَداءَ; **~ is not the right one** لَيْسَ هذا هو الشيءَ المُناسِبَ; **who did ~?** مَنْ فَعَلَ هذا؟; **what did you mean by ~?** ماذا عَنَيتَ بِهَذا؟; **it happened like ~** حَدَثَ على هذا النَحْوِ; **what's all ~?** ما كُلُّ هذا؟; **what's ~ all about?** ماذا يَعْني كُلُّ هذا؟; **at ~ he got up and left** وَعِنْدَ هذا الحَدِّ نَهَضَ وَانْصَرَفَ; **~ is what happens when you don't follow the instructions!** هذا ما يَحْدُثُ عِنْدَما لا تَتَّبِعُ التَعْليماتِ!

B *determiner* (*pl* **these**) هَذا (هَؤُلاءِ; f هَذِهِ; m du هَذانِ; f du هاتانِ); **~ picture/these pictures** هذه الصورة \ الصُوَر; **~ horse/these horses** هذا الحِصان \ هذه الأَحْصِنة; **~ girl/these girls** هذه البِنْت \ هَؤُلاءِ البَنات; **~ boy/these boys** هذا الوَلَد \ هَؤُلاءِ الأَوْلاد; **~ man is dangerous** هذا الرَجُلُ خَطيرٌ; **~ lamp doesn't work** هذا المِصْباحُ لا يَعْمَلُ; **these cakes are delicious/awful** هذا الكَعْكُ لَذيذٌ \ فَظيعٌ; **do it ~ way, not that way** افْعَلْهُ على هذا النَحْوِ، وَلَيْسَ بِتِلْكَ الطَريقةِ; (infml) **then ~ woman came up to me** ثُمَّ اقْتَرَبَتْ مِنّي هذه المَرْأةُ

C *adv* **it's ~ big/small** هو بِهَذا القَدْرِ من الكِبَرِ \ الصِغَرِ; **she was only ~ high** كانَتْ بِهَذا القَدْرِ فَقَطْ من الطولِ; **I can't eat ~ much** لا أَسْتَطيعُ أنْ آكُلَ كُلَّ هذه الكَمِّيّةِ; **I didn't realize it was ~ serious/difficult** لم أُدْرِكْ أنَّهُ كانَ بِهَذِهِ الجِدِّيّةِ \ الصُعوبةِ; **I didn't think it would take ~ long** لم أَكُنْ أَظُنُّ أنَّهُ سَيَسْتَغْرِقُ كُلَّ هذا الوَقْتِ; **we've got ~ far, so it would be a pity to stop now** وَصَلْنا إلى هذا الحَدِّ، وَلِذا سَيَكونُ من المُؤْسِفِ التَوَقُّفُ الآنَ

thistle /ˈθɪs(ə)l/ *n* شَوْك الجَمَل

thong /θɒŋ/ *n* **1** (for fastening) سَيْر (سُيور) **2** (underwear, swimming costume) جي سْتْرينْج (سِرْوال داخِليّ رَفيع بِدونِ تَغْطِيةٍ خَلْفِيّةٍ) **3** (AmE) (sandal) بابوج (بَوابيجُ)

thorax /ˈθɔːraks/ *n* (*pl* **thoraxes** or **thoraces**) قَفَص صَدْرِيّ

thorn /θɔːn/ *n* شَوْك (أَشْواك)

thorny /ˈθɔːni/ *adj* (**thornier, thorniest**) **1** ‹*bush, branch*› شائِك **2** ‹*issue, problem*› شائِك, مُعَقَّد, عَويص

thorough /ˈθʌrə/ *adj* **1** ‹*search, investigation*› مُعَمَّق **2** ‹*person*› دَقيق (دِقاق)

thoroughbred /ˈθʌrəbrɛd/ **A** *adj* ‹*horse, stallion*› أَصيل

B *n* جَواد أَصيل

thoroughfare /ˈθʌrəfɛː/ *n* **1** (route) طَريق (mf; طُرُق, طُرُقات), مَمَرّ (مَمَرّات), مَسْلَك (مَسالِكُ) **2** (street) شارِع عامّ, طَريق رَئيسيّ

thoroughly /ˈθʌrəli/ *adv* **1** ‹*to clean, wash*› بِإتْقانٍ

2 (completely) ‹*to enjoy, recommend*› بالكامِلِ, على نَحْوٍ تامٍّ; **I ~ enjoyed the book** اسْتَمْتَعْتُ جِدًّا بالكِتابِ

those /ðəʊz/ *pl* ▸ **that**

thou /ðaʊ/ *pron* (old use) ▸ **you** 1

though /ðəʊ/ **A** *conj* **1** (despite the fact that) بالرَغْمِ من (أنّ), مع أنّ; **~ small, the apartment was large enough for their needs** بالرَغْمِ من صغَرِ الشَقّة، إلاّ أنّها كانَتْ واسِعةً بِما يَكْفي لِتَلْبِيةِ احْتِياجاتِهِمْ; **strange ~ it may seem, it's true** مع أنّهُ قد يَبْدو غَريباً، إلاّ أنّهُ صَحيحٌ; **talented ~ he is, he's also very lazy** بالرَغْم من أنّهُ مَوْهوبٌ، إلاّ أنّهُ أيْضاً كَسولٌ جِدًّا **2** (but) لَكِنْ; **an unwise ~ courageous act** تَصَرُّفٌ غَيْر حَكيمٍ وَلَكِنَّهُ شُجاعٌ; **it's good, ~ I say it myself!** هو جَيِّدٌ، وَأَقولُها بِكُلِّ تَواضُعٍ!

B *adv* مع ذلك, بالرَغْم من ذلك; **she's not at home; I'll keep trying ~** هي لَيْسَتْ في المَنْزِلِ؛ وَمَعَ ذلك سَأَظَلُّ أُحاوِلُ; **fortunately, ~, they survived** وَلَكِنْ، لِحُسْنِ الحَظِّ، فَقَدْ نَجَوْا

thought /θɔːt/ **A** *past tense, past participle* ▸ **think** A, B

B *n* **1** (idea) فِكْرة (فِكَر); **it was just a ~** كانَتْ مُجَرَّدَ فِكْرةٍ; **what a kind ~!** يا لَها من فِكْرةٍ لَطيفةٍ! **2** [u] (reflection) تَفْكير; **to be deep in ~** كانَ عَميقاً في تَفْكيرِهِ; **after much ~** بعد تَفْكيرٍ عَميقٍ **3** [u] (consideration) اهْتِمام (اهْتِمامات); **to give ~ to sth** أعارَ شَيْئاً اهْتِماماً; **we never gave it much ~** لم نُعِرْهُ اهْتِماماً; **don't give it another ~** لا تُعِرْهُ مَزيداً من الاهْتِمامِ أَبَداً; **to put a lot of ~ into a gift** الكَثيرَ من الاهْتِمامِ; فَكَّرَ كَثيراً في هَدِيّةٍ **4** (intention) **to have no ~ of doing sth** لم يَكُنْ لَدَيْهِ نِيّةٌ في فِعْلِ شَيْءٍ; **I've given up all ~s of moving** لَقَدْ تَخَلَّيْتُ عن فِكْرةِ الانْتِقالِ

C (**thoughts**) *n pl* **1** (mind) أَفْكار; **to collect** *or* **gather one's ~s** جَمَعَ أَفْكارَهُ; **my ~s were elsewhere** كانَتْ أَفْكاري في مَكانٍ آخَرَ **2** (opinions) آراء; **let me have your ~s on this** دَعْني أَسْمَعُ رَأْيَكَ في هذا

thoughtful /ˈθɔːtfʊl/ *adj* **1** (pensive) ‹*person, look*› مُسْتَغْرِق في التَفْكيرِ **2** (considerate) ‹*person*› مُراعٍ لِشُعورِ الآخَرينَ; ‹*gift*› مَدْروس; **it was a ~ gesture** كانَتْ لَفْتةً كَريمةً

thoughtfully /ˈθɔːtf(ə)li/ *adv* **1** (pensively) ‹*to look, frown*› بِتَفَكُّرٍ **2** (considerately) ‹*to provide, place*› بِعِنايةٍ

thoughtless /ˈθɔːtləs/ *adj* ‹*behaviour, comment*› أَهْوَج, طائِش (dipt)

thought-out /θɔːtˈaʊt/ *adj* **a well/poorly ~ plan** خُطّة مَدْروسة بِإتْقانٍ \ غَيْر مَدْروسةٍ

thought-provoking /ˈθɔːtprəvəʊkɪŋ/ *adj* ‹*book, question*› مُثير لِلتَفْكيرِ

thousand /ˈθaʊz(ə)nd/ *n, adj* أَلْف (mf; آلاف, أُلوف); **a/one ~** أَلْف (mf; آلاف, أُلوف); **she died in two ~ and nine** ماتَتْ في عامِ أَلْفَيْنِ وَتِسْعةٍ

thousandth /ˈθaʊz(ə)nθ/ **A** *n* **1** (**the thousandth**) (in a series) الأَلْف **2** (fraction) جُزْء من أَلْفٍ

B *adj* ‹*time, performance*› الأَلْف

thrash /θraʃ/ *vt* **1** (to beat, whip) ضَرَبَ (i; ضَرْب), جَلَدَ (i; جَلْد) ‹*a child, an animal*› **2** (infml) (to defeat) سَحَقَ (a; سَحْق) ‹*an opponent, a rival*›

Phrasal verbs **thrash about**, **thrash around** «captive, fish» تَخَبَّطَ

• **thrash out**: **~ [sth] out, ~ out [sth]** أَشْبعَ [شَيْئاً] نِقاشاً \ بَحْثاً ‹*a problem, an issue*›; تَوَصَّلَ إلى [شَيْءٍ] ‹*a solution, an agreement*›

thrashing /ˈθraʃɪŋ/ *n* ضَرْب

thread /θred/ **A** *n* **1** (of cotton, silk) خَيْط (خُيوط, خيطان) **2** (of a screw) سِنّ (mf; أَسْنان) **3** (of a story, an argument) رابِط بين الأَحْداثِ, خَيْط (خُيوط, خيطان)

B *vt* **1** [أَدْخَلَ الخَيْطَ في الثُقْبِ] ‹*a needle, sewing machine*› **2** (to link) نَظَمَ (في خَيْطٍ أو سِلْكٍ) ‹*the beads*›

threadbare /ˈθredbɛː/ *adj* ‹*carpet, clothes*› بالٍ, رَثّ (رِثاث)

threat /θrɛt/ *n* تَهْديد (تَهْديدات); **to pose a ~ to sth/sb** شَكَّلَ تَهْديداً لِشَيْءٍ \ لِشَخْصٍ; **their way of life is under ~** أُسْلوبُ حَياتِهِمْ مُهَدَّدٌ

threaten /ˈθrɛt(ə)n/ **A** *vt* **1** (to make threats against) هَدَّدَ ‹*a person, sb's life*›; **he ~ed to kill me** هَدَّدَني بالقَتْلِ **2** (to warn of) هَدَّدَ (ب) ‹*legal action, violence*›

B *vi* «storm, danger» شَكَّلَ تَهْديداً

threatening /ˈθrɛtnɪŋ/ *adj* ‹*behaviour, manner*› يَتَّسِمُ بالتَهْديدِ; ‹*letter, phone call*› تَهْديد

three /θriː/ *n, adj* ثَلاثة ▸ see also **five**

three-dimensional /ˌθriːdɪˈmɛnʃ(ə)n(ə)l, ˌθriːdʌɪˈmɛnʃ(ə)n(ə)l/ *adj* ‹*structure, space*› ثُلاثيّ الأَبْعادِ

threefold /ˈθriːfəʊld/ **A** *adj* ‹*increase, reduction*› بِثلاثة أَضْعافٍ **B** *adv* ‹*to increase, decrease*› ثَلاثةَ أَضْعافٍ

three-piece /ˈθriːpiːs/ *adj* **1** **~ suit** بَدْلة (من ثَلاثة قِطَع) **2** **~ suite** طَقْم صالون كامِل

three-quarters /θriːˈkwɔːtəz/ **A** *adv* حتّى \ إلى ثَلاثة أَرْباعِهِ; **~ full/finished** مُمْتَلِئ \ مُنْتَهٍ إلى ثَلاثة أَرْباعِه **B** *pron* ثَلاثة أَرْباعٍ; **~ of an hour** ثَلاثة أَرْباعِ ساعةٍ

thresh /θrɛʃ/ *vt* دَرَسَ (u; دَرْس) ‹*grain, corn*›

threshold /ˈθrɛʃəʊld, ˈθrɛʃhəʊld/ *n* **1** (doorway) عَتَبة (عَتَبات, أَعْتاب); **to be on the ~ of sth** كانَ على عَتَبةِ شَيْءٍ **2** (limit) حَدّ (حُدود)

threw /θruː/ *past tense* ▸**throw**

thrift /θrɪft/ *n* تَوْفير, حُسْن التَدْبيرِ

thrift store, **thrift shop** *n* (AmE) دُكّان يَبيعُ الأَغْراضَ المُسْتَعْمَلةَ لِتَمْويل الأَعْمالِ الخَيْرِيّةِ

thrifty /ˈθrɪfti/ *adj* (**thriftier**, **thriftiest**) ‹*shopper*› غَيْر مُقْتَصِد; ‹*habits*› التَوفيرِ, مُبَذِّر

thrill /θrɪl/ **A** *n* نَشْوة **B** *vt* أَثارَ ‹*crowds, audiences*›

thrilled /θrɪld/ *adj* مُبْتَهِج للغايةِ; **to be ~ with/at sth** كانَ مُبْتَهِجاً للغايةِ لِشَيْءٍ; **she'll be so ~ to see you** سَتَشْعُرُ بِسَعادةٍ غامِرةٍ عند رُؤْيَتِك

thriller /ˈθrɪlə/ *n* (film) فِلْم الإثارةِ; (novel) قِصّة الإثارة

thrilling /ˈθrɪlɪŋ/ *adj* ‹*finish, experience*› مُثير

thrive /θrʌɪv/ *vi* (*past tense* **throve** or **thrived**; *past participle* **thriven** or **thrived**) «person» نَجَحَ (a; نَجاح); «plant» أَيْنَعَ; «business, community» ازْدَهَرَ

thriving /ˈθrʌɪvɪŋ/ *adj* ‹*business, community*› ناجِح, مُزْدَهِر

throat /θrəʊt/ *n* **1** (gullet) حَنْجَرة (حَناجِرُ) **2** (neck) عُنُق (f; أَعْناق)

throb /θrɒb/ *vi* (**-bb-**) **1** (to beat) «heart, pulse» نَبَضَ (i; نَبْض, نَبَضان), خَفَقَ (i-u; خَفْق, خَفَقان); **my head was ~bing with pain** كانَ رَأْسي يَخْفُقُ من الأَلَمِ **2** (with repetitive sound) «engine, drums» ارْتَجَّ

throbbing /ˈθrɒbɪŋ/ *adj* **1** ‹*pain, headache*› مُبَرِّح **2** ‹*music*› إيقاعيّ; ‹*noise*› صاخِب

throes /θrəʊz/ *n pl* (fml) **death ~** غَمَرات \ سَكَرات المَوْتِ
(Idiom) **to be in the throes of sth/doing sth** كانَ في غَمْرةِ شَيْءٍ

thrombosis /θrɒmˈbəʊsɪs/ *n* (*pl* **thromboses** /-siːz/) تَجَلُّط, خُثار, تَخَثُّر

throne /θrəʊn/ *n* عَرْش (عُروش, أَعْراش), كُرْسيّ (كَراسٍ)

throng /θrɒŋ/ **A** *n* (fml) حَشْد (حُشود), جُمْهور (n coll, no singul n; جَماهيرُ) **B** *vt* احْتَشَدَ (في) ‹*the streets, a town*›

throttle /ˈθrɒt(ə)l/ **A** *n* صِمام خانِق **B** *vt* خَنَقَ (u; خَنْق) ‹*a victim*›

through /θruː/ **A** *prep* **1** (from one side to the other) عَبْرَ; **to travel ~ the village/city** سافَرَ عَبْرَ القَرْيةِ \ المَدينةِ **2** (by way of) عَبْرَ; **to go ~ diplomatic channels** مَرَّ عَبْرَ القَنَواتِ الدِبْلوماسيّةِ; **to come in ~ the floor/door** تَسَرَّبَ عَبْرَ الأَرْضِ \ البابِ **3** (past) **to go ~ a red light** اجْتازَ إشارةً ضَوْئيّةً حَمْراءَ; **to go ~ customs** مَرَّ عَبْرَ الجَمارِكِ; **to push one's way ~ the crowd** شَقَّ طَرِيقَهُ وَسْطَ الحَشْدِ **4** (in amongst) **to fly ~ the clouds** «aeroplanes» طارَ ما بين الغُيومِ; **to fly ~ the air** «arrows, bullets» طارَ في الهَواءِ; ▸**go**, ▸**search**, ▸**sort** **5** (by means of) **I heard ~ a friend** سَمِعْتُ عن طَريقِ صَديقٍ; **to send sth ~ the post** أَرْسَلَ شَيْئاً عَبْرَ البَريدِ; **it was ~ him that I got this job** حَصَلْتُ على هذا العَمَلِ من خِلالِهِ; **to speak ~ an interpreter** تَكَلَّمَ عَبْرَ مُتَرْجِمٍ **6** (because of) **they lost ~ inexperience** خَسِروا بِسَبَبِ عَدَمِ الخِبْرةِ; **they failed ~ no fault of their own** فَشِلوا بِسَبَبِ خَطَإٍ لم يَرْتَكِبوهُ **7** (throughout) **to work ~ the night** عَمِلَ طَوالَ اللَيْلِ; **all/right ~ the day** طَوالَ \ على مَدارِ اليَوْمِ; **he talked right ~ the film** كانَ يَتَكَلَّمُ باسْتِمْرارٍ طيلةَ عَرْضِ الفيلْمِ; ▸**live¹**, ▸**see through** **8** (up to and including) لِغايةِ; **from Friday ~ to Sunday, from Friday ~ Sunday** (AmE) من يَوْمِ الجُمْعةِ ولِغايةِ يَوْمِ الأَحَدِ **B** *adv* **1** (from one side to the other) **the water went right ~** تَسَرَّبَ الماءُ من جانِبٍ لِآخَرَ; **to let sb ~** سَمَحَ لِشَخْصٍ بالدُخولِ \ بالمُرورِ **2** (completely) **to be wet/soaked ~**

sb/doubt on sth أَلْقى شُبُهاتٍ حول شَخْصٍ \ الشُكوكَ على شَيْءٍ; she threw the audience a kiss رَمَتْ بِقُبْلَةٍ للجُمْهورِ **3** (to cast) أَلْقى ‹*light, a shadow*› **4** (infml) (to disconcert) أَرْبَكَ; the question completely threw me! لَقَدْ أَرْبَكَني السُؤالُ تَماماً!; to ~ sb into confusion *or* disarray أَرْبَكَ شَخْصاً **5** (to activate) حَرَّكَ ‹*a switch, lever*› **6** (infml) (in rage) to ~ a fit/tantrum أَقامَ ضَجَّةً \ أَثارَ ضَجَّةً **7** (infml) (to organize) to ~ a party أَقامَ حَفْلَةً **8** (in sports) to ~ a game/fight باعَ المُباراةَ \ مُباراةَ المُصارَعةِ **9** (in pottery) to ~ a pot قامَ بِتَشْكيلِ آنِيةٍ فُخّارِيَّةٍ [على عَجَلةِ الخَزّافِ]

B *vi* (*past tense* **threw**; *past participle* **thrown**) رَمى (i; رَمْي, رِماية), قَذَفَ (i; قَذْف)

C *v refl* (*past tense* **threw**; *past participle* **thrown**) to ~ oneself رَمى بِنَفْسِهِ \ ارْتَمى; to ~ oneself off a bridge/in front of a train رَمى \ أَلْقى بِنَفْسِهِ من على الجِسْرِ \ أمامَ القِطارِ; to ~ oneself onto the bed/sofa ارْتَمى على السَريرِ \ على الأَرِيكةِ; to ~ oneself to the ground ارْتَمى على الأَرْضِ; to ~ oneself into one's work انْغَمَسَ في عَمَلِهِ

D *n* **1** (of a javelin, discus, ball, etc) رَمْي; (in wrestling, judo, etc) إِسْقاط; it's United's ~ ضَرْبةُ البِدايةِ لِفَريقِ يونايْتِد **2** (for chairs, sofas, etc) [قِطْعةُ قُماشٍ تُرْمى على أَرِيكةٍ] **3** (infml) at £10/$50 a ~ (each) سِعْرُ كُلِّ واحِدٍ 10 جُنَيْهاتٍ \ 50 دولار

(Idioms) to throw in one's lot with sb رَبَطَ مَصيرَهُ بِشَخْصٍ; to throw in the sponge *or* towel رَفَعَ الرايةَ البَيْضاءَ; to throw money at the problem [أَنْفَقَ المالَ بِلا حِسابٍ لِحَلِّ المُشْكِلةِ]

(Phrasal verbs) **throw around, throw about**: ~ [sth] around **1** to ~ a ball around رَمى كُرةً **2** طَرَحَ [شَيْئاً] لِلنِقاشِ ‹*ideas, names*›; to ~ one's money around بَذَّرَ مالَهُ

• **throw aside** **A** ~ aside [sth], ~ [sth] aside **1** (to discard) رَمى [شَيْئاً] جانِباً ‹*a book, hammer*› **2** (to abandon) تَخَلّى عن [شَيْءٍ] ‹*one's principles, standards*› **B** ~ [sb] aside رَمى [شَخْصاً] جانِباً

• **throw away**: ~ [sth] away, ~ away [sth] **1** أَهْمَلَ [شَيْئاً] ‹*rubbish, old clothes, a photograph*› **2** (to waste) أَضاعَ [شَيْئاً] ‹*a chance, an opportunity*›; بَذَّرَ [شَيْئاً] ‹*money*›; he threw away the advantage he held أَضاعَ المَزايا الّتي كانَ يَتَمَتَّعُ بِها

to be cooked right ~ كانَ مُتَبَّلاً تَماماً; كانَ مَطْهُوّاً على نَحْوٍ تامٍّ **3** (from beginning to end) to read/play sth right ~ قَرَأَ \ عَزَفَ شَيْئاً من أَلِفِهِ إلى يائِهِ; I'm halfway ~ the article أنا في مُنْتَصَفِ المَقالةِ **4** (successful) to go ~ تَقَدَّمَ **5** (connected) you're ~ أَنْتَ على الخَطِّ; you're ~ to Mr Wilkins أَنْتَ على الخَطِّ مع السَيِّدِ ويلْكِنْز

C (**through and through**) *adv phr* to know the area/him ~ and ~ كانَ يَعْرِفُ المِنْطَقةَ \ يَعْرِفُهُ تَمامَ المَعْرِفةِ

D *adj* **1** (infml) (finished) مُنْتَهٍ; I'm ~ انْتَهَيْتُ (من أَمْرٍ); are you ~ with the paper? هل انْتَهَيْتَ من كِتابةِ البَحْثِ؟; as a politician, he's ~ انْتهى (مُسْتَقْبَلُهُ) كَسِياسيٍّ **2** (direct) ‹*train, ticket*› مُباشِر; 'no ~ road' 'طَريقٌ مَسْدودٌ'; a ~ route to the station طَريق مُباشِر إلى المَحَطّةِ; I got the ~ train from London رَكِبْتُ القِطارَ المُباشِرَ من لُنْدُن **3** (successful) to be ~ to the next round انْتَقَلَ إلى الجَوْلةِ التاليةِ بِنَجاحٍ; he went ~ to the next round in straight sets انْتَقَلَ إلى الجَوْلةِ التاليةِ بِدونِ خَسارةِ أَيّةِ جَوْلةٍ سابِقةٍ **4** (BrE) (worn) to be ~ at the knee كانَ بالِياً \ مُهْتَرِئاً

throughout /θruːˈaʊt/ **A** *prep* **1** (all over) في كُلِّ أَنْحاءِ; ~ Europe في كُلِّ أَنْحاءِ أوروبّا **2** (from start to finish) طَوالَ, على مَدارِ \ مَدى; ~ his life طَوالَ حَياتِهِ

B *adv* (in every part) في كُلِّ جُزْءٍ

throughway, **thruway** /ˈθruːweɪ/ *n* (AmE) طَريق سَريع

throve /θrəʊv/ *past tense* ▸ **thrive**

throw /θrəʊ/ **A** *vt* (*past tense* **threw**; *past participle* **thrown**) **1** (to propel) رَمى (i; رَمْي, رِماية), قَذَفَ (i; قَذْف) ‹*a stone, ball, stick*›; to ~ the ball up high رَمى الكُرةَ عالِياً; she threw the ball to him قَذَفَت الكُرةَ إلَيْهِ; he threw the stone at his brother رَمى الحَجَرةَ على أَخيهِ; ~ the ball back to me! أَعِد الكُرةَ إلَيَّ!; she threw her apron over her head لَبِسَتْ مِئْزَرَها \ مِرْيَلَتَها بِسُرْعةٍ; she threw her arms round my neck عانَقَتْني بِقُوّةٍ, طَوَّقَتْ عُنُقي بِذِراعَيْها; he was ~n clear of the car انْقَذَفَ خارِجَ السَيّارةِ تَماماً; he was ~n to the floor by the explosion انْقَذَفَ على الأَرْضِ من جَرّاءِ الانْفِجارِ **2** (to direct) أَلْقى ‹*an insult, a question, glance*›; life has ~n many challenges at us وَضَعَت الحَياةُ الكَثيرَ من التَحَدّياتِ أَمامَنا; to ~ suspicion on

• **throw back**: **~ back [sth], ~ [sth] back** 1 (in sports) أعادَ [شَيْئاً] ‹a ball›; **she threw it back to me** أعادَتْهُ إلَيَّ 2 (in fishing) أعادَ [شَيْئاً] إلى الماءِ ‹a fish› 3 (in body movements) ألْقى \ رَمى ب [شَيْءٍ] إلى الوَراءِ ‹one's head, shoulders›

• **throw in**: **~ in [sth], ~ [sth] in** 1 (infml) (to include) أضافَ [شَيْئاً] 2 (to add) أضافَ [شَيْئاً] ‹herbs, an ingredient›

• **throw off** A **~ off [sth], ~ [sth] off** 1 (to take off) نَزَعَ [شَيْئاً] ‹one's clothes›; أزالَ [شَيْئاً] ‹the bedclothes› 2 (to get free of) تَخلَّصَ من [شَيءٍ] ‹oppression, one's pursuers› 3 تَخلَّصَ من [شَيْءٍ] ‹a cold› 4 (to compose quickly) ارْتَجَلَ [شَيْئاً] ‹a poem, melody› B **~ off [sb], ~ [sb] off** (from trains, buses, planes) تَخلَّصَ من [شَخْصٍ] ‹a passenger, hooligan›

• **throw on**: **~ on [sth], ~ [sth] on** (to put on) لَبِسَ \ ارْتَدى [شَيْئاً] بِسُرْعَةٍ ‹a shirt, pair of trousers›

• **throw open**: **~ open [sth], ~ [sth] open** 1 فَتَحَ [شَيْئاً] عُنْوةً ‹a door, window› 2 (to the public) فَتَحَ أبْواب [شَيْءٍ] للعُمومِ ‹the gardens, a palace›; **to ~ a discussion open** فَتَحَ بابَ النِقاشِ

• **throw out** A **~ out [sth], ~ [sth] out** 1 (to get rid of) تَخَلَّصَ من [شَيْءٍ] ‹rubbish, furniture› 2 (to reject) رَفَضَ [شَيْئاً] ‹a case, plan, an application› 3 (to extend) **~ your arms out in front of you** مُدَّ ذِراعَيْكَ أمامَكَ B **~ out [sb], ~ [sb] out** 1 (from a bar, restaurant) رَمى [شَخْصاً] في الخارِجِ ‹a trouble-maker› 2 (from a club, organization) فَصَلَ [شَخْصاً] ‹a member›; **he was ~n out for breaking the club rules** فُصِلَ لِمُخالَفَتِهِ قَواعِدَ النادي

• **throw over** (infml BrE): **~ over [sb], ~ [sb] over** تَخَلّى عن [شَخْصٍ] ‹one's fiancé, fiancée›

• **throw together**: A **~ [sb] together** «fate, events» جَمَعَ [شَخْصاً] مَعاً ‹people› B **~ [sth] together** مَعاً [رَمى [شَيْئاً] في القِدْرِ ‹the ingredients›; أعَدَّ [شَيْئاً] بِسُرْعةٍ ‹a meal›

• **throw up** A (infml) تَقَيَّأَ B **~ up [sth], ~ [sth] up** 1 (infml) (to abandon) تَخَلّى عن [شَيْءٍ] ‹a job, position› 2 (to reveal) أثارَ الانْتِباهَ إلى [شَيْءٍ] ‹a fact, discovery› 3 (to emit) «waves, volcanoes» انْبَعَثَ من [شَيْءٍ] ‹smoke, spray, lava› 4 (up into the air) قَذَفَ \ رَمى [شَيْئاً] ‹the ball, one's arms› 5 (infml) (to vomit) تَقَيَّأَ [شَيْئاً] ‹one's meal›

throwaway /ˈθrəʊəweɪ/ *adj* 1 (discardable) ‹*camera, cutlery*› يُرْمى بعد اسْتِعْمالِهِ 2 (casual) ‹*remark, reference*› عابِر

throwback /ˈθrəʊbak/ *n* 1 (nostalgic) [مُثير للحَنينِ 2 (ancestral) ارْتِداد وِراثيّ

throw-in /ˈθrəʊɪn/ *n* رَمْية تَماسٍّ

thrown /θrəʊn/ *past participle* ▸**throw** A, B

thrush /θrʌʃ/ *n* 1 (bird) سُمْنة 2 [u] (infection) مَرَض القُلاع, سُلاق

thrust /θrʌst/ A *vt* (*past tense, past participle* **thrust**) **to ~ the knife/letter at sb** دَفَعَ السكّينَ \ الرسالةَ نحو شَخْصٍ; **she ~ the knife into his chest** غَرَزَت السكّينَ في صَدْرِهِ; **to ~ the money into one's bag** دَفَعَ الأمْوالَ بِقوّةٍ في حَقيبَتِه; **to ~ one's head out of the window** أطَلَّ بِرأْسِهِ من الشُبّاكِ

B *v refl* (*past tense, past participle* **thrust**) **to ~ oneself forward** دَفَعَ نَفْسَهُ إلى الأمامِ

C *n* 1 (of engines) قوّة دَفْعٍ 2 (attack) هُجوم 3 (with a sword, etc) طَعْنة (طَعَنات) 4 (of an argument) فَحْوى (f; فَحاوٍ, فَحاوى); **the ~ of his argument/article is that ...** فَحْوى حُجَّتِهِ \ مَقالَتِهِ هو أنّ …

(Phrasal verbs) **thrust aside**: **~ [sth/sb] aside, ~ aside [sth/sb]** 1 دَفَعَ [شَيْئاً] جانِباً ‹an argument, a principle› 2 دَفَعَ [شَيْئاً] \ شَخْصاً] جانِباً ‹a bystander›

• **thrust back**: **~ [sth] back, ~ back [sth]** 1 دَفَعَ [شَيْئاً] إلى الوَراءِ ‹the enemy› 2 أجْبَرَ [شَيْئاً] على العَوْدة ‹an issue, a person›

• **thrust forward**: 1 **~ forward** «crowd» انْدَفَعَ إلى الأمامِ 2 **~ [sth] forward, ~ forward [sth]** دَفَعَ [شَيْئاً] إلى الأمامِ ‹a sword, one's hand›

• **thrust out**: **~ [sth] out, ~ out [sth]** دَفَعَ [شَيْئاً] إلى الأمامِ ‹one's hand, chin›; **he ~ her out of the way** دَفَعَها بَعيداً عن الخطَرِ

• **thrust upon**: **~ [sth] upon sb** فَرَضَ [شَيْئاً] على شَخْصٍ ‹an idea, a task›

thruway (AmE) *n* ▸**throughway**

thud /θʌd/ **A** *n* دَوِيّ

B *vi* (-dd-) «heart» نَبَضَ بِقوّةٍ; «footsteps» أَحْدَثَ دَوِيًّا

thug /θʌg/ *n* بَلْطَجِيّ, مُجْرِم

thumb /θʌm/ **A** *n* إِبْهام (اليَد)

B *vt* **1** (also **thumb through**) تَصَفَّحَ ‹a book, magazine›

2 (infml) **to ~ a lift** [أشارَ بِإِبْهامِهِ إلى سَيّارةٍ لِتَوْصيلِهِ]

(Idioms) **to be under sb's thumb** كانَ تحت سَيْطَرةِ شخصٍ; **to stick out like a sore thumb** بدا شاذًّا عمّا حَوْلَهُ

thumbs down /θʌmz 'daʊn/ *n* (infml) **to give sb/sth the ~** اعْتَرَضَ على شخصٍ \ شَيْءٍ

thumbs up /θʌmz 'ʌp/ *n* (infml) **to give sb/sth the ~** (in support) وافَقَ على شخصٍ \ شَيْءٍ; (of approval) أَيَّدَ شَخْصاً \ شَيْئاً

thumbtack /'θʌmtak/ *n* (AmE) دَبّوس تَثْبيت

thump /θʌmp/ **A** *vt* (infml) خَبَطَ (i; خَبْط), ضَرَبَ (i; ضَرْب) ‹the table›

B *vi* «music, one's heart» دَقَّ (u; دَقّ)

C *n* **1** (blow) ضَرْبة, خَبْطة (باليَد أو بآلةٍ حادّةٍ) **2** (sound) صَوْت ارْتِطامٍ

thunder /'θʌndə/ **A** *n* **1** (after lightning) رَعْد (رُعود) **2** (of hoofs, applause) دَوِيّ

B *v impers* رَعَدَ (a-u; رَعْد); **it's ~ing** السَماءُ تَرْعُدُ

(Idiom) **to steal sb's thunder** [سَرَقَ مُتْعةَ شَخْصٍ في الإعْلانِ عن حَدَثٍ مُهِمٍّ]

thunderbolt /'θʌndəbəʊlt/ *n* صاعِقة (صَواعِقُ)

thunderclap /'θʌndəklap/ *n* دَوِيّ \ هَزيم الرَعْدِ

thunderstorm /'θʌndəstɔːm/ *n* عاصِفة رَعْدِيّة

thunderstruck /'θʌndəstrʌk/ *adj* ‹person› مَشْدوه

thundery /'θʌnd(ə)ri/ *adj* ‹shower, weather› رَعْدِيّ

Thursday /'θəːzdeɪ, 'θəːzdi/ *n* (يَوْم) الخَميسِ; ▸**Wednesday**

thus /ðʌs/ *adv* (fml) **1** (consequently) وَبالتالي, لِذَلِكَ; **~ far** حَتّى \ إلى الآنَ **2** (in this way) هَكَذا, على هذا النَحْوِ; **he described it ~** وَصَفَهُ على هذا النَحْوِ

thwart /θwɔːt/ *vt* (fml) أَحْبَطَ, حالَ (u; حَيْلولة) (دون ‹an attack, a plan›

thy /ðʌɪ/ *determiner* (old use) ▸**your**

thyme /tʌɪm/ *n* زَعْتَر

thyroid /'θʌɪrɔɪd/ *n* (also **thyroid gland**) غُدّة دَرَقِيّة

ti /tiː/ *n* تي (النوتة السابعة في السُلَّمِ الموسيقيِّ الكَبير); ▸**te**

tiara /tɪ'ɑːrə/ *n* [عِصابة مُرَصَّعة بالجَواهِرِ]

Tiberias /tʌɪ'bɪərɪəs/ *pr n* طَبَرِيّا; **Lake ~** بُحَيْرة طَبَرِيّا

Tibet /tɪ'bɛt/ *pr n* التِبت (f)

Tibetan /tɪ'bɛt(ə)n/ *n, adj* تِبتِيّ

tic /tɪk/ *n* **to have a ~** عانى من تَشَنُّجٍ

tick /tɪk/ **A** *n* **1** (of clocks, watches) دَقّة **2** (mark) عَلامة (عَلائِمُ, عَلامات); **to put a ~ against the correct answer** وَضَعَ عَلامةً على الجَوابِ الصَحيحِ **3** (insect) قُراد (n coll; قِرْدان) **4** (infml) (short time) لَحْظة (لَحَظات); **I'll be with you in a ~/two ~s** سَأكونُ مَعَكَ خِلالَ لَحْظةٍ \ لَحْظَتَيْنِ

B *vt* (to mark) وَضَعَ عَلامةً في ‹the box, answer›; **to ~ the box** وَضَعَ عَلامةً في الإطارِ

C *vi* «clocks, bombs» دَقَّ (u; دَقّ); **I know what makes him ~** أَعْرِفُ ما الَّذي يُحَفِّزُهُ

(Phrasal verbs) **tick by** «hours, minutes» مَرَّ (u; مُرور)

• **tick off**: **~ [sth/sb] off, ~ off [sth/sb]** **1** (to mark) وَضَعَ عَلامةً على [شَيْءٍ \ شَخْصٍ] ‹a name, an item› **2** (BrE) (infml) (to reprimand) وَبَّخَ [شَخْصاً] ‹me, her› **3** (AmE) (infml) (to annoy) أَزْعَجَ [شَخْصاً] ‹me, him›

• **tick over** (BrE) «engines, cars» عَمِلَ \ دارَ بِأَقَلِّ سُرْعةٍ مُمْكِنةٍ

ticket /'tɪkɪt/ **A** *n* **1** (for travel, entry) تَذْكِرة (تَذاكِرُ); (to recover items) وَصْل (وُصولات); **a bus ~** تَذْكِرة باصٍ; **admission by ~ only** الدُخولُ بالتَذاكِرِ فَقَطْ; **I have two ~s for the game** عِنْدي تَذْكِرَتانِ لِلْمُقابَلةِ; **for him, football was a ~ to a better life** كانَتْ كُرةُ القَدَمِ, بالنِسْبةِ إليْهِ, تَذْكِرةَ عُبورٍ إلى حَياةٍ أَفْضَلَ **2** (for raffles, lotteries) بِطاقة (بِطاقات) **3** (infml) (fine) مُخالَفة; **a speeding ~** مُخالَفة سُرْعةٍ; **a parking ~** مُخالَفة رَكْنِ سَيّارةٍ **4** (AmE) (policies of a party) سِياسات حِزْبٍ; (candidates of a party) مُرَشَّحو حِزْبٍ; **to be elected on an environmental ~** أُنْتُخِبَ بِسَبَبِ سِياساتِ الحِزْبِ البيئيّةِ; **to run on the Republican ~** تَرَشَّحَ عن الحِزْبِ الجُمْهوريِّ

B *vt* **1** (to label) أَلْصَقَ بِطاقةً على *<the goods, baggage>* **2** (AmE) (infml) (to fine) **to be ~ed** تَحَصَّلَ على مُخالَفةٍ

(Idiom) **that's just the ticket!** (infml) !هذا هو المَطْلوبُ

ticket inspector *n* مُفَتِّش تَذاكِر

ticket office *n* مَكْتَب بَيْع تَذاكِر

tickle /ˈtɪk(ə)l/ **A** *vt* دَغْدَغَ (i; دَغْدَغة) *<sb's feet>*

B *vi* «wool, beards» وَخَزَ (i; وَخْز)

C *n* وَخْز

(Idiom) **to be tickled pink** *or* **to death** (infml) كانَ مَسْروراً أَشَدَّ السُرورِ

ticklish /ˈtɪklɪʃ/ *adj* **1** (liable to laugh) *<feet, person>* سَريع التَدَغْدُغ; **to be ~** كانَ سَريعَ التَدَغْدُغ **2** (infml) (delicate) *<issue, matter>* حَرِج

tidal /ˈtʌɪd(ə)l/ *adj* *<current, power>* المَدِّ والجَزْر

tidal wave *n* تْسونامي, مَوْجة عاتِية

tiddler /ˈtɪdlə/ *n* (BrE) **1** (small fish) [سَمَكة صَغيرة جِدًّا] **2** (infml) (small person) [شَخْص \ طِفْل صَغير جِدًّا]

tide /tʌɪd/ *n* **1** (of the sea) مَدّ وَجَزْر; **high/low ~** أَعْلى مَدٍّ \ أَدْنى جَزْرٍ; **the ~ is in/out** المَدُّ مُرْتَفِعٌ \ مُنْخَفِضٌ; **the ~ is going out/coming in** يَتَراجَعُ \ يَرْتَفِعُ المَدُّ **2** (of opinion) تَيّار, مَدّ (مُدود, مَدّ, تَيّارات); **a rising ~ of radicalism/nationalism** تَيّار مُتَصاعِد في الرَديكاليّةِ \ القَوْميّةِ; **the ~ of history/events** التاريخ \ الأَحْداثِ; **to swim against/with the ~** سَبَحَ ضِدَّ \ مَع التَيّارِ

(Phrasal verb) **tide over**: **~ [sb] over** أَوْصَلَ [شَخْصاً] إلى بَرّ الأَمانِ

tidily /ˈtʌɪdɪli/ *adv* *<to arrange, dress>* بِشَكْلٍ مُنَظَّم \ مُنَسَّق

tidiness /ˈtʌɪdinəs/ *n* حُسْن التَرْتيب

tidy /ˈtʌɪdi/ **A** *adj* (**tidier, tidiest**) **1** *<house, garden, desk, appearance>* مُرَتَّب; **did you leave the room ~?** هل تَرَكْتَ الغُرْفةَ مُرَتَّبةً؟; **he's a very ~ person** هو شَخْصٌ مَرَتَّبٌ جِدًّا **2** (infml) *<amount, salary, portion>* ضَخْم

B *n* (also **tidy up**) (BrE) **to have a ~** قامَ بِتَرْتيبِ المَكانِ

C *vt, vi* (**tidies, tidying, tidied**) ▸ **tidy up**

(Phrasal verbs) **tidy away**: **~ [sth] away, ~ away [sth]** وَضَعَ [شَيْئاً] في مَكانِهِ *<the toys, papers>*

• **tidy up** **A** (to put things away) [رَتَّبَ مَكاناً]; **I always have to ~ up after him** يَجِبُ عَلَيَّ دائماً أَنْ أُنَظِّفَ وَراءَهُ **B** **~ up [sth], ~ [sth] up** رَتَّبَ [شَيْئاً] *<one's desk, papers, hair>*

tie /tʌɪ/ **A** *vt* (*present participle* **tying**) **1** (with string, rope) رَبَطَ (i-u; رَبْط) *<sb's hands, ankles>*; **to ~ sb/sth to sth** رَبَطَ شَخْصاً \ شَيْئاً إلى شَيْءٍ *<a label, an animal, a prisoner>*; **to ~ the parcel with string** رَبَطَ الطَرْدَ البَريديَّ بِخَيْطٍ **2** (to knot) رَبَطَ (i-u; رَبْط) *<a scarf, cravat, one's laces>*; **to ~ a knot in the string** عَقَدَ عُقْدةً في الخَيْطِ **3** (to link) اِرْتَبَطَ, تَعَلَّقَ (ب); **to be ~d to the house** كانَ مُتَعَلِّقاً بالبَيْتِ; **prosperity is ~d to growth** الازْدِهارُ مُرْتَبِطٌ بالنُموّ

B *vi* (*present participle* **tying**) **1** (with string, rope) «string, cord, rope» رُبِطَ; **the apron ~s at the back** تُرْبَطُ المَرْيَلةُ من الخَلْفِ **2** (in matches, competitions, races, election) تَعادَلَ; **to ~ for third place** جاءا مُتَعادِلَيْنِ في المَرْكَزِ الثالِثِ

C *n* **1** (worn on neck) رَبْطة عُنُق **2** (for bags, plants, cables) رِباط (أَرْبِطة) **3** (bond) صِلة, رابِط; **family ~s** رَوابِط عائِليّة **4** (constraint) قَيْد (قُيود) **5** (in competitions) تَعادُل (تَعادُلات); **there is a ~ for second place** هُناكَ تَعادُلٌ في النِقاطِ في المَرْكَزِ الثاني **6** (Sport) (in knockout competitions) مُباراة تَأْهيليّة (دَوْر قبل النِهائيِّ في الكَأْسِ أو البُطولةِ)

(Idiom) **my hands are tied** يَدايَ مُقَيَّدَتانِ

(Phrasal verbs) **tie back**: **~ [sth] back, ~ back [sth]** رَبَطَ [شَيْئاً] *<one's hair, a curtain>*

• **tie down**: **~ [sb/sth] down, ~ down [sb/sth]** **1** (to hold fast) رَبَطَ [شَيْئاً] *<a tarpaulin, load>*; قَيَّدَ [شَخْصاً] *<a prisoner>* **2** (to restrict) قَيَّدَ [شَخْصاً] *<a person>*; **to ~ sb down to a date** قَيَّدَ شَخْصاً بِمَوْعِدٍ; **he doesn't want to be ~d down** لا يُريدُ أَنْ يَكونَ مُقَيَّداً

• **tie in with** **A** **~ in with [sth]** **1** (to tally with) اتَّفَقَ مع [شَيْءٍ] *<a fact, statement>* **2** (to have a link to) ارْتَبَطَ بـ [شَيْءٍ] *<an action, event>* **B** **~ [sth] in with sth, ~ in [sth] with sth** (to combine) رَبَطَ [شَيْئاً] مع شَيْءٍ *<information, a fact>*

• **tie on**: **~ [sth] on, ~ on [sth]** رَبَطَ \ شَدَّ [شَيْئاً] ‹*a label, ribbon, hat*›

• **tie together**: **~ [sth] together, ~ together [sth]** رَبَطَ \ قَيَّدَ [شَيْئاً] ‹*sb's hands, a bundle, the sticks*›

• **tie up** **A** **~ [sb/sth] up, ~ up [sb/sth]** **1** (to secure) رَبَطَ [شَخْصاً \ شَيْئاً] بِإِحْكام ‹*a prisoner, an animal, a parcel*› **2** (Fin) جَمَّدَ [شَيْئاً] ‹*capital, savings*› **3** (to finalize) انْتَهى من [شَيْءٍ] ‹*the details, a deal*› **4** (AmE) (to impede) أعاقَ \ عَرْقَلَ [شَيْئاً] ‹*the traffic, production*›; **to get ~d up** تَعَطَّلَ **B** **to be ~d up** (to be busy) كانَ مَشْغولاً; **he's ~d up in a meeting** هو مَشْغولٌ بِاجْتِماعٍ

tiebreaker /ˈtʌɪbreɪkə/, **tiebreak** *n* (in tennis) وَقْت إِضافيّ (في مُباراةِ التِنِس)

tiepin /ˈtʌɪpɪn/ *n* دَبّوس رَبْطَةِ العُنُق

tier /tɪə/ *n* **1** (row, layer) طَبَقة **2** (in hierarchies) مُسْتَوًى, طَبَقة (مُسْتَوَيات); **to add/cut a ~ of management** أضافَ \ ألْغى طَبَقةً من العامِلينَ في الإدارةِ; **a two-/three- ~ system of supervision** نِظام إشْرافٍ مُزْدَوَج \ ثُلاثيّ المُسْتَوَياتِ

tiff /tɪf/ *n* (infml) شِجار, مُشادّة

tiger /ˈtʌɪgə/ *n* (*pl* **tigers** or **tiger**) نَمِر (نُمور)

tiger moth *n* عُثّة النَمِر

tight /tʌɪt/ **A** *adj* **1** (firm) ‹*lid*› مُحْكَم الإغْلاقِ; ‹*screw, knot*› مَشْدود; **the screw/lid is very ~** البُرْغي مَشْدودٌ \ الغِطاءُ مُحْكَمُ الإغْلاقِ **2** (tense) ‹*rope, string*› مَشْدود **3** (restricted) ‹*space, gap*› ضَيِّق; **space was ~ in our first house** كانَ بَيْتُنا الأَوَّلُ ضَيِّقاً; **with six of us in the car, it was a ~ squeeze** كانَت السَيّارةُ مُزْدَحِمةً جِدًّا لِأَنّنا كُنّا سِتّةَ أَشْخاصٍ في السَيّارة; **a ~ bend/corner** مُنْحَنًى حادّ \ زاوِية حادّة **4** (close) ‹*election, race*› مُتَقارِب **5** (close-fitting) ‹*jacket, shirt, trousers*› ضَيِّق; **these shoes are too ~** هذا الحِذاءُ ضَيِّقٌ جِدًّا; **a pair of ~ jeans** بَنْطَلون جينْز ضَيِّق **6** (muscular) ‹*body*› مَفْتول العَضَلاتِ; ‹*stomach*› مَشْدود **7** (strict) ‹*security*› مُشَدَّد, شَديد; ‹*deadline, budget*› صارِم; **to keep ~ control over sth/sb** واصَلَ فَرْضَ رَقابةٍ مُشَدَّدةٍ على شَيْءٍ \ شَخْصٍ; **to work to a ~ budget** عَمِلَ بِميزانِيةٍ صارِمةٍ; **money is very ~ these days** الأَمْوالُ قَليلةٌ \ نادِرةٌ في هذه الأَيّامِ **8** (busy) ‹*schedule, timetable*› ضَيِّق **9** (infml) (mean) بَخيل (بُخَلاءُ); **to be ~ with one's money** كانَ مُتَقَشِّفاً

B *adv* **1** (firmly) ‹*to hold, grip*› بِشِدّةٍ, بِإِحْكامٍ; **to fasten/close sth ~** شَدَّ \ أَغْلَقَ شَيْئاً بِإِحْكامٍ; **hold ~!** أَمْسِكْ بِإِحْكامٍ!; **he shut his eyes ~** أَغْلَقَ عَيْنَيْهِ بِشِدّةٍ **2** (closely) **to be packed ~** كانَ مُكْتَظًّا بِشَكْلٍ شَديدٍ; **to pull one's coat ~ around oneself** شَدَّ مِعْطَفَهُ حَوْلَهُ بِقُوّةٍ

C **(tights)** *n pl* (BrE) [جَوارِب طَوِيلة ضَيِّقة]

(Idioms) **to be in a tight spot** *or* **corner** كانَ في الزاوِيةِ; **to sit tight** [اكْتَفى بِمُراقَبةِ الوَضْعِ]

tighten /ˈtʌɪt(ə)n/ **A** *vt* **1** (to make tight) شَدَّ (i-u; شَدّ) ‹*a lid, screw*› **2** (to intensify) شَدَّدَ ‹*security, restrictions*›

B *vi* «lips, muscles» تَقَلَّصَ

(Phrasal verb) **tighten up ~ up [sth], ~ [sth] up** شَدَّدَ [شَيْئاً] ‹*the law, rules*›; **to ~ up on fraud** تَشَدَّدَ في قَضايا الاحْتِيالِ

tight-fisted /ˌtʌɪtˈfɪstɪd/ *adj* (infml) ‹*employer*› بَخيل (بُخَلاءُ); (infml) ‹*company*› [يَنْتَهِجُ سِياسةً تَقَشُّفيّةً]

tight-fitting /ˌtʌɪtˈfɪtɪŋ/ *adj* ‹*dress, jeans*› ضَيِّق

tight-knit /ˌtʌɪtˈnɪt/ *adj* ‹*community, family*› مُتَماسِك

tightly /ˈtʌɪtli/ *adv* ‹*to hold, wrap*› بِإِحْكامٍ

tightrope /ˈtʌɪtrəʊp/ *n* حَبْل مَشْدود, حَبْل البَهْلَوانِ; **to walk the ~** سارَ على حَبْلٍ مَشْدودٍ

tightrope walker *n* بَهْلَوان الحَبْلِ

tights /tʌɪts/ *n pl* **1** (BrE) (hosiery) [جَوارِب نِسائيّة طَوِيلة] **2** (for ballet, sports) [مَلابِس رِياضيّة ضَيِّقة]

tigress /ˈtʌɪgrɪs/ *n* نَمِرة

Tigris /ˈtʌɪgrɪs/ *pr n* دِجْلة (dipt)

tilapia /tɪˈlapiə/ *n* (*pl* **tilapia**) بُلْطيّ

tile /tʌɪl/ **A** *n* (for roof) قِرْميد (قَراميدُ); (for floor, wall) بَلاط

B *vt* بَلَّطَ ‹*a floor, bathroom*›

till¹ /tɪl/ ▸**until**

till² /tɪl/ *n* صُنْدوق (نُقودٍ)

till³ /tɪl/ *vt* زَرَعَ (a; زَرْع) ‹*land*›

tiller /'tɪlə/ *n* دَفّة

tilt /tɪlt/ **A** *vt* **1** (to slant) أَمالَ ‹*the mirror, sunshade, chair, one's head*›; **to ~ one's head back/to the side** أَمالَ رَأْسَهُ إلى الخَلْفِ \ جانِباً; **don't ~ your chair!** لا تُمِلْ كُرْسِيَّكَ! **2** (to influence) **to ~ the balance in sb's favour/against sb** قَلَبَ المَوازينَ لِصالِحِ \ ضدّ شَخْصٍ; **the balance has been ~ed in favour of our company's bid** انْقَلَبَت المَوازينُ لِصالِحِ العَرْضِ المُقدَّمِ من شَرِكَتِنا

B *vi* (to slant) «spire, table, ground» مالَ (i; مَيَلان ,مَيْل); **to ~ to the left/to one side** مالَ إلى اليَسارِ \ جانِباً; **the floor ~s on this side** تَميلُ الأَرْضيّةُ إلى هذا الجانِبِ

C *n* **1** (incline) مَيْل (أَمْيال ,مُيول), انْحِناء, انْحِدار (انْحِدارات); **the table has a slight ~** الطاولةُ بِها مَيْلٌ بَسيطٌ **2** (infml) (attack) نَقْد ,هُجوم; **to have a ~ at the organizers** هاجَمَ المُنَظِّمينَ

timber /'tɪmbə/ *n* **1** [u] (material) خَشَب (أَخْشاب) **2** [u] (trees) شَجَر (للاسْتِعْمالِ كَخَشَبِ بِناءٍ) **3** (beam) لَوْح خَشَبيّ, عارِضة (عَوارِض), كَمَرة, رافِدة (رَوافِدُ)

timbre /'tambə/ *n* جَرْس (جُروس), نَبْرة

time /taɪm/ **A** *n* **1** [u] (in the past, present, future) وَقْت, زَمَن; **to travel through ~ and space** سَفَر عَبْرَ الزَمَنِ والمَكانِ; **as ~ goes by/passes** بِمُرورِ الوَقْتِ; **at this point in ~** في الوَقْتِ الحاضِرِ; **the biggest lottery win of all ~** أَكْبَر جائِزة يانَصيب على الإطْلاقِ **2** [u] (specific duration) وَقْت, فَتْرة, مُدّة; **in five days'/weeks' ~** بعد خَمْسةِ أَيّامٍ \ أَسابيعَ; **a long/short ~ ago** منذ وَقْتٍ بَعيدٍ \ قَريبٍ; **she worked most of the ~** عَمِلَتْ مُعْظَمَ الوَقْتِ; **there's plenty of ~, there's all the ~ in the world** هُناكَ مُتَّسَعٌ من الوَقْتِ; **she was lying the whole ~** كانَتْ تَكْذِبُ طوال الوَقْتِ; **take your ~ over it** خُذْ وَقْتَكَ فيهِ; **she spent her ~ painting** قَضَتْ وَقْتَها تَرْسِمُ; **you have (enough) ~ to buy a newspaper** لَدَيْكَ وَقْتٌ كافٍ لِشراءِ جَريدةٍ; **we had to wait for a long ~** اضْطُرِرْنا للانْتِظارِ فَتْرةً طَويلةً; **you took a long ~!, what a long ~ you took!** اسْتَغْرَقْتَ وَقْتاً طَويلاً!; **we haven't heard from her for some ~** لم نَتَلَقَّ أَخْباراً مِنْها منذ زَمَنٍ; **within the agreed ~** خلالَ الوَقْتِ المُتَّفَقِ عَلَيْهِ; **in your own ~** (at your own pace) في الوَقْتِ الّذي يُلائِمُكَ; (outside working hours) في وَقْتِكَ الخاصِّ; **on company ~** في وَقْتِ العَمَلِ **3** [u] (with clocks) وَقْت; **what ~ is it?, what's the ~?** كم الساعة \ الوَقْتُ؟; **the ~ is 11 o'clock** الساعةُ 11; **10 am local ~** 10 صَباحاً بالتَوْقيتِ المَحَلّيِّ; **that clock keeps good ~** تِلْكَ الساعةُ تُبَيِّنُ الوَقْتَ بِدِقّةٍ **4** (in scheduling) وَقْت, مَوْعِد (مَواعِدُ); **we'll meet tomorrow, at the same ~** سَنَتَقابَلُ غَداً، في نَفْسِ الوَقْتِ; **this ~ last/next week** في نَفْسِ هذا الوَقْتِ الأُسْبوعَ الماضِيَ \ القادِمَ; **the trains are running on ~** تَسيرُ القِطاراتُ في مَواعيدِها; **the bus/train ~s** مَواعيد الحافِلاتِ \ القِطاراتِ; **you're just in ~ for lunch** جِئْتَ في الوَقْتِ المُناسِبِ للغَداءِ; **to arrive in good ~** وَصَلَ مُبَكِّراً; **the flight/journey ~ is three hours** مُدّةُ الرِحْلةِ ثَلاثُ ساعاتٍ; **the school must be ready in ~ for the new term** يَجِبُ أنْ تَكونَ المَدْرَسةُ مُسْتَعِدّةً قبل بَدْءِ الفَصْلِ الدِراسيِّ الجَديدِ **5** (era, epoch) عَصْر (عُصور ,أَعْصُر), زَمَن (أَزْمان), وَقْت (أَوْقات), عَهْد (عُهود); **in the ~ of the Pharaohs** في عَصْرِ الفَراعِنةِ; **at that ~** في ذلك العَصْرِ; **at the ~** في ذلك الوَقْتِ; **there was a ~ when one could ...** كانَ هُناكَ وَقْتٌ عِنْدَما كانَ المَرْءُ يَسْتَطيعُ أنْ ...; **to be ahead of the ~s** كانَ سابِقاً لِعَصْرِهِ; **to be behind the ~s** كانَ غَيْرَ مُواكِبٍ للعَصْرِ; **to keep up with the ~s** واكَبَ العَصْرَ; **~s are hard** الظُروفُ صَعْبةٌ; **in happier ~s** في أَوْقاتٍ أَفْضَلَ; **that was before my ~** كانَ ذلك قبل زَماني; **at my ~ of life** في مِثْلِ عُمْري **6** (moment) وَقْت (أَوْقات); **it's ~ to go!** حانَ وَقْتُ الرَحيلِ!; **this is no ~ for jokes** لَيْسَ هذا وَقْتُ المِزاحِ; **at ~s** في بَعْضِ الأَحْيانِ \ الأَوْقاتِ, أَحْياناً; **at all ~s** في جَميعِ الأَوْقاتِ, طوال الوَقْتِ; **come at any ~** تَعالَ في أَيِّ وَقْتٍ; **you've come at the right ~** جِئْتَ في الوَقْتِ المُناسِبِ; **the ~ has come for change/action** حانَ وَقْتُ التَغْييرِ \ الفِعْلِ; **we're expecting him any ~ now** نَتَوَقَّعُ وُصولَهُ في أَيِّ وَقْتٍ الآنَ; **by the ~ she got there the train had gone** عند وُصولِها إلى هُناكَ كانَ القِطارُ قد غادَرَ; **some ~ this week** في وَقْتٍ ما هذا الأُسْبوعَ; **for the ~ being** في الوَقْتِ الراهِنِ; **from the ~ (that) I was 15** منذ أنْ كانَ عُمْري 15 سَنةً; **from that/this ~ on** منذ ذلك الوَقْتِ \ الحينِ; **in ~s of crisis** في أَوْقاتِ الأَزَماتِ; **no more than three passengers at the same ~** مَمْنوعٌ رُكوبُ أَكْثَرَ من ثَلاثةِ

أَفْرادٍ في نَفْسِ الوَقْتِ **7** (occasion) مَرّة (مَرّات ,مِرار); **the first/last/next ~** المَرّة الأولى \ الأخيرة \ التالية; **nine ~s out of ten** تِسْع مَرّاتٍ من كُلّ عَشَرةٍ; **three ~s a month** ثَلاث مَرّاتٍ في الشَهْرِ; **four at a ~** أَرْبَعة في المَرّةِ الواحِدةِ; **~ after ~** مَرّةً تِلْوَ مَرّةٍ, مِراراً وتِكْراراً, الأُخْرى; **she passed first ~ (round)** نَجَحَتْ مِن أَوّلِ مَرّةٍ; **from ~ to ~** من آنٍ \ وَقْتٍ لِآخَرَ **8** (experience) **we had a good/bad ~** قَضَيْنا وَقْتاً طَيِّباً \ سَيِّئاً; **have a good ~!** أَتَمَنّى لَكَ وَقْتاً طَيِّباً!; **she enjoyed her ~ in Canada** اسْتَمْتَعَتْ بِوَقْتِها في كَنَدا **9** (Mus) إيقاع (إيقاعات); **to stay in** *or* **keep ~** حافَظَ على الإيقاعِ **10** (Sport) زَمَن (أَزْمان); **a fast/slow ~** زَمَن سَريع \ بَطيء **11** (in multiplication) **two ~s two is four** اثْنانِ في اثْنَيْنِ يُساوي أَرْبَعةً; **ten ~s longer/stronger** عَشْر مَرّاتٍ أَطْوَلَ \ أَقْوى

B *vt* **(times, timing, timed)** **1** (to schedule) حَدَّدَ الوَقْتَ, أَقَّتَ, وَقَّتَ ‹*an attack, a holiday, meeting*›; **to be well-/badly timed** كانَ في تَوْقيتٍ جَيِّدٍ \ سَيِّئٍ; **the announcement was perfectly ~d** جاءَ الإعْلانُ في تَوْقيتٍ مُناسِبٍ تَماماً **2** (to judge) «batsman, player» اخْتارَ الوَقْتَ ‹*a stroke, shot*›; **to ~ a remark/joke** اخْتارَ وَقْتَ مُلاحَظةٍ \ دُعابةٍ **3** (to measure speed, duration) قاسَ الوَقْتَ ‹*a race, journey*›; **to ~ sb over 100 metres** قاسَ الوَقْتَ الّذي اسْتَغْرَقَهُ شَخْصٌ في عَدْوِ 100 مِترٍ; **to ~ an egg** قاسَ وَقْتَ نُضْجِ بَيْضةٍ

C *v refl* **to ~ oneself** حَسَبَ الوَقْتَ الّذي اسْتَغْرَقَهُ

Idioms **only time will tell** لن تَتَّضِحَ الأُمورُ إلاّ مع الوَقْتِ; **to do time** قَضى حُكْماً بالسَجْنِ; **to have time on one's hands** كانَ لَدَيْهِ الكَثيرُ من وَقْتِ الفَراغِ

time bomb *n* **1** (weapon) قُنْبُلة مَوْقوتة \ زَمَنيّة **2** (situation) قُنْبُلة مَوْقوتة

time-consuming /tʌɪmk(ə)n'sju:mɪŋ/ *adj* ‹*process, task*› يَتَطَلَّبُ وَقْتاً طَويلاً

time difference *n* فارِق زَمَنيّ

time frame *n* إطار زَمَنيّ

timekeeper /'tʌɪmki:pə/ *n* **1** (at sports) ضابِط الوَقْتِ **2** (in punctuality) مُحافِظ على المَواعِيدِ

timeless /'tʌɪmləs/ *adj* ‹*quality, beauty*› سَرْمَديّ, خالِد, أَبَديّ

time limit *n* **1** (deadline) أَجَل (آجال), مُهْلة, حَدّ زَمَنيّ; **to set a time limit for the completion of a job** وَضَعَ حَدّاً زَمَنيّاً لإِنْهاءِ عَمَلٍ **2** (maximum duration) الفَتْرة الزَمَنيّة القُصْوى

timely /'tʌɪmli/ *adj* **(timelier, timeliest)** (fml) ‹*intervention, arrival*› في حينِهِ, في الوَقْتِ المُناسِبِ

time management *n* إدارة الوَقْتِ

time off *n* إجازة

timer /'tʌɪmə/ *n* **1** (to measure time) ساعة تَوْقيتٍ **2** (for activation) تايْمِر

time-saving /'tʌɪmseɪvɪŋ/ *adj before n* ‹*device, technique*› مُوَفِّر \ مُخْتَصِر للوَقْتِ

timescale /'tʌɪmskeɪl/ *n* مُدّة \ فَتْرة زَمَنيّة; **within a 6 month ~** خِلالَ فَتْرةٍ زَمَنيّةٍ لِمُدّةِ سِتّةِ أَشْهُرٍ

timeshare /'tʌɪmʃɛː/ *n* **1** (property) وَحْدة سَكَنيّة بِنِظامِ المُشارَكةِ بالوَقْتِ **2** [u] (arrangement) نِظام المُشارَكةِ بالوَقْتِ

time sheet *n* سِجِلّ الحُضورِ والانْصِرافِ

time signature *n* إيقاع (عَلامة زَمَنيّة موسيقيّة)

time span *n* فَتْرة (فَتَرات), مُدّة (مُدَد)

timetable /'tʌɪmteɪb(ə)l/ **A** *n* (BrE) **1** (for buses, trains) جَدْوَل مَواعيدَ; **a bus/train ~** جَدْوَل مَواعيدِ الباصِ \ القِطارِ **2** (of lessons) جَدْوَل زَمَنيّ \ دِراسيّ **3** (of events) جَدْوَل أَعْمالٍ

B *vt* حَدَّدَ وَقْتاً \ مَوْعِداً لِ ‹*a lesson, meeting*›

time zone *n* مِنْطَقة زَمَنيّة

timid /'tɪmɪd/ *adj* ‹*child, voice*› هَيّاب, خَجِل

timidly /'tɪmɪdli/ *adv* ‹*to ask, smile*› بِتَرَدُّدٍ

timing /'tʌɪmɪŋ/ *n* **1** (choice of time) تَوْقيت **2** (of engines) تَوْقيت الإشْعالِ

timpani /'tɪmp(ə)ni/ *n pl* (also **tympani**) تِمْباني (طَبْل ذو صُنْدوقٍ مُصَوِّتٍ كَبير)

tin /tɪn/ *n* **1** (metal) قَصْدير **2** (BrE) (can) عُلْبة, تَنَكة **3** (for biscuits, cakes) عُلْبة

tin can *n* عُلْبة

tinfoil /'tɪnfɔɪl/ *n* وَرَق أَلومِنيوم

tinge /tɪndʒ/ **A** *vt* **to be ~d with sadness/nostalgia** كانَ مَشوباً بالحُزْنِ \ الحَنينِ

B *n* **1** (of colour) مَسْحة (مَسَحات) **2** (of sadness, regret) مَسْحة (مَسَحات)

tingle /ˈtɪŋg(ə)l/ **A** *vi* «skin, fingers» نَمِلَ (a; نَمَل), خَدِرَ (a; خَدَر)

B *n* خَدَر, نَمَل

tingling /ˈtɪŋglɪŋ/ *n* خَدَر, نَمَل

tinker /ˈtɪŋkə/ *vi* **to ~ with the engine/system** عَبِث بالمُحَرِّكِ \ الجِهازِ

tinkle /ˈtɪŋk(ə)l/ **A** *vi* «chimes, water» طَنْطَنَ (i; طَنْطَنة), رَنَّ (i; رَنين)

B *n* رَنين, خَشْخَشة

tinned /tɪnd/ *adj* ‹*meat, pears*› مُعَلَّب

tinnitus /ˈtɪnɪtəs/ *n* طَنين

tinny /ˈtɪni/ *adj* (**tinnier**, **tinniest**) **1** (of a sound) ‹*speakers, music*› حادّ الصَّوْتِ **2** (badly made) ‹*car, toy*› رديء الصُّنْع

tin opener *n* (BrE) فَتّاحة عُلَبٍ

tinplate /ˈtɪnpleɪt/ *n* صَفيح, تَنك

tinsel /ˈtɪns(ə)l/ *n* (شَريط لامِع للزَّخْرفةِ والزينةِ)

tint /tɪnt/ *n* صِبْغة

tinted /ˈtɪntɪd/ *adj* **1** (of glass) ‹*windows, spectacles*› داكِن **2** (dyed) ‹*hair, eyelashes*› مَصْبوغ

tiny /ˈtʌɪni/ *adj* (**tinier**, **tiniest**) ‹*amount, minority*› ضَئيل, صَغير جِدًّا

tip /tɪp/ **A** *n* **1** (of a stick, nose, tail) طَرَف (أَطْراف); (of a finger) أُنْمُلة (أَنامِلُ); **to stand on the ~s of one's toes** وَقَفَ على أَطْرافِ أَصابِعِهِ; **the southernmost ~ of the peninsula** الطَّرَف الواقِع في أَقْصى جَنوبِ شِبْهِ الجَزيرةِ **2** (protective end of a stick, heel, an umbrella) [قِطْعة من المَعْدِنِ تُثَبَّتُ على طَرَفِ شَيْءٍ لِحِمايَتِهِ] **3** (gratuity) بَقْشيش (بَقاشيش), إكْرامِيّة; **he left a $10 ~** تَرَكَ 10 دولاراتٍ بَقْشيشاً **4** (hint) نَصيحة (نَصائِحُ) **5** (in betting) مَعْلومة سِرِّيّة **6** (BrE) (for waste) مَقْلَب للنُّفاياتِ **7** (BrE) (infml) (mess) فَوْضى (f)

B *vt* (**-pp-**) **1** (to tilt) أَمالَ ‹*a chair, bowl, glass*›; **to ~ one's chair back** أَمالَ كُرْسِيَّهُ للخَلْفِ; **to ~ the box on its side** قَلَبَ الصُّنْدوقَ على جانِبِهِ; **to ~ the scales at 60 kg** سَجَّلَ وَزْنُهُ 60 كجم **2** (to pour, empty) **to ~ sth into/out of sth** فَرَّغَ شَيْئاً في \ من شَيْءٍ ‹*the contents, tea, dirty water*›; **he ~ped the coins onto the table** أَفْرَغَ القِطَعَ النَّقْديّةَ على الطاوِلةِ; **to ~ the water away** أَفْرَغَ الماءَ **3** (for service) أَعْطى بَقْشيشاً ‹*a waiter, driver*›; **to ~ the doorman $10** أَعْطى البَوّابَ بَقْشيشاً 10 دولاراتٍ **4** (in betting) **to ~ a team/horse to win** أَلْمَحَ إلى إمْكانِيّةِ فَوْزِ فَريقٍ \ حِصانٍ; **to ~ sb to be a future president** تَكَهَّنَ أَنَّ شَخْصاً سَيَكونُ رَئيساً في المُسْتَقْبَلِ **5** (to push) دَفَعَ (a; دَفْع); **to ~ the ball over the bar** دَفَعَ الكُرةَ فوق العارِضةِ

C *vi* (**-pp-**) (to tilt) «seats, buckets» مالَ (i; مَيْل, مَيَلان); **to ~ forward/back/onto one side** مالَ للأَمامِ \ للخَلْفِ \ جانِباً

(Phrasal verbs) **tip off**: **~ off [sb]**, **~ [sb] off** أَدْلى بِمَعْلوماتٍ سِرِّيّةٍ إلى [شَخْصٍ] ‹*a crook, reporter, the police*›

• **tip out**: **~ out [sth]**, **~ [sth] out** أَفْرَغَ [شَيْئاً] ‹*a drawer, clothes*›

• **tip over** **A** «bucket, bus» انْقَلَبَ **B** **~ [sth] over** قَلَبَ [شَيْئاً] ‹*a chair, car, box*›

• **tip up** **A** (to tilt) «seats, lids» رَفَعَ [شَيْئاً] لِأَعْلى **B** **~ up [sth]**, **~ [sth] up** رَفَعَ [شَيْئاً] ‹*a cup, bottle*›

tip-off /ˈtɪpɒf/ *n* مَعْلومة سِرِّيّة, وِشاية

tipper /ˈtɪpə/ *n* (person leaving a tip) [شَخص يَدفعُ بَقْشيشاً \ إكْرامِيّةً]; **to be a generous/mean ~** أَعْطى إكْرامِيّةً كَبيرةً \ بَسيطةً

tiptoe /ˈtɪptəʊ/ **A** *n* **on ~** على أَطْرافِ الأَصابِعِ

B *vi* (**tiptoes**, **tiptoeing**, **tiptoed**) «parent, children» مَشى على أَطْرافِ أَصابِعِهِ

tip-top /tɪpˈtɒp/ *adj* (infml) ‹*food, service*› مُمْتاز

tirade /tʌɪˈreɪd/ *n* [خُطْبة مُسْهَبة وَشَديدة اللَّهْجةِ]

tire /tʌɪə/ **A** *n* (AmE) ▸ **tyre**

B *vt* أَتْعَبَ, أَنْهَكَ ‹*a child, dog*›

C *vi* **1** (to get tired) «children, athletes» تَعِبَ (a; تَعَب) **2** (to get bored) **to ~ of sth, to ~ of doing sth** سَئِمَ من شَيْءٍ; **I'm ~d of his jokes** سَئِمْتُ من نِكاتِهِ; **he's ~d of going to work each day** سَئِمَ من ذَهابِهِ إلى العَمَلِ كُلَّ يَوْمٍ

(Phrasal verb) **tire out**: **~ [sb] out** أَشَدَّ التَّعَبِ, أَتْعَبَ [شَخْصاً] ‹*a child, dog*›; **I feel ~d out!** أَشْعُرُ بالتَّعَبِ المُطْلَقِ, أَرْهَقَ [شَخْصاً]

tired /tʌɪəd/ *adj* 1 (weary) ‹*eyes, legs*› تَعِب, مُتْعَب, مُنْهَك; **to feel ~** شَعَرَ بالتَّعَبِ 2 (bored) **to be ~ of sb/sth** مَلَّ من شَخْصٍ \ شَيْءٍ

tiredness /ˈtʌɪədnəs/ *n* تَعَب

tireless /ˈtʌɪələs/ *adj* ‹*efforts, work*› دَؤُوب, لا يَكِلُّ ولا يَمَلُّ

tiresome /ˈtʌɪəs(ə)m/ *adj* ‹*chore, formalities*› مُزْعِج

tiring /ˈtʌɪərɪŋ/ *adj* ‹*journey, activity*› مُتْعِب, مُرْهِق, مُنْهِك

tissue /ˈtɪʃuː/ *n* 1 (handkerchief) مِنْدِيل (مَنادِيلُ) 2 (also **tissue paper**) وَرَق رَقِيق 3 (of animals, plants) نَسِيج (أَنْسِجَة)

tit /tɪt/ *n* 1 (bird) قُرْقُف 2 (infml) (woman's breast) ثَدْي (أَثْداء)

Idiom **tit for tat** واحِدة بواحِدةٍ

titanium /tɪˈteɪniəm/ *n* تيتانيوم

titbit (BrE) /ˈtɪtbɪt/, **tidbit** (AmE) /ˈtɪdbɪt/ *n* 1 (of food) لُقْمة شَهِيّة 2 (of gossip, news) [خَبَر صَغِير مُثِير]

title /ˈtʌɪt(ə)l/ **A** *n* 1 (of a book, painting, etc) عُنْوان (عَناوِينُ) 2 (form of address) لَقَب (أَلْقاب) 3 (in sports) لَقَب (البُطولة); **he won the world ~ in 2007** فازَ بِلَقَبِ البُطولةِ في عام 2007 4 [u] (legal right) حَقّ مِلْكِيّةٍ

B *vt* عَنْوَنَ (i; عَنْوَنة) ‹*a book, play*›

title bar *n* شَرِيط العُنْوانِ

title deed *n* سَنَد \ صَكّ مِلْكِيّةٍ

title-holder /ˈtʌɪtəlˌhəʊldə/ *n* حامِل لَقَبِ البُطولةِ

title page *n* صَفْحة العُنْوانِ

title role *n* [دَوْر الشَخْصِيّةِ الّتي يَحْمِل الفِيلْمُ أو المَسْرَحِيّةُ اسْمَها]

titrate /tʌɪˈtreɪt, tɪˈtreɪt/ *vt* عايَرَ (قاسَ بالمُقارَنة مع مَحْلولٍ عِيارِيٍّ) ‹*a solution*›

titter /ˈtɪtə/ **A** *vi* «class, children» ضَحِكَ ضِحْكاً مَكْتوماً

B *n* ضِحْك مَكْتوم

tittle-tattle /ˈtɪtəltat(ə)l/ *n* (infml) ثَرْثَرة, القِيل والقال

titular /ˈtɪtjʊlə/ *adj* ‹*president, head*› اسْمِيّ

tizzy /ˈtɪzi/ *n* (infml) **to be in a ~** قَلِقَ (a; قَلَق)

T-junction /ˈtiːdʒʌŋkʃ(ə)n/ *n* تَقاطُع ثُلاثِيّ

TN *abbr* = **Tennessee**

to /tə, before a vowel tʊ, tuː, emphat. tuː/ **A** *prep* 1 (expressing direction) إلى ‹*school, the mall*›; **she's gone ~ Mary's** ذَهَبَتْ إلى مَنْزِلِ ماري; **~ town** إلى المَدِينةِ; **to Tripoli/Algeria** إلى طَرابُلُسَ \ الجَزائِرِ; **the road ~ the village** الطَرِيق إلى القَرْيةِ; **trains ~ and from Cairo** القِطارات من وَإلى القاهِرةِ 2 (facing towards) تُجاهَ, بِاتِّجاهِ; **turned ~ the wall** تُجاهَ الحائِطِ; **with his back ~ them** مُعْطِياً إيّاهُمْ ظَهْرَهُ 3 (touching) لِ; **holding the letter ~ his chest** ضامًّا الرِسالةَ إلى صَدْرِهِ; **back ~ back** ظَهْراً لِظَهْرٍ 4 (with limits) إلى; **~ the end/this day** حتّى النِهايةِ \ الآنَ; **50 ~ 60 people** 50 إلى 60 شَخْصاً; **in five ~ ten minutes** في خَمْسٍ إلى عَشْرِ دَقائِقَ; **to count ~ 100** عَدَّ إلى 100 5 (with indirect objects) ‹*to give, offer*› لِ; **give them ~ Sophie** أَعْطِها لِصوفي; **~ me it's not important** بالنِسْبةِ لي الأَمْرُ غَيْرُ مُهِمٍّ; **be nice ~ them** كُنْ لَطِيفاً مَعَهُمْ 6 (in toasts, dedications) في صِحّةِ, على نَخْبِ \ شَرَفِ; **(here's) ~ the happy couple** في صِحّةِ الزَوْجَيْنِ السَعِيدَيْنِ; **~ all my friends and colleagues** في صِحّةِ كُلِّ أَصْدِقائي وَزُمَلائي 7 (in accordance with) **is it ~ your taste?** هل يُناسِبُ ذَوْقَكَ؟; **to dance ~ the music** رَقَصَ على الموسِيقى 8 (in comparisons, relationships) **to win by three goals ~ two** فازَ بِثَلاثةِ أَهْدافٍ مُقابِلَ هَدَفَيْنِ; **perpendicular ~ the ground** مُتَعامِد مع الأَرْضِ; **next door ~ the school** مُجاوِر للمَدْرَسةِ; **drawn ~ scale** مَرْسوم حَسْبَ مِقْياسٍ مُعَيَّنٍ 9 (showing purpose) **to invite sb ~ dinner** دَعا شَخْصاً للعَشاءِ; **~ this end** لِهَذِهِ الغايةِ 10 (belonging to) لِ; **the key ~ the safe** مِفْتاح الخَزْنةِ; **a room ~ myself** غُرْفة لي وَحْدي; **there's no sense ~ it** لَيْسَ مَنْطِقيًّا 11 (showing place) نَحْوَ, إلى; **it's ~ the north of here** إنَّهُ إلى الشَمالِ من هُنا; **place the cursor ~ the left of the word** ضَعِ المُؤَشِّرَ إلى يَسارِ الكَلِمةِ 12 (showing reaction) لِ; **~ his surprise/dismay** لِدَهْشَتِهِ \ لِفَزَعِهِ 13 (Busn) (on invoices) **~ repairing/delivering** للتَصْلِيحِ \ للتَوْزِيعِ

B *infinitive particle* 1 (in infinitives) [أداة تَدُلُّ على المَصْدَرِ المُؤَوَّلِ في اللُغةِ الإنْجِلِيزِيّةِ]; **~ see it is ~ believe it** لن أُصَدِّقَ حتّى أرى بِأُمِّ عَيْني 2 (expressing purpose) لِ; **he did it ~ impress us** فَعَلَهُ لِيُثِيرَ إعْجابَنا; **~ raise the alarm, ring 0909** لِإطْلاقِ صَفّارةِ الإنْذارِ، اتَّصِلْ بِ0909 3 (to avoid verb repetition) **don't go, if you don't want ~** لا تَذْهَبْ، إذا لم تُرِدْ ذلك; **'did you go?'—'no I promised not ~'** 'هل ذَهَبْتَ؟' — 'لا لَقَدْ وَعَدْتُ بِعَدَمِ الذَهابِ' **4** (linking consecutive acts) **he woke up ~ hear the phone ringing** اسْتَيْقَظَ وَسَمِعَ رَنينَ الهاتِفِ **5** (after superlatives) **the youngest ~ qualify was ...** أَصْغَرُ مُتَأَهِّلٍ كانَ ... **6** (following impersonal verbs) **it's difficult ~ say** لا أَدْري بالضَبْطِ; **it would be nice ~ be able to say it's true!** لَيْتَ الأَمْرَ كانَ كَذلك

C /tuː/ *adv* (closed) **to push the door ~** دَفَعَ البابَ إلى أنْ انْغَلَق

Idiom **that's all there is to it** هذا كُلُّ ما في الأَمْرِ

toad /təʊd/ *n* ضِفْدَعٌ (ضَفادِعُ)

toadstool /ˈtəʊdstuːl/ *n* فُطْر (n coll; singul n فُطْرٌ ;فُطور) نَبات فُطْرِيّ

to and fro *adv* <to swing, rush> ذَهاباً وَإياباً

toast /təʊst/ **A** *n* **1** (grilled bread) تُوسْت; خُبْز مُحَمَّص; **to make ~** حَمَّصَ خُبْزاً **2** (tribute) نَخْب (أَنْخاب); **to make a ~ to the happy couple** اقْتَرَحَ نَخْباً لِلزَوْجَيْنِ السَعيدَيْن **3** (popular person) **the ~ of the town** رَجُل الساعةِ; **after winning the medal she was the ~ of the town** بعد أنْ فازَتْ بالميدالية أَصْبَحَتْ مَحَطَّ الأَنْظارِ في المَدينةِ

B *vt* **1** «cook» حَمَّصَ <a slice of bread, sandwich>; **~ the almonds until brown** حَمِّص اللَوْزَ حتّى يُصْبِحَ لَوْنُهُ بُنِّيًّا **2** (in ceremonies) شَرِبَ النَخْبَ <the bride and groom, success>; **the guests rose to their feet to ~ the couple/the success of the venture** وَقَفَ الضُيوفُ لِيَشْرَبوا نَخْبَ الزَوْجَيْنِ \ نَجاحِ المَشْروعِ

C **(toasted)** *adj* <sandwich, chestnuts, sesame seeds> مُحَمَّص

Idiom **to be toast** (infml) انْتَهى أَمْرُهُ

toaster /ˈtəʊstə/ *n* مُحَمِّص خُبْزٍ, مِحْمَصة

tobacco /təˈbakəʊ/ *n* (*pl* **tobaccos**) **1** (plant) تَبْغ (تُبوغ) **2** (for smoking) تِبْغ (تُبوغ), دُخان (أَدْخِنة)

tobacconist /təˈbak(ə)nɪst/ *n* **1** (person) بائِع لَوازِمِ التَدْخينِ **2** **(tobacconist's)** (business) [دُكّان لِبَيْعِ لَوازِمِ التَدْخينِ]

toboggan /təˈbɒg(ə)n/ **A** *n* مِزْلَقة (مَزالِقُ), مِزْلَج (مَزالِجُ)

B *vi* «children» تَزَلَّجَ (بِواسِطةِ مِزْلَقةٍ)

today /təˈdeɪ/ **A** *adv* **1** (this day) اليَوْمَ; **we're going back ~** سَنَعودُ اليَوْمَ; **the exams start a week from ~** سَتَبْدَأُ الامْتِحاناتُ بعد أُسْبوعٍ من اليَوْم; **he arrives later ~** سَيَصِلُ في وَقْتٍ مُتَأَخِّرٍ اليَوْمَ **2** (nowadays) اليَوْمَ, في الوَقْتِ الحاضِرِ; **young people ~ face many challenges** يُواجِهُ الشَبابُ اليَوْمَ العَديدَ من التَحَدِّياتِ

B *n* **1** (this day) اليَوْم; **~ is Friday** اليَوْمُ الجُمْعةُ; **what's ~'s date?** ما تاريخُ اليَوْمِ؟; **I'm starting my diet from ~, I'm starting my diet as from ~** سَأَبْدَأُ نِظامي الغِذائيَّ من اليَوْمِ **2** (the present) اليَوْم, الوَقْت الحاضِر; **~'s citizens** مُواطِنو اليَوْمِ

toddler /ˈtɒdlə/ *n* طِفْل صَغير

toe /təʊ/ *n* **1** (of the foot) إصْبَع قَدَمٍ; **the big/little ~** إصْبَع القَدَمِ الكَبير \ الصَغير **2** (of a sock, shoe) مُقَدِّمة

Idioms **to keep sb on his toes** حَثَّ شَخْصاً على إنجازِ عَمَلٍ; **to toe the line** الْتَزَمَ بالنَهْج

toehold /ˈtəʊhəʊld/ *n* **1** (entry) مَوْطِئ قَدَم; **to get a ~ in the market** حَصَلَ على مَوْطِئِ قَدَمٍ في السوقِ **2** (in climbing) مَوْطِئ قَدَمٍ

toenail /ˈtəʊneɪl/ *n* ظُفْر إصْبَعِ قَدَمٍ

toffee /ˈtɒfi/ *n* توفي (حَلْوى لَزِجة مَطّاطة)

toffee-nosed /ˈtɒfɪnəʊzd/ *adj* (BrE infml pej) <snob> مَغْرور

tofu /ˈtəʊfuː/ *n* توفو (الصويا)

toga /ˈtəʊgə/ *n* [ثَوْب فَضْفاض كان يَرْتَديهِ قُدَماءُ الرومانِ]

together /təˈgeðə/ **A** *adv* **1** (accompanying) مَعاً, مع بَعْضٍ; **they're always ~** هُمْ دائِماً معاً; **to get back ~ again** تَصالَحا; **to sit close ~** جَلَسوا جَنْباً إلى جَنْبٍ; **we're all in this ~** نَحْنُ في هذا سَواءً; **they belong ~** يُناسِبونَ بَعْضُهُم البَعْضَ; **the talks brought the two sides closer ~** قَرَّبَتْ المُحادَثاتُ بين الطَرَفَيْنِ **2** (combining) مَعاً, سَوِيًّا; **the two halves screw ~** يُثَبَّتُ النِصْفانِ مَعاً بِواسِطةِ بُرْغيٍّ; **he nailed the two planks ~** ثَبَّتَ اللَوْحَانِ مَعاً بِالمَساميرِ; **those colours go ~ well** تَتَناسَبُ تِلْكَ الأَلْوانُ على نَحْوٍ جَيِّدٍ; **his argument doesn't hold ~ very well** حُجَّتُهُ غَيْرُ مُتَماسِكةٍ **3** (at the same time) في نَفْسِ الوَقْتِ, في وَقْتٍ \ آنٍ واحِدٍ; **they were all talking ~** كانوا يَتَكَلَّمونَ جَميعاً في وَقْتٍ واحِدٍ; **three busses came ~**

جاءَتْ ثَلاثُ حافلاتٍ في آنٍ واحِدٍ

B *adj* (infml) مُتَماسِك

C **(together with)** *prep phr* (as well as) عِلاوةً ,بالإضافةِ إلى

مَعَ ,على

(Idiom) **to get it together** (infml) نَظَّمَ أُمورَهُ

togetherness /tə'geðənəs/ *n* تآلُف ,شُعور التَضامُنِ

Togo /'təʊgəʊ/ *pr n* توغو

toil /tɔɪl/ **A** *vi* (also **toil away**) كَدَحَ (a; كَدْح ,كَدّ (u; كَدّ

B *n* (liter) كَدْح ,كَدّ

toilet /'tɔɪlɪt/ *n* **1** (bowl) مِرْحاض (مَراحيضُ) **2** (room) دَوْرة (حَمّامات) ,حَمّام (مَراحيضُ) مِرْحاض ,المِياهِ; **public ~(s)** مِرْحاض عامّ; **I need to go to the ~** أنا بِحاجةٍ إلى الذَهابِ إلى الحَمّامِ

toilet bag *n* حقيبة أَدواتِ الزينةِ

toilet brush *n* فُرْشاة مِرْحاضٍ

toilet paper *n* وَرَق تْواليت

toiletries /'tɔɪlɪtriz/ *n pl* أدوات الحَمّامِ \ التَزيِنِ

toilet roll *n* **1** (cardboard tube) [أُنبوب الكَرْتون داخِلَ لَفّةِ لَفّة وَرَقِ تواليت] **2** (paper) [وَرَقِ التَواليت]

toilet water *n* (عِطْر سائِل مُخَفَّف) كولونْيا ,ماء التَواليت

token /'təʊk(ə)n/ **A** *n* **1** (symbol) تَعْبير; **please accept this gift as a ~ of our gratitude** الرَجاءُ أنْ تَقْبَلوا هذه الهَدِيّةَ تَعْبيراً عن امْتِنانِنا **2** (for a machine, phone) عُمْلة رَمْزِيّة (قِرْص يوضَعُ [في آلةٍ ما لِتَشْغيلِها **3** (voucher) وَرَقة بِقيمةٍ مُعَيَّنةٍ لِشراءِ] شَيْءٍ]; **a gift ~** [وَرَقة بِقيمةٍ مُعَيَّنةٍ لِشراءِ هَدِيّةٍ]

B *adj before n* ‹gesture, woman› رَمْزيّ

(Idiom) **by the same token** كَذلِكَ

tokenism /'təʊk(ə)nɪz(ə)m/ *n* (pej) تَفْضيل \ قُبول رَمْزِيّ

Tokyo /'təʊkɪəʊ/ *pr n* طوكِيو (f)

told /təʊld/ *past tense, past participle* ▸ **tell**

tolerable /'tɒlərəb(ə)l/ *adj* **1** (bearable) ‹level, heat› مُحْتَمَل, مَقْبول ,كافٍ **2** (adequate) ‹standard, comfort› مُطاق

tolerance /'tɒlərəns/ *n* تَسامُح; **religious/racial ~** تَسامُح دينيّ \ عِرْقيّ

tolerant /'tɒlərənt/ *adj* ‹society, attitude› مُتَساهِل ,مُتَسامِح

tolerate /'tɒləreɪt/ *vt* **1** (to put up with) تَسامَحَ ‹sb's behaviour, an injustice› **2** (to withstand) تَحَمَّلَ ‹pain, shade›

toleration /tɒlə'reɪʃ(ə)n/ *n* تَسامُح

toll /təʊl/ **A** *n* **1** (in disasters) حَصيلة \ عَدَد الجَرْحى; **the official death ~ is 736** الحَصيلةُ الرَسْميّةُ لِعَدَدِ القَتْلى هي 736 **2** (fee) رَسْم مُرورٍ

B *vt* قَرَعَ (a; قَرْع) ‹a bell›

C *vi* «bells» دَقَّ (u; دَقّ)

(Idiom) **to take its toll (on sb/sth)** أثَّر (على شَخْصٍ \ شَيْءٍ) تَأْثيراً سَلْبِيّاً

tollbooth /'təʊlbuːð/ *n* [كُشْك لِدَفْع رُسومِ المُرورِ]

toll bridge *n* [جِسْر بِرَسْمِ المُرورِ]

toll-free /təʊl'friː/ **A** *adj* ‹call, number› مَجانيّ

B *adv* ‹to phone, call› مَجانِيّاً

toll road *n* [طَريق بِرَسْمِ المُرورِ]

tollway /'təʊlweɪ/ *n* (AmE) [طَريق بَرَسْمِ المُرورِ]

tomato /tə'mɑːtəʊ/ **A** *n* (*pl* **tomatoes**) طَماطِم (n coll, dipt) بَنَدورة (Levant)

B *adj before n* ‹puree, juice› الطَماطِم

tomato ketchup *n* صَلْصة طَماطِمَ

tomb /tuːm/ *n* (أَضْرِحة ,ضَرائِحُ) ضَريح; **the ~ of the unknown soldier** ضَريح الجُنْديِّ المَجْهولِ

tomboy /'tɒmbɔɪ/ *n* فَتاة \ بِنْت مُسْتَرْجِلة

tombstone /'tuːmstəʊn/ *n* بَلاطة قَبْرٍ

tomcat /'tɒmkat/ *n* (قِطَط) قِطّ ,(هِرَرة) هِرّ

tome /təʊm/ *n* (fml) (مُجَلَّدات) مُجَلَّد ,كِتاب كَبير

tomorrow /tə'mɒrəʊ/ **A** *adv* غَداً; **see you ~!** أَراكَ غَداً!; **we'll meet ~ morning/evening** سَنَلْتَقي غَداً صَباحاً \ مَساءً; **all day ~** طَوال يَوْمِ غَدٍ; **can you deliver it first thing ~?** هل يُمْكِنُكَ أنْ تُوَصِّلَهُ غَداً في الصَباحِ الباكِرِ؟; **a week ~, ~ week** بعد أُسْبوعٍ من الغَدِ

B *n* **1** (day) الغَد; **~ is Monday** غَداً هو يَوْمُ الاثْنَيْنِ; **as from ~** بَدْءاً من الغَدِ; **~ is another day** غَداً يَوْمٌ جَديدٌ; **do it by ~** افْعَلْهُ بِحُلولِ يَوْمِ غَدٍ **2** (the future) الغَد ,المُسْتَقْبَل; **the citizens of ~** مُواطِنو الغَدِ

tom-tom /'tɒmtɒm/ *n* طَبْل (أَطْبال, طُبول)

ton /tʌn/ *n* **1** (in weight) (also **metric ton**) طُنّ (أَطْنان) **2** (AmE) (also **net ton** or **short ton**) [وَحْدة وَزْنٍ تُساوي 2000 رَطْلٍ \ 907 كغ] **3** (BrE) (also **gross ton** or **long ton**) [وَحْدة وَزْنٍ تُساوي 2240 رَطْلاً \ 1016 كغ] **4** (infml) (large amount) **it weighs a ~!** هو ثَقيلٌ جِدًّا!; **~s of people** المَلايين من الناسِ

tone /təʊn/ **A** *n* **1** (of sounds) نَغْمة (نَغَمات); **you need to adjust the ~** تَحْتاجُ إلى ضَبْطِ الصَوْتِ **2** (of voices) نَبْرة, لَهْجة (لَهَجات); **they spoke in angry/serious ~s** تَحَدَّثوا بِلَهْجةٍ غاضِبةٍ \ جادّةٍ; **I didn't like his ~ of voice** لم تُعْجِبْني نَبْرةُ صَوْتِهِ **3** (of letters, meetings) أُسْلوب (أَساليبُ); **to lower/raise the ~ of a conversation** انْحَدَرَ \ تَرَفَّعَ في أُسْلوبِ مُحادَثةٍ; **he set an informal/formal ~ to the meeting** حَدَّدَ أُسْلوباً رَسْميًّا \ غَيْرَ رَسْميٍّ للاجْتِماعِ **4** (of a colour) مَسْحة (مَسَحات); **a blue with warm red ~s** لَوْن أَزْرَق بِهِ مَسَحاتٌ من الأَحْمَرِ الدافِئِ **5** (of a phone) نَغْمة (نَغَمات); **please leave your message after the ~** الرَجاءُ تَرْكُ رِسالةٍ بعد سَماعِ الصُفّارةِ **6** (of the body) صَلابة **7** (interval) فاصِل **8** (in speech) نَبْرة; **a rising/falling ~** نَبْرة صاعِدة \ هابِطة

B *vt* (also **tone up**) قَوّى ‹*one's muscles, thighs*›; **an exercise designed to ~ the thigh muscles** تَدْريب مُخَصَّص لِتَقْوِيةِ عَضَلاتِ الفَخْذَيْنِ

C *vi* (also **tone in**) (to blend) «colours» انْسَجَمَ, تَناغَمَ; **I want everything in the room to ~** أُريدُ أَنْ يَتَناغَمَ كُلُّ شَيْءٍ في الغُرْفةِ; **the carpet ~s beautifully with the wallpaper** تَتَلاءَمُ السَجّادةُ بِشَكْلٍ جَذّابٍ مع وَرَقِ الحائطِ

Phrasal verb **tone down: ~ [sth] down, ~ down [sth]** خَفَّفَ من حِدّة [شَيْءٍ] ‹*colours, a statement*›

tone-deaf /təʊn'dɛf/ *adj* **to be ~** لم تَكُنْ لَهُ أُذُنٌ موسيقيّةٌ

Tonga /'tɒŋgə/ *pr n* تونْجا

tongs /tɒŋz/ *n pl* مِلْقَط (مَلاقِطُ)

tongue /tʌŋ/ *n* **1** (in mouth) لِسان (أَلْسِنة, أَلْسُن); **to stick one's ~ out at sb** أَخْرَجَ لِسانَهُ لِشَخْصٍ **2** (fml) (language) لُغة; **their native ~** لُغَتُهُم الأُمّ \ الأَصْليّة **3** (as food) لِسان (أَلْسِنة, أَلْسُن) **4** (on shoes) لِسان (أَلْسِنة, أَلْسُن)

Idioms **to bite one's tongue** عَضَّ على لِسانِهِ; **to lose/find one's tongue** انْعَقَدَ لِسانُهُ \ انْفَكَّتْ عُقْدةُ لِسانِهِ

tongue-in-cheek /tʌŋɪn'tʃiːk/ **A** *adj* ‹*humour, comment*› ساخِر **B** *adv* **to say sth ~** قالَ شَيْئاً ساخِراً

tongue-tied /'tʌŋtʌɪd/ *adj* ‹*child, interviewee*› مَعْقود اللِسانِ

tongue-twister /'tʌŋtwɪstə/ *n* [جُمْلة فيها تَنافُر الحُروفِ]

tonic /'tɒnɪk/ *n* **1** (also **tonic water**) ماء التونيك (مَشْروب غازيّ) **2** (for patients) مُقَوٍّ (مُقَوِّيات)

tonight /tə'nʌɪt/ **A** *adv* **1** (this evening) ‹*to eat, leave*› اللَيْلَةَ, هذه اللَيْلَةَ; **are you going out ~?** هل سَتَخْرُجُ هذه اللَيْلَةَ؟; **what shall we do ~?** ماذا سَنَفْعَلُ اللَيْلَةَ؟ **2** (this night) ‹*to sleep, rain*› اللَيْلَةَ, هذه اللَيْلَةَ; **it's going to rain ~** سَوْفَ تُمطِرُ اللَيْلَةَ

B *n* اللَيْلة, هذه اللَيْلة; **have you seen ~'s news?** هل شاهَدْتَ أَخْبارَ اللَيْلةِ؟

tonne /tʌn/ *n* طُنّ (أَطْنان)

tonsil /'tɒns(ə)l/ *n* لَوْزة; **to remove sb's ~s** اسْتَأْصَلَ لَوْزَتَيْ شَخْصٍ

tonsillectomy /ˌtɒnsɪ'lɛktəmi/ *n* (*pl* **tonsillectomies**) اسْتِئْصال اللَوْزَتَيْنِ

tonsillitis /ˌtɒnsɪ'lʌɪtɪs/ *n* الْتِهاب اللَوْزَتَيْنِ

too /tuː/ *adv* **1** (also) أَيْضاً, كَذَلِكَ; **'I love you'—'I love you ~'** 'أُحِبُّكَ' — 'وَأَنا أَيْضاً أُحِبُّكَ'; **have you been to India ~?** (like me) هل سافَرْتَ أَنْتَ أَيْضاً إلى الهِنْدِ؟; (as well as other countries) هل سافَرْتَ إلى الهِنْدِ أَيْضاً؟; **she's kind but she's strict ~** هي طَيِّبةٌ وَلَكِنَّها أَيْضاً صارِمةٌ **2** (excessively) أَكْثَر مِمّا يَنْبَغي \ من اللازِمِ; **it's ~ early to leave** الوَقْتُ مُبَكِّرٌ جِدًّا لِلمُغادَرةِ; **the coat is ~ big for him** المِعْطَفُ كَبيرٌ جِدًّا عَلَيْهِ; **~ many/~ few people** عدد كَبير \ قَليل جِدًّا من الناسِ; **I ate ~ much** أَكَلْتُ أَكْثَرَ من اللازِمِ; **he was in ~ much of a hurry to talk** كانَ مُتَعَجِّلاً جِدًّا وَلَمْ يَسْتَطِعِ الكَلامَ; **it was ~ little ~ late** كانَ قَليلاً جِدًّا وَمُتَأَخِّراً جِدًّا **3** (expressing indignation) **'they're here'—'about time ~!'** 'لَقَدْ جاؤوا' — 'وَلَكِنْ مُتَأَخِّرينَ جِدًّا!'; **'I'm sorry'—'I should think so ~!'** 'أَنا آسِفٌ' — 'هذا هو المَفْروضُ!'; **... and in front of your mother ~!** ... وَأَمامَ أُمِّكَ أَيْضاً! **4** (fml) (emphatic: very) جِدًّا; **you're**

~ kind! أَنْتَ طَيِّبٌ جِدًّا!; **they'll be only ~ pleased to help** سَيَكونونَ سُعَداءَ جِدًّا بِتَقْديمِ المُساعَدةِ; **she hasn't been ~ well recently** لم تَكُنْ على ما يُرامُ مُؤَخَّراً; ▸ **all**, ▸ **only** 5 (in negatives) جِدًّا; **we're not ~ thrilled** لَسْنا مُتَحَمِّسينَ جِدًّا; **I'm not ~ sure about that** لَسْتُ واثِقاً تَماماً من ذلك; **'they've arrived'—'none ~ soon!'** 'لَقَدْ وَصَلوا' — 'في آخرِ لَحْظةٍ!'

took /tʊk/ *past tense* ▸ **take**

tool /tuːl/ *n* أداة (أَدَوات), وَسيلة (وَسائِل)

Idiom **to down tools** (BrE) تَوَقَّفَ عن العَمَلِ

toolbar /ˈtuːlbɑː/ *n* شَريط أَدَواتٍ

toolbox /ˈtuːlbɒks/ *n* صُنْدوق أَدَواتٍ

toolkit *n* صُنْدوق أَدَواتٍ

tool shed *n* [مَخْزَن الأَدَواتِ]

tooltip /ˈtuːltɪp/ *n* تَلْميح (إطار مَعْلوماتٍ يَصِفُ العُنْصُرَ الّذي يُشيرُ إلَيْهِ مُؤَشِّرُ الفأرةِ)

toot /tuːt/ **A** *n* (by car) صَفير

B *vt* نَفَخَ (a; نَفْخ), أَطْلَقَ ‹*a horn*›

C *vi* «drivers» نَفَخَ في بوقٍ, أَطْلَقَ بوقاً

tooth /tuːθ/ *n* (*pl* **teeth**) 1 (of person, animal) سِنّ (mf; أَسْنان); **the front/back teeth** الأَسْنان الأَماميّة \ الخَلْفيّة 2 (of a comb, saw) سِنّ (mf; أَسْنان)

Idioms **to be long in the tooth** كَبُرَ في السِّنِّ, وَهَنَ عَظْمُهُ; **to get your teeth into sth** انْكَبَّ على شَيْءٍ, تَحَمَّسَ لِشَيْءٍ; **to lie through your teeth** كَذَبَ في وَضَحِ النَّهارِ

toothache /ˈtuːθeɪk/ *n* أَلَم أَسْنانٍ

toothbrush /ˈtuːθbrʌʃ/ *n* فُرْشاة أَسْنانٍ

tooth decay *n* تَسَوُّس الأَسْنانِ

toothpaste /ˈtuːθpeɪst/ *n* مَعْجون أَسْنانٍ

toothpick /ˈtuːθpɪk/ *n* عود أَسْنانٍ

top /tɒp/ **A** *n* 1 (of a ladder, wall, page) أَعْلى (أَعالٍ); (of a mountain, hill, tower) قِمّة (قِمَم); **at the ~ of the stairs/hill** أَعْلى الدَرَجِ \ التَلِّ; **United are at the ~ of the table** يَتَصَدَّرُ يونايْتِد قائمةَ الدَوْرِيِّ; **eight lines from the ~** ثَمانِية أَسْطُرٍ من أَعْلى 2 (in rankings) قِمّة (قِمَم), صَدارة; **to aim for the ~** سَعى للقِمّةِ; **to be/stay on ~** تَرَبَّعَ على القِمّةِ; **she made it to the ~ of her profession** وَصَلَتْ إلى أَعْلى مَرْكَزٍ في مِهْنَتِها; **to be ~ of the class** كانَ الأَفْضَلَ; **to be at the ~ of the agenda** كانَ في صَدارةِ جَدْوَلِ الأَعْمالِ 3 (of a table, liquid) سَطْح (سُطوح, أَسْطُح), أَعْلى (أَعالٍ); **cut the ~s off the carrots** اقْطَعْ رُؤوسَ الجَزَرِ 4 (cap, lid) غِطاء (أَغْطِية) 5 (garment) [قِطْعة مَلابِسَ نِسائيّةٍ تُغَطّي الجُزْءَ العُلْوِيَّ من الجِسْمِ]; **a sleeveless ~** قَميص بِلا أَكْمامٍ 6 (also **top gear**) سُرْعة قُصْوى; **to be in ~** كانَ يَسيرُ بِأَقْصى سُرْعةٍ 7 (toy) نَحْلة دَوّارة; **to spin a ~** لَفَّ نَحْلةً دَوّارةً

B *adj* 1 (highest) ‹*step, layer, bunk*› أَعْلى (f عُلْيا), عُلْوِيّ; **in the ~ left-hand corner** في الجانِبِ العُلْوِيِّ من ناحِيةِ اليَسارِ; **the ~ notes** النَغَمات الموسيقيّة العُلْيا \ المُرْتَفِعة; **to get ~ marks** حَصَلَ على الدَرَجاتِ النِهائيّةِ 2 (in rankings) ‹*adviser, job*› رَفيع; ‹*authority*› أَعْلى (f عُلْيا); ‹*choice*› مُفَضَّل; **to be in the ~ three** كانَ ضِمْنَ الثَلاثةِ الأَفْضَلِ 3 (maximum) ‹*speed, priority, weight*› أَقْصى (f قُصْوى); **to drive at ~ speed** قادَ بِأَقْصى سُرْعةٍ

C (**on top of**) *prep phr* 1 (located on) فَوْقَ ‹*a hill, cupboard, the fridge*›; **they live on ~ of each other** يَعيشونَ مُتَكَدِّسينَ 2 (in addition to) بالإضافةِ إلى ‹*one's workload, wages, an injury*› 3 (in control of) **to be on ~ of the situation** كانَ مُسَيْطِراً على المَوْقِفِ

D *vt* (**-pp-**) 1 (to head) تَصَدَّرَ, جاءَ في المُقَدِّمةِ ‹*the league, table, list*›; **to ~ the polls** تَصَدَّرَ اسْتِطْلاعاتِ الرَأْيِ; **to ~ the bill** تَرَبَّعَ على العَرْشِ \ القِمّةِ; **unemployment ~ped the agenda** تَصَدَّرَت البِطالةُ جَدْوَلَ الأَعْمالِ 2 (to exceed) «sales, imports» تَخَطّى, تَجاوَزَ ‹*a sum, figure*› 3 (to improve on) تَفَوَّقَ (على) ‹*a performance*›; حَسَّنَ ‹*a story*›; **~ that!** افْعَلْ أَفْضَلَ من ذلك! 4 (to finish off) وُضِعَ على القِمّةِ ‹*a building, tower, hill*›; زَيَّنَ ‹*a cake, dish*›; **a golden dome ~ped the mosque** كانَ المَسْجِدُ تَعْلوهُ قُبّةٌ ذَهَبيّةٌ; **each cake was ~ped with a cherry** كانَتْ كُلُّ كَعْكةٍ مُزَيَّنةً بِحَبّةِ كَرَزٍ

E *v refl* (**-pp-**) (infml) **to ~ oneself** قَتَلَ نَفْسَهُ

Idioms **from top to bottom** من أَعْلاهُ إلى أَسْفَلِهِ; **to search the house from ~ to bottom** فَتَّشَ البَيْتَ من أَعْلاهُ إلى أَسْفَلِهِ; **on top of all this, to top it all** فوق كُلِّ هذا; **on ~ of all this,**

I've just got a huge tax bill وفَوْقَ كُلِّ هذا، جاءَتْني للتوِّ فاتورةُ ضَرائِبَ هائِلةٌ; **to get on top of sb** (to overwhelm) أَرْهَقَ شَخْصاً; (to depress) كانَ فوق احْتِمالِ شَخْصٍ; **to be over the top** (infml) كانَ أَكْثَرَ من اللازِمِ; **to go over the top** (Mil) شَنَّ هُجوماً من فَوْقِ حاجِزٍ; (to go too far) تَجاوَزَ حُدودَ المَعْقولِ

(Phrasal verbs) **top off**: **~ off [sth], ~ [sth] off** خَتَمَ [شَيْئاً] ‹*a meal, weekend*›

• **top up** **A** **to ~ up with fuel** أَضافَ المَزيدَ من الوَقودِ **B** **~ up [sth], ~ [sth] up** (to fill) أَكْمَلَ [شَيْئاً] ‹*the tank, sb's glass*›

topaz /'təʊpaz/ *n* توباز

top hat *n* [قُبَّعة رِجاليّة رَسْميّة]

top-heavy /tɒp'hɛvi/ *adj* ‹*structure, bookcase*› [غَير مُسْتَقِرّ بِسَبَبِ ثِقَلِ أَعلاهُ]

topic /'tɒpɪk/ *n* مَوْضوع (مَواضيعُ, مَوْضوعات)

topical /'tɒpɪk(ə)l/ *adj* ‹*allusion, issue*› حاليّ

topless /'tɒpləs/ *adj* ‹*sunbathing, dancer*› عاري الصَّدْرِ

top-level /,tɒp'lɛv(ə)l/ *adj before n* ‹*talks, meeting*› على مُسْتَوًى عالٍ \ رَفيعٍ

topography /tə'pɒgrəfi/ *n* طُبوغْرافيا

topping /'tɒpɪŋ/ *n* [طَبَقة أَكْلٍ فَوْقيّة]

topple /'tɒp(ə)l/ **A** *vt* **1** (to knock over) قَلَبَ (i; قَلْب) ‹*a statue, skyscraper*› **2** (to overthrow) أَطاحَ, أَسْقَطَ (ب) ‹*a regime, dictator*›

B *vi* (also **topple over**) «*trees, vase*» سَقَطَ, انْقَلَبَ (u; سُقوط, مَسْقَط), وَقَعَ (a; وُقوع)

top-ranking /,tɒp'raŋkɪŋ/ *adj* ‹*official, officer*› ذو رُتْبةٍ عاليةٍ \ مَنْصِب كَبيرٍ

top secret *adj* ‹*document, intelligence*› سِرّيّ للغاية

topsoil /'tɒpsɔɪl/ *n* سَطْح التُّرْبة العُلْويّ

topsy-turvy /,tɒpsɪ'tə:vi/ *adj* (infml) ‹*house, world*› مَقْلوب رَأْساً على عَقِبٍ, في فَوْضى

top-up card /'tɒpʌp ,kɑ:d/ *n* بطاقة شَحْنِ الرَّصيد

torch /tɔ:tʃ/ *n* **1** (BrE) (flashlight) كَشّاف ضَوْئيّ \ كَهْرَبائيّ **2** (with flames) مِشْعَل (مَشاعِلُ)

torchlight /'tɔ:tʃlʌɪt/ *n* ضَوْء مَشاعِلَ

torchlight procession *n* مَسيرة مَشاعِلَ

tore /tɔ:/ *past tense* ▸ **tear¹**

torment **A** /'tɔ:mɛnt/ *n* عَذاب (عَذابات)

B /tɔ:'mɛnt/ *vt* عَذَّبَ ‹*a victim, prisoner*›; **he was ~ed by guilt** عَذَّبَهُ الإحْساسُ بالذَنْبِ

tormentor /tɔ:'mɛntə/ *n* (fml) مُعَذِّب

torn /tɔ:n/ *past participle* ▸ **tear¹**

tornado /tɔ:'neɪdəʊ/ *n* (*pl* **tornadoes** or **tornados**) إعْصار (أَعاصيرُ)

torpedo /tɔ:'pi:dəʊ/ **A** *n* (*pl* **torpedoes**) طورْبيد (طَرابيدُ)

B *vt* (**torpedoes, torpedoing, torpedoed**) **1** (to sink) نَسَفَ (i; نَسْف) ‹*a ship, vessel*› **2** (to ruin) أَحْبَطَ ‹*a plan, mission*›

torpor /'tɔ:pə/ *n* (fml) بَلادة, خُمول

torque /tɔ:k/ *n* عَزْم الدَّوَرانِ

torrent /'tɒrənt/ *n* سَيْل (سُيول), وابِل; **a ~ of abuse** وابِل من الإهاناتِ

torrential /tə'rɛnʃ(ə)l/ *adj* ‹*rain, downpour*› جارِف, غَزير

torrid /'tɒrɪd/ *adj* **1** (fml) (very hot) ‹*heat*› لافِح; ‹*climate*› حارّ **2** (passionate) ‹*affair, tale*› مُلْتَهِب **3** (problematic) ‹*day, time*› مَليء بالمَشاكِلِ

torso /'tɔ:səʊ/ *n* (*pl* **torsos**) جِذْع (أَجْذاع, جُذوع), بَدَن (أَبْدان, أَبْدُن)

tort /tɔ:t/ *n* ضَرَر, إساءة (أَضْرار), مُخالَفة

tortoise /'tɔ:təs/ *n* سُلَحْفاة (سَلاحِفُ)

tortoiseshell /'tɔ:təsʃɛl/ *n* عَظْم ظَهْر السُّلَحْفاةِ

tortuous /'tɔ:tʃʊəs/ *adj* ‹*path, route*› مُلْتَوٍ, مُنْعَرِج

torture /'tɔ:tʃə/ **A** *n* تَعْذيب

B *vt* **1** (physically) عَذَّبَ ‹*a prisoner, a suspect*› **2** (mentally) **to be ~d by guilt/doubt** عَذَّبَهُ الإحْساسُ بالذَنْبِ \ الشكُّ

Tory /'tɔ:ri/ *n* (*pl* **Tories**) مُحافِظ

toss /tɒs/ **A** *vt* **1** (to throw) رَمى, أَلْقى (i; رَمْي, رِماية) ‹*a ball, stick*›; **she ~ed her bags into the corner** أَلْقَتْ حَقائِبَها على الجانِبِ; **he ~ed the grenade into the bunker** أَلْقى القُنْبُلَةَ في المَخْبَأِ; **to ~ a coin** أَجْرى قُرْعةً بالعُمْلةِ; **let's ~ a coin for it** دَعْنا نُجْري قُرْعةً بالعُمْلةِ عَلَيْهِ **2** (to stir) قَلَّبَ ‹*a salad, vegetables*› **3** (to flip) [قَلَبَ بِقَذْفِهِ في الهَواءِ] ‹*a pancake*›

4 (to throw back) دَفَعَ للخَلْفِ ‹*one's head, mane*› 5 (to unseat) «horse» أَسْقَطَ ‹*a rider*› 6 (to shake violently) «wind» هَزَّ (u; هَزّ) ‹*branches, leaves*›

B *vi* 1 (restlessly) «person» تَقَلَّبَ; **the trees ~ed in the wind** اهْتَزَّت الأَشْجارُ مع الريحِ 2 (with a coin) أَجْرى قُرْعةً بالعُمْلةِ; **to ~ to see who will kick-off** أَجْرى قُرْعةً بالعُمْلةِ لِتَحْديدِ من يَبْدَأُ اللَعِبِ

C *n* 1 (throw) رَمْية; **a ~ of the dice** رَمْية زَهْرٍ 2 (of a coin) **to win/lose the ~** كَسَبَ \ خَسِرَ القُرْعةَ; **to decide sth on the ~ of a coin** أَجْرى قُرْعةً بالعُمْلةِ على شَيْءٍ 3 (jerky movement) **with a ~ of the head/of her hair** مع هَزِّ الرَأْسِ \ شَعْرِها

(Idiom) **I don't** *or* **couldn't give a toss** (infml) لا يُهِمُّني أَبداً

(Phrasal verbs) **toss about, toss around**: **~ [sth/sb] around** 1 تَبادَلَ [شَيْئاً] ‹*ideas*›; تَقاذَفَ [شَيْئاً \ شَخْصاً] ‹*a ball*› 2 تَقاذَفَ [شَيْئاً \ شَخْصاً] ‹*a passenger, boat*›

• **toss away**: **~ [sth] away, ~ away [sth]** أَلْقى [شَيْئاً] ‹*rubbish, a paper*›

• **toss back**: **~ [sth] back, ~ back [sth]** (to return) أَعادَ [شَيْئاً] ‹*a ball, one's keys, a fish*›

• **toss off**: **~ [sth] off, ~ off [sth]** (infml) أَعَدَّ [شَيْئاً] على عَجَلٍ ‹*an article, a letter*›

• **toss up** «referee» أَجْرى قُرْعةً بالعُمْلةِ; **to ~ up to decide sth** أَجْرى قُرْعةً بالعُمْلةِ لِيُقَرِّرَ شَيْئاً

tot /tɒt/ *n* 1 (infml) (toddler) طِفْل (أَطْفال) 2 (BrE) (of whisky, rum) جُرْعة (جُرَع, جُرْعات)

(Phrasal verb) **tot up** (BrE): **~ up [sth], ~ [sth] up** جَمَعَ [شَيْئاً] ‹*the figures, bill*›

total /'təʊt(ə)l/ **A** *adj before n* 1 (added together) ‹*cost, amount*› إجْماليّ 2 (complete) ‹*disaster, lack*› كامِل, كُلّيّ (كَمَلة)

B *n* مَجْموع (مَجاميعُ); **we will be ten in ~** سَيَكونُ مَجْموعُنا عَشَرةً

C *vt* (-ll- BrE, -l- AmE) 1 (to add up) جَمَعَ (a; جَمْع) ‹*the figures, column*› 2 (to add up to) بَلَغَ (في مَجْموعِهِ) ‹*a thousand dollars*›

totalitarian /təʊtælə'tɛːriən/ *adj* ‹*regime, state*› شُموليّ, توتاليتاريّ

totalizator /'təʊtəlʌɪzeɪtə/ *n* [ماكينة الرِهانِ المُشْتَرَك]

totally /'təʊt(ə)li/ *adv* ‹*to agree, destroy*› حَتْماً, بِكُلّيَّتِهِ, تَماماً

tote /təʊt/ *vt* (infml) حَمَلَ (i; حَمْل), عَتَلَ (i-u; عَتْل) ‹*a rifle, bag*›

totem /'təʊtəm/ *n* طَوْطَم (رَمْز مُقَدَّس)

totem pole *n* عمود طَوْطَم

totter /'tɒtə/ *vi* «drunk, babies» تَمايَلَ, تَرَنَّحَ

toucan /'tuːk(ə)n/ *n* طوقان

touch /tʌtʃ/ **A** *vt* 1 (to come into contact with) لَمَسَ (i-u; لَمْس), مَسَّ (u; مَسّ, مَسيس) ‹*the cable, handle*›; **he ~ed the wound** لَمَسَ الجُرْحَ; **to ~ sb on the shoulder** لَمَسَ كَتِفَ شخصٍ; **the bed is ~ing the wall** السَريرُ يَلْمِسُ الحائطَ 2 (to affect) أَثَّرَ (على) ‹*a house, painting*›; **the tornado didn't ~ our house** لم يَمُسَّ الإعْصارُ بَيْتَنا; **inflation ~es all sections of society** يُؤَثِّرُ التَضخُّمُ على كُلِّ فِئاتِ المُجْتَمَعِ; **I never ~ed him** لم أَمُسَّهُ بِسوءٍ 3 (to affect emotionally) أَثَّرَتْ, حَرَّكَ المَشاعِرَ, أَثَّرَ; **we were ~ed by their kindness** حَرَّكَ طيبَتُهُمْ فينا; **the sight of the grieving family ~ed us all** مَشْهَدُ الأُسْرةِ المَكْلومةِ مَشاعِرَنا جَميعاً 4 (to consume) تَناوَلَ ‹*alcohol, meat, dairy products*›; **I never ~ spirits** لا أَتناوَلُ المُسْكِراتِ أَبَداً; **you've hardly ~ed your food** لم تَتَناوَلْ إلاّ قَدْراً يَسيراً من طَعامِكَ 5 (infml) (to ask for) **to ~ sb for sth** سَأَلَ شَخْصاً أَنْ يُعْطِيَه شَيْئاً 6 (to equal) ضاهى ‹*a rival, an activity, a product*›; **when it comes to tennis, no one can ~ him** عِنْدَما يَتَعلَّقُ الأَمْرُ بالتِنِس، فَلا يَسْتَطيعُ أَحَدٌ أَنْ يُبارِيهِ 7 (to reach) «prices, temperatures» وَصَلَ (i; وُصول) (إلى) ‹*a level, figure*›; **inflation ~ed 5% last month** وَصَلَ التَضخُّمُ إلى 5٪ الشَهرَ الماضِيَ

B *vi* 1 (to come together) «wires, hands» تَماسَّ, تلامَسَ 2 (with one's hands) لَمَسَ (i-u; لَمْس); **'do not ~'** مَمْنوعٌ اللَمْسُ

C *n* 1 (physical) لَمْسة; **it breaks at the slightest ~** يَنْكَسِرُ من أَبْسَطِ لَمْسةٍ; **the ~ of her hand** لَمْسة يَدِها; **I felt a ~ on my shoulder** شَعَرْتُ بِلَمْسةٍ على كَتِفي 2 [u] (sense) لَمْس; **to be soft/rough to the ~** كانَ ناعِمَ \ خَشِنَ المَلْمَسِ; **I found my way by ~** وَجَدْتُ طَريقي عن طَريقِ التَحَسُّسِ 3 [u] (style) لَمْسة; **he has a delicate/light ~** لَدَيْهِ لَمْسةٌ لَطيفةٌ \ خَفيفةٌ;

he lacks the human ~ يَفْتَقِدُ اللَمْسةَ الإنْسانيّةَ **4** [u] (ability) لَمْسة; **to lose one's ~** فَقَدَ قُدْرَتَهُ على تَحْقيقِ النَجاحِ; **he has the magic/golden ~** لَدَيْهِ لَمْسةٌ سِحْرِيّةٌ **5** (detail) لَمْسة; **to add the finishing ~es to sth** وَضَعَ اللَمَساتِ الأَخيرةَ \ النِهائيّةَ على شَيْءٍ; **that was a nice ~** كانَتْ تِلْكَ لَمْسةٌ \ لَفْتةٌ لَطيفةٌ **6** (small amount) **a ~ of salt** مَسْحة من المِلْحِ; **there was a ~ of sadness in her voice** كانَتْ هُناكَ نَبْرةُ حُزْنٍ في صَوْتِها; **he's got a ~ of flu** أُصيبَ بِبَرْدٍ بَسيطٍ **7** [u] (in contact) **to be/get in ~ with sb** كانَ على اتِّصالٍ \ اتَّصَلَ بِشَخْصٍ; **to be out of ~ with sb** لم يَكُنْ على اتِّصالٍ بِشَخْصٍ; **to lose ~ with sb** انْقَطَعَ الاتِّصالُ بَيْنَهُ وَبَيْنَ شَخْصٍ; **he's out of ~ with reality** هو مَعْزولٌ عن الواقِعِ **8** [u] (non-playing area) خارِجَ المَلْعَبِ; **to go into ~** ذَهَبَ خارِجَ المَلْعَبِ

(Idiom) **to be a soft touch** كانَ رَقيقَ القَلْبِ

(Phrasal verbs) **touch down** **1** «planes» هَبَطَ (i-u; هُبوط) **2** (in rugby) سَجَّلَ مُحاوَلةً

• **touch off**: **~ [sth] off, ~ off [sth]** **1** أَثارَ [شَيْئاً] ‹*a riot, debate*› **2** أَحْدَثَ [شَيْئاً] ‹*a fire, an explosion*›

• **touch on**: **~ on [sth]** تَعَرَّضَ ل [شَيْءٍ] بِشَكْلٍ موجَزٍ ‹*a subject, question*›

• **touch up**: **~ [sth/sb] up, ~ up [sth/sb]** **1** (to repair) أَصْلَحَ [شَيْئاً] ‹*the paintwork*› **2** (to edit) حَسَّنَ [شَيْئاً] ‹*a photograph*› **3** (BrE) (infml) (sexually) لَمَسَ جِسْمَ [شَخْصٍ] ‹*a woman, colleague*›

• **touch upon** ▸ **touch on**

touchdown /ˈtʌtʃdaʊn/ *n* **1** (by an aircraft or by a spaceship) هُبوط **2** (in rugby, American football) هَدَف (أَهْداف)

touched /tʌtʃt/ *adj* **to be/feel ~** تَأَثَّرَ

touching /ˈtʌtʃɪŋ/ *adj* ‹*tribute, gesture*› مُؤَثِّر

touchline /ˈtʌtʃlaɪn/ *n* خطّ التَماسّ

touchpad /ˈtʌtʃpad/ *n* لَوْحة لَمْسيّة, لَوْحة تَحَكُّمٍ باللَمْسِ

touchscreen /ˈtʌtʃskriːn/ *n* شاشة لَمْسٍ; **a ~ computer** كُمْبيوتَر بِشاشةِ لَمْسٍ

touch-tone /ˈtʌtʃtəʊn/ *adj* ‹*telephone, technology*› [بِنَغْمةِ اللَمْسِ]

touch-type /ˈtʌtʃtaɪp/ *vi* «journalists, editors» كَتَبَ باللَمْسِ (ضَرَبَ على الآلةِ الكاتِبةِ دون النَظَرِ إلى المَفاتيحِ)

touchy /ˈtʌtʃi/ *adj* (**touchier**, **touchiest**) **1** (easily offended) ‹*type*› شَديد الحَسّاسيّةِ, سَريع الانْفِعالِ; **to be ~ about sth** كانَ شَديدَ الحَسّاسيّةِ تُجاهَ شَيْءٍ **2** (that may offend) ‹*subject, situation*› حَسّاس, دَقيق

tough /tʌf/ **A** *adj* **1** (difficult) ‹*conditions, question, choice*› صَعْب; **to have a ~ time** عاشَ وَقْتاً عَصيباً; **the exam was very ~** كانَ الامْتِحانُ صَعْباً جِدًّا **2** (severe) ‹*policy, measures, law*› مُتَشَدِّد, صارِم; **to be ~ on crime/gangs** كانَ صارِماً مع الجَريمةِ \ العِصاباتِ; **competition is ~** المُنافَسةُ شَرِسةٌ; **to take a ~ line with sb** أَخَذَ مَوْقِفاً مُتَشَدِّداً مع شَخْصٍ **3** (lawless) ‹*neighbourhood, school*› يَتَّسِمُ بالعُنْفِ; **he's a real ~ guy** هو شَخْصٌ عَنيفٌ حَقًّا **4** (unsentimental) ‹*businessman, policeman*› صَعْب المِراسِ, مُتَشَدِّد, قاسٍ, صارِم; **he's a ~ negotiator** هو مُفاوِضٌ صَعْبُ المِراسِ **5** ‹*meat, steak*› قاسٍ, صَعْب المَضْغِ; **the steak is as ~ as old boots** شَريحةُ اللَحْمِ قاسِيةٌ جِدًّا **6** (durable) ‹*shoes, material*› مَتين **7** (resilient) ‹*child, old pensioner, plant*› قادر على التَحَمُّلِ **8** (infml) (unfortunate) **~ luck!** حَظّ سَيِّءٌ!; **that's really ~!** ذلك حَظٌّ عاثِرٌ حَقًّا!; **it was ~ on them** كانَ ذلك صَعْباً عَلَيْهِمْ **B** *n* (infml) (violent person) شَخْص عُدْوانيّ **C** *excl* (infml) حَظّ عاثِر

(Idiom) **to hang tough on sth** (AmE) (infml) ظَلَّ مُتَشَدِّداً بِخُصوصِ شَيْءٍ

(Phrasal verb) **tough out**: **~ [sth] out** (infml) واجَهَ [شَيْئاً] بِإصْرارٍ ‹*a crisis, situation*›

toughen /ˈtʌf(ə)n/ *vt* **1** (to strengthen) قَوّى ‹*glass*›; خَشَّنَ ‹*skin*› **2** (also **toughen up**) (to make more mature) قَوّى ‹*a child*› **3** (also **toughen up**) (to make stricter) شَدَّدَ ‹*a law, penalty*›

toupee /ˈtuːpeɪ/ *n* شَعْر مُسْتَعار (لِلرِجالِ)

tour /tʊə, tɔː/ **A** *n* **1** (around a country) جَوْلة; **a bus *or* coach ~** جَوْلة بالحافِلةِ; **to go on a ~ of Europe/China** ذَهَبَ في جَوْلةٍ في أوروبّا \ الصين **2** (of a town) جَوْلة (سِياحيّة) **3** (of a building) زِيارة, جَوْلة; **a ~ of inspection** جَوْلة تَفْتيشٍ; **we went on a ~ of the factory/mine** ذَهَبْنا في زِيارةٍ إلى المَصْنَعِ \ المَنْجَمِ **4** (by performers, teams) جَوْلة; **a concert/lecture ~**

جَوْلة لِإلْقاءِ مُحاضَراتٍ \ لِإقامةِ حَفَلاتٍ موسيقيّةٍ; **to be/go on ~** كانَ \ ذَهَبَ في جَوْلةٍ **5** (also **tour of duty**) مُهِمّة عَمَلٍ

B *vt* **1** «holidaymakers, visitors» قامَ بِجَوْلةٍ سِياحيّةٍ في ‹*a country, city*› **2** زارَ (u; زَوْر, زِيارة) ‹*a castle, factory*›

3 «team, orchestra» قامَ بِجَوْلةٍ في ‹*a country, continent*›

4 «exhibition, show» تَجَوَّلَ (في), جالَ (u; جَوْل), جابَ (u; جَوْب) ‹*a country, continent*›

C *vi* **1** «family» قامَ بِجَوْلةٍ سِياحيّةٍ **2** «performers, team, show» تَجَوَّلَ

tour guide *n* دَليل سِياحيّ

touring car *n* سَيّارة سِياحيّة

tourism /ˈtʊəriz(ə)m, ˈtɔːriz(ə)m/ *n* سِياحة

tourist /ˈtʊərɪst, ˈtɔːrɪst/ *n* **1** (traveller) سائِح (سُيّاح, سائِحونَ)

2 (also **tourist class**) (cheapest class) دَرَجة سِياحيّة

tourist industry *n* (**the tourist industry**) القِطاع السِياحيّ

tourist trap *n* (infml) [مَكان يَسْتَغِلُّ السُيّاحَ]

touristy /ˈtʊərɪsti, ˈtɔːrɪsti/ *adj* (infml) ‹*spot, beach*› سِياحيّ

tournament /ˈtɔːnəmənt/ *n* بُطولة

tourniquet /ˈtʊənɪkeɪ/ *n* [ضِمادة لِوَقْفِ النَزيفِ]

tousle /ˈtaʊz(ə)l/ *vt* نَكَشَ (u; نَكْش), شَعَّثَ ‹*sb's hair*›

tousled /ˈtaʊzəld/ *adj* ‹*hair*› مَنْكوش; ‹*bedclothes*› مُبَعْثَر

tout /taʊt/ **A** *vt* دَلَّلَ (على) ‹*products, wares*›

B *vi* **to ~ for business** اِجْتَذَبَ الزَبائِنَ

C *n* (also **ticket tout**) (BrE) [بائِع التَذاكِرِ بالسوقِ السَوْداءِ]

tow /təʊ/ **A** *vt* جَرَّ (u; جَرّ), سَحَبَ (a; سَحْب), قَطَرَ (u; قَطْر) ‹*a car, trailer*›; **the car was ~ed away** سُحِبَت السَيّارةُ

B *n* جَرّ, قَطْر, سَحْب; **to give sb a ~** سَحَبَ \ جَرَّ (سَيّارة) شَخْصٍ; **I had three children in ~** كانَ مَعي ثَلاثةُ أطْفالٍ

towards (BrE) /təˈwɔːdz/, **toward** (AmE) /təwɔːd/ *prep*

1 (to) نَحْوَ, إلى; **he was standing with his back ~ me** كانَ واقِفاً خَلْفَهُ إلَيَّ **2** (regarding) تُجاهَ, نَحْوَ; **his behaviour ~ the female employees** تَصَرُّفُهُ نَحْوَ المُوَظَّفاتِ **3** (as a contribution) مِن أجْلِ, لِ; **they gave me £200 ~ it** مَنَحوني 200 جُنَيْهٍ مِن أجْلِهِ **4** (near) قُرْبَ, عِنْدَ, نَحْوَ; **~ the end of his life** نَحْوَ نِهايةِ حَياتِهِ

tow bar *n* قَضيب قَطْرٍ

towel /ˈtaʊəl/ **A** *n* فوطة (فُوَط), مِنْشَفة (مَناشِفُ)

B *vt* (**-ll-** BrE, **-l-** AmE) جَفَّفَ, نَشَّفَ ‹*one's hair, body*›

towelling (BrE), **toweling** (AmE) /ˈtaʊəlɪŋ/ *n* قُماش الفُوَطِ

towel rail *n* فَوّاطة

tower /ˈtaʊə/ **A** *n* بُرْج (بُروج, أبْراج)

B *vi* **to ~ above** *or* **over sth** «cliffs, mountains» عَلا شَيْئاً; **he ~s over his mother** هو أطْوَلُ من أُمِّهِ بِكَثيرٍ

tower block *n* (BrE) عِمارة شاهِقة

towering /ˈtaʊərɪŋ/ *adj* **1** ‹*tree, building*› شاهِق **2** (important) ‹*figure, personality*› مُهِمّ, مُمَيَّز; ‹*achievement*› ساحِق

towline /ˈtəʊlʌɪn/ *n* (Aut) ▸ **tow rope**

town /taʊn/ *n* بَلْدة; **to go into ~** ذَهَبَ إلى وَسَطِ المَدينةِ

(Idioms) **a night on the town** (infml) سَهْرة في المَدينةِ; **to go to town on sth** (infml) عَمِلَ بِجِدٍّ على شَيْءٍ

town centre (BrE), **town center** (AmE) *n* وَسَط بَلْدةٍ \ مَدينةٍ

town council *n* (in the UK) مَجْلِس بَلَديّ

town hall *n* دار بَلَديّة, قَصْر بَلَديّ, قَصْر مَدينةٍ

town house *n* **1** (urban) بَيْت (في مَدينةٍ) **2** (attached) [بَيْت في صَفٍّ من البُيوتِ المُتَلاصِقة]

town planner *n* مُخَطِّط مُدُنٍ

town planning *n* تَخْطيط مُدُنٍ

township /ˈtaʊnʃɪp/ *n* **1** (formerly, in South Africa) [حَيّ \ بَلْدة السودِ] **2** (in Australia, New Zealand) ضَيْعة (ضِياع)

towpath /ˈtəʊpɑːθ/ *n* [طَريق مُحاذٍ لِضِفّةِ نَهْرٍ \ قَناةٍ]

tow rope *n* حَبْل سَحْبٍ \ قَطْرٍ

tow truck *n* شاحِنة رافِعة

toxaemia (BrE), **toxemia** (AmE) /tɒkˈsiːmɪə/ *n* تَسَمُّم الدَمِ

toxic /ˈtɒksɪk/ *adj* **1** (Ecol) ‹*waste, chemical*› سامّ **2** (Fin) ‹*debt, assets*› خَطير

toxicity /tɒkˈsɪsəti/ *n* سُمّيّة

toxin /ˈtɒksɪn/ *n* مادّة سامّة

toxoplasmosis /ˌtɒksəʊplazˈməʊsɪs/ *n* داء المُقَوَّساتِ

toy /tɔɪ/ **A** *n* لُعْبة (لُعَب)

B *vi* **to ~ with the idea of doing sth** «person» فَكَّرَ في فِعْلِ شَيْءٍ; **to ~ with a pen** «person, fingers» عَبِثَ بِقَلَمٍ

C *adj* **1** ‹*gun, car*› لُعْبة **2** (miniature) ‹*dog, poodle*› [صَغير الحَجْمِ]

toyshop /ˈtɔɪʃɒp/ *n* مَحَلّ أَلْعابٍ

trace /treɪs/ **A** *vt* **1** (to locate) اكْتَشَفَ \ حَدَّدَ المَكانَ ‹*a fugitive, phone call*›; **they ~d him to an address in Doha** حَدَّدوا مَوْقِعَهُ في مَكانٍ في الدوحةِ **2** (to uncover) تَتَبَّعَ ‹*the history, development, one's ancestry*› **3** (to monitor) تَتَبَّعَ ‹*an order, the movements*› **4** (to copy) نَسَخَ (a; نَسْخ), شَفَّ (i; شُفوف, شَفيف), اسْتَشَفَّ ‹*a map, drawing*› **5** (to draw) رَسَمَ (u; رَسْم) ‹*a line, pattern*›

B *n* **1** (sign) أَثَر (آثار); **they found no ~ of him/the money** لَم يَجِدوا أَثَراً لَهُ \ للمالِ; **to disappear without ~** اخْتَفَى دون أَثَرٍ **2** (of a chemical, drug) أَثَر (آثار) **3** (of irony, an accent, a smile) عَلامة (عَلامات, عَلائِمُ), أَثَر (آثار)

(Phrasal verb) **trace back**: **~ [sth] back, ~ back [sth]** تَتَبَّعَ [شَيْئاً] ‹*one's ancestry, origins*›

tracer /ˈtreɪsə/ *n* **1** (also **tracer bullet**) طَلْقة كاشِفة **2** (in medicine) كاشِف (كَشَفة)

tracheotomy /ˌtrakɪˈɒtəmi/ *n* (*pl* **tracheotomies**) ثَقْب القَصَبةِ الهَوائيّةِ

tracing paper /ˈtreɪsɪŋ ˌpeɪpə/ *n* وَرَق شَفّاف

track /trak/ **A** *n* **1** (animal's, a person's) أَثَر سَيْرٍ \ أَقْدامٍ **2** (of an animal, a person) آثار أَقْدامٍ; (of a vehicle) آثار سَيْرٍ; **to keep ~ of sb's movements/progress** تَتَبَّعَ تَحَرُّكاتِ \ تَقَدُّمَ شَخْصٍ; **keep ~ of what you spend** سَجِّل ما تُنْفِقُهُ; **to lose ~ of sth** لَم يَتَمَكَّنْ من مُتابَعةِ شَيْءٍ; **to cover one's ~s** أَخْفى آثارَهُ; **we'd better make ~s** من الأَفْضَلِ أَنْ نَرْحَلَ; **to stop (dead) in one's ~s** تَوَقَّفَ مُتَسَمِّراً في مَكانِهِ **3** (course of a storm, missile) مَسار (مَسارات) **4** (path, road) مَسار (مَسارات), مَمَرّ (مَمَرّات), مَسْلَك (مَسالِكُ), طَريق (mf; طُرُق, طُرُقات); **she helped me get back on ~** ساعَدَتْني في العَوْدةِ إلى المَسارِ الصَحيحِ; **to be on the right/wrong ~** كانَ يَسيرُ على الطَريقِ الصَحيحِ \ الخَطأِ **5** (for racing) مِضْمار (مَضاميرُ); **motor-racing ~** (BrE) مِضْمار سِباقِ السَيّاراتِ **6** [u] (track events) سِباقات المِضْمارِ; **~ and field** سِباقات المِضْمارِ والمَيْدانِ **7** (railway line) خَطّ (خُطوط) **8** (song) أُغْنيّة (أَغانيُّ); **the title ~** الأُغْنيّة الرَئيسيّة **9** (of a tank) جَنْزير (جَنازيرُ) **10** (AmE) (ability group) مُسْتَوًى (مُسْتَوَيات); **the first ~** المُسْتَوى الأَوَّلُ

B *vt* **1** اقْتَفى الأَثَرَ, تَعَقَّبَ ‹*a person, an animal*›; **to ~ sb's movements** تَتَبَّعَ تَحَرُّكاتِ شَخْصٍ **2** تَتَبَّعَ ‹*a missile, storm*› **3** تابَعَ, راقَبَ ‹*the progress, performance*›

(Phrasal verb) **track down**: **~ [sb/sth] down, ~ down [sb/sth]** عَثَرَ على [شَخْصٍ \ شَيْءٍ] ‹*the killer, owner, a copy*›

tracker /ˈtrakə/ *n* **1** مُطارِد, مُلاحِق **2** (also **tracker fund**) [صُنْدوق يَتْبَعُ مَسارَ مُؤَشِّرٍ]

tracker dog *n* كَلْب بوليسيّ, كَلْب إِثْرٍ

track event *n* سِباق مِضْمارٍ

tracking /ˈtrakɪŋ/ *n* **1** (of vehicles, animals) تَعَقُّب **2** (AmE) (of pupils) [تَقْسيم تَلاميذَ حَسَبَ القُدُراتِ]

track record *n* سِجِل إِنْجازاتٍ

track shoe *n* حِذاء جَرْيٍ (ذو مَساميرَ)

tracksuit /ˈtraksuːt/ *n* بَدْلة رِياضيّة

tract /trakt/ *n* **1** (of land) بُقْعة, قِطْعة (أَرْضٍ) **2** (in the body) قَناة (قَنَوات), مَجْرًى (مَجارٍ, مَجْرَيات) **3** (pamphlet) نُبْذة (نُبَذ)

traction /ˈtrakʃ(ə)n/ *n* **1** (motive power) جَرّ **2** (on limbs, muscles) شَدّ **3** (grip) احْتِكاك الْتِصاقيّ

tractor /ˈtraktə/ *n* جَرّار (جَرّارات)

tractor trailer *n* (AmE) شاحِنة مَقْطورة

trade /treɪd/ **A** *n* **1** [u] (activity) تِجارة; **~ is bad/good** حَرَكةُ التِجارةِ سَيِّئةٌ \ جَيِّدةٌ; **to do a good ~ in soft drinks** أَدارَ تِجارةً جَيِّدةً في المَشْروباتِ الغازيّةِ **2** [u] (sector of industry) تِجارة; **the motor/book ~** تِجارة السَيّاراتِ \ الكُتُبِ **3** [u] (profession) مِهْنة, حِرْفة; **he's a carpenter by ~** حِرْفَتُهُ النِجارةُ; **to practise/learn a ~** مارَسَ \ تَعَلَّمَ حِرْفةً **4** (transaction) تَعامُل **5** (AmE) (of a player) بَيْع (بُيوع, بُيوعات)

B *vt* **1** (in buying and selling) تاجَرَ (في) ‹*products, commodities, stocks*›; **the two sides ~d hostages** تَبادَلَ الجانِبانِ الرَهائِنَ **2** (to exchange) تَبادَلَ ‹*insults, blows*› **3** (AmE) (to sell) باعَ (i; بَيْع, مَبيع) ‹*a player*›

C *vi* **1** (to buy and sell) «businesses, firms» تاجَرَ; **to ~ in commodities** تاجَرَ في السِلَعِ; **to ~ at a profit/loss** رَبِحَ \ خَسِرَ في تِجارَتِهِ **2** (on financial markets) «stocks, commodities» تَمَّ تَداوُلُهُ; **Saudi Arabian crude oil was trading at a high price** تَمَّ تَداوُلُ النَفْطِ الخام من المَمْلَكَةِ السعوديّةِ بِسِعْرٍ مُرْتَفِعٍ

Phrasal verbs **trade in**: **1** **~ [sth] in, ~ in [sth]** اسْتَبْدَلَ [شَيْئاً] ‹a car, computer› **2** **~ in [sth]** تاجَرَ في [شَيْءٍ] ‹oil futures, foreign exchange›

• **trade off**: **~ [sth] off against sth, ~ off [sth] against sth** وازَنَ بين [شَيْءٍ] وَشَيْءٍ ‹the advantages, profits and losses›

• **trade up** (AmE) ▸ **trade in**

trade agreement *n* مُعاهَدة تِجاريّة

trade deficit *n* عَجْز تجاريّ

trade fair *n* مَعْرِض تِجاريّ

trade-in /'treɪdɪn/ *n* اسْتِبْدال (اسْتِبْدالات)

trade journal *n* مَجَلّة مُتَخَصِّصة (عِلْميّة أو مِهْنيّة)

trademark /'treɪdmɑːk/ *n* **1** (name, symbol) عَلامة تِجاريّة **2** (distinctive characteristic) عَلامة مُمَيِّزة

trade name *n* اسْم تِجاريّ

trade-off /'treɪdɒf/ *n* حَلّ وَسَط

trader /'treɪdə/ *n* تاجر (تجار ,تُجّار)

trade route *n* طَريق تِجاري ,قَناة تِجاريّة

trade secret *n* سِرّ تِجاريّ

tradesman /'treɪdzmən/ *n* (*pl* **-men**) حِرَفيّ

Trades Union Congress *n* (in UK) [مُنَظّمة بريطانيّة للنِقابات]

trade union *n* نِقابة

trade union member *n* عُضْو نِقابة

trading /'treɪdɪŋ/ *n* تِجارة

trading estate *n* (BrE) مِنْطَقة صِناعيّة

tradition /trə'dɪʃ(ə)n/ *n* تَقْليد (تَقاليد); **to keep a ~** حافَظَ على تَقْليدٍ

traditional /trə'dɪʃ(ə)n(ə)l/ *adj* ‹music, method› تَقْليديّ

traditionalism /trə'dɪʃ(ə)nəlɪz(ə)m/ *n* تَقْليديّة

traditionalist /trə'dɪʃ(ə)nəlɪst/ *n, adj* تَقْليديّ

traditionally /trə'dɪʃ(ə)n(ə)li/ *adv* ‹to use, celebrate› على نَحْوٍ تَقْليديٍّ ,تَقْليديًّا

traffic /'trafɪk/ **A** *n* **1** (volume of vehicles) حَرَكة المُرورِ ,مرور; **to direct the ~** نَظَّمَ المُرورَ; **heavy/light ~** حَرَكة مُرورٍ كَثيفة \ خَفيفة; **~ into the city** حَرَكة المُرورِ إلى المَدينةِ; **the volume of ~ has doubled** تَضاعَفَ حَجْمُ حَرَكةِ المُرورِ **2** (of aircraft, ships, etc) حَرَكة; **freight/passenger ~ has increased/decreased** زادَتْ \ قَلَّتْ حَرَكةُ الشَحْنِ \ المُسافِرينَ **3** (in drugs, arms) تِجارة; **~ in drugs and arms** تجارة في المُخَدِّراتِ والأَسْلِحةِ **4** (Tel) حَرَكة

B *vi* (**-ck-**) **to ~ in drugs/arms** تاجَرَ في المُخَدِّراتِ \ الأَسْلِحةِ

traffic accident *n* حادث سَيْرٍ \ مُروريّ

traffic calming *n* إبْطاء حَرَكة السَيْرِ \ المُرورِ

traffic circle *n* (AmE) مَمَرّ دائريّ ,دَوَران ,دَوّار (دَوّارات) (Gulf), صينيّة (صَوانيّ) (Egypt)

traffic cone *n* مَخْروط مُرورٍ

traffic island *n* [مَكان مُرْتَفِع في وَسَطِ الشارعِ]

traffic jam *n* اخْتِناق مُروريّ

trafficker /'trafɪkə/ *n* مُهَرِّب

traffic lights *n* إشارات ضَوْئيّة \ المُرورِ

traffic warden *n* (BrE) شُرْطيّ مُرورٍ \ سَيْرٍ

tragedy /'tradʒɪdi/ *n* (*pl* **tragedies**) **1** (disaster) مَأْساة (مَآسٍ) **2** (play) تراجيديا **3** [u] (genre) تْراجيدِيا

tragic /'tradʒɪk/ *adj* ‹death, consequences› فاجِع ,مَأْساويّ

tragically /'tradʒɪkli/ *adv* ‹to die, end› بِشَكْلٍ مَأْساويٍّ \ فاجِعٍ

tragicomedy /,tradʒɪ'kɒmɪdi/ *n* الدْراما التْراجيديّة الكوميديّة

trail /treɪl/ **A** *n* **1** (path) مَمَرّ (مَمَرّات) ,دَرْب (دُروب ,دِراب); **he spent the day on the campaign ~** قَضى اليَوْمَ في جَوْلةٍ انْتِخابيّةٍ **2** (of blood, slime) أَثَر (آثار); (of smoke) ذَيْل (ذُيول, أَذْيال); **the hurricane left a ~ of destruction in its wake** خَلَّفَ الإعْصارُ وَراءَهُ دَماراً واسِعاً **3** (left by suspect, animal) أَثَر (آثار); **to pick up/lose sb's ~** تَقَفّى \ فَقَدَ أَثَرَ شَخْصٍ; **the police are hot on his ~** تَتَعَقَّبُهُ الشُرْطةُ عن كَثَبٍ

B *vt* **1** (to drag along) جَرَّ وَراءَهُ; **she was ~ing her scarf along the ground** كانَتْ تَجُرُّ وِشاحَها وَراءَها على الأَرْضِ **2** (to follow) اقْتَفى الأَثَرَ ,تَتَبَّعَ ,تَعَقَّبَ ‹an animal, a person›

3 (in a game, opinion poll) تَأَخَّرَ (عن) ‹*the leader, one's opponent*›; **the Liberals are ~ing the Progressives in the polls** جاءَ الليبراليّونَ مُتأَخِّرين عن التقدُّميّينَ في اسْتِطْلاعاتِ الرَأْيِ

C *vi* 1 «scarf, robes» انْجَرَّ 2 «plants» نَما مُتَّجِهاً نحو 3 (to walk slowly) مَشى بِتَثاقُلٍ \ مُتَباطِئاً; **the children ~ed along behind their mother** مَشى الأَطْفالُ بِتَثاقُلٍ خلف أُمِّهِمْ 4 (to be losing) كانَ مُتَأَخِّراً; **we were ~ing 3 -1 at half-time** كُنّا مُتَأَخِّرينَ 3–1 في الشَوْطِ الأَوَّلِ

(Phrasal verb) **trail away, trail off** «voice, speaker» خَفَتَ (u; خُفوت), تَلاشى

trail bike *n* دَرّاجة نارِيّة (خَفيفة للطُرُقِ الوَعْرة)

trailblazer /'treɪlbleɪzə/ *n* رائِد

trailer /'treɪlə/ *n* 1 (for towing) مَقْطورة 2 (AmE) (towed by a car) مَقْطورة سَكَنيّة, كَرَفان 3 (for a film) تْرايْلَر (فيلْم تَرْويجيّ قصير)

train /treɪn/ **A** *vt* 1 دَرَّبَ ‹*staff, students, soldiers*›; **to ~ sb for sth/to do sth** دَرَّبَ شخصاً على شَيْءٍ \ فِعْلِ شَيْءٍ; **they are ~ed in the use of firearms/fire equipment** هُم مُدَرَّبون على اسْتِخْدامِ الأَسْلِحةِ النارِيّةِ \ مُعِدّاتِ الحَريقِ; **they are ~ing as/to be pilots** يَتَدَرَّبونَ لِيُصْبِحوا طَيّارينَ 2 دَرَّبَ ‹*an animal*› 3 (in sport) مَرَّنَ, دَرَّبَ ‹*a horse, team*› 4 (to aim) صَوَّبَ, وَجَّهَ ‹*a gun, binoculars*›; **she ~ed the gun on him** صَوَّبَت السِلاحَ نَحْوَهُ 5 وَجَّهَ النُموَّ الناريَّ ‹*a plant, tree*›

B *vi* 1 (professionally) «students» تَأَهَّلَ, تَدَرَّبَ; **he is ~ing as a/to be a doctor** يَتَأَهَّلُ لِيُصْبِحَ طَبيباً 2 (in sport) «team, athletes» تَمَرَّنَ, تَدَرَّبَ

C *n* 1 (locomotive) قِطار (قِطارات, قُطُر, قُطُرات); **the ~ to London, the London ~** القِطار المُتَّجِه إلى لَنْدَن; **to travel/go by ~** سافَرَ \ ذَهَبَ بالقِطارِ; **I came back/went out on the ~** عُدْتُ \ ذَهَبْتُ بالقِطارِ; **the fast/slow ~ to Alexandria** القِطار السَريع \ البَطيء إلى الإسْكَنْدَرِيّةِ 2 (fml) (sequence) تَتابُع, تَسَلْسُل; **he interrupted my ~ of thought** قَطَعَ حَبْلَ أَفْكاري; **the war brought famine in its ~** حَمَلَت الحَرْبُ مَعَها المَجاعةَ 3 (of camels, mules, vehicles) قافِلة (قَوافِل) 4 (progress, motion) **to set a process in ~** وَضَعَ عَمَليّةً على بِدايةِ الطَريقِ 5 (of a wedding dress) ذَيْل (ذُيول, أَذْيال)

train driver *n* سائِق قِطارٍ

trained /treɪnd/ *adj* 1 ‹*staff, worker*› مُدَرَّب; **a highly ~ workforce** قُوًى عامِلة على دَرَجةٍ عالِيةٍ من التَدْريبِ 2 ‹*nurse, teacher, paramedic*› مُؤَهَّل 3 ‹*animal*› مُدَرَّب 4 ‹*eye, ear, voice*› مُدَرَّب

trainee /treɪ'niː/ *n* مُتَدَرِّب

trainer /'treɪnə/ *n* 1 (person) مُدَرِّب 2 (BrE) (shoe) حِذاء رِياضةٍ

training /'treɪnɪŋ/ *n* 1 (of staff) تَدْريب; **to give ~ in technical skills** أَعْطى تَدْريباً على المَهاراتِ الفَنّيّةِ 2 (in sport) تَدْريب (تَدْريبات), تَمْرين (تَمارينُ, تَمْرينات); **to be in ~ for sth** كانَ يَتَمَرَّنُ من أَجْلِ شَيْءٍ; **to be out of ~** كانَ مُتَوَقِّفاً عن التَمْرينِ

training college *n* (BrE) دار, مَعْهَد تَكْوينِ \ إِعْدادِ المُعَلِّمينَ المُعَلِّمينَ

trainspotter /'treɪnspɒtə/ *n* (BrE) [هاوي مُراقَبةِ القِطاراتِ]

traipse /treɪps/ *vi* [مَشى مُتَثاقِلاً]

trait /treɪt, treɪ/ *n* سِمة, صِفة, ميزة

traitor /'treɪtə/ *n* خائِن (خَوَنة, خُوّان); **to turn ~** أَصْبَحَ خائِناً

trajectory /trə'dʒekt(ə)ri/ *n* (*pl* **trajectories**) مَسار (مَسارات)

tram /tram/ *n* (BrE) تْرام (تْرامات)

tramp /tramp/ **A** *vi* مَشى مُتَثاقِلاً

B *n* مُتَشَرِّد

trample /'tramp(ə)l/ **A** *vt* داسَ (u; دَوْس), على, سَحَقَ (a; سَحْق) ‹*grass, plants*›; **he was ~d to death** سُحِقَ حتّى المَوْتِ

B *vi* **to ~ on sth** داسَ على شَيْءٍ

trampoline /'trampəliːn/ *n* تْرامْبولين

trance /trɑːns/ *n* شِبْه غَيْبوبةٍ

tranquil /'traŋkwɪl/ *adj* ‹*setting, waters*› ساكِن, هادِئ

tranquillize, -ise (BrE), **tranquilize** (AmE) /'traŋkwɪlʌɪz/ *vt* هَدَّأَ ‹*an animal, a patient*›

tranquillizer, -iser (BrE) /'traŋkwɪlʌɪzə/ *n* مُهَدِّئ (مُهَدِّئات)

transaction /tran'zakʃ(ə)n/ *n* صَفْقة (صَفَقات), مُعامَلة

transatlantic /tranzət'lantɪk/ *adj* ‹*flight, relations*› عَبْرَ الأَطْلَسيِّ

transcend /tran'send/ *vt* 1 (to go beyond) تَجاوَزَ, فاقَ (u; فَوْق, فَواق) ‹*boundaries, limits*› 2 (to overcome) تَعَدّى, تَجاوَزَ ‹*barriers, limitations*›

transcribe /tran'skrʌɪb/ *vt* نَقَلَ (u; نَقْل), سَجَّلَ, دَوَّنَ *‹an interview, a tape›*

transcript /'transkrɪpt/ *n* نُسْخة (نُسَخ)

transcription /tran'skrɪpʃ(ə)n/ *n* (P&P) تَدْوين, نَقْل

transfer **A** /trans'fəː/ *vt* (-rr-) **1** (to move) نَقَلَ (u; نَقْل) *‹an employee, a student, production›*; **to ~ production from Europe to Asia** نَقَلَ الإنْتاجَ من أوروبّا إلى آسِيا; **the prisoners were ~red to a more secure jail** نُقِلَ السَجَناءُ إلى سِجْنٍ مُؤَمَّنٍ بِشَكْلٍ أَفْضَلَ **2** (between clubs) نَقَلَ (u; نَقْل) *‹a player›* **3** (to copy) نَقَلَ (u; نَقْل) *‹data, information›*; **to ~ data between IT systems** نَقَلَ البَياناتِ بين أَنْظِمةِ تِقْنِيّةِ المَعْلوماتِ; **it's easy to ~ images from palmtop to desktop** من السَهْلِ نَقْلُ الصُوَرِ من الحاسوبِ الكَفّيِّ إلى حاسوبِ سَطْحِ المَكْتَبِ **4** (to transmit) تَنازَلَ (عن) *‹ownership, a property›*; حَوَّلَ *‹money›*; **he's ~red his wealth/property to his children** تَنازَلَ عن ثَرْوَتِهِ \ مُمْتَلَكاتِهِ لِأَبْنائِهِ; **to ~ $5,000 to a savings account** حَوَّلَ 5000 دولار إلى حِسابِ تَوْفيرٍ **5** (to redirect) حَوَّلَ *‹a call›*

B /trans'fəː/ *vi* (-rr-) **1** (to relocate) «employees, players, civil servants» اِنْتَقَلَ; **I'm ~ring to the Boston branch** سَأَنْتَقِلُ إلى فَرْعِ بوسْطُن; **the play will ~ from Broadway to the West End** سَتَنْتَقِلُ المَسْرَحيّةُ من بْرودْواي إلى ويسْت إنْد **2** «passengers» غَيَّرَ **3** (to change courses) **to ~ from microbiology to medicine** غَيَّرَ اخْتِصاصَهُ من الأَحْياءِ الدَقيقةِ إلى الطِبِّ; (to change institutions) **to ~ from Bristol to York** انْتَقَلَ من جامِعةِ بْرِيسْتول إلى جامِعةِ يورْك

C /'transfəː/ *n* **1** (of heat, skills, power) نَقْل; **the ~ of data from one system to another** نَقْل البَياناتِ من جِهازٍ إلى آخَرَ **2** (of employees, players) نَقْل; **he's on temporary ~ from the ministry of transport** هو مَنْقولٌ بِشَكْلٍ مُؤَقَّتٍ من وِزارةِ المُواصَلاتِ; **Jones has applied for a ~** قَدَّمَ جونز طَلَباً بِنَقْلِهِ **3** (of funds) تَحْويل (تَحْويلات); **the ~ of funds between accounts/banks** تَحْويل الأَمْوالِ بين الحِساباتِ \ البُنوكِ **4** (of assets, property) نَقْل مِلْكيّةٍ; **the ~ of the car to the new owner** نَقْل مِلْكيّةِ السَيّارةِ إلى المالِكِ الجَديدِ **5** (BrE) (to paper, china, etc) مُلْصَق (مُلْصَقات) **6** (between places) انْتِقال (انْتِقالات); **all ~s included** شامِل جَميعِ الانْتِقالاتِ **7** (AmE) (student) طالِب مُحَوَّل \ مَنْقول **8** (AmE) (ticket) تَذْكِرة تَحْويلٍ (تَذْكِرة صالِحة للانْتِقالِ من وَسيلةِ مُواصَلاتٍ إلى أُخرى)

transferable /trans'fəːrəb(ə)l/ *adj* *‹skills, assets, vote›* قابِل للتَحْويلِ; **not ~** غَيْر قابِلٍ للتَحْويلِ

transfix /trans'fɪks/ *vt* «sight, beauty» فَتَنَ (i; فُتون, فَتْن), صَعَقَ (a; صَعْق) *‹audiences, viewers›*

transfixed /trans'fɪkst/ *adj* مَذْهول, مَفْتون, مَصْعوق; **to be ~ with terror** ماتَ خَوْفاً

transform /trans'fɔːm/ *vt* حَوَّلَ *‹sb's life, society›*; **to ~ sth into sth** حَوَّلَ شَيْئاً إلى شَيْءٍ

transformation /transfə'meɪʃ(ə)n/ *n* تَحْويل (تَحْويلات), تَغْيير (تَغْييرات)

transformer /trans'fɔːmə/ *n* مُحَوِّل (مُحَوِّلات)

transfuse /trans'fjuːz/ *vt* نَقَلَ (u; نَقْل) *‹blood, plasma›*

transfusion /trans'fjuːʒ(ə)n/ *n* نَقْل (الدم)

transgender /tranz'dʒɛndə/, **transgendered** /tranz'dʒɛndəd/ *adj* *‹person, issue›* مُتَحَوِّل جِنْسيّاً

transgenic /tranz'dʒɛnɪk/ *adj* *‹plant, animal›* طافِر

transgress /tranz'grɛs/ *vt* (fml) خَرَجَ (u; خُروج; عَلى), خالَفَ, تَجاوَزَ *‹a law, rule, limits›*

transient /'tranzɪənt/ *adj* *‹population, effect›* زائِل, مُؤَقَّت, عابِر

transistor /tran'zɪstə, tran'sɪstə/ *n* **1** (semiconductor) تَرَنْزِسْتُر **2** (also **transistor radio**) تَرَنْزِسْتُر

transit /'tranzɪt, 'transɪt/ *n* **1** (conveyance) نَقْل; **passengers in ~** مُسافِرونَ عابِرونَ; **it was lost in ~** ضاعَ في الشَحْنِ **2** (AmE) (transport system) نَقْل; **to use public ~** اِسْتَخْدَمَ النَقْلَ العامَّ

transition /tran'zɪʃ(ə)n/ *n* انْتِقال (انْتِقالات)

transitional /tran'zɪʃ(ə)n(ə)l, tran'sɪʃ(ə)n(ə)l/ *adj* *‹government, period›* انْتِقاليّ

transitive /'transətɪv/ *adj* *‹verb, use›* مُتَعَدٍّ

translate /tranz'leɪt/ **A** *vt* تَرْجَمَ (i; تَرْجَمة) *‹a word, book›*; **to ~ sth into English/Arabic** تَرْجَمَ شَيْئاً إلى الإنْجْليزيّةِ \ العَرَبيّةِ

B *vi* **1** «person» تَرْجَمَ (i; تَرْجَمة) **2** «name, title» يُمْكِنُ تَرْجَمَتُهُ

translation /tranz'leɪʃ(ə)n/ *n* تَرْجَمة (تَراجِمُ)

translator /tranzˈleɪtə/ *n* مُتَرْجِم

transmission /tranzˈmɪʃ(ə)n/ *n* **1** [u] (act of transmitting) نَقْل **2** (broadcast) إِرْسال (إِرْسالات)

transmit /tranzˈmɪt/ *vt* (**-tt-**) **1** (to pass on) نَقَلَ (u; نَقْل) ‹*a disease, values*› **2** (to broadcast) أَرْسَلَ ‹*a programme, signal*›

transmitter /tranzˈmɪtə/ *n* جِهاز إِرْسالٍ

transparency /transˈparənsi/ *n* (*pl* **-cies**) **1** [u] (openness) شَفّافِيّة **2** (slide) شَريحة (شَرائِح)

transparent /transˈparənt/ *adj* ‹*plastic, glass*› شَفّاف

transpire /tranˈspʌɪə/ *vi* **1** (to be revealed) اِتَّضَحَ; **it ~d that...** ... اِتَّضَحَ أَنَّ **2** (fml) (to happen) وَقَعَ (a; وُقوع), حَدَثَ (u; حُدوث) **3** «leaf, plant» نَتَحَ (a; نَتْح)

transplant /transˈplɑːnt/ **A** *vt* زَرَعَ (a; زَرْع) ‹*an organ, a plant*›
B *n* **1** (operation) زَرْع (زُروع); **to carry out an organ ~** أَجْرى عَمَلِيّةَ زَرْعٍ **2** (organ) عُضْو مَزْروع

transplantation /transplɑːnˈteɪʃ(ə)n/ *n* زَرْع (زُروع)

transport A /tranˈspɔːt/ *vt* نَقَلَ (u; نَقْل) ‹*passengers, freight, a container*›
B /ˈtranspɔːt/ *n* **1** [u] (of goods, passengers) نَقْل; **air and road ~ was disrupted** تَعَطَّلَ النَقْلُ الجَوِّيُّ والبَرِّيُّ; **to travel by public ~** سافَرَ بالمُواصَلاتِ العامّةِ **2** [u] (means of travelling) وَسيلة نَقْلٍ; **do you need ~?** هل تَحْتاجُ إلى وَسيلةِ نَقْلٍ ؟ **3** (also **transport ship**) سَفينة نَقْلٍ (also **transport aircraft**) طائِرة نَقْلٍ; **his car was in collision with a troop ~** اِصْطَدَمَتْ سَيّارَتُهُ بِحافِلةِ نَقْلِ الجُنودِ **4** (liter) (rapture) نَشْوة; **to go into ~s of delight** اِنْتَشى من السَعادةِ

transportation /transpɔːˈteɪʃ(ə)n/ *n* **1** نَقْل; **the cost includes/excludes ~** يَشْمَلُ \ لا يَشْمَلُ الثَمَنُ النَقْلَ **2** (means of travelling) وَسيلة نَقْلٍ

transport costs *n* تَكاليف نَقْلٍ

transporter /tranˈspɔːtə/ *n* شاحِنة نَقْلِ سَيّاراتٍ

transport network *n* شَبَكة نَقْلٍ

transpose /tranˈspəʊz/ *vt* **1** (to interchange) حَوَّلَ ‹*letters, numbers*› **2** (in music) [غَيَّرَ مَقامَهُ] ‹*a piece, song*›

transsexual /tranzˈsɛkʃuːəl/ *n, adj* مُتَحَوِّل جِنْسِيًّا

transvestite /tranzˈvɛstʌɪt/ *n* [مُرْتَدي مَلابِسِ الجِنْسِ الآخَرِ]

trap /trap/ **A** *n* فَخّ (فُخوخ ,فِخاخ)
B *vt* (**-pp-**) **1** (to snare) «poacher, trapper» صادَ (بِفَخٍّ) ‹*an animal*› **2** (to catch, immobilize) حَصَرَ (i-u; حَصْر) ‹*a person, one's finger*›

trapdoor /trapˈdɔː/ *n* دَرْفة, باب مَسْحور (دَرَفات)

trapeze /trəˈpiːz/ *n* [أُرْجوحة لِبَهْلَوانٍ]

trapper /ˈtrapə/ *n* حابِل (صَيّاد حَيَواناتٍ من أَجْلِ فِرائِها)

trappings /ˈtrapɪŋz/ *n pl* **1** (paraphernalia) مَظاهِر; **the ~ of power/success** مَظاهِر القُوّةِ \ النَجاحِ **2** (harness) [عُدّة وَسَرْج مُزَيَّنة (للحُصانِ)]

trash /traʃ/ **A** *n* **1** (AmE) (refuse) زُبالة, قُمامة (قُمامات) **2** (worthless items) فَضَلات **3** (AmE infml) (worthless people) حُثالة
B *vt* (infml) **1** (to vandalize) خَرَّبَ ‹*a place, room*› **2** (to criticize) اِنْتَقَدَ بِحِدّةٍ ‹*a film, sb's reputation*›

trash can *n* (AmE) صُنْدوق قُمامةٍ

trash man *n* (*pl* **-men**) (AmE) زَبّال

trashy /ˈtraʃi/ *adj* (**trashier**, **trashiest**) (infml) ‹*novel, film*› تافِه; ‹*goods*› رَديء

trauma /ˈtrɔːmə/ *n* **1** (emotional) صَدْمة نَفْسيّة **2** (physical) جُرْح (إصابة جَسَديّة بالِغة)

traumatic /trɔːˈmatɪk/ *adj* **1** ‹*event, experience*› يُسَبِّبُ صَدْمةً نَفْسيّةً **2** ‹*injury*› جارِح, جارِح (يَتَسَبَّبُ في جُروحٍ)

traumatize, -ise (BrE) /ˈtrɔːmətʌɪz/ *vt* سَبَّبَ \ أَحْدَثَ صَدْمةً نَفْسيّةً ل ‹*a child, victim*›

travel /ˈtrav(ə)l/ **A** *vt* (**-ll-** BrE, **-l-** AmE) سافَرَ ‹*long distances*›; جابَ (u; جَوْب), جالَ (u; جَوْل), تَجَوَّلَ (في) ‹*the country*›; **we ~led the length and breadth of the country** تَجَوَّلْنا في طولِ البِلادِ وَعَرْضِها
B *vi* (**-ll-** BrE, **-l-** AmE) **1** (to journey) «person» سافَرَ; **to ~ by bus/car** سافَرَ بالحافِلةِ \ بالسَيّارة; **their teacher is ~ling with them** يُسافِرُ مُدَرِّسُهُمْ مَعَهُمْ; **he ~s widely** يُسافِرُ إلى أماكِنَ كَثيرةٍ; **to ~ on a German passport** يُسافِرُ بِجَوازِ سَفَرٍ أَلْمانيٍّ; **they were ~ling abroad** كانوا مُسافِرينَ إلى الخارِجِ; **to ~ light** سافَرَ بأَمْتِعةٍ خَفيفةٍ; **to ~ in style** سافَرَ سَفَراً مُرَفَّهاً; **bad news ~s fast** تَنْتَقِلُ الأَخْبارُ السَيِّئةُ بِسُرْعةٍ **2** (Sci) (to move)

«light, sound» سارَ ,سافَرَ ,انْتَقَل (i; مَسير ,سَيْر); **to ~ at 80 kph** سارَ بِسُرْعَةِ 80 كم في الساعَةِ; **the train was ~ling through a tunnel** كانَ القِطارُ يَسيرُ في نَفَقٍ **3** **to ~ well/badly** «vegetables, produce» تَأَثَّر \ لم يَتَأَثَّر بالسَفَرِ

C *n* سَفَر (أَسْفار); **~ by air/sea is cheap, air/sea ~ is cheap** السَفَرُ عن طَريقِ الجَوِّ \ البَحْرِ رَخيصٌ; **the job involves a lot of ~** تَتَطَلَّبُ الوَظيفةُ الكَثيرَ من السَفَرِ

D (**travels**) *n pl* سَفَريّات ,رِحْلات; **he's off on his ~s again** ذَهَبَ في إحْدى سَفَريّاتِهِ مَرَّةً أُخرى; **in the course of my ~s** أثناء سَفَريّاتي

travel agency, **travel agent's** *n* وكالة سَفَر

travel agent *n* وَكيل سَفَر ,وَكيل سِياحيّ

travel card *n* [بِطاقة نَقْل]

travel expenses *n* تكاليف السَفَرِ

travel insurance *n* تَأمين السَفَرِ

traveller (BrE), **traveler** (AmE) /ˈtrav(ə)lə/ *n* **1** (on a plane, train) مُسافِر **2** (BrE) (itinerant) ابْن سَبيلٍ

traveller's cheque (BrE), **traveler's check** (AmE) *n* شيك سِياحيّ

travelling (BrE), **traveling** (AmE) /ˈtravəlɪŋ/ **A** *n* سَفَر; **she does a lot of ~** تُسافِرُ كَثيراً

B *adj before n* ‹*exhibition, circus*› مُتَجَوِّل ,مُتَنَقِّل

travelling companion *n* رَفيق سَفَرٍ

travelling expenses *n* تَكاليف السَفَرِ

travelling salesman *n* تاجر مُتَجَوِّل

travel-sick /ˈtrav(ə)lsɪk/ *adj* (BrE) يُعاني من دُوارِ السَفَرِ

travel sickness *n* (BrE) دُوار السَفَرِ

traverse /trəˈvəːs/ *vt* (fml) ‹*a distance, country*› اجْتازَ ,قَطَع (a; قَطْع)

trawl /trɔːl/ **A** *vt* **1** (to fish) [صادَ السَمكَ بِشِباكِ الجَرِّ في] ‹*the seas, waters*› **2** (to search through) فَتَّشَ ‹*the Internet, shops*›

B *vi* «fishermen, boats» [اصْطادَ بِشِباكِ الجَرِّ]

trawler /ˈtrɔːlə/ *n* [سَفينة صَيْدٍ بِشِباكِ الجَرِّ]

trawlerman /ˈtrɔːləmən/ *n* (*pl* **-men**) [صَيّاد سَمَكٍ بِشِباكِ الجَرِّ]

tray /treɪ/ *n* صينيّة (صَوانيّ)

treacherous /ˈtretʃ(ə)rəs/ *adj* **1** ‹*person*› خائِن (خَوَنة) **2** ‹*conditions, current*› خَطير ,غَيْر مَأْمونٍ

treachery /ˈtretʃ(ə)ri/ *n* (*pl* **treacheries**) خِيانة

treacle /ˈtriːk(ə)l/ *n* (BrE) دِبْس

tread /tred/ **A** *vt* (*past tense* **trod**; *past participle* **trodden**) **to ~ mud indoors** لَوَّثَ البَيْتَ بالطينِ العالِقِ في حِذائِهِ; **to ~ water** وَطَأَ المِياهَ (وَقَفَ على قَدَمَيْهِ في الماءِ); **a well-trodden path** مَمَرّ مُمَهَّد

B *vi* (*past tense* **trod**; *past participle* **trodden**) (to walk) «person» خَطا (u; خَطْو) ,مَشى (i; مَشْي); **to ~ carefully** مَشى بِتَأَنٍّ; **to ~ on a snail** داسَ على حَلَزونٍ; **to ~ in a puddle** خَطا في بِرْكَةٍ

C *n* **1** [u] (footsteps) وَقْع أَقْدامٍ \ خُطُواتٍ; **they heard his heavy ~ on the stairs** سَمِعوا وَقْعَ خُطُواتِهِ الثَقيلةِ على الدَرَجِ **2** [u] (of tyres) مَداس (سَطْح إطارِ السَيّارةِ) **3** (of stairs) سَطْح (أَسْطُح ,سُطوح ,أَسْطِحة)

treadle /ˈtred(ə)l/ *n* دَوّاسة

treason /ˈtriːz(ə)n/ *n* خِيانة

treasure /ˈtreʒə/ **A** *n* **1** [u] (gold, silver, jewels etc.) كَنْز (كُنوز) **2** (valuable thing) كَنْز (كُنوز) **3** (infml) (valuable person) ذُخْر (أَذْخار)

B *vt* **1** (to cherish) ادَّخَرَ ‹*a memory, gift*› **2** (to value highly) اعْتَزَّ (ب) ‹*a friendship, freedom*›

C (**treasured**) *adj* ‹*possession, memory*› عَزيز ,ثَمين ,قَيِّم

treasurer /ˈtreʒ(ə)rə/ *n* أَمين صُنْدوقٍ

treasure trove *n* كَنْز دَفين

treasury /ˈtreʒ(ə)ri/ *n* (*pl* **treasuries**) **1** ((government department) **the Treasury**) الخِزانة العامّة ,خَزينة الدَوْلةِ; **the Department of the T~** (AmE) وِزارة الماليّة **2** (store of funds) خَزينة (خَزائِنُ)

treat /triːt/ **A** *vt* **1** (to deal with) تَصَرَّفَ (مع) ,تَعامَلَ ,عامَلَ ‹*a person, an animal*›; **to ~ sb well/badly** عامَلَ شَخْصاً بِشَكْلٍ حَسَنٍ \ سَيِّءٍ; **to ~ sb with respect/contempt** عامَلَ شَخْصاً باحْتِرامٍ \ باحْتِقارٍ; **these figures should be ~ed with caution** يَنْبَغي التَعامُلُ مع هذه الأَرْقامِ بِحَذَرٍ; **they ~ me like a child** يُعامِلونَني كَطِفْلٍ; **he ~s our house like a hotel** يَتَعامَلُ مع بَيْتِنا كَفُنْدُقٍ **2** (to handle) تَعامَلَ (مع) ‹*an object*› **3** (to consider) اعْتَبَرَ ,تَعامَلَ (مع) ‹*a situation, problem*›; **she ~ed it as a joke** تَعامَلَتْ مَعَهُ على أَنَّهُ مَزْحةٌ **4** (medically)

عالَجَ <*a patient, disease*>; **to ~ the condition with antibiotics** عالَجَ الحالةَ بالمُضادّاتِ الحَيَويّةِ **5** (for preservation) عالَجَ <*wood, crops*> **6** (for purification) عالَجَ <*sewage, waste water*> **7** (to entertain) اسْتَضافَ; **to ~ sb to a meal** اسْتَضافَ شَخْصاً على وَجْبةٍ

B *v refl* **to ~ oneself to sth** مَتَّعَ نَفْسَهُ بِشَيْءٍ

C *n* **1** (pleasure) [شَيْء مُمْتِع وَغَيْر مُعْتادٍ]; **as a special ~ we went to the zoo** كَمُكافَأَةٍ خاصّةٍ، ذَهَبْنا لِحَديقةِ الحَيَوانِ; **we have a real ~ for you tonight** لَدَيْنا مُفاجَأَةٌ حَقيقيّةٌ لَكَ اللَّيْلَةَ; **the dancing was a ~ to watch** كانَ الرَقْصُ مُتْعةً في المُشاهَدةِ **2** (food item) [طَعام مَخْصوص مَحْبوب] **3** (infml) (offer to pay) **it's my ~** هو على حِسابي

D (**a treat**) *adv phr* (BrE infml) **the plan worked a ~** حَقَّقَت الخُطّةُ نَجاحاً كَبيراً; **the show went down a ~ with the children** اسْتَمْتَعَ الأَطْفالُ بالعَرْضِ بِدَرَجةٍ كَبيرةٍ

treatise /ˈtriːtɪs, ˈtriːtɪz/ *n* أُطْروحة (أَبْحاث ,بُحوث) بَحْث ,(رَسائِل ,رِسالات) رِسالة

treatment /ˈtriːtmənt/ *n* **1** (of a candidate, detainee, etc) مُعامَلة; **she received preferential ~** تَلَقَّت مُعامَلةً تَفْضيليّةً; **the book won't stand rough ~** لن يَتَحَمَّلَ الكِتابُ التَعامُلَ الخَشِنَ **2** (of a theme) مُعالَجة; **the subject gets a more light-hearted ~** يُعالَجُ المَوضوعُ بِشَكْلٍ أَكْثَرَ مَرَحاً **3** (of patients, diseases) عِلاج; **the injured were transferred to hospital for ~** نُقِلَ المُصابونَ إلى المُسْتَشْفى لِتَلَقّي العلاجَ; **to be given a course of ~** أُعْطِيَ دَوْرةً عِلاجيّةً; **a new ~ for cancer** عِلاج جَديد للسَرَطانِ; **to undergo ~** خَضَعَ للعِلاجِ **4** (of wood, metal) مُعالَجة

treaty /ˈtriːti/ *n* (*pl* **treaties**) مُعاهَدة

treble /ˈtrɛb(ə)l/ **A** *adj* **1** <*thickness, measure*> ثُلاثيّ **2** <*voice, instrument*> سوبْرانو

B *n* **1** (voice, singer) سوبْرانو **2** [u] (of an audio system) تَرَدُّدات عالية

C *vt* ضاعَفَ ثَلاثَ مَرّاتٍ <*prices, profits*>

D *vi* «prices, membership» تَضاعَفَ ثَلاثَ مَرّاتٍ

treble clef *n* مِفْتاح الصول

tree /triː/ *n* شَجَر (n coll; أَشْجار)

treeline /ˈtriːlʌɪn/ *n* [آخِر حَدٍّ تَنْمو فيه الأَشْجارُ]

tree-lined /ˈtriːlʌɪnd/ *adj* <*street, avenue*> مَحْفوف بالأَشْجارِ

treetop /ˈtriːtɒp/ *n* أَعْلى شَجَرةٍ

tree trunk *n* جِذْع شَجَرةٍ

trek /trɛk/ **A** *n* (long journey) رِحْلة (طَويلة شاقّة); **it's quite a ~ from the station** إنَّها رِحْلةٌ طَويلةٌ من المَحَطّةِ

B *vi* (**-kk-**) رَحَلَ (على الأَقْدامِ); **to go ~king** قامَ بِرِحْلةٍ

trekking /ˈtrɛkɪŋ/ *n* [التَنَزُّه سَيْراً على الأَقْدامِ (لِمَسافاتٍ طَويلةٍ)]

trellis /ˈtrɛlɪs/ *n* تَعْريشة

tremble /ˈtrɛmb(ə)l/ *vi* «person, hands, voice» ارْتَجَفَ, ارْتَعَشَ, ارْتَعَدَ, اهْتَزَّ; **the leaves ~d** اهْتَزَّت الأَوْراقُ

tremendous /trɪˈmɛndəs/ *adj* **1** (huge) <*amount, pressure*> هائِل, ضَخْم **2** (infml) (very good) <*job, opportunity*> رائِع

tremendously /trəˈmɛndəsli/ *adv* <*important, successful*> للغايةِ, إلى أَبْعَدِ الحُدودِ

tremor /ˈtrɛmə/ *n* **1** (of fear) ارْتِعاش (ارْتِعاشات) **2** (in limbs) رَعْشة (رَعَشات), رَجْفة (رَجَفات) **3** (Geol) ▸ **earth tremor**

trench /trɛntʃ/ *n* **1** (ditch) أُخْدود (dipt; أَخاديدُ), خَنْدَق (خَنادِقُ) **2** (in warfare) خَنْدَق (خَنادِقُ)

trench coat *n* مِعْطَف واقٍ من المَطَرِ

trend /trɛnd/ *n* **1** (tendency) اتِّجاه (اتِّجاهات), نَزْعة (نَزَعات); **an upward/downward ~** اتِّجاه إلى الأَعْلى \ إلى الأَسْفَلِ **2** (fashion) موضة; **the latest ~ in wallpapers** آخِر موضةٍ في وَرَقِ الجُدْرانِ

trendsetter /ˈtrɛndsɛtə/ *n* رائِد الموضة

trendy /ˈtrɛndi/ *adj* (**trendier**, **trendiest**) (infml) <*bar, clothes*> على آخِرِ موضةٍ \ طِرازٍ

trepidation /ˌtrɛpɪˈdeɪʃ(ə)n/ *n* جَزَع, قَلَق

trespass /ˈtrɛspəs/ *vi* «walkers, intruders» تَعَدّى (على عِقارٍ أو مَكانٍ)

trespasser /ˈtrɛspəsə/ *n* مُتَعَدٍّ, مُتَجاوِز (على عِقارٍ أو مَكانٍ); **'~s will be prosecuted'** [سَتَتِمُّ مُقاضاةُ المُتَعَدّينَ]

tress /trɛs/ (liter) **A** *n* (lock of hair) خُصْلة (خُصَل, خُصْلات)

B (**tresses**) *n pl* شَعْر

trestle /ˈtrɛs(ə)l/ *n* حامِل (خَشَبيّ مُزْدَوِج الأَرْجُلِ)

trestle table *n* طاوِلة (مُتَكَوِّنة من سَطْحٍ خَشَبيٍّ على حامِلَيْن)

triage /ˈtriːɑːʒ/ *n* فَرْز المَرْضى

trial /ˈtrʌɪəl/ **A** *n* **1** (in court) مُحاكَمة; **a murder/fraud ~** مُحاكَمة بِتُهْمَةِ القَتْلِ \ الاحْتِيالِ; **a show ~** مُحاكَمة صوريّة; **~ by jury** مُحاكَمة أمام هَيْئَةِ مُحَلَّفين; **to be on ~ for murder** واجَهَ مُحاكَمةً بِتُهْمَةِ القَتْلِ; **to stand ~ for treason** حوكِمَ بِتُهْمَةِ الخِيانةِ **2** (of a drug, process) تَجْرِبة (تَجارِبُ), اخْتِبار (اخْتِبارات); **the drug is on ~** العَقّارُ قَيْدَ التَجْرِبةِ; **to carry out** *or* **conduct a ~ of a product** أَجْرى تَجْرِبةً على مُنْتَجٍ **3** *usu pl* (of players, musicians) اخْتِبار (اخْتِبارات); **to hold ~s for new players/singers** أَجْرى اخْتِباراتٍ للاّعِبينَ \ للمُطْرِبينَ الجُدُدِ; **Olympic ~s** تَصْفيّات تَمْهيديّة لِدَوْرة الألْعابِ الأولِمْبيّةِ **4** (annoyance) مِحْنة (مِحَن), بَلِيّة (بَلايا); **to face the ~s of old age** واجَهَ مِحَنَ كِبَرِ السِنِّ; **she's a ~ for her parents** تُسَبِّبُ مَتاعِبَ جَمّةً لِوالِدَيْها

B *adj* ‹*offer, period*› تَجْريبيّ; **take it on a ~ basis** خُذْهُ على سَبيلِ التَجْرِبةِ

C *vt* (BrE) جَرَّبَ ‹*a method, drug*›

trial run *n* **1** (of a vehicle) قِيادة تَجْريبيّة **2** (of a new system) تَشْغيل تَجْريبيّ

triangle /ˈtrʌɪaŋg(ə)l/ *n* **1** (shape) مُثَلَّث (مُثَلَّثات); **an equilateral ~** مُثَلَّث مُتَساوي الأَضْلاعِ **2** (musical instrument) مُثَلَّث (مُثَلَّثات)

triangular /trʌɪˈaŋgjʊlə/ *adj* ‹*shape, area*› مُثَلَّث

triathlon /trʌɪˈaθlɒn/ *n* سِباق ثُلاثيّ

tribal /ˈtrʌɪb(ə)l/ *adj* ‹*leader, custom*› قَبَليّ

tribe /trʌɪb/ *n* قَبيلة (قَبائِلُ)

tribesman /ˈtrʌɪbzmən/ *n* (*pl* **-men**) رَجُل قَبيلةٍ

tribeswoman /ˈtrʌɪbzwʊmən/ *n* (*pl* **-women**) امْرَأة قَبيلةٍ

tribunal /trʌɪˈbjuːn(ə)l/ *n* مَحْكَمة (خاصّة)

tributary /ˈtrɪbjʊt(ə)ri/ *n* (*pl* **tributaries**) رافِد (رَوافِدُ)

tribute /ˈtrɪbjuːt/ *n* **1** (act of praise) تَكْريم; **to pay ~ to sb/sth** أَشادَ بِذِكْرِ شَخْصٍ \ شَيْءٍ **2** (testimony) شَهادة, دَليل (دَلائِلُ, أَدِلّة); **his recovery is a ~ to his doctor's skill** اسْتِعادةُ صِحَّتِهِ دَليلٌ على مَهارةِ طَبيبِهِ

triceps /ˈtrʌɪseps/ *n* (*pl* **triceps**) عَضَلة ثُلاثيّة الرُؤوسِ

trick /trɪk/ **A** *n* **1** (ruse) حيلة (حِيَل), خُدْعة (خُدْعات, خُدَع); **it's all a ~!** الأَمْرُ كُلُّهُ خُدْعةٌ!; **a ~ of the light** وَهْم بَصَريّ **2** (prank) خُدْعة (خُدْعات, خُدَع), تَخَيُّل (تَخَيُّلات), تَوَهُّم, مَقْلَب (مَقالِبُ); **to play a ~ on sb** خَدَعَ شَخْصاً مَزْحاً; **he's up to his ~s again** يُمارِسُ أَلاعيبَهُ مَرّةً أُخْرى **3** (by a magician, dog) خُدْعة (خُدْعات, خُدَع) **4** (secret) سِرّ (أَسْرار); **the ~ is to cook it very slowly** السِرُّ هو أَنْ تَطْهُوَهُ بِبُطْءٍ شَديدٍ **5** (in cards) نُقْطة في جَوْلة [أَوْراق اللَعِبِ في جَوْلةٍ]; **to win** *or* **take a ~** سَجَّلَ نُقْطةً في جَوْلةٍ

B *vt* «con man» خَدَعَ (a; خَدْع), احْتالَ (على) ‹*a victim, user*›; **she was ~ed out of her life savings** احْتيلَ عَلَيْها وَخَسِرَتْ كُلَّ مُدَّخَراتِها; **to ~ sb into doing sth** خَدَعَ شَخْصاً لِكَيْ يَفْعَلَ شَيْئاً

(Idioms) **the tricks of the trade** أَسْرار المِهْنةِ; **to do the trick** (infml) أَدّى المَطْلوبَ, وَفى بالغَرَضِ

trickle /ˈtrɪk(ə)l/ **A** *vi* **1** (to flow) قَطَرَ (u; قَطْر), تَقاطَرَ; **raindrops ~d down the window** تَساقَطَتْ قَطَراتُ المَطَرِ على النافِذةِ **2** (to come, go) تَوالى \ تَتابَعَ بِبُطْءٍ; **the results are trickling in** تَظْهَرُ النَتائِجُ شَيْئاً فَشَيْئاً; **the ball ~d over the line** تَدَحْرَجَت الكُرةُ بِبُطْءٍ على الخَطِّ; **the crowd started to ~ away** أَخَذَ الحَشْدُ يَتَفَرَّقُ شَيْئاً فَشَيْئاً

B *n* **1** (of blood, water) قَطْر, سَيْل رَقيق, تَقَطُّر **2** (of visitors, voters) عَدَد قَليل; **a steady ~ of orders/complaints** عَدَد قَليل من الطَلَباتِ \ الشكاوى المُتَدَفِّقة بِشَكْلٍ ثابِتٍ

trickster /ˈtrɪkstə/ *n* (infml) مُحْتال, مُخادِع, نَصّاب

tricky /ˈtrɪki/ *adj* (**trickier**, **trickiest**) (infml) **1** (difficult) ‹*task, problem*› عَويص, مُعَقَّد; **it's a ~ business** هي مَسْأَلةٌ عَويصةٌ **2** (sensitive) ‹*matter, decision*› دَقيق, حَسّاس

tricycle /ˈtrʌɪsɪk(ə)l/ *n* دَرّاجة بِثَلاثِ عَجَلاتٍ

tried /trʌɪd/ *past tense, past participle* ▸ **try**

tries /trʌɪz/ **A** (*3rd pers sing pres*) ▸ **try** A, B

B *pl* ▸ **try** C

trifle /ˈtrʌɪf(ə)l/ *n* **1** (triviality) أَمْر تافِه \ شَيْء, نَبْذ (أَنْباذ) **2** (dessert) [حَلْوى مَصْنوعة من الفاكِهةِ والقِشْطةِ والكَعْكِ]

(Phrasal verb) **trifle with**: **~ with sb/sth** اسْتَهانَ بِشَخْصٍ \ بِشَيْءٍ ‹*a person, an issue*›

trifling /ˈtraɪflɪŋ/ *adj* ‹*matter, sum*› تافِه

trigger /ˈtrɪɡə/ **A** *n* زِناد (أَزْنِدة); **to pull the ~** ضَغَطَ على الزِنادِ **B** *vt* (also **trigger off**) أَثارَ ‹*a reaction, crisis*›

trill /trɪl/ *n* رَعْشة (رَعَشات)

trillion /ˈtrɪljən/ *n, adj* تِرِيلْيون

trilogy /ˈtrɪlədʒi/ *n* (*pl* **trilogies**) ثُلاثِيّة

trim /trɪm/ **A** *vt* (**-mm-**) **1** (to cut) قَصَّ (u; قَصّ)، شَذَّبَ، هَذَّبَ ‹*sb's hair, the grass, hedge*›; **~ the fat off the meat** أَزِلِ الدُهْنَ من اللَحْمِ **2** (to reduce) خَفَّضَ ‹*the cost, spending*›; **to ~ the budget by 5%, to ~ 5% off the budget** خَفَّضَ الميزانِيَّةَ بِنِسْبةِ 5٪ **3** (to decorate) زَرْكَشَ (i; زَرْكَشة) ‹*a garment, cushion*› **4** (to adjust) ضَبَطَ (i-u; ضَبْط)، عَدَّلَ ‹*a sail*›
B *n* **1** (of hair, beard) تَهْذيب، قَصّ، تَشْذيب **2** (of a hedge) تَشْذيب، تَقْليم **3** (on clothes, furnishings, etc) زَرْكَشة; **a cream sofa with a brown ~** أَريكة لَوْنُها قِشْدِيٌّ بِحَوافٍّ مُزَرْكَشةٍ بِاللَوْنِ البُنِّيِّ **4** (of a car) كَمالِيّات; **the exterior/interior ~** الكَمالِيّات الخارِجِيّة \ الداخِلِيّة **5** [u] (good condition) حالة جَيِّدة; **to keep oneself in ~** حافَظَ على لِياقَتِهِ البَدَنِيّة
C *adj* (**-mm-**) **1** (neat, smart) ‹*person*› مُهَنْدَم; ‹*garden*› مُنَسَّق، مُرَتَّب **2** (slender) ‹*figure, waist*› نَحيل، نَحيف، رَشيق; **she's still very ~** ما زالَتْ رَشيقةً جِدًّا

trimester /traɪˈmestə/ *n* (AmE) فَصْل (فُصول)

trimming /ˈtrɪmɪŋ/ *n* **1** (decoration) زَرْكَش **2** (**trimmings** *n pl*) (offcuts) قُصاصات

Trinidad /ˈtrɪnɪdad/ *pr n* تْرينيداد (f)

Trinidad and Tobago /ˌtrɪnɪdad ənd təˈbeɪɡəʊ/ *pr n* تْرينيداد وَتوباغو

Trinidadian /trɪnɪˈdadiən/ *n, adj* تْرينيداديّ

Trinity /ˈtrɪnəti/ *n* (**the Trinity**) الثالوث

trinket /ˈtrɪŋkɪt/ *n* [حِلْية تافِهة]

trio /ˈtriːəʊ/ *n* ثُلاثِيّ

trip /trɪp/ **A** *vt* (**-pp-**) **1** (to cause to stumble) أَعْثَرَ، أَوْقَعَ; **the root ~ped me** تَعَثَّرْتُ في الجِذْرِ **2** شَغَّلَ ‹*a switch, an alarm*›
B *vi* (**-pp-**) **1** (to stumble) تَعَثَّرَ; **to ~ on** *or* **over sth** تَعَثَّرَ في شَيْءٍ; **he ~ped on the stairs** تَعَثَّرَ على الدَرَجِ; **she ~ped over the cable** تَعَثَّرَتْ في السِلْكِ **2** (infml) (to move jauntily) **to ~ along** سارَ بِرَشاقةٍ
C *n* **1** (journey) رِحْلة (رِحَل، رِحْلات); **a business/shopping ~** رِحْلة عَمَلٍ \ تَسَوُّقٍ; **to go on a ~** ذَهَبَ في رِحْلةٍ; **I make the ~ several times a year** أَقومُ بالرِحْلةِ عِدّةَ مَرّاتٍ في السَنةِ **2** (excursion) رِحْلة (رِحَل، رِحْلات)، نُزْهة (نُزَه، نُزْهات); **a ~ to the beach** رِحْلة إلى الشاطِئِ **3** (infml) (drug-induced) هَلْوَسة (هَلاوِس)
Phrasal verb **trip up** **A** **1** (to stumble) تَعَثَّرَ **2** (to be mistaken) زَلَّ (i; زَلّ، زُلول)، أَخْطَأَ **B** **~ [sb] up, ~ up [sb]** **1** (to cause to stumble) أَعْثَرَ \ أَوْقَعَ [شَخْصاً] **2** (to catch out) اسْتَدْرَجَ [شَخْصاً] في الكَلامِ ‹*a witness, candidate*›

tripe /traɪp/ *n* **1** (food) كِرْش (كُروش) **2** (infml) (nonsense) كَلام \ شَيْء سَخيف

triple /ˈtrɪp(ə)l/ *adj* ‹*bypass, contest*› ثُلاثِيّ

triple jump *n* قَفْز ثُلاثِيّ

triplet /ˈtrɪplɪt/ *n* واحِد من ثَلاثةِ تَوائِمَ

triplicate /ˈtrɪplɪkət/ (**in triplicate**) *adv phr* «to copy, to fill out» ثَلاثَ مَرّاتٍ

tripod /ˈtraɪpɒd/ *n* حامِل ثُلاثِيّ القَوائِم

Tripoli /ˈtrɪp(ə)li/ *pr n* طَرابُلُس (dipt f)

triptote /ˈtrɪptəʊt/ *n* اسْم مُنْصَرِف

triptotic /trɪpˈtɒtɪk/ *adj* ‹*noun*› مُنْصَرِف

trite /traɪt/ *adj* (**triter, tritest**) ‹*remark, sentiment*› مُبْتَذَل

triumph /ˈtraɪʌmf/ **A** *n* نَصْر، انْتِصار (انْتِصارات)، ظَفَر **B** *vi* «athlete, team» انْتَصَرَ

triumphal /traɪˈʌmf(ə)l/ *adj* ‹*entry, procession*› نَصْرٍ

triumphant /traɪˈʌmf(ə)nt/ *adj* ‹*team, smile*› مُنْتَصِر

trivia /ˈtrɪvɪə/ *n pl* (fml) تَوافِه (dipt)

trivial /ˈtrɪvɪəl/ *adj* (not important) ‹*matter, sum*› تافِه (تَوافِهُ)

triviality /ˌtrɪvɪˈalɪti/ *n* (*pl* **trivialities**) (fml) تَفاهة

trivialize, -ise (BrE) /ˈtrɪvɪəlaɪz/ *vt* بَخَسَ (a; بَخْس)، حَطَّ من الشَأْنِ ‹*an issue, suffering*›

trod /trɒd/ *past tense* ▸ **tread**

trodden /ˈtrɒd(ə)n/ *past participle* ▸ **tread**

trolley /ˈtrɒli/ *n* **1** (BrE) (for luggage) ترولي; (for shopping) عَرَبة تَسَوُّقٍ **2** (BrE) (for food, drinks,) تْرولي **3** (AmE) (tram) (تَرامات) تْرام

trolleybus /ˈtrɒlɪbʌs/ *n* (BrE) تْرولي باص (حافِلة كَهْرَبائيّة)

trolley car *n* (AmE) (تْرامات) تْرام

trombone /trɒmˈbəʊn/ *n* مُتَرَدِّدة ,تْرومْبون (آلة نَفْخٍ موسيقيّة)

troop /truːp/ **A** *n* **1** (unit) (فِرَق) فِرْقة **2** (**troops** *n pl*) (soldiers) قوّات

B *vi* «crowds, children» اِحْتَشَدَ; **to ~ off/in** ذَهَبوا \ جاؤوا في مَجْموعةٍ

troop carrier *n* ناقِلة جُنودٍ.

trooper /ˈtruːpə/ *n* **1** (soldier) (جُنود) جُنْديّ **2** (AmE) (policeman) شُرْطيّ

trophy /ˈtrəʊfi/ *n* (*pl* **trophies**) (جَوائِز) جائِزة ,كَأس (mf; كُؤوس)

tropic /ˈtrɒpɪk/ *n* **1** (line) (مَدارات) مَدار; **the ~ of Cancer/ Capricorn** مَدار السَّرطانِ \ الجَدْيِ **2** (**the Tropics**) المَناطِق الاسْتِوائيّة \ المَداريّة

tropical /ˈtrɒpɪk(ə)l/ *adj* ‹*storm, forest*› مَداريّ ,اِسْتِوائيّ

trot /trɒt/ **A** *vi* (**-tt-**) **1** «horses, dogs» (رَكْض ;u) رَكَضَ **2** «people» هَرْوَلَ (هَرْوَلة ;i), رَكَضَ (رَكْض ;u), سارَ مُسْرِعاً; **he ~ted off to fetch us some drinks** مَضى مُسْرِعاً لِيُحْضِرَ لَنا بَعْضَ المَشْروباتِ

B *n* هَرْوَلة ,رَكْض; **at a ~** راكِضاً; **to break into a ~** «horse, jogger» انْطَلَقَ راكِضاً

C (**the trots**) *n pl* (infml) الإسْهال

Idiom **on the trot** (BrE) (infml) على التَوالي

Phrasal verb **trot out**: **~ out [sth]** (infml) ذَكَرَ [شَيْئاً] مَعْهوداً \ مُعْتاداً ‹*an excuse, argument*›

trouble /ˈtrʌb(ə)l/ **A** *n* **1** [u] (problems) مَتاعِب ,مَشاكِل; **his leg is giving him ~** يُعاني من مَشاكِلَ في رِجْلِهِ; **heart/back ~** مَشاكِل في القَلْبِ \ الظَهْرِ; **to have ~ doing sth** وَجَدَ صُعوبةً في فِعْلِ شَيْءٍ; **to be in/get into ~** كانَ \ وَقَعَ في مُشْكِلةٍ; **to get sb into ~** أَوْقَعَ شَخْصاً في مُشْكِلةٍ; **to cause ~** سَبَّبَ مَشاكِلَ; **to be asking for ~** (infml) جَلَبَ المَشاكِلَ على نَفْسِهِ; **to get sb out of ~** خَلَّصَ شَخْصاً من مُشْكِلةٍ **2** (individual problem) (مَشاكِلُ ,مُشْكِلات) مُشْكِلة; **what's the ~?** ما المُشْكِلةُ؟; **your ~s are over** انْتَهَتْ مَشاكِلُكَ; **the ~ with you is that you never listen** المُشْكِلةُ عِنْدَكَ أَنَّكَ لا تَسْتَمِعُ أَبَداً **3** [u] (effort) عَناء, تَعَب ,مَشَقّة; **it's not worth the ~** لا يَسْتَحِقُّ العَناءَ; **it's no ~** لم يُسَبِّبْ إزْعاجاً على الإطْلاقِ; **he's been no ~ at all** عَناءَ فيهِ; **it's more ~ than it's worth** مَتاعِبُهُ أَكْثَرُ من مَنافِعِهِ; **to take the ~ to do sth, to go to the ~ of doing sth** كَلَّفَ نَفْسَهُ عَناءَ فِعْلِ شَيْءٍ; **to save sb the ~ of doing sth** وَفَّرَ على شَخْصٍ عَناءَ فِعْلِ شَيْءٍ; **nothing is too much ~ for him** لا تَقِفُ جُهودُهُ عند حَدٍّ **4** [u] (disorder) اضْطِرابات ,مَشاكِل; **the police are expecting ~** تَتَوَقَّعُ الشُرْطةُ حُدوثَ بَعْضِ المَشاكِلِ; **to be looking for ~** كانَ يَبْحَثُ عن المَشاكِلِ

B *vt* (**troubles, troubling, troubled**) **1** (to inconvenience, bother) أَزْعَجَ ,ضايَقَ; **could I ~ you for a lift?** هل أُزْعِجُكَ إذا طَلَبْتُ مِنْكَ أنْ تُوَصِّلَني؟ **2** (to worry) «problem, question» أَقْلَقَ; **don't let it ~ you** لا تَدَعْهُ يُقْلِقُكَ **3** (to cause discomfort to) «injury, cough» آلَمَ ,أَزْعَجَ (Form IV; imperf يُؤْلِمُ); **he has been ~d by injury all season** أَزْعَجَتْهُ الإصابةُ طوال المَوْسِمِ

C *vi* **to ~ to do sth** كَلَّفَ نَفْسَهُ فِعْلَ شَيْءٍ

D *v refl* **to ~ oneself to do sth** كَبَّدَ نَفْسَهُ عَناءَ فِعْلِ شَيْءٍ

troubled /ˈtrʌbəld/ *adj* **1** (worried) ‹*teenager, expression*› قَلِق, مَهْموم **2** (disturbed) ‹*region, past*› مُضْطَرِب

trouble-free /ˌtrʌb(ə)lˈfriː/ *adj* ‹*journey, service*› بِدونِ مَشاكِلَ

troublemaker /ˈtrʌbəlmeɪkə/ *n* مُشاغِب

troubleshooter /ˈtrʌb(ə)lʃuːtə/ *n* حَلّال مَشاكِلَ

troublesome /ˈtrʌbəls(ə)m/ *adj* ‹*injury*› (شَواقُّ) شاقّ ,مُتْعِب, مُزْعِج; ‹*neighbour*› عَسير

trouble spot *n* مِنْطَقة مُضْطَرِبة

trough /trɒf/ *n* **1** (for animals) (مَعالِفُ) مِعْلَف **2** (between waves) قاع (المَوْجةِ) **3** (of low pressure) مُنْخَفَض (جَوّيّ)

troupe /truːp/ *n* (فِرَق) فِرْقة; **a circus ~** فِرْقة سيرْك

trousers /ˈtraʊzəz/ *n pl* (BrE) (بَنْطَلونات) بَنْطَلون ,(سَراويلُ) سِرْوال; **a pair of ~** (بَنْطَلونات) بَنْطَلون ,(سَراويلُ) سِرْوال

trouser suit *n* (BrE) بَدْلة نِسائيّة (بِسِرْوالٍ)

trousseau /ˈtruːsəʊ/ *n* (*pl* **trousseaux** or **trousseaus** /-z/) جِهاز العَروسِ

trout /traʊt/ *n* (*pl* **trout**) تَروتة

trowel /ˈtraʊəl/ *n* 1 (for building) مالَج (مَوالِجُ), مُسْطَرين 2 (for gardening) مِجْرَفة (مَجارِفُ)

truancy /ˈtruːənsi/ *n* تَغَيُّب (عن المَدْرَسةِ بدونِ إذْنٍ)

truant /ˈtruːənt/ *n* تِلْميذ مُتَغَيِّب (بِدونِ إذْنٍ); **to play ~** تَغَيَّبَ عن المَدْرَسةِ (بدونِ إذْنٍ)

truce /truːs/ *n* هُدْنة (هُدَن, هُدْنات), مُهادَنة; **to call a ~** أعْلَنَ هُدْنةً

truck /trʌk/ *n* 1 (vehicle) شاحِنة 2 (BrE) (rail wagon) عَرَبة بَضائِعَ (في قِطارٍ)

Idiom **to have no truck with sb/sth** رَفَضَ التَعامُلَ مع شَخْصٍ \ شَيْءٍ

truck driver *n* سائِق شاحِنةٍ

trucker /ˈtrʌkə/ *n* (AmE) سائِق شاحِنةٍ

truck farming *n* (AmE) [زِراعة فَواكِهَ وَخُضْرَواتٍ بِكَمِّيّاتٍ تِجارِيّةٍ]

trucking /ˈtrʌkɪŋ/ *n* (AmE) نَقْل (بالشاحِناتِ)

truculent /ˈtrʌkjʊlənt/ *adj* ‹mood, teenager› شَرِس, مُشاكِس

trudge /trʌdʒ/ *vi* «soldiers, children» مَشَى بِصُعوبةٍ; **we ~d through the snow** [مَشَيْنا عَبْرَ الثلج بِتَثاقُلٍ وَبُطْءٍ]

true /truː/ A *n* **out of ~** مُنْحَرِف عن الوَضْعِ الصَحيحِ
B *adj* 1 (truthful) ‹statement, allegation, rumour› حَقيقيّ, صادِق, صَحيح; **it is ~ to say that ...** يَحِقُ القَوْلُ بأنَّ ...; **that's ~** هذا صَحيحٌ; **to come ~** تَحَقَّقَ; **that can't be ~!** ذلك مُسْتَحيلٌ!; **~, I haven't seen it myself** حَقًّا, لم أرَهُ بِنَفْسي 2 (not fictitious) ‹story› حَقيقيّ, واقِعيّ; **the movie is based on a ~ story** الفيلْم مأْخوذٌ من قِصّةٍ حَقيقيّةٍ 3 (genuine) ‹believer, hero› حَقيقيّ; **~ love** حُبّ حَقيقيّ; **this is not democracy in the ~ sense of the word** لَيْسَتْ هذه ديمُقْراطيّةً بالمَعْنى الحَقيقيِّ للكَلِمةِ 4 (verifiable) ‹cost, identity› حَقيقيّ; ‹copy› طِبْقَ الأَصْلِ 5 (accurate) ‹picture, likeness› دَقيق; **to be ~ to life** «movie, scene» كانَ مُعَبِّراً عن الواقِعِ 6 (loyal) ‹friend, servant› مُخْلِص; **he was ~ to his word/his principles** كانَ صادِقاً في وَعْدِهِ \ مُخْلِصاً لِمَبادِئِهِ 7 (correctly aligned) مَضْبوط, مُتَحاذٍ

Idiom **true to form, he ...** كَما هو مُتَوَقَّعٌ مِنْهُ, فَقَدْ ...

true-life /ˌtruːˈlaɪf/ *adj* ‹adventure, story› حَقيقيّ

true north *n* الشَمال الحَقيقيّ

truffle /ˈtrʌf(ə)l/ *n* 1 (fungus) كَمْء (أكْمُؤ) 2 (chocolate) تْروفِل

truly /ˈtruːli/ *adv* 1 (really) ‹awful, remarkable› حَقًّا, حَقيقةً; **she ~ believed he would return the money** اعْتَقَدَتْ حَقًّا بأنَّهُ سَيُعيدُ المالَ 2 (fml) (as letter ending) **yours ~** مع خالِصِ التَحيّاتِ

trump /trʌmp/ *n* 1 (in card games) وَرَقة رابِحة; **to play a ~ (card)** لَعِبَ وَرَقةً رابِحةً 2 (decider) وَرَقة رابِحة

Idiom **to come/turn up trumps** حالَفَهُ الحَظُّ

trumped-up /trʌmptˈʌp/ *adj before noun* ‹charge, evidence› مُلَفَّق, مُخْتَلَق

trumpet /ˈtrʌmpɪt/ *n* بوق (أبْواق)

Idiom **to blow your own trumpet** امْتَدَحَ نَفْسَهُ

trumpeter /ˈtrʌmpɪtə/ *n* بَوّاق, عازِف على البوقِ

truncheon /ˈtrʌntʃ(ə)n/ *n* هِراوة (هَراوى, هِراوات)

trunk /trʌŋk/ *n* 1 (of a tree) جِذْع (جُذوع, أَجْذاع) 2 (torso) جِذْع (جُذوع, أَجْذاع) 3 (elephant's) خُرْطوم (خَراطيمُ) 4 (for clothes, etc) صُنْدوق (صَناديقُ) 5 (AmE) (of a car) صُنْدوق (صَناديقُ) 6 (**trunks** *n pl*) سِرْوال قَصير (للسِباحةِ); **a pair of ~s** سِرْوال قَصير (للسِباحةِ)

trunk road *n* (BrE) طَريق رَئيسيّ

truss /trʌs/ *n* (also **truss up**) ‹a chicken, pheasant› كَتَّفَ, رَبَطَ (i-u; رَبْط)

Phrasal verb **truss up**: **~ up [sb], ~ [sb] up** (infml) (to tie) كَتَّفَ [شَخْصاً] ‹a captive, victim›

trust /trʌst/ A *n* 1 [u] (faith) ثِقة; **to put one's ~ in sb/sth** وَضَعَ ثِقَتَهُ في شَخْصٍ \ شَيْءٍ; **to take sth on ~** قَبِلَ شَيْئاً بِناءً على الثِقةِ 2 [u] (responsibility) مَسْؤولِيّة; **a position of ~** مَوْقِع مَسْؤولِيّةٍ 3 (for beneficiaries) وِصاية; **to hold sth in ~ for a beneficiary** وَضَعَ شَيْئاً تحت الوِصايةِ لِصالِحِ موصًى عَلَيْهِ 4 (organization) جَمْعِيّة, صُنْدوق (صَناديقُ) 5 (AmE) (collaborating corporations) شَرِكة \ اتِّحاد إدارةِ أمْوالٍ
B *vt* 1 (to have confidence in) وَثِقَ (i; ثِقة, وُثوق ب); **to ~ sb's judgement** وَثِقَ بِرَأْيِ شَخْصٍ; **I can't ~ her to do it** لا أَسْتَطيعُ أنْ أَثِقَ بِها في فِعْلِهِ 2 (to entrust) **to ~ sb with sth**

اِئْتَمَنَ شَخْصاً على شَيْءٍ **3** (fml) (to hope) أَمَلَ (u; أَمَل); **I ~ that this is satisfactory** آمَلُ أنْ يَكونَ هذا مُرْضِياً
C *vi* **to ~ in sb/sth** آمَنَ ب \ وَثِقَ في شَخْصٍ \ شَيْءٍ; **to ~ to luck** اتَّكَلَ على الحَظِّ
D (**trusted**) *adj* ‹*friend, adviser*› مَوْثوق بِهِ

trusted /ˈtrʌstɪd/ *adj before n* ‹*friend, source*› مَوْثوق بِهِ, مُؤْتَمَن

trustee /trʌsˈtiː/ *n* **1** (of assets) وَصِيّ (أَوْصِياءُ) **2** (of a charity) أَمين صُنْدوقٍ

trust fund *n* صُنْدوق ائْتِمانيّ

trusting /ˈtrʌstɪŋ/ *adj* ‹*nature, relationship*› واثِق; ‹*child, soul*› سَريع التَصْديق, بَريء (أَبْرِياءُ)

trust territory *n* إقْليم مَشْمول بالوِصايَةِ

trustworthy /ˈtrʌstwɜːði/ *adj* ‹*friend, source*› مَوْثوق بِهِ

truth /truːθ/ *n* (*pl* **truths** /truːðz/) **1** [u] (real facts) حَقيقة, حَقّ, صِدْق; **he's telling the ~** يُخْبِرُ بالحَقيقَةِ; **the ~ is that I never met him** الحَقيقةُ هي أنّي لم أُقابِلْهُ أَبَداً; **there is some/no ~ in this** هذا بِهِ بَعْضُ \ خالٍ من الصِدْقِ; **to tell you the ~, I have no idea** حَتّى أكونَ صادِقاً مَعَكَ، لَيْسَ لَدَيَّ أَيُّ فِكْرَةٍ; **nothing could be further from the ~** هذا أَبْعَدُ ما يَكونُ عن الحَقيقَةِ
2 [u] (of a statement, story) صِدْق, صِحّة; **the ~ of the matter is hard to establish** من الصَعْبِ التَأَكُّدُ من صِحّةِ الأَمْرِ
3 (accepted fact) حَقيقة (حَقائِقُ)

truthful /ˈtruːθfʊl/ *adj* **1** (honest) ‹*witness, manner*› صادِق **2** (based on fact) ‹*account, answer*› مُطابِق للحَقيقَةِ \ للواقِعِ

try /trʌɪ/ **A** *vt* (*3rd person present sing* **tries**, *past tense, past participle* **tried**) **1** (to attempt) حاوَلَ; **to ~ to do sth, to ~ doing sth** حاوَلَ أنْ يَفْعَلَ شَيْئاً; **she tried to phone him, she tried phoning him** حاوَلَت الاتّصالَ بِهِ; **to ~ hard to do sth** حاوَلَ جاهِداً أنْ يَفْعَلَ شَيْئاً; **to ~ one's hardest** *or* **best to do sth** حاوَلَ بِأَقْصى جُهْدِهِ أنْ يَفْعَلَ شَيْئاً **2** (to test) جَرَّبَ ‹*a recipe, tool, product*›; **I tried the recipe/method, but it didn't work** جَرَّبْتُ الوَصْفةَ \ الطَريقةَ وَلَكِنَّها لم تَنْجَحْ; **I'll ~ anything once** أُحِبُّ أنْ أُجَرِّبَ أَيَّ شَيْءٍ وَلَوْ مَرَّةً واحِدةً; **~ the library/any pharmacy** حاوِلْ أنْ تَسْأَلَ في المَكْتَبةِ \ أَيِّ صَيْدَلِيّةٍ; **to ~ one's hand at pottery/weaving** جَرَّبَ مَوْهِبَتَهُ في أَعْمالِ الفُخّارِ \ النَسيجِ **3** (to sample) ذاقَ, تَذَوَّقَ (u; ذَوْق, ذِواق, مَذاق) ‹*the soup, food, wine*› **4** (to push to limits) اِخْتَبَرَ, اِمْتَحَنَ ‹*sb's faith, tolerance*›; **to ~ sb's patience** اِخْتَبَرَ قُدْرةَ شَخْصٍ على الصَبْرِ **5** «judge» حاكَمَ ‹*a criminal*›; حَكَمَ (u; حُكْم) في ‹*a case*›
B *vi* (*3rd person present sing* **tries**, *past tense, past participle* **tried**) (to attempt sth) «person» حاوَلَ; **he didn't even ~** هو حَتّى لم يُحاوِلْ; **to ~ again** حاوَلَ مَرّةً أُخْرى; **to ~ for a loan/post** حاوَلَ الحُصولَ على قَرْضٍ \ مَنْصِبٍ
C *n* (*pl* **tries**) **1** (attempt) تَجْرِبة, مُحاوَلة; **to have a ~ at doing sth** حاوَلَ أنْ يَفْعَلَ شَيْئاً; **nice ~!** مُحاوَلة جَيِّدة!; **go on, give it a ~** هَيّا، جَرِّبْهُ **2** (in rugby) مُحاوَلة

Phrasal verbs **try on**: **~ [sth] on, ~ on [sth]** قاسَ [شَيْئاً] ‹*a hat, dress*›; **to ~ it on** (infml) خادَعَ
• **try out**: **1** **~ [sth] out, ~ out [sth]** جَرَّبَ [شَيْئاً] ‹*a car, drug, recipe*›; **it's worth ~ing it out** يَسْتَحِقُّ أنْ تُجَرِّبَهُ **2** **~ [sb] out, ~ out [sb]** اِخْتَبَرَ [شَخْصاً]; **they are ~ing out the hopefuls for the first team** يُجْرونَ اختِباراتٍ للمُرَشَّحينَ للفَريقِ الأَوَّلِ

trying /ˈtrʌɪɪŋ/ *adj* ‹*time, child*› شاقّ (شَواقّ), مُجْهِد, مُتْعِب

tsar, **czar** /zɑː/ *n* **1** (ruler) قَيْصَر (روسِيا قَديماً) **2** (government minister) مَسْؤول حُكوميّ

tsetse fly /ˈtsɛtsi flʌɪ/ *n* ذُبابة تْسي تْسي

T-shirt /ˈtiːʃəːt/ *n* تي شيرْت

tsp *abbr* = **teaspoon(s)ful** مِلْعَقة صَغيرة

tsunami /tsuːˈnɑːmi/ *n* تْسونامي

tub /tʌb/ *n* **1** (for water) طَسْت (طُسوت), طَشْت (طُشوت); (for flowers) حَوْض (أَحْواض) **2** (of ice cream, etc) بَرْطَمان (بَرْطَمانات) **3** (AmE) (bath) بانْيو (بانْيوهات)

tuba /ˈtjuːbə/ *n* توبا (آلة نَفْخٍ كَبيرة وَنُحاسيّة)

tubby /ˈtʌbi/ *adj* (**tubbier**, **tubbiest**) (infml) ‹*man, woman*› بَدين (بُدُن)

tube /tjuːb/ *n* **1** (pipe) أُنْبوب (أَنابيبُ) **2** (container) أُنْبوب (أَنابيبُ), عُلْبة (عُلَب); **a ~ of toothpaste** أُنْبوب مَعْجونِ أَسْنانٍ
3 (AmE infml) (TV) (**the tube**) التِلِفِزْيون **4** (infml) (in London) (**the Tube®**) المِتْرو; **to take the T~** رَكِبَ المِتْرو

Idiom **to go down the tubes** (infml) اِنْحَدَرَ إلى الهاوِيةِ

tuber /ˈtjuːbə/ *n* عَسْقَل

tuberculosis /tjʊˌbɜːkjʊˈləʊsɪs/ *n* سُلّ

tubing /ˈtjuːbɪŋ/ *n* أُنبوب (أَنابيبُ)

tubular /ˈtjuːbjʊlə/ *adj* <*steel, shape*> أُنْبوبيّ

tuck /tʌk/ **A** *vt* [أَدْخَل تحت شَيْءٍ]; **to ~ one's shirt into one's trousers** أَدْخَل قميصَهُ تحت بَنْطلونِهِ; **~ the sheets in** ضَع الشَراشِفَ تحت الحَشيّةِ \ المَرْتَبةِ; **she ~ed her hair behind her ears** وَضَعَتْ شَعْرَها خلف أُذُنَيْها; **he had a newspaper ~ed under his arm** تَأَبَّطَ جَريدةً; **she sat with her feet ~ed under her** جَلَسَتْ ثانيةً رِجْلَيْها تَحْتَها

B *n* (in a sleeve, dress) ثَنْيَة (ثَنَيات)

(Phrasal verbs) **tuck away**: **~ [sth] away, ~ away [sth]** **1▸** (to store) ادَّخَرَ [شَيْئًا] <*money, valuables*> **2▸** (to conceal) **to be ~ed away** «village» كانَ مَعْزولاً; «article» كانَ مَنْشوراً في إِحْدى [الصَفحاتِ الداخِليّةِ]

• **tuck in** **A** (infml) أَكَل بِشَهيّةٍ **B** **~ in [sth], ~ [sth] in** **1▸** أَدْخَل [شَيْئًا] تحت البَنْطلون <*one's shirt*> **2▸** أَدْخَل حاشِيةَ [شَيْءٍ] تحت السَرير <*a sheet, blanket*> **C** **~ [sb] in, ~ in [sb]** أَحْكَمَ تَغْطِيةَ [شَخْصٍ] <*a child*>

• **tuck up**: **~ up [sb], ~ [sb] up** أَحْكَمَ تَغْطِيةَ [شَخْصٍ] <*a child*>; **to be ~ed up in bed** كانَ مُغَطًّى بِإِحْكامٍ في السَرير

Tuesday /ˈtjuːzdeɪ, ˈtjuːzdi/ *n* يَوْم الثُلاثاء; ▸ **Wednesday**

tuft /tʌft/ *n* خُصْلة (خُصْلات, خُصَل); **a ~ of hair** خُصْلة شَعْرٍ

tug /tʌg/ **A** *vt* **(-gg-)** شَدَّ (i-u; شَدّ) <*sb's hair, sleeve*>

B *vi* **(-gg-)** **to ~ at/on a rope/cord** «dogs, children» شَدَّ حَبْلاً

C *n* **1▸** (pull) شَدّة **2▸** (also **tug boat**) سَفينة قَطْرٍ

tug of love *n* (infml) [نِزاع بين مُطَلَّقَيْن على وِصايةِ الأَوْلادِ]

tug of war *n* **1▸** (contest) شَدّ الحَبْلِ **2▸** (between factions) تَنازُع (تَنازُعات)

tuition /tjuːˈɪʃ(ə)n/ *n* **1▸** (teaching) تَدْريس, تَعْليم (تَعْليمات, تَعاليمُ) **2▸** (fees) رُسوم دِراسيّة

tuition fees *n* رُسوم دِراسيّة

tulip /ˈtjuːlɪp/ *n* توليب

tumble /ˈtʌmb(ə)l/ **A** *vi* **1▸** (to collapse) «old person, books» سَقَطَ (u; سُقوط), هَوى (i; هُويّ) **2▸** (to fall) «prices, unemployment» انْخَفَض **3▸** (to somersault) «clowns, acrobats» تَشَقْلَبَ

B *n* (fall) سَقْطة (سَقَطات), عَثْرة (عَثَرات)

tumbledown /ˈtʌmbəldaʊn/ *adj* <*cottage, village*> مُتَداعٍ

tumble-dry /tʌmb(ə)lˈdrʌɪ/ *vt* جَفَّفَ (بِواسِطةِ مُجَفِّفِ المَلابِسِ) <*washing, clothes*>

tumble dryer, **tumble drier** *n* نَشّافة

tumbler /ˈtʌmblə/ *n* كَأْس (mf; كُؤوس), قَدَح (أَقْداح)

tummy /ˈtʌmi/ *n* (*pl* **tummies**) (infml) بَطْن (بُطون)

tumour (BrE), **tumor** (AmE) /ˈtjuːmə/ *n* وَرَم (أَوْرام)

tumult /ˈtjuːmʌlt/ *n* (fml) صَخَب, جَلَبة (جَلَب)

tumultuous /tjʊˈmʌltjʊəs/ **A** *adj* (fml) (noisy) <*applause, roar*> صاخِب

B *adj* (confused) <*presidency, marriage*> مُضْطَرِب

tuna /ˈtjuːnə/ *n* (also **tuna fish**) تونة, تُنّ

tundra /ˈtʌndrə/ *n* تونْدرا [إِقليم سُهولٍ بالمِنطقةِ القُطْبيّةِ الشماليّةِ]

tune /tjuːn/ **A** *n* **1▸** (melody) لَحْن (أَلْحان), نَغَم (أَنْغام) **2▸** (regarding pitch) **to be in/out of ~** كانَ مُدَوْزَنًا \ غَيْرَ مُدَوْزَنٍ; **to sing in/out of ~** غَنّى بِشَكْلٍ جَميلٍ \ بِنشازٍ **3▸** (infml) (expressing amounts) **to the ~ of five million dollars** إلى ما يَبْلُغُ مِقْدارُهُ خَمْسةَ مَلايينِ دولار

B *vt* **1▸** دَوْزَنَ (i; دَوْزَنة) <*a piano, guitar*> **2▸** ضَبَطَ (i-u; ضَبْط) <*a radio, television*>; **stay ~d!** اِبْقَوْا مَعَنا! **3▸** ضَبَطَ (i-u; ضَبْط) (على) <*an engine*>

(Idioms) **to call the tune** كانَ صاحِبَ الكَلِمةِ الفَصْلِ; **to change one's tune** غَيَّرَ نَبْرَتَهُ

(Phrasal verbs) **tune in** «viewers, listeners» ضَبَطَ; **to ~ in to a station** ضَبَطَ مِذْياعاً على مَوْجةِ مَحَطّةٍ

• **tune up** «orchestras, musicians» بَدَأَ العَزْفَ

tuneful /ˈtjuːnfʊl/ *adj* <*singing*> رَخيم

tuner /ˈtjuːnə/ *n* **1▸** (of musical instruments) مُدَوْزِن (الآلاتِ الموسيقيّةِ); **a piano ~** مُدَوْزِن بيانو **2▸** (of radios) مُوالِف

tungsten /ˈtʌŋst(ə)n/ *n* تَنْجِسْتِن (عُنْصُر فِلِزّيّ)

tunic /ˈtjuːnɪk/ *n* **1▸** (of a uniform) سُتْرة (سُتَر) **2▸** (in ancient times) تونيك [ثَوْب إِغْريقيّ أو رومانيّ قَديم بِدونِ كُمَّيْنِ]

tuning fork /ˈtjuːnɪŋ ˌfɔːk/ *n* شَوْكة رَنّانة

Tunis /ˈtjuːnɪs/ *pr n* (العاصِمة) تونس

Tunisia /tjuːˈnɪzɪə/ *pr n* تونس (dipt f)

Tunisian /tjuːˈnɪziən/ *n, adj* تونِسيّ

tunnel /ˈtʌn(ə)l/ **A** *n* نَفَق (أَنْفاق)

B *vi* (**-ll-** BrE, **-l-** AmE) (to excavate a passage) «miners, machines» حَفَرَ نَفَقاً; **to ~ through a hillside** حَفَرَ نَفَقاً عَبْرَ تَلٍّ

C *vt* (**-ll-** BrE, **-l-** AmE) (to excavate) حَفَرَ (i; حَفْر) ‹*a passage, one's way*›

tunnel vision *n* رُؤْية نَفَقِيّة

tunny /ˈtʌni/ *n* (*pl* **tunnies** or **tunny**) تُنّ, تونة

turban /ˈtəːb(ə)n/ *n* عِمامة (عَمائِمُ)

turbid /ˈtəːbɪd/ *adj* (liter) ‹*water, river*› كَدِر, عَكِر

turbine /ˈtəːbʌɪn/ *n* عَنَفَة, توربين (توربينات)

turbo /ˈtəːbəʊ/ *n* **1** (also **turbocharger**) شاحِن توربينيّ **2** (car) سَيّارة تيربو

turbocharged /təːbəʊˈtʃɑːdʒd/ *adj* ‹*car, engine*› بِشاحِنٍ توربينيٍّ

turbot /ˈtəːbət/ *n* (*pl* **turbot** or **turbots**) سَمَك التُّرس

turbulence /ˈtəːbjʊləns/ *n* **1** (in the air, water) اضْطِراب (اضْطِرابات), هِياج **2** (turmoil) اضْطِراب, شَغَب (اضْطِرابات)

turbulent /ˈtəːbjʊlənt/ *adj* **1** ‹*air, water*› هائِج, مُضْطَرِب

2 ‹*history, career*› عاصِف, مُضْطَرِب

tureen /təˈriːn/ *n* وِعاء, سُلْطانيّة (أَوْعِية)

turf /təːf/ **A** *n* **1** [u] (grass) أَرْض مُعْشِبة **2** (*pl* **turfs** or **turves**) (square of grass) [قِطْعة من طَبَقة عُشْبيّة]

B *vt* [غَطّى بالعُشْب] ‹*a lawn, football pitch*›

(Phrasal verb) **turf out**: **~ out [sb/sth], ~ [sb/sth] out** (infml) (to eject) طَرَدَ [شَخْصاً] ‹*a protester, guest*›; (to throw away) رَمى [شَيْئاً] ‹*clothes, junk*›

turf accountant *n* وَكيل المُراهَنات

turgid /ˈtəːdʒɪd/ *adj* (fml) ‹*style, prose*› طَنّان

Turk /təːk/ *n* تُرْكيّ (أَتْراك)

turkey /ˈtəːki/ *n* **1** (bird) ديك روميّ **2** (AmE infml) (flop) إخْفاق (إخْفاقات)

Turkey /ˈtəːki/ *pr n* تُرْكيا

Turkish /ˈtəːkɪʃ/ **A** *adj* ‹*border, food*› تُرْكيّ (أَتْراك)

B *n* (language) (اللُّغة) التُّرْكيّة

Turkish bath *n* حَمّام تُرْكيّ

Turkish delight *n* مَلْبَن

Turkmenistan /təːkmɛnɪˈstɑːn/ *pr n* تُرْكْمانِسْتان (f)

turmeric /ˈtəːmərɪk/ *n* زَعْفَران هِنْديّ, كُرْكُم

turmoil /ˈtəːmɔɪl/ *n* اضْطِراب (اضْطِرابات), شَغَب, هَرْج وَمَرْج

turn /təːn/ **A** *vt* **1** (to rotate) أَدارَ ‹*a wheel, handle*›; **to ~ the key in the lock** أَدارَ المِفْتاحَ في القُفْل **2** (to move) أَدارَ ‹*a chair, bed*›; **to ~ one's head** أَدارَ رَأْسَهُ; **she ~ed the patient onto his side** أَدارَت المَريض على جَنْبِهِ; **to ~ the page** قَلَبَ الصَّفْحةَ **3** (upside down) قَلَبَ (i; قَلْب) ‹*a mattress, steak*› **4** (to direct) أَدارَ ‹*one's eyes, a gun*›; **she ~ed her eyes to me** أَدارَتْ عَيْنَيْها إِلَيَّ; **to ~ one's back on sb** أَدارَ ظَهْرَهُ لِشَخْصٍ; **to ~ a gun/hose on sb** صَوَّبَ بُنْدُقيّةً \ خُرطومَ ماءٍ إلى شَخْصٍ **5** (to transform) حَوَّلَ; **to ~ sth into sth** حَوَّلَ شَيْئاً إلى شَيْءٍ; **to ~ water into steam** حَوَّلَ الماءَ إلى بُخارٍ; **he ~ed her into a star** حَوَّلَها إلى نَجْمةٍ **6** (with time, age) بَلَغَ (u; بُلوغ); **he ~ed 80 last month** بَلَغَ 80 سَنةً في الشَّهْرِ الماضي; **it's just ~ed two o'clock** لَقَدْ دَقَّت الساعة الثانيةُ **7** (on a lathe) خَرَطَ (i-u; خَرْط) ‹*a table leg, spindle*›

B *vi* **1** (to rotate) «keys, wheels, planets» دارَ (u; دَوْر, دَوَران) **2** (to change direction) «people, vehicles, roads» دارَ (u; دَوْر, دَوَران); **to ~ in one's seat** دارَ في مَقْعَدِهِ; **~ left at the lights** اتَّجِهْ يَساراً عند الإشارة الضَوْئيّة; **the road ~s north** يَنْعَطِفُ الطَرِيقُ شَمالاً; **to ~ into a street** دَخَلَ شارِعاً **3** (to face the other way) «people, vehicles» اسْتَدارَ; **to ~ and walk out of the room** اسْتَدارَ وَغادَرَ الغُرْفةَ **4** «the tide» تَراجَعَ **5** (in reading) قَلَبَ (i; قَلْب), أَدارَ; **~ to page 19** اذْهَبْ إلى الصَّفْحةِ 19 **6** (to have recourse to) **to ~ to sb for help** لَجَأَ إلى شَخْصٍ طَلَباً للمُساعَدةِ; **to ~ to drink/crime** لَجَأَ إلى الكُحول \ الجَريمةِ; **I didn't know which way to ~** لم أَعْرِفْ إلى أَيْنَ أَذْهَبُ **7** (to focus on) **let us ~ to the question of ...** دَعونا نَتَحَوَّلُ إلى السُّؤالِ ...; **the conversation ~ed to Noelle** تَحَوَّلَ الحَديثُ إلى نَوال **8** (to convert into) **to ~ into sth**

تَحَوَّلَ إلى شَيْءٍ; **the sofa ~s into a bed** تَتَحَوَّلُ الأَرِيكةُ إلى سَرِيرٍ; **he ~ed into a fine athlete** تَحَوَّلَ إلى رِياضيٍّ جَيِّدٍ **9** (to become) أَصْبَحَ; **the lights ~ed green/red** أَصْبَحَت الإشارةُ خَضْراءَ \ حَمْراءَ; **the weather is ~ing cold/warm** يُصْبِحُ الطَّقْسُ بارِداً \ دافِئاً **10** (to go sour) «milk» فَسَدَ (i-u; فَساد) **11** (to change colour) «leaves, trees» تَغَيَّرَ لَوْنُهُ

C *n* **1** (in games, sequences) دَوْر (أَدْوار); **whose ~ is it?** لِمَنْ الدَّوْرُ؟; **to miss a ~** فَوَّتَ دَوْراً; **it's your ~ to make the coffee** إِنَّهُ دَوْرُكَ لِتُعِدَّ القَهْوَةَ; **to have a ~ on the computer** جاءَ دَوْرُهُ لِاسْتِخْدامِ الحاسوبِ; **to take ~s at doing sth** تَناوَبوا على فِعْلِ شَيْءٍ; **she spoke to each of us in ~** تَكَلَّمَتْ مع كُلٍّ مِنّا واحِداً بعد الآخَرِ; **to speak out of ~** تَكَلَّمَ دون انْتِظارِ دَوْرِهِ **2** (circular movement) دَوْرة; **to give sth a ~** (spanner) دَوَّرَ شَيْئاً; (handle/knob) فَتَحَ شَيْئاً; **to take a ~ in the park** قامَ بِجَوْلةٍ قَصيرةٍ في المُنْتَزَهِ **3** (change of direction) انْعِطاف (انْعِطافات); **to make** *or* **do a left ~** دارَ إلى اليَسارِ; **'no right ~'** 'مَمْنوعٌ الاتِّجاهُ \ الانْعِطافُ يَميناً' **4** (bend, curve) مُنْعَطَف (مُنْعَطَفات) **5** (side road) مُنْعَطَف (مُنْعَطَفات); **take the next ~ on the left** *or* **the next left ~** خُذْ المُنْعَطَفَ القادِمَ على اليَسارِ **6** (change) مَنْحًى (مَناحٍ); **the situation took a ~ for the worse** أَخَذَ الوَضْعُ مَنْحًى أَسْوَأَ; **his fortunes took a ~ for the better** تَحَسَّنَتْ حُظوظُهُ; **we were surprised at this ~ of events** تَفاجَأْنا بِهذا التَحَوُّلِ في الأَحْداثِ; **at the ~ of the century** في مَطْلَعِ القَرْنِ **7** (BrE) (infml) (feeling) شُعور مُريع; **it gave me quite a ~** *or* **a nasty ~** انْتابَني شُعورٌ مُريعٌ **8** (act) دَوْر (أَدْوار)

(Idioms) **at every turn** في كُلِّ مُناسَبةٍ; **to be done to a turn** اسْتَوى تَماماً

(Phrasal verbs) **turn about** «soldiers» اسْتَدارَ

• **turn against**: **A** **~ against [sb/sth]** انْقَلَبَ على [شَخْصٍ \ شَيْءٍ] **B** **~ [sb] against sth/sb** حَرَّضَ [شَخْصاً] على شَيْءٍ \ شَخْصٍ

• **turn around** **A** **1** (to face the other way) «people, vehicle» اسْتَدارَ **2** (to rotate) «wheels» دارَ (u; دَوْر, دَوَران) **3** (to improve) «situation» تَحَسَّنَ **B** **~ [sth] around, ~ around [sth]** **1** (facing the other way) غَيَّرَ اتِّجاهَ [شَيْءٍ] ‹*a car, chair*› **2** (in management) أَنْقَذَ وَضْعَ [شَيْءٍ] ‹*a company, team*› **3** (to rephrase) أَعادَ صِياغةَ [شَيْءٍ] ‹*a question, sentence*›

• **turn aside** أَدارَ وَجْهَهُ

• **turn away** **A** أَدارَ وَجْهَهُ **B** **~ [sth] away, ~ away [sth]** أَدارَ [شَيْئاً] ‹*one's face, head*› **C** **~ [sb] away, ~ away [sb]** **1** (to refuse entry to) طَرَدَ [شَخْصاً] ‹*a refugee, visitor*› **2** (to reject) رَفَضَ [شَيْئاً] ‹*business, an applicant*›

• **turn back** **A** **1** (on foot, in a vehicle) اسْتَدارَ; **there's no ~ing back now** لا يُمْكِنُ الرُجوعُ إلى الوَراءِ الآنَ **2** (in a book) رَجَعَ (i; رُجوع) (إلى), عادَ (u; عَوْد, عَوْدة) (إلى); **~ back to page 33** ارْجَعْ \ عُدْ إلى الصَفْحةِ 33 **B** **~ [sth] back, ~ back [sth]** **1** (to reset) أَرْجَعَ [شَيْئاً] إلى الوَراءِ ‹*a watch, clock*›; ▸ **clock** **2** (to fold back) طَوى حاشِيةَ [شَيْءٍ] ‹*a sheet, blanket*› **C** **~ [sb] back, ~ back [sb]** أَعادَ \ أَرْجَعَ [شَخْصاً] ‹*a refugee, vehicle*›

• **turn down** **A** **~ [sth] down, ~ down [sth]** **1** (to reduce) خَفَّضَ في [شَيْءٍ] ‹*the volume, heat, music*› **2** (to fold over) ثَنى [شَيْئاً] ‹*a sheet, one's collar*› **B** **~ [sb/sth] down, ~ down [sb/sth]** رَفَضَ [شَخْصاً \ شَيْئاً] ‹*an offer, applicant, a request*›

• **turn in** **A** (infml) (to go to bed) أَوى إلى الفِراشِ **B** **~ in [sth], ~ [sth] in** (to hand in) سَلَّمَ [شَيْئاً] ‹*an assignment, one's badge*› **C** **~ [sb] in, ~ in [sb]** سَلَّمَ [شَخْصاً] ‹*a suspect, an associate*›; **to ~ oneself in** سَلَّمَ نَفْسَهُ

• **turn off** **A** (to leave a road) انْعَطَفَ; **~ off at the next exit** انْعَطِفْ في المَخْرَجِ القادِمِ **B** **~ off [sth], ~ [sth] off** (to switch off) أَطْفَأَ [شَيْئاً] ‹*a light, TV, an engine*›; (to cut off) أَقْفَلَ [شَيْئاً] ‹*a tap*›; قَطَعَ [شَيْئاً] ‹*the water, gas*› **C** **~ [sb] off** (infml) (to bore) أَضْجَرَ [شَخْصاً]; (to repel) نَفَّرَ [شَخْصاً]

• **turn on** **A** «lights» أَشْعَلَ; «appliances» شَغَّلَ **B** **~ [sth] on, ~ on [sth]** فَتَحَ [شَيْئاً] ‹*a light, TV*›; شَغَّلَ [شَيْئاً] ‹*an engine*›; فَتَحَ [شَيْئاً] ‹*a tap, the water, gas*› **C** **~ [sb] on, ~ on [sb]** **1** (infml) (to excite) أَثارَ [شَخْصاً]; **what ~s you on?** ما الّذي يُثيرُكَ؟ **2** (infml) (sexually) أَثارَ [شَخْصاً] **D** **~ on [sth]** دارَ حولَ [شَيْءٍ] ‹*a question, an issue*› **E** **~ on [sb]** (in revenge) انْقَلَبَ على [شَخْصٍ]

• **turn out** **A** **1** (to end) انْتَهى; **to ~ out well/badly** انْتَهى \ لم

ظَهَرَ أَنَّهُ مُخْطِئٌ \ بَيِّنَتِهِ على ما يُرامُ; **to ~ out to be wrong/right** صَحِيحٌ; **it ~s out that ...** ... ظَهَرَ أنّ **2** (to attend) «voters, fans» حَضَرَ (u; حُضور) **B** **~ [sth] out, ~ out [sth]** **1** (to extinguish) [شَيْئاً] أَطْفَأَ ‹the light› **2** (to empty) [شَيْئاً] أَفْرَغَ ‹one's pockets› **3** (to tip out) [شَيْئاً] أَفْرَغَ ‹a cake, jelly› **4** (to produce) [شَيْئاً] أَنْتَجَ ‹products, graduates› **C** **~ [sb] out, ~ out [sb]** **1** (to eject) [شَخْصاً] طَرَدَ ‹a tenant, lover› **2** (in appearance) **to be well ~ed out** كانَ أَنيقَ المَلْبَسِ

• **turn over** **A** **1** (to roll over) «vehicle» انْقَلَبَ «person» تَقَلَّبَ **2** (to change TV channels) غَيَّرَ القَناةَ **3** «engine» دارَ (u; دَوران, دَوْر) **B** **~ [sth/sb] over, ~ over [sth/sb]** **1** (with books, magazines) [شَيْئاً] قَلَبَ ‹the page›; ▸**leaf** **2** (upside down) [شَخْصاً \ شَيْئاً] قَلَبَ ‹a mattress, card› **3** (to hand over) **to ~ sth/sb over to sb** سَلَّمَ شَيْئاً \ شَخْصاً إلى شَخْصٍ **4** (to reflect on) **to ~ sth over in one's mind** قَلَّبَ جوانِبَ شَيْءٍ في فِكْرِهِ **5** (in sales) [شَيْئاً] بَلَغَ حَجْمُ المَبيعاتِ ‹$20 million›

• **turn round** (BrE) ▸**turn around**

• **turn up** **A** **1** (to arrive, show up) حَضَرَ (u; حُضور); **to ~ up early/late** حَضَرَ باكِراً \ مُتَأَخِّراً **2** (to be found) «lost object» ظَهَرَ (a; ظُهور); **don't worry, your bag will ~ up** لا تَقْلَقْ، سَتَظْهَرُ حَقيبَتُكَ **3** (to present itself) «opportunity, job» أَتى (i; إتْيان) **B** **~ up [sth], ~ [sth] up** **1** (in intensity) رَفَعَ ‹the heating, gas›; (in volume) [شَيْءٍ] رَفَعَ صَوْتَ [شَيْءٍ] في ‹the TV, radio, music› **2** (to shorten) [شَيْئاً] قَصَّرَ ‹trousers, a skirt, a hem› **3** (to point upwards) [شَيْئاً] رَفَعَ ‹one's collar›; ▸**nose** **4** (to discover) [شَيْئاً] كَشَفَ ‹information, facts›

turnabout /'tə:nəbaʊt/, **turnaround** /'tə:nəraʊnd/ *n* **1** (change of direction) اسْتِدارة **2** (in policy, opinion) تَحَوُّل (تَحَوُّلات)

turncoat /'tə:nkəʊt/ *n* (infml) مُرْتَدّ

turning /'tə:nɪŋ/ *n* مُنْعَطَف (مُنْعَطَفات); **to take the next ~** أَخَذَ الشارِعَ القادِمَ

turning circle *n* دائِرة الانْعِطافِ \ اللَّفِّ \ الدَوَرانِ

turning point *n* نُقْطة فاصِلة, نُقْطة تَحَوُّلٍ

turnip /'tə:nɪp/ *n* لِفْت

turn-off /'tə:nɒf/ *n* **1** (on a road) مَخْرَج (مَخارِجُ) **2** (infml) (unattractive feature) **to be a real ~** كانَ مُثيراً للاشْمِئْزازِ تَماماً

turn of phrase *n* صيغة التَعْبيرِ

turnout /'tə:naʊt/ *n* حُضور

turnover /'tə:nəʊvə/ *n* **1** (volume of sales) حَجْم المَبيعاتِ; (of stock) دَوَران المَخْزونِ **2** (of staff) نِسْبة اسْتِبْدالِ عُمّالٍ **3** (pastry) [فَطيرة مَحْشُوّة]

turnpike /'tə:npʌɪk/ *n* **1** (tollgate) [نُقْطة تَحْصيلِ رُسومٍ] **2** (AmE) (toll road) [طَريق بِرُسومِ مُرورٍ]

turn signal *n* (AmE) إشارة انْعِطافٍ

turnstile /'tə:nstʌɪl/ *n* بَوّابة دَوّارة (تَسْمَحُ بالمُرورِ واحِداً واحِداً)

turntable /'tə:nteɪb(ə)l/ *n* فونوغْراف (فونوغْرافات)

turn-up /'tə:nʌp/ *n* (BrE) ثَنْية (البَنْطَلون)

turpentine /'tə:p(ə)ntʌɪn/, **turps** /tə:ps/ *n* تَرْبَنْتين

turquoise /'tə:kwɔɪz/ **A** *n* **1** (colour) اللَوْن الفَيْروزيّ **2** (stone) فَيْروز **B** *adj* ‹waters, sky› فَيْروزيّ

turret /'tʌrɪt/ *n* بُرْج صَغير

turtle /'tə:t(ə)l/ *n* **1** (marine reptile) تِرْسة (تِرْسات, تِرَس) **2** (AmE) (tortoise) سُلَحْفاة (سَلاحِفُ)

turtle dove *n* قُمْريّ

turtleneck /'tə:təlnɛk/ *n* **1** (collar) ياقة عالِية **2** (also **turtleneck sweater**) [بُلوفَر بِياقةٍ عالِيةٍ]

turves /tə:vz/ *n pl* ▸**turf**

Tuscany /'tʌsk(ə)ni/ *pr n* توسْكانا

tusk /tʌsk/ *n* ناب (أَنْياب, نُيوب)

tussle /'tʌs(ə)l/ *n* اشْتِباك (اشْتِباكات), مُناوَشة

tutee /tju:'ti:/ *n* طالِب, تِلْميذ (في تَعْليمٍ خُصوصيٍّ)

tutor /'tju:tə/ *n* **1** (private teacher) مُدَرِّس \ مُعَلِّم خُصوصيّ **2** (BrE) (at university) مُشْرِف دِراسيّ, أُسْتاذ مُشْرِف

tutorial /tju:'tɔ:rɪəl/ *n* **1** (tuition) دَرْس خُصوصيّ **2** (on computers) بَرْنامَج \ دَليل تَعْليميّ

tut-tut /tʌt'tʌt/, **tut** /tʌt/ **A** *excl* ≈ أُفّ **B** *vi* (-tt-) «person» تَأَفَّفَ

tutu /ˈtuːtuː/ *n* تَنّورة توتو (لِراقِصةِ الباليه)

tuxedo /tʌkˈsiːdəʊ/ *n* (*pl* **tuxedos** or **tuxedoes**) (AmE) بَدْلة سْموكِن (زَيّ السَهْرةِ للرِجال)

TV /tiːˈviː/ *n* = **television** تِلِفِزْيون (تِلِفِزْيونات)

TV show *n* بَرْنامَج تِلِفِزْيونيّ

twang /twaŋ/ *n* ① (of a string, guitar) رَنّة ② (of the voice) خُنّة

tweak /twiːk/ *vt* قَرَصَ (u; قَرْص) ‹sb's nose, ear›

twee /twiː/ *adj* (pej) ‹village, poem› [جَميل بِشَكْلٍ مُبالَغٍ فيهِ]

tweed /twiːd/ *n* التَويد (قُماش من الصوف الخَشِنِ المَلْمَسِ)

tweet /twiːt/ **A** *n* (on Twitter) تَغْريدة (على التْويتِر)
B *vi* ① (to chirp) «birds» غَرَّدَ ② (on Twitter) أَرْسَلَ تَغْريدةً (على التْويتِر)

tweezers /ˈtwiːzəz/ *n pl* مِلْقَط (مَلاقِطُ), مِنْتاش

twelfth /twɛlfθ/ **A** *n* ① (in a series) ثانِيَ عَشَرَ ② (fraction) جُزْء من اثْنَيْ عَشَرَ ③ (**the twelfth**) (of a month) الثانِيَ عَشَرَ
B *adj* ‹century, day› ثاني عَشَرَ
C *adv* في المَرْكَزِ الثانِيَ عَشَرَ

Twelfth Night *n* عيد الغِطاسِ

twelve /twɛlv/ *n, adj* اثْنا عَشَرَ

twenties /ˈtwɛntiz/ *n pl* ① (decade) (**the twenties**) العِشْرينات ② (age) **to be in one's ~** كانَ في العِشْريناتِ (من عُمْرِهِ)

twentieth /ˈtwɛntiəθ/ **A** *n* ① (**the twentieth**) (in a series) العِشْرونَ ② (fraction) جُزْء من عِشْرينَ ③ (**the twentieth**) (of a month) العِشْرونَ
B *adj* ‹birthday, anniversary› العِشْرونَ
C *adv* في المَرْكَزِ العِشْرينَ

twenty /ˈtwɛnti/ *n, adj* عِشْرونَ; **we'll leave in ~-sixteen** سَوْفَ نُغادِرُ في أَلْفَيْنِ وَسِتّةَ عَشَرَ

twice /twʌɪs/ *adv* ‹see, win› مَرَّتَيْنِ; **~ a day, ~ daily** مَرَّتَيْنِ في اليَوْمِ; **she earns ~ as much as me** تَكْسِبُ ضِعْفَ ما أَكْسِبُ; **I'm ~ his age** عُمْري ضِعْفُ عُمْرِهِ; **to think ~ about/before doing sth** فَكَّرَ مَرَّتَيْنِ في \ قبل فِعْلِ شَيْءٍ

twiddle /ˈtwɪd(ə)l/ **A** *vt* عَبِثَ (a; عَبَث ب) ‹a knob, dial›; **to ~ one's thumbs** عَبِثَ بِأَصابِعِهِ (أَضاعَ وَقْتَهُ)
B *vi* **to ~ with sth** عَبِثَ بِشَيْءٍ

twig /twɪɡ/ *n* غُصْن (غُصون, أَغْصان)

twilight /ˈtwʌɪlʌɪt/ *n* ① (half light) غَسَق ② (dusk) شَفَق (أَشْفاق) ③ (liter) (final stages) مَراحِل أخيرة

twin /twɪn/ **A** *n* ① (one of two children) تَوْأَم (تَوائِمُ) ② (glove, sock, etc) فَرْدة
B (**twins**) *n pl* تَوْأَمانِ
C *adj before n* ① (related) ‹brother, sister› تَوْأَم (تَوائِمُ); **this is my ~ sister** هذه أُخْتي التَوْأَمُ ② (two) ‹taps, propellers› زَوْج (mf; أَزْواج); **an engine with ~ carburettors** مُحَرِّكٌ بِمُفَحِّمَيْنِ ③ (combined) ‹roles, problems› مُزْدَوِج
D *vt* (**-nn-**) (to link) تَمَّت التَوْأَمةُ ‹towns›; **Birmingham is ~ned with Chicago** تَمَّتْ تَوْأَمةُ مَدينةِ بِرْمِنْغْهام مع مَدينةِ شيكاغو

twin beds *n* سَريرانِ

twine /twʌɪn/ **A** *n* دوبارة (دوبار)
B *vt* جَدَلَ (i-u; جَدْل), لَفَّ (u; لَفّ) ‹ribbon, hair›; **she ~d her arms around his neck** لَفَّتْ ذِراعَيْها حول عُنُقِهِ

twinge /twɪndʒ/ *n* ① (of pain) وَخْز ② (of regret, jealousy) وَخْز الضَميرِ; **a ~ of guilt** شُعور مُفاجِئ

twinkle /ˈtwɪŋk(ə)l/ **A** *vi* ① «lights, stars» تَلأْلأَ, تَأَلَّقَ ② «eyes» بَرَقَ (u; بَرْق), لَمَعَ (a; لَمْع, لَمَعان)
B *n* ① (in sb's eye) بَريق (بَرائِقُ), لَمَعان ② (of a light, star) تَلأْلُؤ (تَلأْلُوات), بَريق (بَرائِقُ)

twinkling /ˈtwɪŋklɪŋ/ *n*
Idiom **in the twinkling of an eye** في لَمْحةِ بَصَرٍ

twin town *n* (BrE) مَدينة شَقيقة \ تَوْأَم

twirl /twəːl/ **A** *vt* فَتَلَ (i; فَتْل) ‹one's hair, moustache›; أَدارَ ‹a baton, an umbrella›
B *vi* «dancers, skirts» دَوَّمَ; **to ~ round** (once) اسْتَدارَ; (repeatedly) دَوَّمَ

twist /twɪst/ **A** *vt* ① (to bend) لوى (i; لَيّ) ‹a wire, rope›; **the ropes had got ~ed** لَقَدْ الْتَوَت الحِبالُ; **his face was ~ed with pain** [تَلَوّى أَلَماً] ② (to turn) بَرَمَ (u; بَرْم), أَدارَ ‹a dial, one's head›; **she ~ed the cap/lid off** بَرَمَت الغِطاءَ ③ (to wind, coil) **to ~ sth around sth** لَفَّ شَيْئاً حول شَيْءٍ; **the yarns/wires are ~ed together** الْتَفَّت الخيوطُ \ الأَسْلاكُ ④ (to distort) شَوَّهَ, حَرَّفَ ‹sb's words, the facts› ⑤ (to injure) **to ~ one's ankle/wrist** الْتَوى كاحِلُهُ \ مِعْصَمُهُ

B *vi* **1** (to turn) **he ~ed around in his chair** تَلَوّى في كُرْسِيِّهِ **2** (to bend) «roads, rivers» اِلْتَوى; **the path ~s and turns up the mountain** يَتَلَوّى الطَرِيقُ وَيَتَعَرَّجُ إلى أعْلى الجَبَلِ

C *n* **1** (action) بَرْم ,لَيّ; **he gave the cap a ~** بَرَمَ الغِطاءَ **2** (in wires, ropes) اعْوِجاج (اعْوِجاجات); (in roads, rivers) مُنْعَطَف (مُنْعَطَفات), مُنْحَنًى (مُنْحَنَيات) **3** (in a story, plot) تَحَوُّل مُفاجِئ في مَجْرى الأَحْداثِ; **cruel/curious ~s of fate** عَجائِبُ القَدَرِ القاسِية \ الغَرِيبة; **his career has taken a new ~** أخَذَتْ مَسيرَتُهُ المِهَنِيَّةُ مُنْعَطَفاً جَديداً **4** (piece) قِطْعة (قِطَع); **a ~ of lemon** قِطْعَة من اللَيْمونِ

twisted /ˈtwɪstɪd/ *adj* **1** ‹*metal, branch*› مُلْتَوٍ **2** ‹*ankle, wrist*› مَوْثوء **3** ‹*logic, mind*› فاسِد (فَسْدى)

twister /ˈtwɪstə/ *n* (AmE infml) إعْصار (أعاصيرُ)

twit /twɪt/ *n* (BrE infml) غَبِيّ (أَغْبِياءُ), أَبْلَه (dipt), عَبيط

twitch /twɪtʃ/ **A** *vi* «lips, ears» ارْتَعَشَ

B *n* ارْتِعاش (ارْتِعاشات)

twitchy /ˈtwɪtʃi/ *adj* (**twitchier, twitchiest**) (infml) مُضْطَرِب

twitter /ˈtwɪtə/ **A** *vi* **1** «birds» زَقْزَقَ (i; زَقْزَقة) **2** «people» ثَرْثَرَ (i; ثَرْثَرة) **3** (on Twitter) وَضَعَ تَغْريدةً (في تويتر)

B *n* (**Twitter**®) تْويتِر

twitterer /ˈtwɪt(ə)rə/ *n* مُغَرِّد (على تْويتِر)

two /tuː/ *n, adj* اثْنانِ (f اثْنَتانِ); **~ books** كِتابانِ; **two by ~** اثْنَيْنِ اثْنَيْنِ ▸ see also **five**

(Idiom) **to put two and two together** تَوَصَّلَ إلى اسْتِنْتاجٍ واضِحٍ

two-bit /ˈtuːbɪt/ *adj* (AmE infml) ‹*town, journalist*› تافِه (تَوافِهُ)

two-dimensional /ˌtuːdaɪˈmɛnʃ(ə)n(ə)l/ *adj* ‹*figure, drawing*› ثُنائيّ البُعْدِ

two-edged /ˈtuːɛdʒd/ *adj* ‹*sword, blade*› ذو حَدَّيْنِ

two-faced /ˌtuːˈfeɪst/ *adj* ‹*liar, hypocrite*› ذو وَجْهَيْنِ

twofold /ˈtuːfəʊld/ **A** *adj* ‹*increase, objective*› مُزْدَوِج

B *adv* ‹*to increase, vary*› ضِعْفَيْنِ

two-piece /tuːˈpiːs/ *n* also **~ suit**; بَدْلة ذات قِطْعَتَيْنِ

two-seater /tuːˈsiːtə/ *n* (car) سَيّارة بِمَقْعَدَيْنِ; (aircraft) طائِرة بِمَقْعَدَيْنِ

twosome /ˈtuːs(ə)m/ *n* زَوْج (mf; أَزْواج)

two-time /ˈtuːtaɪm/ **A** *adj* ‹*champion, winner*› لِمَرَّتَيْنِ

B *vt* (infml) خانَ (u; خِيانة) ‹*one's partner, girlfriend*›

two-tone /ˈtuːtəʊn/ *adj* **1** ‹*shoes, paintwork*› ذو لَوْنَيْنِ **2** ‹*siren, horn*› ذو صَوْتَيْنِ

two-way /tuːˈweɪ/ *adj* **1** ‹*street, traffic*› في اتِّجاهَيْنِ **2** ‹*communication, trade*› مُتَبادَل

two-way mirror *n* مِرْآة عاكِسة شَفّافة

two-way radio *n* جِهاز إرْسالٍ واسْتِقْبالٍ

TX *abbr* = **Texas**

tycoon /taɪˈkuːn/ *n* رَبّ المالِ ثَرِيّ للغايةِ

tying /ˈtaɪɪŋ/ *present participle* ▸ **tie**

tympani /ˈtɪmp(ə)ni/ *n pl* (Mus) ▸ **timpani**

tympanum /ˈtɪmp(ə)nəm/ *n* (*pl* **tympanums** or **tympana**) (Anat) طَبْلة الأُذُنِ

type /taɪp/ **A** *n* **1** (kind, sort) نَوْع (أَنْواع); **hair/skin ~** نَوْعُ الشَعْرِ \ الجِلْدِ; **we treat all ~s of skin condition** نُعالِجُ كُلَّ أَنْواعِ المَشاكِلِ الجِلْدِيّة; **what ~ of work are you looking for?** ما هو نَوْعُ العَمَلِ الّذي تَبْحَثُ عَنْهُ؟; **he's not that ~ of person** هو لَيْسَ من ذلك النَوْعِ من الأَشْخاصِ **2** (special person) شَخْص من نَوْعٍ مُحَدَّدٍ; **she was with some media ~s** كانَتْ مع أَشْخاصٍ من النَوْعِ الّذي يَعْمَلُ في الصَحافةِ; **she's/he's not my ~** لَيْسَتْ \ لَيْسَ من النَوْعِ الّذي يُعْجِبُني **3** (typical example) طَبيعة (طَبائِعُ), طَبْع (طِباع); **to revert to ~** عادَ إلى طَبْعِهِ **4** [u] خَطّ (خُطوط); **printed in small/large ~** مَطْبوع بخَطٍّ صَغيرٍ \ كَبيرٍ

B (**-type**) *suffix* شَبيه (أشْباه); **a cotton-~ material** مادّة شَبيهة بالقُطْنِ

C *vt* «writer» طَبَعَ (a; طَبْع, طِباعة) ‹*a word, letter*›; **to ~ 60 words a minute** طَبَعَ 60 كَلِمةً في الدَقيقةِ; **submissions must be ~d** يَجِبُ أنْ تَكونَ النُصوصُ المُرْسَلةُ مَطْبوعةً

D *vi* طَبَعَ (a; طَبْع, طِباعة)

(Phrasal verbs) **type in**: **~ in** [**sth**], **~** [**sth**] **in** أَدْخَلَ [شَيْئاً] في الحاسوبِ ‹*a word, query*›

• **type out ~ out** [**sth**], **~** [**sth**] **out** طَبَعَ [شَيْئاً] ‹*a letter, report*›

• **type up**: **~** [**sth**] **up** نَسَخَ [شَيْئاً] على الحاسوبِ \ الآلةِ الكاتِبةِ ‹*the notes, report*›

typecast /ˈtʌɪpkɑːst/ *vt* (*past tense, past participle* **typecast**) [أَعْطى نَفْسَ الدَوْرِ على الدَوامِ] <*an actor, a star*>

typeface /ˈtʌɪpfeɪs/ *n* خَطّ طِباعَةٍ

typescript /ˈtʌɪpskrɪpt/ *n* [نَصّ مَطْبوع على آلةٍ كاتِبَةٍ]

typeset /ˈtʌɪpsɛt/ *vt* (*present participle* **-tt-**; *past tense, past participle* **-set**) نَضَّدَ <*a page, magazine*>

typesetter /ˈtʌɪpsɛtə/ *n* مُنَضِّد حُروفِ الطِباعَةِ

typewriter /ˈtʌɪprʌɪtə/ *n* آلة كاتِبَة

typhoid /ˈtʌɪfɔɪd/ *n* التيفوئيد

typhoon /tʌɪˈfuːn/ *n* إِعْصار تَيْفون

typhus /ˈtʌɪfəs/ *n* also **~ fever** تيفوس

typical /ˈtɪpɪk(ə)l/ *adj* <*feature, example*> نَموذَجِيّ

typically /ˈtɪpɪkli/ *adv* <*to occur, involve*> على نَحْوٍ نَموذَجِيٍّ

typify /ˈtɪpɪfʌɪ/ *vt* (**typifies**, **typifying**, **typified**) مَثَّلَ <*sb's work, an area*>

typing /ˈtʌɪpɪŋ/ **A** *n* ضَرْب على الآلَةِ الكاتِبَةِ **B** *adj* الضَرْبِ على الآلَةِ الكاتِبَةِ <*speed*>

typist /ˈtʌɪpɪst/ *n* ضارِب على الآلَةِ الكاتِبَةِ

typographer /tʌɪˈpɒɡrəfə/ *n* مُنَضِّد

typographic /tʌɪpəˈɡrafɪk/, **typographical** /tʌɪpəˈɡrafɪk(ə)l/ *adj* <*error, design*> مَطْبَعِيّ

typography /tʌɪˈpɒɡrəfi/ *n* طِباعة

tyrannical /tɪˈranɪk(ə)l/ *adj* <*regime, dictator*> طاغٍ (طُغاة)، مُسْتَبِدّ، اسْتِبْداديّ

tyrannize, **-ise** (BrE) /ˈtɪrənʌɪz/ *vt* اسْتَبَدَّ (ب) <*a nation, family*>

tyranny /ˈtɪrəni/ *n* اسْتِبْداد، طُغْيان

tyrant /ˈtʌɪrənt/ *n* طاغِية (m) حاكِم مُسْتَبِدّ

tyre (BrE), **tire** (AmE) /ˈtʌɪə/ *n* إطار (إطارات، أُطُر)

tyre pressure (BrE), **tire pressure** (AmE) *n* ضَغْط إطارٍ

Uu

U, u /juː/ **A** *n* (letter) [الحَرْفُ الحادي والعِشْرونَ من الأَبْجَدِيَّةِ الإِنْكْلِيزِيَّةِ]

B *abbr* (**U**) (BrE Cin) = **Universal** [مُناسِبٌ لِكُلِّ الأَعْمارِ]

ubiquitous /juːˈbɪkwɪtəs/ *adj* ‹*presence, feature*› شائِع

udder /ˈʌdə/ *n* ضَرْع (ضُروع)

UFO /juːɛfˈəʊ, ˈjuːfəʊ/ *n* = **unidentified flying object** طَبَق \ جِسْم غامِض \ مَجْهول ,صَحْن طائِر

Uganda /juːˈgandə/ *pr n* أوغَنْدا

Ugandan /juːˈgand(ə)n/ *n, adj* أوغَنْدِيّ

ugly /ˈʌgli/ *adj* (**uglier, ugliest**) ① (in appearance) ‹*person, building*› قَبيح (قِباح, قَبْحى), بَشِع ② (potentially violent) ‹*situation, mood*› خَطِر

UHT /juːeɪtʃˈtiː/ *abbr* (BrE) = **ultra heat treated** مُعالَج بالحَرارةِ الفائِقةِ (مُعَقَّم)

UK /juːˈkeɪ/ *abbr* = **United Kingdom** المَمْلَكة المُتَّحِدة

Ukraine /juːˈkreɪn/ *pr n* أوكْرانِيا

Ukrainian /juːˈkreɪnɪən/ **A** *n* ① (citizen) أوكْرانِيّ ② (language) (اللُغة) الأوكْرانِيّة

B *adj* ‹*leader, border*› أوكْرانِيّ

ukulele /juːkəˈleɪli/ *n* يوكاليلي (قيثارة بِأَرْبَعةِ أَوْتارٍ)

ulcer /ˈʌlsə/ *n* قَرْحة (قِرَح)

ulema, ulama /uːlɪmə, ˈʊləmə/ *n* (*pl* **ulema** or **ulemas**) ① (group of scholars) عُلَماء (dipt) ② (scholar) عالِم (عُلَماءُ)

ulterior /ʌlˈtɪərɪə/ *adj* ‹*purpose, agenda*› خَفِيّ; **~ motive** دافِع خَفِيّ

ultimata /ʌltɪˈmeɪtə/ *n pl* ▸ **ultimatum**

ultimate /ˈʌltɪmət/ **A** *adj* ① (final) ‹*goal, decision*› نِهائِيّ ② (supreme) ‹*sacrifice, authority*› أَعْلى (عُلًى, أَعالٍ; f عُلْيا), أَقْصى (f قُصْوى) ③ (fundamental) ‹*truth, reality*› أَساسِيّ, جَوْهَرِيّ ④ (best) أَفْضَل (dipt; أَفاضِلُ, أَفْضَلونَ; f فُضْلى; f pl فُضْلَيات)

B *n* **the ~ in sth** ذُرْوة شَيْءٍ

ultimately /ˈʌltɪmətli/ *adv* ① (finally) ‹*to decide, succeed*› في النِهايةِ ② (fundamentally) أَساساً, جَوْهَرِيًّا

ultimatum /ʌltɪˈmeɪtəm/ *n* (*pl* **ultimatums**) إِنْذار نِهائِيّ; **to deliver an ~** وَجَّهَ إِنْذاراً نِهائِيًّا

ultra- /ˈʌltrə/ *prefix* ما فَوْقَ, جِدًّا

ultramarine /ˌʌltrəməˈriːn/ *n, adj* أَلْترامارين (أَزْرَق)

ultrasonic /ʌltrəˈsɒnɪk/ *adj* ‹*waves, sensor*› فوق صَوْتِيّ

ultrasound /ˈʌltrəsaʊnd/ *n* ① [u] (Phys) مَوْجات فوق صَوْتِيّةٍ ② (also **ultrasound scan**) تَصْوير بالمَوْجاتِ فوق الصَوْتِيّةِ

ultraviolet /ʌltrəˈvʌɪələt/ *adj* ‹*light, radiation*› فوق بَنَفْسَجِيّ

Umayyad /ʊˈmʌɪjad/ *n* أُمَوِيّ

umbilical /ʌmˈbɪlɪk(ə)l, ˌʌmbɪˈlʌɪk(ə)l/ **A** *adj* سُرِّيّ

B *n* ▸ **umbilical cord**

umbilical cord *n* حَبْل سُرِّيّ

umbrage /ˈʌmbrɪdʒ/ *n* **to take ~ at sth** اسْتاءَ من شَيْءٍ

umbrella /ʌmˈbrɛlə/ *n* مِظَلّة, مَطَرِيّة (NA)

umma, ummah /ˈʊmə/ *n* أُمّة (أُمَم)

umpire /ˈʌmpʌɪə/ *n* حَكَم (حُكّام)

umpteen /ʌmpˈtiːn/ *adj* (infml) ‹*times, chances*› أَلْف (mf; أُلوف, آلاف), عَديد

umpteenth /ʌmpˈtiːnθ/ *adj* (infml) لا يُحْصى; **for the ~ time** لِلمَرّةِ الأَلْفِ

umrah /ˈʊmrɑː/ *n* عُمْرة (عُمَر)

UN /juːˈɛn/ *abbr* = **United Nations**; **the ~** الأُمَم المُتَّحِدة

unable /ʌnˈeɪb(ə)l/ *adj* **to be ~ to do sth** لا يُمْكِنُهُ أَنْ يَفْعَلَ شَيْئاً

unabridged /ʌnəˈbrɪdʒd/ *adj* ‹*version, edition*› كامِل

unacceptable /ʌnəkˈsɛptəb(ə)l/ *adj* ‹*behaviour, risk*› غَيْر مَقْبولٍ

unaccompanied /ʌnəˈkʌmp(ə)nɪd/ *adj* **1** ‹*child, baggage*› غَيْر مَصْحوبٍ **2** ‹*voices, singing*› بِدونِ مُصاحَبةٍ موسيقيّةٍ; ‹*violin, cello*› مُنْفَرِد

unaccounted /ʌnəˈkaʊntɪd/ *adj* (**unaccounted for**) **1** (in emergencies) ‹*people*› مَفْقود, مَجْهول المَصيرِ; **three passengers remain ~ for** لا يَزالُ ثَلاثةُ مُسافِرينَ في عِدادِ المَفْقودينَ **2** (in accounts) ‹*money*› غَيْر مَحْسوبٍ; **that leaves £4,500 ~ for** لا تَزالُ 4,500 جُنَيْهٍ غَيْرَ مُدْرَجةٍ في الحِسابِ

unaccustomed /ʌnəˈkʌstəmd/ *adj* **1** (unused) **to be ~ to sth/to doing sth** لم يَكُنْ مُعْتاداً على شَيْءٍ \ فِعْلِ شَيْءٍ **2** (unusual) ‹*role, exercise*› غَيْر مَألوفٍ \ مَعْهودٍ

unadventurous /ʌnədˈvɛntʃ(ə)rəs/ *adj* ‹*person*› غَيْر مُغامِرٍ; ‹*menu, life*› تَقْليديّ

unaffected /ʌnəˈfɛktɪd/ *adj* **1** (not damaged or changed) **to be ~ by sth** لم يَتَأَثَّرْ بِشَيْءٍ **2** (natural) ‹*manner, person*› غَيْر مُتَكَلِّفٍ

unafraid /ʌnəˈfreɪd/ *adj* **to be ~ of sth/sb** لم يَهَبْ شَيْئاً \ شَخْصاً

unaided /ʌnˈeɪdɪd/ *adv* ‹*to walk, stand*› بِدونِ مُساعَدةٍ

unambiguous /ʌnamˈbɪɡjʊəs/ *adj* ‹*statement, meaning*› لا إِبْهامَ فيهِ, لا يَقْبَلُ الالْتِباسَ

unambitious /ʌnamˈbɪʃəs/ *adj* **1** ‹*employee, candidate*› غَيْر طَموحٍ **2** ‹*plan, goal*› باهِت

unanimous /juːˈnanɪməs/ *adj* ‹*decision, vote*› إِجْماعيّ; **we were ~** كُنّا مُتَّفِقينَ بالإِجْماعِ

unanimously /juːˈnanɪməsli/ *adv* ‹*to vote, agree*› بالإِجْماعِ; **he was elected ~** اُنْتُخِبَ بالإِجْماعِ

unannounced /ʌnəˈnaʊnst/ **A** *adj* ‹*visit, inspection*› غَيْر مُعْلَنٍ عَنْهُ **B** *adv* ‹*to arrive, call*› بِدونِ إِعْلانٍ مُسْبَقٍ

unanswered /ʌnˈɑːnsəd/ *adj* ‹*question, letter*› دونَ إِجابةٍ, لم يَتِمَّ الرَدُّ عَلَيْهِ

unappetizing, -ising (BrE) /ʌnˈapɪtʌɪzɪŋ/ *adj* ‹*meal, food*› غَيْر مُشَهٍّ \ فاتِحٍ لِلشَهيّةِ; ‹*prospect*› غَيْر جَذّابٍ

unappreciative /ʌnəˈpriːʃɪətɪv/ *adj* ‹*audience, employer*› ناكِر للجَميلِ

unapproachable /ʌnəˈprəʊtʃəb(ə)l/ *adj* ‹*person*› يَصْعُبُ الاقْتِرابُ مِنْهُ

unarmed /ʌnˈɑːmd/ *adj* ‹*civilian, protester*› أَعْزَل (dipt; عُزْل); ‹*combat*› بِدونِ سِلاحٍ

unashamedly /ʌnəˈʃeɪmɪdli/ *adv* ‹*to admit, weep*› بِلا حَياءٍ

unasked /ʌnˈɑːskt/ **A** *adj* ‹*question*› غَيْر مَطْروحٍ **B** *adv* ‹*to come, help*› بِدونِ طَلَبٍ \ دَعْوةٍ

unassisted /ʌnəˈsɪstɪd/ *adv* ‹*to walk, breathe*› بِدونِ مُساعَدةٍ

unassuming /ʌnəˈsjuːmɪŋ/ *adj* ‹*person, manner*› مُتَواضِع

unattached /ʌnəˈtatʃt/ *adj* (single) ‹*lady, gentleman*› أَعْزَب (dipt), غَيْر مُرْتَبِطٍ

unattainable /ʌnəˈteɪnəb(ə)l/ *adj* ‹*goal, dream*› بَعيد المَنالِ

unattended /ʌnəˈtɛndɪd/ *adj* **1** (unsupervised) ‹*bags, vehicle*› غَيْر مَصْحوبٍ; **please do not leave baggage ~** الرَجاءَ عَدَمُ تَرْكِ الأَمْتِعةِ دون رَقابةٍ **2** (not dealt with) مُهْمَل

unattractive /ʌnəˈtraktɪv/ *adj* ‹*woman, prospect*› غَيْر جَذّابٍ

unauthorized /ʌnˈɔːθərʌɪzd/ *adj* ‹*access, use*› غَيْر مُصَرَّحٍ بِه

unavailable /ʌnəˈveɪləb(ə)l/ *adj* **1** ‹*data, product*› غَيْر مُتَوَفِّرٍ, غَيْر مُتاحٍ; **that number is ~** لا يُمْكِنُكَ الاتِّصالُ بِهَذا الرَقْمِ **2** ‹*person*› غَيْر مُتَواجِدٍ; **the minister was ~** كانَ الوَزيرُ غَيْرَ مُتَواجِدٍ

unavoidable /ʌnəˈvɔɪdəb(ə)l/ *adj* ‹*consequence, delay*› حَتْميّ, لا مَفَرَّ مِنْهُ

unavoidably /ʌnəˈvɔɪdəbli/ *adv* ‹*absent, late*› حَتْميًّا; **I was ~ delayed** تَأَخَّرْتُ بِشَكْلٍ لا يُمْكِنُ تَجَنُّبُهُ

unaware /ʌnəˈwɛː/ *adj* **to be ~ of sth** لم يُدْرِكْ شَيْئاً; **he is socially/politically ~** هو ساذَجٌ اجْتِماعيًّا \ سِياسيًّا

unawares /ʌnəˈwɛːz/ *adv* **to catch sb ~** أَخَذَ شَخْصاً على (حينِ) غِرّةٍ

unbalanced /ʌnˈbalənst/ *adj* **1** (mentally) ‹*person, mind*› مُخْتَلّ **2** (biased) ‹*reporting, coverage*› مُتَحَيِّز **3** (unideal) ‹*diet, economy*› غَيْر مُتَوازِنٍ

unbearable /ʌnˈbɛːrəb(ə)l/ *adj* ‹*pain, heat*› لا يُطاقُ \ يُحْتَمَلُ

unbeatable /ʌn'bi:təb(ə)l/ *adj* <*opponent, price*> لا يُقْهَرُ

unbeaten /ʌn'bi:t(ə)n/ *adj* <*team, champion*> غَيْرُ مَهْزومٍ; <*record*> غَيْرُ مُحَطَّمٍ

unbeknown /ʌnbɪ'nəʊn/, **unbeknownst** /ʌnbɪ'nəʊnst/ *adv* (fml) **~ to sb** على غَيْرِ عِلْمِ شَخْصٍ

unbelievable /ʌnbɪ'li:vəb(ə)l/ *adj* <*story, amount*> لا يُصَدَّقُ, لا يُمْكِنُ تَصْديقُهُ

unbelievably /ʌnbɪ'li:vəbli/ *adv* <*well, fast*> على نَحْوٍ \ إلى حَدٍّ لا يُصَدَّقُ

unbelieving /ʌnbɪ'li:vɪŋ/ *adj* <*eyes, tone*> مُشَكِّك, غَيْرُ مُصَدِّقٍ

unbending /ʌn'bɛndɪŋ/ *adj* <*will, faith*> صارِم, عَنيد (عُنُد), (صَوارِمُ)

unbiased /ʌn'bʌɪəst/ *adj* <*opinion, observer*> نَزيه, غَيْرُ مُتَحَيِّزٍ (نِزاه, نُزَهاءُ)

unblock /ʌn'blɒk/ *vt* سَلَّكَ <*a drain, sink*>

unbolt /ʌn'bəʊlt/ *vt* فَتَحَ المِزْلاجَ <*a door, gate*>

unborn /ʌn'bɔ:n/ *adj* <*child, baby*> لم يولَدْ بَعْدُ

unbranded /ʌn'brandɪd/ *adj* <*product, goods*> بِدونِ مارْكَةٍ

unbreakable /ʌn'breɪkəb(ə)l/ *adj* <*glass, code*> غَيْرُ قابِلٍ لِلكَسْرِ

unbridled /ʌn'brʌɪdəld/ *adj* <*greed, optimism, power*> غَيْرُ مَحْدودٍ

unbroken /ʌn'brəʊk(ə)n/ *adj* **1** (uninterrupted) <*line, run*> غَيْرُ مُنْقَطِعٍ, مُتَسَلْسِل, مُتَواصِل **2** (intact) <*glass, seal*> سَليم, غَيْرُ مَكْسورٍ

unbuckle /ʌn'bʌk(ə)l/ *vt* فَكَّ (u; فَكّ), حَلَّ (u; حَلّ) <*a belt, seat belt*>

unbutton /ʌn'bʌt(ə)n/ *vt* فَكَّ الأَزْرارَ <*a shirt, coat*>

uncalled-for /ʌn'kɔ:ldfɔ:/ *adj* <*remark, criticism*> لا مُبَرِّرَ لَهُ, في غَيْرِ مَحَلِّهِ

uncanny /ʌn'kani/ *adj* <*resemblance, ability*> شاذّ (شَواذُّ, شُذّاذ), غَريب (غُرَباءُ)

uncaring /ʌn'kɛ:rɪŋ/ *adj* <*attitude, society*> عَديمُ \ فاقِدُ الإحْساسِ

unceremonious /ˌʌnsɛrɪ'məʊnɪəs/ *adj* <*exit, dismissal*> غَيْرُ مُؤَدَّبٍ, فَظّ

uncertain /ʌn'sə:t(ə)n/ **A** *adj* **1** (unsure, doubtful) غَيْرُ واثِقٍ, شاكّ; **to be ~ about sth** كانَ غَيْرَ واثِقٍ بِشَيْءٍ **2** (tentative) <*smile, voice*> مُتَرَدِّد **3** (unpredictable) <*future, times*> لا يُمْكِنُ التَنَبُّؤُ بِهِ

B **(in no uncertain terms)** *phr* بِعِبارةٍ واضِحةٍ

uncertainty /ʌn'sə:t(ə)nti/ *n* (*pl* **uncertainties**) عَدَمُ يَقينٍ, شَكّ (شُكوك)

unchallenged /ʌn'tʃalɪndʒd/ *adj* **1** <*leader, authority*> لا مُنازِعَ لَهُ **2** <*assumption, findings*> مُسَلَّم بِهِ

unchanged /ʌn'tʃeɪndʒd/ *adj* <*team, way of life*> على ما هو عَلَيْهِ; **he is ~ by his success** لم يُغَيِّرْهُ نَجاحُهُ

uncharacteristic /ˌʌnkarəktə'rɪstɪk/ *adj* <*behaviour, error*> غَيْرُ مُعْتادٍ \ مَعْهودٍ

uncharitable /ʌn'tʃarɪtəb(ə)l/ *adj* <*thought, remark*> قاسٍ (قُساة)

unchecked /ʌn'tʃɛkt/ **A** *adj* <*power, growth*> جامِح **B** *adv* <*to continue, grow*> بِدونِ رادِعٍ; **to go ~** لم يَرْدَعْهُ رادِعٌ

uncivilized /ʌn'sɪvɪlʌɪzd/ *adj* **1** <*tribes, peoples*> غَيْرُ مُتَحَضِّرٍ **2** (bad-mannered) <*behaviour, person*> هَمَجيّ (هَمَج)

uncle /'ʌŋk(ə)l/ *n* **1** (brother of your father) عَمّ (أَعْمام, عُموم); (brother of your mother) خال (أَخْوال) **2** (husband of your father's sister) زَوْج عَمّةٍ; (husband of your mother's sister) زَوْج خالةٍ

unclean /ʌn'kli:n/ *adj* **1** (dirty) <*water, hands*> قَذِر **2** (morally wrong) <*thoughts, habits*> نَجِس (أَنْجاس)

unclear /ʌn'klɪə/ *adj* **1** (not obvious) <*reason, future*> غير واضِحٍ, مُبْهَم **2** (confused, doubtful) حائِر, مُتَحَيِّر; **I'm ~ about what we have to do** لَسْتُ على اليَقينِ فيما يَجِبُ عَلَيْنا فِعْلُهُ **3** <*instructions, meaning*> غَيْرُ واضِحٍ

uncoil /ʌn'kɔɪl/ **A** *vt* بَسَطَ (u; بَسْط) <*a rope, wire*> **B** *vi* «rope, snake» انْفَكَّ

uncomfortable /ʌn'kʌmfətəb(ə)l/ *adj* **1** <*chair, shoes*> غَيْرُ مُريحٍ **2** <*silence, feeling*> مُقْلِق, مُزْعِج; **to feel ~** شَعَرَ بالانْزِعاجِ

uncommon /ʌn'kɒmən/ *adj* <*disease, species*> غَيْرُ عاديٍّ \ مَألوفٍ, نادِر; **it is not ~ for the procedure to take a month** لَيْسَ من النادِرِ أنْ يَسْتَغْرِقَ الإجْراءُ شَهْراً كامِلاً

uncommunicative /ʌnkə'mju:nɪkətɪv/ *adj* <*patient, mood*> كَتوم (كُتُم), صَموت (mf)

uncomplaining /ʌnkəm'pleɪnɪŋ/ *adj* ‹*acceptance, person*› مُسْتَسْلِم

uncomplicated /ʌn'kɒmplɪkeɪtɪd/ *adj* ‹*procedure, story*› غَيْر مُعَقَّدٍ, بَسيط (بُسَطاءُ)

uncomplimentary /ˌʌnkɒmplɪ'mɛnt(ə)ri/ *adj* ‹*remark, description*› مُهين

uncompromising /ʌn'kɒmprəmʌɪzɪŋ/ *adj* ‹*attitude, approach*› مُتَصَلِّب

unconcerned /ʌnkən'səːnd/ *adj* **1** (indifferent) غَيْر مُبالٍ **2** (unworried) غَيْر مُكْتَرِثٍ

unconditional /ʌnkən'dɪʃ(ə)n(ə)l/ *adj* ‹*love, surrender*› غَيْر مَشْروطٍ, بِدونِ قَيْدٍ أو شَرْطٍ; **you have my ~ support** لَكَ دَعْمي المُطْلَق

unconfirmed /ʌnkən'fəːmd/ *adj* ‹*reports, rumours*› غَيْر مُؤَكَّدٍ

unconnected /ʌnkə'nɛktɪd/ *adj* ‹*events, incidents*› غَيْر مُتَّصِلٍ; **the two incidents are completely ~** لَيْسَ هُناكَ أَيُّ رابِطٍ بين الحادِثَيْنِ

unconscious /ʌn'kɒnʃəs/ **A** *adj* **1** (insensible) ‹*patient, victim*› فاقِد للوَعْيِ, في غَيْبوبةٍ, مُغْمًى عَلَيْهِ **2** (unaware) ‹*mind, desire*› غَيْر مُدْرِكٍ; **I became ~ of time** فَقَدْتُ الشُعورَ بالوَقْتِ **B** *n* **the ~** اللاوَعْي

unconsciously /ʌn'kɒnʃəsli/ *adv* ‹*to influence, assume*› بِشَكْلٍ غَيْر مُدْرِكٍ

unconstitutional /ˌʌnkɒnstɪ'tjuːʃ(ə)n(ə)l/ *adj* ‹*law, action*› غَيْر دُسْتوريٍّ, مُخالِف للدُسْتورِ

uncontested /ʌnkən'tɛstɪd/ *adj* **1** (without rivals) ‹*election, nomination*› بالتَزْكِيةِ **2** (unchallenged) ‹*divorce*› بالتَراضي; ‹*assertion*› لا يَقْبَلُ الجَدَلَ

uncontrollable /ʌnkən'trəʊləb(ə)l/ *adj* ‹*urge, desire*› جامِح, عارِم; ‹*laughter, shaking*› لا يُمْكِنُ السَيْطَرةُ عَلَيْهِ

uncontrollably /ʌnkən'trəʊləbli/ *adv* ‹*to sob, shake*› بِدونِ سَيْطَرةٍ

uncontrolled /ʌnkən'trəʊld/ *adj* ‹*growth, immigration*› غَيْر مَضْبوطٍ, جامِح

unconventional /ʌnkən'vɛnʃ(ə)n(ə)l/ *adj* ‹*approach, ideas*› غَيْر تَقْليديٍّ, غَيْر مَألوفٍ

unconvinced /ʌnkən'vɪnst/ *adj* غَيْر مُقْتَنِعٍ; **I remain ~ by his arguments** بَقيتُ غَيْر مُقْتَنِعٍ بِحُجَجِهِ

unconvincing /ʌnkən'vɪnsɪŋ/ *adj* ‹*argument, performance*› غَيْر مُقْنِعٍ; ‹*victory*› غَيْر ساحِقٍ

uncooked /ʌn'kʊkt/ *adj* ‹*meat, food*› نِيء

uncooperative /ʌnkəʊ'ɒp(ə)rətɪv/ *adj* ‹*patient, witness*› غَيْر مُتَعاوِنٍ

uncoordinated /ʌnkəʊ'ɔːdɪneɪtɪd/ *adj* **1** (clumsy) ‹*movements, child*› أَخْرَق (dipt; خُرْق) **2** ‹*efforts, service*› غَيْر مُنَسَّقٍ

uncork /ʌn'kɔːk/ *vt* نَزَعَ السَدّادةَ ‹*a bottle, the wine*›

uncorroborated /ʌnkə'rɒbəreɪtɪd/ *adj* ‹*statement, source, evidence*› غَيْر مُؤَيَّدٍ (بالوَقائِعِ)

uncouth /ʌn'kuːθ/ *adj* ‹*behaviour, appearance*› فَظّ (أَفْظاظ), جِلْف (أَجْلاف)

uncover /ʌn'kʌvə/ *vt* **1** (to remove the cover from) رَفَعَ الغِطاءَ عن ‹*furniture, food*› **2** (to find, discover) اكْتَشَفَ, كَشَفَ (عن) (i; كَشْف) ‹*evidence, a secret*› **3** (to expose) كَشَفَ النِقابَ عن ‹*a scandal, crime*›

uncritical /ʌn'krɪtɪk(ə)l/ *adj* ‹*obedience, acceptance*› غَيْر انْتِقاديٍّ, بِدونِ نَقْدٍ

unctuous /'ʌŋktjʊəs/ *adj* ‹*smile, speaker*› مُتَزَلِّف, مُداهِن

uncultivated /ʌn'kʌltɪveɪtɪd/ *adj* ‹*land, fields*› غَيْر مَزْروعٍ

uncurl /ʌn'kəːl/ **A** *vt* بَسَطَ (u; بَسْط), مَدَّ (u; مَدّ) ‹*one's fingers, legs*› **B** *vi* «*snakes, cats*» انْبَسَطَ

uncut /ʌn'kʌt/ *adj* **1** ‹*version, film*› بِدونِ حَذْفٍ **2** ‹*gem*› غَيْر مَقْطوعٍ

undamaged /ʌn'damɪdʒd/ *adj* ‹*building, car*› غَيْر مَعْطوبٍ

undaunted /ʌn'dɔːntɪd/ *adj* ‹*soldier, hero*› شُجاع (شَجْعَة, شُجْعان), باسِل (بَواسِلُ); **she was ~ by the criticism** لم يُثَبِّط النَقْدُ من عَزيمَتِها

undecided /ʌndɪ'sʌɪdɪd/ *adj* **1** ‹*issue, result*› غَيْر مَحْسومٍ **2** ‹*voter, jury*› مُتَرَدِّد

undefeated /ʌndɪ'fiːtɪd/ *adj* ‹*champion, army*› غَيْر مَهْزومٍ

undemanding /ʌndɪ'mɑːndɪŋ/ *adj* ‹*task, work*› لا يَتَطَلَّبُ الكَثيرَ; ‹*child, boss*› قَنوع (قُنُع)

undemocratic /ʌndɛməˈkratɪk/ *adj* ‹*regime, institution*› غَيْر ديموقْراطِيّ

undemonstrative /ʌndɪˈmɒnstrətɪv/ *adj* ‹*child, family*› مُتَحَفِّظ

undeniable /ʌndɪˈnʌɪəb(ə)l/ *adj* ‹*truth, fact*› مُسَلَّم بِهِ, مُؤَكَّد

undeniably /ʌndɪˈnʌɪəbli/ *adv* ‹*impressive, beautiful*› بِدونِ شَكٍّ, بِكُلِّ تَأْكيدٍ

under /ˈʌndə/ **A** *prep* **1** (below) تَحْتَ; **to be ~ the bed/desk** كانَ تحت السَريرِ \ المَكْتَبِ; **it's ~ there** هو تحت ذلك المَكانِ; **to come out from ~ the desk** خَرَجَ من تَحْتِ المَكْتَبِ **2** (less than) **~ $50/two hours** أَقَلّ من $50 \ ساعَتَيْنِ; **children ~ five** الأَطْفال دون الخامِسةِ; **a number ~ ten** عَدَد أَقَلّ من العَشَرةِ; **temperatures ~ 10°C** دَرَجات حَرارةٍ أَقَلّ من 10° مِئَوِيّةٍ **3** (according to) **~ the law** بِمُقْتَضى القانونِ; **to be fined ~ regulation, 6.1** غُرِّمَ بموجِب المادّة, 6.1 **4** (subordinate to) تحت إشْراف \ رئاسة; **I have 50 people ~ me** لَدَيَّ 50 شَخْصاً تَحْتَ إشْرافي **5** (in classifications) **do I look for al-Hakim ~ 'al' or 'Hakim'?** هل أَبْحَثُ عن الحَكيمِ تحت 'ال' أو تحت 'حَكيم'؟
B *adv* **1** (beneath the surface) **to go ~** «diver, swimmer» غَطَسَ تحت الماءِ **2** (less) **£10 and ~** 10 جُنَيْهاتٍ ما دون ذلك; **children of six and ~** الأَطْفال في السادسةِ من العُمْرِ وَما دون ذلك **3** (with anaesthetics) **to put sb ~** خَدَّرَ شَخْصاً (لِأَسْبابٍ طِبِّيّةٍ) **4** (subjugated) **to keep sb ~** أَخْضَعَ شَخْصاً

underachieve /ʌnd(ə)rəˈtʃiːv/ *vi* «students, teams» نَقَصَ (u; نُقْصان, نَقْص)

underachiever /ʌnd(ə)rəˈtʃiːvə/ *n* مَنْ دون المُسْتَوى المَطْلوبِ

underage /ˈʌndərˌeɪdʒ/ *adj* ‹*driver, drinker*› دون السِنِّ القانونِيّةِ, قاصِر; **to be ~** كانَ قاصِراً

underarm /ˈʌndərɑːm/ **A** *adj* **1** ‹*deodorant, hair*› إبْطٍ **2** ‹*service, throw*› [مع عَدَمِ رَفْعِ الذِراعِ فوق مُسْتَوى الكَتِفِ] **B** *adv* ‹*to serve, throw*› [مع عَدَمِ رَفْعِ الذِراعِ فوق مَسْتَوى الكَتِفِ]

undercarriage /ˈʌndəkarɪdʒ/ *n* [u] عَجَلات هُبوطٍ

undercharge /ʌndəˈtʃɑːdʒ/ **A** *vt* [طَلَبَ سِعْراً أَقَلَّ من المُعْتادِ من] ‹*a customer, company*› **B** *vi* «shops, shopkeepers» [طَلَبَ سِعْراً أَقَلَّ من المُعْتادِ]

underclass /ˈʌndəklɑːs/ *n* طَبَقة سُفْلى

underclothes /ˈʌndəkləʊðz/ *n pl* مَلابِس داخِلِيّة

undercoat /ˈʌndəkəʊt/ *n* دِهان أَساسٍ

undercooked /ʌndəˈkʊkt/ *adj* ‹*meat, vegetables*› غَيْر مَطْبوخٍ جَيِّداً

undercover /ʌndəˈkʌvə/ *adj* ‹*operation, agent*› سِرِّيّ

undercurrent /ˈʌndəkʌrənt/ *n* **1** (in the sea) تَيّار تَحْتِيّ **2** (of bitterness, racism) تَيّار خَفِيّ \ تَحْتِيّ

undercut /ʌndəˈkʌt/ *vt* (*present participle* **-tt-**; *past tense, past participle* **undercut**) **1** [طَلَبَ سِعْراً أَقَلَّ من] ‹*a price, competitor*› **2** (to undermine) عَرْقَلَ (i; عَرْقَلة) ‹*sb's efforts*›; أَضْعَفَ ‹*a theory*›

underdeveloped /ʌndədɪˈvɛləpt/ *adj* **1** ‹*child, lungs*› ناقِص النُموِّ **2** ‹*country, economy*› مُتَخَلِّف

underdog /ˈʌndədɒg/ *n* مَغْلوب على أَمْرِهِ

underdone /ʌndəˈdʌn/ *adj* ‹*meat, vegetables*› غَيْر مَطْبوخٍ جَيِّداً

underestimate /ʌndərˈɛstɪmeɪt/ *vt* **1** اسْتَهانَ (ب), اسْتَخَفَّ (ب) ‹*a danger, the opposition*› **2** [لم يُقَدِّر الحَجْمَ] ‹*the cost, losses*›

underexpose /ʌndərɪkˈspəʊz/ *vt* أَنْقَصَ التَعْريضَ ‹*a picture, film*›

underfed /ʌndəˈfɛd/ *adj* ‹*child, population*› يُعاني من نَقْصِ \ سوءِ التَغْذِيةِ

underfoot /ʌndəˈfʊt/ *adv* تحت الأَقْدامِ; **it's wet ~** الأَرْضُ مُبْتَلّةٌ

undergo /ʌndəˈgəʊ/ *vt* (*3rd person present sing* **undergoes**; *past tense* **underwent**; *past participle* **undergone**) خَضَعَ (a; خُضوع; ل) ‹*repairs, treatment*›; **to ~ surgery** خَضَعَ لِعَمَلِيّةٍ جِراحِيّةٍ

undergraduate /ʌndəˈgradjʊət/ *n* طالِب جامِعِيّ

underground **A** /ʌndəˈgraʊnd, ˈʌndəgraʊnd/ *adv* **1** (below ground) ‹*to work, live*› تحت الأَرْضِ **2** ‹*to go, live*› في الخَفاءِ **B** /ˈʌndəgraʊnd/ *adj* **1** (below ground) ‹*explosion, passage*› جَوْفِيّ, تحت الأَرْضِ **2** ‹*newspaper, movement*› سِرِّيّ

3 (avant garde) ‹*movement, comic*› طَلِيعِيّ

C /ˈʌndəgraʊnd/ *n* **(the underground)** **1** (BrE) (metro) مِتْرو أَنْفاقٍ **2** (secret organization) مُقاوَمة سِرِّيّة **3** (artists' organization) حَرَكة فَنِّيّة طَلِيعِيّة

undergrowth /ˈʌndəgrəʊθ/ *n* خميلة (خمائِلُ), غَيْضة

underhand /ˈʌndəhand/ *adj* also **~ed** ‹*method, trick*› مُخادِع, ماكِر (مَكَرة)

underlie /ʌndəˈlʌɪ/ *vt* (*present participle* **underlying**; *past tense* **underlay**; *past participle* **underlain**) **1** (Geol) (to lie below) وَقَعَ (a; وُقوع) تحت ‹*a layer, stratum*› **2** (to support) دَعَمَ (a; دَعْم), سَنَدَ (u; سُنود) ‹*a principle, view*›

underline /ʌndəˈlʌɪn/ *vt* وَضَعَ خَطًّا تحت ‹*text, a word*›

underling /ˈʌndəlɪŋ/ *n* (pej) تابع (تَبَعة, تُبّاع), مَرْؤوس

underlying /ʌndəˈlʌɪɪŋ/ *adj* ‹*problem, cause*› ضِمْنيّ

undermanned /ʌndəˈmand/ *adj* ‹*factory, department*› تَنْقُصُهُ الأَيْدي العامِلةُ

undermine /ʌndəˈmʌɪn/ *vt* أَضْعَفَ ‹*foundations, sb's authority*›

underneath /ʌndəˈniːθ/ **A** *prep* ‹*the table, bridge, floorboards*› تَحْتَ; **she hid it ~ the floor** خَبَّأَتْهُ تحت الأَرْضِ

B *adv* ‹*to crawl*› إلى الأَسْفَلِ; ‹*to live*› في الأَسْفَلِ

C *adj* سُفْلِيّ, تَحْتِيّ ‹*side*›; **the apartment ~** الشقة التي تقعُ في الأَسْفَلِ

D *n* (of a car, stage) جُزْء سُفْليّ \ تَحْتيّ; **clean the ~ regularly** نَظِّف الجُزْءَ السُفْليَّ باسْتِمْرارٍ

undernourished /ʌndəˈnʌrɪʃt/ *adj* ‹*animal, child*› يُعاني من نَقْصِ \ سوءِ التَغْذِيةِ

underpaid /ʌndəˈpeɪd/ **A** *past tense, past participle* ▸ **underpay**

B *adj* ‹*employee, worker*› [يَتَقاضى أَجْراً ناقِصاً]

underpants /ˈʌndəpants/ *n pl* سِرْوال تَحْتيّ

underpass /ˈʌndəpɑːs/ *n* نَفَق (أَنْفاق)

underpay /ʌndəˈpeɪ/ *vt* (*past tense, past participle* **underpaid**) [دَفَعَ أَجْراً ناقِصاً] ‹*an employee, a worker*›

underpin /ʌndəˈpɪn/ *vt* **(-nn-)** **1** (to support) دَعَم, دَعَّمَ (الأَساسَ) ‹*a wall, building*› **2** (to be the basis of) دَعَمَ, عَزَّزَ (a; دَعْم) ‹*a society, theory*›

underprivileged /ʌndəˈprɪvɪlɪdʒd/ *adj* ‹*family, children*› مَحْروم

underrate /ʌndəˈreɪt/ *vt* اسْتَهانَ (ب) ‹*strength, an opponent*›

underscore /ʌndəˈskɔː/ *vt* **1** (to underline) وَضَعَ خَطًّا تحت ‹*a letter, word*› **2** (to emphasize) أَكَّدَ, أَبْرَزَ (على) ‹*importance, a need*›

undersecretary /ʌndəˈsɛkrətri/ *n* (BrE) also **~ of state** وَكيل الوزارة

undersell /ʌndəˈsɛl/ *vt* (*past tense, past participle* **undersold**) **1** (to undercut) باعَ بِسِعْرٍ أَقَلَّ من ‹*a competitor, rival*›; باعَ بِسِعْرٍ أَقَلَّ من قيمَتِهِ ‹*a house, car*› **2** (to underestimate) **to ~ oneself** اسْتَصْغَرَ نَفْسَهُ

undershirt /ˈʌndəʃəːt/ *n* (AmE) قَميص داخِليّ

undershorts /ˈʌndəʃɔːts/ *n pl* (AmE) سِرْوال تَحْتيّ

underside /ˈʌndəsʌɪd/ *n* الجانِب السُفْليّ

underskirt /ˈʌndəskəːt/ *n* تَنّورة داخِليّة

undersold /ʌndəˈsəʊld/ *past tense, past participle* ▸ **undersell**

understaffed /ʌndəˈstɑːft/ *adj* ‹*department, hospital*› يُعاني من نَقْصٍ بالعُمّالِ

understand /ʌndəˈstand/ **A** *vt* (*past tense, past participle* **understood**) **1** (to comprehend) فَهِمَ (a; فَهْم) ‹*a language, the question, importance*›; **I can't ~ why** لا أَسْتَطيعُ أَنْ أَفْهَمَ السَبَبَ; **to make oneself understood** جَعَلَ نَفْسَهُ مَفهوماً; **I can't ~ a word he's saying** لا أَسْتَطيعُ أَنْ أَفْهَمَ كَلِمةً مِمّا يَقولُ **2** (to empathize with) فَهِمَ (a; فَهْم), تَفَهَّمَ ‹*a person, sb's feelings*›; **we ~ each other** نَفْهَمُ بَعْضُنا بَعْضاً; **I can ~ her being annoyed** أَسْتَطيعُ أَنْ أَتَفَهَّمَ انْزِعاجَها **3** (to interpret) فَهِمَ (a; فَهْم); **as I ~ it** كما فَهِمْتُهُ; **what do you ~ by this?** ماذا تَفْهَمُ من هذا؟ **4** (fml) (to believe) اِعْتَقَدَ; **I ~ you're leaving us** أَعْتَقِدُ أَنَّكَ سَتَتْرُكُنا; **I was given to ~ that ...** قيلَ لي جَعَلَني أَعْتَقِدُ أَنَّ ... **5** **to be understood** (mutually accepted) كانَ مَفْهوماً; **I thought (that) that was understood** اعْتَقَدْتُ أَنّ ذلك كانَ مَفْهوماً

B *vi* (*past tense, past participle* **understood**) (to comprehend) فَهِم (a; فَهْم); **I quite ~** أَفْهَمُ جَيِّدًا; **this mustn't happen again, do you ~?** لا يَجِبُ أَنْ يَحْدُثَ هذا مَرّةً أُخْرى، هل تَفْهَمُ؟

understandable /ʌndəˈstandəb(ə)l/ *adj* **1** (comprehensible) مَفْهوم; **his language is easily ~** لُغَتُهُ مَفْهومةٌ بِسُهولةٍ

[2] (reasonable) مَفْهوم ‹*reason, concern, reaction*›; **it's ~ that ...** من المَفْهومِ أنّ ... ; **he took an ~ pride in his achievements** كانَ فَخوراً بِانْجازاتِهِ عن حَقّ

understandably /ʌndəˈstandəbli/ *adv* ‹*reluctant, upset*› بِشَكْلٍ مَفْهومٍ

understanding /ʌndəˈstandɪŋ/ [A] *n* [1] (comprehension) فَهْم (أَفْهام); **to have some/no ~ of a subject** فَهِمَ بَعْضَ المَوْضوعِ \ ما فَهِمَ المَوْضوعَ [2] (of the facts) فَهْم (أَفْهام); **our ~ was that ...** كانَ فَهْمُنا أنّ ... ; **he showed a full/scant ~ of the issues** أَظْهَرَ فَهْماً كامِلاً \ بَسيطاً لِلقَضايا [3] (sympathy) تَفَهُّم; **he preaches tolerance and ~** دَعا إلى التَسامُحِ والتَفَهُّمِ [4] (agreement, arrangement) اتِّفاق (اتِّفاقات); **on the ~ that ...** بِناءً على الاتِّفاقِ أنّ ... ; **there is an ~ that ...** هُناكَ اتِّفاقٌ أنّ [B] *adj* ‹*person, smile*› مُتَفَهِّم; **thank you for being so ~** شُكْراً لِتَفَهُّمِكَ

understate /ʌndəˈsteɪt/ *vt* هَوَّنَ, قَلَّلَ من الأَهَمِّيّةِ ‹*the cost, severity*›

understatement /ˈʌndəsteɪtmənt/ *n* تَعْبير مُلَطَّف

understood /ʌndəˈstʊd/ *past tense, past participle* ▸ **understand**

understudy /ˈʌndəstʌdi/ *n* (*pl* **understudies**) مُمَثِّل احْتِياطيّ (يَأْخُذُ دَوْرَ المُمَثِّلِ الأَساسيِّ عند الحاجةِ)

undertake /ʌndəˈteɪk/ *vt* (*past tense* **undertook**; *past participle* **undertaken**) [1] (to take on) شَرَعَ (ب ;في ;قِيام ;u) قامَ, تَوَلّى (a; شُروع) ‹*a mission, trip*› [2] (to promise) **to ~ to do sth** تَعَهَّدَ بِأَنْ يَفْعَلَ شَيْئاً

undertaker /ˈʌndəteɪkə/ *n* حانوتيّ (حانوتيّة)

undertaking /ʌndəˈteɪkɪŋ/ *n* [1] (venture) مَشْروع (مَشْروعات, مَشاريع) [2] (promise) وَعْد, تَعَهُّد (وُعود)

under-the-counter /ʌndəðəˈkaʊntə/ [A] *adj* ‹*medicines, cigarettes*› غَيْر مَشْروع [B] *adv* (**under the counter**) ‹*to buy, sell*› بِطَريقةٍ غَيْرِ مَشْروعةٍ

undertone /ˈʌndətəʊn/ *n* [1] (low voice) صَوْت خافِت [2] (hint) مَسْحة (مَسَحات)

undervalue /ʌndəˈvaljuː/ *vt* بَخَسَ القيمةَ ‹*an asset, employee*›

underwater /ʌndəˈwɔːtə/ [A] *adj* ‹*cable, exploration*› تحت الماءِ [B] *adv* ‹*to swim, film*› تحت الماءِ

under way *adj* **to get under way** «trains, events» انْطَلَقَ; **to be under way** «trains, ships» كانَ في الطَريقِ; «events, campaigns» جَرى مَجْراهُ

underwear /ˈʌndəweː/ *n* مَلابِس داخِلِيّة

underweight /ʌndəˈweɪt/ *adj* ‹*patient, child*› أَقَلّ من الوَزْنِ الطَبيعيِّ

underwent /ʌndəˈwent/ *past tense* ▸ **undergo**

underworld /ˈʌndəwəːld/ *n* [1] (criminal society) عالَم جَريمةٍ \ إِجْرامٍ [2] (**the Underworld**) (in mythology) العالَم السُفْليّ

underwrite /ʌndəˈraɪt/ *vt* (*past tense* **underwrote**; *past participle* **underwritten**) [1] (in funding) كَفَلَ (a-u; كَفالة) ‹*a project, stadium*› [2] (to guarantee) ضَمِنَ (a; ضَمان) ‹*an insurance policy, a risk*› [3] (in share offers) ضَمِنَ التَغْطِيةَ (تَعَهَّدَ بِشِراءِ ما لا يُباعُ من الأَسْهُمِ) ‹*a share issue*›

undeserving /ʌndɪˈzəːvɪŋ/ *adj* ‹*winner, cause*› غَيْر جَديرٍ, غَيْر مُسْتَحِقٍّ, لا يَسْتَحِقُّ

undesirable /ʌndɪˈzʌɪərəb(ə)l/ *adj* ‹*result, character*› غَيْر مَرْغوبٍ فيهِ

undetected /ʌndɪˈtɛktɪd/ *adv* ‹*to enter, remain*› غَيْر مُلاحَظٍ \ مُدْرَكٍ; **the mistake/cancer went ~** لم يُكْتَشَفِ الخَطَأُ \ مَرَضُ السَرَطانِ

undeterred /ʌndɪˈtəːd/ *adj* **to be ~ by sb/sth** لم يُثَبِّطْ عَزيمَتَهُ شَخْصٌ \ شَيْءٌ

undeveloped /ʌndɪˈvɛləpt/ *adj* ‹*area, oil reserves*› غَيْر مُسْتَثْمَرٍ \ مُسْتَغَلٍّ

undid /ʌnˈdɪd/ *past tense* ▸ **undo**

undignified /ʌnˈdɪgnɪfʌɪd/ *adj* ‹*outburst, behaviour*› غَيْر لائِقٍ \ مُحْرِج, مُحْتَرَم

undisciplined /ʌnˈdɪsɪplɪnd/ *adj* ‹*troops, behaviour*› غَيْر مُنْضَبِطٍ

undiscovered /ʌndɪˈskʌvəd/ *adj* ‹*land, document*› غَيْر مُكْتَشَفٍ

undiscriminating /ʌndɪˈskrɪmɪneɪtɪŋ/ *adj* ‹*client, judge*› لا يُحْسِنُ التَقْديرَ, غَيْر قادِرٍ على التَمْييزِ

undisguised /ʌndɪsˈgʌɪzd/ *adj* ‹*anger, joy*› مَكْشوف

undisputed /ʌndɪˈspjuːtɪd/ *adj* ‹*champion, leader*› بِدونِ مُنازِعٍ; ‹*fact, highlight*› لا جِدالَ فيهِ

undisturbed /ʌndɪ'stə:bd/ *adj* **1** ‹*soil, forest*› مَتْروك على حالِهِ, بِكْر **2** ‹*peace, sleep*› هادِئ, غَيْر مُضْطَرِب

undivided /ʌndɪ'vʌɪdɪd/ *adj* ‹*opposition, loyalty*› غَيْر مُجَزَّأ, كامِل; **to give sb/sth one's ~ attention** أَوْلى شَخْصاً \ شَيْئاً عِنايَتَهُ الكامِلَةَ

undo /ʌn'du:/ *vt* (*3rd person present sing* **undoes**; *past tense* **undid**; *past participle* **undone**) **1** فَكَّ (u; فَكّ) ‹*a button*›; فَكَّ الأَزْرارَ ‹*a jacket*›; حَلَّ (u; حَلّ) ‹*a knot*›; فَتَحَ (a; فَتْح) ‹*a parcel*› **2** أَبْطَلَ, أَلْغى ‹*work, effort*›

undocumented /ʌn'dɒkjʊmɛntɪd/ *adj* **1** ‹*immigrant, worker*› بِدونِ دَليلٍ مُثْبِتٍ **2** ‹*claim, event*› غَيْر مُوَثَّقٍ

undone /ʌn'dʌn/ *adj* **1** مَفْكوك, مَحْلول; **to be/come ~** «buttons, dress» اِنْفَكَّ **2** ‹*work, washing*› غَيْر مُنْجَزٍ

undoubtedly /ʌn'daʊtɪdli/ *adv* ‹*brave, true*› بِلا شَكٍّ \ رَيْبٍ

undress /ʌn'drɛs/ **A** *vt* عَرّى, نَزَعَ \ خَلَعَ المَلابِسَ ‹*a child, patient*›

B *vi* تَعَرّى, تَجَرَّدَ من الثِيابِ

undrinkable /ʌn'drɪnkəb(ə)l/ *adj* ‹*water, wine*› غَيْر صالِحٍ للشُرْبِ, لا يُشْرَبُ

undue /ʌn'dju:/ *adj* ‹*delay, influence*› لا داعِيَ لَهُ

unduly /ʌn'dju:li/ *adv* ‹*optimistic, to worry*› أَكْثَر من اللازِمِ, على نَحْوٍ مُفْرِطٍ \ غَيْر مُلائِمٍ

unearth /ʌn'ə:θ/ *vt* **1** (Archaeol) (to dig up) نَبَشَ (u; نَبْش), اِسْتَخْرَجَ ‹*remains, pottery*› **2** (to find) اِكْتَشَفَ ‹*a photograph, evidence*›

unearthly /ʌn'ə:θli/ *adj* **1** (mysterious) ‹*light, scream*› خارِق للطَبيعةِ, تَقْشَعِرُّ مِنْهُ الأَبْدانُ, مُرْعِب **2** (very early) **at an ~ hour** في ساعةٍ مُبَكِرةٍ جِدًّا

unease /ʌn'i:z/ *n* **1** (anxiety) قَلَق, اِضْطِراب (اِضْطِرابات) **2** (precarious nature) تَوَتُّر (تَوَتُّرات)

uneasily /ʌn'i:zɪli/ *adv* **1** (anxiously) ‹*to wait, enquire*› بِاضْطِرابٍ, بِقَلَقٍ, بِتَوَجُّسٍ **2** (precariously) ‹*to co-exist*› بِصُعوبةٍ

uneasiness /ʌn'i:zinəs/ *n* **1** (anxiety) قَلَق **2** (precarious nature) عَدَم اِرْتِياحٍ

uneasy /ʌn'i:zi/ *adj* (**uneasier, uneasiest**) **1** (anxious) ‹*silence, laugh*› قَلِق, مُضْطَرِب; **to make sb ~** أَقْلَقَ شَخْصاً **2** (precarious) ‹*peace, relationship*› غَيْر مُسْتَقِرٍّ, مُضْطَرِب

uneconomical /ʌni:kə'nɒmɪk(ə)l, ʌnɛkə'nɒmɪk(ə)l/ *adj* ‹*method, factory*› غَيْر اقْتِصاديٍّ, غَيْر مُرْبِحٍ

uneducated /ʌn'ɛdjʊkeɪtɪd/ *adj* ‹*peasant, masses*› غَيْر مُتَعَلِّمٍ \ مُثَقَّفٍ

unemotional /ʌnɪ'məʊʃ(ə)n(ə)l/ *adj* ‹*account, response*› فاتِر (فَواتِرُ), غَيْر انْفِعاليٍّ, بِدونِ انْفِعالٍ

unemployable /ʌnɪm'plɔɪəb(ə)l/ *adj* ‹*candidate, graduate*› غَيْر مُؤَهَّل للعَمَلِ

unemployed /ʌnɪm'plɔɪd/ **A** *n* (**the unemployed** *n pl*) العاطِلونَ (عن العَمَلِ)

B *adj* ‹*worker, teacher*› عاطِل (عن العَمَلِ)

unemployment /ʌnɪm'plɔɪmənt/ *n* بِطالة

unemployment benefit (BrE), **unemployment compensation** (AmE) *n* إعانة \ تَعْويض \ مُخَصَّصات البَطالةِ

unemployment rate *n* مُعَدَّل \ نِسْبة البَطالةِ

unending /ʌn'ɛndɪŋ/ *adj* ‹*series, struggle*› لا نِهايةَ لَهُ, مُسْتَمِرّ, أَبَديّ

unenthusiastic /ˌʌnɪnˌθju:zɪ'astɪk/ *adj* ‹*response, group*› غَيْر مُتَحَمِّسٍ

unenviable /ʌn'ɛnvɪəb(ə)l/ *adj* ‹*position, task*› لا يُحْسَدُ عَلَيْهِ

unequal /ʌn'i:kwəl/ *adj* ‹*amounts, contest*› غَيْر مُتَساوٍ \ مُتَكافِئٍ; **to be ~ to the task** كانَ غَيْرَ كُفْءٍ للمَهَمّةِ

unequivocal /ʌnɪ'kwɪvək(ə)l/ *adj* ‹*statement, evidence*› واضِح, بَيِّن, لا لَبْسَ فيه

UNESCO /ju:'neskəʊ/ *pr n* = **United Nations Educational, Scientific and Cultural Organization** اليونِسْكو (مُنَظَّمة الأُمَمِ المُتَّحِدةِ للتَعْليمِ والعُلومِ والثَقافة)

unethical /ʌn'ɛθɪk(ə)l/ *adj* ‹*behaviour, practice*› غَيْر أَخْلاقيٍّ

uneven /ʌn'i:v(ə)n/ *adj* ‹*surface, wear*› غَيْر مُسْتَوٍ; ‹*distribution, contest*› غَيْر مُنْتَظِمٍ

uneventful /ʌnɪ'vɛntfʊl/ *adj* ‹*day, journey*› لَيْسَ فيه ما يَسْتَحِقُّ الذِكْرَ, عاديّ

unexciting /ʌnɪk'sʌɪtɪŋ/ *adj* ‹*diet, trip*› مُملّ, غَيْر مُثير \ شَيِّق

unexpected /ʌnɪk'spɛktɪd/ *adj* ‹*arrival, outcome*› غَيْر مُتَوقَّع \ مُفاجِئ, مُنْتَظَر

unexpectedly /ʌnɪk'spɛktɪdli/ *adv* ‹*to happen, arrive*› بَغْتَةً; ‹*large, strong*› على نَحْوٍ غَيْر مُتَوقَّع

unexploded /ʌnɪk'spləʊdɪd/ *adj* ‹*bomb, shell*› غَيْر مُنْفَجِر

unexplored /ʌnɪk'splɔːd/ *adj* ‹*region, forest*› غَيْر مُكْتَشَف

unfailing /ʌn'feɪlɪŋ/ *adj* ‹*support, optimism*› ثابت (ثَوابِتُ), لا يَكِلُّ

unfair /ʌn'fɛː/ *adj* ‹*trial, practice*› غَيْر عادِل, غَيْر مُنْصِف, جائر; **that's ~ on the other candidates** ذلك غَيْرُ مُنْصِف للمُرَشَّحينَ الآخَرين; **it's ~ of you to say that** لَيْسَ من الإنْصافِ أنْ تقولَ ذلك

unfair dismissal *n* (in UK) طَرْد تَعَسُّفِيّ

unfairly /ʌn'fɛːli/ *adv* ‹*to treat, punish*› على نَحْوٍ غَيْرِ مُنْصِف, من دونِ حَقّ; **to be ~ dismissed** تَمَّ طَرْدُهُ بِشَكْلٍ تَعَسُّفِيّ

unfairness /ʌn'fɛːnəs/ *n* جَوْر (جَوْرة), ظُلْم

unfaithful /ʌn'feɪθfʊl/ *adj* 1 (to a spouse, partner) خائِن (خَوَنة, خَوّان) 2 (disloyal) ‹*servant, dog*› غَيْر مُخْلِص

unfamiliar /ʌnfə'mɪlɪə/ *adj* 1 ‹*face, situation*› غَيْر مَأْلوف 2 **to be ~ with the language/his work** لم يَكُنْ على مَعْرِفَةٍ باللُّغَةِ \ بِعَمَلِهِ

unfashionable /ʌn'faʃ(ə)nəb(ə)l/ *adj* ‹*dress, club*› مُخالِف للموضة; ‹*opinion, idea*› غَيْر عَصْرِيّ

unfasten /ʌn'fɑːs(ə)n/ *vt* فَكّ (u; فَكّ), حَلّ (u; حَلّ) ‹*one's trousers, seatbelt*›

unfavourable (BrE), **unfavorable** (AmE) /ʌn'feɪv(ə)rəb(ə)l/ *adj* ‹*conditions, weather, outcome*› غَيْر مُؤاتٍ, غَيْر مُلائِم

unfinished /ʌn'fɪnɪʃt/ *adj* ‹*work, building*› غَير مكتمِل \ تامّ

unfit /ʌn'fɪt/ *adj* 1 (in poor physical condition) غَيْر مُسْتَعِدّ بَدَنِيًّا; **I'm too ~ to play** لَسْتُ مُسْتَعِدًّا بَدَنِيًّا لِأَلْعَبَ 2 (ill, injured, etc) ‹*employee*› عاجِز (عَجَزة); ‹*player*› مُصاب; **the accident left her ~ for work** تَرَكَها الحادِثُ عاجِزةً عن العَمَلِ 3 (substandard) ‹*housing, road*› غَيْر مُناسِب; **to be ~ for human habitation** كانَ غَيْرَ مُناسِبٍ للسَكَنِ 4 (not competent) ‹*parent, witness*› غَيْر كُفُؤ; **to be ~ for public office** كانَ كُفُوًا

كانَ مُتْعَباً للوَظيفةِ العامّةِ; **he was so tired, he was ~ to drive** جِدًّا وكانَ غَيْرَ قادِرٍ على قِيادةِ السَيّارةِ

unflagging /ʌn'flagɪŋ/ *adj* ‹*energy, support*› لا يَتْعَبُ, لا يَكِلُّ

unflattering /ʌn'flatərɪŋ/ *adj* ‹*clothes, description*› [لا يُبْرِزُ المَحاسِنَ]

unfold /ʌn'fəʊld/ **A** *vt* بَسَطَ (u; بَسْط) ‹*a map, chair*› **B** *vi* 1 (to open) «leaves, chairs» انْفَتَحَ, انْبَسَطَ 2 (to develop) «stories, events» انْكَشَفَ, تَكَشَّفَ

unforeseeable /ʌnfɔː'siːəb(ə)l/ *adj* ‹*consequences, circumstances*› لا يُمْكِنُ التَنَبُّؤُ بِهِ, غَيْر مُتَوقَّع \ مُنْتَظَر

unforeseen /ʌnfɔː'siːn/ *adj* ‹*problem, circumstances*› غَيْر مُتَوقَّع \ مُنْتَظَر

unforgettable /ʌnfə'gɛtəb(ə)l/ *adj* ‹*experience, moment*› لا يُنْسى

unforgivable /ʌnfə'gɪvəb(ə)l/ *adj* ‹*behaviour, crime*› لا يُغْتَفَرُ

unforgiving /ʌnfə'gɪvɪŋ/ *adj* ‹*environment, terrain*› قاسٍ (قُساة), لا يَرْحَمُ

unfortunate /ʌn'fɔːtʃ(ə)nət/ *adj* 1 (wretched) ‹*victim, children*› تَعيس (تُعَساءُ) 2 (unlucky) ‹*situation, start*› سَيِّئ الحَظِّ 3 (regrettable) ‹*incident, remark*› يُؤْسَفُ لَهُ

unfortunately /ʌn'fɔːtʃ(ə)nətli/ *adv* ‹*named, phrased*› لسوءِ الحَظِّ; **~, I can't help you** لِسوءِ الحَظِّ, لا يُمْكِنُني مُساعَدَتُكَ

unfounded /ʌn'faʊndɪd/ *adj* ‹*allegation, fear*› لا أساسَ لَهُ

unfriend /ʌn'frɛnd/ *vt* أَلْغى الصَداقةَ

unfriendly /ʌn'frɛndli/ *adj* (**unfriendlier**, **unfriendliest**) ‹*neighbour, reception*› فَظّ (أَفْظاظ); ‹*environment, climate*› قاسٍ

unfulfilled /ʌnfʊl'fɪld/ *adj* ‹*ambition, promise*› غَيْر مُنْجَز \ مُحَقَّق; **to feel ~** شَعَرَ بِأَنَّ آمالَهُ لم تَتَحَقَّقْ

unfurl /ʌn'fəːl/ **A** *vt* بَسَطَ (u; بَسْط), نَشَرَ (u; نَشْر) ‹*a banner, sail*› **B** *vi* «sails, flags» انْتَشَرَ, انْبَسَطَ

unfurnished /ʌn'fəːnɪʃt/ *adj* ‹*apartment, rental*› غَيْر مَفْروش

ungainly /ʌn'geɪnli/ *adj* (**ungainlier**, **ungainliest**) ‹*movement, creature*› غَليظ (غِلاظ)

ungracious /ʌn'greɪʃəs/ *adj* ‹*remark, behaviour*› فَظّ (أَفْظاظ)

ungrammatical /ʌngrə'matɪk(ə)l/ *adj* ‹*sentence, English*› مَلْحون

ungrateful /ʌnˈɡreɪtfʊl/ *adj* ‹*child, wretch*› ناكِر للمَعْروفِ \ جاحِد للمَعْروفِ \ للجميلِ ,للجَميلِ

unguarded /ʌnˈɡɑːdɪd/ *adj* 1 (unprotected) ‹*prisoner, frontier*› غَيْر مَحْروسٍ 2 (careless) ‹*remark, criticism*› مُتَهَوِّر, طائِش ,غَيْر مَدْروسٍ; **in an ~ moment** في لَحْظةِ سَهْوٍ

unhappily /ʌnˈhapɪli/ *adv* 1 (sadly) ‹*to stare, end*› بِحُزْنٍ ,ب \ في شَقاءٍ 2 (regrettably) لِلأَسَف ,لِسوءِ الحَظِّ; **~, the marriage only lasted a few months** لِسوءِ الحَظِّ، لم يَسْتَمِرَّ الزَواجُ لِأَكْثَرَ من بِضْعةِ أَشْهُرٍ 3 (expressing dissatisfaction) ‹*to complain, write*› بِاسْتِياءٍ

unhappiness /ʌnˈhapinəs/ *n* 1 (sadness) حُزْن (أَحْزان), عَدَم رِضاً ,(اسْتِياءات) اسْتِياء (dissatisfaction) 2 بُؤْس ,شَقاء 3 (concern) قَلَق

unhappy /ʌnˈhapi/ *adj* (**unhappier**, **unhappiest**) 1 (sad) ‹*life, situation*› تَعيس (تُعَساءُ) ,بائِس (بُؤَساءُ); ‹*face, occasion*› حَزين (حَزانى) ,مُكْتَئِب 2 (regrettable) ‹*coincidence, decision*› سَيِّئ ,الحَظِّ غَيْر مُوَفَّق 3 (dissatisfied) ‹*customer, viewer*› غَيْر راضٍ; **to be ~ with a result/decision** لم يَكُنْ راضِياً على نَتيجةٍ \ قرارٍ 4 (concerned) قَلِق

unharmed /ʌnˈhɑːmd/ *adj* ‹*child, passenger*› سالِم ,سَليم (سُلَماءُ)

unhealthy /ʌnˈhɛlθi/ *adj* (**unhealthier**, **unhealthiest**) 1 (with bad health) ‹*patient, child*› عَليل (أَعِلاّءُ) 2 (causing ill-health) ‹*diet, climate*› ضارّ بالصِحّةِ ,غَيْر صِحِّيّ 3 (obsessive) ‹*interest, curiosity*› غَيْر صِحِّيّ

unheard-of /ʌnˈhəːdɒv/ *adj* 1 (previously unknown) ‹*price, level*› لم يَسْبِقْ لَهُ مَثيلٌ; ‹*actor, brand*› غَيْر مَشْهورٍ \ مَعْروفٍ 2 (shocking) ‹*behaviour, suggestion*› غَيْر لائِقٍ

unheeded /ʌnˈhiːdɪd/ *adj* **to go ~** «warnings, pleas» لم يَعْبَأْ بِهِ أَحَدٌ

unhelpful /ʌnˈhɛlpfʊl/ *adj* ‹*employee, attitude*› غَيْر مُفيدٍ

unhindered /ʌnˈhɪndəd/ *adj* ‹*access, flow*› بلا عائِقٍ

unhinge /ʌnˈhɪndʒ/ *vt* 1 (to remove) ‹*a door, cover*› نَزَعَ من مَفاصِلِهِ 2 (infml) (to upset) ‹*a patient, sb's mind*› خَبَّلَ ,(خَبْل ;u) خَبَلَ

unholy /ʌnˈhəʊli/ *adj* (**unholier**, **unholiest**) 1 (wicked, unnatural) ‹*alliance, pact*› شِرّير (أَشْرار) ,آثِم (أَثَمة) 2 (dreadful) ‹*row, racket*› شَديد (أَشِدّاءُ) ,شِداد ,فَظيع (فُظَعاءُ)

unhook /ʌnˈhʊk/ *vt* حَلَّ (u; حَلّ) ‹*one's skirt, bra*›; فَكَّ (u; فَكّ), نَزَعَ (i; نَزْع) ‹*a picture, calendar*›

unhurried /ʌnˈhʌrɪd/ *adj* ‹*pace, meal*› من غَيْر تَسَرُّعٍ ,مُتَأَنٍّ

unhurt /ʌnˈhəːt/ *adj* ‹*passenger, victim*› سالِم ,سَليم (سُلَماءُ)

unhygienic /ʌnhʌɪˈdʒiːnɪk/ *adj* ‹*conditions, practice*› غَيْر نَظيفٍ

UNICEF /ˈjuːnɪsɛf/ *n* = **United Nations Children's Fund** اليونيسيف (مُنَظَّمة الأُمَمِ المُتَّحِدةِ للطُفولةِ)

unicorn /ˈjuːnɪkɔːn/ *n* أُحاديّ القَرْنِ

unidentified /ʌnʌɪˈdɛntɪfʌɪd/ *adj* ‹*gunman, aircraft*› مَجْهول الهُوِيّةِ

unidentified flying object *n* جِسْم ,طَبَق \ صَحْن طائِر غامِض \ مَجْهول

unification /juːnɪfɪˈkeɪʃ(ə)n/ *n* تَوْحيد

uniform /ˈjuːnɪfɔːm/ **A** *adj* ‹*temperature, speed*› مُتَّسِق ,مُنْتَظِم, مُتَجانِس **B** *n* زِيّ رَسْميّ \ نِظاميّ; **police/school ~** لِباس الشُرْطةِ \ مَدْرَسيّ; **to be in ~** كانَ في زِيِّهِ الرَسْميِّ

uniformity /juːnɪˈfɔːmɪti/ *n* تَجانُس ,اتِّساق ,انْتِظام

uniformly /ˈjuːnɪfɔːmli/ *adv* ‹*to distribute, apply*› بِشَكْلٍ مُنْتَظِمٍ \ مُتَّسِقٍ \ مُتَجانِسٍ

unify /ˈjuːnɪfʌɪ/ *vt* (**unifies**, **unifying**, **unified**) وَحَّدَ ‹*a country, system*›

unilateral /juːnɪˈlat(ə)rəl/ *adj* ‹*action, decision*› أُحاديّ الجانِبِ

unimaginable /ʌnɪˈmadʒɪnəb(ə)l/ *adj* ‹*power, devastation*› لا يُمْكِنُ تَصَوُّرُهُ

unimaginative /ʌnɪˈmadʒɪnətɪv/ *adj* ‹*style, writing*› مُملّ; ‹*artist, writer*› ضَعيف الخَيالِ

unimpeded /ʌnɪmˈpiːdɪd/ *adj* ‹*access*› دونَ عوائِقَ ,غَيْر مَسْدودٍ; ‹*view*› غَيْر مَحْجوبٍ

unimportant /ʌnɪmˈpɔːt(ə)nt/ *adj* ‹*detail, question*› غَيْر مُهِمٍّ, تافِه (تَوافِهُ)

unimpressed /ʌnɪmˈprɛst/ *adj* **to be ~ by sb/sth** لم يَقْتَنِعْ \ يَتَأَثَّرْ بِشَخْصٍ \ شَيْءٍ

uninhabitable /ʌnɪnˈhabɪtəb(ə)l/ *adj* ‹*desert, house*› غَيْر صالِحٍ للسَكَنِ

uninhabited /ʌnɪn'habɪtɪd/ ***adj*** ‹*town*› خالٍ من السُكّانِ \ البَشَرِ; ‹*house*› غَيْر مَسْكونٍ

uninhibited /ʌnɪn'hɪbɪtɪd/ ***adj*** ‹*attitude, person*› بدونِ تَحَرُّجٍ

uninjured /ʌn'ɪndʒəd/ ***adj*** ‹*passenger, onlooker*› لم يُصَبْ

uninspired /ʌnɪn'spʌɪəd/ ***adj*** ‹*performance, speech*› لا روحَ فيه, مُمِلّ, غَيْر مُلْهَمٍ

uninsured /ʌnɪn'ʃʊəd/ ***adj*** ‹*valuables, driver*› غَيْر مُؤَمَّنٍ

unintelligent /ʌnɪn'tɛlɪdʒ(ə)nt/ ***adj*** ‹*response, person*› غَبيّ (أَغْبِياءُ), غَيْر ذَكيٍّ

unintelligible /ʌnɪn'tɛlɪdʒɪb(ə)l/ ***adj*** ‹*speaker, language*› غَيْر مَفْهومٍ

unintended /ʌnɪn'tendɪd/ ***adj*** ‹*consequence, humour*› غَيْر مَقْصودٍ \ مُتَعَمَّدٍ

unintentional /ʌnɪn'tenʃ(ə)n(ə)l/ ***adj*** ‹*humour, mistake*› غَيْر مَقْصودٍ \ مُتَعَمَّدٍ

unintentionally /ʌnɪn'tenʃ(ə)n(ə)li/ ***adv*** ‹*reveal, mislead*› من غَيْر قَصْدٍ

uninterested /ʌn'ɪntərɪstɪd/ ***adj*** ‹*expression, person*› غَيْر مُبالٍ

uninteresting /ʌn'ɪntərɪstɪŋ/ ***adj*** ‹*story, conversation*› مُمِلّ, مُضْجِر

uninvited /ʌnɪn'vʌɪtɪd/ ***adj*** ‹*guest*› غَيْر مَدْعوٍّ

uninviting /ʌnɪn'vʌɪtɪŋ/ ***adj*** ‹*place, prospect*› غَيْر جاذِبٍ; ‹*food*› غَيْر شَهيٍّ

union /'juːniən/ ***n*** ① (also **trade union**) نِقابة عُمّالٍ \ عُمّاليّة; **to join a ~** انْضَمَّ إلى نِقابةٍ عُمّاليّةٍ ② (politically unified whole) اتِّحاد; **the U~ of Socialist Soviet Republics** اتِّحاد الجُمْهوريّاتِ السوفْيتيّةِ الاشْتِراكيّةِ ③ [u] (unification) تَوْحيد ④ (fml) (marriage) زَواج

unionist /'juːniənɪst/ ***n*** ① (in a trade union) نِقابيّ, عُضْو نِقابة عُمّالٍ ② **(Unionist)** (in US history) [مُؤَيِّد لِسِياسةِ اتِّحادِ الوِلاياتِ الشَماليّةِ والجَنوبيّةِ] ③ **(Unionist)** (in UK politics) [مُؤَيِّد لِسِياسةِ اتِّحادِ شَمالِ إيرْلَنْدا وَإنْجِلْترا]

unionize, -ise (BrE) /'juːniənʌɪz/ ***vt*** ‹*a workforce*› [جَمَّعَ في نِقابةٍ]; ‹*a factory*› [جَمَّعَ في نِقابةِ العُمّالِ]

Union Jack, **Union flag** ***pr n*** عَلَمَ المَمْلَكةِ المُتَّحِدةِ

unique /juː'niːk/ ***adj*** ‹*opportunity, feature*› لا مَثيلَ لَهُ, فَريد (من نَوْعِهِ)

uniquely /juː'niːkli/ ***adv*** ① (exceptionally) ‹*talented, privileged*› بِشَكْلٍ اسْتِثْنائيٍّ; ‹*to suit, qualify*› على نَحْوٍ فَريدٍ ② (only) ‹*vulnerable, American*› على وَجْهِ الخُصوصِ, بِشَكْلٍ خاصٍّ

unisex /'juːnɪsɛks/ ***adj*** ‹*clothes, salon*› للنِساءِ والرِجالِ

unison /'juːnɪs(ə)n/ ***n*** **in ~** سَوِيّاً

unit /'juːnɪt/ ***n*** ① (single part) وَحْدة; **a course in ten ~s** بَرْنامَج من عَشْرِ وَحْداتٍ ② (of people) وَحْدة ③ (in measurements) وَحْدة قِياسٍ ④ (department) قِسْم (أَقْسام) ⑤ (module) وَحْدة

unit cost ***n*** سِعْر الوَحْدةِ

unite /juː'nʌɪt/ Ⓐ ***vt*** ‹*a country, party*› وَحَّدَ Ⓑ ***vi*** «parties, countries» تَوَحَّدَ

united /juː'nʌɪtɪd/ ***adj*** ‹*country, front*› مُتَّحِد, مُوَحَّد

United Arab Emirates ***pr n*** **(the United Arab Emirates)** الإمارات العَرَبيّة المُتَّحِدة

United Kingdom ***pr n*** **(the United Kingdom)** المَمْلَكة المُتَّحِدة

United Nations ***n*** **(the United Nations)** الأُمَم المُتَّحِدة

United States ***pr n*** **(the United States of America)** الوِلايات المُتَّحِدة الأَمْريكيّة

unit trust ***n*** صُنْدوق اسْتِثْمارٍ

unity /'juːnɪti/ ***n*** (*pl* **unities**) وَحْدة

universal /juːnɪ'vəːs(ə)l/ ***adj*** ① ‹*suffrage, healthcare*› عامّ; ‹*principle, truth*› كَوْنيّ ② ‹*adaptor, spanner*› عُموميّ, عامّ

universally /juːnɪ'vəːs(ə)li/ ***adv*** ‹*to accept, available*› في كُلِّ مَكانٍ

universe /'juːnɪvəːs/ ***n*** كَوْن (أَكْوان)

university /juːnɪ'vəːsɪti/ ***n*** (*pl* **universities**) جامِعة

unjust /ʌn'dʒʌst/ ***adj*** ‹*law, war*› جائِر, غَيْر عادِلٍ

unjustified /ʌn'dʒʌstɪfʌɪd/ ***adj*** ‹*dismissal, interference*› غَيْر مُبَرَّرٍ

unjustly /ʌn'dʒʌstli/ ***adv*** بِشَكْلٍ غَيْر عادِلٍ

unkempt /ʌn'kɛmpt/ ***adj*** ‹*appearance, hair*› أَشْعَث (dipt; شُعْث)

unkind /ʌn'kʌɪnd/ ***adj*** (**unkinder, unkindest**) ‹*person, remark, word*› قاسٍ (قُساة), فَظّ (أَفْظاظ); **to be ~ to sb** كانَ قاسِياً إزاءَ شَخْصٍ

unknown /ʌn'nəʊn/ **A** *adj* مَجْهول, غَيْر مَعْروفٍ **B** *n* **1** the ~ المَجْهول **2** (person) مَجْهول

unlace /ʌn'leɪs/ *vt* فَكَّ الرِباطَ <*a corset, shoe*>

unlawful /ʌn'lɔːfʊl/ *adj* <*detention, arrest*> غَيْر قانونيٍّ \ مَشْروعٍ

unlawfully /ʌn'lɔːf(ə)li/ *adv* <*to act, kill*> على نَحْوٍ غَيْر قانونيٍّ \ مَشْروعٍ

unleaded /ʌn'lɛdɪd/ *adj* <*petrol, fuel*> خالٍ من الرَصاصِ

unleaded petrol (BrE), **unleaded gasoline** (AmE) *n* بَنْزين خالٍ من الرَصاصِ

unleash /ʌn'liːʃ/ *vt* **1** (to release) أَطْلَقَ <*a dog*>; أَطْلَقَ العِنانَ ل <*aggression, violence*> **2** (to launch) أَطْلَقَ <*a force, campaign*>

unleavened /ʌn'lɛv(ə)nd/ *adj* <*roll, bread*> فَطير (بِدونِ خَميرةٍ)

unless /ʌn'lɛs/ *conj* **1** (but for) ما لم, إلاّ إذا; **she can't take the job ~ she gets a work permit** هي لا تَسْتَطيعُ أَنْ تَحْصُلَ على الوَظيفةِ ما لم تَحْصُلْ على تَصْريحِ عَمَلٍ; **~ I get my passport back, I can't leave the country** لا أَسْتَطيعُ أَنْ أُغادِرَ البَلَدَ, إلاّ إذا اسْتَرْدَدْتُ جوازَ سَفَري; **~ I'm very much mistaken, that's Jim** ما لم أَكُنْ مُخْطِئاً حَقًّا, فَذَلِكَ هو جيم; **~ otherwise agreed ...** إلاّ إذا اتُّفِقَ على خِلافِ ذلك ... **2** (**not unless**) (only if) إلاّ إذا; **are you coming tomorrow? — not ~ you need me** هل سَتأْتي غَداً؟ — لا، إلاّ إذا احْتَجْتَني

unlike¹ /ʌn'lʌɪk/ *prep* **1** (in contrast to) على العَكْسِ من **2** (different from) مُخْتَلِف عن **3** (uncharacteristic of) لَيْسَ من العادةِ; **it's ~ her to do that** لَيْسَ من عادَتِها أَنْ تَفْعَلَ ذلك

unlike² /ʌn'lʌɪk/ *vt* أَلْغى الإعْجاب

unlikely /ʌn'lʌɪkli/ *adj* (**unlikelier**, **unlikeliest**) **1** (improbable) <*event, outcome*> مُسْتَبْعَد, بَعيد الاحْتِمالِ **2** (unexpected) <*candidate, choice*> مُفاجِئ, غَيْر مُتَوَقَّعٍ **3** (probably untrue) <*story, excuse*> غَيْر مَعْقولٍ

unlimited /ʌn'lɪmɪtɪd/ *adj* <*access, supplies*> غَيْر مَحْدودٍ, بِلا حُدودٍ

unlined /ʌn'lʌɪnd/ *adj* **1** <*jacket, curtain*> غَيْر مُبَطَّنٍ **2** <*paper*> غَيْر مُسَطَّرٍ; <*skin*> غَيْر مُجَعَّدٍ

unlisted /ʌn'lɪstɪd/ *adj* **1** (unrecorded) <*model, account*> غَيْر مُسَجَّلٍ (في قائمةٍ) **2** (on stock exchanges) <*company, share*> غَيْر مُدْرَجٍ **3** <*number*> غَيْر مُسَجَّلٍ (بِدَليلِ الهاتِفِ)

unlit /ʌn'lɪt/ *adj* **1** (without light) <*street, room*> غَيْر مُضاءٍ **2** (without flame) <*cigarette, fire*> غَيْر موقَدٍ

unload /ʌn'ləʊd/ **A** *vt* **1** (to empty) فَرَّغَ, أَفْرَغَ <*a truck, ship*> **2** (with bullets, films) فَرَّغَ, أَفْرَغَ <*a gun, camera*> **3** (to remove) فَرَّغَ, أَفْرَغَ <*the cargo, equipment, cotton*> **4** (to sell off) تَخَلَّصَ (من) <*stock, goods*> **B** *vi* **1** (in delivering goods) «trucks, ships» أُفْرِغَتْ حُمولَتُهُ **2** (with bullets, films) «hunter» أَفْرَغَ السِلاحَ; «photographer» أَفْرَغَ الكاميرا

unlock /ʌn'lɒk/ *vt* فَتَحَ القُفْلَ <*a door, suitcase, phone*>

unluckily /ʌn'lʌkɪli/ *adv* لِسوءِ الحَظِّ

unlucky /ʌn'lʌki/ *adj* (**unluckier**, **unluckiest**) **1** (unfortunate) <*contestant, loser, victim*> سَيِّء الحَظِّ **2** <*number, colour*> مَشْؤوم (مَشائِمُ)

unmade /ʌn'meɪd/ *adj* <*bed*> غَيْر مُرَتَّبٍ

unmanageable /ʌn'manɪdʒəb(ə)l/ *adj* <*child, dog*> صَعْب المِراسِ; <*system*> عَسير; <*hair*> صَعْب التَصْفيفِ

unmanned /ʌn'mand/ *adj* <*vehicle, aircraft*> غَيْر مَأْهولٍ; <*crossing*> غَيْر مَحْروسٍ

unmarried /ʌn'marɪd/ *adj* <*woman, couple*> غَيْر مُتَزَوِّجٍ, أَعْزَب (dipt)

unmask /ʌn'mɑːsk/ **A** *vt* كَشَفَ القِناعَ عن, فَضَحَ (a; فَضْح) <*a culprit, villain*> **B** *vi* «revellers» خَلَعَ القِناعَ

unmentionable /ʌn'mɛnʃ(ə)nəb(ə)l/ **A** *adj* **1** (improper to mention) <*subject, disease*> لا يَجوزُ الحَديثُ عَنْهُ **2** (unspeakable) <*suffering*> لا يوصَفُ **B** (**unmentionables**) *n pl* (infml) (underwear) مَلابِس داخِليّة

unmistakable /ʌnmɪ'steɪkəb(ə)l/ *adj* **1** (recognizable) <*sound, smell*> مَعْروف **2** (unambiguous) <*sign, evidence*> واضِح, بَيِّن, لا لَبْسَ فيه

unmotivated /ʌn'məʊtɪveɪtɪd/ *adj* **1** <*student, worker*> غَيْر مُتَحَمِّس **2** <*act, crime*> بِلا دافِعٍ

unmoved /ʌn'muːvd/ *adj* غَيْر مُتَأَثِّرٍ

unnamed /ʌn'neɪmd/ *adj* <*source, narrator*> مَجْهول الاسْمِ

unnatural /ʌn'natʃ(ə)rəl/ *adj* **1** (abnormal) ‹*silence, colour*› غَيْر طَبيعيٍّ, شاذٌّ (شَواذُّ) **2** (affected) ‹*style, laugh*› مُتَكَلَّف, مُتَصَنِّع **3** (unhealthy) ‹*interest, act*› غَيْر صِحّيٍّ

unnecessarily /ʌn'nɛsəs(ə)rəli/ *adv* بلا ضَرورةٍ

unnecessary /ʌn'nɛsəs(ə)ri/ *adj* ‹*suffering, remark*› غَيْر ضَروريٍّ

unnerve /ʌn'nəːv/ *vt* أَقْلَقَ ‹*an investor, opponent*›

unnerving /ʌn'nəːvɪŋ/ *adj* ‹*experience, habit*› مُثير لِلقَلَقِ

unnoticed /ʌn'nəʊtɪst/ *adj* ‹*to go, remain*› غَيْر مَلْحوظٍ; **to go ~** لم يَفْطَنْ لَهُ أَحَدٌ

unobstructed /ʌnəb'strʌktɪd/ *adj* ‹*access*› غَيْر مَسْدودٍ, دونَ عوائِقَ; ‹*view*› غَيْر مَحْجوبٍ

unobtainable /ʌnəb'teɪnəb(ə)l/ *adj* **1** ‹*commodity, parts*› صَعْب المَنالِ, لا يُمْكِنُ الحُصولُ عَلَيْهِ **2** (in phoning) ‹*number*› لا يُمْكِنُ الاتِّصالُ بِهِ

unobtrusive /ʌnəb'truːsɪv/ *adj* ‹*manner, camerawork*› مُتَواضِع

unoccupied /ʌn'ɒkjʊpʌɪd/ *adj* خالٍ, شاغِر (شَواغِرُ)

unofficial /ʌnə'fɪʃ(ə)l/ *adj* غَيْر رَسْميٍّ

unofficially /ʌnə'fɪʃ(ə)li/ *adv* ‹*to tell, estimate*› بِصِفةٍ غَيْر رَسْميّةٍ

unopened /ʌn'əʊp(ə)nd/ *adj* غَيْر مَفْتوحٍ, لم يُفْتَحْ بَعْدُ

unopposed /ʌnə'pəʊzd/ *adj* بِدونِ مُعارَضةٍ; **to be elected ~** أُنْتُخِبَ بِدونِ مُنافَسةٍ

unoriginal /ʌnə'rɪdʒɪn(ə)l/ *adj* ‹*idea, plot*› غَيْر أَصيلٍ, مُبْتَذَل

unorthodox /ʌn'ɔːθədɒks/ *adj* ‹*method, approach*› غَيْر تَقْليديٍّ

unpack /ʌn'pak/ *vt* أَفْرَغَ

unpaid /ʌn'peɪd/ *adj* **1** ‹*bill, debt*› غَيْر مَدْفوعٍ **2** ‹*work, holiday*› بِدونِ أَجْرٍ

unpalatable /ʌn'palətəb(ə)l/ *adj* **1** ‹*truth, choice*› مُرّ, غَيْر مُسْتَساغٍ **2** ‹*food*› غَيْر لَذيذٍ

unparalleled /ʌn'parəlɛld/ *adj* **1** ‹*opportunity, success*› مُنْقَطِع النَظيرِ, فَريد من نَوْعِهِ **2** (unprecedented) ‹*disaster, magnitude*› لم يَسْبِقْ لَهُ مَثيلٌ

unpasteurized /ʌn'pɑːstʃərʌɪzd/ *adj* غَيْر مُبَسْتَرٍ

unperturbed /ʌnpə'təːbd/ *adj* غَيْر مُضْطَرِبٍ, رابِط الجَأْشِ, غَيْر مُنْزَعِجٍ

unplanned /ʌn'pland/ *adj* غَيْر مُخَطَّطٍ لَهُ

unpleasant /ʌn'plɛz(ə)nt/ *adj* ‹*experience, surprise*› مُزْعِج

unpleasantness /ʌn'plɛz(ə)ntnəs/ *n* **1** (of an odour) كَراهة; (of an experience) بَشاعة **2** (bad feeling) نِزاع (نِزاعات), شِقاق

unplug /ʌn'plʌg/ *vt* **(-gg-)** **1** (to disconnect) نَزَعَ القابِسَ ‹*an appliance*›; نَزَعَ (نَزْع) (i; ‹*a cable*› **2** (to unblock) سَلَّكَ ‹*a pipe, sink*›

unpopular /ʌn'pɒpjʊlə/ *adj* ‹*leader, decision*› غَيْر شَعْبيٍّ \ مَحْبوبٍ; **she was ~ with the other girls** لم تَكُنْ مَحْبوبةً من الفَتَياتِ الأُخْرَياتِ

unprecedented /ʌn'prɛsɪdɛntɪd/ *adj* ‹*level, step*› لا سابِقةَ لَهُ, لم يَسْبِقْ لَهُ مَثيلٌ

unpredictable /ʌnprɪ'dɪktəb(ə)l/ *adj* ‹*weather, behaviour*› لا يُمْكِنُ التَنَبُّؤُ \ التَكَهُّنُ بِهِ

unpremeditated /ʌnpriː'mɛdɪteɪtɪd/ *adj* ‹*crime, attack*› غَيْر مُتَعَمَّدٍ

unprepared /ʌnprɪ'pɛːd/ *adj* **1** ‹*person*› غَيْر مُسْتَعِدٍّ; **to be ~ for sth** لم يَكُنْ مُسْتَعِدًّا لِشَيْءٍ **2** ‹*speech*› مُرْتَجَل

unprepossessing /ˌʌnpriːpə'zɛsɪŋ/ *adj* ‹*appearance, building*› غَيْر جَذّابٍ

unpretentious /ʌnprɪ'tɛnʃəs/ *adj* ‹*style, restaurant*› غَيْر مُدَّعٍ, مُتَواضِع

unprincipled /ʌn'prɪnsɪpəld/ *adj* ‹*character, behaviour*› لا مَبادِئَ لَهُ

unproductive /ʌnprə'dʌktɪv/ *adj* ‹*land, debate*› عَقيم (عُقُم, عِقام), غَيْر مُنْتِجٍ

unprofessional /ʌnprə'fɛʃ(ə)n(ə)l/ *adj* ‹*conduct, attitude*› غَيْر مِهْنيٍّ

unprofitable /ʌn'prɒfɪtəb(ə)l/ *adj* ‹*business, store*› غَيْر مُرْبِحٍ

unprotected /ʌnprə'tɛktɪd/ *adj* **1** ‹*surface, wildlife*› غَيْر مَحْميٍّ **2** ‹*sex, intercourse*› غَير آمِنٍ, بِدونِ وِقايةٍ

unprovoked /ʌnprə'vəʊkt/ *adj* ‹*attack, aggression*› لم يَسْبِقْهُ اسْتِفْزازٌ, غَيْر مُبَرَّر

unpublished /ʌn'pʌblɪʃt/ *adj* ‹*manuscript, data*› غَيْر مَنْشورٍ

unpunished /ʌn'pʌnɪʃt/ *adj* ‹*crime*› غَيْر مُعاقَبٍ عَلَيْهِ; ‹*person*› غَيْر مُعاقَبٍ; **to go ~** لم يُعاقَبْ عَلَيْهِ

unqualified /ʌnˈkwɒlɪfʌɪd/ *adj* ① (without qualifications) *‹staff, worker›* غَيْر مُؤَهَّلٍ ② (complete) *‹support, success›* مُطْلَق, (تَوامٌّ) تامّ

unquestionable /ʌnˈkwɛstʃ(ə)nəb(ə)l/ *adj* *‹authority, truth›* لا خِلافَ عَلَيْهِ, لا نِزاعَ \ شَكَّ فيهِ, مُسَلَّم بِهِ

unquestioning /ʌnˈkwɛstʃ(ə)nɪŋ/ *adj* *‹acceptance, obedience›* بِدونِ نِقاشٍ, غَيْر مَشْروطٍ, مُطْلَق

unravel /ʌnˈrav(ə)l/ **A** *vt* (**-ll-** BrE, **-l-** AmE) ① فَكَّ (u; فَكّ), حَلَّ (u; حَلّ) *‹threads, knitting›* ② حَلَّ (u; حَلّ) *‹a mystery, plot›* **B** *vi* (**-ll-** BrE, **-l-** AmE) «threads, knitting» انْفَكَّ, انْحَلَّ

unreadable /ʌnˈriːdəb(ə)l/ *adj* *‹book, writing›* لا يُقْرَأُ

unreal /ʌnˈrɪəl/ *adj* ① (not real) *‹quality, world›* غَيْر حَقيقيٍّ ② (infml) (unbelievable) *‹person›* غَيْر مَعْقولٍ

unrealistic /ˌʌnrɪəˈlɪstɪk/ *adj* *‹expectation, goal›* غَيْر واقِعِيٍّ

unreasonable /ʌnˈriːz(ə)nəb(ə)l/ *adj* *‹behaviour, price›* غَيْر مَعْقولٍ

unrecognizable /ʌnˈrɛkəgnʌɪzəb(ə)l/ *adj* *‹voice, face›* لا يُمْكِنُ التَعَرُّفُ عَلَيْهِ

unrefined /ʌnrɪˈfʌɪnd/ *adj* ① *‹sugar, oil›* غَيْر مُكَرَّرٍ ② *‹person, manners›* غَيْر مُهَذَّبٍ

unrelated /ʌnrɪˈleɪtɪd/ *adj* ① (not connected) *‹incident, matter›* غَيْر مُتَّصِلٍ ② (as family) **to be ~ (to sb)** لا تَرْبُطُهُ صِلةُ قَرابةٍ (بِشَخْصٍ); **they are ~** لا تَرْبُطُهُما صِلةُ قَرابةٍ

unrelenting /ʌnrɪˈlɛntɪŋ/ *adj* *‹heat, pressure›* صارِم, لا يَلينُ (صَوارِمُ)

unreliable /ʌnrɪˈlʌɪəb(ə)l/ *adj* *‹evidence, narrator›* لا يُعْتَمَدُ عَلَيْهِ

unrepeatable /ʌnrɪˈpiːtəb(ə)l/ *adj* ① (unique) *‹bargain, offer›* لا يَتَكَرَّرُ, لا يُمْكِنُ أَنْ يَتَكَرَّرَ ② (vulgar) *‹language, joke›* بَذيء

unrepentant /ʌnrɪˈpɛnt(ə)nt/ *adj* *‹sinner›* غَيْر نادِمٍ \ تائِبٍ

unreported /ʌnrɪˈpɔːtɪd/ *adj* *‹incident, crime›* غَيْر مُبَلَّغٍ عَنْهُ; **to go ~** لم يُبَلَّغْ عَنْهُ

unrepresentative /ˌʌnrɛprɪˈzɛntətɪv/ *adj* *‹sample, opinion›* غَيْر تَمْثيليٍّ

unrequited /ʌnrɪˈkwʌɪtɪd/ *adj* (liter) *‹love›* غَيْر مُتَبادَلٍ, مِن طَرَفٍ واحِدٍ

unresolved /ʌnrɪˈzɒlvd/ *adj* *‹problem, conflict›* لم يُحَلَّ بَعْدُ

unresponsive /ʌnrɪˈspɒnsɪv/ *adj* *‹person, audience›* لا يَسْتَجيبُ

unrest /ʌnˈrɛst/ *n* اضْطِراب (اضْطِرابات)

unrestricted /ʌnrɪˈstrɪktɪd/ *adj* *‹access, power›* لا حَصْرَ لَهُ, مُطْلَق

unrewarded /ʌnrɪˈwɔːdɪd/ *adj* *‹work, efforts›* غَيْر مُكافَأٍ \ مُجازًى

unrewarding /ʌnrɪˈwɔːdɪŋ/ *adj* *‹task, activity›* غَيْر مُجْزٍ \ مُرْبِح

unripe /ʌnˈrʌɪp/ *adj* *‹fruit, banana›* فِجّ, غَيْر ناضِجٍ

unrivalled /ʌnˈrʌɪvəld/ *adj* *‹collection, reputation›* مُنْقَطِع النَظيرِ, لا يُجارى, لا مَثيلَ لَهُ

unroll /ʌnˈrəʊl/ *vt* بَسَطَ (u; بَسْط), فَرَدَ (u; فُرود), نَشَرَ (u; نَشْر) *‹a carpet, sleeping bag, scroll›*

unruffled /ʌnˈrʌfəld/ *adj* *‹composure, attitude›* هادِئ, غَيْر مُضْطَرِبٍ

unruly /ʌnˈruːli/ *adj* (**unrulier**, **unruliest**) ① (disorderly) *‹crowd, child›* غَيْر مُنْضَبِطٍ ② (untidy) *‹hair, beard›* مَنْكوش

unsafe /ʌnˈseɪf/ *adj* ① (dangerous) *‹drinking water, stairs›* خَطِر, غَيْر آمِنٍ ② (threatened) **to feel ~** شَعَرَ بِعَدَمِ الأَمانِ ③ (unreliable) *‹conviction, verdict›* غَيْر سَليمٍ

unsaid /ʌnˈsɛd/ *adj* **to leave a question/objection ~** سَكَتَ عن سُؤالٍ \ اعْتِراضٍ

unsalted /ʌnˈsɔːltɪd/ *adj* *‹butter, peanuts›* غَيْر مُمَلَّحٍ

unsatisfactory /ˌʌnsatɪsˈfakt(ə)ri/ *adj* *‹method, outcome›* غَيْر مُرْضٍ

unsatisfied /ʌnˈsatɪsfʌɪd/ *adj* *‹customer, desire›* غَيْر راضٍ

unsatisfying /ʌnˈsatɪsfʌɪɪŋ/ *adj* *‹experience, outcome›* غَيْر مُرْضٍ

unsaturated /ʌnˈsatʃəreɪtɪd/ *adj* *‹fat, oil›* غَيْر مُشْبَعٍ

unsavoury (BrE), **unsavory** (AmE) /ʌnˈseɪv(ə)ri/ *adj* ① (unappetizing) *‹smell, taste›* كَريه ② (disreputable) *‹character, reputation›* دَنيء (أَدْنياءُ), مُريب

unscathed /ʌnˈskeɪðd/ *adj* *‹reputation, village›* سالِم, لم يَمْسَسْهُ سوءٌ

unscented /ʌnˈsɛntɪd/ *adj* *‹lotion, candle›* غَيْر مُعَطَّرٍ

unscheduled /ʌnˈʃɛdjuːld/ *adj* *‹stop, visit›* غَيْر مُجَدْوَلٍ

unscientific /ˌʌnsʌɪənˈtɪfɪk/ *adj* *‹method, theory›* غَيْر عِلْميٍّ

unscrew /ʌnˈskruː/ *vt* ① (with a screwdriver) فَكَّ (u; فَكّ) *‹a screw, panel›* ② (by twisting) فَكَّ (u; فَكّ), حَلَّ (u; حَلّ) *‹a lid, bulb›*

unscrupulous /ʌn'skruːpjʊləs/ *adj* ‹*behaviour, tactics*› لا ضَميرَ لَهُ, عَديم الضَمير \ الذِمّةِ

unseat /ʌn'siːt/ *vt* ① (to throw off) أَسْقَطَ ‹*a rider, cyclist*› ② (in elections) عَزَلَ (من مَنْصِبِهِ) ‹*the president, mayor*›

unseen /ʌn'siːn/ *adj* ① (invisible) ‹*danger, obstacle*› خَفيّ ② (not seen) ‹*footage, planet*› غَيْر مَرْئيٍّ

unselfconscious /ʌnsɛlf'kɒnʃəs/ *adj* ‹*manner, laughter*› غَيْر خَجولٍ

unselfish /ʌn'sɛlfɪʃ/ *adj* ‹*act, behaviour*› غَيْر أنانيٍّ, إيثاريّ

unsentimental /ˌʌnsɛntɪ'mɛnt(ə)l/ *adj* ‹*account, approach*› واقِعيّ, عَمَليّ, غَيْر عاطِفيٍّ

unsettle /ʌn'sɛt(ə)l/ *vt* بَلْبَلَ (بَلْبَلة ;i) زَعْزَعَ (زَعْزعة ;i), أَقْلَقَ ‹*an audience, investor*›

unsettled /ʌn'sɛtəld/ *adj* ① (unstable) ‹*weather, feeling*› مُضْطَرِب ② (unpaid) ‹*bill, debt*› غَيْر مُسَدَّدٍ

unsettling /ʌn'sɛtlɪŋ/ *adj* ‹*experience, imagery*› مُقْلِق

unshakeable, **unshakable** /ʌn'ʃeɪkəb(ə)l/ *adj* ‹*belief, faith*› لا يَتَزَعْزَعُ, راسِخ

unshaken /ʌn'ʃeɪk(ə)n/ *adj* ‹*confidence, belief*› لم يَتَزَعْزَعْ, راسِخ

unshaven /ʌn'ʃeɪv(ə)n/ *adj* ‹*face, chin*› غَيْر حَليقٍ

unsightly /ʌn'sʌɪtli/ *adj* (**unsightlier**, **unsightliest**) ‹*scar, building*› قَبيح المَنْظَرِ, بَشِع

unsigned /ʌn'sʌɪnd/ *adj* ‹*cheque, letter*› بِلا تَوْقيعٍ, غَيْر مُوَقَّعٍ عَلَيْهِ

unskilled /ʌn'skɪld/ *adj* ① (untrained) ‹*worker, workforce*› غَيْر ماهِرٍ \ مُدَرَّبٍ ② (not needing skill) ‹*work, labour*› لا يَتَطَلَّبُ مَهارةً

unsociable /ʌn'səʊʃəb(ə)l/ *adj* ‹*mood, child*› مُنْعَزِل, انْطِوائيّ

unsocial /ʌn'səʊʃ(ə)l/ *adj* ‹*hours, shift*› [خارِجَ ساعاتِ العَمَلِ العاديّة]

unsold /ʌn'səʊld/ *adj* ‹*stock, tickets*› غَيْر مُباعٍ

unsolicited /ʌnsə'lɪsɪtɪd/ *adj* ‹*advice, mail*› غَيْر مَطْلوبٍ

unsolved /ʌn'sɒlvd/ *adj* ‹*murder, case*› لم يُحَلَّ

unsophisticated /ʌnsə'fɪstɪkeɪtɪd/ *adj* ① (unworldly) ‹*taste, audience*› ساذَج (سُذَّج), بَسيط (بُسَطاءُ) ② (basic) ‹*technology, analysis*› غَيْر مُعَقَّدٍ

unspeakable /ʌn'spiːkəb(ə)l/ *adj* ① (dreadful) ‹*horror, pain*› رَهيب, مُرَوِّع ② (indescribable) ‹*joy, delight*› لا يوصَفُ

unspecified /ʌn'spɛsɪfʌɪd/ *adj* ‹*number, date*› غَيْر مُحَدَّدٍ

unspoiled /ʌn'spɔɪld/, **unspoilt** /ʌn'spɔɪlt/ (BrE) *adj* ‹*countryside, beach*› خالِص (خُلَّص)

unspoken /ʌn'spəʊk(ə)n/ *adj* ‹*agreement, rule*› غَيْر مَنْطوقٍ بِهِ

unstable /ʌn'steɪb(ə)l/ *adj* ① (likely to fall) ‹*structure, load*› غَيْر مُسْتَقِرٍّ ② (changeable) ‹*prices, relationship*› غَيْر ثابِتٍ ③ (unbalanced) ‹*mind, character*› مُتَقَلِّب

unsteadily /ʌn'stɛdɪli/ *adv* ‹*to walk, stand*› مُتَرَنِّحاً

unsteady /ʌn'stɛdi/ *adj* (**unsteadier**, **unsteadiest**) ① (shaky) ‹*hand, chair*› غَيْر ثابِتٍ; **to be ~ on one's feet** تَرَنَّحَ ② (irregular) ‹*voice, flow*› غَيْر مُنْتَظِمٍ

unstoppable /ʌn'stɒpəb(ə)l/ *adj* ‹*rise, momentum*› لا يُمْكِنُ صَدُّهُ \ إيقافُهُ

unstuck /ʌn'stʌk/ *adj* ‹*envelope, label*› غَيْر مُلْصَقٍ; **to come ~** انْفَكَّ

unsubscribe /ʌnsəb'skrʌɪb/ *vi* «members, users» أَلْغى الاشْتِراكَ

unsubstantiated /ʌnsəb'stanʃɪeɪtɪd/ *adj* ‹*claim, report*› لا أَساسَ لَهُ

unsuccessful /ʌnsək'sɛsfʊl/ *adj* ‹*attempt, candidate*› فاشِل, غَيْر مُوَفَّقٍ, خائب; **to be ~ in an attempt/venture** فَشِلَ في مُحاوَلةٍ \ مَشْروعٍ

unsuccessfully /ʌnsək'sɛsf(ə)li/ *adv* ‹*to try, challenge*› بِلا عَبَثاً, جَدْوى

unsuitable /ʌn'suːtəb(ə)l/ *adj* ‹*candidate, accommodation*› غَيْر مُلائِمٍ \ مُناسِبٍ

unsuited /ʌn'suːtɪd/ *adj* **to be ~ to a job** كانَ غَيْرَ مُناسِبٍ لِوَظيفةٍ; **she is ~ to country life** لا تَسْتَطيعُ مُواجَهةَ العَيْشِ في الريفِ

unsupervised /ʌn'suːpəvʌɪzd/ *adj* ‹*swimming, child*› بدونِ إِشْرافٍ \ رَقابةٍ

unsure /ʌn'ʃʊə/ *adj* غَيْر واثِقٍ; **to be ~ of oneself** كانَ غَيْرَ واثِقٍ بِنَفْسِهِ; **to be ~ about sth** كانَ غَيْرَ واثِقٍ من شَيْءٍ

unsurpassed /ʌnsəˈpɑːst/ *adj* (fml) ‹*beauty, knowledge*› لا مَثِيلَ لَهُ

unsuspecting /ʌnsəˈspɛktɪŋ/ *adj* ‹*victim, public*› غَيْر مُرْتابٍ

unsweetened /ʌnˈswiːt(ə)nd/ *adj* ‹*tea, juice*› غَيْر مُحَلًّى

unsympathetic /ˌʌnsɪmpəˈθɛtɪk/ *adj* **1** (uncaring) ‹*manner, attitude*› غَيْر مُتَعاطِفٍ ,(قُساة) قاسٍ **2** (unlikeable) ‹*character, portrayal*› غَيْر وَدودٍ

unsystematic /ˌʌnsɪstəˈmatɪk/ *adj* ‹*method, approach*› غَيْر مُنَظَّمٍ \ مُنْتَظِمٍ \ مَنْهَجِيٍّ

untamed /ʌnˈteɪmd/ *adj* ‹*wilderness, lion*› غَيْر مُرَوَّضٍ

untangle /ʌnˈtaŋg(ə)l/ *vt* **1** (to disentangle) حَلَّ (u; حَلّ), فَكَّ (u; فَكّ) ‹*a knot, thread*› **2** (to solve) حَلَّ (u; حَلّ) ‹*a mystery, difficulty*›

untapped /ʌnˈtapt/ *adj* ‹*resource, potential*› غَيْر مُسْتَثْمَر

untaxed /ʌnˈtakst/ *adj* ‹*income, goods*› مُعْفًى من الضَرائِب

untenable /ʌnˈtɛnəb(ə)l/ *adj* ‹*position, claim*› لا يُمْكِنُ الدِفاعُ عَنْهُ

untended /ʌnˈtɛndɪd/ *adj* **1** (not cared for) ‹*garden, grave*› مُهْمَل **2** (unsupervised) ‹*flock, patient*› بدونِ رِعايةٍ \ رَقابةٍ

unthinkable /ʌnˈθɪŋkəb(ə)l/ *adj* ‹*act, prospect*› لا يُمْكِنُ تَصَوُّرُهُ, لا يَخْطُرُ بِبالٍ; **think the ~** تَخَيَّلْ ما لا يُمْكِنُ تَخَيُّلُهُ

untidily /ʌnˈtʌɪdɪli/ *adv* ‹*to scatter, dress*› من غَيْر تَرْتيبٍ

untidy /ʌnˈtʌɪdi/ *adj* (**untidier, untidiest**) ‹*room, desk, appearance*› غَيْر مُرَتَّبٍ

untie /ʌnˈtʌɪ/ *vt* (*present participle* **untying**) فَكَّ (u; فَكّ), حَلَّ (u; حَلّ) ‹*a knot, shoelaces, rope*›; **to ~ a horse/hostage** فَكَّ حِصانٍ \ رَهينةٍ

until /ənˈtɪl/, **till** /tɪl/ **A** *prep* **1** (up to) حَتّى, إلى; **they're staying ~ Tuesday** سَيَبْقَوْنَ حتّى يَوْمِ الثُلاثاءِ; **it's valid ~ April 2016** هو صالِحٌ حتى أَبْريل 2016 **2** (not before a time) **I didn't wake up ~ 9 a.m.** لم أَسْتَيْقِظْ إلاّ الساعةَ التاسِعةَ صَباحاً **B** *conj* **1** (in time) حَتّى, إلى أَنْ; **she waited ~ he left** انْتَظَرَتْ حتّى خَرَجَ; **we'll stay here ~ she comes back** سَنَبْقى هُنا إلى أَنْ تَعودَ **2** (not before) **they will not be satisfied ~ you apologize** لن يَرْضوا قبل أَنْ تَعْتَذِرَ

untimely /ʌnˈtʌɪmli/ *adj* (fml) **1** (premature) ‹*death, demise*› سابِق لِأَوانِهِ **2** (ill-timed) ‹*announcement, arrival*› في وَقْتٍ غَيْر مُناسِبٍ

unto /ˈʌntʊ/ *prep* (old use) ▸ **to**

untold /ʌnˈtəʊld/ *adj* **1** *before n* (not quantifiable) ‹*wealth, damage*› لا حَصْرَ لَهُ, لا يُحْصى, يَفوقُ الحَصْرِ **2** (not told) ‹*story, secret*› غَيْر مَرْوِيٍّ

untouched /ʌnˈtʌtʃt/ *adj* ‹*decor, meal*› لم يُمَسّ

untoward /ʌntəˈwɔːd/ *adj* ‹*incident, circumstances*› غَيْر مُؤاتٍ

untrained /ʌnˈtreɪnd/ *adj* ‹*teacher, soldier*› غَيْر مُدَرَّبٍ \ مُتَمَرِّسٍ; **to the ~ eye** لِشَخْصٍ غَيْر مُتَمَرِّسٍ

untranslatable /ˌʌntranzˈleɪtəb(ə)l/ *adj* ‹*word, phrase, pun*› غَيْر قابِلٍ للتَرْجَمةِ

untreatable /ʌnˈtriːtəb(ə)l/ *adj* ‹*disease, cancer*› غَيْر قابِلٍ للعِلاجِ

untreated /ʌnˈtriːtɪd/ *adj* **1** (chemically, etc.) ‹*sewage, waste water*› غَيْر مُعالَجٍ **2** (medically) ‹*condition, hypertension*› لا يُعالَجُ

untried /ʌnˈtrʌɪd/ *adj* **1** (not tested) ‹*method, technology*› غَيْر مُجَرَّبٍ \ مُخْتَبَرٍ, لم يُجَرَّبْ بَعْدُ **2** (not brought before court) ‹*prisoner*› لم تَتِمَّ مُحاكَمَتُهُ بَعْدُ

untroubled /ʌnˈtrʌbəld/ *adj* ‹*sleep, face*› هادِئ

untrue /ʌnˈtruː/ *adj* ‹*statement, allegation*› كاذِب, غَيْر صَحيحٍ

untrustworthy /ʌnˈtrʌstwəːði/ *adj* ‹*information, ally*› غَيْر جَديرٍ بالثِقةِ

untruthful /ʌnˈtruːθfʊl/ *adj* **1** (not true) ‹*statement, account*› كاذِب, غَيْر صادِقٍ **2** (lying) ‹*witness, child*› كَذّاب

unused¹ /ʌnˈjuːst/ *adj* **to be ~ to sth/to doing sth** كانَ غَيْرَ مُعْتادٍ على شَيْءٍ \ فِعْلِ شَيْءٍ

unused² /ʌnˈjuːzd/ *adj* ‹*land, leave*› غَيْر مُسْتَعْمَلٍ

unusual /ʌnˈjuːʒʊəl/ *adj* **1** (not normal) ‹*step, circumstance*› نادِر, غَيْر مَأْلوفٍ \ مُعْتادٍ; **it's not ~ for them to work 70 hours a week** لَيْسَ من غَيْرِ المُعْتادِ أَنْ يَعْمَلوا 70 ساعةً في الأُسبوعِ **2** (interesting) ‹*colour, specimen*› اسْتِثْنائِيّ

unusually /ʌnˈjuːʒ(ə)li/ *adv* ‹*high, warm*› خِلافاً للعادةِ

unveil /ʌnˈveɪl/ *vt* «mayor» أَزاحَ السِتارَ عن ‹*a plaque, statue*›

unwanted /ʌnˈwɒntɪd/ *adj* ‹*gift, attention*› غَيْر مَرْغوبٍ فيهِ; **she feels ~** تَشْعُرُ بِأَنَّها غَيْرُ مَرْغوبٍ فيها

unwarranted /ʌn'wɒrəntɪd/ *adj* (not legal) ‹*intrusion*› غير مُرَخَّصٍ; (not justified) ‹*criticism*› لا داعِيَ لَهُ

unwary /ʌn'wɛːri/ *adj* ‹*traveller, prey*› غافِل (غُفَّل, غافِلُونَ), غَيْر حَذِرٍ

unwavering /ʌn'weɪvərɪŋ/ *adj* ‹*support, commitment*› ثابِت, لا يَتَزَعْزَعُ

unwelcome /ʌn'wɛlkəm/ *adj* ‹*guest, attention*› غَيْر مَرْغوبٍ فيهِ; **I felt most ~** شَعَرْتُ بِأَنَّني غَيْرُ مَرْغوبٍ فيهِ

unwell /ʌn'wɛl/ *adj* ‹*patient, child*› مُعْتَلّ الصِحَّةِ, مُتَوَعِّك; **he is feeling ~** يَشْعُرُ بالتَوَعُّكِ

unwholesome /ʌn'həʊls(ə)m/ *adj* ‹*climate, character*› فاسِد (فَسْدى)

unwieldy /ʌn'wiːldi/ *adj* (**unwieldier**, **unwieldiest**) ‹*structure, size*› غَيْر عَمَليٍّ (لِحَجْمِهِ)

unwilling /ʌn'wɪlɪŋ/ *adj* ‹*participant, victim*› رافِض, غَيْر راغِبٍ; **to be ~ to do sth** كانَ غَيْرَ راغِبٍ في فِعْلِ شَيْءٍ

unwillingly /ʌn'wɪlɪŋli/ *adv* ‹*to cooperate, act*› على كُرْهٍ, على مُكْرَهاً, مَضَضٍ

unwillingness /ʌn'wɪlɪŋnəs/ *n* عدم رَغْبةٍ, كُرْه

unwind /ʌn'wʌɪnd/ **A** *vt* (*past tense, past participle* **unwound**) حَلَّ (u; حَلّ) ‹*a cable, bandage*›

B *vi* (*past tense, past participle* **unwound**) «guests, workers» اِسْتَرْخى

unwise /ʌn'wʌɪz/ *adj* ‹*decision, investment*› غَيْر حكيم, طائِش

unwisely /ʌn'wʌɪzli/ *adv* ‹*to choose, act*› بِحَماقةٍ, بِشَكْلٍ طائِشٍ

unwitting /ʌn'wɪtɪŋ/ *adj* (fml) ‹*victim, accomplice*› غَيْر مُدْرِكٍ \ واعٍ

unwittingly /ʌn'wɪtɪŋli/ *adv* ‹*to expose, offend*› من حَيْثُ لا يَدْري

unworthy /ʌn'wəːði/ *adj* (**unworthier**, **unworthiest**) ‹*successor, servant*› غَيْر جَديرٍ; **he considered himself ~ of their praise** اعْتَبَرَ نَفْسَهُ غَيْرَ جَديرٍ بِثَنائِهِمْ

unwound /ʌn'waʊnd/ *past tense, past participle* ▸ **unwind**

unwrap /ʌn'rap/ *vt* (**-pp-**) فَتَحَ (الغِلافَ) ‹*a parcel, present*›

unwritten /ʌn'rɪt(ə)n/ *adj* ‹*rule, agreement*› غَيْر مَكْتوبٍ

unyielding /ʌn'jiːldɪŋ/ *adj* ‹*opposition, commitment*› عَنيد (عُنُد), مُتَصَلِّب, لا يَتَزَعْزَعُ

unzip /ʌn'zɪp/ *vt* (**-pp-**) **1** (to open) فَتَحَ (السَّحّابَ) ‹*one's trousers, a bag*› **2** فَكَّ الضَغْطَ عن ‹*a file*›

up /ʌp/ **A** *adv* **1** (high) **~ here/there** في أَعْلى هذا \ ذلك المَكانِ; **~ in the tree/the clouds** في أَعْلى الشَجَرةِ \ الغُيومِ; **~ on top of the mountain** في أَعْلى الجَبَلِ; **he's going ~ to London** هو ذاهِبٌ إلى لُنْدُن; **she lives ~ in Scotland** تَعيشُ في اسْكُتْلَنْدا; **I live two floors ~** أَعيشُ على بُعْدِ طابِقَيْنِ اثْنَيْنِ; **I'm on my way ~** أَنا صاعِدٌ; **I'll be right ~** سَأَصْعَدُ من هُنا حالاً **2** (leading) مُتَقَدِّماً; **they are two goals/points ~** هُمْ مُتَقَدِّمونَ بِهَدَفَيْنِ \ بِنُقْطَتَيْنِ; **she's 40–15 ~** هي مُتَقَدِّمةٌ 15–40 **3** (upwards) **t-shirts from £5 ~** التيشُرْتات ب £5 وَما فوق; **from (the age of) 14 ~** من (سِنِّ) 14 وَما فوق

B *prep* **1** (at, to higher level) **the cat is ~ the tree** القِطّةُ في أَعْلى الشَجَرةِ; **he's ~ a ladder** هو فوق السُلَّمِ; **the library is ~ the stairs** تَقَعُ المَكْتَبةُ في أَعْلى الدَرَجِ; **he ran ~ the stairs** صَعِدَ الدَرَجَ رَكْضاً; **the road ~ the mountain** الطَريق إلى أَعْلى الجَبَلِ **2** (in direction) **the shops are ~ the road** المَحَلاّت في اتِّجاهِ الشارِعِ; **she lives ~ that road there** تَعيشُ في اتِّجاهِ ذلك الشارِعِ هُناكَ; **he lives just ~ the road** يَعيشُ قَريباً من هُنا; **his office is ~ the corridor from mine** يَقَعُ مَكْتَبُهُ على طولِ الرِواقِ من مَكْتَبي; **he walked ~ the road singing** مَشى على طولِ الطَريقِ وَهُوَ يُغَنّي; **he put it ~ his sleeve** أَخْفاهُ في كُمِّهِ

C (up above) *adv phr, prep phr* في أَعْلى; **it's ~ above the third shelf** إنَّهُ فوق الرَفِّ الثالِثِ

D (up against) *prep phr* **~ against the wall** مُسْتَنِداً إلى الجِدارِ; **to be ~ against strong opposition** واجَهَ مُعارَضةً شَديدةً; **it helps to know what you are ~ against** من المُفيدِ مَعْرِفةُ ماذا تُواجِهُ

E (up and about) *adv phr* **to be ~ and about again** (after illness) وَقَفَ على قَدَمَيْهِ مُجَدَّداً; (out of bed) نَهَضَ من الفِراشِ

F (up and down) *adv phr, prep phr* **1** (to and fro) **to walk** *or* **pace ~ and down** مَشى جيئةً وَذَهاباً **2** (throughout) **~ and down the country** في كُلِّ أَنْحاءِ البِلادِ

G (up and running) *adj phr* **to be ~ and running** «system, project» كانَ يَشْتَغِلُ \ قَيْدَ التَّشْغيلِ; **the system is ~ and running again** الجِهازُ يَشْتَغِلُ مَرّةً أُخرى

H (**up for**) *prep phr* **he's ~ for election** تَرَشَّحَ للانْتِخاباتِ; **the subject ~ for discussion is ...** المَوْضوعُ الّذي سَيُناقَشُ هو ...

I (**up to**) *prep phr* **1** (to particular point) إلى, حَتّى; **~ to here** إلى هُنا; **~ to there** إلى هُناكَ; **I was ~ to my knees in water** بَلَغَ الماءُ رُكْبَتَيَّ **2** (as much, many as) ما يُقارِبُ; **it can cost you ~ to $50** يُمْكِنُ أَنْ يُكَلِّفَكَ ما يُقارِبُ 50 دولاراً; **~ to 500 people arrive every day** يَصِلُ كُلَّ يَوْمٍ ما يُقارِبُ 500 شَخْصٍ; **to work for ~ to 12 hours a day** عَمِلَ ما يُقارِبُ 12 ساعةً في اليَوْمِ; **savings of ~ to 50%** تَوْفيرات تُقارِبُ 50٪ **3** (until) حَتّى; **~ to 2004** حَتّى 2004; **~ to 10.30 pm** حَتّى الـ10:30 مَساءً; **~ to now** حتّى الآنَ **4** (fit enough for) **I'm not ~ to it** لَسْتُ قادِراً عَلَيْهِ; **I'm not ~ to going back to work** لَيْسَ لَدَيَّ الشَّجاعةُ للعَوْدةِ إلى العَمَلِ; **your homework wasn't ~ to your usual standard** كانَ واجِبُكَ المَدْرَسيُّ دونَ مُسْتَواكَ المُعْتادِ; **the play wasn't ~ to much** لم تَكُنِ المَسْرَحيّةُ جَيِّدةً **5** (expressing responsibility) **it's ~ to him to do sth** هو من عَلَيْهِ أَنْ يَفْعَلَ شَيْئاً; **'shall I leave?'—'it's ~ to you!'** 'هَل أُغادِرُ؟' — 'الأَمْرُ يَعودُ لَكَ!'; **if it were ~ to me ...** لو كانَ الأَمْرُ بِيَدي ... **6** (doing) **what is he ~ to?** ماذا يُدَبِّرُ؟; **what are they ~ to?** ماذا يُدَبِّرونَ؟; **they're ~ to something** هُمْ يُدَبِّرونَ شَيْئاً

J *adj* **1** (out of bed) **she's ~** نَهَضَتْ من الفِراشِ; **they're usually ~ early** يَنْهَضونَ من الفِراشِ باكِراً في العادةِ; **we were ~ very late last night** سَهِرْنا إلى ساعةٍ مُتَأَخِّرةٍ لَيْلةَ أَمْسِ; **they were ~ all night** سَهِروا طوال اللَّيْلِ; **I was still ~ at 2 am** كُنْتُ لا أَزالُ مُسْتَيْقِظاً الساعةَ 2 فَجْراً **2** (higher) **sales/production are/is ~ by 10%** ارْتَفَعَتِ المَبيعاتُ \ ارْتَفَعَ الإنْتاجُ بِنِسْبةِ 10٪ **3** (infml) (wrong) **what's ~?** ماذا يَحْدُثُ \ يَجْري؟; **something's ~** شَيْءٌ ما يَحْدُثُ; **what's ~ with him?** ما بالُهُ؟; **there's something ~ with the brakes** هُناكَ مُشْكِلةٌ ما في الفَرامِلِ **4** (in position) **the notice is ~ on the board** الإشْعارُ مُعَلَّقٌ على اللَّوحِ; **is the tent ~?** هل نُصِبَت الخَيْمةُ؟; **the building will soon be ~** سَتُشَيَّدُ البِنايةُ قَريباً **5** (raised) **he had his umbrella ~** كانَتْ شَمْسيَّتُهُ مَفْتوحةً; **when the barrier is ~, you can go through** يُمْكِنُكَ العُبورُ عند رَفْعِ الحاجِزِ; **he had his hand ~** كانَتْ يَدُهُ مَرْفوعةً; **the blinds were ~** كانَت السَّتائِرُ مَرْفوعةً **6** (finished) **'time's ~!'** 'انْتَهى الوَقْتُ!'; **his leave is almost ~** إجازَتُهُ على وَشْكِ الانْتِهاءِ **7** (facing upwards) **'this side ~'** 'هذا الجانِبُ إلى الأَعْلى'; **the body was floating face ~** كانَ الجِسْمُ يَطْفو على ظَهْرِهِ; **the bread landed with the buttered side ~** سَقَطَ الخُبْزُ على الجانِبِ غَيْرِ المَدْهونِ بالزُّبْدةِ **8** (rising) **the river is ~** مَنْسوبُ مِياهِ النَّهْرِ مُرْتَفِعٌ; **the wind is ~** تَهُبُّ الريحُ بِقوّةٍ; **her blood pressure's ~** ضَغْطُ دَمِها مُرْتَفِعٌ **9** (pinned up) **her hair was ~** كانَ شَعْرُها مَرْفوعاً إلى الأَعْلى بِمِشْبَكٍ **10** (being repaired) **the road is ~** يَتِمُّ إصْلاحُ الطَّريقِ **11** (in upward direction) **the ~ escalator** الدَّرَج المُتَحَرِّك الصاعِد **12** (on trial) **to be ~ before the judge** مَثَلَ أمام القاضي; **he's ~ for murder** اتُّهِمَ بِجَريمةِ قَتْلٍ

K *vt* (-pp-) (to increase) رَفَعَ (a; رَفْع) ‹*the price, offer, wages*›

L *vi* (-pp-) (infml) **he ~ped and left** نَهَضَ وَخَرَجَ بِشَكْلٍ مُفاجِئٍ

Idioms **the ups and downs** التَّقَلُّبات; **to be (well) up on** (infml) كانَ ذا مَعْرِفةٍ واسعةٍ; **to be up for it** (infml) كانَ جاهِزاً \ مُسْتَعِدّاً لَهُ; **are you ~ for bungee jumping? — yes, I'm ~ for it/anything** هل أَنْتَ جاهِزٌ للقَفْزِ بالحَبْلِ المَطّاطيِّ؟ — نَعَمْ، أنا مُسْتَعِدٌّ لَهُ \ لِأَيِّ شَيْءٍ; **to be on the up** (infml) كانَ في تَحَسُّنٍ مُسْتَمِرٍّ

up-and-coming /ˌʌp(ə)nˈkʌmɪŋ/ *adj before n* ‹*politician, company*› ذو مُسْتَقْبَلٍ باهِرٍ, واعِد

upbeat /ˈʌpbiːt/ *adj* ‹*mood, assessment*› مُتَفائِل, مُبْتَهِج

upbraid /ʌpˈbreɪd/ *vt* (fml) عَنَّفَ, وَبَّخَ ‹*a student, protester*›

upbringing /ˈʌpbrɪŋɪŋ/ *n* تَنْشِئة, تَرْبِية

upcoming /ʌpˈkʌmɪŋ/ *adj* ‹*election, season*› مُقْبِل, قادِم

update **A** /ʌpˈdeɪt/ *vt* **1** (to inform) أَطْلَعَ على آخِرِ المُسْتَجِدّاتِ ‹*viewers, a person*› **2** (to modernize) حَدَّثَ ‹*software, a website*›

B /ˈʌpdeɪt/ *n* آخِر التَّطَوُّراتِ \ الأَخْبارِ \ المُسْتَجِدّاتِ

upend /ʌpˈɛnd/ *vt* قَلَبَ (i; قَلْب) ‹*a container, barrel*›

upfront /ʌp'frʌnt/ **A** *adv* (infml) ‹*to pay*› مُقَدَّماً

B *adj* **1** (infml) (frank) ‹*manner, organization*› صَريح (صُرَحاءُ)

2 *before n* (in advance) ‹*payment, fee*› مُقَدَّم

upgrade A /ʌp'greɪd/ *vt* **1** (to improve) حَسَّنَ ‹*the specification, comfort*› **2** (in computing) رَقَّى ‹*the software, hardware*› **3** (in status) رَقَّى ‹*one's skills, an employee*›

B /'ʌpgreɪd/ *n* **1** (in category, etc) تَرْقية, رَفْع مُسْتَوًى **2** (of hardware, software) تَرْقِية

upheaval /ʌp'hiːv(ə)l/ *n* اضْطِراب (اضْطِرابات), تَغَيُّر عَنيف

uphill /ʌp'hɪl/ **A** *adv* ‹*to walk, run*› صُعوداً

B *adj* **1** (sloping upwards) ‹*climb, slope*› صاعِد **2** (difficult) ‹*struggle, battle*› مُضْنٍ, مُجْهِد, شاقّ

uphold /ʌp'həʊld/ *vt* (*past tense, past participle* **upheld**) **1** (to support) دَعَمَ (a; دَعْم) ‹*a tradition, principle*› **2** (in law) أَيَّدَ, أَكَّدَ, ثَبَّتَ ‹*a conviction, decision*›

upholster /ʌp'həʊlstə/ *vt* نَجَّدَ ‹*furniture, a chair*›

upholstery /ʌp'həʊlst(ə)ri/ *n* تَنْجيد

upkeep /'ʌpkiːp/ *n* **1** (of a property) صِيانة **2** (of a family) مَعاش (مَعاشات)

uplift /ʌp'lɪft/ *vt* رَفَعَ (a; رَفْع) ‹*spirits, morale*›

uplifting /ʌp'lɪftɪŋ/ *adj* ‹*experience, music*› مُشَجِّع

upload /ʌp'ləʊd/ **A** *vt* حَمَّلَ ‹*a file, photo*›; **to ~ a file to a server** حَمَّلَ ملفًّا إلى خادِمٍ

B *n* **1** (data) مِلَفّ تَحْميلٍ **2** (process) تَحْميل

upmarket (BrE) /ʌp'mɑːkɪt/, **upscale** (AmE) /'ʌpskeɪl/ **A** *adj* ‹*suburb, hotel*› عالي المُسْتَوى, فَخْم, راقٍ

B *adv* ‹*to go, move*› إلى مُسْتَوًى أَعْلى

upon /ə'pɒn/ *prep* (fml) (on) عَلى; **thousands ~ thousands of people** آلاف وآلاف من الناسِ

upper /'ʌpə/ *adj* **1** (higher) ‹*floor, lip*› عُلْوِيّ, أَعْلى (عُلًى; أَعالٍ f عُلْيا); **the ~ floors of the building** الطَوابِق العُلْويّة لِلمَبْنى; **there is no ~ limit to your earnings** لَيْسَ هُناكَ حَدٌّ أَعْلى لِكَسْبِكَ **2** (in status) ‹*rank, echelon*› عُلْوِيّ, سامٍ (سُماة) **3** (geographically) ‹*reaches*› أَعْلى (عُلًى, أَعالٍ; f عُلْيا); **the U~ Nile** أَعالي النيلِ

Idiom **to get/have the upper hand** أَصْبَحَ \ كانَ مُسَيْطِراً

upper case *n* حُروف كَبيرة

upper-case letter *n* حَرْف كَبير

upper class A *n* (**the upper class**), also **the upper classes** الطَبَقة العُلْيا;

B *adj* (*before n* **upper-class**) ‹*accent, Englishman*› ذو الطَبَقةِ العُلْيا

upperclassman /ʌpə'klɑːsmən/ *n* (*pl* **-men**) (AmE) [طالِب في السَنةِ الثالثةِ \ الرابعةِ في المَدْرَسةِ الثانَويّةِ \ الجامِعةِ]

Upper Egypt *pr n* صَعيد مِصْرَ

uppermost /'ʌpəməʊst/ *adj* ‹*branch, rank*› أَعْلى (عُلًى, أَعالٍ; f عُلْيا); أَهَمّ; **that is what is ~ in my mind** هذا أَهَمُّ شَيْءٍ يَشْغَلُ بالي

upper school *n* (BrE) **1** (school) مَدْرَسة ثانَويّة (لِلطَلَبةِ بين سِنِّ الثالِثةَ عَشَرَ والثامِنةَ عَشَرَ) **2** (part of a school) [جُزْء مَدْرَسةٍ لِلطَلَبةِ بين سِنِّ الثالِثةَ عَشَرَ والثامِنةَ عَشَرَ]

upright /'ʌprʌɪt/ **A** *adj* **1** (vertically) ‹*position, posture*› عَموديّ, رَأْسيّ **2** (morally) ‹*citizen, behaviour*› عادِل, مُسْتَقيم, صالِح (صَوالِحُ)

B *adv* ‹*to walk, stand*› عَموديًّا, رَأْسيًّا

uprising /'ʌprʌɪzɪŋ/ *n* انْتِفاضة, ثَوْرة

upriver /ʌp'rɪvə/ *adv* ‹*to travel, swim*› نحو \ في اتِّجاهِ مَنْبَعِ النَهْرِ; **the bridge is ~ from Aswan** الجِسْرُ في اتِّجاهِ مَنْبَعِ النَهْرِ من أَسْوانَ

uproar /'ʌprɔː/ *n* **1** (noise) صَخَب, ضَجيج **2** (dissension) ضَجّة, اهْتِياج

uproot /ʌp'ruːt/ *vt* **1** (from the soil) اقْتَلَعَ, اسْتَأْصَلَ ‹*a tree, weed*› **2** (from home) انْتَزَعَ ‹*a family, child*›

upscale (AmE) /'ʌpskeɪl/ *adj* ▸**upmarket**

upset A /ʌp'set/ *vt* (*present participle* **-tt-**; *past tense, past participle* **upset**) **1** (to distress) أَزْعَجَ, ضايَقَ ‹*a family, child*›; **don't ~ yourself** لا تُزْعِجْ نَفْسَكَ **2** (to offend) أَزْعَجَ ‹*the neighbours, parents*› **3** (to disrupt) أَخَلَّ (ب), أَرْبَكَ ‹*sb's plans, the status quo*›; **to ~ the balance of nature** أَخَلَّ بِتَوازُنِ الطَبيعةِ **4** (to knock over) أَسْقَطَ ‹*a glass, lamp*› **5** (Med) أَزْعَجَ ‹*one's stomach*›

B /'ʌpsɛt/ *n* **1** (in competitions, elections) قَلْب المَوازينِ; **to cause an ~** قامَ بِقَلْبِ المَوازينِ **2** [u] (distress) انْزِعاج

3 (Med) **to have a stomach ~** كانَ عِنْدَهُ تَوَعُّكٌ في المَعِدةِ

C *adj* 1 /ʌp'sɛt/; **they were very ~ when he died** كانوا بُؤَساءَ جِدًّا عِنْدَما ماتَ; **people are ~ by the decision** الناسُ مُنْزَعِجونَ من القَرارِ; **to get upset** (distressed) انْزَعَجَ; (angry) غَضِبَ (a; غَضَب), اغْتاظَ (من) 2 (Med) /'ʌpset/ **to have an ~ stomach** كانَ عِنْدَهُ تَوَعُّكٌ في المَعِدةِ

upsetting /ʌp'sɛtɪŋ/ *adj* <*words, behaviour*> مُقْلِق

upshift /'ʌpʃɪft/ *vi* (AmE) «drivers» [نَقَلَ السُّرْعةَ لِأَعْلى]

upshot /'ʌpʃɒt/ *n* مُحَصِّلة, نَتيجة (نَتائِجُ); **the ~ is that ...** المُحَصِّلة هي أنّ ...

upside /'ʌpsʌɪd/ *n* جانِب إيجابيّ; **being self-employed has its ~** العَمَل الحُرّ لَهُ جانِبُهُ الإيجابيُّ

upside down **A** *adj* <*glass, triangle*> مَقْلوب; **the photo is upside down** الصورةُ مَقْلوبةٌ;

B *adv* <*to hang, lie*> بالمَقْلوبِ, رَأْساً على عَقِبٍ;

Idiom **to turn sth upside down** قَلَبَ شَيْئاً رَأْساً على عَقِبٍ

upstage /ʌp'steɪdʒ/ *vt* غَطّى (على), سَرَقَ الأَضْواءَ من <*a rival, colleague*>

upstairs /ʌp'stɛːz/ **A** *adv* <*to go*> إلى الطابَقِ العُلْويِّ; <*sleep*> في الطابَقِ العُلْويِّ

B *adj before n* <*bedroom, window*> الطابَق العُلْويّ

C *n* **(the upstairs)** الطابَق العُلْويّ

upstart /'ʌpstɑːt/ *n* حَديث نِعْمةٍ

upstate /'ʌpsteɪt/ **A** *adj before n* <*district, farm*> في شَمالِ الوِلايةِ; **to live in ~ New York** عاشَ في شَمالِ وِلايةِ نِيويورْك

B *adv* <*to move, travel*> في شَمالِ الوِلايةِ

upstream /ʌp'striːm/ *adv* <*to swim, head*> ضدّ التَّيّار

upsurge /'ʌpsəːdʒ/ *n* 1 (of interest, support) ارْتِفاع مُفاجِئ; (of anger) فَوْرة, نَوْبة; **she felt a sudden ~ of anger** أُصيبَتْ بِنَوْبةِ غَضَبٍ مُفاجِئةٍ 2 (in demand, sales, etc) زِيادة سَريعة, ارْتِفاع مُفاجِئ

uptake /'ʌpteɪk/ *n*

Idiom **to be quick/slow on the uptake** كانَ سَريعَ \ بَطيءَ الفَهْمِ

uptight /ʌp'tʌɪt/ *adj* (infml) <*guy, lawyer*> مُتَوَتِّر, مُتَشَنِّج; **what are you so ~ about?** ما الّذي يَجْعَلُكَ مُتَشَنِّجاً؟

up to date *adj* (before *n* **up-to-date**) 1 (modern) <*equipment, clothes*> عَصْريّ, حَديث (حُدَثاءُ, حِداث) 2 (current) <*records, timetable*> حاليّ

up to the minute *adj* (before *n* **up-to-the-minute**) <*news, information*> آخِر **(dipt)**

uptown /ʌp'taʊn/ **A** *adj* (AmE) <*train, shop*> [في جُزْءِ المَدينةِ العُلْويِّ]; **~ Manhattan** مانْهاتِن العُلْيا

B *adv* <*to move, head*> [إلى جُزْءِ المَدينةِ العُلْويِّ]

upturn /'ʌptəːn/ **A** *n* انْتِعاش (انْتِعاشات), زِيادة, ارْتِفاع; **there's been an ~ in prices** كانَ هُناكَ ارْتِفاعٌ في الأَسْعارِ

B **(upturned)** *adj* 1 (pointing up) <*nose, palm*> مَرْفوع

2 (upside down) <*boat, bowl*> مَقْلوب

upward /'ʌpwəd/ **A** *adv* (also **downwards**) <*to look, point*> نحو \ إلى الأَعْلى; **to glance ~** أَلْقى نَظْرةً سَريعةً إلى الأَعْلى

B *adj* <*glance, push*> مُتَّجِه إلى الأَعْلى; <*movement*> تَصاعُديّ; **an ~ trend** اتِّجاه تَصاعُديّ; **the ~ path was crowded** كانَ الدَرْبُ العُلْويُّ مُزْدَحِماً

upwardly mobile /ˌʌpwədli 'məʊbʌɪl/ *adj* <*group, family*> [يَسْعى للارْتِقاءِ الاجْتِماعيِّ]

uranium /jʊ'reɪnɪəm/ *n* يورانيوم

Uranus /'jʊərənəs, jʊ'reɪnəs/ *pr n* أورانوس

urban /'əːb(ə)n/ *adj* <*area, design*> حَضَريّ, مَدَنيّ

urbane /əː'beɪn/ *adj* (fml) <*wit, host*> لَبِق, مُؤَدَّب

urbanization, -isation (BrE) /əːb(ə)nʌɪzeɪʃ(ə)n/ *n* تَمْدين

urban planner *n* مُخَطِّط عُمْرانيّ

urban planning *n* تَخْطيط عُمْرانيّ

urban sprawl *n* التَمَدُّد العُمْرانيّ

urchin /'əːtʃɪn/ *n* (infml) ابْن الشارِعِ

Urdu /'ʊəduː/ *n* (اللُغة) الأُرْدِيّة

urge /'əːdʒ/ **A** *vt* 1 (to recommend) حَثَّ (u; حَثّ; على) <*caution, restraint*>; **the Security Council is urging restraint** يَحُثُّ مَجْلِسُ الأَمْنِ على ضَبْطِ النَفْسِ 2 (to exhort) **to ~ sb to do sth** حَثَّ شَخْصاً على أنْ يَفْعَلَ شَيْئاً; **I ~d her not to leave him** حَثَثْتُها على أنْ لا تَتْرُكَهُ

B *n* 1 (strong desire) رَغْبة مُلِحّة; **to have an ~ to do sth** كانَتْ عِنْدَهُ رَغْبةٌ مُلِحّةٌ في أنْ يَفْعَلَ شَيْئاً 2 (sexual) غَريزة (جِنْسيّة)

(Phrasal verb) **urge on**: ~ **on [sb/sth]**, ~ **[sb/sth] on** [1] (to encourage) [حَضَّ \ حَثَّ [شَخْصاً \ شَيْئاً *‹a player, team›*; **to ~ sb on to do sth** حَضَّ شَخْصاً على فِعْلِ شَيْءٍ [2] (to make go faster) «jockey» حَثَّ [شَيْئاً] على الإسْراعِ *‹a horse›*

urgency /ˈəːdʒ(ə)nsi/ *n* [1] (being necessary) اضْطِرار, ضَرورة [2] (regarding speed) ضَرورة الاسْتِعْجال; **I must see you as a matter of ~** من الضَروريِّ أنْ أَراكَ في أَقْرَبِ وَقْتٍ

urgent /ˈəːdʒ(ə)nt/ *adj* [1] (pressing) *‹need, action›* عاجِل, مُلِحّ [2] (insistent) *‹request, tone›* مُلِحّ

urgently /ˈəːdʒ(ə)ntli/ *adv* [1] (speedily) *‹to need, report›* عاجِلاً [2] *‹to whisper, wave›* بِإلْحاحٍ

urinal /jʊəˈrʌɪn(ə)l, ˈjʊərɪn(ə)l/ *n* مِبْوَلة (مَباوِلُ)

urinary /ˈjʊərɪn(ə)ri/ *adj* *‹infection, tract›* بَوْلِيّ

urinate /ˈjʊərɪneɪt/ *vi* (fml) «patients, revellers» تَبَوَّلَ

urine /ˈjʊərɪn/ *n* بَوْل (أَبْوال)

URL /juːɑːrˈɛl/ *n* = **Uniform Resource Locator** عُنْوان إنْتَرْنِت

urn /əːn/ *n* [1] (vase) جَرّة [2] (for ashes) [جَرّة لِحِفْظِ رَمادِ مَيِّتٍ] [3] (for boiling) غَلّاية ماءٍ

urology /jʊˈrɒlədʒi/ *n* مَسالِك بَوْلِيّة

urticaria /əːtɪˈkɛːrɪə/ *n* شَرًى

Uruguay /ˈjʊərəgwʌɪ/ *pr n* أوروغُواي (f)

Uruguayan /jʊərəˈgwʌɪən/ *n, adj* أوروغُوانِيّ

us /ʌs, əs/ *pron* [1] (as direct object) ـنا; **she invited ~** اسْتَدْعَتْنا [2] (as indirect object) ـنا; **he bought ~ an ice cream** اشْتَرى لَنا بوظةً; **give ~ the forms** أَعْطِنا الاسْتِماراتِ [3] (with prep) ـنا; **it's for ~** إنَّهُ لَنا; **both of ~ liked it** كِلانا أَحَبَّهُ; **there are four of ~** ثَمّةَ أَرْبَعةٌ مِنّا; **she's one of ~** إنَّها واحِدةٌ مِنّا [4] (for emphasis) نَحْنُ; **it's ~** إنَّهُ نَحْنُ

US /juːˈɛs/ *abbr* = **United States** الوِلايات المُتَّحِدة

USA /juːɛsˈeɪ/ *abbr* = **United States of America** الوِلايات المُتَّحِدة الأَمْريكيّة

usable /ˈjuːzəb(ə)l/ *adj* *‹space, appliance, data›* قابِل \ صالِح للاسْتِعْمالِ

USAF /juːɛseɪˈɛf/ *abbr* = **United States Air Force** القوّات الجَوّيّة الأَمْريكيّة

usage /ˈjuːsɪdʒ, ˈjuːzɪdʒ/ *n* اسْتِعْمال (اسْتِعْمالات), اسْتِخْدام (اسْتِخْدامات)

USB /juːɛsˈbiː/ *abbr* = **universal serial bus** يو إس بي (ناقِل مُتَسَلْسِل عامّ)

USB flash drive *n* فْلاش يو إس بي

USB port *n* مَنْفَذ يو إس بي

use [A] /juːz/ *vt* [1] (to employ) اسْتَعْمَلَ, اسْتَخْدَمَ *‹a car, method, your knowledge›*; **can I ~ your phone?** هل يُمْكِنُني اسْتِخْدامُ هاتِفِكَ؟ [2] (to consume) اسْتَهْلَكَ *‹fuel, oil›*; **this heater ~s a lot of electricity** تَسْتَهْلِكُ هذه المِدْفَأةُ كَهْرَباءَ عالِيةً [3] (to exploit) اسْتَغَلَّ *‹a colleague, friend›*; **he's just using you** يَسْتَغِلُّكَ فَقَطْ

[B] /juːs/ *modal aux* **he didn't ~ to smoke** لم يَكُنْ مُدَخِّناً; **what did it ~ to look like?** كيف كانَ شَكْلُهُ سابِقاً؟; ▸ **used¹**

[C] /juːs/ *n* [1] (act of using) اسْتِعْمال (اسْتِعْمالات); **a toilet for the ~ of customers** مِرْحاض لِاسْتِعْمالِ الزَبائِنِ; **for my own ~** لِاسْتِعْمالي الخاصِّ; **to make ~ of sth** اسْتَعْمَلَ شَيْئاً; **while the machine is in ~** خلال اسْتِعْمالِ الجِهازِ; **to have the ~ of the car** كانَ لَهُ حَقُّ اسْتِعْمال السَيّارةِ; **to lose the ~ of one's legs** فَقَدَ القُدْرةَ على اسْتِعْمالِ ساقَيْهِ; **this expression is no longer in ~** لم يَعُدْ هذا التَعْبيرُ مُسْتَعْمَلاً [2] (way of using) اسْتِعْمال (اسْتِعْمالات), اسْتِخْدام (اسْتِخْدامات); **to have no further ~ for sb/sth** لم تَعُدْ بِهِ حاجةٌ إلى شَخْصٍ \ شَيْءٍ; **a wide range of industrial ~s** اسْتِعْمالات صِناعيّة واسِعة النِطاقِ; **to put sth to good ~** أَحْسَنَ اسْتِخْدامَ شَيْءٍ [3] (usefulness) **to be of ~ (to sb)** كانَ نافِعاً \ مُفيداً (لِشَخْصٍ); **to be (of) no ~** لَيْسَتْ لَهُ مَنْفَعةٌ \ فائِدةٌ; **what's the ~ of crying?** ما مَنْفَعةُ \ فائِدةُ البُكاءِ؟; **it's no ~** لا فائِدةَ مِنْهُ

(Phrasal verb) **use up**: ~ **[sth] up**, ~ **up [sth]** اسْتَهْلَكَ [شَيْئاً], اسْتَنْزَفَ [شَيْئاً], اسْتَنْفَدَ [شَيْئاً] *‹food›*; **the money was soon ~d up** صُرِفَ المالُ بِسُرْعةٍ

use-by date /ˈjuːzbʌɪ deɪt/ *n* تاريخ الصَلاحيّةِ \ الاسْتِعْمالِ; **to be past its ~** انْتَهى تاريخُ صَلاحيَّتِهِ

used¹ /juːst/ [A] *modal aux* **I ~ to live here** كُنْتُ أَسْكُنُ هُنا; **there ~ to be a factory on the corner** كانَ هُناكَ مَصْنَعٌ في ناصِيةِ الشارِعِ في الماضي

B *adj* (accustomed) **to be ~ to sth** كانَ مُعْتاداً على شَيْءٍ; **I'm not ~ to this heat** لَسْتُ مُعْتاداً على هذه الحَرارة; **you'll get ~ to him** سَوْفَ تَعْتادُ عَلَيْهِ

used² /ju:zd/ **A** *adj* (second hand) ‹*car, syringe, clothes*› مُسْتَعْمَل; **a ~-car salesman** بائِع سَيّاراتٍ مُسْتَعْمَلةٍ

B *past tense, past participle* ▸**use** A, B

useful /ˈju:sfʊl/ *adj* **1** (helpful) ‹*information, tool*› مُفيد, نافِع; **to be ~ for doing sth** كانَ نافِعاً لِفِعْلِ شَيْءٍ; **to be ~ to sb** كانَ مُفيداً لِشَخْصٍ; **to make oneself ~** كانَ خَدوماً; **he made himself ~ around the farm** ساعَدَ في عَمَلِ المَزْرَعةِ **2** (infml) (competent) ‹*footballer, cook*› بارِع, ماهِر; **to be ~ with a gun** كانَ ماهِراً في اسْتِعْمالِ المُسَدَّسِ; **he's a ~ addition to the team** هو إضافةٌ جَيِّدةٌ للفَريقِ

usefulness /ˈju:sfʊlnəs/ *n* صَلاح, فائِدة (فَوائِدُ), مَنْفَعة (مَنافِعُ)

useless /ˈju:sləs/ *adj* **1** (not effective) ‹*junk, gadget*› غَيْر مُجْدٍ, عَديم الفائِدةِ; **it's ~ to protest** لا فائِدةَ من التَظاهُرِ **2** (infml) (incompetent) ‹*fool, cook*› غَيْر قادِر, سَيِّئ, مَيْئُوس مِنْهُ; **he's ~ at tennis/languages** هو سَيِّئٌ في رِياضةِ التِنس \ اللُغاتِ

user /ˈju:zə/ *n* **1** (of products, services) مُسْتَعْمِل, مُسْتَخْدِم **2** (of drugs) مُتَعاطٍ

user-friendly /ju:zəˈfrendli/ *adj* ‹*format, tool*› سَهْل الاسْتِخْدامِ

user group *n* مَجْموعة مُسْتَخْدِمين

username /ˈju:zəneɪm/ *n* اسْم مُسْتَخْدِم

usher /ˈʌʃə/ **A** *n* مُرْشِد, (أَدِلّاءُ) دَليل

B *vt* ‹*a guest, visitor*› أَرْشَدَ, (دَلالة ;u) دَلَّ; **to ~ sb in/out** أَدْخَلَ \ أَخْرَجَ شَخْصاً; **he ~ed us to our seats** دَلَّنا على مَقاعِدِنا

Phrasal verb **usher in**: **~ in [sth]** أَعْلَنَ بِداية [شَيْءٍ] ‹*an era, reforms*›

usherette /ʌʃəˈret/ *n* مُرْشِدة, دَليلة

USN /ju:esˈen/ *abbr* = **United States Navy** بَحْريّة الوِلاياتِ المُتَّحِدةِ

USP /ju:esˈpi:/ *n* = **unique selling point** مَبْدَأ بَيْع فَريد

USS /ju:esˈes/ *abbr* = **United States Ship** سَفينة تابِعة للبَحْريّةِ الأَمْريكيّةِ

USSR /ju:esesˈɑ:/ *pr n* = **Union of Soviet Socialist Republics** اتِّحاد الجُمْهوريّاتِ السوفْيِتيّةِ الاشْتِراكيّةِ

usual /ˈju:ʒʊəl/ **A** *adj* ‹*route, way, procedure*› مَعْهود, مُعْتاد; **let's meet at the ~ time** دَعْنا نَلْتَقي في الوَقْتِ المَعْهودِ; **it's not ~ for patients to have to wait this long** لَيْسَ من المُعْتادِ أنْ يَنْتَظِرَ المَرضى كُلَّ هذا الوَقْتِ; **she was her ~ cheerful self** كانَتْ مَرِحةً كَعادَتِها; **as ~** كالعادةِ; **'business as ~'** 'العَمَلُ مُسْتَمِرٌّ كالمُعْتادِ'; **as is ~ in these cases** كَما هو مَعْهودٌ في مِثْلِ هذه الحالاتِ

B *n* (infml) **the ~** (in a bar) المُعْتاد

usually /ˈju:ʒʊəli/ *adv* ‹*to have, take*› عادةً; **how much do you ~ pay?** كم تَدْفَعُ عادةً؟

usurp /ju:ˈzɜ:p/ *vt* اسْتَوْلى (على) ‹*the power, throne*›

usury /ˈju:ʒ(ə)ri/ *n* (fml) رِباً

UT *abbr* ▸**Utah**

Utah /ˈju:tɔ:, ˈju:tɑ:/ *pr n* يوتا

Utahan /ˈju:tɔ:ən, ˈju:tɑ:ən/ *n, adj* [(شَخْص) من يوتا]

utensil /ju:ˈtens(ə)l/ *n* أَداة (أَدَوات)

uterus /ˈju:t(ə)rəs/ *n* (*pl* **uteri** /ˈju:tərʌɪ/ or **uteruses**) رَحِم (أَرْحام)

utility /ju:ˈtɪlɪti/ *n* **1** [u] (usefulness) فائِدة, مَنْفَعة **2** (company) شَرِكة خِدْماتٍ عامّةٍ, مُؤَسَّسة ذات مَنْفَعةٍ عامّةٍ

utility bill *n* فاتورة الخِدْماتِ

utility company *n* شَرِكة خِدْماتٍ عامّةٍ

utility room *n* غُرْفة غَسيلٍ

utilization, -isation (BrE) /ju:təlʌɪˈzeɪʃ(ə)n/ *n* انْتِفاع, اسْتِفادة, اسْتِخْدام

utilize, -ise (BrE) /ˈju:tɪlʌɪz/ *vt* انْتَفَعَ (ب), اسْتَخْدَمَ, اسْتَفادَ (من) ‹*technology, resources*›

utmost /ˈʌtməʊst/ **A** *adj* ‹*caution, urgency*› أَقْصى (f قُصْوى), أَكْبَر (dipt); **it is of the ~ importance** هو في غايةِ الأَهَمِّيّةِ; **I have the ~ respect for him** أَحْتَرِمُهُ كُلَّ الاحْتِرام

B *n* **to the ~** إلى أَقْصى حَدٍّ; **to do one's ~ to do sth** بَذَلَ قُصارى جُهْدِهِ لِفِعْلِ شَيْءٍ

utopia /ju:ˈtəʊpɪə/ *n* مَدينة فاضِلة, يوطوبيا

utter /ˈʌtə/ **A** *adj* ‹*nonsense, contempt*› مُطْلَق, كُلّيّ, (تَوامٌّ) تامّ

B *vt* نَطَقَ (u; نُطْق; ب) ‹*a word*›; أَطْلَقَ ‹*a cry, sound*›

utterance /ˈʌt(ə)rəns/ *n* تَعْبير (تَعْبيرات), كَلام (n coll, no singul n) قَوْل (أَقْوال)

utterly /ˈʌt(ə)li/ *adv* ‹*different, ridiculous*› تَماماً, للغايةِ

U-turn /ˈjuːtəːn/ *n* ① (in driving) دَوَران للخَلْفِ ② (in policy) انْقِلاب (انْقِلابات); **to do a ~** حَوَّلَ المَسارَ السِياسيَّ

UV /juːˈviː/ *abbr* = **ultraviolet** فوق بَنَفْسَجِيّ

uvula /ˈjuːvjʊlə/ *n* (*pl* **uvulae**) لَهاة (لَهَوات, لَهَيات, لَهاً)

Uzbek /ˈʊzbɛk/ **A** *n* ① (citizen) أوزْبِكِيّ ② (language) (اللُغة) الأوزْبِكيّة

B *adj* ‹*president, border*› أوزْبكِيّ

Uzbekistan /ʊzbɛkɪˈstɑːn, ʊzbɛkɪˈstan/ *pr n* أوزْبِكِسْتان (f)

Vv

V, v /viː/ [A] *n* (letter) [الحَرْف الثاني والعِشْرونَ من الأَبْجَديّةِ الإنْكليزيّةِ]
[B] *abbr* [1] (**v**) = **versus** ضِدَّ [2] (**V**) = **volt(s)** فولْت [3] (**v**; *pl* **vv**) = **verse** (poetry) مَقْطَع (مَقاطِعُ); (in the Bible) آية (آيات)

VA *abbr* [1] (Geog) = **Virginia** [2] (AmE Mil) = **Veterans' Administration** [مُؤَسَّسة للمُحارِبينَ القُدَماءِ]

vacancy /ˈveɪk(ə)nsi/ *n* (*pl* **vacancies**) [1] (job) وَظيفة خالِية \ شاغِرة; **to advertise a ~** أَعْلَنَ عن وَظيفةٍ خالِيةٍ; **to fill a ~** شَغَلَ وَظيفةً خالِيةً [2] (at a hotel) غُرْفة خالِية \ شاغِرة; **'no vacancies'** 'لا توجَدُ غُرَفٌ خالِيةٌ'

vacant /ˈveɪk(ə)nt/ *adj* [1] (unoccupied) <*seat, space*> خالٍ, شاغِر; <*land, plot*> غَيْر مَبْنِيٍّ [2] (available) <*position, post*> خالٍ, شاغِر [3] (blank) <*look, stare*> شارِد, خالٍ من التَعْبير

vacate /vəˈkeɪt/ *vt* [1] (fml) أَخْلى <*a building, premises*> [2] تَخَلّى (عن), تَرَكَ (تَرْك; u) <*a post, position*>

vacation /veɪˈkeɪʃ(ə)n, vəˈkeɪʃ(ə)n/ [A] *n* عُطْلة (عُطَل, عُطْلات), إجازة; **to be/go on ~ in Florida** ذَهَبَ في عُطْلةٍ إلى فلوريدا; **20 days' paid ~** عُطْلة مَدْفوعة الأَجْرِ لِمُدّةِ عِشْرينَ يَوْماً
[B] *vi* قَضى عُطْلةً

vacationer /veɪˈkeɪʃnə, vəˈkeɪʃnə/ *n* (AmE) صاحِب عُطْلةٍ

vaccinate /ˈvaksɪneɪt/ *vt* لَقَّحَ, طَعَّمَ <*a child, animal*>; **to ~ sb against tetanus** طَعَّمَ شَخْصاً ضدّ التيتانوس

vaccination /vaksɪˈneɪʃ(ə)n/ *n* تَلْقيح, تَطْعيم

vaccine /ˈvaksiːn/ *n* لِقاح, طُعْم (طُعوم)

vacillate /ˈvasɪleɪt/ *vi* [1] (to hesitate) تَرَدَّدَ [2] (to waver, sway) تَذَبْذَبَ, تَأَرْجَحَ

vacuum /ˈvakjʊəm/ [A] *n* [1] فَراغ (فَراغات) [2] (infml) ▸ **vacuum cleaner**
[B] *vt* (infml) نَظَّفَ بالمِكْنَسةِ الكَهْرَبائيّةِ <*a room, floor*>
[C] *vi* (infml) نَظَّفَ بالمِكْنَسةِ الكَهْرَبائيّةِ

vacuum cleaner *n* مِكْنَسة كَهْرَبائيّة

vacuum flask (BrE), **vacuum bottle** (AmE) *n* تُرْمُس (تَرامِسُ)

vacuum-pack /ˈvakjuːm,pɑːk/ *vt* عَبَّأَ بِتَفْريغِ الهَواءِ <*meat, cheese*>

vagabond /ˈvagəbɒnd/ *n* مُتَشَرِّد

vagina /vəˈdʒʌɪnə/ *n* مَهْبِل (مَهابِلُ)

vaginal /vəˈdʒʌɪn(ə)l/ *adj* <*delivery, discharge*> مَهْبِليّ

vagrant /ˈveɪgrənt/ *n* مُتَشَرِّد

vague /veɪg/ *adj* [1] (imprecise) <*idea, sense*> مُبْهَم, غامِض (غَوامِضُ); **to be ~ about sth** تَكَلَّمَ عن شَيْءٍ بِشَكْلٍ غامِضٍ; **he was very ~ about the details** تَكَلَّمَ حول التَفاصيلِ بِشَكْلٍ غامِضٍ [2] (distracted) <*person, expression*> غامِض (غَوامِضُ), مُبْهَم; **to look ~** نَظَرَ نَظْرةً مُبْهَمةً; **she was ~ and evasive** كانَ كَلامُها مُبْهَماً وَمُراوِغاً [3] (indistinct) <*outline*> غامِض (غَوامِضُ), مُبْهَم

vaguely /ˈveɪgli/ *adv* [1] (imprecisely) <*to remember*> بِصورةٍ مُبْهَمةٍ, بِغُموضٍ; <*defined, worded*> بِصورةٍ غَيْرِ دَقيقةٍ \ مُمَيَّزةٍ [2] (slightly) <*familiar, uncomfortable*> نَوْعاً ما; **she ~ resembles the Queen** تُشْبِهُ المَلِكةَ نَوْعاً ما [3] (distractedly) <*to smile, gaze*> بِشُرودٍ

vain /veɪn/ [A] *adj* [1] (conceited) <*person*> مَغْرور [2] (futile) <*attempt*> فاشِل; <*effort*> غَيْر مُثْمِرٍ [3] (empty) <*hope, promise*> فارِغ (فُرّاغ)
[B] **(in vain)** *phr* عَبَثاً, سُدًى, دونَ جَدْوى

vainly /ˈveɪnli/ *adv* (futilely) <*to try, seek*> عَبَثاً, سُدًى, دونَ جَدْوى

valency /ˈveɪlənsi/ *n* (*pl* **valencies**) تَكافُؤ

valentine /ˈvaləntʌɪn/ *n* [1] (also **valentine card**) بِطاقة عيدِ الحُبِّ [2] (person) حَبيب (تُرْسَلُ إلَيْهِ بِطاقةُ عيدِ الحُبِّ)

Valentine's Day *n* عيد الحُبِّ

valet /'valɪt, 'valeɪ/ *n* ➊ (man's attendant) خادِم خاصّ, وَصيف (وُصَفاءُ) ➋ (hotel employee) [مُوَظَّف يُنَظِّفُ المَلابِسَ] ➌ (AmE) (parking cars) مُوَظَّف رَكْنِ السَيّاراتِ

valet parking *n* خِدْمة رَكْنِ السَيّاراتِ

valiant /'valɪənt/ *adj* ‹warrior, hero› شُجاع (شُجْعان), مِقْدام, باسِل (بَواسِلُ); ‹effort, attempt› بُطوليّ

valid /'valɪd/ *adj* ➊ (reasonable) ‹reason, argument, point› مَعْقول, وَجيه (وُجَهاءُ), سَليم (سُلَماءُ) ➋ (legally in force) ‹licence, passport› ساري المَفْعولِ

validate /'valɪdeɪt/ *vt* ➊ (to support) أَثْبَتَ الصِحّةَ ‹a claim, theory› ➋ (to confirm) اعْتَمَدَ ‹a ticket, document›

validation /valɪ'deɪʃ(ə)n/ *n* تَحَقُّق من الصِحّةِ

validity /və'lɪdɪti/ *n* (of an argument, claim) صِحّة, سَلامة

valley /'vali/ *n* وادٍ (أَوْدِية, وِدْيان)

valour (BrE), **valor** (AmE) /'valə/ *n* (fml) شَجاعة, إِقْدام, بَسالة

valuable /'valjʊb(ə)l/ *adj* ➊ (precious) ‹commodity, jewellery› قَيِّم, ثَمين, نَفيس; **we are wasting ~ time** نُضَيِّعُ وَقتاً ثَميناً ➋ (useful) ‹information, lesson› قَيِّم, مُفيد

valuables /'valju:əb(ə)lz/ *n pl* أَشْياء ثَمينة, نَفائِس (dipt)

valuation /valjʊ'eɪʃ(ə)n/ *n* تَثْمين

value /'valju:/ **A** *n* ➊ (monetary worth) قيمة, ثَمَن (أَثْمان); **the painting has little ~** قيمةُ اللَوْحةِ ضَئيلةٌ; **they stole goods to the ~ of $7,000** سَرَقوا بِضاعةً تَبْلُغُ قيمَتُها $7000 ➋ [u] (usefulness) فائِدة (فَوائِدُ); **to be of little/great ~ to sb** كانَتْ فائِدَتُهُ صَغيرةً \ كَبيرةً بالنِسْبةِ لِشَخْصٍ; **I see no ~ in continuing this discussion** لا أرى فائِدةً في الاستِمْرارِ في هذا النِقاشِ; **they place a high ~ on formal qualifications** يُقَدِّرونَ المُؤَهَّلاتِ الرَسْميّةَ تَقْديراً عالِياً ➌ [u] (relative to cost) قيمة, ثَمَن (أَثْمان); **to be good/poor ~** كانَ السِعْرُ مُناسِباً \ غَيْرَ مُناسِبٍ; **to get ~ for money** (BrE) حَصَلَ على شَيْءٍ ذي قيمةٍ مُقابِلَ مالِهِ ➍ (in mathematics) قيمة
B (**values**) *n pl* (standards) قِيَم
C *vt* ➊ (to assess the worth of) «assessors» قَيَّمَ, قَدَّرَ ‹a company, property, an asset›; **to have sth ~d** قَدَّرَ قيمةَ شَيْءٍ; **to ~ sth at £150** قَدَّرَ قيمةَ شَيْءٍ بِ £150 ➋ (to esteem) قَدَّرَ ‹one's life, freedom, sb's opinion›; **I ~ him as a friend** أُقَدِّرُهُ كَصَديقٍ

value added tax *n* ضَريبة القيمةِ المُضافةِ

value pack *n* حِزْمة قَيِّمة

valuer /'valjʊə/ *n* (BrE) مُثَمِّن

valve /valv/ *n* صِمام (صِمامات, أَصِمّة)

vampire /'vampʌɪə/ *n* مَصّاص دِماءٍ

van /van/ *n* ➊ (short haul motor vehicle) شاحِنة مُقْفَلة; (long haul motor vehicle) شاحِنة \ سَيّارة نَقْلِ أَثاثٍ ➋ (BrE) (rail vehicle) عَرَبة بِضاعةٍ

vandal /'vand(ə)l/ *n* مُخَرِّب

vandalism /'vandəlɪz(ə)m/ *n* تَخْريب (تَخْريبات)

vandalize, -ise (BrE) /'vandəlʌɪz/ *vt* ‹cars, property› خَرَّبَ

vanguard /'vangɑ:d/ *n* طَليعة (طَلائِعُ)

vanilla /və'nɪlə/ *n* فانيْلِيا

vanish /'vanɪʃ/ *vi* «person, smile» اخْتَفى; **to ~ into thin air** اخْتَفى تَماماً

vanity /'vanɪti/ *n* (*pl* **vanities**) غُرور, زَهْو, خُيَلاء (dipt)

vanquish /'vaŋkwɪʃ/ *vt* (liter) هَزَمَ (i; هَزْم), قَهَرَ (a; قَهْر), تَغَلَّبَ (على) ‹an enemy, evil›

vantage point *n* ➊ (for a view) مَرْقَب (مَراقِبُ) ➋ (for analysis) وُجْهة نَظَرٍ

vaporize, -ise (BrE) /'veɪpərʌɪz/ **A** *vt* ‹a liquid, metal› بَخَّرَ **B** *vi* «liquid, metal» تَبَخَّرَ

vaporizer, -iser (BrE) /'veɪpərʌɪzə/ *n* مِرْذاذ (مَراذيذُ)

vapour (BrE), **vapor** (AmE) /'veɪpə/ *n* بُخار (أَبْخِرة)

vapour trail *n* غيمة طائِرةٍ

variability /vɛ:rɪə'bɪləti/ *n* تَغَيُّر (تَغَيُّرات), تَقَلُّب (تَقَلُّبات)

variable /'vɛ:rɪəb(ə)l/ *adj* ‹rate, number› مُتَغَيِّر, مُتَقَلِّب

variance /'vɛ:rɪəns/ *n* اخْتِلاف (اخْتِلافات), تَبايُن (تَبايُنات), فَرْق (فُروق); **to be at ~ with sth** تَعارَضَ مع شَيْءٍ

variant /'vɛ:rɪənt/ *n* تَنْويعة, شَكْل مُخْتَلِف

variation /vɛ:rɪ'eɪʃ(ə)n/ *n* ➊ (change) اخْتِلاف (اخْتِلافات), تَبايُن (تَبايُنات), فَرْق (فُروق) ➋ (different version) تَنْويع (تَنْويعات) ➌ (in music) تَنْويع (تَنْويعات)

varicose veins /varıkəʊs veınz/ ***n pl*** تَوَسُّع الأَوْرِدةِ

varied /'vɛːrıd/ ***adj*** ‹*programme, diet*› مُتَنوِّع

variegated /'vɛːriəgeıtıd/ ***adj*** ‹*leaf, plant*› مُبَرْقَش; ‹*pattern*› مُتَعَدِّد الأَلْوانِ

variety /və'rʌıəti/ ***n*** (*pl* **varieties**) **1** (diversity) تَنَوُّع (تَنَوُّعات) **2** (range, number) تَشْكيلة; **for a ~ of reasons** لِأَسْبابٍ مُتَنوِّعةٍ **3** (type) ضَرْب (ضُروب), نَوْع (أَنْواع)

variety show ***n*** عَرْض مُنوَّعاتٍ

variola /və'rʌıələ/ ***n*** جُدَريّ

various /'vɛːrıəs/ ***adj*** **1** (different) ‹*forms, reasons*› مُتَنوِّع **2** (several) ‹*people, problems*› عَديد, كَثير

varnish /'vɑːnıʃ/ **A** ***n*** **1** وَرْنيش **2** (BrE) (for nails) طِلاء **B** ***vt*** وَرْنَشَ (i; وَرْنَشة) ‹*floorboards, wood*›; **to ~ one's nails** طَلى أَظافِرَهُ

vary /'vɛːri/ **A** ***vt*** (**varies, varying, varied**) غَيَّرَ ‹*rates, a route*› **B** ***vi*** **1** (to differ) «rates, prices» اِخْتَلَفَ, تَبايَنَ; **opinions ~** تَتَبايَنُ \ تَخْتَلِفُ الآراءُ **2** (to change, fluctuate) «behaviour, weather» تَغَيَّرَ, تَبَدَّلَ

varying /'vɛːriıŋ/ ***adj*** ‹*levels, sizes*› مُتَفاوِت, مُتَبايِن, مُخْتَلِف; **with ~ degrees of success** بِدَرَجاتٍ مُتَفاوِتةٍ من النَجاح

vascular /'vaskjʊlə/ ***adj*** ‹*disease, system*› وِعائيّ

vase /vɑːz, AmE veıs/ ***n*** زَهْريّة, مَزْهَريّة

vasectomy /və'sɛktəmi/ ***n*** (*pl* **vasectomies**) قَطْع الحَبْلِ المَنَويِّ

Vaseline® /'vasəliːn/ ***n*** فازْلين

vast /vɑːst/ ***adj*** **1** (in quantity) ‹*amount, number, difference*› هائِل, ضَخْم; **the ~ majority of people** الأَغْلَبِيّة العُظْمى من الناسِ **2** (in extent) ‹*area, experience*› واسِع

vastly /'vɑːstli/ ***adv*** ‹*different, improved*› إلى حَدٍّ, بِدَرَجةٍ كَبيرةٍ, على نَحْوٍ واسِعٍ, بَعيد

vat /vat/ ***n*** حَوْض (أَحْواض, حِياض, حيضان)

VAT /viːeı'tiː, vat/ ***n*** = **value added tax** ضَريبة القيمةِ المُضافةِ

Vatican /'vatık(ə)n/ ***pr n*** (**the Vatican**) الفاتيكان (f)

Vatican City ***pr n*** مَدينة الفاتيكان (dipt)z

vault /vɔːlt/ **A** ***n*** **1** (strongroom) خِزانة (خِزانات, خَزائِنُ) **2** (crypt) مَدْفِن (مَدافِنُ), مَقْبَرة (مَقابِرُ) **3** (roof) قَبْو (أَقْبِية) **B** ***vt*** قَفَزَ (i; قَفْز, قَفَزان; على) ‹*a barrier, fence*› **C** ***vi*** «athlete, gymnast» قَفَزَ (i; قَفْز), وَثَبَ (i; وَثْب), نَطَّ (u; نَطّ)

VCR /viːsiː'ɑː/ ***n*** = **videocassette recorder** جِهاز فيديو, (تَسْجيلِ) فيديو

VD /viː'diː/ ***n*** = **venereal disease** مَرَض جِنْسيّ

VDT ***n*** (AmE) = **visual display terminal** وِحْدة عَرْضٍ مَرْئيٍّ

VDU /viːdiː'juː/ ***n*** = **visual display unit** وِحْدة عَرْضٍ مَرْئيٍّ

veal /viːl/ ***n*** لَحْم عِجْلٍ, بِتِلّو (Egypt)

vector /'vɛktə/ ***n*** **1** (quantity) مُتَّجِه, كَمِّيّة مُتَّجِهة **2** (organism) ناقِل

veer /vıə/ ***vi*** «vehicle, road, wind» اِنْحَرَفَ, غَيَّرَ اتِّجاهَهُ; **the car ~ed off the road** اِنْحَرَفَت السَيّارةُ عن الطَريقِ; **to ~ off course** «plane, ship» اِنْحَرَفَ عن المَسارِ

vegan /'viːg(ə)n/ ***n, adj*** نَباتيّ صِرْف

veganism /'viːg(ə)niz(ə)m/ ***n*** نَباتيّة صِرْفة

vegetable /'vɛdʒtəb(ə)l/ ***n*** **1** (as food) خُضَر; **green ~s** خَضْراوات خَضْراء **2** (plant) نَبات (n coll; نَباتات)

vegetable garden ***n*** حَديقة خُضْرَواتٍ

vegetable oil ***n*** زَيْت نَباتيّ

vegetarian /vɛdʒı'tɛːrıən/ ***n, adj*** نَباتيّ

vegetarianism /vɛdʒə'tɛːriəniz(ə)m/ ***n*** نَباتيّة

vegetate /'vɛdʒıteıt/ ***vi*** «person, brain» عاشَ حَياةً خامِلةً

vegetation /vɛdʒı'teıʃ(ə)n/ ***n*** غِطاء نَباتيّ, نَباتات

veggie /'vɛdʒi/ ***n*** (infml) **1** (vegetarian) نَباتيّ **2** (vegetable) خُضْرة (خُضَر)

veggie burger ***n*** بُرْجَر نَباتيّ

vehement /'viːımənt/ ***adj*** ‹*opposition, denial*› شَديد (أَشِدّاءُ, شِداد), عَنيف (عُنُف), حادّ

vehemently /'viːəməntli/ ***adv*** ‹*to deny, oppose*› بِشِدّةٍ, بِحِدّةٍ

vehicle /'viːık(ə)l/ ***n*** مَرْكَبة, عَرَبة, سَيّارة

veil /veıl/ **A** ***n*** حِجاب (حُجُب, أَحْجِبة), خِمار (خُمُر), بُرْقُع (بَراقِعُ); **to wear the ~** اِرْتَدى الحِجابَ; **to draw a ~ over sth** أَسْدَلَ السِتارَ على شَيْءٍ **B** ***vt*** حَجَبَ (u; حَجْب) ‹*one's face*›

veiled /veıld/ ***adj*** ‹*threat, reference*› مُبْطَن

vein /veɪn/ *n* 1 (blood vessel) وَريد (أَوْرِدة) 2 (on leaves) عِرْق (عُروق) 3 (in rock) عِرْق (عُروق) 4 (in marble, cheese) عِرْق (عُروق) 5 (style, mood) روح (mf; أَرْواح) قَبيل; **he continued in a similar ~** اسْتَمَرَّ على نَفْسِ المِنْوالِ

velocity /vɪˈlɒsɪti/ *n* (*pl* **velocities**) سُرْعة

velour, **velours** /vəˈlʊə/ *n* فيلور (ضَرْب من المُخْمَلِ \ القَطيفةِ)

velvet /ˈvɛlvɪt/ *n* قَطيفة, مُخْمَل

velvety /ˈvɛlvəti/ *adj* ‹*texture, skin*› مُخْمَليّ

vendetta /vɛnˈdɛtə/ *n* ثَأْر (ثَأْرات), عَداء (عَداءات)

vending machine /ˈvɛndɪŋ məʃiːn/ *n* آلة بَيْعٍ

vendor /ˈvɛndə/ *n* (fml) بائِع (باعة, بائِعونَ)

veneer /vɪˈnɪə/ *n* 1 (covering) قِشْرة (خشبٍ) 2 (appearance) غِطاء (أَغْطِية)

venerate /ˈvɛnəreɪt/ *vt* بَجَّلَ ‹*a saint, an icon*›

venereal disease /vɪˈnɪərɪəl ˌdɪziːz/ *n* مَرَض تناسُليّ \ جِنْسيّ

venetian blind /vəˌniːʃ(ə)n ˈblʌɪnd/ *n* سِتارة مَعْدِنية

Venezuela /ˌvɛnɪˈzweɪlə/ *pr n* فِنِزْويلا

Venezuelan /vɛnəˈzweɪlən/ *n, adj* فِنِزْويليّ

vengeance /ˈvɛndʒ(ə)ns/ *n* ثَأْر (ثَأْرات), انْتِقام

(Idiom) **with a vengeance** (infml) بِعُنْفٍ, بِقوّةٍ, بِشِدّةٍ

vengeful /ˈvɛndʒfʊl/ *adj* (fml) ‹*god, act*› ثَأْريّ, انْتِقاميّ

Venice /ˈvɛnɪs/ *pr n* البُنْدُقيّة

venison /ˈvɛnɪs(ə)n, ˈvɛnɪz(ə)n/ *n* لَحْم أَيِّلٍ

venom /ˈvɛnəm/ *n* 1 (of a snake, scorpion etc.) سَمّ (سُموم) 2 (malice) حِقْد (أَحْقاد)

venomous /ˈvɛnəməs/ *adj* 1 ‹*snake, spider*› سامّ (سَوامُّ) 2 ‹*look, attack*› حاقِد (حَقَدة)

vent /vɛnt/ A *n* فُتْحة (فُتَح, فُتْحات)

B *vt* نَفَّسَ (عن) ‹*one's anger, frustration*›

ventilate /ˈvɛntɪleɪt/ *vt* هَوّى ‹*a room, building*›

ventilation /ˌvɛntɪˈleɪʃ(ə)n/ *n* تَهْوِية

ventilator /ˈvɛntɪleɪtə/ *n* (Med) جِهاز تَنَفُّسٍ

ventricle /ˈvɛntrɪk(ə)l/ *n* بُطَيْن

ventriloquist /vɛnˈtrɪləkwɪst/ *n* مُتَكَلِّم من بَطْنِه

venture /ˈvɛntʃə/ A *n* 1 (undertaking) مُغامَرة 2 (in business) مَشْروع (تجاريّ)

B *vt* عَبَّرَ (عن) ‹*an opinion, a guess*›; **to ~ to do sth** جَرُؤَ على \ خاطَرَ بِفِعْلِ شَيْءٍ

C *vi* «explorers, tourists» خاطَرَ بالسَفَرِ; **to ~ out** غامَرَ بالخُروجِ

venue /ˈvɛnjuː/ *n* مَكان (أَماكِنُ, أَمْكِنة)

Venus /ˈviːnəs/ *pr n* الزُهَرة

veranda, **verandah** /vəˈrandə/ *n* فَرانْدة; **to sit on the ~** جَلَسَ في الفَرانْدةِ

verb /vəːb/ *n* فِعْل (أَفْعال); **a regular/an irregular ~** فِعْل عاديّ \ شاذّ

verbal /ˈvəːb(ə)l/ *adj* 1 ‹*agreement*› شَفَهيّ; ‹*abuse*› لَفْظيّ 2 ‹*use, phrase*› فِعْليّ

verbal noun *n* مَصْدَر (مَصادِرُ)

verbatim /vəːˈbeɪtɪm/ A *adv* ‹*to quote, repeat*› حَرْفيًّا

B *adj* ‹*report, account*› حَرْفيّ

verbose /vəːˈbəʊs/ *adj* (fml) ‹*report, speech*› مُطْنَب, مُسْهَب

verdict /ˈvəːdɪkt/ *n* 1 (jury's decision) قَرار (قرارات), حُكْم (أَحْكام); **to reach a ~ of guilty/not guilty** صَدَرَ الحُكْمُ بالإِدانةِ \ بِعَدَمِ الإِدانةِ 2 (conclusion) رَأْي (آراء)

verge¹ /vəːdʒ/ *n* (BrE) حافّة

verge² /vəːdʒ/ *n* **to be on the ~ of tears** كانَ على حافّةِ البُكاءِ; **on the ~ of death/collapse** على حافّةِ المَوْتِ \ الانْهِيارِ

(Phrasal verb) **verge on: ~ on [sth]** مالَ إلى, اقْتَرَبَ من [شَيْءٍ] [شَيْءٍ] ‹*slander, hysteria*›

verification /ˌvɛrɪfɪˈkeɪʃ(ə)n/ *n* تَحقُّق

verify /ˈvɛrɪfʌɪ/ *vt* (**verifies, verifying, verified**) تَحَقَّقَ من (صِحّةِ) ‹*the facts, a signature*›

veritable /ˈvɛrɪtəb(ə)l/ *adj* (fml) ‹*feast*› حَقيقيّ, فِعْليّ

vermicelli /vəːmɪˈtʃɛli/ *n* شَعْرِيّة

vermilion /vəˈmɪljən/ A *n* لَوْن قِرْمِزيّ

B *adj* ‹*lipstick, sunset*› قِرْمِزيّ

vermin /ˈvəːmɪn/ *n pl* 1 (animals) حَيَوانات \ طُيور ضارّة 2 (lice, insects) هَوامُّ (حَشَرات طُفَيْلِيّة ضارّة)

Vermont /vəˈmɒnt/ *pr n* فيرْمونت (f)

Vermonter /vəˈmɒntə/ *pr n* شَخْص من فيرْمونت

vernacular /vəˈnakjʊlə/ *n* (**the vernacular**) (اللُغة) العامّيّة

verruca /vəˈruːkə/ *n* (*pl* **verrucae** or **verrucas**) ثُؤْلول (ثَآليل)

versatile /ˈvəːsətʌɪl/ *adj* **1** (adaptable) ‹*actor, player*› مُتَعَدِّد **2** (multi-purpose) ‹*vehicle, tool*› مَرِن ,مُتَعَدِّد المَواهِب الاسْتِخْدامات

versatility /vəːsəˈtɪləti/ *n* (of people) مُرونة ,تَعَدُّد المَواهِب; (of objects) تَعَدُّد الاسْتِخْدامات

verse /vəːs/ *n* **1** [u] (poetry) شِعْر (أَشْعار) **2** (of poems, songs) مَقْطَع شِعْريّ **3** (in the Koran, Bible) آية (آيات ,آي)

versed /vəːst/ *adj* (also **well versed**) ‹*scholar, expert*› خَبير (خُبَراءُ); **to be well ~ in a subject** كانَ خَبيراً في مادّةٍ

version /ˈvəːʃ(ə)n/ *n* **1** (of an event) رِواية **2** (form, variant) نُسْخة (نُسَخ)

versus /ˈvəːsəs/ *prep* **1** (against) ضِدَّ **2** (as opposed to) مُقابِلَ

vertebra /ˈvəːtɪbrə/ *n* (*pl* **vertebrae**) فِقْرة (فِقْرات ,فِقَرات), فَقارة (فَقار)

vertebrate /ˈvəːtɪbrət/ *n* حَيَوان فِقْريّ \ فَقاريّ

vertical /ˈvəːtɪk(ə)l/ *adj* ‹*axis, line*› رَأْسيّ ,عَموديّ

vertically /ˈvəːtɪkli/ *adv* ‹*to grow, rise*› رَأْسيًّا ,عَموديًّا

vertigo /ˈvəːtɪgəʊ/ *n* دَوْخة ,دُوار

verve /vəːv/ *n* حَيَويّة ,(أَنْشطة) نَشاط ,حَماس

very /ˈvɛri/ **A** *adv* **1** (extremely) ‹*hot, cold, good*› جِدًّا; **I'm ~ sorry** أنا آسِفٌ جِدًّا; **she's ~ well** هي بِخَيْرٍ تَماماً; **I didn't eat/find ~ much** لم آكُل \ أَجِد الكَثيرَ; **to be ~ much a city dweller** لا يَروقُ لَهُ سِوى حَياةِ المَدينةِ **2** (absolutely) **the ~ best/worst thing** أَفْضَل \ أَسْوَأ شَيْءٍ على الإطْلاقِ; **in the ~ best of health** في أَفْضَل صِحّةٍ وَعافِيةٍ; **at the ~ latest/ earliest** على أَقْصى \ أَقْرَبِ تَقْديرٍ; **at the ~ least, you'll need ...** على الأَقَلّ, سَتَحْتاجُ ...; **you'll be the ~ first/last to know** سَتكونُ أَوَّلَ \ آخِرَ مَنْ يَعْلَمُ على الإطْلاقِ **3** (actually) **the ~ same words** نَفْس الكَلِماتِ بالنَصِّ; **the ~ next day** اليَوْم التالي مُباشَرةً; **the ~ next person I met** الشَخْص الّذي قابَلْتُهُ مُباشَرةً بعد ذلك; **a car of your ~ own** سَيّارة خاصّة بِكَ وَحْدَكَ

B *adj* **1** (actual) بِذاتِهِ ,بِعَيْنِهِ; **this ~ second** في هذه اللَحْظةِ ذاتِها; **those were her ~ words** كانَتْ تِلْكَ هي كَلِماتُها حَرْفيًّا **2** (ideal) **the ~ person/thing I need** الشَخْص \ الشَيْء الّذي أَحْتاجُهُ بالضَبْطِ **3** (precisely at) تَحْديداً; **from the ~ beginning** مِن البِدايةِ الأولى; **at the ~ front** في الواجِهةِ; **to the ~ end** إلى النِهاية; **on the ~ edge** على أَقْصى الحافّةِ **4** (mere) ‹*mention, thought*› مُجَرَّد; **the ~ idea!** كَفى سَخافةً!

vesicle /ˈvɛsɪk(ə)l/ *n* حُوَيْصِلة

vespers /ˈvɛspəz/ *n* + *v sg ou pl* صَلاة المَساءِ

vessel /ˈvɛs(ə)l/ *n* **1** (fml) (ship) سَفينة (سُفُن ,سَفائِنُ), مَرْكَب (مَراكِبُ) **2** (fml) (container) إناء (آنِية ,أَوانٍ), وِعاء (أَوْعِية) **3** (Anat) وِعاء (أَوْعِية)

vest /vɛst/ *n* **1** (underwear) فانِلّة داخِليّة **2** (for sport, fashion) صُدْرة (صُدَر) **3** (AmE) (sleeveless jacket) قَميص (أَقْمِصة)

vested interest /ˌvɛstɪd ˈɪntrɛst/ *n* **to have a ~ in sth/in doing sth** كانَ لَهُ مَصْلَحةٌ خاصّةٌ في شَيْءٍ \ في فِعْل شَيْءٍ

vestige /ˈvɛstɪdʒ/ *n* أَثَر (آثار), بَقيّة (بَقايا)

vestment /ˈvɛstmənt/ *n* رِداء كَهَنوتيّ

vestry /ˈvɛstri/ *n* (*pl* **vestries**) [غُرْفة مَلابِس الكَهَنةِ]

vet /vɛt/ **A** *n* **1** = **veterinary surgeon** (BrE) = **veterinarian** (AmE) طَبيب بَيْطَريّ **2** (AmE infml) = **veteran** مُحارِب قَديم

B *vt* (**-tt-**) فَحَصَ (a; فَحْص) ‹*a candidate, contents*›

veteran /ˈvɛt(ə)rən/ **A** *n* **1** (experienced person) خَبير (خُبَراءُ), مُحارِب قَديم **2** (of war) مُتَمَرِّس

B *adj* ‹*sportsman, politician*› مُتَمَرِّس ,خَبير (خُبَراءُ)

veteran car *n* (BrE) سَيّارة عَتيقة (مَصْنوعة قبل 1919)

Veterans Day *n* (AmE) يَوْم المُحارِبينَ القُدامى

veterinarian /ˌvɛtərɪˈnɛːrɪən/ *n* (AmE) بَيْطار ,طَبيب بَيْطَريّ (بَياطِرة)

veterinary /ˈvɛtrənri/ *adj* ‹*medicine, care*› بَيْطَريّ (بَياطِرة)

veterinary surgeon *n* (BrE) بَيْطار ,طَبيب بَيْطَريّ (بَياطِرة)

veterinary surgery *n* عِيادة بَيْطَريّة

veto /ˈviːtəʊ/ **A** *n* (*pl* **vetoes**) (حَقّ) الفيتو; **to use/exercise one's ~** اسْتَخْدَمَ الفيتو

B *vt* (**vetoes, vetoing, vetoed**) اسْتَخْدَمَ الفيتو ضدّ ‹*a resolution, proposal*›

vetting /ˈvɛtɪŋ/ *n* تَحَرٍّ (تَحَرِّيات)، فَحْص (فُحوص)

vex /vɛks/ *vt* **1** (to annoy) أَغاظَ، ضايَقَ ‹*a person*› **2** (to puzzle) حَيَّرَ، أَرْبَكَ ‹*the scientists, experts*›

vexed /ˈvɛkst/ *adj* ‹*question, issue*› إِشْكاليّ

VHF /viːeɪtʃˈɛf/ *n* = **very high frequency** تَرَدُّد عالٍ جِدًّا

via /ˈvʌɪə/ *prep* **1** (by way of) عن طَريق **2** (by means of) عَبْرَ، بواسِطةِ

viability /vʌɪəˈbɪləti/ *n* [قابِليّة النجاحِ \ التَطْبيقِ \ النموِّ إلخ]

viable /ˈvʌɪəb(ə)l/ *adj* ‹*business, solution*› [قابل للنَجاحِ \ التَطْبيقِ \ النُموِّ إلخ]

viaduct /ˈvʌɪədʌkt/ *n* كوبْري (كَباريّ)، جِسْر (جُسور)

vial /ˈvʌɪəl/ *n* قارورة (قَواريرُ)، قِنّينة (قَنانٍ)

vibes /vʌɪbz/ *n* (infml) مَشاعِر; **to have good/bad ~ about sth** كانَتْ لَهُ مَشاعِرُ إيجابيّةٌ \ سَلْبيّةٌ تُجاهَ شَيْءٍ

vibrant /ˈvʌɪbrənt/ *adj* **1** (full of life) ‹*community, city*› نابِض بالحَياةِ **2** (vivid) ‹*colour*› زاهٍ **3** (resonant) ‹*voice, music*› رَنّان، مُثير

vibraphone /ˈvʌɪbrəfəʊn/ *n* فيبْرافون (آلة نَقْرٍ موسيقيّةٍ)

vibrate /vʌɪˈbreɪt/ *vi* «violin strings, mobile phones» اهْتَزَّ، ارْتَجَّ

vibration /vʌɪˈbreɪʃ(ə)n/ *n* اهْتِزاز (اهْتِزازات)، ارْتِجاج (ارْتِجاجات)

vicar /ˈvɪkə/ *n* قَسّ (قُسوس، قُسُس)

vicarage /ˈvɪkərɪdʒ/ *n* بَيْت \ مَسْكَن القَسِّ

vicarious /vɪˈkɛːriəs/ *adj* (fml) ‹*pleasure, experience*› غَيْر مُباشِرٍ

vice¹ /vʌɪs/ *n* **1** [u] (immorality) رَذيلة (رَذائِلُ) **2** (weakness) نُقْطة ضُعْفٍ

vice², vise (AmE) /vʌɪs/ *n* مِلْزَمة (مَلازِمُ)، مَنْجَلة

vice chancellor *n* نائِب رَئيسِ جامِعةٍ

vice president *n* **1** (of a nation) نائِب رَئيسٍ; **the Vice President of the United States** نائِب رَئيسِ الوِلاياتِ المُتَّحِدةِ **2** (of a corporation) نائِب رَئيسٍ **3** (of a society, club) نائِب رَئيس

vice squad *n* شُرْطة الآدابِ

vice versa *adv* العَكْسُ بالعَكْسِ

vicinity /vɪˈsɪnɪti/ *n* جِوار

vicious /ˈvɪʃəs/ *adj* **1** (violent, savage) ‹*attack, dog*› شَرِس **2** (malicious) ‹*rumour, campaign*› خَبيث (خُبَثاءُ)

vicious circle *n* حَلْقة مُفْرَغة

viciously /ˈvɪʃəsli/ *adv* ‹*to attack, fight*› بِشَراسةٍ، بِضَراوةٍ، بِوَحْشيّةٍ

victim /ˈvɪktɪm/ *n* ضَحيّة (ضَحايا)، فَريسة (فَرائِسُ)

victimization, -isation (BrE) /vɪktɪmʌɪˈzeɪʃ(ə)n/ *n* ظُلْم

victimize, -ise (BrE) /ˈvɪktɪmʌɪz/ *vt* ظَلَمَ (i; ظُلْم) ‹*a worker, minority*›

victor /ˈvɪktə/ *n* (liter) مُنْتَصِر، ظافِر

Victorian /vɪkˈtɔːrɪən/ *adj, n* فيكْتوريّ (خاصّ بِعَهْدِ المَلِكةِ فيكْتوريا)

victorious /vɪkˈtɔːrɪəs/ *adj* ‹*team, army*› مُنْتَصِر، ظافِر

victory /ˈvɪkt(ə)ri/ *n* (*pl* **victories**) نَصْر، انْتِصار (انْتِصارات); **to win a ~ over an opponent** انْتَصَرَ على خَصْمٍ

video /ˈvɪdɪəʊ/ **A** *n* (*pl* **videos**) **1** (also **video film**) فيلْم فيدْيو; **on ~** على الفيدْيو **2** (also **video cassette**) كاسيت فيدْيو **3** (also **video recorder**) جِهاز تَسْجيلِ فيدْيو **B** *vt* (**videos, videoing, videoed**) **1** (from TV) سَجَّلَ على فيدْيو ‹*a programme, film*› **2** (on camcorder) صَوَّرَ على فيدْيو ‹*a wedding, an event*›

video camera *n* كاميرا \ آلة تَصْويرِ فيدْيو

video card *n* بِطاقة فيدْيو

video chat **A** *n* دَرْدَشة الفيدْيو; **B** *vi* (**video-chat**) دَرْدَشَ عن طَريقِ الفيدْيو

videoconference /ˈvɪdɪəʊˌkɒnf(ə)rəns/ *n* مُؤْتَمَر فيدْيو

videoconferencing /ˈvɪdiəʊkɒnf(ə)rənsɪŋ/ *n* نِظام مُؤْتَمَراتِ بالفيدْيو

videodisc /ˈvɪdɪəʊdɪsk/ *n* قُرْص فيدْيو

video game *n* لُعْبة فيدْيو

video nasty *n* [فيلْم فيدْيو إباحيّ \ مُرْعِب]

videophone /ˈvɪdɪəʊfəʊn/ *n* هاتِف فيدْيو

videotape /ˈvɪdɪəʊteɪp/ *n* شَريط فيدْيو

vie /vʌɪ/ *vi* (*present participle* **vying**) «candidates, siblings» تَنافَسَ; **to ~ for attention** تَنافَسَ على الاهْتِمامِ

Vienna /vɪ'ɛnə/ *pr n* فِيينا

Vietnam /vjɛt'nam/ *pr n* فيِتْنام (f)

Vietnamese /ˌvɪɛtnə'miːz/ **A** *adj* ‹*people, restaurant, government*› فيِتْناميّ

B *n* **1** (*pl* **Vietnamese**) (citizen) فيِتْناميّ **2** (language) (اللُغة) الفيِتْناميّة

view /vjuː/ **A** *n* **1** (prospect, scene) مَنْظَرٌ (مَناظِرُ); **the trees cut off the ~** أَخْفَت الأَشْجارُ المَنْظَرَ; **our new room has a better ~** غُرْفَتُنا الجَديدةُ تُطِلُّ على مَنْظَرٍ أَفْضَلَ; **he provided an overall ~ of the situation** أَعْطى صورةً \ فِكْرةً عامّةً عن الوَضْعِ **2** [u] (field of vision) رُؤْيَة; **the paintings will be on ~ from tomorrow** سَتُعْرَضُ اللَوْحاتُ غَداً; **the lake was within ~ of the house** كانَت البُحَيْرةُ على مَرْأى العَيْنِ من البَيْتِ; **you're blocking my ~!** أَنْتَ تَحْجُبُ عنّي الرُؤْيةَ!; **to come into ~** لاحَ (u; لَوْح), أَصْبَحَ مَرْئيًّا; **to be hidden from ~** كانَ مَخْفيًّا عن الأَنْظارِ; **to disappear from ~** اخْتَفى عن الأَنْظارِ; **to keep sth/sb in ~** أَخَذَ شَيْئاً \ شَخْصاً في عَيْنِ الاعْتِبارِ; **to do sth in full ~ of sb** فَعَلَ شَيْئاً أمامَ أَعْيُنِ شَخْصٍ **3** (way of considering) رَأْي (آراء), وِجْهة نَظَرٍ; **in my ~** في نَظَري \ رَأْيي; **she takes the ~ that ...** تَتَبَنّى وِجْهةَ النَظَرِ أنّ ...; **to take the long ~** تَبَنّى نَظْرةً بَعيدةَ المَدى **4** [u] (intention) نيّة (نَوايا, نيّات); **with a ~ to doing sth** بِنيّةِ فِعْلِ شَيْءٍ; **with this end in ~** [لِهَذا الغَرَضِ] **5** (picture, image) مَنْظَرٌ (مَناظِرُ) **6** (visit, inspection) عَرْض (عُروض); ▸ **viewing**

B (**in view of**) *prep phr* باعْتِبارِ

C *vt* **1** (to consider) اعْتَبَرَ ‹*a situation, sb's comments*›; **to ~ sth/sb with suspicion** نَظَرَ إلى شَيْءٍ \ شَخْصٍ بِشَكٍّ; **their activities were ~ed as subversive** اُعْتُبِرَتْ أَنْشِطَتُهُم مُدَمِّرةً **2** (to look at) اطَّلَعَ (على) ‹*an image, exhibition*›; **to ~ the file, visit our website** لِرُؤْيةِ المِلَفِّ، زُرْ مَوْقِعَنا **3** (to inspect) عايَنَ ‹*a property, house*› **4** (to watch) شاهَدَ ‹*a movie, video, programme*›

viewer /'vjuːə/ *n* **1** (of TV) مُشاهِد **2** (of exhibits) زائر (زوّار, زائرون)

viewfinder /'vjuːfʌɪndə/ *n* [جِهاز مُثَبَّت بالكاميرا لِرُؤْيةِ المَنْظَرِ المُصَوَّرِ]

viewing /'vjuːɪŋ/ *n* **1** (of television) مُشاهَدة; **the movie makes for compulsive ~** الفيلْمُ جَديرٌ بالمُشاهَدةِ; **it bears repeated ~s** يَسْتَحِقُّ المُشاهَدةَ أَكْثَرَ من مَرّةٍ **2** (of a house, apartment) مُشاهَدة, مُعايَنة; **'~ by appointment only'** 'المُعايَنةُ بالمَوْعِدِ فَقَطْ' **3** (artworks) عَرْض (عُروض) **4** (of a film) عَرْض (عُروض)

viewpoint /'vjuːpɔɪnt/ *n* وِجْهة نَظَرٍ

vigil /'vɪdʒɪl/ *n* **1** (by sickbed) يَقَظة, سَهَر; **to keep a ~ over a sick person** سَهِرَ بِجانِبِ شَخْصٍ مَريضٍ **2** (by demonstrators) مُظاهَرة صامِتة

vigilance /'vɪdʒɪləns/ *n* يَقَظة, تَيَقُّظ, حَذِر

vigilant /'vɪdʒɪlənt/ *adj* ‹*guard, neighbour*› مُتَيَقِّظ, يَقِظ (أَيْقاظ)

vigilante /ˌvɪdʒɪ'lanti/ *n* [عُضْو لَجْنة أَمْنٍ أَهْليّةٍ]

vigorous /'vɪg(ə)rəs/ *adj* **1** (healthy) ‹*growth, plant*› قَويّ (أَقْوِياءُ) **2** (energetic) ‹*exercise, debate*› قَويّ (أَقْوِياءُ); **he enjoyed a ~ old age** تَمَتَّعَ بِشَيْخوخةٍ مُفْعَمةٍ بالحَيَويّةِ

vigorously /'vɪg(ə)rəsli/ *adv* **1** (healthily) ‹*to grow*› بِنَشاطٍ, بِقوّةٍ **2** (strenuously) ‹*to defend, deny*› بِقوّةٍ, بِشِدّةٍ

vigour (BrE), **vigor** (AmE) /'vɪgə/ *n* قوّة (قُوًى), نَشاط (أَنْشِطة)

Viking /'vʌɪkɪŋ/ *n* فايْكِنْج

vile /vʌɪl/ *adj* (**viler**, **vilest**) **1** (fml) (wicked) ‹*act, crime*› دَنيء (أَدْنِياءُ), خَسيس (أَخِسّاءُ) **2** (foul) ‹*weather, temper*› رَديء (أَرْدِياءُ)

villa /'vɪlə/ *n* فيلاّ (فيلاّت)

village /'vɪlɪdʒ/ *n* قَرْية (قُرًى)

village hall *n* قاعة مُناسَباتٍ (في قَرْيةٍ)

villager /'vɪlɪdʒə/ *n* قَرَويّ

villain /'vɪlən/ *n* **1** (criminal) نَذْل (أَنْذال), وَغْد (أَوْغاد), مُجْرِم **2** (in books, films) شِرّير (أَشْرار, أَشِرّاءُ)

vinaigrette /ˌvɪnɪ'grɛt/ *n* (also **vinaigrette dressing**) صَلْصة خَلٍّ

vindicate /'vɪndɪkeɪt/ *vt* بَرَّأَ ‹*a decision, claim*›

vindictive /vɪn'dɪktɪv/ *adj* ‹*behaviour, policy*› حَقود (حُقُد), انْتِقاميّ

vindictiveness /vɪn'dɪktɪvnəs/ *n* حِقْد (أَحْقاد)

vine /vʌɪn/ *n* **1** (grapevine) كَرْمة (العِنَبِ) **2** (climbing plant) نبات مُتَسَلِّق

vinegar /ˈvɪnɪɡə/ *n* خَلّ (خُلول)

vineyard /ˈvɪnjəd/ *n* كَرْم (كُروم)

vintage /ˈvɪntɪdʒ/ **A** *n* **1** (year) سَنة (إِنْتاج النَبيذِ) **2** (harvest) جَنْي (كَرْمٍ)
B *adj* **1** (of a good year) ‹*wine, port*› [من سَنةٍ ذاتِ مَحْصولٍ جَيِّدٍ] **2** (classic) ‹*clothing, performance*› كْلاسيكيّ

vintage car *n* (BrE) سَيّارة عَتيقة (مَصنوعة ما بين 1919 و1930)

vinyl /ˈvʌɪn(ə)l/ *n* **1** (substance, material) فينيل **2** (record) **on ~** على أُسْطُوانةِ فينيل

viola /vɪˈəʊlə/ *n* كَمان أَوْسَط

violate /ˈvʌɪəleɪt/ *vt* **1** (to contravene) نَكَثَ, أَخَلَّ, انْتَهَكَ (i-u; نَكْث) ‹*a law, one's rights*› **2** (to infringe) خَرَقَ, انْتَهَكَ (i-u; خَرْق) ‹*air space, privacy*›

violation /vʌɪəˈleɪʃ(ə)n/ *n* **1** (of law, rights) انْتِهاك (انْتِهاكات), خَرْق (خُروق), مُخالَفة; **a ~ of the safety regulations** مُخالَفة لِقَواعِدِ السَلامة **2** (of an exclusion zone, no-fly area) انْتِهاك (انْتِهاكات), خَرْق (خُروق)

violence /ˈvʌɪələns/ *n* **1** (of an attack, robbery) عُنْف **2** (of a storm, wave, impact) شِدّة

violent /ˈvʌɪələnt/ *adj* **1** (aggressive) ‹*crime, behaviour*› عَنيف (عُنُف) **2** (powerful, intense) ‹*temper, storm*› حادّ

violently /ˈvʌɪələntli/ *adv* **1** (forcefully) ‹*to attack, to murder*› بِعُنْفٍ **2** (intensely) ‹*to oppose, disagree*› بِشِدّةٍ

violet /ˈvʌɪələt/ **A** *n* **1** (flower) بَنَفْسَج (n coll) **2** (colour) لَون بَنَفْسَجيّ
B *adj* ‹*flower*› بَنَفْسَجيّ

violin /vʌɪəˈlɪn/ *n* كَمان, كَمَنْجة

violinist /vʌɪəˈlɪnɪst/ *n* عازِف كَمانٍ

VIP /viːʌɪˈpiː/ **A** *n* = **very important person** شَخْصيّة مُهِمّة جِدًّا
B *adj before n* ‹*lounge, treatment*› لِلشَخْصيّاتِ المُهِمّةِ

viper /ˈvʌɪpə/ *n* أَفْعى (f; أَفاعٍ)

viral /ˈvʌɪrəl/ *adj* **1** (in medicine) ‹*infection, disease*› فَيروسيّ **2** (in computing) ‹*video, marketing*› فَيْروسيّ; **to go ~** أَصْبَحَ واسِعَ الانْتِشارِ

virgin /ˈvəːdʒɪn/ **A** *n* عَذْراء (f; عَذْراوات, عَذارى), بَتول (f), بِكْر (أَبْكار)
B *adj* **1** (chaste) ‹*bride*› عَذْراء (عَذْراوات, عَذارى); ‹*birth*› عُذْريّ **2** (untouched) ‹*forest*› بِكْر; ‹*snow*› خالِص

Virginia /vəˈdʒɪnɪə/ *pr n* فيرْجينيا

Virginian /vəˈdʒɪnɪən/ *pr n, adj* [(شَخْص) من فيرْجينيا]

virginity /vəˈdʒɪnɪti/ *n* عُذْرِيّة; **to lose one's ~** فَقَدَ عُذْرِيَّتَهُ

Virgo /ˈvəːɡəʊ/ *n* (*pl* **Virgos**) **1** (sign) بُرْج العَذْراءِ **2** (person) [من مَواليدِ بُرجِ العَذْراءِ]

virile /ˈvɪrʌɪl/ *adj* ‹*hero, male*› رُجوليّ

virtual /ˈvəːtʃʊəl/ *adj* **1** (almost complete) ‹*standstill, stranger*› شِبْه كامِلٍ **2** (in cyberspace) ‹*memory, drive*› افْتِراضيّ, ظاهِريّ

virtually /ˈvəːtjʊəli/ *adv* ‹*to admit, promise*› فِعْلِيًّا, عَمَلِيًّا; ‹*impossible, identical*› بِشَكْلٍ شِبْهِ كامِلٍ

virtual reality *n* الواقِع الافْتِراضيّ

virtue /ˈvəːtʃuː/ *n* **1** (goodness) فَضيلة (فَضائِلُ) **2** (advantage) مَزِيّة (مَزايا), ميزة, فائدة (فَوائِدُ) **3** (reason) **by ~ of sth** بِحُكْمِ شَيْءٍ

virtuoso /vəːtʃuːˈəʊsəʊ, vəːtʃuːˈəʊzəʊ/ *n* (*pl* **virtuosos** or **virtuosi**) بارِع \ ماهِر, عازِف عَبْقَريّ (عَبْقَريّونَ, عَباقِرة)

virtuous /ˈvəːtʃuːəs/ *adj* ‹*person, deed*› فاضِل (فاضِلونَ, فُضَلاءُ)

virulent /ˈvɪrʊlənt/ *adj* ‹*strain, pathogen*› عُضال

virus /ˈvʌɪrəs/ *n* **1** (in pathology) فَيْروس (فَيْروسات) **2** (in programming) فَيْروس (فَيْروسات)

visa /ˈviːzə/ *n* فيزا, تَأْشيرة دُخولٍ

vis-à-vis /ˌviːzɑːˈviː/ *prep* بالنِسْبةِ ل

viscose /ˈvɪskəʊz, ˈvɪskəʊs/ *n* فِسْكوز

viscount /ˈvʌɪkaʊnt/ *n* فيكونْت (نَبيل من نُبَلاءِ بَريطانيا)

viscous /ˈvɪskəs/ *adj* ‹*oil, substance*› لَزِج, دَبِق

vise (AmE) *n* ▸ **vice²**

visibility /vɪzɪˈbɪlɪti/ *n* رُؤْية (رُؤًى), مَجال الرُؤْيةِ

visible /ˈvɪzɪb(ə)l/ *adj* **1** (able to be seen) ‹*star, sign*› مَرْئيّ **2** (obvious) ‹*improvement, change*› واضِح, مَلْحوظ, ظاهِر

visibly /ˈvɪzəbli/ *adv* ‹*shaken, annoyed*› على نَحْوٍ ظاهِرٍ

vision /ˈvɪʒ(ə)n/ *n* **1** [u] (ability to see) بَصَر (أَبْصار), رُؤْية (رُؤًى) **2** [u] (foresight) بَصيرة (بَصائِرُ) **3** (idea, mental picture) رُؤْية

(رُؤًى) ,تَصَوُّر (تَصَوُّرات) ,تَخَيُّل (تَخَيُّلات); **his ~ of the future** رُؤْيَتُهُ للمُسْتَقْبَل **4** (dream, revelation) رُؤْيا (رُؤًى)

visionary /ˈvɪʒ(ə)n(ə)ri/ *n* (*pl* **visionaries**) شَخْص ذو بَصيرةٍ

visit /ˈvɪzɪt/ **A** *vt* **1** زارَ (u; زِيارة) ‹*a friend, one's family*›; **she was ~ing relatives in Egypt** كانَتْ تَزورُ أَقارِبَها في مِصْرَ; **to ~ sb in hospital** زارَ شَخْصاً في المُسْتَشْفى **2** **to ~ the doctor/dentist** ذَهَبَ إلى الطَبيبِ \ طَبيبِ الأَسْنانِ **3** (as a traveller) زارَ (u; زِيارة) ‹*a country, museum, an exhibition*› **4** (to inspect) تَفَقَّدَ ‹*a school, workplace*› **5** (to access) زارَ (u; زِيارة) ‹*a website*›
B *vi* **1** (to stay temporarily) زارَ (u; زِيارة); **we're just ~ing** نحن فَقَطْ نَقومُ بزِيارةٍ **2** (AmE) **to ~ with sb** (to pay sb a visit) زارَ شَخْصاً; (to chat) دَرْدَشَ مع شَخْصٍ
C *n* **1** (call) زِيارة; **an official/a state ~** زِيارة رَسْمِيّة; **to pay a ~ to sb, to pay sb a ~** زارَ شَخْصاً; **we had a ~ from the police today** زارَتْنا الشُرْطةُ اليَوْمَ; **the doctor made a home ~** ذَهَبَ الطَبيبُ لِزِيارةِ مَريضٍ في بَيْتِهِ **2** (stay) زِيارة; **I bought it on a ~ to Turkey** اشْتَرَيْتُهُ أثناء زِيارةٍ إلى تُرْكيا; **in 1995 he made a ~ to Venice** 1995 زارَ البُنْدُقِيّةَ سَنة **3** (to a website) زِيارة

visiting card /ˈvɪzɪtɪŋ ˌkɑːd/ *n* بِطاقة تَعْريفٍ

visiting hours /ˈvɪzɪtɪŋ ˌaʊəz/ *n pl* وَقْت الزِيارةِ

visitor /ˈvɪzɪtə/ *n* زائِر (زائِرونَ ,زُوّار; f pl زائِرات)

visitor centre (BrE), **visitor center** (AmE) *n* مَرْكَز زُوّارٍ

visitors' book *n* سِجِلّ الزُوّارِ

visor /ˈvʌɪzə/ *n* **1** (on helmets) واقي وَجْهٍ ,مُقَدِّمة خَوْذةٍ **2** (on caps) حافّة (القُبَّعة) **3** (for cars) حافّة زُجاجِ سَيّارةٍ, حاجِب شَمْسٍ

vista /ˈvɪstə/ *n* مَنْظَر (مَناظِرُ)

visual /ˈvɪʒuːəl/ *adj* ‹*capability, impairment*› بَصَريّ

visual aid *n* وَسيلة بَصَرِيّة

visual arts *n* فُنون مَرْئِيّة \ بَصَرِيّة

visualize, **-ise** (BrE) /ˈvɪʒuːəlʌɪz/ *vt* **1** (to picture) تَصَوَّرَ ‹*a building, scene*› **2** (to foresee) تَوَقَّعَ ‹*a solution, an event*›

visually /ˈvɪʒʊəli/ *adv* ‹*stunning, intrusive*› بَصَرِيًّا

visually impaired *adj* مُعاق بَصَرِيًّا

vital /ˈvʌɪt(ə)l/ *adj* ‹*factor, role*› أَساسيّ ,جَوْهَريّ; **of ~ importance** ذو أَهَمِّيّةٍ جَوْهَرِيّةٍ

vitality /vʌɪˈtalɪti/ *n* حَيَوِيّة

vitally /ˈvʌɪt(ə)li/ *adv* ‹*important, necessary*› على نَحْوٍ أَساسيٍّ

vital organ *n* عُضْو حَيَويّ

vital signs *n* عَلامات حَيَوِيّة

vital statistics *n* **1** (population data) إحْصاءات حَيَوِيّة \ سُكّانِيّة **2** (BrE infml) (woman's) [مَقاييس جِسْمِ مَرْأةٍ]

vitamin /ˈvɪtəmɪn/ *n* فيتامين (فيتامينات)

vitamin C *n* فيتامين سي

viva /ˈvʌɪvə/ *n* امْتِحان شَفَويّ

vivacious /vɪˈveɪʃəs/ *adj* ‹*woman, personality*› مُفْعَم بالحَيَوِيّةِ, مَرِح (مَرْحى)

vivid /ˈvɪvɪd/ *adj* **1** (bright) ‹*colour, green*› زاهٍ ,ناصِع **2** (clear) ‹*memory*› ناصِع; ‹*description*› جَليّ

vividly /ˈvɪvɪdli/ *adv* **1** (brightly) ‹*coloured, to flash*› على نَحْوٍ زاهٍ \ مُشْرِقٍ \ ساطِعٍ **2** (clearly) ‹*to remember, illustrate*› بِوُضوحٍ

vivisection /vɪvɪˈsekʃ(ə)n/ *n* تَشْريح الأَحْياءِ

vixen /ˈvɪks(ə)n/ *n* **1** (Zool) أُنْثى الثَعْلَبِ ,ثَعْلَبة **2** (woman) امْرَأة مُشاكِسة \ شَرِسة

viz /vɪz/ *adv* = **videlicet** (namely) أَيْ

vizier /vɪˈzɪə/ *n* وَزير (وُزَراءُ)

V-neck /ˈviːnɛk/ *n* (neckline) ياقة مُثَلَّثة; (sweater) [قَميص بياقةٍ مُثَلَّثةٍ]

vocabulary /vəʊˈkabjʊləri/ *n* (*pl* **vocabularies**) مُفْرَدات

vocal /ˈvəʊk(ə)l/ **A** *adj* (vociferous) ‹*minority, campaign*› صاخِب
B (**vocals**) *n pl* غِناء

vocal cords *n* حِبال صَوْتِيّة

vocalist /ˈvəʊkəlɪst/ *n* مُغَنٍّ ,مُنْشِد

vocalization, **-isation** (BrE) /vəʊkəlʌɪˈzeɪʃ(ə)n/ *n* **1** (fml) (into words) تَعْبير **2** (writing vowels) تَشْكيل

vocalize, **-ise** (BrE) /ˈvəʊkəlʌɪz/ *vt* **1** نَطَقَ (u; نُطْق ب) ‹*one's thoughts*› **2** شَكَّلَ ‹*a word*›

vocation /vəʊˈkeɪʃ(ə)n/ *n* نِداء (نِداءات)

vocational /vəʊˈkeɪʃ(ə)n(ə)l/ *adj* ‹*qualification, diploma*› مِهَنيّ

vocational course *n* تَعْليم مِهَنيّ

vocational training *n* تَدْريب مِهْنِيّ

vociferous /vəʊ'sɪf(ə)rəs/ *adj* ‹*minority, protest*› صاخِب

vodka /'vɒdkə/ *n* فودْكا

vogue /vəʊg/ *n* موضة

voice /vɔɪs/ **A** *n* **1** (in speech) صَوْت (أَصْوات); **in a loud/low ~** بِصَوْتٍ عالٍ \ مُنْخَفِض; **to raise/lower one's ~** رفَعَ \ خفَض صَوْتَهُ; **keep your ~ down!** اِخْفِضْ صَوْتَكَ!; **to lose one's ~** فَقَدَ صَوْتَهُ; **at the top of one's ~** بِأَعْلى صَوْتِهِ **2** (for singing) صَوْت (أَصْوات); **to have a good singing ~** كانَ صَوْتُهُ جَيِّداً **3** (opinion) صَوْت (أَصْوات); **to make one's ~ heard** جَعَلَ صَوْتَهُ مَسْموعاً; **to speak with one ~** تَكَلَّموا بِصَوْتٍ واحِدٍ **4** (channel) صَوْت (أَصْوات) **5** (in grammar) صيغة الفِعْل; **in the active/passive ~** في صيغةِ المَبْنِيّ للمَعْلومِ \ للمَجْهولِ

B *vt* **1** (fml) (to express) عَبَّرَ (عن) ‹*one's concern, opinion*› **2** «speaker» نَطَقَ بِشَكْلٍ مَجْهورٍ ‹*a consonant, sound*›

voicemail, **voice mail** /'vɔɪsmeɪl/ *n* **1** (system) بَريد صَوْتيّ **2** (message) رِسالة صَوْتِيّة

voice-over /'vɔɪs,əʊvə/ *n* تَعْليق صَوْتيّ

voice recognition *n* التَعَرُّف على الصَوْتِ

void /vɔɪd/ **A** *adj* **1** (of no effect) ‹*contract, agreement*› باطِل **2** (fml) (empty) **to be ~ of life/emotion** اِفْتَقَدَ الحَياةَ \ العاطِفةَ

B *n* **1** (empty space) خَلاء, فَراغ (فَراغات) **2** (emptiness) فَراغ (فَراغات)

VoIP /vɔɪp/ *abbr* = **Voice over Internet Protocol** بُروتوكول الصَوْتِ عَبْرَ الإِنْتَرْنِت

vol *n* = **volume** مُجَلَّد (مُجَلَّدات)

volatile /'vɒlətʌɪl/ *adj* **1** (Chem) ‹*compound, oil*› مُتَطاير **2** (unpredictable) ‹*prices, temper*› مُتَغَيِّر, مُتَقَلِّب

volatility /vɒlə'tɪləti/ *n* **1** (of oils, compounds) قابِلِيّة التَطايُر, تَطايُرِيّة **2** (of prices, situations) عَدَم اسْتِقْرارٍ

volcanic /vɒl'kanɪk/ *adj* ‹*eruption, activity*› بُرْكانيّ

volcano /vɒl'keɪnəʊ/ *n* (*pl* **volcanoes** or **volcanos**) بُرْكان (بَراكينُ); **an active/dormant ~** بُرْكان ثائِر \ خامِد

vole /vəʊl/ *n* فَأْر الحَقْلِ

volition /və'lɪʃ(ə)n/ *n* إرادة

volley /'vɒli/ **A** *n* **1** (in playing the ball) ضَرْب الكُرة قبل هُبوطِها على الأَرْضِ] **2** (of shots, questions) وابِل

B *vt* ضَرَبَ (قبل الهُبوطِ على الأَرْضِ) ‹*the ball*›

C *vi* [ضَرَبَ الكُرَةَ قبل هُبوطِها على الأَرْضِ]

volleyball /'vɒlɪbɔːl/ *n* [u] الكُرة الطائِرة

volt /vəʊlt/ *n* فولْت

voltage /'vəʊltɪdʒ/ *n* فولْتِيّة, جُهْد (كَهْرَبائِيّ)

volume /'vɒljuːm/ *n* **1** (of containers) حَجْم (حُجوم, أَحْجام) **2** (degree of loudness) صَوْت (قوّة) **3** (book) مُجَلَّد (مُجَلَّدات)

Idiom **to speak volumes about sth** دَلَّ دَلالةً واضِحةً على شَيْءٍ

volume control *n* زرّ التَحَكُّم في الصَوْتِ

voluminous /və'ljuːmɪnəs/ *adj* ‹*skirt, documentation*› ضَخْم, كَبير الحَجْمِ

voluntarily /'vɒləntrɪli/ *adv* **1** (willingly) ‹*to leave, surrender*› طَوْعاً, بِمَحْضِ إرادَتِهِ, عن طيبِ خاطِرٍ **2** (without payment) ‹*to work*› مَجّاناً, بِدونِ أَجْرٍ

voluntary /'vɒlənt(ə)ri/ *adj* **1** (willing) ‹*scheme, repatriation*› طَوْعيّ, بِلا أَجْرٍ **2** (unpaid) ‹*work, organization*› تَطَوُّعيّ

volunteer /,vɒlən'tɪə/ **A** *n* مُتَطَوِّع

B *vt* قَدَّمَ ‹*assistance, information*›

C *vi* **1** (for a task) تَطَوَّعَ; **to ~ to do sth** تَطَوَّعَ لِفِعْلِ شَيْءٍ **2** (Mil) تَطَوَّعَ في الجَيْشِ

voluptuous /və'lʌptjʊəs/ *adj* ‹*figure, woman*› شَهْوانيّ

vomit /'vɒmɪt/ **A** *vt, vi* تَقَيَّأَ, اسْتَفْرَغَ

B *n* تَقَيُّؤ

voodoo /'vuːduː/ *n* فودو

voracious /və'reɪʃəs/ *adj* ‹*appetite, predator*› شَرِه, نَهِم

vortex /'vɔːteks/ *n* (*pl* **vortexes** or **vortices**) دَوّامة

vote /vəʊt/ **A** *n* **1** (in elections, etc) صَوْت (أَصْوات), اقْتِراع (اقْتِراعات); **to cast one's ~** أَدْلى بِصَوْتِهِ; **to get 3,500 ~s** نالَ 3500 صَوْتاً; **one man one ~** لِكُلِّ شَخْصٍ صَوْتٌ واحِدٌ; **how many ~s did she get?** كم صَوْتاً نالَتْ؟ **2** (on a motion, issue) تَصْويت; **to take a ~ on the issue** طَرَحَ المَسْأَلَةَ

للتَصْويتِ; **to put the proposal to the ~** طَرَحَ الاقْتِراحَ للتَصْويتِ; **the chairman has the casting ~** رَئيسُ مَجْلِسِ الإدارة لَهُ الصَوْتُ الحاسِمُ **3** (the vote) التَصْويت; **to get the ~** تَحَصَّلَ على حَقِّ التَصْويتِ **4** [u] (ballot) الأَصْوات; **to receive 60% of the ~** نالَ 60٪ من الأَصْواتِ; **the Republican ~ increased by 10%** زادَ عَدَدُ الأَصْواتِ للحِزْبِ الجُمْهوريِّ بِنِسْبةِ 10٪

B *vt* **1** (in elections) انْتَخَبَ ‹*Democrat*›; **how did you ~?** مَن انْتَخَبْتَ؟; **I always ~ Liberal/Republican** أنا دائماً أَنْتَخِبُ الليبراليّينَ \ الجُمْهوريّينَ; **to be ~d best actress/ Miss World** تَمَّ انْتِخابُها كَأَفْضَلِ مُمَثِّلةٍ \ كَمَلِكةِ جَمالِ العالَمِ **2** (to authorize) صَوَّتَ بالمُوافقةِ ‹*the funds, money*› **3** (infml) (to propose) اقْتَرَحَ; **I ~ (that) we say yes to that** أَقْتَرِحُ التَصْويتَ بالإيجابِ على ذلك

C *vi* «electorate, voters» اقْتَرَعَ ,صَوَّتَ; **they're too young to ~** لم يَبْلُغوا سِنَّ التَصْويتِ \ الاقْتِراعِ; **to ~ for/against the reform** صَوَّتَ لِصالِحِ \ ضِدَّ الإصْلاحِ; **let's ~ on it** لِنَقُمْ بِاقْتِراعٍ عَلَيْهِ; **to ~ to raise taxes/expenditure** صَوَّتَ على رَفْعِ الضَرائِبِ \ الإنْفاقِ

(Idiom) **to vote with one's feet** [أَظْهَرَ لامُبالاةً]

(Phrasal verbs) **vote down**: **~ [sth] down, ~ down [sth]** صَوَّتَ ضِدَّ [شَيْءٍ] ‹*a proposal, motion*›

• **vote in**: **~ [sb] in, ~ in [sb]** «electorate, electors» انْتَخَبَ [شَخْصاً] ‹*a candidate, party*›

• **vote out**: **~ [sb/sth] out, ~ out [sb/sth]** «country, electorate» أَسْقَطَ [شَخْصاً \ شَيْئاً] في التَصْويتِ ‹*a politician, the amendment*›

• **vote through**: **~ [sth] through, ~ through [sth]** صَوَّتَ بالمُوافَقةِ على [شَيْءٍ] ‹*the bill, measure*›; **the budget was ~d through without a debate** تَمَّت المُوافَقةُ على الميزانيّةِ دون مُناقَشةٍ

vote of confidence *n* تَصْويت على مَنْحِ الثِقةِ

voter /ˈvəʊtə/ *n* مُصَوِّت, مُنْتَخِب, ناخِب

voting /ˈvəʊtɪŋ/ *n* تَصْويت (تَصْويتات) اقْتِراع (اقْتِراعات)

voting age *n* سِنّ الاقْتِراعِ

voting booth *n* حُجْرة تَصْويتٍ

voucher /ˈvaʊtʃə/ *n* **1** (in exchanges) قَسيمة (قَسائِمُ) **2** (receipt) إيصال (إيصالات)

vouch for /vaʊtʃ/ *vt* ضَمِنَ شَخْصاً \ شَيْئاً ‹*a person, fact*›

vow /vaʊ/ **A** *n* يَمين (f; أَيْمان ,أَيْمُن) قَسَم (أَقْسام) نَذْر (نُذور, نُذورات) عَهْد (عُهود)

B *vt* (i-u; نَذْر ,نُذور) نَذَرَ ‹*love, revenge*›

vowel /ˈvaʊəl/ *n* حَرَكة

voyage /ˈvɔɪɪdʒ/ *n* رِحْلة (رِحَل ,رِحْلات)

voyager /ˈvɔɪɪdʒə/ *n* رَحّالة

voyeur /vɔɪˈəː/ *n* مُتَلَصِّص

vs /ˈvəːsəs/ *prep* = **versus** ضِدَّ

V-sign /ˈviːsʌɪn/ *n* **1** (victory sign) عَلامة النَصْرِ **2** (BrE) (offensive gesture) [إيماءة مُهينة]

VSO /viːesˈəʊ/ *n* = **Voluntary Service Overseas** [جَمْعيّة خَيْريّة بَريطانيّة لِمُساعَدةِ البُلْدانِ النامِيةِ]

VT *abbr* ▸ **Vermont**

vulgar /ˈvʌlgə/ *adj* **1** (rude) ‹*joke, language*› سوقيّ ,فاحِش **2** (lacking refinement) ‹*clothes, person*› سوقيّ

vulgarity /vʌlˈgarɪti/ *n* (*pl* **vulgarities**) **1** (of a joke, sb's language) فَظاظة ,وَقاحة **2** (of clothes, a person) سوقيّة, ابْتِذال

vulnerability /vʌln(ə)rəˈbɪləti/ *n* (*pl* **vulnerabilities**) قابِليّة الإصابةِ ,ضَعْف ,عَدَم حَصانةٍ

vulnerable /ˈvʌln(ə)rəb(ə)l/ *adj* ‹*patient, child*› ضَعيف (ضُعَفاءُ, ضِعاف ,ضَعَفة) ,مُتَعَرِّض

vulture /ˈvʌltʃə/ *n* نَسْر (نُسور)

vulva /ˈvʌlvə/ *n* فَرْج (فُروج)

Ww

W, **w** /ˈdʌbəlju:/ **A** *n* (letter) واو ≈ (الحَرْف الثالث والعشْرونَ من الأبْجَديّة الإنْجليزيّة)

B *abbr* (**W**) **1** = **West** غَرْب **2** = **Watt** واط

WA *abbr* ▸**Washington**

wacky /ˈwaki/ *adj* (**wackier, wackiest**) (infml) ‹*movie, idea*› غَريب (غُرَباءُ)

wad /wɒd/ *n* **1** (of banknotes, paper) رِزْمة (رِزَم) **2** (of cotton wool, padding) كُرة (كُرات ,كُرًى)

waddle /ˈwɒd(ə)l/ *vi* «ducks, people» مَشى مُتَمايِلاً

wade /weɪd/ *vi* (in water) «bathers, children» خاضَ (u; خَوْض)

Phrasal verb **wade into** (infml): **1** ~ **into [sth]** (to start energetically) شَرَعَ في [شَيْءٍ] ‹*a task*› **2** ~ **into [sb]** (to attack) هاجَمَ [شَخْصاً] ‹*demonstrators, a crowd*›

wader /ˈweɪdə/ *n* (Zool) كَراكي (طائِر خائِض ذو قَوائِمَ طَويلةٍ)

waders /ˈweɪdəz/ *n pl* [أَحْذِية للخوضِ في الماءِ]

wading pool /ˈweɪdɪŋ ˌpu:l/ *n* (AmE) حَمّام سِباحةٍ غَيْر عَميقٍ [للأطْفالِ]

wafer /ˈweɪfə/ *n* **1** (Culin) رُقاقة بَسْكَويت **2** (Rel_Chr) خُبْز القُرْبانِ المُقَدَّسِ

wafer-thin /ˌweɪfəˈθɪn/ *adj* **1** ‹*slice, mint*› رَقيق جدًّا **2** ‹*majority, margin*› ضَئيل جدًّا

waffle /ˈwɒf(ə)l/ **A** *vi* (*also* **waffle on**) ثَرْثَرَ (i; ثَرْثَرة), أطالَ الكَلامَ لَغْواً

B *n* **1** (Culin) وافِل **2** [u] (infml) (nonsense) هَذَر

waft /wɒft/ *vi* «scents, smells» انْبَعَثَ

wag /wag/ **A** *vt* (**-gg-**) «dog» هَزَّ (u; هَزّ) ‹*tail*›

B *vi* (**-gg-**) «tails» بَصْبَصَ ,تَهَزْهَزَ (i; بَصْبَصة); **tongues were ~ging** كانَ الناسُ مُنْهَمِكينَ في القيلِ والقالِ

wage /weɪdʒ/ **A** *n* **1** (pay) أُجْرة, راتِب (رَواتِبُ); **to earn a daily/weekly ~** حَصَلَ على راتِبٍ يَوْميٍّ \ أُسْبوعيٍّ **2** (**wages** *n pl*) (cash) أُجور; **to collect one's ~s** قَبَضَ أَجْرَهُ

B *adj before n* ‹*increase, freeze*› راتِبٍ

C *vt* شَنَّ (u; شَنّ) ‹*a campaign, war*›; **to ~ a vendetta on sb** شَنَّ حَمْلةً انْتِقاميّةً ضدّ شَخْصٍ

wage earner *n* أَجير (أُجَراءُ)

wage packet *n* **1** (envelope) ظَرْف الراتِبِ **2** (money) أُجْرة ,(رَواتِبُ) راتِب

wager /ˈweɪdʒə/ **A** *n* مُراهَنة

B *vt* راهَنَ ‹*money, a fortune*›

wage rise (BrE), **wage raise** (AmE) *n* زيادة راتِبٍ

wage slip *n* قَسيمة راتِبٍ

wagon, waggon (BrE) /ˈwag(ə)n/ *n* **1** (horse-drawn) عَرَبة (خَيْلٍ) **2** (BrE) (on railways) عَرَبة (بَضائِعَ) **3** (BrE) (infml) (lorry) شاحِنة **4** (AmE infml) ▸**station wagon**

Idiom **to be on the wagon** لم يَعُدْ يَشْرَبُ الخَمْرِ

Wahhabi, Wahabi /wəˈhɑ:bi/ *n* وَهّابيّ

waif /weɪf/ *n* طِفْل شارِعٍ

wail /weɪl/ **A** *n* (of a baby) بُكاء; (of a mourner) عَويل; (of a siren) دَويّ

B *vi* «babies» بَكى (i; بُكًى ,بُكاء); «mourners» ناحَ (u; نُواح, نِياحة), انْتَحَبَ; «sirens» دَوّى

waist /weɪst/ *n* خَصْر (خُصور)

waistband /ˈweɪstband/ *n* حِزام الخَصْرِ

waistcoat /ˈweɪstkəʊt/ *n* (BrE) صُدْرة (صُدَر)

waistline /ˈweɪstlʌɪn/ *n* **1** (of garments) خَطّ الخَصْرِ **2** (of a person) مُحيط الخَصْرِ

waist measurement *n* قِياس الخَصْرِ

wait /weɪt/ **A** *vt* **1** (to watch for) اِنْتَظَرَ *‹one's turn, chance›* **2** (AmE) **to ~ tables** عَمِلَ كَنادِلٍ

B *vi* **1** (in expectation) «people, trains» اِنْتَظَرَ; **please ~ here** اِنْتَظِرْ هُنا رَجاءً; **to ~ for a friend/taxi** اِنْتَظَرَ صَديقاً \ سَيّارة تاكْسي; **to ~ for sb to do sth** اِنْتَظَرَ شَخْصاً لِيَقومَ بِفِعْلِ شَيْءٍ; **to keep sb ~ing** جَعَلَ شَخْصاً يَنْتَظِرُ; **to ~ for sth to happen** اِنْتَظَرَ حُدوثَ شَيْءٍ; **it was worth ~ing for** اِسْتَحَقَّ الأَمْرُ الانْتِظارَ; **I'm ~ing to use the phone** أَنْتَظِرُ لِكَيْ أَسْتَعْمِلَ الهاتِفَ; **the train ~ing at platform 3, is the 4.15 to London** القِطارُ الّذي يَنْتَظِرُ على الرَصيفِ 3 هو الّذي سَيَتَّجِهُ إلى لَنْدَن في الساعةِ 4.15; **the goods are ~ing to be collected** البَضائِعُ في انْتِظارِ مَنْ يَأْتي لِأَخْذِها **2** (to be postponed) «meal, calls» تَأَجَّلَ; **it can/can't ~** يُمْكِنُ \ لا يُمْكِنُ تَأْجيلُهُ **3** (BrE) (to serve) **to ~ at table** عَمِلَ كَنادِلٍ

C *n* اِنْتِظار; **an hour's ~** اِنْتِظار ساعةٍ; **to have a long/short ~** اِنْتَظَرَ طَويلاً \ لِفَتْرةٍ قَصيرةٍ

(Idioms) **can't wait for sth/until sth** تاقَ لِحُدوثِ شَيْءٍ; **I can't wait for him to be back home** أَتوقُ لِعَوْدَتِهِ إلى البَيْتِ; **I can't wait till we hear the result** أَتوقُ لِمَعْرِفةِ النَتيجةِ; **to lie in wait for sb** تَرَبَّصَ بِشَخْصٍ

(Phrasal verbs) **wait around, wait about** (BrE) اِنْتَظَرَ; **to ~ around for her/the bus to arrive** اِنْتَظَرَها \ انْتَظَرَ وُصولَ الحافِلةِ

• **wait behind** «class» اِنْتَظَرَ بُرْهةً (بعد انْتِهاءِ شَيْءٍ); **to ~ behind for sb** اِنْتَظَرَ شَخْصاً بُرْهةً

• **wait in** (BrE) اِنْتَظَرَ في البَيْتِ; **to ~ in for sb** اِنْتَظَرَ شَخْصاً في البَيْتِ

• **wait on** **A** **~ on [sb]** (to serve) خَدَمَ [شَخْصاً] كَنادِلٍ; **to ~ on sb hand and foot** سَهِرَ على خِدْمةِ شَخْصٍ **B** **~ on [sth]** اِنْتَظَرَ [شَيْئاً] *‹the result, permission›*

• **wait up** **1** (to stay awake) بَقِيَ مُسْتَيْقِظاً; **to ~ up for sb** بَقِيَ مُسْتَيْقِظاً في انْتِظارِ شَخْصٍ **2** (AmE) (to stay patiently) **~ up!** اِنْتَظِرْ!

waiter /ˈweɪtə/ *n* نادِل (نُدُل)

waiting /ˈweɪtɪŋ/ *n* (BrE) وُقوف; **No ~** مَمْنوعٌ الوُقوفُ

waiting game *n* **to play a waiting game** اِنْتَظَرَ

waiting list (BrE), **wait list** (AmE) *n* قائِمة انْتِظارٍ

waiting room *n* قاعة \ غُرْفة انْتِظارٍ

wait list *n* (AmE) ▸**waiting list**

waitress /ˈweɪtrɪs/ *n* نادِلة

waive /weɪv/ *vt* تَنازَلَ (عن) *‹a claim, fine›*

waiver /ˈweɪvə/ *n* إعْفاء (إعْفاءات)

wake /weɪk/ **A** *vt* (*past tense* **woke**; *past participle* **woken**) أَيْقَظَ *‹a baby, the neighbours›*

B *vi* (*past tense* **woke**; *past participle* **woken**) «sleeper» اِسْتَيْقَظَ, صَحا (u; صَحْو); **I woke to find myself in hospital** اِسْتَيْقَظْتُ لِأَجِدَ نَفْسي في المُسْتَشْفى

C *n* **1** (in the sea) [أَثَر حَرَكةِ السَفينةِ في الماءِ]; **in the ~ of sth** في أَعْقابِ شَيْءٍ; **war brings suffering in its ~** الحَرْبُ تُخَلِّفُ المُعاناةَ **2** (before a funeral) [السَهَر على جُثّةِ المَيِّتِ قبل دَفْنِها] (after a funeral) [الاحْتِفاء بِحَياةِ المَيِّتِ بعد دَفْنِهِ]

(Phrasal verb) **wake up** **A** **1** (to stop sleeping) صَحا, اِسْتَيْقَظَ (u; صَحْو) **2** (to become aware) اِنْتَبَهَ; **~ up!** اِنْتَبِهْ!; **to ~ up to sth** اِنْتَبَهَ لِشَيْءٍ **B** **~ up [sb], ~ [sb] up** أَيْقَظَ [شَخْصاً]

wake-up call /ˈweɪkʌp ˌkɔːl/ *n* **1** (telephone call) مُكالَمة إيقاظٍ (من النَوْمِ) **2** (warning) ناقوس خَطَرٍ, عَلامة إنْذارٍ

Wales /weɪlz/ *pr n* ويلْز (f)

walk /wɔːk/ **A** *vt* **1** (to cover on foot) مَشى (i; مَشْي) *‹a distance, the streets›*; **we ~ed 15 miles a day** مَشَيْنا 15 ميلاً في اليَوْمِ; **they ~ long distances to fetch water** يَمْشونَ مَسافاتٍ طَويلةً لِجَلْبِ الماءِ; **shall we take the bus or ~ it?** هل نَسْتَقِلُّ الحافِلةَ أم نَقْطَعُ المَسافةَ مَشْياً؟ **2** (to accompany) رافَقَ; **I ~ed her home** رافَقْتُها إلى البَيْتِ مَشْياً **3** (to exercise) مَشّى *‹a dog›*

B *vi* **1** (to go on foot) مَشى (i; مَشْي); **it's not far, let's ~** هو لَيْسَ بَعيداً، دَعْنا نَمْشي; **I was ~ing down the street** كُنْتُ أَمْشي في الشارِعِ; **to ~ through the door/the woods** مَشى عَبْرَ البابِ \ في الغابةِ; **we ~ed around the city for hours** تَجَوَّلْنا في المَدينةِ لِساعاتٍ; **a policeman ~ed by** مَرَّ شُرْطِيٌّ; **to ~ in one's sleep** مَشى في نَوْمِهِ; **to ~ up and down the room** ذَرَعَ الغُرْفةَ جيئةً وذَهاباً; **'~'** (AmE) (at traffic lights) تَسْتَطيعُ العُبورَ الآنَ **2** (for pleasure) تَمَشّى

C *n* **1** نُزْهة (نُزُهات); **to go for a ~** خَرَجَ لِيَتَمَشّى; **to take a ~** تَمَشّى; **it's about ten minutes' ~** تَبْعُدُ حَوالَيْ عَشْرِ دَقائِقَ

مَشْياً; **the beach is only a short ~ away** الشاطِئُ يَقَعُ على بُعْدِ مَسافةٍ قَصيرةٍ سَيْراً على الأَقْدامِ; **it's a long ~ back to the hotel** يَتَطَلَّبُ الرُجوعُ إلى الفُنْدُقِ المَشْيَ لِفَتْرةٍ طَويلةٍ; **to take the dog for a ~** أَخَذَ الكَلْبَ في نُزْهةٍ **2** (gait) مِشْيَة **3** (pace) مَشْي; **to slow down to a ~** [خَفَّفَ من سُرْعةِ جَرْيِهِ حتّى صارَ يَمْشي] **4** (path) مَمْشى (مَماشٍ); **people from all ~s of life** أُناس من مُخْتَلَفِ مَناحي الحَياةِ **5** (recreational route) مَمْشى (مَماشٍ)

Idioms **to walk all over sb** (infml) أَساءَ مُعامَلةَ شَخْصٍ; **to walk it** (infml) فازَ بِسُهولةٍ

Phrasal verbs **walk away** **1** (to leave) غادَرَ; **she ~ed away without a scratch** خَرَجَتْ من الحادِثِ دون أنْ تُصابَ بِخَدْشٍ **2** (to abdicate responsibility) تَمَلَّصَ من مَسْؤوليّةِ شَيْءٍ; **to ~ away from a problem** هَرَبَ من مُشْكِلةٍ

• **walk in** دَخَلَ (u; دُخول)

• **walk in on**: **~ in on [sb]** دَخَلَ على شَخْصٍ

• **walk into**: **~ into [sth]** **1** (to enter) دَخَلَ [شَيْئاً] *<a room, house>*; **she ~ed into that job** حَصَلَتْ على تِلْكَ الوَظيفةِ بدونِ جُهْدٍ **2** (infml) (to collide with) دَخَلَ في \ اصْطَدَمَ ب [شَيْءٍ] *<a wall, door>* **3** (to become caught in) وَقَعَ في [شَيْءٍ] *<a trap, an ambush>*; **you ~ed straight into the trap!** مَشَيْتَ بِرِجْلَيْكَ إلى الفَخِّ!

• **walk off** **1** (to leave) انْصَرَفَ **2** (infml) **to ~ off with sth** (to steal) سَرَقَ شَيْئاً; (to win) رَبِحَ شَيْئاً (بِسُهولةٍ)

• **walk out** **1** (to leave) خَرَجَ (u; خُروج), غادَرَ; **they ~ed out of the meeting** غادَروا الاجْتِماعَ **2** (to go on strike) أَضْرَبَ

• **walk out on**: **~ out on [sb/sth]** (infml) تَخَلّى عن [شَخْصٍ\ شَيْءٍ] *<one's husband, wife>*

• **walk up** تَوَجَّهَ; **to ~ up to sb/sth** تَوَجَّهَ إلى شَخْصٍ \ شَيْءٍ

walker /ˈwɔːkə/ *n* ماشٍ (مُشاة)

walkie-talkie /wɔːkɪˈtɔːki/ *n* جِهاز لاسِلْكيّ

walk-in /ˈwɔːkɪn/ *adj, modifier* **1** (in housing) *<wardrobe, shower>* [يُمْكِنُ دُخولُهُ] **2** (without appointments) *<centre, clinic>* [لا يَحْتاجُ إلى ميعادٍ مُسْبَقٍ]

walking /ˈwɔːkɪŋ/ *n* مَشْي

walking boots *n* حِذاء المَشْيِ

walking distance *n* **to be within ~** كانَ على مَسافةٍ قَريبةٍ

walking frame *n* إطار مَشْيٍ

walking stick *n* عَصا مَشْيٍ

walk-on /wɔːkˈɒn/ *adj before n* **a ~ part** دَوْر تافِه

walkout /ˈwɔːkaʊt/ *n* (strike) إضْراب (إضْرابات); (from a meeting) انْسِحاب احْتِجاجيّ

walkover /ˈwɔːkəʊvə/ *n* انْتِصار سَهْل

walkway /ˈwɔːkweɪ/ *n* (between buildings) مَمَرّ (مَمَرّات); (path) مَمْشى (مَماشٍ)

wall /wɔːl/ *n* **1** (of a house) حائِط (حَوائِطُ, حيطان), جِدار (جُدْران); (of a city) سور (أَسْوار); **the mirror's on the ~** المِرْآةُ على الجِدارِ \ الحائِطِ **2** (of a tunnel) جِدار (جُدْران) **3** (of internal organs) جِدار (جُدْران) **4** (of a tyre) جِدار (جُدْران) **5** (barrier) جِدار (جُدْران); **the questions were met with a ~ of silence** قوبِلَتِ الأَسْئِلةُ بِجِدارٍ من الصَمْتِ; **a ~ of flames** جِدار من اللَهَبِ

Idioms **to be a fly on the wall** تَلَصَّصَ على غَيْرِهِ; **to be off the wall** (infml) كانَ غَريبَ الأَطْوارِ; **to drive sb up the wall** (infml) أَثارَ غَضَبَ شَخْصٍ; **to go to the wall** أَفْلَسَ, دَخَلَ في حائِطٍ; **to have one's back to the wall** حُشِرَ في الزاوِيةِ

Phrasal verbs **wall in**: **~ in [sth], ~ [sth] in** سَيَّجَ [شَيْئاً] *<the garden, pool>*

• **wall off**: **~ off [sth], ~ [sth] off** (to block up) سَوَّرَ [شَيْئاً] *<a door, suite>*

• **wall up**: **~ up [sth], ~ [sth] up** أَغْلَقَ [شَيْئاً] بِجِدارٍ *<the windows>*; **they decided to ~ up the entrance** قَرَّروا أنْ يُغْلِقوا المَدْخَلَ بِجِدارٍ

wallaby /ˈwɒləbi/ *n* (*pl* **wallabies**) **1** [كَنْغَر صَغير] **2** **(the Wallabies)** [المُنْتَخَب الوَطَنيّ الأُسْترالِيّ للرُجْبي]

wallchart *n* رَسْم بَيانيّ جِداريّ

walled /wɔːld/ *adj* *<city, garden>* مُسَوَّر, مُحاط بِسورٍ

wallet /ˈwɒlɪt/ *n* **1** (for money) مَحْفَظة (مَحْفَظات, مَحافِظُ) **2** (for documents) حافِظة (حَوافِظُ)

wallflower /ˈwɔːlflaʊə/ *n* **1** (plant) مَنْثور **2** (infml) (person) [شَخْص لا يَجِدُ مَنْ يُحادِثُهُ أو يُراقِصُهُ في حَفْلةٍ]

wall light *n* مِصْباح جِداريّ

wall-mounted /ˈwɔːlmaʊntɪd/ *adj* ‹*television, heater*› مُعلَّق على الحائطِ

wallop /ˈwɒləp/ (infml) **A** *vt* لَكَمَ بِقوّةٍ ‹*a person*›; ضَرَبَ بِعُنْفٍ ‹*a ball, punchbag*›

B *n* ضَرْبة \ لَكْمة عَنيفة

wallow /ˈwɒləʊ/ *vi* **1** (to lie, bathe) «animal, person» تَمَرَّغَ

2 (to indulge) غَرِقَ (a; غَرَق); **to ~ in misery/nostalgia** غَرِقَ في الأَحْزانِ \ الحَنينِ

wall painting *n* جِداريّة

wallpaper /ˈwɔːlpeɪpə/ **A** *n* **1** (for walls) وَرَق جُدْرانٍ \ حائِطٍ

2 (for computers) خَلْفيّة

B *vt* أَلْصَقَ وَرَقَ الجُدْرانِ على ‹*the room, ceiling*›

walnut /ˈwɔːlnʌt/ *n* **1** (nut) جَوْز (n coll; أَجْواز) **2** (tree, wood) جَوْز

walrus /ˈwɔːlrəs/ *n* (*pl* **walruses** or **walrus**) فَظّ, كَبْع

waltz /wɔːlts/ **A** *n* فالْس

B *vi* «couples, dancers» رَقَصَ الفالْس

wan /wɒn/ *adj* **1** ‹*face, complexion*› شاحِب (شَواحِبُ) **2** ‹*smile*› باهِت

wand /wɒnd/ *n* عَصاً (سِحْرِيّة)

wander /ˈwɒndə/ **A** *vt* طافَ (u; طَواف), هامَ (i; هَيْم) ‹*the world, town*›; **to ~ the streets** طافَ في الشَوارِعِ

B *vi* **1** (to walk, stroll) تَجَوَّلَ, تَمَشّى, تَنَزَّهَ; **to ~ around town** تَمَشّى \ تَجَوَّلَ في المَدينةِ; **he ~ed in off the street** جاءَ من الشارِعِ **2** (to stray) هامَ (i; هَيْم), شَرَدَ (u; شُرود); **the cows had ~ed into the next field** كانَتْ الأَبْقارُ قد شَرَدَتْ حتّى بَلَغَت الحَقْلَ المُجاوِرَ; **don't ~ off** لا تَذْهَبْ بَعيداً **3** (to drift) «mind, attention» شَرَدَ (u; شُرود); **her mind ~ed back to the previous summer** شَرَدَ ذِهْنُها عائِداً إلى الصَيْفِ الماضِي; **to ~ off the point** *or* **subject** خَرَجَ عن المَوْضوعِ

C *n* (infml) نُزْهة, جَوْلة (نُزْهات); **to go for a ~** خَرَجَ لِيَتَمَشّى

Phrasal verb **wander around, wander about** (BrE) **1** (to stroll) تَجَوَّلَ **2** (when lost) هامَ (i; هَيْم)

wanderer /ˈwɒnd(ə)rə/ *n* دائِم التَنَقُّلِ, هائِم, مُتَشَرِّد

wanderings /ˈwɒndərɪŋz/ *n pl* رِحْلات, تَجْوال

wanderlust /ˈwɒndəlʌst/ *n* حُبّ السَفَرِ \ التَجْوالِ

wane /weɪn/ **A** *n* **to be on the ~** «the moon» كانَ في المُحاقِ; «popularity, influence» تَضاءَلَ

B *vi* **1** «the moon» تَناقَصَ **2** «interest, influence» تَضاءَلَ

▸ see also **wax** C

C (**waning**) *adj* **1** ‹*moon*› في المُحاقِ **2** ‹*interest, influence*› مُتَضائِل

wangle /ˈwaŋg(ə)l/ *vt* (infml) حَصَلَ على (بالحيلةِ) ‹*an invitation, a discount*›

wannabe /ˈwɒnəbi/ *n* (infml) [شَخْص طامِح للشُهْرةِ والنَجاحِ]

want /wɒnt/ **A** *vt* **1** (to desire) أَرادَ, رَغِبَ (في; رَغْبة; a) ‹*money, information*›; **to ~ sb to do sth** أَرادَ من شَخْصٍ أنْ يَقومَ بِشَيْءٍ; **I ~ the job to be finished** أُريدُ لِهَذا العَمَلِ أنْ يَنْتَهِيَ; **I don't ~ to** لا أُريدُ ذلك; **how much** *or* **what do you ~ for this chair?** كم تُريدُ مُقابِلَ هذا الكُرْسيِّ؟; **where do you ~ me?** أَيْنَ تُريدُني؟; **they just don't ~ to know** هُمْ فَقَطْ لا يُريدونَ أنْ يَتَدَخَّلوا; **what do I ~ with a bike?** ماذا عَساني أَفْعَلُ بِدَرّاجةٍ؟ **2** (infml) (to need) احْتاجَ; **you ~ to get that seen to** تَحْتاجُ أنْ تَعْرِضَ ذلك لِلفَحْصِ; **all that's ~ed is your signature** كُلُّ ما هو مَطْلوبٌ مِنْكَ هو أنْ تُوَقِّعَ **3** (to require the presence of) طَلَبَ (u; مَطْلَب, طَلَب); **you're ~ed on the phone** هُناكَ مَنْ يَطْلُبُكَ على الهاتِفِ; **the boss ~s you** الرَئيسُ يُريدُكَ (لِأَمْرٍ ما); **I know when I'm not ~ed** أَعْرِفُ مَتى أُصْبِحُ شَخْصاً غَيْرَ مَرْغوبٍ فيهِ **4** (to seek) **to be ~ed by the police** كانَ مَطْلوباً للشُرْطةِ

B *vi* **to ~ for sth** (liter) احْتاجَ شَيْئاً

C *n* **1** (fml) (need) احْتِياج (احْتِياجات), حاجة, مُتَطَلَّب (مُتَطَلَّبات); **my ~s are few** احْتِياجاتي قَليلةٌ **2** [u] (deprivation) حِرْمان **3** [u] (lack) عَدَم وُجودٍ \ تَوَفُّرٍ; **it's not for ~ of trying** لَيْسَ لِعَدَمِ تَوَفُّرِ المُحاوَلةِ; **for ~ of a better word** لِعَدَمِ وُجودِ كَلِمةٍ دَقيقةٍ

Phrasal verbs **want in** (infml) **1** (to wish to enter) رَغِبَ في الدُخولِ **2** (to wish to participate) رَغِبَ في المُشارَكةِ; **he ~s in on the deal** يَرْغَبُ في المُشارَكةِ في الصَفْقةِ

• **want out** (infml) **1** (to wish to leave) رَغِبَ في المُغادَرةِ \ الخُروجِ **2** (to no longer wish to participate) رَغِبَ في الانْسِحابِ; **she ~ed out of the relationship/business** أَرادَت الانْسِحابَ من العَلاقةِ \ المَشْروعِ التِجاريِّ

wanted /ˈwɒntɪd/ *adj* ‹*man, criminal*› مَطْلوب; **W~ Dead or Alive** مَطْلوب حَيًّا أو مَيِّتاً

wanting /ˈwɒntɪŋ/ *adj* (fml) 1▶ **to be ~** كانَ ناقِصاً 2▶ **to be found ~** وُجِدَ غَيْرَ كُفُؤٍ

wanton /ˈwɒnt(ə)n/ *adj* 1▶ (reckless) ‹*destruction, vandalism*› لا مُبَرِّرَ لَهُ 2▶ (licentious) ‹*behaviour*› داعِر، (فَجَرة، فُجّار) فاجِر (دُعّار)

waqf /vʌkf/ *n* (*pl* **waqf**) وَقْف (أَوْقاف)

war /wɔː/ *n* 1▶ (conflict) حَرْب (f; حُروب); **he was killed in** *or* **during the ~** قُتِلَ في الحَرْبِ; **to go to ~ with sb** دَخَلَ في حَرْبٍ مع شَخْصٍ; **to be at ~ with sb** كانَ في حَرْبٍ مع شَخْصٍ 2▶ (in rivalries) حَرْب (f; حُروب); **a trade ~** حَرْب تِجارِيّة; **a ~ of words** حَرْب كَلامِيّة 3▶ (campaign) حَرْب (f; حُروب); **the ~ on terror/drugs** الحَرْب على الإرْهابِ \ المُخَدِّراتِ

warble /ˈwɔːb(ə)l/ *vi* «birds» غَرَّدَ

war crime *n* جَرِيمة حَرْبٍ

ward /wɔːd/ *n* 1▶ (for patients) جَناح (أَجْنِحة)، عَنْبَر (عَنابِر); **the maternity/paediatric ~** جَناح الوِلادةِ \ الأَطْفالِ 2▶ (electoral) دائِرة انْتِخابِيّة 3▶ (also **ward of court** BrE, **ward of the state** AmE) قاصِر تحت وِصايةِ المَحْكَمةِ

(Phrasal verb) **ward off**: **~ off [sth]** صَدَّ [شَيْئاً] ‹*an attack, a blow*›; وَقَى من [شَيْءٍ] ‹*a disease, infection*›

warden /ˈwɔːd(ə)n/ *n* 1▶ (supervisor of a park) حارِس (حُرّاس); (of a hostel, home) بَوّاب 2▶ (BrE) (of a university, college) عَميد (عُمَداءُ) 3▶ (AmE) (of a prison) آمِر، مَأْمور

warder /ˈwɔːdə/ *n* (BrE) حارِس سِجْنٍ، سَجّان

wardrobe /ˈwɔːdrəʊb/ *n* 1▶ (cupboard) خِزانة مَلابِسَ 2▶ (set of clothes) مَجْموعة مَلابِسَ

warehouse /ˈwɛːhaʊs/ *n* مُسْتَوْدَع (مُسْتَوْدَعات)، مَخْزَن (مَخازِنُ)

warehouseman /ˈwɛːhaʊsmən/ *n* (*pl* **-men**) أَمين مُسْتَوْدَعٍ

wares /wɛːz/ *n pl* (fml) سِلَع

warfare /ˈwɔːfɛː/ *n* حَرْب (f; حُروب)

war game *n* 1▶ (game) لُعْبة حَرْبِيّة 2▶ (military exercise) مُناوَرة عَسْكَرِيّة

warhead /ˈwɔːhɛd/ *n* رَأْس حَرْبِيّ

warily /ˈwɛːrɪli/ *adv* 1▶ (cautiously) ‹*to tread, peer*› بِحَذَرٍ 2▶ (mistrustfully) ‹*to ask, look*› بِعَدَمِ الثِقةِ، بِارْتِيابٍ

warlike /ˈwɔːlʌɪk/ *adj* ‹*tribe, nature*› مُحِبّ للحَرْبِ

warlord /ˈwɔːlɔːd/ *n* أَمير حَرْبٍ

warm /wɔːm/ **A** *adj* (**warmer, warmest**) 1▶ (not cold) ‹*bath, climate, hands*› دافِئ; **to be** *or* **feel ~** شَعَرَ بالدِفْءِ; **are you ~ enough?** هل تَشْعُرُ بالدِفْءِ بِشَكْلٍ كافٍ؟; **it's ~ today** الجَوُّ دافِئٌ اليَوْمَ; **it's ~ for April** الجَوُّ دافِئٌ على غَيْرِ العادةِ في أَبْريل; **it's nice and ~ here** الجَوُّ جَميلٌ ودافِئٌ هُنا; **this is the ~est room in the house** هذه أَدْفَأُ غُرْفةٍ في البَيْتِ; **you need ~ clothes** تَحْتاجُ مَلابِسَ دافِئةً; **cook in a ~ oven** اُطْبُخْ في فُرْنٍ دافِئٍ 2▶ (welcoming) ‹*person, atmosphere, smile*› حارّ; **we gave them a ~ welcome** اسْتَقْبَلْناهُم اسْتِقْبالاً حارًّا 3▶ (in a guessing game) **you're getting ~** أَنْتَ قَريبٌ من الجَوابِ الصَحيحِ 4▶ (deep) ‹*colour, red*› حارّ
B *vt* ‹*the room, plate*› دَفَّأَ; **she was ~ing her hands** كانَتْ تُدَفِّئُ يَدَيْها
C *vi* «soup, room» أَصْبَحَ دافِئاً
D *v refl* **to ~ oneself** تَدَفَّأَ
E *n* (infml) **the ~** دِفْء، المَكان الدافِئ; **come into the ~** تَعالَ إلى الدِفْءِ

(Phrasal verb) **warm up** **A** 1▶ (to become hotter) «rooms, cars» أَصْبَحَ دافِئاً 2▶ «athletes, orchestras» تَمَرَّنَ 3▶ (to become lively) «discussions, audience» سَخُنَ (u; سُخونة، سَخانة) **B** **~ up [sth]**, **~ [sth] up** 1▶ (to heat) سَخَّنَ [شَيْئاً] ‹*a room, water*› 2▶ (to run) سَخَّنَ [شَيْئاً] ‹*an engine, car*› 3▶ (to prepare) سَخَّنَ [شَيْئاً] ‹*an audience*›; **he ~s up the audience before the star comes on stage** يُسَخِّنُ الجُمْهورَ قَبلَ صُعودِ النَجْمِ على المَسْرَحِ

warm-blooded /wɔːmˈblʌdɪd/ *adj* ‹*animal, bird*› ذو دَمٍ حارٍّ

war memorial *n* نُصُب تَذْكارِيّ لِقَتْلى الحَرْبِ

warm-hearted /wɔːmˈhɑːtɪd/ *adj* ‹*generosity, welcome*› وَدود، عَطوف (عُطُف)

warmly /ˈwɔːmli/ *adv* ‹*to welcome, greet*› بِحَرارةٍ; **to smile ~** ابْتَسَمَ ابْتِسامةً دافِئةً

warmth /wɔːmθ/ *n* [1] (heat) دِفْء; **they sat close to the fire for ~** جَلَسوا قُرْبَ النارِ طَلَباً للدِفْءِ [2] (of a welcome, etc) دِفْء, حَرارة [3] (of colours) حَرارة

warm-up /ˈwɔːmʌp/ *n* تَسْخين

warn /wɔːn/ **A** *vt* [1] (to caution) «police, parent, doctor» حَذَّر (من); **she ~ed me not to underestimate him** حَذَّرَني من الاسْتِهانةِ بِهِ; **a programme ~ing schoolchildren about the dangers of drugs** بَرْنامَج يُحَذِّرُ أَطْفالَ المَدارِسِ من مَخاطِرِ المُخَدِّراتِ; **to ~ sb against sth/doing sth** حَذَّرَ شَخْصاً من شَيْءٍ \ من فِعْلِ شَيْءٍ [2] (to alert) «expert, report» حَذَّرَ (من), نَبَّهَ; **he ~ed that time was running out** حَذَّرَ من \ نَبَّهَ إلى أنّ الوَقْتَ يَنْفُذُ

B *vi* **to ~ of sth** حَذَّرَ من شَيْءٍ

(Phrasal verb) **warn off**: **~ [sb] off, ~ off [sb]** أَمَرَ [شَخْصاً] بالابْتِعادِ; **to ~ sb off doing sth** حَذَّرَ شَخْصاً من فِعْلِ شَيْءٍ; **to ~ sb off alcohol/drugs** أَمَرَ شَخْصاً بالابْتِعادِ عن الكُحولِ \ المُخَدِّراتِ

warning /ˈwɔːnɪŋ/ *n* [1] (of danger) تَحْذير (تَحْذيرات); **a flood/tornado ~** تَحْذير بحُدوثِ فَيَضانٍ \ إعْصارٍ; **a health ~** تَحْذير صِحّيّ; **to issue a ~ about sth/against doing sth** أَصْدَرَ تَحْذيراً بِشأْنِ شَيْءٍ \ ضدَّ القِيامِ بِشَيْءٍ [2] (caution) تَحْذير, إنْذار (تَحْذيرات); **an official/a written ~** إنْذار رَسْميّ \ مَكْتوب; **she was let off with a ~** أُخْلِيَ سَبيلُها بعد تَوْجيهِ تَنْبيه [3] [u] (advance notice) تَحْذير (تَحْذيرات), إنْذار لَها (إشْعارات), إشْعار (تَنْبيهات); **to attack/hit out without ~** هاجَمَ \ ضَرَبَ دون تَحْذيرٍ

warning sign *n* [1] (on a road, building) لافِتة تَحْذيريّة [2] (of something bad or unpleasant) عَلامة إنْذارٍ, نَذير (نُذُر)

warning triangle *n* مُثَلَّث تَحْذيرٍ

warp /wɔːp/ **A** *vt* [1] قَوَّسَ ‹wood, metal› [2] شَوَّهَ ‹sb's mind, judgement›

B *vi* «boards, metal» اعْوَجَّ, الْتَوى, تَقَوَّسَ

warped /wɔːpt/ *adj* [1] (distorted) ‹wood, rails› مُقَوَّس [2] (abnormal) ‹mind, sense of humour› مُشَوَّه

warplane /ˈwɔːpleɪn/ *n* طائِرة حَرْبيّة

warrant /ˈwɒrənt/ **A** *n* أَمْر (أوامِرُ), مُذَكِّرة; **to issue an arrest ~** أَصْدَرَ مُذَكِّرةَ اعْتِقالٍ; **to obtain a search ~** اسْتَصْدَرَ أَمْرَ تَفْتيشٍ

B *vt* (fml) [1] (to justify) سَوَّغَ, بَرَّرَ ‹behaviour, action› [2] (to deserve) اسْتَأْهَلَ, اسْتَحَقَّ ‹investigation, attention›

warrant officer *n* مُساعِد

warranty /ˈwɒrənti/ *n* (*pl* **warranties**) كَفالة, ضَمان

warren /ˈwɒrən/ *n* [1] (rabbits') [أَرْض تَكْثُرُ فيها جُحورُ الأرانِبِ] [2] (maze) مَتاهة

warring /ˈwɔːrɪŋ/ *adj before n* ‹factions, families› مُتَحارِب, مُتَناحِر

warrior /ˈwɒrɪə/ *n* مُحارِب

Warsaw /ˈwɔːsɔː/ *pr n* وارْسو (f)

warship /ˈwɔːʃɪp/ *n* سَفينة حَرْبيّة

wart /wɔːt/ *n* ثُؤْلول (ثَآليلُ)

wartime /ˈwɔːtaɪm/ *n* **in ~** في زَمَنِ الحَرْبِ

war-torn /ˈwɔːtɔːn/ *adj* ‹country, region› مَزَّقَتْهُ الحَرْبُ

war veteran *n* مُحارِب قَديم

wary /ˈwɛːri/ *adj* (**warier, wariest**) [1] (cautious) حَذِر, يَقِظ (أَيْقاظ), مُحْتَرِس [2] (mistrustful) ‹look› مُرْتاب; **be ~ of emails from people you don't know** لا تَثِقْ بالبَريدِ من مَجْهولينَ

war zone *n* مِنْطَقة حَرْبٍ

was /wɒz, wəz/ *past tense* ▸**be**

wash /wɒʃ/ **A** *vt* [1] (to clean) غَسَلَ (i; غَسْل), نَظَّفَ ‹the clothes, car, floor›; **to get ~ed** اسْتَحَمَّ, اغْتَسَلَ; **to ~ one's hands/hair** غَسَلَ يَدَيْه \ شَعْرَهُ; **to ~ the dishes** غَسَلَ الأوانيَ [2] (to carry along) لَفَظَ (i; لَفْظ) ‹silt, debris›; **two bodies were ~ed ashore** لَفَظَ البَحْرُ جَسَدَيْنِ على الشاطِئِ; **to ~ sb/sth overboard** سَحَبَ شَخْصاً \ شيْئاً جانِباً [3] (liter) (to lap against) «waves» غَسَلَ (i; غَسْل) ‹the shores›

B *vi* [1] (to clean oneself) اسْتَحَمَّ, اغْتَسَلَ [2] (to clean dishes) غَسَلَ الأواني [3] (to become clean) «fabrics, garments» نَظُفَ (u; نَظافة) [4] (infml) (to be believed) «arguments, stories» كانَ [قابِلاً للتَصْديقِ]; **that excuse doesn't ~** ذلك العُذْرُ لا يُمْكِنُ تَصْديقُهُ

C *v refl* **to ~ oneself** «person» اسْتَحَمَّ, اغْتَسَلَ; **to ~ itself** «animal» نَظَّفَ نَفْسَهُ

D *n* **1** (by a person) اِغْتِسال ,اِسْتِحْمام ,اِغْتِسال; **to have a ~** اِغْتَسَلَ, **to give the car/floor a ~** غَسَلَ السَّيّارةَ \ الأَرْضيّةَ; أَخَذَ حَمّاماً ,اِسْتَحَمَّ **2** (for clothes) غَسيل; **the weekly ~** الغَسيل الأُسْبوعيّ; **your trousers are in the ~** سِرْوالُكَ في الغَسيل **3** (from boats) [أَثَر السَفينةِ العابِرةِ على الماءِ] **4** (for the skin) غَسول

(Idiom) **to wash one's hands of sb/sth** غَسَلَ يَدَيْهِ من شَخْصٍ \ شَيْءٍ

(Phrasal verbs) **wash away** **A** **~ [sth] away, ~ away [sth]** **1** (to clean) جَرَفَ [شَيْئاً] \ أَزالَ [شَيْئاً] ‹*dirt, blood*› **2** (to carry off) غَسَلَ \ أَزالَ [شَيْئاً] ‹*a road, village, bridge*› **B** **~ [sb] away** جَرَفَ [شَخْصاً]

• **wash down**: **~ [sth] down, ~ down [sth]** **1** (to clean) غَسَلَ [شَيْئاً] ‹*a wall, the paintwork*› **2** (to accompany) [شَرِبَ شَيْئاً على [شَيْءٍ]] ‹*a meal, pill*›

• **wash off** **A** «marks, dirt» زالَ (a; زَوال) **B** **~ [sth] off, ~ off [sth]** غَسَلَ \ أَزالَ [شَيْئاً] ‹*blood, dirt*›

• **wash out** **A** «stains, colour» زالَ (a; زَوال) **B** **~ [sth] out, ~ out [sth]** **1** (to remove by cleaning) غَسَلَ \ أَزالَ [شَيْئاً] ‹*a stain*› **2** (to rinse inside) غَسَلَ [شَيْئاً] ‹*a cup, bottle*› **3** (to cause cancellation of) أَلْغى [شَيْئاً] (بِسببِ الطَقسِ السَيِّئِ) ‹*a game, match*›

• **wash over**: **1** **~ over [sth]** غَمَرَ [شَيْئاً] ‹*the deck, floor*›; **everything I say just ~es over him** لا شَيْءَ أَقولُهُ يُؤَثِّرُ فيهِ **2** **~ over [sb]** «relief, disappointment» غَمَرَ [شَخْصاً]

• **wash up** **A** **1** (BrE) (to clean dishes) غَسَلَ الأَوانِيَ **2** (AmE) (to clean oneself) غَسَلَ وَجْهَهُ وَيَدَيْهِ **B** **~ [sth] up, ~ up [sth]** **1** (to clean) غَسَلَ [شَيْئاً] ‹*the dishes, breakfast things*› **2** (to bring ashore) لَفَظَ [شَيْئاً] ‹*a body, debris*›

washable /ˈwɒʃəb(ə)l/ *adj* ‹*fabric, garment*› قابِل للغَسْلِ

washbasin /ˈwɒʃbeɪs(ə)n/ *n* حَوْض غَسيلٍ

washbowl /ˈwɒʃbəʊl/ *n* (AmE) مَغْسَلة ,حَوْض غَسيلٍ (مَغاسِلُ)

washcloth /ˈwɒʃklɒθ/ *n* (AmE) مِنْشَفة وَجْهٍ

washed out /ˌwɒʃt ˈaʊt/ *adj* (*before n* **washed-out**) **1** (faded) ‹*colour, jeans*› باهِت **2** (infml) (tired) مُرْهَق ,مُتْعَب

washed-up /wɒʃtˈʌp/ *adj* (infml) ‹*film star, actor*› مُنْتَهٍ

washer /ˈwɒʃə/ *n* **1** (for a tap) جِلْدة **2** (for a screw) حَلْقة (حَلَقات ,حَلَق) **3** (washing machine) غَسّالة

washer-dryer /ˌwɒʃəˈdrʌɪə/ *n* غَسّالة مُجَفِّف

washing /ˈwɒʃɪŋ/ *n* **1** (laundry) غَسيل (غَسْلى) **2** (act of laundering) غَسْل; **to do the ~** غَسَلَ المَلابِسَ

washing line *n* (BrE) حَبْل غَسيلٍ

washing machine *n* غَسّالة

washing powder *n* (BrE) مَسْحوق غَسيلٍ

Washington /ˈwɒʃɪŋt(ə)n/ *pr n* **1** (also **Washington DC**) (city) واشِنْطُن دي سي \ العاصِمة **2** (state) (وِلاية) واشِنْطُن

Washingtonian /ˌwɒʃɪŋˈtəʊnɪən/ *pr n, adj* [(شَخْص) من واشِنْطُن]

washing-up /wɒʃɪŋˈʌp/ (BrE) *n* **1** (act of washing up) غَسْل \ غَسيل الصُحونِ \ المَواعينِ \ الأَواني; **to do the ~** غَسَلَ الصُحونَ \ المَواعينَ \ الأَوانيَ **2** (dishes, cutlery) الأَواني المُتَّسِخة

washing-up liquid *n* سائِل غَسيلِ الصُحونِ

washout /ˈwɒʃaʊt/ *n* (infml) **1** (failure) إِخْفاق (إِخْفاقات) **2** (due to rain) مُلْغًى (بِسَبَبِ الأَمْطارِ الغَزيرةِ)

washroom /ˈwɒʃruːm/ *n* دَوْرة المِياهِ ,مِرْحاض (مَراحيضُ)

wasn't /ˈwɒz(ə)nt/ *abbr* = **was not** ▸ **be**

wasp /wɒsp/ *n* دَبّور (دَبابيرُ) ,زُنْبور (زَنابيرُ)

Wasp /wɒsp/ *n* = **White Anglo-Saxon Protestant** [مُواطِن أَمريكيّ أَبْيَض وَبْروتِسْتانْتيّ من أَصْلٍ أَنْجِلو سَكْسونيٍّ]

waspish /ˈwɒspɪʃ/ *adj* ‹*remark, humour*› لاذِع (لَواذِعُ)

wastage /ˈweɪstɪdʒ/ *n* **1** (of resources, energy) هَدْر **2** (BrE) (also **natural wastage**) [الاِنْخِفاض \ التَقَلُّص الطَبيعيّ لِحَجْمِ القُوى العامِلةِ بِسَبَبِ التَقاعُدِ والاِسْتِقالاتِ الاِخْتِياريّةِ إِلخ]

waste /weɪst/ **A** *vt* **1** (to squander) أَهْدَرَ ,بَدَّدَ ,ضَيَّعَ ‹*money, resources, food*›; **I've ~d my time here** ضَيَّعْتُ وَقْتي هُنا; **don't ~ your breath** لا تُتْعِبْ نَفْسَكَ في الكَلامِ; **she's ~d on him** لا يُقَدِّرُها قَدْرَها; **it's a shame to ~ all that food** من العارِ تَبْديدُ كُلِّ ذلك الطَعامِ **2** (to make thinner) «hunger, the cancer» أَضْعَفَ ,هَزَّلَ ‹*one's body, limbs*›; **her body had been ~d by the cancer** أَضْعَفَ السَرَطانُ جِسْمَها **B** *vi* «food, materials» تَبَدَّدَ ,ذَهَبَ هَدَراً

C *adj before n* (discarded) ‹*gases, products*› عادِم; **the ~ gases are burned off** يَتِمُّ حَرْقُ الغازاتِ العادِمةِ; **~ water is released into the sea** يَتِمُّ التَخلُّص من مِياهِ الصَرْفِ في البَحْرِ

D *n* **1** (of resources) إهْدار; (of time) إضاعة; **what a ~!** يا لَلْخَسارةِ!; **that was a complete ~ of time** كانَ ذلك مَضْيَعةً للوَقْتِ تَماماً; **it's a ~ of time and money** هو مَضْيَعةٌ للوَقْتِ والمالِ; **it's a ~ of her talents** هو إضاعةٌ لِمَواهِبِها; **to go to ~** أُهْمِلَ **2** [u] (also **wastes**) (refuse) مُخَلَّفات; **industrial ~** مُخَلَّفات صِناعيّة

E (**wastes**) *n pl* (wilderness) بَرِّيّة (بَراريّ); **the frozen ~s of the Antarctic** [المَناطِق القُطْبيّة الجَليديّة الغَيْر مَأْهولةٍ في أَنْتارْكْتيكا]

(Phrasal verb) **waste away** «patients» نَحَلَ (a-u; نُحول)، أُصيبَ بالهُزالِ

wastebasket /ˈweɪstbɑːskɪt/ *n* (AmE) سَلّة المُهْمَلاتِ

waste bin *n* (BrE) **1** (for paper) سَلّة المُهْمَلاتِ **2** (for rubbish) سَلّة النُفاياتِ

wasted /ˈweɪstɪd/ *adj* **1** (lost) ‹*time, money, opportunity*› مُهْدَر **2** (to no purpose) ‹*effort, journey*› غَيْر مُفيدٍ **3** (emaciated) ‹*body, muscles*› ضامِر (ضُمَّر، ضَوامِرُ)

waste disposal *n* التَخلُّص من النُفاياتِ

waste-disposal unit /ˌweɪstdɪsˈpəʊsəl juːnɪt/ *n* (BrE) وَحْدة التَخلُّصِ من النُفاياتِ

wasteful /ˈweɪstfʊl/ *adj* ‹*expenditure, use*› مُهْدِر; ‹*person*› مُبَذِّر

wasteland /ˈweɪstland/ *n* خَراب \ بور \ أَرْض قَفْر

wastepaper /weɪstˈpeɪpə/ *n* نُفايات الوَرَقِ

wastepaper basket, **wastepaper bin** (BrE) *n* سَلّة المُهْمَلاتِ

waste pipe *n* أُنْبوب تَصْريفٍ

wasting /ˈweɪstɪŋ/ *adj before n* ‹*disease*› مُهْلِك، مُضْنٍ

watch /wɒtʃ/ **A** *vt* **1** (to look at) شاهَدَ، تَفَرَّجَ (على) ‹*a movie, game*›; **to ~ TV** شاهَدَ التِلْفازَ; **the fight was ~ed by 9 million people** تَفَرَّجَ 9 مَلايينِ شَخْصٍ على النِزالِ **2** (to observe) راقَبَ ‹*a person, scene*›; **to ~ sb doing** *or* **do sth** راقَبَ شَخْصاً وَهُوَ يَفْعَلُ شَيْئاً **3** (to monitor) تابَعَ ‹*sb's progress, a situation*› **4** (under surveillance) راقَبَ ‹*a house, suspect*› **5** (to be careful about) انْتَبَهَ (إلى) ‹*one's weight, language*›; **~ you don't spill it** انْتَبِهْ حتّى لا تَسْكُبُهُ; **~ where you put that paintbrush!** انْتَبِهْ أَيْنَ تَضَعُ فُرْشاةَ الرَسْمِ تِلْكَ!; **~ it!** (infml) انْتَبِهْ! **6** (to look after) اعْتَنى (ب) ‹*sb's bags, a child*›

B *vi* «observers, viewers» تَرَقَّبَ; **they are ~ing to see what will happen next** يَتَرَقَّبونَ لِيَرَوْا ما سَيَحْصُلُ لاحِقاً

C *v refl* **to ~ oneself** **1** (to look at oneself) نَظَرَ إلى نَفْسِهِ **2** (infml) (to be careful) راقَبَ نَفْسَهُ

D *n* **1** (timepiece) ساعة (يَدٍ) **2** (observation) **to keep ~** راقَبَ; **to keep a close ~ on sb/sth** راقَبَ شَخْصاً \ شَيْئاً عن كَثَبٍ; **to be on the ~ for sb/sth** احْتَرَسَ من شَخْصٍ \ شَيْءٍ **3** (time on duty) حِراسة; **to be on ~** كانَ في الحِراسةِ; **it happened on his ~** حَدَثَ تحت مَسْؤوليَّتِهِ **4** (on ships) نَوْبة الحِراسةِ **5** (guard) حارِس (حَرَس، حُرّاس)

(Phrasal verbs) **watch for**: **~ for [sb/sth]** انْتَبَهَ إلى [شَخْصٍ \ شَيْءٍ] ‹*signs, changes, opportunities*›

• **watch out** **1** (to be careful) أَخَذَ حَذَرَهُ، احْتَرَسَ; **~ out!** احْتَرِسْ! **2** (to be alert for) انْتَظَرَ; **we'll be ~ing out for you** سَنَكونُ في انْتِظارِكَ; **~ out for our next issue!** انْتَظِروا عَدَدَنا التاليَ!

• **watch over**: **~ over [sb/sth]** اعْتَنى ب [شَخْصٍ \ شَيْءٍ] ‹*a child, situation*›

watchable /ˈwɒtʃəb(ə)l/ *adj* ‹*film, actor*› مُمْتِع

watchband /ˈwɒtʃband/ *n* (AmE) حِزام الساعةِ

watch chain *n* سِلْسِلة ساعةٍ

watchdog /ˈwɒtʃdɒg/ *n* **1** (dog) كَلْب حِراسةٍ **2** (organization) لَجْنة مُراقَبةٍ، هَيْئة رَقابةٍ

watcher /ˈwɒtʃə/ *n* (observer) مُراقِب; (spectator) مُشاهِد; **TV ~s** مُشاهِدو التِلفِزْيون

watchful /ˈwɒtʃfʊl/ *adj* ‹*eye, supervision*› يَقِظ (أَيْقاظ)، مُتَنَبِّه

watchmaker /ˈwɒtʃmeɪkə/ *n* ساعاتيّ

watchman /ˈwɒtʃmən/ *n* (*pl* **-men**) حارِس (حَرَس، حُرّاس)، خَفير (خُفَراءُ)

watch strap *n* حِزام الساعةِ

watchtower /ˈwɒtʃtaʊə/ *n* بُرْج مُراقَبة

watchword /ˈwɒtʃwəːd/ *n* شِعار (شِعارات)

water /ˈwɔːtə/ **A** *n* **1** ماء (مِياه); **to travel by ~** (by sea) سافَرَ بَحْراً; (by river) سافَرَ عن طَريقِ النَهْرِ; **to be under ~** غَمَرَتْهُ المِياهُ; **the wine was flowing like ~** كانَ النَبيذُ مُتَوَفِّراً بِكَثْرةٍ **2** **to pass ~** بالَ (u; بَوْل), تَبَوَّلَ

B (**waters**) *n pl* **1** (of a nation) مِياه; **international ~s** مِياه دُوَلِيّة; **we are sailing uncharted ~s** نَقومُ بِعَمَلٍ ريادِيٍّ \ غَيْرِ مَسْبوقٍ **2** (in obstetrics) ماء الجَنين, السائل الأَمْنيوسيّ

C *vt* **1** سَقى (i; سَقْي), رَوى (i; رَيّ, رِيّ) ‹*the plants, crops, garden*› **2** رَوى (i; رَيّ, رِيّ), سَقى (i; سَقْي) ‹*the horses, cattle*›

D *vi* **the smell of cooking makes my mouth ~** رائِحةُ الطَبْخِ تُسيلُ لُعابي; **the smoke/onion made her eyes ~** جَعَلَ الدُخانُ \ البَصَلُ عُيونَها تَدْمَعُ

(Idioms) **like water off a duck's back** ≈ دَخَلَ من أُذُنٍ وَخَرَجَ من الأُخْرى; **to hold water** كانَ مَبْنِيًّا على أَساسٍ سَليمٍ; **to be water under the bridge** لم تَعُدْ لَهُ أَهَمِّيّةٌ ▸ **head**

(Phrasal verb) **water down**: **~ down** [sth], **~** [sth] **down** **1** (to dilute) خَفَّفَ [شَيْئاً] ‹*a drink, whisky*› **2** (to make less effective) خَفَّفَ من حدّة [شَيْءٍ] ‹*a proposal, reform*›

water beetle *n* خُنْفُساء الماءِ

waterbird /ˈwɔːtəbəːd/ *n* طائِر مائيّ

water boatman *n* [حَشَرة مائِيّة]

water bottle *n* زُجاجة مِياهٍ, مَطْرة

water cannon *n* مِدْفَع مائيّ

water chestnut *n* قَسْطَل الماءِ (نَبات مائيّ)

watercolour (BrE), **watercolor** (AmE) /ˈwɔːtəkʌlə/ *n* **1** (paint) لَوْن مائيّ **2** (painting) لَوْحة مائيّة

watercress /ˈwɔːtəkrɛs/ *n* جِرْجير

waterfall /ˈwɔːtəfɔːl/ *n* شَلّال (شَلّالات)

water filter *n* فِلْتِر \ مُرَشِّح ماءٍ

waterfront /ˈwɔːtəfrʌnt/ *n* [الجُزْء المُطِلّ على البَحْرِ \ البُحَيْرة \ النَهْرِ]

water heater *n* سَخّان مِياهٍ

waterhen /ˈwɔːtəhɛn/ *n* (*pl* **waterhen** or **waterhens**) دَجاج ماءٍ

watering can /ˈwɔːtərɪŋ kaːn/ *n* مِرَشّة (مَراشّ)

water jug *n* إِبْريق (أَباريق)

water jump *n* [القَفْز فوق الماءِ (في سِباقِ الخَيْلِ)]

water level *n* مُسْتَوًى \ مَنْسوب ماءٍ

water lily *n* نيلَوْفَر (نَبات مائيّ ذو أَوْراقٍ كَبيرةٍ)

waterlogged /ˈwɔːtəlɒgd/ *adj* ‹*pitch, soil*› مُشْبَع بالماءِ

water main *n* أُنْبوب الماءِ الرَئيسيّ

watermark /ˈwɔːtəmaːk/ *n* عَلامة مائيّة

watermelon /ˈwɔːtəmɛlən/ *n* بِطّيخ (n coll)

water meter *n* عَدّاد المِياه

watermill /ˈwɔːtəmɪl/ *n* طاحونة مائيّة

water on the brain *n* ماء على الدِماغ

water on the knee *n* ماء على الرُكْبةِ

water polo *n* كُرة الماءِ

water power *n* طاقة مائيّة

waterproof /ˈwɔːtəpruːf/ **A** *adj* ‹*jacket, watch*› مُقاوِم للماءِ

B *vt* ‹*a tent, boots*› جَعَلَ مُقاوِماً للماءِ

waterproofs /ˈwɔːtəpruːfs/ *n pl* مَلابِس مُقاوِمة للماءِ

water-resistant /ˈwɔːtərɪzɪst(ə)nt/ *adj* ‹*fabric, coating*› مُقاوِم للماءِ

watershed /ˈwɔːtəʃɛd/ *n* **1** (turning point) نُقْطة تَحَوُّلٍ **2** (divide) خَطّ تَقْسيمِ المِياه **3** (drainage basin) مُسْتَجْمَع مائيّ

waterski /ˈwɔːtəskiː/ **A** *n* لَوْح التَزَحْلُقِ على الماءِ

B *vi* (**waterskis**, **waterskiing**, **waterskied**) «person» تَزَحْلَقَ على الماءِ

water-skiing /ˈwɔːtəskiːɪŋ/ *n* التَزَحْلُق \ التزَلُّج على الماءِ

water slide *n* زُحْلَيْقة مائيّة

water snake *n* ثُعْبان مائيّ

water sport *n* رِياضات مائية

water table *n* مُسْتَوى المِياهِ الجَوْفيّة

watertight /ˈwɔːtətʌɪt/ *adj* **1** ‹*compartment, seal*› مانِع \ مُضادّ للماءِ **2** ‹*case, excuse, argument*› دامِغ

water tower *n* بُرْج مِياهٍ

waterway /ˈwɔːtəweɪ/ *n* مَمَرّ مائيّ

waterwheel /ˈwɔːtəwiːl/ *n* ساقِية (سَواقٍ), ناعورة (نَواعيرُ)

water wings *n* عَوّامات الأَذْرُع

watery /ˈwɔːt(ə)ri/ *adj* **1** (like water) مائيّ **2** ‹*soup, coffee*› خَفيف **3** ‹*eyes*› دامِع

watt /wɒt/ *n* واط

wave /weɪv/ **A** *vt* **1** (gesturing) لَوَّحَ (ب), أشارَ (ب) ‹*one's hand, a flag, stick*›; **to ~ goodbye to sb** لَوَّحَ لِشَخْصٍ مُوَدِّعاً; **the protesters were waving placards** كانَ المُحْتَجّونَ يُلَوِّحونَ بِلافِتاتٍ; **to ~ one's arms in the air** لَوَّحَ بِيَدَيْهِ في الهَواءِ **2** (to direct) وَجَّهَ; **he ~d us on/away** أشارَ لَنا بالمُضيِّ \ بالابْتِعادِ **3** (at a hairdresser's) **to have one's hair ~d** مَوَّجَ شَعْرَهُ **B** *vi* **1** (with one's hand) لَوَّحَ; **he ~d when he saw me** لَوَّحَ بِيَدِهِ عِنْدَما رَآني; **to ~ to *or* at sb** لَوَّحَ بِيَدِهِ لِشَخْصٍ; **she ~d to me to come in** أشارَتْ إِلَيَّ بالدُخولِ **2** (to move gently) «flags» رَفْرَفَ (i; رَفْرَفة); «branches» تَمايَلَ **C** *n* **1** (hand gesture) تَلْويح باليَدِ; **she gave the crowd a ~ as she passed** لَوَّحَتْ للجُمْهورِ عِنْدَما مَرَّتْ; **with a ~ of his hand** بِتَلْويحةٍ من يَدِهِ **2** (of the sea) مَوْج (n coll; أَمْواج) **3** (of attacks, anger) مَوْج (n coll; أَمْواج); **the pain came in ~s** جاءَ الأَلَمُ بِشَكْلٍ مُتَتابِعٍ **4** (in hair) تَمَوُّج (تَمَوُّجات) **5** (Phys) مَوْجة; **low-/high-frequency radio ~s** مَوْجات الراديُو ذات التَرَدُّدِ المُنْخَفِضِ \ العالي

Idiom **to make waves** (to cause a stir) أَحْدَثَ ضَجّةً; (to cause trouble) سَبَّبَ مَشاكِلَ

Phrasal verbs **wave down**: **~ down [sth], ~ [sth] down** أشارَ لِ [شَيْءٍ] بالتَوَقُّفِ ‹*a taxi, car, driver*›

• **wave off**: **~ [sb] off, ~ off [sb]** وَدَّعَ [شَخْصاً] ‹*a friend, passenger*›

waveband /ˈweɪvband/ *n* حُزْمة مَوْجيّة

wave farm *n* مَزْرَعة مَوْجيّة

wavelength /ˈweɪvlɛŋθ/ *n* (of radio transmission) طول مَوْجةٍ

Idiom **to be on the same/a different wavelength** يَتَّفِقونَ \ يَخْتَلِفونَ في أُسْلوبِ التَفْكيرِ

wave power *n* طاقة الأَمْواجِ (لِتَوْليدِ الكَهْرَباءِ)

waver /ˈweɪvə/ *vi* **1** (to falter) «faith, confidence» ضَعُفَ (u; ضَعْف, ضُعْف), تَداعى **2** (in tone) «voice» اضْطَرَبَ **3** (to be indecisive) «person» تَرَدَّدَ

wavy /ˈweɪvi/ *adj* (**wavier**, **waviest**) ‹*hair, line*› مُتَمَوِّج

wax /waks/ **A** *n* **1** (for candles) شَمْع (شُموع) **2** (in the ear) صِمْلاخ (صَماليخ) **B** *vt* **1** شَمَّعَ ‹*a floor, car*› **2** أَزالَ الشَعْرَ من (بالشَمْعِ) ‹*one's legs, chest*› **C** *vi* «moon» ازْدادَ; **his popularity ~ed and waned** شَعْبِيَّتُهُ سادَتْ ثُمَّ بادَتْ

waxed jacket /wakst ˈdʒakɪt/ *n* جاكيت مُشَمَّع

waxed paper /ˌwakst ˈpeɪpə/ *n* وَرَق مُشَمَّع

waxworks /ˈwakswəːks/ *n* (*pl* **waxworks**) مَتْحَف الشَمْعِ

waxy /ˈwaksi/ *adj* (**waxier**, **waxiest**) ‹*texture, substance*› شَمْعيّ

way /weɪ/ **A** *n* **1** (route, road) طَريق (mf; طُرُقات, طُرُق), سَبيل (mf; سُبُل); **the ~ in/out** الطَريق إلى الداخِلِ \ الخارِجِ; **the quickest ~ to town** أَسْرَع طَريقٍ إلى البَلْدةِ; **can you tell me the ~ to the museum?** هل يُمْكِنُكَ أنْ تَدُلَّني على الطَريقِ إلى المَتْحَفِ; **to find one's ~** وَجَدَ طَريقَهُ; **to go the long/short ~** أَخَذَ الطَريقَ الطَويلَ \ القَصيرَ; **I phoned on the ~ back** هاتَفْتُ في طَريقِ العَوْدةِ; **she hit her head on the ~ down** أُصيبَتْ في رَأْسِها وَهِيَ في طَريقِها إلى الأَسْفَلِ; **it's the only ~ out of this situation** هو السَبيلُ الوَحيدُ للخُروجِ من هذا المَوْقِفِ; **I'm on my ~** أنا قادِمٌ; **we stopped on the ~ here** تَوَقَّفْنا للاسْتِراحةِ في الطَريقِ إلى هُنا; **it's not on my ~** هو لَيْسَ في طَريقي; **I must be on my ~** يَجِبُ أنْ أَذْهَبَ الآنَ; **to be on the ~ to victory/disaster** كانَ في طَريقِهِ إلى النَصْرِ \ كارِثةٍ; **an improved version is on the ~** هُناكَ نُسْخةٌ مُحَسَّنةٌ في الطَريقِ; **to go out of one's ~ to do sth** كَلَّفَ نَفْسَهُ بِفِعْلِ شَيْءٍ; **Polston is rather out of the ~** بولْسْتون في مِنْطَقةٍ مُنْعَزِلةٍ; **to go one's own ~** سَلَكَ طَريقَهُ الخاصَّ; **they decided to go their separate ~s** قَرَّرا أنْ يَذْهَبَ كُلٌّ في طَريقِهِ \ إلى حالِ سَبيلِهِ; **to make one's own ~ there/home** اسْتَدَلَّ على الطَريقِ بِنَفْسِهِ إلى هُناكَ \ البَيْتِ; **I'm with you all the ~** أنا مَعَكَ على طولِ الطَريقِ **2** (direction) اتِّجاه (اتِّجاهات); **which ~ did he go?** في أَيِّ اتِّجاهٍ ذَهَبَ؟; **he went that ~** ذَهَبَ في ذلك الاتِّجاهِ; **this ~!** هذا الاتِّجاه \ الطَريق!; **the wrong/right ~ around** بالشَكْلِ المَقْلوبِ \ الصَحيحِ; **if you're ever down our ~** إنْ حَدَثَ وَجِئْتَ إلى مَنْطِقَتِنا **3** (side) جانِب (جَوانِبُ); **'this ~ up'** 'هذا الجانِبُ لِأَعْلى'; **the other ~ up** في وَضْعٍ مَعْكوسٍ; **turn the pieces the right ~ up** أَدِرِ القِطَعَ إلى أَعْلى **4** (expressing obstruction) **to be in sb's ~** اعْتَرَضَ طَريقَ شَخْصٍ; **to be**

in the ~ أَعاقَ الطَرِيقَ; **she won't let anything get in the ~ of her plans** لا تَدَعُ شَيْئاً يَقِفُ في طَرِيقِ خُطَطِها; **to get out of the ~** أَفْسَحَ الطَرِيقَ; **get out of my ~!** ابْتَعِدْ عن طَرِيقي!; **to keep out of the ~** ابْتَعَدَ عن الطَرِيقِ; **to keep/stay out of sb's ~** تَجَنَّبَ شَخْصاً; **to make ~ for sth/sb** أَفْسَحَ المَجالَ لِشَيْءٍ \ لِشَخْصٍ **5** (in time) فَتْرة (فَتَرات); **to be a long ~ off** لا يَزالُ بَعيداً; **to be a short ~ off** اقْتَرَبَ; **my birthday is still some ~ off** لا يَزالُ عيدُ ميلادي بَعيداً بَعْضَ الشَيْءِ; **we still have a long ~ to go** لا يَزالُ الطَرِيقُ أَمامَنا طَوِيلاً **6** (method) طَرِيقة (طَرائِق, طُرُق), أُسْلوب (أَساليبُ); **do it this ~** افْعَلْها بِهَذِهِ الطَرِيقةِ; **let me explain it another ~** دَعْني أَشْرَحُهُ بِطَرِيقةٍ أُخرى; **she doesn't see it that ~** لا تَنْظُرُ إلَيْهِ من هذه الزاوِيةِ; **in the same ~** بِنَفْسِ الطَرِيقةِ; **to my ~ of thinking** من وُجْهةِ نَظَري; **that's the ~!** تِلْكَ هي الطَرِيقةُ الصَحِيحةُ!; **I like the ~ he dresses** تُعْجِبُني طَرِيقةُ لِبْسِهِ; **either ~, she's wrong** كَيْفَما نَظَرْتَ إلى المَوْضوعِ، هي مُخْطِئةٌ; **one ~ and another it's been an eventful day** بِشَكْلٍ أو بِآخَرٍ كانَ اليَوْمُ مَليئاً بالأَحْداثِ; **no two ~s about it** بِدونِ شَكٍّ; **no ~!** (infml) مُسْتَحيل! **7** (respect, aspect) **in a ~ he's right** هو على حَقٍّ من ناحِيةٍ; **in one ~ it's sad** من ناحِيةٍ الأَمْرُ مُحْزِنٌ; **can I help in any ~?** هل بِإمْكاني أنْ أُساعِدَ بِأَيِّ شَكْلٍ؟; **in some ~s they're wrong** هُمْ مُخْطِئونَ من بَعْضِ الجَوانِبِ **8** (custom) طَرِيقة, أُسْلوب (أَساليبُ), (طَرائِق, طُرُق); **~ of life** أُسْلوب حَياةٍ; **that's the modern ~** تِلْكَ هي الطَرِيقةُ العَصْرِيّةُ; **I know all her little ~s** أَعْرِفُ كُلَّ شَيْءٍ عَنْهُ; **it's the ~ of the world** هكذا هي الدُنْيا **9** (talent) **to have a ~ with words** امْتَلَكَ مَوْهِبةَ التَعْبيرِ; **to have a ~ with children/animals** يَعْرِفُ كَيْفِيّةَ التَعامُلِ مع الأَطْفالِ \ الحَيَواناتِ **10** (will, wish) **to get/have one's own ~** فَعَلَ \ حَصَلَ على ما يُريدُ; **if I had my ~ ...** لو خُيِّرْتُ ...; **have it your own ~!** (infml) افْعَلْ ما يَحْلو لَكَ!

B *adv* (infml) **~ back in April/1926** منذ فَتْرةٍ طَوِيلةٍ في شَهْرِ نيسانَ \ في عامِ 1926; **he's ~ ahead of/behind the rest** هو مُتَقَدِّمٌ \ مُتَخَلِّفٌ كَثيراً عن البَقِيّةِ; **the film went ~ over budget** كَلَّفَ الفيلْمُ أَكْثَرَ من ميزانِيَّتِهِ بِكَثيرٍ

C (**by the way**) *adv phr* بالمُناسَبةِ

D (**in the way of**) *prep phr* من حَيْثُ; **there's not much in the ~ of news** لَيْسَ هُناكَ الكَثيرُ من الأَخْبارِ; **what have you got in the ~ of food?** ماذا عِنْدَكَ من الطَعامِ؟

waylay /weɪˈleɪ/ *vt* (*past tense, past participle* **waylaid**) اعْتَرَضَ السَبيلَ ‹*a passer-by, convoy*›

waymark /ˈweɪmɑːk/ *n* مَعْلَم (مَعالِمُ)

way-out /weɪˈaʊt/ *adj* (infml) ‹*clothes, party*› طَليعيّ, غَيْر تَقْليديٍّ

ways and means *n* السُبُل والوَسائِل, الطُرُق والأَساليب

wayside /ˈweɪsʌɪd/ *n* جانِب طَرِيقٍ

Idiom **to fall by the wayside** فَشِلَ (a; فَشَل)

wayward /ˈweɪwəd/ *adj* ‹*child, husband*› عاصٍ (عُصاة)

we /wiː, wi/ *pron* نَحْنُ; **~ left at six** غادَرْنا في السادِسةِ; **~ Scots like the sun** نَحْنُ الاسْكُتْلَنْدِيّونَ نُحِبُّ الشَمْسَ; **~ four have agreed that ...** نَحْنُ الأَرْبَعةُ اتَّفَقْنا على أنّ ...; **~ all make mistakes** كُلُّنا نُخْطِئُ

weak /wiːk/ *adj* **1** (physically) ‹*wrist, muscle, person*› ضَعيف (ضَعَفة, ضِعاف, ضُعَفاءُ) **2** (in health) ‹*eyesight, health, nerves*› ضَعيف (ضَعَفة, ضِعاف, ضُعَفاءُ); **to become/grow ~(er)** أَصْبَحَ ضَعيفاً; **to have a ~ heart** كانَ قَلْبُهُ ضَعيفاً; **to be ~ with** *or* **from hunger** أَصْبَحَ ضَعيفاً بِسَبَبِ الجوعِ **3** (not powerful) ‹*army, government, lens*› ضَعيف (ضَعَفة, ضِعاف, ضُعَفاءُ); **the royal family had grown too ~** كانَت العائِلةُ المالِكةُ قد أَصْبَحَتْ ضَعيفةً جِدًّا; **~ leadership was the party's ruin** كانَت القِيادةُ الضَعيفةُ سَبَبَ دَمارِ الحِزْبِ **4** (unconvincing) ‹*plot, evidence*› ضَعيف (ضَعَفة, ضِعاف, ضُعَفاءُ) **5** (of poor ability) ضَعيف (ضَعَفة, ضِعاف, ضُعَفاءُ); **he's ~ in** *or* **at physics, his physics is ~** هو ضَعيفٌ في الفيزْياءِ; **what are her ~ points?** ما هي نِقاطُ ضَعْفِها؟ **6** ‹*beam, bridge*› ضَعيف **7** (dilute) ‹*acid, tea, solution*› خَفيف; **the ~ rays of the setting sun** خُيوط الشَمْسِ الضَعيفة وَهيَ تَغْرُبُ **8** (in value) ‹*market, demand, currency*› ضَعيف **9** (in English: regular) ‹*form, verb*› قِياسيّ; (in Arabic: having a weak radical) ‹*verb*› مُعْتَلّ

weaken /ˈwiːk(ə)n/ **A** *vt* **1** (to damage) أَضْعَفَ, أَوْهَنَ ‹*a structure, part*› **2** (to undermine) أَضْعَفَ ‹*a government, sb's authority*› **3** (to dilute) خَفَّفَ ‹*a solution, concentration*›

B *vi* **1** (physically) «one's grip, muscles» ضَعُفَ (u; ضُعْف, ضَعْف) **2** (morally) «one's position, resolve» ضَعُفَ (u; ضُعْف, ضَعْف) **3** (in value) «economies, currencies» هَبَطَ (i-u; هُبوط)

weakling /'wi:klɪŋ/ *n* ضَعيف (ضُعَفاءُ, ضِعاف, ضَعَفَة), خَرِع

weakly /'wi:kli/ *adv* **1** (without vigour) ‹*to move, struggle*› بِضَعْفٍ **2** (feebly) ‹*to smile, protest*› بِوَهْنٍ

weakness /'wi:knəs/ *n* **1** [u] (of a person, muscle) ضَعْف **2** [u] (of drinks, solution) خِفَّة **3** (of evidence, argument) نُقْطة ضَعْفٍ **4** [u] (of currencies, economies) ضَعْف, هُبوط **5** (liking) وَلَع; **to have a ~ for cigars/chocolate** كانَ مولَعاً بالسيجاراتِ \ الشوكولاتةِ

weak-willed /wi:k'wɪld/ *adj* ‹*coward, young man*› ضَعيف الإرادةِ

weal /wi:l/ *n* عَلامة حَمْراء مُتَوَرِّمة على الجِلْدِ ناتِجة عن ضَرْبةٍ أو ضَغْطٍ)

wealth /wɛlθ/ *n* **1** (riches) ثَرْوة, غِنًى **2** (large amount) **a ~ of experience/information** ثَرْوة من التَجارِبِ \ المَعْلوماتِ

wealthy /'wɛlθi/ *adj* (**wealthier**, **wealthiest**) ‹*family, businessman*› غَنِيّ (أَغْنِياءُ), ثَرِيّ (أَثْرِياءُ)

wean /wi:n/ *vt* **1** فَطَمَ (i; فَطْم, فِطام) ‹*a baby, puppy*› **2** **to ~ sb off drugs/medication** خَلَّصَ شَخْصاً من إدْمانِ المُخَدِّراتِ \ الدَواءِ]

weapon /'wɛp(ə)n/ *n* سِلاح (أَسْلِحة)

weapon of mass destruction *n* سِلاح الدَمارِ الشامِلِ

weaponry /'wɛp(ə)nri/ *n* أَسْلِحة

wear /wɛ:/ **A** *vt* (*past tense* **wore**; *past participle* **worn**) **1** (to have on) لَبِسَ (a; لُبْس), ارْتَدى ‹*clothes, jewellery, glasses*›; وَضَعَ (a; وَضْع) ‹*make-up, perfume*›; **I haven't got a thing to ~** لَيْسَ لَدَيَّ أَيُّ شَيْءٍ أَرْتَديهِ; **she was ~ing blue** كانَتْ تَلْبَسُ مَلابِسَ زَرْقاءَ; **to ~ make-up** وَضَعَ الماكِياج **2** (normally) لَبِسَ (a; لُبْس), ارْتَدى ‹*glasses, jewellery*›; وَضَعَ (a; وَضْع) ‹*make-up*›; **to ~ one's hair long/short** كانَ شَعْرُهُ طَويلاً \ قَصيراً; **I can't ~ red** الأَحْمَرُ لا يُناسِبُني **3** (to display) بَدا عَلَيْهِ; **she wore a puzzled look** بَدَتْ عَلَيْها نَظْرةُ حيرةٍ **4** (through use) أَبْلى ‹*a carpet, the tread*›; **to ~ a hole in sth** أَحْدَثَ ثُقْباً في شَيْءٍ **5** (BrE) (infml) (to accept) قَبِلَ (a; قَبول, قُبول), سَمَحَ (a; سَماح ;ب); **he won't ~ that** لن يَقْبَلَ \ يَسْمَحَ بذلِكَ

B *vi* (*past tense* **wore**; *past participle* **worn**) **1** (to deteriorate) «garments, parts, carpets» بَلِيَ (a; بِلًى, بَلاء); **my patience is ~ing thin** بَدَأَ صَبْري يَنْفُذُ **2** (to last) **a fabric that ~s well** قُماش شَديد التَحَمُّلِ; **he's worn well** (infml) يَبْدو أَصْغَرَ من سِنِّهِ

C *n* **1** (clothing) مَلْبَس (مَلابِسُ); **casual/evening ~** مَلابِس كاجْوال \ مَسائيّة; **all employees must have appropriate protective ~** على كُلِّ المُوَظَّفينَ أنْ يَرْتَدوا مَلابِسَ واقِيةً **2** (use) اسْتِخْدام; **for everyday ~** للاسْتِخْدامِ اليَوْميِّ مُناسِبةً; **I've had three years' ~ out of these boots** بَقِيَ هذا الحِذاءُ مَعي لِثَلاثِ سَنَواتٍ; **there's still some ~ left in these tyres** ما زالَ من المُمْكِنِ اسْتِخْدامُ هذه الإطاراتِ **3** (damage) بِلًى; **normal ~ and tear** بِلًى عاديّ

(Phrasal verbs) **wear away** **A** «inscription, paint» تآكَلَ **B** **~ away [sth], ~ [sth] away** مَحا [شَيْئاً] ‹*an inscription, paint*›; أَبْلى [شَيْئاً] ‹*the rock, steps*›; **the steps gradually get worn away** تَبْلى دَرَجاتُ السُلَّمِ شَيْئاً فَشَيْئاً

• **wear down** **A** «heels, steps, tread» تآكَلَ **B** **~ down [sth], ~ [sth] down** **1** (to erode) أَبْلى [شَيْئاً] ‹*the stone, pencil, heels*›; **to be worn down** كانَ مُتآكِلاً **2** (to weaken) أَضْعَفَ [شَيْئاً] ‹*sb's defences, the opposition*› **C** **~ [sb] down** أَنْهَكَ [شَخْصاً] ‹*an opponent, the enemy*›

• **wear off** **A** **1** «effect, anaesthetic» فَقَدَ مَفْعولَهُ; **the novelty/shock has worn off now** ذَهَبَ أَثَرُ الحَداثةِ \ الصَدْمةِ الآنَ **2** «paint, coating» بَلِيَ (a; بِلًى, بَلاء), ذَهَبَ (a; ذَهاب, مَذْهَب) **B** **~ [sth] off, ~ off [sth]** مَحا [شَيْئاً] ‹*the paint, varnish*›

• **wear on** «day, evening» مَضى, تَقَدَّمَ (i; مُضِيّ)

• **wear out** **A** «tyres, shoes, clothes» بَلِيَ (a; بِلًى, بَلاء); **my patience is ~ing out** بَدَأَ صَبْري يَنْفُذُ **B** **1** **~ out [sth], ~ [sth] out** اسْتَهْلَكَ [شَيْئاً] ‹*the tyres, one's shoes, clothes*› **2** **~ [sb] out** أَنْهَكَ [شَخْصاً]

• **wear through** «soles, fabric» أَصْبَحَ بِهِ ثُقوبٌ

wearily /'wɪ(ə)rəli/ *adv* ‹*to explain, walk*› بِتَعَبٍ

weariness /'wɪərinəs/ *n* تَعَب (أَتْعاب), إِعْياء

wearing /'wɛ:rɪŋ/ *adj* ‹*job, situation*› مُرْهِق, مُتْعِب, مُجْهِد

weary /ˈwɪəri/ **A** *adj* (**wearier**, **weariest**) **1** (physically) ‹*traveller, legs*› تَعْبان, تَعِب (dipt) **2** (jaded) ‹*sigh, voice*› سَئِم, ضَجِر; **to grow ~ of a job/situation** سَئِمَ من عَمَلٍ \ حالةٍ ضَجِرَ **B** *vi* (**wearies**, **wearying**, **wearied**) سَئِمَ (a; سَأْم), ضَجِرَ (a; ضَجَر ,من ب); **to weary of sb/sth** \ ضَجِرَ من شَخْصٍ شَيْءٍ

weasel /ˈwiːz(ə)l/ *n* ابْن عِرْسٍ

weather /ˈwɛðə/ **A** *n* طَقْس, جَوّ (جِواء ,أَجْواء); **what's the ~ like?** كيف حالُ الطَقْسِ؟; **the ~ here is hot** الجَوُّ هُنا حارٌّ; **in bad/cold ~** في جَوٍّ سَيِّءٍ \ بارِدٍ; **you can't go out in this ~!** لا يُمْكِنُكَ الخُروجُ في هذا الجَوِّ!; **when the ~'s good** عِنْدَما يَكونُ الجَوُّ جَيِّداً; **~ permitting** إذا سَمَحَ الطَقْسُ; **in all ~s** (BrE) في جَميعِ الظُروفِ الجَوِّيّةِ; **whatever the ~** مَهْما كانَتْ حالةُ الجَوِّ **B** *vt* **1** صَمَدَ أمام, قاوَمَ ‹*a storm, the winter*› **2** صَمَدَ أمام ‹*a crisis, recession*›; **to ~ the storm** صَمَدَ في وَجْهِ العاصِفةِ **3** (to erode) تَسَبَّبَ في التَآكُلِ ‹*rock, stone*› **C** *vi* «rock, stone» تَآكَلَ **D** (**weathered**) *adj* ‹*rock, stone*› مُتآكِل

(Idiom) **to be/feel under the weather** (infml) شَعَرَ أَنَّهُ لَيْسَ على ما يُرامُ

weather-beaten /ˈwɛðəbiːt(ə)n/ *adj* ‹*face*› أَسْفَع (dipt; سُفْع); ‹*rocks*› مُتآكِل

weather chart *n* خَريطة الطَقْسِ

weathercock /ˈwɛðəkɒk/ *n* دَوّارة الرِياحِ

weather forecast *n* (weather predictions) تَنَبُّؤات جَوِّيّة; (on radio, TV) نَشْرة جَوِّيّة

weather forecaster *n* مُذيع النَشْرةِ الجَوِّيّةِ

weathergirl /ˈwɛðəɡəːl/ *n* مُذيعة النَشْرةِ الجَوِّيّةِ

weatherman /ˈwɛðəman/ *n* (*pl* **-men**) مُذيع النَشْرةِ الجَوِّيّةِ

weatherproof /ˈwɛðəpruːf/ *adj* **1** ‹*coat, shoes*› ضِدّ الماءِ **2** ‹*paint, shelter*› [صامِد في وَجْهِ الأَحْوالِ الجَوِّيّةِ]

weathervane /ˈwɛðəveɪn/ *n* دَوّارة الرِياحِ

weave /wiːv/ **A** *vt* (*past tense* **wove** or **weaved**; *past participle* **woven** or **weaved**) **1** نَسَجَ (i-u; نَسْج) ‹*cloth, thread, a basket*› **2** صَنَعَ (a; صِناعة) ‹*a garland*› **3** نَسَجَ (i-u; نَسْج), حاكَ (u; حِياكة) ‹*a story, plot*›; **she ~d a fascinating tale** نَسَجَتْ قِصّةً رائِعةً **4** (to twist and turn) **to ~ one's way through sth** شَقَّ طَرِيقَهُ من خِلالِ شَيْءٍ **B** *vi* (*past tense* **wove** or **weaved**; *past participle* **woven** or **weaved**) **1** (to make cloth) «weavers» نَسَجَ (i-u; نَسْج), حاكَ (u; حِياكة) **2** (to twist and turn) «drivers, dancers» تَمايَلَ; **to ~ in and out** ساقَ \ قادَ بِشَكْلٍ مُتَعَرِّجٍ; **she was weaving through the traffic** كانَتْ تَقودُ بِشَكْلٍ مُتَعَرِّجٍ وَسْطَ السَيّاراتِ **C** *n* حِياكة, نَسْج **D** (**woven**) *adj* ‹*fabric, basket*› مَنْسوج

weaver /ˈwiːvə/ *n* حائِك, نَسّاج (حاكة)

weaving /ˈwiːvɪŋ/ *n* نَسْج, حِياكة

web /wɛb/ *n* **1** نَسيج \ بَيْت العَنْكَبوتِ; **to be caught in a ~ of lies** كانَ واقِعاً في شَبَكةٍ من الأَكاذيبِ **2** (also **the World Wide Web**) شَبَكة الإِنْتَرْنت

webbing /ˈwɛbɪŋ/ *n* شَريط \ حِزام التَنْجيدِ

webcam® /ˈwɛbkam/ *n* ويب كام, كاميرا الويب \ الإِنْتَرْنِت

web designer *n* مُصَمِّم مَواقِعِ إِنْتَرْنت

webinar /ˈwɛbɪnɑː/ *n* ويبينار (حَلْقة دِراسيّة عَبْرَ الإِنْتَرْنت)

weblog /ˈwɛblɒɡ/ *n* مُدَوَّنة

webmail /ˈwɛbmeɪl/ *n* بَريد الويب

webmaster /ˈwɛbmɑːstə/ *n* مُدير مَوْقِعِ الويب

web page *n* صَفْحة الويب

web search *n* بَحْث على الويب

website /ˈwɛbsʌɪt/ *n* مَوْقِع الويب

webspace /ˈwɛbspeɪs/ *n* حَيِّز الويب (مِساحة تَخْزينيّة على خادِمِ إِنْتَرْنت)

wed /wɛd/ **A** *n* **the newly ~s** المُتَزَوِّجانِ حَديثاً **B** *vt* (*present participle* **-dd-**; *past tense, past participle* **wed** or **wedded**) (fml) تَزَوَّجَ ‹*one's fiancée, sweetheart*›

we'd /wiːd/ *abbr* = **we would**, = **we had**

wedding /ˈwɛdɪŋ/ *n* زِفاف, زَواج, عُرْس (أَعْراس); **to have a church/civil ~** كانَ زِفافُهُما في الكَنيسةِ \ مَدَنِيًّا

wedding anniversary *n* عيد \ ذِكْرى الزَواجِ

wedding day *n* يَوْم الزِفافِ

wedding dress, **wedding gown** *n* فُسْتان زِفافٍ

wedding reception *n* حَفْلة زِفافٍ \ زَواجٍ

wedding ring *n* خاتَم الزَواجِ

wedge /wɛdʒ/ **A** *n* **1** (for doors) إِسْفين (أَسافينُ); **a ~ of cheese** قِطْعة مُثَلَّثة من الجُبْنِ; **a ~ of lemon** شَريحة من اللَيْمونِ **2** (shoe) [حِذاء نِسائيّ ذو كَعْبٍ عالٍ عَريضٍ]

B *vt* (to make firm) **to ~ sth in** *or* **into place** حَشَرَ \ دَسَّ شَيْئاً في مَكانِهِ; **to ~ a door open/shut** حَشَرَ شَيْئاً في البابِ لِإِبْقائِهِ مَفْتوحاً \ مُغْلَقاً; **I was ~d between a fat man and his fat wife** كُنْتُ مَحْشوراً بين رَجُلٍ سَمينٍ وَزَوْجَتِهِ السَمينةِ

(Idiom) **the thin edge of the wedge** بِداية المَتاعِبِ

Wednesday /ˈwɛnzdeɪ, ˈwɛnzdi/ *n* (يَوْم) الأَرْبعاءِ; **on ~** في يَوْمِ الأَرْبِعاءِ; **next/last ~** الأَرْبِعاء القادِمِ \ الماضي; **it's ~ today** اليَوْمُ هو يَوْمُ الأَرْبعاءِ; **~ morning/afternoon** الأَرْبِعاء صَباحاً \ عَصْراً; **the ~ after next** يَوْم الأَرْبِعاءِ الَّذي يَلي الأَرْبِعاءَ القادِمَ

wee /wiː/ **A** *n* (BrE infml) **to have a ~** تَبَوَّلَ

B *adj* (BrE infml) ‹*boy, drink*› صَغير (صِغار, صُغَراءُ)

C *vi* (BrE infml) تَبَوَّلَ

weed /wiːd/ **A** *n* **1** (wild plant) عُشْب ضارّ **2** (infml) (marijuana) قِنَّب (هِنْديّ)

B *vt* أَزالَ الأَعْشابَ الضارّةَ من ‹*a garden, border*›

(Phrasal verb) **weed out: ~ [sb/sth] out, ~ out [sb/sth]** تَخَلَّصَ من [شَخْصٍ \ شَيْءٍ] ‹*corruption, terrorists*›

weedkiller /ˈwiːdkɪlə/ *n* مُبيد الأَعْشابِ

weedy /ˈwiːdi/ *adj* (**weedier**, **weediest**) (infml) ‹*boy, teenager*› هَزيل (هَزْلى), نَحيل (نَحْلى)

week /wiːk/ *n* أُسْبوع (أَسابيعُ); **what day of the ~ is it?** أَيُّ يَوْمٍ من أَيّامِ الأُسْبوعِ هذا؟; **last/next ~** الأُسْبوعَ الماضي \ القادِمِ; **it's this ~** هو في هذا الأُسْبوعِ; **the ~ before last** الأُسْبوع قبل الماضي; **every ~** كُلَّ أُسْبوعٍ; **every other ~** مَرّةً كُلَّ أُسْبوعَيْنِ; **twice a ~** مَرَّتَيْنِ في الأُسْبوعِ; **to work a forty-hour ~** عَمِلَ أَرْبَعينَ ساعةً في الأُسْبوعِ; **in three ~s' time** في غُضونِ ثَلاثةِ أَسابيعَ; **a ~'s rent** إِيجار أُسْبوعٍ; **to pay by the ~** دَفَعَ أُسْبوعيًّا

weekday /ˈwiːkdeɪ/ *n* يَوْم عَمَلٍ; **on ~s/on a ~** في أَيّامِ العَمَلِ \ يَوْمٍ من أَيّامِ العَمَلِ

weekend /wiːkˈɛnd/ *n* عُطْلة نِهايةِ الأُسْبوعِ; **at** (BrE) *or* **on** (AmE) **the ~** في عُطْلَةِ نِهايةِ الأُسْبوعِ

weekly /ˈwiːkli/ **A** *adj* **1** ‹*trip, service*› أُسْبوعيّ; **on a ~ basis** على أَساسٍ أُسْبوعيٍّ **2** ‹*wage, rate*› أُسْبوعيّ

B *adv* ‹*to pay, meet*› أُسْبوعيًّا, كُلَّ أُسْبوعٍ

C *n* (*pl* **weeklies**) (newspaper, magazine) مَجَلّة \ جَريدة أُسْبوعيّة

weep /wiːp/ *vi* (*past tense, past participle* **wept**) **1** (to cry) بَكى (i; بُكاء), ناحَ (u; نَوْح, نُواح) **2** (to ooze) «blisters, wounds» نَزَّ (i; نَزّ, نَزيز)

weeping willow /ˌwiːpɪŋ ˈwɪləʊ/ *n* صَفْصاف مُسْتَحٍ \ بابِليّ

weepy /ˈwiːpi/ *adj* (**weepier**, **weepiest**) ‹*mood*› سَريع \ بَكّاء; ‹*film*› مُحْزِن, كَثير البُكاءِ

weevil /ˈwiːvɪl/ *n* سوس (n coll; سيسان)

weigh /weɪ/ **A** *vt* **1** وَزَنَ (i; وَزْن, زِنة) ‹*the flour, packet, baby*›; **to ~ 10 kilos** كانَ وَزْنُهُ 10 كيلوغرامات; **how much do you ~?** كم وَزْنُكَ؟ **2** (to consider) «person» دَرَسَ, قَيَّمَ (u; دَرْس) ‹*the advantages, evidence, options*›; **to ~ the evidence, for and against** دَرَسَ الدَليلَ، ما لَهُ وَما عَلَيْهِ **3** (Naut) **to ~ anchor** «ship» رَفَعَ المِرْساةَ; **the ship had already ~ed anchor** كانَتْ السَفينةُ قد رَفَعَتِ المِرْساةَ

B *vi* (fml) **1** (to have influence) **to ~ with sb** «evidence, argument» أَثَّرَ على شَخْصٍ; **this argument will ~ heavily/ very little with him** سَيَكونُ لِهَذِهِ الحُجّةِ ثِقْلاً كَبيراً \ ضَئيلاً **2** (be a burden) **to ~ on sb** أَثْقَلَ كاهِلَ شَخْصٍ عَلَيْهِ; **the responsibility ~s heavily on her** أَثْقَلَتِ المَسْؤوليّةُ كاهِلَها

C *v refl* **to ~ oneself** وَزَنَ نَفْسَهُ

(Phrasal verbs) **weigh down: ~ down [sth/sb], ~ [sth/sb] down** «luggage, load» أَثْقَلَ كاهِلَ [شَخْصٍ \ شَيْءٍ] ‹*the mule, vehicle, tree*›; **the branches/trees were ~ed down with the snow** كانَ الثَلْجُ حِمْلاً ثَقيلاً على الأَغْصانِ \ الأَشْجارِ; **to be ~ed down by debt/responsibilities** أَثْقَلَتِ الدُيونُ \ المَسْؤوليّاتُ كاهِلَهُ

• **weigh in** **1** «boxer, jockey» سَجَّلَ وَزْنَهُ; **to ~ in at 70 kg** سَجَّلَ في فِئةِ 70 كغ **2** (to intervene) ساهَمَ, شارَكَ

• **weigh out** «cook» وَزَنَ (i; وَزْن, زِنة) ‹*a kilo, the ingredients*›

• **weigh up: ~ up [sth/sb], ~ [sth/sb] up** قَيَّمَ [شَيْئاً \ شَخْصاً] ‹*the options, prospects, situation*›

weighing machine /ˈweɪɪŋ məʃiːn/ *n* ميزان (مَوازينُ)

weight /weɪt/ **A** *n* **1** (heaviness) وَزْن (أَوْزان), ثِقْل (أَثْقال); **to lose/put on ~** نَقَصَ \ زادَ وَزْنُهُ; **to be under/over 1 kilo in ~** كانَ وَزْنُهُ أَقَلَّ \ أَكْثَر من 1 كيلو; **what is your ~?** ما وَزْنُكَ؟; **they're the same ~** هُمْ في نَفْسِ الوَزْنِ **2** (in systems of measurement) وَزْن (أَوْزان) **3** (for scales) عِيار (عِيارات); **a 100 gram ~** عِيار وَزْنُهُ 100 غرام **4** (for lifting) ثِقْل (أَثْقال) **5** (influence) تَأْثير; **to carry a lot of/little ~ with sb** كانَ لَهُ قُدْرةٌ كَبيرةٌ \ مَحْدودةٌ على التَّأثيرِ على شَخْصٍ; **to give** *or* **lend ~ to sth** أَعْطى \ أَعارَ وَزْناً لِشَخْصٍ; **to throw one's ~ behind a proposal** أَلْقى بِثِقْلِهِ خلف مُقْتَرَحٍ; **don't attach too much ~ to what he says: he's no expert** لا تُعْطِ وَزْناً زائداً لِما يَقولُ فَهُوَ لَيْسَ خبيراً

B *vt* **1** (to make heavy) «angler, person» ثَقَّلَ, أَثْقَلَ ‹*a net, hem*›; **if you don't ~ the curtain, it won't hang properly** إذا لم تُثْقِلِ السِتارة، فَلَنْ تَنْسَدِلَ بِشَكْلٍ جَيِّدٍ **2** (to bias) **to ~ the evidence/statistics against/in favour of sb** اسْتَعْمَلَ الدَّليلَ \ الإحْصاءاتِ ضِدَّ \ في صالِحِ شَخْصٍ; **everything seemed ~ed against them** بَدا كُلُّ شَيْءٍ ضِدَّهُمْ **3** (in statistics) «person» وَزَنَ, رَجَّحَ (اسْتَخْرَجَ الوَزْنَ المُرَجَّحَ) ‹*an index, the figures*›

Idioms **to pull one's weight** أَدّى ما عَلَيْهِ; **to throw one's weight about** *or* **around** تَسَلَّطَ

Phrasal verb **weight down**: **~ down [sth], ~ [sth] down** أَثْقَلَ [شَيْئاً] ‹*the sack, body*›

weightless /ˈweɪtləs/ *adj* ‹*state, body*› عَديم الوَزْنِ

weightlessness /ˈweɪtlɪsnəs/ *n* انْعِدام الوَزْنِ

weightlifter /ˈweɪtlɪftə/ *n* رافِع أَثْقالٍ

weightlifting /ˈweɪtlɪftɪŋ/ *n* رَفْع الأَثْقالِ

weight training *n* التَّدْريب على رَفْعِ الأَثْقالِ

weighty /ˈweɪti/ *adj* (**weightier, weightiest**) **1** (heavy) ‹*cargo, book*› ثَقيل (ثِقال) **2** (serious) ‹*issue, argument*› ذو أَهَمِّيَّةٍ \ تَأْثيرٍ

weir /wɪə/ *n* هَدّار (سَدّ صَغير)

weird /wɪəd/ *adj* ‹*feeling, creature*› غَريب (غُرَباءُ), عَجيب

welcome /ˈwɛlkəm/ **A** *n* **1** (greeting) تَرْحيب (تَرْحيبات); **to give sb a warm/cool ~** رَحَّبَ بِشَخْصٍ تَرْحيباً حارًا \ فاتِرًا **2** (to proposals, announcements, etc) تَرْحيب (تَرْحيبات)

B *excl* **~!** مَرْحَباً!; **~ home!** مَرْحَباً بِكَ في بَيْتِكَ!

C *vt* **1** (to greet) رَحَّبَ (ب) ‹*a visitor, new member*›; **please ~ our guest tonight, Willie Mays!** رَحِّبوا مَعي بِضَيْفِنا اللَّيْلَةَ، ويلي مايْز! **2** (to receive) رَحَّبَ (ب) ‹*the news, opportunity, decision*›; **we ~ your feedback on this matter** نُرَحِّبُ بِآرائِكُمْ حول هذه القَضيّةِ

D *adj* **1** (gladly received) ‹*guest, visitor*› مُرَحَّب بِهِ; **admission is free and all are ~** الدُخولُ مَجّانيٌّ والكُلُّ مُرَحَّبٌ بِهِ; **to make sb ~** جَعَلَ شَخْصاً يَشْعُرُ بِأَنَّهُ مَوْضِعُ تَرْحيبٍ **2** (pleasing) ‹*change, news*› مُرْضٍ, سارّ; **an open fire is a ~ sight on a cold night** النارُ المُشْتَعِلةُ هي مَنْظَرٌ سارٌّ في لَيْلَةٍ بارِدةٍ **3** (freely permitted) مُرَحَّب بِهِ; **you are ~ to join us** مَرْحَباً بِكَ إذا أَرَدْتَ الانْضِمامَ إِلَيْنا **4** (acknowledging thanks) **you're ~** على الرَحْبِ والسَعةِ

Idioms **to welcome sb/sth with open arms** رَحَّبَ بِشَخْصٍ \ بِشَيْءٍ بِحَفاوةٍ كَبيرةٍ; **to outstay** *or* **overstay one's welcome** أَطالَ في زِيارَتِهِ أَكْثَرَ من اللازِمِ

Phrasal verb **welcome back**: **~ back [sb], ~ [sb] back** رَحَّبَ بِعَوْدةِ [شَخْصٍ]

welcome drink *n* مَشْروب تَرْحيبيّ

welcome speech *n* كَلِمة تَرْحيبٍ

welcoming /ˈwɛlkəmɪŋ/ *adj* ‹*atmosphere, place*› مُرَحِّب

welcoming ceremony *n* حَفْل \ مَراسِم تَرْحيبٍ

welcoming committee *n* لَجْنة تَرْحيبٍ

weld /wɛld/ *vt* لَحَمَ (u; لَحْم) ‹*a plate, the metal*›

welder /ˈwɛldə/ *n* لَحّام, عامِل لِحامٍ

welfare /ˈwɛlfɛː/ *n* **1** (well-being) رَفاهِية, خَيْر **2** (state assistance) مُساعَدة اجْتِماعيّة

welfare state *n* دَوْلة رِعايةٍ اجْتِماعيّةٍ

welfare worker *n* [مُوَظَّف في قِطاعِ الرِعايةِ الاجْتِماعيّةِ]

well[1] /wɛl/ **A** *adv* (*comparative* **better**; *superlative* **best**) **1** (to a high standard) ‹*to play, live*› حَسَناً; **to do ~ at school** نَجَحَ في المَدْرَسةِ; **the operation went ~** نَجَحَتِ العَمَليّةُ; **~ done!** حَسَناً!, أَحْسَنْتَ! **2** (thoroughly) ‹*to clean, mix*› جَيِّداً; **shake ~ before serving** خُضَّ جَيِّداً قبل التَّقْديمِ; **it was ~ worth waiting for** كانَ يَسْتَحِقُّ الانْتِظارَ فِعْلاً **3** (expressing probability) **you may ~ be right** قَدْ تَكونُ على حَقٍّ

B *adj* (*comparative* **better**; *superlative* **best**) **1▸** (in good health) بِخَيْرٍ; **I don't feel ~** لا أَشْعُرُ بِخَيْرٍ; **I hope you are all ~** أَتَمَنّى أَنْ تَكونوا جَميعاً بِخَيْرٍ; **get ~ soon** أَتَمَنّى لَكَ الشِفاءَ العاجِلَ **2▸** (satisfactory) **all is ~** كُلُّ شَيْءٍ على ما يُرامُ \ بِخَيْرٍ \ صَحيحاً \ كَما يَنْبَغي; (introducing negative statement) **that's all very ~, but ...** هذا كُلُّهُ كَلامٌ جَميلٌ، وَلَكِنْ ... **3▸** (convenient) **to be (just) as ~** كانَ مُناسِباً; **we may as ~ go home** فَلْنَذْهَبْ إلى البَيْتِ

C *excl* **1▸** (continuing a conversation) والآنَ, حَسَناً; **~ then, what's the problem?** والآنَ، ما المُشْكِلةُ؟ **2▸** (expressing surprise, anger) حَسَناً; **~, ~, fancy seeing you here!** ها أَنْتَ هُنا، إِنَّهُ لَأَمْرٌ غَريبٌ!; **~, you could have told me!** حَسَناً، كانَ بِإمْكانِكَ أَنْ تُخْبِرَني!

D (**as well**) *phr* (too, also) أَيْضاً; **I saw it as ~** رَأَيْتُهُ أَيْضاً

E (**as well as**) *phr* (in addition to) بالإضافةِ إلى, فَضْلاً عن; **we need money as ~ as food** نَحْتاجُ إلى المالِ بالإضافةِ إلى الطَعام

well² /wɛl/ *n* بِئْر (f; آبار); **to drill a ~** حَفَرَ بِئْراً

Phrasal verb **well up** «tears, water» نَبَعَ (a-i-u; نَبْع)

we'll /wiːl/ *abbr* = **we shall**, = **we will**

well-balanced /wɛl'balənst/ *adj* **1▸** (in personality) ‹personality, child› رَزين, (رِزان), مُتَّزِن **2▸** (in food intake) ‹diet, meal› مُتوازِن

well-behaved /wɛlbɪ'heɪvd/ *adj* ‹child, dog› حَسَن السُلوك

well-being /wɛl'biːɪŋ/ *n* رَفاهِية

well-defined /wɛldɪ'fʌɪnd/ *adj* ‹objective, boundary› واضِح المَعالِم, مُحَدَّد بِدِقّةٍ \ تَحْديداً جَيِّداً

well-deserved /wɛldɪ'zəːvd/ *adj* ‹reputation, holiday› مُسْتَحَقّ عن جَدارة

well disposed *adj* **to be well disposed towards** تَعاطَفَ (مع) ‹person, regime, idea›

well-done /wɛl'dʌn/ *adj* (Culin) ‹steak, meat› مَطْهوّ جَيِّداً

well-dressed /wɛl'drɛst/ *adj* ‹lady, businessman› حَسَن الهِنْدامِ, مُهَنْدَم, مُتأَنِّق

well-educated /wɛl'ɛdʒʊkeɪtɪd/ *adj* ‹child, family› مُثَقَّف, مُتَعَلِّم

well-founded /wɛl'faʊndɪd/ *adj* ‹fear, suspicion› مُحِقّ, راسِخ الأَساسِ

well-groomed /wɛl'gruːmd/ *adj* ‹gentleman, hair› مُهَنْدَم, أَنيق, حَسَن المَظْهَرِ

well-heeled /wɛl'hiːld/ *adj* ‹client, tourist› غَنيّ (أَغْنِياء), ثَرِيّ (أَثْرِياء)

well-informed /wɛlɪn'fɔːmd/ *adj* ‹consumer› واسِع المَعْرِفةِ; ‹decision› مَدْروس

wellington /'wɛlɪŋt(ə)n/, **wellington boot** /ˌwɛlɪŋt(ə)n 'buːt/ *n* (BrE) جَزْمة مَطّاطِيّة

Wellington /'wɛlɪŋt(ə)n/ *pr n* ويلينْغْتون (عاصِمة نِيوزِيلَنْدا)

well-kept /wɛl'kɛpt/ *adj* ‹garden, village› مُرَتَّب

well-known /wɛl'nəʊn/ *adj* ‹actor, fact› مَعْروف, مَشْهور (مَشاهير)

well-liked /wɛl'lʌɪkt/ *adj* ‹student, politician› مَحْبوب

well-made /wɛl'meɪd/ *adj* ‹film, car› جَيِّد الصُنْعِ

well-mannered /wɛl'manəd/ *adj* ‹gentleman, child› مُهَذَّب, مُؤَدَّب

well-meaning /wɛl'miːnɪŋ/ *adj* ‹people, attempt› طَيِّب \ حَسَن \ سَليم النِيّةِ

well-off /wɛl'ɒf/ **A** *n* (**the well-off** *n pl*) الأَغْنِياء, الأَثْرِياء

B *adj* ‹family, businessman› مَيْسور الحال, غَنيّ (أَغْنِياء), ثَرِيّ (أَثْرِياءُ)

well-read /wɛl'rɛd/ *adj* ‹historian, student› مُطَّلِع

well-respected /wɛlrɪ'spɛktɪd/ *adj* ‹historian, newspaper› مُحْتَرَم

well-rounded /wɛl'raʊndɪd/ *adj* ‹education› مُنَوَّع; ‹personality› مَصْقول

well thought out *adj* ‹plan, tactics› مَدْروس, مَوْزون

well-timed /wɛl'tʌɪmd/ *adj* ‹pass, intervention, tackle› حَسَن التَوْقيتِ

well-to-do /wɛltə'duː/ *adj* ‹family, suburb› ثَرِيّ (أَثْرِياءُ), غَنيّ (أَغْنِياءُ), موسِر

well trained /wɛl 'treɪnd/ *adj* مُدَرَّب بِشَكْلٍ جَيِّد

well-wisher /'wɛlwɪʃə/ *n* مُهَنِّئ

well-worn /wɛl'wɔːn/ *adj* ‹*carpet, jacket*› بالٍ

Welsh /wɛlʃ/ **A** *adj* ‹*history, custom*› ويلْزيّ

B *n* **1** (citizens) (**the Welsh**) سُكّان ويلز **2** (language) (اللُغة) الويلْزيّة

Welshman /'wɛlʃmən/ *n* (*pl* **-men**) ويلْزيّ

welt /wɛlt/ *n* (انْتِبارات) انْتِبار

welterweight /'wɛltəweɪt/ *n* وَزْن الويلْتر (مُلاكِم وَزْنُهُ ما بين 63,5–67 كغ)

went /wɛnt/ *past tense* ▸ **go**

wept /wɛpt/ *past tense, past participle* ▸ **weep**

were /wɜː, wə/ *past tense* ▸ **be**

we're /wɪə/ *abbr* = **we are**

weren't /wɜːnt/ *abbr* = **were not** ▸ **be**

west /wɛst/ **A** *n* **1** (compass direction) غَرْب **2** (**the West**) (part of the world, a country) الغَرْب

B *adj* ‹*side, wind*› غَرْبيّ

C *adv* ‹*to face, move*› غَرْباً

Idiom **to go west** (BrE) ضاعَ (i; ضَياع)، تَدَمَّرَ

West Bank *pr n* (**the West Bank**) الضِفّة الغَرْبيّة

westbound /'wɛstbaʊnd/ *adj* ‹*lane, train*› مُتَّجِه غَرْباً

West End *pr n* (**the West End**) الوسْت إنْد (الجُزْء الغَرْبيّ من وَسَطِ لُنْدُن ويَضُمُّ أهَمَّ مَناطِقِ التَسَوُّق والتَرْفيه)

westerly /'wɛst(ə)li/ **A** *adj* ‹*direction, wind*› غَرْبيّ

B *n* (*pl* **westerlies**) ريح غَرْبيّة

western /'wɛst(ə)n/ **A** *adj* **1** ‹*coast, region*› غَرْبيّ; **the ~ Atlantic** غَرْب المُحيطِ الأَطْلَسيّ **2** (also **Western**) ‹*philosophy, culture*› غَرْبيّ

B *n* فيلْم رُعاة البَقَر

westerner /'wɛst(ə)nə/ *n* غَرْبيّ

westernize, -ise (BrE) /'wɛst(ə)nʌɪz/ *vt* غَرَّبَ ‹*a country, society*›; **to become ~d** تَغَرَّبَ، اسْتَغْرَبَ

west-facing /'wɛstfeɪsɪŋ/ *adj* ‹*window, balcony, room*› مُوَجَّه نحو الغَرْبِ

West Indian *n, adj* كاريبيّ

West Indies *pr n pl* (**the West Indies**) جُزُر الهِنْدِ الغَرْبيّةِ

Westminster Abbey /ˌwestmɪnstər 'abi/ *n* كَنيسة ويسْتْمِنِسْتَر أبي

West Virginia *pr n* فِرْجينيا الغَرْبيّة

West Virginian /wɛst və'dʒɪnɪən/ *pr n, adj* [(شَخْص) من فِرجينيا الغَرْبية]

westward /'wɛstwəd/ **A** *adj* ‹*expansion, journey*› مُتَّجِه غَرْباً

B *adv* (also **westwards**) ‹*to travel, move*› غَرْباً

wet /wɛt/ **A** *adj* (**-tt-**) **1** (damp) ‹*clothes, hair, grass*› مُبَلَّل; **to get ~** تَبَلَّلَ; **to get one's feet ~** تَبَلَّلَتْ قَدَماهُ; **to be ~ through** «clothes, person» كانَ مُبَلَّلاً تَماماً; **her face was ~ with tears** تَبَلَّلَ وَجْهُها بالدُموعِ **2** (rainy) ‹*weather, day, conditions*› مُمْطِر، مَطير; **it was too ~ to go out** كانَ الجَوُّ مُمْطِراً جِدًّا لِدَرَجةِ أَنَّنا لم نَسْتَطِع الخُروجَ; **it's been the ~test summer on record** لم يَسْبِقْ أَنْ هَطَلَ هذا الكَمُّ من الأَمْطارِ في صَيْفٍ من قَبْلُ **3** (freshly applied) ‹*cement, plaster*› طَرِيّ، غَيْر جافٍّ; **'~ paint'** 'احْذَر الدِهانَ'; **the ink is still ~** لم يَجِفَّ الحِبْرُ بَعْدُ **4** (BrE) (infml) (feeble) ضَعيف (ضُعَفاءُ، ضِعاف، ضَعَفة; f pl ضَعائِفُ); **don't be so ~!** لا تَكُنْ ضَعيفاً هكذا!

B *vt* (*present participle* **-tt-**; *past tense, past participle* **wet** or **wetted**) **1** (with liquid) بَلَّلَ ‹*one's lips, hair, feet*› **2** (with urine) **to ~ one's pants/the bed** بَلَّلَ سِرْوالَهُ \ الفِراشَ

C *v refl* (*present participle* **-tt-**; *past tense, past participle* **wet** or **wetted**) **to ~ oneself** تَبَوَّلَ على نَفْسه

D *n* [u] (dampness) بَلَل، رُطوبة; **don't leave your bike out in the ~** لا تَتْرُكْ دَرّاجَتَكَ تحت المَطَرِ

wet blanket *n* (infml) مُفْسِد لِلمُتْعة

wetland /'wɛtlənd/ *n* مِنْطَقة رَطِبة، مُسْتَنْقَع (مُسْتَنْقَعات)

wet-look /'wɛtlʊk/ *adj* ‹*boots, skirt*› ذو مَظْهَرٍ رَطْبٍ \ لامِع

wetsuit /'wɛtsuːt/ *n* بَدْلة الغَوّاصينَ

we've /wiːv/ *abbr* = **we have**

whack /wak/ **A** *vt* ضَرَبَ (i; ضَرْب)، صَفَعَ (a; صَفْع)، لَطَمَ (i; لَطْم) ‹*a ball, an opponent*›

B *n* ضَرْبة (ضَرَبات)، صَفْعة، لَطْمة (لَطَمات)

C *excl* [دَويّ ضَرْبةٍ]

whacked /wakt/ *adj* (infml) **to be/feel ~** كانَ مُرْهَقاً \ مُنْهَكاً

whale /weɪl/ *n* (Zool) حوت (حيتان)

Idiom **to have a whale of a time** (infml) قضى وَقْتاً مُمْتِعاً

whaler /ˈweɪlə/ *n* (ship) سَفينة صَيْدِ الحيتانِ

whaling /ˈweɪlɪŋ/ *n* صَيْد الحيتانِ

wharf /wɔːf/ *n* (*pl* **wharves**) رَصيف الميناءِ \ السُفُنِ

what /wɒt/ **A** *pron* **1** (interrogative) (before noun) ما; (before verb) ماذا; **~ is happening?, ~'s happening?** ماذا يَحْدُثُ؟; **~'s wrong?, ~'s the matter?** ما الخَطْبُ؟; **~'s your email address?** ما عُنْوانُ بَريدِكَ الإلِكْتْرونيِّ؟; **~'s this called in Russian?, ~'s the Russian for this?** ماذا يُسَمّى هذا في اللُغَةِ الروسيّةِ؟; **~ are you doing?** ماذا تَفْعَلُ ؟; **~ do you do? — I'm an engineer** ماذا تَعْمَلُ ؟ — أنا مُهَنْدِسٌ; **~ did it cost?** كم كانَ ثَمَنُهُ؟; **~'s that button for?** ما الغَرَضُ من هذا الزِرِّ؟; **'I'm going shopping'—'~ for?'** 'أنا ذاهِبٌ للتَسَوُّقِ' — 'لِتَشْتَريَ ماذا؟' **2** (expressing surprise) **'It will cost $500' - 'What?'** 'سَتُكَلِّفُ 500 دولارٍ' — 'ماذا؟'; **'He asked her to marry him' - 'He did ~?'** 'طَلَبَ مِنْها الزواجَ' — 'طَلَبَ مِنْها ماذا؟'; **and ~ it must have cost!** لا بُدَّ أنّهُ كَلَّفَ كَثيراً! **3** (in rhetorical questions) **~ can we do?** ماذا بِوُسْعِنا أنْ نَفْعَلَ ؟; **~'s the use?** ما الفائِدةُ؟; **~ does he care?** وَهَلْ يُهِمُّهُ شَيْءٌ؟ **4** (whatever) **do ~ you want** افْعَلْ ما تُريدُ; **he always does ~ he wants** يَفْعَلُ دائِماً ما يُريدُ **5** (in indirect speech) (before noun) ما; (before verb) ماذا; **I wonder ~'s happening** أتساءَلُ ماذا يَحْدُثُ; **she's not ~ she was** لَيْسَتْ كَما كانَتْ; **this is ~ is called a 'helix'** هذا هو ما يُسَمّى 'اللَوْلَبُ'; **she asked me ~ I wanted** سَأَلَتْني ماذا أُريدُ; **do you know ~ that is?** هل تَعْرِفُ ما هذا؟; **~ I need is ...** ما أَحْتاجُ إِلَيْهِ هو ...; **he was holding ~ looked like a briefcase** كانَ يَحْمِلُ ما يُشْبِهُ الحَقيبةَ **6** (inviting repetition) **~?, ~ did you say?** ماذا قُلْتَ ؟; **George ~?** جورْج ماذا؟

B *determiner* **1** (which) ما, أيّ; **~ time is it?** كم الساعةُ؟; **~ blogs do you follow?** ما المُدَوَّناتُ الّتي تُتابِعُها؟; **do you know ~ flight he took?** هل تَعْلَمُ أيَّ رِحْلةٍ سافَرَ فيها؟ **2** (in exclamations) يا لَهُ من; **~ a lovely apartment!** يا لَها من شَقّةٍ جَميلةٍ!; **~ a strange thing to do!** يا لَهُ من تَصَرُّفٍ غَريبٍ! **~ awful weather/luck!** يا لَهُ من طَقْسٍ فَظيعٍ \ حَظٍّ تَعيسٍ! **3** (fml) (all of the) **~ little she has, she gives away** تَتَبَرَّعُ بِما لَدَيْها، **~ belongings she had, she left to her niece** مَهْما كانَ قَليلاً; **~ few hotels there were, were full** تَرَكَتْ لِابْنَةِ أَخيها كُلَّ ما كانَ لَدَيْها من مُمْتَلَكاتٍ; كانَتْ كُلُّ الفَنادِقِ القَليلةِ هُناكَ مُمْتَلِئةً

C (**what about**) *phr* **1** (in highlighting) **~ about the email he sent?** وَماذا عن الرِسالةِ الإلِكْتْرونيّةِ الّتي أَرْسَلَها؟; **~ about Jack?** وَماذا عن جاك؟; **~ about the children?** وَماذا عن الأَطْفالِ؟ **2** (in suggestions) **~ about a roast?** ما رَأْيُكَ في شِواءٍ؟; **~ about Tuesday?** ما قَوْلُكَ في يَوْمِ الثُلاثاءِ؟ **3** (in reply) **'~ about your Jack?'—'~ about him?'** 'ماذا عن حَبيبِكِ جاك؟' — 'ماذا عَنْهُ؟'; **'What about your sister?' - 'What about her?'** 'ماذا عن أُخْتِكَ؟' — 'ماذا عَنْها؟'

D (**what if**) *phr* **~ if he doesn't come?** ماذا لو لم يَأْتِ؟; **~ if I bring the food?** ما رَأْيُكَ لو أَحْضَرْتُ الطَعامَ؟

E (**what of**) *phr* **~ of Mr Littlewood?** ماذا حَدَثَ للسَيِّدِ ليتيلوود؟; **~ of it !** (infml) وَماذا إذَنْ؟

F (**what with**) *phr* **~ with one thing and another** بين هذا وَذاكَ; **~ with the my cold and his back** بين إصابَتي بالبَرْدِ وَإصابَتِهِ بِأَلَمٍ في الظَهْرِ

G *excl* ماذا; **~! you can't be serious!** ماذا! لا بُدَّ أنّكَ تَمْزَحُ!; **~! I don't believe it!** ماذا! لا أُصَدِّقُ هذا!

Idiom **and do you know what?** (infml) وَهَلْ تَعْلَمُ ماذا أَيْضاً؟

whatever /wɒtˈevə/ **A** *pron* **1** (that which) ما; **to do ~ is expedient/required** فَعَلَ ما هو مُناسِبٌ \ مَطْلوبٌ **2** (anything that) كُلّ ما; **do ~ you like** افْعَلْ كُلَّ ما تُريدُ; **~ he says goes** كُلُّ ما يَقولُهُ يُنَفَّذُ; **~ you say** (as you like) كَما تَشاءُ \ تُريدُ **3** (no matter what) مَهْما; **~ happens** مَهْما يَحْصُلْ **4** (what on earth) ماذا; **~ do you mean?** ما الّذي تَعْنيه؟ **5** (infml) (the like) ما شاكَلَ ذلك; **to the cinema or ~** إلى السينَما أو ما شاكَلَ ذلك **6** (infml) (expressing no preference) أيّاً كانَ; **I'll call you — ~** سَأَتّصِلُ بِكَ — لا يُهِمُّ; **what do you want to do? — ~** ماذا تُريدُ أنْ تَفْعَلَ؟ — لا فَرْقَ عِنْدي

B *determiner* **1** (any) **take ~ action is needed** اتَّخِذْ أيَّ إجْراءاتٍ لازِمةٍ **2** (no matter what) **~ the events/their arguments** مَهْما كانَت الأَحْداثُ \ حُجَجُهُمْ; **for ~ reason** لِسَبَبٍ ما

C *adv* (at all) **is there any possibility ~ that you can come?** هل هُناكَ أيُّ احْتِمالٍ، ولَوْ كانَ بَسيطاً، أنْ تأْتِيَ؟; **there's no evidence ~** لا يوجَدُ دَليلٌ إطْلاقاً \ البَتَّةَ

what's-her-name /ˈwɒtsəneɪm/ *n* (infml) [فُلانة]

what's-his-name /ˈwɒtsɪzneɪm/ *n* (infml) [فُلان]

whatsoever /wɒtsəʊˈɛvə/ **A** *adv* ▸ **whatever** C; **I have no doubt ~** لا شَكَّ لَدَيَّ إطْلاقاً; **'Is there any possibility you're mistaken?' - 'None ~'** 'هل هُناكَ أيُّ احْتِمالٍ أنْ تكونَ مُخْطِئاً؟' – 'أبَداً إطْلاقاً'

B *pron* (fml) ▸ **whatever** A

wheat /wiːt/ *n* حِنْطة, قَمْح

wheatgerm /ˈwiːtdʒəːm/ *n* بِذْرة الحِنْطةِ

wheatmeal /ˈwiːtmiːl/ *n* دقيق \ طَحين القَمْحِ

wheedle /ˈwiːd(ə)l/ *vt* **to ~ money/a secret out of sb** [نالَ مالاً \ سِرًّا من شَخْصٍ بالتَمَلُّقِ]

wheel /wiːl/ **A** *n* **1** (on vehicles, furniture, etc) دولاب, عَجَلة (دَواليبُ) **2** (in a vehicle, boat) عَجَلة قِيادةٍ, (مَقاوِدُ) مِقْوَد; **to be at** *or* **behind the ~** كانَ وراء المِقْوَدِ \ عَجَلةِ القِيادةِ **3** (in watches, mechanisms, etc) تُرْس, (تُروس, أتْراس)

B (**wheels**) *n pl* (infml) (car) سَيّارة; **have you got ~s?** هل عِنْدَكَ سَيّارةٌ؟

C *vt* **1** (by pushing) دَفَعَ \ جَرَّ (على عَجَلاتٍ) ‹*a bicycle, wheelbarrow*› **2** (on a conveyance) حَمَلَ على عَرَبةٍ ‹*a patient, baby, sack*›; **they ~ed me into the operating theatre** حَمَلوني على عَرَبةٍ إلى غُرْفةِ العَمَلِيّاتِ

D *vi* (also **wheel round**) **1** (to turn sharply) «cars, riders» اسْتَدارَ **2** (to circle) «birds» دارَ (u; دَوْر, دَوَران)

E (**-wheeled**) *in combination* **a four-/six-~ed vehicle** مَرْكَبة ذات أرْبعِ \ سِتِّ عَجَلاتٍ

(Idioms) **to wheel and deal** (infml) لَعِبَ على كُلِّ الحِبالِ [عَقَدَ صَفَقاتٍ كَثيرةً بِشَكْلٍ مُلْتَوٍ]; **to reinvent the wheel** أعادَ اخْتِراعَ العَجَلةِ

(Phrasal verb) **wheel out**: **~ [sth] out, ~ out [sth]** **1** (to bring out) دَفَعَ \ جَرَّ [شَيْئاً] ‹*a bicycle, trolley*› **2** (infml) (to bring forward) أنْتَجَ \ اسْتَخْدَمَ [شَيْئاً] ‹*an argument, excuse, statistics*›

wheelbarrow /ˈwiːlbarəʊ/ *n* عَرَبة اليَدِ

wheelchair /ˈwiːltʃɛː/ *n* كُرْسيّ مُتَحرِّك \ مُقْعَدين

wheel clamp *n* قِفْل عَجَلةٍ, مِشْبَك (للسَيّاراتِ المُخالِفةِ)

wheeler-dealer /wiːləˈdiːlə/ *n* (infml) كائِد, (مَكَرة) ماكِر

wheelie bin /ˈwiːlɪ bɪn/ *n* (BrE) [حاوِية قُمامةٍ بِعَجَلاتٍ]

wheeling and dealing /ˌwiːlɪŋ ən ˈdiːlɪŋ/ *n* (infml) كَيْد (كِياد), دَسيسة (دَسائِسُ)

wheeze /wiːz/ *vi* «asthma sufferer, elderly person» أزَّ صَدْرُهُ, لَهِثَ (a; لَهْث, لُهاث), نَهِجَ (a; نَهْج)

wheezy /ˈwiːzi/ *adj* (**wheezier, wheeziest**) ‹*voice, breathing*› لاهِث, مع أزيزٍ في الصَدْرِ

when /wɛn/ **A** *adv* **1** (in interrogatives) مَتى; **~ are you leaving?** مَتى سَتُغادِرُ؟; **~ is the parade?** مَتى العَرْضُ؟; **~ did he die?** مَتى ماتَ؟; **~ do you use ...?** مَتى تَسْتَخْدِمُ ...؟; **ask him ~ he sent the email** اسْألْهُ مَتى أرْسَلَ البَريدَ الإلِكْترونيَّ; **I wonder ~ they will arrive** أتَساءَلُ مَتى سَيَصِلونَ; **that was ~ I realized that ...** كانَ ذلك عِنْدَما أدْرَكْتُ أنَّ ...; **tell me** *or* **say ~** أخْبِرْني مَتى; **~ do you need to be at the airport?** مَتى يَجِبُ أنْ تَكونَ في المَطارِ؟; **since ~ have they owned the farm?** منذ مَتى وَهُمْ يَمْتَلِكونَ المَزْرَعةَ؟ **2** (as relative) **the year ~ we got married** العام الّذي تَزَوَّجْنا فيهِ; **it was the summer ~ we were away** كانَ هذا في الصَيْفِ الّذي كُنّا فيهِ في الخارِجِ **3** (whenever) عِنْدَما; **he's happiest ~ he's on the farm** يَكونُ في أسْعَدِ أحْوالِهِ عِنْدَما يَكونُ في المَزْرَعةِ; **~ possible avoid using Internet cafes** تَجَنَّبِ اسْتِخْدامَ مَقاهي الإنْتَرْنِت بِقَدْرِ الإمْكانِ

B *conj* **1** (at the time when) عِنْدَما; **I'll ask him ~ I see him** سَأسْألُهُ عِنْدَما أراهُ; **I was upstairs ~ the phone rang** كُنْتُ في الطابَقِ العُلْويِّ عِنْدَما رَنَّ الهاتِفُ **2** (if) إذا; **why buy their products ~ ours are cheaper?** لِماذا تَشْتَري بَضائِعَهُمْ إذا كانَتْ بَضائِعُنا أرْخَصَ؟; **our results look good ~ you compare them to theirs** تَبْدو نَتائِجُنا جَيِّدةً إذا قارَنْتَها بِنَتائِجِهِمْ **3** (although) بالرَغْمِ من أنَّ, مع أنَّ; **she went on the stage ~ she could have been a musician** اشْتَغَلَتْ بالتَمْثيلِ مع أنَّهُ كانَ بِإمْكانِها أنْ تَكونَ موسيقيّةً; **she said she was 18, ~ I know she's only 16** قالَتْ إنَّ عُمْرَها 18 سَنةً مع أنّي أعْلَمُ أنَّ عُمْرَها 16 سَنةً فَقَطْ

whenever /wɛnˈɛvə/ *adv* **1** (no matter when) **~ you want** في أيِّ وَقْتٍ تُريدُ \ تَشاءُ **2** (every time that) كُلَّما; **~ (it is) possible** كُلَّما أمْكَنَ ذلك **3** (expressing doubt) **she promised to return them soon, ~ that might be!** وَعَدَتْ أنْ تُعيدَها قريباً، وَلَكِنَّ اللهَ أعْلَمُ مَتى!

where /wɛː/ **A** *pron* **1** (indicating place) حَيْثُ; **this is ~ we live** هذا هو المَكانُ الّذي نَعيشُ فيهِ; **that's ~ he's mistaken** هُنا يَكْمُنُ خَطَؤُهُ **2** (with prepositions) حَيْثُ; **what can you see from ~ you are?** ماذا يُمْكِنُكَ أنْ تَرى من حَيْثُ أنْتَ؟

B *adv* **1** (in the interrogative) أيْنَ; **~ do you work?** أيْنَ تَعْمَلُ؟; **~'s the nearest bank?** أيْنَ أقْرَبُ بَنْكٍ؟; **~'re you from?** من أيْنَ أنْتَ؟; **~'re we going?** إلى أيْنَ نَحْنُ ذاهِبونَ؟ **2** (in indirect questions) أيْنَ; **ask him ~ he's going** اسْألْهُ إلى أيْنَ هو ذاهِبٌ; **find out ~ he's been** اكْتَشِفْ أيْنَ كانَ **3** (as a relative) حَيْثُ; **the village ~ we live** القَرْيةُ الّتي نَعيشُ فيها; **it's not ~ you said it was** هو لَيْسَ حَيْثُ قُلْتَ **4** (whenever) عِنْدَما; **~ necessary order more stock** أُطْلُبِ المَزيدَ من المَخْزونِ عند الضَرورة

C *conj* **they'll want to save money ~ they can** سَيُريدونَ تَوْفيرَ المالِ كُلَّما أمْكَنَهُمْ ذلك; **she's irrational ~ he's concerned** هي غَيْرُ مَنْطِقيّةٍ عِنْدَما يَتَعَلَّقُ الأمْرُ بِهِ

(Idiom) **to be where it's at** (infml) كانَ في مَرْكَزِ النَشاطِ والحَيَويّةِ; **New York is ~ it's at** نيويورْك هي مَرْكَزُ النَشاطِ والحَيَويّةِ

whereabouts **A** /wɛːrəˈbaʊts/ *adv* أيْنَ; **~ are you living now?** أيْنَ تَسْكُنُ الآنَ؟

B /ˈwɛːrəbaʊts/ *n pl* مَكان (أماكِنُ، أمْكِنة)

whereas /wɛːrˈaz/ *conj* بَيْنَما

whereby /wɛːˈbʌɪ/ *adv* (fml) وِفْقاً لَهُ

wherein /wɛːrˈɪn/ *adv* (fml) في ما

wherever /wɛːrˈɛvə/ *adv* **1** (anywhere) **I'll go ~ she goes** سَأذْهَبُ أيْنَما \ حَيْثُما تَذْهَبُ **2** (whenever) **~ possible** كُلَّما \ حَيْثُما كانَ مُمْكِناً

wherewithal /ˈwɛːwɪðɔːl/ *n* **to have the ~ to do sth** كانَ لَدَيْهِ المالُ الكافي لِفِعْلِ شَيْءٍ

whet /wɛt/ *vt* (-tt-) أثارَ <*sb's curiosity, interest*>; **the book ~ted his appetite for travel** أثارَ الكِتابُ شَهيّتَهُ للسَفَرِ

whether /ˈwɛðə/ *conj* **1** (with uncertainty) ما إذا; **I wonder ~ it's true** أتَساءَلُ ما إذا كانَ هذا صَحيحاً; **I wasn't sure ~ to answer or not, I wasn't sure ~ or not to answer** لم أكُنْ مُتَأكِّداً هل أُجيبُ أم لا; **she was worried about ~ to invite them** كانَتْ مُتَحَيِّرةً أتَدْعوهُمْ أم لا; **the question is ~ anyone is interested** السُؤالُ هو هل هُناكَ أيُّ شَخْصٍ مُهْتَمٌّ **2** (with certainties) **he's going to school ~ he likes it or not!** سَيَذْهَبُ إلى المَدْرَسةِ سَواءً أحَبَّ ذلك أم لا!; **everyone, ~ young or old, can celebrate** يُمْكِنُ للجَميعِ، سَواءٌ كانوا صِغاراً أم كِباراً، أنْ يَحْتَفِلوا; **~ you are in work or not, this tax will affect you** سَواءٌ كُنْتَ تَعْمَلُ أم لا، سَتُؤَثِّرُ عَلَيْكَ هذه الضَريبةُ; **~ or not people are happy is of little importance** لَيْسَ لِسَعادةِ الناسِ أو شَقائِهِمْ أهَمّيّةٌ كَبيرةٌ

whew /fjuː/ *excl* (in relief, fatigue) أُفّ

whey /weɪ/ *n* مَصْلُ الحَليبِ \ اللَبَنِ

which /wɪtʃ/ **A** *pron* **1** (also **which one**) **I don't mind ~ (one)** لا أُمانِعُ في أيٍّ مِنْهُمْ; **~ of the two do you prefer?** أيٌّ مِنْهُما تُفَضِّلُ؟; **~ is the fastest route?** أيُّ الطَريقَيْنِ \ الطُرُقِ أسْرَعُ؟; **~ of you got the answer right?** مَنْ مِنْكُمْ تَوَصَّلَ إلى الإجابةِ الصَحيحةِ؟; **~ of the groups ...?** أيُّ المَجْموعاتِ ...؟; **do you know ~ he chose?** هل تَعْلَمُ أيُّهُما \ أيُّهُم اخْتارَ؟; **can you tell ~ is ~?** هل يُمْكِنُكَ أنْ تُمَيِّزَ بَيْنَهُما؟ **2** الّذي (f التّي; m du اللّذانِ; f du اللّتانِ); **the mirror ~ hangs in the hall** المِرْآةُ المُعَلَّقةُ في القاعةِ; **the car in ~ he was travelling** السَيّارةُ الّتي كانَ يُسافِرُ فيها; **he says he supplied the data, ~ is untrue** يَقولُ إنّهُ قَدَّمَ البَياناتِ، وَهَذا غَيْرُ صَحيحٍ; **~ reminds me ...** وَهُوَ ما يُذَكِّرُني ...; **he's resigned, from ~ we can assume that ...** اسْتَقالَ، وَعَلَيْهِ يُمْكِنُ أنْ نَفْتَرِضَ أنَّ ...

B *determiner* **1** (in questions) أيّ; **~ award did he win?** أيُّ جائِزةٍ فازَ بِها؟; **~ DVDs do you mean?** أيُّ أقْراصِ دي في دي تَقْصِدُ؟; **he told me ~ jacket he'd like** أخْبَرَني أيُّ سُتْرةٍ يُريدُ; **she asked me ~ teams would leave first** سَألَتْني أيُّ الفِرَقِ سَتُغادِرُ أوَّلاً; **~ one of the children ...?** أيُّ واحِدٍ مِنَ الأطْفالِ ...؟ **2** (as a relative) **he arrived at 2.00 p.m., by ~ time ...** وَصَلَ الساعةَ 2:00 بعد الظُهْرِ، في الوَقْتِ الّذي ...; **you may wish to join, in ~ case ...** قد تَرْغَبُ في الانْضِمامِ، ...

وفي هذه الحالةِ ... ; **he left the room, during ~ time no one spoke** غادرَ الغُرْفةَ، وخِلالَ هذه الفَتْرةِ لم يَتكلَّمْ أَحَدٌ

whichever /wɪtʃˈɛvə/ **A** *determiner* **1** (the one that) **we'll buy ~ car is cheapest** سَوْفَ نَشْتَرِي السَيّارة الأَرْخَص **2** (no matter which) **it takes three hours, ~ road you take** يَسْتَغْرِقُ ثَلاثَ ساعاتٍ، سِواءٌ سَلَكْتَ هذا الطَرِيقَ أم ذاكَ

B *pron* **1** (the one that) أَيُّما; **2 or 2.30, ~ suits you best** الساعةَ الثانيةَ أو الثانيةِ والنِصْفِ، أَيُّهُما أَنْسَبُ لَكَ **2** (no matter which one) أَيُّما; **'do you want the big piece or the small piece?'—'~'** 'هل تُرِيدُ القِطْعةَ الكَبِيرةَ أَم الصَغِيرةَ ؟'—'أَيُّهُما'

whiff /wɪf/ *n* نَفْحة (نَفَحات)

while /wʌɪl/ **A** *n* مُدّة (مُدد), فَتْرة (فَتَرات); **we only stayed for a little ~** مَكَثْنا لِفَتْرةٍ قَصِيرةٍ فَقطْ; **a short ~ ago** قبل \ منذ فَتْرةٍ قَصِيرةٍ; **this could take a ~** يُمْكِنُ أَنْ يَسْتَغْرِق مُدّةً طَوِيلةً; **it's the best film I've seen in a long ~** هو أَفْضلُ فِيلم شاهَدْتُهُ منذ وَقْتٍ طَوِيلٍ; **once in a ~** مِن وَقْتٍ لِآخَرَ, مِن حِينٍ إِلى حِينٍ, بين الفَيْنةِ والأُخْرى

B *conj* **1** (during the time that) بَيْنَما; **she fell asleep ~ watching TV** غَفتْ أَثْناءَ مُشاهَدةِ التِلْفِزْيون; **could you get some milk ~ you're about it?** هل يُمْكِنُكَ أَنْ تَشْتَرِيَ حَلِيباً بَيْنَما تَتَسَوَّقُ؟ **2** (although) رَغْمَ أَنَّ, مع أَنَّ **3** (whereas) بَيْنَما

(Phrasal verb) **while away**: **~ away [sth]** قَتَلَ \ أَمْضى [شَيْئاً] ‹the hours, time›; **to ~ away the time we played cards** لَعِبْنا الوَرَقَ لِنَقْتُلَ الوَقْتَ

whilst /wʌɪlst/ *conj* ▸ **while**

whim /wɪm/ *n* نَزْوة (نَزَوات), بَدِيهة; **on a ~** على البَدِيهةِ

whimper /ˈwɪmpə/ **A** *vi* «dog, child» أَنَّ (i; أَنِين)

B *n* أَنِين

whimsical /ˈwɪmzɪk(ə)l/ *adj* **1** (fanciful) ‹style, tale› خَيالِيّ, وَهْمِيّ **2** (capricious) ‹person, nature› مُتَقَلِّب

whine /wʌɪn/ **A** *n* **1** (of a dog) عُواء; (of a person) أَنِين, تَأَوُّه, انْتِحاب **2** (of an engine) طَنِين

B *vi* **1** (to whimper) «dog» عَوى (i; عُواء); «child» انْتَحَبَ, تَأَوَّهَ **2** (to complain) تَذَمَّرَ

whinge /wɪndʒ/ *vi* (*present participle* **whingeing** or **whinging**) (BrE infml) «person» تَذَمَّرَ

whining /ˈwʌɪnɪŋ/ **A** *n* **1** (of a dog) عُواء **2** (complaints) تَذَمُّر (تَذَمُّرات)

B *adj* ‹noise› طَنّان; ‹voice, child› مُتَذَمِّر

whinny /ˈwɪni/ *vi* (**whinnies, whinnying, whinnied**) «horse» صَهَلَ (a-i; صَهِيل), حَمْحَمَ (i; حَمْحَمة)

whip /wɪp/ **A** *n* **1** (for punishment) سَوْط (أَسْواط, سِياط), كُرْباج (كَرابِيجُ) **2** (Pol) (party official) زَعِيم الأَقَلِّيّةِ **3** (dessert) مَخْفُوق

B *vt* (**-pp-**) **1** (to beat) ساطَ (u; سَوْط), جَلَدَ (i; جَلْد), ضَرَبَ بالسَوْطِ ‹a prisoner, a horse› **2** خَفَقَ (i-u; خَفْق, خَفَقان) ‹cream, egg whites› **3** (infml) (to remove) **he ~ped the key out of my hand/off the desk** خَطفَ المِفْتاحَ من يَدي \ من على الطاوِلةِ **4** (infml) (to defeat) «player» هَزَمَ (i; هَزْم) **5** (BrE) (infml) (to steal) اخْتَطَفَ ‹a bicycle, sb's wallet›

C *vi* (**-pp-**) **1** (back and forth) «branches, tails» تَمايَلَ **2** (infml) «person» تَحَرَّكَ بِسُرْعةٍ; **I'll ~ round and get it** سآتي بِسُرْعةٍ وَآخُذُهُ; **two taxis ~ped by** مَرَّتْ سَيّارَتا تاكْسي بِسُرْعةٍ

(Phrasal verbs) **whip away**: **~ away [sth], ~ [sth] away** أَزالَ [شَيْئاً] بِسُرْعةٍ ‹sb's plate, hat›

• **whip off**: **~ off [sth], ~ [sth] off** (infml) نَزَعَ [شَيْئاً] بِسُرْعةٍ ‹one's shirt, shoes›

• **whip out**: **~ out [sth], ~ [sth] out** (infml) أَخْرَجَ [شَيْئاً] بِسُرْعةٍ ‹a gun, knife, one's wallet›

• **whip through**: **~ through [sth]** (infml) انْتَهى من [شَيْءٍ] بِسُرْعةٍ ‹a task, book›

• **whip up**: **~ up [sth], ~ [sth] up** **1** (to incite) «speaker» حَرَّضَ على [شَيْءٍ] ‹hatred, fear, unrest›; **to ~ the crowd up into a frenzy** أَثارَ في الجُمْهورِ مَوْجةً من الحَماسِ **2** (infml) (to produce) حَضَّرَ [شَيْئاً] بِسُرْعةٍ ‹a snack, meal, report› **3** خَفَقَ [شَيْئاً] ‹the cream, eggs›

whiplash /ˈwɪplaʃ/ *n* إِصابة في الرَأْسِ

whip-round /ˈwɪp/ *n* (BrE infml) جَمْع تَبَرُّعاتٍ

whir, whirr /wəː/ *vi* طَنَّ (i; طَنِين), أَزَّ (i-u; أَزِيز)

whirl /wəːl/ **A** *vt* أَدارَ, دَوَّمَ ‹a sword, dance partner›

B *vi* **1** (to go around in circles) «dancer, leaves, dust» دارَ (u; دَوْر, دَوَران), دَوَّمَ **2** (to turn quickly) **to ~ around** اسْتَدارَ بِسُرْعةٍ

C *n* **1** (flurry) اضْطِراب, تَهَيُّج **2** (circular movement) تَدْويم, دَوَران

(Idiom) **to give sth a whirl** (infml) جَرَّبَ شَيْئاً

whirlpool /ˈwɜːlpuːl/ *n* دُرْدور, دَوّامة

whirlwind /ˈwɜːlwɪnd/ *n* زَوْبَعة (زَوابِعُ)

whirlwind romance *n* عَلاقة عاطِفيّة سَريعة

whisk /wɪsk/ **A** *vt* **1** (to beat) خَفَقَ (i-u; خَفْق, خَفَقان) ‹*the sauce, mixture, eggs*› **2** **to ~ a visitor/plate away** أَخَذَ زائِراً \ صَحْناً أُخِذَ بِسُرْعةٍ إلى; **he was ~ed off to the hospital** جانِباً بِسُرْعةٍ المُسْتَشْفى **3** (to flick) نَفَضَ (u; نَفْض) ‹*a crumb, fly*›

B *vi* (to move quickly) «vehicles, people» تَحَرَّكَ بِسُرْعةٍ; **a bicycle ~ed by** *or* **past** مَرَّتْ دَرّاجةٌ بِسُرْعةٍ

C *n* (also **egg whisk**) خَفّاقة بَيْضٍ

whisker /ˈwɪskə/ **A** *n* **1** (single hair) شَعْرة شارِبٍ **2** (infml) (small amount) شَعْرة

B (**whiskers**) *n pl* (of a man) سالِف (سَوالِفُ); (of a cat, rat etc.) شارِب (شَوارِبُ)

whisky /ˈwɪski/, **whiskey** (AmE) *n* (*pl* **whiskies**) ويسْكي

whisper /ˈwɪspə/ **A** *vt* همس (i; هَمْس, ب) ‹*words, a name*›

B *vi* **1** «voice, person» هَمَسَ (i; هَمْس), هَسَّ (i; هَسّ), وَشْوَشَ (i; وَشْوَشة) **2** (liter) «leaves» خَفَّ (i; خَفيف), خَشْخَشَ (i; خَشْخَشة); «wind» هَفَّ (i; هَفّ, هَفيف); «water» خَرَّ (i-u; خَرير)

C *n* **1** (soft voice) هَمْسة, هَسّ; **'let's go,' she said in a ~** 'دَعْنا نَذْهَبْ'، قالَتْ هامِسةً **2** (rumour) إشاعة

whistle /ˈwɪs(ə)l/ **A** *n* **1** (small instrument) صَفّارة; **the referee blew his ~ for a foul/to end the game** أَطْلَقَ الحَكَمُ صَفّارَتَهُ مُعْلِناً مُخالَفةً \ نِهاية المُباراةِ **2** (mechanism) صَفّارة **3** (through lips) تَصْفير **4** (screech) صَفير

B *vt* صَفَّرَ ‹*a tune*›

C *vi* **1** (with one's mouth) صَفَّرَ; **he ~s at all the girls** يُصَفِّرُ على كُلِّ البَناتِ **2** (with an instrument) «referees, traffic policeman» صَفَّرَ **3** (to make a noise) «train, wind, kettle» صَفَّرَ; **the train ~d as it approached the station** صَفَّرَ القِطارُ عِنْدَما اقْتَرَبَ من المَحَطّةِ **4** (to move fast) **to ~ past** *or* **by** «bullets, train» مَرَّ بِسُرْعةٍ

(Idiom) **to blow the whistle on sb/sth** بَلَّغَ عن شَخْصٍ \ شَيْءٍ

white /wʌɪt/ **A** *adj* **1** ‹*paint, shirt, hair*› أَبْيَض (dipt; بِيض); **to go** *or* **turn ~** ابْيَضَّ **2** (Caucasian) ‹*race, child, skin*› أَبْيَض (dipt; بِيض); (culturally) ‹*prejudice, fears*› مُتَعَلِّق بالشَخْصِ الأَبْيَضِ; **a ~ man/woman** رَجُل أَبْيَض \ امْرَأة بَيْضاء **3** (pale) ‹*face, cheeks*› شاحِب (شَواحِبُ); **her skin/she was very ~** كانَ لَوْنُها شاحِباً جِدّاً; **she went ~ when she saw him** أَصْبَحَ لَوْنُها شاحِباً عِنْدَما رَأَتْهُ **4** (BrE) (with milk) ‹*coffee*› بالحَليبِ

B *n* **1** (colour) أَبْيَض (dipt) **2** (of the eye) بَياض (العَيْنِ) **3** (of an egg) بَياض (البَيْضِ) **4** (also **White**) (Caucasian) أَبْيَض (dipt; بِيض) **5** (wine) نَبيذ أَبْيَض **6** (in chess, draughts) أَحْجار بَيْضاء

C (**whites**) *n pl* (clothes) **cricket/tennis/chef's ~s** ملابس لاعِبِ الكْريكِت \ لاعِبِ التِنِس \ الطاهي البَيْضاء

whitebait /ˈwʌɪtbeɪt/ *n* [صِغار الرَنْكةِ وما يُشْبِهُها من السَمَكِ]

whiteboard /ˈwʌɪtbɔːd/ *n* سَبّورة بَيْضاء

white coffee *n* (BrE) قَهْوة مع حَليب

white-collar /wʌɪtˈkɒlə/ *adj* ‹*employee*› [يُؤَدّي عَمَلاً كِتابيّاً]; ‹*job*› [غَيْر يَدَويٍّ]

white elephant *n* [شَيْء لا يُريدُهُ صاحِبُهُ]

white goods *n* أَجْهِزة رَئيسيّة (أَجْهِزة مَنْزِليّة كَبيرة)

white horses *n* [أَمْواج يُغَطّي الزَبَدُ قِمَمَها]

white-hot /ˌwʌɪtˈhɒt/ *adj* ‹*metal, poker*› [مُحَمًّى لِدَرَجةِ الابْيِضاضِ]

White House *n* (**the White House**) البَيْت الأَبْيَض

white-knuckle /ˈwʌɪtnʌk(ə)l/ *adj before n* ‹*ride, experience*› [مُنْتَهى الإثارةِ والخَوْفِ]

white lie *n* كِذْبة بَيْضاء

whiten /ˈwʌɪt(ə)n/ *vt* بَيَّضَ ‹*teeth, skin*›

whitener /ˈwʌɪtnə/ *n* **1** (for teeth, skin) مُبَيِّض **2** (for coffee, tea) حَليب القَهْوة

whiteness /ˈwʌɪtnəs/ *n* بَياض

white sauce *n* صَلْصة بَيْضاء

white spirit *n* كُحول \ سْبيرتو أَبْيَض

whitewash /ˈwʌɪtwɒʃ/ **A** *n* **1** (for walls) طِلاء الجير **2** (cover-up) إخْفاء الجَرائِم **B** *vt* ‹walls› بَيَّض (بِطِلاءِ الجير)

white water *n* أَنْهار صَعْبَة

white wedding *n* زَفاف أَبْيَض

whiting /ˈwʌɪtɪŋ/ *n* (*pl* **whiting**) غُبَر (أَغْبار)

Whitsun /ˈwɪts(ə)n/ *n* العَنْصَرة

Whit Sunday /wɪt ˈsʌndeɪ/ *n* عيد العَنْصَرةِ

whittle /ˈwɪt(ə)l/ *vt* برى (i; بَري), قَلَّم ‹a stick›; حَفَر (i; حَفْر) ‹wood›

(Phrasal verbs) **whittle away**: **~ away [sth]** خَفَّض [شَيْئاً] ‹sb's lead, advantage›; صَرَف [شَيْئاً] ‹funds, resources›; قَلَّل من [شَيْءٍ] ‹sb's rights, powers›

• **whittle down**: **~ down [sth], ~ [sth] down** قَلَّص [شَيْئاً] ‹a list, debt›; قَلَّص عَدَد [شَيْءٍ] ‹applicants›

whizz, **whiz** (AmE) /wɪz/ *vi* **to ~ by** *or* **past** «bullets, cars» مَرَّ [بِسُرْعةٍ]; **I ~ed through the book** قَرَأْتُ الكِتابَ بِسُرْعةٍ

whizz-kid, **whiz kid** (AmE) /ˈwɪzkɪd/ *n* (infml) عَبْقَريّ (عَباقِرة)

who /huː/ *pron* **1** (interrogative) مَنْ; **~ knows the answer?** مَنْ يَعْرِفُ الإجابةَ؟; **~'s going to be there?** مَنْ سَيَكونُ هُناكَ؟; **~ should I say is calling?** مَن المُتَّصِلُ؟; **~ do you think you are?** مَنْ تَظُنُّ نَفْسَكَ؟; **~ did you invite?** مَنْ دَعَوْتَ؟; **~ are you emailing?** إلى مَنْ تَكْتُبُ هذا البَريدَ الإلِكْترونيَّ؟; **~ was she with?** مع مَنْ كانَتْ؟; **~ did you buy it for?** لِمَنْ اشْتَرَيْتَهُ؟; **Adam ~?** آدَمُ مَنْ؟; **I don't know ~ you're referring to** لا أَعْلَمُ مَنْ تَقْصِدُ; **I was in the Post Office and ~ should I see but Diane** كُنْتُ في مَكْتَبِ البَريدِ وَكانت المُفاجَأةُ أنْ رَأَيْتُ دايان **2** (relative) الَّذي (الَّذينَ); f الَّتي; f pl اللاّتي, الَّواتي; m du اللَّذانِ; f du اللَّتانِ), مَنْ; **the boy ~ has the bike** الوَلَد الَّذي لَدَيْه الدَرّاجةُ; **the girl ~ lives opposite** البِنْت الَّتي تَعيشُ في الجِهةِ المُقابِلةِ; **is she the woman ~ wrote it?** هل هذه هي المَرْأةُ الَّتي كَتَبَتْهُ؟; **do you know ~ came?** هل تَعْلَمُ مَنْ أَتى؟; **there is plenty of food for those ~ need it** هُناكَ الكَثيرُ من الطَعامِ لأولائِكَ الَّذينَ يَحْتاجونَهُ; **those ~ are entitled to, should vote now** أولائِكَ الَّذينَ يَحِقُّ لَهُم التَصْويتُ، يَنْبَغي عَلَيْهِم أَنْ يُصَوِّتوا الآنَ **3** (whoever) **bring ~ you like** أَحْضِرْ مَنْ تُحِبُّ

WHO /dʌbljuːeɪtʃəʊ/ *n* = **World Health Organization** مُنَظَّمة الصِحّةِ العالَميّة

who'd /huːd/ *abbr* **1** = **who had** **2** = **who would**

whodunnit, **whodunit** /huːˈdʌnɪt/ *n* (infml) مَن القاتِلُ؟ (قِصّة بوليسيّة)

whoever /huːˈɛvə/ *pron* **1** (no matter who) **~ wins the election will have to deal with the problem** أَيًّا كانَ الفائِزُ في الانْتِخاباتِ سَيَتَعَيَّنُ عَلَيْهِ أنْ يَتَعامَلَ مع المُشْكِلةِ; **~ he is: send him away** كائِناً مَنْ كانَ، أُطْلُبْ مِنْهُ أنْ يُغادِرَ; **it makes no difference ~ it is** لَيْسَ هُناكَ فَرْقٌ أَيًّا كانَ الشَخْصُ **2** (anyone that) أَيّ شَخْصٍ, مَنْ; **I'll tell ~ I want** سَأُخْبِرُ مَنْ أُريدُ; **invite ~ you like** أُدْعُ مَنْ تُحِبُّ; **~ did this deserves to be put in prison** مَنْ فَعَلَ هذا يَسْتَحِقُّ أنْ يُسْجَنَ **3** (who on earth) مَنْ هذا الّذي; **~ said that to you?** مَنْ هذا الّذي قالَ لَكَ ذلك؟

whole /həʊl/ **A** *adj* **1** (entire) ‹week, day› كامِل, كُلّ; **we spent the ~ week at ...** قَضى كامِلَ الأُسْبوعِ في ...; **his ~ body was burned** كانَ كُلُّ جِسْمِهِ مُحْروقاً; **he spent his ~ life in Yemen** قَضى كُلَّ حَياتِهِ في اليَمَنِ **2** (for emphasis) **it's a ~ new way of thinking** إنَّها طَريقةُ تَفْكيرٍ جَديدةٌ بِشَكْلٍ كُلّيٍّ; **that's the ~ point!** ذلك هو بَيْتُ القَصيدِ!; **we waited for three ~ days** انْتَظَرْنا ثَلاثةَ أَيّامٍ كامِلةٍ; **we discussed a ~ range of issues** ناقَشْنا مَجْموعةً كامِلةً من المَواضيعِ **3** (intact) ‹glass, vase› سَليم; **not a plate was left ~** لم يَبْقَ طَبَقٌ سَليماً

B *n* **1** (entire unit) كُلّ; **consider the issue as a ~** أُنْظُرْ إلى المَوْضوعِ كَكُلٍّ; **for the country as a ~** للدَوْلةِ كَكُلٍّ **2** (all) **the ~ of sth** الكُلّ من شَيْءٍ; **the ~ of August** كُلّ شَهْرِ أَغُسْطُس; **the ~ of the city was affected** تَأَثَّرَتْ المَدينةُ كُلُّها

C *adv* ‹to swallow, eat› كامِلاً, كُلَّهُ; **he ate it ~** أَكَلَهُ كُلَّهُ

D (**on the whole**) *adv phr* على العُمومِ; **on the ~, I agree** على العُمومِ، أُوافِقُ

wholefood /ˈhəʊlfuːd/ *n* غِذاء كامِل

wholehearted /həʊlˈhɑːtɪd/ *adj* ‹support, approval› مُخْلِص, صادِق

wholeheartedly /həʊlˈhɑːtɪdli/ *adv* ‹*to agree, support*› من القَلْب ,بِصِدْقٍ ,بِإِخْلاصٍ

wholemeal /ˈhəʊlmiːl/ *adj* (BrE) ‹*bread, flour*› كامِل الحَبَّة

whole milk *n* حَليب كامِل الدَسَم

whole note *n* (AmE) مُسْتَديرة

wholesale /ˈhəʊlseɪl/ **A** *adv* **1** ‹*to sell, buy*› بالجُمْلة **2** (out of hand) ‹*to copy, adopt, to reject*› كُلِّيًّا

B *adj* **1** ‹*price, business*› بالجُمْلة **2** (large-scale) ‹*change, destruction*› على نِطاقٍ واسِعٍ

C *n* ▸ **wholesale trade**

wholesale price *n* سِعْر الجُمْلة

wholesaler /ˈhəʊlseɪlə/ *n* تاجِر الجُمْلة

wholesale trade *n* تِجارة الجُمْلة

wholesome /ˈhəʊls(ə)m/ *adj* **1** (healthy) ‹*food, meal*› صِحّيّ **2** (morally good) ‹*entertainment, image*› أَخْلاقيّ

wholewheat, **whole wheat** (AmE) /ˈhəʊlwiːt/ *adj before n* ‹*bread, flour*› كامِل الحَبّة

who'll /huːl/ *abbr* = **who will**

wholly /ˈhəʊlli/ *adv* ‹*different, inadequate*› تَماماً

whom /huːm/ *pron* (fml) **1** (interrogative) مَنْ; **~ did she meet?** مَنْ قابَلَتْ؟; **to ~ are you referring?** مَنْ تَقْصِدُ؟ **2** (relative) الَّذي ,الَّذينَ (f التي ;f pl اللاّتي ,الّواتي ;m du اللَّذانِ ;f du اللَّتانِ); **my cousin ~ I referred to previously** ابْن عَمّي الّذي أَشَرْتُ إِلَيْهِ سابِقاً; **the person to ~/of ~ I spoke** الشَخْص الّذي تَحَدَّثْتُ مَعَهُ \ عَنْهُ; **... four of ~ are soldiers** ... أَرْبَعةٌ مِنْهُمْ جُنودٌ; **Kirsten and Matthew, both of ~ had ridden before** كيرْسْتين وَماثيو، وَكِلاهُما قد رَكِبَ الخَيْلَ من قَبْلُ

whooping cough /ˈhuːpɪŋ ˌkɒf/ *n* سُعال ديكيّ

whoops /wʊps/ *excl* ≈ يا ساتِرُ

whop, **whap** /wɒp/ *vt* (**-pp-**) (infml) ضَرَبَ (i; ضَرْب) ‹*a person, ball*›

whopper /ˈwɒpə/ *n* (infml) **1** (large thing) [شَيْء ضَخْم \ هائِل] **2** (lie) كَذْبة كَبيرة

whopping /ˈwɒpɪŋ/ *adj* (infml) (also **whopping great**) ‹*increase, fine*› هائِل ,ضَخْم

whore /hɔː/ *n* (pej) عاهِرة (عاهِرات ,عَواهِرُ)

whorl /wɔːl/ *n* حَلَزون (حَلَزونات)

who's /huːz/ *abbr* **1** = **who is** **2** = **who has**

whose /huːz/ **A** *pron* لِمَنْ ,مِلْك مَنْ; **~ is this?** لِمَنْ هذا؟; **~ are these?** لِمَنْ هذه؟; **we don't know ~ it is** لا نَعْرِفُ مِلْكُ مَنْ هذا; **~ is this boat/horse?** مِلْكُ مَنْ هذا القارِبُ \ الحِصانُ؟

B *adj* **1** (interrogative) **~ laptop is that?** مِلْكُ مَنْ ذلك الكُمْبْيوتر النَقّالُ؟; **~ keys are these?** مَفاتيحُ مَنْ هذه؟; **~ coat did you take?** مِعْطَفُ مَنْ أَخَذْتَ؟; **do you know ~ handbag was stolen?** هل تَعْلَمُ حَقيبةُ مَنْ سُرِقَتْ؟ **2** (relative) **the boy ~ bike was stolen** الوَلَدُ الّذي سُرِقَتْ دَرّاجَتُهُ; **the one, ~ name is drawn out first, wins** الشَخْصُ الّذي يُسْحَبُ اسْمُهُ أَوّلاً يَفوزُ

whosoever /huːsəʊˈevə/ *pron* (old use) ▸ **whoever**

who've /huːv/ *abbr* = **who have**

why /wʌɪ/ **A** *adv* **1** (in questions) لِماذا; **~ are you smiling?** لِماذا تَبْتَسِمُ؟; **~ didn't you go?** لِماذا لم تَذْهَبْ؟; **~ bother?** لِماذا تُشْغِلُ بالَكَ؟; **~ the delay?** لِماذا التَأْخيرُ؟; **~ me?** لِماذا أنا؟; **'it's not possible'—'~ not?'** 'لَيْسَ هذا مُمْكِناً' — 'وَلِمَ لا؟'; **'can I apply?'—'I don't see ~ not'** 'هل يُمْكِنُني أنْ أَتَقَدَّمَ بِطَلَبٍ؟' — 'لا أرى مانِعاً لِذَلِكَ' **2** (in suggestions) لِماذا; **~ don't you apply for the job?** لِماذا لا تَتَقَدَّمُ إلى الوَظيفةِ؟; **there's no reason ~ you shouldn't do it** لَيْسَ هُناكَ سَبَبٌ يَمْنَعُكَ من فِعْلِهِ; **~ not sell the car?** لِماذا لا تَبيعُ السَيّارةَ؟ **3** (expressing anger) لِماذا; **~ don't they mind their own business?** لِماذا لا يَهْتَمّونَ بِشُؤونِهِم الخاصّةِ؟; **~ can't you be quiet?** لِماذا لا يُمْكِنُكَ الالْتِزامُ بالصَمْتِ؟; **they are incompetent, that's ~!** هُمْ غَيْرُ أَكْفاءٍ، ذلك هو السَبَبُ! **4** (**whyever**) (BrE) (expressing surprise) **~ever not?** وَلِمَ لا؟; **~ever did you say that?** لِماذا بِحَقِّ السَماءِ قُلْتَ ذلك؟

B *conj* لِذا; **that is ~ they came** لِذَلِكَ جاؤوا; **is that ~ she telephoned?** هل ذلك هو سَبَبُ اتِّصالِها؟; **that's not ~ I asked** لَيْسَ هذا هو سَبَبُ سُؤالي; **one of the reasons ~ they left** أَحَد أَسْبابِ رَحيلِهِمْ

C *excl* (old use) عَجَباً; **~, that's the reason!** عَجَباً، ذلك هو السَبَبُ!

D *n* **the ~s and the wherefores of the issue** أسْباب وَحَيْثِيّات المَسْأَلِةِ

WI *abbr* **A** ▸ **Wisconsin**

B /dʌblju:ʌɪ/ *n* (in UK) = **Women's Institute** جَمْعِيّة \ مُنَظَّمة النِساءِ

wick /wɪk/ *n* فتيلة (فَتيلات, فَتائِلُ), ذُبالة (ذُبال)

wicked /ˈwɪkɪd/ *adj* (**wickeder, wickedest**) **1** (evil) ‹*deed, witch*› شِرّير (أشْرار); **to have a ~ tongue** كانَ لَدَيْهِ لِسانٌ لاذِعٌ \ خَبيثٌ **2** (mischievous) ‹*grin, sense of humour*› لَعوب, عابِث (f; لَعائِبُ)

wicker /ˈwɪkə/ *n* (also **wickerwork**) خَيْزُران (خَيازِرُ)

wicket /ˈwɪkɪt/ *n* **1** (stumps) ويكيت (هَدَف ذو ثَلاثِ قَوائِمَ خَشَبِيّةٍ في الكِريكِت) **2** (playing area) مَلْعَب الكِريكِت **3** (AmE) (transaction window) شُبّاك (لِبَيْعِ التَذاكِرِ إلخ)

wide /wʌɪd/ **A** *adj* **1** (broad) ‹*river, opening, doorway*› واسِع, شاسِع; **it's 30 cm ~** يَبْلُغُ اتِّساعُهُ 30 سم; **they're making the street ~r** يُوَسِّعونَ الطَرِيقَ; **her eyes were ~ with fear** اتَّسَعَتْ عَيْناها من الخَوْفِ; **they won by a ~ margin** فازوا بِفارِقٍ واسِعٍ **2** (extensive) ‹*variety, choice*› واسِع, شاسِع; **a ~ selection of products** اخْتِيار واسِع من المَنْتوجاتِ; **a ~ range of opinions** عَدَد كَبير من الآراءِ **3** (immense) ‹*ocean, desert, sky*› واسِع, شاسِع **4** ‹*shot, ball*› بَعيد; **the shot was ~** كانَتْ القَذْفَةُ بَعيدةً

B *adv* **1** (far apart) بِشَكْلٍ واسِعٍ; **set the posts ~r apart** ضَعِ العَمودَيْنِ بِشَكْلٍ أكْثَرَ تَباعُداً; **to open one's eyes ~** فَتَحَ عَيْنَيْهِ بِشَكْلٍ واسِعٍ; **open ~!** افْتَحْ بِشَكْلٍ واسِعٍ! **2** (to one side) **the shot went ~** اتَّجَهَت الكُرةُ بَعيداً عن الزاوِيةِ; **his estimate is ~ of the mark** تَقْديرُهُ بَعيدٌ عن الصَوابِ

wide-angle lens /ˌwʌɪdˌaŋgəl ˈlɛnz/ *n* عَدَسة مُتَّسعة الزاوِية

wide awake *adj* يَقِظ تَماماً

wide-eyed /ˌwʌɪdˈʌɪd/ *adj* **1** (with surprise, fear) ‹*look, stare*› فاغِر العَيْنَيْنِ **2** (naïve) ‹*innocence, wonder*› ساذَج (سُذَّج), بَسيط (بُسَطاءُ)

widely /ˈwʌɪdli/ *adv* **1** (extensively) ‹*available, sold, used*› على نِطاقٍ \ على نَحْوٍ \ بِشَكْلٍ واسِعٍ; **the product is now ~ available** المُنْتَجُ مُتَوفِّرٌ على نِطاقٍ واسِعِ الآنَ; **he has travelled ~, he is ~ travelled** سافَرَ كَثيراً **2** (commonly) ‹*acknowledged, accepted, used*› على نِطاقٍ \ على نَحْوٍ \ بِشَكْلٍ واسِعٍ; **to be ~ known for sth** كانَ مَعْروفاً على نِطاقٍ واسِعٍ بِشَيْءٍ; **it is ~ believed that ...** يُعْتَقَدُ على نِطاقٍ واسِعٍ أنّ ...; **a country ~ admired for its technology** دَوْلة هي مَحَطُّ إعْجابٍ على نِطاقٍ واسِعٍ بِسَبَبِ تَقْنِيَتِها **3** (significantly) ‹*to differ, vary*› بِشَكْلٍ مَلْحوظٍ **4** (distanced) ‹*spaced, planted*› بِشَكْلٍ مُتَباعِدٍ

widely read /wʌɪdli: ˈrɛd/ *adj* **1** (read by many) ‹*author, book*› مَقْروء على نِطاقٍ واسِعٍ **2** (knowledgeable) ‹*student, scholar*› واسِع الاطِّلاعِ \ المَعْرِفةِ

widen /ˈwʌɪd(ə)n/ **A** *vt* **1** (to make wider) عَرَّضَ, وَسَّعَ ‹*a road, gap*› **2** (to increase) مَدَّدَ, وَسَّعَ ‹*the choice, scope*›

B *vi* «rivers, valleys» تَوَسَّعَ, اتَّسَعَ

widening /ˈwʌɪdnɪŋ/ *adj* ‹*gap, division*› مُتَزايِد, مُتَّسِع

wide open *adj* **1** (fully open) ‹*door*› مَفْتوح على مِصْراعَيْهِ; ‹*eyes*› فاغِر **2** (undecided) ‹*race, election*› [لا يُمْكِنُ التَنَبُّؤُ بِنَتيجَتِهِ]

wide-ranging /wʌɪdˈreɪndʒɪŋ/ *adj* ‹*discussion, interests*› واسِع النِطاقِ

widescreen /ˈwʌɪdskri:n/ *adj* ‹*format, film*› الشاشةِ العَريضةِ

widescreen TV *n* تِلِفِزْيون بِشاشةٍ عَريضةٍ

widespread /ˈwʌɪdsprɛd/ *adj* ‹*devastation, belief*› واسِع الانْتِشارِ

widget /ˈwɪdʒɪt/ *n* **1** (infml) (thing) آلة **2** (in computing) عُنْصُر واجِهةِ مُسْتَخْدِمٍ

widow /ˈwɪdəʊ/ **A** *n* أرْمَلة (أرامِلُ)

B *vt* **to be ~ed** تَرَمَّلَ

widower /ˈwɪdəʊə/ *n* أرْمَل (dipt; أرامِلُ)

width /wɪdθ, wɪtθ/ *n* عَرْض (عُروض); **it's 15 metres in ~** عَرْضُهُ 15 مِتْراً; **to estimate the ~ of the river** قَدَّرَ عَرْضَ النَهْرِ

wield /wi:ld/ *vt* **1** (to brandish) كانَ في يَدِهِ ‹*a knife, gun*› **2** (to exert) مارَسَ ‹*power, influence*›

wife /wʌɪf/ *n* (*pl* **wives** /wʌɪvz/) زَوْجة

Wi-Fi® /ˈwʌɪfʌɪ/ *n* = **Wireless Fidelity** واي فاي (بَثّ لاسِلْكِيّ)

wig /wɪg/ *n* باروكة, شَعْر مُسْتَعار \ اصْطِناعِيّ

wiggle /ˈwɪg(ə)l/ **A** *vt* حَرَّكَ ‹*an eyebrow, ear*›; **to ~ one's hips** هَزَّ وَسَطَهُ; **to ~ one's fingers** حَرَّكَ أصابِعَهُ

B *vi* «snakes, worms» تَلَوّى

C *n* تَلَوٍّ

wild /wʌɪld/ **A** *adj* **1** (not cultivated) ‹*plant, mushroom*› بَرّيّ **2** (undomesticated) ‹*animal, bird*› بَرّيّ **3** (rugged) ‹*landscape, terrain*› وَعْر **4** (turbulent) ‹*wind, waves*› هائِج; **it was a ~ night** كانَتْ لَيْلَةً هائِجَةً **5** (unrestrained) ‹*party, laughter, applause*› صاخِب; **the fans went ~** هاجَ المُعْجَبونَ; **he led a ~ life in Beirut** عاشَ حَياةً صاخِبَةً في بَيْروت; **to drive sb ~** هَيَّجَ شَخْصاً **6** (infml) (enthusiastic) **to be ~ about computers/films** كانَ مُغْرَماً بالحَواسيبِ \ الأَفْلامِ **7** (outlandish) ‹*idea, scheme, promise*› غَريب **8** (infml) (furious) مُغْتاظ; **to drive sb ~** أَغاظَ شَخْصاً; **this computer is driving me ~** هذا الكُمْبيوتَر يَدْفَعُني إلى الجُنونِ

B *adv* **1** «plants» ‹*to grow*› بِشَكْلٍ بَرّيٍّ; «animals» ‹*to live*› بِشَكْلٍ بَرّيٍّ **2** (without restraint) على نَحْوٍ جامِحٍ; **the children were running ~** كانَ الأَطْفالُ يَجْرونَ بِشَكْلٍ جامِحٍ; **let your imagination run ~** أَطْلِقْ لِخَيالِكَ العَنانَ

C *n* (natural habitat) **to be found in the ~** كانَ مَوْجوداً في البَرّيّةِ; **it grows in the ~** يَنْمو في البَرّيّةِ; **the call of the ~** نِداء البَرّيّة

D (**wilds**) *n pl* (remote area) **to live in the ~s of Canada** عاشَ في بَراري كَنَدا

wild boar *n* خِنْزير بَرّيّ

wild card *n* **1** (in cards) [وَرَقة يُمْكِنُ اسْتِعْمالُها كَأَيَّةِ وَرَقةٍ أُخْرى] **2** (also **wildcard**) (in computing) حَرْف بَدَلٍ **3** (unpredictable element) عامِل غَيْر ثابِتٍ **4** (in sport) [حَقّ المُشارَكةِ في بُطولةٍ رَغْمَ عَدَمِ التَأَهُّلِ لَها]

wildcat /ˈwʌɪldkat/ *n* (*pl* **wildcats** or **wildcat**) قِطّ \ سِنَّوْر بَرّيّ

wilderness /ˈwɪldənəs/ *n* **1** (wilds) بَرّيّة (بَراريّ), قَفْر (قِفار) **2** (neglected area) [مِنْطَقة مُهْمَلة]

wild-eyed /ˌwʌɪldˈʌɪd/ *adj* ‹*look, person*› هائِج

wildfire /ˈwʌɪldfʌɪə/ *n* (uncontrolled fire) نار هَوْجاء

(Idiom) **to spread like wildfire** «rumour, news» انْتَشَرَ انْتِشارَ النارِ في الهَشيمِ

wild flower *n* زَهْرة بَرّيّة

wild goose chase *n* (infml) بَحْث بِلا جَدْوى; **to send sb on a ~** أَرْسَلَ شَخْصاً في مَهَمّةٍ غَيْرِ مُجْدِيةٍ

wildlife /ˈwʌɪldlʌɪf/ *n* الحَياة البَرّيّة

wildlife park, **wildlife reserve**, **wildlife sanctuary** *n* مَحْمِيّة الحَياةِ البَرّيّةِ

wildly /ˈwʌɪldli/ *adv* **1** (unrestrainedly) ‹*to spend, talk*› دون قُيودٍ; **the police fired ~ into the crowd** أَطْلَقَت الشُرْطةُ النارَ على الحِشْدِ بِشَكْلٍ عَشْوائيٍّ **2** (violently) ‹*to wave, gesture*› بِعُنْفٍ; **his heart was beating ~** كانَ قَلْبُهُ يَنْبُضُ بِعُنْفٍ; **prices have fluctuated ~** تَقَلَّبَتْ الأَسْعارُ بِشِدّةٍ **3** (without justification) ‹*optimistic, enthusiastic, successful*› إلى أَبْعَدِ الحُدودِ; **a ~ optimistic/inaccurate forecast** تَوَقُّعات مُتَفائِلة \ غَيْر دَقيقةٍ إلى أَبْعَدِ الحُدودِ

wildness /ˈwʌɪldnəs/ *n* **1** (of landscapes) بَرّيّة (بَراريّ) **2** (of wind, waves, weather) هَيَجان **3** (of animals) تَوَحُّش **4** (of behaviour) طَيْش; (of an evening, a party) صَخَب **5** (of ideas, plans, promises) غَرابة

Wild West *n* (**the Wild West**) الغَرْب المُتَوَحِّش (مِنْطَقة غَرْبِ الوِلاياتِ المُتَّحِدةِ)

wiles /wʌɪlz/ *n pl* كَيْد (كِياد)

wilful (BrE), **willful** (AmE) /ˈwɪlfʊl/ *adj* **1** (headstrong) ‹*child, behaviour*› عَنيد (عُنُد) **2** (deliberate) ‹*neglect, damage*› مُتَعَمَّد

wilfully (BrE), **willfully** (AmE) /ˈwɪlf(ə)li/ *adv* **1** (obstinately) ‹*to act, refuse*› بِعِنادٍ **2** (deliberately) ‹*to neglect, disobey*› عَمْداً, عن قَصْدٍ

will[1] /wɪl/ **A** *modal aux* (*present short form* **'ll**, *negative present short form* **won't**, *past or conditional* **would**, *past or conditional short form* **'d**, *negative or conditional short form* **wouldn't**) **1** (expressing the future) **I will/I'll see you tomorrow** سَأَراكَ غَداً; **it will not/won't rain** لَن تُمْطِرَ; **~ there be many people there?** هل سَيَكونُ هُناكَ كَثيرٌ من الناسِ؟; **what ~ you do now?** ماذا سَتَفْعَلُ الآنَ؟ **2** (expressing willingness or intention) **~ you help me?** هل تُساعِدُني؟; **we won't stay too long** لن نَمْكُثَ طَويلاً; **he won't cooperate** لا يُريدُ أَنْ يَتَعاوَنَ **3** (in requests, commands) **~ you pass the salt, please?** هل يُمْكِنُكَ أَنْ تُناوِلَني المِلْحَ، من فَضْلِكَ؟; **~ you please be quiet!** الْزَموا الصَمْتَ من فَضْلِكُمْ! **4** (in invitations) **~ you have some tea?** هل تُريدُ بَعْضَ الشايِ؟; **won't you join us for dinner?** أَلا تَتَناوَلُ العَشاءَ مَعَنا؟; **what ~ you have to drink?** ماذا تُريدُ

أَظُنُّ أنّ تَشْرَبَ؟ **5** (in assumptions) **he'll be about 30 now** أَظُنُّ أنّهُ فرانْك ;عُمْرُهُ حوالَيْ 30 عاماً الآنَ **that will be Frank**

6 (indicating sth predictable or customary) **they ~ ask for a deposit** هذه الأَشْياءُ ;سَيَطْلُبونَ وَديعةً **these things ~ happen** من الوارِدِ حُدوثُها; **they would/they'd go to the movies every week** كانوا يَذْهَبونَ إلى السينما كُلَّ أُسْبوعٍ **7** (in tag questions and short answers) **you'll come again, won't you?** سَوْفَ تَأْتي مَرَّةً أُخرى، أَلَيْسَ كَذٰلِكَ؟ ;**you won't forget, ~ you?** لن تَنْسى، أَلَيْسَ كَذٰلِكَ؟ ;**'~ you call me?'—'yes, I ~'** 'هل سَتَتَّصِلُ بي؟' — 'نَعَمْ، سَأَفْعَلُ' ;**'she'll be furious'—'no, she won't!'** 'سَتَشْتاطُ غَضَباً' — 'كَلاّ، لن تَفْعَلَ!' ;**'I'll do it'—'no you won't!'** 'سَأَفْعَلُ ذلك' — 'كَلاّ، لن تَفْعَلَ!' **8** (to like) **if you ~** إذا جازَ التَّعْبيرُ

B *vt* (*past tense, past participle* **willed**) **1** (to urge mentally) **to ~ sb/sth to do sth** تَمَنّى لِشَخْصٍ \ لِشَيْءٍ أنْ يَفْعَلَ شَيْئاً; **she ~ed him to live** تَمَنَّتْ لَهُ أنْ يَعيشَ **2** (wish, intend) شاءَ (a; مَشيئة); **fate ~ed it differently** شاءَ القَدَرُ خِلافَ ذلك **3** (Law) **to ~ sth to sb** أَوْصى لِشَخْصٍ بِشَيْءٍ

will² /wɪl/ *n* **1** (volition) إرادة; **against my ~** ضِدّ إرادَتي; **to lose the ~ to live** فَقَدَ الرَّغْبةَ في الحَياةِ; **patients come and go at ~** يَأْتي المَرْضى وَيُغادِرونَ كُلَّما أَرادوا ذلك **2** (legal document) وَصيّة (وَصايا); **to make a ~** كَتَبَ وَصيَّةً; **to leave sth to sb in one's ~** أَوْصى بِشَيْءٍ لِشَخْصٍ

willing /wɪlɪŋ/ *adj* **1** (prepared) **to be ~ to help/go** كانَ مُسْتَعِدًّا لِلمُساعَدةِ \ للذَّهابِ **2** (eager) ‹*pupil, helper*› راغِب (رَغْبَة), مُتَحَمِّس

willingly /wɪlɪŋli/ *adv* ‹*to volunteer, give*› طَوْعاً, عن طيبِ خاطِرٍ

willingness /wɪlɪŋnəs/ *n* اسْتِعْداد (اسْتِعْدادات)

willow /wɪləʊ/ *n* (also **willow tree**) صَفْصاف

willpower /wɪlpaʊə/ *n* قوّة الإرادةِ

willy-nilly /wɪli'nɪli/ *adv* **1** (inescapably) ‹*to carry, take*› طَوْعاً أو كَرْهاً **2** (haphazardly) ‹*to carry out, choose*› شاءَ أم أَبى, عَشْوائيًّا, اعْتِباطيًّا

wilt /wɪlt/ *vi* **1** (of plants) «flowers, crops» ذَبَلَ (u; ذُبول), ذَوى (i; ذَويّ) **2** (of people) «spectators, athletes» شَعَرَ بالإرْهاقِ

wily /'wʌɪli/ *adj* (**wilier, wiliest**) ‹*fox, politician*› ماكِر (مَكْرة), مُخادِع

wimp /wɪmp/ *n* (infml) إمَّع, ضَعيف الشَخْصيّةِ

win /wɪn/ **A** *vt* (*present participle* **-nn-**; *past tense, past participle* **won**) **1** انْتَصَرَ (في) ‹*a battle, war, fight*› **2** «candidate» فازَ (u; فَوْز; ب) ‹*an election, sb's vote, a seat*›; **she won more votes than any other candidate** فازَتْ بِأَصْواتٍ أَكْثَر من أيِّ مُرَشَّحٍ آخَرَ **3** فازَ (u; فَوْز; ب) ‹*a race, competition, game*›; **the crew/team won by 2 metres/50 points** فازَ الفَريقُ بِمِتْرَيْنِ \ 50 نُقْطةً **4** كَسَبَ (i; كَسْب), فازَ (u; فَوْز; ب) ‹*a bet, money, a prize*›; **he won $200 on Arabian Brave** كَسَبَ 200$ رِهاناً على الحِصانِ أَرابْيان بْرايْف; **she won third prize in the tombola/talent show/crossword competition** فازَتْ بالجائزةِ الثالثةِ في اليانَصيبِ \ حَفْلةِ المَواهِبِ \ مُسابَقةِ الكَلِماتِ المُتَقاطِعةِ **5** (fml) (to gain) فازَ (u; فَوْز; ب) ‹*sb's sympathy, friendship, a reprieve*›; **to ~ sb's love/respect** فازَ بِحُبِّ \ بِاحْتِرامِ شَخْصٍ

B *vi* (*present participle* **-nn-**; *past tense, past participle* **won**) **1** (in a battle, sport) «army, player, team» فازَ (u; فَوْز), انْتَصَرَ; **to ~ at chess/athletics** فازَ في الشَطْرَنْجِ \ أَلْعابِ القُوى **2** (in an argument) فازَ (u; فَوْز), انْتَصَرَ; **you ~!** انْتَصَرْتَ!; **you just can't ~ with her** لن تَسْتَطيعَ أنْ تَنْتَصِرَ عَلَيْها

C *n* **1** (a victory) انْتِصار (انْتِصارات), فَوْز **2** (in betting) كَسْب

Phrasal verbs **win back**: **~ [sth] back, ~ back [sth]** **1** «team» اسْتَعادَ [شَيْئاً] ‹*a title, position*› **2** «troops» اسْتَعادَ [شَيْئاً] ‹*a position, city*› **3** «politician» اسْتَعادَ [شَيْئاً] ‹*the support, votes*› **4** اسْتَعادَ [شَيْئاً] ‹*sb's affection, respect*›

• **win over, win round**: **~ over [sb], ~ [sb] over** (to persuade) «reason, argument» أَقْنَعَ [شَخْصاً]

• **win through** (to be successful) فازَ رَغْمَ الصُعوباتِ; **to ~ through to the finals** بَلَغَ الأَدْوارَ النِهائيّةَ رَغْمَ الصُعوباتِ

wince /wɪns/ **A** *vi* جَفَلَ (i-u; جُفول, جَفْل), انْكَمَشَ, انْقَبَضَ **B** *n* جُفول, انْكِماش, انْقِباض

winch /wɪntʃ/ **A** *n* وِنْش (وِنْشات), مِرْفاع (مَرافيعُ), رافِعة (رَوافِعُ) **B** *vt* رَفَعَ بِوِنْش ‹*a vehicle, casualty*›; **to ~ sth up** رَفَعَ شَيْئاً بِرافِعةٍ

wind¹ /wɪnd/ **A** *n* **1** (air current) ريح (mf; رِياح); **high** *or* **strong ~s** رِياح قَوِيّة; **a cold north ~** رِياح شَماليّة بارِدة;

the prevailing ~ الرِياح السائِدة; **the ~ was blowing from the south** كانَت الرِياحُ تَهُبُّ من الجَنوب **2** [u] (breath) نَفَس (أَنْفاس); **to knock the ~ out of sb** قَطَعَ أَنْفاسَ شَخْصٍ; **to get a second ~** اسْتَعادَ أَنْفاسَهُ **3** (trend, influence) ريح (mf; رِياح); **the ~ of change** ريح التَغْيير; **there was something in the ~** بَدَأَت ريحُ التَغْيير تَهُبُّ **4** [u] (flatulence) ريح (mf; غاز من المَعِدة) (رِياح); **to break ~** أَطْلَقَ ريحاً **5** [u] (Music) **the ~** [آلات النَفْخ الموسيقيّة في الأوركسْترا]

B *vt* **1** (to make breathless) «punches, falls» قَطَعَ النَفَس <*a person, player*> **2** (to burp) تَجَشَّأَ <*a baby*>

(Idioms) **to get wind of sth** اكْتَشَفَ أَمْرَ شَيْءٍ; **to take the wind out of sb's sails** فاجَأَ شَخْصاً من حَيْثُ لا يَتَوَقَّعُ

wind² /wʌɪnd/ **A** *vt* (*past tense, past participle* **wound**) **1** (to coil) لَفَّ (u; لَفّ) <*a rope, tape, wire*> **2** (to turn) أَدارَ <*a handle*> **3** (also **wind up**) مَلَأَ (a; مَلْء), عَبَّأَ <*a watch, clock, toy*> **4** (to move slowly) **to ~ one's way** «roads, rivers, processions» سارَ بِبُطْءٍ

B *vi* (*past tense, past participle* **wound**) «roads, rivers» تَواصَلَ بَطيئاً

C *n* (of a handle) مَلْء, تَعْبِئة

(Phrasal verbs) **wind down A 1** (to end) «companies, organizations» تَداعى; «production» تَراجَعَ **2** (to relax) «person» اسْتَرْخى **3** «clocks, watches» اسْتَنْفَدَ طاقَتَهُ **B ~ down [sth], ~ [sth] down 1** (to open) فَتَحَ [شَيْئاً] <*a car window*> **2** (to prepare for closure) اسْتَعَدَّ لِإغْلاقِ [شَيْءٍ] <*a business, factory*>

• **wind in**: **~ in [sth], ~ [sth] in** سَحَبَ [شَيْئاً] بالبَكْرة <*a cable, fishing line, fish*>

• **wind up A 1** (to finish) «events, performances, speakers» انْتَهى **2** (infml) (to finish up) «people, cars» **to ~ up somewhere** انْتَهى في مَكانٍ ما; **we wound up in a camp site/sleeping in a barn** انْتَهَيْنا في مَوْقِعٍ للتَخْييم \ نائِمين في اسْطَبْلٍ **B ~ up [sth], ~ [sth] up 1** (to raise) أَغْلَقَ [شَيْئاً] <*a car window*> **2** (to terminate) صَفّى [شَيْئاً] <*a business, factory, organization*> **3** (in inheritance) صَفّى [شَيْئاً] <*sb's estate*> **4** (to activate) عَبَّأَ \ مَلَأَ [شَيْئاً] <*a clock, toy*> **C ~ [sb] up, ~ up [sb] 1** (BrE) (to play a joke on) مازَحَ [شَخْصاً] <*a friend, colleague*> **2** (to annoy) أَزْعَجَ [شَخْصاً] <*an opponent*>; **to be wound up about sth** كانَ غاضِباً بِسَبَبِ شَيْءٍ

wind chimes *n* [أَجْراس تَدُقُّها الرِياحُ]

wind energy *n* طاقة الرِياح

windfall /ˈwɪndfɔːl/ *n* **1** (fruit) [فاكِهة أَسْقَطَتْها الريحُ من الشَجَر] **2** (money) [مَبْلَغ \ إرْث غير مُتَوَقَّع]

windfall profit *n* [رِبْح غَيْر مُتَوَقَّع]

windfall tax *n* ضَريبة المَرّة الواحِدة (بعد رِبْحٍ غَيْرِ مُتَوَقَّع)

wind farm *n* مَزْرَعة \ مَحَطّة رِياحٍ (لِتَوْليدِ الكَهْرَباءِ بِطاقةِ الرِياحِ)

winding /ˈwʌɪndɪŋ/ *adj* <*road, staircase*> مُلْتَوٍ, مُتَعَرِّج

wind instrument *n* آلة نَفْخٍ (موسيقيّة)

windmill /ˈwɪndmɪl/ *n* طاحونة هَوائيّة

window /ˈwɪndəʊ/ *n* **1** (of a house, vehicle) شُبّاك (شَبابيكُ), نافِذة (نَوافِذُ); (of a shop) واجِهة عَرْضٍ; **to look out of the ~** نَظَرَ من الشُبّاكِ; **I'd like a seat by the ~** أُحِبُّ أنْ أَجْلِسَ بِجانِبِ النافذة **2** (on computer screens) نافِذة (نَوافِذُ); **to open/close a ~** فَتَحَ \ أَغْلَقَ نافِذةً **3** (in schedules) فُرْصة (فُرَص); **to provide a ~ of opportunity to do sth** وَفَّرَ فُرْصةً لِفِعْلِ شَيْءٍ **4** (of an envelope) نافِذة (نَوافِذُ)

(Idiom) **to go out the window** اخْتَفى عن الأَنْظار

window blind *n* سِتارة النافِذةِ

window box *n* [حَوْض زُهورٍ يُعَلَّق على عَتَبة النافِذة]

window cleaner *n* مُنَظِّف نَوافِذَ

window display *n* واجِهة عَرْضٍ

window dressing *n* **1** (in shops) تَزْيين واجِهةِ المَحَلّ **2** (deception) تَمْويه

window ledge, window sill *n* عَتَبة نافِذةٍ

windowpane /ˈwɪndəʊpeɪn/ *n* لَوْح زُجاجيّ

window seat *n* مَقْعَد نافِذةٍ

window-shopping /ˈwɪndəʊʃɒpɪŋ/ *n* التَفَرُّج على واجِهاتِ المَحَلّات

windpipe /ˈwɪndpʌɪp/ *n* قَصَبة هَوائيّة

wind power *n* طاقة الرِياحِ

windscreen (BrE) /ˈwɪndskriːn/, **windshield** (AmE) /ˈwɪndʃild/ *n* زُجاج أماميّ

windscreen wiper (BrE), **windshield wiper** (AmE) *n* مَسّاحة الزُجاجِ الأماميّ

windsurf /ˈwɪndsəːf/ *vi* رَكِبَ الأَمْواجَ (بِاسْتِخْدامِ شِراعٍ)

windsurfer /ˈwɪndsəːfə/ *n* **1** (person) راكِب الأَمْواجِ **2** (board) لَوْح التَزَحْلُق على الماءِ (بِاسْتِخْدامِ شِراعٍ)

windsurfing /ˈwɪndsəːfɪŋ/ *n* رُكوب الأَمْواجِ (بِاسْتِخْدامِ شِراعٍ)

windswept /ˈwɪndswɛpt/ *adj* **1** (exposed) ‹*beach, hillside*› [تَهُبُّ فيهِ الرِياحُ بِقوّةٍ] **2** (dishevelled) ‹*hair*› أَشْعَث (dipt)

wind turbine *n* توربين الرِياحِ

windy /ˈwɪndi/ *adj* (**windier, windiest**) ‹*day, place*› عاصِف, شَديد الرِياحِ

wine /wʌɪn/ *n* خَمْر (خُمور), نَبيذ (أَنْبِذة)

winegrower /ˈwʌɪngrəʊə/ *n* مُزارِع الكُرومِ

wine growing *n* زِراعة الكُرومِ

wing /wɪŋ/ **A** *n* **1** (of birds, insects, aircraft) جَناح (أَجْنِحة, أَجْنُح) **2** (of a building) جَناح (أَجْنِحة, أَجْنُح) **3** (of a car) مَصَدّ (مَصَدّات), رَفْرَف (رَفارِف) **4** (of an armchair) [مِسْنَد جانِبيّ للرَأْسِ في أَريكةٍ] **5** (in sports) جَناح (أَجْنِحة, أَجْنُح); **to play on the right/left ~** يَلْعَبُ كَجَناحٍ أَيْمَنَ \ أَيْسَرَ **6** (of a party) جَناح (أَجْنِحة, أَجْنُح) **7** (in the air force) جَناح (أَجْنِحة, أَجْنُح)

B (**wings**) *n pl* **1** (Theat) **the ~s** أَجْنِحة (المَسْرَح); **to be waiting in the ~s** كانَ يَنْتَظِرُ في الأَجْنِحةِ **2** (qualification) **to get one's ~s** حَصَلَ على رُخْصةِ قِيادةِ الطائِرةِ

C *vt* **1** (to injure) جَرَحَ (a; جَرْح) ‹*a bird*› **2** **to ~ one's way to a place** «passengers» سافَرَ بالطائِرةِ

(Idioms) **to take sb under one's wing** أَخَذَ شَخْصاً تحت جَناحِهِ; **to take wing** (liter) «birds, planes» حَلَّقَ عالِياً; **to wing it** (infml) ارْتَجَلَ شَيْئاً ▸ **spread**

wing commander *n* مُقَدِّم طَيّار

winger /ˈwɪŋə/ *n* لاعِب جَناحٍ

wing mirror *n* (BrE) مِرْآة جانِبيّة

wing nut *n* صامولة مُجَنَّحة

wingspan /ˈwɪŋspan/ *n* باع الجَناحِ

wink /wɪŋk/ **A** *vi* **1** (with swift eye-movement) غَمَزَ (بالعَيْنِ); **to ~ at sb** غَمَزَ لِشَخْصٍ بِعَيْنِهِ; **to ~ at a misdemeanour** تَغاضى عن مُخالَفةٍ **2** (to twinkle) «lights, stars» تَلأْلأَ, أَوْمَضَ

B *n* غَمْزة; **to give sb a ~** غَمَزَ بِعَيْنِهِ لِشَخْصٍ; **we didn't get a ~ of sleep all night** لم تَغْمُضْ لَنا عَيْنٌ طوال اللَيْلِ

Winnebago® /ˌwɪnəˈbeɪgəʊ/ *n* [بَيْت مُتَنَقِّل]

winner /ˈwɪnə/ *n* **1** (victor) فائِز **2** (success) **to be a ~** «show, films» كانَ ناجِحاً

winning /ˈwɪnɪŋ/ *adj* **1** (victorious) ‹*team, candidate*› فائِز **2** (charming) ‹*smile, personality*› خَلاّب, جَذّاب

winning post *n* [عَمود نِهاية مِضْمارِ السِباقِ]

winnings /ˈwɪnɪŋz/ *n pl* مَكاسِب, أَرْباح

winning streak *n* **to be on a winning streak** حَقَّقَ سِلْسِلةً من النَجاحاتِ

winter /ˈwɪntə/ **A** *n* شِتاء (شُتيّ, أَشْتِية); **a mild/severe ~** شِتاء مُعْتَدِل \ قارِس

B *adj before n* ‹*clothes, sports, weather*› شِتَوِيّ

C *vi* قَضى الشِتاءَ

Winter Olympics *n* (**the Winter Olympics**) الأَلْعاب الأولِمْبيّة الشِتَويّة

winter sports *n* رِياضة الشِتاءِ

wintertime /ˈwɪntətʌɪm/ *n* فَصْل الشِتاءِ

wintry /ˈwɪntri/ *adj* (**wintrier, wintriest**) ‹*conditions, landscape*› شِتَويّ

wipe /wʌɪp/ **A** *vt* **1** (to rub, clean) مَسَحَ (a; مَسْح) ‹*one's face, the plates*›; **he ~d the table** مَسَحَ الطاوِلةَ; **to ~ the floor clean** نَظَّفَ الأَرْضيّةَ بِمِمْسَحةٍ; **'please ~ your feet'** 'امْسَحْ رِجْلَيْكَ من فَضْلِكَ'; **she ~d her eyes** مَسَحَتْ عَيْنَيْها; **to ~ one's nose** مَسَحَ أَنْفَهُ **2** (to erase) مَسَحَ (a; مَسْح) ‹*data, an image*›

B *n* **1** (rub, clean) مَسْح (a; مَسْح); **to give sth a ~** قامَ بِمَسْحِ شَيْءٍ ‹*the table, work surface*›; قامَ بِغَسْلِ \ بِشَطْفِ شَيْءٍ ‹*the bath, sink*› **2** (disposable cloth) مِنْديل صِحّيّ

(Phrasal verbs) **wipe away**: **~ away [sth], ~ [sth] away** مَسَحَ [شَيْئاً] ‹*tears, sweat, mark*›

• **wipe down**: **~ down [sth], ~ [sth] down** مَسَحَ [شَيْئاً] ‹*a door, table*›

• **wipe off**: ~ **off** [**sth**], ~ [**sth**] **off** 1 (to clean off) نَظَّفَ [شَيْئاً] *<the dirt, a mark, stain>* 2 (to clean off) مَسَحَ [شَيْئاً] *<data, a file, an image>*

• **wipe out** A (infml) (to fall) سَقَطَ (u; مَسْقَط ,سُقوط) B ~ **out** [**sth**], ~ [**sth**] **out** 1 (to kill) أَبادَ [شَيْئاً] *<the enemy, population, a species>* 2 (to eliminate) أَزالَ [شَيْئاً] *<a memory, the past>*; أَلْغى [شَيْئاً] *<a debt, profit>* 3 (to clean) نَظَّفَ [شَيْئاً] بِمِنْديلٍ *<a container, cupboard>* 4 (infml) (to defeat) أَلْحَقَ هَزيمةً ب [شَيْءٍ] *<an opponent, a team, a player>* 5 (infml) (to break) كَسَرَ [شَيْئاً] *<a record, time>*

wiper /ˈwʌɪpə/ *n* ▸ **windscreen wiper**

WIPO /ˈwʌɪpəʊ/ *n* = **World Intellectual Property Organization** المُنَظَّمة العالَميّة لِلمِلْكيّةِ الفِكْريّةِ

wire /wʌɪə/ A *n* 1 (metal strand) سِلْك (أَسْلاك) 2 (AmE) (telegram) بَرْقيّة; (fml) **to send/receive a** ~ أَرْسَلَ \ تَلَقّى بَرْقيّةً
B *vt* 1 (for electricity) وَصَّلَ بِأَسْلاكٍ *<a plug, lamp>*; **to ~ a house** رَكَّبَ الأَسْلاكَ الكَهْرَبائيّةَ في بَيْتٍ 2 (electronic ally) أَبْرَقَ (إلى), أَرْسَلَ بَرْقيّةً *<money, a message>*; **to ~ sb money** أَرْسَلَ إلى شَخْصٍ حَوالةً بَنْكيّةً 3 (in dentistry, surgery) رَبَطَ بِسِلْكٍ *<sb's jaws, bones>*

(Idiom) **down to the wire** (infml) حتّى الرَمَقِ الأَخيرِ

wire cutters *n* مِقْراض أَسْلاكٍ

wireless /ˈwʌɪələs/ A *adj* *<network, technology>* لاسِلْكيّ
B *n* 1 (telecommunication) إرْسال \ اتِّصال لاسِلْكيّ 2 (BrE) (radio) جِهاز الراديو

wire wool *n* سِلْك غَسيلِ الأَواني

wiring /ˈwʌɪərɪŋ/ *n* شَبَكة الأَسْلاكِ الكَهْرَبائيّةِ

wiry /ˈwʌɪəri/ *adj* (**wirier, wiriest**) 1 (athletic) *<physique, man>* قَويّ (وَنَحيل) 2 (coarse) *<hair, grass>* خَشِن

Wisconsin /wɪsˈkɒnsɪn/ *pr n* ويسْكونْسِن (f)

wisdom /ˈwɪzdəm/ *n* حِكْمة

wisdom tooth *n* ضِرْس عَقْلٍ

wise /wʌɪz/ A *adj* 1 (prudent) *<decision, person>* حَكيم (حُكَماءُ) 2 (learned) *<leader, words>* حَكيم (حُكَماءُ); **a ~ old man** رَجُل مُسِنّ حَكيم 3 (infml) (aware) **to be/get ~ to sth** فَطِنَ إلى شَيْءٍ
B (**-wise**); *in combination* 1 (in a particular way) بِ; **length-/width-~** بالطولِ \ بالعَرْضِ 2 (with reference to) فيما يَتَعَلَّقُ ب; **time-/health-~** فيما يَتَعَلَّقُ بالوَقْتِ \ بالصِحّةِ

(Idiom) **to be none the wiser** بَقِيَ على جَهْلِهِ

(Phrasal verb) **wise up** (infml) «person, organization» تَنَبَّهَ

wisecrack /ˈwʌɪzkrak/ *n* (infml) نُكْتة (نُكَت, نِكات)

wise guy *n* (infml) مَزّاح

wisely /ˈwʌɪzli/ *adv* *<to choose, invest>* بِتَبَصُّرٍ, بِحِكْمةٍ, بِتَعَقُّلٍ

wish /wɪʃ/ A *vt* 1 (with desires) تَمَنّى; **I ~ (that) you were here** أَتَمَنّى لو كُنْتَ هُنا; **I just ~ we lived closer** أَتَمَنّى فَقَطْ لو كُنّا نَعيشُ في مَكانٍ أَقْرَبَ; **I ~ they would be quiet** أَتَمَنّى لو أَنَّهُم يَهْدَؤونَ; **he bought it and then ~ed he hadn't** اشْتَراهُ ثُمَّ تَمَنّى لو لم يَفْعَلْ; **I wouldn't ~ it on my worst enemy** لا أَتَمَنّاهُ لِأَسْوَأِ أَعْدائي 2 (with congratulations, greetings) تَمَنّى (ل); **we ~ed them luck** تَمَنَّيْنا لَهُمْ حَظًّا سَعيداً; **to ~ sb happy birthday** تَمَنّى لِشَخْصٍ عيدَ ميلادٍ سَعيداً; **to ~ sb joy or happiness** تَمَنّى لِشَخْصٍ السَعادةَ 3 (fml) (to want) أَرادَ *<an audience>*; **I ~ to leave at once** أُريدُ أَنْ أُغادِرَ حالاً; **I don't ~ to seem unkind but ...** لا أُريدُ أَنْ أَبْدُوَ فَظًّا وَلَكِنْ ...
B *vi* (to desire, want) تَمَنّى; **just as you ~** تَماماً كما تُريدُ; **to ~ for sth** تَمَنّى حُدوثَ شَيْءٍ \ الحُصولَ على شَيْءٍ; **what more could you ~ for?** ماذا يُمْكِنُ أَنْ تَتَمَنّى أَكْثَرَ من ذلك؟
C *n* (desire) أُمْنِيّة; **to make a ~** تَمَنّى أُمْنِيّةً; **her ~ came true** تَحَقَّقَتْ أُمْنِيَتُها; **to grant sb's ~** حَقَّقَ أُمْنِيّةَ شَخْصٍ
D (**wishes**) *n pl* أُمْنِيّات; **with best ~es** مع أَجْمَلِ الأُمْنِيّاتِ; **please give him my best ~es** بَلِّغْهُ أَطْيَبَ أُمْنِيّاتي من فَضْلِكَ

wishful thinking *n* تَفْكير رَغْبَويّ; **that's just wishful thinking** ذلك مُجَرَّدُ تَمَنِّياتٍ

wishy-washy /ˈwɪʃiwɒʃi/ *adj* (infml) *<liberalism, compromise>* مُتَراخٍ, ضَعيف

wisp /wɪsp/ *n* (of hair) خُصْلة (صَغيرة); (of smoke, cloud) خَيْط رَفيع

wispy /ˈwɪspi/ *adj* (**wispier, wispiest**) *<hair>* ناعِم (نَواعِمُ); *<clouds>* رَقيق (رِقاق)

wisteria /wɪˈstɪərɪə/ *n* (*pl* **wisteria** or **wisterias**) حُلْوة (نَبات مُعْتَرِش بالعَناقيد)

wistful /ˈwɪstfʊl/ *adj ‹look, smile›* مَلْهوف

wit /wɪt/ [A] *n* [1] (sense of humour) حِسٌّ فُكاهِيٌّ; **to have a quick/ready ~** كانَ عِنْدَهُ حِسٌّ فُكاهِيٌّ سَريعٌ \ جاهِزٌ; **to have a dry ~** كانَ عِنْدَهُ حِسٌّ فُكاهِيٌّ جافٌّ [2] (person) ظَريف (ظُرَفاءُ)
[B] (**wits**) *n pl* (intelligence) بَديهة; **to collect** *or* **gather one's ~s** اسْتَجْمَعَ أَفْكارَهُ; **to have the ~** *or* **~s to do sth** كانَ حاضِرَ البَديهةِ لِيَفْعَلَ شَيْئاً; **to live by one's ~s** عاشَ مُعْتَمِداً على حَذاقَتِهِ
[C] (**to wit**) *adv phr* (fml) على وَجْهِ التَّحْديدِ

(Idioms) **to be at one's wits' end** أَعْيَتْهُ الحيلةُ; **to be scared** *or* **frightened out of one's wits** أُصيبَ بالذُّعْرِ; **to have** *or* **keep one's wits about one** كانَ حاضِرَ البَديهةِ

witch /wɪtʃ/ *n* ساحِرة

witchcraft /ˈwɪtʃkrɑːft/ *n* سِحْر (أَسْحار)

witch doctor *n* طَبيب ساحِر

witch-hunt /ˈwɪtʃhʌnt/ *n* حَمْلة شَعْواء

with /wɪð, wɪθ/ *prep* [1] (accompanied by) **to travel ~ sb** سافَرَ مع شَخْصٍ; **bring a friend ~ you** أَحْضِرْ مَعَكَ صَديقاً; **to live ~ sb** عاشَ مع شَخْصٍ; **I'll be ~ you in a second** سَأَكونُ مَعَكَ بعد لَحْظةٍ; **you're safe ~ us** أَنْتَ في أمانٍ مَعَنا; **take your umbrella ~ you** خُذْ مَعَكَ شَمْسِيَّتَكَ [2] (involving sb) **a meeting/discussion ~ sb** اجْتِماع \ نِقاش مع شَخْصٍ [3] (indicating an agent) **to cut sth ~ a knife** قَطَعَ شَيْئاً بالسِّكّينِ; **to hit sb ~ a bar** ضَرَبَ شَخْصاً بِقَضيبٍ; **to walk ~ a stick** مَشى بِعَصاً [4] (in descriptions) ذو (ذَوو, أولو; f ذات; f pl ذَوات; m du ذَوا; f du ذاتا; gen ذي; acc ذا); **a girl ~ black hair** فَتاة شَعْرُها أَسْوَدُ; **the boy ~ the broken leg** الفَتى ذو الرِّجْلِ المَكْسورةِ; **a dress ~ a large collar** فُسْتان بِياقةٍ كَبيرةٍ; **a room ~ a basin** غُرْفة بِحَوْضٍ [5] (indicating manner, attitude) **to be delighted ~ sth** كانَ سَعيداً بِشَيْءٍ; **to do sth ~ difficulty/pleasure** فَعَلَ شَيْئاً بِصُعوبةٍ \ بِسُرورٍ; **to be patient ~ sb** صَبَرَ على شَخْصٍ [6] (according to) **to vary ~ the temperature** اخْتَلَفَ بِاخْتِلافِ دَرَجةِ الحَرارةِ; **to fade ~ time** تَلاشى مع الوَقْتِ [7] (owning) **passengers ~ tickets** رُكّاب بِتَذاكِرَ; **only people ~ experience need apply** مَطْلوبٌ أَشْخاصٌ ذَوي خِبْرةٍ فَقَطْ [8] (regarding) **the border ~ Libya** الحُدود مع ليبْيا; **how are things ~ you?** كيفَ أَحْوالُكَ؟; **what do you want ~ another car?** ماذا سَتَفْعَلُ بِسَيّارةٍ أُخْرى؟; **it's a habit ~ her** هذا من عاداتِها [9] (showing support) **I'm ~ you on this matter** أنا مَعَكَ في هذا الأَمْرِ [10] (because of) **sick ~ worry** قَلِق جِدًّا; **to blush ~ embarrassment** احْمَرَّ وَجْهُهُ خَجَلاً \ من الخَجَلِ; **I can't do it ~ you watching** لا أَسْتَطيعُ فِعْلَهُ وَأَنْتَ تُراقِبُني [11] (suffering from) **people ~ Aids/leukaemia** الأَشْخاص المُصابونَ بالإيدْز \ بِسَرَطانِ الدَمِ; **to be ill ~ flu** كانَ مُصاباً بالإنْفلوَنْزا [12] (against) **to compete ~ China** نافَسَ الصين; **to be at war ~ with them** كانَ في حَرْبٍ مَعَهُمْ [13] (with events) **~ the approach of spring** مع اقْتِرابِ (فَصْلِ) الرَبيعِ; **~ the introduction of the reforms** مع إِدْخالِ الإِصْلاحاتِ; **~ two days to go before the election** قبل يَوْمَيْنِ من مَوْعِدِ الانْتِخاباتِ [14] (in **~ that, he left** وَعَلى إِثْرِ ذلك، انْصَرَفَ; paid relationships) **a reporter ~ the Gazette** صُحُفيّ من (جَريدةِ) الجازيت; **he's ~ the UN** يَعْمَلُ في (مُنَظَّمةِ) الأُمَمِ المُتَّحِدةِ; **we're ~ the National Bank** نَتَعامَلُ مع البَنْكِ الوَطَنِيِّ [15] (in the same direction as) **to sail ~ the wind** أَبْحَرَ في اتِّجاهِ الريحِ; **to drift ~ the tide** انْجَرَفَ مع التَيّارِ

withdraw /wɪðˈdrɔː/ [A] *vt* (*past tense* **withdrew**, *past participle* **withdrawn**) [1] سَحَبَ (a; سَحْب) *‹troops, tanks›* [2] (from an account) سَحَبَ (a; سَحْب) *‹money, cash›* [3] (fml) (to pull back) سَحَبَ (a; سَحْب) *‹one's hand, an object›* [4] (to stop) سَحَبَ (a; سَحْب) *‹support, funding›* [5] (fml) (to cancel) سَحَبَ (a; سَحْب) *‹an offer, an application›* [6] (from sale) سَحَبَ (من) الأَسْواقِ (a; سَحْب) *‹a product, model›* [7] (in disputes) سَحَبَ (a; سَحْب) *‹an accusation, allegation›*
[B] *vi* (*past tense* **withdrew**, *past participle* **withdrawn**) [1] (to leave) «troops, tanks» انْسَحَبَ [2] (from games, elections, etc) «competitor, candidate» انْسَحَبَ [3] (socially) انْزَوى, انْعَزَلَ; **to ~ from society** انْعَزَلَ عن المُجْتَمَعِ

withdrawal /wɪðˈdrɔːəl/ *n* [1] (of troops, forces) انْسِحاب (انْسِحابات) [2] (of money) سَحْب; **to make a ~ from an account** سَحَبَ المالَ من حِسابٍ [3] (of support, funding) سَحْب [4] (of a product) سَحْب من الأَسْواقِ [5] (of an accusation, application) سَحْب **6** (of a competitor, candidate) انْسِحاب (انْسِحابات) **7** (from drugs) انْسِحاب (انْسِحابات)

withdrawal symptoms *n* أَعْراض انْسِحابيّة

withdrawn /wɪð'drɔːn/ **A** *past participle* ▸ **withdraw**
B *adj* ‹*personality, child*› مُنْعَزِل

wither /'wɪðə/ *vi* **1** «plants, crops» ذَبُلَ (u; ذُبول) **2** «limb, muscle» ذَوى (i; ذَوِيّ), اضْمَحَلَّ (اضْمِحْلال)

withered /wɪðəd/ *adj* **1** ‹*flowers, grass*› ذابِل **2** ‹*hand, arm*› ذاوٍ, مُصاب بالضُمورِ

withering /'wɪðərɪŋ/ *adj* ‹*look*› جافّ; ‹*attack, criticism*› لاذِع, حادّ, مُؤلِم

withhold /wɪð'həʊld/ *vt* (*past tense, past participle* **withheld**)
1 (fml) (not divulge) حَجَبَ (u; حَجْب) ‹*information, evidence*›; مَنَعَ (a; مَنْع) ‹*consent*› **2** (not pay) امْتَنَعَ عن الدَفْع ‹*payment, rent*› **3** (not give) رَفَضَ (i-u; رَفْض) ‹*consent*›

within /wɪð'ɪn/ **A** *prep* **1** (inside) داخِلَ, ضِمْنَ; **~ a five-mile radius** ضِمْنَ شُعاع 5 أَمْيالٍ; **factions ~ the party** فِئات داخِلَ الحِزْبِ **2** (not beyond) داخِلَ; **the station is ~ walking distance** المَحَطّةُ على مَسافةٍ قَريبةٍ **3** (in less than) في خِلالِ, في أَقَلَّ من, في ظَرْفِ; **he'll be here ~ the hour** سَيَكونُ هُنا في أَقَلِّ من ساعةٍ; **they died ~ a week of each other** ماتا في غُضونِ أُسْبوعٍ من بَعْضِهِما البَعْض
B *adv* في الداخِلِ

without /wɪð'aʊt/ **A** *prep* بِلا, من غَيْرِ, بِدونِ, دونَ; **she went in ~ knocking** دَخَلَتْ من غَيْرِ أَنْ تَطْرُقَ البابَ
B *adv* (not having) **I'll have to manage ~** يَجِبُ أَنْ أُدَبِّرَ أُموري بِدونِ ذلك

withstand /wɪð'stand/ *vt* (*past tense, past participle* **withstood**) تَحَمَّلَ, احْتَمَلَ ‹*pressure, impact*›; قاوَمَ ‹*heat, cold*›; صَمَدَ (u; صُمود) (أَمام) ‹*an attack, a siege*›

witness /'wɪtnəs/ **A** *n* **1** (to an incident) شاهِد (شُهود, أَشْهاد); **she was a ~ to the accident** كانَتْ شاهِدةً على الحادِثِ; **~ for the prosecution/the defence** شاهِد إثْباتٍ \ نَفْيٍ; **to call sb as a ~** اسْتَدْعى شَخْصاً لِيَكونَ شاهِداً **2** (to sb's signature, a document) شاهِد (شُهود, أَشْهاد); **to be a ~ to sb's will** كانَ شاهِداً على وَصيّةِ شَخْصٍ **3** [u] (fml) (testimony) **to bear ~ to sth** شَهِدَ على شَيْءٍ
B *vt* **1** (to see) كانَ شاهِداً على ‹*an attack, incident, accident*› **2** (to confirm) شَهِدَ (a; شَهادة; على) ‹*a will, signature*›

witness box (BrE), **witness stand** (AmE) *n* مِنَصّة الشُهودِ

witticism /'wɪtɪsiz(ə)m/ *n* مُلْحة (مُلَح), نُكْتة (نُكَت, نِكات)

witty /'wɪti/ *adj* (**wittier, wittiest**) ‹*remark, person*› ظَريف (ظُرَفاءُ), فَكِه

wives /wʌɪvz/ *n pl* ▸ **wife**

wizard /'wɪzəd/ *n* **1** (magician) ساحِر (سَحَرة, ساحِرونَ) **2** (expert) خَبير (خُبَراءُ); **a computer/financial ~** خَبير كُمْبيوتَر \ ماليّ

wizened /'wɪz(ə)nd/ *adj* ‹*face, old woman*› ذابِل (ذُبُّل)

wk *abbr* = **week** أُسْبوع (أَسابيعُ)

WMD /dʌblju:ɛm'di:/ *n* = **Weapon of Mass Destruction** سِلاح دَمارٍ شامِلٍ

wobble /'wɒb(ə)l/ *vi* **1** (to sway) «table, cyclist, jelly» تمايَلَ **2** (to quaver) «voice» ارْتَجَفَ, ارْتَعَشَ

wobbly /'wɒbli/ *adj* (**wobblier, wobbliest**) **1** ‹*table, chair, legs*› غَيْر ثابِتٍ; ‹*wheel, tooth*› مُهْتَزّ; **I felt ~** شَعَرْتُ بِعَدَمِ الثَباتِ **2** ‹*voice*› مُرْتَجِف, مُرْتَعِش

woe /wəʊ/ *n* (liter) **1** أَسًى, كَرْب (كُروب), حُزْن (أَحْزان); **~ betide you if you lose it!** الوَيْلُ لَكَ إذا فَقَدْتَهُ **2** (**woes** *n pl*) مَشاكِل, مَتاعِب

woeful /'wəʊfʊl/ *adj* **1** (deplorable) ‹*lack, ignorance*› يُرْثى لَهُ **2** (sorrowful) ‹*tale, cry*› مُحْزِن, مُثير للأَسى

wok /wɒk/ *n* [نَوْع من القُدور]

woke /wəʊk/ *past tense* ▸ **wake**

woken /'wəʊk(ə)n/ *past participle* ▸ **wake**

wolf /wʊlf/ **A** *n* (*pl* **wolves**) ذِئْب (ذِئاب)
B *vt* (infml) الْتَهَمَ

wolf whistle *n* صَفير إعْجابٍ

wolves /wʊlvz/ *n pl* ▸ **wolf**

woman /'wʊmən/ *n* (*pl* **women**) امْرَأة (نِساء); **a young ~** امْرَأة شابّة; **a ~ comes in to clean twice a week** تَأْتي امْرَأةٌ

إِنَّها امْرَأَةٌ مُسْتَقِلَّةٌ ~ ;**she's her own** لِلتَّنْظِيفِ مَرَّتَيْنِ أُسْبوعِيًّا; **to talk ~ to** ~ تَحَدَّثَتْ حَديثَ امْرَأَةٍ لِامْرَأَةٍ

woman doctor *n* دُكْتورة, طَبيبة

woman driver *n* سائِقة

womanizer, **-iser** (BrE) /ˈwʊmənʌɪzə/ *n* زير نِساءٍ

womanly /ˈwʊmənli/ *adj* <*charm, curves*> أُنْثَوِيّ

womb /wuːm/ *n* رَحِم (أَرْحام)

women /ˈwɪmɪn/ *n pl* ▸ **woman**

women's liberation, (infml) **women's lib** *n* تَحْرير المَرْأَةِ

women's movement *n* (**the women's movement**) الحَرَكة النِسائيّة

women's rights *n* حُقوق المَرْأَةِ

won /wʌn/ *past tense, past participle* ▸ **win**

wonder /ˈwʌndə/ **A** *n* **1** (marvel) أُعْجوبة (أَعاجيبُ), عَجيبة (عَجائِبُ); **it's a ~ that no one realized** من العَجيبِ أنّ أَحَداً لم يُدْرِكْ; **no ~ that he felt cheated** لا عَجَبَ في أنْ يَشْعُرَ أَنَّهُ خُدِعَ; **small** *or* **little ~ that ...** لا عَجَبَ أنّ ... ; **to be a ~ with children/horses** كانَ ماهِراً في التَعامُلِ مع الأَطْفالِ \ الخَيْلِ; **to be a ~ with engines/computers** كانَ خَبيراً في المُحَرِّكاتِ \ الحَواسيبِ; **to work ~s with sth** حَقَّقَ نَجاحاً باهِراً في شَيْءٍ; **the ~s of the ancient/modern world** عَجائِب العالَمِ القَديمِ \ الجَديدِ **2** [u] (awe) ذُهول, تَعَجُّب; **to be lost in ~** شَعَرَ بالذُهولِ
B *modifier* <*cure, drug*> مُعْجِزة; **a new ~ cure** دَواء مُعْجِزة
C *vt* (to ask oneself) تَساءَلَ; **I ~ how/why he did it** أَتَساءَلُ كَيفَ \ لِماذا فَعَلَهُ; **I ~ if you could help me?** أَتَساءَلُ إنْ كُنْتَ تَسْتَطيعُ أنْ تُساعِدَني ؟
D *vi* **1** (to think) **to ~ about sth** تَساءَلَ عن شَيْءٍ; **I'm ~ing about my options** أَتَساءَلُ عن اخْتِياراتي **2** (in statements) **it's not to be ~ed at that they are feeling angry** لا عَجَبَ أَنَّهُمْ يَشْعُرونَ بالغَضَبِ; **they'll be late again, I shouldn't ~** سَيَتَأَخَّرونَ مَرّةً أُخْرى, لا يَجِبُ أنْ نَسْتَعْجِبَ

wonderful /ˈwʌndəfʊl/ *adj* <*opportunity, person*> رائِع; **we had a ~ time** قَضَيْنا وَقْتاً مُمْتِعاً للغايةِ

wonderfully /ˈwʌndəf(ə)li/ *adv* <*written, to work*> على نَحْوٍ رائِع, بِصورةٍ رائِعةٍ

wonky /ˈwɒŋki/ *adj* (**wonkier**, **wonkiest**) (BrE infml) **1** (wobbly) <*table, stool*> غَيْر ثابِتٍ **2** (crooked) <*parting*> مُعْوَجّ, مُلْتَوٍ; <*picture*> مائِل

wont /wəʊnt/ *adj* (liter hum) **to be ~ to do sth** كانَ مُعْتاداً أنْ يَفْعَلَ شَيْئاً

won't /wəʊnt/ *abbr* = **will not** ▸ **will[1]**

woo /wuː/ *vt* (**woos**, **wooing**, **wooed**) **1** <*a woman*> اِسْتَمالَ, تَوَدَّدَ (إلى) **2** <*voters, customers*> تَوَدَّدَ (إلى)

wood /wʊd/ *n* **1** (material) خَشَب (أَخْشاب); (firewood) حَطَب (أَحْطاب) **2** (wooded area) غابة (غابات, غاب); **the ~s** الغابة

woodcarver /ˈwʊdkɑːvə/ *n* حَفّار خَشَبٍ

woodcock /ˈwʊdkɒk/ *n* (*pl* **woodcock** *or* **woodcocks**) دَجاجة الأَرْضِ

wooded /ˈwʊdɪd/ *adj* <*area, valley*> مُشَجَّر

wooden /ˈwʊd(ə)n/ *adj* **1** (made of wood) <*floor, spoon*> خَشَبيّ **2** (stiff, awkward) <*acting, performance*> مُتَخَشِّب, جافّ, خَشِن (خِشان)

woodland /ˈwʊdlənd/ *n* أَرْض مُشَجَّرة

woodlouse /ˈwʊdlaʊs/ *n* (*pl* **woodlice** /-lʌɪs/) قَمْل الخَشَبِ

woodpecker /ˈwʊdpɛkə/ *n* نَقّار الخَشَبِ

wood pigeon *n* وَرَشان (وَرْشان)

woodpile /ˈwʊdpʌɪl/ *n* كَوْمة حَطَب

woodshed /ˈwʊdʃɛd/ *n* مَخْزَن الحَطَبِ

woodwind /ˈwʊdwɪnd/ *n pl* آلات نَفْخٍ خَشَبِيّة; **the ~s** آلات النَفْخِ الخَشَبِيّة (في أوركِسْترا)

woodwork /ˈwʊdwəːk/ *n* **1** (wooden fittings) [الأَجْزاء المَصْنوعة من الخَشَبِ في غُرْفة أو بِناية] **2** (BrE) (carpentry) نِجارة

woodworm /ˈwʊdwəːm/ *n* (*pl* **woodworm** *or* **woodworms**) **1** (larva) سوس الخَشَبِ **2** [u] (infestation) تَسْويس

woody /ˈwʊdi/ *adj* (**woodier**, **woodiest**) **1** <*hill, landscape*> مُشْجِر **2** <*plant, stem*> خَشَبِيّ

woof /wʊf/ **A** *n* نُباح
B *excl* عَوْعَوْ

wool /wʊl/ *n* صوف

woollen, **woolen** (AmE) /ˈwʊlən/ **A** *adj* ‹*socks, cloth*› صوفيّ **B** (**woollens** also **woolens** AmE) *n pl* (garments) مَلابِس صوفيّة

woolly, **wooly** (AmE) /ˈwʊli/ **A** *adj* (**woollier**, **woolliest**) **1** ‹*hat, sweater*› صوفيّ **2** ‹*thinking, argument*› غامِض ,مُبْهَم, غير واضِح **B** *n* (*pl* **woollies**) (BrE infml) سُتْرة صوفيّة

word /wəːd/ **A** *n* **1** (verbal expression) كَلِمة; **those were his very ~s** تِلْكَ كانَتْ كَلِماتُهُ بالضَبْطِ; **tell us in your own ~s** أَخْبِرْنا بِأُسْلوبِكَ; **to have no ~s to express sth** لم يَجِد الكَلِماتِ للتَعْبيرِ عن شَيْءٍ; **I couldn't get a ~ in** لم أَسْتَطِعْ أَنْ أَقولَ كَلِمةً واحِدةً; **in other ~s, he's failed** بِعِبارةٍ أُخرى، لَقَدْ فَشِلَ; **the spoken/written ~** الكَلِمة المَنْطوقة \ المَكْتوبة; **by ~ of mouth** مُشافَهةً \ شَفَوِيًّا; **what's the Greek ~ for 'table'?** ما هي الكَلِمةُ اليونانيّةُ ل 'طاولة'؟; **he's a man of few ~s** هو رَجُلٌ قليلُ الكَلامِ; **a ~ of advice/warning** نَصيحة \ تَحْذير; **it's all too awful for ~s** إنَّهُ فَظيعٌ إلى دَرَجةٍ تَعْجِزُ فيها الكَلِماتُ عن وَصْفِهِ; **I believed every ~ he said** صَدَّقْتُ كُلَّ كَلِمةٍ قالَها **2** (anything, something) كَلِمة; **not to hear/understand a ~ of what was said** لم يَسْمَعْ \ يَفْهَمْ كَلِمةً مِمّا قيلَ; **I don't believe a ~ of it** لا أُصَدِّقُ كَلِمةً مِنْهُ; **he won't hear a ~ against her** لن يَسْمَعَ أيّةَ كَلِمةٍ تُقالُ ضِدَّها; **he never has a good ~ to say about anyone** لَيْس لَدَيْهِ أَبَداً أَيّةُ كَلِمةٍ طَيِّبةٍ لِيَقولَها عن أَيِّ شَخْصٍ **3** [u] (information) خَبَر ,مَعْلومة (أَخْبار); **there is no ~ of them** لا خَبَرَ مِنْهُمْ; **~ got out that ...** انْتَشَرت الأَخْبارُ ...; **to spread the ~** نَشَر الخَبَرَ **4** (promise) كَلِمة; **he gave me his ~** أَعْطاني كَلِمَتَهُ; **to keep/break one's ~** حافَظَ على كَلِمَتِهِ \ أَخْلَفَ بِوَعْدِهِ; **it's his ~ against mine** كَلِمَتُهُ ضِدّ كَلِمَتي (لَيْس هُناكَ دَليلٌ); **don't take my ~ for it** لا تَعْتَمِدْ فَقَطْ على ما أَقولُهُ; **he's a man of his ~** هو رَجُلٌ يَحْتَرِمُ كَلِمَتَهُ **5** (rumour) **~ has it that he's a millionaire** يَقولونَ إِنَّهُ مِلْيونير; **~ got round** *or* **around that ...** انْتَشَرت الشائِعاتُ ... **6** (command) أَمْر (أَوامِرُ); **if you need anything just say the ~** أَخْبِرْني إذا أَرَدْتَ أَيَّ شَيْءٍ; **just say the ~ and I'll come** اُطْلُبْني فَقَطْ وَسآتي **B** (**words**) *n pl* **1** (verbiage) إِطْناب; **it's all empty ~s** إنَّهُ مُجَرَّدُ كَلامٍ فارِغٍ **2** (of play) دَوْر (أَدْوار); (of song) كَلِمات (قَصائِدُ) قَصيدة ,الأُغْنِيةِ **C** (**worded**) *in combination* **a carefully ~ed letter** رِسالة مَكْتوبة بِحَذَرٍ; **a strongly ~ed statement** بَيان مَكْتوب بِقُوّةٍ **D** *vt* صاغَ (u; صِياغة) ‹*a reply, letter, statement*›

(Idioms) **to eat one's words** أُجْبِرَ على التَراجُعِ عن أَقْوالِهِ; **the last word in ...** القَوْل الفَصْل في ...; **to take the words out of sb's mouth** قالَ ما كانَ يَجولُ بِخاطِرِ شَخْصٍ

word for word *adv* ‹*to copy, repeat*› كَلِمةً كَلِمةً; ‹*to translate*› حَرْفِيًّا

wording /ˈwəːdɪŋ/ *n* صِياغة; **I suggest changing the ~ to make it clearer** أَقْتَرِحُ تَغْييرَ الصِياغةِ لِجَعْلِهِ أَكْثَرَ وُضوحاً

word list *n* قائِمة كَلِماتٍ

word of mouth *n* مُشافَهة; **by word of mouth** مُشافَهةً

word processing *n* مُعالَجة الكَلِماتِ

word processor *n* مُعالِج كَلِماتٍ

wordy /ˈwəːdi/ *adj* (**wordier**, **wordiest**) ‹*document, writer*› مَليء بالحَشْوِ ,مُسْهَب ,مُطْنَب

wore /wɔː/ *past tense* ▸ **wear** A, B

work /wəːk/ **A** *n* **1** (physical or mental activity) عَمَل (أَعْمال); **to be at ~ on sth** كانَ يَعْمَلُ على شَيْءٍ; **to be hard at ~** كانَ غارِقاً في العَمَلِ; **to go to** *or* **get to ~ on sth** بَدَأَ العَمَلَ على شَيْءٍ; **to put a lot of ~ into sth** عَمِلَ لِساعاتٍ طَويلةٍ على شَيْءٍ ‹*an essay, a meal*›; **to put** *or* **set sb to ~** طَلَبَ من شَخْصٍ القِيامَ بِعَمَلٍ; **we put him to ~ cleaning** طَلَبْنا مِنْهُ أَنْ يَقومَ بالتَنْظيفِ; **it was hard ~ chopping the wood** كانَ تَقْطيعُ الخَشَبِ عَمَلاً صَعْباً; **it's hot/thirsty ~** إنَّهُ عَمَلٌ يُسَبِّبُ الشُعورَ بالحَرارة \ بالعَطَشِ; **your report needs more ~** عَمَلُكَ يَحْتاجُ إلى مَزيدٍ من البَحْثِ; **to make short** *or* **light work of sth** قامَ بِشَيْءٍ كَأَنَّهُ عَمَلٌ خَفيفٌ **2** (employment) عَمَل (أَعْمال); **to be in ~/out of ~** كانَ لَهُ عَمَلٌ \ كانَ عاطِلاً عن العَمَلِ; **to be looking for ~** كانَ يَبْحَثُ عن عَمَلٍ; **to be off ~** كانَ في عُطْلةٍ مَرَضيّةٍ **3** (place of employment) **to go to ~** ذَهَبَ إلى العَمَلِ; **don't phone me at ~** لا تَتَّصِلْ بي في العَمَلِ **4** [u] (construction) أَشْغال **5** [u] (papers, computer files) **to take ~ home** أَكْمَلَ عَمَلَهُ في المَنْزِلِ **6** (assignment, artwork) عَمَل (أعْمال); **is this your ~?** هل هذا عَمَلُكَ ؟; **to mark students' ~** صَحَّحَ واجِباتِ الطُلّابِ; **a ~ of genius** عَمَل عَبْقَرِيّ; **a ~ of reference** عَمَل مَرْجَعِيّ; **this robbery was the ~ of a professional** كانَتْ هذه السَرِقةُ من عَمَلِ شَخْصٍ مُحْتَرِفٍ ⑦ (effect) **to go to ~** «drugs, detergent» قامَ بِمَفْعولِهِ; **the weedkiller did its ~** قامَ مُزيلُ الأَعْشابِ بِمَفْعولِهِ

B (**works**) *n pl* ① (plant, factory) مَعْمَل (مَعامِلُ), مَصْنَع (مَصانِعُ) ② (construction work) أَشْغال ③ (infml) (everything) **the ~s, the full ~s** كُلّ الأَغْراضِ

C *vt* ① (to earn a living by) عَمِلَ (a; عَمَل); **to ~ shifts** عَمِلَ في وَرْدِيّاتٍ مُخْتَلِفةٍ; **to ~ days/nights** عَمِلَ في النَهارِ \ اللَيْلِ; **to ~ a 40 hour week** عَمِلَ 40 ساعةً في الأُسْبوعِ; **we ~ed twelve hours without a break** عَمِلْنا اثْنَتَيْ عَشْرةَ ساعةً دون اسْتِراحةٍ; **to ~ one's way through college** [كانَ يَعْمَلُ ويَدْرُسُ في نَفْسِ الوَقْتِ أثناء الدِراسةِ في الجامِعةِ] ② (by enforcing) **to ~ sb hard** شَغَّلَ شَخْصاً بِشَكْلٍ شاقٍّ ③ (to operate) شَغَّلَ ‹*a computer, the equipment, a machine*› ④ (to exploit) اسْتَخْدَمَ ‹*an oilfield, land, a mine*› ⑤ «sales representatives, pickpockets, prostitutes» مارَسَ عَمَلَهُ في ‹*an area*› ⑥ **to ~ one's way through sth** (finishing: a task, list, document) شَقَّ طَريقَهُ إلى انْتِهاءِ شَيْءٍ; (: food, drink) أَتى على شَيْءٍ; **to ~ one's way through the alphabet** أَنْجَزَ عَمَلَهُ كامِلاً ⑦ (to bring about) **to ~ wonders/miracles** أَتى بالمُعْجِزاتِ ⑧ (to use to one's advantage) اسْتَغَلَّ; **to ~ the system** اسْتَغَلَّ النِظامَ; **how did you manage to ~ it?** كيف تَمَكَّنْتَ من تَشْغيلِهِ؟; **I've ~ed things so that you travel free** لَقَدْ رَتَّبْتُ لَكَ الأُمورَ لِتُسافِرَ مَجّاناً ⑨ (to fashion) شَكَّلَ ‹*the clay, gold*›; شَكَّلَ ‹*the dough*› ⑩ (to manoeuvre) **to ~ sth into a slot/hole** حَرَّكَ شَيْئاً نحو فَتْحةٍ \ ثُقْبٍ; **to ~ a lever up and down** حَرَّكَ رافِعةً صُعوداً وَهُبوطاً ⑪ (to move) **to ~ one's way through a crowd/across a room** شَقَّ طَريقَهُ في الزِحامِ \ عابِراً الغُرْفةَ; **to ~ one's way along a ledge** شَقَّ طَريقَهُ على طولِ السِلْسِلةِ الصَخْرِيّةِ; **start at the top and ~ your way down** ابْدَأْ من الأَعْلى ولا تَتَوَقَّفْ حتّى تَنْتَهِيَ; **it ~ed its way loose, it ~ed itself loose** تَحَرَّكَ حتّى فَكَّ نَفْسَهُ

D *vi* ① (in a job, profession) عَمِلَ (a; عَمَل), اشْتَغَلَ; **to ~ at home** عَمِلَ في البَيْتِ; **to ~ as a midwife/teacher** عَمِلَتْ قابِلةً \ عَمِلَ مُدَرِّساً; **to ~ in sales/publishing** عَمِلَ في المَبيعاتِ \ النَشْرِ ② (on a task, an object) عَمِلَ (a; عَمَل), اشْتَغَلَ; **to ~ on sth** عَمِلَ على شَيْءٍ; **he's ~ing on his speech** يُعِدُّ خِطابَهُ; **I spent the morning ~ing in the garden** قَضَّيْتُ الصَباحَ أَعْمَلُ في الحَديقةِ; **I'm ~ing on the assumption that ...** أَعْمَلُ مُفْتَرِضاً أنّ ... ③ (to use) **he ~s in silver/bronze** يَشْتَغِلُ بالفِضّةِ \ بالبُرونْزِ; **he ~s in oils/watercolours** يَسْتَعْمِلُ الأَلْوانَ الزَيْتِيّةَ \ المائيّةَ ④ (to strive) **to ~ towards a solution/an agreement** عَمِلَ على الوُصولِ إلى حَلٍّ \ اتِّفاقٍ; **to ~ against corruption/globalization** عَمِلَ ضدّ الفَسادِ \ العَوْلَمةِ ⑤ (to function) «equipment, machines, systems» عَمِلَ (a; عَمَل); **the system ~s very well** يَعْمَلُ النِظامُ بِصورةٍ جَيِّدةٍ جِدّاً; **the washing machine isn't ~ing** الغَسّالةُ لا تَعْمَلُ; **to ~ on batteries/off the mains** عَمِلَ على البَطّارِيّاتِ \ مُنْفَصِلاً عن المُوصِلاتِ الكَهْرَبائِيّةِ الرَئيسِيّةِ ⑥ (to turn out) عَمِلَ (a; عَمَل); **it doesn't ~** *or* **things don't ~ like that** لا يَعْمَلُ بِتِلْكَ الطَريقةِ; **to ~ to sb's advantage, to ~ in sb's favour** عَمِلَ لِصالِحِ شَخْصٍ; **to ~ to sb's disadvantage, to ~ against sb** عَمِلَ ضدّ مَصْلَحةِ شَخْصٍ ⑦ (to be successful) «treatments, drugs» كانَ فَعّالاً, أَعْطى مَفْعولَهُ; **does the prescribed medicine ~?** هل أَعْطى الدَواءُ المَوْصوفُ مَفْعولَهُ؟; **the plan never ~ed** لم تَنْجَح الخُطّةُ أَبَداً

E *v refl* ① (to exert oneself) **to ~ oneself too hard** أَجْهَدَ نَفْسَهُ كَثيراً ② (into an emotional state) **to ~ oneself into a rage/frenzy** اغْتاظَ \ دَخَلَ في نَوْبةٍ من الهِياجِ

(Idioms) **to have one's work cut out** كانَ أَمامَهُ عَمَلٌ شاقٌّ; **to work one's way up** شَقَّ طَريقَهُ إلى القِمّةِ

(Phrasal verbs) **work around**: **~ around to [sth]** دارَ حولَ شَيْءٍ ‹*a subject*›; **it took him ages to ~ around to what he wanted to say** ظَلَّ وَقْتاً طويلاً يَدورُ حولَ المَوْضوعِ لِيَتَمَكَّنَ من قَوْلِ ما يُريدُ

• **work in**: **~ in [sth], ~ [sth] in** ① (to incorporate) ضَمَّنَ في [شَيْءٍ] ‹*a joke, reference*›; أَدْرَجَ في [شَيْءٍ] ‹*a fact, name*› ② (to mix in) خَلَطَ في [شَيْءٍ] ‹*an ingredient*›

• **work off**: **~ [sth] off, ~ off [sth]** ① (to remove) أَزالَ [شَيْئاً] ‹*a lid*› ② (to get rid of) تَخَلَّصَ من [شَيْءٍ] ‹*weight, energy,* *one's frustration›* **3** (to repay) [سَدَّدَ [شَيْئاً] مُقابِلَ العَمَلِ] *‹a loan, debt›*

• **work on** **A** (to continue) عَمِلَ وَاصَلَ العَمَلَ **B** **~ on [sb]** (infml) على إقْناعِ [شَخْصٍ]

• **work out** **A** **1** (to exercise) تَمَرَّنَ **2** «plans, marriages» (to go well) نَجَحَ (a; نَجاح) **3** (to add up to) **to ~ out at** (BrE) *or* **to** (AmE) **sth** بَلَغَ سِعْرُهُ \ مَجْموعُهُ شَيْئاً; **so that ~s out at twenty pounds each** ذلك يَعْني أنّ سِعْرَ كُلِّ واحِدٍ عِشْرونَ جُنَيْهاً إذَنْ

B **~ out [sth], ~ [sth] out** **1** (to calculate) تَوَصَّلَ إلى [شَيْءٍ] *‹the answer›*; حَسَبَ [شَيْئاً] *‹the average, total›* **2** (to solve) حَلَّ [شَيْئاً] تَوَصَّلَ إلى [شَيْءٍ] *‹the answer, reason, culprit›*; *‹a riddle, problem, clue›*; **have you ~ed out what it means?** هل تَمَكَّنْتَ من مَعْرِفةِ ما يَعْني؟ **3** (to devise) اسْتَنْبَطَ \ رَسَمَ [شَيْئاً] *‹a plan, route›* **4** (in employment) **to ~ out one's notice** واصَلَ العَمَلَ أثناء المُهْلةِ المُعْطاةِ

• **work over**: **~ [sb] over** (infml) أشْبَعَ [شَخْصاً] ضَرْباً *‹an informer, a victim›*

• **work to**: **~ to [sth]** الْتَزَمَ ب [شَيْءٍ] *‹a budget, schedule›*; **to ~ to a deadline** الْتَزَمَ بِمَوْعِدٍ نِهائيٍّ

• **work up** **A** **~ up [sth]** وَفَّرَ [شَيْئاً] نَمّى [شَيْئاً] *‹interest›*; *‹support›*; **to ~ up the courage to do sth** أصْبَحَ لَدَيْهِ الشَّجاعةُ لِيَفْعَلَ شَيْئاً; **to ~ up an appetite** تَطَوَّرَتْ لَدَيْهِ شَهيّةٌ **B** **~ up to [sth]** تَواصَلَ تَدْريجيًّا حتّى [شَيْءٍ] *‹an announcement, a confession, confrontation›* **C** **~ [sb] up** **1** (to excite) أثارَ [شَخْصاً] *‹a crowd, child›*; **he ~ed the crowd up into a frenzy** أثارَ الجُمْهورَ خالِقاً فيهِ حالةً من الهِياجِ **2** (in annoyance) **to get ~ed up** تَضايَقَ كَثيراً; **to ~ oneself up into a state** بَلَغَ دَرَجةً عالِيةً من الانْفِعالِ

workable /'wə:kəb(ə)l/ *adj ‹solution, plan›* قابِل للتَطْبيقِ

workaholic /wə:kə'hɒlɪk/ *n* (infml) مُدْمِن على العَمَلِ

workbench /'wə:kbɛntʃ/ *n* مِنْضَدة \ طاوِلة عَمَلٍ

workbook /'wə:kbʊk/ *n* كُرّاسة تَمارينَ

work clothes *n* مَلابِس العَمَلِ

workday /'wə:kdeɪ/ *n* **1** (weekday) يَوْم عَمَلٍ **2** (part of the day) يَوْم عَمَلٍ

worker /'wə:kə/ *n* **1** (in manual job) عامِل (عامِلونَ, عُمّال); **a factory/construction ~** عامِل مَصْنَعٍ \ بِناءٍ; **she's a hard ~** هي عامِلةٌ مُجِدّةٌ **2** (bee, ant) شَغّالة, عامِلة

work experience *n* خِبْرة عَمَليّة

workforce /'wə:kfɔ:s/ *n* **1** (working population) القُوى العامِلة **2** (employees) عامِلونَ, مُوَظَّفونَ

working /'wə:kɪŋ/ **A** *adj* **1** (professional) *‹parent, mother, population›* عامِل; **the ~ population has increased/decreased** ارْتَفَعَ \ انْخَفَضَ عَدَدُ السُّكّانِ القادِرينَ على العَمَلِ; **she has two ~ parents** لَدَيْها أبَوانِ عامِلانِ **2** (relating to work) *‹conditions, methods›* عَمَلٍ; **during ~ hours** أثناء ساعاتِ العَمَلِ; **we have a good ~ relationship** لَدَيْنا عِلاقةُ عَمَلٍ جَيِّدةٍ **3** (provisional) *‹title, hypothesis›* مُؤَقَّت **4** (functional) *‹model, farm, mine›* عامِل; **to have a ~ knowledge of Arabic** كانَ على دِرايةٍ باللُغةِ العَرَبيّةِ; **in full/good ~ order** يَعْمَلُ بِشَكْلٍ جَيِّدٍ \ مُمْتازٍ

B *n* (functioning) طَريقة عَمَلٍ

C **(workings)** *n pl* **1** (fml) (functioning) طَريقة عَمَلٍ **2** (calculations) طَريقة الحِسابِ

working capital *n* رَأس مالٍ عامِل

working class **A** *n* **the working class** *or* **classes** الطَبَقة العامِلة;

B **(working-class)** *adj ‹area, background›* عُمّاليّ

working party *n* جَماعة عَمَلٍ

workings /'wə:kɪŋz/ *n pl* طَريقة عَمَلٍ

workload /'wə:kləʊd/ *n* كَمّيّة عَمَلٍ

workman /'wə:kmən/ *n* (*pl* **-men**) عامِل (عُمّال)

workmanlike /'wə:kmənlʌɪk/ *adj ‹performance, effort›* ماهِر (لَكِنْ غَيْر مُلْهَم)

workmanship /'wə:kmənʃɪp/ *n* مَهارة, إتْقان; **an exquisite piece of ~** قِطْعة تَعْكِسُ مَهارةً حِرَفيّةً عالِيةً

workmate /'wə:kmeɪt/ *n* زَميل (زُمَلاءُ)

work of art *n* عَمَل فَنّيّ

workout /'wə:kaʊt/ *n* تَمْرين رِياضيّ

work permit *n* تَأْشيرة عَمَلٍ

workplace /'wə:kpleɪs/ *n* مَكان عَمَلٍ

work-sharing /'wəːkʃɛːrɪŋ/ *n* تقاسُم العَمَل

worksheet /'wəːkʃiːt/ *n* 1 (for learning) وَرَقة عَمَلٍ 2 (in spreadsheets) وَرَقة عَمَلٍ

workshop /'wəːkʃɒp/ *n* 1 (room, building) وَرْشة (وَرْشات, وِرَش), مَشْغَل (مَشاغِلُ) 2 (study group) وَرْشة عَمَلٍ

workstation /'wəːksteɪʃ(ə)n/ *n* مَحَطّة عَمَلٍ

work surface *n* مِنْضَدة (مِنْضَدات, مَناضِدُ)

worktop /'wəːktɒp/ *n* (BrE) سَطْح \ مِنْضَدة عَمَلٍ

work to rule *n* [احْتِجاج عن طَرِيقِ التَباطُؤِ في العَمَلِ بِتَطْبِيقِ القَواعِدِ بِدِقّةٍ]

world /wəːld/ *n* 1 (planet) عالَم (عَوالِمُ, عالَمونَ), دُنْيا (دُنًى), كَوْن (أَكْوان); **the biggest/smallest in the ~** الأَكْبَر \ الأَصْغَر في العالَمِ; **he is known throughout the ~** هو مَعْروفٌ في العالَمِ كُلِّهِ; **the creation of the ~** خَلْق العالَمِ \ الكَوْنِ; **to travel round the ~** سافَرَ حول العالَمِ; **to want sth more than anything in the ~** أَرادَ شَيْئاً أَكْثَرَ من أَيِّ شَيْءٍ آخَرَ في العالَمِ 2 (society) عالَم (عَوالِمُ, عالَمونَ); **to make one's way in the ~** شَقَّ طَرِيقَهُ في الحَياةِ; **in the eyes of the ~** في عُيونِ العالَمِ; **to go up/down in the ~** عَلا \ انْخَفَضَ شَأْنُهُ في المُجْتَمَعِ; **to lead the ~ in electronics** قادَ العالَمَ في الإلِكْتْرونِيّاتِ; **the whole ~ knows that** العالَمُ كُلُّهُ يَعْلَمُ ذلك; **the outside ~** العالَم الخارِجيّ 3 (community) عالَم (عَوالِمُ, عالَمونَ); **the art/business ~** عالَم الفَنِّ \ الأَعْمالِ 4 (part of the earth) عالَم (عَوالِمُ, عالَمونَ); **the developed ~** العالَم المُتَقَدِّمِ 5 (person's environment) عالَم (عَوالِمُ, عالَمونَ); **he lives in a ~ of his own** يَعِيشُ في عالَمِهِ الخاصِّ

Idioms **to be worlds apart** كانا في عالَمَيْنِ مُخْتَلِفَيْنِ; **to do sb a world of good** كانَتْ لَهُ فائِدةٌ كَبِيرةٌ بالنِسْبةِ لِشَخْصٍ; **it's not the end of the world!** (infml) هذا لَيْسَ نِهايةَ العالَمِ!; **to be out of this world** (infml) لَيْسَ لَهُ مَثِيلٌ; **to set the world on fire** قَلَبَ \ أَشْعَلَ الدُنْيا; **to set the world to rights** طَرَحَ حُلولاً لِمَشاكِلِ العالَمِ; **to be the world's worst ...** (infml) كانَ أَسْوَأَ ... في العالَمِ; **there's a world of difference between ...** شَتّانَ بين ...; **to be on top of the world** كانَ في قِمّةِ السَعادةِ; **to get the best of both worlds** حَصَلَ على أَفْضَلِ ما في العالَمَيْنِ; **to think the world of sb** كانَ مُعْجَباً جِدًّا بِشَخْصٍ; **to watch the world go by** تَفَرَّجَ على الدُنْيا; **with the best will in the world** [مَهْما حاوَلَ أَنْ يَكونَ مُنْصِفاً] ▸ **oyster**

World Bank *n* **(the World Bank)** البَنْك الدُوَليّ

world championship *n* بُطولة العالَمِ

world-class /'wəːldklɑːs/ *adj* ‹*player, facility*› من الطِرازِ العالَميِّ, ذو مُسْتَوًى عالَميٍّ

World Cup *n* **(the World Cup)** كَأْس العالَمِ

world fair *n* مَعْرِض عالَميّ

world-famous /wəːld'feɪməs/ *adj* ‹*author, brand*› مَشْهور عالَمِيًّا

World Health Organization *n* **(the World Health Organization)** مُنَظَّمة الصِحّةِ العالَمِيّة

world leader *n* 1 (politician) زَعِيم من زُعَماءِ العالَمِ 2 (company) شَرِكة رائِدة عالَمِيًّا

worldly /'wəːldli/ *adj* 1 (not spiritual) ‹*possessions, concerns*› دُنْيَويّ 2 (experienced) ‹*person*› مُحَنَّك

worldly-wise /ˌwəːldli'wʌɪz/ *adj* ‹*attitude, adviser*› مُحَنَّك

world music *n* موسيقى عالَمِيّة

world power *n* دَوْلة كُبْرى \ عُظْمى

world record *n* رَقْم قِياسيّ عالَميّ

World Series *n* (AmE) **(the World Series)** [بُطولات البيسْبول في شِمالِ أَمْرِيكا]

World Trade Organization *n* **(the World Trade Organization)** مُنَظَّمة التِجارةِ العالَمِيّة

world view *n* رُؤْية العالَمِ

world war *n* حَرْب عالَمِيّة

worldwide /'wəːldwʌɪd/ A *adj* ‹*sales, reputation*› عالَميّ B *adv* ‹*to sell, be known*› حول العالَمِ, في كُلِّ أَنْحاءِ العالَمِ

World Wide Web *n* **(the World Wide Web)** الشَبَكة العَنْكَبوتِيّة العالَمِيّة

worm /wəːm/ A *n* 1 (invertebrate) دود (n coll; ديدان) 2 (in medicine) دود (n coll; ديدان) 3 (infml) (as insult) حَقِير (حُقَراءُ), خَسِيس (أَخِسّاءُ) 4 (computer virus) دودة حاسوبٍ 5 (Comput) = **write-once read many times** [جِهاز تَخْزِينِ مَعْلوماتٍ تَتِمُّ الكِتابةُ عَلَيْهِ مَرّةً واحِدةً]

B *vt* 1 عالَجَ من الديدانِ ‹*an animal*› 2 (to insinuate oneself) to ~ one's way in وَصَلَ بِطُرُقٍ مُلْتَوِيةٍ; **she ~ed her way into a permanent job** حَصَلَتْ على وَظيفةٍ دائِمةٍ بِطُرُقٍ مُلْتَوِيةٍ

(Idiom) **a can of worms** مُعْضِلة عَويصة, مَسْأَلة مُعقَّدة

(Phrasal verb) **worm out**: ~ [sth] **out of sb** اسْتَدْرَجَ شَخْصاً لِلْحُصولِ على [شَيْءٍ]

worn /wɔːn/ **A** *past participle* ▸ **wear** A, B

B *adj* ‹*tyre, jeans*› مُهْتَرِئ, بالٍ; ‹*stone, steps*› مُتَآكِل

worn out *adj* (*before n* **worn-out** /ˈwɔːnaʊt/) **1** ‹*shoes, clothes*› رَثّ, بالٍ **2** ‹*person, animal*› مُرْهَق

worried /ˈwʌrɪd/ *adj* ‹*look, parents*› قَلِق; **to be ~ about sb/sth** قَلِقَ (a; قَلَق) كانَ قَلِقاً على شَخْصٍ \ بِشَأْنِ شَيْءٍ; **to get ~** قَلِقَ (a; قَلَق)

worrier /ˈwʌriə/ *n* [شَخْص مِقْلاق]

worry /ˈwʌri/ **A** *vt* (*3rd person present sing* **worries**, *present participle* **worrying**, *past tense, past participle* **worried**) **1** (to concern) أَقْلَقَ ‹*a person*›; **it worried him that they had not replied** أَقْلَقَهُ عَدَمُ رَدِّهِمْ **2** (to be concerned) قَلِقَ (a; قَلَق); **I ~ that he could be in danger** أَخْشى أَنَّهُ قد يَكونُ في خَطَرٍ **3** (to bother) ضايَقَ ‹*a person*›; **it wouldn't ~ me if I never saw them again** لن أُبالي إذا لم أَرَهُمْ ثانِيةً **4** «dogs» ضايَقَ ‹*sheep*›

B *vi* (*3rd person present sing* **worries**, *present participle* **worrying**, *past tense, past participle* **worried**) (to be anxious) «person» قَلِقَ (a; قَلَق); **to ~ about sth/sb** قَلِقَ على \ من شَيْءٍ \ شَخْصٍ; **to ~ about doing sth** قَلِقَ من فِعْلِ شَيْءٍ; **there's nothing to ~ about** لَيْسَ هُناكَ ما يَسْتَدْعي القَلَقَ; **not to ~, I'll get a taxi** لا تَقْلَقْ، سَوْفَ آخُذُ تاكْسي; **he'll be punished, don't you ~!** سَوْفَ يُعاقَبُ، لا تَقْلَقْ!; **I ~ for his sanity sometimes** أَقْلَقُ على سَلامةِ عَقْلِهِ أَحْياناً

C *v refl* (*3rd person present sing* **worries**, *present participle* **worrying**, *past tense, past participle* **worried**) **to ~ oneself about sb/sth** قَلِقَ على شَخْصٍ \ شَيْءٍ; **I worried myself sick over the results** كُنْتُ في شِدّةِ القَلَقِ على النَّتيجةِ

D *n* (*pl* **worries**) **1** (problem) هَمّ, قَلَق (هُموم); **that's the least of my worries** ذلك أَهْوَنُ هُمومي; **he's a ~ to his parents** هو مَصْدَرُ قَلَقٍ لِوالِدَيْهِ **2** [u] (anxiety) قَلَق; **it caused him a lot of ~** سَبَّبَ لَهُ قَلَقاً كَثيراً

(Idiom) **no worries** لا عَلَيْكَ

worry beads *n* ≈ مِسْبَحة (مَسابِح)

worrying /ˈwʌrɪɪŋ/ *adj* ‹*trend, sign*› مُقْلِق

worse /wɜːs/ **A** *adj* (*comparative of* **bad**) أَسْوَأ; **to get ~** «situation, weather» تَدَهْوَرَ; «patient» تَدَهْوَرَتْ حالَتُهُ; **to make matters ~, it started snowing** والّذي زادَ الطينَ بِلّةً، سُقوطُ الثَّلْجِ

B *adv* (*comparative* **badly**) بِشَكْلٍ أَسْوَأ

C *n* **there is ~ to come** سَتَزيدُ الأُمورُ سوءاً; **things took a turn for the ~** ساءَتِ الأُمورُ; **to look the ~ for wear** (damaged) ظَهَرَ مُتَدَهْوِراً; (drunk) بَدا سَكْراناً

worsen /ˈwɜːs(ə)n/ **A** *vt* فاقَمَ, جَعَلَ أَسْوَأ ‹*a situation, problem*›

B *vi* «condition, situation» تَفاقَمَ, ازْدادَ سوءاً

worsening /ˈwɜːsnɪŋ/ *adj* ‹*situation, crisis*› تَرَدٍّ, تَفاقُم

worse off *adj* (*before n* **worse-off** /ˈwɜːsɒf/) **1** (poorer) أَفْقَر **2** (less favourably placed) في وَضْعٍ أَسْوَأ; **the family is now worse off** العائِلةُ في وَضْعٍ أَسْوَأ الآنَ

worship /ˈwɜːʃɪp/ **A** *n* **1** (of God, a deity) عِبادة; **a place of ~** بَيْت عِبادةٍ **2** (of money, wealth) عِبادة **3** (BrE) (in titles) **Your/His Worship** سِيادَتُكُمْ \ سِيادَتُهُ

B *vt* (**-pp-**, **-p-** AmE) **1** عَبَدَ (u; عِبادة) ‹*God, a deity*› **2** عَبَدَ (u; عِبادة) ‹*money, wealth*›; بَجَّلَ ‹*a person*›

C *vi* (**-pp-**, **-p-** AmE) تَعَبَّدَ

worshipper, **worshiper** (AmE) /ˈwɜːʃɪpə/ *n* عابِد (عابِدونَ, عَبَدة, عُبّاد)

worst /wɜːst/ **A** *adj* (*superlative of* **bad**) **1** (most unsatisfactory, unpleasant) ‹*film, holiday*› الأَسْوَأ; **that's the ~ thing you could have said** هذا أَسْوَأُ شَيْءٍ يُمْكِنُ أَنْ تَقولَهُ **2** (most serious) ‹*case, mistake*› الأَخْطَر, الأَسْوَأ

B *adv* على أَسْوَأِ نَحْوٍ; **the area ~ hit by the earthquake** المِنْطَقة الأَكْثَرِ إصابةً بالزِلْزالِ; **~ of all** الأَسْوَأ من ذلك كُلِّهِ

C *n* **the ~** الأَسْوَأ; **I began to fear the ~** بَدَأْتُ أَخْشى الأَسْوَأَ; **his sister brings out the ~ in him** تَجْعَلُهُ أُخْتُهُ في أَسْوَأ حالاتِهِ العَصَبِيّةِ; **at ~** في أَسْوَأِ الأَحْوالِ; **I'm at my ~ in the mornings** أَكونُ في أَسْوَأ حالاتي في الصَّباحِ; **this is commercialism at its ~** هذه هي الروحُ التِجارِيّةُ في أَسْوَأ حالاتِها

(Idiom) **if the worst comes to the worst** إذا وَقَعَ المَحْظورُ

worth /wɜːθ/ **A** ***adj*** **1** (of financial value) **to be ~ sth** كانَتْ قيمَتُهُ شَيْئاً; **the pound was ~ 1.18 euros** كانَتْ قيمةُ الجُنَيْهِ 1.18 يورو; **what** *or* **how much is it ~?** ما ثَمَنُهُ؟; **it's not ~ much** لَيْسَتْ لَهُ قيمةٌ كَبيرةٌ; **he is ~ millions** تُقَدَّرُ ثَرْوَتُهُ بالمَلايينِ **2** (of abstract value) **to be ~ sth** اسْتَحَقَّ شَيْئاً; **unsubstantiated reports are not ~ much** التَقاريرُ غَيْرُ المُؤَكَّدةِ لَيْسَتْ لَها قيمةٌ كَبيرةٌ; **it's more than my job is ~ to do that** ذلك يَتَعَدّى مُتَطَلِّباتِ وَظيفَتي; **to be ~ a try** كانَ يَسْتَحِقُّ المُحاوَلةَ; **don't get upset, it's not ~ it** لا تَحْزَنْ، فَهُوَ لا يَسْتَحِقُّ ذلك; **his suggestion is ~ considering** يَسْتَحِقُّ اقْتِراحُهُ الاعْتِبارَ

B ***n*** **1** (measure, quantity) **five pounds'/two days' ~ of sth** شَيْء تُعادِلُ قيمَتُهُ خَمْسةَ جُنَيْهاتٍ \ يَوْمَيْنِ; **thousands of dollars' ~ of damage** ضَرَر بِقيمةِ آلافِ الدولاراتِ; **a week's ~ of supplies** مُؤَن تَكْفي أُسْبوعاً; **to get one's money's ~** حَصَلَ على قيمةِ ما دَفَعَ **2** (value) قيمة; **these gems are of little/great ~** هذه الأَحْجارُ الكَريمةُ قَليلةُ \ كَبيرةُ القيمةِ; **to prove one's ~** أَثْبَتَ جَدارَتَهُ

(Idioms) **for what it's worth** لِلعِلْمِ فَقَطْ; **to be worth sb's while** اسْتَحَقَّ العَناءَ من شَخْصٍ

worthless /ˈwɜːθləs/ ***adj*** **1** ‹*shares, junk*› عَديمُ القيمةِ; **to be ~** لا جَدْوى مِنْهُ **2** ‹*person*› حَقير (حُقَراءُ), كانَ عَديمَ القيمةِ

worthwhile /wɜːθˈwaɪl/ ***adj*** ‹*cause, project*› جَدير, مُفيد بالاهْتِمامِ; **to be ~ doing** اسْتَحَقَّ فِعْلُهُ; **it is ~ to remember that** لَيْس من المُفيدِ تَذَكُّرُ ذلك; **he's got nothing ~ to say** لَدَيْهِ كَلامٌ جَديرٌ بالاهْتِمامِ

worthy /ˈwɜːði/ ***adj*** (**worthier, worthiest**) **1** (deserving) **to be ~ of sth/sb** كانَ جَديراً بِشَيْءٍ \ بِشَخْصٍ; **the design is ~ of the prize** يَسْتَحِقُّ التَصْميمُ الجائِزةَ; **he felt he was not ~ of her** شَعَرَ بِأَنَّهُ غَيْرُ جَديرٍ بِها **2** (appropriate) ‹*successor, opponent*› مُناسِب **3** (admirable) ‹*effort, aim, person*› جَدير بالإِعْجابِ; **a ~ cause** قَضيّة جَديرة بالاهْتِمامِ

would /wʊd, wəd/ ***modal aux*** (*also* **'d**; *negative* **wouldn't, would not**) **1** (in past tenses, in reported speech) **she said she ~n't/would not be at the meeting** قالَتْ أَنَّها لن تَحْضُرَ الاجْتِماعَ; **I thought you'd like it/would like it** اعْتَقَدْتُ أَنَّكَ سَتُحِبُّهُ; **they promised they ~ come back** وَعَدوا بِأَنَّهُمْ سَيَعودونَ; **I thought she ~ have forgotten** اعْتَقَدْتُ أَنَّها قد نَسِيَتْ; **I wish he ~ shut the door!** أَتَمَنّى لو أَنَّهُ أَغْلَقَ البابَ! **2** (in conditional statements) **I'm sure she ~ help if you asked her** أنا واثِقٌ أَنَّها سَتُساعِدُكَ إذا طَلَبْتَ مِنها ذلك; **if we'd left earlier we ~ have caught the train** لو أَنَّنا غادَرْنا باكِراً لَكُنّا قد أَدْرَكْنا القِطارَ; **who ~ have believed it?** مَنْ كانَ سَيُصَدِّقُ هذا؟; **you ~n't have thought it possible!** ما كُنْتَ لِتَظُنَّ بِأَنَّ هذا مُمْكِنٌ!; **I ~ have found out sooner or later** كُنْتُ سَأَكْتَشِفُ ذلك عاجِلاً أو آجِلاً; **we ~n't have survived without his help** ما كُنّا لِنَسْتَمِرَّ لَوْلا مُساعَدَتِهِ **3** (expressing willingness to act) **they couldn't find anyone who ~ take the job** لم يَسْتَطيعوا العُثورَ على أَيِّ شَخْصٍ يَقْبَلُ بالوَظيفةِ; **he ~n't hurt a fly** لا يُؤْذي ذُبابةً \ نَمْلةً; **she just ~n't listen** هي بِبَساطةٍ لا تُريدُ أَنْ تَسْتَمِعَ; **the police ~n't give any further details** لم تُرِد الشُرْطةُ إِعْطاءَ أَيِّ تَفاصيلَ أُخْرى; **I asked her to leave but she ~n't** طَلَبْتُ مِنْها أَنْ تُغادِرَ وَلَكِنَّها رَفَضَتْ **4** (expressing inability to function) **the door ~n't close** البابُ لا يَنْغَلِقُ **5** (expressing desire, preference) **we ~ like to stay another night** نُحِبُّ \ نَوَدُّ أَنْ نَبْقى لَيْلةً أُخْرى; **we'd really like to see you** نُحِبُّ \ نَوَدُّ حَقًّا أَنْ نَراكَ; **I ~ much rather travel alone** أُفَضِّلُ أَنْ أُسافِرَ وَحْدي; **she ~ have preferred a puppy** كانَتْ تُفَضِّلُ جَرْواً; **I'd like a coffee** أُريدُ قَهْوةً **6** (in polite requests or proposals) **~ you like something to eat?** هل تُحِبُّ أَنْ تَأْكُلَ شَيْئاً؟; **switch off the light, ~ you?** هل يُمْكِنُكَ أَنْ تُطْفِئَ النورَ؟; **~ you be interested in buying one?** هل تَوَدُّ أَنْ تَشْتَرِيَ واحِداً؟; **~ you like to go to a concert?** هل تُحِبُّ الذَهابَ إلى حَفْلةٍ موسيقيّة؟; **~ you give her a message?** هل يُمْكِنُكَ أَنْ تُبْلِغَها رِسالةً؟; **~ you mind not smoking please?** رَجاءً لا تُدَخِّنْ!; **~ you please be quiet?** هل يُمْكِنُكَ الْتِزامُ الهُدوءِ من فَضْلِكَ؟; **~ you be so kind as to leave?** (fml) هَلا تَفَضَّلْتَ بالمُغادَرةِ؟ **7** (used to attenuate statements) **it ~ seem that he was right** يَبْدو كَما لو أَنَّهُ كانَ مُحِقًّا; **I ~ have thought it was obvious** كانَ يَبْدو لي أَنَّهُ واضِحٌ **8** (when giving advice) **I ~ check the list first** لو كُنْتُ مَكانَكَ لَتَفَحَّصْتُ القائِمةَ أَوَّلاً; **I ~n't do that if I were you** لو كُنْتُ مَكانَكَ لَما فَعَلْتُ ذلك; **I'd phone her in case she isn't**

at home لو كُنْتُ مَكانَكَ لاتَّصَلْتُ بِها في حالِ ما لم تَكُنْ في البَيْتِ 9 (expressing exasperation) **'he denies it'—'well he ~, ~n't he?'** 'هو يُنْكِرُ فِعْلَتَهُ' — 'حَسَناً هذا ما هو مُتَوَقَّعٌ مِنْهُ، أَلَيْسَ كَذلِكَ؟'; **'she put her foot in it'—'she ~!'** 'فَعَلَتْ شَيْئاً مُحْرِجاً' — 'هذا هو المُتَوَقَّعُ مِنْها!' 10 (expressing an assumption) **being so young, you ~n't remember the war** لِأَنَّكَ صَغيرُ السِّنِّ جِدًّا، فَلَنْ تَتَذَكَّرَ الحَرْبَ; **it ~ have been about five years ago** كانَ هذا منذ ما يَقْرُبُ من خَمْسِ سَنَواتٍ مَضَتْ 11 (indicating past habitual events, behaviour) **she ~ sit for hours at the window** كانَتْ تَجْلِسُ لِساعاتٍ أمامَ النافِذَةِ 12 (fml) (if only) **~ that it were true!** أَتَمَنّى لو كانَ هذا صَحيحاً!; **~ to God that ...** (fml) أَتَمَنّى من اللهِ أَنْ ...

would-be /ˈwʊdbi/ *adj*; **a ~ actor/writer** [شَخْص يَطْمَحُ إلى التَّمْثيلِ \ الكِتابَةِ]; **his ~ assassin** [الشَّخْص الّذي كانَ يُخَطِّطُ لِقَتْلِهِ]

wouldn't /ˈwʊd(ə)nt/ *abbr* = **would not** ▸ **would**

would've /ˈwʊdəv/ *abbr* = **would have**

wound¹ /wuːnd/ A *n* 1 (injury) جُرْح (جُروح, جِراح); **a ~ in the leg/head** جُرْح في الساقِ \ الرَّأْسِ; **to die from one's ~s** ماتَ من جُروحِهِ 2 (mental) جُرْح (جُروح, جِراح)
B *vt* جَرَحَ (a; جَرْح) ‹*the guard, corporal*›; **to ~ sb in the leg/stomach** جَرَحَ شَخْصاً في الساقِ \ المَعِدَةِ; **five soldiers were killed and ten ~ed** قُتِلَ خَمْسَةُ جُنودٍ وجُرِحَ عَشَرَةُ
(Idiom) **to lick one's wounds** لَعِقَ جُروحَهُ

wound² /waʊnd/ *past tense, past participle* ▸ **wind²**

wounded /ˈwuːndɪd/ A *n pl* **the ~** الجَرْحى
B *adj* 1 ‹*soldier, animal*› جَريح (جَرْحى), مَجْروح (مَجاريحُ)
2 ‹*pride, look*› مُهان, مَجْروح

wove /wəʊv/ *past tense* ▸ **weave**

woven /ˈwəʊv(ə)n/ *past participle* ▸ **weave**

wow /waʊ/ (infml) A *excl* يا إلَهي, يا لَلعَجَبِ
B *vt* أَثارَ الإعْجابَ, أَدْهَشَ ‹*audiences, fans*›

wpm *abbr* = **words per minute** كَلِمة في الدَّقيقةِ

wrangle /ˈraŋg(ə)l/ A *n* نِزاع (نِزاعات), جِدال (جِدالات)
B *vi* تَجادَلَ, نازَعَ

wrap /rap/ A *vt* (-pp-) 1 (for delivery, sale) غَلَّفَ ‹*food, a present*›; **would you like it ~ped?** هل تُريدُهُ مُغَلَّفاً؟; **to ~ a book in gift paper** غَلَّفَ كِتاباً بِوَرَقِ هَدايا 2 (for warmth, protection) **to ~ a blanket/coat around sb/sth, to ~ sb/sth in a blanket/coat** غَطّى شَخْصاً \ شَيْئاً بِبَطّانِيَّةٍ \ بِمِعْطَفٍ ‹*the baby, one's neck, shoulders*›; **to ~ oneself in a towel** لَفَّ نَفْسَهُ بِمِنْشَفةٍ; **to be ~ped in mystery/silence** اكْتَنَفَهُ \ غَلَّفَهُ الغُموضُ \ الصَّمْتُ 3 (as a seal) لَفَّ (u; لَفّ) ‹*tape, a handkerchief*›; **I ~ped a handkerchief around my finger** لَفَفْتُ مِنْديلاً حول إصْبَعي; **to ~ tape around a joint** لَفَّ شَريطاً حول وَصْلةٍ
B (-wrapped) *in combination* **foil-/plastic-~ped** مُغَلَّف بِوَرَقِ أَلَمِنيوم \ بِغِطاءٍ بْلاسْتيك
C *n* 1 [u] (packaging) غِلاف (أَغْلِفة, غُلُف) 2 (on shoulders) شال (شالات); (at waist) تَنّورة مَلْفوفة 3 (Culin) سَنْدْويتْش مَلْفوف
(Idiom) **to keep sth under wraps** أَبْقى شَيْئاً سِرًّا
(Phrasal verb) **wrap up** A 1 (to dress warmly) ارْتَدى مَلابِسَ ثَقيلةً; **~ up well!** ارْتَدِ مَلابِسَ ثَقيلةً! 2 (BrE) (infml) (to shut up) صَمَتَ (u; صَمْت, صُموت); **~ up!** اخْرَسْ! B **~ up [sth/sb], ~ [sth/sb] up** 1 (for delivery, sale) غَلَّفَ [شَيْئاً] ‹*a parcel, gift, purchase*› 2 (to dress warmly) لَبَّسَ [شَخْصاً] مَلابِسَ ثَقيلةً ‹*a child, patient*› 3 (to end) خَتَمَ \ أَنْهى [شَيْئاً] ‹*a session, meeting, concert*› 4 (to settle) أَبْرَمَ [شَيْئاً] ‹*a deal*›; [شَيْئاً] اخْتَتَمَ ‹*the championship, negotiations*› 5 (to be involved) **to be ~ped up in an activity/a problem** انْهَمَكَ في نَشاطٍ \ مُشْكِلةٍ; **he's very ~ped up in his work** هو مُنْهَمِكٌ جِدًّا في عَمَلِهِ

wrap-around /ˈrapəraʊnd/ *adj* ‹*skirt, dress*› لَفٌّ

wrap-around sunglasses *n* [نَظّارات شَمْسيّة ذات رِباطٍ وراء الرَّأْسِ]

wrap-over /ˈrapəʊvə/ *adj before n* ‹*skirt, dress*› لَفٌّ

wrapper /ˈrapə/ *n* غِلاف (أَغْلِفة, غُلُف)

wrapping /ˈrapɪŋ/ *n* غِلاف (أَغْلِفة, غُلُف)

wrapping paper *n* وَرَق تَغْليفٍ

wrath /rɒθ/ *n* (liter hum) غَيْظ, حَنَق

wreak /riːk/ *vt* **to ~ havoc on sth** عاثَ فَساداً في شَيْءٍ; **to ~ vengeance/revenge on sb** انْتَقَمَ من شَخْصٍ

wreath /riːθ/ *n* إكْليل (أَكاليلُ)

wreck /rɛk/ **A** *n* **1** (destroyed ship) حُطام (سَفينةٍ) **2** (destruction of a ship) تَحطُّم (سَفينةٍ) **3** (of vehicles, etc) حُطام; **it's a complete ~** إنَّهُ مُحطَّمٌ تَماماً **4** (AmE) (crash) حادِث تَحطُّم; **a car/train ~** حادِث تَحطُّمِ سَيّارةٍ \ قِطارٍ **5** (infml) (person) مُنْهار; **I was a complete nervous ~** كُنْتُ في انْهيارٍ عَصَبيٍّ تامٍّ

B *vt* **1** خَرَّبَ, حَطَّمَ ‹a car, building, house› **2** «storm» حَطَّمَ, أَغْرَقَ ‹a ship› **3** دَمَّرَ, خَرَّبَ ‹sb's life, career, marriage›; **the strike ~ed our holiday** خَرَّبَ الإضْرابُ عُطْلَتَنا

wreckage /ˈrɛkɪdʒ/ *n* حُطام

wrecked /rɛkt/ *adj* ‹car, plane, building› مُحطَّم

wrecker /ˈrɛkə/ *n* **1** (person) مُهَدِّم, مُخَرِّب **2** (AmE) (recovery truck) شاحِنة رافِعة

wren /rɛn/ *n* نَمْنَمة

wrench /rɛntʃ/ **A** *n* **1** (pull) نَزْع, خَلْع **2** (distressing experience) عَذاب (عَذابات, أَعْذِبة), إحْساس مُؤْلِم **3** (AmE) (for nuts, bolts) مِفْتاح رَبْط **4** (BrE) (with adjustable jaw) مِفْتاح إنْجليزيّ

B *vt* **1** (to pull) نَزَعَ, خَلَعَ (بِقوّةٍ); (to twist) لَوى (i; لَيّ, لُويّ) ‹sb's arm, a door›; **he ~ed the door open** فَتَحَ البابَ بِقوّةٍ **2** (to injure) لَوى (i; لَيّ, لُويّ) ‹one's knee, ankle›

wrest /rɛst/ *vt* أَخَذَ بِقوّةٍ, انْتَزَعَ ‹control, a weapon›

wrestle /ˈrɛs(ə)l/ **A** *vt* **to ~ sb to the ground** صَرَعَ شَخْصاً على الأَرْضِ

B *vi* **1** صارَعَ; **to ~ with sb** تَصارَعَ مع شَخْصٍ **2** (to struggle) صارَعَ; **to ~ with a problem** تَخَبَّطَ في مُشْكِلةٍ; **to ~ with one's conscience** صارَعَ ضَميرَهُ

wrestler /ˈrɛslə/ *n* مُصارِع

wrestling /ˈrɛslɪŋ/ *n* مُصارَعة

wretch /rɛtʃ/ *n* **1** (unfortunate person) مِسْكين (مَساكينُ, مِسْكينون) **2** (infml) (despicable person) حَقير (حُقَراءُ), خَسيس (أَخِسّاءُ)

wretched /ˈrɛtʃɪd/ *adj* **1** (unhappy) ‹person, life› بائِس (بُؤَساءُ), تَعيس (تُعَساءُ) **2** (very bad) ‹conditions› زَريّ, قاسٍ; ‹luck› سَيِّئ جِدّاً **3** (expressing anger) لَعين (لُعَناءُ), حَقير (حُقَراءُ)

wriggle /ˈrɪɡ(ə)l/ **A** *vt* **1** (to move) **to ~ one's toes/fingers** حَرَّكَ أَصابِعَ رِجْلَيْهِ \ أَصابِعَهُ **2** (to twist and turn) **to ~ one's way out of sth** تَمَلَّصَ من شَيْءٍ

B *vi* (to twist and turn) «worms, snakes, children» تَلَوّى; **to ~ free** تَلَوّى حتّى حَرَّرَ نَفْسَهُ; **to ~ along the ground** تَلَوّى على الأَرْضِ; **to ~ under the fence** زَحَفَ من تَحْتِ السِياجِ

Phrasal verbs **wriggle about, wriggle around** (to twist and turn) «worms, snakes, children» أَخَذَ يَتَلَوّى

• **wriggle out** **1** (to escape) «snakes, hamster» فَرَّ (i; فِرار) **2** (to avoid) **to ~ out of a job/of doing sth** تَمَلَّصَ من العَمَلِ \ عَمَلِ شَيْءٍ

wring /rɪŋ/ *vt* (*past tense, past participle* **wrung**) **1** عَصَرَ (i; عَصْر) ‹a cloth, clothes›; **she wrung the water out of her swimsuit** عَصَرَت الماءَ من لِباسِ سِباحَتِها **2** **to ~ sth from/out of sb** انْتَزَعَ شَيْئاً من شَخْصٍ ‹a confession, money› **3** لَوى (i; لَيّ, لُويّ) ‹an animal's neck›; **sometimes I want to ~ his neck!** أَحْياناً أَوَدُّ أَنْ أَلْوِيَ رَقْبَتَهُ!; **to ~ one's hands** فَرَكَ يَدَيْهِ بِانْفِعالٍ وَعَصَبيّةٍ

Phrasal verb **wring out**: ~ [sth] out, ~ out [sth] عَصَرَ [شَيْئاً] ‹a cloth, garment›

wrinkle /ˈrɪŋk(ə)l/ **A** *n* **1** (in cloth, clothes) غَضْن (غُضون), تَجْعيد (تَجاعيدُ) **2** (in one's skin) تَجْعيد (تَجاعيدُ)

B *vt* ‹skin, fabric› غَضَّنَ, جَعَّدَ; **to ~ one's nose** حَرَّكَ أَنْفَهُ باشْمِئْزازٍ

C *vi* «fabric» تَغَضَّنَ, تَجَعَّدَ

wrinkled /ˈrɪŋk(ə)ld/ *adj* ‹face, clothes› مُغَضَّن, مُجَعَّد, مُتَجَعِّد

wrinkly /ˈrɪŋkli/ *adj* (**wrinklier**, **wrinkliest**) (BrE) (infml) ‹face, clothes› مُغَضَّن, مُجَعَّد, مُتَجَعِّد

wrist /rɪst/ *n* مِعْصَم (مَعاصِمُ)

wristband /ˈrɪstband/ *n* **1** سِوار المِعْصَمِ **2** (part of a sleeve) طَرَف رُدْنِ القَميصِ المُطَوِّق للمِعْصَمِ

wristwatch /ˈrɪstwɒtʃ/ *n* ساعة المِعْصَمِ \ اليَدِ

writ /rɪt/ *n* أَمْر قَضائيّ

write /rʌɪt/ **A** *vt* (*past tense* **wrote**; *past participle* **written**) **1** (to set down on paper) «journalist» كَتَبَ (u; كَتْب, كِتابة) ‹an article, a note, letter›; «author, composer» أَلَّفَ ‹music, book›; **he wrote the music for the film** أَلَّفَ موسيقى الفيلْمِ;

it's written in Modern Standard Arabic هو مَكْتوبٌ باللُغةِ العَرَبيّةِ الفُصْحى; **to ~ the condition into the contract** كَتَبَ الشَرْطَ ضِمْنَ العَقْدِ **2** (to make out) كَتَبَ (u; كِتابة, كَتْب) *‹a cheque, prescription›* **3** (to compile) كَتَبَ (u; كِتابة, كَتْب) *‹software, a program›* **4** (AmE) (to compose a letter to) كَتَبَ رِسالةً لـ *‹a person›*; **~ me when you get back** أُكْتُبْ لي رِسالةً عِنْدَما تعودُ

B *vi* (*past tense* **wrote**; *past participle* **written**) **1** (to form words) كَتَبَ (u; كِتابة, كَتْب); **to ~ in pencil/ink** كَتَبَ بِقَلَمِ رَصاصٍ \ حِبْرٍ; **I wrote home** كَتَبْتُ رِسالةً إلى أَهْلي; **this pen doesn't ~** هذا القَلَمُ لا يَكْتُبُ; **I have nothing to ~ with** لَيْسَ لَدَيَّ ما أَكْتُبُ بِهِ **2** (as a profession) كَتَبَ (u; كِتابة, كَتْب), أَلَّفَ; **he ~s for a living** يَمْتَهِنُ الكِتابةَ; **I ~ for a national newspaper** أَكْتُبُ في صَحيفةٍ وَطَنيّةٍ; **to ~ about current affairs/ecology** كَتَبَ عن الشُؤونِ الراهِنةِ \ عِلْمِ البيئةِ

Phrasal verbs **write away**: (to request) **to ~ away for a catalogue/the details** أَرْسَلَ طَلَباً لِكَتالوج \ للتفاصيل

• **write back A** (to reply) كَتَبَ رَدًّا (على رِسالةٍ) **B ~ back [sth], ~ [sth] back** كَتَبَ [شَيْئاً] كَرَدٍّ *‹a letter, reply›*; **she wrote back that she had been unwell** كَتَبَتْ رَدًّا بِأنّها كانَتْ مَريضةً

• **write down**: **~ [sth] down, ~ down [sth] 1** (to note) كَتَبَ \ دَوَّنَ [شَيْئاً] *‹the details, sb's name›* **2** (to record) كَتَبَ \ دَوَّنَ [شَيْئاً] *‹the results, information›* **3** (in value) خَفَضَ قيمةَ [شَيْءٍ] *‹an asset, a debt, the value›*

• **write in A** «viewers, listeners» أَرْسَلَ; **please ~ in with your suggestions** بِرَجاءِ إرْسالِ اقْتِراحاتِكَ **B ~ [sb] in, ~ in [sb]** (AmE) «voters» أَضافَ اسْمَ [شَخْصٍ] *‹a candidate›*

• **write off A** (to request) أَرْسَلَ طَلَباً; **to ~ off for a catalogue/the details** أَرْسَلَ طَلَباً لِكَتالوج \ للتَفاصيلِ **B ~ [sth] off, ~ off [sth] 1** (to wreck) «drivers» دَمَّرَ [شَيْئاً] *‹a car›* **2** (to make valueless) أَسْقَطَ \ شَطَبَ [شَيْئاً] *‹a debt, loss, an investment›* **3** «insurance company» اعْتَبَرَ [شَيْئاً] عَديمَ القيمةِ *‹a car›* **4** (to consider ended) أَلْغى [شَيْئاً] *‹a project, an operation›* **C ~ [sb] off, ~ off [sb]** (to dismiss) «critics» اعْتَبَرَ [شَخْصاً] غَيْرَ مَقْبولٍ *‹a singer, an athlete, a student›*

• **write out A ~ [sth] out, ~ out [sth] 1** (to put down on paper) كَتَبَ [شَيْئاً] *‹instructions, a list›* **2** نَسَخَ [شَيْئاً] *‹an essay, words›* **B ~ [sb] out** (Radio, TV) (to delete) حَذَفَ دَوْرَ [شَخْصٍ] *‹a character›*

• **write up**: **~ [sth] up, ~ up [sth] 1** (to record) كَتَبَ \ دَوَّنَ [شَيْئاً] *‹the results, notes, one's findings›* **2** (in value) رَفَعَ قيمةَ [شَيْءٍ] *‹an asset›*

write-off /ˈrʌɪtɒf/ *n* **1** (vehicle) [سَيّارة مَعْطوبة جِدًّا غَيْر قابِلةٍ للتَصْليح] **2** (of debts, assets) إلْغاء (إلْغاءات)

write-protect /ˈrʌɪtprəˌtɛkt/ *vt* حَمى ضدّ الكِتابةِ *‹a flash drive›*

writer /ˈrʌɪtə/ *n* **1** (by profession) كاتِب (كَتَبة, كُتّاب) **2** (of an article, a document) كاتِب (كَتَبة, كُتّاب)

writer's block *n* تَوَقُّف ذِهْنِ الكاتِبِ (عَدَم القُدْرةِ على الكِتابةِ بِسَبَبِ نَقْصِ الأفْكار)

write-up /ˈrʌɪtʌp/ *n* **1** (review) انْتِقاد (انْتِقادات) **2** (account) تَقْرير (تَقارير)

writhe /rʌɪð/ *vi* «body, snake» تَلَوّى; **to ~ in agony** تَلَوّى أَلَماً

writing /ˈrʌɪtɪŋ/ *n* **1** (act of writing) كِتابة; **I didn't get any ~ done yesterday** لم أَتَمَكَّنْ من الكِتابةِ أَمْسِ **2** (words and letters) كِتابة, خَطّ (خُطوط); **the ~ was very small** كانَ الخَطُّ صَغيراً جِدًّا; **to put sth in ~** دَوَّنَ شَيْئاً على الوَرَقِ **3** (handwriting) خَطّ (يَدَويّ) **4** (literature) مُؤَلَّفات **5** (**writings** *n pl*) مُؤَلَّفات

writing desk *n* طاوِلة كِتابةٍ, مَكْتَب (مَكاتِبُ)

writing pad *n* دَفْتَر (دَفاتِرُ)

writing paper *n* وَرَق الكِتابةِ

written /ˈrɪt(ə)n/ **A** *past participle* ▸ **write**

B *adj* **1** (in writing) *‹permission, statement›* مَكْتوب **2** (with pen and paper) *‹test, examination›* كِتابيّ

wrong /rɒŋ/ **A** *adj* **1** (incorrect, ill-chosen) *‹answer, direction, choice›* خاطِئ, خَطَأ; **you are ~** أَنْتَ مُخْطِئٌ; **to give a ~ answer** أَعْطى جَواباً خاطِئاً; **their forecast was ~** كانَ تَوَقُّعُهُمْ خاطِئاً; **to take the ~ road** سارَ في الطَريقِ الخَطَأ; **you've got the ~ number** مَعَكَ الرَقْمُ الخاطِئُ; **to get one's facts ~** أَخْطَأَ في الحَقائِقِ; **it's the ~ glue for the job** إنَّه الغِراءُ الخاطِئُ لِهَذا الغَرَضِ; **don't get the ~ idea** لا تُسِئْ فَهْمي **2** (mistaken) **to be ~** كانَ مُخْطِئاً; **that's where you're ~** ذلك مَوْضِعُ

كانَ مُخْطِئاً بِشأْنِ شَخْصٍ \ شَيْءٍ; **she was ~ about him** كانَتْ مُخْطِئةً بِشَأْنِهِ; **to prove sb ~** أَثْبَتَ خطأَ شخصٍ ③ (reprehensible) خطأً, خاطِئ; **she hasn't done anything ~** لم تَفْعَلْ شَيْئاً خاطِئاً; **it is ~ to steal/cheat** السَرِقةُ \ الغِشُّ خطأٌ; **it was ~ of me to do that** كانَ خطأً مِنّي أنْ أَفْعَلَ ذلك; **it's ~ that so few people own so much** لَيْسَ من العَدْلِ أنْ يَمْتَلِكَ عددٌ قليلٌ من الناسِ الكَثيرَ من المُمْتَلَكاتِ; **there's nothing ~ with** *or* **in sth** لا حَرَجَ \ عَيْبَ في شَيْءٍ ④ (not as it should be) خطأً; **there is something badly ~ here** هُناكَ خطأٌ فادِحٌ هُنا; **there's something ~ with my computer** هُناكَ شَيْءٌ خطأٌ في حاسوبي; **what's ~ with your arm?** ماذا أَصابَ ذِراعَكَ؟; **what's ~ with you?** ما خَطْبُكَ؟

B *adv* **to go ~** «cars, plans» تَعَطَّلَ; **you won't go far ~ if ...** لن تُخْطِئَ إنْ ...; **you can't go ~, just follow the blue arrows** لن تُخْطِئَ، فَقَط اتْبَع الأَسْهُمَ الزَرْقاءَ; **to get the date/details ~** أَخْطأَ في التاريخِ \ التفاصيل; **I think you've got it ~** أَعْتَقِدُ أَنَّكَ أَخْطأْتَ; **he spelled my name ~** أَخْطأَ في كِتابةِ اسْمي

C *n* ① [u] (bad, evil) خطأ (أَخْطاء), غَلَط (أَغْلاط); **to be in the ~** كانَ على خَطأٍ; **to have no sense of right or ~** كانَ لا يُمَيِّزُ بين الصَوابِ والخَطَأِ ② (injustice) ظُلْم; **to right a ~** صَحَّحَ خطأً; **the rights and ~s of the matter** جَوانِبُ الصَوابِ والخَطأِ في الأَمْرِ

D *vt* (to treat unjustly) أَساءَ (إلى) ‹*one's wife, family*›

(Idioms) **don't get me wrong** لا تُسِئْ فَهْمي; **to be in the wrong** كانَ على خَطأٍ; **two wrongs don't make a right** [خطأُ الغَيْرِ لا يُبَرِّرُ لَكَ خَطأَكَ]; **you've got me all wrong** أَسَأْتَ فَهْمي تَماماً ▸**stick**

wrongdoer /'rɒŋ,duːə/ *n* مُخالِف القانونِ

wrongdoing /'rɒŋduːɪŋ/ *n* جَريمة, مُخالَفة (جَرائِمُ); **to deny ~** أَنْكَرَ الجَريمةَ

wrong-foot /,rɒŋ'fʊt/ *vt* ① (in games) راوَغَ ‹*a defender, one's opponent*› ② (to disconcert) أَرْبَكَ ‹*the opposition, an expert*›

wrongful /'rɒŋfʊl/ *adj* ‹*arrest, imprisonment, dismissal*› غَيْر قانونيٍّ, غَيْر شَرْعيٍّ, غَيْر مَشْروعٍ

wrongly /'rɒŋli/ *adv* ① (incorrectly) ‹*to spell, translate*› بِشَكْلٍ خاطِئٍ \ غَيْر صَحيح; **he concluded, ~, that ...** اسْتَنْتَجَ خطأً أنّ ... ② (mistakenly) ‹*to convict, accuse*› خطأً, بِطَريقِ الخَطأِ, بِشَكْلٍ خاطِئٍ; **rightly or ~** عن حَقٍّ أو عن باطِلٍ

wrote /rəʊt/ *past tense* ▸**write**

wrought /rɔːt/ **A** (liter) *past tense, past participle* ▸**wreak**; **the destruction ~ by war** الدمار الّذي أَحْدَثَتْهُ الحَرْبُ

B *adj* مُشَكَّل, مَصْنوع; **finely ~ jewellery** مُجَوْهَرات مَشْغولة بِشَكْلٍ دَقيقٍ

wrought iron *n* حَديد مُطاوِع

wrung /rʌŋ/ *past tense, past participle* ▸**wring**

wry /raɪ/ *adj* (**wrier, wriest**) ‹*smile, humour*› ساخِر; **she made a ~ face** قَطَّبَتْ وَجْهَها

WTO /dʌbljuːtiː'əʊ/ *n* = **World Trade Organization** مُنَظَّمة التِجارةِ العالَميّة

wudu /wʊ'duː/ *n* وُضوء

WV *abbr* = **West Virginia**

WWW /dʌbljuːdʌbljuː'dʌbljuː/ *abbr* = **World Wide Web** الشَبَكة العَنْكَبوتيّة العالَميّة

WY *abbr* ▸**Wyoming**

Wyoming /waɪ'əʊmɪŋ/ *pr n* وايومِنْغ (f)

WYSIWYG /'wɪziwɪg/ *adj* = **what you see is what you get** ‹*software, tool*› ما تَراهُ هو ما تَحْصُلُ عَلَيْهِ

X, **x** /ɛks/ *n* 1 (letter) [الحَرْف الرابِع والعِشْرونَ من الأَبْجَدِيّة الإِنْكْليزِيّة] 2 (standing for names) فُلان; (standing for numbers) س (رَمْز للكَمِّيّة المَجْهولةِ في الرِياضِيّاتِ); **Mr X~** السَيِّد فُلان

xenophobia /zɛnəˈfəʊbɪə/ *n* (fear) الخَوْف من الأَجانِب; (loathing) كُرْه \ كَراهِية الأَجانِب

xenophobic /zɛnəˈfəʊbɪk/ *adj* (fearful) ‹*attitude*› خائِف من الأَجانِب; (loathing) ‹*attack*› كارِه للأَجانِبِ

Xerox® /ˈzɪərɒks/ **A** *n* نُسْخة مُصَوَّرة

B (**xerox**) *vt* صَوَّرَ, نَسَخ (a; نَسْخ)

XL /ɛksˈɛl/ *abbr* = **extra large** [كَبير جِدًّا]

Xmas /ˈkrɪsməs, ˈɛksməs/ *n* (infml) = **Christmas** عيد الميلادِ

XML /ɛksɛmˈɛl/ *n* = **Extensible Markup Language** إكْس إم إل (لُغة التَمْييزِ \ التَرْميز القابِلة للامْتِدادِ)

X-ray /ˈɛksreɪ/ **A** *n* 1 (ray) شُعاع سينيّ \ إكْس 2 (image) صورة بالأَشِعّة (السينيّة); **to take an ~ of the fracture** صَوَّرَ الكَسْرَ بالأَشِعّة السينيّة

B *vt* صَوَّرَ بالأَشِعّة السينيّة ‹*a patient, fracture*›

xylophone /ˈzaɪləfəʊn/ *n* إكْسيليفون (آلة موسيقيّة)

Yy

Y, y /wʌɪ/ *n* ياء ≈ [الحَرْف الخامِس والعِشْرونَ من الأَبْجَدِيّةِ الإنْكْليزِيّةِ]

yacht /jɒt/ *n* 1 (sailing boat) يَخْت (بِشِراعٍ) 2 (power boat) يَخْت (يُخوت)

yacht club *n* نادي اليُخوتِ

yachting /ˈjɒtɪŋ/ *n* الإبْحار باليُخوتِ

yacht race *n* سِباق اليُخوتِ

yachtsman /ˈjɒtsmən/ *n* (*pl* **-men**) قائد \ رُبّان يَخْت

yahoo¹ /jɑːˈhuː, jaˈhuː/ *excl* (infml) 1 ها (تَعْبير عن الفَرْحةِ) 2 (**Yahoo!**®) ياهو (شَرِكة خَدَماتِ إنْتَرْنِت)

yahoo² /ˈjɑːhuː, jəˈhuː/ *n* (infml) شَخْص فَظّ, جِلْف (أَجْلاف)

yak /jak/ *n* (*pl* **yak** or **yaks**) ياك, قَطاس (حَيَوان من فَصيلةِ البَقَرِيّاتِ)

Yale lock® /ˈjeɪl lɒk/ *n* قُفْل يِيل (قُفْل أُسْطُوانيّ ذو مِفْتاحٍ مُسَنَّنٍ)

yam /jam/ *n* يام (نَبات كالبَطاطا)

yank /jaŋk/ *vt* ‹sb's arm, a door› جَذَبَ بِشِدّةٍ, نَتَرَ (u; نَتْر)

Yank /jaŋk/ *n* (BrE) (infml) يانْكيّ (أَحَد سُكّانِ الوِلاياتِ المُتَّحِدةِ)

Yankee /ˈjaŋki/ *n* (infml) 1 (person from the USA) يانْكيّ (أَحَد سُكّانِ الوِلاياتِ المُتَّحِدةِ) 2 (soldier) [جُنْديّ من الجُنودِ الفيديراليّينَ خلال الحَرْبِ الأَهْلِيّةِ الأَمْريكيّةِ] 3 (AmE) (person from north-eastern USA) يانْكيّ (أَحَد سُكّانِ الشَمالِ الشَرْقيِّ من الوِلاياتِ المُتَّحِدةِ)

yap /jap/ **A** *vi* (**-pp-**) «dogs» نَبَحَ (a; نُباح)
B *n* نُباح

yard /jɑːd/ *n* 1 (measure) يارْدة 2 (open space) باحة 3 (AmE) (garden) حَديقة (حَدائِقُ) 4 ▸**shipyard**, ▸**boatyard**

yardstick /ˈjɑːdstɪk/ *n* مِقْياس (مَقاييسُ), مِعْيار (مَعاييرُ)

yarn /jɑːn/ *n* 1 (thread) خَيْط (خُيوط, أَخْياط, خيطان) 2 (infml) (tale) [حِكاية طَويلة مُلَفَّقة]

yashmak /ˈjaʃmak/ *n* يَشْمَك (نَوْع من النِقابِ)

yawn /jɔːn/ **A** *vi* «person» تَثاءَبَ
B *n* تَثاؤُب, ثُؤَباء (dipt f)

yawning /ˈjɔːnɪŋ/ *adj* ‹gap, chasm› واسِع

yd *abbr* = **yard** يارْدة

ye /jiː/ (old use) **A** *pron* = **ye** أَنْتُمْ, أَنْتُنَّ, أَنْتُما
B *definite article* = **the** ال

yeah /jɛː/ *excl* (infml) نَعَمْ

year /jɪə, jəː/ **A** *n* 1 (period of time) سَنة (سَنَوات, سِنونَ, سِنينَ), عام (أَعْوام); **over the past ~** خلال السَنةِ الماضِيةِ; **I worked there for two ~s** عَمِلْتُ هُناكَ لِمُدّةِ سَنَتَيْنِ; **all year round** على مَدارِ السَنةِ; **~ after ~, ~ in ~ out** سَنةً بعد سَنةٍ; **she is nine ~s old** هي في التاسِعةِ من عُمْرِها 2 (at school, university) سَنة دِراسيّة
B (**years**) *n pl* (infml) (a long time) **I haven't seen him for** *or* **in ~s** لم أَرَهُ منذ وَقْتٍ طَويلٍ

yearbook /ˈjɪəbʊk/ *n* 1 (directory) حَوْلِيّة 2 (AmE) (of a class) كِتاب مَدْرَسيّ سَنَويّ

year end *n* نِهاية السَنةِ الماليّةِ

year-long /ˈjɪəlɒŋ/ *adj* ‹journey, course› لِمُدّةِ سَنةٍ كامِلةٍ

yearly /ˈjɪəli/ **A** *adj* ‹income, event› سَنَويّ; **on a ~ basis** على أَساسٍ سَنَويٍّ
B *adv* ‹to increase, occur› سَنَويًّا; **twice ~** مَرَّتَيْنِ في العام

yearn /jəːn/ *vi* تاقَ (u; تَوْق, تَوَقان; إلى), تَشَوَّقَ (إلى), حَنَّ (i; حَنين; إلى); **to ~ to do sth** تاقَ إلى فِعْلِ شَيْءٍ; **to ~ for sth** حَنَّ إلى شَيْءٍ

yearning /ˈjəːnɪŋ/ *n* تَوْق, حَنين, اشْتِياق (اشْتِياقات); **their ~ for freedom/to return** تَوْقُهُمْ إلى الحُرِّيّةِ \ الرُجوعِ

yeast /jiːst/ *n* خَميرة (خَمائِرُ)

yell /jɛl/ **A** *n* صَرْخة (صَرَخات), صَيْحة

B *vt* هَتَفَ (i; هُتاف ;ب) ‹*sb's name, abuse*›

C *vi* «child, crowd» صاحَ (i; صِياح, صَيْح), صَرَخَ (u; صُراخ, صَريخ); **to ~ at sb** صاحَ على شَخْصٍ

yellow /ˈjɛləʊ/ **A** *adj* **1** ‹*hair, fields, traffic lights*› أَصْفَر (dipt; صُفْر)

2 (infml) (cowardly) ≈ جَبان

B *n* **1** (colour) أَصْفَر (dipt; صُفْر); **to be wearing ~** لَبِسَ ثِياباً صَفْراءَ; **to go** *or* **turn ~** اصْفَرَّ **2** (signal) إشارة صَفْراء

C *vi* «newspaper, teeth» اصْفَرَّ

yellow-belly /ˈjɛləʊbɛli/ *n* (infml) جَبان

yellow card *n* بِطاقة صَفْراء; **to show a player the yellow card** أَشْهَرَ البِطاقةَ الصَفْراءَ في وَجْهِ لاعِبٍ

yellow fever *n* حُمّى صَفْراء

yellowish /ˈjɛləʊɪʃ/ *adj* ‹*glow, light*› ضارِب إلى الصُفْرة

Yellow Pages® *n* (**the Yellow Pages**) الصَفَحات الصَفْراء

yelp /jɛlp/ **A** *n* صَرْخة (صَرَخات)

B *vi* «dog» عَوى (i; عُواء); «person» صَرَخَ (u; صُراخ, صَريخ)

Yemen /ˈjɛmən/ *pr n* اليَمَن (f)

Yemeni /ˈjɛməni/ *n, adj* يَمَنيّ

yen /jɛn/ *n* **1** (infml) (longing) تَوْق, (رِغاب, رَغَبات) رَغْبة; **to have a ~ for sth/to do sth** تَمَلَّكَتْهُ الرَغْبةُ في شَيْءٍ \ فِعْلِ شَيْءٍ **2** (*pl* **yen**) (currency) يِنّ

yeoman /ˈjəʊmən/ *n* (*pl* **-men**) (also **yeoman farmer**) (Hist) [صاحِب مَزْرَعةٍ صَغيرةٍ في النِظامِ الإقْطاعيِّ القَديمِ]

Yeoman of the Guard *n* [أَحَد أَفْرادِ الحَرَسِ المَلَكيِّ البَريطانيِّ]

yep /jɛp/, **yup** /jʌp/ *excl* (infml) نَعَمْ

yes /jɛs/ *excl, n* نَعَمْ; **to say ~** قالَ نَعَمْ

yes-man /ˈjɛsman/ *n* (*pl* **-men**) (infml) إمَّع

yesterday /ˈjɛstədeɪ, ˈjɛstədi/ **A** *adv* **1** البارِحةَ, أَمْسِ; **it rained ~** تَساقَطَت الأَمْطارُ البارِحةَ; **all day ~** طوالَ يَوْمِ أَمْسِ; **early/late ~** في وَقْتٍ مُبَكِّرٍ \ مُتَأَخِّرٍ بالأَمْسِ **2** (liter) (in the past) في الماضي; **towns that ~ were just villages** مُدُن كانَتْ بالأَمْسِ مُجَرَّدَ قُرًى

B *n* **1** البارِحة, أَمْس; **~ was Friday** كانَ الأَمْسُ يَوْمَ الجُمْعةِ; **~'s newspaper** جَريدة أَمْسِ; **the day before ~** أَوَّل أَمْسِ; **they always want everything ~** لا يَصْبِرونَ على مَطالِبِهِمْ

2 (the past) **~'s fashions** مَوضة قَديمة; **~'s students are tomorrow's employers** طُلّابُ البارِحةِ هُمْ أَصْحابُ العَمَلِ غَداً; **~'s customs and crafts** عادات وَحِرَف قَديمة

yesterday afternoon **A** *n* ظُهْر البارِحةِ;

B *adv* ظُهْرَ البارِحةِ

yesterday evening **A** *n* مَساء البارِحةِ;

B *adv* مَساءَ البارِحةِ

yesterday morning **A** *n* صَباح البارِحةِ;

B *adv* صَباحَ البارِحةِ

yesteryear /ˈjɛstəjɪə/ *n* (liter) (last year) العام الماضي; (the past) الماضي; **stars of ~** نُجوم من الماضي

yes-vote /ˈjɛsvəʊt/ *n* تَصْويت بِنَعَم

yet /jɛt/ **A** *adv* **1** (up till now) حتّى الآنِ; **not ~** لَيْس بَعْدُ; **it's not ready ~** لَيْس جاهِزاً بَعْدُ; **it's the best ~** هو الأَفْضَلُ حتّى الآنِ **2** (in statements) بَعْدُ; **don't go (just) ~** لا تَذْهَبْ الآنَ; **he won't come for hours ~** لن يَأْتِيَ إلّا بعد بِضْعِ ساعاتٍ; **they may ~ come** ما زالَ هُناكَ احْتِمالٌ أَنْ يَأْتوا **3** (in questions) بَعْدُ, حتّى الآنَ; **has he arrived ~?** هل وَصَلَ بَعْدُ؟; **haven't you finished ~?** أَلَمْ تَنْتَهِ بَعْدُ؟ **4** (fml) (even, still) **~ more cars drove by** وَمَرَّتْ سَيّاراتٌ أَكْثَرُ; **~ again, he asked the question** وَطَرَحَ السُؤالَ من جَديدٍ

B *conj* (fml) رَغْمَ \ مع ذلك; **it's a small apartment, ~ it's surprisingly spacious** هي شَقّةٌ صَغيرةٌ، وَرَغْمَ ذلك تُعْطي إحْساساً بالاتِّساعِ; **the car was a write-off, ~ he was unhurt** تَدَمَّرَت السَيّارةُ تَماماً، وَرَغْمَ ذلك لم يُصَبْ بِأَذًى

yew /juː/ *n* **1** (also **yew tree**) طَقْسوس (شَجَرة دائِمة الخُضْرةِ)

2 [u] (wood) خَشَب الطَقْسوس

Y-fronts® /ˈwʌɪfrʌnts/ *n pl* (BrE) [سِرْوال داخِليّ لِلرِجال]

YHA /wʌɪeɪtʃeɪ/ *n* = **Youth Hostels Association** جَمْعيّة بُيوتِ الشَباب

Yiddish /ˈjɪdɪʃ/ **A** *n* (اللُغة) اليِديشيّة

B *adj* ‹*word, literature*› يِديشيّ

yield /jiːld/ **A** *vt* **1** (to produce, bear) «crops» أَثْمَرَ; «land, animals» أَنْتَجَ **2** (to deliver) حَقَّقَ ‹*a return, profit*›; **the bonds ~ 6% per annum** تُحَقِّقُ السَنَداتُ 6٪ كَعائِدٍ سَنَويٍّ **3** (to reveal)

كَشَفَ (i; كَشْف) عن <*a clue, information*> **4** (to give up) تَخَلّى (عن) <*control, a position*>

B *vi* **1** (to give in to force, temptation, threats) «governments, towns» اِسْتَسْلَمَ; **to ~ to the enemy** اِسْتَسْلَمَ إلى العَدوِّ; **to ~ to persuasion** رَضَخَ للإغْراءِ **2** (under pressure) «door, bridge, shelves» مالَ (i; مَيْل، مَيَلان) **3** (to be productive) **to ~ well/poorly** «land, plantation» أَنْتَجَ بكَثْرة \ قليلاً **4** (AmE) «vehicles, drivers» أَفْسَحَ ~ لَهُ أَمامَكَ الطَّريقَ' 'أَوْلَوِيّةُ المُرورِ

C *n* **1** (of a tree, field, crop) مَحْصول (مَحاصيلُ، مَحْصولات), إنْتاج، ناتِج; **the annual milk ~** الإنْتاج السَنَويّ من اللَبَنِ **2** (on shares, bonds) عائِد (عائِدات، عَوائِدُ)

(Phrasal verb) **yield up** كشف (i; كَشْف) عن <*a secret, treasure*>

YMCA /wʌɪɛmsiːˈeɪ/ *n* = **Young Men's Christian Association** جَمْعيّة الشُبّانِ المَسيحيّينَ

yob /jɒb/, **yobbo** /ˈjɒbəʊ/ *n* (BrE) (infml) وَغْد (شَخْص غَليظ الطَبْع)

yodel /ˈjəʊd(ə)l/ *vi* (**-ll-** BrE, **-l-** AmE) «singers, choirs» غَنّى [مُسْرِعاً في الانْتِقالِ إلى الطَبَقاتِ الصَوْتِيّةِ العُلْيا]

yoga /ˈjəʊgə/ *n* يوجا

yogurt, **yoghurt**, **yoghourt** /ˈjɒgət/ *n* لَبَن (رائِب \ زَباديّ)

yoke /jəʊk/ **A** *n* **1** (for oxen, horses) نير (نيران، أَنْيار) **2** (burden, oppression) نير (نيران، أَنيار)

B *vt* قَرَنَ (البَهائِمَ للحَرْثِ أو الجَرِّ) <*the oxen, horses*>

yokel /ˈjəʊk(ə)l/ *n* (infml) ريفيّ \ فَلّاح ساذَج

yolk /jəʊk/ *n* مُحّ (أَمْحاح), صُفار البَيْضِ

Yom Kippur War /jɒm ˈkɪpə/, **October War** *n* حَرْب أُكْتوبر

yonder /ˈjɒndə/ *adv* (old use) هُناكَ

yonks /jɒŋks/ *n pl* (BrE infml) **I haven't seen him for ~** لم أَرَهُ منذ زَمَنٍ بَعيدٍ

you /juː, jə/ *pron* **1** (masc sing) أَنْتَ; (fem sing) أَنْتِ; (masc & fem dual) أَنْتُما; (masc pl) أَنْتُمْ; (fem pl) أَنْتُنَّ; **it's for ~** (masc sing) هو لَكَ; (fem sing) هو لَكِ; (masc & fem dual) هو لَكُما; (masc pl) هو لَكُمْ; (fem pl) هو لَكُنَّ; **~ Egyptians could teach us many lessons** أَنْتُم أَيُّها المِصْريّونَ تَسْتَطيعونَ أَنْ تُعَلِّمونا الكَثيرَ من الدُروسِ; **~ two can stay** أَنْتُما الاثْنانِ تَسْتَطيعانِ أَنْ تَبْقَيا; **~ liar!** (infml) أَنْتَ كَذّابٌ! **2** (as indefinite pronoun) أَحَد; **~ never know!** وَما يُدْريكَ؟; **~ just don't know what will happen!** لا أَحَدَ يَعْرِفُ ما يُمْكِنُ أَنْ يَحْدُثَ!; **~ get malaria from mosquitoes** تَنْتَقِلُ العَدْوى بالمَلارِيا عن طَريقِ البَعوضِ

you'd /juːd/ *abbr* **1** = **you had** **2** = **you would**

you-know-what /juːnəʊˈwɒt/ *pron* (infml) تَعْرِفُ ماذا أَعْني

you-know-who /juːnəʊˈhuː/ *pron* (infml) تَعْرِفُ من أَعْني

you'll /juːl/ *abbr* = **you will**

young /jʌŋ/ **A** *adj* (in age) <*child, tree, animal*> صَغير (صِغار);

to be ~ at heart كانَتْ عِنْدَهُ روحُ الشَبابِ; **she is ten years ~er than him** هي أَصْغَرُ مِنْهُ بِعَشْرِ سَنَواتٍ; **in my ~er days** في (أَيّام) شَبابي; **children as ~ as five years old** أَطْفال من عُمْرِ خَمْسِ سَنَواتٍ; **to marry/die ~** تَزَوَّجَ \ ماتَ صَغيراً; **... is the ~est member of the UN** ... هي أَحْدَثُ عُضْوٍ في الأُمَمِ المُتَّحِدةِ; **~ people** الشَباب; **her ~er brother** أَخوها الأَصْغَر

B *n pl* **1** (**the young**) (young people) الشَباب, الصِغار;

entertainment for ~ and old alike تَرْفيه للصِغارِ والكِبارِ مَعاً **2** (of animals) صِغار

young blood *n* دِماء شابّة

youngish /ˈjʌŋɪʃ/ *adj* <*man, crowd*> صَغير السِنِّ نَوْعاً ما, أَقْرَب إلى الشَبابِ

young professional *n* شابّ مُحْتَرِف \ مِهْنيّ

youngster /ˈjʌŋstə/ *n* حَدَث (أَحْداث), شابّ (شُبّان، شَباب)

your /jɔː, jʊə/ *determiner* (masc sing) ـكَ; (fem sing) ـكِ; (masc & fem dual) ـكُما; (masc pl) ـكُمْ; (fem pl) ـكُنَّ; **I like ~ dress** يُعْجِبُني فُسْتانُكِ; **~ hat has gone** اخْتَفَتْ قُبَّعَتُكَ; **you should always protect ~ passwords** يَجِبُ أَنْ تَحْمِيَ كَلِماتِ السِرِّ الخاصّةِ بِكَ دائِماً

you're /jʊə, jɔː/ *abbr* = **you are**

yours /jɔːz/ *pron* **my car is red but ~ is blue** سَيّارَتي حَمْراءُ لَكِنَّ سَيّارَتَكَ زَرْقاءُ; **which house is ~?** أَيُّ بَيْتٍ هو بَيْتُكَ؟; **he's a colleague of ~** هو زَميلٌ لَكَ; **it's not ~** لَيْسَ لَكَ; **the money wasn't ~ to waste** لم تَكُن الأَمْوالُ لَكَ حتّى تُفَرِّطَ فيها; **where's that dog of ~?** أَيْنَ كَلْبُكُم اللَعينُ ذلكَ؟

yourself /jɔːˈsɛlf/ *pron* **1** (reflexive) (masc) نَفْسَكَ; (fem) نَفْسَكِ; **have you cut ~?** هل جَرَحْتَ نَفْسَكَ؟; **be ~** كُنْ نَفْسَكَ

2 (emphasis) (you yourself) (masc) نَفْسُكَ; (fem) نَفْسُكِ; (by yourself) (masc) بِنَفْسِكَ; (fem) بِنَفْسِكِ; **you ~ said that ...** أَنْتَ نَفْسُكَ قُلْتَ إنّ ...; **did you make it ~?** هل صَنَعْتَهُ بِنَفْسِكَ؟ **3** (after prepositions) **save some for ~** احْتَفِظْ بِقَليلٍ لِنَفْسِكَ **4** (in expressions) **were you (all) by ~?** هل كُنْتَ بِمُفْرَدِكَ؟; **you're not ~ today** لَسْتَ على ما يُرامُ اليَوْمَ; **to have the house all to ~** كانَ البَيْتُ كُلُّهُ لَكَ بِمُفْرَدِكَ

yourselves /jɔ:ˈsɛlvz/ *pron* **1** (reflexive) (masc & fem dual) نَفْسَيْكُما; (masc pl) أَنْفُسَكُمْ; (fem pl) أَنْفُسَكُنَّ; **did you dress ~?** هل لَبِسْتُمْ مُلابِسَكُمْ؟ **2** (emphasis) (you yourselves) (masc & fem dual) نَفْساكُما; (masc pl) أَنْفُسُكُمْ; (fem pl) أَنْفُسُكُنَّ; (by yourselves) (masc & fem dual) بِنَفْسَيْكُما; (masc pl) بِأَنْفُسِكُمْ; (fem pl) بِأَنْفُسِكُنَّ; **you ~ said ...** أَنْتُمْ أَنْفُسُكُمْ قُلْتُمْ إنّ ...; **why don't you do it ~?** لِماذا لا تَفْعَلونَهُ بِأَنْفُسِكُمْ؟ **3** (after prepositions) **save some pizza for ~** احْتَفِظوا بالقَليلِ من البيتْزا لأَنْفُسِكُمْ **4** (in expressions) **were you (all) by ~?** هل كُنْتُمْ بِمُفْرَدِكُمْ؟; **you're not ~ today** لَسْتُمْ على ما يُرامُ اليَوْمَ

youth /ju:θ/ *n* (*pl* **youths** /ju:ðz/) **1** (early life) شَباب **2** [u] (young people) شَباب **3** (young man) شابّ (شَباب, شُبّان, فِتْيَة, فِتْيان) فَتًى

youth club *n* نادٍ لِلشَّبابِ

youthful /ˈju:θfʊl/ *adj* **1** (young) ‹*appearance, audience*› فَتِيّ **2** (typical of youth) ‹*energy, enthusiasm*› خاصّ بالشَّبابِ

youth hostel *n* بَيْت الشَّبابِ

youth worker *n* أَخِصّائيّ رِعايَةِ شَبابٍ

you've /ju:v/ *abbr* = **you have**

yowl /jaʊl/ *vi* «cats» ماءَ (u; مُواء); «child» بَكى (i; بُكاء, بُكِيّ)

yo-yo® /ˈjəʊjəʊ/ *n* يويو

yr *abbr* (*pl* **yrs**) = **year(s)** سَنة (سَنَوات, سِنون, سِنينَ)

yuan /jʊˈɑ:n/ *n* (*pl* **yuan**) يُوان (عُمْلة صينيّة)

yucca /ˈjʌkə/ *n* يوكا

yuck /jʌk/ *excl* (infml) إخس, هذا مُقْرِفٌ

yucky /ˈjʌki/ *adj* (**yuckier**, **yuckiest**) (infml) ‹*food, smell*› مُقْرِف

Yugoslav /ˈju:gəʊslɑ:v/ *n, adj* يوغوسْلافيّ

Yugoslavia /ju:gəʊˈslɑ:vɪə/ *pr n* يوغوسْلافيا

Yugoslavian /ju:gəʊˈslɑ:vɪən/ *n, adj* يوغوسْلافيّ

yule log /ˈju:l ˌlɒg/ *n* [قِطْعة من الخَشَبِ تُحْرَقُ في المِدْفَأةِ في لَيْلَةِ عيد الميلادِ]

yummy /ˈjʌmi/ *adj* (**yummier**, **yummiest**) ‹*food, cake*› لَذيذ (لِذاذ)

yup /jʌp/ *excl* (infml) ▸ **yep**

yuppie /ˈjʌpi/ *n* (*pl* **yuppies**) (infml pej) [شابّ ذو راتِبٍ عالٍ يَعْمَلُ في المَدينة وَيَعيشُ حَياةً فاخِرةً]

YWCA /wʌɪdʌbljuːsiːˈeɪ/ *n* = **Young Women's Christian Association** جَمْعيّة الشّابّاتِ المَسيحيّاتِ

Zz

Z, z /zed/ *n* زاي ≈ (الحَرْف السادِس والعِشْرونَ من الأَبْجَدِيّةِ الإنْكليزيّةِ)

Zaire /zɑɪ'ɪə/ *pr n* زائير (الاسْم القَديم لِجُمْهوريّةِ الكونْغو الديمُقْراطيّةِ)

Zairean /zɑː'ɪrɪən/ *n, adj* زائيريّ

zakat /zə'kɑːt/ *n* زَكاة (زَكَوات)

Zambia /'zambɪə/ *pr n* زامْبِيا

Zambian /'zambiən/ *n, adj* زامْبيّ

zany /'zeɪni/ *adj* (**zanier**, **zaniest**) (infml) ‹*character, humour*› فُكاهيّ, مُضْحِك

zap /zap/ *vt* (**-pp-**) (infml) ضَرَب بِعُنْفٍ, هاجَمَ ‹*a city, an enemy*›

zapper /'zapə/ *n* (infml) **1** (for TV) جِهاز تَحَكُّمٍ عن بُعْدٍ **2** (AmE) (for insects) جِهاز قَتْلِ الحَشَراتِ (الطائِرة)

zeal /ziːl/ *n* حَمِيّة, حَماس

zealot /'zɛlət/ *n* مُتَعَصِّب

zealous /'zɛləs/ *adj* ‹*advocate, supporter*› مُتَحَمِّس

zebra /'zɛbrə, 'ziːbrə/ *n* (*pl* **zebras** or **zebra**) حِمار وَحْشيّ \ مُخَطَّط \ زَرَدٍ

zebra crossing *n* (BrE) مَعْبَر مُشاةٍ (بِخُطوطٍ بَيْضاءَ وَسَوْداءَ)

zenith /'zɛnɪθ/ *n* سَمْت (الرَّأْسِ); **her career reached its ~ in the 1950s** بَلَغَتْ ذُرْوَةَ حَياتِها المِهْنِيّةِ في الخَمْسينيّاتِ

zero /'zɪərəʊ/ **A** *n* (*pl* **zeros** or **zeroes**) صِفْر; **it was 40 degrees below ~** بَلَغَتْ (دَرَجةُ الحَرارةِ) 40 دَرَجةً تحت الصِفْرِ

B *adj* ‹*value, probability*› صِفْريّ, مُنْعَدِم; **~ gravity/growth** انْعِدام الجاذِبِيّةِ \ النُموّ; **he has ~ chance of winning** لَيْسَ لَهُ أيُّ فُرْصةٍ في الفَوْزِ

(Phrasal verb) **zero in**: **to ~ in on sth** (to focus attention) «investigators, the media» رَكَّزَ على شَيْءٍ

zero-carbon /zɪərəʊ'kɑːb(ə)n/ *adj* خالٍ من الكَرْبون; **~ homes** مَنازِل خالية من الكَرْبون

zero hour *n* ساعة الصِفْرِ

zero-rated /ˌzirəʊ'reɪtɪd/ *adj* (BrE) ‹*goods, item*› مَفْروض عَلَيْه ضَريبةٌ (بِمُعَدَّل) الصِفْرِ]

zest /zest/ *n* **1** (enthusiasm) حَيَوِيّة, هِمّة (هِمَم), حَماس **2** (of citrus fruit) قِشْرة (قِشْر)

ziggurat /'zɪgʊrat/ *n* زِقّورة (مَعْبَد مُدَرَّج)

zigzag /'zɪgzag/ **A** *n* خَطّ مُتَعَرِّج

B *vi* (**-gg-**) «person, road» تَعَرَّجَ

zilch /zɪltʃ/ *n* (infml) لا شَيْءَ

Zimbabwe /zɪm'bɑːbwi, zɪm'bɑːbweɪ/ *pr n* زيمْبابْوي

Zimbabwean /zɪm'bɑːbwiən/ *n, adj* زيمْبابْويّ

Zimmer® /'zɪmə/ *n* (also **Zimmer frame**) إطار المَشْيِ

zinc /zɪŋk/ *n* زِنْك

zing /zɪŋ/ *n* (infml) حَيَوِيّة

Zionism /'zʌɪəniz(ə)m/ *n* صَهْيونيّة

Zionist /'zʌɪənɪst/ *n, adj* صَهْيونيّ

zip /zɪp/ **A** *n* **1** (also **zipper**, **zip fastener**) سَحّاب, (أَزِمّة) زِمام (Levant, Iraq), سوسْتة (Egypt); **to do up/undo a ~** غَلَقَ \ فَتَحَ زِماماً **2** (infml) (energy) نَشاط, حَيَوِيّة; **she doesn't have much ~ these days** لا تَتَمَتَّعُ بالحَيَوِيّة كَثيراً هذه الأَيّامَ **3** (sound) أَزيز; **the ~ of a bullet** أَزيز الرَصاصِ **4** (AmE) (infml) (nothing) لا شَيْءَ; **I know ~ about it** لا أَعْرِفُ شَيْئاً عَنْهُ

B *vt* (**-pp-**) **1** (to close) **to ~ sth open/shut** فَتَحَ \ غَلَقَ سَحّابَ شَيْءٍ **2** ضَغَطَ (a; ضَغْط) ‹*a file*›

C *vi* (**-pp-**) **1** (infml) «bag, dress» أُغْلِقَ الزِمامُ; **the dress ~s at the back** يُغْلَقُ زِمامُ الفُسْتانِ من الخَلْفِ **2** **to ~ along, to ~ past** «cars, traffic» مَرَّ بِسُرْعةٍ

(Phrasal verbs) **zip on**: **~ [sth] on** رَبَطَ [شَيْئاً] بِزِمامٍ ‹*the hood, sleeve*›

• **zip through**: **~ through [sth]** (infml) انْتَهى من [شَيْءٍ] بِسُرْعَةٍ ‹*the work, exam*›

• **zip up** 1 «dress, gown» أَغْلَقَ بِزِمامٍ; **it ~s up at the back/front** يُغْلَقُ من الخَلْفِ \ الأَمامِ بِواسِطَةِ زِمامٍ 2 **~ [sb/sth] up, ~ up [sb/sth]** «person» أَغْلَقَ زِمامَ [شَخْصٍ \ شَيْءٍ] ‹*the bag, dress*›; **can you ~ me up, please?** هل يُمْكِنُكَ أَنْ تُغْلِقَ زِمامي، من فَضْلِكَ؟

zip code *n* (AmE) رَمْز بَريديّ

zip fastener *n* ▸**zip** A1

zip file *n* مِلَفّ مَضْغوط

zipper /ˈzɪpə/ *n* (AmE) ▸**zip** A1

zip pocket *n* جَيْب بِسَحّابٍ

zither /ˈzɪðə/ *n* [آلَة وَتَرِيّة تُشْبِهُ القانونَ]

zodiac /ˈzəʊdiak/ *n* (**the zodiac**) دائِرة الأَبْراجِ

zombie /ˈzɒmbi/ *n* زومْبي (جُثّة أُعيدَتْ إلى الحَياةِ)

zone /zəʊn/ *n* مِنْطَقة (مَناطِق)

zonked /zɒŋkt/ *adj* (infml) (also **zonked out**) مُرْهَق

zoo /zuː/ *n* حَديقة حَيَواناتٍ

zookeeper /ˈzuːkiːpə/ *n* حارِس حَديقةِ حَيَواناتٍ

zoologist /zəʊˈɒlədʒɪst/ *n* عالِم الحَيَوانِ

zoology /zəʊˈɒlədʒi/ *n* عِلْم الحَيَوانِ

zoom /zuːm/ **A** *vi* (infml) (move quickly) **to ~ away** «car, driver» انْطَلَقَ بِسُرْعَةٍ

B *n* (also **zoom lens**) عَدَسة زوم \ تَقْريبٍ

(Phrasal verb) **zoom in**: **to ~ in on sth/sb** «camera, cameraman» قَرَّبَ شَيْئاً \ شَخْصاً

zucchini /zʊˈkiːni/ *n* (*pl* **zucchini** or **zucchinis**) (AmE) كوسة، قَرْع صَيْفيّ

Zulu /ˈzuːluː/ **A** *n* 1 (person) زولو 2 (language) (اللُغة) الزولُويّة

B *adj* ‹*warrior, culture*› زولو

Zumba® /ˈzʊmbə/ *n* زومْبا (تَمارين اللِياقةِ البَدَنيّةِ تَعْتَمِدُ على حَرَكاتِ الرَقْصِ اللاتينيِّ)

Zurich /ˈzjʊərɪk/ *pr n* زيورخ (f)

Parts of speech أقسام الكلام

abbr	*abbreviation*	اختصار
adj	*adjective*	صفة
adj phr	*adjectival phrase*	عبارة وصفية
adv	*adverb*	ظرف
adv phr	*adverbial phrase*	عبارة ظرفية
article		أداة تعريف \ تنكير
combining form		صيغة تركيب
conj	*conjunction*	حرف عطف
conj phr	*conjunction phrase*	عبارة ربط
definite article		أداة تعريف
demonstrative pronoun		اسم إشارة
determiner		محدِّد
determiner phr	*determiner phrase*	عبارة تحديد
excl	*exclamation*	أداة تعجب \ نداء
infinitive particle		أداة تنكير
modal aux	*modal auxiliary*	فعل مساعد
modifier		معدِّل
n	*noun*	اسم
n coll	*collective noun*	اسم جمع
n pl	*plural noun*	جمع
n sing	*singular noun*	اسم مفرد
num	*number*	عدد
partic	*particle*	حرف \ أداة
passive		مبني للمجهول
past participle		اسم المفعول
prep	*preposition*	حرف جر
pron	*pronoun*	ضمير
pron phr	*pronoun phrase*	عبارة تبدأ بضمير
relative pron	*relative pronoun*	اسم موصول
suffix		لاحقة
v	*verb*	فعل
v aux	*auxiliary verb*	فعل مساعد
vi	*intransitive verb*	فعل غير متعد
v impers	*impersonal verb*	فعل مبهم
v refl	*reflexive verb*	فعل انعكاسي
vt	*transitive verb*	فعل متعد